Joel Whitburn's

top pop singles

1955 - 2002

Billboard®

Chart Data Compiled From *Billboard's* Pop Singles Charts, 1955-2002.

Cover design by Dean Eggert Design

ISBN 0-89820-155-1

Record Research Inc.
P.O. Box 200
Menomonee Falls, Wisconsin 53052-0200 U.S.A.

Phone: (262) 251-5408
Fax: (262) 251-9452
E-Mail: books@recordresearch.com
Web Site: www.recordresearch.com

THIS IS DEDICATED TO THE ONES I LOVE...

Photo by Jerusha Olsan

My wife Fran, my daughter Kim, my son-in-law David,
my granddaughter Samantha and my grandson Nathaniel.

Special thanks...

...to my Record Research staff: Bill Hathaway, Kim Bloxdorf, Brent Olynick, Jeanne Olynick, Paul Haney, Kay Wagner, Sue Hustad, Fran Whitburn and Nestor Vidotto.

...and to David Dana-Bashian, Jeff Chepp, Dean Eggert, Marv Goldberg, Ferdie Gonzalez, Paul Grein, Peter Grendysa, Jackie Herdocia, Steven Herwitt, John Jayne, Rocky Kruegel, George Moonoogian, Tim Neely, Jerry Osborne, Steve Propes and Bob Pruter, all of whom contributed to the unending task of musical "Trivial Pursuit."

And a very special thanks to Billboard...especially to Howard Appelbaum, Sam Bell, Keith Caulfield, Michael Ellis, Keith Girard, John Kilcullen, Mary Ann Kim, Geoff Mayfield, Gordon Murray, Silvio Pietroluongo, Ken Schlager, Rachel Vilson, and Alex Vitoulis...I've enjoyed every minute of my 33-year relationship with your incomparable magazine.

CONTENTS

THE TOP SINGLES:

ROCK & ROLL HALL OF FAME INDUCTEES 983

#1 HITS 985

A chronological listing, by peak date, of every title to top *Billboard's* pop singles charts (showing the artist's count of total #1 hits).

AUTHOR'S NOTE

One of my main goals while researching this tenth edition of *Top Pop Singles* was to provide at least one line of bio for every artist and to uncover more trivia about the titles. From the very first page of my research, I was greatly encouraged when I found out the following new facts:

- Abaco Dream was actually Sly & The Family Stone!
- The Jewels, as in Billy Abbott And The Jewels, were really The Tymes!
- For The Abbey Tavern Singers, I found more data and a current photo!

With these revelations at the beginning of my project, I became more determined than ever to search out new, verifiable information.

This passion for trivial pursuit is shared by many of you readers. Although it is rarely completely satisfied, it has encouraged me to look at my research from new angles. The results of this fascination are new features to the main section of the book and new special sections devoted to these recent revelations. The additions to my research are outlined in the "What's New With This Edition" and "User's Guide" sections. Following are some fun facts I kept tabs on while working on this book.

#1 Runs:

- June 2, 1958, was the only date that one record was #1 on every *Billboard* singles chart: "All I Have To Do Is Dream" by The Everly Brothers topped all three Pop charts, both R&B charts and both Country charts.
- For seven consecutive weeks, two different versions of "Singing The Blues" held down the #1 spot on seven of *Billboard's* singles charts: Guy Mitchell's version of the song hit #1 on the four Pop charts while the version by Marty Robbins hit #1 on the three Country charts.
- Two versions of "Young Love" by Tab Hunter and Sonny James accomplished this same feat for two consecutive weeks.

Poker Hands:

From 1955-1957 when *Billboard* published four separate Pop singles charts, several records reached consecutive peak positions on the different charts:

- "Blue Suede Shoes" by Carl Perkins peaked at #2, #3, #4, #5.
- "True Love" by Bing Crosby & Grace Kelly peaked at #3, #4, #5, #6.
- "I'm In Love Again" by Fats Domino peaked at #3, #4, #5, #6.
- "Why Do Fools Fall In Love" by Frankie Lymon and The Teenagers peaked at #6, #7, #8, #9.
- "Canadian Sunset" by Andy Williams peaked at #7, #8, #9, #10.
- Only one record hit #1, #2, #3: "Get A Job" by The Silhouettes achieved this in 1958 when *Billboard* published three separate Pop singles charts.

Hot 100 Chart Firsts:

May 23, 1987: first *Airplay-only* hit, "Never Say Goodbye" by Bon Jovi

June 9, 1990: first *Sales-only* hit, "911 Is A Joke" by Public Enemy

March 3, 1979: first *12"-only* hit, "Whole Lotta Love" by The Wonder Band

June 3, 1989: first *cassette-only* hits, "Me Myself And I" by De La Soul and "Right Next To Me" by Whistle

August 21, 1993: first *CD-only* hit, "Few & Far Between" by 10,000 Maniacs

August 26, 2000: first *DVD-only* hit, "Just Be A Man About It" by Toni Braxton

December 5, 1998: highest charted *album cut-only* hit on first Hot 100 that included album cuts, "Iris" by Goo Goo Dolls

Chart Champs:

I have expanded the Top Artist ranking from 500 to 600 and am happy to once again feature a commentary on the ranking by renowned musicologist Paul Grein. Following are a few previously unacknowledged chart feats I found on some of the most well-known chart stars:

- Three artists accumulated the most double-sided Top 10 hits: Elvis Presley, The Beatles and Ricky Nelson. (And from three records, Ricky landed six consecutive Top 10 hits!)
- Three artists peaked at every position in the Top 10: Madonna, Aretha Franklin and Marvin Gaye.
- Elvis Presley peaked at nearly every Top 40 position except for #7, #10, #14, #27 and #37; he also peaked at 62 of the positions #1 through #100. James Brown had the most different peak positions: 63.

I hope you've enjoyed these various details. Whether your favorite artist is Vic Damone, Vic Dana, Dana Dane or just plain Dana, and whether your favorite song is "So Young," "So Tough," "So Rare" or "So What," may you, too, be entertained by the information in the upcoming pages.

JOEL WHITBURN

PAUL GREIN COMMENTARY

For this, our 10th edition of Top Pop Singles, we asked noted musicologist Paul Grein to review our back-of-the-book rankings and comment on key changes since the last edition. He came up with a lot of interesting material. This is his report:

Three female solo artists appear in the Top 10 on Joel Whitburn's newly revised (and expanded) list of the Top 600 artists of the rock era. Madonna jumps to #4, Janet Jackson vaults to #9 and Aretha Franklin dips to #10. It's the first time that three female solo stars have appeared in the Top 10 since Whitburn introduced this tabulation three decades ago.

Madonna's #4 ranking is the highest ever by a female artist. Connie Francis was #5 when the recap was first published in *Top Pop Singles 1955-1972*. Madonna places even higher on a separate list of artists with the most Top 10 hits in the rock era. The pop icon rises to #2, just behind Elvis Presley.

Janet Jackson's surge to #9 on the master list is equally impressive. She is closing in on brother Michael, who has ranked among the Top 10 artists ever since the 1955-1993 edition. The siblings' dual Top 10 rankings constitute the strongest showing for related pop attractions in music history—eclipsing even the Dorsey brothers, who reigned in the pre-rock era. In Joel Whitburn's *Pop Hits Singles & Albums 1940-1954*, Tommy was ranked as the #8 hit-maker of that period and Jimmy was #12.

At the rate she's going, Janet may eventually surpass Michael on the survey of Top 600 artists. She has already pulled ahead of him on the list of artists with the most Top 10 hits. Janet has tallied 29, one more than her brother. This is especially impressive because Michael had a nearly 15-year head start in amassing Top 10 solo hits.

Elvis Presley and The Beatles continue as the #1 and #2 artists of the rock era, positions they have held since the ranking was created. In a sign of their unquestioned dominance, Presley is the top male artist, and The Beatles are the top group, in five key categories—most chart hits, most Top 40 hits, most Top 10 hits, most #1 hits and most weeks at the #1 position.

By contrast, no one female dominates in all of these categories. Aretha Franklin remains the female artist with the most chart hits. Madonna is the female with the most Top 40 hits and the most Top 10 hits. Mariah Carey is the female with the most #1 hits and the most weeks at the #1 position.

Elton John is #3 on the master list of Top 600 artists, a position he has held since the 1955-1996 edition. In the first two editions of this list, Pat Boone was #3. In subsequent editions, James Brown and Stevie Wonder took turns in the #3 spot.

The top four slots are now held by the most successful artists to debut in the '50s, '60s, '70s and '80s—Presley, The Beatles, Elton John and Madonna, respectively. The highest-ranking artist to debut in the 1990s is Mariah Carey, who vaults to #14.

Five artists break into the Top 100 in this edition—Puff Daddy at #66, Duran Duran at #87, Celine Dion at #88, U2 at #94 and Jay-Z at #95. Puff Daddy and Jay-Z have only been charting since 1996, making their high placements especially impressive. Significantly, both of these acts hail from the world of hip-hop, a characteristic they share with many of the acts that have surged in recent editions.

Destiny's Child is the top new entry on the list at #181, followed by Usher at #192, Ja Rule at #199, Missy "Misdemeanor" Elliot at #206, *NSYNC at #220 and Jennifer Lopez at #253.

Eminem's "Lose Yourself" is the biggest hit to emerge since the last edition of *Top Pop Singles.* The Oscar-winning rap smash logged 12 weeks at #1.

Numerous artists have died since the last edition of *Top Pop Singles*. The most noteworthy include George Harrison, Maurice Gibb of the Bee Gees and Aaliyah, who enters the list of Top 600 artists posthumously at #264—higher than such potent new arrivals as Christina Aguilera, Faith Hill and Nelly.

Perry Como, who also died since the last edition, deserves special mention. The crooner, who ranks as the #38 hit-maker of the rock era, was the #3 artist of the pre-rock period, according to *Pop Hits Singles & Albums 1940-1954*. The one-time barber is one of only three artists to rank among the Top 40 artists of both the pre-rock and rock eras. The others are Frank Sinatra and Nat "King" Cole.

Whitburn has added a new feature to this edition—a list showing the ages, at the time of their first hit, of each of the Top 600 artists of the rock era. Tevin Campbell (11) was the youngest male artist at the time of his first hit. Brenda Lee (12) was the youngest female artist. Michael Jackson of the Jackson 5 (11) was the youngest group member. At the other extreme, Willie Nelson (42) was the oldest male artist at the time of his first Hot 100 hit. Tina Turner (45) was the oldest female artist (though she had amassed numerous hits as half of Ike & Tina Turner). Roebuck "Pop" Staples of the Staple Singers (51) was the oldest group member.

Another new feature makes it easy to see at a glance which artists have ranked among the Top 30 artists of the decade the most times. Top marks go to Elvis Presley and Elton John, who each ranked among the Top 10 artists of the decade three times.

The list of the Top 600 artists of the rock era concludes with the Intruders, an R&B group that notched 14 chart hits in the late 1960s and early 1970s. Only three of the group's singles made the Top 40. Only one ("Cowboys To Girls") made the Top 10. But chart victories stand forever—and Joel Whitburn never forgets.

Paul Grein

RESEARCHING BILLBOARD'S POP CHARTS

Top Pop Singles 1955-2002 features the research of over 25,000 hits and over 6,000 artists, and begins with 1955 — the year rock 'n' roll scored its first mainstream success with the chart-topping hit "Rock Around The Clock" by Bill Haley & His Comets. At that time, *Billboard* magazine published three main pop singles charts: Best Sellers In Stores, Most Played By Jockeys and Most Played In Juke Boxes. The chart research begins with the issue of *Billboard* dated January 1, 1955, and includes all of the songs on the above-mentioned charts, even if they first charted in 1954. In November of 1955, *Billboard* introduced its first 100-position pop chart, the Top 100. These four charts reported on different aspects of the sales and radio airplay of the hottest pop singles in America. Each of these charts is researched to impart an intricate picture of popular music of the mid-1950s.

On August 4, 1958, *Billboard* introduced the Hot 100, its first chart to fully integrate the hottest-selling and most-played pop singles. The Hot 100 has since hosted every type of music that falls under the wide umbrella of the popular song, from reggae to rock to doo-wop to country to rap to novelty and more. The history of *Billboard's* Hot 100 through 2002 constitutes the bulk of the chart data in this book.

For the Hot 100's first four decades, an essential qualification for a song's placement on the chart was its commercial availability in America as a single. The record industry's practice of releasing singles for consumers declined dramatically in the 1990s. More and more radio hits were ineligible to chart on the Hot 100 as they were never released commercially as singles. The Hot 100 Airplay and Hot 100 Singles Sales charts that *Billboard* created in 1984 became valued accompaniments to the Hot 100 chart in providing a thorough picture of each week's biggest hits. For this reason, the hits of *Billboard's* Hot 100 Airplay and Hot 100 Singles Sales charts that did not appear on the Hot 100 chart are included. Throughout the 1990s, *Billboard* adjusted the compilation method of their Hot 100 in order to keep pace with a rapidly changing music marketplace. On December 5, 1998, *Billboard* debuted a completely revised Hot 100, which included for the first time, songs that were not commercially available in America as singles.

The standard configuration for the pop singles chart from 1955-1989 is the 7" 45 rpm vinyl single, referred to hereafter as the "45". All singles within these three and one-half decades were released commercially as "45s" unless otherwise indicated. The vinyl symbol ("v") is not shown in the symbol column of titles that charted during these years, as it would accompany nearly every one of these titles.

On July 28, 1990, the cassette single replaced the "45" as the standard configuration on the Hot 100. From 1990 through November 1998, the label and number of all singles refers to the cassette single release, unless otherwise indicated.

On June 27, 1998, the CD single replaced the cassette single as the standard configuration on the Hot 100. The starting point for the CD single as the configuration referred to in the label and number column is December 5, 1998, the date that *Billboard* introduced its most revised Hot 100 ever. From this point on, the label and number refer to the CD single. If the song is not commercially available, then "album cut" is listed in the label and number column.

All chart data within *Top Pop Singles* is from the charts listed below. The beginning dates researched are also the debut dates of most charts, with the exception of Best Sellers, Jockeys and Juke Box charts, all of which debuted before 1955. As "# of Positions" indicates, the size of certain charts varied from week to week. The main pop singles charts appear in bold type.

Chart Title	Dates Researched	# of Positions
Best Sellers In Stores	**1/1/55 - 10/13/58 ***	**20-50**
Most Played By Jockeys	**1/1/55 - 7/28/58 ***	**20-25**
Most Played In Juke Boxes	**1/1/55 - 6/17/57 ***	**20**
Top 100	**11/12/55 - 7/28/58 ***	**100**
Honor Roll Of Hits**	1/1/55 - 11/16/63 *	20-30
Coming Up Strong**	7/16/55 - 7/28/58 *	10
Hot 100	**8/4/58 - 12/28/02**	**100**
Christmas Singles (seasonal chart)	1963 - 1973	3-38
" "	1983 - 1985 *	10
Hot 100 Singles Sales	**10/20/84 - 12/28/02**	**30-75**
Hot 100 Airplay	**10/20/84 - 12/28/02**	**30-75**
Top 40 Radio Monitor	12/8/90 - 7/10/93 *	75

*: date of final chart

** researched only for songs that appeared exclusively on these charts

CHART METHODOLOGY

Radio airplay and record sales have always been the two combined factors of a song's ranking on *Billboard's* Hot 100 chart. To better reflect the hottest songs of the ever-changing radio and record industry, *Billboard* has continually revised its compilation method over the years. From 1958-91, *Billboard* compiled the Hot 100 from playlists reported by radio stations and surveys of retail sales outlets. On November 30, 1991, *Billboard* brought the Hot 100 into the computer age in determining the chart by a combination of actual radio airplay monitored electronically by Nielsen Broadcast Data Systems (BDS), additional playlists from small-market stations, and actual point-of-sale information provided by Nielsen SoundScan. The increasing abundance of popular songs not commercially available as singles necessitated the most dramatic change to the Hot 100 on December 5, 1998, when *Billboard* unveiled the first Hot 100 chart to include songs not commercially available as singles.

Before publishing these and any other alterations to the compilation method of the Hot 100, *Billboard* ran unpublished test charts. When *Billboard* unveiled a new Hot 100 based on a new process, it continued the previous weeks positions and weeks charted tally for each entry from its unpublished test chart rather than the Hot 100 published in the prior week's issue. All of the research within this book is of published charts. No research is from *Billboard's* test charts of the 1990s.

The maze of configurations available for singles in the 1990s required that we create a new set of symbols to show singles availability. For further explanation, see CONFIGURATION SYMBOLS on page xix.

MULTIPLE POP CHARTS, 1955-1958

The single's "DEBUT" date is taken from the chart on which it first appeared if it hit more than one of the following pop singles charts published from 1955-58: Best Sellers In Stores, Most Played By Jockeys, Most Played In Juke Boxes, Top 100 or Hot 100. The date shown is *Billboard's* actual issue date, and is not taken from the "week ending" dates as shown on the various charts when they were originally published. (The issue and week ending dates were different until January 13, 1962, when *Billboard* began using one date system for both the magazine and the charts.)

If a song did not hit the Hot 100 but did hit one or more of the other pop singles charts active from 1955-58, then a chart-by-chart breakdown is listed to the right of the song title. In such cases, that single's highest position listed in the peak position column is taken from the chart on which it achieved its highest ranking. Also, that single's total weeks charted and weeks at positions #1 or #2 are taken from the chart on which it achieved its highest total.

HOT 100 SALES AND AIRPLAY

The data used to compile each week's Hot 100 chart is also used to compile the weekly Hot 100 Singles Sales and Hot 100 Airplay charts. The early Sales chart was compiled from the best-selling records based on reports from record stores, and the early Airplay chart was compiled from the most-played songs based on radio station playlists. From June 8, 1991 through November 23, 1991, the Sales and Airplay charts were not compiled from the same data as the Hot 100. During that period *Billboard* began compiling the Sales and Airplay charts from data provided by BDS and SoundScan. As of November 30, 1991, *Billboard* also began compiling the Hot 100 via BDS and SoundScan; the charts were once again directly related. The songs that hit the Sales and Airplay charts, but did not hit the Hot 100, are denoted by the letters 'A' (Airplay chart) and 'S' (Sales chart), in the peak position column. The Sales and Airplay peak positions of songs that crossed over to the Hot 100 are listed to the right of the song title.

TOP 40 RADIO MONITOR

Billboard compiled their Top 40 Radio Monitor pop chart from actual monitored airplay data provided by Broadcast Data systems (BDS). From December 8, 1990 through June 1, 1991, *Billboard* published both the Hot 100 Airplay chart (compiled from radio station playlists) and the Top 40 Radio Monitor chart. As of June 8, 1991, *Billboard* dropped the Hot 100 Airplay chart in favor of the Top 40 Radio Monitor chart. On July 17, 1993, the Top 40 Radio Monitor chart was renamed the Hot 100 Airplay chart. During the overlap period of the Top 40 Radio Monitor chart and the early Airplay chart (December 8, 1990 through June 1, 1991), the only Top 40 Radio Monitor chart hits included herein are those that did not also make either the Hot 100, Hot 100 Sales or Hot 100 Airplay charts. Songs that hit the Top 40 Radio Monitor chart exclusively appear in the main artist section and are denoted by the superscript letter 'A' following their peak position.

CHRISTMAS SINGLES

From 1963 through 1972, and from 1983 through 1985, *Billboard* published a seasonal Christmas Singles chart, and did not chart Christmas singles on the Hot 100. The only exception came in 1984, when *Billboard* charted two new Christmas singles on the Hot 100, and did not list them on the special Christmas Singles chart.

Songs that hit *Billboard's* Christmas Singles chart exclusively appear in the main artist section, and are denoted by the superscript letter 'X' following their peak position.

If a song hit this seasonal chart more than once but never hit the Hot 100, the song is listed only the first time that it charted. Each of the song's peak positions/years charted are noted below the title. All of its weeks charted are tallied in the total weeks column.

If a song hit *Billboard's* Hot 100 and special Christmas Singles chart, its peak position and weeks charted on the latter chart appear below the title. If such a song hit both charts more than once, its overall peak position and total weeks charted and all of its peak positions/years on the Christmas Singles charts are noted below the title of its final Hot 100 charting.

HONOR ROLL OF HITS / COMING UP STRONG

The Honor Roll Of Hits chart was a weekly ranking that included all versions of a popular song as one listing. The Coming Up Strong chart was a continuation of *Billboard's* Best Sellers In Stores chart. We researched the Honor Roll Of Hits and Coming Up Strong charts only for records which made these charts but did not make any of the other *Billboard* pop charts. The 26 songs that hit the Honor Roll and Coming Up charts exclusively appear in the main artist section, and are denoted by the superscript letters 'HR' (Honor Roll chart) and 'CU' (Coming Up chart), following their peak position.

ISSUE DATE vs. COLLECTION DATE

All dates within *Top Pop Singles* refer to the issue dates of *Billboard* magazine. Keep in mind that the Hot 100 chart reports on singles activity from the seven-day periods ending 11 to 13 days prior. For example, *Billboard* compiled its Hot 100 chart dated September 6, 1997 (Saturday) on August 27 (Wednesday). The radio airplay reports for this Hot 100 covered a seven-day period ending August 26 (Tuesday). Its sales reports covered a seven-day period ending August 24 (Sunday). Delivery of the September 6 issue began on August 29 (Friday). *Billboard's* timing has changed slightly over the years, so as a general guide, subtract 11 to 13 days from the chart debut (issue) date to determine the beginning of a song's national popularity.

Billboard used a Saturday issue date for all of the research herein, except from April 29, 1957 to December 25, 1961, when they changed to a Monday issue date. On January 6, 1962, *Billboard* reverted to a permanent Saturday issue date.

WHAT'S NEW WITH THIS EDITION

RED TYPE

For the first time ever, key information is now highlighted in **red type**. You can quickly spot: **artist names**, **Top 3 or 5 hits of top artists**, **peak chart year of every artist**, **all Top 10 hits**, **special symbols (picture sleeve**, **cassette**, **CD and "45" vinyl symbols**), and much more!

NEW SYMBOLS

The 'Pic' column, which was exclusively devoted to picture sleeve information in the previous edition, is now named 'Sym' (as in symbols) and features even more data about the songs. Two new pieces of information appear in that column: the DVD symbol (◗) and the enchanced CD symbol (+). Also, the vinyl symbol (v) and the maxi cassette or maxi CD symbol (*) now appear in that column.

A new letter symbol has also been added for 'Live' (L) recordings, which appears to the right of the title.

A heavy underline below a debut date (ex.: <u>4/27/85</u>) indicates a five-year (or more) gap between this date and the year of the debut date of the artist's next hit. This general indication is based strictly on year and not a 60-month span of time.

LP is now one of the Chart Abbreviation symbols that are listed across from artist name headings, and indicates that the artist charted an album on The Billboard 200.

ENHANCEMENTS

Numerous artists and/or groups that had their own listings in the past edition are now combined with their related artist or group. For example, the solo hits of Agnetha Fältskog and her bandmate Frida now appear under ABBA. Cross references are used throughout to find these artists.

If the artist name on a title varies slightly from their main artist name, it is now listed across from the title (Ex.: ***[HERB ALPERT]***). This is not used for duets, etc. which still appear in bold type below the title.

Biographical information now appears for every artist, although for some obscure artists it's very limited. With this in mind, we certainly would appreciate any <u>verifiable</u> artist information you can provide.

The chart information for a title that hit #1 on other charts (Adult Contemporary, R&B, Country, and Rock Tracks) is now listed in red type to the right of the title rather than in a title note. For example AC^3 to the right of a title indicates the title hit #1 on the Adult Contemporary chart for three weeks.

The promotional CD symbol (✪) and its label number and related title notes are no longer shown; instead, "album cut" is shown in the Label & Number column for Hot 100 hits that were not released as commercial singles.

The Song Title Section now includes special key word headings — such as "Rock," "Love," "How," "Let" — that help you quickly find sections of listings in which multiple titles begin with that word or a variation of it. Also, all Top 10 peak positions are highlighted in **red**.

Criteria for an artist's top hit and Top 3 or 5 hit has changed. See the explanation on page xxii.

Criteria for Hot Streaks has changed (explanation on page xxiii). A bold underline below a debut date indicates a five-year or more gap between an artist's hits, which now breaks a Top 40 streak and ends the shading.

The age of nearly every Top 600 Artist at the time of his or her debut on the pop singles chart is now shown in red type in the "Top 600 Artist Debuts" section on page 958.

The #1 Hits section now indicates the chronological position (such as **9 of 18**) in red type for each #1 hit in the artist's total string of #1s.

Two slight changes to the alphabetization of artists' names have been implemented: "The" in a group name is not considered in alphabetizing. For example, "Church, The" now appears before "Church, Eugene." Also, artists whose first names are initials now appear before artists who use full first names. For example, "Jackson, J.J." appears before "Jackson, Janet."

USER'S GUIDE

The artist section lists each artist's charted hits in chronological order. Each of an artist's song titles is sequentially numbered. All Top 10 singles are now highlighted in **red**.

EXPLANATION OF COLUMNAR HEADINGS & SYMBOLS

DEBUT: Date single first charted

PEAK: Highest charted position (highlighted in bold type).

❶ #1 song

WKS: Total weeks charted (currently a song is automatically dropped from the Hot 100 if it charted 20 weeks or more and drops below position 50)

Gold: ● Gold single ①

▲ Platinum single ① (additional million units sold are indicated by a numeral following the symbol)

A-side: Song title of chart hit

B-side: Flip side of vinyl single or additional track(s) on a charted cassette or CD single

$: Current value of near-mint commercial single

Sym: ■ Custom picture sleeve was originally issued commercially with the record ②

□ Promotional picture sleeve was distributed to radio stations and the press ②

⊙ One-page insert was issued inside the record sleeve

▮ Cassette single ③

★ CD single ④

T 12" vinyl single ④

◗ DVD single

V 7" 45 rpm vinyl single ④

* Maxi cassette or maxi CD — asterisk follows cassette or CD symbol ④

+ Enhanced CD (follows CD symbol)

Label & Number: Original label and number of single when charted — "album cut" is shown in the label column for Hot 100 hits that were never released as commercial singles. The album from which the hit attained its airplay is noted below the title along with the album label and number.

① The primary source used to determine gold and platinum singles is the Recording Industry Association of America (RIAA), which began certifying gold singles in 1958 and platinum singles in 1976. From 1958 through 1988, RIAA required sales of one million units for a gold single and two million units for a platinum single; however, as of January 1, 1989, RIAA lowered the certification requirements for gold singles to sales of 500,000 units and for platinum to one million units. Certification of DVD-only singles require sales of 25,000 units for gold and 50,000 units for platinum. Some record labels have never requested RIAA certifications for their hits. In order to fill in the gaps, especially during the period before 1958, various other trade publications and reports were used to supplement RIAA's certifications.

② ■ and □ apply only to 7" vinyl records from 1955-1989. From 1990 on, picture sleeves issued with vinyl records are indicated after the song's label and number.

③ ▮ applies to cassette singles released from 1/6/90 through 11/28/98. For the few titles from 1989, symbol indicates that the single was only available on cassette and not available on vinyl.

④ Refer to CONFIGURATION SYMBOLS on page xix for further explanation.

EXPLANATION OF SYMBOLS

★60★ Number next to an artist name denotes an artist's ranking among the Top 600 Artists (see ranking on page 950)

12/3/84 An underlined debut date indicates a five-year (or more) gap between this date and the debut date of the artist's next hit

+ Indicates single peaked in the year after it first charted

- Indicates a holiday single that peaked in January, but is considered a holiday hit in the previous year (as shown in our Pop Annual 1955-1999 book).

↑: Indicates the weeks charted data are subject to change since the single was still charted as of the 8/9/03 research cut-off date

/ Divides a two-sided hit. Complete chart data (debut date, peak position, etc.) is shown for both sides if each side achieved its own peak position. If a title charted only as the B-side, then only the debut date and weeks it charted as a "tag along" side are listed.

PEAK POSITION SYMBOLS

2^3 Superior number to the right of a #1 or #2 peak position is the total weeks the single held that position

The following superscript letters following the peak position in the "PEAK" column apply to songs that did not hit *Billboard's* Hot 100 chart but hit one of the charts below. These letter designations indicate that the peak position in the "PEAK" column is from the following charts:

A: Hot 100 Airplay or Top 40 Radio Monitor (10/20/84-12/28/02)
S: Hot 100 Singles Sales (10/20/84-12/28/02)
X: Christmas Singles (1963-73 and 1983-85)
HR: Honor Roll Of Hits (1/1/55-11/16/63)
CU: Coming Up Strong (7/16/55-7/28/58)

Before the debut of the Hot 100 chart on August 4, 1958, *Billboard* published four primary weekly pop singles charts (Most Played By Jockeys, Best Sellers In Stores, Most Played in Juke Boxes, and Top 100). The peak position shown in the "PEAK" column for the pre-Hot 100 pop singles charts is taken from the chart on which it achieved its highest position. No letter designation for the peak's particular chart appears in the "PEAK" column. The individual peak positions attained on these four pre-Hot 100 pop singles charts are listed to the right of the A-side title, preceded by:

A: Airplay (Most Played By Jockeys)
S: Sales (Best Sellers In Stores)
J: Most Played In Juke Boxes
T: Top 100

LETTER(S) IN BRACKETS AFTER TITLES

C - Comedy
F - Foreign language
I - Instrumental
L - Live
N - Novelty
R - Re-entry, reissue, remix or re-release of a previously charted song by that artist*
S - Spoken
X - Christmas

* Includes singles that re-entered following an absence of at least six months from the charts, and singles re-issued with a new label and number.

CONFIGURATION SYMBOLS

★ CD single commercially available. Symbol refers only to singles from December 5, 1998 on.

▮ Cassette single. Symbol refers only to singles from 1990 until December 5, 1998.

* Maxi Cassette single or maxi CD single

\+ Enhanced CD single

◗ DVD single

T 12" vinyl single

v A 7" vinyl 45 rpm single is commercially available. Symbol refers only to singles from 1990 on.

"45" In title notes indicates availability of 7" 45 rpm vinyl single for singles from 1990 on.

7" VINYL SINGLES

The 7" vinyl 45 rpm single is the standard configuration for *Billboard's* pop singles charts and of the research for all charted titles from 1955-1989. A label and number in this book from these three and one-half decades is taken from the original commercial release of its 7" vinyl 45 rpm single, unless otherwise indicated. As the vast majority of the titles of these years are 7" vinyl 45 rpm singles, their vinyl availability is not specified with a **v** in the symbol column or "45" in title notes.

The main configuration for records on the Hot 100 chart and for the research from 1990-98 is the cassette single. The CD single replaced the cassette single as the main configuration of the Hot 100 on June 27, 1998, and is listed as the main configuration in this book as of December 5, 1998. From 1990 on, if a charted cassette or CD single was also released as a 7" vinyl 45 rpm single, a **v** follows the cassette or CD symbol. A "45" in title notes shows the B-side or other information about the 7" vinyl single. According to *Billboard's* current chart methodology a song's main configuration is listed as an "album cut," even if it is available as a "45."

12" VINYL SINGLES

Songs released exclusively to retail as 12" vinyl singles are indicated with a **T** in the symbol column. The 12" single usually contains four to seven mixes of the same tune; and, therefore, is priced higher than the 7" single.

CASSETTE SINGLES

From 1990 until December 5, 1998, the cassette single is the standard configuration referred to in the label and number column in this book. The cassette symbol ▮ is used for those years. It is also used in 1989 to indicate the cassette-only commercial release of some titles, which were not commercially released on 7" vinyl.

An asterisk * to the right of the cassette symbol indicates that it is a cassette maxi-single, which usually consists of four to six tracks, is packaged in a hard plastic case with a custom picture insert, and is priced higher than a regular cassette single.

CD SINGLES

The CD single ★ is the standard configuration for all titles on and after the pivotal Hot 100 chart of December 5, 1998. Unless otherwise indicated, all labels and numbers from December 5, 1998 to December 28, 2002, refer to the CD single. For the few singles exclusively available commercially on CD single before December 5, 1998, a ★ symbol indicates such CD singles.

An asterisk * to the right of the CD symbol indicates that it is a CD maxi-single, which usually consists of four to six tracks and is priced higher than a regular CD single.

A plus + to the right of the CD symbol indicates that it is an enhanced CD single usually featuring song lyrics, videos, photos and other information accessible via computer.

DVD SINGLES

A DVD single ◗ features a music video of the song and other miscellaneous content such as artist interviews, biographies, outtakes, etc. The first DVD single did not chart until 2000.

PICTURES OF THE TOP ARTISTS

A picture of each of the Top 200 artists is shown next to their listing in the artist section. Each Top 200 artist's overall ranking is listed to the right of their name. In addition, any "Super Hot Artist" (as explained on page 947) with a rank of #201-300 is also pictured.

CHART ABBREVIATIONS

The abbreviations listed to the right of an artist's name indicate other Record Research books, plus their corresponding annual updates in the *Music Yearbooks* through 2002, in which the artist has additional chart hits that are not listed in this book. The abbreviations are:

MEM: *Pop Memories 1890-1954**
POP: *Pop Hits Singles & Albums 1940-1954*
BUB: *Bubbling Under The Hot 100 1959-2002*
R&B: *Top R&B Singles 1942-2002*
C&W: *Top Country Singles 1944-2002*
AC: *Top Adult Contemporary 1961-2002*
ROK: *Mainstream (Album) Rock Tracks 1981-2002* & *Modern Rock Tracks 1988-2002*
LP: *Top Pop Albums 1955-2002*

*Shown only when more titles by an artist can be found prior to 1940.

PICTURE SLEEVE GUIDE

If a picture sleeve was issued in the 1990s the vinyl symbol v follows the cassette symbol ▮ and the picture sleeve symbol ■ is shown after the label number.

ARTIST'S TOP YEAR

The year of an artist's peak popularity (based on yearly Hot 100 chart performance) is listed to the right of the artist's name. The same point system used to determine an artist's overall rank (see page 948) is also used to determine the artist's top year. The year of a record's popularity is based on its peak year and not the year it first charted. For example, an artist may have charted a record with a debut date of 11/28/64+. The plus sign after the date indicates the record peaked in 1965; and, therefore, the record is considered a 1965 hit.

Although the year from which an artist generates the most points is generally considered the top year, some exceptions are made. For example, if an artist had a lone major hit in one year, and a few minor hits in another year which collectively accumulate more points, the year of the major hit is considered the artist's top year. For artists who charted before 1955, their entire pop-chart histories were evaluated, based on their hits in our *Pop Hits Singles & Albums 1940-1954* and *Pop Memories 1890-1954* books. For example, Patti Page's peak year on the charts is 1950, well before her chart hits listed in this book.

ARTIST'S BIGGEST HITS

For an artist that charted five or more singles, the artist's highest-charting single is shaded and considered their top hit. The top hit is a reflection of chart performance only and may or may not relate to an artist's best seller over the years. A tie is broken based on total weeks at the peak position, then total weeks in the Top 10, total weeks in the Top 40, and total weeks charted. If an artist's top hit has two or more hits at the same peak position and with the same peak weeks, then the first tiebreaker will be a platinum single ranking over a gold single. When selecting a top hit, all Top 10 Hot 100 hits are considered first, then Top 10 airplay or sales hits. Unlike our previous edition, an artist must be the lead artist or share equal billing in order for a title to be considered the artist's top hit. Titles are not eligible if the artist is listed as "featured" and not the main artist (or group member's solo hits that are listed within the group's hits). Christmas chart-only hits are not eligible to be an artist's top hit.

The Top 3 hits of every artist with 10 to 19 charted hits and the Top 5 hits of every artist with 20 or more charted hits are listed in **red type** right below the artist's biography. The selection of Top 3 and Top 5 hits follow the same eligibility rules as those used to determine an artist's top hit.

Because of the shrinking availability of singles in the 1990s (especially with the revised Hot 100 rules for the 12/5/98 chart), Sales-only entries from that point on are not eligible for inclusion as an artist's top hit or Top 3 or 5 hits — unless the majority of an artist's hits are Sales only.

ARTIST & TITLE NOTES

Below every artist name are biographical notes about the artist. Directly under some song titles are notes indicating backing vocalists, guest instrumentalists, the title of the movie in which the song was featured, the name of a famous songwriter or producer, etc. Duets and other important name variations are shown in bold capital letters. Also, names of artists mentioned in the artist and title notes of other Hot 100 artists are highlighted in bold type if they have their own discographies elsewhere in this book. A name is only shown bold the first time it appears in an artist's biography. All movie, TV and album titles, and other major works are shown in italics. "Bubbled Under" refers to *Billboard's* Bubbling Under The Hot 100 chart. As always, we welcome any corrections/updates to our artist biographies or title notes. Please include solid evidence.

#1 HITS ON OTHER CHARTS

Songs that peaked at #1 on the Adult Contemporary, R&B, and Country singles charts, and the Mainstream (Album) Rock and Modern Rock tracks charts are indicated by the following letter symbols highlighted in red to the right of the song title:

AC = Adult Contemporary
RB = R&B/Hip-Hop Singles and Tracks
CW = Country Singles and Tracks
AR = Mainstream (Album) Rock Tracks
MR = Modern Rock Tracks

The peak weeks at #1 are shown in superscript next to the letter symbol (ex.: **AC**^{3})

TOP 40 HIT STREAKS

The peak positions of an artist's string of five or more consecutive Top 40 hits are shaded in a red box, so you can quickly spot their hot streaks. Reissues or early label affiliation releases, EP releases, B-side chart hits, recordings with other artists, a group member's solo releases, Christmas, Hot 100 Airplay or Sales chart hits and album cuts that did not hit the Top 40 do not break a string but can count within a string. The peak position of a non-Top 40 B-side chart hit (of a Top 40 A-side chart hit) is shaded in a string even if it appears at the end of a string. A string is broken if there is at least a five-year gap between hits (see underline symbol described in the "Explanation Of Symbols").

B-SIDES

A-side herein refers to the chart hit side, even though the record label may label it as the B-side. During the 1990s, record labels often released a "45" of an earlier hit (and usually a bigger hit) as the B-side of a current release.

B-sides of cassette and CD singles often contain one or more mixes of the A-side along with another title, which may also include one or more mixes. Mixes are shown in parentheses in small letters in the B-side column — ex.: (instrumental), (live), (remix), (album version). A diagonal symbol (/) is used to separate A-side mixes from the other titles on the cassette [ex.: (album version) / Gonna Love You Right]. Often an A-side and a B-side are on the same side of the cassette single. Occasionally, cassette singles repeat the same program on both sides of the cassette. Unless otherwise noted, singles issued on both cassette and vinyl have the same B-sides and label and number. If a cassette single has multiple B-side listings and a "45" is available with the same label and number, then the B-side of the "45", unless otherwise noted in title notes, is the last title listed in the B-side column.

If a single's A-side is recorded by a duo and a solo artist records its B-side, then the solo artist's name is shown in parentheses after the B-side, and vice versa.

If a B-side made *Billboard's* Bubbling Under the Hot 100 chart, its peak position is shown in parentheses to the right of the B-side. If a B-side made *Billboard's* Country Singles, R&B Singles, Adult Contemporary Singles, Modern Rock Tracks, Album (Mainstream) Rock Tracks or pre-1955 pop charts, an indication of the chart (C&W, R&B, AC, ROK, Pop) and its peak position are shown in parentheses to the right of the B-side [ex.: *Love Will Rain On You* (R&B #25)].

FOUR OR MORE HITS FROM AN ALBUM

If an artist charted four or more singles from an album, the album title is shown in the title notes. These title notes are generally applicable to singles that charted after 1963. From 1955 to 1963, singles greatly outsold albums. The arrival of The Beatles on the music scene in 1964 ushered in the rock album era. Soon album sales exploded and eventually outpaced the sales and releases of singles.

VERSIONS OF SAME SONG

Various versions of a song title charting within this era are listed together under one title in the Song Title Section. Cross-references under a version of the same song are not shown in title notes in the Artist Section.

RECORD PRICE GUIDE

This is the fifth edition of *Top Pop Singles* to feature a price guide and also includes the price of a chart hit's earlier release. The current price of a record's earlier release is noted below the title along with its label and number. Also noted are the current prices of valuable versions of that song by different artists; usually such versions are rare originals and never charted. Picture sleeves are not included in record price!

With new each edition of *Top Pop Singles* record prices continue to change. The current prices of many 1950s and 1960s records, valued at $10-$15 in our last edition, are now as high as $25 — and hundreds of chart hits are now priced at $50 and up.

The prices reflect the current estimated value of an original commercial copy in near-mint condition. You will note that the very collectable records such as the doo-wop, novelty, R&B groups and rockabilly singles reflect a much higher price than most. When evaluating the more common singles, the age of the record is a major determining factor. Generally, older records are scarcer and more difficult to find in good condition and thus command a higher value.

Often, the prices within this book for near-mint copies of high- and low-charting records of the same era are very close. Although it may be easier to find a copy of a million-selling hit of the past, it is difficult to find one in near-mint condition; because popular records are usually played more, they sustain more scratching and damage. Lower-charting and less popular records are, generally, handled significantly less, thereby remaining in great condition. For example, Bobby Darin's "Queen Of The Hop," a Top 10 hit in 1958, is more sought after than his 1960 hit, "Beachcomber." However, finding a near-mint copy of "Queen Of The Hop" would be much more difficult than finding the obscure "Beachcomber" in near-mint condition.

Estimates of a record's value differ, especially when considering geographics. A $10 record in this book may be worth $20 in New York City, but only $5 in the South. Also, variations of the original commercial release, such as promotional copies, mistakes or differentiations on the label, colored vinyl, etc. can vastly increase, or in rare cases, decrease the price of a record. The purpose of this guide is to give a ballpark figure to aid in determining the value of chart hits.

ARTIST SECTION

Lists, alphabetically by artist name, every song in chronological sequence that charted on *Billboard's* pop singles charts from January 1, 1955 through December 28, 2002.

KEY

Here's a quick reference guide to our symbols. Refer to *RESEARCHING BILLBOARD'S POP SINGLES CHARTS* and *USER'S GUIDE* for complete descriptions. (The artist and titles below are NOT real.)

1. Artist's ranking within the Top 600 artists
2. More hits in other Record Research books
3. Artist's peak year of popularity
4. Five-year or more gap between hits
5. Artist's top 3 or top 5 hits
6. Peak position on Juke Box (**J**), Best Sellers (**S**), Top 100 (**T**) and Disk Jockey (**A**) charts
7. Peaked in the following year (**+**)
8. #1 Country hit (or #1s on other Billboard charts)
9. Promotional picture sleeve (□)
10. Commercial picture sleeve (■)
11. One-page insert (inside sleeve) (⊙)
12. Cassette single (▮)
13. Maxi Cassette single (*)
14. Hot 100 Airplay Chart-only hit (**A**)
15. Hot 100 Sales Chart-only hit (**S**)
16. Christmas/Novelty song **[X-N]** (or other specialty recordings)
17. 2-sided hit separator (**/**)
18. Also issued on a vinyl "45" (**V**)
19. Enhanced CD single (**+**)
20. DVD single (◗)
21. Peak position on Hot 100 Airplay (**A**) and Hot 100 Sales (**S**) charts
22. Top 40 hit streak (shaded)
23. Gold single ●
24. Platinum single ▲
25. Top 10 hit in **red**
26. Artist's top hit (shaded)
27. Current value of near-mint commercial single
28. 12" single

A

DEBUT	PEAK	WKS	Gold	A-side (Chart Hit)...B-side	$	Sym	Label & Number
				A+ '96			
				Born Andre Levins on 8/29/82 in Hempstead, New York. Male rapper.			
8/3/96	**66**	14		1 **All I See** ...S:47 *(instrumental) / Alpha 2 Omega*	$3	▌	Kedar/Universal 56003
				Shakira Atily (female vocal)			
11/14/98	**63**	3		2 **Enjoy Yourself**...S:47 *(instrumental) / Up Top New York*	$3	▌	Kedar/Universal 56212
				Keanne Henson (female vocal); samples "A Fifth Of Beethoven" by **Walter Murphy**			
				AALIYAH ★264★ R&B/BUB/LP '94			
				Born Aaliyah Dana Haughton on 1/16/79 in Brooklyn, New York; raised in Detroit, Michigan. Died in a plane crash on 8/25/2001 (age 22). Female R&B singer/actress. Acted in the movies *Romeo Must Die* and *Queen Of The Damned*. Married **R. Kelly** on 7/31/94 (marriage later annulled). Also see **Timbaland & Magoo**'s "Up Jumps Da Boogie" and **Kris Kross**'s "Live And Die For Hip Hop."			
				1)Try Again 2)Miss You 3)Back & Forth			
4/30/94	**5**	24	●	1 **Back & Forth**...RB^3 S:3 / A:7 *(remix)*	$4	▌	Blackground 42174
9/3/94	**6**	20	●	2 **At Your Best (You Are Love)**...S:4 / A:11 *(2 remixes)*	$4	▌	Blackground 42239
				written by **The Isley Brothers** (from their 1976 album *Harvest For The World*)			
1/14/95	**75**	8		3 **Age Ain't Nothing But A Number**...S:59 *I'm Down*	$4	▌	Blackground 42273
				R. Kelly produced all of above, wrote #1 & 3, and rapped on #1			
12/16/95	**60^S**	2		4 **I Need You Tonight**...BUB:103 *Realms Of Junior M.A.F.I.A. (Part II)*	$4	▌	Undeas/Big Beat 98097
				JUNIOR M.A.F.I.A. Featuring Aaliyah			
				Lil' Kim, Trife and Klepto (rap); samples "I Wonder If I Take You Home" by **Lisa Lisa and Cult Jam**			
8/31/96	**11**	20		5 **If Your Girl Only Knew**...RB^2 S:7 / A:43 *(remix)*	$4	▌	Blackground 98067
12/28/96+	**25^A**	20		6 **One In A Million**...RB^{6A}			album cut
4/12/97	**59^A**	6		7 **4 Page Letter**...			album cut
				Timbaland and **Missy Elliott** (ad-libs, above 3); Elliott also co-wrote above 3			
10/4/97	**9**	20	●	8 **The One I Gave My Heart To**...S:6 / A:41 *Hot Like Fire* (R&B #31^A)	$4	▌	Blackground 98002
				above 4 from the album *One In A Million* on Blackground 92715; re-entered the Sales chart (#68) for 1 week on 9/15/01			
7/4/98	**4^A**	30		9 **Are You That Somebody?**...RB^{8A} HOT:21(8 wks)			album cut
				Timbaland (male rapper); from the movie *Dr. Dolittle* starring **Eddie Murphy** (soundtrack on Blackground 83113)			
1/29/00	**35**	20		10 **I Don't Wanna**...A:26			album cut
				from the movie *Next Friday* starring **Ice Cube**			
3/18/00	**❶^1**	32		11 **Try Again** A:❶^9 *(3 versions)*	$6	T^V	Blackground 38722
				above 2 from the movie *Romeo Must Die* starring Jet Li and Aaliyah; "45" B-side: "Come Back In One Piece" (with **DMX**)			
6/2/01	**59**	16		12 **We Need A Resolution**...A:50 *(3 versions)*	$6	T^V	Blackground 38781
				AALIYAH feat. Timbaland			
				"45" B-side: (instrumental)			
9/8/01	**14**	25		13 **Rock The Boat**...A:13		V	album cut
2/2/02	**25**	24		14 **More Than A Woman**...A:21		V	album cut
				"45" issued for above 2 on Blackground 38814			
8/24/02	**16**	20		15 **I Care 4 U**...A:15			album cut
				above 4 from the album *Aaliyah* on Blackground 10082; **Timbaland** (producer: #5-7, 9, 11, 12, 14 & 15)			
11/30/02+	**3**	30		16 **Miss You**...S:3 / A:3 *(remix w/***Jay-Z***)*	$4	★	Blackground 000384
				ABACO DREAM — see SLY & THE FAMILY STONE			
				ABBA ★132★ BUB/AC '77			
				Pop group formed in Stockholm, Sweden: Anni-Frid "**Frida**" (see #21 below) Lyngstad (born on 11/15/45) and **Agnetha Fältskog** (see #22 & 23 below) (born on 4/5/50; vocals), Bjorn Ulvaeus (born on 4/24/45; guitar) and Benny Andersson (born on 12/16/45; keyboards). All members born in Sweden, except Frida who was born in Norway. ABBA is an acronym of members' first initials. Benny and Bjorn recorded together in 1966. Bjorn and Agnetha were married from 1971-79. Benny and Frida were married from 1978-81. Disbanded in 1982. Bjorn and Benny co-wrote the musical project *Chess* with Tim Rice (featuring "One Night In Bangkok").			
				1)Dancing Queen 2)Take A Chance On Me 3)Waterloo 4)The Winner Takes It All 5)The Name Of The Game			
6/1/74	**6**	17		1 **Waterloo** *[ABBA (Bjorn, Benny, Anna & Frida)]*...*Watch Out*	$6		Atlantic 3035
9/14/74	**27**	10		2 **Honey, Honey**...*Dance (While The Music Still Goes On)*	$5		Atlantic 3209
8/9/75	**15**	17		3 **SOS**...*Man In The Middle*	$5		Atlantic 3265
				only chart hit where both title and artist are palindromes			
2/14/76	**15**	15		4 **I Do, I Do, I Do, I Do, I Do**...*Bang-A Boomerang*	$5		Atlantic 3310
5/22/76	**32**	9		5 **Mamma Mia**...AC^2 *Tropical Loveland*	$5		Atlantic 3315
				title of a stage musical based on the songs of Abba, which opened in London in 1999			
9/4/76	**13**	16		6 **Fernando**...AC^2 *Rock Me*	$5		Atlantic 3346
				also issued with "Tropical Loveland" as the B-side			
12/11/76+	**❶^1**	22	●	7 **Dancing Queen** *That's Me*	$5		Atlantic 3372
				ABBA:			
5/14/77	**14**	15		8 **Knowing Me, Knowing You**...*Happy Hawaii (Why Did It Have To Be Me)*	$5	■	Atlantic 3387
10/22/77	**56**	7		9 **Money, Money, Money**...*Crazy World*	$5	■	Atlantic 3434
12/24/77+	**12**	16		10 **The Name Of The Game**...*I Wonder (Departure)*	$5		Atlantic 3449
4/22/78	**3**	18	●	11 **Take A Chance On Me**...*I'm A Marionette*	$5	■	Atlantic 3457
5/19/79	**19**	14		12 **Does Your Mother Know**...*Kisses Of Fire*	$5	■	Atlantic 3574
9/22/79	**64**	5		13 **Angeleyes /**			
9/1/79	**80**	3		14 **Voulez-Vous**...	$5	■	Atlantic 3609
11/10/79+	**29**	12		15 **Chiquitita**...*Lovelight*	$5		Atlantic 3629
				Spanish version released on Atlantic 3630; above 4 from the album *Voulez-Vous*			

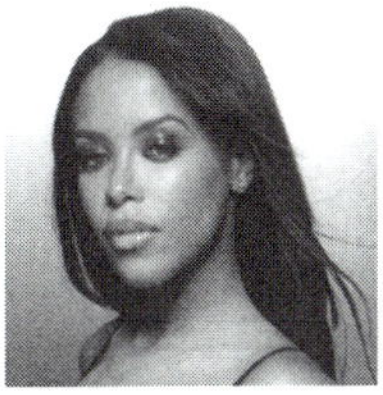

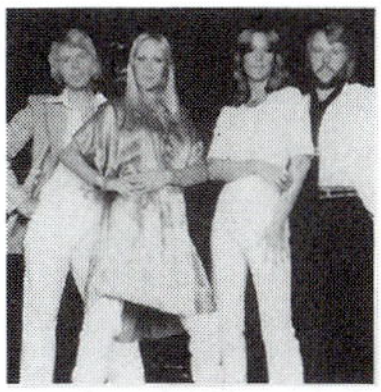

DEBUT	PEAK	WKS	Gold	A-side (Chart Hit)..............B-side	$	Sym	Label & Number

ABBA — Cont'd

DEBUT	PEAK	WKS	Gold	A-side (Chart Hit)..............B-side	$	Sym	Label & Number
11/22/80+	8	26		16 The Winner Takes It All ....AC[2] *Elaine*	$5		Atlantic 3776
4/4/81	45	11		17 Super Trouper.......... *The Piper*	$5	■	Atlantic 3806
6/27/81	90	6		18 On And On And On .... *Lay All Your Love On Me*	$4		Atlantic 3826
1/9/82	27	14		19 When All Is Said And Done .... *Should I Laugh Or Cry*	$4	■	Atlantic 3889
4/17/82	63	8		20 The Visitors .... *Head Over Heels*	$4	■	Atlantic 4031
				all of above written and produced by Benny & Bjorn			
11/6/82+	13	29		21 I Know There's Something Going On .... *Threnody*	$3		Atlantic 89984
				FRIDA			
				produced by **Phil Collins**			
8/27/83	29	15		22 Can't Shake Loose.......... *Man*	$3	■	Polydor 815230
				AGNETHA FÄLTSKOG			
				above 2 written by **Russ Ballard** (**Argent**)			
4/23/88	93	3		23 I Wasn't The One (Who Said Goodbye) .... *If You Need Somebody Tonight* (Fältskog)	$3	■	Atlantic 89145
				AGNETHA FÄLTSKOG AND PETER CETERA			

ABBEY TAVERN SINGERS, The — '66

Traditional seven-member Irish group that performed at The Abbey Tavern near Dublin, Ireland.

DEBUT	PEAK	WKS	Gold	A-side (Chart Hit)..............B-side	$	Sym	Label & Number
9/24/66	94	2		Off To Dublin In The Green .... *The Gallant Forty Twa'* [L]	$10		HBR 498

ABBOTT, Billy, And The Jewels — '63

Born William Vaughn in Camden, New Jersey (changed last name so as not to be confused with orchestra leader Billy Vaughn). First recorded on ABC-Paramount in 1962 with the R&B group The Corvells ("Take My Love"). The Jewels were actually Parkway Records vocal group **The Tymes**.

DEBUT	PEAK	WKS	Gold	A-side (Chart Hit)..............B-side	$	Sym	Label & Number
7/20/63	55	8		Groovy Baby.......... *Come On And Dance With Me*	$25		Parkway 874

ABBOTT, Gregory — R&B/AC/LP '87

Born on 4/2/54 in Harlem, New York. R&B singer/songwriter (wrote and produced both of his hits). Formerly married to **Freda Payne**.

DEBUT	PEAK	WKS	Gold	A-side (Chart Hit)..............B-side	$	Sym	Label & Number
10/18/86+	❶[1]	22	▲	1 Shake You Down ....RB[2] A:❶[1] / S:2 *Wait Until Tomorrow*	$3	■	Columbia 06191
2/21/87	56	11		2 I Got The Feelin' (It's Over) .... *Rhyme And Reason*	$3	■	Columbia 06632

ABC — LP '85

Electro-pop/dance group from Sheffield, Yorkshire, England: Martin Fry (vocals), Mark White (guitar), Stephen Singleton (sax), Mark Lickley (bass) and David Palmer (drums). At the end of 1983, the latter three left, leaving duo of Fry and White.

DEBUT	PEAK	WKS	Gold	A-side (Chart Hit)..............B-side	$	Sym	Label & Number
9/11/82+	18	25		1 The Look Of Love (Part One) .... *Theme From Mantrap*	$4	■	Mercury 76168
1/29/83	25	15		2 Poison Arrow.......... *Tears Are Not Enough*	$4	■	Mercury 810340
				above 2 produced by Trevor Horn (**Yes**, **The Buggles**)			
2/4/84	89	3		3 That Was Then But This Is Now.......... *Vertigo*	$4	■	Mercury 814631
8/24/85	9	22		4 Be Near Me ....S:10 / A:10 *A To Z*	$3	■	Mercury 880626
1/18/86	20	14		5 (How To Be A) Millionaire ....S:17 / A:26 *Tower Of London*	$3	■	Mercury 884382
5/17/86	91	4		6 Vanity Kills .... *Judy's Jewels*	$3		Mercury 884714
7/4/87	5	19		7 When Smokey Sings S:5 / A:6 *Chicago (Part 1)*	$3	■	Mercury 888604
				a tribute to **Smokey Robinson**; all of above co-written by Martin Fry and Mark White			

ABDUL, Paula ★149★ — BUB/LP '89

Born on 6/19/62 in San Fernando, California. Pop-dance singer/choreographer. Former cheerleader for the NBA's Los Angeles Lakers. Choreographed **Janet Jackson**'s *Control* videos and **Tracey Ullman**'s TV show. Started own Captive label. Married to actor Emilio Estevez from 1992-94. Starred in the 1997 TV movie *Touched By Evil*. One of the judges on TV's *American Idol*.

1)Rush, Rush 2)Straight Up 3)Opposites Attract

DEBUT	PEAK	WKS	Gold	A-side (Chart Hit)..............B-side	$	Sym	Label & Number
6/18/88	41	13		1 Knocked Out..........S:39 *(instrumental)*	$3	■	Virgin 99329
11/12/88	88	5		2 (It's Just) The Way That You Love Me .... *(dub mix)*	$3	■	Virgin 99282
				also see re-entry (#6 below)			
12/3/88+	❶[3]	25	▲	3 Straight Up..........A:❶[3] / S:❶[1] *Cold Hearted*	$3		Virgin 99256
				reissued with a new mix of "Straight Up" as the B-side in 1989			
3/11/89	❶[2]	22	●	4 Forever Your Girl ....A:❶[2] / S:2 *Next To You*	$3	■	Virgin 99230
6/24/89	❶[1]	21	●	5 Cold Hearted ....S:❶[1] / A:❶[1] *One Or The Other*	$3	■	Virgin 99196
				first released as the B-side of #3 above			
9/23/89	3	20		6 (It's Just) The Way That You Love Me..........A:2 / S:4 *(dub mix)* [R]	$3		Virgin 99282
				re-entry of #2 above; reissue is on an orange label (without a picture sleeve - original label color is black)			
12/16/89+	❶[3]	23	●	7 Opposites Attract ....A:❶[4] / S:❶[3] *One Or The Other*	$4	■	Virgin 99158
				PAULA ABDUL (with The Wild Pair) (Marv Gunn & Bruce Christian)			
				Derrick Delite (of The Soul Purpose; rap); all of above from the album *Forever Your Girl*			
5/11/91	❶[5]	19	●	8 Rush, Rush AC[5] A:❶[8] / S:3 *(dub mix)*	$3	▮V	Virgin 98828
7/20/91	❶[1]	16		9 The Promise Of A New Day..........A:5 / S:25 *(12" mix)*	$3	▮V	Captive/Virgin 98752
10/19/91	6	20		10 Blowing Kisses In The Wind ....A:5 / S:15 *Spellbound*	$3	▮V	Captive/Virgin 98683
1/18/92	16	14		11 Vibeology..........A:16 / S:22 *(dub mix)*	$3	▮V	Captive/Virgin 98737
4/4/92	19	13		12 Will You Marry Me? ....A:13 / S:61 *Goodnight, My Love*	$3	▮V	Captive/Virgin 98584
				Sandra St. Victor (backing vocals: above 5, except #10); **Stevie Wonder** (harmonica); above 5 from the album *Spellbound*			
6/17/95	28	13		13 My Love Is For Real ....S:24 / A:44 *(2 versions) / Didn't I Say I Love You*	$3	▮V	Captive/Virgin 38493 ■
				Ofra Haza (backing vocal)			
9/9/95	58	9		14 Crazy Cool ....A:68 / S:73 *(2 remixes) / The Choice Is Yours*	$3	▮V	Captive/Virgin 38510
				"45": Virgin 18850			

AB LOGIC — '92

Techno-rave studio group assembled by Belgian producers Jacko Bultinck and Peter Gillis, featuring singer Marianne and rapper K-Swing.

DEBUT	PEAK	WKS	Gold	A-side (Chart Hit)..............B-side	$	Sym	Label & Number
8/1/92	60	20		1 The Hitman ....A:41 / S:68 *(instrumental mix)*	$4	▮	Interscope 98506
12/26/92+	83	11		2 Get Up (Move Boy Move)..........A:59 *(album version)*	$4	▮	Interscope 98453

DEBUT	PEAK	WKS	Gold	A-side (Chart Hit)...B-side	$	Sym	Label & Number
				ABOVE THE LAW R&B/BUB/LP **'02**			
				Rap trio from Pamona, California: Don Hutchinson, Kevin Gulley and Anthony Stewart. Hutchinson is the nephew of **Willie Hutch**.			
8/10/02	6^{S}	17		**Sex, Money, & Music** ...*(3 versions) / Ghetto Platinum*	$8	★*	WestWorld 70837
				ABRAMS, Miss AC **'70**			
				Born Rita Abrams on 8/30/43 in Cleveland, Ohio. Taught grade school in Mill Valley, California.			
8/1/70	90	3		**Mill Valley** ...*The Happiest Day Of My Life*	$6	■	Reprise 0928
				MISS ABRAMS AND THE STRAWBERRY POINT SCHOOL THIRD GRADE CLASS			
				A.B. SKHY **'69**			
				Rock group from San Francisco, California: Dennis Geyer (vocals, guitar), Howard Wales (keyboards), Jim Marcotte (bass) and Terry Andersen (drums).			
12/6/69	100	1		**Camel Back** ...*Just What I Need* [I]	$8	■	MGM 14086
				ABSOLUTE R&B/BUB **'00**			
				Male R&B vocal duo: Corey (from Washington DC) and Yaroo (from Atlanta, Georgia).			
9/23/00	26^{S}	17		**Is It Really Like That?** ...*(2 album snippets) / (interview)*	$6	★+	Noontime/Atlantic 84942
				ABSTRAC' **'90**			
				Female dance trio from the Bronx, New York: Mary, Marsha and Topaz.			
12/23/89+	89	6		**Right And Hype** ...*(acappella version)*	$4	■	Reprise 22872
				ACCENTS, The **'59**			
				R&B vocal group from Philadelphia, Pennsylvania: Robert Draper (lead), Robert Armstrong, Billy Hood, James Jackson, Arvid Garrett and Israel Goudeau. Garrett had been in the R&B vocal group Three Sharps & A Flat.			
12/22/58+	51	12		**Wiggle, Wiggle** ...*Dreamin' And Schemin'*	$25		Brunswick 55100
				melody is simlar to **Bobby Day**'s "Little Bitty Pretty One"			
				AC/DC ROK/BUB/LP **'80**			
				Hard-rock group from Sydney, Australia: brothers Angus and Malcolm Young (guitars), Ron Belford "Bon" Scott (vocals), Mark Evans (bass) and Phil Rudd (drums). Cliff Williams replaced Evans in 1977. Bon Scott died of alcohol abuse on 2/19/80 (age 33) and was replaced by Brian Johnson. Simon Wright replaced Rudd in 1985. Wright joined Dio in 1989, replaced by Chris Slade of **The Firm**. Rudd returned in 1995. Angus and Malcolm are the younger brothers of George Young of **The Easybeats** and **Flash & The Pan**. Group inducted into the Rock and Roll Hall of Fame in 2003.			
10/13/79	47	10		1 **Highway To Hell** ...*Night Prowler*	$6		Atlantic 3617
9/6/80	35	16		2 **You Shook Me All Night Long** ...*Have A Drink On Me*	$5		Atlantic 3761
12/20/80+	37	15		3 **Back In Black** ...*What Do You Do For Money Honey*	$5		Atlantic 3787
1/16/82	44	9		4 **Let's Get It Up** ...*Snowballed*	$5	■	Atlantic 3894
				all of above produced by Robert John "Mutt" Lange			
10/1/83	84	5		5 **Guns For Hire** ...*Landslide*	$5	■	Atlantic 89774
12/8/90+	23	16		6 **Moneytalks** S:16 / A:30 *Borrowed Time*	$5	▮V	Atco 98881
7/3/93	65	11		7 **Big Gun** ...AR[2] S:39 *Back In Black (live)*	$5	▮	Atco 98406
				from the movie *Last Action Hero* starring Arnold Schwarzenegger; Angus and Malcolm Young co-wrote all of their hits			
				ACE LP **'75**			
				Pub-rock group from Sheffield, Yorkshire, England: **Paul Carrack** (vocals), Phil Harris and Alan King (guitars), Terry Comer (bass) and Fran Byrne (drums). Disbanded in 1977. Carrack joined **Squeeze** in 1981, then **Mike + The Mechanics** in 1985.			
3/8/75	3	16		1 **How Long** ...*Sniffin' About*	$5		Anchor 21000
7/26/75	71	4		2 **Rock & Roll Runaway** ...*Know How It Feels*	$5		Anchor 21002
				ACE, Johnny R&B **'55**			
				Born John Alexander on 6/9/29 in Memphis, Tennessee. Shot himself playing Russian Roulette backstage at the City Auditorium in Houston, Texas, on 12/24/54; died the following day (age 25). R&B singer/pianist/organist/songwriter. Worked with the **B.B. King** band, then formed The Beale Streeters with **Bobby Bland** and Earl Forrest before going solo.			
2/19/55	17	9		**Pledging My Love** ...RB[10] S:17 / J:17 / A:19 *No Money*	$50		Duke 136
				Johnny Board (orch.); also issued with "Anymore" as the B-side			
	★383★			**ACE OF BASE** BUB/LP **'94**			
				Pop-dance group from Gothenburg, Sweden: vocalists/sisters Jenny (born on 5/19/72) and Linn (born on 10/31/70) Berggren with keyboardists Jonas "Joker" Berggren (born on 3/25/67; their brother) and Ulf "Buddha" Ekberg (born on 12/6/70). Also see **Yaki-Da**'s "I Saw You Dancing."			
9/18/93	2^{3}	36	▲	1 **All That She Wants** ...S:❶[3] / A:2 *(Banghra version)*	$3	▮V	Arista 12614
1/1/94	❶^{6}	41	▲	2 **The Sign** A:❶[13] / S:2 *Young And Proud*	$3	▮	Arista 12653
5/7/94	4	31	●	3 **Don't Turn Around** ...A:❷[2] / S:6 *Dancer In A Daydream*	$3	▮V	Arista 12691
				co-written by **Albert Hammond**; #55 R&B hit for **Luther Ingram** in 1987; #45 R&B hit for Aswad in 1988; #19 Adult Contemporary hit for **Neil Diamond** in 1992; "45" issued for #1 & 3 on Arista 12705			
10/22/94	20	20		4 **Living In Danger** ...A:16 / S:42 *(remix)*	$3	▮	Arista 12754
				all of above from the album *The Sign*			
11/11/95	15	20		5 **Beautiful Life** ...S:11 / A:21 *(radio edit)*	$3	▮V	Arista 12889
2/24/96	30	17		6 **Lucky Love** ...A:35 / S:38 *(**Frankie Knuckles** edit)*	$3	▮V	Arista 12979
				"45": Arista 12981; above 3: #1 Dance Club Play hits			
7/18/98	10	20	●	7 **Cruel Summer** ...S:10 / A:40 *(remix)*	$3	▮	Arista 13505
10/31/98	76	5		8 **Whenever You're Near Me** ...S:57 *He Decides*	$3	▮	Arista 13553
				all of above (except #3 & 7) written by keyboardist Jonas Berggren			
				ACE SPECTRUM LP **'74**			
				R&B vocal group from Harlem, New York: Ed Zant, Aubrey Johnson, Elliot Isaac and Rudy Gay.			
9/28/74	57	6		**Don't Send Nobody Else** ...*Don't Let Me Be Lonely Tonight*	$6		Atlantic 3012
				written by **Ashford & Simpson**			
				ACKLIN, Barbara R&B/BUB/LP **'68**			
				Born on 2/28/42 in Chicago, Illinois. Died of pneumonia on 11/27/98 (age 56). R&B singer/songwriter. Cousin to Monk Higgins, who produced her first sessions for Special Agent in 1966 (as Barbara Allen). Backup vocalist at Chess Records in the mid-1960s. Formerly married to Eugene Record of **The Chi-Lites**.			
7/13/68	15	12		1 **Love Makes A Woman** ...*Come And See Me Baby*	$12		Brunswick 55379
10/19/68	57	8		2 **From The Teacher To The Preacher** ...*Anywhere But Nowhere*	$12		Brunswick 55387
				GENE CHANDLER And BARBARA ACKLIN			

DEBUT	PEAK	WKS	Gold	A-side (Chart Hit)	B-side	$	Sym	Label & Number
				ACKLIN, Barbara — Cont'd				
11/16/68+	67	9		3 **Just Ain't No Love**	*Please Sunrise, Please*	$12	■	Brunswick 55388
2/22/69	79	3		4 **Am I The Same Girl**	*Be By My Side*	$12		Brunswick 55399
				instrumental track is the same one recorded by **Young-Holt Unlimited** for their 1968 hit "Soulful Strut"				

ADAM & THE ANTS — see ANT, Adam

ADAMS, Bryan ★58★ ROK/AC/BUB/LP '85

Born on 11/5/59 in Kingston, Ontario, Canada. Rock singer/songwriter/guitarist. Lead singer of **Sweeney Todd** in 1976. Teamed with Jim Vallance in 1977 in songwriting partnership. Cameo appearance in the movie *Pink Cadillac*. Also see **Glass Tiger**'s "Don't Forget Me (When I'm Gone)."

1)(Everything I Do) I Do It For You 2)Have You Ever Really Loved A Woman? 3)All For Love 4)Heaven 5)Can't Stop This Thing We Started

DEBUT	PEAK	WKS	Gold	A-side (Chart Hit)	B-side	$	Sym	Label & Number
3/13/82	84	2		1 **Lonely Nights**	*Don't Look Now*	$5		A&M 2359
3/12/83	10	19		2 **Straight From The Heart**	*One Good Reason*	$5	■	A&M 2536
6/11/83	15	14		3 **Cuts Like A Knife**	*Lonely Nights*	$5	■	A&M 2553
9/3/83	24	12		4 **This Time**	*Fits Ya Good* (ROK #15)	$5	■	A&M 2574
11/3/84+	6	19		5 **Run To You** AR[4] A:6 / S:7	*I'm Ready* (ROK #26)	$5	■	A&M 2686
2/2/85	11	17		6 **Somebody** AR[2] A:10 / S:14	*Long Gone*	$5	■	A&M 2701
4/20/85	❶[2]	19		7 **Heaven** S:❶[2] / A:2	*Heaven "Live"*	$5	■	A&M 2729
6/29/85	5	17		8 **Summer Of '69** A:4 / S:5	*The Best Was Yet To Come*	$5	■	A&M 2739
9/14/85	13	15		9 **One Night Love Affair** A:10 / S:15	*Lonely Nights*	$5	■	A&M 2770
11/23/85+	15	14		10 **It's Only Love** A:14 / S:16	*The Only One* (Adams)	$5	■	A&M 2791
				BRYAN ADAMS/TINA TURNER				
				above 6 from the album *Reckless*				
12/21/85	4[X]	2		11 **Christmas Time**	*Reggae Christmas* [X]	$6	■	A&M 8651
				issued on green vinyl; a different picture sleeve was issued in 1986				
3/28/87	6	16		12 **Heat Of The Night** S:4 / A:6	*Another Day* (ROK #33)	$4	■	A&M 2921
				the first "45" also issued as a cassette single				
6/13/87	26	13		13 **Hearts On Fire** S:23 / A:26	*The Best Was Yet To Come*	$4	■	A&M 2948
8/22/87	32	12		14 **Victim Of Love** S:29 / A:30	*Into The Fire* (ROK #6)	$4	■	A&M 2964
				all of above produced by Bryan Adams and Bob Clearmountain				
6/29/91	❶[7]	22	▲[3]	15 **(Everything I Do) I Do It For You** AC[8] S:❶[17] / A:❶[8]	*(album version)*	$3	▮V	A&M 1567
				from the movie *Robin Hood: Prince Of Thieves* starring Kevin Costner				
9/14/91	2[1]	20	●	16 **Can't Stop This Thing We Started** S:11 / A:14	*(Everything I Do) I Do It For You*	$3	▮V	A&M 1576
12/21/91+	31	15		17 **There Will Never Be Another Tonight** A:48 / S:72	*Heat Of The Night (live)*	$3	▮	A&M 1588
3/14/92	13	20		18 **Thought I'd Died And Gone To Heaven** A:14 / S:24	*Summer Of '69 (live)*	$3	▮	A&M 1592
8/1/92	11	20		19 **Do I Have To Say The Words?** A:10 / S:29	*Cuts Like A Knife (live)*	$3	▮	A&M 1611
				above 5 from the album *Waking Up The Neighbours*				
10/23/93	7	28		20 **Please Forgive Me** A:3 / S:8	*Can't Stop This Thing We Started (live)*	$3	▮V	A&M 0422
				"45" B-side: "Cuts Like A Knife"				
11/27/93+	❶[3]	22	▲	21 **All For Love** S:❶[5] / A:3	*(instrumental)*	$3	▮V	A&M 0476
				BRYAN ADAMS ROD STEWART STING				
				from the movie *The Three Musketeers* starring Kiefer Sutherland and Charlie Sheen				
4/15/95	❶[5]	24		22 **Have You Ever Really Loved A Woman?** AC[5] S:❶[1] / A:3	*Low Life*	$3	▮V	A&M 1028
				Paco de Lucia (acoustic guitar); from the movie *Don Juan DeMarco* starring Johnny Depp				
11/25/95	73	4		23 **Rock Steady**	*Come To Me* (Raitt) [L]	$3	▮	Capitol 58500
				BONNIE RAITT BRYAN ADAMS				
5/25/96	52	12		24 **The Only Thing That Looks Good On Me Is You** S:58 / A:66	*Hey Elvis*	$4	▮V	A&M 1578 ■
8/31/96	24	23		25 **Let's Make A Night To Remember** A:26 / S:28	*Star*	$3	▮V	A&M 1862
11/23/96	8	20	●	26 **I Finally Found Someone** S:7 / A:20	*Evergreen (Spanish version* - Streisand)	$3	▮	Columbia 78480
				BARBRA STREISAND and BRYAN ADAMS				
				from the movie *The Mirror Has Two Faces* starring Streisand				
4/12/97	59[A]	10		27 **I'll Always Be Right There**				album cut
				from the album *18 Til I Die* on A&M 0551				
12/27/97+	42[A]	9		28 **Back To You**	[L]			album cut
				from the album *MTV Unplugged* on A&M 0831; Adams wrote or co-wrote all of his hits				

ADAMS, Johnny R&B/BUB '69

Born Lathan John Adams on 1/5/32 in New Orleans, Louisiana. Died of cancer on 9/14/98 (age 66). R&B singer nicknamed "The Tan Canary." First recorded on the Ric label in 1959 with "I Won't Cry."

DEBUT	PEAK	WKS	Gold	A-side (Chart Hit)	B-side	$	Sym	Label & Number
12/14/68	82	3		1 **Release Me**	*You Make A New Man Out Of Me*	$15		SSS Int'l. 750
				originally released on the Watch label in 1968				
6/28/69	28	8		2 **Reconsider Me**	*If I Could See You One More Time*	$15		SSS Int'l. 770
10/11/69	89	2		3 **I Can't Be All Bad**	*In A Moment Of Weakness*	$15		SSS Int'l. 780

ADAMS, Oleta R&B/AC/LP '91

Born on 5/4/62 in Seattle, Washington. Female R&B singer/pianist. Backing singer on **Tears For Fears**' *Seeds Of Love* album and tour.

DEBUT	PEAK	WKS	Gold	A-side (Chart Hit)	B-side	$	Sym	Label & Number
12/15/90+	5	23		**Get Here** S:2 / A:13	*(3 album snippets) / Watch What Happens*	$3	▮V	Fontana 878476
				"45" issued on Mercury 878476; written and recorded by **Brenda Russell** in 1988				

ADAMS, Yolanda R&B/LP '00

Born on 10/21/63 in Houston, Texas. Black female gospel singer.

DEBUT	PEAK	WKS	Gold	A-side (Chart Hit)	B-side	$	Sym	Label & Number
8/26/00	57	20		**Open My Heart** A:53	*(4 versions)*	$6	T	Elektra 67118

DEBUT	PEAK	WKS	Gold		A-side (Chart Hit)	B-side	$	Sym	Label & Number

ADDERLEY, "Cannonball"   LP '67

Born Julian Edwin Adderley on 9/15/28 in Tampa, Florida. Died of a stroke on 8/8/75 (age 46). Nickname derived from "cannibal," in tribute to his love of eating. Alto saxophonist/leader of jazz combo featuring brother Nat Adderley (cornet) and Joe Zawinul (piano; left in 1971 to form Weather Report; replaced by **George Duke**).

DEBUT	PEAK	WKS	Gold		A-side (Chart Hit)	B-side	$	Sym	Label & Number
4/10/61	41	6		1	**African Waltz** *[CANNONBALL ADDERLEY Orchestra]*	*Kelly Blue* [I]	$12		Riverside 45457
2/16/63	66	7		2	**The Jive Samba** *[CANNONBALL ADDERLEY Sextet]*	*Lillie* [I-L]	$12		Riverside 4541
1/7/67	11	11		3	**Mercy, Mercy, Mercy**	*Games* [I-L]	$8		Capitol 5798
4/8/67	73	5		4	**Why? (Am I Treated So Bad)**	*I'm On My Way* [I-L]	$8		Capitol 5877
1/17/70	86	3		5	**Country Preacher** *[CANNONBALL ADDERLEY QUINTET]*	*Hummin'* [I]	$7		Capitol 2698

ADDRISI BROTHERS, The   BUB/AC/LP '77

Pop singing/songwriting duo from Winthrop, Massachusetts. Dick was born on 7/4/41. Don was born on 12/14/38; died on 11/13/84 (age 45). Wrote **The Association**'s "Never My Love."

DEBUT	PEAK	WKS	Gold		A-side (Chart Hit)	B-side	$	Sym	Label & Number
6/1/59	62	6		1	**Cherrystone**	*Lilies Grow High*	$30		Del-Fi 4116
1/22/72	25	12		2	**We've Got To Get It On Again**	*You Make It All Worthwhile*	$7		Columbia 45521
4/9/77	20	15		3	**Slow Dancin' Don't Turn Me On**	*(long version)*	$5		Buddah 566
9/17/77	74	4		4	**Does She Do It Like She Dances**	*Baby, Love Is A Two Way Street*	$5		Buddah 579
12/10/77	80	4		5	**Never My Love**	*Emergency*	$5		Buddah 587
8/11/79	45	8		6	**Ghost Dancer**	*Part II*	$5	□	Scotti Brothers 500
					Dick and Don Addrisi wrote all of their hits (except #4)				

ADKINS, Trace   C&W/BUB/LP '01

Born on 1/13/62 in Springhill, Louisiana. Male country singer/songwriter/guitarist.

DEBUT	PEAK	WKS	Gold		A-side (Chart Hit)	B-side	$	Sym	Label & Number
11/23/96+	78	9		1	**Every Light In The House** S:53	*If I Fall (You're Goin' With Me)*	$4	▮V	Capitol 58574
					"45": Capitol 19224				
10/18/97	70	16		2	**The Rest Of Mine** S:49	*Dreamin' Out Loud*	$4	▮V	Capitol 58680
					"45": Capitol 19698; B-side: "Wayfaring Stranger"				
4/29/00	65	11		3	**More** A:57			V	album cut
					from the album *More..* on Capitol 96618; "45": Capitol 38701; B-side: "The Night He Can't Remember"				
10/20/01	44	20		4	**I'm Tryin'** A:42			V	album cut
					"45": Capitol 77667; B-side: "Chrome"				
7/20/02	80	4		5	**Help Me Understand** A:75				album cut
					above 2 from the album *Chrome* on Capitol 30618				

AD LIBS, The   R&B '65

Black doo-wop group from Newark, New Jersey: Mary Ann Thomas (lead), Hugh Harris, Danny Austin, Norman Donegan and Dave Watt. First recorded for T-Kay in 1962. Originally called the Creators.

DEBUT	PEAK	WKS	Gold		A-side (Chart Hit)	B-side	$	Sym	Label & Number
1/16/65	8	10		1	**The Boy From New York City**	*Kicked Around*	$20		Blue Cat 102
5/1/65	100	1		2	**He Ain't No Angel**	*Ask Anybody*	$20		Blue Cat 114

ADVENTURES, The   LP '88

Pop group from Belfast, Ireland: Terry Sharpe (vocals), husband-and-wife Patrick (guitar) and Eileen (vocals) Gribben, Gerard "Spud" Murphy (guitar), Tony Ayre (bass) and Paul Crowder (drums).

DEBUT	PEAK	WKS	Gold		A-side (Chart Hit)	B-side	$	Sym	Label & Number
4/30/88	95	3			**Broken Land**	*Don't Stand On Me*	$3	■	Elektra 69414

ADVENTURES OF STEVIE V   '90

Black dance group from Bedfordshire, England. Assembled by producer Stevie Vincent. Includes singer Melodie Washington and multi-instrumentalist Mick Walsh.

DEBUT	PEAK	WKS	Gold		A-side (Chart Hit)	B-side	$	Sym	Label & Number
7/21/90	25	19		1	**Dirty Cash (Money Talks)** S:13 / A:31	*(remix)*	$4	▮	Mercury 875802
1/19/91	94	6		2	**Jealousy**	*(3 album snippets) / (w/o rap)*	$4	▮V	Mercury 878662

AEROSMITH ★72★   ROK/BUB/LP '90

Hard-rock group formed in Boston, Massachusetts: Steven Tyler (vocals; born Steven Tallarico on 3/26/48), Joe Perry (guitar; born on 9/10/50), Brad Whitford (guitar; born on 2/23/52), Tom Hamilton (bass; born on 12/31/51) and Joey Kramer (drums; born on 6/21/50). Perry left for own Joe Perry Project in 1979; replaced by Jimmy Crespo. Whitford left in 1981; replaced by Rick Dufay. Original band reunited in April 1984. Tyler's daughter is actress/model Liv Tyler. Group inducted into the Rock and Roll Hall of Fame in 2001.

1)I Don't Want To Miss A Thing 2)Angel 3)Janie's Got A Gun 4)Love In An Elevator 5)Dream On

DEBUT	PEAK	WKS	Gold		A-side (Chart Hit)	B-side	$	Sym	Label & Number
10/20/73	59	9		1	**Dream On**	*Somebody*	$7		Columbia 45894
					also see re-entry (#3 below)				
6/14/75	36	8		2	**Sweet Emotion**	*Uncle Salty*	$6		Columbia 10155
					made the Album Rock charts in 1991 (#36)				
1/10/76	6	20		3	**Dream On**	*Somebody* [R]	$6		Columbia 10278
					#3 is a longer version (4:28) than #1 above (3:25)				
6/12/76	21	15		4	**Last Child**	*Combination*	$6		Columbia 10359
9/25/76	71	4		5	**Home Tonight**	*Pandora's Box*	$6		Columbia 10407
11/20/76+	10	17		6	**Walk This Way**	*Uncle Salty*	$6		Columbia 10449
					first issued in 1975 on Columbia 10206 (with "Round And Round" as the B-side); revived in 1986 as a "rap" hit by **Run-D.M.C.** (with Tyler & Perry)				
4/9/77	38	8		7	**Back In The Saddle**	*Nobody's Fault*	$6		Columbia 10516
10/22/77	42	11		8	**Draw The Line**	*Bright, Light, Fright*	$5		Columbia 10637
3/11/78	70	5		9	**Kings And Queens**	*Critical Mass*	$5		Columbia 10699
8/5/78	23	12		10	**Come Together**	*Kings And Queens*	$5		Columbia 10802
					from the movie *Sgt. Pepper's Lonely Hearts Club Band* starring **Peter Frampton** and the **Bee Gees**				
1/20/79	77	3		11	**Chip Away The Stone**	*S.O.S./Chip Away The Stone (live)*	$5		Columbia 10880
					all of above (except #1 & 3) produced by Jack Douglas				
1/12/80	67	6		12	**Remember (Walking In The Sand)**	*Bone To Bone (Coney Island White Fish Boy)*	$5		Columbia 11181
10/3/87	14	20		13	**Dude (Looks Like A Lady)** S:10 / A:15	*Simoriah*	$3	■	Geffen 28240
1/30/88	3	25		14	**Angel** S:2 / A:4	*Girl Keeps Coming Apart*	$3	■	Geffen 28249
6/4/88	17	17		15	**Rag Doll** S:15 / A:20	*St. John*	$3	■	Geffen 27915
9/2/89	5	16	●	16	**Love In An Elevator** AR[2] S:2 / A:7	*Young Lust*	$3	■	Geffen 22845
11/25/89+	4	18		17	**Janie's Got A Gun** S:3 / A:7	*Voodoo Medicine Man*	$4	▮	Geffen 22727

DEBUT	PEAK	WKS	Gold	A-side (Chart Hit)..................B-side	$	Sym	Label & Number
				AEROSMITH — Cont'd			
3/17/90	9	17		18 **What It Takes**..........AR[1] S:7 / A:10 *Monkey On My Back* (ROK #17)	$4	▮V	Geffen 19944
6/23/90	22	15		19 **The Other Side**..........AR[2] A:19 / S:24 *My Girl*	$4	▮V	Geffen 19927
				above 4 from the album *Pump*			
4/10/93	18	20		20 **Livin' On The Edge**..........AR[9] S:16 / A:38 *Don't Stop*	$4	▮V	Geffen 19149
7/31/93	12	26	●	21 **Cryin'**..........AR[6] S:9 / A:23 *Walk On Down*	$4	▮V	Geffen 19256
12/4/93+	24	21		22 **Amazing**..........S:24 / A:26 *Fever* (ROK #5)	$4	▮V	Geffen 19264
				Don Henley (backing vocal); includes a brief snippet of the actual 1945 recording of "Who Threw The Whiskey In The Well" by Lucky Millinder & His Orchestra (#1 R&B hit in 1945)			
5/21/94	17	23		23 **Crazy**..........A:18 / S:21 *Gotta Love It*	$4	▮V	Geffen 19267
				above 4 from the album *Get A Grip*; #13-23: produced by Bruce Fairbairn (died on 5/17/99)			
11/12/94	48	14		24 **Blind Man**..........A:56 / S:70 *Head First*	$4	▮V	Geffen 19377
3/1/97	35	15	●	25 **Falling In Love (Is Hard On The Knees)**..........AR[5] S:25 *Fall Together*	$3	▮V	Columbia 78499 ■
8/23/97	51	11		26 **Hole In My Soul**..........S:29 *Falling Off*	$3	▮V	Columbia 78569 ■
				Desmond Child co-wrote #13, 14, 18, 23 & 26			
2/28/98	27	13		27 **Pink**..........AR[4] S:21 / A:65 *Taste Of India* (ROK #3)	$3	▮	Columbia 78830
9/5/98	❶[4]	20	●	28 **I Don't Want To Miss A Thing**..........S:❶[2] / A:❶[1] *Taste Of India / Animal Crackers*	$4	★V	Columbia 78952 ■
				from the movie *Armageddon* starring **Bruce Willis**; re-entered Sales chart (see #30 below)			
1/27/01	7	20		29 **Jaded**..........AR[5] S:8 / A:11 *(2 mixes) / Under My Skin / Angel's Eye* (ROK #4)	$8	★*V	Columbia 79555
				"45": Columbia 79572			
3/23/02	10[S]	37		30 **I Don't Want To Miss A Thing**..........*Animal Crackers / Taste Of India* [R]	$4	★	Columbia 79691
				reissue of #28 above on Columbia's "Platinum Hits" series; Tyler wrote or co-wrote all of their hits (except #10-12, 28 & 30)			
				AFRIQUE LP '73			
				R&B-jazz studio group formed in Los Angeles, California: David T. Walker and Arthur Wright (guitars), Charles Kynard (organ), Joe Kelso, Paul Jeffery and Steve Kravitz (horns), King Errisson, **Paul Humphrey**, Wallace Snow, Charles Taggart and Chino Valdes (percussion), Chuck Rainey (bass) and Ray Pound (drums).			
6/9/73	47	9		**Soul Makossa**..........*Hot Mud* [F-I]	$6		Mainstream 5542
				AFROMAN LP '01			
				Born Joseph Foreman in Los Angeles, California; later based in Hattiesburg, Mississippi. Novelty rapper/songwriter.			
8/18/01	13	10		**Because I Got High**..........A:11 / S:56 *(2 versions) / She Won't Let Me F**k / Tall Cans* [N]	$6	TV	Universal 015310
				"45": Universal 015282; from the movie *Jay And Silent Bob Strike Back* starring Jason Mewes			
				AFTERNOON DELIGHTS, The '81			
				Female studio vocal group from Boston, Massachusetts: Rebecca Hall, Suzanne Boucher, Janet Powell and Robalee Barnes. Group named after **Starland Vocal Band**'s #1 hit from 1976.			
7/25/81	33	16		**General Hospi-Tale**..........*(instrumental)* [N]	$4		MCA 51148
				parody of the TV soap *General Hospital*			
	★509★			**AFTER 7** R&B/AC/LP '90			
				R&B vocal trio from Indianapolis, Indiana: Keith Mitchell with brothers Melvin and **Kevon Edmonds** (see #11 below). Keith is the cousin of Mark "L.A. Reid" Rooney. Kevon and Melvin are the brothers of **Babyface**. Keith left in 1997. Also see **Babyface**'s "And Our Feelings."			
				1)Can't Stop 2)Ready Or Not 3)Heat Of The Moment			
10/21/89	74	12		1 **Heat Of The Moment**..........*(instrumental)*	$3	■	Virgin 99204
				also see re-entry (#4 below)			
3/31/90	7	21	●	2 **Ready Or Not**..........RB[2] S:5 / A:9 *(instrumental)*	$3	▮V	Virgin 98995
7/28/90	6	25	●	3 **Can't Stop**..........RB[1] A:6 / S:10 *(instrumental)*	$3	▮V	Virgin 98961
11/24/90+	19	18		4 **Heat Of The Moment**..........A:18 / S:20 *(instrumental)* [R]	$3	▮	Virgin 99204
				#4 is a longer version (6:10) than #1 above (4:20); no "45" issued for longer version; all of above from the album *After 7*			
5/25/91	24	15		5 **Nights Like This**..........S:36 / A:36 *Baby Stop Running Around*	$3	▮	Virgin 98798
				from the movie *The Five Heartbeats* starring Robert Townsend			
8/15/92	45	13		6 **Kickin' It**..........A:36 / S:46 *Nights Like This*	$3	▮	Virgin 12594
11/7/92	55	18		7 **Baby I'm For Real/Natural High**..........S:36 / A:51 *He Said, She Said*	$3	▮V	Virgin 12623
				includes a 20-second segment of **Bloodstone**'s "Natural High"; **Marvin Gaye** co-wrote "Baby I'm For Real"			
4/17/93	67[S]	4		8 **Can He Love U Like This**..........BUB:103 *One Night / My Only Woman* (R&B #36)	$3	▮V	Virgin 12643
				"45" issued for above 2 on Virgin 56954			
4/16/94	87	6		9 **Gonna Love You Right**..........S:48 *(album version)*	$4	▮V	Fox/Beacon 10006
				from the movie *Sugar Hill* starring Wesley Snipes			
7/8/95	31	22		10 **'Til You Do Me Right**..........S:20 / A:59 *(album version) / Gonna Love You Right*	$3	▮V	Virgin 38494
				"45" issued for above 2 on Virgin 18587			
11/6/99	10	20	●	11 **24/7**..........S:4 / A:45 *I Want You More*	$4	★	RCA 65924
				KEVON EDMONDS			
				Shanice, Jason Edwards and IveyGirl (backing vocals)			
				AFTERSHOCK '91			
				Hip-hop duo from Staten Island, New York: rapper Guy Charles Routte and singer Jose Rivera.			
3/30/91	52	16		**Going Through The Motions**..........A:63 *(Spanish edit)*	$5	▮	Virgin 98868
				AFTER THE FIRE LP '83			
				Rock group from England: Andy Piercy (vocals, bass), John Russell (guitar), Peter Banks (keyboards/guitar; **Yes**, **Flash**) and Pete King (drums).			
2/12/83	5	21		1 **Der Kommissar**..........*Dancing In The Shadows*	$4		Epic 03559
				Kommissar is German for "detective"			
5/28/83	85	3		2 **Dancing In The Shadows**..........*Starflight*	$4		Epic 03908
				AFU-RA R&B/LP '01			
				Born Aaron Phillip in Brooklyn, New York. Male rapper.			
5/12/01	25[S]	11		**Bigacts Littleacts**..........*(5 mixes)*	$6	★*	D&D/Koch 8263
				AFU-RA featuring GZA			
				AGEE, LeVert '02			
				Born in Atlanta, Georgia. Male rapper.			
3/16/02	33[S]	8		**Stop Playin'**..........*(4 versions)*	$5	★	KnightStar 1237
				LEVERT AGEE Feat Mr. Low Down & Evol (CD cover shows "ATL Bomb Squad Compilation")			

AGUILERA, Christina ★269★ — LP '00

Born on 12/18/80 in Staten Island, New York (of Irish and Ecuadorian descent); raised in Wexford, Pennsylvania. Pop-dance singer/songwriter. Regular on TV's *The Mickey Mouse Club* (1992-93). Won the 1999 Best New Artist Grammy Award.

1)Genie In A Bottle 2)Lady Marmalade 3)Come On Over Baby (all I want is you)

DEBUT	PEAK	WKS	Gold	A-side (Chart Hit)...B-side	$	Sym	Label & Number
7/3/99	❶^{5}	25	▲	1 Genie In A Bottle S:❶^{4} / A:❶^{3} *Blessed* "45": RCA 65813; B-side: "So Emotional"; also see re-entry (#8 below)	$4	★^{V}	RCA 65692
11/27/99+	❶^{2}	24	●	2 What A Girl Wants ...S:❶^{2} / A:2 *We're A Miracle* "45": RCA 65968; B-side: "Genie In A Bottle (Eddie Arroyo rhythm mix)"	$4	★^{V}	RCA 65960
12/18/99	18	4		3 The Christmas Song (Chestnuts Roasting On An Open Fire) ...S:6 *Genie In A Bottle (Arroyo remix)* [X]	$5	★	RCA 65943
4/15/00	3	22		4 I Turn To You ...S:❶^{1} / A:14 *Por Siempre Tu*	$5	★$^{+V}$	RCA 60251
8/5/00	❶^{4}	21	●	5 Come On Over Baby (all I want is you) ...S:❶^{6} / A:4 *Ven Conmigo (solamente tú)* "45": RCA 60346; all of above (except #3) from the album *Christina Aguilera*; also see re-entry (#9 below)	$4	★^{V}	RCA 60341
1/27/01	13	20		6 Nobody Wants To Be Lonely ...A:10 **RICKY MARTIN with CHRISTINA AGUILERA** "45": Columbia 79573; B-side: "Solo Quiero Amarte (Nobody Wants To Be Lonely)"		V	album cut
4/14/01	❶^{5}	20		7 Lady Marmalade ...A:❶^{6} *(3 mixes)* **CHRISTINA AGUILERA, LIL' KIM, MÝA and P!NK** co-produced by **Missy "Misdemeanor" Elliott**; from the movie *Moulin Rouge* starring Nicole Kidman and Ewan McGregor	$6	T	Interscope 497066
12/8/01	17^{S}	21		8 Genie In A Bottle / [R]			
12/8/01		21		9 Come On Over Baby (all I want is you) ... [R] above 2 reissued on RCA's "Double-Play CD Single"; re-entry of #1 & 5 above	$4	★	RCA 60506
9/21/02	48	20		10 Dirrty ...S:2 / A:49 *Make Over* **CHRISTINA AGUILERA Featuring Redman**	$4	★	RCA 60669
11/23/02+	2^{1}	27		11 Beautiful ...A:2 *(3 remixes)* "45": RCA 50960; B-side: "Fighter"	$6	T^{V}	RCA 51195

A-HA — AC/BUB/LP '85

Pop trio from Oslo, Norway: Morten Harket (vocals), Pal Waaktaar (guitar) and Magne "Mags" Furuholmen (keyboards).

DEBUT	PEAK	WKS	Gold	A-side (Chart Hit)...B-side	$	Sym	Label & Number
7/13/85	❶^{1}	27		1 Take On Me ...A:❶^{2} / S:3 *Love Is Reason* issued with a regular picture sleeve and a promotional 8-page booklet sleeve	$3	■	Warner 29011
11/30/85+	20	17		2 The Sun Always Shines On T.V. ...A:17 / S:21 *Driftwood*	$3	■	Warner 28846
1/24/87	50	10		3 Cry Wolf ...*Maybe Maybe*	$3	■	Warner 28500

AHMAD — '94

Born Ahmad Lewis on 10/12/75 in Los Angeles, California. Male hip-hop artist. Member of **4th Avenue Jones**'.

DEBUT	PEAK	WKS	Gold	A-side (Chart Hit)...B-side	$	Sym	Label & Number
5/28/94	26	20	●	Back In The Day ...S:13 / A:39 *(remix)* samples "Let's Do It Again" by **The Staple Singers** (written by **Curtis Mayfield**)	$3	▮	Giant 18217

★226★ **AIR SUPPLY** — AC/LP '81

Pop vocal duo from Melbourne, Australia: Russell Hitchcock (born on 6/15/49 in Melbourne) and Graham Russell (born on 6/1/50 in Nottingham, England). Their regular backing band included David Moyse and Rex Goh (guitars), Frank Esler-Smith (keyboards), David Green (bass) and Ralph Cooper (drums).

1)The One That You Love 2)All Out Of Love 3)Making Love Out Of Nothing At All

DEBUT	PEAK	WKS	Gold	A-side (Chart Hit)...B-side	$	Sym	Label & Number
2/9/80	3	23		1 Lost In Love ...AC^{6} *I Don't Want To Lose You*	$3		Arista 0479
6/14/80	2^{4}	27	●	2 All Out Of Love ...*Old Habits Die Hard*	$3		Arista 0520
10/25/80+	5	22		3 Every Woman In The World ...*Having You Near Me* also released with "My Best Friend" as the B-side	$3		Arista 0564
5/16/81	❶^{1}	19	●	4 The One That You Love *I Want To Give It All*	$3	■	Arista 0604
9/26/81	5	20		5 Here I Am (Just When I Thought I Was Over You) ...AC^{3} *Don't Turn Me Away*	$3		Arista 0626
12/12/81+	5	20		6 Sweet Dreams ...*Don't Turn Me Away*	$3		Arista 0655
6/12/82	5	18		7 Even The Nights Are Better ...AC^{4} *One Step Closer*	$3	■	Arista 0692
9/18/82	38	9		8 Young Love ...*She Never Heard Me Call*	$3		Arista 1005
11/13/82+	38	14		9 Two Less Lonely People In The World ...*What Kind Of Girl*	$3		Arista 1004
7/30/83	2^{3}	25	●	10 Making Love Out Of Nothing At All ...*Late Again (live)*	$3	■	Arista 9056
5/25/85	19	15		11 Just As I Am ...S:16 / A:22 *Crazy Love*	$3	■	Arista 9353
8/10/85	68	6		12 The Power Of Love (You Are My Lady) ...*Sunset*	$3	■	Arista 9391
8/9/86	76	8		13 Lonely Is The Night ...*I'd Die For You*	$3	■	Arista 9521

AIRWAVES — '78

Pop trio from Wales: Ray Martinez (vocals, guitar), John David (bass) and Dave Charles (drums).

DEBUT	PEAK	WKS	Gold	A-side (Chart Hit)...B-side	$	Sym	Label & Number
6/3/78	62	6		So Hard Livin' Without You ...*Hope You Won't*	$6		A&M 2032

AKENS, Jewel — BUB '65

Born on 9/12/40 in Houston, Texas. Male R&B singer/producer.

DEBUT	PEAK	WKS	Gold	A-side (Chart Hit)...B-side	$	Sym	Label & Number
1/23/65	3	14		1 The Birds And The Bees ...*Tic Tac Toe*	$15		Era 3141
5/1/65	68	5		2 Georgie Porgie ...*Around The Corner (From My House)*	$15		Era 3142

AKINYELE — R&B/LP '99

Born Akinyele Adams in 1970 in Queens, New York. Male hardcore rapper.

DEBUT	PEAK	WKS	Gold	A-side (Chart Hit)...B-side	$	Sym	Label & Number
9/18/99	45^{S}	10		Take A Lick ...*Three* from the "X-rated" movie *Aktapuss*	$6	★	Volcano 34281

DEBUT	PEAK	WKS	Gold	A-side (Chart Hit)........B-side	$	Sym	Label & Number
	★588★			**ALABAMA** C&W/BUB/AC/LP '82			
				Country group from Fort Payne, Alabama: Randy Owen (vocals, guitar; born on 12/13/49), Jeff Cook (keyboards, fiddle; born on 8/27/49), Teddy Gentry (bass, vocals; born on 1/22/52) and Mark Herndon (drums, vocals; born on 5/11/55). Randy, Jeff and Teddy are cousins. Earlier incarnation of group known as Wildcountry, 1969-77. Charted 78 Country hits, 1977-02.			
				1)Love In The First Degree 2)Take Me Down 3)Feels So Right			
6/6/81	20	22		1 **Feels So Right**....CW^{2} *See The Embers, Feel The Flame*	$5		RCA 12236
11/14/81+	15	21		2 **Love In The First Degree** CW^{2} *Ride The Train*	$5		RCA 12288
5/22/82	18	13		3 **Take Me Down**....CW^{1} *Lovin' You Is Killin' Me*	$4		RCA 13210
				first recorded by **Exile** in 1980 ("Bubbled Under" at #102)			
9/4/82	65	12		4 **Close Enough To Perfect**....CW^{1} *Fantasy*	$4		RCA 13294
5/7/83	38	11		5 **The Closer You Get**....CW^{1} *You Turn Me On*	$4		RCA 13524
				first recorded by **Rita Coolidge** in 1981 ("Bubbled Under" at #103)			
10/29/83	76	6		6 **Lady Down On Love**....CW^{1} *Lovin' Man*	$4		RCA 13590
12/17/83	3^{X}	4		7 **Christmas In Dixie**....*Never Be One* [X]	$4		RCA 13664
				X: 3/'83; 8/'85; #35 Country hit in 1982 on RCA 13358			
5/19/84	72	10		8 **When We Make Love**....CW^{1} *Carolina Mountain Dewe*	$4		RCA 13763
1/17/87	71	8		9 **Deep River Woman**....*Ballerina Girl* (Richie)	$3	■	Motown 1873
				LIONEL RICHIE with Alabama			
12/5/98	82	5		10 **How Do You Fall In Love**....A:71		V	album cut
2/6/99	69	8		11 **Keepin' Up**....A:50		V	album cut
				above 2 from the album *For The Record* on RCA 67633; "45" issued for above 2 on RCA 65561			
5/29/99	29	20		12 **God Must Have Spent A Little More Time On You**....A:22 / S:23 *Sad Lookin' Moon* (Alabama)	$4	★^{V}	RCA 65759
				ALABAMA (featuring *NSYNC)			
				ALAIMO, Chuck, Quartet '57			
				Rock and roll band from Rochester, New York: Chuck Alaimo (sax; since deceased), Tommy Rossi (drums), Pat Magnolia (bass) and Bill Irvine (piano).			
4/29/57	92	1		**Leap Frog**....T:92 *That's My Desire* [I]	$25		MGM 12449
				B-side is a rock and roll remake of **Frankie Laine**'s 1947 hit (vocal by Alaimo)			
				ALAIMO, Steve BUB '63			
				Born on 12/6/39 in Rochester, New York. Star of TV's *Where The Action Is*, 1965-66. Member of **The Unknowns**. Appeared in the movies *Stanley* and *Wild Rebels*. President of Vision Records in Miami since 1987. Cousin of Jimmy Alaimo of **The Mojo Men**. Steve had the most pop hits by any artist without a top 40 hit.			
3/17/62	81	1		1 **Mashed Potatoes (Part 1)**....*(Part 2)*	$15		Checker 1006
1/5/63	46	10		2 **Every Day I Have To Cry** *Little Girl (Please Take A Chance With Me)*	$15		Checker 1032
10/5/63	100	1		3 **Michael - Pt. 1**....*Pt. 2*	$15		Checker 1054
11/16/63	74	6		4 **Gotta Lotta Love**....*Happy Pappy*	$15		Imperial 66003
3/6/65	77	2		5 **Real Live Girl**....*Need You*	$12		ABC-Paramount 10620
				from the Broadway musical *Little Me* starring Sid Caesar			
6/26/65	89	2		6 **Cast Your Fate To The Wind**....*Mais Oui*	$12		ABC-Paramount 10680
5/21/66	92	2		7 **So Much Love**....*Truer Than True*	$12		ABC-Paramount 10805
6/26/71	72	6		8 **When My Little Girl Is Smiling**....*Gemini*	$6		Entrance 7501
4/29/72	79	3		9 **Amerikan Music**....*Nobody's Fool* [N]	$6		Entrance 7507
				Amerikan: pronounced am-er-ee-can			
				ALARM, The ROK/BUB/LP '89			
				Rock group from Rhyl, Wales: Mike Peters (vocals), Dave Sharp (guitar), Eddie MacDonald (bass) and Nigel Twist (drums).			
12/28/85+	61	10		1 **Strength**....*Majority*	$5	■	I.R.S. 52736
12/19/87+	71	8		2 **Rain In The Summertime**....*Rose Beyond The Wall*	$4	■	I.R.S. 53219
3/26/88	77	6		3 **Presence Of Love**....*My Land Your Land*	$4	■	I.R.S. 53259
10/7/89	50	13		4 **Sold Me Down The River**....S:37 *Black Sun / How The Mighty Fall*	$4	▮	I.R.S. 73002
				ALBERT, Eddie, & Sondra Lee BUB '56			
				Born Edward Albert Heimberger on 4/22/08 in Rock Island, Illinois. Played "Oliver Wendell Douglas" on TV's *Green Acres*. Appeared in over 75 movies. Sondra Lee is Eddie's daughter.			
2/18/56	56	4		**Little Child**....T:56 *Jenny Kissed Me* (Albert)	$15	■	Kapp 134
				adapted from the French title "Little Boy And The Old Man"			
				ALBERT, Morris LP '75			
				Born Morris Albert Kaisermann on 9/7/51 in Brazil. Singer/songwriter.			
6/21/75	6	32	●	1 **Feelings**....*This World Today Is A Mess*	$4		RCA Victor 10279
2/7/76	93	2		2 **Sweet Loving Man**....*Christine*	$4		RCA Victor 10437
				ALBERTI, Willy '59			
				Born Carel Verbrugge on 10/14/26 in Amsterdam, Netherlands. Died of cancer on 2/18/85 (age 58).			
11/30/59	42	8		**Marina**....*Cerasella (Canzone Allegra)* [F]	$12		London 1888
				AL B. SURE! R&B/LP '88			
				Born Al Brown in 1969 in Boston, Massachusetts; raised in Mt. Vernon, New York. R&B singer/songwriter. Also see **Usher**'s "The Many Ways."			
4/9/88	7	21		1 **Nite And Day** RB^{3} S:6 / A:8 *Nuit Et Jour*	$3	■	Warner 28192
				French version is on the B-side; Spanish version is on the B-side of #2 below			
8/6/88	45	12		2 **Off On Your Own (Girl)**....RB^{2} *Noche Y Dia*	$3	■	Warner 27870
11/19/88	80	11		3 **Killing Me Softly**....*(instrumental)*	$3	■	Warner 27772
3/10/90	31	13	●	4 **The Secret Garden (Sweet Seduction Suite)**....RB^{1} S:20 *(instrumental)*	$3	▮^{V}	Qwest 19992 ■
				QUINCY JONES/Al B. Sure!/James Ingram/El DeBarge/Barry White			
10/13/90	42	14		5 **Missunderstanding**....RB^{1} S:31 *(radio edit)*	$3	▮^{V}	Warner 19590
8/29/92	47	20		6 **Right Now**....RB^{1} S:26 / A:55 *(instrumental)*	$3	▮	Warner 18819
4/16/94	flip	16		7 **I'm Still In Love With You**....S:40 / A:65 *Part Time Lover* (**H-Town** - #57)	$4	▮	Death Row 98283
				from the movie *Above The Rim* starring **2 Pac**; "I'm Still In Love With You" and "Part Time Lover" by **H-Town** were issued on the same cassette single and were listed together at one chart position each week ("Part Time Lover" was always listed first)			

DEBUT	PEAK	WKS	Gold	A-side (Chart Hit)...B-side	$	Sym	Label & Number
				ALESSI '82			
				Pop duo of identical twin brothers Billy and Bobby Alessi. Born on 7/12/53 in West Hempstead, New York.			
5/1/82	71	4		**Put Away Your Love** ... *Long Time Friends*	$4		Qwest 50055
				Christopher Cross (co-producer)			
				ALEXANDER, Arthur BUB/R&B '62			
				Born on 5/10/40 in Florence, Alabama. Died of a heart attack on 6/9/93 (age 53). R&B singer/songwriter. Teamed with Rick Hall in studio work at Muscle Shoals. First recorded for Judd in 1960. Only rock-era artist to have his compositions recorded by **The Beatles**, **The Rolling Stones** and **Bob Dylan**.			
2/24/62	24	12		1 **You Better Move On** ... *A Shot Of Rhythm And Blues*	$20		Dot 16309
				recorded by **The Rolling Stones** on their 1965 album *December's Children*			
5/26/62	58	8		2 **Where Have You Been (All My Life)** ... *Soldiers Of Love*	$20		Dot 16357
10/27/62	68	6		3 **Anna (Go To Him)** ... *I Hang My Head And Cry*	$20		Dot 16387
				record was the subject for an episode on TV's *Married With Children*; recorded by **The Beatles** on their 1964 album *Introducing The Beatles*			
9/13/75	45	9		4 **Every Day I Have To Cry Some** ... *Everybody Needs Somebody To Love*	$8		Buddah 492
				ALFI AND HARRY — see SEVILLE, David			
				ALI, Tatyana R&B/BUB/LP '98			
				Born on 1/24/79 in North Bellmore, Long Island, New York. Singer/actress. Played "Ashley Banks" on TV's *The Fresh Prince Of Bel-Air*.			
8/8/98	6	17	●	1 **Daydreamin'** ... S:5 / A:43 *(Part II)*	$3	▮	MJJ Music/Work 78855
				samples "Black Cow" by **Steely Dan**			
7/10/99	31^S	12		2 **Everytime** ... BUB:118 *(Cutfather & Joe edit)*	$4	★	MJJ Music/Work 79198
				ALIAS ROK/LP '90			
				Rock group formed in Los Angeles, California, by former **Sheriff** bandmates Freddy Curci (vocals) and Steve DeMarchi (guitar), with former **Heart** members Roger Fisher (guitar), Steve Fossen (bass) and Mike Derosier (drums).			
9/8/90	2[1]	23		1 **More Than Words Can Say** ... A:3 / S:4 *Say What I Wanna Say*	$4	▮	EMI 50324
1/19/91	13	17		2 **Waiting For Love** ... A:13 / S:20 *True Emotion*	$4	▮	EMI 50337
7/6/91	90	4		3 **Perfect World** ... *Bitter* (Terrell)	$4	▮	Giant 19249
				from the movie *Don't Tell Mom The Babysitter's Dead* starring Christina Applegate			
				ALICE DEEJAY LP '00			
				Techno-dance act from Amsterdam, Netherlands. Featuring Judy (Alice Deejay).			
4/8/00	27	20		**Better Off Alone** ... A:28 *(3 versions)*	$6	T	Republic 156798
				ALICE IN CHAINS ROK/BUB/LP '94			
				Male hard-rock group formed in Seattle, Washington: Layne Staley (vocals), Jerry Cantrell (guitar), Mike Starr (bass) and Sean Kinney (drums). Starr replaced by Mike Inez (former bassist for **Ozzy Osbourne**) by 1994. In 1995, Inez recorded with Slash's Snakepit and Staley recorded with Mad Season. Staley died of a drug overdose on 4/5/2002 (age 34).			
2/19/94	48^A	15		1 **No Excuses** ... AR[2]			album cut
				from the album *Jar Of Flies* on Columbia 57628			
1/27/96	52^A	11		2 **Heaven Beside You** ...			album cut
				from the album *Alice In Chains* on Columbia 67248			
				ALICE WONDER LAND '63			
				Alice Faye Henderson was discovered by songwriter Stephen Schlaks, the co-owner of Bardell Records (wrote **Kenny Dino**'s "Your Ma Said You Cried In Your Sleep Last Night"). Alice was his neighbor's maid.			
9/14/63	62	7		**He's Mine (I Love Him, I Love Him, I Love Him)** ... *Cha Linde*	$25		Bardell 774
				ALIEN ANT FARM ROK/LP '01			
				Rock group from Los Angeles, California: Dryden Mitchell (vocals), Terry Corso (guitar), Tye Zamora (bass) and Mike Cosgrove (drums).			
8/25/01	23	20		**Smooth Criminal** ... MR[4] A:23			album cut
				from the album *ANThology* on New Noize 450293			
				ALISHA BUB/R&B/LP '86			
				Born in Brooklyn, New York. White female dance singer.			
12/21/85+	68	17		1 **Baby Talk** ... *One Little Lie*	$4		Vanguard 35262
8/22/87	97	1		2 **Into My Secret** ... *Do You Dream About Me*	$4	■	RCA 5219
				remixed version released on RCA 5278			
5/26/90	54	8		3 **Bounce Back** ... *(no B-side)*	$4	▮V	MCA 53802
				originally recorded in 1988 by the dance band Fire On Blonde; "45": MCA 79021; B-side: "I Need Forever"			
				ALIVE AND KICKING LP '70			
				Pop-rock group from Brooklyn, New York: Pepe Cardona (male vocals) and Sandy Toder (female vocals), John Parisio (guitar), Bruce Sudano (organ), Thomas "Woody" Wilson (bass) and Vito Albano (drums). Sudano married **Donna Summer** on 7/16/80 and was a member of **Brooklyn Dreams**.			
6/6/70	7	14		1 **Tighter, Tighter** ... *Sunday Morning*	$7		Roulette 7078
				co-written and co-produced by **Tommy James**			
9/26/70	69	5		2 **Just Let It Come** *[ALIVE 'N KICKIN']* ... *Mother Carey's Chicken*	$7		Roulette 7087
				ALKAHOLIKS, Tha R&B/BUB/LP '97			
				Rap trio from Los Angeles, California: James "J-Ro" Robinson, Rico "Tash" Smith and Eric "E-Swift" Brooks. Changed name to **Tha Liks** in 2001.			
6/28/97	66	9		**Hip Hop Drunkies** ... S:49 *(remix)*	$4	▮	Loud/RCA 64882
				THA ALKAHOLIKS Featuring Ol' Dirty Bastard			
				ALKATRAZ — see FLEXX G.			
				ALLAN, Davie, And The Arrows LP '67			
				Born in Los Angeles, California. Began as a session guitarist for **Mike Curb**. While in high school at Van Nuys, California, formed The Arrows: Allan (Fender lead guitar), Drew Bennett (bass), Jared Hendler (keyboards) and Larry Brown (drums).			
2/13/65	64	7		1 **Apache '65** *[THE ARROWS Featuring Davie Allan]* ... *Blue Guitar* [I]	$15		Tower 116
				first released on Sidewalk 1 in 1964 ($30)			
11/12/66	99	2		2 **Theme From The Wild Angels** ... *U.F.O.* [I]	$15		Tower 267

DEBUT	PEAK	WKS	Gold	A-side (Chart Hit)....................B-side	$	Sym	Label & Number
				ALLAN, Davie, And The Arrows — Cont'd			
4/22/67	**37**	17		3 **Blue's Theme** .... *Bongo Party* [I]	$15		Tower 295
				originally released as by **THE ARROWS Featuring Davie Allen**; above 2 from the movie *The Wild Angels* starring Peter Fonda			
7/29/67	**97**	1		4 **Devil's Angels** ***[DAVIE ALLEN AND THE ARROWS]*** .... *Cody's Theme* [I]	$15		Tower 341
				title song from the movie starring John Cassavetes; above 3 written and produced by **Mike Curb**			
				ALLAN, Gary C&W/BUB/LP **'02**			
				Born Gary Herzberg on 12/5/67 in Montebello, California; raised in La Mirada, California. Country singer/songwriter/guitarist.			
1/22/00	**76**	5		1 **Smoke Rings In The Dark** A:64		v	album cut
				"45": MCA Nashville 72109; B-side: "Right Where I Need To Be"			
4/7/01	**42**	20		2 **Right Where I Need To Be** A:36		v	album cut
				"45": MCA Nashville72180; B-side: "Don't Tell Mama"; above 2 from the album *Smoke Rings In The Dark* on MCA Nashville 70101			
5/18/02	**37**	20		3 **The One** A:32		v	album cut
				"45": MCA Nashville 72232; B-side: "I'm Doin' My Best"; from the album *Alright Guy* on MCA Nashville 70201			
				ALL CITY R&B **'98**			
				Rap duo from Brooklyn, New York: J. Mega and Greg Valentine.			
7/11/98	**75**	4		**The Actual** .... S:50 *Priceless*	$4	▮	MCA 55445
				ALLEN, Deborah C&W/LP **'84**			
				Born Deborah Lynn Thurmond on 9/30/53 in Memphis, Tennessee. Country singer/songwriter.			
10/15/83+	**26**	21		**Baby I Lied** .... *Time Is Taking You Away From Me*	$5	■	RCA 13600
				ALLEN, Donna R&B/LP **'87**			
				Born in Key West, Florida; raised in Tampa, Florida. R&B singer. Former cheerleader for the Tampa Bay Buccaneers.			
2/14/87	**21**	18		**Serious** .... A:19 / S:21 *Bad Love*	$4		21 Records 99497
				ALLEN, Lee, And His Band BUB **'58**			
				Born on 7/2/27 in Pittsburg, Kansas. Died of cancer on 10/18/94 (age 67). Black saxophonist; played on hits by **Fats Domino**, **Little Richard** and others. Played tenor sax on The Blasters' first three albums.			
1/13/58	**54**	11		1 **Walkin' With Mr. Lee** .... T:54 *Promenade* [I]	$25		Ember 1027
				title inspired by **The Bobbettes**' 1957 hit "Mr. Lee"			
9/29/58	**92**	1		2 **Tic Toc** .... H:92 *Chuggin'* [I]	$25		Ember 1039
				ALLEN, Peter AC/BUB/LP **'81**			
				Born Peter Allen Woolnough on 2/10/44 in Tenterfield, Australia. Died of AIDS on 6/18/92 (age 48). Cabaret-style performer/songwriter. Married to Liza Minnelli from 1967-73. Co-writer of "Arthur's Theme" and "I Honestly Love You."			
1/10/81	**55**	8		**Fly Away** .... *Simon*	$5		A&M 2288
				ALLEN, Rex C&W/POP **'62**			
				Born on 12/31/20 in Willcox, Arizona. Died after being struck by a car on 12/17/99 (age 78). Western singer/guitarist/actor. Starred in numerous western movies in the 1950s. Narrator for numerous Walt Disney documentaries during the 1960s and 1970s. Own TV series, *Frontier Doctor*, in 1954. His son, Rex Jr., was a top country signer from 1973-87.			
9/15/62	**17**	8		**Don't Go Near The Indians** .... *Touched So Deeply*	$12		Mercury 71997
				The Merry Melody Singers (backing vocals)			
				ALLEN, Richie **'60**			
				Born Richard Podolor. Record producer/songwriter. Also see **The Hondells** and **The Pets**.			
11/21/60	**90**	2		**Stranger From Durango** .... *Redskin* [I]	$20		Imperial 5683
				B-side is a guitar instrumental in the **Duane Eddy** 'twangy' style			
				ALLEN, Steve BUB/LP **'55**			
				Born on 12/26/21 in New York City, New York; raised in Chicago, Illinois. Died of heart failure on 10/30/2000 (age 78). Comedian/actor/songwriter/author. In 1954, became the first host of TV's *Tonight Show*. Played title role in the 1956 movie *The **Benny Goodman** Story*. Hosted own variety and talk shows, 1956-80. Married actress Jayne Meadows on 7/31/54.			
11/12/55	**35**	12		1 **Autumn Leaves** T:35 *High And Dry* (Cates) [I]	$15		Coral 61485
				STEVE ALLEN with GEORGE CATES And His Orchestra & Chorus			
12/17/55+	**56**	8		2 **What Is A Wife** .... T:56 *Memories Of You* [N-S]	$15		Coral 61542
				parody of the 1951 hit "What Is A Boy" (also see **Tom Edwards**' "What Is A Teenage Girl/Boy?")			
<u>8/18/56</u>	**75**	4		3 **Lola's Theme** .... T:75 *Conversation (On The Telephone)* [I]	$12		Coral 61681
				from the movie *Trapeze* starring Burt Lancaster and Tony Curtis			
4/27/63	**64**	7		4 **Gravy Waltz** .... *Preacherman* [I]	$10		Dot 16457
				Don Trenner (orch.)			
10/12/63	**85**	5		5 **Cuando Calienta El Sol (When The Sun Is Hot)** .... *Leave It To Me* (Allen) [F]	$10		Dot 16507
				STEVE ALLEN and His Orchestra with The Copacabana Trio			
				English version of tune is known as "Love Me With All Your Heart"; above 2 reissued in 1965 on Dot 240 with a picture sleeve promoting Lamb Knit sweaters			
				ALLEY CATS, The **'63**			
				Black vocal group from Los Angeles, California: Bobby Sheen (of **Bob B. Soxx & The Blue Jeans**), Gary and Chester Pipkin, Sheridan Spencer, Brice Coefield and James Barker.			
1/12/63	**43**	7		**Puddin N' Tain (Ask Me Again, I'll Tell You the Same)** .... *Feel So Good*	$40		Philles 108
				produced by Phil Spector			
				ALLEY LIFE **'01**			
				Born in Detroit, Michigan. Male hip-hop artist.			
5/19/01	**44**S	6		**That's The Way We Roll** .... *(dirty version) / 313 (2 versions)*	$7	★	Farmclub.com 497419
	★587★			**ALL-4-ONE** BUB/R&B/AC/LP **'94**			
				Male interracial vocal group from Los Angeles, California: Jamie Jones (born on 11/25/71), Delious Kennedy (born on 12/2/73), Alfred Nevarez (born on 5/18/72) and Tony Borowiak (born on 10/12/72).			
1/1/94	**5**	22	●	1 **So Much In Love** .... S:4 / A:6 *Something About You*	$3	▮v	Blitzz/Atlantic 87271
				originally released on Blitzz 15001 in 1993			
4/23/94	❶11	30	▲	2 **I Swear** A:❶9 / S:❶7 *Here If You're Ready*	$3	▮v	Blitzz/Atlantic 87243
				"45" issued for above 2 on Blitzz/Atlantic 87243			
1/7/95	**57**	20		3 **(She's Got) Skillz** .... S:49 / A:72 *(remix)*	$3	▮	Blitzz/Atlantic 87223

DEBUT	PEAK	WKS	Gold	A-side (Chart Hit)..................B-side	$	Sym	Label & Number
				ALL-4-ONE — Cont'd			
6/17/95	5	29	●	4 **I Can Love You Like That**.................A:3 / S:10 *All-4-1*	$3	▮V	Blitzz/Atlantic 87134
				"45": Blitzz/Atlantic 87097; B-side: "I'm Your Man" ("Bubbled Under" #116); #2 & 4: #1 Country hits for **John Michael Montgomery**			
6/29/96	30	15	●	5 **Someday**.................S:15 *(album version)*	$3	▮	Hollywood 64011
				from the Disney animated movie *The Hunchback Of Notre Dame*			
				ALLISON, Brooke '01			
				Born on 9/26/86 in Lampasas, Texas. Female pop singer.			
4/21/01	28[S]	13		**The Kiss Off (Goodbye)**.................*(4 remixes)*	$4	★	2KSounds 20001
				samples "Goodbye" by Elwood Edwards; co-produced by **Robert Palmer**			
				ALLISON, Gene R&B '58			
				Born on 8/29/34 in Nashville, Tennessee. R&B singer. First recorded for Calvert in 1956.			
12/16/57+	36	17		1 **You Can Make It If You Try**.................S:36 / T:37 *Hey, Hey, I Love You*	$25		Vee-Jay 256
5/5/58	73	6		2 **Have Faith**.................T:73 *My Heart Remembers*	$25		Vee-Jay 273
				ALLISONS, The '63			
				American female group — not related to the British male duo.			
12/14/63	93	1		**Surfer Street**.................*Money*	$30		Tip 1011
				tune is similar to "Big Boy Pete" by **The Olympics** and "The Jolly Green Giant" by **The Kingsmen**			
	★552★			**ALLMAN BROTHERS BAND, The** ROK/BUB/LP '73			
				Southern-rock group formed in Macon, Georgia: brothers Duane (lead guitar; born on 11/20/46) and **Gregg Allman** (see #6 below) (keyboards; born on 12/8/47), Dickey Betts (guitar; born on 12/12/43), Berry Oakley (bass; born on 4/4/48), and the drum duo of Butch Trucks (born on 5/11/47) and Jai Johnny Johanson (born on 7/8/44). Duane and Gregg known earlier as the Allman Joys and Hour Glass. Duane was the top session guitarist at Muscle Shoals studio; killed in a motorcycle crash on 10/29/71 (age 24). Oakley died in another cycle accident on 11/11/72 (age 24); replaced by Lamar Williams (died on 1/25/83). Chuck Leavell (keyboards) added in 1972. Group split up in 1976. Gregg formed **The Gregg Allman Band** (see #14 below). Betts formed Great Southern. Leavell, Williams and Johanson formed the fusion-rock band **Sea Level** (see #10 below). Allman and Betts reunited with a new Allman Brothers lineup in 1978. Disbanded in 1981. Allman, Betts, Trucks and Johanson regrouped with Warren Haynes (guitar), Allen Woody (bass) and Johnny Neel (keyboards) in 1989. Neel left in 1990, replaced by Mark Quinones. Woody died on 8/26/2000 (age 44). Original group inducted into the Rock and Roll Hall of Fame in 1995.			
				1)Ramblin Man 2)Midnight Rider 3)Crazy Love			
1/9/71	92	3		1 **Revival (Love Is Everywhere)**.................*Leave My Blues At Home*	$6		Capricorn 8011
4/29/72	77	4		2 **Ain't Wastin' Time No More**.................*Melissa*	$6		Capricorn 0003
8/12/72	86	2		3 **Melissa**.................*Blue Sky*	$6		Capricorn 0007
12/2/72	86	4		4 **One Way Out**.................*Standback*	$6		Capricorn 0014
				written by Rock & Roll Hall Of Fame blues-great, Elmore James			
8/25/73	2[1]	16		5 **Ramblin Man** *Pony Boy*	$6		Capricorn 0027
12/22/73+	19	12		6 **Midnight Rider**.................*Multi-Colored Lady*	$6		Capricorn 0035
				GREGG ALLMAN			
				originally released by **The Allman Brothers Band** on the 1970 album *Idlewild South*			
1/19/74	65	6		7 **Jessica**.................*Come And Go Blues* [I]	$6		Capricorn 0036
11/15/75	67	3		8 **Nevertheless** /			
11/15/75	78	3		9 **Louisiana Lou And Three Card Monty John**.................	$6		Capricorn 0246
2/25/78	50	10		10 **That's Your Secret**.................*Storm Warning*	$5		Capricorn 0287
				SEA LEVEL			
3/24/79	29	9		11 **Crazy Love**.................*Just Ain't Easy*	$5		Capricorn 0320
9/13/80	58	8		12 **Angeline**.................*So Long*	$4		Arista 0555
8/8/81	39	11		13 **Straight From The Heart**.................*Leavin'*	$4	■	Arista 0618
4/4/87	49	10		14 **I'm No Angel**.................AR[1] *Lead Me On*	$4		Epic 06998
				THE GREGG ALLMAN BAND			
				ALL SAINTS LP '98			
				Female interracial vocal group from London, England: sisters Natalie and Nicky Appleton, with Shaznay Lewis and Melanie Blatt.			
1/31/98	36	18		1 **I Know Where It's At**.................S:31 / A:53 *(radio mix)*	$3	▮V	London 570112
				samples "The Fez" by **Steely Dan**			
7/25/98	4	19		2 **Never Ever**.................S:3 / A:12 *(remix) / I Remember*	$3	▮V	London 570178
				melody is similar to "Amazing Grace"			
				ALL SPORTS BAND '82			
				Pop-rock group dressed up in various athletic uniforms: Michael John Toste (vocals), Cy Sulack (guitar), Chuck Kentis (keyboards), Alfonso Carey (bass) and Jimmy "The Boxer" Clark (drums).			
11/28/81	93	2		1 **I'm Your Superman**.................*Can't Give Up The Feeling*	$4		Radio 3871
2/6/82	78	3		2 **Opposites Do Attract**.................*Lovestruck*	$4		Radio 3892
				ALL STAR TRIBUTE — see ARTISTS AGAINST AIDS			
				ALLURE LP '97			
				Female R&B vocal group from New York City, New York: Alia Davis, Akissa Mendez, Lalisha McLean and Linnie Belcher.			
3/15/97	35	15		1 **Head Over Heels**.................S:32 / A:61 *(3 versions)*	$3	▮	Crave 78522
				ALLURE featuring Nas			
				samples "The Bridge" by MC Shan			
8/30/97	4	25	●	2 **All Cried Out**.................S:6 / A:8 *Head Over Heels* (w/Tone & **AZ**)	$3	▮	Crave 78678
				ALLURE featuring 112			
				above 2 co-produced by **Mariah Carey** (on her own label, Crave)			
8/18/01	10[S]	25		3 **Enjoy Yourself**.................*(instrumental)*	$4	★	MCA 155860
				ALMOND, Marc — see SOFT CELL			

DEBUT	PEAK	WKS	Gold	A-side (Chart Hit)	B-side	$	Sym	Label & Number

ALPERT, Herb/The Tijuana Brass ★79★ AC/BUB/R&B/LP '66

Born on 3/31/35 in Los Angeles, California. Trumpeter/bandleader/producer/composer. Played trumpet since age eight. A&R for Keen Records. Produced first **Jan & Dean** session. Wrote "Wonderful World" hit for **Sam Cooke**. Recorded as Dore Alpert in 1962. Formed A&M Records with Jerry Moss in 1962. Used studio musicians until early 1965, then formed own band. Alpert and Moss formed the Almo Sounds label in 1994. Alpert is the only artist of the rock era to hit #1 on the "Hot 100" with a vocal and with an instrumental record.

1)This Guy's In Love With You 2)Rise 3)Diamonds 4)The Lonely Bull 5)Taste Of Honey

DEBUT	PEAK	WKS	Gold	A-side (Chart Hit)	B-side	$	Sym	Label & Number
				THE TIJUANA BRASS Featuring Herb Alpert:				
10/27/62	6	14		1 **The Lonely Bull** (El Solo Torro)	*Acapulco 1922* [I]	$10		A&M 703
				HERB ALPERT'S TIJUANA BRASS:				
3/30/63	96	1		2 **Marching Thru Madrid**	*Struttin' With Maria (#102)* [I]	$8		A&M 706
3/28/64	77	5		3 **Mexican Drummer Man** — **The Blossoms** (backing vocals)	*The Great Manolete (La Virgen de La Macarena)*	$10		A&M 732
6/27/64	85	5		4 **The Mexican Shuffle** — tune used for a Teabury gum commercial: "The Cinnamint Shuffle"	*Numero Cinco* [I]	$8		A&M 742
2/20/65	68	10		5 **Whipped Cream**	*Las Mañanitas* [I]	$8		A&M 760
				HERB ALPERT & THE TIJUANA BRASS:				
9/25/65	7	16		6 **Taste Of Honey** / AC[5] [I] — tune written and introduced by **Bobby Scott** in the 1960 Broadway show *A Taste of Honey*; 1965 Grammy winner: Record of the Year				
9/11/65	47	6		7 **3rd Man Theme** — #1 hit for both Anton Karas and Guy Lombardo in 1950	[I]	$7		A&M 775
12/25/65+	11	12		8 **Zorba The Greek** / [I] — title song from the movie starring Anthony Quinn				
12/25/65+	38	8		9 **Tijuana Taxi**	[I]	$7		A&M 787
3/19/66	24	8		10 **What Now My Love** / [I] — written in France in 1962 by Gilbert Becaud as "Et Maintenant"				
3/19/66	27	7		11 **Spanish Flea** — theme song from TV's *The Dating Game*; above 5 (except #10) from the album *Going Places*	[I]	$7	■	A&M 792
7/2/66	18	8		12 **The Work Song** — written in 1960 by jazz artist Nat Adderley	*Plucky* [I]	$6	■	A&M 805
9/3/66	28	6		13 **Flamingo** — #13 hit for Duke Ellington in 1941	*So What's New?* [I]	$6	■	A&M 813
11/19/66	19	8		14 **Mame** — title song from the Broadway musical starring Angela Lansbury	*Our Day Will Come*	$6	■	A&M 823
3/11/67	37	5		15 **Wade In The Water**	*Mexican Road Race* [I]	$6	■	A&M 840
4/8/67	27	9		16 **Casino Royale** AC[2] — title song from the movie starring David Niven and Peter Sellers	*The Wall Street Rag* [I]	$6	■	A&M 850
7/8/67	32	5		17 **The Happening** — title song from the movie starring Anthony Quinn	*Town Without Pity* [I]	$6	■	A&M 860
9/9/67	35	6		18 **A Banda** (Ah Bahn-da) AC[2]	*Miss Frenchy Brown* [I]	$6	■	A&M 870
1/13/68	51	6		19 **Carmen** — adapted from Bizet's opera *Carmen*	*Love So Fine* [I]	$6	■	A&M 890
4/20/68	72	6		20 **Cabaret** — title song from the Broadway musical starring Jill Haworth	[I]	$6	■	A&M 925
5/18/68	❶[4]	14	●	21 **This Guy's In Love With You** *[HERB ALPERT]* AC[10]	*A Quiet Tear* (& Tijuana Brass)	$6	■	A&M 929
8/31/68	51	6		22 **To Wait For Love** *[HERB ALPERT]*	*Bud* (& Tijuana Brass)	$6	■	A&M 964
12/7/68	❶[3X]	4		23 **The Christmas Song** *[HERB ALPERT]* / [X] — issued with 2 different photos on the B-side of the picture sleeve				
12/14/68	45	6		24 **My Favorite Things** — from the Rodgers & Hammerstein musical *The Sound of Music*	[X-I]	$6	■	A&M 1001
3/29/69	78	5		25 **Zazueira** (Za-zoo-wher-a)	*Treasure Of San Miguel* [F]	$6	■	A&M 1043
5/31/69	63	6		26 **Without Her** *[HERB ALPERT]* — written by **Nilsson**	*Sandbox* (& Tijuana Brass)	$6	■	A&M 1065
10/17/70	74	4		27 **Jerusalem**	*Strike Up The Band* [I]	$6	■	A&M 1225
3/10/73	77	8		28 **Last Tango In Paris** *[HERB ALPERT & THE TJB]* — title song from the movie starring Marlon Brando	*Fire And Rain* [I]	$5		A&M 1420
5/18/74	84	6		29 **Fox Hunt** *[HERB ALPERT & THE TJB]*	*I Can't Go On Living Baby Without You* [I]	$5		A&M 1526
				HERB ALPERT:				
7/28/79	❶[2]	25	●	30 **Rise** AC[1]	*Aranjuez (Mon Amour)* [I]	$4		A&M 2151
11/17/79+	30	13		31 **Rotation** — picture sleeve has a center-cut hole and shows only Alpert's name and the song title	*Angelina* [I]	$4	■	A&M 2202
6/28/80	50	8		32 **Beyond**	*Keep It Goin'* [I]	$4	■	A&M 2246
9/5/81	79	5		33 **Magic Man**	*Fantasy Island* [I]	$4	■	A&M 2356
6/26/82	37	10		34 **Route 101**	*Angel* [I]	$4	■	A&M 2422
8/20/83	81	4		35 **Garden Party**	*Oriental Eyes* [I]	$4		A&M 2562
12/10/83	77	5		36 **Red Hot**	*Sundown* [I]	$4		A&M 2593
9/15/84	90	2		37 **Bullish** *[HERB ALPERT TIJUANA BRASS]*	*Oriental Eyes* (Alpert) [I]	$4	■	A&M 2655
2/28/87	46	10		38 **Keep Your Eye On Me** S:31	*Our Song*	$3	■	A&M 2915
4/11/87	5	19		39 **Diamonds** RB[2] S:5 / A:7 — **HERB ALPERT (with Janet Jackson)**	*African Flame*	$3	■	A&M 2929
7/18/87	35	14		40 **Making Love In The Rain** S:35 / A:39 — **Lisa Keith** (backing vocal, above 3)	*Rocket To The Moon*	$3	■	A&M 2949

ALPHA TEAM '93

Electronic-rave duo from Chicago, Illinois: Dane Roewade and D.J. Attack.

DEBUT	PEAK	WKS	Gold	A-side (Chart Hit)	B-side	$	Sym	Label & Number
1/30/93	74	8		**Speed** S:49 / A:61 — samples theme and dialog from the 1960s animated TV series *Speed Racer*	*(radio edit) / Hardcore* [N]	$8	■*	Strictly Hype 106

DEBUT	PEAK	WKS	Gold	A-side (Chart Hit)	B-side	$	Sym	Label & Number
				ALPHAVILLE LP **'85**				
				Male pop trio from Berlin, Germany: Marian Gold (vocals), Frank Mertens (keyboards) and Bernhard Lloyd (drums).				
11/24/84+	66	10		1 **Big In Japan**	*Seeds*	$3	■	Atlantic 89665
3/23/85	93	4		2 **Forever Young**	*Lies*	$3		Atlantic 89578
10/29/88	65	14		3 **Forever Young**	*Lies* [R]	$3	■	Atlantic 89013
				above 2 are the same version				
				AL-SHID **'02**				
				Born Alpha Sesay-Harrell in Queens, New York. Male rapper.				
4/13/02	66S	1		**Ign'ant**	*(2 versions) / Fight Club* (w/Hug)	$7	T	Old Maid 2008
				A.L.T. And The Lost Civilization BUB **'92**				
				Born Al Trivette in Los Angeles, California. French-Mexican rapper. Formerly with **Latin Alliance**. A.L.T.: Another Latin Timebomb.				
7/11/92	48	14		**Tequila** S:32 / A:48	*Refried Beans*	$6	▮V	Atco 98533
				rap version of **The Champs**' 1958 instrumental hit				
				AMANDA **'01**				
				Born Amanda Lameche in 1985 in France; raised in Taby, Sweden. Female pop singer. Her sister, Anais Lameche, is a member of **Play**.				
5/12/01	81	6		**Everybody Doesn't** S:18	*(remix)*	$5	★+	Maverick 16771
				AMAZING RHYTHM ACES, The C&W/BUB/LP **'75**				
				Country-rock group from Memphis, Tennessee: Howard Russell Smith (vocals, guitar), Barry "Byrd" Burton (guitar, dobro), Billy Earhart III (keyboards), Jeff Davis (bass) and David "Butch" McDade (drums). Disbanded in 1980. McDade died of cancer on 11/29/98 (age 52).				
6/21/75	14	16		1 **Third Rate Romance**	*Mystery Train*	$6		ABC 12078
12/20/75+	72	8		2 **Amazing Grace (Used To Be Her Favorite Song)**	*The Beautiful Lie*	$6		ABC 12142
9/18/76	42	10		3 **The End Is Not In Sight (The Cowboy Tune)**	*Same Ole' Me*	$6		ABC 12202
				AMAZULU **'87**				
				Female reggae-styled trio formed in London, England: Ann Marie Ruddock (vocals), Sharon Bailey (percussion) and Lesley Beach (saxophone).				
7/25/87	90	4		**Montego Bay**	*Only Love*	$5		Mango 121
				AMBER **'97**				
				Born Marie-Claire Cremers in Holland; raised in Germany. Female dance singer/songwriter.				
6/15/96+	24	40		1 **This Is Your Night** A:14 / S:61	*(radio mix)*	$4	▮	Tommy Boy 7735
1/18/97	74	10		2 **Colour Of Love**	*(radio edit)*	$4	▮	Tommy Boy 7748
10/18/97+	58	20		3 **One More Night** A:68	*(album version)*	$4	▮	Tommy Boy 7786
8/29/98	52	15		4 **If You Could Read My Mind** S:55	*(instrumental)*	$4	★	Tommy Boy 7497
				STARS ON 54: ULTRA NATÉ, AMBER, JOCELYN ENRIQUEZ				
				from the movie *54* starring Ryan Phillippe; originally charted its first 5 weeks as a CD maxi-single on Tommy Boy 497, then charted 9 more weeks as a cassette single; re-entered *Hot 100* on 2/27/99 at #99 for 1 more week as a regular CD single				
7/17/99+	42	29		5 **Sexual (Li Da Di)** S:25 / A:46	*(6 versions)*	$7	★*	Tommy Boy 381
				charted for 8 weeks (#93); re-entered *Hot 100* 3 more times: 1 week on 9/25/99 (#99); 5 weeks on 10/9/99 (#96); 15 weeks on 11/20/99 (#42)				
2/5/00	51S	15		6 **Above The Clouds**	*(7 remixes)*	$7	★*	Tommy Boy 2053
10/27/01	33S	21		7 **Yes!**	*(4 versions)*	$7	★*	Tommy Boy 2272
				chorus inspired by poet James Joyce's "Ulysses"				
8/24/02	30S	6		8 **The Need To Be Naked**	*(4 versions)*	$7	★*	Tommy Boy 2366
12/28/02	28S	7		9 **Anyway (men are from mars)**	*(5 remixes)*	$7	★*	Tommy Boy 2386
				AMBOY DUKES, The BUB/LP **'68**				
				Hard-rock group from Detroit, Michigan: John Drake (vocals), **Ted Nugent** and Steve Farmer (guitars), Rick Lober (keyboards), Bill White (bass) and Dave Palmer (drums). Numerous personnel changes with Nugent the only constant. Disbanded in 1975.				
6/29/68	16	12		**Journey To The Center Of The Mind**	*Mississippi Murderer*	$15		Mainstream 684
				AMBROSIA BUB/ROK/AC/LP **'80**				
				Pop group formed in Los Angeles, California: **David Pack** (see #8 below) (vocals, guitar), Joe Puerta (vocals, bass), Christopher North (keyboards) and Burleigh Drummond (drums). Group disbanded in 1984. Puerta joined **Bruce Hornsby & The Range**.				
6/14/75	17	14		1 **Holdin' On To Yesterday**	*Make Us All Aware*	$5		20th Century 2207
11/8/75	63	5		2 **Nice, Nice, Very Nice**	*Lover Arrive*	$5		20th Century 2244
				inspired by Kurt Vonnegut's book *Cat's Cradle* (Vonnegut listed as co-writer of the song)				
2/26/77	39	8		3 **Magical Mystery Tour**	*Cowboy Star*	$5		20th Century 2327
				featuring the **London Symphony Orch.** and the **Royal Philharmonic Orch.**; from the documentary movie *All This And World War II*				
9/2/78	3	21		4 **How Much I Feel**	*Ready For Camarillo*	$4		Warner 8640
4/5/80	3	19		5 **Biggest Part Of Me**	*Livin' On My Own*	$4		Warner 49225
7/12/80	13	18		6 **You're The Only Woman (You & I)**	*Shape I'm In*	$4		Warner 49508
6/5/82	86	4		7 **How Can You Love Me**	*Still Not Satisfied*	$4		Warner 29996
1/25/86	95	3		8 **Prove Me Wrong**	*(instrumental)*	$3		Warner 28802
				DAVID PACK				
				from the movie *White Nights* starring Mikhail Baryshnikov; Pack wrote all of above (except #3)				
	★213★			**AMERICA** AC/BUB/LP **'72**				
				Soft-rock trio formed in London, England. Consisted of Americans **Dan Peek** (born on 11/1/50; see #15 below) and Gerry Beckley (born on 9/12/52), with Englishman Dewey Bunnell (born on 1/19/51). All played guitars. Met at U.S. Air Force base. Moved to the U.S. in February 1972. Won the 1972 Best New Artist Grammy Award. Continued as a duo after Peek left in 1976 and became a popular Contemporary Christian act.				
				1)A Horse With No Name 2)Sister Golden Hair 3)Tin Man				
2/19/72	❶3	14	●	1 **A Horse With No Name**	*Everyone I Meet Is From California*	$6		Warner 7555
5/20/72	9	10		2 **I Need You**	*Riverside*	$6	■	Warner 7580
10/21/72	8	12		3 **Ventura Highway**	*Saturn Nights*	$6		Warner 7641
1/27/73	35	8		4 **Don't Cross The River**	*To Each His Own*	$6		Warner 7670

DEBUT	PEAK	WKS	Gold	A-side (Chart Hit)......B-side	$	Sym	Label & Number
				AMERICA — Cont'd			
4/28/73	62	5		5 **Only In Your Heart**......*Moon Song*	$6		Warner 7694
8/18/73	67	8		6 **Muskrat Love**......*Cornwall Blank*	$6		Warner 7725
8/24/74	4	18		7 **Tin Man**......AC[1] *In The Country* charted first 6 weeks on Warner 7839; remaining weeks on 8014	$6		Warner 8014
12/28/74+	5	14		8 **Lonely People**......AC[1] *Mad Dog*	$6	■	Warner 8048
4/5/75	1[1]	16		9 **Sister Golden Hair**......*Midnight*	$6		Warner 8086
7/19/75	20	13		10 **Daisy Jane**......*Tomorrow*	$6		Warner 8118
11/29/75+	44	9		11 **Woman Tonight**......*Bell Tree*	$6		Warner 8157
5/15/76	23	12		12 **Today's The Day**......AC[2] *Hideaway Part II*	$6		Warner 8212
8/21/76	75	4		13 **Amber Cascades**......*Who Loves You* #7-13: produced by **George Martin** (**The Beatles**' producer)	$6		Warner 8238
3/24/79	56	5		14 **California Dreamin'**......*See It My Way* (FDR) from the beach movie *California Dreaming* starring Dennis Christopher	$6	□	American Int'l. 700
9/15/79	78	5		15 **All Things Are Possible**......*He's All That's Right* **DAN PEEK**	$6		Lamb & Lion 817
7/31/82	8	20		16 **You Can Do Magic**......*Even The Score*	$4		Capitol 5142
11/27/82+	45	13		17 **Right Before Your Eyes**......*Inspector Mills*	$4	■	Capitol 5177
6/18/83	33	12		18 **The Border**......*Sometimes Lovers*	$4	■	Capitol 5236
				AMERICAN BREED, The BUB/LP **'68** Interracial pop-rock group from Chicago, Illinois: Gary Loizzo (vocals, guitar), Al Ciner (guitar), Chuck Colbert (bass) and Lee Graziano (drums). Later members Kevin Murphy (keyboards) and Andre Fischer (drums) went on to form **Rufus**.			
6/3/67	24	9		1 **Step Out Of Your Mind**......*Same Old Thing*	$12		Acta 804
12/2/67+	5	14	●	2 **Bend Me, Shape Me**......*Mindrocker*	$12		Acta 811
2/24/68	39	7		3 **Green Light**......*Don't It Make You Cry*	$12	■	Acta 821
5/25/68	84	3		4 **Ready, Willing and Able**......*Take Me If You Want Me*	$12		Acta 824
8/3/68	88	4		5 **Anyway That You Want Me**......*Master Of My Fate*	$12		Acta 827
				AMERICAN COMEDY NETWORK, The **'84** Group of former DJ's headed by Andy Goodman. DJ Bob Rivers contributed song parodies to the group.			
2/4/84	70	5		**Breaking Up Is Hard On You (a/k/a Don't Take Ma Bell Away From Me)**......*(3 "Krapco" novelty segments)* [N] parody of **Neil Sedaka**'s "Breaking Up Is Hard To Do"	$5		Critique 704
				AMERICAN FLYER LP **'76** Veteran folk-rock group: Craig Fuller (**Pure Prairie League**), Eric Kaz (**Blues Magoos**), Steve Katz (**Blood, Sweat & Tears**) and Doug Yule (The Velvet Underground).			
10/30/76	80	4		**Let Me Down Easy**......*Queen Of All My Days*	$6		United Artists 874
				AMERICAN HI-FI ROK/LP **'01** Male rock group from Boston, Massachusetts: Stacy Jones (vocals), Jaime Arentzen (guitar), Drew Parsons (bass) and Brian Nolan (drums). Jones was drummer with **Letters To Cleo**.			
6/23/01	41	20		**Flavor Of The Weak**......A:37 from the album *American Hi-Fi* on Island 542871			album cut
				AMERIE R&B/LP **'02** Born Amerie Rogers in 1980 in Brooklyn, New York (Korean mother/African-American father); raised in Washington DC. Female R&B singer.			
6/8/02	23	19		1 **Why Don't We Fall In Love**......S:17 / A:22 *(6 versions)* **AMERIE (featuring Ludacris)**	$6	T	Rise/Columbia 79774
12/7/02	51	15		2 **Talkin' To Me**......S:30 / A:47 *(7 remixes;* 3 w/**Foxy Brown**)	$6	T	Rise/Columbia 79849
12/14/02+	36	15		3 **Paradise**......S:33 / A:36 *(2 versions) / After School* (w/**P. Diddy**) **LL COOL J feat. Amerie** samples "Rising To The Top" by Keni Burke	$6	T	Def Jam 063820
				AMES, Ed AC/BUB/LP **'67** Born Ed Urick on 7/9/27 in Malden, Massachusetts. Lead singer of **The Ames Brothers**. Played the Native American "Mingo" on the TV series *Daniel Boone*.			
1/23/65	73	6		1 **Try To Remember**......*Love Is Here To Stay* from the off-Broadway musical *The Fantasticks* starring Jerry Orbach	$7		RCA Victor 8483
1/21/67	8	13		2 **My Cup Runneth Over**......AC[4] *It Seems A Long Long Time* from the off-Broadway musical *I Do, I Do* starring Mary Martin and Robert Preston; title based on Psalms 23:5	$7		RCA Victor 9002
5/6/67	61	7		3 **Time, Time**......AC[1] *One Little Girl At A Time*	$6		RCA Victor 9178
9/30/67	98	2		4 **When The Snow Is On The Roses**......AC[4] *Let Me So Love*	$6		RCA Victor 9319
12/16/67+	19	8		5 **Who Will Answer?**......*My Love Is Gone From Me*	$6	■	RCA Victor 9400
5/11/68	79	6		6 **Apologize**......*The Wind Will Change Tomorrow (Cuando Sali de Cuba)* **Perry Botkin, Jr.** (orch., above 5)	$6		RCA Victor 9517
5/31/69	92	4		7 **Son Of A Travelin' Man**......*"2001"*	$6		RCA Victor 0156
				AMES, Nancy BUB/LP **'66** Born Nancy Alfaro in 1937 in Washington DC. Singer/actress. Her grandfather was president of Panama. Cast as the "TW3 Girl" on the American TV series *That Was The Week That Was*.			
3/19/66	89	3		1 **He Wore The Green Beret**......*War Is A Card Game* answer song to "Ballad Of The Green Berets" by **SSgt. Barry Sadler**	$8		Epic 10003
10/8/66	95	4		2 **Cry Softly**......*I Don't Want To Talk About It*	$12		Epic 10056

DEBUT	PEAK	WKS	Gold	A-side (Chart Hit)...B-side	$	Sym	Label & Number
	★287★			**AMES BROTHERS, The** MEM/POP/BUB/LP '50			
				Pop vocal group from Malden, Massachusetts. Formed in 1947. Family name Urick. Consisted of lead singer **Ed Ames** (born on 7/9/27) and his brothers Gene (born on 2/13/25), Joe (born on 5/3/24) and Vic (born on 5/20/25; died on 1/23/78, age 52). Charted 23 pop hits, 1948-54; including 3 #1 hits: "Rag Mop," "Sentimental Me" and "You You You." Own TV series in 1955. Ed recorded solo and acted on Broadway and TV.			
				1)The Naughty Lady Of Shady Lane 2)Tammy 3)Melodie D'Amour 4)It Only Hurts For A Little While 5)My Bonnie Lassie			
11/20/54	3	15	●	1 **The Naughty Lady Of Shady Lane** S:3 / A:3 / J:3 *Addio*	$15	□	RCA Victor 5897
				picture sleeve is a "This Is Their Life" comic strip-styled sleeve			
9/24/55	11	11		2 **My Bonnie Lassie** ....S:11 / T:11 / A:14 / J:16 *So Will I*	$15		RCA Victor 6208
				tune charted in 1961 by **The Cambridge Strings** and **Mitch Miller** as "Tunes Of Glory" (adapted from "Scotland The Brave")			
2/25/56	35	12		3 **Forever Darling /** T:35			
				title song from the movie starring Lucille Ball and Desi Arnaz			
3/3/56	84	2		4 **I'm Gonna Love You**........T:84	$15		RCA Victor 6400
5/5/56	11	24		5 **It Only Hurts For A Little While /** J:11 / T:15 / A:15 / S:16			
6/30/56	89	1		6 **If You Wanna See Mamie Tonight**........T:89	$15		RCA Victor 6481
				from the movie *The Revolt of Mamie Stover* starring Jane Russell			
9/8/56	49	7		7 **49 Shades Of Green /** T:49			
9/8/56	67	6		8 **Summer Sweetheart**........T:67	$12		RCA Victor 6608
11/24/56	51	9		9 **I Saw Esau**........T:51 *The Game Of Love*	$12		RCA Victor 6720
7/1/57	5	24		10 **Tammy /** A:5 / S:24 / T:29			
				from the movie *Tammy and The Bachelor* starring **Debbie Reynolds**			
6/10/57	64	13		11 **Rockin' Shoes**........T:64 / S:flip	$12		RCA Victor 6930
				Joe Reisman (orch., above 2)			
10/7/57	5	20		12 **Melodie D'Amour (Melody of Love)**........A:5 / T:12 / S:12 *So Little Time*	$12		RCA Victor 7046
				French song written by Henri Salvador in 1949			
2/24/58	67	2		13 **Little Gypsy**........T:67 *In Love*	$12		RCA Victor 7142
3/31/58	23	11		14 **A Very Precious Love**........A:23 / T:65 *Don't Leave Me Now*	$12		RCA Victor 7167
				from the movie *Marjorie Morningstar* starring Natalie Wood			
8/4/58	90	1		15 **Stay /** H:90			
8/4/58	98	1		16 **Little Serenade**........H:98	$10		RCA Victor 7268
9/29/58	17	15		17 **Pussy Cat /** H:17 / S:20			
9/29/58	45	9		18 **No One But You (In My Heart)**........H:45 / S:flip	$10		RCA Victor 7315
12/29/58+	37	10		19 **Red River Rose**........*When The Summer Comes Again*	$10		RCA Victor 7413
				Hugo Winterhalter (orch., all of above - except #10 & 11)			
5/18/59	78	4		20 **Someone To Come Home To**........*Mason-Dixon Line*	$10		RCA Victor 7526
				Ray Martin (orch.)			
2/1/60	38	13		21 **China Doll**........*Christopher Sunday*	$10	■	RCA Victor 7655
				AMESBURY, Bill '74			
				Born in 1948 in Toronto, Ontario, Canada. Pop singer/songwriter/guitarist.			
2/16/74	59	9		**Virginia (Touch Me Like You Do)**........*That Close To Me*	$5		Casablanca 0001
				AMIL — see JAY-Z / TAMAR			
				AMOROSI, Vanessa '02			
				Born on 8/8/81 in Melbourne, Australia. Pop singer.			
2/9/02	48^S	2		**Absolutely Everybody**........*Shine*	$4	★	Universal 015082
				AMOS, Tori BUB/ROK/LP '98			
				Born Myra Ellen Amos on 8/22/63 in Newton, North Carolina; raised in Baltimore, Maryland. Alternative pop-rock singer/songwriter/pianist.			
2/19/94	72	12		1 **God**........MR^2 A:64 / S:73 *Sister Janet*	$5	▮	Atlantic 87250
1/20/96	60	13		2 **Caught A Lite Sneeze**........S:47 / A:64 *(medley of 4 "Silly Songs")*	$8	★*	Atlantic 85519
3/22/97	65	20		3 **Silent All These Years**........A:66 *(live version)*	$5	▮	Atlantic 83001
				from her 1992 album *Little Earthquakes*			
6/27/98	49	14		4 **Spark** S:60 / A:65 *Purple People*	$5	▮V	Atlantic 84104
10/3/98	54	5		5 **Jackie's Strength**........S:33 *Never Seen Blue / Beulah Land*	$5	▮	Atlantic 84163
12/12/98	38^S	3		6 **Raspberry Swirl**........*(remix) / Spark (remix) / Cruel*	$6	★V	Atlantic 84412
9/11/99	91	2		7 **Bliss**........S:16 *Hey Jupiter (live)*	$6	★V	Atlantic 84532
9/25/99	22^S	9		8 **1000 Oceans**........*Baker Baker (live)*	$6	★V	Atlantic 84534
2/26/00	48^S	3		9 **Concertina**........*Famous Blue Raincoat / Twinkle (both live)*	$7	★**	Atlantic 84651
				all of above written and produced by Amos			
				AMYTH '99			
				R&B vocal group from Baton Rouge, Louisiana: Wayne Spears, Otis Jupiter, Jelani Phillips and Stephen Joyce.			
10/23/99	59^S	4		**1*2*3**........*(instrumental)*	$6	★	Rock The Bells 16948
				ANA LP '90			
				Born Ana Rodriguez on 2/22/72 in Cuba; raised in Orlando, Florida. Female dance singer.			
7/11/87	94	3		1 **Shy Boys**........*Love Is The Winner*	$4	■	Parc 07056
5/19/90	66	7		2 **Got To Tell Me Something**........*What Could I Do*	$4	▮	Parc 73317
				ANACOSTIA — see PRESIDENTS, The			
				ANASTACIA BUB/LP '00			
				Born Anastacia Newkirk on 9/17/75 in Brooklyn, New York; raised in Chicago, Illinois. Female pop-dance singer.			
4/1/00	92	3		**I'm Outta Love**........S:16 *(remix) / Baptize My Soul*	$4	★V	Daylight/Epic 79343
				ANDERSON, Bill C&W/BUB/LP '63			
				Born James William Anderson III on 11/1/37 in Columbia, South Carolina. Country singer/songwriter/actor (charted 80 hits, 1958-91). Hosted Nashville Network's TV game show *Fandango*. Member of the *Grand Ole Opry* since 1961. Known as "Whispering Bill."			
10/27/62	89	4		1 **Mama Sang A Song**........CW^7 *On And On And On* [S]	$10		Decca 31404
4/13/63	8	15		2 **Still** CW^7 *You Made It Easy*	$10		Decca 31458
8/24/63	53	6		3 **8 X 10**........*One Mile Over - Two Miles Back*	$10	■	Decca 31521

DEBUT	PEAK	WKS	Gold	A-side (Chart Hit)	B-side	$	Sym	Label & Number
				ANDERSON, Bill — Cont'd				
12/28/68	18^{X}	1		4 **Po' Folks' Christmas**	*Christmas Time's A-Coming* [X]	$10	■	Decca 32417
				BILL ANDERSON And The Po' Boys				
11/21/70	93	3		5 **Where Have All Our Heroes Gone**	*Loving A Memory* [S]	$8		Decca 32744
7/15/78	80	4		6 **I Can't Wait Any Longer**	*Joanna*	$5		MCA 40893
				ANDERSON, Carl — see LORING, Gloria				
				ANDERSON, Elton '60				
				Born in 1932 in Lake Charles, Louisiana. Black singer who sang and played guitar with the Sid Lawrence Combo. Sid played bass guitar and was killed in a car crash in 1956.				
1/25/60	88	4		**Secret Of Love**	*Cool Down Baby*	$25		Mercury 71542
				ELTON ANDERSON with Sid Lawrence Combo				
				recorded in 1955 and originally released on Eddie Shuler's (the song's co-writer) Goldband label				
				ANDERSON, Ernestine LP '61				
				Born on 11/11/28 in Houston, Texas. Jazz singer. Formerly with **Eddie Heywood** and Lionel Hampton.				
2/27/61	98	1		**A Lover's Question**	*That's All I Want From You*	$25		Mercury 71772
				ANDERSON, Jade '02				
				Born in 1981 in London, England. Female singer. Daughter of **Jon Anderson** (lead singer of **Yes**).				
5/25/02	96	2		**Sugarhigh**	S:16 *Dive Deeper Medley*	$4	★	Columbia 79757
				ANDERSON, Jesse '70				
				R&B singer/songwriter.				
4/25/70	95	2		**I Got A Problem**	*Mighty Mighty*	$10		Thomas 805
				ANDERSON, John C&W/LP '83				
				Born on 12/13/54 in Orlando, Florida; raised in Apopka, Florida. Country singer/songwriter/guitarist. Charted 57 Country hits, 1977-2000.				
3/5/83	43	13	●	**Swingin'**	CW^{1} *A Honky Tonk Saturday Night*	$5		Warner 29788
				ANDERSON, Jon — see JON & VANGELIS				
				ANDERSON, Lale '61				
				Born on 3/23/10 in Bremerhaven, Germany. Died on 8/29/72 (age 62). Female singer.				
4/24/61	88	4		**(A Ship Will Come) Ein Schiff Wird Kommen**	*Manchmal Traum Ich Vom Kornfeld* [F]	$12		King 5478
				German vocal of the movie title song *Never On Sunday* (starring Melina Mercouri)				
				ANDERSON, Lynn C&W/BUB/LP '71				
				Born on 9/26/47 in Grand Forks, North Dakota; raised in Sacramento, California. Country singer. Daughter of country singer Liz Anderson. An accomplished equestrian, Lynn was the California Horse Show Queen in 1966. Charted 60 Country hits, 1966-89.				
11/28/70+	3	17	●	1 **Rose Garden**	CW^{5} *Nothing Between Us*	$6		Columbia 45252
				"Bubbled Under" (#119) for **Dobie Gray** in 1969 on White Whale 300				
5/15/71	63	6		2 **You're My Man**	CW^{2} *I'm Gonna Write A Song*	$6		Columbia 45356
8/21/71	63	7		3 **How Can I Unlove You**	CW^{3} *Don't Say Things You Don't Mean*	$5		Columbia 45429
1/29/72	71	5		4 **Cry**	*Simple Words*	$5		Columbia 45529
				#1 hit for **Johnnie Ray** in 1951				
6/30/73	74	10		5 **Top Of The World**	*I Wish I Was A Little Boy Again*	$5		Columbia 45857
1/4/75	93	3		6 **What A Man, My Man Is**	CW^{1} *Everything's Falling In Place (For Me And You)*	$5		Columbia 10041
				ANDERSON, Sunshine R&B/LP '01				
				Born on 10/26/73 in Charlotte, North Carolina. Female R&B singer.				
3/10/01	18	20		**Heard It All Before**	A:12 / S:51 *(3 versions)*	$6	T^{V}	Soulife 95524
				Mikey Dan (male vocal); "45": Soulife 97985; B-side: "Lunch Or Dinner"				
				ANDERSON, Vicki — see BROWN, James				
				ANDREONE, Leah '97				
				Born on 5/24/73 in San Diego, California. Female pop singer/pianist.				
1/25/97	57	20		**It's Alright, It's OK**	A:51 *Hate You Didn't Try*	$4	▮	RCA 64662
				ANDREWS, Chris '66				
				Born on 10/15/38 in Romford, London, England. White male singer/songwriter.				
1/1/66	94	1		**Yesterday Man**	*Too Bad You Don't Want Me*	$10		Atco 6385
				ANDREWS, Jessica C&W/BUB/LP '01				
				Born on 12/29/83 in Huntingdon, Tennessee. Country singer.				
4/17/99	66^{S}	9		1 **I Will Be There For You**	BUB:108 *(4 album snippets)*	$4	★^{V}	DreamWorks 59021
				"45" B-side: (same version)				
4/15/00	25^{S}	16		2 **Unbreakable Heart**	BUB:110 *(2 versions)*	$4	★^{V}	DreamWorks 59042
				"45" B-side: (acapella version)				
1/27/01	28	20		3 **Who I Am**	CW^{3} A:20		V	album cut
				"45": DreamWorks 50918; B-side: "Helplessly, Hopelessly" (C&W #31); from the album *Who I Am* on DreamWorks 50248				
				ANDREWS, Julie AC/LP '65				
				Born Julia Wells on 10/1/35 in Walton-on-Thames, England. Noted Broadway and movie actress. Starred in the acclaimed Broadway productions of *My Fair Lady* and *Camelot*. Won 1964's Best Actress Oscar for *Mary Poppins*.				
4/24/65	66	5		**Super-cali-fragil-istic-expi-ali-docious**	*A Spoonful Of Sugar* (Andrews) [N]	$8	■	Buena Vista 434
				JULIE ANDREWS - DICK VAN DYKE and THE PEARLIES				
				from the Disney movie *Mary Poppins* starring Andrews and Van Dyke				
				ANDREWS, Lee, And The Hearts '57				
				Born Arthur Lee Andrew Thompson in 1938 in Goldsboro, North Carolina; raised in Philadelphia, Pennsylvania. Formed vocal group The Hearts in 1952. First recorded for Rainbow in 1954. Group on Chess included Thomas "Butch" Curry, Ted Weems, Roy and Wendell Calhoun.				
8/12/57	45	10		1 **Long Lonely Nights**	T:45 *The Clock*	$50		Chess 1665
				first released on Main Line 102 in 1957 ($400-green label)				
11/25/57	20	17		2 **Tear Drops**	S:20 / T:20 / A:21 *The Girl Around The Corner*	$40		Chess 1675
6/2/58	33	11		3 **Try The Impossible**	S:33 / T:33 *Nobody's Home*	$30		United Artists 123
				first released on Casino 452 in 1958 ($800-'playing cards' label)				

DEBUT	PEAK	WKS	Gold	A-side (Chart Hit)	B-side	$	Sym	Label & Number

ANDREWS, Patty — POP '49

Born on 2/26/18 in Minneapolis, Minnesota. Member of the **Andrews Sisters**. Appeared in 15 movies including *Private Buckaroo* (1942) and *Road To Rio* (1947). The Andrews Sisters charted 71 pop hits, 1940-51.

DEBUT	PEAK	WKS	Gold	A-side (Chart Hit)	B-side	$	Sym	Label & Number
11/12/55	69	5		**Suddenly There's A Valley** T:69 — Harold Mooney (orch.)	*Booga-Da-Woog*	$15		Capitol 3228

ANDREWS, Ruby — R&B/BUB '67

Born Ruby Stackhouse on 3/12/47 in Hollandale, Mississippi. R&B singer who sang backup with **The C.O.D.'s** in 1965.

DEBUT	PEAK	WKS	Gold	A-side (Chart Hit)	B-side	$	Sym	Label & Number
8/26/67	51	9		1 **Casonova (Your Playing Days Are Over)**	*I Just Don't Believe It*	$12		Zodiac 1004
1/20/68	92	1		2 **Hey Boy Take A Chance On Love**	*Come To Me*	$12		Zodiac 1006
8/2/69	96	2		3 **You Made A Believer (Out Of Me)**	*Where Have You Gone*	$12		Zodiac 1015

ANGEL — LP '78

Hard-rock group from Washington DC: Frank DiMino (vocals), Edwin "Punky" Meadows (guitar; **The Cherry People**), Gregg Giuffria (keyboards; **Giuffria**, **House Of Lords**), Mickey Jones (bass) and Barry Brandt (drums). Felix Robinson replaced Jones by 1978.

DEBUT	PEAK	WKS	Gold	A-side (Chart Hit)	B-side	$	Sym	Label & Number
4/23/77	77	6		1 **That Magic Touch**	*Big Boy (Let's Do It Again)*	$6		Casablanca 878
4/1/78	44	8		2 **Ain't Gonna Eat Out My Heart Anymore**	*Flying With Broken Wings (Without You)*	$6		Casablanca 914

ANGELICA — '92

Born Angelica Garcia on 5/21/72 in El Monte, California. Latin pop-dance singer.

DEBUT	PEAK	WKS	Gold	A-side (Chart Hit)	B-side	$	Sym	Label & Number
10/19/91+	29	20		**Angel Baby** S:19 / A:40 — a portion of the song is sung in Spanish	*(all English version)*	$4	▮	Quality/Ultra 15171

ANGELINA — BUB '96

Born Angelina Camarillo in Union City, California. Latin pop-dance singer/songwriter.

DEBUT	PEAK	WKS	Gold	A-side (Chart Hit)	B-side	$	Sym	Label & Number
3/23/96	52	20		1 **Release Me** A:46	*(radio edit)*	$4	▮	Upstairs 0115
10/19/96	69	11		2 **I Don't Need Your Love** A:70	*(release edit)*	$4	▮	Upstairs 0120
2/15/97	82	15		3 **Without Your Love**	*(haus-a-holic mix)*	$4	▮	Upstairs 0123
8/16/97	89	4		4 **Tide Is High**	*(dance mix)*	$4	▮	Upstairs 0127

ANGELS, The — BUB/LP '63

Female pop trio from Orange, New Jersey. Formed as The Starlets with sisters Phyllis "Jiggs" & Barbara Allbut, and Linda Jansen (lead singer). Jansen was replaced by Peggy Santiglia (later of **Dusk**) in 1962. Studio backing vocalists for **Lou Christie** and others in the mid-1960s. Barbara replaced by Lana Shaw, formerly of **The Serendipity Singers**. Peggy replaced by Debbie Swisher, formerly of **The Pixies Three**.

DEBUT	PEAK	WKS	Gold	A-side (Chart Hit)	B-side	$	Sym	Label & Number
10/16/61+	14	14		1 **'Til**	*A Moment Ago*	$20		Caprice 107
2/17/62	38	11		2 **Cry Baby Cry** — **Hutch Davie** (orch., above 2)	*That's All I Ask Of You*	$20		Caprice 112
8/3/63	1 [3]	14		3 **My Boyfriend's Back**	*(Love Me) Now*	$15		Smash 1834
10/26/63	25	7		4 **I Adore Him** / — co-written by Jan Berry (of **Jan & Dean**)				
12/7/63	84	3		5 **Thank You And Goodnight**		$15	▮	Smash 1854
1/18/64	41	7		6 **Wow Wow Wee (He's The Boy For Me)**	*Snowflakes And Teardrops*	$15		Smash 1870

ANIMALS, The — BUB/LP '64

★212★

Rock group formed in Newcastle-upon-Tyne, England, as the **Alan Price Combo**. Consisted of **Eric Burdon** (vocals; born on 5/11/41), Alan Price (keyboards; born on 4/19/42), Bryan "Chas" Chandler (bass; born on 12/18/38), Hilton Valentine (guitar; born on 5/21/43) and John Steel (drums; born on 2/4/41). Price left in May 1965; replaced by Dave Rowberry (died of heart failure on 6/6/2003, age 62). Chandler pursued a management career and discovered **Jimi Hendrix** in 1966; died in his sleep of an apparent heart attack on 7/17/96 (age 57). Steel left in 1966; replaced by Barry Jenkins. Group disbanded in July 1968. After a period with **War**, Burdon and the other originals reunited in 1976 and again in 1983. Inducted into the Rock and Roll Hall of Fame in 1994.

1)The House Of The Rising Sun 2)San Franciscan Nights 3)See See Rider

DEBUT	PEAK	WKS	Gold	A-side (Chart Hit)	B-side	$	Sym	Label & Number
8/8/64	1 [3]	11		1 **The House Of The Rising Sun**	*Talkin' 'Bout You*	$15	▮	MGM 13264
9/12/64	57	3		2 **Gonna Send You Back To Walker (Gonna Send You Back To Georgia)**	*Baby Let Me Take You Home (#102)*	$15		MGM 13242
9/26/64	19	9		3 **I'm Crying** — picture sleeve variation shows B-side as "Take It Easy"	*Take It Easy Baby*	$15	▮	MGM 13274
12/5/64+	43	7		4 **Boom Boom**	*Blue Feeling*	$15	▮	MGM 13298
2/6/65	15	10		5 **Don't Let Me Be Misunderstood**	*Club A-GoGo*	$15		MGM 13311
5/15/65	32	6		6 **Bring It On Home To Me**	*For Miss Caulker*	$15	▮	MGM 13339
8/14/65	13	11		7 **We Gotta Get Out Of This Place**	*I Can't Believe It*	$15		MGM 13382
11/6/65+	23	12		8 **It's My Life** — above 4 from the album *Animal Tracks*; all of above produced by Mickie Most	*I'm Going To Change The World*	$15		MGM 13414
2/26/66	34	7		9 **Inside-Looking Out**	*You're On My Mind*	$12		MGM 13468
5/21/66	12	10		10 **Don't Bring Me Down**	*Cheating*	$12		MGM 13514
				ERIC BURDON & THE ANIMALS:				
9/17/66	10	10		11 **See See Rider** — #14 hit for Ma Rainey in 1925 (as "See See Rider Blues")	*She'll Return It*	$10		MGM 13582
11/26/66	29	9		12 **Help Me Girl**	*That Ain't Where It's At*	$10		MGM 13636
4/8/67	15	9		13 **When I Was Young**	*A Girl Named Sandoz*	$10		MGM 13721
8/5/67	9	10		14 **San Franciscan Nights**	*Good Times*	$10	▮	MGM 13769
12/16/67+	15	9		15 **Monterey** — story-in-song of the famed Monterey International Pop Festival, June 16-18, 1967	*Ain't It So*	$10	▮	MGM 13868
4/13/68	80	4		16 **Anything**	*It's All Meat*	$10		MGM 13917
6/1/68	14	14		17 **Sky Pilot (Part One)** — #9-17: produced by Tom Wilson	*(Part Two)*	$10		MGM 13939
11/23/68	67	8		18 **White Houses**	*River Deep, Mountain High*	$10		MGM 14013
8/13/83	48	10		19 **The Night** *[THE ANIMALS]*	*No John No*	$6		I.R.S. 9920

ANIMOTION

LP **'85**

Techno-pop group: Astrid Plane (female vocals), Bill Wadhams (male vocals, keyboards), Don Kirkpatrick (guitar), Charles Ottavio (bass) and Frency O'Brien (drums). Plane and Wadhams left by 1988, replaced by Cynthia Rhodes and Paul Engemann. Rhodes was an actress (in movies *Staying Alive* and *Dirty Dancing*). Engemann was formerly with **Device**. Rhodes married **Richard Marx** on 1/8/89. Plane and Ottavio married on 10/13/90.

DEBUT	PEAK	WKS	Gold	A-side (Chart Hit)	B-side	$	Sym	Label & Number
1/26/85	6	24		1 **Obsession**	S:5 / A:5 *Turn Around*	$4	■	Mercury 880266
6/1/85	39	13		2 **Let Him Go**	*Holding You*	$4	■	Mercury 880737
3/8/86	76	6		3 **I Engineer**	*The Essence*	$3	■	Casablanca 884433
5/17/86	84	4		4 **I Want You**	*Staring Down The Demons*	$3	■	Casablanca 884729
2/18/89	9	18		5 **Room To Move**	A:9 / S:12 *Send It Over*	$3	■	Polydor 871418
				from the movie *My Stepmother Is An Alien* starring Dan Aykroyd and Kim Basinger				
6/10/89	53	9		6 **Calling It Love**	*The Way Into Your Heart*	$3	■	Polydor 889054
				written by **Desmond Child** and drummer Anton Fig of David Letterman's *Late Show* CBS Orchestra				

ANITA AND TH' SO-AND-SO'S

'62

Group is actually the Anita Kerr Singers. Anita was born Anita Jean Grilli on 10/31/27 in Memphis, Tennessee. One of the most prolific studio backup vocal groups of the 1950s and 1960s. Also see **The Little Dippers**.

DEBUT	PEAK	WKS	Gold	A-side (Chart Hit)	B-side	$	Sym	Label & Number
2/17/62	91	3		**Joey Baby**	*Rinky Tinky Rhythm*	$15		RCA Victor 7974

ANKA, Paul ★29★

BUB/AC/LP **'59**

Born on 7/30/41 in Ottawa, Ontario, Canada. Performer since age 12. Father financed first recording, "I Confess," on RPM 472 in 1956. Wrote "It Doesn't Matter Anymore" (**Buddy Holly**), "She's A Lady" (**Tom Jones**) and the English lyrics to "My Way" (**Frank Sinatra**). Also wrote theme for TV's *Tonight Show.* Own TV variety show in 1973. Appeared in the 1959 move *Girls Town*, the 1962 movie *The Longest Day* and the 1992 movie *Captain Ron*. Longtime popular entertainer in Las Vegas.

1)Lonely Boy 2)(You're) Having My Baby 3)Diana 4)Put Your Head On My Shoulder 5)Puppy Love

DEBUT	PEAK	WKS	Gold	A-side (Chart Hit)	B-side	$	Sym	Label & Number
7/15/57	❶[1]	29	●	1 **Diana** RB[2]	S:❶[1] / T:2 / A:2 *Don't Gamble With Love*	$25		ABC-Paramount 9831
				Diana was the Anka family's babysitter				
12/16/57	97	1		2 **I Love You, Baby**	T:97 *Tell Me That You Love Me*	$30		ABC-Paramount 9855
1/20/58	7	17		3 **You Are My Destiny**	T:7 / S:9 / A:9 *When I Stop Loving You (That'll Be The Day)*	$20		ABC-Paramount 9880
4/21/58	15	14		4 **Crazy Love /**	S:15 / T:19			
4/21/58	16	13		5 **Let The Bells Keep Ringing**	S:16 / A:18 / T:30	$20		ABC-Paramount 9907
7/28/58	69	5		6 **Midnight**	H:69 *Verboten! (Forbidden)*	$20		ABC-Paramount 9937
10/6/58	80	5		7 **Just Young**	H:80 *So It's Goodbye*	$20		ABC-Paramount 9956
12/1/58+	29	8		8 **The Teen Commandments**	*If You Learn To Pray* (**Don Costa** Chorus) [S]	$25		ABC-Paramount 9974
				PAUL ANKA-GEO. HAMILTON IV-JOHNNY NASH				
				Bill Givens (narrative); inspirational talk from the three ABC-Paramount artists				
12/22/58+	15	17		9 **(All of a Sudden) My Heart Sings**	*That's Love*	$20		ABC-Paramount 9987
				#7 hit for Johnnie Johnston in 1945				
3/30/59	33	9		10 **I Miss You So**	*Late Last Night*	$20	■	ABC-Paramount 10011
				#20 hit for The Cats and the Fiddle in 1940				
6/1/59	❶[4]	15	●	11 **Lonely Boy**	*Your Love*	$20		ABC-Paramount 10022
				from the movie *Girls Town* starring Mamie Van Doren and Anka				
8/31/59	2[3]	18		12 **Put Your Head On My Shoulder**	*Don't Ever Leave Me*	$20	■	ABC-Paramount 10040
11/23/59	4	15		13 **It's Time To Cry**	*Something Has Changed Me*	$20	■	ABC-Paramount 10064
2/22/60	2[2]	14		14 **Puppy Love /**				
4/4/60	90	2		15 **Adam And Eve**		$15	■	ABC-Paramount 10082
				from the movie *The Private Lives of Adam & Eve* starring Mamie Van Doren and Mickey Rooney				
5/23/60	8	13		16 **My Home Town /**				
5/30/60	41	9		17 **Something Happened**		$15	■	ABC-Paramount 10106
8/1/60	23	12		18 **Hello Young Lovers /**				
				from the Rodgers & Hammerstein musical *The King And I* starring Yul Brynner				
8/1/60	40	11		19 **I Love You In The Same Old Way**		$15	■	ABC-Paramount 10132
9/26/60	11	11		20 **Summer's Gone**	*I'd Have To Share*	$15	■	ABC-Paramount 10147
1/16/61	16	8		21 **The Story Of My Love**	*Don't Say You're Sorry (#108)*	$15	■	ABC-Paramount 10168
3/13/61	13	11		22 **Tonight My Love, Tonight**	*I'm Just A Fool Anyway*	$15	■	ABC-Paramount 10194
				melody adapted from "Caro Nome" from Verdi's opera *Rigoletto*				
5/29/61	10	10		23 **Dance On Little Girl**	*I Talk To You (On The Telephone)*	$15	■	ABC-Paramount 10220
8/28/61	35	7		24 **Kissin' On The Phone /**				
9/11/61	70	4		25 **Cinderella**		$15	■	ABC-Paramount 10239
2/24/62	12	12		26 **Love Me Warm And Tender**	*I'd Like To Know*	$12	■	RCA Victor 7977
5/26/62	13	10		27 **A Steel Guitar And A Glass Of Wine**	*I Never Knew Your Name*	$12	■	RCA Victor 8030
8/25/62	46	6		28 **Every Night (Without You)**	*There You Go*	$12	■	RCA Victor 8068
8/25/62	94	1		29 **I'm Coming Home**	*Cry*	$15		ABC-Paramount 10338
11/3/62	19	8		30 **Eso Beso (That Kiss!)**	*Give Me Back My Heart*	$12	■	RCA Victor 8097
1/19/63	26	8		31 **Love (Makes the World Go 'Round)**	*Crying In The Wind*	$12	■	RCA Victor 8115
4/13/63	39	8		32 **Remember Diana**	*At Night*	$12	■	RCA Victor 8170
6/29/63	97	1		33 **Hello Jim**	*You've Got The Nerve To Call This Love*	$12	■	RCA Victor 8195
12/14/63	89	3		34 **Did You Have A Happy Birthday?**	*For No Good Reason At All*	$12	■	RCA Victor 8272
1/4/69	27	10		35 **Goodnight My Love**	*This Crazy World*	$10		RCA Victor 9648
				#7 R&B hit for **Jesse Belvin** in 1956				
3/22/69	64	6		36 **In The Still Of The Night**	*Pickin' Up The Pieces*	$10		RCA Victor 0126
5/31/69	80	4		37 **Sincerely**	*Next Year*	$10		RCA Victor 0164
				written by legendary DJ Alan Freed and Harvey Fuqua (of **The Moonglows**)				
11/22/69	86	3		38 **Happy**	*Can't Get You Out Of My Mind*	$10		RCA Victor 9767
10/2/71	53	11		39 **Do I Love You**	*So Long City*	$7		Buddah 252
3/25/72	65	9		40 **Jubilation**	*Everything's Been Changed*	$7		Buddah 294

DEBUT	PEAK	WKS	Gold	A-side (Chart Hit)..........B-side	$	Sym	Label & Number
				ANKA, Paul — Cont'd			
1/5/74	80	8		41 **Let Me Get To Know You**..........*Flashback*	$6		Fame 345
7/6/74	❶ 3	15	●	42 **(You're) Having My Baby**..........*Papa (Anka)*	$5		United Artists 454
11/9/74+	7	16		43 **One Man Woman/One Woman Man**..........*Let Me Get To Know You (Anka)*	$5		United Artists 569
3/15/75	8	15		44 **I Don't Like To Sleep Alone**..........*How Can Anything Be Beautiful-After You (Anka)*	$5	■	United Artists 615
7/26/75	15	13		45 **(I Believe) There's Nothing Stronger Than Our Love**...*Today I Became A Fool (Anka)*	$5		United Artists 685
				PAUL ANKA with Odia Coates (above 4)			
11/15/75+	7	20		46 **Times Of Your Life**..........AC[1] *Water Runs Deep*	$5	■	United Artists 737
				tune adapted from a Kodak jingle			
4/3/76	33	9		47 **Anytime (I'll Be There)**..........*Something About You*	$5		United Artists 789
12/18/76+	60	7		48 **Happier**..........*Closing Doors*	$5		United Artists 911
4/30/77	80	2		49 **My Best Friend's Wife**..........*Never Gonna Fall In Love Again (Like I Fell In Love With You)*	$5		United Artists 972
7/16/77	75	4		50 **Everybody Ought To Be In Love**..........*Tonight*	$5		United Artists 1018
10/7/78	35	11		51 **This Is Love**..........*I'm By Myself Again*	$4		RCA 11395
4/18/81	48	9		52 **I've Been Waiting For You All Of My Life**..........*Think I'm In Love Again*	$4		RCA 12225
6/18/83	40	16		53 **Hold Me 'Til The Mornin' Comes**..........*This Is The First Time*	$4	■	Columbia 03897
				Peter Cetera (backing vocal); Anka wrote all of his hits (except #7-10, 17, 18, 24, 30, 35-38, 46, 51 & 52); Anka's musical arrangers and conductors: Stan Applebaum (#24, 25), Charles Calello (#49, 50), Michel Colombier (#48), **Don Costa** (#1-13, 17, 21, 34, 35, 37), **Ray Ellis** (#26-28), Sid Feller (#14-16, 18-20, 22, 23, 29), **David Foster** (#53), Rick Hall (#44, 45), Johnny Harris (#40, 42, 46), Jimmie Haskell (#41, 43, 47), **Bill Justis** (#52), Sammy Lowe (#32, 33), **Teddy Randazzo** (#36), **Joe Sherman** (#30, 31), John Tartaglia (#38), David Van DePitte (#39) and David Wolfert (#51)			
				ANNETTE BUB/LP **'60**			
				Born Annette Funicello on 10/22/42 in Utica, New York. Became America's most popular Mouseketter after her debut on the TV series *The Mickey Mouse Club* in 1955. Acted in several teen movies in the early 1960s. Co-starred with **Frankie Avalon** in many movies, the last being *Back To The Beach* in 1987. Diagnosed with multiple sclerosis in 1987.			
				1)Tall Paul 2)O Dio Mio 3)Pineapple Princess			
1/5/59	7	15		1 **Tall Paul** *Ma - He's Making Eyes At Me*	$25		Disneyland 118
4/13/59	73	4		2 **Jo-Jo The Dog-Faced Boy**..........*Love Me Forever*	$20		Buena Vista 336
				some pressings released with "Lonely Guitar" as the B-side ($25)			
7/6/59	50	11		3 **Lonely Guitar**..........*Wild Willie*	$20	■	Buena Vista 339
				written by the leader of the original TV series *The Mickey Mouse Club*, Jimmie Dodd			
10/26/59+	20	18		4 **First Name Initial /**			
10/26/59	74	3		5 **My Heart Became Of Age**..........	$20	■	Buena Vista 349
				originally released in 1959 on Buena Vista 344 (B-side: "Especially For You")			
2/22/60	10	12		6 **O Dio Mio**..........*It Took Dreams*	$20	■	Buena Vista 354
6/6/60	36	8		7 **Train Of Love**..........*Tell Me Who's The Girl*	$20	■	Buena Vista 359
				picture sleeve issued with either a gold or silver title strip across the top of the sleeve			
8/15/60	11	14		8 **Pineapple Princess**..........*Luau Cha Cha Cha*	$20	■	Buena Vista 362
12/26/60	92	2		9 **Talk To Me Baby**..........*I Love You Baby*	$20	■	Buena Vista 369
				#7 & 9: written by **Paul Anka**			
2/20/61	87	2		10 **Dream Boy**..........*Please, Please, Signoré*	$20	■	Buena Vista 374
				ANNETTE with the Afterbeats (#1, 4, 5 & 7-10)			
				based on the 1880 Italian song "Funiculi-Funicula"			
				ANN-MARGRET BUB/LP **'61**			
				Born Ann-Margret Olsson on 4/28/41 in Valsjöbyn, Jämtland, Sweden; raised in Wilmette, Illinois. Actress/dancer/singer. Starred in many movies (including *Viva Las Vegas* with **Elvis Presley**) and Broadway shows. Married **Roger Smith** on 5/8/67.			
7/24/61	17	12		1 **I Just Don't Understand**..........*I Don't Hurt Anymore*	$15	■	RCA Victor 7894
11/13/61	97	3		2 **It Do Me So Good**..........*Gimme Love*	$15	■	RCA Victor 7952
				written by blues-great Willie Dixon			
3/24/62	82	5		3 **What Am I Supposed To Do**..........*Let's Stop Kidding Each Other*	$15	■	RCA Victor 7986
				ANOTHER BAD CREATION R&B/LP **'91**			
				Pre-teen R&B-rap vocal group from Atlanta, Georgia: Chris Sellers, Dave Shelton, Romell Chapman, with brothers Marliss and Demetrius Pugh. Appeared in the movie *The Meteor Man.*			
1/12/91	9	23	●	1 **Iesha**..........S:2 / A:18 *(no B-side)*	$4	■V	Motown 2070
				Michael Bivins (rap)			
4/27/91	10	17		2 **Playground**..........S:9 / A:27 *(acappella mix)*	$4	■V	Motown 2088
				Boyz II Men (backing vocals, above 2); "45" issued for above 2 on Motown 2132			
				ANOTHER LEVEL **'99**			
				Interracial male vocal group from London, England: Mark Baron, Dane Bowers, Bobak Kianoush and Wayne Williams.			
8/21/99	42S	8		**Summertime**..........*I Can See You In My Mind*	$4	★	Arista 13696
				ANOTHER LEVEL featuring TQ			
				ANT, Adam ROK/LP **'83**			
				Born Stuart Leslie Goddard on 11/3/54 in London, England. Formed romantic-punk group Adam And The Ants in 1976. Three original Ants left to join **Bow Wow Wow**; Ant headed new lineup in 1980. Ant went solo in 1982. Acted in the movies *World Gone Wild* and *Slam Dance*, and several TV shows, including *The Equalizer.*			
11/13/82+	12	21		1 **Goody Two Shoes** *Crackpot History*	$4		Epic 03367
3/12/83	66	8		2 **Desperate But Not Serious**..........*Place In The Country*	$4		Epic 03688
2/4/84	42	13		3 **Strip**..........*Yours, Yours, Yours*	$4	■	Epic 04337
				co-produced by **Phil Collins**			
3/10/90	17	16		4 **Room At The Top**..........S:15 / A:16 *Bruce Lee*	$3	■V	MCA 53679
4/1/95	39	19		5 **Wonderful**..........A:37 / S:69 *Goes Around*	$3	■V	Capitol 58239
				"45": Capitol 18393; all of above written by Ant			
				ANTELL, Pete BUB **'62**			
				Born Peter Blaise Antonio in Queens, New York. Later a composer for TV movies.			
12/8/62	100	1		**Night Time**..........*Something About You*	$20		Cameo 234

DEBUT	PEAK	WKS	Gold	A-side (Chart Hit)...B-side	$	Sym	Label & Number
				ANTHONY, Marc BUB/AC/LP **'00**			
				Born Marco Antonio Muniz on 9/16/69 in the Bronx, New York. Latin singer/actor. Starred in **Paul Simon**'s Broadway musical *The Capeman* and in the movie *Bringing Out The Dead*.			
9/11/99	**3**	40	●	1 **I Need To Know** ....S:4 / A:5 *Dimelo (I Need To Know)*	$4	★^{V}	Columbia 79250
2/26/00	**2^2**	32		2 **You Sang To Me**....AC^7 S:❶^3 / A:12 *Muy Dentro De Mi (You Sang To Me)*	$4	★^{V}	Columbia 79406
				"45" issued for above 2 on Columbia 79250			
9/16/00	**70**	20		3 **My Baby You**....A:68			album cut
				above 3 from the album *Marc Anthony* on Columbia 69726			
7/6/02	**81**	14		4 **I've Got You** ....S:37 *(6 remixes)*	$8	★*	Columbia 79751
				ANTHONY, Ray MEM/POP/BUB/AC/LP **'50**			
				Born Raymond Antonini on 1/20/22 in Bentleyville, Pennsylvania; raised in Cleveland, Ohio. Big band leader/trumpeter. Joined Al Donahue in 1939, then with Glenn Miller and **Jimmy Dorsey** from 1940-42. Led U.S. Army band. Own band in 1946. Own TV series in the 1950s. Appeared in the movie *Daddy Long Legs* with Fred Astaire in 1955. Wrote "Bunny Hop." Married to actress Mamie Van Doren from 1955-61. Charted 22 pop hits, 1949-54, including the #2 hits "At Last" and "Dragnet."			
1/22/55	**19**	4		1 **Melody Of Love**....A:19 *I'm Gonna Live Till I Die*	$20		Capitol 3018
				FRANK SINATRA and RAY ANTHONY And His Orchestra			
				music written in 1903, lyrics added in 1954 by **Tom Glazer**			
9/10/55	**28^{HR}**	3		2 **Pete Kelly's Blues**....*DC-7* [I]	$15		Capitol 3176
				title song from the movie starring Jack Webb			
1/5/59	**8**	17		3 **Peter Gunn** *Tango For Two (mmm Shall We Dance?)* [I]	$12		Capitol 4041
4/20/59	**96**	1		4 **Walkin' To Mother's**....*The Bunny Hop* [I]	$12		Capitol 4176
				above 2 written by **Henry Mancini** and from the *Peter Gunn* TV series starring Craig Stevens			
6/30/62	**74**	8		5 **Worried Mind**....*Al Di La* [I]	$8		Capitol 4742
				country song written and recorded in 1940 by Ted Daffan			
12/15/62	**96**	2		6 **Let Me Entertain You**....*The Wishing Star* [I]	$8		Capitol 4876
				from the movie *Gypsy* starring Rosalind Russell; Jimmie Haskell (orch., above 2)			
				ANTON, Susan — see KNOBLOCK, Fred			
				ANYTHING BOX **'90**			
				Dance trio led by New Jersey native Claude Strilio (vocals) with Dania Morales and Paul Rijnders.			
2/17/90	**65**	10		**Living In Oblivion**....*(pop radio mix)*	$3	▮	Epic 73231
				APACHE LP **'93**			
				Born Anthony Teaks in Jersey City, New Jersey. Male rapper.			
1/30/93	**67**	10		**Gangsta Bitch**....S:31 *(3 versions) / Apache Ain't Shit*	$7	▮*^{V}	Tommy Boy 541
				produced by **A Tribe Called Quest**; "45": Tommy Boy/Collectables 541; B-side: (same version)			
				APOLLONIA 6 LP **'84**			
				Female R&B trio formed by **Prince**. Led by Patty "Apollonia" Kotero (co-star of movie *Purple Rain* and cast member of TV's *Falcon Crest*, 1985-86). With former **Vanity** 6 members Brenda Bennett and Susan Moonsie. Also see **Prince**'s "Take Me With U."			
10/20/84	**85**	6		**Sex Shooter**....*In A Spanish Villa*	$4	■	Warner 29182
				from the movie *Purple Rain* starring **Prince** and Apollonia			
				APOLLO 100 AC/LP **'72**			
				Studio group from England: Tom Parker, Clem Cattini, Vic Flick, Jim Lawless and Brian Odgers.			
1/1/72	**6**	14		1 **Joy**....*Exercise In A Minor* [I]	$6		Mega 0050
				based upon Johann Sebastian Bach's *Jesu, Joy of Man's Desiring*			
4/15/72	**94**	3		2 **Mendelssohn's 4th (Second Movement)**....*Reach For The Sky* [I]	$6		Mega 0069
				based upon Felix Mendelssohn's opening melody of the 2nd movement of his 4th symphony			
				APPALACHIANS, The **'63**			
				Folk group. Included Priscilla Mitchell Hubbard (married to **Jerry Reed**) and **Stan Robinson** (father of Chris and Rich Robinson of **The Black Crowes**).			
3/30/63	**62**	8		**Bony Moronie**....*It Takes A Man*	$12		ABC-Paramount 10419
				arrangement similar to "Walk Right In" by **The Rooftop Singers**			
				APPLE, Fiona ROK/LP **'97**			
				Born Fiona Apple Maggart on 9/13/77 in Manhattan, New York. Adult Alternative pop-rock singer/songwriter/pianist. Daughter of singer Diane McAfee and actor Brandon Maggart.			
10/4/97	**21**	20		**Criminal**....A:21 / S:25 *Sleep To Dream (live)* (ROK #28)	$4	▮^{V}	Clean Slate 78595
				APPLEJACKS, The BUB **'58**			
				Studio band led by Dave Appell (born on 3/24/22 in Philadelphia, Pennsylvania). Also see **John Zacherle**'s "Dinner With Drac."			
9/15/58	**16**	15		1 **Mexican Hat Rock**....H:16 / S:29 *Stop! Red Light!* [I]	$20		Cameo 149
				adaptation of the 1919 song "Mexican Hat Dance"; also released with "Sophisticated Swing" as the B-side			
12/22/58+	**38**	10		2 **Rocka-Conga**....*Am I Blue*	$20		Cameo 155
				early pressings issued as "Rocka-Tonga" ($25)			
2/23/59	**70**	4		3 **Bunny Hop**....*Night Train Stroll* [I]	$20		Cameo 158
				#13 hit for **Ray Anthony** in 1952			
				APRIL **'91**			
				Female dance singer April Kelly.			
6/8/91	**55^{A}**	12		**You're The One For Me**....*(5 versions)*	$6	▮*	Metropolitan 4467
				APRIL WINE ROK/BUB/LP **'81**			
				Rock group from Montreal, Quebec, Canada: Myles Goodwyn (vocals, guitar), Brian Greenway and Gary Moffet (guitars), Steve Lang (bass) and Jerry Mercer (drums; **Mashmakhan**).			
3/25/72	**32**	11		1 **You Could Have Been A Lady**....*Teacher*	$6		Big Tree 133
3/3/79	**34**	11		2 **Roller**....*Right Down To It*	$4		Capitol 4660
2/9/80	**86**	3		3 **I Like To Rock**....*Babes In Arms*	$4		Capitol 4828
2/7/81	**21**	16		4 **Just Between You And Me** *Big City Girls*	$4	■	Capitol 4975
				issued with a regular picture sleeve and a foldout poster sleeve			
5/30/81	**57**	8		5 **Sign Of The Gypsy Queen**....*Crash And Burn*	$4	■	Capitol 5001
7/3/82	**50**	8		6 **Enough Is Enough**....*Ain't Got Your Love*	$4	■	Capitol 5133
2/11/84	**58**	6		7 **This Could Be The Right One**....*Really Don't Want Your Love*	$4	■	Capitol 5319

DEBUT	PEAK	WKS	Gold	A-side (Chart Hit)..........B-side	$	Sym	Label & Number
				AQUA LP **'97**			
				Pop-dance group from Denmark: Lene Grawford Nystrom, Rene Dif, Claus Norreen and Soren Rasted.			
9/6/97	7	16		1 **Barbie Girl**..........S:5 / A:24 *(no B-side)* [N]	$3	▮	MCA 55392
12/13/97+	23	17		2 **Lollipop (Candyman)**..........S:18 *Good Morning Sunshine*	$6	▮	MCA 55410
				cassette issued in a special flip-top box with 2 Aqua trading cards			
2/28/98	49[A]	9		3 **Turn Back Time**..........			album cut
				above 3 from the album *Aquarium* on MCA 11705			
				AQUATONES, The BUB **'58**			
				White doo-wop group formed in Valley Stream, Long Island, New York: Lynn Nixon and Larry Vannata (lead singers), David Goddard and Eugene McCarthy. Female lead Nixon trained as an operatic soprano.			
4/28/58	21	12		**You**..........T:21 / S:24 *She's The One For Me*	$30		Fargo 1001
				ARBORS, The BUB/AC/LP **'69**			
				Pop vocal group formed in Ann Arbor, Michigan, by two pairs of brothers: Edward and Fred Farran, and Scott and Tom Herrick. Edward Farran died of kidney failure on 1/2/2003 (age 64).			
10/15/66	51	10		1 **A Symphony For Susan**..........*Love Is The Light*	$10		Date 1529
6/17/67	59	4		2 **Graduation Day**..........*I Win The Whole Wide World*	$10		Date 1561
2/22/69	20	10		3 **The Letter**..........*Most Of All*	$10		Date 1638
5/31/69	67	5		4 **I Can't Quit Her**..........*Lovin' Tonight (Maybe Tonight)*	$10		Date 1645
				first recorded by **Blood, Sweat & Tears** on their 1968 album *Child Is Father To The Man*			
				ARCADIA LP **'85**			
				Pop-rock trio from England: **Duran Duran**'s Simon LeBon (vocals), Nick Rhodes (keyboards) and Roger Taylor (drums).			
10/26/85	6	16		1 **Election Day**..........S:4 / A:6 *She's Moody And Grey, She's Mean And She's Restless*	$3	■	Capitol 5501
				Grace Jones (narration)			
2/1/86	33	10		2 **Goodbye Is Forever**..........S:29 *Missing*	$3	■	Capitol 5542
				ARCHER, Tasmin LP **'93**			
				Born in 1964 in Bradford, Yorkshire, England (of Jamaican parentage). Black female singer.			
4/17/93	32	15		**Sleeping Satellite**..........A:29 / S:73 *(acoustic version)*	$3	▮[V]	SBK 50426
				"45": SBK 17397; B-side: "Lords Of The New Church"			
				ARCHIES, The BUB/LP **'69**			
				Studio group created by Don Kirshner; based on the Saturday morning cartoon television series. Lead vocalist Ron Dante (born Carmine Granito on 8/22/45 in Staten Island, New York) was also the voice of **The Cuff Links** and co-producer of many of **Barry Manilow**'s hits. All tunes written and produced by Jeff Barry, who was half of a prolific hit-writing partnership with his then-wife **Ellie Greenwich**. Other vocalists included Greenwich, **Toni Wine**, Tony Passalacqua and **Andy Kim** (who co-wrote 4 of their 6 hits). The cartoon characters' names are Archie, Betty, Veronica, Jughead and Reggie.			
9/28/68	22	13		1 **Bang-Shang-A-Lang**..........*Truck Driver*	$8	■	Calendar 1006
12/28/68+	53	8		2 **Feelin' So Good (S.k.o.o.b.y-D.o.o)**..........*Love Light*	$8	■	Calendar 1007
7/26/69	1[4]	22	●	3 **Sugar, Sugar** *Melody Hill*	$8		Calendar 1008
11/29/69+	10	13	●	4 **Jingle Jangle**..........*Justine*	$8		Kirshner 5002
3/7/70	40	7		5 **Who's Your Baby?**..........*Senorita Rita*	$8		Kirshner 5003
7/4/70	57	7		6 **Sunshine**..........*Over And Over*	$8		Kirshner 1009
				ARDEN, Jann AC/LP **'96**			
				Born Jann Arden Richards on 3/27/62 in Calgary, Alberta, Canada. Female singer/songwriter.			
2/10/96	12	40		**Insensitive**..........A:8 / S:20 *Gasoline (live)*	$3	▮[V]	A&M 1274
				from the movie *Bed Of Roses* starring Christian Slater; "45": A&M 1972; B-side: "Good Mother"			
				ARDEN, Toni POP **'50**			
				Born Antoinette Aroizzone in New York City, New York. Female vocalist. Sang with Al Trace in 1945 and Joe Reichman in 1946. Hit #7 on the pop charts in 1950 with "I Can Dream, Can't I?"			
2/4/56	78	1		1 **Are You Satisfied?**..........T:78 *I Forgot To Remember To Forget*	$15		RCA Victor 6346
5/26/58	13	14		2 **Padre**..........A:13 / T:18 / S:19 *All At Once*	$12		Decca 30628
				Jack Pleis (orch.)			
				ARENA, Tina BUB/LP **'96**			
				Born Philopina Arena on 11/1/67 in Melbourne, Australia. Female singer.			
4/20/96	38	12		**Chains**..........A:30 / S:48 *Greatest Gift*	$3	▮	Epic 78281
				ARGENT BUB/LP **'72**			
				Rock group from England: Rod Argent (vocals, keyboards; **Zombies**), Jim Rodford (bass; Argent's cousin), Robert Henrit (drums) and **Russ Ballard** (guitar; later a successful songwriter/producer). Henrit later joined **Charlie**. Rodford and Henrit were later with **The Kinks**.			
6/17/72	5	15		**Hold Your Head Up**..........*Keep On Rollin'*	$8		Epic 10852
				also released with "Closer To Heaven" as the B-side			
				ARKADE **'71**			
				Pop trio from Los Angeles, California: Michael Price, Dan Walsh and **Austin Roberts** (**Buchanan Brothers**).			
8/22/70	99	1		1 **Sing Out The Love (In My Heart)**..........*Susan*	$6		Dunhill/ABC 4247
2/13/71	60	6		2 **The Morning Of Our Lives**..........*Rhythm Of The People*	$6	■	Dunhill/ABC 4268
				ARMATRADING, Joan BUB/ROK/LP **'83**			
				Born on 12/9/50 in St. Kitts, West Indies; raised in Birmingham, England. Black singer/songwriter/guitarist.			
5/28/83	78	6		**Drop The Pilot**..........*Business Is Business*	$4	■	A&M 2538
				ARMEN, Kay MEM/POP **'44**			
				Born Armen Manoogian on 11/2/20 in Chicago, Illinois. Singer/actress. Appeared in the 1955 movie musical *Hit The Deck*. Hit #7 on the pop charts in 1944 with "The Dreamer."			
12/9/57	91	1		**Ha! Ha! Ha! (Chella Lla!)**..........T:91 *Till*	$15		Decca 30474
				Jack Pleis (orch.)			

DEBUT	PEAK	WKS	Gold	A-side (Chart Hit)...B-side	$	Sym	Label & Number

ARMENIAN JAZZ SEXTET '57

New York-based group of Armenian descent: Aram Manoogian, Berge Minasian, Cory Tosoian, Eddie Arvanigian, Thomas Minasian and Arthur Melkonian.

DEBUT	PEAK	WKS	Gold	A-side (Chart Hit)...B-side	$	Sym	Label & Number
4/29/57	67	6		**Harem Dance**...T:67 *Pretty Girl* [I] **Ralph Marterie**'s hit of this song was entitled "Shish-Kebab" (both charted on the same date)	$15		Kapp 181

ARMS, Russell '57

Born on 2/3/29 in Berkeley, California. One of the regulars on TV's *Your Hit Parade*, 1952-57.

DEBUT	PEAK	WKS	Gold	A-side (Chart Hit)...B-side	$	Sym	Label & Number
1/12/57	22	15		**Cinco Robles (Five Oaks)**...S:22 / T:23 / A:23 *The World Is Made Of Lisa* Pete King (orch.)	$15		Era 1026

ARMSTRONG, Louis MEM/POP/R&B/BUB/LP '32

Born Daniel Louis Armstrong on 8/4/01 in New Orleans, Louisiana. Died of heart failure on 7/6/71 (age 69). Nickname: "Satchmo." Joined the legendary band of Joe "King" Oliver in Chicago in 1922. By 1929, had become the most widely known black musician in the world. Influenced dozens of singers and trumpet players, both black and white. Numerous appearances on radio, TV and in movies. Won Grammy's Lifetime Achievement Award in 1972. Inducted into the Rock and Roll Hall of Fame in 1990. Charted 72 pop hits, 1926-54, including his #1 hit "All Of Me" in 1932.

DEBUT	PEAK	WKS	Gold	A-side (Chart Hit)...B-side	$	Sym	Label & Number
2/11/56	20	15		1 **A Theme From The Threepenny Opera (Mack The Knife)**...T:20 *Back O' Town Blues* **LOUIS ARMSTRONG & HIS ALL-STARS**	$20		Columbia 40587
10/13/56	88	4		2 **Now You Has Jazz**...T:88 *High Society Calypso* (Armstrong) [N] **BING CROSBY and LOUIS ARMSTRONG** Johnny Green (MGM Studio Orch.); from the movie *High Society* starring Crosby and **Grace Kelly**	$20		Capitol 3506
11/3/56	29	11		3 **Blueberry Hill**...T:29 *That Lucky Old Sun* (#19/'49) **LOUIS ARMSTRONG And GORDON JENKINS And His Orchestra and Chorus** first released in 1949 on Decca 24752; #2 hit for Glenn Miller in 1940	$20		Decca 30091
2/15/64	❶[1]	22		4 **Hello, Dolly!** AC[9] *A Lot Of Livin' To Do* from the Broadway musical starring Carol Channing (also #6 below); a court ruling found this song to be based on the 1949 hit "Sunflower" (the state song of Kansas)	$8	■	Kapp 573
6/20/64	45	7		5 **I Still Get Jealous**...*Someday* **LOUIS ARMSTRONG And The All Stars** (above 2) from the 1947 Broadway musical *High Button Shoes* starring Phil Silvers; #21 hit for the Three Suns in 1947	$8	■	Kapp 597
10/3/64	56	6		6 **So Long Dearie**...*Pretty Little Missy*	$8	■	Mercury 72338
5/21/66	81	4		7 **Mame**...*Tin Roof Blues* title song from the Broadway musical starring Angela Lansbury	$8	■	Mercury 72574
2/20/88	32	11		8 **What A Wonderful World** ..S:29 / A:38 *Game Of Love* (**Wayne Fontana & The Mindbenders**) featured in the movie *Good Morning, Vietnam* starring Robin Williams; originally hit the Adult Contemporary chart (#12) in 1967 and "Bubbled Under" (#116) in 1968 on ABC 10982	$4	■	A&M 3010
8/14/99	53[S]	15		9 **What A Wonderful World**...*Desafinado* (Kenny G) [R] **LOUIS ARMSTRONG With KENNY G** same recording as #8 above with Kenny G's sax overdubbed into the original recording	$4	★	Arista 13710

ARNELL, Ginny BUB '64

Born on 11/2/42 in New Haven, Connecticut. Female singer.

DEBUT	PEAK	WKS	Gold	A-side (Chart Hit)...B-side	$	Sym	Label & Number
11/16/63+	50	12		**Dumb Head**...*How Many Times Can One Heart Break*	$15		MGM 13177

ARNO, Audrey '61

Vocalist Arno and group leader Hazy Osterwald (born on 2/18/22 in Switzerland) were German TV stars.

DEBUT	PEAK	WKS	Gold	A-side (Chart Hit)...B-side	$	Sym	Label & Number
4/10/61	87	2		**La Pachanga**...*Bei Mir Ist Nix Amore So Im Vorubergehn* [F] **AUDREY ARNO And The Hazy Osterwald Sextet**	$12		Decca 31238

ARNOLD, Calvin R&B '68

R&B singer/songwriter.

DEBUT	PEAK	WKS	Gold	A-side (Chart Hit)...B-side	$	Sym	Label & Number
1/13/68	72	8		**Funky Way**...*Snatchin' Back*	$10		Venture 605

ARNOLD, Eddy C&W/MEM/POP/BUB/AC/LP '48

★409★

Born Richard Edward Arnold on 5/15/18 in Henderson, Tennessee. Ranked as the #1 artist in *Joel Whitburn's Top Country Singles 1944-2001* book (charted 146 hits, 1945-99). Became popular on Nashville's *Grand Ole Opry* as a singer with Pee Wee King (1940-43). Nicknamed "The Tennessee Plowboy." Elected to the Country Music Hall of Fame in 1966.

1)Make The World Go Away 2)I Wouldn't Know Where To Begin 3)I Want To Go With You 4)The Last Word In Lonesome Is Me 5)The Tip Of My Fingers

DEBUT	PEAK	WKS	Gold	A-side (Chart Hit)...B-side	$	Sym	Label & Number
11/19/55	69	1		1 **The Cattle Call**...CW[2] T:69 *The Kentuckian Song* (C&W #8) new version of the B-side of Arnold's first Country hit in 1945 "Each Minute Seems A Million Years"	$20		RCA Victor 6139
12/10/55	99	1		2 **The Richest Man (In the World)**...T:99 *I Walked Alone Last Night* (C&W #6) **Hugo Winterhalter** (orch., above 2)	$20		RCA Victor 6290
11/24/56	22	8		3 **I Wouldn't Know Where To Begin**...A:22 / T:64 *The Ballad Of Wes Tancred*	$20		RCA Victor 6699
12/1/56	47	9		4 **Mutual Admiration Society**...T:47 *If'n* **EDDY ARNOLD and JAYE P. MORGAN** from the musical *Happy Hunting* starring Ethel Merman	$20		RCA Victor 6708
6/3/57	51	6		5 **Gonna Find Me A Bluebird**...T:51 *Little Bit* **Charlie Grean** (orch.)	$20		RCA Victor 6905
3/9/59	97	2		6 **Chip Off The Old Block**...*I'll Hold You In My Heart* B-side is a new version of Arnold's #1 hit (for 21 weeks) in 1947	$15		RCA Victor 7435
7/13/59	48	10		7 **Tennessee Stud**...*What's The Good (Of All This Love)*	$15		RCA Victor 7542
12/22/62	98	1		8 **Does He Mean That Much To You?**...*Tender Touch*	$10	■	RCA Victor 8102
5/15/65	60	9		9 **What's He Doing In My World**...CW[2] *Laura Lee*	$8		RCA Victor 8516
10/16/65	6	14		10 **Make The World Go Away** CW[3] / AC[4] *The Easy Way* #2 Country hit for **Ray Price** in 1963	$8	■	RCA Victor 8679
2/5/66	36	11		11 **I Want To Go With You**...CW[6] / AC[3] *You'd Better Stop Tellin' Lies (About Me)*	$8	■	RCA Victor 8749
5/14/66	40	7		12 **The Last Word In Lonesome Is Me**...*Mary Claire Melvina Rebecca Jane* written by **Roger Miller**	$8	■	RCA Victor 8818
7/23/66	43	7		13 **The Tip Of My Fingers**...*Long, Long Friendship*	$8	■	RCA Victor 8869
10/15/66	53	6		14 **Somebody Like Me**...CW[4] *Taking Chances*	$8	■	RCA Victor 8965
3/18/67	87	2		15 **Lonely Again**...CW[2] *Love On My Mind*	$7		RCA Victor 9080
5/6/67	57	8		16 **Misty Blue**...*Calling Mary Names* #4 Country hit for Wilma Burgess in 1966	$7		RCA Victor 9182

DEBUT	PEAK	WKS	Gold	A-side (Chart Hit)..........B-side	$	Sym	Label & Number
				ARNOLD, Eddy — Cont'd			
8/19/67	**66**	8		17 **Turn The World Around**..........CW[1] *The Long Ride Home*	$7		RCA Victor 9265
12/2/67	**91**	4		18 **Here Comes Heaven**..........*Baby That's Living*	$7		RCA Victor 9368
2/10/68	**74**	4		19 **Here Comes The Rain, Baby**..........*The World I Used To Know*	$7		RCA Victor 9437
5/18/68	**74**	7		20 **It's Over**..........*No Matter Whose Baby You Are*	$7		RCA Victor 9525
9/7/68	**84**	4		21 **Then You Can Tell Me Goodbye**..........CW[2] *Apples, Raisins And Roses*	$7		RCA Victor 9606
12/7/68	**99**	2		22 **They Don't Make Love Like They Used To**..........*What A Wonderful World*	$7		RCA Victor 9667
				all of above produced by **Chet Atkins**			
				AROUND THE WAY '92			
				R&B vocal trio from New York City, New York: Lena Fraticelli, Michael Bertot and Kashu Myles (from Jamaica). Also features rapper Kenny Diaz.			
11/7/92	**89**	5		**Really Into You**..........A:61 *(radio mix)*	$3	▮	Atlantic 87427
				samples "Just The Two Of Us" by **Grover Washington Jr.**			
				ARPEGGIO LP '79			
				Disco studio group assembled by producer Simon Soussan.			
3/10/79	**70**	5		**Love And Desire (Part I)**..........*(Part II)*	$4		Polydor 14535
				ARRESTED DEVELOPMENT R&B/LP '92			
				Hip-hop group from Atlanta, Georgia: Todd "Speech" Thomas, **Dionne Farris**, Aerlee Taree, Tim Barnwell, Montsho Eshe, Rasa Don and Baba Oje. Won the 1992 Best New Artist Grammy Award.			
4/11/92	**6**	22	●	1 **Tennessee**..........RB[1] S:4 / A:10 *(2 remixes) / Natural* (R&B #90)	$3	▮V	Chrysalis 23829
8/15/92	**8**	23	●	2 **People Everyday**..........S:5 / A:10 *(remix) / Children Play With Earth*	$3	▮V	Chrysalis 50397
				contains chorus to **Sly & The Family Stone**'s "Everyday People"; "45" issued for above 2 on Chrysalis 57882			
12/12/92+	**90**	6		3 **Revolution**..........S:61 *(4 versions)*	$5	★*V	Chrysalis 24812
				from the movie *Malcolm X* starring Denzel Washington			
12/19/92+	**6**	24	●	4 **Mr. Wendal** A:6 / S:7 *Revolution*	$3	▮V	Chrysalis 24810
				"45" issued for above 2 on EMI 56800			
5/14/94	**45**	12		5 **Ease My Mind**..........S:31 / A:44 *Shell*	$3	▮V	Chrysalis 58158
				samples "Open All Night Drums" (written by **George Clinton**); "45": Chrysalis 17931			
				ARRINGTON, Steve — see SLAVE			
				ARROWS, The — see ALLAN, Davie			
				ARTFUL DODGER UK — see DAVID, Craig			
				ARTIE THE 1 MAN PARTY '95			
				Born Artie Yanez in Juarez, Mexico. Later moved to California. Dance DJ/producer/singer.			
9/30/95	**65**	19		1 **A Mover La Colita**..........A:57 *(remix)* [F]	$4	▮	Scotti Brothers 78048
				title is Spanish for "move your butt"			
3/23/96	**74**	14		2 **Esa Nena Linda**..........*(remix)* [F]	$4	▮	Scotti Brothers 78065
				D.J. JUANITO presents ARTIE THE 1 MAN PARTY (above 2)			
				title is Spanish for "this pretty girl"			
				ARTISTICS, The R&B/BUB '67			
				R&B vocal group formed in 1958 at Marshall High School in Chicago, Illinois. Backup work for **Major Lance**. First recorded for Okeh in 1963, with Curt Thomas, Larry Johnson, Jessie Bolian and Aaron Floyd. Lead singer Robert Dobyne added in 1963; replaced by Marvin Smith (ex-**El Dorados**) in 1964. Smith left in 1967, but sang on studio recordings. Other lead singers were Tommy Green and Fred Pettis. Disbanded in 1973. Bolian died on 8/24/94 (age 53). Also see **Ted Taylor**.			
12/17/66+	**55**	10		1 **I'm Gonna Miss You**..........*Hope We Have*	$10		Brunswick 55301
3/18/67	**69**	6		2 **Girl I Need You**..........*Glad I Met You*	$10		Brunswick 55315
				ARTISTS AGAINST AIDS LP '01			
				All-star group organized to benefit worldwide AIDS research. Featured performers include **Christina Aguilera**, **Backstreet Boys**, **Mary J. Blige**, **Destiny's Child**, **Eve**, **Nelly Furtado**, **Ja Rule**, **Jagged Edge**, **Alicia Keys**, **Lil' Kim**, **Jennifer Lopez**, **Nas**, **Nelly**, ***NSYNC**, **P. Diddy**, **Britney Spears** and **Usher**.			
10/6/01	**27**	10		**What's Going On**..........A:26 *(3 versions)*	$6	TV	Play-Tone 79670
				ARTISTS AGAINST AIDS Featuring All-Star Lineup			
				"45": Columbia 79663; a portion of the proceeds donated to the September 11th Fund of the United Way			
				ARTISTS UNITED AGAINST APARTHEID LP '85			
				Benefit group of 49 superstar artists formed to protest the South African apartheid government; proceeds went to political prisoners in South Africa. Organized by **Little Steven** and **Arthur Baker**. Featuring **Pat Benatar**, Bono (**U2**), **Jackson Browne**, **Jimmy Cliff**, **Bob Dylan**, **Peter Gabriel**, **Bonnie Raitt**, **Lou Reed**, **Bruce Springsteen**, and many others.			
11/2/85	**38**	13		**Sun City**..........S:25 *Not So Far Away*	$5	■	Manhattan 50017
				ART N' SOUL R&B '96			
				R&B trio from Oakland, California: Tracy (vocals, bass), Lattrel (keyboards) and Dion (drums).			
3/16/96	**72**	14		**Ever Since You Went Away**..........S:48 *(album version)*	$4	▮	Big Beat 98112
				ART OF NOISE, The R&B/BUB/LP '86			
				Techno-pop trio from England: Anne Dudley (keyboards), J.J. Jeczalik (keyboards, programmer) and Gary Langan (engineer). All three were part of Trevor Horn's production team in the early 1980s. Worked with **ABC**, **Frankie Goes To Hollywood**, **Enigma** and others. Disbanded in mid-1990.			
5/17/86	**50**	11		1 **Peter Gunn**..........*Something Always Happens* (Art Of Noise) [I]	$6	■	China 42986
				THE ART OF NOISE Featuring Duane Eddy			
				also see **Duane Eddy**'s charted version in 1960			
8/16/86	**34**	12		2 **Paranoimia**..........A:33 / S:37 *Why Me?* (Art Of Noise)	$5	■	China 43002
				THE ART OF NOISE with MAX HEADROOM			
				Max Headroom is a British "computer-generated" celebrity voiced by actor Matt Frewer			
12/3/88+	**31**	11		3 **Kiss**..........S:23 / A:35 *E.F.L.* (Art Of Noise)	$5	■	China 871038
				THE ART OF NOISE Featuring Tom Jones			
				ARVON, Bobby BUB/AC '78			
				Born Robert Arvonio on 9/13/41 in Scranton, Pennsylvania. Singer/songwriter/pianist.			
12/3/77+	**72**	16		**Until Now**..........*Stay A Little Longer*	$6		First Artists 41000

DEBUT	PEAK	WKS	Gold	A-side (Chart Hit)..................B-side	$	Sym	Label & Number
	★378★			**ASHANTI** R&B/LP **'02**			
				Born Ashanti Douglas on 10/13/80 in Glen Cove, Long Island, New York. Female hip-hop singer.			
11/17/01+	❶^{2}	27		1 **Always On Time** ....RB^{8} A:❶^{2} / S:27 *(2 versions) / Worldwide Gangsta* **JA RULE (feat. Ashanti)**	$6	T	Def Jam 588795
2/16/02	❶^{10}	32		2 **Foolish** RB^{10} A:❶^{10} / S:15 *(2 versions)* samples "Stay With Me" by **DeBarge**	$6	T	Murder Inc. 588986
2/16/02	2^{7}	28		3 **What's Luv?** ....A:2 / S:20 *(2 versions) / Definition Of A Don (w/Remy)* **FAT JOE Featuring Ashanti**	$6	T	Atlantic 85233
6/1/02	8	23		4 **Happy** ....A:8 / S:32 *(2 versions) / Call* contains an interpolation of "Outstanding" by **The Gap Band**	$6	T	Murder Inc. 582935
6/22/02	6	20		5 **Down 4 U** ....A:6 **IRV GOTTI PRESENTS THE INC. Featuring Ja Rule, Ashanti, Charli Baltimore & Vita** from the album *Irv Gotti Presents The Inc.* on Murder Inc. 062033			album cut
7/27/02	15	22		6 **Baby** ....A:14 / S:61 *(4 versions)* **ASHANTI feat. Crooked I** samples "Mary Jane" by **Scarface**; #2, 4 & 6: from the album *Ashanti* on Murder Inc. 586830	$6	T	Murder Inc. 063851
12/28/02+	2^{1}	20		7 **Mesmerize**..........A:2 / S:23 *(2 versions) / Pop N****s* **JA RULE feat. Ashanti** samples "Stop, Look, Listen" by **The Stylistics**	$6	T	Murder Inc. 063773
				ASHE, Clarence **'64**			
				Soul singer/songwriter.			
6/6/64	99	1		**Trouble I've Had** ....*Dancing In A Dream World* [S] originally released on J&S 1466 in 1964 ($15)	$15		Chess 1896
				ASHFORD & SIMPSON R&B/BUB/LP **'85**			
				Husband-and-wife R&B vocal/songwriting duo: Nickolas Ashford (born on 5/4/43 in Fairfield, South Carolina) and **Valerie Simpson** (born on 8/26/46 in Brooklyn, New York). Recorded as Valerie & Nick in 1964 ("Bubbled Under"). Team wrote for **Chuck Jackson** and **Maxine Brown**. Joined staff at Motown and wrote and produced for many of the label's top stars. Valerie recorded solo in 1972 (see #1 below). They married in 1974. Valerie sang female part on the **Marvin Gaye/Tammi Terrell** duets "Good Lovin' Ain't Easy To Come By," "What You Gave Me" and "The Onion Song," due to Terrell's ailing health. Valerie's brother, Ray Simpson, was the lead singer of **Village People**. Charted 35 R&B hits, 1973-97.			
12/9/72+	63	9		1 **Silly Wasn't I** ....*I Believe I'm Gonna Take This Ride* **VALERIE SIMPSON**	$6		Tamla 54224
1/19/74	88	3		2 **(I'd Know You) Anywhere** ....*I'm Determined*	$6		Warner 7745
3/11/78	79	9		3 **Don't Cost You Nothing**..........*Let Love Use Me*	$5		Warner 8514
8/18/79	36	13		4 **Found A Cure** ....*You Always Could*	$5		Warner 8870
6/5/82	56	10		5 **Street Corner** ....*Make It Work Again*	$4	■	Capitol 5109
11/10/84+	12	24		6 **Solid** RB^{3} S:8 / A:15 *(dub version)*	$3	■	Capitol 5397
9/27/86	84	4		7 **Count Your Blessings**..........*Side Effect*	$3	■	Capitol 5598
				ASHTON, GARDNER & DYKE LP **'71**			
				Pop trio from England: Tony Ashton (vocals, keyboards), Kim Gardner (bass) and Roy Dyke (drums). Ashton died of cancer on 5/28/2001 (age 55). Gardner died of cancer on 10/24/2001 (age 53).			
6/19/71	40	10		**Resurrection Shuffle** ....*I'm Your Spiritual Breadman*	$6		Capitol 3060
				ASIA ROK/LP **'82**			
				All-star rock group from England: John Wetton (vocals, bass; **King Crimson**, **Uriah Heep**), Steve Howe (keyboards; **Yes**, **The Buggles**) and Carl Palmer (drums; **Emerson, Lake & Palmer**). Mandy Meyer (**Krokus**), replaced Howe in 1985. Pat Thrall (**Automatic Man**, **Pat Travers Band**, **Hughes/Thrall**) replaced Meyer in 1990.			
4/17/82	4	18		1 **Heat Of The Moment** AR^{6} *Ride Easy*	$4	■	Geffen 50040
7/24/82	17	14		2 **Only Time Will Tell**..........*Time Again* (ROK #43)	$4	■	Geffen 29970
7/30/83	10	13		3 **Don't Cry**..........AR^{1} *Daylight* (ROK #24)	$4	■	Geffen 29571
10/15/83	34	13		4 **The Smile Has Left Your Eyes**..........*Lying To Yourself*	$4	■	Geffen 29475
12/7/85+	46	11		5 **Go**..........*After The War*	$4	■	Geffen 28872
9/29/90	64	7		6 **Days Like These** ....*Voice Of America*	$3	▮	Geffen 19677
				ASSEMBLED MULTITUDE, The **'70**			
				Studio group from Philadelphia, Pennsylvania. Arranged by Tom Sellers (died on 3/9/88 in a fire in his hometown of Wayne, Pennsylvania, age 39).			
6/27/70	16	13		1 **Overture From Tommy (A Rock Opera)**..........*Mud* [I]	$6		Atlantic 2737
10/3/70	79	4		2 **Woodstock**..........*Mr. Peppercorn* [I] written by **Joni Mitchell** about the legendary 1969 rock festival	$6		Atlantic 2764
2/6/71	95	2		3 **Medley From "Superstar" (A Rock Opera)** ....*Where The Woodbine Twineth* [I] re-entered the *Hot 100* for 1 week on 12/25/71 (#100)	$5		Atlantic 2780
	★350★			**ASSOCIATION, The** BUB/LP **'67**			
				Pop group from Los Angeles, California: Gary Alexander (born on 9/25/43), Russ Giguere (born on 10/18/43), and Jim Yester (born on 11/24/39; guitars), Terry Kirkman (born on 12/12/41; keyboards), Brian Cole (born on 9/8/42; died of a drug overdose on 8/2/72, age 29; bass) and Ted Bluechel (born on 12/2/42; drums). All shared vocals. Larry Ramos (guitar) joined in 1967. Richard Thompson replaced Giguere in 1970.			
				1)Windy 2)Cherish 3)Never My Love			
6/4/66	7	11		1 **Along Comes Mary** ....*Your Own Love*	$10		Valiant 741
8/27/66	❶^{3}	14	●	2 **Cherish**..........*Don't Blame It On Me*	$10		Valiant 747
11/26/66	35	7		3 **Pandora's Golden Heebie Jeebies** ....*Standing Still* title refers to the Sunset Strip nightclub Pandora's Box	$10	■	Valiant 755
2/4/67	51	7		4 **No Fair At All** ....*Looking Glass* (#113)	$10		Valiant 758
5/27/67	❶^{4}	14	●	5 **Windy** *Sometime*	$8		Warner 7041
8/26/67	2^{2}	14	●	6 **Never My Love** /			
9/2/67	100	2		7 **Requiem For The Masses**	$8	■	Warner 7074
2/3/68	10	9		8 **Everything That Touches You**..........*We Love Us*	$8		Warner 7163
5/18/68	39	8		9 **Time For Livin'**..........*Birthday Morning* #6 & 9: written by **The Addrisi Brothers**	$8		Warner 7195
8/24/68	47	6		10 **Six Man Band** ....*Like Always*	$7		Warner 7229

DEBUT	PEAK	WKS	Gold	A-side (Chart Hit)......B-side	$	Sym	Label & Number
				ASSOCIATION, The — Cont'd			
3/15/69	80	11		11 **Goodbye Columbus** ...... *The Time It Is Today*	$7		Warner 7267
				originally charted for 4 weeks; re-entered on 8/16/69 (#88); title song from the movie starring Richard Benjamin			
2/24/73	91	5		12 **Names, Tags, Numbers & Labels** ...... *Rainbows Bent*	$6		Mums 6016
1/31/81	66	5		13 **Dreamer** ...... *You Turn The Light On*	$4		Elektra 47094
				ASTLEY, Jon LP '88			
				Born in Manchester, England. Noted rock producer (**The Who**, **Eric Clapton** and **Corey Hart**). No relation to **Rick Astley**.			
6/27/87	77	10		1 **Jane's Getting Serious** ...... *The Animal*	$3	■	Atlantic 89258
10/15/88	74	8		2 **Put This Love To The Test** ...... *Been There, Done That*	$3	■	Atlantic 89027
	★478★			**ASTLEY, Rick** AC/LP '88			
				Born on 2/6/66 in Warrington, England. Pop singer/guitarist. No relation to **Jon Astley**.			
12/19/87+	❶^{2}	24	●	1 **Never Gonna Give You Up** AC^{3} S:❶^{1} / A:❶^{1} *(instrumental)*	$3	■	RCA 5347
4/16/88	❶^{1}	18		2 **Together Forever** ...... S:❶^{1} / A:❶^{1} *I'll Never Set You Free*	$3	■	RCA 8319
7/16/88	10	16		3 **It Would Take A Strong Strong Man** ...... AC^{1} S:8 / A:12 *You Move Me*	$3	■	RCA 8663
12/17/88+	6	18		4 **She Wants To Dance With Me** ...... S:6 / A:6 *(instrumental)*	$3	■	RCA 8838
4/15/89	38	10		5 **Giving Up On Love** ...... S:34 / A:40 *I'll Be Fine*	$3	■	RCA 8872
8/19/89	89	3		6 **Ain't Too Proud To Beg** ...... *I Don't Want To Be Your Lover*	$3	■	RCA 9030
2/16/91	7	20		7 **Cry For Help** ...... AC^{1} S:7 / A:7 *Behind The Smile*	$3	▮^{V}	RCA 2774
6/22/91	81	5		8 **Move Right Out** ...... *The Bottom Line*	$3	▮^{V}	RCA 2839
				"45": RCA 62067; B-side: "Cry For Help"			
9/4/93	28	20		9 **Hopelessly** ...... A:21 / S:64 *Stop Breaking Your Heart*	$3	▮	RCA 62597
				ASTORS, The '65			
				R&B vocal group from Memphis, Tennessee: Curtis Johnson (lead), Eddie Stanback, Richard Harris and Sam Byrnes.			
7/10/65	63	9		**Candy** ...... *I Found Out*	$25		Stax 170
				melody based on Grofe's *On The Trail* from *Grand Canyon Suite*; lyrics written by **Isaac Hayes**			
				ASTRONAUTS, The BUB/LP '63			
				Surf-rock group from Boulder, Colorado. Guitarists Bob Demmon, Dennis Lindsey, Rich Fifield and Storm Patterson, with drummer Jim Gallagher. Fifield and Patterson share vocals. Lindsey died of heart failure in 1991.			
7/27/63	94	1		**Baja** ...... *Kuk* [I]	$25		RCA Victor 8194
				ATC LP '01			
				Pop vocal group: Joe (from New Zealand), Sarah (from Australia), Tracey (from England) and Livio (from Italy). ATC: A Touch of Class.			
2/10/01	28	18		**Around The World (La La La La La)** ...... A:29 *(5 mixes)*	$6	T	Republic 158610
				A*TEENS LP '01			
				Teen **Abba** tribute group from Stockholm, Sweden: Dhani Lennevald, Sara Lumholdt, Amit Paul and Marie Serenholt.			
1/1/00	63^{S}	4		1 **Mamma Mia** ...... *(extended version)*	$4	★^{V}	Stockholm/MCA 561415
7/8/00	95	5		2 **Dancing Queen** ...... S:13 *(extended version)*	$4	★^{V}	Stockholm/MCA 156704
				"45" issued for above 2 on Stockholm 561415			
1/6/01	93	3		3 **Bouncing Off The Ceiling (Upside Down)** ...... S:12 *Super Trouper*	$5	★$^{+}$	Stockholm/MCA 157585
				above 2 include a foldout poster			
11/3/01	61^{S}	10		4 **...To The Music** ...... *Bouncing Off The Ceiling / Halfway Around The World (video)*	$7	★**	Stockholm/MCA 015367
				ATHENAEUM '98			
				Alternative-rock group from Greensboro, North Carolina: Mark Kano (vocals), Grey Brewster (guitar), Alex McKinney (bass) and Nic Brown (drums).			
8/1/98	58	14		**What I Didn't Know** ...... A:75 *(2 album excerpts)*	$3	▮	Atlantic 84144
				ATKINS, Chet C&W/BUB/LP '59			
				Born on 6/20/24 in Luttrell, Tennessee. Died of cancer on 6/30/2001 (age 77). Revered guitarist. Began recording for RCA in 1947. Moved to Nashville in 1950 and became prolific studio musician/producer. RCA's A&R manager in Nashville from 1960-68; RCA Vice President from 1968-82. Entered the Country Music Hall of Fame in 1973 as its youngest inductee (age 49). Won Grammy's Lifetime Achievement Award in 1993. Recipient of *Billboard's* Century Award in 1997. Inducted into the Rock and Roll Hall of Fame in 2002.			
2/25/56	52	9		1 **The Poor People Of Paris (Jean's Song)** ...... T:52 *Honey* [I]	$15		RCA Victor 6366
9/28/59	49	8		2 **Boo Boo Stick Beat** *Django's Castle* [I]	$15		RCA Victor 7589
2/15/60	73	3		3 **Teensville** / [I]			
1/4/60	82	6		4 **One Mint Julep** ...... [I]	$15		RCA Victor 7684
				#2 R&B hit for **The Clovers** in 1952			
7/17/65	98	2		5 **Yakety Axe** ...... *Letter Edged In Black* [I]	$10		RCA Victor 8590
				guitar version of **Boots Randolph**'s "Yakety Sax" (inspired by **The Coasters**' "Yakety Yak")			
				ATKINS, Christopher '82			
				Born on 2/21/61 in Rye, New York. Teen movie actor; starred in *The Blue Lagoon* and *The Pirate Movie*.			
8/7/82	71	7		**How Can I Live Without Her** ...... *I Am A Pirate King* (Ted Hamilton & The Pirates)	$4	■	Polydor 2210
				from the movie *The Pirate Movie* starring Atkins and **Kristy McNichol**			
				ATL ALL-STARS, The '99			
				Male rap group from Atlanta, Georgia. Features Cecil Glenn ("DC The Brain Supreme") from **Tag Team**.			
2/6/99	56^{S}	2		**The Dirty Bird Groove** ...... *(3 mixes)*	$8	★*	CLG 71999
				THE ATL ALL-STARS Featuring DC The Brain Supreme			
				song celebrates the NFL's Atlanta Falcons (nicknamed "The Dirty Birds"); CD single issued without a picture insert			
				ATLANTA DISCO BAND, The BUB/R&B/LP '76			
				Disco studio group from Atlanta, Georgia, assembled by producer Dave Crawford. Includes members of **MFSB**.			
1/10/76	94	4		**Bad Luck** ...... *Ole Goat* [I]	$5		Ariola America 7611

DEBUT	PEAK	WKS	Gold	A-side (Chart Hit)	B-side	$	Sym	Label & Number

ATLANTA RHYTHM SECTION ★448★ BUB/C&W/LP '78

Group formed by musicians from Studio One, Doraville, Georgia, in 1971. Consisted of Rodney Justo (vocals), Barry Bailey (born on 6/12/48) and J.R. Cobb (guitars; born on 2/5/44), Paul Goddard (bass; born on 6/23/45), Dean Daughtry (keyboards; born on 9/8/46) and Robert Nix (drums). Justo, Daughtry and Nix were with **Roy Orbison**'s band, **The Candymen**. Cobb, Daughtry and band manager/producer Buddy Buie were with the **Classics IV**. Justo left after first album; replaced by Ronnie Hammond. Nix left in late 1979; replaced by Roy Yeager.

1)So In To You 2)Imaginary Lover 3)I'm Not Gonna Let It Bother Me Tonight

DEBUT	PEAK	WKS	Gold	A-side (Chart Hit)	B-side	$	Sym	Label & Number
10/5/74	35	8		1 **Doraville**	*Who You Gonna Run To*	$6		Polydor 14248
2/22/75	79	5		2 **Angel (What In The World's Come Over Us)**	*Help Yourself*	$6		Polydor 14262
6/5/76	82	4		3 **Jukin**	*Beautiful Dreamers*	$6		Polydor 14323
				song includes a few bars of "San Antonio Rose"				
8/21/76	85	3		4 **Free Spirit**	*Police! Police!*	$6		Polydor 14339
1/29/77	7	19		5 **So In To You**	*Everybody Gotta Go*	$5		Polydor 14373
6/4/77	42	7		6 **Neon Nites**	*Don't Miss The Message*	$5		Polydor 14397
9/3/77	64	5		7 **Dog Days**	*Cuban Crisis*	$5		Polydor 14411
10/15/77	68	6		8 **Georgia Rhythm**	*Hitch-Hikers' Hero*	$5		Polydor 14432
3/4/78	7	17		9 **Imaginary Lover**	*Silent Treatment*	$5		Polydor 14459
6/10/78	14	13		10 **I'm Not Gonna Let It Bother Me Tonight**	*The Ballad Of Lois Malone*	$5		Polydor 14484
9/16/78	43	9		11 **Champagne Jam**	*The Great Escape*	$5		Polydor 14504
5/26/79	19	14		12 **Do It Or Die**	*My Song*	$5		Polydor 14568
8/11/79	17	14		13 **Spooky**	*It's Only Music*	$5		Polydor 2001
8/29/81	29	15		14 **Alien**	*Southern Exposure*	$5		Columbia 02471
				all of above co-written and produced by Buddy Buie				

ATLANTIC STARR ★468★ R&B/BUB/LP '87

R&B group from White Plains, New York: brothers David (guitar; born on 9/8/58), Wayne (keyboards; born on 4/13/57) and Jonathan (trumpet) Lewis, with **Sharon Bryant** (vocals; born on 8/14/56; see #8 & 9 below), Cliff Archer (bass) and Porter Carroll (drums). Barbara Weathers replaced Bryant in 1984. Rachel Oliver replaced Weathers in 1991. Charted 27 R&B hits, 1978-94.

1)Always 2)Secret Lovers 3)Masterpiece

DEBUT	PEAK	WKS	Gold	A-side (Chart Hit)	B-side	$	Sym	Label & Number
3/27/82	38	11		1 **Circles**	*Does It Matter*	$4	■	A&M 2392
				picture sleeve has a center-cut hole and shows only the name Atlantic Starr on a blue background				
12/10/83	87	7		2 **Touch A Four Leaf Clover**	*Circles*	$4	■	A&M 2580
5/25/85	90	6		3 **Freak-A-Ristic**	*Island Dream*	$4	■	A&M 2718
12/28/85+	3	23		4 **Secret Lovers** AC[1]	S:2 / A:2 *Thank You*	$3		A&M 2788
4/19/86	57	12		5 **If Your Heart Isn't In It**	*One Love*	$3	■	A&M 2822
3/28/87	❶[1]	22		6 **Always** RB[2] / AC[2]	A:❶[1] / S:2 *(instrumental)*	$3	■	Warner 28455
8/15/87	58	13		7 **One Lover At A Time**	*I'm In Love*	$3	■	Warner 28327
8/19/89	34	13		8 **Let Go**	S:32 / A:35 *Saturday Nite*	$3	■	Wing 871722
12/16/89	90	5		9 **Foolish Heart**	*Saturday Nite*	$3		Wing 889878
				SHARON BRYANT (above 2)				
11/23/91	75	8		10 **Love Crazy**	A:59 *Under Your Spell*	$3	▮	Reprise 19150
2/1/92	3	20	●	11 **Masterpiece**	A:4 / S:6 *Bring It Back Home Again*	$3	▮V	Reprise 19076
				written by **Kenny Nolan**				
6/4/94	55	13		12 **I'll Remember You**	S:54 *Let's Just Sneak Around*	$3	▮	Arista 12678
				also released as a cassette single on Arista 12742 in 1994				

ATMOSPHERE R&B/LP '02

Rap trio from Minneapolis, Minnesota: Sean "Slug" Daley (rapper), Anthony "Ant" Davis (producer) and Mr. Dibbs (DJ).

DEBUT	PEAK	WKS	Gold	A-side (Chart Hit)	B-side	$	Sym	Label & Number
5/11/02	32[S]	3		1 **Modern Man's Hustle**	*Onemosphere / Twomosphere / Threemosphere*	$8	T	RSE/Fat Beats 2001
5/11/02	69[S]	1		2 **RPM Revolutions Per Minute Pt. 2.1**	*(3 versions) / Afterburner* (Serum & Induce)	$8	T	Counterflow 022
				SLUG AND EL-P				

ATTITUDES '76

Group of top session musicians: **David Foster** (keyboards), Danny Kortchmar (guitar), Paul Stallworth (bass) and Jim Keltner (drums).

DEBUT	PEAK	WKS	Gold	A-side (Chart Hit)	B-side	$	Sym	Label & Number
9/4/76	94	6		**Sweet Summer Music**	*If We Want To*	$6		Dark Horse 10011

AUDIENCE LP '71

Rock group from London, England: Howard Werth (vocals, guitar), Keith Gemmell (sax), Trevor Williams (bass) and Tony Connor (drums).

DEBUT	PEAK	WKS	Gold	A-side (Chart Hit)	B-side	$	Sym	Label & Number
7/17/71	74	5		**Indian Summer**	*It Brings A Tear*	$6		Elektra 45732

AUDIOSLAVE ROK/LP '02

Group of former **Rage Against The Machine** members Tom Morello (guitar), Tim Commerford (bass) and Brad Wilk (drums), with Chris Cornell (vocals; **Soundgarden**).

DEBUT	PEAK	WKS	Gold	A-side (Chart Hit)	B-side	$	Sym	Label & Number
11/23/02	69	15		**Cochise**	A:68		V	album cut
				from the album *Audioslave* on Epic 86968; "45": Epic 79810; B-side: (same version)				

AUDREY '56

Label shows artist billing as 'with love from AUDREY'.

DEBUT	PEAK	WKS	Gold	A-side (Chart Hit)	B-side	$	Sym	Label & Number
9/22/56	87	1		**Dear Elvis (Pages 1 & 2)**	T:87 [N]	$100		Plus 104
				"break-in" novelty record featuring bits of 16 hits, including 4 by **The Platters** and 2 **Elvis Presley** Sun Recordings: "Baby Let's Play House" and "I Don't Care If The Sun Don't Shine"				

AUGER, Brian, & The Trinity BUB/LP '70

Born on 7/18/39 in Bihar, India; raised in London, England. Jazz-rock keyboardist.

DEBUT	PEAK	WKS	Gold	A-side (Chart Hit)	B-side	$	Sym	Label & Number
10/10/70	100	2		**Listen Here**	*I Wanna Take You Higher* [I]	$6		RCA Victor 0381

AUGUST, Jan — see HAYMAN, Richard

AURRA — see SLAVE

DEBUT	PEAK	WKS	Gold	A-side (Chart Hit)	B-side	$	Sym	Label & Number

AUSTIN, Gene — MEM '28

Born on 6/24/1900 in Gainesville, Texas. Died on 1/24/72 (age 71). The most popular singer of the late 1920's. His 1928 hit "My Blue Heaven" sold over five million copies. Godfather of Country singer **David Houston**. Charted 55 pop hits, 1925-34.

DEBUT	PEAK	WKS	Gold	A-side (Chart Hit)	B-side	$	Sym	Label & Number
5/27/57	75	3		**Too Late** ... T:75 from the Goodyear TV Playhouse production *The Gene Austin Story*	*That's Love*	$12	■	RCA Victor 6880

AUSTIN, Patti — R&B/AC/BUB/LP '83

Born on 8/10/48 in Harlem, New York. R&B-jazz singer. Her father, Gordon, was a big band trombonist. **Dinah Washington** and **Quincy Jones** proclaimed themselves her godparents. Debuted at Harlem's Apollo Theatre at age four. Signed to a record contract with RCA at age five. By the late 1960s was a prolific session and commercial jingle singer. In the 1988 movie *Tucker*. Charted 20 R&B hits, 1969-91. Also see **Yutaka**'s "Love Light."

DEBUT	PEAK	WKS	Gold	A-side (Chart Hit)	B-side	$	Sym	Label & Number
12/12/81+	62	8		1 **Every Home Should Have One** also see re-entry (#3 below)	*Solero*	$4		Qwest 49854
4/24/82+	❶2	32	●	2 **Baby, Come To Me** AC^3 **PATTI AUSTIN (with James Ingram)** originally charted for 4 weeks (#73); re-entered on 10/16/82	*Solero*	$3		Qwest 50036
3/19/83	69	7		3 **Every Home Should Have One** remixed version of #1 above	*Solero* [R]	$3		Qwest 29727
5/14/83	45	17		4 **How Do You Keep The Music Playing** **JAMES INGRAM AND PATTI AUSTIN** theme from the movie *Best Friends* starring **Burt Reynolds** and Goldie Hawn	*(long version)*	$3		Qwest 29618
2/11/84	82	4		5 **It's Gonna Be Special** from the movie *Two Of A Kind* starring **John Travolta** and **Olivia Newton-John**	*Solero*	$3		Qwest 29373
5/3/86	55	9		6 **The Heat Of Heat**	*Hot! In The Flames Of Love*	$3		Qwest 28788

AUSTIN, Sherrié — C&W/LP '99

Born on 8/28/70 in Sydney, Australia; raised in Townsville, Australia. Country singer/actress. Played "Pippa McKenna" on TV's *The Facts Of Life* (1987-88). Former member of **Colourhaus** (as Sherrié Krenn).

DEBUT	PEAK	WKS	Gold	A-side (Chart Hit)	B-side	$	Sym	Label & Number
7/31/99	89	10		1 **Never Been Kissed** ... S:28	*Words*	$5	★+V	Arista 13140
11/27/99	47^{S}	12		2 **Little Bird**	*Never Been Kissed*	$4	★V	Arista 13184

AUSTIN, Sil — '56

Born Sylvester Austin on 9/17/29 in Dunnellon, Florida. Died of cancer on 9/1/2001 (age 71). R&B tenor saxophonist. Played with Tiny Bradshaw Band before forming own group.

DEBUT	PEAK	WKS	Gold	A-side (Chart Hit)	B-side	$	Sym	Label & Number
11/10/56	17	14		1 **Slow Walk** ... J:17 / T:19 / S:20	*Wildwood* [I]	$15		Mercury 70963
2/16/57	74	1		2 **Birthday Party** ... T:74	*The Last Time* [I]	$15		Mercury 71027
6/1/59	59	12		3 **Danny Boy** based on the traditional Irish song "Londonderry Air" written in 1855	*The Hungry Eye* [I]	$12		Mercury 71442

AUTECHRE — '02

Experimental techno duo from Sheffield, Yorkshire, England: Sean Booth and Rob Brown.

DEBUT	PEAK	WKS	Gold	A-side (Chart Hit)	B-side	$	Sym	Label & Number
8/24/02	53^{S}	1		**Gantz Graf**	*Dial / Cap IV* [I]	$10	★*	Warp 256

AUTOGRAPH — ROK/LP '85

Hard-rock group from Los Angeles, California: Steve Plunkett (vocals, guitar), Steve Lynch (guitar), Steven Isham (keyboards), Randy Rand (bass) and Keni Richards (drums).

DEBUT	PEAK	WKS	Gold	A-side (Chart Hit)	B-side	$	Sym	Label & Number
12/22/84+	29	19		**Turn Up The Radio** ... S:25	*Thrill Of Love*	$5	■	RCA 13953

AUTOMATIC MAN — LP '77

Rock group formed in San Francisco, California, by Michael Shrieve (drums; **Santana**). Included Bayete (vocals, keyboards), Pat Thrall (guitar; **Pat Travers Band**,**Hughes/Thrall**, **Asia**) and Donni Harvey (bass).

DEBUT	PEAK	WKS	Gold	A-side (Chart Hit)	B-side	$	Sym	Label & Number
2/12/77	97	2		**My Pearl**	*Newspapers*	$6		Island 063

AUTRY, Gene — C&W/MEM/POP/AC '50

Born Orvon Gene Autry on 9/29/07 in Tioga, Texas. Died of respiratory failure on 10/2/98 (age 91). The first cowboy singing star of the movies. Formed Challenge Records. Former owner of the California (Anaheim) Angels baseball team. Elected to the Country Music Hall of Fame in 1969. Charted 24 pop hits, 1933-53.

DEBUT	PEAK	WKS	Gold	A-side (Chart Hit)	B-side	$	Sym	Label & Number
12/30/57	70	3		**Rudolph The Red-Nosed Reindeer** ... T:70 Carl Cotner (orch.); new version on Autry's own label of his #1 hit from 1949; reissued in 1958 on Challenge 59030 with a picture sleeve	*Here Comes Santa* [X-R]	$30		Challenge 1010

AVALON, Frankie ★136★ — BUB/LP '59

Born Francis Avallone on 9/18/39 in Philadelphia, Pennsylvania. Teen idol managed by Bob Marcucci. Worked in bands in 1953 in Atlantic City, New Jersey. Performed on radio and TV with Paul Whiteman, mid-1950s. Singer/trumpet player with Rocco & His Saints in 1956 which included **Bobby Rydell**. Co-starred in many movies with **Annette**. Appeared in the movies *Jamboree!*, *Guns Of The Timberland*, and *The Alamo*. Owner of Frankie Avalon Products, a line of health supplement products.

1)Venus 2)Why 3)Just Ask Your Heart 4)Dede Dinah 5)Bobby Sox To Stockings

DEBUT	PEAK	WKS	Gold	A-side (Chart Hit)	B-side	$	Sym	Label & Number
1/20/58	7	15		1 **DeDe Dinah** ... T:7 / S:9 / A:24	*Ooh La La*	$25		Chancellor 1011
4/14/58	49	9		2 **You Excite Me** ... T:49 / S:50	*Darlin'*	$25		Chancellor 1016
7/21/58	9	13		3 **Ginger Bread** ... H:9 / S:11 **The Four Dates** (backing vocals)	*Blue Betty*	$25	■	Chancellor 1021
10/13/58	15	17		4 **I'll Wait For You /** H:15				
10/13/58	79	2		5 **What Little Girl** ... H:79		$25	■	Chancellor 1026
2/9/59	❶5	17	●	6 **Venus** also see re-entry (#25 below)	*I'm Broke*	$25	■	Chancellor 1031
5/25/59	8	13		7 **Bobby Sox To Stockings /**				
5/25/59	10	14		8 **A Boy Without A Girl**		$20	■	Chancellor 1036
8/31/59	7	16		9 **Just Ask Your Heart /**				
9/21/59	54	5		10 **Two Fools**		$20	■	Chancellor 1040
11/23/59	❶1	16		11 **Why /**				
12/21/59+	39	6		12 **Swingin' On A Rainbow** issued with 2 different picture sleeves: with a blue background and with a red background		$20	■	Chancellor 1045
3/14/60	22	10		13 **Don't Throw Away All Those Teardrops**	*Talk, Talk, Talk*	$20	■	Chancellor 1048

DEBUT	PEAK	WKS	Gold	A-side (Chart Hit)...B-side	$	Sym	Label & Number
				AVALON, Frankie — Cont'd			
6/13/60	**32**	12		14 **Where Are You /**			
6/13/60	**82**	2		15 **Tuxedo Junction**	$20	■	Chancellor 1052
				#1 million-selling hit for Glenn Miller & His Orchestra in 1940			
9/19/60	**26**	13		16 **Togetherness /**			
10/10/60	**85**	2		17 **Don't Let Love Pass Me By**	$20	■	Chancellor 1056
12/12/60+	**47**	6		18 **A Perfect Love /**			
12/12/60	**56**	7		19 **The Puppet Song** [N]	$20	■	Chancellor 1065
2/27/61	**70**	4		20 **All Of Everything**...*Call Me Anytime* (#102)	$20	■	Chancellor 1071
5/29/61	**82**	2		21 **Who Else But You**...*Gotta Get A Girl*	$20		Chancellor 1077
9/25/61	**90**	2		22 **True, True Love**...*Married* (#112)	$20	■	Chancellor 1087
3/24/62	**26**	11		23 **You Are Mine**...*Ponchinello*	$20	■	Chancellor 1107
7/14/62	**75**	6		24 **A Miracle**...*Don't Let Me Stand In Your Way* (#111)	$20	■	Chancellor 1115
1/24/76	**46**	11		25 **Venus**...AC[1] *(disco version)* [R]	$6	■	De-Lite 1578
				disco version of #6 above; Avalon's arrangers and conductors: **Don Costa** (#23, 24), Peter DeAngelis (#1-15, 17-19), Russ Faith (#16, 21), Ian Freebairn-Smith (#22), Jerry Ragovoy (#20) and Joe Renzetti (#25)			
				AVANT LP **'00**			
				Born Myron Avant on 4/26/76 in Cleveland, Ohio. Male R&B singer.			
4/29/00	**23**	20		1 **Separated** RB[1] S:2 / A:22 *(remix w/***Kelly Rowland***)*	$4	★	Magic Johnson 155725
11/4/00	**26**	20		2 **My First Love**...A:21 **AVANT Featuring Ketara Wyatt** from the album *My Thoughts* on Magic Johnson 112069			album cut
1/5/02	**27**	20		3 **Nothing In This World**...A:25 **KEKE WYATT featuring Avant** from the album *Soul Sista* on MCA 112609			album cut
3/23/02	**27**	20		4 **Makin' Good Love**...A:27 from the album *Ecstasy* on Magic Johnson 112809			album cut
9/28/02	**96**	4		5 **Don't Say No, Just Say Yes**...*(3 versions)*	$4	★	Magic Johnson 113996
				AVANT-GARDE, The BUB **'68**			
				Duo of Chuck Woolery and Elkin "Bubba" Fowler. Woolery was the original host of TV's *Wheel of Fortune* and *Love Connection*.			
8/31/68	**40**	10		**Naturally Stoned**...*Honey And Gall*	$8		Columbia 44590
				AVERAGE, Johnny, Band **'81**			
				Born in Nottingham, Nottinghamshire, England. Rock guitarist. His wife, Nikki Wills, was the featured vocalist.			
2/21/81	**53**	7		**Ch Ch Cherie**...*Gotta Go Home* **THE JOHNNY AVERAGE BAND Featuring Nikki Wills**	$5		Bearsville 49671
				AVILA, Bobby Ross R&B **'93**			
				Born on 3/7/75 in San Bernardino, California. Singer/songwriter.			
5/1/93	**86**	3		**La La Love**...A:51 *Tu Amor (La La Love)*	$4	▮	Perspective 7422
				AWB (AVERAGE WHITE BAND) R&B/BUB/LP **'75**			
				White funk group from Scotland: Alan Gorrie (vocals, bass), Onnie McIntyre (guitar, vocals), Hamish Stuart (guitar, vocals), Malcolm Duncan (sax), Roger Ball (sax, keyboards) and Robbie McIntosh (drums). Gorrie and McIntyre were members of Forever More. McIntosh died of a drug overdose on 9/23/74 (age 24), replaced by Steve Ferrone. McIntosh and Ferrone were members of **Brian Auger's Oblivion Express**. Stuart later joined **Paul McCartney**'s touring band.			
				AWB:			
12/7/74+	❶[1]	17	●	1 **Pick Up The Pieces** *Work To Do* [I]	$5		Atlantic 3229
4/12/75	**10**	15		2 **Cut The Cake**...*Person To Person*	$5		Atlantic 3261
8/23/75	**39**	8		3 **If I Ever Lose This Heaven**...*High Flyin' Woman*	$5		Atlantic 3285
11/29/75	**33**	7		4 **School Boy Crush**...*Groovin' The Night Away*	$5		Atlantic 3304
9/4/76	**40**	8		5 **Queen Of My Soul** *[AVERAGE WHITE BAND]*...*Would You Stay* all of above produced by Arif Mardin	$5		Atlantic 3354
4/14/79	**92**	3		6 **Walk On By**...*Too Late To Cry*	$5		Atlantic 3563
6/21/80	**53**	8		7 **Let's Go 'Round Again** *[AVERAGE WHITE BAND]*...*Help Is On The Way*	$4		Arista 0515
				AXE BUB/ROK/LP **'82**			
				Rock group from Gainesville, Florida: Bobby Barth (vocals, guitar), Michael Osborne (guitar), Edgar Riley (keyboards), Wayne Haner (bass) and Ted Mueller (drums). Disbanded in 1984. Group made the Adult Contemporary chart in 1976 as Babyface. Osborne died in a car crash on 7/21/84 (age 34).			
7/24/82	**64**	6		1 **Now Or Never**...*Video Inspiration*	$5		Atco 7408
10/22/83	**94**	2		2 **I Think You'll Remember Tonight**...*Let The Music Come Back*	$5		Atco 99823
				AXTON, Hoyt C&W/BUB/LP **'74**			
				Born on 3/25/38 in Duncan, Oklahoma. Died of a heart attack on 10/26/99 (age 61). Son of songwriter Mae Axton ("Heartbreak Hotel"; died on 4/16/97, age 82). Appeared in the movies *The Black Stallion* and *Gremlins*. Wrote hits "Greenback Dollar" for **The Kingston Trio**, "The Pusher" for **Steppenwolf**, and "Joy To The World" and "Never Been To Spain" for **Three Dog Night**. Started own Jeremiah label in 1978.			
6/1/74	**54**	6		**When The Morning Comes**...*Billie's Theme* **Linda Ronstadt** (harmony vocal)	$6		A&M 1497
				AZ R&B/BUB/LP **'95**			
				Born Anthony Cruz in Brooklyn, New York. Male rapper. First pressings show artist as AZ The Visualiza.			
7/15/95	**25**	20	●	**Sugar Hill**...S:11 / A:64 *Rather Unique* **missjones** (female vocal); rap version of "Sugar Free" by Juicy (#13 R&B hit in 1986)	$3	▮	EMI 58407
				AZAR, Steve C&W **'02**			
				Born on 4/11/64 in Greenville, Mississippi. Country singer/songwriter/guitarist.			
4/6/02	**35**	20		**I Don't Have To Be Me ('Til Monday)**...A:32 from the album *Waitin' On Joe* on Mercury 170269; "45": Mercury 172230; B-side: "You Don't Know How It Feels"		V	album cut

DEBUT	PEAK	WKS	Gold	A-side (Chart Hit)..........B-side	$	Sym	Label & Number
				AZUL AZUL '01			
				Latin group from Bolivia: Fabio Zambrana (vocals), Ricardo Fries (guitar), Ademar Villagomez (bass) and Boris Anzoategui (drums). Group name is Spanish for "blue blue."			
4/7/01	70	20		**La Bomba** ....S:10 *(Bomba mix)*	$4	★	Sony Discos 84464
				CD single also issued with 2 additional remixes and a different picture cover on Sony Discos 84285			
				AZ YET LP '97			
				R&B vocal group from Philadelphia, Pennsylvania: Dion Allen, Darryl Anthony, Marc Nelson, Shawn Rivera and Kenny Terry.			
8/24/96	9	29	●	1 **Last Night** ....RB[1] / CW[1] S:5 / A:40 *(instrumental)*	$3	▮V	LaFace 24181
				written and produced by **Babyface**; from the movie *The Nutty Professor* starring **Eddie Murphy**			
2/22/97	8	34	▲	2 **Hard To Say I'm Sorry** ....S:6 / A:15 *(**david foster**'s remix)*	$3	▮V	LaFace 24223
				AZ YET Featuring Peter Cetera			
				"45" B-side: "Last Night" (no credit to Cetera)			
10/18/97	77	10		3 **You're The Inspiration** ....S:56 *Do You Love Me That Much / (3 album snippets)*	$4	▮	River North 3018
				PETER CETERA featuring Az Yet			

B

DEBUT	PEAK	WKS	Gold	A-side (Chart Hit)..........B-side	$	Sym	Label & Number
				BABY R&B/LP '03			
				Born Brian Williams in New Orleans, Louisiana. Male rapper/songwriter. Member of **Big Tymers** and **Cash Money Millionaires**.			
11/16/02+	33	20		**Do That...** ....S:22 / A:33 *(3 versions)*	$6	T	Cash Money 060079
				BABY (AKA DA #1 STUNNA) Featuring P. Diddy			
	★236★			**BABYFACE** R&B/BUB/LP '94			
				Born Kenneth Edmonds on 4/10/59 in Indianapolis, Indiana. R&B vocalist/instrumentalist. Formerly with Manchild and **The Deele**. Dubbed "Babyface" by Bootsy Collins. Brother of Melvin and **Kevon Edmonds** of **After 7**. With Mark "L.A. Reid" Rooney (The Deele), co-wrote **Pebbles**' "Girlfriend" and **The Whispers**' "Rock Steady"; they also did writing/production work for **Paula Abdul**, **Bobby Brown**, **The Boys**, **The Jacksons**, **Midnight Star** and **Karyn White**; they co-founded LaFace Records in Atlanta in 1989. Babyface's wife, Tracey, was president of Yab Yum Records. Also see **Milestone**.			
				1)When Can I See You 2)Every Time I Close My Eyes 3)This Is For The Lover In You			
8/12/89	7	18		1 **It's No Crime** ....RB[2] A:7 / S:8 *(instrumental)*	$3		Solar 68966
11/18/89+	14	17		2 **Tender Lover** ....RB[1] S:8 / A:18 *(instrumental)*	$3	▮V	Solar 74003
				Troop (backing vocals)			
2/24/90	6	18		3 **Whip Appeal** ....S:6 / A:6 *(instrumental)*	$3	▮V	Solar 74007
6/16/90	30	13		4 **My Kinda Girl** ....A:24 / S:38 *(instrumental)*	$3	▮V	Solar 74515
				above 4 from the album *Tender Lover*			
7/25/92	29	16		5 **Give U My Heart** ....A:29 / S:39 *(album version)*	$4	▮	LaFace 24026
				BABYFACE (Featuring Toni Braxton)			
				from the movie *Boomerang* starring **Eddie Murphy**			
8/14/93	81	9		6 **For The Cool In You** ....S:57 *(remix)*	$3	▮V	Epic 77109
10/23/93+	15	23		7 **Never Keeping Secrets** ....A:15 / S:18 *For The Cool In You (remix)*	$3	▮V	Epic 77264
3/5/94	21	20		8 **And Our Feelings** ....A:26 / S:29 *Never Keeping Secrets*	$3	▮V	Epic 77394
				After 7 (backing vocals)			
6/18/94	4	36	●	9 **When Can I See You** A:4 / S:9 *(R&B remix)*	$3	▮V	Epic 77550
				"45": Epic 77608; above 4 from the album *For The Cool In You*;			
10/1/94	68[S]	2		10 **Where Is My Love?** ....BUB:106 *Starlight, Moonlight, Candlelight*	$3	▮V	Reprise 18140
				EL DeBARGE featuring Babyface			
4/29/95	10	30	●	11 **Someone To Love** ....S:9 / A:16 *(3 album snippets)*	$3	▮V	Yab Yum 77895
				JON b featuring BABYFACE			
				from the movie *Bad Boys* starring Martin Lawrence and **Will Smith** (**Fresh Prince**); "45" B-side: "Pretty Girl"			
4/20/96	68	9		12 **Slow Jams** ....S:43 *(remix)*	$3	▮V	Qwest 17673
				QUINCY JONES Featuring Babyface and Tamia with Portrait and Barry White			
10/26/96	6	20	▲	13 **This Is For The Lover In You** ....S:3 / A:37 *(remix)*	$3	▮V	Epic 78443
				BABYFACE Featuring LL Cool J, Howard Hewett, Jody Watley and Jeffrey Daniels			
				#17 R&B hit for **Shalamar** in 1981 (Hewett, Watley and Daniels were members of **Shalamar**)			
2/1/97	6	26	●	14 **Every Time I Close My Eyes** ....S:5 / A:10 *Lady, Lady*	$3	▮V	Epic 78485
				Mariah Carey (backing vocal); **Sheila E.** (percussion); **Kenny G** (saxophone)			
6/14/97	47[A]	11		15 **How Come, How Long**			album cut
				BABYFACE Featuring Stevie Wonder			
				above 3 from the album *The Day* on Epic 67293			
10/25/97	95	2		16 **Sunshine** ....*(2 versions)*	$6	T	Roc-A-Fella 574923
				JAY-Z featuring Babyface and Foxy Brown			
5/12/01	31	15		17 **There She Goes** ....S:3 *(instrumental) / (5 album snippets)*	$4	★	Arista 13988
9/22/01	80	15		18 **What If** ....*(instrumental) / Lover And Friend*	$6	T	Arista 15034
				all of above (except #12, 13 & 16) written by **Babyface**			
				BABY JANE & THE ROCKABYES '63			
				Black female vocal group: Madelyn Moore, Yvonne DeMunn, Estelle McEwan and Yolanda Robinson. Name inspired by the movie *Whatever Happened To Baby Jane.*			
1/5/63	69	7		**How Much Is That Doggie In The Window** ....*My Boy John*	$20		United Artists 560
				#1 hit for **Patti Page** in 1953			
				BABY RAY '66			
				Male R&B singer Ray Eddlemon.			
12/3/66	69	6		**There's Something On Your Mind** ....*The House On Soul Hill* [N]	$15		Imperial 66216
				BABY S '01			
				Born in Los Angeles, California. Male rapper.			
10/20/01	51[S]	2		**I'm Ghetto** ....*(instrumental) / (6 album snippets* hosted by Bubba Loc)	$5	★	Blast/Ruthless 79654

DEBUT	PEAK	WKS	Gold	A-side (Chart Hit)........B-side	$	Sym	Label & Number
				BABYS, The LP **'79**			
				Rock group from England: **John Waite** (vocals), Walt Stocker (guitar), Mike Corby (guitar, keyboards) and Tony Brock (drums). By 1980, keyboardist **Jonathan Cain** (later of **Journey**) had replaced Corby, and bassist Ricky Phillips joined group. In 1989, Waite formed **Bad English** with Phillips and Cain.			
3/19/77	88	2		1 **If You've Got The Time**........*Head Above The Waves*	$6		Chrysalis 2132
10/8/77	13	16		2 **Isn't It Time** *Give Me Your Love*	$5		Chrysalis 2173
2/4/78	53	7		3 **Silver Dreams**........*And If You Could See Me Fly*	$5	⊙	Chrysalis 2201
1/6/79	13	16		4 **Every Time I Think Of You**........*Please Don't Leave Me Here* also issued with "Head First" as the B-side	$5		Chrysalis 2279
5/26/79	77	3		5 **Head First**........*California*	$5		Chrysalis 2323
1/19/80	33	12		6 **Back On My Feet Again**........*Turn Around In Tokyo*	$5	■	Chrysalis 2398
5/3/80	72	4		7 **Midnight Rendezvous**........*Love Is Just A Mystery*	$5		Chrysalis 2425
11/15/80	42	12		8 **Turn And Walk Away**........*Darker Side Of Town*	$5		Chrysalis 2467
				BABY TALK **'98**			
				Studio group assembled by producer David Hummer.			
5/30/98	71	6		**Hooked On A Feeling (Ooga-Chaka)**........S:49 *(3 versions)* from the TV show *Ally McBeal* starring Calista Flockhart; "Multi-Image" CD case shows title as "Dancing Baby"	$8	★*	Peter Pan 4409
				BACHARACH, Burt AC/BUB/LP **'63**			
				Born on 5/12/28 in Kansas City, Missouri. Conductor/arranger/composer. With lyricist Hal David wrote "Close To You," "Raindrops Keep Falling On My Head," "This Guy's In Love With You," "What's New Pussycat" and most of **Dionne Warwick**'s hits. Married to actress Angie Dickinson from 1966-80. Married to songwriter **Carole Bayer Sager** from 1982-90.			
7/27/63	93	3		1 **Saturday Sunshine**........*And So Goodbye My Love*	$7		Kapp 532
7/5/69	93	2		2 **I'll Never Fall In Love Again**........*Pacific Coast Highway* from the Broadway musical *Promises, Promises* starring Jerry Orbach; Bacharach does not sing on above 2 (vocals by a chorus)	$6		A&M 1064
				BACHELORS, The AC/LP **'64**			
				Pop vocal trio from Dublin, Ireland: brothers Declan and Conleth Cluskey, with John Stokes. Formed in 1958 as a barbershop trio, The Harmony Chords.			
4/18/64	10	13		1 **Diane** *Happy Land* #2 hit for the Nat Shilkret Orchestra in 1928	$12		London 9639
6/27/64	33	8		2 **I Believe**........*Sweet Lullabies* #2 hit for **Frankie Laine** in 1953	$12	■	London 9672
9/12/64	69	6		3 **I Wouldn't Trade You For The World**........*Beneath The Willow Tree*	$12	■	London 9693
12/26/64+	27	10		4 **No Arms Can Ever Hold You**........*Oh, Samuel Don't Die*	$12		London 9724
6/12/65	15	10		5 **Marie**........*You Can Tell* #1 hit for **Tommy Dorsey** in 1937; written by Irving Berlin in 1928	$10		London 9762
10/9/65	32	7		6 **Chapel In The Moonlight**........*The Old Wishing Well* #1 hit for Shep Fields in 1936	$10	■	London 9793
4/16/66	38	6		7 **Love Me With All Of Your Heart**........*There's No Room In My Heart*	$10		London 9828
7/2/66	49	6		8 **Can I Trust You?**........*My Girl*	$10		London 20010
1/7/67	83	3		9 **Walk With Faith In Your Heart**........*Queen Of Ireland - Molly Malone*	$10		London 20018
				BACHMAN, Tal LP **'99**			
				Born on 8/13/69 in Vancouver, British Columbia, Canada. Male rock singer/songwriter/guitarist. Son of Randy Bachman (of **Bachman-Turner Overdrive**).			
6/19/99	14	28		**She's So High**........A:10 from the album *Tal Bachman* on Columbia 67956			album cut
	★505★			**BACHMAN-TURNER OVERDRIVE** LP **'74**			
				Hard-rock group from Vancouver, British Columbia, Canada: brothers Randy (vocals, guitar; born on 9/27/43) and Robbie (drums; born on 2/18/53) Bachman, with C. Fred Turner (vocals, bass; born on 10/16/43) and Blair Thornton (guitar; born on 7/23/50). Originally known as Brave Belt. Randy had been in **The Guess Who** and recorded solo. Randy left in 1977 to form **Ironhorse**; regrouped with Turner in 1984. Randy is the father of **Tal Bachman**. *1)You Ain't Seen Nothing Yet 2)Takin' Care Of Business 3)Roll On Down The Highway*			
12/1/73	68	6		1 **Blue Collar**........*Hold Back The Water*	$6		Mercury 73417
2/23/74	23	15		2 **Let It Ride**........*Tramp*	$6		Mercury 73457
5/18/74	12	20		3 **Takin' Care Of Business**........*Stonegates*	$6		Mercury 73487
9/21/74	❶[1]	17	●	4 **You Ain't Seen Nothing Yet /**			
12/7/74		6		5 **Free Wheelin'**........[I] dedicated to **Duane Allman**	$5		Mercury 73622
1/18/75	14	11		6 **Roll On Down The Highway**........*Sledgehammer*	$5		Mercury 73656
5/17/75	21	12		7 **Hey You**........*Flat Broke Love*	$5		Mercury 73683
12/6/75+	43	7		8 **Down To The Line**........*She's A Devil*	$5	■	Mercury 73724
2/7/76	33	7		9 **Take It Like A Man**........*Woncha Take Me For A While* **Little Richard** (backing vocal)	$5		Mercury 73766
4/24/76	65	6		10 **Lookin' Out For #1**........*Find Out About Love*	$5		Mercury 73784
9/18/76	70	5		11 **Gimme Your Money Please**........*Four Wheel Drive*	$5		Mercury 73843
2/24/79	60	7		12 **Heartaches** *[BTO]*........*Heaven Tonight*	$5		Mercury 74046
	★215★			**BACKSTREET BOYS** LP **'98**			
				"Boy band" formed in Orlando, Florida: Nick Carter (born on 1/28/80 in Jamestown, New York), Howie Dorough (born on 8/22/73 in Orlando, Florida), Brian Littrell (born on 2/20/75 in Lexington, Kentucky), A.J. McLean (born on 1/9/78 in West Palm Beach, Florida) and Kevin Richardson (born on 10/3/71 in Lexington, Kentucky). Carter is the older brother of singers **Aaron Carter** and **Leslie Carter**. *1)Quit Playing Games (With My Heart) 2)Everybody (Backstreet's Back) 3)All I Have To Give*			
10/28/95	69	20		1 **We've Got It Goin' On**........*(remix) / (album medley)* cassette single issued with 1 of 5 different picture trading cards	$5	▮	Jive 42329
6/28/97	2[2]	43	▲	2 **Quit Playing Games (With My Heart)** A:2 / S:3 *Lay Down Beside Me*	$3	▮V	Jive 42453
11/1/97+	4[A]	56		3 **As Long As You Love Me**........			album cut
4/18/98	4	22	▲	4 **Everybody (Backstreet's Back)**........S:4 / A:27 *(remix)* "45" issued for above 2 on Jive 42510	$3	▮V	Jive 42510

DEBUT	PEAK	WKS	Gold	A-side (Chart Hit)...B-side	$	Sym	Label & Number
				BACKSTREET BOYS — Cont'd			
7/18/98	4^{A}	22		5 **I'll Never Break Your Heart**...AC^{7} HOT:35(2 wks) CD and cassette single only available at select discount merchants for a short time	$15	★	Jive 42528
1/30/99	5	21	▲	6 **All I Have To Give**...S:3 / A:16 *(Part II - The Conversation Mix)* all of above from the album *Backstreet Boys* on Jive 41589	$4	$★^{V}$	Jive 42562
4/24/99	6	31		7 **I Want It That Way**...AC^{10} A:❶^{3}		V	album cut
9/18/99	25	19		8 **Larger Than Life**...A:20 B-sides for above 2 "45s" are the same as the A-sides		V	album cut
1/1/00	6	24		9 **Show Me The Meaning Of Being Lonely**...A:2			album cut
5/27/00	30	15		10 **The One**...A:30 above 4 from the album *Millennium* on Jive 41672			album cut
10/14/00	9	20		11 **Shape Of My Heart**...A:7 *(same version)*	$6	T^{V}	Jive 42758
2/17/01	52	6		12 **The Call**...A:57			album cut
5/26/01	27	20		13 **More Than That**...A:23 above 3 from the album *Black & Blue* on Jive 41743			album cut
10/20/01	28	20		14 **Drowning**...A:33 from the album *The Hits - Chapter One...* on Jive 41779			album cut
				BACKUS, Jim, and Friend '58 Born on 2/25/13 in Cleveland, Ohio. Died of pneumonia on 7/3/89 (age 76). Actor, starred in dozens of movies. Played "Thurston Howell III" on TV's *Gilligan's Island.* Also famous as the voice of "Mr. Magoo" in the cartoon series. Label misspelled last name as Bakus on some pressings.			
7/14/58	40	5		**Delicious!**...S:40 / T:42 *I Need A Vacation* [N] Appleknocker And His Group (instrumental backing)	$20		Jubilee 5330
				BAD AZZ R&B/LP '99 Born in 1975 in Los Angeles, California. Male rapper.			
3/13/99	58^{S}	4		**We Be Puttin' It Down**...*(instrumental) / Ghetto Star* **BAD AZZ featuring Snoop Dogg** clean version available on No Limit 53467	$4	★	No Limit 53465
				BAD BOYS BLUE BUB '93 Dance trio formed in Cologne, Germany: John McInerney (from Liverpool, lead vocals), Andrew Thomas (from Los Angeles) and Ova Standing (from Zaire).			
3/13/93	81	7		**Save Your Love**...A:59 *(12" mix)*	$4	▮	Zoo 14081
	★343★			**BAD COMPANY** ROK/LP '75 Rock group from England: Paul Rodgers (vocals; born on 12/17/49), Mick Ralphs (guitar; born on 3/31/44), Raymond "Boz" Burrell (bass; born on 8/1/46) and Simon Kirke (drums; born on 7/28/49). Rodgers and Kirke from **Free**; Ralphs from **Mott The Hoople**; and Burrell from **King Crimson**. Rodgers, who left group in late 1982, was a member of **The Firm** (1984-86) and The Law (in 1991). Vocalist Brian Howe joined in 1986. Burrell left in 1987. Dave "Bucket" Colwell (guitar) and Rick Wills (of **Foreigner**; bass) joined in late 1992. Howe left in early 1995; replaced by Robert Hart. Band named after a 1972 Jeff Bridges movie. *1)Can't Get Enough 2)Feel Like Makin' Love 3)Rock 'N' Roll Fantasy*			
8/17/74	5	15		1 **Can't Get Enough** *Little Miss Fortune*	$6		Swan Song 70015
1/18/75	19	10		2 **Movin' On**...*Easy On My Soul*	$6		Swan Song 70101
4/19/75	36	8		3 **Good Lovin' Gone Bad**...*Whiskey Bottle*	$6		Swan Song 70103
7/5/75	10	15		4 **Feel Like Makin' Love**...*Wild Fire Woman*	$6		Swan Song 70106
3/20/76	20	13		5 **Young Blood**...*Do Right By Your Woman*	$6		Swan Song 70108
7/10/76	59	6		6 **Honey Child**...*Fade Away*	$6		Swan Song 70109
5/21/77	78	4		7 **Burnin' Sky**...*Everything I Need*	$6		Swan Song 70112
3/17/79	13	20	●	8 **Rock 'N' Roll Fantasy**...*Crazy Circles*	$6	■	Swan Song 70119
8/4/79	56	6		9 **Gone, Gone, Gone**...*Take The Time*	$6	■	Swan Song 71000
10/2/82	74	4		10 **Electricland**...*Untie The Knot*	$6	■	Swan Song 99966
10/18/86	85	5		11 **This Love**...*Tell It Like It Is*	$4	■	Atlantic 89355
4/22/89	82	8		12 **Shake It Up**...*Dangerous Age*	$4	■	Atlantic 88939
7/14/90	89	6		13 **Holy Water**...AR^{2} *I Can't Live Without You*	$3	$▮^{V}$	Atco 98944
11/10/90+	16	24		14 **If You Needed Somebody**...A:14 / S:18 *Dead Of The Night* "45" issued for above 2 on Atlantic Oldies Series 94936 in 1993	$3	$▮^{V}$	Atco 98914
8/24/91	28	17		15 **Walk Through Fire**...A:54 *Lay Your Love On Me*	$3	▮	Atco 98748
9/12/92	38	13		16 **How About That**...AR^{6} A:55 *Brokenhearted*	$3	$▮^{V}$	Atco 98509
12/19/92	87	8		17 **This Could Be The One**...*Both Feet In The Water* "45" issued for above 2 on Atco 98463	$3	$▮^{V}$	Atco 98463
				BAD ENGLISH ROK/AC/LP '89 Rock supergroup: **John Waite** (vocals), Ricky Phillips (bass), **Jonathan Cain** (keyboards), Neal Schon (guitar) and Deen Castronovo (drums). Waite, Phillips and Cain were members of **The Babys**. Cain and Schon (ex-**Santana**) were members of **Journey**. Schon and Castronovo joined Hardline in 1992.			
7/22/89	45	11		1 **Forget Me Not**...A:38 *Lay Down*	$3		Epic 68946
9/16/89	❶^{2}	22	●	2 **When I See You Smile** S:❶^{2} / A:❶^{2} *Rockin' Horse*	$3		Epic 69082
12/23/89+	5	19		3 **Price Of Love**...A:5 / S:7 *The Restless Ones*	$3	$▮^{V}$	Epic 73094
4/14/90	66	9		4 **Heaven Is A 4 Letter Word**...*Lay Down*	$3	▮	Epic 73307
6/9/90	21	17		5 **Possession**...A:14 / S:34 *Tough Times Don't Last* all of above from the album *Bad English*	$3	$▮^{V}$	Epic 73398
8/31/91	42	13		6 **Straight To Your Heart**...A:69 *Make Love Last*	$3	▮	Epic 73982

DEBUT	PEAK	WKS	Gold	A-side (Chart Hit)...B-side	$	Sym	Label & Number

BADFINGER — BUB/LP '70

Rock group from Swansea, Wales, originally known as **The Iveys**. Consisted of Pete Ham (guitar), Tom Evans (bass), Joey Molland (guitar; joined in late 1968, after band recorded "Maybe Tomorrow") and Mike Gibbins (drums). All but Gibbins shared vocals. After Ham committed suicide on 4/23/75 (age 27), group disbanded. Molland and Evans reunited in 1978 with Glen Sherba (guitar), Tony Kaye (keyboards, **Yes**) and Richard Bryan (drums). Evans committed suicide on 11/23/83 (age 36).

DEBUT	PEAK	WKS	Gold	A-side (Chart Hit)...B-side	$	Sym	Label & Number
2/15/69	67	6		1 **Maybe Tomorrow** ... *Daddy's A Millionaire* **THE IVEYS**	$20		Apple 1803
2/7/70	7	15		2 **Come And Get It** ... *Rock Of All Ages* written and produced by **Paul McCartney**; from the movie *The Magic Christian* starring Peter Sellers	$15		Apple 1815
10/31/70	8	12		3 **No Matter What** ... *Carry On Till Tomorrow*	$15		Apple 1822
12/4/71+	4	14	●	4 **Day After Day** *Money* **George Harrison** (guitar, producer); **Leon Russell** (piano)	$15		Apple 1841
3/25/72	14	10		5 **Baby Blue** ... *Flying* produced by **Todd Rundgren**	$15	■	Apple 1844
4/7/79	69	4		6 **Love Is Gonna Come At Last** ... *Sail Away*	$6		Elektra 46025
2/28/81	56	8		7 **Hold On** ... *Passin' Time*	$6		Radio 3793

BADLEES, The — ROK '96

Rock group from Philadelphia, Pennsylvania: Pete Palladino (vocals), Bret Alexander and Jeff Feltenberger (guitars), Paul Smith (bass) and Ron Simasek (drums).

DEBUT	PEAK	WKS	Gold	A-side (Chart Hit)...B-side	$	Sym	Label & Number
7/6/96	67	11		**Angeline Is Coming Home** ... A:59 *Fear Of Falling (live)* (ROK #31)	$4	▮	Atlas/A&M 6412

BAD SEED, The — R&B '01

Born Corey Pierson in 1975 in Brooklyn, New York. Male rapper.

DEBUT	PEAK	WKS	Gold	A-side (Chart Hit)...B-side	$	Sym	Label & Number
2/3/01	42^{S}	10		**Uhhnnh** ... *(2 versions) / Would You Luh Me? / War & Peace*	$6	T	J Grand/Rawkus 299

BADU, Erykah — R&B/BUB/LP '97

Born Erica Wright on 2/26/71 in Dallas, Texas. R&B singer/songwriter/actress. Played "Rose Rose" in the movie *The Cider House Rules.*

DEBUT	PEAK	WKS	Gold	A-side (Chart Hit)...B-side	$	Sym	Label & Number
1/25/97	12	19	●	1 **On&On** ... RB^{2} S:7 / A:58 *(2 versions) / (4 album snippets)*	$3	▮^{V}	Kedar/Universal 56002
5/24/97	61^{A}	7		2 **Next Lifetime** ... RB^{2A} from the album *Baduizm* on Kedar/Universal 53027			album cut
12/6/97	62^{A}	5		3 **Tyrone** ... RB^{6A} [L] from the album *Live* on Kedar/Universal 53109; "45" issued for #1 & 3 on Kedar/Universal 56189		V	album cut
2/13/99	39	14		4 **You Got Me** ... A:24 *(5 versions)* **THE ROOTS featuring Erykah Badu**	$6	T	MCA 55539
8/28/99	76	6		5 **Southern Gul** ... S:16 *(2 versions)* **ERYKAH BADU featuring Rahzel**	$4	★	Motown 56360
8/19/00	6	20		6 **Bag Lady** RB^{7} S:3 / A:21 *(main version)* samples "Bumpy's Lament" by **Isaac Hayes**	$4	★	Motown 158326
9/7/02+	9	27		7 **Love Of My Life (An Ode To Hip Hop)** ... A:9 / S:27 *(3 versions)* **ERYKAH BADU Featuring Common** from the movie *Brown Sugar* starring Taye Diggs	$6	T	Fox/MCA 113987

BAEZ, Joan — AC/LP '71

Born Joan Chandos Baez on 1/9/41 in Staten Island, New York, to a Mexican father and British mother. Pre-eminent folk song stylist. Became a political activist while attending Boston University in the late 1950s. Made her professional debut in July 1959 at the first Newport Folk Festival. Orientation changed from traditional to popular folk songs in the early '60s. Influential in fostering career of **Bob Dylan**.

DEBUT	PEAK	WKS	Gold	A-side (Chart Hit)...B-side	$	Sym	Label & Number
11/9/63	90	1		1 **We Shall Overcome** ... *What Have They Done To The Rain* [L] recorded at Miles College in Birmingham, Alabama; based on the music from an early hymn of 1794	$10		Vanguard 35023
9/11/65	50	7		2 **There But For Fortune** ... *Daddy You Been On My Mind*	$10	□	Vanguard 35031
12/10/66	16^{X}	3		3 **The Little Drummer Boy** ... *Cantique De Noel* [X] Peter Schickele (orch.)	$10	■	Vanguard 35046
4/26/69	86	4		4 **Love Is Just A Four-Letter Word** ... *Love Minus Zero/No Limit* written by **Bob Dylan**	$10		Vanguard 35088
8/14/71	3	15	●	5 **The Night They Drove Old Dixie Down** AC^{5} *When Time Is Stolen* written by Robbie Robertson (leader of **The Band**; B-side of the group's 1969 hit "Up On Cripple Creek")	$8		Vanguard 35138
11/13/71	49	8		6 **Let It Be** ... *Poor Wayfaring Stranger* (w/Mimi Fariña)	$8		Vanguard 35145
7/29/72	69	8		7 **In The Quiet Morning** ... *To Bobby* written by Mimi Fariña (Joan's sister) for **Janis Joplin**	$5	■	A&M 1362
7/12/75	57	5		8 **Blue Sky** ... *Dida* first recorded by **The Allman Brothers Band** on their 1972 album *Eat A Peach*	$5		A&M 1703
9/20/75	35	11		9 **Diamonds And Rust** ... *Winds Of The Old Days* autobiographical song about Baez and **Bob Dylan**	$5		A&M 1737

BAGBY, Doc — '57

Born Harold Bagby in Philadelphia, Pennsylvania. Black organist. Owner of the Red Top label.

DEBUT	PEAK	WKS	Gold	A-side (Chart Hit)...B-side	$	Sym	Label & Number
9/30/57	69	4		**Dumplin's** ... T:69 *Sylvia's Callin'* [I]	$20		Okeh 7089

BAHAMA MAMA'S — '01

Female vocal duo from Miami, Florida: Yvey and Shevy Green.

DEBUT	PEAK	WKS	Gold	A-side (Chart Hit)...B-side	$	Sym	Label & Number
1/6/01	32^{S}	11		**Who Let The Dogs Out** ... *(4 mixes)* [N] cover version of the **Baha Men**'s original version below	$6	★*	Truly Hype 71211

BAHA MEN — LP '00

R&B group from the Bahamas: Rick Carey and Omerit Hield (vocals), Marvin Prosper (rapper), Herschel Small and Patrick Carey (guitars), Tony Flowers (percussion), Jeff Cher (keyboards), Isaiah Taylor (bass) and Colyn Grant (drums).

DEBUT	PEAK	WKS	Gold	A-side (Chart Hit)...B-side	$	Sym	Label & Number
7/22/00	40	20		1 **Who Let The Dogs Out** ... S:15 / A:35 *Get Ya Party On* [N]	$4	★	S-Curve 751050
2/3/01	94	4		2 **You All Dat** ... S:12 *(dance remix) / Who Let The Dogs Out* **BAHA MEN with Imani Coppola** samples "The Lion Sleeps Tonight" by **The Tokens**	$5	★$^{+}$	S-Curve 151002
3/2/02	5^{S}	21		3 **Move It Like This** ... *Break Away* "45": S-Curve/Capitol 77687; B-side: (remix)	$4	★^{V}	S-Curve 77687

DEBUT	PEAK	WKS	Gold	A-side (Chart Hit)	B-side	$	Sym	Label & Number
				BAILEY, Philip R&B/LP '85				
				Born on 5/8/51 in Denver, Colorado. Co-lead singer of **Earth, Wind & Fire**. Recorded Christian music from 1984-90.				
11/24/84+	2^2	23	●	1 Easy Lover S:❶^1 / A:2	*Woman* (Bailey)	$3	■	Columbia 04679
				PHILIP BAILEY (with Phil Collins)				
4/6/85	46	12		2 Walking On The Chinese Wall	*Children Of The Ghetto*	$3	■	Columbia 04826
				above 2 produced by **Phil Collins**				
				BAILEY, Razzy C&W/AC/LP '74				
				Born Rasie Michael Bailey on 2/14/39 in Five Points, Alabama. Country singer/songwriter. Charted 31 Country hits, 1976-89. Wrote **Dickey Lee**'s hit "9,999,999 Tears."				
5/25/74	67	6		I Hate Hate	*Singing Other People's Songs*	$6		MGM 14728
				RAZZY				
				first released on Aquarian 601 as by: RAZZY And The Neighborhood Kids ($10)				
				BAINBRIDGE, Merril BUB/LP '96				
				Born on 6/2/68 in Melbourne, Australia. Female singer/songwriter.				
9/7/96	4	30	●	1 Mouth A:5 / S:9	*Julie*	$3	▮	Universal 56018
3/22/97	91	6		2 Under The Water	*Mouth (alternate take)*	$3	▮	Universal 56112
				Chris Wilson (male vocal)				
				BAIRD, Dan — see GEORGIA SATELLITES				
				BAJA MARIMBA BAND AC/BUB/LP '64				
				Group led by marimbist Julius Wechter (born on 5/10/35 in Chicago; died of cancer on 2/1/99, age 63). Group featured various studio musicians with Wechter the only constant. Wechter also played with **Herb Alpert** and **Martin Denny**.				
12/21/63+	41	9		1 Comin' In The Back Door	*December's Child* [I]	$8		Almo Int'l. 201
11/26/66	52	6		2 Ghost Riders In The Sky	*Sabor A Mi (Be True To Me)* [I]	$6		A&M 824
				#1 hit for **Vaughn Monroe** in 1949				
4/29/67	98	1		3 Georgy Girl	*Cabeza Arriba! (Heads Up!)* [I]	$6		A&M 843
				title song from the movie starring Lynn Redgrave and James Mason				
8/5/67	96	2		4 Along Comes Mary	*Wall Street Rag* [I]	$6	■	A&M 862
	★523★			**BAKER, Anita** R&B/AC/BUB/LP '88				
				Born on 12/20/57 in Toledo, Ohio; raised in Detroit, Michigan. R&B/jazz-styled singer. Female lead singer of Chapter 8 from 1976-83.				
				1)Giving You The Best That I Got 2)Sweet Love 3)Just Because				
8/16/86	8	22		1 Sweet Love S:6 / A:9	*Watch Your Step*	$3		Elektra 69557
11/29/86+	37	18		2 Caught Up In The Rapture S:37 / A:40	*Mystery*	$3	■	Elektra 69511
3/21/87	44	14		3 Same Ole Love (365 Days A Year) S:35	*(live version)*	$3	■	Elektra 69484
8/22/87	44	17		4 No One In The World S:37	*Watch Your Step*	$3	■	Elektra 69456
				all of above from the album *Rapture*				
9/24/88	3	22		5 Giving You The Best That I Got RB^2 / AC^1 S:2 / A:3	*Good Enough*	$3	■	Elektra 69371
1/21/89	14	16		6 Just Because RB^1 A:11 / S:14	*Good Enough*	$3	■	Elektra 69327
6/23/90	44	13		7 Talk To Me S:37	*Good Enough*	$3	▮V	Elektra 64964
9/22/90	72	7		8 Soul Inspiration	*Good Enough*	$3	▮V	Elektra 64935
9/3/94	36	20		9 Body & Soul S:19 / A:52	*Baby*	$3	▮	Elektra 64520
12/31/94+	74	12		10 I Apologize S:47	*Baby*	$3	▮	Elektra 64497
				BAKER, Arthur R&B '92				
				Born on 4/22/55 in Boston, Massachusetts. Prolific producer. Since producing **Afrika Bambaataa**'s "Planet Rock" in 1982, has produced or mixed for **New Order**, **Bob Dylan**, **New Edition**, **Bruce Springsteen**, **Fine Young Cannibals**, **The Rolling Stones**, **U2**, **Paul McCartney** and many others. Co-produced/co-wrote the **Artists United Against Apartheid** project. Formed own labels, Streetwise and Minimal.				
3/21/92	93	4		I O U A:56	*Give In To The Rhythm*	$3	▮	RCA 62208
				ARTHUR BAKER featuring Nikeeta				
				BAKER, George, Selection BUB/LP '70				
				Baker is Johannes Bouwens (born on 12/9/44), leader of pop group from Holland that includes Jan Hop, Jacobus Anthonius Greuter, George The and Jan Gerbrand Visser. Female singer Nelleke Brzoskowsky joined in 1975 (heard on "Paloma Blanca").				
3/21/70	21	13		1 Little Green Bag	*Pretty Little Dreamer*	$6		Colossus 112
6/20/70	93	2		2 Dear Ann	*Fly*	$6	■	Colossus 117
11/29/75+	26	15		3 Paloma Blanca AC^1	*Dreamboat*	$5		Warner 8115
				title means "White Dove"				
				BAKER('S), Ginger, Air Force LP '70				
				Born Peter Baker on 8/19/39 in Lewisham, England. Drummer for **Cream** and Blind Faith. Got start as replacement for Charlie Watts (who left to join **The Rolling Stones**) in Alexis Korner's Blues Inc. (**C.C.S.**) in 1962. Then with the Graham Bond Organization. Air Force featured **Steve Winwood**, Denny Laine (**Moody Blues**, **Wings**) and Rick Grech (Family, **Traffic**, Blind Faith). Joined Masters Of Reality in 1992.				
5/23/70	85	2		Man Of Constant Sorrow	*Doin' It*	$7		Atco 6750
				Denny Laine (vocal); traditional song featured in the 2001 movie *O Brother, Where Art Thou?*				
	★404★			**BAKER, LaVern** R&B/BUB '59				
				Born Delores Williams on 11/11/29 in Chicago, Illinois. Died of heart failure on 3/10/97 (age 67). Recorded as "Little Miss Share Cropper" and "Bea Baker." One of the most popular female R&B singers of the early rock era. After working with the Todd Rhodes Orchestra, 1952-53, toured Europe, solo. Signed with Atlantic Records in 1953. Backing group: The Gliders. Moved to the Philippines in 1969 and for 20 years worked as an entertainer and manager at a servicemen's club in Subic Bay. Inducted into the Rock and Roll Hall of Fame in 1991.				
				1)I Cried A Tear 2)Tweedlee Dee 3)Jim Dandy 4)I Can't Love You Enough 5)I Waited Too Long				
1/15/55	14	11		1 Tweedlee Dee *[LaVERN BAKER and The Gliders]* J:14 / S:22	*Tomorrow Night*	$50		Atlantic 1047
10/6/56	22	11		2 I Can't Love You Enough / A:22 / T:48				
1/5/57	97	1		3 Still T:97		$30		Atlantic 1104
12/29/56+	17	19		4 Jim Dandy *[LaVERNE BAKER and The Gliders]* / RB^1 S:17 / A:20 / T:22				
12/15/56	94	1		5 Tra La La *[LaVERNE BAKER and The Gliders]* T:94		$30		Atlantic 1116
				from the movie *Rock, Rock, Rock* starring Tuesday Weld				
7/1/57	76	2		6 Jim Dandy Got Married T:76	*The Game Of Love (A-One and A-Two)*	$30		Atlantic 1136

DEBUT	PEAK	WKS	Gold	A-side (Chart Hit)...B-side	$	Sym	Label & Number
				BAKER, LaVern — Cont'd			
9/16/57	71	7		7 **Humpty Dumpty Heart** ....T:71 *Love Me Right* from the movie *Mr. Rock & Roll* starring Alan Freed	$30		Atlantic 1150
12/8/58+	6	21	●	8 **I Cried A Tear** *Dix-A-Billy*	$25		Atlantic 2007
4/20/59	33	11		9 **I Waited Too Long** .... *You're Teasing Me* written by **Neil Sedaka**	$20		Atlantic 2021
7/27/59	52	10		10 **So High So Low /** based on the spiritual "Bosom Of Abraham" (also known as "Oh, Rock My Soul")			
8/17/59	79	2		11 **If You Love Me** .... #4 hit for **Kay Starr** in 1954	$20		Atlantic 2033
11/2/59	63	9		12 **Tiny Tim** .... *For Love Of You*	$20		Atlantic 2041
5/2/60	83	4		13 **Wheel Of Fortune /** #1 hit for **Kay Starr** in 1952			
5/23/60	83	4		14 **Shadows Of Love**	$20		Atlantic 2059
11/14/60	46	11		15 **Bumble Bee** .... *My Time Will Come*	$20		Atlantic 2077
2/13/61	81	3		16 **You're The Boss** .... *I'll Never Be Free* (#103) **LaVERN BAKER & JIMMY RICKS** (of The Ravens; died on 7/2/74)	$20		Atlantic 2090
4/10/61	37	7		17 **Saved** .... *Don Juan*	$15		Atlantic 2099
12/1/62+	34	11		18 **See See Rider** .... *The Story Of My Love (I Had A Dream)* #14 hit for Ma Rainey in 1925 (as "See See Rider Blues")	$15		Atlantic 2167
2/13/65	84	2		19 **Fly Me To The Moon** .... *Ain't Gonna Cry No More* written in 1954 as "In Other Words"	$12		Atlantic 2267
1/15/66	93	1		20 **Think Twice** .... *Please Don't Hurt Me* (#128) **JACKIE WILSON And LaVERN BAKER**	$12		Brunswick 55287
				BALANCE LP **'81** Pop-rock trio from the Bronx, New York: Peppy Castro (vocals; **Blues Magoos**), Bob Kulick (guitar; brother of Bruce Kulick of **Kiss**) and Doug Katsaros (keyboards).			
7/11/81	22	17		1 **Breaking Away** .... *It's So Strange*	$4		Portrait 02177
11/21/81+	58	11		2 **Falling In Love** .... *Fly Through The Night*	$4		Portrait 02608
				BALDRY, Long John LP **'71** Born on 1/12/41 in London, England. Influential blues rocker. Formed Steampacket with **Rod Stewart**, and Bluesology with **Elton John**.			
1/13/68	88	2		1 **Let The Heartaches Begin** .... *Hey Lord You Made The Night Too Long*	$8		Warner 7098
8/21/71	73	7		2 **Don't Try To Lay No Boogie-Woogie On The King Of Rock And Roll** *[JOHN BALDRY]* .... *Mr. Rubin* (**Elton John**, producer) produced by **Rod Stewart**	$8		Warner 7506
8/11/79	89	3		3 **You've Lost That Lovin' Feelin'** .... *Baldry's Out* (Baldry) **LONG JOHN BALDRY & Kathi MacDonald**	$5	■	EMI America 8018
				BALIN, Marty AC/BUB/LP **'81** Born Martyn Buchwald on 1/30/42 in Cincinnati, Ohio. Co-founder of **Jefferson Airplane/Starship** and **KBC Band**.			
5/23/81	8	21		1 **Hearts** .... *Freeway*	$4	■	EMI America 8084
9/19/81	27	13		2 **Atlanta Lady (Something About Your Love)** .... *Lydia!*	$4		EMI America 8093
2/19/83	63	6		3 **What Love Is** .... *Will You Forever*	$4	■	EMI America 8153
				BALL, David C&W/BUB/LP **'01** Born on 7/9/53 in Rock Hill, South Carolina. Country singer/songwriter/guitarist.			
7/2/94	40	12		1 **Thinkin' Problem** ....S:18 *Down At The Bottom Of A Broken Heart*	$4	▮V	Warner 18250
10/27/01	36	20		2 **Riding With Private Malone** ....A:33 from the album *Amigo* on Dualtone 01109; "45": Dualtone 1120; B-side: "Missing Her Blues"		V	album cut
				BALL, Kenny, and His Jazzmen BUB/LP **'62** Born on 5/22/30 in Ilford, Essex, England. Trumpet player. His Jazzmen: Diz Disley (banjo), Johnny Bennett (trombone), Dave Jones (clarinet), Colin Bates (piano), Vic Pitts (bass) and Ron Bowden (drums).			
2/3/62	2^1	14		1 **Midnight In Moscow** ....AC^3 *American Patrol* [I] original Russian title: "Padmoskoveeye Vietchera"	$10		Kapp 442
4/14/62	88	1		2 **March Of The Siamese Children** .... *Vilia* [I] from the Rodgers & Hammerstein musical *The King And I* starring Yul Brynner	$10		Kapp 451
6/2/62	87	6		3 **The Green Leaves Of Summer** .... *I Shall Not Be Moved* [I] from the movie *The Alamo* starring John Wayne	$10		Kapp 460
				BALLADS, The **'68** R&B vocal group from Oakland, California: Nathan Robertson, Jon Foster, Rico Thompson and Lesley LaPalma.			
7/20/68	65	7		**God Bless Our Love** .... *My Baby Knows How To Love Her Man* some pressings label group name as: THE BALLARDS ($20)	$15		Venture 615
				BALLARD, Ashley **'01** Born in 1985 in Mission Viejo, California. Female pop singer.			
3/24/01	25^S	17		**Hottie** .... *(3 album snippets)*	$4	★	Atlantic 84941
	★538★			**BALLARD, Hank, And The Midnighters** R&B/BUB **'60** R&B vocal group from Detroit, Michigan. Formed in 1952 as The Royals: Henry Booth, Charles Sutton, Lawson Smith and Sonny Woods. In late 1953, Henry "Hank" Ballard (born John Kendricks on 11/18/27 in Detroit; died of cancer on 3/2/2003, age 75) replaced Smith and became lead singer. Name changed to The Midnighters in 1954. Had the original recording of "The Twist," written by Ballard. After group disbanded in 1965, re-formed with Frank Stadford, Walter Miller and Wesley Hargrove. Worked in the **James Brown** Revue. Ballard inducted into the Rock and Roll Hall of Fame in 1990. *1)Let's Go, Let's Go, Let's Go 2)Finger Poppin' Time 3)The Hoochi Coochi Coo*			
3/9/59	87	3		1 **Teardrops On Your Letter** .... *The Twist*	$30		King 5171
5/4/59	72	7		2 **Kansas City** .... *I'll Keep You Happy*	$25		King 5195
5/16/60	7	26		3 **Finger Poppin' Time** .... *I Love You, I Love You So-o-o*	$25		King 5341
7/18/60	28	16		4 **The Twist** .... *Teardrops On Your Letter* B-side of #1 above; melody is the same as the 1955 R&B hit "WhatCha Gonna Do" by **Clyde McPhatter & The Drifters**	$30		King 5171
9/19/60	6	16		5 **Let's Go, Let's Go, Let's Go** RB^3 *If You'd Forgive Me* also see #13 below	$25		King 5400

DEBUT	PEAK	WKS	Gold	A-side (Chart Hit)...B-side	$	Sym	Label & Number
				BALLARD, Hank, And The Midnighters — Cont'd			
12/5/60+	23	11		6 **The Hoochi Coochi Coo** ... *I'm Thinking Of You*	$20		King 5430
2/20/61	39	6		7 **Let's Go Again (Where We Went Last Night)** ... *Deep Blue Sea*	$20		King 5459
4/3/61	33	8		8 **The Continental Walk** ... *What Is This I See*	$20	■	King 5491
6/26/61	26	7		9 **The Switch-A-Roo /**			
6/19/61	92	1		10 **The Float** ...	$20		King 5510
8/21/61	49	3		11 **Nothing But Good /**			
8/21/61	66	5		12 **Keep On Dancing** ...	$20		King 5535
2/10/62	87	4		13 **Do You Know How To Twist** ... *Broadway*	$20		King 5593
				melody is the same as #5 above; Ballard wrote all of above (except #1, 2 & 8)			
				BALLARD, Russ ROK/BUB/LP **'80**			
				Born on 10/31/45 in Waltham Cross, Hertfordshire, England. Pop-rock singer/songwriter/producer. Guitarist of **Argent**, 1969-74. Wrote "Come And Get Your Love," "Since You've Been Gone" and others.			
6/14/80	58	8		**On The Rebound** ... *Riding With The Angels*	$5		Epic 50883
				BALLIN' JACK LP **'71**			
				Interracial jazz-rock group from San Francisco, California: Jim Walters (vocals, trumpet), Glenn Thomas (guitar), Jim Coile (sax), Tim McFarland (trombone), Luther Rabb (bass) and Ronnie Hammond (drums). Rabb and Hammond joined **War** in 1979.			
2/13/71	93	4		**Super Highway** ... *Only A Tear*	$6		Columbia 45312
				BALLOON FARM, The **'68**			
				Psychedelic-rock group from New Jersey: Mike Appel, Ed Schnug, Don Henny and Jay Saks. Appel went on to manage **Bruce Springsteen**.			
2/24/68	37	8		**A Question Of Temperature** ... *Hurtin' For Your Love*	$12		Laurie 3405
				first pressings show last word in title as "Tempature"			
				BALTIMORA LP **'86**			
				Born Jimmy McShane on 5/23/57 in Londonderry, Northern Ireland. Died of AIDS on 3/28/95 (age 37). Pop singer.			
10/19/85+	13	26		1 **Tarzan Boy** ... S:11 / A:17 *(dub version)*	$3	■	Manhattan 50018
				same version re-charted at #3 below			
4/12/86	87	4		2 **Living In The Background** ... *Chinese Restaurant*	$3		Manhattan 50029
3/27/93	51	12		3 **Tarzan Boy** ... S:40 / A:51 *(1993 remix)* [R]	$3	▮V	SBK 50424
				featured in the movie *Teenage Mutant Ninja Turtles III* starring Elias Koteas; tune also featured in a Listerine TV commercial; "45": SBK 17320 (green vinyl); B-side: "Rockin' Over The Beat" by **Technotronic** (#95/'90)			
				BALTIMORE, Charli R&B **'99**			
				Born Tiffany Lane on 10/11/73 in Philadelphia, Pennsylvania. Female rapper.			
4/25/98	70[A]	1		1 **Money** ... *(3 versions)*	$6	T	Untertainment 78937
				samples "For The Love Of Money" by **The O'Jays**; from the movie *Woo* starring Jada Pinkett Smith			
3/13/99	54[S]	9		2 **Stand Up** ... *(2 versions) / Pimp Da One U Love*	$4	★	Untertainment 79094
				CHARLI BALTIMORE Featuring Ghostface Killah			
				samples "We Want To Party, Party, Party" and "Me And My Baby Got Our Own Thing Going" both by **Lyn Collins**			
4/13/02	21	19		3 **Down A** Chick** ... A:20 / S:63 *Smokin And Ridin* (w/Jodi Mack & 0-1)	$4	★	Def Jam 063946
				JA RULE feat. Charli "Chuck" Baltimore			
6/22/02	6	20		4 **Down 4 U** ... A:6			album cut
				IRV GOTTI PRESENTS THE INC. Featuring Ja Rule, Ashanti, Charli Baltimore & Vita			
				from the album *Irv Gotti Presents The Inc.* on Murder Inc. 062033			
				BALTIMORE AND OHIO MARCHING BAND, The LP **'67**			
				Studio group assembled by producers Joey Day and Alan Dischel.			
10/28/67	94	3		**Lapland** ... *Condition Red* [I]	$7		Jubilee 5592
				Lapland: region of extreme Northern Europe			
				BAMA **'79**			
				Session group from Muscle Shoals, Alabama. Headed by songwriters Terry Skinner and J.L. Wallace.			
10/6/79	86	5		**Touch Me When We're Dancing** ... *Turning The Tables*	$5		Free Flight 11629
				BAMBAATAA, Afrika R&B **'82**			
				Born Kevin Donovan on 4/10/60 in South Bronx, New York. Pioneering funk DJ/rapper. Also known as Khayan Aasim. The Soul Sonic Force is rappers M.C. G.L.O.B.E. (John B. Miller), Mr. Biggs (Ellis Williams) and Pow Wow (Robert Allen) with D.J. Jazzy Jay.			
7/17/82	48	11		**Planet Rock** ... *(instrumental)*	$7		Tommy Boy 823
				Afrika Bambaataa & the SOUL SONIC FORCE			
				includes riffs from "Trans-Europe Express" by **Kraftwerk**			
				BANANARAMA BUB/ROK/LP **'86**			
				Pop-rock "girl group" from London, England: Sarah Dallin, Keren Woodward and Siobhan Fahey. Group name is a combination of the children's TV show **The Banana Splits** and the **Roxy Music** song "Pyjamarama." Fahey married **Dave Stewart** (**Eurythmics**) on 8/1/87; left group in early 1988, replaced by Jacqui O'Sullivan (who left in mid-1991). Fahey later formed duo **Shakespear's Sister**.			
				1)Venus 2)I Heard A Rumour 3)Cruel Summer			
7/2/83	83	4		1 **Shy Boy (Don't It Make You Feel Good)** ... *Give Us Back Our Cheap Fares*	$5	■	London 810112
5/19/84	95	2		2 **Robert DeNiro's Waiting** ... *Push!*	$5	■	London 820033
7/21/84	9	18		3 **Cruel Summer** ... S:17 *Cruel dub*	$4		London 810127
11/10/84	70	8		4 **The Wild Life** ... *State I'm In*	$4	■	London 882019
				title song from the movie starring Christopher Penn			
6/28/86	❶[1]	19		5 **Venus** ... S:❶[2] / A:3 *White Train*	$3	■	London 886056
10/18/86	73	5		6 **More Than Physical** ... *Scarlett*	$3	■	London 886080
12/27/86+	76	7		7 **A Trick Of The Night** ... *Cut Above The Rest*	$3	■	London 886119
				included in the 1986 movie *Jumpin' Jack Flash* starring Whoopi Goldberg			
7/18/87	4	19		8 **I Heard A Rumour** ... S:3 / A:5 *Clean Cut Boy*	$3	■	London 886165
				from the movie *Disorderlies* starring the **Fat Boys** and Ralph Bellamy			
11/21/87+	47	13		9 **I Can't Help It** ... *Mr. Sleaze*	$3	■	London 886212
3/19/88	48	10		10 **Love In The First Degree** ... S:40 *Ecstasy*	$3	■	London 886255
11/26/88	89	3		11 **Love, Truth & Honesty** ... *Strike It Rich*	$3	■	London 886362

DEBUT	PEAK	WKS	Gold	A-side (Chart Hit)...B-side	$	Sym	Label & Number

BANANA SPLITS, The — '69

Saturday morning TV series featuring four live-action animals: Fleegle (dog), Drooper (lion), Bingo (gorilla) and Snorky (elephant). Actual vocals on the records were performed by songwriters Ritchie Adams and Mark Barkan.

DEBUT	PEAK	WKS	Gold	A-side (Chart Hit)...B-side	$	Sym	Label & Number
2/8/69	96	1		**The Tra La La Song (One Banana, Two Banana)**...*Toy Piano Melody*	$10	■	Decca 32429

BAND, The — BUB/LP '70

Rock group formed in Woodstock, New York: Robbie Robertson (vocals, guitar), Levon Helm (vocals, drums), Rick Danko (bass), Richard Manuel and Garth Hudson (keyboards). All from Canada (except Helm from Arkansas) and all were with **Ronnie Hawkins**' Hawks. Group's "farewell concert" on Thanksgiving Day in 1976 was documented in the Martin Scorcese movie *The Last Waltz*. Manuel committed suicide on 3/4/86 (age 42). Helm, Danko and Hudson reunited in 1993 with Jim Weider (guitar), Richard Bell (piano) and Randy Ciarlante (drums). Worked on albums and tours as **Bob Dylan**'s backup band. Inducted into the Rock and Roll Hall of Fame in 1994. Danko died on 12/10/99 (age 56).

DEBUT	PEAK	WKS	Gold	A-side (Chart Hit)...B-side	$	Sym	Label & Number
8/31/68	63	7		1 **The Weight**...*I Shall Be Released* **JAIME ROBBIE ROBERTSON, RICK DANKO, RICHARD MANUEL, GARTH HUDSON, LEVON HELM**	$10		Capitol 2269
11/1/69+	25	14		2 **Up On Cripple Creek** *The Night They Drove Old Dixie Down*	$8		Capitol 2635
2/14/70	57	8		3 **Rag Mama Rag**...*The Unfaithful Servant*	$8	■	Capitol 2705
10/10/70	77	4		4 **Time To Kill**...*The Shape I'm In* (#121)	$8		Capitol 2870
10/16/71	72	6		5 **Life Is A Carnival**...*The Moon Struck One*	$8		Capitol 3199
9/16/72	34	11		6 **Don't Do It**...*Rag Mama Rag (live)* [L] #27 hit in 1964 for **Marvin Gaye** as "Baby Don't You Do It"	$8		Capitol 3433
11/24/73	73	7		7 **Ain't Got No Home**...*Get Up Jake*	$6		Capitol 3758
8/10/74	66	5		8 **Most Likely You Go Your Way (And I'll Go Mine)**...*Stage Fright* (The Band) [L] **BOB DYLAN/THE BAND**	$8		Asylum 11043
3/20/76	62	4		9 **Ophelia**...*Hobo Jungle*	$5		Capitol 4230

BAND AID — '84

A benefit recording to assist famine relief in Ethiopia. Organized by **Bob Geldof** of **The Boomtown Rats**, all-star group also included **Bananarama**, **Phil Collins**, **Culture Club**, **Duran Duran**, **Frankie Goes To Hollywood**, **Heaven 17**, **Kool & The Gang**, **Paul McCartney**, **Spandau Ballet**, **Status Quo**, **Sting**, **The Style Council**, **Ultravox**, **U2**, **Wham!** and **Paul Young**.

DEBUT	PEAK	WKS	Gold	A-side (Chart Hit)...B-side	$	Sym	Label & Number
12/22/84	13	9	●	1 **Do They Know It's Christmas?**...S:6 *Feed The World* [X]	$5	■	Columbia 04749
1/3/98-	49^A	2		2 **Do They Know It's Christmas**...[X-R] from the Australian import album *Christmas Wishes* on Dino 147 (also see "Last Christmas" by **George Michael & Wham!**); above 2 are the same version			album cut

BANDIT — '79

Rock group from England: Gerry Trew (vocals), Danny McIntosh (guitar), Tony Lester (bass) and Theodore Thunder (drums).

DEBUT	PEAK	WKS	Gold	A-side (Chart Hit)...B-side	$	Sym	Label & Number
3/10/79	77	4		**One Way Love**...*I'm A Rocker*	$5		Ariola America 7731

BAND OF GOLD — '84

Dutch session vocalists and musicians assembled by producers **Pete Wingfield** and Paco Saval.

DEBUT	PEAK	WKS	Gold	A-side (Chart Hit)...B-side	$	Sym	Label & Number
10/13/84	64	7		**Medley: Love Songs Are Back Again**...*Love Songs Are Back Again (vocal theme)* Let's Put It All Together/Betcha By Golly Wow/Side Show/ Have You Seen Her/Reunited/You Make Me Feel Brand New/ Kiss And Say Goodbye/Love Songs Are Back Again	$4		RCA 13866

BAND OF THE BLACK WATCH, The — LP '76

Military unit from Canada. Led by pipe major Bruce Bolton.

DEBUT	PEAK	WKS	Gold	A-side (Chart Hit)...B-side	$	Sym	Label & Number
1/31/76	75	9		**Scotch On The Rocks**...*Let's Go To Jersey* [I]	$5		Private Stock 45,055

BANG — LP '72

Rock trio from Florida: Frank Ferrara (vocals, bass), Frank Gilcken (guitar) and Tony D'Lorio (drums).

DEBUT	PEAK	WKS	Gold	A-side (Chart Hit)...B-side	$	Sym	Label & Number
4/22/72	90	6		**Questions**...*Future Shock*	$6		Capitol 3304

BANG — '90

Pop duo formed in London, England. Paul Calliris (vocals) and Billy Adams (keyboards) were born in Athens, Greece.

DEBUT	PEAK	WKS	Gold	A-side (Chart Hit)...B-side	$	Sym	Label & Number
8/11/90	93	2		**Holding My Heart**...*(remix)*	$4	▮	Vendetta 1504

B ANGIE B — R&B/LP '91

Born Angela Boyd in Morton, Mississippi. Black singer/dancer/songwriter with **M.C. Hammer**'s posse.

DEBUT	PEAK	WKS	Gold	A-side (Chart Hit)...B-side	$	Sym	Label & Number
4/27/91	54	8		**I Don't Want To Lose Your Love**...S:33 *(2 remixes)* #51 hit in 1976 for **The Emotions** as "I Don't Wanna Lose Your Love"	$4	▮	Bust It/Capitol 44658

★314★ BANGLES — ROK/LP '86

Female pop-rock group from Los Angeles, California: sisters Vicki (lead guitar; born on 1/11/58) and Debbi (drums; born on 8/22/61) Peterson, Michael Steele (bass; born on 6/2/55) and **Susanna Hoffs** (see #9 & 10 below) (guitar; born on 1/17/59). Originally named The Bangs. Steele was previously in The Runaways. Hoffs starred in the 1987 movie *The Allnighter*. Disbanded in October 1989. Also see **Cyndi Lauper**'s "Change Of Heart."

1)Walk Like An Egyptian 2)Eternal Flame 3)Hazy Shade Of Winter

DEBUT	PEAK	WKS	Gold	A-side (Chart Hit)...B-side	$	Sym	Label & Number
1/25/86	2^1	20		1 **Manic Monday**...S:3 / A:4 *In A Different Light* written by **Prince** under the pseudonym "Christopher"	$4	■	Columbia 05757
5/10/86	29	14		2 **If She Knew What She Wants**...A:27 / S:29 *Not Like You*	$4	■	Columbia 05886
9/27/86	❶^4	23	●	3 **Walk Like An Egyptian** S:❶^4 / A:❶^4 *Angels Don't Fall In Love*	$4		Columbia 06257
2/14/87	11	16		4 **Walking Down Your Street**...S:9 / A:10 *Let It Go* all of above from the album *Different Light*	$4	■	Columbia 06674
11/14/87+	2^1	21		5 **Hazy Shade Of Winter**...S:2 / A:3 *She Lost You* (**Joan Jett & The Blackhearts**) written by **Paul Simon**; from the movie *Less Than Zero* starring Andrew McCarthy	$4	■	Def Jam 07630
10/15/88+	5	20		6 **In Your Room**...S:4 / A:9 *Bell Jar*	$3	■	Columbia 08090
2/4/89	❶^1	19	●	7 **Eternal Flame**...AC^2 A:❶^1 / S:2 *What I Meant To Say*	$3		Columbia 68533
5/6/89	30	12		8 **Be With You**...S:29 / A:29 *Let It Go*	$3		Columbia 68744
2/2/91	30	11		9 **My Side Of The Bed**...A:28 / S:32 *Made Of Stone*	$3	▮	Columbia 73529
11/30/96+	77	12		10 **All I Want**...*Those Days Are Over* **SUSANNA HOFFS** (above 2)	$3	▮	London 850686

DEBUT	PEAK	WKS	Gold	A-side (Chart Hit)........................B-side	$	Sym	Label & Number
				BANKS, Darrell BUB **'66**			
				Born Darrell Eubanks in 1938 in Mansfield, Ohio; raised in Buffalo, New York. Shot to death in March 1970 in Detroit, Michigan (age 31). R&B singer/songwriter.			
7/23/66	27	12		1 **Open The Door To Your Heart** .... *Our Love (Is In The Pocket)*	$20		Revilot 201
10/15/66	55	8		2 **Somebody (Somewhere) Needs You** .... *Baby What'cha You Got (For Me)*	$20		Revilot 203
				BANKS, Phatty — see MIDWEST MAFIA			
				BANZAII **'75**			
				Disco studio group from France.			
10/11/75	98	1		**Chinese Kung Fu** .... *(disco version)* [I]	$5		Scepter 12407
				BARBARA AND THE BROWNS **'64**			
				R&B family group: sisters Barbara (lead vocals), Roberta, Betty and Maurice Brown.			
5/2/64	97	2		**Big Party** .... *You Belong To Her*	$20		Stax 150
				BARBARA And THE UNIQUES **'71**			
				R&B vocal trio from Chicago, Illinois: sisters Barbara and Gwen Livsey with Doris Lindsey.			
1/2/71	91	3		**There It Goes Again** .... *What's The Use*	$15		Arden 3001
				BARBARIANS, The BUB **'65**			
				Garage-rock band from Provincetown, Massachusetts: Victor "Moulty" Moulton (vocals, drums), Jeff Morris and Bruce Benson (guitars), and Jerry Causi (bass). Regulars on TV's *Shindig* and *The T.A.M.I. Show.* Moulton had a hook in place of his left hand which he lost in an explosion from a homemade lead-pipe-and-gasoline bomb.			
9/25/65	55	6		1 **Are You A Boy Or Are You A Girl** .... *Take It Or Leave It*	$20		Laurie 3308
2/26/66	90	4		2 **Moulty** .... *I'll Keep On Seeing You*	$25		Laurie 3326
				The Elegants (backing vocals); autobiographical tune by the band's drummer, Victor "Moulty" Moulton			
				BARBER('S), Chris, Jazz Band **'59**			
				Born on 4/17/30 in Welwyn Garden City, Hertfordshire, England. Trombone player. His band featured Monty Sunshine on clarinet.			
1/12/59	5	15	●	**Petite Fleur (Little Flower)** .... *Wild Cat Blues* [I]	$15	■	Laurie 3022
				written in 1952 by jazz great Sidney Bechet			
				BARBER, Frank, Orch. LP **'82**			
				Big band led by British arranger/conductor Frank Barber.			
5/8/82	61	12		**Hooked On Big Bands** .... *Hooked On Big Bands (Duke Ellington Medley)* [I]	$5		Victory 1001
				Glenn Miller medley: In The Mood/Pennsylvania 6-5000/ I've Got A Gal In Kalamazoo/Moonlight Serenade/ Little Brown Jug/Chattanooga Choo Choo/At Last/American Patrol/ In The Mood			
				BARBOUR, Keith LP **'69**			
				Born on 1/21/41 in New York. Pop singer/songwriter. Formerly with **The New Christy Minstrels**. Married to TV actress Deidre Hall (*Our House* and *Days of Our Lives*) from 1972-77.			
9/27/69	40	9		**Echo Park** .... *Here I Am Losing You*	$7		Epic 10486
				written by **Buzz Clifford**			
				BARBUSTERS, The — see JETT, Joan			
				BARCLAY, Eddie, and His Orch. **'55**			
				Born on 1/26/21 in Paris, France. Head of the French recording company Compagnie Phonographique Francaise and own Barclay label.			
7/16/55	18	1		**The Bandit (O'Cangaceiro)** .... J:18 *Neu Piao* [I]	$25		Tico 45-249
				theme from the Brazilian movie *O'Cangaceiro*			
				BARDEUX R&B/LP **'88**			
				Female dance duo from Los Angeles, California: Stacy "Acacia" Smith and Jaz. Melanie Taylor replaced Jaz in 1989. Bardeux (pronounced: bar-DO) is plural for Bardot (as in actress Brigitte Bardot).			
2/27/88	81	7		1 **Magic Carpet Ride** .... *When We Kiss*	$4	■	Enigma 75016
4/16/88	36	13		2 **When We Kiss** .... A:32 / S:40 *Magic Carpet Ride*	$4	■	Enigma 75018
9/16/89	68	10		3 **I Love To Bass** .... *(dance mix)*	$4		Enigma 75047
				12" pressings show title as "I Love The Bass"			
				BARE, Bobby C&W/BUB/LP **'63**			
				Born on 4/7/35 in Ironton, Ohio. Country singer/songwriter/guitarist. Drafted by the Army in 1958; left a demo tape of "The All American Boy" with Fraternity Records. The song was released erroneously as by Bill Parsons. Wrote songs for the movie *Teenage Millionaire* (1961). Acted in the movie *A Distant Trumpet* in 1964. Own TV series in the mid-1980s. Charted 70 Country hits, 1962-86.			
12/22/58+	2[1]	16		1 **The All American Boy** .... *Rubber Dolly* [N]	$40		Fraternity 835
				BILL PARSONS			
7/21/62	23	12		2 **Shame On Me** .... *Above And Beyond*	$12		RCA Victor 8032
6/15/63	16	12		3 **Detroit City** .... *Heart Of Ice*	$12	■	RCA Victor 8183
				written by Mel Tillis			
10/5/63	10	11		4 **500 Miles Away From Home** .... *It All Depends On Linda*	$12		RCA Victor 8238
2/8/64	33	7		5 **Miller's Cave** .... *Jeannie's Last Kiss*	$12		RCA Victor 8294
				#9 Country hit for **Hank Snow** in 1960			
5/16/64	94	1		6 **Have I Stayed Away Too Long** .... *More Than A Poor Boy Can Give*	$12		RCA Victor 8358
				#14 hit for **Perry Como** in 1944			
10/31/64	60	7		7 **Four Strong Winds** .... *Take Me Home*	$12		RCA Victor 8443
				written by Ian Tyson of the Canadian folk duo Ian & Sylvia			
1/5/74	41	8		8 **Daddy What If** .... *A Restless Wind* [N]	$6		RCA Victor 0197
				with 5-year-old son, Bobby, Jr.; written by Shel Silverstein			
				BARENAKED LADIES ROK/LP **'98**			
				Alternative-rock group from Toronto, Ontario, Canada: Steven Page (vocals), Ed Robertson (guitar), Kevin Hearn (keyboards), Jim Creeggan (bass) and Tyler Stewart (drums).			
5/10/97	88	6		1 **The Old Apartment** .... *Lovers In A Dangerous Time*	$4	▮V	Reprise 17499
11/22/97+	68	20		2 **Brian Wilson** .... *Back / Break Your Heart*	$4	▮V	Reprise 17290
				first released on their 1992 album *Gordon*; **Brian Wilson** is the leader of **The Beach Boys**			
10/3/98	❶[1]	20		3 **One Week** MR[5] A:2 / S:3 *Shoe Box (live) / When You Dream (home demo)*	$4	★V	Reprise 17174

DEBUT	PEAK	WKS	Gold	A-side (Chart Hit)...B-side	$	Sym	Label & Number
				BARENAKED LADIES — Cont'd			
12/26/98+	**44**	12		4 **It's All Been Done**...A:39 "45": Reprise 16936 (B-side of "Call And Answer"); above 2 from the album *Stunt* on Reprise 46963		V	album cut
9/9/00	**15**	21		5 **Pinch Me**...S:14 / A:17 *Powder Blue* "45" B-side: "Falling For The First Time"	$4	★V	Reprise 16827
4/7/01	**86**	4		6 **Too Little Too Late**...S:50 *Pinch Me (Injeti Remix)*	$5	★+V	Reprise 16774
				BAR-KAYS R&B/BUB/LP **'67** Funk group from Memphis, Tennessee: Jimmy King (guitar), Ronnie Caldwell (organ), Phalon Jones (sax), Ben Cauley (trumpet), James Alexander (bass) and Carl Cunningham (drums). The plane crash that killed **Otis Redding** (on 12/10/67 in Madison, Wisconsin) also claimed the lives of all the Bar-Kays except Alexander (not on the plane) and Cauley (survived the crash). Alexander re-formed the group with Larry Dodson (vocals), Barry Wilkins (guitar), Harvey Henderson (sax), Winston Stewart (organ) and Willie Hall (drums). Charted 32 R&B hits, 1967-95. Also see the **Mar-Keys** and **The Parkays**.			
5/20/67	**17**	15	●	1 **Soul Finger /** [I]			
9/2/67	**76**	4		2 **Knucklehead**... [I] co-written by Booker T. Jones of **Booker T. & The MG's**	$10		Volt 148
10/14/67	**91**	4		3 **Give Everybody Some**...*Don't Do That* [I]	$10		Volt 154
12/25/71+	**53**	10		4 **Son Of Shaft**...*Sang And Dance*	$8		Volt 4073
10/16/76+	**23**	16		5 **Shake Your Rump To The Funk**...*Summer Of Our Love*	$5		Mercury 73833
2/12/77	**74**	4		6 **Too Hot To Stop (Pt. 1)**...*Bang, Bang (Stick'em Up)*	$5		Mercury 73888
12/8/79+	**57**	7		7 **Move Your Boogie Body**...*Love's What It's All About*	$5		Mercury 76015
3/22/80	**60**	5		8 **Today Is The Day**...*Loving You Is My Occupation*	$5		Mercury 76036
5/26/84	**73**	8		9 **Freakshow On The Dance Floor**...*Lovers Should Never Fall In Love* from the movie *Breakin'* starring Lucinda Dickey and break-dancer Adolfo Quinones	$4		Mercury 818631
				BARLOW, Gary — see TAKE THAT			
				BARNES, Cheryl **'79** Singer/actress. Co-starred in the movie *Hair*.			
4/28/79	**64**	7		**Easy To Be Hard**...*Good Morning Starshine* **HAIR (Original Soundtrack Recording)**	$5		RCA 11548
				BARNES, J.J. R&B **'67** Born James Jay Barnes on 11/30/43 in Detroit, Michigan. First recorded for Kable in 1960. Member of **The Holidays**, 1966.			
4/9/66	**80**	5		1 **Real Humdinger**...*I Ain't Gonna Do It*	$20		Ric-Tic 110
5/20/67	**61**	10		2 **Baby Please Come Back Home**...*Chains Of Love*	$20		Groovesville 1006
				BARNES, Jimmy **'59** Born in Newark, New Jersey. R&B singer.			
3/9/59	**90**	2		**No Regrets**...*Keep Your Love Handy*	$30		Gibraltar 101
				BARNES, Jimmy ROK/LP **'87** Born on 4/28/56 in Glasgow, Scotland; raised in Australia. Lead singer of Cold Chisel.			
3/22/86	**74**	8		1 **Working Class Man**...*Boys Cry Out For War* from the movie *Gung Ho* starring Michael Keaton	$3		Geffen 28749
6/20/87	**47**	13		2 **Good Times**...*Laying Down The Law* **INXS AND JIMMY BARNES** from the movie *The Lost Boys* starring Kiefer Sutherland	$3	■	Atlantic 89237
7/9/88	**91**	2		3 **Too Much Ain't Enough Love**...*Do Or Die*	$3	■	Geffen 27920
				BARNUM, H.B. **'61** Born on 7/15/36 in Houston, Texas; raised in Los Angeles, California. Songwriter/producer/arranger. Member of **The Dyna-Sores**.			
1/9/61	**35**	7		**Lost Love**...*Hallelujah* [I]	$20		Eldo 111
				BARRETT, Richard **'59** Born in Philadelphia, Pennsylvania. Black singer/songwriter/pianist/producer. Key figure in the Philly soul sound. Discovered **Frankie Lymon & The Teenagers**, **The Chantels**, **Little Anthony & The Imperials**, and **The Isley Brothers**. Lead singer with the Valentines which included **Dave "Baby" Cortez** and Ronnie Bright (of "Mr. Bass Man" fame). Managed **The Three Degrees**.			
4/28/58	**94**	1		1 **(When Your Heart's On Fire) Smoke Gets In Your Eyes**...T:94 *Remember Me* Morty Craft (orch.); #1 hit for Paul Whiteman's Orchestra in 1934	$40		MGM 12616
7/20/59	**93**	2		2 **Summer's Love**...*All Is Forgiven* **RICHARD BARRETT With The Chantels**	$75		Gone 5060
				BARRETTO, Ray **'63** Born on 4/29/29 in Brooklyn, New York. Latin percussionist. Member of **The Blackout Allstars**.			
4/27/63	**17**	9		**El Watusi**...*Ritmo Sabroso* [F-N]	$15		Tico 419
				BARRON KNIGHTS, The **'79** Novelty group from England: Anthony Osmond and Richard Palmer (vocals), Peter Langford (guitar), Butch Baker (bass) and Dave Ballinger (drums).			
8/25/79	**70**	3		**The Topical Song**...*The Big V-Asectomy* [N] parody of **Supertramp**'s "The Logical Song"	$6		Epic 50755
				BARRY, Claudja R&B/LP **'79** Born in Jamaica; raised in Toronto, Ontario, Canada. Black dance singer/actress. Appeared in the musicals *Hair* and *Catch My Soul*.			
2/25/78	**72**	9		1 **Dancin' Fever**...*Long Lost Friend*	$6		Salsoul 2058
4/14/79	**56**	12		2 **Boogie Woogie Dancin' Shoes**...*Love Of The Hurtin' Kind*	$6		Chrysalis 2313
				BARRY, Joe **'61** Born Joe Barrios on 7/13/39 in Cut Off, Louisiana. Singer/guitarist.			
4/24/61	**24**	12		1 **I'm A Fool To Care**...*I Got A Feeling* first released on JIN 144 in 1961 ($15); #6 hit for **Les Paul & Mary Ford** in 1954	$12		Smash 1702
7/31/61	**63**	5		2 **Teardrops In My Heart**...*For You, Sunshine* #4 Country hit for Sons Of The Pioneers in 1947	$12	■	Smash 1710

DEBUT	PEAK	WKS	Gold	A-side (Chart Hit)	B-side	$	Sym	Label & Number
				BARRY, John, and His Orchestra BUB **'65**				
				Born on 11/3/33 in York, England. Prolific movie soundtrack composer/conductor. Married to **Jane Birken** from 1965-68.				
3/13/65	72	3		**Goldfinger**	*Troubadour* [I]	$8		United Artists 791
				title song from the James Bond movie starring Sean Connery; Barry also conducted **Shirley Bassey**'s vocal version				
				BARRY, Len BUB/LP **'65**				
				Born Leonard Borisoff on 6/12/42 in Philadelphia, Pennsylvania. Lead singer of **The Dovells** from 1957-63.				
5/29/65	84	4		1 **Lip Sync (To The Tongue Twisters)**	*At The Hop "65"*	$12		Decca 31788
9/25/65	2[1]	15		2 **1-2-3**	*Bullseye*	$12		Decca 31827
1/1/66	27	9		3 **Like A Baby**	*Happiness (Is A Girl Like You)*	$10		Decca 31889
3/19/66	26	8		4 **Somewhere**	*It's A Cryin' Shame*	$10		Decca 31923
				from the musical *West Side Story*				
6/18/66	91	3		5 **It's That Time Of The Year**	*Happily Ever After*	$10		Decca 31969
9/17/66	98	2		6 **I Struck It Rich**	*Love Is*	$10		Decca 32011
				BARRY And The TAMERLANES BUB **'63**				
				Pop vocal trio from Los Angeles, California: songwriters **Barry DeVorzon**, Terry Smith and Bodie Chandler. Arranged by **Perry Botkin, Jr.** DeVorzon founded the Valiant label and began his ongoing prolific songwriting career in the mid-1950s.				
10/19/63	21	10		**I Wonder What She's Doing Tonight**	*Don't Go*	$15		Valiant 6034
				BARTLEY, Chris BUB **'67**				
				Born on 4/17/49 in Harlem, New York. Male R&B singer.				
7/22/67	32	7		**The Sweetest Thing This Side Of Heaven**	*Love Me Baby*	$15		Vando 101
				written and produced by **Van McCoy**				
				BASE, Rob — see ROB				
				BASEMENT JAXX LP **'02**				
				Electro-dance/rock production duo from England: Simon Ratcliffe and Felix Buxton.				
1/19/02	43[S]	10		1 **Where's Your Head At**	*(4 versions) / Just 1 Kiss / Twilite / Romeo*	$8	★**	XL/Astralwerks 38803
				samples "This Wreckage" and "M.E.", both by **Gary Numan**				
7/27/02	56[S]	4		2 **Get Me Off**	*(3 versions) / Do Your Thing / Broken Dreams*	$8	★*	XL/Astralwerks 38836
				BASIA AC/LP **'88**				
				Born Basia Trzetrzelewska on 9/30/59 in Jaworzno, Poland. Female pop singer.				
7/23/88	26	20		1 **Time And Tide**	S:21 / A:28 *Run For Cover*	$3		Epic 07730
12/10/88+	53	11		2 **New Day For You**	*Freeze Thaw*	$3		Epic 08112
4/7/90	29	12		3 **Cruising For Bruising**	A:27 / S:34 *Come To Heaven*	$3	▮	Epic 73239
				BASIE, Count MEM/POP/R&B/AC/LP **'47**				
				Born William Basie on 8/21/04 in Red Bank, New Jersey. Died of cancer on 4/26/84 (age 79). Legendary jazz, big band leader/pianist/organist. Appeared in many movies. Won Grammy's Lifetime Achievement Award in 2002. Hit #1 on the pop charts in 1947 with "Open The Door, Richard!"				
1/14/56	28	13		1 **April In Paris**	T:28 *Roll 'Em Pete* [I]	$20		Clef 89162
				written in 1932; Grammy Hall of Fame Award winner in 1985				
8/18/58	100	1		2 **Going To Chicago Blues**	H:100 *Swingin' The Blues*	$15		Roulette 4088
				Joe Williams, Jon Hendrix, Dave Lambert and Annie Ross (vocals)				
1/13/62	94	2		3 **The Basie Twist**	*The Trot* [I]	$15		Roulette 4403
6/1/63	77	9		4 **I Can't Stop Loving You**	*Nice 'N' Easy* [I]	$12		Reprise 20170
2/17/68	49	7		5 **For Your Precious Love**	*Uptight (Everything's Alright)*	$10		Brunswick 55365
4/27/68	84	5		6 **Chain Gang**	*Funky Broadway*	$10		Brunswick 55373
				JACKIE WILSON And COUNT BASIE (above 2)				
				BASIL, Toni LP **'82**				
				Born Antonia Basilotta on 9/22/43 in Philadelphia, Pennsylvania. Choreographer/actress/video director. Worked on the TV shows *Shindig* and *Hullabaloo*. Choreographed the movie *American Grafitti*. Appeared in the movie *Easy Rider*.				
9/4/82	❶[1]	27	▲	1 **Mickey**	*Thief On The Loose*	$4	■	Chrysalis 2638
				cheering provided by the 1981 Dorsey High School (Los Angeles) cheerleaders				
2/26/83	77	4		2 **Shoppin' From A To Z**	*Time After Time*	$4	■	Chrysalis 03537
1/21/84	81	6		3 **Over My Head**	*Best Performance*	$4	■	Chrysalis 42753
				BASKERVILLE HOUNDS, The **'69**				
				Rock group from Cleveland, Ohio: Dante Rossi (vocals), Larry Meese (guitar), Jack Topper (organ), Bill Emery (bass) and Michael Macron (drums). Named after the famous Sherlock Holmes work by Sir Arthur Conan Doyle.				
10/11/69	88	2		**Hold Me**	*Here I Come Miami* [L]	$10		Avco Embassy 4504
				originally released on Tema 135 in 1967 ($15)				
				BASS, Fontella R&B/LP **'65**				
				Born on 7/3/40 in St. Louis, Missouri. R&B vocalist/pianist/organist. Mother was a member of the Clara Ward Gospel Troupe. Sang in church choirs; with Oliver Sain's band, St. Louis; with **Little Milton**'s blues show to 1964. Married to trumpet player Lester Bowie.				
2/6/65	33	11		1 **Don't Mess Up A Good Thing**	*Jerk Loose* (Oliver Sain)	$12		Checker 1097
5/29/65	91	2		2 **You'll Miss Me (When I'm Gone)**	*Don't Jump*	$12		Checker 1111
				FONTELLA BASS & BOBBY McCLURE (above 2)				
10/2/65	4	13		3 **Rescue Me**	RB[4] *Soul Of The Man*	$15		Checker 1120
12/25/65+	37	8		4 **Recovery**	*Leave It In The Hands Of Love*	$10		Checker 1131
3/26/66	78	6		5 **I Surrender**	*I Can't Rest* (R&B #31)	$10		Checker 1137
8/27/66	100	1		6 **Safe And Sound**	*You'll Never Ever Know* (R&B #34)	$10		Checker 1147
				BASSEY, Shirley AC/BUB/LP **'65**				
				Born on 1/8/37 in Cardiff, Wales. R&B singer. Began professional career at age 16 as a member of the touring show *Memories Of Al Jolson*. Became a popular club attraction in America in 1961.				
1/30/65	8	13		1 **Goldfinger**	*Strange How Love Can Be*	$8		United Artists 790
				John Barry (orch.); also see Barry's instrumental version				
9/19/70	55	9		2 **Something**	*What Are You Doing The Rest Of Your Life?*	$5		United Artists 50698

DEBUT	PEAK	WKS	Gold	A-side (Chart Hit)..........B-side	$	Sym	Label & Number
				BASSEY, Shirley — Cont'd			
1/29/72	57	9		3 **Diamonds Are Forever** .... *For The Love Of Him* #1 & 3: title songs from James Bond movies starring Sean Connery	$5		United Artists 50845
6/2/73	48	11		4 **Never, Never, Never (Grande, Grande, Grande)** .... *Day By Day*	$5	□	United Artists 211
				BATDORF & RODNEY LP **'75** Pop duo: John Batdorf and Mark Rodney. Batdorf formed the group **Silver** in 1976.			
8/9/75	87	7		1 **You Are A Song** .... *Another Part Of Me* originally written and recorded by **Jim Weatherly**	$5		Arista 0132
12/13/75	69	3		2 **Somewhere In The Night** .... *Ain't It Like Home*	$5		Arista 0159
				BATEY, Nikie **'02** Female R&B singer.			
11/2/02	32^{S}	13		**It Just Happened** .... *(street version)* song ends with a gunshot	$6	★	AVS 670842
				BAXTER, Duke **'69** Born in Australia. White pop singer/songwriter.			
7/26/69	52	6		**Everybody Knows Matilda** .... *I Ain't No School Boy*	$15		VMC 740
				BAXTER, Les, his Chorus and Orchestra MEM/POP/LP **'56** Born on 3/14/22 in Mexia, Texas. Died of a heart attack on 1/15/96 (age 73). Orchestra leader/arranger. Began as a conductor on radio shows in the 1930s. Member of **Mel Torme**'s vocal group, the Mel-Tones. Musical arranger for Capitol Records (**Nat King Cole**, **Margaret Whiting** and others) in the 1950s. Composed over 250 scores for radio, television and movies. Hit #2 on the pop charts in 1953 with "April In Portugal."			
4/9/55	❶^{2}	21		1 **Unchained Melody** / A:❶^{2} / S:2 / J:3 from the movie *Unchained* starring football star Elroy "Crazylegs" Hirsch			
4/30/55		1		2 **Medic** .... S:flip [I] theme from the TV series *Medic* starring Richard Boone; song also known as "Blue Star"	$15		Capitol 3055
8/13/55	5	12		3 **Wake The Town And Tell The People** ....A:5 / J:8 / S:10 / T:24 *I'll Never Stop Loving You* The Notables (vocals)	$15		Capitol 3120
2/11/56	❶^{6}	24	●	4 **The Poor People Of Paris** T:❶^{6} / A:❶^{6} / S:❶^{4} / J:❶^{3} *Theme From "Helen Of Troy"* [I] French song written in 1954 as "Le Goualante De Pauvre Jean" ("Jean's Song")	$15		Capitol 3336
2/11/56	80	3		5 **The Trouble With Harry** .... T:80 *Havana* inspired by the Alfred Hitchcock movie starring John Forsythe and Shirley MacLaine	$15		Capitol 3291
5/19/56	44	9		6 **Tango Of The Drums** / T:44 [I]			
6/30/56	82	1		7 **Sinner Man** .... T:82 Will Holt (vocal)	$12		Capitol 3404
10/20/56	63	5		8 **Giant** .... T:63 *There's Never Been Anyone Else But You* title song from the movie starring Elizabeth Taylor, Rock Hudson and James Dean (died before filming completed)	$12		Capitol 3526
12/22/56	82	1		9 **The Left Arm Of Buddha** .... T:82 *(What Happens In) Buenos Aires* [I]	$12		Capitol 3573
	★589★			**BAY CITY ROLLERS** LP **'76** Pop-rock group from Edinburgh, Scotland: Les McKeown (vocals; born on 11/12/55), brothers Alan (guitar; born on 6/20/53) and Derek (drums; born on 3/19/55) Longmuir, Eric Faulkner (guitar; born on 10/21/55) and Stuart "Woody" Wood (bass; born on 2/25/57). Alan Longmuir left in mid-1976; returned in 1978. Ian Mitchell (guitar) joined briefly in 1976.			
10/11/75+	❶^{1}	17	●	1 **Saturday Night** *Marlina*	$5	■	Arista 0149
2/7/76	9	15		2 **Money Honey** .... *Maryanne*	$5	■	Arista 0170
5/1/76	28	9		3 **Rock And Roll Love Letter** .... *Shanghai'd In Love* originally written and recorded by **Tim Moore**	$5		Arista 0185
9/4/76	12	16		4 **I Only Want To Be With You** .... *Write A Letter*	$5		Arista 0205
12/11/76+	54	7		5 **Yesterday's Hero** .... *My Lisa*	$5		Arista 0216
2/12/77	60	7		6 **Dedication** .... *Rock N' Roller*	$5	■	Arista 0233
6/4/77	10	17		7 **You Made Me Believe In Magic** .... *Dance Dance Dance*	$5		Arista 0256
10/15/77+	24	17		8 **The Way I Feel Tonight** .... *Love Power* also released with "Sweet Virginia" as the B-side	$5		Arista 0272
				BAZUKA R&B **'75** Instrumental studio group assembled by producer Tony Camillo.			
4/12/75	10	20		**Dynomite-Part I** .... *Part II* [I] **Tony Camillo's BAZUKA** song inspired by an exclamation used by J.J. Walker on the TV series *Good Times*	$5		A&M 1666
				BBMAK AC/BUB/LP **'00** Male pop trio from Liverpool, England: Mark Barry (born on 10/26/78), Christian Burns (born on 1/18/74) and Steve McNally (born on 7/4/78).			
4/29/00	13	31		1 **Back Here** .... AC^{7} S:4 / A:11 *Miss You More / (3 album snippets)*	$4	★	Hollywood 64040
12/30/00+	54	9		2 **Still On Your Side** .... A:62 from the album *Sooner Or Later* on Hollywood 62260			album cut
8/17/02	56	8		3 **Out Of My Heart (Into Your Head)** .... S:15 / A:63	$5	◗	Hollywood 69012
				B. BUMBLE & THE STINGERS **'61** Los Angeles sessionmen that included **Ernie Freeman** (piano), Tommy Tedesco (guitar), Earl Palmer (drums) and Red Callender (bass) on their first two hits. "Nut Rocker" was first recorded by Freeman, Palmer and René Hall (guitar) as Jack B. Nimble And The Quicks ("Bubbled Under" at #115 in 1962 on Del-Rio); Rendezvous then released their newly recorded version featuring Palmer, Hall and Ali Hazan on piano. Pianist R.C. Gamble led a touring trio from Oklahoma as B. Bumble & The Stingers.			
3/27/61	21	10		1 **Bumble Boogie** .... *School Days Blues* [I] adaptation of Rimsky-Korsakov's *Flight Of The Bumble Bee*; #7 hit for Freddy Martin (Jack Fina, piano) in 1946	$20		Rendezvous 140
7/10/61	89	1		2 **Boogie Woogie** .... *Near You* [I] written in 1928 by pianist Clarence "Pinetop" Smith; #3 hit for **Tommy Dorsey** (Howard Smith, piano) in 1938	$20		Rendezvous 151
3/3/62	23	11		3 **Nut Rocker** .... *Nautilus* [I] adapted from Tchaikovsky's *The Nutcracker* Suite	$20		Rendezvous 166

B.C. — see IV XAMPLE

BEACH BOYS, The ★17★

BUB/AC/C&W/LP '66

The most popular American rock and roll group was formed in 1961 in Hawthorne, California. Consisted of brothers **Brian Wilson** (see #26 below) (keyboards, bass; born on 6/20/42), **Carl Wilson** (see #53 below) (guitar; born on 12/21/46) and Dennis Wilson (drums; born on 12/4/44); their cousin Mike Love (lead vocals, saxophone; born on 3/15/41), and Al Jardine (guitar; born on 9/3/42). Known in high school as Kenny & The Cadets, Carl & The Passions, then The Pendletones. First recorded for X/Candix in 1961. Ignited the surf-rock craze. Jardine replaced by David Marks from March 1962 to March 1963. Brian quit touring with group in December 1964, replaced briefly by **Glen Campbell** until Bruce Johnston (of **Bruce And Terry**) joined permanently in April 1965. Johnston and Campbell also recorded in the studio band **Sagittarius** in 1967. Love formed **Celebration** in 1977. Brian continued to write for and produce group, returned to stage in 1983. Daryl Dragon (of **Captain & Tennille**) was a keyboardist in their stage band. Dennis Wilson drowned on 12/28/83 (age 39). Lineup of Carl, Brian, Mike, Alan and Bruce continued to perform. Carl Wilson died of cancer on 2/6/98 (age 51). Carnie and Wendy Wilson, daughters of Brian Wilson, were members of **Wilson Phillips**. Group was inducted into the Rock and Roll Hall of Fame in 1988. Won Grammy's Lifetime Achievement Award in 2001. Also see **The Flame**.

1)I Get Around 2)Help Me, Rhonda 3)Good Vibrations 4)Kokomo 5)Barbara Ann

DEBUT	PEAK	WKS	Gold	#	A-side (Chart Hit)	B-side	$	Sym	Label & Number
2/17/62	75	6		1	**Surfin**	*Luau*	$250		Candix 331
					first released on X 301 ($1000) and then on Candix 301 ($400) in 1961				
8/11/62	14	17		2	**Surfin' Safari /**				
10/13/62	76	1		3	**409**		$25	■	Capitol 4777
12/1/62+	49	8		4	**Ten Little Indians**	*County Fair*	$40	■	Capitol 4880
					above 4 from the album *Surfin' Safari*				
3/23/63	3	17		5	**Surfin' U.S.A. /**				
					also see #43 below				
4/27/63	23	13		6	**Shut Down**		$25		Capitol 4932
8/3/63	7	14		7	**Surfer Girl /**				
8/17/63	15	11		8	**Little Deuce Coupe**		$25		Capitol 5009
					a new Beach Boys' version featuring James House made the Country charts in 1996 on River North 3014				
11/2/63	6	12		9	**Be True To Your School /**				
					featuring cheerleading by The Honeys and the University of Wisconsin "fight" song "On Wisconsin"; #3, 6, 8 & 9: from the album *Little Deuce Coupe*				
11/2/63	23	11		10	**In My Room**		$25		Capitol 5069
12/21/63	3^{X}	6		11	**Little Saint Nick**	*The Lord's Prayer* [X]	$30		Capitol 5096
					X: 3/'63; 6/'64				
2/15/64	5	11		12	**Fun, Fun, Fun**	*Why Do Fools Fall In Love* (#120)	$25	■	Capitol 5118
5/23/64	❶^{2}	15	●	13	**I Get Around /**				
5/30/64	24	10		14	**Don't Worry Baby**		$25	■	Capitol 5174
					a new Beach Boys' version featuring **Lorrie Morgan** made the Country charts in 1996 as an album cut				
9/5/64	9	10		15	**When I Grow Up (To Be A Man)**	*She Knows Me Too Well* (#101)	$25	■	Capitol 5245
10/17/64	44	6		16	**Wendy /**	*Don't Back Down*			
10/17/64	65	5		17	**Little Honda**	*Hushabye* [EP]	$75	■	Capitol R-5267
					above 2 from the EP *4-By The Beach Boys*				
11/7/64	8	11		18	**Dance, Dance, Dance**	*The Warmth Of The Sun*	$25	■	Capitol 5306
12/5/64	3^{X}	4		19	**The Man With All The Toys**	*Blue Christmas* [X]	$30		Capitol 5312
2/27/65	12	8		20	**Do You Wanna Dance? /**				
3/6/65	52	5		21	**Please Let Me Wonder**		$20	■	Capitol 5372
4/17/65	❶^{2}	14		22	**Help Me, Rhonda**	*Kiss Me, Baby*	$20	■	Capitol 5395
					the "45" hit version is on the album *Summer Days (And Summer Nights!!)*; #15, 18 & 20-22: from the album *The Beach Boys Today!*				
7/24/65	3	11		23	**California Girls**	*Let Him Run Wild*	$20	■	Capitol 5464
11/27/65+	20	8		24	**The Little Girl I Once Knew**	*There's No Other (Like My Baby)*	$20	■	Capitol 5540
1/1/66	2^{2}	11		25	**Barbara Ann**	*Girl Don't Tell Me*	$20	■	Capitol 5561
					Dean Torrence (of **Jan & Dean**; lead vocals); "Bubbled Under" (#101) in 1975 on Capitol 4110				
3/26/66	32	7		26	**Caroline, No**	*Summer Means New Love*	$25		Capitol 5610
					BRIAN WILSON				
4/2/66	3	11		27	**Sloop John B**	*You're So Good To Me*	$20	■	Capitol 5602
					originally a folk song ("The Wreck Of The John B. Sails") from the West Indies in 1927				
7/30/66	8	11		28	**Wouldn't It Be Nice /**				
					"Bubbled Under" (#103) in 1975 on Brother 1336				
8/13/66	39	8		29	**God Only Knows**		$20		Capitol 5706
					above 4 from the album *Pet Sounds*				
10/22/66	❶^{1}	14	●	30	**Good Vibrations**	*Let's Go Away For Awhile*	$20	■	Capitol 5676
					#7-30: Brian Wilson shown as producer (also #38, 45 & 46 below)				
8/5/67	12	7		31	**Heroes And Villains**	*You're Welcome*	$15	■	Brother 1001
					an unreleased issue in the U.S. on Capitol 5826 featured a full-color picture sleeve				
11/4/67	31	6		32	**Wild Honey**	*Wind Chimes*	$15		Capitol 2028
12/23/67+	19	9		33	**Darlin'**	*Here Today*	$15	■	Capitol 2068
4/20/68	47	7		34	**Friends**	*Little Bird*	$12		Capitol 2160
7/27/68	20	10		35	**Do It Again**	*Wake The World*	$12		Capitol 2239
					#1-35 (except #20, 25 & 27): Brian Wilson shown as songwriter (also #38, 39, 41, 44, 46 & 48-50 below)				
12/14/68	61	6		36	**Bluebirds Over The Mountain**	*Never Learn Not To Love*	$12		Capitol 2360
3/8/69	24	10		37	**I Can Hear Music**	*All I Want To Do*	$12		Capitol 2432
7/5/69	63	6		38	**Break Away**	*Celebrate The News*	$12		Capitol 2530
3/7/70	64	5		39	**Add Some Music To Your Day**	*Susie Cincinnati*	$10		Brother/Reprise 0894
10/30/71	89	5		40	**Long Promised Road**	*'Til I Die*	$25		Brother/Reprise 1047
					first released on Brother/Reprise 1015 in 1971 ($25)				
2/24/73	79	7		41	**Sail On Sailor**	*Only With You*	$12		Brother/Reprise 1138
					also see #44 below				
5/12/73	84	4		42	**California Saga (On My Way To Sunny Californ-i-a)**	*Funky Pretty*	$12		Brother/Reprise 1156
8/17/74	36	8		43	**Surfin' U.S.A.**	*The Warmth Of The Sun* [R]	$7		Capitol 3924
					same version as #5 above; song now credited as written by **Chuck Berry** ("Sweet Little Sixteen")				
4/12/75	49	10		44	**Sail On Sailor**	*Only With You* [R]	$10		Brother/Reprise 1325
					same version as #41 above				

DEBUT	PEAK	WKS	Gold	A-side (Chart Hit)..............B-side	$	Sym	Label & Number
				BEACH BOYS, The — Cont'd			
6/5/76	5	17		45 **Rock And Roll Music**............*The T M Song*	$5		Brother/Reprise 1354
8/21/76	29	10		46 **It's O.K.**............*Had To Phone Ya*	$5		Brother/Reprise 1368
9/9/78	59	6		47 **Peggy Sue**............*Hey Little Tomboy*	$5		Brother/Reprise 1394
3/3/79	44	8		48 **Here Comes The Night**............*Baby Blue*	$5		Caribou 9026
				disco remake of a track from their 1967 *Wild Honey* album			
4/28/79	40	10		49 **Good Timin'**............*Love Surrounds Me*	$5		Caribou 9029
4/12/80	83	3		50 **Goin' On**............*Endless Harmony*	$5		Caribou 9032
7/25/81	12	18		51 **The Beach Boys Medley**............*God Only Knows*	$5		Capitol 5030
				Good Vibrations/Help Me, Rhonda/I Get Around/Shut Down/ Surfin' Safari/Barbara Ann/Surfin' USA/Fun, Fun, Fun			
11/21/81+	18	15		52 **Come Go With Me**............*Don't Go Near The Water*	$5		Caribou 02633
5/14/83	72	6		53 **What You Do To Me**............*Time*	$5		Caribou 03590
				CARL WILSON			
5/25/85	26	12		54 **Getcha Back**............A:24 / S:29 *Male Ego*	$5	■	Caribou 04913
8/3/85	82	5		55 **It's Gettin' Late**............*It's OK*	$5	■	Caribou 05433
6/28/86	68	6		56 **Rock 'N' Roll To The Rescue**............*Good Vibrations (live in London)*	$5	■	Capitol 5595
9/20/86	57	10		57 **California Dreamin'**............*Lady Liberty*	$5		Capitol 5630
				Roger McGuinn (of **The Byrds**; electric 12-string guitar solo)			
7/11/87	12	19		58 **Wipeout**............S:4 / A:20 *Crushin'* (Fat Boys)	$3	■	Tin Pan Apple 885960
				FAT BOYS (with The Beach Boys)			
9/3/88	❶[1]	28	▲	59 **Kokomo**............A:❶[2] / S:❶[1] *Tutti Frutti* (**Little Richard**)	$3		Elektra 69385
				from the movie *Cocktail* starring Tom Cruise			
8/26/89	93	3		60 **Still Cruisin'**............*Kokomo*	$3	▮[V]	Capitol 44445
				from the movie *Lethal Weapon 2* starring Mel Gibson; "45" promo: Capitol 79789; B-side: (same)			
				BEAR WITNEZ! '02			
				Male rapper from Washington DC.			
12/15/01+	18[S]	20		**Can I Get That?!!?**............*What If God Was One Of Us / We Want More / 50 Point Game*	$15	★*	Eargasm 3511
				BEASTIE BOYS R&B/ROK/BUB/LP '87			
				White rap-punk trio from Brooklyn, New York: Adam Horovitz, Adam Yauch and Mike Diamond. Horovitz starred in the movie *Lost Angels*; was married to actress Ione Skye (daughter of **Donovan**) from 1991-99. **DJ Hurricane** was their DJ. Group started own Grand Royal record label.			
12/20/86+	7	18		1 **(You Gotta) Fight For Your Right (To Party!)** S:4 / A:9 *Paul Revere*	$5		Def Jam 06595
3/21/87	48	10		2 **Brass Monkey**............*Posse In Effect*	$5		Def Jam 07020
8/5/89	36	10		3 **Hey Ladies**............S:25 *Shake Your Rump*	$5		Capitol 44454
7/4/92	93	5		4 **So What 'Cha Want**............S:49 *(3 versions) / The Skills To Pay The Bills / Groove Holmes*	$6	▮*	Capitol 15847
7/23/94	69[S]	3		5 **Get It Together**............BUB:101 *Sabotage* (#115/ROK #18)	$5	▮[V]	Grand R./Cap. 58219
				sample "Headless Heroes" by Eugene McDaniels; "45": Capitol 18042 (white vinyl); B-side: "Futterman's Rule"			
8/1/98	28	18		6 **Intergalactic**............A:32 *(5 versions)*	$6	T[V]	Grand R./Cap. 58705
				samples "Prelude C# Minor" by **Les Baxter** and elements from **The Jazz Crusaders**' album *Powerhouse*; "45": Capitol 19973; B-side: "Peanut Butter & Jelly"			

BEATLES, The ★2★ BUB/LP '64

The world's #1 rock group was formed in Liverpool, England, in the late 1950s. Known in early forms as The Quarrymen, Johnny & the Moondogs, The Rainbows, and the Silver Beatles. Named The Beatles in 1960. Originally consisted of **John Lennon** (born on 10/9/40), **Paul McCartney** (born on 6/18/42) and **George Harrison** (guitars; born on 2/24/43), Stu Sutcliffe (bass) and Pete Best (drums). Sutcliffe left in April 1961 (died of a brain hemorrhage on 4/10/62); McCartney moved to bass. Best replaced by **Ringo Starr** (born on 7/7/40) in August 1962. Group managed by Brian Epstein (died of a sleeping-pill overdose on 8/27/67) and produced by **George Martin** (born on 1/3/26) (see #25 below). First U.S. tour in February 1964. Won the 1964 Best New Artist Grammy Award. Group starred in the movies *A Hard Day's Night* (1964), *Help* (1965), *Magical Mystery Tour* (1967) and *Let It Be* (1970); contributed soundtrack to the animated movie *Yellow Submarine* (1968). Own Apple label in 1968. McCartney publicly announced group's dissolution on 4/10/70. Won the Grammy's Trustees Award in 1972. Lennon was shot to death on 12/8/80 (age 40). Harrison died of cancer on 11/29/2001 (age 58). Group inducted into the Rock and Roll Hall of Fame in 1988. On 11/19/95, ABC-TV began airing three-night documentary, *The Beatles Anthology*, which featured two new Beatles recordings (studio reunion of McCartney, Harrison and Starr with original demos by Lennon).

Here, in chronological order, are the Beatles' singles released in the U.S. prior to 1964:
1) 4/23/62: My Bonnie/The Saints...Decca 31382 (Tony Sheridan And The Beat Brothers) ($15,000)
2) 2/25/63: Please Please Me/Ask My Way...Vee-Jay 498 (The Beatles) ($1500)
3) 5/27/63: From Me To You (#116)/Thank You Girl...Vee-Jay 522 ($900)
4) 9/16/63: She Loves You/I'll Get You...Swan 4152 ($600 - white label)

1)Hey Jude 2)I Want To Hold Your Hand 3)Get Back 4)Can't Buy Me Love 5)Yesterday 6)Hello Goodbye 7)We Can Work It Out 8)I Feel Fine 9)Help! 10)She Loves You

DEBUT	PEAK	WKS	Gold	A-side (Chart Hit)..............B-side	$	Sym	Label & Number
1/18/64	❶[7]	15	●	1 **I Want To Hold Your Hand** /			
				John Lennon & **Paul McCartney** wrote all of The Beatles' hits (except #6, 7, 9, 17, 18, 20, 28, 29, 34, 39, 55, 62, 65, 70 & 71)			
2/8/64	14	11		2 **I Saw Her Standing There**............	$30	■	Capitol 5112
1/25/64	❶[2]	15		3 **She Loves You**............*I'll Get You*	$50	■	Swan 4152
				reissue (black label) of September 1963 release; also see #19 below (German version)			
2/1/64	3	13		4 **Please Please Me** /			
				recorded November 1962			
3/7/64	41	6		5 **From Me To You**............	$50	■	Vee-Jay 581
				originally "Bubbled Under" (#116) on 8/3/63 on Vee-Jay 522 ($900); from the album *Jolly What! The Beatles & Frank Ifield*; a promotional sleeve was also issued ($2000)			
2/15/64	26	6		6 **My Bonnie (My Bonnie Lies Over The Ocean)**..*The Saints (When The Saints Go Marching In)*	$50	■	MGM 13213
				THE BEATLES With Tony Sheridan			
				originally released in 1962 on Decca (see 4/23/62 chronological note above)			

DEBUT	PEAK	WKS	Gold	A-side (Chart Hit)......B-side	$	Sym	Label & Number
				BEATLES, The — Cont'd			
3/14/64	2[4]	11		7 **Twist And Shout** /			
				song first recorded by the Top Notes in 1961 (Atlantic 2115-$30); also see #70 below			
4/11/64	74	1		8 **There's A Place**	$50		Tollie 9001
3/21/64	68	4		9 **Roll Over Beethoven** ......*Please Mister Postman*	$60		Capitol 72133
3/28/64	45	6		10 **All My Loving** ......*This Boy*	$60		Capitol 72144
				above 2 singles released by Capitol Records of Canada; above 2 titles and their B-sides also issued on #18 below (same versions); #1, 2 & 10: from the album *Meet The Beatles!*			
3/28/64	❶[5]	10	●	11 **Can't Buy Me Love** /			
4/4/64	48	4		12 **You Can't Do That**	$30	■	Capitol 5150
3/28/64	2[1]	11		13 **Do You Want To Know A Secret** /			
4/4/64	35	7		14 **Thank You Girl**	$50	■	Vee-Jay 587
				#3, 9, 12 & 14: from *The Beatles' Second Album*			
4/11/64	❶[1]	14		15 **Love Me Do** /			
5/9/64	10	8		16 **P.S. I Love You**	$50	■	Tollie 9008
				above 2 recorded September 1962 (with Andy White on drums, Ringo on tambourine); #2, 4, 7, 8, 13, 15 & 16: from the album *Introducing...The Beatles*			
4/18/64	88	1		17 **Why** ......*Cry For A Shadow*	$150	■	MGM 13227
				THE BEATLES With TONY SHERIDAN			
				#6 & 17: recorded May 1961 (Tony Sheridan-vocal, Pete Best-drums, Lennon, McCartney, Harrison); from the album *The Beatles with Tony Sheridan and Their Guests*			
6/13/64	92	3		18 **Four By The Beatles** ...... [EP]	$400	■	Capitol EAP 1-2121
				4-track EP: "All My Loving"/"This Boy" (from the album *Meet The Beatles*)/"Roll Over Beethoven"/"Please Mr. Postman" (from *The Beatles Second Album*); unless otherwise notated, above EP and Swan, Vee-Jay, Tollie and Capitol Records of Canada titles were recorded between February and July 1963			
6/27/64	97	1		19 **Sie Liebt Dich (She Loves You)** *[DIE BEATLES]*......*I'll Get You* [F-R]	$150		Swan 4182
				released in 1980 on the album *Rarities*; June 1964 release on Atco 6302: "Sweet Georgia Brown"/"Take Out Some Insurance On Me Baby" (The Beatles With Tony Sheridan-$200)			
7/18/64	19	9		20 **Ain't She Sweet** ......*Nobody's Child* (w/Tony Sheridan)	$50	■	Atco 6308
				recorded May 1961 (Pete Best, Lennon, McCartney, Harrison); released in 1970 on the album *The Beatles featuring Tony Sheridan-In The Beginning*; #1 hit for Ben Bernie in 1927; Atco and MGM releases recorded in Germany			
7/18/64	❶[2]	13	●	21 **A Hard Day's Night** /			
7/25/64	53	4		22 **I Should Have Known Better**	$30	■	Capitol 5222
7/25/64	12	9		23 **And I Love Her** /			
8/1/64	53	9		24 **If I Fell**	$30	■	Capitol 5235
7/25/64	53	8		25 **Ringo's Theme (This Boy)** ......*And I Love Her* (#105) [I]	$25	■	United Artists 745
				GEORGE MARTIN AND HIS ORCH.			
8/1/64	25	7		26 **I'll Cry Instead** /			
8/1/64	95	1		27 **I'm Happy Just To Dance With You**	$30	■	Capitol 5234
				above 7 from the album and movie *A Hard Day's Night*			
9/5/64	17	8		28 **Matchbox** /			
				written and recorded by **Carl Perkins** in 1956 on Sun 261 ($50); original lyrics by Blind Lemon Jefferson			
9/5/64	25	7		29 **Slow Down**	$30	■	Capitol 5255
				written and recorded by **Larry Williams** in 1958 on Specialty 626 ($40); #23, 24 & 26-29: from the album *Something New*			
12/5/64	❶[3]	11	●	30 **I Feel Fine** /			
12/5/64	4	9		31 **She's A Woman**	$30	■	Capitol 5327
2/20/65	❶[2]	10	●	32 **Eight Days A Week** /			
2/20/65	39	6		33 **I Don't Want To Spoil The Party**	$30	■	Capitol 5371
2/27/65	68	5		34 **4 - By The Beatles** ...... [EP]	$275	■	Capitol R-5365
				4-track EP: "Honey Don't"/"I'm A Loser"/"Mr. Moonlight"/ "Everybody's Trying To Be My Baby"; #30, 31 & 34: from the album *Beatles '65*			
4/24/65	❶[1]	11		35 **Ticket To Ride** /			
5/1/65	46	4		36 **Yes It Is**	$30	■	Capitol 5407
				#32, 33 & 36: from the album *Beatles VI*			
8/7/65	❶[3]	13	●	37 **Help!** ......*I'm Down* (#101)	$30	■	Capitol 5476
				#35 & 37: from the album and movie *Help* (originally titled *Eight Arms To Hold You*)			
9/25/65	❶[4]	11	●	38 **Yesterday** /			
				there have been more than 2500 recorded versions of this song			
9/25/65	47	7		39 **Act Naturally**	$30	■	Capitol 5498
				#1 Country hit for **Buck Owens** in 1963; October 1965, 6 records released on Capitol Records' "The Star Line" series: "Twist And Shout"/"There's A Place" (6061); "Love Me Do"/"P.S. I Love You" (6062); "Please Please Me"/"From Me To You" (6063); "Do You Want To Know A Secret"/"Thank You Girl" (6064); "Roll Over Beethoven"/"Misery" (6065); "Boys" (#102)/"Kansas City" (6066-$125 each)			
12/18/65+	❶[3]	12	●	40 **We Can Work It Out** /			
12/18/65+	5	10		41 **Day Tripper**	$30	■	Capitol 5555
3/5/66	3	9	●	42 **Nowhere Man** /			
3/12/66	81	2		43 **What Goes On**	$30	■	Capitol 5587
				#38-43: from the album *Yesterday...And Today*			
6/11/66	❶[2]	10	●	44 **Paperback Writer** /			
6/11/66	23	7		45 **Rain**	$30	■	Capitol 5651
8/20/66	2[1]	9	●	46 **Yellow Submarine** /			
				title song of The Beatles' animated movie, released in 1968			
8/27/66	11	8		47 **Eleanor Rigby**	$30	■	Capitol 5715
				above 2 from the album *Revolver*			
2/25/67	❶[1]	10	●	48 **Penny Lane** /			
2/25/67	8	9		49 **Strawberry Fields Forever**	$30	■	Capitol 5810
7/22/67	❶[1]	11	●	50 **All You Need Is Love** /			
				intro is from "La Marseillaise" (the French national anthem)			
7/29/67	34	5		51 **Baby You're A Rich Man**	$30	■	Capitol 5964
12/2/67	❶[3]	11	●	52 **Hello Goodbye** /			
12/9/67	56	4		53 **I Am The Walrus**	$30	■	Capitol 2056
				from The Beatles' movie *Magical Mystery Tour*; above 6 from the album *Magical Mystery Tour*			

DEBUT	PEAK	WKS	Gold	A-side (Chart Hit)..........B-side	$	Sym	Label & Number
				BEATLES, The — Cont'd			
3/23/68	4	11	▲	54 Lady Madonna /			
3/30/68	96	1		55 The Inner Light	$30	■	Capitol 2138
				released in 1980 on the album *Rarities*; written by **George Harrison** (also #62 & 65 below)			
9/14/68	1[9]	19	▲[4]	56 Hey Jude /			
9/14/68	12	11		57 Revolution	$20		Apple 2276
5/10/69	1[5]	12	▲[2]	58 Get Back /			
5/10/69	35	4		59 Don't Let Me Down	$20		Apple 2490
				THE BEATLES with Billy Preston (above 2)			
6/14/69	8	9	●	60 The Ballad Of John And Yoko..........*Old Brown Shoe*	$20	■	Apple 2531
				#44, 45, 54, 56, 57, 59 & 60: from the album *Hey Jude*			
10/18/69	1[1]	16	▲[2]	61 Come Together /			
10/18/69	3	16		62 Something	$20		Apple 2654
				above 2 from the album *Abbey Road*; #56, 58 & 61: issued in plain black 1/2 sleeves with the writing "The Beatles on Apple"			
3/21/70	1[2]	14	▲[2]	63 Let It Be..........AC[4] *You Know My Name (Look Up My Number)*	$20	■	Apple 2764
5/23/70	1[2]	10	▲	64 The Long And Winding Road /			
5/23/70		10		65 For You Blue	$20	■	Apple 2832
				above 3 songs from The Beatles' documentary movie *Let It Be*; #58 & 63-65: from the album *Let It Be*; 18 of The Beatles 23 regular Capitol/Apple releases were #1 hits			
6/12/76	7	16	●	66 Got To Get You Into My Life..........*Helter Skelter*	$10	■	Capitol 4274
				from the 1966 album *Revolver*			
11/20/76	49	7		67 Ob-La-Di, Ob-La-Da..........*Julia*	$10	■	Capitol 4347
				from the 1968 *The Beatles [White Album]*			
9/16/78	71	7		68 Sgt. Pepper's Lonely Hearts Club Band/With A Little Help From My Friends..........*A Day In The Life*	$8	■	Capitol 4612
				from the 1967 album *Sgt. Pepper's Lonely Hearts Club Band*			
3/27/82	12	11		69 The Beatles' Movie Medley..........*I'm Happy Just To Dance With You*	$5	■	Capitol 5107
				Magical Mystery Tour/All You Need Is Love/You've Got To Hide Your Love Away/I Should Have Known Better/ A Hard Day's Night/Ticket To Ride/Get Back			
8/9/86	23	15		70 Twist And Shout..........S:20 / A:29 *There's A Place* [R]	$5		Capitol 5624
				revived through inclusion in the movies *Ferris Bueller's Day Off* starring Matthew Broderick and *Back To School* starring **Rodney Dangerfield**; same version as #7 above			
4/22/95	67	4		71 Baby It's You..........S:26 *I'll Follow The Sun / Devil In Her Heart / Boys* [EP]	$5	▮[V]	Apple 58348 ■
				recorded on 6/1/63 for The Beatles' appearance on London's BBC radio program *Pop Go The Beatles*; from the album *Live At The BBC*			
12/30/95+	6	11	●	72 Free As A Bird..........S:5 / A:60 *Christmas Time (Is Here Again)*	$4	▮[V]	Apple 58497 ■
				original demo recorded by **John Lennon** in 1977, with new vocals and instrumentation added by the other Beatles; from the album *Anthology 1*			
3/23/96	11	7	●	73 Real Love..........S:5 *Baby's In Black (live)*	$4	▮[V]	Apple 58544 ■
				original demo recorded by **John Lennon** in 1979, with new vocals and instrumentation added by the other Beatles; from the album *Anthology 2*; "45" issued with small center hole for above 2			
				BEATNUTS, The R&B/LP **'99**			
				Latin rap trio from Queens, New York: Les Fernandez, Jerry Tineo and Bert Smalls (left in 1996).			
9/27/97	86	3		1 Off The Books..........*(3 versions)*	$5	▮	Relativity 1646
				THE BEATNUTS Featuring Big Punisher & Cuban Link			
6/26/99	84	12		2 Watch Out Now..........S:22 *(2 versions) / Turn It Out* (w/Greg Nice)	$5	★	Relativity 1795
				THE BEATNUTS Featuring Yellaklaw			
3/3/01	66[S]	2		3 No Escapin' This..........*(2 versions) / It's Da Nuts* (w/Al Tariq)	$6	T	Loud 1983
6/8/02	35[S]	1		4 Duck Season..........*(2 versions) / Ducky Boy* (**Jurassic 5**)	$7	T	Sequence 8005
				THE BEATNUTS Featuring Al' Tariq			
				BEATS INTERNATIONAL LP **'90**			
				Dance group from England: Lester Noel and Lindy Layton (vocals), Andy Boucher (keyboards), Norman Cook (bass) and Luke Creswell (drums). Cook (who later recorded as **Fatboy Slim**) was bassist of The Housemartins and assembled **The Mighty Dub Kats**.			
4/14/90	76	5		1 Dub Be Good To Me..........*Invasion Of The Estate Agents*	$4	▮	Elektra 64970
				#55 hit for **The S.O.S. Band** in 1983 as "Just Be Good To Me"			
8/25/90	76	8		2 Won't Talk About It..........*(7" Beats International Theme)*	$4	▮	Elektra 64948
				BEATTY, E.C. **'59**			
				Born in Charlotte, North Carolina. Pop singer/songwriter.			
9/21/59	50	6		Ski King..........*I'm A Lucky Man* [N]	$25		Colonial 7003
				BEAU, Toby — see TOBY			
				BEAU BRUMMELS, The LP **'65**			
				Rock group from San Francisco, California: Sal Valentino (vocals; born Sal Spanminato), Ron Elliott (guitar), Ron Meagher (bass) and John Petersen (drums). Petersen left in 1966 to join **Harpers Bizzare**.			
1/2/65	15	12		1 Laugh, Laugh..........*Still In Love With You Baby*	$15		Autumn 8
4/17/65	8	12		2 Just A Little..........*They'll Make You Cry*	$15		Autumn 10
7/24/65	38	7		3 You Tell Me Why..........*I Want You*	$12		Autumn 16
10/9/65	52	8		4 Don't Talk To Strangers..........*In Good Time*	$12		Autumn 20
12/25/65	97	1		5 Good Time Music..........*Sad Little Girl*	$12		Autumn 24
6/4/66	95	3		6 One Too Many Mornings..........*She Reigns*	$10		Warner 5813
				written by **Bob Dylan** (from his 1964 album *The Times They Are A-Changin'*)			
				BEAU COUP **'87**			
				Rock group from Cleveland, Ohio: brothers Frank and Tommy Amato, with Dennis Lewin and Bill March. Lewin is a distant cousin of **Eric Carmen**.			
10/31/87	80	6		Sweet Rachel..........*Hold On Me*	$4		Amherst 318
				BEAU-MARKS, The **'60**			
				Rock and roll group from Montreal, Quebec, Canada: Ray Hutchinson (vocals, guitar), Mike Robitaille (guitar), Joey Frechette (leader, piano) and Gilles Tailleur (drums).			
5/16/60	45	14		Clap Your Hands..........*Daddy Said*	$25		Shad 5017

DEBUT	PEAK	WKS	Gold	A-side (Chart Hit)...B-side	$	Sym	Label & Number

BEAUMONT, Jimmy — see SKYLINERS, The

BEAUVOIR, Jean — LP '86

Born in Chicago of Haitian parentage; raised in Brooklyn, New York. Male singer/bassist. Member of the Plasmatics and **Little Steven and the Disciples Of Soul**.

DEBUT	PEAK	WKS	Gold	A-side (Chart Hit)...B-side	$	Sym	Label & Number
6/14/86	73	8		**Feel The Heat** ....*Standing In The Line Of Fire* from the movie *Cobra* starring Sylvester Stallone	$4	■	Columbia 05904

BECK — ROK/LP '94

Born Beck David Campbell (later changed his last name to his mother's maiden name of Hansen) on 7/8/70 in Los Angeles, California. Alternative-rock singer/songwriter/guitarist.

DEBUT	PEAK	WKS	Gold	A-side (Chart Hit)...B-side	$	Sym	Label & Number
1/29/94	10	24	●	1 **Loser** MR[5] S:3 / A:31 *Alcohol* samples "I Walk On Guilded Splinters" by **Dr. John**	$3	▮V	DGC/Bong Load 19270
6/29/96	61	19		2 **Where It's At** ....A:40 *(4 remixes)* samples "Get Up And Dance" by **Mantronix**	$6	T	DGC/Bong Load 22214
11/9/96	94	4		3 **Devils Haircut** ....*(3 remixes) / Clock* samples "Out Of Sight" by **Them** and "Soul Drums" by **Pretty Purdie**	$6	T	DGC/Bong Load 22222
5/31/97	78	7		4 **The New Pollution** ....A:51 *(3 remixes) / Lemonade*	$6	T	DGC/Bong Load 22300
9/13/97	73	10		5 **Jack-Ass** ....A:74 *(2 remixes) / Brother* samples "It's All Over Now Baby Blue" by **Them** (written by **Bob Dylan** on his 1965 album *Bringing It All Back Home*); above 4 from the album *Odelay*	$6	T	DGC/Bong Load 22303

BECK, Jeff — ROK/BUB/LP '85

Born on 6/24/44 in Wallington, Surrey, England. Prolific rock guitarist. With **The Yardbirds** from 1964-66. **Rod Stewart** and **Ron Wood** (**Faces**, **Rolling Stones**) were members of the Jeff Beck Group from 1967-69. Member of supergroup **The Honeydrippers**.

DEBUT	PEAK	WKS	Gold	A-side (Chart Hit)...B-side	$	Sym	Label & Number
8/2/69	36	7		1 **Goo Goo Barabajagal (Love Is Hot)** ....*Trudi* **DONOVAN (With The Jeff Beck Group)**	$8	■	Epic 10510
6/15/85	48	10		2 **People Get Ready** ....*Back On The Street* (Beck w/Karen Lawrence) **JEFF BECK and ROD STEWART**	$4	■	Epic 05416

BECK, Jimmy, & His Orchestra — '59

Born on 12/30/29 in Cleveland, Ohio. R&B saxophonist.

DEBUT	PEAK	WKS	Gold	A-side (Chart Hit)...B-side	$	Sym	Label & Number
4/20/59	82	2		**Pipe Dreams** ....*Blue Night* [I]	$25		Champion 1002

BECKHAM, Bob — C&W/BUB '59

Born on 7/8/27 in Stratford, Oklahoma. Pop-country singer.

DEBUT	PEAK	WKS	Gold	A-side (Chart Hit)...B-side	$	Sym	Label & Number
8/10/59	32	21		1 **Just As Much As Ever** ....*Your Sweet Love*	$12	■	Decca 30861
1/4/60	36	13		2 **Crazy Arms** ....*Beloved*	$12	■	Decca 31029

BECKMEIER BROTHERS — '79

Duo from San Francisco, California: Freddie and Stevie Beckmeier. Freddie was a member of the Paul Butterfield Blues Band.

DEBUT	PEAK	WKS	Gold	A-side (Chart Hit)...B-side	$	Sym	Label & Number
7/28/79	53	6		**Rock And Roll Dancin'** ....*You Can Love*	$5		Casablanca 1000

BEDINGFIELD, Daniel — LP '02

Born in 1980 in New Zealand; raised in England. Pop singer/songwriter.

DEBUT	PEAK	WKS	Gold	A-side (Chart Hit)...B-side	$	Sym	Label & Number
7/27/02	10	21		**Gotta Get Thru This** ....A:13 *(4 versions)* 12" issued on white vinyl	$6	T	Island 570976

BEECHER, Johnny — '63

Born John Johnson on 7/21/31 in Donaldsonville, Louisiana. Also known as Plas Johnson. Alto saxophonist. Heard on several of **Duane Eddy**'s hits and "The Pink Panther Theme" by **Henry Mancini**.

DEBUT	PEAK	WKS	Gold	A-side (Chart Hit)...B-side	$	Sym	Label & Number
3/2/63	65	8		**Sax Fifth Avenue** ....*Jack Sax The City* [I] **JOHNNY BEECHER and his Buckingham Road Quintet** Bert Kendricks (organ); originally released on Omega 116 in 1962 ($15)	$12		Warner 5341

BEE GEES ★15★ — BUB/AC/C&W/LP '78

Trio of brothers from Manchester, England: **Barry Gibb** (see #36, 38 & 44 below) (born on 9/1/46) and twins Maurice and **Robin Gibb** (see #32, 37 & 43 below) (born on 12/22/49). First performed in December 1955. To Australia in 1958, performed as the Gibbs, later as BG's, finally the Bee Gees. First recorded for Leedon/Festival in 1963. Returned to England in February 1967, with guitarist Vince Melouney and drummer Colin Peterson. Toured Europe and the U.S. in 1968. Melouney left in December 1968; Robin left for solo career in 1969. When Peterson left in August 1969, Barry and Maurice went solo. After eight months, the brothers reunited. Maurice was married to **Lulu** from 1969-73. Composed soundtracks for *Saturday Night Fever* and *Staying Alive*. Acted in the movie *Sgt. Pepper's Lonely Hearts Club Band*. Youngest brother, **Andy Gibb**, was a successful solo singer (died on 3/10/88). Maurice died of heart failure on 1/12/2003 (age 53). Trio inducted into the Rock and Roll Hall of Fame in 1997. Also see **Samantha Sang**'s "Emotion."

1)Night Fever 2)Stayin' Alive 3)How Can You Mend A Broken Heart 4)How Deep Is Your Love 5)Too Much Heaven

DEBUT	PEAK	WKS	Gold	A-side (Chart Hit)...B-side	$	Sym	Label & Number
5/27/67	14	7		1 **New York Mining Disaster 1941 Have You Seen My Wife, Mr. Jones** ....*I Can't See Nobody* (#128)	$10		Atco 6487
7/15/67	17	9		2 **To Love Somebody** ....*Close Another Door*	$10		Atco 6503
9/30/67	16	9		3 **Holiday** ....*Every Christian Lion Hearted Man Will Show You*	$10		Atco 6521
11/11/67	11	8		4 **(The Lights Went Out In) Massachusetts** ....*Sir Geoffrey Saved The World*	$10		Atco 6532
1/20/68	15	11		5 **Words** ....*Sinking Ships*	$10		Atco 6548
4/6/68	57	6		6 **Jumbo** ....*The Singer Sang His Song* (#116)	$10		Atco 6570
8/17/68	8	13		7 **I've Gotta Get A Message To You** ....*Kitty Can*	$8		Atco 6603
12/21/68+	6	11		8 **I Started A Joke** ....*Kilburn Towers*	$8		Atco 6639
3/22/69	37	7		9 **First Of May** ....*Lamplight*	$8		Atco 6657
5/31/69	54	6		10 **Tomorrow Tomorrow** ....*Sun In My Morning*	$8		Atco 6682
9/20/69	73	3		11 **Don't Forget To Remember** ....*The Lord*	$8		Atco 6702
3/28/70	91	3		12 **If Only I Had My Mind On Something Else** ....*Sweetheart* insert features a photo of Maurice and Barry Gibb	$8	⊙	Atco 6741
7/11/70	94	1		13 **I.O.I.O.** ....*Then You Left Me*	$8		Atco 6752
12/5/70+	3	14	●	14 **Lonely Days** ....*Man For All Seasons*	$7		Atco 6795
6/26/71	❶[4]	15	●	15 **How Can You Mend A Broken Heart** ....*Country Woman*	$7		Atco 6824

DEBUT	PEAK	WKS	Gold	A-side (Chart Hit)...B-side	$	Sym	Label & Number
				BEE GEES — Cont'd			
10/23/71	53	7		16 **Don't Wanna Live Inside Myself**...*Walking Back To Waterloo*	$7		Atco 6847
1/29/72	16	8		17 **My World**...*On Time*	$7		Atco 6871
7/29/72	16	12		18 **Run To Me**...*Road To Alaska*	$7		Atco 6896
11/18/72	34	7		19 **Alive**...*Paper Mache, Cabbages And Kings*	$7		Atco 6909
3/24/73	94	3		20 **Saw A New Morning**...*My Life Has Been A Song*	$6		RSO 401
3/9/74	93	3		21 **Mr. Natural**...*It Doesn't Matter Much To Me*	$6		RSO 408
5/31/75	1^{2}	17	●	22 **Jive Talkin'**...*Wind Of Change*	$5		RSO 510
10/4/75	7	16		23 **Nights On Broadway**...*Edge Of The Universe*	$5		RSO 515
12/27/75+	12	16		24 **Fanny (Be Tender With My Love)**...*Country Lanes*	$5		RSO 519
7/4/76	1^{1}	20	●	25 **You Should Be Dancing**...*Subway*	$5		RSO 853
9/18/76	3	23	●	26 **Love So Right**...*You Stepped Into My Life*	$5		RSO 859
				B-side was a #47 hit in 1979 for **Melba Moore**			
1/15/77	12	15		27 **Boogie Child**...*Lovers*	$5		RSO 867
7/23/77	26	13		28 **Edge Of The Universe**...*Words (live)*	$5		RSO 880
				studio version is on the B-side of #23 above			
9/24/77	1^{3}	33	●	29 **How Deep Is Your Love**...AC[6] *Can't Keep A Good Man Down*	$4		RSO 882
12/10/77+	1^{4}	27	▲	30 **Stayin' Alive**...*If I Can't Have You*	$4		RSO 885
				B-side was a #1 hit in 1978 for **Yvonne Elliman**			
2/4/78	1^{8}	20	▲	31 **Night Fever** *Down The Road*	$4		RSO 889
				above 3 from the album and movie *Saturday Night Fever* starring **John Travolta**			
8/12/78	15	12		32 **Oh! Darling**...*She's Leaving Home* (**Bee Gees**, Jay MacIntosh, John Whee)	$4		RSO 907
				ROBIN GIBB			
				from the movie *Sgt. Pepper's Lonely Hearts Club Band* starring **Peter Frampton** and the **Bee Gees**; tune introduced on **The Beatles**' 1969 album *Abbey Road*			
11/18/78+	1^{2}	21	▲	33 **Too Much Heaven**...*Rest Your Love On Me* (C&W #39)	$4		RSO 913
2/10/79	1^{2}	20	▲	34 **Tragedy**...*Until*	$4		RSO 918
4/21/79	1^{1}	19	●	35 **Love You Inside Out**...*I'm Satisfied*	$4		RSO 925
11/1/80+	3	22	●	36 **Guilty**...*Life Story* (Streisand)	$4		Columbia 11390
				BARBRA STREISAND & BARRY GIBB			
11/8/80	50	10		37 **Help Me!**...*(instrumental)*	$4	■	RSO 1047
				MARCY LEVY AND ROBIN GIBB			
				from the movie *Times Square* starring **Tim Curry**; Levy: see **Shakespear's Sister**			
1/31/81	10	16		38 **What Kind Of Fool**...AC[4] *The Love Inside* (Streisand)	$4		Columbia 11430
				BARBRA STREISAND & BARRY GIBB			
9/26/81	30	8		39 **He's A Liar**...*(instrumental)*	$4		RSO 1066
11/7/81	45	10		40 **Living Eyes**...*I Still Love You*	$4		RSO 1067
5/21/83	24	11		41 **The Woman In You**...*Stayin' Alive*	$4	■	RSO 813173
				B-side is the original long version (4:48) of #30 above (3:29)			
8/20/83	49	6		42 **Someone Belonging To Someone**...*I Love You Too Much*	$4	■	RSO 815235
				above 2 from the movie *Staying Alive* starring **John Travolta**			
6/2/84	37	12		43 **Boys Do Fall In Love**...*Diamonds*	$4	■	Mirage 99743
				ROBIN GIBB			
9/1/84	37	10		44 **Shine Shine**...*She Says*	$4	■	MCA 52443
				BARRY GIBB			
9/19/87	75	6		45 **You Win Again**...*Backtafunk*	$3	■	Warner 28351
7/29/89	7	14		46 **One**...AC[2] S:8 / A:9 *Wing And A Prayer*	$3	■	Warner 22899
10/23/93	74	9		47 **Paying The Price Of Love**...A:74 *(3 remixes)*	$3	▮	Polydor 859164
				includes the bonus cassette "Decadance"			
6/7/97	28	20		48 **Alone**...S:23 / A:49 *Stayin' Alive (live)*	$3	▮[V]	Polydor 571006
				"45" B-side: "How Deep Is Your Love" (longer version [3:58] than #29 above [3:30])			
12/13/97	57	9		49 **Still Waters (Run Deep)**...S:49 *Love Never Dies*	$3	▮	Polydor 569218
				all of their hits (except #32) written by one or more of the three Gibb brothers			
				BEELOW LP **'02**			
				Born Bruce Moore in Baton Rouge, Louisiana. Male rapper.			
3/30/02	13^{S}	10		**Do Yo Thang**...*Iron Yo Ass / Twerk / Ho Ass Nigga / Bring It On / Out Your Clothes*	$15	T	Ballin 12164
				samples "Jungle Boogie" by **Kool & The Gang**			
				BEENIE MAN R&B/LP **'02**			
				Born Moses Davis on 8/22/73 in Kingston, Jamaica. Reggae singer/rapper. Beenie is Jamaican slang for little.			
8/16/97	90	3		1 **Dancehall Queen**...*(edit)*	$4	▮	Island 572036
				BEENIE MAN FEATURING CHEVELLE FRANKLYN			
				title song from the movie starring Audrey Reid			
3/14/98	40	20		2 **Who Am I "Sim Simma"**...S:26 / A:74 *(3 versions)*	$4	▮	VP 6160
10/21/00	54	15		3 **Girls Dem Sugar**...A:54		V	album cut
				BEENIE MAN featuring Mýa			
				from the album *Art And Life* on Virgin 49093; "45" B-side: (instrumental)			
5/18/02	50^{S}	3		4 **Fresh From Yard**...*(2 versions) / Bossman* (w/**Lady Saw** & **Sean Paul**)	$6	T	Shocking Vibes 38827
				BEENIE MAN & LIL' KIM			
				samples "Flex" by **Mad Cobra** and "Roots & Culture" by **Shabba Ranks**			
8/3/02	28	12		5 **Feel It Boy** S:12 / A:30 *(3 remixes)*	$4	★	Virgin 38846
				BEENIE MAN feat. JANET			
				BEFORE DARK R&B **'99**			
				Female R&B vocal trio from Los Angeles, California: sisters Arike and Jeni Rice, with Mia LeFleur. Arike Rice was a member of **Voices**.			
6/26/99	57^{S}	6		1 **Baby**...*Secrets*	$5	★[+]	RCA 65761
5/20/00	77	9		2 **Monica**...S:8 *Push N Shove*	$4	★	RCA 65999

DEBUT	PEAK	WKS	Gold	A-side (Chart Hit)....B-side	$	Sym	Label & Number
				BEGA, Lou LP **'99**			
				Born David Lubega on 4/13/75 in Munich, Germany (Sicilian mother/Ugandan father).			
8/28/99	3	22		1 **Mambo No. 5 (A Little Bit Of...)** ....A:❶[6] *(3 versions)*	$6	T[V]	RCA 65842
				new lyrics added to **Perez Prado**'s 1950 recording on RCA 3782 (also see "7-11" by the **Gone All Stars**); "45": RCA 65851; B-side: "Beauty On The TV-Screen"			
1/29/00	74	3		2 **Tricky Tricky** A:70			album cut
12/22/01+	40[S]	7		3 **Mambo No. 5 (A Little Bit Of...)** / [R]			
12/22/01		7		4 **Tricky Tricky** .... [R]	$4	★	RCA 60504
				above 2 reissued on RCA's "Double-Play CD Single"; all of above from the album *A Little Bit Of Mambo* on RCA 67887			
				BEGINNING OF THE END, The **'71**			
				R&B group from the Bahamas: brothers Ray (organ), Roy (guitar) and Frank (drums) Munnings, with Fred Henfield (bass).			
5/8/71	15	14		**Funky Nassau-Part I** ....*Part II*	$7		Alston 4595
				BELAFONTE, Harry MEM/AC/POP/LP **'57**			
				Born on 3/1/27 in Harlem, New York (Jamaican mother and West Indian father). Calypso singer/actor/activist. Rode the crest of the calypso craze to worldwide stardom. Starred in several movies. Became UNICEF goodwill ambassador in 1987. Father of actress Shari Belafonte. Won Grammy's Lifetime Achievement Award in 2000. Hit #19 on the pop charts in 1953 with "Gomen Nasai (Forgive Me)."			
10/20/56+	14	26		1 **Jamaica Farewell**....A:14 / S:17 / T:17 / J:17 *Once Was*	$15	■	RCA Victor 6663
				adaptation of a West Indian folk song			
12/22/56	12	5		2 **Mary's Boy Child**....S:12 / A:12 / T:15 *Venezuela* [X]	$15	■	RCA Victor 6735
				William Lorin (orch., above 2)			
1/12/57	5	20	●	3 **Banana Boat (Day-O)** A:5 / S:5 / T:5 / J:5 *Star-O*	$15	■	RCA Victor 6771
				Tony Scott (orch. and chorus); based on a Jamaican folk song brought to the U.S. in the late 1940s			
3/9/57	84	4		4 **Hold 'Em Joe** / T:84 [R]			
				from the Broadway show *John Murray Anderson's Almanac* starring Belafonte; originally charted in 1954 on RCA Victor 5617 (#30)			
2/2/57		3		5 **I'm Just A Country Boy** ....CU:flip	$12	■	RCA Victor 0322
				Hugo Winterhalter (orch., above 2)			
3/23/57	11	20		6 **Mama Look At Bubu** / S:11 / T:13 / A:14 / J:18			
				some pressings show title as "Mama Look A Boo Boo (Shut You Mouth-Go Away)"			
4/20/57	90	2		7 **Don't Ever Love Me** T:90	$12	■	RCA Victor 6830
				adaptation of a West Indian folk song (better known as "Yellow Bird"); all of above picture sleeves feature the same photo of Belafonte			
6/3/57	25	10		8 **Cocoanut Woman** / S:25 / T:48			
6/3/57	30	18		9 **Island In The Sun** ....S:30 / T:42	$12		RCA Victor 6885
				title song from the movie starring Belafonte; Bob Corman (orch., above 4)			
				BELEW, Adrian ROK/LP **'89**			
				Born Robert Steven Belew on 12/23/49 in Covington, Kentucky. Prolific rock guitarist. Discovered by **Frank Zappa**. Sideman with **Talking Heads**, **David Bowie**, **Tom Tom Club**, **Laurie Anderson**, **Paul Simon** and others. Member of **King Crimson** from 1981-84.			
8/5/89	58	8		**Oh Daddy**....*Peaceable Kingdom*	$3	■	Atlantic 88904
				Adrian's daughter, Audie (vocal backing)			
				BELL, Archie, & The Drells R&B/BUB/LP **'68**			
				Born on 9/1/44 in Henderson, Texas. Lead singer of the Drells, an R&B vocal group from Leo Smith Junior High School in Houston. Charted 21 R&B hits, 1968-81. First recorded for Ovid in 1967. Recorded "Tighten Up" with group consisting of Bell, Huey "Billy" Butler, Joe Cross and James Wise. Bell was in U.S. Army at time of hit. Later recordings consisted of Bell, Wise, Lee Bell and Willie Parnell. Still active in "beach music" scene.			
				1)Tighten Up 2)I Can't Stop Dancing 3)There's Gonna Be A Showdown			
3/30/68	❶[2]	15	●	1 **Tighten Up** RB[2] *Part II*	$8		Atlantic 2478
				originally released on Ovide 228 in 1967 ($25)			
7/20/68	9	10		2 **I Can't Stop Dancing** ....*You're Such A Beautiful Child*	$8		Atlantic 2534
9/28/68	44	7		3 **Do The Choo Choo** ....*Love Will Rain On You* (R&B #25)	$8		Atlantic 2559
12/14/68+	21	11		4 **There's Gonna Be A Showdown** ....*Go For What You Know*	$8		Atlantic 2583
3/29/69	94	3		5 **I Love My Baby**....*Just A Little Closer* (#128)	$8		Atlantic 2612
6/21/69	59	7		6 **Girl You're Too Young** ....*Do The Hand Jive*	$8		Atlantic 2644
9/13/69	87	4		7 **My Balloon's Going Up**....*Giving Up Dancing*	$8		Atlantic 2663
				above 4 from the album *There's Gonna Be A Showdown*			
12/27/69+	90	2		8 **A World Without Music**....*Here I Go Again* (#112)	$8		Atlantic 2693
4/18/70	100	1		9 **Don't Let The Music Slip Away** ....*Houston Texas*	$8		Atlantic 2721
12/12/70	93	2		10 **Wrap It Up**....*Deal With Him*	$8		Atlantic 2768
				co-written by **Isaac Hayes**			
3/17/73	61	9		11 **Dancing To Your Music** ....*Count The Ways*	$6		Glades 1707
				BELL, Benny **'75**			
				Born Benjamin Samberg on 3/27/06 in Brooklyn, New York. Died on 9/1/99 (age 93). Risque singer/songwriter.			
3/8/75	30	11		**Shaving Cream** ....*The Girl From Chicago* [N]	$7		Vanguard 35183
				Paul Wynn (born Phil Winston; vocal); originally released on Cocktail Party Songs 202 in 1946 ($30)			
				BELL, Madeline **'68**			
				Born on 7/23/42 in Newark, New Jersey. Singer/actress. In cast of *Black Nativity*; toured England in the mid-1960s and remained there. Formed group **Blue Mink**, 1969-73. Commercial jingle singer since then. Also see **Space**.			
2/10/68	26	9		**I'm Gonna Make You Love Me**....*Picture Me Gone*	$8		Philips 40517
				BELL, Maggie LP **'74**			
				Born on 1/12/45 in Glasgow, Scotland. Lead singer of the rock band Stone The Crows.			
5/11/74	97	3		**After Midnight**....*Souvenirs*	$6		Atlantic 3018
				BELL, Randy **'84**			
				Pop-rock singer/songwriter.			
7/7/84	90	3		**Don't Do Me** ....*Someone's Fantasy*	$4	■	Epic 04497

BELL, Vincent
LP '70

Born Vincent Gambella on 7/28/35 in Brooklyn, New York. Veteran studio guitarist. Formerly with the East Coast vocal group **The Gallahads**. His "water sound" guitar was featured in **Ferrante & Teicher**'s hit "Midnight Cowboy." Not to be confused with Vincent Lee Bell of **The Ramrods**.

DEBUT	PEAK	WKS	Gold	A-side (Chart Hit)..........B-side	$	Sym	Label & Number
4/11/70	31	8		**Airport Love Theme (Gwen And Vern)** ....*Marilyn's Theme* [I] from the movie *Airport* starring Burt Lancaster	$8		Decca 32659

BELL, William
R&B/BUB/LP '77

Born William Yarborough on 7/16/39 in Memphis, Tennessee. R&B singer. Own Peachtree and Wilbe labels. With **Rufus Thomas** band in 1953.

DEBUT	PEAK	WKS	Gold	A-side (Chart Hit)..........B-side	$	Sym	Label & Number
4/28/62	95	1		1 **You Don't Miss Your Water** ....*Formula Of Love*	$15		Stax 116
4/15/67	95	2		2 **Everybody Loves A Winner** ....*You're Such A Sweet Thang*	$12		Stax 212
4/27/68	86	6		3 **A Tribute To A King**..........*Every Man Oughta Have A Woman* (#115) a tribute to **Otis Redding**	$10		Stax 248
8/31/68	75	6		4 **Private Number**..........*Love-Eye-Tis* **JUDY CLAY & WILLIAM BELL**	$10		Stax 0005
1/4/69	45	9		5 **I Forgot To Be Your Lover**..........*Bring The Curtain Down* #6 hit for **Billy Idol** in 1986 as "To Be A Lover"; above 4 co-written by Booker T. Jones of **Booker T. & The MG's**	$10		Stax 0015
2/19/77	10	15	●	6 **Tryin' To Love Two** RB[1] *If Sex Was All We Had*	$6		Mercury 73839

BELLAMY BROTHERS
C&W/AC/LP '76

Country duo from Darby, Florida: brothers Howard (see #1 below) (born on 2/2/46; guitar) and **David Bellamy** (born on 9/16/50; guitar, keyboards). Charted 46 Country hits, 1976-94. Made their professional debut in 1958. David wrote "Spiders And Snakes" hit for **Jim Stafford**. Moved to Los Angeles in 1973.

DEBUT	PEAK	WKS	Gold	A-side (Chart Hit)..........B-side	$	Sym	Label & Number
9/20/75	77	6		1 **Nothin' Heavy**..........*Baby, You're Not A Legend* **DAVID BELLAMY**	$5		Warner/Curb 8123
1/31/76	❶[1]	19		2 **Let Your Love Flow** *Inside Of My Guitar*	$5		Warner/Curb 8169
7/10/76	70	3		3 **Hell Cat**..........*I'm The Only Sane Man Left Alive*	$5		Warner/Curb 8220
9/11/76	73	3		4 **Satin Sheets**..........*Rainy, Windy, Sunshine (Roadeo Road)*	$5		Warner/Curb 8248
5/26/79	39	11		5 **If I Said You Have A Beautiful Body Would You Hold It Against Me** ....CW[3] *Make Me Over*	$5		Warner/Curb 8790

BELL & JAMES
R&B/BUB/LP '79

R&B duo of Leroy Bell and Casey James. Began as songwriting team for Bell's uncle, producer Thom Bell.

DEBUT	PEAK	WKS	Gold	A-side (Chart Hit)..........B-side	$	Sym	Label & Number
1/27/79	15	16	●	**Livin' It Up (Friday Night)** ....*Don't Let The Man Get You*	$6		A&M 2069

BELL BIV DeVOE
★542★

R&B/BUB/LP '90

R&B trio of **New Edition** members: Ricky Bell (born on 9/18/67), Michael Bivins (born on 8/10/68) and Ronnie DeVoe (born on 11/17/67). Bivins produced **Another Bad Creation**, **Boyz II Men** and **M.C. Brains**, formed own record label, Biv 10, and assembled **East Coast Family**.

DEBUT	PEAK	WKS	Gold	A-side (Chart Hit)..........B-side	$	Sym	Label & Number
4/7/90	3	22	▲	1 **Poison** RB[2] S:❶[3] / A:3 *(no B-side)* "45" B-side: (instrumental)	$3	▮[V]	MCA 53772
6/30/90	3	22		2 **Do Me!** ....S:❶[1] / A:4 *(no B-side)* "45": MCA 79045; B-side: (instrumental)	$3	▮[V]	MCA 53848
10/13/90	26	15		3 **B.B.D. (I Thought It Was Me)?** ....RB[1] S:18 / A:39 *(instrumental)*	$3	▮[V]	MCA 53897
1/19/91	63	8		4 **When Will I See You Smile Again?**..........*(no B-side)*	$3	▮	MCA 53976
6/8/91	63[S]	2		5 **She's Dope!** ....*(no B-side)* all of above from the album *Poison*	$3	▮	MCA 54064
8/31/91	37[A]	19		6 **Word To The Mutha!**.......... **New Edition** (guest vocals); from the album *WBBD - Bootcity! The Remix Album* on MCA 10345			album cut
5/30/92	10	20		7 **The Best Things In Life Are Free** ....RB[1] A:5 / S:16 *(3 album snippets)* **LUTHER VANDROSS and JANET JACKSON with BBD and Ralph Tresvant** from the movie *Mo' Money* starring Damon Wayans; "45" B-side: (edit-no rap)	$3	▮[V]	Perspective 0010
11/14/92+	21	17		8 **Gangsta** ....S:10 / A:29 *(instrumental)*	$3	▮[V]	MCA 54555
8/21/93	38	19		9 **Something In Your Eyes** ....S:26 / A:54 *(instrumental)*	$3	▮[V]	MCA 54725

BELLE, Regina
R&B/AC/LP '93

Born on 7/17/63 in Englewood, New Jersey. Featured female vocalist with **The Manhattans**, 1986-87.

DEBUT	PEAK	WKS	Gold	A-side (Chart Hit)..........B-side	$	Sym	Label & Number
7/18/87	68	9		1 **Show Me The Way**..........*(instrumental)*	$3		Columbia 07080
2/6/88	89	3		2 **Without You**..........*The Higher You Climb* (Bryson) **PEABO BRYSON & REGINA BELLE** love theme from the movie *Leonard Pt. 6* starring **Bill Cosby**	$3	■	Elektra 69426
10/14/89	60	9		3 **Baby Come To Me** ....RB[1] *This Is Love*	$3		Columbia 68969
2/24/90	43	11		4 **Make It Like It Was** ....RB[1] A:38 / S:40 *Special Part Of Me*	$3	▮[V]	Columbia 73022
12/19/92+	❶[1]	23	●	5 **A Whole New World (Aladdin's Theme)** AC[6] A:❶[4] / S:2 *After The Kiss (instrumental)* **PEABO BRYSON and REGINA BELLE** from the Disney animated movie *Aladdin*	$3	▮[V]	Columbia 74751
4/3/93	52	17		6 **If I Could** ....S:35 / A:59 *Love*	$3	▮[V]	Columbia 74864

BELLE AND SEBASTIAN
LP '01

Pop group from Scotland: Stuart Murdoch and Isobel Campbell (vocals), Stevie Jackson (guitar), Chris Geddes (keyboards), Stuart David (bass) and Richard Colburn (drums). Named after a French children's TV series.

DEBUT	PEAK	WKS	Gold	A-side (Chart Hit)..........B-side	$	Sym	Label & Number
6/3/00	47[S]	4		1 **Legal Man**..........*Judy Is A Dick Slap / Winter Wooskie* **BELLE AND SEBASTIAN Featuring The Maisonettes**	$5	★	Jeepster/Matador 448
6/30/01	30[S]	3		2 **Jonathan David** ....*Take Your Carriage Clock And Shove It / The Loneliness Of A Middle Distance Runner*	$5	★[V]	Jeepster/Matador 510 ■
12/8/01	17[S]	8		3 **I'm Waking Up To Us**..........*I Love My Car / Marx and Engels*	$5	★	Jeepster/Matador 511

BELLE EPOQUE
'78

Female disco trio from Paris, France: Marcia Briscue, Evelyne Lenton and Judy Lisboa.

DEBUT	PEAK	WKS	Gold	A-side (Chart Hit)..........B-side	$	Sym	Label & Number
3/11/78	92	4		**Miss Broadway**..........*Losing You*	$5		Big Tree 16109

DEBUT	PEAK	WKS	Gold	A-side (Chart Hit)..................B-side	$	Sym	Label & Number
				BELLE STARS, The LP **'89**			
				Female group from England: Jennie McKeown (vocals), Sarah-Jane Owen and Stella Barker (guitars), Miranda Joyce and Clare Hirst (saxophones), Lesley Shone (bass) and Judy Parsons (drums).			
5/7/83	75	4		1 **Sign Of The Times**..................*Madness*	$4	■	Warner 29672
3/4/89	14	18		2 **Iko Iko**..................S:6 / A:18 *Las Vegas* (Hans Zimmer)	$4		Capitol 44343
				from the movie *Rain Man* starring Dustin Hoffman and Tom Cruise; earlier version featured on their 1983 album *The Belle Stars*			
				BELL NOTES, The **'59**			
				Rock and roll group from Long Island, New York: Carl Bonura (vocals, sax), Ray Ceroni (vocals, guitar), Lenny Giamblavo (bass), Peter Kane (piano) and John Casey (drums). Discovered by WADO DJ Alan Fredericks.			
1/26/59	6	16		1 **I've Had It**..................*Be Mine*	$25		Time 1004
5/4/59	76	7		2 **Old Spanish Town**..................*She Went That-A-Way*	$25		Time 1010
8/29/60	96	2		3 **Shortnin' Bread**..................*To Each His Own*	$25		Madison 136
				based on a traditional folk song from 1905			
				BELLS, The LP **'71**			
				Pop group from Montreal, Quebec, Canada: Jacki Ralph and Cliff Edwards (vocals), Charles Clarke (guitar), Dennis Will (keyboards), Michael Waye (bass) and Douglas Gravelle (drums).			
1/9/71	95	5		1 **Fly Little White Dove Fly**..................*Follow The Sun*	$5		Polydor 15016
3/6/71	7	14	●	2 **Stay Awhile**..................*Sing A Song Of Freedom*	$5		Polydor 15023
6/26/71	64	5		3 **I Love You Lady Dawn**..................*Rain*	$5		Polydor 15027
				BELLUS, Tony **'59**			
				Born Anthony Bellusci on 4/17/36 in Chicago, Illinois. Pop singer/accordionist. First recorded for Shi-Fi in 1958.			
4/27/59	25	26		**Robbin' The Cradle**..................*Valentine Girl*	$25		NRC 023
				BELLY ROK/BUB/LP **'93**			
				Alternative-rock group from Newport, Rhode Island: Tanya Donelly (vocals, guitar) with brothers Thomas (guitar) and Chris (drums) Gorman. Gail Greenwood (bass) joined by mid-1993. Donelly was a member of Throwing Muses (with stepsister Kristin Hersh) and **The Breeders**.			
5/15/93	95	4		**Feed The Tree**..................MR[3] *Star*	$4	▮[V]	Sire/Reprise 18570
				BELMONTS, The BUB/LP **'61**			
				Doo-wop trio from the Bronx, New York: Angelo D'Aleo, Fred Milano and Carlo Mastrangelo. Sang with **Dion** from 1957-60. Named after Belmont Avenue in the Bronx, New York. Frank Lyndon replaced Mastrangelo in May 1962.			
5/22/61	18	11		1 **Tell Me Why** *Smoke From Your Cigarette*	$30		Sabrina 500
				first released on Surprise 1000 in 1961 ($125); original version by Norman Fox & The Rob-Roys in 1957 on Back Beat 501 ($50)			
9/4/61	57	9		2 **Don't Get Around Much Anymore**..................*Searching For A New Love*	$30		Sabrina 501
				written in 1940 by Duke Ellington; #2 hit for the Ink Spots in 1943			
12/25/61+	75	4		3 **I Need Some One**..................*That American Dance*	$30		Sabina 502
7/21/62	28	14		4 **Come On Little Angel**..................*How About Me*	$25		Sabina 505
11/17/62	53	6		5 **Diddle-Dee-Dum (What Happens When Your Love Has Gone)**..................*Farewell*	$25		Sabina 507
4/20/63	86	3		6 **Ann-Marie**..................*Ac-cent-tchu-ate The Positive*	$25		Sabina 509
9/26/81	81	4		7 **Let's Put The Fun Back In Rock N Roll**..................*Your Mama Ain't Always Right*	$7		MiaSound 1002
				FREDDY CANNON & THE BELMONTS			
				BELUSHI, John — see BLUES BROTHERS			
				BELVIN, Jesse R&B **'59**			
				Born on 12/15/33 in Texarkana, Texas; raised in Los Angeles, California. Died in a car crash on 2/6/60 (age 26). Recorded with Marvin Phillips as "Jesse & Marvin." A pivotal figure in the development of the R&B sound on the West Coast. His classic recording of "Goodnight My Love" was a #7 R&B hit in 1956. Co-wrote "Earth Angel" with Curtis Williams of **The Penguins**. Also see **The Cliques**, **The Chargers**, and **The Shields**.			
12/29/58+	81	4		1 **Funny**..................*Pledging My Love*	$25		RCA Victor 7387
3/30/59	31	13		2 **Guess Who**..................*My Girl Is Just Enough Woman For Me*	$25		RCA Victor 7469
				written by Jesse's wife, Jo Anne Belvin; Shorty Rogers (orch. and chorus, above 2)			
	★210★			**BENATAR, Pat** ROK/LP **'85**			
				Born Patricia Andrzejewski on 1/10/53 in Lindenhurst, Long Island, New York. Rock singer. Married her producer/guitarist Neil Geraldo on 2/20/82. Acted in the movie *Union City* and the 1989 ABC afterschool TV special *Torn Between Two Fathers*.			
				1)We Belong 2)Love Is A Battlefield 3)Hit Me With Your Best Shot			
12/22/79+	23	18		1 **Heartbreaker**..................*My Clone Sleeps Alone*	$5	■	Chrysalis 2395
4/5/80	27	14		2 **We Live For Love**..................*So Sincere*	$5	■	Chrysalis 2419
7/26/80	42	11		3 **You Better Run**..................*Out-A-Touch*	$5		Chrysalis 2450
10/4/80	9	24	●	4 **Hit Me With Your Best Shot**..................*Prisoner Of Love*	$4	■	Chrysalis 2464
1/17/81	18	18		5 **Treat Me Right**..................*Never Wanna Leave You*	$4	■	Chrysalis 2487
7/18/81	17	15		6 **Fire And Ice**..................*Hard To Believe*	$4	■	Chrysalis 2529
10/3/81	38	11		7 **Promises In The Dark**..................*Evil Genius*	$4	■	Chrysalis 2555
10/16/82	13	16		8 **Shadows Of The Night**..................*The Victim* (ROK #23)	$4	■	Chrysalis 2647
2/5/83	20	14		9 **Little Too Late**..................*Fight It Out*	$4	■	Chrysalis 03536
4/23/83	39	10		10 **Looking For A Stranger**..................*I'll Do It*	$4	■	Chrysalis 42688
9/24/83	5	22	●	11 **Love Is A Battlefield**..................AR[4] *Hell Is For Children (live)*	$4	■	Chrysalis 42732
10/27/84+	5	20		12 **We Belong** A:2 / S:3 *Suburban King*	$4	■	Chrysalis 42826
1/19/85	36	9		13 **Ooh Ooh Song**..................*La Cancion Ooh Ooh*	$4	■	Chrysalis 42843
7/6/85	10	17	●	14 **Invincible**..................S:9 / A:9 *(instrumental)*	$4	■	Chrysalis 41507
				theme from the movie *Legend of Billie Jean* starring Helen Slater			
11/23/85+	28	13		15 **Sex As A Weapon**..................A:28 *Red Vision*	$4	■	Chrysalis 42927
2/15/86	54	8		16 **Le Bel Age**..................*Walking In The Underground*	$4		Chrysalis 42968
				French title (pronounced: lah-bel-awj) translates as "the best year"			
7/2/88	19	17		17 **All Fired Up**..................S:11 / A:30 *Cool Zero*	$4	■	Chrysalis 43268
12/29/01+	37[S]	2		18 **Christmas in America**..................*(instrumental) / Please Come Home For Christmas* [X]	$7	★	Gold Circle 58804

DEBUT	PEAK	WKS	Gold	A-side (Chart Hit)...B-side	$	Sym	Label & Number

BENÉT, Eric

R&B/BUB/LP **'99**

Born Eric Benét Jordan on 10/5/69 in Milwaukee, Wisconsin. R&B singer/songwriter. Married actress Halle Berry on 1/19/2001.

DEBUT	PEAK	WKS	Gold	A-side (Chart Hit)...B-side	$	Sym	Label & Number
3/20/99	**55**	14		1 **Georgy Porgy**...A:32 / S:50 *(4 remixes)* **ERIC BENÉT featuring Faith Evans**	$7	★*V	Warner 44612
7/3/99	**21**	22	●	2 **Spend My Life With You**...RB^2 S:11 / A:34 *Georgy Porgy* (w/**Faith Evans**) **ERIC BENÉT featuring Tamia** "45" issued for above 2 on Warner 16958	$4	★V	Warner 16958

BENNETT, Boyd, And His Rockets

'55

Born on 12/7/24 in Muscle Shoals, Alabama. Died on 6/2/2002 (age 77). Attended high school in Tennessee; formed first band there. Later became a DJ in Kentucky.

DEBUT	PEAK	WKS	Gold	A-side (Chart Hit)...B-side	$	Sym	Label & Number
7/9/55	**5**	17		1 **Seventeen**...S:5 / J:8 / A:9 / T:28 *Little Ole You-All*	$40		King 1470
11/12/55	**39**	8		2 **My Boy-Flat Top**...T:39 *Banjo Rock And Roll* Joe "Big Moe" Muzey (vocal, above 2)	$40		King 1494
4/14/56	**63**	10		3 **Blue Suede Shoes**...T:63 *Mumbles Blues*	$35		King 4903
9/21/59	**73**	4		4 **Boogie Bear** *[BOYD BENNETT]*...*A Boy Can Tell* [N] novelty tune based on the *Yogi Bear* (with Boo Boo) cartoon series	$20		Mercury 71479

BENNETT, Joe, and The Sparkletones

BUB **'57**

Teen rock and roll band from Spartanburg, South Carolina: Joe Bennett (vocals, guitar; born in 1941), Howard Childress (guitar), Wayne Arthur (bass) and Irving Denton (drums).

DEBUT	PEAK	WKS	Gold	A-side (Chart Hit)...B-side	$	Sym	Label & Number
8/26/57	**17**	19		1 **Black Slacks**...T:17 / S:18 / A:21 *Boppin' Rock Boogie*	$30		ABC-Paramount 9837
12/23/57	**42**	8		2 **Penny Loafers And Bobby Socks**...S:42 / T:43 *Rocket*	$30		ABC-Paramount 9867

BENNETT, Tony ★178★

MEM/POP/AC/BUB/LP **'51**

Born Anthony Dominick Benedetto on 8/3/26 in Queens, New York. One of the top jazz vocalists of the past 40 years. Worked local clubs while in high school, sang in U.S. Army bands. Breakthrough with Bob Hope in 1949 who suggested that he change his then-stage name, Joe Bari, to Tony Bennett. Audition record of "Boulevard Of Broken Dreams" earned a Columbia contract in 1950. Appeared in the movie *The Oscar*. Won Grammy's Lifetime Achievement Award in 2001. Charted 3 huge #1 hits from 1951-53: "Because Of You," "Cold, Cold Heart" and "Rags To Riches."

1)In The Middle Of An Island 2)From The Candy Store On The Corner 3)I Wanna Be Around 4)Can You Find It In Your Heart 5)The Good Life

DEBUT	PEAK	WKS	Gold	A-side (Chart Hit)...B-side	$	Sym	Label & Number
4/14/56	**16**	19		1 **Can You Find It In Your Heart**...S:16 / J:18 / T:19 / A:20 *Forget Her*	$15		Columbia 40667
8/18/56	**11**	12		2 **From The Candy Store On The Corner To The Chapel On The Hill /**...A:11 / T:33 Lois Winter (female vocal)			
8/18/56	**38**	14		3 **Happiness Street (Corner Sunshine Square)**...T:38	$15		Columbia 40726
11/10/56	**18**	8		4 **The Autumn Waltz /** A:18 / T:41			
11/10/56	**46**	14		5 **Just In Time**...T:46 from the Broadway show *Bells Are Ringing* starring Judy Holliday	$15		Columbia 40770
5/20/57	**49**	9		6 **One For My Baby (And One More For The Road)**...T:49 *No Hard Feelings* from the 1943 movie *The Sky's The Limit* starring Fred Astaire	$15		Columbia 40907
8/5/57	**9**	21		7 **In The Middle Of An Island /** S:9 / T:9 / A:13			
8/19/57	**93**	1		8 **I Am**...T:93 / S:flip	$15		Columbia 40965
11/18/57	**22**	2		9 **Ca, C'est L'amour**...A:22 / T:96 *I Never Felt More Like Falling In Love* written by Cole Porter; from the movie *Les Girls* starring Gene Kelly	$12		Columbia 41032
6/23/58	**23**	8		10 **Young And Warm And Wonderful**...A:23 / S:42 / T:57 *Now I Lay Me Down To Sleep*	$12		Columbia 41172
9/8/58	**20**	13		11 **Firefly**...H:20 / S:45 *The Night That Heaven Fell*	$12	■	Columbia 41237
8/17/59	**73**	6		12 **Smile**...*You Can't Love Them All* written in 1936 by Charlie Chaplin for his movie *Modern Times*; #10 hit for **Nat "King" Cole** in 1954	$12		Columbia 41434
12/21/59+	**74**	5		13 **Climb Ev'ry Mountain**...*Ask Anyone In Love* from the Rodgers & Hammerstein Broadway musical *The Sound Of Music* starring Mary Martin	$12		Columbia 41520
8/11/62	**19**	21		14 **I Left My Heart In San Francisco**...*Once Upon A Time* new lyrics to this song written in 1954; issued with 2 different picture sleeves; 1962 Grammy winner: Record of the Year	$10	■	Columbia 42332
1/12/63	**14**	16		15 **I Wanna Be Around /**			
1/5/63	**85**	8		16 **I Will Live My Life For You**...	$10		Columbia 42634
5/11/63	**18**	10		17 **The Good Life /**			
6/8/63	**92**	2		18 **Spring In Manhattan**...	$10		Columbia 42779
7/20/63	**70**	7		19 **This Is All I Ask /** written in 1958 by band leader **Gordon Jenkins**			
7/27/63	**99**	2		20 **True Blue Lou**...	$10		Columbia 42820
10/12/63	**54**	7		21 **Don't Wait Too Long**...*Limehouse Blues*	$10		Columbia 42886
12/21/63+	**52**	9		22 **The Little Boy**...*The Moment Of Truth* (#127)	$10		Columbia 42931
3/21/64	**94**	5		23 **When Joanna Loved Me**...*The Kid's A Dreamer*	$10	□	Columbia 42996
8/22/64	**94**	3		24 **A Taste Of Honey /** tune written and introduced by **Bobby Scott** in the 1960 Broadway show *A Taste of Honey*			
7/11/64	**99**	1		25 **It's A Sin To Tell A Lie**... [L] #1 hit for Fats Waller in 1936; recorded in Las Vegas	$8	■	Columbia 43073
10/3/64	**33**	10		26 **Who Can I Turn To (When Nobody Needs Me)**...*Waltz For Debby* from the Broadway musical *The Roar Of The Greasepaint* starring **Anthony Newley**	$8	□	Columbia 43141
2/13/65	**34**	9		27 **If I Ruled The World**...*Take The Moment* The Will Bronson Chorus (backing vocals); from the Broadway musical *Pickwick* starring Harry Secombe	$8	□	Columbia 43220
7/24/65	**84**	4		28 **Fly Me To The Moon (In Other Words)**...*How Insensitive* The Ralph Sharon Trio (backing vocals); written in 1954 with the title "In Other Words"	$8		Columbia 43331
11/13/65	**95**	6		29 **Love Theme From"The Sandpiper" (The Shadow Of Your Smile)**...*I'll Only Miss Her When I Think Of Her* Academy Award-winning song from the movie *The Sandpiper* starring Elizabeth Taylor and **Richard Burton**	$8	□	Columbia 43431

DEBUT	PEAK	WKS	Gold	A-side (Chart Hit)...B-side	$	Sym	Label & Number
				BENNETT, Tony — Cont'd			
7/23/66	89	4		30 **Georgia Rose** ... *The Very Thought Of You* Urbie Green (trombone solo)	$8		Columbia 43715
10/28/67	91	5		31 **For Once In My Life** ... *How Do You Say Auf Wiedersehn* Bennett's musical arrangers and conductors: Ralph Burns (#12, 19, 20, 30), **Ray Conniff** (#6), **Don Costa** (#18, 27, 28), **Frank DeVol** (#10, 13), **Ray Ellis** (#7, 8, 11), **Percy Faith** (#1-5), **Neal Hefti** (#9), **Dick Hyman** (#21, 22, 24), Johnny Mandel (#29), Marty Manning (#14-17, 23), Ralph Sharon (#25), George Siravo (#26) and Torrie Zito (#31)	$8		Columbia 44258
	★349★			**BENSON, George** R&B/BUB/AC/LP **'80** Born on 3/22/43 in Pittsburgh, Pennsylvania. R&B-jazz guitarist. Played guitar from age eight. Played in **Brother Jack McDuff**'s trio in 1963. House musician at CTI Records to early 1970s. Influenced by **Wes Montgomery**. Member of Fuse One. *1)Give Me The Night 2)Turn Your Love Around 3)On Broadway*			
6/12/76	10	19		1 **This Masquerade** ... *Lady* written by **Leon Russell** (B-side of his 1972 hit single "Tight Rope"); 1976 Grammy winner: Record of the Year	$5		Warner 8209
10/16/76	63	6		2 **Breezin'** ... *Six To Four* [I] written by **Bobby Womack**	$5		Warner 8268
7/2/77	71	5		3 **Gonna Love You More** ... *Valdez In The Country*	$5		Warner 8377
7/30/77	24	14		4 **The Greatest Love Of All** ... *Ali's Theme* (Michael Masser) from the movie *The Greatest* starring Muhammad Ali	$5	■	Arista 0251
3/11/78	7	18		5 **On Broadway** ... *We As Love* also issued with a promo sleeve (Warner 0370)	$4	■	Warner 8542
2/24/79	18	15		6 **Love Ballad** ... *You're Never Too Far From Me*	$4	■	Warner 8759
7/5/80	4	23		7 **Give Me The Night** RB[3] *Dinorah, Dinorah*	$4	■	Warner 49505
10/18/80	61	6		8 **Love X Love** ... *Love Dance*	$4		Warner 49570
8/29/81	46	10		9 **Love All The Hurt Away** ... *Whole Lot Of Me* (Franklin) **ARETHA FRANKLIN AND GEORGE BENSON**	$4		Arista 0624
10/24/81+	5	22		10 **Turn Your Love Around** ... RB[1] *Nature Boy*	$4	■	Warner 49846
2/20/82	52	9		11 **Never Give Up On A Good Thing** ... *Livin' Inside Your Love*	$4	■	Warner 50005
5/14/83	43	10		12 **Inside Love (So Personal)** ... *In Search Of A Dream*	$4	■	Warner 29649
7/23/83	30	13		13 **Lady Love Me (One More Time)** ... *Being With You*	$4		Warner 29563
12/15/84+	48	13		14 **20/20** ... *Shark Bite*	$4	■	Warner 29120
				BENSON, Jo Jo — see SCOTT, Peggy			

DEBUT	PEAK	WKS	Gold	A-side (Chart Hit)...B-side	$	Sym	Label & Number
				BENTON, Brook ★46★ R&B/BUB/AC **'60** Born Benjamin Franklin Peay on 9/19/31 in Camden, South Carolina. Died of spinal meningitis on 4/9/88 (age 56). R&B singer/songwriter. In The Camden Jubilee Singers. To New York in 1948, joined Bill Langford's Langfordaires. With Jerusalem Stars in 1951. First recorded under own name for Okeh in 1953. Wrote "Looking Back," "A Lover's Question," "It's Just A Matter Of Time" and "Endlessly." *1)The Boll Weevil Song 2)It's Just A Matter Of Time 3)Hotel Happiness 4)Rainy Night In Georgia 5)Baby (You've Got What It Takes)*			
3/10/58	82	4		1 **A Million Miles From Nowhere** ... T:82 *Devoted*	$25		Vik 0311
1/26/59	3	18	●	2 **It's Just A Matter Of Time /** RB[9]			
2/23/59	78	4		3 **Hurtin' Inside** ...	$20		Mercury 71394
4/20/59	12	13		4 **Endlessly /**			
5/18/59	38	7		5 **So Close** ...	$20		Mercury 71443
7/13/59	16	14		6 **Thank You Pretty Baby /** RB[4]			
7/20/59	82	1		7 **With All Of My Heart** ...	$20		Mercury 71478
10/19/59	6	16		8 **So Many Ways** ... RB[3] *I Want You Forever*	$20		Mercury 71512
12/21/59	66	5		9 **This Time Of The Year** ... *Nothing In The World* [X] released on Mercury 71558 in 1959; reissued in 1960 on Mercury 71730 with a picture sleeve	$20		Mercury 71554
1/25/60	5	15	●	10 **Baby (You've Got What It Takes)** ... RB[10] *I Do* **DINAH WASHINGTON & BROOK BENTON**	$20		Mercury 71565
4/11/60	37	9		11 **The Ties That Bind /**			
4/18/60	58	6		12 **Hither And Thither And Yon** ...	$20	■	Mercury 71566
5/23/60	7	13		13 **A Rockin' Good Way (To Mess Around And Fall In Love)** ... RB[4] *I Believe* **DINAH WASHINGTON & BROOK BENTON** tune first recorded by **The Spaniels** in 1958	$20	■	Mercury 71629
8/8/60	7	17		14 **Kiddio /** RB[9] tune introduced by **Teddy Randazzo** in the 1957 movie *Mr. Rock And Roll* starring Alan Freed			
8/22/60	16	12		15 **The Same One** ...	$20	■	Mercury 71652
11/14/60	24	10		16 **Fools Rush In (Where Angels Fear To Tread) /** #3 hit for Glenn Miller in 1940			
12/26/60	93	1		17 **Someday You'll Want Me To Want You** ... #5 hit for the **Mills Brothers** in 1949	$15	■	Mercury 71722
2/13/61	11	12		18 **Think Twice /**			
2/6/61	28	8		19 **For My Baby** ...	$15	■	Mercury 71774
5/15/61	2[3]	16		20 **The Boll Weevil Song** AC[3] *Your Eyes* [N] The Mike Stewart Singers (backing vocals); adaptation of a traditional American folk song	$15	■	Mercury 71820
8/21/61	20	8		21 **Frankie And Johnny /** version of mid-19th century traditional folk song			
10/2/61	45	5		22 **It's Just A House Without You** ...	$15	■	Mercury 71859
11/20/61+	15	10		23 **Revenge** ... *Really, Really*	$15	■	Mercury 71903
1/13/62	19	9		24 **Shadrack /** written in 1931 as "Shadrack, Meshack, Abednigo" (friends of Daniel, in The Bible)			
1/13/62	77	2		25 **The Lost Penny** ... [S]	$15	■	Mercury 71912
2/17/62	43	7		26 **Walk On The Wild Side** ... *Somewhere In The Used To Be* title song from the movie starring Laurence Harvey; issued with 2 different picture sleeves	$15	■	Mercury 71925

DEBUT	PEAK	WKS	Gold	A-side (Chart Hit)..........B-side	$	Sym	Label & Number
				BENTON, Brook — Cont'd			
5/5/62	45	8		27 **Hit Record** .... *Thanks To The Fool* (#106)	$12	■	Mercury 71962
				issued with 2 different picture sleeves (a blue background and an orange background)			
8/25/62	13	10		28 **Lie To Me** .... *With The Touch Of Your Hand* (#120)	$12	■	Mercury 72024
11/24/62+	3	12		29 **Hotel Happiness** /			
12/8/62	89	1		30 **Still Waters Run Deep**	$12	■	Mercury 72055
				The Merry Melody Singers (backing vocals, above 3)			
3/16/63	28	8		31 **I Got What I Wanted** /			
3/9/63	59	8		32 **Dearer Than Life**	$12	■	Mercury 72099
6/15/63	22	9		33 **My True Confession** .... *Tender Years*	$12	■	Mercury 72135
9/7/63	32	10		34 **Two Tickets To Paradise** .... *Don't Hate Me*	$12	■	Mercury 72177
				issued with 2 different picture sleeves (a glossy sleeve and a thin paper sleeve)			
11/30/63	3^{X}	6		35 **You're All I Want For Christmas** .... *This Time Of The Year* [X]	$12	■	Mercury 72214
				X: 3/'63; 21/'64; different song than the same-titled hit by **Frankie Laine** in 1948			
1/25/64	35	7		36 **Going Going Gone** .... *After Midnight*	$12	■	Mercury 72230
5/9/64	43	8		37 **Too Late To Turn Back Now** /			
5/16/64	47	7		38 **Another Cup Of Coffee**	$12	■	Mercury 72266
				issued with 2 different picture sleeves			
7/18/64	75	7		39 **A House Is Not A Home** .... *Come On Back*	$12	■	Mercury 72303
				title song from the movie starring Shelley Winters			
10/3/64	53	7		40 **Lumberjack** .... *Don't Do What I Did (Do What I Say)*	$12	■	Mercury 72333
12/19/64+	67	4		41 **Do It Right** .... *Please, Please Make It Easy* (#119)	$10	■	Mercury 72365
7/3/65	100	1		42 **Love Me Now** .... *A Sleepin' At The Foot Of The Bed*	$10		Mercury 72446
11/13/65	53	7		43 **Mother Nature, Father Time** .... *You're Mine (And I Love You)*	$10	■	RCA Victor 8693
8/19/67	78	4		44 **Laura (Tell Me What He's Got That I Ain't Got)** .... *You're The Reason I'm Living*	$10		Reprise 0611
10/26/68	99	2		45 **Do Your Own Thing** .... *I Just Don't Know What To Do With Myself*	$8		Cotillion 44007
7/5/69	74	6		46 **Nothing Can Take The Place Of You** .... *Woman Without Love*	$8		Cotillion 44034
1/10/70	4	15	●	47 **Rainy Night In Georgia** .... RB[1] *Where Do I Go From Here*	$8		Cotillion 44057
				written by **Tony Joe White**			
4/18/70	72	6		48 **My Way** .... *A Little Bit Of Soap*	$8		Cotillion 44072
5/30/70	45	7		49 **Don't It Make You Want To Go Home** .... *I've Gotta Be Me*	$8		Cotillion 44078
12/26/70+	67	6		50 **Shoes** .... *Let Me Fix It*	$8		Cotillion 44093
				BROOK BENTON With The Dixie Flyers (above 2)			
				Benton's musical arrangers and conductors: Stan Applebaum (#21, 26), Luchi DeJesus (#35, 36, 40, 41), Malcolm Dodds (#23-25, 27, 34), **Ray Ellis** (#38), Belford Hendricks (#2-10, 13-20, 22, 37), **Bill Justis** (#31-33), Jerry Kennedy (#28-30), Andy Lorber (#39), Arif Mardin (#46-50), **Billy Mure** (#1), Fred Norman (#11, 12), Clyde Otis (#43), Mike Stoller (#45), **Billy Strange** (#44) and Teacho Wiltshire (#42)			
				BENZINO LP '02			
				Born Raymond Scott in Boston, Massachusetts. Male rapper/producer.			
2/2/02	75^{S}	1		1 **Bootee** .... *(3 versions)*	$7	T	Surrender 015631
				BENZINO f/ Fabolous & G-Dep			
				samples "The Bertha Butt Boogie" by **The Jimmy Castor Bunch**			
10/12/02	82	18		2 **Rock The Party** .... S:32 *(3 versions)*	$6	T	Elektra 67330
				BERGEN, Polly LP '58			
				Born Nellie Burgin on 7/4/30 in Knoxville, Tennessee. Singer/actress. Not related to actress Candice Bergen.			
12/15/58	67	6		**Come Prima (Koma Preema)** .... *Au Revoir Again*	$12		Columbia 41275
				Glenn Osser (orch); translation of this Italian song: "For The First Time"			
				BERLIN LP '86			
				Electro-pop group from Los Angeles, California: Terri Nunn (vocals), Rick Olsen (guitar), Matt Reid and David Diamond (keyboards), John Crawford (bass) and Rob Brill (drums). Pared down to a trio in 1985 with Nunn, Crawford and Brill. Nunn was a teen actress, appearing on such TV shows as *Lou Grant*.			
3/5/83	62	7		1 **Sex (I'm A...)** .... *Tell Me Why*	$4	■	Geffen 29747
5/28/83	58	10		2 **The Metro** .... *World Of Smiles*	$4	■	Geffen 29638
9/24/83	82	3		3 **Masquerade** .... *Live Sex*	$4	■	Geffen 29504
3/10/84	23	17		4 **No More Words** .... *Rumor Of Love*	$4	■	Geffen 29360
				also on the B-side of "Crazy For You" by **Madonna**			
6/30/84	74	4		5 **Now It's My Turn** .... *Lost In The Crowd*	$4	■	Geffen 29283
6/21/86	❶[1]	21	●	6 **Take My Breath Away** S:❶[1] / A:2 *Radar Radio* (**Giorgio Moroder** w/Joe Pizzulo)	$3	■	Columbia 05903
				love theme from the movie *Top Gun* starring Tom Cruise; also see re-entry at #8 below			
10/25/86	82	5		7 **Like Flames** .... *Hideaway*	$3	■	Geffen 28563
1/11/92	60^{A}	9		8 **Take My Breath Away** .... [R]			album cut
				BERLIN featuring TERRI NUNN			
				remix of #6 above (available as a promo CD single on Geffen 4369)			
				BERLIN PHILHARMONIC '70			
				Symphony orchestra conducted by Karl Böhm (died on 8/14/81, age 86).			
1/3/70	90	4		**Theme Music For The Film "2001" A Space Odyssey from Also Sprach Zarathustra** ..... *Elvira Madigan Theme* (Geza Anda) [I]	$7		Polydor 15009
				theme from the movie *"2001" A Space Odyssey* starring a computer: HAL 9000			
				BERMUDAS, The '64			
				White "girl group": Rickie Page (wife of producer George Motola) and her two daughters. Rickie was one of The Crypt-Kickers with **Bobby "Boris" Pickett**.			
4/18/64	62	10		**Donnie** .... *Chu Sen Ling*	$15		Era 3125
				BERNARD, Crystal — see CETERA, Peter			
				BERNARD, Rod BUB '59			
				Born on 8/12/40 in Opelousas, Louisiana. Rock and roll singer/guitarist.			
3/9/59	20	12		1 **This Should Go On Forever** .... *Pardon, Mr. Gordon*	$25		Argo 5327
				first released on JIN 105 in 1958 ($50)			
11/9/59	74	9		2 **One More Chance** .... *Shedding Teardrops Over You*	$20		Mercury 71507
				written by J.P. Richardson (**The Big Bopper**)			

DEBUT	PEAK	WKS	Gold	A-side (Chart Hit)...B-side	$	Sym	Label & Number

BERNSTEIN, Elmer, and Orchestra — BUB '56

Born on 4/4/22 in New York City, New York. Composer/conductor for over 60 movie soundtracks.

DEBUT	PEAK	WKS	Gold	A-side (Chart Hit)...B-side	$	Sym	Label & Number
3/24/56	16	15		**"Main Title" From "The Man With The Golden Arm"**....S:16 / T:32 *Clark Street* [I]	$15		Decca 29869
				Shelly Manne (drums); title song from the movie *The Man With The Golden Arm* starring **Frank Sinatra**			

BERRY, Chuck ★123★ — R&B/BUB/LP '58

Born Charles Edward Anderson Berry on 10/18/26 in St. Louis, Missouri. Acclaimed as one of rock and roll's most influential artists. Muddy Waters introduced Berry to Leonard Chess (Chess Records) in Chicago. First recording, "Maybellene," was an instant success. Appeared in the movie *Rock, Rock, Rock* in 1956 and several others. Incarcerated for violating the Mann Act (1962-63) and income tax evasion (1979). Won Grammy's Lifetime Achievement Award in 1984. Inducted into the Rock and Roll Hall of Fame in 1986. Movie documentary/concert tribute to Berry, *Hail! Hail! Rock 'N' Roll*, released in 1987.

1)My Ding-A-Ling 2)Sweet Little Sixteen 3)School Day 4)Maybellene 5)Johnny B. Goode

DEBUT	PEAK	WKS	Gold	A-side (Chart Hit)...B-side	$	Sym	Label & Number
8/20/55	5	11		1 **Maybellene**....RB[11] S:5 / J:6 / A:13 / T:42 *Wee Wee Hours* (R&B #10)	$50		Chess 1604
6/30/56	29	5		2 **Roll Over Beethoven**....T:29 *Drifting Heart*	$50		Chess 1626
				CHUCK BERRY and His Combo (above 2)			
				above 2 are Grammy Hall of Fame Award winners			
4/6/57	3	26		3 **School Day**....RB[5] S:3 / T:5 / A:6 / J:7 *Deep Feeling*	$50		Chess 1653
				some pressings show title as "School Day (Ring! Ring! Goes The Bell)"			
7/29/57	57	7		4 **Oh Baby Doll**....T:57 *Lajaunda*	$50		Chess 1664
11/11/57	8	19		5 **Rock & Roll Music**....T:8 / S:9 *Blue Feeling*	$30		Chess 1671
2/17/58	2[3]	16		6 **Sweet Little Sixteen**....RB[3] S:2 / T:2 / A:5 *Reelin And Rocking*	$30		Chess 1683
				also see **The Beach Boys**' hit "Surfin' U.S.A." in 1974; see #37 below for a live version of the B-side			
4/28/58	8	15		7 **Johnny B. Goode**....T:8 / S:9 / A:16 *Around & Around*	$30		Chess 1691
7/28/58	81	2		8 **Beautiful Delilah**....H:81 *Vacation Time*	$30		Chess 1697
8/25/58	18	10		9 **Carol**....H:18 / S:29 *Hey Pedro*	$30		Chess 1700
11/10/58	47	9		10 **Sweet Little Rock And Roll /**			
11/17/58	83	5		11 **Joe Joe Gun**....	$30		Chess 1709
12/15/58	69	3		12 **Run Rudolph Run /** [X]			
12/15/58	71	3		13 **Merry Christmas Baby**.... [X]	$40		Chess 1714
				#3 R&B hit in 1947 for Johnny Moore's Three Blazers (w/**Charles Brown**)			
2/16/59	60	5		14 **Anthony Boy**....*That's My Desire*	$30		Chess 1716
3/30/59	32	13		15 **Almost Grown /**			
4/13/59	80	4		16 **Little Queenie**....	$30		Chess 1722
				from the movie *Go Johnny Go* starring Alan Freed			
6/22/59	37	8		17 **Back In The U.S.A.**....*Memphis, Tennessee*	$30		Chess 1729
				Berry had 5 non-charted Chess "45s" during the '50s: "Thirty Days"/"Together" (1610); "No Money Down"/"Down Bound Train" (1615); "Too Much Monkey Business"/"Brown Eyed Handsome Man" (1635); "You Can't Catch Me"/"Havana Moon" (1645); and "Broken Arrow"/"Childhood Sweetheart" (1737)			
2/15/60	42	6		18 **Too Pooped To Pop "Casey" /**			
2/1/60	64	8		19 **Let It Rock**....	$30		Chess 1747
3/7/64	23	10		20 **Nadine (Is It You?)**....*O Rangutang*	$20		Chess 1883
5/23/64	10	11		21 **No Particular Place To Go**....*You Two*	$20	■	Chess 1898
8/1/64	14	9		22 **You Never Can Tell**....*Brenda Lee*	$20	■	Chess 1906
10/24/64	54	6		23 **Little Marie**....*Go, Bobby Soxer*	$20	■	Chess 1912
				answer song to Berry's (and **Johnny Rivers**') hit "Memphis" (see B-side of #17 above)			
12/12/64+	41	7		24 **Promised Land**....*Things I Used To Do*	$20	■	Chess 1916
				above 4 picture sleeves feature the same photo of Berry			
4/3/65	95	4		25 **Dear Dad**....*Lonely School Days*	$20		Chess 1926
8/5/72	❶[2]	17	●	26 **My Ding-A-Ling** *Johnny B. Goode (live)* [L-N]	$7		Chess 2131
				Average White Band (backing band); original version recorded by Dave Bartholomew in 1952 on King 4544 ($200); then by The Bees in 1954 on Imperial 5314 ($300) as "Toy Bell"; recorded by Berry in 1966 as "My Tambourine"			
12/2/72+	27	13		27 **Reelin' & Rockin'**....*Let's Boogie* [L]	$7		Chess 2136
				above 2 recorded in Coventry, England; Berry wrote all of his hits (except #12, 13, 18 & 26)			

BERRY, John — C&W/LP '96

Born on 9/14/59 in Aiken, South Carolina; raised in Atlanta, Georgia. Country singer/songwriter/guitarist. Survived a motorcycle crash in 1981 and brain surgery in 1994.

DEBUT	PEAK	WKS	Gold	A-side (Chart Hit)...B-side	$	Sym	Label & Number
11/16/96	75[S]	1		**Change My Mind**....BUB:103 *Standing On The Edge Of Goodbye*	$4	■[V]	Capitol 58577
				"45": Capitol 19251; B-side: "Time To Be A Man"			

BERTRAND, Plastic — '78

Born Roger Jouret on 2/24/58 in Brussels, Belgium. Male punk rocker.

DEBUT	PEAK	WKS	Gold	A-side (Chart Hit)...B-side	$	Sym	Label & Number
4/29/78	47	10		**Ca Plane Pour Moi**....*Pogo Pogo* [F]	$6	■	Sire 1020
				translation of French song: "It's Fine With Me"			

BETTERS, Harold — '64

Born in Connellsville, Pennsylvania. Black jazz trombonist.

DEBUT	PEAK	WKS	Gold	A-side (Chart Hit)...B-side	$	Sym	Label & Number
11/14/64	74	8		**Do Anything You Wanna (Part I)**....*(Part II)* [I]	$12		Gateway 747

BETTER THAN EZRA — ROK/BUB/LP '95

Rock trio from New Orleans, Louisiana: Kevin Griffin (vocals, guitar, songwriter), Tom Drummond (bass) and Cary Bonnecaze (drums). Travis McNabb replaced Bonnecaze by 1996.

DEBUT	PEAK	WKS	Gold	A-side (Chart Hit)...B-side	$	Sym	Label & Number
7/1/95	30	20		1 **Good** MR[5] A:21 / S:40 *Circle Of Friends (live)*	$3	■	Elektra 64428
7/29/95	48[A]	20		2 **In The Blood**....			album cut
11/25/95	71	12		3 **Rosealia**....A:67 *In The Blood (live)*	$3	■	Elektra 64352
				above 3 from the album *Deluxe* on Elektra 61784			
8/10/96	62[A]	10		4 **King Of New Orleans**....			album cut

DEBUT	PEAK	WKS	Gold	A-side (Chart Hit)...B-side	$	Sym	Label & Number
				BETTER THAN EZRA — Cont'd			
12/21/96+	**48**	20		5 **Desperately Wanting** ....A:51 *Palace Hotel*	$3	▮	Elektra 64228
				above 2 from the album *Friction, Baby* on Elektra 61944			
3/13/99	**78**	4		6 **At The Stars** A:69			album cut
				from the album *How Does Your Garden Grow?* on Elektra 62247			
				BETTY BOO '90			
				Born Allison Clarkson on 3/6/70 in London, England. Female dance singer.			
11/3/90	**90**	4		**Doin' The Do** ....*Shame*	$4	▮	Sire 19570
				BEVERLEY SISTERS, The '57			
				Vocal trio from London, England: sisters Joy, Babs and Teddie Beverley. Babs and Teddie are twins.			
12/29/56+	**41**	9		**Greensleeves** ....T:41 *I'll See You In My Dreams*	$15		London 1703
				Roland Shaw (orch.); one of the oldest published songs (from 16th-century England)			
				BEVERLY '00			
				Born Beverly Crowder in Atlanta, Georgia. Female R&B singer.			
1/29/00	**35[S]**	17		**You Came Along** ....*I Really Do Love You*	$4	★	Yab Yum 64037
				BEWITCHED — see B*WITCHED			
				B-52's, The ROK/LP '90			
				New-wave dance group from Athens, Georgia: Cindy Wilson (guitar, vocals) and her brother Ricky Wilson (guitar; died of AIDS on 10/12/85, age 32), Kate Pierson (organ, vocals), **Fred Schneider** (see #7 below) (keyboards, vocals) and Keith Strickland (drums; moved to guitar after Ricky's death). Cindy left in 1991, replaced on tour by Julee Cruise. Appeared as **the B.C. 52's** in the movie *The Flintstones*. B-52 is slang for the bouffant hairstyle worn by Kate and Cindy.			
4/19/80	**56**	8		1 **Rock Lobster** ....*6060-842* [N]	$4	■	Warner 49173
				originally released on Boo-Fant 52 in 1978 with a picture sleeve			
10/18/80	**74**	5		2 **Private Idaho** ....*Party Out Of Bounds*	$4	■	Warner 49537
7/16/83	**81**	4		3 **Legal Tender** ....*Moon 83*	$4	■	Warner 29579
9/2/89	**3**	27	●	4 **Love Shack** MR[4] S:2 / A:6 *Channel Z* (ROK #1)	$3	■	Reprise 22817
12/23/89+	**3**	20	●	5 **Roam** ....S:2 / A:2 *Bushfire*	$3	▮[V]	Reprise 22667
4/21/90	**30**	11		6 **Deadbeat Club** ....A:25 *Planet Claire (live)*	$3	▮[V]	Reprise 19938
7/6/91	**85**	4		7 **Monster** ....*Summer In Hell* [N]	$3	▮	Reprise 19262
				FRED SCHNEIDER			
				Kate Pierson (backing vocal); remastered version of his 1984 Dance-Club Play chart hit (#25)			
6/20/92	**28**	13		8 **Good Stuff** ....MR[4] A:25 / S:46 *Bad Influence*	$3	▮[V]	Reprise 18895
5/21/94	**33**	8		9 **(Meet) The Flintstones** *[the B.C. 52's]*....A:32 / S:50 *(Barney's edit)* [N]	$3	▮[V]	MCA 54839
				from the movie *The Flintstones* starring John Goodman (theme song of the TV series)			
				B.G. R&B/LP '99			
				Born Christopher Dorsey in 1980 in New Orleans, Louisiana. Male rapper. B.G.: Baby Gangsta. Also see **Hot Boy$**.			
9/18/99	**36**	19		1 **Bling Bling** ....A:25 / S:72 *(3 versions)*	$6	T	Cash Money 156483
				B.G. Feat. Baby, Turk, Mannie Fresh, Juvenile and Lil Wayne			
12/4/99+	**72**	11		2 **Tha Block Is Hot** ....A:57 *(3 versions)*	$6	T	Cash Money 156546
				LIL WAYNE (featuring Juvenile and B.G.)			
				B.G. THE PRINCE OF RAP '91			
				Born Bernard Greene in Washington DC. Male rapper.			
8/17/91	**72**	9		**This Beat Is Hot** ....S:44 / A:57 *(edit)*	$4	▮[V]	Epic 73950
				B.I. R&B '02			
				Born in Houston, Texas. Male rapper.			
11/16/02	**62[S]**	3		**Precious** ....*(street version) / Weekend*	$6	★	Young Life 71225
				BIDDU ORCHESTRA LP '75			
				Born Biddu Appaiah in Bangalore, India. Male dance songwriter/producer/arranger. To England, worked as a baker. In 1969, began producing for Beacon Records.			
10/4/75	**57**	6		1 **Summer Of '42** ....*Northern Dancer* [I]	$5		Epic 50139
				disco version of the movie theme			
1/10/76	**72**	4		2 **I Could Have Danced All Night /** [I]			
				from the musical *My Fair Lady*			
1/10/76		4		3 **Jump For Joy** .... [I]	$5		Epic 50173
				BIG AUDIO DYNAMITE II ROK/LP '91			
				Rock group from England: Mick Jones (vocals, guitar), Nick Hawkins (guitar), Gary Stonadge (bass) and Chris Kavanagh (drums). Jones was co-founder of **The Clash**; not to be confused with Mick Jones of Foreigner.			
9/21/91	**32**	17		1 **Rush** ....MR[4] S:53 / A:75 *Kool-Aid*	$4	▮	Columbia 73987
				borrows organ riff from **The Who**'s "Baba O'Riley"			
2/15/92	**72**	10		2 **The Globe** ....S:73 *Rush (club version)*	$4	▮	Columbia 74149
				borrows shouts from **The Clash**'s "Should I Stay Or Should I Go?"			
				BIG BOPPER '58			
				Born Jiles Perry Richardson on 10/24/30 in Sabine Pass, Texas. DJ at KTRM in Beaumont, Texas. Wrote "Running Bear" for **Johnny Preston**. Died with **Buddy Holly** and **Ritchie Valens** in the 2/3/59 plane crash (age 28).			
8/4/58	**6**	25		1 **Chantilly Lace** ....H:6 / S:13 *Purple People Eater Meets Witch Doctor* [N]	$25		Mercury 71343
				first released on "D" 1008 in 1958 ($300)			
12/8/58	**38**	7		2 **Big Bopper's Wedding /** [N]			
12/1/58	**72**	4		3 **Little Red Riding Hood** .... [N]	$25		Mercury 71375
				BIG BROTHER & THE HOLDING COMPANY — see JOPLIN, Janis			
				BIG BUB LP '97			
				Born Frederick Lee Drakeford in Englewood, New Jersey. Black male singer/rapper.			
9/6/97	**70**	5		**Need Your Love** ....S:50 *(2 versions) / (4 album snippets)*	$3	▮	Kedar/Universal 56129
				BIG BUB featuring Queen Latifah & Heavy D			
				samples "I Want Your Love" by **Chic**			

DEBUT	PEAK	WKS	Gold	A-side (Chart Hit)..................B-side	$	Sym	Label & Number
				BIG "C" '02			
				Born Christopher McMurray in Atlanta, Georgia. Male rapper/songwriter.			
11/2/02	12^{S}	23		**Shady**..................*(2 versions) / Got What It Takes*	$6	★	Southpaw 001
				BIG COUNTRY ROK/LP '83			
				Pop-rock group from Dunfermline, Scotland: Stuart Adamson (vocals, guitar), Bruce Watson (guitar), Tony Butler (bass) and Mark Brzezicki (drums). Adamson committed suicide on 12/16/2001 (age 43).			
10/22/83	17	15		1 **In A Big Country**..................*All Of Us*	$4	■	Mercury 814467
2/4/84	52	6		2 **Fields Of Fire**..................*Angle Park*	$4	■	Mercury 811450
				picture sleeve is a foldout poster sleeve			
6/2/84	86	2		3 **Wonderland**..................*Lost Patrol (live)*	$4	■	Mercury 818834
				BIGGA FIGGAZ '01			
				Male rap duo from San Francisco, California: Jevon Roberson and Kenneth King.			
5/12/01	26^{S}	9		1 **Who's Gonna Love Ya'**..................*(club version) / Up In Da' Club*	$8	★*	King B 3002
10/27/01	14^{S}	9		2 **Get Mo**..................*(2 versions) / Fryed Ryde (w/Daz Dillinger, Tex Mex)*	$8	★	Dean's List 001
				SHERM (feat. Bigga Figgas)			
				BIG GIPP — see DJ HURRICANE			
				BIG JIM '01			
				Born James Wright in Cincinnati, Ohio. R&B singer. Backing vocalist for **Mary J. Blige**.			
11/3/01	55^{S}	4		**Little Sister**..................*(2 versions) / Whole Lot Of Woman*	$6	★	Platinum Soul 530231
				BIG L LP '00			
				Born Lamont Coleman on 5/30/74 in Harlem, New York. Shot to death in New York City on 2/15/99 (age 24). Male rapper.			
6/17/00	20^{S}	14		**Flamboyant**..................*(instrumental) / On The Mic*	$6	★	Rawkus 38707
				BIG LEW '01			
				Born Lew Powell in Washington DC. Male rapper.			
9/29/01	14^{S}	9		**How We Do**..................*(4 versions)*	$15	★	Col-Beast 22172
				BIG LEW Betta Known As "POPEYE REDS" Featuring: Nonchalant			
				BIG LOGIC '02			
				Born Daniel Peterson in Los Angeles, California. Male rapper.			
4/27/02	30^{S}	9		**Hyde Ha**..................*Don't Stop / Where da Ladies At / (3 album snippets)*	$8	★	Goodinvision 90409
				BIG MAYBELLE R&B '67			
				Born Mabel Louise Smith on 5/1/24 in Jackson, Tennessee. Died of diabetes on 1/23/72 (age 47). R&B singer/pianist.			
1/14/67	96	3		**96 Tears**..................*That's Life*	$20		Rojac 112
				BIG MOUNTAIN LP '94			
				Multi-cultural reggae band from San Diego, California: Quino (vocals, rhythm guitar), Jerome Cruz (guitar), Manfred Reinke (keyboards), Gregory Blakney (percussion), Lance Rhodes (drums) and Lynn Copeland (bass).			
4/10/93	51	20		1 **Touch My Light**..................A:28 / S:70 *(Spanglish verison) / Llena Mi Vida*	$5	▮	Quality 19120
2/26/94	6	28	●	2 **Baby, I Love Your Way**..................A:2 / S:12 *Baby, Te Quiero Ati*	$4	▮	RCA 62780
				from the movie *Reality Bites* starring Winona Ryder			
8/6/94	80	6		3 **Sweet Sensual Love**..................A:73 *(English version) / (Spanish version)*	$4	▮	Giant 18120
12/16/95+	44	13		4 **Get Together**..................A:38 *Todo Mundo De La Mano*	$4	▮	Giant 17750
				BIG NOISE '89			
				Pop band group from Birmingham, England: Anthony Fenelle (vocals), Huw Lucas (guitar), Paul Johnson (keyboards), Linton Levy (sax), Tony Jones (percussion), Gary Thompson (bass) and Tony Lahiffe (drums).			
11/4/89	97	3		**Name And Number**..................*Ain't No Doubt*	$3		Atco 99168
				BIG PIG LP '88			
				Rock group from Australia: male singers Nick Disbray, Tony Antoniades, Tim Rosewarne and Oleh Witer, with female singer Sherine, and drummers Adrian Scaglione and Neil Baker.			
3/19/88	60	10		**Breakaway**..................*Hell Bent Heaven*	$4	■	A&M 3014
				#62 R&B hit for **Chuck Jackson** in 1973 as "I Can't Break Away"			
				BIG PUNISHER R&B/BUB/LP '98			
				Born Christopher Rios on 11/9/71 in the Bronx, New York. Died of a heart attack on 2/7/2000 (age 28). Male rapper. Also see **Brandy**'s "Have You Ever?" and **Fat Joe**'s "Firewater."			
9/27/97	86	3		1 **Off The Books**..................*(3 versions)*	$5	▮	Relativity 1646
				THE BEATNUTS Featuring Big Punisher & Cuban Link			
11/1/97	57	20		2 **I'm Not A Player**..................S:40 *Wishful Thinking*	$4	▮	Loud/RCA 64910
				samples "Darlin' Darlin' Baby" by **The O'Jays**			
6/13/98	24	23		3 **Still Not A Player** A:23 *(instrumental) / Twinz (Deep Cover 98)*	$6	T	Loud/RCA 65478
				BIG PUNISHER (Featuring Joe)			
2/19/00	51	17		4 **Feelin' So Good**..................S:7 / A:48 *(album version)*	$4	★V	Epic/Work 79387 ■
				JENNIFER LOPEZ (Featuring Big Pun & Fat Joe)			
				samples "Set It Off" by Strafe			
4/22/00	75	15		5 **It's So Hard**..................A:63 *(3 versions) / Leatherface*	$6	T	Loud 79350
				BIG PUN Featuring Donell Jones			
				Tony Sunshine (backing vocal)			
				BIG RIC '83			
				Rock group from Los Angeles, California: Joel Porter (vocals), John Pondel (guitar), Kevin DiSimone (keyboards) and Bud Harner (drums).			
9/3/83	91	3		**Take Away**..................*Or What*	$4		Scotti Brothers 04084
				BIG SAMBO and The House Wreckers '62			
				Born James Young on 8/3/37 in Beaumont, Texas. Died on 6/10/83 (age 45). Black saxophonist/vocalist.			
3/10/62	74	7		**The Rains Came**..................*At The Party*	$15		Eric 7003
				BIG SISTER '96			
				Born Vicki Walker in New Orleans, Louisiana; raised in Chicago, Illinois. Dance singer.			
4/6/96	91	2		**'Round We Go**..................*(3 remixes)*	$7	▮*	SOS 1019
				produced by **20 Fingers**			

DEBUT	PEAK	WKS	Gold	A-side (Chart Hit)...B-side	$	Sym	Label & Number
				BIG TROUBLE '87			
				Female pop group formed in Los Angeles, California: Bobbi Eakes (vocals), Rebecca Ryan (keyboards), Julia Farey (bass) and Suzy Zarow (drums). Formed by TV network executive Fred Silverman. Eakes was Miss Georgia 1982 and later played "Macy Alexander" on TV's *The Bold & The Beautiful.*			
10/17/87	71	7		**Crazy World** ...*Lipstick*	$3	■	Epic 07432
				BIG TYMERS R&B/BUB/LP '02			
				Rap duo from New Orleans, Louisiana: Mannie Fresh and Brian "**Baby**" Williams. Members of **Cash Money Millionaires**.			
4/13/02	11	24		1 **Still Fly** ...A:11 / S:28 *(main version)*	$4	★	Cash Money 060072
8/31/02	46	18		2 **Oh Yeah!** ...S:35 / A:47 *(3 versions)*	$6	T	Cash Money 060065
				BIG TYMERS featuring Tazee, Boo & Gotti			
11/16/02+	33	20		3 **Do That...** ...S:22 / A:33 *(3 versions)*	$6	T	Cash Money 060079
				BABY (AKA DA #1 STUNNA) Featuring P. Diddy			
				BILAL R&B/BUB/LP '01			
				Born Bilal Oliver in 1979 in Philadelphia, Pennsylvania. Male R&B singer.			
1/27/01	71	14		1 **Soul Sista** ...S:8 *(2 versions) / (3 album snippets)*	$4	★	Moyo/Interscope 497409
				produced by **Raphael Saadiq**			
7/14/01	18[S]	36		2 **Love It** ...*(2 versions) / (3 album snippets)*	$4	★	Moyo/Interscope 497584
10/5/02	39[S]	7		3 **Waitin' For The DJ** ...*(2 versions) / Guerrilla Monsoon Rap* (w/Black Thought, **Pharoahe Monch** & Kanye West)	$6	T	Rawkus 113974
				TALIB KWELI Featuring Bilal			
				BILK, Mr. Acker BUB/AC/LP '62			
				Born Bernard Stanley Bilk on 1/28/29 in Pensford, Somerset, England. Clarinetist/composer. Cowrote **Monty Kelly**'s "Summer Set."			
3/17/62	❶[1]	21	●	1 **Stranger On The Shore** ...AC[7] *Cielito Lindo* [I]	$10		Atco 6217
				title song from the British TV show starring Richard Vernon; originally titled "Jenny"			
7/14/62	59	6		2 **Above The Stars** ...*Soft Sands* [I]	$10		Atco 6230
				from the movie *The Wonderful World Of The Brothers Grimm* starring Laurence Harvey			
12/1/62	92	3		3 **Limelight** ...*Lonely* [I]	$10		Atco 6238
				written in 1952 by Charlie Chaplin (also known as "Terry's Theme from *Limelight* and as "Eternally")			
2/2/63	77	3		4 **Only You (And You Alone)** ...*A Taste Of Honey* [I]	$10		Atco 6247
				all of above with the Leon Young String Chorale			
				BILLIE BUB '99			
				Born Billie Piper on 9/22/82 in Swindon, Wiltshire, England. White female dance singer.			
5/8/99	49[S]	15		**She Wants You** ...BUB:123 *(2 versions) / Because We Want To*	$5	★[V]	Virgin 38658
				B-side is the "Theme for 1999 Women's World Cup"; "45": Virgin 38672			
				BILLY & LILLIE '58			
				Vocal duo of Billy Ford (born on 3/9/25 in Bloomfield, New Jersey) and Lillie Bryant (born on 2/14/40 in Newburg, New York). Backing group: Billy Ford's Thunderbirds.			
1/6/58	9	13		1 **La Dee Dah** ...T:9 / S:10 / A:23 *The Monster* (Billy Ford & Thunderbirds)	$25		Swan 4002
5/5/58	56	4		2 **Happiness** ...T:56 *Creepin', Crawlin', Cryin'*	$20		Swan 4005
12/22/58+	14	13		3 **Lucky Ladybug** ...*I Promise You*	$20		Swan 4020
7/13/59	88	6		4 **Bells, Bells, Bells (The Bell Song)** ...*Honeymoonin'*	$20		Swan 4036
				BILLY & THE BEATERS — see VERA, Billy			
				BILLY JOE & THE CHECKMATES '62			
				Born Louis Bideu on 3/21/19 in El Paso, Texas. Worked as a comedian. Hosted own local *Lew Bedell Show* in New York. Dubbed himself Billy Joe Hunter in the early 1960s.			
1/13/62	10	13		**Percolator (Twist)** ...*Round & Round & Round & Round* [I]	$15		Dore 620
				based on the "perky" tune used in a Maxwell House coffee jingle			
				BILLY SATELLITE LP '84			
				Rock group from Oakland, California: Monty Byrom (vocals), Danny Chauncey (guitar), Ira Walker (bass) and Tom Falletti (drums).			
8/18/84	64	6		1 **Satisfy Me** ...*Turning Point*	$4	■	Capitol 5356
12/8/84	78	5		2 **I Wanna Go Back** ...*Rockin' Down The Highway*	$4	■	Capitol 5409
				BIMBO JET '75			
				Disco studio group from France. Assembled by producer Laurent Rossi.			
5/24/75	43	10		**El Bimbo** ...*(disco version)* [I]	$5		Scepter 12406
				#1 song in 6 different European countries			
				BINGOBOYS '91			
				Dance trio of DJs from Vienna, Austria: Klaus Biedermann, Paul Pfab and Helmut Wolfgruber. Princessa is a female rapper from New York.			
2/16/91	25	14		1 **How To Dance** ...S:23 / A:31 *(instrumental)*	$3	▮	Atlantic 87756
				BINGOBOYS Featuring Princessa			
				samples "Dance, Dance, Dance" by **Chic**, "Dance (Disco Heat)" by **Sylvester** and "Kiss" by **Art Of Noise Featuring Tom Jones**			
6/29/91	71	6		2 **Borrowed Love** ...A:64 *(instrumental)*	$3	▮	Atlantic 87676
				featuring Arnold Jarvis and Princessa			
				BIRDLEGS & PAULINE '63			
				R&B group from Chicago: husband-and-wife Sidney Banks (born on 10/13/29 in Chicago, Illinois) and Pauline Shivers Banks (born on 4/28/33 in Memphis, Tennessee), with brothers Mack and Floyd Murphy.			
7/6/63	94	2		**Spring** ...*In So Many Ways*	$12		Vee-Jay 510
				BIRDLEGS & PAULINE And Their Versatility Birds			
				originally issued on Cuca 1125 in 1963 ($40)			
				BIRKIN, Jane, & Serge Gainsbourg LP '70			
				Actress Birkin was born on 12/14/46 in London, England. Married to **John Barry** from 1965-68. Singer/songwriter Lucien "Serge" Gainsbourg was born on 4/2/28 in Paris, France. Died of heart failure on 3/2/91 (age 62). Birkin and Gainsbourg were married from 1968-80.			
11/29/69+	58	10		**Je T'Aime...Moi Non Plus** ...*Jane B* (Birkin) [F]	$8		Fontana 1665
				sexual recording was banned on many radio shows worldwide; #1 hit in England			

DEBUT	PEAK	WKS	Gold	A-side (Chart Hit)...B-side	$	Sym	Label & Number
				BISCUIT '90			
				Born Steve Walker in Oakland, California. Male rapper. Began as a bodyguard for **New Kids On The Block**.			
10/27/90	85	3		**Biscuit's In The House** ...*(3 album snippets)*	$3	▮	Columbia 73585
				samples **Free**'s 1970 hit "All Right Now"			
				BISHOP '01			
				Born Travis Kendrick in Brooklyn, New York. Male rapper.			
6/23/01	38S	10		**U Know U Ghetto** ...*(2 versions) / (3 album snippets)*	$6	★	Tony Mercedes 8306
				BISHOP, Elvin LP '76			
				Born on 10/21/42 in Tulsa, Oklahoma. Lead guitarist with The Paul Butterfield Blues Band (1965-68).			
10/5/74	61	6		1 **Travelin' Shoes** ...*Fishin'*	$5		Capricorn 0202
6/28/75	83	5		2 **Sure Feels Good** ...*Arkansas Line*	$5		Capricorn 0237
3/6/76	3	17	●	3 **Fooled Around And Fell In Love** *Have A Good Time*	$5		Capricorn 0252
				Mickey Thomas (of **Starship**; lead vocal)			
7/24/76	68	4		4 **Struttin' My Stuff** ...*Grab All The Love*	$5		Capricorn 0256
12/25/76+	93	8		5 **Spend Some Time** ...*Sugar Dumplin'*	$5		Capricorn 0266
				ELVIN BISHOP Featuring Mickey Thomas			
				BISHOP, Stephen AC/BUB/LP '77			
				Born on 11/14/51 in San Diego, California. Pop-rock singer/songwriter. Wrote several movie themes. Cameo role as the "Charming Guy With Guitar" in *National Lampoon's Animal House.*			
12/11/76+	22	15		1 **Save It For A Rainy Day** ...*Careless*	$5		ABC 12232
				Chaka Khan (background vocal); **Eric Clapton** (guitar solo)			
5/7/77	11	28		2 **On And On** *Little Italy*	$5		ABC 12260
				a promotional picture sleeve was issued for the above 2 in September 1977			
9/16/78	32	13		3 **Everybody Needs Love** ...*Only The Heart Within You*	$5		ABC 12406
12/23/78+	73	5		4 **Animal House** ...*Dream Girl* [N]	$5	■	ABC 12435
				title song from the movie starring **John Belushi**			
1/29/83	25	20		5 **It Might Be You** ...AC2 *Metamorphosis Blues (It Might Be You)* (Dave Grusin)	$4		Warner 29791
				theme from the movie *Tootsie* starring Dustin Hoffman			
3/31/84	87	3		6 **Unfaithfully Yours (One Love)** ...*It's Only Love*	$4		Warner 29345
				from the remake of the 1948 movie *Unfaithfully Yours* starring Dudley Moore			
				BIZARRE INC featuring Angie Brown '93			
				Techno-dance trio of DJs from England: Andrew Meecham, Dean Meredith and Carl Turner. Featuring female session singer Angie Brown.			
1/23/93	47	23		**I'm Gonna Get You** ...A:23 / S:54 *(remix)*	$4	▮	Columbia 74814
				also see the B-side of **The Blackout Allstars**			
				BIZ MARKIE R&B/LP '90			
				Born Marcel Hall on 4/8/64 in Harlem, New York. Rapper/actor. Appeared in the movie *The Meteor Man.* Also see **Usher**'s "Think Of You."			
1/20/90	9	22	▲	**Just A Friend** ...S:5 / A:19 *(instrumental)*	$3	■V	Cold Chillin' 22784
				re-entered the R&B Sales chart on 8/10/02 (#56) due to the popularity of **Mario**'s "Just A Friend 2002"			
				BJÖRK ROK/BUB/LP '94			
				Born Björk Gudmundsdottir on 11/12/65 in Reykjavik, Iceland. Female lead singer of the dance group The Sugarcubes.			
2/12/94	88	5		1 **Big Time Sensuality** ...*There's More To Life Than This*	$3	▮	Elektra 64561
				produced by Nellee Hooper of **Soul II Soul**			
9/1/01	50S	3		2 **Hidden Place** ...*Generous Palmstroke / Verandi*	$8	◗	Elektra 40228
	★364★			**BLACK('S), Bill, Combo** C&W/BUB/LP '60			
				Born on 9/17/26 in Memphis, Tennessee. Died of a brain tumor on 10/21/65 (age 39). White bass guitarist/songwriter. Session work in Memphis; backed **Elvis Presley** (with Scotty Moore, guitar; D.J. Fontana, drums) on most of his early records. Formed own band in 1959. Labeled as "The Untouchable Sound." Larry Rogers and Bob Tucker led group after Black's death; recorded well into the 1970s.			
				1)White Silver Sands 2)Don't Be Cruel 3)Blue Tango			
11/30/59+	17	12	●	1 **Smokie -- Part 2** ...RB4 *Part 1* [I]	$20		Hi 2018
3/7/60	9	14	●	2 **White Silver Sands** RB4 *The Wheel* [I]	$20		Hi 2021
6/27/60	18	10	●	3 **Josephine** ...*Dry Bones* [I]	$15	■	Hi 2022
				#3 hit for Wayne King's Orchestra in 1937			
9/12/60	11	13		4 **Don't Be Cruel** ...*Rollin'* [I]	$15	■	Hi 2026
				Black played bass on **Elvis Presley**'s original 1956 hit			
11/28/60	16	10		5 **Blue Tango** ...*Willie* [I]	$15	■	Hi 2027
				#1 hit for Leroy Anderson in 1952			
2/20/61	20	8		6 **Hearts Of Stone** ...*Royal Blue* [I]	$15		Hi 2028
6/5/61	25	8		7 **Ole Buttermilk Sky** ...*Yogi* [I]	$12	■	Hi 2036
				written and popularized in 1946 by Hoagy Carmichael			
9/25/61	41	7		8 **Movin'** / [I]			
9/25/61	92	2		9 **Honky Train** ... [I]	$12		Hi 2038
12/18/61+	26	9		10 **Twist-Her** ...*My Girl Josephine* [I]	$12		Hi 2042
5/5/62	92	2		11 **-twistin'-White Silver Sands** ...*My Babe* [I-R]	$12	■	Hi 2052
				twist version of #2 above			
8/11/62	78	7		12 **So What** ...*Blues For The Red Boy* [I]	$12		Hi 2055
4/27/63	51	8		13 **Do It - Rat Now** ...*Little Jasper* [I]	$12		Hi 2064
10/5/63	47	6		14 **Monkey-Shine** ...*Long Gone* [I]	$12		Hi 2069
2/1/64	67	5		15 **Comin' On** ...*Soft Winds* [I]	$12		Hi 2072
5/16/64	91	3		16 **Tequila** ...*Raunchy* (#118) [I]	$12		Hi 2077
10/3/64	73	4		17 **Little Queenie** ...*Boo-Ray* [I]	$12		Hi 2079
1/2/65	89	1		18 **So What** ...*Blues For The Red Boy* [I-R]	$12		Hi 2055
				reissue of #12 above (same version)			
6/22/68	82	6		19 **Turn On Your Love Light** ...*Ribbon Of Darkness* [I]	$10		Hi 2145

DEBUT	PEAK	WKS	Gold	A-side (Chart Hit)..........B-side	$	Sym	Label & Number
				BLACK, Cilla BUB **'64**			
				Born Priscilla White on 5/27/43 in Liverpool, England. Discovered by **The Beatles**' manager Brian Epstein while she was working as a coat checker/singer at Liverpool's Cavern Club.			
7/4/64	**26**	7		1 **You're My World**..........*Suffer Now I Must*	$15		Capitol 5196
9/19/64	**79**	3		2 **It's For You**..........*He Won't Ask Me* written by **John Lennon** and **Paul McCartney** (McCartney plays piano)	$12		Capitol 5258
8/27/66	**95**	3		3 **Alfie**..........*Night Time Is Here* title song from the movie starring Michael Caine	$12		Capitol 5674
				BLACK, Clint C&W/LP **'93**			
				Born on 2/4/62 in Long Branch, New Jersey; raised in Houston, Texas. Country singer/guitarist (charted 47 hits, 1989-02). Former construction worker. Married actress Lisa Hartman on 10/20/91.			
6/12/93	**43**	11		1 **A Bad Goodbye**..........S:19 *The Hard Way* (Black) **CLINT BLACK (with Wynonna)**	$4	▮V	RCA 62503
1/1/94	**70**^{S}	3		2 **State Of Mind**..........BUB:102 *Tuckered Out* (C&W #74)	$4	▮V	RCA 62700
12/20/97	**76**	9		3 **Something That We Do**..........S:64 *(acoustic version)* "45": RCA 64961; B-side: "Bitter Side Of Sweet"	$4	▮V	RCA 65336
10/16/99	**31**	20		4 **When I Said I Do** CW^2 A:19 **CLINT BLACK (with Lisa Hartman Black)** "45": RCA 65897; B-side: "You Don't Need Me Now" (C&W #29)		V	album cut
2/19/00	**44**	20		5 **Been There**..........A:36 **CLINT BLACK with Steve Wariner** "45": RCA 65966; B-side: (same as #4 above); above 2 from the album *D'lectrified* on RCA 67823		V	album cut
				BLACK, Jay — see JAY & THE AMERICANS			
				BLACK, Jeanne **'60**			
				Born Gloria Jeanne Black on 10/25/37 in Pomona, California. Country-pop singer. Discovered by **Cliffie Stone**; sang with her sister Janie on Stone's TV show *Hometown Jamboree.*			
5/2/60	**4**	11	●	1 **He'll Have To Stay**..........*Under Your Spell Again* (Jeanne & Janie) answer song to **Jim Reeves**'s "He'll Have To Go"; promo sleeve features a photo of Jeanne and Janie	$12	□	Capitol 4368
7/25/60	**43**	9		2 **Lisa**..........*Journey Of Love* (Jeanne & Janie)	$12		Capitol 4396
12/26/60+	**63**	5		3 **Oh, How I Miss You Tonight**..........*A Little Bit Lonely* #1 hit for Ben Selvin's Orchestra in 1925; Billy Liebert (orch., all of above)	$12		Capitol 4492
				BLACK, Oscar **'61**			
				R&B singer.			
4/24/61	**94**	1		**I'm A Fool To Care**..........*I Got A Feeling* #6 hit for **Les Paul & Mary Ford** in 1954	$15		Savoy 1600
				BLACK, Sunni **'01**			
				Male rapper.			
12/16/00+	**56**^{S}	6		**No! No! No!**..........*(3 versions) / (4 album snippets)* **SUNNI BLACK Featuring Mother Superia**	$6	★	King Pin Station 197
				BLACK, Terry **'72**			
				Born on 2/3/49 in North Vancouver, British Columbia, Canada. Male singer. Married female singer Laurel Ward in 1970.			
11/21/64	**99**	2		1 **Unless You Care**..........*Can't We Go Somewhere?*	$12		Tollie 9026
2/12/72	**57**	8		2 **Goin' Down (On The Road To L.A.)**..........*Oh Babe* **TERRY BLACK AND LAUREL WARD**	$6	■	Kama Sutra 540
				BLACKALICIOUS R&B/LP **'02**			
				Rap duo from Sacramento, California: Xavier "Chief Xcel" Mosley and Tim "The Gift of Gab" Parker.			
6/8/02	**69**^{S}	1		**Make You Feel That Way**..........*(2 versions) / Sky Is Falling*	$7	T	MCA 155934
				BLACK BOX LP **'91**			
				Male Italian dance trio of producer Daniele Davoli and musicians Mirko Limoni and Valerio Semplici. Videos feature French model Katrin Quinol as lead singer; however, **Martha Wash** is the uncredited lead vocalist on all of the group's hits.			
8/4/90	**8**	19		1 **Everybody Everybody**..........S:5 / A:15 *(2 versions)* "45": Collectables 4704; B-side: "Ride On Time"	$3	▮V	RCA 2628
12/8/90+	**23**	14		2 **I Don't Know Anybody Else**..........S:15 *Ride On Time*	$3	▮V	RCA 2735
4/6/91	**8**	18		3 **Strike It Up**..........A:10 / S:14 *(hard core remix)* "45" issued for above 2 on Collectables 4776; all of above: #1 Dance Club Play hits	$3	▮V	RCA 2794
				BLACKBYRDS, The R&B/BUB/LP **'75**			
				R&B group formed by **Donald Byrd** (see #1 below) (born on 12/9/32 in Detroit, Michigan) while teaching jazz at Howard University in Washington DC. Core members: Joe Hall (vocals, bass), Kevin Toney (vocals, keyboards) and Keith Killgo (vocals, drums).			
6/9/73	**88**	6		1 **Black Byrd**..........*Slop Jar Blues* [I] **DONALD BYRD**	$6		Blue Note 212
9/7/74	**69**	6		2 **Do It, Fluid**..........*Summer Love* (#101)	$5		Fantasy 729
2/8/75	**6**	17		3 **Walking In Rhythm** *The Baby*	$5		Fantasy 736
8/2/75	**70**	4		4 **Flyin' High**..........*All I Ask*	$5		Fantasy 747
3/6/76	**19**	13		5 **Happy Music**..........*Love So Fine*	$5		Fantasy 762
7/17/76	**93**	3		6 **Rock Creek Park**..........*Thankful 'Bout Yourself*	$5		Fantasy 771
3/12/77	**95**	3		7 **Time Is Movin'**..........*Lady*	$5		Fantasy 787
				BLACK CROWES, The ROK/BUB/LP **'91**			
				Rock group from Atlanta, Georgia. Led by brothers Chris (vocals) and Rich (guitar) Robinson. Includes Jeff Cease (guitar), Johnny Colt (bass) and Steve Gorman (drums). Cease left in late 1991, replaced by Marc Ford (ex-Burning Tree). By 1994, Eddie Harsch (keyboards) joined. Chris Robinson married actress Kate Hudson (daughter of Goldie Hawn) on 12/31/2000. The Robinson brothers are the sons of **Stan Robinson**.			
5/12/90	**75**	9		1 **Jealous Again**..........*Thick N' Thin*	$3	▮	Def American 19697
10/27/90	**45**	15		2 **Hard To Handle**..........AR^2 A:26 / S:36 *Jealous Again (acoustic version)*	$3	▮	Def American 19668
3/16/91	**30**	16		3 **She Talks To Angels**..........AR^1 A:28 / S:33 *(live video version)*	$3	▮V	Def American 19403
6/22/91	**26**	14		4 **Hard To Handle** *Waitin' Guilty* [R] same version as #2 above	$3	▮V	Def American 19245

DEBUT	PEAK	WKS	Gold	A-side (Chart Hit)..................B-side	$	Sym	Label & Number
				BLACK CROWES, The — Cont'd			
6/13/92	**48**	9		5 **Remedy**..................AR[11] S:45 *Darling Of The Underground Press*	$3	▮[V]	Def American 18877 ■
9/5/92	**80**	6		6 **Thorn In My Pride**..................AR[4] *Sting Me* (ROK #1)	$3	▮[V]	Def American 18803
				BLACK EYED PEAS R&B/LP '01			
				Rap trio from Los Angeles, California: Will.I.Am, Alp.De.Ap and Taboo.			
3/31/01	**63**	8		**Request Line**..................S:6 *(3 versions)*	$5	★	Interscope 497498
				BLACK EYED PEAS featuring Macy Gray			
				BLACKFOOT ROK/BUB/LP '79			
				Rock group from Jacksonville, Florida: Rickey Medlocke (vocals, guitar), Charlie Hargrett (guitar), Greg Walker (bass) and Jakson Spires (drums). Medlocke and Walker were original members of **Lynyrd Skynyrd**.			
6/23/79	**26**	14		1 **Highway Song**..................*Road Fever*	$5		Atco 7104
10/20/79	**38**	14		2 **Train, Train**..................*Baby Blue*	$5		Atco 7207
6/20/81	**42**	12		3 **Fly Away**..................*Good Morning*	$5		Atco 7331
				BLACKFOOT, J. '84			
				Born John Colbert on 11/20/46 in Greenville, Mississippi. R&B singer. Formerly with **The Soul Children**.			
3/3/84	**90**	5		**Taxi**..................*Where Is Love*	$7		Sound Town 0004
				BLACKGIRL R&B/BUB '94			
				Black female R&B vocal trio from Atlanta, Georgia: Nycolia "Tye-V" Turman, Pamela Copeland and Rochelle Stuart.			
2/12/94	**91**	3		1 **Krazy**..................*(3 album snippets)*	$3	▮	Kaper/RCA 62665
7/2/94	**71**	13		2 **90's Girl**..................S:45 *(2 versions)*	$3	▮	Kaper/RCA 62865
				BLACKHAWK C&W/BUB/LP '99			
				Country vocal trio: **Henry Paul** (**Outlaws**), **Van Stephenson** and Dave Robbins. Stephenson died of cancer on 4/8/2001 (age 47).			
3/12/94	**73**[S]	3		1 **Goodbye Says It All**..................BUB:111 *Let 'Em Whirl*	$4	▮[V]	Arista 12568
9/30/95	**66**[S]	6		2 **I'm Not Strong Enough To Say No**..................BUB:104 *A Kiss Is Worth A Thousand Words*	$4	▮[V]	Arista 12857
12/5/98+	**41**	14		3 **There You Have It**..................A:35 / S:73 *When I Find It, I'll Know It*	$4	★[V]	Arista 13134
				BLACKJACK LP '79			
				Rock group from New York City, New York: Michael Bolotin (vocals), Bruce Kulick (guitar), Jimmy Haslip (bass) and Sandy Gennaro (drums). Bolotin began solo career in 1983 as **Michael Bolton**. Kulick joined **Kiss** in 1985.			
7/21/79	**62**	6		**Love Me Tonight**..................*Heart Of Mine*	$8		Polydor 14572
				BLACK LAB ROK '98			
				Rock group from Berkeley, California: Paul Durham (vocals), Michael Belfer (guitar), Geoff Stanfield (bass) and Bryan Head (drums).			
6/13/98	**75**[A]	1		**Time Ago**..................			album cut
				from the album *Your Body Above Me* on DGC 25127			
				BLACK MOON R&B/BUB/LP '93			
				Rap trio from Brooklyn, New York: Kenyatta "Buckshot Shorty" Blake (lead vocals), 5 Ft. Excellerator and DJ Evil Dee of the Beat Minerz. Black Moon stands for Brothers Lyrically Acting, Combining Kicking Music Out On Nations. Buckshot Shorty is also a member of **The Crooklyn Dodgers**.			
2/27/93	**86**	6		1 **Who Got The Props**..................S:61 *F**k It Up*	$4	▮	Nervous 20026
4/23/94	**93**	10		2 **I Got Cha Opin**..................S:71 *(instrumental)*	$4	▮	Wreck 20083
				samples "Playing Your Game, Baby" by **Barry White**			
				BLACK OAK ARKANSAS LP '74			
				Rock group from Black Oak, Arkansas: Jim "Dandy" Mangrum (vocals), Ricky Reynolds, Jimmy Henderson and Stan Knight (guitars), Pat Daugherty (bass) and Wayne Evans (drums).			
12/15/73+	**25**	13		1 **Jim Dandy**..................*Red Hot Lovin'*	$6		Atco 6948
				Ruby Starr (backing vocal; born Constance Mierzwiak; died of cancer on 1/14/95)			
1/10/76	**89**	2		2 **Strong Enough To Be Gentle**..................*Ace In The Hole*	$5		MCA 40496
				BLACKOUT ALLSTARS, The '97			
				All-star Latin group: **Ray Barretto**, **Sheila E.**, Tito Puente, Tito Nieves, Paquito D'Rivera, Dave Valentin and **Grover Washington Jr.** Washington died of a heart attack on 12/17/99 (age 56). Puente died of heart failure on 5/31/2000 (age 77).			
12/7/96+	**25**	22		**I Like It**..................A:26 / S:46 *Joy* (Staxx Of Joy) / *Reach* (Robi Rob's Clubworld) / *I'm Gonna Get You* (**Bizarre Inc.**)	$4	▮	Columbia 78455
				recorded for the 1994 movie *I Like It Like That* starring Lauren Velez; renewed popularity due to inclusion in a Burger King commercial			
				BLACK ROB LP '00			
				Born Robert Ross in 1970 in Harlem, New York. Male rapper.			
3/4/00	**43**	17		1 **Whoa!**..................A:38 / S:61 *(3 versions)*	$6	T	Bad Boy 79297
5/26/01	**80**	9		2 **Let's Get It**..................S:58 / A:74 *(3 versions)*	$6	T	Bad Boy 79383
				THREE THE... G. Dep, P. Diddy & Black Rob			
				samples "Love & Happiness" by **Al Green**			
7/28/01	**33**	12		3 **Bad Boy For Life**..................A:30 / S:49 *(3 versions)*	$6	T	Bad Boy 79400
				P. DIDDY, BLACK ROB & MARK CURRY			
				BLACK SABBATH ROK/LP '72			
				Hard-rock group from Birmingham, England: **Ozzy Osbourne** (vocals), Tony Iommi (guitar), Terry "Geezer" Butler (bass) and William Ward (drums). Osbourne fired from band in January 1979; replaced by Ronnie James Dio. Numerous personnel changes over the years.			
11/28/70	**61**	8		1 **Paranoid**..................*The Wizard*	$10		Warner 7437
1/29/72	**52**	10		2 **Iron Man**..................*Electric Funeral*	$10		Warner 7530
				BLACK SHEEP R&B/LP '92			
				Rap duo from the Bronx, New York: Andres Titus and William McLean.			
2/29/92	**57**	19		1 **The Choice Is Yours**..................S:27 / A:58 *(album version)*	$4	▮	Mercury 866086
				samples Johnny Hammond's "Big Sur Suite"			
7/4/92	**80**	8		2 **Strobelite Honey**..................S:59 / A:67 *(same version)*	$4	▮	Mercury 866868
				samples "The Glow Of Love" by **Change** (featuring **Luther Vandross**)			
9/26/92	**52**	11		3 **Work To Do**..................A:36 *(3 album snippets) / (radio mix w/rap)*	$3	▮[V]	Wing 863540
				VANESSA WILLIAMS (featuring Black Sheep)			
10/22/94	**73**[S]	1		4 **Without A Doubt**..................BUB:103 *(2 versions) / (2 album snippets)*	$3	▮	Mercury 856170

DEBUT	PEAK	WKS	Gold	A-side (Chart Hit)..........B-side	$	Sym	Label & Number

BLACK STAR — see KWELI, Talib / MOS DEF

BLACKstreet — ★347★ — R&B/BUB/LP '96

R&B/hip-hop group: **Teddy Riley** (vocals), Chauncey Hannibal, Levi Little and **Dave Hollister**. Riley, a prolific producer (**Michael Jackson**, **Keith Sweat**, **Bobby Brown** and more) and originator of the "new jack swing" style was a member of **Guy** and Kids At Work. Hollister is the cousin of **K-Ci & JoJo** of **Jodeci**. Hollister and Little left in late 1995; replaced by **Eric Williams** and Mark Middleton.

1)No Diggity 2)I Get Lonely 3)Before I Let You Go

DEBUT	PEAK	WKS	Gold	A-side (Chart Hit)..........B-side	$	Sym	Label & Number
6/25/94	34	20		1 **Booti Call**..........S:21 / A:71 *I Like The Way You Work* samples "Atomic Dog" by **George Clinton** and "Heartbreaker" by **Zapp**	$4	▌	Interscope 98255
10/22/94+	7	27		2 **Before I Let You Go**..........S:5 / A:14 *Baby Be Mine*	$3	▌	Interscope 98211
4/1/95	43	13		3 **Joy**..........S:36 / A:63 *(album version-no rap)* Menton Smith (rap); co-written by **Michael Jackson**	$3	▌	Interscope 98164
8/19/95	80	7		4 **Tonight's The Night**..........S:43 *(remix w/SWV &* **Craig Mack***)* **BLACKstreet (featuring SWV)** all of above from the album *BLACKstreet*	$3	▌	Interscope 98118
10/12/96	❶^{4}	31	▲	5 **No Diggity** RB^{4} S:❶^{6} / A:9 *Billie Jean* **BLACKstreet (Featuring Dr. Dre)** **Queen Pen** (female rap); samples "Grandma's Hands" by **Bill Withers**; also see the B-side of **Queen Pen**'s "All My Love"	$3	▌	Interscope 97007
11/30/96+	42^{A}	13		6 **Get Me Home**.......... **FOXY BROWN Featuring BLACKstreet** samples "Gotta Get You Home Tonight" by **Eugene Wilde**; from Brown's album *Ill Na Na* on Def Jam 533684			album cut
2/15/97	12^{A}	29		7 **Don't Leave Me**..........RB^{3A} from the album *Another Level* on Interscope 90071			album cut
8/2/97	58	10		8 **Fix**..........S:49 *(5 mixes) / Man Behind The Music* (**Queen Pen**) **BLACKstreet Featuring Ol Dirty Bastard and Slash**	$8	★*	Interscope 95011
1/31/98	52	20		9 **The City Is Mine**..........S:32 *(TV track) / A Million And One Questions* (Jay-Z) **JAY-Z (Featuring BlackStreet)** samples "You Belong To The City" by **Glenn Frey** and "You Gonna Make Me Love Somebody Else" by **The Jones Girls**	$3	▌	Roc-A-Fella 568592
5/23/98	3	20	●	10 **I Get Lonely**..........RB^{2} S:2 / A:24 *(2 edits)* **JANET (Featuring BLACKstreet)**	$3	▌^{V}	Virgin 38631
12/5/98+	14	17		11 **Take Me There**..........A:8 **BLACKSTREET & MÝA featuring MA$E & BLINKY BLINK** samples "I Want You Back" by **The Jackson 5**; from the animated movie *The RugRats Movie*			album cut
3/13/99	47	11		12 **Girlfriend/Boyfriend**..........A:28 *(2 versions) / Take Me There* **BLACKSTREET With Janet** **Ja Rule** and **Eve** (rap vocals)	$6	T	Interscope 95043

BLACKWELL — '69

Pop-rock group from Houston, Texas: Glenn Gibson (vocals), Jimmy Smith (guitar), John Bundrick (keyboards), Terry Wilson (bass) and Randy Dehart (drums).

DEBUT	PEAK	WKS	Gold	A-side (Chart Hit)..........B-side	$	Sym	Label & Number
10/25/69	89	2		**Wonderful**..........*Dirty Story*	$10		Astro 1000

BLACKWELL, Charlie — '59

Born on 5/11/21 in Seattle, Washington. Percussionist, top sideman with many jazz greats (**Stan Kenton**, **Dave Brubeck**, Charlie Barnett and others).

DEBUT	PEAK	WKS	Gold	A-side (Chart Hit)..........B-side	$	Sym	Label & Number
2/9/59	55	9		**Midnight Oil**..........*None Of 'Em Glow Like You* [I]	$12		Warner 5031

BLADES OF GRASS, The — '67

Pop group from New Jersey: Dave Gordon, Frank Dichiara, Bruce Ames and Marc Black.

DEBUT	PEAK	WKS	Gold	A-side (Chart Hit)..........B-side	$	Sym	Label & Number
7/15/67	87	4		**Happy**..........*That's What A Boy Likes*	$8		Jubilee 5582

BLAHZAY BLAHZAY — R&B/BUB '95

Rap duo from Brooklyn, New York: rapper Out Loud and producer DJ P.F. Cuttin.

DEBUT	PEAK	WKS	Gold	A-side (Chart Hit)..........B-side	$	Sym	Label & Number
10/7/95	46	20		**Danger**..........S:33 / A:54 *(TV track)* samples "Rockin' Chair" by **Gwen McCrae**	$5	▌	Fader 127049

BLAIR — '98

Born Blair MacKichan in 1970 in London, England. White male dance-pop singer.

DEBUT	PEAK	WKS	Gold	A-side (Chart Hit)..........B-side	$	Sym	Label & Number
5/23/98	86	4		**Have Fun, Go Mad**..........*More Love* (**Brand New Heavies**) from the movie *Sliding Doors* starring Gwyneth Paltrow	$3	▌	Jersey/MCA 55444

BLANCHARD, Jack, & Misty Morgan — C&W/LP '70

Husband-and-wife country duo. Both born in Buffalo, New York. Jack (born on 5/8/42) plays saxophone and keyboards. Misty (born on 5/23/45) plays keyboards. Met and married while working in Florida.

DEBUT	PEAK	WKS	Gold	A-side (Chart Hit)..........B-side	$	Sym	Label & Number
2/28/70	23	13		1 **Tennessee Bird Walk**..........CW^{2} *The Clock Of St. James* [N]	$7		Wayside 010
6/27/70	78	6		2 **Humphrey The Camel**..........*A Place In My Mind* [N]	$7		Wayside 013

BLAND, Billy — BUB '60

Born on 4/5/32 in Wilmington, North Carolina. R&B singer. Formed group the Four Bees in 1954. First recorded solo for Old Town in 1955.

DEBUT	PEAK	WKS	Gold	A-side (Chart Hit)..........B-side	$	Sym	Label & Number
2/15/60	7	20		1 **Let The Little Girl Dance**..........*Sweet Thing*	$25		Old Town 1076
6/27/60	94	2		2 **You Were Born To Be Loved**..........*Pardon Me* (#102)	$20		Old Town 1082
10/10/60	91	2		3 **Harmony**..........*Make Believe Lover* written by **Gene Pitney**	$20		Old Town 1088
8/7/61	90	4		4 **My Heart's On Fire**..........*Can't Stop Her From Dancing*	$20		Old Town 1105

BLAND, Bobby — ★202★ — R&B/BUB/LP '64

Born on 1/27/30 in Rosemark, Tennessee. Blues singer/guitarist. Nicknamed "Blue." Sang in gospel group The Miniatures in Memphis, late 1940s. Member of the Beale Streeters which included **Johnny Ace**, **B.B. King**, **Rosco Gordon**, Earl Forest and Willie Nix in 1949. Driver and valet for B.B. King; appeared in the Johnny Ace Revue, early 1950s. First recorded in 1952 for the Modern label. Charted 63 R&B hits, 1957-85. Inducted into the Rock and Roll Hall of Fame in 1992. Won Grammy's Lifetime Achievement Award in 1997.

1)Ain't Nothing You Can Do 2)Call On Me 3)Turn On Your Love Light 4)That's The Way Love Is 5)This Time I'm Gone For Good

DEBUT	PEAK	WKS	Gold	A-side (Chart Hit)..........B-side	$	Sym	Label & Number
8/5/57	43	21		1 **Farther Up The Road**..........RB^{2} T:43 *Sometime Tomorrow* **BOBBY "BLUE" BLAND**	$30		Duke 170

DEBUT	PEAK	WKS	Gold	A-side (Chart Hit)	B-side	$	Sym	Label & Number
				BLAND, Bobby — Cont'd				
1/25/60	**89**	3		2 **I'll Take Care Of You**	*That's Why*	$25		Duke 314
				written by **Brook Benton**				
11/7/60	**71**	5		3 **Cry Cry Cry**	*I've Been Wrong So Long*	$25		Duke 327
2/20/61	**46**	7		4 **I Pity The Fool** RB[1]	*Close To You*	$25		Duke 332
8/7/61	**71**	7		5 **Don't Cry No More**	*Saint James Infirmary*	$25		Duke 340
12/4/61+	**28**	10		6 **Turn On Your Love Light**	*You're The One (That I Need)*	$20		Duke 344
3/31/62	**76**	4		7 **Who Will The Next Fool Be**	*Blue Moon*	$20		Duke 347
				written by **Charlie Rich**				
3/31/62	**86**	1		8 **Ain't That Loving You**	*Jelly, Jelly, Jelly*	$25		Duke 338
8/11/62	**56**	8		9 **Yield Not To Temptation**	*How Does A Cheating Woman Feel*	$20		Duke 352
9/8/62	**43**	13		10 **Stormy Monday Blues**	*Your Friends*	$20		Duke 355
				#5 R&B hit in 1948 for T-Bone Walker as "Call It Stormy Monday"				
1/5/63	**22**	12		11 **Call On Me /**				
1/19/63	**33**	10		12 **That's The Way Love Is** RB[2]		$20		Duke 360
7/20/63	**56**	6		13 **Sometimes You Gotta Cry A Little**	*You're Worth It All*	$15		Duke 366
12/28/63+	**91**	3		14 **The Feeling Is Gone**	*I Can't Stop Singing (#106)*	$15		Duke 370
3/7/64	**20**	9		15 **Ain't Nothing You Can Do**	*Honey Child*	$15		Duke 375
6/13/64	**42**	9		16 **Share Your Love With Me**	*After It's Too Late (#111)*	$15		Duke 377
10/24/64	**49**	6		17 **Ain't Doing Too Bad (Part 1)**	*(Part 2)*	$15		Duke 383
1/9/65	**78**	3		18 **Blind Man /**				
1/2/65	**99**	1		19 **Black Night**		$15		Duke 386
4/24/65	**93**	1		20 **Ain't No Telling**	*Dust Got In Daddy's Eyes (#125)*	$15		Duke 390
8/28/65	**63**	8		21 **These Hands (Small But Mighty)**	*Today*	$15		Duke 385
1/8/66	**62**	6		22 **I'm Too Far Gone (To Turn Around)**	*If You Could Read My Mind*	$15		Duke 393
5/21/66	**75**	6		23 **Good Time Charlie**	*Good Time Charlie (Working His Groove Bag)*	$10		Duke 402
9/17/66	**65**	5		24 **Poverty**	*Building A Fire With Rain*	$10		Duke 407
4/22/67	**88**	2		25 **You're All I Need**	*Deep In My Soul*	$10		Duke 416
3/9/68	**96**	3		26 **Driftin' Blues**	*A Piece Of Gold*	$10		Duke 432
				#2 R&B hit in 1946 for Johnny Moore's Three Blazers				
11/16/68+	**58**	10		27 **Rockin' In The Same Old Boat**	*Wouldn't You Rather Have Me*	$10		Duke 440
6/14/69	**91**	3		28 **Gotta Get To Know You**	*Baby, I'm On My Way*	$10		Duke 447
9/13/69	**60**	7		29 **Chains Of Love**	*Ask Me 'Bout Nothing (But The Blues)*	$10		Duke 449
				#2 R&B hit in 1951 for **Joe Turner**				
2/14/70	**96**	2		30 **If You've Got A Heart**	*Sad Feeling*	$10		Duke 458
12/5/70	**89**	3		31 **Keep On Loving Me (You'll See The Change)**	*I've Just Got To Forget About You*	$10		Duke 464
6/19/71	**97**	1		32 **I'm Sorry**	*Yum Yum Tree*	$10		Duke 466
				#19 R&B hit in 1958 for Kenny Martin				
2/26/72	**64**	5		33 **Do What You Set Out To Do**	*Ain't Nothing You Can Do*	$10		Duke 472
11/17/73+	**42**	13		34 **This Time I'm Gone For Good**	*Where Baby Went*	$5		Dunhill/ABC 4369
				#3-6, 8, 9, 11-18, 20, 21, 23, 27, 28, 30, 33 & 34: written by Deadric Malone				
3/2/74	**69**	6		35 **Goin' Down Slow**	*Up And Down World*	$5		Dunhill/ABC 4379
				BOBBY BLUE BLAND (above 2)				
8/10/74	**91**	7		36 **Ain't No Love In The Heart Of The City**	*Twenty-Four Hour Blues*	$5		Dunhill/ABC 15003
11/23/74	**88**	7		37 **I Wouldn't Treat A Dog (The Way You Treated Me)**	*I Ain't Gonna Be The First To Cry*	$5		Dunhill/ABC 15015
				BLANE, Marcie '62				
				Born on 5/21/44 in Brooklyn, New York. Pop singer.				
10/20/62	**3**	16		1 **Bobby's Girl**	*A Time To Dream*	$20		Seville 120
2/23/63	**82**	3		2 **What Does A Girl Do?**	*How Can I Tell Him?*	$20		Seville 123
				Billy Mure (orch., above 2)				
				BLAQ, Rufus '98				
				Born Rufus Moore in Youngstown, Ohio. Male rapper.				
5/2/98	**97**	4		**Out Of Sight (Yo)**	*Credentials*	$4	▮	Perspective 587594
				BLAQTHOVEN — see EASTSIDAZ				
				BLAQUE R&B/LP '99				
				Female R&B vocal trio from Atlanta, Georgia: Shamari Fears, Natina Reed and Brandi Williams.				
4/17/99	**8**	20	●	1 **808**	S:4 / A:22 *(instrumental)*	$4	★V	Track Masters 78857
				written and produced by **R. Kelly**; "45" B-side: "I Do"				
10/23/99+	**5**	29		2 **Bring It All To Me**	A:4			album cut
				BLAQUE (Feat. *NSYNC)				
				above 2 from the album *Blaque* on Track Masters 68987				
				BLAZE '76				
				Five-member pop-rock group from Cincinnati, Ohio.				
12/11/76	**95**	2		**Silver Heels**	*Rock N' Roll Madness*	$5		Epic 50292
				first recorded by **Fleetwood Mac** on their 1974 album *Heroes Are Hard To Find*				
				BLEND, The '78				
				Rock group from Portland, Maine: Jim Drown (vocals, guitar), Steven Dore (guitar), Donnie Pomber (keyboards), Ken Holt (bass) and Skip Smith (drums). Drown died on 12/3/2002 (age 55).				
12/16/78	**91**	5		**I'm Gonna Make You Love Me**	*I Hope You Find Somethin'*	$5		MCA 40961
				BLENDELLS, The '64				
				Latin rock group from Los Angeles, California: Sal Murillo (vocals), Rudy Valona and Tommy Esparza (guitars), Don Cardenas (sax), Mike Rincon (bass) and Ron Chipres (drums).				
9/12/64	**62**	8		**La La La La La**	*Huggie's Bunnies*	$20		Reprise 0291
				first released on Rampart 641 in 1964 ($30); first recorded by **Stevie Wonder** in 1963				

DEBUT	PEAK	WKS	Gold	A-side (Chart Hit)..........B-side	$	Sym	Label & Number
				BLENDERS, The '63			
				R&B vocal group from Chicago, Illinois: Hilliard "Johnny" Jones (formerly with the Five Chances), Albert Hunter, Goldie Coates, Delores Johnson and Gail Mapp (lead). Later recorded as The Candles on the Nike label.			
7/6/63	61	8		**Daughter**.......... *Everybody's Got A Right*	$25		Witch 114
				BLESSID UNION OF SOULS LP '95			
				Interracial Adult Alternative group from Cincinnati, Ohio: Eliot Sloan (vocals, piano), Jeff Pence (guitar), Charly Roth (keyboards), Tony Clark (bass) and Eddie Hedges (drums). Group name taken from a line in the TV show *M*A*S*H*.			
2/18/95	8	31		1 **I Believe** A:3 / S:14 *(album version) / Heaven*	$3	▮V	EMI 58320
8/5/95	29	20		2 **Let Me Be The One** ....A:28 / S:66 *Who's To Blame*	$3	▮V	EMI 58443
				"45" issued for above 2 on EMI 18737			
2/17/96	54^A	7		3 **Oh Virginia**			album cut
7/13/96	70	14		4 **All Along** ....A:65 *Home / I Believe (acoustic version)*	$3	▮V	EMI 58576
				"45": EMI 19205; all of above from the album *Home* on EMI 31836			
5/10/97	39	20		5 **I Wanna Be There**..........A:47 / S:55 *Walk Away*	$3	▮V	EMI 58643
				"45": EMI 19562			
2/14/98	48	19		6 **Light In Your Eyes** ....A:50 / S:57 *I Believe (acoustic version)*	$3	▮V	Capitol 58670
				"45": EMI 19850; B-side: "I Wanna Be There"			
6/12/99	33	20		7 **Hey Leonardo (she likes me for me)**..........A:28			album cut
				from the album *Walking Off The Buzz* on Push 27047			
				BLEYER, Archie, Orchestra and Chorus POP '54			
				Born on 6/12/09 in Corona, New York. Died of Parkinson's disease on 3/20/89 (age 79). Arranger/music director for the radio and TV show *Arthur Godfrey and His Friends* from 1949-54. Founded Cadence Records. Married **Chordettes** member Janet Ertel in 1954. Hit #2 on the pop charts in 1954 with "Hernando's Hideaway."			
12/4/54+	17	6		1 **The Naughty Lady Of Shady Lane** ..A:17 / J:20 / S:26 *While The Vesper Bells Were Ringing*	$15		Cadence 1254
6/30/56	61	3		2 **The Rockin' Ghost**..........T:61 *Sleep, Sleep, Daughter*	$15		Cadence 1293
				written by **Steve Allen**			
				BLIGE, Mary J. ★116★ R&B/BUB/LP '01			
				Born Mary Jane Blige on 1/11/71 in Atlanta, Georgia; raised in Yonkers, New York. R&B singer. Also see **Case**'s "Touch Me Tease Me."			
				1)Family Affair 2)Not Gon' Cry 3)I'll Be There For You/You're All I Need To Get By 4)Real Love 5)Rainy Dayz			
6/20/92	29	20	●	1 **You Remind Me** ....RB^1 S:17 / A:37 *(instrumental)*	$3	▮	Uptown/MCA 54327
				from the movie *Strictly Business* starring Tommy Davidson			
8/29/92	7	31	●	2 **Real Love** ....RB^2 A:4 / S:12 *(hip hop version)*	$3	▮V	Uptown/MCA 54455
12/19/92	57	20		3 **Reminisce**..........A:46 / S:48 *(instrumental)*	$3	▮V	Uptown/MCA 54526
2/13/93	28	20		4 **Sweet Thing** ....A:16 / S:43 *Slow Down*	$3	▮V	Uptown/MCA 54586
5/15/93	44	16		5 **Love No Limit**..........A:30 / S:49 *(instrumental)*	$3	▮V	Uptown/MCA 54639
				all of above from the album *What's The 411?*			
1/1/94	63	13		6 **You Don't Have To Worry**..........S:53 *(remix w/rap)*	$3	▮	Uptown/MCA 54701
				samples "Papa Don't Take No Mess" by **James Brown**; contains excerpts from "Ode To Billie Joe" as performed by **Lou Donaldson**			
11/5/94	29	20		7 **Be Happy** ....S:21 / A:48 *(acappella version)*	$3	▮	Uptown/MCA 54927
				samples "You're Too Good To Me" by **Curtis Mayfield**			
4/8/95	22	14		8 **I'm Goin' Down**..........S:11 / A:22 *(remix)*	$3	▮	Uptown/MCA 55008
5/6/95	3	20	▲	9 **I'll Be There For You/You're All I Need To Get By**..........RB^3 S:❶^1 / A:33 *(Puff Daddy mix)*	$3	▮	Def Jam 851878
				METHOD MAN featuring Mary J. Blige			
				medley of 2 songs written by **Ashford & Simpson**			
6/17/95	57	19		10 **You Bring Me Joy /**			
				samples "It's Ecstasy When You Lay Down Next To Me" by **Barry White**			
7/1/95	65	17		11 **I Love You**	$3	▮	Uptown/MCA 55029
				#7, 8, 10 & 11: from the album *My Life*			
10/28/95	95	2		12 **(You Make Me Feel Like A) Natural Woman**..........S:65 *Jeeps, Lex Coups, Bimaz & Benz* (**Lost Boyz**)	$3	▮	Uptown/MCA 55139
				from the TV show *New York Undercover* starring Michael DeLorenzo			
1/27/96	2^2	20	▲	13 **Not Gon' Cry** ....RB^5 S:❶^5 / A:19 *My Funny Valentine* (**Chaka Khan**)	$3	▮V	Arista 12957
				from the movie *Waiting To Exhale* starring **Whitney Houston**			
3/29/97	43^A	12		14 **Love Is All We Need**			album cut
7/26/97	28	19		15 **I Can Love You** ....S:18 / A:75 *Love Is All We Need* (w/**Foxy Brown**)	$3	▮	MCA 55362
				samples "Queen Bitch" by **Lil' Kim**			
9/27/97	24	20		16 **Everything**..........S:23 / A:40 *(radio edit)*	$3	▮	MCA 55353
				samples "You Are Everything" by **The Stylistics**, "The Payback" by **James Brown** and "Sukiyaki" by **A Taste Of Honey**			
3/7/98	71^A	1		17 **Seven Days**			album cut
				above 4 from the album *Share My World* on MCA 11606			
12/5/98	79	5		18 **Lean On Me**..........A:67			album cut
				KIRK FRANKLIN featuring Mary J. Blige, Bono, R. Kelly, Crystal Lewis and The Family			
				from the album *The Nu Nation Project* on Gospo Centric 90178			
7/24/99	44	14		19 **All That I Can Say**..........A:33			album cut
				written and produced by **Lauryn Hill**			
11/13/99+	63	15		20 **Deep Inside** A:46			album cut
				Elton John (acoustic piano); samples "Bennie And The Jets"			
4/15/00	68	9		21 **Give Me You** ....A:58 *(remix) / Let No Man Put Asunder*	$6	T	MCA 155708
				above 3 from the album *Mary* on MCA 11929			
10/7/00	38	19		22 **911** ....A:30 / S:61 *(5 versions)*	$6	T	Columbia 79460
				WYCLEF JEAN Featuring Mary J. Blige			
				samples "The Payback" by **James Brown** and "What I Am" by **Edie Brickell & New Bohemians**			

DEBUT	PEAK	WKS	Gold	A-side (Chart Hit)..........B-side	$	Sym	Label & Number
				BLIGE, Mary J. — Cont'd			
7/28/01	$❶^{6}$	41		23 **Family Affair** RB^{2} A:$❶^{5}$ / S:4 *(3 versions) / Checkin' For Me*	$7	★*	MCA 155894
				produced by **Dr. Dre**; second cut on CD single is a remix featuring **Jadakiss** and **Fabolous**			
12/15/01+	15	20		24 **No More Drama** ....A:15 / S:24 *(5 versions)*	$6	T	MCA 155929
				samples "Nadia's Theme (The Young And The Restless)" by **Barry DeVorzon & Perry Botkin, Jr.**			
3/30/02	12	20		25 **Rainy Dayz** ....A:10 / S:60 *(3 versions)*	$6	T	MCA 155972
				MARY J. BLIGE Featuring Ja Rule			
12/21/02+	65	15		26 **Come Close To Me** ....S:37 / A:65 *(2 versions) / I Got A Right Ta*	$6	T	MCA 113957
				COMMON Featuring Mary J. Blige			
				BLIND MELON ROK/LP **'93**			
				Male rock group formed in Los Angeles, California: Shannon Hoon (vocals), Rogers Stevens and Christopher Thorn (guitars), Brad Smith (bass) and Glen Graham (drums). Stevens, Smith and Graham are from West Point, Mississippi. Hoon died of a drug overdose on 10/21/95 (age 28).			
8/21/93	20	23		1 **No Rain** ....AR^{2} / MR^{3} A:16 / S:66 *(live) / Drive / Soak The Sin*	$6	★*V	Capitol 15994
				"45": Capitol 17590 (black or yellow vinyl); B-side: "Tones Of Home" (ROK #10); cassette single (Capitol 44939-$30) issued early in 1993 and in very limited distribution			
8/19/95	54^{A}	8		2 **Galaxie**		V	album cut
				from the album *Soup* on Capitol 28732; "45": Capitol 18726; B-side: "Toes Across The Floor"			
				BLINK-182 ROK/BUB/LP **'00**			
				Rock trio from San Diego, California: Tom DeLonge (vocals, guitar), Mark Hoppus (vocals, bass) and Scott Raynor (drums). Travis Barker replaced Raynor in 1998.			
1/24/98	61^{A}	9		1 **Dammit (Growing Up)**			album cut
				from the album *Dude Ranch* on Cargo 11624			
7/17/99	58	20		2 **What's My Age Again?** A:49			album cut
12/4/99+	6	23		3 **All The Small Things** MR^{8} S:5 / A:18 *M&M's*	$4	★	MCA 155606
				above 2 from the album *Enema Of The State* on MCA 11950			
7/28/01	71	9		4 **The Rock Show** A:71			album cut
				from the album *Take Off Your Pants And Jacket* on MCA 112627			
12/8/01+	34^{S}	7		5 **I Won't Be Home For Christmas** ...*All The Small Things / Josie / Please Take Me Home* [X]	$8	★*	MCA 155886
				BLINKY — see STARR, Edwin			
				BLOCKA BOYZ, The **'01**			
				Rap group from Orlando, Florida.			
10/27/01	50^{S}	3		**Whatcha Wants To Do** ....*(instrumental)*	$10	★	Malachi 17742
	★338★			**BLONDIE** ROK/BUB/LP **'80**			
				New-wave rock group formed in New York City, New York: **Debbie Harry** (vocals; born on 7/1/45), Chris Stein (born on 1/5/50) and Frank Infante (guitars), Jimmy Destri (keyboards; born on 4/13/54), Nigel Harrison (bass; born on 4/24/51) and Clem Burke (drums; born on 11/24/55). Harry had been in the folk-rock group Wind In The Willows. Disbanded in 1982; reunited in 1999.			
				1)Call Me 2)Rapture 3)The Tide Is High			
2/17/79	$❶^{1}$	21	●	1 **Heart Of Glass** *11:59*	$5	■	Chrysalis 2295
6/2/79	24	14		2 **One Way Or Another** ....*Just Go Away*	$5		Chrysalis 2336
9/29/79	27	14		3 **Dreaming** ....*Living In The Real World*	$5		Chrysalis 2379
2/2/80	84	3		4 **The Hardest Part** ....*Sound-A-Sleep*	$5	■	Chrysalis 2408
2/16/80	$❶^{6}$	25	●	5 **Call Me** *(instrumental)* (**Giorgio Moroder**)	$5	■	Chrysalis 2414
				theme from the movie *American Gigolo* starring Richard Gere; issued with 2 different picture sleeves			
5/17/80	39	9		6 **Atomic** ....*Die Young Stay Pretty*	$5	■	Chrysalis 2410
11/15/80+	$❶^{1}$	26	●	7 **The Tide Is High** ....*Suzy And Jeffrey*	$5	■	Chrysalis 2465
				first recorded by Jamaican reggae band, The Paragons (not to be confused with the doo-wop group listed in this book)			
1/31/81	$❶^{2}$	20	●	8 **Rapture** ....*Walk Like Me*	$5	■	Chrysalis 2485
5/29/82	37	10		9 **Island Of Lost Souls** ....*Dragonfly*	$5	■	Chrysalis 2603
				all of above produced by Mike Chapman (except #5: **Giorgio Moroder**)			
4/10/99	82	6		10 **Maria** ....S:47 *(3 versions)*	$8	★*	Logic/Beyond 78040
				BLOODHOUND GANG ROK/LP **'00**			
				Electro-rock group from Philadelphia, Pennsylvania: Jimmy Pop Ali (vocals), Lupus (guitar), Q-Ball (DJ), Evil Jared (bass) and Spanky G (drums).			
3/18/00	52	12		**The Bad Touch** A:50			album cut
				from the album *Hooray For Boobies* on Republic 490455			
				BLOODROCK LP **'71**			
				Rock group from Fort Worth, Texas: Jim Rutledge (vocals), Lee Pickens and Nick Taylor (guitars), Stevie Hill (keyboards), Eddie Grundy (bass) and Rick Cobb (drums). Rutledge headed own production company in the 1970s; produced **Meri Wilson**'s "Telephone Man."			
1/2/71	36	13		**D.O.A.** ....*Children's Heritage*	$8		Capitol 3009
				BLOODSTONE R&B/BUB/LP **'73**			
				R&B vocal group from Kansas City, Missouri: Charles Love, Willis Draffen, Charles McCormick and Harry Williams. Group starred in the 1975 movie *Train Ride To Hollywood*. Draffen died on 2/8/2002 (age 56).			
4/21/73	10	19	▲	1 **Natural High** *Peter's Jones*	$6		London 1046
9/15/73	43	14		2 **Never Let You Go** ....*You Know We've Learned*	$6		London 1051
2/23/74	34	14		3 **Outside Woman** ....*Dumb Dude*	$6		London 1052
7/27/74	82	6		4 **That's Not How It Goes** ....*Everybody Needs Love*	$6		London 1055
3/29/75	57	7		5 **My Little Lady** ....*Loving You Is Just A Pastime*	$6		London 1061
	★492★			**BLOOD, SWEAT & TEARS** BUB/AC/LP **'69**			
				Rock-jazz group formed by Al Kooper (keyboards; born on 2/5/44; **Royal Teens, Blues Project**) in 1967. Nucleus consisted of Kooper, Steve Katz (guitar; born on 5/9/45; **American Flyer**; Blues Project), Bobby Colomby (drums; born on 12/20/44) and Jim Fielder (bass; born on 10/4/47). Kooper replaced by lead singer David Clayton-Thomas (born on 9/13/41) by 1969. Clayton-Thomas replaced by Jerry Fisher in 1972. Katz left in 1973. Clayton-Thomas rejoined in 1974. Colomby later worked as a television music reporter and an executive with Epic, Capitol, EMI and CBS.			
				1)Spinning Wheel 2)You've Made Me So Very Happy 3)And When I Die			
3/1/69	2^{3}	13	●	1 **You've Made Me So Very Happy** ....*Blues - Part II*	$6		Columbia 44776

DEBUT	PEAK	WKS	Gold	A-side (Chart Hit)...B-side	$	Sym	Label & Number
				BLOOD, SWEAT & TEARS — Cont'd			
5/31/69	2^3	13	●	2 **Spinning Wheel** AC^2 *More And More*	$6		Columbia 44871
				ends with the 1815 Austrian tune "O Du Lieber Augustin" ("Did You Ever See A Lassie")			
10/18/69	2^1	13	●	3 **And When I Die** ... *Sometimes In Winter*	$6		Columbia 45008
				written by **Laura Nyro**			
8/1/70	**14**	8		4 **Hi-De-Ho** ... *The Battle*	$6		Columbia 45204
10/3/70	**29**	7		5 **Lucretia Mac Evil** ... *Lucretia's Reprise*	$6		Columbia 45235
7/31/71	**32**	8		6 **Go Down Gamblin'** ... *Valentine's Day*	$6	■	Columbia 45427
10/30/71	**73**	6		7 **Lisa, Listen To Me** ... *Cowboys And Indians*	$6		Columbia 45477
9/30/72	**44**	11		8 **So Long Dixie** ... *Alone*	$6	■	Columbia 45661
6/29/74	**83**	4		9 **Tell Me That I'm Wrong** ... *Rock Reprise*	$5		Columbia 46059
6/14/75	**62**	6		10 **Got To Get You Into My Life** ... *Naked Man*	$5		Columbia 10151
				BLOOM, Bobby BUB/LP **'70**			
				Born in 1945 in New York City, New York. Died from an accidental shooting on 2/28/74 (age 28). Pop singer/songwriter. Much session work in the 1960s.			
9/12/70	**8**	16		1 **Montego Bay** ... *Try A Little Harder*	$8		L&R/MGM 157
1/9/71	**84**	4		2 **Where Are We Going** ... *Of Yesterday*	$8		Roulette 7095
1/16/71	**80**	6		3 **Make Me Happy** ... *This Thing I've Gotten Into*	$8		MGM 14212
6/26/71	**93**	4		4 **We're All Goin' Home** ... *Careful Not To Break The Spell*	$8		MGM 14246
				BLOSSOMS, The R&B/BUB **'61**			
				Female R&B backing vocal group for **Elvis Presley**, **Paul Anka**, **Duane Eddy**, **Bobby Darin**, **Mamas & Papas**, **Beach Boys**, **Herb Alpert**, **Dionne Warwick** and many others. Regulars on TV's *Shindig.* Members **Darlene Love**, Fanita James (nee Barrett) and Gloria Jones were members of **Bob B. Soxx & The Blue Jeans**. Also included twins Annette and Nanette Williams. Grazia Nitzsche (wife of **Jack Nitzsche**) sang on the sessions. Love also sang lead on two hits by **The Crystals**.			
5/8/61	**79**	4		**Son-In-Law** ... *I'll Wait*	$25		Challenge 9109
				answer song to **Ernie K-Doe**'s "Mother-In-Law"			
				BLOUNT, Tanya R&B **'94**			
				Born on 9/25/77 in Washington DC. Female R&B singer.			
10/8/94	**90**	6		**Through The Rain** ... *(radio edit)*	$3	▮	Polydor 853314
				BLOW, Kurtis R&B/LP **'85**			
				Born Kurt Walker on 8/9/59 in Harlem, New York. Pioneering rapper. Began as a disco DJ. Appeared in the movie *Krush Groove.*			
9/6/80	**87**	6		1 **The Breaks (Part 1)** ... *(Part 2)*	$6		Mercury 76075
				a new version with Nadanuf was a #58 R&B hit in 1997			
4/13/85	**71**	6		2 **Basketball** ... *(It's) The Game* (**Ralph MacDonald**) [N]	$6		Polydor 881529
				BLOW MONKEYS, The LP **'86**			
				Pop-rock group from England: "Dr. Robert" Howard (vocals, guitar), Neville Henry (saxophone), Mick Anker (bass) and Tony Kiley (drums).			
5/3/86	**14**	19		**Digging Your Scene** ... S:12 / A:16 *(U.K. mix)*	$4	■	RCA 14325
				BLUE **'77**			
				Pop-rock group from Glasgow, Scotland: brothers Hugh (guitar) and David (keyboards) Nicholson, Ian McMillan (bass) and Charlie Smith (drums).			
5/7/77	**88**	5		**Capture Your Heart** ... *The Shepherd*	$6		Rocket 40706
				co-produced by **Elton John**			
				BLUE, David **'73**			
				Born Stuart David Cohen on 2/18/41 in Providence, Rhode Island. Died while jogging on 12/2/82 (age 41).			
5/12/73	**94**	4		**Outlaw Man** ... *Troubadour Song*	$6		Asylum 11015
				produced by **Graham Nash**			
				BLUE-BELLES, The — see LaBELLE, Patti / STARLETS			
				BLUE CHEER LP **'68**			
				Hard-rock trio from San Francisco, California: Dickie Peterson (vocals, bass), Leigh Stephens (guitar) and Paul Whaley (drums). One of the first "heavy metal" bands.			
3/2/68	**14**	13		1 **Summertime Blues** ... *Out Of Focus*	$15	■	Philips 40516
7/6/68	**92**	4		2 **Just A Little Bit** ... *Gypsy Ball*	$12		Philips 40541
				BLUE DIAMONDS, The **'60**			
				Vocal duo from Indonesia: brothers Rudy (born on 12/5/41; died on 12/18/2000, age 59) and Riem DeWolff (born on 4/15/43). Immigrated to Holland in 1949.			
11/28/60	**72**	5		**Ramona** ... *All Of Me*	$12		London 1954
				#1 hit for both **Gene Austin** and Paul Whiteman in 1928			
				BLUE HAZE **'73**			
				Reggae group from England.			
11/11/72+	**27**	14		**Smoke Gets In Your Eyes** ... *Anna Rosanna*	$6		A&M 1357
				#1 hit for Paul Whiteman in 1934 (from the1933 Jerome Kern musical *Roberta* starring Bob Hope)			
				BLUE JAYS, The **'61**			
				R&B vocal group from Los Angeles, California: Leon Peels, Van Richardson, Alex Manigo and Leonard Davidson. Peels died of cancer on 4/12/99 (age 62).			
8/14/61	**31**	9		**Lover's Island** ... *You're Gonna Cry*	$40		Milestone 2008
				BLUE MAGIC R&B/BUB/LP **'74**			
				R&B vocal group from Philadelphia, Pennsylvania: Theodore Mills (lead), Vernon Sawyer, Wendell Sawyer, Keith Beaton and Richard Pratt.			
2/2/74	**74**	6		1 **Stop To Start** ... *Where Have You Been*	$7		Atco 6949
5/18/74	**8**	21	●	2 **Sideshow** ... RB^1 *Just Don't Want To Be Lonely*	$7		Atco 6961
10/19/74	**36**	9		3 **Three Ring Circus** ... *Welcome To The Club*	$7		Atco 7004

DEBUT	PEAK	WKS	Gold	A-side (Chart Hit)...B-side	$	Sym	Label & Number
				BLUE MERCEDES LP '88			
				Pop duo from London, England: David Titlow (vocals) and Duncan Millar (keyboards).			
3/5/88	66	6		**I Want To Be Your Property** ...*(instrumental)*	$3	■	MCA 53262
				BLUE MINK '70			
				Pop group from England: **Madeline Bell** and Roger Cook (vocals), Alan Parker (guitar), Roger Coulman (keyboards), Herbie Flowers (bass) and Barry Morgan (drums). Cook was half of **David & Jonathan** duo and co-founder of **White Plains**.			
9/26/70	64	6		**Our World**...*Respects To Mr. Jones*	$8		Philips 40686
				BLUENOTES, The '60			
				White male vocal group from Asheboro, North Carolina: Ralph Harrington, Pat Patterson, Tom Underwood and Joe Tanner (later an arranger/publisher; since deceased). Did backing vocals for **George Hamilton IV**.			
9/8/58	73	4		1 **My Lucky Love** ...H:73 *Drizzlin' Rain*	$20		Colonial 7777
				DOUG FRANKLIN with the Bluenotes			
12/14/59+	61	9		2 **I Don't Know What It Is**...*Summer Love*	$25		Brooke 111
				BLUE NOTES, The — see MELVIN, Harold			
				BLUE ÖYSTER CULT ROK/LP '76			
				Hard-rock group from Long Island, New York: Eric Bloom (vocals), Donald "Buck Dharma" Roeser (guitar), Allen Lanier (keyboards), and brothers Joe (bass) and Albert (drums) Bouchard. Rick Downey replaced Albert Bouchard in 1982. Downey left in 1984. Tommy Zvoncheck (keyboards) and Jimmy Wilcox (drums) joined in 1985. Bloom is a cousin of DJ Howard Stern.			
7/31/76	12	20		1 **(Don't Fear) The Reaper** ...*Tattoo Vampire*	$6		Columbia 10384
9/8/79	74	4		2 **In Thee** ...*Lonely Teardrops*	$4		Columbia 11055
8/15/81	40	14		3 **Burnin' For You** ...AR[2] *Vengeance (The Pact)*	$4	■	Columbia 02415
2/11/84	83	3		4 **Shooting Shark** ...*Dragon Lady*	$4	■	Columbia 04298
				BLUE RIDGE RANGERS — see FOGERTY, John			
				BLUES BROTHERS BUB/LP '79			
				Duo of comedians **John Belushi** (see #1 below) (as "Jake Blues") and Dan Aykroyd (as "Elwood Blues"). Originally created for TV's *Saturday Night Live*. Starred in their own movie. Belushi was born on 1/24/49 in Wheaton, Illinois. Died of a drug overdose on 3/5/82 (age 33). Aykroyd was born on 7/1/52 in Ottawa, Ontario, Canada. Backing band included **Paul Shaffer**, and Steve Cropper and Donald "Duck" Dunn of **Booker T. & The MG's**. Actor John Goodman replaced Belushi for the *Blues Brothers 2000* movie.			
9/30/78	89	4		1 **Louie, Louie**...*Money (That's What I Want)*	$5		MCA 40950
				JOHN BELUSHI			
				from the movie *National Lampoon's Animal House* starring Belushi			
12/9/78+	14	15		2 **Soul Man** *Excusez Moi Mon Cherie*	$5	■	Atlantic 3545
3/3/79	37	8		3 **Rubber Biscuit** ...*"B" Movie Box Car Blues* [N]	$5		Atlantic 3564
				gibberish tune introduced by The Chips in 1956 (Josie 803-$100)			
5/31/80	18	14		4 **Gimme Some Lovin'**...*She Caught The Katy*	$5	■	Atlantic 3666
				from the soundtrack *The Blues Brothers*			
12/20/80+	39	11		5 **Who's Making Love**...*Perry Mason Theme*	$5		Atlantic 3785
				BLUES IMAGE LP '70			
				Rock group from Tampa, Florida: **Mike Pinera** (vocals, guitar; **Iron Butterfly**), Frank "Skip" Konte (keyboards; **Three Dog Night**), Joe Lala (percussion), Malcolm Jones (bass) and Manuel Bertematti (drums).			
5/9/70	4	15	●	1 **Ride Captain Ride**...*Pay My Dues*	$8		Atco 6746
9/26/70	81	4		2 **Gas Lamps And Clay** ...*Running The Water*	$8		Atco 6777
				BLUES MAGOOS BUB/LP '67			
				Psychedelic-rock group from the Bronx, New York: Emil "Peppy Castro" Thielhelm (vocals, guitar), Mike Esposito (guitar), Ralph Scala (keyboards), Ronnie Gilbert (bass) and Geoff Daking (drums). Originally known as the Bloos Magoos. Castro later became lead singer of **Balance**.			
12/10/66+	5	14		1 **(We Ain't Got) Nothin' Yet**...*Gotta Get Away*	$20		Mercury 72622
3/18/67	60	6		2 **Pipe Dream** /			
4/8/67	81	2		3 **There's A Chance We Can Make It** ...	$15	■	Mercury 72660
6/10/67	71	5		4 **One By One**...*Dante's Inferno*	$15	■	Mercury 72692
				BLUES PROJECT, The LP '67			
				Blues-rock group from New York City, New York: Danny Kalb (guitar) and Roy Blumenfeld (drums). Vocalist Tommy Flanders left group in 1966. Guitarist Steve Katz and organist Al Kooper took over vocals. Katz and Kooper left to form **Blood, Sweat & Tears** in 1968.			
4/1/67	96	2		**No Time Like The Right Time** ...*Steve's Song*	$15		Verve Folkways 5040
				BLUE STARS '56			
				Pop-jazz group formed in Paris, France. Lead vocals by Blossom Dearie (born on 4/28/26 in East Durham, New York), a former big-band singer who sang with King Pleasure on his 1952 R&B hit "Moody Mood For Love."			
12/17/55+	16	20		**Lullaby Of Birdland** ...A:16 / S:20 / T:20 *That's My Girl* [F]	$15		Mercury 70742
				arranged by **Michel Legrand**; composed by George Shearing in 1952			
				BLUES TRAVELER ROK/LP '95			
				Blues-rock group from New York City, New York: John Popper (vocals, harmonica), Chan Kinchla (guitar), Bobby Sheehan (bass) and Brendan Hill (drums). Sheehan died of a drug overdose on 8/20/99 (age 31); replaced by Chan's brother, Tad Kinchla.			
3/25/95	8	49		1 **Run-Around**...A:3 / S:27 *Trust In Trust*	$3	■[V]	A&M 0982
10/7/95+	23	34		2 **Hook**...A:18 / S:50 *Love & Greed*	$3	■[V]	A&M 1176
				"45" issued for above 2 on A&M 1174			
7/20/96	36[A]	19		3 **But Anyway** ... [L]			album cut
				from the album *Live From The Fall* on A&M 0515 (first recorded on their 1991 studio album *Blues Traveler* on A&M 5308)			
10/18/97	74[A]	1		4 **Most Precarious**...			album cut
				from the album *Straight On Till Morning* on A&M 0750			

DEBUT	PEAK	WKS	Gold	A-side (Chart Hit)...B-side	$	Sym	Label & Number
				BLUE SWEDE LP '74			
				Pop group from Sweden: Bjorn Skifs (vocals), Michael Areklew (guitar), Anders Berglund (keyboards), Hinke Ekestubbe (sax), Thomas Berglund (trumpet), Bosse Liljedahl (bass) and Jan Guldback (drums).			
2/16/74	❶[1]	17	●	1 Hooked On A Feeling ... *Gotta Have Your Love*	$6		EMI 3627
				also released on Capitol 3627 in 1974; "oogachuga" arrangement borrowed from **Jonathan King**'s 1971 British hit of the same title			
6/15/74	71	4		2 **Silly Milly** ... *Lonely Sunday Afternoon*	$6	■	EMI 3893
8/24/74	7	11		3 Never My Love ... *Pinewood Rally*	$6	■	EMI 3938
2/22/75	61	5		4 **Hush/I'm Alive** ... *Lonely Sunday Afternoon*	$6		EMI 4029
				medley of the **Deep Purple** hit and the B-side of **Tommy James & The Shondells**' hit "Crystal Blue Persuasion"			
				BLUE TRAIN '91			
				Rock group from Nottingham, Nottinghamshire, England: Tony Osborne (vocals), Alan Fearn (guitar), Simon Husbands (keyboards) and Paul Betts (drums).			
10/5/91	46	13		**All I Need Is You** ... A:68 *(remix)*	$4	▮	Zoo 14018
				BLUE ZONE U.K. — see STANSFIELD, Lisa			
				BLUR ROK/LP '94			
				Techno-rock group from London, England: Damon Albarn (vocals), Graham Coxon (guitar), Alex James (bass) and Dave Rowntree (drums).			
1/11/92	82	6		1 **There's No Other Way** ... *Explain*	$3	▮	SBK/Food 07374
6/25/94	59	15		2 **Girls & Boys** ... A:61 / S:63 *(**Pet Shop Boys** radio edit) / Maggie May*	$3	▮	SBK/Food 58155
5/17/97	55[A]	11		3 **Song 2** ...		V	album cut
				from the album *Blur* on SBK/Food 42876; "45": Virgin 19581; B-side: "Get Out Of Cities"			
				BMU (BLACK MEN UNITED) '94			
				All-star gathering of top R&B stars: **R. Kelly**, **Tevin Campbell**, **Aaron Hall**, **Brian McKnight**, **Boyz II Men**, **Tony Toni Toné**, **Silk**, **Keith Sweat**, Stokley (**Mint Condition**), **H-Town**, **Christopher Williams**, **Portrait**, **Gerald Levert**, **Al B. Sure!**, Damion Hall, Lil' Joe (**Rude Boys**), **Intro**, **D.R.S.**, **El DeBarge**, **After 7**, **Usher**, Sovory, **Joe**, **D'Angelo** and **Lenny Kravitz** (guitar).			
10/8/94	28	20		**U Will Know** ... S:12 *(extended version) / (3 album snippets)*	$4	▮V	Mercury 856200
				from the movie *Jason's Lyric* starring Forest Whitaker; "45": Mercury 856272; B-side: (same version)			
				BO, Eddie '69			
				Born Edwin Bocage on 9/20/30 in New Orleans, Louisiana. R&B singer/pianist/producer. Nicknamed "Spider."			
8/2/69	73	9		**Hook And Sling-Part I** ... *Part II*	$8		Scram 117
				BOB & EARL R&B/BUB '64			
				R&B vocal duo: Bob Relf & Earl Nelson. **Bobby Day** sang with Earl Nelson (as Bob & Earl) in 1960, however, Day was not involved in either of Bob & Earl's charted hits. Earl Lee Nelson (wife's name was Jackie) recorded the hit "The Duck" as **Jackie Lee**. Earl was also lead singer on the **Hollywood Flames**' hit "Buzz-Buzz-Buzz."			
10/20/62	85	4		1 **Don't Ever Leave Me** ... *Fancy Free*	$25		Tempe 102
12/21/63+	44	11		2 **Harlem Shuffle** ... *I'll Keep Running Back*	$20		Marc 104
				BOBBETTES, The BUB '57			
				Female R&B vocal group from Harlem, New York: sisters Emma and Jannie Pought, Laura Webb, Helen Gathers and Heather Dixon. Jannie Pought died in a car crash in September 1980 (age 36). Webb died of cancer on 1/8/2001 (age 59).			
8/5/57	6	24		1 Mr. Lee RB[4] T:6 / A:6 / S:7 *Look At The Stars*	$30		Atlantic 1144
				song inspired by the group's 5th grade teacher			
7/4/60	52	8		2 **I Shot Mr. Lee** ... *Billy*	$25		Triple-X 104
				also released on Atlantic 2069 in 1960 ($25; B-side: "Untrue Love")			
10/10/60	66	8		3 **Have Mercy Baby** /			
				#1 R&B hit in 1952 for **The Dominoes**			
10/24/60	95	1		4 **Dance With Me Georgie** ...	$25		Triple-X 106
				twist version of **Georgia Gibbs**' 1955 hit "Dance With Me Henry"			
9/4/61	72	4		5 **I Don't Like It Like That** ... *Mr. Johnny Q*	$25		Gone 5112
				answer song to **Chris Kenner**'s "I Like It Like That"; originally released on End 1095 in 1961 ($30)			
				BOB B. SOXX And The Blue Jeans '63			
				Vocal trio formed by producer Phil Spector (**The Teddy Bears**). Bobby Sheen (**The Alley Cats**) with **Darlene Love** and Fanita James (both formerly with **The Blossoms**). Love and James later replaced by Gloria Jones (also with The Blossoms) and Carolyn Willis. Sheen died of pneumonia on 11/23/2000 (age 58).			
11/17/62+	8	13		1 Zip-A-Dee Doo-Dah ... *Flip And Nitty*	$25		Philles 107
				Academy Award winning song introduced in the 1947 Disney movie *Song Of The South*			
2/16/63	38	9		2 **Why Do Lovers Break Each Other's Heart?** ... *Dr. Kaplan's Office*	$25		Philles 110
6/8/63	63	6		3 **Not Too Young To Get Married** ... *Annette*	$25		Philles 113
				all of above produced by Phil Spector and arranged by **Jack Nitzsche**			
				BoDEANS ROK/LP '96			
				Folk-rock group from Waukesha, Wisconsin: Sam Llanas and Kurt Neumann (vocals, guitars), Michael Ramos (keyboards), Bob Griffin (bass) and Nick Kitsos (drums).			
3/9/96	16	20		**Closer To Free** ... A:6 *(live album version)*	$3	▮V	Slash 17674
				featured in the TV show *Party Of Five* starring Scott Wolf			
				BOHANNON, Hamilton R&B/BUB/LP '75			
				Born on 3/7/42 in Newnan, Georgia. **Stevie Wonder**'s drummer from 1965-67. Bandleader/arranger for Motown tours until the mid-1970s.			
9/13/75	98	2		**Foot Stompin Music** ... *Dance With Your Parno*	$6		Dakar 4544
				BOLGER, Ray '50			
				Born Raymond Bulcao on 1/10/04 in Dorchester, Massachusetts. Died of cancer on 1/15/87 (age 83). One of Broadway's best-loved dancers and comedians, featured in 11 productions from 1926-69. Made his permanent mark on movie history as "The Scarecrow" in *The Wizard Of Oz*.			
12/28/63	10[X]	1		L'il Elfy ... *Frosty The Snowman* [X-N]	$8	■	Armour 7799
				Gene Garf (orch.)			

DEBUT	PEAK	WKS	Gold	A-side (Chart Hit)...B-side	$	Sym	Label & Number

BOLTON, Michael ★121★ AC/ROK/BUB/LP '90

Born Michael Bolotin on 2/26/53 in New Haven, Connecticut. First recorded for Epic in 1968. Lead singer of **Blackjack** in the late 1970s. Began recording as Michael Bolton in 1983.

1)How Am I Supposed To Live Without You 2)When A Man Loves A Woman 3)How Can We Be Lovers 4)Love Is A Wonderful Thing 5)Said I Loved You...But I Lied

DEBUT	PEAK	WKS	Gold	A-side (Chart Hit)...B-side	$	Sym	Label & Number
5/14/83	82	3		1 **Fools Game** ...*Fighting For My Life*	$4		Columbia 03800
9/5/87	19	25		2 **That's What Love Is All About** ...A:17 / S:18 *Take A Look At My Face*	$4	⊙	Columbia 7322
1/23/88	11	17		3 **(Sittin' On) The Dock Of The Bay** ...S:7 / A:12 *Call My Name*	$4	■	Columbia 07680
				a special promotional picture sleeve also issued with a message from **Otis Redding**'s widow on the back of the sleeve			
5/28/88	79	6		4 **Wait On Love** ...*I Almost Believed You*	$4	■	Columbia 07794
7/1/89	17	17		5 **Soul Provider** ...S:18 / A:21 *The Hunger*	$4		Columbia 68909
10/28/89+	❶3	23		6 **How Am I Supposed To Live Without You** AC2 A:❶2 / S:❶1 *Forever Eyes*	$3	▮V	Columbia 73017
3/3/90	3	18		7 **How Can We Be Lovers** ...A:3 / S:4 *That's What Love Is All About*	$3	▮V	Columbia 73257
				"45": Columbia 73318			
5/26/90	7	19		8 **When I'm Back On My Feet Again** ...AC3 A:5 / S:14 *Walk Away*	$3	▮V	Columbia 73342
8/25/90	36	10		9 **Georgia On My Mind** ...A:30 / S:39 *Take A Look At My Face*	$3	▮V	Columbia 73490
				sax solo by **Kenny G** on single version, Michael Brecker (of **The Brecker Brothers**) on album version; tune written in 1930 by Hoagy Carmichael; #10 hit for Frankie Trumbauer in 1931; above 5 from the album *Soul Provider*			
4/20/91	4	17		10 **Love Is A Wonderful Thing** ...AC4 A:2 / S:11 *Soul Provider*	$3	▮V	Columbia 73719
				a 1994 court ruling found that Bolton took "significant" elements from **The Isley Brothers**' same-named song of 1966			
7/13/91	7	18		11 **Time, Love And Tenderness** ...AC2 A:15 / S:39 *That's What Love Is All About*	$3	▮V	Columbia 73889
10/12/91	❶1	20		12 **When A Man Loves A Woman** ...AC4 A:❶3 / S:8 *Save Me*	$3	▮V	Columbia 74020
1/25/92	12	20		13 **Missing You Now** ...AC3 A:10 / S:33 *It's Only My Heart* (Bolton)	$3	▮V	Columbia 74184
				MICHAEL BOLTON Featuring Kenny G			
5/16/92	16A	20		14 **Steel Bars** ...			album cut
				written by Bolton and **Bob Dylan**; above 5 from the album *Time, Love & Tenderness* on Columbia 46771			
10/17/92	11	20		15 **To Love Somebody** ...AC5 A:13 / S:16 *Now That I Found You*	$3	▮V	Columbia 74733
11/28/92	73A	1		16 **Reach Out I'll Be There** ...		V	album cut
1/9/93	73A	1		17 **White Christmas** ... [X]		V	album cut
				above 3 from the album *Timeless (The Classics)* on Columbia 52783; "45" issued for above 2 on Columbia 74798			
11/6/93+	6	24	●	18 **Said I Loved You...But I Lied** ...AC12 A:7 / S:10 *Soul Provider*	$3	▮V	Columbia 77260
3/19/94	32	15		19 **Completely** ...A:32 / S:51 *That's What Love Is All About (live)*	$3	▮V	Columbia 77376
6/25/94	30A	8		20 **Ain't Got Nothing If You Ain't Got Love** ...		V	album cut
				"45" and cassette issued with #21 below; above 3 from the album *The One Thing* on Columbia 53567			
9/2/95	27	14		21 **Can I Touch You...There?** ...S:26 / A:36 *Ain't Got Nothing If You Ain't Got Love*	$3	▮V	Columbia 77991
6/7/97	24	20	●	22 **Go The Distance** ...AC3 S:16 / A:62 *Soul Of My Soul*	$3	▮	Columbia 78554
				from the Disney animated movie *Hercules*			
11/29/97	65A	8		23 **The Best Of Love** ...			album cut
				from the album *All That Matters* on Columbia 68510			

BOND, Johnny C&W/LP '60

Born Cyrus Whitfield Bond on 6/1/15 in Enville, Oklahoma. Died of a heart attack on 6/12/78 (age 63). Country singer/songwriter/actor/author. Appeared in several movies.

DEBUT	PEAK	WKS	Gold	A-side (Chart Hit)...B-side	$	Sym	Label & Number
8/8/60	26	10		1 **Hot Rod Lincoln** ...*Five Minute Love Affair* [N-S]	$15		Republic 2005
				original version by Tiny Hill charted (#29) in 1951 as "Hot Rod Race"			
3/13/65	43	8		2 **10 Little Bottles** ...*Let It Be Me* [L-N-S]	$15		Starday 704
				originally released by Bond in 1954 on Columbia 21222 ($20)			

BONDS, Gary (U.S.) ★414★ BUB/LP '61

Born Gary Anderson on 6/6/39 in Jacksonville, Florida; raised in Norfolk, Virginia. Black rock and roll singer/songwriter.

1)Quarter To Three 2)School Is Out 3)New Orleans

DEBUT	PEAK	WKS	Gold	A-side (Chart Hit)...B-side	$	Sym	Label & Number
10/17/60	6	14		1 **New Orleans** *[U.S. BONDS]* ...*Please Forgive Me*	$25		Legrand 1003
5/22/61	❶2	15	●	2 **Quarter To Three** *[U.S. BONDS]* *Time Ole Story*	$20	■	Legrand 1008
				melody is the same as The Church Street Five's "A Night With Daddy G" ("Bubbled Under" at #111 in 1961)			
7/24/61	5	11		3 **School Is Out** ...*One Million Tears*	$20	■	Legrand 1009
10/23/61	28	5		4 **School Is In** ...*Trip To The Moon*	$20		Legrand 1012
12/11/61+	9	16		5 **Dear Lady Twist** ...*Havin' So Much Fun*	$20		Legrand 1015
3/31/62	9	10		6 **Twist, Twist Senora** ...*Food Of Love*	$20		Legrand 1018
				inspired by the calypso song "Shake Shake Senora (Jump In The Line)"			
6/23/62	27	7		7 **Seven Day Weekend** ...*Gettin' A Groove*	$20		Legrand 1019
				from the movie *It's Trad-Dad* starring **Helen Shapiro**			
8/25/62	92	3		8 **Copy Cat** ...*I'll Change That Too*	$20		Legrand 1020
4/25/81	11	18		9 **This Little Girl** ...*Way Back When*	$5	■	EMI America 8079
				written by **Bruce Springsteen** (also #11 below)			
7/18/81	65	6		10 **Jolé Blon** ...*Just Like A Child*	$5		EMI America 8089
				#2 Country hit for Moon Mullican in 1947			
6/12/82	21	16		11 **Out Of Work** ...*Bring Her Back*	$5	■	EMI America 8117
				Clarence Clemons (sax solo); above 3 produced by **Bruce Springsteen** and Miami Steve (**Little Steven**) Van Zandt			

BONES — see PEPPERMINT TROLLEY COMPANY, The

DEBUT	PEAK	WKS	Gold	A-side (Chart Hit).................B-side	$	Sym	Label & Number

BONE THUGS-N-HARMONY ★388★ R&B/BUB/LP '96

Male rap group from Cleveland, Ohio: Anthony Henderson ("**Krayzie Bone**"; born on 6/17/74) (see # 7 & 10 below), Charles Scruggs ("**Wish Bone**"; born on 2/26/77), Bryon McCane ("Bizzy Bone"; born on 9/12/76) (see #10 below) and brothers Steven Howse ("Layzie Bone"; born on 9/23/77) and Stanley Howse ("Flesh-N-Bone"; born on 6/24/75; went solo in 1996). Steven and Stanley are brothers; Scruggs is their cousin. Discovered by **Eazy-E**. Previously known as Bone Enterprise.

1)Tha Crossroads 2)Look Into My Eyes 3)1st Of Tha Month

DEBUT	PEAK	WKS	Gold	A-side (Chart Hit).................B-side	$	Sym	Label & Number
9/17/94	22	20	●	1 **thuggish-ruggish-Bone**.................S:10 / A:53 *(instrumental)* Shatasha Williams (female vocal)	$3	▮	Ruthless 5527
2/25/95	41	14		2 **Foe Tha Love Of $**.................S:18 *Moe Cheese / Thuggish Ruggish Bone / Moe $* **BONE THUGS N HARMONY Featuring Eazy-E**	$3	▮	Ruthless 5540
8/26/95	14	20	●	3 **1st Of Tha Month**.................S:9 / A:35 *(radio edit w/Tré) / Die Die Die*	$3	▮	Ruthless 6331
12/9/95+	62	13		4 **East 1999**.................S:34 *(remix) / Buddah Lovaz*	$3	▮	Ruthless 6332
5/11/96	❶[8]	20	▲[2]	5 **Tha Crossroads** RB[7] S:❶[9] / A:8 *Crossroad (album version)* contains an interpolation of **The Isley Brothers**' "Make Me Say It Again Girl"	$3	▮	Ruthless 6335
9/7/96	39[A]	14		6 **Days Of Our Livez**.................*Let It Go* (**Ray J** - #25) from the movie *Set It Off* starring Jada Pinkett	$3	▮	EastWest 64206
2/15/97	77	10		7 **Take Your Time**.................S:60 *Thug Devotion* (Mo Thugs Family) **TRÉ Featuring Krayzie Bone**	$3	▮	Mo Thugs 1586
6/21/97	4	20	▲	8 **Look Into My Eyes**.................S:2 / A:72 *(instrumental)* from the movie *Batman & Robin* starring George Clooney	$3	▮	Ruthless 6343
10/18/97	27	20	●	9 **If I Could Teach The World**.................S:14 *(3 versions) / Body Rott*	$3	▮	Ruthless 6344
3/7/98	53[A]	3		10 **Breakdown**.................*My All* (Carey - #1) **MARIAH CAREY (Featuring Krayzie Bone & Wish Bone)**	$3	▮[V]	Columbia 78821 ■
11/21/98+	15	20	●	11 **Ghetto Cowboy**.................S:5 *(album version) / (4 album snippets)* **MO THUGS FAMILY AND BONE THUGS N HARMONY** clean version available on Mo Thugs/Relativity 1747; Mo Thugs Family: Powder, Thug Queen and Felecia	$4	★	Mo Thugs/Relativity 1707

BONEY M R&B/BUB/LP '78

Vocal group created in Germany by producer/composer Frank Farian. Farian sang solo on first recording in 1975, group formed later. Consisted of Marcia Barrett, Maizie Williams, Liz Mitchell and Bobby Farrell. All were from the West Indies. Farian created the **Far Corporation** in 1986 and **Milli Vanilli** in 1988.

DEBUT	PEAK	WKS	Gold	A-side (Chart Hit).................B-side	$	Sym	Label & Number
1/22/77	65	5		1 **Daddy Cool**.................*Lovin' Or Leavin'*	$6		Atco 7063
8/27/77	96	3		2 **Ma Baker**.................*A Woman Can Change A Man* Ma Baker voice: Lorraine Pollack; radio voice: Bill Swisher	$5		Atlantic 3422
6/3/78	30	17		3 **Rivers Of Babylon**.................*Brown Girl In The Ring* lyrics based on Psalm 137 from the Bible	$5		Sire 1027
12/23/78	85	5		4 **Mary's Boy Child/Oh My Lord**.................*Dancing In The Streets* (#103) [X]	$5		Sire 1036

BONHAM ROK/LP '90

British hard-rock quartet led by drummer Jason Bonham, the son of **Led Zeppelin**'s drummer, the late John Bonham. Includes Daniel MacMaster (vocals), Ian Hatton (guitar) and John Smithson (keyboards, bass).

DEBUT	PEAK	WKS	Gold	A-side (Chart Hit).................B-side	$	Sym	Label & Number
11/25/89+	55	15		**Wait For You**.................*Cross Me And See*	$3	▮	WTG 73034

BONHAM, Tracy ROK/LP '96

Born on 3/16/67 in Eugene, Oregon. Female rock singer/songwriter/guitarist.

DEBUT	PEAK	WKS	Gold	A-side (Chart Hit).................B-side	$	Sym	Label & Number
4/20/96	32[A]	15		**Mother Mother**.................MR[3] from the album *The Burdens Of Being Upright* on Island 524187			album cut

BON JOVI ★75★ ROK/LP '89

Rock group from Sayreville, New Jersey: **Jon Bon Jovi** (vocals; born on 3/2/62), **Richie Sambora** (see #17 below) (guitar; born on 7/11/59), Dave Bryan (keyboards; born on 2/7/62), Alec John Such (bass; born on 11/14/56) and Tico Torres (drums; born on 10/7/53). Such left in November 1994. Jon also pursued acting with roles in movies *Moonlight and Valentino* (1995) and *U571* (2000) and on TV's *Ally McBeal*. Sambora married actress Heather Locklear on 12/17/94.

1)Livin' On A Prayer 2)Bad Medicine 3)Blaze Of Glory 4)You Give Love A Bad Name 5)I'll Be There For You

DEBUT	PEAK	WKS	Gold	A-side (Chart Hit).................B-side	$	Sym	Label & Number
2/25/84	39	13		1 **Runaway**.................*Love Lies*	$5	■	Mercury 818309
5/26/84	48	11		2 **She Don't Know Me**.................*Burning For Love*	$5	■	Mercury 818958
4/20/85	54	8		3 **Only Lonely**.................*Always Run To You*	$5	■	Mercury 880736
8/3/85	69	6		4 **In And Out Of Love**.................*Breakout (Japanese live version)*	$5		Mercury 880951
9/6/86	❶[1]	24		5 **You Give Love A Bad Name**.................S:❷[2] / A:5 *Raise Your Hands*	$3	■	Mercury 884953
12/13/86+	❶[4]	21		6 **Livin' On A Prayer** AR[2] A:❶[4] / S:❶[3] *Wild In The Streets*	$3	■	Mercury 888184
4/11/87	7	17		7 **Wanted Dead Or Alive**.................S:6 / A:6 *I'd Die For You*	$3	■	Mercury 888467
5/23/87	28[A]	6		8 **Never Say Goodbye**................. above 4 from the album *Slippery When Wet* on Mercury 830264			album cut
10/17/87	38[A]	1		9 **Edge Of A Broken Heart**................. from the movie *Disorderlies* starring the **Fat Boys** (soundtrack album on Polydor 833274); above 2 were the first *Hot 100 Airplay*-only album cuts			album cut
9/24/88	❶[2]	20		10 **Bad Medicine**.................S:2 / A:2 *99 In The Shade*	$3	■	Mercury 870657
11/26/88+	3	20		11 **Born To Be My Baby**.................A:2 / S:3 *Love For Sale*	$3	■	Mercury 872156
3/4/89	❶[1]	22		12 **I'll Be There For You**.................S:❶[1] / A:❶[1] *Homebound Train*	$3	■	Mercury 872564
6/3/89	7	16		13 **Lay Your Hands On Me**.................S:7 / A:7 *Runaway (live)*	$3	■	Mercury 874452
10/7/89	9	19		14 **Living In Sin**.................A:9 / S:10 *Love Is War* above 5 from the album *New Jersey*; #5-14: produced by Bruce Fairbairn (died on 5/17/99)	$3	■	Mercury 876070
7/21/90	❶[1]	21	▲	15 **Blaze Of Glory** *[JON BON JOVI]*..AR[1] S:❸[3] / A:2 *You Really Got Me Now* (w/**Little Richard**) with **Jeff Beck** and **Aldo Nova** (guitars) and Randy Jackson (bass)	$3	▮[V]	Mercury 875896
10/27/90	12	16		16 **Miracle** *[JON BON JOVI]*.................S:11 / A:12 *Blood Money* above 2 from the movie *Young Guns II* starring Emilio Estevez and Kiefer Sutherland	$3	▮[V]	Mercury 878392
9/28/91	63	7		17 **Ballad Of Youth**.................*Wind Cries Mary* **RICHIE SAMBORA**	$3	▮	Mercury 868790

DEBUT	PEAK	WKS	Gold	A-side (Chart Hit)....................B-side	$	Sym	Label & Number
				BON JOVI — Cont'd			
1/11/92	64[A]	7		18 **Levon** *[JON BON JOVI]*........			album cut
				from the tribute album *Two Rooms - Celebrating The Songs Of* **Elton John** & *Bernie Taupin* on Polydor 845750			
10/24/92	29	16		19 **Keep The Faith**........AR[1] S:31 / A:39 *I Wish Everyday Could Be Like Christmas*	$3	▮V	Jambco 864432
1/23/93	10	20		20 **Bed Of Roses**........S:10 / A:20 *Lay Your Hands On Me (live)*	$3	▮V	Jambco 864852
5/8/93	27	16		21 **In These Arms**........A:27 / S:46 *(live version) / Save A Prayer*	$3	▮V	Jambco 862088
8/14/93	97	4		22 **I'll Sleep When I'm Dead**........*Never Say Goodbye (live)*	$3	▮V	Jambco 862428
				above 4 from the album *Keep The Faith*			
10/1/94	4	32	▲	23 **Always**........S:2 / A:3 *Never Say Goodbye / Edge Of A Broken Heart*	$3	▮V	Mercury 856227
				"45": Mercury 856226; B-side: "Living In Sin"			
6/10/95	14	20		24 **This Ain't A Love Song**........S:15 / A:27 *Prostitute / Always (live)*	$3	▮V	Mercury 856824
9/23/95	76	9		25 **Something For The Pain** / S:70			
11/25/95	88	4		26 **Lie To Me**........	$3	▮V	Mercury 852296
6/21/97	57[A]	5		27 **Midnight In Chelsea** *[JON BON JOVI]*........			album cut
				from the album *Destination Anywhere* on Mercury 534903			
8/12/00	33	20		28 **It's My Life**........A:27			album cut
				"45": Island 562801; B-side: "Next 100 Years"			
2/17/01	57	10		29 **Thank You For Loving Me**........A:60		V	album cut
				"45" issued on red vinyl (Island 572770); B-side: "Bed Of Roses"; above 2 from the album *Crush* on Island 542474			
				BONNIE AND THE TREASURES '65			
				Born Charlotte Ann Matheny in 1945. Died of cancer in 1976 (age 31). Also recorded as Charlotte O'Hara and Bonnie Graham.			
8/28/65	77	5		**Home Of The Brave**........*Our Song*	$60		Phi-Dan 5005
				BONNIE LOU C&W '55			
				Born Mary Kath on 10/27/24 in Towanda, Illinois. Country singer/guitarist.			
11/12/55	14	15		**Daddy-O**........J:14 / S:25 / T:28 *Dancing In My Socks*	$40		King 4835
				BONNIE SISTERS '56			
				Doo-wop "girl group" from New York City, New York: Pat, Jean and Sylvia Bonnie. All were nurses at Bellevue Hospital. One of the first white female rock and roll vocal groups.			
2/18/56	18	7		**Cry Baby**........S:18 / T:35 *Broken*	$60		Rainbow 328
				BONOFF, Karla BUB/AC/LP '82			
				Born on 12/27/51 in Los Angeles, California. Pop singer/songwriter/pianist.			
2/11/78	76	4		1 **I Can't Hold On**........*Falling Star*	$5		Columbia 10618
3/1/80	69	7		2 **Baby Don't Go**........*The Letter*	$5		Columbia 11206
5/1/82	19	18		3 **Personally**........*Dream*	$4	■	Columbia 02805
				#92 R&B hit for **Jackie Moore** in 1978			
9/25/82	63	7		4 **Please Be The One**........*Just Walk Away*	$4		Columbia 03172
				BOOBAKAW '02			
				Male hip-hop artist from Washington DC.			
12/29/01+	30[S]	4		**Rock Em**........*Ha Ha Ha Ha Ha / Talkin Down / (5 album snippets)*	$10	★	Whitestone 12772
				BOOBAKAW AND THE WILD YOUNGINZ Featuring Vita			
				BOOKER, Chuckii R&B/LP '89			
				Born in 1966 in Los Angeles, California. R&B multi-instrumentalist. Session keyboard work with **Vanessa Williams**, Gerald Albright and **Troop**. Godson of **Barry White**.			
7/8/89	42	14		1 **Turned Away**........RB[1] *Keep Your Guard Up*	$3		Atlantic 88917
11/21/92	68	12		2 **Games**........RB[1] S:44 *(3 album snippets)*	$3	▮	Atlantic 87448
				BOOKER, James '60			
				Born on 12/17/39 in New Orleans, Louisiana. Died on 11/8/83 (age 43). R&B-jazz pianist/organist. Nicknamed "Little Booker." First recorded for Imperial in 1954. With **Dee Clark**'s band in 1960. Session work at Duke/Peacock in Houston.			
11/7/60	43	11		**Gonzo**........*Cool Turkey* [I]	$15		Peacock 1697
	★381★			**BOOKER T. & THE MG'S** R&B/BUB/AC/LP '69			
				Interracial R&B band formed by sessionmen from Stax Records in Memphis, Tennessee. Consisted of Booker T. Jones (keyboards; born on 11/12/44 in Memphis, Tennessee), Steve Cropper (guitar), Donald "Duck" Dunn (bass) and Al Jackson, Jr. (drums; murdered on 10/1/75, age 39). MG stands for Memphis Group. Jones was in a band with classmate **Maurice White** of **Earth, Wind & Fire**. Cropper and Dunn had been in the **Mar-Keys**. Much session work. Recordings included horns by Andrew Love, Wayne Jackson and Joe Arnold, plus **Isaac Hayes**, piano. Group disbanded in 1971, and reorganized for a short time in 1973. Cropper and Dunn joined the **Blues Brothers**. Jones received music degree from Indiana University; married Priscilla Coolidge (sister of Rita); and did production work for **Rita Coolidge**, Earl Klugh, **Bill Withers** and **Willie Nelson** (his *Stardust* album). Group inducted into the Rock and Roll Hall of Fame in 1992.			
				1)Green Onions 2)Time Is Tight 3)Hang 'Em High			
8/11/62	3	16	●	1 **Green Onions** RB[4] *Behave Yourself* [I]	$15		Stax 127
				originally released on Volt 102 in 1962 ($30)			
12/22/62+	82	5		2 **Jellybread**........*Aw' Mercy* [I]	$12		Stax 131
7/27/63	78	7		3 **Chinese Checkers**........*Plum-Nellie* [I]	$12		Stax 137
2/22/64	97	3		4 **Mo-Onions**........*Tic-Tac-Toe (#109)* [I]	$12		Stax 142
				also released on Stax 142 with "Fannie Mae" as the B-side ($15)			
8/15/64	95	2		5 **Soul Dressing**........*MG Party* [I]	$10		Stax 153
6/5/65	58	10		6 **Boot-Leg**........*Outrage* [I]	$10		Stax 169
9/3/66	85	5		7 **My Sweet Potato**........*Booker-Loo* [I]	$10		Stax 196
12/17/66	20[X]	2		8 **Jingle Bells**........*Winter Wonderland* [X-I]	$12		Stax 203
3/25/67	37	13		9 **Hip Hug-Her**........*Summertime* [I]	$10		Stax 211
8/5/67	21	12		10 **Groovin'** / [I]			
7/29/67	70	5		11 **Slim Jenkin's Place**........[I]	$10		Stax 224
7/13/68	17	10	●	12 **Soul-Limbo**........*Heads Or Tails* [I]	$8		Stax 0001
11/9/68+	9	18		13 **Hang 'Em High**........*Over Easy* [I]	$8		Stax 0013
				title song from the movie starring **Clint Eastwood**			
3/15/69	6	13	●	14 **Time Is Tight**........*Johnny, I Love You* [I]	$8	□	Stax 0028
				from the movie *Up Tight* starring Ruby Dee			

DEBUT	PEAK	WKS	Gold	A-side (Chart Hit)...B-side	$	Sym	Label & Number
				BOOKER T. & THE MG'S — Cont'd			
6/7/69	**37**	8		15 **Mrs. Robinson**...*Soul Clap '69* [I]	$8		Stax 0037
				from the movie *The Graduate* starring Dustin Hoffman and Anne Bancroft			
9/6/69	**88**	4		16 **Slum Baby**...*Meditation* [I]	$8		Stax 0049
7/25/70	**76**	4		17 **Something**...*Sunday Sermon* [I]	$8		Stax 0073
3/20/71	**45**	16		18 **Melting Pot**...*Kinda Easy Like* [I]	$8		Stax 0082
				BOOK OF LOVE ROK/LP '88			
				Electro-dance/pop quartet formed in New York City, New York: Susan Ottaviano (lead vocals), Ted Ottaviano and Lauren Roselli (keyboards), and Jade Lee (percussion). The Ottavianos are not related.			
9/3/88	**90**	4		1 **Pretty Boys And Pretty Girls**...*Tubular Bells*	$4	■	Sire 27858
2/17/01	**63**^{S}	1		2 **Boy**...*(8 versions)*	$8	★*	Reprise 44928
				BOOM, Taka R&B/LP '79			
				Born Yvonne Stevens in 1954 in Chicago, Illinois. R&B singer. Sister of **Chaka Khan**.			
5/5/79	**74**	4		**Night Dancin'**...*Cloud Dancer*	$5		Ariola America 7748
				BOOMTOWN RATS, The ROK/LP '80			
				Post-punk group from Dun Laoghaire, Ireland: **Bob Geldof** (see #2 below) (vocals; born on 10/5/54), Gerry Cott and Garry Roberts (guitars), Johnnie Fingers (keyboards), Pete Briquette (bass) and Simon Crowe (drums). Geldof organized **Band Aid**.			
2/2/80	**73**	5		1 **I Don't Like Mondays**...*It's All The Rage*	$5		Columbia 11117
				based on the case of a San Diego teenager, Brenda Spencer, who shot two people to death on a Monday (1/29/79)			
12/13/86+	**82**	6		2 **This Is The World Calling**...*Talk Me Up*	$3	■	Atlantic 89341
				BOB GELDOF			
				BOONE, Daniel LP '72			
				Born Peter Lee Stirling on 7/31/42 in Birmingham, England. Pop singer/songwriter.			
6/3/72	**15**	20		1 **Beautiful Sunday**...*Truly Julie*	$5		Mercury 73281
11/11/72	**86**	5		2 **Annabelle**...*Sleepyhead*	$5		Mercury 73339
5/24/75	**93**	3		3 **Run Tell The People**...*Rock And Roll Bum*	$5		Pye 71011
				BOONE, Debby C&W/AC/LP '77			
				Born on 9/22/56 in Leonia, New Jersey. Third daughter of Shirley and **Pat Boone** and granddaughter of Red Foley. Worked with the Boone Family from the mid-1960s, sang with sisters in the Boone Girls Gospel Quartet. Went solo in 1977. Winner of three Grammys including Best New Artist of 1977. Popular Contemporary Christian artist. Married Gabriel Ferrer, the son of **Rosemary Clooney** and actor Jose Ferrer, on 9/1/79.			
9/3/77	❶^{10}	25	▲	1 **You Light Up My Life**...AC[1] *Hasta Mañana*	$5		Warner/Curb 8455
				title song from the movie starring Didi Conn; first released on Warner 8446 (B-side: "He's A Rebel")			
2/11/78	**50**	5		2 **California**...*Hey Everybody*	$5	■	Warner/Curb 8511
5/27/78	**74**	7		3 **God Knows** /			
				co-written by Peter Noone (of **Herman's Hermits**)			
5/27/78		3		4 **Baby, I'm Yours**...	$5	■	Warner/Curb 8554
				BOONE, Pat ★11★ C&W/BUB/AC/LP '57			
				Born Charles Eugene Boone on 6/1/34 in Jacksonville, Florida. To Tennessee in 1936. Direct descendant of Daniel Boone. Married Country singer Red Foley's daughter, Shirley, on 11/7/53. Won on *Arthur Godfrey's Talent Scouts* in 1954. First recorded for Republic Records in 1954. Graduated from New York's Columbia University in 1958. Hosted own TV show, *The Pat Boone-Chevy Showroom*, 1957-60. Appeared in 15 movies. Wrote several books. Toured with wife and daughters Cherry, Linda, Laura and **Debby Boone** in the mid-1960s. Hosted own syndicated show on Christian radio. Recording artist **Nick Todd** is his younger brother. Pat's trademark: white buck shoes. Comeback on charts in 1997 with an album covering heavy-metal tunes. Also see **The Fontane Sisters**' "Voices."			
				1)Love Letters In The Sand 2)April Love 3)I Almost Lost My Mind 4)Ain't That A Shame 5)Don't Forbid Me			
4/2/55	**16**	12		1 **Two Hearts**...S:16 / J:16 *Tra-La-La*	$20		Dot 15338
				#8 R&B hit for **The Charms** in 1955			
7/9/55	❶^{2}	20	●	2 **Ain't That A Shame**...J:❶^{2} / S:2 / A:2 / T:21 *Tennessee Saturday Night*	$20		Dot 15377
10/29/55	**7**	14		3 **At My Front Door (Crazy Little Mama)** / T:7 / J:7 / S:8 / A:10			
11/12/55	**26**	11		4 **No Other Arms**...T:26 / S:flip / J:flip	$20		Dot 15422
				tune better known as "No Arms Can Ever Hold You"			
12/17/55+	**19**	10		5 **Gee Whittakers!**...J:19 / T:27 *Take The Time*	$20		Dot 15435
				#14 R&B hit for **The Five Keys** in 1956			
2/4/56	**4**	22	●	6 **I'll Be Home** / A:4 / J:4 / T:5 / S:6			
				#5 R&B hit for **The Flamingos** in 1956			
1/28/56	**12**	18		7 **Tutti' Frutti**...T:12 / J:13 / S:15 / A:15	$20		Dot 15443
4/14/56	**8**	15		8 **Long Tall Sally** / J:8 / T:18 / S:23 / A:23			
4/28/56	**76**	3		9 **Just As Long As I'm With You**...T:76	$20		Dot 15457
				written by **Billy Vaughn**			
6/2/56	❶^{4}	23	●	10 **I Almost Lost My Mind** / J:❶^{4} / T:❶^{2} / S:2 / A:2			
				#1 R&B hit for **Ivory Joe Hunter** in 1950			
6/9/56	**57**	7		11 **I'm In Love With You**...T:57 / S:flip	$20		Dot 15472
9/15/56	**5**	24	●	12 **Friendly Persuasion (Thee I Love)** / A:5 / T:8 / J:8 / S:9			
				title song from the movie *Friendly Persuasion* starring Gary Cooper and Dorothy McGuire			
9/15/56	**10**	14		13 **Chains Of Love**...J:10 / S:15 / T:20	$20		Dot 15490
				#2 R&B hit for **Joe Turner** in 1951; all of above are on the maroon Dot label			
12/22/56+	❶^{1}	22	●	14 **Don't Forbid Me** / T:❶^{1} / J:❶^{1} / A:2 / S:3			
12/22/56+	**37**	18		15 **Anastasia**...T:37 / S:flip	$15		Dot 15521
				title song from the movie starring Ingrid Bergman and Yul Brynner			
3/16/57	**5**	21	●	16 **Why Baby Why** / S:5 / T:6 / A:7 / J:7			
3/16/57	**27**	10		17 **I'm Waiting Just For You**...T:27 / S:flip / J:flip	$15		Dot 15545
				#2 R&B hit for Lucky Millinder in 1951			
5/6/57	❶^{7}	34	●	18 **Love Letters In The Sand** / A:❶^{7} / S:❶^{5} / T:❶^{5} / J:2			
				#6 hit for Ted Black & His Orchestra in 1931; picture sleeve issued with an orange or purple tinted background			
5/6/57	**14**	25		19 **Bernardine**...A:14 / T:23 / S:flip / J:flip	$15	■	Dot 15570
				above 2 from the movie *Bernardine* starring Boone and Janet Gaynor			

DEBUT	PEAK	WKS	Gold	A-side (Chart Hit)..........B-side	$	Sym	Label & Number
				BOONE, Pat — Cont'd			
8/12/57	6	21	●	20 **Remember You're Mine** / A:6 / S:10 / T:20			
8/19/57	14	14		21 **There's A Gold Mine In The Sky** ....S:14 / A:20 / T:28	$15		Dot 15602
				#5 hit for Horace Heidt in 1938			
10/28/57	❶[6]	26	●	22 **April Love** / A:❶[6] / S:❶[2] / T:❶[1]			
				title song from the movie starring Boone and Shirley Jones			
11/4/57	80	3		23 **When The Swallows Come Back To Capistrano** ....T:80 / S:flip	$15		Dot 15660
				Top 10 hit in 1940 for both Glenn Miller and The Ink Spots			
2/17/58	4	19	●	24 **A Wonderful Time Up There** / S:4 / A:7 / T:10			
				originally titled "Gospel Boogie" (1947)			
2/17/58	4	16		25 **It's Too Soon To Know** ....S:4 / A:11 / T:13	$15		Dot 15690
				#1 R&B hit for The Orioles in 1948			
5/5/58	5	14		26 **Sugar Moon** / A:5 / S:10 / T:11			
5/19/58	63	5		27 **Cherie, I Love You** ....T:63 / S:flip	$15	■	Dot 15750
				#4 hit for Ben Bernie in 1926			
7/14/58	7	13		28 **If Dreams Came True** / A:7 / S:11 / H:12			
7/14/58	39	9		29 **That's How Much I Love You** ....H:39 / S:flip	$15		Dot 15785
				#10 hit for **Frank Sinatra** in 1947; #4 Country hit for Boone's father-in-law, Red Foley, in 1947			
9/22/58	21	9		30 **Gee, But It's Lonely** / S:21 / H:31			
				written by Phil Everly (of **The Everly Brothers**)			
9/22/58	23	11		31 **For My Good Fortune** ....H:23 / S:29	$15		Dot 15825
10/27/58	34	11		32 **I'll Remember Tonight** ....*The Mardi Gras March*	$15	■	Dot 15840
				from the movie *Mardi Gras* starring Boone and **Tommy Sands**			
1/12/59	21	14		33 **With The Wind And The Rain In Your Hair** /			
				Top 10 hit in 1940 for both Bob Crosby and Kay Kyser			
1/12/59	49	8		34 **Good Rockin' Tonight**	$15		Dot 15888
				written by **Roy Brown**; #1 R&B hit for Wynonie Harris in 1948			
3/23/59	23	11		35 **For A Penny** /			
4/20/59	62	4		36 **The Wang Dang Taffy-Apple Tango (Mambo Cha Cha Cha)**	$15		Dot 15914
6/15/59	17	11		37 **Twixt Twelve And Twenty** ....*Rock-Boll-Weevil*	$15	■	Dot 15955
				also the title of Boone's best-selling book			
9/14/59	29	9		38 **Fools Hall Of Fame** ....*Brightest Wishing Star*	$15	■	Dot 15982
11/30/59	71	5		39 **Beyond The Sunset** ....*My Faithful Heart*	$15		Dot 16006
				#7 Country hit for The Three Suns in 1950			
2/22/60	18	12		40 **(Welcome) New Lovers** /			
3/21/60	94	1		41 **Words**	$12	■	Dot 16048
				new lyrics to the 1873 song "Silver Threads Among The Gold"			
5/23/60	44	8		42 **Walking The Floor Over You** /			
				written and popularized in 1941 by Ernest Tubb			
5/30/60	50	8		43 **Spring Rain**	$12	■	Dot 16073
8/22/60	66	3		44 **Delia Gone** /			
				arrangement is similar to **Bobby Darin**'s "Mack The Knife"			
8/22/60	72	3		45 **Candy Sweet**	$12		Dot 16122
10/24/60	44	8		46 **Dear John** /			
				#1 Country hit for **Jean Shepard** & **Ferlin Husky** in 1953			
10/24/60	47	8		47 **Alabam**	$12		Dot 16152
1/23/61	64	6		48 **The Exodus Song (This Land Is Mine)** ....*There's A Moon Out Tonight*	$12		Dot 16176
				Boone wrote the words to this theme from the Otto Preminger movie *Exodus* starring Paul Newman			
5/1/61	❶[1]	15		49 **Moody River** ....*A Thousand Years*	$12		Dot 16209
8/21/61	19	9		50 **Big Cold Wind** ....*That's My Desire*	$12		Dot 16244
11/13/61+	35	10		51 **Johnny Will** ....*(If I'm Dreaming) Just Let Me Dream (#114)*	$12		Dot 16284
1/27/62	32	9		52 **I'll See You In My Dreams** /			
				4 versions of this tune hit the Top 10 in 1925			
2/10/62	77	4		53 **Pictures In The Fire**	$12		Dot 16312
5/19/62	95	1		54 **Quando, Quando, Quando (Tell Me When)** ....*Willing And Eager (#113)*	$12		Dot 16349
6/16/62	6	13		55 **Speedy Gonzales** ....*The Locket* [N]	$12		Dot 16368
				featuring the voice of Mel Blanc as "Speedy Gonzales"; first released by David Dante in 1962 on RCA 8056 ($15)			
9/22/62	45	7		56 **Ten Lonely Guys** ....*Lover's Lane*	$12		Dot 16391
				co-written by **Neil Diamond**			
3/9/63	91	1		57 **Meditation (Meditacao)** ....*Days Of Wine And Roses (#117)*	$10		Dot 16439
9/26/64	72	5		58 **Beach Girl** ....*Little Honda*	$40		Dot 16658
				Bruce Johnston and Terry Melcher (of **Bruce & Terry**, **The Rip Chords**; writers, producers and backing vocals)			
10/22/66	49	8		59 **Wish You Were Here, Buddy** ....*Love For Love*	$8		Dot 16933
<u>4/19/69</u>	100	2		60 **July You're A Woman** ....*Break My Mind*	$6		Tetragrammaton 1516
				written by **John Stewart** (**Kingston Trio**);			
				Boone's arrangers and conductors: Lew Douglas (#1), **Ernie Freeman** (#59), Jimmie Haskell (#55, 56), Mort Lindsey (#37, 40, 41, 43, 45), Milt Rogers (#48, 50), Vic Schoen (#44) and **Billy Vaughn** (#2-36, 38, 39, 42, 46, 47, 49, 51-53)			
11/23/02	15[S]	16		61 **Under God** ....*(no B-side)*	$5	★	The Gold Label 2117
				BORN JAMERICANS R&B/BUB/LP **'98**			
				Dancehall reggae duo: Horace "Edley Shine" Payne and Norman "Natch" Howell. Both were born in U.S. to Jamaican parents. Payne was raised in Washington DC; Howell was raised in Hartford, Connecticut.			
1/29/94	84	4		1 **Boom Shak A-Tack** ....S:65 *(dancehall remix)*	$4	▮	Delicious Vinyl 98373
				samples "Pot Belly" by **Lou Donaldson**			
2/7/98	72	10		2 **Send My Love/Send One Your Love** ....S:73 *(reprise) / Gotta Get Mine* (w/**Mad Lion**, Shinehead, Sleepy Wonder)	$4	▮	Delicious Vinyl 71903
				samples "Send One Your Love" by **Stevie Wonder**			
				BORN PREDATORS **'02**			
				Male rap duo: Tone Bone and DJ Skills.			
10/26/02	13[S]	7		**Product Of Our Environment** ....*(2 versions) / Tellem*	$4	★	Three Gems 9021

DEBUT	PEAK	WKS	Gold	A-side (Chart Hit)...B-side	$	Sym	Label & Number
				BOSS R&B/BUB/LP **'93**			
				Female rap duo based in Los Angeles, California: Lichelle "Boss" Laws and Irene "Dee" Moore.			
4/24/93	**65**	13		**Deeper**...S:32 *(instrumental)*	$4	▮	DJ West/Chaos 74853
				samples "I'm Gonna Love You Just A Little Bit More Baby" by **Barry White** and "Dub Fire" by Aswad			
				BOSSON **'00**			
				Born Staffan Olsson in 1974 in Gothenburg, Sweden. Male pop singer.			
3/11/00	**47^S**	8		**We Live**...*(2 versions) / Happy*	$4	★^{V}	MNW/Capitol 58813
	★444★			**BOSTON** ROK/LP **'86**			
				Rock group from Boston, Massachusetts, spearheaded by Tom Scholz (guitars, keyboards, songwriter; born on 3/10/47). His homemade demo tapes became the basis of Boston's first album in 1976 with Scholz recruiting members Brad Delp (vocals; born on 6/12/51), Barry Goudreau (guitar; born on 11/29/51), Fran Sheehan (bass; born on 3/26/49) and Sib Hashian (drums; born on 8/17/49). Goudreau formed **Orion The Hunter** in 1982. After a long; absence from the charts, Boston returned in 1986 as a duo: Scholz and Delp. Delp and Goudreau spearheaded **RTZ** in 1991. Scholz's 1994 Boston lineup: Fran Cosmo (Orion The Hunter) and Tommy Funderburk (vocals), Gary Pihl (guitar), David Sikes (bass) and Doug Huffman (drums). Scholz is an avid inventor with several patented inventions.			
				1)Amanda 2)Don't Look Back 3)More Than A Feeling			
9/18/76	**5**	19		1 **More Than A Feeling**...*Smokin'*	$4		Epic 50266
1/29/77	**22**	10		2 **Long Time**...*Let Me Take You Home Tonight*	$4		Epic 50329
5/14/77	**38**	8		3 **Peace Of Mind**...*Foreplay*	$4		Epic 50381
8/19/78	**4**	13		4 **Don't Look Back**...*The Journey*	$4		Epic 50590
11/18/78+	**31**	12		5 **A Man I'll Never Be**...*Don't Be Afraid*	$4		Epic 50638
3/24/79	**46**	7		6 **Feelin' Satisfied**...*Used To Bad News*	$4		Epic 50677
9/27/86	**❶^2**	18		7 **Amanda** AR^3 A:❶^3 / S:❶^2 *My Destination*	$3	■	MCA 52756
12/6/86+	**9**	15		8 **We're Ready**...S:8 / A:9 *The Launch: Countdown/Ignition/Third Stage Separation*	$3	■	MCA 52985
3/7/87	**20**	13		9 **Can'tcha Say (You Believe In Me)/Still In Love**...S:20 / A:24 *Cool The Engines* (ROK #4)	$3	■	MCA 53029
6/11/94	**51**	10		10 **I Need Your Love**...S:62 *We Can Make It*	$3	▮^{V}	MCA 54803
				BOSTON POPS ORCHESTRA MEM/POP/LP **'38**			
				An American institution founded in 1885 by Henry Lee Higginson, conductor of the Boston Symphony Orchestra. Arthur Fiedler (born on 12/17/1894 in Boston, Massachusetts; trained in Germany; died on 7/10/79, age 84) joined the orchestra in 1915 as a violist; began his reign as its conductor in 1930 and remained until his death. Local radio broadcasts of concerts began in 1952, then syndicated nationally from 1962-92. National public TV program *Evening at Pops* began in 1969. **John Williams** succeeded Fiedler in 1980. Keith Lockhart (former Cincinnati Pops conductor) succeeded Williams in 1995.			
7/4/64	**55**	6		**I Want To Hold Your Hand**...*Hello, Dolly!* [I]	$10	■	RCA Victor 8378
				a **Richard Hayman** arrangement of **The Beatles**' first U.S. hit			
				BOTKIN, Perry Jr. — see DeVORZON, Barry			
				BOUNTY KILLER LP **'98**			
				Born Rodney Pryce on 6/26/72 in Riverton City, Jamaica. Reggae singer.			
3/15/97	**81**	5		1 **Hip-Hopera**...S:64 *Living Dangerously* (w/Barrington Levy)	$5	▮	TVT/Blunt 1464
				BOUNTY KILLER Featuring The Fugees			
10/10/98	**79**	7		2 **Deadly Zone**...S:66 *(instrumental)*	$5	▮	TVT Soundtrax 8215
				BOUNTY KILLER Featuring Mobb Deep & Rappin' Noyd from the movie *Blade* starring Wesley Snipes			
12/8/01+	**5**	20		3 **Hey Baby**...A:5			album cut
				NO DOUBT Featuring Bounty Killer from the album *Rock Steady* on Interscope 493158			
				BOURGEOIS TAGG AC/LP **'87**			
				Rock group from Los Angeles, California: **Brent Bourgeois** (see #3 below) (vocals, keyboards), Larry Tagg (vocals, bass), Lyle Workman (guitar), Scott Moon (synthesizer) and Michael Urbano (drums). Bourgeois was named vice president of A&R for Word Records in 1997.			
4/12/86	**62**	10		1 **Mutual Surrender (What A Wonderful World)**...*The Move Up*	$3		Island 99558
10/10/87	**38**	17		2 **I Don't Mind At All**...S:35 *Pencil & Paper*	$3		Island 99409
				produced by **Todd Rundgren**			
4/28/90	**32**	13		3 **Dare To Fall In Love**...A:25 *My Little Island*	$3	▮	Charisma 98971
				BRENT BOURGEOIS			
				BOWEN, Jimmy **'57**			
				Born on 11/30/37 in Santa Rita, New Mexico. Formed The Rhythm Orchids at West Texas State University with **Buddy Knox**, Don Lanier and Dave "**Dicky Doo**" Alldred. Bowen became a producer and top record executive on the West Coast. Produced 20 of **Dean Martin**'s hits, 1964-69. In 1977, moved to Nashville. In 1984, became president of MCA Records in Nashville (renamed Universal Records in 1988).			
				JIMMY BOWEN with the Rhythm Orchids:			
2/23/57	**14**	17		1 **I'm Stickin' With You /** T:14 / J:15 / S:16 / A:20			
				originally released on Triple-D 798 in 1956; flip side was "Party Doll" by **Buddy Knox** ($900)			
3/9/57	**63**	6		2 **Ever Lovin' Fingers**...T:63	$40		Roulette 4001
5/20/57	**57**	7		3 **Warm Up To Me Baby**...T:57 *I Trusted You*	$25		Roulette 4010
7/28/58	**50**	9		4 **By The Light Of The Silvery Moon**...H:50 *The Two Step*	$20		Roulette 4083
				#1 hit for Billy Murray & The Haydn Quartet in 1910			

DEBUT	PEAK	WKS	Gold	A-side (Chart Hit)...B-side	$	Sym	Label & Number

BOWIE, David ★122★ ROK/BUB/LP '83

Born David Robert Jones on 1/8/47 in London, England. Left pupil paralyzed in a childhood fight resulting in appearance of different-colored eyes. From 1964-66, recorded with the bands King Bees, Manish Boys and Lower Third. First recorded solo in 1966. Joined Lindsay Kemp Mime Troupe in 1967. Formed short-lived trio Feathers in 1968. Adopted new personas (Ziggy Stardust, Alladin Sane, Thin White Duke) to accompany several of his musical phases. Married to Angie Barnett, the subject of **The Rolling Stones**' song "Angie," from 1970-80. Acted in several movies including *The Man Who Fell To Earth* (1976), *Labyrinth* (1986), and *Absolute Beginners* (1986); starred in *The Elephant Man* (1980) on Broadway. Formed the group Tin Machine in 1988. Married Somalian actress/supermodel Iman on 4/24/92. Inducted into the Rock and Roll Hall of Fame in 1996. Launched own Internet service provider, Bowienet, in 1998.

1)Fame 2)Let's Dance 3)Dancing In The Street 4)Blue Jean 5)Golden Years

DEBUT	PEAK	WKS	Gold	A-side (Chart Hit)...B-side	$	Sym	Label & Number
4/15/72	66	7		1 **Changes**...*Andy Warhol*	$10		RCA Victor 0605
7/1/72	65	9		2 **Starman**...*Suffragette City*	$8	■	RCA Victor 0719
11/25/72	71	5		3 **The Jean Genie**...*Hang On To Yourself* — title is a pun on playwright Jean Genet's name; song is about **Iggy Pop**	$8		RCA Victor 0838
1/27/73	15	14		4 **Space Oddity**...*The Man Who Sold The World* — same version "Bubbled Under" (#124) on Mercury 72949 in 1969 ($60); also see **Peter Schilling**'s "Major Tom"	$8	■	RCA Victor 0876
6/1/74	64	8		5 **Rebel Rebel** *[BOWIE]*...*Lady Grinning Soul*	$8		RCA Victor 0287
12/7/74+	41	11		6 **Changes**...*Andy Warhol* [R] — Rick Wakeman (of **Yes**; piano); issued on grey label (#1 above on orange label - same version)	$8		RCA Victor 0605
3/15/75	28	11		7 **Young Americans**...*Knock On Wood* — **Luther Vandross** (backing vocal); **David Sanborn** (saxophone)	$8		RCA Victor 10152
6/28/75	❶[2]	21	●	8 **Fame**...*Right* — **John Lennon** (backing vocal and song's co-writer)	$6		RCA Victor 10320
12/13/75+	10	21		9 **Golden Years**...*Can You Hear Me*	$6		RCA Victor 10441
5/22/76	64	5		10 **TVC 15**...*We Are The Dead*	$6		RCA Victor 10664
4/9/77	69	6		11 **Sound And Vision**...*A New Career In A New Town*	$5		RCA 10905
12/6/80+	70	9		12 **Fashion**...*Scream Like A Baby*	$5	■	RCA 12134
11/7/81+	29	15		13 **Under Pressure**...*Soul Brother* (Queen) — **QUEEN & DAVID BOWIE**; also see "Ice Ice Baby" by **Vanilla Ice**	$5	■	Elektra 47235
4/17/82	67	10		14 **Cat People (Putting Out Fire)**...*Paul's Theme (Jogging Chase)* (**Giorgio Moroder**) — from the movie *Cat People* starring Nastassia Kinski	$5	■	Backstreet 52024
3/26/83	❶[1]	20	●	15 **Let's Dance**...*Cat People (Putting Out Fire)*	$4	■	EMI America 8158
6/4/83	10	18		16 **China Girl**...*Shake It*	$4	■	EMI America 8165
9/17/83	14	13		17 **Modern Love**...*(live version)*	$4	■	EMI America 8177
3/10/84	73	4		18 **Without You**...*Criminal World* (ROK #31) — **Stevie Ray Vaughan** (guitar, above 4); above 4 from the album *Let's Dance*	$4	■	EMI America 8190
9/15/84	8	18		19 **Blue Jean**...S:7 / A:10 *Dancing With The Big Boys*	$4	■	EMI America 8231
12/1/84	53	9		20 **Tonight**...*Tumble And Twirl* — **Tina Turner** (backing vocal); picture sleeve is a foldout poster	$4	■	EMI America 8246
2/2/85	32	12		21 **This Is Not America**...S:27 *(instrumental)* (Pat Metheny Group) — **DAVID BOWIE/PAT METHENY GROUP**; theme from the movie *The Falcon And The Snowman* starring Timothy Hutton and Sean Penn	$4	■	EMI America 8251
8/31/85	7	14		22 **Dancing In The Street**...S:5 / A:8 *(instrumental)* — **MICK JAGGER/DAVID BOWIE**; from the Live-Aid project for Africa	$4	■	EMI America 8288
3/29/86	53	9		23 **Absolute Beginners**...*(dub mix)* — title song from the movie starring Bowie and Patsy Kensit	$3	■	EMI America 8308
4/4/87	21	12		24 **Day-In Day-Out**...S:17 / A:24 *Julie*	$3	■	EMI America 8380
8/8/87	27	11		25 **Never Let Me Down**...S:23 / A:32 *'87 And Cry*	$3	■	EMI America 43031
10/14/95	92	2		26 **The Hearts Filthy Lesson**...*(alt. mix) / Nothing To Be Desired*	$3	▮	Virgin 38518
11/22/97	66	16		27 **I'm Afraid Of Americans**...S:68 *(5 versions)* — produced by **Nine Inch Nails**; all of above written or co-written by Bowie (except #22)	$8	★*	Virgin 38618
12/23/00	58^S	3		28 **Peace On Earth/Little Drummer Boy**...*(no B-side)* [X] — originally performed on the 1977 TV Christmas special *Bing Crosby's Merrie Olde Christmas*; "45" issued in 1982 on RCA 13400 with a picture sleeve; the CD single contains an additional 1:45 of dialogue	$10	★+	Oglio 85001
12/29/01	75^S	1		29 **Peace On Earth/Little Drummer Boy**...*(no B-side)* [X-R]	$10	★+	Oglio 85001
12/21/02	43^S	4		30 **Peace On Earth/Little Drummer Boy**...*(no B-side)* [X-R] — **DAVID BOWIE & BING CROSBY** (above 3)	$10	★+	Oglio 85001

BOWLES, Rick '82

Born in Shelby, North Carolina. Pop singer/songwriter. Later co-wrote several country hits.

DEBUT	PEAK	WKS	Gold	A-side (Chart Hit)...B-side	$	Sym	Label & Number
7/3/82	77	3		**Too Good To Turn Back Now**...*Mr. Right*	$4		Polydor 2209

BOW WOW WOW BUB/LP '82

New-wave group assembled in London, England, by Malcolm McLaren (former Sex Pistols manager). Consisted of Annabella Lwin (vocals; born Myant Myant Aye in Burma), Matthew Ashman (guitar), Leroy Gorman (bass) and Dave Barbarossa (drums). The latter three were members of **Adam And The Ants** until 1980. **Boy George** had a brief stint with the group. Ashman died of diabetes on 11/21/95 (age 35).

DEBUT	PEAK	WKS	Gold	A-side (Chart Hit)...B-side	$	Sym	Label & Number
5/29/82	62	7		1 **I Want Candy**...*Elimination Dancing*	$5	■	RCA 13204
4/23/83	77	4		2 **Do You Wanna Hold Me?**...*What's The Time (Hey Buddy)*	$4		RCA 13467

★494★ BOX TOPS, The LP '67

Pop-rock group from Memphis, Tennessee: Alex Chilton (vocals; born on 12/28/50), Gary Talley (guitar; born on 8/17/47), John Evans (organ), Bill Cunningham (bass; born on 1/23/50) and Danny Smythe (drums). Evans and Smythe left in late 1967; replaced by Rick Allen and Tom Boggs. Disbanded in 1970. Chilton later formed the power-pop band Big Star. Cunningham is the brother of B.B. Cunningham of **The Hombres**.

1)The Letter 2)Cry Like A Baby 3)Soul Deep

DEBUT	PEAK	WKS	Gold	A-side (Chart Hit)...B-side	$	Sym	Label & Number
8/12/67	❶[4]	16	●	1 **The Letter**...*Happy Times*	$10		Mala 565
11/11/67	24	9		2 **Neon Rainbow**...*Everything I Am*	$10		Mala 580
3/2/68	2[2]	15	●	3 **Cry Like A Baby**...*The Door You Closed To Me*	$10		Mala 593

DEBUT	PEAK	WKS	Gold	A-side (Chart Hit)...B-side	$	Sym	Label & Number
				BOX TOPS, The — Cont'd			
6/1/68	**26**	8		4 **Choo Choo Train** ... *Fields Of Clover*	$10		Mala 12005
9/14/68	**37**	6		5 **I Met Her In Church** ... *People Gonna Talk*	$10		Mala 12017
12/28/68+	**28**	15		6 **Sweet Cream Ladies, Forward March** ... *I See Only Sunshine* some pressings show title as just "Sweet Cream Ladies"	$10		Mala 12035
4/26/69	**67**	5		7 **I Shall Be Released** ... *I Must Be The Devil* written by **Bob Dylan**	$10		Mala 12038
7/5/69	**18**	14		8 **Soul Deep** ... *(The) Happy Song*	$10		Mala 12040
10/18/69	**58**	7		9 **Turn On A Dream** ... *Together*	$10		Mala 12042
3/21/70	**92**	2		10 **You Keep Tightening Up On Me** ... *Come On Honey*	$8		Bell 865
				BOYCE, Tommy, & Bobby Hart BUB/LP '68			
				Top songwriting duo/production team. Writers of "Pretty Little Angel Eyes," "Come A Little Bit Closer," much of **The Monkees** material and others. Toured and recorded with The Monkees' **Davy Jones** and **Mickey Dolenz** in 1975. Boyce (see #1 below) was born on 9/29/39 in Charlottesville, Virginia. Died of a self-inflicted gunshot wound on 11/23/94 (age 55). Hart was born on 2/18/39 in Phoenix, Arizona.			
10/13/62	**80**	3		1 **I'll Remember Carol** ... *Too Late For Tears* **TOMMY BOYCE**	$20		RCA Victor 8074
7/15/67	**39**	7		2 **Out & About** ... *My Little Chickadee*	$10	■	A&M 858
12/23/67+	**8**	14		3 **I Wonder What She's Doing Tonite** ... *The Ambushers*	$10	■	A&M 893
4/6/68	**53**	6		4 **Goodbye Baby (I Don't Want To See You Cry)** ... *Where Angels Go, Trouble Follows*	$10	■	A&M 919
7/6/68	**27**	10		5 **Alice Long (You're Still My Favorite Girlfriend)** ... *P.O. Box 9847*	$10	■	A&M 948
				BOYER, Bonnie '79			
				Disco singer.			
7/28/79	**43**	8		**Got To Give In To Love** ... *Never, Never*	$4		Columbia 11028
				BOY GEORGE — see CULTURE CLUB			
				BOY KRAZY '93			
				Female pop vocal group from New York: Kimberly Blake, Johnna Lee Cummings, Josselyne Jones and Ruth Ann Roberts (a former Miss Junior America).			
1/23/93	**18**	20		1 **That's What Love Can Do** ... A:11 / S:40 *One Thing Leads To Another*	$3	▮V	Next Plateau 857024
5/29/93	**59**	9		2 **Good Times With Bad Boys** ... A:54 *That's What Love Can Do* "45 issued for above 2 on Collectables 4928	$3	▮V	Next Plateau 857136
				BOY MEETS GIRL LP '88			
				Songwriting/recording duo from Seattle, Washington: Shannon Rubicam and George Merrill. Married in 1988. Wrote **Whitney Houston**'s hits "How Will I Know" and "I Wanna Dance With Somebody."			
4/6/85	**39**	13		1 **Oh Girl** ... *Kissing, Falling, Flying*	$3	■	A&M 2713
9/10/88	**5**	25		2 **Waiting For A Star To Fall** ... AC[1] S:4 / A:6 *No Apologies*	$3	■	RCA 8691
1/28/89	**49**	11		3 **Bring Down The Moon** ... S:31 *Restless Dreamer*	$3	■	RCA 8807
				BOYS, The R&B/LP '89			
				R&B vocal group from Northridge, California: brothers Khiry, Hakeem, Tajh and Bilal Samad. All were members of performing gymnastic troupes. Ages 9-14 in 1988. Also see **Classic Example**'s "It's Alright."			
12/10/88+	**13**	19		1 **Dial My Heart** ... RB[1] S:11 / A:17 *(instrumental)*	$3	■	Motown 53301
8/25/90	**29**	15		2 **Crazy** ... RB[1] S:17 *(no B-side)* "45": Motown 924; B-side: (radio mix)	$3	▮V	Motown 2053
				BOYS BAND, The '82			
				Country-rock trio from Hendersonville, Tennessee: Greg Gordon (vocals), B. James Lowry (guitar, vocals) and Rusty Golden (keyboards, vocals; son of William Golden of the **Oak Ridge Boys**).			
3/6/82	**61**	8		**Don't Stop Me Baby (I'm On Fire)** ... *We're Lovers*	$4	■	Elektra 47406
				BOYS CLUB AC/LP '89			
				Duo formed in Minneapolis, Minnesota: vocalists Joe Pasquale and Gene Hunt (born Eugene Wolfgramm; formerly with his family group, **The Jets**).			
10/22/88+	**8**	21		**I Remember Holding You** ... S:6 / A:11 *It's Alright*	$3	■	MCA 53430
				BOYS DON'T CRY LP '86			
				Pop-rock group from England: Nick Richards (vocals), Nico Ramsden (guitar), Brian Chatton (keybaords), Mark Smith (bass) and Jeff Seopardi (drums).			
4/5/86	**12**	19		**I Wanna Be A Cowboy** ... S:11 / A:11 *(instrumental)*	$4		Profile 5084
				BOYS IN THE BAND, The R&B/BUB '70			
				Studio group led by Herman Lewis Griffin, the first husband of **Mary Wells**. Griffin (born on 11/25/36 in Selma, Alabama; died of a heart attack on 11/11/89, age 52) recorded in 1957, on H.O.B., the first song of Berry Gordy's Jobete Publishing.			
6/6/70	**48**	10		**(How Bout A Little Hand For) The Boys In The Band** ... *Sumpin Heavy* from the movie *The Phynx* starring A. Michael Miller	$6		Spring 103
				BOYZ-N-GIRLZ UNITED '00			
				Interracial pop vocal group formed in Florida: Daniel Dix, Robbie Carrico, Criss Ruiz and Rina Mayo.			
6/17/00	**66**S	5		**Messed Around** ... *(remix) / (3 album snippets)*	$5	★	Edel America 58372

DEBUT	PEAK	WKS	Gold	A-side (Chart Hit)..............B-side	$	Sym	Label & Number

BOYZ II MEN ★57★ R&B/BUB/AC/LP '94

R&B vocal group from Philadelphia, Pennsylvania: Wanya Morris (born on 7/29/74), Michael McCary (born on 12/16/72), **Shawn Stockman** (see #15 below) (born on 9/26/73) and **Nathan Morris** (see #16 below) (born on 6/18/72). Discovered by Michael Bivins (**New Edition**, **Bell Biv DeVoe**). Appeared in the 1992 TV mini-series **The Jacksons**: An American Dream. Boyz II Men hold down 3 of the top 6 all-time hits of the rock era ('55-'02)! Also see **Another Bad Creation**, **Brandy**'s "Brokenhearted", **MC Brains**, **Uncle Sam** and **LL Cool J**'s "Hey Lover."

1)One Sweet Day 2)I'll Make Love To You 3)End of the Road 4)On Bended Knee 5)4 Seasons Of Loneliness

DEBUT	PEAK	WKS	Gold	A-side (Chart Hit)..............B-side	$	Sym	Label & Number
6/15/91	3	24	▲	1 **Motownphilly** ....S:2 / A:3 *(5 album snippets)* Michael Bivins (rap)	$3	▮V	Motown 2090
9/21/91	2[4]	22	●	2 **It's So Hard To Say Goodbye To Yesterday** ....RB[1] S:2 / A:5 *(5 album snippets)* #38 R&B hit for G.C. Cameron in 1975; "45": Motown 2168; B-side: "Sympin'" (R&B #72)	$3	▮V	Motown 2136
12/14/91+	16	20		3 **Uhh Ahh** ....RB[1] S:14 / A:19 *(instrumental)*	$3	▮V	Motown 2141
4/4/92	49	20		4 **Please Don't Go** ....A:38 / S:46 *(instrumental)* "45" issued for above 2 on Motown 2162	$3	▮V	Motown 2155
7/18/92	❶[13]	32	▲	5 **End of the Road** ....RB[4] A:❶[13] / S:❶[12] *(instrumental)* from the movie *Boomerang* starring **Eddie Murphy**; "45" B-side: "1-4-All-4-1" by **East Coast Family**; above 5 from the album *Cooleyhighharmony*	$3	▮V	Motown 2178
11/28/92+	3	20	▲	6 **In The Still Of The Nite (I'll Remember)** ....A:2 / S:3 *(5 album snippets)* from the TV mini-series **The Jacksons**: An American Dream; "45" B-side: "Who's Lovin' You" by **The Jackson 5**	$3	▮V	Motown 2193
12/11/93	32	7		7 **Let It Snow** ....S:27 / A:40 *Silent Night* [X] **Brian McKnight** (guest vocal/co-writer/co-producer)	$3	▮V	Motown 2218
8/13/94	❶[14]	33	▲	8 **I'll Make Love To You** ....RB[9] / AC[3] A:❶[12] / S:❶[11] *(instrumental)* "45" issued with #10 below as the B-side	$3	▮V	Motown 2257
11/19/94	❶[6]	27	▲	9 **On Bended Knee** ....A:❶[11] / S:2 *(instrumental)* "45": Motown 0284; B-side: "I'll Make Love To You" (sexy version)	$3	▮V	Motown 0244
2/25/95	21	20		10 **Thank You** ....S:21 / A:28 *Fallin'* samples "La-Di-Da-Di" by Doug E. Fresh	$3	▮V	Motown 0274
4/29/95	2[1]	28	●	11 **Water Runs Dry** ....A:❶[1] / S:8 *(mood mix)*	$3	▮V	Motown 0358
9/2/95	56	14		12 **Vibin'** ....S:28 *(remix w/Treach, **Craig Mack**, **Busta Rhymes**, **Method Man**)* "45" issued for above 2 on Motown 0422; above 5 from the album *II*	$3	▮V	Motown 0406
12/2/95	❶[16]	27	▲[2]	13 **One Sweet Day** AC[13] A:❶[13] / S:❶[11] *(live version)* **MARIAH CAREY & BOYZ II MEN** "45": Columbia 78072; B-side: "I Am Free"; also see re-entry at #21 below	$3	▮V	Columbia 78074
12/2/95+	46	11		14 **I Remember** ....S:24 *(4 album snippets)*	$3	▮	Motown 0480
1/13/96	45	15		15 **Visions Of A Sunset** ....S:18 *(string mix)* **SHAWN STOCKMAN** from the movie *Mr. Holland's Opus* starring Richard Dreyfuss	$3	▮	Polydor 0962
7/27/96	86	5		16 **Wishes** ....*(instrumental)* **NATHAN MORRIS (of Boyz II Men)** samples "For What It's Worth" by **The Buffalo Springfield**; from the movie *Kazaam* starring **Shaquille O'Neal**	$3	▮	Perspective 7550
9/27/97	❶[1]	20	▲	17 **4 Seasons Of Loneliness** ....S:❶[1] / A:12 *(remix)* "45": Motown 0714	$3	▮V	Motown 0684
12/13/97+	7	20	▲	18 **A Song For Mama** ....RB[2] S:5 / A:30 *(instrumental)* from the movie *Soul Food* starring **Vanessa Williams**; "45": Motown 0744	$3	▮V	Motown 0720
1/16/99	32	9	●	19 **I Will Get There** ....S:8 *(3 versions)* from the animated movie *The Prince Of Egypt*	$4	★	DreamWorks 59018
12/30/00+	80	4		20 **Thank You In Advance** ....S:19 *Leaders Of The Pack*	$4	★	Universal 158443
3/23/02	35[S]	18		21 **One Sweet Day** ....*(live version)* [R] **MARIAH CAREY & BOYZ II MEN** reissue of #13 above on Columbia's "Platinum Hits" series	$4	★	Columbia 79699

BRADLEY, Jan '63

Born Addie Bradley on 7/6/43 in Byhalia, Mississippi; raised in Robbins, Illinois. R&B singer. First recorded for Formal in 1962. Became a social worker in 1976.

DEBUT	PEAK	WKS	Gold	A-side (Chart Hit)..............B-side	$	Sym	Label & Number
1/5/63	14	14		1 **Mama Didn't Lie** ....*Lovers Like Me* written by **Curtis Mayfield**; first released on Formal 1044 in 1962 ($200)	$12		Chess 1845
2/6/65	93	3		2 **I'm Over You** ....*The Brush Off*	$10		Chess 1919

BRADLEY, Owen, Quintet POP/C&W '49

Born on 10/21/15 in Westmoreland, Tennessee. Died on 1/7/98 (age 82). Band leader/producer/organist/combo leader. Country A&R director for Decca from 1958-68. Vice president of MCA from 1968. His quintet included Hank Garland (guitar), E.R. "Dutch" McMillan (tenor horn), **Bob Moore** (bass) and Buddy Harmon (drums). Elected to the Country Music Hall of Fame in 1974. Hit #11 on the pop charts in 1949 with "Blues Stay Away From Me."

DEBUT	PEAK	WKS	Gold	A-side (Chart Hit)..............B-side	$	Sym	Label & Number
7/29/57	18	5		1 **White Silver Sands** ....A:18 / T:68 *Midnight Blues* Anita Kerr Quartet (vocals)	$15		Decca 30363
3/3/58	46	8		2 **Big Guitar** ....T:46 / S:48 *Sentimental Dream* [I]	$15		Decca 30564

BRADSHAW, Terry C&W '76

Born on 9/2/48 in Shreveport, Louisiana. Pro football quarterback with the Pittsburgh Steelers from 1970-83. In the movies *Hooper*, *Smokey and the Bandit II* and *Cannonball Run*. Current TV football analyst (on Fox's *NFL Sunday*).

DEBUT	PEAK	WKS	Gold	A-side (Chart Hit)..............B-side	$	Sym	Label & Number
3/6/76	91	5		**I'm So Lonesome I Could Cry** ....*Making Plans* written by Hank Williams in 1949	$5		Mercury 73760

BRAIDS, The '96

Female R&B vocal duo from Oakland, California: Caitlin Cornwell and Zoe Ellis.

DEBUT	PEAK	WKS	Gold	A-side (Chart Hit)..............B-side	$	Sym	Label & Number
10/19/96	42	17		**Bohemian Rhapsody** ....S:30 / A:51 *(instrumental)* from the movie *High School High* starring Jon Lovitz	$4	▮	Big Beat 98055

DEBUT	PEAK	WKS	Gold	A-side (Chart Hit)..........B-side	$	Sym	Label & Number

BRAINSTORM — R&B/LP '77

Disco group from Detroit, Michigan: Belita Karen "B.B." Woods (vocals), Charles Overton, Jeryl Bright, Larry H. "Leap" Sims, Gerald "Jumpin' Jerry" Kent, Trenita Womack, E. Lamont "Stro" Johnson, Willie Wooten and Renell Gonsalves (son of famous Duke Ellington saxman Paul Gonsalves).

DEBUT	PEAK	WKS	Gold	A-side (Chart Hit)..........B-side	$	Sym	Label & Number
3/12/77	86	3		**Wake Up And Be Somebody** ..... *We Know A Place*	$6		Tabu 10811

BRAITHWAITE, Daryl — '91

Born on 1/11/49 in Melbourne, Australia; raised in Randwick, Australia. Former lead singer of the **Sherbs**.

DEBUT	PEAK	WKS	Gold	A-side (Chart Hit)..........B-side	$	Sym	Label & Number
6/1/91	47	10		**Higher Than Hope** ..... *I Can See Higher Than Before*	$3	▮	Epic/Associated 73788

BRAM TCHAIKOVSKY — BUB/LP '79

Rock trio from Lincolnshire, England: Peter Bramall (vocals, guitar; **The Motors**), Micky Broadbent (bass) and Keith Boyce (drums).

DEBUT	PEAK	WKS	Gold	A-side (Chart Hit)..........B-side	$	Sym	Label & Number
7/7/79	37	12		**Girl Of My Dreams** ..... *Sarah Smiles*	$5		Polydor 14575

BRANCH, Michelle — LP '02

Born on 7/2/83 in Sedona, Arizona. Adult Alternative pop-rock singer/songwriter/guitarist.

DEBUT	PEAK	WKS	Gold	A-side (Chart Hit)..........B-side	$	Sym	Label & Number
9/1/01	12	20		1 **Everywhere** A:12			album cut
2/23/02	6	28		2 **All You Wanted** A:6			album cut
8/31/02	21	20		3 **Goodbye To You** A:26			album cut
				above 3 from the album *The Spirit Room* on Maverick 47985			
10/5/02	5	37		4 **The Game Of Love** ..... A:5 / S:19 *(instrumental)*	$4	★^{V}	Arista 15203
				SANTANA featuring Michelle Branch			
				"45": Arista 50980; B-side: "Nothing At All" (featuring **Musiq**)			

BRAND NEW HEAVIES, The — R&B/LP '94

Funk group from London, England: N'Dea Davenport (vocals), Simon Bartholomew (guitar), Andrew Levy (bass) and Jan Kincaid (drums). Davenport left in 1996; replaced by **Siedah Garrett**. Also see the B-side of **Blair**'s "Have Fun, Go Mad."

DEBUT	PEAK	WKS	Gold	A-side (Chart Hit)..........B-side	$	Sym	Label & Number
9/7/91	54	8		1 **Never Stop** ..... A:52 *(remix) / (3 album snippets)*	$4	▮	Delicious Vinyl 868552
				THE BRAND NEW HEAVIES featuring N'Dea Davenport			
3/19/94	51	11		2 **Dream on Dreamer** ..... A:41 *(remix) / (3 album snippets)*	$4	▮	Delicious Vinyl 98321
5/17/97	88	5		3 **Sometimes** ..... *(remix w/***Q-Tip***)*	$4	▮	Delicious Vinyl 4009

BRAND NUBIAN — R&B/LP '98

Rap trio from New Rochelle, New York: Maxwell Dixon ("**Grand Puba**"), Derek Murphy **"Sadat X"**) and Lorenzo DeChalus ("Lord Jamar"). Dixon left in 1992, replaced by Terence Perry ("Sincere Allah"). Dixon returned in 1998.

DEBUT	PEAK	WKS	Gold	A-side (Chart Hit)..........B-side	$	Sym	Label & Number
1/2/93	77	10		1 **Punks Jump Up To Get Beat Down** ..... S:45 *(remix w/Diamond)*	$4	▮	Elektra 64687
4/3/93	92	3		2 **Love Me Or Leave Me Alone** ..... S:71 *The Travel Jam*	$4	▮	Elektra 64661
10/29/94	94	2		3 **Word Is Bond** ..... *Straight Off The Head / Return Of The Dred*	$6	▮*	Elektra 66191
				samples "I'm The One" by **Average White Band**; above title used as a connection with the police in the 2002 Washington DC-area sniper rampage			
10/24/98	54	6		4 **Don't Let It Go To Your Head** ..... S:37 *The Return*	$3	▮	Arista 13571
				samples "Don't Let It Go To Your Head" by Jean Carn; clean version available on Arista 13573			

BRANDON — '91

Born in San Jose, California (of Latin and Danish parentage). Dance singer/multi-instrumentalist.

DEBUT	PEAK	WKS	Gold	A-side (Chart Hit)..........B-side	$	Sym	Label & Number
5/11/91	64	10		**Kisses In The Night** ..... A:74 *Destiny*	$4	▮	Alpha International 70718

BRANDON, Bill — R&B '78

Born in 1944 in Huntsville, Alabama. Black vocalist/trumpeter/bassist/drummer.

DEBUT	PEAK	WKS	Gold	A-side (Chart Hit)..........B-side	$	Sym	Label & Number
2/25/78	80	7		**We Fell In Love While Dancing** ..... *(long version)*	$5		Prelude 71102

BRANDT, Paul — C&W/LP '96

Born on 7/21/72 in Calgary, Alberta, Canada. Country singer/songwriter/guitarist.

DEBUT	PEAK	WKS	Gold	A-side (Chart Hit)..........B-side	$	Sym	Label & Number
10/12/96	63^{S}	5		**I Do** ..... BUB:102 *(instrumental)*	$4	▮^{V}	Reprise 17616
				"45" B-side: "One And Only One"			

BRANDY ★179★ — R&B/LP '98

Born Brandy Norwood on 2/11/79 in McComb, Mississippi; raised in Los Angeles, California. Singer/actress. Star of the TV series *Moesha*. Played "Karla Wilson" in the 1998 movie *I Still Know What You Did Last Summer*. Sister of **Ray J**.

1)The Boy Is Mine 2)Have You Ever? 3)Sittin' Up In My Room

DEBUT	PEAK	WKS	Gold	A-side (Chart Hit)..........B-side	$	Sym	Label & Number
10/1/94	6	28	●	1 **I Wanna Be Down** ..... RB^{4} S:4 / A:10 *(3 album snippets)*	$3	▮^{V}	Atlantic 87225
2/4/95	4	20	▲	2 **Baby** ..... RB^{4} S:❶^{5} / A:19 *I Wanna Be Down (remix)*	$3	▮^{V}	Atlantic 87173
				"45" issued for above 2 on Atlantic 87173			
6/3/95	34	20		3 **Best Friend** ..... S:25 / A:51 *Movin' On*	$3	▮	Atlantic 87148
9/9/95	9	20	●	4 **Brokenhearted** ..... S:5 / A:21 *(album version)*	$3	▮	Atlantic 87150
				Wanya Morris (of **Boyz II Men**; male vocal); above 4 from the album *Brandy*			
12/30/95+	2^{2}	33	▲	5 **Sittin' Up In My Room** ..... S:2 / A:8 *My Love, Sweet Love* (**Patti LaBelle**)	$3	▮^{V}	Arista 12929
				from the movie *Waiting To Exhale* starring **Whitney Houston**; remix version with guest rapper **LL Cool J** issued on Arista 12972			
8/24/96	25	20		6 **Missing You** ..... S:15 *(acappella version) / So Right, For Life* (Michael Speaks)	$3	▮^{V}	EastWest 64262
				BRANDY, TAMIA, GLADYS KNIGHT & CHAKA KHAN			
				from the movie *Set It Off* starring Jada Pinkett and **Queen Latifah**			
5/30/98	❶^{13}	27	▲^{2}	7 **The Boy Is Mine** ..... RB^{8} S:❶^{9} / A:2 *(instrumental)*	$3	▮^{V}	Atlantic 84089
				BRANDY & MONICA			
7/4/98	44^{A}	16		8 **Top Of The World**			album cut
				BRANDY (Featuring Mase)			
12/5/98+	❶^{2}	22		9 **Have You Ever?** ..... A:❶^{9} / S:3 *Top Of The World (remix w/***Fat Joe** & **Big Pun***)*	$3	★^{V}	Atlantic 84198
12/5/98+	72	14		10 **Angel In Disguise** A:58			album cut
				Joe (backing vocal)			
4/24/99	16	20		11 **Almost Doesn't Count** A:7			album cut

DEBUT	PEAK	WKS	Gold	A-side (Chart Hit)...B-side	$	Sym	Label & Number
				BRANDY — Cont'd			
10/23/99	**79**	6		12 **U Don't Know Me (Like U Used To)**....S:33 *(2 versions) / Almost Doesn't Count / Top Of The World*	$8	★*	Atlantic 84508
				BRANDY Featuring Shaunta & Da Brat			
				above 6 from the album *Never S-a-y Never* on Atlantic 83039			
11/24/01	**71^{S}**	1		13 **Formal Invite**....*(5 remixes)*	$6	T	Atlantic 85182
				RAY J (Featuring Brandy, Teddy Riley & Shorty Mack)			
1/26/02	**7**	18		14 **What About Us?**....A:6 / S:25 *(3 versions)*	$6	T^{V}	Atlantic 85217
5/4/02	**18**	20		15 **Full Moon**....S:16 / A:17 *(11 extended remixes)*	$8	$★^{*V}$	Atlantic 85269
				above 2 from the album *Full Moon* on Atlantic 83493; "45" issued for above 2 on Atlantic 85267			
	★367★			**BRANIGAN, Laura** AC/LP **'82**			
				Born on 7/3/57 in Brewster, New York. Pop singer/actress. Played "Monica" in the 1984 movie *Delta Pi.*			
				1)Gloria 2)Self Control 3)Solitaire			
3/20/82	**69**	7		1 **All Night With Me**....*I Wish We Could Be Alone*	$4		Atlantic 4023
7/10/82	**2^{3}**	36	▲	2 **Gloria** *Living A Lie*	$3		Atlantic 4048
				tune first popularized in Italy in 1979 by the song's composer, Umberto Tozzi			
3/19/83	**7**	17		3 **Solitaire**....*I'm Not The Only One*	$3	■	Atlantic 89868
7/2/83	**12**	20		4 **How Am I Supposed To Live Without You**....AC^{3} *Mama*	$3	■	Atlantic 89805
4/14/84	**4**	25		5 **Self Control**....*Silent Partners*	$3	■	Atlantic 89676
8/4/84	**20**	15		6 **The Lucky One**....*Breaking Out*	$3	■	Atlantic 89636
				from the TV movie *An Uncommon Love* starring Barry Bostwick			
11/3/84	**55**	12		7 **Ti Amo**....*Satisfaction*	$3	■	Atlantic 89608
7/27/85	**40**	11		8 **Spanish Eddie**....*Tenderness*	$3	■	Atlantic 89531
10/19/85	**82**	4		9 **Hold Me**....*Tenderness*	$3	■	Atlantic 89496
3/1/86	**90**	6		10 **I Found Someone**....*When*	$3	■	Atlantic 89451
				#4 & 10: written by **Michael Bolton**			
7/4/87	**48**	10		11 **Shattered Glass**....S:37 *Statue In The Rain*	$3	■	Atlantic 89245
10/24/87+	**26**	18		12 **Power Of Love**....S:19 / A:32 *Spirit Of Love*	$3	■	Atlantic 89191
3/31/90	**59**	9		13 **Moonlight On Water**....*Reverse Psychology*	$3	▮	Atlantic 87969
				BRASS CONSTRUCTION R&B/BUB/LP **'76**			
				Disco group from Brooklyn, New York: Randy Muller (vocals, keyboards), Joe Wong (guitar), Wayne Parris, Morris Price, Jesse Ward and Mickey Grudge (horn section), Sandy Billups (congas), Wade Williamston (bass) and Larry Payton (drums). Muller later formed **Skyy**.			
4/3/76	**14**	16		1 **Movin'**....RB^{1} *Talkin'* [I]	$5		United Artists 775
12/25/76+	**51**	12		2 **Ha Cha Cha (Funktion)**....*Sambo (Conditions)* [I]	$5		United Artists 921
				BRASS RING, The BUB/AC/LP **'66**			
				Studio group assembled by producer/arranger/saxophonist Phil Bodner (born on 6/13/21).			
3/12/66	**32**	9		1 **The Phoenix Love Theme (Senza Fine)**....*Lightening Bug* [I]	$7		Dunhill 4023
				from the movie *The Flight Of The Phoenix* starring James Stewart			
2/4/67	**36**	7		2 **The Dis-Advantages Of You**....*The Dating Game* [I]	$7		Dunhill 4065
				melody taken from a Benson & Hedges cigarette jingle; B-side is the TV game show theme			
				BRAT PACK, The **'90**			
				Male dance vocal duo from New Jersey: Patrick Donovan and Ray Frazier.			
2/3/90	**36**	12		1 **You're The Only Woman**....A:33 *(remix)*	$4	$▮^{V}$	Vendetta 1447
6/30/90	**71**	7		2 **I'm Never Gonna Give You Up**....*(remix)*	$4	▮	Vendetta 1502
				above 2 produced by **Clivilles & Cole**			
				BRAUN, Bob BUB/LP **'62**			
				Born Robert Brown on 4/20/29 in Ludlow, Kentucky. Died of Parkinson's disease on 1/15/2001 (age 71). Hosted own TV show in Cincinnati.			
7/21/62	**26**	10		**Till Death Do Us Part**....*So It Goes* [S]	$8	■	Decca 31355
				BRAVO ALL STARS **'98**			
				Collaboration of **Backstreet Boys**, The Boyz, Blümchen, **Aaron Carter**, Gil, The Moffatts, Mr. President, **'N Sync**, R'N'G, Scooter, Sqeezer, and Touché. Benefitting the Nordoff-Robbins Music Therapy Foundation.			
11/7/98	**60**	4		**Let The Music Heal Your Soul**....S:53 *(unplugged version)*	$6	▮	Edel America 4329
				additional chorus vocals by **Sarah Brightman**; with the London Session Orchestra			
				BRAXTON, Toni **★141★** AC/R&B/LP **'96**			
				Born on 10/7/68 in Severn, Maryland. Female R&B singer. Recorded in 1990 with her younger sisters as **The Braxtons**. Married Keri Lewis (of **Mint Condition**) on 4/21/2001. Won the 1993 Best New Artist Grammy Award.			
				1)Un-Break My Heart 2)You're Makin' Me High 3)He Wasn't Man Enough			
7/25/92	**29**	16		1 **Give U My Heart**....A:29 / S:39 *(album version)*	$4	▮	LaFace 24026
				BABYFACE (Featuring Toni Braxton)			
11/14/92+	**33**	20		2 **Love Shoulda Brought You Home**....S:25 / A:36 *(slow sensual mix)*	$4	▮	LaFace 24035
				above 2 from the movie *Boomerang* starring **Eddie Murphy**			
7/3/93	**7**	26	●	3 **Another Sad Love Song**....A:8 / S:14 *(instrumental)*	$3	▮	LaFace 24047
10/16/93+	**3**	35	●	4 **Breathe Again**....A:❶[1] / S:6 *(instrumental)*	$3	▮	LaFace 24054
11/27/93+	**48^{A}**	12		5 **Seven Whole Days**....RB^{5A}			album cut
4/2/94	**7**	31	●	6 **You Mean The World To Me**....A:3 / S:14 *Seven Whole Days (live)*	$3	$▮^{V}$	LaFace 24064
11/26/94+	**28**	13		7 **I Belong To You** / S:31 / A:35			
10/1/94	**35**	21		8 **How Many Ways**....S:27 / A:54	$3	▮	LaFace 24081
				above 7 from the album *Toni Braxton* on LaFace 26007			

DEBUT	PEAK	WKS	Gold	A-side (Chart Hit)............B-side	$	Sym	Label & Number
				BRAXTON, Toni — Cont'd			
6/8/96	❶[1]	41	▲	9 **You're Makin' Me High** / RB[2] / DC[2] S:2 / A:6			
6/8/96		41		10 **Let It Flow** ....S:flip	$3	▮[V]	LaFace 24160
				from the movie *Waiting To Exhale* starring **Whitney Houston**; #1-6, 9 & 10: written by **Babyface**			
10/26/96	❶[11]	42	▲	11 **Un-Break My Heart** AC[14] / DC[4] A:❶[2] / S:❶[1] *(Spanish version)*	$3	▮[V]	LaFace 24200
				Shanice Wilson (backing vocal)			
3/29/97	19	20	●	12 **I Don't Want To** / S:18 / A:34			
				written and produced by **R. Kelly**; #9, 11 & 12: #1 Dance Club Play hits			
4/12/97		18		13 **I Love Me Some Him**............	$3	▮	LaFace 24229
				above 5 from the album *Secrets*			
3/18/00	2[2]	37	●	14 **He Wasn't Man Enough**............RB[4] S:❶[5] / A:9 *(instrumental)*	$4	★	LaFace 24463
7/29/00	32	20		15 **Just Be A Man About It**............A:19	$8	◗	LaFace 24517
				Dr. Dre (backing vocal)			
12/2/00	98	3		16 **Spanish Guitar**............*(8 versions)*	$6	T	LaFace 24499
11/9/02	86	14		17 **Hit The Freeway**............S:42 *(3 versions)*	$6	T[V]	Arista 15196
				TONI BRAXTON Featuring Loon			
				"45": Arista 50973; B-side: "A Better Man"			
				BRAXTONS, The R&B/BUB/LP **'96**			
				Vocal trio of sisters from Severn, Maryland: Tamar, Trina and Towanda Braxton. Began as a quintet, with Traci and **Toni Braxton**. Toni went solo in 1992; Traci went solo in 1995.			
8/3/96	83	8		**So Many Ways**............S:54 *(instrumental)*	$4	▮	Atlantic 87056
				from the movie *High School High* starring Jon Lovitz			
	★281★			**BREAD** LP **'70**			
				Soft-rock group formed in Los Angeles, California. Consisted of leader **David Gates** (vocals, guitar, keyboards; born on 12/11/40), James Griffin (guitar), Robb Royer (guitar) and Jim Gordon (drums). Originally called Pleasure Faire. Griffin and Royer co-wrote the award-winning hit "For All We Know" with Fred Karlin in 1969. Mike Botts replaced Gordon after first album. Royer replaced by Larry Knechtel (top sessionman, member of **Duane Eddy**'s Rebels) in 1971. Disbanded in 1973; reunited briefly in 1976. All hits written and produced by Gates.			
				1)Make It With You 2)Baby I'm-A Want You 3)If			
6/13/70	❶[1]	17	●	1 **Make It With You** *Why Do You Keep Me Waiting*	$6		Elektra 45686
9/26/70	10	11		2 **It Don't Matter To Me**............*Call On Me*	$6	■	Elektra 45701
1/2/71	28	10		3 **Let Your Love Go**............*Too Much Love*	$6		Elektra 45711
3/27/71	4	12		4 **If**............AC[3] *Take Comfort*	$6	■	Elektra 45720
7/17/71	37	9		5 **Mother Freedom**............*Live In Your Love*	$6		Elektra 45740
10/23/71	3	12	●	6 **Baby I'm - A Want You**............AC[1] *Truckin'*	$6		Elektra 45751
1/29/72	5	13		7 **Everything I Own**............*I Don't Love You*	$6		Elektra 45765
4/22/72	15	11		8 **Diary**............*Down On My Knees*	$6		Elektra 45784
				above 4 from the album *Baby I'm - A Want You*			
7/29/72	11	10		9 **The Guitar Man**............AC[1] *Just Like Yesterday*	$6		Elektra 45803
11/11/72	15	11		10 **Sweet Surrender**............AC[2] *Make It By Yourself*	$6		Elektra 45818
2/3/73	15	11		11 **Aubrey**............*Didn't Even Know Her Name*	$6		Elektra 45832
11/27/76+	9	16		12 **Lost Without Your Love**............*Change Of Heart*	$5		Elektra 45365
4/16/77	60	7		13 **Hooked On You**............*Our Lady Of Sorrow*	$5		Elektra 45389
				BREAKFAST CLUB LP **'87**			
				Pop-dance group from Manhattan, New York: brothers Dan (vocals) and Eddie (guitar) Gilroy, Gary Burke (bass) and Stephen Bray (drums). **Madonna** was with the group for a short time in 1979 as the drummer. Bray co-produced Madonna's *True Blue* album.			
3/14/87	7	19		1 **Right On Track**............S:5 / A:12 *(**Jellybean** remix)*	$3	■	MCA 52954
7/11/87	48	9		2 **Kiss And Tell**............S:37 *Right On Track (uptown dub)*	$3	■	MCA 53128
				BREATHE AC/LP **'88**			
				Pop group from London, England: David Glasper (vocals), Marcus Lillington (guitar), Michael Delahunty (bass) and Ian Spice (drums). Delahunty left in 1988.			
4/16/88	2[2]	29		1 **Hands To Heaven** S:❶[2] / A:2 *Life And Times*	$3	■	A&M 2991
9/10/88	3	22		2 **How Can I Fall?**............AC[2] S:❶[1] / A:3 *Monday Morning Blues*	$3	■	A&M 1224
1/14/89	10	16		3 **Don't Tell Me Lies**............A:9 / S:13 *Liberties Of Love*	$3	■	A&M 1267
8/25/90	21	15		4 **Say A Prayer**............A:15 / S:30 *(save my soul 7")*	$3	▮	A&M 1519
11/17/90+	34	13		5 **Does She Love That Man?**............A:32 *Say It*	$3	▮	A&M 1535
				BREATHE featuring David Glasper			
				BREATHLESS **'80**			
				Rock group from Cleveland, Ohio: Jonah Koslen (vocals; **Michael Stanley Band**), Alan Greene (guitar), Mark Avsec (keyboards; **Wild Cherry**), Bob Benjamin (bass), and Rodney Psyka and Kevin Valentine (drums).			
1/12/80	92	4		**Takin' It Back**............*Alibis*	$5		EMI America 8020
				BRECKER BROTHERS, The R&B/LP **'75**			
				White jazz-funk duo of Philadelphia-born brothers Randy (trumpet; born on 11/27/45) and Michael (reeds; born on 3/29/49) Brecker. Both are prolific sessionmen. The brothers began recording together in their group, Dreams; also with **Spyro Gyra**.			
6/7/75	58	9		**Sneakin' Up Behind You**............*Sponge* [I]	$5		Arista 0122
				BREEDERS, The ROK/BUB/LP **'94**			
				Rock group from Dayton, Ohio: twin sisters/guitarists/vocalists Kim and Kelley Deal, bassist Josephine Wiggs (native of Bedfordshire, England) and drummer Jim MacPherson. Kim was a member of the Pixies. Tanya Donelly (Throwing Muses, **Belly**) was an early member.			
12/4/93+	44	20		**Cannonball**............S:35 / A:52 *Lord Of The Thighs / Cro-Aloha*	$3	▮[V]	4AD/Elektra 64566
				"45": 4AD/Elektra 64565; B-side: "Divine Hammer" (ROK #28)			
				BREMERS, Beverly BUB/LP **'72**			
				Born on 3/10/50 in Chicago, Illinois. Pop singer/actress.			
12/18/71+	15	16		1 **Don't Say You Don't Remember**............*Get Smart Girl*	$6		Scepter 12315
4/29/72	40	15		2 **We're Free**............*Colors Of Love*	$5	■	Scepter 12348
9/16/72	63	9		3 **I'll Make You Music**............*I Made A Man Out Of You, Jimmy*	$5		Scepter 12363

DEBUT	PEAK	WKS	Gold	A-side (Chart Hit)	B-side	$	Sym	Label & Number

BRENDA & THE TABULATIONS — R&B/BUB/LP '67

R&B vocal group from Philadelphia, Pennsylvania: Brenda Payton, Jerry Jones, Eddie Jackson and Maurice Coates. Bernard Murphy was added in 1969. Reorganized in 1970 with vocalists Payton, Pat Mercer and Deborah Martin. Payton died on 6/14/92.

1)Dry Your Eyes 2)Right On The Tip Of My Tongue 3)The Touch Of You

DEBUT	PEAK	WKS	Gold	A-side (Chart Hit)	B-side	$	Sym	Label & Number
2/25/67	20	11		1 Dry Your Eyes	*The Wash*	$15		Dionn 500
5/20/67	66	7		2 Stay Together Young Lovers /				
6/10/67	66	6		3 Who's Lovin' You — written by **Smokey Robinson**		$12		Dionn 501
8/12/67	97	2		4 Just Once In A Lifetime — above 4 from the album *Dry Your Eyes*	*Hey Boy*	$12		Dionn 503
11/4/67	58	7		5 When You're Gone	*Hey Boy*	$12		Dionn 504
3/16/68	86	4		6 Baby You're So Right For Me	*To The One I Love* (R&B #45)	$12		Dionn 507
1/17/70	50	8		7 The Touch Of You	*Stop Sneaking Around*	$8		Top & Bottom 401
5/9/70	64	8		8 And My Heart Sang (Tra La La)	*Lies Lies Lies*	$8		Top & Bottom 403
8/22/70	77	3		9 Don't Make Me Over	*You've Changed*	$8		Top & Bottom 404
4/3/71	23	13		10 Right On The Tip Of My Tongue	*Always & Forever*	$8		Top & Bottom 407
8/28/71	94	5		11 A Part Of You	*Where There's A Will (There's A Way)*	$8		Top & Bottom 408

BRENNAN, Walter — LP '62

Born on 7/25/1894 in Swampscott, Massachusetts. Died of emphysema on 9/21/74 (age 80). Famous character actor. Appeared in several movies and TV shows.

DEBUT	PEAK	WKS	Gold	A-side (Chart Hit)	B-side	$	Sym	Label & Number
4/25/60	30	12		1 Dutchman's Gold — **WALTER BRENNAN With BILLY VAUGHN and his Orchestra**	*Back To The Farm* [S]	$12	■	Dot 16066
4/7/62	5	11		2 Old Rivers	*The Epic Ride Of John H. Glenn* [S]	$10		Liberty 55436
8/4/62	100	1		3 Houdini	*The Old Kelly Place* [S]	$10	■	Liberty 55477
10/20/62	38	8		4 Mama Sang A Song — **The Johnny Mann Singers** (backing vocals, above 3)	*Who Will Take Gramma* [S]	$10		Liberty 55508

BREWER, Teresa — MEM/POP/BUB/LP '53

★230★

Born Theresa Breuer on 5/7/31 in Toledo, Ohio. Pop singer. Debuted on *Major Bowes Amateur Hour* at age five, toured with show until age 12. Appeared on *Pick & Pat* radio show. First recorded for London in 1949. In the movie *Those Redheads From Seattle* (1953). Charted two huge #1 hits from 1950-53: "Music! Music! Music!" and "Till I Waltz Again With You."

1)A Tear Fell 2)Let Me Go, Lover! 3)A Sweet Old Fashioned Girl 4)You Send Me 5)Empty Arms

DEBUT	PEAK	WKS	Gold	A-side (Chart Hit)	B-side	$	Sym	Label & Number
12/18/54+	6	12		1 Let Me Go, Lover! (J:6 / A:7 / S:8) — **TERESA BREWER with The Lancers**; written in 1953 as "Let Me Go Devil" and first recorded by **Georgie Shaw**	*The Moon Is On Fire*	$20		Coral 61315
2/26/55	19[HR]	1		2 I Gotta Go Get My Baby — written by **Marvin Rainwater**	*What More Is There To Say*	$15		Coral 61339
3/19/55	17	3		3 Pledging My Love / (A:17 / J:18 / S:30)				
5/7/55		1		4 How Important Can It Be? (J:flip)		$15		Coral 61362
6/4/55	20	1		5 Silver Dollar (J:20) — **Jack Pleis** (orch., all of above)	*I Don't Want To Be Lonely Tonight*	$15		Coral 61394
7/30/55	15	4		6 The Banjo's Back In Town (J:15)	*How To Be Very, Very Popular*	$15		Coral 61448
11/19/55	66	3		7 Shoot It Again (T:66) — introduced on the TV program *U.S. Steel Hour*	*You're Telling Our Secrets*	$15		Coral 61528
2/25/56	5	23		8 A Tear Fell / (J:5 / T:7 / S:9 / A:9) — #15 R&B hit for **Ivory Joe Hunter** in 1956				
3/3/56	17	15		9 Bo Weevil (T:17 / A:20 / S:flip / J:flip)		$15		Coral 61590
6/9/56	7	20		10 A Sweet Old Fashioned Girl (J:7 / T:9 / A:11 / S:12)	*Goodbye, John*	$15		Coral 61636
9/22/56	87	3		11 I Love Mickey (T:87) [N] — **MICKEY MANTLE And TERESA BREWER** (Mantle died on 8/13/95)	*Keep Your Cotton Pickin' Paddies Offa My Heart* (Brewer)	$30		Coral 61700
11/10/56	21	14		12 Mutual Admiration Society / (T:21 / S:24 / A:24) — from the musical *Happy Hunting* starring Ethel Merman				
11/24/56	73	5		13 Crazy With Love (T:73)		$15		Coral 61737
4/6/57	13	17		14 Empty Arms (J:13 / T:18 / A:19 / S:23)	*The Ricky-Tick Song*	$15		Coral 61805
6/17/57	64	7		15 Teardrops In My Heart (T:64) — #4 Country hit for the Sons of the Pioneers in 1947	*Lula Rock-A-Hula*	$15		Coral 61850
11/11/57	8	12		16 You Send Me (A:8 / S:27 / T:31)	*Would I Were*	$15		Coral 61898
9/1/58	99	1		17 Pickle Up A Doodle (H:99)	*The Rain Falls On Ev'rybody*	$12		Coral 62013
10/6/58	38	5		18 The Hula Hoop Song (H:38)	*So Shy*	$12		Coral 62033
1/5/59	75	5		19 The One Rose (That's Left In My Heart) — #8 hit in 1937 for 3 different artists	*Satellite*	$12		Coral 62057
3/16/59	40	8		20 Heavenly Lover	*Fair Weather Sweetheart*	$12		Coral 62084
2/1/60	66	4		21 Peace Of Mind	*Venetian Sunset*	$10	■	Coral 62167
8/8/60	31	16		22 Anymore — #3 Country hit for **Roy Drusky** in 1960	*That Piano Man*	$10	■	Coral 62219
11/28/60	84	5		23 Have You Ever Been Lonely (Have You Ever Been Blue) — #8 hit for Ted Lewis & His Band in 1933	*When Do You Love Me*	$10		Coral 62236
5/22/61	74	4		24 Milord — **Dick Jacobs** (orch.: #6-24)	*I've Got My Fingers Crossed*	$10		Coral 62265

BREWER & SHIPLEY — LP '71

Folk-rock duo formed in Los Angeles, California: Mike Brewer (born in 1944 in Oklahoma City, Oklahoma) and Tom Shipley (born in 1942 in Mineral Ridge, Ohio).

DEBUT	PEAK	WKS	Gold	A-side (Chart Hit)	B-side	$	Sym	Label & Number
2/13/71	10	14		1 One Toke Over The Line — Jerry Garcia (of **Grateful Dead**; steel guitar)	*Oh Mommy*	$7		Kama Sutra 516
5/15/71	55	8		2 Tarkio Road	*Seems Like A Long Time*	$6		Kama Sutra 524
2/5/72	98	3		3 Shake Off The Demon	*Indian Summer*	$6	■	Kama Sutra 539

DEBUT	PEAK	WKS	Gold	A-side (Chart Hit)..........B-side	$	Sym	Label & Number
				B RICH LP **'02**			
				Born Brian Rich in Baltimore, Maryland. Male rapper.			
5/18/02	98	2		**Whoa Now** ....S:58 *(2 versions)*	$6	T	Atlantic 85296
				samples "Movin' On Up" (theme from TV's *The Jeffersons*) by Janet DuBois			
				BRICK R&B/BUB/LP **'77**			
				Black disco-jazz group from Atlanta, Georgia: Jimmy Brown (sax), Reggie Hargis (guitar), Don Nevins (keyboards), Ray Ransom (bass) and Eddie Irons (drums). All share vocals. Session work in the early 1970s.			
10/23/76+	3	21		1 **Dazz** ....RB^4 *Southern Sunset*	$5		Bang 727
				title is short for disco-jazz; also see **Dazz Band**			
9/3/77	18	18		2 **Dusic** ....*Happy*	$5		Bang 734
				title is short for disco-music			
1/28/78	92	4		3 **Ain't Gonna' Hurt Nobody** ....*Honey Chile*	$5		Bang 735
				BRICKELL, Edie ROK/LP **'89**			
				Born on 3/10/66 in Oak Cliff, Texas. Pop singer/songwriter. New Bohemians: Kenny Withrow (guitar), Brad Houser (bass) and John Bush (drums). Group disbanded in 1991. Brickell married **Paul Simon** on 5/30/92.			
11/26/88+	7	19		1 **What I Am** ....S:4 / A:9 *I Do*	$3	■	Geffen 27696
4/8/89	48	10		2 **Circle** ....*Now*	$3	■	Geffen 27580
				EDIE BRICKELL & NEW BOHEMIAMS (above 2)			
8/20/94	60	8		3 **Good Times** ....A:56 *Picture Perfect Morning*	$3	▮V	Geffen 19273
				Barry White (guest vocal); co-produced by **Paul Simon**			
				BRICKMAN, Jim **'97**			
				Born on 11/20/61 in Cleveland, Ohio. New Age pianist/songwriter.			
11/1/97	50	16		1 **Valentine** ....S:36 / A:65 *A Broken Wing* (McBride - #61)	$4	V	RCA 64963
				MARTINA McBRIDE with Jim Brickman			
12/27/97+	65^A	7		2 **The Gift** .... [X]			album cut
				COLLIN RAYE with Jim Brickman			
				from Raye's album *The Best Of Collin Raye - Direct Hits* on Epic 67893			
				BRIDGES, Alicia LP **'78**			
				Born on 7/15/53 in Lawndale, North Carolina. Disco singer/songwriter.			
7/8/78	5	31	●	1 **I Love The Nightlife (Disco 'Round)** ....*Self Applause*	$4		Polydor 14483
4/7/79	86	2		2 **Body Heat** ....*We Are One*	$4		Polydor 14539
				BRIGGS, Lillian **'55**			
				Born Lillian Biggs in Allentown, Pennsylvania. Died of cancer on 4/11/98 (age 64). White big band-styled singer. Discovered by Alan Freed while working in Joy Cayler's All-Girl Orchestra in New York City.			
9/17/55	18	3		**I Want You To Be My Baby** ....A:18 / J:19 / S:23 / T:53 *Don't Stay Away Too Long*	$25		Epic 9115
				O.B. Masingill (orch.); originally recorded by Louis Jordan in 1953 on Decca 28883			
				BRIGHT, Larry **'60**			
				Born Julian Ferebee Bright on 8/17/34 in Norfolk, Virginia; raised in Corpus Christi, Texas. White soul singer/guitarist.			
5/16/60	90	3		**Mojo Workout (Dance)** ....*I'll Change My Ways*	$20		Tide 006
				BRIGHTER SIDE OF DARKNESS R&B **'73**			
				R&B vocal group from Chicago, Illinois: Darryl Lamont, Ralph Eskridge, Randolph Murphy and Larry Washington.			
12/9/72+	16	13	●	**Love Jones** ....*I'm The Guy*	$6		20th Century 2002
				also see **Cheech & Chong**'s parody "Basketball Jones"			
				BRIGHTMAN, Sarah LP **'01**			
				Born on 8/14/60 in London, England. Adult Contemporary singer/actress. Starred in Broadway's *The Phantom Of The Opera*. Married to Andrew Lloyd Webber from 1984-90.			
6/23/01	34^S	12		**A Whiter Shade Of Pale** ....*(4 mixes) / A Question Of Honour*	$8	★**	Angel 79374
				BRILEY, Martin ROK/LP **'83**			
				Born on 6/10/52 in England. Rock singer/songwriter/guitarist.			
5/21/83	36	15		**The Salt In My Tears** ....*Dumb Love*	$4		Mercury 812165
				BRILL **'02**			
				Born Jabreel Shakir in Los Angeles, California. Male rapper.			
4/6/02	48^S	3		**I've Been Real** ....*Keep It Real*	$4	★	Motown 158051
				BRISTOL, Johnny R&B/BUB/LP **'74**			
				Born on 2/3/39 in Morganton, North Carolina. R&B singer/composer/producer. Teamed with Jackey Beavers, recorded as Johnny & Jackey for Tri-Phi, 1961. Teamed with **Harvey Fuqua** as Motown producers until 1973.			
6/29/74	8	17		1 **Hang On In There Baby** ....*Take Care Of You For Me*	$5		MGM 14715
11/16/74	48	7		2 **You And I** ....*It Don't Hurt No More*	$5		MGM 14762
11/27/76+	43	11		3 **Do It To My Mind** ....*Love To Have A Chance To Taste The Wine*	$5		Atlantic 3360
8/30/80	63	8		4 **My Guy/My Girl** ....*Now*	$5		Handshake 5300
				AMII STEWART & JOHNNY BRISTOL			
				medley of #1 tunes by **Mary Wells** and **The Temptations** (both written by **Smokey Robinson**)			
				BRITISH LIONS LP **'78**			
				Rock group from Birmingham, England: John Fiddler (vocals), Ray Major (guitar), Morgan Fisher (keyboards), Pete "Overend" Watts (bass) and Dale "Buffin" Griffin (drums). Fisher, Watts and Griffin were members of **Mott The Hoople**.			
7/22/78	87	4		**Wild In The Streets** ....*Booster*	$6		RSO 898
				first recorded by **Garland Jeffreys** in 1974 ("Bubbled Under" #115)			
				BRITNY FOX ROK/LP **'88**			
				Hard-rock group from Philadelphia, Pennsylvania: "Dizzy" Dean Davidson (vocals), Michael Kelly Smith (guitar), Billy Childs (bass) and Johnny Dee (drums).			
10/1/88	100	2		**Long Way To Love** ....*Livin' On The Edge*	$4		Columbia 07926
				BROADWAY R&B **'76**			
				R&B group led by vocalist Patti Williams.			
7/17/76	86	4		**You To Me Are Everything** ....*Our Love Has Come To An End*	$6		Granite 540

DEBUT	PEAK	WKS	Gold	A-side (Chart Hit)...B-side	$	Sym	Label & Number
				BROCK, Chad C&W/BUB/LP **'00**			
				Born on 7/31/63 in Ocala, Florida. Country singer/songwriter/guitarist.			
2/20/99	**39**	17		1 **Ordinary Life**...A:23 / S:70 *My Memory Ain't What It Used To Be*	$4	★V	Warner 17136
8/21/99	**86**	12		2 **Lightning Does The Work**...S:68 / A:74 *Evangeline* (C&W #51)	$4	★V	Warner 16984
1/1/00	**75**	3		3 **A Country Boy Can Survive (Y2K Version)**...S:25 *Going The Distance*	$4	★V	Warner 16895
				CHAD BROCK (With Hank Williams, Jr. & George Jones)			
				#2 Country hit for **Hank Williams, Jr.** in 1982			
4/8/00	**22**	20		4 **Yes!**...CW3 S:23 / A:24 *Tell Me Your Secret*	$4	★V	Warner 16876
				B-ROCK & THE BIZZ **'97**			
				B-Rock is rap producer Baron Agee from Mobile, Alabama. The Bizz is a studio group assembled by Agee.			
4/19/97	**10**	19	●	**MyBabyDaddy**...S:3 / A:65 *(bassed out club mix)*	$4	▮	Tony Mercedes 24221
				Kitty Thomas (female vocal); samples "Best Of My Love" by **The Emotions**			
				BRONSKI BEAT — see SOMERVILLE, Jimmy			
				BROOD, Herman LP **'79**			
				Born on 11/5/46 in Zwolle, Holland. Committed suicide on 7/11/2001 (age 54). Leader of Dutch rock band Wild Romance.			
7/14/79	**35**	11		**Saturdaynight**...*Back (In Y'r love)*	$5	□	Ariola America 7754
				BROOKLYN BOUNCE **'98**			
				Dance group is actually German producers Matthias Menck and Dennis Böhn. Represented on stage by male singer Damon and female dancers Ulrica and Maeva.			
4/11/98	**95**	4		**Get Ready To Bounce**...*(same version)*	$4	▮	Edel America 3722
				BROOKLYN BRIDGE BUB/AC/LP **'69**			
				Pop group from Long Island, New York, made up of a vocal quartet and seven-piece band. The Del-Satins are **Johnny Maestro** (lead vocals, **The Crests**), Fred Ferrara, Les Cauchi and Mike Gregorie (backing vocals). The Rhythm Method are Richie Macioce (guitar), Tom Sullivan and Joe Ruvio (saxophones), Shelly Davis (trumpet), Carolyn Wood (organ), Jimmy Rosica (bass) and Artie Catanzarita (drums).			
12/21/68+	**3**	12	●	1 **Worst That Could Happen** *Your Kite, My Kite*	$8		Buddah 75
3/8/69	**45**	6		2 **Blessed Is The Rain /**			
5/10/69	**48**	9		3 **Welcome Me Love**...	$8		Buddah 95
				THE BROOKLYN BRIDGE Featuring Johnny Maestro (above 2)			
7/19/69	**46**	8		4 **Your Husband - My Wife**...*Everybody's Cookin'*	$8		Buddah 126
10/4/69	**51**	6		5 **You'll Never Walk Alone**...*Minstral Sunday*	$8		Buddah 139
				from the Rodgers & Hammerstein musical *Carousel*			
7/11/70	**91**	2		6 **Down By The River**...*Look Again*	$8		Buddah 179
				written by **Neil Young**			
10/3/70	**98**	2		7 **Day Is Done**...*Easy Way*	$8		Buddah 193
				B-side of promo pressings shown as "Opposites" (same song as "Easy Way")			
				BROOKLYN DREAMS LP **'79**			
				Disco trio from Brooklyn, New York: **Joe "Bean" Esposito** (see #5 below) (vocals, guitar), Bruce Sudano (keyboards; **Alive And Kicking**) and Eddie Hokenson (drums). Sudano married **Donna Summer** on 7/16/80. Also see **Brenda Russell**'s "Piano In The Dark."			
11/12/77	**63**	5		1 **Sad Eyes**...*Hollywood Circles*	$5		Millennium 606
3/25/78	**57**	8		2 **Music, Harmony And Rhythm**...*Old Fashioned Girl*	$5		Millennium 610
1/13/79	**4**	19	●	3 **Heaven Knows** *Only One Man* (Summer)	$5		Casablanca 959
				DONNA SUMMER with Brooklyn Dreams			
2/24/79	**69**	4		4 **Make It Last**...*Long Distance*	$5		Casablanca 962
10/22/83	**86**	2		5 **Lady, Lady, Lady**...*To Turn The Stone*	$4		Casablanca 814430
				JOE "BEAN" ESPOSITO			
				from the movie *Flashdance* starring Jennifer Beals			
				BROOKS, Donnie BUB **'60**			
				Born John Abahosh in Dallas, Texas; raised in Ventura, California. Pop singer.			
6/13/60	**7**	20		1 **Mission Bell**...*Do It For Me*	$20		Era 3018
11/28/60	**31**	10		2 **Doll House**...*Round Robin* (#115)	$15	■	Era 3028
3/13/61	**90**	2		3 **Memphis**...*That's Why*	$15	■	Era 3042
				BROOKS, Garth C&W/AC/BUB/LP **'99**			
				Born Troyal Garth Brooks on 2/7/62 in Luba, Oklahoma; raised in Yukon, Oklahoma. Country singer/guitarist (charted 86 hits, 1989-02). Attended Oklahoma State on a track scholarship (javelin). His immense popularity contributed to a resurgence of Country music in the 1990's.			
7/9/94	**45**A	9		1 **Hard Luck Woman**...			album cut
				from the tribute album *Kiss My Ass: Classic Kiss Regrooved* on Mercury 522123			
5/30/98	**56**	20		2 **One Heart At A Time**...S:33 *(same version)*	$4	▮	Atlantic 84117
				GARTH BROOKS, BILLY DEAN, FAITH HILL, OLIVIA NEWTON-JOHN, NEAL McCOY, MICHAEL McDONALD, VICTORIA SHAW, BRYAN WHITE			
12/5/98	**62**	5		3 **It's Your Song**...A:47 [L]			album cut
				from the album *Double Live* on Capitol 97424			
9/11/99	**5**	10		4 **Lost In You** S:2	$4	★V	Capitol 58788
				GARTH BROOKS AS CHRIS GAINES			
				Gaines is a fictional character created for a proposed movie *The Lamb* starring Brooks			
2/19/00	**69**	6		5 **Do What You Gotta Do**...A:60		V	album cut
				from the album *Sevens* on Capitol 56599; "45": Capitol 58845; B-side: "A Friend To Me" (C&W #68)			
12/23/00+	**50**	14		6 **Wild Horses**...A:43			album cut
				from the 1990 album *No Fences* on Capitol 93866			
10/27/01	**22**S	12		7 **Call Me Claus**...*'Zat You, Santa Claus? / Mary Had A Little Lamb* [X]	$5	★V	Capitol 77669
				theme song from the TV movie starring Whoopi Goldberg; "45": "'Zat You, Santa Claus?" / "Mary Had A Little Lamb" on Capitol 77678			
10/27/01	**46**	20		8 **Wrapped Up In You**...A:46			album cut
				from the album *Scarecrow* on Capitol 31330			

DEBUT	PEAK	WKS	Gold	A-side (Chart Hit)...B-side	$	Sym	Label & Number
				BROOKS, Meredith LP **'97**			
				Born on 6/12/58 in Oregon City, Oregon. Female rock singer/guitarist. Former member of **The Graces**.			
4/26/97	**2**[4]	30	●	1 **Bitch** ...S:2 / A:6 *Down By The River*	$3	▮	Capitol 58634
2/28/98	**46**	10		2 **What Would Happen**...A:44 / S:52 *Every Time She Walks Away*	$3	▮V	Capitol 58681
				"45": Capitol 19722; B-Side: "My Little Town"			
				BROOKS, Nancy **'79**			
				Pop-rock singer.			
3/3/79	**66**	4		**I'm Not Gonna Cry Anymore** ...*Let's Go Whoop Ti Hoo*	$5		Arista 0385
				BROOKS & DUNN C&W/BUB/LP **'01**			
				Country duo of Kix Brooks (born on 5/12/55 in Shreveport, Louisiana) and Ronnie Dunn (born on 6/1/53 in Coleman, Texas). Charted 41 Country hits, 1991-02.			
				1)Ain't Nothing 'Bout You 2)Only In America 3)Husbands And Wives			
7/25/92	**50**	15		1 **Boot Scootin' Boogie** ...CW[4] S:20 *(album version)*	$4	▮V	Arista 12440
				originally released as the B-side of their #1 hit in 1981 "My Next Broken Heart" on Arista 12337; "45" B-side: "Lost And Found" (C&W #6)			
3/5/94	**97**	3		2 **Rock My World (Little Country Girl)**...S:56 *(club mix)*	$4	▮V	Arista 12636
				"45" B-side: "Our Time Is Coming"			
4/27/96	**79**	12		3 **My Maria**...CW[3] S:44 *Mama Don't Get Dressed Up For Nothing* (C&W #13)	$4	▮V	Arista 12993
12/5/98	**36**	9		4 **Husbands And Wives** ...CW[1] A:28		V	album cut
				"45": Arista Nashville 13143; B-side: "How Long Gone" (C&W #1)			
2/13/99	**51**	11		5 **I Can't Get Over You** ...A:35		V	album cut
				"45": Arista Nashville 13152; B-side: "Way Gone"; above 2 from the album *If You See Her* on Arista 18865			
10/16/99	**75**	3		6 **Missing You** ...A:63		V	album cut
				"45": Arista Nashville 13179; B-side: "The Trouble With Angels"			
6/10/00	**55**	19		7 **You'll Always Be Loved By Me**...A:47 *Don't Look Back Now*	$4	▮V	Arista 13198
				commercial single available on cassette only; above 2 from the album *Tight Rope* on Arista 18895			
3/10/01	**25**	20		8 **Ain't Nothing 'Bout You** CW[6] A:16		V	album cut
				"45": Arista 69048; B-side: "Husbands And Wives"			
7/21/01	**33**	20		9 **Only In America**...CW[1] A:29		V	album cut
12/22/01+	**39**	20		10 **The Long Goodbye** ...CW[1] A:35		V	album cut
				"45" issued for above 2 on Arista Nashville 69130			
5/25/02	**48**	13		11 **My Heart Is Lost To You** ...A:46			album cut
12/7/02	**75**	5		12 **Every River**...A:72			album cut
				above 5 from the album *Steers & Stripes* on Arista Nashville 67003			
				BROS LP **'88**			
				Pop trio from London, England: twin brothers Matt (vocals) and Luke (drums) Goss, with Craig Logan (bass). Group's name rhymes with "cross."			
6/25/88	**83**	5		**When Will I Be Famous?** ...*Love To Hate You*	$3	■	Epic 07905
				BROTHER BEYOND **'90**			
				Pop group from England: Nathan Moore (vocals), David White (guitar), Carl Fysh (keyboards) and Steve Alexander (drums).			
6/23/90	**27**	15		**The Girl I Used To Know** ...S:26 / A:28 *Universal*	$3	▮	EMI 50287
				BROTHERHOOD CREED R&B **'92**			
				Rap duo from Los Angeles, California: Tyrone Ward and Sean McDuffie.			
4/18/92	**53**	18		**Helluva**...S:32 / A:67 *(radio mix)*	$4	▮	Gasoline Alley 54350
				samples "Groovin'" by **The Young Rascals**			
				BROTHERHOOD OF MAN, The LP **'70**			
				Studio group from England featuring **Tony Burrows**, Johnny Goodison and Sunny Leslie (female singer). Burrows was lead singer of **Edison Lighthouse**, **First Class**, **The Pipkins** and **White Plains**. 1976 hit featured new members: Nicky Stevens, Sandra Stevens, Martin Lee and Lee Sheridan.			
4/18/70	**13**	15		1 **United We Stand**...*Say A Prayer*	$6		Deram 85059
8/22/70	**61**	7		2 **Where Are You Going To My Love**...*Living In The Land Of Love*	$6		Deram 85065
5/1/71	**77**	3		3 **Reach Out Your Hand**...*A Better Tomorrow*	$6		Deram 85073
5/8/76	**27**	11		4 **Save Your Kisses For Me** ...AC[1] *Let's Live Together*	$5		Pye 71066
				BROTHERS FOUR, The AC/BUB/LP **'60**			
				Folk-pop group formed at the University of Washington: Dick Foley, Bob Flick, John Paine and Mike Kirkland.			
2/22/60	**2**[4]	20		1 **Greenfields** *Angelique-O*	$10	■	Columbia 41571
				written in 1956 by **Terry Gilkyson & The Easy Riders**			
7/4/60	**50**	7		2 **My Tani** ...*Ellie Lou*	$10	■	Columbia 41692
10/31/60	**65**	7		3 **The Green Leaves Of Summer**...*Beautiful Brown Eyes*	$10	■	Columbia 41808
				from the movie *The Alamo* starring John Wayne			
4/10/61	**32**	5		4 **Frogg**...*Sweet Rosyanne* [N]	$8	■	Columbia 41958
				new version of tune written back in 1580 as "Frog Went A Courtin'"			
1/20/62	**68**	8		5 **Blue Water Line**...*Summer Days Alone*	$8	■	Columbia 42256
12/14/63	**89**	3		6 **Hootenanny Saturday Night**...*Across The Sea*	$8		Columbia 42927
				theme from the TV folk music variety show *Hootenanny*			
11/6/65	**91**	3		7 **Try To Remember**...*Sakura*	$8		Columbia 43404
				from the off-Broadway musical *The Fantasticks* starring Jerry Orbach			
12/17/66	**26**[X]	2		8 **I'll Be Home For Christmas**...*'Twas The Night Before Christmas* [X]	$8		Columbia 43919
				#3 hit for **Bing Crosby** in 1943			
				BROTHERS IN RHYTHM **'91**			
				Duo of dance remixers: Steve Anderson and Dave Seaman.			
8/10/91	**64**[A]	5		**Such A Good Feeling**...*(2 versions)*	$5	▮*	4th & B'way 440538

DEBUT	PEAK	WKS	Gold	A-side (Chart Hit)...B-side	$	Sym	Label & Number

BROTHERS JOHNSON, The — R&B/BUB/LP '76

R&B-funk duo from Los Angeles, California: brothers George (born on 5/17/53) and Louis (born on 4/13/55) Johnson. Own band, the Johnson Three + 1, with brother Tommy and cousin Alex Weir. With **Billy Preston**'s band to 1975. Duo split up in 1982.

DEBUT	PEAK	WKS	Gold	A-side (Chart Hit)...B-side	$	Sym	Label & Number
10/11/75	70	10		1 **Is It Love That We're Missin'** ... *Cry Baby* **QUINCY JONES (featuring The Brothers Johnson)**	$5	■	A&M 1743
5/1/76	3	17	●	2 **I'll Be Good To You** RB[1] *The Devil*	$5	■	A&M 1806
8/14/76	30	15		3 **Get The Funk Out Ma Face** ... *Tomorrow*	$5	■	A&M 1851
7/2/77	5	19	●	4 **Strawberry Letter 23** ... RB[1] *Dancin' And Prancin'* **Lee Ritenour** (guitar solo)	$5	■	A&M 1949
3/15/80	7	19		5 **Stomp!** ... RB[2] *Let's Swing*	$5		A&M 2216
8/16/80	73	4		6 **Treasure** ... *Smilin' On Ya*	$4		A&M 2254
6/27/81	67	6		7 **The Real Thing** ... *I Want You*	$4		A&M 2343

BROTHER TO BROTHER — R&B '74

R&B group from St. Louis, Missouri: Michael Burton (vocals), Billy Jones (guitar), Frankie Prescott (bass) and Yogi Horton (drums).

DEBUT	PEAK	WKS	Gold	A-side (Chart Hit)...B-side	$	Sym	Label & Number
10/12/74	46	7		**In The Bottle** ... *The Affair*	$7		Turbo 039

BROWN, Al — '60

Born on 5/22/30 in Fairmont, West Virginia. Black singer/songwriter/producer. The Tunetoppers backing band formed in 1953.

DEBUT	PEAK	WKS	Gold	A-side (Chart Hit)...B-side	$	Sym	Label & Number
4/4/60	23	12		**The Madison** ... *Mo' Madison* **AL BROWN'S TUNETOPPERS featuring COOKIE BROWN**	$25		Amy 804

BROWN, Alex — R&B '85

Female R&B singer.

DEBUT	PEAK	WKS	Gold	A-side (Chart Hit)...B-side	$	Sym	Label & Number
5/4/85	76	6		**(Come On) Shout** ... *Technique* (Rainey) from the movie *Girls Just Want To Have Fun* starring Sarah Jessica Parker	$5		Mercury 880694

BROWN, Arthur — BUB/LP '68

Born Arthur Wilton on 6/24/44 in Whitby, England. White theatrical rock singer. His band consisted of Sean Nicholas (guitar), Vince Crane (organ) and Carl Palmer (drums; Atomic Rooster, **Emerson, Lake & Palmer**, **Asia**). Since 1992, has been a partner in a music therapy practice known as Healing Songs Therapy. Crane committed suicide on 2/14/89 (age 44).

DEBUT	PEAK	WKS	Gold	A-side (Chart Hit)...B-side	$	Sym	Label & Number
9/7/68	2[1]	13	●	**Fire** ... *Rest Cure* **THE CRAZY WORLD OF ARTHUR BROWN**	$10		Atlantic 2556

BROWN, Bobby ★195★ — R&B/LP '89

Born on 2/5/69 in Roxbury, Massachusetts. Member of **New Edition**. Appeared in the movies *Ghostbusters II*, *Panther* and *A Thin Line Between Love & Hate*. Established own Bosstown recording studio and label in Atlanta in 1991. Married **Whitney Houston** on 7/18/92.

1)She Ain't Worth It 2)My Prerogative 3)On Our Own

DEBUT	PEAK	WKS	Gold	A-side (Chart Hit)...B-side	$	Sym	Label & Number
12/20/86+	57	9		1 **Girlfriend** ... RB[2] *(sing-a-long version)*	$4	■	MCA 52866
7/23/88	8	26	●	2 **Don't Be Cruel** ... RB[2] S:3 / A:13 *(instrumental)*	$3	■	MCA 53327
10/22/88+	❶[1]	24	●	3 **My Prerogative** ... RB[2] S:❶[1] / A:2 *(instrumental)*	$3	■	MCA 53383
1/7/89	3	17		4 **Roni** ... A:3 / S:4 *(instrumental)*	$3	■	MCA 53463
3/25/89	3	21	●	5 **Every Little Step** ... RB[1] S:2 / A:3 *(w/rap)*	$3	■	MCA 53618
6/10/89	2[3]	20	▲	6 **On Our Own** ... RB[1] S:❶[2] / A:2 *(w/o rap)* from the movie *Ghostbusters II* starring Bill Murray and Dan Aykroyd	$3		MCA 53662
8/26/89	7	21	●	7 **Rock Wit'cha** ... A:6 / S:8 *(instrumental)* #2-7 (except #6): from the album *Don't Be Cruel*	$3		MCA 53652
5/19/90	❶[2]	18	●	8 **She Ain't Worth It** A:❶[3] / S:4 *(no B-side)* **GLENN MEDEIROS Featuring Bobby Brown** "45": MCA 79047; B-side: "Victim Of Love" (Medeiros)	$3	▮[V]	MCA 53831
8/8/92	3	20	●	9 **Humpin' Around** ... RB[2] S:4 / A:4 *(3 album snippets)*	$3	▮[V]	MCA 54342
10/17/92	7	23	●	10 **Good Enough** ... A:5 / S:7 *(3 album snippets)* **Whitney Houston** (backing vocal)	$3	▮[V]	MCA 54517
1/16/93	14	16		11 **Get Away** ... S:15 / A:18 *(w/o rap)*	$3	▮[V]	MCA 54511
4/24/93	57	9		12 **That's The Way Love Is** ... A:50 *(instrumental)* above 4 from the album *Bobby*	$3	▮[V]	MCA 54618
11/20/93	32[A]	9		13 **Something In Common** ... **BOBBY BROWN With WHITNEY HOUSTON** from Brown's album *Remixes N The Key Of B* on MCA 10974			album cut
11/23/02	42	10		14 **Thug Lovin'** ... S:24 / A:42 *(3 versions)* **JA RULE feat. Bobby Brown** contains an interpolation of "Knocks Me Off My Feet" by **Stevie Wonder**	$6	T	Murder Inc. 063838

BROWN, Boots, And His Blockbusters — '58

Brown was actually black jazz trumpeter Shorty Rogers. Born Milton Rajonsky on 4/14/24 in Lee, Massachusetts. Died of liver failure on 11/7/94 (age 70). Worked with the big bands of **Woody Herman** and **Stan Kenton**.

DEBUT	PEAK	WKS	Gold	A-side (Chart Hit)...B-side	$	Sym	Label & Number
8/11/58	23	8		**Cerveza** ... S:23 / H:62 *Juicy* [I] tune is very similar to **The Champs**' "Tequila"	$20		RCA Victor 7269

BROWN, Buster — BUB '60

Born Wayman Glasco on 8/15/11 in Cordele, Georgia. Died on 1/31/76 (age 64). R&B singer/harmonica player.

DEBUT	PEAK	WKS	Gold	A-side (Chart Hit)...B-side	$	Sym	Label & Number
2/1/60	38	17		1 **Fannie Mae** ... RB[1] *Lost In A Dream*	$30		Fire 1008
9/19/60	81	3		2 **Is You Is Or Is You Ain't My Baby** ... *Don't Dog Your Woman* #3 R&B hit for Louis Jordan in 1944	$25		Fire 1023
2/3/62	99	2		3 **Sugar Babe** ... *I'm Going-But I'll Be Back*	$25		Fire 507

DEBUT	PEAK	WKS	Gold	A-side (Chart Hit)..........B-side	$	Sym	Label & Number

BROWN, Charles — R&B/BUB/LP '61

Born on 9/13/22 in Texas City, Texas. Died of heart failure on 1/21/99 (age 76). R&B singer/pianist. Joined Johnny Moore's Three Blazers in 1944. Charted 24 R&B hits from 1945-52 as a solo artist and with Johnny Moore's Three Blazers. Inducted into the Rock and Roll Hall of Fame in 1999 as an early influence.

DEBUT	PEAK	WKS	Gold	A-side (Chart Hit)..........B-side	$	Sym	Label & Number
12/25/61	76	2		1 **Please Come Home For Christmas**..........X:❶[1] *Christmas (Comes But Once A Year)* (Amos Milburn) [X] #21 R&B hit in 1960; "Bubbled Under" (#108) in 1962; Christmas charts: [#1[1]-35 weeks] 4/'63; 3/'64; 2/'65; 3/'66; 3/'67; 3/'68; 4/'69; 3/'70; 1/'72; 9/'73	$15		King 5405
12/12/64	4^{X}	5		2 **Merry Christmas Baby**..........*I Lost Everything* [X] X: 4/'64; 10/'65 (Imperial version first released in 1962)	$12		Imperial 5902
12/18/65	2^{1X}	16		3 **Merry Christmas Baby**..........*Sleigh Ride* (Lloyd Glenn) [X] **CHARLES BROWN With Johnny Moore's 3 Blazers** X: 5/'65; 4/'66; 6/'67; 2/'68; 4/'69; 8/'70 (this original version was a #3 R&B hit in 1947 on Exclusive 254)	$20		Hollywood 1021
12/15/73	2^{1X}	2		4 **Merry Christmas Baby**..........*Let's Make Every Day A Christmas Day* [X] above 3 are different versions of the same song (King version first released in 1968)	$10		King 6194

BROWN, Chuck, & The Soul Searchers — R&B/LP '79

Funk group from Washington DC: Chuck Brown (vocals, guitar), John Buchanan and Curtis Johnson (keyboards), Don Tillery (trumpet), Leroy Fleming (sax), Gregory Gerran (congas), Jerry Wilder (bass) and Ricky Wellman (drums).

DEBUT	PEAK	WKS	Gold	A-side (Chart Hit)..........B-side	$	Sym	Label & Number
2/3/79	34	12	●	**Bustin' Loose Part 1**..........RB[4] *Part 2*	$5		Source 40967

BROWN, Don — '78

Born in 1949 in Minneapolis, Minnesota. Pop singer/songwriter/producer.

DEBUT	PEAK	WKS	Gold	A-side (Chart Hit)..........B-side	$	Sym	Label & Number
3/18/78	74	5		**Sitting In Limbo**..........*Romance And Magic* written by **Jimmy Cliff**	$6		1st American 102

BROWN, Foxy — R&B/BUB/LP '97

Born Inga Marchand on 9/6/79 in Brooklyn, New York. Female rapper. Guest rapper on songs by **Toni Braxton**, **Case**, **Jay-Z**, **L.L. Cool J** and **Total**. "Foxy Brown" was an action movie character of the 1970s played by actress Pam Grier.

DEBUT	PEAK	WKS	Gold	A-side (Chart Hit)..........B-side	$	Sym	Label & Number
11/30/96+	42^{A}	13		1 **Get Me Home**.......... **FOXY BROWN Featuring BLACKstreet** samples "Gotta Get You Home Tonight" by **Eugene Wilde**; from Brown's album *Ill Na Na* on Def Jam 533684			album cut
2/15/97	7	20	●	2 **I'll Be** S:2 / A:52 *La Familia* **FOXY BROWN Featuring Jay-Z** samples "I'll Be Good" by **Rene & Angela**	$3	▮	Violator 574028
8/16/97	53	15		3 **Big Bad Mamma**..........A:51 *(2 versions)* **FOXY BROWN Featuring Dru Hill** samples "She's A Bad Mama Jama" by **Carl Carlton**; from the movie *Def Jam's How To Be A Player* starring Bill Bellamy	$6	T	Violator 571441
10/25/97	95	2		4 **Sunshine**..........*(2 versions)* **JAY-Z featuring Babyface and Foxy Brown**	$6	T	Roc-A-Fella 574923
1/23/99	91	6		5 **Hot Spot**..........*(2 versions) / BWA* (w/**Mia X** & **Gangsta Boo**)	$6	T	Violator 566499
9/8/01	59^{S}	2		6 **Candy**..........BUB:124 *(2 versions) / 730* **FOXY BROWN (Feat. Kelis)** a limited edition 12" single issued on pink vinyl ($20)	$6	T	Def Jam 588738

BROWN, Horace — R&B/BUB/LP '96

Born in Charlotte, North Carolina. R&B singer.

DEBUT	PEAK	WKS	Gold	A-side (Chart Hit)..........B-side	$	Sym	Label & Number
3/30/96	62	12		1 **One For The Money**..........S:55 *(instrumental)* samples "Flava In Ya Ear" by **Craig Mack** and "7 Mo Beats To Break/Old Days"	$4	▮	Motown 0512
8/10/96	95	1		2 **Things We Do For Love**..........*(instrumental)* contains elements from "Blues & Pants" by **James Brown**	$4	▮	Motown 0360
6/1/02	52^{S}	1		3 **Friday Night**..........*(3 versions)* **MR. CHEEKS featuring Horace Brown** samples "Fly Robin Fly" by **Silver Convention**	$6	T	Universal 015975

BROWN, James ★6★ — R&B/BUB/LP '65

Born on 5/3/33 in Barnwell, South Carolina; raised in Augusta, Georgia. Formed own vocal group, the Famous Flames with **Bobby Byrd**. Cut a demo record of own composition "Please Please Please" in November 1955 at radio station WIBB in Macon. Signed to King/Federal Records in January 1956 and re-recorded the song. Cameo appearances in movies *The* ***Blues Brothers*** and *Rocky IV*. One of the originators of "Soul" music, variously billed on Polydor hits as "Soul I," "The Creator," "The Godfather of Soul," "The Hit Man" and "Minister of New New Super Heavy Funk." His backing group, **The JB's**, featured various personnel, including **Nat Kendrick**, Bootsy Collins, **Maceo** Parker and **Fred Wesley**. On 12/15/88, received a six-year prison sentence after leading police on an interstate car chase; released from prison on 2/27/91. Inducted into the Rock and Roll Hall of Fame in 1986. Won Grammy's Lifetime Achievement Award in 1992. Ranked as the #1 artist in *Joel Whitburn's Top R&B Singles 1942-1999* book. Also see **Lyn Collins**.

1)I Got You (I Feel Good) 2)Living In America 3)I Got The Feelin' 4)Cold Sweat 5)Papa's Got A Brand New Bag 6)It's A Man's Man's Man's World 7)Say It Loud - I'm Black And I'm Proud 8)Mother Popcorn 9)Super Bad 10) Licking Stick - Licking Stick

DEBUT	PEAK	WKS	Gold	A-side (Chart Hit)..........B-side	$	Sym	Label & Number
12/15/58+	48	13		1 **Try Me**..........RB[1] *Tell Me What I Did Wrong* also see #26 below	$50		Federal 12337
5/2/60	33	8		2 **Think** / #9 R&B hit for **The "5" Royales** in 1957; also see #37, 85 & 86 below			
6/27/60	86	1		3 **You've Got The Power**.......... Bea Ford (female vocal)	$30		Federal 12370
8/29/60	79	5		4 **This Old Heart**..........*Wonder When You're Coming Home*	$30		Federal 12378
11/14/60	68	6		5 **The Bells**..........*And I Do Just What I Want* #3 R&B hit for **Billy Ward & His Dominoes** in 1953	$20		King 5423
2/27/61	40	8		6 **Bewildered**..........*If You Want Me* #1 R&B hit for both Amos Milburn and the Red Miller Trio in 1948	$20		King 5442
5/15/61	47	8		7 **I Don't Mind**..........*Love Don't Love Nobody*	$20		King 5466
8/21/61	49	4		8 **Baby, You're Right**..........*I'll Never, Never Let You Go*	$20		King 5524
12/18/61+	48	10		9 **Lost Someone**..........*Cross Firing* also see #28 below	$20		King 5573
4/14/62	35	11		10 **Night Train**..........*Why Does Everything Happen To Me* #1 R&B hit for Jimmy Forest in 1952 (riff borrowed from Duke Ellington's 1946 tune "Happy-Go-Lucky Local")	$20		King 5614

DEBUT	PEAK	WKS	Gold		A-side (Chart Hit)	B-side	$	Sym	Label & Number
					BROWN, James — Cont'd				
7/7/62	61	4		11	**Shout And Shimmy**	*Come Over Here*	$20		King 5657
9/29/62	82	2		12	**Mashed Potatoes U.S.A.**	*You Don't Have To Go*	$20		King 5672
12/8/62	93	3		13	**Three Hearts In A Tangle**	*I've Got Money*	$20		King 5701
					#2 Country hit for **Roy Drusky** in 1961				
2/9/63	99	1		14	**Every Beat Of My Heart**	*Like A Baby* (R&B #24) [I]	$20		King 5710
4/20/63	18	11		15	**Prisoner Of Love**	*Choo-Choo*	$20		King 5739
					#1 hit for **Perry Como** in 1946				
7/27/63	55	6		16	**These Foolish Things**	*(Can You) Feel It Part 1*	$20		King 5767
					#1 hit for **Benny Goodman** in 1936				
10/12/63	77	5		17	**Signed, Sealed, And Delivered**	*Waiting In Vain*	$20		King 5803
					#2 Country hit for **Cowboy Copas** in 1948				
1/25/64	23	10		18	**Oh Baby Don't You Weep (Part 1)**	*(Part 2)*	$20	■	King 5842
2/15/64	95	2		19	**Please, Please, Please**	*In The Wee Wee Hours (Of The Nite)* (#125) [L]	$20		King 5853
					same version (with "live" effects dubbed in) as Brown's #5 1956 R&B hit on Federal 12258 ($75)				
5/2/64	95	2		20	**Caldonia**	*Evil*	$15	■	Smash 1898
					some pressings titled as "Caledonia"; #1 R&B hit for Louis Jordan in 1945				
7/4/64	99	1		21	**The Things That I Used To Do**	*Out Of The Blue*	$15	■	Smash 1908
					#1 R&B hit for Guitar Slim in 1954				
8/15/64	24	10		22	**Out Of Sight**	*Maybe The Last Time* (#107)	$15	■	Smash 1919
					JAMES BROWN And His Orchestra (above 3)				
12/26/64+	92	2		23	**Have Mercy Baby**	*Just Won't Do Right (I Stay In The Chapel Every Night)*	$15		King 5968
					#1 R&B hit for **The Dominoes** in 1952				
7/17/65	8	13		24	**Papa's Got A Brand New Bag Part I**	RB[8] *Part II*	$15		King 5999
11/13/65	3	12		25	**I Got You (I Feel Good)**	RB[6] *I Can't Help It (I Just Do-Do-Do)*	$15		King 6015
11/20/65	63	8		26	**Try Me** *[JAMES BROWN At The Organ]*	*Papa's Got A Brand New Bag* [I] [I-R]	$15		Smash 2008
					instrumental version of #1 above				
2/19/66	73	2		27	**I'll Go Crazy /**	[L]			
					#15 R&B hit for Brown in 1960 on Federal 12369 ($30)				
2/5/66	94	2		28	**Lost Someone**	[L-R]	$12		King 6020
3/5/66	42	7		29	**Ain't That A Groove Part 1**	*Part 2*	$12		King 6025
4/30/66	8	9		30	**It's A Man's Man's Man's World**	RB[2] *Is It Yes Or Is It No?*	$12		King 6035
7/30/66	53	9		31	**Money Won't Change You Part 1**	*Part 2*	$12		King 6048
10/8/66	50	7		32	**Don't Be A Drop-Out**	*Tell Me That You Love Me*	$12		King 6056
12/10/66	8[X]	4		33	**Sweet Little Baby Boy (Part 1)**	*(Part 2)* [X]	$15		King 6065
					X: 8/'66; 23/'67				
12/17/66	12[X]	4		34	**The Christmas Song (Version 1)**	*(Version 2)* [X]	$15		King 6064
					X: 12/'66; 20/'68				
1/7/67	29	8		35	**Bring It Up**	*Nobody Knows*	$12		King 6071
3/4/67	55	5		36	**Kansas City**	*Stone Fox*	$12		King 6086
4/8/67	100	1		37	**Think**	*Nobody Cares* (Anderson) [R]	$12		King 6091
					VICKI ANDERSON And JAMES BROWN				
					also see #2 above and #85 & 86 below				
5/6/67	46	7		38	**Let Yourself Go**	*Good Rockin' Tonight*	$12		King 6100
7/15/67	7	12		39	**Cold Sweat - Part 1**	RB[3] *Part 2*	$12		King 6110
10/28/67	40	6		40	**Get It Together (Part 1)**	*(Part 2)*	$12		King 6122
12/9/67	13[X]	4		41	**Let's Make This Christmas Mean Something This Year (Part 1)**	*(Part 2)* [X]	$15		King 6072
					first released in 1966				
12/9/67+	28	9		42	**I Can't Stand Myself (When You Touch Me) /**				
1/20/68	36	8		43	**There Was A Time**		$12		King 6144
3/16/68	6	12		44	**I Got The Feelin'**	RB[2] *If I Ruled The World*	$12		King 6155
5/25/68	14	8		45	**Licking Stick - Licking Stick (Part 1)**	*(Part 2)*	$12		King 6166
5/25/68	52	7		46	**America Is My Home - Pt. 1**	*Pt. 2* [S]	$12		King 6112
7/27/68	55	6		47	**I Guess I'll Have To Cry, Cry, Cry**	*Just Plain Funk*	$12		King 6141
					JAMES BROWN And The Famous Flames (all of above except #5, 20-22, 26 & 37)				
9/7/68	10	11		48	**Say It Loud - I'm Black And I'm Proud (Part 1)**	RB[6] *(Part 2)*	$12		King 6187
11/9/68	31	7		49	**Goodbye My Love**	*Shades Of Brown*	$12		King 6198
12/14/68	4[X]	6		50	**Santa Claus Go Straight To The Ghetto**	*You Know It* [X]	$15		King 6203
					X: 4/'68; 6/'69				
12/21/68	86	4		51	**Tit For Tat (Ain't No Taking Back)**	*Believers Shall Enjoy (Non Believers Shall Suffer)*	$12		King 6204
1/25/69	15	9		52	**Give It Up Or Turnit A Loose**	RB[2] *I'll Lose My Mind*	$12		King 6213
4/5/69	20	8		53	**I Don't Want Nobody To Give Me Nothing (Open Up The Door, I'll Get It Myself)**	*(Part 2)*	$12		King 6224
5/31/69	30	9		54	**The Popcorn**	*The Chicken* [I]	$12		King 6240
6/14/69	11	12		55	**Mother Popcorn (You Got To Have A Mother For Me) Part 1**	RB[2] *Part 2*	$10		King 6245
8/23/69	41	6		56	**Lowdown Popcorn**	*Top Of The Stack* [I]	$10		King 6250
9/13/69	37	7		57	**World (Part 1)**	*(Part 2)*	$10		King 6258
10/11/69	21	8		58	**Let A Man Come In And Do The Popcorn Part One**	*Sometime*	$10		King 6255
11/22/69+	24	11		59	**Ain't It Funky Now (Part 1)**	*(Part 2)* [I]	$10		King 6280
12/20/69+	40	8		60	**Part Two (Let A Man Come In And Do The Popcorn)**	*Gittin' A Little Hipper (Part 2)*	$10		King 6275
2/14/70	32	8		61	**It's A New Day (Part 1) & (Part 2)**	*Georgia On My Mind*	$10		King 6292
3/21/70	51	5		62	**Funky Drummer (Part 1)**	*(Part 2)*	$10		King 6290
5/2/70	32	8		63	**Brother Rapp (Part 1) & (Part 2)**	*Bewildered*	$10		King 6310
7/18/70	15	9		64	**Get Up I Feel Like Being Like A Sex Machine (Part 1)**	*(Part 2)*	$10		King 6318
					also see #95 below				
10/3/70	13	10		65	**Super Bad (Part 1 & Part 2)**	RB[2] *(Part 3)*	$10		King 6329
					first pressings show title as "Call Me Super Bad"				
12/19/70	7[X]	1		66	**Santa Claus Is Definitely Here To Stay**	*Hey America* [X]	$10	■	King 6340
1/2/71	34	8		67	**Get Up, Get Into It, Get Involved Pt. 1**	*Pt. 2*	$10		King 6347
2/27/71	29	9		68	**Soul Power Pt. 1**	*Pt. 2 & Pt. 3*	$10		King 6368

DEBUT	PEAK	WKS	Gold	A-side (Chart Hit)	B-side	$	Sym	Label & Number
				BROWN, James — Cont'd				
3/6/71	90	2		69 **Spinning Wheel Pt. 1**	*Pt. 2* [I]	$10		King 6366
5/8/71	50	6		70 **I Cried**	*World Pt. 2*	$10		King 6363
6/12/71	35	6		71 **Escape-ism (Part 1)**	*(Part 2 & 3)* [S]	$10		People 2500
7/3/71	15	11		72 **Hot Pants Pt. 1 (She Got To Use What She Got To Get What She Wants)**	RB[1] *Pt. 2 & 3*	$10		People 2501
8/28/71	22	9		73 **Make It Funky (Part 1)**	RB[2] *(Part 2)*	$8		Polydor 14088
10/23/71	68	6		74 **My Part/Make It Funky-Part 3** above 2 are different versions of the same tune	*Part 4* [I]	$8		Polydor 14098
11/13/71	35	8		75 **I'm A Greedy Man - Part I**	*Part II*	$8		Polydor 14100
2/12/72	27	7		76 **Talking Loud And Saying Nothing - Part I** first released in 1971 on King 6359	RB[1] *Part II*	$8		Polydor 14109
3/4/72	40	7		77 **King Heroin** issued with 2 different picture sleeves	*Theme From King Heroin* (Dave Matthews) [S]	$8	■	Polydor 14116
5/6/72	43	7		78 **There It Is Part 1**	*Part 2*	$8		Polydor 14125
6/24/72	44	8		79 **Honky Tonk - Part 1** *[THE JAMES BROWN SOUL TRAIN]*	*Part 2* [I]	$8		Polydor 14129
8/5/72	18	14	●	80 **Get On The Good Foot-Part 1**	RB[4] *Part 2*	$8		Polydor 14139
11/18/72	44	7		81 **I Got A Bag Of My Own**	*Public Enemy #1 - Part 1*	$8		Polydor 14153
12/23/72+	56	7		82 **What My Baby Needs Now Is A Little More Lovin'** **JAMES BROWN-LYN COLLINS**	*This Guy-This Girl's In Love*	$8		Polydor 14157
1/20/73	27	8		83 **I Got Ants In My Pants - Part 1 and i want to dance**	*Part 15 & 16*	$7		Polydor 14162
3/10/73	50	7		84 **Down And Out In New York City** from the movie *Black Caesar* starring Fred Williamson	*Mama's Dead*	$7		Polydor 14168
5/19/73	77	5		85 **Think**	*Something* [R]	$7		Polydor 14177
8/11/73	80	2		86 **Think** above 2 are different versions of the same song; also see #2 & 37 above	*Something* [R]	$7		Polydor 14185
8/18/73	50	8		87 **Sexy, Sexy, Sexy** from the movie *Slaughter's Big Rip-Off* starring Jim Brown	*Slaughter Theme*	$6		Polydor 14194
12/1/73+	58	11		88 **Stoned To The Bone - Part 1** some pressings issued as "Stone To The Bone - Part 1"	*Stoned To The Bone (Some More)*	$6		Polydor 14210
3/23/74	26	13	●	89 **The Payback - Part I**	RB[2] *Part II*	$6	■	Polydor 14223
6/22/74	29	13		90 **My Thang**	RB[2] *Public Enemy #1 - Part I*	$6		Polydor 14244
8/24/74	31	11		91 **Papa Don't Take No Mess Part I**	RB[1] *Part II*	$6		Polydor 14255
11/9/74	44	10		92 **Funky President (People It's Bad)** /				
12/7/74		6		93 **Coldblooded**		$6		Polydor 14258
2/22/75	80	4		94 **Reality**	*I Need Your Love So Bad*	$6		Polydor 14268
5/17/75	61	5		95 **Sex Machine Part I** new version of #64 above	*Part II* [R]	$6		Polydor 14270
8/14/76	45	7		96 **Get Up Offa That Thing**	*Release The Pressure*	$6		Polydor 14326
2/26/77	88	3		97 **Bodyheat (Part 1)** Brown's face is pictured on the record label from #55-97 (except #79 & 87)	*(Part 2)*	$6		Polydor 14360
12/7/85+	4	19		98 **Living In America** from the movie *Rocky IV* starring Sylvester Stallone	S:4 / A:6 *Farewell* (Vince DiCola)	$4	■	Scotti Brothers 05682
10/18/86	93	2		99 **Gravity**	*(dub mix)*	$4	■	Scotti Brothers 06275

BROWN, Jim Ed — see BROWNS, The

BROWN, Jocelyn R&B **'84**

Born in North Carolina. Female R&B singer. Backing vocalist for **Luther Vandross**, **George Benson**, **John Lennon** and many others. Singer with the dance groups Inner Life and **Salsoul Orchestra**.

DEBUT	PEAK	WKS	Gold	A-side (Chart Hit)	B-side	$	Sym	Label & Number
6/16/84	75	10		**Somebody Else's Guy**	*(instrumental)*	$6		Vinyl Dreams 71

BROWN, Louise **'61**

Born in Chicago, Illinois. Black lounge singer/pianist.

DEBUT	PEAK	WKS	Gold	A-side (Chart Hit)	B-side	$	Sym	Label & Number
5/8/61	76	5		**Son-In-Law**	*You Gave Me Misery*	$50		Witch 101

BROWN, Maxine R&B/BUB/LP **'61**

Born on 4/27/32 in Kingstree, South Carolina. R&B singer. With gospel groups The Manhattans and The Royaltones in New York City in the late 1950s. Starred in the Broadway musical *Wild Women Don't Have The Blues*.

1)All In My Mind 2)Oh No Not My Baby 3)Funny

DEBUT	PEAK	WKS	Gold	A-side (Chart Hit)	B-side	$	Sym	Label & Number
12/31/60+	19	12		1 **All In My Mind**	*Harry Let's Marry*	$20		Nomar 103
3/27/61	25	10		2 **Funny** reissued on Musictone 1117 in 1963; above 2 reissued on Wham 7036 with a picture sleeve	*Now That You've Gone*	$20		Nomar 106
6/30/62	98	1		3 **My Time For Cryin'**	*Wanting You*	$15		ABC-Paramount 10327
4/6/63	75	5		4 **Ask Me**	*Yesterday's Kisses*	$15	■	Wand 135
1/4/64	99	2		5 **Coming Back To You**	*Since I Found You*	$15		Wand 142
10/24/64+	24	13		6 **Oh No Not My Baby** **Dee Dee Warwick** (harmony vocal)	*You Upset My Soul*	$15		Wand 162
2/13/65	56	7		7 **It's Gonna Be Alright**	*You Do Something To Me*	$15		Wand 173
4/24/65	55	9		8 **Something You Got** **CHUCK JACKSON & MAXINE BROWN**	*Baby Take Me*	$15		Wand 181
7/3/65	55	8		9 **One Step At A Time**	*Anything For A Laugh*	$15		Wand 185
8/21/65	91	4		10 **Can't Let You Out Of My Sight** **CHUCK JACKSON & MAXINE BROWN**	*Don't Go*	$15		Wand 191
10/23/65	98	1		11 **I Need You So** **CHUCK JACKSON and MAXINE BROWN** written by **Ivory Joe Hunter**	*'Cause We're In Love*	$15		Wand 198
12/11/65+	63	9		12 **If You Gotta Make A Fool Of Somebody**	*You're In Love*	$15		Wand 1104
2/18/67	91	4		13 **Hold On I'm Coming** **CHUCK JACKSON & MAXINE BROWN**	*Never Had It So Good*	$15		Wand 1148

DEBUT	PEAK	WKS	Gold	A-side (Chart Hit)...B-side	$	Sym	Label & Number
				BROWN, Maxine — Cont'd			
5/6/67	91	1		14 **Daddy's Home**...*Don't Go*	$15		Wand 1155
				CHUCK JACKSON & MAXINE BROWN			
9/27/69	73	8		15 **We'll Cry Together**...*Darling, Be Home Soon*	$8		Common. United 3001
				BROWN, Nappy R&B '55			
				Born Napoleon Brown Culp on 10/12/29 in Charlotte, North Carolina. R&B-gospel singer.			
4/30/55	25	4		1 **Don't Be Angry**...S:25 *It's Really You*	$35		Savoy 1155
1/19/57	57	9		2 **Little By Little**...T:57 *I'm Getting Lonesome*	$30		Savoy 1506
				with the Zippers Quartet			
11/10/58	89	2		3 **It Don't Hurt No More**...*My Baby*	$25		Savoy 1551
				with Teacho Wiltshire's Orchestra			
				BROWN, Oscar Jr. '74			
				Born on 10/10/26 in Chicago, Illinois. R&B-jazz singer. Radio actor while still a teenager. Hosted the TV series *Jazz Scene* in 1962.			
5/18/74	69	6		**The Lone Ranger**...*Feel The Fire*	$6		Atlantic 3001
				BROWN, Peter R&B/BUB/LP '78			
				Born on 7/11/53 in Blue Island, Illinois. Disco singer/keyboardist.			
9/17/77	18	14		1 **Do Ya Wanna Get Funky With Me**...*Burning Love Breakdown*	$6		Drive 6258
				Wildflower (backing vocals, also on #3 below)			
3/4/78	8	28		2 **Dance With Me** *For Your Love*	$6		Drive 6269
9/23/78	54	8		3 **You Should Do It**...*Without Love*	$6		Drive 6272
				PETER BROWN with Betty Wright (above 2)			
8/18/79	86	6		4 **Crank It Up (Funk Town) Pt. 1**...*Pt. 2*	$5		Drive 6278
12/15/79+	59	8		5 **Stargazer**...*Penguin*	$5		Drive 6281
				BROWN, Polly R&B '75			
				Born on 4/18/47 in Birmingham, England. White soul singer. Lead vocalist of **Pickettywitch** and **Sweet Dreams**.			
1/4/75	16	13		**Up In A Puff Of Smoke**...*I'm Saving All My Love*	$6		GTO 1002
				BROWN, Randy R&B '79			
				Born in Memphis, Tennessee. R&B singer/songwriter.			
3/31/79	72	4		**You Says It All**...*Crazy 'Bout You Baby*	$5		Parachute 523
				BROWN, Roy R&B/C&W '57			
				Born on 9/10/25 in New Orleans, Louisiana. Died of a heart attack on 5/25/81 (age 55). R&B vocalist/pianist. One of the originators of the New Orleans R&B sound. Wrote "Good Rockin' Tonight" in 1948.			
4/29/57	89	2		1 **Party Doll**...T:89 *I'm Stickin' With You*	$30		Imperial 5427
7/1/57	29	15		2 **Let The Four Winds Blow**...S:29 / T:38 *Diddy-Y-Diddy-O*	$30		Imperial 5439
				BROWN, Ruth R&B/MEM '58			
				Born Ruth Weston on 1/30/28 in Portsmouth, Virginia. R&B pioneer. Married singer/trumpeter Jimmy Brown in 1945. In late 1946, sang for one month with Lucky Millinder's band, then fired. Later heard by Duke Ellington, who alerted Herb Abramson of the then-new Atlantic Records. Abramson signed her to a contract. Became Atlantic Records' top-selling artist of the 1950s. Married for a time to Willis Jackson. In later years, had acting roles in the TV shows *Hello, Larry* and *Checking In*, plus several Broadway and Las Vegas musicals. Appeared in the movies *Under The Rainbow* (1981) and *Hairspray* (1988). Starred in the 1988 musical *Black And Blue*. Inducted into the Rock and Roll Hall of Fame in 1993.			
2/23/57	25	9		1 **Lucky Lips**...S:25 / A:25 / T:26 *My Heart Is Breaking Over You*	$30		Atlantic 1125
9/22/58	24	10		2 **This Little Girl's Gone Rockin'** H:24 *Why Me* (R&B #17)	$30		Atlantic 1197
				King Curtis (sax solo); written by **Bobby Darin**			
6/1/59	96	2		3 **Jack O'Diamonds**...*I Can't Hear A Word You Say*	$25		Atlantic 2026
10/12/59	64	6		4 **I Don't Know**...*Papa Daddy*	$25		Atlantic 2035
				written by **Brook Benton**			
3/14/60	62	8		5 **Don't Deceive Me**...*I Burned Your Letter*	$25		Atlantic 2052
				#6 R&B hit for **Chuck Willis** in 1953			
6/23/62	97	2		6 **Shake A Hand**...*Say It Again*	$15		Philips 40028
				#1 R&B hit for Faye Adams in 1953			
9/8/62	99	1		7 **Mama (He Treats Your Daughter Mean)**...*Hold My Hand*	$15		Philips 40056
				The Milestone Singers (backing vocals); remake of Ruth's #1 R&B hit in 1953 on Atlantic 986			
				BROWN, Sam '89			
				Born on 10/7/64 in London, England. White female singer/songwriter. Backing vocalist for **Small Faces**, Mark Knopfler, **Spandau Ballet** and others since her teens. Daughter of U.K. singer/guitarist Joe Brown and singer Vicki Brown.			
4/15/89	65	10		**Stop**...*Blue Soldier*	$3	■	A&M 1234
				BROWN, Shirley R&B/BUB/LP '74			
				Born on 1/6/47 in West Memphis, Arkansas; raised in St. Louis, Missouri. R&B singer.			
11/2/74	22	14		1 **Woman To Woman**...RB[2] *Yes Sir Brother*	$6		Truth 3206
5/10/75	94	2		2 **It Ain't No Fun**...*I've Got To Go On Without You*	$6		Truth 3223
	★286★			**BROWNE, Jackson** ROK/BUB/AC/LP '78			
				Born on 10/9/48 in Heidelberg, Germany (U.S. Army base); raised in Los Angeles. Pop-rock singer/songwriter/guitarist/pianist. With Tim Buckley and Nico in 1967 in New York City. Returned to Los Angeles, concentrated on songwriting. His songs were recorded by **Linda Ronstadt**, Tom Rush, **Joe Cocker**, **The Byrds**, **Johnny Rivers**, **Bonnie Raitt**, and many others. Worked with the **Eagles**. Produced **Warren Zevon**'s first album. Wife, Phyllis, committed suicide on 3/25/76. A prominent activist against nuclear power.			
				1)Somebody's Baby 2)Doctor My Eyes 3)Running On Empty			
3/18/72	8	12		1 **Doctor My Eyes**...*Looking Into You*	$6		Asylum 11004
8/5/72	48	9		2 **Rock Me On The Water**...*Something Fine*	$6		Asylum 11006
9/29/73	85	10		3 **Redneck Friend**...*These Times You've Come*	$6		Asylum 11023
				Glenn Frey (harmony vocal); Rockaday Johnnie (**Elton John**; piano)			
2/5/77	23	9		4 **Here Come Those Tears Again**...*Linda Paloma*	$5		Asylum 45379
				Bonnie Raitt (harmony vocal); **John Hall** (of **Orleans**; guitar solo)			
5/21/77	58	5		5 **The Pretender**...*Daddy's Tune*	$5		Asylum 45399
				David Crosby and **Graham Nash** (harmony vocals)			

DEBUT	PEAK	WKS	Gold	A-side (Chart Hit)..........B-side	$	Sym	Label & Number
				BROWNE, Jackson — Cont'd			
2/11/78	11	17		6 **Running On Empty** ....*Nothing But Time*	$5	■	Asylum 45460
6/10/78	20	15		7 **Stay** / David Lindley (falsetto vocal); Rosemary Butler (female vocal)			
7/8/78		8		8 **The Load-Out** .... originally issued with "Rosie" as the B-side of "Stay" (picture sleeve shows "Stay" b/w "Rosie")	$5	■	Asylum 45485
7/5/80	19	16		9 **Boulevard**..........*Call It A Loan*	$4	■	Asylum 47003
9/20/80	22	13		10 **That Girl Could Sing**..........*Of Missing Persons*	$4		Asylum 47036
7/31/82	7	19		11 **Somebody's Baby** *The Crow On The Cradle* (w/Graham Nash & David Lindley) from the movie *Fast Times At Ridgemont High* starring Sean Penn	$4	■	Asylum 69982
7/9/83	13	15		12 **Lawyers In Love**..........*Say It Isn't True*	$4	■	Asylum 69826
9/24/83	25	17		13 **Tender Is The Night** ....*On The Day*	$4	■	Asylum 69791
1/14/84	45	9		14 **For A Rocker** ....*Downtown*	$4	■	Asylum 69764
10/26/85+	18	19		15 **You're A Friend Of Mine**..........A:17 / S:20 *Let The Music Say It* (Clemons) **CLARENCE CLEMONS And Jackson Browne** includes vocals by actress Daryl Hannah (Browne's then-girlfriend)	$3	■	Columbia 05660
3/1/86	30	12		16 **For America**..........A:27 *Till I Go Down*	$3	■	Asylum 69566
6/7/86	70	7		17 **In The Shape Of A Heart** ....*Voice Of America*	$3	■	Asylum 69543
				BROWNS, The C&W/BUB/AC **'59** Vocal trio from Sparkman, Arkansas: **Jim Ed Brown** (see #8 below) (born on 4/1/34) and his sisters Maxine and Bonnie. Charted 21 Country hits, 1954-67. Jim hosted Nashville Network's TV talent show *You Can Be A Star!*. Member of the *Grand Ole Opry* since 1963.			
7/27/59	1^{4}	17	●	1 **The Three Bells** CW^{10} *Heaven Fell Last Night* French tune written in 1945 as "Les Trois Cloches"; #14 hit for **Les Compagnons De La Chanson** in 1952	$15		RCA Victor 7555
11/2/59	13	14		2 **Scarlet Ribbons (For Her Hair)**..........*Blue Bells Ring* #14 hit for **Jo Stafford** in 1950	$12		RCA Victor 7614
				THE BROWNS featuring Jim Edward Brown:			
3/14/60	5	15		3 **The Old Lamplighter** / #1 hit for **Sammy Kaye**'s Orchestra in 1946			
3/28/60	47	7		4 **Teen-Ex**..........	$12	■	RCA Victor 7700
11/14/60	56	7		5 **Send Me The Pillow You Dream On** ....*You're So Much A Part Of Me* #5 Country hit for **Hank Locklin** in 1958	$12		RCA Victor 7804
12/19/60	97	1		6 **Blue Christmas**..........*Greenwillow Christmas (Carol)* [X] #1 Country hit for Ernest Tubb in 1950	$12		RCA Victor 7820
4/10/61	97	2		7 **Ground Hog**..........*Angel's Dolly* written by **Homer & Jethro**; also see **John D. Loudermilk**'s "Road Hog"; all of above produced by **Chet Atkins**	$12		RCA Victor 7866
11/14/70	47	11		8 **Morning** ....*How To Lose A Good Woman* **JIM ED BROWN**	$6		RCA Victor 9909
				BROWNSTONE R&B/BUB/LP **'95** Female R&B vocal trio from Los Angeles, California: Monica Doby, Nichole Gilbert and Charmayne Maxwell. Doby left group for health reasons in June 1995; replaced by **Kina** Cosper.			
12/10/94+	8	27	●	1 **If You Love Me**..........S:5 / A:9 *(radio edit)* samples "Spellbound" by K-Solo	$3	■V	MJJ Music 77732
4/29/95	49	15		2 **Grapevyne**..........S:28 *(album version)* "45" issued for above 2 on MJJ Music 77864	$3	■V	MJJ Music 77864
7/15/95	54	13		3 **I Can't Tell You Why** ....S:31 *If You Love Me (remix w/***Craig Mack***)*	$3	■V	MJJ Music 77848
5/17/97	39	16		4 **5 Miles To Empty** ....S:25 *Revenge*	$3	■V	MJJ Music 78496
				BROWN SUGAR BUB **'76** Born Clydie King on 8/21/43 in Atlanta, Georgia. Female R&B singer. Formerly in **The Raeletts**.			
2/28/76	79	4		**The Game Is Over (What's The Matter With You)** ....*I'm Going Through Changes Now*	$5		Capitol 4198
				BROWNSVILLE STATION LP **'74** Rock trio from Ann Arbor, Michigan: Michael Lutz (vocals, bass), Michael "Cub" Koda (guitar) and Henry Weck (drums). Koda died of kidney failure on 7/1/2000 (age 51).			
12/23/72+	96	3		1 **The Red Back Spider**..........*Rock With The Music* [N]	$6		Big Tree 156
3/3/73	57	8		2 **Let Your Yeah Be Yeah**..........*Mister Robert* written by **Jimmy Cliff**	$6		Big Tree 161
10/27/73+	3	19	●	3 **Smokin' In The Boy's Room** *Barefootin'*	$6		Big Tree 16011
5/25/74	48	8		4 **I'm The Leader Of The Gang**..........*Meet Me On The Fourth Floor* written and recorded by **Gary Glitter** in 1973	$6		Big Tree 15005
8/31/74	31	9		5 **Kings Of The Party** ....*Ostrich*	$6		Big Tree 16001
6/4/77	46	10		6 **Lady (Put The Light On Me)** ....*Rockers' N' Rollers*	$5		Private Stock 45,149
8/20/77	59	7		7 **The Martian Boogie**..........*Mr. Johnson Sez* [N]	$5		Private Stock 45,167
				BRUBECK, Dave, Quartet BUB/LP **'61** Born David Warren on 12/6/20 in Concord, California. Leader of jazz quartet consisting of Brubeck (piano), Paul Desmond (alto sax), Joe Morello (drums) and Eugene Wright (bass). One of America's all-time most popular jazz groups on college campuses. Desmond died on 5/30/77 (age 52). Brubeck won Grammy's Lifetime Achievement Award in 1996.			
9/11/61	25	12		1 **Take Five** ....*Blue Rondo A La Turk* [I] trend-setting jazz classic played in 5/4 time	$12		Columbia 41479
12/4/61+	74	6		2 **Unsquare Dance** ....*It's A Raggy Waltz* [I]	$10	■	Columbia 42228
1/5/63	69	7		3 **Bossa Nova U.S.A.**..........*This Can't Be Love* [I]	$10	■	Columbia 42651
				BRUCE AND TERRY — see RIP CHORDS, The			
				BRYANT, Anita BUB/LP **'60** Born on 3/25/40 in Barnsdale, Oklahoma. As Miss Oklahoma, she was second runner-up to Miss America in 1958. Pop singer. *1)Paper Roses 2)In My Little Corner Of The World 3)Wonderland By Night*			
6/29/59	30	13		1 **Till There Was You** ....*Little George (Got The Hiccoughs)* from the Broadway musical *The Music Man* starring Robert Preston and **Shirley Jones**	$10		Carlton 512
9/21/59	62	6		2 **Six Boys And Seven Girls**..........*The Blessings Of Love*	$10		Carlton 518

DEBUT	PEAK	WKS	Gold	A-side (Chart Hit)..........B-side	$	Sym	Label & Number
				BRYANT, Anita — Cont'd			
12/28/59+	78	3		3 **Promise Me A Rose (A Slight Detail) /** from the Broadway musical *Take Me Along* starring **Jackie Gleason**			
12/28/59	94	1		4 **Do-Re-Mi** from the Broadway musical *The Sound Of Music* starring Mary Martin	$10		Carlton 523
4/11/60	5	17		5 **Paper Roses** .... *Mixed Emotions* **Monty Kelly** (orch., all of above)	$10		Carlton 528
7/11/60	10	14		6 **In My Little Corner Of The World** .... *Anyone Would Love You*	$10		Carlton 530
10/10/60	62	7		7 **One Of The Lucky Ones** .... *Love Look Away*	$8		Carlton 535
12/5/60+	18	10		8 **Wonderland By Night** .... *Pictures* Lew Douglas (orch.)	$8		Carlton 537
2/13/61	85	4		9 **A Texan And A Girl From Mexico** .... *He's Not Good Enough For You*	$8		Carlton 538
5/15/61	87	2		10 **I Can't Do It By Myself** .... *An Angel Cried*	$8		Carlton 547
5/16/64	59	8		11 **The World Of Lonely People** .... *It's Better To Cry Today Than To Cry Tomorrow*	$6	□	Columbia 43037
				BRYANT, Ray R&B/BUB/LP **'60** Born Raphael Bryant on 12/24/31 in Philadelphia, Pennsylvania. R&B-jazz pianist/bandleader. Uncle of *Tonight Show* guitarist Kevin Eubanks. Also see **Aretha Franklin**'s first chart hit.			
4/11/60	30	9		1 **The Madison Time - Part I** .... *Part II* [I-S] dance calls: Eddie Morrison (died on 2/28/87); sleeve included a foldout insert with dance instructions	$15	■	Columbia 41628
9/30/67	89	2		2 **Ode To Billy Joe** .... *Ramblin'* [I]	$8		Cadet 5575
				BRYANT, Sharon — see ATLANTIC STARR			
	★435★			**BRYSON, Peabo** R&B/BUB/AC/LP **'93** Born Robert Peabo Bryson on 4/13/51 in Greenville, South Carolina. R&B singer/producer (charted 45 hits, 1976-93). First solo recording for Bang in 1970. Married Juanita Leonard, former wife of boxer Sugar Ray Leonard, in 1992. *1)A Whole New World (Aladdin's Theme) 2)Beauty And The Beast 3)If Ever You're In My Arms Again*			
3/20/76	94	3		1 **Do It With Feeling** .... *This Is The Life* **MICHAEL ZAGER'S MOON BAND Featuring Peabo Bryson** re-entered the R&B charts in 1978 on Bang 737 (#76)	$6		Bang 720
2/28/81	54	9		2 **Lovers After All** .... *Happier Than I've Ever Been* (Manchester) **MELISSA MANCHESTER AND PEABO BRYSON**	$4		Arista 0587
1/9/82	42	12		3 **Let The Feeling Flow** .... *Move Your Body*	$4		Capitol 5065
7/9/83	16	29		4 **Tonight, I Celebrate My Love** .... *Born To Love* **PEABO BRYSON/ROBERTA FLACK**	$4	■	Capitol 5242
12/24/83+	58	11		5 **You're Looking Like Love To Me** .... *Let Me Be The One You Need* (Bryson) **PEABO BRYSON/ROBERTA FLACK**	$4	■	Capitol 5307
5/12/84	10	25		6 **If Ever You're In My Arms Again** .... AC[4] *There's No Getting Over You*	$3		Elektra 69728
9/29/84	82	4		7 **Slow Dancin'** .... *Love Means Forever*	$3		Elektra 69699
6/29/85	78	6		8 **Take No Prisoners (In The Game Of Love)** .... *Love Means Forever*	$3	■	Elektra 69632
2/6/88	89	3		9 **Without You** .... *The Higher You Climb* (Bryson) **PEABO BRYSON & REGINA BELLE** love theme from the movie *Leonard Pt. 6* starring **Bill Cosby**	$3	■	Elektra 69426
6/22/91	52	15		10 **Can You Stop The Rain** .... RB[2] S:40 *I Wish You Love*	$3	▮[V]	Columbia 73745
1/18/92	9	20	▲	11 **Beauty And The Beast** .... S:8 / A:17 *The Beast Lets Belle Go* [I] **CELINE DION and PEABO BRYSON** title song from the Disney animated movie	$3	▮[V]	Epic 74090
12/19/92+	❶[1]	23	●	12 **A Whole New World (Aladdin's Theme)** AC[6] A:❶[4] / S:2 *After The Kiss (instrumental)* **PEABO BRYSON and REGINA BELLE** from the Disney animated movie *Aladdin*	$3	▮[V]	Columbia 74751
5/22/93	25	20		13 **By The Time This Night Is Over** .... AC[2] A:24 / S:57 *Homeland* (Kenny G) **KENNY G with Peabo Bryson**	$3	▮	Arista 12565
				BSK **'01** Born Bum Soo Kim (BSK) on 1/26/79 in Masan, South Korea. Male pop vocalist.			
12/22/01	51[S]	1		**Hello, Goodbye, Hello** .... *(2 versions)*	$15	★	KukDo 7101
				B.T. EXPRESS R&B/LP **'74** R&B-disco group from Brooklyn, New York. Earlier known as Brooklyn Trucking Express. Core members: Barbara Joyce Lomas (female vocals; left by 1977), brothers Louis (vocals, bass) and Bill (sax) Risbrook, Richard Thompson (guitar), Carlos Ward (flute) and Dennis Rowe (congas). Keyboardist Michael Jones, who was with the group from 1976-79, later recorded solo as techno-funk musician **Kashif**.			
9/28/74	2[2]	18	●	1 **Do It ('Til You're Satisfied)** RB[1] *(disco remix)*	$6		Scepter 12395
1/25/75	4	15	●	2 **Express** .... RB[1] *(disco mix)* [I]	$5		Roadshow 7001
9/13/75	31	13		3 **Peace Pipe /**			
8/9/75	40	6		4 **Give It What You Got**	$5		Roadshow 7003
1/24/76	82	4		5 **Close To You** .... *Whatcha Think About That?*	$5		Roadshow 7005
6/5/76	52	4		6 **Can't Stop Groovin' Now, Wanna Do It Some More** .... *Herbs*	$4		Columbia 10346
				B2K R&B/BUB/LP **'02** Male R&B vocal group from Los Angeles, California: Jarell "J-Boog" Houston, Mario "Raz-B" Thornton, Dreux "Lil Fizz" Frederic and Omari Grandberry.			
1/5/02	37	22		1 **Uh Huh** .... S:❶[10] / A:41 *(2 remixes) / (3 album snippets)*	$8	★[+V]	Epic 79686
4/27/02	34	18		2 **Gots Ta Be** .... S:6 / A:35 *Uh Huh* "45" issued for above 2 on Epic 79742	$8	◗[V]	Epic 79719
11/2/02	73	4		3 **Why I Love You** .... A:71 above 3 from the album *B2K* on Epic 85457			album cut
11/30/02+	❶[1]	22		4 **Bump, Bump, Bump** .... A:❷[2] / S:24 *(instrumental)* **B2K & P. DIDDY** produced and co-written by **R. Kelly**	$4	★	Epic 79842

DEBUT	PEAK	WKS	Gold	A-side (Chart Hit)	B-side	$	Sym	Label & Number
				BUBBLE PUPPY, The BUB/LP '69				
				Psychedelic-rock group from Houston, Texas: Rod Price (vocals), Todd Potter (guitar), Roy Cox (bass) and David Fore (drums). Later recorded as Demian.				
2/15/69	14	12		**Hot Smoke & Sasafrass**	*Lonely*	$25		Int'l. Artists 128
				BUCHANAN and ANCELL — see GOODMAN, Dickie				
				BUCHANAN & GOODMAN — see GOODMAN, Dickie				
				BUCHANAN BROTHERS — see CASHMAN & WEST				
				BUCKETHEADS, The '95				
				Group is actually solo dance producer Kenny "Dope" Gonzalez (from Brooklyn, New York).				
7/1/95	49	18		**The Bomb! (These Sounds Fall Into My Mind)** samples "Street Player" by **Chicago**	A:46 / S:67 *(remix)*	$4	■	Big Beat 98140
				BUCKEYE '79				
				Rock group from Cleveland, Ohio: Ronn Price (vocals, bass), Thom Fowle (guitar), Gabriel Katona (keyboards) and Beaver Parker (drums).				
8/25/79	63	5		**Where Will Your Heart Take You**	*That Kind Of Man*	$5		Polydor 14578
				BUCKINGHAM, Lindsey ROK/BUB/AC/LP '82				
				Born on 10/3/49 in Palo Alto, California. Rock guitarist/singer/songwriter. In group Fritz from 1967-71; with **Stevie Nicks** (Fritz lead singer) formed duo, Buckingham Nicks, in early 1970s. Both joined **Fleetwood Mac** in 1975. Buckingham left Fleetwood Mac in 1987. His grandfather founded Keystone Coffee; his father founded Alta Coffee. Buckingham's brother Gregg won a silver medal in swimming in the 1968 Olympics. Reunited with Fleetwood Mac in 1997.				
10/24/81+	9	19		1 **Trouble**	*Mary Lee Jones*	$4	■	Asylum 47223
8/6/83	82	5		2 **Holiday Road** from the movie *National Lampoon's Vacation* starring Chevy Chase	*The Trip (Theme From Vacation)* (Ralph Burns)	$4		Warner 29570
7/28/84	23	16		3 **Go Insane**	*Play In The Rain*	$4	■	Elektra 69714
	★595★			**BUCKINGHAMS, The** BUB/LP '67				
				Pop-rock group from Chicago, Illinois: Dennis Tufano (vocals; born on 9/11/46), Carl Giammarese (guitar; born on 8/21/47), Dennis Miccoli (keyboards), Nick Fortuna (bass; born on 5/1/46) and Jon Poulos (drums; born on 3/31/47; died of a drug overdose on 3/26/80, age 32). Martin Grebb (born on 9/2/46) replaced Miccoli in 1967. **Tufano and Giammarese** (see #8 below) recorded as a duo in 1973. Grebb formed **The Fabulous Rhinestones**.				
12/31/66+	❶[2]	13		1 **Kind Of A Drag**	*You Make Me Feel So Good*	$15		U.S.A. 860
3/11/67	41	6		2 **Laudy Miss Claudy** some pressings titled as "Lawdy Miss Clawdy" (B-side: "I Call Your Name"); #1 R&B hit for **Lloyd Price** in 1952	*Making Up & Breakin' Up*	$15		U.S.A. 869
3/11/67	6	14		3 **Don't You Care**	*Why Don't You Love Me*	$8	■	Columbia 44053
6/17/67	5	12		4 **Mercy, Mercy, Mercy**	*You Are Gone*	$8	■	Columbia 44182
9/9/67	12	10		5 **Hey Baby (They're Playing Our Song)**	*And Our Love*	$8	■	Columbia 44254
12/9/67+	11	12		6 **Susan**	*Foreign Policy*	$8	■	Columbia 44378
6/8/68	57	6		7 **Back In Love Again**	*You Misunderstand Me*	$8	■	Columbia 44533
4/28/73	68	8		8 **Music Everywhere** TUFANO & GIAMMARESE	*Just A Dream Away*	$5		Ode 66033
				BUCKNER & GARCIA BUB/LP '82				
				Novelty duo from Atlanta, Georgia: Jerry Buckner (keyboards) and Gary Garcia (vocals). Also recorded as **Willis "The Guard" & Vigorish**.				
12/27/80	82	3		1 **Merry Christmas In The NFL** WILLIS "THE GUARD" & VIGORISH	*(instrumental)* [X-N]	$7		Handshake 5308
1/9/82	9	19	●	2 **Pac-Man Fever** inspired by the video game; originally released on BGO 1001 in 1981 ($10)	*(instrumental)* [N]	$4		Columbia 02673
				BUCKWHEAT LP '72				
				Pop group from Los Angeles, California: **Debbie Campbell** (see #2 below) (vocals), Michael Smotherman (vocals, keyboards), Randy James (guitar), Mark Durham (bass) and Timmy Harrison (drums).				
4/1/72	84	5		1 **Simple Song Of Freedom** written by **Bobby Darin**	*I Got To Boogie*	$6		London 176
7/5/75	84	5		2 **Please Tell Him That I Said Hello** DEBBIE CAMPBELL	*You Better Wait*	$6		Playboy 6037
				BUD AND TRAVIS LP '60				
				Folk duo from San Francisco, California: Bud Dashiel and Travis Edmonson. Dashiel died on 6/2/89.				
10/17/60	64	9		**Ballad Of The Alamo** from the movie *The Alamo* starring John Wayne	*The Green Leaves Of Summer*	$12		Liberty 55284
				BUENA VISTAS, The BUB '66				
				Three-man, one-woman band that also recorded as Kathy Lynn & Play Boys. Kathy Lynn is Kathy Lynn Keppen.				
7/2/66	87	4		1 **Hot Shot**	*T.N.T.* [I]	$15		Swan 4255
6/1/68	88	4		2 **Here Come Da Judge** title inspired by a recurrent gag line on TV's *Rowan & Martin's Laugh-In*	*Big Red* [I]	$12		Marquee 443
				BUFFALO SPRINGFIELD, The BUB/LP '67				
				Superstar group formed in Los Angeles, California: **Stephen Stills**, **Neil Young**, **Richie Furay**, Dewey Martin and Bruce Palmer (replaced by **Jim Messina** after first two albums). Disbanded in 1968. Stills and Young with **Crosby, Stills, Nash & Young**. Furay and Messina formed **Poco**. Group inducted into the Rock and Roll Hall of Fame in 1997.				
1/28/67	7	15		1 **For What It's Worth (Stop, Hey What's That Sound)**	*Do I Have To Come Right Out And Say It*	$15		Atco 6459
7/15/67	58	7		2 **Bluebird**	*Mr. Soul*	$15		Atco 6499
9/30/67	44	7		3 **Rock 'N' Roll Woman** above 3 written by **Stephen Stills**	*A Child's Claim To Fame*	$12		Atco 6519
1/13/68	98	2		4 **Expecting To Fly**	*Everydays*	$12		Atco 6545
10/12/68	82	3		5 **On The Way Home** above 2 written by **Neil Young**	*Four Days Gone*	$12		Atco 6615

DEBUT	PEAK	WKS	Gold	A-side (Chart Hit)...B-side	$	Sym	Label & Number
				BUFFETT, Jimmy C&W/BUB/AC/ROK/LP '77			
				Born on 12/25/46 in Pascagoula, Mississippi; raised in Mobile, Alabama. Has BS degree in journalism from the University of Southern Mississippi. After working in New Orleans, moved to Nashville in 1969. Nashville correspondent for *Billboard* magazine, 1969-70. Settled in Key West in 1971.Author of several books. Appeared in the 1978 movie *FM.* Faithful fans known as "Parrotheads."			
				1)Margaritaville 2)Come Monday 3)Cheeseburger In Paradise			
5/18/74	**30**	14		1 **Come Monday** ...*The Wino And I Know*	$6		Dunhill/ABC 4385
4/2/77	**8**	22		2 **Margaritaville** AC[1] *Miss You So Badly*	$5		ABC 12254
				a duet version with **Alan Jackson** made the Country charts in 1999 and 2000			
9/17/77	**37**	10		3 **Changes In Latitudes, Changes In Attitudes** ...*Landfall*	$5	■	ABC 12305
4/22/78	**32**	11		4 **Cheeseburger In Paradise** ...*African Friend* [N]	$5		ABC 12358
8/12/78	**52**	6		5 **Livingston Saturday Night** ...*Cowboy In The Jungle*	$5		ABC 12391
12/2/78	**84**	6		6 **Mañana** ...*Coast Of Marseilles*	$5		ABC 12428
9/8/79	**35**	11		7 **Fins** ...*Dreamsicle*	$4		MCA 41109
12/22/79+	**66**	7		8 **Volcano** ...*Stranded On A Sandbar*	$4		MCA 41161
3/8/80	**77**	5		9 **Survive** ...*Boat Drinks*	$4		MCA 41199
				all of above written by Buffett			
2/21/81	**57**	8		10 **It's My Job** ...*Little Miss Magic*	$4		MCA 51061
				written by **Mac McAnally**; #2-10: produced by Norbert Putnam			
				BUFFY ROK '96			
				Female Latin pop-rock singer.			
3/16/96	**78**	9		**Give Me...A Reason** ...*(old school mix)*	$5	■	Velocity 0629
				BUGGLES, The LP '79			
				New-wave duo from England: Geoff Downes and Trevor Horn. Both joined the group **Yes** in 1980. Downes joined **Asia** in 1981. Horn became a prolific producer. Also see **The Jags**.			
11/10/79	**40**	10		**Video Killed The Radio Star** ...*Kid Dynamo*	$6		Island 49114
				the premiere video on MTV's first show (8/1/81)			
				BULL & THE MATADORS '68			
				R&B trio from St. Louis, Missouri: JaMell "Bull" Parks (born on 6/7/45), Milton Hardy and James Otis Love.			
8/24/68	**39**	14		**The Funky Judge** ...*(instrumental)*	$10		Toddlin' Town 108
				BULLDOG BUB/LP '72			
				Rock group from New York City, New York: Billy Hocher (vocals, bass), Eric Thorngren and Gene Cornish (guitars), John Turi (keyboards) and Dino Danelli (drums). Cornish and Danelli were members of **The Rascals**. Thorngren later became a prolific record mixer. Also see **Fotomaker**.			
10/14/72	**44**	15		**No** ...*Good Times Are Comin'*	$6		Decca 32996
				BULLENS, Cindy '79			
				Born on 11/30/57 in West Newbury, Massachusetts. Pop-rock singer/guitarist.			
2/3/79	**56**	7		1 **Survivor** ...*Finally Rockin'*	$4		United Artists 1261
1/12/80	**90**	3		2 **Trust Me** ...*Holding Me Crazy*	$4		Casablanca 2217
				BULLET BUB '72			
				Rock duo from London, England: John Cann (vocals) and Paul Hammond (drums).			
11/6/71+	**28**	13		1 **White Lies, Blue Eyes** ...*Changes Of Mind*	$6		Big Tree 123
3/11/72	**96**	2		2 **Willpower Weak, Temptation Strong** ...*Hittin' On You*	$6		Big Tree 131
				BULLETBOYS ROK/LP '89			
				Hard-rock group from Los Angeles, California: Marq Torien (vocals), Mick Sweda (guitar), Lonnie Vencent (bass) and Jimmy D'Anda (drums).			
4/29/89	**78**	6		1 **For The Love Of Money** ...*Crank Me Up*	$3	■	Warner 27554
7/22/89	**71**	10		2 **Smooth Up** ...*Badlands*	$3		Warner 22876
				BUMBLE BEE UNLIMITED '77			
				Disco group from New York City, New York. Led by singer/songwriter Patrick Adams.			
12/11/76+	**92**	5		**Love Bug** ...*(long disco version)*	$5		Mercury 73864
				BUMPY KNUCKLES — see FOXXX, Freddie			
				BUOYS, The '71			
				Rock group from Wilkes-Barre, Pennsylvania: Bill Kelly (vocals), Carl Siracuse (guitar), Fran Brozena (keyboards), Jerry Hludzik (bass) and Chris Hanlon (drums). **Rupert Holmes** (**Street People**) was their composer/arranger.			
1/2/71	**17**	17		1 **Timothy** ...*It Feels Good*	$10	■	Scepter 12275
6/19/71	**84**	3		2 **Give Up Your Guns** ...*The Prince Of Thieves*	$8		Scepter 12318
				BURBANK, Gary, with Band McNally '80			
				Burbank is a DJ at WLW in Cincinnati, Ohio; was a DJ at WHAS in Louisville, Kentucky, at the time of his hit.			
6/28/80	**67**	5		**Who Shot J.R.?** ...*Honkin'* (Tennessee Valley Authority) [N]	$5		Ovation 1150
				inspired by the J.R. shooting episode on TV's *Dallas*			
				BURDON, Eric, And War BUB/LP '70			
				Born on 5/11/41 in Walker, Newcastle, England. After leaving **The Animals**, Burdon teamed up with the funk band **War** for two albums. Starred in the movie *Comeback* and made a cameo appearance in *The Doors.*			
5/23/70	**3**	21	●	1 **Spill The Wine** ...*Magic Mountain*	$8	■	MGM 14118
12/19/70+	**50**	8		2 **They Can't Take Away Our Music** ...*Home Cookin'* (#108)	$8		MGM 14196
				Sharon Scott (female vocal)			

DEBUT	PEAK	WKS	Gold	A-side (Chart Hit)..................B-side	$	Sym	Label & Number

BURKE, Solomon

★334★ R&B/BUB/LP **'65**

Born on 2/22/36 in Philadelphia, Pennsylvania. Soul singer. Preached and broadcast from own church, "Solomon's Temple," in Philadelphia from 1945-55 as the "Wonder Boy Preacher." Church was founded for him by his grandmother. First recorded for Apollo in 1954. Left music to attend mortuary school; returned in 1960. Inducted into the Rock and Roll Hall of Fame in 2001. Also see **The Soul Clan**.

1)Got To Get You Off My Mind 2)Just Out Of Reach 3)Tonight's The Night 4)Goodbye Baby (Baby Goodbye) 5)If You Need Me

DEBUT	PEAK	WKS	Gold	A-side (Chart Hit)..................B-side	$	Sym	Label & Number
9/18/61	24	17		1 **Just Out Of Reach (Of My Two Open Arms)** .... *Be Bop Grandma*	$20		Atlantic 2114
1/27/62	44	10		2 **Cry To Me** .... *I Almost Lost My Mind*	$20		Atlantic 2131
5/26/62	71	8		3 **Down In The Valley /**			
7/7/62	85	2		4 **I'm Hanging Up My Heart For You**	$15		Atlantic 2147
9/8/62	93	3		5 **I Really Don't Want To Know** .... *Tonight My Heart She Is Crying (Love Is A Bird)* #11 hit for **Les Paul & Mary Ford** in 1954	$15		Atlantic 2157
4/20/63	37	11		6 **If You Need Me** .... *You Can Make It If You Try*	$15		Atlantic 2185
7/20/63	66	6		7 **Can't Nobody Love You** .... *Stupidity*	$15		Atlantic 2196
11/2/63	49	8		8 **You're Good For Me** .... *Beautiful Brown Eyes*	$15		Atlantic 2205
2/8/64	51	8		9 **He'll Have To Go** .... *Rockin' Soul*	$15		Atlantic 2218
4/18/64	33	10		10 **Goodbye Baby (Baby Goodbye)** .... *Someone To Love Me*	$15		Atlantic 2226
7/18/64	58	8		11 **Everybody Needs Somebody To Love** .... *Looking For My Baby*	$15		Atlantic 2241
10/10/64	92	3		12 **Yes I Do** .... *Won't You Give Him (One More Chance)*	$15		Atlantic 2254
11/28/64	57	5		13 **The Price** .... *More Rockin' Soul* [I]	$15		Atlantic 2259
3/6/65	22	10		14 **Got To Get You Off My Mind** RB[3] *Peepin'*	$15		Atlantic 2276
5/29/65	28	10		15 **Tonight's The Night** .... *Maggie's Farm*	$12		Atlantic 2288
8/21/65	89	4		16 **Someone Is Watching** .... *Dance, Dance, Dance*	$12		Atlantic 2299
11/27/65	94	2		17 **Only Love (Can Save Me Now)** .... *Little Girl That Loves Me*	$12		Atlantic 2308
1/8/66	96	2		18 **Baby Come On Home** .... *(No, No, No) Can't Stop Lovin' You Now*	$12		Atlantic 2314
4/9/66	97	2		19 **I Feel A Sin Coming On** .... *Mountain Of Pride*	$12		Atlantic 2327
2/11/67	64	5		20 **Keep A Light In The Window Till I Come Home** .... *Time Is A Thief*	$12		Atlantic 2378
7/1/67	49	5		21 **Take Me (Just As I Am)** .... *I Stayed Away Too Long*	$12		Atlantic 2416
5/4/68	68	8		22 **I Wish I Knew (How It Would Feel To Be Free)** .... *It's Just A Matter Of Time*	$12		Atlantic 2507
5/3/69	45	7		23 **Proud Mary** .... *What Am I Living For*	$10		Bell 783
5/1/71	96	2		24 **The Electronic Magnetism (That's Heavy, Baby)** .... *Bridge Of Life*	$6		MGM 14221
4/15/72	89	5		25 **Love's Street And Fool's Road** .... *I Got To Tell It* from the movie *Cool Breeze* starring Thalmus Rasulala	$6		MGM 14353
3/22/75	96	2		26 **You And Your Baby Blues** .... *I'm Leaving On That Late, Late Train*	$5		Chess 2159

BURNETTE, Billy

C&W **'80**

Born on 5/8/53 in Memphis, Tennessee. Son of **Dorsey Burnette**, nephew of **Johnny Burnette**, and cousin of **Rocky Burnette**. Member of **Fleetwood Mac** from 1987-1993. Writer of many Country hits.

DEBUT	PEAK	WKS	Gold	A-side (Chart Hit)..................B-side	$	Sym	Label & Number
11/1/80	68	5		**Don't Say No** .... *Rockin' L.A.*	$5		Columbia 11380

BURNETTE, Dorsey

C&W/BUB **'60**

Born on 12/28/32 in Memphis, Tennessee. Died of a heart attack on 8/19/79 (age 46). Older brother of **Johnny Burnette** and father of **Billy Burnette**. Recorded with brother Johnny as **The Texans** (see Johnny Burnette) in 1961.

DEBUT	PEAK	WKS	Gold	A-side (Chart Hit)..................B-side	$	Sym	Label & Number
2/1/60	23	15		1 **(There Was A) Tall Oak Tree** .... *Juarez Town*	$20		Era 3012
6/6/60	48	11		2 **Hey Little One** .... *Big Rock Candy Mountain (#102)*	$20		Era 3019
1/25/69	67	6		3 **The Greatest Love** .... *Thin Little, Simple Little, Plain Little Girl* written by **Joe South**	$10		Liberty 56087

BURNETTE, Johnny

BUB **'60**

Born on 3/25/34 in Memphis. Died in a boating accident on Clear Lake in California on 8/1/64 (age 30). Johnny, younger brother **Dorsey Burnette**, and Paul Burlison formed the Johnny Burnette Rock 'N Roll Trio, 1953-57. Recorded with brother Dorsey as **The Texans** (see #4 below) in 1961. Father of **Rocky Burnette**.

DEBUT	PEAK	WKS	Gold	A-side (Chart Hit)..................B-side	$	Sym	Label & Number
7/25/60	11	15		1 **Dreamin'** .... *Cincinnati Fireball*	$20		Liberty 55258
10/31/60	8	15		2 **You're Sixteen** *I Beg Your Pardon*	$20	■	Liberty 55285
2/6/61	17	9		3 **Little Boy Sad** .... *(I Go) Down To The River*	$15	■	Liberty 55298
3/27/61	100	1		4 **Green Grass Of Texas** .... *Bloody River* [I] **THE TEXANS**	$30		Infinity 001
5/1/61	58	7		5 **Big Big World** .... *Ballad Of The One Eyed Jacks*	$15	■	Liberty 55318
10/16/61	18	9		6 **God, Country And My Baby** .... *Honestly I Do* **Johnny Mann Singers** (backing vocals)	$15		Liberty 55379

BURNETTE, Rocky

BUB/LP **'80**

Born Jonathan Burnette on 6/12/53 in Memphis, Tennessee. Son of **Johnny Burnette**, nephew of **Dorsey Burnette** and cousin of **Billy Burnette** (of **Fleetwood Mac**).

DEBUT	PEAK	WKS	Gold	A-side (Chart Hit)..................B-side	$	Sym	Label & Number
5/10/80	8	19		**Tired Of Toein' The Line** .... *Boogie Down In Mobile, Alabama*	$5		EMI America 8043

BURNS, George

C&W/MEM/LP **'33**

Born Nathan Birnbaum on 1/20/1896 in New York City, New York. Died on 3/9/96 (age 100). Popular radio, movie and TV comedian. Starred in several movies including *The Sunshine Boys* and *Oh God*. His only other charted record was in 1933 - the all-time longest span between charted hits (47 years).

DEBUT	PEAK	WKS	Gold	A-side (Chart Hit)..................B-side	$	Sym	Label & Number
1/19/80	49	10		**I Wish I Was Eighteen Again** .... *One Of The Mysteries Of Life*	$5	■	Mercury 57011

BURRELL, Kenny

BUB/LP **'65**

Born on 7/31/31 in Detroit, Michigan. Jazz guitarist. Veteran sessionman with Blue Note and Prestige. Featured guitarist on albums by **Jimmy Smith** and **Kai Winding**.

DEBUT	PEAK	WKS	Gold	A-side (Chart Hit)..................B-side	$	Sym	Label & Number
10/2/65	92	3		1 **The Organ Grinder's Swing** .... *I'll Close My Eyes* [I] **JIMMY SMITH With KENNY BURRELL And GRADY TATE** #2 hit for Jimmie Lunceford in 1936	$8		Verve 10363
12/30/67	21[X]	1		2 **The Little Drummer Boy** .... *Silent Night* [X-I]	$8		Cadet 5555

DEBUT	PEAK	WKS	Gold	A-side (Chart Hit)...B-side	$	Sym	Label & Number
				BURROWS, Tony '70			
				Born on 4/14/42 in Exeter, England. Lead singer for the following groups: **White Plains**, **First Class**, **Brotherhood Of Man**, **Edison Lighthouse** and **The Pipkins**.			
6/6/70	87	4		**Melanie Makes Me Smile** ... *I'll Get Along Somehow Girl*	$6		Bell 884
				BURTNICK, Glen — see STYX			
				BURTON, Jenny R&B/BUB/LP '84			
				Born on 11/18/57 in Brooklyn, New York. Female R&B singer.			
1/28/84	81	6		1 **Remember What You Like** ... *Players*	$4		Atlantic 89748
6/9/84	54	7		2 **Strangers In A Strange World** ... *(instrumental)* **JENNY BURTON & PATRICK JUDE** love theme from the movie *Beat Street* starring Rae Dawn Chong	$4	■	Atlantic 89660
				BURTON, Richard '65			
				Born Richard Jenkins on 11/10/25 in Pontrydyfen, Wales. Died of a cerebral hemorrhage on 8/5/84 (age 58). Leading actor from 1948-83. Twice married to and divorced from actress Elizabeth Taylor.			
1/30/65	64	5		**Married Man** ... *Finding Words For Spring* (**Richard Hayman**) [S] from the Broadway musical *Baker Street* starring Fritz Weaver	$8	■	MGM 13307
				BURTON, Richard '02			
				Born in Los Angeles, California. R&B singer.			
8/3/02	58^S	1		**Baller** ... *(instrumental)* **RICHARD BURTON Featuring Ruff Endz**	$5	★	MCA 155855
				BUS BOYS, The R&B/LP '84			
				R&B group from Los Angeles, California: Gus Louderman (vocals), brothers Brian (keyboards) and Kevin (bass) O'Neal, Victor Johnson (guitar), Michael Jones (keyboards) and Steve Felix (drums). Group appeared in the movie *48 HRS.*			
8/4/84	68	5		**Cleanin' Up The Town** ... *New Shoes* from the movie *Ghostbusters* starring Dan Aykroyd and Bill Murray	$4	■	Arista 9229
				BUSCH, Lou, and His Orchestra MEM '56			
				Born on 7/18/10 in Louisville, Kentucky. Died on 9/19/79 (age 69). Pianist/orchestra leader. Also recorded as **Joe "Fingers" Carr** (#7 pop hit in 1950 "Sam's Song").			
12/24/55+	75	6		1 **Zambezi** ... T:75 *Rainbow's End* [I] adaptation of a South African song	$12		Capitol 3272
2/25/56	35	11		2 **11th Hour Melody** ... T:35 *The Charming Mademoiselle From Paris, France*	$12		Capitol 3349
5/19/56	19	16		3 **Portuguese Washerwomen** ... A:19 / T:25 / S:25 *Lucky Pierre* [I] **JOE "FINGERS" CARR**	$10		Capitol 3418
				BUSH ROK/BUB/LP '96			
				Rock group from London, England: Gavin Rossdale (vocals, guitar, songwriter), Nigel Pulsford (guitar), Dave Parsons (bass) and Robin Goodridge (drums). Rossdale married Gwen Stefani (lead singer of **No Doubt**) on 9/14/2002.			
1/14/95	40^A	15		1 **Everything Zen** ...			album cut
4/29/95	46^A	13		2 **Little Things** ... *(live version) / Bud*	$8	★+	Trauma 95745
9/2/95	30	20		3 **Comedown** ... MR² A:25 / S:68 *(album version) / Testosterone*	$5	▮	Trauma 98134
1/27/96	28	20		4 **Glycerine** MR² A:28 / S:33 *Solomon's Bones*	$5	▮	Trauma 98088
4/13/96	43	20		5 **Machinehead** ... A:24 / S:58 *Alien (live)* from the movie *Fear* starring Mark Wahlberg (**Marky Mark**); all of above from the album *Sixteen Stone* on Trauma 92531	$5	▮	Trauma 98079
11/2/96	27^A	15		6 **Swallowed** ... MR⁷			album cut
1/18/97	41^A	14		7 **Greedy Fly** ... above 2 from the album *Razorblade Suitcase* on Trauma 90091			album cut
10/25/97	63^A	10		8 **Mouth** ... from the movie soundtrack album *An American Werewolf In Paris* on Hollywood 62131			album cut
10/2/99	67	20		9 **The Chemicals Between Us** ... MR⁵ A:58 from the album *The Science Of Things* on Trauma 490483			album cut
				BUSH, Kate ROK/BUB/LP '85			
				Born on 7/30/58 in Bexleyheath, Kent, England. Discovered by **David Gilmour** of **Pink Floyd**. Signed to EMI at age 16 while still at St. Joseph's Convent Grammar School. In 1993, directed movie *The Line, The Curve and The Cross* which was based on six songs from her album *The Red Shoes*.			
2/17/79	85	4		1 **The Man With The Child In His Eyes** ... *Moving*	$7		EMI America 8006
9/7/85	30	20		2 **Running Up That Hill** ... S:26 *Under The Ivy*	$6	■	EMI America 8285
4/4/87	72	6		3 **Don't Give Up** ... *Curtains* (Gabriel) **PETER GABRIEL/KATE BUSH**	$4	■	Geffen 28463
12/25/93	88	6		4 **Rubberband Girl** ... *This Woman's Work*	$4	▮	Columbia 77280
				BUSHWICK BILL — see GETO BOYS, The			
	★369★			**BUSTA RHYMES** R&B/BUB/LP '98			
				Born Trevor Smith on 5/20/72 in Brooklyn, New York. Male rapper. Founder of rap group Leaders Of The New School and member of Flipmode Squad. Played "Freddie Harris" in the 2002 movie *Halloween: Resurrection.* *1)What's It Gonna Be?! 2)Woo-Hah!! Got You All In Check 3)Dangerous*			
3/9/96	8	20	▲	1 **Woo-Hah!! Got You All In Check /** S:5 / A:52 samples "Space" by Galt MacDermot			
4/6/96		16		2 **Everything Remains Raw** ... S:flip	$3	▮	Elektra 64335
7/13/96	52	13		3 **It's a Party** ... S:32 *Ill Vibe* (w/**Q-Tip**) **BUSTA RHYMES (featuring Zhané)**	$4	▮	Elektra 64268
9/6/97	37^A	21		4 **Put Your Hands Where My Eyes Could See** ... from the album *When Disaster Strikes...* on Elektra 62064; also see #14 below			album cut
1/10/98	9	19	●	5 **Dangerous** ... S:6 / A:60 *You Won't Tell, I Won't Tell* samples "E.T. Boogie" by Extra T'S	$3	▮	Elektra 64131
3/21/98	19	20	●	6 **Victory** ... S:11 *(remix) / Bad Boy's Been Around The World Remix* (w/**Mase**) **PUFF DADDY & THE FAMILY Featuring The Notorious B.I.G. & Busta Rhymes** samples "Alone In The Ring" (from the movie *Rocky*) by **Bill Conti**	$3	▮	Bad Boy 79155
5/9/98	10	20	●	7 **Turn It Up [Remix]/Fire It Up** ... S:5 *Rhymes Galore* samples the theme from TV's *Knight Rider*	$3	▮	Elektra 64104

DEBUT	PEAK	WKS	Gold	A-side (Chart Hit)...B-side	$	Sym	Label & Number
				BUSTA RHYMES — Cont'd			
3/13/99	3	20	●	8 **What's It Gonna Be?!** RB[1] S:2 / A:9 *Tear Da Roof Off* **BUSTA RHYMES Featuring Janet** Antoinette Roberson (backing vocal)	$5	★[+]	Elektra 64051
3/17/01	63[S]	1		9 **Ante Up** (Remix)...*(2 versions) / Cold As Ice* **M.O.P. (feat. Busta Rhymes, Tephlon, and Remy Martin)**	$7	T	Loud 1984
6/30/01	63	14		10 **What It Is**...S:56 / A:60 *(2 versions)* **Kelis** (additional vocals); originally released on the various artists album *Violator The Album V2.0*	$6	T	Violator 79600
11/10/01+	26	20		11 **Break Ya Neck**...A:21 / S:39 *(3 versions)* samples "Give It Away" by **Red Hot Chili Peppers**	$6	T	J Records 21061
12/8/01	42[S]	3		12 **As I Come Back**...*(2 versions)* samples "Scenario" by **A Tribe Called Quest**	$7	T	J Records 21118
3/2/02	11	20		13 **Pass The Courvoisier Part II**...A:10 / S:14 *(5 versions)* **BUSTA RHYMES featuring P. Diddy & Pharrell** above 4 from the album *Genesis*	$6	T	J Records 21154
8/31/02	53[S]	9		14 **Tonight I'm Gonna Let Go**...*(5 versions)* **SYLEENA JOHNSON Featuring Busta Rhymes, Rampage, Sham & Spliff Star** samples #4 above and "Sweet Green Fields" by **Seals & Crofts**	$6	T	Jive 40042
11/9/02+	46	20		15 **Make It Clap**...S:15 / A:43 *(3 versions)* **BUSTA RHYMES (feat. Spliff Star)**	$6	T	J Records 21236
12/14/02	17[S]	7		16 **Gimme The Light (Remix)**...*(2 versions)* **SEAN PAUL Featuring Busta Rhymes** "45": VP/Atlantic 8809; B-side: (clean radio edit)	$6	T[V]	Atlantic 85422

BUSTERS, The — '63

Rock and roll band from Springfield, Massachusetts: Alan Orkins, John Chappel and Freddie Cole (guitars), Al Marczyk (sax), Jack Baker (bass) and Fran Parda (drums). Originally known as the Northern Lights, recorded "Typhoid" which was released as "Bust Out" by The Busters. Baker and Parda put together a new Busters touring group.

DEBUT	PEAK	WKS	Gold	A-side (Chart Hit)...B-side	$	Sym	Label & Number
9/7/63	25	10		**Bust Out**...*Astronaut's* [I]	$25		Arlen 735

BUTANES, The — '61

Black doo-wop group backed by Teddy McRae's Orchestra.

DEBUT	PEAK	WKS	Gold	A-side (Chart Hit)...B-side	$	Sym	Label & Number
7/31/61	96	3		**Don't Forget I Love You**...*That My Desire*	$25		Enrica 1007

BUTCHER, Jon — ROK/LP '85

Born in Boston, Massachusetts. Black rock singer/guitarist. The Axis included Thom Gimbel (keyboards), Jimmy Johnson (bass) and Derek Blevins (drums).

DEBUT	PEAK	WKS	Gold	A-side (Chart Hit)...B-side	$	Sym	Label & Number
11/30/85	94	3		**Sounds Of Your Voice**...*Stop* (ROK #31) **THE JON BUTCHER AXIS**	$4	■	Capitol 5534

BUTLER, Billy, & The Chanters — R&B/BUB '65

Born on 6/7/45 in Chicago, Illinois. R&B singer/songwriter/guitarist. Younger brother of **Jerry Butler**.

DEBUT	PEAK	WKS	Gold	A-side (Chart Hit)...B-side	$	Sym	Label & Number
7/3/65	60	6		**I Can't Work No Longer**...*Tomorrow Is Another Day* written by **Curtis Mayfield**	$15		Okeh 7221

BUTLER, Carl — C&W/LP '63

Born on 6/2/27 in Knoxville, Tennessee. Died on 9/4/92 (age 65). Country singer. His wife, Pearl, who sang harmony, died on 3/1/89 (age 61).

DEBUT	PEAK	WKS	Gold	A-side (Chart Hit)...B-side	$	Sym	Label & Number
2/9/63	88	2		**Don't Let Me Cross Over**...CW[11] *Wonder Drug*	$12	□	Columbia 42593

BUTLER, Champ — POP '51

Born on 12/21/26 in St. Louis, Missouri; raised in Los Angeles, California. Died on 3/8/92 (age 65). Pop singer. Hit #17 on the pop charts in 1951 with "Down Yonder."

DEBUT	PEAK	WKS	Gold	A-side (Chart Hit)...B-side	$	Sym	Label & Number
11/19/55	77	4		**Someone On Your Mind**...T:77 *I Want To Love You* **CHAMP BUTLER With GEORGE CATES And His Chorus and Orchestra**	$15		Coral 61496

BUTLER, Jerry ★105★ — R&B/BUB/LP '69

Born on 12/8/39 in Sunflower, Mississippi. Older brother of **Billy Butler**. Sang in the Northern Jubilee Gospel Singers, with **Curtis Mayfield**. Later with the Quails. In 1957, Butler and Mayfield joined the Roosters with Sam Gooden and brothers Arthur and Richard Brooks. Changed name to **The Impressions** in 1957. Left for solo career in autumn of 1958. Also worked as the Cook County Commissioner in Illinois. Dubbed "The Ice Man." Host of the popular PBS TV "Doo Wop" specials.

1)Only The Strong Survive 2)Let It Be Me 3)He Will Break Your Heart 4)Moon River 5)For Your Precious Love

DEBUT	PEAK	WKS	Gold	A-side (Chart Hit)...B-side	$	Sym	Label & Number
6/16/58	11	12		1 **For Your Precious Love**...S:11 / T:11 / A:25 *Sweet Was The Wine* **JERRY BUTLER and The Impressions** originally released on Vee-Jay 280 ($6000), then on Falcon 1013 ($50) and then on Abner 1013; also see #17 below	$50		Abner 1013
10/31/60	7	15		2 **He Will Break Your Heart**...RB[7] *Thanks To You*	$20		Vee-Jay 354
3/6/61	27	10		3 **Find Another Girl**...*When Trouble Calls*	$15		Vee-Jay 375
7/24/61	25	8		4 **I'm A Telling You**...*I See A Fool*	$15		Vee-Jay 390
10/9/61	11	17		5 **Moon River**...*Aware Of Love* (#105) from the movie *Breakfast At Tiffany's* starring Audrey Hepburn	$15		Vee-Jay 405
7/7/62	20	11		6 **Make It Easy On Yourself**...*It's Too Late*	$15		Vee-Jay 451
10/13/62	63	7		7 **You Can Run** (But You Can't Hide)...*I'm The One*	$15		Vee-Jay 463
12/15/62	100	1		8 **Theme From Taras Bulba (The Wishing Star)**...*You Go Right Through Me* title song from the movie *Taras Bulba* starring Tony Curtis	$15	■	Vee-Jay 475
3/30/63	68	6		9 **Whatever You Want**...*You Won't Be Sorry*	$15		Vee-Jay 486
11/23/63+	31	11		10 **Need To Belong**...*Give Me Your Love*	$15		Vee-Jay 567
4/4/64	56	6		11 **Giving Up On Love**...*I've Been Trying*	$12		Vee-Jay 588
8/1/64	61	6		12 **I Stand Accused** /			
6/27/64	95	2		13 **I Don't Want To Hear Anymore**... written by **Randy Newman**	$12	■	Vee-Jay 598
9/5/64	5	13		14 **Let It Be Me**...*Ain't That Loving You Baby* (#108) **BETTY EVERETT & JERRY BUTLER**	$15		Vee-Jay 613

DEBUT	PEAK	WKS	Gold	A-side (Chart Hit)...B-side	$	Sym	Label & Number
				BUTLER, Jerry — Cont'd			
12/5/64+	42	7		15 **Smile**...*Love Is Strange* **BETTY EVERETT & JERRY BUTLER** written in 1936 by Charlie Chaplin for his movie *Modern Times*; #10 hit for **Nat "King" Cole** in 1954	$15		Vee-Jay 633
3/6/65	64	4		16 **Good Times**...*I've Grown Accustomed To Her Face*	$12		Vee-Jay 651
3/26/66	99	2		17 **For Your Precious Love**...*Give It Up* [R] new version of #1 above	$12		Vee-Jay 715
1/21/67	60	9		18 **I Dig You Baby**...*Some Kinda Magic*	$10		Mercury 72648
10/21/67	38	7		19 **Mr. Dream Merchant**...*Cause I Love You So*	$10		Mercury 72721
12/30/67+	62	6		20 **Lost**...*You Don't Know What You Got Until You Lose It* different song from Butler's 1959 R&B hit "Lost"	$10		Mercury 72764
5/4/68	20	14		21 **Never Give You Up**...*Beside You*	$10		Mercury 72798
8/31/68	16	13		22 **Hey, Western Union Man**...RB[1] *Just Can't Forget About You*	$10		Mercury 72850
12/7/68+	39	10		23 **Are You Happy**...*(Strange) I Still Love You*	$10		Mercury 72876
3/1/69	4	13	●	24 **Only The Strong Survive** RB[2] *Just Because I Really Love You*	$8		Mercury 72898
5/31/69	24	10		25 **Moody Woman**...*Go Away - Find Yourself*	$8		Mercury 72929
8/30/69	20	10		26 **What's The Use Of Breaking Up**...*A Brand New Me* (#109)	$8		Mercury 72960
11/15/69	44	8		27 **Don't Let Love Hang You Up**...*Walking Around In Teardrops*	$8		Mercury 72991
1/24/70	62	5		28 **Got To See If I Can't Get Mommy (To Come Back Home)**...*I Forgot To Remember*	$8		Mercury 73015
3/21/70	46	5		29 **I Could Write A Book**...*Since I Lost You Lady*	$8		Mercury 73045
8/22/70	95	1		30 **Where Are You Going**...*You Can Fly* from the movie *Joe* starring Peter Boyle	$8		Mercury 73101
1/2/71	94	3		31 **You Just Can't Win (By Making The Same Mistake)**...*Sho Is Grooving* **GENE & JERRY** (Gene Chandler)	$8		Mercury 73163
3/6/71	69	8		32 **If It's Real What I Feel**...*Why Are You Leaving Me* also released with artist credited as **JERRY BUTLER Featuring Brenda Lee**	$7		Mercury 73169
7/10/71	85	3		33 **How Did We Lose It Baby**...*Do You Finally Need A Friend*	$7		Mercury 73210
10/9/71	93	2		34 **Walk Easy My Son**...*Let Me Be*	$7		Mercury 73241
12/11/71+	21	18	●	35 **Ain't Understanding Mellow**...*Windy City Soul* (Butler) **JERRY BUTLER and BRENDA LEE EAGER**	$7		Mercury 73255
5/20/72	85	4		36 **I Only Have Eyes For You**...*A Prayer* #2 hit for Ben Selvin in 1934 (from the movie musical *Dames* starring Joan Blondell)	$7		Mercury 73290
9/9/72	91	3		37 **(They Long To Be) Close To You**...*You Can't Always Tell* (Butler) **JERRY BUTLER Featuring Brenda Lee Eager**	$7		Mercury 73301
11/4/72	52	7		38 **One Night Affair**...*Life's Unfortunate Sons*	$7		Mercury 73335
3/12/77	51	11		39 **I Wanna Do It To You**...*I Don't Wanna Be Reminded*	$5		Motown 1414
				BUTLER, Jonathan R&B/AC/BUB **'87** Born in Capetown, South Africa. R&B guitarist/singer/songwriter. Migrated to London in 1984 (at age 21).			
6/27/87	27	14		**Lies**...S:21 / A:30 *Haunted By Your Love*	$4	■	Jive 1038
				BUTTERFLYS, The — see RAINDROPS, The			
				BUTTHOLE SURFERS ROK/LP **'96** Punk-rock group from San Antonio, Texas: Gibby Haynes (vocals), Paul Leary (guitar), Jeff Pinkus (bass) and King Coffey (drums).			
5/25/96	26[A]	20		**Pepper**...MR[3] from the album *Electriclarryland* on Capitol 29842; "45": Capitol 19200; B-side: "Birds"		V	album cut
				B*WITCHED LP **'99** Female vocal group from Dublin, Ireland: twin sisters Edele and Keavy Lynch, with Sinead O'Carroll and Lindsay Armaou.			
2/20/99	9	15	●	1 **C'est La Vie**...S:4 *B*Witched Quiz Show / (3 album snippets) / Get Happy* title is French for "That's Life"	$3	★V	Epic 79084
6/19/99	67	8		2 **Rollercoaster**...S:10 *C'est La Vie (remix) / B*Witched Go To The Moon / B*Witched Megamix / Together We'll Be Fine*	$3	★V	Epic 79179
				BYRD, Bobby R&B/BUB **'64** Born on 8/15/34 in Toccoa, Georgia. Founder/leader of **James Brown**'s vocal group, The Famous Flames.			
4/4/64	52	6		1 **Baby Baby Baby**...*(instrumental* - Sammy Lowe) **ANNA KING-BOBBY BYRD**	$20		Smash 1884
10/24/70	69	5		2 **I Need Help (I Can't Do It Alone) Pt. 1**...*Pt. 2*	$10		King 6323
9/25/71	85	4		3 **Hot Pants - I'm Coming, Coming, I'm Coming**...*Hang It Up*	$8		BrownStone 4203
2/26/72	88	3		4 **Keep On Doin' What You're Doin'**...*Let Me Know* all of above produced by **James Brown**	$8		BrownStone 4205
				BYRD, Charlie AC/LP **'62** Born on 9/16/25 in Chuckatuch, Virginia. Died of cancer on 11/30/99 (age 74). Jazz and classical guitar virtuoso. Studied under classical master guitarist Segovia. With **Woody Herman** in 1959.			
9/29/62	15	16		1 **Desafinado**...*Theme From Dr. Kildare* (Getz) [I] **STAN GETZ/CHARLIE BYRD**	$12		Verve 10260
1/26/63	66	9		2 **Meditation (Meditacao)**...*O Barquinho (Little Boat)* [I] Walter Raim Strings (orchestral backing); above 2 written by Brazilian composer Antonio Carlos Jobim	$10		Riverside 4544
				BYRD, Donald — see BLACKBYRDS, The			
				BYRD, Jerry POP/C&W **'50** Born on 3/9/20 in Lima, Ohio. Steel guitarist. Member of the guitar session band The Nashville Guitars. Hit #19 on the pop charts in 1950 with "Harbor Lights."			
8/1/60	97	1		1 **Theme From Adventures In Paradise**...*Indian Love Call* [I] **JERRY BYRD and His Steel Guitar** theme from the TV series *Adventures In Paradise* starring Gardner McKay	$10		Monument 419
3/17/62	74	9		2 **Memories Of Maria**...*Invitation (To Love)* [I] **The Music of JERRY BYRD** written by **Roy Orbison**	$10		Monument 449

DEBUT	PEAK	WKS	Gold	A-side (Chart Hit)...B-side	$	Sym	Label & Number

BYRD, Russell — '61

Born Bertrand Berns on 11/8/29 in New York City, New York. Died of a heart attack on 12/31/67 (age 38). Producer/songwriter/co-owner of Bang Records. Wrote "Twist And Shout" and "Hang On Sloopy."

DEBUT	PEAK	WKS	Gold	A-side (Chart Hit)...B-side	$	Sym	Label & Number
5/8/61	50	5		**You'd Better Come Home** ... *Let's Tell Him All About It*	$12		Wand 107

BYRD, Tracy — C&W/BUB/LP '02

Born on 12/17/66 in Beaumont, Texas; raised in Vidor, Texas. Male country singer.

DEBUT	PEAK	WKS	Gold	A-side (Chart Hit)...B-side	$	Sym	Label & Number
10/22/94	81	5		1 **Watermelon Crawl** ... S:48 *You Never Know Just How Good You've Got It*	$4	■V	MCA 54889
4/1/95	68	7		2 **The Keeper Of The Stars** ... S:29 *Pink Flamingos*	$4	■V	MCA 54988
8/12/95	92	3		3 **Walking To Jerusalem** ... S:61 *Down On The Bottom*	$4	■V	MCA 55049
4/4/98	63	18		4 **I'm From The Country** ... S:44 *For Me It's You*	$4	■V	MCA 72040
1/29/00	76	8		5 **Put Your Hand In Mine** ... A:65 from the album *It's About Time* on RCA 67881; "45": RCA 65907; B-side: "It's About Time"		V	album cut
1/12/02	64	10		6 **Just Let Me Be In Love** ... A:61 "45": RCA 69106; B-side: "Somebody's Dream"		V	album cut
7/6/02	26	20		7 **Ten Rounds With José Cuervo** CW[1] A:25 "45": RCA 69171; B-side: "Somebody's Dream"; above 2 from the album *Ten Rounds* on RCA 67009		V	album cut

BYRDS, The — ★389★ — BUB/ROK/LP '65

Folk-rock group formed in Los Angeles, California. Consisted of James McGuinn (12-string guitar; born on 7/13/42), **David Crosby** (guitar; born on 8/14/41), Gene Clark (percussion; born on 11/17/41), Chris Hillman (bass; born on 12/4/42) and Mike Clarke (drums; born on 6/3/44). McGuinn, who changed his first name to Roger in 1968, had been with **Bobby Darin** and the **Chad Mitchell Trio**. Clark had been with the **New Christy Minstrels**. All except Clarke had folk music background. First recorded as the Beefeaters for Elektra in 1964. Also recorded as the Jet Set. Professional debut in March 1965. Clark left after "Eight Miles High." Crosby left in 1968 to form **Crosby, Stills & Nash**. Re-formed in 1968 with McGuinn, Hillman, Kevin Kelly (drums) and Gram Parsons (guitar). Hillman and Parsons left that same year to form the Flying Burrito Brothers. McGuinn again re-formed with Clarence White (guitar), John York (bass) and Gene Parsons (drums). Reunions with original members in 1973 and 1979. Gram Parsons died of a heroin overdose on 9/19/73 (age 26). Hillman with **The Souther, Hillman, Furay Band** in 1974. **McGuinn, Clark & Hillman** later recorded as a trio. In 1986, Hillman formed popular Country group The Desert Rose Band. McGuinn, Crosby and Hillman reunited on stage on 2/24/90 for a **Roy Orbison** tribute. Gene Clark died of natural causes on 5/24/91 (age 46). Mike Clarke, also with the Flying Burrito Brothers and **Firefall**, died of liver failure on 12/19/93 (age 49). Group inducted into the Rock and Roll Hall of Fame in 1991.

1)Turn! Turn! Turn! 2)Mr. Tambourine Man 3)Eight Miles High

DEBUT	PEAK	WKS	Gold	A-side (Chart Hit)...B-side	$	Sym	Label & Number
5/15/65	❶[1]	13		1 **Mr. Tambourine Man** ... *I Knew I'd Want You*	$15	□	Columbia 43271
7/3/65	40	10		2 **All I Really Want To Do** ... *I'll Feel A Whole Lot Better* (#103)	$15		Columbia 43332
10/23/65	❶[3]	14		3 **Turn! Turn! Turn! (To Everything There Is A Season)** *She Don't Care About Time* lyrics adapted by **Pete Seeger** from the Bible: Ecclesiastes 3:1-8	$15		Columbia 43424
2/12/66	63	5		4 **It Won't Be Wrong /**			
2/5/66	79	4		5 **Set You Free This Time** ...	$12		Columbia 43501
4/9/66	14	9		6 **Eight Miles High** ... *Why*	$12	■	Columbia 43578
7/16/66	44	5		7 **5 D (Fifth Dimension)** ... *Captain Soul* [I]	$12		Columbia 43702
9/24/66	36	7		8 **Mr. Spaceman** ... *What's Happening?!?!*	$12		Columbia 43766
1/28/67	29	7		9 **So You Want To Be A Rock 'N' Roll Star** ... *Everybody's Been Burned*	$12		Columbia 43987
4/1/67	30	7		10 **My Back Pages** ... *Renaissance Fair*	$12		Columbia 44054
6/10/67	74	4		11 **Have You Seen Her Face** ... *Don't Make Waves*	$10	■	Columbia 44157
8/19/67	82	2		12 **Lady Friend** ... *Old John Robertson*	$10		Columbia 44230
11/18/67	89	3		13 **Goin' Back** ... *Change Is Now*	$10		Columbia 44362
5/11/68	74	5		14 **You Ain't Going Nowhere** ... *Artificial Energy* #1, 2, 10 & 14: written by **Bob Dylan**	$10		Columbia 44499
11/1/69	65	6		15 **Ballad Of Easy Rider** ... *Oil In My Lamp* from the movie *Easy Rider* starring Peter Fonda	$10		Columbia 44990
2/7/70	97	1		16 **Jesus Is Just Alright** ... *It's All Over Now, Baby Blue* #1-5, 15 & 16: produced by Terry Melcher (of **Bruce & Terry**)	$10		Columbia 45071

BYRNES, Edward — '59

Born Edward Breitenberger on 7/30/33 in New York City, New York. Best known as "Kookie" on TV's *77 Sunset Strip.*

DEBUT	PEAK	WKS	Gold	A-side (Chart Hit)...B-side	$	Sym	Label & Number
4/20/59	4	13	●	1 **Kookie, Kookie (Lend Me Your Comb)** ... *You're The Top* (Byrnes) [N] **EDWARD BYRNES And CONNIE STEVENS**	$20	■	Warner 5047
8/10/59	42	9		2 **Like I Love You** ... *Kookie's Mad Pad* (Byrnes) [N] **EDD BYRNES and FRIEND** The Big Sound of **Don Ralke** (backing band, above 2)	$15	■	Warner 5087

C

CABOOSE, The — '70

Gospel-rock group: Gary Johns and Patricia Karr (vocals), Jackie Cook (guitar), Walt Ramsey (keyboards), Tom Cathey (bass) and Joel Williams (drums).

DEBUT	PEAK	WKS	Gold	A-side (Chart Hit)...B-side	$	Sym	Label & Number
8/1/70	79	3		**Black Hands White Cotton** ... *In My Hour Of Need*	$6		Enterprise 9015

CADETS, The/THE JACKS — '56

R&B vocal group from Los Angeles, California: Aaron Collins, **Ted Taylor**, William "Dub" Jones (bass man for **The Coasters**; died on 1/16/00), Willie Davis and Lloyd McCraw. Recorded as both The Jacks on RPM with Davis as lead and The Cadets on Modern with Collins or Jones as lead. Collins and Davis joined **The Flares** in 1961. Collins' sisters, Betty and Rosie, recorded as **The Teen Queens**.

DEBUT	PEAK	WKS	Gold	A-side (Chart Hit)...B-side	$	Sym	Label & Number
11/12/55	82	3		1 **Why Don't You Write Me?** ... T:82 *My Darling* **THE JACKS**	$80		RPM 428
7/14/56	15	11		2 **Stranded In The Jungle** ... S:15 / A:16 / J:16 / T:18 *I Want You* [N] **THE CADETS**	$50		Modern 994

DEBUT	PEAK	WKS	Gold	A-side (Chart Hit)	B-side	$	Sym	Label & Number

CADILLACS, The
R&B/BUB **'56**

R&B vocal group formed in 1953 at P.S. 139 in Harlem, New York, as the Carnations. The first R&B vocal group to extensively use choreography in their stage routines. Consisted of Earl "Speedoo" Carroll (lead), LaVerne Drake, Earl Wade, Charles Brooks and Robert Phillips. By 1958, Drake and Brooks replaced by James Bailey and Bobby Spencer. Varying membership. Carroll joined **The Coasters** in 1961. Spencer was later the lead voice for **Crazy Elephant**. Bailey died in 1980 (age 48).

DEBUT	PEAK	WKS	Gold	A-side (Chart Hit)	B-side	$	Sym	Label & Number
12/10/55+	**17**	17		1 **Speedoo** S:17 / T:30 Jesse Powell (orch.); song's title is lead singer Earl Carroll's nickname	*Let Me Explain*	$80		Josie 785
12/8/58+	**28**	10		2 **Peek-A-Boo** Osie Johnson (orch.)	*Oh, Oh, Lolita*	$40		Josie 846

CAESAR, Shirley
'75

Born on 10/13/38 in Durham, North Carolina. Billed as the "First Lady of Gospel Music."

DEBUT	PEAK	WKS	Gold	A-side (Chart Hit)	B-side	$	Sym	Label & Number
5/17/75	**91**	5		**No Charge** #1 Country hit for **Melba Montgomery** in 1974	*(gospel version)*	$5		HOB/Scepter 12402

CAFFERTY, John
ROK/LP **'84**

Rock group from Narragansett, Rhode Island: John Cafferty (vocals, guitar), Gary Gramolini (guitar), Robert Cotoia (keyboards), Michael Antunes (saxophone), Pat Lupo (bass) and Kenny Jo Silva (drums). Wrote and recorded the music for the soundtrack *Eddie And The Cruisers.*

1)On The Dark Side 2)C-I-T-Y 3)Tough All Over

DEBUT	PEAK	WKS	Gold	A-side (Chart Hit)	B-side	$	Sym	Label & Number
				EDDIE AND THE CRUISERS:				
10/8/83	**64**	9		1 **On The Dark Side**	*Wild Summer Nights*	$6		Scotti Brothers 04107
				JOHN CAFFERTY AND THE BEAVER BROWN BAND:				
1/28/84	**78**	5		2 **Tender Years**	*Down On My Knees*	$6		Scotti Brothers 04327
8/18/84	**7**	18		3 **On The Dark Side** AR^{5} A:6 / S:11 same version as #1 above	*Wild Summer Nights* [R]	$4		Scotti Brothers 04594
11/17/84+	**31**	14		4 **Tender Years** S:28 / A:28 same version as #2 above; all of above from the movie *Eddie And The Cruisers* starring Tom Berenger	*Down On My Knees* [R]	$4	■	Scotti Brothers 04682
5/11/85	**22**	15		5 **Tough All Over** AR^{2} A:13 / S:26	*Strangers In Paradise*	$4	■	Scotti Brothers 04891
8/10/85	**18**	15		6 **C-I-T-Y** S:19 / A:19	*Where The Action Is*	$4	■	Scotti Brothers 05452
11/9/85	**64**	10		7 **Small Town Girl**	*More Than Just One Of The Boys*	$4	■	Scotti Brothers 05668
3/1/86	**76**	6		8 **Heart's On Fire** **JOHN CAFFERTY** from the movie *Rocky IV* starring Sylvester Stallone	*Small Town Girl* (w/Beaver Brown Band)	$4	■	Scotti Brothers 05774
6/14/86	**62**	8		9 **Voice Of America's Sons** from the movie *Cobra* starring Sylvester Stallone	*Dixieland*	$3	■	Scotti Brothers 06048
7/29/89	**66**	7		10 **Pride & Passion** from the movie *Eddie And The Cruisers II* starring Michael Pare	*Heat Of The Night*	$3		Scotti Brothers 68999

CAGE
R&B/LP **'00**

Born Christian Palko in 1970 on a U.S. military base in West Germany; raised in Brooklyn, New York. Male rapper. Member of **Smut Peddlers** (see #1 below).

DEBUT	PEAK	WKS	Gold	A-side (Chart Hit)	B-side	$	Sym	Label & Number
12/2/00	**56^{S}**	2		1 **That Smut** **SMUT PEDDLERS**	*(2 versions) / Medicated Minutes*	$6	T	Rawkus 273
1/27/01	**63^{S}**	3		2 **Suicidal Failure**	*(2 versions) / Dust Vs. Ecstacy / The Weather Report* (w/Copywrite)	$7	T	Eastern/Rawkus 287

CAGE, Athena
'96

Born in Atlanta, Georgia. Female R&B singer. Former member of **Kut Klose**.

DEBUT	PEAK	WKS	Gold	A-side (Chart Hit)	B-side	$	Sym	Label & Number
10/5/96	**3**	35	▲	1 **Nobody** RB^{3} S:3 / A:10 **KEITH SWEAT Featuring Athena Cage** **Kut Klose** (backing vocals)	*In The Mood*	$3	▮V	Elektra 64245
7/21/01	**22^{S}**	14		2 **Hey Hey**	*(radio edit) / (2 album snippets)*	$4	★	Priority 50205

CAGLE, Chris
C&W/LP **'02**

Born Christian Cagle on 12/31/69 in Louisiana; raised in Houston, Texas. Male country singer/songwriter/guitarist.

DEBUT	PEAK	WKS	Gold	A-side (Chart Hit)	B-side	$	Sym	Label & Number
10/21/00	**76**	11		1 **My Love Goes On And On** S:65	*Play It Loud*	$4	★V	Virgin 58867
7/7/01	**60**	12		2 **Laredo** A:52 "45": Capitol 58979; B-side: "Lovin' You Lovin' Me"			V	album cut
2/9/02	**35**	20		3 **I Breathe In, I Breathe Out** CW^{1} A:34 "45": Capitol 77696; B-side: "Country By The Grace Of God"; all of above from the album *Play It Loud* on Capitol 34170			V	album cut

CAIN, Jonathan
'76

Born on 2/26/50 in Chicago, Illinois. Former keyboardist with **The Babys**. Joined **Journey** in 1981. Co-founded **Bad English** in 1989. Formerly married to **Tané Cain**.

DEBUT	PEAK	WKS	Gold	A-side (Chart Hit)	B-side	$	Sym	Label & Number
1/10/76	**44**	9		**'Til It's Time To Say Goodbye**	*Ladies' Night*	$5		October 1001

CAIN, Tané
BUB/LP **'82**

Born Tané McClure on 6/8/59 in Pacific Palasades, California. Female singer/songwriter. Daughter of actor Doug McClure. Formerly married to **Jonathan Cain**. First name pronounced: tawnee.

DEBUT	PEAK	WKS	Gold	A-side (Chart Hit)	B-side	$	Sym	Label & Number
8/14/82	**37**	11		**Holdin' On**	*Hurtin' Kind*	$4		RCA 13287

CAIOLA, Al, And His Orchestra
BUB **'61**

Born on 9/7/20 in Jersey City, New Jersey. Prolific studio guitarist.

DEBUT	PEAK	WKS	Gold	A-side (Chart Hit)	B-side	$	Sym	Label & Number
12/5/60+	**35**	12		1 **The Magnificent Seven** title song from the movie starring Yul Brynner; tune used for Marlboro cigarette commercials (also see "Sweet Soul Music")	*The Lonely Rebel* [I]	$12		United Artists 261
4/3/61	**19**	10		2 **Bonanza** title song from the TV series starring **Lorne Greene**; above 2 produced by **Don Costa**	*Bounty Hunter* [I]	$10		United Artists 302

CAKE
ROK/BUB/LP **'99**

Rock group from Sacramento, California: John McCrea (vocals, guitar), Greg Brown (guitar), Vince DiFiore (trumpet), Victor Damiani (bass) and Todd Roper (drums).

DEBUT	PEAK	WKS	Gold	A-side (Chart Hit)	B-side	$	Sym	Label & Number
10/26/96	**35^{A}**	14		1 **The Distance** from the album *Fashion Nugget* on Capricorn 532867				album cut
12/5/98+	**78**	17		2 **Never There** MR^{3} A:43 from the album *Prolonging The Magic* on Capricorn 538092				album cut

DEBUT	PEAK	WKS	Gold	A-side (Chart Hit)......B-side	$	Sym	Label & Number

CALDWELL, Bobby R&B/BUB/AC/LP **'79**

Born on 8/15/51 in New York City, New York; raised in Miami, Florida. Multi-instrumentalist/songwriter. Wrote tracks for *New Mickey Mouse Club* TV show, commercials, and **Peter Cetera** and **Amy Grant**'s "The Next Time I Fall."

DEBUT	PEAK	WKS	Gold	A-side (Chart Hit)......B-side	$	Sym	Label & Number
12/23/78+	9	20		1 **What You Won't Do For Love**......*Love Won't Wait* a special heart-shaped red vinyl "45" issued on Clouds HSS1	$5		Clouds 11
4/19/80	42	10		2 **Coming Down From Love**......*Open Your Eyes*	$5		Clouds 21
9/11/82	77	6		3 **All Of My Love**......*Sunny Hills*	$4		Polydor 2212

CALE, J.J. LP **'72**

Born Jean Jacques Cale on 12/5/38 in Oklahoma City, Oklahoma. Rock singer/songwriter/guitarist. Wrote **Eric Clapton**'s "After Midnight" and "Cocaine." In high school bands with **Leon Russell**. Worked with Phil Spector and **Delaney & Bonnie**. Session work with **Art Garfunkel**, **Bob Seger** and **Neil Young**.

DEBUT	PEAK	WKS	Gold	A-side (Chart Hit)......B-side	$	Sym	Label & Number
1/29/72	22	14		1 **Crazy Mama**......*Don't Go To Strangers*	$6		Shelter 7314
5/20/72	42	11		2 **After Midnight**......*Crying Eyes*	$6		Shelter 7321
11/4/72	42	8		3 **Lies**......*Riding Home*	$6		Shelter 7326
12/25/76	96	3		4 **Hey Baby**......*Cocaine*	$5		Shelter 62002

CALEN, Frankie **'61**

Teen pop singer in the style of **Frankie Avalon**.

DEBUT	PEAK	WKS	Gold	A-side (Chart Hit)......B-side	$	Sym	Label & Number
6/12/61	78	6		**Joanie**......*Pa I Passed My Drivin' Test*	$50		Spark 902

CALHOUN, Slimm LP **'00**

Born in College Park, Georgia. Male rapper.

DEBUT	PEAK	WKS	Gold	A-side (Chart Hit)......B-side	$	Sym	Label & Number
10/21/00	18S	18		**It's OK**......*(instrumental)* **SLIMM CALHOUN (Featuring Andre 3000 of Outkast)**	$5	★	Aquemini/EastWest 67091

CALI, Dena **'01**

Born in 1979 in Pasadena, California. Black female rapper/singer.

DEBUT	PEAK	WKS	Gold	A-side (Chart Hit)......B-side	$	Sym	Label & Number
10/13/01	21S	10		**I'm Your Girl**......*(3 remixes)*	$6	★	ES3/Treydan 0119

CALIFORNIA RAISINS, The LP **'88**

Studio group produced by Ross Vannelli (producer of **Earth, Wind & Fire** and **Howard Hewett**; brother of **Gino Vannelli**). Features R&B vocalist/drummer **Buddy Miles** and vocalist Alfie Silas. Based on the Claymation characters of a California Raisin Growers' television commercial.

DEBUT	PEAK	WKS	Gold	A-side (Chart Hit)......B-side	$	Sym	Label & Number
1/23/88	84	4		**I Heard It Through The Grapevine**......*You Can't Hurry Love* **Buddy Miles** (lead vocal)	$4	■	Priority 9719

CALL, The ROK/LP **'89**

Rock group from California: Michael Been (vocals, guitar), Tom Ferrier (guitar), Greg Freeman (bass) and Scott Musick (drums). Jim Goodwin (keyboards) replaced Freeman in 1984. Hit #2 on the Contemporary Christian charts in 1986 with "I Still Believe."

DEBUT	PEAK	WKS	Gold	A-side (Chart Hit)......B-side	$	Sym	Label & Number
5/7/83	74	5		1 **The Walls Came Down**......*Upperbirth*	$5	■	Mercury 811487
7/22/89	51	9		2 **Let The Day Begin**......AR1 *Uncovered*	$4		MCA 53658

CALLENDER, Bobby **'63**

Teen pop singer/songwriter.

DEBUT	PEAK	WKS	Gold	A-side (Chart Hit)......B-side	$	Sym	Label & Number
3/16/63	95	2		**Little Star**......*Love And Kisses (I'll Give To You)*	$25		Roulette 4471

CALLING, The LP **'02**

Rock group from Los Angeles, California: Alex Band (vocals), Aaron Kamin and Sean Woolstenhulme (guitars), Billy Mohler (bass) and Nate Wood (drums).

DEBUT	PEAK	WKS	Gold	A-side (Chart Hit)......B-side	$	Sym	Label & Number
11/10/01+	5	45		**Wherever You Will Go**......S:3 / A:5 *(acoustic version) / (3 album snippets)* "45": RCA 60553; B-side: "Adrienne" (#116)	$4	★+V	RCA 60518

CALLOWAY, Cab MEM/POP/R&B **'31**

Born Cabell Calloway on 12/25/07 in Rochester, New York; raised in Baltimore, Maryland. Died of a stroke on 11/18/94 (age 86). Nicknamed "His Hi-De-Ho Highness Of Jive." Vocalist/bandleader/alto saxophonist/drummer. Gained fame at New York's Cotton Club in the 1930s. Appeared in many movies, including *The Blues Brothers*. Signature song is his 1931 hit "Minnie The Moocher." Charted 43 pop hits, 1930-45.

DEBUT	PEAK	WKS	Gold	A-side (Chart Hit)......B-side	$	Sym	Label & Number
2/18/56	62	2		1 **Little Child**......T:62 *The Voice* (Cab Calloway) **LAEL & CAB CALLOWAY** (Lael is Cab's 8-year-old daughter) **Don Costa** (orch.); adapted from the French title "Little Boy And The Old Man"; a picture sleeve was issued on ABC-Paramount's Children's Series (CX-1)	$15		ABC-Paramount 9671
4/16/66	89	3		2 **History Repeats Itself**......*After Taxes* [S] an accounting of "coincidental" parallels between the careers and deaths of Presidents Lincoln and Kennedy	$10		Boom 60,006

CAMBRIDGE STRINGS AND SINGERS, The **'61**

British studio assemblage conducted and arranged by Dick Rowe and Malcolm Lockyer (died on 6/28/76, age 53). Also see **The Knightsbridge Strings**.

DEBUT	PEAK	WKS	Gold	A-side (Chart Hit)......B-side	$	Sym	Label & Number
2/13/61	60	6		**Theme from Tunes Of Glory**......*Love theme from "The World Of Suzie Wong"* [I] title song from the movie starring Alec Guinness; charted in 1955 by **The Ames Brothers** as "My Bonnie Lassie" (adapted from "Scotland The Brave")	$10		London 1960

CAMEO R&B/BUB/LP **'86**

R&B-funk group founded by Larry Blackmon (vocals, drums, producer) as The New York City Players. Originally contained several members. In late 1982, Blackmon relocated the group to Atlanta, Georgia. Pared the group down to a trio of Blackmon, Tomi Jenkins and Nathan Leftenant. Charted 38 R&B hits, 1977-95.

DEBUT	PEAK	WKS	Gold	A-side (Chart Hit)......B-side	$	Sym	Label & Number
4/7/84	47	11		1 **She's Strange**......RB4 *Tribute To Bob Marley*	$4		Atlanta Artists 818384
9/13/86	6	21		2 **Word Up** RB3 S:2 / A:8 *Urban Warrior*	$3	■	Atlanta Artists 884933
12/27/86+	21	17		3 **Candy**......RB2 S:19 / A:28 *She's Strange (long version)*	$3	■	Atlanta Artists 888193
4/25/87	50	8		4 **Back And Forth**......*You Can Have The World*	$3	■	Atlanta Artists 888385
11/5/88	85	5		5 **You Make Me Work**......*DKWIG*	$3	■	Atlanta Artists 870587

CAMILLO, Tony — see BAZUKA

CAMOUFLAGE ROK/LP **'89**

Dance trio from Germany: Marcus Meyn (vocals), Heiko Maile (keyboards) and Oliver Kreyssig (backing vocals; left band in 1990).

DEBUT	PEAK	WKS	Gold	A-side (Chart Hit)......B-side	$	Sym	Label & Number
12/24/88+	59	12		**The Great Commandment**......*Pompeji*	$3	■	Atlantic 89031

DEBUT	PEAK	WKS	Gold	A-side (Chart Hit)..........B-side	$	Sym	Label & Number

CAMP, Hamilton — '68

Born on 10/30/34 in London, England. Singer/actor. Cast member of the TV shows *He & She, Just Our Luck, Story Theater* and *Turn-On.*

DEBUT	PEAK	WKS	Gold	A-side (Chart Hit)..........B-side	$	Sym	Label & Number
5/4/68	76	5		**Here's To You**..........*Leavin' Anyhow*	$8		Warner 7165

CAMPBELL, Debbie — see BUCKWHEAT

CAMPBELL, Glen ★76★ — C&W/AC/BUB/LP '69

Born on 4/22/36 in Delight, Arkansas. Country singer/songwriter/guitarist. With his uncle Dick Bills' band, 1954-58. To Los Angeles; recorded with **The Champs** in 1960. Became prolific studio musician; with **The Hondells** in 1964, **The Beach Boys** in 1965 and **Sagittarius** in 1967. Own TV show *The Glen Campbell Goodtime Hour*, 1968-72. In movies *True Grit, Norwood* and *Strange Homecoming*; voice in the animated movie *Rock-A-Doodle.* Charted 75 Country hits and 42 Adult Contemporary hits, 1962-93.

1)Rhinestone Cowboy 2)Southern Nights 3)Wichita Lineman 4)Galveston 5)It's Only Make Believe

DEBUT	PEAK	WKS	Gold	A-side (Chart Hit)..........B-side	$	Sym	Label & Number
10/30/61	62	10		1 **Turn Around, Look At Me**..........*Brenda*	$20		Crest 1087
8/25/62	76	2		2 **Too Late To Worry - Too Blue To Cry**..........*How Do I Tell My Heart Not To Break* #1 Country hit for Al Dexter in 1944	$15		Capitol 4783
9/25/65	45	7		3 **The Universal Soldier**..........*Spanish Shades* written by **Buffy St. Marie**	$10		Capitol 5504
7/8/67	62	7		4 **Gentle On My Mind**..........*Just Another Man* also see #9 below (same version)	$8		Capitol 5939
10/28/67	26	11		5 **By The Time I Get To Phoenix**..........*You've Still Got A Place In My Heart*	$7		Capitol 2015
1/20/68	54	7		6 **Hey Little One**..........*My Baby's Gone*	$7	■	Capitol 2076
4/6/68	36	12		7 **I Wanna Live**..........CW[3] *That's All That Matters*	$7		Capitol 2146
7/6/68	32	8		8 **Dreams Of The Everyday Housewife**..........*Kelli Hoedown*	$7		Capitol 2224
9/14/68	39	9		9 **Gentle On My Mind**..........*Just Another Man* [R]	$8		Capitol 5939
10/26/68	74	6		10 **Mornin' Glory**..........*Less Of Me* (C&W #44) **BOBBIE GENTRY & GLEN CAMPBELL**	$6		Capitol 2314
11/2/68+	3	15	●	11 **Wichita Lineman**..........CW[2] / AC[6] *Fate Of Man*	$6		Capitol 2302
12/14/68	7[X]	3		12 **Christmas Is For Children**..........*There's No Place Like Home* [X]	$8		Capitol 2336
1/25/69	36	9		13 **Let It Be Me**..........*Little Green Apples* **GLEN CAMPBELL AND BOBBIE GENTRY**	$6		Capitol 2387
3/1/69	4	12	●	14 **Galveston**..........CW[3] / AC[6] *How Come Every Time I Itch I Wind Up Scratchin' You*	$6		Capitol 2428
5/3/69	26	8		15 **Where's The Playground Susie**..........*Arkansas*	$6		Capitol 2494
7/26/69	35	7		16 **True Grit**..........*Hava Nagila* title song from the movie starring John Wayne and Campbell	$6		Capitol 2573
10/11/69	23	11		17 **Try A Little Kindness**..........AC[1] *Lonely My Lonely Friend*	$6		Capitol 2659
1/17/70	19	9		18 **Honey Come Back**..........*Where Do You Go* #5, 11, 14, 15 & 18: written by Jimmy Webb	$6		Capitol 2718
2/14/70	27	10		19 **All I Have To Do Is Dream**..........*Less Of Me* **BOBBIE GENTRY & GLEN CAMPBELL**	$6		Capitol 2745
4/11/70	40	8		20 **Oh Happy Day**..........*Someone Above*	$6		Capitol 2787
7/4/70	52	8		21 **Everything A Man Could Ever Need**..........*Norwood (Me And My Guitar)* written by **Mac Davis**; from the movie *Norwood* starring Campbell	$6		Capitol 2843
9/5/70	10	12		22 **It's Only Make Believe**..........*Pave Your Way Into Tomorrow*	$6		Capitol 2905
3/13/71	31	7		23 **Dream Baby (How Long Must I Dream)**..........*Here And Now*	$6		Capitol 3062
6/26/71	61	7		24 **The Last Time I Saw Her**..........*Bach Talk* written by **Gordon Lightfoot**	$6		Capitol 3123
10/23/71	81	5		25 **I Say A Little Prayer/By The Time I Get To Phoenix**..........*All Through The Night* **GLEN CAMPBELL/ANNE MURRAY** #4-25: **Al DeLory** (producer, arranger, conductor)	$6		Capitol 3200
8/26/72	61	7		26 **I Will Never Pass This Way Again**..........*We All Pull The Load*	$6		Capitol 3411
12/9/72+	78	7		27 **One Last Time**..........*All My Tomorrows* written by **The Addrisi Brothers**	$6		Capitol 3483
3/17/73	45	12		28 **I Knew Jesus (Before He Was A Star)**..........*On This Road*	$5		Capitol 3548
2/9/74	68	6		29 **Houston (I'm Comin' To See You)**..........*Honestly Love*	$5		Capitol 3808
5/31/75	❶[2]	23	●	30 **Rhinestone Cowboy**..........CW[3] / AC[1] *Lovelight* #24 Adult Contemporary hit for Larry Weiss (song's writer) in 1974	$5		Capitol 4095
11/8/75+	11	14		31 **Country Boy (You Got Your Feet In L.A.)**..........AC[1] *Record Collector's Dream*	$5		Capitol 4155
3/27/76	27	10		32 **Don't Pull Your Love/Then You Can Tell Me Goodbye**..........AC[1] *I Miss You Tonight*	$5		Capitol 4245
2/12/77	❶[1]	21	●	33 **Southern Nights**..........CW[2] / AC[4] *William Tell Overture*	$5		Capitol 4376
7/9/77	39	11		34 **Sunflower**..........AC[1] *How High Did We Go* written by **Neil Diamond**	$5		Capitol 4445
10/21/78	38	11		35 **Can You Fool**..........*Let's All Sing A Song About It* originally released earlier in 1978 on Capitol 4584 with "Another Fine Mess" as the B-side (C&W #21)	$5		Capitol 4638
5/17/80	42	10		36 **Somethin' 'Bout You Baby I Like**..........*Late Night Confession* (Campbell) **GLEN CAMPBELL and RITA COOLIDGE**	$5		Capitol 4865
1/24/81	65	5		37 **I Don't Want To Know Your Name**..........*Daisy A Day*	$5		Capitol 4959
8/22/81	94	3		38 **I Love My Truck**..........*Melody's Melody* (David Shire) from the movie *The Night The Lights Went Out In Georgia* starring **Kristy McNichol**	$5		Mirage 3845

CAMPBELL, Jim — '70

Pop singer.

DEBUT	PEAK	WKS	Gold	A-side (Chart Hit)..........B-side	$	Sym	Label & Number
7/18/70	93	2		**The Lights Of Tucson**..........*Child Of Clay*	$7		Laurie 3546

DEBUT	PEAK	WKS	Gold	A-side (Chart Hit)	B-side	$	Sym	Label & Number

CAMPBELL, Jo Ann — '62

Born on 7/20/38 in Jacksonville, Florida. First recorded for El Dorado in 1957. In the movies *Johnny Melody*, *Go Johnny Go* and *Hey, Let's Twist*. Married Country singer Troy Seals (cousin of **Dan Seals**) in the early 1960s; recorded together as **Jo Ann & Troy** in 1964.

DEBUT	PEAK	WKS	Gold	A-side (Chart Hit)	B-side	$	Sym	Label & Number
8/15/60	61	9		1 **A Kookie Little Paradise**	*Bobby, Bobby, Bobby* [N]	$35		ABC-Paramount 10134
8/18/62	38	7		2 **(I'm The Girl On) Wolverton Mountain** answer song to **Claude King**'s "Wolverton Mountain"; some pressings titled as "I'm The Girl From Wolverton Mountain"	*Sloppy Joe*	$25		Cameo 223
4/27/63	88	3		3 **Mother, Please!**	*Waitin' For Love*	$25		Cameo 249
12/12/64+	67	6		4 **I Found A Love Oh What A Love** **JO ANN & TROY**	*Who Do You Love*	$15		Atlantic 2256

CAMPBELL, Naomi — see VANILLA ICE

★451★ CAMPBELL, Tevin — R&B/LP '94

Born on 11/12/76 in Waxahachie, Texas. R&B singer. Had first chart hit at the age of 13. Won role in 1988 for the TV show *Wally & The Valentines*. Discovered by **Quincy Jones**. Appeared in the movie *Graffiti Bridge*.

1)Tell Me What You Want Me To Do 2)Can We Talk 3)I'm Ready

DEBUT	PEAK	WKS	Gold	A-side (Chart Hit)	B-side	$	Sym	Label & Number
5/26/90	75	5		1 **Tomorrow (A Better You, Better Me)** RB^{1} **QUINCY JONES Featuring Tevin Campbell**	*(instrumental)*	$4	▮V	Qwest 19881
12/8/90+	12	29	●	2 **Round And Round** A:12 / S:13 written and produced by **Prince**; from the movie *Graffiti Bridge* starring **Prince**; "45": Paisley Park 19748	*(soul dub)*	$3	▮V	Paisley Park 21740
8/10/91	88	5		3 **Just Ask Me To** A:72 **Chubb Rock** (rap); from the movie *Boyz N The Hood* starring **Ice Cube**	*(hip hop mix)*	$3	▮	Qwest 19275
11/9/91+	6	25	●	4 **Tell Me What You Want Me To Do** RB^{1} A:6 / S:8	*(instrumental)*	$3	▮V	Qwest 19131
4/11/92	85	12		5 **Goodbye** S:55	*Just Ask Me To* (w/**Chubb Rock**)	$3	▮	Qwest 19008
6/6/92	53	9		6 **Strawberry Letter 23** A:46	*(single remix)*	$3	▮	Qwest 18919
10/17/92	72	11		7 **Alone With You** RB^{1} S:47 #2-7: from the album *T.E.V.I.N.*; #3, 5 & 7: produced by **Al B. Sure!**	*Just Ask Me To* (w/**Chubb Rock**)	$3	▮	Qwest 18874
10/16/93+	9	26	●	8 **Can We Talk** RB^{3} S:9 / A:9	*Look What We'd Have (If You Were Mine)*	$3	▮V	Qwest 18346
12/18/93+	45^{A}	14		9 **Shhh** written by **Prince**			V	album cut
3/12/94	9	22		10 **I'm Ready** A:8 / S:15 "45" issued for above 2 on Qwest 18264	*(instrumental)*	$3	▮V	Qwest 18264
6/25/94	20	20		11 **Always In My Heart** A:22 / S:24	*(album version)*	$3	▮V	Qwest 18260
12/31/94+	71	7		12 **Don't Say Goodbye Girl** above 5 from the album *I'm Ready* on Qwest 45388	*The Halls Of Desire*	$3	▮V	Qwest 18254
6/22/96	47	9		13 **Back To The World** S:41 / A:49	*(instrumental)*	$3	▮V	Qwest 17629
1/30/99	100	2		14 **Another Way** S:41	*(instrumental)*	$4	★	Qwest 17178

CAMP LO — R&B/BUB/LP '97

Hip-hop duo from the Bronx, New York: Salahadeen Wallace and Saladine Wilds.

DEBUT	PEAK	WKS	Gold	A-side (Chart Hit)	B-side	$	Sym	Label & Number
1/4/97	50	17		**Luchini aka (this is it)** S:29 samples "Adventures In The Land Of Music" by **Dynasty**	*Swing* (w/Ish)	$5	▮	Profile 5458

CAM'RON — R&B/LP '02

Born Cameron Giles on 2/4/76 in Harlem, New York. Male rapper. Also see **Diplomats**.

DEBUT	PEAK	WKS	Gold	A-side (Chart Hit)	B-side	$	Sym	Label & Number
7/18/98	41	17		1 **Horse & Carriage** A:46 **CAM'RON featuring Mase**	*(4 versions) / F**k You*	$6	T	Untertainment 78938
6/26/99	99	2		2 **Let Me Know** S:20 samples the Theme to *Monday Night Football* titled "Superstar" aka "Heavy Action" by Johnny Pearson	*(2 versions)*	$5	★	Untertainment 79170
10/14/00	83	10		3 **What Means The World To You** samples "Roxanne" by **The Police**	*(3 versions)/That's Me*	$6	T	Epic 79434
4/20/02	4	21		4 **Oh Boy** RB^{5} A:4 / S:17 **CAM'RON feat. Juelz Santana** samples "I'm Going Down" by **Rose Royce**	*(2 versions) / The Roc (Just Fire)*	$6	T	Roc-A-Fella 582864
6/29/02	35^{S}	6		5 **Welcome To New York City** **CAM'RON feat. Jay-Z and Juelz Santana**	*(3 versions)*	$6	T	Roc-A-Fella 582970
8/31/02	3	21		6 **Hey Ma** A:3 / S:21 **CAM'RON (feat. Juelz Santana, Freekey Zekey and Toya)**	*(instrumental) / Boy Boy*	$6	T	Roc-A-Fella 063958
12/14/02	57^{S}	2		7 **Boy (I Need You)** **MARIAH CAREY Feat. Cam'ron** samples "I'm Going Down" by **Rose Royce**	*Irresistible* (w/**West Side Connection**) / *You Got Me* (w/**Jay-Z** & **Freeway**)	$6	T	Monarc 063794

★520★ C & C MUSIC FACTORY — R&B/LP '91

Dance group led by producers/songwriters Robert **Clivilles** (percussion; born on 8/30/64) & David **Cole** (keyboards; born on 6/3/62). Featured vocalists include **Freedom Williams** and Deborah Cooper (Fatback, **Change**). **Martha Wash** (Two Tons O' Fun, **The Weather Girls**) is the actual vocalist of "Gonna Make You Sweat," lip-synched in video by Liberian-born Zelma Davis. Cole died of spinal meningitis on 1/24/95 (age 32). Also see **Taylor Dayne**'s "Can't Get Enough Of Your Love."

1)Gonna Make You Sweat (Everybody Dance Now) 2)Here We Go 3)Things That Make You Go Hmmmm...

DEBUT	PEAK	WKS	Gold	A-side (Chart Hit)	B-side	$	Sym	Label & Number
11/17/90+	❶^{2}	25	▲	1 **Gonna Make You Sweat (Everybody Dance Now)** RB^{1} / DC^{5} S:❶^{4} / A:3 **C & C MUSIC FACTORY Featuring Freedom Williams** (see bio note) "45": Columbia 73772	*(club mix)*	$3	▮V	Columbia 73604
3/2/91	3	20	●	2 **Here We Go** S:3 / A:5 **C + C MUSIC FACTORY Presents Freedom Williams and Zelma Davis**	*(radio mix)*	$3	▮V	Columbia 73690
7/20/91	4	16	●	3 **Things That Make You Go Hmmmm** A:10 / S:12 **C + C MUSIC FACTORY featuring Freedom Williams**	*(radio mix 2)*	$3	▮V	Columbia 73687
11/9/91	50	14		4 **Just A Touch Of Love** A:40 above 4 from the album *Gonna Make You Sweat*	*(hot radio mix)*	$3	▮	Columbia 74033
1/25/92	44	15		5 **A Deeper Love /** S:47 / A:55				
1/11/92	54	17		6 **Pride (In The Name Of Love)** A:48 / S:64 **CLIVILLES & COLE** (above 2) Paul Pesco and Deborah Cooper (vocals, above 2)		$3	▮	Columbia 74136

DEBUT	PEAK	WKS	Gold	A-side (Chart Hit)...B-side	$	Sym	Label & Number
				C & C MUSIC FACTORY — Cont'd			
8/15/92	**83**	6		7 **Keep It Comin' (Dance Till You Can't Dance No More!)** ....A:65 / S:67 *(pop radio mix)*	$3	▮	Columbia 74432
				C + C MUSIC FACTORY Featuring Q-Unique and Deborah Cooper			
				from the movie *Buffy The Vampire Slayer* starring Kristy Swanson			
6/5/93	**74**	4		8 **Voice Of Freedom** ....A:40 *(edited version)*	$3	▮	Columbia 77061
				FREEDOM WILLIAMS			
				samples **George Michael**'s "Freedom" (1990 version)			
7/30/94	**40**	20		9 **Do You Wanna Get Funky** ....S:21 / A:47 *(Mark the 45 King remix)*	$3	▮	Columbia 77582
				all of above (except #6 & 8): #1 Dance Club Play hits			
8/5/95	**70^{A}**	3		10 **Robi-Rob's Boriqua Anthem** ....BUB:102 *I Found Love* [F]	$3	▮	Columbia 78048
				CANDI '88			
				Dance group from Toronto, Ontario, Canada: Candy Pennella (vocals), Nino Milazzo (bass), Rich Imbrogno (keyboards) and Paul Russo (drums).			
10/22/88	**68**	7		**Dancing Under A Latin Moon** ....*Luna Latina Tu Y Yo*	$4	■	I.R.S. 53436
				CANDLEBOX ROK '94			
				Rock group from Seattle, Washington: Kevin Martin (vocals), Peter Klett (guitar), Bardi Martin (bass) and Scott Mercado (drums). The Martins are not related.			
3/19/94	**78**	18		1 **You** ....S:70 *Pull Away*	$4	▮V	Maverick/Sire 18304
8/27/94	**18**	23		2 **Far Behind** ....S:13 / A:23 *You (live)*	$4	▮	Maverick/Sire 18118
9/16/95	**60^{A}**	3		3 **Simple Lessons**			album cut
				from the album *Lucy* on Maverick/Sire 45962			
				CANDY AND THE KISSES '65			
				Black vocal trio from Port Richmond, New York: sisters Candy (lead) and Suzanne Nelson, with schoolmate Jeanette Johnson.			
11/21/64+	**51**	10		**The 81** ....*Two Happy People*	$20		Cameo 336
				CANDYMAN LP '90			
				Born on 6/25/68 in Los Angeles, California. Male rapper.			
9/1/90	**9**	23	▲	1 **Knockin' Boots** ....S:2 / A:28 *Keep On Watcha Doin'*	$3	▮V	Epic 73450
				samples **Rose Royce**'s "Ooh Boy" and **Betty Wright**'s "Tonight Is The Night"			
12/15/90+	**69**	11		2 **Melt In Your Mouth** ....*The Mack Is Back*	$3	▮V	Epic 73652
				rap to the melody of the **Spinners**' "Could It Be I'm Falling In Love"			
4/13/91	**91**	4		3 **Nightgown** ....*(album version)*	$3	▮	Epic 73721
				CANDYMEN, The LP '67			
				Former backing band for **Roy Orbison**: Rodney Justo (vocals), John Adkins (guitar), Dean Daughtry (piano), Billy Gilmore (bass) and Bob Nix (drums). Daughtry joined the **Classics IV**. Justo, Daughtry and Nix later joined the **Atlanta Rhythm Section**. Adkins died in June 1989 (age 47).			
11/18/67	**81**	5		**Georgia Pines** ....*Movies In My Mind*	$8		ABC 10995
				CANE, Gary, And His Friends '60			
				Cane was a 17-year-old from Brooklyn, New York, with 16 of his teenaged friends.			
6/6/60	**99**	1		**The Yen Yet Song** ....*I'll Walk The Earth* [N]	$20		Shell 719
				CANIBUS R&B/LP '98			
				Born Germaine Williams in New Jersey. Male rapper.			
12/27/97	**75**	12		1 **4, 3, 2, 1** ....*(5 versions)*	$6	T	Def Jam 568321
				LL COOL J Featuring Method Man, Redman, DMX, Canibus and Master P			
				samples "Fight For Your Right" by **Beastie Boys**, "Rock The Bells" by **LL Cool J** and "Shut 'Em Down" by **Public Enemy**			
4/11/98	**28**	15		2 **Second Round K.O.** ....S:18 *(2 versions) / How We Roll*	$3	▮	Universal 56175
				CANNED HEAT BUB/LP '68			
				Blues-rock group from Los Angeles, California: Bob "The Bear" Hite (vocals, harmonica), Al "Blind Owl" Wilson (guitar, harmonica, vocals), Henry Vestine (guitar), Larry Taylor (bass) and Frank Cook (drums). Cook replaced by Fito de la Parra in 1968. Vestine replaced by Harvey Mandel in 1969. Wilson died of a drug overdose on 9/3/70 (age 27). Hite died of a drug-related heart attack on 4/6/81 (age 36). Vestine died of heart failure on 10/20/97 (age 52).			
8/10/68	**16**	11		1 **On The Road Again** ....*Boogie Music*	$10		Liberty 56038
12/7/68+	**11**	11		2 **Going Up The Country** *One Kind Favor*	$10	■	Liberty 56077
12/21/68	**18^{X}**	2		3 **Christmas Blues** ....*The Chipmunk Song* (w/**The Chipmunks**) [X]	$75		Liberty 56079
				The Chipmunks (although credited on the label and on the charts) do not perform on this tune (see B-side)			
3/15/69	**67**	5		4 **Time Was** ....*Low Down*	$10		Liberty 56097
10/10/70	**26**	11		5 **Let's Work Together** ....*I'm Her Man*	$10		Liberty 56151
				originally released in 1962 by **Wilbert Harrison** as "Let's Stick Together"			
3/18/72	**88**	5		6 **Rockin' With The King** ....*I Don't Care What You Tell Me*	$7		United Artists 50892
				Little Richard (piano, vocal)			
				CANNIBAL AND THE HEADHUNTERS BUB/LP '65			
				Latino vocal group from Los Angeles, California: Frankie "Cannibal" Garcia, brothers Robert and Joe Jaramillo, and Richard Lopez. Garcia died on 1/21/96 (age 49). Joe Jaramillo died on 5/24/2000 (age 51).			
2/27/65	**30**	14		**Land Of 1000 Dances** ....*I'll Show You How To Love Me*	$20		Rampart 642
				"Bubbled Under" (#106) on 9/3/66 on Date 1525 ($20)			
				CANNON, Ace BUB/C&W/LP '62			
				Born on 5/4/34 in Grenada, Mississippi. White saxophonist/songwriter. Worked with **Bill Black's Combo**.			
12/25/61+	**17**	16		1 **Tuff** *"Sittin' Tight"* [I]	$15		Hi 2040
				first issued on **Bill Black**'s label, Louis 2001 in 1961 ($30)			
4/14/62	**36**	7		2 **Blues (Stay Away From Me)** ....*Blues In My Heart* [I]	$12		Hi 2051
				#11 hit for **Owen Bradley** in 1949			
4/14/62	**92**	1		3 **Sugar Blues** ....*38 Special* [I]	$15		Santo 503
				Clyde McCoy's famous theme song and #2 hit from 1931			
6/22/63	**67**	7		4 **Cottonfields** ....*Mildew* [I]	$12	■	Hi 2065
				traditional American ballad, copyrighted in 1850			
3/14/64	**84**	2		5 **Searchin'** ....*Love Letters In The Sand* [I]	$12		Hi 2074

DEBUT	PEAK	WKS	Gold	A-side (Chart Hit)...B-side	$	Sym	Label & Number
	★249★			**CANNON, Freddy** BUB/LP **'60**			
				Born Frederick Picariello on 12/4/39 in Lynn, Massachusetts. Local work with own band, Freddy Karmon & The Hurricanes. Nickname "Boom Boom" came from big bass drum-sound on his records. Band arrangements by **Frank Slay** on all Swan recordings. Also see **The G-Clefs**' "Ka-Ding Dong."			
				1)Palisades Park 2)Way Down Yonder In New Orleans 3)Tallahassee Lassie 4)Action 5)Abigail Beecher			
5/11/59	6	15		1 **Tallahassee Lassie** ...*You Know*	$20		Swan 4031
8/24/59	43	9		2 **Okefenokee**...*Kookie Hat*	$20		Swan 4038
11/23/59+	3	15	●	3 **Way Down Yonder In New Orleans**...*Fractured*	$20	■	Swan 4043
				#9 hit for the Peerless Quartet in 1922			
2/22/60	34	7		4 **Chattanooga Shoe Shine Boy**...*Boston "My Home Town"*	$15	■	Swan 4050
				#1 hit for Red Foley in 1950			
5/9/60	28	10		5 **Jump Over /**			
5/16/60	60	3		6 **The Urge**...	$15	■	Swan 4053
7/25/60	83	5		7 **Happy Shades Of Blue**...*(Kwa-Na-Va-Ka) Cuernavaca Choo Choo*	$15	■	Swan 4057
				FREDDIE CANNON (#2, 3 & 7)			
10/10/60	59	4		8 **Humdinger**...*My Blue Heaven*	$15	■	Swan 4061
1/9/61	54	6		9 **Muskrat Ramble**...*Two Thousand-88*	$15	■	Swan 4066
				#8 hit for **Louis Armstrong** in 1926			
5/1/61	51	8		10 **Buzz Buzz A-Diddle-It**...*Opportunity* (#114)	$15		Swan 4071
7/31/61	35	8		11 **Transistor Sister**...*Walk To The Moon*	$15	■	Swan 4078
10/16/61	71	6		12 **For Me And My Gal**...*Blue Plate Special*	$15		Swan 4083
				#1 hit for Van & Schenck in 1917			
1/6/62	68	5		13 **Twistin' All Night Long**...*Some Kind Of Nut* [N]	$20		Swan 4092
				DANNY AND THE JUNIORS with Freddy Cannon			
2/3/62	92	2		14 **Teen Queen Of The Week**...*Wild Guy*	$15		Swan 4096
5/12/62	3	15		15 **Palisades Park** *June, July, and August*	$15		Swan 4106
				written by Chuck Barris (host of TV's *The Gong Show*)			
9/8/62	45	4		16 **What's Gonna Happen When Summer's Done**...*Broadway*	$15		Swan 4117
11/10/62	67	5		17 **If You Were A Rock And Roll Record**...*The Truth, Ruth*	$15		Swan 4122
5/4/63	65	7		18 **Patty Baby**...*Betty Jean*	$15		Swan 4139
8/3/63	52	7		19 **Everybody Monkey**...*Oh Gloria*	$25		Swan 4149
2/1/64	16	8		20 **Abigail Beecher**...*All American Girl*	$12		Warner 5409
				all of above produced by **Frank Slay**			
8/14/65	13	9		21 **Action**...*Beachwood City*	$12		Warner 5645
				from Dick Clark's daily ABC-TV show *Where The Action Is*; #104 hit for Ricky Lyons in 1960 as "Shim Sham Shuffle"			
2/19/66	41	6		22 **The Dedication Song**...*Come On, Come On*	$12		Warner 5693
9/26/81	81	4		23 **Let's Put The Fun Back In Rock N Roll**...*Your Mama Ain't Always Right*	$7		MiaSound 1002
				FREDDY CANNON & THE BELMONTS			
				CANTINA BAND, The — see CHRISTIE, Lou / MECO			
				CANTRELL, Blu R&B/LP **'01**			
				Born Tiffany Cantrell in 1976 in Providence, Rhode Island. Female R&B singer.			
5/5/01	2^2	34		**Hit 'Em Up Style (Oops!)**...S:❶^1 / A:3 *(instrumental) / (5 album snippets)*	$4	★	Arista 13974
				CANTRELL, Lana AC/LP **'75**			
				Born on 8/7/43 in Sydney, Australia. Female singer/actress.			
2/22/75	63	5		**Like A Sunday Morning**...*Good Times*	$5		Polydor 14261
				CANYON **'75**			
				Pop vocal group: Richard Carmichael, Randy Davidson, Bill Frazier and Mark Lance.			
7/5/75	98	1		**Top Of The World (Make My Reservation)**...*Boogie Down Broadway*	$5		Magna-Glide 323
				CAPALDI, Jim ROK/BUB/AC/LP **'83**			
				Born on 8/24/44 in Evesham, Worcestershire, England. Rock singer/drummer. Member of **Traffic**.			
4/8/72	91	4		1 **Eve**...*Going Down Slow All The Way*	$6		Island 1204
1/18/75	55	7		2 **It's All Right**...*Whale Meat Again*	$5		Island 003
12/13/75	97	1		3 **Love Hurts**...*Sugar Honey*	$5		Island 045
				first released in 1960 on **The Everly Brothers**' album *A Date With The Everly Brothers*			
4/30/83	28	13		4 **That's Love** *Runaway*	$4	■	Atlantic 89849
8/27/83	75	5		5 **Living On The Edge**...*Gifts Of Unknown Things*	$4		Atlantic 89799
				CAPITOLS, The BUB/R&B/LP **'66**			
				R&B vocal trio from Detroit, Michigan: Sam George (vocals, drums), Donald Storball (guitar) and Richard McDougall (keyboards). George was murdered on 3/17/82 (age 39).			
4/30/66	7	14		1 **Cool Jerk**...*Hello Stranger*	$15		Karen 1524
8/27/66	74	4		2 **I Got To Handle It**...*Zig-Zagging*	$12		Karen 1525
11/12/66	65	6		3 **We Got A Thing That's In The Groove**...*Tired Running From You*	$12		Karen 1526
				CAPLETON R&B/BUB **'95**			
				Born Clifton Bailey on 4/13/67 in Islington, St. Mary, Jamaica. Male dancehall-reggae DJ/singer/songwriter.			
2/4/95	57	14		1 **Tour**...S:44 *(original yard mix)*	$5	▮	Signet 162
10/28/95	79	10		2 **Wings Of The Morning**...S:57 *(album version)*	$6	▮	African Star 577198
				CAPLETON (Featuring Method Man)			
				contains an interpolation of **Otis Redding**'s "Hard To Handle"			
				CAPONE — see TRAGEDY			
				CAPONIAC **'01**			
				Born in Los Angeles, California. Male rapper.			
4/14/01	46^S	6		**Da B.O.M.B.**...*(2 mixes)*	$10	★	Tomoboom 1108
				CAPPADONNA — see RZA			

DEBUT	PEAK	WKS	Gold	A-side (Chart Hit)...B-side	$	Sym	Label & Number

CAPRIS, The — '61

Italian-American doo-wop group from Queens, New York: Nick Santamaria (lead), Mike Mincieli (1st tenor), Frank Reina (2nd tenor), Vinny Naccarato (baritone) and John Apostol (bass). Disbanded in 1959, re-formed when song "There's A Moon Out Tonight" was reissued on Lost-Nite in 1960 and became a hit in 1961.

DEBUT	PEAK	WKS	Gold	A-side (Chart Hit)...B-side	$	Sym	Label & Number
12/31/60+	3	14		1 **There's A Moon Out Tonight**...*Indian Girl* originally released on Planet 1010 in 1959 ($1000) and on Lost-Nite 101 in 1960 ($75)	$30		Old Town 1094
3/27/61	74	4		2 **Where I Fell In Love**...*Some People Think*	$40		Old Town 1099
9/18/61	92	1		3 **Girl In My Dreams**...*My Island In The Sun*	$50		Old Town 1107
8/18/62	99	1		4 **Limbo**...*From The Vine Came The Grape*	$25		Mr. Peeke 118

CAPTAIN & TENNILLE — AC/BUB/LP '75

★245★

Pop duo: Daryl "The Captain" Dragon (born on 8/27/42 in Los Angeles, California) and his wife, Toni Tennille (born on 5/8/43 in Montgomery, Alabama). They married in 1974. Dragon is the son of noted conductor Carmen Dragon. Keyboardist with **The Beach Boys**, nicknamed "The Captain" by **Mike Love**. Duo had own TV show on ABC from 1976-77.

1)Love Will Keep Us Together 2)Do That To Me One More Time 3)Lonely Night (Angel Face)

DEBUT	PEAK	WKS	Gold	A-side (Chart Hit)...B-side	$	Sym	Label & Number
4/19/75	1^{4}	23	●	1 **Love Will Keep Us Together** AC^{1} *Gentle Stranger* first recorded by **Neil Sedaka** (on his 1974 album *Sedaka's Back*); 1975 Grammy winner: Record of the Year	$5	■	A&M 1672
8/16/75	49	6		2 **Por Amor Viviremos**...*Broddy Bounce* [F-R] Spanish version of "Love Will Keep Us Together"	$6		A&M 1715
9/27/75	4	17	●	3 **The Way I Want To Touch You**...AC^{2} *Broddy Bounce* first released on Butterscotch Castle 001 ($50), then on Joyce 101 ($40), then on A&M 1624, all in 1974; Spanish version released on A&M 1774 in 1975	$5	■	A&M 1725
1/24/76	3	19	●	4 **Lonely Night (Angel Face)**...AC^{1} *Smile For Me One More Time* first recorded by **Neil Sedaka** (on his 1975 album *The Hungry Years*)	$5	■	A&M 1782
5/1/76	4	16	●	5 **Shop Around**...AC^{1} *Butterscotch Castle* above 2 reissued with a 4-color picture sleeve on A&M 8600 in 1977	$5	■	A&M 1817
9/25/76	4	20	●	6 **Muskrat Love**...AC^{4} *Honey Come Love Me*	$5	■	A&M 1870
3/19/77	13	12		7 **Can't Stop Dancin'**...*Mis Canciones (The Good Songs)* written by **Ray Stevens**	$5	■	A&M 1912
6/11/77	61	7		8 **Come In From The Rain**...*We Never Really Say Goodbye* originally recorded by **Melissa Manchester** (on her 1976 album *Better Days & Happy Endings*)	$5	■	A&M 1944
4/22/78	74	6		9 **I'm On My Way**...*We Never Really Say Goodbye*	$5	■	A&M 2027
8/5/78	10	22		10 **You Never Done It Like That**..."*D" Keyboard Blues* first recorded by **Neil Sedaka** (on his 1977 album *A Song*); #1, 2, 4 & 10: written by **Neil Sedaka**	$5	■	A&M 2063
12/9/78+	40	10		11 **You Need A Woman Tonight**...*Love Me Like A Baby*	$5	■	A&M 2106
10/20/79+	1^{1}	27	●	12 **Do That To Me One More Time**...*Deep In The Dark*	$4		Casablanca 2215
3/8/80	55	7		13 **Love On A Shoestring**...*How Can You Be So Cold*	$4		Casablanca 2243
5/10/80	53	6		14 **Happy Together (A Fantasy)**...*Baby You Still Got It*	$4		Casablanca 2264

CAPTAIN HOLLYWOOD PROJECT — BUB '93

Captain Hollywood is dance producer Tony Harrison. Born on 8/9/62 in Newark, New Jersey; raised in Detroit, Michigan. While in the Army, was stationed in Nuremburg, Germany, where he began entertainment career as a choreographer.

DEBUT	PEAK	WKS	Gold	A-side (Chart Hit)...B-side	$	Sym	Label & Number
5/1/93	17	20		**More And More**...A:12 / S:21 *(Underground mix)* Nina (lead vocal)	$4	■V	Imago 25029

CARA, Irene — LP '83

★485★

Born Irene Escalera on 3/18/59 in the Bronx, New York. Dance singer/actress/pianist. Appeared in several movies and TV shows.

DEBUT	PEAK	WKS	Gold	A-side (Chart Hit)...B-side	$	Sym	Label & Number
6/14/80	4	26		1 **Fame**...*Never Alone* (Contemporary Gospel Chorus)	$4		RSO 1034
8/16/80	19	23		2 **Out Here On My Own**...*(piano and vocal version)* co-written by **Lesley Gore**; above 2 from the movie *Fame* starring Cara	$4		RSO 1048
11/28/81+	42	18		3 **Anyone Can See**...*Why*	$4		Network 47950
4/2/83	1^{6}	25	●	4 **Flashdance...What A Feeling** *Love Theme From "Flashdance"* (Helen St. John) from the movie *Flashdance* starring Jennifer Beals	$3		Casablanca 811440
10/22/83	13	15		5 **Why Me?**...*Talk Too Much*	$3	■	Geffen 29464
12/10/83+	37	14		6 **The Dream (Hold On To Your Dream)**...*Receiving* from the movie *D.C. Cab* starring Cara and Mr. T.	$3		Geffen 29396
3/24/84	8	19		7 **Breakdance**...*Cue Me Up*	$3		Geffen 29328
7/28/84	78	5		8 **You Were Made For Me**...*Receiving* above 5 from the album *What A Feelin'*	$3		Geffen 29257

CARAVELLES, The — LP '63

Female pop vocal duo from England: Andrea Simpson (born on 9/12/45) and Lois Wilkinson (born on 4/3/44).

DEBUT	PEAK	WKS	Gold	A-side (Chart Hit)...B-side	$	Sym	Label & Number
11/2/63	3	13		1 **You Don't Have To Be A Baby To Cry**...*The Last One To Know* #10 Country hit for Ernest Tubb in 1950	$12		Smash 1852
2/8/64	94	4		2 **Have You Ever Been Lonely (Have You Ever Been Blue)**...*Don't Blow Your Cool* #8 hit for Ted Lewis in 1933	$12		Smash 1869

CARDENAS, Luis — '86

Born in Los Angeles, California. Rock singer/drummer.

DEBUT	PEAK	WKS	Gold	A-side (Chart Hit)...B-side	$	Sym	Label & Number
9/20/86	83	5		**Runaway**...*Still Waiting*	$5	■	Allied Artists 72500

CARDIGANS, The — ROK/LP '97

Pop-rock group from Malmo, Sweden: Nina Persson (vocals), Peter Svensson (guitar), Lars-Olof Johansson (keyboards), Magnus Sveningsson (bass) and Bengt Lagersburg (drums).

DEBUT	PEAK	WKS	Gold	A-side (Chart Hit)...B-side	$	Sym	Label & Number
12/7/96+	2^{8A}	49		**Lovefool**... from the album *First Band On The Moon* on Stockholm/Mercury 533117			album cut

CAREFREES, The — '64

Female vocal trio from England: Lyn Cornell, Betty Prescott and Barbara Kay.

DEBUT	PEAK	WKS	Gold	A-side (Chart Hit)...B-side	$	Sym	Label & Number
3/21/64	39	5		**We Love You Beatles**...*Hot Blooded Lover* [N] new lyrics to "We Love You Conrad" from the musical *Bye Bye Birdie* starring Chita Rivera	$25	■	London Int'l. 10614

CARREY, Mariah ★14★

R&B/BUB/AC/LP **'95**

Born on 3/27/70 in Greenlawn, Long Island, New York. Her mother is Patricia Carey, former singer with the New York City Opera. Mariah sang backup for **Brenda K. Starr**. Won the 1990 Best New Artist Grammy Award. Married Tommy Mottola, president of Sony Music Entertainment, on 6/5/93; divorced on 3/4/98. Starred in the 2001 movie *Glitter*. Also see **Babyface**'s "Every Time I Close My Eyes."

1)One Sweet Day 2)Fantasy 3)Dreamlover 4)Hero 5)Vision Of Love

DEBUT	PEAK	WKS	Gold	A-side (Chart Hit)..........B-side	$	Sym	Label & Number
6/2/90	❶[4]	22	●	1 **Vision Of Love** ....RB[2] / AC[3] A:❶[3] / S:❶[2] *(3 album snippets)*	$3	▮[V]	Columbia 73348
9/15/90	❶[3]	26	●	2 **Love Takes Time**..........RB[1] / AC[1] S:❶[2] / A:❶[2] *Sent From Up Above*	$3	▮[V]	Columbia 73455
1/19/91	❶[2]	19	●	3 **Someday**..........A:❶[4] / S:2 *Alone In Love*	$3	▮[V]	Columbia 73561
4/6/91	❶[2]	19		4 **I Don't Wanna Cry**..........AC[1] A:❶[2] / S:3 *You Need Me* above 4 from the album *Mariah Carey*	$3	▮[V]	Columbia 73743
8/31/91	❶[3]	20	●	5 **Emotions**..........RB[1] A:❶[4] / S:10 *Vanishing*	$3	▮[V]	Columbia 73977
11/16/91+	2[1]	20		6 **Can't Let Go**..........AC[3] A:2 / S:8 *To Be Around You*	$3	▮[V]	Columbia 74088
2/22/92	5	20		7 **Make It Happen**..........A:2 / S:18 *Emotions (special edit)*	$3	▮[V]	Columbia 74239
5/30/92	❶[2]	20		8 **I'll Be There**..........AC[2] A:❶[8] / S:3 *So Blessed* [L] **Trey Lorenz** (male vocal: #5, 7 & 8); recorded on MTV's *Unplugged EP*; also see #35 below	$3	▮[V]	Columbia 74330
8/7/93	❶[8]	29	▲	9 **Dreamlover**..........A:❶[11] / S:2 *Do You Think Of Me* samples "Blind Alley" (from **The Emotions**' album *Untouched*)	$3	▮[V]	Columbia 77080
10/23/93	❶[4]	30	▲	10 **Hero**..........A:❶[10] / S:2 *Everything Fades Away* also see #33 below	$3	▮[V]	Columbia 77224
1/29/94	3	23	●	11 **Without You** / A:2 / S:3			
2/12/94		21		12 **Never Forget You**.......... **Babyface** (co-writer and backing vocal)	$3	▮[V]	Columbia 77358
5/28/94	12	21		13 **Anytime You Need A Friend**..........A:8 / S:19 *Music Box* above 5 from the album *Music Box*	$3	▮[V]	Columbia 77499
9/10/94	2[1]	20	●	14 **Endless Love**..........S:2 / A:5 *(instrumental)* **LUTHER VANDROSS & MARIAH CAREY**	$3	▮[V]	Columbia 77629
12/24/94	12[A]	3		15 **All I Want For Christmas Is You**.......... [X] from the album *Merry Christmas* on Columbia 64222 (also see #18, 21 & 30 - same versions)			album cut
9/30/95	❶[8]	25	▲[2]	16 **Fantasy**..........RB[6] A:❶[7] / S:❶[5] *(remix w/**Ol Dirty Bastard**)* samples "Genius Of Love" by **Tom Tom Club**	$3	▮[V]	Columbia 78043
12/2/95	❶[16]	27	▲[2]	17 **One Sweet Day** AC[13] A:❶[13] / S:❶[11] *(live version)* **MARIAH CAREY & BOYZ II MEN** "45": Columbia 78072; B-side: "I Am Free"; also see #34 below	$3	▮[V]	Columbia 78074
12/30/95	35[A]	2		18 **All I Want For Christmas Is You**.......... [X-R]			album cut
4/6/96	❶[2]	32	▲	19 **Always Be My Baby**..........RB[1] S:❶[1] / A:2 *(remix w/**Da Brat** & **Xscape**) / Slipping Away* "45" B-side: "Long Ago"	$3	▮[V]	Columbia 78276 ■
6/29/96	9[A]	20		20 **Forever**.......... #16, 17, 19 & 20: from the album *Daydream* on Columbia 66700			album cut
1/4/97-	35[A]	1		21 **All I Want For Christmas Is You**.......... [X-R]			album cut
9/13/97	❶[3]	20	▲	22 **Honey**..........S:❶[3] / A:11 *(remix w/**Mase** & **The Lox**)* samples "The Body Rock" by Treacherous 3 and "Hey D.J." by **Lighter Shade Of Brown**	$3	▮[V]	Columbia 78648 ■
10/4/97	16[A]	14		23 **Butterfly**..........			album cut
5/9/98	❶[1]	20	▲	24 **My All** / S:❶[2] / A:15		V	
3/7/98	53[A]	3		25 **Breakdown**.......... **MARIAH CAREY (Featuring Krayzie Bone & Wish Bone)** above 4 from the album *Butterfly* on Columbia 67835	$3	▮[V]	Columbia 78821 ■
12/5/98+	15	17	●	26 **When You Believe**..........S:7 / A:38 *(instrumental)* **WHITNEY HOUSTON and MARIAH CAREY** from the animated movie *The Prince Of Egypt*	$4	★	DreamWorks 59022
2/6/99	4	20	▲	27 **I Still Believe**..........S:3 / A:20 *I Still Believe/Pure Imagination* (w/**Krayzie Bone** & **Da Brat**) B-side is a special mix on both the "45" and CD single that hit #3 on the R&B charts	$4	★[V]	Columbia 79093 ■
9/4/99	❶[2]	20	●	28 **Heartbreaker**..........RB[2] S:❶[2] / A:8 *(remix w/**Da Brat** & **Missy Elliott**)* **MARIAH CAREY (Featuring Jay-Z)** samples "Attack Of The Name Game" by **Stacy Lattisaw**	$4	★[V]	Columbia 79260
12/11/99+	❶[1]	20	●	29 **Thank God I Found You**..........RB[1] S:❶[3] / A:15 *(remix)* **MARIAH With Joe & 98°** remix versions with **Nas** and **Joe** issued on Columbia 79339	$4	★[V]	Columbia 79338
1/8/00-	83	1		30 **All I Want For Christmas Is You**..........A:62 [X-R]			album cut
6/24/00	28	7		31 **Crybaby**..........S:2 *Can't Take That Away / Love Hangover/Heartbreaker* **MARIAH CAREY Featuring Snoop Dogg** samples "Piece Of My Love" by **Guy**; "45" B-side: "Can't Take That Away (Mariah's Theme)"	$4	★[V]	Columbia 79348
6/23/01	2[2]	14	●	32 **Loverboy**..........RB[2] S:❶[4] / A:50 *(remix w/**Da Brat** & **Ludacris** [R&B #1])* samples "Candy" by **Cameo**; from the movie *Glitter* starring Carey	$4	★	Virgin 38791
12/29/01	81	3		33 **Never Too Far/Hero Medley**..........S:3 *There For Me* see #10 above for the original version of "Hero"; "Never Too Far" (from the movie *Glitter*) "Bubbled Under" in 2001 (#105)	$4	★	Virgin 38813
3/23/02	35[S]	18		34 **One Sweet Day**..........*(live version)* [R] **MARIAH CAREY & BOYZ II MEN** reissue of #17 above on Columbia's "Platinum Hits" series	$4	★	Columbia 79699
3/23/02	54[S]	3		35 **I'll Be There**..........*So Blessed* [L-R] **MARIAH CAREY Featuring Trey Lorenz** reissue of #8 above on Columbia's "Platinum Hits" series; all of above written by Carey (except #8, 11, 14, 26, 27 & 35)	$4	★	Columbia 79698
12/14/02	57[S]	2		36 **Boy (I Need You)**..........*Irresistible* (w/**West Side Connection**) / *You Got Me* (w/**Jay-Z** & **Freeway**) **MARIAH CAREY Feat. Cam'ron** samples "I'm Going Down" by **Rose Royce**	$6	T	Monarc 063794
12/28/02+	81	9		37 **Through The Rain**..........S:❶[2] *(radio edit) / Bringin' On The Heartbreak* "45": Monarc 063904; B-side: (same version)	$4	★[V]	Monarc 063904

DEBUT	PEAK	WKS	Gold	A-side (Chart Hit)...B-side	$	Sym	Label & Number

CARLISLE — CARMEN

CAREY, Tony — LP '84

Born on 10/16/52 in Watsonville, California. Later settled in West Germany. Ex-keyboardist with **Rainbow** and lead singer of **Planet P**.

DEBUT	PEAK	WKS	Gold	A-side (Chart Hit)	B-side	$	Sym	Label & Number
3/26/83	79	7		1 **I Won't Be Home Tonight**	*Sing Along*	$5		Rocshire 95030
7/2/83	64	9		2 **West Coast Summer Nights**	*Sing Along*	$5	■	Rocshire 95037
				above 2 first released on Rocshire 001A and 001C, respectively, in 1982				
3/3/84	22	15		3 **A Fine Fine Day** ...AR^1	*Say It's All Over*	$4	■	MCA 52343
6/9/84	33	11		4 **The First Day Of Summer**	*One More Goodbye*	$4		MCA 52388

CARGILL, Henson — C&W/LP '68

Born on 2/5/41 in Oklahoma City, Oklahoma. Country singer.

DEBUT	PEAK	WKS	Gold	A-side (Chart Hit)	B-side	$	Sym	Label & Number
12/23/67+	25	12		**Skip A Rope** ...CW^5	*A Very Well Traveled Man*	$8		Monument 1041

CARLISLE, Belinda — LP '88

★502★

Born on 8/17/58 in Hollywood, California. Lead singer of the **Go-Go's**, 1978-84. Married to Morgan Mason, son of the late actor James Mason.

DEBUT	PEAK	WKS	Gold	A-side (Chart Hit)	B-side	$	Sym	Label & Number
5/17/86	3	21		1 **Mad About You** ...S:2 / A:4	*I Never Wanted A Rich Man*	$4	■	I.R.S. 52815
				Andy Taylor (of **Duran Duran**; guitar solo)				
9/20/86	82	5		2 **I Feel The Magic**	*From The Heart*	$4	■	I.R.S. 52889
9/26/87	❶^1	21		3 **Heaven Is A Place On Earth** S:❶^2 / A:❶^1	*We Can Change*	$3	■	MCA 53181
1/16/88	2^1	16		4 **I Get Weak** ...S:❶^1 / A:3	*Should I Let You In?*	$3	■	MCA 53242
4/16/88	7	17		5 **Circle In The Sand** ...S:6 / A:9	*We Can Change*	$3	■	MCA 53308
7/30/88	88	4		6 **I Feel Free**	*Should I Let You In?*	$4	■	MCA 53377
				"Bubbled Under" (#116) for **Cream** in 1967; above 4 from the album *Heaven On Earth*				
9/30/89	11	18		7 **Leave A Light On** ...S:11 / A:13	*Shades Of Michaelangelo*	$6		MCA 53706
				George Harrison (slide guitar solo)				
1/20/90	30	13		8 **Summer Rain** ...S:23 / A:35	*Shades Of Michaelangelo*	$3	▮^{V}	MCA 53783
10/26/91	73	6		9 **Do You Feel Like I Feel?**	*World Of Love*	$3	▮	MCA 54183

CARLISLE, Bob — LP '97

Born on 9/29/56 in Santa Ana, California. Singer/songwriter/guitarist. Recorded Christian music on the Sparrow label since 1993.

DEBUT	PEAK	WKS	Gold	A-side (Chart Hit)	B-side	$	Sym	Label & Number
5/10/97	10^A	15		**Butterfly Kisses** ...AC^7 S:65	*(instrumental) / You Must Have Been An Angel*	$20	★^{V}	Diadem 1221
				"Limited Edition Collector's CD Gift Box" single available only in Christian bookstores (therefore ineligible for the main *Hot 100* chart; "45": Diadem/Jive 42456; B-side: (Country remix)				

CARLISLE, Steve — '81

Pop background and radio jingle singer. Appeared in several movies.

DEBUT	PEAK	WKS	Gold	A-side (Chart Hit)	B-side	$	Sym	Label & Number
11/21/81	65	10		**WKRP In Cincinnati**	*You Told A Lie*	$5		MCA 51205
				produced by **Buckner & Garcia**; main theme from the TV series starring Gary Sandy and Loni Anderson				

CARLTON, Carl — R&B/BUB/LP '74

Born on 10/22/52 in Detroit, Michigan. R&B singer/songwriter.

DEBUT	PEAK	WKS	Gold	A-side (Chart Hit)	B-side	$	Sym	Label & Number
6/29/68	75	8		1 **Competition Ain't Nothin'**	*Three Way Love*	$8		Back Beat 588
7/11/70	78	6		2 **Drop By My Place**	*Two Timer*	$8		Back Beat 613
				LITTLE CARL CARLTON (above 2)				
9/21/74	6	15		3 **Everlasting Love**	*I Wanna Be Your Main Squeeze*	$6		Back Beat 27001
2/15/75	91	4		4 **Smokin' Room**	*Signed, Sealed, Delivered I'm Yours*	$5		ABC 12059
8/22/81	22	21	●	5 **She's A Bad Mama Jama (She's Built, She's Stacked)**	*This Feeling's Rated X-tra*	$4		20th Century 2488

CARLTON, Larry — AC/LP '81

Born on 3/2/48 in Torrance, California. Top session guitarist. Frequent guest guitarist of **The Crusaders**, 1972-77. Fully recovered from a near-fatal gunshot wound suffered in a robbery attack in 1988. Married to Contemporary Christian artist Michelle Pillar.

DEBUT	PEAK	WKS	Gold	A-side (Chart Hit)	B-side	$	Sym	Label & Number
8/22/81	10	22		1 **The Theme From Hill Street Blues**	*Aaron's Tune* [I]	$4	■	Elektra 47186
				MIKE POST featuring Larry Carlton				
				theme from the TV series starring Daniel J. Travanti				
2/27/82	74	8		2 **Sleepwalk**	*Frenchman's Flat* [I]	$4		Warner 50019

CARLTON, Vanessa — LP '02

Born on 8/16/80 in Milford, Pennsylvania. Adult Contemporary singer/songwriter/pianist.

DEBUT	PEAK	WKS	Gold	A-side (Chart Hit)	B-side	$	Sym	Label & Number
3/2/02	5	41		1 **A Thousand Miles** ...AC^7 S:2 / A:5	*Twilight*	$4	★	A&M 497676
8/24/02	30	18		2 **Ordinary Day** ...A:38	*Parade*	$4	★	A&M 497761

CARMEN, Eric — C&W/LP '76

★405★

Born on 8/11/49 in Cleveland, Ohio. Classical training at Cleveland Institute of Music from early years to mid-teens. Lead singer of the **Raspberries** from 1970-74. Wrote "That's Rock 'N' Roll" and "Hey Deanie" for **Shaun Cassidy**.

1)All By Myself 2)Make Me Lose Control 3)Hungry Eyes

DEBUT	PEAK	WKS	Gold	A-side (Chart Hit)	B-side	$	Sym	Label & Number
12/20/75+	2^3	19	●	1 **All By Myself**	*Everything*	$5		Arista 0165
				interlude based on Rachmaninov's "Piano Concerto No.2"				
5/1/76	11	15		2 **Never Gonna Fall In Love Again** ...AC^1	*No Hard Feelings*	$5		Arista 0184
				melody based on Rachmaninov's *Second Symphony*				
8/14/76	34	10		3 **Sunrise**	*My Girl*	$5		Arista 0200
8/27/77	23	16		4 **She Did It**	*Someday*	$5	■	Arista 0266
12/24/77+	88	3		5 **Boats Against The Current**	*Take It Or Leave It*	$5	□	Arista 0295
9/16/78	19	16		6 **Change Of Heart**	*Hey Deanie*	$5		Arista 0354
1/27/79	62	5		7 **Baby, I Need Your Lovin'**	*Heaven Can Wait*	$5		Arista 0384
7/12/80	75	2		8 **It Hurts Too Much**	*You Need Some Lovin'*	$5		Arista 0506
1/19/85	35	11		9 **I Wanna Hear It From Your Lips**	*Spotlight*	$3	■	Geffen 29118
4/20/85	87	3		10 **I'm Through With Love**	*Maybe My Baby*	$3	■	Geffen 29032
11/7/87+	4	25		11 **Hungry Eyes** ...S:4 / A:4	*Where Are You Tonight* (Tom Johnston)	$3		RCA 5315
				from the movie *Dirty Dancing* starring **Patrick Swayze**				

DEBUT	PEAK	WKS	Gold	A-side (Chart Hit)...B-side	$	Sym	Label & Number
				CARMEN, Eric — Cont'd			
5/21/88	3	20		12 Make Me Lose Control ...AC³ S:❶¹ / A:4 *That's Rock 'N Roll*	$3	■	Arista 9686
10/8/88	87	3		13 Reason To Try ...*Sunrise*	$3	■	Arista 9746
				tune used by NBC-TV for the 1988 Summer Olympics; all of above written by Carmen (except #7, 11 & 13)			
	★218★			**CARNES, Kim** ROK/C&W/AC/LP '81			
				Born on 7/20/45 in Los Angeles, California. Female vocalist/pianist/composer. Member of **The New Christy Minstrels** with husband/co-writer Dave Ellingson and **Kenny Rogers**, late 1960s. Wrote and performed vocals for the **Sugar Bears**. Wrote for and performed in commercials. Co-wrote "Love Comes From Unexpected Places," which won the American Song Festival in 1977 and was later recorded by **Barbra Streisand**.			
				1)Bette Davis Eyes 2)Don't Fall In Love With A Dreamer 3)More Love			
6/17/78	36	12		1 You're A Part Of Me ...*Shine On (You Got To Shine On Your Light)* (Cotton)	$5		Ariola America 7704
				GENE COTTON with Kim Carnes			
				Carnes's solo version made the Adult Contemporary charts in 1976 on A&M 1767 (#32)			
2/24/79	56	5		2 It Hurts So Bad ...*Lookin' For A Big Night*	$5		EMI America 8011
3/29/80	4	19		3 Don't Fall In Love With A Dreamer ...*Goin' Home To The Rock/Gideon Tanner* (Rogers)	$5	■	United Artists 1345
				KENNY ROGERS with Kim Carnes			
5/31/80	10	19		4 More Love...*Changin'*	$5	■	EMI America 8045
10/4/80	44	8		5 Cry Like A Baby...*In The Chill Of The Night*	$5		EMI America 8058
3/28/81	❶⁹	26	●	6 Bette Davis Eyes *Miss You Tonite*	$4	■	EMI America 8077
				written by **Jackie DeShannon** and Donna Weiss; 1981 Grammy winner: Record of the Year			
8/8/81	28	12		7 Draw Of The Cards...*Break The Rules Tonite (Out Of School)* (ROK #46)	$4	■	EMI America 8087
10/24/81	60	6		8 Mistaken Identity ...*Jamaica Sunday Morning*	$4	■	EMI America 8098
8/21/82	29	12		9 Voyeur ...*Thrill Of The Grill*	$4	■	EMI America 8127
11/6/82+	36	13		10 Does It Make You Remember ...*Take It On The Chin*	$4	■	EMI America 8147
10/15/83	40	13		11 Invisible Hands...*I'll Be Here Where The Heart Is*	$4	■	EMI America 8181
1/21/84	54	8		12 You Make My Heart Beat Faster (And That's All That Matters) ...*Hangin' On By A Thread (A Sad Affair Of The Heart)*	$4	■	EMI America 8191
5/19/84	74	5		13 I Pretend ...*Hurricane*	$4	■	EMI America 8202
9/15/84	15	19		14 What About Me? ...AC² A:14 / S:16 *The Rest Of Last Night* (Rogers)	$3	■	RCA 13899
				KENNY ROGERS with KIM CARNES and JAMES INGRAM			
12/15/84+	51	10		15 Make No Mistake, He's Mine ...*Clear Sailing* (Streisand)	$3	■	Columbia 04695
				BARBRA STREISAND (WITH KIM CARNES)			
1/19/85	68	6		16 Invitation To Dance ...*Breakthrough* (Haven)	$3	■	EMI America 8250
				from the anthology movie *That's Dancing!*			
5/11/85	15	16		17 Crazy In The Night (Barking At Airplanes) ...S:14 / A:20 *Oliver (Voice On The Radio)*	$3	■	EMI America 8267
8/3/85	67	4		18 Abadabadango ...*He Makes The Sun Rise (Orpheus)*	$3	■	EMI America 8281
5/24/86	79	5		19 Divided Hearts ...*You Say You Love Me (But I Know You Don't)*	$3	■	EMI America 8322
				CAROSONE, Renato '58			
				Born on 1/2/20 in Naples, Italy. Died on 5/20/2001 (age 81). Male singer.			
5/5/58	18	13		Torero...A:18 / T:19 / S:20 *Chello Lla (That One There)* [F]	$12		Capitol 71080
				CARPENTER, Mary Chapin C&W/AC/LP '93			
				Born on 2/21/58 in Princeton, New Jersey. Country singer/guitarist. Moved to Washington DC in 1974. Graduated from Brown University with an American Civilization degree. Charted 27 Country hits, 1989-01.			
2/13/93	57	11		1 Passionate Kisses ...A:53 / S:72 *Middle Ground*	$4	▌V	Columbia 74795
10/29/94	90	6		2 Shut Up And Kiss Me ...CW¹ S:50 *End Of My Pirate Days*	$4	▌V	Columbia 77696
7/17/99	85	7		3 Almost Home...*Dancing In The Dark (live)*	$4	★	Columbia 79148
				CARPENTER, Thelma '61			
				Born on 1/15/20 in Brooklyn, New York. Died on 5/15/97 (age 77). Black singer with Teddy Wilson, Coleman Hawkins and **Count Basie** bands. On Eddie Cantor's radio show, 1945-46. Starred in Broadway's *Hello, Dolly!* In the movies *The Wiz* and *The Cotton Club*.			
12/31/60+	55	6		Yes, I'm Lonesome Tonight...*Gimme A Little Kiss (Will Ya, Huh?)*	$12		Coral 62241
				Henry Jerome (orch.); answer song to **Elvis Presley**'s "Are You Lonesome To-night?"			
				CARPENTERS ★60★ AC/BUB/LP '70			
				Brother-sister duo originally from New Haven, Connecticut: Richard (born on 10/15/46) and Karen Carpenter (born on 3/2/50; died of heart failure due to anorexia nervosa on 2/4/83, age 32). To Downey, California, in 1963. Richard played piano from age nine. Karen played drums in group with Richard and bass player Wes Jacobs in 1965. The trio recorded for RCA in 1966. After a period with the band Spectrum, the Carpenters recorded as a duo for A&M in 1969. Won the 1970 Best New Artist Grammy Award. Hosts of the TV variety show *Make Your Own Kind Of Music* in 1971. 1988 TV movie *The Karen Carpenter Story* was based on Karen's life.			
				1)(They Long To Be) Close To You 2)Top Of The World 3)Please Mr. Postman 4)We've Only Just Begun 5)Superstar			
2/14/70	54	12		1 Ticket To Ride ...*Your Wonderful Parade*	$8		A&M 1142
6/20/70	❶⁴	17	●	2 (They Long To Be) Close To You AC⁶ *I Kept On Loving You*	$6		A&M 1183
				first released as the B-side of **Richard Chamberlain**'s 1963 hit "Blue Guitar"			
9/12/70	2⁴	17	●	3 We've Only Just Begun ...AC⁷ *All Of My Life*	$6	■	A&M 1217
				adapted from a commercial jingle for Crocker Bank of California			
12/19/70	❶³ˣ	12		4 Merry Christmas Darling ...*Mr. Guder* [X]	$6	■	A&M 1236
				X: 1/'70; 1/'71; 4/'72; 1/'73; 5/'83; reissued in 1974 on A&M 1648 (B-side: "Santa Claus Is Coming To Town") and in 1977 on A&M 1991 (B-side: "Christmas Song") (both with different picture sleeves)			
2/6/71	3	13	●	5 For All We Know ...AC³ *Don't Be Afraid*	$6	■	A&M 1243
				from the movie *Lovers And Other Strangers* starring Bea Arthur; issued with a textured background picture sleeve and with a plain background sleeve			
5/15/71	2²	12	●	6 Rainy Days And Mondays ...AC⁴ *Saturday*	$6	■	A&M 1260
9/4/71	2²	13	●	7 Superstar / AC²			
				written by **Leon Russell** and Bonnie Bramlett (of **Delaney & Bonnie**)			
11/20/71+	67	10		8 Bless The Beasts And Children ...	$6	■	A&M 1289
				title song from the movie starring Billy Mumy; there are 2 picture sleeve variations			

DEBUT	PEAK	WKS	Gold	A-side (Chart Hit)	B-side	$	Sym	Label & Number
				CARPENTERS — Cont'd				
1/15/72	2[2]	12	●	9 **Hurting Each Other** AC[2]	*Maybe It's You*	$6	■	A&M 1322
				first recorded by **Jimmy Clanton** in 1965 on Mala 500				
4/29/72	12	10		10 **It's Going To Take Some Time**	*Flat Baroque*	$6	■	A&M 1351
				written by **Carole King** (on her 1971 album *Music*)				
7/15/72	7	10		11 **Goodbye To Love**	*Crystal Lullaby*	$6	■	A&M 1367
				all of above produced by Jack Daugherty				
2/24/73	3	14	●	12 **Sing** AC[2]	*Druscilla Penny*	$6	■	A&M 1413
				featured on the *Sesame Street* TV show				
6/2/73	2[1]	14	●	13 **Yesterday Once More** AC[3]	*Road Ode*	$6	■	A&M 1446
10/6/73	❶[2]	20	●	14 **Top Of The World**	*Heather*	$5	■	A&M 1468
4/13/74	11	12		15 **I Won't Last A Day Without You** AC[1]	*One Love*	$5	■	A&M 1521
				written by **Paul Williams** (his version "Bubbled Under" (#106) in 1973); #8-11, 14 & 15: from the album *A Song For You*				
11/23/74+	❶[1]	17	●	16 **Please Mr. Postman** AC[1]	*This Masquerade*	$5	■	A&M 1646
3/29/75	4	13		17 **Only Yesterday** AC[1]	*Happy*	$5	■	A&M 1677
8/2/75	17	10		18 **Solitaire** AC[1]	*Love Me For What I Am*	$5	■	A&M 1721
				written by **Neil Sedaka** (on his 1974 album *Sedaka's Back*)				
2/28/76	12	13		19 **There's A Kind Of Hush (All Over The World)** AC[2]	*(I'm Caught Between) Goodbye And I Love You*	$5	■	A&M 1800
6/12/76	25	11		20 **I Need To Be In Love** AC[1]	*Sandy*	$5		A&M 1828
9/4/76	56	5		21 **Goofus**	*Boat To Sail*	$5		A&M 1859
				there were 4 Top 20 versions of this tune in 1932				
5/21/77	35	10		22 **All You Get From Love Is A Love Song**	*I Have You*	$5	■	A&M 1940
10/8/77	32	14		23 **Calling Occupants Of Interplanetary Craft**	*Can't Smile Without You*	$5	■	A&M 1978
				(The Recognized Anthem of World Contact Day)				
2/4/78	44	13		24 **Sweet, Sweet Smile**	*I Have You*	$5	■	A&M 2008
				written by **Juice Newton**				
12/9/78	68	5		25 **I Believe You**	*B'wanna She No Home*	$5		A&M 2097
				written by **The Addrisi Brothers**				
6/20/81	16	14		26 **Touch Me When We're Dancing** AC[2]	*Because We Are In Love (The Wedding Song)*	$4	■	A&M 2344
9/12/81	72	8		27 **(Want You) Back In My Life Again**	*Somebody's Been Lyin'*	$4		A&M 2370
12/19/81+	63	6		28 **Those Good Old Dreams**	*When It's Gone (It's Just Gone)*	$4		A&M 2386
4/24/82	74	4		29 **Beechwood 4-5789**	*Two Sides*	$4		A&M 2405
				above 5 from the album *Made In America*; #12-29: produced by Richard Carpenter				
				CARR, Cathy	BUB **'56**			
				Born Angela Helen Catherine Cordovano on 6/28/36 in the Bronx, New York. Died in November 1988 (age 52).				
3/24/56	2[1]	24		1 **Ivory Tower** J:2 / T:6 / S:7 / A:9	*Please, Please Believe Me*	$20		Fraternity 734
7/28/56	67	4		2 **Heart Hideaway** T:67	*The Boy On Page Thirty-Five*	$20		Fraternity 743
				Dan Belloc (orch., above 2)				
1/26/59	42	12		3 **First Anniversary**	*With Love*	$12		Roulette 4125
				Hugo Peretti (of **Hugo & Luigi**; orch.)				
6/8/59	63	4		4 **I'm Gonna Change Him**	*The Little Things You Do*	$12		Roulette 4152
				Joe Reisman (orch.)				
				CARR, James	R&B/BUB **'66**			
				Born on 6/13/42 in Memphis, Tennessee. Died of cancer on 1/7/2001 (age 58). Former gospel singer.				
4/9/66	63	6		1 **You've Got My Mind Messed Up**	*That's What I Want To Know*	$15		Goldwax 302
7/30/66	99	1		2 **Love Attack**	*Coming Back To Me Baby*	$15		Goldwax 309
10/22/66	85	4		3 **Pouring Water On A Drowning Man**	*Forgetting You*	$15		Goldwax 311
2/25/67	77	6		4 **The Dark End Of The Street**	*Lovable Girl*	$15		Goldwax 317
9/23/67	97	3		5 **I'm A Fool For You**	*Gonna Send You Back To Georgia*	$15		Goldwax 328
				Betty Harris (female vocal)				
1/6/68	63	10		6 **A Man Needs A Woman**	*Stronger Than Love*	$15		Goldwax 332
				CARR, Joe "Fingers" — see BUSCH, Lou				
				CARR, Valerie	**'58**			
				Born in 1936 in New York. Black singer.				
6/9/58	19	2		**When The Boys Talk About The Girls** A:19 / T:84	*Padre*	$15		Roulette 4066
				Hugo Peretti (of **Hugo & Luigi**; orch.)				
				CARR, Vikki	AC/BUB/LP **'67**			
				Born Florencia Martinez Cardona on 7/19/41 in El Paso, Texas. Regular on TV's **Ray Anthony** Show in 1962.				
9/2/67	3	15		1 **It Must Be Him** AC[3]	*That's All*	$7		Liberty 55986
12/23/67+	34	8		2 **The Lesson** AC[1]	*One More Mountain*	$7	■	Liberty 56012
3/30/68	91	5		3 **Your Heart Is Free Just Like The Wind /**				
				from the French song "Le vent et la jeunesse"				
3/23/68	99	3		4 **She'll Be There**		$7		Liberty 56026
5/3/69	35	13		5 **With Pen In Hand**	*Can't Take My Eyes Off You*	$7		Liberty 56092
				written by **Bobby Goldsboro**				
10/4/69	79	4		6 **Eternity**	*I Will Wait For Love*	$7		Liberty 56132
				introduction borrowed from Mozart's 40th Symphony				
1/23/71	96	4		7 **I'll Be Home**	*Call My Heart Your Home*	$6		Columbia 45296
				written by **Randy Newman**				
				CARRACK, Paul	ROK/AC/LP **'88**			
				Born on 4/22/51 in Sheffield, Yorkshire, England. Lead singer of **Ace** (1973-76), **Squeeze** (1981, 1993) and **Mike + The Mechanics** (1985-1992). Keyboardist with **Roxy Music** (1978-80). With **Nick Lowe & His Cowboy Outfit** in 1985.				
9/4/82	37	13		1 **I Need You**	*Call Me Tonight*	$4		Epic 03146
				produced by **Nick Lowe**				
11/14/87+	9	24		2 **Don't Shed A Tear** S:6 / A:9	*Merilee*	$3	■	Chrysalis 43164
3/19/88	28	13		3 **One Good Reason** S:25 / A:25	*All Your Love Is In Vain*	$3	■	Chrysalis 43204

DEBUT	PEAK	WKS	Gold	A-side (Chart Hit)......B-side	$	Sym	Label & Number
				CARRACK, Paul — Cont'd			
6/18/88	90	3		4 **When You Walk In The Room** ......*If You See Her Walkin'*	$3	■	Chrysalis 43252
				written by **Jackie DeShannon**			
9/10/88	91	3		5 **Button Off My Shirt** ......*Double It Up*	$3		Chrysalis 43288
				above 4 from the album *One Good Reason*			
10/28/89	31	13		6 **I Live By The Groove** ......S:28 / A:31 *Tailfinder*	$3		Chrysalis 23427
9/13/97	72^A	1		7 **For Once In Our Lives**		V	album cut
				from the album *Blue Views* on Ark 21 10007; "45": Ark 21 19940; B-side: "Eyes Of Blue"			
				CARRADINE, Keith LP **'76**			
				Born on 8/8/49 in San Mateo, California. Leading actor in several movies including *Pretty Baby, Nashville, The Long Riders* and others. Son of actor John Carradine; half-brother of actor David Carradine.			
5/8/76	17	19		**I'm Easy** ......AC[1] *200 Years* (Henry Gibson)	$5		ABC 12117
				from the movie *Nashville* starring Carradine			
				CARROLL, Andrea **'63**			
				Born Andrea DeCapite on 10/3/46 in Cleveland, Ohio. Teen pop singer.			
7/20/63	45	9		**It Hurts To Be Sixteen** ......*Why Am I So Shy*	$20		Big Top 3156
				The Chiffons (backing vocals); Andrea was "Sixteen" when she recorded this song			
				CARROLL, Bernadette **'64**			
				Teen pop singer.			
5/16/64	47	9		**Party Girl** ......*I Don't Wanna Know*	$15		Laurie 3238
				CARROLL, Bob MEM/POP **'53**			
				Born on 6/18/18 in New York City, New York. White baritone singer. Sang with Charlie Barnet and **Jimmy Dorsey** in the 1940s. Hit #14 on the pop charts in 1953 with "Say It With Your Heart."			
3/2/57	61	7		**Butterfly** ......T:61 *Look What You've Done To Me*	$25		Bally 1028
				Lew Douglas (orch.)			
				CARROLL, Cathy **'62**			
				Teen pop singer.			
8/4/62	91	3		**Poor Little Puppet** ......*Love And Learn*	$20		Warner 5284
				CARROLL, David, And His Orchestra BUB/MEM/LP **'55**			
				Born Nook Schrier on 10/15/13 in Chicago, Illinois. Arranger/conductor since 1951 for many top Mercury artists.			
1/8/55	8	17		1 **Melody Of Love** A:8 / S:9 / J:12 *La Golondrina* [I]	$10		Mercury 70516
				music written in 1903; narrative (Paul Tremaine) version on Mercury 70521 ($10)			
11/26/55	20	16		2 **It's Almost Tomorrow** ......A:20 / T:34 *You Are Mine*	$10		Mercury 70717
				Jack Halloran Singers (vocals)			
3/23/57	65	3		3 **The Ship That Never Sailed** ......T:65 *I Love You Truly* [S]	$10		Mercury 71069
				Franklyn MacCormack (narration); written by 1930s bandleader Art Kassel			
9/2/57	56	7		4 **Fascination** ......T:56 *Swingin' Sweethearts* [I]	$10		Mercury 71152
				from the movie *Love In The Afternoon* starring Gary Cooper and Audrey Hepburn			
10/24/60	98	1		5 **Midnight Lace** ......*Juke Box Jingle* [I]	$8		Mercury 71703
				title song from the movie starring **Doris Day**			
2/24/62	61	7		6 **The White Rose Of Athens** ......*Theme From Slaughter On Tenth Avenue* [I]	$7		Mercury 71917
				from the German documentary movie *Dreamland of Desire*			
				CARROLL, Dina BUB **'93**			
				Born on 8/21/68 in Newmarket, Suffolk, England (African-American father and Scottish mother). R&B singer.			
4/17/93	95	2		**So Close** ......*Why Did I Let You Go / (2 album snippets)*	$3	▮	A&M 0206
				CARROLL, Jimmy — see COREY, Jill			
				CARROLL, Ronnie **'63**			
				Born Ronald Cleghorn on 8/18/34 in Belfast, Ireland. Male singer.			
6/8/63	91	4		**Say Wonderful Things** ......*Please Tell Me Your Name*	$12		Philips 40110
				Wally Stott (orch. and chorus)			
				CARROLL BROS. **'62**			
				Rock and roll band formed at Frankford High School in Philadelphia, Pennsylvania: Pete Carroll (guitar), Dick Noble (organ/sax), Jimmy Chick (drums), Kenneth Dorn (sax) and Billy McGraw (bass).			
8/18/62	100	1		**Sweet Georgia Brown** ......*Boot It!* [I]	$20		Cameo 221
				written in 1925; theme song of the Harlem Globetrotters basketball team			
				CARS, The ★150★ ROK/LP **'84**			
				Rock group from Boston, Massachusetts: **Ric Ocasek** (see #9, 17 & 19 below) (vocals, guitar; born on 3/23/49), **Benjamin Orr** (see #18 below) (bass, vocals; born on 8/9/47), Elliot Easton (guitar; born on 12/18/53), Greg Hawkes (keyboards; born on 3/15/50) and David Robinson (drums; born on 4/2/53). Ocasek, Orr and Hawkes had been in trio in the early 1970s. Group named by Robinson; got start at the Rat Club in Boston. Disbanded in 1988. Ocasek appeared in the 1987 movie *Made In Heaven.* Married supermodel/actress Paulina Porizkova on 8/23/89. His son Christopher Otcasek is leader of Glamour Camp. Orr died of cancer on 10/3/2000 (age 53).			
				1)Drive 2)Shake It Up 3)You Might Think 4)Tonight She Comes 5)Magic			
6/17/78	27	17		1 **Just What I Needed** ......*I'm In Touch With Your World*	$5	■	Elektra 45491
10/21/78	35	15		2 **My Best Friend's Girl** ......*Don't Cha Stop*	$5		Elektra 45537
3/17/79	41	10		3 **Good Times Roll** ......*All Mixed Up*	$5		Elektra 46014
6/30/79	14	15		4 **Let's Go** ......*That's It*	$5		Elektra 46063
10/13/79	41	10		5 **It's All I Can Do** ......*Got A Lot On My Head*	$5	■	Elektra 46546
9/6/80	37	11		6 **Touch And Go** ......*Down Boys*	$5		Elektra 47039
11/21/81+	4	22		7 **Shake It Up** ......*Cruiser* (ROK #37)	$5	■	Elektra 47250
3/27/82	41	9		8 **Since You're Gone** ......*Think It Over*	$5	■	Elektra 47433
				all of above produced by Roy Thomas Baker			

DEBUT	PEAK	WKS	Gold	A-side (Chart Hit)....B-side	$	Sym	Label & Number
				CARS, The — Cont'd			
2/12/83	47	9		9 **Something To Grab For**....*Connect Up To Me*	$4	■	Geffen 29784
				RIC OCASEK			
3/10/84	7	17		10 **You Might Think**....AR[3] *Heartbeat City*	$4	■	Elektra 69744
5/19/84	12	17		11 **Magic**....AR[1] *I Refuse*	$4		Elektra 69724
8/4/84	3	19		12 **Drive** AC[3] S:3 / A:8 *Stranger Eyes*	$4		Elektra 69706
10/27/84	20	15		13 **Hello Again**....S:17 / A:17 *(dub version)*	$4		Elektra 69681
1/26/85	33	17		14 **Why Can't I Have You**....A:28 *Breakaway* (ROK #19)	$4		Elektra 69657
				above 5 from the album *Heartbeat City*			
11/2/85+	7	17		15 **Tonight She Comes**....AR[3] A:7 / S:10 *Just What I Needed*	$4		Elektra 69589
2/1/86	32	11		16 **I'm Not The One**....A:30 *Heartbeat City*	$4		Elektra 69569
				originally released on the group's 1981 album *Shake It Up*			
9/6/86	15	19		17 **Emotion In Motion**....AR[1] / MR[1] S:16 / A:17 *P.F.J.*	$3	■	Geffen 28617
				RIC OCASEK			
11/8/86+	24	20		18 **Stay The Night**....A:18 / S:26 *That's The Way*	$3	■	Elektra 69506
				BENJAMIN ORR			
12/20/86+	75	8		19 **True To You**....*Hello Darkness*	$3	■	Geffen 28504
				RIC OCASEK			
8/29/87	17	14		20 **You Are The Girl**....A:16 / S:19 *Ta Ta Wayo Wayo*	$3	■	Elektra 69446
11/14/87	85	4		21 **Strap Me In**....*Door To Door*	$3		Elektra 69427
1/23/88	74	5		22 **Coming Up You**....*Double Trouble* (ROK #42)	$3	■	Elektra 69432
				all of above (except #18) written by Ric Ocasek			
				CARSON, Jeff C&W/BUB/LP **'95**			
				Born Jeff Herndon on 12/16/64 in Tulsa, Oklahoma; raised in Gravette, Arkansas. Country singer/songwriter/guitarist.			
9/16/95	97	2		**Not On Your Love**....CW[1] S:61 *Betty's Takin' Judo*	$4	■V	MCG/Curb 76954
				CARSON, Kit **'56**			
				Born Lisa Morrow. Vocalist on **Benny Goodman**'s 1946 #2 hit "Symphony."			
11/19/55	11	22		**Band Of Gold**....A:11 / T:17 *Cast Your Bread Upon The Waters*	$15		Capitol 3283
				Dick Hyman (orch.)			
				CARSON, Mindy MEM/POP **'50**			
				Born on 7/16/27 in New York City, New York. Sang with Paul Whiteman in the 1940s. Hit #6 on the pop charts in 1950 with "My Foolish Heart."			
8/27/55	13	8		1 **Wake The Town And Tell The People**....A:13 / J:13 / S:20 / T:33 *Hold Me Tight*	$15		Columbia 40537
				Norman Leyden (orch.)			
12/17/55+	53	13		2 **Memories Are Made Of This**....T:53 *Cryin' For Your Kisses*	$15		Columbia 40573
				The Columbians (male backing chorus)			
12/8/56+	34	12		3 **Since I Met You Baby**....T:34 *Goodnight My Love (Pleasant Dreams)*	$15		Columbia 40789
				Ray Conniff (orch., above 2)			
				CARTER, Aaron LP **'00**			
				Born on 12/7/87 in Tampa, Florida. White teen rapper. Younger brother of Nick Carter of the **Backstreet Boys** and **Leslie Carter**.			
8/26/00	35	15	●	1 **Aaron's Party (Come Get It)**....S:4 *(2 album snippets) / Jump Jump*	$4	★	Jive 42691
4/28/01	96	2		2 **That's How I Beat Shaq**....S:12 *One For The Summer* [N]	$5	★	Jive 42873
				Shaq: **Shaquille O'Neal** of the NBA's Los Angeles Lakers			
				CARTER, Betty — see CHARLES, Ray			
				CARTER, Carlene — see ORRALL, Robert Ellis			
	★464★			**CARTER, Clarence** R&B/BUB/LP **'70**			
				Born on 1/14/36 in Montgomery, Alabama. R&B vocalist/guitarist/songwriter. Blind since age one; self-taught on guitar at age 11. Teamed with vocalist/pianist Calvin Scott as Clarence & Calvin, recorded for Fairlane in the early 1960s. Carter went solo in 1966. Married for a time to **Candi Staton**.			
				1)Patches 2)Slip Away 3)Too Weak To Fight			
6/24/67	98	1		1 **Thread The Needle**....*Don't Make My Baby Cry*	$12		Fame 1013
1/20/68	62	8		2 **Looking For A Fox**....*I Can't See Myself (Crying About You)*	$8		Atlantic 2461
7/13/68	6	16	●	3 **Slip Away** /			
6/1/68	88	3		4 **Funky Fever**....	$8		Atlantic 2508
				above 4 from the album *This Is Clarence Carter*			
11/9/68+	13	15	●	5 **Too Weak To Fight**....*Let Me Comfort You*	$8		Atlantic 2569
12/14/68	4[X]	3		6 **Back Door Santa**....*That Old Time Feeling* [X]	$8		Atlantic 2576
3/1/69	31	10		7 **Snatching It Back**....*Making Love (At The Dark End Of The Street)*	$8		Atlantic 2605
6/21/69	65	6		8 **The Feeling Is Right**....*You Can't Miss What You Can't Measure*	$8		Atlantic 2642
9/27/69	46	9		9 **Doin' Our Thing**....*I Smell A Rat*	$8		Atlantic 2660
2/14/70	94	4		10 **Take It Off Him And Put It On Me**....*The Few Troubles I've Had*	$8		Atlantic 2702
4/11/70	42	14		11 **I Can't Leave Your Love Alone**....*Devil Woman*	$8		Atlantic 2726
7/18/70	4	14	●	12 **Patches** *Say It One More Time*	$8		Atlantic 2748
11/7/70	51	9		13 **It's All In Your Mind**....*Till I Can't Take It Anymore*	$8		Atlantic 2774
5/8/71	61	6		14 **The Court Room**....*Getting The Bills (But No Merchandise)* [N]	$8		Atlantic 2801
8/7/71	84	5		15 **Slipped, Tripped And Fell In Love**....*I Hate To Love & Run*	$8		Atlantic 2818
7/7/73	65	8		16 **Sixty Minute Man** /			
				#1 R&B hit for **The Dominoes** in 1951			
6/9/73	80	5		17 **Mother-In-Law**....	$6		Fame 250
				all of above produced by Rick Hall			

DEBUT	PEAK	WKS	Gold	A-side (Chart Hit)...B-side	$	Sym	Label & Number
				CARTER, Deana C&W/LP **'96**			
				Born on 1/4/66 in Nashville, Tennessee. Country singer/songwriter. Daughter of prominent session musician Fred Carter, Jr.			
10/5/96	**65**	10		1 **Strawberry Wine** ....CW[2] S:40 *Before We Ever Heard Goodbye* "45": Capitol Nashville 19223	$4	▮V	Capitol 58585
2/8/97	**72**	9		2 **We Danced Anyway** ....CW[2] S:45 *Rita Valentine*	$4	▮V	Capitol 58626
12/13/97+	**85**	6		3 **Did I Shave My Legs For This?** ....S:74 *(live version)* "45" issued for above 2 on Capitol Nashville 19450	$4	▮V	Capitol 58672
12/5/98	**83**	2		4 **Absence Of The Heart** ....A:72 from the album *Everything's Gonna Be Alright* on Capitol 21142; "45": Capitol Nashville 58738		V	album cut
				CARTER, June — see CASH, Johnny			
				CARTER, Leslie **'01**			
				Born on 6/6/86 in Tampa, Florida. Pop singer. Younger sister of Nick Carter of the **Backstreet Boys**. Older sister of **Aaron Carter**.			
4/28/01	**99**	1		**Like, Wow!** ....S:15 *True* CD package includes a pull-out sticker	$5	★	DreamWorks 50927
				CARTER, Mel AC/BUB/LP **'65**			
				Born on 4/22/39 in Cincinnati, Ohio. R&B singer/actor. Sang on local radio from age four; with Lionel Hampton on stage show at age nine. With **Paul Gayten**, Jimmy Scott bands. Joined Raspberry Singers gospel group in the early '50s. With his mother's gospel group, The Carvetts, in the mid-1950s. Named Top Gospel Tenor in 1957. Recorded in late '50s for Tri-State, Arwin, then Mercury. With Gospel Pearls in the early '60s. Acted on TV's *Quincy*, *Sanford And Son*, *Marcus Welby, MD* and *Magnum P.I.*			
7/6/63	**44**	10		1 **When A Boy Falls In Love** ....*So Wonderful* co-written by **Sam Cooke**	$15		Derby 1003
6/26/65	**8**	15		2 **Hold Me, Thrill Me, Kiss Me** AC[1] *A Sweet Little Girl* #5 hit for **Karen Chandler** in 1953	$10		Imperial 66113
10/30/65	**38**	7		3 **(All Of A Sudden) My Heart Sings** ....*When I Hold The Hand Of The One I Love* #7 hit for Johnnie Johnston in 1945	$10		Imperial 66138
1/22/66	**50**	8		4 **Love Is All We Need** ....*I Wish I Didn't Love You So*	$10		Imperial 66148
4/9/66	**32**	8		5 **Band Of Gold** ....AC[2] *Detour*	$10		Imperial 66165
7/16/66	**49**	7		6 **You You You** ....*If You Lose Her* #1 hit for **The Ames Brothers** in 1953	$10		Imperial 66183
10/1/66	**78**	5		7 **Take Good Care Of Her** ....*Tar And Cement* #2-7: produced by **Nick DeCaro**	$10		Imperial 66208
				CARTER, Ralph R&B **'75**			
				Born on 5/30/61 in Harlem, New York. Black dance singer/actor. Played "Michael Evans" on the TV series *Good Times*.			
9/6/75	**95**	3		**When You're Young And In Love** ....*(disco version)*	$5		Mercury 73695
				CARTER, Torrey **'00**			
				Born on 8/7/76 in Detroit, Michigan. R&B singer/rapper.			
6/24/00	**86**	7		**Take That** ....S:10 *(instrumental) / (3 album snippets)* **TORREY CARTER (Featuring Missy "Misdemeanor" Elliott)**	$5	★	The Gold Mind 67036
				CARTER, Valerie — see MONEY, Eddie			
				CARTOUCHE **'91**			
				Dance duo from Belgium: Myrelle Tholen and Jean-Paul Visser. Cartouche means "bullet" in French.			
4/13/91	**66**	10		**Feel The Groove** ....*(Sergosonic mix)*	$4	▮	Scotti Brothers 5281
				CARTRIDGE, Flip **'66**			
				Born William Meshel on 5/5/46 in Brooklyn, New York. Later became an executive at Ariola America Records.			
8/20/66	**91**	2		**Dear Mrs. Applebee** ....*Don't Take The Lovers From The World*	$10		Parrot 306
				CASCADES, The BUB/LP **'63**			
				Pop group from San Diego, California: John Gummoe (vocals), Eddie Snyder (piano), David Wilson (sax), David Stevens (bass) and David Zabo (drums). Snyder hit the country charts in 1989 as "Eddie Preston." Wilson died of cancer on 11/14/2000 (age 63).			
1/12/63	**3**	16		1 **Rhythm Of The Rain** AC[2] *Let Me Be*	$20		Valiant 6026
5/11/63	**60**	5		2 **The Last Leaf /**			
4/27/63	**91**	4		3 **Shy Girl**	$20		Valiant 6028
12/28/63+	**86**	3		4 **For Your Sweet Love** ....*Jeannie*	$15		RCA Victor 8268
8/16/69	**61**	6		5 **Maybe The Rain Will Fall** ....*Naggin' Cries*	$10		Uni 55152
				CASE R&B/BUB/LP **'01**			
				Born Casey Woodard on 1/10/73 in Harlem, New York. Male R&B singer/songwriter.			
5/11/96	**14**	20	●	1 **Touch Me Tease Me** ....S:7 / A:50 *(instrumental)* **Mary J. Blige** and **Foxy Brown** (backing vocals); samples "P.S.K. What Does It Mean" by Schooly D; from the movie *The Nutty Professor* starring **Eddie Murphy**	$3	▮	Def Jam 854620
12/26/98+	**10**	20		2 **Faded Pictures** ....S:8 / A:56 *(TV track) / (5 album snippets* - Case) **CASE & JOE** from the movie *Rush Hour* starring Jackie Chan	$4	★	Def Jam 566494
6/5/99	**15**	20		3 **Happily Ever After** ....S:8 / A:23 *Where Did Our Love Go?*	$4	★	Def Jam 566954
1/8/00	**77**	12		4 **The Best Man I Can Be** ....A:67 **GINUWINE, R.L., TYRESE, CASE** from the movie *The Best Man* starring Taye Diggs (soundtrack on Columbia 69924)			album cut
5/13/00	**91**	4		5 **Love Sets You Free** ....S:18 *It's Gonna Rain* (Price) **KELLY PRICE & FRIENDS (Dru Hill, Montell Jordan, Case, Playa, Kandice Love, Lovher)** from the movie *The Hurricane* starring Denzel Washington	$4	★	Def Soul 562683
2/10/01	**4**	22		6 **Missing You** RB[4] S:3 / A:24 *(Bedtime remix) / Not Your Friend*	$5	★+	Def Soul 572839
9/1/01	**6**	25		7 **Livin' It Up** ....A:6 / S:29 *(2 versions) / The Inc.* (w/Caddillac Tah & Black Child) **JA RULE (feat. Case)** samples "Do I Do" by **Stevie Wonder**	$6	T	Def Jam 588741

DEBUT	PEAK	WKS	Gold	A-side (Chart Hit)...B-side	$	Sym	Label & Number

CASEY, Al
BUB **'63**

Born on 10/26/36 in Long Beach, California. Guitarist/pianist/bandleader/producer. Much session work with **Lee Hazlewood** productions, including **Sanford Clark** and **Duane Eddy**. Not to be confused with black guitarist of the same name. Also see **Ray Sharpe**.

DEBUT	PEAK	WKS	Gold	A-side (Chart Hit)...B-side	$	Sym	Label & Number
4/7/62	92	2		1 **Cookin'** ...*Hotfoot* [I] originally released on Blue Horizon 925 in 1962 ($30)	$20		Stacy 925
7/28/62	71	6		2 **Jivin' Around**...*Doin' The Shotish* [I] **AL CASEY COMBO** (above 2) originally released on United Artists 494 in 1962 ($25)	$20		Stacy 936
7/13/63	48	8		3 **Surfin' Hootenanny**...*Easy Pickin'* K-C-Ettes (female vocals); Casey imitates guitarists **Dick Dale**, **The Ventures** and **Duane Eddy**	$25		Stacy 962

CASH, Alvin
BUB **'65**

Born Alvin Welch on 2/15/39 in St. Louis, Missouri. Died on 11/21/99 (age 60). Soul-funk singer/dancer. Formed song/dance troupe The Crawlers in 1960, with brothers Robert, Arthur and George (ages 8 to 10). They never sang on any of Alvin's hits. Alvin moved to Chicago in 1963. First recorded for Mar-V-Lus in 1964. Cut "Twine Time" with backing band the Nightlighters from Louisville, who changed their name to the Registers.

DEBUT	PEAK	WKS	Gold	A-side (Chart Hit)...B-side	$	Sym	Label & Number
				ALVIN CASH & THE CRAWLERS:			
1/2/65	14	11		1 **Twine Time** *The Bump* [I]	$15		Mar-V-Lus 6002
3/27/65	59	7		2 **The Barracuda**...*Do It One More Time (The Twine)*	$12		Mar-V-Lus 6005
				ALVIN CASH & THE REGISTERS:			
7/30/66	49	9		3 **The Philly Freeze**...*No Deposit - No Return*	$12		Mar-V-Lus 6012
11/26/66	74	6		4 **Alvin's Boo-Ga-Loo**...*Let's Do Some Good Timing*	$12		Mar-V-Lus 6014
11/23/68	66	5		5 **Keep On Dancing** *[ALVIN CASH]*...*(instrumental)* Scott Bros. (orch.)	$10		Toddlin' Town 111

CASH, Johnny ★85★
C&W/BUB/AC/LP **'58**

Born on 2/26/32 in Kingsland, Arkansas. Country singer/songwriter/guitarist. Brother Roy led the Dixie Rhythm Ramblers band in late 1940s. In U.S. Air Force, 1950-54. Formed trio with Luther Perkins (guitar) and Marshall Grant (bass) in 1955. First recorded for Sun in 1955. On *Louisiana Hayride* and *Grand Ole Opry* in 1957. Own TV show for ABC from 1969-71. Worked with **June Carter** from 1961; married her in March 1968. **Carl Perkins** and **The Statler Brothers** were members of his touring troupe from 1968-75. Ranks within the top three male vocalists in the history of the Country charts. Charted 136 Country hits, 1955-98. Daughter **Rosanne Cash** and stepdaughter **Carlene Carter** had successful singing careers. June Carter died of heart failure on 5/15/2003 (age 73). Elected to the Country Music Hall of Fame in 1980. Inducted into the Rock and Roll Hall of Fame in 1992. Won Grammy's Lifetime Achievement Award in 1999.

1)A Boy Named Sue 2)Guess Things Happen That Way 3)Ballad Of A Teenage Queen 4)Ring Of Fire 5)I Walk The Line

DEBUT	PEAK	WKS	Gold	A-side (Chart Hit)...B-side	$	Sym	Label & Number
9/15/56	17	22		1 **I Walk The Line**...CW[6] S:17 / J:17 / T:19 / A:25 *Get Rhythm* (C&W flip)	$40		Sun 241
7/1/57	99	2		2 **Next In Line**...T:99 *Don't Make Me Go*	$40		Sun 266
10/14/57	88	4		3 **Home Of The Blues**...T:88 *Give My Love To Rose* (C&W #13)	$40		Sun 279
2/3/58	14	19		4 **Ballad Of A Teenage Queen** / CW[10] A:14 / S:16 / T:16			
3/17/58		7		5 **Big River**...S:flip re-entered the Country charts on 12/5/70 on Sun 1121 (#41)	$30		Sun 283
6/2/58	11	16		6 **Guess Things Happen That Way** / CW[8] S:11 / T:11 / A:18			
6/2/58	66	9		7 **Come In Stranger**...T:66 / S:flip	$30	■	Sun 295
8/25/58	24	11		8 **The Ways Of A Woman In Love** / H:24 / S:26 written by **Charlie Rich** and **Bill Justis**			
9/8/58		6		9 **You're The Nearest Thing To Heaven**...S:flip	$25		Sun 302
10/6/58	38	11		10 **All Over Again** / H:38			
10/20/58	52	8		11 **What Do I Care**...	$20	■	Columbia 41251
12/15/58+	47	7		12 **It's Just About Time** /			
12/15/58	85	1		13 **I Just Thought You'd Like To Know**... written by **Charlie Rich**	$25		Sun 309
1/19/59	32	12		14 **Don't Take Your Guns To Town**...CW[6] *I Still Miss Someone*	$20	■	Columbia 41313
4/27/59	57	7		15 **Frankie's Man, Johnny**...*You Dreamer You* (C&W #13) version of mid-19th century traditional folk song "Frankie & Johnny"	$15		Columbia 41371
7/13/59	66	8		16 **Katy Too**...*I Forgot To Remember To Forget*	$20		Sun 321
8/3/59	43	11		17 **I Got Stripes** /			
8/24/59	76	3		18 **Five Feet High And Rising**...	$15		Columbia 41427
12/21/59	63	3		19 **The Little Drummer Boy**...*I'll Remember You* [X]	$15	■	Columbia 41481
3/14/60	84	2		20 **Straight A's In Love**...*I Love You Because* (C&W #20)	$20		Sun 334
7/4/60	79	4		21 **Second Honeymoon** /			
7/25/60	92	1		22 **Honky-Tonk Girl**... #9 Country hit for **Hank Thompson** in 1954	$15		Columbia 41707
7/11/60	85	3		23 **Down The Street To 301**...*The Story Of A Broken Heart* (#107) **JOHNNY CASH And The Tennessee Two** (all of above Sun Records)	$20		Sun 343
12/31/60+	93	2		24 **Oh Lonesome Me**...*Life Goes On* Gene Lowery Singers (backing vocals)	$20		Sun 355
11/13/61	84	6		25 **Tennessee Flat-Top Box**...*Tall Men*	$12	■	Columbia 42147
9/15/62	94	1		26 **Bonanza!**...*Pick A Bale O' Cotton* title song from the TV series starring **Lorne Greene**	$12	■	Columbia 42512
6/1/63	17	13		27 **Ring Of Fire**...CW[7] *I'd Still Be There* issued with 3 different picture sleeves: with a guitar background, a train background, and with a promo sleeve	$10	■	Columbia 42788
10/26/63	44	7		28 **The Matador**...*Still In Town*	$10	■	Columbia 42880
2/15/64	35	8		29 **Understand Your Man**...CW[6] *Dark As A Dungeon* (#119)	$10	□	Columbia 42964
10/31/64	58	8		30 **It Ain't Me, Babe**...*Time And Time Again* **June Carter** (harmony vocal); written by **Bob Dylan**	$10	□	Columbia 43145
2/13/65	80	6		31 **Orange Blossom Special**...*All Of God's Children Ain't Free* bluegrass tune written in 1938	$10		Columbia 43206
2/26/66	46	6		32 **The One On The Right Is On The Left**...*Cotton Pickin' Hands* [N]	$10		Columbia 43496

DEBUT	PEAK	WKS	Gold	A-side (Chart Hit)...B-side	$	Sym	Label & Number
				CASH, Johnny — Cont'd			
7/2/66	96	2		33 **Everybody Loves A Nut** ...*Austin Prison* [N]	$10		Columbia 43673
1/27/68	91	2		34 **Rosanna's Going Wild** ...*Roll Call*	$8	■	Columbia 44373
5/25/68	32	12		35 **Folsom Prison Blues** ...CW^{4} *The Folk Singer* [L] recorded at Folsom Prison; studio version hit #4 on the Country charts in 1956 on Sun 232 ($40)	$8	■	Columbia 44513
12/28/68+	42	10		36 **Daddy Sang Bass** ...CW^{6} *He Turned The Water Into Wine* **The Statler Brothers** (backing vocals); written by **Carl Perkins**; includes some lines from "Will The Circle Be Unbroken"	$8		Columbia 44689
7/26/69	2^{3}	12	●	37 **A Boy Named Sue** CW^{5} / AC^{2} *San Quentin* [L-N] recorded at San Quentin prison	$8		Columbia 44944
11/22/69	50	6		38 **Blistered** /			
11/8/69	75	8		39 **See Ruby Fall** ...	$8		Columbia 45020
11/15/69	60	6		40 **Get Rhythm** ...*Hey Porter* [L] same tune as the B-side of #1 above (with "live" effects dubbed in)	$8		Sun 1103
1/24/70	36	8		41 **If I Were A Carpenter** ...*'Cause I Love You* **JOHNNY CASH & JUNE CARTER**	$8		Columbia 45064
2/28/70	93	1		42 **Rock Island Line** ...*Next In Line* originated in the mid-1930s as an Arkansas prison song; long associated with folk legend Leadbelly; all Sun titles recorded from 1956-58	$8		Sun 1111
4/11/70	19	8		43 **What Is Truth** ...*Sing A Traveling Song* [S]	$8		Columbia 45134
8/29/70	46	7		44 **Sunday Morning Coming Down** ...CW^{2} *I'm Gonna Try To Be That Way* written by **Kris Kristofferson**	$8		Columbia 45211
12/12/70+	54	7		45 **Flesh And Blood** ...CW^{1} *This Side Of The Law* from the movie *I Walk The Line* starring Gregory Peck	$8		Columbia 45269
3/20/71	58	6		46 **Man In Black** ...*Little Bit Of Yesterday* all of above written by Cash (except #4, 6, 8, 12, 13, 15, 19, 21-24, 26, 27, 30-34, 36-38, 41 & 44)	$8		Columbia 45339
5/13/72	75	7		47 **Kate** ...*The Miracle Man* written by **Marty Robbins**	$8		Columbia 45590
4/17/76	29	10		48 **One Piece At A Time** ...CW^{2} *Go On Blues* [N] **JOHNNY CASH And The Tennessee Three** (above 2)	$6		Columbia 10321
				CASH, Rosanne C&W/AC/BUB/LP **'81** Born on 5/24/56 in Memphis, Tennessee. Daughter of **Johnny Cash** and Vivian Liberto. Raised by her mother in California, then moved to Nashville after high school graduation. Worked in the Johnny Cash Road Show. Married to **Rodney Crowell** from 1979-92. Moved to New York. Married producer John Leventhal in 1995. Released short-story collection *Bodies Of Water* in 1996. Charted 24 Country hits, 1979-91.			
4/25/81	22	20		**Seven Year Ache** ...CW^{1} *Blue Moon With Heartache* B-side hit #1 on the Country charts in 1982 on Columbia 02659	$4	□	Columbia 11426
				CASH, Tommy C&W **'70** Born on 4/5/40 in Dyess, Arkansas. Brother of **Johnny Cash**.			
12/13/69+	79	6		**Six White Horses** ...*I Owe The World To You* tribute to John F. Kennedy, Robert Kennedy and **Martin Luther King**	$8		Epic 10540
				CASH & COMPUTA **'01** Rap duo from New York City, New York.			
11/17/01	28^{S}	11		**Ground Zero (In Our Hearts You Will Remain)** ...*(3 versions)* opens with President Bush's speech at "Ground Zero"; proceeds benefit the Twin Towers Fund	$5	★	Select 25076
				CASHMAN & WEST AC/LP **'69** Duo of pop record producers/songwriters/singers Dennis "**Terry Cashman**" (see #6 below) Minogue (born on 7/5/41) and Thomas "Tommy West" Picardo, Jr. (born on 8/17/42). Produced all of **Jim Croce**'s recordings. Recorded as **Buchanan Brothers** (see #1 & 2 below) and **Morning Mist** (see #3 below).			
5/3/69	22	11		1 **Medicine Man (Part I)** *(Part II)*	$8		Event 3302
9/20/69	61	6		2 **Son Of A Lovin' Man** ...*I'll Never Get Enough* **BUCHANAN BROTHERS** (above 2)	$8		Event 3305
8/7/71	96	3		3 **California On My Mind** ...*All The Time It Was You* **MORNING MIST** tune used in a commercial for Kodak cameras	$7		Event 206
9/23/72	27	11		4 **American City Suite** ...*I Belong To You* Sweet City Song/All Around The Town/A Friend Is Dying	$6	■	Dunhill/ABC 4324
12/30/72+	59	7		5 **Songman** ...*If You Were A Rainbow*	$6		Dunhill/ABC 4333
11/27/76	79	2		6 **Baby, Baby I Love You** ...*We'll Be Together* **TERRY CASHMAN** all of above written by Cashman & West	$4		Lifesong 45015
				CASH MONEY MILLIONAIRES LP **'01** Rap collective of Cash Money label artists: **Big Tymers**, **Juvenile** and **Lil' Wayne**.			
12/16/00+	47	13		**Project Chick** ...A:39 / S:59 *(2 versions* / I Don't Know from the movie *Baller Blockin'* starring **B.G.** and **Juvenile**	$7	T	Cash Money 860919
				CASINOS, The BUB **'67** Pop vocal group from Cincinnati, Ohio: Gene Hughes (lead), Pete Bolton, Bob Armstrong, Tom Mathews, Ray White, Mickey Denton, Glen Hughes, Joe Patterson and Bill Hawkins.			
1/14/67	6	13		1 **Then You Can Tell Me Goodbye** ...*I Still Love You*	$12		Fraternity 977
4/29/67	65	4		2 **It's All Over Now** ...*Tailor Made* written by Don Everly of **The Everly Brothers**; also issued as "It's All Over"	$12		Fraternity 985
				CASLONS, The BUB **'61** White pop vocal group from Brooklyn, New York.			
9/11/61	89	2		**Anniversary Of Love** ...*The Quiet One*	$30		Seeco 6078
				CASSIDY, David BUB/AC/LP **'71** Born on 4/12/50 in New York City, New York. Son of actor Jack Cassidy and actress Evelyn Ward. Played "Keith Partridge", the lead singer of TV's **The Partridge Family**. Married to actress Kay Lenz from 1977-83. Co-starred with his half-brother **Shaun Cassidy** on Broadway's *Blood Brothers* in 1993.			
11/6/71	9	12	●	1 **Cherish** AC^{1} *All I Wanna Do Is Touch You*	$5	■	Bell 45,150
2/19/72	37	9		2 **Could It Be Forever** ...*Blind Hope*	$5	■	Bell 45,187

DEBUT	PEAK	WKS	Gold	A-side (Chart Hit)...B-side	$	Sym	Label & Number
				CASSIDY, David — Cont'd			
5/20/72	25	9		3 **How Can I Be Sure** ...*Ricky's Tune*	$5		Bell 45,220
9/9/72	38	8		4 **Rock Me Baby**...*Two Time Loser*	$5		Bell 45,260
9/22/90	27	16		5 **Lyin' To Myself**...S:26 / A:26 *I'll Believe You Again*	$3	▮	Enigma 75084
				CASSIDY, Shaun LP **'77**			
				Born on 9/27/59 in Los Angeles, California. Son of actor Jack Cassidy and actress Shirley Jones of TV's ***The Partridge Family***. Played "Joe Hardy" on TV's *The Hardy Boys*. Co-starred with his half-brother **David Cassidy** on Broadway's *Blood Brothers* in 1993. Cast member of the TV soap *General Hospital* in 1987. Married to model Ann Pennington, 1979-91.			
5/14/77	❶[1]	22	●	1 **Da Doo Ron Ron** *Holiday*	$4	■	Warner/Curb 8365
7/23/77	3	24	●	2 **That's Rock 'N' Roll**...*I Wanna Be With You*	$4	■	Warner/Curb 8423
11/12/77+	7	16	●	3 **Hey Deanie**...*Strange Sensation*	$4	■	Warner/Curb 8488
				above 2 written by **Eric Carmen**			
3/25/78	31	10		4 **Do You Believe In Magic**...*Teen Dream*	$4	■	Warner/Curb 8533
9/9/78	80	3		5 **Our Night**...*Right Before Your Skies*	$4	■	Warner/Curb 8634
				CASTAWAYS, The BUB **'65**			
				Rock and roll garage band of teens from St. Paul, Minnesota: Richard Roby (vocals, bass), Robert Folschow and Roy Hensley (guitars), James Donna (keyboards) and Dennis Craswell (drums). Craswell later joined **Crow**.			
8/14/65	12	14		**Liar, Liar**...*Sam*	$15		Soma 1433
				CASTELLS, The BUB **'61**			
				Adult Contemporary vocal group from Santa Rosa, California: Bob Ussery, Tom Hicks, Joe Kelly and Chuck Girard (later with **The Hondells**).			
5/29/61	20	12		1 **Sacred**...*I Get Dreamy*	$20		Era 3048
10/9/61	98	2		2 **Make Believe Wedding**...*My Miracle*	$20		Era 3057
4/14/62	21	13		3 **So This Is Love**...*On The Street Of Tears*	$20		Era 3073
8/25/62	91	2		4 **Oh! What It Seemed To Be**...*Stand There Mountain*	$20		Era 3083
				#1 hit for both **Frank Sinatra** and Frankie Carle in 1946			
				CASTLE, David **'77**			
				Born on 11/28/52 in Overton, Texas. Pop singer/songwriter.			
9/24/77	68	7		1 **Ten To Eight**...*Finally*	$5		Parachute 501
1/7/78	89	2		2 **The Loneliest Man On The Moon**...*Pretending*	$5		Parachute 505
				CASTLEMAN, Boomer — see LEWIS & CLARKE EXPEDITION, The			
				CASTLE SISTERS, The **'62**			
				Pop vocal trio similar in style to **The McGuire Sisters**.			
7/21/62	100	1		**Goodbye Dad**...*Wishing Star*	$15	■	Terrace 7506
				Billy Mure (orch.)			
				CASTOR, Jimmy R&B/BUB/LP **'72**			
				Born on 6/22/43 in New York City, New York. R&B singer/saxophonist/composer/arranger. Formed the Jimmy Castor Bunch in 1972: Gerry Thomas (keyboards), Doug Gibson (bass), Harry Jensen (guitar), Lenny Fridie, Jr. (congas) and Bobby Manigault (drums).			
12/31/66+	31	9		1 **Hey, Leroy, Your Mama's Callin' You**...*Ham Hocks Espanol* [I]	$8		Smash 2069
				THE JIMMY CASTOR BUNCH:			
5/13/72	6	12	●	2 **Troglodyte** (Cave Man)...*I Promise To Remember* [N]	$6		RCA Victor 48-1029
2/22/75	16	13		3 **The Bertha Butt Boogie-Part 1**...*Part II* [N]	$5		Atlantic 3232
10/18/75	69	7		4 **King Kong - Pt. I**...*Pt. II* [N]	$5		Atlantic 3295
				CASWELL, Johnny — see CRYSTAL MANSION			
				CATE BROS. LP **'76**			
				White pop-rock duo of twins Ernie (vocals, piano) and Earl (guitar) Cate. Born on 12/26/42 in Fayetteville, Arkansas.			
2/7/76	24	20		1 **Union Man**...*Easy Way Out*	$5		Asylum 45294
7/24/76	91	3		2 **Can't Change My Heart**...*Time For Us*	$5		Asylum 45326
				CATES, George, And His Orchestra **'56**			
				Born on 10/19/11 in New York City, New York. Died on 5/10/2002 (age 90). Arranger for **Bing Crosby**, **Teresa Brewer**, The Andrews Sisters and others. Musical director of TV's ***Lawrence Welk** Show* for 25 years.			
11/12/55	35	12		1 **Autumn Leaves**...T:35 *High And Dry* (Cates) [I]	$15		Coral 61485
				STEVE ALLEN with GEORGE CATES And His Orchestra & Chorus			
11/19/55	77	4		2 **Someone On Your Mind**...T:77 *I Want To Love You*	$15		Coral 61496
				CHAMP BUTLER With GEORGE CATES And His Chorus and Orchestra			
4/14/56	4	22		3 **Moonglow And Theme From "Picnic"**...T:4 / A:4 / S:5 / J:7 *Rio Batucada* [I]	$15		Coral 61618
				featuring The Stan Wrightsman Quartet: from the movie *Picnic* starring William Holden; 4 Top 10 versions of "Moonglow" charted in 1934			
9/15/56	75	2		4 **Where There's Life**...T:75 *One Night In Monte Carlo* [I]	$12		Coral 61683
				melody based on a Budweiser beer jingle			
				CATHY And JOE **'64**			
				Pop vocal duo from New Orleans, Louisiana: Catherine Anne Bunn and Joseph J. Wegman. Similar in style to **Paul & Paula**.			
10/10/64	82	2		**I See You**...*It's All Over Now*	$12		Smash 1929
				CATHY JEAN and THE ROOMMATES BUB **'61**			
				Cathy Jean was born on 9/8/45 in Brooklyn, New York. The Roommates were a vocal quartet from Queens, New York: Steve Susskind (lead), Jack Sailson and Felix Alvarez (tenors) and Bob Minsky (bass).			
2/27/61	12	12		1 **Please Love Me Forever**...*Canadian Sunset* (Cathy Jean)	$25	□	Valmor 007
4/10/61	49	9		2 **Glory Of Love**...*Never Knew*	$20	□	Valmor 008
				THE ROOMMATES			
				#1 hit for **Benny Goodman** in 1936			
				CAT MOTHER and The All Night News Boys BUB/LP **'69**			
				Rock group from New York produced by **Jimi Hendrix**: Larry Packer (guitar), Bob Smith (piano), Charley Chin (banjo), Roy Michaels (bass) and Michael Equine (drums). All share vocals.			
6/28/69	21	8		**Good Old Rock 'N Roll**...*Bad News*	$8		Polydor 14002
				Sweet Little Sixteen/Long Tall Sally/Chantilly Lace/ Whole Lotta Shakin' Goin On/Blue Suede Shoes/Party Doll			

DEBUT	PEAK	WKS	Gold	A-side (Chart Hit)..........B-side	$	Sym	Label & Number
				CAUSE & EFFECT LP **'92**			
				Pop duo based in Northern California: Sean Rowley (keyboards) and British-born Robert Rowe (vocals, guitar). Joined on tour by drummer Evan Parandes, then Richard Shepherd. Rowley died of asthma-related cardiac arrest on 11/12/92 (age 23). Rowe, Shepherd and Keith David Milo continued as a trio.			
2/29/92	**38**	20		1 **You Think You Know Her** ....A:33 *New World*	$3	▮	SRC/Zoo 14025
7/18/92	**75**	6		2 **Another Minute** ....A:64 *Unholy Day*	$3	▮	SRC/Zoo 14036
6/25/94	**67**	11		3 **It's Over Now (It's Alright)** ....A:65 *Words To Hold On To*	$3	▮	Zoo 14146
				CAVALIERE, Felix — see RASCALS, The			
				CAZZ **'78**			
				Born Robert Lewis in Texas. R&B singer.			
2/18/78	**70**	5		**Let's Live Together** ....*This Is My Music*	$5		Number 1 Record 210
				produced by **Dale Hawkins**			
				C.C. & COMPANY — see C.J. & CO.			
				C COMPANY Featuring TERRY NELSON **'71**			
				Group of studio musicians led by DJ/singer Terry Nelson from Russellville, Alabama.			
4/24/71	**37**	4	●	**Battle Hymn Of Lt. Calley** ....*Routine Patrol* [S]	$6		Plantation 73
				Lt. William Calley Jr. was court-martialed for the massacre of unarmed civilians in My Lai, Vietnam, committed by his Army company			
				C.C.S. LP **'71**			
				Jazz-rock collective from England. Put together by a core trio of vocalists Alexis Korner and Peter Thorup, with arranger John Cameron. Name stands for Collective Consciousness Society. Korner's Blues Inc., a pioneer blues-rock band of the early 1960s, featured **Mick Jagger**, **Ginger Baker**, Jack Bruce and other rock notables. Korner died of lung cancer on 1/1/84 (age 55).			
2/6/71	**58**	4		**Whole Lotta Love** ....*Boom Boom* [I]	$8		Rak 4501
				CEBALLO, Kevin **'02**			
				Born in New York City, New York (Puerto Rican parents). Latin singer/songwriter.			
12/29/01+	**50**[S]	8		**My First Love** ....*(remix)*	$4	★	Universal 015563
				CEE-LO LP **'02**			
				Born on 5/30/75 in Atlanta, Georgia. Male rapper. Member of **Goodie Mob**.			
4/6/02	**98**	3		1 **Closet Freak** ....*(2 versions)*	$6	T	Arista 15086
7/13/02	**70**	18		2 **In Da Wind** ....S:55 / A:66 *(3 versions)*	$6	T	Slip n Slide 85333
				TRICK DADDY feat. Cee-Lo & Big Boi			
				CELEBRATION featuring MIKE LOVE **'78**			
				Pop group formed in Los Angeles, California: Mike Love (vocals), Ron Altback (keyboards), Charles Lloyd (sax) and Dave "Doc" Robinson (bass). Love is lead singer of **The Beach Boys**. Altback and Robinson were members of **King Harvest**.			
4/29/78	**28**	12		**Almost Summer** ....*Lookin' Good* (w/Charles Lloyd)	$8		MCA 40891
				title song from the movie starring Bruno Kirby			
				CELI BEE & THE BUZZY BUNCH LP **'77**			
				Disco group from Puerto Rico. Led by female vocalist Celinas Soto.			
6/11/77	**41**	13		**Superman** ....*Hurt Me, Hurt Me*	$6		APA 17001
				CELLARFUL OF NOISE **'88**			
				Rock group from Cleveland, Ohio. Led by singer/songwriter/keyboardist Mark Avsec (**Wild Cherry**).			
3/5/88	**69**	7		**Samantha (What You Gonna Do?)** ....*Shuck And Jive*	$4		CBS Associated 07731
				CELLOS, The **'57**			
				Black doo-wop group from Queens, New York: Cliff "Monk" Williams (lead), Robert Thomas, Alton Campbell, William Montgomery and Alvin Williams.			
5/27/57	**62**	10		**Rang Tang Ding Dong (I Am The Japanese Sandman)** ...T:62 *You Took My Love*	$40		Apollo 510
				CENTRAL LINE R&B/LP **'81**			
				R&B group from London, England: Linton Beckles (vocals, drums), Henry Defoe (guitar), Lipson Francis (keyboards) and Camelle Hinds (bass).			
11/14/81	**84**	6		**Walking Into Sunshine** ....*We Chose Love*	$4		Mercury 76126
				CERRONE R&B/LP **'77**			
				Born Jean-Marc Cerrone in 1952 in St. Michel, France. Dance composer/producer/drummer. A pioneer of the Euro-disco sound. Also see **Kongas**.			
2/26/77	**36**	8		1 **Love In 'C' Minor - Pt. I** ....*Pt. II* [I]	$4		Cotillion 44215
1/21/78	**70**	5		2 **Supernature** ....*Sweet Drums*	$4		Cotillion 44230
	★**359**★			**CETERA, Peter** AC/ROK/LP **'86**			
				Born on 9/13/44 in Chicago, Illinois. Lead singer/bass guitarist of **Chicago** from 1967-85. Also see **Paul Anka**'s "Hold Me 'Til The Mornin' Comes."			
				1)Glory Of Love 2)The Next Time I Fall 3)One Good Woman			
6/7/86	❶[2]	21		1 **Glory Of Love** AC[5] A:❶[2] / S:2 *On The Line*	$3	■	Full Moon 28662
				theme from the movie *The Karate Kid Part II* starring Ralph Macchio; issued with a full-color and a 2-color picture sleeve			
9/20/86	❶[1]	21		2 **The Next Time I Fall** ....AC[2] A:2 / S:3 *Holy Moly* (Cetera)	$3	■	Full Moon 28597
				PETER CETERA w/AMY GRANT			
1/24/87	**61**	6		3 **Big Mistake** ....*Livin' In The Limelight*	$3	■	Full Moon 28507
4/23/88	**93**	3		4 **I Wasn't The One (Who Said Goodbye)** ....*If You Need Somebody Tonight* (Fältskog)	$3	■	Atlantic 89145
				AGNETHA FÄLTSKOG AND PETER CETERA			
7/23/88	**4**	18		5 **One Good Woman** ....AC[4] A:3 / S:6 *One More Story*	$3	■	Full Moon 27824
10/29/88	**59**	8		6 **Best Of Times** ....*Only Love Knows Why*	$3	■	Full Moon 27712
3/11/89	**6**	20	●	7 **After All** ....AC[4] S:4 / A:9 *Dangerous Times* (Cher)	$3	■	Geffen 27529
				CHER and PETER CETERA			
				love theme from the movie *Chances Are* starring Cybill Shepherd and Robert Downey, Jr.			
7/11/92	**35**	20		8 **Restless Heart** ....AC[2] A:30 / S:48 *Dip Your Wings*	$3	▮	Warner 18897
1/23/93	**71**	8		9 **Feels Like Heaven** ....A:70 *World Falling Down* (Cetera)	$3	▮[V]	Warner 18651
				PETER CETERA with Chaka Khan			
7/17/93	**68**	13		10 **Even A Fool Can See** ....A:42 *Where There's No Tomorrow*	$3	▮	Warner 18561

DEBUT	PEAK	WKS	Gold		A-side (Chart Hit)	B-side	$	Sym	Label & Number
					CETERA, Peter — Cont'd				
10/21/95	86	8		11	(I Wanna Take) **Forever Tonight** **PETER CETERA with Crystal Bernard** Bernard was a cast member of TV's *Wings*	*The Lucky Ones* (Cetera)	$3	■	River North 3005
2/22/97	8	34	▲	12	**Hard To Say I'm Sorry** **AZ YET Featuring Peter Cetera** "45" B-side: "Last Night" (no credit to Cetera)	S:6 / A:15 (*david foster's remix*)	$3	■V	LaFace 24223
10/18/97	77	10		13	**You're The Inspiration** **PETER CETERA Featuring Az Yet** above 2 charted by **Chicago** (featuring Cetera) in 1982 and 1984, respectively	S:56 *Do You Love Me That Much / (3 album snippets)*	$4	■	River North 3018
					CHACKSFIELD, Frank, And His Orch. POP/LP '53 Born on 5/9/14 in Battle, Sussex, England. Died on 6/9/95 (age 81). Pianist/bandleader. Hit #2 on the pop charts in 1953 with "Ebb Tide."				
1/25/60	47	8			**On The Beach** title song from the movie starring Gregory Peck; written by **Steve Allen** and Ernest Gold	*A Paris Valentine* [I]	$10		London 1901
					CHAD & JEREMY BUB/LP '64 Soft-rock duo from London, England: Chad Stuart (born on 12/10/43) and Jeremy Clyde (born on 3/22/44). Broke up in 1967. Re-formed briefly in 1982. *1)A Summer Song 2)Willow Weep For Me 3)Before And After*				
5/23/64	21	9		1	**Yesterday's Gone**	*Lemon Tree*	$10		World Artists 1021
8/15/64	7	14		2	**A Summer Song**	*No Tears For Johnnie*	$10		World Artists 1027
11/14/64+	15	13		3	**Willow Weep For Me** #2 hit for Paul Whiteman in 1933	AC[1] *If She Was Mine*	$10	■	World Artists 1034
2/20/65	23	9		4	**If I Loved You** from the Rodgers & Hammerstein musical *Carousel*	*Donna Donna*	$10	■	World Artists 1041
4/10/65	51	8		5	**What Do You Want With Me** **CHAD STUART AND JEREMY CLYDE** (#1, 2 & 5)	*A Very Good Year*	$10		World Artists 1052
5/15/65	17	9		6	**Before And After**	*Fare Thee Well (I Must Be Gone)*	$8	□	Columbia 43277
7/10/65	97	2		7	**From A Window** written by **John Lennon** and **Paul McCartney**	*My Coloring Book*	$10		World Artists 1056
8/7/65	35	7		8	**I Don't Wanna Lose You Baby** #6 & 8 issued with the same "Columbia Records Proudly Introduces..." promo picture sleeve	*Pennies*	$8	□	Columbia 43339
10/30/65	91	2		9	**I Have Dreamed** from the Rodgers & Hammerstein musical *The King And I* starring Yul Brynner	*Should I* (#128)	$8		Columbia 43414
7/9/66	30	9		10	**Distant Shores**	*Last Night*	$8	■	Columbia 43682
10/8/66	87	4		11	**You Are She**	*I Won't Cry*	$8	■	Columbia 43807
					CHAIRMEN OF THE BOARD R&B/BUB/LP '70 R&B vocal group from Detroit, Michigan: General Norman Johnson, Danny Woods, Harrison Kennedy and Eddie Curtis. First recorded for Invictus in 1969. Johnson was leader of **The Showmen** from 1961-67; wrote "Patches," hit for **Clarence Carter**. Johnson went solo in 1976.				
1/17/70	3	15	●	1	**Give Me Just A Little More Time**	*Since The Days Of Pigtails (and Fairy Tales)*	$6		Invictus 9074
5/2/70	38	9		2	(You've Got Me) **Dangling On A String**	*I'll Come Crawling*	$6		Invictus 9078
8/1/70	38	9		3	**Everything's Tuesday**	*Patches*	$6		Invictus 9079
11/14/70+	13	13		4	**Pay To The Piper**	*Bless You*	$6	■	Invictus 9081
2/13/71	42	8		5	**Chairman Of The Board**	*When Will She Tell Me She Needs Me*	$6		Invictus 9086
6/9/73	59	9		6	**Finder's Keepers** **CHAIRMAN OF THE BOARD** (#3 & 6)	*(instrumental)*	$6		Invictus 1251
					CHAKACHAS, The LP '72 Studio group from Belgium. Featuring saxophonist Victor Ingevald.				
1/15/72	8	15	●		**Jungle Fever**	*Cha Ka Cha* [I]	$6		Polydor 15030
					CHAMBERLAIN, Richard LP '62 Born George Richard Chamberlain on 3/31/35 in Beverly Hills, California. Leading movie, theater and TV actor. Played lead role in TV's *Dr. Kildare*, 1961-66.				
6/2/62	10	14		1	**Theme From Dr. Kildare (Three Stars Will Shine Tonight)** **David Rose** (orch.)	*A Kiss To Build A Dream On*	$8	■	MGM 13075
10/6/62	21	9		2	**Love Me Tender** adapted from the 1861 tune "Aura Lee"	*All I Do Is Dream Of You*	$8	■	MGM 13097
2/9/63	14	12		3	**All I Have To Do Is Dream /**				
2/16/63	64	5		4	**Hi-Lili, Hi-Lo** from the 1953 movie *Lili* starring Leslie Caron and Mel Ferrer		$8	■	MGM 13121
7/6/63	65	7		5	**I Will Love You /**				
7/27/63	98	1		6	**True Love** Cole Porter song from the movie *High Society*; all of above from the album *Richard Chamberlain Sings*		$8	■	MGM 13148
9/28/63	42	8		7	**Blue Guitar** B-side became a #1 hit for the **Carpenters** in 1970	*They Long To Be Close To You*	$8	■	MGM 13170
12/5/64	99	1		8	**Rome Will Never Leave You** performed on the TV series *Dr. Kildare*	*You Always Hurt The One You Love*	$8	■	MGM 13285
					CHAMBERS BROTHERS, The BUB/R&B/LP '68 Group of brothers from Lee County, Mississippi: Willie (guitar), Joe (guitar), Lester (harmonica) and George (bass) Chambers, with Brian Keenan (drums).				
8/10/68	11	14		1	**Time Has Come Today**	*People Get Ready*	$10		Columbia 44414
11/23/68	37	8		2	**I Can't Turn You Loose** written by **Otis Redding**	*Do Your Thing*	$10	■	Columbia 44679
12/21/68+	83	5		3	**Shout! - Part 1**	*Part 2*	$15		Vault 945
7/12/69	92	2		4	**Wake Up** from the movie *The April Fools* starring Jack Lemmon	*Everybody Needs Someone*	$10		Columbia 44890
2/28/70	96	1		5	**Love, Peace And Happiness**	*If You Want Me To*	$10		Columbia 45088

DEBUT	PEAK	WKS	Gold	A-side (Chart Hit)......B-side	$	Sym	Label & Number

CHAMPAGNE '77

Pop group from Rotterdam, Holland: Paulette Bronkhorst, Trudie Huysdens, Jan Vredenburg and Bert van der Wiel.

DEBUT	PEAK	WKS	Gold	A-side (Chart Hit)......B-side	$	Sym	Label & Number
3/26/77	83	4		Rock And Roll Star ......*Kiss You Baby*	$5	■	Ariola America 7658

CHAMPAIGN R&B/BUB/LP '81

R&B group from Champaign, Illinois: Pauli Carman and Rena Jones (vocals), Leon Reeder (guitar), Michael Day and Dana Walden (keyboards), Michael Reed (bass) and Rocky Maffit (drums).

DEBUT	PEAK	WKS	Gold	A-side (Chart Hit)......B-side	$	Sym	Label & Number
2/14/81	12	23		1 How 'Bout Us......AC[2] *Lighten Up*	$4		Columbia 11433
				also released with "Spinnin'" as the B-side			
4/2/83	23	20		2 Try Again ......*International Feel*	$4		Columbia 03563

CHAMPLIN, Bill — see SONS OF CHAMPLIN

CHAMPS, The BUB '58

Rock and roll instrumental group from Los Angeles, California. Named after **Gene Autry**'s horse, Champ. Originally consisted of studio musicians Dave Burgess (rhythm guitar), Buddy Bruce (lead guitar), Danny Flores (sax; later changed name to Chuck Rio), Cliff Hils (bass) and Gene Alden (drums). Shortly after "Tequila" became a hit, Bruce and Hils were replaced by Dale Norris and Joe Burnas. Eight months after recording "Tequila," Flores and Alden left, replaced by Jimmy Seals (sax) & Dash Crofts (drums), later a hit recording duo (**Seals & Crofts**). Other personnel changes followed; in 1960, guitarist **Glen Campbell** spent some time in the group. Also see **Kuf-Linx**.

DEBUT	PEAK	WKS	Gold	A-side (Chart Hit)......B-side	$	Sym	Label & Number
2/24/58	1[5]	19	●	1 Tequila RB[4] S:1[5] / T:1[5] / A:1[2] *Train To Nowhere* [I]	$25		Challenge 1016
5/26/58	30	10		2 El Rancho Rock / T:30 / S:31 [I]			
				based on the 1934 tune "Alla En El Rancho Grande"; #6 hit for **Bing Crosby** in 1939			
8/11/58	94	1		3 Midnighter......H:94 [I]	$20		Challenge 59007
8/11/58	59	7		4 Chariot Rock ......H:59 *Subway* [I]	$20		Challenge 59018
				based on the American spiritual "Swing Low, Swing Chariot"			
1/18/60	30	11		5 Too Much Tequila ......*Twenty Thousand Leagues* [I]	$20		Challenge 59063
5/26/62	40	13		6 Limbo Rock / [I]			
2/3/62	99	1		7 Tequila Twist...... [I-R]	$20		Challenge 9131
				twist version of #1 above			
10/20/62	97	1		8 Limbo Dance......*Latin Limbo*	$20		Challenge 9162

CHAMPS' BOYS ORCHESTRA, The '76

Instrumental group from France.

DEBUT	PEAK	WKS	Gold	A-side (Chart Hit)......B-side	$	Sym	Label & Number
5/29/76	98	2		Tubular Bells ......*Fleur* [I]	$6		Janus 259
				theme from the movie *The Exorcist* starring Linda Blair			

★270★ CHANDLER, Gene R&B/BUB/LP '62

Born Eugene Dixon on 7/6/40 in Chicago, Illinois. R&B singer/producer. Took last name from his favorite movie star, Jeff Chandler. Joined the Gaytones at Englewood High School in 1955. Joined his neighborhood vocal group **The Dukays** (see #1, 3 & 4 below) in 1956. In the U.S. Army, Germany, 1957-60. Rejoined The Dukays in 1960; they first recorded for NAT in 1961. Group recorded "Duke Of Earl" while under contract to NAT; however, Vee-Jay purchased the recording and released the record as by Gene Chandler. Own label, Mr. Chand, 1969-73. Charted 36 R&B hits, 1962-86. Gene, **Jerry Butler**, **Lloyd Price** and **Ben E. King** formed a corporation "The 4 Kings of Rhythm & Blues" in 1999.

1)Duke Of Earl 2)Groovy Situation 3)Nothing Can Stop Me 4)Just Be True 5)Bless Our Love

DEBUT	PEAK	WKS	Gold	A-side (Chart Hit)......B-side	$	Sym	Label & Number
5/15/61	64	13		1 The Girl's A Devil *[THE DUKAYS]*......*The Big Lie*	$20		NAT 4001
1/13/62	1[3]	15	●	2 Duke Of Earl RB[5] *Kissin' In The Kitchen*	$25		Vee-Jay 416
				song is actually by **The Dukays** (with Gene Chandler, lead singer)			
1/20/62	73	5		3 Nite Owl *[DUKAYS]*......*Festival Of Love*	$20		NAT 4002
3/31/62	88	1		4 Nite Owl *[DUKAYS]*......*Festival Of Love*	$20		Vee-Jay 430
				above 2 are the same version (recorded at the same session as "Duke Of Earl")			
4/28/62	91	2		5 Walk On With The Duke *[THE DUKE OF EARL]*......*London Town*	$20		Vee-Jay 440
2/23/63	47	12		6 Rainbow /			
11/24/62	49	8		7 You Threw A Lucky Punch	$20		Vee-Jay 468
				Cal Carter and Friends (backing vocals); answer song to **Mary Wells**' "You Beat Me To The Punch"			
8/10/63	71	7		8 Man's Temptation ......*Baby That's Love*	$20		Vee-Jay 536
5/2/64	92	2		9 Soul Hootenanny Pt. I ......*Pt. II*	$15		Constellation 114
7/11/64	19	10		10 Just Be True......*A Song Called Soul*	$15		Constellation 130
9/26/64	39	9		11 Bless Our Love......*London Town*	$15		Constellation 136
12/5/64+	40	8		12 What Now ......*If You Can't Be True (Find a Part Time Love)*	$15		Constellation 141
3/6/65	92	1		13 You Can't Hurt Me No More ......*Everybody Lets Dance*	$15		Constellation 146
4/17/65	18	12		14 Nothing Can Stop Me ......*The Big Lie*	$15		Constellation 149
8/21/65	92	3		15 Good Times ......*No One Can Love You (Like I Do)*	$15		Constellation 160
11/27/65+	69	8		16 Rainbow '65 Part I ......*Part II* [L-R]	$15		Constellation 158
				studio version on #6 above; #6, 8, 10 & 12-16: written by **Curtis Mayfield**			
3/19/66	88	2		17 (I'm Just A) Fool For You......*Buddy Ain't It A Shame*	$15		Constellation 167
11/26/66+	45	8		18 I Fooled You This Time ......*Such A Pretty Thing*	$15		Checker 1155
2/25/67	66	9		19 Girl Don't Care......*My Love*	$12		Brunswick 55312
6/10/67	94	4		20 To Be A Lover......*After The Laughter*	$12		Checker 1165
9/2/67	98	1		21 There Goes The Lover......*Tell Me What Can I Do*	$12		Brunswick 55339
9/21/68	82	3		22 There Was A Time ......*Those Were The Good Old Days*	$12		Brunswick 55383
10/19/68	57	8		23 From The Teacher To The Preacher ......*Anywhere But Nowhere*	$12		Brunswick 55387
				GENE CHANDLER And BARBARA ACKLIN			
7/11/70	12	15	●	24 Groovy Situation ......*Not The Marrying Kind*	$8		Mercury 73083
11/7/70	75	5		25 Simply Call It Love......*Give Me A Chance*	$8		Mercury 73121
1/2/71	94	3		26 You Just Can't Win (By Making The Same Mistake) ......*Sho Is Grooving*	$8		Mercury 73163
				GENE & JERRY (Jerry Butler)			
1/6/79	53	9		27 Get Down ......*I'm The Traveling Kind*	$5		Chi-Sound 2386
10/6/79	99	2		28 When You're #1......*I'll Remember You*	$5		20th Century 2411
				first pressings issued on Chi-Sound 2411 in 1979			

CHANDLER, Karen
MEM/POP '53

Born Eva Nadauld in Rexburg, Idaho. Sang with **Benny Goodman** under the name Eve Young in 1946. Hit #5 on the pop charts in 1953 with "Hold Me, Thrill Me, Kiss Me."

DEBUT	PEAK	WKS	Gold	A-side (Chart Hit)...B-side	$	Sym	Label & Number
9/29/56	49	9		**Tonight You Belong To Me** ....T:49 *Crazy Arms* **KAREN CHANDLER & JIMMY WAKELY** Karen's husband, **Jack Pleis** (orch.); #1 hit for **Gene Austin** in 1927	$20		Decca 30040

CHANDLER, Kenny
BUB '63

Born Kenneth Bolognese on 11/21/40 in Harrisburg, Pennsylvania. White pop singer. Also recorded as Kenny Beau.

DEBUT	PEAK	WKS	Gold	A-side (Chart Hit)...B-side	$	Sym	Label & Number
4/6/63	64	7		**Heart** ....*Wait For Me*	$15		Laurie 3158

CHANELS — see 5 CHANELS

CHANGE
R&B/LP '80

European-American dance group formed in Italy by producers Jacques Fred Petrus and Mauro Malavasi. Led by Paolo Gianolio (guitar) and David Romani (bass). **Luther Vandross** sang lead on several songs of group's first charted album. Later group, based in New York, included lead vocals by James Robinson and Deborah "Crab" Cooper (later with **C & C Music Factory**). One-time band member Rick Gallwey married **Sharon Bryant**, former lead singer of **Atlantic Starr**.

DEBUT	PEAK	WKS	Gold	A-side (Chart Hit)...B-side	$	Sym	Label & Number
5/17/80	40	13		1 **A Lover's Holiday** ....*The End*	$5		RFC 49208
6/6/81	80	4		2 **Paradise** ....*Your Move*	$4		RFC/Atlantic 3809
8/8/81	89	2		3 **Hold Tight** ....*Stop For Love*	$4		RFC/Atlantic 3832
5/29/82	84	5		4 **The Very Best In You** ....*You're My Girl*	$4		RFC/Atlantic 4027

CHANGING FACES
R&B/BUB/LP '94

Female R&B vocal duo from Brooklyn, New York: Charisse Rose and Cassandra Lucas.

DEBUT	PEAK	WKS	Gold	A-side (Chart Hit)...B-side	$	Sym	Label & Number
7/30/94	3	21	▲	1 **Stroke You Up** S:2 / A:12 *(remix edit)*	$3	▌	Big Beat 98279
11/19/94+	38	20		2 **Foolin' Around** ....S:19 / A:68 *Feeling All This Love*	$3	▌	Big Beat 98207
5/10/97	8	25	▲	3 **G.H.E.T.T.O.U.T.** ....RB[4] S:4 / A:31 *Goin' Nowhere*	$3	▌	Big Beat 98026
11/8/97	65	12		4 **All Of My Days** ....S:54 *(instrumental)* **CHANGING FACES (Featuring Jay-Z)** from the movie *Space Jam* starring Michael Jordan; all of above written and produced by **R. Kelly**	$3	▌	Big Beat 98000
9/30/00	64	11		5 **That Other Woman** ....S:24 / A:61 *(5 versions)* produced by **Joe**	$8	★**	Atlantic 84939

CHANGIN' TIMES, The
'65

Songwriting/producing duo: Artie Kornfeld and Steve Duboff.

DEBUT	PEAK	WKS	Gold	A-side (Chart Hit)...B-side	$	Sym	Label & Number
11/13/65	87	3		**Pied Piper** ....*Thank You Babe*	$20		Philips 40320

CHANNEL, Bruce
BUB/LP '62

Born on 11/28/40 in Jacksonville, Texas. Pop singer.

DEBUT	PEAK	WKS	Gold	A-side (Chart Hit)...B-side	$	Sym	Label & Number
1/27/62	1 (3)	15	●	1 **Hey! Baby** *Dream Girl* **Delbert McClinton** (harmonica player); first released on Le Cam 953 in 1961 ($40)	$20		Smash 1731
4/28/62	52	7		2 **Number One Man** ....*If Only I Had Known*	$15		Smash 1752
7/28/62	98	2		3 **Come On Baby** ....*Mine Exclusively*	$12		Smash 1769
2/29/64	89	3		4 **Going Back To Louisiana** ....*Forget Me Not*	$12		Le Cam 122
12/23/67	90	2		5 **Mr. Bus Driver** ....*It's Me* produced by **Dale Hawkins**	$10		Mala 579

CHANNEL LIVE
LP '95

Rap duo from New Jersey: Tuffy and Hakeem.

DEBUT	PEAK	WKS	Gold	A-side (Chart Hit)...B-side	$	Sym	Label & Number
2/4/95	54	12		**Mad Izm** ....S:28 *(2 versions)*	$3	▌	Capitol 58313

CHANSON
R&B/LP '79

Disco studio group. Lead vocals by James Jamerson, Jr. and David Williams. Jamerson's father was a prominent Motown bassist. Group name is French for song.

DEBUT	PEAK	WKS	Gold	A-side (Chart Hit)...B-side	$	Sym	Label & Number
11/11/78+	21	16		**Don't Hold Back** ....*Did You Ever*	$4		Ariola America 7717

CHANTAY'S
LP '63

Teen surf-rock group from Santa Ana, California: Bob Spickard (lead guitar), Brian Carman (rhythm guitar), Rob Marshall (piano), Warren Waters (bass) and Bob Welsh (drums).

DEBUT	PEAK	WKS	Gold	A-side (Chart Hit)...B-side	$	Sym	Label & Number
3/2/63	4	16		**Pipeline** ....*Move It* [I] Pipeline is a surfing term for the curl of the wave before it breaks; "Bubbled Under" on 10/1/66 on Dot 145 (#106); first released on Downey 104 in 1962 ($50)	$20		Dot 16440

CHANTELS, The
BUB '58

Female R&B vocal group from the Bronx, New York. Formed in high school, with lead Arlene Smith, Sonia Goring, Rene Minus, Jackie Landry and Lois Harris. Group name taken from that of a rival school, St. Francis de Chantelle. Auditioned for **Richard Barrett**, who became their manager and obtained a contract with Gone/End Records. Landry died of cancer on 12/23/97 (age 56). **Carol Douglas** was a member in the early 1970s.

DEBUT	PEAK	WKS	Gold	A-side (Chart Hit)...B-side	$	Sym	Label & Number
9/30/57	71	6		1 **He's Gone** ....T:71 *The Plea*	$75		End 1001
1/20/58	15	18		2 **Maybe** ....T:15 / S:16 *Come My Little Baby* "Bubbled Under" (#116) on 12/6/69 on Roulette 7064 ($10)	$50		End 1005
3/31/58	39	13		3 **Every Night (I Pray)** ....S:39 / T:40 *Whoever You Are*	$50		End 1015
6/16/58	42	7		4 **I Love You So** ....T:42 / S:44 *How Could You Call It Off*	$50		End 1020
7/20/59	93	2		5 **Summer's Love** ....*All Is Forgiven* **RICHARD BARRETT With The Chantels**	$75		Gone 5060
8/28/61	14	12		6 **Look In My Eyes** *Glad To Be Back*	$20		Carlton 555
11/13/61	29	9		7 **Well, I Told You** ....*Still* answer song to **Ray Charles**' "Hit The Road Jack"	$20		Carlton 564
3/23/63	77	2		8 **Eternally** ....*Swamp Water* Charlie Chaplin penned the melody, originally known as "Terry's Theme" from the 1952 movie *Limelight* starring Chaplin	$40		Ludix 101

CHANTERS, The
'61

Black teen doo-wop group from Queens, New York: Larry Pendergrass (lead), Fred Paige, Bud Johnson, Elliot Green and Bobby Thompson. Johnson's father is famous bandleader **Buddy Johnson**, who arranged their sessions. Group disbanded in the early 1960s. Not to be confused with Billy Butler's Chanters.

DEBUT	PEAK	WKS	Gold	A-side (Chart Hit)...B-side	$	Sym	Label & Number
6/19/61	41	9		**No, No, No** ....*I Make This Pledge (To You)*	$50		DeLuxe 6191

DEBUT	PEAK	WKS	Gold	A-side (Chart Hit)...B-side	$	Sym	Label & Number
				CHAPIN, Harry AC/BUB/LP **'74**			
				Born on 12/7/42 in Long Island, New York. Died in a car crash on 7/16/81 (age 38). Folk-rock singer/songwriter/guitarist.			
3/11/72	24	16		1 **Taxi** ... *Empty*	$6		Elektra 45770
10/21/72	75	6		2 **Sunday Morning Sunshine** ... *Burning Herself*	$6		Elektra 45811
1/5/74	36	13		3 **WOLD** ... *Short Stories*	$6		Elektra 45874
10/5/74	❶[1]	19	●	4 **Cat's In The Cradle** *Vacancy*	$5		Elektra 45203
				lyrics from a poem by Harry's wife, Sandy			
2/15/75	44	9		5 **I Wanna Learn A Love Song** ... *She Sings Songs Without Words*	$5		Elektra 45236
6/26/76	86	3		6 **Better Place To Be (Parts 1 & 2)** ... [L]	$5		Elektra 45327
				studio version "Bubbled Under" (#118) on 2/3/73 on Elektra 45828			
11/1/80	23	14		7 **Sequel** ... *I Finally Found It Sandy*	$4		Boardwalk 5700
				sequel to 1972's "Taxi"			
				CHAPLAIN, Paul, and his Emeralds **'60**			
				Rock and roll group from Webster, Massachusetts: Paul Chaplain, George Dibonaventura, Bob Prince and Bill Hickman.			
8/29/60	82	4		**Shortnin' Bread** ... *Nicotine*	$30		Harper 100
				based on a traditional folk song from 1905			
				CHAPMAN, Tracy BUB/LP **'88**			
				Born on 3/20/64 in Cleveland, Ohio. Folk-R&B singer/songwriter/guitarist. Won the 1988 Best New Artist Grammy Award.			
6/4/88	6	21		1 **Fast Car** ... S:4 / A:7 *For You*	$3		Elektra 69412
10/1/88	75	4		2 **Talkin' Bout A Revolution** ... *Behind The Wall*	$3	■	Elektra 69383
11/5/88	48	12		3 **Baby Can I Hold You** ... *If Not Now...*	$3	■	Elektra 69356
10/28/89	90	4		4 **Crossroads** ... *Born To Fight*	$3	■	Elektra 69273
4/6/96	3	39	▲	5 **Give Me One Reason** A:2 / S:5 *The Rape of the World*	$3	■V	Elektra 64346
				CHARGERS, The **'58**			
				R&B vocal group from Los Angeles, California: Benny Easley, brothers Dunbar and Johnny White, Jimmy Scott and Mitchell Alexander. Founded by **Jesse Belvin**.			
9/1/58	95	1		**Old MacDonald** ... H:95 *Dandilyon*	$30		RCA Victor 7301
				Shorty Rogers (orch.); adaptation of children's song originating in the early 1700's			
				CHARLENE LP **'82**			
				Born Charlene D'Angelo on 6/1/50 in Hollywood, California. Pop-R&B singer.			
3/5/77	97	4		1 **It Ain't Easy Comin' Down** ... *On My Way To You*	$5		Prodigal 0632
				"Bubbled Under" (#109) on 7/24/82 on Motown 1621			
5/14/77	96	3		2 **Freddie** ... *(instrumental)*	$5	■	Prodigal 0633
9/24/77	97	3		3 **I've Never Been To Me** ... *It's Really Nice To Be In Love Again*	$10		Prodigal 0636
3/6/82	3	20		4 **I've Never Been To Me** *Somewhere In My Life* [R]	$4		Motown 1611
				re-released after DJ Scott Shannon began playing the song on WRBQ-FM in Tampa, Florida; same version as #3 above			
10/30/82	46	11		5 **Used To Be** ... *I Want To Come Back As A Song* (Charlene)	$4	□	Motown 1650
				CHARLENE & STEVIE WONDER			
				CHARLES, Jimmy **'60**			
				Born in 1942 in Paterson, New Jersey. R&B singer. Won Apollo Amateur Contest in 1958.			
8/22/60	5	15		1 **A Million To One** ... *Hop Scotch Hop*	$20		Promo 1002
				The Revelletts (backing vocals); first released on Glenville 1002 in 1960 ($50)			
12/5/60+	47	12		2 **The Age For Love** ... *Follow The Swallow*	$20	■	Promo 1003
				Phil Medley (orch., above 2)			
				CHARLES, Ray ★18★ R&B/BUB/C&W/AC/LP **'62**			
				Born Ray Charles Robinson on 9/23/30 in Albany, Georgia; raised in Greenville, Florida. Partially blind at age five, completely blind at seven (glaucoma). Studied classical piano and clarinet at State School for Deaf and Blind Children, St. Augustine, Florida, 1937-45. With local Florida bands; moved to Seattle in 1948. Formed the McSon Trio (also known as the Maxim Trio and the Maxine Trio) with Gossady McGhee (guitar) and Milton Garred (bass). First recordings were very much in the King Cole Trio style. Formed own band in 1954. **The Raeletts** were Ray's credited and uncredited backing vocalists. Inducted into the Rock and Roll Hall of Fame in 1986. Won Grammy's Lifetime Achievement Award in 1987. Popular performer, with many TV and movie appearances.			
				1)I Can't Stop Loving You 2)Hit The Road Jack 3)Georgia On My Mind 4)You Don't Know Me 5)Busted			
10/28/57	34	15		1 **Swanee River Rock (Talkin' 'Bout That River)** ... S:34 / T:42 *I Want A Little Girl*	$30		Atlantic 1154
				Mongo Santamaria (congo drums); based on Stephen Foster's "Old Folks At Home"			
12/22/58	79	2		2 **Rockhouse (Part 2)** ... *(Part 1)* [I]	$20		Atlantic 2006
2/9/59	95	1		3 **(Night Time Is) The Right Time** ... *Tell All The World About You*	$20		Atlantic 2010
				original version by **Nappy Brown** in 1957 on Savoy 1525 ($25)			
7/6/59	6	15		4 **What'd I Say (Part I)** ... RB[1] *(Part II)*	$20		Atlantic 2031
11/9/59	40	10		5 **I'm Movin' On** ... *I Believe To My Soul*	$15		Atlantic 2043
				#1 Country hit for **Hank Snow** in 1950			
1/11/60	78	3		6 **Let The Good Times Roll** /			
				#2 R&B hit for Louis Jordan in 1947			
2/8/60	95	2		7 **Don't Let The Sun Catch You Cryin'** ...	$15		Atlantic 2047
				#3 R&B hit for Louis Jordan in 1946			
6/27/60	40	8		8 **Sticks And Stones** ... *Worried Life Blues*	$15		ABC-Paramount 10118
9/26/60	❶[1]	13		9 **Georgia On My Mind** ... *Carry Me Back To Old Virginny*	$15		ABC-Paramount 10135
				written by Hoagy Carmichael; #10 hit for Frankie Trumbauer in 1931			
11/21/60	28	9		10 **Ruby** /			
				from the movie *Ruby Gentry* starring Charlton Heston; there were 4 Top 30 versions of this tune in 1953			
11/21/60	55	4		11 **Hardhearted Hannah** ...	$15		ABC-Paramount 10164
				#3 hit for Dolly Kay in 1924			
11/28/60	83	2		12 **Come Rain Or Come Shine** ... *Tell Me You'll Wait For Me*	$15		Atlantic 2084
				#17 hit for **Margaret Whiting** in 1946; from the musical *St. Louis Woman* starring Pearl Bailey; also see #57 below			
1/16/61	58	6		13 **Them That Got** ... *I Wonder*	$12		ABC-Paramount 10141
3/6/61	8	13		14 **One Mint Julep** ... RB[1] *Let's Go* [I]	$12		Impulse! 200
				#2 R&B hit for **The Clovers** in 1952			

DEBUT	PEAK	WKS	Gold	A-side (Chart Hit)	B-side	$	Sym	Label & Number
				CHARLES, Ray — Cont'd				
6/19/61	66	5		15 I've Got News For You /				
6/19/61	84	2		16 I'm Gonna Move To The Outskirts Of Town		$12		Impulse! 202
				#17 hit for Jimmie Lunceford in 1942				
9/11/61	1[2]	13		17 Hit The Road Jack RB[5]	*The Danger Zone*	$12		ABC-Paramount 10244
11/27/61+	9	12		18 Unchain My Heart / RB[2]				
12/11/61+	72	4		19 But On The Other Hand Baby		$12		ABC-Paramount 10266
3/3/62	91	2		20 Baby It's Cold Outside	*We'll Be Together Again*	$12		ABC-Paramount 10298
				RAY CHARLES and BETTY CARTER				
				#3 hit for **Margaret Whiting** & Johnny Mercer in 1949; from the movie *Neptune's Daughter* starring Esther Williams; Carter was born Lillie Mae Jones on 5/16/30 in Flint, Michigan and sang with Lionel Hampton's band from 1948-51				
4/7/62	20	7		21 Hide 'Nor Hair /				
3/31/62	44	7		22 At The Club		$12		ABC-Paramount 10314
5/5/62	1[5]	18	●	23 I Can't Stop Loving You / RB[10] / AC[5]				
5/12/62	41	9		24 Born To Lose		$12		ABC-Paramount 10330
				#3 Country hit for Ted Daffan's Texans in 1944				
7/28/62	2[1]	11		25 You Don't Know Me / AC[3]				
7/28/62	60	4		26 Careless Love		$12		ABC-Paramount 10345
				new lyrics to the traditional blues standard; above 4 from the album *Modern Sounds In Country And Western Music*				
11/17/62	7	12		27 You Are My Sunshine / RB[3]				
				#20 hit for **Bing Crosby** in 1941				
11/17/62	29	9		28 Your Cheating Heart		$12		ABC-Paramount 10375
				#1 Country hit for Hank Williams in 1953				
2/23/63	20	8		29 Don't Set Me Free /				
3/9/63	92	2		30 The Brightest Smile In Town		$12		ABC-Paramount 10405
4/13/63	8	11		31 Take These Chains From My Heart	*No Letter Today* (#105)	$12		ABC-Paramount 10435
				#1 Country hit for Hank Williams in 1953				
6/22/63	21	8		32 No One /				
6/22/63	29	7		33 Without Love (There Is Nothing)		$12		ABC-Paramount 10453
9/7/63	4	12		34 Busted	*Making Believe* (#102)	$12		ABC-Paramount 10481
				#13 Country hit for **Johnny Cash** earlier in 1963				
12/7/63+	20	9		35 That Lucky Old Sun	*Ol' Man Time*	$12		ABC-Paramount 10509
				#1 hit for **Frankie Laine** in 1949				
2/29/64	38	7		36 My Heart Cries For You /				
				there were 8 Top 30 versions of this tune in 1951				
2/22/64	39	7		37 Baby, Don't You Cry (The New Swingova Rhythm)		$12		ABC-Paramount 10530
5/30/64	51	6		38 My Baby Don't Dig Me	*Something's Wrong*	$10		ABC-Paramount 10557
				#17, 19, 21, 22 & 38: written by **Percy Mayfield**				
8/1/64	50	5		39 A Tear Fell /				
				#15 R&B hit for **Ivory Joe Hunter** in 1956				
7/18/64	55	6		40 No One To Cry To		$10		ABC-Paramount 10571
				#6 Country hit in 1946 for the Sons Of The Pioneers; Gene Lowell Singers (backing vocals, above 2)				
9/26/64	52	7		41 Smack Dab In The Middle	*I Wake Up Crying*	$10		ABC-Paramount 10588
				tune recorded in 1955 by **Count Basie** (Joe Williams, vocal)				
12/12/64+	46	8		42 Makin' Whoopee	*(instrumental)*	$10		ABC-Paramount 10609
				#2 hit for Eddie Cantor in 1929				
2/6/65	58	7		43 Cry	*Teardrops From My Eyes* (#112)	$10		ABC-Paramount 10615
				#1 hit for **Johnnie Ray** in 1951				
4/17/65	79	3		44 I Gotta Woman (Part One)	*(Part Two)*	$10		ABC-Paramount 10649
				Charles' original version hit #1 on the R&B charts in 1955				
7/17/65	84	4		45 I'm A Fool To Care	*Love's Gonna Live Here (Swingova)*	$10		ABC-Paramount 10700
				#6 hit for **Les Paul & Mary Ford** in 1954				
12/11/65+	6	15		46 Crying Time AC[3]	*When My Dreamboat Comes Home*	$10		ABC-Paramount 10739
				#28, 31 & 46: **Jack Halloran Singers** (backing vocals)				
3/26/66	19	8		47 Together Again / AC[3]				
				above 2 written by **Buck Owens**				
3/26/66	91	2		48 You're Just About To Lose Your Clown		$10		ABC-Paramount 10785
5/28/66	31	9		49 Let's Go Get Stoned RB[1]	*The Train*	$8		ABC 10808
9/3/66	32	7		50 I Chose To Sing The Blues	*Hopelessly*	$8		ABC 10840
				#3, 8, 17, 18, 27, 29, 32, 38, 41, 46, 49 & 50: **The Raeletts** (backing vocals)				
11/12/66	64	6		51 Please Say You're Fooling /				
11/26/66	72	4		52 I Don't Need No Doctor		$8		ABC/TRC 10865
				#49 & 52: written by **Ashford & Simpson**; #2, 4, 5, 8, 13, 17-19, 21, 22, 29, 30, 34, 37, 38, 41, 44, 51 & 52 shown as: **RAY CHARLES And His Orchestra**				
3/18/67	98	1		53 I Want To Talk About You	*Something Inside Me* (#112)	$8		ABC/TRC 10901
				written by **Billy Eckstine**				
5/20/67	15	12		54 Here We Go Again	*Somebody Ought To Write A Book About It* (#105)	$8		ABC/TRC 10938
8/26/67	33	7		55 In The Heat Of The Night	*Something's Got To Change*	$8		ABC/TRC 10970
				title song from the movie starring Sidney Poitier				
11/11/67	25	7		56 Yesterday	*Never Had Enough Of Nothing Yet*	$8		ABC/TRC 11009
1/20/68	98	2		57 Come Rain Or Come Shine	*Tell Me You'll Wait For Me* [R]	$12		Atlantic 2470
				reissue on "Atlantic Classic's Revisited" (see #12 above - same version)				
2/24/68	64	8		58 That's A Lie	*Go On Home*	$8	■	ABC/TRC 11045
6/8/68	35	10		59 Eleanor Rigby /				
				#56 & 59: written by **John Lennon** & **Paul McCartney**				
6/15/68	46	12		60 Understanding		$8		ABC/TRC 11090
9/28/68	83	2		61 Sweet Young Thing Like You /				
10/19/68	92	2		62 Listen, They're Playing My Song		$8		ABC/TRC 11133
1/4/69	77	6		63 If It Wasn't For Bad Luck	*When I Stop Dreaming* (Charles - #112)	$8		ABC/TRC 11170
				RAY CHARLES & JIMMY LEWIS				
5/17/69	94	2		64 Let Me Love You	*I'm Satisfied*	$8		ABC/TRC 11213

DEBUT	PEAK	WKS	Gold	A-side (Chart Hit)	B-side	$	Sym	Label & Number
				CHARLES, Ray — Cont'd				
3/14/70	98	2		65 **Laughin And Clownin** written by **Sam Cooke**	*That Thing Called Love*	$8		ABC/TRC 11259
10/3/70+	41	18		66 **If You Were Mine**	*Till I Can't Take It Anymore*	$8		ABC/TRC 11271
3/13/71	36	11		67 **Don't Change On Me** #50, 58, 60, 64 & 67: written by **Jimmy Holiday**	*Sweet Memories*	$8		ABC/TRC 11291
3/20/71	36	12		68 **Booty Butt** **THE RAY CHARLES ORCHESTRA**	*Sidewinder* [I]	$10		Tangerine 1015
8/28/71	68	8		69 **Feel So Bad** #8 R&B hit for **Chuck Willis** in 1954	*Your Love Is So Doggone Good*	$7		ABC/TRC 11308
12/25/71+	54	7		70 **What Am I Living For**	*Tired Of My Tears*	$7		ABC/TRC 11317
7/8/72	65	6		71 **Look What They've Done To My Song, Ma**	*America The Beautiful*	$7		ABC/TRC 11329
6/9/73	81	4		72 **I Can Make It Thru The Days (But Oh Those Lonely Nights)**	*Ring Of Fire*	$7		ABC/TRC 11351
11/17/73	82	6		73 **Come Live With Me**	*Everybody Sing*	$6		CrossOver 973
9/13/75	91	3		74 **Living For The City**	*Then We'll Be Home*	$6		CrossOver 981
4/4/87	75	7		75 **Baby Grand** **BILLY JOEL Featuring Ray Charles**	*Big Man On Mulberry Street* (Joel)	$3	■	Columbia 06994
11/18/89+	18	16		76 **I'll Be Good To You** RB[2] S:13 / A:26 **QUINCY JONES Featuring Ray Charles and Chaka Khan** Charles' musical conductors and arrangers: Ralph Burns (#9, 12, 15, 57), Sid Feller (#13, 17, 18, 21, 22, 34-37, 39-45), **Quincy Jones** (#14, 16), Marty Paich (#10, 11, 20, 23-25, 28, 31) and Gerald Wilson (#26, 27, 29, 30, 32, 33, 38)	*(instrumental)*	$3	■V	Qwest 22697
7/20/02	9[S]	11		77 **Mother**	*New Orleans*	$5	★	CrossOver 0026
				CHARLES, Ray, Singers AC/BUB/LP **'64** Born Charles Raymond Offenberg on 9/13/18 in Chicago, Illinois. Arranger/conductor for many TV shows including the ***Perry Como** Show*, ***Glen Campbell** Goodtime Hour* and ***Sha-Na-Na***. Winner of two Emmys.				
11/12/55	55	8		1 **Autumn Leaves** T:55	*Early Autumn*	$12		MGM 12068
4/11/64	3	15		2 **Love Me With All Your Heart (Cuando Calienta El Sol)** AC[4]	*Sweet Little Mountain Bird*	$6		Command 4046
7/11/64	29	6		3 **Al-Di-La** / from the movie *Rome Adventure* starring Troy Donahue				
9/19/64	83	3		4 **Till The End Of Time** #1 hit for **Perry Como** in 1945; melody based on Chopin's "Polonaise"		$6		Command 4049
11/14/64+	32	10		5 **One More Time**	*Bluesette*	$6		Command 4057
2/27/65	72	4		6 **This Is My Prayer**	*A Toy For A Boy*	$6		Command 4059
6/13/70	99	1		7 **Move Me, O Wondrous Music**	*I'll Fly Away*	$6		Command 4135
				CHARLES, Sonny R&B/BUB/LP **'69** Born in Fort Wayne, Indiana. R&B singer. Leader of **The Checkmates, Ltd.** which includes Bobby Stevens, Harvey Trees, Bill Van Buskirk and Marvin Smith.				
4/5/69	65	7		1 **Love Is All I Have To Give** **THE CHECKMATES, LTD.**	*Never Should Have Lied*	$8		A&M 1039
5/10/69	13	13		2 **Black Pearl** **SONNY CHARLES and THE CHECKMATES, LTD.** originally released only as **SONNY CHARLES**	*Lazy Susan*	$8		A&M 1053
10/18/69	69	4		3 **Proud Mary** **THE CHECKMATES, LTD. featuring SONNY CHARLES** all of above produced by Phil Spector	*Spanish Harlem*	$8		A&M 1127
11/13/82+	40	14		4 **Put It In A Magazine** **SONNY CHARLES**	*The Week-End Father Song*	$5		Highrise 2001
				CHARLES, Tommy **'56** Born on 11/29/29 in Chattanooga, Tennessee. Died on 8/8/96 (age 66). Pop singer.				
2/11/56	43	14		1 **Our Love Affair** T:43 **Jack Halloran** Chorus (backing vocals)	*If You Were Me (And I Were You)*	$20		Decca 29717
7/21/56	92	3		2 **After School** T:92 The Anita Kerr Singers (backing vocals); Cliff Parman (orch., above 2)	*I'll Wait For Your Call*	$20		Decca 29946
				CHARLES & EDDIE BUB/LP **'92** R&B vocal duo: Charles Pettigrew (from Philadelphia, Pennsylvania) and Eddie Chacon (from Oakland, California). Pettigrew died of cancer on 4/6/2001 (age 37).				
8/22/92	13	26		**Would I Lie To You?** A:14 / S:15 "45": Capitol 57986; B-side: "N.Y.C."	*Unconditional*	$3	▮V	Capitol 44809
				CHARLIE LP **'83** Rock group from England: Terry Thomas (guitar), Julian Colbeck (guitar), John Anderson (bass) and Steve Gadd (drums). Varying membership also included Bob Henrit (drums; **Argent**; joined by 1983) and Terry Slesser (vocals; joined in 1980). Henrit joined **The Kinks** by 1984.				
8/20/77	96	2		1 **Turning To You**	*Pressure Point*	$6		Janus 270
8/5/78	54	7		2 **She Loves To Be In Love**	*Life So Cruel*	$6		Janus 276
9/8/79	60	6		3 **Killer Cut**	*The End Of It All*	$5	■	Arista 0449
6/25/83	38	11		4 **It's Inevitable**	*Can't Wait 'Till Tomorrow*	$4	■	Mirage 99862
				CHARM **'92** Born in Brooklyn, New York. Male rapper.				
1/18/92	91	3		**Butt Naked** A:69	*(4 remixes)*	$7	▮*	Turnstyle 96251
				CHARMETTES, The **'63** Female R&B vocal trio from Brooklyn, New York: Clara Byrd, Mittie Ponder and Betty Simmons.				
11/23/63	100	1		**Please Don't Kiss Me Again**	*What Is A Tear*	$30		Kapp 547
				CHARM FARM **'96** Techno-pop group from Detroit, Michigan: Dennis White (vocals), Steve Zuccaro (guitar), Ken Roberts (keyboards), Dino Zoyes (bass) and Eric Meyer (drums).				
9/21/96	89	4		**Superstar**	*(2 remixes)*	$4	▮	PRA/Mercury 578470

DEBUT	PEAK	WKS	Gold	A-side (Chart Hit)..........B-side	$	Sym	Label & Number

CHARMS, The — R&B/POP '55

R&B vocal group from Cincinnati, Ohio: **Otis Williams**, Richard Parker, Donald Peak, Joe Penn and Rolland Bradley. Group first recorded for Rockin' in 1953. Otis, not to be confused with the same-named member of The Temptations, later recorded country music.

DEBUT	PEAK	WKS	Gold	A-side (Chart Hit)..........B-side	$	Sym	Label & Number
11/27/54+	15	15		1 **Hearts Of Stone** .... RB[9] S:15 / J:15 / A:20 *Who Knows*	$100		DeLuxe 6062
1/15/55	26	3		2 **Ling, Ting, Tong** .... S:26 *Bazoom (I Need Your Lovin') (R&B #15)*	$75		DeLuxe 6076
				OTIS WILLIAMS And His New Group:			
1/28/56	48	9		3 **That's Your Mistake** .... T:48 *Too Late I Learned*	$30		DeLuxe 6091
				OTIS WILLIAMS And His CHARMS:			
3/31/56	11	21		4 **Ivory Tower** A:11 / T:12 / S:13 / J:19 *In Paradise*	$30		DeLuxe 6093
3/13/61	95	3		5 **Little Turtle Dove** .... *So Can I*	$20		King 5455
9/18/61	99	1		6 **Panic** .... *Pardon Me*	$20		King 5527

CHARTBUSTERS, The — BUB '64

Rock and roll band from Washington DC: Vernon Sandusky (vocals, guitar), Vince Gideon (guitar), John Dubas (bass) and Mitch Corday (drums).

DEBUT	PEAK	WKS	Gold	A-side (Chart Hit)..........B-side	$	Sym	Label & Number
7/11/64	33	8		1 **She's The One** .... *Slippin Thru Your Fingers*	$15		Mutual 502
11/14/64	92	2		2 **Why (Doncha Be My Girl)** .... *Stop The Music*	$15		Mutual 508

CHARTS, The — BUB '57

R&B vocal group from Brooklyn, New York: Joe Grier (lead), Leroy Binns and Steven Brown (tenors), Glenmore Jackson (baritone) and Ross Buford (bass). Brown died on 1/20/89 (age 48). Also see **Les Cooper**.

DEBUT	PEAK	WKS	Gold	A-side (Chart Hit)..........B-side	$	Sym	Label & Number
7/15/57	88	4		**Deserie** .... T:88 *"Zoop"*	$100		Everlast 5001
				originally charted for 3 weeks (#89); re-entered on 10/7/57; "Bubbled Under" (#132) on 3/26/66 on Wand 1112 ($25)			

CHASE — BUB/LP '71

Jazz-rock band organized by trumpeter Bill Chase (born in 1935 in Chicago, Illinois; formerly with **Woody Herman** and **Stan Kenton**). Varying lineup. Chase along with bandmates John Emma, Wallace Yohn and Walter Clark were killed in a plane crash on 8/9/74 near Jackson, Minnesota.

DEBUT	PEAK	WKS	Gold	A-side (Chart Hit)..........B-side	$	Sym	Label & Number
5/22/71	24	13		1 **Get It On** .... *River*	$5		Epic 10738
9/11/71	84	5		2 **Handbags And Gladrags** .... *Open Up Wide*	$5		Epic 10775
12/18/71+	81	5		3 **So Many People** .... *Paint It Sad*	$5		Epic 10806

CHASE, Ellison — '76

Born in 1952 in Ohio. Male dance-rock singer. Backing vocalist for **Patty Smyth**.

DEBUT	PEAK	WKS	Gold	A-side (Chart Hit)..........B-side	$	Sym	Label & Number
8/28/76	92	3		**Let's Rock** .... *To The Disco*	$5		Big Tree 16072

CHATER, Kerry — see PUCKETT, Gary

CHEAP TRICK — ★289★ — ROK/BUB/LP '88

Rock group from Rockford, Illinois: **Robin Zander** (vocals; born on 1/23/52), Rick Nielsen (guitar; born on 12/22/46), Tom Petersson (bass; born on 5/9/50) and Bun E. Carlos (drums; born Brad Carlson on 6/12/51). Discovered by **Aerosmith**'s producer Jack Douglas. Petersson replaced by Jon Brant in 1980; returned in 1988, replacing Brant.

1)The Flame 2)Don't Be Cruel 3)I Want You To Want Me

DEBUT	PEAK	WKS	Gold	A-side (Chart Hit)..........B-side	$	Sym	Label & Number
7/22/78	62	8		1 **Surrender** .... *Auf Wiedersehen*	$8		Epic 50570
4/28/79	7	19	●	2 **I Want You To Want Me** .... *Clock Strikes Ten* [L]	$5	■	Epic 50680
				studio version on the 1977 *In Color* album			
8/4/79	35	10		3 **Ain't That A Shame** .... *ELO Kiddies* [L]	$5		Epic 50743
				above 2 recorded on 4/28/78 at the Budokan concert hall in Japan			
10/6/79	26	10		4 **Dream Police** .... *Heaven Tonight*	$4	□	Epic 50774
12/8/79+	32	11		5 **Voices** .... *The House Is Rockin' (With Domestic Problems)*	$4	■	Epic 50814
5/24/80	44	10		6 **Everything Works If You Let It** .... *Way Of The World*	$4		Epic 50887
				from the movie *Roadie* starring **Meat Loaf**			
11/8/80	48	12		7 **Stop This Game** .... *Who D' King*	$4		Epic 50942
6/5/82	45	11		8 **If You Want My Love** .... *Four Letter Word*	$4		Epic 02968
10/9/82	65	7		9 **She's Tight** .... *All I Really Want To Do*	$4	■	Epic 03233
7/27/85	44	17		10 **Tonight It's You** .... *Wild Wild Women*	$3	■	Epic 05431
4/9/88	❶[2]	27		11 **The Flame** A:❷[2] / S:❶[1] *Through The Night*	$3	■	Epic 07745
7/30/88	4	17		12 **Don't Be Cruel** .... S:3 / A:4 *I Know What I Want (live)*	$3	■	Epic 07965
11/5/88	33	14		13 **Ghost Town** .... A:32 / S:34 *Wrong Side Of Love*	$3	■	Epic 08097
2/18/89	75	6		14 **Never Had A Lot To Lose** .... *All We Need Is A Dream*	$3		Epic 68563
				above 4 from the album *Lap Of Luxury*			
7/21/90	12	14		15 **Can't Stop Fallin' Into Love** .... A:13 / S:15 *You Drive, I'll Steer*	$3	▮V	Epic 73444
10/27/90	50	10		16 **Wherever Would I Be** .... *Busted*	$3	▮V	Epic 73580

CHECKER, Chubby — ★67★ — BUB/ROK/LP '62

Born Ernest Evans on 10/3/41 in Andrews, South Carolina; raised in Philadelphia, Pennsylvania. Did impersonations of famous singers. First recorded for Parkway in 1959. Dick Clark's then-wife Bobbie suggested that Evans change his name to Chubby Checker due to his resemblance to a teenage **Fats Domino**. Cover version of **Hank Ballard**'s "The Twist" started worldwide dance craze. On 4/12/64, married Miss World 1962, Dutch-born Catharina Lodders ("Loddy Lo" written for her). In the movies *Don't Knock The Twist* and *Twist Around The Clock*.

1)The Twist 2)Pony Time 3)Limbo Rock 4)Slow Twistin' 5)The Fly

DEBUT	PEAK	WKS	Gold	A-side (Chart Hit)..........B-side	$	Sym	Label & Number
5/18/59	38	7		1 **The Class** .... *Schooldays, Oh, Schooldays* [N]	$30		Parkway 804
				imitations of **Fats Domino**, **The Coasters**, **Elvis Presley**, **Cozy Cole** and **The Chipmunks** parodying "Mary Had A Little Lamb"			
8/1/60	❶[1]	18	●	2 **The Twist** *Toot*	$30		Parkway 811
				melody is the same as "What'cha Gonna Do" by **Clyde McPhatter & The Drifters** (1955 #2 R&B hit); also see #10 and #35 below			
10/10/60	14	13		3 **The Hucklebuck** /			
				#5 hit for **Tommy Dorsey** and #10 hit for **Frank Sinatra** in 1949			
10/10/60	42	8		4 **Whole Lotta Shakin' Goin' On**	$20		Parkway 813

DEBUT	PEAK	WKS	Gold	A-side (Chart Hit)...B-side	$	Sym	Label & Number
				CHECKER, Chubby — Cont'd			
1/23/61	❶[3]	16		5 **Pony Time** ...RB[2] *Oh, Susannah*	$20		Parkway 818
				tune is similar to **The Midnighters**' 1954 R&B hit "Sexy Ways"			
4/24/61	24	7		6 **Dance The Mess Around** /			
				remake of Richard Berry's "The Mess Around" (1958-Flip 336-$40)			
4/17/61	43	6		7 **Good, Good Lovin'**	$15		Parkway 822
				co-written by **James Brown**			
6/19/61	8	23	●	8 **Let's Twist Again** ...*Everything's Gonna' Be All Right*	$15	■	Parkway 824
				originally charted for 12 weeks; re-entered on 11/20/61 (#22)			
9/25/61	7	13		9 **The Fly** ...*That's The Way It Goes*	$15	■	Parkway 830
11/13/61+	❶[2]	21	●	10 **The Twist** / [R]			
				the only record of the rock era to re-enter the charts and return to the #1 position; same version as #2 above			
12/11/61	68	3		11 **Twistin' U.S.A.**	$20	■	Parkway 811
12/11/61	21	5		12 **Jingle Bell Rock** ...*Jingle Bells Imitations* [X]	$15	■	Cameo 205
				BOBBY RYDELL CHUBBY CHECKER			
3/3/62	3	14		13 **Slow Twistin'** /			
				CHUBBY CHECKER (with Dee Dee Sharp)			
3/17/62	72	2		14 **La Paloma Twist**	$15	■	Parkway 835
				adapted from a Spanish tango written in 1864			
6/23/62	12	10		15 **Dancin' Party** ...*Gotta Get Myself Together*	$15	■	Parkway 842
9/8/62	2[2]	23	●	16 **Limbo Rock** /			
9/15/62	10	13		17 **Popeye The Hitchhiker**	$15	■	Parkway 849
12/15/62	92	2		18 **Jingle Bell Rock** ...*Jingle Bell Imitations* [X-R]	$15	■	Cameo 205
				BOBBY RYDELL CHUBBY CHECKER			
2/23/63	15	12		19 **Twenty Miles** /			
2/16/63	20	10		20 **Let's Limbo Some More**	$15	■	Parkway 862
5/18/63	12	9		21 **Birdland** /			
				remake of **Huey "Piano" Smith**'s "We Like Birdland" (1958-Ace 548-$20)			
6/15/63	98	1		22 **Black Cloud**	$15	■	Parkway 873
7/20/63	25	8		23 **Twist It Up** /			
7/13/63	55	6		24 **Surf Party**	$15	■	Parkway 879
11/2/63	12	13		25 **Loddy Lo** /			
				adapted from the Bahamian folk song "Hey Li-Lee, Hey Li-Lee Lo"; originally issued with "Everything's Gonna Be All Right" as the B-side			
12/7/63+	17	14		26 **Hooka Tooka**	$15	■	Parkway 890
3/14/64	23	9		27 **Hey, Bobba Needle** ...*Spread Joy*	$15	■	Parkway 907
6/6/64	40	7		28 **Lazy Elsie Molly** ...*Rosie (#116)*	$15	■	Parkway 920
				written by **Tommy Boyce & Bobby Hart**			
8/29/64	50	7		29 **She Wants T' Swim** ...*You Better Believe It Baby*	$12	■	Parkway 922
1/2/65	70	4		30 **Lovely, Lovely (Loverly, Loverly)** ...*The Weekend's Here*	$12	■	Parkway 936
4/3/65	40	9		31 **Let's Do The Freddie** ...*(At The) Discotheque*	$12		Parkway 949
				#1, 6, 8, 11, 15, 17, 19-21, 23-25, 27, 29 & 31: written by Kal Mann and/or Dave Appell (**The Applejacks**)			
7/2/66	76	5		32 **Hey You! Little Boo-Ga-Loo** ...*Pussy Cat*	$12		Parkway 989
4/5/69	82	5		33 **Back In The U.S.S.R.** ...*Windy Cream*	$10		Buddah 100
				written by **John Lennon** and **Paul McCartney** (recorded on **The Beatles**' 1968 *"White Album"*)			
2/20/82	91	5		34 **Running** ...*Is Tonight The Night*	$5		MCA 51233
6/18/88	16	15		35 **The Twist (Yo, Twist!)** ...S:12 / A:17 *(buffapella version)* [R]	$3	■	Tin Pan Apple 887571
				FAT BOYS (with Chubby Checker)			
				CHECKMATES, LTD., The — see CHARLES, Sonny			
				CHEECH & CHONG LP **'74**			
				Comedians Richard "Cheech" Marin (born on 7/13/46 in Watts, California) and Thomas Chong (born on 5/24/38 in Edmonton, Alberta, Canada). Starred in movies since 1978. Chong, the father of actress Rae Dawn Chong, was the guitarist of **Bobby Taylor & The Vancouvers**. Duo split in the late 1980s. Cheech was a cast member of TV's *Golden Palace* and *Nash Bridges*.			
12/25/71	3[X]	7		1 **Santa Claus And His Old Lady** ...*Dave* [X-C]	$8	■	Ode 66021
				X: 4/'71; 3/'72; 3/'73; made the Album Rock chart on 1/10/98 (#38) on Rhino Records			
9/8/73	15	11		2 **Basketball Jones Featuring Tyrone Shoelaces** ...*Don't Bug Me* [N]	$6	■	Ode 66038
				parody of "Love Jones" by **Brighter Side Of Darkness**; all-star band includes **George Harrison**, **Carole King**, **Billy Preston**, **Tom Scott**, and **Darlene Love** and Michelle Phillips (**The Mamas & The Papas**) as cheerleaders			
11/24/73+	24	12		3 **Sister Mary Elephant (Shudd-Up!)** ...*Wink Dinkerson* [C]	$6	■	Ode 66041
8/10/74	9	13		4 **Earache My Eye (Featuring Alice Bowie)** *Turn That Thing Down (Featuring Alice Bowie)* [C]	$6	■	Ode 66102
11/9/74	55	6		5 **Black Lassie (Featuring Johnny Stash)** ...*Coming Attractions* [C]	$6	■	Ode 66104
10/18/75	54	5		6 **(How I Spent My Summer Vacation) Or A Day At The Beach With Pedro & Man - Parts I & II** ... [C]	$6		Ode 66115
6/12/76	41	8		7 **Framed** ...*Pedro's Request* [N]	$6		Ode 66124
				tune is the B-side of **Ritchie Valens**' 1958 hit "Come On, Let's Go"			
11/12/77+	41	10		8 **Bloat On Featuring the Bloaters** ...*Just Say "Right On"* [C]	$6	■	Ode 50471
				parody of "Float On" by **The Floaters**			
9/21/85	48	11		9 **Born In East L.A.** ...S:29 *I'm A (Modern) Man* [N]	$3	■	MCA 52655
				parody of **Bruce Springsteen**'s "Born In The U.S.A."; in 1987 Cheech starred in the movie *Born In East L.A.*			
				CHEE-CHEE and PEPPY R&B **'71**			
				Black teen duo of Keith "Chee-Chee" Bolling (born in 1957 in Frankfort, Pennsylvania) and Dorothy "Peppy" Moore (born in 1959 in Morristown, Pennsylvania). Duo formed by producer **Jesse James**.			
5/29/71	49	14		**I Know I'm In Love** ...*My Love Will Never Fade Away*	$7		Buddah 225
				CHEEKS, Judy **'78**			
				Born in Miami, Florida. Dance singer. Daughter of gospel singer/preacher Rev. Julius Cheeks. Cousin of Genobia Jeter.			
10/7/78	65	5		**Mellow Lovin'** ...*Darling, That's Me*	$5		Salsoul 2063

DEBUT	PEAK	WKS	Gold	A-side (Chart Hit)..........B-side	$	Sym	Label & Number

CHEERS, The — POP '55

Pop vocal trio from Los Angeles, California: Bert Convy, Gil Garfield and Sue Allen. Convy later became a popular TV personality; died of a brain tumor on 7/15/91 (age 58). Hit #15 on the pop charts in 1954 with "(Bazoom) I Need Your Lovin'."

DEBUT	PEAK	WKS	Gold	A-side (Chart Hit)..........B-side	$	Sym	Label & Number
9/24/55	6	11		Black Denim Trousers ....S:6 / A:6 / T:13 / J:20 *Some Night In Alaska*	$30		Capitol 3219
				Les Baxter (orch. and chorus)			

CHEMAY, Joe, Band — BUB '81

Born on 3/22/50 in Baltimore, Maryland. Pop-rock singer/bassist. Band included Billy Walker (guitar), John Hobbs (piano), Mike Meros (organ), Louis Conte (percussion) and Paul Leim (drums).

DEBUT	PEAK	WKS	Gold	A-side (Chart Hit)..........B-side	$	Sym	Label & Number
2/14/81	68	8		Proud ....*Once In A Life*	$5		Unicorn 95001

CHEMICAL BROTHERS, The — BUB/ROK/LP '97

Techno-dance DJ duo from England: Tom Rowlands and Ed Simons.

DEBUT	PEAK	WKS	Gold	A-side (Chart Hit)..........B-side	$	Sym	Label & Number
1/25/97	80	5		1 Setting Sun ....S:64 *(2 versions) / Buzz Tracks*	$5	■	Astralwerks 6187
				Noel Gallagher of **Oasis** (vocal)			
9/29/01	42[S]	4		2 It Began In Afrika ....*(long version) / Hot Acid Rhythm 1* [I]	$5	★	Astralwerks 38798
				samples "Drumbeat" by Jim Ingram			
2/2/02	38[S]	6		3 Star Guitar ....*(3 versions) / Base 6* [I]	$8	★*	Astralwerks 88122

CHER ★54★ — BUB/AC/C&W/LP '89

Born Cherilyn Sarkisian on 5/20/46 in El Centro, California. Adopted by stepfather at age 15 and last name changed to La Piere. Worked as backup singer for Phil Spector (**The Teddy Bears**). Recorded as "Bonnie Jo Mason" and "Cherilyn" in 1964. Recorded with **Sonny** Bono (born on 2/16/35; died on 1/5/98) as "Caesar & Cleo" in 1963, then as **Sonny & Cher** from 1965-73. Married to Bono from 1963-75. Married to **Gregg Allman** from 1975-78. Own TV series with Bono from 1971-74, 1976-77. Member of the group Black Rose in 1980. Acclaimed movie actress (won the 1987 Best Actress Oscar for *Moonstruck*).

1)Believe 2)Gypsys, Tramps & Thieves 3)Half-Breed 4)Dark Lady 5)Bang Bang (My Baby Shot Me Down)

DEBUT	PEAK	WKS	Gold	A-side (Chart Hit)..........B-side	$	Sym	Label & Number
7/3/65	15	12		1 All I Really Want To Do ....*I'm Gonna Love You*	$12		Imperial 66114
				written by **Bob Dylan**			
10/16/65	25	7		2 Where Do You Go ....*See See Blues*	$10		Imperial 66136
3/12/66	2[1]	11		3 Bang Bang (My Baby Shot Me Down) ....*Needles And Pins*	$10		Imperial 66160
7/30/66	32	6		4 Alfie ....*She's No Better Than Me*	$10		Imperial 66192
				title song from the movie starring Michael Caine			
11/26/66	97	1		5 Behind The Door ....*Magic In The Air*	$10		Imperial 66217
9/9/67	94	2		6 Hey Joe ....*Our Day Will Come*	$10		Imperial 66252
10/28/67	9	13		7 You Better Sit Down Kids ....*Mama (When My Dollies Have Babies)*	$10		Imperial 66261
				B-side "Bubbled Under" (#124) in 1966 on Imperial 66223			
9/18/71	❶[2]	16	●	8 Gypsys, Tramps & Thieves ....*He'll Never Know*	$6		Kapp 2146
1/29/72	7	13		9 The Way Of Love ....*Don't Put It On Me*	$6		Kapp 2158
5/20/72	22	8		10 Living In A House Divided ....*One Honest Man*	$6		Kapp 2171
9/9/72	46	8		11 Don't Hide Your Love ....*The First Time*	$6		Kapp 2184
				written by **Neil Sedaka**			
8/4/73	❶[2]	20	●	12 Half-Breed ....*Melody*	$5		MCA 40102
1/19/74	❶[1]	16	●	13 Dark Lady ....*Two People Clinging To A Thread*	$5		MCA 40161
5/25/74	27	11		14 Train Of Thought ....*Dixie Girl*	$5		MCA 40245
8/10/74	42	9		15 I Saw A Man And He Danced With His Wife ....*I Hate To Sleep Alone*	$5		MCA 40273
1/15/77	93	2		16 Pirate ....*Send The Man Over*	$5		Warner 8311
2/10/79	8	19	●	17 Take Me Home ....*My Song (Too Far Gone)*	$4		Casablanca 965
6/2/79	49	7		18 Wasn't It Good ....*It's Too Late To Love Me Now* (C&W #87)	$4		Casablanca 987
9/15/79	59	5		19 Hell On Wheels ....*Git Down (Guitar Groupie)*	$4		Casablanca 2208
11/21/87+	10	26		20 I Found Someone ....S:8 / A:11 *Dangerous Times*	$3	■	Geffen 28191
				written and produced by **Michael Bolton**			
4/9/88	14	15		21 We All Sleep Alone ....A:12 / S:14 *Working Girl*	$3	■	Geffen 27986
				co-written and co-produced by **Jon Bon Jovi**			
7/30/88	79	4		22 Skin Deep ....*Perfection*	$3	■	Geffen 27894
3/11/89	6	20	●	23 After All ....AC[4] S:4 / A:9 *Dangerous Times* (Cher)	$3	■	Geffen 27529
				CHER and PETER CETERA			
				love theme from the movie *Chances Are* starring Cybill Shepherd and Robert Downey, Jr.			
7/8/89	3	23	●	24 If I Could Turn Back Time ....AC[1] S:2 / A:4 *Some Guys*	$3	■	Geffen 22886
10/21/89	8	18		25 Just Like Jesse James ....S:6 / A:11 *Starting Over*	$3		Geffen 22844
2/10/90	20	14		26 Heart Of Stone ....S:21 / A:27 *All Because Of You*	$3	■[V]	Geffen 19953
				above 4 from the album *Heart Of Stone*			
11/24/90+	33	16		27 The Shoop Shoop Song (It's In His Kiss) ....S:23 *Love On A Rooftop*	$3	■[V]	Geffen 19659
				from the movie *Mermaids* starring Cher			
6/15/91	17	15		28 Love And Understanding ....A:38 / S:45 *Trail Of Broken Hearts*	$3	■[V]	Geffen 19023
10/19/91+	37	20		29 Save Up All Your Tears ....A:40 / S:59 *A World Without Heroes*	$3	■[V]	Geffen 19105
6/15/96	52	14		30 One By One ....A:52 / S:64 *I Wouldn't Treat A Dog (The Way You Treated Me)*	$3	■[V]	Reprise 17695
12/19/98+	❶[4]	31	▲	31 Believe ....S:❶[4] / A:2 *(remix)*	$4	★[V]	Warner 17119
5/22/99	57	12		32 Strong Enough ....S:35 / A:70 *(9 versions)*	$8	★*	Warner 44644
11/20/99	38[S]	6		33 All Or Nothing ....*(3 mixes) / Dov'e L'Amore*	$8	★*	Warner 44774
4/6/02	85	6		34 Song For The Lonely ....S:7 *(6 versions)*	$8	★*	Warner 42422
8/31/02	11[S]	13		35 A Different Kind Of Love Song ....*(6 versions) / The Music's No Good Without You*	$8	★*	Warner 42455

CHERI — R&B '82

Female dance duo from Montreal, Quebec, Canada: Rosalind Hunt and Lyn Cullerier.

DEBUT	PEAK	WKS	Gold	A-side (Chart Hit)..........B-side	$	Sym	Label & Number
4/10/82	39	12		Murphy's Law ....*(instrumental)* [N]	$4		Venture 149

DEBUT	PEAK	WKS	Gold	A-side (Chart Hit)	B-side	$	Sym	Label & Number
				CHERRELLE R&B/LP '86				
				Born Cheryl Norton on 10/13/58 in Los Angeles, California. R&B singer. Cousin of singer **Pebbles**.				
7/7/84	79	9		1 **I Didn't Mean To Turn You On**	*I Need You Now*	$4		Tabu 04406
2/15/86	26	17		2 **Saturday Love** S:19	*Will You Satisfy?* (Cherrelle)	$3	■	Tabu 05767
				CHERRELLE with ALEXANDER O'NEAL				
1/23/88	28	14		3 **Never Knew Love Like This** A:26 / S:28	*What's Missing* (O'Neal)	$3	■	Tabu 07646
				ALEXANDER O'NEAL featuring Cherrelle				
				CHERRY, Don POP/BUB/AC/C&W/LP '56				
				Born on 1/11/24 in Wichita Falls, Texas. Studied voice after the service in mid-1940s. Vocalist with Jan Garber band in the late 1940s. Accomplished professional golfer. Hit #4 on the pop charts in 1950 with "Thinking Of You."				
12/3/55+	4	22		1 **Band Of Gold** A:4 / S:5 / T:5 / J:5	*Rumble Boogie*	$15		Columbia 40597
4/7/56	29	12		2 **Wild Cherry /** T:29				
4/21/56	72	1		3 **I'm Still A King To You** T:72		$12		Columbia 40665
7/14/56	22	14		4 **Ghost Town /** A:22 / T:26				
8/25/56	78	1		5 **I'll Be Around** T:78		$12		Columbia 40705
				#17 hit for the **Mills Brothers** in 1943; **Ray Conniff** (orch. and chorus, all of above)				
10/6/56	65	8		6 **Namely You** T:65	*If I Had My Druthers*	$12		Columbia 40746
				David Terry (orch.); from the Broadway show *Li'l Abner* starring Edie Adams and Peter Palmer				
				CHERRY, Eagle-Eye LP '99				
				Born on 5/7/69 in Stockholm, Sweden. Son of trumpeter Don Cherry. Half-brother of **Neneh Cherry**.				
12/5/98+	5	28		**Save Tonight** A:2				album cut
				Hot 100 Airplay debut: 8/1/98; from the album *Desireless* on Work 69434				
				CHERRY, Neneh ROK/LP '89				
				Born on 3/10/63 in Stockholm, Sweden; raised in Brooklyn, New York. R&B-dance singer. Stepdaughter of jazz trumpeter Don Cherry. Half-sister of **Eagle-Eye Cherry**. Married composer/musician Cameron "Booga Bear" McVey in December 1990.				
4/1/89	3	24	●	1 **Buffalo Stance** S:❶² / A:4	*(electro ski mix)*	$3	■	Virgin 99231
				from the movie *Slaves Of New York* starring **Bernadette Peters**				
7/22/89	8	14		2 **Kisses On The Wind** S:9 / A:10	*Buffalo Blues*	$3	■	Virgin 99183
12/9/89+	73	8		3 **Heart**	*Phony Ladies*	$3		Virgin 99153
3/27/93	43	12		4 **Buddy X** A:29	*Move With Me*	$3	▮V	Virgin 12648
				samples "Sugar Free" by Juicy (#13 R&B hit in 1986); "45": Virgin 56975; B-side: "Trout" (w/Michael Stipe) (ROK #2)				
10/8/94	98	4		5 **7 Seconds**	*Mame Bamba* (N'Dour)	$3	▮	Chaos/Columbia 77483
				YOUSSOU N'DOUR & NENEH CHERRY				
				Cherry sings in English; N'Dour sings in French and Wolof				
				CHERRY PEOPLE, The BUB '68				
				Pop-rock group from Washington DC: brothers Doug (vocals) and Chris (guitar) Grimes, Edwin "Punky" Meadows (guitar), Jan Zukowski (bass) and Rocky Isaac (drums). Meadows later joined **Angel**.				
7/20/68	45	8		**And Suddenly**	*Imagination*	$8	■	Heritage 801
				CHERRY POPPIN' DADDIES LP '98				
				Retro-swing group from Eugene, Oregon: Steve Perry (vocals, guitar), Jason Moss (guitar), Dana Heitman, Sean Flannery and Ian Early (horns), Darren Cassidy (bass) and Tim Donahue (drums).				
4/11/98	41^A	17		**Zoot Suit Riot**				album cut
				from the album *Zoot Suit Riot* on Mojo 53081				
	★579★			**CHESNEY, Kenny** C&W/BUB/LP '02				
				Born on 3/26/68 in Knoxville, Tennessee; raised in Luttrell, Tennessee. Country singer/songwriter/guitarist.				
				1)The Good Stuff 2)Don't Happen Twice 3)How Forever Feels				
5/9/98	79	7		1 **That's Why I'm Here** S:57	*A Chance* (C&W #11)	$4	▮V	BNA 65399
10/3/98	71^S	5		2 **I Will Stand** BUB:101	*She Always Said It First*	$4	▮V	BNA 65570
2/6/99	27	21		3 **How Forever Feels** CW⁶ A:17 / S:31	*You Win, I Win, We Lose*	$4	★V	BNA 65666
7/10/99	34	20		4 **You Had Me From Hello** CW¹ A:25			V	album cut
				"45": BNA 65745; B-side: "Everywhere We Go"				
11/20/99	74	12		5 **She Thinks My Tractor's Sexy** A:61			V	album cut
				"45": BNA 65934; B-side: "You Had Me From Hello"				
4/1/00	56	17		6 **What I Need To Do** A:48			V	album cut
				"45": BNA 65964; B-side: "She Thinks My Tractor's Sexy"; above 4 from the album *Everywhere We Go* on BNA 67655				
10/21/00	34	20		7 **I Lost It** A:30			V	album cut
				Pam Tillis (backing vocal); "45": BNA 69007; B-side: "The Tin Man" (C&W #19)				
3/10/01	26	20		8 **Don't Happen Twice** CW¹ A:20			V	album cut
				"45": BNA 69035; B-side: "I Lost It"; above 2 from the album *Greatest Hits* on BNA 67976				
2/9/02	35	20		9 **Young** A:33			V	album cut
				"45": BNA 69131; B-side: "For The First Time"				
6/8/02	22	20		10 **The Good Stuff** CW⁷ A:20			V	album cut
11/30/02	55	15		11 **A Lot Of Things Different** A:52			V	album cut
				"45" available for above 2 on BNA 69172; above 3 from the album *No Shoes, No Shirt, No Problems* on BNA 67038				
				CHESNUTT, Mark C&W/BUB/LP '99				
				Born on 9/6/63 in Beaumont, Texas. Country singer/guitarist.				
12/19/98+	17	20		1 **I Don't Want To Miss A Thing** CW² S:14 / A:21	*Wherever You Are* (C&W #45)	$4	★V	Decca 72078
8/10/02	62	11		2 **She Was** A:58				album cut
				from the album *Mark Chesnutt* on Columbia 86540				
				CHEVELLE ROK/LP '03				
				Rock trio from Chicago, Illinois: brothers Pete (vocals, guitar), Joe (bass) and Sam (drums) Loeffler.				
11/30/02+	56	20		**The Red** A:55	*Wonder What's Next*	$4	★	Epic 79818

DEBUT	PEAK	WKS	Gold	A-side (Chart Hit)..........B-side	$	Sym	Label & Number
	★466★			**CHIC** R&B/BUB/LP **'78**			

R&B-disco group formed in New York City, New York, by prolific producers Bernard Edwards (bass; born on 10/31/52) and **Nile Rodgers** (see #11 below) (guitar; born on 9/19/52). Featured drummer Tony Thompson and vocalists Luci Martin and Norma Jean Wright. Wright began solo career in 1978 as Norma Jean; replaced by Alfa Anderson. Edwards recorded with the studio group Roundtree in 1978. Rodgers joined **The Honeydrippers** in 1984. Thompson joined the **Power Station** in 1985, and Edwards became their producer. Wright, along with supporting Chic member Raymond Jones, formed State Of Art in 1991. Rodgers and Edwards regrouped as Chic in 1992 with female lead vocalists/South Carolina natives Sylvester Logan Sharp and Jenn Thomas. Edwards died of pneumonia on 4/18/96 (age 43). Pronounced: sheek.

1)Le Freak 2)Good Times 3)Dance, Dance Dance (Yowsah, Yowsah, Yowsah)

DEBUT	PEAK	WKS	Gold	A-side (Chart Hit)..........B-side	$	Sym	Label & Number
10/29/77+	6	28	●	1 **Dance, Dance, Dance (Yowsah, Yowsah, Yowsah)** ....*Sao Paulo* first released on Buddah 583 in 1977 ($8)	$5		Atlantic 3435
4/22/78	38	10		2 **Everybody Dance**..........*Est-Ce Que C'est Chic* **Luther Vandross** (backing vocal, above 2)	$5		Atlantic 3469
10/28/78	❶ 6	25	▲	3 **Le Freak** RB[5] *Savoir Faire*	$4	■	Atlantic 3519
2/10/79	7	19	●	4 **I Want Your Love**..........*(Funny) Bone*	$4	■	Atlantic 3557
6/16/79	❶ 1	19	●	5 **Good Times**..........RB[6] *A Warm Summer Night*	$4	■	Atlantic 3584
10/6/79	43	9		6 **My Forbidden Lover**..........*What About Me*	$4		Atlantic 3620
8/30/80	61	6		7 **Rebels Are We**..........*Open Up*	$4		Atlantic 3665
11/15/80	79	3		8 **Real People** /			
11/22/80		2		9 **Chip Off The Old Block**..........	$4		Atlantic 3768
6/5/82	80	6		10 **Soup For One**..........*Burn Hard* title song from the movie starring Saul Rubinek	$4		Mirage 4032
6/1/85	88	3		11 **Let's Go Out Tonight**..........*Doll Squad* **NILE RODGERS**	$3	■	Warner 29049

CHICAGO ★22★ AC/R&B/LP **'71**

Jazz-oriented rock group from Chicago, Illinois: **Peter Cetera** (vocals, bass; born on 9/13/44), Terry Kath (vocals, guitar; born on 1/31/46), Robert Lamm (vocals, keyboards; born on 10/13/44), James Pankow (trombone; born on 8/20/47), Lee Loughnane (trumpet; born on 10/21/46), Walt Parazaider (sax; born on 3/14/45) and Danny Seraphine (drums; born on 8/28/48). Known as the Big Thing, then moved to Los Angeles in 1969 and changed name to Chicago Transit Authroity, then simply to Chicago later that year. Kath died of a self-inflicted gunshot on 1/23/78 (age 31); replaced by Donnie Dacus (guitar, vocals; 1978-80). **Bill Champlin** (**Sons Of Champlin**; guitar, keyboards, vocals) joined in 1981. Cetera left in 1985; replaced by Jason Scheff (bass, vocals). Seraphine left in 1990. Original members Lamm, Loughnane, Pankow and Parazaider still performing as Chicago with Champlin, Scheff, Tris Imboden (drums) and Keith Howland (guitar).

1)If You Leave Me Now 2)Hard To Say I'm Sorry 3)Look Away 4)Hard Habit To Break 5)You're The Inspiration

DEBUT	PEAK	WKS	Gold	A-side (Chart Hit)..........B-side	$	Sym	Label & Number
8/9/69	71	3		1 **Questions 67 And 68**..........*Listen* longer version (4:45) than #9 below (3:25)	$10	■	Columbia 44909
4/4/70	9	14		2 **Make Me Smile**..........*Colour My World* (same as #8 below)	$7	■	Columbia 45127
7/25/70	4	12		3 **25 Or 6 To 4**..........*Where Do We Go From Here* also see #39 below	$7		Columbia 45194
11/7/70+	7	13		4 **Does Anybody Really Know What Time It Is?**..........*Listen*	$7	■	Columbia 45264
2/20/71	20	9		5 **Free**..........*Free Country*	$7	■	Columbia 45331
5/8/71	35	8		6 **Lowdown**..........*Loneliness Is Just A Word*	$7	■	Columbia 45370
6/26/71	7	13		7 **Beginnings** / AC[1] originally released in 1969 on Columbia 45011 with "Poem 58" as the B-side			
7/3/71		12		8 **Colour My World**..........	$7	■	Columbia 45417
10/9/71	24	10		9 **Questions 67 And 68** / [R]			
10/9/71	49	10		10 **I'm A Man**.......... #1, 4, 7, 9 & 10: from the 1969 album *Chicago Transit Authority*	$7		Columbia 45467
8/5/72	3	12	●	11 **Saturday In The Park**..........*Alma Mater*	$7		Columbia 45657
10/28/72	24	10		12 **Dialogue (Part I & II)**..........*Now That You've Gone* charted for 1 week on Columbia 45683; remaining weeks on 45717; picture sleeve issued with both numbers	$7	■	Columbia 45717
6/23/73	10	16		13 **Feelin' Stronger Every Day**..........*Jenny*	$6		Columbia 45880
9/29/73	4	19	●	14 **Just You 'N' Me**..........*Critic's Choice*	$6		Columbia 45933
3/16/74	9	15		15 **(I've Been) Searchin' So Long**..........*Byblos*	$6		Columbia 46020
6/22/74	6	15		16 **Call On Me**..........AC[1] *Prelude To Aire*	$6		Columbia 46062
10/19/74	11	15		17 **Wishing You Were Here**..........AC[1] *Life Saver* Carl Wilson, Dennis Wilson and Al Jardine (of **The Beach Boys**; backing vocals)	$6		Columbia 10049
2/22/75	13	9		18 **Harry Truman**..........*Till We Meet Again*	$6	■	Columbia 10092
4/26/75	5	11		19 **Old Days**..........*Hideaway*	$6		Columbia 10131
9/6/75	61	5		20 **Brand New Love Affair (Part I & II)**..........*Hideaway*	$6		Columbia 10200
6/26/76	32	9		21 **Another Rainy Day In New York City**..........*Hope For Love*	$6		Columbia 10360
8/14/76	❶ 2	21	▲	22 **If You Leave Me Now** AC[1] *Together Again*	$5		Columbia 10390
4/9/77	49	7		23 **You Are On My Mind**..........*Gently I'll Wake You*	$5		Columbia 10523
9/24/77	4	17		24 **Baby, What A Big Surprise**..........*Takin' It On Uptown*	$5	■	Columbia 10620
2/11/78	44	9		25 **Little One**..........*Till The End Of Time*	$5		Columbia 10683
5/20/78	63	5		26 **Take Me Back To Chicago**..........*Policeman* all of above produced by James William Guercio	$5		Columbia 10737
10/21/78	14	13		27 **Alive Again**..........*Love Was New*	$5		Columbia 10845
12/23/78+	14	15		28 **No Tell Lover**..........*Take A Chance*	$5		Columbia 10879
4/14/79	73	3		29 **Gone Long Gone**..........*The Greatest Love On Earth*	$5		Columbia 10935
9/1/79	83	5		30 **Must Have Been Crazy**..........*Closer To You*	$5		Columbia 11061
8/23/80	56	9		31 **Thunder And Lightning**..........*I'd Rather Be Rich*	$5		Columbia 11345
6/5/82	❶ 2	24	●	32 **Hard To Say I'm Sorry**..........AC[3] *Sonny Think Twice* from the movie *Summer Lovers* starring Daryl Hannah	$4		Full Moon 29979
9/25/82	22	15		33 **Love Me Tomorrow**..........*Bad Advice*	$4		Full Moon 29911
1/29/83	81	5		34 **What You're Missing**..........*Rescue You*	$4		Full Moon 29798
5/5/84	16	17		35 **Stay The Night**..........*Only You*	$3	■	Warner/Full Moon 29306

DEBUT	PEAK	WKS	Gold	A-side (Chart Hit)..........B-side	$	Sym	Label & Number
				CHICAGO — Cont'd			
8/4/84	3	25		36 **Hard Habit To Break**..........A:2 / S:3 *Remember The Feeling*	$3	■	Warner/Full Moon 29214
11/17/84+	3	22		37 **You're The Inspiration**..........AC^{2} A:❶^{1} / S:5 *Once In A Lifetime*	$3		Warner/Full Moon 29126
2/23/85	14	16		38 **Along Comes A Woman**..........A:7 / S:25 *We Can Stop The Hurtin'*	$3		Warner/Full Moon 29082
				above 4 from the album *Chicago 17*			
9/6/86	48	8		39 **25 Or 6 To 4**..........*One More Day* [R]	$3	■	Warner/Full Moon 28628
				new version of #3 above; also on the B-side of #40 & 47 below			
11/15/86+	3	23		40 **Will You Still Love Me?**..........A:2 / S:4 *25 Or 6 To 4*	$3		Warner/Full Moon 28512
3/21/87	17	19		41 **If She Would Have Been Faithful...**..........A:11 / S:22 *Forever*	$3	■	Warner/Full Moon 28424
7/11/87	91	3		42 **Niagara Falls**..........*I Believe*	$3	■	Warner/Full Moon 28283
				above 4 from the album *Chicago 18*; #32-42: produced by **David Foster**			
6/4/88	3	21		43 **I Don't Wanna Live Without Your Love**..........A:2 / S:3 *I Stand Up*	$3	■	Reprise/Full Moon 27855
9/24/88	❶^{2}	24	●	44 **Look Away**..........AC^{1} A:❶^{3} / S:❶^{1} *Come In From The Night*	$3	■	Reprise/Full Moon 27766
1/21/89	10	17		45 **You're Not Alone**..........A:8 / S:13 *It's Alright*	$3	■	Reprise/Full Moon 27757
5/13/89	55	12		46 **We Can Last Forever**..........*One More Day*	$3		Reprise/Full Moon 22985
12/2/89+	5	18		47 **What Kind Of Man Would I Be?**..........A:4 / S:6 *25 Or 6 To 4*	$3	■	Reprise/Full Moon 22741
				above 5 from the album *Chicago 19*			
7/28/90	75	5		48 **Hearts In Trouble**..........*Car Building* (Hans Zimmer)	$3	▮	DGC 19679
				from the movie *Days Of Thunder* starring Tom Cruise; all of above (except #10, 34, 36 & 40-45) written by various members of Chicago			
1/26/91	39	11		49 **Chasin' The Wind**..........S:37 / A:38 *Only Time Can Heal The Wounded*	$3	▮^{V}	Reprise 19466
6/7/97	59^{A}	10		50 **Here In My Heart**..........AC^{1}			album cut
				from the album *The Heart Of Chicago* on Reprise 46554			
				CHICAGO BEARS SHUFFLIN' CREW, The '86			
				Actual members of the Chicago Bears football team (Super Bowl XX Champs) rapping about themselves. Featuring (in order): Walter Payton, Willie Gault, Mike Singletary, Jim McMahon, Otis Wilson, Steve Fuller, Mike Richardson, Richard Dent, Gary Fencik and William ("The Refrigerator") Perry.			
1/11/86	41	9	●	**Superbowl Shuffle**..........S:28 *(instrumental)* [N]	$5	■	Red Label 71012
				CHICAGO LOOP, The '66			
				Rock group from Chicago, Illinois: Bob Slawson and Judy Navy (vocals), John Savanna (guitar), Barry Goldberg (piano), Carmen Riole (bass) and Jack Siomoms (drums).			
11/5/66	37	7		**(When She Needs Good Lovin') She Comes To Me**..........*This Must Be The Place*	$10		DynoVoice 226
				some pressings titled "(When She Wants Good Lovin') My Baby Comes To Me" (see B-side of **The Coasters**' "Idol With The Golden Head")			
				CHICORY '72			
				Rock group from Maidstone, Kent, England: Peter Hewson (vocals), Rick Foster (guitar), Barry Mayger (bass) and Brian Shearer (drums). Known in England as Chicory Tip.			
3/11/72	91	3		**Son Of My Father**..........*Pride Comes Before A Fall*	$7		Epic 10837
	★540★			**CHIFFONS, The** BUB/LP '63			
				Female R&B vocal group from the Bronx, New York. Formed while high school classmates; worked as backup singers in 1960. Consisted of Judy Craig, Barbara Lee Jones (born on 5/16/47), Patricia Bennett (born on 4/7/47) and Sylvia Peterson (born on 9/30/46). Jones died of a heart attack on 5/15/92 (age 44). Also recorded as **The Four Pennies** on the Rust label. Also see **Andrea Carroll**.			
				1)He's So Fine 2)One Fine Day 3)Sweet Talkin' Guy			
9/12/60	76	4		1 **Tonight's The Night**..........*Do You Know*	$100		Big Deal 6003
2/23/63	❶^{4}	15		2 **He's So Fine**..........RB^{4} *Oh My Lover*	$20		Laurie 3152
				a 1976 court ruling found **George Harrison** guilty of "subconscious plagiarism" of song when writing "My Sweet Lord"			
6/1/63	5	10		3 **One Fine Day**..........*Why Am I So Shy*	$20		Laurie 3179
6/22/63	67	5		4 **My Block**..........*Dry Your Eyes*	$25		Rust 5071
				THE FOUR PENNIES			
9/7/63	40	9		5 **A Love So Fine**..........*Only My Friend*	$15		Laurie 3195
11/9/63	95	1		6 **When The Boy's Happy (The Girl's Happy Too)**..........*Hockaday Part I*	$25		Rust 5070
				THE FOUR PENNIES			
11/16/63+	36	10		7 **I Have A Boyfriend**..........*I'm Gonna Dry My Eyes*	$15		Laurie 3212
8/1/64	81	3		8 **Sailor Boy**..........*When Summer's Through*	$15		Laurie 3262
6/19/65	49	9		9 **Nobody Knows What's Goin' On (In My Mind But Me)**..........*The Real Thing*	$15		Laurie 3301
				also released with "Did You Ever Go Steady" as the B-side			
5/7/66	10	10		10 **Sweet Talkin' Guy**..........*Did You Ever Go Steady*	$15		Laurie 3340
8/6/66	67	4		11 **Out Of This World**..........*Just A Boy*	$15		Laurie 3350
10/1/66	85	2		12 **Stop, Look And Listen**..........*March*	$15		Laurie 3357
				CHILD, Desmond AC/LP '91			
				Born John Charles Barrett Jr. on 10/28/53 in Miami, Florida (Cuban mother/Hungarian father). Prolific producer/songwriter. Formed vocal group Rouge with Diane Grasselli, Myriam Valle and **Maria Vidal** in 1974. Wrote "We All Sleep Alone," "Livin' On A Prayer" and "Dude (Looks Like A Lady)."			
1/20/79	51	11		1 **Our Love Is Insane**..........*City In Heat*	$4		Capitol 4669
				DESMOND CHILD and ROUGE			
6/22/91	40	12		2 **Love On A Rooftop**..........A:66 *A Ray Of Hope*	$3	▮^{V}	Elektra 64883
10/5/91	74	6		3 **You're The Story Of My Life**..........*Do Me Right*	$3	▮	Elektra 64850
				CHILD, Jane LP '90			
				Born on 2/15/69 in Toronto, Ontario, Canada. Singer/songwriter/keyboardist.			
2/10/90	2^{3}	21	●	1 **Don't Wanna Fall In Love**..........A:❶^{2} / S:3 *World Lullabye*	$3	▮^{V}	Warner 19933
6/2/90	49	9		2 **Welcome To The Real World**..........*Hey Mr. Jones*	$3	▮^{V}	Warner 19834
				CHILDS, Toni LP '88			
				Born on 7/20/60 in Orange, California. Female rock singer.			
8/13/88	72	7		**Don't Walk Away**..........*Hush*	$3	■	A&M 1237

DEBUT	PEAK	WKS	Gold	A-side (Chart Hit)...B-side	$	Sym	Label & Number
	★336★			**CHI-LITES, The** R&B/BUB/LP '72			

R&B vocal group from Chicago, Illinois: Eugene Record (lead; born on 12/23/40), Robert "Squirrel" Lester (tenor), Marshall Thompson (baritone) and Creadel "Red" Jones (bass). First recorded as the Hi-Lites on Daran in 1963. Eugene Record (husband of **Barbara Acklin**) went solo in 1976. Charted 43 R&B hits, 1969-98.

1)Oh Girl 2)Have You Seen Her 3)(For God's Sake) Give More Power To The People 4)Stoned Out Of My Mind 5)A Letter To Myself

DEBUT	PEAK	WKS	Gold	A-side (Chart Hit)...B-side	$	Sym	Label & Number
3/1/69	88	6		1 **Give It Away**...*What Do I Wish For*	$8		Brunswick 55398
8/2/69	94	3		2 **Let Me Be The Man My Daddy Was**...*The Twelfth Of Never* (#122)	$8		Brunswick 55414
8/15/70	72	6		3 **I Like Your Lovin' (Do You Like Mine)**...*You're No Longer Part Of My Heart*	$8		Brunswick 55438
12/19/70+	72	7		4 **Are You My Woman? (Tell Me So)**...*Troubles A' Comin*	$8		Brunswick 55442
4/10/71	26	11		5 **(For God's Sake) Give More Power To The People**...*Troubles A' Comin*	$8		Brunswick 55450
7/24/71	70	5		6 **We Are Neighbors**...*What Do I Wish For*	$8		Brunswick 55455
10/23/71	3	14		7 **Have You Seen Her**...RB^2 *Yes I'm Ready (If I Don't Get To Go)*	$8		Brunswick 55462
				a new version made the R&B charts in 1981 on Chi-Sound 2481 (#48)			
11/6/71	95	3		8 **I Want To Pay You Back (For Loving Me)**...*Love Uprising*	$8		Brunswick 55458
				above 4 from the album *(For God's Sake) Give More Power To The People*			
4/8/72	❶^1	15		9 **Oh Girl** RB^2 *Being In Love*	$8		Brunswick 55471
7/15/72	47	9		10 **The Coldest Days Of My Life (Part 1)**...*(Part 2)*	$8		Brunswick 55478
9/30/72	57	5		11 **A Lonely Man /**			
9/30/72		5		12 **The Man & The Woman (The Boy & The Girl)**...	$8		Brunswick 55483
				above 4 from the album *A Lonely Man*			
12/2/72	61	6		13 **We Need Order**...*Living In The Footsteps Of Another Man*	$7		Brunswick 55489
2/10/73	33	11		14 **A Letter To Myself**...*Sally*	$7		Brunswick 55491
6/9/73	92	4		15 **My Heart Just Keeps On Breakin'**...*Just Two Teenage Kids (Still In Love)*	$7		Brunswick 55496
8/4/73	30	13		16 **Stoned Out Of My Mind**...*Someone Elses Arms*	$7		Brunswick 55500
11/17/73	47	10		17 **I Found Sunshine**...*Marriage License*	$7		Brunswick 55503
2/9/74	54	8		18 **Homely Girl**...*I Never Had It So Good (And Felt So Bad)*	$7		Brunswick 55505
6/15/74	63	7		19 **There Will Never Be Any Peace (Until God Is Seated At The Conference Table)**...*Too Good To Beforgotten*	$7		Brunswick 55512
8/31/74	83	3		20 **You Got To Be The One**...*Happiness Is Your Middle Name*	$7		Brunswick 55514
3/1/75	78	7		21 **Toby /**			
				#2, 6, 7, 16 & 21: co-written by **Barbara Acklin**			
3/1/75		7		22 **That's How Long**...	$7		Brunswick 55515
				above 4 from the album *Toby*			
11/8/75	94	3		23 **It's Time For Love**...*Here I Am* (R&B #87)	$7		Brunswick 55520
				all of above (except #22) written and produced by Eugene Record			

CHILLDRIN OF DA GHETTO LP '99

Male rap trio from Chicago, Illinois: Goldiiz, Bad Seed and P-Child.

DEBUT	PEAK	WKS	Gold	A-side (Chart Hit)...B-side	$	Sym	Label & Number
9/25/99	53^S	4		**Luv At First Sight**...*(instrumental)*	$6	★	Hoo-Bangin' 53564
				CHILLDRIN OF DA GHETTO featuring Soultré			

CHILLIWACK BUB/ROK/LP '81

Rock group from Vancouver, British Columbia, Canada: Bill Henderson (vocals, guitar, songwriter), Brian MacLeod (guitar), Ab Bryant (bass) and Rick Taylor (drums). Bryant and MacLeod later joined **Headpins**. Bryant was also with **Prism**. MacLeod died of cancer on 4/25/92.

DEBUT	PEAK	WKS	Gold	A-side (Chart Hit)...B-side	$	Sym	Label & Number
2/5/72	75	3		1 **Lonesome Mary**...*Ridin'*	$8		A&M 1310
12/28/74+	98	6		2 **Crazy Talk**...*In And Out*	$6		Sire 716
4/30/77	75	6		3 **Fly At Night**...*Mary Lou & Me*	$5		Mushroom 7024
8/5/78	67	6		4 **Arms Of Mary**...*I Wanna Be The One*	$5		Mushroom 7033
9/26/81	22	19		5 **My Girl (Gone, Gone, Gone)** *Sign Here*	$4		Millennium 11813
1/16/82	33	11		6 **I Believe**...*Living In Stereo*	$4		Millennium 13102
10/23/82	41	13		7 **Whatcha Gonna Do**...*Really Don't Mind*	$4		Millennium 13110

CHIMES, The '61

Vocal group from Brooklyn, New York: Len Cocco, Pat DePrisco, Richard Mercado, Joe Croce and Pat McGuire.

DEBUT	PEAK	WKS	Gold	A-side (Chart Hit)...B-side	$	Sym	Label & Number
10/31/60+	11	18		1 **Once In Awhile**...*Summer Night*	$50		Tag 444
				#1 hit for **Tommy Dorsey** in 1937; originally issued with "Oh How I Love You So" by the BiTones as the B-side ($75)			
3/27/61	38	9		2 **I'm In The Mood For Love**...*Only Love*	$40		Tag 445
				#1 hit for Little Jack Little in 1935			

CHIMES, The R&B/LP '90

Dance trio from Scotland: Pauline Henry (vocals), Mike Peden (bass) and James Locke (drums).

DEBUT	PEAK	WKS	Gold	A-side (Chart Hit)...B-side	$	Sym	Label & Number
2/3/90	86	5		**1-2-3**...*Underestimate*	$3	▌	Columbia 73087

CHIPMUNKS, The — see SEVILLE, David

CHOCOLATE BANDIT '01

Born William Green in Los Angeles, California. Male rapper.

DEBUT	PEAK	WKS	Gold	A-side (Chart Hit)...B-side	$	Sym	Label & Number
11/10/01	52^S	4		**Gotta Have It**...*(2 versions)*	$10	★	Countryboy 303

CHOCOLATE MILK R&B/BUB/LP '75

R&B group from New Orleans, Louisiana: Frank Richard (vocals), Mario Tio (guitar), Robert Dabon (keyboards), Amadee Castanell (sax), Joe Foxx (trumpet) and Dwight Richards (drums).

DEBUT	PEAK	WKS	Gold	A-side (Chart Hit)...B-side	$	Sym	Label & Number
7/12/75	69	5		**Action Speaks Louder Than Words**...*Ain't Nothin' But A Thing*	$6		RCA Victor 10290

CHOICE FOUR, The R&B/BUB '75

R&B vocal group from Washington DC: Bobby Hamilton (lead), Ted Maduro, Pete Marshall and Charles Blagmore.

DEBUT	PEAK	WKS	Gold	A-side (Chart Hit)...B-side	$	Sym	Label & Number
8/30/75	91	4		**When You're Young And In Love**...*I Can't Make You Love Me*	$6		RCA Victor 10342

CHOIR, The '67

Rock group from Cleveland, Ohio: Wally Bryson (vocals, guitar; **Fotomaker**), David Smalley (guitar), James Skeen (bass) and Jim Bonfanti (drums). Bryson, Smalley and Bonfanti went on to form the **Raspberries** with **Eric Carmen**.

DEBUT	PEAK	WKS	Gold	A-side (Chart Hit)...B-side	$	Sym	Label & Number
6/3/67	68	6		**It's Cold Outside**...*I'm Going Home*	$15		Roulette 4738
				first released on Canadian American 203 in 1967 ($40)			

DEBUT	PEAK	WKS	Gold	A-side (Chart Hit)...B-side	$	Sym	Label & Number
				CHOIRBOYS '89			
				Rock group from Sydney, Australia: Mark Gable (vocals), Brett Williams (guitar), Ian Hulme (bass) and Lindsay Tebbutt (drums).			
3/11/89	80	7		**Run To Paradise** ... *Gasoline*	$4		WTG 68564
	★408★			**CHORDETTES, The** POP '54			
				Female vocal group from Sheboygan, Wisconsin: Janet Ertel, Carol Buschman, Lynn Evans and Margie Needham. With Arthur Godfrey from 1949-53. Ertel married Cadence owner **Archie Bleyer** in 1954; her daughter Jackie was married to Phil Everly of **The Everly Brothers**. Ertel died of cancer on 11/22/88 (age 75).			
				1)Mr. Sandman 2)Lollipop 3)Born To Be With You			
10/30/54	❶[7]	20	●	1 **Mr. Sandman** S:❶[7] / A:❶[7] / J:❶[4] *I Don't Wanna See You Cryin'*	$20		Cadence 1247
1/14/56	91	2		2 **The Wedding** ... T:91 *I Don't Know-I Don't Care*	$15		Cadence 1273
3/10/56	14	12		3 **Eddie My Love** ... A:14 / S:17 / T:18 *Whistlin' Willie (Our Melody)*	$15		Cadence 1284
6/2/56	5	20		4 **Born To Be With You** ... T:5 / A:5 / J:5 / S:7 *Love Never Changes*	$15		Cadence 1291
9/29/56	16	18		5 **Lay Down Your Arms /** T:16 / J:16 / S:18 / A:20			
10/20/56	45	11		6 **Teen Age Goodnight** ... T:45 / S:flip	$15		Cadence 1299
9/9/57	8	15		7 **Just Between You And Me /** A:8 / S:15 / T:19			
9/16/57	73	6		8 **Soft Sands** ... T:73 / S:flip	$15		Cadence 1330
3/10/58	2[2]	15		9 **Lollipop** ... A:2 / S:2 / T:2 *Baby Come-A Back-A*	$15		Cadence 1345
5/19/58	17	11		10 **Zorro** ... T:17 / S:18 / A:22 *Love Is A Two-Way Street*	$15	■	Cadence 1349
				theme from the Disney TV series starring Guy Williams			
3/2/59	27	11		11 **No Other Arms, No Other Lips** ... *We Should Be Together*	$15		Cadence 1361
8/17/59	89	3		12 **A Girl's Work Is Never Done** ... *No Wheels*	$12	■	Cadence 1366
				issued with a black-&-white and a full-color picture sleeve			
6/19/61	13	12		13 **Never On Sunday /**			
				title song from the movie starring Melina Mercouri			
9/25/61	90	1		14 **Faraway Star** ...	$12		Cadence 1402
				Archie Bleyer (orch., all of above)			
				CHRISTIAN, Chris AC '81			
				Born on 2/7/51 in Abilene, Texas. Singer/songwriter/producer. Member of **Cotton, Lloyd and Christian**. Began recording Christian music in 1977.			
9/27/75	66	5		1 **I Go To Pieces** ... *Mr. Rock 'N' Roll*	$5		20th Century 2217
				COTTON, LLOYD and CHRISTIAN			
				written by **Del Shannon**			
10/3/81	37	14		2 **I Want You, I Need You** ... *I Don't Believe You*	$4	■	Boardwalk 126
8/28/82	88	3		3 **Ain't Nothing Like The Real Thing/You're All I Need To Get By** ... *Houston* (Christian)	$4		Boardwalk 149
				CHRIS CHRISTIAN (with Amy Holland)			
				CHRISTIE LP '70			
				Pop-rock trio from England: Jeff Christie (vocals, bass), Vic Elmes (guitar) and Mike Blakely (drums). Blakely's brother, Alan, was a member of **The Tremeloes**.			
7/18/70	23	23		1 **Yellow River** ... *Down The Mississippi Line*	$6		Epic 10626
1/30/71	100	1		2 **San Bernadino** ... *Here I Am*	$6		Epic 10695
				CHRISTIE, Dean '62			
				Teen pop singer/songwriter.			
11/3/62	87	4		**Heart Breaker** ... *I'm A Loser*	$20		Select 715
				first released on SWL 1607 in 1962 ($25); tune is similar to **Dion**'s "Runaround Sue"; B-side similar to **Elton John**'s "Crocodile Rock"			
	★530★			**CHRISTIE, Lou** BUB/AC/LP '66			
				Born Lugee Sacco on 2/19/43 in Glen Willard, Pennsylvania. Joined vocal group the Classics; first recorded for Starr in 1960. Started long association with songwriter Twyla Herbert. Recorded as Lugee & The Lions for Robbee in 1961. Sang lead for **Meco**'s **The Cantina Band** in 1981.			
				1)Lightnin' Strikes 2)Two Faces Have I 3)I'm Gonna Make You Mine			
1/5/63	24	13		1 **The Gypsy Cried** ... *Red Sails In The Sunset*	$15		Roulette 4457
				first released on C&C 102 in 1962 ($150)			
3/30/63	6	15		2 **Two Faces Have I** ... *All That Glitters Isn't Gold*	$15		Roulette 4481
7/20/63	46	5		3 **How Many Teardrops** ... *You And I (Have A Right To Cry)*	$15		Roulette 4504
12/25/65+	❶[1]	15	●	4 **Lightnin' Strikes** *Cryin' In The Streets*	$12		MGM 13412
3/5/66	45	8		5 **Outside The Gates Of Heaven** ... *All That Glitters Isn't Gold*	$15		Co & Ce 235
3/19/66	95	1		6 **Big Time** ... *Cryin' On My Knees*	$20	■	Colpix 799
3/26/66	16	8		7 **Rhapsody In The Rain** ... *Trapeze*	$15	■	MGM 13473
				early pressings include the lyrics "we were makin' out in the rain"; reissued as "we fell in love in the rain"; melody inspired by Tchaikovsky's *Romeo and Juliet*			
6/25/66	81	5		8 **Painter** ... *Du Ronda*	$12	■	MGM 13533
				melody inspired by "One Fine Day" from Puccini's opera *Madame Butterfly*; **The Angels** (backing vocals, above 2)			
4/29/67	95	2		9 **Shake Hands And Walk Away Cryin'** ... *Escape*	$15		Columbia 44062
8/23/69	10	12		10 **I'm Gonna Make You Mine** ... *I'm Gonna Get Married*	$8		Buddah 116
12/20/69+	73	4		11 **Are You Getting Any Sunshine?** ... *It'll Take Time*	$8		Buddah 149
2/16/74	80	10		12 **Beyond The Blue Horizon** ... *Saddle The Wind*	$8		Three Brothers 402
				sung by Jeanette MacDonald in the 1930 movie *Monte Carlo*			
7/25/81	81	3		13 **Summer '81 medley** ... *Out In California*	$8		Millennium 11818
				THE CANTINA BAND (featuring Lou Christie)			
				Beach Boys' medley: Surfer Girl/Fun, Fun, Fun/409/I Get Around/ Dance, Dance, Dance/California Girls/ Wouldn't It Be Nice/Help Me, Rhonda/Good Vibrations			
				CHRISTIE, Susan '66			
				Born Beatrice Hill. White teen pop singer.			
6/11/66	63	8		**I Love Onions** ... *Take Me As You Find Me* [N]	$12	■	Columbia 43595

DEBUT	PEAK	WKS	Gold	A-side (Chart Hit)..........B-side	$	Sym	Label & Number

CHRISTIÓN — R&B/BUB/LP '97
R&B vocal duo from Oakland, California: Kenny Ski and Allen Anthony.

DEBUT	PEAK	WKS	Gold	A-side (Chart Hit)..........B-side	$	Sym	Label & Number
4/26/97	53	18		1 **Full Of Smoke**..........S:33 *Aftermath* samples "Trouble Man" by **Marvin Gaye**	$4	▮	Roc-A-Fella 573786
6/6/98	86	4		2 **I Wanna Get Next To You**..........S:65 *(TV track) / Where I'm From*	$4	▮	Roc-A-Fella 568476

CHRISTOPHER, Gavin — R&B/LP '86
Born in Chicago, Illinois. R&B singer/composer/producer. Brother of **Shawn Christopher**.

DEBUT	PEAK	WKS	Gold	A-side (Chart Hit)..........B-side	$	Sym	Label & Number
5/24/86	22	17		**One Step Closer To You**..........S:18 / A:27 *(instrumental)*	$3	■	Manhattan 50028

CHRISTOPHER, Shawn — R&B '91
Born in Chicago, Illinois. Sister of **Gavin Christopher**. Touring vocalist with **Chaka Khan** from 1982-85. Also see **Lil Louis**.

DEBUT	PEAK	WKS	Gold	A-side (Chart Hit)..........B-side	$	Sym	Label & Number
2/16/91	67	7		1 **Another Sleepless Night**..........*(jazzy dub)* **MIKE "Hitman" WILSON featuring SHAWN CHRISTOPHER** (original label credit) "45" B-side: "I'll Do Ya Right"	$3	▮[V]	Arista 2148
2/29/92	71	8		2 **Don't Lose the Magic**..........A:44 *(Morales' 7")* above 2: #1 Dance Club Play hits	$3	▮	Arista 12416

CHUBB ROCK — R&B/LP '91
Born Richard Simpson on 5/28/68 in Jamaica; raised in Brooklyn, New York. Male rapper.

DEBUT	PEAK	WKS	Gold	A-side (Chart Hit)..........B-side	$	Sym	Label & Number
5/18/91	95	2		**Treat 'Em Right**..........S:44 *(3 remixes)*	$6	▮*	Select 5009

CHUCK D. — see KOOL MOE DEE

CHUCKLEBUTT — '98
Group of studio musicians from New Jersey led by producer Adam Marano.

DEBUT	PEAK	WKS	Gold	A-side (Chart Hit)..........B-side	$	Sym	Label & Number
1/31/98	87	6		**Tubthumping**..........S:69 *(remix)* cover version of **Chumbawamba**'s hit (see below)	$6	▮	Under The Cover 977

CHUCK-N-BLOOD — '02
Male rap duo from Miami, Florida: Chuck Dondada and Blood Vessel.

DEBUT	PEAK	WKS	Gold	A-side (Chart Hit)..........B-side	$	Sym	Label & Number
7/6/02	7^S	13		**My Dogs**..........*(instrumental)* **CHUCK-N-BLOOD Featuring Wolverine & Mad Dreadz**	$6	★	Forealah Jamz 2071

CHUMBAWAMBA — BUB/LP '97
Post-punk rock group from Leeds, England: Alice Nutter, Lou Watts, Danbert Nubacon, Paul Greco, Jude Abbott, Dunstan Bruce, Neil Ferguson and Harry Hamer.

DEBUT	PEAK	WKS	Gold	A-side (Chart Hit)..........B-side	$	Sym	Label & Number
9/13/97	6	31		1 **Tubthumping**..........MR[7] A:❶[9] / S:30 *(2 remixes) / Farewell To The Crown / Football Song* Tubthumping is slang for unsolicited sermonizing	$6	★[V]	Republic 56146
3/28/98	60^A	5		2 **Amnesia**..........BUB:101 *(2 versions) / Tubthumping (remix)* "45" issued for above 2 on Republic 56191	$6	T[V]	Republic 56181

CHUNKY A — R&B/LP '89
Chunkston Arthur Hall is actually actor/comedian Arsenio Hall. Born on 2/12/57 in Cleveland, Ohio. Hosted own late night talk show (1989-1994) and starred in own sitcom (1997). Acted in the movies *Coming To America* and *Harlem Nights*. Hosted the 2002 revival of TV's *Star Search*.

DEBUT	PEAK	WKS	Gold	A-side (Chart Hit)..........B-side	$	Sym	Label & Number
12/2/89	77	6		**Owwww!**..........*(plumpapella version)* samples "Word Up" by **Cameo**	$4	■	MCA 53736

CHURCH, The — ROK/LP '88
Folk-rock group from Canberra, Australia: Steve Kilbey (vocals, bass), Peter Koppes and Marty Willson-Piper (guitars), and Richard Ploog (drums).

DEBUT	PEAK	WKS	Gold	A-side (Chart Hit)..........B-side	$	Sym	Label & Number
4/9/88	24	15		**Under The Milky Way**..........S:19 / A:29 *Musk*	$4	■	Arista 9673

CHURCH, Eugene — BUB/R&B '59
Born on 1/23/38 in St. Louis, Missouri; raised in Los Angeles, California. Died of AIDS on 4/16/93 (age 55). R&B singer/songwriter. Recorded with **Jesse Belvin** as **The Cliques**. Later worked in Texas as a hairdresser and sang gospel music.

DEBUT	PEAK	WKS	Gold	A-side (Chart Hit)..........B-side	$	Sym	Label & Number
12/15/58+	36	15		1 **Pretty Girls Everywhere**..........*For The Rest Of My Life* **EUGENE CHURCH and The Fellows** (Gaynel Hodge, Tommy Williams and **Jesse Belvin**)	$25		Class 235
8/3/59	67	5		2 **Miami**..........*I Ain't Goin' For That*	$20		Class 254

CINDERELLA — ROK/LP '87
Hard-rock group from Philadelphia, Pennsylvania: Tom Keifer (vocals, guitar), Jeff LaBar (guitar), Eric Brittingham (bass) and Fred Coury (drums).

DEBUT	PEAK	WKS	Gold	A-side (Chart Hit)..........B-side	$	Sym	Label & Number
11/8/86+	13	21		1 **Nobody's Fool**..........S:11 / A:22 *Push, Push*	$3	■	Mercury 884851
4/25/87	66	7		2 **Somebody Save Me**..........*Hell On Wheels*	$3	■	Mercury 888483
9/3/88	12	22		3 **Don't Know What You Got (Till It's Gone)** S:9 / A:16 *Fire And Ice*	$3	■	Mercury 870644
1/21/89	36	10		4 **The Last Mile**..........S:34 / A:39 *Long Cold Winter*	$3	■	Mercury 872148
4/8/89	20	17		5 **Coming Home**..........S:18 / A:20 *Take Me Back*	$3	■	Mercury 872982
8/5/89	51	7		6 **Gypsy Road**..........*Jumpin' Jack Flash (live)* above 4 from the album *Long Cold Winter*	$3		Mercury 874578
12/8/90+	36	13		7 **Shelter Me**..........A:35 / S:37 *Electric Love*	$3	▮[V]	Mercury 878700
3/16/91	44	11		8 **Heartbreak Station**..........*Love Gone Bad*	$3	▮	Mercury 878796

CIRCA '58 — see P-NUT GALLERY

CIRCUS — '73
Rock group from Cleveland, Ohio: Dan Hrdlicka (vocals, guitar), Mick Sabol (guitar), Phil Alexander (keyboards), Frank Salle (bass) and Tommy Dobeck (drums). Dobeck later joined the **Michael Stanley Band**.

DEBUT	PEAK	WKS	Gold	A-side (Chart Hit)..........B-side	$	Sym	Label & Number
2/24/73	91	4		**Stop, Wait & Listen**..........*I Need Your Love*	$6		Metromedia 265

CISYK, Kacey — AC '77
Born in 1953 in Brooklyn, New York. Died of cancer on 3/29/98 (age 44). Session singer.

DEBUT	PEAK	WKS	Gold	A-side (Chart Hit)..........B-side	$	Sym	Label & Number
11/12/77	80	4		**You Light Up My Life**..........*You Light Up My Life* (Joe Brooks) **ORIGINAL CAST** (Cisyk uncredited on label) Joe Brooks (orch.); title song from the movie starring Didi Conn	$5		Arista 0287

DEBUT	PEAK	WKS	Gold	A-side (Chart Hit)..........B-side	$	Sym	Label & Number
				CITIZEN KING '99			
				Rock group from Milwaukee, Wisconsin: Matt Sims (vocals, bass), Kristian Riley (guitar), Malcolm Michiles (DJ), Dave Cooley (keyboards) and DJ Brooks (drums).			
5/29/99	25	20		**Better Days (and the bottom drops out)** ....A:31 / S:32 *Basement Show*	$4	★V	Warner 16965
				contains a spoken excerpt from "(Intro To) Radar" by the Legendary Stardust Cowboy			
				CITY BOY LP '78			
				Pop-rock group from Birmingham, England: Lol Mason (vocals), Mike Slamer (guitar), Max Thomas (keyboards), Steve Broughton (percussion), Chris Dunn (bass) and Roy Ward (drums).			
8/12/78	27	12		**5.7.0.5.** ....*Bad For Business*	$5	■	Mercury 73999
				CITY HIGH LP '01			
				Black hip-hop trio from Willingboro, New Jersey: Claudette Ortiz, Robby Pardlo and Ryan Toby.			
3/24/01	8	28		1 **What Would You Do?** ....S:❶² / A:9 *(instrumental) / (3 album snippets)*	$4	★	Booga Basement 497489
				co-produced by **Wyclef Jean**			
10/13/01+	18	24		2 **Caramel** ....A:18 *(5 versions)*	$6	T	Booga Basement 497608
				CITY HIGH Featuring Eve			
				C.J. & CO. R&B/BUB/LP '77			
				Disco group from Detroit, Michigan: Cornelius Brown, Curtis Durden, Joni Tolbert, Connie Durden and Charles Clark.			
1/3/76	91	8		1 **Daydreamer**....*Would You Believe It?*	$5		Westbound 5016
				C.C. & COMPANY			
5/21/77	36	29		2 **Devil's Gun**....*Free To Be Me*	$5		Westbound 55400
				CLANTON, Ike '60			
				Born in Baton Rouge, Louisiana. Brother of **Jimmy Clanton**. Touring bassist in 1959 with **Duane Eddy**'s Rebels.			
5/23/60	91	2		1 **Down The Aisle** ....*(I Guess) I'm Sorry*	$15		Ace 583
				tune recorded in 1961 by **Jimmy Clanton** and Mary Ann Mobley on Ace 616			
8/4/62	95	2		2 **Sugar Plum** ....*I'm Guilty (Of Loving You)*	$12		Mercury 71975
	★519★			**CLANTON, Jimmy** BUB '58			
				Born on 9/2/40 in Baton Rouge, Louisiana. Brother of **Ike Clanton**. Played in local bands, discovered by Ace Records while making a demo at Cosimo Matassa's studio in New Orleans. Recorded with famous New Orleans sessionmen, including **Huey "Piano" Smith**, Earl King (guitar) and **Lee Allen** (tenor sax). Toured with Dick Clark's Caravan Of Stars. Starred in the movie *Go, Johnny, Go!* in 1958. DJ in Lancaster, Pennsylvania, from 1972-76.			
				1)Just A Dream 2)Go, Jimmy, Go 3)Venus In Blue Jeans			
7/14/58	4	18		1 **Just A Dream** RB¹ S:4 / H:4 *You Aim To Please*	$25		Ace 546
				JIMMY CLANTON And His Rockets			
10/20/58	25	12		2 **A Letter To An Angel /**			
11/3/58	38	7		3 **A Part Of Me**	$20		Ace 551
8/3/59	33	12		4 **My Own True Love** ....*Little Boy In Love*	$20	■	Ace 567
				melody is "Tara's Theme" from the movie *Gone With The Wind* starring Clark Gable and Vivien Leigh			
12/7/59+	5	16		5 **Go, Jimmy, Go** ....*I Trusted You*	$20	■	Ace 575
4/25/60	22	13		6 **Another Sleepless Night** ....*I'm Gonna Try*	$20	■	Ace 585
8/22/60	63	8		7 **Come Back /**			
9/26/60	91	3		8 **Wait**	$20	■	Ace 600
1/9/61	50	6		9 **What Am I Gonna Do** ....*If I*	$20	■	Ace 607
8/18/62	7	13		10 **Venus In Blue Jeans** ....*Highway Bound*	$20		Ace 8001
				#6, 9 & 10: written by **Neil Sedaka**			
1/5/63	77	4		11 **Darkest Street In Town** ....*Dreams Of A Fool*	$15		Ace 8005
11/15/69	97	3		12 **Curly** ....*I'll Never Forget Your Love*	$10		Laurie 3508
				**CLAPTON, Eric** ★108★ ROK/AC/BUB/LP '92			
				Born Eric Patrick Clapp on 3/30/45 in Ripley, England. Prolific rock-blues guitarist/vocalist. With The Roosters in 1963, **The Yardbirds**, 1963-65, and **John Mayall**'s Bluesbreakers, 1965-66. Formed **Cream** with Jack Bruce and **Ginger Baker** in 1966. Formed Blind Faith in 1968; worked with **John Lennon**'s Plastic Ono Band, and **Delaney & Bonnie**. Formed **Derek and The Dominos** in 1970. After two years of reclusion (1971-72), Clapton performed his comeback concert at London's Rainbow Theatre in January 1973. Began actively recording and touring again in 1974. Nicknamed "Slowhand" in 1964 while with The Yardbirds. Inducted into the Rock and Roll Hall of Fame in 2000.			
				1)I Shot The Sheriff 2)Tears In Heaven 3)Lay Down Sally 4)Change The World 5)Promises			
2/21/70	84	3		1 **Comin' Home**....*Groupie (Superstar)*	$10		Atco 6725
				DELANEY & BONNIE AND FRIENDS FEATURING ERIC CLAPTON			
10/17/70	18	12		2 **After Midnight**....*Easy Now*	$8		Atco 6784
2/27/71	91	2		3 **Bell Bottom Blues** ....*Keep On Growing*	$8		Atco 6803
				also see #7 below			
3/27/71	51	10		4 **Layla**....*I Am Yours*	$8		Atco 6809
				Duane **Allman** (guitar); Layla: nickname of Pattie Boyd, married to **George Harrison** from 1966-74 and Clapton from 1979-88			
5/13/72	10	15		5 **Layla** ....*I Am Yours* [R]	$8	⊙	Atco 6809
				DEREK AND THE DOMINOS (above 3)			
				longer version (7:10) than #4 above (2:43); also see #26 below; sleeve insert was a memo to radio dated 4/18/72			
9/23/72	48	13		6 **Let It Rain**....*Easy Now*	$7		Polydor 15049
2/17/73	78	5		7 **Bell Bottom Blues** ....*Little Wing* [R]	$7	□	Polydor 15056
				same recording (longer version) as Derek & The Dominos' 1971 hit above; #3-7 (except #6): from the Derek & The Dominos album *Layla*			
7/13/74	❶¹	14	●	8 **I Shot The Sheriff** *Give Me Strength*	$5		RSO 409
				Yvonne Elliman (backing vocal); written by **Bob Marley**; also released on RSO 500			
11/2/74	26	9		9 **Willie And The Hand Jive**....*Mainline Florida*	$5		RSO 503
10/16/76	24	14		10 **Hello Old Friend**....*All Our Pastimes*	$5		RSO 861
1/7/78	3	23	●	11 **Lay Down Sally** ....*Next Time You See Her*	$5		RSO 886
5/13/78	16	17		12 **Wonderful Tonight** ....*Peaches And Diesel*	$5		RSO 895
				written for Clapton's wife-to-be, Pattie Boyd; **Yvonne Elliman** and **Marcy Levy** (backing vocals, above 3)			

DEBUT	PEAK	WKS	Gold	A-side (Chart Hit)...B-side	$	Sym	Label & Number
				CLAPTON, Eric — Cont'd			
10/14/78+	9	18		13 **Promises** /			
2/24/79	40	7		14 **Watch Out For Lucy**	$5		RSO 910
6/21/80	30	14		15 **Tulsa Time** / [L]			
				studio version on the 1978 *Backless* album; #1 Country hit for **Don Williams** in 1978			
7/5/80		12		16 **Cocaine** [L]	$5		RSO 1039
				studio version on the 1977 *Slowhand* album; #2 & 16: written by **J.J. Cale**			
11/8/80	76	5		17 **Blues Power** ... *Early In The Morning* [L]	$4		RSO 1051
				studio version on the 1970 *Eric Clapton* album			
2/28/81	10	17		18 **I Can't Stand It** ... AR^{2} *Black Rose*	$4		RSO 1060
6/13/81	78	5		19 **Another Ticket** ... *Rita Mae* (ROK #18)	$4	■	RSO 1064
				ERIC CLAPTON AND HIS BAND (#13-19)			
1/29/83	18	16		20 **I've Got A Rock N' Roll Heart** ... *Man In Love*	$4		Duck/Warner 29780
3/9/85	26	12		21 **Forever Man** ... AR^{2} A:20 / S:30 *Too Bad*	$3	■	Duck/Warner 29081
6/29/85	89	2		22 **See What Love Can Do** ... *She's Waiting*	$3		Duck/Warner 28986
11/18/89	55	11		23 **Pretending** ... AR^{6} *Before You Accuse Me* (ROK #9)	$3	■	Duck/Reprise 22732
				Chaka Khan (backing vocal)			
3/10/90	88	5		24 **Bad Love** ... AR^{3} *Hard Times*	$3	▮	Duck/Reprise 19980
				Phil Collins (backing vocal)			
2/8/92	2^{4}	26	▲	25 **Tears In Heaven** ... AC^{3} S:❶^{3} / A:3 *Tracks And Lines*	$3	▮^{V}	Duck/Reprise 19038
				from the movie *Rush* starring Jason Patric; Clapton wrote this song for his son, Conor, who fell to his death on 3/20/91 (age 4) from a New York City apartment window on the 53rd floor; 1992 Grammy winner: Record of the Year			
10/3/92	12	20		26 **Layla** ... A:12 / S:16 *Signe* [L-R]	$3	▮^{V}	Duck/Reprise 18787
				"live" acoustic version (also see #4 & 5 above)			
7/20/96	5	43	●	27 **Change The World** ... AC^{13} A:2 / S:9 *Danny Boy*	$3	▮^{V}	Reprise 17621
				from the movie *Phenomenon* starring **John Travolta**; 1996 Grammy winner: Record of the Year			
2/21/98	16^{A}	22		28 **My Father's Eyes**			album cut
				from the album *Pilgrim* on Duck 46577; Clapton wrote all of above (except #2, 8, 9, 13, 15, 16, 20-23 & 27)			

CLARK, Claudine — '62

Born on 4/26/41 in Macon, Georgia; raised in Philadelphia, Pennsylvania. Black singer/songwriter. First recorded for Herald in 1958. Also recorded for Swan as Joy Dawn.

DEBUT	PEAK	WKS	Gold	A-side (Chart Hit)...B-side	$	Sym	Label & Number
6/30/62	5	15		**Party Lights** ... *Disappointed*	$20		Chancellor 1113

CLARK, Dave, Five ★125★ — BUB/LP '64

Rock and roll band formed in Tottenham, England. By 1961 established lineup: Dave Clark (drums; born on 12/15/42), Mike Smith (vocals, keyboards; born on 12/6/43), Lenny Davidson (guitar; born on 5/30/44), Denny Payton (sax; born on 8/11/43) and Rick Huxley (bass; born on 8/5/42). Clark had been a movie stuntman. First recorded for Ember and Piccadilly in 1962. In May 1964 made first of 18 appearances on *The Ed Sullivan Show*. In the movie *Having A Wild Weekend* (released abroad as *Catch Us If You Can*) in 1965. Announced breakup in August 1970; Clark and Smith recorded as Dave Clark & Friends until 1973. Clark co-wrote and produced the 1986 London stage musical *Time*.

1)Over And Over 2)Because 3)Bits And Pieces 4)Catch Us If You Can 5)Can't You See That She's Mine

DEBUT	PEAK	WKS	Gold	A-side (Chart Hit)...B-side	$	Sym	Label & Number
2/15/64	6	14		1 **Glad All Over** ... *I Know You*	$15	■	Epic 9656
4/4/64	4	11		2 **Bits And Pieces** ... *All Of The Time*	$15		Epic 9671
4/25/64	53	8		3 **I Knew It All The Time** ... *That's What I Said*	$20	■	Congress 212
				recorded in 1963			
5/2/64	11	10		4 **Do You Love Me** ... *Chaquita*	$15		Epic 9678
6/13/64	4	10		5 **Can't You See That She's Mine** ... *No Time To Lose*	$15	■	Epic 9692
8/1/64	3	10		6 **Because** ... *Theme Without A Name*	$15	■	Epic 9704
10/3/64	15	8		7 **Everybody Knows (I Still Love You)** ... *Ol' Sol*	$15	■	Epic 9722
11/14/64+	14	12		8 **Any Way You Want It** ... *Crying Over You*	$15		Epic 9739
2/6/65	14	9		9 **Come Home** ... *Your Turn To Cry*	$15	■	Epic 9763
4/17/65	23	9		10 **Reelin' And Rockin'** ... *I'm Thinking* (#128)	$15		Epic 9786
6/19/65	7	11		11 **I Like It Like That** ... *Hurting Inside*	$15	■	Epic 9811
8/21/65	4	11		12 **Catch Us If You Can** ... *On The Move*	$15	■	Epic 9833
				from the movie *Having A Wild Weekend* (originally titled *Catch Us If You Can*) starring the Dave Clark Five			
11/13/65	❶^{1}	12		13 **Over And Over** *I'll Be Yours (My Love)*	$15	■	Epic 9863
				issued with a regular picture sleeve and with a promotional sleeve featuring a photo of the group on stage			
2/5/66	18	7		14 **At The Scene** ... *I Miss You*	$15	■	Epic 9882
4/2/66	12	8		15 **Try Too Hard** ... *All Night Long*	$15	■	Epic 10004
6/11/66	28	7		16 **Please Tell Me Why** ... *Look Before You Leap* (#101)	$15	■	Epic 10031
8/13/66	50	6		17 **Satisfied With You** ... *Don't Let Me Down*	$15	■	Epic 10053
10/22/66	48	6		18 **Nineteen Days** ... *Sitting Here Baby*	$15	■	Epic 10076
1/7/67	44	7		19 **I've Got To Have A Reason** ... *Good Time Woman*	$15	■	Epic 10114
4/1/67	7	10		20 **You Got What It Takes** ... *Doctor Rhythm*	$15	■	Epic 10144
6/10/67	35	6		21 **You Must Have Been A Beautiful Baby** ... *Man In The Pin Stripe Suit*	$15	■	Epic 10179
				#1 hit for **Bing Crosby** in 1938			
8/12/67	67	4		22 **A Little Bit Now** ... *You Don't Play Me Around*	$15	■	Epic 10209
11/18/67	89	2		23 **Red And Blue** ... *Concentration Baby*	$15		Epic 10244
				Clark wrote or co-wrote all of above (except #3, 4, 10, 11, 13 & 20-22)			
12/16/67+	43	8		24 **Everybody Knows** ... *Inside And Out*	$15	■	Epic 10265
				different song from #7 above; all of above picture sleeves feature feature black-&-white photos of the group			

DEBUT	PEAK	WKS	Gold	A-side (Chart Hit)..........B-side	$	Sym	Label & Number

CLARK, Dee ★586★ BUB '61

Born Delecta Clark on 11/7/38 in Blytheville, Arkansas. Died of a heart attack on 12/7/90 (age 52). Male R&B singer. To Chicago in 1941. In Hambone Kids with Sammy McGrier and Ronny Strong; first recorded for Okeh in 1952. Joined R&B vocal group the Goldentones in 1953. Group became the Kool Gents; billed as The Delegates for Vee-Jay in 1956. First solo recording for Falcon in 1957.

1)Raindrops 2)Just Keep It Up 3)Hey Little Girl

DEBUT	PEAK	WKS	Gold	A-side (Chart Hit)..........B-side	$	Sym	Label & Number
12/1/58+	21	17		1 **Nobody But You**.......*When I Call On You*	$25		Abner 1019
5/4/59	18	15		2 **Just Keep It Up**.......*Whispering Grass*	$25		Abner 1026
8/24/59	20	15		3 **Hey Little Girl**.......*If It Wasn't For Love*	$25	■	Abner 1029
12/7/59+	33	11		4 **How About That**.......*Blues Get Off My Shoulder* (#109)	$25		Abner 1032
3/14/60	56	7		5 **At My Front Door**.......*Cling A Ling*	$25		Abner 1037
8/15/60	43	10		6 **You're Looking Good**.......*Gloria*	$20		Vee-Jay 355
2/6/61	34	9		7 **Your Friends**.......*Because I Love You* (#105)	$20		Vee-Jay 372
5/1/61	2[1]	16		8 **Raindrops** *I Want To Love You*	$20		Vee-Jay 383
10/6/62	52	7		9 **I'm Going Back To School**.......*Nobody But You* Riley Hampton (orch., all of above)	$20		Vee-Jay 462
11/2/63	92	5		10 **Crossfire Time**.......*I'm Going Home*	$15		Constellation 108

CLARK, Louis — see ROYAL PHILHARMONIC ORCHESTRA

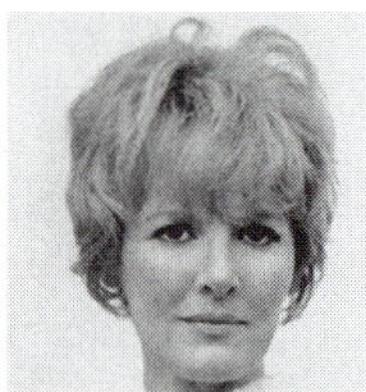

CLARK, Petula ★154★ AC/LP '65

Born on 11/15/32 in Epsom, Surrey, England. Adult Contemporary singer/actress. On radio at age nine; own show *Pet's Parlour* at age 11. TV series in England in 1950. First U.S. record release for Coral in 1953. Appeared in over 20 British movies from 1944-57; revived her movie career in the late 1960s, starring in *Finian's Rainbow* and *Goodbye Mr. Chips*.

1)Downtown 2)My Love 3)I Know A Place 4)This Is My Song 5)Don't Sleep In The Subway

DEBUT	PEAK	WKS	Gold	A-side (Chart Hit)..........B-side	$	Sym	Label & Number
12/19/64+	❶[2]	15	●	1 **Downtown** *You'd Better Love Me*	$10		Warner 5494
3/20/65	3	12		2 **I Know A Place**.......*Jack And John*	$10		Warner 5612
7/10/65	22	9		3 **You'd Better Come Home**.......*Heart*	$10		Warner 5643
10/9/65	21	8		4 **Round Every Corner**.......*Two Rivers*	$10		Warner 5661
12/25/65+	❶[2]	13		5 **My Love**.......*Where Am I Going*	$10		Warner 5684
3/26/66	11	8		6 **A Sign Of The Times**.......*Time For Love*	$10		Warner 5802
7/16/66	9	9		7 **I Couldn't Live Without Your Love**.......AC[1] *Your Way Of Life*	$10		Warner 5835
10/22/66	21	7		8 **Who Am I**.......*Love Is A Long Journey*	$10		Warner 5863
12/24/66+	16	9		9 **Color My World**.......*Take Me Home Again* all of above written and produced by Tony Hatch	$10		Warner 5882
3/4/67	3	12		10 **This Is My Song**.......*High* written by Charlie Chaplin; from the movie *A Countess From Hong Kong* starring Marlon Brando	$8		Warner 7002
6/3/67	5	10		11 **Don't Sleep In The Subway**.......AC[3] *Here Comes The Morning*	$8		Warner 7049
9/2/67	26	7		12 **The Cat In The Window (The Bird In The Sky)**.......*Fancy Dancin' Man*	$8		Warner 7073
12/2/67	31	7		13 **The Other Man's Grass Is Always Greener**.......*At The Crossroads*	$8		Warner 7097
2/17/68	15	11		14 **Kiss Me Goodbye**.......*I've Got Love Going For Me*	$8		Warner 7170
7/20/68	37	7		15 **Don't Give Up**.......*Every Time I See A Rainbow*	$8		Warner 7216
11/23/68	59	8		16 **American Boys**.......*Look To The Sky* some pressings show title as "American Boy"	$8		Warner 7244
4/12/69	62	5		17 **Happy Heart**.......*Love Is The Only Thing*	$8		Warner 7275
8/9/69	89	3		18 **Look At Mine**.......*You And I*	$8		Warner 7310
11/29/69	93	1		19 **No One Better Than You**.......*Things Bright And Beautiful*	$8		Warner 7343
6/10/72	70	13		20 **My Guy**.......*Little Bit Of Lovin'*	$6		MGM 14392
10/7/72	61	10		21 **Wedding Song (There Is Love)**.......*Song Without End*	$6		MGM 14431
2/6/82	66	6		22 **Natural Love**.......*Because I Love Him*	$4		Scotti Brothers 02676

CLARK, Roy C&W/BUB/AC/LP '69

Born on 4/15/33 in Meherrin, Virginia. Country singer/guitarist. Charted 52 Country hits, 1963-89. Acted in the TV series *The Beverly Hillbillies*, appearing as both "Cousin Roy" and Roy's mother, "Big Mama Halsey." Clark and **Buck Owens** hosted TV's *Hee Haw* from 1969-86.

DEBUT	PEAK	WKS	Gold	A-side (Chart Hit)..........B-side	$	Sym	Label & Number
6/29/63	45	8		1 **Tips Of My Fingers**.......*Spooky Movies*	$10		Capitol 4956
6/14/69	19	10		2 **Yesterday, When I Was Young** *Just Another Man* written by singer/actor Charles Aznavour	$8		Dot 17246
1/24/70	94	3		3 **Then She's A Lover**.......*Say Amen*	$8		Dot 17335
10/31/70	90	3		4 **Thank God And Greyhound**.......*Strangers*	$8		Dot 17355
5/26/73	89	3		5 **Come Live With Me**.......CW[1] *Darby's Castle*	$8		Dot 17449
12/15/73+	81	5		6 **Somewhere Between Love And Tomorrow**.......*I'll Paint You A Song*	$8		Dot 17480

CLARK, Sanford '56

Born on 10/24/35 in Tulsa, Oklahoma. Male singer/songwriter/guitarist.

DEBUT	PEAK	WKS	Gold	A-side (Chart Hit)..........B-side	$	Sym	Label & Number
7/28/56	7	21		1 **The Fool**.......S:7 / J:7 / T:9 / A:16 *Lonesome For A Letter* first released on MCI 1003 in 1956 ($125)	$50		Dot 15481
12/8/56	74	3		2 **A Cheat**.......T:74 *Usta Be My Baby* **Al Casey** (guitar, above 2)	$40		Dot 15516

CLARK, Terri C&W/BUB/LP '02

Born Terri Sauson (Clark is her stepfather's last name) on 8/5/68 in Montreal, Quebec, Canada; raised in Medicine Hat, Alberta, Canada. Female country singer/guitarist.

DEBUT	PEAK	WKS	Gold	A-side (Chart Hit)..........B-side	$	Sym	Label & Number
5/23/98	72	13		1 **Now That I Found You**.......S:48 *Getting Even With The Blues*	$4	▮V	Mercury 568746
12/5/98	40	12		2 **You're Easy On The Eyes**.......CW[3] A:30 "45": Mercury 566218; B-side: "That's Me Not Loving You"		V	album cut

DEBUT	PEAK	WKS	Gold	A-side (Chart Hit)	B-side	$	Sym	Label & Number
				CLARK, Terri — Cont'd				
4/3/99	69	8		3 **Everytime I Cry**	A:49		V	album cut
				"45": Mercury 566848; B-side: "Till I Get There"; all of above from the album *How I Feel* on Mercury 558211				
12/16/00	75	6		4 **A Little Gasoline**	A:73		V	album cut
				from the album *Fearless* on Mercury 170157; "45": Mercury 172178; B-side: "Empty"				
11/9/02+	27	20		5 **I Just Wanna Be Mad**	A:26 *Three Mississippi*	$4	★V	Mercury 172262
				CLARKE, Allan — see HOLLIES				
				CLARKE, Rozlyne '90				
				Born in Brooklyn, New York. Female dance singer.				
12/8/90	74^A	2		**Eddy Steady Go**	*(new age mix)*	$7	▮	Atlantic 87803
				CLARKE, Stanley R&B/AC/LP '81				
				Born on 6/30/51 in Philadelphia, Pennsylvania. R&B-jazz bassist/violinist/cellist. With Chick Corea in Return To Forever in 1973. Much session work, solo debut in 1974. Member of Fuse One in 1982 and Animal Logic in 1989.				
5/2/81	19	20		**Sweet Baby**	*Never Judge A Cover By Its Book*	$4		Epic 01052
				STANLEY CLARKE/GEORGE DUKE				
				CLARKE, Tony '65				
				Born in New York City, New York; raised in Detroit, Michigan. Died in 1970. Soul singer/songwriter. Acted in the movie *They Call Me Mr. Tibbs.*				
3/14/64	88	1		1 **(The Story Of) Woman, Love And A Man (Part 1)**	*(Part 2)*	$12		Chess 1880
3/27/65	31	9		2 **The Entertainer**	*This Heart Of Mine*	$12		Chess 1924
				CLARK FAMILY EXPERIENCE, The C&W '00				
				Bluegrass group from Rocky Mount, Virginia: brothers Alan (guitar), Ashley (fiddle), Austin (dobro), Adam (mandolin), Aaron (bass) and Andrew (drums) Clark.				
11/18/00	80	12		**Meanwhile Back At The Ranch**	S:37 *Restless*	$5	★	Curb 73118
				co-produced by **Tim McGraw**; B-side was a #20 Country hit for **Carl Perkins** in 1969				
				CLARKSON, Kelly '02				
				Born on 4/24/82 in Burleson, Texas. Female pop singer. Winner on TV's first *American Idol* talent series.				
9/21/02	❶^2	20	●	**A Moment Like This**	S:❶^5 / A:8 *Before Your Love*	$4	★V	RCA 60622
				"45": RCA 60646				
				CLASH, The ROK/LP '83				
				Eclectic new wave rock group from London, England: John "Joe Strummer" Mellor (vocals), Mick Jones (guitar), Paul Simonon (bass) and Nicky "Topper" Headon (drums). Political activists, who wrote songs protesting racism and oppression. Headon left in May 1983; replaced by Peter Howard. Jones (not to be confused with Mick Jones of Foreigner) left band in 1984 to form **Big Audio Dynamite**. Strummer disbanded The Clash in early 1986, and appeared in the 1987 movie *Straight To Hell.* Strummer died of heart failure on 12/22/2002 (age 50). Group inducted into the Rock and Roll Hall of Fame in 2003.				
3/22/80	23	14		1 **Train In Vain (Stand By Me)**	*London Calling*	$6		Epic 50851
7/17/82	45	13		2 **Should I Stay Or Should I Go**	*First Night Back In London*	$6	■	Epic 03061
				originally released on Epic 03006 (B-side: "Inoculated City"); also see #4 below				
10/2/82+	8	24		3 **Rock The Casbah**	*Long Time Jerk*	$5		Epic 03245
2/19/83	50	10		4 **Should I Stay Or Should I Go?**	*Cool Confusion* [R]	$5	■	Epic 03547
				same version as #2 above				
				CLASSIC EXAMPLE '92				
				Male R&B vocal group from Boston, Massachusetts: Darin Campbell, Jami Thompson, Gerald Alston, Marvin Harris and Bunny Rose. Alston is no relation to the same-named lead singer of The Manhattans.				
11/14/92	68	14		**It's Alright**	A:52 *(remix)*	$4	▮	Hollywood Basic 64690
				The Boys (backing vocals); from the movie *South Central* starring Glenn Plummer				
				CLASSICS, The BUB/R&B '63				
				Italian-American doo-wop group from Brooklyn, New York: Emil Stucchio (lead), Johnny Gambale, Tony Victor and Jamie Troy. First known as the Perennials. First recorded for Dart in 1959.				
3/6/61	50	5		1 **Blue Moon**	*Little Boy Lost* (Lance)	$40		Promo 1010
				HERB LANCE & THE CLASSICS				
				there were 3 Top 10 versions of this Rodgers & Hart tune in 1935				
6/22/63	20	9		2 **Till Then**	*Enie Minie Mo*	$30		Musicnote 1116
				#8 hit for **The Mills Brothers** in 1944; #10 hit for **The Hilltoppers** in 1954				
	★511★			**CLASSICS IV** BUB/AC/LP '68				
				Soft-rock group from Jacksonville, Florida: **Dennis Yost** (vocals), J.R. Cobb and Wally Eaton (guitars), Joe Wilson (bass) and Kim Venable (drums). Wilson was replaced by Dean Daughtry (of **The Candymen**). Cobb, Daughtry and producer Buddy Buie later joined the **Atlanta Rhythm Section**.				
				1)Traces 2)Spooky 3)Stormy				
12/23/67+	3	15		1 **Spooky**	*Poor People*	$8		Imperial 66259
5/4/68	90	3		2 **Soul Train**	*Strange Changes*	$8		Imperial 66293
				CLASSICS IV Featuring Dennis Yost:				
10/26/68	5	15	●	3 **Stormy**	*24 Hours Of Loneliness*	$8		Imperial 66328
2/8/69	2^1	12		4 **Traces**	*Mary, Mary Row Your Boat*	$8		Imperial 66352
5/3/69	19	11		5 **Everyday With You Girl**	*Sentimental Lady*	$8		Imperial 66378
				DENNIS YOST AND THE CLASSICS IV:				
8/2/69	49	7		6 **Change Of Heart**	*Rainy Day*	$7		Imperial 66393
11/15/69	58	8		7 **Midnight**	*The Comic*	$7		Imperial 66424
3/28/70	59	5		8 **The Funniest Thing**	*Nobody Loves You But Me*	$7		Imperial 66439
10/24/70	69	8		9 **Where Did All The Good Times Go**	*Ain't It The Truth*	$6		Liberty 56200
10/21/72	39	13		10 **What Am I Crying For?**	*All In Your Mind*	$6		MGM South 7002
3/10/73	95	3		11 **Rosanna**	*One Man Show*	$6		MGM South 7012
				all of above written by Buddy Buie and J.R. Cobb				
4/5/75	94	2		12 **My First Day Without Her**	*Lovin' Each Other*	$5		MGM 14785

DEBUT	PEAK	WKS	Gold	A-side (Chart Hit)..................B-side	$	Sym	Label & Number
				CLASS 2000 **'00**			
				Studio group from New York City, New York. Formed to "cover" the **Vitamin C** hit by issuing a commercial CD single.			
6/3/00	69^{S}	2		**Graduation (Friends Forever)** ....*(2 versions)*	$8	★	Pure Music/Wasco 9917
				melody based on Pachelbel's Canon in D Major"			
				CLAY, Judy BUB/R&B **'68**			
				Born Judy Guion on 9/12/38 in Fayetteville, North Carolina. Died of kidney failure on 7/19/2001 (age 62). Black singer. In backup group with **Cissy Houston**, **Dionne Warwick** and **Dee Dee Warwick**, for **Don Covay**, **Wilson Pickett** and many others.			
12/2/67+	**54**	9		1 **Storybook Children** ....*Really Together*	$10		Atlantic 2445
				BILLY VERA & JUDY CLAY			
2/17/68	**36**	6		2 **Country Girl - City Man** ....*So Good (To Be Together)*	$10		Atlantic 2480
				BILLY VERA & JUDY CLAY			
8/31/68	**75**	6		3 **Private Number** ....*Love-Eye-Tis*	$10		Stax 0005
				JUDY CLAY & WILLIAM BELL			
				CLAY, Otis R&B/BUB **'68**			
				Born on 2/11/42 in Waxhaw, Mississippi. R&B singer.			
8/24/68	**97**	3		**She's About A Mover** ....*You Don't Miss Your Water*	$10		Cotillion 44001
				CLAY, Tom LP **'71**			
				Born Thomas Clague on 8/20/29 in Binghamton, New York. Died of cancer on 11/22/95 (age 66). Was a DJ at KGBS in Los Angeles when he created this recording.			
7/10/71	**8**	9		**What The World Needs Now Is Love/Abraham, Martin and John** ....*The Victors* [S]	$6	□	Mowest 5002
				The Blackberries (vocal accompaniment); picture sleeve issued "compliments of KGBS Radio"			
				CLAYTON, Adam — see U2			
				CLAYTON, Merry R&B/BUB/LP **'88**			
				Born Mary Clayton on 12/25/48 in New Orleans, Louisiana. Session singer. In **The Raeletts**, **Ray Charles**' backing vocal group from 1967-69. Acted in the 1987 movie *Maid To Order.*			
6/6/70	**73**	7		1 **Gimme Shelter** ....*Good Girls*	$5		Ode 66003
				Clayton sang on **The Rolling Stones**' version of this song from their album *Let It Bleed*			
12/11/71+	**71**	7		2 **After All This Time** ....*Whatever*	$5		Ode 66018
12/23/72+	**72**	6		3 **Oh No, Not My Baby** ....*Suspicious Minds*	$5		Ode 66030
				above 2 written by **Carole King**			
7/26/75	**45**	9		4 **Keep Your Eye On The Sparrow** ....*Loving Grows Up Slow*	$5		Ode 66110
				from the TV series *Baretta* starring Robert Blake			
3/5/88	**45**	11		5 **Yes** *In The Still Of The Night* (**Five Satins**)	$3		RCA 6989
				from the movie *Dirty Dancing* starring **Patrick Swayze**			
				CLEAN LIVING **'72**			
				Country-rock group: Norman Schell (vocals, guitar), Al Anderson, Robert LaMountain and Robert LaPalm (guitars), Frank Shaw (bass) and Tim Griffin (drums). Anderson was also with **The Wildweeds** and **NRBQ**.			
11/4/72	**49**	12		**In Heaven There Is No Beer** ....*Backwoods Girl* [N]	$6		Vanguard 35162
				CLEFS OF LAVENDER HILL BUB **'66**			
				Rock and roll vocal group from Miami, Florida: brothers Fred and Bill Moss with Joseph Ximenes and his sister Lorraine. The Ximenes legally changed their names to Travis and Coventry Fairchild.			
6/25/66	**80**	6		**Stop! - Get A Ticket** ....*First Tell Me Why*	$20		Date 1510
				originally issued on the Thames label in 1966 ($30)			
				CLEFTONES, The **'61**			
				R&B vocal group from Queens, New York: Herbie Cox (lead), Charlie James (first tenor), Berman Patterson (second tenor), William McClain (baritone) and Warren Corbin (bass). Originally called the Silvertones.			
2/18/56	**78**	1		1 **You Baby You** ....T:78 *I Was Dreaming*	$75		Gee 1000
4/28/56	**57**	12		2 **Little Girl Of Mine** ....T:57 *You're Driving Me Mad*	$60		Gee 1011
				Jimmy Wright (orch., above 2)			
5/22/61	**18**	10		3 **Heart And Soul** *How Do You Feel*	$30		Gee 1064
				#1 hit for Larry Clinton in 1938			
9/4/61	**60**	6		4 **For Sentimental Reasons** ....*'Deed I Do*	$30		Gee 1067
				#1 hit for **Nat "King" Cole** in 1946			
12/29/62	**95**	1		5 **Lover Come Back To Me** ....*There She Goes*	$30		Gee 1079
				#3 hit for Paul Whiteman in 1929			
				CLEMONS, Clarence LP **'86**			
				Born on 1/11/42 in Norfolk, Virginia. Black saxophonist in **Bruce Springsteen**'s E Street Band. Nicknamed "The Big Man." Also see **Michael Stanley Band**.			
10/26/85+	**18**	19		**You're A Friend Of Mine** ....A:17 / S:20 *Let The Music Say It* (Clemons)	$3	■	Columbia 05660
				CLARENCE CLEMONS And Jackson Browne			
				includes vocals by actress Daryl Hannah (Browne's then-girlfriend)			
				CLEOPATRA LP **'98**			
				Black teen vocal trio from Manchester, England: sisters Cleopatra, Zainam and Yonah Higgins.			
7/4/98	**26**	19		1 **Cleopatra's Theme** ....S:14 *(remix)*	$3	▮	Maverick 17229
10/31/98	**81**	5		2 **Life Ain't Easy** ....S:45 *(remix)*	$3	▮	Maverick 17159
9/9/00	68^{S}	3		3 **U Got It** ....*(remix)*	$5	★	Maverick 16830
				CLICK, The R&B/LP **'95**			
				Collaboration of top rappers: **E-40**, B-Legit, Suga-T and D-Shot.			
7/16/94	**94**	2		1 **Captain Save A Hoe** ....S:66 *(remix) / Practice Looking Hard*	$4	▮	Sick Wid' It/Jive 42230
				E-40 (Featuring The Click)			
				first week charted as "Captain Save Them Thoe" (clean version released to radio only)			
11/11/95	**63**	13		2 **Hurricane** ....S:48 *Actin' Bad*	$4	▮	Sick Wid' It/Jive 42335
4/6/96	72^{S}	2		3 **Scandalous** ....BUB:101 *Wolf Tickets / (2 album snippets)*	$4	▮	Sick Wid' It/Jive 42366

DEBUT	PEAK	WKS	Gold	A-side (Chart Hit)...B-side	$	Sym	Label & Number
				CLIFF, Jimmy R&B/BUB/AC/LP '70			
				Born James Chambers on 4/1/48 in St. James, Jamaica. Reggae singer/songwriter. Starred in the movies *The Harder They Come* (1975) and *Club Paradise* (1986).			
12/6/69+	25	11		1 **Wonderful World, Beautiful People** ... *Waterfall*	$8	■	A&M 1146
3/14/70	89	3		2 **Come Into My Life** ... *Viet Nam*	$8	■	A&M 1167
11/6/93+	18	25		3 **I Can See Clearly Now** ... A:11 / S:33 *Sweet Jamaica* (Tony Rebel)	$5	■V	Chaos/Columbia 77207
				from the movie *Cool Runnings* starring John Candy; "45": Collectables 4688; B-side: "Worker Man" by **Patra** (#53)			
				CLIFFORD, Buzz BUB '61			
				Born Reese Francis Clifford III on 10/8/42 in Berwyn, Illinois. Teen pop-novelty singer.			
1/9/61	6	14		**Baby Sittin' Boogie** ... *Driftwood* [N]	$20	■	Columbia 41876
				babies' voices are by the children (boy & girl) of the producer; originally titled "Baby Sitter Boogie" ($30)			
				CLIFFORD, Linda R&B/LP '78			
				Born in 1944 in Brooklyn, New York. R&B-dance singer.			
7/1/78	76	11		1 **Runaway Love** ... *Broadway Gypsy Lady*	$4		Curtom 0138
8/26/78	54	8		2 **If My Friends Could See Me Now** ... *Please Darling, Don't Say Goodbye*	$4		Curtom 0140
				from the Neil Simon musical *Sweet Charity* starring Gwen Verdon			
3/24/79	41	6		3 **Bridge Over Troubled Water** ... *Hold Me Close*	$4		RSO 921
8/9/80	41	11		4 **Red Light** ... *Ralph And Monty* (Michael Gore)	$4		RSO 1041
				from the movie *Fame* starring **Irene Cara**			
				CLIFFORD, Mike '62			
				Born on 11/6/43 in Los Angeles, California. White pop singer/actor. In the 1970s Broadway production of *Grease*.			
9/15/62	12	13		1 **Close To Cathy** ... *She's Just Another Girl*	$12		United Artists 489
12/29/62+	68	7		2 **What To Do With Laurie** ... *That's What They Said*	$12		United Artists 557
5/11/63	96	1		3 **One Boy Too Late** ... *Danny's Dream*	$12		United Artists 588
				Alan Lorber (orch., all of above)			
				CLIMAX AC/LP '72			
				White pop group from Los Angeles, California: Sonny Geraci (vocals, **The Outsiders**), Walter Nims (guitar), Virgil Weber (keyboards), Steve York (bass) and Robert Neilson (drums).			
1/1/72	3	15	●	1 **Precious And Few** ... *Park Preserve*	$5		Rocky Road 30055
				originally released on Carousel 30055 ($6) in 1971			
5/6/72	52	15		2 **Life And Breath** ... *If It Feels Good-Do It*	$5		Rocky Road 30061
				CLIMAX featuring Sonny Geraci			
				CLIMAX BLUES BAND BUB/LP '77			
				Blues-rock group from Stafford, England: Colin Cooper (vocals, sax), Peter Haycock (guitar, vocals), Derek Holt (bass) and John Cuffley (drums).			
2/19/77	3	22		1 **Couldn't Get It Right** ... *Sav'ry Gravy*	$5		Sire 736
7/8/78	91	4		2 **Makin' Love** ... *The Gospel Singer*	$5		Sire 1026
11/15/80	47	12		3 **Gotta Have More Love** ... *One For Me And You*	$4		Warner 49605
2/21/81	12	27		4 **I Love You** ... *Horizontalized*	$4		Warner 49669
				CLIMIE FISHER LP '88			
				Pop-rock duo. Simon Climie (vocals) was born on 4/7/60 in Fulham, London, England. Rob Fisher (keyboards) was born on 11/5/59 in Cheltenham, Gloucestershire, England; died of complications following stomach surgery on 8/25/99 (age 39). Fisher was a member of **Naked Eyes**.			
5/14/88	23	18		**Love Changes (Everything)** ... S:22 / A:24 *Never Close To The Show*	$3	■	Capitol 44137
				CLINE, Patsy C&W/BUB/LP '61			
				Born Virginia Patterson Hensley on 9/8/32 in Gore, Virginia. Killed in a plane crash (age 30) with **Cowboy Copas** and **Hawkshaw Hawkins** on 3/5/63 near Camden, Tennessee. Elected to the Country Music Hall of Fame in 1973. Jessica Lange portrayed Cline in the 1985 biographical movie *Sweet Dreams*. Won Grammy's Lifetime Achievement Award in 1995.			
				1)Crazy 2)Walkin' After Midnight 3)I Fall To Pieces			
2/23/57	12	16		1 **Walkin' After Midnight** ... J:12 / T:17 / S:21 / A:22 *A Poor Man's Roses (Or A Rich Man's Gold)* (C&W #14)	$20	■	Decca 30221
				reissue on Everest 2020 "Bubbled Under" (#108) in 1963			
5/22/61	12	20		2 **I Fall To Pieces** ... CW² *Lovin' In Vain*	$12		Decca 31205
				2 other Cline versions made the Country charts in 1980 (#67) and 1982 (#54 w/**Jim Reeves**)			
10/23/61	9	11		3 **Crazy** /			
				written by **Willie Nelson**			
10/23/61	99	1		4 **Who Can I Count On** ...	$12		Decca 31317
1/27/62	14	13		5 **She's Got You** / CW⁵			
2/10/62	97	2		6 **Strange** ...	$12		Decca 31354
5/19/62	53	6		7 **When I Get Thru With You (You'll Love Me Too)** /			
5/12/62	90	2		8 **Imagine That** ...	$12	■	Decca 31377
8/25/62	85	1		9 **So Wrong** ... *You're Stronger Than Me* (#107)	$12		Decca 31406
				written by **Carl Perkins**			
10/13/62	73	7		10 **Heartaches** ... *Why Can't He Be You* (#103)	$12		Decca 31429
				#12 hit for Guy Lombardo in 1931; #1 hit for Ted Weems in 1947			
1/26/63	83	5		11 **Leavin' On Your Mind** ... *Tra Le La Le La Triangle*	$12	■	Decca 31455
4/20/63	44	10		12 **Sweet Dreams (Of You)** ... *Back In Baby's Arms*	$12		Decca 31483
				written by **Don Gibson**; #2 Country hit for **Faron Young** in 1956			
8/31/63	96	3		13 **Faded Love** ... *Blue Moon Of Kentucky*	$12		Decca 31522
				#8 Country hit for Bob Wills in 1950			

CLINTON, George — see FORSHÉ / ICE CUBE / PARLIAMENT/FUNKADELIC

DEBUT	PEAK	WKS	Gold	A-side (Chart Hit)...B-side	$	Sym	Label & Number

CLIPSE — LP '02

Male rap duo from Virginia Beach, Virginia: brothers Gene "Malice" and Terrance "Pusha T" Thornton. Also see **Justin Timberlake**.

DEBUT	PEAK	WKS	Gold	A-side (Chart Hit)...B-side	$	Sym	Label & Number
5/25/02	30	20		1 **Grindin'** ...S:11 / A:30 *(2 versions)*	$6	T	Arista 15078
9/14/02	19	21		2 **When The Last Time**...S:18 / A:19 *(3 versions) / I'm Not You*	$6	T	Arista 15154
12/28/02+	13^{S}	23		3 **Star** ...*(instrumental) / (3 album snippets) / (3 album snippets - Latif)* **702 Featuring Clipse**	$4	★	Motown 019583

CLIQUE, The — BUB/LP '69

Pop-rock group from Beaumont, Texas: Randy Shaw (vocals), David Dunham, Sid Templeton, Tommy Pena, John Kanesaw and Jerry Cope.

DEBUT	PEAK	WKS	Gold	A-side (Chart Hit)...B-side	$	Sym	Label & Number
8/30/69	22	11		1 **Sugar On Sunday**...*Superman*	$12		White Whale 323
11/22/69	45	7		2 **I'll Hold Out My Hand**...*Soul Mates*	$12		White Whale 333
2/28/70	100	1		3 **Sparkle And Shine** ...*I'm Alive* #1 & 3: written by **Tommy James**	$12		White Whale 338

CLIQUES, The — '56

R&B vocal duo: **Jesse Belvin** and **Eugene Church**.

DEBUT	PEAK	WKS	Gold	A-side (Chart Hit)...B-side	$	Sym	Label & Number
5/19/56	45	1		**The Girl In My Dreams** ...T:45 *I Wanna Know Why*	$60		Modern 987

CLIVILLÉS & COLE — see C & C Music Factory

C-LOC — see SONS OF FUNK

CLOCKS — '82

Rock group from Wichita, Kansas: Jerry Sumner (vocals, bass), Lance Threet (guitar), Gerald Graves (keyboards) and Steve Swaim (drums).

DEBUT	PEAK	WKS	Gold	A-side (Chart Hit)...B-side	$	Sym	Label & Number
8/28/82	67	5		**She Looks A Lot Like You** ...*Feeling This Way*	$5		Boulevard 03075

CLOONEY, Rosemary — MEM/POP/BUB/AC/LP '54

Born on 5/23/28 in Maysville, Kentucky. Died of cancer on 6/29/2002 (age 74). Sang with her sister Betty in Tony Pastor's orchestra in the late 1940s. Became one of the most popular singers of the early 1950s. Acted in several movies including *White Christmas*. Re-emerged in the late 70's as a successful jazz and ballad singer and as a TV commercial actress. Married for a time to actor Jose Ferrer; their son Gabriel married **Debby Boone**, and their other son, actor Miguel, starred in the TV series *Lateline*. Her brother, Nick Clooney, is a popular TV broadcaster, and his son, George Clooney, is a popular TV and movie actor. Won Grammy's Lifetime Achievement Award in 2002. Charted 2 #1 hits, 1951-52: "Come On-a My House" and "Half As Much."

1)Hey There 2)This Ole House 3)Mambo Italiano

DEBUT	PEAK	WKS	Gold	A-side (Chart Hit)...B-side	$	Sym	Label & Number
7/17/54	❶ 6	27	●	1 **Hey There** / S:❶6 / A:❶5 / J:❶4 from the Broadway musical *The Pajama Game* starring John Raitt			
8/7/54	❶ 3	27		2 **This Ole House** ...J:❶3 / S:❶1 / A:5 #2 Country hit for **Stuart Hamblen** in 1954	$15		Columbia 40266
11/13/54	9	12	●	3 **Mambo Italiano** ...J:9 / S:10 / A:13 *We'll Be Together Again* The Mellomen (backing vocals); Buddy Cole (orch., above 3)	$15		Columbia 40361
11/12/55	62	9		4 **Pet Me, Poppa**...T:62 *Wake Me* **Ray Conniff** (orch.); from the movie *Guys and Dolls* starring Marlon Brando	$15		Columbia 40579
1/21/56	82	3		5 **The Key To My Heart**...T:82 *A Little Girl At Heart* Jimmy Carroll (orch.); Buddy Weed (harpsichord)	$15		Columbia 40619
1/28/56	20	8		6 **Memories Of You** ...J:20 / T:52 *It's Bad For Me* **THE BENNY GOODMAN TRIO with ROSEMARY CLOONEY** from the movie *The Benny Goodman Story* starring **Steve Allen** (originally from the 1930 all-black revue *Blackbirds*)	$15		Columbia 40616
5/19/56	49	13		7 **I Could Have Danced All Night** / T:49			
5/26/56	70	6		8 **I've Grown Accustomed To Your Face**...T:70 Paul Weston & his Music From Hollywood (orch.); above 2 from Broadway's *My Fair Lady* starring **Julie Andrews**	$15		Columbia 40676
3/16/57	10	16		9 **Mangos** ...A:10 / S:23 / T:25 *Independent (On My Own)* Frank Comstock (orch.); from the musical revue *Ziegfeld Follies 1957*	$15		Columbia 40835
8/29/60	84	3		10 **Many A Wonderful Moment** ...*Vaya Vaya (Go, My Darling, Go)* Dick Reynolds (orch.)	$10	■	RCA Victor 7754

CLOUT — '78

Rock group from Johannesburg, South Africa: Cindi Alter (vocals), Sandie Robbie and Inge Herbst (guitars), Jennie Garson (keyboards), Lee Tomlinson (bass) and Bones Brettell (drums).

DEBUT	PEAK	WKS	Gold	A-side (Chart Hit)...B-side	$	Sym	Label & Number
9/2/78	67	10		**Substitute**...*When Will You Be Mine*	$5		Epic 50591

CLOVERS, The — R&B/BUB '59

R&B vocal group from Washington DC: John "Buddy" Bailey (lead), Matthew McQuater, Harold Lucas, Harold Winely and Bill Harris. Charted 21 R&B hits, 1951-59. Bailey entered the U.S. Army in 1952, replaced by Billy Mitchell. Upon Bailey's return, Mitchell stayed in the group. Harris died of pancreatic cancer on 12/10/88 (age 63). A Clovers unit with Lucas performed until 1992. Lucas died of cancer on 1/6/94 (age 61). Mitchell died of a stroke on 11/5/2002 (age 71).

DEBUT	PEAK	WKS	Gold	A-side (Chart Hit)...B-side	$	Sym	Label & Number
6/23/56	30	13		1 **Love, Love, Love** ...T:30 *Your Tender Lips*	$75		Atlantic 1094
9/14/59	23	17		2 **Love Potion No. 9**...*Stay Awhile*	$30		United Artists 180

CLUB DRAMA — '01

Rap group from Cleveland, Ohio.

DEBUT	PEAK	WKS	Gold	A-side (Chart Hit)...B-side	$	Sym	Label & Number
11/3/01	22^{S}	4		**The Bedrock**...*(album version) / That's My Style / I'm The Man / (8 album snippets)* **Phatty Banks Presents CLUB DRAMA**	$15	★*	Divided We Fall 70804

CLUB HOUSE — '83

Italian dance-disco studio group.

DEBUT	PEAK	WKS	Gold	A-side (Chart Hit)...B-side	$	Sym	Label & Number
8/20/83	75	5		**Do It Again/Billie Jean**...*Infusion*	$4		Atlantic 89795

CLUBLAND — '92

Dance collaboration assembled by Swedish producer Jan Ekholm and British drummer Morgan King. Features female vocalist Zemya (pronounced: zem-i-ah) Hamilton (of Jamaican and Swedish parentage).

DEBUT	PEAK	WKS	Gold	A-side (Chart Hit)...B-side	$	Sym	Label & Number
1/4/92	79	12		1 **Hold On (Tighter To Love)**...A:53 *(4 remixes)*	$7	▮*	Great Jones 530611
5/23/92	90	4		2 **Set Me Free**...A:56 *(2 remixes)* **CLUBLAND featuring ZEMYA HAMILTON**	$7	▮*	Great Jones 530615

DEBUT	PEAK	WKS	Gold	A-side (Chart Hit)...B-side	$	Sym	Label & Number

CLUB NOUVEAU — R&B/LP '87

Dance group from Sacramento, California. Formed and fronted by Jay King producer/owner of King Jay Records; founded the **Timex Social Club**). Early lineup: vocalists Valerie Watson and Samuelle Prater with Denzil Foster and Thomas McElroy. Prater, Foster and McElroy left in 1988, replaced by David Agent and Kevin Irving. Agent left in 1989. Foster and McElroy formed a prolific production duo and also recorded as **FMob** (see **En Vogue**'s "Runaway Love").

DEBUT	PEAK	WKS	Gold	A-side (Chart Hit)...B-side	$	Sym	Label & Number
2/14/87	❶[2]	17	●	1 **Lean On Me** ... A:❷[2] / S:❶[1] *Pump It Up (reprise)* King Jay/Warner 7" sold 600,000 units; Tommy Boy 12" sold 400,000	$3		King Jay/Warner 28430
5/30/87	39	13		2 **Why You Treat Me So Bad** ... S:37 *(edit version)*	$3		King Jay/Warner 28360

CLUB 69 — '98

Dance group assembled by Austrian producer **Peter Rauhofer**. Lead vocals by Suzanne Palmer and Kim Cooper. Also see **Pet Shop Boys**.

DEBUT	PEAK	WKS	Gold	A-side (Chart Hit)...B-side	$	Sym	Label & Number
1/24/98	95	3		1 **Much Better** ... *Drama (w/Kim Cooper)* **CLUB 69 featuring Suzanne Palmer**	$4	▮	Twisted/MCA 55402
2/13/99	59[S]	2		2 **Tainted Love** ... *(3 versions)* **SOFT CELL vs. CLUB 69** 1982 hit by **Soft Cell** remixed by **Club 69**'s producer **Peter Rauhofer**	$6	★	Twisted 55530

C NOTE — LP '99

Male pop vocal group from Orlando, Florida: Jose Martinez, Raul Molina, David Perez and Andrew Rogers.

DEBUT	PEAK	WKS	Gold	A-side (Chart Hit)...B-side	$	Sym	Label & Number
4/10/99	33[S]	18		**Wait Till I Get Home** ... BUB:104 *Come Over Tonight* samples "I Can't Go For That" by **Daryl Hall & John Oates**	$5	★	Trans Continental 79145

★239★ COASTERS, The — R&B '59

R&B vocal group formed in Los Angeles, California, in late 1955 from elements of **The Robins**. Originally consisted of Carl Gardner (lead; ex-Robins; born on 4/29/28), Leon Hughes (tenor), Billy Guy (baritone lead; born on 6/20/36), Bobby Nunn (bass; ex-Robins; born on 9/20/25) and Adolph Jacobs (guitar). Noted for serio-comic recordings, primarily of Leiber & Stoller songs. Cornelius Gunter (early member of The Flairs; brother of Shirley Gunter; born on 11/14/38) joined in 1957, left in 1961. Will "Dub" Jones (ex-**Cadets**) replaced Nunn in late 1958 and is heard on "Charlie Brown" and "Along Came Jones." Earl "Speedoo" Carroll (ex-**Cadillacs**) joined group in 1961. Bobby Nunn died of a heart attack on 11/5/86 (age 61). Gunter was shot to death on 2/26/90 (age 51) in his car at an intersection in North Las Vegas. Jones died on 1/16/2000 (age 71). Guy died of a heart attack on 11/5/2002 (age 66). Group inducted into the Rock and Roll Hall of Fame in 1987.

1)Yakety Yak 2)Charlie Brown 3)Searchin' 4)Poison Ivy 5)Young Blood

DEBUT	PEAK	WKS	Gold	A-side (Chart Hit)...B-side	$	Sym	Label & Number
12/10/55	79	1		1 **Smokey Joe's Cafe** ... T:79 *Just Like A Fool* **THE ROBINS** title of the Broadway musical featuring the songs of Jerry Leiber & Mike Stoller; first released on Spark 122 in 1955 ($300)	$60		Atco 6059
9/22/56	73	1		2 **One Kiss Led To Another** ... T:73 *Brazil*	$60		Atco 6073
5/13/57	3	26	●	3 **Searchin'** / RB[12] S:3 / T:5 / A:6 / J:10			
5/6/57	8	24		4 **Young Blood** ... RB[1] T:8 / A:10 / J:12 / S:14	$40		Atco 6087
10/21/57	64	6		5 **Idol With The Golden Head** ... T:64 *(When She Wants Good Lovin') My Baby Comes To Me*	$40		Atco 6098
6/2/58	❶[1]	16	●	6 **Yakety Yak** RB[7] T:❶[1] / S:2 / A:2 *Zing! Went The Strings Of My Heart*	$25		Atco 6116
2/2/59	2[3]	15	●	7 **Charlie Brown** ... *Three Cool Cats* [N] **King Curtis** (saxophone, above 2)	$25		Atco 6132
5/18/59	9	12		8 **Along Came Jones** ... *That Is Rock & Roll* [N]	$25		Atco 6141
8/24/59	7	16	●	9 **Poison Ivy** / RB[4]			
9/7/59	38	8		10 **I'm A Hog For You** ...	$25		Atco 6146
12/21/59+	36	8		11 **Run Red Run** /			
12/7/59+	47	10		12 **What About Us** ...	$25		Atco 6153
5/2/60	70	3		13 **Besame Mucho (Part I)** ... *(Part II)* #1 hit for the **Jimmy Dorsey Orchestra** in 1944 (Mexican song)	$20		Atco 6163
6/20/60	51	9		14 **Wake Me, Shake Me** ... *Stewball*	$20		Atco 6168
10/3/60	83	4		15 **Shoppin' For Clothes** ... *The Snake And The Book Worm* [N]	$20		Atco 6178
1/30/61	37	8		16 **Wait A Minute** ... *Thumbin' A Ride* written by **Bobby Darin** and Don Kirshner	$20		Atco 6186
4/24/61	23	12		17 **Little Egypt (Ying-Yang)** ... *Keep On Rolling* [N]	$20		Atco 6192
8/14/61	96	2		18 **Girls Girls Girls (Part II)** ... *(Part I)* recorded in 1962 by **Elvis Presley** as the title song for his movie *Girls! Girls! Girls!*	$20		Atco 6204
3/28/64	64	6		19 **T'ain't Nothin' To Me** ... *Speedo's Back In Town* [N]	$15		Atco 6287
12/11/71+	76	6		20 **Love Potion Number Nine** ... *D.W. Washburn* all of above (except #13, 14, 16 & 19) written and produced by Leiber and Stoller	$7		King 6385

COATES, Odia — AC '75

Born on 11/13/41 in Mississippi. Died of cancer on 5/19/91 (age 49). Black female singer. Member of the **Edwin Hawkins Singers**. Sang with **Paul Anka** on four of his hits (1974-75).

DEBUT	PEAK	WKS	Gold	A-side (Chart Hit)...B-side	$	Sym	Label & Number
3/1/75	71	6		1 **Showdown** /			
4/19/75	91	3		2 **Don't Leave Me In The Morning** ... written by **Paul Anka**; originally titled and recorded as "Leave Me In The Morning"	$5		United Artists 601

COBB, Joyce — BUB/R&B '80

Born in Okmulgee, Oklahoma. R&B singer/songwriter.

DEBUT	PEAK	WKS	Gold	A-side (Chart Hit)...B-side	$	Sym	Label & Number
11/24/79+	42	12		**Dig The Gold** ... *Don't Be Mad At Me*	$7		Cream 7939

COCCIANTE, Richard — '76

Born in 1946 in Saigon, Vietnam (Italian father/French mother); raised in Rome, Italy. Adult Contemporary singer/songwriter.

DEBUT	PEAK	WKS	Gold	A-side (Chart Hit)...B-side	$	Sym	Label & Number
4/10/76	41	6		**When Love Has Gone Away** ... *If I Were*	$6		20th Century 2275

COCHISE — '71

Rock group from England: John Gilbert (vocals), Mick Grabham and B.J. Cole (guitars), Rick Wills (bass) and Willie Wilson (drums). Wills also a member of **Foreigner**, **Roxy Music** and **Small Faces**. Wilson also a member of **Sutherland Brothers & Quiver**.

DEBUT	PEAK	WKS	Gold	A-side (Chart Hit)...B-side	$	Sym	Label & Number
5/29/71	96	4		**Love's Made A Fool Of You** ... *Words Of A Dying Man* written in 1958 by **Buddy Holly**; picture sleeve has a center-cut hole and is designed like the record label	$7	■	United Artists 50756

DEBUT	PEAK	WKS	Gold	A-side (Chart Hit)......B-side	$	Sym	Label & Number

COCHRAN, Anita
C&W/LP **'98**

Born on 2/6/67 in Pontiac, Michigan. Country singer/songwriter/guitarist.

DEBUT	PEAK	WKS	Gold	A-side (Chart Hit)......B-side	$	Sym	Label & Number
1/3/98	59	15		**What If I Said** ....CW[1] S:40 *Daddy Can You See Me* (Cochran - C&W #69)) **ANITA COCHRAN with Steve Wariner**	$4	■V	Warner 17263

COCHRAN, Eddie
BUB **'58**

Born Edward Ray Cochrane on 10/3/38 in Oklahoma City, Oklahoma; raised in Albert Lea, Minnesota. Killed in a car crash on 4/17/60 (age 21) in Chippenham, Wiltshire, England; accident also injured **Gene Vincent**. Influential rock and roll singer/guitarist. Moved to Bell Gardens, California, in 1953. Teamed with Hank Cochran (no relation) as the Cochran Brothers; first recorded as Country act for Ekko Records in 1954. Appeared in movies *The Girl Can't Help It*, *Untamed Youth* and *Go, Johnny, Go!* Inducted into the Rock and Roll Hall of Fame in 1987.

DEBUT	PEAK	WKS	Gold	A-side (Chart Hit)......B-side	$	Sym	Label & Number
3/23/57	18	13		1 **Sittin' In The Balcony** ....T:18 / A:18 / J:20 / S:22 *Dark Lonely Street*	$50		Liberty 55056
9/16/57	82	6		2 **Drive In Show** ....T:82 *Am I Blue*	$50		Liberty 55087
3/10/58	94	1		3 **Jeannie Jeannie Jeannie**....T:94 *Pocketful Of Hearts*	$50		Liberty 55123
8/4/58	8	16		4 **Summertime Blues** H:8 / S:13 *Love Again*	$50		Liberty 55144
11/24/58+	35	12		5 **C'mon Everybody**....*Don't Ever Let Me Go*	$40		Liberty 55166
3/16/59	99	1		6 **Teenage Heaven** ....*I Remember* rock adaptation of the melody from "Home On The Range"	$40		Liberty 55177
8/31/59	58	9		7 **Somethin Else** ....*Boll Weevil Song* song's writer, Sharon Sheeley, was injured in Cochran's fatal car crash	$40		Liberty 55203

COCHRAN, Tammy
C&W/BUB **'01**

Born on 1/30/70 in Austinburg, Ohio. Country singer/songwriter.

DEBUT	PEAK	WKS	Gold	A-side (Chart Hit)......B-side	$	Sym	Label & Number
7/1/00	68[S]	3		1 **If You Can** ....*When Love Was Enough*	$4	★	Epic 79415
10/6/01	73	11		2 **Angels In Waiting** ....A:66 from the album *Tammy Cochran* on Epic 69736			album cut

COCHRANE, Tom/RED RIDER
ROK/BUB/LP **'92**

Born on 5/13/53 in Lynn Lake, Manitoba, Canada. Rock singer/songwriter. Formed **Red Rider** in 1976 with Ken Greer (guitar), Peter Boynton (keyboards), Jeff Jones (bass) and Rob Baker (drums). Steve Sexton replaced Boynton in 1982; left in early 1984.

DEBUT	PEAK	WKS	Gold	A-side (Chart Hit)......B-side	$	Sym	Label & Number
4/5/80	48	7		1 **White Hot**....*Avenue "A"*	$4	■	Capitol 4845
6/16/84	71	6		2 **Young Thing, Wild Dreams (Rock Me)** ....*Among The Ruins (I'll Be Here)* **RED RIDER** (above 2)	$4	■	Capitol 5335
5/16/92	6	26	●	3 **Life Is A Highway** ....S:7 / A:7 *Emotional Truth* "45": Capitol 57780	$3	■V	Capitol 44815
11/14/92	88	4		4 **Washed Away**....*Lunatic Fringe (live)* "45": Capitol 57987; all of above written by Cochrane	$3	■V	Capitol 44879

COCKBURN, Bruce
ROK/BUB/LP **'80**

Born on 5/27/45 in Ottawa, Ontario, Canada. Pop-rock singer/songwriter. Pronounced: CO-burn.

DEBUT	PEAK	WKS	Gold	A-side (Chart Hit)......B-side	$	Sym	Label & Number
3/22/80	21	17		1 **Wondering Where The Lions Are** ....*After The Rain*	$4		Millennium 11786
2/9/85	88	3		2 **If I Had A Rocket Launcher** ....*Nicaragua*	$4		Gold Mountain 82013

COCKER, Joe
★257★ ROK/AC/BUB/LP **'70**

Born John Robert Cocker on 5/20/44 in Sheffield, Yorkshire, England. Own skiffle band, the Cavaliers, late 1950s, later reorganized as Vance Arnold & The Avengers. Assembled the Grease Band in the mid-1960s. Performed at Woodstock in 1969. Successful tour with 43-piece revue, Mad Dogs & Englishmen, in 1970. Notable spastic stage antics were based on **Ray Charles**'s movements at the piano.

1)Up Where We Belong 2)You Are So Beautiful 3)The Letter 4)Cry Me A River 5)When The Night Comes

DEBUT	PEAK	WKS	Gold	A-side (Chart Hit)......B-side	$	Sym	Label & Number
11/16/68	68	6		1 **With A Little Help From My Friends** ....*Something's Coming On* Jimmy Page (guitar); written by **John Lennon** and **Paul McCartney**	$10		A&M 991
6/21/69	69	6		2 **Feeling Alright**....*Sandpaper Cadillac* **Brenda Holloway** and **Merry Clayton** (backing vocals); also see #9 below (same version); written by **Dave Mason**	$8		A&M 1063
10/4/69	69	6		3 **Delta Lady** ....*She's So Good To Me* written by **Leon Russell** for his former girlfriend **Rita Coolidge**	$8		A&M 1112
12/6/69+	30	12		4 **She Came In Through The Bathroom Window** ....*Change In Louise* written by **John Lennon** and **Paul McCartney**	$8	■	A&M 1147
4/18/70	7	12		5 **The Letter** ....*Space Captain* [L] **JOE COCKER with Leon Russell & The Shelter People**	$7	■	A&M 1174
10/10/70	11	9		6 **Cry Me A River**....*Give Peace A Chance* [L] recorded at Fillmore East, New York on 3/27/70	$7	■	A&M 1200
5/22/71	22	11		7 **High Time We Went** /			
6/12/71	8	8		8 **Black-Eyed Blues**	$7	■	A&M 1258
1/8/72	33	9		9 **Feeling Alright**....*Sandpaper Cadillac* [R]	$7		A&M 1063
9/16/72	27	8		10 **Midnight Rider** / originally released by the **Allman Brothers Band** on their 1970 album *Idlewild South*			
12/2/72+	56	9		11 **Woman To Woman** .... **JOE COCKER and The Chris Stainton Band** (above 2)	$7	■	A&M 1370
2/17/73	51	8		12 **Pardon Me Sir** ....*St. James Infirmary Blues* #7, 8 & 10-12: from the album *Joe Cocker* on A&M 4368	$6	■	A&M 1407
6/22/74	46	12		13 **Put Out The Light**....*If I Love You*	$6	■	A&M 1539
1/11/75	5	17		14 **You Are So Beautiful** / co-written by **Billy Preston**			
1/18/75		4		15 **It's A Sin When You Love Somebody**	$5		A&M 1641
10/21/78	43	8		16 **Fun Time**....*Watching The River Flow*	$4	■	Asylum 45540
9/26/81	97	3		17 **I'm So Glad I'm Standing Here Today**....*Standing Tall* (Crusaders) **CRUSADERS Guest Artist: JOE COCKER**	$4		MCA 51177
8/21/82	1[3]	23	▲	18 **Up Where We Belong** *Sweet Li'l Woman* (Cocker) **JOE COCKER and JENNIFER WARNES** love theme from the movie *An Officer And A Gentleman* starring Richard Gere	$4	■	Island 99996
10/20/84	69	7		19 **Edge Of A Dream**....*Tempted* theme from the movie *Teachers* starring Nick Nolte	$4	■	Capitol 5412
3/8/86	91	4		20 **Shelter Me**....*Tell Me There's A Way*	$4		Capitol 5557

DEBUT	PEAK	WKS	Gold	A-side (Chart Hit)...B-side	$	Sym	Label & Number
				COCKER, Joe — Cont'd			
10/28/89+	11	20		21 **When The Night Comes** ...A:9 / S:15 *One Night Of Sin*	$4	▮V	Capitol 44437
				"45" promo: Capitol 79711; "45" also issued in 1992 on Capitol 57988; #19 & 21 co-written by **Bryan Adams**			
6/23/90	96	1		22 **What Are You Doing With A Fool Like Me** ...*Another Mind Gone*	$4	▮V	Capitol 44543
				"45" promo: Capitol 79025			
				COCK ROBIN LP '85			
				Pop group from Los Angeles, California: Peter Kingsbery (vocals, bass), Anna LaCazio (vocals, keyboards), Clive Wright (guitars) and Louis Molino (drums).			
6/15/85	35	16		**When Your Heart Is Weak**...*Because It Keeps On Working*	$4	■	Columbia 04875
				COCOA BROVAZ R&B/BUB/LP '94			
				Rap duo from Brooklyn, New York: Tek and Steele (formerly **Smif-N-Wessun**).			
5/28/94	93	5		1 **Bucktown** ...S:75 *(instrumental) / Let's Git It On*	$6	▮*	Wreck 20069
				SMIF-N-WESSUN			
2/10/01	58S	6		2 **Get Up**...*(3 versions) / Let's Grow* (**Royce Da 5'9"**)	$7	T	Rawkus 295
				C.O.D.'s, The BUB '66			
				R&B vocal trio from Chicago, Illinois: Larry Brownlee, Robert Lewis and Carl Washington. Brownlee (died in 1978) wrote all of the group's songs; later became a member of **The Lost Generation** and Mystique. **Ruby Andrews** was a backing vocalist.			
11/27/65+	41	12		**Michael**...*Cry No More*	$12		Kellmac 1003
				COFFEY, Dennis, And The Detroit Guitar Band R&B/LP '72			
				Born in Detroit, Michigan. White session guitarist for Motown. Also see **Al Kent**.			
10/30/71+	6	17	●	1 **Scorpio**...*Sad Angel* [I]	$6		Sussex 226
2/19/72	18	12		2 **Taurus**...*Can You Feel It* [I]	$6		Sussex 233
6/3/72	93	4		3 **Getting It On /** [I]			
6/3/72		4		4 **Ride, Sally, Ride** *[DENNIS COFFEY]* ... [I]	$6		Sussex 237
				COFFEY, Kellie C&W/LP '02			
				Born on 4/22/78 in Moore, Oklahoma. Female country singer/songwriter.			
6/1/02	54	18		**When You Lie Next To Me** ...A:52			album cut
				from the album *When You Lie Next To Me* on BNA 67040			
				COHN, Marc BUB/AC/LP '91			
				Born on 7/5/59 in Cleveland, Ohio. Pop-rock singer/songwriter/pianist. Won the 1991 Best New Artist Grammy Award.			
3/30/91	13	23		1 **Walking In Memphis**...A:27 / S:30 *Dig Down Deep*	$3	▮V	Atlantic 87747
				"45" issued in 1993 on Atlantic Oldies 84882; B-side: "Ghost Train"			
8/10/91	63	8		2 **Silver Thunderbird** ...*Strangers In A Car*	$3	▮	Atlantic 87678
11/2/91	80	5		3 **True Companion** ...*Miles Away*	$3	▮	Atlantic 87583
				COKO — see SWV			
				COLD BLOOD BUB/LP '70			
				Rock group from San Francisco, California. Core members: Lydia Pense (vocals), Michael Sasaki (guitar), Raul Matute (piano), Rod Ellicott (bass), Max Haskett (trumpet) and Danny Hull (sax). Haskett later joined **Rubicon**.			
1/24/70	52	6		**You Got Me Hummin**...*If You Will*	$7		San Francisco 60
				co-written by **Isaac Hayes**			
				COLDER, Ben — see WOOLEY, Sheb			
				COLDPLAY ROK/BUB/LP '01			
				Rock group from Edinburgh, Scotland: Chris Martin (vocals), Jon Buckland (guitar), Guy Berryman (bass) and Will Champion (drums).			
3/10/01	48	20		**Yellow**...A:48		V	album cut
				from the album *Parachutes* on Nettwerk/Capitol 30162; "45": Nettwerk/Capitol 58980; B-side: "Trouble" (ROK #28)			
				COLE, Ann R&B '62			
				Born Cynthia Coleman on 1/24/34 in Newark, New Jersey. Also see **Fats Domino**'s "When I See You."			
11/24/62	99	1		**Don't Stop The Wedding** ...*Have Fun* (R&B #21)	$20		Roulette 4452
				COLE, Bobby '68			
				Singer/songwriter/pianist. Musical director for Judy Garland's final Palace Theatre performace. Died from a fall in New York City on 12/19/97.			
8/3/68	79	3		**Mister Bo Jangles** ...*Bus 22 To Bethlehem*	$10		Date 1613
				COLE, Cozy R&B/BUB '58			
				Born William Randolph Cole on 10/17/09 in East Orange, New Jersey. Died of cancer on 1/29/81 (age 71). Lead drummer for many swing bands, including Benny Carter, Willie Bryant, **Cab Calloway** and **Louis Armstrong**.			
8/25/58	3	21	●	1 **Topsy II** / RB6 H:3 / S:10 [I]			
				#14 hit for **Benny Goodman** in 1938			
9/15/58	27	13		2 **Topsy I** ...H:27 / S:45 [I]	$20		Love 5004
12/1/58	36	8		3 **Turvy II** ...*Turvy I* [I]	$20		Love 5014
				written by **Dick Hyman**			
				COLE, Gardner '88			
				Born on 2/7/62 in Flint, Michigan. White songwriter/singer/producer. Wrote **Madonna**'s "Open Your Heart," **Jody Watley**'s "Most Of All" and "Strange But True" for **Times Two**.			
10/15/88	91	3		**Live It Up** ...*Got Me Curious*	$3	■	Warner 27793
				COLE, Jude BUB/ROK/AC/LP '90			
				Born on 6/18/60 in Carbon Cliff, Illinois; raised in East Moline, Illinois. Male singer/guitarist. Member of the rock band **The Records** from 1979-81.			
4/14/90	16	18		1 **Baby, It's Tonight** A:12 / S:21 *Heart Of Blues*	$3	▮V	Reprise 19869
8/4/90	32	15		2 **Time For Letting Go** ...A:26 *Prove Me Wrong*	$3	▮V	Reprise 19743
12/1/90+	69	15		3 **House Full Of Reasons** ...*(3 album snippets)*	$3	▮	Reprise 19530
9/12/92	71	7		4 **Start The Car**...*A Place In The Line*	$3	▮	Reprise 18793
1/23/93	57	12		5 **Tell The Truth**...A:51 *It Comes Around* (ROK #19)	$3	▮V	Reprise 18673

DEBUT	PEAK	WKS	Gold	A-side (Chart Hit)..........B-side	$	Sym	Label & Number

COLE, Nat "King" ★36★ MEM/POP/R&B/BUB/AC/C&W/LP '55

Born Nathaniel Adams Coles on 3/17/19 in Montgomery, Alabama; raised in Chicago, Illinois. Died of lung cancer on 2/15/65 (age 45). Own band, the Royal Dukes, at age 17. First recorded in 1936 in band led by brother Eddie. Toured with "Shuffle Along" musical revue, lived in Los Angeles. Formed The King Cole Trio in 1939: Nat (piano), Oscar Moore (guitar; later joined brother's group, Johnny Moore's Three Blazers) and Wesley Prince (bass; replaced several years later by Johnny Miller). Began solo career in 1950. In movies *St. Louis Blues*, *Cat Ballou*, and many other movie appearances. The first major African-American performer to star in a network (NBC) TV variety series (1956-57). Charted 45 pop hits, 1943-54 of which 4 were #1 hits: "For Sentimental Reasons," "Nature Boy," "Mona Lisa" and "Too Young." Stopped performing in 1964 due to ill health. His daughter **Natalie Cole** is a recording star. Won Grammy's Lifetime Achievement Award in 1990. Inducted into the Rock and Roll Hall of Fame in 2000 as an early influence.

1)Ramblin' Rose 2)A Blossom Fell 3)Looking Back 4)Send For Me 5)Those Lazy-Hazy-Crazy Days Of Summer

DEBUT	PEAK	WKS	Gold	A-side (Chart Hit)..........B-side	$	Sym	Label & Number
11/13/54	14	7		1 **Hajji Baba (Persian Lament)** ....S:14 / A:16 / J:19 *Unbelievable* from the movie *The Adventures of Hajji Baba* starring John Derek	$20		Capitol 2949
3/5/55	7	16		2 **Darling Je Vous Aime Beaucoup** / A:7 / S:10 / J:14 #21 hit for Hildegarde in 1943 (her theme song)			
3/5/55	23	13		3 **The Sand And The Sea** ....S:23 / J:flip	$20		Capitol 3027
5/7/55	2[1]	20		4 **A Blossom Fell** / S:2 / J:2 / A:3			
5/21/55	8	10		5 **If I May** ....A:8 / S:flip / J:flip **NAT "KING" COLE and THE FOUR KNIGHTS**	$20		Capitol 3095
7/16/55	24	2		6 **My One Sin** ....S:24 *The Blues From Kiss Me Deadly*	$20		Capitol 3136
10/22/55	13	13		7 **Someone You Love** / S:13 / A:19 / T:21			
10/22/55	13	11		8 **Forgive My Heart** ....S:13 / T:21	$20		Capitol 3234
12/31/55+	47	8		9 **Take Me Back To Toyland** / T:47 [X]			
1/14/56	57	5		10 **I'm Gonna Laugh You Right Out Of My Life** T:57	$20		Capitol 3305
2/11/56	18	11		11 **Ask Me** / A:18 / T:25			
2/25/56	72	6		12 **Nothing Ever Changes My Love For You** T:72	$15		Capitol 3328
4/7/56	21	12		13 **Too Young To Go Steady** / A:21 / T:31 from the musical *Strip For Action*			
4/21/56	79	6		14 **Never Let Me Go** ....T:79 from the movie *The Scarlet Hour* starring Carol Ohmart; above 2 issued with a special tri-fold insert	$15	⊙	Capitol 3390
7/7/56	16	20		15 **That's All There Is To That** / J:16 / S:17 / T:18 / A:18 **NAT "KING" COLE and THE FOUR KNIGHTS**			
7/7/56	59	8		16 **My Dream Sonata** T:59	$20		Capitol 3456
10/27/56	11	18		17 **Night Lights** / A:11 / T:16 / S:17			
10/27/56	25	13		18 **To The Ends Of The Earth** ....S:25 / A:25 / T:39	$15		Capitol 3551
2/9/57	18	13		19 **Ballerina** / A:18 / T:36 #1 hit for **Vaughn Monroe** in 1947			
2/9/57	65	6		20 **You Are My First Love** ....T:65 from the movie *It's Great To Be Young* starring John Mills	$15		Capitol 3619
4/29/57	48	7		21 **When Rock And Roll Come To Trinidad** ....T:48 *China Gate* **Nelson Riddle** (orch., all of above)	$20		Capitol 3702
5/6/57	79	4		22 **Stardust** ....T:79 [EP] **Gordon Jenkins** (orch.); written in 1927; from the EP *Love Is The Thing* (other cuts: "When Sunny Gets Blue" / "Maybe It's Because I Love You Too Much" / "It's All In The Game")	$25	■	Capitol E.P. 824
6/17/57	6	27		23 **Send For Me** / RB[2] S:6 / T:7 / A:9			
6/17/57	21	15		24 **My Personal Possession** ....A:21 / T:63 / S:flip **NAT "KING" COLE and THE FOUR KNIGHTS**	$20		Capitol 3737
9/23/57	30	14		25 **With You On My Mind** / S:30 / T:33 McCoy's Boys (backing vocals: #23 & 25); **Billy May** (orch.: #23 & 25)			
11/11/57		4		26 **The Song Of Raintree County** ....S:flip from the movie *Raintree County* starring Elizabeth Taylor; Johnny Green (MGM Studio Orch.); picture sleeve is a 4-page foldout promo sleeve for *Raintree County*	$15	□	Capitol 3782
1/27/58	33	13		27 **Angel Smile** ....S:33 / T:35 *Back In My Arms*	$15		Capitol 3860
4/14/58	5	19		28 **Looking Back** / S:5 / T:5 / A:9 a new version "Bubbled Under" on 12/11/65 on Capitol 5549 (#123)			
4/14/58	67	6		29 **Do I Like It** ....T:67 / S:flip	$15		Capitol 3939
7/21/58	38	11		30 **Come Closer To Me (Acercate Mas)** / S:38 / H:41 Armando Romeu, Jr. (orch. - 1940 Mexican song)			
8/11/58	99	1		31 **Nothing In The World** ....H:99 #28 & 31 co-written by **Brook Benton**	$15		Capitol 4004
10/13/58	45	11		32 **Non Dimenticar (Don't Forget)** ....H:45 *Bend A Little My Way* melody composed for the 1951 Italian movie *Anna* starring Silvana Mangano	$15		Capitol 4056
2/2/59	82	4		33 **Give Me Your Love** /			
2/2/59	85	3		34 **Madrid**	$15		Capitol 4125
5/4/59	45	9		35 **You Made Me Love You** / #1 hit for Al Jolson in 1913			
5/25/59	69	4		36 **I Must Be Dreaming**	$15		Capitol 4184
8/3/59	51	12		37 **Midnight Flyer** /			
8/31/59	96	2		38 **Sweet Bird Of Youth** .... title taken from the Tennessee Williams' play (a 1962 movie); melody is similar to **The Four Lads**' hit of "The Mocking Bird"	$15	■	Capitol 4248
2/1/60	30	8		39 **Time And The River** /			
3/7/60	92	2		40 **Whatcha' Gonna Do** .... [I] Nat "King" Cole (piano solo); Dave Cavanaugh (orch.: #28, 29, 34 & 36-40)	$12		Capitol 4325
8/1/60	47	8		41 **My Love** ....*Steady* **NAT KING COLE-STAN KENTON**	$12		Capitol 4393
12/12/60	80	2	●	42 **The Christmas Song (Merry Christmas To You)** ....*The Little Boy That Santa Claus Forgot* [X-R] original version by The King Cole Trio charted in 1946 on Capitol 311 (#3); new version released in 1954 on Capitol 2955 (with **Nelson Riddle** orch.); final version recorded in 1961 (with Ralph Carmichael orch.)	$10		Capitol 3561

DEBUT	PEAK	WKS	Gold	A-side (Chart Hit)..........B-side	$	Sym	Label & Number
				COLE, Nat "King" — Cont'd			
12/31/60+	**86**	2		43 **If I Knew** .... *The World In My Arms*	$10		Capitol 4481
				from Broadway's *The Unsinkable Molly Brown* starring Tammy Grimes			
6/26/61	**71**	7		44 **Take A Fool's Advice** .... *Make It Last*	$10		Capitol 4582
				Ralph Carmichael (orch., above 2)			
9/18/61	**73**	4		45 **Let True Love Begin** .... *Cappuccina* (#115)	$10		Capitol 4623
				Richard Wess (orch.)			
8/4/62	**2**[2]	16	●	46 **Ramblin' Rose** AC[5] *The Good Times*	$10	■	Capitol 4804
11/10/62	**13**	11		47 **Dear Lonely Hearts** .... *Who's Next In Line?*	$10	■	Capitol 4870
12/15/62	**65**	3		48 **The Christmas Song (Merry Christmas To You)** .... X:❶[2] *The Little Boy That Santa Claus Forgot* [X-R]	$8		Capitol 3561
				#42 above on purple label (same version); above on yellow/orange swirl label; **Nelson Riddle** (orch.: #24, 27, 31-33, 35, 42 & 48); Christmas charts: [#1[2]-34 weeks] 13/'63; 6/'64; 4/'65; 5/'66; 4/'67; 2/'68; 1/'69; 9/'70; 1/'72; 13/'73; 5/'83; 7/'84; 6/'85			
3/2/63	**42**	9		49 **All Over The World /** RB[2]			
3/2/63	**87**	3		50 **Nothing Goes Up (Without Coming Down)**	$8		Capitol 4919
				Belford Hendricks (orch.: #46, 47, 49 & 50)			
5/11/63	**6**	12		51 **Those Lazy-Hazy-Crazy Days Of Summer** .... *In The Cool Of The Day*	$8	■	Capitol 4965
8/31/63	**12**	13		52 **That Sunday, That Summer /**			
9/14/63	**92**	3		53 **Mr. Wishing Well**	$8		Capitol 5027
2/22/64	**49**	6		54 **My True Carrie, Love** .... *A Rag, A Bone And A Hank Of Hair*	$8		Capitol 5125
4/25/64	**22**	9		55 **I Don't Want To Be Hurt Anymore /**			
				Merry Young Souls (backing vocals, above 2)			
4/11/64	**100**	1		56 **People**	$8		Capitol 5155
				from the Broadway musical *Funny Girl* starring **Barbra Streisand**			
9/19/64	**34**	9		57 **I Don't Want To See Tomorrow /**			
9/26/64	**81**	4		58 **L-O-V-E**	$8		Capitol 5261
				Ralph Carmichael (orch.: #51-58); written by **Bert Kaempfert**			
8/6/66	**90**	4		59 **Let Me Tell You, Babe** .... *For The Want Of A Kiss*	$8		Capitol 5683
7/13/91	**14**	17	●	60 **Unforgettable** .... S:9 / A:37 *Cottage For Sale* (Natalie Cole)	$3	▮[V]	Elektra 64875
				NATALIE COLE with Nat "King" Cole			
				Nat's vocals are dubbed in from his 1961 remake version of his original 1952 hit (#12); 1991 Grammy winner: Record of the Year			
	★**241**★			**COLE, Natalie** R&B/AC/BUB/LP **'88**			
				Born Stephanie Natalie Cole on 2/6/50 in Los Angeles, California. Daughter of **Nat "King" Cole**. Professional debut at age 11. Married for a time to her producer, Marvin Yancey, Jr. Later married Andre Fischer, former drummer of **Rufus** and producer for **Brenda Russell**, **Michael Franks** and Andrae Crouch, until 1992. Natalie won the 1975 Best New Artist Grammy Award. Hosted own syndicated variety TV show *Big Break* in 1990.			
				1)Pink Cadillac 2)I've Got Love On My Mind 3)This Will Be			
8/30/75	**6**	17		1 **This Will Be** .... RB[2] *Joey*	$4		Capitol 4109
12/13/75+	**32**	17		2 **Inseparable** .... RB[1] *How Come You Won't Stay Here*	$4		Capitol 4193
5/29/76	**25**	16		3 **Sophisticated Lady (She's A Different Lady)** .... RB[1] *Good Morning Heartache*	$4		Capitol 4259
9/11/76	**49**	12		4 **Mr. Melody** .... *Not Like Mine*	$4		Capitol 4328
1/29/77	**5**	21	●	5 **I've Got Love On My Mind** .... RB[5] *Unpredictable You*	$4		Capitol 4360
7/23/77	**79**	4		6 **Party Lights** .... *Peaceful Living*	$4		Capitol 4439
1/14/78	**10**	21	●	7 **Our Love** .... RB[2] *La Costa*	$4		Capitol 4509
6/21/80	**21**	21		8 **Someone That I Used To Love** .... *Don't Look Back*	$4		Capitol 4869
5/4/85	**57**	10		9 **Dangerous** .... *Love Is On The Way*	$3	■	Modern 99648
9/7/85	**81**	6		10 **A Little Bit Of Heaven** .... *When I Need It Bad, You Got It Good*	$3		Modern 99630
7/25/87	**13**	18		11 **Jump Start** .... S:12 / A:16 *More Than The Stars*	$3	■	Manhattan 50073
11/7/87+	**13**	22		12 **I Live For Your Love** .... S:11 / A:17 *More Than The Stars*	$3	■	Manhattan 50094
3/5/88	**5**	17		13 **Pink Cadillac** S:2 / A:6 *I Wanna Be That Woman*	$3		EMI-Manhattan 50117
				written and recorded by **Bruce Springsteen** in 1984 (B-side of "Dancing In The Dark")			
8/27/88	**95**	1		14 **When I Fall In Love** .... *Pink Cadillac*	$3	■	EMI-Manhattan 50138
				recorded by **Nat "King" Cole** on his 1957 #1 album *Love Is The Thing*; above 4 from the album *Everlasting*			
4/15/89	**7**	19		15 **Miss You Like Crazy** .... RB[1] / AC[1] S:5 / A:8 *Good To Be Back*	$3	■	EMI 50185
2/24/90	**34**	10		16 **Wild Women Do** .... S:25 *(remix)*	$3	▮	EMI 50275
				from the movie *Pretty Woman* starring Julia Roberts and Richard Gere			
7/13/91	**14**	17	●	17 **Unforgettable** .... S:9 / A:37 *Cottage For Sale* (Natalie Cole)	$3	▮[V]	Elektra 64875
				NATALIE COLE with Nat "King" Cole			
				Nat's vocals are dubbed in from his 1961 remake version of his original 1952 hit (#12); 1991 Grammy winner: Record of the Year			
10/11/97	**84**	5		18 **A Smile Like Yours** .... *Unforgettable*	$3	▮	Elektra 64146
				title song from the movie starring Greg Kinnear and Lauren Holly			
				COLE, Paula BUB/LP **'97**			
				Born on 4/5/68 in Rockport, Massachusetts. Adult Alternative singer/songwriter. Won the 1997 Best New Artist Grammy Award.			
4/12/97	**8**	21		1 **Where Have All The Cowboys Gone?** .... A:6 / S:17 *hush, hush, hush.*	$3	▮[V]	Warner 17373
11/1/97+	**11**	56		2 **I Don't Want To Wait** .... A:5 / S:33 *Hitler's Brothers*	$3	▮[V]	Warner 17318
3/7/98	**35**[A]	16		3 **Me**			album cut
				all of above from the album *This Fire* on Imago 46424			
				COLE, Samantha **'97**			
				Born on 10/31/75 in Long Island, New York. Former dancer on MTV's *The Grind*. Singer/songwriter similar in style to **Mariah Carey**.			
8/30/97	**78**	5		**Happy With You** .... *Shadow Of Love*	$3	▮	Universal 56122
				COLE, Tony **'72**			
				Adult Contemporary singer/guitarist/songwriter from England.			
10/28/72	**97**	4		**Suite: Man And Woman** .... *All I Meant To Do*	$6		20th Century 2001

DEBUT	PEAK	WKS	Gold	A-side (Chart Hit)...B-side	$	Sym	Label & Number
				COLLAGE '94			
				Dance project assembled by Adam Marano, who spearheaded **T.P.E.** in 1991. Featured singer was Tony Monte. Both were students at Philadelphia's Temple University in 1993.			
11/30/91	91	2		1 **Then Came You** ...A:74 *(3 versions)*	$6	▮*	MicMac 2564
				T.P.E.			
11/27/93+	56	20		2 **I'll Be Loving You**...A:46 *Te Amare*	$5	▮	Viper 0102
7/4/98	59	20		3 **Can't We Try**...S:62 *(remix)*	$5	▮V	Robbins 72025
				ROCKELL (With Collage)			
				"45" B-side: "In A Dream" by Rockell (#72)			
				COLLAY and the Satellites '60			
				Collay is rock and roll singer/songwriter Anthony Callais (from New Orleans, Louisiana).			
4/25/60	82	3		**Last Chance**...*Little Girl Next Door*	$40		Sho-Biz 1002
				COLLECTIVE SOUL ROK/BUB/LP '95			
				Rock group from Stockbridge, Georgia: brothers Ed (vocals) and Dean (guitar) Roland with Ross Childress (guitar), Will Turpin (bass) and Shane Evans (drums).			
5/7/94	11	29	●	1 **Shine** AR[8] A:8 / S:11 *(remix album version)*	$3	▮V	Atlantic 87237
				"45" B-side: "Breathe" (ROK #12)			
2/4/95	49[A]	9		2 **Gel**...		V	album cut
				from the movie soundtrack album *The Jerky Boys* on Select/Atlantic 82708; also on the *Collective Soul* album			
5/13/95	20	39		3 **December** ...AR[9] A:11 / S:57 *Where The River Flows* (ROK #1)	$3	▮V	Atlantic 87157
				"45" issued for above 2 on Atlantic 87157			
11/18/95+	19	34		4 **The World I Know**...AR[4] A:9 / S:51 *When The Water Falls*	$3	▮V	Atlantic 87088
				"45" B-side: "Smashing Young Man" (ROK #8)			
4/5/97	65	10		5 **Precious Declaration**...AR[4] A:56 *Link*	$3	▮V	Atlantic 83003
6/28/97	72	11		6 **Listen** ...AR[5] *Crowded Head*	$3	▮V	Atlantic 84006
				"45" B-side: "Precious Declaration"			
3/6/99	73	20		7 **Heavy** ...AR[15] A:56			album cut
3/13/99	76	7		8 **Run** ...A:64			album cut
				from the movie *Varsity Blues* starring James Van Der Beek; above 2 from the album *Dosage* on Atlantic 83162			
				COLLEGE BOYZ, The R&B/LP '92			
				Male rap group from Los Angeles, California: Rom, Squeak, The Q and DJ B-Selector.			
5/23/92	68	15		**Victim Of The Ghetto** ...S:40 *Rigamarole/Politics Of A Gangster*	$3	▮	Virgin 98635
				COLLEY, Keith BUB '63			
				Pop singer from Connell, Washington. Later a record executive with the Challenge label.			
9/14/63	66	8		**Enamorado** ...*No-Joke* [F]	$15		Unical 3006
				title is Spanish for "In Love"			
				COLLIER, Mitty R&B '64			
				Born on 6/21/41 in Birmingham, Alabama. R&B singer. Toured with gospel group the Hayes Ensemble. Moved to Chicago in 1959. Won Al Benson's Talent Contest at the Regal Theater. First recorded for Chess in 1961.			
9/26/64	41	10		1 **I Had A Talk With My Man** ...*Free Girl (In The Morning)*	$12		Chess 1907
1/9/65	91	5		2 **No Faith, No Love**...*Together*	$12		Chess 1918
3/19/66	97	2		3 **Sharing You**...*Walk Away*	$12		Chess 1953
				COLLINS, Dave And Ansil '71			
				Reggae duo from Jamaica: Dave Barker (vocals) and Ansil Collins (keyboards).			
6/12/71	22	11		**Double Barrel** ...*(instrumental)*	$6		Big Tree 115
				COLLINS, Dorothy '55			
				Born Marjorie Chandler on 11/18/26 in Windsor, Ontario, Canada. Died of a heart attack on 7/21/94 (age 67). Star of TV's *Your Hit Parade*. Married to orchestra leader Raymond Scott from 1952-mid 1960s.			
11/12/55	16	15		1 **My Boy - Flat Top**...J:16 / T:22 *In Love*	$12		Coral 61510
1/28/56	17	10		2 **Seven Days**...J:17 / T:25 *Manuello (His Head Is In The Shade)*	$12		Coral 61562
				Dick Jacobs (orch., above 2)			
12/21/59+	43	10		3 **Baciare Baciare (Kissing Kissing)**...*In The Good Old Days*	$10		Top Rank 2024
				Bill Sanford (orch.)			
6/13/60	79	3		4 **Banjo Boy** ...*The Happy Heart Of Paris*	$10		Top Rank 2052
				with Milton DeLugg's Children's Chorus			
				COLLINS, Edwyn LP '95			
				Born on 8/23/59 in Edinburgh, Scotland. Pop-rock singer/songwriter.			
10/28/95	32	9		**A Girl Like You** ...A:31 *If You Could Love Me*	$5	▮	Bar None/A&M 1234
				from the movie *Empire Records* starring Anthony LaPaglia			
				COLLINS, Judy BUB/AC/LP '68			
				Born on 5/1/39 in Seattle, Washington. Contemporary folk singer/songwriter. Began studying classical piano at age five. Moved to Los Angeles, then to Denver at age nine, where her father, Chuck Collins, was a radio personality. Classical debut at 13, playing with the Denver Businessmen's Symphony Orchestra. Discovered folk music at 15. Signed to Elektra in 1961. Her cover versions gave exposure to then-unknown songwriters Leonard Cohen, **Joni Mitchell**, **Randy Newman** and Sandy Denny. **Stephen Stills** wrote "Suite: Judy Blue Eyes" for her. Appeared in the New York Shakespeare Festival's production of *Peer Gynt*. Nominated for a 1974 Academy Award for co-directing *Antonia: A Portrait of the Woman*, a documentary about Judy's former classical mentor and a pioneer female orchestra conductor, Dr. Antonia Brico.			
				1)Both Sides Now 2)Amazing Grace 3)Send In The Clowns			
1/21/67	97	2		1 **Hard Lovin' Loser** ...*I Think It's Going To Rain Today*	$8		Elektra 45610
11/9/68	8	11		2 **Both Sides Now** *Who Knows Where The Time Goes*	$8		Elektra 45639
2/1/69	55	6		3 **Someday Soon** ...*My Father*	$8		Elektra 45649
8/9/69	78	4		4 **Chelsea Morning**...*Pretty Polly*	$8	■	Elektra 45657
				#2 & 4: written by **Joni Mitchell**			
11/29/69	69	7		5 **Turn! Turn! Turn!/To Everything There Is A Season**...*Pack Up Your Sorrows*	$8		Elektra 45680
				lyrics adapted by **Pete Seeger** from the *Book of Ecclesiastes*			
12/12/70+	15	15		6 **Amazing Grace** ...*Nightingale I*	$7		Elektra 45709
				recorded at St. Paul's Chapel, Columbia University; Rev. John Newton wrote the words in 1779; William Walker composed the melody in 1844			

DEBUT	PEAK	WKS	Gold	A-side (Chart Hit)...B-side	$	Sym	Label & Number

COLLINS, Judy — Cont'd

DEBUT	PEAK	WKS	Gold	A-side (Chart Hit)...B-side	$	Sym	Label & Number
12/18/71+	90	7		7 **Open The Door (Song For Judith)** ... *Innisfree*	$7		Elektra 45755
2/10/73	32	11		8 **Cook With Honey** ... *So Begins The Task*	$6		Elektra 45831
6/21/75	36	11		9 **Send In The Clowns** ... *Houses*	$5		Elektra 45253
				from the Broadway musical *A Little Night Music* starring Glynis Johns			
9/24/77	19	16		10 **Send In The Clowns** ... *Houses* [R]	$5		Elektra 45253
				above 2 are the same version			
3/17/79	66	6		11 **Hard Times For Lovers** ... *Happy End*	$5	■	Elektra 46020

COLLINS, Lyn

R&B '72

Born on 6/12/48 in Lexington, Texas. With Charles Pikes & The Scholars in the mid-1960s. Joined the **James Brown** Revue in 1969. Billed as "The Female Preacher" and later as "The Sultry Siren of Funk."

DEBUT	PEAK	WKS	Gold	A-side (Chart Hit)...B-side	$	Sym	Label & Number
9/2/72	66	7		1 **Think (About It)** ... *Ain't No Sunshine*	$8		People 608
				tune sampled on **Rob Base & D.J. E-Z Rock**'s 1988 hit "It Takes Two"			
12/2/72	86	4		2 **Me And My Baby Got A Good Thing Going** ... *I'll Never Let You Break My Heart Again*	$8		People 615
12/23/72+	56	7		3 **What My Baby Needs Now Is A Little More Lovin'** ... *This Guy-This Girl's In Love*	$8		Polydor 14157
				JAMES BROWN-LYN COLLINS			
				all of above written and produced by **James Brown**			

COLLINS, Phil ★52★

ROK/AC/BUB/LP '85

Born on 1/31/51 in Chiswick, London, England. Pop vocalist/multi-instrumentalist/composer. Stage actor as a young child; played the "Artful Dodger" in the London production of *Oliver*. With group Flaming Youth in 1969. Joined **Genesis** as its drummer in 1970, became lead singer in 1975. Also with jazz-rock group Brand X. First solo album in 1981. Starred in the 1988 movie *Buster* and appeared in *Hook* and *Frauds*. Left Genesis in April 1996.

1)Another Day In Paradise 2)Against All Odds 3)Two Hearts 4)Groovy Kind Of Love 5)One More Night

DEBUT	PEAK	WKS	Gold	A-side (Chart Hit)...B-side	$	Sym	Label & Number
3/21/81	19	16		1 **I Missed Again** ... *I'm Not Moving*	$4	■	Atlantic 3790
5/30/81	19	17	●	2 **In The Air Tonight** ... *The Roof Is Leaking*	$4	■	Atlantic 3824
				"Bubbled Under" (#102) in 1984 on Atlantic Oldies 13231 due to play on TV's *Miami Vice* starring **Don Johnson**			
11/6/82+	10	21		3 **You Can't Hurry Love** ... *Do You Know, Do You Care?* (ROK #41)	$4	■	Atlantic 89933
2/12/83	39	11		4 **I Don't Care Anymore** ... *The West Side*	$4	■	Atlantic 89877
5/14/83	79	4		5 **I Cannot Believe It's True** ... *Thru These Walls* (ROK #34)	$4		Atlantic 89864
2/25/84	❶[3]	24	●	6 **Against All Odds (Take A Look At Me Now)** ... AR[1] *The Search* (Larry Carlton & Michel Colombier)	$3	■	Atlantic 89700
				title song from the movie *Against All Odds* starring Jeff Bridges			
11/24/84+	2[2]	23	●	7 **Easy Lover** ... S:❶[1] / A:2 *Woman* (Bailey)	$3	■	Columbia 04679
				PHILIP BAILEY (with Phil Collins)			
2/9/85	❶[2]	18	●	8 **One More Night** ... AC[3] A:❶[2] / S:❶[1] *The Man With The Horn* (ROK #38)	$3	■	Atlantic 89588
5/11/85	❶[1]	17	●	9 **Sussudio** ... A:❶[4] / S:2 *I Like The Way*	$3	■	Atlantic 89560
7/20/85	4	18		10 **Don't Lose My Number** ... A:2 / S:7 *We Said Hello Goodbye*	$3	■	Atlantic 89536
10/5/85	❶[1]	21		11 **Separate Lives** ... AC[3] A:❶[2] / S:2 *I Don't Wanna Know* (Collins - ROK #42)	$3	■	Atlantic 89498
				PHIL COLLINS and MARILYN MARTIN			
				love theme from the movie *White Nights* starring Mikhail Baryshnikov; issued with 2 different picture sleeves			
3/15/86	7	16		12 **Take Me Home** ... A:3 / S:10 *Only You Know And I Know*	$3	■	Atlantic 89472
				Peter Gabriel and **Sting** (backing vocals); #8-10 & 12: from the album *No Jacket Required*			
9/3/88	❶[2]	25	●	13 **Groovy Kind Of Love** ... AC[3] A:❶[2] / S:❶[1] *Big Noise* [I]	$3	■	Atlantic 89017
11/19/88+	❶[2]	18		14 **Two Hearts** ... AC[5] A:❶[3] / S:❶[1] *The Robbery* (Anne Dudley)	$3	■	Atlantic 88980
				above 2 from the movie *Buster* starring Collins			
11/4/89	❶[4]	18	●	15 **Another Day In Paradise** AC[5] A:❶[5] / S:2 *Heat On The Street*	$3	■	Atlantic 88774
				David Crosby (backing vocal); 1990 Grammy winner: Record of the Year			
2/3/90	3	17		16 **I Wish It Would Rain Down** ... A:3 / S:4 *You've Been In Love (That Little Bit Too Long)*	$3	■V	Atlantic 88738
				Eric Clapton (guitar)			
4/28/90	4	19		17 **Do You Remember?** ... AC[5] A:4 / S:9 *I Wish It Would Rain Down (demo version)*	$3	■V	Atlantic 87955
8/4/90	4	22		18 **Something Happened On The Way To Heaven** ... A:❶[2] / S:10 *Lionel (Do You Remember? - demo)*	$3	■V	Atlantic 87885
11/10/90+	23	13		19 **Hang In Long Enough** ... A:24 / S:26 *Separate Lives (live)*	$3	■V	Atlantic 87800
				above 5 from the album *...But Seriously*			
2/2/91	73	5		20 **Who Said I Would** ... [L]		V	album cut
				from the album *Serious Hits...Live!* on Atlantic 82157; "45" issued in 1993 on Atlantic Oldies 84881; B-side: "Another Day In Paradise"			
5/8/93	44	20		21 **Hero** ... A:31 / S:47 *Coverage* (Crosby)	$4	■V	Atlantic 87360
				DAVID CROSBY & PHIL COLLINS			
10/30/93	25	17		22 **Both Sides Of The Story** ... A:22 *Always (live)*	$3	■	Atlantic 87299
1/29/94	24	20		23 **Everyday** ... A:16 *Don't Call Me Ashley*	$3	■	Atlantic 87300
10/26/96	45	16		24 **Dance Into The Light** ... A:39 / S:69 *Take Me Down / It's Over*	$3	■	Face Value/Atlantic 87043
2/15/97	77	14		25 **It's In Your Eyes** ... A:69 *Easy Lover (live) / Separate Lives (live)*	$3	■	Face Value/Atlantic 87016
11/21/98	66[A]	2		26 **True Colors** ... BUB:112			album cut
				Babyface (backing vocal/producer); from the album *...Hits* on Atlantic 83139			
7/3/99	21	20		27 **You'll Be In My Heart** ... AC[19] S:9 / A:50 *(no B-side)*	$3	★	Walt Disney 60025
				from the animated movie *Tarzan*; all of above (except #3, 11, 13 & 26) written by Collins			

COLLINS, Susan — see DAVIS, Paul

COLLINS, Tyler

R&B/LP '90

Born in Harlem, New York; raised in Detroit, Michigan. Female R&B singer.

DEBUT	PEAK	WKS	Gold	A-side (Chart Hit)...B-side	$	Sym	Label & Number
4/28/90	6	21		1 **Girls Nite Out** ... A:3 / S:9 *(2 remixes)*	$3	■V	RCA 2630
9/1/90	53	9		2 **Second Chance** ... *(hip house version)*	$3	■	RCA 2639
9/19/92	88	3		3 **It Doesn't Matter** ... *Yesterday's Song*	$3	■V	RCA 62325
12/2/95	48	2		4 **Never Alone (Eeyore's Lullaby)** ... S:15 *The Kanga-Roo Hop* (Kathie Lee Gifford)	$3	■	Walt Disney 60345
				Eeyore is the donkey in the children's story *Winnie The Pooh*			

DEBUT	PEAK	WKS	Gold	A-side (Chart Hit)..........B-side	$	Sym	Label & Number

COLOR ME BADD ★324★ R&B/BUB/LP '91

Vocal group from Oklahoma City, Oklahoma: Bryan Abrams (born on 11/16/69), Sam Watters (born on 7/23/70), Mark Calderon (born on 9/27/70) and Kevin Thornton (born on 6/17/69). Formed while in high school in Oklahoma City.

1)I Adore Mi Amor 2)All 4 Love 3)I Wanna Sex You Up

DEBUT	PEAK	WKS	Gold	A-side (Chart Hit)..........B-side	$	Sym	Label & Number
4/6/91	2^{4}	23	▲^{2}	1 I Wanna Sex You Up..........RB^{2} S:❶^{3} / A:2 *(album version)* from the movie *New Jack City* starring Wesley Snipes and **Ice-T**	$3	▮V	Giant 19382
7/27/91	❶^{2}	20	●	2 I Adore Mi Amor RB^{1} A:❶^{3} / S:4 *(international mix)*	$3	▮V	Giant 19204
11/9/91+	❶^{1}	28	●	3 All 4 Love..........A:❶^{4} / S:4 *Color Me Badd (R&B #56)*	$3	▮V	Giant 19236
2/1/92	16	20		4 Thinkin' Back..........A:15 / S:33 *(XXX version)*	$3	▮V	Giant 19074
5/9/92	18	20		5 Slow Motion..........A:12 / S:43 *(main mix 2)* samples "Spinning Wheel" by **Blood, Sweat & Tears**; all of above from the album *C.M.B.*	$3	▮V	Giant 18908
9/26/92	15	18		6 Forever Love..........A:9 / S:16 *(album version)* from the movie *Mo' Money* starring Damon and Marlon Wayans	$3	▮V	Giant 18727
10/30/93	23	19		7 Time And Chance..........S:19 / A:44 *(instrumental)* samples "My Philosophy" by Boogie Down Productions	$3	▮V	Giant 18339
1/15/94	23	17		8 Choose..........A:20 / S:42 *(album version)*	$3	▮V	Giant 18270
5/4/96	21	22		9 The Earth, The Sun, The Rain..........A:20 / S:31 *Soft N' Easy*	$3	▮V	Giant 17654
7/25/98	48	13		10 Remember When..........S:32 *(instrumental)*	$3	▮	Epic 78924

COLOURHAUS '92

Pop duo of Australian vocalist Sherrié Krenn and British producer/guitarist Phil Radford (writer of "The Flame" by **Cheap Trick**). Krenn later became known as country singer **Sherrié Austin**.

DEBUT	PEAK	WKS	Gold	A-side (Chart Hit)..........B-side	$	Sym	Label & Number
5/2/92	50	10		Innocent Child..........A:60 *We Talk To The Angels*	$4	▮	Interscope 98613

COLTER, Jessi C&W/LP '75

Born Mirriam Johnson on 5/25/43 in Phoenix, Arizona. Country singer/songwriter. Married to **Duane Eddy** from 1961-68. Married **Waylon Jennings** in October 1969.

DEBUT	PEAK	WKS	Gold	A-side (Chart Hit)..........B-side	$	Sym	Label & Number
4/5/75	4	17		1 I'm Not Lisa..........CW^{1} *For The First Time*	$6		Capitol 4009
10/11/75	57	5		2 What's Happened To Blue Eyes /			
9/6/75	64	7		3 You Ain't Never Been Loved (Like I'm Gonna Love You).......... all of above written by Jessi and produced by **Waylon Jennings**	$5		Capitol 4087

COLTRANE, Chi BUB/LP '72

Born on 11/16/48 in Racine, Wisconsin. Female rock singer/pianist. Pronounced: shy.

DEBUT	PEAK	WKS	Gold	A-side (Chart Hit)..........B-side	$	Sym	Label & Number
9/2/72	17	13		Thunder And Lightning..........*Time To Come In*	$5		Columbia 45640

COLUMBO, Chris, Quintet '63

Born on 6/17/1902 in Atlantic City, New Jersey. Jazz drummer; recorded with Duke Ellington and Louis Jordan.

DEBUT	PEAK	WKS	Gold	A-side (Chart Hit)..........B-side	$	Sym	Label & Number
6/29/63	93	2		Summertime..........*Minerology* [I] #12 hit for Billie Holiday in 1936; from Gershwin's folk opera *Porgy And Bess*	$12		Strand 25056

COLVIN, Shawn ROK/AC/LP '97

Born Shanna Colvin on 1/10/58 in Vermillion, South Dakota. Female folk singer.

DEBUT	PEAK	WKS	Gold	A-side (Chart Hit)..........B-side	$	Sym	Label & Number
7/12/97	7	32		Sunny Came Home..........AC^{4} A:❶^{4} / S:29 *What I Get Paid For* 1997 Grammy winner: Record of the Year	$3	▮	Columbia 78528

COMING OF AGE '93

Male vocal group from Los Angeles, California: Terrance ("**TQ**" Quaites, Israel Spencer, Ivan Shaw, Tee Kese and Marthony Tabb.

DEBUT	PEAK	WKS	Gold	A-side (Chart Hit)..........B-side	$	Sym	Label & Number
12/4/93	74^{S}	2		Coming Home To Love..........BUB:101 *(album version)*	$4	▮	Zoo 14099

COMMANDER CODY And His Lost Planet Airmen LP '72

Born George Frayne on 7/19/44 in Boise, Idaho; raised in Brooklyn, New York. Singer/keyboardist. His Lost Planet Airmen consisted of John Tichy, Dove Bolton and Bill Kirchen (guitars), Andy Stein (fiddle, sax), Bruce Barlow (bass) and Lance Dickerson (drums).

DEBUT	PEAK	WKS	Gold	A-side (Chart Hit)..........B-side	$	Sym	Label & Number
3/25/72	9	14		1 Hot Rod Lincoln *My Home In My Hand* [N] original version by Tiny Hill charted in 1951 as "Hot Rod Race" (#29)	$7		Paramount 0146
7/22/72	81	7		2 Beat Me Daddy Eight To The Bar..........*Daddy's Gonna Treat You Right* #2 hit for Will Bradley in 1940	$7	■	Paramount 0169
7/7/73	94	5		3 Smoke! Smoke! Smoke! (That Cigarette)..........*Rock That Boogie* [N] #1 Country and Pop hit for Tex Williams in 1947	$7	■	Paramount 0216
12/22/73	19^{X}	1		4 Daddy's Drinking Up Our Christmas..........*Honeysuckle Honey* [X] **COMMANDER CODY**	$7		Dot 17487
2/22/75	56	6		5 Don't Let Go..........*Keep On Lovin' Her*	$5		Warner 8073

COMMITMENTS, The LP '91

Group of Irish actors/musicians who starred in the movie of the same name: Robert Arkin, Michael Aherne, Angeline Ball, Maria Doyle, Dave Finnegan, Bronagh Gallagher, Felim Gormley, Glen Hansard, Dick Massey, Kenneth McCluskey, Johnny Murphy and Andrew Strong. All did their own performing.

DEBUT	PEAK	WKS	Gold	A-side (Chart Hit)..........B-side	$	Sym	Label & Number
10/26/91	67	4		Try A Little Tenderness..........*Mr. Pitiful* from the movie *The Commitments*; "45": Beacon/MCA 54260; B-side: "Do Right Woman, Do Right Man"; one in a series of 7 "45s", all from *The Commitments* soundtrack, and issued as a set with custom jukebox title strips and a photo of the group	$5	▮V	Beacon/MCA 54128

COMMODORES ★99★ R&B/AC/LP '79

R&B group formed in Tuskegee, Alabama: **Lionel Richie** (vocals, saxophone; born on 6/20/49), William King (trumpet; born on 1/29/49), Thomas McClary (guitar; born on 10/6/50), Milan Williams (keyboards; born on 3/28/48), Ronald LaPread (bass; born on 9/4/50) and Walter "Clyde" Orange (drums; born on 12/9/46). First recorded for Motown in 1972. In the movie *Thank God It's Friday*. Richie left group in 1982.

1)Three Times A Lady 2)Still 3)Nightshift 4)Oh No 5)Sail On

DEBUT	PEAK	WKS	Gold	A-side (Chart Hit)..........B-side	$	Sym	Label & Number
6/15/74	22	13		1 Machine Gun..........*There's A Song In My Heart* [I]	$6		Motown 1307
11/16/74	75	8		2 I Feel Sanctified..........*It Is As Good As You Make It*	$6		Motown 1319

DEBUT	PEAK	WKS	Gold	A-side (Chart Hit)..................B-side	$	Sym	Label & Number
				COMMODORES — Cont'd			
5/10/75	19	15		3 **Slippery When Wet**..................RB^{1} *The Bump*	$5		Motown 1338
12/27/75+	5	23		4 **Sweet Love**..................*Better Never Than Forever*	$5		Motown 1381
9/18/76	7	16		5 **Just To Be Close To You**..................RB^{2} *Thumpin' Music*	$5		Motown 1402
1/8/77	39	9		6 **Fancy Dancer**..................*Cebu*	$5		Motown 1408
6/4/77	4	22		7 **Easy**..................RB^{1} *Can't Let You Tease Me*	$5		Motown 1418
8/27/77	5	16		8 **Brick House**..................*Captain Quick Draw*	$5		Motown 1425
12/17/77+	24	12		9 **Too Hot Ta Trot**..................RB^{1} *Funky Situation*	$5		Motown 1432
6/17/78	❶^{2}	20		10 **Three Times A Lady** RB^{2} / AC^{3} *Look What You've Done To Me*	$4		Motown 1443
9/23/78	38	10		11 **Flying High**..................*X-Rated Movie*	$4		Motown 1452
8/11/79	4	17		12 **Sail On**..................*Thumpin' Music*	$4		Motown 1466
9/29/79	❶^{1}	20		13 **Still**..................RB^{1} *Such A Woman*	$4		Motown 1474
12/15/79+	25	15		14 **Wonderland**..................*Lovin' You*	$4		Motown 1479
6/21/80	20	16		15 **Old-Fashion Love**..................*Sexy Lady*	$4		Motown 1489
9/20/80	54	9		16 **Heroes**..................*Funky Situation*	$4		Motown 1495
6/20/81	8	22		17 **Lady (You Bring Me Up)**..................*Gettin' It*	$4		Motown 1514
9/26/81	4	20		18 **Oh No**..................*Lovin' You*	$4		Motown 1527
2/6/82	66	5		19 **Why You Wanna Try Me**..................*X-Rated Movie*	$4		Motown 1604
				Lionel Richie's last song as the group's lead singer			
12/4/82+	70	6		20 **Painted Picture**..................*Reach High*	$3		Motown 1651
				all of above (except #2) produced by James Carmichael and Commodores			
9/17/83	54	13		21 **Only You**..................*Cebu*	$3		Motown 1694
1/26/85	3	22		22 **Nightshift**..................RB^{4} S:3 / A:4 *I Keep Running*	$3	■	Motown 1773
				a tribute to **Marvin Gaye** and **Jackie Wilson**			
5/25/85	43	9		23 **Animal Instinct**..................*Lightin' Up The Night*	$3		Motown 1788
9/21/85	87	4		24 **Janet**..................*I'm In Love*	$3	■	Motown 1802
11/1/86	65	12		25 **Goin' To The Bank**..................*Serious Love*	$3	■	Polydor 885358
				COMMON R&B/BUB **'00**			
				Born Lonnie Rashied Lynn in 1971 in Chicago, Illinois. Male rapper. Originally performed as Common Sense.			
4/17/99	35^{S}	10		1 **One-Nine-Nine-Nine**..................BUB:110 *(instrumental) / Like They Used To Say*	$5	★	Rawkus 53474
				COMMON feat. Sadat X			
				clean version available on Rawkus 53475			
8/5/00	44	19		2 **The Light** A:40 / S:67 *(2 versions) / Funky For You*	$6	T	MCA 155763
				samples "Open Your Eyes" by **Bobby Caldwell**			
6/23/01	50^{S}	7		3 **The Sun God**..................*(3 versions) / Get Back Pt. 2* (w/**Talib Kweli** & DCQ)	$6	T	Rawkus 320
				HI-TEK feat. Common & Vinia Mojica			
9/7/02+	9	27		4 **Love Of My Life (An Ode To Hip Hop)**..................A:9 / S:27 *(3 versions)*	$6	T	Fox/MCA 113987
				ERYKAH BADU Featuring Common			
				from the movie *Brown Sugar* starring Taye Diggs			
12/21/02+	65	15		5 **Come Close To Me**..................S:37 / A:65 *(2 versions) / I Got A Right Ta*	$6	T	MCA 113957
				COMMON Featuring Mary J. Blige			
				COMMUNARDS — see SOMERVILLE, Jimmy			

				COMO, Perry ★38★ MEM/POP/AC/BUB/C&W/LP **'46**			
				Born Pierino Como on 5/18/12 in Canonsburg, Pennsylvania. Died on 5/12/2001 (age 88). Owned barbershop in hometown. With Freddy Carlone band in 1933; with Ted Weems from 1936-42. In the movies *Something For The Boys*, *Doll Face*, *If I'm Lucky* and *Words And Music*, 1944-48. Own *Supper Club* radio series to late 1940s. Own TV shows (15 minutes) from 1948-55. Host of hourly TV shows from 1955-63. Winner of five Emmys. One of the most popular singers of the 20th century. Charted 84 pop hits, 1943-54. Won Grammy's Lifetime Achievement Award in 2002.			
				1)Round And Round 2)Hog Diggity 3)Catch A Falling Star 4)Ko Ko Mo 5)More			
10/2/54	4	18	●	1 **Papa Loves Mambo**..................S:4 / A:4 / J:4 *The Things I Didn't Do (#27/'54)*	$20		RCA Victor 5857
12/25/54	8	3		2 **There's No Place Like Home For The Holidays**..................A:8 / S:18 *Silk Stockings* [X]	$20		RCA Victor 5950
				The Fontane Sisters (backing vocals)			
2/5/55	2^{3}	14		3 **Ko Ko Mo (I Love You So)**..................A:2 / S:4 / J:5 *You'll Always Be My Lifetime Sweetheart*	$20		RCA Victor 5994
				#6 R&B hit for **Gene & Eunice** in 1955			
6/11/55	12	5		4 **Chee Chee-oo Chee (Sang the Little Bird)** / A:12 / J:14 / S:24			
6/25/55	18	1		5 **Two Lost Souls**..................A:18 / S:flip	$15		RCA Victor 6137
				PERRY COMO and JAYE P. MORGAN (above 2)			
				from the Broadway musical *Damn Yankees* starring Gwen Verdon			
8/13/55	5	14		6 **Tina Marie** / A:5 / S:6 / J:8 / T:12			
8/13/55	20	1		7 **Fooled**..................A:20 / S:flip	$15		RCA Victor 6192
				melody based on a classical theme by Franz Lehar			
11/12/55+	11	17		8 **All At Once You Love Her** / A:11 / T:24			
				from the Broadway musical *Pipe Dream* starring Helen Traubel			
11/12/55	79	4		9 **The Rose Tattoo**..................T:79	$15		RCA Victor 6294
				written for, but not included in the movie *The Rose Tattoo* starring Burt Lancaster			
3/10/56	❶^{1}	23	●	10 **Hot Diggity (Dog Ziggity Boom)** / A:❶^{1} / T:2 / S:2 / J:2			
				adapted from the 1883 orchestral rhapsody *Espana* by French composer Chabrier			
3/10/56	10	17		11 **Juke Box Baby**..................T:10 / A:11 / S:flip / J:flip	$15		RCA Victor 6427
6/16/56	4	18		12 **More** / S:4 / J:6 / A:8 / T:9			
6/9/56	8	17		13 **Glendora**..................A:8 / T:14 / S:flip / J:flip	$15		RCA Victor 6554
7/28/56	18	10		14 **Somebody Up There Likes Me** / J:18 / A:22 / T:26			
				title song from the movie starring Paul Newman			
7/28/56	85	5		15 **Dream Along With Me (I'm On My Way To A Star)**..................T:85	$15	■	RCA Victor 6590
				Como's famous opening song for his TV shows			

DEBUT	PEAK	WKS	Gold	A-side (Chart Hit)...B-side	$	Sym	Label & Number
				COMO, Perry — Cont'd			
11/3/56	42	9		16 **Moonlight Love** / T:42 based on the classic tune "Clair de Lune" by Debussy (1905)			
11/10/56	59	8		17 **Chincherinchee** T:59	$12		RCA Victor 6670
2/23/57	❶[2]	29	●	18 **Round And Round** / A:❶[2] / S:❶[1] / T:❶[1] / J:3			
3/9/57	50	7		19 **Mi Casa, Su Casa (My House Is Your House)**....T:50 / S:flip	$12		RCA Victor 6815
5/20/57	13	14		20 **The Girl With The Golden Braids** / A:13 / T:15 / S:26			
5/27/57	48	7		21 **My Little Baby** ....T:48 / S:flip	$12		RCA Victor 6904
9/2/57	76	4		22 **Dancin'** ....T:76 *Marching Along To The Blues*	$12		RCA Victor 6991
10/14/57	12	17		23 **Just Born (To Be Your Baby)** / S:12 / A:13 / T:19			
10/21/57	18	15		24 **Ivy Rose** ....A:18 / T:32 / S:flip	$12		RCA Victor 7050
12/30/57	74	2		25 **Jingle Bells** ....T:74 [X-EP] Russ Case (orch.); from the EP *Merry Christmas Music*, originally recorded in 1946 (other cuts: "Rudolph The Red-Nosed Reindeer" / "Santa Claus Is Comin' To Town" / "Frosty The Snow Man" / "Winter Wonderland")	$25	■	RCA Victor EPA-920
1/13/58	❶[1]	23	●	26 **Catch A Falling Star** / A:❶[1] / S:3 / T:9 #18, 25 & 26: issued with picture sleeves on RCA's Bluebird children's series			
1/20/58	4	16		27 **Magic Moments** ....A:4 / T:27 / S:42	$12		RCA Victor 7128
4/14/58	6	16		28 **Kewpie Doll** / A:6 / S:12 / T:12			
5/5/58	19	1		29 **Dance Only With Me**....A:19 from the Broadway musical *Say Darling* starring David Wayne	$12		RCA Victor 7202
7/28/58	28	10		30 **Moon Talk** ....S:28 / H:29 *Beats There A Heart So True*	$10		RCA Victor 7274
10/13/58	33	10		31 **Love Makes The World Go 'Round** / H:33			
10/27/58	47	10		32 **Mandolins In The Moonlight**	$10		RCA Victor 7353
2/23/59	29	9		33 **Tomboy** ....*Kiss Me And Kiss Me And Kiss Me*	$10		RCA Victor 7464
6/8/59	47	9		34 **I Know** ....*You Are In Love*	$10	■	RCA Victor 7541
2/8/60	22	11		35 **Delaware** / [N]			
2/8/60	81	2		36 **I Know What God Is**....	$10		RCA Victor 7670
12/26/60	80	2		37 **Make Someone Happy** ....*Gone Is My Love* from the Broadway musical *Do Re Mi* starring Phil Silvers	$10		RCA Victor 7812
11/20/61	92	3		38 **You're Following Me** ....*Especially For The Young*	$8		RCA Victor 7962
3/31/62	23	12		39 **Caterina**....*The Island Of Forgotten Lovers*	$8	■	RCA Victor 8004
6/1/63	39	9		40 **(I Love You) Don't You Forget It** ....*One More Mountain* Mitchell Ayres (orch., all of above - except #25)	$8	■	RCA Victor 8186
4/10/65	25	10		41 **Dream On Little Dreamer** ....*My Own Peculiar Way*	$8	■	RCA Victor 8533
7/31/65	88	4		42 **Oowee, Oowee**....*Summer Wind* The Anita Kerr Quartet (backing vocals, above 2)	$8		RCA Victor 8636
5/20/67	92	4		43 **Stop! And Think It Over** ....AC[1] *How Beautiful The World Can Be*	$6		RCA Victor 9165
3/16/68	92	2		44 **The Father Of Girls** ....*Somebody Makes It So*	$6		RCA Victor 9448
12/28/68	28[X]	1		45 **There Is No Christmas Like A Home Christmas** ....*Christmas Eve* [X] original version released in 1950 on RCA Victor 3933; **Ray Charles Singers** (backing vocals, all of above - except #2, 5, 7, 9, 20, 21, 25, 37, 41, 42 & 44); Nick Perito (orch., above 3)	$6		RCA Victor 9683
4/12/69	38	10		46 **Seattle**.... from the TV series *Here Come The Brides* starring **Bobby Sherman**	$5		RCA Victor 9722
11/14/70+	10	17		47 **It's Impossible** ....AC[4] *Long Life, Lots Of Happiness*	$5		RCA Victor 0387
3/20/71	53	8		48 **I Think Of You** ....*El Condor Pasa*	$5		RCA Victor 0444
4/14/73	29	16		49 **And I Love You So**....AC[1] *Love Looks So Good On You* written by **Don McLean**; some pressings list title as "And I Love Her So"	$5		RCA Victor 0906
12/21/74	92	2		50 **Christmas Dream** ....*Christ Is Born* [X] from the movie *The Odessa File* starring Jon Voight	$5		RCA Victor 10122
				COMPAGNONS DE LA CHANSON — see LES COMPAGNONS			
				COMPANY B LP '87 Female dance trio from Miami, Florida: Lori L, Lezlee Livrano and Susan Johnson.			
3/21/87	21	18		**Fascinated**....S:17 / A:27 *(dub version)*	$3		Atlantic 89294
				COMPTON'S MOST WANTED — see MC EIHT			
				COMSTOCK, Bobby, & The Counts '63 Born on 12/29/41 in Ithaca, New York. Rock and roll singer/songwriter/guitarist.			
10/26/59	52	7		1 **Tennessee Waltz**....*Sweet Talk* #1 hit for **Patti Page** in 1950	$25		Blaze 349
3/7/60	90	4		2 **Jambalaya**....*Let's Talk It Over* #1 Country hit for Hank Williams in 1952	$20		Atlantic 2051
2/16/63	57	6		3 **Let's Stomp** *[BOBBY COMSTOCK]* ....*I Want To Do It*	$15		Lawn 202
9/14/63	98	2		4 **Your Boyfriend's Back** ....*This Little Love Of Mine* answer song to **The Angels**' "My Boyfriend's Back"	$20		Lawn 219
				CONCRETE BLONDE ROK/LP '90 Rock trio from Los Angeles, California: Johnette Napolitano (vocals, bass), James Andrew Mankey (guitar) and Paul Thompson (drums).			
8/18/90	19	21		**Joey**....MR[4] S:14 / A:30 *I Want You*	$5	■	I.R.S. 73014
				CONDUCTOR '82 Rock group from Los Angeles, California. Led by singer Judy Comden.			
1/30/82	63	5		**Voice On The Radio** ....*Conductor Overture*	$5		Montage 1210
				CON FUNK SHUN R&B/BUB/LP '78 Funk group from Vallejo, California: **Michael Cooper** (see #5 below) (vocals, guitar; born on 11/15/52), Danny Thomas (keyboards), Karl Fuller, Paul Harrell and Felton Pilate (horns), Cedric Martin (bass) and Louis McCall (drums). Charted 26 R&B hits, 1977-96.			
12/17/77+	23	13		1 **Ffun** RB[2] *Indian Summer Love* [I]	$5		Mercury 73959
8/26/78	60	6		2 **Shake And Dance With Me**....*I'll Set You Out O.K.*	$5		Mercury 74008
1/24/81	40	10		3 **Too Tight**....*Play Widit*	$4		Mercury 76089

DEBUT	PEAK	WKS	Gold	A-side (Chart Hit)	B-side	$	Sym	Label & Number
				CON FUNK SHUN — Cont'd				
1/7/84	76	5		4 **Baby, I'm Hooked (Right Into Your Love)**	*Thinking About You, Baby*	$4		Mercury 814581
3/13/93	67	9		5 **Shoop Shoop (Never Stop Givin' You Love)** A:49 / S:60	*Fun, Fun, Fun*	$3	▮	Reprise 18649
				MICHAEL COOPER				
				CONLEY, Arthur BUB/R&B/LP **'67**				
				Born on 4/1/46 in Atlanta, Georgia. Soul singer/songwriter. Discovered by **Otis Redding** in 1965 (recorded for Redding's Jotis label). First recorded for NRC as Arthur & The Corvets. Also see **The Soul Clan**.				
3/11/67	2[1]	15	●	1 **Sweet Soul Music**	*Let's Go Steady*	$10		Atco 6463
				originally written by **Sam Cooke** as "Yeah Man"				
6/10/67	31	7		2 **Shake, Rattle & Roll**	*You Don't Have To See Me*	$10		Atco 6494
				#1 R&B hit for **Joe Turner** in 1954				
11/4/67	73	3		3 **Whole Lotta Woman**	*Love Comes And Goes*	$10		Atco 6529
				above 3 produced by **Otis Redding**				
3/16/68	14	12		4 **Funky Street**	*Put Our Love Together*	$8		Atco 6563
6/22/68	58	5		5 **People Sure Act Funny**	*Burning Fire*	$8		Atco 6588
10/26/68	85	4		6 **Aunt Dora's Love Soul Shack**	*Is That You Love*	$8		Atco 6622
1/4/69	51	6		7 **Ob-La-Di, Ob-La-Da**	*Otis Sleep On*	$8		Atco 6640
				written by **John Lennon** and **Paul McCartney**				
				CONNICK, Harry Jr. AC/LP **'95**				
				Born on 9/11/67 in New Orleans, Louisiana. Jazz-pop pianist/vocalist. Studied jazz under Ellis Marsalis, the father of Wynton and Branford Marsalis. Acted in the movies *Memphis Belle*, *Little Man Tate*, *Independence Day* and *Hope Floats*. Married model/actress Jill Goodacre in 1994.				
10/22/94+	67	20		**(I Could Only) Whisper Your Name** A:51	*Trouble*	$3	▮	Columbia 77718
				CONNIFF, Ray AC/BUB/LP **'66**				
				Born on 11/6/16 in Attleboro, Massachusetts. Died of a stroke on 10/12/2002 (age 85). Trombonist/arranger with Bunny Berigan, Bob Crosby, Harry James, **Vaughn Monroe** and Artie Shaw bands. Arranger/conductor for many of Columbia Records' top vocalists during the 1950s and 1960s (**Guy Mitchell**, **Johnny Mathis**, **Marty Robbins**, etc.). Charted 51 pop albums, 1957-73.				
3/16/57	73	4		1 **'S Wonderful** T:73	*Wagon Wheels* [I]	$10		Columbia 40827
				from the Gershwin musical *Funny Face* starring Fred Astaire; #5 hit for Frank Crumit in 1928				
10/17/60	92	4		2 **Midnight Lace - Part I**	*Part II* [I]	$8		Columbia 41800
				Eddy Manson (harmonica solo); from the movie *Midnight Lace* starring **Doris Day**				
				RAY CONNIFF And The Singers:				
7/18/64	57	10		3 **Invisible Tears**	*Singing The Blues*	$6	□	Columbia 43061
				#13 Country hit for **Ned Miller** in 1964				
12/25/65	19[X]	1		4 **The Real Meaning Of Christmas**	*Go Tell It On The Mountain* [X]	$8		Columbia 43448
6/18/66	9	12		5 **Somewhere, My Love** AC[4]	*Midsummer In Sweden*	$6		Columbia 43626
				Lara's Theme from the movie *Dr. Zhivago* starring Omar Sharif				
10/8/66	94	2		6 **Lookin' For Love**	*It Takes Two*	$6		Columbia 43814
				CONNOR, Chris **'57**				
				Born on 11/8/27 in Kansas City, Missouri. Female jazz-styled singer; with **Stan Kenton** from 1952-53.				
10/27/56+	34	28		1 **I Miss You So** T:34	*My Heart Is So Full Of You*	$20		Atlantic 1105
				#20 hit for The Cats and the Fiddle in 1940				
6/10/57	95	1		2 **Trust In Me** T:95	*Mixed Emotions*	$20		Atlantic 1138
				#4 hit for Mildred Bailey in 1937; **Ray Ellis** (orch., above 2)				
				CONNORS, Norman R&B/BUB/LP **'76**				
				Born on 3/1/48 in Philadelphia, Pennsylvania. Jazz drummer with Archie Shepp, John Coltrane, Pharoah Sanders and others. Own group on Buddah in 1972. **Michael Henderson** was born on 7/7/51 in Yazoo City, Mississippi. R&B singer/bass player. Featured vocalist on Connors' records.				
1/3/76	97	3		1 **Valentine Love**	*Akia*	$5		Buddah 499
				Michael Henderson and Jean Carn (vocals)				
8/28/76	27	16		2 **You Are My Starship**	*Bubbles*	$5		Buddah 542
				Michael Henderson (vocal)				
10/14/78	88	3		3 **Take Me I'm Yours**	*Let Me Love You*	$5		Buddah 597
				MICHAEL HENDERSON				
				CONQUEST, June — see HATHAWAY, Donny				
				CONSCIOUS DAUGHTERS, The R&B/BUB/LP **'94**				
				Female rap duo from Oakland, California: Carla Green and Karryl Smith.				
3/19/94	42	15		**Something To Ride To (Fonky Expedition)** S:35 / A:48	*(3 remixes)*	$5	▮	Scarface/Priority 53851
				CONSUMER RAPPORT **'75**				
				Dance group from New York, featuring Frank Floyd (pit singer in the musical *The Wiz*).				
4/19/75	42	12		**Ease On Down The Road**	*Go On With Your Bad Self*	$6		Wing & A Prayer 101
				from the Broadway musical *The Wiz* starring **Stephanie Mills**				
				CONTI, Bill **'77**				
				Born on 4/13/42 in Providence, Rhode Island. Composer/conductor for the first three *Rocky* movies; also for *The Karate Kid*, *Private Benjamin*, *For Your Eyes Only*, and an Oscar-winning score for *The Right Stuff*.				
4/23/77	❶[1]	20	●	1 **Gonna Fly Now**	*Reflections* [I]	$5		United Artists 940
				theme from the movie *Rocky* starring Sylvester Stallone				
11/6/82	52	9		2 **Theme From Dynasty**	*Theme From Falcon Crest* [I]	$5		Arista 1021
				theme from the TV series *Dynasty* starring Joan Collins and John Forsythe				
				CONTINENTAL 4, The R&B **'71**				
				R&B vocal group: Freddie Kelly (falsetto lead), Ronnie McGregor and Larry McGregor (tenors), and Anthony Burke (baritone).				
6/19/71	84	5		**Day By Day (Every Minute of The Hour)**	*What You Gave Us*	$8		Jay Walking 011
				CONTINENTAL MINIATURES **'78**				
				Pop group from Los Angeles, California: Kevin McCarthy (vocals), Rich Bytnar and Eric Ramon (guitars), Matt Walker (bass), David Kendrick (drums).				
5/13/78	90	3		**Stay Awhile**	*Glad All Over*	$5	■	London 266

DEBUT	PEAK	WKS	Gold	A-side (Chart Hit).....B-side	$	Sym	Label & Number

CONTINO, Dick

POP '54

Born on 1/17/30 in Fresno, California. Accordion virtuoso. Discovered by bandleader Horace Heidt and featured on his radio show in the late 1940s.

DEBUT	PEAK	WKS	Gold	A-side (Chart Hit).....B-side	$	Sym	Label & Number
4/20/57	42	8		**Pledge Of Love** .....T:42 *Two Loves Have I* **David Carroll** (orch.)	$12		Mercury 71079

CONTOURS, The

R&B '62

R&B vocal group from Detroit, Michigan: Billy Gordon, Billy Hoggs, Joe Billingslea, Sylvester Potts, Huey Davis (guitar; died on 2/23/2002, age 63) and Hubert Johnson (died on 7/11/81). **Dennis Edwards**, a member in 1967, joined **The Temptations** in 1968. Gordon was married to Georgeanna Tillman of **The Marvelettes**. Johnson was the cousin of **Jackie Wilson**.

DEBUT	PEAK	WKS	Gold	A-side (Chart Hit).....B-side	$	Sym	Label & Number
8/11/62	3	18	●	1 **Do You Love Me** RB[3] *Move, Mr. Man* also see #9 below	$20		Gordy 7005
12/22/62+	43	9		2 **Shake Sherry** .....*You Better Get In Line*	$15		Gordy 7012
4/6/63	64	6		3 **Don't Let Her Be Your Baby** .....*It Must Be Love*	$15		Gordy 7016
4/4/64	41	6		4 **Can You Do It** .....*I'll Stand By You*	$15		Gordy 7029
12/19/64+	47	7		5 **Can You Jerk Like Me** .....*That Day When She Needed Me* (R&B #37)	$15		Gordy 7037
8/14/65	57	8		6 **First I Look At The Purse** .....*Searching For A Girl* written and produced by **Smokey Robinson**	$15		Gordy 7044
5/28/66	85	2		7 **Just A Little Misunderstanding** .....*Determination* co-written by **Stevie Wonder**	$15		Gordy 7052
4/15/67	79	3		8 **It's So Hard Being A Loser** .....*Your Love Grows More Precious Everyday*	$15		Gordy 7059
6/4/88	11	16		9 **Do You Love Me** .....A:7 / S:15 *Shake, Sherrie* [R] same version as #1 above; featured in the movie *Dirty Dancing* starring **Patrick Swayze**	$6	■	Motown Yesteryear 448

CONWELL, Tommy, And The Young Rumblers

ROK/LP '89

Born in Philadelphia, Pennsylvania. Rock singer/guitarist. The Young Rumblers: Chris Day (guitar), Rob Miller (keyboards; **Hooters**), Paul Slivka (bass) and Jim Hannum (drums).

DEBUT	PEAK	WKS	Gold	A-side (Chart Hit).....B-side	$	Sym	Label & Number
9/24/88	74	7		1 **I'm Not Your Man** .....AR[1] *Workout (Part II)*	$5	■	Columbia 07980
12/17/88+	48	11		2 **If We Never Meet Again** .....*Everything They Say Is True*	$5		Columbia 08505

COO COO CAL

LP '01

Born Calvin Bellamy on 4/30/70 in Milwaukee, Wisconsin. Male rapper.

DEBUT	PEAK	WKS	Gold	A-side (Chart Hit).....B-side	$	Sym	Label & Number
8/4/01	81	9		1 **My Projects** .....S:7 *(2 versions) / Dedication* (w/Do It To Death)	$8	★*	Tommy Boy 2225
7/20/02	14[S]	12		2 **Throw It Up** .....*(2 versions)* **ILLICIT BIZNEZ Feat. Coo Coo Cal**	$5	★	Felonious 80012

COOKE, Sam ★50★

BUB/LP '60

Born on 1/22/31 in Clarksdale, Mississippi; raised in Chicago, Illinois. Died from a gunshot wound on 12/11/64 (age 33); shot by a female motel manager under mysterious circumstances. Son of a Baptist minister. Sang in choir from age six. Joined gospel group the Highway Q.C.'s. Lead singer of the Soul Stirrers from 1950-56. First recorded secular songs in 1956 as "Dale Cook" on Specialty. String of hits on Keen label led to contract with RCA. Nephew is singer **R.B. Greaves**. Inducted into the Rock and Roll Hall of Fame in 1986. Won Grammy's Lifetime Achievement Award in 1999. Revered as the definitive soul singer.

1)You Send Me 2)Chain Gang 3)Shake 4)Twistin' The Night Away 5)Another Saturday Night

DEBUT	PEAK	WKS	Gold	A-side (Chart Hit).....B-side	$	Sym	Label & Number
10/21/57	1[3]	26	●	1 **You Send Me** / RB[6] T:1[3] / S:1[2] / A:1[1] written by Sam's brother, Charles "L.C." Cooke			
11/4/57	81	4		2 **Summertime** .....T:81 / S:flip #12 hit for Billie Holiday in 1936; from Gershwin's folk opera *Porgy And Bess*; "Bubbled Under" (#106) on 8/24/59 on Keen 8-2101	$30		Keen 3-4013
12/23/57+	18	14		3 **I'll Come Running Back To You** / RB[1] S:18 / T:22			
12/23/57	60	5		4 **Forever** .....T:60 / S:flip different version released on Specialty 596 as by Dale Cook ($40); Rene Hall (orch., above 2)	$30		Specialty 619
12/30/57+	17	11		5 **(I Love You) For Sentimental Reasons** / .....S:17 / T:43 #1 hit for **Nat "King" Cole** in 1946			
12/30/57+	47	12		6 **Desire Me** .....T:47 / S:48	$30		Keen 3-4002
3/17/58	26	13		7 **Lonely Island** / S:26 / T:39			
3/24/58	27	7		8 **You Were Made For Me** .....S:27 / T:39 #3-8: released earlier in 1957	$30		Keen 3-4009
8/4/58	22	17		9 **Win Your Love For Me** .....S:22 / H:33 *Love Song From "Houseboat" (Almost In Your Arms)*	$30		Keen 3-2006
11/17/58	26	16		10 **Love You Most Of All** .....*Blue Moon* Bumps Blackwell (orch.: #1, 2, 7, 8 & 10)	$30		Keen 3-2008
3/9/59	31	13		11 **Everybody Likes To Cha Cha Cha** .....*Little Things You Do*	$25		Keen 3-2018
6/8/59	28	10		12 **Only Sixteen** .....*Let's Go Steady Again*	$25		Keen 3-2022
11/9/59	81	5		13 **There, I've Said It Again** .....*One Hour Ahead Of The Posse* **Don Ralke** (orch.); #1 hit for **Vaughn Monroe** in 1945; song introduced in 1941 by the Benny Carter Orch. (Bluebird 11090)	$25		Keen 8-2105
3/14/60	50	7		14 **Teenage Sonata** .....*If You Were The Only Girl*	$20		RCA Victor 7701
5/9/60	12	15		15 **Wonderful World** .....*Along The Navajo Trail*	$20		Keen 8-2112
8/15/60	2[2]	16		16 **Chain Gang** .....*I Fall In Love Every Day* Glenn Osser (orch.: #14 & 16)	$15	■	RCA Victor 7783
12/5/60	29	8		17 **Sad Mood** .....*Love Me*	$15		RCA Victor 7816
3/6/61	31	8		18 **That's It - I Quit - I'm Movin' On** .....*What Do You Say* Sammy Lowe (orch., above 2)	$15		RCA Victor 7853
6/5/61	17	12		19 **Cupid** .....*Farewell, My Darling*	$15	■	RCA Victor 7883
9/25/61	56	7		20 **Feel It** / also see #42 below (same version)			
9/25/61	93	1		21 **It's All Right** ..... Stan Applebaum (orch., above 2 and #42 below)	$15	■	RCA Victor 7927
2/3/62	9	15		22 **Twistin' The Night Away** .....RB[3] *One More Time*	$15		RCA Victor 7983

DEBUT	PEAK	WKS	Gold	A-side (Chart Hit)..................B-side	$	Sym	Label & Number
				COOKE, Sam — Cont'd			
6/23/62	13	11		23 **Bring It On Home To Me /**			
5/26/62	17	15		24 **Having A Party**	$15		RCA Victor 8036
				Lou Rawls (backing vocal, above 2)			
9/29/62	12	11		25 **Nothing Can Change This Love /**			
10/27/62	70	6		26 **Somebody Have Mercy**	$15	■	RCA Victor 8088
1/26/63	13	9		27 **Send Me Some Lovin' /**			
2/2/63	66	7		28 **Baby, Baby, Baby**	$15	■	RCA Victor 8129
				Horace Ott (orch., above 2)			
4/20/63	10	11		29 **Another Saturday Night** RB[1] *Love Will Find A Way (#105)*	$15	■	RCA Victor 8164
7/27/63	14	11		30 **Frankie And Johnny** *Cool Train*	$15	■	RCA Victor 8215
				Ralph Burns (orch.); version of mid-19th century traditional folk song			
10/26/63	11	10		31 **Little Red Rooster** *You Gotta Move*	$15	■	RCA Victor 8247
				#5 R&B hit for Margie Day in 1951; also recorded by **The Rolling Stones**, **The Grateful Dead** and **The Doors**			
1/25/64	11	10		32 **Good News** *Basin Street Blues*	$15		RCA Victor 8299
6/6/64	11	10		33 **Good Times /**			
6/13/64	35	8		34 **Tennessee Waltz**	$15		RCA Victor 8368
				#1 hit for **Patti Page** in 1950; **Hugo & Luigi** produced all of above RCA Victor recordings			
9/26/64	31	12		35 **Cousin Of Mine /**			
				originally charted for 8 weeks; re-entered on 1/16/65 (#73)			
10/10/64	93	3		36 **That's Where It's At**	$15		RCA Victor 8426
1/9/65	7	11		37 **Shake /**			
1/30/65	31	7		38 **A Change Is Gonna Come**	$15		RCA Victor 8486
				written by Sam in response to **Bob Dylan**'s "Blowin' In The Wind"			
4/10/65	41	7		39 **It's Got The Whole World Shakin'** *(Somebody) Ease My Troublin' Mind (#115)*	$15		RCA Victor 8539
6/5/65	52	5		40 **When A Boy Falls In Love** *The Piper*	$12		RCA Victor 8586
				Rene Hall (orch.: #19, 22-26, 29, 31-33 & 40)			
7/24/65	32	9		41 **Sugar Dumpling** *Bridge Of Tears*	$12	■	RCA Victor 8631
2/19/66	95	2		42 **Feel It** *That's All* [R]	$12		RCA Victor 8751
				#3, 8, 9, 16, 17, 19-26, 28, 29, 32, 33 & 35-42: written by Cooke			
4/30/66	97	1		43 **Let's Go Steady Again** *Trouble Blues*	$12		RCA Victor 8803
				same version is on the B-side of #12 above			
				COOKER '74			
				Born Norman DesRosiers in Chicago, Illinois. Pop singer/songwriter.			
2/2/74	88	5		**Try (Try To Fall In Love)** *The Ah-Ah Song*	$6		Scepter 12388
				COOKIE & HIS CUPCAKES '59			
				Swamp-rock group from Louisiana: Huey "Cookie" Thierry (vocals, saxophone), Shelton Dunaway, Sidney Reynaud, Marshall Laday, Ernest Jacobs, Joe Landry and Ivory Jackson. Cookie died on 9/23/97 (age 61).			
1/19/59	47	15		1 **Matilda** *Married Life*	$30		Judd 1002
				first released as "Mathilda" on Khoury 703 in 1958 ($50)			
5/4/63	94	4		2 **Got You On My Mind** *I've Been So Lonely*	$15		Chess 1848
				first released on Lyric 1004 in 1963 ($25)			
				COOKIES, The R&B '63			
				Female R&B vocal trio from Brooklyn, New York. Much backup work for Atlantic in mid-'50s, then for **Neil Sedaka** and **Carole King** in early '60s. Formed in 1954 with Dorothy Jones, her cousin Beulah Roberston and Ethel "Darlene" McCrea. Margie Hendrix replaced Beulah in 1956. Margie and Darlene joined the **The Raeletts** in 1958. Darlene's sister **Earl-Jean** (see #5 below) McCrea and Margaret Ross joined Dorothy in 1960. Margie died of a drug overdose in 1966. Beulah died of cancer in 1987.			
11/10/62	17	12		1 **Chains** *Stranger In My Arms*	$20		Dimension 1002
3/2/63	7	13		2 **Don't Say Nothin' Bad (About My Baby)** *Softly In The Night*	$20		Dimension 1008
7/6/63	72	5		3 **Will Power** *I Want A Boy For My Birthday*	$20		Dimension 1012
11/30/63+	33	11		4 **Girls Grow Up Faster Than Boys** *Only To Other People*	$20		Dimension 1020
6/27/64	38	8		5 **I'm Into Somethin' Good** *We Love And Learn*	$15		Colpix 729
				EARL-JEAN			
				COOL BREEZE LP '99			
				Born Freddy Calhoun in Atlanta, Georgia. Male rapper.			
1/30/99	73	10		**Watch For The Hook** S:20 *(instrumental)*	$4	★	Organized Noize 97046
				COOL BREEZE Featuring OutKast, Goodie Mob & Witchdoctor			
				samples **Neil Young**'s "Southern Man" as performed by **Merry Clayton**			
				COOLEY, Eddie, And The Dimples '56			
				Born in New York City, New York. R&B singer/songwriter. Wrote "Fever" (hit for **Little Willie John**, **Peggy Lee**, **Rita Coolidge** and **The McCoys**). The Dimples were a black female trio.			
10/27/56	20	13		**Priscilla** S:20 / J:20 / T:26 *Got A Little Woman*	$30		Royal Roost 621
				COOL HEAT '70			
				Group of New York studio musicians led by Bo Gentry and Kenny Laguna.			
8/15/70	89	3		**Groovin' With Mr. Bloe** *Are You Nuts?* [I]	$10		Forward 152
				originally released as the B-side of "Make Believe" by **Wind** (**Tony Orlando**)			
	★438★			**COOLIDGE, Rita** AC/C&W/BUB/LP '77			
				Born on 5/1/44 in Nashville, Tennessee. Had own group, R.C. and the Moonpies, at Florida State University. Moved to Los Angeles in the late 1960s. Did backup work for **Delaney & Bonnie**, **Leon Russell**, **Joe Cocker** and **Eric Clapton**. With **Kris Kristofferson** from 1971, married to him from 1973-80. Known as "The Delta Lady," for whom Leon Russell wrote the song of the same name. In the 1983 movie *Club Med.*			
				1)(Your Love Has Lifted Me) Higher And Higher 2)We're All Alone 3)The Way You Do The Things You Do			
5/10/69	96	1		1 **Turn Around And Love You** *Walkin' In The Mornin'*	$10		Pepper 443
12/30/72+	76	7		2 **Fever /**			
1/13/73		2		3 **My Crew**	$5	■	A&M 1398
				written by Booker T. Jones (of **Booker T. & The MG's**)			
11/17/73	49	10		4 **A Song I'd Like To Sing** *From The Bottle To The Bottom*	$5	■	A&M 1475

DEBUT	PEAK	WKS	Gold	A-side (Chart Hit)	B-side	$	Sym	Label & Number
				COOLIDGE, Rita — Cont'd				
3/23/74	86	5		5 **Loving Arms** **KRIS KRISTOFFERSON & RITA COOLIDGE** (above 2)	*I'm Down (But I Keep Falling)*	$5		A&M 1498
5/7/77	2^1	27	●	6 (Your Love Has Lifted Me) **Higher And Higher**	*Who's To Bless And Who's To Blame*	$5	■	A&M 1922
9/17/77	7	20	●	7 **We're All Alone** AC[1] written by **Boz Scaggs**	*Southern Lady*	$5	■	A&M 1965
1/14/78	20	11		8 **The Way You Do The Things You Do**	*I Feel The Burden (Being Lifted Off My Shoulders)*	$5	■	A&M 2004
7/1/78	25	12		9 **You**	*Only You Know And I Know*	$5	■	A&M 2058
11/4/78	68	7		10 **Love Me Again**	*The Jealous Kind* (C&W #63)	$5		A&M 2090
9/1/79	66	7		11 **One Fine Day**	*Sweet Emotion*	$5		A&M 2169
11/17/79+	38	10		12 **I'd Rather Leave While I'm In Love**	*Sweet Emotion*	$5		A&M 2199
5/17/80	42	10		13 **Somethin' 'Bout You Baby I Like** **GLEN CAMPBELL and RITA COOLIDGE**	*Late Night Confession* (Campbell)	$5		Capitol 4865
12/13/80+	46	12		14 **Fool That I Am**	*Can She Keep You Satisfied*	$5		A&M 2281
7/2/83	36	13		15 **All Time High** AC[4] from the James Bond movie *Octopussy* starring Roger Moore	*(instrumental–***John Barry***)*	$4	■	A&M 2551
	★537★			**COOLIO** R&B/BUB/LP '95 Born Artis Ivey on 8/1/63 in Los Angeles, California. Male rapper. Former member of **WC And The MAAD Circle**.				
6/4/94	3	25	▲	1 **Fantastic Voyage** S:❶[4] / A:11 rap version of **Lakeside**'s "Fantastic Voyage"; "45": Tommy Boy/Collectables 617	*(Timber radio edit)*	$3	▮V	Tommy Boy 7617
8/19/95	$❶^3$	38	$▲^3$	2 **Gangsta's Paradise** S:❶[7] / A:7 **COOLIO featuring L.V.** rap version of "Pastime Paradise" by **Stevie Wonder**; from the movie *Dangerous Minds* starring Michelle Pfeiffer	*(instrumental)*	$3	▮V	MCA Soundtracks 55104
12/9/95+	24	15		3 **Too Hot** S:13 "45" issued for above 2 on Tommy Boy 718	*Exercise Yo Game*	$3	▮V	Tommy Boy 7718
3/9/96	5	21	●	4 **1,2,3,4 (Sumpin' New)** S:4 / A:16 contains elements of "Wikka Wrap" by The Evasions and "Thighs High" by Tom Browne; "45": Tommy Boy 721	*(clean album version)*	$3	▮V	Tommy Boy 7721
6/1/96	29	18	●	5 **It's All The Way Live (Now)** S:17 from the movie *Eddie* starring Whoopi Goldberg; "45": Tommy Boy/Collectables 731; B-side: (instrumental)	*1,2,3,4 Sumpin' New (Timber mix)*	$3	▮V	Tommy Boy 7731
7/5/97	12	20	●	6 **C U When U Get There** S:6 **COOLIO Featuring 40 Thevz** contains an interpolation of Pachelbel's "Canon In D Major"; from the movie *Nothing To Lose* starring Martin Lawrence	*(remix)*	$3	▮	Tommy Boy 7785
12/16/00	61^S	1		7 **Tears Of A Clown** **BRANDY MOSS-SCOTT (Featuring Coolio)**	*(2 versions)*	$6	★	Heavenly 2000
	★235★			**COOPER, Alice** ROK/LP '72 Born Vincent Furnier on 2/4/48 in Detroit, Michigan. Formed hard-rock band, Alice Cooper, in Phoenix in 1965: Furnier (vocals), Glen Buxton (guitar), Michael Bruce (keyboards), Dennis Dunaway (bass) and Neal Smith (drums). Furnier went on to assume the Alice Cooper (a 17th-century witch) name for himself. Band split in 1974. Cooper went solo and became known for his bizarre stage antics. Appeared in the movies *Prince Of Darkness* and *Wayne's World*, among others. Buxton died on 10/19/97 (age 49). *1)School's Out 2)Poison 3)You And Me 4)How You Gonna See Me Now 5)Only Women*				
2/20/71	21	13		1 **Eighteen**	*Body*	$6		Warner 7449
6/12/71	94	3		2 **Caught In A Dream**	*Hallowed Be My Name*	$6		Warner 7490
12/25/71+	59	8		3 **Under My Wheels**	*Desperado*	$6		Warner 7529
3/11/72	49	10		4 **Be My Lover**	*Yeah, Yeah, Yeah*	$6		Warner 7568
6/3/72	7	13		5 **School's Out**	*Gutter Cat*	$6	■	Warner 7596
10/7/72	26	8		6 **Elected**	*Luney Tune*	$6	■	Warner 7631
2/3/73	35	10		7 **Hello Hurray**	*Generation Landslide*	$6		Warner 7673
4/14/73	25	12		8 **No More Mr. Nice Guy**	*Raped And Freezin'*	$6		Warner 7691
8/4/73	57	6		9 **Billion Dollar Babies** **Donovan** (guest vocal); above 4 from the album *Billion Dollar Babies*	*Mary Ann*	$6		Warner 7724
12/29/73+	48	8		10 **Teenage Lament '74**	*Hard Hearted Alice*	$6		Warner 7762
4/5/75	12	16		11 **Only Women**	*Cold Ethyl*	$4		Atlantic 3254
8/16/75	67	4		12 **Department Of Youth**	*Some Folks*	$4		Atlantic 3280
10/25/75	45	6		13 **Welcome To My Nightmare**	*Cold Ethyl*	$4		Atlantic 3298
7/4/76+	12	27	●	14 **I Never Cry**	*Go To Hell*	$4		Warner 8228
4/30/77	9	21		15 **You And Me**	*It's Hot Tonight*	$4	■	Warner 8349
10/21/78	12	16		16 **How You Gonna See Me Now**	*No Tricks* (w/**Betty Wright**)	$4		Warner 8695
5/17/80	40	9		17 **Clones (We're All)**	*Model Citizen*	$4	■	Warner 49204
9/23/89	7	19	●	18 **Poison** S:5 / A:12	*Trash*	$3		Epic 68958
1/20/90	56	9		19 **House Of Fire** co-written by **Joan Jett** and **Desmond Child**	*Ballad Of Dwight Fry*	$4	▮V	Epic 73085
4/28/90	89	3		20 **Only My Heart Talkin'**	*Under My Wheels (live)*	$4	▮	Epic 73268
7/27/91	78	5		21 **Hey Stoopid** **Ozzy Osbourne** (backing vocal); Slash (of **Guns N' Roses**; guitar)	*It Rained All Night*	$4	▮V	Epic 73845
				COOPER, Les, and the Soul Rockers '63 Born on 3/15/31 in Norfolk, Virginia. Pianist/arranger. Member of the doo-wop groups The Empires and The Whirlers.				
10/6/62+	22	16		**Wiggle Wobble** Joe Grier (former lead singer of **The Charts**; tenor sax solo)	*Dig Yourself* [I]	$15		Everlast 5019
				COOPER, Michael — see CON FUNK SHUN				
				COOPER BROTHERS '78 Pop-rock group from Ottawa, Ontario, Canada: brothers Richard (guitar) and Brian (bass) Cooper, Terry King and Darryl Alguire (guitars), Charles Robinson III (flute), Al Serwa (keyboards), and Glenn Bell (drums). All but Serwa share vocals.				
10/28/78	48	13		1 **The Dream Never Dies**	*Crazy Sundays*	$5		Capricorn 0308
6/30/79	79	4		2 **I'll Know Her When I See Her** **COOPER BROTHERS BAND**	*Heroes*	$5		Capricorn 0325
				COPACABANA TRIO — see ALLEN, Steve				

DEBUT	PEAK	WKS	Gold	A-side (Chart Hit)..................B-side	$	Sym	Label & Number
				COPAS, Cowboy C&W/MEM **'60**			
				Born Lloyd Estel Copas on 7/15/13 in Blue Creek, Ohio. Died on 3/5/63 (age 49) in the plane crash that also killed **Patsy Cline** and **Hawkshaw Hawkins**. Country singer/fiddler/guitarist.			
9/26/60	63	12		**Alabam** ....CW[12] *I Can*	$15		Starday 501
				COPE, Julian ROK/LP **'87**			
				Born on 10/21/57 in Bargoed, Wales; raised in Tamworth, England. Former lead singer/songwriter/bassist of the British group the Teardrop Explodes.			
3/21/87	84	4		**World Shut Your Mouth** ....*Umpteenth Unnatural Blues*	$4	■	Island 99479
				COPELAND, Ken **'57**			
				Born on 5/25/37 in Gainesville, Texas. Later became a televangelist with own Kenneth Copeland Ministries.			
4/6/57	12	15		**Pledge Of Love** ....A:12 / T:17 / S:23 *Night Air* (The Mints) first released on LIN 5007 in 1957 ($50)	$25		Imperial 5432
				COPPOLA, Imani **'97**			
				Born in Long Island, New York. Female singer/rapper.			
9/13/97	36	20		1 **Legend Of A Cowgirl** ....S:41 / A:41 *(remix)* samples "Sunshine Superman" by **Donovan**	$4	▮	Columbia 78651
2/3/01	94	4		2 **You All Dat** ....S:12 *(dance remix) / Who Let The Dogs Out* **BAHA MEN with Imani Coppola** samples "The Lion Sleeps Tonight" by **The Tokens**	$5	★+	S-Curve 151002
				COREY LP **'02**			
				Born Corey Hodges on 11/13/88 in Atlanta, Georgia. Teen R&B singer.			
1/26/02	63	13		**Hush Lil' Lady** ....S:2 *(2 versions) / (5 album snippets)* **COREY featuring Lil' Romeo** contains an interpolation of the folk song "Hush Little Baby"	$5	★	Motown 015474
				COREY, Jill MEM **'57**			
				Born Norma Jean Speranza on 9/30/35 in Avonmore, Pennsylvania. Married major league baseball player Don Hoak. Regular on TV's *Your Hit Parade* from 1957-58.			
12/22/56+	21	16		1 **I Love My Baby (My Baby Loves Me)** ....A:21 / T:28 *Egghead* #6 hit for Fred Waring's Pennsylvanians in 1926	$12		Columbia 40794
4/20/57	57	7		2 **Let It Be Me /** T:57 French song; English version introduced by Jill on the CBS-TV dramatic series *Climax*			
4/29/57	95	1		3 **Make Like A Bunny, Honey** ....T:95 [N] **JILL COREY with JIMMY CARROLL** (above 2)	$12		Columbia 40878
8/5/57	11	13		4 **Love Me To Pieces** S:11 / A:11 / T:18 *Love* performed by Corey on the 7/15/57 *Studio One Summer Theatre* TV production of *Love Me To Pieces*; Jimmy Carroll (orch., all of above)	$12		Columbia 40955
9/1/58	96	2		5 **Big Daddy** ....H:96 *Wherefore Art Thou, Romeo?* Glenn Osser (orch.)	$12		Columbia 41202
				CORINA **'91**			
				Born Corina Ayala on 10/14/63 in Manhattan, New York. Female dance singer.			
5/18/91	6	21		1 **Temptation** ....A:2 / S:24 *Loving You Like Crazy*	$3	▮	Cutting/Atco 98775
9/28/91	51	20		2 **Whispers** ....A:42 *Give Me Back My Heart*	$3	▮	Cutting/Atco 98709
5/9/92	72[A]	2		3 **Now That You're Gone** ....*(4 versions)*	$6	▮*	Cutting 259
7/5/97	86	8		4 **Summertime Summertime** ....*(5 versions)* samples "122 BPM" by Jive Rhythm Tracks	$6	T	So So Def 78567
				CORLEY, Al **'85**			
				Born on 5/22/56 in Wichita, Kansas. Pop-rock singer/songwriter/actor. Played the original "Steven Carrington" on TV's *Dynasty*.			
5/11/85	80	5		**Square Rooms** ....*Don't Play With Me*	$5	■	Mercury 822241
				CORLEY, Bob **'55**			
				White stand-up comedian with a southern drawl.			
11/19/55	95	1		**Number One Street (Sides 1 & 2)** ....T:95 [C-L] released in 1957 on RCA Victor 6946 ($20)	$50		Stars, Inc. 4773
				CORNBREAD & BISCUITS **'60**			
				Black comedy duo.			
11/14/60	75	5		**The Big Time Spender (Parts I & II)** .... [C-L] Lea Lendon (backing music); also released on Anna 102 in 1960 ($40)	$30		Maske 102
				CORNELIUS BROTHERS & SISTER ROSE R&B/BUB/LP **'72**			
				R&B family trio from Dania, Florida: Edward, Carter and Rose Cornelius. Carter died of a heart attack on 11/7/91 (age 43).			
4/10/71	3	18	●	1 **Treat Her Like A Lady** ....*Over At My Place* first released on Platinum 105 in 1970 ($15)	$5		United Artists 50721
5/27/72	2[2]	14	●	2 **Too Late To Turn Back Now** *Lift Your Love Higher*	$5		United Artists 50910
9/2/72	23	11		3 **Don't Ever Be Lonely (A Poor Little Fool Like Me)** ....*I'm So Glad (To Be Loved By You)*	$5		United Artists 50954
12/23/72+	37	9		4 **I'm Never Gonna Be Alone Anymore** ....*Let's Stay Together*	$5		United Artists 50996
4/28/73	96	2		5 **Let Me Down Easy** ....*Gonna Be Sweet For You* all of above from the album *Cornelius Brothers & Sister Rose*	$5		United Artists 208
				CORNELL, Don MEM/POP **'52**			
				Born on 4/21/19 in New York City, New York. Popular singer/guitarist. From the late 1930s, worked with Al Kavelin and Red Nichols. Achieved great success with **Sammy Kaye**, charting 14 hits from 1942-50. Hit #3 as a solo artist in 1952 with "I'm Yours." *1)Hold My Hand 2)The Bible Tells Me So 3)Most Of All*			
9/11/54	2[1]	18	●	1 **Hold My Hand** A:2 / S:5 / J:7 *I'm Blessed* Jerry Carr (orch.); from the movie *Susan Slept Here* starring Dick Powell and **Debbie Reynolds**	$20		Coral 61206
5/14/55	14	6		2 **Most Of All /** A:14 / S:20 #5 R&B hit for **The Moonglows** in 1955			
5/21/55		2		3 **The Door Is Still Open To My Heart** ....S:flip #4 R&B hit for The Cardinals in 1955	$20		Coral 61393

DEBUT	PEAK	WKS	Gold	A-side (Chart Hit)...B-side	$	Sym	Label & Number

CORNELL, Don — Cont'd

DEBUT	PEAK	WKS	Gold	A-side (Chart Hit)...B-side	$	Sym	Label & Number
9/10/55	7	13		4 The Bible Tells Me So / S:7 / J:8 / A:18 / T:31 written by **Roy Rogers**' wife, Dale Evans			
9/24/55	26	9		5 Love Is A Many-Splendored Thing ...T:26 / S:flip / J:flip title song from the movie starring William Holden	$15		Coral 61467
11/12/55	25	2		6 Young Abe Lincoln ...T:25 *Dream World*	$15		Coral 61521
2/18/56	80	5		7 Teenage Meeting (Gonna Rock It Up Right) ...T:80 *I Still Have A Prayer*	$20		Coral 61584
4/14/56	59	8		8 Rock Island Line ...T:59 *Na-Ne Na-Na* Carretta (orch.: #5 & 8); originated in the mid-1930s as an Arkansas prison song; long associated with folk legend Leadbelly	$15		Coral 61613
11/10/56	57	6		9 See-Saw / T:57			
10/20/56		1		10 From The Bottom Of My Heart ...CU:flip original version by **The Clovers** in 1956 on Atlantic 1107 ($50); #3 & 10: written by **Chuck Willis**	$15		Coral 61721
4/27/57	47	8		11 Mama Guitar ...T:47 *A Face In The Crowd* from the movie *A Face In The Crowd* starring **Andy Griffith**; **Dick Jacobs** (orch.: #2-4, 6, 7 & 9-11)	$15		Coral 61819

CORO '91

Born Jose Coro in New York; raised in Miami, Florida. Black singer/actor. Appeared in **Don Johnson**'s "Heartbeat" video and TV's *Miami Vice.*

DEBUT	PEAK	WKS	Gold	A-side (Chart Hit)...B-side	$	Sym	Label & Number
7/13/91	54	11		My Fallen Angel ...A:33 *Where Are You Tonight*	$4	▮	Cutting/Charisma 98772

CORONA LP '95

Dance duo: Italian producer Francesco Bontempi and Brazilian singer Olga DeSouza.

DEBUT	PEAK	WKS	Gold	A-side (Chart Hit)...B-side	$	Sym	Label & Number
11/12/94+	11	27		1 The Rhythm Of The Night ...A:10 / S:18 *(Rapino Brothers radio version)*	$4	▮	EastWest 98192
5/13/95	57	17		2 Baby Baby ...A:51 / S:70 *(Robyx piano remix edit)*	$4	▮	EastWest 64438

CORRS, The AC/BUB/LP '01

Sibling pop group from Ireland: Andrea (lead vocals), Jim (guitar), Sharon (violin) and Caroline (drums) Corr.

DEBUT	PEAK	WKS	Gold	A-side (Chart Hit)...B-side	$	Sym	Label & Number
10/14/95	68	11		1 Runaway ...A:75 *Leave Me Alone / (3 album snippets)*	$4	▮	143/Lava 98133
1/27/01	34	20		2 Breathless ...A:30 from the album *In Blue* on 143/Lava 83352			album cut

CORSAIRS Featuring Jay "Bird" Uzzell '62

R&B vocal group from La Grange, North Carolina: brothers Jay "Bird" (lead), James and "King" Moe Uzzell, with cousin George Wooten.

DEBUT	PEAK	WKS	Gold	A-side (Chart Hit)...B-side	$	Sym	Label & Number
12/25/61+	12	15		1 Smoky Places ...*Thinkin' (Maybe She's Changed Her Ways)*	$20		Tuff 1808
4/14/62	68	8		2 I'll Take You Home ...*Sittin' On Your Doorstep*	$15		Tuff/Chess 1818

CORTEZ, Dave "Baby" BUB/R&B/LP '59

Born David Cortez Clowney on 8/13/38 in Detroit, Michigan. R&B keyboardist/composer. Played organ and sang with the vocal group The Pearls from 1955-57, and also with the Valentines, which included **Richard Barrett** and Ronnie Bright (of "Mr. Bass Man" fame), from 1956-57. Frequent session work in New York. First recorded (as David Clooney) for Ember in 1956.

DEBUT	PEAK	WKS	Gold	A-side (Chart Hit)...B-side	$	Sym	Label & Number
3/16/59	❶[1]	17		1 The Happy Organ *Love Me As I Love You* [I]	$20		Clock 1009
6/8/59	61	8		2 The Whistling Organ ...*I'm Happy* [I]	$20		Clock 1012
7/14/62	10	14		3 Rinky Dink ...*Getting Right* [I]	$25		Julia/Chess 1829
10/13/62	67	7		4 Happy Weekend ...*Fiddle Sticks* [I]	$15		Chess 1834
11/17/62	96	2		5 Fiesta ...*Hey - Hey - Hey* [I]	$15		Emit 301
4/13/63	91	2		6 Hot Cakes! 1st Serving...*2nd Serving* [I]	$12		Chess 1850
8/24/63	76	3		7 Organ Shout...*Precious You* [I]	$12		Chess 1861
6/4/66	91	3		8 Count Down...*Summertime (Cha-Cha-Cha)* [I]	$10		Roulette 4679

CORY '77

Born Cory Braverman on 12/16/49 in Brooklyn, New York. Female singer/songwriter.

DEBUT	PEAK	WKS	Gold	A-side (Chart Hit)...B-side	$	Sym	Label & Number
3/5/77	89	3		Fire Sign ...*Party King*	$5		Phantom 10856

COSBY, Bill BUB/R&B/LP '67

Born William Henry Cosby, Jr. on 7/12/38 in Philadelphia, Pennsylvania. Top comedian. Starred in several movies and TV shows.

DEBUT	PEAK	WKS	Gold	A-side (Chart Hit)...B-side	$	Sym	Label & Number
9/2/67	4	11		1 Little Ole Man (Uptight-Everything's Alright) *Hush Hush* [N]	$8		Warner 7072
12/2/67	71	6		2 Hooray For The Salvation Army Band ...*Ursalena* [N]	$8		Warner 7096
3/2/68	91	3		3 Funky North Philly ...*Stop, Look & Listen* [N]	$8		Warner 7171
5/2/70	70	3		4 Grover Henson Feels Forgotten...*(instrumental)* [S]	$6		Uni 55223
5/8/76	46	10		5 Yes, Yes, Yes ...*Ben* [C]	$5		Capitol 4258

COSTA, Don, And His Orchestra And Chorus BUB/AC '60

Born on 6/10/25 in Boston, Massachusetts. Died on 1/19/83 (age 57). Arranger for **Vaughn Monroe**, **Frank Sinatra**, **Vic Damone**, **The Ames Brothers** and many more. A&R director of ABC-Paramount Records, then for United Artists Records.

DEBUT	PEAK	WKS	Gold	A-side (Chart Hit)...B-side	$	Sym	Label & Number
11/16/59	59	6		1 I'll Walk The Line...*Catwalk* [I] instrumental version of **Johnny Cash**'s "I Walk The Line"	$15		United Artists 190
5/2/60	27	13		2 Theme From "The Unforgiven" (The Need For Love) ...*Streets Of Paris* [I] from the movie *The Unforgiven* starring Burt Lancaster and Audrey Hepburn	$12	⊙	United Artists 221
8/8/60	19	26		3 Never On Sunday...*The Sound Of Love* [I] title song from the movie starring Melina Mercouri; originally charted for 15 weeks; re-entered on 5/8/61 (#37)	$12	■	United Artists 234

COSTELLO, Elvis ROK/BUB/LP '89

Born Declan MacManus on 8/25/54 in Paddington, London, England; raised in Liverpool, England. Leading eclectic rock singer. Adopted stage name Elvis Costello in 1976; Costello is his mother's maiden name. In 1977, formed backing band The Attractions: Steve "Nieve" Nason (keyboards), Bruce Thomas (bass; **Sutherland Brothers & Quiver**) and Peter Thomas (drums). Appeared in the 1987 movie *Straight To Hell.* Married Cait O'Riordan, former bassist with The Pogues, on 5/16/86. Inducted into the Rock and Roll Hall of Fame in 2003.

DEBUT	PEAK	WKS	Gold	A-side (Chart Hit)...B-side	$	Sym	Label & Number
8/20/83	36	14		1 Everyday I Write The Book...*Heathen Town*	$5	■	Columbia 04045
7/28/84	56	9		2 The Only Flame In Town...*Turning The Town Red* **ELVIS COSTELLO & THE ATTRACTIONS** (above 2) **Daryl Hall** (backing vocal)	$5	■	Columbia 04502
2/11/89	19	14		3 Veronica ...MR[2] S:15 / A:28 *You're No Good* **Paul McCartney** (co-writer, bass guitar)	$4	■	Warner 22981

DEBUT	PEAK	WKS	Gold	A-side (Chart Hit)..B-side	$	Sym	Label & Number
				COTTON, Gene '78			
				Born on 6/30/44 in Columbus, Ohio. Pop-rock singer/songwriter/guitarist. Recording since 1967.			
11/16/74	79	5		1 **Sunshine Roses** ....*Mrs. Oliver*	$6		Myrrh 137
				also released on Myrrh 136 in 1974			
5/24/75	73	3		2 **Damn It All** ....*Country Spirit*	$5		ABC 12087
12/4/76+	33	11		3 **You've Got Me Runnin'** ....*It's Over Goodbye*	$5		ABC 12227
2/4/78	23	14		4 **Before My Heart Finds Out** *Like A Sunday In Salem*	$5		Ariola America 7675
6/17/78	36	12		5 **You're A Part Of Me**....................*Shine On (You Got To Shine On Your Light)* (Cotton)	$5		Ariola America 7704
				GENE COTTON with Kim Carnes			
9/30/78	40	10		6 **Like A Sunday In Salem (The Amos & Andy Song)**....................*Shine On (You Got To Shine On Your Light)*	$5		Ariola America 7723
3/13/82	76	8		7 **If I Could Get You (into my Life)** ....*Rained On Before*	$5		Knoll 5002
				COTTON, Josie LP '82			
				Born Kathleen Josey on 5/15/51 in Dallas, Texas. Pop-rock singer/actress. Appeared in the movie *Valley Girl*.			
8/21/82	74	7		1 **He Could Be The One** ....*Systematic Way*	$5	■	Elektra 47481
4/7/84	82	4		2 **Jimmy Loves Maryann**....................*No Pictures Of Dad*	$5	■	Elektra 69748
				COTTON, LLOYD and CHRISTIAN — see CHRISTIAN, Chris			
				COUGAR, John — see MELLENCAMP			
				COUNT FIVE BUB/LP '66			
				Psychedelic garage-rock band from San Jose, California: Kenn Ellner (vocals), John Michalski and Sean Byrne (guitars), Roy Chaney (bass) and Craig Atkinson (drums). Atkinson died on 10/13/98 (age 50).			
9/10/66	5	12		**Psychotic Reaction** ....*They're Gonna Get You*	$15		Double Shot 104
				COUNTING CROWS ROK/LP '94			
				Rock group from San Francisco, California: Adam Duritz (vocals), David Bryson (guitar), Charlie Gillingham (piano), Matt Malley (bass) and Steve Bowman (drums). Ben Mize replaced Bowman in 1994. Guitarist Dan Vickrey joined in 1996.			
1/22/94	5^{A}	47		1 **Mr. Jones**			album cut
6/18/94	31^{A}	23		2 **Round Here**			album cut
8/6/94	45^{A}	20		3 **Einstein On The Beach (For An Eggman)** ....MR^{1}			album cut
				from the various artists album *DGC Rarities Vol. 1* on DGC 24704			
12/10/94	66^{A}	4		4 **Rain King**....................			album cut
				#1, 2 & 4: from the album *August and Everything After* on DGC 24528			
10/12/96	45^{A}	9		5 **Angels Of The Silences**....................			album cut
12/7/96+	6^{A}	28		6 **A Long December**....................		V	album cut
5/31/97	51^{A}	9		7 **Daylight Fading**....................			album cut
				above 3 from the album *Recovering The Satellites* on DGC 24975			
11/6/99+	28	20		8 **Hanginaround** A:19		V	album cut
				from the album *This Desert Life* on DGC 490415; "45" issued for #6 & 8 on DGC 97216			
				COUNTRY COALITION '70			
				Country-rock group: Peggie Moje, Dick Bradley, Tom Riney and John Kurtz.			
3/21/70	96	3		**Time To Get It Together** ....*How Do I Love You*	$6		BluesWay 61034
				COUNTRY JOE AND THE FISH BUB/LP '76			
				Born Joseph McDonald on 1/1/42 in El Monte, California. Highly political rock singer/guitarist. The Fish: Barry Melton and David Cohen (guitars), Bruce Barthol (bass) and Chicken Hirsch (drums). Disbanded in 1970.			
8/5/67	95	2		1 **Not So Sweet Martha Lorraine**....................*The Masked Marauder*	$10		Vanguard 35052
11/29/75+	92	7		2 **Breakfast For Two**....................*Lost My Connection*	$5		Fantasy 758
				COUNTRY JOE McDONALD			
				COUNTY, Jayne '02			
				Born Wayne Rogers in 1947 in Dallas, Georgia. Punk-rock singer. Began performing as Wayne County in New York City. Underwent a sex change in the late 1970s and became Jayne County.			
5/18/02	72^{S}	1		**F**k Off 2000** ....*(3 versions)*	$10	★*	Royalty 85008
				original version "F**k Off" released in 1980 on Attic Records			
				COURTNEY, Lou R&B '67			
				Born in Buffalo, New York. R&B singer/songwriter.			
1/28/67	71	6		1 **Skate Now**....................*I Can Always Tell*	$12		Riverside 4588
4/8/67	80	3		2 **Do The Thing** ....*The Man Is Lonely*	$12		Riverside 4589
				COURTSHIP, The '72			
				Pop-rock group from Texas.			
6/24/72	93	2		**It's The Same Old Love** ....*Last Row, First Balcony*	$6		Tamla 54217
				COVAY, Don R&B/BUB '73			
				Born on 3/24/38 in Orangeburg, South Carolina. R&B singer/songwriter. Member of the Rainbows in 1955. Recorded as "Pretty Boy" with **Little Richard**'s band for Atlantic in 1957. Formed **The Goodtimers** in 1960. Also see **The Soul Clan**.			
1/23/61	60	9		1 **Pony Time**....................*Love Boat* [I]	$50		Arnold 1002
				THE GOODTIMERS			
12/29/62+	75	7		2 **The Popeye Waddle**....................*One Little Boy Had Money*	$20		Cameo 239
9/5/64	35	10		3 **Mercy, Mercy** ....*Can't Stay Away*	$20		Rosemart 801
				Jimi Hendrix (guitar)			
12/26/64	97	2		4 **Take This Hurt Off Me** ....*Please Don't Let Me Know*	$15		Rosemart 802
11/13/65	44	9		5 **Seesaw**....................*I Never Get Enough Of Your Love*	$10		Atlantic 2301
				DON COVAY & THE GOODTIMERS (#3 & 5)			
7/7/73	29	10		6 **I Was Checkin' Out She Was Checkin' In** *Money (That's What I Want)*	$6		Mercury 73385
7/13/74	63	6		7 **It's Better To Have (And Don't Need)**....................*Leave Him - Part 1*	$6		Mercury 73469

DEBUT	PEAK	WKS	Gold	A-side (Chart Hit)......B-side	$	Sym	Label & Number
				COVEN '71			
				Pop group: Jinx Dawson (female vocals), Oz (male vocals), Christopher Nelson (guitar), John Hobbs (keyboards) and Steve Ross (drums).			
9/18/71	26	12		1 **One Tin Soldier, The Legend of Billy Jack** ......*I Think You Always Knew* from the movie *Billy Jack* starring Tom Laughlin; same version re-charted at #3 below	$5		Warner 7509
7/21/73	79	6		2 **One Tin Soldier (The Legend of Billy Jack)** ......*I Guess It's A Beautiful Day (Least I Think It Is)* [R] new version (both conducted by Mundell Lowe)	$5		MGM 14308
12/29/73+	73	6		3 **One Tin Soldier, The Legend of Billy Jack** ......*Johnnie* (Teresa Kelly) [R] reissue of the original version (#1 above)	$5		Warner 0101
	★533★			**COVER GIRLS, The** BUB/LP '90			
				Female dance trio from New York City, New York: Louise Sabater, Caroline Jackson and Sunshine Wright (replaced by Margo Urban in 1989). New 1992 lineup: Jackson, Evelyn Escalera and Michelle Valentine.			
				1)We Can't Go Wrong 2)Wishing On A Star 3)Because Of You			
2/28/87	44	18		1 **Show Me** ......S:31 *Drumapella*	$4		Fever 1911
8/1/87	98	1		2 **Spring Love** ......*(Spring mix)*	$4		Fever 1913
11/28/87+	27	20		3 **Because Of You** ......S:24 / A:28 *(Percapella version)*	$4	■	Fever 1914
3/26/88	40	19		4 **Promise Me** ......S:33 *One Night Affair*	$4	■	Fever 1917
7/23/88	55	13		5 **Inside Outside** ......S:37 *(instrumental)* all of above from the album *Show Me*	$4	■	Fever 1916
9/9/89	38	14		6 **My Heart Skips A Beat** ......S:36 *Spring Love* "45" promo: Capitol 79705; B-side: (same)	$3	▮V	Capitol 44436
12/9/89+	8	19		7 **We Can't Go Wrong** A:7 / S:9 *(edit) / Love Mission* "45" promo: Capitol 79884; B-side: (album version)	$3	▮V	Capitol 44498
4/7/90	49	12		8 **All That Glitters Isn't Gold** ......*(2 remixes)* "45" promo: Capitol 79000; B-side: (same)	$3	▮V	Capitol 44545
2/9/91	55	11		9 **Funk Boutique /** A:65			
1/12/91	63^{A}	3		10 **Don't Stop Now**	$3		Epic 73698
5/30/92	9	20		11 **Wishing On A Star** ......A:2 / S:16 *Funk Boutique*	$3	▮V	Epic 74343
8/29/92	75	8		12 **Thank You** ......A:62 *Wishing On A Star (Spanish version)*	$3	▮V	Epic 74438
				COVERVERSIONS.COM '01			
				Studio group from Los Angeles, California.			
11/10/01	33^{S}	13		**Because I Got High** ......*(Party mix)* [N] cover version of **Afroman**'s hit	$5	★	CoverVersions.com 1001
				COWBOY CHURCH SUNDAY SCHOOL, The '55			
				Producer **Stuart Hamblen**'s family: his daughters Veeva Susanne (age 18) and Obee Jane "Lisa" (age 16) with his wife Suzy, plus two of the girls' friends. Recorded at 33-1/3 rpm so that the record sounds like children's voices at 45 rpm. Veeva married actor Harve Presnell.			
1/1/55	8	21		**Open Up Your Heart (And Let The Sunshine In)** ......S:8 / A:18 / J:19 *The Lord Is Counting On You* a picture sleeve was issued for Decca's Children's Series (1-299)	$15		Decca 29367
				COWBOY JUNKIES ROK/LP '94			
				Alternative-rock group from Toronto, Ontario, Canada: siblings Margo (vocals), Michael (guitar) and Peter (drums) Timmins, and Alan Anton (bass).			
10/29/94	52^{A}	9		1 **Sweet Jane** ...... from the movie soundtrack album *Natural Born Killers* on Nothing 92460; released as a "45" in 1988 (ROK #5) on RCA 8879 with a picture sleeve; B-side: "200 More Miles"; written and recorded by Velvet Underground in 1970			album cut
4/20/96	75^{A}	1		2 **A Common Disaster** ...... from the album *Lay It Down* on Geffen 24952			album cut
				COWSILLS, The BUB/LP '68			
				Family pop group from Newport, Rhode Island: brothers Bill, Bob, Paul, Barry and John, with their younger sister Susan and mother Barbara (died on 1/31/85, age 56). Bob, Paul, John and Susan reunited for touring in 1990. Susan married Peter Holsapple of The dB's on 4/18/93. Group was the inspiration for TV's **The Partridge Family**.			
9/30/67	2^{2}	16	●	1 **The Rain, The Park & Other Things** ......*River Blue*	$8	■	MGM 13810
1/13/68	21	9		2 **We Can Fly** ......*A Time For Rememberance*	$8	■	MGM 13886
3/16/68	54	6		3 **In Need Of A Friend** ......*Mister Flynn*	$8	■	MGM 13909
6/1/68	10	13		4 **Indian Lake** ......*Newspaper Blanket*	$8	■	MGM 13944
9/14/68	44	6		5 **Poor Baby** ......*Meet Me At The Wishing Well*	$8		MGM 13981
3/15/69	2^{2}	15	●	6 **Hair** *What Is Happy?* from the rock musical *Hair* starring Steve Curry	$8		MGM 14026
6/21/69	75	4		7 **The Prophecy Of Daniel and John The Divine (Six-Six-Six)** ......*Gotta Get Away From It All*	$8		MGM 14063
10/11/69	74	7		8 **Silver Threads And Golden Needles** ......*Love American Style*	$8	■	MGM 14084
	★561★			**COX, Deborah** LP '98			
				Born on 7/13/74 in Toronto, Ontario, Canada. R&B singer/songwriter. Also see **Tami Davis**'s "How Do I Say I'm Sorry.".			
				1)Nobody's Supposed To Be Here 2)We Can't Be Friends 3)Who Do U Love			
9/9/95	27	20		1 **Sentimental** ......S:9 *My Radio*	$3	▮V	Arista 12852
2/3/96	17	20		2 **Who Do U Love** ......S:12 / A:62 *(Morales mix)* "45" issued for above 2 on Arista 12950	$3	▮V	Arista 12950
7/6/96	48	14		3 **Where Do We Go From Here** ......S:25 *Call Me*	$3	▮	Arista 13223
1/4/97	97	4		4 **The Sound Of My Tears** ......*It Could've Been You*	$3	▮	Arista 13277
7/5/97	56	17		5 **Things Just Ain't The Same** ......S:34 / A:70 *(remix)* samples "You Are Everything" by **The Stylistics**; from the movie *Money Talks* starring Chris Tucker	$3	▮	Arista 13380
10/3/98	2^{8}	29	▲	6 **Nobody's Supposed To Be Here** RB[14] S:❶[1] / A:6 *(dance mix)*	$3	★	Arista 13550
5/22/99	70	6		7 **It's Over Now** ......S:41 *(6 versions) / Nobody's Supposed To Be Here (remix)*	$6	★*	Arista 13656

DEBUT	PEAK	WKS	Gold	A-side (Chart Hit)...B-side	$	Sym	Label & Number
				COX, Deborah — Cont'd			
9/11/99	8	20		8 **We Can't Be Friends** ...RB[2] S:5 / A:36 *It's Over Now (2 versions)*	$3	★	Arista 13724
				DEBORAH COX with R.L. from Next			
				Montell Jordan (backing vocal)			
6/17/00	70	9		9 **Same Script, Different Cast** ...A:64 *(4 remixes)*	$6	T	Arista 13860
				WHITNEY HOUSTON & DEBORAH COX			
11/2/02	67[S]	1		10 **Up & Down (In & Out)** ...*(5 versions)*	$6	T	J Records 21204
				DEBORAH COX (feat. Jadakiss)			
				COYOTE SISTERS, The AC **'84**			
				White female vocal trio: Marty Gwinn, Leah Kunkel (sister of **Mama Cass**) and Renee Armand.			
7/28/84	66	10		**Straight From The Heart (Into Your Life)** ...*Echo*	$4	■	Morocco 1742
				COZIER, Jimmy LP **'01**			
				Born on 10/15/77 in Brooklyn, New York. R&B singer/songwriter.			
6/16/01	26	15		**She's All I Got** ...S:6 / A:51 *(remix* w/**E-40**)	$4	★	J Records 21069
				CRABBY APPLETON BUB/LP **'70**			
				Pop-rock group from Los Angeles, California: Michael Fennelly (vocals, guitar), Casey Foutz (keyboards), Flaco Falcon (percussion), Hank Harvey (bass) and Phil Jones (drums). Named for the cartoon character on the original Captain Kangaroo TV show.			
5/9/70	36	14		**Go Back** ...*Try*	$7		Elektra 45687
				CRACKER ROK/BUB/LP **'94**			
				Rock trio from Redlands, California: David Lowery (vocals; Camper Van Beethoven), John Hickman (guitar) and Davey Faragher (bass). Faragher left by 1996; Bob Rupe (**Faragher Bros.**; bass) and Charlie Quintana (drums) joined.			
4/9/94	64	13		1 **Low** ...S:56 / A:69 *Nostalgia*	$4	▮V	Virgin 38427
				"45": Virgin 17910			
4/6/96	67[A]	3		2 **I Hate My Generation** ...		V	album cut
				from the album *The Golden Age* on Virgin 41498; "45": Virgin 19118; B-side: "Big Dipper"			
				CRADDOCK, Billy "Crash" C&W/BUB/LP **'74**			
				Born on 6/13/39 in Greensboro, North Carolina. Country-rock singer. First recorded for Colonial in 1957. Nickname "Crash" came from his stock car racing hobby. Charted 41 Country hits, 1971-89.			
11/9/59	94	1		1 **Don't Destroy Me** ...*Boom Boom Baby*	$25	■	Columbia 41470
				CRASH CRADDOCK			
				also issued with a special promotional 8-page booklet-type picture sleeve			
6/29/74	16	15		2 **Rub It In** ...CW[2] *It's Hard To Love A Hungry, Worried Man*	$5		ABC 12013
11/23/74+	33	9		3 **Ruby, Baby** ...CW[1] *Walk When Love Walks*	$5		ABC 12036
				#10 R&B hit for **The Drifters** in 1956			
12/13/75+	54	8		4 **Easy As Pie** ...*She's Mine*	$5		ABC/Dot 17584
				CRAMER, Floyd BUB/AC/C&W/MEM/LP **'61**			
				Born on 10/27/33 in Samti, Louisiana; raised in Huttig, Arkansas. Died of cancer on 12/31/97 (age 64). Nashville's top session pianist. Played piano from age five. Moved to Nashville in 1955. Worked with **Elvis Presley**, **Johnny Cash**, **Perry Como**, **Chet Atkins** and many others.			
				1)Last Date 2)On The Rebound 3)San Antonio Rose			
4/28/58	87	2		1 **Flip Flop And Bop** ...T:87 *Sophisticated Swing* [I]	$15		RCA Victor 7156
10/10/60	2[4]	20	●	2 **Last Date** *Sweetie Baby* [I]	$12		RCA Victor 7775
3/6/61	4	13		3 **On The Rebound** ...*Mood Indigo* [I]	$10	■	RCA Victor 7840
6/5/61	8	12		4 **San Antonio Rose** ...*I Can Just Imagine* [I]	$10		RCA Victor 7893
				written by Bob Wills in 1938			
9/25/61	63	7		5 **Your Last Goodbye** / [I]			
10/2/61	95	2		6 **Hang On** ... [I]	$8	■	RCA Victor 7907
1/20/62	36	8		7 **Chattanooga Choo Choo** / [I]			
				#1 hit for Glenn Miller in 1941 (from the movie *Sun Valley Serenade* starring Sonja Henie)			
2/3/62	90	2		8 **Let's Go** ... [I]	$8		RCA Victor 7978
4/14/62	87	3		9 **Lovesick Blues** ...*The First Hurt* [I]	$8		RCA Victor 8013
				#1 Country hit for Hank Williams in 1949			
7/7/62	63	4		10 **Hot Pepper** ...*For Those That Cry* [I]	$8		RCA Victor 8051
12/29/62+	49	11		11 **Java** ...*Melissa* [I]	$8		RCA Victor 8116
				all of above produced by **Chet Atkins**			
				CRAMPTON SISTERS, The **'64**			
				White doo-wop duo of sisters from Bloomfield, New Jersey. Peggy Crampton is one of the sisters.			
2/8/64	92	2		**I Didn't Know What Time It Was** ...*I Cried When I Found You Gone*	$20		DCP 1001
				this Rodgers & Hart song originally hit #6 in 1939 for **Benny Goodman**; DCP record label is owned by **Don Costa**			
				CRANBERRIES, The ROK/LP **'94**			
				Pop-rock group from Limerick, Ireland: Dolores O'Riordan (vocals), brothers Noel (guitar) and Mike (bass) Hogan, and Fergal Lawler (drums). Group formed in 1990 as the Cranberry Saw Us. O'Riordan joined in 1991 and group shortened name to The Cranberries. O'Riordan married Don Burton, assistant tour manager for **Duran Duran**, on 7/18/94.			
10/23/93+	8	24	●	1 **Linger** A:14 / S:16 *How*	$4	▮V	Island 862800
4/2/94	42	20		2 **Dreams** ...A:38 / S:57 *What You Were*	$4	▮V	Island 864436
				"45" issued for above 2 on Island 858172			
10/1/94	22[A]	26		3 **Zombie** ...MR[6]		V	album cut
2/18/95	39[A]	14		4 **Ode To My Family** ...		V	album cut
				above 2 from the album *No Need To Argue* on Island 524050; "45" issued for above 2 on Island 854206			
4/13/96	21[A]	12		5 **Salvation** ...MR[4]			album cut
11/23/96+	22	20		6 **When You're Gone** / S:23 / A:50			
11/23/96	48	20		7 **Free To Decide** ...A:22 / S:51	$4	▮V	Island 854802
				above 3 from the album *To The Faithful Departed* on Island 524234			

CRANE, Les
LP '71

Born on 12/3/35 in San Francisco, California. Hosted TV talk show *ABC's Nightlife* in 1964. Married to actress Tina Louise from 1966-70.

DEBUT	PEAK	WKS	Gold	A-side (Chart Hit)	B-side	$	Sym	Label & Number
10/9/71	8	12		Desiderata originally a piece of prose written in 1906 by Max Ehrmann	*A Different Drummer* [S]	$5	■	Warner 7520

CRASH TEST DUMMIES
LP '94

Pop-rock group from Winnipeg, Manitoba, Canada: brothers Brad (vocals) and Dan (bass) Roberts, with Ellen Reid (keyboards), Benjamin Darvill (harmonica) and Mitch Dorge (drums).

DEBUT	PEAK	WKS	Gold	A-side (Chart Hit)	B-side	$	Sym	Label & Number
10/5/91	56	6		1 Superman's Song	*The Voyage*	$3	■	Arista 12339
1/29/94	4	24	●	2 Mmm Mmm Mmm Mmm	MR[1] S:2 / A:15 *Superman's Song*	$3	■	Arista 12654
7/9/94	66	10		3 Afternoons & Coffeespoons above 2 co-produced by Jerry Harrison of **Talking Heads**	S:70 *Mmm Mmm Mmm Mmm (live)*	$3	■	Arista 12706

CRAWFORD, Johnny
BUB/LP '62

Born on 3/26/46 in Los Angeles, California. One of the original Mouseketeers. Played Chuck Connors' son ("Mark McCain") on TV's *The Rifleman*, 1958-63.

DEBUT	PEAK	WKS	Gold	A-side (Chart Hit)	B-side	$	Sym	Label & Number
6/12/61	70	4		1 Daydreams	*So Goes The Story*	$15	■	Del-Fi 4162
3/3/62	43	9		2 Patti Ann	*Donna*	$15		Del-Fi 4172
5/12/62	8	13		3 Cindy's Birthday	*Something Special*	$15	■	Del-Fi 4178
8/11/62	14	9		4 Your Nose Is Gonna Grow	*Mr. Blue*	$15	■	Del-Fi 4181
11/3/62	12	10		5 Rumors	*No One Really Loves A Clown*	$15	■	Del-Fi 4188
1/5/63	29	8		6 Proud	*Lonesome Town*	$15		Del-Fi 4193
9/7/63	72	7		7 Cindy's Gonna Cry	*Debbie*	$15		Del-Fi 4221
1/11/64	95	3		8 Judy Loves Me	*Living In The Past*	$15		Del-Fi 4231

CRAWFORD, Randy — see CRUSADERS / SPRINGFIELD, Rick

CRAWLER
LP '77

Rock group from England formerly known as Back Street Crawler; shortened name after death of leader Paul Kossoff (**Free**; died of drug-induced heart failure on 3/19/76). Consisted of Terry Wilson-Slesser (vocals), Geoff Whitehorn (guitar), John Bundrick (keyboards), Terry Wilson (bass) and Tony Braunagel (drums).

DEBUT	PEAK	WKS	Gold	A-side (Chart Hit)	B-side	$	Sym	Label & Number
10/15/77	65	7		Stone Cold Sober	*One Too Many Lovers*	$5		Epic 50442

CRAY, Robert, Band
ROK/LP '87

Born on 8/1/53 in Columbus, Georgia. Blues-rock guitarist/vocalist. Played bass with fictional band, Otis Day & The Knights, in the movie *Animal House*. Band formed in 1974 as backing tour group for bluesman Albert Collins. Lineup from 1986-89: Peter Boe (keyboards), Richard Cousins (bass) and David Olson (drums).

DEBUT	PEAK	WKS	Gold	A-side (Chart Hit)	B-side	$	Sym	Label & Number
2/7/87	22	14		1 Smoking Gun	S:21 / A:33 *Fantasized*	$3	■	Mercury 888343
5/16/87	80	6		2 Right Next Door (Because of Me)	*New Blood*	$3	■	Mercury 888327
9/24/88	74	6		3 Don't Be Afraid Of The Dark	*At Last*	$3	■	Mercury 870569

CRAZY ELEPHANT
BUB '69

Bubblegum studio concoction by producers Jerry **Kasenetz** and Jeff **Katz**. Robert Spencer (**The Cadillacs**) on lead vocals. Joey Levine (**Ohio Express**, **Reunion**) on backing vocals. Touring group formed later.

DEBUT	PEAK	WKS	Gold	A-side (Chart Hit)	B-side	$	Sym	Label & Number
3/1/69	12	13		Gimme Gimme Good Lovin' first released on Sphere Sound 77005 in 1968 ($20)	*Dark Part Of My Mind*	$10		Bell 763

CRAZY OTTO
LP '55

Born Fritz Schulz-Reichel on 7/4/12 in Meiningen, Germany. Died on 2/14/90 (age 77). Honky-tonk pianist. Wrote original German version of 1954 hit "The Man With The Banjo." Also see **Johnny Maddox**' 1955 hit "The Crazy Otto."

DEBUT	PEAK	WKS	Gold	A-side (Chart Hit)	B-side	$	Sym	Label & Number
3/5/55	19	5		1 Glad Rag Doll / #10 hit for Ted Lewis in 1929	S:19 [I]			
2/26/55	21	3		2 Smiles #1 hit for Joseph C. Smith's Orchestra in 1918; Decca 29403 originally released as by Happy Otto	S:21 [I]	$12		Decca 29403

CRAZY TOWN
LP '01

White rock-rap group from Los Angeles, California: Seth "Shifty Shellshock" Binzer and Bret "Epic" Mazur (vocals), DJ AM (DJ), Craig Tyler and Anthony Valli (guitars), Doug Miller (bass) and James Bradley (drums).

DEBUT	PEAK	WKS	Gold	A-side (Chart Hit)	B-side	$	Sym	Label & Number
1/6/01	❶[2]	23		Butterfly samples "Pretty Little Ditty" by the **Red Hot Chili Peppers**; "45": Columbia 79570; B-side: "Revolving Door"	MR[2] S:3 / A:4 *(4 versions)*	$8	★*V	Columbia 79549

CREAM
BUB/LP '68

All-star rock trio from England: **Eric Clapton** (guitar), Jack Bruce (bass) and **Ginger Baker** (drums). Baker and Bruce had been in Alexis Korner's Blues Inc. (**C.C.S.**) and the Graham Bond Organization. Clapton and Bruce were in **John Mayall**'s Bluesbreakers. After Cream disbanded, Clapton and Baker formed Blind Faith. Cream inducted into the Rock and Roll Hall of Fame in 1993.

DEBUT	PEAK	WKS	Gold	A-side (Chart Hit)	B-side	$	Sym	Label & Number
1/13/68	5	26	●	1 Sunshine Of Your Love originally charted for 14 weeks (#36); re-entered on 7/6/68	*SWLABR*	$10		Atco 6544
5/11/68	64	5		2 Anyone For Tennis theme from the movie *The Savage Seven* starring Robert Walker	*Pressed Rat And Warthog*	$10		Atco 6575
10/5/68	6	11		3 White Room	*Those Were The Days*	$10		Atco 6617
1/25/69	28	8		4 Crossroads written and recorded in 1936 by influential bluesman Robert Johnson as "Cross Road Blues"	*Passing The Time* [L]	$10		Atco 6646
4/5/69	60	5		5 Badge written by **George Harrison** and **Eric Clapton**; all of above produced by Felix Pappalardi	*What A Bringdown*	$10		Atco 6668

CREATIVE SOURCE
R&B/BUB/LP '74

Vocal R&B-dance group from Los Angeles, California: Don Wyatt, Celeste Rhodes, Steve Flanagan, Barbara Berryman and Barbara Lewis. Formed in 1972 by Ron Townson of **The 5th Dimension**.

DEBUT	PEAK	WKS	Gold	A-side (Chart Hit)	B-side	$	Sym	Label & Number
4/6/74	69	7		Who Is He And What Is He To You written by **Bill Withers**	*(instrumental)*	$7		Sussex 509

DEBUT	PEAK	WKS	Gold	A-side (Chart Hit)...B-side	$	Sym	Label & Number

★525★ CREED — ROK/BUB/LP '00

Rock group from Tallahassee, Florida: Scott Stapp (vocals), Mark Tremonti (guitar), Brian Marshall (bass) and Scott Phillips (drums).

DEBUT	PEAK	WKS	Gold	A-side (Chart Hit)...B-side	$	Sym	Label & Number
2/21/98	54[A]	13		1 My Own Prison			album cut
2/27/99	70	20		2 One ...A:49 above 2 from the album *My Own Prison* on Wind-Up 13049			album cut
9/11/99+	7	57		3 Higher ...AR[17] / MR[3] A:6			album cut
5/13/00	❶[1]	47		4 With Arms Wide Open ...AR[4] A:2 / S:13 *(2 versions)* above 2 from the album *Human Clay* on Wind-Up 13053	$6	★+	Wind-Up 18004
10/27/01+	4	29		5 My Sacrifice ...AR[9] A:4			album cut
6/8/02	6	34		6 One Last Breath ...A:5 from the album *Weathered* on Wind-Up 13075			album cut
11/2/02	6[S]	19		7 Don't Stop Dancing ...*(acoustic version) / With Arms Wide Open (acoustic version)* above 3 from the album *Weathered* on Wind-Up 13075	$5	★+	Wind-Up 18010

CREEDENCE CLEARWATER REVIVAL ★170★ — C&W/LP '69

Rock group formed in El Cerrito, California: **John Fogerty** (vocals, guitar; born on 5/28/45), brother Tom Fogerty (guitar; born on 11/9/41), Stu Cook (keyboards, bass; born on 4/25/45) and Doug Clifford (drums; born on 4/24/45). First recorded as the Blue Velvets for the Orchestra label in 1959. Recorded as the Golliwogs for Fantasy in 1964. Renamed Creedence Clearwater Revival in 1967. Tom Fogerty left for a solo career in 1971 and group disbanded in October 1972. Tom Fogerty died of respiratory failure on 9/6/90 (age 48). Group inducted into the Rock and Roll Hall of Fame in 1993. Also see **Don Harrison Band**.

1)Proud Mary 2)Travelin' Band 3)Green River 4)Lookin' Out My Back Door 5)Bad Moon Rising

DEBUT	PEAK	WKS	Gold	A-side (Chart Hit)...B-side	$	Sym	Label & Number
9/7/68	11	12	●	1 Suzie Q. (Part One) ...*(Part Two)*	$8		Fantasy 616
11/9/68	58	9		2 I Put A Spell On You ...*Walk On The Water* written and recorded by Screamin' Jay Hawkins (died on 2/12/2000) in 1956 on Okeh 7072 ($50)	$8		Fantasy 617
1/25/69	2[3]	14	▲	3 Proud Mary ...*Born On The Bayou*	$6		Fantasy 619
5/3/69	2[1]	14	▲	4 Bad Moon Rising /			
5/3/69	52	4		5 Lodi	$6		Fantasy 622
8/2/69	2[1]	13	●	6 Green River /			
8/2/69	30	8		7 Commotion above 4 from the album *Green River*	$6		Fantasy 625
10/25/69	3	15	▲	8 Down On The Corner /			
11/1/69	14	14		9 Fortunate Son	$6	■	Fantasy 634
1/31/70	2[2]	10	▲	10 Travelin' Band /			
1/31/70		10		11 Who'll Stop The Rain	$6	■	Fantasy 637
4/25/70	4	11	●	12 Up Around The Bend /			
4/25/70		11		13 Run Through The Jungle	$6	■	Fantasy 641
8/8/70	2[1]	13	▲	14 Lookin' Out My Back Door /			
8/8/70		13		15 Long As I Can See The Light	$6	■	Fantasy 645
1/30/71	8	10	●	16 Have You Ever Seen The Rain /			
1/30/71		5		17 Hey Tonight	$6		Fantasy 655
7/17/71	6	9	●	18 Sweet Hitch-Hiker ...*Door To Door*	$6	■	Fantasy 665
5/6/72	25	8		19 Someday Never Comes ...*Tearin' Up The Country* #3-19: written by **John Fogerty**	$6		Fantasy 676
1/31/76	43	8		20 I Heard It Through The Grapevine ...*Good Golly Miss Molly* #10-15 & 20: from the 1970 album *Cosmo's Factory*	$5	■	Fantasy 759

CRENSHAW, Marshall — ROK/BUB/LP '82

Born on 11/11/53 in Detroit, Michigan. Rockabilly singer/guitarist. Played **John Lennon** in the road show of *Beatlemania* in 1976. Appeared in the movie *Peggy Sue Got Married* and portrayed **Buddy Holly** in the 1987 movie *La Bamba*.

DEBUT	PEAK	WKS	Gold	A-side (Chart Hit)...B-side	$	Sym	Label & Number
7/10/82	36	11		Someday, Someway ...*You're My Favorite Waste Of Time* from the movie *Night Shift* starring Michael Keaton and Henry Winkler	$6		Warner 29974

CRESCENDOS, The — '58

White vocal group from Nashville, Tennessee: cousins George Lanius and James Lanius, Ken Brigham, Tom Fortner and Jim Hall.

DEBUT	PEAK	WKS	Gold	A-side (Chart Hit)...B-side	$	Sym	Label & Number
1/6/58	5	18		Oh Julie ...T:5 / S:6 / A:7 *My Little Girl* Janice Green (female vocal); picture sleeve has a center-cut hole with pictures of the group members (label shown as Nashboro)	$25	■	Nasco 6005

CRESCENTS, The — '64

Rock and roll instrumental group from Oxnard, California. Led by female guitar teacher Chiyo Ishii.

DEBUT	PEAK	WKS	Gold	A-side (Chart Hit)...B-side	$	Sym	Label & Number
12/28/63+	69	10		Pink Dominos ...*Breakout* [I] first released on Break Out 3 in 1963 (Chiyo & The Crescents - $30)	$20		Era 3116

CRESPO, Elvis — LP '98

Born on 7/30/71 in Brooklyn, New York. Latin singer/songwriter.

DEBUT	PEAK	WKS	Gold	A-side (Chart Hit)...B-side	$	Sym	Label & Number
11/21/98	84	2		Suavemente ...S:57 *(5 remixes)* regular CD single also issued (2 bonus mixes) on Sony Discos 83047	$7	★+	Sony Discos 82795

★483★ CRESTS, The — BUB '59

Interracial doo-wop group formed in Manhattan, New York: **Johnny Maestro** (see #11-13 below) (born Johnny Mastrangelo on 5/7/39; shown as Mastro on all The Crests' hits; joined as lead singer in 1956), Harold Torres, Talmadge Gough, J.T. Carter and Patricia Van Dross. Discovered by Al Browne; first recorded for Joyce in 1957. Van Dross (older sister of **Luther Vandross**) left group in 1958. Maestro left for solo work in 1960; replaced by James Ancrum. Maestro later joined **Brooklyn Bridge**.

1)16 Candles 2)Step By Step 3)Trouble In Paradise

DEBUT	PEAK	WKS	Gold	A-side (Chart Hit)...B-side	$	Sym	Label & Number
7/15/57	86	2		1 Sweetest One ...T:86 *My Juanita* **CREST'S** Al Browne (orch.); some pressings show an oversize Y in the label name ($300)	$75		Joyce 103
11/24/58+	2[2]	21		2 16 Candles ...*Beside You*	$50		Coed 506
3/23/59	28	13		3 Six Nights A Week ...*I Do*	$40		Coed 509
6/8/59	79	6		4 Flower Of Love ...*Molly Mae*	$40		Coed 511

DEBUT	PEAK	WKS	Gold	A-side (Chart Hit)...B-side	$	Sym	Label & Number
				CRESTS, The — Cont'd			
8/17/59	22	16		5 **The Angels Listened In** ... *I Thank The Moon*	$40		Coed 515
12/7/59+	42	10		6 **A Year Ago Tonight** ... *Paper Crown*	$40		Coed 521
2/29/60	14	15		7 **Step By Step** ... *Gee (But I'd Give The World)*	$35		Coed 525
6/13/60	20	13		8 **Trouble In Paradise** ... *Always You*	$35		Coed 531
				THE CRESTS featuring Johnny Mastro:			
9/12/60	81	4		9 **Journey Of Love** ... *If My Heart Could Write A Letter*	$30		Coed 535
10/24/60	100	1		10 **Isn't It Amazing** ... *Molly Mae*	$30		Coed 537
2/6/61	20	12		11 **Model Girl** ... *We've Got To Tell Them* **JOHNNY MASTRO The Voice Of The Crests**	$25		Coed 545
4/24/61	33	9		12 **What A Surprise** ... *The Warning Voice* **JOHNNY MAESTRO The Voice Of The Crests**	$25		Coed 549
7/24/61	57	5		13 **Mr. Happiness** ... *Test Of Love* **JOHNNY MAESTRO with The Coeds**	$25		Coed 552
				CRETONES, The LP **'80** Rock group from Los Angeles, California: Mark Goldenberg (vocals, guitar), Steve Leonard (keyboards), Peter Bernstein (bass) and Steve Beers (drums).			
5/3/80	79	6		**Real Love** ... *Ways Of The Heart*	$5	■	Planet 45911
	★469★			**CREW-CUTS, The** MEM/POP **'54** Pop vocal group from Toronto, Ontario, Canada: brothers John (lead; born on 8/28/31) and Ray (bass; born on 11/28/32) Perkins, Pat Barrett (tenor; born on 9/15/31), and Rudi Maugeri (baritone; born on 1/27/31). First called the Canadaires, changed name in 1954. Maugeri did vocal arrangements for the group. The group's huge #1 hit (9 weeks) in the summer of 1954, "Sh-Boom," helped to usher in the rock & roll era. Disbanded in 1963. One of the first white vocal groups to "cover" R&B hits. *1)Earth Angel 2)Ko Ko Mo (I Love You So) 3)Gum Drop*			
2/5/55	3	13		1 **Earth Angel /** A:3 / S:8 / J:8			
1/29/55	6	14		2 **Ko Ko Mo (I Love You So)** ... J:6 / S:10 / A:11 #6 R&B hit for **Gene & Eunice** in 1955	$20		Mercury 70529
4/30/55	14	8		3 **Don't Be Angry /** S:14 / A:14 / J:19			
4/30/55		8		4 **Chop Chop Boom** ... S:flip #10 R&B hit for The Danderliers in 1955	$20		Mercury 70597
6/25/55	16	7		5 **A Story Untold** ... S:16 *Carmen's Boogie* #2 R&B hit for The Nutmegs in 1955	$20		Mercury 70634
8/27/55	10	8		6 **Gum Drop** ... S:10 / A:14 / J:20 / T:80 *Song Of The Fool* recorded by the R&B group **Otis Williams & His New Group** in 1955 ($30)	$20		Mercury 70668
12/10/55+	11	18		7 **Angels In The Sky /** S:11 / T:13 / J:13 / A:16 song first recorded in 1954 by **Tony Martin** (RCA Victor 5757)			
12/24/55+	31	12		8 **Mostly Martha** ... T:31 / S:flip / J:flip based on "M'Appari" from the Flotow opera *Martha*; #2 hit for Larry Clinton in 1938	$20		Mercury 70741
2/4/56	18	11		9 **Seven Days** ... A:18 / T:20 *That's Your Mistake*	$15		Mercury 70782
6/30/56	45	5		10 **Tell Me Why** ... T:45 *Rebel In Town*	$15		Mercury 70890
1/12/57	17	12		11 **Young Love** ... A:17 / J:17 / T:24 *Little By Little* **David Carroll** (orch., all of above)	$15		Mercury 71022
				CREWE, Bob BUB/AC/LP **'67** Born on 11/12/37 in Newark, New Jersey. Wrote many hit songs beginning with "Silhouettes" in 1957. One of the top producers of the 1960s. Wrote and produced most of the hits by **The 4 Seasons**. Head of several labels, publishing and production companies. Assembled The Bob Crewe Generation, an aggregation of studio musicians.			
2/1/60	96	2		1 **The Whiffenpoof Song** ... *Let's Pretend* Ralph Burns (orch.); theme song of the Yale University Glee Club since 1909	$15		Warwick 519
				THE BOB CREWE GENERATION:			
12/31/66+	15	10		2 **Music To Watch Girls By** ... *Girls On The Rocks* [I] **Hutch Davie** (orch.); tune used in a Diet Pepsi commercial	$8		DynoVoice 229
10/28/67	89	2		3 **Birds Of Britain** ... *I Will Wait For You* [I]	$7		DynoVoice 902
3/6/76	56	6		4 **Street Talk** *[B.C.G. (B.C. Generation)]* ... *(Var. II)* [I]	$5		20th Century 2271
				CRICKETS, The — see HOLLY, Buddy / VEE, Bobby			
				CRIMEWAVE **'01** Rap group from Brooklyn, New York: Shamus, Flu, Karachi-Raw, Skar and Maximillan.			
4/21/01	54^S	5		1 **What Side You On** ... *(2 versions) / Street Smart "50 Bars" / Dan-Sin Teardrops* **CRIMEWAVE Featuring Shamus, Flu, Karachi-Raw, Skar & Maximillan**	$8	★*	CrimeWave 2001
10/20/01+	27^S	20		2 **Think Big** ... *(2 versions) / Certified Killaz*	$8	★*	CrimeWave 2002
				CRITTERS, The BUB/LP **'66** Pop group from Plainfield, New Jersey: Don Ciccone (vocals, guitar), Jimmy Ryan (guitar), Chris Darway (organ), Kenny Gorka (bass) and Jack Decker (drums). Ciccone later joined **The 4 Seasons**.			
5/28/66	42	9		1 **Younger Girl** ... *Gone For Awhile* first recorded by **The Lovin' Spoonful** on their 1965 debut album	$12		Kapp 752
8/13/66	17	11		2 **Mr. Dieingly Sad** ... *It Just Won't Be That Way* picture sleeve issued with either a full-color picture on front or with a white title strip across top of picture	$12	■	Kapp 769
12/3/66	55	6		3 **Bad Misunderstanding** ... *Forever Or No More*	$10		Kapp 793
7/8/67	39	8		4 **Don't Let The Rain Fall Down On Me** ... *Walk Like A Man Again*	$10		Kapp 838
	★412★			**CROCE, Jim** BUB/LP **'73** Born on 1/10/43 in Philadelphia, Pennsylvania. Killed in a plane crash on 9/20/73 (age 30) in Natchitoches, Louisiana. Singer/songwriter/guitarist. Recorded with wife Ingrid for Capitol in 1968. Lead guitarist on his hits, Maury Muehleisen, was killed in the same crash. *1)Bad, Bad Leroy Brown 2)Time In A Bottle 3)You Don't Mess Around With Jim*			
7/1/72	8	13		1 **You Don't Mess Around With Jim** ... *Photographs And Memories*	$6		ABC 11328
10/14/72	17	12		2 **Operator (That's Not the Way it Feels)** ... *Rapid Roy (The Stock Car Boy)*	$6		ABC 11335
2/3/73	37	10		3 **One Less Set Of Footsteps** ... *It Doesn't Have To Be That Way*	$6		ABC 11346

DEBUT	PEAK	WKS	Gold	A-side (Chart Hit)...B-side	$	Sym	Label & Number
				CROCE, Jim — Cont'd			
4/21/73	1[2]	22	●	4 **Bad, Bad Leroy Brown** *A Good Time Man Like Me Ain't Got No Business (Singin' the Blues)*	$6		ABC 11359
10/6/73	10	17		5 **I Got A Name** ... *Alabama Rain*	$6		ABC 11389
				from the movie *The Last American Hero* starring Jeff Bridges			
11/17/73	1[2]	15	●	6 **Time In A Bottle** ... AC[2] *Hard Time Losin' Man*	$6		ABC 11405
12/29/73	64	5		7 **It Doesn't Have To Be That Way** ... *Roller Derby Queen* [X]	$6	■	ABC 11413
				picture sleeve shows tune as "His Christmas Love Song"; also released as the B-side of #3 above			
3/2/74	9	14		8 **I'll Have To Say I Love You In A Song** ... AC[1] *Salon And Saloon*	$6		ABC 11424
6/8/74	32	11		9 **Workin' At The Car Wash Blues** ... *Thursday*	$6		ABC 11447
				also released on ABC 12015 in 1974; all of above (except #5) written by Croce			
1/3/76	63	9		10 **Chain Gang Medley** ... *Stone Walls*	$5		Lifesong 45001
				Chain Gang/He Don't Love You/Searchin'; all of above produced by **Terry Cashman & Tommy West**			
				CROCHET, Cleveland, and Band '61			
				Born on 6/6/21 in Hathaway, Louisiana. White fiddle player with his cajun band, the Hillbilly Ramblers.			
12/31/60+	80	5		**Sugar Bee** ... *Drunkard's Dream*	$20		Goldband 1106
				Jesse "Jay" Stutes (vocal)			
				CROCKETT, G.L. '65			
				Born George Crockett on 9/18/28 in Carrollton, Mississippi. Died on 2/15/67 (age 38). Blues singer.			
8/7/65	67	6		**It's A Man Down There** ... *Every Hour, Every Day*	$15		4 Brothers 445
				CROOKLYN DODGERS, The '94			
				Rap group from Brooklyn, New York. Created by director Spike Lee for his movies *Crooklyn* and *Clockers*.			
5/21/94	60	12		1 **Crooklyn** ... S:32 *(instrumental)*	$4	▌	MCA 54837
				THE CROOKLYN DODGERS featuring Special Ed, Buckshot and Masta Ace			
				title song from the Spike Lee movie starring Alfre Woodard; produced by **A Tribe Called Quest**; samples "The Place Where We Dwell" by **Gang Starr** and "Who Got The Props" by **Black Moon**; contains Bob Wolff's broadcast of Jackie Robinson's game-winning base hit during the 1956 World Series			
9/16/95	96	2		2 **Return Of The Crooklyn Dodgers** ... S:70 *(instrumental)*	$5	▌	MCA 55114
				CROOKLYN DODGERS '95			
				from the Spike Lee movie *Clockers* starring Harvey Keitel			
	★342★			**CROSBY, Bing** MEM/POP/AC/C&W/BUB/R&B/LP '44			
				One of the most popular entertainers of the 20th century. Born Harry Lillis Crosby on 5/3/03 in Tacoma, Washington. Died of a heart attack on 10/14/77 (age 74) on a golf course near Madrid, Spain. Bing and singing partner Al Rinker were hired in 1926 by Paul Whiteman; with Harry Barris they became the Rhythm Boys and gained an increasing following. The trio split from Whiteman in 1930, and Bing sang briefly with Gus Arnheim's band. It was his early-1931 smash with Arnheim, "I Surrender, Dear," which earned Bing a CBS radio contract and launched an unsurpassed solo career. Over the next three decades the resonant Crosby baritone and breezy persona sold more than 300 million records and was featured in over 50 movies (won Academy Award for *Going My Way*, 1944). Won Grammy's Lifetime Achievement Award in 1962. Ranked as the #1 artist in three of Joel Whitburn's books: *Pop Memories 1890-1954* (340 hits, 1931-54), *Pop Hits 1940-1954* (135 hits, 1940-54) and *A Century Of Pop Music*. Married to actress Dixie Lee from 1930 until her death in 1952; their son Gary (died on 8/24/95, age 62) began recording in 1950. Married to actress Kathryn Grant from 1957 until his death; their daughter Mary became an actress. Bing's youngest brother, Bob Crosby (died on 3/9/93, age 80), was a popular swing-era bandleader. Besides "White Christmas," Bing's biggest 2 hits were each #1 for 10 weeks: "Pennies From Heaven" in 1936 and "Sweet Leilani" in 1937.			
				1)True Love 2)White Christmas 3)Around The World 4)Adeste Fideles 5)In A Little Spanish Town			
12/25/54	13	3	●	1 **White Christmas** ... A:13 / J:19 / S:21 *God Rest Ye Merry Gentlemen* [X-R]	$10		Decca 23778
				with the Ken Darby Singers and John Scott Trotter's Orchestra; original version hit #1 in October 1942; new version recorded in 1947; made pop charts for 20 Christmas seasons			
12/24/55	7	3		2 **White Christmas** ... A:7 / T:18 *God Rest Ye Merry Gentlemen* [X-R]	$10		Decca 23778
4/7/56	49	7		3 **In A Little Spanish Town ('Twas On A Night Like This)** ... T:49 *Ol' Man River*	$15		Decca 29850
				BING CROSBY And The BUDDY COLE TRIO (pianist Cole was Crosby's orchestra leader; died on 11/5/64, age 47)			
				#1 hit for Paul Whiteman in 1927			
9/8/56	3	31	●	4 **True Love** / A:3 / T:4 / S:5 / J:6			
				BING CROSBY and GRACE KELLY (famed American actress and Princess of Monaco; died on 9/14/82 in an auto accident, age 52)			
9/22/56	92	2		5 **Well Did You Evah?** ... T:92 [N]	$20		Capitol 3507
				BING CROSBY and FRANK SINATRA			
				originally from the 1939 Cole Porter Broadway musical *DuBarry Was A Lady* starring Ethel Merman			
10/13/56	88	4		6 **Now You Has Jazz** ... T:88 *High Society Calypso* (Armstrong) [N]	$20		Capitol 3506
				BING CROSBY and LOUIS ARMSTRONG			
				Johnny Green (MGM Studio Orch., above 3); above 3 from the movie *High Society* starring Crosby and Sinatra			
12/29/56	65	1		7 **White Christmas** ... T:65 *God Rest Ye Merry Gentlemen* [X-R]	$10	■	Decca 23778
5/20/57	25	31		8 **Around The World** ... S:25 / T:54 *(Main Theme) Around The World* (**Victor Young** - #13)	$12	■	Decca 30262
				Buddy Cole (orch.); from the movie *Around The World In 80 Days* starring David Niven; first released on Decca 30120 in 1956			
12/16/57	34	6		9 **White Christmas** ... T:34 / S:36 *God Rest Ye Merry Gentlemen* [X-R]	$10		Decca 23778
12/30/57	54	3		10 **Silent Night** ... T:54 *Adeste Fideles* [X-R]	$10		Decca 23777
				first recorded by Crosby with Paul Whiteman's orchestra in 1928; Crosby's first solo version recorded and charted in 1935; re-recorded in 1942, and above version recorded in 1947			
12/30/57	78	2		11 **Silver Bells** ... X:22 / T:78 *That Christmas Feeling* [X]	$12		Decca 27229
				BING CROSBY AND CAROL RICHARDS			
				from the movie *The Lemon Drop Kid* starring Bob Hope; recorded and first released by Crosby & Richards in 1950; Christmas charts: #22/'66 (2 weeks)			
12/30/57	97	1		12 **How Lovely Is Christmas** ... T:97 *My Own Individual Star* [X]	$15	■	Kapp 196
				Arthur Norman (choir and orch.)			
12/22/58	66	2		13 **White Christmas** ... *God Rest Ye Merry Gentlemen* [X-R]	$10		Decca 23778
12/28/59	59	1		14 **White Christmas** ... *God Rest Ye Merry Gentlemen* [X-R]	$10	■	Decca 23778
				all '50s Decca records have black labels; '60s have multi-colored labels; first "White Christmas" picture sleeve was issued in 1959			
12/12/60	26	3		15 **White Christmas** ... *God Rest Ye Merry Gentlemen* [X-R]	$8	■	Decca 23778
12/12/60	45	3		16 **Adeste Fideles (Oh, Come, All Ye Faithful)** / [X]			
				above version recorded by Crosby in 1942 (previously uncharted)			
12/19/60	54	2		17 **Silent Night** ... X:13 [X-R]	$8	■	Decca 23777
				John Scott Trotter (orch.) and Max Terr's Mixed Chorus (above 2); Christmas charts: [#13-9 weeks] 13/'65; 13/'66; 19/'67; 15/'70			
12/11/61	12	4		18 **White Christmas** ... *God Rest Ye Merry Gentlemen* [X-R]	$8	■	Decca 23778

DEBUT	PEAK	WKS	Gold	A-side (Chart Hit)....................B-side	$	Sym	Label & Number
				CROSBY, Bing — Cont'd			
12/15/62	38	3		19 **White Christmas**..........X:❷[2] *God Rest Ye Merry Gentlemen* [X-R]	$8	■	Decca 23778
				Christmas charts: [#1[2]-36 weeks] 3/'63; 3/'64; 3/'65; 3/'66; 2/'67; 3/'68; 1/'69; 5/'70; 5/'72; 8/'73; 1/'83; 2/'84; 2/'85 (reissued in 1980 on MCA 65022); all are the same 1947 version			
12/14/63	2^{1X}	5		20 **Do You Hear What I Hear?**..........*Christmas Dinner Country Style* [X]	$10		Capitol 5088
				X: 2/'63; 12/'64; 15/'65; Ralph Carmichael (chorus and orch.)			
<u>12/25/65</u>	20^{X}	1		21 **The White World Of Winter**..........*The Secret Of Christmas* (w/Fred Waring) [X]	$10		Reprise 0424
				Sonny Burke (orch.)			
12/23/00	58^{S}	3		22 **Peace On Earth/Little Drummer Boy**..........*(no B-side)* [X]	$10	★[+]	Oglio 85001
				originally performed on the 1977 TV Christmas special *Bing Crosby's Merrie Olde Christmas*; "45" issued in 1982 on RCA 13400 with a picture sleeve; the CD single contains an additional 1:45 of dialogue			
12/29/01	75^{S}	1		23 **Peace On Earth/Little Drummer Boy**..........*(no B-side)* [X-R]	$10	★[+]	Oglio 85001
12/21/02	43^{S}	4		24 **Peace On Earth/Little Drummer Boy**..........*(no B-side)* [X-R]	$10	★[+]	Oglio 85001
				DAVID BOWIE & BING CROSBY (above 3)			
				CROSBY, Chris BUB **'64**			
				Nephew of **Bing Crosby**. Son of the late bandleader Bob Crosby.			
2/15/64	53	7		**Young And In Love**..........*Raindrops In My Heart*	$10		MGM 13191
				from the TV series *Dr. Kildare* starring **Richard Chamberlain**			
				CROSBY, David BUB/ROK/LP **'72**			
				Born on 8/14/41 in Los Angeles, California. Singer/guitarist with **The Byrds** from 1964-68 and later **Crosby, Stills & Nash**. Son of cinematographer Floyd Crosby (*High Noon*). Frequent troubles with the law due to drug charges. Movie cameos in *Backdraft*, *Hook* and *Thunderheart*; appeared on TV's *Roseanne*. Underwent a successful liver transplant on 11/19/94. In early 2000, it was announced that he was the biological father (via artificial insemination) of two children for the couple of **Melissa Etheridge** and Julie Cypher. Also see **Hootie & The Blowfish**'s "Hold My Hand."			
5/1/71	95	1		1 **Music Is Love**..........*Laughing*	$6		Atlantic 2792
				Graham Nash and **Neil Young** (backing vocals)			
				GRAHAM NASH & DAVID CROSBY:			
5/6/72	36	9		2 **Immigration Man**..........*Whole Cloth*	$6		Atlantic 2873
8/12/72	99	2		3 **Southbound Train**..........*The Wall Song*	$6		Atlantic 2892
11/15/75	52	6		4 **Carry Me**..........*Mama Lion*	$5		ABC 12140
<u>8/7/76</u>	89	3		5 **Out Of The Darkness**..........*Broken Bird*	$5		ABC 12199
5/8/93	44	20		6 **Hero**..........A:31 / S:47 *Coverage* (Crosby)	$4	▮[V]	Atlantic 87360
				DAVID CROSBY & PHIL COLLINS			
	★391★			**CROSBY, STILLS & NASH** ROK/AC/C&W/LP **'70**			
				Folk-rock trio formed in Laurel Canyon, California. Consisted of **David Crosby** (guitar; born on 8/14/41), **Stephen Stills** (guitar, keyboards, bass; born on 1/3/45) and **Graham Nash** (guitar; born on 2/2/42). Crosby had been in **The Byrds**, Stills had been in **Buffalo Springfield**, and Nash was with **The Hollies**. Won the 1969 Best New Artist Grammy Award. **Neil Young** (guitar; born on 11/12/45), formerly with Buffalo Springfield, joined group in 1970; left in 1974. Reunion in 1988. Trio inducted into the Rock and Roll Hall of Fame in 1997. Crosby, Stills, Nash & Young reunited for a tour and album in 2000.			
				1)Just A Song Before I Go 2)Wasted On The Way 3)Woodstock			
				CROSBY, STILLS & NASH:			
7/19/69	28	8		1 **Marrakesh Express**..........*Helplessly Hoping*	$7		Atlantic 2652
10/4/69	21	12		2 **Suite: Judy Blue Eyes**..........*Long Time Gone*	$7		Atlantic 2676
				written by **Stephen Stills** for **Judy Collins**			
				CROSBY, STILLS, NASH & YOUNG:			
3/28/70	11	11		3 **Woodstock**..........*Helpless*	$7		Atlantic 2723
				written by **Joni Mitchell** about the legendary 1969 rock festival			
6/6/70	16	11		4 **Teach Your Children**..........*Carry On*	$7		Atlantic 2735
				Jerry Garcia (of **Grateful Dead**; steel guitar)			
6/27/70	14	9		5 **Ohio**..........*Find The Cost Of Freedom*	$7	■	Atlantic 2740
				written by **Neil Young** after 4 students were killed at Kent State by National Guardsmen during an antiwar demonstration on 5/4/70			
<u>9/19/70</u>	30	9		6 **Our House**..........*Deja Vu*	$7		Atlantic 2760
				CROSBY, STILLS & NASH:			
5/28/77	7	21		7 **Just A Song Before I Go**..........*Dark Star*	$5	■	Atlantic 3401
<u>10/1/77</u>	43	9		8 **Fair Game**..........*Anything At All*	$5		Atlantic 3432
6/26/82	9	15		9 **Wasted On The Way**..........*Delta*	$4	■	Atlantic 4058
				with **Timothy B. Schmit**			
9/18/82	18	17		10 **Southern Cross**..........*Into The Darkness*	$4	■	Atlantic 89969
1/29/83	69	6		11 **Too Much Love To Hide**..........*Song For Susan*	$4		Atlantic 89888
<u>6/25/83</u>	45	9		12 **War Games**..........*Shadow Captain*	$4	■	Atlantic 89812
2/4/89	69	8		13 **Got It Made**..........AR[2] *This Old House* (C&W #92)	$4	■	Atlantic 88966
				CROSBY, STILLS, NASH & YOUNG			
	★355★			**CROSS, Christopher** AC/LP **'80**			
				Born Christopher Geppert on 5/3/51 in San Antonio, Texas. Pop-rock singer/songwriter/guitarist. Formed own group with Rob Meurer (keyboards), Andy Salmon (bass) and Tommy Taylor (drums) in 1973. Won the 1980 Best New Artist Grammy Award.			
				1)Arthur's Theme (Best That You Can Do) 2)Sailing 3)Ride Like The Wind			
2/16/80	2^{4}	21		1 **Ride Like The Wind**..........*Minstrel Gigolo*	$4		Warner 49184
				Michael McDonald (backing vocal)			
6/14/80	❶[1]	21		2 **Sailing**..........*Poor Shirley*	$4		Warner 49507
				1980 Grammy winner: Record of the Year			
10/11/80	15	19		3 **Never Be The Same**..........AC[2] *The Light Is On*	$4		Warner 49580
3/28/81	20	14		4 **Say You'll Be Mine**..........*Spinning*	$4		Warner 49705
				Nicolette Larson (backing vocal); above 4 from the album *Christopher Cross*			
8/15/81	❶[3]	24	●	5 **Arthur's Theme (Best That You Can Do)**..........AC[4] *Minstrel Gigolo*	$4	■	Warner 49787
				from the movie *Arthur* starring Dudley Moore			
1/22/83	12	16		6 **All Right**..........*Long World*	$4	■	Warner 29843
5/7/83	33	10		7 **No Time For Talk**..........*Words Of Wisdom*	$4		Warner 29662
12/10/83+	9	17		8 **Think Of Laura**..........AC[4] *Words Of Wisdom*	$4		Warner 29658
				popularized through play on TV's *General Hospital*			

DEBUT	PEAK	WKS	Gold	A-side (Chart Hit)...B-side	$	Sym	Label & Number
				CROSS, Christopher — Cont'd			
6/16/84	76	5		9 **A Chance For Heaven**...*Talking In My Sleep* swimming theme from the Official Music of the XXIIIrd Olympiad Los Angeles 1984	$3	■	Columbia 04492
10/26/85	68	5		10 **Charm The Snake**...*Open Your Heart* all of above written by Cross and produced by Michael Omartian	$3	■	Warner 28864
				CROSS, Jimmy '65 Born on 11/17/38 in Philadelphia, Pennsylvania. Died of a heart attack on 10/8/78 (age 39). Produced the syndicated radio series *Country Concert*.			
1/30/65	92	3		**I Want My Baby Back**...*Play The Other Side* [I] [N]	$20		Tollie 9039
				CROSS COUNTRY — see TOKENS, The			
				CROW BUB/LP '70 Rock-blues group from Minneapolis, Minnesota: Dave Waggoner (vocals), Dick Weigand (guitar), Kink Middlemist (organ), Larry Weigand (bass) and Denny Craswell (drums; **The Castaways**).			
10/25/69+	19	15		1 **Evil Woman Don't Play Your Games With Me**...*Gonna Leave A Mark*	$8		Amaret 112
5/16/70	56	14		2 **Cottage Cheese**...*Slow Down* (#103)	$8		Amaret 119
10/24/70	52	9		3 **Don't Try To Lay No Boogie Woogie On The "King Of Rock & Roll"**...*Satisfied*	$8		Amaret 125
	★361★			**CROW, Sheryl** LP '94 Born on 2/11/62 in Kennett, Missouri. Adult Alternative rock singer/songwriter/guitarist. After attending the University of Missouri, worked as a grade school music teacher, until moving to Los Angeles in 1986. Worked as backing singer for **Michael Jackson**, **Don Henley**, **George Harrison** and others. Crow's compositions covered by **Eric Clapton** and **Wynonna Judd**. Won the 1994 Best New Artist Grammy Award. *1)All I Wanna Do 2)Strong Enough 3)If It Makes You Happy*			
4/23/94	60	10		1 **Leaving Las Vegas**...A:60 *The Na-Na Song*	$4	▮V	A&M 0582
8/6/94	2^{6}	33	●	2 **All I Wanna Do** AC^{8} A:2 / S:7 *Solidify* 1994 Grammy winner: Record of the Year; "45" issued for above 2 on A&M 0836	$3	▮V	A&M 0702
12/31/94+	5	26		3 **Strong Enough**...A:2 / S:11 *What I Can Do For You* "45": A&M 0932; B-side: "Run, Baby, Run"	$3	▮V	A&M 0798
7/8/95	36	18		4 **Can't Cry Anymore**...A:30 / S:69 *We Do What We Can* all of above from the album *Tuesday Night Music Club*	$3	▮V	A&M 0638
9/21/96+	10	27		5 **If It Makes You Happy**...A:7 / S:17 *Keep On Growing* "45" B-side: "I'm Going To Be A Wheel Someday"	$3	▮V	A&M 1874
3/29/97	11	20		6 **Everyday Is A Winding Road**...A:6 / S:27 *Sad Sad World*	$3	▮V	A&M 2032
5/24/97	19^{A}	20		7 **A Change Would Do You Good**... above 3 from the album *Sheryl Crow* on A&M 0587			album cut
9/5/98	9^{A}	23		8 **My Favorite Mistake**...HOT:20(10 wks) "45": A&M 2776; B-side: "There Goes The Neighborhood"		V	album cut
4/10/99	49	13		9 **Anything But Down**...A:41 "45": A&M 0867; B-side: "The Difficult Kind"; above 2 from the album *The Globe Sessions* on A&M 540959		V	album cut
4/13/02	17	29		10 **Soak Up The Sun**...A:18			album cut
9/14/02	88	5		11 **Steve McQueen**...*If It Makes You Happy (live)* above 2 from the album *C'mon, C'mon* on A&M 493260; all of above written by Crow	$5	★	A&M 497762
11/30/02+	4	34	●	12 **Picture**...S:❶^{12} / A:6 *(2 versions)* **KID ROCK Featuring ALLISON MOORER or SHERYL CROW** commercial single features Moorer; the vast majority of radio stations played the original album version featuring Crow	$4	★	Universal South 172274
				CROWDED HOUSE ROK/BUB/LP '87 Pop trio from New Zealand: Neil Finn (vocals, guitar, piano), Nick Seymour (bass) and Paul Hester (drums). Finn and Hester were former members of **Split Enz**.			
1/17/87	2^{1}	24		1 **Don't Dream It's Over** S:2 / A:2 *That's What I Call Love*	$3	■	Capitol 5614
5/2/87	7	21		2 **Something So Strong**...S:7 / A:7 *I Walk Away*	$3	■	Capitol 5695
8/8/87	65	8		3 **World Where You Live**...*Hole In The River*	$3	■	Capitol 44033
7/9/88	42	11		4 **Better Be Home Soon**...S:32 *Kill Eye*	$3	■	Capitol 44164
10/19/91	75	6		5 **Fall At Your Feet**...*Whispers And Moans* all of above written by Neil Finn	$3	▮	Capitol 44747
				CROWELL, Rodney C&W/BUB/LP '80 Born on 8/7/50 in Houston, Texas. Country singer/songwriter/guitarist. Married to **Rosanne Cash** from 1979-92. Wrote the **Dirt Band**'s "American Dream" and many other Country hits. Charted 23 Country hits, 1978-95.			
5/10/80	37	11		**Ashes By Now**...*Blues In The Daytime*	$5		Warner 49224
				CROWN HEIGHTS AFFAIR R&B/BUB/LP '76 R&B-disco group from New York City, New York: Phil Thomas (vocals), William Anderson (guitar), Howard Young (keyboards), Bert Reid, James Baynard and Raymond Reid (horn section), Muki Wilson (bass), and Raymond Rock (drums).			
8/16/75	43	13		1 **Dreaming A Dream**...*(disco version)*	$5		De-Lite 1570
12/6/75+	83	8		2 **Every Beat Of My Heart**...*(new disco version)*	$5		De-Lite 1575
5/22/76	49	12		3 **Foxy Lady**...*Picture Show* [I]	$5		De-Lite 1581
2/19/77	42	13		4 **Dancin'**...*Love Me*	$5		De-Lite 1588
				CRU LP '97 Rap trio from Brooklyn, New York: Chadio, Yogi and Mighty Ha.			
7/5/97	68	8		**Just Another Case**...S:58 *(remix) / Pronto* **CRU Featuring Slick Rick** samples "Mona Lisa" by **Slick Rick**, "The World Is A Place" by Rhythm and "Everybody Plays The Fool" by **The Main Ingredient**	$4	▮	Violator 573856
				CRUCIAL CONFLICT R&B/LP '96 Hip-hop group from Chicago, Illinois: Corey Johnson, Marrico King, Ralph Levertson and Wondosas Martin.			
5/11/96	18	20	●	**Hay**...S:6 *(2 versions) / Showdown*	$4	▮	Pallas/Universal 56008
				CRUISE, Erin '92 Born in Chicago, Illinois. Female dance singer.			
1/25/92	90	7		**Cold Shower**...A:75 *(2 remixes)*	$5	▮	Critique 15479

DEBUT	PEAK	WKS	Gold	A-side (Chart Hit)	B-side	$	Sym	Label & Number

CRUSADERS, The — R&B/BUB/AC/LP '79

Instrumental jazz-oriented group formed in Houston, Texas, as the Swingsters, in the early 1950s. To California in the early 1960s, name changed to **The Jazz Crusaders**. Became The Crusaders in 1971. Included Joe Sample (keyboards), Wilton Felder (reeds), Nesbert "Stix" Hooper (drums) and Wayne Henderson (trombone; left in 1975). **Larry Carlton** was a frequent guest guitarist from 1972-77.

DEBUT	PEAK	WKS	Gold	A-side (Chart Hit)	B-side	$	Sym	Label & Number
4/2/66	95	1		1 **Uptight (Everything's Alright)**	*Scratch* [I]	$8		Pacific Jazz 88125
12/26/70+	90	3		2 **Way Back Home**	*Jackson!* [I]	$7		Chisa 8010
				THE JAZZ CRUSADERS (above 2)				
7/15/72	52	9		3 **Put It Where You Want It**	*Mosadi (Woman)* [I]	$6		Blue Thumb 208
5/12/73	86	5		4 **Don't Let It Get You Down**	*Journey From Within* [I]	$5		Blue Thumb 225
4/27/74	81	6		5 **Scratch**	*Way Back Home* [I]	$5		Blue Thumb 249
8/25/79	36	16		6 **Street Life**	*The Hustler*	$4		MCA 41054
				Randy Crawford (vocal)				
9/26/81	97	3		7 **I'm So Glad I'm Standing Here Today**	*Standing Tall* (Crusaders)	$4		MCA 51177
				CRUSADERS Guest Artist: JOE COCKER				

CRUSH — '96

Female pop-rock vocal duo from England: Donna Air and Jayni Hoy.

DEBUT	PEAK	WKS	Gold	A-side (Chart Hit)	B-side	$	Sym	Label & Number
8/17/96	72	21		**Jellyhead**	A:74 *(7" edit)*	$5	▮	Robbins 72002

CRYAN' SHAMES, The — BUB/LP '66

Pop-rock group from Chicago, Illinois: Tom Doody (vocals), Jim Fairs and Jerry Stone (guitars), Jim Pilster (tambourine), Dave Purple (bass) and Dennis Conroy (drums).

DEBUT	PEAK	WKS	Gold	A-side (Chart Hit)	B-side	$	Sym	Label & Number
7/23/66	49	9		1 **Sugar And Spice**	*Ben Franklin's Almanac*	$15		Destination 624
11/26/66	85	4		2 **I Wanna Meet You**	*We Could Be Happy*	$10		Columbia 43836
8/5/67	85	8		3 **It Could Be We're In Love**	*I Was Lonely When*	$10	■	Columbia 44191
4/6/68	85	3		4 **Up On The Roof**	*The Sailing Ship*	$10		Columbia 44457
6/22/68	99	2		5 **Young Birds Fly**	*Sunshine Psalm*	$10		Columbia 44545
				written by **Oliver**				

CRYSTAL, Billy — LP '85

Born on 3/14/47 in Long Beach, Long Island, New York. Actor/comedian. Cast member of TV's *Soap*, 1977-81, and a regular on *Saturday Night Live*, 1984-85. Star of the movies *Throw Momma From The Train*, *City Slickers I & II*, *When Harry Met Sally* and others.

DEBUT	PEAK	WKS	Gold	A-side (Chart Hit)	B-side	$	Sym	Label & Number
7/27/85	58	12		**You Look Marvelous**	*(dub version)* [N]	$4	■	A&M 2764
				humorous impersonation of Fernando Lamas (died on 10/9/82); written by Crystal and **Paul Shaffer**				

CRYSTAL MANSION — '70

Pop group: **Johnny Caswell** (see #1 below) (vocals), Ron Gentile (guitar), Sam Rota (keyboards), Jerry Marlow (bass) and Rick Morley (drums).

DEBUT	PEAK	WKS	Gold	A-side (Chart Hit)	B-side	$	Sym	Label & Number
8/3/63	97	1		1 **At The Shore**	*Gotta Dance*	$12		Smash 1833
				JOHNNY CASWELL				
12/21/68+	84	5		2 **The Thought Of Loving You**	*Hallelujah*	$6		Capitol 2275
11/7/70	73	6		3 **Carolina In My Mind**	*If I Live*	$6		Colossus 128

CRYSTALS, The — LP '62

R&B-rock and roll "girl group" from Brooklyn, New York: Barbara Alston, Dee Dee Kennibrew, Mary Thomas, Patricia Wright and Myrna Gerrard. La La Brooks replaced Gerrard in 1962. Thomas left in 1962. Wright was replaced by Frances Collins in 1964. Alston died of a heart attack on 5/15/92 (age 48). The Crystals and **The Ronettes** were producer Phil Spector's most successful 1960s "girl groups."

DEBUT	PEAK	WKS	Gold	A-side (Chart Hit)	B-side	$	Sym	Label & Number
11/20/61+	20	11		1 **There's No Other (Like My Baby)**	*Oh Yeah, Maybe Baby*	$40		Philles 100
3/31/62	13	13		2 **Uptown**	*What A Nice Way To Turn Seventeen*	$40		Philles 102
				Barbara Alston (lead vocal, above 2)				
9/8/62	❶[2]	18		3 **He's A Rebel**	*I Love You Eddie*	$40		Philles 106
				written by **Gene Pitney**				
12/29/62+	11	12		4 **He's Sure The Boy I Love**	*Walkin' Along (La La La)*	$30		Philles 109
				Darlene Love (lead vocal); above 2 actually recorded by **The Blossoms**				
4/27/63	3	13		5 **Da Doo Ron Ron (When He Walked Me Home)**	*Git' It*	$30		Philles 112
8/17/63	6	12		6 **Then He Kissed Me**	*Brother Julius*	$30		Philles 115
2/1/64	92	3		7 **Little Boy**	*Harry (From W. Va.) & Milt*	$30		Philles 119
8/1/64	98	1		8 **All Grown Up**	*Irving (Jaggered Sixteenths)*	$30		Philles 122
				La La Brooks (lead vocal, above 4); all of above produced by Phil Spector				

C.3.O — '02

Born Cameron Stevens in Dayton, Ohio. Male rapper.

DEBUT	PEAK	WKS	Gold	A-side (Chart Hit)	B-side	$	Sym	Label & Number
7/13/02	32[S]	9		**Bigger Than Life**	*(album version) / Bounce Baby*	$10	★	Mama's Boy 2000

CUBA, Joe, Sextet — R&B/BUB/LP '66

Born Gilberto Calderon in Harlem, New York. Latin conga player. Other members of his sextet: Jose "Cheo" Feliciano (vocals, not to be confused with the solo star), Tommy Berrios (vibes), Nick Jimenez (piano), Jules Cordero (bass) and Jimmy Sabater (drums).

DEBUT	PEAK	WKS	Gold	A-side (Chart Hit)	B-side	$	Sym	Label & Number
10/22/66	63	8		1 **"Bang" "Bang"**	*Push, Push, Push* [F]	$7		Tico 475
1/7/67	62	5		2 **Oh Yeah!**	*Sock It To Me*	$7		Tico 490

CUBAN LINK — R&B '00

Born Felix Delgado on 12/18/74 in Cuba; raised in Brooklyn, New York. Male rapper.

DEBUT	PEAK	WKS	Gold	A-side (Chart Hit)	B-side	$	Sym	Label & Number
6/24/00	18[S]	17		**Flowers For The Dead**	*(instrumental)*	$5	★	Atlantic 84685
				tribute to **Big Punisher** (died on 2/7/2000); samples "Nadia's Theme" by **Barry DeVorzon & Perry Botkin Jr.**				

CUES, The — '57

R&B vocal group from Brooklyn, New York: Jimmy Breedlove, Ollie Jones and Abel DeCosta (tenors), Robie Kirk ("Winfield Scott"; baritone) and Eddie Barnes (bass). Backing vocal group for many artists on Atlantic Records.

DEBUT	PEAK	WKS	Gold	A-side (Chart Hit)	B-side	$	Sym	Label & Number
11/19/55	86	1		1 **Burn That Candle**	T:86 *Oh My Darlin'*	$40		Capitol 3245
1/19/57	77	1		2 **Why**	T:77 *Prince Or Pauper*	$40		Capitol 3582

DEBUT	PEAK	WKS	Gold	A-side (Chart Hit)...B-side	$	Sym	Label & Number
				CUEVAS, Chris '92			
				Born on 2/8/73 in Long Beach, Mississippi. White male pop singer. Junior Vocalist winner on TV's *Star Search.*			
2/1/92	58	11		**You Are The One**...S:59 / A:68 *Give Our Love A Chance*	$3	▮	Atlantic 87563
				CUFF LINKS, The AC/LP '69			
				Group is actually the overdubbed voice of pop singer Ron Dante (**The Archies**).			
9/13/69	9	12		1 **Tracy**...*Where Do You Go?*	$6	□	Decca 32533
12/13/69+	41	9		2 **When Julie Comes Around**...*Sally Ann (You're Such A Pretty Baby)*	$6		Decca 32592
3/7/70	76	6		3 **Run Sally Run**...*I Remember*	$6		Decca 32639
				CUGINI '80			
				Born Donald Cugini on 5/7/59 in Los Angeles, California. Pop singer/songwriter.			
12/22/79+	88	4		**Let Me Sleep Alone**...*You Give Good Boogie*	$4		Scotti Brothers 503
				CULT, The ROK/BUB/LP '89			
				Rock group from England. Nucleus of evercharging lineup included Ian Astbury (vocals; born Ian Lindsay), Billy Duffy (guitar), Jamie Stewart (bass) and Les Warner (drums). Warner left in 1988; replaced by Matt Sorum (**Guns N' Roses**).			
5/27/89	46	11		1 **Fire Woman**...*Automatic Blues*	$4	■	Sire 27543
9/30/89	93	4		2 **Edie (Ciao Baby)**...*Love Removal Machine (live)*	$4		Sire 22873
				CULTURE BEAT BUB '94			
				Dance group assembled by Germans Torsten Fenslau (DJ/producer; died in a car accident on 11/6/93, age 29), Juergen "Nosie" Katzmann (composer/guitarist) and Peter Zweier (composer/engineer). Includes London vocalist Lana Evans and New Jersey rapper Jay Supreme.			
2/23/91	56^A	7		1 **I Like You**...*(4 versions)* CULTURE BEAT Featuring Lana E. And Jay Supreme	$6	T	Epic 73600
11/6/93+	17	20	●	2 **Mr. Vain**...A:17 / S:19 *(edit w/o rap)* "45": 550 Music/Epic 77372; B-side: "Got To Get It"	$3	▮V	550 Music/Epic 77259
	★258★			**CULTURE CLUB** R&B/LP '83			
				Pop group formed in London, England: George "**Boy George**" (see #11 & 12 below) O'Dowd (vocals; born on 6/14/61), Roy Hay (guitar, keyboards; born on 8/12/61), Michael Craig (bass; born on 2/15/60) and Jon Moss (drums; born on 9/11/57). Designer Sue Clowes originated distinctive costuming for the group. Won the 1983 Best New Artist Grammy Award. Boy George went solo in 1987. *1)Karma Chameleon 2)Do You Really Want To Hurt Me 3)Time (Clock Of The Heart)*			
12/4/82+	2^3	25		1 **Do You Really Want To Hurt Me**...*You Know I'm Not Crazy*	$4		Epic/Virgin 03368
4/16/83	2^2	18		2 **Time (Clock Of The Heart)**...*Romance Beyond The Alphabet*	$4	■	Epic/Virgin 03796
7/2/83	9	16		3 **I'll Tumble 4 Ya**...*Mystery Boy*	$4	■	Epic/Virgin 03912
10/22/83	10	17		4 **Church Of The Poison Mind**...*Mystery Boy*	$4	■	Epic/Virgin 04144
12/3/83+	❶^3	22	●	5 **Karma Chameleon** *That's The Way (I'm Only Trying To Help You)*	$3	■	Virgin/Epic 04221
3/3/84	5	16		6 **Miss Me Blind**...*Colour By Numbers* **Jermaine Stewart** (backing vocal)	$3	■	Virgin/Epic 04388
5/12/84	13	13		7 **It's A Miracle**...*Love Twist* above 4 from the album *Colour By Numbers*	$3	■	Virgin/Epic 04457
10/6/84	17	13		8 **The War Song**...S:18 / A:18 *La Cancion De Guerra*	$3	■	Virgin/Epic 04638
12/15/84+	33	13		9 **Mistake No. 3**...A:29 *Don't Go Down That Street*	$3		Virgin/Epic 04727
4/5/86	12	14		10 **Move Away**...S:11 / A:14 *Sexuality*	$3	■	Virgin/Epic 05847
				BOY GEORGE:			
12/26/87+	40	12		11 **Live My Life**...S:37 / A:39 *(soul remix)* from the movie *Hiding Out* starring Jon Cryer	$3		Virgin 99390
3/13/93	15	17		12 **The Crying Game**...S:18 / A:22 *The Crying Game* (Dave Berry) title song from the movie starring Stephen Rea; produced by the **Pet Shop Boys**; "45": SBK 56996 (red vinyl); B-side: "Stand By Your Man" by Lyle Lovett (C&W #82/'89)	$3	▮V	SBK 50437
				CUMMINGS, Burton AC/C&W/LP '77			
				Born on 12/31/47 in Winnipeg, Manitoba, Canada. Lead singer of **The Guess Who**. Acted in the 1982 movie *Melanie.*			
10/9/76+	10	21	●	1 **Stand Tall** *Burch Magic*	$5		Portrait 70001
2/19/77	61	5		2 **I'm Scared**...*Sugartime Flashback Joys*	$5		Portrait 70002
9/10/77	74	4		3 **My Own Way To Rock**...*A Song For Him*	$5		Portrait 70007
7/15/78	85	5		4 **Break It To Them Gently**...*Roll With The Punches*	$5	■	Portrait 70016
9/12/81	37	11		5 **You Saved My Soul**...*Real Good* from the movie *Melanie* starring Glynnis O'Connor	$4	■	Alfa 7008
				CUNHA, Rick '74			
				Born on 7/19/45 in Los Angeles, California. Session guitarist.			
4/27/74	61	7		**(I'm A) YoYo Man**...*Wild Side Of Life*	$6		GRC 2016
				CUPIDS, The '63			
				White doo-wop group from Brooklyn, New York. Group dissolved after the untimely death of its lead singer. The Camelots fulfilled the rest of The Cupids' recording obligations.			
7/6/63	57	6		**Brenda**...*For You* first released on Aanko 1002 in 1963 ($100)	$50		KC 115
				CURB, Mike, Congregation AC/BUB/LP '72			
				Born on 12/24/44 in Savannah, Georgia. Pop music mogul and politician. President of MGM Records, 1969-73. Elected lieutenant governor of California in 1978; served as governor of California, 1980. Formed own company, Sidewalk Records, in 1964; became Curb Records in 1974. Currently resides in Nashville, Tennessee.			
11/7/70+	34	17		1 **Burning Bridges**...*We'll Sing In The Sunshine* from the movie *Kelly's Heroes* starring **Clint Eastwood**	$5		MGM 14151
3/11/72	❶^3	21	●	2 **The Candy Man**...AC^2 *I Want To Be Happy* (Davis) **SAMMY DAVIS, JR. with The Mike Curb Congregation** from the movie *Willy Wonka And The Chocolate Factory* starring Gene Wilder; originally recorded as by The Mike Curb Congregation; Davis's vocals dubbed in later	$5		MGM 14320

DEBUT	PEAK	WKS	Gold	A-side (Chart Hit)...B-side	$	Sym	Label & Number
				CURB, Mike, Congregation — Cont'd			
4/22/72	**38**	10		3 **Long Haired Lover From Liverpool** ... *Mother Of Mine* (#101) **LITTLE JIMMY OSMOND with The Mike Curb Congregation** first released in 1970 as by **The Mike Curb Congregation** on MGM 14140	$5		MGM 14376
10/21/72	**92**	5		4 **The People Tree** ... *Mr. Bojangles* (Davis) **SAMMY DAVIS, JR. (with The Mike Curb Congregation)**	$5		MGM 14426
	★**491**★			**CURE, The** ROK/BUB/LP **'89** Techno-rock group formed in England by Robert Smith (vocals, guitar; born on 4/21/59) and Laurence "Lol" Tolhurst (drums; born on 2/3/59). Since 1983, members have included Smith, Tolhurst (until 1990), Porl Thompson, Simon Gallup, Andy Anderson (1984), Boris Williams and Roger O'Donnell (1989). Perry Bamonte joined in 1992. Smith was also a touring member of **Siouxsie And The Banshees** in the early 1980s. *1)Love Song 2)Friday I'm Love 3)Just Like Heaven*			
2/15/86	**99**	1		1 **In Between Days (Without You)** ... *Stop Dead* first released in July 1985	$5	■	Elektra 69604
6/20/87	**54**	12		2 **Why Can't I Be You?** ... *A Japanese Dream*	$5	■	Elektra 69474
10/10/87+	**40**	19		3 **Just Like Heaven** ... A:37 *Breathe*	$5	■	Elektra 69443
3/5/88	**65**	7		4 **Hot Hot Hot!!!** ... *Hey You!!!*	$4	■	Elektra 69424
5/13/89	**46**	11		5 **Fascination Street** ... MR[7] S:37 *Babble*	$4	■	Elektra 69300
8/12/89	**2**[1]	17		6 **Love Song** S:3 / A:7 *2 Late*	$3		Elektra 69280
12/2/89	**74**	8		7 **Lullaby** ... *Homesick*	$3		Elektra 69249
4/21/90	**71**	8		8 **Pictures Of You** ... *Prayers For Rain* above 4 from the album *Disintegration*	$3	▮	Elektra 64974
11/3/90	**72**	4		9 **Never Enough** ... MR[3] *Harold And Joe*	$3	▮V	Fiction/Elektra 64928
1/19/91	**97**	3		10 **Close To Me** ... *Just Like Heaven (dizzy mix)* remix of a track from their 1985 album *The Head On The Door*	$3	▮	Fiction/Elektra 64911
4/4/92	**42**	12		11 **High** ... MR[4] S:18 / A:46 *This Twilight Garden*	$3	▮	Fiction/Elektra 64766
6/13/92	**18**	20		12 **Friday I'm In Love** ... MR[4] A:16 / S:28 *Halo*	$3	▮	Fiction/Elektra 64742
12/18/93	**66**[A]	6		13 **Purple Haze** ... from the album *Stone Free: A Tribute To Jimi Hendrix* on Reprise 45438			album cut
5/11/96	**44**	4		14 **The 13th** ... S:30 / A:61 *Adonais*	$3	▮	Fiction/Elektra 64292
7/20/96	**58**	5		15 **Mint Car** ... A:51 *Home*	$3	▮	Fiction/Elektra 64275
10/25/97	**64**[A]	8		16 **Wrong Number** ... from the album *Galore* on Fiction/Elektra 62117			album cut
				CURIOSITY KILLED THE CAT LP **'87** Pop-rock group formed in London, England: Ben Volpeliere-Pierrot (vocals), Julian Brookhouse (guitar), Nick Thorpe (bass) and Miguel Drummond (drums).			
8/1/87	**42**	13		**Misfit** ... S:37 *Man*	$3	■	Mercury 888674
				CURRENT **'77** Disco session group assembled by producer Joe Saraceno (**The T-Bones**).			
4/30/77	**94**	3		**Theme From "Rocky" (Gonna Fly Now)** ... *Peter's Theme* [I]	$5		Playboy 6098
				CURRIE, Cherie & Marie **'79** Identical twins born on 11/30/59 in Encino, California. Cherie (formerly with the rock band The Runaways) appeared in the movies *Foxes* and *Wavelength.*			
10/20/79	**95**	3		**Since You've Been Gone** ... *Longer Than Forever*	$5	■	Capitol 4754
				CURRY, Clifford **'67** Born on 11/4/40 in Knoxville, Tennessee. R&B singer.			
5/6/67	**95**	3		**She Shot A Hole In My Soul** ... *We're Gonna Hate Ourselves In The Morning*	$20		Elf 90,002
				CURRY, Mark — see PUFF DADDY			
				CURRY, Tim LP **'79** Born on 4/19/46 in Cheshire, England. Actor/singer. Starred in several movies.			
11/3/79	**91**	3		**I Do The Rock** ... *Hide This Face*	$6	□	A&M 2166
				CURTIE AND THE BOOMBOX **'85** Female vocal group from Holland: Curtie Fortune (lead), Patricia Balrak, Judith Landry and Denise van der Hek.			
7/27/85	**81**	4		**Black Kisses (Never Make You Blue)** ... *(special version)*	$3		RCA 14103
				CURTIS — see KING CURTIS			
				CURTOLA, Bobby **'62** Born on 4/17/44 in Port Arthur, Ontario, Canada. Teen pop singer.			
5/5/62	**41**	14		1 **Fortuneteller** ... *Johnny Take Your Time*	$20		Del-Fi 4177
10/27/62	**92**	3		2 **Aladdin** ... *I Don't Want To Go On Without You*	$20	■	Del-Fi 4185
				CUT 'N' MOVE **'91** Dance group from Denmark: producer/musicians Per Holm and Jorn Kristensen with rapper Jens "M.C. Zipp" Larsen and female vocalist Thera Hoeymanss.			
8/3/91	**76**	6		**Get Serious** ... *(cut the crap clean version)*	$3	▮	Epic 73878
				CUTTING CREW AC/LP **'87** Pop-rock group formed in England: Nick Van Eede (vocals), Kevin MacMichael (guitar), Colin Farley (bass) and Martin Beedle (drums). MacMichael died of cancer on 12/31/2002 (age 51).			
3/7/87	**❶**[2]	19		1 **(I Just) Died In Your Arms** ... A:❶[2] / S:2 *For The Longest Time*	$3	■	Virgin 99481
6/6/87	**38**	11		2 **One For The Mockingbird** ... A:32 *Mirror And A Blade (live)*	$3	■	Virgin 99464
9/5/87	**9**	21		3 **I've Been In Love Before** ... A:8 / S:11 *Life In A Dangerous Time*	$3	■	Virgin 99425
5/13/89	**77**	5		4 **(Between A) Rock And A Hard Place** ... *Card House*	$3	■	Virgin 99215

DEBUT	PEAK	WKS	Gold	A-side (Chart Hit)...B-side	$	Sym	Label & Number
				CYCLONES '58			
				Instrumental rock and roll band led by Bill Taylor.			
9/29/58	83	2		**Bullwhip Rock**...H:83 *Nelda Jane* (Bill Taylor & Cyclones) [I]	$50		Trophy 500
				CYMANDE R&B/BUB/LP '73			
				Afro-rock band from the West Indies: Ray King (vocals), Pat Patterson (guitar), Peter Serreo and Derek Gibbs (saxophones), Mike Rose (flute), Joe Dee and Pablo Gonsales (percussion), and Sam Kelly (drums).			
1/20/73	48	10		**The Message**...*Zion I*	$6		Janus 203
				CYMARRON LP '71			
				Male pop vocal trio from Memphis, Tennessee: Richard Mainegra, Rick Yancey and Sherrill Parks.			
6/12/71	17	12		1 **Rings**...*Like Children*	$7		Entrance 7500
10/2/71	96	4		2 **Valerie**...*Across The Kansas Sky*	$7		Entrance 7502
				CYMBAL, Johnny BUB '63			
				Born on 2/3/45 in Ochitree, Scotland. Died of a heart attack on 3/16/93 (age 48). Pop singer/songwriter/producer. Also recorded as **Derek** (see #4 & 5 below).			
2/16/63	16	13		1 **Mr. Bass Man**...*Sacred Lovers Vow* [N]	$20		Kapp 503
				Ronnie Bright (bass singer; member of the Valentines)			
5/11/63	58	6		2 **Teenage Heaven**...*Cinderella Baby*	$15		Kapp 524
8/3/63	77	4		3 **Dum Dum Dee Dum**...*(Surfin' At) Tia Juana*	$15		Kapp 539
				DEREK:			
10/26/68+	11	15		4 **Cinnamon** *This Is My Story*	$8		Bang 558
2/22/69	59	6		5 **Back Door Man**...*Sell Your Soul*	$8		Bang 566
				CYNTHIA BUB '90			
				Born Cynthia Torres on 5/6/68 in New York. Dance singer. Recorded duet with Johnny Ortiz. Also see **Sa-Fire**'s "Make Up My Mind."			
9/1/90	53	15		1 **Dream Boy-Dream Girl**...*(4 versions)*	$6	▮*	MicMac 2539
				CYNTHIA & JOHNNY 'O'			
6/22/91	70	8		2 **Break Up To Make Up**...A:74 *(background vocal mix)*	$4	▮	MicMac 3558
9/12/92	75^A	1		3 **Love Me Tonight**...*(3 versions)*	$6	▮*	MicMac 2580
10/17/98	83	7		4 **If I Had The Chance**...*(radio edit)*	$4	★	Timber! 7746
				CYPRESS HILL R&B/BUB/ROK/LP '93			
				Rap trio from Los Angeles, California: Senen "Sen Dog" Reyes (Cuban-born; older brother of **Mellow Man Ace**), Louis "B-Real" Freese and Lawrence "Mixmaster Muggs" Muggerud (former member of The 7A3). Band named for Cypress Street in the Southgate section of Los Angeles. Appeared in the movie *The Meteor Man.*			
				1)Insane In The Brain 2)Throw Your Set In The Air 3)We Ain't Goin' Out Like That			
2/22/92	77	7		1 **How I Could Just Kill A Man /** S:39			
2/15/92	94	8		2 **The Phuncky Feel One**...	$5	▮	Ruffhouse 73930
4/11/92	72^S	2		3 **Hand On The Pump**...*Real Estate*	$5	▮	Ruffhouse 74105
7/10/93	19	20	●	4 **Insane In The Brain** S:10 / A:35 *Stoned Is The Way Of The Walk*	$4	▮	Ruffhouse 77135
1/8/94	65	7		5 **We Ain't Goin' Out Like That**...S:38 *Hits From The Bong*	$4	▮	Ruffhouse 77307
				samples "The Wizard" by **Black Sabbath**			
10/14/95	45	18		6 **Throw Your Set In The Air**...S:21 *Killa Hill*	$4	▮	Ruffhouse 78042
6/22/96	87	3		7 **Boom Biddy Bye Bye**...S:75 *(album version)*	$4	▮	Ruffhouse 78339
9/26/98	70	7		8 **Tequila Sunrise /** S:50			
9/19/98	72	4		9 **Dr. Greenthumb**...S:50	$8	★*	Ruffhouse 79024
3/16/02	57^S	6		10 **Lowrider**...*(instrumental) / Psychodelic Vision / (Rap) Superstar / (Rock) Superstar* (ROK #18)	$7	★*	Columbia 79709
				CYRKLE, The BUB/LP '66			
				Pop group formed in Easton, Pennsylvania: Don Dannemann (vocals, guitar), Mike Losekamp (keyboards), Tom Dawes (bass) and Marty Fried (drums). Signed to Columbia and managed by **The Beatles**' manager Brian Epstein; named by **John Lennon**.			
5/21/66	2^1	13		1 **Red Rubber Ball** *How Can I Leave Her*	$10	■	Columbia 43589
8/13/66	16	8		2 **Turn-Down Day**...*Big, Little Woman*	$10	■	Columbia 43729
12/3/66	59	5		3 **Please Don't Ever Leave Me**...*Money To Burn*	$10		Columbia 43871
2/4/67	70	4		4 **I Wish You Could Be Here**...*The Visit (She Was Here)*	$10	■	Columbia 43965
				#1 & 4: written by **Paul Simon** and Bruce Woodley (of **The Seekers**)			
5/13/67	72	5		5 **We Had A Good Thing Goin'**...*Two Rooms*	$10		Columbia 44108
				written by **Neil Sedaka** and Howard Greenfield			
9/2/67	95	1		6 **Penny Arcade**...*The Words*	$10		Columbia 44224
				CYRUS, Billy Ray C&W/AC/LP '92			
				Born on 8/25/61 in Flatwoods, Kentucky. Country singer. Plays "Dr. Clint Cassidy" on the PAX-TV series *Doc.*			
5/9/92	4	25	▲	1 **Achy Breaky Heart** CW^5 S:2 / A:38 *(3 album snippets)*	$4	▮V	Mercury 866522
				recorded by The Marcy Brothers in 1991 as "Don't Tell My Heart"; "45" B-side: "Wher'm I Gonna Live?" (C&W #23)			
10/10/92	72	9		2 **Could've Been Me**...S:35 *(album version) / I'm So Miserable*	$4	▮V	Mercury 866998
3/13/93	70	9		3 **She's Not Cryin' Anymore**...S:36 *Achy Breaky Heart (live)*	$4	▮V	Mercury 864778
				"45" B-side: "Someday, Somewhere, Somehow"			
7/31/93	76	10		4 **In The Heart Of A Woman**...S:47 *Right Face Wrong Time*	$4	▮V	Mercury 862448
1/8/94	71^S	2		5 **Somebody New**...BUB:104 *Only Time Will Tell*	$4	▮V	Mercury 862754
1/23/99	46	17		6 **Busy Man**...A:31		V	album cut
				from the album *Shot Full Of Love* on Mercury 558347; "45": Mercury 566582; B-side: "Touchy Subject"			
9/23/00	80	13		7 **You Won't Be Lonely Now**...S:41 *Southern Rain* (C&W #45/'01)	$4	★V	Monument 79440
				"45": Monument 79528; B-side: "We The People" (C&W #60)			

RARE 45s

Audrey
Dear Elvis

The Blue Notes
My Hero

Bonnie And The Treasures
Home Of The Brave

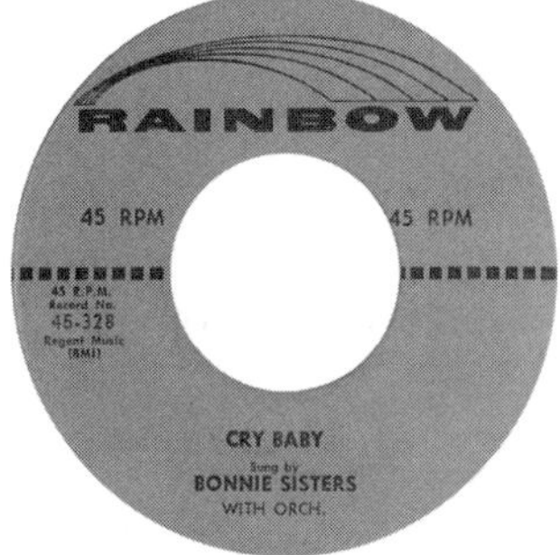

Bonnie Sisters
Cry Baby

The Chantels
He's Gone

The Charts
Deserie

The Chiffons
Tonight's The Night

The Cleftones
You Baby You

Crest's
Sweetest One

Debbie Dean
Don't Let Him Shop Around

The Dubs
Don't Ask Me (To Be Lonely)

The Goodtimers
Pony Time

RARE 45s

The Harptones
What Will I Tell My Heart

Adrian Kimberly — *The Graduation Song...*
Pomp And Circumstance

Herb Lance & The Classics
Blue Moon

The Ly-Dells
Wizard Of Love

Shamus M'Cool
American Memories

The Royal Jokers
You Tickle Me Baby

The Silva-Tones
That's All I Want From You

Tico And The Triumphs
Motorcycle

The Turbans
When You Dance

Valadiers
Greetings (This Is Uncle Sam)

The Velours
Can I Come Over Tonight

Willows
Church Bells May Ring

DEBUT	PEAK	WKS	Gold	A-side (Chart Hit)..................B-side	$	Sym	Label & Number

D

				DA BEATMINERZ LP **'01**			
				Rap production group: Mr. Walt, Rich Blak, Evil Dee, Baby Paul and Chocolate Ty.			
7/14/01	41S	4		**Take That**................*(2 versions) / Extreme Situation* (**Cocoa Brovaz** & Blackhearted Skavengers)	$7	T	Rawkus 300
				DA BEATMINERZ feat. Flipmode Squad & Vinia Mojica			
	★387★			**DA BRAT** R&B/LP **'94**			
				Born Shawntae Harris on 4/14/74 in Chicago, Illinois. Female rapper. Discovered by her producer/songwriter **Jermaine Dupri** at a **Kris Kross** concert in Chicago. Also see **Total**'s "No One Else."			
				1)Funkdafied 2)Ghetto Love 3)Give It 2 You			
6/4/94	6	20	▲	1 **Funkdafied** S:3 / A:17 *(instrumental)*	$3	▮	So So Def 77532
				samples "Between The Sheets" by **The Isley Brothers**			
10/15/94	37	18		2 **Fa All Y'all**..................S:20 *(remix)*	$3	▮	So So Def 77594
4/15/95	26	18	●	3 **Give It 2 You**..................S:15 / A:43 *(EP version)*	$3	▮	So So Def 77836
				Trey Lorenz (backing vocal)			
10/12/96	30	16	●	4 **Sittin' On Top Of The World**..................S:15 *(instrumental)*	$3	▮	So So Def 78426
				contains a replay of "Mary Jane" by **Rick James**			
3/22/97	16	15	●	5 **Ghetto Love**..................S:8 *(4 album snippets)*	$3	▮	So So Def 78527
				DA BRAT Featuring T-Boz			
				samples "All This Love" by **DeBarge** and "Public Enemy No. 1" by **Public Enemy**			
7/12/97	6	21	▲	6 **Not Tonight**..................S:3 / A:39 *(instrumental)*	$3	▮	Undeas/Big Beat 98019
				LIL' KIM Featuring Da Brat, Left Eye, Missy "Misdemeanor" Elliott and Angie Martinez			
				samples "Ladies Night" by **Kool & The Gang**; from the movie *Nothing To Lose* starring Martin Lawrence			
9/20/97	65	9		7 **The Way That You Talk**..................S:59 *(4 album snippets)*	$3	▮	So So Def 78639
				JAGGED EDGE featuring Da Brat & JD			
10/18/97	12	20	●	8 **Sock It 2 Me**..................S:7 / A:36	$3	▮	EastWest 64144
				MISSY "MISDEMEANOR" ELLIOTT Featuring Da Brat			
				samples "Ready Or Not Here I Come" by **The Delfonics**			
3/7/98	29	19	●	9 **The Party Continues**..............S:16 *We Just Wanna Party With You* (w/**Snoop Doggy Dogg**)	$3	▮	So So Def 78807
				JD & DA BRAT			
				Usher (backing vocal); samples "She's Strange" by **Cameo**			
10/23/99	79	6		10 **U Don't Know Me (Like U Used To)**..................S:33 *(2 versions) / Almost Doesn't Count / Top Of The World*	$8	★*	Atlantic 84508
				BRANDY Featuring Shaunta & Da Brat			
6/3/00	26	20		11 **What'Chu Like** / A:19			
				DA BRAT Featuring Tyrese			
2/26/00	56	18		12 **That's What I'm Looking For**..................A:49 / S:75	$6	T	So So Def 79330
5/18/02	50S	6		13 **Put It Inside**..................*(2 versions)*	$6	★	TNO/Orpheus 90412
				WON-G (featuring) Da Brat			
				DADDY DEWDROP **'71**			
				Born Richard Monda in Cleveland, Ohio. Pop singer. Songwriter for the TV cartoon series *Sabrina & The Groovy Ghoulies.*			
3/6/71	9	16		**Chick-A-Boom (Don't Ya Jes' Love It)**..................*John Jacob Jingleheimer Smith* [N]	$7		Sunflower 105
				DADDY-O'S, The **'58**			
				Novelty session group produced by guitarist Billy Mure (of **The Trumpeteers**).			
6/16/58	39	8		**Got A Match?**..................S:39 / T:40 *Have A Cigar!* [I-N]	$20		Cabot 122
				DA EN TOURAGE **'02**			
				Male rap group from Lafayette, Louisiana: Paul "Bunny B" Brown, Tomosa "Toemas" Griffin, Damon "Red Boy" Spencer and Travis "Alley Cat" Zeno.			
1/26/02	18S	9		**Bunny Hop**..................*(5 versions)*	$10	★*	Red Boy 7183
				DAFT PUNK BUB/LP **'97**			
				Electronica-dance duo from Paris, France: Thomas Bangalter (**Stardust**) and Guy-Manuel de Homem-Christo.			
8/30/97	61	20		1 **Around The World**..................S:54 *(3 versions)* [I]	$3	▮V	Virgin 38608
				"45": Virgin 19730; B-side: (remix)			
2/10/01	61	16		2 **One More Time**..................S:17 / A:71 *(2 versions)*	$4	★	Virgin 38758
				D'AGOSTINO, Gigi **'01**			
				Born Luigino Di Agostino in Italy. Electronica-dance DJ/remixer/producer.			
8/4/01	78	13		**I'll Fly With You (L'Amour Toujours)**..................A:74 *(edit) / Bla Bla Bla*	$6	T	Arista 13998
				DAHL, Steve, And Teenage Radiation **'79**			
				Born on 11/20/54 in La Canada, California. DJ in Chicago. Organized the controversial "disco sucks demolition" at Chicago's Comiskey Park on 7/12/79.			
9/22/79	58	6		**Do You Think I'm Disco?**..................*Coho Lip Blues* [N]	$5	■	Ovation 1132
				parody of **Rod Stewart**'s "Da Ya Think I'm Sexy?"; picture sleeve issued with either red or black lettering			
				DAILY, E.G. **'86**			
				Born Elizabeth Daily on 9/11/62 in Los Angeles, California. R&B-dance singer/actress. Acted in the movies *Pee-Wee's Big Adventure* and *Valley Girl.* Performs voices for the animated TV series *Rugrats.*			
4/26/86	70	10		**Say It, Say It**..................*Don't Let Them Take The Child Away*	$3	■	A&M 2825
				DAKOTA MOON AC **'98**			
				Black pop group formed in Los Angeles, California: Ty Taylor (vocals), Joe Dean (guitar), Ray Artis (bass) and Malloy (drums).			
3/21/98	69	13		**A Promise I Make**..................*Snow In July*	$3	▮	Elektra 64116
				DALE, Alan MEM/POP/BUB **'55**			
				Born Aldo Sigismondi on 7/9/28 in Brooklyn, New York. Died of heart failure on 4/20/2002 (age 73). Baritone singer formerly with Carmen Cavallaro. Hosted his own TV shows beginning in 1948. Starred in the 1956 movie *Don't Knock The Rock.*			
4/30/55	14	7		1 **Cherry Pink (And Apple Blossom White)**..................J:14 / A:19 / S:27 *I'm Sincere*	$15		Coral 61373
				from the movie *Underwater!* starring Jane Russell			
7/2/55	10	7		2 **Sweet And Gentle**..................A:10 / S:12 / J:14 *You Still Mean The Same To Me*	$15		Coral 61435
				Cuban song ("Me Lo Dijo Adela"); **Dick Jacobs** (orch., above 2)			

DEBUT	PEAK	WKS	Gold	A-side (Chart Hit)...B-side	$	Sym	Label & Number
				DALE, Dick, and The Del-Tones BUB/LP **'62**			
				Born Richard Monsour on 5/4/37 in Boston, Massachusetts. Later based in Southern California. Influential surf-rock guitarist.			
11/27/61+	60	9		1 **Let's Go Trippin'** ...*Del-Tone Rock* [I]	$35		Deltone 5017
10/26/63	98	1		2 **The Scavenger** ...*Wild Ideas*	$25		Capitol 5048
				DALE & GRACE BUB/LP **'63**			
				Pop vocal duo: Dale Houston (of Ferriday, Louisiana) and Grace Broussard (of Prairieville, Louisiana).			
10/5/63	❶[2]	15		1 **I'm Leaving It Up To You** ...AC[2] *That's What I Like About You* written and recorded by Don & Dewey in 1957 on Specialty 610 ($30)	$12		Montel 921
1/25/64	8	9		2 **Stop And Think It Over** ...*Bad Luck*	$12		Montel 922
5/2/64	65	5		3 **The Loneliest Night** ...*I'm Not Free* above 3 first released on Michelle 921, 923 & 928, respectively ($20 each)	$12		Montel 928
				DALLARA, Tony **'59**			
				Born on 6/30/36 in Campobasso, Italy. Adult Contemporary singer.			
12/8/58+	60	7		**Come Prima** ...*Condannami* [F] also released under the name Tony Dalardo	$12		Mercury 71327
				DALTON, Kathy AC/LP **'74**			
				Born in Memphis, Tennessee. Pop-country singer.			
9/14/74	72	5		**Boogie Bands And One Night Stands** ...*Pour Your Wine All Over Me*	$6		DiscReet 1210
				DALTREY, Roger ROK/BUB/LP **'80**			
				Born on 3/1/44 in Hammersmith, London, England. Formed band The Detours, which later became **The Who**; Daltrey was The Who's lead singer. Starred in the movies *Tommy*, *Lisztomania*, *The Legacy* and *McVicar*.			
6/2/73	83	7		1 **Giving It All Away** ...*Way Of The World*	$6		Track 40053
10/4/75	68	8		2 **Come And Get Your Love** ...*Heart-s Right*	$5		MCA 40453
10/8/77	88	3		3 **Avenging Annie** ...*The Prisoner*	$5		MCA 40800
7/5/80	53	10		4 **Free Me** ...*McVicar*	$4	■	Polydor 2105
9/13/80	20	19		5 **Without Your Love** *Escape Part I* above 2 from the movie *McVicar* starring Daltrey	$4		Polydor 2121
2/18/84	62	9		6 **Walking In My Sleep** ...*Somebody Told Me*	$3	■	Atlantic 89704
9/14/85	48	13		7 **After The Fire** ...*It Don't Satisfy Me*	$3	■	Atlantic 89491
12/28/85+	86	4		8 **Let Me Down Easy** ...*Fallen Angel* written by **Bryan Adams**	$3	■	Atlantic 89471
				DAMAGE **'97**			
				Male R&B vocal group from London, England: Andrez, Coree, Jade, Noel and Ras.			
7/5/97	82	4		**Love II Love** ...*(same version)*	$4	▮	Critique 15608
				DAMIAN, Michael AC/LP **'89**			
				Born Michael Damian Weir on 4/26/62 in San Diego, California. While performing on *American Bandstand*, was discovered by the producers of TV soap opera *The Young & The Restless* and won the role of "Danny Romalotti" in 1981.			
5/30/81	69	6		1 **She Did It** ...*I Love How You Love Me*	$5	■	LEG 007
3/18/89	❶[1]	21	●	2 **Rock On** A:❶[1] / S:2 *Where Is She?* (Blue Future) from the movie *Dream A Little Dream* starring Corey Feldman	$3		Cypress 1420
6/17/89	31	12		3 **Cover Of Love** ...A:29 / S:34 *(instrumental)*	$3	■	Cypress 1430
10/28/89+	24	21		4 **Was It Nothing At All** ...S:22 / A:22 *Photograph*	$3	▮	Cypress 1451
6/8/91	60	8		5 **What A Price To Pay** ...*(7" remix)* "45": A&M/Collectables 8715; B-side: "Rock On"	$3	▮V	A&M 1559
7/6/02	40S	8		6 **Shadows In The Night** ...*(4 remixes)*	$5	★	Modern Voices 002
				DAMIAN DAME R&B **'91**			
				Black male/female duo. Damian was born Bruce Broadus in Battle Creek, Michigan. Died of cancer on 6/27/96 (age 29). Dame was born Debra Hurd in Houston, Texas. Died in a car crash on 7/4/94 (age 36).			
5/18/91	42	12		1 **Exclusivity** ...RB[2] S:68 *(instrumental)*	$4	▮V	LaFace 4000
12/14/91	90	6		2 **Right Down To It** ...*(album version)*	$4	▮V	LaFace 24002
				DAMIANO, Joe **'59**			
				Born on 1/29/39 in Philadelphia, Pennsylvania. White pop singer. Brother of Peter DeAngelis (produced for **Frankie Avalon** and **Fabian**).			
8/31/59	91	3		**I Cried** ...*Sittin' On A Shelf*	$15		Chancellor 1039
				DAMITA JO BUB/AC/MEM/LP **'61**			
				Born Damita Jo DuBlanc on 8/5/30 in Austin, Texas. Died on 12/25/98 (age 68). R&B singer/songwriter. With **Steve Gibson & The Red Caps** (married to Gibson) from 1951-53 and 1959-60. Regular on Redd Foxx's TV variety series in 1977.			
10/24/60	22	12		1 **I'll Save The Last Dance For You** ...*Forgive* Cliff Parman (orch.); answer song to **The Drifters**' "Save The Last Dance For Me"	$15		Mercury 71690
2/6/61	75	5		2 **Keep Your Hands Off Of Him** ...*Hush, Somebody's Calling My Name* Mike Stewart Singers (backing vocals); Belford Hendricks (orch.); #1 R&B hit in 1955 by Jay McShann's Orchestra with Priscilla Bowman as "Hands Off"	$15		Mercury 71760
7/3/61	12	9		3 **I'll Be There** ...*Love Laid Its Hands On Me* Chuck Sagle (orch.); answer song to **Ben E. King**'s "Stand By Me"	$15	■	Mercury 71840
12/10/66+	68	10		4 **If You Go Away** ...*When The Fog Rolls In To San Francisco* Leroy Glover (orch.); French song with English lyrics by **Rod McKuen**	$8	□	Epic 10061
				DAMN YANKEES ROK/LP **'90**			
				Superstar rock group: guitarist **Ted Nugent** (**Amboy Dukes**), bassist/vocalist Jack Blades (**Night Ranger**), guitarist/vocalist **Tommy Shaw** (**Styx**) and drummer Michael Cartellone. Shaw and Blades recorded as a duo in 1995.			
4/21/90	60	12		1 **Coming Of Age** ...AR[1] *Tell Me How You Want It*	$3	▮	Warner 19838
9/22/90+	3	29	●	2 **High Enough** S:2 / A:4 *Piledriver*	$3	▮V	Warner 19595
4/20/91	50	10		3 **Come Again** ...*(single mix)*	$3	▮V	Warner 19408
10/10/92	20	20		4 **Where You Goin' Now** ...A:28 / S:37 *This Side Of Hell*	$3	▮V	Warner 18728
4/17/93	62	10		5 **Silence Is Broken** ...A:71 *Double Coyote* from the movie *Nowhere To Run* starring Jean-Claude van Damme	$3	▮V	Warner 18612

DEBUT	PEAK	WKS	Gold	A-side (Chart Hit)...B-side	$	Sym	Label & Number
				DAMON('S), Liz, Orient Express AC/LP '71			
				Damon is the leader of the three-woman, six-man Adult Contemporary vocal/instrumental group from Hawaii.			
12/26/70+	33	12		**1900 Yesterday**...*You're Falling In Love*	$6		White Whale 368
				DAMONE, Vic MEM/POP/AC/BUB/LP '49			
				Born Vito Farinola on 6/12/28 in Brooklyn, New York. Damone is among the most popular of postwar ballad singers. Charted 32 pop hits, 1947-53, including the #1 hit "You're Breaking My Heart" in 1949. Appeared in the movies *Kismet*, *Meet Me In Las Vegas* and *Hell To Eternity*. Hosted own TV series (1956-57). Married to actress Diahann Carroll from 1987-96.			
11/19/55	73	4		1 **Por Favor**...T:73 *Born To Sing The Blues* Hugo Peretti (of **Hugo & Luigi**; orch.)	$12		Mercury 70699
4/21/56	4	25		2 **On The Street Where You Live** A:4 / T:8 / S:8 / J:13 *We All Need Love* **Percy Faith** (orch.); from the Broadway musical *My Fair Lady* starring **Julie Andrews**	$15		Columbia 40654
9/22/56	59	10		3 **War And Peace**...T:59 *Speak, My Love* David Terry (orch.); title song from the movie starring Audrey Hepburn	$12		Columbia 40733
4/13/57	62	10		4 **Do I Love You (Because You're Beautiful)**...T:62 *The Legend Of The Bells* Marty Manning (orch.); from the CBS-TV musical *Cinderella* starring **Julie Andrews**	$12		Columbia 40858
9/9/57	16	16		5 **An Affair To Remember (Our Love Affair)**...A:16 / T:35 *In The Eyes Of The World* from the movie *An Affair To Remember* starring **Cary Grant** and Deborah Kerr	$12		Columbia 40945
5/5/58	88	1		6 **Gigi**...T:88 *Life Does A Man A Favor* title song from the movie starring Leslie Caron; **Percy Faith** (orch., above 2)	$12		Columbia 41122
4/17/65	30	10		7 **You Were Only Fooling (While I Was Falling In Love)**...*Please Help Me, I'm Falling* **Ernie Freeman** (orch.); #8 hit for the Ink Spots in 1949	$7		Warner 5616
				DAMOZEL '02			
				Female R&B vocal group from Los Angeles, California: Brandy, Lisa, Tamisha and Tasha.			
8/3/02	70S	1		**Everyday's A Party**...*(instrumental)*	$6	★	MCA 155838
				DANA '97			
				Born Dana Harris in Tampa, Florida. Female R&B singer.			
8/30/97	59	11		**As We Lay**...S:41 *(instrumental)*	$4	▮	Tony Mercedes 24252
	★527★			**DANA, Vic** AC/BUB/LP '65			
				Born on 8/26/42 in Buffalo, New York. Adult Contemporary singer. Moved to California as a teen. Replaced Tony Butala (of **The Lettermen**) in the Los Angeles group Eddie Laurence & The Whatnotts in 1960. *1)Red Roses For A Blue Lady 2)Shangri-La 3)I Love You Drops*			
11/27/61	45	8		1 **Little Altar Boy**...X:13 *Hello, Roommate* [X] **Hank Levine** (orch.); Christmas charts: #13/'65 (2 weeks)	$12		Dolton 48
3/31/62	47	9		2 **I Will**...*Proud*	$8	■	Dolton 51
5/25/63	96	2		3 **Danger**...*Heart, Hand And Teardrop* written by **Bob Beckham**	$8	■	Dolton 73
8/10/63	42	11		4 **More**...*That's Why I'm Sorry* theme from the Italian documentary movie *Mondo Cane*	$8		Dolton 81
3/28/64	27	10		5 **Shangri-La**...*Warm And Tender*	$8		Dolton 92
7/11/64	53	7		6 **Love Is All We Need**...*I Need You Now*	$8	■	Dolton 95
10/17/64	97	3		7 **Garden In The Rain**...*Stairway To The Stars* #15 hit for **Gene Austin** in 1929; #14 hit for the **Four Aces** in 1952	$8	■	Dolton 99
2/6/65	10	12		8 **Red Roses For A Blue Lady** *Blue Ribbons (For Her Curls)* #3 hit for **Vaughn Monroe** in 1949	$8		Dolton 304
5/22/65	66	6		9 **Bring A Little Sunshine (To My Heart)**...*That's All*	$8	■	Dolton 305
8/7/65	51	9		10 **Moonlight And Roses (Bring Mem'ries Of You)**...*What'll I Do* #3 hit for John McCormack in 1925	$8		Dolton 309
12/4/65	51	7		11 **Crystal Chandelier**...*What Now My Love* Tommy Oliver (orch., above 2)	$8		Dolton 313
5/7/66	30	8		12 **I Love You Drops**...*Sunny Skies* #4 Country hit for **Bill Anderson** in 1966	$8		Dolton 319
8/6/66	71	3		13 **A Million And One**...*My Baby Wouldn't Leave Me* #2 Country hit for **Billy Walker** in 1966; **Ernie Freeman** (orch.: #2-9, 12 & 13)	$8		Dolton 322
1/10/70	47	12		14 **If I Never Knew Your Name**...*Sad Day Song*	$7		Liberty 56150
5/16/70	72	6		15 **Red Red Wine**...*Another Dream Shot Down* Al Capps (orch., above 2); above 2 written by **Neil Diamond**	$7		Liberty 56163
				DANA DANE LP '95			
				Born in Brooklyn, New York. Male rapper.			
2/18/95	74S	1		**Record Jock**...BUB:115 *(remix)*	$5	▮	Maverick/Sire 18055
				DANCER, PRANCER AND NERVOUS '59			
				Novelty production of "The Singing Reindeer" (similar to **The Chipmunks**).			
12/7/59	34	6		**The Happy Reindeer**...*Dancer's Waltz* [X-N]	$12	■	Capitol 4300
				DANDELION '95			
				Rock group from Philadelphia, Pennsylvania: brothers Kevin (vocals, guitar) and Mike (bass) Morpurgo, Carl Hinds (guitar) and Dante Cimino (drums).			
8/26/95	74A	1		**Weird-Out**... from the album *Dyslexicon* on Ruffhouse 64194			album cut
				D'ANGELO R&B/BUB/LP '96			
				Born Michael D'Angelo Archer on 2/11/74 in Richmond, Virginia. R&B singer/songwriter. Also see **GZA/Genius**'s "Cold World."			
7/1/95	27	20		1 **Brown Sugar**...S:16 / A:63 *(2 mixes) / (3 album snippets)*	$3	▮V	EMI 58360
11/4/95	53	18		2 **Cruisin'**...S:30 *(album version)*	$3	▮	EMI 58468
3/2/96	10	20	●	3 **Lady** S:7 / A:43 *(2 versions)* "45": EMI 19019; B-side: (remix w/**AZ**)	$3	▮V	EMI 58543
10/5/96	74	6		4 **Me And Those Dreamin' Eyes Of Mine**...S:55 *(2 versions) / Can't Hide Love* all of above from the album *Brown Sugar*; "45" issued for #1 & 4 on EMI 19170	$3	▮V	EMI 58570
2/27/99	98	2		5 **Break Ups 2 Make Ups**...*(2 versions) / Suspect Chin Music* (w/Streetlife) **METHOD MAN featuring D'Angelo**	$6	T	Def Jam 563405

DEBUT	PEAK	WKS	Gold	A-side (Chart Hit)..........B-side	$	Sym	Label & Number
				D'ANGELO — Cont'd			
12/11/99+	70	5		6 **Left & Right** ....S:20 *(w/o rap version)*	$4	★V	Virgin 38678
				D'ANGELO featuring Method Man and Redman			
				"45": Virgin 58836; B-side: "Untitled (How Does It Feel)" (**D'Angelo** - #25)			
1/22/00	25	17		7 **Untitled (How Does It Feel)** A:17		V	album cut
				from the album *Voodoo* on Virgin 48499; "45" issued for above 2 on Virgin 58836			
4/27/02	99	2		8 **Be Here** ....S:72 *(3 versions)*	$6	T	Universal 015788
				RAPHAEL SAADIQ f/ D'Angelo			

DANGER, Harvey — see HARVEY DANGER

DANGER DANGER — LP '90

Hard-rock group from Queens, New York: Ted Poley (vocals), Andy Timmons (guitar), Kasey Smith (keyboards), Bruno Ravel (bass) and Steve West (drums).

DEBUT	PEAK	WKS	Gold	A-side (Chart Hit)..........B-side	$	Sym	Label & Number
6/2/90	49	13		**Bang Bang** ....*Boys Will Be Boys*	$4	▮	Imagine/Epic 73380

DANGERFIELD, Rodney — LP '84

Born Jacob Cohen on 11/22/21 in Babylon, Long Island, New York. Popular stand-up comedian/actor who "gets no respect."

DEBUT	PEAK	WKS	Gold	A-side (Chart Hit)..........B-side	$	Sym	Label & Number
12/3/83+	83	8		**Rappin' Rodney** ....*Funiculi, Funicula* [C]	$5	■	RCA 13656
				Dangerfield "raps" to a musical background			

DANIELS, Charlie, Band — C&W/BUB/ROK/LP '79

Born on 10/28/36 in Wilmington, North Carolina. Country-rock singer/fiddle player. His band: Tom Crain (guitar), Joe "Taz" DiGregorio (keyboards), Charles Hayward (bass), and James W. Marshall & Fred Edwards (drums). Marshall and Edwards left in 1986; replaced by Jack Gavin. Daniels led the Jaguars from 1958-67. Went solo in 1968 and worked as a session musician in Nashville. Played on **Bob Dylan**'s *Nashville Skyline* album. Group appeared in the movie *Urban Cowboy*. Began recording Christian music in 1994.

DEBUT	PEAK	WKS	Gold	A-side (Chart Hit)..........B-side	$	Sym	Label & Number
6/30/73	9	12		1 **Uneasy Rider** *[CHARLIE DANIELS]*..........*Funky Junky* [N]	$6		Kama Sutra 576
2/8/75	29	10		2 **The South's Gonna Do It** ....*New York City, King Size Rosewood Bed*	$6		Kama Sutra 598
5/10/75	56	8		3 **Long Haired Country Boy** ....*I've Been Down*	$6		Kama Sutra 601
				with Dickey Betts (**The Allman Brothers Band**) on dobro			
2/7/76	91	4		4 **Texas** ....*Everything Is Kinda Allright*	$6		Kama Sutra 607
6/23/79	3	18	▲	5 **The Devil Went Down To Georgia** CW[1] *Rainbow Ride*	$5		Epic 50700
				re-entered the Country charts (#60) in 1998 as an album cut			
5/31/80	11	15		6 **In America** ....*Blue Star*	$4		Epic 50888
8/16/80	31	14		7 **The Legend Of Wooley Swamp** ....*Money*	$4		Epic 50921
3/27/82	22	12		8 **Still In Saigon** ....*Blowing Along With The Wind*	$4		Epic 02828
11/11/00+	47S	9		9 **All Night Long** ....*Merry Christmas From The Family* (C&W #38)	$4	★V	Columbia 79515
				MONTGOMERY GENTRY Featuring Charlie Daniels			

DANIELS, Jeffrey — see BABYFACE

DANKWORTH, Johnny, and His Orchestra — BUB '56

Born on 9/20/27 in London, England. Alto saxophonist/jazz bandleader/composer. Married singer Cleo Laine in 1958.

DEBUT	PEAK	WKS	Gold	A-side (Chart Hit)..........B-side	$	Sym	Label & Number
8/25/56	61	4		**Experiments With Mice** ....T:61 *Applecake* [I] [N]	$15		Capitol 3499
				Dankworth narrates and plays a tribute to the big bands of **Billy May**, **Benny Goodman**, Glenn Miller, **Stan Kenton**, Sauter-Finegan and Gerry Mulligan to the tune "3 Blind Mice"			

DANLEERS, The — '58

Black doo-wop group from Brooklyn, New York: Jimmy Weston (lead; died on 6/10/93), Johnny Lee (first tenor), Willie Ephraim (second tenor), Nat McCune (baritone) and Roosevelt Mays (bass). Group was named after their manager, Danny Webb, who wrote "One Summer Night." Not to be confused with the R&B group, The Danderliers.

DEBUT	PEAK	WKS	Gold	A-side (Chart Hit)..........B-side	$	Sym	Label & Number
6/30/58	7	13		**One Summer Night** ....A:7 / S:14 / H:16 *Wheelin' And A-Dealin'*	$25		Mercury 71322
				originally released on AMP-3 2115 in 1958 as by The Dandleers ($150)			

DANNY & THE JUNIORS — '58

White doo-wop group from Philadelphia, Pennsylvania: Danny Rapp (lead; born on 5/10/41; committed suicide on 4/5/83, age 41), David White (first tenor), Frank Maffei (second tenor) and Joe Terranova (baritone). White later joined **The Spokesmen**. Group appeared in the 1958 movie *Let's Rock*.

DEBUT	PEAK	WKS	Gold	A-side (Chart Hit)..........B-side	$	Sym	Label & Number
12/9/57+	❶7	21	●	1 **At The Hop** RB5 T:❶7 / S:❶5 / A:❶3 *Sometimes (When I'm All Alone)*	$30		ABC-Paramount 9871
				song originally written as "Do The Bop"; first released on Singular 711 in 1957 ($800)			
3/3/58	19	11		2 **Rock And Roll Is Here To Stay** ....S:19 / T:19 *School Boy Romance*	$30		ABC-Paramount 9888
6/23/58	39	6		3 **Dottie** ....S:39 / T:41 *In The Meantime*	$30		ABC-Paramount 9926
				Artie Singer (orch., all of above)			
9/19/60	27	9		4 **Twistin' U.S.A.** ....*A Thousand Miles Away*	$20		Swan 4060
2/20/61	60	7		5 **Pony Express** ....*Daydreamer*	$20		Swan 4068
9/18/61	80	5		6 **Back To The Hop** ....*The Charleston Fish*	$20		Swan 4082
1/6/62	68	5		7 **Twistin' All Night Long** ....*Some Kind Of Nut* [N]	$20		Swan 4092
				DANNY AND THE JUNIORS with Freddy Cannon			
4/14/62	93	1		8 **Doin' The Continental Walk** ....*Do The Mashed Potatoes*	$20		Swan 4100
				Frank Slay (orch.: #4-8)			
1/19/63	99	2		9 **Oo-La-La-Limbo** ....*Now And Then*	$25		Guyden 2076

DANNY BOY — '97

Born in Chicago, Illinois; raised in Los Angeles, California. R&B singer.

DEBUT	PEAK	WKS	Gold	A-side (Chart Hit)..........B-side	$	Sym	Label & Number
5/31/97	70S	3		**It's Over Now** ....BUB:101 *(instrumental)*	$5	▮	Death Row 97017
				written by **Babyface**; from the movie *Gridlock'd* starring Tupac Shakur (**2 Pac**)			

DANNY WILSON — AC/LP '87

Pop trio from Dundee, Scotland: brothers Gary (vocals, guitar) and Kit (keyboards, percussion) Clark, with Ged Grimes (bass). Group named after the 1952 **Frank Sinatra** movie *Meet Danny Wilson*.

DEBUT	PEAK	WKS	Gold	A-side (Chart Hit)..........B-side	$	Sym	Label & Number
6/6/87	23	20		**Mary's Prayer** ....S:22 / A:22 *Monkey's Shiney Day*	$4	■	Virgin 99465

DEBUT	PEAK	WKS	Gold	A-side (Chart Hit)........B-side	$	Sym	Label & Number

DANTÉ and the EVERGREENS — BUB '60

Born Donald Drowty on 9/8/41 in Los Angeles, California. Pop singer. The Evergreens: Bill Young, future record producer Tony Moon and future Beverly Hills lawyer Frank D. Rosenthal.

DEBUT	PEAK	WKS	Gold	A-side (Chart Hit)........B-side	$	Sym	Label & Number
5/30/60	15	13		1 **Alley-Oop**........*The Right Time* [N]	$25		Madison 130
9/12/60	73	6		2 **Time Machine**........*Dream Land* [N]	$25		Madison 135
				above 2 produced by **Herb Alpert** and Lou Adler			

DANZIG — ROK/LP '94

Born Glenn Danzig on 6/23/59 in Lodi, New Jersey. Hard-rock singer/songwriter. His group: John Crist (guitar), Eerie Von (bass) and Chuck Biscuits (drums).

DEBUT	PEAK	WKS	Gold	A-side (Chart Hit)........B-side	$	Sym	Label & Number
2/12/94	43	15		**Mother**........S:12 *(live version)*	$5	▮	American 18256
				remix of song from Danzig's self-titled 1988 debut album			

D'ARBY, Terence Trent — R&B/BUB/ROK/LP '88

Born on 3/15/62 in Brooklyn, New York; later based in London, England. R&B-pop singer/songwriter/producer. Last name originally spelled Darby. Was a member of the U.S. Army boxing team.

DEBUT	PEAK	WKS	Gold	A-side (Chart Hit)........B-side	$	Sym	Label & Number
10/24/87	68	8		1 **If You Let Me Stay**........*Loving You Is Another Word For Lonely*	$3	■	Columbia 07398
1/16/88	❶[1]	25	●	2 **Wishing Well** RB[1] S:❶[1] / A:2 *Elevators & Hearts*	$3	■	Columbia 07675
5/28/88	4	21		3 **Sign Your Name**........S:4 / A:5 *Greasy Chicken*	$3	■	Columbia 07911
9/10/88	30	11		4 **Dance Little Sister (Part One)**........S:26 / A:30 *(Part Two)*	$3	■	Columbia 08023
				all of above from the album *Introducing The Hardline According To Terence Trent D'Arby*			
8/28/93	74	8		5 **Delicate**........A:70 *She Kissed Me* (ROK #5)	$3	▮	Columbia 77128
				Des'ree (female vocal)			

DARENSBOURG, Joe, and his Dixie Flyers — '58

Born on 7/9/06 in Baton Rouge, Louisiana. Died on 5/24/85 (age 78). Black clarinetist with Jack Teagarden and **Louis Armstrong**.

DEBUT	PEAK	WKS	Gold	A-side (Chart Hit)........B-side	$	Sym	Label & Number
1/27/58	43	9		**Yellow Dog Blues**........S:43 / T:45 *Martinque* [I]	$12		Lark 452
				written in 1928 by legendary composer W.C. Handy			

DARIAN, Fred — '61

Born on 6/16/27 in Detroit, Michigan. Pop singer/songwriter/producer. Co-writer of the #1 hit "Mr. Custer." Produced records for **Dobie Gray**.

DEBUT	PEAK	WKS	Gold	A-side (Chart Hit)........B-side	$	Sym	Label & Number
2/27/61	100	1		1 **Battle Of Gettysburg**........*Legend Of The Ghost Stage* [S]	$12		JAF 2020
9/25/61	96	1		2 **Johnny Willow**........*Strong Man*	$12		JAF 2023

DARIN, Bobby ★56★ — BUB/LP '59

Born Walden Robert Cassotto on 5/14/36 in the Bronx, New York. Died of heart failure on 12/20/73 (age 37). Pop-rock-swing vocalist/pianist/songwriter/entertainer. First recorded in 1956 with The Jaybirds (Decca). First appeared on TV in March 1956 on *The* **Tommy Dorsey** *Show*. Won the 1959 Best New Artist Grammy Award. Married to actress Sandra Dee from 1960-67. Nominated for an Oscar for his performance in the movie *Captain Newman, MD* (1963). Formed own record company, Direction. Inducted into the Rock and Roll Hall of Fame in 1990.

1)Mack The Knife 2)Dream Lover 3)You're The Reason I'm Living 4)Splish Splash 5)Things

DEBUT	PEAK	WKS	Gold	A-side (Chart Hit)........B-side	$	Sym	Label & Number
6/23/58	3	15	●	1 **Splish Splash**........RB[2] H:3 / S:4 / A:5 *Judy, Don't Be Moody*	$25		Atco 6117
7/28/58	24	10		2 **Early In The Morning**........H:24 / S:24 *Now We're One*	$40		Atco 6121
				THE RINKY-DINKS			
				originally issued on Brunswick 55073 ($150) as by the Ding Dongs (to conceal Darin's identity; he was under contract to Atco)			
10/6/58	9	19	●	3 **Queen Of The Hop**........H:9 *Lost Love*	$25		Atco 6127
1/26/59	38	9		4 **Plain Jane**........*While I'm Gone*	$20	■	Atco 6133
				adapted from the 1844 song "Buffalo Gals"			
4/20/59	2[1]	17	●	5 **Dream Lover**........*Bullmoose*	$15	■	Atco 6140
8/24/59	❶[9]	26	●	6 **Mack The Knife** *Was There A Call For Me*	$15	■	Atco 6147
				written in 1928 as "Moritat" or "Theme From The Threepenny Opera"; 1959 Grammy winner: Record of the Year			
1/18/60	6	14		7 **Beyond The Sea**........*That's The Way Love Is*	$15	■	Atco 6158
				introduced by **Benny Goodman** in 1948 (from the 1945 French song "La Mer")			
3/21/60	21	9		8 **Clementine**........*Tall Story*	$15	■	Atco 6161
				folk tune written in 1884 as "Oh, My Darling Clementine"			
5/23/60	19	11		9 **Won't You Come Home Bill Bailey /**			
				#1 hit for Arthur Collins in 1902			
7/11/60	79	2		10 **I'll Be There**........	$15	■	Atco 6167
9/5/60	100	1		11 **Beachcomber**........*Autumn Blues* [I]	$15	■	Atco 6173
				BOBBY DARIN at the Piano			
9/26/60	20	12		12 **Artificial Flowers /**			
				from the musical *Tenderloin* starring **Eileen Rodgers**			
9/26/60	45	9		13 **Somebody To Love**........	$15	■	Atco 6179
12/19/60	51	3		14 **Christmas Auld Lang Syne /** [X]			
12/26/60	95	1		15 **Child Of God**........[X]	$25	■	Atco 6183
2/6/61	14	10		16 **Lazy River**........*Oo-ee Train*	$15	■	Atco 6188
				#19 hit for Hoagy Carmichael in 1932			
6/12/61	40	6		17 **Nature Boy**........*Look For My True Love*	$15	■	Atco 6196
				#1 hit for **Nat King Cole** in 1948			
9/4/61	5	11		18 **You Must Have Been A Beautiful Baby**........*Sorrow Tomorrow*	$15	■	Atco 6206
				#1 hit for **Bing Crosby** in 1938			
12/11/61+	15	13		19 **Irresistible You /**			
12/18/61+	30	10		20 **Multiplication**........	$15	■	Atco 6214
				from the movie *Come September* starring Darin and Sandra Dee			
3/31/62	24	8		21 **What'd I Say (Part 1)**........*(Part II)*	$15	■	Atco 6221
7/7/62	3	12		22 **Things**........*Jailer Bring Me Water*	$15		Atco 6229

DEBUT	PEAK	WKS	Gold	A-side (Chart Hit)..........B-side	$	Sym	Label & Number
				DARIN, Bobby — Cont'd			
9/29/62	**32**	8		23 **If A Man Answers**..........*A True, True Love* (#105)	$12	■	Capitol 4837
				title song from the movie starring Darin and Sandra Dee; a Capitol custom record and picture sleeve issued with a special Scripto pen offer for the above A & B-sides plus 2 more songs			
9/29/62	**42**	7		24 **Baby Face**..........*You Know How*	$12		Atco 6236
				#1 hit for Jan Garber in 1926; #3 hit for **Art Mooney** in 1948			
12/15/62	**90**	1		25 **I Found A New Baby**..........*Keep A Walkin'*	$12		Atco 6244
				#19 hit for **The Mills Brothers** in 1934			
1/19/63	**3**	14		26 **You're The Reason I'm Living**..........*Now You're Gone*	$10	■	Capitol 4897
5/11/63	**10**	10		27 **18 Yellow Roses**..........*Not For Me*	$10	■	Capitol 4970
8/24/63	**43**	9		28 **Treat My Baby Good**..........*Down So Long*	$10		Capitol 5019
11/23/63	**64**	7		29 **Be Mad Little Girl**..........*Since You Been Gone*	$10		Capitol 5079
3/7/64	**93**	3		30 **I Wonder Who's Kissing Her Now**..........*As Long As I'm Singing*	$10		Capitol 5126
				#1 hit for Henry Burr in 1909; #2 hit for **Perry Como** in 1947			
5/16/64	**45**	9		31 **Milord**..........*Golden Earrings* [F]	$12		Atco 6297
10/3/64	**86**	3		32 **The Things In This House**..........*Wait By The Water*	$10		Capitol 5257
2/6/65	**79**	3		33 **Hello, Dolly!**..........*Goodbye, Charlie*	$10		Capitol 5359
				a court ruling found this song to be based on the 1949 hit "Sunflower"			
4/30/66	**53**	7		34 **Mame**..........*Walkin In The Shadow Of Love*	$8		Atlantic 2329
				above 2 are title songs from Broadway musicals			
9/24/66	**8**	11		35 **If I Were A Carpenter**..........*Rainin'*	$8		Atlantic 2350
12/10/66	**66**	5		36 **The Girl That Stood Beside Me**..........*Reason To Believe*	$8		Atlantic 2367
1/14/67	**32**	8		37 **Lovin' You**..........*Amy*	$8		Atlantic 2376
4/8/67	**62**	5		38 **The Lady Came From Baltimore**..........*I Am*	$8		Atlantic 2395
7/29/67	**93**	2		39 **Darling Be Home Soon**..........*Hello Sunshine*	$8		Atlantic 2420
2/8/69	**79**	3		40 **Long Line Rider**..........*Change*	$10		Direction 350
				#1, 2, 5, 10, 11, 13, 20, 22, 23, 26-29, 32 & 40: written by Darin			
1/6/73	**67**	8		41 **Happy**..........*Something In Her Love*	$6		Motown 1217
				love theme from the movie *Lady Sings The Blues* starring **Diana Ross**; Darin's musical conductors: Richard Behrke (#12, 16), **Perry Botkin, Jr.** (#34), Bob Halley (#37), Jimmy Haskell (#19-21, 23-26, 28, 29, 32), **Jack Nitzsche** (#27), Donald Peake (#35, 36), **Shorty Rogers** (#11), **Bobby Scott** (#9, 14, 15) and Richard Wess (#6-8, 10, 13, 33)			
				DARKSIDE BALLAZ '00			
				Rap duo from Chicago, Illinois: Lo and Sko.			
12/16/00	**50^{S}**	4		**Peace Of Mind**..........*(album version) / Grand Finale* (Legit Ballaz & Twista)	$10	★	Legit Ballin 25014
				DARKSIDE BALLAZ Feat. Twista			
				DARLIN, Florraine BUB '62			
				Born Florraine Panza on 1/20/44 in Pittsburgh, Pennsylvania. Pop singer similar in style to **Connie Francis**.			
8/25/62	**62**	7		**Long As The Rose Is Red**..........*I Don't Know*	$12		Epic 9529
				Robert Mersey (orch.); answer song to **Bobby Vinton**'s "Roses Are Red"			
				DARREN, James BUB/AC/C&W/LP '62			
				Born James Ercolani on 6/8/36 in Philadelphia, Pennsylvania. Pop singer/actor. Moved to Hollywood in 1955. In the movies *Rumble On The Docks, The Brothers Rico, Operation Mad Ball, Gunman's Walk, The Guns Of Navarone, Because They're Young* and *Let No Man Write My Epitaph.* Played "Moondoggie," Gidget's boyfriend, in *Gidget, Gidget Goes Hawaiian* and *Gidget Goes To Rome.* In the TV series *The Time Tunnel* from 1966-67 and *T.J. Hooker* from 1983-86.			
				1)Goodbye Cruel World 2)Her Royal Majesty 3)Conscience			
4/27/59	**41**	12		1 **Gidget**..........*"You"*	$20		Colpix 113
				title song from the movie starring Darren and Sandra Dee			
8/3/59	**47**	8		2 **Angel Face**..........*I Don't Wanna Lose Ya*	$20		Colpix 119
				JIMMY DARREN (above 2)			
10/16/61	**3**	17		3 **Goodbye Cruel World**..........*Valerie*	$15	■	Colpix 609
				originally released on Colpix 181 in 1961 ($20)			
2/3/62	**6**	11		4 **Her Royal Majesty**..........*If I Could Only Tell You*	$15		Colpix 622
4/14/62	**11**	10		5 **Conscience**..........*Dream Big*	$15		Colpix 630
6/30/62	**39**	8		6 **Mary's Little Lamb**..........*The Life Of The Party*	$15		Colpix 644
10/13/62	**97**	1		7 **Hail To The Conquering Hero**..........*To Young To Go Steady*	$12		Colpix 655
2/9/63	**54**	6		8 **Pin A Medal On Joey**..........*Diamond Head*	$12		Colpix 672
1/14/67	**35**	8		9 **All**..........*Misty Morning Eyes*	$8		Warner 5874
				from the movie *Run For Your Wife* starring Frankie Randall			
3/19/77	**52**	9		10 **You Take My Heart Away**..........*(disco version)*	$5		Private Stock 45,136
				from the movie *Rocky* starring Sylvester Stallone			
				DARTELLS, The LP '63			
				Rock and roll band from Oxnard, California: Doug Phillips (vocals, bass), Dick Burns, Corky Wilkie, Rich Peil, Randy Ray and Gary Peeler. Phillips died on 5/5/95 (age 50).			
4/13/63	**11**	11		1 **Hot Pastrami**..........*Dartell Stomp*	$20		Dot 16453
				first released on Arlen 509 in 1962 ($30); revision of **Nat Kendricks**'s "(Do The) Mashed Potatoes"			
8/24/63	**99**	1		2 **Dance, Everybody, Dance**..........*The Scoobie Song*	$20		Dot 16502
				first released on Arlen 513 in 1962 ($30)			
				DARUDE '01			
				Born Ville Virtanen on 1/28/75 in Finland. Techno-dance DJ/producer.			
7/21/01	**83**	10		**Sandstorm**..........S:57 *(3 mixes)* [I]	$8	★*	Groovilicious 37127
				DAS EFX R&B/BUB/LP '92			
				Hip-hop duo of Andre "Dray" Weston (born on 9/9/70) and Willie "Skoob" Hines (born on 11/27/70) formed at Virginia State. DAS is an acronym for Dray And Skoob (which is "books" spelled backward).			
5/9/92	**25**	20	●	1 **They Want EFX** S:12 / A:35 *Jussummen*	$3	▌	EastWest 98600
7/31/93	**20**	20	▲	2 **Check Yo Self**..........RB^1 S:9 / A:47 *(instrumental) / It Was A Good Day / 24 With a L*	$5	▌*	Priority 53830
				ICE CUBE featuring DAS EFX			
				samples "The Message" by **Grandmaster Flash & The Furious Five**			
11/13/93	**43**	12		3 **Freakit**..........S:22 *Gimme Dat Microphone*	$3	▌	EastWest 98341

DEBUT	PEAK	WKS	Gold	A-side (Chart Hit)......B-side	$	Sym	Label & Number
				DAS EFX — Cont'd			
9/23/95	**61**	10		4 **Real Hip-Hop** ......S:42 *No Diggedy*	$3	▮	EastWest 64387
2/17/96	**86**	3		5 **Microphone Master** ......S:48 *(album version)*	$3	▮	EastWest 64309
				DAS EFX featuring Mobb Deep			
				samples "Come Clean" by **Jeru The Damaja** and "Neva Go Back" by **Special Ed**			
				DASH, Sarah R&B/LP **'79**			
				Born on 8/18/43 in Trenton, New Jersey. R&B singer. Original member of **The Blue-Belles** and **LaBelle**.			
2/17/79	**71**	4		**Sinner Man** ......*Look But Don't Touch*	$5		Kirshner 4278
				DAVE DEE, DOZY, BEAKY, MICK AND TICH BUB/LP **'68**			
				Pop group from Wiltshire, England: "Dave Dee" Harmon (vocals), Trevor "Dozy" Davies (guitar), John "Beaky" Dymond (guitar), Michael "Mick" Wilson (bass) and Ian "Tich" Amey (drums).			
1/6/68	**52**	6		**Zabadak** ......*The Sun Goes Down* [F]	$10		Imperial 66270
				DAVID, Craig BUB/LP **'02**			
				Born on 5/5/81 in Southampton, England. R&B singer/songwriter.			
6/9/01	**15**	27		1 **Fill Me In** ......S:3 / A:17 *(Full Crew Mix) / (3 album snippets)*	$5	★+V	Wildstar/Atlantic 88101
12/8/01+	**10**	20		2 **7 Days** ......S:8 / A:10 *(5 remixes - w/**Mos Def** & **Fat Joe**)*	$8	★++V	Wildstar/Atlantic 85232
				"45" issued for above 2 on Atlantic 88101			
4/13/02	**65**S	1		3 **Re-Rewind** ......*(2 remixes)*	$6	★	Republic 156916
				ARTFUL DODGER UK			
				remix by Mark Hill and Peter Devereux (Artful Dodger UK) of David's recording "Rewind" from his 2001 album *Born To Do It*			
5/25/02	**44**	20		4 **Walking Away** ......A:48 *(5 versions)*	$6	TV	Wildstar 85329
				"45": Atlantic 85322; B-side "Time To Party"			
				DAVID, F.R. **'83**			
				Born Robert Fitoussi on 1/1/54 in Tunisia, Africa; raised in Paris, France. White pop singer/songwriter.			
7/23/83	**62**	9		**Words** ......*Rocker Blues*	$4		Carrere 101
				DAVID & DAVID ROK/LP **'86**			
				Pop-rock duo from Los Angeles, California: David Baerwald and David Ricketts.			
10/4/86	**37**	16		1 **Welcome To The Boomtown** ......S:31 *A Rock For The Forgotten*	$3	■	A&M 2857
1/24/87	**51**	11		2 **Ain't So Easy** ......*Swimming In The Ocean*	$3	■	A&M 2905
				Toni Childs (backing vocal)			
				DAVID & JONATHAN BUB **'66**			
				Songwriting/producing/vocal duo from Bristol, England: Roger Greenaway (David) and Roger Cook (Jonathan). Both later were production team for **White Plains**. Cook founded **Blue Mink**. Greenaway also in **The Pipkins**.			
1/8/66	**18**	9		**Michelle** ......*How Bitter The Taste Of Love*	$12		Capitol 5563
				George Martin (orch.); written by **John Lennon** and **Paul McCartney** (from **The Beatles**' *Rubber Soul* album)			
				DAVIDSON, Clay C&W/BUB **'00**			
				Born in Saltville, Virginia. Country singer/guitarist.			
3/25/00	**49**	20		**Unconditional** ......A:44 / S:53 *My Best Friend And Me*	$4	★V	Virgin 38690
				"45": Virgin 58838			
				DAVIE, Hutch, and his Honky Tonkers **'58**			
				Born Robert Davie. Leading musical arranger during the 1950s and 1960s. Pianist on **Jim Lowe**'s hit "The Green Door."			
6/2/58	**51**	7		**Woodchopper's Ball** ......T:51 *Honky Tonk Train* [I]	$15		Atco 6110
				#9 hit for **Woody Herman** in 1939			
				DAVINA LP **'97**			
				Born Davina Bussey in Detroit, Michigan. Female R&B singer/songwriter.			
11/1/97	**60**	19		1 **So Good** ......S:40 *(4 versions w/**Raekwon** & **Xzibit**)*	$3	▮	Loud/RCA 65303
				samples "Django" by Cal Tjader; from the movie *Hoodlum* starring Laurence Fishburne			
4/18/98	**81**	9		2 **Come Over To My Place** ......S:61 *(instrumental) / So Good (w/**Ol' Dirty Bastard**)*	$3	▮	Loud/RCA 65448
				DAVIS, Alana LP **'98**			
				Born on 5/6/74 in Manhattan, New York. Female pop-rock singer/songwriter.			
12/6/97+	**37**	20		**32 Flavors** ......S:43 / A:52 *Lullaby*	$3	▮	Elektra 64129
				DAVIS, Jimmy, & Junction LP **'87**			
				Born in Memphis, Tennessee. Rock singer/guitarist. His band Junction: Tommy Burroughs (guitar), John Scott (piano) and Chuck Reynolds (drums).			
11/7/87	**67**	6		**Kick The Wall** ......*Over The Top*	$4	■	QMI Music 53107
				DAVIS, John, And The Monster Orchestra R&B/BUB **'79**			
				Born on 8/31/52 in Philadelphia, Pennsylvania. Dance singer/songwriter/producer/arranger. In U.S. Naval Academy Band. Wrote score for the Broadway musical *Gotta Go Disco*. Also see **Arthur Prysock**'s "When Love Is New."			
12/23/78+	**89**	4		**Ain't That Enough For You** ......*Disco Fever*	$5		Sam 5011
	★421★			**DAVIS, Mac** C&W/AC/BUB/LP **'72**			
				Born on 1/21/42 in Lubbock, Texas. Country-pop singer/songwriter/actor. Worked as a regional rep for Vee-Jay and Liberty Records. Wrote "In The Ghetto" and "Don't Cry Daddy" for **Elvis Presley**. Host of own musical variety TV series from 1974-76. Appearances in several movies, including *North Dallas Forty* in 1979.			
				1)Baby Don't Get Hooked On Me 2)Stop And Smell The Roses 3)One Hell Of A Woman			
5/16/70	**53**	8		1 **Whoever Finds This, I Love You** ......*Half And Half (Song For Sarah)*	$6	■	Columbia 45117
2/27/71	**92**	2		2 **Beginning To Feel The Pain** ......*Butterfly Girl*	$6		Columbia 45302
7/1/72	**①**3	18	●	3 **Baby Don't Get Hooked On Me** AC3 *Poem For My Little Lady*	$5		Columbia 45618
11/25/72	**63**	7		4 **Everybody Loves A Love Song** ......*Friend, Lover, Woman, Wife*	$5		Columbia 45727
2/17/73	**73**	7		5 **Dream Me Home** ......*Spread Your Love On Me*	$5		Columbia 45773
				all of above (except #2) from the album *Baby Don't Get Hooked On Me*			
5/5/73	**88**	6		6 **Your Side Of The Bed** ......*(Hope You Didn't) Chop No Wood*	$5		Columbia 45839
3/30/74	**11**	28		7 **One Hell Of A Woman** ......*A Poor Man's Gold*	$5		Columbia 46004
8/24/74	**9**	14		8 **Stop And Smell The Roses** ......AC1 *Poor Boy Boogie*	$5		Columbia 10018
				co-written by Doc Severinsen			
12/7/74+	**15**	11		9 **Rock N' Roll (I Gave You The Best Years Of My Life)** ......*Emily Suzanne*	$5		Columbia 10070

DEBUT	PEAK	WKS	Gold	A-side (Chart Hit)..........B-side	$	Sym	Label & Number
				DAVIS, Mac — Cont'd			
4/5/75	54	4		10 **(If You Add) All The Love In The World** ..... *Smiley*	$5		Columbia 10111
5/31/75	53	8		11 **Burnin' Thing** ..... *A Special Place In Heaven*	$5		Columbia 10148
4/10/76	76	5		12 **Forever Lovers** ..... *The Love Lamp*	$5		Columbia 10304
3/22/80	43	12		13 **It's Hard To Be Humble** ..... *The Greatest Gift Of All* [N]	$4		Casablanca 2244
10/18/80	51	9		14 **Texas In My Rear View Mirror** ..... *Sad Songs* all of above (except #9, 10 & 12) written by Davis	$4		Casablanca 2305
7/11/81	76	6		15 **Secrets** ..... *Remember When (Beverly's Song)*	$4		Casablanca 2336
				DAVIS, Martha — see MOTELS, The			
	★353★			**DAVIS, Paul** C&W/BUB/LP **'82** Born on 4/21/48 in Meridian, Mississippi. Pop-country singer/songwriter/producer. Survived a shooting in Nashville on 7/30/86. *1)'65 Love Affair 2)I Go Crazy 3)Cool Night*			
4/18/70	52	12		1 **A Little Bit Of Soap** ..... *Three Little Words*	$7		Bang 576
9/12/70	51	9		2 **I Just Wanna Keep It Together** ..... *Pollyana*	$7		Bang 579
12/23/72+	68	9		3 **Boogie Woogie Man** ..... *Johnny Poverty*	$6		Bang 599
10/12/74+	23	18		4 **Ride 'Em Cowboy** ..... *I'm The Only Sinner (In Salt Lake City)*	$5		Bang 712
7/5/75	90	2		5 **Keep Our Love Alive** ..... *I Got A Yearning*	$5		Bang 718
4/24/76	45	10		6 **Thinking Of You** ..... *Karma Baby*	$5		Bang 724
8/7/76	35	9		7 **Superstar** ..... *Magnolia Blues* tribute to **Elton John**, **Stevie Wonder**, **Linda Ronstadt** and **Joni Mitchell**	$5		Bang 726
8/27/77+	7	40		8 **I Go Crazy** ..... *Reggae Kinda Way*	$5		Bang 733
5/20/78	51	6		9 **Darlin'** ..... *You're Not Just A Rose* **PAUL DAVIS Featuring Susan Collins**	$5		Bang 736
8/26/78	17	21		10 **Sweet Life** ..... *Bad Dream* a new version as a duet with **Marie Osmond** made the Country charts in 1988 (#47)	$5		Bang 738
3/8/80	23	14		11 **Do Right** ..... *He Sang Our Love Songs*	$4		Bang 4808
7/19/80	78	4		12 **Cry Just A Little** ..... *Do You Believe In Love*	$4		Bang 4811
11/7/81+	11	19		13 **Cool Night** ..... *One More Time For The Lonely*	$4		Arista 0645
2/27/82	6	20		14 **'65 Love Affair** ..... *We're Still Together* all of above (except #1 & 9) written by Davis	$4		Arista 0661
7/17/82	40	10		15 **Love Or Let Me Be Lonely** ..... *Oriental Eyes*	$4		Arista 0697
	★331★			**DAVIS, Sammy Jr.** BUB/AC/MEM/POP/C&W/LP **'55** Born on 12/8/25 in Harlem, New York. Died of cancer on 5/16/90 (age 64). One of America's all-time great entertainers. With father and uncle in dance act the Will Mastin Trio from the early 1940s. First recorded for Capitol in 1950. Lost his left ey e and had his nose smashed in an auto accident near San Bernardino, California, on 11/19/54; returned to performing in January 1955. Frequent appearances on TV, Broadway and in movies. Won Grammy's Lifetime Achievement Award in 2001. First hit the pop charts in 1954 with "Hey There" (#16). *1)The Candy Man 2)Something's Gotta Give 3)I've Gotta Be Me*			
6/4/55	9	11		1 **Something's Gotta Give** / S:9 / J:16 / A:20 from the movie *Daddy Long Legs* starring Fred Astaire; a picture sleeve was issued promoting 2 songs from the movie *Daddy Long Legs* (**Sammy Davis, Jr.**'s and **The Four Aces**'s "Sluefoot")		□	
5/28/55	12	12		2 **Love Me Or Leave Me** ..... S:12 / A:20 #2 hit in 1929 for Ruth Etting and title song of her 1955 biopic starring **Doris Day**	$15		Decca 29484
7/2/55	13	6		3 **That Old Black Magic** ..... A:13 / S:16 / J:18 *A Man With A Dream* #1 hit for Glenn Miller in 1943 (from the movie *Star-Spangled Rhythm* starring **Bing Crosby**)	$15		Decca 29541
11/26/55+	87	3		4 **I'll Know** ..... T:87 *Adelaide* from the movie *Guys And Dolls* starring Marlon Brando and **Frank Sinatra**	$12		Decca 29672
7/14/56	71	3		5 **Five** ..... T:71 *You're Sensational*	$12		Decca 29976
9/8/56	46	13		6 **Earthbound** ..... *Just One Of Those Things*	$12		Decca 30035
11/17/56	59	4		7 **New York's My Home** ..... T:59 *Never Like This* from **Gordon Jenkins**' 1946 musical narrative *Manhattan Tower*	$12		Decca 30111
9/1/62	17	15		8 **What Kind Of Fool Am I** ..... *Gonna Build A Mountain* from the Broadway musical *Stop The World-I Want To Get Off* starring **Anthony Newley**	$10		Reprise 20,048
12/1/62	64	6		9 **Me And My Shadow** / **FRANK SINATRA and SAMMY DAVIS JR.** #1 hit for "Whispering" Jack Smith in 1927			
12/22/62	94	3		10 **Sam's Song** ..... [N] **DEAN MARTIN and SAMMY DAVIS JR.** #3 hit for Gary & **Bing Crosby** in 1950	$15	■	Reprise 20,128
1/26/63	59	9		11 **As Long As She Needs Me** ..... *Song From "Two For The Seesaw"* from Broadway's *Oliver!* starring Clive Revill	$10		Reprise 20,138
11/30/63+	17	17		12 **The Shelter Of Your Arms** ..... *This Was My Love*	$10		Reprise 20,216
5/27/67	37	9		13 **Don't Blame The Children** ..... *She Believes In Me* [S]	$7		Reprise 0566
5/25/68	93	3		14 **Lonely Is The Name** ..... *Flash, Bang, Wallop!*	$7		Reprise 0673
12/14/68+	11	16		15 **I've Gotta Be Me** ..... AC⁷ *Bein' Natural Bein' Me* from the Broadway musical *Golden Rainbow* starring **Steve Lawrence** and **Eydie Gorme**	$7		Reprise 0779
3/11/72	❶³	21	●	16 **The Candy Man** ..... AC² *I Want To Be Happy* (Davis) from the movie *Willy Wonka And The Chocolate Factory* starring Gene Wilder; originally recorded as by The Mike Curb Congregation; Davis's vocals dubbed in later	$5		MGM 14320
10/21/72	92	5		17 **The People Tree** ..... *Mr. Bojangles* (Davis) **SAMMY DAVIS, JR. with The Mike Curb Congregation** (above 2) Davis's musical arrangers and conductors: **H.B. Barnum** (#13, 14), **Perry Botkin, Jr.** (#12), **Don Costa** (#16, 17), **Billy May** (#9, 10), Sy Oliver (#1, 2), Marty Paich (#8, 11), **Jack Pleis** (#4, 6, 7), Morty Stevens (#3, 5) and Richard Wess (#15)	$5		MGM 14426

DEBUT	PEAK	WKS	Gold	A-side (Chart Hit)	B-side	$	Sym	Label & Number

DAVIS, Skeeter
C&W/BUB/LP '63

Born Mary Frances Penick on 12/30/31 in Dry Ridge, Kentucky. Country singer. Recorded with friend Betty Jack Davis as the Davis Sisters until Betty Jack was killed in a car accident on 8/2/53. Married to TV's *Nashville Now* host, Ralph Emery (1960-64). Married to Joey Spampinato, the bassist of jazz-rock band **NRBQ** (1983-96). Charted 41 Country hits, 1958-76.

DEBUT	PEAK	WKS	Gold	A-side (Chart Hit)	B-side	$	Sym	Label & Number
8/22/60	39	7		1 **(I Can't Help You) I'm Falling Too**	*No Never*	$12		RCA Victor 7767
				answer song to **Hank Locklin**'s "Please Help Me, I'm Falling"				
12/12/60+	26	8		2 **My Last Date (With You)**	*Someone I'd Like To Forget*	$12		RCA Victor 7825
				vocal version of **Floyd Cramer**'s "Last Date"				
1/26/63	2^1	17		3 **The End Of The World** AC^4	*Somebody Loves You*	$12		RCA Victor 8098
				the most successful "crossover" hit on *Billboard's* 4 major singles charts: AC #1^4 / C&W #2^3 / Hot 100 #2^1 / R&B #4				
5/11/63	41	7		4 **I'm Saving My Love**	*Somebody Else On Your Mind*	$12		RCA Victor 8176
9/7/63	7	13		5 **I Can't Stay Mad At You**	*It Was Only A Heart*	$12	■	RCA Victor 8219
1/25/64	47	7		6 **He Says The Same Things To Me /**				
2/22/64	92	1		7 **How Much Can A Lonely Heart Stand**		$12		RCA Victor 8288
5/2/64	48	7		8 **Gonna Get Along Without You Now**	*Now You're Gone*	$12		RCA Victor 8347
				#25 hit for **Teresa Brewer** in 1952; all of above (except #4) produced by **Chet Atkins**				

DAVIS, Spencer, Group
BUB/LP '67

Born on 7/14/41 in Swansea, South Wales. Rock singer/rhythm guitarist. Formed his R&B-styled rock group in Birmingham, England in 1963. Featured **Steve Winwood** (lead vocals, lead guitar, keyboards), his brother Muff Winwood (bass) and Pete York (drums). Steve Winwood left in 1967 to form the group **Traffic**; later, a successful solo artist. Muff became senior director of A&R at CBS Records, U.K.

DEBUT	PEAK	WKS	Gold	A-side (Chart Hit)	B-side	$	Sym	Label & Number
3/5/66	76	4		1 **Keep On Running**	*High Time Baby*	$15		Atco 6400
12/31/66+	7	13		2 **Gimme Some Lovin'**	*Blues In F*	$12		United Artists 50108
3/25/67	10	9		3 **I'm A Man**	*Can't Get Enough Of It*	$12		United Artists 50144
6/17/67	47	7		4 **Somebody Help Me**	*On The Green Light*	$10		United Artists 50162
9/16/67	100	1		5 **Time Seller**	*Don't Want You No More*	$10	■	United Artists 50202

DAVIS, Tami
'98

Born in Charleston, South Carolina. Female R&B singer.

DEBUT	PEAK	WKS	Gold	A-side (Chart Hit)	B-side	$	Sym	Label & Number
7/4/98	63	14		1 **How Do I Say I'm Sorry** S:41	*Why You Wanna Do Me Like This / (3 album snippets)*	$4	▮	Red Ant/BMG 15308
				Deborah Cox (backing vocal; co-writer); first released on Red Ant/Mercury 119008				
11/28/98	93	1		2 **Only You** S:47	*(2 versions)*	$4	▮	Red Ant/BMG 15325

DAVIS, Tim
'72

Born on 11/29/43 in Milwaukee, Wisconsin. Died on 9/20/88 (age 44). Pop singer/drummer.

DEBUT	PEAK	WKS	Gold	A-side (Chart Hit)	B-side	$	Sym	Label & Number
9/16/72	91	3		**Buzzy Brown**	*On The Rocks* [N]	$6		Metromedia 253

DAVIS, Tyrone
★479★ R&B/BUB/LP '70

Born on 5/4/38 in Greenville, Mississippi; raised in Saginaw, Michigan. R&B singer. To Chicago in 1959. Worked as valet/chauffeur for **Freddy King** until 1962. Working local clubs when discovered by Harold Burrage. First recorded for Four Brothers in 1965 as Tyrone The Wonder Boy. His younger sister, Jean Davis, was a member of the group **Facts Of Life**. Charted 43 R&B hits, 1968-88.

1)Turn Back The Hands Of Time 2)Can I Change My Mind 3)There It Is

DEBUT	PEAK	WKS	Gold	A-side (Chart Hit)	B-side	$	Sym	Label & Number
12/21/68+	5	13	●	1 **Can I Change My Mind** RB^3	*A Woman Needs To Be Loved*	$8		Dakar 602
3/22/69	34	7		2 **Is It Something You've Got**	*Undying Love*	$8		Dakar 605
3/21/70	3	13	●	3 **Turn Back The Hands Of Time** RB^2	*I Keep Coming Back*	$8		Dakar 616
6/27/70	53	9		4 **I'll Be Right Here**	*Just Because Of You*	$7		Dakar 618
10/3/70	58	8		5 **Let Me Back In**	*Love Bones*	$7		Dakar 621
3/20/71	60	7		6 **Could I Forget You**	*Just My Way Of Loving You*	$7		Dakar 623
7/3/71	75	7		7 **One-Way Ticket**	*We Got A Love*	$7		Dakar 624
11/20/71	94	3		8 **You Keep Me Holding On**	*We Got A Love No One Can Deny*	$7		Dakar 626
3/25/72	61	9		9 **I Had It All The Time**	*You Wouldn't Believe*	$7		Dakar 4501
4/21/73	64	9		10 **Without You In My Life**	*How Could I Forget You*	$7		Dakar 4519
7/28/73	32	9		11 **There It Is**	*You Wouldn't Believe*	$7		Dakar 4523
2/2/74	57	9		12 **I Wish It Was Me**	*You Don't Have To Beg Me To Stay*	$7		Dakar 4529
				all of above produced by **Willie Henderson**				
7/6/74	89	2		13 **What Goes Up (Must Come Down)**	*There's Got To Be An Answer*	$7		Dakar 4532
9/25/76	38	11		14 **Give It Up (Turn It Loose)**	*You're Too Much*	$6		Columbia 10388
12/25/82+	57	6		15 **Are You Serious**	*Overdue*	$5		Highrise 2005

DAWN — see ORLANDO, Tony

DAY, Arlan
'81

Born in Manchester, England. White pop-jazz pianist/singer.

DEBUT	PEAK	WKS	Gold	A-side (Chart Hit)	B-side	$	Sym	Label & Number
10/17/81	71	7		**I Surrender**	*The Only Woman*	$5		Pasha 02480

DAY, Bobby
BUB '58

Born Robert Byrd on 7/1/30 in Ft. Worth, Texas. Died of cancer on 7/15/90 (age 60). R&B singer/songwriter. To Watts, Los Angeles in 1948. Formed the **Hollywood Flames** in 1950. Group also recorded as The Flames in 1950. Day recorded with various Flames members as the Hollywood Four Flames, Jets, Tangiers, and The Satellites until 1957. Day then recorded solo, and later in duo **Bob & Earl** in 1960.

DEBUT	PEAK	WKS	Gold	A-side (Chart Hit)	B-side	$	Sym	Label & Number
11/18/57	57	8		1 **Little Bitty Pretty One** T:57	*When The Swallows Come Back To Capistrano*	$30		Class 211
				BOBBY DAY and The Satellites				
8/4/58	2^2	21	●	2 **Rock-in Robin /** RB^3 H:2 / S:4				
8/4/58	41	11		3 **Over And Over** H:41 / S:flip		$30		Class 229
12/29/58+	54	6		4 **The Bluebird, The Buzzard & The Oriole**	*Alone Too Long*	$25		Class 241
4/20/59	98	1		5 **That's All I Want**	*Say Yes*	$25		Class 245
6/22/59	82	1		6 **Gotta New Girl**	*Mr. & Mrs. Rock-'N-Roll*	$25		Class 252

DEBUT	PEAK	WKS	Gold	A-side (Chart Hit)..........B-side	$	Sym	Label & Number
	★507★			**DAY, Doris** MEM/POP/BUB/AC/LP **'48** Born Doris Kappelhoff on 4/3/22 in Cincinnati, Ohio. Sang briefly with Bob Crosby in 1940 and shortly thereafter became a major star with the Les Brown band (she had 12 charted hits with Brown including the #1 hits "Sentimental Journey" and "My Dreams Are Getting Better All The Time"). Her great solo recording success was soon transcended by Hollywood as Day became the #1 box office star of the late 1950s and early 1960s. Star of own popular TV series from 1968-73. Her husband, Marty Melcher, owned Arwin Records; their son, Terry, was a member of **The Rip Chords** and **Bruce And Terry**, and a prolific producer (**The Beach Boys**). Charted 32 pop hits, 1948-54, including 3 #1 hits: "Love Somebody," "A Guy Is A Guy" and "Secret Love." *1)Whatever Will Be, Will Be (Que Sera, Sera) 2)If I Give My Heart To You 3)Everybody Loves A Lover*			
9/11/54	3	17		1 **If I Give My Heart To You** ....J:3 / S:4 / A:4 *Anyone Can Fall In Love* The Mellomen (backing vocals)	$15		Columbia 40300
7/23/55	13	9		2 **I'll Never Stop Loving You** ....A:13 / S:15 / T:93 *Never Look Back* **Percy Faith** (orch.); from the movie *Love Me Or Leave Me* starring Day	$15		Columbia 40505
11/26/55	83	6		3 **Ooh Bang Jiggilly Jang** ....T:83 *Jimmy Unknown*	$12		Columbia 40581
1/7/56	51	7		4 **Let It Ring** ....T:51 *Love's Little Island* Paul Weston (orch., above 2 & #7 below)	$12		Columbia 40618
6/23/56	2^{3}	27	●	5 **Whatever Will Be, Will Be (Que Sera, Sera)** T:2 / A:2 / J:3 / S:3 *I've Gotta Sing Away These Blues* from the movie *The Man Who Knew Too Much* starring Day and James Stewart	$12		Columbia 40704
10/20/56	64	10		6 **Julie** / T:64 Leith Stevens (orch.); title song from the movie starring Day			
10/20/56	79	4		7 **Love In A Home** ....T:79 from the Broadway musical *L'il Abner* starring Edie Adams and Peter Palmer	$10		Columbia 40758
12/22/56+	63	11		8 **The Party's Over**..........T:63 *Whad'ja Put In That Kiss* from the Broadway musical *Bells Are Ringing* starring Judy Holliday	$10		Columbia 40798
4/20/57	68	6		9 **Twelve O'Clock Tonight** ....T:68 *Today Will Be Yesterday Tomorrow!*	$10		Columbia 40870
4/21/58	56	12		10 **Teacher's Pet** ....T:56 *A Very Precious Love* title song from the movie starring Day and Clark Gable; also released on Columbia 41103 in 1958	$8		Columbia 41123
7/21/58	6	14		11 **Everybody Loves A Lover** ....A:6 / H:14 / S:17 *Instant Love*	$8	■	Columbia 41195
10/27/58	43	8		12 **Tunnel Of Love**..........*Run Away, Skidaddle, Skidoo* title song from the movie starring Day	$8	■	Columbia 41252
5/11/59	100	1		13 **Love Me In The Daytime** ....*He's So Married*	$8		Columbia 41354
2/22/60	50	7		14 **Anyway The Wind Blows**..........*Soft As The Starlight* from the movie *Please Don't Eat The Daisies* starring Day	$8		Columbia 41569
4/7/62	98	1		15 **Lover Come Back**..........*Falling* title song from the movie starring Day and Rock Hudson; **Frank DeVol** (orch.: #5 & 8-15)	$8		Columbia 42295
				DAY, Jennifer **'00** Born on 8/22/79 in McAlpin, Florida. Country singer/songwriter.			
2/19/00	46^{S}	12		**The Fun Of Your Love**..........*(3 album snippets)* "45": BNA 65939; B-side: "What If It's Me" (C&W #67)	$5	★^{V}	BNA 65931
				DAY, Morris — see TIME, The			
				DAYBREAK **'70** Pop vocal group from Canada.			
6/13/70	94	3		**Good Morning Freedom** ....*I Could Have Heard The Crying*	$5		Uni 55234
				DAYE, Cory — see DR. BUZZARD			
	★307★			**DAYNE, Taylor** BUB/LP **'90** Born Leslie Wunderman on 3/7/62 in Baldwin, Long Island, New York. White female dance-pop singer. *1)Love Will Lead You Back 2)Don't Rush Me 3)I'll Always Love You*			
10/10/87+	7	25	●	1 **Tell It To My Heart** ....S:5 / A:10 *(instrumental)* issued with 2 different picture sleeves: a text sleeve and a photo sleeve	$3	■	Arista 9612
2/20/88	7	18		2 **Prove Your Love** ....S:7 / A:9 *Upon The Journey's End* (w/Billy T. Scott)	$3	■	Arista 9676
6/11/88	3	30	●	3 **I'll Always Love You** ....S:2 / A:5 *Where Does That Boy Hang Out*	$3	■	Arista 9700
11/5/88+	2^{1}	20		4 **Don't Rush Me** ....S:2 / A:2 *In The Darkness* above 4 from the album *Tell It To My Heart*	$3	■	Arista 9722
10/21/89	5	18		5 **With Every Beat Of My Heart** ....A:3 / S:6 *All I Ever Wanted*	$3	■	Arista 9895
1/27/90	❶^{1}	20	●	6 **Love Will Lead You Back** AC^{4} A:❷^{2} / S:❶^{1} *You Meant The World To Me*	$3	▮^{V}	Arista 9938
5/5/90	4	18		7 **I'll Be Your Shelter**..........A:3 / S:9 *Ain't No Good*	$3	▮^{V}	Arista 2005
8/4/90	12	16		8 **Heart Of Stone** ....A:11 / S:18 *Wait For Me* above 4 from the album *Can't Fight Fate*; all of above produced by Ric Wake	$3	▮^{V}	Arista 2057
6/5/93	20	20		9 **Can't Get Enough Of Your Love** ....A:17 / S:27 *Let's Spend The Night Together* produced by **Clivilles & Cole**	$3	▮^{V}	Arista 12582
10/2/93	50	14		10 **Send Me A Lover**..........S:58 / A:62 *Someone Like You*	$3	▮^{V}	Arista 12603
				DA YOUNGSTA'S R&B/BUB/LP **'94** Hip-hop trio from Philadelphia, Pennsylvania: brothers Taji and Qur'an Goodman, with Tarik Dawson.			
9/24/94	68	9		**Hip Hop Ride** ....A:72 *No Mercy* samples "Hip Hop Vs. Rap" by **KRS-One** and "Just Rhymin' With Biz" by **Big Daddy Kane**	$4	▮	EastWest 98240
				DAYS OF THE NEW ROK/BUB/LP **'97** Rock group from Louisville, Kentucky: Travis Meeks (vocals), Todd Whitener (guitar), Jesse Vest (bass) and Matt Taul (drums).			
11/15/97	57^{A}	17		**Touch, Peel And Stand**..........AR^{16} from the album *Days Of The New* on Outpost/Geffen 30004			album cut
				DAYTON R&B **'82** Funk group from Dayton, Ohio: Chris Jones (male vocals), Jennifer Matthews (female vocals), Shawn Sandridge (guitar), Craig Robinson (bass) and Kevin Hurt (drums).			
7/24/82	58	7		**Hot Fun In The Summertime**..........*(instrumental)*	$5		Liberty 1468
				DAZE **'98** Dance trio from Greve, Denmark: Trine Bix (female vocals), Jesper Tonnov and Lucas Sieber.			
5/23/98	88	3		**Superhero** ....*(3 album snippets)*	$3	▮	Columbia 78867

DEBUT	PEAK	WKS	Gold	A-side (Chart Hit)...B-side	$	Sym	Label & Number

DAZZ BAND — R&B/BUB/LP '82

Funk-dance band from Cleveland, Ohio: Bobby Harris (vocals, sax), Eric Fearman (guitar), Kevin Frederick (keyboards), Kenny Pettus (percussion), Pierre DeMudd and Sennie "Skip" Martin (horns), Michael Wiley (bass), and Isaac Wiley (drums). "Dazz" means "disco- jazz." Martin joined **Kool & The Gang** in 1988.

DEBUT	PEAK	WKS	Gold	A-side (Chart Hit)...B-side	$	Sym	Label & Number
4/24/82	5	23		1 **Let It Whip** ... RB^5 *Everyday Love*	$4		Motown 1609
2/11/84	61	11		2 **Joystick** ... *Don't Get Caught In The Middle*	$4		Motown 1701
12/1/84	84	7		3 **Let It All Blow** ... *Now That I Have You*	$4		Motown 1760

D-CRU — '00

R&B-pop vocal trio from Vancouver, British Columbia, Canada: Tanessa Tompkins, Tito Chipman and Craig Smart.

DEBUT	PEAK	WKS	Gold	A-side (Chart Hit)...B-side	$	Sym	Label & Number
9/2/00	73^S	1		**I Will Be Waiting** ...	$5	★	Elektra 67084

DC TALK — BUB/LP '96

Contemporary rock/hip-hop Christian trio from Washington DC: Toby McKeehan, Michael Tait and Kevin Smith.

DEBUT	PEAK	WKS	Gold	A-side (Chart Hit)...B-side	$	Sym	Label & Number
11/16/96	29	19		**Just Between You And Me** ... A:21 / S:56 *So Help Me God* "45": Virgin 19564; B-side: "Colored People"	$4	▮^{V}	Virgin 38575

D-DON — '00

Born Don Diesel in Newark, New Jersey. Male rapper.

DEBUT	PEAK	WKS	Gold	A-side (Chart Hit)...B-side	$	Sym	Label & Number
10/7/00	69^S	3		**And You Know That** ... *(2 versions) / Blazin* (w/Govna-Mattic) **D-DON (Featuring Redman)** samples "Catch The Beat" by Ski Valley	$6	★	Lock Down 54398

DEADEYE DICK — '94

Pop-rock trio from New Orleans, Louisiana: Caleb Guillotte (guitar), Mark Miller (bass) and Billy Landry (drums). All share vocals. Group name taken from a Kurt Vonnegut novel.

DEBUT	PEAK	WKS	Gold	A-side (Chart Hit)...B-side	$	Sym	Label & Number
8/27/94+	27	27	●	**New Age Girl** ... S:18 / A:48 *Sentimental Crap* from the movie *Dumb And Dumber* starring Jim Carrey; "45" released on purple, multi-colored vinyl; B-side: "Perfect Family"	$4	▮^{V}	Ichiban 232

DEADLY NIGHTSHADE, The — '76

Female disco band: Helen Hooke, Anne Bowen and Pamela Brandt.

DEBUT	PEAK	WKS	Gold	A-side (Chart Hit)...B-side	$	Sym	Label & Number
7/17/76	79	4		**Mary Hartman, Mary Hartman** ... *Dance, Mr. Big, Dance* theme from the TV serial starring Louise Lasser	$6		Phantom 10709

DEAD OR ALIVE — LP '85

Dance group from Liverpool, England: Pete Burns (vocals), Tim Lever (keyboards), Mike Percy (bass) and Steve Coy (drums).

DEBUT	PEAK	WKS	Gold	A-side (Chart Hit)...B-side	$	Sym	Label & Number
6/1/85	11	18		1 **You Spin Me Round (Like A Record)** A:11 / S:12 *Misty Circles*	$3		Epic 04894
9/21/85	75	7		2 **Lover Come Back To Me** ... *Far Too Hard*	$3	■	Epic 05607
11/29/86+	15	22		3 **Brand New Lover** ... S:15 / A:15 *In Too Deep (live)*	$3	■	Epic 06374
4/25/87	85	6		4 **Something In My House** ... *D.J. Hit That Button*	$3	■	Epic 07022
7/1/89	69	8		5 **Come Home With Me Baby** ... *(Deadhouse dub 7" edit)*	$3		Epic 68885

DEAL, Bill, & The Rhondels — BUB/LP '69

Brassy-rock band from Virginia Beach, Virginia: Bill Deal (vocals, organ), Bob Fisher (guitar), Mike Kerwin, Jeff Pollard, Ronny Rosenbaum and Ken Dawson (horns), Don Queinsenburry (bass) and Ammon Tharp (drums).

DEBUT	PEAK	WKS	Gold	A-side (Chart Hit)...B-side	$	Sym	Label & Number
1/18/69	39	10		1 **May I** ... *Day By Day My Love Grows Stronger* first recorded in 1965 by **Maurice Williams**	$10		Heritage 803
4/19/69	35	10		2 **I've Been Hurt** ... *I've Got My Needs*	$10	■	Heritage 812
8/16/69	23	9		3 **What Kind Of Fool Do You Think I Am** *Are You Ready For This*	$10		Heritage 817
11/15/69	85	5		4 **Swingin' Tight** ... *Tuck's Theme*	$10	■	Heritage 818
3/21/70	62	7		5 **Nothing Succeeds Like Success** ... *Swingin' Tight* **Jimmy Soul** (organ, all of above)	$10		Heritage 821

DEAN, Billy — see BROOKS, Garth / ROGERS, Kenny

DEAN, Debbie — '61

Born Reba Jeanette Smith on 2/1/28 in Corbin, New York. Also recorded as Penny Smith, Debra Dixon and Debbie Stevens. Signed by Berry Gordy as the first white artist to any of his Motown labels.

DEBUT	PEAK	WKS	Gold	A-side (Chart Hit)...B-side	$	Sym	Label & Number
2/6/61	92	2		**Don't Let Him Shop Around** ... *A New Girl* answer song to **The Miracles**' "Shop Around"	$75		Motown 1007

DEAN, Jimmy — ★453★ — C&W/BUB/AC/LP '61

Born on 8/10/28 in Plainview, Texas. Country singer/pianist/guitarist. With Tennessee Haymakers in Washington, D.C. in 1948. Own Texas Wildcats in 1952. Recorded for Four Star in 1952. Own CBS-TV series, 1957-58; ABC-TV series, 1963-66. Business interests include a restaurant chain and a line of pork sausage. Married Country singer Donna Meade on 10/27/91.

1)Big Bad John 2)P.T. 109 3)The Cajun Queen

DEBUT	PEAK	WKS	Gold	A-side (Chart Hit)...B-side	$	Sym	Label & Number
10/14/57	67	8		1 **Deep Blue Sea** ... T:67 *Love Me So I'll Know*	$15		Columbia 40995
12/23/57	32	5		2 **Little Sandy Sleighfoot** ... T:32 / S:37 *When They Ring The Golden Bells* [X-N] **Ray Ellis** (orch., above 2)	$15	■	Columbia 41025
10/2/61	1^5	16	●	3 **Big Bad John** CW^2 / AC^{10} *I Won't Go Huntin' With You Jake* [S]	$10	■	Columbia 42175
1/6/62	24	7		4 **Dear Ivan** ... *Smoke, Smoke, Smoke That Cigarette* [S] background music: "Battle Hymn Of The Republic"	$10	■	Columbia 42259
1/27/62	22	8		5 **The Cajun Queen** / [S]			
1/20/62	26	9		6 **To A Sleeping Beauty** ... [S] background music: "Memories"; soliloquy first recorded by **Jackie Gleason** in 1957; a new version made the Country charts (#85) in 1976 on Casino 074	$10	■	Columbia 42282
3/31/62	8	11		7 **P.T. 109** ... *Walk On, Boy* based on the sinking of President John F. Kennedy's torpedo boat on 8/2/43	$10	■	Columbia 42338
6/23/62	41	8		8 **Steel Men** ... *Little Bitty Big John*	$10	■	Columbia 42483
9/15/62	29	9		9 **Little Black Book** ... *Please Pass The Biscuits*	$10	■	Columbia 42529
12/1/62	73	6		10 **Gonna Raise A Rukus Tonight** ... *A Day That Changed The World*	$10	■	Columbia 42600
6/26/65	91	3		11 **The First Thing Ev'ry Morning** (And The Last Thing Ev'ry Night) ... CW^2 *Awkward Situation*	$8		Columbia 43263

DEBUT	PEAK	WKS	Gold	A-side (Chart Hit)..................B-side	$	Sym	Label & Number
				DEAN, Jimmy — Cont'd			
12/25/65	14[X]	1		12 **Yes, Patricia, There Is A Santa Claus**..............*Blue Christmas* [X-S]	$10		Columbia 43457
				inspired by the famous 1897 newspaper article "Yes, Virginia, There Is A Santa Claus"			
5/15/76	35	4	●	13 **I.O.U.**..............*Let's Pick Up The Pieces (And Start Over Again)* [S]	$5		Casino 052
				an ode of thanks to mother; hit the Country charts on Mother's Day in 1976, 1977 & 1983			
				DEAN AND JEAN BUB **'64**			
				Rock and roll vocal duo of Welton "Dean" Young and Brenda Lee "Jean" Jones from Dayton, Ohio. Jones died of cancer on 8/4/2001 (age 63).			
11/2/63+	35	13		1 **Tra La La La Suzy**..............*I Love The Summertime*	$15		Rust 5067
2/22/64	32	8		2 **Hey Jean, Hey Dean**..............*Please Don't Tell Me Now*	$15		Rust 5075
5/30/64	91	5		3 **I Wanna Be Loved**..............*Thread Your Needle* (#123)	$15		Rust 5081
				#1 hit for the Andrews Sisters in 1950			
				DEAN AND MARC — see NEWBEATS, The			
	★384★			**DeBARGE/El DeBarge** R&B/BUB/AC/LP **'85**			
				R&B family group from Grand Rapids, Michigan: Eldra "El" (vocals, keyboards; born on 6/4/61), Mark (trumpet, saxophone; born on 6/19/59), James (keyboards; born on 8/22/63), Randy (bass; born on 8/6/58) and Bunny (vocals; born on 3/15/55). Brothers Bobby and Tommy were in **Switch**. James was briefly married to **Janet Jackson** in 1984. Also see **Tone Loc**.			
				1)Rhythm Of The Night 2)Who's Johnny 3)Who's Holding Donna Now			
				DeBARGE:			
2/5/83	31	17		1 **I Like It**..............*Hesitated*	$4		Gordy 1645
4/23/83	17	19		2 **All This Love**..............AC[3] *I'm In Love With You*	$4		Gordy 1660
10/15/83+	18	21		3 **Time Will Reveal**..............RB[5] *I'll Never Fall In Love Again*	$4		Gordy 1705
3/17/84	45	11		4 **Love Me In A Special Way**..............*Dance The Night Away*	$4		Gordy 1723
2/16/85	3	22		5 **Rhythm Of The Night** RB[1] / AC[1] S:3 / A:3 *Queen Of My Heart*	$3	■	Gordy 1770
				from the Berry Gordy movie *The Last Dragon* starring **Vanity**			
6/1/85	6	19		6 **Who's Holding Donna Now**..............AC[3] A:6 / S:7 *Be My Lady*	$3	■	Gordy 1793
				EL DeBARGE with DeBARGE:			
8/31/85	46	10		7 **You Wear It Well**..............*Baby, Won't Cha Come Quick*	$3	■	Gordy 1804
12/7/85+	75	7		8 **The Heart Is Not So Smart**..............*Share My World*	$3	■	Gordy 1822
				above 4 from the DeBarge album *Rhythm Of The Night*			
				EL DeBARGE:			
4/26/86	3	19		9 **Who's Johnny**..............RB[1] A:3 / S:4 *Love Me In A Special Way*	$3	■	Gordy 1842
				theme from the movie *Short Circuit* starring Ally Sheedy			
8/9/86	43	12		10 **Love Always**..............*The Walls (Came Tumbling Down)*	$3	■	Gordy 1857
12/27/86+	70	9		11 **Someone**..............*Stop! Don't Tease Me*	$3	■	Gordy 1867
3/10/90	31	13	●	12 **The Secret Garden (Sweet Seduction Suite)**..............RB[1] S:20 *(instrumental)*	$3	▮[V]	Qwest 19992 ■
				QUINCY JONES/Al B. Sure!/James Ingram/El DeBarge/Barry White			
10/1/94	68[S]	2		13 **Where Is My Love?**..............BUB:106 *Starlight, Moonlight, Candlelight*	$3	▮[V]	Reprise 18140
				EL DeBARGE featuring Babyface			
				written and produced by **Babyface**			
				DeBARGE, Chico R&B/BUB/LP **'87**			
				Born Jonathan DeBarge on 6/23/66 in Grand Rapids, Michigan. DeBarge sibling, but not a member of the group **DeBarge**. Served six years in prison in the early 1990s for conspiracy to sell drugs.			
11/8/86+	21	20		1 **Talk To Me**..............A:17 / S:22 *If It Takes All Night*	$3	■	Motown 1858
3/20/99	56[S]	4		2 **Soopaman Lover**..............*(2 versions) / Superman/Virgin* (R&B #97)	$8	★*	Motown 56233
				CHICO DeBARGE Featuring Erick Sermon & Redman			
				samples "Superman Lover" by **Johnny "Guitar" Watson**			
10/23/99	71	13		3 **Give You What You Want (Fa Sure)**..............S:23 *(5 album snippets)*	$3	★	Motown 156443
				DeBURGH, Chris AC/BUB/LP **'87**			
				Born Christopher Davidson on 10/15/48 in Buenos Aires, Argentina (Irish parents). Adult Contemporary singer/songwriter. DeBurgh was his mother's maiden name.			
4/30/83	34	14		1 **Don't Pay The Ferryman**..............*All The Love I Have Inside*	$4		A&M 2511
8/20/83	71	5		2 **Ship To Shore**..............*The Getaway*	$4		A&M 2565
6/30/84	44	13		3 **High On Emotion**..............*Much More Than This*	$4		A&M 2643
2/14/87	3	26		4 **The Lady In Red**..............S:❶[1] / A:4 *The Vision*	$3	■	A&M 2848
				originally issued with "The Spirit Of Man" as the A-side and with a different picture sleeve			
				DeCARO, Nick AC/LP **'69**			
				Prolific record producer/arranger/conductor.			
1/11/69	95	1		**If I Only Had Time**..............*Caroline, No* [I]	$6		A&M 1000
				DeCASTRO SISTERS, The **'55**			
				Female vocal trio from Cuba: Peggy, Babette and Cherie DeCastro.			
10/9/54+	2[1]	20		1 **Teach Me Tonight** J:2 / A:3 / S:3 *It's Love*	$25		Abbott 3001
5/7/55	17	4		2 **Boom Boom Boomerang**..............J:17 / S:24 *Let Your Love Walk In*	$20		Abbott 3003
				Thurl Ravenscroft (bass voice)			
12/17/55+	66	6		3 **Too Late Now**..............T:66 *Give Me Time*	$20		Abbott 3011
				from the 1951 movie *Royal Wedding* starring Fred Astaire			
12/31/55	84	1		4 **Snowbound For Christmas**..............T:84 *Christmas Is A-Comin'* [X]	$20		Abbott 3012
				Skip Martin (orch., all of above)			
10/20/56	74	5		5 **It's Yours**..............T:74 *Don't Call Me Sweetie*	$12		RCA Victor 6661
				Joe Reisman (orch.)			
8/18/58	99	1		6 **Who Are They To Say**..............H:99 *When You Look At Me*	$10		ABC-Paramount 9932
1/5/59	76	4		7 **Teach Me Tonight Cha Cha**..............*The Things I Tell My Pillow* [R]	$10		ABC-Paramount 9988
				new version of #1 above; **Don Costa** (orch., above 2)			
				DEE, Daisy R&B **'91**			
				Born Desiree Rollocks in 1970 in Curacao, Brazil. Female dance singer.			
3/30/91	73	11		**Crazy**..............A:39 *(instrumental)*	$4	▮	LMR/RCA 2812

DEBUT	PEAK	WKS	Gold	A-side (Chart Hit)......B-side	$	Sym	Label & Number
				DEE, Dave — see DAVE DEE, DOZY, BEAKY, MICK AND TICH			
				DEE, Jimmy, And The Offbeats '58			
				Jimmy Dee Fore (who later managed the Houston Astrodome) led this Texas rock and roll band.			
1/6/58	47	10		**Henrietta** ......S:47 / T:53 *Don't Cry No More (w/The Montclairs)*	$40		Dot 15664
				first released on TNT 148 in 1957 ($75)			
				DEE, Joey, & the Starliters BUB/LP '62			
				Born Joseph DiNicola on 6/11/40 in Passaic, New Jersey. High school classmate of **The Shirelles**. Joey first recorded for the Bonus and Scepter labels in 1960. Joey & the Starliters became the house band at the Peppermint Lounge, New York City in September 1960. Actor Joe Pesci played guitar with band briefly in 1961. Own club, The Starliter, in New York City in 1964. Band then included, for a time, three members who later formed **The Young Rascals**, and **Jimi Hendrix** on guitar, 1965-66. In the movies *Hey, Let's Twist* and *Two Tickets To Paris*.			
11/20/61+	❶[3]	18	●	1 **Peppermint Twist - Part I** ...... *Part II*	$20		Roulette 4401
				inspired by New York City's Peppermint Lounge club			
2/17/62	20	6		2 **Hey, Let's Twist /**			
3/10/62	74	3		3 **Roly Poly**	$20	■	Roulette 4408
3/24/62	6	12		4 **Shout - Part I** ...... *Part II*	$20	■	Roulette 4416
				above 3 from the movie *Hey, Let's Twist!* starring Dee			
8/25/62	18	10		5 **What Kind Of Love Is This** ...... *Wing-Ding*	$15	■	Roulette 4438
				from the movie *Two Tickets To Paris* starring Dee			
11/3/62	61	7		6 **I Lost My Baby** *[JOEY DEE]* ...... *Keep Your Mind On What You're Doin'*	$15	■	Roulette 4456
				above 2 written by **Johnny Nash**			
2/16/63	100	1		7 **Baby, You're Driving Me Crazy** *[JOEY DEE]* ...... *Help Me Pick Up The Pieces*	$15		Roulette 4467
4/27/63	36	7		8 **Hot Pastrami With Mashed Potatoes - Part I** ...... *Part II*	$15		Roulette 4488
				all of above produced by Henry Glover			
7/20/63	89	3		9 **Dance, Dance, Dance** *[JOEY DEE]* ...... *Let's Have A Party*	$15		Roulette 4503
				DEE, Johnny — see LOUDERMILK, John D.			
				DEE, Kiki BUB/LP '76			
				Born Pauline Matthews on 3/6/47 in Yorkshire, England. Female pop-rock singer.			
3/27/71	87	3		1 **Love Makes The World Go Round** ...... *Jimmy*	$7		Rare Earth 5025
9/14/74	12	20		2 **I've Got The Music In Me** *[THE KIKI DEE BAND]* ...... *Simple Melody*	$6		Rocket 40293
5/24/75	74	3		3 **How Glad I Am** ...... *Peter*	$5		Rocket 40401
3/6/76	82	4		4 **Once A Fool** ...... *Someone To Me*	$5		Rocket 40506
				ELTON JOHN and KIKI DEE:			
7/4/76	❶[4]	20	●	5 **Don't Go Breaking My Heart** AC[1] *Snow Queen*	$5	■	Rocket 40585
11/27/93	56	12		6 **True Love** ......S:54 *Runaway Train* (**Elton John** & **Eric Clapton** - ROK #10)	$3	▮V	MCA 54762
				written by Cole Porter in 1956 for the movie *High Society*			
				DEE, Lenny LP '55			
				Born Leonard DeStoppelaire on 1/5/23 in Chicago, Illinois. Male organist. Released over 60 organ instrumental albums from 1955-78.			
2/12/55	19	15		**Plantation Boogie** ......J:19 / S:23 *The Birth Of The Blues* [I]	$12		Decca 29360
				DEE, Lola MEM '55			
				White pop vocalist.			
11/12/55	72	2		**Paper Roses** ......T:72 *Only You (And You Alone)*	$20		Wing 90015
				Jack Halloran Choir (backing vocals); Lew Douglas (orch.); different song than **Anita Bryant**'s 1960 hit			
				DEE, Tommy '59			
				Born Thomas Donaldson on 7/15/36 in Vicker, Virginia. DJ at KFXM-San Bernadino at the time of his only hit (first recorded by **Eddie Cochran**). Currently a producer/promoter/record company executive in Nashville.			
3/30/59	11	12		**Three Stars** ...... *I'll Never Change* (Carol Kay & the Teen-Aires) [S]	$25		Crest 1057
				Tommy Dee (narration); Carol Kay and the Teen-Aires (vocals); a tribute to **Buddy Holly**, **Ritchie Valens** and the **Big Bopper**			
				DEEE-LITE LP '90			
				Dance trio formed in New York: Super DJ Dmitry Brill (from Kiev, Soviet Union), Jungle DJ Towa "Towa" Tei (from Tokyo, Japan) and vocalist Lady Miss Kier (Kier Kirby from Youngstown, Ohio). Group's name inspired by the tune "It's De-lovely" from the 1936 Cole Porter musical *Red, Hot & Blue*. Brill and Kier are married.			
9/15/90	4	23	●	1 **Groove Is In The Heart** ......S:❶[2] / A:6 *What Is Love?*	$3	▮V	Elektra 64934
				Bootsy Collins (backing vocal); **Q-Tip** (of **A Tribe Called Quest**; rap); "45" issued in 1993 on Elektra 65939; B-side: "Power Of Love"			
1/5/91	47	10		2 **Power Of Love** ...... *(album version) / Deee-Lite Theme*	$3	▮V	Elektra 64912
				DEEJAY, Alice — see ALICE DEEJAY			
				DEE JAY And The Runaways '66			
				Rock and roll group from Spirit Lake, Iowa: "Dee" Denny Storey (drums) and "Jay" John Senn (bass), with Gary Lind (vocals), Chuck Colegrove (guitar), Bob Godfredson (guitar) and Tom Vallie (organ).			
5/7/66	45	11		**Peter Rabbit** ...... *Are You Ready*	$15		Smash 2034
				first released on IGL 103 in 1966 ($50; B-side: "Three Steps To Heaven")			
				DEELE, The R&B/BUB/LP '88			
				R&B group from Cincinnati, Ohio: Darnell Bristol and Carlos Greene (vocals), Stanley Burke, Kenneth "**Babyface**" Edmonds, Mark "L.A. Reid" Rooney and Kevin Roberson. Babyface and L.A. Reid later formed LaFace Records.			
1/21/84	77	8		1 **Body Talk** ...... *(instrumental)*	$4		Solar 69785
2/27/88	10	21		2 **Two Occasions** ......A:8 / S:13 *(instrumental)*	$3		Solar 70015
				DEEP BLUE SOMETHING BUB/LP '95			
				Pop-rock group from Dallas, Texas: brothers Todd (vocals, bass) and Toby (guitar) Pipes, Kirk Tatom (guitar) and John Kirtland (drums).			
8/19/95+	5	36		**Breakfast At Tiffany's** ......A:4 / S:15 *(2 versions) / A Water Prayer*	$3	▮	Interscope 98138
				DEEP FOREST LP '94			
				French keyboardist Michel Sanchez and Brussels-based producer Dan Lacksman.			
2/26/94	78	8		**Sweet Lullaby** ......A:75 *(Round the World mix)* [F]	$3	▮V	Epic 77095
				made *Billboard's* Dance Club Play charts in May 1993 (#6); reissued later in 1994 on Epic 77371 with a picture sleeve (B-side: "Forest Hymn")			

DEBUT	PEAK	WKS	Gold	A-side (Chart Hit)..........B-side	$	Sym	Label & Number

DEEP PURPLE — ROK/BUB/LP '68

Hard-rock group from England: Rod Evans (vocals), Ritchie Blackmore (guitar), Jon Lord (keyboards), Nicky Simper (bass) and Ian Paice (drums). Evans and Simper left in 1969, replaced by Ian Gillan (vocals) and Roger Glover (bass). Evans formed Captain Beyond. Gillan and Glover left in late 1973, replaced by David Coverdale (vocals) and Glenn Hughes (bass). Blackmore left in early 1975 to form **Rainbow** (which Glover later joined); replaced by American Tommy Bolin (ex-**James Gang** guitarist; died on 12/4/76). Band split in July 1976. Coverdale formed **Whitesnake**. Blackmore, Lord, Paice, Gillan and Glover reunited in 1984. Hughes joined **Black Sabbath** as vocalist in 1986. Gillan left in 1989 to form Garth Rockett & The Moonshiners; replaced by Joe Lynn Turner (ex-Rainbow), then returned in 1992 to take Turner's place.

DEBUT	PEAK	WKS	Gold	A-side (Chart Hit)..........B-side	$	Sym	Label & Number
8/17/68	4	10		1 **Hush** ... *One More Rainy Day*	$10	□	Tetragrammaton 1503
11/9/68	38	8		2 **Kentucky Woman** ... *Hard Road*	$10	■	Tetragrammaton 1508
1/25/69	53	5		3 **River Deep-Mountain High** ... *Listen, Learn, Read On*	$10		Tetragrammaton 1514
12/5/70	66	6		4 **Black Night** ... *Into The Fire*	$8		Warner 7405
4/21/73	60	6		5 **Woman From Tokyo** ... *Super Trouper* first charted for 2 weeks (#80) on Warner 7672; re-charted on 9/29/73	$6		Warner 7737
5/26/73	4	16	●	6 **Smoke On The Water** ... *(longer version)* inspired by the burning of the Montreux Casino on 12/3/71 during a **Frank Zappa** show for which Deep Purple opened	$6		Warner 7710
3/23/74	91	4		7 **Might Just Take Your Life** ... *Coronarias Redig*	$6		Warner 7784
1/5/85	61	7		8 **Knocking At Your Back Door** ... *Wasted Sunsets*	$4	■	Mercury 880477

DEES, Rick, And His Cast Of Idiots — BUB/LP '76

Born Rigdon Dees on 3/14/50 in Jacksonville, Florida. DJ working at WMPS-Memphis when he conceived idea for "Disco Duck." Currently one of America's top radio DJs (*Weekly Top 40*). Host of TV's *Solid Gold* (1984) and his own late-night talk show *Into The Night* (1990).

DEBUT	PEAK	WKS	Gold	A-side (Chart Hit)..........B-side	$	Sym	Label & Number
8/14/76	❶[1]	25	▲	1 **Disco Duck (Part I)** ... *(Part II)* [N]	$4		RSO 857
1/15/77	56	6		2 **Dis-Gorilla (Part 1)** ... *(Part 2)* [I] [N]	$4		RSO 866
12/15/84	75	5		3 **Eat My Shorts** *[RICK DEES]* ... *Get Nekked* (#104) [N]	$4	■	Atlantic 89601

DEFAULT — ROK/LP '02

Rock group from Vancouver, British Columbia, Canada: Dallas Smith (vocals), Jeremy Hora (guitar), Dave Benedict (bass) and Dan Craig (drums).

DEBUT	PEAK	WKS	Gold	A-side (Chart Hit)..........B-side	$	Sym	Label & Number
1/5/02	13	35		**Wasting My Time** ... A:13 from the album *The Fallout* on TVT 2310			album cut

DEFINITION OF SOUND — '91

Dance group featuring lead vocalist Elaine Vassel.

DEBUT	PEAK	WKS	Gold	A-side (Chart Hit)..........B-side	$	Sym	Label & Number
4/6/91	68[A]	6		**Now Is Tomorrow** ... *(12" version) / (2* **De La Soul** *remixes)*	$8	▮*	Cardiac 4010

DEF LEPPARD ★159★ — ROK/BUB/LP '88

Hard-rock group from Sheffield, Yorkshire, England: Joe Elliott (vocals; born on 8/1/59), Steve Clark (born on 4/23/60) and Pete Willis (guitars; born on 2/16/60), Rick Savage (bass; born on 12/2/60) and Rick Allen (drums; born on 11/1/63; lost his left arm in an auto accident on 12/31/84). Phil Collen (born on 12/8/57) replaced Willis in late 1982. Clark died of alcohol-related respiratory failure on 1/8/91 (age 30). Guitarist Vivian Campbell (**Whitesnake**, Dio, Riverdogs, Shadow King) joined in April 1992.

1)Love Bites 2)Pour Some Sugar On Me 3)Armageddon It

DEBUT	PEAK	WKS	Gold	A-side (Chart Hit)..........B-side	$	Sym	Label & Number
3/12/83	12	17		1 **Photograph** ... AR[6] *Action! Not Words* (ROK #42)	$4	■	Mercury 811215
6/11/83	16	15		2 **Rock Of Ages** ... AR[1] *Billy's Got A Gun* (ROK #33)	$4		Mercury 812604
9/3/83	28	14		3 **Foolin'** ... *Comin' Under Fire* (ROK #24)	$4		Mercury 814178
6/9/84	61	8		4 **Bringin' On The Heartbreak** ... *Me & My Wine* remix of song originally released on their 1981 album *High 'n' Dry*	$4	■	Mercury 818779
8/22/87	80	5		5 **Women** ... *Tear It Down*	$4	■	Mercury 888757
10/10/87	19	19		6 **Animal** ... S:16 / A:24 *I Wanna Be Your Hero*	$3	■	Mercury 888832
1/23/88	10	16		7 **Hysteria** ... S:10 / A:11 *Ride Into The Sun*	$3	■	Mercury 870004
4/23/88	2[1]	24		8 **Pour Some Sugar On Me** ... A:2 / S:3 *Ring Of Fire*	$3	■	Mercury 870298
8/13/88	❶[1]	23		9 **Love Bites** ... A:❶[2] / S:2 *Billy's Got A Gun (live)*	$3	■	Mercury 870402
11/19/88+	3	18		10 **Armageddon It** ... S:❶[1] / A:3 *Release Me* (Stumpus Maximus & The Good Ol' Boys)	$3	■	Mercury 870692
3/4/89	12	13		11 **Rocket** ... S:11 / A:13 *Women (live)* #5-11: from the album *Hysteria*; all of above produced by Robert John "Mutt" Lange	$3	■	Mercury 872614
4/11/92	15	18		12 **Let's Get Rocked** ... AR[1] S:10 / A:43 *Only After Dark*	$3	▮V	Mercury 866568
6/27/92	36	10		13 **Make Love Like A Man** ... S:41 / A:57 *Miss You In A Heartbeat* B-side charted at #18 below	$3	▮V	Mercury 864038
8/22/92	12	20		14 **Have You Ever Needed Someone So Bad** ... S:14 / A:21 *Elected (live)* (ROK #22)	$3	▮V	Mercury 864136
12/12/92+	34	15		15 **Stand Up (Kick Love Into Motion)** ... AR[5] A:50 *From The Inside* (The Acoustic Hippies From Hell)	$3	▮V	Mercury 864604
4/3/93	62	9		16 **Tonight** ... *She's Too Tough* #12-16: from the album *Adrenalize*	$3	▮V	Mercury 862016
9/11/93	12	20		17 **Two Steps Behind** ... A:17 / S:18 *Tonight (acoustic version)* from the movie *Last Action Hero* starring Arnold Schwarzenegger	$3	▮	Columbia 77116
12/11/93+	39	17		18 **Miss You In A Heartbeat** ... A:53 / S:54 *(acoustic version) / Let's Get Rocked (live)*	$3	▮V	Mercury 858080
12/2/95+	58	14		19 **When Love & Hate Collide** ... S:71 / A:73 *Can't Keep Away From The Flame*	$3	▮V	Mercury 852424

DeFRANCO FAMILY Featuring Tony DeFranco — BUB/LP '73

Family teen pop vocal group from Port Colborne, Ontario, Canada: Tony (born on 8/31/59), Merlina (born on 7/20/57), Nino (born on 10/19/56), Marisa (born on 7/23/55) and Benny (born on 7/11/54) DeFranco.

DEBUT	PEAK	WKS	Gold	A-side (Chart Hit)..........B-side	$	Sym	Label & Number
9/8/73	3	17	●	1 **Heartbeat - It's A Lovebeat** ... *Sweet, Sweet Loretta*	$5	■	20th Century 2030
12/29/73+	32	12		2 **Abra-Ca-Dabra** ... *Same Kind A' Love*	$5	■	20th Century 2070
5/4/74	18	13		3 **Save The Last Dance For Me** ... *Because We Both Are Young*	$5	■	20th Century 2088

DEGREES OF MOTION — '92

Dance group from Brooklyn, New York: Biti, Kit West, Balle Legend and Mariposa.

DEBUT	PEAK	WKS	Gold	A-side (Chart Hit)..........B-side	$	Sym	Label & Number
3/7/92	94	2		**Do You Want It Right Now** ... A:65 *(2 mixes)*	$6	▮	Esquire 182

DEBUT	PEAK	WKS	Gold	A-side (Chart Hit)...B-side	$	Sym	Label & Number
				DÉJA — see SLAVE			
				DEJA VU '98			
				Dance group from England featuring female singer Tasmin.			
3/14/98	58	17		**My Heart Will Go On (love theme from Titanic)** ...S:37 *(radio edit)*	$5	▮	Interhit 54020
				dance version of the love theme from the movie *Titanic* starring Leonardo DiCaprio			
				DeJOHN SISTERS '55			
				Pop vocal duo from Chester, Pennsylvania: Julie (born on 3/18/31) and Dux (born on 1/21/33) DeGiovanni.			
12/25/54+	6	13		1 **(My Baby Don't Love Me) No More**...A:6 / S:8 / J:11 *Theresa (The Little Flower)*	$20		Epic 9085
				O.B. Masingill (orch.)			
11/26/55	97	1		2 **C'est La Vie**...T:97 *Uninvited Love*	$15		Epic 9131
				Ray Ellis (orch.)			
8/18/58	73	2		3 **Straighten Up & Fly Right**...H:73 *Wrong Guy* [N]	$15		Sunbeam 106
				Arnie Goland (orch.); written and charted (#9 in 1944) by **Nat King Cole**; from the 1943 movie *Here Comes Elmer*			
				DEKKER, Desmond, & The Aces BUB/LP '69			
				Born Desmond Dacris on 7/16/41 in Kingston, Jamaica. Leader of reggae group.			
5/17/69	9	10		**Israelites**...*My Precious World (The Man)*	$7		Uni 55129
				DELACARDOS, The '61			
				R&B vocal group from Charlotte, North Carolina: Vernon Hill, Harold Ford, Robert Gates and Christopher Harris.			
6/5/61	78	5		**Hold Back The Tears**...*Mr. Dillon*	$20		United Artists 310
				DEL AMITRI BUB/LP '95			
				Pop-rock group from Glasgow, Scotland: Justin Currie (vocals, bass), David Cummings and Iain Harvie (guitars), and Brian McDermott (drums).			
5/19/90	35	11		1 **Kiss This Thing Goodbye**...S:31 / A:33 *The Return Of Maggie Brown*	$3	▮	A&M 1485
8/15/92	30	17		2 **Always The Last To Know**...A:31 / S:71 *Be My Downfall*	$3	▮	A&M 1604
7/8/95	10	36		3 **Roll To Me**...A:6 / S:50 *Long Way Down*	$3	▮V	A&M 1114
				"45": A&M 1322; B-side: "Tell Her This" ("Bubbled Under" at #117 in 1996)			
				DELANEY & BONNIE BUB/LP '71			
				Vocal duo: Delaney Bramlett (born on 7/1/39 in Pontotoc County, Mississippi) and wife Bonnie Lynn Bramlett (born on 11/8/44 in Acton, Illinois). Married in 1967. Backing artists (Friends) included, at various times, **Leon Russell**, **Rita Coolidge**, **Dave Mason**, **Eric Clapton**, Duane Allman (**Allman Brothers Band**) and many others. Friends Bobby Whitlock, Carl Radle and Jim Gordon later became Eric Clapton's Dominos. Delaney & Bonnie dissolved their marriage and group in 1972. Their daughter Bekka was lead vocalist of The Zoo, then joined **Fleetwood Mac** in 1993. Also see **The Shindogs**.			
2/21/70	84	3		1 **Comin' Home**...*Groupie (Superstar)*	$10		Atco 6725
				DELANEY & BONNIE AND FRIENDS FEATURING ERIC CLAPTON			
8/15/70	43	8		2 **Soul Shake** /			
5/23/70	75	4		3 **Free The People**...	$8		Atco 6756
5/22/71	13	15		4 **Never Ending Song Of Love** *Don't Deceive Me (Please Don't Go)*	$8		Atco 6804
				DELANEY & BONNIE & FRIENDS (above 3)			
9/25/71	20	10		5 **Only You Know And I Know**...*God Knows I Love You*	$8		Atco 6838
1/22/72	59	5		6 **Move 'Em Out**...*Sing My Way Home*	$8		Atco 6866
4/29/72	99	2		7 **Where There's A Will There's A Way**...*Lonesome And A Long Way From Home*	$8		Atco 6883
				DE LA SOUL R&B/BUB/LP '89			
				Alternative-rap trio from Amityville, Long Island, New York: Kelvin Mercer, David Jolicoeur and Vincent Mason.			
6/3/89	34	17	●	1 **Me Myself And I**...RB[1] S:21 *(instrumental)*	$8	▮	Tommy Boy 7926
				samples **Funkadelic**'s "(not just) Knee Deep"; the first Top 40 cassette-only single (no "45")			
9/18/93	76	5		2 **Breakadawn**...S:60 *En Focus*	$3	▮V	Tommy Boy 7586
				samples "I Can't Help It" by **Michael Jackson**, "Quiet Storm" by **Smokey Robinson** and "Song And Dance" by the **Bar-Kays**; "45": Tommy Boy/Collectables 586			
7/22/00	68S	4		3 **Oooh.**...BUB:125 *(2 versions) / Foolin*	$6	T	Tommy Boy 2118
				DE LA SOUL Feat: Redman			
				samples "Enter The Dragon" By **Chubb Rock**			
12/23/00	96	3		4 **All Good?**...S:43 *(4 remixes)*	$8	★*	Tommy Boy 2178
				DE LA SOUL Feat: Chaka Khan			
				DELBERT & GLEN — see McCLINTON, Delbert			
				DELEGATES, The '72			
				Novelty trio of Bob DeCarlo, Nick Cenci and Nick Kousaleous. DeCarlo was a DJ in Tampa, Florida. Cenci and Kousaleous owned the Co & Ce record label.			
10/21/72	8	8		**Convention '72**...*Funky Butt* [N]	$10		Mainstream 5525
				"break-in" novelty record; some pressings have the hit side on both the A & B-sides			
				DELEGATION R&B/LP '79			
				R&B-disco trio based in England: Jamaicans Ricky Bailey and Ray Patterson, with Texan, Bruce Dunbar.			
2/3/79	45	12		**Oh Honey**...*Let Me Take You To The Sun*	$6		Shady Brook 1048
				DELERIUM '01			
				Eclectic-ambient duo from England: producers/keyboardists Rhys Fulber and Bill Leeb. Also recorded as Frontline Assembly.			
1/20/01	58S	17		1 **Silence**...*(3 remixes) / Aria*	$8	★*	Nettwerk 33111
				DELERIUM Featuring Sarah McLachlan			
				recorded in 1997; featured in the movies *Breakdown Palace* starring Claire Danes and *Bounce* starring Ben Affleck			
7/7/01	57S	3		2 **Innocente**...*(4 remixes)*	$8	★*	Nettwerk 33130
				DELERIUM featuring Leigh Nash (of Sixpence None The Richer)			

DEBUT	PEAK	WKS	Gold	A-side (Chart Hit)	B-side	$	Sym	Label & Number

★490★ DELFONICS, The — R&B/BUB/LP '68

R&B vocal group from Philadelphia, Pennsylvania: brothers William (born on 1/17/45) and Wilbert (born on 10/19/47) Hart, Ritchie Daniels and Randy Cain (born on 5/2/45). First recorded for Moon Shot in 1967. Daniels left for the service in 1968, group continued as a trio. Cain was replaced by **Major Harris** in 1971. Harris went solo in 1974.

1)La - La - Means I Love You 2)Didn't I (Blow Your Mind This Time) 3)Break Your Promise

DEBUT	PEAK	WKS	Gold	A-side (Chart Hit)	B-side	$	Sym	Label & Number
2/3/68	4	15		1 **La - La - Means I Love You**	*Can't Get Over Losing You*	$10		Philly Groove 150
4/27/68	42	9		2 **I'm Sorry**	*You're Gone*	$10		Philly Groove 151
5/4/68	92	4		3 **He Don't Really Love You**	*Without You*	$15		Moon Shot 6703
8/31/68	35	10		4 **Break Your Promise**	*Alfie*	$10		Philly Groove 152
12/7/68+	35	9		5 **Ready Or Not Here I Come (Can't Hide From Love) /**				
2/22/69	72	3		6 **Somebody Loves You**		$10		Philly Groove 154
6/14/69	94	2		7 **Funny Feeling**	*My New Love*	$10		Philly Groove 156
8/16/69	40	10		8 **You Got Yours And I'll Get Mine**	*Loving Him*	$10		Philly Groove 157
1/10/70	10	14	●	9 **Didn't I (Blow Your Mind This Time)**	*Down Is Up, Up Is Down*	$8		Philly Groove 161
6/6/70	40	9		10 **Trying To Make A Fool Of Me**	*Baby I Love You*	$8		Philly Groove 162
9/19/70	53	8		11 **When You Get Right Down To It**	*I Gave To You*	$8		Philly Groove 163
				all of above produced by Thom Bell				
6/19/71	52	7		12 **Hey! Love /**				
6/19/71	58	8		13 **Over And Over**		$8		Philly Groove 166
				#7, 9-11 & 13: from the album *The Delfonics*				
10/30/71	81	6		14 **Walk Right Up To The Sun**	*Round And Round*	$8		Philly Groove 169
6/24/72	86	3		15 **Tell Me This Is A Dream**	*I'm A Man*	$8		Philly Groove 172
6/9/73	91	4		16 **I Don't Want To Make You Wait**	*Baby I Miss You*	$8		Philly Groove 176

DEL FUEGOS, The — ROK/LP '86

Rock group from Boston, Massachusetts: Dan Zanes (vocals, guitar), Warren Zanes (guitar), Tom Lloyd (bass) and Woody Giessman (drums).

DEBUT	PEAK	WKS	Gold	A-side (Chart Hit)	B-side	$	Sym	Label & Number
5/31/86	87	4		**I Still Want You**	*Hand In Hand*	$4	■	Slash 28822

DELINQUENT HABITS — LP '96

Latino hip-hop trio from Los Angeles, California: Kemo (David Thomas) and Ives (Ivan Martin) with DJ/producer O.G. Style (Alejandro Martinez).

DEBUT	PEAK	WKS	Gold	A-side (Chart Hit)	B-side	$	Sym	Label & Number
4/27/96	35	20		**Tres Delinquentes** S:22 / A:71	*What It Be Like*	$5	▮	Loud/RCA 64526
				contains a replayed sample from **Herb Alpert**'s "The Lonely Bull"				

DELIVERANCE — '80

Pop vocal trio from Three Hills, Alberta, Canada: brothers Paul, Danny and Ken Janz. Similar in style to the **Bee Gees**.

DEBUT	PEAK	WKS	Gold	A-side (Chart Hit)	B-side	$	Sym	Label & Number
8/30/80	71	5		**Leaving L.A.**	*Prince Of The Galaxies*	$4		Columbia 11320

DELIVERANCE Soundtrack — see WEISSBERG, Eric

★302★ DELLS, The — R&B/BUB/LP '68

R&B vocal group from Harvey, Illinois: Johnny Funches (lead), Marvin Junior (baritone lead; born on 1/31/36), Verne Allison (tenor; born on 6/22/36), Mickey McGill (baritone; born on 2/17/37) and Chuck Barksdale (bass; born on 6/11/35). First recorded as the El-Rays for Checker in 1953. Signed with Vee-Jay in 1955. Group remained intact into the 1980s, with the exception of Funches, who was replaced by Johnny Carter (ex-**Flamingos**; born on 6/2/34) in 1960. Funches died on 1/23/98 (age 62). Charted 47 R&B hits, 1956-92.

1)Stay In My Corner 2)Oh, What A Night 3)Always Together 4)There Is 5)I Can Sing A Rainbow/Love Is Blue

DEBUT	PEAK	WKS	Gold	A-side (Chart Hit)	B-side	$	Sym	Label & Number
12/22/62	97	3		1 **The (Bossa Nova) Bird**	*Eternally*	$15		Argo 5428
11/4/67	61	10		2 **O-O, I Love You**	*There Is*	$8		Cadet 5574
1/20/68	20	11		3 **There Is**	*Show Me*	$8		Cadet 5590
4/13/68	44	8		4 **Wear It On Our Face**	*Please Don't Change Me Now*	$8		Cadet 5599
6/29/68	10	13		5 **Stay In My Corner** RB[3]	*Love Is So Simple*	$8		Cadet 5612
				original version was a #23 R&B hit on Vee-Jay 674 in 1965 ($15)				
10/12/68	18	8		6 **Always Together**	*I Want My Momma*	$8		Cadet 5621
12/28/68+	38	9		7 **Does Anybody Know I'm Here**	*Make Sure (You Have Someone Who Loves You)*	$8		Cadet 5631
3/8/69	92	4		8 **Hallways Of My Mind /**				
4/12/69	98	2		9 **I Can't Do Enough**		$8		Cadet 5636
5/24/69	22	10		10 **I Can Sing A Rainbow/Love Is Blue**	*Hallelujah Baby*	$8		Cadet 5641
8/16/69	10	11		11 **Oh, What A Night** RB[1]	*Believe Me*	$8		Cadet 5649
				original version was a #4 R&B hit on Vee-Jay 204 in 1956 ($100)				
11/1/69	42	8		12 **On The Dock Of The Bay**	*When I'm In Your Arms* (#108)	$8		Cadet 5658
1/24/70	43	8		13 **Oh What A Day**	*The Change We Go Thru (For Love)*	$8		Cadet 5663
4/18/70	51	8		14 **Open Up My Heart /**				
5/9/70		4		15 **Nadine**		$8		Cadet 5667
7/18/70	74	4		16 **Long Lonely Nights**	*A Little Understanding*	$8		Cadet 5672
2/6/71	92	2		17 **The Glory Of Love**	*A Whiter Shade Of Pale*	$8		Cadet 5679
				re-entered the R&B charts in 1975 (#59); #1 hit for **Benny Goodman** in 1936; all of above (except #1) produced by Bobby Miller				
8/14/71	30	12		18 **The Love We Had (Stays On My Mind)**	*Freedom Means*	$7		Cadet 5683
2/26/72	94	3		19 **It's All Up To You**	*Oh, My Dear* (R&B #36)	$7		Cadet 5689
4/21/73	34	16	●	20 **Give Your Baby A Standing Ovation**	*Closer*	$7		Cadet 5696
10/6/73	51	8		21 **My Pretending Days Are Over**	*Let's Make It Last*	$7		Cadet 5698
1/19/74	60	7		22 **I Miss You**	*Don't Make Me A Storyteller*	$7		Cadet 5700
7/6/74	94	2		23 **I Wish It Was Me You Loved**	*Two Together Is Better Than One*	$7		Cadet 5702
10/26/74	87	3		24 **Bring Back The Love Of Yesterday**	*Learning To Love You Was Easy* (R&B #18)	$7		Cadet 5703
				later pressings replaced above title with "Sweeter As The Days Go By"				

DEBUT	PEAK	WKS	Gold	A-side (Chart Hit)...B-side	$	Sym	Label & Number
				DELL-VIKINGS, The BUB '57			
				Interracial doo-wop group formed at the Air Force Serviceman's Club in 1955 in Pittsburgh, Pennsylvania. "Come Go With Me" featured lead singer Norman Wright with Corinthian "Kripp" Johnson, Don Jackson, Clarence Quick (wrote #1 & 2 below) and David Lerchey (the only white member). "Whispering Bells" featured Kripp Johnson as lead singer with Gus Backus (white tenor) replacing Don Jackson. Mercury signed the group (as Del Vikings) in May, 1957 with Gus Backus as lead singer and William Blakely replacing Kripp Johnson (died on 6/22/90, age 57). Many personnel changes thereafter, including successful R&B singer **Chuck Jackson**. Quick died of a heart attack on 5/5/83 (age 46).			
2/16/57	**4**	31	●	1 **Come Go With Me** ...S:4 / T:5 / J:6 / A:6 *How Can I Find True Love*	$30		Dot 15538
				first released on Fee Bee 205 in 1956 ($500); new version by Del Vikings "Bubbled Under" (#112) in 1973 on Scepter 12367 ($10)			
7/8/57	**9**	18		2 **Whispering Bells**...T:9 / S:10 / A:19 *Don't Be A Fool*	$30		Dot 15592
				THE DELL-VIKINGS Featuring Kripp Johnson			
				first released on Fee Bee 214 in 1956 ($400)			
7/15/57	**12**	13		3 **Cool Shake**...A:12 / T:46 *Jitterbug Mary*	$30		Mercury 71132
				DEL VIKINGS featuring Gus Backus			
				DeLORY, Al AC '70			
				Born on 1/31/30 in Los Angeles, California. Prolific producer/arranger/conductor. Sang in the pop trio The Balladeers.			
6/13/70	**70**	12		**Song From M*A*S*H**...*Feeling Of Love* [I]	$6		Capitol 2811
				theme from the movie and TV series *M*A*S*H*; song's real title: "Suicide Is Painless"			
				DELPHS, Jimmy '68			
				Born in Toledo, Ohio. R&B singer.			
5/25/68	**96**	4		**Don't Sign The Paper Baby (I Want You Back)**...*Almost*	$12		Karen 1538
				DEL THE FUNKY HOMOSAPIEN R&B/LP '02			
				Born Teren Jones on 8/12/72 in Oakland, California. Male rapper. Cousin of **Ice Cube**.			
5/11/02	**66**S	1		**One Big Trip**...*(instrumental) / The High Road* (Swollen Members)	$10	T	Hiero Imp. 230013
				DeMARCO, Ralph '59			
				Born on 1/22/43 in the Bronx, New York. Pop singer.			
11/9/59	**91**	2		**Old Shep**...*More Than Riches*	$20	■	Guaranteed 202
				written by Red Foley in 1933			
				DeMATTEO, Nicky '60			
				Born in 1942 in Philadelphia, Pennsylvania. Male teen pop singer.			
3/7/60	**90**	2		**Suddenly**...*I Couldn't Sleep A Wink Last Night*	$20		Guyden 2024
				Norman Baker (orch.)			
				DEMENSIONS, The '60			
				White pop vocal group from the Bronx, New York: Lenny Del Giudice (Lenny Dell), Marisa Martelli, Howard Margolin and Charlie Peterson.			
7/4/60	**16**	15		1 **Over The Rainbow**...*Nursery Rhime Rock*	$30		Mohawk 116
				Irv Spice (orch.); first sung by Judy Garland in the 1939 movie *The Wizard Of Oz*; some pressings show artist as The Dimensions			
3/2/63	**95**	3		2 **My Foolish Heart**...*Just One More Chance*	$30	■	Coral 62344
				Henry Jerome (orch.); #3 hit for **Gordon Jenkins** in 1950			
				DEM GHETTO PLAYA$ '02			
				Rap trio from Atlanta, Georgia.			
6/1/02	**53**S	5		**Ghetto Millionaire**...*(3 versions) / Wutcha Be*	$10	★	Deep End 1985
				DEMUS, Chaka, & Pliers R&B/BUB '93			
				Male dancehall reggae duo from Jamaica: John "Chaka Demus" Taylor and Everton "Pliers" Banner.			
1/2/93	**57**	17		**Murder She Wrote**...S:30 / A:51 *(Nigar mix)*	$5	▮	Mango 530131
				DENINE BUB '96			
				Born Denine Latanzo in Philadelphia, Pennsylvania. White female dance singer.			
1/20/96	**72**	11		**All Cried Out**...A:75 *I Only Wanted To Love You*	$6	▮	Viper 201
				DENINE f/ Adam Marano			
				DENNEY, Kevin C&W/LP '02			
				Born in Monticello, Kentucky. Country singer/songwriter/guitarist.			
2/2/02	**76**	17		**That's Just Jessie**...S:16 *Correct Me If I'm Right*	$5	★+	Lyric Street 64063
				DENNIS, Cathy AC/LP '91			
				Born on 3/25/69 in Norwich, Norfolk, England. White dance-pop singer/songwriter. Vocalist for producer Dancin' Danny D's **D-Mob**. Also see **PM Dawn**'s "Looking Through Patient Eyes."			
12/16/89+	**10**	21		1 **C'mon And Get My Love**...A:10 / S:12 *(12" remix)*	$4	▮	FFRR 886798
				D MOB Introducing Cathy Dennis			
				from the movie *She-Devil* starring Meryl Streep and Roseanne Barr			
4/28/90	**59**	9		2 **That's The Way Of The World**...*(long version) / (3 album snippets)*	$4	▮	FFRR 886980
				D MOB with Cathy Dennis			
10/27/90+	**9**	22		3 **Just Another Dream**...S:8 / A:8 *(hot mix)*	$3	▮V	Polydor 877962
3/2/91	**2**2	20		4 **Touch Me (All Night Long)** A:2 / S:3 *(hot mix)*	$3	▮V	Polydor 879466
				#70 R&B hit for Wish Featuring Fonda Rae in 1985			
7/6/91	**8**	20		5 **Too Many Walls**...AC2 A:13 / S:35 *(acappella version)*	$3	▮V	Polydor 867134
12/14/91	**90**	3		6 **Everybody Move**...A:68 *(3 mixes)*	$5	▮*	Polydor 867989
				all of above (except #2) from the album *Move To This*			
9/5/92	**32**	13		7 **You Lied To Me**...A:25 / S:65 *Touch Me (All Night Long) / (3 album snippets)*	$3	▮	Polydor 863452
12/26/92+	**61**	12		8 **Irresistible**...A:65 *Too Many Walls / (3 album snippets)*	$3	▮	Polydor 861210
				DENNIS DA MENACE '01			
				Born in Washington DC. Male rapper.			
9/29/01	**14**S	34		**Buster**...*Ball*	$10	★	1st Avenue 0001

DEBUT	PEAK	WKS	Gold	A-side (Chart Hit)..................B-side	$	Sym	Label & Number

DENNY, Martin (The Exotic Sounds of) — BUB/LP '59

Born on 4/10/21 in Manhattan, New York. Composer/arranger/pianist. Originated "The Exotic Sounds of Martin Denny" in Hawaii, featuring **Arthur Lyman** and Julius Wechter (**Baja Marimba Band**) on vibes and marimba.

DEBUT	PEAK	WKS	Gold	A-side (Chart Hit)..................B-side	$	Sym	Label & Number
4/13/59	4	16	●	1 **Quiet Village** .... *Llama Serenade* [I] written and first recorded in 1952 by **Les Baxter** (Capitol 2225)	$10		Liberty 55162
7/20/59	88	2		2 **Martinique** .... *Sake Rock* (pronounced "Socky") [I]	$10		Liberty 55199
10/26/59	28	8		3 **The Enchanted Sea** .... *Stranger In Paradise* [I]	$10		Liberty 55212
7/14/62	50	15		4 **A Taste Of Honey** .... *The Brighter Side* [I] **MARTIN DENNY and His Orchestra** tune introduced by **Bobby Scott** in the 1960 Broadway show *A Taste of Honey*	$8	■	Liberty 55470

DENVER, John ★81★ — C&W/AC/BUB/LP '74

Born Henry John Deutschendorf on 12/31/43 in Roswell, New Mexico. Died at the controls of a light plane which crashed off the California coast on 10/12/97 (age 53). To Los Angeles in 1964. With the **Chad Mitchell Trio** from 1965-68. Wrote "Leaving On A Jet Plane." Starred in the 1977 movie *Oh, God.* Won an Emmy in 1975 for the TV special *An Evening with John Denver.*

1)Annie's Song 2)Sunshine On My Shoulders 3)Thank God I'm A Country Boy 4)I'm Sorry 5)Calypso

DEBUT	PEAK	WKS	Gold	A-side (Chart Hit)..................B-side	$	Sym	Label & Number
4/10/71	2[1]	23	●	1 **Take Me Home, Country Roads** .... *Poems, Prayers And Promises* Fat City (Bill Danoff & Taffy Nivert of **Starland Vocal Band**; backing vocals)	$7		RCA Victor 0445
11/6/71	47	11		2 **Friends With You** .... *Starwood In Aspen*	$6		RCA Victor 0567
3/11/72	81	3		3 **Everyday** .... *City Of New Orleans* written by **Buddy Holly**	$6		RCA Victor 0647
7/22/72	88	6		4 **Goodbye Again** .... *The Eagle And The Hawk*	$6		RCA Victor 0737
11/25/72+	9	19		5 **Rocky Mountain High** .... *Spring*	$5		RCA Victor 0829
5/26/73	62	10		6 **I'd Rather Be A Cowboy** .... *Sunshine On My Shoulders*	$5		RCA Victor 0955
9/15/73	89	5		7 **Farewell Andromeda (Welcome To My Morning)** .... *Whiskey Basin Blues*	$5		RCA Victor 0067
12/22/73	69	5		8 **Please, Daddy** .... X:7 *Rocky Mountain Suite (Cold Nights in Canada)* [X] Christmas charts: #7/'73 (3 weeks)	$5		RCA Victor 0182
1/26/74	❶[1]	18	●	9 **Sunshine On My Shoulders** .... AC[2] *Around And Around* first released as the B-side of #6 above	$5		RCA Victor 0213
6/1/74	❶[2]	17	●	10 **Annie's Song** AC[3] *Cool An' Green An' Shady* written by Denver for his then-wife Annie Martell (married 1967-83)	$5		RCA Victor 0295
9/21/74	5	16	●	11 **Back Home Again** .... CW[1] / AC[2] *It's Up To You*	$5		RCA Victor 10065
12/28/74+	13	11		12 **Sweet Surrender** .... AC[1] *Summer* [L]	$5		RCA Victor 10148
3/22/75	❶[1]	19	●	13 **Thank God I'm A Country Boy** .... CW[1] *My Sweet Lady* [L] above 2 recorded at the Universal City Amphitheater, California; both were originally studio cuts from the album *Back Home Again*	$5		RCA Victor 10239
8/16/75	❶[1]	18	●	14 **I'm Sorry** / CW[1] / AC[2]			
10/11/75	2[4]	10		15 **Calypso** .... dedicated to Jacques Cousteau and his ship "Calypso"	$5		RCA Victor 10353
12/6/75+	13	12		16 **Fly Away** .... AC[2] *Two Shots* **Olivia Newton-John** (backing vocal)	$5		RCA Victor 10517
12/13/75	58	4		17 **Christmas For Cowboys** .... *Silent Night, Holy Night* [X]	$5		RCA Victor 10464
3/6/76	29	8		18 **Looking For Space** .... AC[1] *Windsong* #14-16 & 18: from the album *Windsong*	$5		RCA Victor 10586
5/8/76	60	4		19 **It Makes Me Giggle** .... *Spirit*	$5		RCA Victor 10687
9/11/76	36	7		20 **Like A Sad Song** .... AC[1] *Pegasus*	$4		RCA 10774
12/25/76+	65	7		21 **Baby, You Look Good To Me Tonight** .... *Wrangle Mountain Song*	$4		RCA 10854
3/12/77	32	11		22 **My Sweet Lady** .... *Welcome To My Morning (Farewell Andromeda)* recorded in 1971 on his *Poems, Prayers & Promises* album (also see the 'live' version on the B-side of #13 above)	$4		RCA 10911
11/26/77+	44	10		23 **How Can I Leave You Again** .... *To The Wild Country*	$4		RCA 11036
3/4/78	59	7		24 **It Amazes Me** .... *Druthers*	$4		RCA 11214
4/29/78	55	5		25 **I Want To Live** .... *Tradewinds*	$4		RCA 11267
2/23/80	52	10		26 **Autograph** .... *The Mountain Song*	$4	■	RCA 11915
6/21/80	97	3		27 **Dancing With The Mountains** .... *American Child* all of above produced by Milton Okun	$4		RCA 12017
6/13/81	36	20		28 **Some Days Are Diamonds (Some Days Are Stone)** .... *Country Love*	$4		RCA 12246
10/31/81	66	7		29 **The Cowboy And The Lady** .... *Till You Opened My Eyes* written by **Bobby Goldsboro**	$4		RCA 12345
1/16/82	59	7		30 **Perhaps Love** .... *Annie's Song* (Domingo) **PLACIDO DOMINGO AND JOHN DENVER** Denver's solo version is on his 1982 album *Seasons Of The Heart*	$4		Columbia 02679
3/6/82	31	14		31 **Shanghai Breezes** .... AC[1] *What One Man Can Do*	$4		RCA 13071
7/31/82	78	5		32 **Seasons Of The Heart** .... *Islands*	$4		RCA 13270
11/10/84	85	4		33 **Love Again** .... *It's About Time* (Denver) **JOHN DENVER and SYLVIE VARTAN** all of above (except #2, 3, 8, 13, 17, 21, 28 & 29) written by Denver	$4		RCA 13931

DEODATO — AC/R&B/LP '73

Born Eumir Deodato on 6/21/42 in Rio de Janeiro, Brazil. Dance keyboardist/composer/producer/arranger. **Kool & The Gang**'s producer from 1979-82.

DEBUT	PEAK	WKS	Gold	A-side (Chart Hit)..................B-side	$	Sym	Label & Number
2/3/73	2[1]	12		1 **Also Sprach Zarathustra (2001)** .... *Spirit Of Summer* [I] theme from the movie *2001: A Space Odyssey*; written by classical composer Richard Strauss in 1896	$5		CTI 12
8/25/73	41	8		2 **Rhapsody In Blue** .... *Super Strut* [I] the classic George Gershwin tune; a hit for Paul Whiteman (with piano solo by Gershwin) in 1924	$5	■	CTI 16
10/23/76	84	6		3 **Peter Gunn** .... *Amani* [I] title theme from the TV series starring Craig Stevens; written by **Henry Mancini**	$4		MCA 40631
6/19/82	70	5		4 **Happy Hour** .... *Sweet Magic* Kelly Barretto (lead vocal)	$4		Warner 29984

DEBUT	PEAK	WKS	Gold	A-side (Chart Hit)..........B-side	$	Sym	Label & Number

DEPECHE MODE

★341★ ROK/LP **'90**

All-synthesized electro-pop group formed in Basildon, England: singer Dave Gahan (born on 5/9/62) and synthesizer players Martin L. Gore (born on 7/23/61), Vince Clarke (born on 7/3/60) and Andy Fletcher (born on 7/8/61). Clarke left in 1982 (formed **Yaz**, then **Erasure**), replaced by Alan Wilder (born on 6/1/59; left in 1995). Group name is French for fast fashion. From 1997-on, group consists of Gahan, Gore and Fletcher.

1)Enjoy The Silence 2)People Are People 3)Policy Of Truth

DEBUT	PEAK	WKS	Gold	A-side (Chart Hit)..........B-side	$	Sym	Label & Number
5/25/85	13	18		1 **People Are People**..........A:11 / S:16 *In Your Memory*	$4	■	Sire 29221
9/7/85	87	3		2 **Master And Servant**..........*(Set Me Free) Remotivate Me*	$4	■	Sire 28918
7/25/87	76	6		3 **Strangelove**..........*Fpmip*	$4	■	Sire 28366
12/26/87+	63	10		4 **Never Let Me Down Again**..........*Pleasure, Little Treasure*	$4	■	Sire 28189
5/7/88	61	11		5 **Route 66/Behind The Wheel**..........*Behind The Wheel*	$4	■	Sire 27991
				"Route 66" was a #11 hit for **Nat "King" Cole** in 1946			
9/10/88	50	9		6 **Strangelove**..........*Nothing* [R]	$4	■	Sire 27777
				new mix of #3 above; above 4 from the album *Music For The Masses*			
12/9/89+	28	20	●	7 **Personal Jesus**..........S:20 *Dangerous* (ROK #13)	$3	▮V	Sire/Reprise 19941
				"45": Sire 18889; B-side: "Policy Of Truth"			
4/14/90	8	24	●	8 **Enjoy The Silence** MR^{3} A:4 / S:10 *Memphisto*	$3	▮V	Sire/Reprise 19885
8/11/90	15	16		9 **Policy Of Truth**..........MR^{1} A:11 / S:22 *Kaleid*	$3	▮V	Sire/Reprise 19842
11/24/90	52	10		10 **World In My Eyes**..........*Happiest Girl / Sea Of Sin*	$3	▮V	Sire/Reprise 19580
				"45": Sire 18890; B-side: "Enjoy The Silence"; above 4 from the album *Violator*			
3/6/93	37	12	●	11 **I Feel You**..........MR^{5} S:14 / A:59 *One Caress*	$3	▮V	Sire/Reprise 18600
6/5/93	69	8		12 **Walking In My Shoes**..........MR^{1} A:61 *My Joy*	$3	▮V	Sire/Reprise 18506
2/22/97	47	5		13 **Barrel Of A Gun**..........S:36 / A:65 *(3 phase mix) / Painkiller*	$3	▮V	Mute/Reprise 17409
5/17/97	38	20		14 **It's No Good**..........A:44 / S:58 *(remix) / Slowblow*	$3	▮V	Mute/Reprise 17390
12/6/97	88	3		15 **Home**..........*(remix) / Useless*	$3	▮V	Mute/Reprise 17314
10/3/98	61	9		16 **Only When I Lose Myself**..........S:54 *(remix) / Headstar / Surrender*	$8	★*	Mute/Reprise 44546
5/12/01	85	10		17 **Dream On**..........S:11 *(3 mixes) / Easy Tiger (Bertrand Burgalat)*	$8	★*V	Mute/Reprise 44982
8/18/01	32^{S}	9		18 **I Feel Loved**..........*(3 versions) / Dirt*	$8	★*V	Mute/Reprise 42398
				"45" issued for above 2 on Mute/Reprise 16732			
12/29/01	28^{S}	7		19 **Freelove**..........*(5 remixes)*	$8	★*	Mute/Reprise 42419
				all of above (except #5 "Route 66") written by Martin Gore			

DEREK — see CYMBAL, Johnny

DEREK AND THE DOMINOS — see CLAPTON, Eric

DERRINGER, Rick

LP **'74**

Born Richard Zehringer on 8/5/47 in Celina, Ohio. Lead singer/guitarist of the rock band **The McCoys**. Performed on and produced sessions for both **Edgar** and **Johnny Winter**'s bands; also a producer for **"Weird Al" Yankovic**.

DEBUT	PEAK	WKS	Gold	A-side (Chart Hit)..........B-side	$	Sym	Label & Number
1/19/74	23	14		1 **Rock And Roll, Hoochie Koo**..........*Time Warp* [I]	$5		Blue Sky 2751
4/27/74	80	5		2 **Teenage Love Affair**..........*Slide On Over Slinky*	$5		Blue Sky 2752
				A-side label number misprinted as 2572			
4/5/75	94	4		3 **Hang On Sloopy**..........*Skyscraper Blues*	$5		Blue Sky 2755
				also see **The McCoys** (Derringer's group) #1 hit from 1965			
8/28/76	86	2		4 **Let Me In** *[DERRINGER]*..........*You Can Have Me*	$5		Blue Sky 2765

DeSANTO, Sugar Pie

R&B **'64**

Born Umpeylia Balinton on 10/16/35 in Brooklyn, New York; raised in San Francisco, California. Female R&B singer. Member of the **James Brown** Revue.

DEBUT	PEAK	WKS	Gold	A-side (Chart Hit)..........B-side	$	Sym	Label & Number
4/18/64	48	5		1 **Slip-In Mules (No High Heel Sneakers)**..........*Mr. & Mrs.*	$15		Checker 1073
				answer song to **Tommy Tucker**'s "Hi-Heel Sneakers"			
12/18/65	96	1		2 **Do I Make Myself Clear**..........*Somewhere Down The Line*	$12		Cadet 5519
8/13/66	97	2		3 **In The Basement - Part 1**..........*Part 2* (DeSanto)	$12		Cadet 5539
				ETTA JAMES & SUGAR PIE DeSANTO (above 2)			

DeSARIO, Teri

LP **'80**

Born in Miami, Florida. Female dance-pop singer/songwriter. Began recording Christian music in 1983.

DEBUT	PEAK	WKS	Gold	A-side (Chart Hit)..........B-side	$	Sym	Label & Number
7/1/78	43	12		1 **Ain't Nothing Gonna Keep Me From You**..........*Sometime Kind Of Thing*	$4		Casablanca 929
				written and produced by **Barry Gibb** of the **Bee Gees**			
				TERI DeSARIO with K.C.:			
11/17/79+	2^{2}	23	●	2 **Yes, I'm Ready**..........AC^{2} *With Your Love* (DeSario)	$4		Casablanca 2227
6/28/80	66	6		3 **Dancin' In The Streets**..........*Moonlight Madness* (DeSario)	$4		Casablanca 2278

DeSHANNON, Jackie

BUB/AC/LP **'69**

Born Sharon Myers on 8/21/44 in Hazel, Kentucky. Soft-rock singer/songwriter. On radio at age six. First recorded (as Sherry Lee Myers) for Glenn in 1959. To Los Angeles in 1960. Attained prominence as a prolific songwriter (over 600 to date). Co-writer of mega-pop hit "Bette Davis Eyes." Toured with **The Beatles** for 26 concerts in 1964. In the movies *Surf Party*, *C'mon Let's Live A Little* and *Hide And Seek*. Married to **Randy Edelman**.

1)Put A Little Love In Your Heart 2)What The World Needs Now Is Love 3)Love Will Find A Way

DEBUT	PEAK	WKS	Gold	A-side (Chart Hit)..........B-side	$	Sym	Label & Number
2/23/63	97	2		1 **Faded Love**..........*Dancing Silhouettes*	$20	■	Liberty 55526
				#8 Country hit for Bob Wills in 1950			
5/18/63	84	4		2 **Needles And Pins**..........*Did He Call Today, Mama?*	$20		Liberty 55563
				written by **Sonny** Bono and **Jack Nitzsche**			
1/25/64	99	1		3 **When You Walk In The Room**..........*Till You Say You'll Be Mine*	$20		Liberty 55645
5/22/65	7	13		4 **What The World Needs Now Is Love**..........*I Remember The Boy*	$10		Imperial 66110
10/2/65	66	6		5 **A Lifetime Of Loneliness**..........*Don't Turn Your Back On Me*	$10		Imperial 66132
5/28/66	83	3		6 **Come And Get Me**..........*Splendor In The Grass*	$10		Imperial 66171
				above 3 written and produced by **Burt Bacharach** and Hal David			
9/10/66	68	6		7 **I Can Make It With You**..........*To Be Myself*	$10		Imperial 66202
8/24/68	55	8		8 **The Weight**..........*Effervescent Blue*	$10		Imperial 66313
6/28/69	4	14	●	9 **Put A Little Love In Your Heart**..........*Always Together*	$8		Imperial 66385
11/1/69	40	8		10 **Love Will Find A Way**..........*I Let Go Completely*	$8		Imperial 66419
3/7/70	82	4		11 **Brighton Hill**..........*You Can Come To Me*	$8		Imperial 66438

DEBUT	PEAK	WKS	Gold	A-side (Chart Hit)...B-side	$	Sym	Label & Number
				DeSHANNON, Jackie — Cont'd			
5/30/70	96	1		12 **You Keep Me Hangin' On/Hurt So Bad** ...*What Was Your Day Like*	$8		Imperial 66452
8/8/70	84	7		13 **It's So Nice** ...*Mediterranean Sky*	$8		Liberty 56187
6/3/72	76	9		14 **Vanilla Ólay** ...*Only Love Can Break Your Heart* (AC #38)	$8		Atlantic 2871
10/29/77	68	10		15 **Don't Let The Flame Burn Out** ...*I Don't Think I Can Wait* #3, 9-11, 14 & 15: written by DeShannon	$10		Amherst 725
3/8/80	86	5		16 **I Don't Need You Anymore** ...*Find Love* **TOGETHER? (Original Soundtrack Recording) Featuring Jackie DeShannon** from the movie *Together?* starring Jacqueline Bisset; written and produced by **Paul Anka** and **Burt Bacharach**	$6		RCA 11902
				DESMOND, Johnny MEM/POP '55 Born Giovanni Desimons on 11/14/20 in Detroit, Michigan. Died on 9/6/85 (age 64). Pop singer. Sang with **Bob Crosby**, **Gene Krupa** and **Glenn Miller**'s military band. Featured on the *Breakfast Club* radio show and TV's *Your Hit Parade.* Charted 12 pop hits from 1947-54.			
3/26/55	6	11		1 **Play Me Hearts And Flowers (I Wanna Cry)** ...A:6 / J:11 / S:16 *I'm So Ashamed* Don Jacoby (orch.); introduced by Desmond on 3/6/55 on TV's *Philco Playhouse*	$15		Coral 61379
8/13/55	3	16		2 **The Yellow Rose Of Texas** ...A:3 / J:4 / S:6 / T:16 *You're In Love With Someone* adaptation of a Civil War campfire song	$15		Coral 61476
11/19/55	17	11		3 **Sixteen Tons** ...A:17 / T:50 *Ballo Italiano*	$15		Coral 61529
5/27/57	62	2		4 **A White Sport Coat (And A Pink Carnation)** ...T:62 *Just Lookin'* **Dick Jacobs** (orch., above 3)	$12		Coral 61835
				DES'REE LP '95 Born Des'ree Weeks on 11/30/68 in London, England (West Indian parentage). Black female singer/songwriter. Also see **Terence Trent D'Arby**'s "Delicate."			
9/3/94+	5	44		1 **You Gotta Be** ...A:2 / S:17 *Competitive World*	$3	▮V	550 Music/Epic 77551
4/1/95	67	11		2 **Feel So High** ...*Living In The City* "45" issued for above 2 on 550 Music/Epic 77693	$3	▮V	550 Music/Epic 77693
				 **DESTINY'S CHILD** ★181★ R&B/BUB/LP '00 Female R&B vocal group from Houston, Texas: **Beyoncé Knowles** (born on 9/4/81), **Kelly Rowland** (born on 2/11/81), LaTavia Roberson (born on 11/1/81) and LeToya (**Toya**) Luckett (born on 3/11/81). Roberson and Luckett left in early 2000; replaced by Farrah Franklin (born on 5/3/81) and Michelle Williams (born on 7/23/80). Franklin left shortly thereafter, leaving trio of Knowles, Rowland and Williams. Knowles played "Foxxy Cleopatra" in the movie *Austin Powers in Goldmember.* *1)Independent Women Part I 2)Say My Name 3)Bootylicious*			
11/29/97+	3	35	▲	1 **No, No, No Part 2** ...RB[1] S:❶[1] / A:22 *(Part 1)* **DESTINY'S CHILD (featuring Wyclef Jean)**	$3	▮	Columbia 78618
3/21/98	57	16		2 **Just Be Straight With Me** ...S:40 *(instrumental)* **SILKK the SHOCKER Featuring Master P, Destiny's Child, O'Dell, Mo B. Dick** rap version with new lyrics of "Just Be Good To Me" by **The S.O.S. Band**; clean version available on No Limit 53313	$5	▮	No Limit 53305
6/19/99	❶[1]	20	●	3 **Bills, Bills, Bills** ...RB[9] S:❶[1] / A:4 *(3 album snippets)*	$4	★	Columbia 79175
9/25/99	33	20		4 **Bug A Boo** ...A:22			album cut
12/25/99+	❶[3]	32	●	5 **Say My Name** ...RB[3] S:❷[2] / A:❶[1] *(**Timbaland** remix)*	$4	★	Columbia 79342
5/13/00	3	32		6 **Jumpin', Jumpin'** ...A:❶[7] / S:16 *(3 remixes) / Upside Down* above 4 from the album *The Writing's On The Wall* on Columbia 69870	$8	★*	Columbia 79446
9/23/00	❶[11]	28		7 **Independent Women Part I** RB[3] A:❶[9] / S:3 *(3 remixes) / 8 Days Of Christmas (#102/'01)* from the movie *Charlie's Angels* starring Drew Barrymore	$8	★*	Columbia 79493
3/17/01	2[7]	20		8 **Survivor** ...A:❶[5] / S:3 *(4 remixes)* "45": Columbia 79582; CD-maxi single and "45" B-side contain a remix of the track featuring **Da Brat**	$8	★*V	Columbia 79566
6/9/01	❶[2]	19		9 **Bootylicious** ...S:2 / A:5 *(4 remixes)* samples "Edge Of Seventeen" by **Stevie Nicks**; from the TV movie *MTV's Hip Hopera: Carmen* starring **Beyoncé Knowles**	$8	★*	Columbia 79622
9/29/01	10	20		10 **Emotion** ...A:10 *(9 remixes)* 12" single issued with 2 discs (10 total versions); above 4 from the album *Survivor*	$10	T	Columbia 79672
				DETERGENTS, The '65 Novelty vocal trio from New York: Ron Dante (of **The Archies** and **The Cuff Links**), Tommy Wynn and Danny Jordan.			
12/5/64+	19	8		1 **Leader Of The Laundromat** ...*Ulcers* [N] parody of **The Shangri-Las**' "Leader Of The Pack"	$20	■	Roulette 4590
3/20/65	89	3		2 **Double-O-Seven** ...*The Blue Kangaroo* [N] parody of James Bond movies	$15		Roulette 4603
				DETROIT EMERALDS R&B/BUB/LP '72 R&B vocal group from Little Rock, Arkansas: brothers Abrim, Ivory, Cleophus and Raymond Tilmon. In 1970, group reduced to trio of Abrim, Ivory and friend James Mitchell. 1977 group consisted of Abrim Tilmon, Paul Riser, Johnny Allen and Maurice King. "Sweet" James Epps, of the **Fantastic Four**, was a cousin of the Tilmon brothers. The group's backing band, from 1971-73, later recorded as Chapter 8. Abrim Tilmon died of a heart attack in July 1982 (age 37).			
3/30/68	89	5		1 **Show Time** ...*(instrumental)*	$15		Ric-Tic 135
2/20/71	43	14		2 **Do Me Right** ...*Just Now And Then*	$8		Westbound 172
8/14/71	91	4		3 **Wear This Ring (With Love)** ...*I Bet You Get The One (Who Loves You)*	$8		Westbound 181
1/8/72	36	13		4 **You Want It, You Got It** ...*Till You Decide To Come Home*	$8		Westbound 192
5/27/72	24	17		5 **Baby Let Me Take You (In My Arms)** *I'll Never Sail The Sea Again*	$8		Westbound 203
5/14/77	90	5		6 **Feel The Need** ...*Love Has Come To Me* original version "Bubbled Under" (#110) on 11/11/72 as "Feel The Need In Me" on Westbound 209	$6		Westbound 55401
				DeVAUGHN, William R&B/LP '74 Born in 1948 in Washington DC. R&B singer/songwriter/guitarist.			
5/4/74	4	18	●	1 **Be Thankful For What You Got** ...RB[1] *Part 2*	$7		Roxbury 0236
9/7/74	43	9		2 **Blood Is Thicker Than Water** ...*Part II*	$7		Roxbury 2001

DEBUT	PEAK	WKS	Gold	A-side (Chart Hit)....................B-side	$	Sym	Label & Number

DEVICE — LP '86

Pop-rock trio from Los Angeles, California: Paul Engemann (vocals), **Holly Knight** (keyboards, bass, vocals) and Gene Black (guitar). Engemann joined **Animotion** in 1988. Prolific songwriter Knight was a member of **Spider**.

DEBUT	PEAK	WKS	Gold	A-side (Chart Hit)....................B-side	$	Sym	Label & Number
6/14/86	35	14		1 **Hanging On A Heart Attack** ....A:26 / S:37 *(extended version)*	$4	■	Chrysalis 42996
9/27/86	79	6		2 **Who Says** ....*Pieces On The Ground*	$4		Chrysalis 43063

DEVO — BUB/ROK/LP '80

Robotic rock-dance group from Akron, Ohio: brothers Mark (synthesizers) and Bob (vocals, guitar) Mothersbaugh, brothers Jerry (bass) and Bob (guitar) Casale, and Alan Myers (drums).

DEBUT	PEAK	WKS	Gold	A-side (Chart Hit)....................B-side	$	Sym	Label & Number
8/30/80	14	25	●	1 **Whip It** ....*Turn Around*	$5		Warner 49550
9/5/81	43	12		2 **Working In The Coal Mine** ....*Planet Earth* from the animated movie *Heavy Metal*	$4	■	Full Moon 47204
5/21/83	59	6		3 **Theme From Doctor Detroit** ....*King Of Soul* (**James Brown**) from the movie *Doctor Detroit* starring Dan Aykroyd	$4		Backstreet 52215

DeVOL, Frank — POP/AC/LP '50

Born Herman Frank DeVol on 9/20/11 in Moundsville, West Virginia; raised in Canton, Ohio. Died of heart failure on 10/27/99 (age 88). Composer/conductor/arranger for many top singers, radio and TV shows. Composed the TV theme for *My Three Sons*. Married to singer Helen O'Connell from 1991-93.

DEBUT	PEAK	WKS	Gold	A-side (Chart Hit)....................B-side	$	Sym	Label & Number
5/16/60	77	6		**La Montana (If She Should Come To You)** ....*The Key Theme* [I] **FRANK DeVOL and his Rainbow Strings**	$10	■	Columbia 41620

DEVONÉ — '96

Born Devoné Shuford in Los Angeles, California. Male dance singer.

DEBUT	PEAK	WKS	Gold	A-side (Chart Hit)....................B-side	$	Sym	Label & Number
1/20/96	70	9		**Energy** ....A:71 *(acid trip mix)*	$5	▮	Aqua Boogie 852636

DeVORZON, Barry, and Perry Botkin, Jr. — LP '76

Songwriting/producing/arranging duo based in California. DeVorzon was born on 7/31/34 in Brooklyn, New York. Founded Valiant Records. Leader of **Barry And The Tamerlanes**. Began prolific songwriting career in the mid-1950s. Botkin was born on 4/16/33 in Manhattan, New York. Son of orchestra leader Perry Botkin, Sr.

DEBUT	PEAK	WKS	Gold	A-side (Chart Hit)....................B-side	$	Sym	Label & Number
8/28/76	8	22	●	1 **Nadia's Theme (The Young And The Restless)** ....*Down The Line* [I] originally written as "Cotton's Dream" for the movie *Bless The Beasts And Children*, then used as the theme song for TV's *The Young and The Restless*, and finally as the music for then-Romanian gymnast Nadia Comaneci in the 1976 summer Olympics; picture sleeve issued with a green, blue or black border	$4	■	A&M 1856
1/22/77	82	5		2 **Bless The Beasts And Children** ....*Down The Line* [I] title song from the movie starring Billy Mumy	$4		A&M 1890

DEVOTIONS, The — '64

White doo-wop group from Queens, New York: Ray Sanchez, Bob Weisbrod, Bob Hovorka, Frank Pardo and Joe Pardo.

DEBUT	PEAK	WKS	Gold	A-side (Chart Hit)....................B-side	$	Sym	Label & Number
2/8/64	36	10		**Rip Van Winkle** ....*(I Love You) For Sentimental Reasons* [N] first released on Delta 1001 ($150) in 1961 and then on Roulette 4406 ($40) in 1962	$25		Roulette 4541

DEXTER, Terry — '99

Born in 1978 in Detroit, Michigan. Black female singer/songwriter.

DEBUT	PEAK	WKS	Gold	A-side (Chart Hit)....................B-side	$	Sym	Label & Number
8/21/99	99	1		1 **Better Than Me** ....S:38 *(instrumental)*	$4	★	University 16950
2/19/00	59[S]	3		2 **Strayed Away** ....*(instrumental)*	$4	★	University 16907

DEXYS MIDNIGHT RUNNERS — LP '83

Pop-rock group from Birmingham, England: Kevin Rowland (vocals), Billy Adams (guitar), Brian Maurice (sax), Paul Speare (flute), Jimmy Patterson (trombone), Micky Billingham (piano), Giorgio Kilkenny (bass) and Seb Shelton (drums). Billingham was later with **General Public**.

DEBUT	PEAK	WKS	Gold	A-side (Chart Hit)....................B-side	$	Sym	Label & Number
1/22/83	❶[1]	23		1 **Come On Eileen** ....*Let's Make This Precious*	$4	■	Mercury 76189
5/28/83	86	4		2 **The Celtic Soul Brothers** ....*Reminisce Part 1*	$4	■	Mercury 811142

DEY, Tracey — BUB '64

Born in Yonkers, New York. Girl-group-styled solo singer. Also recorded as the "voice" of **The Rag Dolls**.

DEBUT	PEAK	WKS	Gold	A-side (Chart Hit)....................B-side	$	Sym	Label & Number
9/14/63	75	5		1 **Teenage Cleopatra** ....*Who's That (A Dream Smiled At Me)*	$20		Liberty 55604
12/28/63	93	3		2 **Here Comes The Boy** ....*Teddy's The Boy I Love*	$15		Amy 894
4/25/64	51	8		3 **Gonna' Get Along Without You Now** ....*Go Away* #25 hit for **Teresa Brewer** in 1952	$15		Amy 901

DeYOUNG, Cliff — '74

Born on 2/12/46 in Los Angeles, California. Adult Contemporary singer/actor. Starred in the movie *Shock Treatment*.

DEBUT	PEAK	WKS	Gold	A-side (Chart Hit)....................B-side	$	Sym	Label & Number
1/5/74	17	15		**My Sweet Lady** ....*Sunshine* written by **John Denver**; from the TV soundtrack *Sunshine*; some pressings show artist as: CLIFF DeYOUNG with BILL MUMY & COREY FISCHER; some pressings show B-side title as "Sunshine On My Shoulders"	$5	■	MCA 40156

DeYOUNG, Dennis — AC/LP '84

Born on 2/18/47 in Chicago, Illinois. Lead singer/keyboardist of **Styx**.

DEBUT	PEAK	WKS	Gold	A-side (Chart Hit)....................B-side	$	Sym	Label & Number
9/8/84	10	22		1 **Desert Moon** ....A:6 / S:12 *Gravity*	$3	■	A&M 2666
12/8/84	83	4		2 **Don't Wait For Heroes** ....*Gravity*	$3		A&M 2692
3/15/86	54	11		3 **Call Me** ....*Please*	$3	■	A&M 2816
6/28/86	93	3		4 **This Is The Time** ....*Southbound Ryan* from the movie *The Karate Kid Part II* starring Ralph Macchio	$3		A&M 2839

DFC — see MC BREED

DIAMOND, Joel — '81

Born on 2/20/43 in Passaic, New Jersey. Producer/songwriter/record industry executive. Producer for **Engelbert Humperdinck** for 11 years. Worked in music publishing for Mercury, CBS, and his own company, Silver Blue Records/Productions. Appeared in the movie *Crossover Dreams*.

DEBUT	PEAK	WKS	Gold	A-side (Chart Hit)....................B-side	$	Sym	Label & Number
2/21/81	82	3		**Theme From Raging Bull (Cavalleria Rusticana)** ....*Joey's Theme* [I] from the movie *Raging Bull* starring Robert DeNiro; theme is "Intermezzo" from the opera *Cavalleria Rusticana* by Pietro Mascagni	$6		Motown 1504

DIAMOND, Leo — POP '53

Born on 6/29/15 in Brooklyn, New York. Died on 9/15/66 (age 51). Arranger/lead harmonica player for The Borrah Minevitch Harmonica Rascals, 1930-46. Hit #14 on the pop charts in 1953 with "Off Shore."

DEBUT	PEAK	WKS	Gold	A-side (Chart Hit)....................B-side	$	Sym	Label & Number
2/19/55	30	1		**Melody Of Love** ....S:30 *The Phantom Gaucho* [I] music written in 1903; lyrics added in 1954 by **Tom Glazer**	$12		RCA Victor 5973

DIAMOND, Neil ★24★

AC/LP **'70**

Born on 1/24/41 in Brooklyn, New York. Pop-rock singer/guitarist/prolific composer. Worked as songplugger/staff writer in New York City; also wrote under pseudonym Mark Lewis. His real name is Neil Diamond, however he considered changing his name to Noah Kaminsky early in his career. First recorded for Duel in 1960. Wrote for **The Monkees** TV show. Wrote score for the movie *Jonathan Livingston Seagull.* Starred in and composed the music for *The Jazz Singer* in 1980. America's top male vocalist from 1966-86.

1)You Don't Bring Me Flowers 2)Cracklin' Rosie 3)Song Sung Blue 4)Love On The Rocks 5)Sweet Caroline

DEBUT	PEAK	WKS	Gold	A-side (Chart Hit)	B-side	$	Sym	Label & Number
5/21/66	55	10		1 **Solitary Man**	*Do It*	$15		Bang 519
8/20/66	6	12		2 **Cherry, Cherry**	*I'll Come Running*	$12		Bang 528
				also see "live" version at #31 below				
11/12/66	16	8		3 **I Got The Feelin' (Oh No No)**	*The Boat I Row*	$12		Bang 536
1/28/67	18	8		4 **You Got To Me**	*Someday Baby*	$12		Bang 540
4/8/67	10	11		5 **Girl, You'll Be A Woman Soon**	*You'll Forget*	$12		Bang 542
7/15/67	13	11		6 **I Thank The Lord For The Night Time**	*The Long Way Home*	$12		Bang 547
				some pressings show title as "Thank The Lord For The Night Time"				
10/14/67	22	8		7 **Kentucky Woman**	*The Time Is Now*	$12		Bang 551
1/6/68	51	6		8 **New Orleans**	*Hanky Panky*	$12		Bang 554
4/13/68	62	3		9 **Red Red Wine**	*Red Rubber Ball*	$12		Bang 556
				all Bang recordings produced by Jeff Barry and **Ellie Greenwich**				
5/11/68	58	6		10 **Brooklyn Roads**	*Holiday Inn Blues*	$8		Uni 55065
7/13/68	66	6		11 **Two-Bit Manchild**	*Broad Old Woman (6 A.M. Insanity)*	$8	■	Uni 55075
10/5/68	68	5		12 **Sunday Sun**	*Honey-Drippin' Times*	$8		Uni 55084
2/22/69	22	13		13 **Brother Love's Travelling Salvation Show**	*A Modern Day Version Of Love*	$8		Uni 55109
6/28/69	4	14	▲	14 **Sweet Caroline (Good Times Never Seemed So Good)**	*Dig In*	$7		Uni 55136
11/1/69	6	14	▲	15 **Holly Holy**	*Hurtin' You Don't Come Easy*	$7		Uni 55175
2/7/70	24	14		16 **Shilo**	*La Bamba*	$10		Bang 575
				first issued on Bang 561 in 1968				
2/21/70	53	6		17 **Until It's Time For You To Go**	*And The Singer Sings His Song*	$7		Uni 55204
				written by **Buffy Sainte-Marie** in 1965				
5/2/70	30	7		18 **Soolaimón (African Trilogy II)**	*And The Grass Won't Pay No Mind*	$7	■	Uni 55224
7/11/70	21	14		19 **Solitary Man**	*The Time Is Now* [R]	$10		Bang 578
				same version as #1 above				
8/22/70	❶[1]	15	▲	20 **Cracklin' Rosie**	*Lordy*	$7		Uni 55250
11/7/70	20	11		21 **He Ain't Heavy...He's My Brother**	*Free Life*	$7		Uni 55264
				famous slogan of Father Flanagan's Boys Town in Nebraska				
11/7/70	36	10		22 **Do It**	*Hanky Panky*	$10		Bang 580
				also see the B-side of #1 above; #1-3, 8, 19 & 22: from the 1966 album *The Feel Of Neil Diamond*				
3/27/71	4	10		23 **I Am...I Said /**				
6/5/71	65	5		24 **Done Too Soon**		$7		Uni 55278
				#18, 20, 21 & 24: from the album *Tap Root Manuscript*				
6/26/71	51	8		25 **I'm A Believer**	*Crooked Street*	$10		Bang 586
11/13/71	14	9		26 **Stones /**				
1/8/72	1	1		27 **Crunchy Granola Suite**		$7		Uni 55310
5/6/72	❶[1]	13	●	28 **Song Sung Blue** AC[7]	*Gitchy Goomy*	$7		Uni 55326
8/12/72	11	11		29 **Play Me**	*Porcupine Pie*	$7		Uni 55346
11/11/72	17	12		30 **Walk On Water**	*High Rolling Man*	$7		Uni 55352
3/17/73	31	10		31 **"Cherry Cherry" from Hot August Night**	*Morningside* [L-R]	$6		MCA 40017
				studio version on #2 above				
8/11/73	91	3		32 **The Long Way Home**	*Monday, Monday*	$8		Bang 703
				also see the B-side of #6 above; #1, 2, 4-6, 9, 16, 19, 25 & 32: from the 1967 album *Just For You*				
8/25/73	56	6		33 **The Last Thing On My Mind**	*Canta Libre*	$6		MCA 40092
				#23, 26, 27 & 33: from the album *Stones*; "Bubbled Under" (#117) for **The Vejtables** in 1965				
10/27/73	34	9		34 **Be**	*Flight Of The Gull*	$5	■	Columbia 45942
3/16/74	75	4		35 **Skybird**	*Lonely Looking Sky*	$5		Columbia 45998
				above 2 from the movie *Jonathan Livingston Seagull*				
10/5/74	5	15		36 **Longfellow Serenade** AC[1]	*Rosemary's Wine*	$5		Columbia 10043
2/1/75	34	7		37 **I've Been This Way Before** AC[1]	*Reggae Strut*	$5		Columbia 10084
				most of above hits (Uni, MCA, Columbia) produced by Tom Catalano				
6/19/76	11	12		38 **If You Know What I Mean** AC[2]	*Street Life*	$5		Columbia 10366
9/11/76	43	8		39 **Don't Think....Feel**	*Home Is A Wounded Heart*	$5		Columbia 10405
				above 2 produced by Robbie Robertson (of **The Band**)				
12/3/77+	16	14		40 **Desirée** AC[1]	*Once In A While*	$5		Columbia 10657
10/28/78	❶[2]	17	▲	41 **You Don't Bring Me Flowers**	*(instrumental)*	$4		Columbia 10840
				BARBRA & NEIL				
				Diamond's solo version is on his 1977 album *I'm Glad You're Here With Me Tonight*				
1/27/79	20	11		42 **Forever In Blue Jeans**	*Remember Me*	$4		Columbia 10897
5/19/79	55	7		43 **Say Maybe**	*Diamond Girls*	$4		Columbia 10945
12/22/79+	17	16		44 **September Morn'**	*I'm A Believer*	$4		Columbia 11175
4/5/80	67	6		45 **The Good Lord Loves You**	*Jazz Time*	$4		Columbia 11232
11/1/80+	2[3]	20		46 **Love On The Rocks**	*Acapulco*	$4	■	Capitol 4939
1/31/81	6	16		47 **Hello Again**	*Amazed And Confused*	$4	■	Capitol 4960
4/25/81	8	17		48 **America** AC[3]	*Songs Of Life*	$4	■	Capitol 4994
				above 3 from the movie *The Jazz Singer* starring Diamond				
11/7/81+	11	15		49 **Yesterday's Songs** AC[6]	*Guitar Heaven*	$3	■	Columbia 02604
2/13/82	27	10		50 **On The Way To The Sky**	*Save Me*	$3	■	Columbia 02712

DEBUT	PEAK	WKS	Gold	A-side (Chart Hit)..................B-side	$	Sym	Label & Number
				DIAMOND, Neil — Cont'd			
5/22/82	35	11		51 **Be Mine Tonight**........*Right By You*	$3		Columbia 02928
9/11/82	5	19		52 **Heartlight**........AC⁴ *You Don't Know Me*	$3	■	Columbia 03219
				inspired by the movie *E.T.* starring Henry Thomas			
1/15/83	35	12		53 **I'm Alive**........*Lost Among The Stars*	$3		Columbia 03503
4/23/83	65	8		54 **Front Page Story**........*I'm Guilty*	$3	■	Columbia 03801
8/18/84	62	8		55 **Turn Around**........*Brooklyn On A Saturday Night*	$3	■	Columbia 04541
5/24/86	53	10		56 **Headed For The Future**........*Angel*	$3	■	Columbia 05889
				all of above (except #8, 17, 21, 33 & 45) composed by Diamond			
				DIAMOND REO BUB **'75**			
				Rock group from Pittsburgh, Pennsylvania: Bob McKeag (vocals, guitar), Frank Czuri (keyboards), Norm Nardini (bass) and Robbie Johns (drums).			
1/11/75	44	6		**Ain't That Peculiar**........*(From Here To) Infinity*	$5		Big Tree 16030
				DIAMOND RIO C&W/BUB/LP **'02**			
				Country group formed in Nashville, Tennessee: Marty Roe (vocals), Jimmy Olander (guitar), Gene Johnson (mandolin), Dan Truman (piano), Dana Williams (bass) and Brian Prout (drums).			
2/4/95	72^S	1		1 **Night Is Fallin' In My Heart**........BUB:107 *Down By The Riverside*	$5	▮V	Arista 12764
4/8/95	71^S	5		2 **Bubba Hyde**........BUB:102 *(dance mix)*	$5	▮V	Arista 12787
12/19/98+	36	20		3 **Unbelievable**........A:24		V	album cut
				from the album *Unbelievable* on Arista 18866; "45": Arista 13138; B-side: "You're Gone" (C&W #4)			
1/20/01	29	20		4 **One More Day**........CW² A:21		V	album cut
				from the album *One More Day* on Arista 67999; "45": Arista 69036; B-side: "Stuff" (C&W #36)			
8/10/02	28	20		5 **Beautiful Mess** CW² A:27			album cut
				from the album *Completely* on Arista 67046			
	★240★			**DIAMONDS, The** C&W **'57**			
				White doo-wop group from Toronto, Ontario, Canada: Dave Somerville (lead; born on 4/8/34), Ted Kowalski (tenor; born on 6/17/35), Phil Levitt (baritone; born on 9/6/34) and Bill Reed (bass; born on 11/24/34). Recorded for Coral in 1955. Debuted on Mercury in January 1956. Michael Douglas replaced Levitt in early 1958. Reed and Kowalski replaced in 1959 by Evan Fisher and John Felten (killed in a plane crash in 1982). Frequent personnel changes. Dave teamed with **Four Preps**' co-founder, Bruce Belland, as a duo from 1962-69. Bob Duncan (lead) joined in 1978 and re-formed the group, after Felten's death, with new lineup. Group hit the Country charts in 1987. The Diamonds and The Crew-Cuts (both from Toronto and both on Mercury) were two of the first white vocal groups to "cover" R&B hits.			
				1)Little Darlin' 2)The Stroll 3)Silhouettes			
2/18/56	12	19		1 **Why Do Fools Fall In Love**........A:12 / T:16 / S:18 / J:19 *You Baby You*	$20		Mercury 70790
4/21/56	14	17		2 **The Church Bells May Ring**........S:14 / J:15 / A:17 / T:20 *Little Girl Of Mine*	$20		Mercury 70835
6/23/56	30	14		3 **Love, Love, Love**........T:30 *Ev'ry Night About This Time*	$20		Mercury 70889
9/22/56	34	8		4 **Soft Summer Breeze** / T:34			
9/8/56	35	9		5 **Ka-Ding-Dong**........T:35	$20		Mercury 70934
3/16/57	2⁸	26	●	6 **Little Darlin'** S:2 / J:2 / T:2 / A:2 *Faithful And True*	$30		Mercury 71060
6/24/57	13	2		7 **Words Of Love**........A:13 / T:76 *Don't Say Goodbye*	$20		Mercury 71128
				written by **Buddy Holly**			
8/26/57	16	11		8 **Zip Zip**........A:16 / T:45 *Oh, How I Wish*	$20		Mercury 71165
				David Carroll (orch., all of above)			
11/4/57	10	11		9 **Silhouettes**........A:10 / T:60 *Daddy Cool*	$20		Mercury 71197
12/30/57+	4	21	●	10 **The Stroll**........A:4 / T:5 / S:7 *Land Of Beauty*	$25	⊙	Mercury 71242
				sleeve insert features a photo of each group member and instructions on how to do "The Stroll"			
4/14/58	37	12		11 **High Sign**........S:37 / T:38 *Don't Let Me Down*	$20	■	Mercury 71291
7/28/58	16	8		12 **Kathy-O** / A:16 / S:41 / H:45			
				title song from the movie starring Patty McCormack			
8/4/58	73	4		13 **Happy Years**........H:73 / S:flip	$20		Mercury 71330
10/27/58	29	12		14 **Walking Along**........*Eternal Lovers*	$20		Mercury 71366
				original 1957 R&B version is by the Solitaires on Old Town 1034 ($125)			
1/26/59	18	14		15 **She Say (Oom Dooby Doom)**........*From The Bottom Of My Heart*	$20		Mercury 71404
7/3/61	22	9		16 **One Summer Night**........*It's A Doggone Shame*	$20		Mercury 71831
				DIBANGO, Manu R&B/BUB/LP **'73**			
				Born on 2/10/34 in Cameroon, Africa. Jazz-R&B saxophonist/pianist.			
6/23/73	35	9		**Soul Makossa**........*Lily* [I]	$5		Atlantic 2971
				DICK AND DEEDEE BUB **'61**			
				Pop vocal duo formed in Santa Monica, California: Dick St. John Gosting and Deedee Sperling.			
7/31/61	2²	15		1 **The Mountain's High** *I Want Someone*	$15		Liberty 55350
				first released on Lama 7778 in 1961 ($30)			
3/17/62	22	14		2 **Tell Me**........*Will You Always Love Me*	$15		Liberty 55412
				first released on Lama 7783 in 1961 ($30)			
3/16/63	17	11		3 **Young And In Love**........*Say To Me*	$12		Warner 5342
10/5/63	93	1		4 **Where Did The Good Times Go**........*Guess Our Love Must Show*	$10		Warner 5383
11/23/63+	27	9		5 **Turn Around**........*Don't Leave Me*	$10		Warner 5396
				folk tune introduced in 1959 by **Harry Belafonte**			
2/22/64	89	3		6 **All My Trials**........*Don't Think Twice, It's All Right*	$10		Warner 5411
				traditional West Indian lullaby			
11/21/64+	13	13		7 **Thou Shalt Not Steal**........*Just 'Round The River Bend*	$10	□	Warner 5482
				a special picture sleeve was issued promoting Triumph motorcycles			
3/13/65	87	3		8 **Be My Baby**........*Room 404*	$10		Warner 5608
				all of above produced by **Don Ralke** and The Wilder Bros.			
				DICKENS, "Little" Jimmy C&W/BUB **'65**			
				Born on 12/19/20 in Bolt, West Virginia. Country singer/guitarist.			
10/16/65	15	10		**May The Bird Of Paradise Fly Up Your Nose**........CW² *My Eyes Are Jealous* [N]	$8		Columbia 43388

DEBUT	PEAK	WKS	Gold	A-side (Chart Hit)...B-side	$	Sym	Label & Number
				DICKY DOO AND THE DON'TS '58			
				White vocal group founded by **Gerry Granahan** in Brooklyn, New York. Group named after the nickname of Dick Clark's son, Dicky Doo. Group featured Harvey Davis (bass), Ray Gangi (guitar), Al Ways (sax) and Dave Alldred (ex-drummer of **Buddy Knox** and **Jimmy Bowen**'s Rhythm Orchids).			
2/10/58	28	14		1 **Click-Clack** T:28 / S:29 *Did You Cry* **DICKEY DOO And The Don'ts**	$25		Swan 4001
5/5/58	40	8		2 **Nee Nee Na Na Na Na Nu Nu /** T:40 / S:42 [I-N]			
6/9/58	46	8		3 **Flip Top Box**...S:46 / T:61 [N]	$25		Swan 4006
9/29/58	44	9		4 **Leave Me Alone (Let Me Cry)**...H:44 *Wild Party* melody based on the "Battle Hymn Of The Republic"	$20		Swan 4014
2/2/59	61	6		5 **Teardrops Will Fall**...*Come With Us* based on the collegiate tune "Our Boys Will Shine Tonight"	$20		Swan 4025
				DIDDLEY, Bo R&B/BUB/LP '59			
				Born Otha Ellas Bates McDaniel on 12/30/28 in McComb, Mississippi; raised in Chicago, Illinois. Unique and influential R&B-rock & roll guitarist/vocalist. Adopted as an infant by his mother's cousin, Mrs. Gussie McDaniel. Began recording in 1955 with the Chess/Checker label. Name "bo diddley" is a one-stringed African guitar. His first record was a two-sided #1 hit on the R&B charts in 1955: "Bo Diddley"/"I'm A Man." Inducted into the Rock and Roll Hall of Fame in 1987. Won Grammy's Lifetime Achievement Award in 1998.			
7/6/59	62	5		1 **Crackin Up**...*The Great Grandfather*	$30		Checker 924
9/21/59	20	12		2 **Say Man** *The Clock Strikes Twelve* [N] Diddley trades insults with maracas player Jerome Green; picture sleeve is a paper sleeve produced from Diddley's Checker 5125 EP	$30	■	Checker 931
2/29/60	75	6		3 **Road Runner**...*My Story*	$25		Checker 942
8/18/62	48	10		4 **You Can't Judge A Book By The Cover**...*I Can Tell* written by Rock & Roll Hall Of Fame inductee Willie Dixon; some pressings show "A Book By The Cover You Can't Judge"	$25		Checker 1019
1/21/67	88	7		5 **Ooh Baby**...*Back To School*	$15		Checker 1158
				DIDO BUB/LP '01			
				Born Dido Armstrong on 12/25/71 in London, England. Female Adult Alternative pop-rock singer/songwriter.			
11/4/00	51	15		1 **Stan**...A:48 **EMINEM (Featuring Dido)** samples "Thankyou" by Dido; from the **Eminem** album *The Marshall Mathers LP* on Aftermath 490629			album cut
1/13/01	3	39		2 **Thankyou**...AC[4] A:3 / S:36 *(3 versions)*	$8	★*	Arista 13996
				DIESEL BUB/LP '81			
				Rock group from Holland: Rob Vunderink (vocals, guitar), Mark Boon (guitar), Frank Papendrecht (bass) and Pim Koopman (drums).			
9/12/81	25	18		**Sausalito Summernight**...*Bite Back* first released on Regency 96001 in 1981	$5		Regency 7339
				DIFFIE, Joe C&W/BUB/LP '99			
				Born on 12/28/58 in Tulsa, Oklahoma; raised in Duncan, Oklahoma. Country singer/songwriter/guitarist. Charted 35 Country hits, 1990-02.			
12/25/93+	69	11		1 **John Deere Green**...S:36 *Somewhere Under The Rainbow*	$4	▮V	Epic 77235
9/10/94	84	9		2 **Third Rock From The Sun**...CW[2] S:40 *(dance mix)* "45" B-side: "From Here On Out"	$4	▮V	Epic 77577
12/24/94+	60	5		3 **Pickup Man**...CW[4] S:31 *From Here On Out*	$4	▮V	Epic 77715
4/8/95	84	7		4 **So Help Me Girl**...S:46 *The Cows Came Home*	$4	▮V	Epic 77808
5/15/99	38	20		5 **A Night To Remember** A:32 / S:46 *Don't Our Love Look Natural* "45" B-side: "Texas Size Heartache" (C&W #4)	$4	★V	Epic 79118
1/1/00	90	6		6 **The Quittin' Kind**...*Don't Our Love Look Natural*	$4	★	Epic 79268
8/12/00	57	14		7 **It's Always Somethin'**...A:48 from the album *A Night To Remember* on Epic 69815			album cut
1/19/02	66	11		8 **In Another World**...A:63 from the album *In Another World* on Monument 85373			album cut
				DIGABLE PLANETS R&B/BUB/LP '93			
				Rap outfit from Washington DC: Ishmael "Butterfly" Butler, Mary Ann "Ladybug" Vierra and Craig "Doodle Bug" Irving.			
1/16/93	15	20	●	1 **Rebirth Of Slick (Cool Like Dat)**...S:5 / A:26 *(album version)*	$3	▮V	Pendulum 64674
5/22/93	68[S]	2		2 **Where I'm From**...BUB:106 *(original mix)* samples "Ain't Nothin' Wrong" by **K.C. And The Sunshine Band**; "45" issued for above 2 on Pendulum 64674	$3	▮V	Pendulum 64648
10/15/94	80	7		3 **9th Wonder (blackitolism)**...S:48 *(Accpeltier version)* samples "Supperrappin' Theme" by **Grandmaster Flash And The Furious Five**	$3	▮	Pendulum 58159
				DIGITAL ALLIES '01			
				White male electronica trio featuring vocals by Richard Luzzi.			
8/18/01	43[S]	6		**Without You**...*(7 versions)* **DIGITAL ALLIES Featuring Richard Luzzi**	$10	★*	Xtreme 831
				DIGITAL UNDERGROUND R&B/LP '90			
				Hip-hop group from Oakland, California: Gregory Jacobs (aka "Humpty-Hump" and "Shock-G"), Ron Brooks (aka "Money B"), Earl Cook (aka "Schmoovy-Schmoov"), James Dight (aka "Chopmaster J") and DJ Fuze. Tupac (**2Pac**) Shakur was a member in 1991. Group appeared in the movie *Nothing But Trouble*.			
3/17/90	11	23	▲	1 **The Humpty Dance**...S:5 / A:25 *(Humpstrumental mix)* [N] "45": Tommy Boy/Collectables 944; B-side: (same version)	$3	▮V	Tommy Boy 7944
2/23/91	61[A]	11		2 **Same Song**... samples "Theme From The Black Hole" by **Parliament**; from the movie soundtrack album *Nothing But Trouble* on Warner 26491			album cut
11/16/91+	40	20	●	3 **Kiss You Back**...S:23 / A:50 *(3 mixes)* samples **Funkadelic**'s "(not just) Knee Deep"	$5	▮*	Tommy Boy 993
				DILLARDS, The BUB/LP '71			
				Country-rock group from Salem, Missouri: Rodney Dillard (vocals, guitar), Billy Ray Latham (banjo), Dean Webb (mandolin), Mitch Jayne (bass) and Paul York (drums).			
7/31/71	92	2		**It's About Time**...*One A.M.* (#111)	$7		Anthem 101

DEBUT	PEAK	WKS	Gold	A-side (Chart Hit)	B-side	$	Sym	Label & Number

DILLMAN BAND, The — LP '81

Country-rock group: Steve Solmonson (vocals), Pat Frederick and Steve Seamans (guitars), Dik Shopteau (bass) and Dan Flaherty (drums).

DEBUT	PEAK	WKS	Gold	A-side (Chart Hit)	B-side	$	Sym	Label & Number
5/9/81	45	9		**Lovin' The Night Away**	*C.O.D.*	$5		RCA 12206

DINNING, Mark — '60

Born on 8/17/33 in Drury, Oklahoma. Died of a heart attack on 3/22/86 (age 52). Pop singer. Brother of the Dinning Sisters vocal trio. First recorded for MGM in 1957.

DEBUT	PEAK	WKS	Gold	A-side (Chart Hit)	B-side	$	Sym	Label & Number
12/21/59+	❶[2]	18	●	1 **Teen Angel** written by Mark's sister, Jeannie	*Bye Now Baby*	$20		MGM 12845
4/18/60	68	6		2 **A Star Is Born (A Love Has Died)**	*You Win Again*	$20	■	MGM 12888
8/22/60	84	6		3 **The Lovin' Touch**	*Come Back To Me (My Love)*	$20	■	MGM 12929
2/20/61	81	6		4 **Top Forty, News, Weather And Sports**	*Suddenly (There's Only You)* [N]	$20		MGM 12980

DINO — BUB/LP '89

Born Dino Esposito on 7/20/63 in Encino, California; raised in Hawaii and Connecticut. Pop-dance singer.

DEBUT	PEAK	WKS	Gold	A-side (Chart Hit)	B-side	$	Sym	Label & Number
7/16/88	50	12		1 **Summergirls**	*(instrumental)*	$4		4th & B'way 7468
2/4/89	42	14		2 **24/7**	A:39 / S:40 *Nightime Lovekind*	$4	■	4th & B'way 7471
5/13/89	7	25	●	3 **I Like It**	S:6 / A:7 *(instrumental)*	$3		4th & B'way 7483
9/9/89	23	15		4 **Sunshine**	A:23 / S:25 *(instrumental)*	$3	■	4th & B'way 7489
12/16/89+	61	9		5 **Never 2 Much Of U** all of above from the album *24/7*	*In The City*	$3	▮V	4th & B'way 7495
8/11/90	6	18		6 **Romeo** all of above written and produced by Dino	A:7 / S:8 *(dub version)*	$3	▮V	Island 878012
11/10/90+	31	14		7 **Gentle** Delona Tanner (female vocal)	S:28 / A:38 *(album version)*	$3	▮	Island 878472
7/10/93	27	20		8 **Ooh Child**	A:16 / S:62 *(3 album snippets)*	$3	▮	EastWest 98398

DINO, Kenny — '61

Born on 9/12/39 in Hicksville, Long Island, New York. Pop singer.

DEBUT	PEAK	WKS	Gold	A-side (Chart Hit)	B-side	$	Sym	Label & Number
11/6/61	24	11		**Your Ma Said You Cried In Your Sleep Last Night**	*Dream A Girl*	$20		Musicor 1013

DINO, Paul — '61

Born Paul Dino Bertuccini, Jr. on 3/2/35 in Philadelphia, Pennsylvania. Married for a time to Justine Correlli, a regular on TV's *American Bandstand.*

DEBUT	PEAK	WKS	Gold	A-side (Chart Hit)	B-side	$	Sym	Label & Number
1/23/61	38	12		**Ginnie Bell**	*Bye-Bye*	$20		Promo 2180

DINO, DESI & BILLY — BUB/LP '65

Dino (**Dean Martin**'s son, Dean Martin, Jr.), Desi (Lucille Ball and Desi Arnaz's son, Desiderio Arnaz IV) & Billy (a schoolmate from Beverly Hills, William Hinsche). Dino (formerly married to actress Olivia Hussey and to Olympic skater Dorothy Hamill) was killed on 3/21/87 (age 35) when his Air National Guard jet crashed.

DEBUT	PEAK	WKS	Gold	A-side (Chart Hit)	B-side	$	Sym	Label & Number
6/26/65	17	12		1 **I'm A Fool**	*So Many Ways*	$12	■	Reprise 0367
9/18/65	25	9		2 **Not The Lovin' Kind**	*Chimes Of Freedom*	$12	■	Reprise 0401
12/11/65+	60	7		3 **Please Don't Fight It**	*The Rebel Kind*	$12	■	Reprise 0426
3/5/66	94	2		4 **Superman** all of above produced by **Lee Hazlewood**	*I Can't Get Her Off My Mind*	$12		Reprise 0444
6/17/67	99	1		5 **Two In The Afternoon**	*Good Luck, Best Wishes To You*	$12		Reprise 0579
8/10/68	92	4		6 **Tell Someone You Love Them**	*General Outline*	$12		Reprise 0698

DINOSAUR JR. — ROK/LP '94

Rock group formed in 1984 in Amherst, Massachusetts: Joseph Mascis (vocals, guitar), Mike Johnson (guitar) and Murph (drums). Murph left in late 1993; replaced by George Berz. Mascis acted in the movie *Gas Food Lodging.*

DEBUT	PEAK	WKS	Gold	A-side (Chart Hit)	B-side	$	Sym	Label & Number
10/1/94	62[A]	6		**Feel The Pain** from the album *Without A Sound* on Sire/Reprise 45719				album cut

DION (Dion and The Belmonts) ★77★ — AC/BUB/LP '62

Born Dion DiMucci on 7/18/39 in the Bronx, New York. First recorded as Dion & The Timberlanes on Mohawk in 1957. Formed doo-wop group, Dion & The Belmonts, in the Bronx in 1958. Consisted of Dion (lead), Angelo D'Aleo (first tenor), Fred Milano (second tenor) and Carlo Mastrangelo (bass). Named for Belmont Avenue in the Bronx. D'Aleo was in the Navy in 1959 and missed some recording and picture sessions. Dion went solo in 1960 as did **The Belmonts**. Brief reunion with The Belmonts in 1967 and 1972, periodically since then. Began recording Christian music in 1981. Inducted into the Rock and Roll Hall of Fame in 1989.

1)Runaround Sue 2)Ruby Baby 3)The Wanderer 4)Where Or When 5)Lovers Who Wander

DION and THE BELMONTS:

DEBUT	PEAK	WKS	Gold	A-side (Chart Hit)	B-side	$	Sym	Label & Number
5/19/58	22	13		1 **I Wonder Why**	T:22 / S:24 *Teen Angel*	$30		Laurie 3013
8/25/58	19	16		2 **No One Knows**	S:19 / H:24 *I Can't Go On (Rosalie)*	$30		Laurie 3015
12/22/58+	40	12		3 **Don't Pity Me**	*Just You*	$30		Laurie 3021
4/20/59	5	15		4 **A Teenager In Love**	*I've Cried Before*	$25		Laurie 3027
9/14/59	48	8		5 **Every Little Thing I Do /**				
10/19/59	73	3		6 **A Lover's Prayer**		$25	■	Laurie 3035
12/28/59+	3	16		7 **Where Or When** #1 hit for Hal Kemp & His Orchestra in 1937 (from the Rodgers & Hart musical *Babes In Arms* starring Mitzi Green)	*That's My Desire*	$25	■	Laurie 3044
4/25/60	30	9		8 **When You Wish Upon A Star** from the Disney animated movie *Pinocchio*; #1 hit for Glenn Miller in 1940	*Wonderful Girl*	$25	■	Laurie 3052
7/18/60	38	7		9 **In The Still Of The Night** the Cole Porter classic; #3 hit for **Tommy Dorsey** in 1937	*A Funny Feeling*	$25	■	Laurie 3059

DION:

DEBUT	PEAK	WKS	Gold	A-side (Chart Hit)	B-side	$	Sym	Label & Number
10/17/60	12	16		10 **Lonely Teenager /**				
12/5/60	96	1		11 **Little Miss Blue**		$20	■	Laurie 3070
2/6/61	42	6		12 **Havin' Fun**	*North East End Of The Corner*	$20	■	Laurie 3081
5/1/61	82	3		13 **Kissin Game**	*Heaven Help Me*	$20	■	Laurie 3090

DEBUT	PEAK	WKS	Gold		A-side (Chart Hit)...B-side	$	Sym	Label & Number
					DION — Cont'd			
9/25/61	❶[2]	14	●	14	**Runaround Sue** ...*Runaway Girl*	$20	■	Laurie 3110
12/4/61+	2[1]	18		15	**The Wanderer** /			
12/4/61	36	8		16	**The Majestic** ...	$20	■	Laurie 3115
4/21/62	3	12		17	**Lovers Who Wander** /			
4/21/62	42	7		18	**(I was) Born To Cry** ...	$20	■	Laurie 3123
7/7/62	8	11		19	**Little Diane** ...*Lost For Sure*	$20	■	Laurie 3134
11/10/62	10	11		20	**Love Came To Me** ...*Little Girl*	$20		Laurie 3145
1/19/63	2[3]	13		21	**Ruby Baby** ...*He'll Only Hurt You*	$15	■	Columbia 42662
					#10 R&B hit for **The Drifters** in 1956; 2 different promotional sleeves were also issued			
3/2/63	21	11		22	**Sandy** ...*Faith*	$20		Laurie 3153
4/20/63	21	8		23	**This Little Girl** ...*The Loneliest Man In The World*	$15	⊙	Columbia 42776
6/15/63	48	6		24	**Come Go With Me** ...*King Without A Queen*	$20		Laurie 3171
7/6/63	31	7		25	**Be Careful Of Stones That You Throw** ..*I Can't Believe (That You Don't Love Me Anymore)*	$15		Columbia 42810
					recorded in 1952 by Hank Williams (as Luke The Drifter) on MGM 11309			
9/14/63	6	11		26	**Donna The Prima Donna** ...*You're Mine*	$15	□	Columbia 42852
11/16/63	6	11		27	**Drip Drop** ...*No One's Waiting For Me*	$15		Columbia 42917
					Del Satins (backing vocals, #14-27 - except #25)			
8/22/64	71	4		28	**Johnny B. Goode** ...*Chicago Blues*	$15		Columbia 43096
					DION DI MUCI (above 3)			
10/26/68	4	14	●	29	**Abraham, Martin And John** ...*Daddy Rollin' (In Your Arms)*	$12		Laurie 3464
					a tribute to Abraham Lincoln, **Martin Luther King**, and John and Robert Kennedy			
1/25/69	63	4		30	**Purple Haze** ...*The Dolphins*	$12		Laurie 3478
4/26/69	91	2		31	**From Both Sides Now** ...*Sun Fun Song*	$12		Laurie 3495
6/27/70	75	3		32	**Your Own Back Yard** ...*Sit Down, Old Friend*	$10		Warner 7401
8/5/89	75	5		33	**And The Night Stood Still** ...*Tower Of Love*	$4	■	Arista 9797
					Dave Edmunds, **Patty Smyth** and Mark Lennon (backing vocals)			

DION, Celine ★88★ AC/BUB/LP '96

Born on 3/30/68 in Charlemagne, Quebec, Canada. Adult Contemporary singer. Youngest of 14 children. Began performing at age five. Wrote first song at age 12. Married her longtime manager, Rene Angelil, on 12/17/94.

1)Because You Loved Me 2)I'm Your Angel 3)The Power Of Love 4)My Heart Will Go On (Love Theme From 'Titanic') 5)It's All Coming Back To Me Now

DEBUT	PEAK	WKS	Gold		A-side (Chart Hit)...B-side	$	Sym	Label & Number
12/8/90+	4	24		1	**Where Does My Heart Beat Now** ...A:3 / S:9 *I Feel Too Much*	$3	▮V	Epic 73536
4/6/91	35	12		2	**(If There Was) Any Other Way** ...A:28 *I'm Loving Every Moment With You*	$3	▮V	Epic 73665
					"45" issued for above 2 on Epic 73665			
1/18/92	9	20	▲	3	**Beauty And The Beast** ...S:8 / A:17 *The Beast Lets Belle Go* [I]	$3	▮V	Epic 74090
					CELINE DION and PEABO BRYSON			
					title song from the Disney animated movie			
4/25/92	4	22		4	**If You Asked Me To** ...AC[3] A:3 / S:11 *Love You Blind*	$3	▮V	Epic 74277
					"45" B-side: "Where Does My Heart Beat Now"			
8/1/92	29	20		5	**Nothing Broken But My Heart** ...AC[1] A:35 / S:49 *Unison*	$3	▮V	Epic 74336
11/21/92+	36	17		6	**Love Can Move Mountains** ...A:35 *Cry Just A Little*	$3	▮V	Epic 74337
					above 4 from the album *Celine Dion*			
7/17/93	23	20		7	**When I Fall In Love** ...A:28 / S:31 *If I Were You* (Dion)	$3	▮V	Epic Soundtrax 77021
					CELINE DION CLIVE GRIFFIN			
					from the movie *Sleepless In Seattle* starring Tom Hanks and Meg Ryan; #20 hit for **Doris Day** in 1952			
11/27/93+	❶[4]	33	▲	8	**The Power Of Love** ...AC[4] S:❶[5] / A:2 *No Living Without Loving You*	$3	▮V	550 Music/Epic 77230
4/30/94	23	19		9	**Misled** ...A:22 / S:52 *Real Emotion*	$3	▮V	550 Music/Epic 77344
8/20/94	95	5		10	**Think Twice** ...*L'Amour Existe Encore*	$3	▮V	550 Music/Epic 77545
1/21/95	93	3		11	**Only One Road** ...*The Power Of Love (live)*	$3	▮	550 Music/Epic 77661
					above 5 from the album *The Colour Of My Love*			
3/9/96	❶[6]	33	▲	12	**Because You Loved Me** AC[19] A:❶[14] / S:❶[6] *I Don't Know*	$3	▮V	550 Music/Epic 78237
					theme from the movie *Up Close & Personal* starring Robert Redford			
8/17/96	2[5]	30	▲	13	**It's All Coming Back To Me Now** ...AC[5] A:❶[2] / S:3 *The Power Of The Dream*	$3	▮V	550 Music/Epic 78345
3/29/97	4	20	●	14	**All By Myself** ...AC[3] S:5 / A:7 *Because You Loved Me (live)*	$3	▮V	550 Music/Epic 78529
10/25/97	58[A]	6		15	**Tell Him** ...			album cut
					CELINE DION & BARBRA STREISAND			
2/28/98	❶[2]	20	●	16	**My Heart Will Go On (Love Theme From 'Titanic')** ...AC[10] A:❶[10] / S:❶[2] *Rose* (**James Horner**)	$3	▮	550 Music/Epic 78825
					from the all-time top box office movie *Titanic* starring Leonardo DiCaprio; 1998 Grammy winner: Record of the Year			
5/30/98	11[A]	24		17	**To Love You More** ...AC[8]			album cut
					above 3 from the album *Let's Talk About Love* on 550 Music/Epic 68861			
12/5/98	❶[6]	18	▲	18	**I'm Your Angel** ...AC[12] S:❶[6] / A:22 *(no B-side)*	$4	★V	Jive 42557
					R. KELLY & CELINE DION			
					"45" B-side is the same as the A-side			
11/13/99+	6	28		19	**That's The Way It Is** ...AC[1] A:2 / S:62		V	album cut
					from the album *All The Way...A Decade Of Song* on Epic/550 Music 63760; "45": Epic/550 Music 79309; B-side: (same as A-side)			
3/2/02	22	20	●	20	**A New Day Has Come** ...AC[21] S:16 / A:22	$8	▶V	Epic 79728
					"45": Epic 79740; B-side: "I'm Alive" (BUB #111)			

DIPLOMATS, The BUB '64

R&B vocal group from Washington DC: Ervan L. Waters, William Collier, Samuel Culley and Tom Price.

DEBUT	PEAK	WKS	Gold		A-side (Chart Hit)...B-side	$	Sym	Label & Number
2/1/64	89	3			**Here's A Heart** ...*He's Got You Now*	$20		Arock 1004

DEBUT	PEAK	WKS	Gold	A-side (Chart Hit)..........B-side	$	Sym	Label & Number
				DIPLOMATS R&B/LP **'02**			
				Rap group from Harlem, New York: **Cam'ron** Giles, Jimmy Jones, Ezekiel "Freaky Zeeky" Jiles and LeRon "Juelz Santana" James.			
10/19/02	54[S]	1		**Bout It Bout It... Part III**....*(2 versions) / I'm Ready* (w/**Cam'ron**, Jimmy Jones & **Juelz Santana**) **THE DIPLOMATS Feat. Master P** samples "Bout It Bout It II" by **Master P**	$6	T	Roc-A-Fella 063918
				DIRE STRAITS ROK/BUB/LP **'85**			
				Rock group formed in London, England: Mark Knopfler (vocals, guitar) and his brother David (guitar), with John Illsley (bass) and Pick Withers (drums). David left in mid-1980, replaced by Hal Lindes (left in 1985). Added keyboardist Alan Clark in 1982. Terry Williams replaced Withers in 1983. Guitarist Guy Fletcher added in 1984. Mark and Guy were also members of The Notting Hillbillies in 1990.			
2/10/79	4	15		1 **Sultans Of Swing**..........*Southbound Again*	$4		Warner 8736
7/28/79	45	7		2 **Lady Writer**..........*Where Do You Think You're Going?*	$4	■	Warner 49006
12/20/80+	58	10		3 **Skateaway**..........*Solid Rock* (ROK #56)	$4	■	Warner 49632
1/8/83	75	4		4 **Industrial Disease**..........*Badges, Posters, Stickers, T-Shirts*	$4		Warner 29880
7/13/85	❶[3]	22		5 **Money For Nothing** AR[3] A:❶[3] / S:❶[2] *Love Over Gold (live)* **Sting** (backing vocal, co-writer)	$3	■	Warner 28950
11/2/85+	7	21		6 **Walk Of Life**..........A:6 / S:8 *One World* (ROK #8) first released in 1985 on Warner 29013	$3	■	Warner 28878
3/1/86	19	14		7 **So Far Away**..........A:17 / S:26 *If I Had You*	$3	■	Warner 28789
				DIRKSEN, Senator Everett McKinley LP **'67**			
				Born on 1/4/1896 in Pekin, Illinois. Died on 9/7/69 (age 73). U.S. senator from Illinois, 1950-69. Oldest person (age 71 on 1/7/67) to make the top 40 of the *Hot 100* (not posthumously). Also see **Senator Bobby**.			
12/24/66+	29	6		**Gallant Men**..........*The New Colossus (Statue of Liberty)* [S] John Cacavas (orch.); words written by CBS News Commentator, Charles Osgood	$7	■	Capitol 5805
				DIRT BAND, The — see NITTY GRITTY DIRT BAND			
				DIRTY VEGAS LP **'02**			
				Electronica trio from England: producers Ben Harris, Paul Harris and Steve Smith.			
5/11/02	14	20		**Days Go By**..........A:15 / S:26 *(3 versions)* tune featured in a 2002 Mitsubishi Eclipse TV ad campaign	$6	T	Capitol 77742
				DISCO TEX & HIS SEX-O-LETTES BUB/LP **'75**			
				Disco studio group assembled by producer **Bob Crewe**. Featuring lead voice Sir Monti Rock III (real name: Joseph Montanez).			
11/23/74+	10	15		1 **Get Dancin'**..........*Part II*	$5		Chelsea 3004
4/19/75	23	11		2 **I Wanna Dance Wit' Choo (Doo Dat Dance), Part I**..........*Part II*	$5		Chelsea 3015
8/30/75	80	3		3 **Jam Band**..........*Jam Band Reprise*	$5		Chelsea 3026
7/4/76	60	9		4 **Dancin' Kid**..........*(long version)* **DISCO-TEX & THE SEX-O-LETTES Featuring Sir Monti Rock III** (#1, 2 & 4)	$5		Chelsea 3045
				DISHWALLA ROK/LP **'96**			
				Pop-rock group from Santa Barbara, California: J.R. Richards (vocals), Rodney Browning (guitar), Scot Alexander (bass) and George Pendergast (drums).			
4/6/96	15	48		**Counting Blue Cars**..........MR[1] A:5 / S:41 *The Other Side Of The World*	$4	▮	A&M 1462
				DIS 'N' DAT BUB/R&B **'95**			
				R&B duo of sisters Tishea (Dis) and Tenesia (Dat) Bennett.			
12/10/94	71[S]	4		1 **Party**..........BUB:102 *(5 mixes)* **69 Boyz** (backing vocals); samples "Do You Wanna Go Party" By **KC And The Sunshine Band**	$5	▮*	Epic Street 77400
5/6/95	60	18		2 **Freak Me Baby**..........S:36 *(2 mixes) / (3 album snippets)* featuring **95 South**, **69 Boyz** and K-Nock	$4	▮	Epic Street 77845
				DISTURBED LP **'02**			
				Hard-rock group from Chicago, Illinois: David Draiman (vocals), Dan Donegan (guitar), Steve "Fuzz" Kmak (bass) and Mark Wengren (drums).			
9/28/02	58	20		**Prayer**..........A:56 from the album *Believe* on Reprise 48320			album cut
				DIVINE LP **'98**			
				Female R&B vocal trio from New Jersey: Nikki Bratcher, Kia Thornton and Tonia Tash.			
9/12/98	❶[1]	27	▲	1 **Lately**..........S:❷[2] / A:8 *(instrumental) / My Love / (3 album snippets)*	$4	★	Red Ant 15316
4/3/99	29	9		2 **One More Try**..........S:15 *(2 versions)*	$4	★	Red Ant 15330
				DIVING FOR PEARLS **'89**			
				Pop-rock group from New York: Danny Malone (vocals), Yul Vazquez (guitar), Jack Moran (keyboards), David Weeks (bass) and Peter Clemente (drums).			
12/9/89	84	6		**Gimme Your Good Lovin'**..........*The Girl Can't Stop It*	$4	▮	Epic 69036
				DIVINYLS ROK/LP **'91**			
				Rock group from Australia: Christina Amphlett (vocals), Mark McEntee (guitar), Bjarne Olin (keyboards), Richard Grossman (bass) and J.J. Harris (drums). By 1991, group reduced to a duo of Amphlett and McEntee.			
1/25/86	76	7		1 **Pleasure And Pain**..........*Heart Telegraph*	$4	■	Chrysalis 42916
3/9/91	4	18		2 **I Touch Myself**..........S:2 / A:7 *Follow Through*	$4	▮[V]	Virgin 98873
				DIXIEBELLES, The BUB **'63**			
				Black female trio from Memphis, Tennessee: Shirley Thomas, Mary Hunt and Mildred Pratcher. Backed by pianist **Jerry Smith** (as Cornbread & Jerry).			
9/28/63	9	13		1 **(Down At) Papa Joe's**..........*Rock, Rock, Rock*	$10		Sound Stage 7 2507
1/18/64	15	8		2 **Southtown, U.S.A.**..........*Why Don't You Set Me Free*	$10		Sound Stage 7 2517

DEBUT	PEAK	WKS	Gold	A-side (Chart Hit)...B-side	$	Sym	Label & Number
	★403★			**DIXIE CHICKS** C&W/BUB/LP **'02**			
				Female country trio from Lubbock, Texas: sisters Emily Robison (guitar, banjo; born on 8/16/72) and Martie Maguire (fiddle, mandolin; born on 10/12/69), with Natalie Maines (lead vocals; born on 10/14/74). Several radio stations banned their songs after Maines made a controversial statement about President Bush in March 2003.			
				1)Long Time Gone 2)Landslide 3)Goodbye Earl			
1/31/98	**77**	7		1 **I Can Love You Better**...S:61 *Give It Up Or Let Me Go*	$4	▮	Monument 78746
5/16/98	**36**	16		2 **There's Your Trouble**...CW^2 S:23 *Give It Up Or Let Me Go*	$4	▮^{V}	Monument 78899
9/5/98	**41**	20		3 **Wide Open Spaces**...CW^4 A:33 / S:52 *I Can Love You Better*	$4	★^{V}	Monument 79003
				"45" issued for above 2 on Monument 79047			
1/23/99	**34**	20		4 **You Were Mine**...CW^2 A:20			album cut
5/15/99	**46**	16		5 **Tonight The Heartache's On Me**...A:34		V	album cut
				"45": Monument 79204; B-side: "Give It Up Or Let Me Go"; all of above from the album *Wide Open Spaces* on Monument 68195			
7/24/99	**39**	18		6 **Ready To Run**...A:27			album cut
				from the movie *Runaway Bride* starring Julia Roberts and Richard Gere			
11/27/99+	**27**	20		7 **Cowboy Take Me Away**...CW^3 A:22		V	album cut
3/18/00	**19**	15	●	8 **Goodbye Earl**...S:4 / A:60 *Stand By Your Man*	$4	★^{V}	Monument 79352
				"45" issued for above 2 on Monument 79352			
6/24/00	**65**	10		9 **Cold Day In July**...A:57			album cut
10/7/00	**31**	20		10 **Without You**...CW^1 A:27			album cut
3/17/01	**38**	18		11 **If I Fall You're Going Down With Me**...A:31			album cut
1/19/02	**55**	19		12 **Some Days You Gotta Dance**...A:53			album cut
				above 7 from the album *Fly* on Monument 69678			
6/22/02	**7**	20		13 **Long Time Gone** S:❶^5 / A:28 *Don't Waste Your Heart*	$4	★^{V}	Monument 79790
9/21/02+	**7**	29		14 **Landslide**...S:3 / A:8 *(remix)*	$4	★^{V}	Monument 79857
				"45" issued for above 2 on Columbia 79791			
				DIXIE CUPS, The BUB/LP **'64**			
				Black female "girl group" from New Orleans, Louisiana: Barbara Ann Hawkins, her sister Rosa Lee Hawkins and their cousin Joan Marie Johnson. Discovered and managed by singer/producer **Joe Jones**.			
5/2/64	❶^3	13		1 **Chapel Of Love** RB^3 *Ain't That Nice*	$25		Red Bird 001
7/18/64	**12**	9		2 **People Say**...*Girls Can Tell*	$20		Red Bird 006
10/24/64	**39**	6		3 **You Should Have Seen The Way He Looked At Me**...*No True Love*	$20		Red Bird 012
12/19/64+	**51**	9		4 **Little Bell**...*Another Boy Like Mine*	$20		Red Bird 017
4/3/65	**20**	10		5 **Iko Iko**...*Gee Baby Gee*	$20		Red Bird 024
				recorded by James "Sugar Boy" Crawford in 1953 as "Jock-O-Mo" on Checker 787 ($100)			
				DIXIE DRIFTER, The R&B **'65**			
				Born Enoch Gregory on 12/13/36 in Harlem, New York. Died on 4/29/2000 (age 63). Black male DJ.			
9/4/65	**99**	2		**Soul Heaven**...*Three Chairs Theme* [S]	$10		Roulette 4641
				a spoken tribute to **Dinah Washington**, **Nat King Cole** and **Sam Cooke**			
				DIXIE FLYERS, The — see BENTON, Brook / FRANKLIN, Aretha / LULU / WARWICK, Dee Dee			
				DJ COMPANY **'97**			
				Techno-dance group from Germany: producers Stefan Benz, Paul Strand and Louis Lasky, with January Ordu (female singer), and Michael Fielder and Brian Thomas (dancers).			
6/14/97	**53**	19		**Rhythm Of Love**...A:53 *(rap version)*	$4	▮	Crave 78578
				DJ ENCORE (feat.) ENGELINA LP **'02**			
				White electronica duo from Copenhagen, Denmark: DJ Andreas Hemmeth and pop singer Engelina.			
1/19/02	**51**^{S}	3		1 **I See Right Through To You**...*(3 remixes)*	$5	★	MCA 015120
8/3/02	**53**^{S}	2		2 **Walking In The Sky**...*(4 versions)*	$5	★	MCA 019126
				D.J. E-Z ROCK — see ROB BASE			
				DJ HURRICANE **'00**			
				Born Wendall Fite in Queens, New York. Black rapper/DJ/producer/songwriter. Former DJ with the **Beastie Boys**.			
6/19/99	**57**^{S}	9		1 **Come Get It**...*(instrumental) / For The Thugs* (**Trick Daddy**)	$5	★	TVT 8311
				DJ HURRICANE featuring Flipmode Squad's Rah Digga, Rampage and Lord Have Mercy			
9/9/00	**52**^{S}	8		2 **Connect**...*(2 versions) / The Life* (w/**Kool G Rap**)	$5	★	TVT 6451
				DJ HURRICANE w/Xzibit, Big Gipp & Pharoahe Monch			
				D.J. JAZZY JEFF & THE FRESH PRINCE R&B/LP **'91**			
				Rap duo from Philadelphia, Pennsylvania: D.J. Jeff Townes (born on 1/22/65) and rapper/actor **Will Smith** (born on 9/25/68). Also see **The Simpsons**.			
5/21/88	**12**	19	●	1 **Parents Just Don't Understand**...S:6 / A:19 *(instrumental)*	$3	■	Jive 1099
7/30/88	**15**	16		2 **A Nightmare On My Street**...S:10 / A:22 *(instrumental)*	$3	■	Jive 1124
10/29/88	**57**	12		3 **Girls Ain't Nothing But Trouble**...*Brand New Funk* (R&B #76) [N]	$3	■	Jive 1147
				features the theme from TV's *I Dream Of Jeannie* starring Barbara Eden; original version made the R&B charts in 1986 on Word-Up 001			
11/4/89	**58**	9		4 **I Think I Can Beat Mike Tyson**...S:34 *(instrumental)* [N]	$3	■	Jive 1282
				Tyson: heavyweight boxing champ from 1986-90			
6/15/91	**4**	18	▲	5 **Summertime** RB^1 S:2 / A:10 *(D.J. Jazzy Jeff's mix)*	$3	▮	Jive 1465
				samples **Kool & The Gang**'s "Summer Madness"			
10/12/91	**20**	19	●	6 **Ring My Bell**...S:9 / A:54 *(Hula & K. Fingers radio mix)*	$3	▮	Jive 42024
				JAZZY JEFF & FRESH PRINCE:			
8/7/93	**13**	20	●	7 **Boom! Shake The Room**...S:3 / A:51 *From Da South*	$3	▮	Jive 42108
				samples "Funky Worm" by the **Ohio Players**			
12/4/93	**79**	7		8 **I'm Looking For The One (To Be With Me)**...S:57 *Get Hyped*	$3	▮	Jive 42183
				samples "Tell Me If You Still Care" by **The S.O.S. Band**			
				D.J. JUANITO — see ARTIE THE 1 MAN PARTY			

DEBUT	PEAK	WKS	Gold	A-side (Chart Hit)...B-side	$	Sym	Label & Number
				DJ KOOL R&B/BUB/LP **'97**			
				Born John Bowman in Washington DC. Male rapper.			
2/1/97	30	20	●	1 **Let Me Clear My Throat**..........S:21 *(remix* w/Doug E. Fresh & **Biz Markie**) [L]	$4	▮V	American 17441
				samples "Hollywood Swinging" by **Kool & The Gang** and "The 900 Number" by DJ Mark; "45": Collectables 5218			
5/19/01	97	2		2 **Let's Get Dirty (I Can't Get In Da Club)**..........S:48 *(3 versions)*	$6	T	Def Jam 572917
				REDMAN Feat. DJ Kool			
				DJ MIKO **'94**			
				Born Monier Quartrarro in Milan, Italy. Male DJ.			
6/18/94	58	20		**What's Up**..........A:51 *(extended clap attack)*	$5	▮	ZYX 6691
				dance version of the 1993 hit by **4 Non Blondes**; features British vocalist Louise Gard			
				DJ QUIK R&B/LP **'91**			
				Born David Blake on 1/18/70 in Compton, California. Male rapper. Produced **2nd II None**.			
6/8/91	49S	5		1 **Born And Raised In Compton**..........*(radio version)*	$4	▮	Profile 5323
8/24/91	49	9		2 **Tonite**..........S:42 *(remix)*	$4	▮	Profile 5338
7/25/92	62	11		3 **Jus Lyke Compton**..........S:32 *(radio version)*	$4	▮V	Profile 5372
				"45" B-side: "Tonite"			
4/1/95	81	10		4 **Safe + Sound**..........*Diggin' U Out*	$4	▮	Profile 5432
10/20/01	9S	8		5 **Nothing's Wrong**..........*(3 versions)*	$5	★	TNO/EMG 70021
				WON-G Featuring DJ Quik			
				DJ SAMMY LP **'02**			
				Born on 10/29/69 in Mallorca, Spain. Electronica dance producer.			
6/1/02	8	27		1 **Heaven**..........S:2 / A:12 *(5 versions)*	$8	★*	Robbins 72057
				DJ SAMMY & YANOU featuring DO			
12/28/02+	52S	6		2 **The Boys Of Summer**..........*(4 versions) / Appalachian Fall*	$8	★*	Robbins 72075
				DJ SAMMY featuring Loona			
				DJ SHADOW LP **'02**			
				Born Josh Davis in 1972 in Los Angeles, California; later based in England. Male electronica DJ/producer.			
6/1/02	9S	7		1 **You Can't Go Home Again!**..........*Disavowed / Treach Battle Beat* [I]	$5	★	MCA 582896
11/2/02	10S	6		2 **Six Days**..........*(2 versions) / 100 Metre Dash*	$8	★**	MCA 063874
				DJ SHADOW featuring Mos Def			
				samples "Six Day War" by Colonel Bagshot and "I Cry In The Morning" by Dennis Olivieri			
				DJ TAZ **'97**			
				Born Tino Santron McIntosh in Atlanta, Georgia. Male DJ/rapper.			
4/5/97	51	20		**That's Right**..........S:40 *(2 versions)*	$4	▮	Breakaway/EMI 58641
				DJ TAZ Featuring Raheem The Dream			
				samples "Tonight" by **Ready For The World**			
				DJ TIËSTO **'02**			
				Born Tijs Verwerst on 1/17/69 in Holland. Dance DJ.			
5/11/02	63S	2		**In My Memory**..........*(3 remixes) / Urban Train* (w/Kirsty Hawkshaw)	$7	★*	Nettwerk 36327
				DJ TIËSTO Featuring Nicola Hitchcock From Mandalay			
				D MOB — see DENNIS, Cathy			
	★591★			**DMX** R&B/BUB/LP **'00**			
				Born Earl Simmons on 12/18/70 in Baltimore, Maryland; raised in Yonkers, New York. Male rapper/actor. DMX is short for Dark Man X. Acted in the movies *Belly*, *Romeo Must Die*, *Exit Wounds* and *Cradle 2 The Grave*.			
				1)Party Up (Up In Here) 2)Get At Me Dog 3)What You Want			
12/27/97	75	12		1 **4, 3, 2, 1**..........*(5 versions)*	$6	T	Def Jam 568321
				LL COOL J Featuring Method Man, Redman, DMX, Canibus and Master P			
				samples "Fight For Your Right" by **Beastie Boys**, "Rock The Bells" by **LL Cool J** and "Shut 'Em Down" by **Public Enemy**			
2/21/98	70	6		2 **Nothin' Move But The Money**...S:62 *Usual Suspects* (w/**DMX**, **Ja Rule**, **The Lox** & Khadafi)	$5	▮	Blunt 4939
				MIC GERONIMO featuring DMX & Black Rob			
2/28/98	39	20	●	3 **Get At Me Dog**..........S:28 *Stop Being Greedy*	$4	▮	Def Jam 568862
				DMX (featuring Sheek of The Lox)			
				samples "Everything Good To You" by **B.T. Express**; B-side charted as a 12" single (see #5 below)			
4/4/98	17	20	●	4 **Money, Power & Respect**..........S:10 / A:65 *(instrumental)*	$4	▮	Bad Boy 79156
				THE LOX [Feat. DMX & Lil' Kim]			
				samples "New Beginning" by Dexter Wansel			
8/15/98	79	6		5 **Stop Being Greedy**..........*React* (**Onyx**) / *Full Cooperation* (Def Squad)	$6	T	Def Jam 568989
				12" single titled as "Survival Of The Illest"			
9/26/98	70	10		6 **How's It Goin' Down?**..........*Countdown* (Lil' Jamal & **PMD**) / *Broke Willies* (**Onyx**)	$6	T	Def Jam 566243
				DMX Feat. Faith Evans			
				12" single titled as "Survival Of The Illest, Vol. 2"; also see the B-side of #7 below			
2/20/99	94	4		7 **Ruff Ryders' Anthem**..........*(2 versions) / How's It Goin' Down?* (w/**Faith Evans**)	$7	T	Def Jam 566217
				charted 1 week (#94) on 2/20/99; 2 weeks (#97) on 4/10/99; 1 week (#96) on 5/8/99; a remix version by DJ Clue "Bubbled Under" (#124) on 4/3/99; #3 & 5-7: from the album *It's Dark And Hell Is Hot*			
1/15/00	67	11		8 **What's My Name**..........A:59 *(3 versions)*	$6	T	Def Jam 562540
2/26/00	27	21		9 **Party Up (Up In Here)** A:22 / S:68 *(2 versions) / D-X-L (Hard White)* (w/**The Lox & Drag-On**)	$6	T	Def Jam 562605
7/1/00	49	20		10 **What You Want**..........A:42 *(2 versions) / Fame*	$6	T	Def Jam 562808
				DMX (featuring Sisqó)			
11/11/00	91	7		11 **Do You**..........*(2 versions) / Rush* (w/Lady Luck)	$6	T	Loud/Def Jam 1967
				FUNKMASTER FLEX Featuring DMX			
9/15/01	36S	5		12 **We Right Here**..........BUB:117 *(2 versions) / You Could Be Blind*	$6	T	Def Jam 588746
10/13/01	60	12		13 **Who We Be**..........S:37 / A:59 *(3 versions)*	$6	T	Def Jam 572720
2/2/02	86	7		14 **I Miss You**..........*(2 versions) / Number 11*	$6	T	Def Jam 588874
				DMX featuring Faith Evans			
				contains strains of the hymn "Amazing Grace"			
				D.N.A. — see VEGA, Suzanne			

DEBUT	PEAK	WKS	Gold	A-side (Chart Hit)...B-side	$	Sym	Label & Number

DOBKINS, Carl Jr. '59

Born Carl Edward Dobkins on 1/13/41 in Cincinnati, Ohio. Teen pop singer/songwriter. "Junior" added to last name when Carl started singing at age 16. First recorded for Fraternity in 1958. Left music, mid-1960s.

DEBUT	PEAK	WKS	Gold	A-side (Chart Hit)...B-side	$	Sym	Label & Number
4/13/59	3	24		1 My Heart Is An Open Book ... *My Pledge To You*	$20		Decca 30803
10/12/59	67	3		2 If You Don't Want My Lovin' ... *Love Is Everything* The Seniors (backing vocals); The Orbits (instrumental backing); first released in May of 1958	$20		Decca 30656
12/7/59+	25	17		3 Lucky Devil ... *(There's A Little Song A-Singing) In My Heart*	$20	■	Decca 31020
5/16/60	62	8		4 Exclusively Yours ... *One Little Girl*	$15	■	Decca 31088

DOC BOX & B. FRESH '90

Male rap duo from Jacksonville, Florida. Discovered by producer **Joyce "Fenderella" Irby** (of **Klymaxx**).

DEBUT	PEAK	WKS	Gold	A-side (Chart Hit)...B-side	$	Sym	Label & Number
7/21/90	51	15		Slow Love ... *(after hours edit)*	$4	▮V	Motown 2028

DR. ALBAN '93

Born Alban Nwapa on 8/26/57 in Nigeria; later based in Stockholm, Sweden. Dance DJ.

DEBUT	PEAK	WKS	Gold	A-side (Chart Hit)...B-side	$	Sym	Label & Number
4/24/93	88	11		It's My Life ... A:72 *(ragga mix)*	$5	▮	Logic/Arista 12491

DOCTOR AND THE MEDICS LP '86

Glam-rock group from London, England: Clive "Doctor" Jackson (lead vocals), brothers Wendi and Collette Anadin (backing vocals), Steve Maguire (guitar), Richard Searle (bass) and Vom (drums).

DEBUT	PEAK	WKS	Gold	A-side (Chart Hit)...B-side	$	Sym	Label & Number
8/2/86	69	11		Spirit In The Sky ... *Laughing At The Pieces*	$5	■	I.R.S. 52880

DR. BUZZARD'S ORIGINAL SAVANNAH BAND R&B/LP '76

Big-band swing-disco band formed in Brooklyn, New York, by brothers Stony Browder (guitar) and Thomas "August Darnell" Browder (bass). Featuring **Cory Daye** (see #3 below) (vocals), Andy Hernandez (vibraphone) and Mickey Sevilla (drums). Darnell and Hernandez left in 1980 to form **Kid Creole & The Coconuts** (see **Barry Manilow**'s "Hey Mambo").

DEBUT	PEAK	WKS	Gold	A-side (Chart Hit)...B-side	$	Sym	Label & Number
9/25/76	80	3		1 I'll Play The Fool ... *Sunshower*	$4		RCA 10762
11/6/76+	27	20		2 Whispering/Cherchez La Femme/Se Si Bon ... *Sunshower* "Whispering" was a #1 hit for Paul Whiteman in 1920; "Se Si Bon" was a #8 hit for Eartha Kitt in 1953 as "C'est Si Bon"	$4		RCA 10827
10/27/79	76	3		3 Pow Wow ... *Green Light* **CORY DAYE**	$4		New York Int'l. 11748

DR. DRE R&B/BUB/LP '93

★380★

Born Andre Young on 2/18/65 in Compton, California. Rapper/producer. Co-founder of N.W.A. and **World Class Wreckin' Cru**. Produced several artists. Founded Death Row Records in 1992. Half-brother of **Warren G.**

1)Nuthin' But A "G" Thang 2)Dre Day 3)Keep Their Heads Ringin'

DEBUT	PEAK	WKS	Gold	A-side (Chart Hit)...B-side	$	Sym	Label & Number
6/6/92	57^S	3		1 Deep Cover ... *(instrumental)* **DR. DRE Introducing Snoop Doggy Dogg** title song from the movie starring Jeff Goldblum	$6	▮	Solar/Epic 74547
1/30/93	2^1	27	▲	2 Nuthin' But A "G" Thang RB^2 S:❶^1 / A:10 *(instrumental)* "G": Gangsta; samples **Leon Haywood**'s "I Want'a Do Something Freaky To You"	$3	▮	Death Row 53819
5/15/93	8	20	●	3 Dre Day ... S:4 / A:17 *(instrumental)* **DR. DRE (featuring Snoop Doggy Dogg)** (above 2)	$3	▮	Death Row 53827
9/25/93	34	18		4 Let Me Ride ... S:26 / A:44 *(extended club mix)* **George Clinton** (special guest); Val Young (female vocal); samples **Parliament**'s "Mothership Connection (Star Child)"	$3	▮	Death Row 53839
3/18/95	10	20	●	5 Keep Their Heads Ringin' ... S:6 / A:31 *Take A Hit* (**Mack 10**) from the movie *Friday* starring **Ice Cube**	$3	▮	Priority 53188
6/15/96	6	24		6 California Love ... S:3 / A:19 *How Do U Want It* (**2 PAC w/KC & JoJo** - #1) **2 PAC (featuring Dr. Dre and Roger Troutman)** samples "So Ruff So Tuff" by **Roger** and "Woman To Woman" by **Joe Cocker**	$3	▮	Death Row 854652
10/12/96	❶^4	31	▲	7 No Diggity ... RB^4 S:❶^6 / A:9 *Billie Jean* **BLACKstreet (Featuring Dr. Dre)** **Queen Pen** (female rap); samples "Grandma's Hands" by **Bill Withers**	$3	▮	Interscope 97007
11/27/99	93	5		8 Still D.R.E. ... S:73 *(3 versions)* **DR. DRE Featuring Snoop Dogg**	$6	T	Aftermath 497192
1/22/00	25	20		9 Forgot About Dre ... A:20 **DR. DRE Featuring Eminem** from the album *2001* on Aftermath 90486			album cut
5/27/00	23	20		10 The Next Episode ... A:16 / S:62 *(3 versions)* **DR. DRE Featuring Snoop Dogg** **Kurupt** (backing vocal)	$6	T	Aftermath 497333
3/9/02	98	3		11 Knoc ... S:39 *(4 versions)* **KNOC-TURN'AL w/ Dr. Dre and Missy "Misdemeanor" Elliott**	$6	T	LA Confidential 67290

DOCTOR DRE & ED LOVER R&B/BUB '94

Rap duo from Queens, New York: Andre "Doctor Dre" Brown and James "Ed Lover" Roberts. Hosted TV show *Yo! MTV Raps.* Starred in the movie *Who's The Man.*

DEBUT	PEAK	WKS	Gold	A-side (Chart Hit)...B-side	$	Sym	Label & Number
11/19/94	85	7		Back Up Off Me! ... *It's Like That Ya'll* contains elements from "Ain't No Stoppin' Us Now" by **McFadden & Whitehead**	$4	▮	Relativity 1236

DR. FEELGOOD AND THE INTERNS '62

Group is actually bluesman Willie "Piano Red" Perryman. Born on 10/19/11 in Hampton, Georgia. Died of cancer on 7/25/85 (age 73).

DEBUT	PEAK	WKS	Gold	A-side (Chart Hit)...B-side	$	Sym	Label & Number
4/21/62	66	9		1 Doctor Feel-Good ... *Mister Moonlight* B-side recorded by **The Beatles** on their *Beatles '65* album	$15		Okeh 7144
8/4/62	84	3		2 Right String But The Wrong Yo-Yo ... *What's Up, Doc* #10 R&B hit for Piano Red in 1951 on RCA Victor 50-0106 ($50)	$15		Okeh 7156

DEBUT	PEAK	WKS	Gold	A-side (Chart Hit)..........B-side	$	Sym	Label & Number

DR. HOOK ★209★ C&W/LP '79

Pop-rock group formed in Union City, New Jersey: **Ray Sawyer** (see #9 below) (vocals; born on 2/1/37; dubbed "Dr. Hook" because of eye patch), Dennis Locorriere (vocals, guitar; born on 6/13/49), George Cummings (born on 7/28/38) and Rik Elswit (guitars; born on 7/6/45), William Francis (keyboards; born on 1/16/42), Jance Garfat (bass; born on 3/3/44) and Jay David (drums; born on 8/8/42). John Wolters replaced David in 1973. Bob Henke replaced Cummings in 1975. Group appeared in and performed the music for the movie *Who Is Harry Kellerman And Why Is He Saying Those Terrible Things About Me?*. Wolters died of cancer on 6/16/97 (age 52).

1)Sexy Eyes 2)Sylvia's Mother 3)Sharing The Night Together 4)When You're In Love With A Beautiful Woman 5)Only Sixteen

DR. HOOK AND THE MEDICINE SHOW:

DEBUT	PEAK	WKS	Gold	A-side (Chart Hit)..........B-side	$	Sym	Label & Number
4/1/72	5	15	●	1 **Sylvia's Mother**..........*Makin' It Natural*	$6		Columbia 45562
9/9/72	71	6		2 **Carry Me, Carrie**..........*I Call That True Love*	$6	■	Columbia 45667
12/2/72+	6	20	●	3 **The Cover Of "Rolling Stone"**..........*Queen Of The Silver Dollar* [N]	$6		Columbia 45732
				group was actually featured on the cover of *Rolling Stone* magazine on 3/29/73			
7/7/73	83	4		4 **Roland The Roadie And Gertrude The Groupie**..........*Put A Little Bit On Me* [N]	$6		Columbia 45878
9/29/73	68	7		5 **Life Ain't Easy**..........*The Wonderful Soup Stone*	$6		Columbia 45925
				all of above written by Shel Silverstein (also #13 below)			

DR. HOOK:

DEBUT	PEAK	WKS	Gold	A-side (Chart Hit)..........B-side	$	Sym	Label & Number
8/23/75	95	5		6 **The Millionaire**..........*Cooky And Lila* [N]	$5	□	Capitol 4104
				promo sleeve and record "A Free Stimu From Dr. Hook" featured samples from their album *Bankrupt*			
1/3/76	6	22	●	7 **Only Sixteen**..........*Let Me Be Your Lover*	$5		Capitol 4171
6/19/76	11	24		8 **A Little Bit More**..........*A Couple More Years* (C&W #51)	$5		Capitol 4280
11/6/76	81	3		9 (One More Year Of) **Daddy's Little Girl**..........*I Need The High*	$5		Capitol 4344
				RAY SAWYER			
11/27/76	55	11		10 **If Not You**..........*Bad Eye Bill*	$5		Capitol 4364
6/25/77	46	10		11 **Walk Right In**..........*Sexy Energy*	$5		Capitol 4423
9/16/78+	6	22	●	12 **Sharing The Night Together**..........*You Make My Pants Want To Get Up And Dance*	$4		Capitol 4621
2/3/79	54	7		13 **All The Time In The World**..........*Dooley Jones*	$4		Capitol 4677
4/14/79	6	25	●	14 **When You're In Love With A Beautiful Woman**..........*Knowing She's There*	$4		Capitol 4705
10/13/79+	12	19		15 **Better Love Next Time**..........*Mountain Mary*	$4		Capitol 4785
2/16/80	5	21	●	16 **Sexy Eyes** *Help Me Mama*	$4		Capitol 4831
7/5/80	51	9		17 **Years From Now**..........*I Don't Feel Much Like Smilin'*	$4	■	Capitol 4885
11/1/80	34	14		18 **Girls Can Get It**..........*Doin' It*	$4		Casablanca 2314
4/11/81	69	4		19 **That Didn't Hurt Too Bad**..........*99 And Me*	$4		Casablanca 2325
2/27/82	25	12		20 **Baby Makes Her Blue Jeans Talk**..........*The Turn On*	$4	■	Casablanca 2347
6/12/82	60	10		21 **Loveline**..........*Pity The Fool*	$4		Casablanca 2351
				co-written by **Eddie Rabbitt**; all of above produced by Ron Haffkine			

DR. JOHN BUB/R&B/LP '73

Born Malcolm Rebennack on 11/20/42 in New Orleans, Louisiana. Swamp-rock singer/pianist.

DEBUT	PEAK	WKS	Gold	A-side (Chart Hit)..........B-side	$	Sym	Label & Number
4/15/72	71	5		1 **Iko Iko**..........*Huey Smith Medley*	$8		Atco 6882
4/14/73	9	20		2 **Right Place Wrong Time**..........*I Been Hoodood*	$7		Atco 6914
9/15/73	42	9		3 **Such A Night**..........*Cold Cold Cold*	$7		Atco 6937
5/11/74	92	4		4 **(Everybody Wanna Get Rich) Rite Away**..........*Mos' Scocious*	$7		Atco 6957

DR. WEST'S MEDICINE SHOW and JUNK BAND '66

'Jug band' from California: **Norman Greenbaum** (vocals, guitar), Bonnie Wallach (vocals), George Ducay (harmonica), Jack Carrington (bass) and Evan Engber (drums).

DEBUT	PEAK	WKS	Gold	A-side (Chart Hit)..........B-side	$	Sym	Label & Number
11/26/66	52	7		**The Eggplant That Ate Chicago**..........*You Can't Fight City Hall Blues* [N]	$15		Go Go 100

DODD, Deryl C&W '99

Born on 4/12/64 in Comanche, Texas; raised in Dallas, Texas. Country singer/songwriter/guitarist.

DEBUT	PEAK	WKS	Gold	A-side (Chart Hit)..........B-side	$	Sym	Label & Number
1/2/99	88	7		**A Bitter End**..........*Time On My Hands*	$4	★	Columbia 79013

DODDS, Nella '64

Born in Philadelphia, Pennsylvania. R&B singer.

DEBUT	PEAK	WKS	Gold	A-side (Chart Hit)..........B-side	$	Sym	Label & Number
11/14/64	74	3		1 **Come See About Me**..........*You Don't Love Me Anymore*	$12		Wand 167
1/9/65	96	2		2 **Finders Keepers, Losers Weepers**..........*A Girl's Life*	$12		Wand 171

DOGGETT, Bill R&B '56

Born on 2/16/16 in Philadelphia, Pennsylvania. Died on 11/13/96 (age 80). Leading jazz-R&B organist/pianist. Formed own band in 1938, recorded with the Jimmy Mundy Band in 1939. With the Ink Spots, Illinois Jacquet, Lucky Millinder, Louis Jordan, **Ella Fitzgerald**, **Louis Armstrong**, Coleman Hawkins and many others. Formed own combo in 1952.

DEBUT	PEAK	WKS	Gold	A-side (Chart Hit)..........B-side	$	Sym	Label & Number
8/18/56	2^3	29	●	1 **Honky Tonk (Parts 1 & 2)** RB^{13} J:2 / S:2 / T:2 / A:6 [I]	$25		King 4950
				Clifford Scott (saxophone; died in May 1993, age 65); also see #9 below			
11/24/56+	26	12		2 **Slow Walk**..........T:26 *Hand In Hand* [I]	$20		King 5000
2/16/57	67	7		3 **Ram-Bunk-Shush**..........T:67 *Blue Largo* [I]	$20		King 5020
11/4/57	35	14		4 **Soft**..........S:35 / T:51 *Hot Ginger* [I]	$20		King 5080
				#3 R&B hit for Tiny Bradshaw in 1953			
8/4/58	82	2		5 **Blip Blop**..........H:82 *Tanya* [I]	$15		King 5138
11/10/58	92	1		6 **Hold It**..........*Birdie* [I]	$15		King 5149
1/4/60	95	2		7 **Smokie-Part 2**..........*Evening Dreams* [I]	$15		King 5310
12/26/60	66	3		8 (Let's Do) **The Hully Gully Twist**..........*Jackrabbit* [I]	$12		Warner 5181
1/30/61	57	10		9 **Honky Tonk (Part 2)**..........*Floyd's Guitar Blues* [I-R]	$12		King 5444
				same version as Part 2 of #1 above			

DEBUT	PEAK	WKS	Gold	A-side (Chart Hit)...B-side	$	Sym	Label & Number
				DOGG POUND, Tha R&B/LP **'96**			
				Rap duo from Los Angeles, California: Delmar "Dat Nigga Daz" Arnaud and Ricardo "Kurupt The Kingpin" Brown. Arnaud is a cousin of **Nate Dogg** and **Snoop Dogg**.			
1/6/96	45	16		1 **Let's Play House**...S:18 *(instrumental)*	$3	▮	Death Row 53230
				THA DOGG POUND Featuring Michel'le			
10/5/96	51	16		2 **Music Makes Me High**...S:36 *(album version)*	$3	▮	Universal 56022
				LOST BOYZ (featuring Tha Dogg Pound)			
				samples "Bounce, Rock, Skate, Roll" by **Vaughan Mason & Crew**			
12/14/96+	38	20		3 **Nothin' But The Cavi Hit**...S:22 *Is There A Heaven 4 A Gangsta?* (**Master P**)	$3	▮	Priority 53263
				MACK 10 & THA DOGG POUND			
				from the rap documentary movie *Rhyme & Reason*			
				DOGGYS ANGELS LP **'00**			
				Female rap trio assembled by **Snoop Dogg**: Big Chan, Coniyac and Kola.			
11/18/00	18[S]	16		**Baby If You're Ready**...*(3 versions)*	$5	★	TVT 2132
				Snoop Dogg Presents DOGGYS ANGELS (Featuring Toi)			
				DOG'S EYE VIEW LP **'96**			
				Rock group from Manhattan, New York: Peter Stuart (vocals, guitar), Oren Bloedow (guitar), John Abbey (bass) and Alan Bezozi (drums).			
3/9/96	14[A]	32		1 **Everything Falls Apart**...			album cut
				from the album *Happy Nowhere* on Columbia 66882			
9/28/96	66	14		2 **Everything Falls Apart** / [L]			
				'stripped down' version of #1 above			
9/28/96		14		3 **Small Wonders**...	$4	▮	Columbia 78415
				DOKKEN ROK/BUB/LP **'85**			
				Hard-rock group from Los Angeles, California: Don Dokken (vocals), George Lynch (guitar), Juan Croucier (bass) and Mick Brown (drums). Jeff Pilson replaced Croucier in late 1983. Disbanded in 1988. Lynch and Brown formed Lynch Mob in 1990. Dokken, Lynch, Pilson and Brown reunited as Dokken in early 1995.			
5/4/85	64	11		1 **Alone Again**...*Tooth And Nail*	$4		Elektra 69650
2/22/86	77	7		2 **In My Dreams**...*Til The Livin' End*	$4		Elektra 69563
12/19/87+	72	8		3 **Burning Like A Flame**...*Lost Behind The Wall*	$4	■	Elektra 69435
				DOLBY, Thomas ROK/LP **'83**			
				Born Thomas Morgan Dolby Robertson on 10/14/58 in Cairo, Egypt (British parents); raised in London, England. New-wave singer/songwriter/keyboardist. Married actress Kathleen Beller (played "Kirby Colby" on TV's *Dynasty*) in 1988.			
2/19/83	5	22		1 **She Blinded Me With Science**...*Flying North*	$4		Capitol 5204
				features brief spoken-word interludes by British scientist/TV personality Magnus Pyke (died on 10/19/92, age 83); first released on Harvest 5204 in 1982			
6/18/83	67	5		2 **Europa And The Pirate Twins**...*Radio Silence*	$4	■	Capitol 5238
2/25/84	62	7		3 **Hyperactive**...*Get Out Of My Mix* (Dolby's Cube)	$4	■	Capitol 5321
				DOLCE, Joe LP **'81**			
				Born in 1947 in Painesville, Ohio. Novelty singer/songwriter.			
5/2/81	53	14		**Shaddap You Face**...*Ain't In No Hurry* [N]	$4		MCA 51053
				portrays the Italian character Giuseppi in this novelty recording			
				DOLENZ, Micky **'67**			
				Born on 3/8/45 in Tarzana, California. Singer/drummer of **The Monkees**. Son of actor George Dolenz. Father of actress Amy Dolenz. Under the name Mickey Braddock, played "Corky" in the TV series *Circus Boy* from 1956-58.			
3/4/67	75	6		**Don't Do It**...*Plastic Symphony III* [I]	$20	■	Challenge 59353
				DOLLAR **'80**			
				Rock duo from England: David Van Day and Theresa Bazzar.			
12/22/79+	74	6		**Shooting Star**...*Star Control*	$5		Carrere 7208
				DOLPHINS, The **'65**			
				Pop vocal trio: Carl Edmonson (lead), Paul Singleton and Marvin Lockhard. Edmonson was married to Linda Parrish of **2 Of Clubs**.			
12/19/64+	69	7		**Hey-Da-Da-Dow**...*I Don't Want To Go On Without You*	$15		Fraternity 937
				with The Driving Wind Orch. (Carl Edmonson, Tom Dooley, Panny Sarakatsannis and Gene Lawson)			
				DOMINGO, Plácido LP **'82**			
				Born on 1/21/41 in Madrid, Spain. One of the world's leading operatic tenors. Emigrated to Mexico in 1950. Debuted at the New York Metropolitan Opera in 1968.			
1/16/82	59	7		**Perhaps Love**...*Annie's Song* (Domingo)	$4		Columbia 02679
				PLACIDO DOMINGO AND JOHN DENVER			
				DOMINO R&B/BUB/LP **'94**			
				Born Shawn Ivy in 1972 in St. Louis, Missouri; raised in Long Beach, California. Male rapper.			
11/27/93+	7	20	●	1 **Getto Jam** S:3 / A:27 *(radio edit)*	$3	▮	OutBurst 77298
4/9/94	27	19		2 **Sweet Potatoe Pie**...S:18 / A:40 *(radio version)*	$3	▮	OutBurst 77350
5/27/95	56[S]	5		3 **Tales From The Hood**...BUB:103 *I'm Talkin' To Myself* (NME & Grench The Mean 1)	$4	▮	MCA Soundtracks 55038
				Chill (rap); title song from the movie starring Corbin Bernsen			
3/9/96	87	6		4 **Physical Funk**...S:58 *Do You Qualify*	$4	▮	OutBurst 577794
3/3/01	66[S]	4		5 **Like That**...*(radio edit)*	$5	★	Getto Jam 1041
				DOMINO Featuring Diamonique			

DEBUT	PEAK	WKS	Gold		A-side (Chart Hit)..........B-side	$	Sym	Label & Number

DOMINO, Fats ★23★ R&B/BUB/MEM/C&W/LP '57

Born Antoine Domino on 2/26/28 in New Orleans, Louisiana. Classic New Orleans R&B piano-playing vocalist; heavily influenced by Fats Waller and Albert Ammons. Joined the Dave Bartholomew band, mid-1940s. Signed to Imperial record label in 1949. His first recording "The Fat Man" reportedly was a million seller. Fats had a dozen Top 10 R&B hits (1950-55) prior to his first pop hit. Heard on many sessions cut by other R&B artists, including **Lloyd Price** and **Joe Turner**. In the movies *Shake, Rattle And Rock!*, *Jamboree!*, *The Big Beat* and *The Girl Can't Help It*. Teamed with co-writer Dave Bartholomew on majority of his hits. Inducted into the Rock and Roll Hall of Fame in 1986. Won Grammy's Hall of Fame and Lifetime Achievement Awards in 1987.

1)Blueberry Hill 2)I'm In Love Again 3)I'm Walkin' 4)Blue Monday 5)Whole Lotta Loving

DEBUT	PEAK	WKS	Gold		A-side (Chart Hit)..........B-side	$	Sym	Label & Number
7/16/55	10	13	●	1	**Ain't It A Shame** ....RB^{11} J:10 / S:16 / T:86 *La-La*	$40		Imperial 5348
					title of song better known as "Ain't That A Shame"			
3/3/56	35	9	●	2	**Bo Weevil** ....T:35 *Don't Blame It On Me* (R&B #9)	$25		Imperial 5375
4/28/56	3	23	●	3	**I'm In Love Again** / RB^{9} J:3 / S:4 / T:5 / A:6			
4/28/56	19	20		4	**My Blue Heaven** ....J:19 / T:21 / S:flip	$25		Imperial 5386
					#1 hit for both **Gene Austin** and Paul Whiteman in 1927			
7/28/56	14	16		5	**When My Dreamboat Comes Home** / J:14 / S:21 / T:22			
					#3 hit for Guy Lombardo in 1937			
7/28/56	44	13		6	**So-Long** ....T:44 / S:flip / J:flip	$25		Imperial 5396
10/6/56+	2^{3}	27	●	7	**Blueberry Hill** RB^{11} J:2 / S:3 / T:4 / A:7 *Honey Chile* (R&B #2)	$25		Imperial 5407
					Grammy Hall of Fame Award winner in 1987; #2 hit for Glenn Miller in 1940			
1/5/57	5	18	●	8	**Blue Monday** / RB^{8} J:5 / S:9 / T:9 / A:9			
					recorded on 3/30/55; from the movie *The Girl Can't Help It* starring Jayne Mansfield			
1/12/57	50	10		9	**What's The Reason I'm Not Pleasing You** ....T:50 / S:flip / J:flip	$25		Imperial 5417
					#1 hit for Guy Lombardo in 1935			
3/9/57	4	25	●	10	**I'm Walkin'** ....RB^{6} A:4 / J:5 / S:5 / T:5 *I'm In The Mood For Love*	$25	■	Imperial 5428
5/27/57	6	12	●	11	**It's You I Love** / S:6 / T:22			
5/13/57	8	18		12	**Valley Of Tears** ....S:8 / T:13 / A:13	$25		Imperial 5442
8/12/57	29	10		13	**When I See You** / S:29 / T:36			
					Ann Cole (female vocal)			
8/12/57	64	6		14	**What Will I Tell My Heart** ....T:64 / S:flip	$25		Imperial 5454
					#2 hit for Andy Kirk in 1937; all of above are on red or maroon labels			
10/21/57	23	13	●	15	**Wait And See** / S:23 / T:27			
					from the movie *Jamboree!* starring Kay Medford			
10/21/57	79	4		16	**I Still Love You** ....T:79 / S:flip	$25		Imperial 5467
12/23/57+	26	9		17	**The Big Beat** / S:26 / T:36			
					title song from the movie starring William Reynolds			
12/30/57+	32	11		18	**I Want You To Know** ....S:32 / T:48	$25	■	Imperial 5477
3/17/58	55	7		19	**Yes, My Darling** ....T:55 *Don't You Know I Love You*	$25		Imperial 5492
5/5/58	22	11		20	**Sick And Tired** / S:22 / T:30			
					original version recorded in 1957 by **Chris Kenner** on Imperial 5448 ($30)			
5/5/58	55	7		21	**No, No** ....T:55 / S:flip	$25		Imperial 5515
7/7/58	48	6		22	**Little Mary** ....S:48 / T:49 *Prisoner's Song*	$25		Imperial 5526
9/22/58	92	1		23	**Young School Girl** ....H:92 *It Must Be Love*	$25		Imperial 5537
11/17/58+	6	15	●	24	**Whole Lotta Loving** /			
11/17/58	92	1		25	**Coquette**	$25		Imperial 5553
					#6 hit in 1928 for Guy Lombardo (his theme song)			
2/16/59	50	9		26	**Telling Lies** /			
					recorded on 1/25/57			
2/16/59	50	8		27	**When The Saints Go Marching In**	$20		Imperial 5569
					written in 1896 by Katharine Purvis and James Black			
5/11/59	16	11		28	**I'm Ready** /			
5/11/59	51	8		29	**Margie**	$20		Imperial 5585
					#1 hit for Eddie Cantor in 1921			
8/10/59	8	13		30	**I Want To Walk You Home** / RB^{1}			
7/27/59	17	13		31	**I'm Gonna Be A Wheel Some Day**	$20		Imperial 5606
					original version recorded in 1957 by Bobby Mitchell on Imperial 5475 ($40)			
10/26/59	8	14		32	**Be My Guest** /			
10/26/59	33	9		33	**I've Been Around**	$20	■	Imperial 5629
2/1/60	25	10		34	**Country Boy** /			
2/15/60	98	1		35	**If You Need Me**	$20		Imperial 5645
4/25/60	51	7		36	**Tell Me That You Love Me** /			
5/9/60	84	2		37	**Before I Grow Too Old**	$20		Imperial 5660
6/20/60	6	14		38	**Walking To New Orleans** /			
6/27/60	21	11		39	**Don't Come Knockin'**	$20		Imperial 5675
9/5/60	15	11		40	**Three Nights A Week** /			
9/5/60	58	6		41	**Put Your Arms Around Me Honey**	$20		Imperial 5687
					#1 hit for Arthur Collins & Byron Harlan in 1911			
10/24/60	14	15		42	**My Girl Josephine** /			
10/31/60	38	9		43	**Natural Born Lover**	$20		Imperial 5704
1/23/61	22	9		44	**What A Price** /			
1/23/61	33	8		45	**Ain't That Just Like A Woman**	$20		Imperial 5723
					#17 hit for Louis Jordan in 1946			
3/20/61	32	7		46	**Shu Rah** /			
3/20/61	32	6		47	**Fell In Love On Monday**	$20		Imperial 5734
5/15/61	23	11		48	**It Keeps Rainin'** ....*I Just Cry*	$20		Imperial 5753
7/24/61	15	11		49	**Let The Four Winds Blow** ....*Good Hearted Man*	$20		Imperial 5764

DEBUT	PEAK	WKS	Gold	A-side (Chart Hit)...B-side	$	Sym	Label & Number
				DOMINO, Fats — Cont'd			
10/2/61	**22**	8		50 **What A Party** /			
10/16/61	**83**	1		51 **Rockin' Bicycle**	$20		Imperial 5779
12/11/61+	**30**	7		52 **Jambalaya (On The Bayou)** / #1 Country hit for Hank Williams in 1952			
12/4/61	**67**	2		53 **I Hear You Knocking** recorded on 11/4/58; #2 R&B hit for Smiley Lewis in 1955	$15		Imperial 5796
2/24/62	**22**	10		54 **You Win Again** / #10 Country hit for Hank Williams and #13 pop hit for **Tommy Edwards** in 1952			
3/3/62	**90**	2		55 **Ida Jane** recorded on 5/25/56	$15		Imperial 5816
5/12/62	**59**	7		56 **My Real Name** ... *My Heart Is Bleeding*	$15		Imperial 5833
6/30/62	**77**	5		57 **Nothing New (Same Old Thing)** /			
7/21/62	**98**	1		58 **Dance With Mr. Domino**	$15		Imperial 5863
10/6/62	**79**	5		59 **Did You Ever See A Dream Walking** ... *Stop The Clock (#103)* #1 hit for Eddy Duchin in 1933	$15		Imperial 5875
5/18/63	**59**	7		60 **There Goes (My Heart Again)** ... *Can't Go On Without You (#123)*	$12		ABC-Paramount 10444
9/21/63	**35**	8		61 **Red Sails In The Sunset** ... *Song For Rosemary* [I] #1 hit for both **Bing Crosby** and Guy Lombardo in 1935	$12		ABC-Paramount 10484
1/4/64	**63**	5		62 **Who Cares** ... *Just A Lonely Man (#108)*	$12		ABC-Paramount 10512
2/29/64	**86**	2		63 **Lazy Lady** ... *I Don't Want To Set The World On Fire (#122)*	$12		ABC-Paramount 10531
9/19/64	**99**	2		64 **Sally Was A Good Old Girl** ... *For You* #20 Country hit for Hank Cochran in 1962	$12		ABC-Paramount 10584
10/31/64	**99**	2		65 **Heartbreak Hill** ... *Kansas City*	$12		ABC-Paramount 10596
9/7/68	**100**	2		66 **Lady Madonna** ... *One For The Highway* all of above (except #4, 5, 7, 9, 14, 25, 27, 29, 41, 45, 52-54, 59, 61, 62, 64 & 66) written by Domino (most with co-writer and producer, Dave Bartholomew)	$15		Reprise 0763
				DOMINOES — see WARD, Billy			
				DONALD & The Delighters — see JENKINS, Donald			
				DONALDS, Andru '95 Born in Kingston, Jamaica. Male reggae singer.			
12/10/94+	**38**	19		**Mishale** ... A:49 *Cryin' In The Rain* "45": Metro Blue 18551; B-side: "Tryin' To Tell Ya"	$5	■ V	Metro Blue 58256
				DONALDSON, Bo, And The Heywoods LP '74 Pop group from Cincinnati, Ohio: Bo Donaldson (keyboards), Mike Gibbons (vocals), Scott Baker (guitar), Gary Coveyou (reeds), Rick Joswick (percussion), David Krock (bass) and Nicky Brunetti (drums).			
10/28/72	**64**	8		1 **Special Someone** ... *I Wish I Could* **THE HEYWOODS**	$6		Family 0911
4/20/74	①2	19	●	2 **Billy, Don't Be A Hero** ... *Don't Ever Look Back* also released in 1974 on ABC 12011	$4		ABC 11435
7/27/74	**15**	12		3 **Who Do You Think You Are** ... *Fool's Way Of Lovin'*	$4		ABC 12006
11/16/74	**39**	7		4 **The Heartbreak Kid** ... *Girl Don't Make Me Wait*	$4	■	ABC 12039
7/5/75	**95**	2		5 **Our Last Song Together** ... *Make The Most Of This World* written by **Neil Sedaka** and Howard Greenfield	$4		ABC 12108
				DONALDSON, Lou LP '67 Born on 11/1/26 in Badin, North Carolina. Black jazz alto saxophonist. Leader of small combos in the East.			
11/4/67	**93**	4		**Alligator Bogaloo** ... *Rev. Moses* [I]	$8		Blue Note 1934
				DON & JUAN '62 R&B vocal duo from Brooklyn, New York: Roland "Don" Trone and Claude "Juan" Johnson of **The Genies**. Don died in May 1982 (age 45). Juan died on 10/31/2002 (age 67).			
2/10/62	**7**	13		1 **What's Your Name** ... *Chicken Necks*	$25		Big Top 3079
10/27/62	**91**	3		2 **Magic Wand** ... *What I Really Meant To Say*	$30		Big Top 3121
				DON AND THE GOODTIMES LP '67 Pop-rock group from Portland, Oregon: Don Gallucci (vocals, piano; **The Kingsmen**), Joey Newman (guitar), Jeff Hawks (tambourine), Buzz Overman (bass) and Bobby Holden (drums).			
4/22/67	**56**	7		1 **I Could Be So Good To You** ... *And It's So Good*	$10	■	Epic 10145
7/29/67	**98**	1		2 **Happy And Me** ... *If You Love Her, Cherish Her And Such*	$10	■	Epic 10199
				DON, DICK N' JIMMY MEM/POP '54 "Cocktail music" trio: Don Sutton (piano; baritone), Dick Rock (bass; tenor) and Jimmy Cook (acoustic guitar; lead singer). Hit #14 on the pop charts in 1954 with "That's What I Like."			
12/3/55	**96**	2		**Love Is A Many Splendored Thing** ... T:96 *In Madrid* title song from the movie starring William Holden	$20		Crown 158
				DONEGAN, Lonnie, And His Skiffle Group '56 Born Anthony Donegan on 4/29/31 in Glasgow, Scotland. Died on 11/3/2002 (age 71). England's "King of Skiffle." Member of **Chris Barber's Jazz Band** in 1954.			
3/24/56	**8**	17		1 **Rock Island Line** ... S:8 / T:10 / A:10 / J:13 *John Henry* **THE LONNIE DONEGAN Skiffle Group** originated in the mid-1930s as an Arkansas prison song; long associated with folk legend Leadbelly	$35		London 1650
6/9/56	**58**	2		2 **Lost John** ... T:58 *Stewball*	$25		Mercury 70872
8/7/61	**5**	11		3 **Does Your Chewing Gum Lose It's Flavor (On The Bedpost Over Night)** ... *Aunt Rhody* [N] #9 hit in 1924 for Ernest Hare & Billy Jones as "Does The Spearmint Lose Its Flavor On The Bedpost Overnight?"; originally released on Dot 15911 in February 1959	$20		Dot 15911

DONNER, Ral
BUB **'61**

Born on 2/10/43 in Chicago, Illinois. Died of cancer on 4/6/84 (age 41). Pop vocalist similar in style to **Elvis Presley**. Narrator for the movie *This Is Elvis*.

DEBUT	PEAK	WKS	Gold	A-side (Chart Hit)...B-side	$	Sym	Label & Number
4/17/61	19	11		1 **Girl Of My Best Friend**...*It's Been A Long Long Time* **RAL DONNER & The Starfires** recorded by **Elvis Presley** in 1960 on his *Elvis Is Back!* album	$40		Gone 5102
7/10/61	4	12		2 **You Don't Know What You've Got (Until You Lose It)** *So Close To Heaven*	$30		Gone 5108
9/25/61	39	9		3 **Please Don't Go**...*I Didn't Figure On Him (To Come Back)*	$25		Gone 5114
12/25/61+	18	11		4 **She's Everything (I Wanted You To Be)**...*Because We're Young*	$25		Gone 5121
3/24/62	74	7		5 **(What A Sad Way) To Love Someone**...*Will You Love Me In Heaven*	$25		Gone 5125

DONNIE and THE DREAMERS
'61

Italian-American doo-wop group from the Bronx, New York: Louis "Donnie" Burgio, Andy Catalano, Frank Furstaci and Pete Vecchiarelli.

DEBUT	PEAK	WKS	Gold	A-side (Chart Hit)...B-side	$	Sym	Label & Number
5/1/61	35	10		1 **Count Every Star**...*Dorothy* #4 hit for **Ray Anthony** in 1950	$30		Whale 500
7/17/61	79	3		2 **My Memories Of You**...*Teenage Love*	$40		Whale 505

DONOVAN
★274★ BUB/LP **'66**

Born Donovan Leitch on 5/10/46 in Glasgow, Scotland; raised in London, England. Pop-rock-folk singer/songwriter/guitarist. Appeared in the movies *The Pied Piper Of Hamlin* (1972) and *Brother Sun, Sister Moon* (1973). Father of actress Ione Skye and actor Donovan Leitch, Jr.

1)Sunshine Superman 2)Mellow Yellow 3)Hurdy Gurdy Man

DEBUT	PEAK	WKS	Gold	A-side (Chart Hit)...B-side	$	Sym	Label & Number
5/15/65	23	10		1 **Catch The Wind**...*Why Do You Treat Me Like You Do*	$15		Hickory 1309
8/14/65	61	7		2 **Colours**...*Josie*	$15		Hickory 1324
9/25/65	53	7		3 **Universal Soldier**...*Do You Hear Me Now* written by **Buffy St. Marie**	$15		Hickory 1338
7/30/66	1^1	13		4 **Sunshine Superman** *The Trip* Jimmy Page (guitar)	$10	■	Epic 10045
11/12/66	2^3	12	●	5 **Mellow Yellow**...*Sunny South Kensington* **Paul McCartney** (whispers)	$10	■	Epic 10098
2/11/67	19	7		6 **Epistle To Dippy**...*Preachin' Love*	$8	■	Epic 10127
8/12/67	11	9		7 **There Is A Mountain**...*Sand And Foam*	$8		Epic 10212
11/25/67	23	7		8 **Wear Your Love Like Heaven**...*Oh Gosh*	$8	■	Epic 10253
3/9/68	26	9		9 **Jennifer Juniper**...*Poor Cow*	$8	■	Epic 10300
6/22/68	5	12		10 **Hurdy Gurdy Man**...*Teen Angel*	$8	■	Epic 10345
10/5/68	33	6		11 **Lalena**...*Aye My Love*	$8	■	Epic 10393
4/5/69	7	13		12 **Atlantis** / Atlantis: legendary sunken continent in the Atlantic Ocean			
2/8/69	35	6		13 **To Susan On The West Coast Waiting**...	$8	■	Epic 10434
8/2/69	36	7		14 **Goo Goo Barabajagal (Love Is Hot)**...*Trudi* **DONOVAN (With The Jeff Beck Group)** all of above Epic hits produced by Mickie Most	$8	■	Epic 10510
8/22/70	55	8		15 **Riki Tiki Tavi**...*Roots Of Oak* title of chapter 9 of Rudyard Kipling's 1894 classic *The Jungle Book*	$8	■	Epic 10649
2/27/71	84	3		16 **Celia Of The Seals**...*The Song Of The Wandering Aengus*	$8	■	Epic 10694
4/28/73	66	8		17 **I Like You**...*Earth Sign Man* all of above (except #3) written by Donovan	$6		Epic 10983

DONZ, The
'01

R&B vocal duo from Jersey City, New Jersey: Jeff Oakes and Larry Poteat.

DEBUT	PEAK	WKS	Gold	A-side (Chart Hit)...B-side	$	Sym	Label & Number
4/7/01	27^S	11		1 **Cry No More**...*(no B-Side listed)*	$5	★	Heartless 14780
8/25/01	13^S	10		2 **Give**...*(instrumental)*	$5	★	Heartless 13069

DOOBIE BROTHERS, The
★102★ ROK/BUB/AC/LP **'79**

Pop-rock group formed in San Jose, California: **Patrick Simmons** (see #26 & 27 below) (vocals, guitar; born on 1/23/50), **Tom Johnston** (see #20 below) (lead vocals, guitar, keyboards; born on 8/15/48), Tiran Porter (bass) and John Hartman (drums; born on 3/18/50). Mike Hossack (percussion; born on 9/18/50) added in 1972 (later replaced by Keith Knudsen). Jeff "Skunk" Baxter (slide guitar; born on 12/13/48), formerly with **Steely Dan**, added in 1974. **Michael McDonald** (lead vocals, keyboards), added in 1975. Johnston left in 1978. Baxter and Hartman replaced by Cornelius Bumpus (keyboards, saxophone), John McFee (guitar) and Chet McCracken (drums) in 1979. Johnston wrote majority of hits from 1972-75; McDonald, from 1976-83. Disbanded in 1983. Re-formed in early 1988 with Johnston, Simmons, Hartman, Porter, Hossack, and Bobby LaKind (percussion; died of cancer on 12/24/92). Also see **Carly Simon**'s "It Keeps You Runnin'."

1)What A Fool Believes 2)Black Water 3)Real Love 4)Long Train Runnin' 5)The Doctor

DEBUT	PEAK	WKS	Gold	A-side (Chart Hit)...B-side	$	Sym	Label & Number
9/2/72	11	13		1 **Listen To The Music**...*Toulouse Street*	$6		Warner 7619
12/16/72+	35	11		2 **Jesus Is Just Alright**...*Rockin' Down The Highway*	$6		Warner 7661
4/21/73	8	18		3 **Long Train Runnin'**...*Without You*	$5		Warner 7698
8/18/73	15	13		4 **China Grove**...*Evil Woman*	$5		Warner 7728
4/20/74	32	10		5 **Another Park, Another Sunday**...*Black Water*	$5		Warner 7795
7/27/74	52	8		6 **Eyes Of Silver**...*You Just Can't Stop It* also released in 1974 on Warner 8011	$5		Warner 7832
11/2/74	58	6		7 **Nobody**...*Flying Cloud* originally "Bubbled Under" (#122) on 7/17/71 on Warner 7495	$5		Warner 8041
12/21/74+	1^1	17	●	8 **Black Water**...*Song To See You Through* first released as the B-side of #5 above	$5		Warner 8062
5/3/75	11	12		9 **Take Me In Your Arms (Rock Me)**...*Slat Key Soquel Rag*	$5		Warner 8092
8/2/75	40	7		10 **Sweet Maxine**...*Double Dealin' Four Flusher*	$5		Warner 8126
12/27/75+	60	4		11 **I Cheat The Hangman**...*Music Man*	$5		Warner 8161
4/17/76	13	14		12 **Takin' It To The Streets**...*For Someone Special*	$5		Warner 8196
8/28/76	87	2		13 **Wheels Of Fortune**...*Slat Key Soquel Rag*	$5		Warner 8233

DEBUT	PEAK	WKS	Gold	A-side (Chart Hit)	B-side	$	Sym	Label & Number
				DOOBIE BROTHERS, The — Cont'd				
11/13/76+	37	14		14 **It Keeps You Runnin'**	*Turn It Loose*	$5		Warner 8282
7/30/77	48	7		15 **Little Darling (I Need You)**	*Losin' End*	$5		Warner 8408
10/8/77	66	7		16 **Echoes Of Love**	*There's A Light*	$5		Warner 8471
1/20/79	❶[1]	20	●	17 **What A Fool Believes**	*Don't Stop To Watch The Wheels*	$4	■	Warner 8725
				written by **Kenny Loggins** and **Michael McDonald**; 1979 Grammy winner: Record of the Year				
5/5/79	14	14		18 **Minute By Minute**	*Sweet Feelin'*	$4		Warner 8828
8/11/79	25	12		19 **Dependin' On You**	*How Do The Fools Survive?*	$4		Warner 49029
11/17/79+	34	12		20 **Savannah Nights**	*Outlaw*	$4		Warner 49096
				TOM JOHNSTON				
9/6/80	5	16		21 **Real Love**	*Thank You Love*	$4	■	Warner 49503
11/22/80+	24	14		22 **One Step Closer**	*South Bay Strut*	$4		Warner 49622
1/24/81	76	4		23 **Wynken, Blynken And Nod**	*In Harmony* (Kate Taylor)	$5	■	Sesame Street 49642
				from the children's album *In Harmony* by various artists; lyrics are from a favorite children's poem by Eugene Field				
2/14/81	62	5		24 **Keep This Train A-Rollin'**	*Just In Time*	$4		Warner 49670
2/6/82	65	5		25 **Here To Love You**	*Wynken, Blynken And Nod*	$4		Warner 50001
				#17-19 & 25: from the album *Minute By Minute*				
3/19/83	30	13		26 **So Wrong**	*If You Want A Little Love*	$4		Elektra 69839
6/18/83	75	5		27 **Don't Make Me Do It**	*Sue Sad*	$4		Elektra 69817
				PATRICK SIMMONS (above 2)				
				written by **Huey Lewis**				
7/30/83	79	4		28 **You Belong To Me**	*South City Midnight Lady* [L]	$4	■	Warner 29552
				all of above (except #23, 26 & 27) produced by Ted Templeman				
5/20/89	9	14		29 **The Doctor** AR[3] S:9 / A:11	*Too High A Price*	$3	■	Capitol 44376
8/12/89	45	9		30 **Need A Little Taste Of Love**	*I Can Read Your Mind*	$4	▌	Capitol 44441
				written and recorded by **The Isley Brothers** on their 1974 album *Live It Up*				
				DOOLITTLE BAND, The '80				
				Pop-country studio musicians from Nashville, Tennessee: Hilke Cornelious, Jeff Tweel and Jack 'Stackatrack' Groshmal.				
10/11/80	49	7		**Who Were You Thinkin' Of**	*Arizona Highways*	$5		Columbia 11355
				early pressings credit artist as: DANDY & THE DOOLITTLE BAND				
				DO OR DIE R&B/LP '96				
				Male rap trio from Chicago, Illinois: AK 47, N.A.R.D. and Belo Zero.				
8/3/96	22	20	●	1 **Po Pimp** S:10	*Promise*	$4	▌	Rap-A-Lot 38559
				DO OR DIE featuring Twista				
3/28/98	62	14		2 **Still Po' Pimpin'** S:47	*(3 versions)*	$4	▌[V]	Rap-A-Lot 38636
				DO OR DIE featuring Johnny P and Twista				
				"45": Virgin 19949; B-side: "Promise"				
	★293★			**DOORS, The** BUB/LP '67				
				Rock group formed in Los Angeles, California: Jim Morrison (vocals; born on 12/8/43), Ray Manzarek (keyboards; born on 2/12/35), Robby Krieger (guitar; born on 1/8/46) and John Densmore (drums; born on 12/1/44). Controversial onstage performances by Morrison caused several arrests and cancellations. Group appeared in the 1969 movie *A Feast Of Friends*. Morrison left group on 12/12/70; died of heart failure in Paris on 7/3/71 (age 27). Group disbanded in 1973. 1991 movie based on group's career, *The Doors*, starred Val Kilmer as Morrison. Group inducted into the Rock and Roll Hall of Fame in 1993.				
				1)Light My Fire 2)Hello, I Love You 3)Touch Me				
6/3/67	❶[3]	17	●	1 **Light My Fire**	*The Crystal Ship*	$12		Elektra 45615
				also see re-entry at #6 below				
9/23/67	12	9		2 **People Are Strange**	*Unhappy Girl*	$12	■	Elektra 45621
12/9/67+	25	7		3 **Love Me Two Times**	*Moonlight Drive*	$12		Elektra 45624
3/30/68	39	8		4 **The Unknown Soldier**	*We Could Be So Good Together*	$12	■	Elektra 45628
7/6/68	❶[2]	12	●	5 **Hello, I Love You**	*Love Street*	$12		Elektra 45635
				early pressings show title as "Hello, I Love You, Won't You Tell Me Your Name?" ($20)				
8/31/68	87	6		6 **Light My Fire**	*The Crystal Ship* [R]	$12		Elektra 45615
12/28/68+	3	13	●	7 **Touch Me**	*Wild Child*	$12		Elektra 45646
3/29/69	44	6		8 **Wishful Sinful**	*Who Scared You*	$10		Elektra 45656
6/14/69	57	9		9 **Tell All The People**	*Easy Ride*	$10	■	Elektra 45663
9/6/69	64	6		10 **Runnin' Blue**	*Do It*	$10		Elektra 45675
				above 4 from the album *The Soft Parade*				
4/11/70	50	6		11 **You Make Me Real /**				
4/11/70		6		12 **Roadhouse Blues**		$10		Elektra 45685
				all of above produced by Paul Rothchild				
4/10/71	11	11		13 **Love Her Madly**	*(You Need Meat) Don't Go No Further*	$8		Elektra 45726
7/3/71	14	12		14 **Riders On The Storm**	*Changeling*	$8		Elektra 45738
				debuted on the *Hot 100* the same day Morrison died				
11/27/71	71	7		15 **Tightrope Ride**	*Variety Is The Spice Of Life*	$8		Elektra 45757
9/30/72	85	4		16 **The Mosquito**	*It Slipped My Mind*	$8		Elektra 45807
				above 2 are without Jim Morrison				
12/3/83+	71	7		17 **Gloria**	*Moonlight Drive*	$5		Elektra 69770
				recorded as a "soundcheck" in 1969				
				DORE, Charlie LP '80				
				Born in 1956 in London, England. Female pop singer/songwriter/actress.				
2/23/80	13	17		**Pilot Of The Airwaves**	*Sleepless*	$5		Island 49166
				DORMAN, Harold '60				
				Born on 12/23/26 in Drew, Mississippi; raised in Sledge, Mississippi. Died on 10/8/88 (age 61). Rock and roll singer.				
2/29/60	21	19		**Mountain Of Love**	*To Be With You*	$25		Rita 1003

DEBUT	PEAK	WKS	Gold	A-side (Chart Hit)..............B-side	$	Sym	Label & Number
				DORSEY, Jimmy, Orchestra MEM/POP/LP **'41**			
				Born on 2/29/04 in Shenandoah, Pennsylvania. Died of cancer on 6/12/57 (age 53). Esteemed alto sax and clarinet soloist/bandleader. Recorded with his brother **Tommy Dorsey** in the Dorsey Brothers Orchestra, 1928-35 and 1953-56. Many big band #1 hits, including "Amapola," "Green Eyes," "Tangerine," "Besame Mucho" and "Maria Elena."			
2/23/57	2^4	38	●	1 **So Rare** ....A:2 / T:2 / S:3 / J:6 *Sophisticated Swing*	$20		Fraternity 755
				Jimmy Dorsey (sax); #1 hit for Guy Lombardo in 1937			
8/19/57	21	11		2 **June Night** / A:21 / S:27 / T:39			
				Dick Stabile (sax); Arthur Malvin Singers (vocals, above 2); #2 hit for Ted Lewis in 1924			
8/26/57	77	9		3 **Jay-Dee's Boogie Woogie** ....T:77 / S:flip [I]	$15		Fraternity 777
				based on **Tommy Dorsey**'s "Boogie-Woogie"; above 2 cut 5 days after Jimmy's death, under the direction of Lee Castle (died on 11/16/90)			
				DORSEY, Lee BUB/R&B/LP **'66**			
				Born Irving Lee Dorsey on 12/24/24 in New Orleans, Louisiana. Died of emphysema on 12/1/86 (age 61). R&B singer. Prizefighter in the early 1950s as "Kid Chocolate." Major hits produced by Allen Toussaint and Marshall Sehorn.			
9/11/61	7	13		1 **Ya Ya** RB^1 *Give Me You*	$15		Fury 1053
12/18/61+	27	9		2 **Do-Re-Mi**..........*People Gonna Talk*	$15		Fury 1056
7/3/65	28	9		3 **Ride Your Pony**..........*The Kitty Cat Song*	$10		Amy 927
1/1/66	44	10		4 **Get Out Of My Life, Woman**..........*So Long*	$10		Amy 945
7/23/66	8	12		5 **Working In The Coal Mine**..........*Mexico*	$10		Amy 958
10/22/66	23	9		6 **Holy Cow**..........*Operation Heartache*	$10		Amy 965
				above 4 from the album *The New Lee Dorsey*			
5/13/67	97	1		7 **My Old Car**..........*Why Wait Until Tomorrow*	$10		Amy 987
10/21/67	62	6		8 **Go-Go Girl**..........*I Can Hear You Callin'*	$10		Amy 998
6/28/69	95	3		9 **Everything I Do Gonh Be Funky (From Now On)**..........*There Should Be A Book*	$8		Amy 11,055
				DORSEY, Marc **'99**			
				Born in Washington DC. R&B singer.			
6/5/99	59^S	7		**If You Really Wanna Know**..........*(album version) / (remix w/Jane Blaze)*	$4	★	Jive 42564
				DORSEY, Tommy, Orchestra MEM/POP/LP **'37**			
				Born on 11/19/05 in Mahanoy Plane, Pennsylvania. Choked to death on 11/26/56 (age 51). Esteemed trombonist/band leader. Tommy and brother **Jimmy Dorsey** recorded together as the Dorsey Brothers Orchestra from 1928-35 and 1953-56. They hosted a musical variety TV show, *Stage Show*, 1954-56. Warren Covington fronted band after Tommy's death. Many classic big band #1 hits, including "Alone," "Once In A While," "I'll Never Smile Again," "There Are Such Things" and "In The Blue Of Evening."			
				THE TOMMY DORSEY ORCHESTRA STARRING WARREN COVINGTON:			
9/1/58	7	20	●	1 **Tea For Two Cha Cha**..........H:7 / S:8 *My Baby Just Cares For Me* [I]	$12		Decca 30704
				"Tea For Two" was a #1 hit for Marion Harris in 1925			
12/1/58	70	3		2 **I Want To Be Happy Cha Cha**..........*Satan Takes A Holiday*	$10		Decca 30790
				"I Want To Be Happy" was a #2 hit for Vincent Lopez in 1925; above 2 from the 1924 Broadway musical *No No Nanette* starring Louise Groody			
				DOUBLE AC/LP **'86**			
				Pop duo from Switzerland: Felix Haug (vocals, guitar) and Kurt Maloo (keyboards).			
6/28/86	16	18		**The Captain Of Her Heart**..........S:10 / A:19 *Your Prayer Takes Me Off Part II*	$3	■	A&M 2838
				DOUBLE DEE featuring Dany **'90**			
				Dance duo from Italy: Davide Domenella and Donato "Dany" Losito.			
12/22/90	64^A	3		**Found Love**..........*(5 mixes)*	$7	T	Epic 73548
				DOUBLE EXPOSURE R&B/BUB/LP **'76**			
				Disco group from Philadelphia, Pennsylvania: James Williams, Leonard "Butch" Davis, Charles Whittington and Joseph Harris.			
6/19/76	54	9		**Ten Percent**..........*Pick Me*	$5		Salsoul 2008
				DOUBLE IMAGE **'83**			
				Techno-rock band.			
7/2/83	92	3		**Night Pulse**..........*S.O.S.*	$5		CBS Assoc./Curb 03942
				DOUCETTE BUB/LP **'78**			
				Rock group from Montreal, Quebec, Canada: Jerry Doucette (vocals, guitar), Mark Olson (keyboards), Donnie Cummings (bass) and Duris Maxwell (drums).			
4/8/78	72	8		**Mama Let Him Play**..........*All Over You*	$5		Mushroom 7030
				DOUGLAS, Carl LP **'74**			
				Born in 1942 in Jamaica; raised in California. Disco singer.			
10/12/74	❶^2	18	●	1 **Kung Fu Fighting**..........RB^1 *Gamblin' Man*	$5		20th Century 2140
2/15/75	48	7		2 **Dance The Kung Fu**..........*Changing Times*	$5		20th Century 2168
				DOUGLAS, Carol BUB/LP **'75**			
				Born Carol Strickland on 4/7/48 in Brooklyn, New York. Disco singer. Member of **The Chantels** in the early 1970s. Cousin of **Sam Cooke**.			
11/30/74+	11	16		1 **Doctor's Orders**..........*Baby Don't Let This Good Love Die*	$5		Midland Int'l. 10113
4/12/75	81	2		2 **A Hurricane Is Coming Tonite**..........*I Fell In Love With Love*	$5		Midland Int'l. 10229
				DOUGLAS, Mike MEM/AC/BUB/LP **'66**			
				Born Michael Dowd on 8/11/25 in Chicago, Illinois. Singer with Kay Kyser's band from 1945-50. Hosted own TV talk show from 1961-80.			
12/25/65+	6	9		**The Men In My Little Girl's Life**..........*Stranger On The Shore*	$7		Epic 9876
				DOUGLAS, Ronny **'61**			
				Born Ralph Bruce Douglas. Now deceased. Black singer/songwriter, similar in style to **Sam Cooke**.			
7/31/61	75	3		**Run, Run, Run**..........*You Say*	$20		Everest 19413
				DOVALE, Debbie **'63**			
				Twelve-year-old pop singer from Pittsburgh, Pennsylvania.			
11/16/63	81	4		**Hey Lover**..........*This World We Love In*	$20		Roulette 4521
				first released on Ricky Records 105 in 1963 ($50)			

DEBUT	PEAK	WKS	Gold	A-side (Chart Hit)..........B-side	$	Sym	Label & Number
	★306★			**DOVE, Ronnie** C&W/BUB/LP **'65** Born on 9/7/35 in Herndon, Virginia; raised in Baltimore, Maryland. Adult Contemporary singer. Nearly all of Dove's hits were produced by Phil Kahl (vice president of Diamond Records). First recording on own Dove label in 1958 as Ronnie Dove and the Bell-Tones. *1)One Kiss For Old Simes' Sake 2)Right Or Wrong 3)A Little Bit Of Heaven 4)Cry 5)When Liking Turns To Loving*			
7/18/64	40	11		1 **Say You**..........*Let Me Stay Today* first recorded by Jamie Coe in 1960 on ABC-Paramount 10149 ($20)	$10		Diamond 167
10/24/64	14	10		2 **Right Or Wrong**..........*Baby, Put Your Arms Around Me*	$8		Diamond 173
1/9/65	54	7		3 **Hello Pretty Girl**..........*Keep It A Secret*	$8		Diamond 176
3/13/65	14	11		4 **One Kiss For Old Times' Sake** *No Greater Love*	$8		Diamond 179
6/5/65	16	10		5 **A Little Bit Of Heaven**..........*If I Live To Be A Hundred*	$8		Diamond 184
8/28/65	21	9		6 **I'll Make All Your Dreams Come True**..........*I Had To Lose You (To Find That I Need You)*	$8		Diamond 188
11/6/65	25	8		7 **Kiss Away**..........*Where In The World* above 4 (& #16 below): arranged by **Ray Stevens**	$8		Diamond 191
1/22/66	18	9		8 **When Liking Turns To Loving**..........*I'm Learning How To Smile Again*	$8		Diamond 195
4/16/66	20	8		9 **Let's Start All Over Again**..........*That Empty Feeling*	$8		Diamond 198
6/18/66	27	8		10 **Happy Summer Days**..........*Long After*	$8	■	Diamond 205
9/3/66	22	9		11 **I Really Don't Want To Know**..........*Years Of Tears* #11 hit for **Les Paul & Mary Ford** in 1954	$8		Diamond 208
11/26/66	18	9		12 **Cry**..........*Autumn Rhapsody* #1 hit for **Johnnie Ray** in 1951	$8		Diamond 214
2/18/67	45	6		13 **One More Mountain To Climb**..........*All*	$7		Diamond 217
4/22/67	50	6		14 **My Babe**..........*Put My Mind At Ease* written and produced by **Neil Diamond**	$7		Diamond 221
8/5/67	54	5		15 **I Want To Love You For What You Are**..........*I Thank You For Your Love*	$7		Diamond 227
12/16/67	87	3		16 **Dancin' Out Of My Heart**..........*Back from Baltimore*	$7		Diamond 233
3/16/68	99	3		17 **In Some Time**..........*Livin' For Your Lovin'*	$7		Diamond 240
6/8/68	67	6		18 **Mountain Of Love**..........*Never Gonna Cry (The Way I'll Cry Tonight)*	$7		Diamond 244
9/21/68	96	3		19 **Tomboy**..........*Tell Me Tomorrow* #1-3, 8-13, 15, 18 & 19: arranged by **Bill Justis**	$7		Diamond 249
5/31/69	93	2		20 **I Need You Now**..........*Bluebird*	$7		Diamond 260
				DOVELLS, The BUB/LP **'61** Rock and roll vocal group from Philadelphia, Pennsylvania. Originally called the Brooktones. Consisted of Leonard Borisoff ("**Len Barry**"; born on 6/12/42), Arnie Silver, Jerry Gross ("Jerry Summers"), Mike Freda ("Mike Dennis") and Jim Meeley ("Danny Brooks"). Brooks left in 1962. Barry left in late 1963 and recorded solo. Group continued as a trio. Recorded as **The Magistrates** (see #9 below) for MGM in 1968.			
9/11/61	2^{2}	16		1 **Bristol Stomp** *Letters Of Love* Bristol: town near Philadelphia	$15		Parkway 827
1/27/62	37	10		2 **Do The New Continental**..........*Mope-Itty Mope Stomp*	$15	■	Parkway 833
5/19/62	27	11		3 **Bristol Twistin' Annie**..........*The Actor*	$15	■	Parkway 838
8/11/62	25	12		4 **Hully Gully Baby**..........*Your Last Chance*	$15	■	Parkway 845
11/24/62	82	3		5 **The Jitterbug**..........*Kissin' In The Kitchen*	$15	■	Parkway 855
4/27/63	3	14		6 **You Can't Sit Down**..........*Wildwood Days*	$15	■	Parkway 867
8/31/63	50	7		7 **Betty In Bermudas**..........*Dance The Froog*	$15	■	Parkway 882
11/9/63	94	2		8 **Stop Monkeyin' Aroun'**..........*No No No* #1, 2, 4, 7 & 8: written by Kal Mann and Dave Appell	$15	■	Parkway 889
6/1/68	54	7		9 **Here Come The Judge**..........*Girl* [N] **THE MAGISTRATES** Jean Hillary (female voice); title inspired by a recurrent gag line on TV's *Rowan & Martin's Laugh-In*	$12		MGM 13946
				DOVE SHACK LP **'95** R&B-rap vocal trio from Long Beach, California: Mark Makonie, Anthony Blount and Gary Brown.			
8/12/95	54	20		**Summertime In The LBC**..........S:40 *Bomb Drop* from the rap concert movie *The Show!*	$4	▮	RAL/Def Jam 579382
				DOWELL, Joe BUB **'61** Born on 1/23/40 in Bloomington, Indiana. Pop singer. Signed to Mercury's Smash label by Shelby Singleton, Jr.			
6/26/61	❶[1]	16		1 **Wooden Heart**..........AC[3] *Little Bo Peep* based on the German folk song "Muss I Denn"; originally sung by **Elvis Presley** in the 1960 movie *G.I. Blues*	$12	■	Smash 1708
10/16/61	50	7		2 **The Bridge Of Love**..........*Just Love Me*	$12	■	Smash 1717
6/23/62	23	9		3 **Little Red Rented Rowboat**..........*The One I Left For You* Stephen Scott Singers (backing vocals); Jerry Kennedy (orch.)	$12	■	Smash 1759
				DOWNING, Al C&W/BUB/R&B **'63** Born on 1/9/40 in Centralia, Oklahoma; raised in Lenapah, Oklahoma. Black singer/songwriter/pianist. Session work with **Wanda Jackson**. First recorded for White Rock in 1958. Later pursued a country career (charted 15 Country hits from 1978-89).			
4/27/63	73	2		1 **You Never Miss Your Water (Till The Well Runs Dry)**....*If You Want It (I've Got It)* (#129) **"LITTLE ESTHER" PHILLIPS & "BIG AL" DOWNING**	$15		Lenox 5565
2/22/75	85	4		2 **I'll Be Holding On**..........*Baby Let's Talk It Over* (R&B #68)	$7		Chess 2158
				DOZIER, Lamont — see HOLLAND-DOZIER-HOLLAND			
				DRAFI **'66** Born Drafi Deutscher on 5/9/46 in Berlin, Germany. Male pop singer/producer.			
5/14/66	80	3		**Marble Breaks And Iron Bends**..........*Amanda*	$8		London 10825
				DRAG-ON R&B/BUB/LP **'00** Born Melvin Smalls in 1980 in the Bronx, New York. Male rapper.			
12/4/99+	35^{S}	21		1 **Down Bottom**..........BUB:118 *(remix) / Spit These Bars / C'mon, C'mon* **DRAG-ON Featuring Yung Wun**	$8	★*	Ruff Ryders 497186
9/9/00	72^{S}	7		2 **Let Me Be The One**..........*(4 versions)* **RAM-Z (Featuring Drag-On)** samples "Rockin' Chair" by **Gwen McCrae**	$4	★	TVT 6473

DEBUT	PEAK	WKS	Gold	A-side (Chart Hit)	B-side	$	Sym	Label & Number
				DRAGON '84 Pop-rock group from Auckland, New Zealand: Marc Hunter (vocals), Robert Taylor (guitar), Ivan Thompson and Paul Hewson (keyboards), Todd Hunter (bass), and Neil Story (drums). Hewson died of a drug overdose in 1985. Hunter died of cancer on 7/17/98 (age 44).				
8/18/84	88	4		Rain	*Moroxy Bind*	$5		Polydor 817292
				DRAKE, Charlie '62 Born Charles Springall on 6/19/25 in London, England. Actor/comedian.				
1/13/62	21	12		My Boomerang Won't Come Back original pressings use the refrain "black in the face" ($25); later pressings: "blue in the face"	*She's My Girl* [N]	$15		United Artists 398
				DRAKE, Guy '70 Born on 7/24/04 in Weir, Kentucky. Died on 6/17/84 (age 79). Country singer/comedian.				
1/31/70	63	14		Welfare Cadilac	*Keep Off My Grass* [N-S]	$7		Royal American 1
				DRAKE, Pete BUB/LP '64 Born Roddis Franklin Drake on 10/8/32 in Atlanta, Georgia. Died on 7/29/88 (age 55). Session steel guitarist.				
3/7/64	25	11		Forever **PETE DRAKE And His Talking Steel Guitar**	*Sleep Walk*	$8		Smash 1867
				DRAMA LP '00 Born in 1980 in Atlanta, Georgia. Male rapper. Drama stands for Drastic Retaliation Against My Adversaries.				
2/12/00	73	13		Left/Right	S:21 *(3 versions) / I'm Ballin' Man*	$8	★*	Tight 2 Def 4501
				DRAMATICS, The R&B/BUB/LP '72 R&B vocal group from Detroit, Michigan: Ron Banks, William Howard, Larry Demps, Willie Ford and Elbert Wilkins. Howard and Wilkins replaced by L.J. Reynolds and Lenny Mayes in 1973. Charted 36 R&B hits, 1967-96. *1)In The Rain 2)Whatcha See Is Whatcha Get 3)Hey You! Get Off My Mountain*				
7/3/71	9	15		1 Whatcha See Is Whatcha Get	*Thankful For Your Love*	$10		Volt 4058
12/11/71+	78	7		2 Get Up And Get Down	*Fall In Love, Lady Love*	$8		Volt 4071
2/26/72	5	13		3 In The Rain	RB[4] *(Gimme Some) Good Soul Music*	$8		Volt 4075
8/26/72	67	9		4 Toast To The Fool	*Your Love Was Strange*	$8		Volt 4082
5/5/73	43	12		5 Hey You! Get Off My Mountain	*The Devil Is Dope*	$8		Volt 4090
10/27/73	45	10		6 Fell For You	*Now You Got Me Loving You*	$8		Volt 4099
8/24/74	62	6		7 Door To Your Heart	*Choosing Up On You* (R&B #30)	$6		Cadet 5704
5/3/75	47	9		8 Me And Mrs. Jones	*I Cried All The Way Home* [L]	$5		ABC 12090
11/22/75	81	3		9 (I'm Going By) The Stars In Your Eyes **RON BANKS AND THE DRAMATICS** (above 2)	*Trying To Get Over Losing You*	$5		ABC 12125
1/17/76	87	3		10 You're Fooling You #1-3, 5-7, 9 & 10: written by Tony Hester (also produced #1-3 & 5-7)	*I'll Make It So Good*	$5		ABC 12150
1/8/77	53	15		11 Be My Girl	*Richest Man Alive*	$5		ABC 12235
10/22/77	76	6		12 Shake It Well	*That Heaven Kind Of Feeling*	$5		ABC 12299
	★559★			**DRAPER, Rusty** C&W/MEM/POP/BUB '55 Born Farrell Draper on 1/25/23 in Kirksville, Missouri. Died of pneumonia on 3/28/2003 (age 80). Male singer/songwriter/guitarist. Known as "Ol' Redhead." Hit #6 on the pop charts in 1953 with "Gambler's Guitar." *1)The Shifting, Whispering Sands 2)Freight Train 3)Are You Satisfied?*				
8/20/55	18	4		1 Seventeen	S:18 / T:88 *Can't Live Without Them Anymore*	$15		Mercury 70651
10/1/55	3	16		2 The Shifting, Whispering Sands	J:3 / S:6 / T:7 / A:14 *Time*	$15		Mercury 70696
12/17/55+	11	18		3 Are You Satisfied?	S:11 / J:11 / T:12 *Wabash Cannonball*	$15		Mercury 70757
4/7/56	50	8		4 Held For Questioning	T:50 *Forty-Two*	$15		Mercury 70818
9/1/56	20	14		5 In The Middle Of The House **Jack Halloran Singers** (backing vocals, above 4); **David Carroll** (orch., all of above)	T:20 / A:24 *Pink Cadillac* [N]	$25		Mercury 70921
2/16/57	88	2		6 Tiger Lily	T:88 *Confidential*	$15		Mercury 70989
2/23/57	53	6		7 Let's Go Calypso Hugo (**Hugo & Luigi**) Peretti (orch., above 2)	T:53 *Should I Ever Love Again*	$15		Mercury 71039
5/20/57	6	18		8 Freight Train Dick Noel Singers (backing vocals); Carl Stevens (orch.); folk song composed in the early 1900s	A:6 / T:11 / S:17 *Seven Come Eleven*	$15		Mercury 71102
7/18/60	54	7		9 Please Help Me, I'm Falling	*Mule Skinner Blues* (#105)	$12		Mercury 71634
9/11/61	91	2		10 Signed, Sealed And Delivered #2 Country hit for **Cowboy Copas** in 1948	*Scared To Go Home*	$12		Mercury 71854
9/28/63	57	8		11 Night Life **Bob Moore** (orch.); written by **Willie Nelson**	*That's Why I Love You Like I Do*	$8		Monument 823
				DREAM LP '00 Female pop vocal group from Los Angeles, California: Holly Arnstein, Melissa Schuman, Ashley Poole and Diana Ortiz.				
9/30/00	2^2	28	●	1 He Loves U Not	S:❶[4] / A:7 *(instrumental)*	$4	★	Bad Boy 79338
5/12/01	39	20		2 This Is Me Kain (rap); samples "Take Me To The Mardi Gras" by **Paul Simon**; produced by **Puff Daddy**	S:4 / A:44 *(Mike Rizzo's Hyper Mix)*	$4	★	Bad Boy 79402
				DREAM ACADEMY, The ROK/LP '86 Pop-rock trio from England: Nick Laird-Clowes (guitar, vocals), Gilbert Gabriel (keyboards) and Kate St. John (vocals).				
11/30/85+	7	21		1 Life In A Northern Town	A:4 / S:7 *Test Tape No. 3*	$3	■	Warner 28841
4/19/86	36	11		2 The Love Parade	A:32 *Girl In A Million (For Edie Sedgwick)*	$3	■	Reprise 28750
				DREAMLOVERS, The BUB '61 R&B vocal group from Philadelphia, Pennsylvania: Tommy Ricks, Cleveland Hammock, Morris Gardner, and brothers Cliff and Ray Dunn. Backup vocal group for most of **Chubby Checker**'s hits. Named after **Bobby Darin**'s hit record.				
7/31/61	10	12		1 When We Get Married	*Just Because*	$25		Heritage 102
6/30/62	62	5		2 If I Should Lose You	*I Miss You* (#115)	$25		End 1114

DEBUT	PEAK	WKS	Gold	A-side (Chart Hit)....B-side	$	Sym	Label & Number

DREAM STREET — LP '01

Teen male vocal group from New York: Matt Ballinger, Frankie Galasso, Jesse McCartney, Greg Raposo and Chris Trousdale.

DEBUT	PEAK	WKS	Gold	A-side (Chart Hit)....B-side	$	Sym	Label & Number
7/21/01	48^{S}	4		1 **It Happens Every Time** ....*(4 album snippets)* available only with the purchase of Dreamstreet Magazine #2	$8	★$^{+}$	Edel/UEG 183052
12/1/01	24^{S}	10		2 **I Say Yeah** ....*Sugar Rush* first released as an enchanced CD on Edel/UEG 183222 (available only with the purchase of Dreamstreet Magazine #3)	$5	★	Edel/UEG 183252

DREAM WEAVERS, The — '56

Adult Contemporary vocal group from Miami, Florida: Wade Buff, Gene Adkinson, Lee Turner, Eddie Newson, Sally Sanborn, Mary Carr and Mary Rude.

DEBUT	PEAK	WKS	Gold	A-side (Chart Hit)....B-side	$	Sym	Label & Number
11/12/55+	7	23		1 **It's Almost Tomorrow** J:7 / S:8 / T:8 / A:10 *You've Got Me Wondering*	$20		Decca 29683
				THE DREAM WEAVERS Featuring Wade Buff:			
3/10/56	82	6		2 **Into The Night** / T:82			
4/7/56	100	1		3 **You're Mine** ....T:100 **Jack Pleis** (orch., above 2)	$15		Decca 29818
5/5/56	33	9		4 **A Little Love Can Go A Long, Long Way** / T:33 from the Goodyear TV Playhouse Production *Joey*			
5/19/56	87	2		5 **Is There Somebody Else** ....T:87 Sy Oliver (orch., above 2)	$15		Decca 29905

DRESSLAR, Len — '56

Born in 1924 in Evanston, Illinois. Singer/actor. The memorable voice ("Ho Ho Ho") of the Jolly Green Giant commercials.

DEBUT	PEAK	WKS	Gold	A-side (Chart Hit)....B-side	$	Sym	Label & Number
2/18/56	78	1		1 **Chain Gang** / T:78			
2/18/56	81	2		2 **These Hands** ....T:81 **Jack Halloran Singers** and **David Carroll** (backing vocals and orch., above 2)	$20		Mercury 70774

DREW, Patti — R&B/BUB '68

Born on 12/29/44 in Charleston, South Carolina; raised in Evanston, Illinois. Lead singer of black vocal group **The Drew-Vels** (see #1 below); included her sisters Lorraine and Erma Drew, and bass singer Carlton Black (married to Erma). Patti first recorded under her own name for Quill in 1966. Left music in 1971.

DEBUT	PEAK	WKS	Gold	A-side (Chart Hit)....B-side	$	Sym	Label & Number
2/8/64	90	2		1 **Tell Him** ....*Just Because* **THE DREW-VELS**	$12		Capitol 5055
8/26/67	85	8		2 **Tell Him** ....*Turn Away From Me* solo version which also features Carlton Black (bass voice); Don Caron (orch., above 2)	$10		Capitol 5861
8/3/68	62	11		3 **Workin' On A Groovy Thing** ....*Without A Doubt* co-written by **Neil Sedaka**	$8		Capitol 2197
11/16/68	93	2		4 **Hard To Handle** ....*Just Can't Forget About You*	$8		Capitol 2339

DREWS, J.D. — '81

Born Jurgen Drews on 4/2/48 in Berlin, Germany. Progressive rock singer.

DEBUT	PEAK	WKS	Gold	A-side (Chart Hit)....B-side	$	Sym	Label & Number
12/27/80+	79	6		**Don't Want No-Body** ....*Here I Am Again*	$6		Unicorn 95000

DREW-VELS, The - see DREW, Patti

DRIFTERS, The ★89★ — R&B/BUB/MEM/LP '60

R&B vocal group formed to showcase lead singer **Clyde McPhatter** on Atlantic in 1953. Included Gerhart and Andrew Thrasher, Bill Pinkney and McPhatter (who went solo in 1955). The Drifters had 11 Top 10 R&B hits (1953-55) prior to their first pop hit. Group continued with various lead singers through 1958. In 1959, manager George Treadwell disbanded the group and brought in The Five Crowns and renamed them The Drifters. New lineup included **Ben E. King** (lead; born on 9/23/38), Doc Green (baritone; born on 10/8/34), Charlie Thomas (tenor; born on 4/7/37) and Elsbeary Hobbs (bass; born on 8/4/36). Green died on 3/10/89 (age 54). Hobbs died on 5/31/96 (age 59). The majority of The Drifters' pop hits were sung with three different lead singers: **Ben E. King** (1959-60), Rudy Lewis (1961-63) and Johnny Moore (1957, 1964-66). Lewis died of a heart attack on 5/20/64 (age 27). Moore died of respiratory failure on 12/30/98 (age 64). Leiber & Stoller produced their hits from 1959-63. Many personnel changes throughout career and several groups have used the name in later years. Group inducted into the Rock and Roll Hall of Fame in 1988.

1)Save The Last Dance For Me 2)There Goes My Baby 3)Under The Boardwalk 4)Up On The Roof 5)On Broadway

DEBUT	PEAK	WKS	Gold	A-side (Chart Hit)....B-side	$	Sym	Label & Number
12/31/55	80	1		1 **White Christmas** ....T:80 *The Bells of St. Mary's* **THE DRIFTERS featuring Clyde McPhatter and Bill Pinckney** recorded November 1953; #2 R&B hit in 1954	$60	[X]	Atlantic 1048
3/9/57	69	4		2 **Fools Fall In Love** ....T:69 *It Was A Tear*	$30		Atlantic 1123
7/1/57	79	2		3 **Hypnotized** ....T:79 *Drifting Away From You*	$30		Atlantic 1141
8/11/58	58	2		4 **Drip Drop** / H:58			
6/23/58	72	5		5 **Moonlight Bay** ....T:72 #1 hit for the American Quartet in 1912	$30		Atlantic 1187
6/1/59	2^{1}	19	●	6 **There Goes My Baby** ....RB^{1} *Oh My Love*	$25		Atlantic 2025
10/12/59	15	15	●	7 **Dance With Me** /			
11/2/59	33	11		8 **(If You Cry) True Love, True Love**	$20		Atlantic 2040
2/22/60	16	11		9 **This Magic Moment** ....*Baltimore*	$20		Atlantic 2050
5/23/60	54	9		10 **Lonely Winds** ....*Hey Senorita*	$20		Atlantic 2062
9/5/60	1^{3}	18	●	11 **Save The Last Dance For Me** RB^{1} *Nobody But Me*	$20		Atlantic 2071
12/19/60+	17	11		12 **I Count The Tears** ....*Suddenly There's A Valley* **Ben E. King** (lead singer, #6-12 - except #8)	$20		Atlantic 2087
12/19/60	96	1		13 **White Christmas** ....*The Bells of St. Mary's* #1 above on yellow and black label; reissues on red and black label	$20	[X-R]	Atlantic 1048
3/20/61	32	11		14 **Some Kind Of Wonderful** ....*Honey Bee*	$20		Atlantic 2096
6/5/61	14	12		15 **Please Stay** ....*No Sweet Lovin'*	$20		Atlantic 2105
9/11/61	16	11		16 **Sweets For My Sweet** ....*Loneliness Or Happiness*	$20		Atlantic 2117
12/18/61	72	5		17 **Room Full Of Tears** ....*Somebody New Dancin' With You*	$15		Atlantic 2127
2/24/62	28	10		18 **When My Little Girl Is Smiling** ....*Mexican Divorce* Charlie Thomas (lead singer, above 3)	$15		Atlantic 2134
5/12/62	73	1		19 **Stranger On The Shore** ....*What To Do*	$15		Atlantic 2143
11/3/62+	5	20		20 **Up On The Roof** ....*Another Night With The Boys*	$15		Atlantic 2162

DEBUT	PEAK	WKS	Gold	A-side (Chart Hit)...B-side	$	Sym	Label & Number
				DRIFTERS, The — Cont'd			
12/22/62	88	1		21 **White Christmas** ...X:4 *The Bells of St. Mary's* [X-R]	$20		Atlantic 1048
				Christmas charts: [#4-10 weeks] 17/'63; 4/'64; 13/'65; 17/'66; 14/'67			
3/23/63	9	10		22 **On Broadway** ...*Let The Music Play*	$15		Atlantic 2182
				Phil Spector (guitar solo)			
6/15/63	71	6		23 **Rat Race** ...*If You Don't Come Back* (#101)	$15		Atlantic 2191
9/7/63	25	10		24 **I'll Take You Home** ...*I Feel Good All Over*	$15		Atlantic 2201
2/1/64	43	7		25 **Vaya Con Dios** ...*In The Land Of Make Believe*	$15		Atlantic 2216
				#1 hit for **Les Paul & Mary Ford** in 1953; Rudy Lewis (lead singer, #14-25 - except #16-18, 21 & 24)			
5/2/64	56	7		26 **One Way Love** ...*Didn't It*	$15		Atlantic 2225
6/27/64	4	14		27 **Under The Boardwalk** ...*I Don't Want To Go On Without You*	$15		Atlantic 2237
9/26/64	33	7		28 **I've Got Sand In My Shoes** ...*He's Just A Playboy* (#115)	$12		Atlantic 2253
11/14/64	18	9		29 **Saturday Night At The Movies** ...*Spanish Lace*	$12	■	Atlantic 2260
1/30/65	43	6		30 **At The Club** ...*Answer The Phone*	$12		Atlantic 2268
4/24/65	60	5		31 **Come On Over To My Place /**			
4/24/65	90	2		32 **Chains Of Love** ...	$12		Atlantic 2285
7/3/65	91	3		33 **Follow Me** ...*The Outside World*	$12		Atlantic 2292
8/14/65	51	6		34 **I'll Take You Where The Music's Playing** ...*Far From The Maddening Crowd*	$12		Atlantic 2298
3/19/66	48	7		35 **Memories Are Made Of This** ...*My Islands In The Sun*	$12		Atlantic 2325
12/3/66	62	7		36 **Baby What I Mean** ...*Aretha*	$12		Atlantic 2366
				Johnny Moore (lead singer, #26-36 - except #32); The Drifters' musical arrangers: Stan Applebaum (#9-12, 16, 17), Artie Butler (#35), **Ray Ellis** (#5, 14, 15), Bob Gallo (#36), Bert Keyes (#31-33), Claus Ogermann (#18, 19), Gene Page (#34), Gary Sherman (#20, 22-26) and Teacho Wiltshire (#28-30)			
				DROPLINE '02			
				Rock group formed in Los Angeles, California: Steve Sulikowski (vocals, guitar), Jonathan Berry (guitar), Eric Houlihan (bass) and Chad Norris (drums).			
6/22/02	68[S]	2		**Fly Away From Here (Graduation Day)** ...*Fallen Angel*	$5	★[V]	143/Reprise 16703
				D.R.S. R&B/LP '93			
				Male R&B vocal group from Sacramento, California: Endo, Pic, Jail Bait, Deuce Deuce and Blunt. D.R.S.: Dirty Rotten Scoundrels.			
10/16/93	4	20	▲	**Gangsta Lean** ...RB[6] S:2 / A:13 *(2 versions)*	$3	▮	Capitol 44958
				DRU DOWN R&B/LP '95			
				Born Danyle Robinson in Oakland, California. Male rapper.			
12/24/94+	65	16		1 **Pimp Of The Year** ...S:54 *Mack Of The Year / 911 Rescue*	$4	▮	Relativity 1223
8/31/96	92	5		2 **Can You Feel Me** ...S:67 *Deal Went Bad*	$4	▮	Relativity 1567
				contains replayed elements from the **Fat Boys**' "Can You Feel It"			
	★395★			**DRU HILL** R&B/LP '97			
				Male R&B vocal group from Baltimore, Maryland: Mark "**Sisqo**" Andrews (born on 11/9/78), James "Woody" Green, Tamir "Nokio" Ruffin (born on 1/21/79) and Larry "Jazz" Anthony. Green left in March 1999. Group named after Druid Hill Park in Baltimore.			
				1)How Deep Is Your Love 2)In My Bed 3)Never Make A Promise			
8/31/96	18	23	●	1 **Tell Me** ...S:10 / A:62 *(2 mixes) / (3 album snippets)*	$3	▮	Island 854660
				from the movie *Eddie* starring Whoopi Goldberg			
1/11/97	4	25	▲	2 **In My Bed** ...RB[3] S:3 / A:36 *Tell Me (remix* w/Big Dex)	$3	▮[V]	Island 854854
				"45": Island 572210; B-side: "5 Steps"			
8/9/97	7	20	●	3 **Never Make A Promise** ...RB[4] S:3 / A:61 *In My Bed (remix* w/**Da Brat** & **Jermaine Dupri**)	$3	▮	Island 572082
8/16/97	53	15		4 **Big Bad Mamma** ...A:51 *(2 versions)*	$6	T	Violator 571441
				FOXY BROWN Featuring Dru Hill			
				samples "She's A Bad Mama Jama" by **Carl Carlton**; from the movie *Def Jam's How to Be A Player* starring Bill Bellamy			
12/13/97+	13	20	●	5 **We're Not Making Love No More** ...S:8 *(instrumental)*	$3	▮	LaFace 24295
				Babyface (backing vocal, writer and producer); from the movie *Soul Food* starring **Vanessa Williams**			
10/10/98	3	20	●	6 **How Deep Is Your Love** RB[3] S:❶[2] / A:16 *(w/o rap) / (3 album snippets)*	$4	★	Island 572424
				DRU HILL Featuring REDMAN			
12/5/98+	21	21		7 **These Are The Times** ...A:12 / S:15 *(instrumental) / (3 album snippets)*	$4	★[V]	Island 572588
				"45": Island 572482; B-side: "You Are Everything"			
5/22/99	❶[1]	17	●	8 **Wild Wild West** ...S:❶[1] / A:2 *Y'All Know* (Smith)	$4	★	Overbrook 79157
				WILL SMITH featuring Dru Hill and Kool Mo Dee			
				samples "Wild, Wild West" by **Kool Moe Dee** and "I Wish" by **Stevie Wonder**; title song from the movie starring Smith and Kevin Kline			
6/19/99	84	10		9 **You Are Everything** ...*(5 versions)*	$6	T[V]	Def Soul 562021
				12" single includes remixes featuring **Ja Rule**; "45" issued for #7 & 9 on Island 572482			
9/25/99	79	12		10 **Beauty** ...A:68			album cut
				above 5 (except #8) from the album *Enter The Dru* on Island 524542			
5/13/00	91	4		11 **Love Sets You Free** ...S:18 *It's Gonna Rain* (Price)	$4	★	Def Soul 562683
				KELLY PRICE & FRIENDS (Dru Hill, Montell Jordan, Case, Playa, Kandice Love, Lovher)			
				from the movie *The Hurricane* starring Denzel Washington			
12/7/02+	25	17		12 **I Should Be...** ...A:22		V	album cut
				from the album *Dru World Order* on Def Soul 063377; "45": Def Soul 063865; B-side: same version			
				DRUNKEN MASTER '01			
				Born in Brooklyn, New York. Rapper/producer. Name taken from the Jackie Chan movie *The Legend Of Drunken Master.*			
8/25/01	44[S]	9		**50 Playaz Deep** ...*(2 versions) / (album sampler)*	$5	★	FB/Universal 015111
				DRUNKEN MASTER Featuring Lola Damone			
				samples "Summer Madness" by **Kool & The Gang**			
				DRUPI '73			
				Born Giampiero Anelli in 1949 in Pavia, Italy. Male singer.			
11/3/73	88	4		**Vado Via** ...*Un Letto E. Lei* [F]	$5		A&M 1460
				DRUSKY, Roy C&W '61			
				Born on 6/22/30 in Atlanta, Georgia. Country singer/guitarist. Charted 42 Country hits, 1960-77.			
4/10/61	35	16		**Three Hearts In A Tangle** ...*I'd Rather Loan You Out* (C&W #10)	$12		Decca 31193

DEBUT	PEAK	WKS	Gold	A-side (Chart Hit)....................B-side	$	Sym	Label & Number
				DSD (The Dirty South Divas) '02			
				Female rap duo from Tampa, Florida.			
5/25/02	42	18		1 **My Neck, My Back (Lick It)** ....A:41 / S:61 *(4 versions) / The K-Wang*	$6	T	Dirty Down 751136
				KHIA Featuring: DSD			
11/23/02	13^S	14		2 **Play Wit It**....................*(4 versions)*	$8	★*	Dirty Down 316
				DSD (The Dirty South Divas) featuring Khia			
				"D" TRAIN R&B/LP '84			
				R&B-dance duo from Brooklyn, New York: James "D Train" Williams (vocals) and Hubert Eaves III (keyboards).			
1/7/84	79	6		**Something's On Your Mind**....................*(instrumental)*	$5		Prelude 8080
				D-12 LP '01			
				Rap group from Detroit, Michigan: Marshall Mathers ("**Eminem**"), DeShaun Holton ("**Proof**"), Denine Porter ("Kon Artis"), Rufus Johnson ("Bizzare"), Oscar Moore ("Swift") and Von Carlisle ("Kuniva"). D-12 is short for Dirty Dozen.			
12/16/00+	31^S	21		1 **$#!* On You**....................*(3 versions)*	$5	★*	Shady 497344
6/23/01	19	15		2 **Purple Hills**....................S:3 / A:40 *(instrumental)*	$5	★	Shady 497583
				12" (Shady 497569) contains "dirty" version (title shown as "Purple Pills"); above 2 produced by **Eminem**			
				DUALS '61			
				Rock and roll instrumental duo from Los Angeles, California: Henry Bellinger and Johnny Lageman.			
9/11/61	25	11		**Stick Shift**....................*Cruising* [I]	$30		Sue 745
				first released on Star Revue 1031 in 1961 ($300)			
				DUBS, The '57			
				R&B vocal group from Harlem, New York: Richard Blandon, Cleveland Still, Bill Carlyle, Tommy Grate and Jim Miller. Blandon died on 12/20/91 (age 57).			
7/15/57	72	4		1 **Don't Ask Me (To Be Lonely)**....................T:72 *Darling*	$125		Gone 5002
				first released on Johnson 102 in 1957 ($1500)			
11/4/57	23	16		2 **Could This Be Magic**....................S:23 / T:24 *Such Lovin'*	$125		Gone 5011
8/24/59	74	6		3 **Chapel Of Dreams**....................*Is There A Love For Me*	$60		Gone 5046
				also issued on Gone 5069 in 1959 (charted for 5 weeks on 5046 and 1 week on 5069)			
				DUCENT, Ricardo — see SHAGGY			
				DUDLEY, Dave C&W/BUB '63			
				Born David Pedruska on 5/3/28 in Spencer, Wisconsin. Country singer/guitarist (charted 41 hits, 1961-80).			
6/8/63	32	11		1 **Six Days On The Road**....................*I Feel A Cry Coming On*	$12		Golden Wing 3020
10/12/63	95	1		2 **Cowboy Boots**....................*I Think I'll Cheat (A Little Tonight)*	$12		Golden Ring 3030
				DUICE LP '93			
				Male rap duo: LA Sno (from Los Angeles) and Creo-D (from Barbados).			
1/9/93	12	40	▲^{2}	**Dazzey Duks**....................S:8 / A:18 *(remix)*	$3	▮	TMR/Bellmark 72501
				title inspired by the short shorts worn by Daisy Duke of TV's *Dukes Of Hazzard*			
				DUKAYS, The — see CHANDLER, Gene			
				DUKE, Doris R&B/BUB '70			
				Born Doris Curry in Sandersville, Georgia. R&B singer. Recorded as Doris Willingham for Hy-Monty in 1967.			
2/28/70	50	9		**To The Other Woman (I'm The Other Woman)**....................*I Don't Care Anymore*	$8		Canyon 28
				DUKE, George R&B/LP '81			
				Born on 1/12/46 in San Rafael, California. Jazz-rock keyboardist. Own group in San Francisco during the mid-1950s. With the Don Ellis Big Band and Jean-Luc Ponty. With **Frank Zappa**'s Mothers Of Invention from 1971-75. Also with **Cannonball Adderley** from 1972-75. Own group from 1977. With **Stanley Clarke** in the Clarke/Duke Project. **The California Raisins**' lead vocalist.			
1/7/78	54	6		1 **Reach For It**....................*Just For You*	$4		Epic 50463
5/2/81	19	20		2 **Sweet Baby**....................*Never Judge A Cover By Its Book*	$4		Epic 01052
				STANLEY CLARKE/GEORGE DUKE			
2/20/82	41	9		3 **Shine On**....................*Positive Energy*	$4		Epic 02701
				DUKE, Patty LP '65			
				Born Anna Marie Duke on 12/14/46 in Elmhurst, New York. Movie and TV actress. Married to actor John Astin from 1972-85.			
6/26/65	8	11		1 **Don't Just Stand There**....................*Everything But Love*	$10	■	United Artists 875
10/2/65	22	8		2 **Say Something Funny** /			
9/25/65	77	5		3 **Funny Little Butterflies**....................	$10	■	United Artists 915
				from the movie *Billie* starring Duke			
2/26/66	64	5		4 **Whenever She Holds You**....................*Nothing But You*	$10		United Artists 978
				female version of **Bobby Goldsboro**'s hit "Whenever He Holds You"			
				DUKE & THE DRIVERS '75			
				Rock group from Boston, Massachusetts: Tom Swift (vocals), Sam Deluxe and Cadillac Jack (guitars), Rhinestone Mudflaps (sax), Koko Dee (bass) and Bobby Blue Sky (drums).			
8/16/75	95	4		**What You Got**....................*Like I Want It*	$5		ABC 12110
				DUKE JUPITER BUB/LP '82			
				Rock group from Rochester, New York: Marshall James Styler (vocals, keyboards), Greg Walker (guitar), George Barajas (bass) and David Corcoran (drums). Barajas died on 8/17/82 (age 33). Rickey Ellis (bass) joined in 1983.			
3/27/82	58	7		1 **I'll Drink To You**....................*Begin Again*	$5		Coast to Coast 02801
5/12/84	68	7		2 **Little Lady**....................*(I've Got A) Little Black Book*	$5		Morocco 1736
				DULFER, Candy — see STEWART, David A.			
				DUNDAS, David '76			
				Born on 4/2/45 in Oxford, England. Pop singer/actor/commercial jingle writer.			
10/9/76+	17	21		**Jeans On**....................*Sleepy Serena*	$5		Chrysalis 2094
				originally a jingle in England for Brutus Jeans			
				DUNN & McCASHEN '70			
				Rock duo of singers/guitarists/songwriters Don Dunn and Tony McCashen.			
11/7/70	91	2		**Alright In The City**....................*Man On The Corner*	$8		Capitol 2935

DEBUT	PEAK	WKS	Gold	A-side (Chart Hit)...B-side	$	Sym	Label & Number
				DUPREE, Robbie LP **'80**			
				Born Robert Dupuis on 12/23/46 in Brooklyn, New York. Soft-rock singer/songwriter.			
4/12/80	6	23		1 **Steal Away** ... *I'm No Stranger*	$4		Elektra 46621
7/19/80	15	18		2 **Hot Rod Hearts** ... *Love Is A Mystery*	$4		Elektra 47005
5/23/81	54	7		3 **Brooklyn Girls** ... *Lonely Runner*	$4	■	Elektra 47145
				DUPREES, The BUB/LP **'62**			
				Italian-American doo-wop group from Jersey City, New Jersey: Joey Vann, Mike Arnone, Tom Bialablow, Joe Santollo and John Salvato. Santollo died of a heart attack on 6/3/81 (age 37). Vann died on 2/28/84 (age 40). Group also recorded as **I.A.P. CO.** (see #9 below).			
8/4/62	7	13		1 **You Belong To Me** *Take Me As I Am*	$20		Coed 569
				#1 hit for **Jo Stafford** in 1952			
10/20/62	13	10		2 **My Own True Love** ... *Ginny*	$20		Coed 571
				melody is "Tara's Theme" from the movie *Gone With The Wind* starring Clark Gable and Vivien Leigh			
1/26/63	91	4		3 **I'd Rather Be Here In Your Arms** ... *I Wish I Could Believe You*	$20		Coed 574
3/23/63	89	2		4 **Gone With The Wind** ... *Let's Make Love Again*	$20		Coed 576
				#1 hit for Horace Heidt in 1937 (not from the movie; inspired by the novel)			
8/24/63	37	7		5 **Why Don't You Believe Me** ... *My Dearest One*	$15		Coed 584
				#1 hit for **Joni James** in 1952			
11/9/63	18	10		6 **Have You Heard** ... *Love Eyes*	$15		Coed 585
				#4 hit for **Joni James** in 1953			
1/25/64	74	5		7 **(It's No) Sin** ... *The Sand And The Sea*	$15		Coed 587
				THE DUPREES featuring Joey Vann (above 4)			
				#1 hit for **Eddy Howard** in 1951			
7/24/65	91	2		8 **Around The Corner** ... *They Said It Couldn't Be Done*	$12		Columbia 43336
5/2/70	97	2		9 **Check Yourself** ... *The Sky's The Limit*	$6	■	Colossus 110
				I.A.P. CO. (The Italian Asphalt & Pavement Company)			
				DUPRI, Jermaine R&B/BUB/LP **'98**			
				Born on 9/23/73 in Atlanta, Georgia. Black producer of many top rap and R&B acts, including **Xscape**, **Da Brat** and **Kris Kross** on his own label So So Def Recordings. Also produced **Mariah Carey** and **TLC**.			
3/7/98	29	19	●	1 **The Party Continues** S:16 *We Just Wanna Party With You* (w/**Snoop Doggy Dogg**)	$3	▮	So So Def 78807
				JD & DA BRAT			
				Usher (backing vocal); samples "She's Strange" by **Cameo**			
7/4/98	52	20		2 **Money Ain't A Thang** ... A:62 *(3 versions)*	$6	T	So So Def 78864
				JD Featuring JAY-Z			
10/23/99	52^S	9		3 **Get None** ... *(2 versions) / Don't Cry*	$4	★	DreamWorks 59025
				TAMAR featuring J.D. & Amil			
10/20/01	95	5		4 **Ballin' Out Of Control** ... S:53 *(3 versions) / Hate Blood* (w/**Jadakiss** & **Freeway**)	$6	T	So So Def 79590
				JERMAINE DUPRI featuring Nate Dogg			
12/29/01+	35	20		5 **Welcome To Atlanta** ... A:36			album cut
				JERMAINE DUPRI • LUDACRIS			
				from the Dupri album *Instructions* on So So Def 85830 and the Ludacris album *Word Of Mouf* on Def Jam 586446			
4/20/02	91	5		6 **Tell Me What's It Gonna Be** ... S:65 *(3 versions)*	$6	T	Motown 015880
				BRIAN McKNIGHT Featuring Jermaine Dupri			
				samples "Hydra" by **Grover Washington, Jr.**			

DEBUT	PEAK	WKS	Gold	A-side (Chart Hit)...B-side	$	Sym	Label & Number
				DURAN DURAN ★87★ ROK/BUB/LP **'84**			
				Synth-pop-dance band from Birmingham, England: Simon LeBon (vocals; born on 10/27/58), **Andy Taylor** (see #11 & 12 below) (guitar; born on 2/16/61), Nick Rhodes (keyboards; born Nicholas James Bates on 6/8/62), **John Taylor** (see #10 below) (bass; born on 6/20/60) and Roger Taylor (drums; born on 4/26/60). None of the Taylors are related. Group named after a villain in the Jane Fonda movie *Barbarella*. In 1984, Andy and Roger left the group. In 1985, Andy and John recorded with supergroup **The Power Station**; Simon, Nick and Roger recorded as **Arcadia**. Duran Duran reduced to a trio in 1986 of Simon, Nick and John. Expanded to a quintet in 1990 with the addition of guitarist Warren Cuccurullo (**Missing Persons**) and drummer Sterling Campbell (left by 1993; joined **Soul Asylum** in 1995). Huge popularity helped by their distinctive MTV music videos.			
				1)The Reflex 2)A View To A Kill 3)The Wild Boys 4)Notorious 5)Ordinary World			
12/25/82+	3	23	●	1 **Hungry Like The Wolf** ... AR[3] *(long version)*	$4	■	Harvest 5195
				first released on Harvest 5134 in 1982 (B-side: "Careless Memories")			
4/2/83	14	13		2 **Rio** ... *Hold Back The Rain*	$3	■	Capitol 5215
				first released on Harvest 5175 in 1982			
6/4/83	4	17		3 **Is There Something I Should Know** ... *Careless Memories*	$3	■	Capitol 5233
11/5/83	3	17		4 **Union Of The Snake** ... *Secret Oktober*	$3	■	Capitol 5290
1/14/84	10	16		5 **New Moon On Monday** ... *Tiger Tiger*	$3	■	Capitol 5309
4/21/84	❶[2]	21	●	6 **The Reflex** *New Religion*	$3	■	Capitol 5345
				picture sleeve is a foldout poster			
11/3/84	2[4]	18	●	7 **The Wild Boys** ... S:❶[2] / A:2 *(I'm Looking For) Cracks In The Pavement*	$3	■	Capitol 5417
2/2/85	16	14		8 **Save A Prayer** ... A:12 / S:21 *(live version)*	$3	■	Capitol 5438
				from the 1982 album *Rio*			
5/18/85	❶[2]	17		9 **A View To A Kill** ... S:❶[3] / A:2 *A View To A Kill* (**John Barry**)	$3	■	Capitol 5475
				title song from the James Bond movie starring Roger Moore			
3/8/86	23	12		10 **I Do What I Do...(Theme for 9 1/2 Weeks)** ... S:18 / A:26 *Jazz*	$3	■	Capitol 5551
				John TAYLOR Jonathan ELIAS			
				from the movie *9 1/2 Weeks* starring Mickey Rourke and Kim Basinger			
5/31/86	24	17		11 **Take It Easy** ... A:23 / S:24 *Angel Eyes*	$3	■	Atlantic 89414
10/25/86	73	6		12 **When The Rain Comes Down** ... *Broken Windows*	$3	■	MCA 52946
				ANDY TAYLOR (above 2)			
11/1/86+	2[1]	17		13 **Notorious** ... S:❶[1] / A:3 *Winter Marches On*	$3	■	Capitol 5648
1/31/87	39	9		14 **Skin Trade** ... S:30 *We Need You*	$3	■	Capitol 5670
5/2/87	70	5		15 **Meet El Presidente** ... *Vertigo (Do The Demolition)*	$3	■	Capitol 44001
				picture sleeve is a foldout poster			
10/15/88	4	16		16 **I Don't Want Your Love** ... S:3 / A:4 *(album version)*	$3	■	Capitol 44237

DEBUT	PEAK	WKS	Gold	A-side (Chart Hit)...B-side	$	Sym	Label & Number
				DURAN DURAN — Cont'd			
12/24/88+	22	13		17 **All She Wants Is** ....S:18 / A:25 *I Believe/All I Need To Know (medley)* above 2: #1 Dance Club Play hits	$3	■	Capitol 44287
3/18/89	72	5		18 **Do You Believe In Shame?**....*(The Krush Brothers LSD edit)* from the movie *Tequila Sunrise* starring Mel Gibson	$3	■	Capitol 44337
9/1/90	64	7		19 **Violence Of Summer (Love's Taking Over)** ....*Yo Bad Azizi* **DURANDURAN** (above 4)	$4	▮	Capitol 44608
1/9/93	3	22	●	20 **Ordinary World** ....A:3 / S:6 *(acoustic version) / Save A Prayer (live)* "45": Capitol 56945; B-side: "Save A Prayer"	$3	▮V	Capitol 44908
4/17/93	7	25		21 **Come Undone** ....A:6 / S:15 *(mix 2 master) / Time For Temptation* "45": Capitol 17316; B-side: "Skin Trade"	$3	▮V	Capitol 44918
9/4/93	45	11		22 **Too Much Information** ....S:49 / A:63 *First Impression / Come Undone (new mix)* sold with bonus cassette "No Ordinary EP" (Hungry Like The Wolf/Notorious/Come Undone); recorded 'live' at Tower Records, L.A.; "45": Capitol 17438; B-side: "Drowning Man"	$5	▮V	Capitol 44955
3/18/95	67^A	6		23 **White Lines** .... from the album *Thank You* on Captiol 29419; "Bubbled Under" (#101) in 1983 for **Grandmaster & Melle Mel**, who also perform on this version; "45": Capitol 18488; B-side: "Watching The Detectives"		V	album cut
10/11/97	52	9		24 **Electric Barbarella** ....A:54 *(2 mixes) / Sinner And Saint / Out Of My Mind* "45": Capitol 19721	$8	★*+V	Capitol 58674
				DURANTE, Jimmy MEM/POP/AC/BUB/LP **'34** Born on 2/10/1893 in Brooklyn, New York. Died of pneumonia on 1/29/80 (age 86). Legendary comedian. Appeared in numerous movies and TV shows.			
9/7/63	51	8		**September Song** ....*Young At Heart* introduced in the 1938 Broadway musical *Knickerbocker Holiday* by actor Walter Huston	$8		Warner 5382
				DURST, Fred — see STAIND			
				DUSK BUB **'71** Studio group created by **Dawn**'s producers, Hank Medress and Dave Appell. Lead vocals by Peggy Santiglia of **The Angels**.			
2/6/71	57	9		1 **Angel Baby** ....*If We Just Leave Today*	$6		Bell 961
6/12/71	53	13		2 **I Hear Those Church Bells Ringing** ....*I Cannot See To See You*	$6		Bell 990
				DUVALL, Huelyn **'59** Born on 8/18/39 in Garner, Texas; raised in Huckabay, Texas. Male rockabilly singer.			
6/15/59	88	3		**Little Boy Blue** ....*Three Months To Kill* record released in June 1958	$50		Challenge 59014
				DYKE AND THE BLAZERS R&B/BUB/LP **'69** R&B-funk group from Buffalo, New York: Arlester "Dyke" Christian (vocals; songwriter), Alvester "Pig" Jacobs (guitar), Bernard Williams and Clarence Towns (saxophones), Alvin Battle (bass) and Willie Earl (drums). Dyke was shot to death in Phoenix on 3/30/71 (age 28).			
4/15/67	65	15		1 **Funky Broadway Part I** ....*Part II*	$10		Original Sound 64
4/13/68	67	5		2 **Funky Walk Part I (East)** ....*Part II (West)*	$8		Original Sound 79
5/17/69	35	10		3 **We Got More Soul** ....*Shotgun Slim*	$8		Original Sound 86
9/20/69	36	11		4 **Let A Woman Be A Woman - Let A Man Be A Man**....*Uhh (#118)*	$8		Original Sound 89
				DYLAN, Bob ★193★ ROK/BUB/LP **'65** Born Robert Zimmerman on 5/24/41 in Duluth, Minnesota; raised in Hibbing, Minnesota. Highly influential singer/songwriter/guitarist/harmonica player. Innovator of folk-rock style. Took stage name from poet Dylan Thomas. To New York City in December 1960. Worked Greenwich Village folk clubs. Signed to Columbia Records in October 1961. Motorcycle crash on 7/29/66 led to short retirement. Subject of documentaries *Don't Look Back* (1965) and *Eat The Document* (1969). Acted in movies *Pat Garrett And Billy The Kid* (1973), *Renaldo And Clara* (1978; also directed) and *Hearts Of Fire* (1987). Newly-found Christian faith reflected in his recordings of 1979-81. Member of the supergroup **Traveling Wilburys**. His son Jakob is lead singer of **The Wallflowers**. Inducted into the Rock and Roll Hall of Fame in 1988. Won Grammy's Lifetime Achievement Award in 1991. *1)Like A Rolling Stone 2)Rainy Day Women #12 & 35 3)Lay Lady Lay 4)Positively 4th Street 5)Knockin' On Heaven's Door*			
4/3/65	39	8		1 **Subterranean Homesick Blues** ....*She Belongs To Me* B-side was a #33 hit for **Rick Nelson** in 1969	$20	□	Columbia 43242
7/24/65	2^2	12		2 **Like A Rolling Stone** *Gates Of Eden* features Al Kooper (later of **Blood, Sweat & Tears**) on organ	$20		Columbia 43346
10/2/65	7	9		3 **Positively 4th Street** ....*From A Buick 6*	$20	■	Columbia 43389
1/1/66	58	6		4 **Can You Please Crawl Out Your Window?**....*Highway 61 Revisited*	$20		Columbia 43477
4/16/66	2^1	10		5 **Rainy Day Women #12 & 35** ....*Pledging My Time*	$15		Columbia 43592
7/2/66	20	7		6 **I Want You** ....*Just Like Tom Thumb's Blues*	$15	■	Columbia 43683
9/10/66	33	6		7 **Just Like A Woman**....*Obviously 5 Believers*	$15		Columbia 43792
5/20/67	81	4		8 **Leopard-Skin Pill-Box Hat** ....*Most Likely You Go Your Way And I'll Go Mine* above 4 from the album *Blonde On Blonde*	$15		Columbia 44069
5/17/69	85	5		9 **I Threw It All Away**....*Drifter's Escape*	$10		Columbia 44826
7/12/69	7	14		10 **Lay Lady Lay** ....*Peggy Day* written for his wife Sarah Lowndes (married 1965-77)	$10		Columbia 44926
11/1/69	50	7		11 **Tonight I'll Be Staying Here With You** ....*Country Pie*	$10		Columbia 45004
7/25/70	41	7		12 **Wigwam**....*Copper Kettle (The Pale Moonlight)* [I] #3-12: produced by Bob Johnston	$10		Columbia 45199
6/26/71	41	8		13 **Watching The River Flow** ....*Spanish Is The Loving Tongue* **Leon Russell** (piano)	$10		Columbia 45409
12/4/71+	33	8		14 **George Jackson** ....*(big band version)* Jackson: black militant shot to death in a prison riot at San Quentin on 8/21/71	$10		Columbia 45516
9/1/73	12	16		15 **Knockin' On Heaven's Door**....*Turkey Chase* Roger McGuinn (of **The Byrds**; guitar); from the movie *Pat Garrett And Billy The Kid* starring Dylan	$8		Columbia 45913
12/15/73+	55	7		16 **A Fool Such As I** ....*Lily Of The West* #3 Country hit for **Hank Snow** in 1953	$8		Columbia 45982

DEBUT	PEAK	WKS	Gold	A-side (Chart Hit)..........B-side	$	Sym	Label & Number
				DYLAN, Bob — Cont'd			
2/23/74	**44**	6		17 **On A Night Like This**............*You Angel You*	$8		Asylum 11033
				B-side was a hit for **Manfred Mann** in 1979			
8/10/74	**66**	5		18 **Most Likely You Go Your Way (And I'll Go Mine)**.......*Stage Fright* (The Band) [L]	$8		Asylum 11043
				BOB DYLAN/THE BAND			
				Dylan's studio version is on the B-side of #8 above			
3/8/75	**31**	7		19 **Tangled Up In Blue**............*If You See Her, Say Hello*	$7		Columbia 10106
11/29/75+	**33**	11		20 **Hurricane (Part I)**............*(Part II)*	$7	■	Columbia 10245
				dedicated to boxer Rubin "Hurricane" Carter, a convicted murderer			
3/13/76	**54**	5		21 **Mozambique**............*Oh, Sister*	$7		Columbia 10298
9/8/79	**24**	12		22 **Gotta Serve Somebody**............*Trouble In Mind*	$5		Columbia 11072
				Mark Knopfler (of **Dire Straits**; guitar)			
12/17/83+	**55**	9		23 **Sweetheart Like You**............*Union Sundown*	$4	■	Columbia 04301
				all of Dylan's hits were written by him (except #16)			
				DYNAMICS, The R&B '63			
				R&B group from Detroit, Michigan: Samuel Stevenson, Isaac "Zeke" Harris, George White and Fred "Sonny" Baker.			
11/2/63	**44**	10		1 **Misery**............*I'm The Man*	$15		Big Top 3161
3/22/69	**59**	7		2 **Ice Cream Song**............*The Love That I Need*	$10		Cotillion 44021
				DYNAMIC SUPERIORS R&B/BUB/LP '74			
				R&B-dance group from Washington DC: Tony Washington, George Spann, George Peterbark, Michael McCalphin and Maurice Washington.			
11/2/74	**68**	7		**Shoe Shoe Shine**............*Release Me*	$6		Motown 1324
				written and produced by **Ashford & Simpson**			
				DYNA-SORES, The '60			
				R&B group featuring **H.B. Barnum**, **Jimmy Norman** and guitarist/vocalist/arranger Réne Hall.			
6/6/60	**59**	3		**Alley-Oop**............*Jungle Walk* [N]	$25		Rendezvous 120
				DYNASTY R&B/BUB/LP '80			
				R&B-dance trio from Los Angeles, California: Kevin Spencer, Nidra Beard and Linda Carriere.			
9/13/80	**87**	6		**I've Just Begun To Love You**............*When You Feel Like Giving Love (Dial My Number)*	$4		Solar 12021
				DYNATONES, The '66			
				White instrumental pop group from Clarksburgh, West Virginia: Ray Figlar (fife, sax), Gary Van Scyoc (bass), Eddie Evans (piano; replaced by Pat Wallace) and Jack Wolfe (drums).			
9/3/66	**53**	8		**The Fife Piper**............*And I Always Will* [I]	$12		HBR 494
				first released on St. Clair 117 in 1966 ($30)			
				DYSHON & SQUABBLE '02			
				Male hip-hop duo from Philadelphia, Pennsylvania.			
12/7/02	**14**S	12		**Thug Lady**............*(instrumental) / (3 album snippets)*	$8	★	Romeo 73583
				DYSON, Ronnie R&B/LP '70			
				Born on 6/5/50 in Washington DC; raised in Brooklyn, New York. Died of heart failure on 11/10/90 (age 40). R&B singer. Acted in the Broadway musical *Hair* and the movie *Putney Swope*.			
6/20/70	**8**	14		1 **(If You Let Me Make Love To You Then) Why Can't I Touch You?** *Girl Don't Come*	$6		Columbia 45110
				from the off-Broadway musical *Salvation* starring Peter Link			
10/17/70	**50**	8		2 **I Don't Wanna Cry**............*She's Gone*	$6		Columbia 45240
7/24/71	**94**	2		3 **When You Get Right Down To It**............*Sleeping Sun*	$6		Columbia 45387
2/17/73	**28**	13		4 **One Man Band (Plays All Alone)**............*I Think I'll Tell Her*	$5	■	Columbia 45776
8/11/73	**60**	7		5 **Just Don't Want To Be Lonely**............*Point Of No Return*	$5		Columbia 45867
7/31/76	**62**	12		6 **The More You Do It (The More I Like It Done To Me)**............*You And Me*	$5		Columbia 10356
				D'ZYRE '91			
				Dance duo from Glendale, Illinois: Troy Guy and Andrea Salazar.			
6/8/91	**77**	9		**Forever Amo'r**............A:36 *(club mix)*	$4	▮	Atlantic 87685
				originally released on DJC 964 (maxi-cassette) in 1990			

EAGER, Brenda Lee — see BUTLER, Jerry

EAGLE-EYE CHERRY — see CHERRY, Eagle-Eye

EAGLES ★106★ AC/ROK/C&W/LP '75

Soft-rock group formed in Los Angeles, California: **Glenn Frey** (vocals, guitar; born on 11/6/48), **Don Henley** (vocals, drums; born on 7/22/47), **Randy Meisner** (bass; born on 3/8/46) and Bernie Leadon (guitar; born on 7/19/47). Meisner founded **Poco**; Leadon had been in the Flying Burrito Brothers; and Frey and Henley were with **Linda Ronstadt**. Debut album recorded in England in 1972. **Don Felder** (guitar; born on 9/21/47) added in 1975. Leadon replaced by **Joe Walsh** (born on 11/20/47) in 1975. Meisner replaced by **Timothy B. Schmit** (born on 10/30/47) in 1977. Frey and Henley were the only members to play on all recordings. Disbanded in 1982. Henley, Frey, Felder, Walsh and Schmit reunited in 1994. Group inducted into the Rock and Roll Hall of Fame in 1998.

1)One Of These Nights 2)Heartache Tonight 3)Hotel California 4)New Kid In Town 5)Best Of My Love

DEBUT	PEAK	WKS	Gold	A-side (Chart Hit)..........B-side	$	Sym	Label & Number
6/3/72	**12**	11		1 **Take It Easy**............*Get You In The Mood*	$6		Asylum 11005
9/9/72	**9**	13		2 **Witchy Woman**............*Earlybird*	$6		Asylum 11008
12/30/72+	**22**	12		3 **Peaceful Easy Feeling**............*Trying*	$6		Asylum 11013
6/23/73	**64**	8		4 **Tequila Sunrise**............*Twenty-One*	$6		Asylum 11017
9/15/73	**59**	8		5 **Outlaw Man**............*Certain Kind Of Fool*	$6		Asylum 11025
				all of above produced by Glyn Johns			
5/4/74	**32**	15		6 **Already Gone**............*Is It True?*	$6		Asylum 11036

DEBUT	PEAK	WKS	Gold	A-side (Chart Hit)...B-side	$	Sym	Label & Number
				EAGLES — Cont'd			
9/21/74	77	5		7 **James Dean** ... *Good Day In Hell*	$6		Asylum 45202
				#1 & 7: written by **Jackson Browne** and **Glenn Frey**			
11/30/74+	❶[1]	19		8 **Best Of My Love** ... AC[1] *Ol' '55*	$5		Asylum 45218
5/31/75	❶[1]	17		9 **One Of These Nights** ... *Visions*	$5		Asylum 45257
9/13/75	2[2]	14		10 **Lyin' Eyes** ... *Too Many Hands*	$5		Asylum 45279
12/20/75+	4	23		11 **Take It To The Limit** ... *After The Thrill Is Gone*	$5		Asylum 45293
12/18/76+	❶[1]	15	●	12 **New Kid In Town** ... *Victim Of Love*	$5		Asylum 45373
2/26/77	❶[1]	19	●	13 **Hotel California** ... *Pretty Maids All In A Row*	$5		Asylum 45386
5/14/77	11	14		14 **Life In The Fast Lane** ... *The Last Resort*	$5		Asylum 45403
12/9/78	18	8		15 **Please Come Home For Christmas** ... *Funky New Year* [X]	$5	■	Asylum 45555
10/6/79	❶[1]	15	●	16 **Heartache Tonight** ... *Teenage Jail*	$5		Asylum 46545
				written by **Bob Seger**, **J.D. Souther**, **Don Henley** and **Glenn Frey**			
12/8/79+	8	15		17 **The Long Run** ... *The Disco Strangler*	$5		Asylum 46569
2/23/80	8	16		18 **I Can't Tell You Why** ... *The Greeks Don't Want No Freaks*	$5		Asylum 46608
				from the movie *Inside Moves* starring John Savage			
12/20/80+	21	14		19 **Seven Bridges Road** ... *The Long Run (live)*	$5		Asylum 47100
				recorded at the Santa Monica Civic Auditorium on 7/28/80; #6-19: produced by Bill Szymczyk			
10/29/94	31	14		20 **Get Over It** ... A:40 / S:57 *(live version)*	$4	▮[V]	Geffen 19376
12/31/94+	22[A]	28		21 **Love Will Keep Us Alive** ... AC[3]			album cut
6/24/95	61[A]	5		22 **Learn To Be Still** ...			album cut
				above 3 from the album *Hell Freezes Over* on Geffen 24725; all of above (except #3, 5, 6, 15, 19 & 21) written by at least one of the Eagles			

EARL, Stacy — '92

Born on 12/28/62 in Boston, Massachusetts. Female dance-pop singer.

DEBUT	PEAK	WKS	Gold	A-side (Chart Hit)...B-side	$	Sym	Label & Number
11/16/91+	26	19		1 **Love Me All Up** ... A:18 *(3 album snippets)*	$3	▮[V]	RCA 62116
				"45" B-side: "Can't Go On This Way"			
2/22/92	27	12		2 **Romeo & Juliet** ... A:22 / S:75 *Sho 'Nuf A Star*	$3	▮[V]	RCA 62192
				STACY EARL (Featuring The Wild Pair) (Marv Gunn & Bruce Christian)			
6/20/92	52	9		3 **Slowly** ... A:56 *(3 album snippets)*	$3	▮[V]	RCA 62271
				"45" B-side: "Do You Really Want My Love"			

EARL-JEAN — see COOKIES, The

EARLS, The — BUB '63

White doo-wop group from the Bronx, New York: Larry Chance, Bob Del Din, Eddie Harder, and Jack Wray.

DEBUT	PEAK	WKS	Gold	A-side (Chart Hit)...B-side	$	Sym	Label & Number
12/15/62+	24	9		**Remember Then** ... *Let's Waddle*	$25		Old Town 1130

EARTH OPERA — LP '69

Pop-rock group from Boston, Massachusetts: Peter Rowan (vocals, guitar; **The Rowans**), David Grisman (mandolin), John Nagy (bass) and Paul Dillon (drums).

DEBUT	PEAK	WKS	Gold	A-side (Chart Hit)...B-side	$	Sym	Label & Number
4/26/69	97	1		**Home To You** ... *Alfie Finney*	$8		Elektra 45650

EARTH, WIND & FIRE ★73★ — R&B/BUB/AC/LP '79

R&B group formed in Los Angeles, California, by Chicago-bred producer/songwriter/vocalist/percussionist/kalimba player **Maurice White** (see #31 & 32 below) (born on 12/19/44). In 1969, White, former session drummer for Chess Records and member of **The Ramsey Lewis Trio**, formed the Salty Peppers; recorded for Capitol. Maurice's brother Verdine White (born on 7/25/51) was the group's bassist. Eighteen months later, the brothers hired a new band and recorded as Earth, Wind & Fire — named for the three elements of Maurice's astrological sign. Co-lead singer **Philip Bailey** (born on 5/8/51) joined in 1971. Group generally contained 8 to 10 members, with frequent personnel shuffling. In the movies *That's the Way of the World* (1975) and *Sgt. Pepper's Lonely Hearts Club Band* (1978). Elaborate stage shows featured an array of magic acts and pyrotechnics. Group inducted into the Rock and Roll Hall of Fame in 2000. Also see **Wade Flemons** and **Ronnie Laws**.

1)Shining Star 2)After The Love Has Gone 3)Let's Groove 4)Sing A Song 5)Boogie Wonderland

DEBUT	PEAK	WKS	Gold	A-side (Chart Hit)...B-side	$	Sym	Label & Number
7/3/71	93	5		1 **Love Is Life** ... *This World Today*	$6		Warner 7492
8/4/73	50	11		2 **Evil** ... *Clover*	$5		Columbia 45888
11/17/73+	52	11		3 **Keep Your Head To The Sky** ... *Build Your Nest*	$5		Columbia 45953
3/9/74	29	15		4 **Mighty Mighty** ... *Drum Song*	$5	■	Columbia 46007
7/13/74	55	9		5 **Kalimba Story** ... *Tee Nine Chee Bit*	$5		Columbia 46070
9/28/74	33	7		6 **Devotion** ... *Fair But So Uncool*	$5		Columbia 10026
1/18/75	50	6		7 **Hot Dawgit** ... *Tambura* (Lewis) [I]	$5		Columbia 10056
				RAMSEY LEWIS and EARTH, WIND & FIRE			
2/15/75	❶[1]	20	●	8 **Shining Star** ... RB[2] *Yearnin', Learnin'*	$5	■	Columbia 10090
3/22/75	44	7		9 **Sun Goddess** ... *Jungle Strut* (Lewis) [I]	$5		Columbia 10103
				RAMSEY LEWIS and EARTH, WIND & FIRE			
7/5/75	12	16		10 **That's The Way Of The World** ... *Africano*	$5		Columbia 10172
11/22/75+	5	17	●	11 **Sing A Song** ... RB[2] *(instrumental)*	$5		Columbia 10251
3/27/76	39	9		12 **Can't Hide Love** ... *Gratitude*	$5		Columbia 10309
7/17/76	12	19	●	13 **Getaway** ... RB[2] *(instrumental)*	$5	■	Columbia 10373
11/20/76+	21	15		14 **Saturday Nite** ... *Departure*	$5		Columbia 10439
10/29/77+	13	18		15 **Serpentine Fire** ... RB[7] *(instrumental)*	$5		Columbia 10625
3/4/78	32	15		16 **Fantasy** ... *Runnin'*	$5		Columbia 10688
7/22/78	9	13	●	17 **Got To Get You Into My Life** ... RB[1] *I'll Write A Song For You*	$5		Columbia 10796
				from the movie *Sgt. Pepper's Lonely Hearts Club Band* starring **Peter Frampton** and the **Bee Gees**			
11/18/78+	8	17	●	18 **September** ... RB[1] *Love's Holiday*	$5		ARC 10854
5/12/79	6	16	●	19 **Boogie Wonderland** ... *(instrumental)*	$5		ARC 10956
				EARTH, WIND & FIRE WITH THE EMOTIONS			
				also released on Columbia 10956 in 1979			
7/7/79	2[2]	17	●	20 **After The Love Has Gone** ... *Rock That!*	$5		ARC 11033
10/20/79	58	7		21 **In The Stone** ... *You And I*	$4		ARC 11093

DEBUT	PEAK	WKS	Gold	A-side (Chart Hit)...B-side	$	Sym	Label & Number
				EARTH, WIND & FIRE — Cont'd			
12/22/79+	64	6		22 **Star** ... *You And I*	$4		ARC 11165
				above 4 from the album *I Am*			
9/20/80	44	9		23 **Let Me Talk** ... *(instrumental)*	$4	■	ARC 11366
11/22/80	48	12		24 **You** ... *Share Your Love*	$4		ARC 11407
2/7/81	59	7		25 **And Love Goes On** ... *Win Or Lose*	$4		ARC 11434
10/3/81	3	24	●	26 **Let's Groove** ... RB[8] *(instrumental)*	$4		ARC 02536
				also see "3-2-1 Pump" by **Redhead Kingpin**			
1/23/82	51	7		27 **Wanna Be With You** ... *Kalimba Tree* [I]	$4		ARC 02688
1/22/83	17	16		28 **Fall In Love With Me** ... *Lady Sun*	$4	■	Columbia 03375
5/14/83	76	4		29 **Side By Side** ... *Something Special*	$4		Columbia 03814
11/12/83	57	9		30 **Magnetic** ... *Speed Of Love*	$4	■	Columbia 04210
8/31/85	50	13		31 **Stand By Me** ... *Can't Stop Love*	$3	■	Columbia 05571
2/8/86	95	1		32 **I Need You** ... *Believe In Magic*	$3	■	Columbia 05726
				MAURICE WHITE (above 2)			
10/31/87	60	13		33 **System Of Survival** ... RB[1] / DC[3] *Writing On The Wall*	$3	■	Columbia 07608
2/13/88	67	8		34 **Thinking Of You** ... *Money Tight*	$3	■	Columbia 07695
				above 2: #1 Dance Club Play hits			
8/28/93	53	10		35 **Sunday Morning** ... A:48 *The L Word*	$3	▮	Reprise 18461
				all of above (except #12, 13, 17, 19, 20 & 30-33) co-written by **Maurice White**; all of above (except #1-3) produced or co-produced by **Maurice White**			
				EAST COAST FAMILY LP **'92**			
				Grouping of artists assembled by Michael Bivins (**New Edition**, **Bell Biv DeVoe**). Features Bivins, **Another Bad Creation**, **Boyz II Men**, and **M.C. Brains**, plus newcomers Whytgize, Yvette Brown, Hayden Hajdu, Cali Brock, Tam Rock, Lady V, Tom Boyy, 1010, Fruit Punch, Anthony Velasquez, and Mark Finesse.			
8/22/92	81	6		**1-4-All-4-1** ... S:43 *(instrumental)*	$3	▮[V]	Biv 10 2171
				co-produced by Michael Bivins and **Boyz II Men**; "45": Motown 2178; B-side: "End Of The Road" by **Boyz II Men**			
				EASTERHOUSE **'89**			
				Rock duo from Manchester, England: brothers Andy (vocals) and Ivor (guitar) Perry.			
4/1/89	82	4		**Come Out Fighting** ... *New World In The Morning*	$3		Columbia 68552
				EAST L.A. CAR POOL **'75**			
				Disco group led by conga player Jack J. Gold.			
8/2/75	72	6		**Like They Say In L.A.** ... *Linda Chicana*	$5		GRC 2064

EASTON, Sheena ★143★ R&B/LP **'81**

Born Sheena Orr on 4/27/59 in Bellshill, Scotland. Pop singer/actress. Won the 1981 Best New Artist Grammy Award. Acted on TV's *Miami Vice*.

1)Morning Train (Nine To Five) 2)The Lover In Me 3)For Your Eyes Only 4)We've Got Tonight 5)Strut

DEBUT	PEAK	WKS	Gold	A-side (Chart Hit)...B-side	$	Sym	Label & Number
2/14/81	1[2]	21	●	1 **Morning Train (Nine To Five)** AC[2] *Calm Before The Storm*	$4	■	EMI America 8071
				originally titled "Nine To Five," except in U.S. to avoid confusion with **Dolly Parton**'s hit			
5/9/81	18	18		2 **Modern Girl** ... *Summer's Over*	$4	■	EMI America 8080
7/25/81	4	25		3 **For Your Eyes Only** ... *(instrumental)*	$4		Liberty 1418
				title song from the James Bond movie starring Roger Moore			
11/28/81+	15	18		4 **You Could Have Been With Me** ... *Savoir Faire*	$4	■	EMI America 8101
4/3/82	30	15		5 **When He Shines** ... *Family Of One*	$4		EMI America 8113
9/4/82	57	7		6 **Machinery** ... *So We Say Goodbye*	$4	■	EMI America 8131
10/30/82	64	7		7 **I Wouldn't Beg For Water** ... *Some Of Us Will*	$4		EMI America 8142
				all of above produced by Christopher Neil			
1/29/83	6	18		8 **We've Got Tonight** ... CW[1] *You Are So Beautiful* (Rogers)	$4	■	Liberty 1492
				KENNY ROGERS and SHEENA EASTON			
8/20/83	9	22		9 **Telefone (Long Distance Love Affair)** ... *Wish You Were Here Tonight*	$4	■	EMI America 8172
12/10/83+	25	20		10 **Almost Over You** ... *I Don't Need Your Word*	$4		EMI America 8186
4/14/84	79	3		11 **Devil In A Fast Car** ... *Sweet Talk*	$4	■	EMI America 8201
8/25/84	7	25		12 **Strut** ... S:4 / A:10 *Letters From The Road*	$3	■	EMI America 8227
12/22/84+	9	17		13 **Sugar Walls** ... S:4 / A:12 *Straight Talking*	$3	■	EMI America 8253
				written and co-produced by **Prince** (as Alexander Nevermind)			
3/23/85	80	6		14 **Swear** ... *Fallen Angels*	$3	■	EMI America 8263
				#9-14: produced by Greg Mathieson			
10/26/85	29	14		15 **Do It For Love** ... S:27 / A:29 *Can't Wait Till Tomorrow*	$3	■	EMI America 8295
2/8/86	65	6		16 **Jimmy Mack** ... *Money Back Guarantee*	$3	■	EMI America 8309
8/2/86	43	12		17 **So Far So Good** ... S:38 / A:40 *Magic Of Love*	$3	■	EMI America 8332
				from the movie *About Last Night* starring Rob Lowe and Demi Moore			
11/5/88+	2[1]	25		18 **The Lover In Me** ... S:2 / A:4 *(instrumental)*	$3	■	MCA 53416
10/21/89	36	14		19 **The Arms Of Orion** ... A:35 / S:37 *I Love U In Me* (Prince)	$3	■	Warner 22757
				PRINCE with Sheena Easton			
				from the movie *Batman* starring Michael Keaton			
3/30/91	19	15		20 **What Comes Naturally** ... A:18 / S:19 *(no B-side)*	$3	▮[V]	MCA 53742
				"45": Collectables/MCA 90204; B-side: "101"			

DEBUT	PEAK	WKS	Gold	A-side (Chart Hit)............B-side	$	Sym	Label & Number
				EASTSIDAZ, Tha R&B/LP **'00**			
				Rap duo from Long Beach, California: Tray Deee and Goldie Loc. Proteges of **Snoop Dogg**.			
1/8/00	**47**	14		1 **G'd Up**............S:12 *(3 versions)* **SNOOP DOGG PRESENTS THA EASTSIDAZ**	$5	★	Dogg House/TVT 2041
7/1/00	**99**	2		2 **Got Beef**............*(3 versions) / Ghetto* (w/Kokane, Kam & **Nate Dogg**) **SNOOP DOGG PRESENTS THA EASTSIDAZ featuring Jayo Felony & Blaqthoven**	$6	T	Dogg House/TVT 2044
3/24/01	**50**	19		3 **Lay Low**............A:44 / S:53 *Wrong Idea* (w/**Bad Azz**, Kokane & Lil Half Dead - R&B #75) **SNOOP DOGG (featuring Master P, Nate Dogg, Butch Cassidy & Tha Eastsidaz)**	$6	T	No Limit 50174
				EASTWOOD, Clint — see SHEPPARD, T.G.			
				EASYBEATS, The LP **'67**			
				Rock group formed in Sydney, Australia: Steven Wright (vocals), George Young and Harry Vanda (guitars), Dick Diamonde (bass) and Gordon Fleet (drums). Young is the older brother of **AC/DC**'s Angus and Malcolm Young. Young and Vanda went on to form **Flash & The Pan**.			
3/18/67	**16**	14		1 **Friday On My Mind**............*Made My Bed: Gonna Lie In It*	$15		United Artists 50106
11/15/69	**100**	1		2 **St. Louis**............*Can't Find Love*	$15		Rare Earth 5009
				EASY RIDERS, The — see GILKYSON, Terry / LAINE, Frankie / MARTIN, Dean			
				EASY STREET **'76**			
				Rock group from England: Peter Marsh (vocals), Ken Nicol (guitar), Jim Hall (bass) and Richard Burgess (drums).			
7/4/76	**81**	5		**I've Been Lovin' You**............*Gonna Wait For Summer*	$5		Capricorn 0255
				EAZY-E R&B/BUB/LP **'94**			
				Born Eric Wright on 9/7/63 in Compton, California. Died of AIDS on 3/26/95 (age 31). Rapper/producer. Formerly with N.W.A.			
11/13/93+	**42**	16		1 **Real Muthaphuckkin G's**............S:20 *Any Last Werdz* featuring Gangsta Dresta and BG. Knocc Out	$3	▮	Ruthless 5508
6/4/94	**63**[S]	4		2 **Luv 4 Dem Gangsta'z**............BUB:103 *(remix)*	$3	▮	MCA 54870
2/25/95	**41**	14		3 **Foe Tha Love Of $**............S:18 *Moe Cheese / Thuggish Ruggish Bone / Moe $* **BONE THUGS N HARMONY Featuring Eazy-E**	$3	▮	Ruthless 5540
12/23/95+	**45**	12		4 **Just Tah Let U Know**............S:22 *(radio mix) / The Muthaphu**in' Real*	$3	▮	Ruthless 5532
				EBONYS, The R&B **'71**			
				R&B vocal group from Camden, New Jersey: Jenny Holmes, David Beasley, James Tuten and Clarence Vaughan.			
6/12/71	**51**	7		1 **You're The Reason Why**............*Sexy Ways*	$8		Philadelphia I. 3503
7/7/73	**68**	6		2 **It's Forever**............*Sexy Ways*	$8		Philadelphia I. 3529
				ECHOES, The BUB **'61**			
				White vocal trio from Brooklyn, New York: Tommy Duffy, Harry Doyle and Tom Morrissey.			
3/6/61	**12**	12		1 **Baby Blue**............*Boomerang* first released on SRG 101 in 1960 ($200)	$25		Seg-Way 103
6/12/61	**88**	3		2 **Sad Eyes (Don't You Cry)**............*It's Rainin'*	$25		Seg-Way 106
				ECKSTINE, Billy MEM/POP/R&B/LP **'50**			
				Born on 7/8/14 in Pittsburgh, Pennsylvania. Died of heart failure on 3/8/93 (age 78). R&B singer/guitarist/trumpeter. One of the most distictive baritones in popular music. Nicknamed "Mr. B." His son Ed was the president of Mercury Records. Had six gold singles from 1945-51, including "My Foolish Heart," "I Apologize" and "I Wanna Be Loved."			
3/10/56	**76**	4		1 **The Bitter With The Sweet**............T:76 *Grapevine* **Hugo Winterhalter** (orch.)	$15		RCA Victor 6436
7/29/57	**82**	7		2 **Passing Strangers**............T:82 *The Door Is Open* **SARAH VAUGHAN & BILLY ECKSTINE**	$12		Mercury 71122
				ECSTASY, PASSION & PAIN R&B/BUB **'74**			
				R&B-dance group from New York: Barbara Roy (vocals, guitar), Billy Gardner (organ), Alan Tizer (percussion), Joseph Williams (bass) and Althea "Cookie" Smith (drums).			
7/6/74	**93**	4		1 **Good Things Don't Last Forever**............*Born To Lose You*	$6		Roulette 7156
10/19/74	**52**	8		2 **Ask Me**............*I'll Take The Blame*	$6		Roulette 7159
3/29/75	**48**	6		3 **One Beautiful Day**............*Try To Believe Me*	$6		Roulette 7163
6/5/76	**98**	2		4 **Touch And Go**............*I'll Do Anything For You* **ECSTASY, PASSION & PAIN FEATURING BARBARA ROY**	$6		Roulette 7182
				EDDIE, John LP **'86**			
				Born in 1959 in Virginia; raised in New Jersey. Pop-rock singer/songwriter.			
6/7/86	**52**	10		**Jungle Boy**............*Mary's Ghost*	$4	■	Columbia 05858
				EDDIE and BETTY **'59**			
				Black husband-and-wife pop-jazz piano and vocal duo: Eddie and Betty Cole. Eddie is an older brother of **Nat King Cole**, who made his recording debut with Eddie Cole's Solid Swingers in 1936 on Decca. Eddie played "The Baron" on TV's *Bourbon Street Beat*.			
6/29/59	**87**	4		**Sweet Someone**............*Saturday Night Fish Fry* first released on Six Thousand 601 in 1957 ($20) and then on Lark 4512 in 1959 ($15)	$15		Warner 5054
				EDDIE & DUTCH **'70**			
				Comedy duo from Chicago, Illinois: Eddie Mascari and Erwin "Dutch" Wenzlaff. Wrote **The Mark IV** 1959 novelty hit "I Got A Wife."			
4/4/70	**52**	7		**My Wife, The Dancer**............*Can't Help Lovin' That Girl* [N]	$6		Ivanhoe 502
				EDDIE AND THE CRUISERS — see CAFFERTY, John			
				EDDIE AND THE TIDE **'85**			
				Rock group from Berkeley, California: Eddie Rice (vocals), Johnny Perri (guitar), Cazz McCaslin (keyboards), George Diebold (bass) and Scott Mason (drums).			
9/21/85	**85**	2		**One In A Million**............*Looking For Excitement*	$4		Atco 99617

DEBUT	PEAK	WKS	Gold	A-side (Chart Hit)	B-side	$	Sym	Label & Number
				 **EDDY, Duane** ★158★ BUB/AC/C&W/LP **'58** Born on 4/26/38 in Corning, New York. Began playing guitar at age five. At age 13, moved to Tucson, then to Coolidge, Arizona. To Phoenix in 1955; began long association with producer/songwriter **Lee Hazlewood**. First recorded as Jimmy & Duane (Jimmy Delbridge) in 1955 on Hazlewood's label, Eb X. Preston. Eddy's backing band, The Rebels, included top sessionmen: pianist Larry Knechtel (later with **Bread**); saxmen Plas Johnson, Jim Horn and Steve Douglas (died on 4/19/93, age 55); guitarists **Al Casey**, his wife Corki Casey and **Donnie Owens**; and drummers Jimmy Troxel and Mike Bermani. Billed on most of his records as: **DUANE EDDY His 'Twangy' Guitar And The Rebels**. Appeared in movies *Because They're Young*, *A Thunder Of Drums*, *The Wild Westerners*, *The Savage Seven* and *Kona Coast*. Married to **Jessi Colter** from 1961-68. Eddy originated the "twangy" guitar sound with his '56 red Gretsch 6120 guitar. Rock 'n' roll's all-time #1 instrumentalist. Inducted into the Rock and Roll Hall of Fame in 1994. Also see **Ray Sharpe**, **Donnie Owens**, **B.J. Thomas** and **Foreigner**.				
				1)Because They're Young 2)Rebel-'Rouser 3)Forty Miles Of Bad Road 4)(Dance With The) Guitar Man 5)Cannonball				
3/17/58	72	3		1 **Moovin' N' Groovin'**	T:72 *Up And Down* [I]	$30		Jamie 1101
6/30/58	6	14		2 **Rebel-'Rouser** The Sharps (later known as **The Rivingtons**, rebel yells); a few early pressings show the fictitious note "From the Production Rebel-Rouser Starring John Buck"	S:6 / H:6 / A:14 *Stalkin'* [I]	$30		Jamie 1104
8/25/58	27	8		3 **Ramrod** different version released in 1957 on Ford 500 as by Duane Eddy and His Rock-A-Billies ($1500)	S:27 / H:28 *The Walker* [I]	$25		Jamie 1109
11/3/58	15	12		4 **Cannonball**	*Mason Dixon Lion* [I]	$25		Jamie 1111
1/19/59	23	13		5 **The Lonely One** all of above from the album *Have 'Twangy' Guitar-Will Travel*	*Detour* [I]	$25		Jamie 1117
3/30/59	30	9		6 **"Yep!"**	*Three-30-Blues* [I]	$25	■	Jamie 1122
6/15/59	9	15		7 **Forty Miles Of Bad Road /**	[I]			
6/29/59	46	8		8 **The Quiet Three**	[I]	$20	■	Jamie 1126
10/5/59	37	8		9 **Some Kind-A Earthquake /** the shortest (1:17) record to chart in the Top 40	[I]			
9/28/59	59	9		10 **First Love, First Tears**	[I]	$20	■	Jamie 1130
12/28/59+	26	9		11 **Bonnie Came Back** traditional Scottish tune "My Bonnie Lies Over The Ocean"	*Lost Island* [I]	$20	■	Jamie 1144
3/21/60	45	7		12 **Shazam!** titled after an expression by comic book hero Captain Marvel	*The Secret Seven* [I]	$20	■	Jamie 1151
5/23/60	4	15		13 **Because They're Young** above 2 from the movie *Because They're Young* starring Dick Clark and Tuesday Weld	*Rebel Walk* [I]	$20	■	Jamie 1156
8/22/60	78	6		14 **Kommotion**	*Theme For Moon Children* [I]	$15	■	Jamie 1163
10/10/60	27	9		15 **Peter Gunn** written by **Henry Mancini**; title song from the TV series starring Craig Stevens; also see #28 below	*Along The Navajo Trail* [I]	$15	■	Jamie 1168
12/19/60+	18	12		16 **"Pepe"** title song from the movie starring Cantinflas; issued with 2 different picture sleeves	*Lost Friend* [I]	$15	■	Jamie 1175
3/20/61	39	7		17 **Theme From Dixie** Anita Kerr Singers & The Jordanaires (vocals); written in 1860	*Gidget Goes Hawaiian* (#101) [I]	$15	■	Jamie 1183
5/29/61	84	3		18 **Ring Of Fire** title song from the movie starring David Janssen	*Bobbie* [I]	$15	■	Jamie 1187
7/17/61	87	2		19 **Drivin' Home**	*Tammy* [I]	$15	■	Jamie 1195
8/28/61	50	5		20 **My Blue Heaven** #1 hit for both **Gene Austin** and Paul Whiteman in 1927	*Along Came Linda* [I]	$15	■	Jamie 1200
4/21/62	78	5		21 **Deep In The Heart Of Texas** #3 hit in 1942 for Alvino Rey & His Orchestra	*Saints And Sinners* [I]	$15	■	RCA Victor 7999
7/7/62	33	9		22 **The Ballad Of Paladin** theme from the TV series *Have Gun-Will Travel* starring Richard Boone	*The Wild Westerners* [I]	$15	■	RCA Victor 8047
10/6/62	12	16		23 **(Dance With The) Guitar Man**	*Stretchin' Out*	$15	■	RCA Victor 8087
2/9/63	28	9		24 **Boss Guitar**	*The Desert Rat*	$12	■	RCA Victor 8131
5/18/63	82	5		25 **Lonely Boy, Lonely Guitar**	*Joshin'*	$12	■	RCA Victor 8180
8/24/63	93	2		26 **Your Baby's Gone Surfin'** **Darlene Love** & **The Blossoms** (labeled as The Rebelettes, vocals, above 4)	*Shuckin'*	$12	■	RCA Victor 8214
1/4/64	97	2		27 **The Son Of Rebel Rouser** all of above (except #3, 11, 13, 15-17 & 20-22) written or co-written by Eddy	*The Story Of Three Loves* [I]	$12	■	RCA Victor 8276
5/17/86	50	11		28 **Peter Gunn** **THE ART OF NOISE Featuring Duane Eddy**	*Something Always Happens* (Art Of Noise) [I-R]	$6	■	China 42986
				EDELMAN, Randy BUB/AC **'75** Born on 6/10/47 in Paterson, New Jersey. Pop singer/songwriter/pianist. Married to **Jackie DeShannon**.				
3/8/75	92	4		**Everybody Wants To Find A Bluebird**	*Pistol Packin' Melody*	$5		20th Century 2155
				EDEN'S CRUSH LP **'01** Female pop-dance vocal group: Ana Maria Lombo (from Columbia), Ivette Sosa (from New Jersey), Maile Misajon (from California), Nicole Scherzinger (from Hawaii) and Rosanna Tavarez (from New York). Group assembled for TV series *PopStars*.				
3/31/01	8	14	●	**Get Over Yourself**	S:❶[2] *(2 versions) / (5 personal messages)*	$4	★	143/London 35063
				EDISON LIGHTHOUSE **'70** Studio group from England. Featuring lead singer **Tony Burrows** (also of **The Brotherhood Of Man**, **First Class**, **The Pipkins** and **White Plains**).				
2/21/70	5	13	●	1 **Love Grows (Where My Rosemary Goes)**	*Every Lonely Day*	$6		Bell 858
1/9/71	72	6		2 **It's Up To You Petula**	*Let's Make It Up*	$6		Bell 960
				EDMONDS, Kevon — see AFTER 7				
				EDMUNDS, Dave ROK/BUB/LP **'71** Born on 4/15/44 in Cardiff, Wales. Rock and roll singer/songwriter/guitarist/producer. Formed Love Sculpture in 1967. Formed rockabilly band **Rockpile** in 1976. Produced for Shakin' Stevens, Brinsley Schwarz and **Stray Cats**.				
12/26/70+	4	12		1 **I Hear You Knocking** #2 R&B hit for Smiley Lewis in 1955	*Black Bill*	$8		MAM 3601
5/1/71	75	4		2 **I'm Comin' Home**	*Country Roll*	$7		MAM 3608
9/1/79	65	6		3 **Girls Talk** written by **Elvis Costello**	*The Creature From The Black Lagoon*	$5		Swan Song 71001

DEBUT	PEAK	WKS	Gold	A-side (Chart Hit)...B-side	$	Sym	Label & Number
				EDMUNDS, Dave — Cont'd			
5/9/81	**54**	8		4 **Almost Saturday Night** ... *You'll Never Get Me Up (In One Of Those)*	$5	■	Swan Song 72000
5/14/83	**39**	15		5 **Slipping Away** ... *Don't Call Me Tonight* written and produced by **Jeff Lynne** (**ELO**)	$4		Columbia 03877
4/20/85	**91**	2		6 **High School Nights** ... *Porky's Revenge* from the movie *Porky's Revenge!* starring Dan Monahan	$4	■	Columbia 04762
				EDSELS, The '61 Black doo-wop group from Campbell, Ohio: George Jones, Marshall Sewell, James Reynolds, and brothers Larry and Harry Green.			
5/1/61	**21**	11		**Rama Lama Ding Dong** ... *Bells* original version released on Dub 2843 in 1958 as "Lama Rama Ding Dong" ($70), then as "Rama Lama Ding Dong" ($50)	$25		Twin 700
				EDWARD BEAR BUB/LP '73 Pop trio from Toronto, Ontario, Canada: Larry Evoy (vocals, drums), Roger Ellis (guitar) and Paul Weldon (keyboards). Took name from a character in *Winnie The Pooh.*			
5/30/70	**68**	4		1 **You, Me And Mexico** ... *Sinking Ship*	$6		Capitol 2801
12/16/72+	**3**	18	●	2 **Last Song** ... AC[2] *Best Friend*	$5	■	Capitol 3452
4/14/73	**37**	12		3 **Close Your Eyes** ... *Cachet County*	$5	■	Capitol 3581
				EDWARDS, Bobby C&W '61 Born Robert Moncrief on 1/18/26 in Anniston, Alabama. Country singer.			
8/28/61	**11**	17		1 **You're The Reason** ... *I'm A Fool For Loving You* Four Young Men (backing vocals)	$12		Crest 1075
1/13/62	**71**	6		2 **What's The Reason** ... *Walk Away Slowly*	$10		Capitol 4674
				EDWARDS, Dennis R&B/LP '84 Born on 2/3/43 in Birmingham, Alabama. Lead singer of **The Contours** in 1967. Lead singer of **The Temptations** from 1968-77, 1980-84 and 1987-present.			
4/28/84	**72**	6		**Don't Look Any Further** ... *I Thought I Could Handle It* **DENNIS EDWARDS (featuring Siedah Garrett)**	$4		Gordy 1715
				EDWARDS, Jimmy '58 Born James Bullington on 2/9/33 in Senath, Missouri. Rock and roll singer/songwriter.			
1/20/58	**78**	3		**Love Bug Crawl** ... T:78 *Honey Lovin'* a different version released in 1957 on Wednesday Records as by Jim Bullington ($400)	$35		Mercury 71209
				EDWARDS, Jonathan BUB/C&W/LP '72 Born on 7/28/46 in Aitkin, Minnesota; raised in Virginia. Pop-country singer/songwriter. Formed bluegrass band Sugar Creek in 1965.			
11/13/71+	**4**	16	●	**Sunshine** ... *Emma* first released on Atco 8021 in 1971 ($10)	$6		Capricorn 8021
				EDWARDS, Tom '57 DJ at WERE Radio in Cleveland, Ohio, 1951-59. Owner of Record Heaven record store in Cleveland. Died on 7/24/81 (age 58).			
2/2/57	**57**	5		1 **What Is A Teenage Girl?** / T:57 [N-S]			
2/9/57	**96**	1		2 **What Is A Teenage Boy?** ... T:96 [N-S] Mort Garson (orch., above 2); both are parodies of the 1951 hit "What Is A Boy" (also see **Steve Allen**'s "What Is A Wife")	$15		Coral 61773
	★398★			**EDWARDS, Tommy** MEM/POP/R&B '58 Born on 2/17/22 in Richmond, Virginia. Died on 10/23/69 (age 47). Black Adult Contemporary singer/pianist/songwriter. Began performing at age nine. First recorded for Top in 1949. *1)It's All In The Game 2)Please Mr. Sun 3)Love Is All We Need*			
8/18/58	❶[6]	22	●	1 **It's All In The Game** / RB[3] S:❶[3] / H:❶[6] melody written in 1912 by U.S. Vice President Charles Dawes (under Calvin Coolidge, 1925-29); original version was a #18 pop hit in 1951 on MGM 11035 ($25)			
10/20/58	**61**	3		2 **Please Love Me Forever** ...	$15		MGM 12688
10/27/58	**15**	16		3 **Love Is All We Need** ... *Mr. Music Man*	$15		MGM 12722
2/16/59	**11**	13		4 **Please Mr. Sun** / original version was a #22 pop hit in 1952 on MGM 11134 ($25); #6 hit for **Johnnie Ray** in 1952			
3/2/59	**27**	12		5 **The Morning Side Of The Mountain** ... original version was a #24 pop hit in 1951 on MGM 10989 ($25); #16 hit for Paul Weston in 1951	$15		MGM 12757
5/18/59	**26**	8		6 **My Melancholy Baby** / this song charted in 6 separate decades from 1915-1962			
6/1/59	**86**	3		7 **It's Only The Good Times** ...	$15		MGM 12794
8/10/59	**53**	10		8 **I've Been There** /			
8/24/59	**100**	1		9 **I Looked At Heaven** ...	$15		MGM 12814
11/16/59+	**47**	9		10 **(New In) The Ways Of Love** /			
11/2/59	**65**	8		11 **Honestly And Truly** ...	$12		MGM 12837
2/22/60	**45**	8		12 **Don't Fence Me In** ... *I'm Building Castles Again* #1 hit for **Bing Crosby** & The Andrews Sisters in 1944	$12		MGM 12871
5/23/60	**18**	13		13 **I Really Don't Want To Know** ... *Unloved* #11 hit for **Les Paul & Mary Ford** in 1954	$12	■	MGM 12890
10/10/60	**78**	2		14 **It's Not The End Of Everything** ... *Blue Heartaches* written by **Bill Anderson**; **LeRoy Holmes** (orch., all of above)	$12		MGM 12916
				EDWARDS, Vincent BUB/AC/LP '62 Born Vincent Edward Zoine on 7/7/28 in Brooklyn, New York. Died of cancer on 3/11/96 (age 67). Actor/singer. Star of TV's *Ben Casey.*			
7/7/62	**68**	6		1 **Why Did You Leave Me?** *[VINCE EDWARDS]* ... *Squeelin Parrot (Twist)* recorded by **Perry Como** in 1952 (RCA Victor 4687)	$15		Russ-Fi 7001
8/11/62	**72**	2		2 **Don't Worry 'Bout Me** ... *And Now* **Dick Jacobs** (orch.); #5 hit for Hal Kemp in 1939	$10	■	Decca 31413

DEBUT	PEAK	WKS	Gold	A-side (Chart Hit)..........B-side	$	Sym	Label & Number
				EELS ROK/LP **'96**			
				Rock trio formed in Los Angeles, California: Mark Everett (vocals, guitar), Tommy Walter (bass) and Butch Norton (drums).			
8/31/96	39[A]	15		**Novocaine For The Soul** ....MR[2] from the album *Beautiful Freak* on Dreamworks 50001			album cut
				E-40 R&B/LP **'97**			
				Born Earl Stevens in Vallejo, California. Male rapper. Member of **The Click**.			
7/16/94	94	2		1 **Captain Save A Hoe** ....S:66 *(remix) / Practice Looking Hard* **E-40 (Featuring The Click)** first week charted as "Captain Save Them Thoe" (clean version released to radio only)	$4	▮	Sick Wid' It/Jive 42230
2/25/95	71	14		2 **1-Luv** ....S:36 *(studio remix) / Fed / 40 Flava* **E-40 (Featuring Leviti)**	$4	▮	Sick Wid' It/Jive 42289
6/24/95	44	13		3 **Sprinkle Me** ....S:33 *(remix)* **E-40 (Featuring Suga T)**	$4	▮	Sick Wid' It/Jive 42298
2/1/97	29	14		4 **Things'll Never Change /** S:17 **E-40 featuring Bo-Rock** samples "The Way It Is" by **Bruce Hornsby**			
2/1/97		14		5 **Rappers' Ball** .... **E-40 featuring Too $hort and K-Ci** samples "Playboy $hort" by **Too $hort**	$4	▮	Sick Wid' It/Jive 42436
				EGAN, Walter LP **'78**			
				Born on 7/12/48 in Jamaica, New York. Pop-rock singer/guitarist/songwriter.			
6/11/77	82	6		1 **Only The Lucky** ....*I'd Rather Have Fun* produced by **Lindsey Buckingham** and **Stevie Nicks**	$5		Columbia 10531
5/27/78	8	22	●	2 **Magnet And Steel** ....*Tunnel O' Love* **Lindsey Buckingham** and **Stevie Nicks** (backing vocals)	$5		Columbia 10719
10/14/78	55	7		3 **Hot Summer Nights** ....*She's So Tough*	$5		Columbia 10824
4/9/83	46	10		4 **Fool Moon Fire** ....*Tammy Ann*	$4	■	Backstreet 52200
				EIFFEL 65 LP **'00**			
				Male dance trio from Italy: Jeffrey Jey, Maurizio Lobina and Gabry Ponte.			
12/11/99+	6	20		**Blue (Da Ba Dee)** ....A:6 *(3 versions)* "45": Republic 156662; B-side: "Move Your Body"	$6	T[V]	Republic 156638
				8TH DAY, The R&B/LP **'71**			
				R&B group from Detroit, Michigan: Lynn Harter (vocals), Melvin Davis (vocals, drums), Michael Anthony and Bruce Nazarian (guitars), Carole Stallings (electric violin), Anita Sherman (vibes), Jerry Paul (percussion) and Tony Newton (bass).			
5/15/71	11	13	●	1 **She's Not Just Another Woman** ....*I Can't Fool Myself*	$6		Invictus 9087
9/18/71	28	11		2 **You've Got To Crawl (Before You Walk)** ....*It's Instrumental To Be Free*	$6		Invictus 9098
1/8/72	79	4		3 **If I Could See The Light** ....*(instrumental)*	$6		Invictus 9107
				EIGHTH WONDER **'89**			
				Pop-dance group from England: Patsy Kensit (vocals), Jamie Kensit (guitar), Geoff Beauchamp (bass) and Steve Grantley (drums). Patsy acted in the movies *Absolute Beginners* and *Lethal Weapon II*; married to Dan Donovan (**Big Audio Dynamite**) from 1988-91, Jim Kerr (**Simple Minds**) from 1992-96 and Liam Gallagher (**Oasis**) from 1997-2000.			
11/19/88+	56	16		1 **Cross My Heart** ....*Let Me In*	$3	■	WTG 08036
4/1/89	84	5		2 **Baby Baby** ....*My Baby's Heartbeat*	$3		WTG 68610
				EIGHT SECONDS **'87**			
				Pop-rock group from Canada: Andres del Castillo (vocals), Marc Parent (guitar), Frank Levin (keyboards), March Cesare (bass) and Scott Milks (drums).			
1/31/87	72	8		**Kiss You (When It's Dangerous)** ....*Land Of The Monster*	$3	■	Polydor 885352
				812 SOULJAZ **'01**			
				Rap trio from Indianapolis, Indiana.			
4/21/01	60[S]	7		**Did That!** ....*(instrumental) / Miss Me / Penitentiary Chances* (w/**Rappin 4-Tay**) **812 Souljaz Feat. Whoo Whee** samples the opening riff of "Dragnet"	$6	★	Lay It Down 2011
				ELASTICA ROK/LP **'95**			
				Rock group from London, England: Justine Frischmann (vocals), Donna Matthews (guitar), Annie Holland (bass) and Justin Welch (drums). Holland left in the fall of 1995.			
3/25/95	53	20		1 **Connection** ....A:42 *Gloria*	$4	▮	DGC 19385
7/22/95	67	9		2 **Stutter** ....A:57 *Rockunroll / 2:1 / Annie*	$5	★	DGC 22001
				ELBERT, Donnie R&B/BUB/LP **'71**			
				Born on 5/25/36 in New Orleans, Louisiana; raised in Buffalo, New York. Died on 1/26/89 (age 52). R&B singer/songwriter.			
7/8/57	61	6		1 **What Can I Do** ....T:61 *Hear My Plea*	$25		DeLuxe 6125
11/28/70	98	2		2 **Can't Get Over Losing You** ....*I Got To Get Myself Together*	$8		Rare Bullet 101
10/16/71	15	13		3 **Where Did Our Love Go** *That's If You Love Me*	$8		All Platinum 2330
1/22/72	92	4		4 **Sweet Baby** ....*Can't Get Over Losing You*	$8		All Platinum 2333
1/29/72	22	9		5 **I Can't Help Myself (Sugar Pie, Honey Bunch)** ....*Love Is Here And Now You're Gone*	$6		Avco 4587
				EL CHICANO BUB/LP **'70**			
				Latin group formed in Los Angeles, California. Core members: Mickey Lesperon (guitar), Andre Baeza (congas), Bobby Espinosa (organ), Freddie Sanchez (bass) and Johnny De Luna (drums). Singers included Ersi Arvizu, and brothers Rudy, Steve and Jerry Salas. Rudy and Steve Salas later formed **Tierra**.			
4/11/70	28	9		1 **Viva Tirado - Part I** ....*Part II* [I] first released on Gordo 703 in 1970 ($10)	$6		Kapp 2085
6/17/72	45	7		2 **Brown Eyed Girl** ....*Mas Zacate*	$5		Kapp 2173
11/17/73	40	10		3 **Tell Her She's Lovely** ....*(Se Fue Mi) Chachita*	$5		MCA 40104

DEBUT	PEAK	WKS	Gold	A-side (Chart Hit)...B-side	$	Sym	Label & Number

EL COCO — LP '78

Disco studio group led by producers Laurin Rinder and W. Michael Lewis.

DEBUT	PEAK	WKS	Gold	A-side (Chart Hit)...B-side	$	Sym	Label & Number
10/23/76	61	8		1 **Lets Get It Together** ...*Fait Le Chat (Do The Cat)* [I]	$6		AVI 115
11/26/77+	44	15		2 **Cocomotion** ...*Love To The World* [I]	$5		AVI 147
10/28/78	91	6		3 **Dancing In Paradise** ...*Love In Your Life*	$5		AVI 203

EL DORADOS, The — R&B '55

R&B vocal group from Chicago, Illinois: Pirkle Lee Moses (lead), Arthur Bassett, Louis Bradley, Jewel Jones and James Maddox. Moses died of a brain tumor on 12/16/2000 (age 63).

DEBUT	PEAK	WKS	Gold	A-side (Chart Hit)...B-side	$	Sym	Label & Number
10/15/55	17	11		**At My Front Door** ...RB[1] S:17 / T:35 *What's Buggin' You Baby*	$75		Vee-Jay 147

ELECTRIC BOYS — ROK/LP '90

Male rock group from Sweden: Conny Bloom (vocals), Franco Santunione (guitar), Andy Christell (bass) and Niclas Sigevall (drums).

DEBUT	PEAK	WKS	Gold	A-side (Chart Hit)...B-side	$	Sym	Label & Number
7/14/90	76	6		**All Lips N' Hips** ...*Halleluja! I'm On Fire*	$4	■	Atco 98973

ELECTRIC EXPRESS, The — '71

R&B-funk band produced by Slack Johnson.

DEBUT	PEAK	WKS	Gold	A-side (Chart Hit)...B-side	$	Sym	Label & Number
7/31/71	81	4		**It's The Real Thing - Pt. I** ...*Pt. II* [I]	$8		Linco 1001

ELECTRIC INDIAN, The — LP '69

Instrumental group assembled from top Philadelphia studio musicians. Some members later joined **MFSB**.

DEBUT	PEAK	WKS	Gold	A-side (Chart Hit)...B-side	$	Sym	Label & Number
8/2/69	16	11		1 **Keem-O-Sabe** ...*Broad Street* [I] — first released on Marmaduke 4001 in 1969 ($20)	$8		United Artists 50563
12/13/69	95	1		2 **Land Of 1000 Dances** ...*Geronimo* [I]	$7		United Artists 50613

ELECTRIC LIGHT ORCHESTRA ★110★ — BUB/AC/LP '79

Orchestral rock band formed in Birmingham, England, by Roy Wood (born on 11/8/46), Bev Bevan (born on 11/25/46) and **Jeff Lynne** (see #27 below) (**The Move**; born on 12/30/47). Wood left after first album, leaving Lynne as group's leader. Much personnel shuffling from then on. From a group size of eight in 1971, the 1986 ELO consisted of three members: Lynne (vocals, guitar, keyboards), Bevan (drums) and Richard Tandy (keyboards, guitar). Bevan also recorded with **Black Sabbath** in 1987. Lynne was a member of the supergroup **Traveling Wilburys**.

1)Don't Bring Me Down 2)Telephone Line 3)Shine A Little Love 4)Xanadu 5)Can't Get It Out Of My Head

DEBUT	PEAK	WKS	Gold	A-side (Chart Hit)...B-side	$	Sym	Label & Number
10/28/72	93	5		1 **Do Ya** ...*California Man* — **THE MOVE** — also see #10 below	$8		United Artists 50928
4/28/73	42	16		2 **Roll Over Beethoven** ...*Queen Of The Hours*	$6		United Artists 173
12/1/73+	53	11		3 **Showdown** ...*In An Old England Town* [I] — also see re-entry at #8 below	$6		United Artists 337
5/4/74	87	5		4 **Daybreaker** ...*Ma-Ma-Ma Belle* [I]	$6		United Artists 405
12/21/74+	9	16		5 **Can't Get It Out Of My Head** ...*Illusions In G Major*	$5	■	United Artists 573
11/15/75+	10	17		6 **Evil Woman** ...*10538 Overture*	$5		United Artists/Jet 729
3/13/76	14	14		7 **Strange Magic** ...*New World Rising*	$5	■	United Artists/Jet 770
8/7/76	59	7		8 **Showdown** ...*Daybreaker (live)* [R] — same version as #3 above	$5		United Artists/Jet 842
10/23/76+	13	18		9 **Livin' Thing** ...*Ma-Ma-Ma Belle*	$5		United Artists/Jet 888
2/5/77	24	12		10 **Do Ya** ...*Nightrider* [R] — new version of #1 above	$5		United Artists/Jet 939
6/11/77	7	23	●	11 **Telephone Line** ...*Poorboy (The Greenwood)* — some pressings issued on green vinyl (picture sleeve came only with this version)	$5	■	United Artists/Jet 1000
11/19/77+	13	15		12 **Turn To Stone** ...*Mister Kingdom*	$5	■	Jet 1099
2/18/78	17	16		13 **Sweet Talkin' Woman** ...*Fire On High*	$5	■	Jet 1145
6/24/78	35	12		14 **Mr. Blue Sky** ...*One Summer Dream*	$5		Jet 5050
10/28/78	75	4		15 **It's Over** ...*The Whale* — above 4 from the album *Out Of The Blue*	$5		Jet 5052
5/19/79	8	15		16 **Shine A Little Love** ...*Jungle*	$5	■	Jet 5057
8/4/79	4	15	●	17 **Don't Bring Me Down** *Dreaming Of 4000*	$5		Jet 5060
10/20/79	37	8		18 **Confusion** ...*Poker*	$5		Jet 5064
12/8/79+	39	11		19 **Last Train To London** ...*Down Home Town* — above 4 from the album *Discovery*	$5		Jet 5067
5/24/80	16	15	●	20 **I'm Alive** ...*Drum Dreams*	$4	■	MCA 41246
8/2/80	13	16		21 **All Over The World** ...*Drum Dreams*	$4	■	MCA 41289
8/9/80	8	17		22 **Xanadu** ...*Whenever You're Away From Me* (Newton-John & Gene Kelly) — **OLIVIA NEWTON-JOHN/ELECTRIC LIGHT ORCHESTRA** — above 3 from the movie *Xanadu* starring Newton-John	$4		MCA 41285
7/25/81	10	19		23 **Hold On Tight** ...*When Time Stood Still*	$4		Jet 02408
10/24/81	38	11		24 **Twilight** ...*Julie Don't Live Here*	$4		Jet 02559
6/25/83	19	13		25 **Rock 'N' Roll Is King** ...*After All*	$4		Jet 03964
10/1/83	86	2		26 **Four Little Diamonds** ...*Letter From Spain* — **ELO** (above 4)	$4		Jet 04130
8/18/84	85	3		27 **Video!** ...*Sooner Or Later* — **JEFF LYNNE** — from the movie *Electric Dreams* starring Virginia Madsen	$4		Virgin/Epic 04570
2/1/86	18	15		28 **Calling America** ...S:19 / A:21 *Caught In A Trap* — all of above written (except #2) and produced by **Jeff Lynne**	$3	■	CBS Associated 05766

DEBUT	PEAK	WKS	Gold	A-side (Chart Hit)........B-side	$	Sym	Label & Number
				ELECTRIC PRUNES, The BUB/LP **'67**			
				Psychedelic-rock group from Seattle, Washington: James Lowe (vocals), Ken Williams and James Spagnola (guitars), Mark Tulin (bass) and Preston Ritter (drums).			
12/10/66+	11	14		1 **I Had Too Much To Dream (Last Night)**........*Luvin*	$20		Reprise 0532
4/1/67	27	8		2 **Get Me To The World On Time**........*Are You Lovin' Me More*	$20		Reprise 0564
				ELECTRONIC ROK/LP **'90**			
				Dance duo from Manchester, England: Bernard Sumner (of **New Order**) and Johnny Marr (of The Smiths).			
3/31/90	38	12		**Getting Away With It**........A:33 / S:39 *Lucky Bag*	$4	▮[V]	Warner 19880
				ELEGANTS, The **'58**			
				White doo-wop from Staten Island, New York: Vito Picone (lead), Arthur Venosa, Frank Tardogna, Carmen Romano and James Moschella. All were veterans of other groups. Also see **The Barbarians**' "Moulty."			
7/21/58	❶[1]	19	●	**Little Star**........RB[4] H:❶[1] / S:2 *Getting Dizzy*	$40		Apt 25005
				tune adapted from Mozart's (age 5) "Twinkle Twinkle Little Star"			
				ELEPHANT'S MEMORY BUB/LP **'70**			
				Jazz-rock group from New York: Michal Shapiro (female vocals), Stan Bronstein (male vocals, sax), Richard Ayers (guitar), Richard Sussman (piano), Myron Yules (trombone), John Ward (bass) and Rick Frank (drums). Backing band for **John Lennon**.			
8/8/70	50	14		**Mongoose**........*I Couldn't Dream*	$8	■	Metromedia 182
				ELEVENTH HOUR, The **'75**			
				Disco group featuring lead singers Michael Gray and Kenneth Kerr.			
4/6/74	94	2		1 **So Good**........*My Bed*	$5		20th Century 2076
8/30/75	55	15		2 **Hollywood Hot**........*Hollywood Hotter* [I]	$5		20th Century 2215
				above 2 written and produced by **Bob Crewe**			
				ELGART, Larry, And His Manhattan Swing Orchestra LP **'82**			
				Born on 3/20/22 in New London, Connecticut. Alto saxophonist. Brother of **Les Elgart**.			
6/5/82	31	12		**Hooked On Swing**........*Hooked On The Big Bands* [I]	$5		RCA 13219
				In the Mood/Cherokee/American Patrol/Sing, Sing, Sing/Don't Be That Way/Little Brown Jug/Opus #1/ Zing Went the Strings of My Heart/String of Pearls			
				ELGART, Les, & his Orch. LP **'56**			
				Born on 8/3/18 in New Haven, Connecticut. Died on 7/29/95 (age 76). Trumpeter/bandleader. Brother of **Larry Elgart**.			
4/7/56	56	10		**Main Title - Golden Arm**........T:56 *D.J. Jamboree* [I]	$15		Columbia 40664
				from the Otto Preminger movie *The Man With The Golden Arm* starring **Frank Sinatra**			
				ELGINS, The **'66**			
				R&B vocal group from Detroit, Michigan: Saundra Mallett Edwards, Johnny Dawson, Cleotha Miller, Robert Fleming and Norbert McClean. Originally called The Downbeats.			
3/19/66	72	8		1 **Darling Baby /**			
2/19/66	92	4		2 **Put Yourself In My Place**........	$20		V.I.P. 25029
				V.I.P. 25029 first released as by The Downbeats ($200)			
10/22/66	50	8		3 **Heaven Must Have Sent You**........*Stay In My Lonely Arms*	$20		V.I.P. 25037
7/29/67	92	1		4 **It's Been A Long Long Time**........*I Understand My Man*	$20		V.I.P. 25043
				ELLEDGE, Jimmy C&W **'61**			
				Born on 1/8/43 in Nashville, Tennessee. Discovered by **Chet Atkins**. Regular at The Pillars nightclub in Biloxi, Mississippi.			
11/13/61+	22	14		**Funny How Time Slips Away**........*Hey Jimmy Joe John Jim Jack*	$12		RCA Victor 7946
				written by **Willie Nelson**; produced by **Chet Atkins**			
				ELLIMAN, Yvonne BUB/AC/LP **'78**			
				Born on 12/29/51 in Honolulu, Hawaii. Played "Mary Magdalene" for the concept album and in the rock opera and movie *Jesus Christ Superstar*. Backing singer for **Eric Clapton**.			
4/24/71	28	10		1 **I Don't Know How To Love Him**........*Overture: Jesus Christ Superstar* (Alan Doggett)	$6		Decca 32785
9/25/71	92	6		2 **Everything's Alright**........*Heaven On Their Minds* (Various Artists)	$6		Decca 32870
				above 2 from *Jesus Christ Superstar* A Rock Opera			
10/2/76	14	19		3 **Love Me**........*(I Don't Know Why) I Keep Hangin' On*	$5		RSO 858
3/19/77	15	16		4 **Hello Stranger**........AC[4] *She'll Be The Home*	$5		RSO 871
1/28/78	❶[1]	22	●	5 **If I Can't Have You** *Good Sign*	$5		RSO 884
				from the movie *Saturday Night Fever* starring **John Travolta**; #3 & 5: written by the **Bee Gees**			
12/23/78+	59	6		6 **Moment By Moment**........*Sailing Ships*	$5	■	RSO 915
				title song from the movie starring **John Travolta**			
10/13/79	34	13		7 **Love Pains**........*Rock Me Slowly*	$5		RSO 1007
				ELLIOTT, Alecia C&W **'00**			
				Born on 12/25/82 in Muscle Shoals, Alabama. Female country singer.			
11/6/99+	42[S]	17		**I'm Diggin' It**........*(dance mix)*	$4	★[V]	MCA 172121
				ELLIOTT, Missy "Misdemeanor" ★206★ R&B/LP **'02**			
				Born on 7/1/71 in Portsmouth, Virginia. Female rapper/singer/songwriter/producer. Former member of the group Sista. Also see **Raven-Symoné**, **702**, **SWV** and **Timbaland**.			
				1)Work It 2)Hot Boyz 3)Get Ur Freak On 4)Gossip Folks 5)Sock It 2 Me			
7/12/97	6	21	▲	1 **Not Tonight**........S:3 / A:39 *(instrumental)*	$3	▮	Undeas/Big Beat 98019
				LIL' KIM Featuring Da Brat, Left Eye, Missy "Misdemeanor" Elliott and Angie Martinez			
				samples "Ladies Night" by **Kool & The Gang**; from the movie *Nothing To Lose* starring Martin Lawrence			

DEBUT	PEAK	WKS	Gold	A-side (Chart Hit)...B-side	$	Sym	Label & Number
				ELLIOTT, Missy "Misdemeanor" — Cont'd			
10/18/97	12	20	●	2 **Sock It 2 Me** / S:7 / A:36 **MISSY "MISDEMEANOR" ELLIOTT Featuring Da Brat** samples "Ready Or Not Here I Come" by **The Delfonics**			
7/5/97	51^{A}	9		3 **The Rain (Supa Dupa Fly)** samples "I Can't Stand The Rain" by **Ann Peebles**	$3	▮	EastWest 64144
6/27/98	5	23	●	4 **Make It Hot** ...S:2 / A:39 *(2 versions)* **NICOLE Featuring Missy "Misdemeanor" Elliott and Mocha**	$3	▮	The Gold Mind 64110
11/7/98+	7	20	●	5 **Trippin'** ...S:6 / A:49 *(**Missy** mix)* **TOTAL (Feat. Missy Elliott)**	$4	★	Bad Boy 79185
12/5/98	92	4		6 **Here We Come** ...A:75 **TIMBALAND featuring Missy "Misdemeanor" Elliott & Magoo** from the album *Tim's Bio: Life From Da Bassment* on Blackground 92815			album cut
5/15/99	90	6		7 **She's A Bitch** ...*(3 versions)*	$6	T	The Gold Mind 63751
7/24/99	64	14		8 **All N My Grill** ...A:54 **MISSY "MISDEMEANOR" ELLIOTT (Featuring Big Boi of Outkast & Nicole)**			album cut
10/2/99	26^{S}	10		9 **Ya Di Ya** ...BUB:124 *Take My Number Down* **GINA THOMPSON featuring Missy "Misdemeanor" Elliott**	$4	★	EastWest 64033
11/27/99+	5	21	▲	10 **Hot Boyz** ...RB^{6} S:2 / A:24 *U Can't Resist* (w/**Juvenile** & **B.G.**) **MISSY "MISDEMEANOR" ELLIOTT [featuring NAS, EVE & Q-TIP]** **Lil' Mo** (vocal ad libs); #7, 8 & 10: from the album *Da Real World* on The Gold Mind 62232	$4	★	The Gold Mind 64029
6/24/00	86	7		11 **Take That** ...S:10 *(instrumental) / (3 album snippets)* **TORREY CARTER (Featuring Missy "Misdemeanor" Elliott)**	$5	★	The Gold Mind 67036
12/16/00+	68	13		12 **Is That Your Chick** ...S:55 / A:62 *(2 versions) / All Types Of S**** **MEMPHIS BLEEK (feat. Jay-Z and Missy Elliott)**	$6	T	Roc-A-Fella 562865
3/24/01	7	24		13 **Get Ur Freak On** ...A:6 / S:46 *(4 versions)*	$6	T	Goldmind 67190
5/19/01	74^{S}	1		14 **Lick Shots** ...*(2 versions) / Get Ur Freak On (2 mixes)*	$7	T	Goldmind 67221
7/14/01	15	21		15 **One Minute Man** ...A:13 **MISSY "MISDEMEANOR" ELLIOTT (featuring Ludacris)**			album cut
11/24/01	28	12		16 **Son Of A Gun (I Betcha Think This Song Is About You)** ...A:26 *(3 versions)* **JANET Featuring Missy Elliott and P. Diddy with Carly Simon** samples "You're So Vain" by **Carly Simon**	$6	T	Virgin 46171
12/15/01+	45	20		17 **Take Away** ...A:44 **MISSY "MISDEMEANOR" ELLIOTT (feat. Ginuwine & introducing Tweet)** #13-15 & 17: from the album *Miss E...So Addictive* on Goldmind 62639			album cut
3/9/02	98	3		18 **Knoc** ...S:39 *(4 versions)* **KNOC-TURN'AL w/ Dr. Dre and Missy "Misdemeanor" Elliott**	$6	T	LA Confidential 67290
8/17/02	60	15		19 **Burnin' Up** ...A:56 **FAITH EVANS Featuring Missy "Misdemeanor" Elliott** from the album *Faithfully* on Bad Boy 73041			album cut
9/7/02	41^{S}	7		20 **Crew Deep** ...*(2 versions) / Imagine* **SKILLZ feat. Missy "Misdemeanor" Elliott and Kandi** samples "Rapper's Delight" by **Sugarhill Gang**	$6	T	Rawkus 113991
9/14/02	2^{10}	25		21 **Work It** RB^{5} A:2 / S:10 *(4 versions - 2 w/**50 Cent**) / P***ycat*	$6	T	Goldmind 67340
12/28/02+	8	20		22 **Gossip Folks** ...A:6 / S:11 *(4 versions)* **MISSY ELLIOTT (Featuring Ludacris)** samples "Double Dutch Bus" by **Frankie Smith**; all of above (except #9, 16 & 19) written or co-written by Elliott	$6	T	Goldmind 67356
				ELLIS, Joey B., And Tynetta Hare '91 Rapper/producer Ellis was born in Philadelphia, Pennsylvania. Female singer Hare was born in Charlotte, North Carolina (member of Soft Touch).			
12/8/90+	66	8		**Go For It! (Heart And Fire)** ...S:38 *(2 versions)* produced by **M.C. Hammer**; from the movie *Rocky V* starring Sylvester Stallone	$3	▮	Capitol 44667
				ELLIS, Ray, And His Orchestra '61 Born on 7/28/23 in Philadelphia, Pennsylvania. Saxophonist/arranger/conductor.			
10/17/60	84	4		1 **Midnight Lace** ...*Theme From "Grand Jury"* [I] title song from the movie starring **Doris Day**	$10		MGM 12942
7/3/61	81	5		2 **La Dolce Vita (The Sweet Life)** ...*Parlami Di Me (Speak To Me)* [I] from the Federico Fellini movie *La Dolce Vita* starring Marcello Mastroianni	$10	■	RCA Victor 7888
				ELLIS, Shirley BUB '65 Born Shirley Elliston in 1941 in the Bronx, New York. R&B singer/songwriter.			
11/16/63+	8	14		1 **The Nitty Gritty** ...*Give Me A List* promo copies released as "The Real Nitty Gritty" by Shirley Elliston ($20)	$15		Congress 202
2/22/64	72	6		2 **(That's) What The Nitty Gritty Is** ...*Get Out* Jim Dandy (bass voice); **Hutch Davie** (orch., above 2)	$12		Congress 208
12/12/64+	3	14		3 **The Name Game** *Whisper To Me Wind*	$12	■	Congress 230
3/20/65	8	9		4 **The Clapping Song (Clap Pat Clap Slap)** ...*This Is Beautiful*	$12	■	Congress 234
5/29/65	78	5		5 **The Puzzle Song (A Puzzle In Song)** ...*I See It, I Like It, I Want It* all of above written by Shirley's manager and husband, Lincoln Chase	$12		Congress 238
2/25/67	67	6		6 **Soul Time** ...*Waitin'*	$8		Columbia 44021
				ELLIS, Terry — see EN VOGUE			
				ELLIS BEXTOR, Sophie '02 Born on 4/10/79 in London, England. Dance singer/songwriter.			
11/16/02	39^{S}	8		**Murder On The Dancefloor** ...*(3 versions)*	$4	★	Universal 065913
				ELLISON, Lorraine BUB/R&B '66 Born in 1935 in Philadelphia, Pennsylvania. Died on 8/17/85 (age 50). R&B singer/songwriter.			
10/8/66	64	8		1 **Stay With Me** ...*I Got My Baby Back*	$8		Warner 5850
10/7/67	89	2		2 **Heart Be Still** ...*Cry Me A River*	$8		Loma 2074
				ELMO & ALMO '67 Duo of songwriters Gary "Elmo" Bonner and Alan "Almo" Gordon. Wrote "Happy Together" for **The Turtles**.			
6/3/67	98	2		**When The Good Sun Shines** ...*Part II*	$8		Daddy Best 2501

DEBUT	PEAK	WKS	Gold	A-side (Chart Hit)..........B-side	$	Sym	Label & Number

ELMO & PATSY
BUB/C&W/LP **'84**

Husband-and-wife team of Elmo Shropshire and Patsy Trigg, originally known as The Homestead Act. First performed "Grandma Got Run Over By A Reindeer" in 1979, recorded in San Francisco. In movie *The Right Stuff.* Divorced in 1985. Elmo also practices part-time as a veterinarian.

DEBUT	PEAK	WKS	Gold	A-side (Chart Hit)..........B-side	$	Sym	Label & Number
12/17/83	❶[1X]	2		1 **Grandma Got Run Over By A Reindeer** *[ELMO 'N PATSY]* ....*Christmas* [X-N] originally released on Oink 2984 in 1979 ($7); first issued on Soundwaves in 1982	$6		Soundwaves 4658
12/15/84	❶[3X]	4		2 **Grandma Got Run Over By A Reindeer** ....*Percy, The Puny Poinsettia* [X-N-R] X: #1[2]/'84; #1[1]/'85; new version of #1 above	$4	■	Epic 04703
1/10/98-	87	1		3 **Grandma Got Run Over By A Reindeer** ....*Percy, The Puny Poinsettia* [X-N-R] "Bubbled Under" (#112) in 1992; above 2 are the same version	$4	▮[V]	Epic 05479

EL-P
R&B/LP **'02**

Born Jaime Meline in 1974 in Queens, New York. White male rapper/producer. El-P is short for El-Producto. Member of the hip-hop group Company Flow.

DEBUT	PEAK	WKS	Gold	A-side (Chart Hit)..........B-side	$	Sym	Label & Number
4/27/02	32[S]	3		1 **Deep Space 9mm** ....*(2 versions) / Tuned Mass Damper*	$8	T	Definitive Jux 25
5/11/02	55[S]	1		2 **Dead Light**..........*(2 versions) / Train Buffer* (Aesop Rock)	$8	T	Chocolate Ind. 028
5/11/02	69[S]	1		3 **RPM Revolutions Per Minute Pt. 2.1**..........*(3 versions) / Afterburner* (Serum & Induce) **SLUG AND EL-P**	$8	T	Counterflow 022

ELUSION
'98

Black female vocal group from California consisting of two sets of identical twins: Tamica and Tonya Johnson (from Los Angeles) and Michelle and Marie Harris (from San Diego).

DEBUT	PEAK	WKS	Gold	A-side (Chart Hit)..........B-side	$	Sym	Label & Number
3/14/98	75	11		**Reality** ....S:55 *(instrumental)*	$4	▮	RCA 64933

EMERSON DRIVE
C&W/BUB/LP **'02**

Country group from Grande Prairie, Alberta, Canada: Brad Mates (vocals), Danick Dupelle (guitar), Chris Hartman (keyboards), Pat Allingham (fiddle), Jeff Loberg (bass) and Mike Melancon (drums).

DEBUT	PEAK	WKS	Gold	A-side (Chart Hit)..........B-side	$	Sym	Label & Number
3/16/02	35	20		1 **I Should Be Sleeping**..........S:19 / A:37 *(2 versions) / Hollywood Kiss*	$4	★[V]	DreamWorks 50362
11/16/02+	34	20		2 **Fall Into Me**..........A:34 above 2 from the album *Emerson Drive* on DreamWorks 450272			album cut

EMERSON, LAKE & PALMER
ROK/LP **'72**

Classical-oriented rock trio from England: Keith Emerson (with The Nice; keyboards), **Greg Lake** (see #5-7 below) (**King Crimson**; vocals, bass, guitars; born on 11/10/48) and Carl Palmer (Atomic Rooster, **Crazy World of Arthur Brown**; drums). Group split up in 1979, with Palmer joining supergroup **Asia**. Emerson and Lake re-grouped in 1986 with new drummer **Cozy Powell** (**Whitesnake**). Palmer returned in 1987, replacing Powell, who joined **Black Sabbath** in 1990. Powell died in a car crash on 4/5/98 (age 50).

DEBUT	PEAK	WKS	Gold	A-side (Chart Hit)..........B-side	$	Sym	Label & Number
3/13/71	48	12		1 **Lucky Man**..........*Knife's Edge* also see #4 below	$6		Cotillion 44106
3/18/72	70	6		2 **Nutrocker**..........*The Great Gates Of Kiev* [I] adapted from Tchaikovsky's *The Nutcracker Suite*	$6		Cotillion 44151
8/26/72	39	11		3 **From The Beginning** *Living Sin*	$6		Cotillion 44158
12/30/72+	51	7		4 **Lucky Man** ....*Knife's Edge* [R] same version as #1 above	$6		Cotillion 44106
12/20/75	95	3		5 **I Believe In Father Christmas** ....*Humbug* [X]	$6	■	Atlantic 3305
9/3/77	91	2		6 **C'est La Vie**..........*Jeremy Bender* (Emerson, Lake & Palmer) from the **Emerson, Lake & Palmer** album *Works, Volume 1*	$5		Atlantic 3405
11/21/81	48	10		7 **Let Me Love You Once**..........*Retribution Drive* **GREG LAKE** (above 3)	$5		Chrysalis 2571
6/21/86	60	8		8 **Touch & Go** ....*Learning To Fly* **EMERSON, LAKE AND POWELL**	$4	■	Polydor 885101

EMF
ROK/LP **'91**

Dance-rock-techno-funk group from Forest of Dean, Gloucestershire, England: James Atkin (vocals), Ian Dench (guitar), Derry Brownson (keyboards, percussion), Zac Foley (bass) and Mark Decloedt (drums). Foley died of a drug overdose on 1/3/2002 (age 31).

DEBUT	PEAK	WKS	Gold	A-side (Chart Hit)..........B-side	$	Sym	Label & Number
4/13/91	❶[1]	23	●	1 **Unbelievable**..........S:3 / A:4 *(Cin City Sex mix)* "45": EMI 57799; B-side: "Search & Destroy"	$3	▮[V]	EMI 50350
9/28/91	18	14		2 **Lies.** ....A:64 / S:69 *Strange Brew (live)*	$3	▮	EMI 50363

EMILIA
'98

Born Emilia Rydberg on 1/5/78 in Sweden. Female dance singer.

DEBUT	PEAK	WKS	Gold	A-side (Chart Hit)..........B-side	$	Sym	Label & Number
11/28/98	92	2		**Big Big World** ....*(4 versions)*	$6	★	Universal 56228

EMINEM
★363★ R&B/BUB/LP **'02**

Born Marshall Mathers III on 10/17/72 in Kansas City, Missouri; raised in Detroit, Michigan. White male rapper/actor. Protege of **Dr. Dre**. First recorded with the rap group Soul Intent in 1995. Created his alter ego, Slim Shady, for his 1999 album *The Slim Shady LP*. Starred in the 2002 movie *8 Mile.* Also see **D-12** and **Sway & King Tech**.

1)Lose Yourself 2)Without Me 3)The Real Slim Shady

DEBUT	PEAK	WKS	Gold	A-side (Chart Hit)..........B-side	$	Sym	Label & Number
1/23/99	36[S]	11		1 **Just Don't Give A F*****..........BUB:114 *(3 versions) / Brain Damage*	$6	▮	Aftermath 95037
2/27/99	36	10		2 **My Name Is**..........A:23 / S:66 *(3 versions)* [N] samples "I Got The" by Labi Siffre; co-written and produced by **Dr. Dre**	$7	T	Aftermath 95040
1/22/00	25	20		3 **Forgot About Dre**..........A:20 **DR. DRE Featuring Eminem** from the **Dr. Dre** album *2001* on Aftermath 90486			album cut
5/6/00	4	19		4 **The Real Slim Shady** ....A:2 / S:42 *(3 versions)*	$6	T	Aftermath 497334
8/26/00	58	10		5 **The Way I Am**..........A:52 *(3 versions)*	$6	T	Aftermath 497399
11/4/00	51	15		6 **Stan**..........A:48 **EMINEM (Featuring Dido)** samples "Thankyou" by Dido; above 3 from the album *The Marshall Mathers LP* on Aftermath 490629			album cut
5/11/02	2[5]	20		7 **Without Me** A:2			album cut

DEBUT	PEAK	WKS	Gold	A-side (Chart Hit)...B-side	$	Sym	Label & Number
				EMINEM — Cont'd			
8/3/02	4	20		8 Cleanin' Out My Closet ...A:4			album cut
				above 2 from the album *The Eminem Show* on Aftermath 10798			
10/5/02	❶[12]	23		9 Lose Yourself A:❶[11] / S:11 *(3 versions)*	$6	T	Shady 497815
				from the movie *8 Mile* starring Eminem; all of above written or co-written by Eminem			
				EMMERSON, Les — see FIVE MAN ELECTRICAL BAND			
				EMOTIONS, The BUB '63			
				White doo-wop group from Brooklyn, New York: Joe Favale (lead), Tony Maltese, Larry Cusamanno, Joe Nigro and Dom Colluri.			
12/1/62+	76	6		Echo ...*Come Dance Baby*	$25		Kapp 490
				EMOTIONS, The R&B/BUB/LP '77			
				Female R&B trio from Chicago, Illinois: sisters Wanda (lead), Sheila and Jeanette Hutchinson. First worked as a child gospel group called the Heavenly Sunbeams. Left gospel, became The Emotions in 1968. Jeanette replaced by cousin Theresa Davis in 1970, and later by sister Pamela. Jeanette returned to the group in 1978. Charted 30 R&B hits, 1969-84.			
5/24/69	39	10		1 So I Can Love You ...*Got To Be The Man*	$8		Volt 4010
11/6/71+	52	14		2 Show Me How ...*Boss Love Maker*	$7		Volt 4066
7/22/72	93	5		3 I Could Never Be Happy ...*I've Fallen In Love*	$7		Volt 4083
3/23/74	73	6		4 Put A Little Love Away ...*I Call This Loving You*	$7		Volt 4106
11/6/76	51	12		5 I Don't Wanna Lose Your Love /			
10/9/76	87	10		6 Flowers ...	$5		Columbia 10347
				originally charted for 4 weeks; re-entered on 1/15/77 as the "tag-along" B-side			
6/11/77	❶[5]	23	▲	7 Best Of My Love RB[4] *A Feeling Is*	$5		Columbia 10544
10/29/77	44	13		8 Don't Ask My Neighbors ...*Love's What's Happenin'*	$5		Columbia 10622
5/12/79	6	16	●	9 Boogie Wonderland ...*(instrumental)*	$5		ARC 10956
				EARTH, WIND & FIRE WITH THE EMOTIONS			
				also released on Columbia 10956 in 1979; #5-9: produced by **Maurice White** (**Earth, Wind & Fire**)			
				EMPEROR'S, The '67			
				R&B group from Harrisburg, Pennsylvania: Edgar Moore (vocal), Donald Brantley, Calvin Tyrone "Ty" Moss, Ronnie Bowers, Milton Brown Jr. and Steve Stephens.			
12/3/66+	55	9		Karate ...*I've Got To Have Her*	$20		Mala 543
				EMPTY MYND '01			
				Born in Los Angeles, California. Black male rapper.			
10/20/01	75[S]	1		Funk ...*(2 versions)*	$6	★	Orpheus 70564
				ENCHANTERS, The '61			
				White doo-wop group.			
3/6/61	96	2		I Lied To My Heart ...*Talk While You Walk*	$40		Musitron 1072
				Dave McRae (orch.)			
				ENCHANTERS, The — see MIMMS, Garnet			
				ENCHANTMENT R&B/BUB/LP '77			
				R&B vocal group from Detroit, Michigan: Ed Clanton, Bobby Green, Davis Banks, Emanuel Johnson and Joe Thomas.			
1/29/77	25	13		1 Gloria ...*Dance To The Music*	$5		Roadshow/U.A. 912
8/6/77	45	10		2 Sunshine ...*Sexy Lady*	$5	■	Roadshow/U.A. 991
				issued with 2 different picture sleeves			
2/4/78	33	11		3 It's You That I Need ...RB[1] *Sunny Shine Feeling*	$5		Roadshow/U.A. 1124
				ENEA, Laura '92			
				Born on 11/16/66 in White Plains, New York (of Italian parentage). Began singing in Italy; won the Miss Italia Pagent Talent Competition.			
3/28/92	70	14		This Is The Last Time ...A:35 *(same version)*	$4	▮	Next Plateau 324
	★455★			**ENGLAND DAN & JOHN FORD COLEY** AC/BUB/C&W/LP '76			
				Pop duo from Austin, Texas: **Dan Seals** (see #10 & 11 below) (born on 2/8/50) and John Ford Coley (born on 10/13/51). In the late 1960s, both were members of **Southwest F.O.B.** Dan, later a top Country artist, is the brother of Jim Seals of **Seals & Crofts** and cousin of Country singers Johnny Duncan, Troy Seals (**Jo Ann & Troy**) and **Brady Seals** (**Little Texas**). Coley appeared in the 1987 movie *Scenes From The Goldmine.*			
				1)I'd Really Love To See You Tonight 2)We'll Never Have To Say Goodbye Again 3)Nights Are Forever Without You			
6/12/76	2[2]	24	●	1 I'd Really Love To See You Tonight AC[1] *It's Not The Same*	$5		Big Tree 16069
10/9/76	10	16		2 Nights Are Forever Without You ...*Showboat Gambler*	$5		Big Tree 16079
				above 2 written by **Parker McGee**			
5/7/77	21	16		3 It's Sad To Belong ...AC[5] *The Time Has Come*	$4		Big Tree 16088
10/1/77	23	14		4 Gone Too Far ...*Where Do I Go From Here*	$4		Big Tree 16102
2/25/78	9	14		5 We'll Never Have To Say Goodbye Again ...AC[6] *Calling For You Again*	$4		Big Tree 16110
6/3/78	49	8		6 You Can't Dance ...*Wanting You Desperately*	$4		Big Tree 16117
3/10/79	10	18		7 Love Is The Answer ...AC[2] *Running After You*	$4		Big Tree 16131
				written by **Todd Rundgren**			
10/27/79	50	6		8 What Can I Do With This Broken Heart ...*Caught Up In The Middle*	$4		Big Tree 17000
3/8/80	75	4		9 In It For Love ...*Who's Lonely Now*	$4		Big Tree 17002
				all of above produced by Kyle Lehning			
8/16/80	57	6		10 Late At Night ...*Lullaby*	$4		Atlantic 3674
				ENGLAND DAN SEALS			
1/25/86	42	15		11 Bop ...CW[1] *In San Antone*	$4		EMI America 8289
				DAN SEALS			
				ENGLISH, Jackie '81			
				Female dance singer/songwriter.			
12/20/80+	94	4		Once A Night ...*Please Let Me Be The Other Woman*	$5		Venture 135
				from the movie *Hopscotch* starring Walter Matthau			

DEBUT	PEAK	WKS	Gold	A-side (Chart Hit)........B-side	$	Sym	Label & Number
				ENGLISH, Kim '02			
				Born in Chicago, Illinois. Black electronica singer/songwriter.			
2/9/02	44^{S}	3		**Everyday**......*(2 remixes) / Treat Me Right*	$6	★	Nervous 20487
				ENGLISH, Scott '64			
				American pop singer/songwriter based in London, England.			
2/22/64	77	5		1 **High On A Hill**......*When* (w/The Dedications)	$30		Spokane 4003
				The Accents (backing vocals); first released on Sultan 4003 in 1963 ($50)			
3/4/72	91	2		2 **Brandy**......*Lead Me Back*	$15		Janus 171
				recorded in 1974 by **Barry Manilow** as "Mandy"			
				ENGLISH CONGREGATION, The BUB '72			
				Pop vocal group from England. Led by singer Brian Keith.			
1/22/72	29	10		**Softly Whispering I Love You**......*When Susie Takes The Plane*	$6		Atco 6865
				ENGVALL, Bill C&W/LP '97			
				Born on 7/27/57 in Galveston, Texas. Country comedian/actor. Played "Bill Pelton" on TV's *The* ***Jeff Foxworthy*** *Show*.			
2/22/97	43	20	●	**Here's Your Sign (Get The Picture)**......S:29 *Things Have Changed* [C]	$4	▮V	Warner 17491
				BILL ENGVALL with Travis Tritt			
				ENIGMA LP '91			
				Born Michael Cretu on 5/18/57 in Bucharest, Romania. Dance producer. Moved to Germany in 1975. Worked with **Vangelis** and **The Art Of Noise**. Featured vocalist is Cretu's wife, Sandra.			
2/9/91	5	18	●	1 **Sadeness Part 1**......S:❶^2 / A:6 *(meditation mix)* [F]	$3	▮V	Charisma 98864
				features traditional Gregorian chants backed by a dance rhythm; sadeness (pronounced: sadness) refers to 18th-century French author/libertine, the Marquis de Sade			
6/8/91	54^{S}	3		2 **Mea Culpa Part II (Catholic Mix)**......*(Orthodox version)*	$3	▮V	Charisma 98806
3/5/94	4	26	●	3 **Return To Innocence**......S:5 / A:7 *(380 midnight mix)*	$3	▮V	Charisma 38423
				"45": Virgin 17911			
11/30/96	81	3		4 **Beyond The Invisible**......S:48 *Almost Full Moon*	$3	▮	Virgin 38572
				ENRIQUEZ, Jocelyn BUB/LP '96			
				Born on 12/28/74 in San Francisco, California. Female R&B-dance singer.			
4/2/94	80	11		1 **I've Been Thinking About You**......A:60 *(3 versions)*	$3	▮	Classified 0200
8/20/94	75^{A}	1		2 **Make This Last Forever**......BUB:101 *Lovely*	$3	▮	Classified 0203
7/27/96	49	23		3 **Do You Miss Me** A:38 / S:61 *(freefloor radio mix)*	$3	▮	Classified 0227
				remixes released in 1996 on Classified 7186 (cassette single)			
4/5/97	55	20		4 **A Little Bit Of Ecstasy**......S:59 *(remix)*	$3	▮	Classified 7190
8/29/98	52	15		5 **If You Could Read My Mind**......S:55 *(instrumental)*	$4	★	Tommy Boy 7497
				STARS ON 54: ULTRA NATÉ, AMBER, JOCELYN ENRIQUEZ			
				from the movie *54* starring Ryan Phillippe; originally charted its first 5 weeks as a CD maxi-single on Tommy Boy 497, then charted 9 more weeks as a cassette single; re-entered *Hot 100* on 2/27/99 at #99 for 1 more week as a regular CD single			
5/27/00	70^{S}	1		6 **When I Get Close To You**......*(7 remixes)*	$8	★*	Tommy Boy 2090
				ENRIQUEZ, Joy '00			
				Born in 1979 in Whittier, California. Female Latin-dance-pop singer.			
10/21/00	46^{S}	23		**Tell Me How You Feel**......*(3 album snippets)*	$4	★	LaFace 13909
				samples "Mellow Mellow Right On" by Lowrell			
				ENTOUCH R&B/LP '90			
				Male R&B vocal duo of Eric McCaine (from Mt. Vernon, New York) and Free (from the Bronx, New York).			
1/13/90	71	7		**All Nite**......*(acappella version)*	$3	▮V	Vintertainment 69260
				ENTOUCH (Featuring Keith Sweat)			
				ENUFF Z'NUFF ROK/LP '90			
				Rock group from Chicago, Illinois: Chip Z'Nuff (bass), Donnie Vie (vocals), Derek Frigo (guitar) and Vikki Foxx (drums).			
10/21/89	67	7		1 **New Thing**......*Kiss The Clown*	$4	■	Atco 99207
1/27/90	47	13		2 **Fly High Michelle**......S:40 *Finger On The Trigger*	$4	▮	Atco 99135
				EN VOGUE ★189★ R&B/LP '92			
				Female R&B vocal group from San Francisco, California: **Terry Ellis** (see #12 below) (born on 9/5/66), **Dawn Robinson** (see #18 below) (born on 11/28/68; **Lucy Pearl**), Cindy Herron (born on 9/26/65) and Maxine Jones (born on 1/16/66). Herron married pro baseball player Glenn Braggs in June of 1993 and acted in the movie *Juice*. Reduced to a trio when Robinson went solo in 1997.			
				1)Don't Let Go (Love) 2)My Lovin' (You're Never Gonna Get It) 3)Hold On			
5/5/90	2^{1}	25	▲	1 **Hold On**......RB^2 S:❶^2 / A:8 *Luv Lines*	$3	▮V	Atlantic 87984
8/25/90	38	11		2 **Lies**......RB^1 S:32 *(album version)*	$3	▮V	Atlantic 87893
12/22/90+	57^{A}	8		3 **You Don't Have To Worry**......RB^1 *(album version)*	$3	▮	Atlantic 87816
3/21/92	2^{3}	30	●	4 **My Lovin' (You're Never Gonna Get It)**......RB^2 A:❶^4 / S:6 *Part Of Me*	$3	▮V	EastWest 98586
				"45" B-side is a Radio Active remix			
6/6/92	6	24	●	5 **Giving Him Something He Can Feel**......RB^1 A:4 / S:10 *My Lovin' (You're Never Gonna Get It) (remix)*	$3	▮V	EastWest 98560
				#28 hit for **Aretha Franklin** in 1976 as "Something He Can Feel"			
9/12/92	8	20	●	6 **Free Your Mind**......S:13 / A:14 *Just Can't Stay Away*	$3	▮V	EastWest 98487
9/12/92	73^{A}	1		7 **Yesterday**......			album cut
12/5/92+	15	20		8 **Give It Up, Turn It Loose**......A:12 / S:47 *You Don't Have To Worry*	$3	▮	EastWest 98455
3/27/93	36	16		9 **Love Don't Love You**......A:28 *Yesterday*	$3	▮	EastWest 98432
				#4-9: from the album *Funky Divas* on EastWest 92121			
10/16/93	51	10		10 **Runaway Love**......A:19 / S:55 ***(FMob** Instrumental)*	$3	▮	EastWest 98354
				EN VOGUE featuring FMob (FMob is producers/keyboardists Thomas McElroy and Denzil Foster, both of **Club Nouveau**)			

DEBUT	PEAK	WKS	Gold	A-side (Chart Hit)...B-side	$	Sym	Label & Number
				EN VOGUE — Cont'd			
1/22/94	3	29	▲	11 **Whatta Man** ...S:2 / A:4 *(7" edit)* **SALT 'N' PEPA with En Vogue** samples "What A Man" by Linda Lyndell (#50 R&B hit in 1968); "45": Next Plateau/London 857356	$3		Next Plateau 857390
11/4/95	52	20		12 **Where Ever You Are**...S:25 *(unplugged version)* **TERRY ELLIS**	$3		EastWest 64361
11/9/96+	2^{4}	35	▲	13 **Don't Let Go (Love)** RB[1] S:3 / A:3 *Hold On* from the movie *Set It Off* starring Jada Pinkett and **Queen Latifah**	$3		EastWest 64231
7/19/97	16	15	●	14 **Whatever**...S:15 / A:20	$3		EastWest 64174
10/11/97	33	17		15 **Too Gone, Too Long**...S:28 / A:58 *Eyes Of A Child*	$3		EastWest 64150
10/10/98	57	8		16 **No Fool No More**...S:34 *Get Contact* (**Missy "Misdemeanor" Elliott** & **Busta Rhymes**) from the movie *Why Do Fools Fall In Love* starring Halle Berry	$3		EastWest 64082
6/17/00	92	4		17 **Riddle**...*(7 versions)*	$6	T	EastWest 67047
12/8/01+	38^{S}	14		18 **Envious**...*(3 album snippets)* **DAWN ROBINSON**	$4	★	Q/Atlantic 97986

ENYA

BUB/AC/LP **'01**

Born Eithne Ni Bhraonain (Gaelic spelling of Brennan) on 5/17/61 in County Donegal, Ireland. From 1980-82, she was a member of her siblings' folk-rock group, Clannad.

DEBUT	PEAK	WKS	Gold	A-side (Chart Hit)...B-side	$	Sym	Label & Number
1/21/89	24	17		1 **Orinoco Flow (Sail Away)**...S:19 / A:28 *Out Of The Blue* Orinoco is a river in South America	$4		Geffen 27633
2/29/92	79	8		2 **Caribbean Blue**...A:71 *Orinoco Flow*	$4		Reprise 19089
1/3/98	88	3		3 **Only If...**...*Willows On The Water / Oíche Chiún (Silent Night)*	$4		Reprise 17266
12/30/00	71^{S}	1		4 **Oíche Chiún (Silent Night)**...*Oriel Window / 'S fagaim mo bhaile* [X-F] also see #6 & 7 and the B-sides of #3 & 5 below	$8	★*	Reprise 40660
7/14/01	10	31		5 **Only Time** AC[6] S:2 / A:9 *Oíche Chiún (Silent Night) / Willows On The Water* from the movie *Sweet November* starring Keanu Reeves and Charlize Theron; "45": Reprise 16719; B-side: "May It Be"	$8	★*V	Reprise 42420
12/1/01	29^{S}	6		6 **Oíche Chiún (Silent Night)**...*Oriel Window / 'S fagaim mo bhaile* [X-F-R]	$8	★*	Reprise 40660
11/30/02	11^{S}	7		7 **Oíche Chiún (Silent Night)**...*Oriel Window / 'S fagaim mo bhaile* [X-F-R]	$8	★*	Reprise 40660

E.O.L.

R&B **'98**

R&B vocal group from Washington DC: Ike, John, Priest and Scooter.

DEBUT	PEAK	WKS	Gold	A-side (Chart Hit)...B-side	$	Sym	Label & Number
7/11/98	79	6		**Love The Way**...S:53 *(rapless edit)* Shelene (rap); written by **112**	$4		RCA 65369

EPIC SPLENDOR, The

'68

Pop-rock group from Long Island, New York: Paul Masarti (vocals), Vic Canone (guitar), Charlie (organ), Larry Jack (bass) and Eddie Garguilo (drums).

DEBUT	PEAK	WKS	Gold	A-side (Chart Hit)...B-side	$	Sym	Label & Number
12/16/67+	87	7		**A Little Rain Must Fall**...*Cowboys And Indians* **Trade Martin** (arranger and conductor); Hot Biscuit label manufactured by Capitol	$10		Hot Biscuit 1450

EPMD — see SERMON, Erick

EPPS, Preston

LP **'59**

Born in 1931 in Oakland, California. Black bongo player.

DEBUT	PEAK	WKS	Gold	A-side (Chart Hit)...B-side	$	Sym	Label & Number
5/18/59	14	13		1 **Bongo Rock**...*Bongo Party* [I]	$20		Original Sound 4
8/15/60	78	3		2 **Bongo Bongo Bongo**...*Hully Gully Bongo* [I]	$20		Original Sound 9

EQUALS, The

'68

Interracial British-Jamaican rock group: twin brothers Derv (vocals) and Lincoln (guitar) Gordon, with **Eddy Grant** and Patrick Lloyd (guitars), and John Hall (drums).

DEBUT	PEAK	WKS	Gold	A-side (Chart Hit)...B-side	$	Sym	Label & Number
9/7/68	32	9		**Baby, Come Back**...*Hold Me Closer*	$10		RCA Victor 9583

ERASURE

ROK/BUB/LP **'88**

Techno-rock-dance duo from England: Andy Bell (vocals) and Vince Clarke (instruments). Clarke was a member of **Depeche Mode** and half of the duo **Yaz**.

DEBUT	PEAK	WKS	Gold	A-side (Chart Hit)...B-side	$	Sym	Label & Number
7/30/88	12	20		1 **Chains Of Love** S:10 / A:10 *Don't Suppose*	$4		Sire 27844
12/10/88+	14	17		2 **A Little Respect**...S:13 / A:14 *Like Zsa Zsa Zsa Gabor*	$4		Sire 27738
7/22/89	97	2		3 **Stop!**...*Ship Of Fools*	$4		Sire 22879
8/10/91	83	11		4 **Chorus (Fishes In The Sea)**...S:52 / A:67 *Snappy*	$4		Sire 19202
9/19/92	51^{A}	11		5 **Take A Chance On Me**... from the mini-album **Abba**-esque on Mute/Elektra 61386			album cut
4/30/94	20	23		6 **Always**...A:17 / S:40 *Tragic*	$3		Mute/Elektra 64552
5/24/97	55	8		7 **In My Arms**...A:58 *Heart Of Glass (live)*	$3		Mute/Maverick 17371

ERIC B. & RAKIM

R&B/BUB/LP **'92**

Rap duo: DJ Eric Barrier (from Elmhurst, New York) and rapper William Griffin, Jr. (from Long Island, New York).

DEBUT	PEAK	WKS	Gold	A-side (Chart Hit)...B-side	$	Sym	Label & Number
6/17/89	9	18		1 **Friends**...S:5 / A:14 *Private Life* (Watley) **JODY WATLEY (With Eric B. & Rakim)**	$3		MCA 53660
2/22/92	96	4		2 **Juice (know the ledge)**...S:52 *(instrumental)* from the movie *Juice* starring Omar Epps	$3		Soul/MCA 54333

ERNIE — see HENSON, Jim

ERUPTION

LP **'78**

Techno-funk-dance group of Jamaican natives based in London: Precious Wilson and Lintel (vocals), brothers Gregory and Morgan Petrineau (guitars), Horatio McKay (keyboards), and Eric Kingsley (drums).

DEBUT	PEAK	WKS	Gold	A-side (Chart Hit)...B-side	$	Sym	Label & Number
3/11/78	18	22		**I Can't Stand The Rain**...*Be Yourself*	$5		Ariola/Hansa 7686

ESCAPE CLUB, The

LP **'88**

Rock group formed in London, England: Trevor Steel (vocals), John Holliday (guitar), Johnnie Christo (bass) and Milan Zekavica (drums).

DEBUT	PEAK	WKS	Gold	A-side (Chart Hit)...B-side	$	Sym	Label & Number
8/20/88	$❶^{1}$	27	●	1 **Wild, Wild West** S:❶[1] / A:❶[1] *We Can Run*	$3		Atlantic 89048
12/10/88+	28	14		2 **Shake For The Sheik**...S:24 / A:28 *Working For The Fatman*	$3		Atlantic 88983
3/25/89	81	6		3 **Walking Through Walls**...*Standing On A Bridge*	$3		Atlantic 88951

DEBUT	PEAK	WKS	Gold	A-side (Chart Hit)	B-side	$	Sym	Label & Number

ESCAPE CLUB, The — Cont'd

DEBUT	PEAK	WKS	Gold	A-side (Chart Hit)	B-side	$	Sym	Label & Number
2/23/91	44	10		4 Call It Poison A:33	*Keep The Motor Running*	$3	■V	Atlantic 87759
				features a sample of **Deep Purple**'s "Strange Kind Of Woman"				
5/25/91	8	25	●	5 I'll Be There ....S:6 / A:14	*Lately*	$3	■V	Atlantic 87683
				"45" issued for above 2 in 1993 on Atlantic Oldies 84878				

ESPN Presents — LP '97

ESPN is America's leading sports cable network. The medley below is based on their best-selling series of albums.

DEBUT	PEAK	WKS	Gold	A-side (Chart Hit)	B-side	$	Sym	Label & Number
5/10/97	31	25	●	The Jock Jam ....S:25 / A:43	*(same)*	$4	■V	Tommy Boy 7780
				"Let's Get Ready To Rumble" (Michael Buffer), "Everybody Everybody" (**Black Box**), "This Is Your Night" (**Amber**), "I Like To Move It" (**Reel 2 Real**), "Give It Up" (**The Goodmen**), "The Bomb" (**The Bucketheads**), "Boom Boom Boom" (**The Outhere Brothers**), "Get Ready 4 This" (**2 Unlimited**), "Whoomp! There It Is" (**Tag Team**), "Strike It Up" (**Black Box**), "Tootsee Roll" (**69 Boyz**), "It Takes Two" (**Rob Base**), "Gonna Make You Sweat" (**C&C Music Factory**), "Pump Up The Jam" (**Technotronic**), "YMCA" (**Village People**), "Twilight Zone" (**2 Unlimited**) and "Rock And Roll Part 2" (**Gary Glitter**); "45": Tommy Boy/Collectables 780				

ESPOSITO, Joe "Bean" — see BROOKLYN DREAMS

ESQUIRES, The — R&B/BUB '67

R&B vocal group from Milwaukee, Wisconsin: brothers Gilbert and Alvis Moorer, Millard Edwards, Sam Pace and Shawn Taylor.

DEBUT	PEAK	WKS	Gold	A-side (Chart Hit)	B-side	$	Sym	Label & Number
8/19/67	11	15		1 Get On Up	*Listen To Me*	$12		Bunky 7750
11/25/67	22	8		2 And Get Away	*Everybody's Laughing*	$12		Bunky 7752
12/28/68+	91	5		3 You've Got The Power	*No Doubt About It*	$12		Wand 1193

ESSEX, The — LP '63

R&B vocal group formed by members of the U.S. Marine Corps at Camp LeJeune, North Carolina: Anita Humes, Walter Vickers, Rodney Taylor, Billy Hill and Rudolph Johnson.

DEBUT	PEAK	WKS	Gold	A-side (Chart Hit)	B-side	$	Sym	Label & Number
6/8/63	1[2]	13		1 Easier Said Than Done ....RB[2]	*Are You Going My Way*	$15		Roulette 4494
8/24/63	12	10		2 A Walkin' Miracle	*What I Don't Know Won't Hurt Me*	$12		Roulette 4515
11/16/63	56	5		3 She's Got Everything	*Out Of Sight, Out Of Mind*	$12		Roulette 4530
				THE ESSEX Featuring Anita Humes (above 2)				

ESSEX, David — BUB/LP '74

Born David Cook on 7/23/47 in London, England. Portrayed "Christ" in the London production of *Godspell*. Star of British movies since 1970.

DEBUT	PEAK	WKS	Gold	A-side (Chart Hit)	B-side	$	Sym	Label & Number
11/10/73+	5	25	●	1 Rock On	*On And On*	$5	■	Columbia 45940
6/1/74	71	5		2 Lamplight	*We All Insane*	$5	■	Columbia 46041

ESTEFAN, Gloria/Miami Sound Machine ★65★ — BUB/AC/LP '88

Latin pop-dance group from Miami, Florida: **Gloria Estefan** (born Gloria Fajardo on 12/1/57 in Havana, Cuba; raised in Miami), her husband Emilio Estefan (keyboards), Juan Avila (bass) and Enrique Garcia (drums). Group later grew to nine members. Gloria and Emilio married on 9/2/78; both were involved in a serious bus crash on 3/20/90. Gloria played "Isabel Vasquez" in the movie *Music Of The Heart*.

1)Anything For You 2)Coming Out Of The Dark 3)Don't Wanna Lose You 4)Music Of My Heart 5)1-2-3

DEBUT	PEAK	WKS	Gold	A-side (Chart Hit)	B-side	$	Sym	Label & Number
				MIAMI SOUND MACHINE:				
10/19/85+	10	27	●	1 Conga ....S:7 / A:12	*Mucho Money*	$3	■	Epic 05457
3/8/86	8	19	●	2 Bad Boy ....S:4 / A:9	*Surrender Paradise*	$3	■	Epic 05805
6/14/86	5	24		3 Words Get In The Way ....AC[2] S:5 / A:8	*Movies*	$3		Epic 06120
11/1/86+	25	16		4 Falling In Love (Uh-Oh) ....A:23 / S:27	*Primitive Love*	$3	■	Epic 06352
				above 4 from the album *Primitive Love*				
				GLORIA ESTEFAN and MIAMI SOUND MACHINE:				
5/30/87	5	17		5 Rhythm Is Gonna Get You ....S:3 / A:6	*Give It Up*	$3	■	Epic 07059
9/5/87	36	11		6 Betcha Say That ....S:33 / A:33	*Love Toy*	$3	■	Epic 07371
11/21/87+	6	23		7 Can't Stay Away From You ....AC[1] S:6 / A:6	*Let It Loose*	$3	■	Epic 07641
3/12/88	1[2]	23	●	8 Anything For You ....AC[3] S:1[2] / A:1[2]	*(Spanish version)*	$3	■	Epic 07759
6/4/88	3	19		9 1-2-3 ....AC[1] S:3 / A:5	*(instrumental)*	$3	■	Epic 07921
				above 5 from the album *Let It Loose*				
				GLORIA ESTEFAN:				
7/8/89	1[1]	18	●	10 Don't Wanna Lose You ....S:1[1] / A:1[1]	*Si Voy A Perderte*	$3		Epic 68959
9/30/89	11	17		11 Get On Your Feet ....A:8 / S:13	*Words Get In The Way (live)*	$3		Epic 69064
12/16/89+	6	21		12 Here We Are ....AC[5] S:8 / A:8	*1-2-3 (live)*	$3	■V	Epic 73084
4/7/90	48	7		13 Oye Mi Canto (Hear My Voice)	*(Spanish version)*	$3	■V	Epic 73269
6/30/90	44	14		14 Cuts Both Ways ....AC[1]	*Nothin' New*	$3	■V	Epic 73395
				above 5 from the album *Cuts Both Ways*				
1/26/91	1[2]	19		15 Coming Out Of The Dark ....AC[2] A:1[1] / S:3	*(Spanish version)*	$3	■V	Epic 73666
				backing vocalists include **Jon Secada** and **Betty Wright**				
4/20/91	53	7		16 Seal Our Fate	*(album version)*	$3	■V	Epic 73769
6/8/91	43	13		17 Can't Forget You A:59	*Light Of Love*	$3	■	Epic 73864
10/12/91	22	20		18 Live For Loving You ....A:15 / S:61	*(underground club edit)*	$3	■V	Epic 73962
				above 4 from the album *Into The Light*				
10/31/92	81	6		19 Always Tomorrow	*Words Get In The Way (live)*	$3	■V	Epic 74472
				royalties benefit the South Florida victims of Hurricane Andrew (8/24/92)				
2/20/93	48	17		20 I See Your Smile ....A:36 / S:51	*Megamix*	$3	■V	Epic 74847
				#15, 17 & 20: co-written by **Jon Secada**				
9/24/94	13	25	●	21 Turn The Beat Around ....A:13 / S:15	*(7" remix)*	$3	■V	Crescent Moon 77630
				from the movie *The Specialist* starring Sylvester Stallone				
1/28/95	27	20		22 Everlasting Love ....A:20 / S:59	*(7" remix)*	$3	■V	Epic 77756
				"45" issued for above 2 on Epic 77756				
4/20/96	42	20		23 Reach ....S:28 / A:60	*(gold medal single edit)*	$3	■V	Epic 78285
				one of the songs selected for the 1996 Olympic Games in Atlanta				
9/7/96	70	10		24 You'll Be Mine (Party Time) S:64	*(2 versions)*	$3	■	Epic 78378

DEBUT	PEAK	WKS	Gold	A-side (Chart Hit)...B-side	$	Sym	Label & Number
				ESTEFAN, Gloria — Cont'd			
12/7/96+	40	19		25 **I'm Not Giving You Up** ....A:48 / S:57 *(single remix) / Higher*	$3	▮V	Epic 78464
5/23/98	27	20		26 **Heaven's What I Feel** ....S:22 / A:56 *Corazón Prohibido / Gloria's Hitmix*	$3	▮V	Epic 78875
11/21/98	76	2		27 **Don't Let This Moment End** ....S:47 *(ballad version) / The 70's "Moment" Medley*	$3	▮V	Epic 79058
9/4/99	2[1]	20		28 **Music Of My Heart** ....S:❶[1] / A:26 *(remix)*	$4	★	Miramax/Epic 79245
				***NSYNC and GLORIA ESTEFAN**			
				from the movie *Music Of The Heart* starring Meryl Streep			
6/10/00	77	1		29 **No Me Dejes De Querer** ....A:70 [F]		V	album cut
				title is Spanish for "Don't Stop Loving Me"; from the album *Alma Caribena* on Epic 62163; "45": Epic 79367; B-side: (radio edit)			
5/12/01	22[S]	12		30 **Out Of Nowhere** ....*(7 mixes) / Y-Tu-Conga (unreleased mix)*	$8	★*	Epic 79576
				all of above (except #28) produced by Emilio Estefan, Jr.; all of above (except #1, 2, 4, 6, 11, 17, 20-22, 24, 26, 28 & 30) written or co-written by Gloria Estefan			
				ESTES, Toni '00			
				Born in 1980 in Tulsa, Oklahoma. Female R&B singer.			
9/9/00	70[S]	2		**Hot** ....*(TV track) / (5 album snippets)*	$5	★	Priority 53584
				ESTUS, Deon R&B/AC/LP '89			
				Born in Detroit, Michigan. R&B singer/bassist.			
2/25/89	5	16		**Heaven Help Me** ....S:4 / A:6 *It's A Party*	$3	■	Mika 871538
				DEON ESTUS (with George Michael)			
				ETERNAL R&B/LP '94			
				Female R&B vocal group from London, England: sisters Easther and Vernie Bennett, with Louise Nurding and Kelle Bryan.			
1/15/94	19	20		**Stay** ....A:16 / S:24 *Don't Say Goodbye*	$3	▮	EMI/1st Avenue 58113
				#6 R&B hit for **Glenn Jones** in 1990			
				ETERNALS, The '59			
				White doo-wop group from the Bronx, New York: Charles Girona (lead), Ernest Sierra and Fred Hodge (tenors), Arnie Torres (baritone) and Alex Miranda (bass).			
7/13/59	78	3		**Rockin' In The Jungle** ....*Rock 'N' Roll Cha-Cha* [N]	$50		Hollywood 68
				ETERNITY'S CHILDREN BUB '68			
				Pop group from Biloxi, Mississippi: Linda Lawley (vocals), Jerry Bounds and Johnny Walker (guitars), Bruce Blackman (keyboards), **Charlie Ross** (bass) and Roy Whitaker (drums). Blackman later formed **Starbuck** and **Korona**.			
7/13/68	69	7		**Mrs. Bluebird** ....*Little Boy*	$12	■	Tower 416
				picture sleeve also issued with "Long Version" shown in large red letters across the front			
	★585★			**ETHERIDGE, Melissa** ROK/AC/LP '95			
				Born on 5/29/61 in Leavenworth, Kansas. Adult Alternative pop-rock singer/songwriter/guitarist.			
				1)I'm The Only One 2)If I Wanted To 3)I Want To Come Over			
4/8/89	94	4		1 **Similar Features** ....*Bring Me Some Water* (ROK #10)	$4	■	Island 99251
11/4/89	95	3		2 **No Souvenirs** ....*(live version)*	$4	■	Island 99176
2/26/94	25	44		3 **Come To My Window** ....A:10 *Ain't It Heavy (live)*	$3	▮V	Island 858028
8/6/94+	8	40		4 **I'm The Only One** AC[2] A:5 / S:36 *Maggie May (live)*	$3	▮V	Island 854068
2/18/95	16	20		5 **If I Wanted To** / A:18 / S:43			
				"45" issued for #3 & 5 on Island 854238			
2/18/95	42	20		6 **Like The Way I Do** ....A:57 / S:67	$3	▮	Island 854238
				from the 1988 album *Melissa Etheridge*			
10/21/95	47[A]	8		7 **Your Little Secret**		V	album cut
				"45": Island 854426; B-side: "All American Girl" (live)			
2/17/96	22	20		8 **I Want To Come Over** ....A:21 / S:29 *Your Little Secret*	$3	▮V	Island 854528
				"45" issued for #4 & 8 on Island 854580			
10/12/96	40	19		9 **Nowhere To Go** ....A:31 / S:65 *Bring Me Some Water (live w/***Joan Osborne***)*	$3	▮	Island 854664
				above 3 from the album *Your Little Secret* on Island 524154			
9/18/99	51	11		10 **Angels Would Fall** ....S:25 / A:57 *Beloved / Into The Dark*	$8	★*+V	Island 562345
				"45": Island 562344; all of above written by Etheridge			
				ETTA & HARVEY — see JAMES, Etta			
				E.U. R&B/LP '88			
				Funk group from Washington DC. Led by singer/bassist Gregory Elliott. E.U.: Experience Unlimited.			
4/16/88	35	12		**Da'Butt** ....RB[1] S:26 *(dub version)*	$3	■	EMI-Manhattan 50115
				from the movie *School Daze* starring Spike Lee			
				EUBANKS, Jack '61			
				Country session guitarist/producer from Nashville, Tennessee. Made the Country Albums chart as a member of The Nashville Guitars.			
11/27/61	83	4		**Searching** ....*Take A Message To Mary* [I]	$10		Monument 451
				JACK EUBANKS and The Sound of the South			
				harmonica instrumental of **The Coasters**' 1957 hit "Searchin'"			
				EUCLID BEACH BAND '79			
				Pop duo from Cleveland, Ohio: Richard Reising and Peter Hewlett.			
3/31/79	81	5		**I Need You** ....*Hard To Say Goodbye*	$4		Epic 50676
				written and produced by **Eric Carmen**			
				EUROGLIDERS LP '84			
				Pop-rock group from Perth, Australia: Grace Knight (vocals), Crispin Akerman (guitar), Amanda Vincent and Bernie Lynch (keyboards), Ron Francois (bass) and John Bennetts (drums).			
11/10/84	65	6		**Heaven (Must Be There)** ....*Waiting For You*	$4		Columbia 04626
				EUROPE LP '87			
				Hard-rock group from Stockholm, Sweden: Joey Tempest (vocals), Kee Marcello (guitar), Mic Michaeli (keyboards), John Leven (bass) and Ian Haugland (drums). Founding guitarist John Norum went solo in 1987.			
1/24/87	8	18		1 **The Final Countdown** ....S:6 / A:8 *On Broken Wings*	$3		Epic 06416
				featured in the movie *Rocky IV* starring Sylvester Stallone			
5/2/87	30	13		2 **Rock The Night** ....S:30 / A:31 *Seven Doors Hotel*	$3	■	Epic 07091

DEBUT	PEAK	WKS	Gold	A-side (Chart Hit)...B-side	$	Sym	Label & Number
				EUROPE — Cont'd			
8/1/87	3	19		3 **Carrie** A:❶[1] / S:5 *Love Chaser*	$3	■	Epic 07282
11/28/87	72	10		4 **Cherokee** ... *Heart Of Stone* all of above from the album *The Final Countdown*	$3	■	Epic 07638
8/13/88	31	13		5 **Superstitious** ... S:29 / A:31 *Lights And Shadows*	$3	■	Epic 07979
	★304★			**EURYTHMICS** ROK/BUB/LP **'83** Synth-pop duo: **Annie Lennox** (born on 12/25/54 in Aberdeen, Scotland; vocals, keyboards, flute, composer) and **David A. Stewart** (born on 9/9/52 in England; keyboards, guitar, synthesizer, composer). Both had been in **The Tourists** from 1977-80. Formed duo in December 1980. Stewart, also a prolific producer, married Siobhan Fahey of **Bananarama** on 8/1/87. Duo split in 1990. *1)Sweet Dreams (Are Made Of This) 2)Here Comes The Rain Again 3)Would I Lie To You?*			
5/14/83	❶[1]	26	●	1 **Sweet Dreams (Are Made of This)** *I Could Give You (A Mirror)*	$3	■	RCA 13533
9/17/83	23	13		2 **Love Is A Stranger** ... *Monkey, Monkey* issued with 2 different color photos of duo on cover of picture sleeve	$3	■	RCA 13618
1/28/84	4	20		3 **Here Comes The Rain Again** ... *Paint A Rumour*	$3	■	RCA 13725
5/5/84	21	13		4 **Who's That Girl?** ... *Aqua*	$3	■	RCA 13800
7/21/84	29	12		5 **Right By Your Side** ... *(party mix)*	$3	■	RCA 13695
11/24/84	81	4		6 **Sexcrime (Nineteen Eighty-Four)** ... *I Did It Just The Same*	$3	■	RCA 13956
4/27/85	5	19		7 **Would I Lie To You?** ... S:4 / A:6 *Here Comes That Sinking Feeling*	$3	■	RCA 14078
8/3/85	22	11		8 **There Must Be An Angel (Playing With My Heart)** ... S:20 / A:25 *Grown Up Girls* **Stevie Wonder** (harmonica)	$3	■	RCA 14160
10/19/85	18	15		9 **Sisters Are Doin' It For Themselves** ... S:16 / A:25 *I Love You Like A Ball And Chain* **(Eurythmics - ROK #36)** **EURYTHMICS and ARETHA FRANKLIN**	$3	■	RCA 14214
2/15/86	78	6		10 **It's Alright (Baby's Coming Back)** ... *Conditioned Soul* above 4 from the album *Be Yourself Tonight*	$3	■	RCA 14284
7/26/86	14	16		11 **Missionary Man** ... AR[1] S:13 / A:17 *Take Your Pain Away*	$3	■	RCA 14414
11/15/86	68	9		12 **Thorn In My Side** ... *In This Town*	$3	■	RCA 5058
12/19/87+	46	10		13 **I Need A Man** ... S:38 *Heaven*	$3	■	RCA 5361
5/28/88	64	7		14 **You Have Placed A Chill In My Heart** ... *Wide Eyed Girl*	$3	■	RCA 8619
9/30/89	40	9		15 **Don't Ask Me Why** ... S:31 *Rich Girl* all of above produced by **David Stewart** and written by Stewart and **Annie Lennox**	$3	■	Arista 9880
				EVAN AND JARON BUB/LP **'01** Pop-rock duo of identical twin brothers: Evan and Jaron Lowenstein. Born on 3/18/74 in Atlanta, Georgia.			
11/4/00+	15	23		**Crazy For This Girl** ... S:7 / A:17 *(acoustic version)* "45": Columbia 79484; B-side: "From My Head To My Heart" (#124)	$4	★V	Columbia 79484
				**EVANS, Faith** ★185★ R&B/BUB/LP **'99** Born on 6/10/73 in Newark, New Jersey. Female R&B singer/songwriter. Married to rapper **The Notorious B.I.G.** from 1994-97. Also see **Usher**'s "Think Of You." *1)I'll Be Missing You 2)Love Like This 3)All Night Long*			
7/1/95	24	20	●	1 **You Used To Love Me** *[FAITH]* ... S:13 / A:58 *(2 remixes)* "45" shown as **Faith Evans**: B-side: (club 2 mix)	$3	▮V	Bad Boy 79025
12/9/95+	21	20	●	2 **Soon As I Get Home** ... S:10 / A:64 *You Used To Love Me* (**Puff Daddy** mix) remix released in 1996 on Bad Boy 79048 (cassette single)	$3	▮	Bad Boy 79040
4/13/96	67	16		3 **Ain't Nobody /** S:41			
4/13/96		16		4 **Kissing You** ... S:flip from the movie *Waiting To Exhale* starring **Whitney Houston**	$4	▮V	Bad Boy 79055
6/14/97	❶[11]	33	▲[3]	5 **I'll Be Missing You** RB[8] S:❶[9] / A:4 *We'll Always Love Big Poppa* (**The Lox**) / *Cry On* (112) **PUFF DADDY & FAITH EVANS (Featuring 112)** "tribute to **The Notorious B.I.G.**"; melody is from "Every Breath You Take" by **The Police**; also see #14 below	$6	▮*	Bad Boy 79097
9/26/98	70	10		6 **How's It Goin' Down?** ... *Countdown* (Lil' Jamal & **PMD**) / *Broke Willies* (**Onyx**) **DMX Feat. Faith Evans** 12" single titled as "Survival Of The Illest, Vol. 2"	$6	T	Def Jam 566243
11/14/98	7	20	●	7 **Love Like This** ... S:9 / A:17 *(3 album snippets)* samples "Chic Cheer" by **Chic**	$4	★	Bad Boy 79117
12/26/98+	2[3]	28	▲	8 **Heartbreak Hotel** ... RB[7] S:2 / A:5 *(dance mix) / It's Not Right But It's Okay* (Houston - #4) **WHITNEY HOUSTON (Feat. Faith Evans & Kelly Price)**	$4	★	Arista 13619
2/6/99	9	19		9 **All Night Long** ... S:9 / A:29 *Life Will Pass You By* **FAITH EVANS (feat. Puff Daddy)** samples "I Hear Music In The Streets" by Unlimited Touch	$4	★	Bad Boy 79203
3/20/99	55	14		10 **Georgy Porgy** ... A:32 / S:50 *(4 remixes)* **ERIC BENÉT featuring Faith Evans**	$7	★*V	Warner 44612
7/10/99	17	20		11 **Never Gonna Let You Go** ... RB[1] S:7 / A:45 *(instrumental)* **Babyface**, Kenya Ivey, Tavia Ivey (backing vocals)	$4	★	Bad Boy 79252
1/8/00	34	16		12 **Love Is Blind** ... A:26 **EVE Featuring Faith Evans** from the **Eve** album *Ruff Ryders' First Lady* on Ruff Ryders 490453			album cut
5/5/01	56	20		13 **Can't Believe** ... A:48 / S:65 *(3 versions)* **FAITH EVANS Featuring Carl Thomas** samples "Phone Tap" by The Firm	$6	T	Bad Boy 79370
6/2/01	56[S]	8		14 **I'll Be Missing You** ... *We'll Always Love Big Poppa* (**The Lox**) / Cry On (112) [R] **PUFF DADDY & FAITH EVANS (Featuring 112)** reissue of #5 above on Bad Boy/Arista's "Maximum Hits" series	$8	★*	Bad Boy 79097
10/6/01	38	20		15 **You Gets No Love** ... A:34 / S:56 *(4 versions)*	$4	★	Bad Boy 79438

DEBUT	PEAK	WKS	Gold	A-side (Chart Hit)..........B-side	$	Sym	Label & Number
				EVANS, Faith — Cont'd			
1/26/02	**14**	21		16 **I Love You** ....A:13 / S:35 *(instrumental) / You Gets No Love* (w/**G. Dep**)	$6	T	Bad Boy 79425
2/2/02	**86**	7		17 **I Miss You**..........*(2 versions) / Number 11*	$6	T	Def Jam 588874
				DMX featuring Faith Evans			
				contains strains of the hymn "Amazing Grace"			
8/17/02	**60**	15		18 **Burnin' Up** A:56			album cut
				FAITH EVANS Featuring Missy "Misdemeanor" Elliott			
				#13, 15, 16 & 18: from the album *Faithfully* on Bad Boy 73041			
9/7/02	**55**^{S}	3		19 **Brown Sugar (Extra Sweet)** ....*(5 versions)*	$6	T	Fox/MCA 113986
				MOS DEF Featuring Faith Evans			
				from the movie *Brown Sugar* starring Taye Diggs			
				EVANS, Paul C&W **'60**			
				Born on 3/5/38 in Brooklyn, New York. Pop singer/songwriter. First recorded for RCA in 1957. Wrote hits "When" for the **Kalin Twins**, "Roses Are Red" for **Bobby Vinton**, "I Gotta Know" and "The Next Step Is Love" for **Elvis Presley**. Wrote the score for the Broadway show *Loot* and the movie *Live Young*.			
9/14/59	**9**	18		1 **Seven Little Girls Sitting In The Back Seat** ....*Worshipping An Idol* [N]	$20		Guaranteed 200
				with the Curls (female backing duo: Sue Singleton and Sue Terry)			
1/25/60	**16**	13		2 **Midnite Special**..........*Since I Met You Baby*	$15		Guaranteed 205
				written and recorded by Leadbelly in 1941 on Victor 27266; #12 R&B hit for Tiny Grimes in 1948			
5/2/60	**10**	14		3 **Happy-Go-Lucky-Me** ....*Fish In The Ocean (Bubbly Bum Bum)*	$15		Guaranteed 208
8/8/60	**81**	4		4 **The Brigade Of Broken Hearts**..........*Twins*	$15		Guaranteed 210
				EVANS, Sara C&W/BUB/LP **'00**			
				Born on 2/5/71 in Boonville, Missouri; raised in Boonesboro, Missouri. Country singer/songwriter.			
12/12/98+	**37**	19		1 **No Place That Far** ....CW^{1} A:27 / S:29 *Cryin' Game* (C&W #56)	$4	★^{V}	RCA 65584
				Vince Gill (backing vocal)			
10/21/00	**34**	20		2 **Born To Fly** ....CW^{1} A:30		V	album cut
4/21/01	**35**	20		3 **I Could Not Ask For More** A:30		V	album cut
				"45" issued for above 2 on RCA 69008			
7/20/02	**35**	19		4 **I Keep Looking**..........A:32			album cut
				above 3 from the album *Born To Fly* on RCA 67964			
	★**424**★			**EVE** R&B/BUB/LP **'02**			
				Born Eve Jeffers on 11/10/78 in Philadelphia, Pennsylvania. Female rapper/songwriter. Star of the Fox TV series *The Opposite Sex*. Also see **BLACKstreet**'s "Girlfriend/Boyfriend."			
				1)Gangsta Lovin' 2)Let Me Blow Ya Mind 3)Gotta Man			
7/3/99	**29**	20		1 **What Ya Want** A:18			album cut
				EVE & NOKIO			
9/18/99	**26**	16		2 **Gotta Man** ....A:19 *(3 versions)*	$6	T	Ruff Ryders 97085
11/27/99+	**5**	21	▲	3 **Hot Boyz**..........RB^{6} S:2 / A:24 *U Can't Resist* (w/**Juvenile** & **B.G.**)	$4	★	The Gold Mind 64029
				MISSY "MISDEMEANOR" ELLIOTT [featuring NAS, EVE & Q-TIP]			
				Lil' Mo (vocal ad libs)			
1/8/00	**34**	16		4 **Love Is Blind** A:26			album cut
				EVE Featuring Faith Evans			
				#1, 2 & 4: from the album *Ruff Ryders' First Lady* on Ruff Ryders 490453			
3/18/00	**73**	7		5 **Ryde Or Die, Chick**..........A:65			album cut
				LOX Featuring Timbaland and Eve			
				from the **Lox** album *We Are The Streets* on Ruff Ryders 490599			
7/15/00	**88**	5		6 **Got It All** ....*(3 versions)*	$6	T	Ruff Ryders 497360
				EVE & JADAKISS			
2/17/01	**47**	18		7 **Who's That Girl?** ....A:44 / S:52 *(4 versions)*	$6	T	Ruff Ryders 497488
4/28/01	**2**^{1}	33		8 **Let Me Blow Ya Mind** ....A:❶^{4} / S:46 *(2 versions) / That's What It Is* (w/Styles of **The Lox**)	$6	T	Ruff Ryders 497562
				EVE Featuring Gwen Stefani (lead singer of **No Doubt**)			
10/13/01+	**18**	24		9 **Caramel** ....A:18 *(5 versions)*	$6	T	Booga Basement 497608
				CITY HIGH Featuring Eve			
7/13/02	**2**^{4}	22		10 **Gangsta Lovin'** A:2 / S:6 *(4 album snippets)*	$4	★	Ruff Ryders 497817
				EVE Feat. Alicia Keys			
				samples "Don't Stop The Music" by **Yarbrough & Peoples**			
11/30/02+	**27**	16		11 **Satisfaction** A:25			album cut
				above 2 from the album *EVE-Olution* on Ruff Ryders 493381			
				EVERCLEAR ROK/BUB/LP **'00**			
				Rock trio formed in Portland, Oregon: Art Alexakis (vocals, guitar), Craig Montoya (bass) and Greg Eklund (drums).			
12/16/95+	**29**^{A}	28		1 **Santa Monica (Watch The World Die)** ....AR^{3}		V	album cut
				"45": Capitol 19018; B-side: "Heroin Girl" (ROK #34)			
5/18/96	**85**	7		2 **Heartspark Dollarsign** ....A:74 *Heroin Girl / Happy Hour / Sin City*	$8	★*^{V}	Capitol 58538
				"45": Capitol 19166; B-side: "Queen Of The Air"; above 2 from the album *Sparkle And Fade* on Capitol 30929			
9/20/97	**43**^{A}	20		3 **Everything To Everyone** ....MR^{1}			album cut
2/28/98	**33**^{A}	26		4 **I Will Buy You A New Life**		V	album cut
				"45": Capitol 19900; B-side: "Like A California King"			
8/22/98	**46**^{A}	29		5 **Father Of Mine**..........HOT:70(17 wks)			album cut
				above 3 from the album *So Much For The Afterglow* on Capitol 36503			
7/8/00	**11**	21		6 **Wonderful** S:6 / A:17 *Father Of Mine (remix) / I'm On Your Time*	$4	★^{V}	Capitol 58870
				"45": Capitol 58856; B-side: "Unemployed Boyfriend"			
				EVERETT, Betty R&B/BUB/LP **'64**			
				Born on 11/23/39 in Greenwood, Mississippi. Died on 8/19/2001 (age 61). R&B singer/pianist. Performed in gospel choirs. To Chicago in the late 1950s. First recorded for Cobra in 1958. Toured England in the mid-1960s.			
				1)Let It Be Me 2)The Shoop Shoop Song (It's In His Kiss) 3)There'll Come A Time			
11/23/63+	**51**	10		1 **You're No Good**..........*Chained To Your Love*	$20		Vee-Jay 566
2/29/64	**6**	13		2 **The Shoop Shoop Song (It's In His Kiss)** ....*Hands Off*	$20		Vee-Jay 585
6/27/64	**66**	5		3 **I Can't Hear You**..........*Can I Get To Know You*	$15		Vee-Jay 599
9/5/64	**5**	13		4 **Let It Be Me** *Ain't That Loving You Baby* (#108)	$15		Vee-Jay 613
				BETTY EVERETT & JERRY BUTLER			

DEBUT	PEAK	WKS	Gold	A-side (Chart Hit)...B-side	$	Sym	Label & Number

EVERETT, Betty — Cont'd

DEBUT	PEAK	WKS	Gold	A-side (Chart Hit)...B-side	$	Sym	Label & Number
11/28/64+	65	6		5 **Getting Mighty Crowded** ... *Chained To A Memory (Why Am I?)*	$15		Vee-Jay 628
12/5/64+	42	7		6 **Smile** ... *Love Is Strange*	$15		Vee-Jay 633
				BETTY EVERETT & JERRY BUTLER written in 1936 by Charlie Chaplin for his movie *Modern Times*; #10 hit for **Nat "King" Cole** in 1954			
1/18/69	26	11		7 **There'll Come A Time** ... *Take Me*	$8		Uni 55100
4/26/69	78	4		8 **I Can't Say No To You** ... *Better Tomorrow Than Today*	$8		Uni 55122
12/20/69	96	2		9 **It's Been A Long Time** ... *Just A Man's Way*	$8		Uni 55174
12/26/70+	96	4		10 **I Got To Tell Somebody** ... *Why Are You Leaving Me*	$8		Fantasy 652

EVERLAST

ROK/BUB/LP **'99**

Born Erik Schrody on 8/18/69 in Valley Stream, New York. White rock-hip-hop singer/songwriter. Former member of **House Of Pain**. Played "Rhodes" in the movie *Judgment Night*.

DEBUT	PEAK	WKS	Gold	A-side (Chart Hit)...B-side	$	Sym	Label & Number
12/19/98+	13	33		**What It's Like** ... AR[1] / MR[9] A:5			album cut
				from the album *Whitey Ford Sings The Blues* on Tommy Boy 1236			

EVERLY BROTHERS, The ★45★

BUB/C&W/AC/LP **'58**

Rock and roll-pop-country vocal duo/guitarists/songwriters/brothers. Don was born Isaac Donald on 2/1/37 in Brownie, Kentucky; Phil was born on 1/19/39 in Chicago, Illinois. Parents were folk and country singers. Don (beginning at age eight) and Phil (age six) sang with parents through high school. Invited to Nashville by **Chet Atkins** and first recorded there for Columbia in 1955. Signed to **Archie Bleyer**'s Cadence Records in 1957. Phil married for a time to the daughter of Janet Bleyer (**Chordettes**). Duo split up in July 1973 and reunited in September 1983. Inducted into the Rock and Roll Hall of Fame in 1986. Won Grammy's Lifetime Achievement Award in 1997. Don's daughter Erin was married for a short time to Axl Rose of **Guns N' Roses** in 1990. Also see **Adrian Kimberly** and **Paul Simon**'s "Graceland."

1)All I Have To Do Is Dream 2)Cathy's Clown 3)Wake Up Little Susie 4)Bird Dog 5)Bye Bye Love

DEBUT	PEAK	WKS	Gold	A-side (Chart Hit)...B-side	$	Sym	Label & Number
5/20/57	2^{4}	27	●	1 **Bye Bye Love** / CW[7] S:2 / T:2 / A:2 / J:9			
7/8/57		1		2 **I Wonder If I Care As Much** ... S:flip	$30		Cadence 1315
9/30/57	❶^{4}	26	●	3 **Wake Up Little Susie** ... RB[1] / CW[8] A:❶[4] / T:❷[2] / S:❶[1] *Maybe Tomorrow*	$30	■	Cadence 1337
2/10/58	26	9		4 **This Little Girl Of Mine** / S:26 / T:28			
				#9 R&B hit for **Ray Charles** in 1955			
3/17/58		1		5 **Should We Tell Him** ... S:flip	$25		Cadence 1342
4/21/58	❶^{5}	17	●	6 **All I Have To Do Is Dream** / RB[5] / CW[3] A:❶[5] / S:❶[4] / T:❶[3]			
				also see #27 below			
5/5/58	30	10		7 **Claudette** ... T:30 / S:flip	$25		Cadence 1348
				written by **Roy Orbison** for his wife			
8/4/58	❶^{1}	18	●	8 **Bird Dog** / CW[6] S:❶[1] / H:2			
8/11/58	10	14		9 **Devoted To You** ... H:10 / S:flip	$25		Cadence 1350
11/10/58	2^{1}	15		10 **Problems** /			
11/24/58	40	6		11 **Love Of My Life** ...	$25	■	Cadence 1355
3/30/59	16	13		12 **Take A Message To Mary** /			
3/30/59	22	12		13 **Poor Jenny** ...	$25		Cadence 1364
8/17/59	4	16		14 **('Til) I Kissed You** ... *Oh, What A Feeling*	$25	■	Cadence 1369
				The Crickets (backing band)			
1/11/60	7	15		15 **Let It Be Me** ... *Since You Broke My Heart*	$25	■	Cadence 1376
4/18/60	❶^{5}	17	●	16 **Cathy's Clown** / RB[1]			
5/16/60	56	6		17 **Always It's You** ...	$20	■	Warner 5151
5/30/60	8	13		18 **When Will I Be Loved** /			
7/11/60	74	5		19 **Be Bop A-Lula** ...	$25		Cadence 1380
9/5/60	7	12		20 **So Sad (To Watch Good Love Go Bad)** /			
9/5/60	21	10		21 **Lucille** ...	$20	■	Warner 5163
10/31/60	22	10		22 **Like Strangers** ... *Brand New Heartache (#109)*	$25		Cadence 1388
				#1, 3, 6, 8-13, 17 & 22: written by Boudleaux & Felice Bryant			
2/6/61	7	13		23 **Walk Right Back** /			
1/30/61	8	12		24 **Ebony Eyes** ...	$20	■	Warner 5199
5/29/61	27	6		25 **Temptation** /			
				#3 hit for **Bing Crosby** in 1934			
6/5/61	41	4		26 **Stick With Me Baby** ...	$20	■	Warner 5220
7/24/61	96	2		27 **All I Have To Do Is Dream** ... *Claudette* [R]	$25		Cadence 1348
				same version as #6 above			
9/25/61	20	8		28 **Don't Blame Me** /			
				#6 hit for Ethel Waters in 1933 (from the musical *Clowns In Clover*)			
10/2/61	82	4		29 **Muskrat** ...	$25	■	Warner 5501 (+2)
				above 2 released as a 7" EP with shortened versions of the B-sides			
1/13/62	6	13		30 **Crying In The Rain** ... *I'm Not Angry*	$20	■	Warner 5250
5/12/62	9	11		31 **That's Old Fashioned (That's The Way Love Should Be)** /			
5/26/62	75	3		32 **How Can I Meet Her?** ...	$20	■	Warner 5273
10/13/62	76	6		33 **I'm Here To Get My Baby Out Of Jail** ... *Lightning Express*	$25		Cadence 1429
10/20/62	48	7		34 **Don't Ask Me To Be Friends** ... *No One Can Make My Sunshine Smile (#117)*	$20	■	Warner 5297
6/20/64	72	6		35 **The Ferris Wheel** ... *Don't Forget To Cry*	$15		Warner 5441
10/17/64	31	10		36 **Gone, Gone, Gone** ... *Torture*	$15		Warner 5478
				#2, 5, 14, 16, 18, 20 & 36: written by Don and/or Phil Everly			
5/27/67	40	8		37 **Bowling Green** ... *I Don't Want To Love You*	$15		Warner 7020
9/1/84	50	12		38 **On The Wings Of A Nightingale** ... *Asleep*	$5		Mercury 880213
				written by **Paul McCartney**; produced by **Dave Edmunds**			

EVERY FATHER'S TEENAGE SON

'67

Bill Dean recites a teenager's response to **Victor Lundberg**'s Top 10 hit.

DEBUT	PEAK	WKS	Gold	A-side (Chart Hit)...B-side	$	Sym	Label & Number
11/25/67	93	4		**A Letter To Dad** ... *Josephine's Song* [S]	$8		Buddah 25
				reply to "An Open Letter To My Teenage Son" by **Victor Lundberg**			

DEBUT	PEAK	WKS	Gold	A-side (Chart Hit)...B-side	$	Sym	Label & Number
				EVERY MOTHERS' SON LP '67			
				Pop-rock group from New York: brothers Dennis (vocals) and Larry (guitar) Larden, Bruce Milner (organ), Schuyler Larsen (bass) and Christopher Augustine (drums).			
5/6/67	6	15		1 **Come On Down To My Boat** ... *I Believe In You*	$10		MGM 13733
8/26/67	46	7		2 **Put Your Mind At Ease** ... *The Proper Four Leaf Clover*	$8	■	MGM 13788
11/11/67	93	2		3 **Pony With The Golden Mane** ... *Dolls In The Clock*	$8		MGM 13844
1/27/68	96	3		4 **No One Knows** ... *What Became Of Mary*	$8		MGM 13887
				EVERYTHING LP '98			
				Ska-rock group from Sperryville, Virginia: Craig Honeycutt (vocals, guitar), Rich Bradley, Wolfe Quinn and Steve Van Dam (horns), David Slankard (bass) and Nate Brown (drums).			
8/1/98	34A	21		**Hooch** ... HOT:69(7 wks) from the album *Super Natural* on Blackbird 38003			album cut
				EVERYTHING BUT THE GIRL AC/ROK/R&B/LP '96			
				Pop-dance duo formed in London, England: Tracey Thorn (vocals) and Ben Watt (guitar, keyboards, vocals). Group name taken from a furniture store sign on England's Hull University campus.			
8/12/95+	2¹	55	●	1 **Missing** A:❶⁵ / S:12 *(album version)*	$3	▮	Atlantic 87124
6/1/96	68	10		2 **Wrong** ... S:73 *(2 remixes)*	$3	▮	Atlantic 87059
10/2/99	64S	2		3 **Five Fathoms** ... *(4 mixes) / Firewall*	$8	★*	Atlantic 84530
3/11/00	66S	1		4 **Temperamental** ... *(7 mixes)*	$8	★*	Atlantic 84657
12/23/00	69S	1		5 **Lullaby Of Clubland** ... *(7 mixes)*	$8	★*	Atlantic 85009
				EVERYTHING is EVERYTHING '69			
				Pop-rock duo of Danny Weiss and Chris Hills.			
2/8/69	69	5		**Witchi Tai To** ... *Oooh Baby* [F]	$8		Vanguard A. 35082
				EVE 6 ROK/BUB/LP '98			
				Rock trio from Los Angeles, California: Max Collins (vocals, bass), Jon Siebels (guitar) and Tony Fagenson (drums).			
12/5/98	28	14		1 **Inside Out** ... MR⁴ A:21 *Hot 100 Airplay* debut: 6/13/98; from the album *Eve 6* on RCA 67617			album cut
6/9/01	30	20		2 **Here's To The Night** ... A:25 from the album *Horrorscope* on RCA 67713			album cut
				EXCELLENTS, The '63			
				White doo-wop group from Brooklyn, New York: John Kuse (lead), George Kuse, Denis Kestenbaum, Joel Feldman, Phil Sanchez and Chuck Epstein.			
11/24/62+	51	9		**Coney Island Baby** ... *You Baby You*	$50		Blast 205
				EXCELS, The '61			
				Doo-wop group from the Bronx, New York: Fred Orange (lead), Benito Travieso, Raphael Diaz, Harry Hilliard and Joe Robles.			
6/5/61	100	1		**Can't Help Lovin' That Girl Of Mine** ... *'Til You Were Gone* from the musical *Show Boat* (as "Can't Help Lovin' Dat Man")	$75		RSVP 111
				EXCITERS, The R&B '63			
				R&B vocal group from Jamaica, New York: Herb Rooney, his wife Brenda Reid, Carol Johnson and Lillian Walker.			
12/1/62+	4	13		1 **Tell Him** *Hard Way To Go*	$15		United Artists 544
3/2/63	57	8		2 **He's Got The Power** ... *Drama Of Love*	$12		United Artists 572
6/22/63	76	3		3 **Get Him** ... *It's So Exciting*	$12		United Artists 604
1/4/64	78	4		4 **Do-Wah-Diddy** ... *If Love Came Your Way* all of above produced by Leiber & Stoller	$12		United Artists 662
1/16/65	98	1		5 **I Want You To Be My Boy** ... *Tonight, Tonight* female version of "I Want You To Be My Girl" by **Frankie Lymon & The Teenagers**	$12	■	Roulette 4591
1/29/66	58	6		6 **A Little Bit Of Soap** ... *I'm Gonna Get Him Someday*	$12		Bang 515
				EX-GIRLFRIEND R&B '91			
				Female R&B vocal group from Brooklyn, New York: Julia Roberson, Monica Boyd, Tisha Hunter and Stacy Francis.			
9/7/91	78	8		**Why Can't You Come Home** ... A:57 / S:68 *Come Home (The Confrontation mix)*	$3	▮	Reprise 19327
				EXHALE '02			
				Female R&B vocal trio from Washington DC: Natasha Belton, Tokiko George and LaToya Watson.			
9/15/01	20S	12		1 **Chillin' In Your Benz** ... *(2 versions)*	$5	★	Real Deal 70635
4/13/02	9S	14		2 **Still Not Over You** ... *(4 versions)*	$8	★*	Real Deal 90300
				EXILE C&W/BUB/AC/LP '78			
				Pop-country group formed in Richmond, Kentucky: Jimmy Stokley (vocals), J.P. Pennington (vocals, guitar), Buzz Cornelison (keyboards), Sonny Lemaire (bass) and Steve Goetzman (drums). Charted 21 Country hits, 1983-91.			
3/5/77	97	3		1 **Try It On** ... *Show Me What You Got*	$5		Atco 7072
7/8/78	❶⁴	23	●	2 **Kiss You All Over** ... *Don't Do It*	$4		Warner/Curb 8589
11/25/78+	40	11		3 **You Thrill Me** ... *One Step At A Time*	$4		Warner/Curb 8711
4/28/79	88	2		4 **How Could This Go Wrong** ... *Being In Love With You Is Easy*	$4		Warner/Curb 8796
	★299★			**EXPOSÉ** BUB/LP '87			
				Female dance trio based in Miami, Florida: Ann Curless (born on 10/7/65), Jeanette Jurado (born on 11/14/66) and Gioia Bruno (born on 6/11/65). Assembled by producer/songwriter Lewis Martineé. Kelly Moneymaker replaced Bruno in 1992. Also see **Sandeé**. *1)Seasons Change 2)Come Go With Me 3)Point Of No Return*			
1/24/87	5	19		1 **Come Go With Me** ... S:4 / A:6 *December*	$3	■	Arista 9555
5/9/87	5	17		2 **Point Of No Return** ... S:5 / A:6 *Extra Extra* new version of group's 1985 Dance/Disco hit (#1) on Arista 9326	$3	■	Arista 9579
8/15/87	7	22		3 **Let Me Be The One** ... S:4 / A:7 *Love Is Our Destiny*	$3	■	Arista 9617
11/28/87+	❶¹	20		4 **Seasons Change** AC¹ S:❶¹ / A:2 *December* above 4 from the album *Exposure*	$3	■	Arista 9640
5/20/89	8	15	●	5 **What You Don't Know** ... S:8 / A:10 *Walk Along With Me* issued with a regular picture sleeve and a foldout poster sleeve	$3	■	Arista 9836

DEBUT	PEAK	WKS	Gold	A-side (Chart Hit)..........B-side	$	Sym	Label & Number
				EXPOSÉ — Cont'd			
8/19/89	10	20		6 **When I Looked At Him**..........A:6 / S:11 *(acoustic version)*	$3	■	Arista 9868
12/9/89+	9	15		7 **Tell Me Why**..........S:7 / A:13 *Let Me Down Easy*	$3	■	Arista 9916
				all of above written and produced by Lewis Martineé			
3/31/90	17	16		8 **Your Baby Never Looked Good In Blue**..........A:11 / S:19 *Now That I Found You*	$3	▮V	Arista 2011
				above 4 from the album *What You Don't Know*			
10/31/92	28	15		9 **I Wish The Phone Would Ring**..........A:21 / S:56 *I'll Never Get Over You (Getting Over Me)*	$3	▮	Arista 12466
3/27/93	8	29	●	10 **I'll Never Get Over You (Getting Over Me)**.....AC[1] A:4 / S:14 *Give Me All Your Love*	$3	▮	Arista 12518
10/16/93	55	14		11 **As Long As I Can Dream**..........A:61 / S:62 *Face To Face*	$3	▮V	Arista 12600
				co-written by **Roy Orbison**			
4/9/94	84	6		12 **In Walked Love**..........A:74 *The Same Love*	$3	▮	Arista 12679
				above 4 from the album *Exposé*			
				EXTREME ROK/LP **'91**			
				Rock group from Boston, Massachusetts: Gary Cherone (vocals), Nuno Bettencourt (guitar; born in Portugal), Pat Badger (bass) and Paul Geary (drums). Cherone became lead singer of **Van Halen** in September 1996.			
3/23/91	❶[1]	24	●	1 **More Than Words**..........S:❶[4] / A:3 *(remix)*	$3	▮V	A&M 1552
				"45" B-side: "Get The Funk Out" (ROK #34)			
8/3/91	4	20		2 **Hole Hearted**..........A:6 / S:19 *Suzi (Wants Her All Day What?)*	$3	▮V	A&M 1564
				"45": A&M/Collectables 8716; B-side: "Get The Funk Out"			
10/24/92	96	3		3 **Rest In Peace**..........AR[2] *Peacemaker Die*	$3	▮	A&M 0055
2/20/93	95	3		4 **Stop The World**..........*Warheads*	$3	▮	A&M 0120
				EYC BUB **'99**			
				Male pop vocal trio from Los Angeles, California: Damon Butler, David Loeffler and Trey Parker (not to be confused with the co-creator of TV's *South Park*). E.Y.C.: Express Yourself Clearly.			
4/17/99	30[S]	8		1 **This Thing Called Love**..........BUB:118 *(3 album snippets) / How Could I Let You Go*	$3	★	Red Ant 15335
8/28/99	35[S]	8		2 **Only A Dream**..........*(3 album snippets)*	$3	★	Red Ant 15338
				EYE TO EYE LP **'82**			
				Pop duo: vocalist Deborah Berg from Seattle, Washington, and pianist Julian Marshall (of **Marshall Hain**) from England.			
5/22/82	37	13		1 **Nice Girls**..........*Time Flys*	$4		Warner 50050
10/29/83	88	2		2 **Lucky**..........*Something Good*	$4		Warner 29455
				EYE TO EYE — see I TO I			

F

DEBUT	PEAK	WKS	Gold	A-side (Chart Hit)..........B-side	$	Sym	Label & Number
				FABARES, Shelley BUB/LP **'62**			
				Born Michele Fabares on 1/19/44 in Santa Monica, California. Pop singer/actress. Niece of actress Nanette Fabray. Starred with **Elvis Presley** in three of his movies. Played "Mary Stone" on *The Donna Reed Show*. Married to record producer Lou Adler from 1964-67. Cast member of several TV series since 1972, among them *One Day At A Time* and *Coach*. Married actor Mike Farrell on 1/31/84.			
3/3/62	❶[2]	15		1 **Johnny Angel**..........*Where's It Gonna Get Me?*	$20	■	Colpix 621
				The Blossoms (backing vocals)			
6/9/62	21	10		2 **Johnny Loves Me**..........*I'm Growing Up*	$20	■	Colpix 636
9/15/62	46	6		3 **The Things We Did Last Summer**..........*Breaking Up Is Hard To Do*	$20		Colpix 654
				#10 hit for **Jo Stafford** in 1946			
4/27/63	72	5		4 **Ronnie, Call Me When You Get A Chance**..........*I Left A Note To Say Goodbye*	$20		Colpix 682
				FAB 5, The R&B/BUB **'96**			
				Gathering of rap acts **Heltah Skeltah** and Originoo Gunn Clappaz.			
2/3/96	75	8		**LeFlaur LeFlah Eshkoshka**..........S:66 *Blah* (#103)	$3	▮	Priority 53223
				THE FABULOUS FIVE Featuring: Heltah Skeltah And Originoo Gunn Clappaz			
				contains elements from "Uzuri" by The Catalysts; Eshkoshka: an ancient warrior yell			
	★551★			**FABIAN** LP **'59**			
				Born Fabiano Forte on 2/6/43 in Philadelphia, Pennsylvania. Discovered at age 14 (because of his good looks and intriguing name) by a chance meeting with Bob Marcucci, owner of Chancellor Records. Began acting career in 1959 with the movie *Hound Dog Man*. His son, Christian Forte, wrote the screenplay for the 1997 movie *Albino Alligator*.			
				1)Tiger 2)Turn Me Loose 3)Hound Dog Man			
1/12/59	31	10		1 **I'm A Man**..........*Hypnotized*	$25	■	Chancellor 1029
				first picture sleeves showed title as "I Am A Man"			
3/30/59	9	13		2 **Turn Me Loose**..........*Stop Thief!*	$25	■	Chancellor 1033
6/15/59	3	13		3 **Tiger** *Mighty Cold (To a warm warm heart)*	$20	■	Chancellor 1037
				picture sleeve issued with an orange or white title strip			
9/7/59	29	8		4 **Come On And Get Me** /			
9/21/59	54	5		5 **Got The Feeling**..........	$20	■	Chancellor 1041
				issued with 3 different picture sleeves			
11/16/59	9	15		6 **Hound Dog Man** /			
11/23/59	12	13		7 **This Friendly World**..........	$20	■	Chancellor 1044
				above 2 from the movie *Hound Dog Man* starring Fabian; issued with 2 different picture sleeves			
2/29/60	31	7		8 **About This Thing Called Love** /			
2/22/60	39	8		9 **String Along**..........	$20	■	Chancellor 1047
				all of above produced by Peter de Angelis			
10/31/60	91	2		10 **Kissin' And Twistin'**..........*Long Before*	$20	■	Chancellor 1061
				FABIAN, Lara AC/LP **'00**			
				Born Lara Crockaert on 1/9/70 in Bruxelles, Belgium; raised in Italy. Female Adult Contemporary singer/songwriter.			
6/10/00	32	17		**I Will Love Again**..........A:35 / S:36 *(3 versions)*	$8	★*	Columbia 79375

DEBUT	PEAK	WKS	Gold	A-side (Chart Hit).....B-side	$	Sym	Label & Number
				FABOLOUS R&B/LP **'02**			
				Born John Jackson on 11/18/79 in Brooklyn, New York. Male rapper. The first artist signed to DJ Clue's label, Desert Storm.			
3/31/01	11	22		1 **Superwoman Pt. II**.....S:2 / A:22 *Superwoman*	$4	★	EastWest 67171
				LIL MO (Featuring Fabolous)			
				charted first 7 weeks as "Superwoman"			
7/21/01	25	20		2 **Can't Deny It**.....A:24 *(4 versions)*	$6	T	Desert Storm 67231
				FABOLOUS featuring Nate Dogg			
				Lil' Mo (background vocals); samples "Ambitionz Az A Ridah" by **2Pac**			
12/1/01+	33	20		3 **Young'n (Holla Back)**.....A:33 / S:41 *(3 versions)*	$6	T	Desert Storm 67265
2/2/02	75S	1		4 **Bootee**.....*(3 versions)*	$7	T	Surrender 015631
				BENZINO f/ Fabolous & G-Dep			
				samples "The Bertha Butt Boogie" by **The Jimmy Castor Bunch**			
8/17/02	20	18		5 **Trade It All (Part 2)** A:13			album cut
				FABOLOUS featuring P. DIDDY & JAGGED EDGE			
				from the movie *Barbershop* starring **Ice Cube** (soundtrack on Epic 86575)			
10/26/02+	5S	31		6 **This Is My Party**.....*(3 album snippets)*	$4	★	Desert Storm 67355
				FABRIC, Bent, and His Piano BUB/LP **'62**			
				Born Bent Fabricius-Bjerre on 12/7/24 in Copenhagen, Denmark. Male pianist.			
7/28/62	7	18	●	1 **Alley Cat**.....*Markin' Time* [I]	$8		Atco 6226
				Danish title: "Omkring et Flygel" ("Around The Piano")			
1/12/63	63	8		2 **Chicken Feed**.....*That Certain Party* (#117) [I]	$8		Atco 6245
				FABU **'95**			
				Female R&B duo: Janine Williams and Christina Hayes.			
5/20/95	88	2		**Just Roll**.....S:56 *(instrumental)*	$4	▮	Big Beat 98175
				FABULOUS COUNTS R&B **'70**			
				R&B group from Detroit, Michigan: Mose Davis (vocals), Demetrus Cates, Raoul Keith Mangrum, Andrew Gibson and Leroy Emmanuel. Recorded as The Counts for Westbound Records.			
4/25/70	88	4		**Get Down People**.....*Lunar Funk*	$8		Moira 108
				FABULOUS POODLES LP **'79**			
				Rock group from England: Tony DeMeur (vocals, guitar), Bobby Valentino (violin), Richie Robertson (bass) and Bryn Burrows (drums).			
4/28/79	81	4		**Mirror Star**.....*Tit Photographer Blues*	$5		Epic 50666
				FABULOUS RHINESTONES, The LP **'72**			
				Rock trio from Chicago, Illinois: Kal David (vocals, guitar), Harvey Brooks (bass) and Martin Grebb (vocals, keyboards; **The Buckinghams**).			
8/5/72	78	4		**What A Wonderful Thing We Have**.....*Nothing New*	$6	■	Just Sunshine 500
				FABULOUS THUNDERBIRDS, The ROK/LP **'86**			
				Male blues-rock group from Austin, Texas: Kim Wilson (vocals, harmonica), Jimmie Vaughan (guitar; older brother of Stevie Ray Vaughan), Keith Ferguson (bass) and Fran Christina (drums). Preston Hubbard replaced Ferguson in late 1981. Vaughan appeared in the 1989 movie *Great Balls Of Fire* and recorded with Stevie Ray as **The Vaughan Brothers** in 1990. Ferguson died of liver failure on 4/29/97 (age 49).			
4/19/86	10	19		1 **Tuff Enuff**.....S:11 / A:12 *Look At That, Look At That* (ROK #20)	$3	■	CBS Associated 05838
8/9/86	50	10		2 **Wrap It Up**.....*True Love*	$3	■	CBS Associated 06270
7/4/87	76	5		3 **Stand Back**.....*It Takes A Big Man To Cry*	$3	■	CBS Associated 07230
				all of above produced by **Dave Edmunds**			
8/27/88	65	7		4 **Powerful Stuff**.....*Tutti Frutti* (**Little Richard**)	$3		Elektra 69384
				from the movie *Cocktail* starring Tom Cruise			
				FACENDA, Tommy **'59**			
				Born on 11/10/39 in Norfolk, Virginia. Backup vocals with **Gene Vincent** from 1957-58. Nicknamed "Bubba." Discovered by Frank Guida, who wrote Facenda's hit and discovered **Gary (U.S.) Bonds**. First recorded for Nasco in 1958. Later became a firefighter in Virginia.			
10/19/59	28	13		**High School U.S.A. (Area)**.....*Plea Of Love* [N]	$40		Atlantic 51 to 78
				first released as "High School U.S.A. Virginia" on Legrand 1001 ($40; B-side: "Give Me Another Chance"); Atlantic then released 28 different versions of this record, each mentioning the names of high schools in the following areas: Virginia (Atlantic 51), New York City, North & South Carolina, Washington D.C., Philadelphia, Detroit, Pittsburgh, Minneapolis & St. Paul, Florida, Newark, Boston, Cleveland, Buffalo, Hartford, Nashville, Indianapolis, Chicago, New Orleans, St. Louis & Kansas City, Georgia & Alabama, Cincinnati, Memphis, Los Angeles, San Francisco, Texas, Seattle & Portland, Denver, and Oklahoma (Atlantic 78)			
				FACES — see SMALL FACES			
				FACE TO FACE ROK/LP **'84**			
				Rock group from Boston, Massachusetts: Laurie Sargent (vocals), brothers Angelo and Stuart Kimball (guitars), John Ryder (bass) and William Beard (drums).			
6/2/84	38	15		**10-9-8**.....*Heaven On Earth*	$4	■	Epic 04430
				FACHIN, Eria **'88**			
				Born in 1950 in Hamilton, Ontario, Canada. Died of cancer on 5/9/96 (age 36). Female dance singer.			
2/27/88	50	10		**Savin' Myself**.....*(instrumental)*	$4	■	Critique 99356
				FACTS OF LIFE R&B/LP **'77**			
				R&B vocal trio formed by **Millie Jackson**, originally known as The Gospel Truth: Jean Davis (younger sister of **Tyrone Davis**), Keith William (Imperials, **Flamingos**) and Chuck Carter.			
3/5/77	31	10		**Sometimes**.....*Love Is The Final Truth*	$7		Kayvette 5128
				produced by **Millie Jackson**; #1 Country hit for **Bill Anderson** & Mary Lou Turner in 1976			

DEBUT	PEAK	WKS	Gold	A-side (Chart Hit)...B-side	$	Sym	Label & Number

FAGEN, Donald — ROK/BUB/AC/LP '82

Born on 1/10/48 in Passaic, New Jersey. Backup keyboardist/vocalist with **Jay & The Americans**. At New York's Bard College, formed band with Walter Becker and drummer-turned-comic actor Chevy Chase. Fagen and Becker formed **Steely Dan** in 1972.

DEBUT	PEAK	WKS	Gold	A-side (Chart Hit)...B-side	$	Sym	Label & Number
10/9/82	26	14		1 **I.G.Y. (What A Beautiful World)** ... *Walk Between Raindrops* I.G.Y.: International Geophysical Year (Jul '57-Dec '58)	$4	■	Warner 29900
1/29/83	70	6		2 **New Frontier** ... *Maxine*	$4		Warner 29792
4/2/88	83	5		3 **Century's End** ... *Shanghai Confidential* from the movie *Bright Lights, Big City* starring Michael J. Fox	$3	■	Warner 27972

FAGIN, Joe — '82

Born in Liverpool, England. Pop singer/songwriter/bassist.

DEBUT	PEAK	WKS	Gold	A-side (Chart Hit)...B-side	$	Sym	Label & Number
7/31/82	80	3		**Younger Days** ... *Do You Give A Damn*	$6		Millennium 13107

FAIR, Yvonne — R&B '76

Born in 1942 in Virginia. Died on 3/6/94 (age 51). R&B-dance singer. Toured with **James Brown** Revue. Appeared in the movie *Lady Sings The Blues*. Married to Sammy Strain of **The O'Jays**.

DEBUT	PEAK	WKS	Gold	A-side (Chart Hit)...B-side	$	Sym	Label & Number
4/24/76	85	5		**It Should Have Been Me** ... *Tell Me Something Good*	$6		Motown 1384

FAIRCHILD, Barbara — C&W '73

Born on 11/12/50 in Knobel, Arkansas. Country singer/songwriter (charted 30 hits, 1969-86).

DEBUT	PEAK	WKS	Gold	A-side (Chart Hit)...B-side	$	Sym	Label & Number
2/24/73	32	19		1 **Teddy Bear Song** ... CW[2] *(You Make Me Feel Like) Singing A Song*	$5		Columbia 45743
8/25/73	95	5		2 **Kid Stuff** ... *Make No Mistakes*	$5		Columbia 45903

FAIRGROUND ATTRACTION — LP '89

Pop group from England: Eddi Reader (female vocals), Mark Nevin (guitar), Simon Edwards (bass) and Roy Dodds (drums).

DEBUT	PEAK	WKS	Gold	A-side (Chart Hit)...B-side	$	Sym	Label & Number
12/17/88+	80	6		**Perfect** ... *Mythology*	$4	■	RCA 8789

FAIRWEATHER — '02

Punk-rock group from Washington DC: Jay, Ben, Shane and Peter.

DEBUT	PEAK	WKS	Gold	A-side (Chart Hit)...B-side	$	Sym	Label & Number
10/12/02	70[S]	1		**Alaska** ... *Still Paradise / Who Brings A Knife To A Gunfight? / Blood On The Pages*	$10	★*	Equal Vision 76

FAITH — see EVANS, Faith

FAITH, Adam — '65

Born Terence Nelhams on 6/23/40 in Acton, London, England. Died of a heart attack on 3/7/2003 (age 62). Pop singer/actor.

DEBUT	PEAK	WKS	Gold	A-side (Chart Hit)...B-side	$	Sym	Label & Number
1/16/65	31	8		1 **It's Alright** ... *I Just Don't Know* **ADAM FAITH With The Roulettes**	$15		Amy 913
4/17/65	97	2		2 **Talk About Love** ... *Stop Feeling Sorry For Yourself*	$15		Amy 922

FAITH, Percy, and his Orchestra — MEM/POP/AC/BUB/LP '53

Born on 4/7/08 in Toronto, Ontario, Canada. Died of cancer on 2/9/76 (age 67). Orchestra leader. Moved to the U.S. in 1940. Joined Columbia Records in 1950 as conductor/arranger for company's leading singers (**Tony Bennett**, **Doris Day**, **Rosemary Clooney**, **Johnny Mathis** and others). Had two huge #1 hits in the early '50s: "Delicado" and "The Song From Moulin Rouge."

DEBUT	PEAK	WKS	Gold	A-side (Chart Hit)...B-side	$	Sym	Label & Number
2/18/56	53	5		1 **Valley Valparaiso** ... T:53 *Bluebell*	$12		Columbia 40633
4/14/56	67	4		2 **We All Need Love** ... T:67 *Carmellita* originally charted for 3 weeks (#93); re-entered on 6/30/56	$12		Columbia 40644
7/21/56	82	3		3 **With A Little Bit Of Luck** ... T:82 *The Rain In Spain* [I] from the Broadway musical *My Fair Lady* starring **Julie Andrews** and Rex Harrison	$12		Columbia 40696
4/13/57	63	13		4 **Till** ... T:63 *The Last Dance* originally charted for 11 weeks; re-entered on 10/21/57 (#84)	$12		Columbia 40826
1/11/60	❶[9]	21	●	5 **The Theme From "A Summer Place"** *Go-Go-Po-Go* [I] from the movie *A Summer Place* starring Troy Donahue and Sandra Dee; a vocal version hit #111 in 1969 and a disco version hit #13 on the AC charts in 1975; 1960 Grammy winner: Record of the Year	$10	■	Columbia 41490
5/9/60	35	10		6 **Theme For Young Lovers** ... *Bimini Goombay* [I] reissued in 1963 as a special promotional "45" with a text sleeve (Columbia 75662)	$8	■	Columbia 41655

FAITH BAND — '79

Pop-rock group from Indianapolis, Indiana: Carl Storie (vocals), David Bennett (guitar), John Cascella (keyboards), Mark Cawley (bass) and David Barnes (drums).

DEBUT	PEAK	WKS	Gold	A-side (Chart Hit)...B-side	$	Sym	Label & Number
12/16/78+	54	9		1 **Dancin' Shoes** ... *Desire* originally released on Village Records 202 in 1978 ($7)	$5		Mercury 74037
6/23/79	76	4		2 **You're My Weakness** ... *Forever*	$5		Mercury 74068

FAITHFULL, Marianne — BUB/LP '65

Born on 12/29/46 in Hampstead, London, England. Discovered by **The Rolling Stones**' manager, Andrew Loog Oldham. Involved in a long, tumultuous relationship with **Mick Jagger**. Acted in several stage and screen productions. Married British art gallery owner John Dunbar, Vibrators bassist Ben Brierly and American playwright Giorgio Dellaterza.

DEBUT	PEAK	WKS	Gold	A-side (Chart Hit)...B-side	$	Sym	Label & Number
11/28/64+	22	9		1 **As Tears Go By** *Greensleeves*	$12		London 9697
2/27/65	26	9		2 **Come And Stay With Me** ... *What Have I Done Wrong* written by **Jackie DeShannon**	$12		London 9731
6/5/65	32	8		3 **This Little Bird** ... *Morning Sun*	$12		London 9759
8/14/65	24	9		4 **Summer Nights** ... *The Sha La La Song*	$12		London 9780
12/11/65	89	3		5 **Go Away From My World** ... *Oh Look Around You*	$12	■	London 9802

FAITH, HOPE & CHARITY — R&B/BUB/LP '70

R&B-dance vocal trio from Tampa, Florida: Brenda Hilliard, Albert Bailey and Zulema Cusseaux. Cusseaux went solo in 1971. Hilliard and Bailey continued as a duo until 1974 when joined by Diane Destry.

DEBUT	PEAK	WKS	Gold	A-side (Chart Hit)...B-side	$	Sym	Label & Number
5/16/70	51	11		1 **So Much Love** ... *Let's Try It Over*	$6		Maxwell 805
9/26/70	96	2		2 **Baby Don't Take Your Love** ... *Make Love To Me*	$6		Maxwell 808
8/16/75	50	15		3 **To Each His Own** ... RB[1] *Find A Way* all of above written and produced by **Van McCoy**	$5		RCA Victor 10343

FAITHLESS — '97

Electronica-dance group from London, England: Rollo Armstrong, Sister Bliss, Jamie Catto and Maxi Jazz.

DEBUT	PEAK	WKS	Gold	A-side (Chart Hit)...B-side	$	Sym	Label & Number
3/29/97	62	19		**Insomnia** ... S:60 *(armand's european vacation mix)*	$4	▮	Arista 13332

DEBUT	PEAK	WKS	Gold	A-side (Chart Hit)	B-side	$	Sym	Label & Number
				FAITH NO MORE ROK/LP **'90**				
				Rock group from San Francisco, California: Michael "Vlad Dracula" Patton (vocals), Jim Martin (guitar), Roddy Bottum (keyboards), Billy Gould (bass) and Mike Bordin (drums).				
6/23/90	**9**	21	●	1 **Epic** ...S:4 / A:19	*Edge Of The World*	$3	▮V	Slash 19813
11/10/90	**92**	3		2 **Falling To Pieces**	*Zombie Eaters*	$3	▮V	Slash 19563
				"45": Slash "Back To Back Hits" 18891; B-side: "Epic" (remix)				
3/20/93	**58**	8		3 **Easy** ...S:45	*Das Schutzenfest*	$3	▮V	Slash 18569
				FALCO ROK/LP **'86**				
				Born Johann Holzel on 2/19/57 in Vienna, Austria. Died in a car crash on 2/6/98 (age 40). Male dance singer/songwriter. Took his name from professional skier Falco Weissflog.				
2/8/86	**❶**3	17		1 **Rock Me Amadeus** ...S:❶3 / A:❶3	*(Canadian version)*	$3		A&M 2821
				tribute to classical composer Wolfgang Amadeus Mozart (1756-1791)				
4/26/86	**18**	14		2 **Vienna Calling** ...A:17 / S:18	*Tango The Night*	$3	■	A&M 2832
				FALCON, Billy **'91**				
				Born on 7/13/56 in Valley Stream, New York. Rock singer/songwriter/guitarist.				
8/17/91	**35**	14		**Power Windows** ...S:73 / A:74	*Oh Boy*	$3	▮V	Jambco 868672
				co-produced by **Jon Bon Jovi**				
				FALCONS, The R&B/BUB **'59**				
				R&B vocal group from Detroit, Michigan: **Eddie Floyd** (lead vocals; replaced in 1961 by **Wilson Pickett**), Bonny "Mack" Rice, Joe Stubbs (brother of the **Four Tops**' Levi Stubbs), Willie Schofield and Lance Finney. Stubbs died on 1/19/98 (age 57). Backing band, Ohio Untouchables, later became **Ohio Players**.				
4/20/59	**17**	20		1 **You're So Fine**	*Goddess Of Angels*	$40		Unart 2013
				Joe Stubbs (lead singer); originally released on Flick 001 in 1959 ($250)				
3/31/62	**75**	9		2 **I Found A Love**	*Swim*	$40		Lu Pine 1003
				THE FALCONS & Band (Ohio Untouchables) **Wilson Pickett** (lead singer)				
				FALTERMEYER, Harold **'85**				
				Born on 10/5/52 in Munich, Germany. Keyboardist/songwriter/arranger/producer. Arranged and played keyboards on the movie scores of *Midnight Express* and *American Gigolo*.				
3/30/85	**3**	19		**Axel F** ...AC2 S:2 / A:4	*Shoot Out* [I]	$3	■	MCA 52536
				from the movie *Beverly Hills Cop* starring **Eddie Murphy** (played Axel Foley)				
				FÄLTSKOG, Agnetha — see ABBA				
				FAME, Georgie LP **'68**				
				Born Clive Powell on 6/26/43 in Leigh, Lancashire, England. Began as a pianist with Billy Fury's backup group, The Blue Flames (became their lead singer in 1962 after Fury dropped them).				
2/13/65	**21**	8		1 **Yeh, Yeh**	*Preach And Teach*	$12		Imperial 66086
5/1/65	**97**	2		2 **In The Meantime**	*Let The Sunshine In*	$10		Imperial 66104
8/20/66	**70**	7		3 **Get Away**	*El Bandido*	$10		Imperial 66189
				GEORGIE FAME And The Blue Flames (above 3)				
2/17/68	**7**	14		4 **The Ballad Of Bonnie And Clyde**	*Beware Of The Dog*	$10		Epic 10283
				inspired by, but not included in, the 1967 movie *Bonnie And Clyde* starring Warren Beatty and Faye Dunaway				
				FAMILY, The — see TIME, The				
				FANCY **'74**				
				Pop-rock group from England: Helen Court (vocals), Ray Fenwick (guitar), Alan Hawkshaw (keyboards), Mo Foster (bass) and Henry Spinetti (drums). Court and Spinetti left after "Wild Thing"; replaced by Annie Kavanagh (vocals) and Les Binks (drums).				
6/15/74	**14**	17		1 **Wild Thing**	*Fancy*	$6		Big Tree 15004
10/12/74	**19**	10		2 **Touch Me**	*I Don't Need Your Love*	$6		Big Tree 16026
				FANNY LP **'75**				
				Female rock group from Los Angeles, California: sisters June (vocals, guitar) and Jean (vocals, bass) Millington, Nicole Barclay (keyboards) and Alice DeBuhr (drums). Jean and Alice left in 1974, replaced by Patti Quatro (bass; sister of **Suzi Quatro**) and Brie Howard (drums).				
9/18/71	**40**	10		1 **Charity Ball**	*Place In The Country*	$6		Reprise 1033
4/29/72	**85**	3		2 **Ain't That Peculiar**	*Think About The Children*	$6		Reprise 1080
6/8/74	**79**	7		3 **I've Had It**	*The First Time*	$5		Casablanca 0009
2/1/75	**29**	11		4 **Butter Boy**	*Beggar Man*	$5		Casablanca 814
				FANTASTIC FOUR R&B/BUB/LP **'67**				
				R&B vocal group from Detroit, Michigan: "Sweet" James Epps, Robert and Joseph Pruitt, and Toby Childs. Robert Pruitt and Childs later replaced by Cleveland Horne and Ernest Newsome. Epps was cousin of the Tilmon brothers of the **Detroit Emeralds**. Horne died of a heart attack on 4/13/2000.				
3/25/67	**63**	9		1 **The Whole World Is A Stage**	*Ain't Love Wonderful*	$20		Ric-Tic 122
5/27/67	**55**	7		2 **You Gave Me Something (And Everything's Alright)**	*Romeo And Juliet's "I Don't Wanna Live Without You (Play)"*	$20		Ric-Tic 128
9/23/67	**68**	5		3 **To Share Your Love**	*As Long As I Live (I Live For You)* (R&B #38)	$20		Ric-Tic 130
9/21/68	**56**	9		4 **I Love You Madly**	*(instrumental)*	$15		Soul 35052
7/26/75	**74**	8		5 **Alvin Stone (The Birth & Death Of A Gangster)**	*I Believe In Miracles (I Believe In You)*	$7		Westbound 5009
				FANTASTIC JOHNNY C, The BUB **'67**				
				Born Johnny Corley on 4/28/43 in Greenwood, South Carolina. R&B singer. Produced and managed by **Jesse James**.				
10/7/67	**7**	18		1 **Boogaloo Down Broadway**	*Look What Love Can Make You Do*	$10		Phil-L.A. 305
2/10/68	**56**	6		2 **Got What You Need**	*New Love*	$10		Phil-L.A. 309
6/29/68	**34**	9		3 **Hitch It To The Horse**	*Cool Broadway*	$10		Phil-L.A. 315
11/16/68	**87**	2		4 **(She's) Some Kind Of Wonderful**	*Baby, I Need You*	$10		Phil-L.A. 320
				FANTASTICS, The BUB **'72**				
				R&B group from Brooklyn, New York: Don Haywood, Jerome Ramos, John Cheetom and Alfred Pitts. Don, Jerome and John were members of **The Velours**.				
2/19/72	**86**	4		(Love Me) **Love The Life I Lead**	*Old Rags And Tatters*	$15		Bell 45,157

DEBUT	PEAK	WKS	Gold	A-side (Chart Hit)..............B-side	$	Sym	Label & Number

FANTASY — LP '70

Rock group from Miami, Florida: Vincent DeMeo (guitar), Lydia Miller (female vocals), Mario Russo (organ), David Robbins (bass) and Greg Kimple (drums).

DEBUT	PEAK	WKS	Gold	A-side (Chart Hit)..............B-side	$	Sym	Label & Number
9/19/70	77	11		**Stoned Cowboy** ....*Understand* [I]	$8		Liberty 56190

FARAGHER BROS., The — AC '79

Soft-rock group from Redlands, California: brothers Danny, Jimmy, Tommy, Davey, Marty and Pammy Faragher. Davey joined **Cracker** in 1992. Also see **Bones** and **The Peppermint Trolley Co.**

DEBUT	PEAK	WKS	Gold	A-side (Chart Hit)..............B-side	$	Sym	Label & Number
2/24/79	50	7		**Stay The Night** ....*That's A Start*	$5		Polydor 14533

FAR CORPORATION — '86

Far: name of producer Frank Farian's studio in Rosbach, Germany. This assemblage of European and American musicians contains three members of **Toto**: Bobby Kimball (lead vocals), Steve Lukather (guitars) and David Paich (keyboards). Robin McAuley (**McAuley Schenker Group**) was also a member. Farian created **Boney M** and **Milli Vanilli**.

DEBUT	PEAK	WKS	Gold	A-side (Chart Hit)..............B-side	$	Sym	Label & Number
10/4/86	89	4		**Stairway To Heaven** ....*Financial Controller* this is the only charted version of the classic 1971 **Led Zeppelin** song	$5	■	Atco 99509

FARDON, Don — '68

Born Donald Maughn on 8/19/43 in Coventry, West Midlands, England. Lead singer of British rock group The Sorrows ("Bubbled Under" in 1965).

DEBUT	PEAK	WKS	Gold	A-side (Chart Hit)..............B-side	$	Sym	Label & Number
8/31/68	20	9		1 **(The Lament Of The Cherokee) Indian Reservation** ....*Dreaming Room* written by **John D. Loudermilk**	$10		GNP Crescendo 405
3/24/73	86	5		2 **Delta Queen** ....*Hometown Baby*	$7		Chelsea 0115

FARGO, Donna — C&W/AC/LP '72

Born Yvonne Vaughan on 11/10/45 in Mount Airy, North Carolina. Recorded for Ramco in 1969. Worked as a high school teacher until June 1972. Fargo was stricken with multiple sclerosis in 1979. Charted 38 Country hits, 1972-91.

DEBUT	PEAK	WKS	Gold	A-side (Chart Hit)..............B-side	$	Sym	Label & Number
5/27/72	11	16	●	1 **The Happiest Girl In The Whole U.S.A.** ....CW^{3} *The Awareness Of Nothing*	$5	■	Dot 17409
9/30/72+	5	20	●	2 **Funny Face** CW^{3} *How Close You Came (To Being Gone)*	$5		Dot 17429
2/24/73	41	9		3 **Superman** ....CW^{1} *Forever Is As Far As I Could Go*	$5		Dot 17444
6/16/73	93	7		4 **You Were Always There** ....CW^{1} *He Can Have All He Wants*	$5		Dot 17460
10/6/73	57	10		5 **Little Girl Gone** ....*Just Call Me*	$5	■	Dot 17476
6/29/74	57	13		6 **You Can't Be A Beacon (If Your Light Don't Shine)** ...CW^{1} *Just A Friend Of Mine*	$5		Dot 17506
11/9/74	86	4		7 **U.S. Of A.** ....*A Woman's Prayer*	$5	■	ABC/Dot 17523
3/22/75	98	2		8 **It Do Feel Good** ....*Only The Strong* all of above (except #6) written by Fargo; all of above produced by Donna's husband, Stan Silver	$5		ABC/Dot 17541

FARM, The — ROK '91

Pop-rock-dance group from Liverpool, England: Peter Hooton (vocals), Steve Grimes and Keith Mullin (guitars), Ben Leach (keyboards), Carl Hunter (bass) and Roy Boulter (drums).

DEBUT	PEAK	WKS	Gold	A-side (Chart Hit)..............B-side	$	Sym	Label & Number
9/28/91	41	16		**Groovy Train** ....A:57 *Stepping Stone*	$3	▮V	Sire 19209

FARNHAM, John — see LITTLE RIVER BAND

FARRIS, Dionne — R&B/BUB/LP '95

Born in 1969 in Bordentown, New Jersey. Female R&B singer. Former member of **Arrested Development**.

DEBUT	PEAK	WKS	Gold	A-side (Chart Hit)..............B-side	$	Sym	Label & Number
1/28/95	4	38		**I Know** ....A:❶^{7} / S:22 *Human* "45": Columbia 77905; B-side: "Don't Ever Touch Me Again" ("Bubbled Under" #121)	$3	▮V	Columbia 77750

FARROW, Cee — '83

Born in Germany. Male synth-pop-dance singer.

DEBUT	PEAK	WKS	Gold	A-side (Chart Hit)..............B-side	$	Sym	Label & Number
9/24/83	82	6		**Should I Love You** ....*Paint It Blue*	$5	■	Rocshire 95032

FASCINATIONS, The — R&B/BUB '67

Female R&B vocal group: Shirley Walker, Joanne Levell, Bernadine Boswell and Fern Bledsoe.

DEBUT	PEAK	WKS	Gold	A-side (Chart Hit)..............B-side	$	Sym	Label & Number
2/11/67	92	3		**Girls Are Out To Get You** ....*You'll Be Sorry* written and produced by **Curtis Mayfield** (on his own label)	$15		Mayfield 7714

FASTBALL — BUB/LP '98

Rock trio from Austin, Texas: Miles Zuniga (vocals, guitar), Tony Scalzo (vocals, bass) and Joey Shuffield (drums).

DEBUT	PEAK	WKS	Gold	A-side (Chart Hit)..............B-side	$	Sym	Label & Number
3/7/98	5^{A}	39		1 **The Way** ....MR^{7} "45": Hollywood 5298 (same B-side)		V	album cut
12/5/98	86	8		2 **Fire Escape** ....A:59 "45": Hot Hits 0001; B-side: "The Hardest Part" by The Pistoleros		V	album cut
7/3/99	20	20		3 **Out Of My Head** ....A:13 above 3 from the album *All The Pain Money Can Buy* on Hollywood 62130			album cut

FASTER PUSSYCAT — ROK/LP '90

Hard-rock group from Los Angeles, California: Taime Downe (vocals), Greg Steele and Brent Muscat (guitars), Eric Stacy (bass), and Mark Michals (drums). Group name taken from the 1965 action movie *Faster Pussycat! Kill! Kill!*

DEBUT	PEAK	WKS	Gold	A-side (Chart Hit)..............B-side	$	Sym	Label & Number
2/24/90	28	21		**House Of Pain** ....S:20 / A:39 *Slip Of The Tongue*	$3	▮V	Elektra 64995

FAT BOYS — R&B/BUB/LP '88

Rap trio from Brooklyn, New York: Mark "**Prince Markie Dee**" (see #4 below) Morales (born on 2/19/60), Darren "The Human Beat Box" Robinson and Damon "Kool Rock-ski" Wimbley. Combined weight of over 750 pounds. Appeared in the 1987 movie *Disorderlies.* Robinson died of cardiac arrest on 12/10/95 (age 28).

DEBUT	PEAK	WKS	Gold	A-side (Chart Hit)..............B-side	$	Sym	Label & Number
7/11/87	12	19		1 **Wipeout** ....S:4 / A:20 *Crushin'* (Fat Boys) **FAT BOYS (with The Beach Boys)**	$3	■	Tin Pan Apple 885960
6/18/88	16	15		2 **The Twist (Yo, Twist!)** ....S:12 / A:17 *(buffapella version)* **FAT BOYS (with Chubby Checker)**	$3	■	Tin Pan Apple 887571
10/15/88	89	3		3 **Louie, Louie** ....*All Day Lover*	$3	■	Tin Pan Apple 871010
4/3/93	64	14		4 **Typical Reasons (Swing My Way)** ....A:48 / S:51 *(still swingin' version)* **PRINCE MARKIE DEE & The Soul Convention** samples **The Gap Band**'s "Outstanding"	$3	▮	Columbia 74866

DEBUT	PEAK	WKS	Gold	A-side (Chart Hit)..................B-side	$	Sym	Label & Number
				FATBOY SLIM ROK/LP '99			
				Born Norman Cook on 7/31/63 in Brighton, Sussex, England. Techno-house instrumentalist. Former member of The Housemartins, **Beats International** and **The Mighty Dub Kats**.			
8/8/98	78	15		1 **The Rockafeller Skank** ....S:61 *(remix) / Always Read The Label / Tweakers Delight*	$4	▮V	Astralwerks 66242
3/13/99	36	20		2 **Praise You** ....A:36 / S:45 *Sho Nuff / The Rockafeller Skank (remix)*	$8	★*V	Astralwerks 66254
				samples "Take Yo Praise" by Camille Yarborough			
11/6/99+	76	12		3 **The Rockafeller Skank** ...A:64 / S:65 *(remix) / Always Read The Label / Tweakers Delight* [R]	$4	★V	Astralwerks 66242
				same version as #1 above; "45" issued for above 3 on Astralwerks 38659			
5/26/01	62^{S}	4		4 **Star 69 (What The F**k)**..........................*(5 mixes) / Weapon Of Choice (video)* (ROK #33)	$8	★**	Astralwerks 38777
				samples "I Get Deep" by Roland Clark			
				FATHER MC R&B/BUB/LP '91			
				Born Timothy Brown in New York City, New York. Dancehall reggae singer. Dropped the MC from his name in mid-1993. Also see **Or-N-More**.			
1/12/91	20	17	●	1 **I'll Do 4 U**..........................S:14 / A:32 *(no B-side)*	$3	▮	Uptown/MCA 53914
				samples "Got To Be Real" by **Cheryl Lynn**			
12/5/92+	37	20		2 **Everything's Gonna Be Alright**..........................S:19 / A:39 *(instrumental)*	$3	▮V	Uptown/MCA 54523
				samples "Good Times" by **Chic**			
				FAT JOE R&B/BUB/LP '02			
				Born Joseph Cartagena on 3/22/65 in the Bronx, New York. Male rapper.			
10/9/93	89	2		1 **Flow Joe** ....*(2 versions) / Livin' Fat*	$4	▮	Violator/Relativity 1185
3/16/96	76	8		2 **Firewater** / S:54			
				featuring **Raekwon**, **Big Punisher** and Armageddon			
3/16/96	85	8		3 **Envy** ....S:flip	$4	▮	Violator/Relativity 1546
				contains elements from "Sexual Healing" by **Marvin Gaye**			
2/19/00	51	17		4 **Feelin' So Good**..........................S:7 / A:48 *(album version)*	$4	★V	Epic/Work 79387 ■
				JENNIFER LOPEZ (Featuring Big Pun & Fat Joe)			
				samples "Set It Off" by Strafe			
10/27/01+	15	20		5 **We Thuggin**..........................A:15 / S:39 *(2 versions) / My Lifestyle* (R&B #94)	$6	T	Atlantic 85174
				FAT JOE Featuring R. Kelly			
2/16/02	2^{7}	28		6 **What's Luv?** A:2 / S:20 *(2 versions) / Definition Of A Don* (w/Remy)	$6	T	Atlantic 85233
				FAT JOE Featuring Ashanti			
8/3/02	48^{S}	1		7 **Live Big** ....*(3 versions)*	$6	T	Elektra 67319
				SACARIO Featuring Angie Martinez & Fat Joe			
10/19/02	77	7		8 **Crush Tonight**..........................S:32 *(2 versions) / It's Nothing* (w/Tony Sunshine)	$6	T	Atlantic 85402
				FAT JOE Featuring Ginuwine			
				FAT PAT '98			
				Born Patrick Hawkins in Houston, Texas. Shot to death on 2/3/98 (age 27). Male rapper.			
12/5/98	75^{S}	1		**Tops Drop**..........................BUB:110 *(2 versions) / Ghetto Dreams*	$6	▮*	Wreckshop 2221
				Dana Jackson (female vocal)			
				FAVORITE ANGEL '90			
				Pop duo from Boston, Massachusetts: songwriter/guitarist Joe McGee and singer Gigi.			
8/11/90	69	7		**Only Women Bleed**..........................*Lucky One*	$3	▮	Columbia 73476
				FEATHER '70			
				Pop group from Los Angeles, California: Steve Woodard, Barry Collings, Roger White, Larry Sims and Peter Bregante. Woodard died of respiratory failure on 10/8/2000 (age 53).			
5/30/70	79	5		**Friends**..........................*Salli*	$6		White Whale 353
				FELDER, Don ROK/BUB/LP '81			
				Born on 9/21/47 in Gainesville, Florida. Guitarist with the **Eagles**.			
7/25/81	43	17		**Heavy Metal (Takin' A Ride)**..........................*All Of You*	$5	■	Full Moon/Asylum 47175
				from the animated movie *Heavy Metal*			
				FELDMAN, Victor, Quartet '62			
				Born on 4/7/34 in London, England. Died on 5/12/87 (age 53). Jazz pianist/vibist. Worked with **Cannonball Adderley** and Miles Davis. Quartet consisted of Feldman (piano), Buddy Collette (sax), Leroy Vinnegar (bass) and Ron Jefferson (drums).			
9/1/62	88	1		**A Taste Of Honey**..........................*Valerie* [I]	$10		Infinity 020
				tune written and introduced by **Bobby Scott** in the 1960 Broadway show *A Taste of Honey*			
				FELICIANO, José BUB/AC/R&B/C&W/LP '68			
				Born on 9/8/45 in Lares, Puerto Rico; raised in the Bronx, New York. Blind since birth. Virtuoso acoustic guitarist. First performed at age nine. First recorded for Spanish language TV series in the mid-1960s. Appeared in several TV shows and own specials. Composed score for TV's *Chico & The Man*. Won the 1968 Best New Artist Grammy Award.			
				1)Light My Fire 2)Hi-Heel Sneakers 3)The Star-Spangled Banner			
7/27/68	3	12		1 **Light My Fire** *California Dreamin'*	$8		RCA Victor 9550
10/19/68	25	8		2 **Hi-Heel Sneakers** /			
10/12/68	77	3		3 **Hitchcock Railway**	$6		RCA Victor 9641
11/2/68	50	5		4 **The Star-Spangled Banner** ....*And I Love Her* [L]	$8		RCA Victor 9665
				recorded at the 5th game of the World Series in Detroit on 10/7/68			
1/25/69	71	5		5 **Hey! Baby** /			
2/8/69	87	1		6 **My World Is Empty Without You**	$6		RCA Victor 9714
				#2, 3, 5 & 6: from the album *Souled*			
5/3/69	70	4		7 **Marley Purt Drive**..........................*Old Turkey Buzzard*	$6		RCA Victor 9739
				written by the **Bee Gees**			
8/23/69	76	5		8 **Rain** ....*She's A Woman* (#103)	$6		RCA Victor 9757
7/4/70	83	2		9 **Destiny** /			
7/4/70	84	2		10 **Susie-Q**	$6		RCA Victor 0358
1/25/75	96	2		11 **Chico And The Man** ....*Hard Times In El Barrio*	$6		RCA Victor 10145
				main theme (written by Feliciano) from the NBC-TV series starring Freddie Prinze (died on 1/28/77, age 22)			
1/10/98-	70^{A}	1		12 **Feliz Navidad** ....*The Little Drummer Boy* [X]	$4	▮V	RCA 6834
				recorded in 1970; "45": EMI Latin 18214 (red vinyl); B-side: "Blue Christmas" by **Glen Campbell**; cassette single first issued in 1987; #12 AC hit in 1999; #105 hit in 2000; all of above (except #4 & 11) produced by Rick Jarrard			

DEBUT	PEAK	WKS	Gold	A-side (Chart Hit)..........B-side	$	Sym	Label & Number
				FELLER, Dick C&W/BUB/AC **'74**			
				Born on 1/2/43 in Bronaugh, Missouri. Country singer/songwriter/guitarist.			
7/27/74	85	5		**Makin' The Best Of A Bad Situation**..........*She's Taken A Gentle Lover* [N]	$5		Asylum 11037
				FELLINI, Suzanne **'80**			
				Born on 8/6/55 in Manhattan, New York. Rock singer/actress.			
3/15/80	87	2		**Love On The Phone**..........*Bad Boy*	$5		Casablanca 2242
				FELONY LP **'83**			
				Rock group from Los Angeles, California: brothers Jeffrey Scott (vocals) and Curly Joe (guitar) Spry, Danny Sands (keyboards), Louis Ruiz (bass) and Arty Blea (drums).			
2/12/83	42	12		**The Fanatic**..........*The Girl Ain't Straight*	$5		Rock 'n' Roll 03497
				from the movie *The Lonely Lady* starring **Pia Zadora**			
				FELONY, Jayo — see EASTSIDAZ			
				FELTS, Narvel C&W **'75**			
				Born Albert Narvel Felts on 11/11/38 near Keiser, Arkansas; raised near Bernie, Missouri. Rockabilly-country singer/songwriter/guitarist. Charted 42 Country hits, 1973-87.			
2/8/60	90	2		1 **Honey Love**..........*Genavee*	$30		Pink 702
				#1 R&B hit for **The Drifters featuring Clyde McPhatter** in 1954			
5/24/75	67	6		2 **Reconsider Me**..........*Foggy Misty Morning*	$6		ABC/Dot 17549
5/22/76	62	4		3 **Lonely Teardrops**..........*I Remember You*	$6		ABC/Dot 17620
				FENDER, Freddy C&W/BUB/LP **'75**			
				Born Baldemar Huerta on 6/4/37 in San Benito, Texas. Mexican-American singer/guitarist. First recorded in Spanish under his real name for Falcon in 1956. In the movie *The Milagro Beanfield War*. Joined the Texas Tornados in 1990. Charted 21 Country hits, 1975-83.			
2/1/75	❶[1]	21	●	1 **Before The Next Teardrop Falls** CW[2] *Waiting For Your Love*	$6		ABC/Dot 17540
6/21/75	8	19	●	2 **Wasted Days And Wasted Nights**..........CW[2] *I Love My Rancho Grande*	$6		ABC/Dot 17558
				originally released on Duncan 1001 in 1959 ($30), Talent Scout 1013 in 1960 ($30) and Imperial 5670 in 1960 ($20)			
10/18/75	20	11		3 **Secret Love**..........CW[1] *Loving Cajun Style*	$6		ABC/Dot 17585
				#1 hit for **Doris Day** in 1954			
10/18/75	45	8		4 **Since I Met You Baby**..........*Little Mama*	$8		GRT 031
				originally released on Duncan 1004 in 1959 ($30)			
2/14/76	32	10		5 **You'll Lose A Good Thing**..........CW[1] *I'm To Blame*	$6		ABC/Dot 17607
5/29/76	59	6		6 **Vaya Con Dios**..........*My Happiness*	$6		ABC/Dot 17627
				#1 hit for **Les Paul & Mary Ford** in 1953			
10/30/76	72	4		7 **Living It Down**..........*Take Her A Message! I'm Lonely*	$6		ABC/Dot 17652
				all of above (except #4) produced by Huey P. Meaux			
				FENDERMEN, The BUB **'60**			
				Rock and roll duo of Phil Humphrey (from Stoughton, Wisconsin) and Jim Sundquist (from Niagara, Wisconsin); both were born on 11/26/37. Formed at the University of Wisconsin-Madison. Named after the Fender guitar.			
5/23/60	5	18		**Mule Skinner Blues**..........*Torture*	$30		Soma 1137
				written in 1931 by country great Jimmie Rodgers; originally released on Cuca 1003 in 1959 ($200)			
				FERGUSON, Helena **'67**			
				Female R&B singer.			
11/11/67	90	5		**Where Is The Party**..........*My Terms*	$10		Compass 7009
				Ohio Players (backing band)			
				FERGUSON, Jay ROK/LP **'78**			
				Born on 5/10/43 in San Fernando Valley, California. Before going solo, formed and led the rock groups **Spirit** and **Jo Jo Gunne**.			
12/17/77+	9	21		1 **Thunder Island**..........*Magic Moment*	$6		Asylum 45444
5/5/79	31	14		2 **Shakedown Cruise**..........*City Of Angels*	$6		Asylum 46041
				FERGUSON, Johnny **'60**			
				Born on 3/22/37 in Nashville, Tennessee. Pop singer. Worked as a DJ in the late 1950s.			
2/22/60	27	15		**Angela Jones**..........*Blue Serge And White Lace*	$20		MGM 12855
				written by **John D. Loudermilk**			
				FERGUSON, Maynard BUB/LP **'77**			
				Born on 5/4/28 in Verdun, Quebec, Canada. Jazz trumpeter. Moved to the U.S. in 1949. Played for Charlie Barnet and then **Stan Kenton**'s Band (1950-56). **Chuck Mangione** played in Ferguson's band.			
4/23/77	28	13		1 **Gonna Fly Now (Theme From "Rocky")**..........*The Fly* [I]	$5		Columbia 10468
				from the movie *Rocky* starring Sylvester Stallone			
8/4/79	82	4		2 **Rocky II Disco**..........*Gabriel*	$5		Columbia 11037
				disco version of #1 above; featuring a line of dialogue by Sylvester Stallone			
				FERKO STRING BAND MEM **'55**			
				String band from Philadelphia, Pennsylvania; directed by William Connors. String bands parade annually in Philadelphia's famed New Year's Day Mummers Parade. **The Nu Tornados** and the **Quaker City Boys** were also Philadelphia string bands.			
6/18/55	14	6		1 **Alabama Jubilee**..........J:14 / S:18 *Sing A Little Melody* [I]	$15		Media 1010
				#2 hit for Arthur Collins & Byron Harlan in 1915			
8/20/55	29[CU]	2		2 **You Are My Sunshine**..........*Ma-(She's Makin' Eyes At Me)*	$15		Media 1013
				classic country song written in 1940 by Jimmie Davis, former governor of Louisiana; #20 hit for **Bing Crosby** in 1941			
				FERRANTE & TEICHER AC/BUB/LP **'61**			
				Piano duo: Arthur Ferrante (born on 9/7/21 in Manhattan, New York) and Louis Teicher (born on 8/24/24 in Wilkes-Barre, Pennsylvania). Met as children while attending Manhattan's performing arts academy Juilliard School. First recorded for Columbia in 1953. Charted 31 albums from 1961-72.			
				1)Exodus 2)Tonight 3)Theme From The Apartment			
7/25/60	10	20		1 **Theme From The Apartment**..........*Lonely Room* [I]	$12	■	United Artists 231
				from the Billy Wilder movie *The Apartment* starring Jack Lemmon; 1949 tune originally entitled "Jealous Lover"			
11/14/60+	2[1]	21	●	2 **Exodus** *Twilight* [I]	$12	■	United Artists 274
				theme from the Otto Preminger movie starring Paul Newman			

DEBUT	PEAK	WKS	Gold	A-side (Chart Hit)..................B-side	$	Sym	Label & Number
				FERRANTE & TEICHER — Cont'd			
3/20/61	**37**	7		3 **Love Theme From One Eyed Jacks** .... *(Tara's Theme From) Gone With The Wind* [I] from the movie *One Eyed Jacks* starring Marlon Brando	$10	■	United Artists 300
6/12/61	**85**	4		4 **Theme From "Goodbye Again"** .... *Possessed* [I] melody based on Brahms's "Symphony No. 3 - Third Movement"; from the movie *Goodbye Again* starring Ingrid Bergman	$10		United Artists 319
10/16/61	**8**	13		5 **Tonight** .... *Dream Of Love* [I] from the movie *West Side Story*; there is a 30-second vocal chorus near the end of the recording; **Don Costa** (orch., all of above)	$10		United Artists 373
3/17/62	**94**	3		6 **Smile** .... *Street Of Palms* [I] written in 1936 by Charlie Chaplin for his movie *Modern Times*; #10 hit for **Nat "King" Cole** in 1954	$8		United Artists 431
6/16/62	**98**	2		7 **Lisa** .... *Negligee* [I] title song from the movie starring Stephen Boyd and Dolores Hart	$8		United Artists 470
2/2/63	**84**	12		8 **Theme From Lawrence Of Arabia** .... *Paris Joy Ride* [I] Garry Sherman (orch.); from the David Lean movie *Lawrence Of Arabia* starring Peter O'Toole	$8		United Artists 563
6/29/63	**83**	5		9 **Antony And Cleopatra Theme** .... *Caesar And Cleopatra Theme* [I] **Leroy Holmes** (orch.); from the movie *Cleopatra* starring Elizabeth Taylor	$8		United Artists 607
11/1/69+	**10**	15		10 **Midnight Cowboy** .... *Rock-A-Bye Baby* [I] featuring the "water sound" guitar of **Vincent Bell**; title song from the movie starring Jon Voight and Dustin Hoffman	$6		United Artists 50554
4/4/70	**99**	1		11 **Lay Lady Lay** .... *The Theme From "Z" (To Yelasto Pedi)* [I] Nick Perito (orch.: #6, 7, 10 & 11)	$6		United Artists 50646
				FERRY, Bryan ROK/BUB/AC/LP **'88** Born on 9/26/45 in County Durham, England. Pop-rock singer/songwriter. Lead singer of **Roxy Music**. Married to socialite Lucy Helmore from 1982-2003.			
12/11/76	**86**	4		1 **Heart On My Sleeve** .... *Re-Make/Re-Model* written by **Gallagher and Lyle**	$5		Atlantic 3364
2/27/88	**31**	13		2 **Kiss And Tell** .... S:24 / A:34 *Zamba* from the movie *Bright Lights, Big City* starring Michael J. Fox	$3	■	Reprise 28117
				FESTIVAL LP **'80** Disco studio group assembled by producer Boris Midney.			
3/8/80	**72**	8		**Don't Cry For Me Argentina** .... *Eva's Theme: Lady Woman* from Broadway's *Evita* starring Patti LuPone (based on the true life story of Argentina's former first lady, Eva Peron)	$5		RSO 1020
				FEVER TREE LP **'68** Psychedelic-rock group from Houston, Texas: Dennis Keller (vocals), Michael Knust (guitar), Rob Landes (piano), E.E. Wolfe (bass) and John Tuttle (drums).			
6/1/68	**91**	6		**San Francisco Girls (Return of the Native)** .... *Come With Me (Rainsong)*	$12		Uni 55060
				FEW GOOD MEN, A R&B/BUB **'96** R&B vocal group from Atlanta, Georgia: Aaron Hilliard, David Morris, Tony Amey and Demail Burks.			
3/23/96	**76**	10		**Have I Never** .... S:53 *(instrumental)* written and produced by **Babyface**	$3	▮V	LaFace 24142
				FIDELITY'S, The **'58** Black male doo-wop group from Harlem, New York. Featuring lead singer **Buddy Miles** (later a prominent session drummer).			
6/9/58	**60**	3		**The Things I Love** .... T:60 *Hold On To What'cha Got (And Get One More)* Teacho Wiltshire (orch.); based on Tchaikovsky's *Melody, Op. 42, No. 3*; #7 hit for **Jimmy Dorsey** in 1941	$30		Baton 252
				FIELD, Sally LP **'67** Born on 11/6/46 in Pasadena, California. Leading TV/movie actress. Star of TV's *Gidget* and *The Flying Nun*. Oscar winner for *Norma Rae* and *Places In The Heart*. Emmy winner for TV's *Sybil*; recurring guest role on *ER*.			
11/18/67	**94**	4		**Felicidad** .... *Find Yourself A Rainbow*	$10	■	Colgems 1008
				FIELD MOB R&B/LP **'02** Male rap duo from Albany, Georgia: Boondox Blax and Kalage.			
12/14/02+	**18**	20		**Sick Of Being Lonely** .... A:17 / S:75 *(3 versions)*	$4	★	MCA 000574
				FIELDS, Ernie, Orch. **'59** Born on 8/26/05 in Nacogdoches, Texas. Died on 5/11/97 (age 91). Black trombonist/pianist/bandleader/arranger.			
9/21/59	**4**	19		1 **In The Mood** .... *Christopher Columbus* [I] #1 hit for Glenn Miller in 1940	$15		Rendezvous 110
2/29/60	**54**	8		2 **Chattanooga Choo Choo** .... *Workin' Out* [I] #1 hit for Glenn Miller in 1941	$12		Rendezvous 117
6/19/61	**47**	10		3 **The Charleston** .... *12th Street Rag* [I] #1 hit for Arthur Gibbs in 1924	$12		Rendezvous 150
				FIELDS, Richard "Dimples" R&B/LP **'82** Born in San Francisco, California. Died of a stroke on 1/15/2000 (age 52). R&B singer/songwriter/producer.			
4/3/82	**47**	10		**If It Ain't One Thing...It's Another** .... RB3 *Mr. Look So Good*	$4		Boardwalk 139
				FIEND — see MASTER P			
				FIESTAS, The BUB **'59** R&B vocal group from Newark, New Jersey: Tommy Bullock (lead), Eddie Morris (tenor), Sam Ingalls (baritone) and Preston Lane (bass).			
4/6/59	**11**	16		1 **So Fine** .... *Last Night I Dreamed*	$30		Old Town 1062
8/25/62	**81**	6		2 **Broken Heart** .... *The Railroad Song*	$25		Old Town 1122

DEBUT	PEAK	WKS	Gold	A-side (Chart Hit)	B-side	$	Sym	Label & Number

5TH DIMENSION, The ★82★ R&B/BUB/AC/LP '69

Adult Contemporary-R&B vocal group formed in Los Angeles, California: **Marilyn McCoo** (born on 9/30/43), **Billy Davis, Jr.** (born on 6/26/40), Florence LaRue (born on 2/4/44), Lamont McLemore (born on 9/17/40) and Ron Townson (born on 1/20/33). McLemore and McCoo had been in the Hi-Fi's; Townson and Davis had been with groups in St. Louis. First called the Versatiles (recorded on the Bronco label in 1966). McCoo and Davis were married on 7/26/69 and recorded as a duo since 1976. Townson died of kidney failure on 8/2/2001 (age 68).

1)Aquarius/Let The Sunshine In 2)Wedding Bell Blues 3)One Less Bell To Answer 4)Stoned Soul Picnic 5)Up -- Up And Away

DEBUT	PEAK	WKS	Gold	A-side (Chart Hit)	B-side	$	Sym	Label & Number
1/14/67	16	10		1 **Go Where You Wanna Go**	*Too Poor To Die*	$8	■	Soul City 753
4/29/67	45	6		2 **Another Day, Another Heartache**	*Rosecrans Blvd.*	$8	■	Soul City 755
6/3/67	7	12		3 **Up -- Up And Away**	*Which Way To Nowhere*	$8		Soul City 756
				1967 Grammy winner: Record of the Year; above 3 produced by **Johnny Rivers** (Soul City is his own label)				
11/4/67	34	7		4 **Paper Cup**	*Poor Side Of Town*	$8		Soul City 760
2/3/68	29	9		5 **Carpet Man**	*The Magic Garden*	$8		Soul City 762
6/1/68	3	16	▲	6 **Stoned Soul Picnic**	*The Sailboat Song*	$8	■	Soul City 766
9/28/68	13	10		7 **Sweet Blindness**	*Bobbie's Blues (Who Do You Think Of?)*	$8	■	Soul City 768
12/21/68+	25	9		8 **California Soul**	*It'll Never Be The Same Again*	$8		Soul City 770
				written by **Ashford & Simpson**				
3/8/69	❶[6]	17	▲	9 **Aquarius/Let The Sunshine In (The Flesh Failures)** AC[2]	*Don'tcha Hear Me Callin' To Ya*	$8	■	Soul City 772
				medley from the off-Broadway rock musical *Hair* starring Steve Curry; also issued with a promotional picture sleeve; 1969 Grammy winner: Record of the Year				
7/19/69	20	10		10 **Workin' On A Groovy Thing**	*Broken Wing Bird*	$8		Soul City 776
9/27/69	❶[3]	15	▲	11 **Wedding Bell Blues** AC[2]	*Lovin' Stew*	$8		Soul City 779
				Laura Nyro's original version "Bubbled Under" (#103) in 1966				
1/3/70	21	9		12 **Blowing Away**	*Skinny Man*	$8		Soul City 780
				above 4 from the album *The Age Of Aquarius*				
2/28/70	60	4		13 **A Change Is Gonna Come & People Gotta Be Free /**				
				medley of a 1965 **Sam Cooke** hit and a 1968 **Rascals** hit				
2/21/70	64	5		14 **The Declaration**		$7		Bell 860
				"The Declaration of Independence" set to music; from the play *Bread, Beans & Things*				
4/4/70	43	8		15 **The Girls' Song**	*It'll Never Be The Same Again*	$8		Soul City 781
4/18/70	24	8		16 **Puppet Man**	*A Love Like Ours*	$6	■	Bell 880
				#10 & 16: written by **Neil Sedaka**				
6/13/70	27	8		17 **Save The Country**	*Dimension 5*	$6		Bell 895
				#6, 7, 11, 12 & 17: written by **Laura Nyro**				
8/22/70	54	6		18 **On The Beach (In The Summertime)**	*This Is Your Life*	$6		Bell 913
10/24/70	2[2]	19	▲	19 **One Less Bell To Answer** AC[1]	*Feelin' Alright?*	$5		Bell 940
				#13, 14, 16, 17 & 19: from the album *Portrait*				
2/27/71	19	10		20 **Love's Lines, Angles And Rhymes**	*The Singer*	$5		Bell 965
5/22/71	44	8		21 **Light Sings**	*Viva! (Viva Tirado)*	$5		Bell 999
				from the Broadway musical *The Me Nobody Knows* starring Melanie Henderson				
9/18/71	12	11		22 **Never My Love** AC[1]	*A Love Like Ours* [L]	$5		Bell 45,134
1/1/72	37	10		23 **Together Let's Find Love**	*I Just Wanta Be Your Friend* [L]	$5		Bell 45,170
4/1/72	8	16	▲	24 **(Last Night) I Didn't Get To Sleep At All**	*The River Witch*	$5		Bell 45,195
9/9/72	10	15		25 **If I Could Reach You** AC[1]	*Tomorrow Belongs To The Children*	$5		Bell 45,261
1/6/73	32	9		26 **Living Together, Growing Together**	*What Do I Need To Be Me*	$5		Bell 45,310
				from the movie *Lost Horizon* starring Peter Finch				
4/14/73	70	4		27 **Everything's Been Changed**	*There Never Was A Day*	$5		Bell 45,338
				written by **Paul Anka**				
8/25/73	52	10		28 **Ashes To Ashes**	*The Singer*	$5		Bell 45,380
12/15/73+	82	9		29 **Flashback**	*Diggin' For A Livin'*	$5		Bell 45,425
				#4-29: produced by Bones Howe				
4/3/76	80	4		30 **Love Hangover**	*Will You Be There*	$4		ABC 12181

FIFTH ESTATE, The BUB '67

Pop group from Stamford, Connecticut: Wayne Wadhams (vocals, keyboards), Rick Engler and Bill Shute (guitars), Doug Ferrara (bass), and Ken Evans (drums).

DEBUT	PEAK	WKS	Gold	A-side (Chart Hit)	B-side	$	Sym	Label & Number
5/20/67	11	10		**Ding Dong! The Witch Is Dead**	*The Rub-A-Dub*	$12		Jubilee 5573
				song originally appeared in the 1939 movie *The Wizard Of Oz* starring Judy Garland				

50 CENT R&B/BUB/LP '03

Born Curtis Jackson on 7/6/76 in Jamaica, Queens, New York. Male rapper/songwriter.

DEBUT	PEAK	WKS	Gold	A-side (Chart Hit)	B-side	$	Sym	Label & Number
11/30/02+	13	20		**Wanksta**	A:13 / S:68 *(3 versions)*	$6	T	Shady 497816
				from the movie *8 Mile* starring **Eminem**				

FIGURES ON A BEACH ROK '89

Techno-rock group from Boston, Massachusetts: Anthony Kaczynski (vocals), John Rolski (guitar), Christopher Ewen (keyboards), Percy Tell (bass) and Michael Smith (drums).

DEBUT	PEAK	WKS	Gold	A-side (Chart Hit)	B-side	$	Sym	Label & Number
4/8/89	67	7		**You Ain't Seen Nothing Yet**	*Independence Day*	$4	■	Sire 27628

FILTER ROK/LP '00

Industrial-rock duo from Cleveland, Ohio: Richard Patrick (vocals, guitar, bass) and Brian Liesegang (keyboards, drums). Both worked with Trent Reznor in **Nine Inch Nails**.

DEBUT	PEAK	WKS	Gold	A-side (Chart Hit)	B-side	$	Sym	Label & Number
8/5/95	76	7		1 **Hey Man Nice Shot**	A:68 *(3 remixes) / White Like That*	$8	★*	Reprise 43531
11/27/99+	12	20		2 **Take A Picture**	S:14 / A:14 *(live version)*	$8	★+V	Reprise 16889
7/27/02	94	5		3 **Where Do We Go From Here**	S:67 *(3 remixes)*	$8	★*	Reprise 42444

DEBUT	PEAK	WKS	Gold	A-side (Chart Hit)..................B-side	$	Sym	Label & Number

FINE YOUNG CANNIBALS — LP '89

Rock trio from Birmingham, England: Roland Gift (vocals) and English Beat members David Steele (bass) and Andy Cox (guitar). Band name taken from the 1960 movie *All The Fine Young Cannibals*. Group appeared in the movie *Tin Men*. Gift acted in the movies *Sammy And Rosie Get Laid* and *Scandal*.

DEBUT	PEAK	WKS	Gold	A-side (Chart Hit)..................B-side	$	Sym	Label & Number
4/5/86	76	5		1 **Johnny Come Home** .... *Love For Sale*	$4	■	I.R.S. 52760
1/28/89	❶[1]	23	●	2 **She Drives Me Crazy** S:❶[1] / A:2 *Pull The Sucker Off*	$3	■	I.R.S./MCA 53483
5/6/89	❶[1]	17		3 **Good Thing** .... A:❶[2] / S:2 *Social Security* from the 1987 movie *Tin Men* starring Richard Dreyfuss and Danny DeVito	$3		I.R.S./MCA 53639
8/12/89	11	12		4 **Don't Look Back** .... S:8 / A:18 *As Hard As It Is*	$3		I.R.S./MCA 53695
11/11/89	54	6		5 **I'm Not The Man I Used To Be** .... *Don't Let It Get You Down*	$3		I.R.S./MCA 53686
2/24/90	90	3		6 **I'm Not Satisfied** .... *Wade In The Water* above 5 from the album *The Raw & The Cooked*	$3	▮V	I.R.S./MCA 53789

FINNEGAN, Larry — BUB '62

Born John Lawrence Finneran on 8/10/38 in Brooklyn, New York. Died of a brain tumor on 7/22/73 (age 34). Pop singer/songwriter.

DEBUT	PEAK	WKS	Gold	A-side (Chart Hit)..................B-side	$	Sym	Label & Number
2/24/62	11	14		**Dear One** .... *Candy Lips*	$15		Old Town 1113

FINNIGAN, Michael — see STILLS, Stephen

FIONA — LP '90

Born Fiona Flanagan on 9/13/61 in Manhattan, New York. Female rock singer/actress. Co-starred in the 1987 movie *Hearts Of Fire*.

DEBUT	PEAK	WKS	Gold	A-side (Chart Hit)..................B-side	$	Sym	Label & Number
4/13/85	64	7		1 **Talk To Me** .... *James*	$3		Atlantic 89572
11/25/89+	52	12		2 **Everything You Do (You're Sexing Me)** .... *Calling On You* **FIONA with Kip Winger**	$3	■	Atlantic 88823

FIORILLO, Elisa — LP '90

Born on 2/28/69 in Philadelphia, Pennsylvania. Female dance singer.

DEBUT	PEAK	WKS	Gold	A-side (Chart Hit)..................B-side	$	Sym	Label & Number
7/11/87	16	15		1 **Who Found Who** A:13 / S:14 *The Real Thing Part II (w/Steven Dante)* **JELLYBEAN/Elisa Fiorillo**	$3	■	Chrysalis 43120
1/23/88	60	8		2 **How Can I Forget You** .... *More Than Love*	$3	■	Chrysalis 43189
5/7/88	49	12		3 **Forgive Me For Dreaming** .... *More Than Love*	$3	■	Chrysalis 43237
9/29/90+	27	19		4 **On The Way Up** .... S:23 / A:36 *(album version)*	$3	▮	Chrysalis 23497
3/9/91	90	4		5 **Oooh This I Need** .... *Purpose In Your Life* written and produced by **Prince** (also co-writer on #4 above)	$3	▮	Chrysalis 23670

FIRE AND RAIN — '73

Pop duo: Patti McCarron and Manny Freiser. Named after **James Taylor**'s 1970 hit.

DEBUT	PEAK	WKS	Gold	A-side (Chart Hit)..................B-side	$	Sym	Label & Number
6/30/73	100	3		**Hello Stranger** .... *Somebody To Love*	$6		Mercury 73373

FIREBALLS, The — LP '63 — ★514★

Rock and roll band from Raton, New Mexico: Chuck Tharp (vocals; born on 2/3/41), George Tomsco (lead guitar; born on 4/24/40), Dan Trammell (rhythm guitar; born on 7/14/40), Stan Lark (bass; born on 7/27/40) and Eric Budd (drums; born on 10/23/38). First recorded for Kapp in 1958. Trammell left group in 1959. Doug Roberts (died on 11/18/81) replaced Budd in 1962. Tharp quit group in 1960 and was replaced by Jimmy Gilmer (vocals, piano). Gilmer was introduced to The Fireballs by their record producer **Norman Petty** at his famed studio in Clovis, New Mexico.

1)Sugar Shack 2)Bottle Of Wine 3)Daisy Petal Pickin'

DEBUT	PEAK	WKS	Gold	A-side (Chart Hit)..................B-side	$	Sym	Label & Number
9/28/59	39	13		1 **Torquay** .... *Cry Baby* [I]	$20		Top Rank 2008
1/11/60	24	12		2 **Bulldog** .... *Nearly Sunrise* [I]	$20		Top Rank 2026
8/29/60	99	1		3 **Vaquero (Cowboy)** .... *Chief Whoopin-Koff* [I]	$20		Top Rank 2054
6/26/61	27	10		4 **Quite A Party** .... *Gunshot* [I] all of above written by lead guitarist George Tomsco	$20		Warwick 644
9/21/63	❶[5]	15	●	5 **Sugar Shack** RB[1] *My Heart Is Free*	$12		Dot 16487
12/14/63+	15	11		6 **Daisy Petal Pickin'** .... *When My Tears Have Dried*	$12		Dot 16539
3/14/64	53	7		7 **Ain't Gonna Tell Anybody** .... *Young Am I* **JIMMY GILMER and THE FIREBALLS** (above 3)	$12		Dot 16583
12/30/67+	9	14		8 **Bottle Of Wine** .... *Can't You See I'm Tryin'*	$10		Atco 6491
4/13/68	79	4		9 **Goin' Away** .... *Groovy Motions*	$10		Atco 6569
11/2/68	63	8		10 **Come On, React!** .... *Woman, Help Me!*	$10		Atco 6614
2/22/69	73	7		11 **Long Green** .... *Light In The Window* first recorded by **The Kingsmen** in 1964 (on the B-side of "The Jolly Green Giant")	$10		Atco 6651

FIREFALL — BUB/AC/LP '76 — ★508★

Soft-rock group from Boulder, Colorado: Rick Roberts (vocals; born on 8/31/49), Larry Burnett (born on 11/8/51) and Jock Bartley (guitars; born on 5/16/50), Mark Andes (**Spirit**, **Jo Jo Gunne**; bass; born on 2/19/48), and Mike Clarke (**Byrds**; drums; born on 6/3/46). David Muse (keyboards; born on 7/27/49) joined in 1977. Andes joined **Heart** in 1980. Roberts and Clarke were members of the Flying Burrito Brothers. Clarke died of liver failure on 12/19/93 (age 49).

1)You Are The Woman 2)Strange Way 3)Just Remember I Love You

DEBUT	PEAK	WKS	Gold	A-side (Chart Hit)..................B-side	$	Sym	Label & Number
6/5/76	42	8		1 **Livin' Ain't Livin'** .... *Love Isn't All*	$5		Atlantic 3333
8/21/76	9	22		2 **You Are The Woman** *Sad Ol' Love Song*	$5		Atlantic 3335
3/26/77	34	10		3 **Cinderella** .... *Dolphin's Lullaby*	$4		Atlantic 3392
8/13/77	11	21		4 **Just Remember I Love You** .... AC[2] *Just Think* **Timothy B. Schmit** (backing vocal)	$4		Atlantic 3420
1/14/78	48	6		5 **So Long** .... *Piece Of Paper*	$4		Atlantic 3452
9/30/78	11	19		6 **Strange Way** .... *Anymore*	$4	■	Atlantic 3518
1/20/79	43	9		7 **Goodbye, I Love You** .... *Baby*	$4	■	Atlantic 3544
4/12/80	35	9		8 **Headed For A Fall** .... *Just What You Need*	$4		Atlantic 3657
6/28/80	50	9		9 **Love That Got Away** .... *Business Is Business* all of above (except #3) written by Rick Roberts	$4		Atlantic 3670
1/24/81	37	9		10 **Staying With It** .... *Dreamers* Lisa Nemzo (female vocal)	$4		Atlantic 3791
1/15/83	59	13		11 **Always** .... *In The Dead Of The Night*	$4		Atlantic 89916

DEBUT	PEAK	WKS	Gold	A-side (Chart Hit)...B-side	$	Sym	Label & Number
				FIREFLIES '59			
				White doo-wop group formed by **Gerry Granahan** (**Dicky Doo And The Don'ts**) and Lee Reynolds (died of cancer). Varying membership included Ritchie Adams (lead), Vinnie Reynolds (died of a heart attack at age 22), Paul Giacalone and Johnny Viscelli. Adams (born Richard Adam Ziegler) wrote "Tossin' And Turnin'" for **Bobby Lewis**.			
9/7/59	**21**	16		1 **You Were Mine**...*Stella Got A Fella*	$25		Ribbon 6901
1/25/60	**90**	3		2 **I Can't Say Goodbye**...*What Did I Do Wrong* **THE FIREFLIES Featuring Ritchie Adams**	$20		Ribbon 6904
				FIREFLY '75			
				Studio disco group assembled by **Kenny Nolan**.			
10/18/75	**67**	9		**Hey There Little Firefly Part I**...*Part II*	$5		A&M 1736
				FIREHOUSE BUB/LP '91			
				Pop-rock group from North Carolina: C.J. Snare (vocals), Bill Leverty (guitar), Perry Richardson (bass) and Michael Foster (drums).			
3/9/91	**19**	23		1 **Don't Treat Me Bad**...S:11 / A:19 *Overnight Sensation*	$3	▮V	Epic 73676
6/29/91	**5**	22	●	2 **Love Of A Lifetime** S:6 / A:10 *Helpless* "45" B-side: "Don't Treat Me Bad"	$3	▮V	Epic 73771
11/16/91+	**58**	14		3 **All She Wrote**...S:49 *Love Of A Lifetime (acoustic version)*	$3	▮V	Epic 73984
7/4/92	**83**	5		4 **Reach For The Sky**...*Don't Treat Me Bad (live) / Shake & Tumble (live)*	$3	▮V	Epic 74335
8/15/92	**8**	20		5 **When I Look Into Your Eyes**...S:11 / A:20 *(2 album snippets)* "45" B-side: "Life In The Real World"	$3	▮V	Epic 74440
12/26/92+	**78**	8		6 **Sleeping With You**...*(acoustic version)* all of above produced by David Prater	$3	▮V	Epic 74323
2/25/95	**26**	20		7 **I Live My Life For You**...S:27 / A:36 *What's Wrong / Love Of A Lifetime (acoustic version)*	$3	▮V	Epic 77812
				FIRE INC. '84			
				Rock group assembled for the movie *Streets Of Fire*.			
6/2/84	**80**	5		**Tonight Is What It Means To Be Young**...*Hold That Snake* (Ry Cooder) written and produced by **Jim Steinman**; from the movie *Streets Of Fire* starring Michael Pare and Diane Lane	$4	■	MCA 52377
				FIRM, The ROK/LP '85			
				All-star rock group from England: Paul Rodgers (**Free**, **Bad Company**), Jimmy Page (**Yardbirds**, **Led Zeppelin**, **Honeydrippers**; guitar), Tony Franklin (bass) and Chris Slade (**Manfred Mann**; drums). Disbanded in 1986. Franklin joined Blue Murder in 1989. Slade joined **AC/DC** in 1990. Rodgers joined The Law in 1991.			
2/9/85	**28**	15		1 **Radioactive**...AR[1] S:23 / A:28 *Together*	$3	■	Atlantic 89586
5/4/85	**73**	5		2 **Satisfaction Guaranteed**...*Closer* (ROK #19)	$3	■	Atlantic 89561
2/15/86	**61**	8		3 **All The Kings Horses**...AR[4] *Fortune Hunter*	$3	■	Atlantic 89458
				FIRST CHOICE R&B/BUB/LP '73			
				Female R&B-dance vocal trio from Philadelphia, Pennsylvania: Rochelle Fleming, Annette Guest and Joyce Jones. By 1977, Jones left and Ursula Herring joined.			
3/10/73	**28**	14		1 **Armed And Extremely Dangerous** *Gonna Keep On Lovin Him*	$6		Philly Groove 175
11/17/73	**56**	8		2 **Smarty Pants**...*One Step Away*	$6		Philly Groove 179
3/2/74	**97**	2		3 **Newsy Neighbors**...*This Little Woman*	$6		Philly Groove 183
9/14/74	**70**	8		4 **The Player - Part 1**...*Part 2*	$6		Philly Groove 200
9/17/77	**41**	9		5 **Doctor Love**...*I Love You More Than Before*	$5		Gold Mind 4004
				FIRST CLASS '74			
				Pop studio group formed in England: **Tony Burrows** (lead vocals), John Carter, Del John and Chas Mills (backing vocals), Spencer James (guitar), Robin Shaw (bass) and Eddie Richards (drums). Burrows was also the vocalist on hits by **The Brotherhood Of Man**, **Edison Lighthouse**, **The Pipkins** and **White Plains**.			
7/20/74	**4**	17		1 **Beach Baby**...*Both Sides Of The Story*	$5		UK 49022
11/23/74	**83**	4		2 **Dreams Are Ten A Penny**...*Lavender Man*	$5		UK 49028
5/24/75	**74**	7		3 **Funny How Love Can Be**...*Surfer Queen* **Danny Hutton**'s original version "Bubbled Under" (#120) in 1966	$5		UK 49033
				FIRST EDITION, The — see ROGERS, Kenny			
				FISCHER, Lisa R&B/AC/LP '91			
				Born in Brooklyn, New York. R&B-dance singer.			
4/13/91	**11**	20		1 **How Can I Ease The Pain**...RB[2] S:19 / A:29 *Reachin' 4/U*	$3	▮	Elektra 64897
9/7/91	**74**	6		2 **Save Me**...A:63 *Chain Of Broken Hearts*	$3	▮	Elektra 64854
				FISCHOFF, George AC '74			
				Born on 8/3/38 in South Bend, Indiana. Pianist/songwriter. Wrote "98.6" for **Keith** and "Lazy Day" for **Spanky & Our Gang**.			
6/1/74	**93**	5		**Georgia Porcupine**...*I'll Never Forget You* [I]	$5		United Artists 410
	★278★			**FISHER, Eddie** MEM/POP/BUB/AC/LP '52			
				Born Edwin Jack Fisher on 8/10/28 in Philadelphia, Pennsylvania. At Copacabana night club in New York at age 17. With **Buddy Morrow** and Charlie Ventura in 1946. On Eddie Cantor's radio show in 1949. In the Armed Forces Special Services, 1952-53. Married to **Debbie Reynolds** from 1955-59. Other marriages to Elizabeth Taylor (1959-64) and **Connie Stevens** (1967-69). Daughter with Debbie is actress/author Carrie Fisher. Daughters with Connie are singer **Tricia Leigh Fisher** and actress Joely Fisher. Own *Coke Time* 15-minute TV series, 1953-57. In movies *All About Eve* (1950), *Bundle Of Joy* (1956) and *Butterfield 8* (1960). Fisher was the #1 idol of bobbysoxers during the early 1950's. Charted 36 pop hits, 1948-54, which included 3 #1 hits: "Oh! My Pa-Pa," "I'm Walking Behind You" and "Wish You Were Here."			
				1)I Need You Now 2)Count Your Blessings 3)Heart 4)Dungaree Doll 5)Cindy, Oh Cindy			
9/4/54	**❶3**	24	●	1 **I Need You Now** S:❶3 / A:❶2 / J:❶2 *Heaven Was Never Like This* picture sleeve is a half sleeve crediting Fisher as the star of *Coke Time* (used for many of his records during his 1953-57 TV show)	$15	■	RCA Victor 5830
10/30/54+	**5**	15		2 **Count Your Blessings (Instead of Sheep)**...S:5 / J:9 / A:10 *Fanny* from the movie *White Christmas* starring **Bing Crosby**	$15		RCA Victor 5871
3/5/55	**16**	2		3 **A Man Chases A Girl (Until She Catches Him)** / A:16 / J:20 / S:27 from the movie *There's No Business Like Show Business* starring Ethel Merman; above 2 written by Irving Berlin			
4/2/55	**20**	1		4 **(I'm Always Hearing) Wedding Bells**...J:20 promo picture sleeve is a *This Is His Life* comic strip-styled sleeve	$15	□	RCA Victor 6015

DEBUT	PEAK	WKS	Gold	A-side (Chart Hit)...B-side	$	Sym	Label & Number
				FISHER, Eddie — Cont'd			
5/14/55	6	13		5 **Heart** ...A:6 / J:13 / S:15 *Near To You*	$15		RCA Victor 6097
				from the Broadway musical *Damn Yankees* starring Gwen Verdon			
8/27/55	11	8		6 **Song Of The Dreamer /** J:11 / S:16 / A:16 / T:43			
9/3/55		4		7 **Don't Stay Away Too Long** ...S:flip / J:flip	$15		RCA Victor 6196
11/12/55	52	4		8 **Magic Fingers /** T:52			
				written by **Don Robertson**			
11/12/55	75	2		9 **I Wanna Go Where You Go, Do What You Do (Then I'll Be Happy)** ...T:75	$15		RCA Victor 6264
				#9 hit for "Whispering" Jack Smith in 1926			
12/17/55+	7	19		10 **Dungaree Doll /** T:7 / J:7 / S:8 / A:9			
12/17/55	20	12		11 **Everybody's Got A Home But Me** ...A:20 / T:41	$15		RCA Victor 6337
				from the Rodgers & Hammerstein Broadway musical *Pipe Dream* starring Helen Traubel			
4/7/56	41	7		12 **Without You /** T:41			
4/14/56	65	8		13 **No Other One** ...T:65	$15		RCA Victor 6470
				written by **Ivory Joe Hunter**			
6/9/56	18	15		14 **On The Street Where You Live /** J:18 / T:28			
				from the Broadway musical *My Fair Lady* starring **Julie Andrews** and Rex Harrison			
6/2/56	42	12		15 **Sweet Heartaches** ...T:42 / J:flip	$15		RCA Victor 6529
9/8/56	80	1		16 **Oh My Maria** ...T:80 *If I'm Elected*	$15		RCA Victor 6615
10/20/56	10	19		17 **Cindy, Oh Cindy** ...S:10 / T:10 / A:10 / J:10 *Around The World*	$15		RCA Victor 6677
				adapted from a sailor's sea chantey			
1/26/57	94	1		18 **Some Day Soon** ...T:94 *All About Love*	$12		RCA Victor 6746
				Henri Rene (orch.); from the movie *Bundle of Joy* starring Fisher and **Debbie Reynolds**			
4/20/57	96	1		19 **Tonight My Heart Will Be Crying** ...T:96 *Blues For Me*	$12		RCA Victor 6849
6/10/57	94	1		20 **Sunshine Girl** ...T:94 *Did You Close Your Eyes?*	$12		RCA Victor 6913
				from the Broadway musical *New Girl In Town* starring Gwen Verdon; **Hugo Winterhalter** (orch., all of above - except #18)			
11/6/61	44	6		21 **Tonight** ...*Breezin' Along With The Breeze*	$10		7 Arts 719
				from the movie *West Side Story* starring Natalie Wood			
10/29/66	45	9		22 **Games That Lovers Play** ...*Mame*	$8		RCA Victor 8956
2/11/67	97	3		23 **People Like You** ...*Come Love*	$8		RCA Victor 9070
				Nelson Riddle (orch., above 2)			
				FISHER, Mary Ann '61			
				Soul singer. Backing vocalist on several **Ray Charles** recordings.			
8/28/61	92	3		**I Can't Take It** ...*Forever More*	$20		Seg-way 1001
				FISHER, Miss Toni '59			
				Born in 1931 in Los Angeles, California. Died of a heart attack on 2/12/99 (age 67). Pop singer.			
11/16/59	3	17		1 **The Big Hurt** ...*Memphis Belle*	$15		Signet 275
				first hit recording to feature an electronic "phasing" gimmick			
4/11/60	93	2		2 **How Deep Is The Ocean** ...*Blue Blue Blue*	$12		Signet 276
				there were 3 Top 10 versions of this Irving Berlin tune in 1932			
5/26/62	37	11		3 **West Of The Wall** *[TONI FISHER]* ...*What Did I Do*	$12		Big Top 3097
				lyrics inspired by the Berlin Wall crisis (8/13/61)			
				FISHER, Tricia Leigh '90			
				Born on 12/26/68 in Burbank, California. Pop singer/actress. Daughter of **Connie Stevens** and **Eddie Fisher**. Acted in the movies *Stick* and *Book of Love*. Half sister of actress Carrie Fisher.			
8/25/90	72	8		**Empty Beach** ...*(Coney Island mix)*	$3	▮	Atco 98932
				FITZGERALD, Ella MEM/POP/R&B/BUB/AC/C&W/LP '44			
				Born on 4/25/18 in Newport News, Virginia. Died of diabetes on 6/15/96 (age 78). The most-honored jazz singer of all time. Discovered after winning on the *Harlem Amateur Hour* in 1934, she was hired by Chick Webb and in 1938 created a popular sensation with "A-Tisket, A-Tasket." Following Webb's death in 1939, Ella took over the band for three years. Won Grammy's Lifetime Achievement Award in 1967. Winner of the *Down Beat* poll as top female vocalist more than 20 times and winner of 12 Grammys, she remains among the undisputed royalty of 20th-century popular music. Charted 49 pop hits, 1936-54, including back-to-back #1 hits in 1944 with the Ink Spots: "Into Each Life Some Rain Must Fall" and "I'm Making Believe."			
7/28/56	74	5		1 **A Beautiful Friendship** ...T:74 *Stay There*	$15		Verve 2012
				Buddy Bregman (orch.)			
5/2/60	27	14		2 **Mack The Knife** ...*Lorelei* [L]	$12		Verve 10209
				written in 1928 as "Moritat" or "Theme From The Threepenny Opera"			
8/15/60	76	5		3 **How High The Moon Part 1** ...*Part 2* [L]	$10		Verve 10220
				#1 hit for **Les Paul & Mary Ford** in 1951; above 2 recorded "live" in concert in West Berlin with the Paul Smith Quartet			
4/6/63	75	3		4 **Bill Bailey, Won't You Please Come Home** ...*Ol' Man Mose* [L]	$10		Verve 10288
				recorded at The Crescendo with the Paul Smith Trio; #1 hit for Arthur Collins in 1902			
				FIVE LP '98			
				Pop vocal group from England: Rich Neville, Scott Robinson, Richard Breen, Jason Brown and Sean Conlon.			
6/6/98	10	26	●	1 **When The Lights Go Out** ...S:7 / A:41 *Straight Up Funk*	$3	▮	Arista 13495
11/14/98	53	10		2 **It's The Things You Do** ...S:21 *Don't You Want It*	$4	★	Arista 13569
4/17/99	86	2		3 **Slam Dunk** ...S:24 *Satisfied*	$6	★+	Arista 13623
				samples "Clap Your Hands" by Herbie			
				FIVE AMERICANS, The BUB/LP '67			
				Rock and roll band from Dallas, Texas: Michael Rabon (vocals; **Gladstone**), Norman Ezell (guitar), John Durrill (keyboards), James Grant (bass) and James Wright (drums). Wright married Robin of **Jon & Robin And The In Crowd** in 1970.			
1/1/66	26	11		1 **I See The Light** ...*The Outcast*	$15		HBR 454
				first released on Abnak 109 in 1965 ($20)			
4/16/66	52	9		2 **Evol-Not Love** ...*Don't Blame Me*	$15	■	HBR 468
3/4/67	5	12		3 **Western Union** *Now That It's Over*	$12		Abnak 118
5/20/67	36	8		4 **Sound Of Love** ...*Sympathy*	$12		Abnak 120
8/12/67	36	7		5 **Zip Code** ...*Sweet Bird Of Youth*	$12		Abnak 123
				above 3 produced by **Dale Hawkins**			
1/27/68	96	2		6 **7:30 Guided Tour** ...*See-Saw-Man*	$12	■	Abnak 126

DEBUT	PEAK	WKS	Gold	A-side (Chart Hit)..........B-side	$	Sym	Label & Number
				FIVE BLOBS, The '58			
				Group is actually the overdubbed vocals of Bernie Nee (born on 12/4/22; died in February 1974, age 51).			
10/6/58	33	10		**The Blob**..........H:33 *Saturday Night In Tiajuana*	$25		Columbia 41250
				title song from the movie starring Steve McQueen			
				FIVE BY FIVE BUB '68			
				Rock group from Magnolia, Arkansas: Ron Plants (vocals, guitar), Larry Andrew (guitar), Tim Milam (organ), Bill Merritt (bass) and Doug Green (drums).			
11/2/68	52	7		**Fire**..........*Hang Up*	$20		Paula 302
				written by **Jimi Hendrix** (from his 1967 album *Are You Experienced?*)			
				5 CHANELS, The '58			
				Black female doo-wop group from New York. Changed name from The Chanels to The 5 Chanels to avoid confusion with the Harlem doo-wop group The Channels.			
12/22/58	98	1		**The Reason**..........*Skiddily Doo*	$40		Deb 500
				originally released as by The Chanels on Deb 500 ($60)			
				FIVE DU-TONES, The '63			
				R&B vocal group from St. Louis, Missouri: Andrew Butler (lead), Willie Guest, LeRoy Joyce, Frank McCurrey and James West. Also see **South Shore Commission**.			
5/18/63	51	12		**Shake A Tail Feather**..........*Divorce Court*	$15		One-derful! 4815
				FIVE EMPREES, The '65			
				Pop-rock group from Benton Harbor, Michigan: Don Cook (vocals), Ron Pelkey and Tony Cantania (guitars), Bill Schueneman (bass), and Mike DeRose (drums).			
9/11/65	74	6		**Little Miss Sad**..........*Hey Lover*	$15		Freeport 1001
				originally recorded by **The Addrisi Brothers** in 1964 on Valiant 6058 ($25); first pressings label group as: The Five Empressions ($20)			
				FIVE FLIGHTS UP '70			
				Black male pop group. Featuring lead singer J.B. Bingham.			
8/22/70	37	11		1 **Do What You Wanna Do**..........*Black Cat*	$8		T-A 202
12/12/70	89	3		2 **After The Feeling Is Gone**..........*Where Are You Going, Girl?*	$8		T-A 207
				FIVE FOR FIGHTING LP '01			
				Group is actually Adult Contemporary singer/songwriter/guitarist John Ondrasik (born in Los Angeles, California). Group name refers to a penalty in hockey.			
9/1/01	14	35		**Superman (It's Not Easy)**..........A:15		V	album cut
				from the album *America Town* on Aware 63759; "45": Aware 79661; B-side: "America Town"			
				FIVE KEYS, The R&B '56			
				R&B vocal group from Newport News, Virginia: brothers Rudy and Bernie West, Ripley Ingram, Maryland Pierce and Ramon Loper. Ingram died on 3/23/95 (age 65). Rudy West died of a heart attack on 5/14/98 (age 65).			
12/25/54	28	2		1 **Ling, Ting, Tong**..........S:28 *I'm Alone*	$60	⊙	Capitol 2945
9/15/56	23	15		2 **Out Of Sight, Out Of Mind**..........S:23 / T:27 *That's Right*	$50	⊙	Capitol 3502
12/15/56+	35	12		3 **Wisdom Of A Fool**..........T:35 *Now Don't That Prove I Love You*	$50		Capitol 3597
				Van Alexander (orch.)			
3/30/57	69	5		4 **Let There Be You**..........T:69 *Tiger Lily*	$50		Capitol 3660
				Dave Cavanaugh (orch.: #2 & 4)			
				FIVE MAN ELECTRICAL BAND LP '71			
				Rock group from Ottawa, Ontario, Canada: **Les Emmerson** (vocals, guitar) (see #4 below), Ted Gerow (piano), Brian Rading (bass) and brothers Rick (percussion) and Mike (drums) Belanger.			
5/29/71	3	18	●	1 **Signs** *Hello Melinda Goodbye*	$6		Lionel 3213
				originally released on MGM 14182 in 1970 ($10)			
10/16/71	26	8		2 **Absolutely Right**..........*(You And I) Butterfly*	$6		Lionel 3220
9/9/72	72	5		3 **Money Back Guarantee**..........*Find The One*	$6		Lion 127
1/13/73	51	9		4 **Control Of Me**..........*Goin' Through The Motions*	$6		Lion 141
				LES EMMERSON			
4/21/73	76	7		5 **I'm A Stranger Here**..........*Doin' The Best We Can Rag*	$6		Lion 149
3/30/74	64	8		6 **Werewolf**..........*Country Angel*	$5		Polydor 14221
				all of above written by Les Emmerson			
				504 BOYZ R&B/LP '00			
				All-star rap trio from New Orleans, Louisiana: **Master P** ("Nino Brown"), **Silkk The Shocker**("Vito") and **Mystikal** ("G Money"). 504 is the area code for New Orleans.			
4/15/00	17	18		1 **Wobble Wobble**..........S:3 / A:56 *(2 versions) / Don't Play No Games*	$6	★	No Limit 38698
11/2/02	69S	1		2 **Tight Whips**..........*(3 versions)*	$8	T	New No Limit 019401
				"5" ROYALES, The R&B/BUB '57			
				R&B vocal group from Winston-Salem, North Carolina: cousins Lowman Pauling, Clarence Pauling and Windsor King, with brothers Eugene and John Tanner. Lowman Pauling died in December 1973 (age 47). Eugene Tanner died on 12/29/94 (age 58). Clarence Pauling died on 5/6/95 (age 67).			
8/5/57	66	12		1 **Think**..........T:66 *I'd Better Make A Move*	$50		King 5053
1/23/61	81	4		2 **Dedicated To The One I Love**..........*Miracle Of Love*	$30		King 5453
				originally released in 1958 on King 5098 ($50)			
				FIVE SATINS, The BUB '56			
				R&B vocal group from New Haven, Connecticut: Fred Parris (lead), Al Denby, Jim Freeman, Eddie Martin and Jessie Murphy (piano). Parris was stationed in the Army in Japan when "In The Still Of The Nite" charted, and the group re-formed with Bill Baker (died of lung cancer on 8/10/94, age 58) as lead singer. Parris returned in January 1958, replacing Baker. Also see **The New Yorkers**.			
9/8/56	24	19	●	1 **In The Still Of The Nite** S:24 / T:29 *The Jones Girl*	$60		Ember 1005
				written by Fred Parris and recorded in a New Haven church basement; originally released on Standord 200 in 1956 ($1000)			
7/22/57	25	17		2 **To The Aisle**..........S:25 / T:25 *Wish I Had My Baby*	$50		Ember 1019
11/30/59	87	3		3 **Shadows** *[5 SATINS]*..........*Toni My Love*	$40		Ember 1056
1/4/60	81	4		4 **In The Still Of The Nite**..........*The Jones Girl* [R]	$40		Ember 1005

DEBUT	PEAK	WKS	Gold	A-side (Chart Hit)..........B-side	$	Sym	Label & Number
				FIVE SATINS, The — Cont'd			
5/9/60	**79**	6		5 **I'll Be Seeing You** .... *A Night Like This* from the 1938 Broadway musical *Right This Way*; #1 hit for **Bing Crosby** in 1944	$40		Ember 1061
1/23/61	**99**	1		6 **In The Still Of The Night/"I'll Remember"** .... *The Jones Girl* [R] #1 above: red label; #4: multi-colored "logs" label; #6: black label (all 3 are the same version)	$40		Ember 1005
2/27/82	**71**	5		7 **Memories Of Days Gone By** .... *Loving You (Would Be The Sweetest Thing)* **FRED PARRIS & THE FIVE SATINS** medley: Sixteen Candles/Earth Angel/Only You (And You Alone)/ A Thousand Miles Away/ Tears On My Pillow/Since I Don't Have You/In The Still Of The Night (I'll Remember)	$20		Elektra 47411
				FIVE SPECIAL R&B/LP '79 R&B vocal group from Detroit, Michigan: Bryan Banks (lead), Steve Harris, Greg Finley, Mike Pettilo and Steve Boyd. Banks is the brother of Ron Banks of **The Dramatics**.			
7/28/79	**55**	5		**Why Leave Us Alone** .... *(instrumental)*	$5		Elektra 46032
				FIVE STAIRSTEPS, The R&B/BUB/LP '70 R&B group from Chicago, Illinois: brothers Clarence, Jr., James, Kenneth and Dennis Burke with their sister Alohe. Later joined by their five-year-old brother Cubie. Managed by their father and produced by **Curtis Mayfield**; later became **The Invisible Man's Band** (see #18 below). *1)O-o-h Child 2)All Night Thing 3)World Of Fantasy*			
5/21/66	**94**	2		1 **You Waited Too Long** .... *Don't Waste Your Time* A-side label number mistakenly listed as 061	$15		Windy C 601
8/6/66	**49**	8		2 **World Of Fantasy** .... *Playgirl's Love*	$15		Windy C 602
11/5/66	**61**	6		3 **Come Back** .... *You Don't Love Me*	$15		Windy C 603
1/14/67	**89**	5		4 **Danger! She's A Stranger** .... *Behind Curtains*	$15		Windy C 604
4/15/67	**87**	2		5 **Ain't Gonna Rest (Till I Get You)** .... *You Can't See*	$15		Windy C 605
5/27/67	**63**	6		6 **Oooh, Baby Baby** .... *The Girl I Love* #1-4 & 6: from the album *The Five Stairsteps*	$15		Windy C 607
				FIVE STAIRSTEPS & CUBIE:			
12/2/67+	**88**	6		7 **Something's Missing** .... *Tell Me Who*	$8	■	Buddah 20
1/27/68	**68**	6		8 **A Million To One** .... *Tell Me Who*	$8	■	Buddah 26
4/20/68	**94**	1		9 **The Shadow Of Your Love** .... *Bad News*	$8		Buddah 35
8/24/68	**59**	9		10 **Don't Change Your Love** .... *New Dance Craze*	$8		Curtom 1931
12/21/68	**91**	2		11 **Stay Close To Me** .... *I Made A Mistake*	$8		Curtom 1933
10/18/69	**88**	3		12 **We Must Be In Love** .... *Little Young Lover*	$8		Curtom 1945
				THE 5 STAIRSTEPS:			
5/2/70	**8**	16	●	13 **O-o-h Child** / originally released with "Who Do You Belong To" on the B-side			
3/21/70	**66**	8		14 **Dear Prudence** .... written by **John Lennon** and **Paul McCartney** (from **The Beatles**' 1968 *"White Album"*)	$7		Buddah 165
10/10/70	**83**	2		15 **America/Standing** / medley: "America" originally recorded on **Steppenwolf**'s 1969 album *Monster*			
10/10/70		1		16 **Because I Love You**	$7		Buddah 188
2/6/71	**81**	6		17 **Didn't It Look So Easy** *[THE STAIRSTEPS]* .... *Peace Is Gonna Come*	$7		Buddah 213
5/17/80	**45**	10		18 **All Night Thing** .... *(instrumental)* **THE INVISIBLE MAN'S BAND**	$5		Mango 103
				FIVE STAR R&B/LP '86 Family R&B-dance vocal group from Romford, Essex, England: Deniece (lead singer), Stedman, Doris, Lorraine and Delroy Pearson. Their father, Buster Pearson, was a guitarist with **Otis Redding**.			
9/14/85	**65**	11		1 **All Fall Down** .... *First Avenue*	$4		RCA 14108
2/8/86	**59**	9		2 **Let Me Be The One** .... *(Philadelphia remix)*	$4	■	RCA 14229
9/13/86	**41**	14		3 **Can't Wait Another Minute** .... S:35 *Don't You Know I Love It*	$4	■	RCA 14421
12/27/86+	**67**	11		4 **If I Say Yes** .... *Let Me Down Easy*	$4	■	RCA 5083
				5000 VOLTS '75 Disco trio from England: Tina Charles, Martin Jay and Tony Eyers.			
10/18/75	**26**	10		**I'm On Fire** .... *Still On Fire*	$6		Philips 40801
				FIXX, The ROK/BUB/LP '83 Techno-pop group from London, England: Cy Curnin (vocals), Jamie West-Oram (guitar), Rupert Greenall (keyboards), Charlie Barrett (bass) and Adam Woods (drums). Barrett left in early 1983; replaced by Alfred Agies. Agies left in 1985; replaced by Dan Brown.			
10/30/82	**76**	8		1 **Stand Or Fall** .... *Sinking Island*	$4		MCA 52106
5/28/83	**20**	16		2 **Saved By Zero** .... *Going Overboard*	$4	■	MCA 52213
8/27/83	**4**	19		3 **One Thing Leads To Another** *Opinions*	$4	■	MCA 52264
11/26/83+	**32**	13		4 **The Sign Of Fire** .... *Saved By Zero (live)*	$4	■	MCA 52316
8/18/84	**15**	15		5 **Are We Ourselves?** .... AR[2] S:13 / A:21 *Deeper And Deeper* (ROK #3)	$4	■	MCA 52444
11/17/84	**69**	5		6 **Sunshine In The Shade** .... *Question*	$4	■	MCA 52498
5/24/86	**19**	14		7 **Secret Separation** .... AR[2] S:18 / A:29 *Sense The Adventure* all of above produced by Rupert Hine	$4		MCA 52832
2/25/89	**55**	10		8 **Driven Out** .... AR[4] *Shred Of Evidence*	$3	■	RCA 8837
3/30/91	**35**	11		9 **How Much Is Enough** .... S:35 / A:35 *(3 album snippets)*	$3	▮	Impact 54028

FLACK, Roberta ★151★ R&B/BUB/AC/LP '72

Born on 2/10/39 in Asheville, North Carolina; raised in Arlington, Virginia. Played piano from an early age. Music scholarship to Howard University at age 15; classmate of **Donny Hathaway**. Worked as a high school music teacher in North Carolina. Discovered by jazz musician **Les McCann**. Signed to Atlantic in 1969.

1)The First Time Ever I Saw Your Face 2)Killing Me Softly With His Song 3)Feel Like Makin' Love

DEBUT	PEAK	WKS	Gold	A-side (Chart Hit)	B-side	$	Sym	Label & Number
6/12/71	29	12		1 **You've Got A Friend**	*Gone Away*	$7		Atlantic 2808
10/23/71	71	6		2 **You've Lost That Lovin' Feelin'**	*Be Real Black For Me*	$7		Atlantic 2837
				ROBERTA FLACK & DONNY HATHAWAY (above 2)				
1/22/72	76	5		3 **Will You Still Love Me Tomorrow**	*Go Up Moses*	$7		Atlantic 2851
3/4/72	1^{6}	18	●	4 **The First Time Ever I Saw Your Face** AC^{6}	*Trade Winds*	$5		Atlantic 2864
				written in 1962; recorded on Flack's 1969 album *First Take*; popularized because of inclusion in the movie *Play Misty For Me*; 1972 Grammy winner: Record of the Year				
6/10/72	5	13	●	5 **Where Is The Love** RB^{1} / AC^{1}	*Mood*	$5		Atlantic 2879
				ROBERTA FLACK & DONNY HATHAWAY				
1/27/73	1^{5}	16	●	6 **Killing Me Softly With His Song**	*Just Like A Woman*	$5		Atlantic 2940
				originally recorded by Lori Lieberman in 1972 on Capitol 3379; 1973 Grammy winner: Record of the Year				
9/22/73	30	9		7 **Jesse**	*No Tears (In The End)*	$5		Atlantic 2982
				written by **Janis Ian**; all of above produced by Joel Dorn				
6/22/74	1^{1}	16	●	8 **Feel Like Makin' Love** RB^{5} / AC^{2}	*When You Smile*	$5		Atlantic 3025
				also released in 1974 on Atlantic 3203				
6/14/75	76	3		9 **Feelin' That Glow**	*Some Gospel According To Matthew*	$5		Atlantic 3271
2/18/78	2^{2}	20	●	10 **The Closer I Get To You** RB^{2}	*Love Is The Healing* (Flack)	$5		Atlantic 3463
				ROBERTA FLACK with DONNY HATHAWAY				
5/20/78	24	13		11 **If Ever I See You Again** AC^{3}	*I'd Like To Be Baby To You*	$5		Atlantic 3483
				title song from the movie starring Joe Brooks				
2/16/80	47	11		12 **You Are My Heaven**	*I'll Love You Forever And Ever* (Flack)	$5		Atlantic 3627
				co-written by **Stevie Wonder**				
5/17/80	56	8		13 **Back Together Again**	*God Don't Like Ugly* (Flack)	$5		Atlantic 3661
				ROBERTA FLACK with DONNY HATHAWAY (above 2)				
3/6/82	13	21		14 **Making Love**	*Jesse*	$4	■	Atlantic 4005
				title song from the movie starring Kate Jackson				
7/24/82	42	11		15 **I'm The One**	*'Til The Morning Comes*	$4		Atlantic 4068
7/9/83	16	29		16 **Tonight, I Celebrate My Love**	*Born To Love*	$4	■	Capitol 5242
12/24/83+	58	11		17 **You're Looking Like Love To Me**	*Let Me Be The One You Need* (Bryson)	$4	■	Capitol 5307
				PEABO BRYSON/ROBERTA FLACK (above 2)				
9/21/91	6	20		18 **Set The Night To Music** A:23 / S:25	*Natural Thing* (Flack)	$3	▮^{V}	Atlantic 87607
				ROBERTA FLACK with Maxi Priest				

FLAME, The '70

Pop-rock group from Durban, South Africa: brothers Rikki, Steve and Brother Fataar, with Terry "Blondie" Chaplin. Rikki (drums) and Blondie (guitar) also played with **The Beach Boys**, 1971-75.

DEBUT	PEAK	WKS	Gold	A-side (Chart Hit)	B-side	$	Sym	Label & Number
11/7/70	95	2		**See The Light**	*Get Your Mind Made Up*	$15		Brother 3500
				produced by **Carl Wilson** (of **The Beach Boys**)				

FLAMING EMBER, The BUB/R&B/LP '70

White R&B-rock group from Detroit, Michigan: Joe Sladich (guitar), Bill Ellis (piano), Jim Bugnel (bass) and Jerry Plunk (drums).

DEBUT	PEAK	WKS	Gold	A-side (Chart Hit)	B-side	$	Sym	Label & Number
9/27/69	26	14		1 **Mind, Body and Soul**	*Filet de Soul*	$7		Hot Wax 6902
1/17/70	88	5		2 **Shades Of Green**	*Don't You Wanna Wanna*	$7		Hot Wax 6907
5/23/70	24	14		3 **Westbound #9**	*Why Don't You Stay*	$7		Hot Wax 7003
10/17/70	34	13		4 **I'm Not My Brothers Keeper**	*Deserted Village*	$7		Hot Wax 7006

FLAMING LIPS, The LP '95

Rock group from Oklahoma City, Oklahoma: Wayne Coyne (vocals), Ron Jones (guitar), Michael Ivins (bass) and Steven Drozd (drums).

DEBUT	PEAK	WKS	Gold	A-side (Chart Hit)	B-side	$	Sym	Label & Number
12/17/94+	55	20		**She Don't Use Jelly** S:46 / A:60	*Turn It On (Bluegrass version)*	$3	▮^{V}	Warner 18131

FLAMINGOS, The R&B/BUB '59

R&B vocal group from Chicago, Illinois: cousins Zeke and Jake Carey, **Tommy Hunt**, Nate Nelson, Johnny Carter and Paul Wilson. Carter replaced Johnny Funches in **The Dells** in 1960. Hunt went solo in 1961. Nelson joined **The Platters** in 1966; died of heart disease on 6/1/84 (age 52). Wilson died in May 1988 (age 53). Jake Carey died of a heart attack on 12/10/97 (age 74). Zeke Carey died of cancer on 12/24/99 (age 66). Group inducted into the Rock and Roll Hall of Fame in 2001.

1)I Only Have Eyes For You 2)Nobody Loves Me Like You 3)Time Was

DEBUT	PEAK	WKS	Gold	A-side (Chart Hit)	B-side	$	Sym	Label & Number
1/19/59	52	10		1 **Lovers Never Say Goodbye**	*That Love Is You*	$40		End 1035
				originally entitled "Please Wait For Me" ($60); re-entered the "Bubbling Under" chart on 10/9/61 (#117)				
6/1/59	11	13		2 **I Only Have Eyes For You**	*At The Prom*	$30		End 1046
				#2 hit for Ben Selvin in 1934; from the movie musical *Dames* starring Joan Blondell; also released with "Love Walked In" and "Goodnight Sweetheart" as the B-sides				
10/5/59	88	3		3 **Love Walked In**	*Yours*	$25		End 1055
				#1 hit in 1938 for **Sammy Kaye** & His Orchestra; from the movie *The Goldwyn Follies* starring Adolphe Menjou				
1/25/60	71	6		4 **I Was Such A Fool (To Fall In Love With You)**	*Heavenly Angel*	$25		End 1062
4/18/60	30	10		5 **Nobody Loves Me Like You**	*Besame Mucho*	$25		End 1068
				written by **Sam Cooke**; also released with "You, Me And The Sea" as the B-side				
7/18/60	74	6		6 **Mio Amore**	*At Night*	$25		End 1073
				translation of Italian title: "My Love"; first released on End 1065 in 1960				
12/19/60+	54	5		7 **Your Other Love**	*Lovers Gotta Cry*	$25		End 1081
3/13/61	92	3		8 **Kokomo**	*That's Why I Love You*	$25		End 1085
				original version released by The Flamingos in 1955 on Parrot 812 ($800); #6 R&B hit for **Gene & Eunice** in 1955				

DEBUT	PEAK	WKS	Gold	A-side (Chart Hit)...B-side	$	Sym	Label & Number

FLAMINGOS, The — Cont'd

DEBUT	PEAK	WKS	Gold	A-side (Chart Hit)...B-side	$	Sym	Label & Number
7/3/61	45	8		9 Time Was ... *Dream Girl* Mexican song written as "Duerme"; #10 hit for **Jimmy Dorsey**'s orchestra in 1941	$25		End 1092
3/19/66	93	2		10 The Boogaloo Party ... *The Nearness Of You*	$15		Philips 40347
4/4/70	86	2		11 Buffalo Soldier ... *(long version)*	$10		Polydor 14019

FLARES, The — BUB '61

R&B vocal group from Los Angeles, California: Aaron Collins (lead), Willie Davis, Tommy Miller and George Hollis. Collins and Davis had been in **The Cadets/The Jacks**; Miller and Hollis had been in The Ermines and The Flairs. Produced by **The Platters** manager/songwriter, Buck Ram.

DEBUT	PEAK	WKS	Gold	A-side (Chart Hit)...B-side	$	Sym	Label & Number
9/4/61	25	15		Foot Stomping - Part 1 ... *Part 2* [I] (The Ramrocks)	$20		Felsted 8624

FLASH — LP '72

Rock group from England: Colin Carter (vocals), Peter Banks (guitar; **Yes**, **After The Fire**), Ray Bennett (bass) and Michael Hough (drums).

DEBUT	PEAK	WKS	Gold	A-side (Chart Hit)...B-side	$	Sym	Label & Number
6/24/72	29	12		Small Beginnings ... *Morning Haze*	$6		Capitol 3345

FLASH AND THE PAN — LP '79

Pop duo formed in Australia: George Young and Harry Vanda (both formerly with **The Easybeats**). George's younger brothers, Angus and Malcolm Young, are members of **AC/DC**.

DEBUT	PEAK	WKS	Gold	A-side (Chart Hit)...B-side	$	Sym	Label & Number
7/28/79	76	4		Hey, St. Peter ... *Walking In The Rain* first released on Midland International 10934 in 1977 ($6)	$5		Epic 50715

FLASH CADILLAC & THE CONTINENTAL KIDS — BUB '76

Fifties-styled rock and roll act from Colorado: Sam "Flash Cadillac" McFadin (vocals, guitar), Linn "Spike" Phillips (guitar), Kris "Angelo" Moe (keyboards), Dwight "Spider" Bement (sax), Warren "Butch" Knight (bass) and Jeff "Wally" Stewart (drums; replaced in 1975 by Paul "Wheaty" Wheatbread). Bement and Wheatbread were with **Gary Puckett & The Union Gap**. Group appeared as the prom band in the movie *American Graffiti*. McFadin died of a heart attack on 8/31/2001 (age 49).

DEBUT	PEAK	WKS	Gold	A-side (Chart Hit)...B-side	$	Sym	Label & Number
5/25/74	93	3		1 Dancin' (On A Saturday Night) ... *The Way I Feel Tonight*	$7		Epic 11102
2/1/75	41	8		2 Good Times, Rock & Roll ... *It's Hard (To Break The Ice)*	$6		Private Stock 45,006
8/28/76	29	14		3 Did You Boogie (With Your Baby) ... *Maybe It's All In My Mind* with spoken interludes by **Wolfman Jack** (some pressings omit these interludes)	$6	⊙	Private Stock 45,079

FLATT & SCRUGGS — C&W/BUB/LP '63

Influential bluegrass duo. Lester Flatt (guitar) was born on 6/28/14 in Overton County, Tennessee; died on 5/11/79 (age 64). Earl Scruggs (banjo) was born on 1/6/24 in Cleveland County, North Carolina. Duo formed in 1948 while both were members of Bill Monroe's band. Regulars on TV's *Beverly Hillbillies*. Separated in early 1969.

DEBUT	PEAK	WKS	Gold	A-side (Chart Hit)...B-side	$	Sym	Label & Number
12/8/62+	44	11		1 The Ballad Of Jed Clampett ... CW[3] *Coal Loadin' Johnny* **LESTER FLATT, EARL SCRUGGS & The Foggy Mountain Boys** from the TV series *The Beverly Hillbillies* starring Buddy Ebsen; also issued with a promo sleeve: "A Business Of Exceptions"	$15	■	Columbia 42606
3/2/68	55	12		2 Foggy Mountain Breakdown ... *Down In The Flood* (C&W #45) [I] theme from the movie *Bonnie & Clyde* starring Warren Beatty and Faye Dunaway	$12		Columbia 44380
3/2/68	55	12		3 Theme From Bonnie & Clyde (Foggy Mountain Breakdown) ... *My Cabin In Caroline* [I] above 2 were listed together as one entry ("Foggy Mountain Breakdown") on the *Hot 100* (all 12 weeks); the Columbia version was recorded in 1968, the Mercury version in 1949	$12	■	Mercury 72739

FLAVOR — '68

Rock trio from Frederick, Maryland: Gary St. Clair (vocals, bass), Demetri Callas (guitar) and Danny Conway (drums).

DEBUT	PEAK	WKS	Gold	A-side (Chart Hit)...B-side	$	Sym	Label & Number
8/3/68	95	5		Sally Had A Party ... *Shop Around*	$7		Columbia 44521

FLAVOR UNIT MCs, The — '93

Rap ensemble assembled by **Queen Latifah**, CEO of Flavor Unit Records. Features **Heavy D**, **Treach** (**Naughty By Nature**), Dres (**Black Sheep**), D-Nice, Chip-Fu (**Fu-Schnickens**), **Freddie Foxx**, and The Almighty RSO.

DEBUT	PEAK	WKS	Gold	A-side (Chart Hit)...B-side	$	Sym	Label & Number
4/3/93	86	4		Roll Wit Tha Flava ... S:48 *(3 versions) / Badd Boyz* (Almighty R.S.O.)	$7	■*	Epic/Flavor Unit 74897

FLEETWOOD MAC ★104★ — ROK/BUB/AC/LP '77

Pop-rock group formed in England by Peter Green (guitar; born on 10/29/46), Mick Fleetwood (drums; born on 6/24/47) and John McVie (bass; born on 11/26/45), along with guitarist Jeremy Spencer (born on 7/4/48). Many lineup changes followed as group headed toward rock superstardom. Green and Spencer left in 1970. **Christine McVie** (keyboards; born on 7/12/43) joined in August 1970. **Bob Welch** (guitar; born on 7/31/46) joined in April 1971, stayed through 1974. Group relocated to California in 1974, whereupon Americans **Lindsey Buckingham** (guitar; born on 10/3/49) and **Stevie Nicks** (vocals; born on 5/26/48) joined in January 1975. Buckingham left in summer of 1987. Guitarists/vocalists **Billy Burnette** (son of **Dorsey Burnette**) and Rick Vito joined in July 1987. Christine McVie and Nicks quit touring with the band at the end of 1990. Vito left in 1991. In early 1993, Nicks and Burnette left. In late 1993, Bekka Bramlett (leader of The Zoo and daughter of **Delaney & Bonnie** Bramlett) and **Dave Mason** joined Mick, John and Christine in band. The classic lineup of Fleetwood, John & Christine McVie, Buckingham and Nicks reunited in May 1997. Christine McVie retired from the group prior to their 2003 album and tour. Inducted into the Rock and Roll Hall of Fame in 1998.

1)Dreams 2)Don't Stop 3)Hold Me 4)Little Lies 5)Big Love

DEBUT	PEAK	WKS	Gold	A-side (Chart Hit)...B-side	$	Sym	Label & Number
1/31/70	55	10		1 Oh Well - Pt. I ... *Pt. II* [I] includes 20 seconds of vocal; from their 1969 album *Then Play On*; written and guitar solo by Peter Green	$20		Reprise 0883
11/8/75+	20	14		2 Over My Head ... *I'm So Afraid*	$6		Reprise 1339
3/6/76	11	18		3 Rhiannon (Will You Ever Win) ... *Sugar Daddy*	$6		Reprise 1345
7/4/76	11	19		4 Say You Love Me ... *Monday Morning*	$6		Reprise 1356
1/8/77	10	15		5 Go Your Own Way ... *Silver Springs*	$8		Warner 8304
4/16/77	1[1]	19	●	6 Dreams ... *Songbird*	$4		Warner 8371
7/9/77	3	18		7 Don't Stop ... *Never Going Back Again*	$4	■	Warner 8413
10/15/77	9	14		8 You Make Loving Fun ... *Gold Dust Woman* above 4 from the album *Rumours*	$4		Warner 8483
10/6/79	8	15		9 Tusk ... *Never Make Me Cry* [L] with U.S.C. Trojan Marching Band, recorded at Dodger Stadium; issued with 2 different picture sleeves	$4	■	Warner 49077
12/15/79+	7	14		10 Sara ... *That's Enough For Me*	$4	■	Warner 49150
3/8/80	20	13		11 Think About Me ... *Save Me A Place*	$4	■	Warner 49196
6/7/80	86	3		12 Sisters Of The Moon ... *Walk A Thin Line* above 4 from the album *Tusk*	$4		Warner 49500

DEBUT	PEAK	WKS	Gold	A-side (Chart Hit)...B-side	$	Sym	Label & Number
				FLEETWOOD MAC — Cont'd			
2/7/81	60	6		13 **Fireflies**...*Over My Head (live)* [L]	$4	■	Warner 49660
6/19/82	4	17		14 **Hold Me**...*Eyes Of The World*	$4	■	Warner 29966
9/4/82	12	14		15 **Gypsy**...*Cool Water*	$4	■	Warner 29918
11/27/82+	22	14		16 **Love In Store**...*Can't Go Back*	$4		Warner 29848
3/28/87	5	16		17 **Big Love**...A:4 / S:6 *You And I, Part I*	$3	■	Warner 28398
6/20/87	19	13		18 **Seven Wonders**...S:17 / A:17 *Book Of Miracles* [I]	$3	■	Warner 28317
8/29/87	4	21		19 **Little Lies**...AC[4] S:3 / A:5 *Ricky*	$3	■	Warner 28291
11/28/87+	14	18		20 **Everywhere**...AC[3] A:12 / S:13 *When I See You Again*	$3	■	Warner 28143
4/2/88	90	4		21 **Family Man**...*Down Endless Street*	$3	■	Warner 28114
				above 5 from the album *Tango In The Night*			
12/3/88+	43	14		22 **As Long As You Follow**...AC[1] *Oh Well (live)*	$3	■	Warner 27644
4/7/90	33	11		23 **Save Me**...A:28 / S:33 *Another Woman (live)*	$3	■V	Warner 19866
9/6/97	41A	16		24 **Silver Springs**... [L]		V	album cut ■
				studio version released in 1977 as the B-side of #5 above; from the album *The Dance* on Reprise 46702; "45": Reprise 17300 (with a picture sleeve); B-side: "Go Your Own Way" (live)			
7/18/98	51	20		25 **Landslide**...A:48 *(3 versions)* [L]	$8	★*	Reprise 44540
				studio version released on the 1975 album *Fleetwood Mac*; songwriters: **Christine McVie** (#2, 4, 7, 8, 11, 14, 16, 19, 20, 22 & 23), **Stevie Nicks** (#3, 6, 10, 12, 13, 15, 18, 24 & 25), **Lindsey Buckingham** (#5, 9, 17 & 21)			
	★437★			**FLEETWOODS, The** BUB/LP '59			
				Pop vocal trio from Olympia, Washington: Gary Troxel (born on 11/28/39), Gretchen Christopher (born on 2/29/40) and Barbara Ellis (born on 2/20/40).			
				1)Come Softly To Me 2)Mr. Blue 3)Tragedy			
3/9/59	❶4	16	●	1 **Come Softly To Me** *I Care So Much*	$25		Dolphin 1
				also released on Liberty 55188 in 1959 ($25)			
5/18/59	39	8		2 **Graduation's Here**...*Oh Lord Let It Be Me*	$20		Dolton 3
9/7/59	❶1	20	●	3 **Mr. Blue** /			
10/26/59	84	2		4 **You Mean Everything To Me**...	$20		Dolton 5
2/15/60	28	9		5 **Outside My Window**...*Magic Star* (#113)	$20		Dolton 15
5/23/60	23	13		6 **Runaround**...*Truly Do*	$20	■	Dolton 22
10/17/60	96	1		7 **The Last One To Know**...*Dormilona*	$20		Dolton 27
4/17/61	10	12		8 **Tragedy**...*Little Miss Sad One*	$15		Dolton 40
9/11/61	30	8		9 **(He's) The Great Impostor**...*Poor Little Girl*	$15		Dolton 45
				co-written by **Jackie DeShannon**			
10/13/62	36	10		10 **Lovers By Night, Strangers By Day**...*They Tell Me It's Summer*	$15		Dolton 62
6/1/63	32	11		11 **Goodnight My Love**...*Jimmy Beware*	$15		Dolton 75
				#7 R&B hit for **Jesse Belvin** in 1956			
				FLEMONS, Wade R&B/BUB '60			
				Born on 9/25/40 in Coffeyville, Kansas. Died of cancer on 10/13/93 (age 53). Black electric pianist of **Maurice White**'s pre-**Earth, Wind & Fire** group, the Salty Peppers, 1969.			
12/22/58+	80	5		1 **Here I Stand**...*My Baby Likes To Rock*	$30		Vee-Jay 295
				WADE FLEMONS and the Newcomers			
2/15/60	94	2		2 **What's Happening**...*Good Nite, It's Time To Go*	$30		Vee-Jay 335
4/25/60	70	4		3 **Easy Lovin'**...*Woops Now*	$30		Vee-Jay 344
				FLETCHER, Darrow R&B '66			
				Born on 1/23/51 in Inkster, Michigan. Male R&B singer/songwriter.			
1/15/66	89	3		**The Pain Gets A Little Deeper**...*My Judgement Day*	$15		Groovy 3001
				FLETCHER, Lois '74			
				Pop-folk singer. Former member of The Back Porch Majority.			
3/30/74	64	7		**I Am What I Am**...*One More Time*	$6		Playboy 50049
				FLEXX G. '99			
				Black male rapper.			
11/13/99	70S	1		**A Whole Lot Of Gangstas Die**...*(instrumental)*	$6	★	Shanty Town 1005
				FLEXX G. featuring Kurupt and Alkatraz			
				FLINT, Shelby BUB '61			
				Born on 9/17/39 in North Hollywood, California. Pop singer/songwriter.			
12/26/60+	22	12		1 **Angel On My Shoulder**...*Somebody*	$12		Valiant 6001
8/13/66	61	7		2 **Cast Your Fate To The Wind**...*The Lilly*	$10		Valiant 743
				FLIRTATIONS, The BUB '69			
				Female R&B vocal group: Shirley and Earnestine Pearce from South Carolina and Viola Billups from Alabama. The Pearce sisters had been in the Gypsies from 1962-65.			
3/8/69	34	14		**Nothing But A Heartache**...*How Can You Tell Me?*	$8		Deram 85038
				FLOATERS, The R&B/BUB/LP '77			
				R&B vocal group from Detroit, Michigan: brothers Paul and Ralph Mitchell, Charles Clarke and Larry Cunningham.			
7/9/77	2²	16	●	**Float On**...RB[6] *Everything Happens For A Reason*	$5	■	ABC 12284
				also see **Cheech & Chong**'s parody "Bloat On"			
				FLOCK OF SEAGULLS, A LP '82			
				New wave group from Liverpool, England: brothers Mike (vocals, keyboards) and Ali (drums) Score, Paul Reynolds (guitar) and Frank Maudsley (bass).			
7/10/82	9	22		1 **I Ran (So Far Away)**...*Pick Me Up*	$4		Jive 102
11/13/82+	30	18		2 **Space Age Love Song**...*Windows*	$4	■	Jive 2003
5/14/83	26	14		3 **Wishing (If I Had A Photograph Of You)**...*Committed*	$4	■	Jive 2006
				also released on Jive 9018 in 1983			
8/11/84	56	9		4 **The More You Live, The More You Love**...*Lost Control*	$4	■	Jive 9220

DEBUT	PEAK	WKS	Gold	A-side (Chart Hit)	B-side	$	Sym	Label & Number

FLOOD, Dick — '59

Born on 11/13/32 in Philadelphia, Pennsylvania. Pop-country singer/songwriter. Performed with **Billy Graves** on **Jimmy Dean**'s CBS-TV show as The Country Lads.

DEBUT	PEAK	WKS	Gold	A-side (Chart Hit)	B-side	$	Sym	Label & Number
8/31/59	23	8		**The Three Bells (The Jimmy Brown Story)** — French tune written in 1945 as "Les Trois Cloches"; #14 hit for **Les Compagnons De La Chanson** in 1952	*Far Away*	$15		Monument 408

FLOYD, Eddie — R&B/BUB '68

Born on 6/25/35 in Montgomery, Alabama; raised in Detroit, Michigan. R&B singer/songwriter. Original member of **The Falcons**, 1955-61. Eddie's uncle, Robert West, founded the Lu Pine record label.

1)Bring It On Home To Me 2)Knock On Wood 3)I've Never Found A Girl (To Love Me Like You Do)

DEBUT	PEAK	WKS	Gold	A-side (Chart Hit)	B-side	$	Sym	Label & Number
9/10/66	28	17	●	1 **Knock On Wood** RB^1	*Got To Make A Comeback*	$10		Stax 194
2/4/67	79	6		2 **Raise Your Hand**	*I've Just Been Feeling Bad*	$10		Stax 208
7/1/67	98	1		3 **Don't Rock The Boat**	*This House*	$10		Stax 219
8/26/67	97	1		4 **Love Is A Doggone Good Thing**	*Hey Now*	$10		Stax 223
10/28/67	92	4		5 **On A Saturday Night**	*Under My Nose*	$10		Stax 233
7/27/68	40	9		6 **I've Never Found A Girl (To Love Me Like You Do)**	*I'm Just The Kind Of Fool*	$7		Stax 0002
10/19/68	17	13		7 **Bring It On Home To Me**	*Sweet Things You Do*	$7		Stax 0012
6/28/69	73	7		8 **Don't Tell Your Mama (Where You've Been)**	*Consider Me*	$7		Stax 0036
11/1/69	98	2		9 **Why Is The Wine Sweeter (On The Other Side)**	*People, Get It Together*	$7		Stax 0051
2/21/70	45	12		10 **California Girl**	*Woodman*	$7		Stax 0060

FLOYD, King — R&B/BUB/LP '71

Born on 2/13/45 in New Orleans, Louisiana. R&B singer/songwriter. First recorded for Original Sound in 1965.

DEBUT	PEAK	WKS	Gold	A-side (Chart Hit)	B-side	$	Sym	Label & Number
10/24/70+	6	20	●	1 **Groove Me** RB^4	*What Our Love Needs*	$6		Chimneyville 435
3/13/71	29	11		2 **Baby Let Me Kiss You**	*Please Don't Leave Me Lonely*	$6	■	Chimneyville 437
9/16/72	53	12		3 **Woman Don't Go Astray**	*Everybody Needs Somebody*	$6		Chimneyville 443

FLYING LIZARDS, The — LP '80

New wave group from England: Patti Palladin (vocals), David Cunningham (guitar, keyboards), Steve Beresford (bass) and J.J. Johnson (drums).

DEBUT	PEAK	WKS	Gold	A-side (Chart Hit)	B-side	$	Sym	Label & Number
12/1/79+	50	10		**Money**	*Money B* [I] [N]	$5	■	Virgin 67003

FLYING MACHINE, The — LP '69

Studio project of British pop songwriters/producers Tony MacAuley and Geoff Stephens. Touring group featured Tony Newman as lead vocalist. Not to be confused with James Taylor's group.

DEBUT	PEAK	WKS	Gold	A-side (Chart Hit)	B-side	$	Sym	Label & Number
10/4/69	5	14	●	1 **Smile A Little Smile For Me**	*Maybe We've Been Loving Too Long*	$8		Congress 6000
2/21/70	87	2		2 **Baby Make It Soon**	*There She Goes*	$8		Congress 6012

FMob — see EN VOGUE

FOCUS — LP '73

Progressive-rock group formed in Amsterdam, Holland: Jan Akkerman (guitar), Thijs van Leer (keyboards, flute), Martin Dresdan (bass) and Hans Cleuver (drums).

DEBUT	PEAK	WKS	Gold	A-side (Chart Hit)	B-side	$	Sym	Label & Number
3/3/73	9	19		1 **Hocus Pocus**	*Hocus Pocus II* [I]	$6		Sire 704
7/28/73	89	5		2 **Sylvia**	*Love Remembered* [I]	$5		Sire 708

FOGELBERG, Dan — AC/C&W/ROK/LP '81

★313★

Born on 8/13/51 in Peoria, Illinois. Soft-rock singer/songwriter. Worked as a folk singer in Los Angeles. With **Van Morrison** in the early 1970s. Session work in Nashville. Fogelberg's backing group is **Fools Gold**.

1)Longer 2)Hard To Say 3)Leader Of The Band

DEBUT	PEAK	WKS	Gold	A-side (Chart Hit)	B-side	$	Sym	Label & Number
2/1/75	31	9		1 **Part Of The Plan** — **Graham Nash** (harmony vocal); **Joe Walsh** (lead guitar; producer)	*Song From Half Mountain*	$5		Epic 50055
10/14/78	24	14		2 **The Power Of Gold** — **DAN FOGELBERG/TIM WEISBERG**; **Don Henley** (harmony vocal)	*Lahaina Luna*	$4		Full Moon 50606
12/15/79+	2^2	22		3 **Longer** AC^1	*Along The Road*	$4		Full Moon 50824
3/22/80	21	13		4 **Heart Hotels** — **Tom Scott** (sax solo)	*Beggar's Game*	$4		Full Moon 50862
12/13/80+	9	18		5 **Same Old Lang Syne**	*Hearts And Crafts*	$4	■	Full Moon 50961
8/29/81	7	19		6 **Hard To Say** — **Glenn Frey** (harmony vocal)	*The Innocent Age*	$4		Full Moon 02488
11/28/81+	9	20		7 **Leader Of The Band** AC^2	*Times Like These*	$4		Full Moon 02647
4/3/82	18	14		8 **Run For The Roses** — above 4 from the album *The Innocent Age*	*The Sand And The Foam*	$4		Full Moon 02821
10/9/82	23	16		9 **Missing You**	*Hearts And Crafts*	$4		Full Moon 03289
2/5/83	29	16		10 **Make Love Stay** AC^1	*Hearts And Crafts*	$4		Full Moon 03525
2/4/84	13	14		11 **The Language Of Love**	*Windows And Walls*	$3	■	Full Moon 04314
4/28/84	48	9		12 **Believe In Me** AC^1	*Windows And Walls*	$3		Full Moon 04447
3/23/85	85	4		13 **Go Down Easy**	*High Country Snows*	$4		Full Moon 04835
5/30/87	84	6		14 **She Don't Look Back** — all of above (except #13) written by Fogelberg	*It Doesn't Matter*	$3	■	Full Moon 07044

FOGERTY, John — ROK/BUB/C&W/LP '85

Born on 5/28/45 in Berkeley, California. Rock singer/songwriter/multi-instrumentalist. With his brother Tom in the Blue Velvets in 1959. Group became the Golliwogs and recorded for Fantasy in 1964. Group renamed **Creedence Clearwater Revival** in 1967. Went solo in 1972 and recorded as **The Blue Ridge Rangers** (see #1 & 2 below).

DEBUT	PEAK	WKS	Gold	A-side (Chart Hit)	B-side	$	Sym	Label & Number
12/2/72+	16	16		1 **Jambalaya (On the Bayou)** — #1 Country hit for Hank Williams in 1952	*Workin' On A Building*	$6		Fantasy 689
3/31/73	37	12		2 **Hearts Of Stone** — **THE BLUE RIDGE RANGERS** (above 2)	*Somewhere Listening (For My Name)*	$6		Fantasy 700
9/6/75	27	11		3 **Rockin' All Over The World**	*The Wall*	$5		Asylum 45274
12/13/75	78	3		4 **Almost Saturday Night**	*Sea Cruise*	$5		Asylum 45291
5/1/76	87	4		5 **You Got The Magic**	*Evil Thing*	$5		Asylum 45309

DEBUT	PEAK	WKS	Gold	A-side (Chart Hit)..........B-side	$	Sym	Label & Number
				FOGERTY, John — Cont'd			
12/22/84+	10	18		6 **The Old Man Down The Road** AR^{3} A:8 / S:12 *Big Train (From Memphis)* (C&W #38) picture sleeve issued with photo in either blue or black ink	$4	■	Warner 29100
3/16/85	20	12		7 **Rock And Roll Girls /** A:19 / S:21			
5/25/85	44	13		8 **Centerfield**	$4	■	Warner 29053
9/6/86	81	4		9 **Eye Of The Zombie** .... *I Confess* (w/Bobby King) all of above written (except #1 & 2) and produced by Fogerty	$4	■	Warner 28657
				FOGHAT ROK/BUB/LP **'76** Rock group formed in England: "Lonesome" Dave Peverett (vocals, guitar), Rod Price (guitar), Tony Stevens (bass) and Roger Earl (drums). Peverett, Stevens and Earl were with **Savoy Brown**. Peverett died of pneumonia on 2/7/2000 (age 57). *1)Slow Ride 2)Third Time Lucky 3)I Just Want To Make Love To You ("live")*			
10/7/72	83	7		1 **I Just Want To Make Love To You** .... *A Hole To Hide In* #4 R&B hit in 1954 for Muddy Waters (as "Just Make Love To Me"); B-side of **Etta James**' 1961 hit "At Last"	$6		Bearsville 0008
4/28/73	82	6		2 **What A Shame** .... *Helping Hand* above 2 produced by **Dave Edmunds**	$6		Bearsville 0014
12/13/75+	20	17		3 **Slow Ride** *Save Your Loving (For Me)*	$5		Bearsville 0306
6/5/76	45	7		4 **Fool For The City** .... *Take It Or Leave It*	$5		Bearsville 0307
11/27/76+	34	10		5 **Drivin' Wheel** .... *Night Shift*	$5		Bearsville 0313
3/26/77	67	3		6 **I'll Be Standing By** .... *Take Me To The River*	$5		Bearsville 0315
9/10/77	33	10		7 **I Just Want To Make Love To You** .... *Fool For The City (live)* [L-R]	$5		Bearsville 0319
5/20/78	36	10		8 **Stone Blue** .... *Chevrolet*	$5		Bearsville 0325
11/17/79+	23	15		9 **Third Time Lucky (First Time I Was A Fool)** .... *Love In Motion*	$5	■	Bearsville 49125
8/2/80	81	3		10 **Stranger In My Home Town** .... *Be My Woman*	$5		Bearsville 49510
				FOLDS, Ben, Five ROK/LP **'98** Born on 9/12/66 in Winston-Salem, North Carolina. Singer/songwriter/pianist. His trio included Robert Sledge (bass) and Darren Jessee (drums).			
12/13/97+	19^{A}	22		**Brick** .... from the album *Whatever And Ever Amen* on 550 Music 67762; "45": 550 Music 79018; B-side: "Fair"		V	album cut
				FOLEY, Ellen LP **'79** Born in 1951 in St. Louis, Missouri. Rock singer/actress. Vocalist on **Meat Loaf**'s *Bat Out Of Hell* album. Acted in several movies and TV shows.			
11/17/79	92	4		**What's A Matter Baby** .... *Hideaway*	$5		Epic 50770
				FOLKER, Jessica **'01** Born on 7/9/77 in Sweden (African father/Swedish mother). Female dance singer.			
10/6/01	40^{S}	5		**To Be Able To Love** .... *(3 remixes)* originally released as a 12" single on Nervous Records 20501 in 2001	$4	★	Jive 42972
				FOLK IMPLOSION **'96** Rock duo from San Francisco, California: Lou Barlow (vocals, bass) and John Davis (guitar, drums).			
12/9/95+	29	20		**Natural One** .... S:32 / A:33 *Cabride* from the movie *Kids* starring Leo Fitzpatrick	$3	▌	London 0430
				FONTAINE, Eddie **'58** Born on 3/6/34 in Jersey City, New Jersey. Rock and roll singer/actor. Played "Pete D'Angelo" on TV's *The Gallant Men.*			
9/22/58	64	3		**Nothin' Shakin'** .... H:64 *Don't Ya Know* first released on Sunbeam 105 in 1958 ($60)	$30		Argo 5309
				FONTANA, Wayne — see MINDBENDERS, The			
	★285★			**FONTANE SISTERS, The** MEM/POP **'55** Pop vocal trio from New Milford, New Jersey: sisters Marge, Bea and Geri, whose family name is Rosse. Backed **Perry Como** on many of his hits from 1949-52, including his #1 hits "A-You're Adorable" and "Hoop-Dee-Doo." *1)Hearts Of Stone 2)Seventeen 3)Eddie My Love*			
12/11/54+	❶^{3}	20	●	1 **Hearts Of Stone** J:❶^{3} / S:❶^{1} / A:2 *Bless Your Heart*	$20		Dot 15265
2/26/55	13	8		2 **Rock Love** .... J:13 / S:19 *You're Mine*	$15		Dot 15333
6/4/55	13	6		3 **Rollin' Stone /** J:13 #8 R&B hit for The Marigolds in 1955			
6/18/55		2		4 **Playmates** .... J:flip #2 hit for Kay Kyser in 1940	$15		Dot 15370
8/20/55	3	15		5 **Seventeen** .... J:3 / S:6 / A:7 / T:15 *If I Could Be With You (One Hour Tonight)*	$15		Dot 15386
11/12/55	11	16		6 **Daddy-O /** T:11 / J:11 / S:13 / A:18			
11/19/55	71	11		7 **Adorable** .... T:71 #1 R&B hit for **The Drifters** in 1955	$15		Dot 15428
12/17/55	36	4		8 **Nuttin' For Christmas** .... T:36 *Silver Bells* [X-N] verse melody based on traditional 19th century French song "Vive La Companie"	$15		Dot 15434
3/10/56	11	17		9 **Eddie My Love** .... J:11 / T:12 / A:13 / S:15 *Yum Yum*	$15		Dot 15450
5/26/56	38	14		10 **I'm In Love Again** .... T:38 *You Always Hurt The One You Love*	$15		Dot 15462
7/28/56	47	7		11 **Voices /** T:47 **Pat Boone** (narration)			
8/11/56	93	2		12 **Lonesome Lover Blues** T:93	$15		Dot 15480
10/13/56	55	7		13 **Please Don't Leave Me /** T:55 #3 R&B hit for **Fats Domino** in 1953			
10/13/56	86	6		14 **Still** T:86	$12		Dot 15501
12/29/56+	13	18		15 **The Banana Boat Song** .... A:13 / J:14 / T:22 *Honolulu Moon*	$12		Dot 15527
5/6/57	72	2		16 **I'm Stickin' With You** .... T:72 *Let The Rest Of The World Go By*	$12		Dot 15555
4/28/58	12	9		17 **Chanson D'Amour (Song Of Love)** .... A:12 / T:68 *Cocoanut Grove* **Billy Vaughn** (orch., all of above)	$12		Dot 15736
11/10/58	94	1		18 **Jealous Heart** .... *Encore d'Amour* Milton DeLugg (orch.); #2 Country hit for **Tex Ritter** in 1945; #4 pop hit for Al Morgan in 1949	$12		Dot 15853

FOO FIGHTERS — ROK/LP '00

Rock group formed in Seattle, Washington: Dave Grohl (vocals, guitar), Pat Smear (guitar), Nate Mendel (bass) and William Goldsmith (drums). Taylor Hawkins replaced Goldsmith in 1997. Franz Stahl replaced Smear in 1998. Grohl was drummer for **Nirvana**. Group name taken from the fiery UFO-like apparitions seen by U.S. pilots during World War II.

DEBUT	PEAK	WKS	Gold	A-side (Chart Hit)...B-side	$	Sym	Label & Number
7/8/95	35^{A}	11		1 **This Is A Call**			album cut
10/7/95	51^{A}	11		2 **I'll Stick Around**			album cut
2/17/96	13^{A}	20		3 **Big Me** "Big Me" also available on a mini-album (Roswell/Capitol 58530); above 3 from the album *Foo Fighters* on Roswell/Capitol 34027			album cut
5/17/97	58^{A}	9		4 **Monkey Wrench** "45": Capitol 19543; B-side: "The Colour And The Shape"		V	album cut
8/9/97	42^{A}	20		5 **Everlong**			album cut
2/14/98	59^{A}	14		6 **My Hero** "45": Capitol 19865; B-side: "Dear Lover"; above 3 from the album *The Colour And The Shape* on Roswell/Capitol 55832		V	album cut
10/16/99+	19	21		7 **Learn To Fly** MR^{1} A:13 from the album *There Is Nothing Left To Lose* on Roswell/RCA 67892			album cut
11/2/02	43	20		8 **All My Life** ...A:41 from the album *One By One* on Roswell/RCA 68008; "45" (33 1/3): Sessions/RCA 031; B-side: "Danny Says"		V	album cut ■

FOOLS, The — LP '81

Rock group from Boston, Massachusetts: Mike Girard (vocals), brothers Stacey (guitar) and Chris (drums) Pedrick, Rich Bartlett (guitar) and Doug Forman (bass).

DEBUT	PEAK	WKS	Gold	A-side (Chart Hit)...B-side	$	Sym	Label & Number
4/19/80	67	4		1 **It's A Night For Beautiful Girls** ...*Sold Out*	$5		EMI America 8036
3/7/81	50	7		2 **Running Scared** ...*Alibi*	$5		EMI America 8072

FOOLS GOLD — LP '76

Backing group for **Dan Fogelberg**: Denny Henson (vocals, guitar), Doug Livingston (piano), Tom Kelly (bass) and Ron Grinel (drums).

DEBUT	PEAK	WKS	Gold	A-side (Chart Hit)...B-side	$	Sym	Label & Number
5/29/76	76	7		**Rain, Oh Rain** ...*One By One* produced by **Glenn Frey**	$6		Morning Sky 700

FORBERT, Steve — ROK/LP '80

Born in 1954 in Meridian, Mississippi. Folk-rock singer/songwriter. Moved to New York City in 1976.

DEBUT	PEAK	WKS	Gold	A-side (Chart Hit)...B-side	$	Sym	Label & Number
12/1/79+	11	19		1 **Romeo's Tune** ...*Make It All So Real*	$5		Nemperor 7525
4/12/80	85	3		2 **Say Goodbye To Little Jo** ...*You're Darn Right*	$5		Nemperor 7529

FORCE M.D.'S — R&B/BUB/LP '86

R&B vocal group from Staten Island, New York: brothers Stevie and Antoine Lundy, Jesse Daniels, Trisco Pearson and Charles Nelson. Nelson died of a heart attack on 3/10/95 (age 30). Antoine Lundy died of ALS on 1/18/98 (age 33). M.D.: Musical Diversity.

DEBUT	PEAK	WKS	Gold	A-side (Chart Hit)...B-side	$	Sym	Label & Number
2/1/86	10	19		1 **Tender Love** ...A:7 / S:12 *(instrumental)* from the all-rap musical movie *Krush Groove* starring **Sheila E.**	$3	■	Warner 28818
8/29/87	78	9		2 **Love Is A House** ...RB^{2} *(instrumental)*	$3	■	Tommy Boy 28300

FORD, Frankie — '59

Born Frank Guzzo on 8/4/39 in Gretna, Louisiana. Rock and roll singer. Appeared with Sophie Tucker, Ted Lewis and Carmen Miranda at local shows at an early age. Appeared in the movie *American Hot Wax*.

DEBUT	PEAK	WKS	Gold	A-side (Chart Hit)...B-side	$	Sym	Label & Number
2/9/59	14	17		1 **Sea Cruise** ...*Roberta*	$30		Ace 554
8/3/59	97	2		2 **Alimony** ...*Can't Tell My Heart (What To Do)* **Huey "Piano" Smith** (orch., above 2)	$25		Ace 566
1/18/60	75	6		3 **Time After Time** ...*I Want To Be Your Man* #16 hit for **Frank Sinatra** in 1947	$25		Ace 580
9/26/60	87	4		4 **You Talk Too Much** ...*If You've Got Troubles*	$15		Imperial 5686
3/20/61	72	5		5 **Seventeen** ...*Dog House*	$15		Imperial 5735

FORD, Lita — ROK/LP '89

Born on 9/23/59 in London, England; raised in Los Angeles, California. Rock singer/guitarist. Member of The Runaways from 1975-79.

DEBUT	PEAK	WKS	Gold	A-side (Chart Hit)...B-side	$	Sym	Label & Number
4/2/88	12	23		1 **Kiss Me Deadly** ...S:8 / A:14 *Broken Dreams*	$3	■	RCA 6866
3/4/89	8	25	●	2 **Close My Eyes Forever** ...S:4 / A:13 *Under The Gun* (Ford) **LITA FORD (with Ozzy Osbourne)**	$3	■	RCA 8899
7/14/90	98	1		3 **Hungry** ...*Big Gun*	$3	▮	RCA 2607
11/2/91	45	14		4 **Shot Of Poison** ...*(3 album snippets)*	$3	▮	RCA 62074

★554★ FORD, "Tennessee" Ernie — C&W/POP/LP '55

Born Ernest Jennings Ford on 2/13/19 in Bristol, Tennessee. Died of liver disease on 10/17/91 (age 72). Country singer (charted 29 hits, 1949-76). Revered as America's favorite hymn singer; his 1957 album *Hymns* peaked at #2 and charted for 277 weeks. Began career as a DJ. Host of musical variety TV shows, 1955-65. Hit #3 on the pop charts in 1950 with "I'll Never Be Free" (duet with **Kay Starr**). Favorite expression: "Bless your little pea-pickin' hearts."

1)Sixteen Tons 2)Ballad Of Davy Crockett 3)That's All

DEBUT	PEAK	WKS	Gold	A-side (Chart Hit)...B-side	$	Sym	Label & Number
3/19/55	5	17		1 **Ballad Of Davy Crockett** ...J:5 / S:6 / A:7 *Farewell* from the ABC-TV *Disneyland* series which featured 3 "Davy Crockett" segments (Dec. '54 - Feb. '55); re-issued later in 1955 on Capitol 3229 ("Learning is Fun!" series) with a picture sleeve	$20		Capitol 3058
11/12/55	❶^{8}	22	●	2 **Sixteen Tons /** CW^{10} J:❶^{8} / S:❶^{7} / T:❶^{6} / A:❶^{6} written in 1947 by Country singer/guitarist Merle Travis			
1/21/56	78	1		3 **You Don't Have To Be A Baby To Cry** ...T:78 #10 Country hit for Ernest Tubb in 1950	$20		Capitol 3262
2/25/56	17	8		4 **That's All** ...A:17 / T:44 *Bright Lights And Blonde-Haired Women*	$20		Capitol 3343
5/19/56	60	6		5 **The Rovin' Gambler** ...T:60 *John Henry*	$15		Capitol 3421
11/3/56	46	11		6 **First Born** ...T:46 *Have You Seen Her*	$15		Capitol 3553
3/9/57	87	2		7 **The Watermelon Song /** T:87			
3/9/57	93	3		8 **One Suit** ...T:93	$15		Capitol 3649
8/26/57	23	12		9 **In The Middle Of An Island /** A:23 / T:56			
8/19/57		1		10 **Ivy League** ...CU:flip Jack Fascinato (orch.: #2-10)	$15		Capitol 3762

DEBUT	PEAK	WKS	Gold	A-side (Chart Hit)...B-side	$	Sym	Label & Number

FORD, "Tennessee" Ernie — Cont'd

DEBUT	PEAK	WKS	Gold	A-side (Chart Hit)...B-side	$	Sym	Label & Number
8/11/58	97	1		11 **Sunday Barbecue** ...H:97 *Love Makes The World Go 'Round* #12 hit in 1952 for the Sauter-Finegan Orchestra as "Doodletown Fifers"	$12		Capitol 3997
2/23/59	100	1		12 **Glad Rags** ...*Sleepin' At The Foot Of The Bed* written by **Johnny Bond**; **Cliffie Stone** (orch.: #1, 11 & 12)	$12		Capitol 4107

FORD, Willa

LP **'01**

Born Amanda Lee Williford on 1/22/81 in Tampa, Florida. Female pop singer.

DEBUT	PEAK	WKS	Gold	A-side (Chart Hit)...B-side	$	Sym	Label & Number
6/9/01	22	20		**I Wanna Be Bad** ...S:6 / A:34 *(rap and vocoder version* (w/Royce Da 5' 9")	$5	★+	Lava/Atlantic 85103

FOREIGNER ★101★

ROK/BUB/LP **'78**

British-American rock group formed in New York City, New York: Mick Jones (guitar; born on 12/27/44), **Lou Gramm** (vocals; born on 5/2/50), Ian McDonald (guitar, keyboards; born on 6/25/46), Ed Gagliardi (bass; born on 2/13/52), Al Greenwood (keyboards; born on 10/20/51) and Dennis Elliott (drums; born on 8/18/50). Gagliardi, Gramm and Greenwood are from New York. Most of material written by Jones (Spooky Tooth) and Gramm. Rick Wills (**Cochise**, **Roxy Music**, **Small Faces**) replaced Gagliardi in 1979. Greenwood and McDonald (**King Crimson**) left in 1980. Gramm left in 1991 to form Shadow King; replaced by Johnny Edwards. Gramm returned in mid-1992. Wills left in 1992 to join **Bad Company**; Elliott left to open woodworking business. Jones not to be confused with Mick Jones of The Clash and Big Audio Dynamite.

1)I Want To Know What Love Is 2)Waiting For A Girl Like You 3)Double Vision 4)Hot Blooded 5)Urgent

DEBUT	PEAK	WKS	Gold	A-side (Chart Hit)...B-side	$	Sym	Label & Number
3/26/77	4	22		1 **Feels Like The First Time** ...*Woman Oh Woman*	$4		Atlantic 3394
7/23/77	6	21		2 **Cold As Ice** ...*I Need You*	$4		Atlantic 3410
12/10/77+	20	14		3 **Long, Long Way From Home** ...*The Damage Is Done*	$4		Atlantic 3439
7/1/78	3	17	●	4 **Hot Blooded** ...*Tramontane*	$4		Atlantic 3488
9/23/78	2^{2}	20	●	5 **Double Vision** ...*Lonely Children*	$4	■	Atlantic 3514
12/23/78+	15	14		6 **Blue Morning, Blue Day** ...*I Have Waited So Long*	$4		Atlantic 3543
9/8/79	12	14		7 **Dirty White Boy** ...*Rev On The Red Line*	$4	■	Atlantic 3618
11/10/79	14	14		8 **Head Games** ...*Do What You Like*	$4	■	Atlantic 3633
2/16/80	41	9		9 **Women** ...*The Modern Day*	$4		Atlantic 3651
7/4/81	4	23		10 **Urgent** ...AR^{4} *Girl On The Moon* **Jr. Walker** (sax solo)	$4	■	Atlantic 3831
10/10/81	2^{10}	23	●	11 **Waiting For A Girl Like You** ...AR^{1} *I'm Gonna Win*	$4	■	Atlantic 3868
2/13/82	26	13		12 **Juke Box Hero** ...*Night Life* (ROK #14)	$4	■	Atlantic 4017
5/15/82	26	13		13 **Break It Up** ...*Head Games (live)*	$4	■	Atlantic 4044
7/31/82	75	6		14 **Luanne** ...*Fool For You Anyway* above 5 from the album *Foreigner 4*	$4		Atlantic 4072
12/8/84+	❶^{2}	21	●	15 **I Want To Know What Love Is** AR^{1} A:❶^{2} / S:❶^{1} *Street Thunder* New Jersey Mass Choir and **Jennifer Holliday** (backing vocals)	$3	■	Atlantic 89596
3/16/85	12	15		16 **That Was Yesterday** ...A:12 / S:17 *Two Different Worlds*	$3	■	Atlantic 89571
6/1/85	54	8		17 **Reaction To Action** ...*She's Too Tough*	$3	■	Atlantic 89542
8/17/85	54	8		18 **Down On Love** ...*Growing Up The Hard Way* above 4 from the album *Agent Provocateur*	$3		Atlantic 89493
12/5/87+	6	19		19 **Say You Will** ...AR^{4} S:5 / A:8 *A Night To Remember*	$3	■	Atlantic 89169
3/19/88	5	17		20 **I Don't Want To Live Without You** ...AC^{1} A:4 / S:6 *Face To Face*	$3	■	Atlantic 89101
7/16/88	56	10		21 **Heart Turns To Stone** ...*Counting Every Minute*	$3	■	Atlantic 89046
3/18/95	42	16		22 **Until The End Of Time** ...A:38 *Under The Gun* (ROK #28) **Duane Eddy** (lead guitar); all of above written by Mick Jones and **Lou Gramm**	$3	▮	Rhythm Safari 53183

FOREST FOR THE TREES

LP **'97**

Group is actually solo alternative pop-rock singer/songwriter/producer Carl Stephenson (co-writer of **Beck**'s "Loser").

DEBUT	PEAK	WKS	Gold	A-side (Chart Hit)...B-side	$	Sym	Label & Number
11/1/97	72	3		**Dream** ...A:68 samples "Substitution" by Melvin Bliss	$6	T	DreamWorks 58005

FORMATIONS, The

'68

R&B vocal group from Philadelphia, Pennsylvania: Victor Drayton, Jerry Akines, Ernie Brooks, Reggie Turner and John Bellman.

DEBUT	PEAK	WKS	Gold	A-side (Chart Hit)...B-side	$	Sym	Label & Number
3/16/68	83	5		**At The Top Of The Stairs** ...*Magic Melody* first released on Bank 1007 in 1967 ($30)	$10		MGM 13899

FOR REAL

R&B/BUB **'96**

Female R&B vocal group from Los Angeles, California: Josina Elder, Wendi Williams, LaTanyia Baldwin and Necia Bray.

DEBUT	PEAK	WKS	Gold	A-side (Chart Hit)...B-side	$	Sym	Label & Number
10/15/94	88	4		1 **You Don't Know Nothin'** ...*Easy To Love Pt. II*	$3	▮	A&M 0776
10/19/96	72	8		2 **Like I Do** ...S:50 *Free*	$3	▮V	Rowdy 35079 ■

FORSHÉ

'99

Black female vocal group.

DEBUT	PEAK	WKS	Gold	A-side (Chart Hit)...B-side	$	Sym	Label & Number
11/13/99	66^{S}	2		**Dog Food** ...*(3 versions)* **George Clinton** (guest vocals)	$6	★	Holland Group 2204

FOR SQUIRRELS

LP **'96**

Rock group from Gainesville, Florida: John Francis Vigliatura (vocals), Travis Michael Tooke (guitar), William Richard White (bass) and Thomas Jacob Griego (drums). Vigliatura (age 20) and White (age 22) were killed in a car crash on 9/8/95. Tooke and Griego went on to form Subrosa.

DEBUT	PEAK	WKS	Gold	A-side (Chart Hit)...B-side	$	Sym	Label & Number
1/13/96	70^{A}	4		**Mighty K.C.** ... K.C.: Kurt Cobain (of **Nirvana**); from the album *Example* on 550 Music/Epic 67150			album cut

FORTÉ, John

LP **'98**

Born in Brooklyn, New York. Male rapper. Member of the **Refugee Camp All-Stars**.

DEBUT	PEAK	WKS	Gold	A-side (Chart Hit)...B-side	$	Sym	Label & Number
5/30/98	59	16		**Ninety Nine (Flash The Message)** ...S:40 *Hot* produced by **Wyclef Jean**; samples "Mash It Up" by Just Ice; contains resung elements from "99 Luftballons" by **Nena**	$4	▮	Ruffhouse 78769

FORTUNE

'86

Male pop-rock group: Larry Greene (vocals), Bobby Birch, Richard Fortune, Nick Fortune and Roger Scott Craig.

DEBUT	PEAK	WKS	Gold	A-side (Chart Hit)...B-side	$	Sym	Label & Number
12/21/85+	80	6		**Stacy** ...*Lonely Hunter*	$3	■	MCA/Camel 52727

DEBUT	PEAK	WKS	Gold	A-side (Chart Hit)...B-side	$	Sym	Label & Number
				FORTUNES, The LP '65			
				Pop group formed in England: Glen Dale Garforth and Barry Pritchard (vocals, guitars), David Carr (keyboards), Rod Allen Bainbridge (bass) and Andy Brown (drums). Pritchard died of heart failure on 1/12/99 (age 54).			
8/21/65	7	11		1 **You've Got Your Troubles** *I've Gotta Go*	$12		Press 9773
11/6/65	27	8		2 **Here It Comes Again** ... *Things I Should Have Known*	$10		Press 9798
2/19/66	82	4		3 **This Golden Ring** ... *Someone To Care*	$10		Press 9811
5/16/70	62	8		4 **That Same Old Feeling** ... *Lifetime Of Love*	$8		World Pacific 77937
5/15/71	15	14		5 **Here Comes That Rainy Day Feeling Again** ... *I Gotta Dream* also released with "Bad Side Of Town" as the B-side	$6		Capitol 3086
10/2/71	72	5		6 **Freedom Comes, Freedom Goes** ... *There's A Man*	$6		Capitol 3179
				49ERS '90			
				Dance group from Italy featuring producer/DJ Gianfranco Bortolotti and vocalist Dawn Mitchell.			
6/16/90	78	9		**Don't You Love Me** ... *(Hip House mix)* "45": Island/Collectables 2606; B-side: Touch Me" (#1 Dance Club Play)	$4	▮V	4th & B'way 447506
				FORUM, The '67			
				Pop-folk trio from Pasadena, California: Phil Campos, Rene Nole and Riselle Bain.			
7/8/67	45	8		**The River Is Wide** ... *I Fall In Love (All Over Again)* first released on Penthouse 504 in 1966 ($25)	$15		Mira 232
				FOR XAMPLE — see IV (Four) XAMPLE			
				FOSTER, Bruce '77			
				Born in Trenton, New Jersey. Pop-rock singer/songwriter/keyboardist. Claims to be a descendant of composer Stephen Foster.			
7/2/77	63	5		**Platinum Heroes** ... *I Remember (The Revolution)* a tribute to **The Beatles**	$7	□	Millennium 602
				FOSTER, David AC/LP '85			
				Born in 1950 in Victoria, British Columbia, Canada. Keyboardist/composer/arranger. Member of the groups **Skylark** and **Attitudes**. Wrote and produced hits for **Chicago**, **Barbra Streisand** and others. Married songwriter/actress Linda Thompson in 1991. Also see **Voices That Care**.			
8/24/85	15	22		1 **Love Theme From St. Elmo's Fire** ... S:14 / A:15 *Georgetown* [I] from the movie *St. Elmo's Fire* starring Rob Lowe and Demi Moore	$3	■	Atlantic 89528
6/14/86	80	8		2 **The Best Of Me** ... *Sajé* (Foster) **DAVID FOSTER AND OLIVIA NEWTON-JOHN**	$3	■	Atlantic 89420
2/27/88	85	3		3 **Winter Games** ... *Piano Concerto In G* [I] theme song used during ABC's telecast of the 1988 Winter Olympics	$3	■	Atlantic 89140
				FOTOMAKER BUB/LP '78			
				Pop-rock group from New York: Wally Bryson and Lex Marchesi (guitars), Frankie Vinci (keyboards), Gene Cornish (bass) and Dino Danelli (drums). All share vocals. Bryson was a member of **The Raspberries**. Cornish and Danelli were members of **The Rascals** and **Bulldog**.			
4/22/78	81	6		1 **Where Have You Been All My Life** ... *Say The Same For You*	$4		Atlantic 3471
12/2/78	63	6		2 **Miles Away** ... *Snowblind*	$4		Atlantic 3531
				FOUNDATIONS, The BUB/LP '69			
				Interracial R&B-pop group formed in England: Clem Curtis (vocals), Allan Warner (guitar), Eric Allendale, Pat Burke and Michael Elliott (horns), Anthony Gomez (keyboards), Peter McBeth (bass) and Tim Harris (drums). Colin Young replaced Curtis in 1968. Group disbanded in 1970.			
12/23/67+	11	13		1 **Baby, Now That I've Found You** ... *Come On Back To Me*	$7		Uni 55038
3/9/68	59	6		2 **Back On My Feet Again** ... *I Can Take Or Leave Your Loving*	$7		Uni 55058
1/4/69	3	15	●	3 **Build Me Up Buttercup** *New Direction*	$7		Uni 55101
4/5/69	51	7		4 **In The Bad, Bad Old Days (Before You Loved Me)** ... *Give Me Love*	$7		Uni 55117
7/5/69	99	2		5 **My Little Chickadee** ... *Soloman Grundy*	$7		Uni 55137
				FOUNTAIN, Pete AC/BUB/LP '62			
				Born on 7/3/30 in New Orleans, Louisiana. Top jazz clarinetist. With **Al Hirt**, 1956-57. Performed on **Lawrence Welk**'s weekly TV show, 1957-59. Own club in New Orleans, The French Quarter Inn.			
2/8/60	93	3		1 **A Closer Walk** ... *Do You Know What It Means To Miss New Orleans* [I] traditional hymn; #9 Country hit for Red Foley in 1950 as "Just A Closer Walk With Thee"	$10		Coral 62154
2/24/62	69	6		2 **Yes Indeed** ... *While We Danced At The Mardi Gras* Charles Bud Dant (orch.); arrangement based on **Ray Charles**' 1958 version (Atlantic 1180); #4 hit for **Tommy Dorsey** in 1941; label is Coral's "Silver Star Series"	$10		Coral 65549
				FOUNTAIN, Roosevelt '63			
				Black funk-jazz band leader.			
1/5/63	78	3		**Red Pepper I** ... *Red Pepper II* [I] **ROOSEVELT FOUNTAIN AND PENS OF RHYTHM**	$20		Prince-Adams 447
				FOUNTAINS OF WAYNE ROK '97			
				Pop-rock duo from New York: Chris Collingwood (vocals, guitar) and Adam Schlesinger (keyboards, drums).			
12/28/96+	71[A]	2		**Radiation Vibe** ... from the album *Fountains Of Wayne* on Scratchie/Tag 92725			album cut
	★243★			**FOUR ACES** MEM/POP '55			
				Vocal group from Chester, Pennsylvania: Al Alberts (lead; born on 3/28/28), Dave Mahoney (tenor; born on 7/7/28), Sol Vaccaro (baritone; born on 10/1/31) and Lou Silvestri (bass; born on 6/10/30). Worked Ye Olde Mill near Philadelphia, late 1940s. First recorded for Victoria in 1951. Group has undergone several personnel changes over the years. Charted 16 pop hits, 1951-54, including the #2 hit "Tell Me Why" and the #1 hit "Three Coins In The Fountain."			
				1)Love Is A Many-Splendored Thing 2)Melody Of Love 3)Mister Sandman 4)Heart 5)A Woman In Love			
				FOUR ACES Featuring Al Alberts:			
11/27/54+	5	14		1 **Mister Sandman** ... A:5 / J:6 / S:9 *(I'll Be With You) In Apple Blossom Time*	$15		Decca 29344
1/15/55	3	21		2 **Melody Of Love** ... J:3 / A:9 / S:11 *There Is A Tavern In The Town* music written in 1903; lyrics added in 1954 by **Tom Glazer**	$15		Decca 29395
5/28/55	13	6		3 **Heart** ... A:13 / J:20 / S:23 *Sluefoot* from the Broadway musical *Damn Yankees* starring Gwen Verdon; also see note for **Sammy Davis, Jr.**'s "Something's Gotta Give"	$15	□	Decca 29476

DEBUT	PEAK	WKS	Gold	A-side (Chart Hit)...B-side	$	Sym	Label & Number
				FOUR ACES — Cont'd			
8/27/55	❶[6]	21	●	4 **Love Is A Many-Splendored Thing** A:❶[6] / T:❶[3] / J:❶[3] / S:❶[2] *Shine On Harvest Moon*	$15		Decca 29625
				title song from the movie starring William Holden and Jennifer Jones			
11/19/55	**14**	17		5 **A Woman In Love /** A:14 / T:19 / S:20			
				from the movie *Guys and Dolls* starring Marlon Brando			
12/3/55	**56**	4		6 **Of This I'm Sure**....T:56	$15		Decca 29725
2/18/56	**62**	8		7 **If You Can Dream /** T:62			
3/24/56	**91**	1		8 **The Gal With The Yaller Shoes**....T:91	$12		Decca 29809
				above 2 from the movie *Meet Me In Las Vegas* starring Dan Dailey			
5/5/56	**43**	16		9 **To Love Again**....T:43 *Charlie Was A Boxer*	$12		Decca 29889
				based on Chopin's E Flat Nocturne; from the movie *The Eddy Duchin Story* starring Tyrone Power			
7/28/56	**22**	11		10 **I Only Know I Love You /** A:22 / T:35			
7/14/56	**86**	3		11 **Dreamer**....T:86	$12		Decca 29989
				Jud Conlon's Rhythmaires (backing vocals, above 2)			
10/20/56	**20**	6		12 **You Can't Run Away From It /** A:20 / T:70			
				title song from the movie starring Jack Lemmon and June Allyson			
9/22/56	**45**	18		13 **Friendly Persuasion (Thee I Love)**....T:45	$12		Decca 30041
				title song from the movie *Friendly Persuasion* starring Gary Cooper and Dorothy McGuire			
12/1/56	**47**	7		14 **Someone To Love /** T:47			
12/15/56+	**61**	15		15 **Written On The Wind**....T:61	$12		Decca 30123
				title song from the movie starring Rock Hudson and Lauren Bacall			
3/30/57	**53**	6		16 **Bahama Mama /** T:53			
3/30/57	**76**	4		17 **You're Mine**....T:76	$12		Decca 30242
3/24/58	**66**	7		18 **Rock And Roll Rhapsody**....T:66 *I Wish I May, I Wish I Might*	$12		Decca 30575
				THE FOUR ACES:			
11/24/58	**63**	4		19 **The World Outside**....*How Can You Forget*	$12		Decca 30764
				introduced as "Warsaw Concerto" in the 1942 movie *Suicide Squadron* starring Anton Walbrook			
3/2/59	**74**	5		20 **No Other Arms, No Other Lips**....*The Inn Of The Sixth Happiness*	$12		Decca 30822
				Jack Pleis (orch., all of above)			
				4 BY FOUR R&B/LP **'87**			
				R&B vocal group from Queens, New York: brothers Damen and Lance Heyward, Steve Gray, and Jeraude Jackson.			
6/13/87	**79**	6		**Want You For My Girlfriend**....*(Girlfriend dub)*	$4	■	Capitol 5690
				FOUR COINS, The MEM/BUB **'57**			
				Vocal group from Canonsburg, Pennsylvania: brothers Michael and George Mahramas, George Mantalis, and Jim Gregorakis. In the 1957 movie *Jamboree!*			
1/15/55	**28**	1		1 **I Love You Madly**....S:28 *Maybe*	$15		Epic 9082
				first recorded by R&B duo Charlie and Ray in 1954 on Herald 438 ($50)			
11/26/55	**22**	16		2 **Memories Of You**....S:22 / T:28 *Tear Down The Fence*	$15		Epic 9129
				from the movie *The* **Benny Goodman** Story starring **Steve Allen**; **Don Costa** (orch., above 2)			
5/27/57	**11**	21		3 **Shangri-La** A:11 / S:22 / T:23 *First In Line*	$12		Epic 9213
9/23/57	**28**	15		4 **My One Sin**....S:28 / T:29 *This Life*	$12		Epic 9229
9/22/58	**72**	3		5 **Wendy, Wendy**....H:72 *Be Still My Heart*	$12		Epic 9286
11/10/58	**21**	11		6 **The World Outside**....*Roselle*	$12		Epic 9295
				introduced as "Warsaw Concerto" in the 1942 movie *Suicide Squadron* starring Anton Walbrook; Marion Evans (orch., above 4)			
6/8/59	**82**	4		7 **One Love, One Heart**....*My First Love* (#106)	$12		Epic 9314
				Joe Sherman (orch.); #4 hit for both Enrico Caruso in 1913 and **Perry Como** in 1948 as "Because"			
				FOUR DATES, The **'58**			
				Pop vocal backing group for **Frankie Avalon** and **Fabian**. Johnny October, lead singer.			
5/12/58	**87**	1		**I'm Happy**....T:87 *Eloise*	$20		Chancellor 1014
				FOUR ESQUIRES, The **'58**			
				Vocal group from Boston, Massachusetts: Bill Courtney, Frank Mahoney, Bob Golden and Wally Gold (died of heart failure on 6/7/98, age 70).			
5/5/56	**55**	7		1 **Look Homeward Angel**....T:55 *Santo Domingo*	$25		London 1652
				Ben Bennett (orch.)			
11/18/57	**25**	10		2 **Love Me Forever**....A:25 / S:44 / T:51 *I Ain't Been Right Since You Left*	$20		Paris 509
				Sid Bass (orch.)			
9/22/58	**21**	17		3 **Hideaway**....H:21 *Repeat After Me* (w/Rosemary June)	$20		Paris 520
				Richard Hayman (orch.)			
				FOUR-EVERS, The BUB **'64**			
				White vocal group from Brooklyn, New York: Joe Di Benedetto (lead), John Capriani, Steve Tudanger and Nick Zagami.			
5/30/64	**75**	4		**Be My Girl**....*If I Were A Magician*	$15		Smash 1887
				first released as "Please Be Mine" on Smash 1887 ($25); a **4 Seasons** sound-alike tune			
				FOUR EXAMPLE — see IV (Four) XAMPLE			
				FOUR FRESHMEN, The MEM/POP/AC/LP **'56**			
				Jazz-styled vocal/instrumental group from Indianapolis, Indiana: brothers Ross and Don Barbour, their cousin Bob Flanigan and Ken Albers. Don Barbour died in a car crash on 10/5/61 (age 32).			
11/12/55	**72**	7		1 **Day By Day**....T:72 *How Can I Tell Her*	$15		Capitol 3154
				#5 hit for **Frank Sinatra** in 1946			
12/10/55+	**69**	7		2 **Charmaine**....T:69 *In This Whole Wide World*	$15		Capitol 3292
				#1 hit for Guy Lombardo in 1927; B-side is one of 7 tunes parodied by **The Four Preps** in their hit "More Money For You And Me"			
5/12/56	**17**	13		3 **Graduation Day**....A:17 / S:25 / T:27 *Lonely Night In Paris*	$15		Capitol 3410
				Dick Reynolds (orch., all of above)			
				FOUR JACKS AND A JILL AC/BUB/LP **'68**			
				Pop group from South Africa: Glenys "Jill" Lynne (vocals), Bruce Bark (guitar), Till Hannamann (keyboards), Clive Harding (bass) and Anthony Hughes (drums).			
3/30/68	**18**	14		1 **Master Jack**....*I Looked Back*	$7		RCA Victor 9473
8/10/68	**96**	2		2 **Mister Nico**....*Hamba Liliwam*	$7		RCA Victor 9572

DEBUT	PEAK	WKS	Gold	A-side (Chart Hit)..........B-side	$	Sym	Label & Number

FOUR KNIGHTS, The — MEM/POP '54

Black vocal group from Charlotte, North Carolina: Gene Alford (lead; died in 1960), Clarence Dixon (baritone), Oscar Broadway (bass) and John Wallace (tenor; died in 1978). Hit #2 on the pop charts in 1954 with "I Get So Lonely (Oh Baby Mine)."

DEBUT	PEAK	WKS	Gold	A-side (Chart Hit)..........B-side	$	Sym	Label & Number
5/21/55	8	10		1 **If I May** ....A:8 / S:flip / J:flip *A Blossom Fell* (Cole - #2)	$20		Capitol 3095
7/7/56	16	20		2 **That's All There Is To That** ....J:16 / S:17 / T:18 / A:18 *My Dream Sonata* (Cole - #59)	$20		Capitol 3456
6/17/57	21	15		3 **My Personal Possession** ....A:21 / T:63 / S:flip *Send For Me* (Cole - #6)	$20		Capitol 3737
				NAT "KING" COLE and THE FOUR KNIGHTS (above 3)			
				Nelson Riddle (orch., above 3)			
1/12/59	83	3		4 **O' Falling Star** ....*Foolish Tears*	$20		Coral 62045
				Charles Bud Dant (orch.)			

★205★ FOUR LADS, The — MEM/POP/AC/LP '56

Vocal group from Toronto, Ontario, Canada: Bernie Toorish (lead tenor), Jimmie Arnold (second tenor), Frankie Busseri (baritone) and Connie Codarini (bass). Sang in choir at St. Michael's Cathedral in Toronto. Worked local hotels and clubs. Worked Le Ruban Bleu in New York City. Signed as backup singers by Columbia in 1950. Backed **Johnnie Ray** on several of his hits, including his #1 hit "Cry." Hit the Top 10 on the pop charts in 1953 with "Istanbul" and in 1954 with "Skokiaan."

1)Moments To Remember 2)No, Not Much! 3)Standing On The Corner

DEBUT	PEAK	WKS	Gold	A-side (Chart Hit)..........B-side	$	Sym	Label & Number
9/3/55	2^6	25	●	1 **Moments To Remember** A:2 / S:3 / T:3 / J:4 *Dream On, My Love Dream On*	$20		Columbia 40539
1/21/56	2^4	24	●	2 **No, Not Much!** / A:2 / T:3 / S:4 / J:4			
2/25/56	52	5		3 **I'll Never Know** T:52	$20		Columbia 40629
4/28/56	3	20		4 **Standing On The Corner** / A:3 / T:3 / S:3 / J:3			
				from the Broadway musical *The Most Happy Fella* starring Robert Weede			
4/28/56	22	16		5 **My Little Angel** ....S:22 / A:24 / T:30 / J:flip	$20		Columbia 40674
5/19/56	67	3		6 **The Mocking Bird** ....T:67 *I May Hate Myself In The Morning* [R]	$20		Epic 9150
				originally charted in 1952 on Okeh 6885 (#23-$30); also see #15 below; melody better known as "Goin' Home" from Dvorak's New World Symphony; also see **Nat King Cole**'s "The Sweet Bird Of Youth"			
9/1/56	16	13		7 **A House With Love In It** / S:16 / A:20 / T:23			
8/25/56	17	13		8 **The Bus Stop Song (A Paper Of Pins)** ....A:17 / S:22 / T:23	$15		Columbia 40736
				from the movie *Bus Stop* starring Marilyn Monroe			
1/26/57	9	21		9 **Who Needs You** / A:9 / S:13 / T:14 / J:17			
1/19/57		4		10 **It's So Easy To Forget** ....CU:flip	$15	■	Columbia 40811
5/6/57	17	12		11 **I Just Don't Know** ....A:17 / T:22 *Golly*	$15		Columbia 40914
12/9/57+	8	14		12 **Put A Light In The Window** ....A:8 / T:35 / S:39 *The Things We Did Last Summer*	$12		Columbia 41058
4/7/58	10	12		13 **There's Only One Of You** ....A:10 / T:41 / S:43 *Blue Tattoo*	$12		Columbia 41136
6/30/58	12	12		14 **Enchanted Island** ....A:12 / H:29 / S:32 *Guess What The Neighbors'll Say*	$12	■	Columbia 41194
				title song from the movie starring **Jane Powell**			
11/3/58	32	10		15 **The Mocking Bird** ....*Won'cha (Give Me Somethin' In Return)* [R]	$12		Columbia 41266
				Joe Mele (orch.); new version of group's 1952 and 1956 hit (#6 above)			
1/5/59	52	10		16 **The Girl On Page 44** ....*Sunday*	$12		Columbia 41310
5/4/59	90	2		17 **The Fountain Of Youth** ....*Meet Me Tonight In Dreamland*	$10		Columbia 41365
				Ray Ellis (orch., all of above - except #6 & 15)			
11/9/59	77	5		18 **Happy Anniversary** ....*Who Do You Think You Are?*	$10	■	Columbia 41497
				Joe Sherman (orch.); title song from the movie starring David Niven			

FOUR LOVERS, The — see 4 SEASONS, The

4 NON BLONDES — ROK/BUB/LP '93

Pop-rock group from San Francisco, California: Linda Perry (vocals), Roger Rocha (guitar), Christa Hillhouse (bass) and Dawn Richardson (drums).

DEBUT	PEAK	WKS	Gold	A-side (Chart Hit)..........B-side	$	Sym	Label & Number
4/24/93	14	26	●	**What's Up** ....S:10 / A:30 *Train*	$3	▌	Interscope 98430

4 OF US, The — '90

Rock group from Newry, Ireland: brothers Brendan (vocals), Paul (keyboards) and Declan (drums) Murphy, with John McCandless (bass).

DEBUT	PEAK	WKS	Gold	A-side (Chart Hit)..........B-side	$	Sym	Label & Number
4/21/90	77	5		**Drag My Bad Name Down** ....*One Strong Hammer*	$4	▌	Columbia 73243

FOUR PENNIES, The — see CHIFFONS, The

4 P.M. (For Positive Music) — BUB/R&B/LP '95

R&B vocal group from Baltimore, Maryland: brothers Rene and Roberto Pena, with Larry McFarland and Marty Ware.

DEBUT	PEAK	WKS	Gold	A-side (Chart Hit)..........B-side	$	Sym	Label & Number
9/17/94+	8	32	●	**Sukiyaki** ....S:10 / A:10 *(radio mix) / For What More*	$3	▌V	Next Plateau 857736
				"45": Next Plateau/London 857970; B-side: "Lay Down Your Love" ("Bubbled Under" #107)			

4.0 — '97

R&B vocal group from Atlanta, Georgia: Tony "T-Bone" Hightower, Sammy "Cat Daddy" Crumbley, Jason "JJ" Sylvain and Ron "Hollywood" Jackson. Pronounced: Four Point Oh.

DEBUT	PEAK	WKS	Gold	A-side (Chart Hit)..........B-side	$	Sym	Label & Number
8/23/97	46	20		**Have A Little Mercy** ....S:27 *(remix)*	$4	▌	Savvy/Perspective 7580

★488★ FOUR PREPS, The — BUB/LP '58

Vocal group from Hollywood, California: Bruce Belland, Glen Larson, Ed Cobb and Marvin Inabnett (born on 7/29/38). Belland, who was later in duo with Dave Somerville of **The Diamonds**, is the father of Tracey and Melissa Belland of **Voice Of The Beehive**. Larson's production company was a creative force behind numerous TV series during the '70s. Inabnett died of a heart attack on 3/7/99 (age 60). Cobb died of leukemia on 9/19/99 (age 61).

1)26 Miles (Santa Catalina) 2)Big Man 3)Down By The Station

DEBUT	PEAK	WKS	Gold	A-side (Chart Hit)..........B-side	$	Sym	Label & Number
12/22/56+	56	12		1 **Dreamy Eyes** ....T:56 *Fools Will Be Fools*	$15		Capitol 3576
				Van Alexander (orch.)			
1/20/58	2^3	20	●	2 **26 Miles (Santa Catalina)** A:2 / T:4 / S:5 *It's You*	$15		Capitol 3845
5/5/58	3	14		3 **Big Man** ....A:3 / T:5 / S:6 *Stop, Baby*	$15		Capitol 3960
8/18/58	21	10		4 **Lazy Summer Night** / H:21 / S:34			
				from the movie *Andy Hardy Comes Home* starring Mickey Rooney			
9/1/58		5		5 **Summertime Lies** ....S:flip	$15		Capitol 4023
11/17/58	69	7		6 **Cinderella** ....*Gidget*	$15		Capitol 4078
				from the movie *Gidget* starring Sandra Dee			
9/14/59	79	2		7 **I Ain't Never** ....*Memories, Memories*	$15		Capitol 4256
				Morty Corb (orch.)			

DEBUT	PEAK	WKS	Gold	A-side (Chart Hit)...B-side	$	Sym	Label & Number
				FOUR PREPS, The — Cont'd			
12/28/59+	13	15		8 **Down By The Station** ... *Listen Honey (I'll Be Home)* new version of tune written in 1948	$12		Capitol 4312
4/18/60	24	10		9 **Got A Girl** ... *(Wait Till You) Hear It From Me* [N]	$12		Capitol 4362
2/6/61	96	2		10 **Calcutta** ... *Gone Are The Days*	$12		Capitol 4508
8/14/61	17	11		11 **More Money For You And Me** ... *Swing Down Chariot* [L-N] medley: Mr. Blue/Alley Oop/Smoke Gets In Your Eyes/In This Whole Wide World/A Worried Man/Tom Dooley/A Teenager In Love; a special promotional picture sleeve was also issued	$15	■	Capitol 4599
3/31/62	61	6		12 **The Big Draft** ... *Suzy Cocroach* [L-N] medley: I'll Never Smile Again/Love Is A Many-Splendored Thing/ The Mountain's High/Heartaches/Anchors Aweigh/Michael/ Runaround Sue; Lincoln Mayorga (orch.: #2-6 & 8-12)	$15	■	Capitol 4716
3/21/64	85	3		13 **A Letter To The Beatles** ... *College Cannonball* [N] Ray Pohlman (orch.)	$25		Capitol 5143

4 SEASONS, The ★31★ BUB/LP '62

Vocal group formed in Newark, New Jersey. In 1955, lead singer **Frankie Valli** (Francis Castelluccio; born on 5/3/37) formed the Variatones with brothers Nick and Tommy (born on 6/19/36) DeVito, and Hank Majewski. Changed name to **The Four Lovers** in 1956. Bob Gaudio (of **The Royal Teens**; born on 11/17/42) joined as keyboardist/songwriter in 1959, replacing Nick DeVito. Nick Massi (born on 9/19/27) replaced Majewski, and their 1961 lineup was set: Valli, Gaudio, Massi and Tommy DeVito. Group had been doing session work for their producer **Bob Crewe** and took their new name from a New Jersey bowling alley, The Four Seasons. In 1965, Nick Massi was replaced by the group's arranger Charlie Calello and then by Joe Long. In 1971, Tommy DeVito retired, and Gaudio left (as a performer) the following year. Numerous personnel changes from then on. The songwriting/producing/arranging team of Bob Crewe, Bob Gaudio and Charlie Calello and the "sound" of Frankie Valli helped rank The 4 Seasons as one of the top American groups of the '60s. Massi died of cancer on 12/24/2000 (age 73). Group inducted into the Rock and Roll Hall of Fame in 1990. Also recorded as **The Wonder Who?** (see #25, 29, 30 & 35). Also see **Gidea Park**.

1)Big Girls Don't Cry 2)Sherry 3)Walk Like A Man 4)December, 1963 5)Rag Doll

DEBUT	PEAK	WKS	Gold	A-side (Chart Hit)...B-side	$	Sym	Label & Number
5/26/56	62	5		1 **You're The Apple Of My Eye** ... T:62 *The Girl In My Dreams* **THE FOUR LOVERS** re-recorded by The 4 Seasons in 1964 as "Apple Of My Eye" on Vee-Jay 618 ("Bubbled Under" #106)	$40		RCA Victor 6518
8/25/62	❶5	14	●	2 **Sherry** ... RB1 *I've Cried Before*	$20		Vee-Jay 456
10/20/62	❶5	16	●	3 **Big Girls Don't Cry** ... RB3 *Connie - O*	$20		Vee-Jay 465
12/15/62	23	3		4 **Santa Claus Is Coming To Town** ... *Christmas Tears* [X] #12 hit for George Hall in 1934	$20		Vee-Jay 478
1/26/63	❶3	13		5 **Walk Like A Man** ... *Lucky Ladybug*	$15		Vee-Jay 485
4/20/63	22	9		6 **Ain't That A Shame!** /			
5/11/63	77	7		7 **Soon (I'll Be Home Again)** ... **THE 4 SEASONS Featuring Frankie Valli**	$15		Vee-Jay 512
7/6/63	3	13		8 **Candy Girl** /			
7/13/63	36	8		9 **Marlena** ...	$15		Vee-Jay 539
10/5/63	36	7		10 **New Mexican Rose** /			
10/5/63	88	3		11 **That's The Only Way** ...	$15		Vee-Jay 562
2/1/64	3	13		12 **Dawn (Go Away)** ... *No Surfin' Today*	$15		Philips 40166
2/15/64	16	11		13 **Stay** ... *Goodnight My Love* #6-11 & 13: from the album *Ain't That A Shame and 11 others*	$15		Vee-Jay 582
4/11/64	6	10		14 **Ronnie** ... *Born To Wander*	$12	■	Philips 40185
6/6/64	28	9		15 **Alone** ... *Long Lonely Nights (#102)*	$15	■	Vee-Jay 597
6/20/64	❶2	12	●	16 **Rag Doll** ... *Silence Is Golden* picture sleeve issued with either a green or a yellow background	$12	■	Philips 40211
8/29/64	10	8		17 **Save It For Me** ... *Funny Face*	$12		Philips 40225
8/29/64	75	4		18 **Sincerely** ... *One Song* legendary DJ Alan Freed listed as co-writer; #3, 5, 15 & 18: from the album *Big Girls Don't Cry and Twelve others*	$15		Vee-Jay 608
11/7/64	20	7		19 **Big Man In Town** ... *Little Angel*	$12	■	Philips 40238
12/26/64	19X	1		20 **I Saw Mommy Kissing Santa Claus** ... *Christmas Tears* [X]	$20	■	Vee-Jay 626
1/16/65	12	9		21 **Bye, Bye, Baby (Baby, Goodbye)** ... *Searching Wind*	$12	■	Philips 40260
4/10/65	64	5		22 **Toy Soldier** ... *Betrayed*	$12	■	Philips 40278
6/19/65	30	7		23 **Girl Come Running** ... *Cry Myself To Sleep*	$12	■	Philips 40305
10/9/65	3	16		24 **Let's Hang On!** ... *On Broadway Tonight*	$12		Philips 40317
11/6/65	12	11		25 **Don't Think Twice** ... *Sassy* **THE WONDER WHO?**	$12	■	Philips 40324
12/25/65+	60	6		26 **Little Boy (In Grown Up Clothes)** ... *Silver Wings* all Vee-Jay hits recorded 1962-63	$15		Vee-Jay 713
1/29/66	9	9		27 **Working My Way Back To You** ... *Too Many Memories*	$12		Philips 40350
5/21/66	13	8		28 **Opus 17 (Don't You Worry 'Bout Me)** ... *Beggars Parade*	$12	■	Philips 40370
7/2/66	87	3		29 **On The Good Ship Lollipop** / from the movie *Bright Eyes* starring Shirley Temple; #4 hit for Rudy Vallee in 1935			
7/16/66	96	1		30 **You're Nobody Till Somebody Loves You** ... **THE WONDER WHO?** (above 2) #14 hit for **Russ Morgan** in 1946	$12	■	Philips 40380
9/3/66	9	10		31 **I've Got You Under My Skin** ... *Huggin' My Pillow* written by Cole Porter; from the movie *Born To Dance* starring James Stewart; #3 hit in 1936 for Ray Noble	$12	■	Philips 40393
12/10/66+	10	10		32 **Tell It To The Rain** ... *Show Girl*	$12	■	Philips 40412
3/4/67	16	9		33 **Beggin'** ... *Dody*	$12	■	Philips 40433
6/10/67	9	10		34 **C'mon Marianne** ... *Let's Ride Again*	$12	■	Philips 40460
7/29/67	89	4		35 **Lonesome Road** ... *Around And Around* (4 Seasons) **THE WONDER WHO?** #3 hit for Ted Lewis in 1930	$12	■	Philips 40471
10/28/67	30	7		36 **Watch The Flowers Grow** ... *Raven*	$10	■	Philips 40490
2/24/68	24	8		37 **Will You Love Me Tomorrow** ... *Around And Around*	$10		Philips 40523

DEBUT	PEAK	WKS	Gold	A-side (Chart Hit).......B-side	$	Sym	Label & Number
				4 SEASONS, The — Cont'd			
12/28/68+	61	6		38 **Electric Stories** .... *Pity*	$10		Philips 40577
				all of above 4 Seasons' Philips records (except "Dawn") labeled as: **Featuring the "sound" of Frankie Valli**			
4/5/69	95	2		39 **Idaho /**			
3/29/69	98	1		40 **Something's On Her Mind**	$8	■	Philips 40597
				4 SEASONS Featuring Frankie Valli (above 2)			
9/13/69	45	7		41 **And That Reminds Me (My Heart Reminds Me)** .... *The Singles Game*	$8	■	Crewe 333
				lyric version of the Italian instrumental "Autumn Concerto"			
5/9/70	94	2		42 **Patch Of Blue** .... *She Gives Me Light*	$8	■	Philips 40662
				Frankie Valli & The 4 SEASONS			
8/23/75	3	20		43 **Who Loves You** .... *(disco version)*	$5		Warner/Curb 8122
12/27/75+	❶[3]	27	●	44 **December, 1963 (Oh, What a Night)** .... *Slip Away*	$5		Warner/Curb 8168
				also see #48 below			
5/29/76	38	8		45 **Silver Star** .... *Mystic Mr. Sam*	$5		Warner/Curb 8203
7/16/77	65	6		46 **Down The Hall** .... *I Believe In You*	$5		Warner/Curb 8407
12/13/80	91	5		47 **Spend The Night In Love** .... *Slip Away*	$5		Warner/Curb 49597
8/13/94	14	27		48 **December 1963 (Oh, What A Night)** .... A:8 / S:30 *(2 radio edits)* [R]	$3	▌	Curb 76917
				dance remix version of #44 above; lead vocals on above 5 by Gerri Polci (drummer)			
				4SHADES '01			
				R&B vocal group from Atlanta, Georgia: brothers Darryl and Willie Cannon, with Fred Frazier and Caesar Riley.			
6/9/01	34[S]	8		**Crave** .... *(2 versions)*	$5	★	Real Deal 70633
				co-executive producer: heavyweight boxing champion Evander Holyfield			
				FOUR SONICS, The '68			
				R&B vocal group from Detroit, Michigan: Willie Frazier, Steve Gaston, Eddy Daniels and James "Jay" Johnson.			
2/10/68	89	2		**You Don't Have To Say You Love Me** .... *It Takes Two*	$30		Sport 110
				FOUR SPORTSMEN, The '61			
				R&B vocal group.			
8/14/61	76	5		**Pitter-Patter** .... *Git Up Paint*	$30		Sunnybrook 4
				4TH AVENUE JONES' R&B '01			
				Hip-hop group from Los Angeles, California: **Ahmad** and Jabu (male vocals), Tena Jones (female vocals), Woodstiff (guitar), Gaily (violin), Greg B (bass) and Drummy Dave (drums).			
2/24/01	66[S]	2		**R.E.S.P.E.C.T.** .... *(2 versions) / Rules Of The Game*	$5	★	Lookalive 74592
				samples "C.R.E.A.M." by **Wu-Tang Clan**			
				4 THE CAUSE '98			
				R&B vocal group from Chicago, Illinois: brother-and-sister J-Man and Ms. Lady, with cousins Shorty and Bennie.			
8/22/98	82	5		**Stand By Me** .... S:67 *We Got U*	$4	▌	RCA 65532

FOUR TOPS ★49★ R&B/BUB/AC/LP '65

Legendary R&B vocal group from Detroit, Michigan: Levi Stubbs (lead singer; born on 6/6/36), Renaldo "Obie" Benson (born on 6/14/36), Lawrence Payton (born on 3/2/38) and Abdul "Duke" Fakir (born on 12/26/35). First recorded for Chess in 1956, then Red Top and Columbia, before signing with Motown in 1963. Stubbs was the voice of Audrey II (the voracious vegetation) in the 1986 movie *Little Shop of Horrors*. Payton died on 6/20/97 (age 59). Group inducted into the Rock and Roll Hall of Fame in 1990. **The Supremes**, **The Temptations**, **The Miracles** and the Four Tops were the "big 4" of the Motown "group sound."

1)Can't Help Myself 2)Reach Out I'll Be There 3)Ain't No Woman 4)Bernadette 5)It's The Same Old Song

DEBUT	PEAK	WKS	Gold	A-side (Chart Hit).......B-side	$	Sym	Label & Number
8/15/64	11	12		1 **Baby I Need Your Loving** .... *Call On Me*	$15		Motown 1062
11/28/64	43	5		2 **Without The One You Love (Life's Not Worth While)** .... *Love Has Gone*	$15		Motown 1069
2/6/65	24	8		3 **Ask The Lonely** .... *Where Did You Go*	$15	■	Motown 1073
5/15/65	❶[2]	14		4 **I Can't Help Myself** RB[9] *Sad Souvenirs*	$15		Motown 1076
7/31/65	5	9		5 **It's The Same Old Song** .... *Your Love Is Amazing*	$15		Motown 1081
7/31/65	93	1		6 **Ain't That Love** .... *Lonely Summer*	$30		Columbia 43356
				originally released in 1960 on Columbia 41755 ($50)			
11/13/65	19	7		7 **Something About You** .... *Darling, I Hum Our Song*	$15		Motown 1084
2/19/66	18	9		8 **Shake Me, Wake Me (When It's Over)** .... *Just As Long As You Need Me*	$15		Motown 1090
5/28/66	45	8		9 **Loving You Is Sweeter Than Ever** .... *I Like Everything About You*	$15		Motown 1096
				co-written by **Stevie Wonder**			
9/3/66	❶[2]	15	●	10 **Reach Out I'll Be There** .... RB[2] *Until You Love Someone*	$12	■	Motown 1098
12/17/66+	6	10		11 **Standing In The Shadows Of Love** .... *Since You've Been Gone*	$12		Motown 1102
3/11/67	4	10		12 **Bernadette** .... *I Got A Feeling*	$12		Motown 1104
5/20/67	14	8		13 **7 Rooms Of Gloom /**			
7/15/67	76	5		14 **I'll Turn To Stone**	$12		Motown 1110
9/16/67	19	8		15 **You Keep Running Away** .... *If You Don't Want My Love*	$12		Motown 1113
2/3/68	14	8		16 **Walk Away Renee** .... *Your Love Is Wonderful*	$12		Motown 1119
4/27/68	20	10		17 **If I Were A Carpenter** .... *Wonderful Baby*	$12		Motown 1124
				#10-14, 16 & 17: from the album *Four Tops Reach Out*			
7/20/68	49	6		18 **Yesterday's Dreams** .... *For Once In My Life*	$10		Motown 1127
10/5/68	51	6		19 **I'm In A Different World** .... *Remember When*	$10		Motown 1132
				all of above written by **Holland, Dozier, Holland** (except #3, 6, 9 & 16-18) and produced by **Holland & Dozier** (except #3, 6, 9 & 18)			
5/10/69	53	7		20 **What Is A Man** .... *Don't Bring Back Memories*	$10		Motown 1147
12/6/69	45	7		21 **Don't Let Him Take Your Love From Me** .... *The Key*	$10		Motown 1159
4/25/70	24	13		22 **It's All In The Game** .... *Love (Is The Answer)*	$10	■	Motown 1164
8/29/70	11	14		23 **Still Water (Love)** .... *Still Water (Peace)*	$10		Motown 1170
11/28/70+	14	10		24 **River Deep - Mountain High** .... *Together We Can Make Such Sweet Music*	$10		Motown 1173
				THE SUPREMES & FOUR TOPS			
1/23/71	40	8		25 **Just Seven Numbers (Can Straighten Out My Life)** .... *I Wish I Were Your Mirror*	$10	■	Motown 1175

DEBUT	PEAK	WKS	Gold	A-side (Chart Hit)	B-side	$	Sym	Label & Number
				FOUR TOPS — Cont'd				
6/5/71	**55**	5		26 **You Gotta Have Love In Your Heart**	*I'm Glad About It*	$10		Motown 1181
				THE SUPREMES & FOUR TOPS				
7/3/71	**70**	4		27 **In These Changing Times**	*Right Before My Eyes*	$10		Motown 1185
9/11/71	**38**	8		28 **MacArthur Park (Part II)**	*(Part I)*	$10		Motown 1189
2/5/72	**90**	3		29 **A Simple Game**	*L.A. (My Town)*	$10		Motown 1196
9/9/72	**53**	9		30 **(It's The Way) Nature Planned It**	*I'll Never Change*	$10		Motown 1210
11/11/72+	**10**	12		31 **Keeper Of The Castle**	*Jubilee With Soul*	$6		Dunhill/ABC 4330
2/3/73	**4**	15	●	32 **Ain't No Woman (Like The One I've Got)**	*The Good Lord Knows*	$6		Dunhill/ABC 4339
6/23/73	**15**	13		33 **Are You Man Enough**	*Peace Of Mind*	$6		Dunhill/ABC 4354
				from the movie *Shaft In Africa* starring Richard Roundtree				
10/13/73	**33**	9		34 **Sweet Understanding Love**	*Main Street People*	$6		Dunhill/ABC 4366
1/26/74	**62**	8		35 **I Just Can't Get You Out Of My Mind**	*Am I My Brother's Keeper*	$6		Dunhill/ABC 4377
5/4/74	**41**	8		36 **One Chain Don't Make No Prison**	*Turn On The Light Of Your Love*	$6	⊙	Dunhill/ABC 4386
8/17/74	**55**	7		37 **Midnight Flower**	*All My Love*	$6	⊙	Dunhill/ABC 15005
5/24/75	**71**	4		38 **Seven Lonely Nights**	*I Can't Hold On Much Longer*	$5		ABC 12096
12/6/75	**97**	1		39 **We All Gotta Stick Together**	*(It Would Almost) Drive Me Out Of My Mind*	$5		ABC 12123
10/30/76	**71**	6		40 **Catfish**	*Look At My Baby*	$5		ABC 12214
8/15/81	**11**	22		41 **When She Was My Girl** RB[2]	*Something To Remember*	$4		Casablanca 2338
5/15/82	**71**	7		42 **Back To School Again**	*Rock-A-Hula-Luau (Summer Is Coming)* (Cast)	$4	■	RSO 1069
				from the movie *Grease 2* starring Michelle Pfeiffer				
8/28/82	**84**	3		43 **Sad Hearts**	*I Believe In You And Me* (R&B #40)	$4		Casablanca 2353
10/22/83	**71**	9		44 **I Just Can't Walk Away**	*Hang*	$4		Motown 1706
8/20/88	**35**	11		45 **Indestructible** S:31 / A:38	*Are You With Me*	$3	■	Arista 9706
				tune used by NBC-TV for the 1988 Summer Olympics				
				FOUR VOICES, The '56				
				Male vocal group: Allan Chase (tenor), Frank Fosta (bass), Sal Mayo (tenor) and Bill McBride (baritone). **Mitch Miller** signed the group to Columbia after seeing them on *Arthur Godfrey's Talent Scouts* TV show. Recorded original version of "Sealed With A Kiss" in 1960 (Columbia 41699).				
3/10/56	**20**	16		1 **Lovely One** S:20 / T:30	*Geronimo*	$20		Columbia 40643
3/24/58	**50**	6		2 **Dancing With My Shadow** S:50 / T:51	*Bon Bon*	$20		Columbia 41076
				Ray Conniff (orch., above 2)				
				IV XAMPLE R&B '95				
				R&B vocal group from Los Angeles, California: brothers Robert (**B.C.**) and Raymond Chevis, with Andre Allen and Lucious.				
3/11/95	**44**	20		1 **I'd Rather Be Alone** S:43 / A:47	*(instrumental)*	$3	▮	MCA 54992
3/13/99	**64**[S]	3		2 **Why-O-Why**	*(instrumental) / (3 album snippets)*	$4	★	Red Ant 15307
				B.C.				
				FOX '75				
				Pop group from England: Noosha Fox (vocals), Herbie Armstrong and Kenny Young (guitars), Pete Solley (keyboards), Gary Taylor (bass) and Jim Frank (drums).				
8/23/75	**53**	8		**Only You Can**	*Out Of My Body*	$5		Ariola America 7601
				FOX, Charles '81				
				Born on 10/30/40 in Manhattan, New York. Composer/conductor/pianist.				
1/24/81	**75**	4		**Seasons**	*Pachelbel's Canon in D Major* [I]	$5		Handshake 5307
				melody based on Pachelbel's *Canon in D Major* and used as the theme from the movie *Ordinary People* starring Donald Sutherland				
				FOX, Samantha LP '88				
				Born on 4/15/66 in London, England. Dance singer. Rose to stardom as a topless model for the U.K. *Daily Sun* newspaper.				
11/1/86+	**4**	23		1 **Touch Me (I Want Your Body)** S:3 / A:6	*Drop Me A Line*	$3	■	Jive 1006
				issued with a regular picture sleeve and a foldout poster sleeve				
3/14/87	**87**	5		2 **Do Ya Do Ya (Wanna Please Me)**	*Want You To Want Me*	$3	■	Jive 1031
10/10/87	**80**	5		3 **Nothing's Gonna Stop Me Now**	*Dream City*	$3	■	Jive 1072
2/27/88	**3**	27		4 **Naughty Girls (Need Love Too)** S:2 / A:5	*(U.K. mix)*	$3	■	Jive 1089
				also issued with "Dream City" as the B-side				
11/12/88+	**8**	23	●	5 **I Wanna Have Some Fun** S:4 / A:11	*Don't Cheat On Me*	$3	■	Jive 1154
				above 2 written, arranged and produced by **Full Force**				
3/18/89	**31**	13		6 **I Only Wanna Be With You** S:24 / A:38	*Confession*	$3	■	Jive 1192
				FOXWORTHY, Jeff C&W/BUB/LP '96				
				Born on 9/6/58 in Atlanta, Georgia; raised in Hapeville, Georgia. Comedian/actor. Starred in won TV sitcom, 1995-97. Began hosting own radio countdown show in April 1999.				
12/10/94+	**75**	10		1 **Redneck Stomp** S:48	*Words In The South* [C-L]	$4	▮V	Warner 18116
8/19/95	**60**[S]	5		2 **Party All Night** BUB:101	*Southern Accent* (Foxworthy) [L-N]	$4	▮V	Warner 17806
				JEFF FOXWORTHY With Little Texas and Scott Rouse				
6/29/96	**66**	10		3 **Redneck Games** S:34	*NASA & Alabama & Fishing Shows* (Foxworthy) [L-N]	$4	▮V	Warner 17648
				JEFF FOXWORTHY with ALAN JACKSON				
				FOXX, Inez R&B/BUB '63				
				Born on 9/9/42 in Greensboro, North Carolina. Sang with the Gospel Tide Chorus. Accompanied vocally on all hits by her brother Charlie Foxx. Charlie died of leukemia on 9/18/98 (age 68).				
6/22/63	**7**	18		1 **Mockingbird**	*Jaybirds*	$20		Symbol 919
				INEZ FOXX with Charlie Foxx				
				adapted from the same traditional folk lyrics as was the song "Bo Diddley"				
12/7/63	**98**	1		2 **Hi Diddle Diddle**	*Talk With Me*	$15		Symbol 924
1/25/64	**91**	3		3 **Ask Me**	*I See You My Love*	$15		Symbol 926
4/25/64	**54**	9		4 **Hurt By Love**	*Confusion*	$15		Symbol 20-001
1/13/68	**76**	5		5 **(1-2-3-4-5-6-7) Count The Days**	*A Stranger I Don't Know (Wish It Was You)*	$12		Dynamo 112
				INEZ & CHARLIE FOXX				

DEBUT	PEAK	WKS	Gold	A-side (Chart Hit)...B-side	$	Sym	Label & Number

FOXX, Jamie
R&B/LP **'94**

Born Eric Bishop on 12/13/67 in Terrell, Texas. R&B singer/actor/comedian. Acted in several movies and TV shows.

DEBUT	PEAK	WKS	Gold	A-side (Chart Hit)...B-side	$	Sym	Label & Number
7/30/94	92	2		**Infatuation** ...S:51 *(album version)*	$4	▮	Fox 62886

FOXXX, Freddie
R&B/LP **'00**

Born Fred Campbell in 1969 in Westbury, New York. Male rapper. Member of **The Flavor Unit MCs**. Also records as **Bumpy Knuckles**.

DEBUT	PEAK	WKS	Gold	A-side (Chart Hit)...B-side	$	Sym	Label & Number
12/2/00	43^S	6		**R.N.S.** ...*The ChanceSellor / The Mastas* (w/**M.O.P.**) **FREDDIE FOXXX (BUMPY KNUCKLES)** RNS: Real Nigga Shit	$6	★	KJAC 005

FOXY
R&B/LP **'78**

Latino dance band from Miami, Florida: Ish "Angel" Ledesma (vocals, guitar), Charlie Murciano (keyboards), Richie Puente (percussion), Arnold Paseiro (bass) and Joe Galdo (drums). Four of group's five members came to Florida with the Cuban emigres of 1959. Ledesma later founded and produced **Oxo** and **Company B**. Puente is son of luminary Latin bandleader Tito Puente.

DEBUT	PEAK	WKS	Gold	A-side (Chart Hit)...B-side	$	Sym	Label & Number
7/22/78	9	21		1 **Get Off** ...RB^2 *You Make Me Hot* Wildflower (background vocals)	$6		Dash 5046
3/31/79	21	15		2 **Hot Number** ...*Call It Love*	$6		Dash 5050

FRAGMA
'00

Trio of electronic dance producers from Europe: brothers Dirk and Marco Duderstadt with Ramon Zenker.

DEBUT	PEAK	WKS	Gold	A-side (Chart Hit)...B-side	$	Sym	Label & Number
10/28/00	99	1		**Toca's Miracle** ...S:53 *(4 remixes)* combines vocals from the 1997 CoCo single "It's A Miracle" with Fragma's "Toca Me"	$6	★	Groovilicious 222

FRAMPTON, Peter
★558★ ROK/LP **'76**

Born on 4/22/50 in Beckenham, Kent, England. Rock singer/songwriter/guitarist. Joined British band The Herd at age 16 before forming **Humble Pie** in 1969, which he left in 1971 to form Frampton's Camel. Went solo in 1974. Played "Billy Shears" in the 1978 movie *Sgt. Pepper's Lonely Hearts Club Band.* Near-fatal car crash on 6/29/78 temporarily sidelined his career.

DEBUT	PEAK	WKS	Gold	A-side (Chart Hit)...B-side	$	Sym	Label & Number
2/21/76	6	18		1 **Show Me The Way** ...*Shine On* [L]	$5	■	A&M 1795
6/26/76	12	16		2 **Baby, I Love Your Way** ...*It's A Plain Shame* [L] studio versions of above 2 released in 1975 on A&M 1693 and 1738, respectively ($7 each); above 2 reissued with a 4-color picture sleeve on A&M 8595 in 1977	$5	■	A&M 1832
9/18/76	10	18		3 **Do You Feel Like We Do** ...*Penny For Your Thoughts* [L] all of above recorded at San Francisco's Winterland	$5		A&M 1867
5/28/77	2^3	20		4 **I'm In You** *St. Thomas (Know How I Feel)*	$5	■	A&M 1941
8/27/77	18	16		5 **Signed, Sealed, Delivered (I'm Yours)** ...*Rocky's Hot Club*	$5	■	A&M 1972
12/10/77+	41	8		6 **Tried To Love** ...*You Don't Have To Worry* **Mick Jagger** (backing vocal)	$6	■	A&M 1988
5/26/79	14	13		7 **I Can't Stand It No More** ...*May I Baby*	$4	■	A&M 2148
2/1/86	74	8		8 **Lying** ...*Into View* all of above written (except #5) and produced by Frampton	$3	■	Atlantic 89463

FRANCIS, Connie
★27★ BUB/AC/C&W/LP **'60**

Born Concetta Rosa Maria Franconero on 12/12/38 in Newark, New Jersey. First recorded for MGM in 1955. From 1961-65, appeared in the movies *Where The Boys Are, Follow The Boys, Looking For Love* and *When The Boys Meet The Girls.* Connie stopped performing after she was raped on 11/8/74. Began comeback with a performance on *Dick Clark's Live Wednesday* TV show in 1978. Pop music's #1 female vocalist from the late 1950s to the mid-1960s.

1)My Heart Has A Mind Of Its Own 2)Everybody's Somebody's Fool 3)Don't Break The Heart That Loves You 4)My Happiness 5)Who's Sorry Now

DEBUT	PEAK	WKS	Gold	A-side (Chart Hit)...B-side	$	Sym	Label & Number
12/2/57	93	1		1 **The Majesty Of Love** ...T:93 *You, My Darlin', You* **MARVIN RAINWATER and CONNIE FRANCIS**	$25		MGM 12555
2/24/58	4	22	●	2 **Who's Sorry Now** ...T:4 / S:5 / A:6 *You Were Only Fooling (While I Was Falling In Love)* there were 3 Top 10 versions of this tune in 1923	$20		MGM 12588
5/12/58	36	12		3 **I'm Sorry I Made You Cry** ...T:36 / S:39 *Lock Up Your Heart* #1 hit for Henry Burr in 1918	$20		MGM 12647
7/28/58	14	14		4 **Stupid Cupid** ...S:14 / H:17 *Carolina Moon*	$20		MGM 12683
10/13/58	30	10		5 **Fallin'** ...H:30 *Happy Days And Lonely Nights*	$20		MGM 12713
12/8/58+	2^2	18	●	6 **My Happiness** ...*Never Before* there were 3 Top 10 versions of this tune in 1948 (written in 1933); picture sleeve issued with either a pink or a white background	$20	■	MGM 12738
3/2/59	22	11		7 **If I Didn't Care** ...*Toward The End Of The Day* #2 hit for the Ink Spots in 1939	$20	■	MGM 12769
5/18/59	5	17		8 **Lipstick On Your Collar** /			
5/18/59	9	15		9 **Frankie** ...	$20		MGM 12793
8/31/59	34	10		10 **You're Gonna Miss Me** /			
9/21/59	69	7		11 **Plenty Good Lovin'** ...	$20		MGM 12824
11/23/59	7	15	●	12 **Among My Souvenirs** / #1 hit for Paul Whiteman in 1928			
11/16/59	36	11		13 **God Bless America** ... written by Irving Berlin and popularized by Kate Smith in 1939	$15		MGM 12841
2/22/60	8	13	●	14 **Mama** / Italian song written in 1941 (English lyrics added in 1946)			
2/29/60	17	11		15 **Teddy** ... written by **Paul Anka**	$15		MGM 12878
5/9/60	1^2	18	●	16 **Everybody's Somebody's Fool** /			
5/23/60	19	11		17 **Jealous Of You (Tango Della Gelosia)** ... [F]	$15	■	MGM 12899
8/15/60	1^2	17		18 **My Heart Has A Mind Of Its Own** /			
8/22/60	42	9		19 **Malagueña** ... [F] written in 1929 by Cuban composer Ernesto Lecuona; from the suite *Andalucia*	$15	■	MGM 12923

FRANCIS, Connie — Cont'd

DEBUT	PEAK	WKS	Gold	#	A-side (Chart Hit)	B-side	$	Sym	Label & Number
11/7/60	7	13	●	20	Many Tears Ago /				
11/7/60	87	1		21	Senza Mamma (With No One)		$15	■	MGM 12964
1/16/61	4	15	●	22	Where The Boys Are /				
					title song from the movie starring George Hamilton; #4, 5, 9 & 22: written by **Neil Sedaka** and Howard Greenfield				
1/16/61	34	8		23	No One		$15	■	MGM 12971
4/17/61	7	10		24	Breakin' In A Brand New Broken Heart	*Someone Else's Boy*	$15	■	MGM 12995
6/26/61	6	11	●	25	Together /	AC[1]			
					#1 hit for Paul Whiteman in 1928				
7/17/61	72	2		26	Too Many Rules		$15	■	MGM 13019
9/25/61	14	9		27	(He's My) Dreamboat /				
9/25/61	42	7		28	Hollywood		$15	■	MGM 13039
					above 2 written by **John D. Loudermilk**				
11/20/61+	10	12		29	When The Boy In Your Arms (Is The Boy In Your Heart) /				
12/11/61	26	5		30	Baby's First Christmas	X:13 [X]	$15	■	MGM 13051
					"Bubbled Under" (#113) on 12/22/62; Christmas charts: #13/'65 (2 weeks)				
2/10/62	❶[1]	13		31	Don't Break The Heart That Loves You	AC[4] *Drop It Joe*	$15	■	MGM 13059
5/12/62	7	9		32	Second Hand Love	*Gonna Git That Man*	$15	■	MGM 13074
					written by Phil Spector				
7/28/62	9	9		33	Vacation	*The Biggest Sin Of All* (#116)	$15	■	MGM 13087
10/6/62	24	9		34	I Was Such A Fool (To Fall In Love With You) /				
10/6/62	57	8		35	He Thinks I Still Care		$12	■	MGM 13096
					#1 Country hit for **George Jones** in 1962 as "She Thinks I Still Care"				
12/15/62+	18	11		36	I'm Gonna' Be Warm This Winter /				
1/5/63	90	5		37	Al Di La	[F]	$12	■	MGM 13116
					from the movie *Rome Adventure* starring Troy Donahue				
3/2/63	17	10		38	Follow The Boys	*Waiting For Billy* (#127)	$12	■	MGM 13127
					title song from the movie starring Francis				
5/18/63	23	9		39	If My Pillow Could Talk	*You're The Only One Can Hurt Me*	$12	■	MGM 13143
8/10/63	36	7		40	Drownin' My Sorrows	*Mala Femmena* (#114)	$12	■	MGM 13160
10/19/63	28	7		41	Your Other Love	*Whatever Happened To Rosemarie*	$12	■	MGM 13176
12/28/63+	46	6		42	In The Summer Of His Years	*My Buddy*	$12	■	MGM 13203
					a tribute to President John F. Kennedy, as introduced by Millicent Martin on the BBC-TV series *That Was The Week That Was*				
2/15/64	24	9		43	Blue Winter	*You Know You Don't Want Me*	$12	■	MGM 13214
5/9/64	25	8		44	Be Anything (But Be Mine)	*Tommy*	$12	■	MGM 13237
					#7 hit for **Eddy Howard** in 1952				
7/18/64	45	7		45	Looking For Love	*This Is My Happiest Moment*	$12	■	MGM 13256
					title song from the movie starring Francis				
10/24/64	42	7		46	Don't Ever Leave Me	*We Have Something More (Than A Summer Love)* (#128)	$12	■	MGM 13287
1/23/65	43	7		47	Whose Heart Are You Breaking Tonight	*Come On Jerry*	$10	■	MGM 13303
3/6/65	48	6		48	For Mama (La Mamma)	*She'll Be Comin' 'Round The Mountain*	$10		MGM 13325
5/1/65	57	7		49	Wishing It Was You	*You're Mine (Just When You're Lonely)*	$10	■	MGM 13331
6/26/65	79	7		50	Forget Domani	*No One Ever Sends Me Roses*	$10		MGM 13363
					from the movie *The Yellow Rolls Royce* starring Rex Harrison and Ingrid Bergman				
9/11/65	80	4		51	Roundabout	*Bossa Nova Hand Dance*	$10		MGM 13389
11/27/65	47	8		52	Jealous Heart	*Can I Rely On You*	$10		MGM 13420
					#2 Country hit for **Tex Ritter** in 1945; #4 pop hit for Al Morgan in 1949				
3/19/66	66	6		53	Love Is Me, Love Is You	*I'd Let You Break My Heart All Over Again*	$10	■	MGM 13470
11/5/66	99	2		54	Spanish Nights And You	*Games That Lovers Play*	$10	■	MGM 13610
4/15/67	94	1		55	Time Alone Will Tell	*Born Free*	$10		MGM 13718
3/8/69	91	4		56	The Wedding Cake	*Over Hill Underground*	$8		MGM 14034
					Francis's musical arrangers and conductors: Stan Applebaum (#17, 20, 22-24), Sid Bass (#1), Artie Butler (#46), **Don Costa** (#29-31, 48, 50), Morty Craft (#5), **Ray Ellis** (#7-13), Tony Hatch (#51, 53), **Leroy Holmes** (#4, 38), **Bill Justis** (#40), Gus Levene (#15), Guilio Libano (#37), Joe Lipman (#2, 3), Alan Lorber (#43-45, 54), Marty Manning (#39), Bill McElhiney (#33), **Billy Mure** (#49), Claus Ogermann (#41, 42, 47, 52), Tony Osborne (#14, 21), Cliff Parman (#25-28), Bill Ramal (#36), **David Rose** (#6), **Joe Sherman** (#16, 55) and Shelby Singleton, Jr. (#56)				

FRANKE & THE KNOCKOUTS — ROK/LP '81

Soft-rock group from New Brunswick, New Jersey: Franke Previte (vocals), Billy Elworthy (guitar), Blake Levinsohn (keyboards), Leigh Foxx (bass) and Claude LeHenaff (drums).

DEBUT	PEAK	WKS	Gold	#	A-side (Chart Hit)	B-side	$	Sym	Label & Number
3/7/81	10	19		1	Sweetheart	*Don't Stop*	$4		Millennium 11801
7/4/81	27	13		2	You're My Girl	*Tell Me Why*	$4		Millennium 11808
4/3/82	24	15		3	Without You (Not Another Lonely Night)	*Shakedown*	$4		Millennium 13105

FRANKIE GOES TO HOLLYWOOD — LP '85

Dance-rock group from Liverpool, England: **Holly Johnson** and Paul Rutherford (vocals), Brian Nash (guitar), Mark O'Toole (bass) and Peter Gill (drums). Group's name inspired by publicity recounting **Frank Sinatra**'s move into the movie industry.

DEBUT	PEAK	WKS	Gold	#	A-side (Chart Hit)	B-side	$	Sym	Label & Number
4/7/84	67	7		1	Relax	*One September Monday*	$3	■	Island 99805
					the video of above song was banned by the BBC in England; featured in the movie *Body Double* starring Melanie Griffith				
10/20/84	43	15		2	Two Tribes	*One February Friday*	$3	■	Island 99695
					sold nearly 2 million copies in England				
1/19/85	10	16	●	3	Relax	S:9 / A:10 *One September Monday* [R]	$3	■	Island 99805
					different mix from #1 above (also issued with a "clean" picture sleeve)				
4/6/85	48	8		4	Welcome To The Pleasuredome	*Relax International (live)*	$3	■	Island 99653

FRANKLIN, Aretha ★10★ R&B/BUB/AC/LP '67

Born on 3/25/42 in Memphis, Tennessee; raised in Detroit, Michigan. Revered as the all-time Queen of Soul Music. Daughter of famous gospel preacher Rev. Cecil L. Franklin, pastor of Detroit's New Bethel Baptist Church. Greatly influenced as a child by family friends/gospel stars Rev. James Cleveland and Clara Ward. First recorded for JVB/Battle in 1956. Signed to Columbia Records in 1960 by legendary talent scout John Hammond. Dramatic turn in style and success after signing with Atlantic in 1966 and working with producer Jerry Wexler. Her sisters Carolyn and **Erma Franklin** also recorded. Married to her manager/cowriter Ted White, 1961-1969, and actor Glynn Turman, 1978-84. Appeared in the 1980 movie *The Blues Brothers*. Inducted into the Rock and Roll Hall of Fame in 1987. Won Grammy's Lifetime Achievement Award in 1994.

1)Respect 2)I Knew You Were Waiting (For Me) 3)Chain Of Fools 4)Spanish Harlem 5)Until You Come Back To Me (That's What I'm Gonna Do)

DEBUT	PEAK	WKS	Gold		A-side (Chart Hit)	B-side	$	Sym	Label & Number
2/27/61	76	3		1	**Won't Be Long**	*Right Now*	$12		Columbia 41923
					Ray Bryant Combo (backing band)				
10/9/61	37	9		2	**Rock-A-Bye Your Baby With A Dixie Melody**	*Operation Heartbreak* (R&B #6)	$12		Columbia 42157
					#1 hit for Al Jolson in 1918				
2/3/62	87	5		3	**I Surrender, Dear** /				
					#3 hit for Gus Arnheim in 1931				
2/10/62	94	1		4	**Rough Lover**		$12	■	Columbia 42266
7/21/62	92	1		5	**Don't Cry, Baby**	*Without The One You Love*	$12	■	Columbia 42456
9/29/62	100	1		6	**Try A Little Tenderness**	*Just For A Thrill* (#111)	$12	■	Columbia 42520
					#6 hit for Ted Lewis in 1933				
12/15/62+	86	5		7	**Trouble In Mind**	*God Bless The Child*	$12		Columbia 42625
					blues standard written in 1926				
9/19/64	57	10		8	**Runnin' Out Of Fools**	*It's Just A Matter Of Time*	$12		Columbia 43113
1/30/65	96	2		9	**Can't You Just See Me**	*Little Miss Raggedy Ann*	$12		Columbia 43203
3/4/67	9	11	●	10	**I Never Loved A Man (The Way I Love You)** RB[7]	*Do Right Woman-Do Right Man* (R&B #37)	$8		Atlantic 2386
4/29/67	1[2]	12	●	11	**Respect** RB[8]	*Dr. Feelgood*	$8		Atlantic 2403
					King Curtis (sax); written by **Otis Redding**				
7/22/67	4	11	●	12	**Baby I Love You** RB[2]	*Going Down Slow*	$8		Atlantic 2427
9/2/67	56	8		13	**Take A Look**	*Follow Your Heart*	$10		Columbia 44270
9/30/67	8	9		14	**A Natural Woman (You Make Me Feel Like)**	*Baby, Baby, Baby*	$8		Atlantic 2441
12/9/67+	2[2]	12	●	15	**Chain Of Fools** RB[4]	*Prove It*	$8		Atlantic 2464
					Joe South (blues guitar intro); written by **Don Covay** (also #24 below)				
12/23/67	94	2		16	**Mockingbird**	*A Mother's Love*	$10		Columbia 44381
					adapted from the same traditional folk lyrics as was the song "Bo Diddley"				
2/24/68	83	3		17	**Soulville**	*If Ever I Would Leave You*	$10		Columbia 44441
					originally "Bubbled Under" (#121) on 5/9/64 on Columbia 43009; all Columbia hits recorded 1960-66				
3/2/68	5	12	●	18	**(Sweet Sweet Baby) Since You've Been Gone** / RB[3]				
4/6/68	16	8		19	**Ain't No Way**		$8		Atlantic 2486
					#14, 15, 18 & 19: from the album *Aretha: Lady Soul*				
5/18/68	7	10	●	20	**Think** / RB[3]				
6/15/68	56	6		21	**You Send Me**		$8		Atlantic 2518
8/17/68	6	9	●	22	**The House That Jack Built** /				
8/17/68	10	11		23	**I Say A Little Prayer**		$8		Atlantic 2546
11/23/68	14	8	●	24	**See Saw** /				
					originally written and recorded by **Don Covay** on his 1967 album *See-Saw*				
11/30/68+	31	7		25	**My Song**		$8		Atlantic 2574
2/22/69	19	7		26	**The Weight** /				
					Duane **Allman** (slide guitar)				
3/15/69	71	6		27	**Tracks Of My Tears**		$8		Atlantic 2603
4/19/69	28	8		28	**I Can't See Myself Leaving You** /				
					#20, 21, 23, 24 & 28: from the album *Aretha Now*				
5/10/69	76	3		29	**Gentle On My Mind**		$8		Atlantic 2619
8/2/69	13	10		30	**Share Your Love With Me** RB[5]	*Pledging My Love/The Clock*	$8		Atlantic 2650
11/8/69	17	8		31	**Eleanor Rigby**	*It Ain't Fair*	$8		Atlantic 2683
2/7/70	13	12		32	**Call Me** / RB[2]				
2/14/70	2	2		33	**Son Of A Preacher Man**		$8		Atlantic 2706
					#26 & 30-33: from the album *This Girl's In Love With You*				
5/23/70	23	8		34	**Spirit In The Dark**	*The Thrill Is Gone* (R&B flip)	$8		Atlantic 2731
8/8/70	11	10	●	35	**Don't Play That Song** RB[3]	*Let It Be*	$8		Atlantic 2751
11/21/70	37	7		36	**Border Song (Holy Moses)** /				
12/19/70		1		37	**You And Me**		$8		Atlantic 2772
					ARETHA FRANKLIN With The Dixie Flyers (#34, 35 & 37)				
2/20/71	19	9		38	**You're All I Need To Get By**	*Pullin'*	$7		Atlantic 2787
4/17/71	6	12	●	39	**Bridge Over Troubled Water** / RB[2]				
6/12/71		4		40	**Brand New Me**		$7		Atlantic 2796
7/31/71	2[2]	12	●	41	**Spanish Harlem** RB[3]	*Lean On Me*	$7		Atlantic 2817
					Dr. John (keyboards)				
10/30/71	9	9	●	42	**Rock Steady** /				
1/15/72	73	4		43	**Oh Me Oh My (I'm A Fool For You Baby)**		$7		Atlantic 2838
3/18/72	5	12	●	44	**Day Dreaming** RB[2]	*I've Been Loving You Too Long*	$7		Atlantic 2866
6/3/72	26	8		45	**All The King's Horses**	*April Fools* (R&B flip)	$7		Atlantic 2883
					#36, 40 & 42-45: from the album *Young, Gifted & Black*				
8/19/72	81	4		46	**Wholy Holy**	*Give Yourself To Jesus*	$7		Atlantic 2901
					with James Cleveland & The Southern California Community Choir; **Marvin Gaye** (co-writer)				
2/10/73	33	10		47	**Master Of Eyes (The Deepness Of Your Eyes)**	*Moody's Mood For Love*	$6		Atlantic 2941
7/7/73	20	13		48	**Angel** RB[2]	*Sister From Texas*	$6		Atlantic 2969
					#19 & 48: written by Aretha's sister, Carolyn (died on 4/25/88)				

DEBUT	PEAK	WKS	Gold	A-side (Chart Hit)...B-side	$	Sym	Label & Number
				FRANKLIN, Aretha — Cont'd			
11/24/73+	3	21	●	49 **Until You Come Back To Me (That's What I'm Gonna Do)**....RB^{1} *If You Don't Think*	$6		Atlantic 2995
				co-written by **Stevie Wonder**; Aretha was the first artist to have a hit at each peak position from #1-10 (the others were **Marvin Gaye** and **Madonna**)			
4/6/74	19	13		50 **I'm In Love**....RB^{2} *Oh Baby*	$6		Atlantic 2999
8/31/74	47	7		51 **Ain't Nothing Like The Real Thing**....*Eight Days On The Road*	$6		Atlantic 3200
11/16/74	45	8		52 **Without Love**....*Don't Go Breaking My Heart*	$6		Atlantic 3224
9/20/75	53	5		53 **Mr. D.J. (5 For The D.J.)**....*As Long As You Are There*	$6		Atlantic 3289
				all of above Atlantics (except #47 & 48) produced by Jerry Wexler			
6/12/76	28	12		54 **Something He Can Feel**....RB^{4} *Loving You Baby*	$6		Atlantic 3326
10/2/76	72	5		55 **Jump**....*Hooked On Your Love* (R&B flip)	$6		Atlantic 3358
2/5/77	82	4		56 **Look Into Your Heart**....*Rock With Me*	$6		Atlantic 3373
				above 3 written and produced by **Curtis Mayfield**			
6/18/77	85	2		57 **Break It To Me Gently**....RB^{1} *Meadows Of Springtime*	$6		Atlantic 3393
12/27/80+	56	8		58 **United Together**....*Take Me With You*	$4		Arista 0569
5/30/81	84	3		59 **Come To Me**....*School Days*	$4		Arista 0600
8/29/81	46	10		60 **Love All The Hurt Away**....*Whole Lot Of Me* (Franklin)	$4		Arista 0624
				ARETHA FRANKLIN AND GEORGE BENSON			
8/21/82	24	12		61 **Jump To It**....RB^{4} *Just My Daydream*	$4		Arista 0699
7/30/83	61	8		62 **Get It Right**....RB^{2} *Giving In*	$4		Arista 9034
				above 2 written and produced by **Luther Vandross**			
6/22/85	3	19		63 **Freeway Of Love**....RB^{5} S:2 / A:5 *Until You Say You Love Me*	$3	■	Arista 9354
9/28/85	7	19		64 **Who's Zoomin' Who**....S:6 / A:7 *Sweet Bitter Love*	$3	■	Arista 9410
10/19/85	18	15		65 **Sisters Are Doin' It For Themselves**....S:16 / A:25 *I Love You Like A Ball And Chain* (Eurythmics - ROK #36)	$3	■	RCA 14214
				EURYTHMICS and ARETHA FRANKLIN			
1/18/86	22	14		66 **Another Night**....S:19 / A:24 *Kind Of Man*	$3		Arista 9453
				above 4 from the album *Who's Zoomin' Who?*			
9/27/86	21	11		67 **Jumpin' Jack Flash**....S:14 / A:25 *Integrity*	$3	■	Arista 9528
				produced by Keith Richards; title song from the movie starring Whoopi Goldberg			
12/6/86+	28	13		68 **Jimmy Lee**....S:23 / A:34 *If You Need My Love Tonight* (w/**Larry Graham**)	$3	■	Arista 9546
				also released on Arista 9557 with "An Angel Cries" as the B-side			
2/21/87	❶^{2}	17		69 **I Knew You Were Waiting (For Me)**....S:❶^{2} / A:❶^{1} *(instrumental)*	$3	■	Arista 9559
				ARETHA FRANKLIN AND GEORGE MICHAEL			
6/20/87	82	4		70 **Rock-A-Lott**....*Look To The Rainbow*	$3	■	Arista 9574
				above 4 from the album *Aretha*			
4/15/89	16	11		71 **Through The Storm**....S:13 / A:19 *Come To Me* (Franklin)	$3	■	Arista 9809
				ARETHA FRANKLIN AND ELTON JOHN			
7/1/89	41	8		72 **It Isn't, It Wasn't, It Ain't Never Gonna Be**....S:35 *If Ever A Love There Was* (Franklin)	$3	■	Arista 9850
				ARETHA FRANKLIN AND WHITNEY HOUSTON			
2/12/94	63	9		73 **A Deeper Love**....S:43 *(Tribesman edit)*	$3	▮	Arista 12657
				written and produced by **C + C Music Factory**; from the movie *Sister Act 2: Back In The Habit* starring Whoopi Goldberg			
5/14/94	26	20		74 **Willing To Forgive**....S:16 / A:57 *Jump To It*	$3	▮	Arista 12680
3/14/98	26	18	●	75 **A Rose Is Still A Rose**....S:14 *(4 album snippets)*	$3	▮	Arista 13465
				samples "What I Am" by **Edie Brickell & New Bohemians**; written and produced by **Lauryn Hill**			
7/18/98	76	11		76 **Here We Go Again**....S:53 *In The Morning / Nessun Dorma*	$4	▮	Arista 13502
				Trina Broussard (backing vocal); samples "The Glow Of Love" by **Change**			
				FRANKLIN, Doug, with the Bluenotes '58			
				Teen pop singer with a white male vocal quartet from North Carolina.			
9/8/58	73	4		**My Lucky Love**....H:73 *Drizzlin' Rain*	$20		Colonial 7777
				FRANKLIN, Erma R&B/BUB/LP '67			
				Born on 3/13/38 in Memphis, Tennessee; raised in Detroit, Michigan. Died of cancer on 9/7/2002 (age 64). Sister of **Aretha Franklin**.			
11/4/67	62	8		**Piece Of My Heart**....*Baby, What You Want Me To Do*	$12		Shout 221
				FRANKLIN, Kirk R&B/LP '98			
				Born on 1/26/70 in Fort Worth, Texas. Gospel singer/choir leader.			
7/12/97	52^{A}	11		1 **Stomp**....			album cut
				GOD'S PROPERTY (featuring Kirk Franklin & "Salt")			
				samples "One Nation Under A Groove" by **Funkadelic**; from the album *God's Property* on B-Rite 90093			
12/5/98	79	5		2 **Lean On Me**....A:67			album cut
				KIRK FRANKLIN featuring Mary J. Blige, Bono, R. Kelly, Crystal Lewis and The Family			
				from the album *The Nu Nation Project* on Gospo Centric 90178			
				FRANKLYN, Chevelle — see BEENIE MAN			
				FRANKS, Michael R&B/AC/LP '76			
				Born on 9/18/44 in La Jolla, California. Jazz-pop singer/songwriter.			
8/7/76	43	8		**Popsicle Toes**....*I Don't Know Why I'm So Happy I'm Sad*	$5		Reprise 1360
				FRANTICS, The '59			
				Instrumental rock and roll group from Seattle, Washington: Ron Petersen (guitar), Chuck Schoning (piano), Bob Hosko (sax), Jim Manolides (bass) and Don Fulton (drums).			
5/25/59	91	3		1 **Straight Flush**....*Young Blues* [I]	$20		Dolton 2
9/14/59	93	1		2 **Fog Cutter**....*Black Sapphire* [I]	$20		Dolton 6
2/29/60	83	2		3 **Werewolf**....*No Werewolf* [I]	$20		Dolton 16
				FRASER, Andy ROK/BUB '84			
				Born on 8/7/52 in London, England. Rock bassist. Formerly with **John Mayall**'s Bluesbreakers and **Free**.			
3/3/84	82	5		**Do You Love Me**....*Palm Of My Hand*	$4	■	Island 99784
				FRASER, Wendy — see SWAYZE, Patrick			

DEBUT	PEAK	WKS	Gold	A-side (Chart Hit)...B-side	$	Sym	Label & Number

FRAZIER, Dallas
C&W/BUB **'66**

Born on 10/27/39 in Spiro, Oklahoma. Country singer/songwriter/multi-instrumentalist. Wrote "Alley-Oop."

DEBUT	PEAK	WKS	Gold	A-side (Chart Hit)...B-side	$	Sym	Label & Number
4/30/66	72	4		**Elvira** ...*That Ain't No Stuff*	$10		Capitol 5560

FREAK NASTY
R&B/LP **'97**

Born Carlito Timmons in Puerto Rico; raised in New Orleans, Louisiana. Male rapper.

DEBUT	PEAK	WKS	Gold	A-side (Chart Hit)...B-side	$	Sym	Label & Number
1/4/97	15	33	▲	**Da' Dip** ...S:12 / A:35 *Down Low (remix) / Bump That Rump*	$3	▮	Power 0112

FREBERG, Stan
MEM/POP/LP **'53**

Born on 8/7/26 in Pasadena, California. Began career doing impersonations on **Cliffie Stone**'s radio show in 1943. Did cartoon voices for the major movie studios. His first in a long string of brilliant satirical recordings was "John And Marsha" in 1951. Launched highly successful advertising career in early 1960s; winner of numerous Clio Awards (outstanding achievement award of the radio and TV ad industry). Hit #1 on the pop charts in 1953 with "St. George And The Dragonet."

DEBUT	PEAK	WKS	Gold	A-side (Chart Hit)...B-side	$	Sym	Label & Number
10/22/55	16	9		1 **The Yellow Rose Of Texas** A:16 / T:47 *Rock Around Stephen Foster* [C] Jud Conlon's Rhythmaires (vocal backing); Alvin Stoller (Yankee Snare Drumming)	$25		Capitol 3249
12/24/55	53	3		2 **Nuttin' For Christmas** ...T:53 *The Night Before Christmas* [X-C] verse melody based on traditional 19th century French song "Vive La Companie"	$25	⊙	Capitol 3280
7/21/56	79	2		3 **Heartbreak Hotel** ...T:79 *Rock Island Line* [C]	$30		Capitol 3480
4/13/57	25	7		4 **Banana Boat (Day-O)** ...S:25 / T:43 *Tele-Vee-Shun* [C] Peter Leeds (interruptions)	$25	⊙	Capitol 3687
11/11/57	32	9		5 **Wun'erful, Wun'erful! (Sides uh-one & uh-two)** ...S:32 / T:36 [C] **Lawrence Welk** parody featuring a medley of tunes: Bubbles In The Wine/Thank You/Louise/Please/Moonlight and Shadows; featuring The Lemon Sisters, Peggy Taylor and Daws Butler	$25	□	Capitol 3815
12/29/58	44	2		6 **Green Chritma** ...*The Meaning Of Christmas* [X-C] Jud Conlon Chorale (vocals); featuring Daws Butler, Marvin Miller and Wil Wright	$25	■	Capitol 4097
2/29/60	99	1		7 **The Old Payola Roll Blues (Side I)** ...*(Side II)* [C] featuring the "Maytag" man, Jesse White (died on 1/8/97); **Billy May** (orch., all of above)	$20	■	Capitol 4329

FRED, John, & His Playboy Band
BUB/LP **'68**

Born John Fred Gourrier on 5/8/41 in Baton Rouge, Louisiana. Formed The Playboys in 1956 as a white band playing R&B music. John played basketball and baseball at LSU and Southeastern Louisiana University.

DEBUT	PEAK	WKS	Gold	A-side (Chart Hit)...B-side	$	Sym	Label & Number
2/23/59	82	5		1 **Shirley** ...*My Love For You* **JOHN FRED and the Playboys**	$20		Montel 1002
11/25/67+	❶[2]	16	●	2 **Judy In Disguise (With Glasses)** ...*When The Lights Go Out* a parody of **The Beatles**' "Lucy In The Sky With Diamonds"	$8		Paula 282
2/24/68	57	6		3 **Hey Hey Bunny** ...*No Letter Today*	$8		Paula 294

FREDDIE AND THE DREAMERS
BUB/LP **'65**

Lead singer Freddie Garrity was born on 11/14/40 in Manchester, England. Formed The Dreamers in 1961 with Derek Quinn (lead guitar), Roy Crewsdon (guitar), Peter Birrell (bass) and Bernie Dwyer (drums). Dwyer died of cancer on 12/4/2002 (age 62).

DEBUT	PEAK	WKS	Gold	A-side (Chart Hit)...B-side	$	Sym	Label & Number
3/13/65	❶[2]	11		1 **I'm Telling You Now** *What Have I Done To You* first released on Capitol 5053 in 1963 ($20)	$15		Tower 125
3/13/65	36	9		2 **I Understand (Just How You Feel)** ...*I Will* melody is from "Auld Lang Syne"; #6 hit for The Four Tunes in 1954	$10		Mercury 72377
4/24/65	18	8		3 **Do The Freddie** ...*Tell Me When* also released with "A Love Like You" as the B-side	$10		Mercury 72428
5/1/65	21	7		4 **You Were Made For Me** ...*So Fine* (Beat Merchants) first released on Capitol 5137 in 1964 ($20)	$15		Tower 127
7/31/65	48	7		5 **A Little You** ...*Things I'd Like To Say*	$10		Mercury 72462

FREDO, Michael
'99

Born on 7/17/79 in Elmira, New York. Pop singer/songwriter/multi-instrumentalist.

DEBUT	PEAK	WKS	Gold	A-side (Chart Hit)...B-side	$	Sym	Label & Number
8/28/99	21[S]	14		**This Time Around** ...*(3 album snippets)* samples "No More Words" by **Berlin**; "45": Qwest 16935; B-side: "Love All Over Again"	$3	★[V]	Qwest 16956

FREE
BUB/LP **'70**

Rock group formed in England: Paul Rodgers (vocals), Paul Kossoff (guitar), **Andy Fraser** (bass) and Simon Kirke (drums). Kossoff and Fraser left in 1972, replaced by Tetsu Yamauchi (bass, later with **Faces**) and John "Rabbit" Bundrick (keyboards). Kossoff (died of drug-induced heart failure on 3/19/76) formed Back Street **Crawler**. Rodgers and Kirke formed **Bad Company** in 1974. Rodgers was lead singer of **The Firm** (1984-85) and The Law (1991).

DEBUT	PEAK	WKS	Gold	A-side (Chart Hit)...B-side	$	Sym	Label & Number
8/15/70	4	16		1 **All Right Now** ...*Mouthful Of Grass*	$6		A&M 1206
11/28/70+	49	8		2 **Stealer** ...*Broad Daylight*	$6	■	A&M 1230

FREEMAN, Bobby
BUB **'58**

Born on 6/13/40 in San Francisco, California. R&B-rock and roll singer. Formed vocal group the Romancers, at age 14, and later formed R&B group the Vocaleers.

DEBUT	PEAK	WKS	Gold	A-side (Chart Hit)...B-side	$	Sym	Label & Number
5/12/58	5	17		1 **Do You Want To Dance** T:5 / S:6 / A:11 *Big Fat Woman*	$25		Josie 835
8/4/58	37	9		2 **Betty Lou Got A New Pair Of Shoes** ...H:37 / S:40 *Starlight*	$25		Josie 841
11/24/58	54	5		3 **Need Your Love** ...*Shame On You Miss Johnson*	$20		Josie 844
6/1/59	90	2		4 **Mary Ann Thomas** ...*Love Me*	$20		Josie 863
12/14/59	93	1		5 **Ebb Tide** ...*Sinbad* #2 hit for **Frank Chacksfield** & His Orchestra in 1953	$20		Josie 872
8/15/60	37	13		6 **(I Do The) Shimmy Shimmy** ...*You Don't Understand Me*	$20		King 5373
4/17/61	89	2		7 **The Mess Around** ...*So Much To Do*	$20		Josie 887
7/11/64	5	12		8 **C'mon And Swim** ...*Part 2*	$12		Autumn 2
10/31/64	56	6		9 **S-W-I-M** ...*That Little Old Heartbreaker Me* above 2 written and produced by Sly Stone (**Sly & The Family Stone**)	$12		Autumn 5

FREEMAN, Ernie
R&B/BUB **'57**

Born on 8/16/22 in Cleveland, Ohio. Died of a heart attack on 5/16/81 (age 58). Black pianist/arranger/producer. Prominent sessionman; on recordings by **Frank Sinatra**, **Dean Martin**, **Sammy Davis, Jr.** and **Connie Francis**. Recorded as "**B. Bumble**" on all records under that name except "Nut Rocker." Musical director at Reprise Records for 10 years. Retired in the late '70s. Also see **Sir Chauncey** and **Joiner, Arkansas Junior High School Band**.

DEBUT	PEAK	WKS	Gold	A-side (Chart Hit)...B-side	$	Sym	Label & Number
9/23/57	75	7		1 **Dumplin's** ...T:75 *Beautiful Weekend* [I]	$15		Imperial 5461
11/18/57	4	18		2 **Raunchy** RB[2] A:4 / S:11 / T:12 *Puddin'* [I]	$25		Imperial 5474

DEBUT	PEAK	WKS	Gold	A-side (Chart Hit)...B-side	$	Sym	Label & Number
				FREEMAN, Ernie — Cont'd			
6/16/58	59	5		3 **Indian Love Call** ...T:59 *Summer Serenade* [I]	$15		Imperial 5518
				from the 1924 musical *Rose Marie* starring Mary Ellis; #8 hit for Jeanette MacDonald & Nelson Eddy in 1937			
10/24/60	70	6		4 **Theme from "The Dark At The Top Of The Stairs"** ...*Come On Home* [I]	$12		Imperial 5693
				title song from the movie starring Robert Preston and Dorothy McGuire			
1/6/62	93	1		5 **The Twist** ...*Shine On Harvest Moon* [I]	$12		Imperial 5793
				FREE MOVEMENT, The LP '71			
				R&B vocal group from Los Angeles, California: brothers Adrian and Claude Jefferson, Godoy Colbert, Cheryl Conley, Josephine Brown and Jennifer Gates.			
5/22/71	5	26		1 **I've Found Someone Of My Own** ...*I Can't Convince My Heart*	$6		Decca 32818
12/11/71+	50	10		2 **The Harder I Try (The Bluer I Get)** ...*Comin' Home*	$5		Columbia 45512
				FREEWAY R&B '02			
				Born Leslie Pridgen in Philadelphia, Pennsylvania. Male rapper.			
2/23/02	55	19		1 **Roc The Mic** ...A:52			album cut
				BEANIE SIGEL & FREEWAY			
				from the movie *State Property* starring Sigel (soundtrack on Roc-A-Fella 586671)			
6/22/02	36^S	6		2 **Line 'Em Up** ...*(2 versions) / Roc The Mic* (w/**Beanie Sigel**, **Nelly** & Murphy Lee)	$6	T	Roc-A-Fella 582947
				FREEWAY featuring Young Chris			
				FREHLEY, Ace — see KISS			
				FRENCH, Don '59			
				Born on 3/31/40 in Wayne, Pennsylvania. Pop singer/guitarist. Later became a stockbroker.			
5/25/59	72	3		**Lonely Saturday Night** ...*Goldilocks*	$30		Lancer 104
				FRENCH, Nicki LP '95			
				Born in Carlisle, England. Female dance singer.			
4/1/95	2[1]	27	●	**Total Eclipse Of The Heart** ...A:2 / S:6 *Pride And Passion*	$3	▌	Critique 15539
				FRENTE! ROK/BUB/LP '94			
				Pop-rock group from Melbourne, Australia: Angie Hart (vocals), Simon Austin (guitar), Tim O'Connor (bass) and Mark Picton (drums). Band name is Spanish for "Front."			
4/23/94	49	15		**Bizarre Love Triangle** ...A:45 / S:54 *Testimony/Risk*	$4	▌	Mammoth 98274
				recorded by **New Order** on their 1986 album *Brotherhood*			
	★400★			**FREY, Glenn** ROK/BUB/AC/LP '85			
				Born on 11/6/48 in Detroit, Michigan. Soft-rock singer/songwriter/guitarist. Founding member of the **Eagles**. Appeared in episodes of TV's *Miami Vice* and *Wiseguy*; starred in the short-lived CBS series *South of Sunset* in 1993. Formed Longbranch Pennywhistle with **J.D. Souther**.			
				1)You Belong To The City 2)The Heat Is On 3)Smuggler's Blues			
6/5/82	31	13		1 **I Found Somebody** ...*She Can't Let Go*	$4	■	Asylum 47466
8/21/82	15	17		2 **The One You Love** ...*All Those Lies*	$4		Asylum 69974
12/11/82+	41	12		3 **All Those Lies** ...*That Girl*	$4		Asylum 69857
6/30/84	20	15		4 **Sexy Girl** ...*Better In The U.S.A.*	$3	■	MCA 52413
9/29/84	54	6		5 **The Allnighter** ...*Smuggler's Blues*	$3	■	MCA 52461
12/8/84+	2[1]	24		6 **The Heat Is On** ...S:❶[1] / A:4 *Shoot Out* (**Harold Faltermeyer**)	$3	■	MCA 52512
				from the movie *Beverly Hills Cop* starring **Eddie Murphy**			
4/6/85	12	19		7 **Smuggler's Blues** ...S:7 / A:16 *New Love*	$3	■	MCA 52546
				originally released as the B-side of #5 above			
9/14/85	2[2]	21		8 **You Belong To The City** AR[3] S:❶[2] / A:3 *Smuggler's Blues*	$3	■	MCA 52651
				above 2 from TV's *Miami Vice* soundtrack			
8/20/88	13	15		9 **True Love** ...S:12 / A:15 *Working Man*	$3	■	MCA 53363
3/18/89	90	4		10 **Livin' Right** ...*Soul Searchin'*	$3		MCA 53497
5/11/91	55	13		11 **Part Of Me, Part Of You** ...*(no B-side)*	$3	▌	MCA 54060
				from the movie *Thelma & Louise* starring Susan Sarandon and Geena Davis			
7/25/92	91	3		12 **I've Got Mine** ...*A Walk In The Dark*	$3	▌	MCA 54429
				FRIDA — see ABBA			
				FRIEDMAN, Dean LP '77			
				Born on 4/21/55 in Paramus, New Jersey. Pop singer/songwriter/pianist.			
4/16/77	26	22		**Ariel** ...*Funny Papers*	$5		Lifesong 45022
				FRIEND AND LOVER '68			
				Husband-and-wife pop vocal duo: Jim (from Houston, Texas) and Cathy (from Chicago, Illinois) Post.			
5/18/68	10	14		1 **Reach Out Of The Darkness** ...*Time On Your Side (You're Only 15 Years Old)*	$8		Verve Forecast 5069
8/31/68	86	2		2 **If Love Is In Your Heart** ...*Zig Zag*	$8		Verve Forecast 5091
				FRIENDS OF DISTINCTION, The LP '69			
				R&B vocal group from Los Angeles, California: Floyd Butler, Harry Elston, Jessica Cleaves and Barbara Jean Love. Butler died of a heart attack on 4/29/90 (age 49).			
4/5/69	3	16	●	1 **Grazing In The Grass** *I Really Hope You Do*	$6		RCA Victor 0107
8/16/69	15	20	●	2 **Going In Circles /**			
7/26/69	63	5		3 **Let Yourself Go** ...	$6		RCA Victor 0204
3/7/70	6	13		4 **Love Or Let Me Be Lonely** ...*This Generation*	$6		RCA Victor 0319
10/10/70	60	8		5 **Time Waits For No One** ...*New Mother Nature*	$5		RCA Victor 0385
				co-written by **Neil Sedaka**			
1/23/71	79	5		6 **I Need You** ...*Check It Out*	$5		RCA Victor 0416
				FRIJID PINK LP '70			
				Male rock group from Detroit, Michigan: Kelly Green (vocals), Gary Thompson (guitar), Tom Beaudry (bass) and Rich Stevens (drums).			
2/7/70	7	13	●	1 **House Of The Rising Sun** ...*Drivin' Blues*	$8		Parrot 341
7/25/70	55	7		2 **Sing A Song For Freedom** ...*End Of The Line*	$8		Parrot 349
12/12/70+	72	5		3 **Heartbreak Hotel** ...*Bye Bye Blues*	$8		Parrot 352

DEBUT	PEAK	WKS	Gold	A-side (Chart Hit)...B-side	$	Sym	Label & Number
				FRIZZELL, Lefty C&W/POP **'51**			
				Born William Orville Frizzell on 3/31/28 in Corsicana, Texas. Died of a stroke on 7/19/75 (age 47). Country singer/songwriter/guitarist (charted 39 hits, 1950-75). Elected to the County Music Hall of Fame in 1982. His brother David was also a top country star. Hit #29 on the pop charts in 1951 with "I Want To Be With You Always."			
1/18/64	85	5		**Saginaw, Michigan**...CW^{4} *When It Rains The Blues*	$12		Columbia 42924
				FROGMEN, The **'61**			
				Instrumental rock and roll band from Los Angeles, California: Dennis Fowley, Larry Bartone, Ray Sullivan, Michael Anderson, Larry Wnuk and Jim Young.			
4/3/61	44	8		**Underwater**...*The Mad Rush* [I]	$25		Candix 314
				first released on Scott 102 in 1961 ($50); reissued on Astra 1009 in 1965 ($12)			
				FROST R&B/BUB/LP **'90**			
				Born Arturo Molina on 5/31/64 in East Los Angeles, California. Raised on military bases in Guam and Germany. Hispanic rapper. Formerly known as **Kid Frost**. Member of **Latin Alliance**.			
7/7/90	42	18		1 **La Raza**...S:28 *In The City*	$3	▮	Virgin 98947
4/18/92	95	3		2 **No Sunshine**...S:59 *The Volo*	$3	▮	Virgin 98583
				KID FROST (above 2)			
				rap version of **Bill Withers**' 1971 hit "Ain't No Sunshine"			
10/28/95	73	14		3 **East Side Rendezvous**...S:66 *Look At What I See*	$3	▮	Ruthless/Relativity 1534
				featuring **A.L.T.** & O.G.Enius; Diane Gordon (additional vocal)			
3/2/96	77	9		4 **La Familia**...*Youseemurda*	$3	▮	Ruthless/Relativity 1547
				Rich Garcia (backing vocal); samples "Family Affair" by **Sly & The Family Stone**			
				FROST, Max, And The Troopers BUB **'68**			
				Studio rock group produced by **Mike Curb**. Paul Wybier was the lead singer.			
9/7/68	22	12		**Shape Of Things To Come**...*Free Lovin'*	$15	□	Tower 419
				from the movie *Wild In The Streets* starring Christopher Jones (as Max Frost)			
				FROST, Thomas & Richard **'69**			
				Born Thomas and Richard Martin in San Mateo, California. Pop singing/songwriting duo of brothers.			
10/25/69	83	4		**She's Got Love**...*The Word Is Love*	$8		Imperial 66405
				FROZEN GHOST ROK/LP **'87**			
				Pop-rock duo from Canada: Arnold Lanni (vocals, guitar, keyboards) and Wolf Hassel (bass). Both were members of the group **Sheriff**.			
4/11/87	69	10		**Should I See**...*Suspended Humanation*	$3		Atlantic 89279
				FRUIT DE LA PASSION **'98**			
				Dance group featuring lead singer Joe Pugas.			
2/7/98	81	8		**Tic Tic Tac**...*(2 versions)*	$4	▮	Aureus 414
				FUEL ROK/LP **'01**			
				Rock group from Harrisburg, Pennsylvania: Brett Scallions (vocals), Carl Bell (guitar), Jeff Abercrombie (bass) and Kevin Miller (drums).			
9/12/98	42	12		1 **Shimmer**...S:41 / A:51 *Walk The Sky / Sunday Girl*	$6	★$^{+V}$	550 Music 79019
				"45": 550 Music 79045; B-side: "Bittersweet" (ROK #15)			
10/28/00+	30	22		2 **Hemorrhage (In My Hands)**...MR^{12} A:24			album cut
7/28/01	64	20		3 **Bad Day**...A:65			album cut
				above 2 from the album *Something Like Human* on 550 Music 69436			
				FUGAZI LP **'01**			
				Punk-rock group from Washington DC: Ian MacKaye (vocals, guitar), Guy Picciotto (guitar), Joe Lally (bass) and Brendan Canty (drums).			
11/3/01	17^{S}	3		**Furniture**...*Number 5 / Hello Morning*	$5	★^{V}	Dischord 129 ■
				FUGEES R&B/BUB/AC/LP **'96**			
				Two-man, one-woman hip-hop outfit: rappers/producers/cousins **Wyclef Jean** and **Pras Michel** (both are of Haitian descent), and rapper/singer **Lauryn Hill** (from East Orange, New Jersey). Fugees is short for refugees. Also see **John Forté**.			
				1)Killing Me Softly 2)Fu-Gee-La 3)Avenues			
7/2/94	49	16		1 **Nappy Heads**...S:37 / A:67 *(instrumental)*	$5	▮	Ruffhouse 77643
				FUGEES (Tranzlator Crew)			
				samples "I Think About Lovin' You" by **Earth, Wind & Fire** and "Heaven At Once" by **Kool & The Gang**			
12/30/95+	29	20	●	2 **Fu-Gee-La**...S:16 / A:66 *How Many Mics*	$4	▮	Ruffhouse 78195
				FUGEES (Refugee Camp)			
				samples "Ooh La La La" by **Teena Marie**			
3/9/96	2^{3A}	35		3 **Killing Me Softly** RB^{5A}			album cut
				FUGEES (feat. Lauryn Hill)			
4/27/96	69^{A}	5		4 **Ready Or Not**...			album cut
6/15/96	38^{A}	16		5 **No Woman, No Cry**...			album cut
				first recorded by **Bob Marley** on the 1975 album *Natty Dread*; above 4 from the album *The Score* on Ruffhouse 67147			
3/15/97	81	5		6 **Hip-Hopera**...S:64 *Living Dangerously* (w/Barrington Levy)	$5	▮	TVT/Blunt 1464
				BOUNTY KILLER Featuring The Fugees			
				REFUGEE CAMP ALL-STARS:			
5/10/97	61^{A}	2		7 **The Sweetest Thing**...			album cut
				REFUGEE CAMP ALL-STARS Featuring Lauryn Hill			
				from the movie *Love Jones* starring Larenz Tate (soundtrack on Columbia 67917)			
6/14/97	45	12		8 **We Trying To Stay Alive**...S:34 *Anything Can Happen / (3 album snippets)*	$6	▮*	Ruffhouse 78602
				samples "Stayin' Alive" by the **Bee Gees** and "Top Billin'" by Audio Two			
9/6/97	62^{A}	7		9 **Guantanamera**...			album cut
				WYCLEF JEAN Featuring Refugee Allstars (above 2)			
				from the album *Wyclef Jean Presents The Carnival* on Ruffhouse 67974			
9/20/97	35	14		10 **Avenues**...S:24 *Back In You Again* (**Rick James** w/**Lil Cease**)	$4	▮	Arista 13411
				REFUGEE CAMP ALL-STARS Featuring Pras (With Ky-Mani)			
				from the movie *Money Talks* starring Chris Tucker; rap version of **Eddy Grant**'s "Electric Avenue"			

DEBUT	PEAK	WKS	Gold	A-side (Chart Hit)...B-side	$	Sym	Label & Number
				FULLER, Bobby, Four BUB/LP **'66**			
				Born on 10/22/43 in Baytown, Texas. Died mysteriously of asphyxiation on 7/18/66 (age 22). Band, formed in El Paso, consisted of Bobby (vocals, guitar) and his brother Randy (bass), with Jim Reese (guitar) and DeWayne Quirico (drums).			
1/29/66	9	11		1 **I Fought The Law** ...*Little Annie Lou*	$15		Mustang 3014
				original version first released on Exeter 124 in 1964 ($300) as by Bobby Fuller (written by Sonny Curtis in 1961)			
4/16/66	26	6		2 **Love's Made A Fool Of You**...*Don't Ever Let Me Know*	$15		Mustang 3016
				written in 1958 by **Buddy Holly**			
				FULLER, Jerry C&W/AC **'59**			
				Born Jerrell Lee Fuller on 11/19/38 in Fort Worth, Texas. First recorded for Lin in 1958. Moved to Los Angeles in the late 1950s. Wrote **Ricky Nelson**'s hits "Travelin' Man," "Young World" and "A Wonder Like You". Produced **Mark Lindsay**, **O.C. Smith** and **Gary Puckett & The Union Gap** (for whom he wrote "Young Girl," "Lady Willpower" and "Over You").			
8/31/59	90	2		1 **Betty My Angel**...*Memories Of You*	$30		Challenge 59052
10/19/59	63	6		2 **Tennessee Waltz** ...*Charlene*	$25		Challenge 59057
				#1 hit for **Patti Page** in 1950			
4/24/61	71	4		3 **Shy Away**...*Heavenly*	$20		Challenge 59104
10/9/61	94	2		4 **Guilty Of Loving You** ...*First Love Never Dies*	$20		Challenge 9114
				FULL FORCE — see LISA LISA AND CULT JAM			
				FULSOM, Lowell R&B/BUB **'67**			
				Born on 3/31/21 in Tulsa, Oklahoma. Died of heart failure on 3/7/99 (age 77). Blues vocalist/guitarist. Also known as Tulsa Red. First recorded for Big Town in 1946. Teamed up with pianist Lloyd Glenn. His band, at one time, included **Ray Charles**, Stanley Turrentine and Billy Brooks.			
12/26/64	6[X]	15		1 **Lonesome Christmas (Part 1)**...*(Part 2)* [X]	$20		Hollywood 1022
				LOWELL FULSON			
				X: 17/'64; 9/'65; 6/'66; 12/'67; 8/'68; 12/'70; originally a #7 hit on the R&B charts on Swingtime 242 in 1950			
12/25/65+	91	3		2 **Black Nights** ...*Little Angel*	$10		Kent 431
1/14/67	52	7		3 **Tramp**...*Pico*	$10		Kent 456
4/1/67	97	2		4 **Make A Little Love**...*I'm Sinking*	$10	■	Kent 463
				FUN AND GAMES, The **'69**			
				Rock group from Houston, Texas: brothers Rock (trumpet) and Joe (bass) Romano, Paul Guille (guitar), Joe Dugan (keyboards), Sam Irwin (tambourine) and Carson Graham (drums). All share vocals.			
1/18/69	78	4		**The Grooviest Girl In The World**...*It Must Have Been The Wind*	$10		Uni 55098
				FUN FACTORY **'95**			
				Dance group: French vocalist Marie-Annette with rapper Rod D., Italian dancer Toni Cottura and German dancer Steve Browarczyk.			
3/18/95	46	20		1 **Close To You** ...A:43 / S:62 *(trouble mix)*	$4	▮	Curb-edel 76945
7/22/95	45	20		2 **I Wanna B With U** A:45 / S:60 *We Are The World*	$4	▮	Curb-edel 76963
1/13/96	88	12		3 **Celebration** /			
1/13/96		12		4 **Take Your Chance** ...	$4	▮	Curb-edel 76972
11/2/96	93	4		5 **Don't Go Away**...*Do Wah Diddy*	$4	▮	Curb-edel 73003
				FUNKADELIC — see PARLIAMENT/FUNKADELIC			
				FUNKDOOBIEST BUB/LP **'93**			
				Rap trio from Los Angeles, California: Ralph "DJ Ralph M" Medrano, Jason "Sondoobie" Vasquez and Tyrone "Tomahawk Funk" Pachenco.			
4/24/93	89	5		**Bow Wow Wow** ...*(radio edit) / I'm Shittin' On 'Em / I'm Flippin' On 'Em*	$6	▮*	Immortal 74852
				FUNKMASTER FLEX R&B/BUB/LP **'98**			
				Born Aston Taylor in Brooklyn, New York. Black rap DJ/producer.			
8/22/98	72	14		1 **Here We Go**...*(instrumental)*	$6	T	Loud/RCA 65542
				FUNKMASTER FLEX Presents Kadejia featuring Product			
				co-written and produced by **Wyclef Jean**			
11/11/00	91	7		2 **Do You**...*(2 versions) / Rush (w/Lady Luck)*	$6	T	Loud/Def Jam 1967
				FUNKMASTER FLEX Featuring DMX			
				FUNKSTAR DE LUXE — see MARLEY, Bob			
				FUNKY COMMUNICATION COMMITTEE LP **'79**			
				Country-pop group: Dennis Clifton (vocals, guitar), J.B. Christman (vocals, keyboards), Steve Gooch (guitar), Lonnie Ledford (bass) and Jim "Be-Bop" Evans (drums).			
7/14/79	47	10		**Baby I Want You**...*That Didn't Hurt Too Bad*	$5		Free Flight 11595
				FUNKY GREEN DOGS **'97**			
				Techno-dance trio from New York: producers Oscar Gaetan and Ralph Falcon, with singer Pamela Williams.			
2/8/97	80	14		**Fired Up!** ...*(4 versions)*	$4	▮	Twisted/MCA 55324
				FUNKY KINGS **'77**			
				Rock group formed in Los Angeles, California: **Jules Shear**, Jack Tempchin and Richard Stekol (vocals, guitars), Mike Finnigan (keyboards), Bill Bodine (bass) and Frank Cotinola (drums).			
11/6/76+	61	11		**Slow Dancing**...*Nothing Was Exchanged*	$5		Arista 0209
				FUN LOVIN' CRIMINALS LP **'96**			
				Eclectic hip-hop trio from Syracuse, New York: Huey Morgan (vocals, guitar), Brian Leiser (bass, keyboards) and Steve Borgovini (drums).			
11/9/96	73[A]	1		**Scooby Snacks** ...		V	album cut
				samples "Movement Of Fear" by Tones on Tail; from the album *Come Find Yourself* on EMI 35703; "45": EMI 19335; B-side: "King Of New York"			
				FUQUA, HARVEY — see JAMES, Etta / MOONGLOWS, The			
				FURAY, Richie BUB/LP **'79**			
				Born on 5/9/44 in Yellow Springs, Ohio. Member of **Buffalo Springfield**, **Poco**, and **The Souther, Hillman, Furay Band**. Began recording Christian music in 1976.			
10/27/79	39	11		**I Still Have Dreams** ...*Headin' South*	$5		Asylum 46534

DEBUT	PEAK	WKS	Gold	A-side (Chart Hit)....................B-side	$	Sym	Label & Number
				FURTADO, Nelly R&B/BUB/LP **'01**			
				Born on 12/2/78 in Victoria, British Columbia, Canada (Portugese parents). Female singer/songwriter.			
3/3/01	9	24		1 **I'm Like A Bird**....A:9			album cut
8/18/01	5	25		2 **Turn Off The Light**....A:5 *(3 mixes) / I'm Like A Bird*	$6	T	DreamWorks 459093
				12" single features a remix with **Ms. Jade** and **Timbaland**; above 2 from the album *Whoa, Nelly!* on DreamWorks 450217			
12/7/02	46S	2		3 **Ching Ching**....BUB:114 *(2 versions) / Jade's The Champ*	$7	T	Beat Club 497820
				MS. JADE Featuring Timbaland & Nelly Furtado			
				FURYS, The **'63**			
				Black vocal group from Los Angeles, California: Jerome Evans (lead singer), Jimmy Green, Melvin White, George Taylor and Robert Washington.			
2/9/63	92	2		**Zing! Went The Strings Of My Heart**....*Never More*	$35		Mack IV 112
				from the 1935 musical revue *Thumbs Up*; #22 hit for Judy Garland in 1943			
				FU-SCHNICKENS R&B/LP **'93**			
				Hip-hop trio from Brooklyn, New York: Larry "Poc-Fu" Maturine, Roderick "Chip-Fu" Roachford (**The Flavor Unit Mcs**) and James "Moc-Fu" Jones. FU stands for "For Unity" and Schnicken is a term invented by the group to signify coalition.			
6/13/92	62S	5		1 **La Schmoove**....*Movie Scene*	$4	▮	Jive 42062
7/3/93	39	17	●	2 **What's Up Doc? (Can We Rock?)**....S:21 / A:66 *(instrumental)*	$4	▮	Jive 42164
				FU-SCHNICKENS with Shaquille O'Neal (Shaq-Fu)			
10/22/94	67	20		3 **Breakdown**....S:35 *(remix) / Sneakin' Up On Ya*	$4	▮	Jive 42244
				samples "Dance Floor" by **Zapp**			
				FUZZ, The LP **'71**			
				Female R&B vocal trio from Washington DC: Sheila Young, Barbara Gilliam and Val Williams.			
1/23/71	21	20		1 **I Love You For All Seasons**....*(instrumental)*	$6		Calla 174
7/31/71	77	3		2 **Like An Open Door**....*Leave It All Behind Me*	$6		Calla 177
10/9/71	95	3		3 **I'm So Glad**....*All About Love*	$6		Calla 179

G

DEBUT	PEAK	WKS	Gold	A-side (Chart Hit)....................B-side	$	Sym	Label & Number
				GABRIEL **'78**			
				Rock group from Seattle, Washington: Terry Lauber (vocals), Frank Butorac (guitar), Gary Ruhl (bass) and Michael Kinder (drums).			
10/7/78	73	4		**Martha (Your Lovers Come And Go)**....*Didn't I Love You?*	$5		Epic/Sweet City 50594
	★515★			**GABRIEL, Peter** ROK/BUB/LP **'86**			
				Born on 2/13/50 in London, England. Lead singer of **Genesis** from 1966-75. Scored movies *Birdy* and *The Last Temptation Of Christ*. In 1982, financed the World of Music Arts and Dance (WOMAD) festival.			
				1)Sledgehammer 2)Big Time 3)In Your Eyes			
4/30/77	68	5		1 **Solsbury Hill**....*Moribund The Burgermeister*	$8		Atco 7079
				also see the "live" version at #4 below			
8/16/80	48	11		2 **Games Without Frontiers**....*Lead A Normal Life*	$5	■	Mercury 76063
				Kate Bush (backing vocal); also see a remix version on the B-side of #11 below			
10/23/82+	29	18		3 **Shock The Monkey**....AR2 *Soft Dog*	$5		Geffen 29883
8/27/83	84	3		4 **Solsbury Hill**....*I Go Swimming (live)* (ROK #38) [L-R]	$5		Geffen 29542
5/10/86	❶1	21		5 **Sledgehammer** AR2 S:❶1 / A:2 *Don't Break This Rhythm*	$3	■	Geffen 28718
8/30/86	26	14		6 **In Your Eyes**....AR1 S:26 / A:27 *(special mix)*	$3	■	Geffen 28622
				also see a shorter version re-entry at #9 below			
11/29/86+	8	23		7 **Big Time**....A:4 / S:8 *We Do What We're Told*	$3	■	Geffen 28503
				Stewart Copeland (of **The Police**; drums)			
4/4/87	72	6		8 **Don't Give Up**....*Curtains* (Gabriel)	$4	■	Geffen 28463
				PETER GABRIEL/KATE BUSH			
5/20/89	41	14		9 **In Your Eyes**....S:39 / A:39 *Skankin' To The Beat* (Fishbone) [R]	$3		WTG 68936
				theme from the movie *Say Anything* starring John Cusack; shorter version than #6 above; above 5 from the album *So*			
10/3/92	52	11		10 **Digging in the Dirt**....AR1 / MR2 A:66 / S:75 *Quiet Steam*	$3	▮V	Geffen 19136
12/19/92+	32	15		11 **Steam**....MR5 A:33 / S:73 *Games Without Frontiers (remix)*	$3	▮V	Geffen 19145
				all of above written by Gabriel			
				GABRIEL And The Angels **'62**			
				Rock and roll band from Camden, New Jersey: Rick Kellis (aka Gabriel, lead vocals), George Jones (guitar), Pete Colangelo (trumpet, vocals), Richie Bruno (bass) and Al Hobbs (drums). Backing vocals by a black female trio named The Swans.			
11/10/62	51	11		**That's Life (That's Tough)**....*Don't Wanna Twist No-More*	$20		Swan 4118
				based on the riddle "What's Tough - Life - What's Life? - A Magazine..."			
				GABRIELLE BUB **'94**			
				Born Louise Gabrielle Bobb on 4/16/70 in London, England. Black female dance singer.			
10/9/93+	26	28		1 **Dreams**....S:24 / A:26 *(dignity mix)*	$3	▮	Go!/London 857298
4/30/94	52	14		2 **I Wish**....A:46 *(2 versions) / Dreams (live)*	$3	▮	Go!/London 857520
				GADA **'02**			
				Rap duo from West Palm Beach, Florida: Ray Millines and Christopher Wright.			
6/8/02	59S	1		**So High**....*(3 versions)*	$6	★	Nuff Nuff 90202
				GADABOUTS, The **'56**			
				R&B vocal group from Chicago, Illinois: Johnnie Barr, Eddie Hayes, Larry Craig and Bill Putnam.			
7/21/56	39	8		**Stranded In The Jungle**....T:39 *Blues Train* [N]	$25		Mercury 70898
				GADSON, Mel **'60**			
				Born on 7/21/37 in Sarasota, Florida. Pop singer.			
5/30/60	69	5		**Comin' Down With Love**....*I'm Gettin Sentimental Over You*	$25		Big Top 3034

DEBUT	PEAK	WKS	Gold	A-side (Chart Hit)..........B-side	$	Sym	Label & Number

GAGNON, Andre, (The Disco Sound of) '76

Born in 1942 in Pacome-de-Kamouraska, Quebec, Canada. Dance pianist/composer.

DEBUT	PEAK	WKS	Gold	A-side (Chart Hit)..........B-side	$	Sym	Label & Number
3/6/76	95	3		**Wow**..........*Ta Samba* [I]	$5		London 230

GAIL, Eyra '02

Born in Miami, Florida. White female electronica-dance singer.

DEBUT	PEAK	WKS	Gold	A-side (Chart Hit)..........B-side	$	Sym	Label & Number
4/27/02	61^{S}	4		**Heaven**..........*(5 versions)*	$8	★*	24/7 Artemis 872475

GAINES, Chris — see BROOKS, Garth

GALE, Sunny MEM/POP '52

Born Selma Segal on 2/20/27 in Clayton, New Jersey; raised in Philadelphia, Pennsylvania. At age 16, placed in the finals of the Miss Philadelphia Beauty Contest. Began career with Hal McIntyre's band. Charted 5 Top 20 pop hits, 1952-54.

DEBUT	PEAK	WKS	Gold	A-side (Chart Hit)..........B-side	$	Sym	Label & Number
1/8/55	17	1		1 **Let Me Go, Lover!** / A:17			
1/29/55	14^{HR}	8		2 **Unsuspecting Heart**.......... **Hugo Winterhalter** (orch., above 2)	$12		RCA Victor 5952
11/26/55	85	8		3 **C'est La Vie**..........T:85 *Looking Glass*	$12		RCA Victor 6286
4/21/56	66	3		4 **Rock And Roll Wedding**..........T:66 *Winner Take All* **Joe Reisman** (orch., above 2)	$12		RCA Victor 6479

GALENS, The '63

Pop vocal group from Los Angeles, California: Galen, Bob Hubener, Charlene Knight (lead singer) and George Ross.

DEBUT	PEAK	WKS	Gold	A-side (Chart Hit)..........B-side	$	Sym	Label & Number
11/23/63	70	5		**Baby I Do Love You**..........*Love Bells* adaptation of the German folk song "Du Du Liegst Mir Im Herzen"; #17 hit in 1949 for **Russ Morgan** as "You, You, You Are The One"	$15		Challenge 9212

GALLAGHER AND LYLE BUB/AC '76

Pop-rock duo from Largs, Ayrshire, Scotland: Benny Gallagher & Graham Lyle. Both formerly with **McGuiness Flint**.

DEBUT	PEAK	WKS	Gold	A-side (Chart Hit)..........B-side	$	Sym	Label & Number
4/10/76	49	14		1 **I Wanna Stay With You**..........*Fifteen Summers*	$4		A&M 1778
8/21/76	67	8		2 **Heart On My Sleeve**..........*Storm In My Soul* originally charted for 5 weeks (#83); re-entered on 11/27/76	$4		A&M 1850

GALLAHADS, The '56

White vocal group from New Jersey: Frank Kreisel, Jackie Vincent, Bob Alexander and Vincent Gambella (later recorded as **Vincent Bell**).

DEBUT	PEAK	WKS	Gold	A-side (Chart Hit)..........B-side	$	Sym	Label & Number
8/18/56	62	9		**The Fool**..........T:62 *The Morning Mail* **Billy Mure** (orch.)	$30		Jubilee 5252

GALLERY BUB/AC/LP '72

Pop group from Detroit, Michigan: Jim Gold (vocals), Brent Anderson (lead guitar), Cal Freeman (steel guitar), Bill Nova (percussion), Dennis Korvarik (bass) and Danny Brucato (drums).

DEBUT	PEAK	WKS	Gold	A-side (Chart Hit)..........B-side	$	Sym	Label & Number
2/26/72	4	22	●	1 **Nice To Be With You**..........*Ginger Haired Man*	$5		Sussex 232
8/12/72	22	16		2 **I Believe In Music**..........*Someone* written by **Mac Davis**	$5	■	Sussex 239
12/30/72+	23	15		3 **Big City Miss Ruth Ann**..........*Lover's Hideaway*	$5		Sussex 248

GALLOP, Frank AC '66

Born on 6/30/1900 in Brooklyn, New York. Died in May 1988 (age 87). Best known as the announcer on **Perry Como**'s TV shows during the 1950s.

DEBUT	PEAK	WKS	Gold	A-side (Chart Hit)..........B-side	$	Sym	Label & Number
6/23/58	57	7		1 **Got A Match?**..........T:57 *I Beg Your Pardon!* [I-N] **FRANK GALLUP** **Don Costa** (orch.)	$15		ABC-Paramount 9931
4/16/66	34	9		2 **The Ballad Of Irving**..........*Would You Believe It?* (Phil Leeds) [C-L] parody of **Lorne Greene**'s "Ringo"; Irving: "the 142nd fastest gun in the West"	$10		Kapp 745

GAMMA LP '80

Rock group formed by guitarist Ronnie Montrose after breakup of Montrose. Also included Davey Pattison (vocals), Mitchell Froom (keyboards), Glenn Letsch (bass) and Denny Carmassi (drums). Carmassi left in late 1982 to join **Heart**. Froom, also a record producer, married **Suzanne Vega** on 3/17/95.

DEBUT	PEAK	WKS	Gold	A-side (Chart Hit)..........B-side	$	Sym	Label & Number
1/5/80	60	6		1 **I'm Alive**..........*Solar Heat*	$4		Elektra 46555
4/3/82	77	5		2 **Right The First Time**..........*No Way Out*	$4		Elektra 47423

GANGSTA BOO R&B/LP '99

Black female rapper. Former member of Three 6 Mafia.

DEBUT	PEAK	WKS	Gold	A-side (Chart Hit)..........B-side	$	Sym	Label & Number
5/1/99	55^{S}	7		**Nasty Trick**..........*(instrumental) / Where Dem Dollas At* (R&B #49)	$5	★	Relativity 1784

GANG STARR R&B/BUB/LP '94

Rap duo from Brooklyn, New York: Christopher "DJ Premier" Martin and Keith "Guru" Elam. Also see **Jeru The Damaja**.

DEBUT	PEAK	WKS	Gold	A-side (Chart Hit)..........B-side	$	Sym	Label & Number
3/5/94	67	11		1 **Mass Appeal**..........S:52 / A:73 *(radio version)* re-entered the R&B Sales charts in 2001 (#66)	$4	▮	Chrysalis 58111
12/6/97+	76	13		2 **You Know My Steez**..........S:63 *(raw version) / So Wassup?!*	$4	▮	Noo Trybe 38624
11/23/02	18^{S}	14		3 **Skills**..........*(2 versions) / Natural*	$6	T	Rap-A-Lot 38849

GANTS, The '65

Garage-rock band from Greenwood, Mississippi: Sid Herring (vocals), Johnny Sanders (guitar), Vince Montgomery (bass) and Don Wood (drums).

DEBUT	PEAK	WKS	Gold	A-side (Chart Hit)..........B-side	$	Sym	Label & Number
9/25/65	46	12		**Road Runner**..........*My Baby Don't Care* first released on Statue 605 in 1965 ($50)	$15		Liberty 55829

GAP BAND, The R&B/BUB/LP '82

R&B-funk trio from Tulsa, Oklahoma: brothers Ronnie, Robert and **Charlie Wilson** (lead singer) (also see #6 & 7 below). Charted 33 R&B hits, 1977-95. Group named for three streets in Tulsa: Greenwood, Archer and Pine. Cousins of Bootsy Collins. Charlie was a member of the **Eurythmics**' backing band.

DEBUT	PEAK	WKS	Gold	A-side (Chart Hit)..........B-side	$	Sym	Label & Number
2/28/81	84	8		1 **Burn Rubber (Why You Wanna Hurt Me)**..........RB^{2} *Nothin' Comes To Sleepers*	$4		Mercury 76091
5/23/81	60	7		2 **Yearning For Your Love**..........*When I Look In Your Eyes*	$4		Mercury 76101
5/22/82	24	14		3 **Early In The Morning** RB^{3} *I'm In Love*	$4	■	Total Experience 8201
8/14/82	31	13		4 **You Dropped A Bomb On Me**..........*Lonely Like Me*	$4		Total Experience 8203
3/12/83	51	8		5 **Outstanding**..........RB^{1} *The Boys Are Back In Town*	$4		Total Experience 8205

DEBUT	PEAK	WKS	Gold	A-side (Chart Hit)..........B-side	$	Sym	Label & Number
				GARBAGE ROK/BUB/LP **'96**			
				Rock group formed in Madison, Wisconsin: Shirley Manson (vocals, guitar; native of Edinburgh, Scotland), Doug Erikson (guitar, bass, keyboards), Steve Marker (guitar) and Butch Vig (drums). Vig produced albums for **Nirvana**, **Soul Asylum**, **Sonic Youth** and **Smashing Pumpkins**.			
7/29/95	97	2		1 **Vow** .... *(torn apart version)*	$5	▮	Almo Sounds 89000
10/7/95	57[A]	9		2 **Queer**			album cut
3/9/96	55	20		3 **Only Happy When It Rains** ....A:54 / S:61 *Girl Don't Come / Sleep*	$4	▮	Almo Sounds 89002
7/27/96	24	20		4 **Stupid Girl** A:26 / S:33 *(radio mix) / Driving Lesson*	$4	▮	Almo Sounds 89004
				samples "Train In Vain" by **The Clash**; all of above from the album *Garbage* on Almo Sounds 80004			
11/30/96+	29[A]	16		5 **#1 Crush** ....MR[4]			album cut
				from the movie *Romeo & Juliet* starring Leonardo DiCaprio and Claire Danes (soundtrack on Capitol 37715)			
5/9/98	52	18		6 **Push It** ....A:56 / S:63 *(remix) / Thirteen*	$6	★	Almo Sounds 89014
				samples "Push It" by **Salt-N-Pepa** and "Don't Worry Baby" by **The Beach Boys**			
8/15/98	70[A]	6		7 **I Think I'm Paranoid** .... *(dub mix) / Push It (2 mixes)*	$6	T	Almo Sounds 88005
3/27/99	52	13		8 **Special** A:42			album cut
				inspired by the 1980 hit "Brass In Pocket (I'm Special)" by **The Pretenders**; above 3 from the album *Version 2.0* on Almo Sounds 80018			
				GARCIA, Jerry — see GRATEFUL DEAD			
				GARCIA, Lilian **'02**			
				Born on 8/19/73 in Florence, South Carolina. Ring announcer for WWE's *Monday Night Raw* TV wrestling show.			
10/26/02+	36[S]	8		**Shout** .... *(instrumental)*	$4	★	Universal 019372
				written and produced by **Meredith Brooks**			
				GARDNER, Dave LP **'57**			
				Born on 6/11/26 in Jackson, Tennessee. Died of a heart attack on 9/22/83 (age 57). "Brother Dave" had six comedy albums chart in the early 1960s.			
7/15/57	22	10		**White Silver Sands** ....S:22 / T:28 *Fat Charlie*	$20		OJ 1002
				GARDNER, Don, and Dee Dee Ford BUB/R&B **'62**			
				R&B vocal duo from Philadelphia, Pennsylvania. Gardner formed his own group, the Sonotones with **Jimmy Smith**, in 1953 and recorded for Gotham and Bruce. Ford also plays organ and piano.			
6/2/62	20	13		1 **I Need Your Loving** .... *Tell Me*	$15		Fire 508
8/11/62	75	5		2 **Glory Of Love** .... *Deed I Do*	$15		KC 106
				#1 hit for **Benny Goodman** in 1936			
8/25/62	66	7		3 **Don't You Worry** .... *I'm Coming Home To Stay*	$15		Fire 513
				GARFUNKEL, Art AC/BUB/LP **'73**			
				Born on 11/5/41 in Forest Hills, New York. Half of **Simon & Garfunkel** duo. Appeared in movies *Catch 22*, *Carnal Knowledge* and *Bad Timing*. Has Master's degree in mathematics from Columbia University.			
9/15/73	9	14		1 **All I Know** AC[4] *Mary Was An Only Child*	$5	■	Columbia 45926
12/29/73+	38	9		2 **I Shall Sing** .... *Feuilles-Oh/Do Space Men Pass Dead Souls On Their Way To The Moon?*	$5		Columbia 45983
				written by **Van Morrison**			
9/21/74	34	8		3 **Second Avenue** .... *Woyaya*	$5		Columbia 10020
				GARFUNKEL (above 3)			
8/23/75	18	18		4 **I Only Have Eyes For You** ....AC[1] *Looking For The Right One*	$5		Columbia 10190
				from the movie musical *Dames* starring Joan Blondell; #2 hit for Ben Selvin in 1934			
12/27/75+	39	11		5 **Break Away** ....AC[1] *Disney Girls*	$5		Columbia 10273
1/21/78	17	14		6 **(What A) Wonderful World** ....AC[5] *Wooden Planes* (Garfunkel)	$5		Columbia 10676
				ART GARFUNKEL with JAMES TAYLOR & PAUL SIMON			
6/9/79	53	8		7 **Since I Don't Have You** .... *When Someone Doesn't Want You*	$5		Columbia 10999
8/8/81	66	9		8 **A Heart In New York** .... *Is This Love*	$4	■	Columbia 02307
				GARI, Frank **'61**			
				Born on 4/1/42 in New York City, New York. Teen pop singer.			
12/19/60+	27	14		1 **Utopia** .... *I Ain't Got A Girl*	$15		Crusade 1020
4/10/61	23	12		2 **Lullaby Of Love** .... *Tonight Is Our Last Night*	$15	■	Crusade 1021
7/3/61	30	10		3 **Princess** .... *The Last Bus Left At Midnight*	$15	■	Crusade 1022
				GARNETT, Gale BUB/LP **'64**			
				Born on 7/17/42 in Auckland, New Zealand. Came to the U.S. in 1951. Made singing debut in 1960. Acted in several movies and TV shows.			
8/8/64	4	17		1 **We'll Sing In The Sunshine** ....AC[7] *Prism Song*	$10		RCA Victor 8388
12/5/64+	54	9		2 **Lovin' Place** .... *I Used To Live Here*	$8	■	RCA Victor 8472
				Sid Bass (orch., above 2)			
				GARRETT, Lee **'76**			
				Born in Mississippi. R&B singer/songwriter. Blind since birth. Teamed with **Stevie Wonder** to write "It's A Shame" hit for the **Spinners**.			
5/22/76	58	6		**You're My Everything** .... *Love Enough For Two*	$6		Chrysalis 2112
				GARRETT, Leif LP **'78**			
				Born on 11/8/61 in Hollywood, California. Teen pop singer/actor. Appeared in several movies, including all three *Walking Tall* movies.			
				1)I Was Made For Dancin' 2)Runaround Sue 3)Surfin' USA			
8/27/77	20	15		1 **Surfin' USA** .... *Special Kind Of Girl*	$4	■	Atlantic 3423
11/12/77+	13	14		2 **Runaround Sue** .... *I Wanna Share A Dream With You*	$4	■	Atlantic 3440
3/4/78	58	7		3 **Put Your Head On My Shoulder** .... *Kari*	$4		Atlantic 3466
4/22/78	49	7		4 **The Wanderer** .... *Love On The Run*	$4	■	Atlantic 3476
				all of above from the album *Leif Garrett*			
11/11/78+	10	21		5 **I Was Made For Dancin'** *Living Without Your Love*	$4	■	Scotti Brothers 403
5/5/79	57	8		6 **Feel The Need** .... *New York City Nights*	$4	■	Scotti Brothers 407
11/3/79	78	5		7 **When I Think Of You** .... *New York City Nights*	$4		Scotti Brothers 502
12/15/79+	60	9		8 **Memorize Your Number** .... *Moonlight Dancin'*	$4		Scotti Brothers 510

DEBUT	PEAK	WKS	Gold	A-side (Chart Hit)...B-side	$	Sym	Label & Number
				GARRETT, Leif — Cont'd			
4/12/80	78	5		9 **I Was Looking For Someone To Love** ... *Little Things You Do* all of above produced by Michael Lloyd	$4		Scotti Brothers 516
12/5/81	84	6		10 **Runaway Rita** ... *Just Like A Brother*	$4	■	Scotti Brothers 02579
				GARRETT, Scott '59 Born on 11/5/32 in Pittsburgh, Pennsylvania. Pop singer.			
3/30/59	92	1		**A House Of Love** ... *So Far So Good* Elise Bretton (female backing vocal); Sid Bass (orch.)	$20		Laurie 3023
				GARRETT, Siedah R&B/AC '84 Born on 6/24/60 in Los Angeles, California. Black female singer/songwriter. Joined the **Brand New Heavies** in 1996. Also see **Michael Jackson**'s "I Just Can't Stop Loving You" and "Man In The Mirror."			
4/28/84	72	6		1 **Don't Look Any Further** ... *I Thought I Could Handle It* **DENNIS EDWARDS (featuring Siedah Garrett)**	$4		Gordy 1715
7/16/88	97	1		2 **K.I.S.S.I.N.G.** ... *Taboo*	$3	■	Qwest 27928
				GARY, John AC/BUB/LP '64 Born John Gary Strader on 11/29/32 in Watertown, New York. Died of cancer on 1/4/98 (age 65). Adult Contemporary singer on Don McNeill's radio program, *Breakfast Club.*			
9/12/64	89	4		**Soon I'll Wed My Love** ... *The Young Lovers* Claus Ogerman (orch.)	$8		RCA Victor 8413
				GARY & DAVE '73 Pop singing/songwriting duo from Canada: Gary Weeks and Dave Beckett.			
12/15/73	92	4		**Could You Ever Love Me Again** ... *Where Do We Go From Here?*	$5		London 200
				GARY AND THE HORNETS BUB '66 Pop-rock band of brothers from Franklin, Ohio: Gary (age 11 in 1966), Gregg (13) and Steve (6) Calvert.			
11/19/66	96	2		**Hi Hi Hazel** ... *Patty Girl*	$15	■	Smash 2061
				GARY O' ROK '81 Born Gary O'Connor in Toronto, Ontario, Canada. Rock singer/songwriter.			
7/18/81	70	5		**Pay You Back With Interest** ... *Just A Little Love*	$4		Capitol 5018
				GARY'S GANG LP '79 Dance group from Queens, New York: Gary Turnier (drums), Eric Matthew (vocals, guitar), Al Lauricella and Rino Minetti (keyboards), Bill Catalano (percussion), Bob Forman (sax) and Jay Leon (trombone).			
2/17/79	41	10		**Keep On Dancin'** ... *Do It At The Disco*	$4		Columbia 10884
				GASKIN, Barbara — see STEWART, Dave			
				GATES, David AC/LP '78 Born on 12/11/40 in Tulsa, Oklahoma. Began career as a session musician, then a songwriter/producer before becoming the lead singer of **Bread**. Wrote **The Murmaids**' hit "Popsicles & Icicles."			
7/14/73	47	8		1 **Clouds** ... *I Use The Soap*	$5	■	Elektra 45857
10/20/73	50	8		2 **Sail Around The World** ... *Help Is On The Way*	$5		Elektra 45868
1/18/75	29	10		3 **Never Let Her Go** ... *Watch Out*	$5		Elektra 45223
12/17/77+	15	24		4 **Goodbye Girl** *Sunday Rider* title song from the Neil Simon movie starring Richard Dreyfuss; issued with 2 different picture sleeves: a photo sleeve and a title sleeve	$4	■	Elektra 45450
8/12/78	30	14		5 **Took The Last Train** ... *Ann*	$4		Elektra 45500
2/9/80	46	8		6 **Where Does The Lovin' Go** ... *Starship Ride*	$4		Elektra 46588
9/26/81	62	7		7 **Take Me Now** ... *It's What You Say*	$4		Arista 0615
				GATLIN, Larry C&W/AC/BUB/LP '74 Born on 5/2/48 in Seminole, Texas. Country singer/songwriter/guitarist. Leader of The Gatlin Brothers; charted 42 Country hits, 1973-90.			
9/14/74	84	4		**Delta Dirt** ... *Those Also Love*	$6		Monument 8622
				GAYE, Marvin ★12★ R&B/BUB/LP '68 Born on 4/2/39 in Washington DC. Fatally shot by his father after a quarrel on 4/1/84 (one day before his 45th birthday). Sang in his father's Apostolic church. In vocal groups the Rainbows and Marquees. Joined **Harvey Fuqua** in the re-formed **Moonglows**. To Detroit in 1960. Session work as a drummer at Motown; married to Berry Gordy's sister Anna, 1961-75. First recorded under own name for Tamla in 1961. In seclusion for several months following the death of **Tammi Terrell** in 1970. Problems with drugs and the IRS led to his moving to Europe for three years. Inducted into the Rock and Roll Hall of Fame in 1987. His daughter **Nona Gaye** also recorded. Won Grammy's Lifetime Achievement Award in 1996. *1)I Heard It Through The Grapevine 2)Let's Get It On 3)Got To Give It Up 4)What's Going On 5)Sexual Healing*			
10/20/62	46	9		1 **Stubborn Kind Of Fellow** ... *It Hurt Me Too*	$25		Tamla 54068
1/12/63	30	12		2 **Hitch Hike** ... *Hello There Angel*	$20		Tamla 54075
5/18/63	10	14		3 **Pride And Joy** ... *One Of These Days* **Martha & The Vandellas** (backing vocals, above 3)	$20		Tamla 54079
10/19/63	22	16		4 **Can I Get A Witness /** **The Supremes** (backing vocals)			
10/19/63	77	3		5 **I'm Crazy 'Bout My Baby** ...	$20		Tamla 54087
3/14/64	15	10		6 **You're A Wonderful One** ... *When I'm Alone I Cry* **The Supremes** (backing vocals)	$20		Tamla 54093
5/16/64	17	10		7 **What's The Matter With You Baby /**			
5/2/64	19	9		8 **Once Upon A Time** ... **MARVIN GAYE & MARY WELLS** (above 2)	$20	■	Motown 1057
6/6/64	15	11		9 **Try It Baby** ... *If My Heart Could Sing* **The Temptations** (backing vocals)	$15	■	Tamla 54095
9/19/64	27	9		10 **Baby Don't You Do It** ... *Walk On The Wild Side*	$15	■	Tamla 54101
10/24/64	61	6		11 **What Good Am I Without You** ... *I Want You 'Round* **MARVIN GAYE & KIM WESTON**	$15		Tamla 54104

DEBUT	PEAK	WKS	Gold	A-side (Chart Hit)..................B-side	$	Sym	Label & Number
				GAYE, Marvin — Cont'd			
11/21/64+	6	14		12 **How Sweet It Is To Be Loved By You** ...*Forever*	$15		Tamla 54107
3/20/65	8	12		13 **I'll Be Doggone** ...RB[1] *You've Been A Long Time Coming*	$15		Tamla 54112
7/10/65	25	7		14 **Pretty Little Baby** ...*Now That You've Won Me*	$15		Tamla 54117
10/9/65	8	12		15 **Ain't That Peculiar** ...RB[1] *She's Got To Be Real*	$15		Tamla 54122
2/19/66	29	8		16 **One More Heartache** ...*When I Had Your Love*	$15		Tamla 54129
5/21/66	44	8		17 **Take This Heart Of Mine** ...*Need Your Lovin (Want You Back)*	$15		Tamla 54132
				#13 & 15-17: produced by **Smokey Robinson**			
8/20/66	47	7		18 **Little Darling, I Need You** ...*Hey Diddle Diddle*	$15		Tamla 54138
1/7/67	14	12		19 **It Takes Two** ...*It's Got To Be A Miracle (This Thing Called Love)*	$15		Tamla 54141
				MARVIN GAYE & KIM WESTON			
5/13/67	19	12		20 **Ain't No Mountain High Enough** ...*Give A Little Love*	$12		Tamla 54149
				MARVIN GAYE & TAMMI TERRELL			
7/1/67	33	7		21 **Your Unchanging Love** ...*I'll Take Care Of You*	$12		Tamla 54153
				#13, 15-18 & 21: from the album *Moods Of Marvin Gaye*			
9/9/67	5	13		22 **Your Precious Love** ...*Hold Me Oh My Darling*	$12		Tamla 54156
12/2/67+	10	11		23 **If I Could Build My Whole World Around You** ...	$12		Tamla 54161
1/13/68	34	7		24 **You** ...*Change What You Can*	$12		Tamla 54160
3/2/68	68	6		25 **If This World Were Mine** ...	$12		Tamla 54161
				MARVIN GAYE & TAMMI TERRELL (above 3)			
				#20 & 22-24: from the album *United*			
4/13/68	8	13		26 **Ain't Nothing Like The Real Thing** ...RB[1] *Little Ole Boy, Little Ole Girl*	$12		Tamla 54163
7/27/68	7	12		27 **You're All I Need To Get By** ...RB[5] *Two Can Have A Party*	$12		Tamla 54169
				MARVIN GAYE & TAMMI TERRELL (above 2)			
9/14/68	32	10		28 **Chained** ...*At Last (I Found A Love)*	$10		Tamla 54170
10/12/68	24	7		29 **Keep On Lovin' Me Honey** ...*You Ain't Livin' Till You're Lovin'*	$10		Tamla 54173
				MARVIN GAYE & TAMMI TERRELL			
11/23/68	1[7]	15		30 **I Heard It Through The Grapevine** RB[7] *You're What's Happening (In The World Today)*	$10		Tamla 54176
2/1/69	30	7		31 **Good Lovin' Ain't Easy To Come By** ...*Satisfied Feelin'*	$10		Tamla 54179
				MARVIN GAYE & TAMMI TERRELL			
4/26/69	4	15		32 **Too Busy Thinking About My Baby** ...RB[6] *Wherever I Lay My Hat (That's My Home)*	$10		Tamla 54181
				first recorded by **The Temptations** on their 1966 album *Gettin' Ready*			
8/23/69	7	12		33 **That's The Way Love Is** ...*Gonna Keep On Tryin' Till I Win Your Love*	$10		Tamla 54185
11/29/69	49	8		34 **What You Gave Me** ...*How You Gonna Keep It (After You Get It)*	$10		Tamla 54187
				MARVIN GAYE & TAMMI TERRELL			
1/10/70	41	7		35 **How Can I Forget /**			
3/7/70	67	6		36 **Gonna Give Her All The Love I've Got** ...	$10		Tamla 54190
4/18/70	50	7		37 **The Onion Song /**			
				Valerie Simpson actually sang the female part on #31, 34 & 37 due to Tammi's poor health			
4/25/70	56	6		38 **California Soul** ...	$10		Tamla 54192
				MARVIN GAYE & TAMMI TERRELL (above 2)			
				all of above Gaye & Terrell titles written (except #23 & 24) and produced (except #20 & 22-24) by **Ashford & Simpson**			
6/13/70	40	7		39 **The End Of Our Road** ...*Me And My Lonely Room*	$10		Tamla 54195
2/20/71	2[3]	15		40 **What's Going On** ...RB[5] *God Is Love*	$8		Tamla 54201
7/3/71	4	12		41 **Mercy Mercy Me (The Ecology)** ...RB[2] *Sad Tomorrows*	$8		Tamla 54207
10/9/71	9	9		42 **Inner City Blues (Make Me Wanna Holler)** ...RB[2] *Wholy Holy*	$8		Tamla 54209
5/20/72	50	5		43 **You're The Man (Part 1)** ...*(Part 2)*	$8		Tamla 54221
12/16/72+	7	12		44 **Trouble Man** ...*Don't Mess With Mister "T"*	$6		Tamla 54228
				title song from the movie starring Robert Hooks			
7/14/73	1[2]	19		45 **Let's Get It On** ...RB[6] *I Wish It Would Rain*	$6		Tamla 54234
10/6/73	12	12		46 **You're A Special Part Of Me** ...*I'm Falling In Love With You*	$6		Motown 1280
				DIANA ROSS & MARVIN GAYE			
11/3/73	21	13		47 **Come Get To This** ...*Distant Lover*	$6		Tamla 54241
1/26/74	50	6		48 **You Sure Love To Ball** ...*Just To Keep You Satisfied*	$6		Tamla 54244
2/23/74	19	16		49 **My Mistake (Was To Love You)** ...*Include Me In Your Life*	$6		Motown 1269
7/13/74	46	9		50 **Don't Knock My Love** ...*Just Say, Just Say*	$6		Motown 1296
				DIANA ROSS & MARVIN GAYE (above 2)			
9/28/74	28	9		51 **Distant Lover** ...*Trouble Man (live)* [L]	$6		Tamla 54253
				studio version is on the B-side of #47 above			
4/24/76	15	13		52 **I Want You** ...RB[1] *(instrumental)*	$5		Tamla 54264
8/14/76	74	5		53 **After The Dance** ...*Feel All My Love Inside*	$5		Tamla 54273
4/16/77	1[1]	18		54 **Got To Give It Up (Pt. I)** ...RB[5] *(Pt. II)* [L]	$5	■	Tamla 54280
				recorded at the London Palladium			
1/20/79	59	8		55 **Pops, We Love You (A Tribute To Father)** ...*(instrumental)*	$5		Motown 1455
				DIANA ROSS, MARVIN GAYE, SMOKEY ROBINSON & STEVIE WONDER			
				song commemorates Berry Gordy Sr.'s death at age 90			
10/30/82+	3	21	▲	56 **Sexual Healing** ...RB[10] *(instrumental)*	$4		Columbia 03302
6/2/01	22	20		57 **Music** ...A:17 / S:31 *(3 versions)* / *Stick 'Em (Cha Cha)*	$6	T	NY.LA 497578
				ERICK SERMON featuring MARVIN GAYE			
				samples **Marvin Gaye**'s "Turn On Some Music" from his 1982 *Midnight Love* album; from the movie *What's The Worst That Could Happen?* starring Martin Lawrence			
				GAYE, Nona R&B/BUB **'92**			
				Born on 9/17/74 in Los Angeles, California. Daughter of **Marvin Gaye**.			
10/10/92	86	6		1 **I'm Overjoyed** ...A:64 *Love Is All You Need For The Future*	$4	▮	Third Stone 98486
8/6/94	72[A]	1		2 **Love Sign** ...			album cut
				NONA GAYE & ♀			
				from the various artists album *1-800-New-Funk* on NPG 71006			

DEBUT	PEAK	WKS	Gold	A-side (Chart Hit)...B-side	$	Sym	Label & Number
	★548★			**GAYLE, Crystal** C&W/AC/LP '77			
				Born Brenda Gail Webb on 1/9/51 in Paintsville, Kentucky; raised in Wabash, Indiana. Sister of country singers **Loretta Lynn**, Jay Lee Webb and Peggy Sue. Charted 52 Country hits, 1970-90.			
				1)Don't It Make My Brown Eyes Blue 2)You And I 3)Half The Way			
6/12/76	71	6		1 **I'll Get Over You** ....CW[1] *High Time*	$5		United Artists 781
8/13/77	2[3]	26	●	2 **Don't It Make My Brown Eyes Blue** CW[4] *It's All Right With Me*	$4		United Artists 1016
2/25/78	52	10		3 **Ready For The Times To Get Better** ....CW[1] *Beyond You*	$4		United Artists 1136
7/29/78	18	18		4 **Talking In Your Sleep** ....CW[2] *Paintin' This Old Town Blue*	$4		United Artists 1214
7/7/79	84	3		5 **When I Dream** ....*Hello I Love You*	$4		United Artists 1288
				remake of Gayle's 1975 album version			
9/29/79	15	16		6 **Half The Way** ....*Room For One More*	$4		Columbia 11087
2/23/80	63	6		7 **It's Like We Never Said Goodbye** ....CW[1] *Don't Go My Love*	$4		Columbia 11198
6/7/80	81	8		8 **The Blue Side** ....*Danger Zone*	$4		Columbia 11270
12/5/81	76	6		9 **The Woman In Me** ....*Crying In The Rain*	$4		Columbia 02523
				all of above produced by Allen Reynolds			
10/9/82+	7	29		10 **You And I** ....CW[1] *All My Life, All My Love* (Rabbitt)	$4		Elektra 69936
				EDDIE RABBITT with CRYSTAL GAYLE			
9/10/83	83	5		11 **Baby, What About You** ....CW[1] *He Is Beautiful To Me*	$4		Warner 29582
12/10/83	84	5		12 **The Sound Of Goodbye** ....CW[1] *Take Me Home*	$4		Warner 29452
				GAYLORDS, The MEM/POP/LP '54			
				Italian-American vocal trio: Ronnie Gaylord (Vincent), Burt Holiday (Bonaldi) and Don Rea. Formed trio while students at the University of Detroit. Had 2 #2 pop hits: "Tell Me You're Mine" in 1953 and "The Little Shoemaker" in 1954.			
11/12/55	67	8		1 **No Arms Can Ever Hold You** ....T:67 *Bring Me A Bluebird*	$12		Mercury 70706
				George Annis (orch.)			
8/18/58	97	1		2 **Ma Ma Ma Marie** ....H:97 *Buona Serra*	$10		Mercury 71337
				from the Italian song "Oh Marie"			
11/10/58	98	1		3 **Flamingo L'Amore** ....*I'm Longin' For Love* [F]	$10		Mercury 71369
				Eddie Chamblee (sax solo); Dick Marx (orch.); Italian version of Duke Ellington's 1941 hit "Flamingo"			
3/6/76	72	6		4 **Eh! Cumpari** ....*The Little Shoemaker* [N]	$6		Prodigal 0622
				GAYLORD & HOLIDAY			
				#2 hit for **Julius LaRosa** in 1953; B-side is a new version of The Gaylords' #2 1954 hit			
				GAYNOR, Gloria R&B/BUB/LP '79			
				Born Gloria Fowles on 9/7/49 in Newark, New Jersey. Dance-disco singer.			
11/2/74+	9	17		1 **Never Can Say Goodbye** ....*We Just Can't Make It*	$5		MGM 14748
3/22/75	60	5		2 **Reach Out, I'll Be There** ....*Searchin'*	$5		MGM 14790
6/28/75	98	1		3 **Walk On By** ....*Real Good People*	$5		MGM 14808
10/25/75	98	2		4 **(If You Want It) Do It Yourself** ....*I'm Still Yours*	$5		MGM 14823
11/29/75	75	5		5 **How High The Moon** ....*My Man's Gone*	$5		MGM 14838
				#1 hit for **Les Paul & Mary Ford** in 1951			
12/16/78+	❶[3]	27	▲	6 **I Will Survive** *Substitute* (#107)	$4		Polydor 14508
9/22/79	42	13		7 **Let Me Know (I Have A Right)** ....*One Number One*	$4		Polydor 2021
				Doc Severinsen (trumpet solo)			
8/17/02	45[S]	3		8 **I Never Knew** ....*(3 remixes) / LP Medley*	$8	★*	Logic 95068
				GAYTEN, Paul R&B/MEM '59			
				Born on 1/29/20 in Kentwood, Louisiana. Died of bleeding ulcers on 3/26/91 (age 71). R&B vocalist/pianist/bandleader. Backup singer on many R&B hits for such artists as **Clarence Henry**, **Annie Laurie** and Bobby Charles.			
12/2/57	68	4		1 **Nervous Boogie** ....T:68 *Flatfoot Sam* (Oscar Wills) [I]	$35		Argo 5277
				PAUL GAYTEN And his Band			
7/21/58	78	2		2 **Windy** ....T:78 *Tickle Toe* [I]	$25		Argo 5300
10/26/59	68	7		3 **The Hunch** ....*Hot Cross Buns* [I]	$25		Anna 1106
				G-CLEFS, The '61			
				R&B vocal group from Roxbury, Massachusetts: brothers Teddy, Chris, Timmy and Arnold Scott, with Ray Gibson.			
7/28/56	24	13		1 **Ka-Ding Dong** ....S:24 / T:53 *Darla, My Darlin'*	$40		Pilgrim 715
				Freddy Cannon (lead guitar)			
9/18/61	9	16		2 **I Understand (Just How You Feel)** ....*Little Girl I Love You*	$20		Terrace 7500
				#6 hit for The Four Tunes in 1954; melody is from "Auld Lang Syne"			
3/10/62	81	5		3 **A Girl Has To Know** ....*(There never was a Dog like) Lad*	$20		Terrace 7503
				G. DEP LP '01			
				Born in Harlem, New York. Male rapper.			
5/26/01	80	9		1 **Let's Get It** ....S:58 / A:74 *(3 versions)*	$6	T	Bad Boy 79383
				THREE THE... G. Dep, P. Diddy & Black Rob			
				samples "Love & Happiness" by **Al Green**			
12/1/01	39[S]	5		2 **Special Delivery** ....*(2 versions) / Child Of The Ghetto*	$6	T	Bad Boy 79409
2/2/02	75[S]	1		3 **Boottee** ....*(3 versions)*	$7	T	Surrender 015631
				BENZINO f/ Fabolous & G-Dep			
				samples "The Bertha Butt Boogie" by **The Jimmy Castor Bunch**			
				GEDDES, David '75			
				Born on 7/1/50 in Michigan. Pop singer.			
8/2/75	4	13		1 **Run Joey Run** ....*Honey Don't Blow It*	$5		Big Tree 16044
11/15/75	18	8		2 **The Last Game Of The Season (A Blind Man In The Bleachers)** ....*Wise Up Girl*	$5		Big Tree 16052
				GEGGY TAH '96			
				Rock trio from Los Angeles, California: singers/multi-instrumentalists Tommy Jordan and Greg Kurstin, with drummer Daren Hahn.			
10/5/96	67[A]	4		**Whoever You Are**			album cut
				from the album *Sacred Cow* on Luaka Bop/Warner 46113			

DEBUT	PEAK	WKS	Gold	A-side (Chart Hit)	B-side	$	Sym	Label & Number

★291★ GEILS, J., Band — BUB/R&B/ROK/LP '82

Rock group from Boston, Massachusetts: Jerome Geils (guitar; born on 2/20/46), **Peter Wolf** (vocals; born on 3/7/46), Magic Dick Salwitz (harmonica; born on 5/13/45), Seth Justman (keyboards; born on 1/27/51), Danny Klein (bass; born on 5/13/46) and Stephen Jo Bladd (drums; born on 7/13/42). Wolf left for a solo career in January 1983.

1)Centerfold 2)Freeze-Frame 3)Must Of Got Lost

DEBUT	PEAK	WKS	Gold	A-side (Chart Hit)	B-side	$	Sym	Label & Number
12/4/71+	39	10		1 **Looking For A Love**	*Whammer Jammer*	$6		Atlantic 2844
3/31/73	30	16		2 **Give It To Me**	*Hold Your Loving*	$6		Atlantic 2953
9/8/73	98	2		3 **Make Up Your Mind**	*Southside Shuffle*	$6	■	Atlantic 2974
11/9/74+	12	11		4 **Must Of Got Lost**	*Funky Judge*	$5		Atlantic 3214
4/17/76	68	6		5 **Where Did Our Love Go**	*What's Your Hurry*	$5		Atlantic 3320
8/20/77	83	3		6 **You're The Only One** *[Geils]*	*Wreckage*	$5		Atlantic 3411
11/18/78+	35	13		7 **One Last Kiss**	*Revenge*	$4	■	EMI America 8007
3/10/79	67	6		8 **Take It Back**	*I Can't Believe You*	$4		EMI America 8012
2/2/80	32	12		9 **Come Back**	*Takin' You Down*	$4		EMI America 8032
4/12/80	38	12		10 **Love Stinks**	*Till The Walls Come Tumblin' Down*	$4	■	EMI America 8039
7/12/80	78	5		11 **Just Can't Wait**	*No Anchovies, Please*	$4		EMI America 8047
11/7/81+	❶[6]	25	●	12 **Centerfold** AR[3]	*Rage In The Cage*	$3	■	EMI America 8102
2/20/82	4	16	●	13 **Freeze-Frame**	*Flamethrower* (R&B #25/ROK #30)	$3	■	EMI America 8108
5/22/82	40	11		14 **Angel In Blue**	*River Blindness*	$3	■	EMI America 8100
11/20/82+	24	14		15 **I Do**	*Sanctuary (live)* [L]	$3	■	EMI America 8148
				original studio version released in 1977 on Atlantic 3454 as by **Geils** with a picture sleeve				
2/26/83	60	6		16 **Land Of A Thousand Dances**	*Jus' Can't Stop Me* [L]	$3		EMI America 8156
11/3/84	63	7		17 **Concealed Weapons**	*Tell 'Em, Jonesy*	$3	■	EMI America 8242
8/10/85	91	2		18 **Fright Night**	*Boppin' Tonight* (Fabulous Fontaines)	$3	■	Private I 05462
				title song from the movie starring Roddy McDowall				

GELDOF, Bob — see BOOMTOWN RATS, The

GENE & DEBBE — BUB '68

Pop duo of **Gene Thomas** and Debbe Neville.

DEBUT	PEAK	WKS	Gold	A-side (Chart Hit)	B-side	$	Sym	Label & Number
				GENE THOMAS:				
10/30/61	53	7		1 **Sometime**	*Every Night*	$12		United Artists 338
				originally released on Venus 1439 in 1961 ($30); "Bubbled Under" (#131) for **Paul Revere And The Raiders** in 1965 as "Sometimes"				
11/16/63+	84	5		2 **Baby's Gone**	*Stand By Love*	$12		United Artists 640
				written by **Roy Orbison** and **Bobby Goldsboro**				
				GENE & DEBBE:				
10/14/67	78	6		3 **Go With Me**	*The Torch I Carry*	$8		TRX 5002
				originally released on San 1519 in 1967 ($15)				
2/17/68	17	16		4 **Playboy**	*I'll Come Running*	$8		TRX 5006
6/29/68	81	4		5 **Lovin' Season**	*Love Will Give Us Wings*	$8		TRX 5010

GENE & EUNICE — R&B '59

Black duo of Forest Gene Wilson (from San Antonio, Texas) and Eunice Levy (from Texarkana, Texas). Gene also recorded as "Gene Forrest." Eunice died on 5/26/2002 (age 71).

DEBUT	PEAK	WKS	Gold	A-side (Chart Hit)	B-side	$	Sym	Label & Number
8/24/59	48	13		**Poco-Loco**	*Go-On Kokomo*	$30		Case 1001

GENE & JERRY — see CHANDLER, Gene / BUTLER, Jerry

GENE LOVES JEZEBEL — ROK/LP '90

Techno-rock group formed in England: twin brothers Jay and Michael Aston (vocals), James Stevenson (guitar), Peter Rizzo (bass) and Chris Bell (drums). Michael Aston left in early 1989.

DEBUT	PEAK	WKS	Gold	A-side (Chart Hit)	B-side	$	Sym	Label & Number
2/6/88	87	3		1 **The Motion Of Love**	*Bugg's Bruises*	$3	■	Geffen 28183
8/18/90	68	10		2 **Jealous** MR[2]	*Last Year*	$3	▮	Geffen 19688

GENERAL PUBLIC — BUB/LP '94

Pop group from Birmingham, England: Dave Wakeling (vocals, guitar), Ranking Roger (vocals, keyboards), Kevin White (guitar), Micky Billingham (keyboards; **Dexys Midnight Runners**), Horace Panter (bass) and Stoker (drums). Wakeling and Roger had been in English Beat. General Public disbanded in March 1987. Wakeling and Roger reunited in 1994.

DEBUT	PEAK	WKS	Gold	A-side (Chart Hit)	B-side	$	Sym	Label & Number
11/17/84+	27	18		1 **Tenderness** S:20 / A:26	*Limited Balance*	$3	■	I.R.S. 9934
4/9/94	22	20		2 **I'll Take You There** A:19 / S:46	*Save It For Later (live)*	$3	▮	Epic Soundtrax 77452
				from the movie *Threesome* starring Lara Flynn Boyle and Stephen Baldwin				
5/6/95	93	3		3 **Rainy Days**	*Blowhard*	$3	▮[V]	Epic 77866
				produced by Jerry Harrison (**Talking Heads**)				

GENESIS ★118★ — ROK/LP '86

Formed as a progressive-rock group in England: **Peter Gabriel** (vocals; born on 2/13/50), Anthony Phillips (guitar), Tony Banks (keyboards; born on 3/27/50), Mike Rutherford (guitar, bass; born on 10/2/50) and Chris Stewart (drums; replaced by John Silver in 1968, then John Mayhew in 1969). Phillips and Mayhew left in 1970, replaced by Steve Hackett (guitar) and **Phil Collins** (drums; born on 1/31/51). Gabriel left in June 1975, with Collins replacing him as new lead singer. Hackett went solo in 1977, leaving group as a trio: Collins, Rutherford and Banks. Added regular members for touring: Americans Chester Thompson (drums), in 1977, and Daryl Stuermer (guitar), in 1978. Collins also recorded in jazz-fusion group Brand X. Rutherford also in own group, **Mike + The Mechanics**, formed in 1985. Hackett later formed group **GTR**. Collins announced his departure from the group in April 1996; Ray Wilson joined as lead singer in June 1997.

1)Invisible Touch 2)In Too Deep 3)Tonight, Tonight, Tonight 4)Throwing It All Away 5)Land Of Confusion

DEBUT	PEAK	WKS	Gold	A-side (Chart Hit)	B-side	$	Sym	Label & Number
3/12/77	62	5		1 **Your Own Special Way**	*In That Quiet Earth'*	$8		Atco 7076
4/22/78	23	16		2 **Follow You Follow Me**	*Inside & Out*	$5		Atlantic 3474
5/24/80	14	18		3 **Misunderstanding**	*Behind The Lines*	$4	■	Atlantic 3662
9/6/80	58	8		4 **Turn It On Again**	*Evidence Of Autumn*	$4		Atlantic 3751
9/26/81	29	18		5 **No Reply At All**	*Dodo*	$4		Atlantic 3858
				features the **Earth, Wind & Fire** horn section				
12/26/81+	26	14		6 **Abacab**	*Who Dunnit?*	$4	■	Atlantic 3891

DEBUT	PEAK	WKS	Gold	A-side (Chart Hit)..........B-side	$	Sym	Label & Number
				GENESIS — Cont'd			
3/20/82	**40**	11		7 **Man On The Corner** .... *Submarine*	$4	■	Atlantic 4025
6/5/82	**32**	14		8 **Paperlate** .... *You Might Recall* (ROK #40)	$4	■	Atlantic 4053
10/1/83	**73**	9		9 **Mama** .... *It's Gonna Get Better* (ROK #16)	$4	■	Atlantic 89770
11/26/83+	**6**	20		10 **That's All!** .... *Second Home By The Sea* (ROK #24)	$4	■	Atlantic 89724
				both a full sleeve and a half sleeve issued showing only "That's All" By Genesis			
3/10/84	**44**	10		11 **Illegal Alien** .... *Turn It On Again (live)*	$4	■	Atlantic 89698
6/16/84	**50**	12		12 **Taking It All Too Hard** .... *Silver Rainbow*	$4	■	Atlantic 89656
				above 4 from the album *Genesis*			
5/31/86	**❶[1]**	17		13 **Invisible Touch** AR[3] A:❶[3] / S:4 *The Last Domino* (ROK #29)	$3	■	Atlantic 89407
8/16/86	**4**	16		14 **Throwing It All Away** .... AC[2] / AR[3] A:2 / S:7 *Do The Neurotic*	$3	■	Atlantic 89372
11/1/86+	**4**	21		15 **Land Of Confusion** .... A:3 / S:5 *Feeding The Fire*	$3	■	Atlantic 89336
2/14/87	**3**	15		16 **Tonight, Tonight, Tonight** .... S:3 / A:3 *In The Glow Of The Night (Part One)*	$3	■	Atlantic 89290
				issued with 2 different picture sleeves: one in color and one in black & white			
4/25/87	**3**	17		17 **In Too Deep** .... AC[3] S:3 / A:3 *I'd Rather Be You*	$3	■	Atlantic 89316
				above 5 from the album *Invisible Touch*			
11/2/91+	**12**	20		18 **No Son Of Mine** .... A:10 / S:31 *Living Forever*	$3	■[V]	Atlantic 87571
2/1/92	**7**	20		19 **I Can't Dance** .... A:11 / S:13 *On The Shoreline*	$3	■[V]	Atlantic 87532
5/2/92	**12**	20		20 **Hold On My Heart** .... AC[5] A:9 / S:41 *Way Of The World*	$3	■[V]	Atlantic 87481
8/1/92	**23**	20		21 **Jesus He Knows Me** .... A:21 / S:72 *Hearts On Fire*	$3	▮	Atlantic 87454
11/7/92+	**21**	20		22 **Never A Time** .... A:22 *Tonight, Tonight, Tonight (live) / Invisible Touch (live)*	$3	▮	Atlantic 87411
				above 5 from the album *We Can't Dance*; all of above written by Collins, Rutherford and Banks			
				GENIES, The '59			
				R&B vocal group from Brooklyn, New York: Roy Hammond (lead), Claude Johnson, Bill Gains, Alexander Faison and Fred Jones. Claude ("Juan") Johnson later teamed with Roland ("Don") Trone as **Don & Juan**.			
3/30/59	**71**	6		**Who's That Knocking** .... *The First Time*	$30		Shad 5002
				GENIUS/GZA — see GZA/GENIUS			
				GENTLE PERSUASION '83			
				Female R&B vocal group.			
2/26/83	**82**	4		**Please Mr. Postman** .... *I Believe In You*	$4		Capitol 5207
				GENTRY, Bobbie C&W/BUB/AC/LP '67			
				Born Roberta Streeter on 7/27/44 in Chickasaw County, Mississippi; raised in Greenwood, Mississippi. Country singer/songwriter/guitarist. Won the 1967 Best New Artist Grammy Award. Married to **Jim Stafford** (1978-79).			
				1)Ode To Billie Joe 2)All I Have To Do Is Dream 3)Fancy			
8/5/67	**❶[4]**	14	●	1 **Ode To Billie Joe** *Mississippi Delta*	$8		Capitol 5950
				also see #10 & 11 below			
11/25/67	**54**	4		2 **Okolona River Bottom Band** .... *Penduli Pendulum*	$6	■	Capitol 2044
4/20/68	**100**	1		3 **Louisiana Man** .... *Courtyard*	$6		Capitol 2147
				#10 Country hit for Rusty & Doug in 1961			
10/26/68	**74**	6		4 **Mornin' Glory** .... *Less Of Me* (C&W #44)	$6		Capitol 2314
				BOBBIE GENTRY & GLEN CAMPBELL			
1/25/69	**36**	9		5 **Let It Be Me** .... *Little Green Apples*	$6		Capitol 2387
				GLEN CAMPBELL AND BOBBIE GENTRY			
11/22/69+	**31**	14		6 **Fancy** .... *Courtyard*	$6		Capitol 2675
2/14/70	**27**	10		7 **All I Have To Do Is Dream** .... *Less Of Me*	$6		Capitol 2745
				BOBBIE GENTRY & GLEN CAMPBELL			
4/11/70	**71**	5		8 **He Made A Woman Out Of Me** .... *Billy The Kid*	$6		Capitol 2788
7/11/70	**81**	6		9 **Apartment 21** .... *Seasons Come, Seasons Go*	$6		Capitol 2849
7/17/76	**54**	6		10 **Ode To Billie Joe** .... *Mississippi Delta* [R]	$5		Capitol 4294
				reissue of #1 above			
7/31/76	**65**	4		11 **Ode To Billy Joe - Main Title** .... *There'll Be Time (Love Theme)* (**Michel LeGrand**) [R]	$5	■	Warner 8210
				new version of #1 & 10 above; from the movie *Ode To Billy Joe* starring Robby Benson			
				GENTRYS, The BUB/LP '65			
				Garage-rock band from Memphis, Tennessee: Larry Raspberry, Jimmy Hart and Bruce Bowles (vocals), Bobby Fisher (guitar), Jimmy Johnson (trumpet), Pat Neal (bass) and Larry Wall (drums). Hart later became a professional wrestling manager, known as "The Mouth of The South."			
9/11/65	**4**	13		1 **Keep On Dancing** *Make Up Your Mind*	$15		MGM 13379
				first released on Youngstown 601 in 1965 ($30)			
1/1/66	**50**	8		2 **Spread It On Thick** .... *Brown Paper Sack* (#101)	$12	■	MGM 13432
5/14/66	**77**	5		3 **Everyday I Have To Cry** .... *Don't Let It Be (This Time)*	$12		MGM 13495
2/7/70	**61**	6		4 **Why Should I Cry** .... *I Need Love*	$6		Sun 1108
4/18/70	**52**	12		5 **Cinnamon Girl** .... *I Just Got The News*	$6		Sun 1114
2/27/71	**97**	2		6 **Wild World** .... *Sunshine*	$6		Sun 1122
				GEORGE, Barbara BUB '62			
				Born on 8/16/42 in New Orleans, Louisiana. R&B singer/songwriter.			
11/13/61+	**3**	19		1 **I Know (You Don't Love Me No More)** .... RB[4] *Love (Is Just A Chance You Take)*	$15		A.F.O. 302
				Melvin Lastie (cornet solo)			
3/31/62	**46**	6		2 **You Talk About Love** .... *Whip O Will*	$12		A.F.O. 304
9/8/62	**96**	1		3 **Send For Me** (If you need some Lovin) .... *Bless You*	$12		Sue 766
				GEORGE, Robin '85			
				Born in Wolverhampton, England. Rock guitarist. Also see **Notorious**.			
4/13/85	**92**	2		**Heartline** .... *The Dangerous Music Story - An Audiobiography*	$4	■	Bronze 99658
				GEORGE & GENE — see JONES, George / PITNEY, Gene			

DEBUT	PEAK	WKS	Gold	A-side (Chart Hit).....B-side	$	Sym	Label & Number
				GEORGIA SATELLITES ROK/LP **'87**			
				Rock group from Atlanta, Georgia: **Dan Baird** (born on 12/12/53) (see #4 below) and Rick Richards (vocals, guitars), Rich Price (bass), and Mauro Magellan (drums). Group disbanded in 1991. Richards joined Izzy Stradlin & The Ju Ju Hounds.			
11/22/86+	2^1	20		1 **Keep Your Hands To Yourself**.....S:❶^1 / A:6 *Can't Stand The Pain*	$3	■	Elektra 69502
3/28/87	86	5		2 **Battleship Chains**.....*Golden Light*	$3	■	Elektra 69497
10/22/88	45	14		3 **Hippy Hippy Shake**.....S:37 *Hand To Mouth*	$3		Elektra 69366
				from the movie *Cocktail* starring Tom Cruise; reissued as the B-side of "Sheila" (not charted) with a picture sleeve on Elektra 69328			
12/5/92+	26	16		4 **I Love You Period**.....S:36 / A:46 *Lost Highway*	$3	▮V	Def American 18724
				DAN BAIRD			
				GEORGIO R&B/LP **'87**			
				Born Georgio Allentini in San Francisco, California. Black dance-funk singer/songwriter/keyboardist/guitarist.			
2/28/87	58	9		1 **Sexappeal**.....*(instrumental)*	$3	■	Motown 1882
8/29/87	96	2		2 **Tina Cherry**.....*Menage A Trois*	$3	■	Motown 1892
12/5/87	59	12		3 **Lover's Lane**.....*I Won't Change*	$3	■	Motown 1906
				GERARD, Danyel **'72**			
				Born Gerard Daniel Kherlakian on 3/7/39 in Paris, France. Pop singer/songwriter.			
6/10/72	78	9		**Butterfly**.....*Let's Love*	$5	■	MGM/Verve 10670
				different version released on Columbia 45468 in 1971 ($6)			
				GERARDO LP **'91**			
				Born Gerardo Mejia on 4/16/65 in Guayaquil, Ecuador; raised in Glendale, California. Latino rapper/actor. Raps in Spanglish (half Spanish, half English). Appeared in the movies *Can't Buy Me Love* and *Colors*. A&R director for Interscope Records.			
2/2/91	7	18	●	1 **Rico Suave**.....S:5 / A:15 *(Spanglish version)*	$3	▮V	Interscope 98871
5/4/91	16	11		2 **We Want The Funk**.....S:22 / A:26 *Fandango*	$3	▮V	Interscope 98815
				samples **Parliament**'s "Tear The Roof Off The Sucker (Give Up The Funk)"; "45" issued for above 2 on Atlantic Oldies/Interscope 94940			
8/24/91	98	2		3 **When The Lights Go Out**.....*(album version)*	$3	▮	Interscope 98734
				GERONIMO, Mic R&B/BUB/LP **'98**			
				Born in Queens, New York. Male rapper.			
2/21/98	70	6		**Nothin' Move But The Money** ...S:62 *Usual Suspects* (w/**DMX**, **Ja Rule**, **The Lox** & Khadafi)	$5	▮	Blunt 4939
				MIC GERONIMO featuring DMX & Black Rob			
				GERRARD, Donny R&B/BUB/AC **'76**			
				Born in Canada. Black lead singer of the pop group **Skylark**.			
3/27/76	87	6		**Words (Are Impossible)**.....*Stand Up*	$5		Greedy 101
	★545★			**GERRY AND THE PACEMAKERS** BUB/LP **'64**			
				Merseybeat pop-rock group from Liverpool, England: Gerry Marsden (vocals, guitar; born on 9/24/42), Leslie Maguire (piano; born on 12/27/41), John Chadwick (bass; born on 5/11/43) and Freddie Marsden (drums; born on 10/23/40). The Marsden brothers had been in skiffle bands; Gerry had own rock band, Mars-Bars. Signed in 1962 by **The Beatles**' manager, Brian Epstein.			
				1)Don't Let The Sun Catch You Crying 2)Ferry Cross The Mersey 3)How Do You Do It?			
5/23/64	4	12		1 **Don't Let The Sun Catch You Crying**.....*Away From You*	$15		Laurie 3251
				reissued in 1970 and "Bubbled Under" (#112)			
7/11/64	9	11		2 **How Do You Do It?**.....*You'll Never Walk Alone*	$15		Laurie 3261
				first released on Laurie 3162 in 1963 ($20); also see the B-side of #3 below			
7/11/64	82	2		3 **I'm The One**.....*How Do You Do It?*	$15		Laurie 3233
				released February 1964 on Laurie 3233 with 2 other B-sides: "You've Got What I Like" and "It's All Right"			
9/26/64	17	9		4 **I Like It**.....*Jambalaya*	$15		Laurie 3271
				first released on Laurie 3196 in 1963 ($20)			
12/12/64+	14	10		5 **I'll Be There**.....*You You You*	$15		Laurie 3279
				written by **Bobby Darin**			
2/6/65	6	11		6 **Ferry Cross The Mersey**.....*Pretend*	$15		Laurie 3284
				some pressings show title as: "Ferry Across The Mersey"			
4/10/65	23	8		7 **It's Gonna Be Alright**.....*Skinny Minnie*	$15		Laurie 3293
				above 2 from the movie *Ferry Cross The Mersey* starring Gerry And The Pacemakers			
6/5/65	48	6		8 **You'll Never Walk Alone**.....*Away From You*	$12		Laurie 3302
				from the musical *Carousel*; first released on Laurie 3218 in 1964 ($20) and as the B-side of #2 above			
8/14/65	68	6		9 **Give All Your Love To Me**.....*You're The Reason* (#117)	$12		Laurie 3313
4/2/66	90	3		10 **La La La**.....*Without You*	$12		Laurie 3337
				all of above (except #2, 4, 5 & 8) written by Gerry Marsden			
9/10/66	28	9		11 **Girl On A Swing**.....*The Way You Look Tonight*	$12		Laurie 3354
				GESTURES, The **'64**			
				Garage-rock band from Mankato, Minnesota: Dale Menten (vocals, guitar), Gus Dewey (guitar), Tom Klugherz (bass) and Bruce Waterson (drums).			
11/14/64	44	8		**Run, Run, Run**.....*It Seems To Me*	$15		Soma 1417
				GETO BOYS, The R&B/BUB/LP **'92**			
				Rap group from Houston, Texas: Richard "**Bushwick Bill**" Shaw (see #2 below), William "**Willie D**" Dennis (see #6 below), Brad "**Scarface**" Jordan, and Collins "DJ Ready Red" Lyaseth (left group in early 1991; replaced by "Big Mike" Barnett). Shaw, a Jamaican-born dwarf, lost his right eye in a shooting on 5/10/91.			
10/5/91+	23	20	●	1 **Mind Playing Tricks On Me**.....S:6 *(2 versions)*	$4	▮	Rap-A-Lot 7241
9/12/92	60^S	5		2 **Ever So Clear**.....*(instrumental) / Call Me Crazy*	$5	▮*	Rap-A-Lot 53807
				BUSHWICK BILL			
3/20/93	75^S	1		3 **Crooked Officer**.....BUB:111 *(2 versions)*	$4	▮	Rap-A-Lot 53818
5/8/93	40	15		4 **Six Feet Deep**.....S:20 / A:49 *(instrumental)*	$4	▮	Rap-A-Lot 53823
				samples "Easy" by the **Commodores** and "What's Going On" by **Marvin Gaye**			
5/4/96	82	7		5 **The World Is A Ghetto**.....S:44 *(radio edit) / Still (2 versions)*	$4	▮	Rap-A-Lot 38544
				GETO BOYS featuring Flaj			
				from the movie *Original Gangstas* starring Fred Williamson			
3/2/02	12^S	12		6 **Dear God**.....*(2 versions) / The Real Freaky Deaky*	$5	★	Relentless 6000
				WILLIE D			
				originally released in 2000 on his *Loved By Few, Hated By Many* album			

DEBUT	PEAK	WKS	Gold	A-side (Chart Hit)..........B-side	$	Sym	Label & Number
				GET WET '81			
				Pop group featuring lead singer Sherri Beachfront.			
4/25/81	39	9		**Just So Lonely**..........*Turn On Your Lights*	$4	■	Boardwalk 02018
				GETZ, Stan BUB/LP '64			
				Born Stan Gayetzsky on 2/2/27 in Philadelphia, Pennsylvania. Died of cancer on 6/6/91 (age 64). Legendary jazz tenor saxophonist. Played with **Stan Kenton** (1944-45), **Jimmy Dorsey** (1945-46), **Benny Goodman** (1946) and **Woody Herman** (1947-49). Leader of the Brazilian-born "Bossa Nova" rage of the 1960s.			
9/29/62	15	16		1 **Desafinado**..........*Theme From Dr. Kildare* (Getz) [I]	$12		Verve 10260
				STAN GETZ/CHARLIE BYRD			
6/6/64	5	12		2 **The Girl From Ipanema**..........AC[2] *Blowin' In The Wind* (Getz - #110)	$10		Verve 10323
				GETZ/GILBERTO (Astrud Gilberto, vocal)			
				1964 Grammy winner: Record of the Year; above 2 written by Brazilian composer Antonio Carlos Jobim			
				GHOSTFACE KILLAH LP '99			
				Born Dennis Coles on 5/9/70 in Brooklyn, New York. Male rapper. Member of **Wu-Tang Clan**. Also see **Raekwon**.			
3/13/99	54S	9		1 **Stand Up**..........*(2 versions) / Pimp Da One U Love*	$4	★	Untertainment 79094
				CHARLI BALTIMORE Featuring Ghostface Killah			
				samples "We Want To Party, Party, Party" and "Me And My Baby Got Our Own Thing Going" both by **Lyn Collins**			
8/5/00	98	1		2 **Cherchez LaGhost**..........S:26 *(2 versions)*	$6	★	Wu-Tang 79464
				samples "Cherchez La Femme" by **Dr. Buzzard's Original "Savannah" Band** and "Jack of Spades" by Boogie Down Productions			
2/9/02	63S	1		3 **Ghost Showers**..........*(2 versions) / Never Be The Same Again* (R&B #65)	$6	★	Epic 79712
				samples "Sunshowers" by **Dr. Buzzard** and "This Is Something For The Radio" by **Biz Markie**			
				GHOST TOWN DJ'S '96			
				DJ rap-dance duo from Atlanta, Georgia: Rodney Terry and Carlton Mahoney.			
7/6/96	31	31		**My Boo**..........A:13 *(5 versions)*	$6	T	So So Def 78358
				GIANT ROK/LP '90			
				Rock group formed in Nashville, Tennessee: brothers Dan (vocals, guitar) and David (drums) Huff, Mike Brignardello (bass) and Alan Pasqua (keyboards).			
9/30/89	56	10		1 **I'm A Believer**..........*No Way Out*	$3		A&M 1454
3/24/90	20	20		2 **I'll See You In My Dreams**..........A:18 / S:22 *Stranger To Me*	$3	▮	A&M 1495
				GIANT STEPS LP '88			
				British pop duo: vocalist Colin Campsie and multi-instrumentalist George McFarlane. Both initially worked together as members of the British band Grand Hotel, then as Quick.			
8/20/88	13	22		1 **Another Lover**..........A:12 / S:13 *Adrenalin*	$3		A&M 1226
1/28/89	58	8		2 **Into You**..........*Give It Up*	$3		A&M 1256
	★273★			**GIBB, Andy** LP '78			
				Born Andrew Roy Gibb on 3/5/58 in Manchester, England. Died of heart failure on 3/10/88 (age 30). Moved to Australia when six months old, then back to England at age nine. Youngest brother of **Barry Gibb**, **Robin Gibb** and Maurice Gibb (the **Bee Gees**). Hosted TV's *Solid Gold* from 1981-82.			
				1)Shadow Dancing 2)I Just Want To Be Your Everything 3)(Love Is) Thicker Than Water			
4/23/77	❶4	31	●	1 **I Just Want To Be Your Everything**..........*In The End*	$4	■	RSO 872
11/5/77+	❶2	29	●	2 **(Love Is) Thicker Than Water**..........*Words And Music*	$4		RSO 883
4/15/78	❶7	25	▲	3 **Shadow Dancing**..........*Let It Be Me*	$4		RSO 893
7/15/78	5	16	●	4 **An Everlasting Love**..........*Flowing Rivers*	$4		RSO 904
10/14/78	9	18	●	5 **(Our Love) Don't Throw It All Away**..........*One More Look At The Night*	$4	■	RSO 911
1/26/80	4	15		6 **Desire**..........*Waiting For You*	$4		RSO 1019
3/29/80	12	13		7 **I Can't Help It**..........*Someone I Ain't* (Gibb)	$4		RSO 1026
				ANDY GIBB AND OLIVIA NEWTON-JOHN			
11/22/80+	15	17		8 **Time Is Time**..........*I Go For You*	$4		RSO 1059
3/14/81	40	8		9 **Me (Without You)**..........*Melody*	$4		RSO 1056
8/15/81	51	8		10 **All I Have To Do Is Dream**..........*Good Feeling* (Gibb)	$4	■	RSO 1065
				ANDY GIBB AND VICTORIA PRINCIPAL ("Pamela Ewing" on TV's *Dallas*)			
				GIBB, Barry — see BEE GEES			
				GIBB, Robin — see BEE GEES			
				GIBBONS, Steve, Band '76			
				Rock group from England: Steve Gibbons (vocals, guitar), Bob Wilson (guitar), Trevor Burton (bass) and Bob Lamb (drums).			
6/5/76	72	4		**Johnny Cool**..........*Strange World*	$5		MCA 40551
	★379★			**GIBBS, Georgia** MEM/POP/BUB/AC '55			
				Born Fredda Gibbons on 8/17/20 in Worcester, Massachusetts. Sang on the *Lucky Strike* radio show from 1937-38. With Hudson-DeLange band, then with Frankie Trumbauer (1940) and Artie Shaw (1942). On the *Garry Moore-Jimmy Durante* radio show in the late '40s, where Moore dubbed her "Her Nibs, Miss Gibbs." Hit #1 in 1952 with "Kiss Of Fire."			
				1)Dance With Me Henry (Wallflower) 2)Tweedle Dee 3)Sweet And Gentle			
1/29/55	2[1]	19	●	1 **Tweedle Dee**..........A:2 / S:3 / J:3 *You're Wrong, All Wrong*	$15		Mercury 70517
3/26/55	❶3	20	●	2 **Dance With Me Henry (Wallflower)** J:❶3 / S:2 / A:3 *Every Road Must Have A Turning*	$15		Mercury 70572
				revised version of **The Midnighters**' #1 1954 R&B hit "Work With Me Annie" and **Etta James**'s #1 1955 R&B hit "The Wallflower"			
7/9/55	12	4		3 **Sweet And Gentle**..........A:12 *Blueberries*	$12		Mercury 70647
				Cuban song ("Me Lo Dijo Adela")			
9/17/55	14	4		4 **I Want You To Be My Baby**..........A:14 / S:22 / T:48 *Come Rain Or Come Shine*	$12		Mercury 70685
				originally recorded by Louis Jordan in 1953 on Decca 28883			
12/3/55	51	12		5 **Goodbye To Rome (Arrivederci Roma)** / T:51			
12/10/55	74	8		6 **24 Hours A Day (365 A Year)**..........T:74	$12		Mercury 70743
3/17/56	36	9		7 **Rock Right**..........T:36 *The Greatest Thing*	$12		Mercury 70811
5/12/56	30	13		8 **Kiss Me Another**..........T:30 *Fool Of The Year*	$12		Mercury 70850
8/18/56	20	16		9 **Happiness Street**..........A:20 / T:25 *Happiness Is A Thing Called Joe*	$12		Mercury 70920
12/8/56	24	7		10 **Tra La La**..........A:24 / T:39 *Morning, Noon And Night*	$12		Mercury 70998
				from the movie *Rock, Rock, Rock* starring Tuesday Weld			

DEBUT	PEAK	WKS	Gold	A-side (Chart Hit)...B-side	$	Sym	Label & Number
				GIBBS, Georgia — Cont'd			
3/16/57	68	3		11 **Silent Lips**...T:68 *Pretty Pretty* Glenn Osser (orch.: #1 & 8-11)	$12		Mercury 71058
6/3/57	92	1		12 **I'm Walking The Floor Over You**...T:92 *Sugar Candy* **Joe Reisman** (orch.); written and popularized in 1941 by Ernest Tubb	$15		RCA Victor 6922
10/6/58	32	5		13 **The Hula Hoop Song**...H:32 / S:42 *Keep In Touch* Hugo Peretti (of **Hugo & Luigi**; orch.: #2-7 & 13)	$12		Roulette 4106
				GIBBS, Terri C&W/LP '81 Born on 6/15/54 in Miami, Florida; raised in Augusta, Georgia. Female country singer/pianist. Blind since birth.			
1/17/81	13	22		1 **Somebody's Knockin'**...*Some Days It Rains All Night Long*	$4		MCA 41309
6/20/81	89	5		2 **Rich Man**...*I Won't Cry In Dallas Anymore*	$4		MCA 51119
	★325★			**GIBSON, Debbie** LP '89 Born on 8/31/70 in Brooklyn, New York; raised in Merrick, Long Island, New York. Pop singer/songwriter/pianist/actress. Playing piano since age five and songwriting since age six. Acted in the Broadway shows *Les Miserables* and *Grease*. *1)Lost In Your Eyes 2)Foolish Beat 3)Out Of The Blue*			
5/9/87	4	28	●	1 **Only In My Dreams**...S:3 / A:3 *(dub version)*	$3	■	Atlantic 89322
10/3/87	4	22		2 **Shake Your Love**...S:4 / A:4 *(dub version)*	$3	■	Atlantic 89187
1/30/88	3	17		3 **Out Of The Blue**...S:3 / A:3 *(dub version)*	$3	■	Atlantic 89129
4/23/88	❶[1]	20		4 **Foolish Beat**...A:❶[2] / S:❶[1] *(instrumental)*	$3	■	Atlantic 89109
8/6/88	22	12		5 **Staying Together**...S:19 / A:26 *(dub version)* all of above from the album *Out Of The Blue*	$3	■	Atlantic 89034
1/21/89	❶[3]	19	●	6 **Lost In Your Eyes** A:❶[3] / S:❶[2] *Silence Speaks (A Thousand Words)*	$3	■	Atlantic 88970
4/1/89	11	13	●	7 **Electric Youth**...S:8 / A:12 *We Could Be Together*	$3	■	Atlantic 88919
6/17/89	17	14		8 **No More Rhyme**...S:15 / A:17 *Over The Wall*	$3	■	Atlantic 88885
9/23/89	71	6		9 **We Could Be Together**...*No More Rhyme (acoustic version)* first released as the B-side of #7 above; above 4 from the album *Electric Youth*	$3	■	Atlantic 88896
11/17/90+	26	12		10 **Anything Is Possible**...A:26 / S:28 *So Close To Forever*	$3	■V	Atlantic 87793
2/6/93	86	5		11 **Losin' Myself**...*(radio mix) / Love Or Lust*	$3	■	Atlantic 87392
	★584★			**GIBSON, Don** C&W/BUB/LP '58 Born on 4/3/28 in Shelby, North Carolina. Country singer/songwriter/guitarist. Joined the *Grand Ole Opry* in 1958. Charted 82 Country hits, 1956-76. *1)Oh Lonesome Me 2)Blue Blue Day 3)Sea Of Heartbreak*			
3/10/58	7	21		1 **Oh Lonesome Me /** CW[8] S:7 / T:8 / A:10			
2/24/58	81	6		2 **I Can't Stop Lovin' You**...T:81 / S:flip	$15		RCA Victor 7133
6/30/58	20	13		3 **Blue Blue Day**...CW[2] A:20 / H:32 / S:32 *Too Soon To Know* originally released in 1957	$15		RCA Victor 7010
9/29/58	46	10		4 **Give Myself A Party /** H:46			
9/29/58	58	10		5 **Look Who's Blue**...H:58	$15		RCA Victor 7330
1/19/59	43	9		6 **Who Cares**...*A Stranger To Me* (C&W #27)	$15		RCA Victor 7437
5/4/59	71	3		7 **Lonesome Old House**...*I Couldn't Care Less*	$15		RCA Victor 7505
8/10/59	85	3		8 **Don't Tell Me Your Troubles**...*Heartbreak Avenue*	$15		RCA Victor 7566
3/7/60	29	11		9 **Just One Time**...*I May Never Get To Heaven*	$15		RCA Victor 7690
8/1/60	72	5		10 **Far, Far Away**...*A Legend In My Time*	$15		RCA Victor 7762
11/14/60	93	4		11 **Sweet Dreams**...*The Same Street* new version of Gibson's 1956 #9 Country hit on MGM 12194 ($30)	$15		RCA Victor 7805
2/13/61	100	1		12 **What About Me**...*The World Is Waiting For The Sunrise* (#108)	$15		RCA Victor 7841
6/19/61	21	14		13 **Sea Of Heartbreak**...*I Think It's Best (To Forget Me)*	$15		RCA Victor 7890
12/4/61	59	4		14 **Lonesome Number One**...*The Same Old Trouble* Gibson wrote all of above (except #13); all produced by **Chet Atkins**	$15		RCA Victor 7959
				GIBSON, Ginny MEM '56 Pop singer on TV's *Your Hit Parade*, 1957-58.			
11/3/56	68	6		**Miracle Of Love**...T:68 *Two Innocent Hearts* **Don Costa** (orch.)	$15		ABC-Paramount 9739
				GIBSON, Johnny BUB '62 Born in Detroit, Michigan. R&B instrumentalist. Also recorded as the Johnny Gibson Trio.			
2/3/62	76	4		**Midnight**...*Chuck-A-Luck* [I]	$20		Big Top 3088
				GIBSON, Steve, And The Red Caps MEM/POP '44 Born on 10/17/14 in Lynchburg, Virginia. Began recording with the Five Red Caps in 1943. The Red Caps: Romaine Brown, Emmett Matthews, Dave Patillo and Jimmy Springs. Gibson's wife **Damita Jo** was featured singer, 1951-53 and 1959-60. Charted 4 Top 10 R&B hits in 1944.			
10/21/57	63	5		**Silhouettes**...T:63 *Flamingo*	$25		ABC-Paramount 9856
				GIBSON BROTHERS LP '79 Dance trio of brothers from the West Indies: Chris (guitar, percussion), Patrick (vocals, drums) and Alex (vocals, keyboards) Gibson.			
6/23/79	81	5		**Cuba**...*(instrumental)*	$5		Island 8832
				GIDEA PARK featuring Adrian Baker '82 Group is actually British singer/producer Adrian Baker.			
1/23/82	82	3		**Seasons Of Gold**...*Lolita* **4 Seasons** medley: Sherry/Big Girls Don't Cry/Walk Like A Man/ I've Got You Under My Skin/Working My Way Back To You/ Opus 17/Dawn/Let's Hang On/The Joy and The Tears/Who Loves You?	$6		Profile 5003
				GIGGLES '92 Born Maria Respeto on 11/6/70 in the Bronx, New York. Female dance singer.			
1/25/92	47	20		**What Goes Around Comes Around**...A:24 *(3 versions)*	$6	■*	Cutting 256
				GILBERTO, Astrud — see GETZ, Stan			

DEBUT	PEAK	WKS	Gold	A-side (Chart Hit)...B-side	$	Sym	Label & Number

GILDER, Nick
LP '78

Born on 11/7/51 in London, England. Moved to Vancouver, British Columbia, Canada, at age 10. Founding member of the rock band **Sweeney Todd**.

DEBUT	PEAK	WKS	Gold	A-side (Chart Hit)...B-side	$	Sym	Label & Number
6/10/78	1[1]	31	▲	1 **Hot Child In The City** ... *Backstreet Noise*	$4		Chrysalis 2226
10/28/78	44	8		2 **Here Comes The Night** ... *Rockaway*	$4	■	Chrysalis 2264
6/16/79	57	6		3 **Rock Me** ... *Got To Get Out*	$4		Chrysalis 2332

GILKYSON, Terry, and The Easy Riders
'57

Folk trio: Terry Gilkyson, Rich Dehr and Frank Miller. Gilkyson died of an aneurysm on 10/15/99 (age 83). Also see **Frankie Laine** and **Dean Martin**.

DEBUT	PEAK	WKS	Gold	A-side (Chart Hit)...B-side	$	Sym	Label & Number
2/2/57	4	19		1 **Marianne** ... J:4 / T:5 / A:5 / S:6 *Goodbye Chiquita* adapted from a Bahamian folk song	$15	■	Columbia 40817
5/27/57	96	2		2 **Tina** ... T:96 *Strollin' Blues* **THE EASY RIDERS**	$12		Columbia 40910

GILL, Johnny
★564★ R&B/BUB/LP '90

Born on 5/22/66 in Washington DC. Sang in family gospel group, Wings Of Faith, from age five. Joined **New Edition** in 1988. His brother Randy and cousin Jermaine Mickey are members of **II D Extreme**. Also see **LSG**.

1)Rub You The Right Way 2)My, My, My 3)Fairweather Friend

DEBUT	PEAK	WKS	Gold	A-side (Chart Hit)...B-side	$	Sym	Label & Number
3/10/84	75	9		1 **Perfect Combination** ... *Heartbreak Look* **STACY LATTISAW & JOHNNY GILL**	$4		Cotillion 99785
5/12/90	3	23	●	2 **Rub You The Right Way** RB[1] A:2 / S:4 *(radio edit w/***C.L. Smooth***)* "45": Motown 1982; B-side: (album version)	$3	▮V	Motown 2045
8/4/90	10	16		3 **My, My, My** ... RB[2] S:9 / A:13 *(no B-side)* **After 7** (backing vocals); "45": Motown 919; B-side: (same as A-side)	$3	▮V	Motown 2033
10/20/90	28	16		4 **Fairweather Friend** ... S:23 / A:33 *(no B-side)*	$3	▮	Motown 2049
3/23/91	84	4		5 **Wrap My Body Tight** ... RB[1] *(Soul mix)* above 4 from the album *Johnny Gill*	$3	▮	Motown 2077
4/25/92	31	17		6 **Silent Prayer** ... A:29 / S:33 *(instrumental)* **SHANICE featuring Johnny Gill** "45": Motown 2169; B-side: "Loving You"	$3	▮V	Motown 2165
10/24/92+	33	19	●	7 **Slow And Sexy** ... S:14 / A:63 *Ting-A-Ling* (Ranks) **SHABBA RANKS (featuring Johnny Gill)**	$3	▮	Epic 74741
5/22/93	56	10		8 **The Floor** ... S:39 / A:45 *(5 album snippets)* **Mint Condition** ("floor" chants)	$3	▮V	Motown 2202
9/21/96	53	18		9 **Let's Get The Mood Right** ... S:28 *(5 album snippets)*	$3	▮	Motown 0510
12/14/96+	43	19		10 **It's Your Body** ... S:16 *(instrumental)* **JOHNNY GILL Featuring Roger Troutman**	$3	▮	Motown 0462

GILL, Vince
C&W/BUB/AC/LP '94

Born on 4/12/57 in Norman, Oklahoma. Country singer/guitarist (charted 53 hits, 1984-02). Member of **Pure Prairie League** from 1979-83. Married to Janis Oliver of the Sweethearts Of The Rodeo from 1980-97. Married **Amy Grant** on 3/10/2000. Also see **Sara Evans**.

DEBUT	PEAK	WKS	Gold	A-side (Chart Hit)...B-side	$	Sym	Label & Number
2/26/94	88	2		1 **Tryin' To Get Over You** ... CW[1] S:56 *Nothing Like A Woman*	$4	▮V	MCA 54706
5/21/94	72	10		2 **Whenever You Come Around** ... S:31 *South Side Of Dixie*	$4	▮V	MCA 54833
11/26/94+	37	21		3 **House Of Love** ... S:38 / A:41 *(remix)* **AMY GRANT with Vince Gill** "45": A&M 0864; B-side: "Good For Me" (Grant)	$3	▮V	A&M 0802
7/4/98	60	13		4 **If You Ever Have Forever In Mind** ... S:40 *Given More Time*	$4	▮V	MCA Nashville 72055
9/2/00	52	20		5 **Feels Like Love** A:46 *When I Look Into Your Heart* (w/**Amy Grant**) from the album *Let's Make Sure We Kiss Goodbye* on MCA 170098; "45": MCA 172168		V	album cut

GILLETTE
LP '95

Born Sandra Gillette on 9/16/73 in Chicago, Illinois. Female rapper.

DEBUT	PEAK	WKS	Gold	A-side (Chart Hit)...B-side	$	Sym	Label & Number
9/10/94+	14	30	●	1 **Short Dick Man** ... S:4 / A:55 *Short Dick (bass mix)* [N] **20 FINGERS featuring GILLETTE** clean version available on Zoo 14193 as "Short Short Man"	$3	▮	SOS/Zoo 14194
3/4/95	42	18		2 **Mr. Personality** ... S:26 / A:67 *(radio mix)* produced by **20 Fingers**	$4	▮	SOS/Zoo 14209

GILLEY, Mickey
C&W/BUB/AC/LP '80

Born on 3/9/36 in Natchez, Mississippi; raised in Ferriday, Louisiana. Country singer/pianist (charted 46 hits, 1968-89). First cousin to both **Jerry Lee Lewis** and TV evangelist Jimmy Swaggart. Co-owner of Gilley's nightclub in Pasadena, Texas, from 1971-89. Gilley and the club were featured in the movie *Urban Cowboy*.

DEBUT	PEAK	WKS	Gold	A-side (Chart Hit)...B-side	$	Sym	Label & Number
6/8/74	50	11		1 **Room Full Of Roses** ... CW[1] *She Called Me Baby* #2 hit for **Sammy Kaye**'s orchestra in 1949	$5		Playboy 50056
5/17/80	22	18		2 **Stand By Me** ... CW[1] *Cotton Eyed Joe* (The Unstrung Heroes) from the movie *Urban Cowboy* starring **John Travolta** and Debra Winger	$4	■	Full Moon 46640
8/16/80	66	7		3 **True Love Ways** ... CW[1] *The More I Turn The Bottle Up* written by **Buddy Holly** and **Norman Petty**	$4		Epic 50876
7/11/81	55	12		4 **You Don't Know Me** ... CW[1] *Jukebox Argument*	$4		Epic 02172

GILMAN, Billy
C&W/LP '00

Born on 5/24/88 in Westerly, Rhode Island; raised in Hope Valley, Rhode Island. Country singer (age 12 in 2000).

DEBUT	PEAK	WKS	Gold	A-side (Chart Hit)...B-side	$	Sym	Label & Number
6/17/00	38	19		1 **One Voice** ... S:8 *'Til I Can Make It On My Own*	$4	★V	Epic 79396
11/11/00+	63	13		2 **Oklahoma** ... S:10 *Warm & Fuzzy* (C&W #50) "45" issued for above 2 on Epic 79527	$4	★V	Epic 79503

GILMER, Jimmy — see FIREBALLS

GILMOUR, David — see PINK FLOYD

GILREATH, James
'63

Born on 11/14/39 in Prairie, Mississippi. Pop singer/songwriter/guitarist.

DEBUT	PEAK	WKS	Gold	A-side (Chart Hit)...B-side	$	Sym	Label & Number
3/23/63	21	12		**Little Band Of Gold** ... *I'll Walk With You*	$15		Joy 274

DEBUT	PEAK	WKS	Gold	A-side (Chart Hit)...B-side	$	Sym	Label & Number
				GILSTRAP, Jim R&B/LP '75			
				Born in Texas. R&B singer.			
3/8/75	55	9		1 **Swing Your Daddy** ... *Pt. 2*	$5		Roxbury 2006
8/16/75	93	3		2 **House Of Strangers** ... *Take Your Daddy For A Ride*	$5		Roxbury 2013
10/25/75	78	8		3 **I'm On Fire** ... *Pt. II*	$5		Roxbury 2016
				GINA G '97			
				Born Gina Gardiner in 1971 in Australia. Female dance singer.			
11/30/96+	12	30		1 **Ooh Aah...Just A Little Bit** ... A:10 / S:22 *(contest version)*	$3	▮V	Eternal/Warner 17455
6/14/97	46	11		2 **Gimme Some Love** ... A:40 *(Eurobeat mix)*	$3	▮V	Eternal/Warner 17355
				GINA GO-GO '89			
				Born Gina Gomez in London, England. Female dance singer.			
2/25/89	78	11		**I Can't Face The Fact** ... *(TV track)*	$3		Capitol 44233
				GIN BLOSSOMS ROK/LP '96			
				Alternative-rock group from Tempe, Arizona: Robin Wilson (vocals), Jesse Valenzuela and Scott Johnson (guitars), Bill Leen (bass) and Phillip Rhodes (drums). Early guitarist Doug Hopkins, writer of "Hey Jealousy" and "Found Out About You," died of a self-inflicted gunshot wound on 12/5/93 (age 32).			
7/24/93	25	22		1 **Hey Jealousy** ... S:28 / A:31 *29*	$4	▮V	A&M 0242
11/20/93+	25	34		2 **Found Out About You** ... MR[1] A:14 *Hands Are Tied*	$4	▮V	A&M 0418
				"45" issued for above 2 on A&M 0418			
5/14/94	21[A]	43		3 **Until I Fall Away** ...		V	album cut
10/22/94	24[A]	20		4 **Allison Road** ...		V	album cut
				"45" issued for above 2 on A&M 0862; above 4 from the album *New Miserable Experience* on A&M 5403			
2/10/96	9	46		5 **Follow You Down /** A:7 / S:45			
2/10/96	11	46		6 **Til I Hear It From You** ... A:8 / S:49	$3	▮V	A&M 1380
				from the movie *Empire Records* starring Anthony LaPaglia			
8/17/96	75	8		7 **As Long As It Matters** ... *Allison Road (live)*	$3	▮V	A&M 1672
				GINO & GINA '58			
				Brother-sister pop vocal duo from Brooklyn, New York: Aristedes and Irene Giosasi. Aristedes co-wrote "Sorry (I Ran All The Way Home)."			
5/19/58	20	12		**(It's Been A Long Time) Pretty Baby** ... A:20 / T:34 / S:39 *Love's A Carousel*	$20		Mercury 71283
				some pressings show title only as "Pretty Baby"			
	★371★			**GINUWINE** R&B/BUB/LP '01			
				Born Elgin Lumpkin on 10/15/75 in Washington DC. Male R&B singer/songwriter.			
				1)Differences 2)I Need A Girl (Part Two) 3)Pony			
9/7/96	6	27	▲	1 **Pony** ... RB[2] S:4 / A:24 *(3 versions)*	$3	▮	550 Music 78373
3/29/97	55[A]	10		2 **Tell Me Do U Wanna** ...			album cut
				above 2 from the album *Ginuwine...The Bachelor* on 550 Music 67685			
8/29/98	67[A]	10		3 **Same Ol' G** ...			album cut
				from the movie *Dr. Dolittle* starring **Eddie Murphy** (soundtrack on Blackground 83113)			
2/20/99	49	19		4 **What's So Different?** ... A:32			album cut
7/17/99	16	20		5 **So Anxious** ... A:10			album cut
				Playa (backing vocals)			
12/11/99+	48	15		6 **None Of Ur Friends Business** ... A:43			album cut
				above 4 from the album *100% Ginuwine* on 550 Music 69598			
1/8/00	77	12		7 **The Best Man I Can Be** ... A:67			album cut
				GINUWINE, R.L., TYRESE, CASE			
				from the movie *The Best Man* starring Taye Diggs (soundtrack on Columbia 69924)			
3/25/00	59	16		8 **You Owe Me** ... A:49			album cut
				NAS (Featuring Ginuwine)			
				from the album *Nastradamus* on Columbia 63930			
4/7/01	66	10		9 **There It Is** ... A:60		V	album cut
7/28/01	4	30		10 **Differences** RB[4] A:4 / S:63 *(4 versions)*	$4	★V	Epic 79711
				above 2 from the album *The Life* on Epic 69622; and both on "45": Epic 79664			
12/15/01+	45	20		11 **Take Away** ... A:44			album cut
				MISSY "MISDEMEANOR" ELLIOTT (feat. Ginuwine & introducing Tweet)			
				from Elliott's album *Miss E...So Addictive* on Goldmind 62639			
6/8/02	4	26		12 **I Need A Girl (Part Two)** ... A:4 / S:17 *(instrumental) / So Complete*	$6	T	Bad Boy 79441
				P. DIDDY AND GINUWINE Featuring Loon, Mario Winans & Tammy Ruggeri			
8/3/02	33	20		13 **Stingy** ... A:32 *Hell Yeah*	$4	★	Epic 79772
				from the movie *Barbershop* starring **Ice Cube**			
10/19/02	77	7		14 **Crush Tonight** ... S:32 *(2 versions) / It's Nothing* (w/Tony Sunshine)	$6	T	Atlantic 85402
				FAT JOE Featuring Ginuwine			
				GIORGIO — see MORODER, Giorgio			
				GIRLFRIENDS, The '64			
				Female R&B vocal trio from Los Angeles, California: Gloria Goodson, Nannette Jackson and Carolyn Willis (**Bob B. Soxx & The Blue Jeans**, **The Honey Cone**).			
12/28/63+	49	7		**My One And Only, Jimmy Boy** ... *For My Sake*	$25		Colpix 712
				written by **David Gates** of **Bread**			
				GIUFFRIA ROK/LP '85			
				Rock group from California: Gregg Giuffria (keyboards; **Angel**), David Glen Eisley (vocals), Craig Goldy (guitar), Chuck Wright (**Quiet Riot**; bass) and Alan Krigger (drums). Lanny Cordola (**Ozzy Osbourne**'s band) and David Sikes replaced Goldy and Wright in late 1985. Giuffria, Wright and Cordola joined **House Of Lords** in 1988.			
11/10/84+	15	19		1 **Call To The Heart** ... S:12 / A:25 *Out Of The Blue (Too Far Gone)*	$3	■	MCA/Camel 52497
3/23/85	57	8		2 **Lonely In Love** ... *Do Me Right*	$3	■	MCA/Camel 52558
5/3/86	52	10		3 **I Must Be Dreaming** ... *Tell It Like It Is*	$3		MCA/Camel 52794
				GLADIOLAS, The — see WILLIAMS, Maurice, & The Zodiacs			

DEBUT	PEAK	WKS	Gold	A-side (Chart Hit)...B-side	$	Sym	Label & Number
				GLADSTONE '72			
				Pop group from Tyler, Texas: H.L. Voelker (vocals), Michael Rabon and Doug Rhone (guitars), Jerry Scheff (bass) and Ron Tutt (drums). Rabon was leader of **The Five Americans**.			
8/26/72	45	11		**A Piece Of Paper** ...*Livin' In The Country*	$6		ABC 11327
				GLAHÉ, Will, and His Orchestra MEM/POP '39			
				Born on 2/12/02 in Elberfeld, Germany. Died on 11/21/89 (age 87). Accordionist/composer/conductor. Hit #1 hit in 1939 with "Beer Barrel Polka."			
11/18/57	16	23		1 **Liechtensteiner Polka** ...S:16 / A:18 / T:19 *Schweizer Kanton-Polka* [F]	$12		London 1755
4/7/58	91	1		2 **Sweet Elizabeth** ...T:91 *Tavern In The Town* [F]	$10		London 1788
				GLASER BROTHERS, Tompall & The C&W/BUB '69			
				Country vocal trio from Spalding, Nebraska: brothers Tompall (born on 9/3/33), Chuck and Jim Glaser. All three have had solo hits on the country charts.			
4/5/69	92	4		**California Girl (And The Tennessee Square)** ...*All That Keeps Ya Goin'*	$7		MGM 14036
				GLASS BOTTLE, The BUB '71			
				Pop group from New Jersey: Gary Criss (male vocals), Carol Denmark (female vocals), Dennis Dees (guitar), Charles Moore (keyboards) and Jon Melia (drums).			
7/17/71	36	13		1 **I Ain't Got Time Anymore** ...*Things*	$7		Avco Embassy 4575
12/4/71	87	2		2 **The Girl Who Loved Me When** ...*Because She's Mine Again*	$7		Avco 4584
				THE GLASS BOTTLE featuring GARY CRISS			
				above 2 produced by novelty artist **Dickie Goodman**			
				GLASS HOUSE, The R&B/BUB '69			
				R&B vocal group from Detroit, Michigan: Larry Mitchell, Pearl Jones, Scherrie Payne, Ty Hunter and Eric Dunham. Hunter (born in 1943; died on 2/24/81) was in **The Originals**. Payne was in **The Supremes** and is the sister of **Freda Payne**.			
10/18/69	59	9		1 **Crumbs Off The Table** ...*Bad Bill Of Goods*	$7		Invictus 9071
7/18/70	90	5		2 **I Can't Be You (You Can't Be Me)** ...*He's In My Life*	$7		Invictus 9076
				GLASS MOON BUB/LP '82			
				Pop-rock group: Dave Adams (vocals, keyboards), Jaime Glaser (guitar), Nestor Nunez (bass) and Chris Jones (drums).			
3/13/82	50	7		**On A Carousel** ...*She Was Magic*	$5		Radio Records 4022
				GLASS TIGER LP '86			
				Pop-rock group from Canada: Alan Frew (vocals), Al Connelly (guitar), Sam Reid (keyboards), Wayne Parker (bass) and Michael Hanson (drums).			
7/12/86	2^1	24		1 **Don't Forget Me (When I'm Gone)** ...S:❶[1] / A:6 *Ancient Evenings*	$3	■	Manhattan 50037
				Bryan Adams (response vocal)			
11/1/86+	7	21		2 **Someday** ...S:7 / A:7 *Vanishing Tribe*	$3	■	Manhattan 50048
2/28/87	34	11		3 **I Will Be There** ...A:28 / S:37 *Do You Wanna Dance (With Me)*	$3	■	Manhattan 50066
4/9/88	31	11		4 **I'm Still Searching** ...S:26 / A:30 *Suffer In Silence*	$3	■	EMI-Manhattan 50116
				GLAZER, Tom LP '63			
				Born on 9/3/14 in Philadelphia, Pennsylvania. Died on 2/21/2003 (age 88). Novelty folk singer. Hosted own ABC radio program, 1945-47. Composed score for the 1957 movie *A Face In The Crowd*.			
6/1/63	14	9		**On Top Of Spaghetti** ...*Battle Hymn Of The Children* [N]	$8	■	Kapp 526
				TOM GLAZER AND THE DO-RE-MI CHILDREN'S CHORUS			
				parody of the traditional folk song "On Top Of Old Smokey"			
				GLEASON, Jackie, and His Orchestra MEM/LP '55			
				Born Herbert John Gleason on 2/26/16 in Brooklyn, New York. Died of cancer on 6/24/87 (age 71). Legendary movie and TV comedian. Father of actress Linda Miller. Grandfather of actor Jason Patric. From 1953-56, had 11 consecutive Top 10 hit albums of lushly-recorded orchestral "mood music."			
11/12/55	50	9		**Autumn Leaves** ...T:50 *Oo! What You Do To Me* [I]	$12		Capitol 3223
				Bobby Hackett (trumpet solo)			
				GLENCOVES, The '63			
				Folk trio from Long Island, New York: singers/guitarists Don Connors and Bill Byrne, with singer Brian Bolger.			
6/15/63	38	9		**Hootenanny** ...*It's Sister Ginny's Turn To Throw The Bomb*	$10		Select 724
				Hootenanny: an exuberant folk-music gathering and the name of an ABC-TV series 1963-64			
				GLITTER, Gary LP '72			
				Born Paul Gadd on 5/8/44 in Banbury, Oxfordshire, England. Glam-rock singer. Backing band is **The Glitter Band** (see #3 below).			
7/22/72	7	11		1 **Rock And Roll Part 2** ...*Part 1* [I]	$6		Bell 45,237
				tune has become "The Sports Anthem" ("The Hey Song") across the USA; also see **The Timelords**' "Doctorin' The Tardis"			
11/4/72	35	9		2 **I Didn't Know I Loved You (Till I Saw You Rock And Roll)** ...*Shakey Sue*	$5		Bell 45,276
11/6/76	91	6		3 **Makes You Blind** ...*People Like You And People Like Me* [I]	$5		Arista 0207
				THE GLITTER BAND			
				GLORIES, The BUB '67			
				Female R&B vocal trio from Harlem, New York: Francis Yvonne Gearing, Betty Stokes and Mildred Vaney.			
6/17/67	74	5		**I Stand Accused (Of Loving You)** ...*Wish They Could Write A Song*	$15		Date 1553
				GOANNA LP '83			
				Rock group from Australia: Shane Howard (vocals), Warrick Harwood and Graham Davidge (guitars), Peter Coughlan (bass) and Robert Ross (drums).			
6/11/83	71	7		**Solid Rock** ...*Four Weeks Gone*	$4	■	Atco 99895
				GODDESS '92			
				Female dance singer from Amsterdam, Netherlands. Former backing singer for **Joe Cocker** and **Falco**.			
12/12/92	74	10		**Sexual** ...A:73 *(instrumental)*	$3	▮	Big Beat 98457
				GODLEY & CREME LP '85			
				Duo from Manchester, England: Kevin Godley (born on 10/7/45) and Lol Creme (born on 9/19/47). Both were members of **Hotlegs** and **10cc**.			
7/20/85	16	17		**Cry** ...A:15 / S:16 *Love Bombs*	$4	■	Polydor 881786

DEBUT	PEAK	WKS	Gold	A-side (Chart Hit)	B-side	$	Sym	Label & Number

GODSPELL — LP '72

The original cast from the Broadway rock musical *Godspell*.

DEBUT	PEAK	WKS	Gold	A-side (Chart Hit)	B-side	$	Sym	Label & Number
5/20/72	13	14		Day By Day original cast member Robin Lamont (lead vocal)	*Bless The Lord*	$6		Bell 45,210

GOFFIN, Louise — AC/LP '79

Born in Brooklyn, New York. Pop singer/songwriter. Daughter of one of pop music's most prolific songwriting teams, Gerry Goffin and **Carole King**.

DEBUT	PEAK	WKS	Gold	A-side (Chart Hit)	B-side	$	Sym	Label & Number
8/18/79	43	9		Remember (Walking In The Sand)	*Trapeze*	$5		Asylum 46521

GO-GO'S — ROK/BUB/LP '82

Female rock group formed in Los Angeles, California: **Belinda Carlisle** (vocals), **Jane Wiedlin** (guitar), Charlotte Caffey (guitar), Kathy Valentine (bass) and Gina Schock (drums). Disbanded in 1984. Reunited briefly in 1990 and again in 1994. Caffey formed **The Graces** in 1989.

DEBUT	PEAK	WKS	Gold	A-side (Chart Hit)	B-side	$	Sym	Label & Number
8/29/81	20	30		1 Our Lips Are Sealed	*Surfing and Spying*	$5	■	I.R.S. 9901
1/30/82	2^{3}	19	●	2 We Got The Beat	*Can't Stop The World*	$5	■	I.R.S. 9903
7/3/82	8	14		3 Vacation	*Beatnik Beach*	$5	■	I.R.S. 9907
9/25/82	50	9		4 Get Up And Go issued with a regular picture sleeve and a sleeve with a cut-out center hole and the words: "the Go-Go's"	*Speeding*	$5	■	I.R.S. 9910
3/17/84	11	16		5 Head Over Heels	*Good For Gone*	$5	■	I.R.S. 9926
6/16/84	32	14		6 Turn To You	*I'm With You*	$5	■	I.R.S. 9928
9/22/84	84	3		7 Yes Or No	*Mercenary*	$5		I.R.S. 9933

GOLD, Andrew — LP '77

Born on 8/2/51 in Burbank, California. Pop-rock singer/songwriter. Son of soundtrack composer Ernest Gold (*Exodus*) and singer Marni Nixon. Session and arranging work for **Linda Ronstadt** since the early 1970s. In pop duo **Wax** in 1986.

DEBUT	PEAK	WKS	Gold	A-side (Chart Hit)	B-side	$	Sym	Label & Number
1/3/76	68	5		1 That's Why I Love You	*A Note From You*	$5		Asylum 45286
3/19/77	7	21		2 Lonely Boy **Linda Ronstadt** (backing vocal)	*Must Be Crazy*	$5	■	Asylum 45384
2/11/78	25	15		3 Thank You For Being A Friend song later adapted as the theme for the TV series *The Golden Girls* starring Bea Arthur and Betty White	*Still You Linger On*	$5		Asylum 45456
6/17/78	67	8		4 Never Let Her Slip Away	*Genevieve*	$5	■	Asylum 45489

GOLDE, Frannie — '79

Born in Chicago, Illinois. Pop singer/songwriter.

DEBUT	PEAK	WKS	Gold	A-side (Chart Hit)	B-side	$	Sym	Label & Number
7/7/79	76	3		Here I Go (Fallin' In Love Again)	*Tell Me What's Goin' On*	$4		Portrait 70031

GOLDEN EARRING — ROK/BUB/LP '83

Rock group from The Hague, Holland: Barry Hay (vocals), George Kooymans (guitar), Rinus Gerritsen (bass) and Cesar Zuiderwijk (drums).

DEBUT	PEAK	WKS	Gold	A-side (Chart Hit)	B-side	$	Sym	Label & Number
5/11/74	13	20		1 Radar Love	*Just Like Vince Taylor*	$6		Track/MCA 40202
10/19/74	91	4		2 Candy's Going Bad	*She Flies On Strange Wings*	$5		Track/MCA 40309
11/27/82+	10	27		3 Twilight Zone AR[1]	*King Dark*	$4		21 Records 103
4/23/83	79	4		4 The Devil Made Me Do It	*Chargin' Up My Batteries*	$4		21 Records 108
3/24/84	76	4		5 When The Lady Smiles	*Orwell's Year*	$4	■	21 Records 112

GOLDFINGER — ROK/LP '96

Rock group from Santa Monica, California: John Feldman (vocals, guitar), Charlie Paulson (guitar), Simon Williams (bass) and Darrin Pfeiffer (drums).

DEBUT	PEAK	WKS	Gold	A-side (Chart Hit)	B-side	$	Sym	Label & Number
4/6/96	47^{A}	17		Here In Your Bedroom from the album *Goldfinger* on Mojo 53007				album cut

GOLDSBORO, Bobby ★177★ — BUB/AC/C&W/LP '68

Born on 1/18/41 in Marianna, Florida. Pop singer/songwriter/guitarist. To Dothan, Alabama, in 1956. Toured with **Roy Orbison**, 1962-64. Own syndicated TV show from 1972-75, *The Bobby Goldsboro Show*.

1)Honey 2)See The Funny Little Clown 3)Watching Scotty Grow 4)Little Things 5)Autumn Of My Life

DEBUT	PEAK	WKS	Gold	A-side (Chart Hit)	B-side	$	Sym	Label & Number
12/22/62+	70	7		1 Molly	*Honey Baby*	$15		Laurie 3148
1/11/64	9	13		2 See The Funny Little Clown	*Hello Loser*	$10		United Artists 672
4/18/64	39	8		3 Whenever He Holds You	*If She Was Mine*	$10	■	United Artists 710
8/8/64	74	6		4 Me Japanese Boy I Love You	*Everyone But Me*	$10		United Artists 742
1/23/65	13	12		5 Little Things	*I Can't Go On Pretending*	$10		United Artists 810
5/1/65	27	11		6 Voodoo Woman	*It Breaks My Heart*	$10		United Artists 862
9/25/65	60	8		7 If You've Got A Heart /				
8/21/65	75	5		8 If You Wait For Love		$8		United Artists 908
12/18/65+	53	7		9 Broomstick Cowboy	*Ain't Got Time For Happy*	$8		United Artists 952
2/19/66	23	8		10 It's Too Late	*I'm Goin' Home*	$8		United Artists 980
5/14/66	56	5		11 I Know You Better Than That	*When Your Love Has Gone*	$8	■	United Artists 50018
9/3/66	70	5		12 It Hurts Me	*Pity The Fool*	$8		United Artists 50056
12/10/66+	35	9		13 Blue Autumn all of above produced by Jack Gold	*I Just Don't Love You Anymore*	$8		United Artists 50087
3/23/68	1^{5}	15	●	14 Honey CW[3] / AC[2] written by **Bobby Russell**	*Danny*	$7		United Artists 50283
6/29/68	19	9		15 Autumn Of My Life	*She Chased Me*	$7	■	United Artists 50318
10/26/68	36	8		16 The Straight Life	*Tomorrow Is Forgotten*	$7		United Artists 50461
12/14/68	11^{X}	3		17 A Christmas Wish	*Look Around You (It's Christmas Time)* [X]	$7		United Artists 50470
2/8/69	61	6		18 Glad She's A Woman	*Letter To Emily*	$7		United Artists 50497

DEBUT	PEAK	WKS	Gold	A-side (Chart Hit)...B-side	$	Sym	Label & Number
				GOLDSBORO, Bobby — Cont'd			
4/19/69	46	10		19 **I'm A Drifter** ...*Hoboes And Kings*	$7		United Artists 50525
8/16/69	53	9		20 **Muddy Mississippi Line** ...*Richer Man Than I*	$7		United Artists 50565
1/10/70	78	5		21 **Mornin Mornin** ...*Requiem*	$7		United Artists 50614
4/4/70	75	6		22 **Can You Feel It** ...*Time Good, Time Bad*	$7		United Artists 50650
12/26/70+	11	13		23 **Watching Scotty Grow**...AC[6] *Water Color Days* written by **Mac Davis**	$7		United Artists 50727
5/8/71	83	6		24 **And I Love You So**...*The Gentle Of A Man*	$7		United Artists 50776
7/24/71	69	6		25 **Come Back Home** ...*I'll Remember You*	$6		United Artists 50807
9/16/72	94	5		26 **With Pen In Hand** ...*Southern Fried Singin' Sunday Mornin'*	$6		United Artists 50938
8/25/73	21	14		27 **Summer (The First Time)**...*Childhood -- 1949* all of above written by Goldsboro (except #1, 4, 14, 16, 18, 21, 23 & 24); Goldsboro's musical conductors and arrangers: **Burt Bacharach** (#4), Chuck Cochran (#24, 25), Arnie Goland (#8), **Bill Justis** (#5-7, 9-13), **Billy Mure** (#1), Garry Sherman (#2, 3), Timmy Tappan (#27) and Don Tweedy (#14-23, 26)	$6	■	United Artists 251
				GOMM, Ian ROK/LP '79 Born on 3/17/47 in Ealing, London, England. Pop-rock singer/songwriter/guitarist.			
9/1/79	18	12		**Hold On** ...*Another Year*	$6		Stiff/Epic 50747
				GONE ALL STARS '58 Instrumental rock and roll-R&B studio band arranged by record company mogul George Goldner.			
2/24/58	30	9		**"7-11"** ...S:30 / T:31 *Down Yonder Rock* [I] rock version of the **Perez Prado** tune "Mambo No. 5"	$30		Gone 5016
				GONZALEZ LP '79 Disco group formed in London, England: Linda Taylor and Alan Marshall (vocals), Jim Cansfield (guitar), Roy Davies (keyboards), Bobby Stignac (percussion), Mick Eve, Chris Mercer, Bud Beadle, Colin Jacas, Ron Carthy and Martin Drover (horn section), Hugh Bullen (bass) and Sergio Castillo (drums).			
1/6/79	26	12		**Haven't Stopped Dancing Yet**...*Just Let It Lay* a different version "Bubbled Under" on 11/18/78 on Capitol 4647 (#106; B-side: "Baby, Baby, Baby")	$5		Capitol 4674
				GOOD BAD UGLY '02 Rap trio from Sugarland, Texas: Bucko-5 ("Good"), Big J ("Bad") and Tony Mac ("Ugly").			
8/31/02	8[S]	13		**Over The Years** ...*(instrumental) / Drop To The Floor*	$8	★*	Paper Down 80042
				GOOD CHARLOTTE ROK/LP '03 Rock group from Waldorf, Maryland: twin brothers Joel (vocals) and Benji (guitar) Madden, with Billy Martin (guitar), Paul Thomas (bass) and Aaron (drums).			
12/14/02+	20	20		**Lifestyles Of The Rich And Famous** ...A:20 from the album *The Young And The Hopeless* on Daylight 86486			album cut
				GOODEES, The '69 Female pop vocal trio from Memphis, Tennessee: Judy Williams, Kay Evans and Sandra Johnson.			
12/21/68+	46	11		**Condition Red** ...*Didn't Know Love Was So Good* tune is similar to "Leader Of The Pack" by **The Shangri-Las**	$10		Hip 8005
				GOODFELLAZ R&B/BUB '97 R&B vocal trio from Brooklyn, New York: Angel Vasquez, DeLouie Avant and Ray Vencier.			
12/14/96+	64	10		**Sugar Honey Ice Tea**...S:52 *(instrumental)* Kahron (rap)	$3	▮	Avatar/Polydor 581914
				GOODIE MOB R&B/BUB/LP '95 Male rap group from Atlanta, Georgia: **Cee-Lo**, Khujo, T-Mo and Big Gipp.			
11/19/94	75[S]	1		1 **Git Up, Git Out** ...BUB:109 *(instrumental)* **OUTKAST (featuring The Goodie Mob)**	$4	▮	LaFace 24085
10/14/95	39	20		2 **Cell Therapy** S:14 *(instrumental) / Soul Food / Benz Or Beamer* (**Outkast**)	$3	▮[V]	LaFace 24113
3/30/96	64	9		3 **Soul Food**...S:36 *(instrumental)* "45" issued for above 2 on LaFace 24145	$3	▮[V]	LaFace 24145
8/31/96	92	3		4 **Dirty South**...S:57 *What Chu Know*	$3	▮	LaFace 24173
6/27/98	50	15		5 **Black Ice (Sky High)** ...S:31 *(**Goodie Mob** version) / (instrumental)* **GOODIE MOB featuring Outkast** clean version available on LaFace 24332	$3	▮	LaFace 24337
1/30/99	73	10		6 **Watch For The Hook** ...S:20 *(instrumental)* **COOL BREEZE Featuring OutKast, Goodie Mob & Witchdoctor** samples **Neil Young**'s "Southern Man" performed by **Merry Clayton**	$4	★	Organized Noize 97046
				GOODIES, The '75 Comedy trio from England: Graeme Garden, Tim Brooke-Taylor and Bill Oddie. Had own show on BBC-TV from 1970-81.			
5/3/75	79	4		**The Funky Gibbon** ...*The Inbetweenies* [N]	$6		20th Century 2189
				GOODMAN, Benny — see CLOONEY, Rosemary			
	★429★			**GOODMAN, Dickie** BUB/LP '56 Born Richard Goodman on 4/19/34 in Brooklyn, New York. Died of a self-inflicted gunshot on 11/6/89 (age 55). Goodman and partner Bill Buchanan originated the novelty "break-in" recordings featuring bits of the original versions of Top 40 hits interwoven throughout the recording (all of the hits listed below are "break-in" records). Goodman was also a comedy writer for Jackie Mason and head of music department at 20th Century Fox. Buchanan died of cancer on 8/1/96 (age 66). Also see the following artists for other "break-in" hits: **Audrey**, **The Delegates**, **Grand Canyon**, **John & Ernest**, **Mickey Shorr**, **Spencer & Spencer** and **Vik Venus**. *1)The Flying Saucer (Parts 1 & 2) 2)Mr. Jaws 3)Flying Saucer The 2nd*			
				BUCHANAN and GOODMAN:			
8/4/56	3	13	●	1 **The Flying Saucer Parts 1 & 2** S:3 / T:7 / A:9 / J:9 [N] originally titled "Back To Earth" on Luniverse 101 ($200)	$60		Luniverse 101
11/17/56	80	1		2 **Buchanan and Goodman On Trial**...T:80 *Crazy* [N]	$50		Luniverse 102
7/22/57	18	13		3 **Flying Saucer The 2nd** ...S:18 / T:19 *Martian Melody* (Martian Symphony Orch.) [N]	$50		Luniverse 105

DEBUT	PEAK	WKS	Gold	A-side (Chart Hit)...B-side	$	Sym	Label & Number
				GOODMAN, Dickie — Cont'd			
12/9/57	85	5		4 **The Creature (From A Science Fiction Movie)**....T:85 *Meet The Creature* [N]	$50		Flying Saucer 501
				BUCHANAN and ANCELL			
12/23/57	32	5		5 **Santa And The Satellite (Parts I & II)**....T:32 / S:36 [X-N]	$50		Luniverse 107
				disc jockey Paul Sherman (narration)			
				DICKIE GOODMAN:			
2/20/61	60	7		6 **The Touchables**....*Martian Melodies* [N]	$25		Mark-X 8009
4/24/61	42	6		7 **The Touchables In Brooklyn**....*Mystery* [N]	$25		Mark-X 8010
12/25/61	99	1		8 **Santa & The Touchables**....*North Pole Rock* [X-N]	$30		Rori 701
				above 3 inspired by the TV series *The Untouchables* starring Robert Stack			
7/14/62	44	6		9 **Ben Crazy**....*Flip Side* [N]	$20		Diamond 119
				first released on JMD 001 in 1962 ($25); inspired by the TV series *Ben Casey* starring **Vincent Edwards**			
5/28/66	70	3		10 **Batman & His Grandmother**....*Suspense* [N]	$20		Red Bird 10058
6/28/69	45	8		11 **On Campus**....*Mombo Suzie* (Johnny Colon) [N]	$10		Cotique 158
9/6/69	95	2		12 **Luna Trip**....*My Victrola* (Joey Pastrana) [N]	$10		Cotique 173
6/16/73	42	7		13 **Watergrate**....*Friends* [N]	$10		Rainy Wednesday 202
2/2/74	33	8		14 **Energy Crisis '74**....*Ruthie's Theme* [N]	$10		Rainy Wednesday 206
				also issued with "The Mistake" as the B-side			
6/15/74	73	4		15 **Mr. President**....*Popularity* [N]	$10		Rainy Wednesday 207
9/6/75	4	10	●	16 **Mr. Jaws**....*Irv's Theme* [N]	$7		Cash 451
2/5/77	48	6		17 **Kong**....*Ed's Tune* [N]	$7		Shock 6
				inspired by the 1976 remake of the movie *King Kong*			
				GOODMEN, The '93			
				Techno-dance instrumental collaboration of producers DJ Zki and Dobre from Amsterdam, Netherlands.			
11/27/93	71	14		**Give It Up**....A:66 *(Batacuda Refrescante version) / Land Of Haze* [I]	$5	▮*	FFRR 350039
				GOOD QUESTION '88			
				R&B-dance duo from Philadelphia, Pennsylvania: brothers Sean and Marc Douglas.			
10/22/88	86	5		**Got A New Love**....*One More Time*	$3	■	Paisley Park 27861
				GOODTIMERS, The — see COVAY, Don			
				GOOD 2 GO '92			
				Female pop-rap vocal group from Los Angeles, California: Melissa Miller, Natalie Fernie, Kathy Webb, Cindy Shows and Missy Newman.			
5/9/92	64	14		**Never Satisfied**....A:45 / S:63 *(club mix)*	$3	▮	Giant 18981
				GOODWIN, Don '73			
				Pop singer/songwriter. Discovered by **Paul Anka** in Las Vegas.			
12/8/73	86	8		**This Is Your Song**....*Help It Along*	$6		Silver Blue 806
				written and co-produced by **Paul Anka**			
				GOODWIN, Ron, and His Orchestra '57			
				Born on 2/17/25 in Plymouth, England. Died on 1/8/2003 (age 77). Arranger/composer/conductor.			
9/9/57	52	8		**Swinging Sweethearts**....T:52 *I'll Find You* [I]	$12		Capitol 3748
				GOODY GOODY '78			
				Disco production by Vincent Montana (Montana Orchestra/**Salsoul Orchestra**) featuring Denise Montana, lead singer.			
11/18/78	82	5		**#1 Dee Jay**....*You Know How Good It Is*	$5		Atlantic 3504
	★418★			**GOO GOO DOLLS** ROK/BUB/LP '98			
				Rock trio from Buffalo, New York: Johnny Rzeznik (vocals, guitar), Robby Takac (bass) and Mike Malinin (drums).			
10/14/95+	5	36		1 **Name**....AR5 / MR4 A:2 / S:31 *Burnin' Up / Hit Or Miss*	$3	▮	Warner 17758
1/6/96	47A	15		2 **Naked**....			album cut
				above 2 from the album *A Boy Named Goo* on Warner 45750			
4/18/98	❶18A	47		3 **Iris** MR5 HOT:9(14 wks)			album cut
				from the movie *City Of Angels* starring Nicolas Cage (soundtrack on Warner Sunset 46867)			
12/5/98+	8	35		4 **Slide**....MR2 A:❶1			album cut
				Hot 100 Airplay debut: 9/26/98			
7/10/99	16	34		5 **Black Balloon**....A:18 / S:22 *Slide (live version)*	$4	★V	Warner 16946
4/22/00	24	20		6 **Broadway**....A:24			album cut
				above 4 from the album *Dizzy Up The Girl* on Warner 47058			
3/23/02	18	20		7 **Here Is Gone**....A:18		V	album cut
9/7/02	64	6		8 **Big Machine**....A:69		V	album cut
				above 2 from the album *Gutterflower* on Warner 48206; "45" issued for above 2 on Warner 16705			
				GOOSE CREEK SYMPHONY LP '72			
				Country-rock group: Ritchie Hart (vocals, guitar), Paul Howard (guitar), Bob Henke (keyboards), Ellis Schweid (fiddle), Chris Mostert (sax), Dave Birkett (bass) and Dennis Kenmore (drums).			
1/29/72	64	9		**(Oh Lord Won't You Buy Me A) Mercedes Benz**....*Rush On Love*	$6		Capitol 3246
				written by **Janis Joplin**			
				GORDON, Barry '55			
				Born on 12/21/48 in Brookline, Massachusetts. Acted in several TV shows.			
12/17/55	6	4	●	1 **Nuttin' For Christmas**....S:6 / T:7 / J:9 / A:10 *Santa Claus Looks Just Like Daddy* [X-N]	$20	■	MGM 12092
				ART MOONEY And His ORCHESTRA with Barry Gordon			
				verse melody based on traditional 19th century French song "Vive La Companie"; picture sleeve issued Christmas, 1956			
2/11/56	52	5		2 **Rock Around Mother Goose**....T:52 *Seven* [N]	$20		MGM 12166
				Art Mooney (orch.); **Ray Charles Singers** (backing vocals, above 2)			
				GORDON, Lonnie '91			
				Born in the Bronx, New York. Female dance singer.			
8/31/91	79	6		1 **Gonna Catch You**....A:52 *(acappella/sax mix)*	$3	▮	SBK 07365
				from the movie *Cool As Ice* starring **Vanilla Ice**			
11/13/93	98	2		2 **Happenin' All Over Again**....*(2 remixes)*	$3	▮	SBK 58010
				above 2: #1 Dance Club Play hits			

DEBUT	PEAK	WKS	Gold	A-side (Chart Hit)...B-side	$	Sym	Label & Number
				GORDON, Robert C&W/LP **'81**			
				Born in 1947 in Washington DC. Rockabilly singer. Lead singer of the New York punk band Tuff Darts.			
10/1/77	83	3		1 **Red Hot**...*Sweet Surrender*	$7		Private Stock 45,156
				ROBERT GORDON With Link Wray			
				rockabilly song originally recorded in 1955 by Billy "The Kid" Emerson on Sun 219 ($150)			
6/27/81	76	4		2 **Someday, Someway**...*Drivin' Wheel*	$5		RCA 12239
				written by **Marshall Crenshaw**			
				GORDON, Rosco R&B **'60**			
				Born on 4/10/28 in Memphis, Tennessee. Died of a heart attack on 7/11/2002 (age 74). R&B singer/guitarist/pianist.			
2/15/60	64	7		**Just A Little Bit**...*Goin' Home*	$25		Vee-Jay 332
	★246★			**GORE, Lesley** BUB/AC/LP **'63**			
				Born on 5/2/46 in Manhattan, New York; raised in Tenafly, New Jersey. Discovered by **Quincy Jones** while singing at a hotel in Manhattan. In the movies *Girls On The Beach*, *Ski Party* and *The T.A.M.I. Show*. Sister of **Michael Gore**.			
				1)It's My Party 2)You Don't Own Me 3)Judy's Turn To Cry			
5/11/63	❶[2]	13		1 **It's My Party** RB[3] *Danny*	$15	■	Mercury 72119
7/6/63	5	11		2 **Judy's Turn To Cry**...*Just Let Me Cry*	$15	■	Mercury 72143
				sequel to "It's My Party"			
9/28/63	5	15		3 **She's A Fool**...*The Old Crowd*	$15	■	Mercury 72180
12/28/63+	2[3]	13		4 **You Don't Own Me**...*Run Bobby, Run*	$15	■	Mercury 72206
3/28/64	12	9		5 **That's The Way Boys Are**...*That's The Way The Ball Bounces*	$15	■	Mercury 72259
5/23/64	37	5		6 **I Don't Wanna Be A Loser**...*It's Gotta Be You*	$15	■	Mercury 72270
7/25/64	14	10		7 **Maybe I Know**...*Wonder Boy*	$15	■	Mercury 72309
10/17/64	76	6		8 **Hey Now /**			
10/31/64	86	4		9 **Sometimes I Wish I Were A Boy**...	$12	■	Mercury 72352
12/26/64+	27	9		10 **Look Of Love**...*Little Girl Go Home*	$12	■	Mercury 72372
				above 4 from the album *Girl Talk*			
3/27/65	71	6		11 **All Of My Life**...*I Cannot Hope For Anyone*	$12	■	Mercury 72412
6/19/65	13	11		12 **Sunshine, Lollipops And Rainbows**...*You've Come Back*	$12	■	Mercury 72433
				from the movie *Ski Party* starring **Frankie Avalon**			
9/11/65	32	8		13 **My Town, My Guy And Me**...*A Girl In Love*	$12	■	Mercury 72475
				all of above produced by **Quincy Jones**			
12/4/65	80	3		14 **I Won't Love You Anymore (Sorry)**...*No Matter What You Do*	$12	■	Mercury 72513
2/5/66	76	3		15 **We Know We're In Love**...*That's What I'll Do*	$12		Mercury 72530
3/26/66	50	6		16 **Young Love**...*I Just Don't Know If I Can*	$12		Mercury 72553
2/4/67	16	14		17 **California Nights**...*I'm Going Out (The Same Way I Came In)*	$12		Mercury 72649
				#12 & 17: co-written by **Marvin Hamlisch**			
6/10/67	65	7		18 **Summer And Sandy**...*I'm Fallin' Down*	$12	■	Mercury 72683
10/21/67	82	4		19 **Brink Of Disaster**...*On A Day Like Today*	$12		Mercury 72726
				Gore's musical arrangers and conductors: Al Capps (#19), **Don Costa** (#13), **Hutch Davie** (#17, 18), Alan Lorber (#14-16) and Claus Ogermann (#1-12)			
				GORE, Michael **'84**			
				Born on 3/5/51 in Manhattan, New York; raised in Tenafly, New Jersey. Prolific songwriter. Brother of **Lesley Gore**.			
4/14/84	84	6		**Theme from "Terms Of Endearment"**...*This Is My Moment* [I]	$4		Capitol 5334
				from the movie *Terms Of Endearment* starring Shirley MacLaine and Jack Nicholson			
				GORILLAZ ROK/LP **'01**			
				Alternative hip-hop/rock group created by Jamie Hewlett and Dan Nakamura: 2-D (vocals, keyboards), Noodle (guitar), Murdoc (bass) and Russel (drums).			
8/25/01	57	11		**Clint Eastwood**...A:56		V	album cut
				from the album *Gorillaz* on Parlophone 33748; "45": Virgin 77673; B-side: "19-2000" (ROK #23)			
				GORKY PARK ROK/LP **'90**			
				Rock group from Russia: Nikolai Noskov (vocals), Alexei Belov and Jan Ianenkov (guitars), "Big" Sasha Minkov (bass) and "Little" Sasha Lvov (drums). Group named after a famous park in Moscow.			
4/28/90	81	6		**Try To Find Me**...*Bang* (ROK #41)	$4	▌	Mercury 876488
	★401★			**GORME, Eydie** AC/BUB/MEM/LP **'63**			
				Born on 8/16/31 in the Bronx, New York. Vocalist with the big bands of Tommy Tucker and Tex Beneke in the late 1940s. Featured on **Steve Allen**'s *Tonight Show* from 1953. Married **Steve Lawrence** on 12/29/57. They recorded as the duo Parker & Penny in 1979.			
				1)Blame It On The Bossa Nova 2)You Need Hands 3)Love Me Forever			
4/21/56	39	14		1 **Too Close For Comfort**...T:39 *That's How*	$12		ABC-Paramount 9684
				from the Broadway musical *Mr. Wonderful* starring **Sammy Davis Jr.**			
7/28/56	34	11		2 **Mama, Teach Me To Dance**...T:34 *You Bring Out The Lover In Me*	$12		ABC-Paramount 9722
4/13/57	65	11		3 **I'll Take Romance**...T:65 *First Impression*	$12		ABC-Paramount 9780
				title song from the 1937 movie starring Grace Moore; #19 hit for Rudy Vallee in 1938			
6/17/57	53	2		4 **Your Kisses Kill Me**...T:53 *Kiss In Your Eyes*	$12		ABC-Paramount 9817
12/16/57	24	2		5 **Love Me Forever**...A:24 / T:86 *Let Me Be Loved*	$12		ABC-Paramount 9863
				Bernie Glow (trumpet solo)			
5/26/58	11	11		6 **You Need Hands**...A:11 / S:32 / T:32 *Dormi-Dormi-Dormi*	$12		ABC-Paramount 9925
8/4/58	63	7		7 **Gotta Have Rain**...H:63 *To You, From Me*	$12		ABC-Paramount 9944
12/29/58	88	1		8 **The Voice In My Heart**...*Separate Tables*	$12		ABC-Paramount 9971
1/19/63	7	15		9 **Blame It On The Bossa Nova** *Guess I Should Have Loved Him More*	$8	■	Columbia 42661
				The Cookies (backing vocals); also issued with a promotional sleeve (text only)			
6/1/63	53	7		10 **Don't Try To Fight It, Baby**...*(Theme From) "Light Fantastic" (My Secret World)*	$8		Columbia 42790
7/20/63	28	11		11 **I Want To Stay Here**...*Ain't Love*	$8	□	Columbia 42815
				STEVE & EYDIE			
9/28/63	80	6		12 **Everybody Go Home**...*The Message*	$8		Columbia 42854
12/21/63+	35	9		13 **I Can't Stop Talking About You**...*To The Movies We Go*	$8		Columbia 42932
				STEVE And EYDIE			

DEBUT	PEAK	WKS	Gold	A-side (Chart Hit)...B-side	$	Sym	Label & Number
				GORME, Eydie — Cont'd			
7/25/64	43	8		14 **I Want You To Meet My Baby /**			
8/29/64	87	3		15 **Can't Get Over (The Bossa Nova)**	$8		Columbia 43082
11/29/69+	45	12		16 **Tonight I'll Say A Prayer** ... *Wild One*	$6		RCA Victor 0250
9/16/72	68	10		17 **We Can Make It Together** ... *E Fini* (Steve & Eydie)	$6	■	MGM 14383
				STEVE & EYDIE featuring The Osmonds			
				Gorme's musical conductors and arrangers: **Don Costa** (#1, 3-8, 16, 17), Marion Evans (#9-13), Sid Feller (#2) and Robert Mersey (#14, 15)			
				GOT'TI, John '01			
				Born in New Orleans, Louisiana. Male rapper.			
9/22/01	47^S	7		**Cut Throat** ... *(2 versions)*	$6	★	Big Pocket/Orpheus 5632
				GOTTI, Suave '01			
				Born in Ohio. Male rapper.			
10/6/01	54^S	5		**Rolla Man** ... *Ohio Love / Up & Down*	$10	★	1 Duck/Strong Arm 80006
				GOULET, Robert AC/BUB/LP '65			
				Born on 11/26/33 in Lawrence, Massachusetts (French Canadian parents). Began concert career in Edmonton, Alberta, Canada. Broadway/movie/TV actor. Launched career as "Sir Lancelot" in the hit Broadway musical *Camelot.* Won the 1962 Best New Artist Grammy Award.			
10/6/62	89	2		1 **What Kind Of Fool Am I?** ... *Where Do I Go From Here?*	$7	■	Columbia 42519
				from the Broadway musical *Stop The World-I Want To Get Off* starring **Anthony Newley**; also issued with a special promo sleeve			
10/24/64+	16	15		2 **My Love, Forgive Me (Amore, Scusami)** ... *I'd Rather Be Rich* (#131)	$7	□	Columbia 43131
6/5/65	58	7		3 **Summer Sounds** ... *The More I See Of Mimi*	$7		Columbia 43301
12/21/68	19^X	2		4 **Hurry Home For Christmas** ... *A Wonderful World Of Christmas* [X]	$7	■	Columbia 44710
				written by **Steve Lawrence** and **Eydie Gorme**			
				GO WEST LP '90			
				Pop-rock duo from England: Peter Cox (vocals) and Richard Drummie (guitar, vocals).			
2/23/85	41	15		1 **We Close Our Eyes** ... *Missing Persons*	$3	■	Chrysalis 42850
6/1/85	54	14		2 **Call Me** ... *Haunted*	$3	■	Chrysalis 42865
9/28/85	73	7		3 **Eye To Eye** ... *Man In My Mirror*	$3	■	Chrysalis 42903
8/1/87	39	13		4 **Don't Look Down - The Sequel** ... A:37 *Let's Build A Boat*	$3	■	Chrysalis 43141
				new version of a track from the group's 1985 *Go West* album			
5/19/90	8	24		5 **King Of Wishful Thinking** ... A:4 / S:15 *(power mix)*	$3	▌^{V}	EMI 50307
				from the movie *Pretty Woman* starring Richard Gere and Julia Roberts			
11/7/92+	14	20		6 **Faithful** ... A:13 / S:47 *I Want You Back / King Of Wishful Thinking*	$3	▌^{V}	EMI 50411
				"45" issued for above 2 on EMI 56948			
3/13/93	55	11		7 **What You Won't Do For Love** ... A:52 *(2 versions)*	$3	▌	EMI 50428
				GQ R&B/BUB/LP '79			
				R&B-dance group from New York City, New York: Emmanuel Rahiem LeBlanc (vocals, guitar), Herb Lane (keyboards), Keith Crier (bass) and Paul Service (drums). Group became a trio with the departure of Service in 1980.			
3/17/79	12	18	●	1 **Disco Nights (Rock-Freak)** ... RB^2 *Boogie Oogie Oogie*	$4		Arista 0388
6/30/79	20	17		2 **I Do Love You** ... *Make My Dreams A Reality* (R&B #8)	$4		Arista 0426
3/13/82	93	2		3 **Sad Girl** ... *Shy Baby*	$4		Arista 0659
				GRACES, The LP '89			
				Female rock vocal trio formed in Los Angeles, California: Charlotte Caffey (guitarist of the **Go-Go's**), **Meredith Brooks** and Gia Ciambotti.			
8/12/89	56	9		**Lay Down Your Arms** ... *Out In The Fields*	$5	▌	A&M 1440
				GRACIE, Charlie '57			
				Born Charles Graci on 5/14/36 in Philadelphia, Pennsylvania. Rock and roll singer/guitarist. Began playing the guitar in 1946. Appeared on the *Paul Whiteman Teen Show* in 1950. First recorded for Cadillac in 1951. Regular on *Bandstand* (later: *American Bandstand*) from 1952-58. Toured England in 1957 and 1979.			
2/16/57	❶^2	17	●	1 **Butterfly** ... J:❶^2 / S:3 / T:7 / A:13 *Ninety-Nine Ways*	$30		Cameo 105
5/6/57	16	15		2 **Fabulous** ... S:16 / T:26 *Just Lookin'*	$25		Cameo 107
8/12/57	71	3		3 **I Love You So Much It Hurts** ... T:71 *Wanderin' Eyes*	$25		Cameo 111
				#1 Country hit for **Jimmy Wakely** in 1948; **Bernie Lowe** (orch., all of above)			
				GRADUATES BUB '59			
				White doo-wop group from Buffalo, New York: John Cappello, Bruce Hammond, Fred Mancuso and Jack Scorsone.			
3/9/59	74	3		**Ballad Of A Girl And Boy** ... *Care*	$30		Shan-Todd 0055
				GRAHAM, Larry R&B/BUB/LP '80			
				Born on 8/14/46 in Beaumont, Texas; raised in Oakland, California. Bass player with **Sly & The Family Stone** from 1966-72. Formed **Graham Central Station** in 1973: Graham (vocals, bass), David Vega (guitar), Hershall Kennedy and Robert Sam (keyboards), Willie Sparks and Patrice Banks (percussion). Graham went solo in 1980.			
				GRAHAM CENTRAL STATION:			
5/4/74	49	8		1 **Can You Handle It?** ... *Ghetto*	$5		Warner 7782
8/9/75	38	9		2 **Your Love** ... RB^1 *I Believe In You*	$5		Warner 8105
11/29/75	92	2		3 **It's Alright** ... *Luckiest People*	$5		Warner 8148
2/21/76	63	6		4 **The Jam** ... *(long version)* [I]	$5		Warner 8175
				LARRY GRAHAM:			
6/28/80	9	20	●	5 **One In A Million You** ... RB^2 *The Entertainer*	$4	■	Warner 49221
10/25/80	76	4		6 **When We Get Married** ... *Tonight*	$4		Warner 49581
9/5/81	67	5		7 **Just Be My Lady** ... *Feels Like Love*	$4		Warner 49744

DEBUT	PEAK	WKS	Gold	A-side (Chart Hit)..........B-side	$	Sym	Label & Number

GRAMM, Lou
ROK/LP **'87**

Born Lou Grammatico on 5/2/50 in Rochester, New York. Lead singer of **Foreigner**.

DEBUT	PEAK	WKS	Gold	A-side (Chart Hit)..........B-side	$	Sym	Label & Number
1/31/87	5	20		1 Midnight Blue..........AR[5] S:6 / A:6 *Chain Of Love*	$3	■	Atlantic 89304
5/9/87	54	12		2 Ready Or Not..........*Lover Come Back*	$3	■	Atlantic 89269
10/28/89+	6	21		3 Just Between You And Me..........A:3 / S:9 *Tin Soldier*	$3	▮V	Atlantic 88781
2/17/90	40	11		4 True Blue Love..........A:35 *Day One*	$3	▮	Atlantic 88768

GRAMMER, Billy
C&W **'59**

Born on 8/28/25 in Benton, Illinois. Country singer/guitarist. Performed regularly on *The* ***Jimmy Dean*** *Show*, CBS-TV, 1957-58. Prominent session musician in Nashville.

DEBUT	PEAK	WKS	Gold	A-side (Chart Hit)..........B-side	$	Sym	Label & Number
11/24/58+	4	20		1 Gotta Travel On..........*Chasing A Dream* based on a 19th-century tune that originated in the British Isles	$15		Monument 400
4/13/59	50	9		2 Bonaparte's Retreat / written by Pee Wee ("Slow Poke") King; #4 hit for **Kay Starr** in 1950			
4/13/59	60	7		3 The Kissing Tree..........	$15		Monument 403

GRANAHAN, Gerry
BUB **'58**

Born on 6/17/39 in Pittston, Pennsylvania. To New York City at age 17. First recorded for Atco as Jerry Grant. Formed **Dicky Doo And The Don'ts** and **The Fireflies**. Formed Caprice Records in 1958 and produced many top hits.

DEBUT	PEAK	WKS	Gold	A-side (Chart Hit)..........B-side	$	Sym	Label & Number
6/9/58	23	11		No Chemise, Please..........T:23 / S:25 *Girl Of My Dreams* [N] Arnie Goland (orch.); tune inspired by the '50s "sack dress" clothing fad	$30		Sunbeam 102

GRANATA, Rocco
'59

Born on 8/16/38 in Figline Vigliaturo, Italy; moved to Belgium at age 10. Singer/songwriter/accordionist.

DEBUT	PEAK	WKS	Gold	A-side (Chart Hit)..........B-side	$	Sym	Label & Number
11/9/59	31	11		Marina..........*Manuela* [F] **ROCCO GRANATA and the International Quintet** picture sleeve issued with 2 versions: black & white, and with a pink title strip	$12	■	Laurie 3041

GRAND CANYON
'74

Novelty duo from Atlanta, Georgia: Ed Brown and Jeff McKee.

DEBUT	PEAK	WKS	Gold	A-side (Chart Hit)..........B-side	$	Sym	Label & Number
11/2/74	72	5		Evil Boll-Weevil..........*Got To Find My Way Back* [N] "break-in" record; inspired by daredevil stunt driver Evel Knievel	$8		Bang 713

GRAND FUNK RAILROAD
★217★ BUB/LP **'74**

Hard-rock group formed in Flint, Michigan: Mark Farner (guitar; born on 9/29/48), Mel Schacher (bass; born on 4/3/51) and Don Brewer (drums; born on 9/3/48). Band name inspired by Michigan landmark the Grand Trunk Railroad. Brewer and Farner had been in **Terry Knight and The Pack** (see #1 below); Schacher was bassist with **? & The Mysterians**. Knight became producer/manager for Grand Funk, until his firing in March 1972. Craig Frost (keyboards) added in 1973. Disbanded in 1976. Re-formed in 1981, with Farner, Brewer and Dennis Bellinger (bass). Disbanded again shortly thereafter. Farner began recording Christian music in 1988.

1)The Loco-Motion 2)We're An American Band 3)Some Kind Of Wonderful 4)Bad Time 5)Shinin' On

DEBUT	PEAK	WKS	Gold	A-side (Chart Hit)..........B-side	$	Sym	Label & Number
11/12/66+	46	10		1 I (Who Have Nothing)..........*Numbers* **TERRY KNIGHT and THE PACK**	$15		Lucky Eleven 230
9/27/69	48	11		2 Time Machine..........*High On A Horse*	$7		Capitol 2567
12/20/69	97	2		3 Mr. Limousine Driver..........*High Falootin' Woman*	$7		Capitol 2691
2/14/70	72	6		4 Heartbreaker..........*Please Don't Worry*	$7		Capitol 2732
8/15/70	22	12		5 Closer To Home..........*Aimless Lady*	$7		Capitol 2877
12/12/70+	47	8		6 Mean Mistreater..........*Mark Say's Alright* [L]	$7		Capitol 2996
5/1/71	54	6		7 Feelin' Alright..........*I Want Freedom* written by **Dave Mason**	$7		Capitol 3095
8/28/71	61	6		8 Gimme Shelter..........*I Can Feel Him In The Morning* first recorded by **The Rolling Stones** on their 1969 album *Let It Bleed*	$7	■	Capitol 3160
1/8/72	29	11		9 Footstompin' Music..........*I Come Tumblin'* silver-colored sleeve issued as a full sleeve and as a half-sleeve for above 2	$6	■	Capitol 3255
4/29/72	73	5		10 Upsetter..........*No Lies* all of above produced by **Terry Knight**	$6		Capitol 3316
9/23/72	29	13		11 Rock 'N Roll Soul..........*Flight Of The Phoenix*	$6		Capitol 3363
				GRAND FUNK:			
7/28/73	❶ 1	17	●	12 We're An American Band..........*Creepin'* some pressings issued on gold vinyl	$5	■	Capitol 3660
11/24/73+	19	12		13 Walk Like A Man..........*The Railroad*	$5	■	Capitol 3760
3/9/74	❶ 2	20	●	14 The Loco-Motion..........*Destitute & Losin'*	$5	■	Capitol 3840
7/13/74	11	11		15 Shinin' On..........*Mr. Pretty Boy* above 4 produced by **Todd Rundgren**	$5	■	Capitol 3917
12/14/74+	3	13		16 Some Kind Of Wonderful..........*Wild*	$5	■	Capitol 4002
4/5/75	4	15		17 Bad Time..........*Good & Evil*	$5		Capitol 4046
				GRAND FUNK RAILROAD:			
1/24/76	53	5		18 Take Me..........*Genevieve*	$5	■	Capitol 4199
3/20/76	69	4		19 Sally..........*Love Is Dyin'*	$5	■	Capitol 4235
8/14/76	45	7		20 Can You Do It..........*1976* produced by **Frank Zappa**	$5	■	MCA 40590

GRANDMASTER FLASH
R&B/LP **'82**

Grandmaster Flash is pioneer rap DJ/producer Joseph Saddler (born in Barbados; raised in the Bronx, New York). Rapper Melle Mel (Melvin Glover) was part of the original Furious Five rap/dance posse with Kidd Creole (Nathaniel Glover — no relation to the August Darnell character), Rahiem (Guy Todd Williams), Cowboy (Keith Wiggins; died on 9/8/89) and Scorpio. Also see **Chaka Khan**'s "I Feel For You" and **Duran Duran**'s "White Lines."

DEBUT	PEAK	WKS	Gold	A-side (Chart Hit)..........B-side	$	Sym	Label & Number
10/16/82	62	7		1 The Message..........*(instrumental)* **GRAND MASTER FLASH & THE FURIOUS FIVE Featuring: Melle Mel and Duke Bootee** available commercially only as a 12" single; "45" (Sugar Hill 787) issued for promotion use only	$8	TV	Sugar Hill 584
8/4/84	86	2		2 Beat Street Breakdown - Part I..........*Part II* **GRANDMASTER MELLE MEL & THE FURIOUS FIVE** from the movie *Beat Street* starring Rae Dawn Chong; above 2 produced by **Sylvia** (**Mickey & Sylvia**)	$4	■	Atlantic 89659

DEBUT	PEAK	WKS	Gold	A-side (Chart Hit)....B-side	$	Sym	Label & Number
				GRANDMASTER SLICE R&B **'91**			
				Born in South Boston, Virginia. Male rapper.			
10/26/91	85	6		**Thinking Of You** ....*Turn Up The Music*	$4	▮	Jive 42034
				Marianne Tutalo (female vocal)			
				GRAND PUBA R&B/BUB/LP **'92**			
				Born Maxwell Dixon on 3/4/66 in the Bronx, New York; raised in New Rochelle, New York. Male rapper. Former member of **Brand Nubian**.			
10/17/92	68	14		1 **360° (What Goes Around)** ....S:43 *(SD50 remix)*	$3	▮	Elektra 64708
				samples "Don't Burn Down The Bridge" by **Gladys Knight & The Pips**			
6/3/95	91	9		2 **I Like It (I Wanna Be Where You Are)** ....*(3 versions) / A Little Of This*	$6	T	Elektra 66131
				features "I Like It" by **DeBarge** and samples the **Willie Hutch** tune "I Wanna Be Where You Are"			
	★283★			**GRANT, Amy** AC/LP **'91**			
				Born on 11/25/60 in Augusta, Georgia. Pop singer/songwriter. Began career as a top Contemporary Christian singer. Married to singer/songwriter Gary Chapman from 1982-99. Married **Vince Gill** on 3/10/2000.			
				1)Baby Baby 2)The Next Time I Fall 3)Every Heartbeat			
5/18/85	29	16		1 **Find A Way** ....A:28 *Angels*	$3	■	A&M 2734
				#1 Contemporary Christian hit for 14 weeks; B-side #1 for 13 weeks in 1984			
8/17/85	66	9		2 **Wise Up** ....*Straight Ahead*	$3	■	A&M 2762
9/20/86	❶^{1}	21		3 **The Next Time I Fall**....AC^{2} A:2 / S:3 *Holy Moly* (Cetera)	$3	■	Full Moon 28597
				PETER CETERA w/AMY GRANT			
8/6/88	96	2		4 **Lead Me On** ....*Sure Enough*	$3	■	A&M 1218
2/23/91	❶^{2}	21		5 **Baby Baby** AC^{3} A:❶^{4} / S:❶^{1} *(remix)*	$3	▮V	A&M 1549
				song inspired by Grant's 6-week-old daughter Millie			
6/15/91	2^{1}	19		6 **Every Heartbeat**....A:2 / S:20 *(remix)*	$3	▮V	A&M 1557
9/28/91	7	20		7 **That's What Love Is For** ....AC^{3} A:9 / S:31 *(album version)*	$3	▮V	A&M 1566
1/18/92	8	20		8 **Good For Me**....A:6 / S:62 *(remix)*	$3	▮V	A&M 1573
4/25/92	20	20		9 **I Will Remember You**....A:25 / S:37 *(remix)*	$3	▮V	A&M 1600
				above 5 from the album *Heart In Motion*			
8/13/94	18	20		10 **Lucky One** ....A:17 / S:30 *(remix)*	$3	▮V	A&M 0724
				"45" issued for above 2 on A&M 0726			
11/26/94+	37	21		11 **House Of Love** ....S:38 / A:41 *(remix)*	$3	▮V	A&M 0802
				AMY GRANT with Vince Gill			
				"45" issued for #8 & 11 on A&M 0864			
6/17/95	67	15		12 **Big Yellow Taxi**....*(album version)*	$3	▮	A&M 0976
8/30/97	21^{A}	24		13 **Takes A Little Time**....			album cut
				from the album *Behind The Eyes* on A&M 0760			
				GRANT, Cary **'67**			
				Born Archibald Leach on 1/18/04 in Bristol, England. Died on 11/29/86 (age 82). One of Hollywood's top leading men. Movies include *Arsenic And Old Lace*, *The Bishop's Wife* and *North By Northwest*.			
12/23/67	33^{X}	2		**Christmas Lullaby** ....*Here's To You* [X-S]	$25		Columbia 44377
				written by **Peggy Lee**			
				GRANT, Earl LP **'58**			
				Born on 1/2/31 in Idabelle, Oklahoma. Died in a car crash on 6/10/70 (age 39). Black singer/songwriter/pianist.			
9/15/58	7	19		1 **The End** H:7 / S:26 *Hunky Dunky Doo*	$15		Decca 30719
				some pressings show title as "(At) The End (Of A Rainbow)"			
1/26/59	63	7		2 **Evening Rain** ....*(instrumental)*	$10		Decca 30819
				Charles Bud Dant (orch., above 2)			
3/28/60	88	3		3 **House Of Bamboo**....*Two Loves Have I*	$10		Decca 31044
5/26/62	44	11		4 **Swingin' Gently** ....*Beyond The Reef* [I]	$10		Decca 25560
9/8/62	55	8		5 **Sweet Sixteen Bars** ....*Learnin' The Blues* [I]	$10		Decca 25574
				written by **Ray Charles**			
10/23/65	75	7		6 **Stand By Me** ....*After Hours* [I]	$7		Decca 25674
12/17/66	3^{X}	16		7 **Silver Bells** ....*Jingle Bells* [X]	$7		Decca 25703
				X: 15/'66; 4/'67; 6/'68; 3/'69; 4/'70; 8/'72			
				GRANT, Eddy R&B/LP **'83**			
				Born Edmond Grant on 3/5/48 in Plaisance, Guyana; raised in London, England. Rock-reggae singer. Member of **The Equals**.			
4/16/83	2^{5}	22	▲	1 **Electric Avenue** ....*Time Warp*	$4		Portrait 03793
8/13/83	53	7		2 **I Don't Wanna Dance** ....*(acappella version)*	$4		Portrait 04039
5/19/84	26	17		3 **Romancing The Stone**....*My Turn To Love You*	$4	■	Portrait 04433
				written for, but not included in, the movie *Romancing The Stone* starring Michael Douglas and Kathleen Turner			
				GRANT, Gogi AC **'56**			
				Born Audrey Arinsberg on 9/20/24 in Philadelphia, Pennsylvania. Female pop singer.			
10/1/55	9	11	●	1 **Suddenly There's A Valley** ....A:9 / S:14 / T:14 / J:19 *Love Is*	$20		Era 1003
2/4/56	62	7		2 **Who Are We**....T:62 *We Believe In Love*	$20		Era 1008
4/28/56	❶^{8}	28	●	3 **The Wayward Wind** A:❶^{8} / T:❶^{7} / S:❶^{6} / J:❶^{4} *No More Than Forever*	$25		Era 1013
				same version reissued at #7 below			
9/15/56	69	7		4 **You're In Love /** T:69			
				from the movie *Accused of Murder* starring David Brian			
9/15/56	75	2		5 **When The Tide Is High**....T:75	$20		Era 1019
8/25/58	80	3		6 **Strange Are The Ways Of Love** ....H:80 *Marjolaina*	$15		RCA Victor 7294
				Bill Thompson Singers (backing vocals); from the movie *The Young Land* starring Pat Wayne			
4/24/61	50	9		7 **The Wayward Wind** ....*When The Tide Is High* [R]	$15		Era 3046
				label shows "Original Special Demand Release"; Buddy Bregman (orch., all of above)			

DEBUT	PEAK	WKS	Gold	A-side (Chart Hit)	B-side	$	Sym	Label & Number

GRANT, Janie — '61

Born Rose Marie Casilli on 9/27/44 in Jersey City, New Jersey. Teen pop singer/songwriter.

DEBUT	PEAK	WKS	Gold	A-side (Chart Hit)	B-side	$	Sym	Label & Number
3/27/61	**29**	13		1 **Triangle**	*She's Going Steady With You*	$15		Caprice 104
8/28/61	**75**	3		2 **Romeo**	*Roller Coaster*	$15		Caprice 109
6/23/62	**74**	4		3 **That Greasy Kid Stuff**	*Trying To Forget You* [N]	$15		Caprice 115
				inspired by a hair tonic jingle; **Hutch Davie** (orch., all of above)				

GRAPEFRUIT — BUB '68

Psychedelic-rock group from England: John Perry (vocals), brothers Pete (guitar) and Geoff (drums) Swettenham, and George Alexander (bass).

DEBUT	PEAK	WKS	Gold	A-side (Chart Hit)	B-side	$	Sym	Label & Number
3/2/68	**98**	1		**Dear Delilah**	*Dead Boot*	$20		Equinox 70000
				produced by Terry Melcher of **Bruce And Terry** and **The Rip Chords**				

★223★ GRASS ROOTS, The — BUB/LP '71

Pop-rock group formed in San Francisco, California: Rob Grill (vocals, bass; born on 11/30/44), Warren Entner (born on 7/7/44) and Creed Bratton (guitars; born on 2/8/43), and Rick Coonce (drums; born on 8/1/47). New lineup in 1971 included Entner, Grill, Reed Kailing and Virgil Webber (guitars), and Joel Larson (drums).

1)Midnight Confessions 2)Let's Live For Today 3)Sooner Or Later 4)I'd Wait A Million Years 5)Temptation Eyes

DEBUT	PEAK	WKS	Gold	A-side (Chart Hit)	B-side	$	Sym	Label & Number
6/18/66	**28**	9		1 **Where Were You When I Needed You**	*(These Are) Bad Times*	$15		Dunhill 4029
9/10/66	**96**	2		2 **Only When You're Lonely**	*This Is What I Was Made For*	$15		Dunhill 4043
5/13/67	**8**	12		3 **Let's Live For Today**	*Depressed Feeling*	$12		Dunhill 4084
8/12/67	**23**	8		4 **Things I Should Have Said**	*Tip Of My Tongue*	$10	■	Dunhill 4094
10/28/67	**68**	5		5 **Wake Up, Wake Up**	*No Exit*	$10		Dunhill 4105
				#1 & 3-5: from the album *Let's Live For Today*				
8/31/68	**5**	15	●	6 **Midnight Confessions**	*Who Will You Be Tomorrow*	$8		Dunhill/ABC 4144
				first recorded by The Evergreen Blues in 1967 on Mercury 72756				
11/30/68+	**28**	9		7 **Bella Linda**	*Hot Bright Lights*	$8		Dunhill/ABC 4162
				some pressings issued as "Della Linda"				
2/15/69	**49**	7		8 **Lovin' Things**	*You & Love Are The Same*	$8		Dunhill/ABC 4180
4/12/69	**31**	11		9 **The River Is Wide**	*(You Gotta) Live For Love*	$8		Dunhill/ABC 4187
7/5/69	**15**	15		10 **I'd Wait A Million Years**	*Fly Me To Havana*	$8		Dunhill/ABC 4198
11/8/69	**24**	10		11 **Heaven Knows**	*Don't Remind Me*	$8		Dunhill/ABC 4217
2/14/70	**44**	8		12 **Walking Through The Country**	*Truck Drivin' Man*	$8		Dunhill/ABC 4227
5/9/70	**35**	10		13 **Baby Hold On**	*Get It Together*	$8	■	Dunhill/ABC 4237
9/19/70	**61**	6		14 **Come On And Say It**	*Something's Comin' Over Me*	$8	■	Dunhill/ABC 4249
12/26/70+	**15**	18		15 **Temptation Eyes**	*Keepin' Me Down*	$8		Dunhill/ABC 4263
6/5/71	**9**	11		16 **Sooner Or Later**	*I Can Turn Off The Rain*	$8		Dunhill/ABC 4279
10/9/71	**16**	11		17 **Two Divided By Love**	*Let It Go*	$8		Dunhill/ABC 4289
2/12/72	**34**	10		18 **Glory Bound**	*Only One*	$8		Dunhill/ABC 4302
6/17/72	**39**	9		19 **The Runway**	*Move Along*	$8		Dunhill/ABC 4316
1/27/73	**55**	10		20 **Love Is What You Make It**	*Someone To Love*	$8		Dunhill/ABC 4335
				all of above produced by Steve Barri				
8/2/75	**71**	11		21 **Mamacita**	*The Last Time Around*	$6		Haven/Capitol 7015

GRATEFUL DEAD — ROK/LP '87

Legendary improvisatory-style rock group formed in San Francisco, California: **Jerry Garcia** (vocals, guitar; born on 8/1/42), **Bob Weir** (vocals, guitar; born on 10/16/47), Ron "Pigpen" McKernan (organ, harmonica), Phil Lesh (bass) and Bill Kreutzmann (drums). Mickey Hart (2nd drummer) and Tom Constanten (keyboards) added in 1968. Constanten left in 1970; Hart in 1971. Keith Godchaux (piano) and his wife Donna (vocals) joined in 1972. Pigpen died of a liver ailment on 3/8/73 (age 27). Hart returned in 1975. Brent Mydland (keyboards) added in 1979, replacing Keith and Donna Godchaux. Mydland was a member of **Silver**. Keith Godchaux died on 7/23/80 (age 32) from injuries suffered in a motorcycle accident. Weir and Mydland also recorded as Bobby & The Midnites. Mydland died on 7/26/90 (age 37) of a drug overdose; **Bruce Hornsby** then took over keyboards on tour until **Tubes** keyboardist Vince Welnick joined band. Garcia died on 8/9/95 (age 53) of a heart attack. Incessant touring band with faithful followers known as "Deadheads." Inducted into the Rock and Roll Hall of Fame in 1994.

DEBUT	PEAK	WKS	Gold	A-side (Chart Hit)	B-side	$	Sym	Label & Number
8/8/70	**69**	7		1 **Uncle John's Band**	*New Speedway Boogie*	$15		Warner 7410
11/27/71	**64**	8		2 **Truckin'**	*Ripple*	$15		Warner 7464
4/15/72	**94**	2		3 **Sugaree**	*Eep Hour*	$15		Warner 7569
				JERRY GARCIA				
2/3/73	**91**	2		4 **Sugar Magnolia**	*Mr. Charlie*	$15		Warner 7667
10/25/75	**81**	5		5 **The Music Never Stopped**	*Help On The Way*	$15		Grateful Dead 718
3/18/78	**70**	5		6 **Bombs Away**	*Easy To Slip*	$6		Arista 0315
				BOB WEIR				
6/21/80	**68**	6		7 **Alabama Getaway**	*Far From Me*	$5	■	Arista 0519
7/25/87	**9**	15		8 **Touch Of Grey** AR^3 S:8 / A:15	*My Brother Esau*	$5	■	Arista 9606
				most pressings on grey vinyl; picture sleeve is a foldout poster (came only with grey vinyl copies)				

GRAVEDIGGAZ — R&B/BUB/LP '94

Male rap group: Robert Diggs (a.k.a. **RZA**; also of **Wu-Tang Clan**), Anthony Berkeley, Paul Huston and Arnold Hamilton. Huston also produced **De La Soul**. Berkeley died of cancer on 7/15/2001 (age 35).

DEBUT	PEAK	WKS	Gold	A-side (Chart Hit)	B-side	$	Sym	Label & Number
7/9/94	**82**	7		**Diary Of A Madman** S:52	*Constant Elevation*	$5	▮	Gee Street 854062

GRAVES, Billy — '59

Born in Delaware. Rock and roll singer. Performed with **Dick Flood** on **Jimmy Dean**'s CBS-TV show as The Country Lads.

DEBUT	PEAK	WKS	Gold	A-side (Chart Hit)	B-side	$	Sym	Label & Number
1/26/59	**53**	9		**The Shag (Is Totally Cool)**	*Uncertain*	$20		Monument 401
				some pressings show title only as "The Shag"				

GRAVES, Carl — BUB/R&B '75

Born in Calgary, Alberta, Canada. R&B singer. With the group **Skylark** in 1973.

DEBUT	PEAK	WKS	Gold	A-side (Chart Hit)	B-side	$	Sym	Label & Number
12/7/74+	**50**	9		1 **Baby, Hang Up The Phone**	*Walk Softly*	$6		A&M 1620
4/16/77	**83**	5		2 **Sad Girl**	*Walk In Love*	$5		Ariola America 7660

DEBUT	PEAK	WKS	Gold	A-side (Chart Hit).....B-side	$	Sym	Label & Number
				GRAVITY KILLS ROK/LP **'96**			
				Techno-rock group from Jefferson City, Missouri: Jeff Scheel (vocals), Matt Dudenhoeffer (guitar), Douglas Firley (keyboards) and Kurt Kerns (bass, drums).			
4/13/96	86	20		**Guilty** ..... *(9 versions) / Goodbye*	$8	★*	TVT 5912
				from the movie *Seven* starring Brad Pitt			
				GRAY, Claude C&W **'61**			
				Born on 1/25/32 in Henderson, Texas. Country singer/guitarist (charted 27 hits, 1960-86). Standing 6'5", known as "The Tall Texan."			
4/10/61	84	2		**I'll Just Have A Cup Of Coffee (Then I'll Go)**..... *I Just Want To Be Alone*	$12		Mercury 71732
				GRAY, David LP **'01**			
				Born in 1968 in Manchester, England; raised in Solva, Wales. Folk-rock singer/songwriter/guitarist.			
12/2/00+	57	18		**Babylon** A:56			album cut
				from the album *White Ladder* on ATO/RCA 69351			
				GRAY, Dobie C&W/BUB/LP **'73**			
				Born Lawrence Darrow Brown on 7/26/40 in Brookshire, Texas. Black singer/songwriter. Acted in the Los Angeles production of *Hair*.			
1/12/63	91	2		1 **Look At Me**..... *Walkin And Whistlin*	$15		Cordak 1602
1/9/65	13	9		2 **The "In" Crowd** ..... *Be A Man*	$10		Charger 105
4/3/65	69	7		3 **See You At The "Go-Go"**..... *Walk With Love*	$10		Charger 107
				above 3 produced by **Fred Darian**			
2/24/73	5	21	●	4 **Drift Away** *City Stars*	$6		Decca 33057
8/4/73	61	11		5 **Loving Arms**..... *Now That I'm Without You*	$6		MCA 40100
				above 2 produced by Mentor Williams (**Paul Williams**' brother)			
2/14/76	78	7		6 **If Love Must Go**..... *Lover's Sweat*	$5		Capricorn 0249
10/23/76	94	2		7 **Find 'Em, Fool 'Em & Forget 'Em**..... *Mellow Man*	$5		Capricorn 0259
12/23/78+	37	11		8 **You Can Do It** ..... *Sharing The Night Together*	$4		Infinity 50,003
				GRAY, Macy R&B/BUB/LP **'00**			
				Born Natalie McIntyre on 9/9/70 in Canton, Ohio. Female R&B singer/songwriter.			
2/19/00	5	27		1 **I Try** A:4		V	album cut ■
				from the album *On How Life Is* on Epic 69490; "45": Epic 79421; B-side: (same)			
3/31/01	63	8		2 **Request Line** .....S:6 *(3 versions)*	$5	★	Interscope 497498
				BLACK EYED PEAS featuring Macy Gray			
				GRAY, Maureen **'62**			
				Born in 1949 in Philadelphia, Pennsylvania. Teen R&B singer.			
6/9/62	91	3		**Dancin' The Strand**..... *"Oh My"*	$25		Landa 689
				GREAN, Charles Randolph, Sounde AC/BUB/LP **'69**			
				Born on 10/1/13 in Manhattan, New York. Conductor/arranger. Married singer **Betty Johnson**.			
6/14/69	13	11		**Quentin's Theme** ..... *#1 At The "Blue Whale"* [I]	$7		Ranwood 840
				from the cult daytime TV serial *Dark Shadows*			
				GREAT WHITE ROK/LP **'89**			
				Hard-rock group formed in Los Angeles, California: Jack Russell (vocals), Mark Kendall (guitar), Lorne Black (bass) and Gary Holland (drums). Audie Desbrow replaced Holland in 1986. Michael Lardie (keyboards) joined in 1987. Tony Montana replaced Black in 1987. Many personnel changes since 1991. The band's pyrotechnic show at a Rhode Island club set off a fire that killed nearly 100 people on 2/21/03, including the band's guitarist, Ty Longley.			
8/22/87	60	14		1 **Rock Me** ..... *Fast Road*	$3	■	Capitol 44042
1/23/88	57	12		2 **Save Your Love** ..... *Mistreater*	$3	■	Capitol 44104
5/13/89	5	26	●	3 **Once Bitten Twice Shy** S:4 / A:6 *Slow Ride*	$3	■	Capitol 44366
				first released in 1975 on **Ian Hunter**'s self-titled album			
9/30/89	30	21		4 **The Angel Song** .....S:27 / A:35 *Run Away*	$3		Capitol 44449
3/17/90	83	5		5 **House Of Broken Love** ..... *Red House / Bitches And Other Women*	$3	▮	Capitol 44491
3/9/91	53	8		6 **Call It Rock N' Roll**..... *Need Your Love Tonight / Down At The Doctor*	$3	▮	Capitol 44676
				GREAVES, R.B. BUB/R&B/LP **'69**			
				Born Ronald Bertram Greaves on 11/28/44 at the USAF Base in Georgetown, British Guyana. Half Native American raised on a Seminole reservation in California. Nephew of **Sam Cooke**.			
10/18/69	2[1]	15	●	1 **Take A Letter Maria** *Big Bad City*	$8		Atco 6714
1/24/70	27	8		2 **Always Something There To Remind Me**..... *Oh When I Was A Boy*	$7		Atco 6726
4/25/70	82	3		3 **Fire & Rain**..... *Ballad Of Leroy*	$7		Atco 6745
9/19/70	88	2		4 **Georgia Took Her Back** ..... *Oh When I Was A Boy*	$7		Atco 6778
12/12/70	82	2		5 **Whiter Shade Of Pale**..... *Show Me The Way To Go*	$7		Atco 6789
				melody based on the Bach cantata *Sleepers Awake*			
				GRECCO, Cyndi **'76**			
				Born on 5/19/52 in Manhattan, New York. Pop singer.			
5/8/76	25	12		**Making Our Dreams Come True**..... *Watching You*	$6		Private Stock 45,086
				theme from the TV series **LaVerne & Shirley** starring Penny Marshall and Cindy Williams			
				GRECO, Buddy MEM/AC/POP/BUB **'47**			
				Born Armando Greco on 8/14/26 in Philadelphia, Pennsylvania. Former pianist/vocalist with **Benny Goodman**. Hit #15 in 1947 with "Ooh! Look-A There, Ain't She Pretty."			
9/22/62	64	11		**Mr. Lonely** ..... *Sentimental Fool*	$15		Epic 9536
				Epic used the same music track on **Bobby Vinton**'s #1 version in 1964			

DEBUT	PEAK	WKS	Gold	A-side (Chart Hit)	B-side	$	Sym	Label & Number

GREEN, Al ★163★ R&B/BUB/LP '72

Born on 4/13/46 in Forrest City, Arkansas. Soul singer/songwriter. With gospel group the Greene Brothers. To Grand Rapids, Michigan in 1959. First recorded for Fargo in 1960. In group The Creations from 1964-67. Sang with his brother Robert Green and Lee Virgins in the group Soul Mates from 1967-68. Went solo in 1969. Wrote most of his songs. Returned to gospel music in 1980. Inducted into the Rock and Roll Hall of Fame in 1995. Won Grammy's Lifetime Achievement Award in 2002.

1)Let's Say Together 2)You Ought To Be With Me 3)I'm Still In Love With You 4)Look What You Done For Me 5)Sha-La-La (Make Me Happy)

DEBUT	PEAK	WKS	Gold	A-side (Chart Hit)	B-side	$	Sym	Label & Number
12/9/67+	41	12		1 **Back Up Train** — AL GREENE & The Soul Mate's	*Don't Leave Me*	$25		Hot Line 15,000
11/21/70+	60	10		2 **I Can't Get Next To You**	*Ride Sally Ride*	$8		Hi 2182
7/24/71	11	19	●	3 **Tired Of Being Alone**	*Get Back Baby*	$6		Hi 2194
12/4/71+	1[1]	16	●	4 **Let's Stay Together** RB[9]	*Tomorrow's Dream*	$6		Hi 2202
4/1/72	4	12	●	5 **Look What You Done For Me**	*La-La For You*	$6		Hi 2211
7/8/72	3	12	●	6 **I'm Still In Love With You** RB[2]	*Old Time Lovin'*	$6		Hi 2216
9/30/72	69	7		7 **Guilty**	*Let Me Help You*	$7		Bell 45,258
10/21/72	3	15	●	8 **You Ought To Be With Me** RB[1]	*What Is This Feeling*	$6		Hi 2227
1/20/73	71	5		9 **Hot Wire** — #7 & 9: recorded in 1967	*Don't Leave Me*	$7		Bell 45,305
2/17/73	10	11	●	10 **Call Me (Come Back Home)**	*What A Wonderful Thing Love Is*	$6		Hi 2235
7/7/73	10	15	●	11 **Here I Am (Come And Take Me)** — except for #7 & 9, the song titles from #2-11 tell a story	*I'm Glad You're Mine*	$6		Hi 2247
12/8/73+	19	11		12 **Livin' For You** RB[1]	*It Ain't No Fun To Me*	$6		Hi 2257
3/30/74	32	11		13 **Let's Get Married**	*So Good To Be Here*	$6		Hi 2262
9/28/74	7	19	●	14 **Sha-La-La (Make Me Happy)**	*School Days*	$6		Hi 2274
3/1/75	13	12		15 **L-O-V-E (Love)** RB[2]	*I Wish You Were Here*	$6		Hi 2282
7/5/75	48	6		16 **Oh Me, Oh My (Dreams In My Arms)**	*Strong As Death (Sweet As Love)*	$5		Hi 2288
11/8/75	28	11		17 **Full Of Fire** RB[1]	*Could I Be The One*	$5		Hi 2300
10/23/76+	37	14		18 **Keep Me Cryin'** — all of above Hi recordings produced by **Willie Mitchell**	*There Is Love*	$5		Hi 2319
1/7/78	83	5		19 **Belle**	*Chariots Of Fire*	$5	■	Hi 77505
11/5/88+	9	17		20 **Put A Little Love In Your Heart** A:8 / S:11 — ANNIE LENNOX & AL GREEN — from the movie *Scrooged* starring Bill Murray; picture sleeve has a center-cut hole and pictures of Bill Murray	*A Great Big Piece Of Love* (The Spheres Of Celestial Influence)	$3	■	A&M 1255

GREEN, Garland R&B/BUB '69

Born Garfield Green on 6/24/42 in Leland, Mississippi. R&B singer/pianist.

DEBUT	PEAK	WKS	Gold	A-side (Chart Hit)	B-side	$	Sym	Label & Number
9/13/69	20	10		**Jealous Kind Of Fella**	*I Can't Believe You Quit Me*	$10		Uni 55143

GREENBAUM, Norman LP '70

Born on 11/20/42 in Malden, Massachusetts. Pop-rock singer/songwriter. Member of **Dr. West's Medicine Show & Junk Band**.

DEBUT	PEAK	WKS	Gold	A-side (Chart Hit)	B-side	$	Sym	Label & Number
2/28/70	3	15	●	1 **Spirit In The Sky**	*Milk Cow*	$8		Reprise 0885
6/13/70	46	6		2 **Canned Ham**	*Junior Cadillac*	$6		Reprise 0919
5/15/71	93	6		3 **California Earthquake**	*Rhode Island Red*	$6		Reprise 1008

GREENBERG, Steve '69

Pop-novelty singer. Not to be confused with Steven Greenberg of Lipps, Inc.

DEBUT	PEAK	WKS	Gold	A-side (Chart Hit)	B-side	$	Sym	Label & Number
7/26/69	97	3		**Big Bruce** — "gay" parody of "Big Bad John" by **Jimmy Dean**; also see "Small Sad Sam" by **Phil McLean**	*Run To You* [N]	$25		Trip 3000

GREEN DAY ROK/BUB/LP '95

Punk-rock trio formed in Berkeley, California: Billie Joe Armstrong (vocals, guitar), Mike Dirnt (bass; born Mike Pritchard) and Frank "Tre Cool" Wright (drums).

1)When I Come Around 2)Good Riddance (Time Of Your Life) 3)J.A.R. (Jason Andrew Relva)

DEBUT	PEAK	WKS	Gold	A-side (Chart Hit)	B-side	$	Sym	Label & Number
5/7/94	36[A]	18		1 **Long View** MR[1]				album cut
8/6/94	26[A]	33		2 **Basket Case** MR[5]			v	album cut
11/5/94	56[A]	5		3 **Welcome To Paradise**				album cut
12/10/94+	6[A]	40		4 **When I Come Around** MR[7] — "45" issued for #2 & 4 on Reprise 17941			v	album cut
4/22/95	41[A]	17		5 **She** — all of above from the album *Dookie* on Reprise 45529				album cut
7/22/95	22[A]	12		6 **J.A.R. (Jason Andrew Relva)** MR[1] — from the movie soundtrack album *Angus* on Reprise 45960				album cut
10/7/95	27[A]	9		7 **Geek Stink Breath**				album cut
12/16/95+	35[A]	20		8 **Brain Stew/Jaded** — titles segued together on album and received airplay as a medley				album cut
7/6/96	70[A]	4		9 **Walking Contradiction** — above 3 from the album *Insomniac* on Reprise 46046				album cut
9/13/97	59[A]	12		10 **Hitchin' A Ride**				album cut
12/6/97+	11[A]	43		11 **Good Riddance (Time Of Your Life)** — above 2 from the album *Nimrod* on Reprise 46794				album cut

GREENE, Barbara '68

Born in Chicago, Illinois. R&B singer.

DEBUT	PEAK	WKS	Gold	A-side (Chart Hit)	B-side	$	Sym	Label & Number
6/22/68	86	6		**Young Boy** — first released on Vivid 105 (as: BARBARA GREEN) in 1968 ($20)	*I Should Have Treated You Right*	$15		Renee 5001

DEBUT	PEAK	WKS	Gold	A-side (Chart Hit)..........B-side	$	Sym	Label & Number
				GREENE, Jack C&W/BUB/LP **'67**			
				Born on 1/7/30 in Maryville, Tennessee. Country singer/songwriter/guitarist. Known as the "Jolly Green Giant." Charted 36 Country hits, 1965-84.			
1/7/67	65	9		**There Goes My Everything** ....CW^{7} *The Hardest Easy Thing*	$8		Decca 32023
				GREENE, Lorne AC/BUB/C&W/LP **'64**			
				Born on 2/12/14 in Ottawa, Ontario, Canada. Died of heart failure on 9/11/87 (age 73). Acted in several movies. Starred on TV's *Bonanza* and *Battlestar Galactica*.			
10/31/64	❶^{1}	12		1 **Ringo**..........AC^{6} *Bonanza* [S]	$8		RCA Victor 8444
1/30/65	72	3		2 **The Man**..........*Pop Goes The Hammer*	$8		RCA Victor 8490
				Joe Reisman (orch., above 2)			
				GREEN EYEZ R&B **'02**			
				Born Peter Peterson in Los Angeles, California. Male rapper.			
4/6/02	18^{S}	8		**Mama's Baby, Poppa's Maybe**..........*Stop That / Unkept Promises*	$6	★	Bigg Mony 2003
				vocal backing by a children's chorus			
				GREEN JELLÝ LP **'93**			
				Novelty hard-rock group formed in Kenmore, New York: Moronic Dictator (lead vocals), Joey Blowey, Rootin', Jesus Quisp, Coy Roy, Sadistica, Hotsy Menshot, Tin Titty, Sven Seven, Reason Clean, Mother Eucker, Roof D.H. and Daddy Longlegs.			
3/27/93	17	20	●	**Three Little Pigs**..........S:5 *Obey The Cowgod* [N]	$3	■ V	Zoo 14088
				originally released as by **Green Jellö**; "45": Zoo 14093; B-side: "Electric Harley House (Of Love)"			
				GREENWICH, Ellie — see RAINDROPS, The			
				GREENWOOD, Lee C&W/AC/LP **'01**			
				Born on 10/27/42 in Los Angeles, California. Country singer/songwriter/multi-instrumentalist. Charted 34 Country hits, 1981-01.			
5/28/83	53	11		1 **I.O.U.**..........*Another You*	$4	■	MCA 52199
10/1/83	96	2		2 **Somebody's Gonna Love You**..........CW^{1} *You're The Woman I Love*	$4		MCA 52257
6/8/91	30^{S}	13		3 **God Bless The USA**..........*This Old Bed*	$4	■ V	MCA 52386
				#7 Country hit in 1984 on MCA 52386 (vinyl)			
9/29/01	16	17		4 **God Bless The USA**..........S:❶^{3} / A:14 *Amazing Grace* [R]	$4	★ V	Curb 73128
				"45" reissue: MCA/Collectables 90226; B-side: "Dixie Road" (C&W #1/'85)			
				GREENWOOD COUNTY SINGERS, The **'66**			
				Folk group from Los Angeles, California (consisting of seven men and two women). Brothers Van Dyke and C. Carson Parks were members.			
8/1/64	75	5		1 **Frankie And Johnny**..........*Climb Up Sunshine Mountain*	$8	■	Kapp 591
				version of mid-19th century traditional folk song; some pressings show title as "The New 'Frankie And Johnnie' Song"			
4/30/66	64	5		2 **Please Don't Sell My Daddy No More Wine** *[THE GREENWOODS]* ...*Southbound*	$8		Kapp 742
				GREGG, Bobby, and His Friends BUB **'62**			
				Born Robert Grego. White jazz-R&B drummer from Philadelphia, Pennsylvania. Performed with **Steve Gibson & The Red Caps** from 1955-60. Also performed on several **Bob Dylan** albums.			
3/17/62	29	10		1 **The Jam** Part 1..........*Part 2* [I]	$15		Cotton 1003
				Roy Buchanan (guitar)			
6/30/62	89	4		2 **Potato Peeler**..........*Sweet Georgia Brown* [I]	$15		Cotton 1006
				GREY & HANKS R&B/BUB **'79**			
				R&B vocal duo from Chicago, Illinois: Zane Grey and Len Ron Hanks.			
3/10/79	83	2		**Dancin'**..........*How Can You Live Without Love*	$5		RCA 11460
				GRIFFIN, Clive **'93**			
				Born in London, England; raised in Reigate, Surrey, England. Former session singer.			
7/17/93	23	20		1 **When I Fall In Love**..........A:28 / S:31 *If I Were You* (Dion)	$3	■ V	Epic Soundtrax 77021
				CELINE DION CLIVE GRIFFIN			
				from the movie *Sleepless In Seattle* starring Tom Hanks and Meg Ryan; #20 hit for **Doris Day** in 1952			
11/20/93	96	3		2 **Commitment Of The Heart**..........*Sensual Feelings*	$3	■ V	550 Music/Epic 77221
				GRIFFIN, Merv POP/BUB **'51**			
				Born on 7/6/25 in San Mateo, California. Popular TV talkshow host/TV producer. Owner of TV game shows *Jeopardy!* and *Wheel Of Fortune*, and an Atlantic City casino. Featured singer with Freddy Martin, 1948-52 (I've Got A Lovely Bunch of Coconuts").			
4/10/61	69	4		**The Charanga**..........*Along Came Joe*	$10		Carlton 545
				Sid Bass (orch. and chorus)			
				GRIFFITH, Andy MEM/POP/LP **'54**			
				Born on 6/1/26 in Mount Airy, North Carolina. Actor/comedian. Starred in several movies and Broadway shows. Star of TV's *The Andy Griffith Show* and *Matlock*. Hit #9 on the pop charts in 1954 with "What It Was, Was Football."			
4/2/55	26	1		**Make Yourself Comfortable**..........S:26 *Ko Ko Mo (I Love You So)* [C]	$25	⊙	Capitol 3057
				Jean Wilson (vocal); Burt Massengale (orch.); foldout insert features a photo of Andy			
				GRIFFITHS, Marcia **'90**			
				Born in 1954 in Kingston, Jamaica. Reggae singer. Member of **Bob Marley**'s backing vocal group, the I Threes, from 1974-81.			
12/9/89+	51	11		**Electric Boogie**..........*(instrumental)*	$5	■ V	Mango 126
				popular dance song better known as the "Electric Slide"			
				GRIGGS, Andy C&W/BUB/LP **'99**			
				Born on 8/13/73 in Monroe, Louisiana. Country singer/songwriter/guitarist.			
3/27/99	28	20		1 **You Won't Ever Be Lonely**..........A:22 / S:69 *(3 album snippets)*	$4	★	RCA 65646
10/2/99	65	10		2 **I'll Go Crazy**..........A:52		V	album cut
3/11/00	37	20		3 **She's More**..........A:33		V	album cut
				"45" issued for above 2 on RCA 65936; above 3 from the album *You Won't Ever Be Lonely* on RCA 67596			
6/29/02	52	12		4 **Tonight I Wanna Be Your Man**..........A:49		V	album cut
				from the album *Freedom* on RCA 67006; "45": RCA 69132; B-side: "How Cool Is That" (C&W #22)			
				GRIN BUB/LP **'72**			
				Rock trio formed in New York: Nils Lofgren (vocals, guitar), Bob Gordon (bass) and Bob Berberich (drums). Lofgren was a member of **Bruce Springsteen**'s E Street Band, 1984-85.			
2/5/72	75	6		**White Lies**..........*Just To Have You*	$7		Spindizzy 4005

DEBUT	PEAK	WKS	Gold	A-side (Chart Hit)..........B-side	$	Sym	Label & Number
				GROCE, Larry LP **'76**			
				Born on 4/22/48 in Dallas, Texas. Pop-folk singer/songwriter. Wrote children's songs for Walt Disney Records.			
1/10/76	9	15		**Junk Food Junkie** ....*Muddy Boggy Banjo Man* [L-N]	$5		Warner/Curb 8165
				recorded at McCabe's nightclub in Santa Monica; first released on Peaceable Records in 1975 with a black-and-white cartoon picture sleeve			
				GROOVE ARMADA **'00**			
				Electronic dance duo from London, England: Tom Findlay and Andy Cato.			
2/5/00	69[S]	1		**I See You Baby** ....*(3 mixes) / If Everybody Looked The Same / Inside My Mind*	$8	★**	Jive 42649
				Gram'ma Funk (female vocal)			
				GROOVE THEORY R&B/LP **'95**			
				Male/female R&B duo: Bryce Wilson and **Amel Larrieux**. Wilson, then known as Bryce Luvah, was a member of **Mantronix**.			
8/26/95	5	33	●	1 **Tell Me** ....S:4 / A:10 *(instrumental)*	$3	▮	Epic 77961
				Trey Lorenz (backing vocal)			
2/10/96	64	12		2 **Keep Tryin'** ....S:56 / A:71 *(instrumental)*	$3	▮	Epic 78197
8/3/96	65	11		3 **Baby Luv**..........A:66 / S:74 *(album version) / Keep Tryin'*	$3	▮	Epic 78359
				contains elements from "Rappa, Dappa, Snappa" by Edwin Birdsong			
				GROSS, Henry BUB/LP **'76**			
				Born on 4/1/51 in Brooklyn, New York. Pop-rock singer/songwriter/guitarist.			
4/26/75	93	3		1 **One More Tomorrow**..........*Evergreen*	$6		A&M 1682
2/28/76	6	20	●	2 **Shannon** ....*Pokey*	$5		Lifesong 45002
				song is a tale about the death of a pet dog			
7/10/76	37	10		3 **Springtime Mama** ....*Overton Square*	$5		Lifesong 45008
10/30/76	85	3		4 **Someday (I Didn't Want To Have to be the One)** ....*Lincoln Road*	$5		Lifesong 45014
				all of above produced by **Terry Cashman & Tommy West**			
				GROUP HOME R&B/BUB **'95**			
				Rap duo from Brooklyn, New York: James "Melachi The Nutcracker" Felder and James "Lil' Dap" Heath.			
2/4/95	85	5		**Supa Star** ....*(2 versions)*	$5	▮	Payday 127019
				GTR LP **'86**			
				Rock group formed in England: Max Bacon (vocals), Steve Hackett and Steve Howe (guitars), Phgil Spalding (bass) and Jonathan Mover (drums). Hackett was with **Genesis**. Howe was with **Yes** and **Asia**. Group name is short for guitar.			
5/10/86	14	16		1 **When The Heart Rules The Mind** ....S:9 / A:19 *Reach Out (Never Say No)*	$3	■	Arista 9470
8/23/86	85	6		2 **The Hunter**..........*Sketches In The Sun*	$3	■	Arista 9512
				GUARALDI, Vince, Trio LP **'63**			
				Born on 7/17/32 in San Francisco, California. Died of a heart attack on 2/6/76 (age 43). Pianist/leader of own jazz trio. Formerly with **Woody Herman** and **Cal Tjader**. Wrote the music for the *Peanuts* TV specials.			
12/8/62+	22	18		**Cast Your Fate To The Wind** ....*Samba De Orpheus* [I]	$12		Fantasy 563
				**GUESS WHO, The** ★188★ BUB/LP **'70**			
				Rock group formed in Winnipeg, Manitoba, Canada: Allan "Chad Allan" Kobel (vocals, guitar), Randy Bachman (guitar; born on 9/27/43), Bob Ashley (piano), Jim Kale (bass; born on 8/11/43) and Garry Peterson (drums; born on 5/26/45). Recorded as The Reflections, and Chad Allan & The Expressions. Ashley replaced by new lead singer **Burton Cummings** (born on 12/31/47) in 1966. Allan left shortly thereafter. Bachman left in 1970 to form **Bachman-Turner Overdrive**; replaced by Kurt Winter and Greg Leskiw (guitars). Leskiw and Kale left in 1972, replaced by Don McDougall (guitar) and Bill Wallace (bass). Domenic Troiano (guitar; **The James Gang**) replaced both Winter and McDougall in 1973. Group disbanded in 1975; several reunions since then. Winter died of a bleeding ulcer on 12/14/97 (age 51).			
				1)American Woman 2)No Time 3)These Eyes 4)Clap For The Wolfman 5)Share The Land			
5/8/65	22	11		1 **Shakin' All Over** *[GUESS WHO?]*..........*Till We Kissed*	$20		Scepter 1295
				group is actually Chad Allan & The Expressions			
4/5/69	6	14	●	2 **These Eyes** ....*Lightfoot*	$7		RCA Victor 0102
7/12/69	10	11	●	3 **Laughing** /			
10/18/69	22	10		4 **Undun**	$7		RCA Victor 0195
12/20/69+	5	14		5 **No Time** ....*Proper Stranger*	$7		RCA Victor 0300
3/21/70	1[3]	15	●	6 **American Woman** /			
4/4/70		13		7 **No Sugar Tonight**	$7		RCA Victor 0325
				all of above include Randy Bachman before his departure			
7/18/70	17	11		8 **Hand Me Down World**..........*Runnin' Down The Street*	$7		RCA Victor 0367
10/24/70	10	10		9 **Share The Land** ....*Bus Rider*	$7	■	RCA Victor 0388
1/30/71	43	7		10 **Hang On To Your Life**..........*Do You Miss Me Darlin'*	$6	■	RCA Victor 0414
4/17/71	29	13		11 **Albert Flasher** /			
4/17/71	55	11		12 **Broken**	$6		RCA Victor 0458
8/14/71	19	12		13 **Rain Dance**..........*One Divided*	$6		RCA Victor 0522
11/27/71+	50	9		14 **Sour Suite** ....*Life In The Bloodstream*	$6		RCA Victor 0578
3/4/72	47	7		15 **Heartbroken Bopper**..........*Arrivederci Girl*	$6		RCA Victor 0659
5/20/72	70	6		16 **Guns, Guns, Guns**..........*Heaven Only Moved Once Yesterday*	$6		RCA Victor 0708
10/14/72	96	3		17 **Runnin' Back To Saskatoon**..........*New Mother Nature* [L]	$6		RCA Victor 0803
2/3/73	61	7		18 **Follow Your Daughter Home**..........*Bye Bye Babe*	$6		RCA Victor 0880
2/16/74	39	19		19 **Star Baby** ....*Musicione*	$6		RCA Victor 0217
7/20/74	6	16		20 **Clap For The Wolfman**..........*Road Food*	$6		RCA Victor 0324
				featuring bits of dialogue by **Wolfman Jack**			
11/23/74+	28	11		21 **Dancin' Fool**..........*Seems Like I Can't Live With You, But I Can't Live Without You*	$6		RCA Victor 10075
				all of above (except #1) produced by Jack Richardson			
				GUIDRY, Greg LP **'82**			
				Born on 1/23/50 in St. Louis, Missouri. Pop singer/songwriter/pianist.			
2/13/82	17	16		1 **Goin' Down** ....*Darlin' It's You*	$4		Columbia 02691
7/17/82	92	2		2 **Into My Love** ....*Are You Ready For Love*	$4		Columbia 02984

DEBUT	PEAK	WKS	Gold	A-side (Chart Hit)........B-side	$	Sym	Label & Number
				GUITAR, Bonnie C&W '57			
				Born Bonnie Buckingham on 3/25/23 in Seattle, Washington. Own group in the early 1950s. Worked as session guitarist in Los Angeles in the mid-1950s. Owner of Dolphin/Dolton Records in Seattle in 1958. Played on several **Fleetwoods**' recordings.			
4/13/57	6	22		1 **Dark Moon**........A:6 / T:8 / S:10 / J:11 *Big Mike*	$20		Dot 15550
				first released on Fabor 4018 in 1956 ($40)			
10/28/57	71	8		2 **Mister Fire Eyes**........T:71 *There's A New Moon Over My Shoulder*	$15		Dot 15612
12/14/59	97	2		3 **Candy Apple Red**........*Come To Me I Love You (Akaka Falls)*	$15		Dolton 10
				released on Dolton 19 in 1960 ($15)			
4/2/66	99	2		4 **I'm Living In Two Worlds**........*Goodtime Charlie*	$8		Dot 16811
				GUNHILL ROAD '73			
				Pop-rock trio: Glenn Leopold, Gil Roman and Steven Goldrich.			
3/31/73	40	15		**Back When My Hair Was Short**........*We Can't Ride The Roller Coaster Anymore*	$6		Kama Sutra 569
	★344★			**GUNS N' ROSES** ROK/LP '88			
				Hard-rock group formed in Los Angeles, California: William "Axl Rose" Bailey (vocals; born on 2/6/62), Saul "Slash" Hudson (born on 7/23/65) and Jeffrey "Izzy Stradlin" Isbell (born on 4/8/62; guitars), Michael "Duff" McKagan (bass; born on 2/5/64) and Steven Adler (drums; born on 1/22/65). Axl Rose married Erin Everly (daughter of Don Everly of **The Everly Brothers**) on 4/27/90; she filed for divorce three weeks later. Adler left in 1990; replaced by Matt Sorum (who had toured with **The Cult**). Keyboardist Dizzy Reed joined in 1990. Stradlin' left in late 1991; replaced by Gilby Clarke (of Kill For Thrills). Slash was married to model Renee Surran from 1992-97. Clarke left band in January 1995. Slash, Sorum and Clarke recorded in 1995 in Slash's Snakepit.			
				1)Sweet Child O' Mine 2)November Rain 3)Patience			
6/25/88	❶²	24	●	1 **Sweet Child O' Mine** S:❶² / A:❶² *It's So Easy*	$5	■	Geffen 27963
				written by Rose for his then-girlfriend Erin Everly			
10/22/88	7	17		2 **Welcome To The Jungle**........S:3 / A:11 *Mr. Brownstone*	$5	■	Geffen 27759
				a promotional text-only ("Don't Report This Record.") sleeve was also issued			
1/14/89	5	17		3 **Paradise City**........S:5 / A:5 *Move To The City*	$5	■	Geffen 27570
4/8/89	4	18	●	4 **Patience**........S:3 / A:5 *Rocket Queen*	$5	■	Geffen 22996
7/29/89	93	5		5 **Nightrain**........*Reckless Life*	$5		Geffen 22869
				all of above (except #4) from the album *Appetite For Destruction*			
7/13/91	29	15	●	6 **You Could Be Mine**........S:2 *Civil War* (ROK #4)	$4	▮V	Geffen 19039
				from the movie *Terminator 2-Judgment Day* starring Arnold Schwarzenegger			
9/21/91	10	20	●	7 **Don't Cry**........S:5 / A:52 *(alternate version)*	$4	▮V	Geffen 19027
12/21/91+	33	16		8 **Live And Let Die**........S:19 *(live version)*	$4	▮V	Geffen 19114
				title song from the James Bond movie starring Roger Moore			
6/27/92	3	20	●	9 **November Rain**........S:4 / A:12 *Sweet Child O' Mine*	$4	▮V	Geffen 19067
11/21/92	72	10		10 **Yesterdays**........S:47 *(live version)*	$4	▮V	Geffen 19142
				#7-9: from the album *Use Your Illusion I*; #6 & 10: from the album *Use Your Illusion II*			
3/5/94	69	9		11 **Since I Don't Have You**........S:37 *You Can't Put Your Arms Around A Memory*	$4	▮V	Geffen 19266
12/31/94+	55	8		12 **Sympathy For The Devil**........S:29 *Escape To Paris* (Elliot Goldenthal)	$4	▮V	Geffen 19381
				first recorded by **The Rolling Stones** on their 1968 album *Beggars Banquet*; from the movie *Interview With The Vampire* starring Tom Cruise; all of above (except #11) produced by Mike Clink			
				GUTHRIE, Arlo BUB/AC/LP '72			
				Born on 7/10/47 in Brooklyn, New York. Folk singer/songwriter. Son of Woody Guthrie. Starred as himself in the 1969 movie *Alice's Restaurant* which was based on his 1967 song "Alice's Restaurant Massacree." Often performed in concert with **Pete Seeger**.			
12/13/69	97	2		1 **Alice's Rock & Roll Restaurant**........*Coming In To Los Angeles*	$12		Reprise 0877
				short version of his 18-minute tale "Alice's Restaurant Massacree"			
7/29/72	18	16		2 **The City Of New Orleans**........*Days Are Short*	$7		Reprise 1103
				composed on the train of the same name by folk singer Steve Goodman (his version "Bubbled Under" at #113 in 1972)			
				GUTHRIE, Gwen R&B/BUB/LP '86			
				Born on 7/9/50 in Newark, New Jersey. Died of cancer on 2/4/99 (age 48). R&B-dance singer/songwriter. Background vocalist for many top artists.			
8/2/86	42	13		**Ain't Nothin' Goin' On But The Rent**........RB¹ S:33 *Passion Eyes*	$4	■	Polydor 885106
				GUY R&B/LP '00			
				R&B trio from Harlem, New York: **Teddy Riley**, with brothers Damion and **Aaron Hall**. By age 20, in 1988, Riley (ex-member of R&B group Kids At Work) was already a renowned producer. Trio disbanded in 1991; reunited in 1999. Riley formed **BLACKstreet** in 1993.			
5/6/89	70	7		1 **I Like**........*(remix)*	$3		Uptown/MCA 53490
9/23/89	62	6		2 **My Fantasy**........RB¹ *(instrumental)*	$3		Motown 1968
				TEDDY RILEY FEATURING GUY			
				from the movie *Do The Right Thing* starring Spike Lee			
11/10/90	50	15		3 **I Wanna Get With U**........S:35 *(3 album snippets)*	$3	▮	MCA 53928
2/23/91	41	15		4 **Let's Chill**........A:38 / S:62 *(3 versions)*	$5	▮*	MCA 54051
7/6/91	73ˢ	4		5 **Do Me Right**........*(3 versions)*	$5	▮*	MCA 54097
12/18/99+	19	11		6 **Dancin'** S:12 *(3 album snippets)*	$3	★	MCA 155657
				GUY, Jasmine R&B/LP '91			
				Born on 3/10/64 in Boston, Massachusetts; raised in Atlanta, Georgia. Black female actress/singer. Played "Whitley Gilbert" on TV's *A Different World*. Began career with the Alvin Ailey Dance Troupe. Dancer in TV show *Fame*. Starred in several off-Broadway shows. In movies *School Daze* and *Harlem Nights*.			
3/23/91	66	10		1 **Another Like My Lover**........*(instrumental)*	$3	▮	Warner 19486
8/3/91	34	20		2 **Just Want To Hold You**........A:34 / S:52 *I Don't Have To Justify*	$3	▮V	Warner 19330
				GUYS NEXT DOOR '91			
				Pop group formed for their own Saturday morning NBC-TV show: Patrick J. Dancy, Eddie Garcia, Bobby Leslie, Damon Sharpe and Chris Wolfe.			
1/5/91	42	11		**I've Been Waiting For You**........S:31 *Telephone Talking*	$3	▮	SBK 07340
				G-WIZ '93			
				Rap group from Los Angeles, California: Jamahl Harris, Ron Martin, Craig Cummins and Kevin Williams.			
7/3/93	73	11		**Teddy Bear**........A:59 / S:68 *Let Your Love Fall Down*	$3	▮	Scotti Brothers 75360

DEBUT	PEAK	WKS	Gold	A-side (Chart Hit)...B-side	$	Sym	Label & Number

GYPSY
BUB/LP **'71**

Rock group formed in Los Angeles, California: James "Owl" Walsh (vocals, keyboards), James Johnson and Enrico Rosenbaum (guitars), Doni Larson (bass), and Jay Epstein (drums). Walsh re-formed the group in 1978 as the **James Walsh Gypsy Band**.

DEBUT	PEAK	WKS	Gold	A-side (Chart Hit)...B-side	$	Sym	Label & Number
12/5/70+	62	8		1 **Gypsy Queen - Part 1** ...*Dead And Gone*	$6		Metromedia 202
10/28/78	71	7		2 **Cuz It's You, Girl** *[JAMES WALSH GYPSY BAND]* ...*Bring Yourself Around*	$5		RCA 11403

GYRL
R&B **'97**

Female R&B vocal group: sisters Miyoko and Jamila, with Tai and Jeanae.

DEBUT	PEAK	WKS	Gold	A-side (Chart Hit)...B-side	$	Sym	Label & Number
6/21/97	91	5		**Get Your Groove On** ...*(remix)* samples "Five Minutes Of Funk" by **Whodini**; from the movie *B.A.P.S.* starring Halle Berry	$4	▮	Silas/MCA 55334

GZA/GENIUS
R&B/BUB/LP **'95**

Born Gary Grice on 8/22/66 in Brooklyn, New York. Male rapper. Member of **Wu-Tang Clan**. Pronounced: jizz-ah.

DEBUT	PEAK	WKS	Gold	A-side (Chart Hit)...B-side	$	Sym	Label & Number
10/28/95	48	7		1 **Liquid Swords** S:18 *Labels* **GENIUS/GZA**	$4	▮	Geffen 19390
12/30/95	97	3		2 **Cold World** ...S:64 *(2 versions) / I Gotcha Back* **GENIUS/GZA Featuring Inspektah Deck a.k.a. Rollie Fingers** samples "Rocket Love" by **Stevie Wonder** and "Love Me In A Special Way" by **DeBarge**; remix later released on Geffen 19394 featuring **D'Angelo**	$4	▮	Geffen 19391
4/6/96	67	13		3 **Shadowboxin'** ...S:56 *(instrumental) / 4th Chamber* **GENIUS/GZA Featuring Method Man**	$4	▮	Geffen 19396
5/12/01	25^S	11		4 **Bigacts Littleacts** ...*(5 mixes)* **AFU-RA featuring GZA**	$6	★*	D&D/Koch 8263
4/13/02	42^S	4		5 **Fame** ...*(3 versions)*	$6	T	MCA 155938
11/2/02	65^S	1		6 **Knock Knock** ...*(2 versions)* samples "I Must Be Living For A Broken Heart" by the **Spinners**	$6	T	MCA 113967

H

HACKETT, Buddy
MEM **'56**

Born on 8/31/24 in Brooklyn, New York. Died of diabetes on 6/30/2003 (age 78). Popular comedian.

DEBUT	PEAK	WKS	Gold	A-side (Chart Hit)...B-side	$	Sym	Label & Number
4/7/56	87	2		**Chinese Rock And Egg Roll** ...T:87 *Ting Me A Tong (Sing Me A Song)* [C] **Dick Jacobs** (orch.); sequel to Hackett's 1953 hit "The Chinese Waiter"	$20		Coral 61594

HADDAWAY
LP **'93**

Born Nester Haddaway on 1/9/65 in Tobago, West Indies; raised in Chicago, Illinois. Black dance singer/choreographer.

DEBUT	PEAK	WKS	Gold	A-side (Chart Hit)...B-side	$	Sym	Label & Number
8/28/93	11	26	●	1 **What Is Love** ...A:11 / S:13 *Sing About Love* song used in recurring "Roxbury" skit (bobbing-head disco guys) on TV's *Saturday Night Live*	$4	▮	Arista 12575
12/25/93+	41	16		2 **Life (Everybody Needs Somebody To Love)** ...A:39 / S:62 *Shout*	$3	▮	Arista 12646

HAGAR, Sammy
★581★ ROK/BUB/LP **'83**

Born on 10/13/47 in Monterey, California. Rock singer/songwriter/guitarist. Lead singer of Montrose (1973-75) and **Van Halen** (1985-96). Also recorded in a quartet with Neal Schon (**Journey**), Kenny Aaronson (**Stories**) and Michael Shrieve (**Santana**).

1)Your Love Is Driving Me Crazy 2)Give To Live 3)I Can't Drive 55

DEBUT	PEAK	WKS	Gold	A-side (Chart Hit)...B-side	$	Sym	Label & Number
12/10/77+	62	8		1 **You Make Me Crazy** ...*Reckless*	$5		Capitol 4502
4/7/79	65	5		2 **(Sittin' On) The Dock Of The Bay** ...*I've Done Everything For You* Brad Delp and Barry Goudreau (of **Boston**; backing vocals)	$5	■	Capitol 4699
9/15/79	77	7		3 **Plain Jane** ...*Wounded In Love*	$5		Capitol 4757
1/30/82	43	10		4 **I'll Fall In Love Again** ...*Satisfied*	$4		Geffen 49881
5/15/82	73	4		5 **Piece Of My Heart** ...*Sweet Hitchhiker*	$4	■	Geffen 50059
12/11/82+	13	19		6 **Your Love Is Driving Me Crazy** *I Don't Need Love* (ROK #24)	$4		Geffen 29816
3/26/83	46	8		7 **Never Give Up** ...*Fast Times At Ridgemont High* (ROK #21)	$4	■	Geffen 29718
5/19/84	94	2		8 **Whiter Shade Of Pale** ...*Hot And Dirty* **HAGAR, SCHON, AARONSON, SHRIEVE** melody based on the Bach cantata *Sleepers Awake*	$4	■	Geffen 29280
7/14/84	38	12		9 **Two Sides Of Love** ...*Burnin' Down The City*	$3	■	Geffen 29246
9/29/84	26	16		10 **I Can't Drive 55** ...A:26 / S:27 *Dick In The Dirt*	$3	■	Geffen 29173
2/14/87	54	14		11 **Winner Takes It All** ...*The Fight* (**Giorgio Moroder**) from the movie *Over The Top* starring Sylvester Stallone	$3	■	Columbia 06647
6/20/87	23	17		12 **Give To Live** ...AR³ S:23 / A:23 *When The Hammer Falls*	$3	■	Geffen 28314
10/24/87	82	13		13 **Eagles Fly** ...*Hands And Knees* above 3 co-produced by Eddie **Van Halen**; all of above (except #2, 5, 7, 8 & 11) written by Hagar	$3	■	Geffen 28185

HAGGARD, Merle
C&W/BUB/LP **'73**

Born on 4/6/37 in Bakersfield, California. Country singer/songwriter/guitarist. Served nearly three years in San Quentin prison on a burglary charge, 1957-60. Signed to Capitol Records in 1965 and then formed backing band, The Strangers. One of the top male vocalists of the Country charts with 38 #1 Country singles (out of 103 charted, 1963-94).

DEBUT	PEAK	WKS	Gold	A-side (Chart Hit)...B-side	$	Sym	Label & Number
11/1/69+	41	14		1 **Okie From Muskogee** ...CW⁴ *If I Had Left It Up To You*	$8	■	Capitol 2626
2/14/70	92	3		2 **The Fightin' Side Of Me** ...CW³ *Every Fool Has A Rainbow*	$8	■	Capitol 2719
3/20/71	90	3		3 **Soldier's Last Letter** ...*The Farmer's Daughter* #1 Country hit for Ernest Tubb in 1944	$8	■	Capitol 3024
12/4/71+	58	7		4 **Carolyn** ...CW³ *When The Feelin' Goes Away*	$8		Capitol 3222
9/1/73	62	8		5 **Everybody's Had The Blues** ...CW² *Nobody Knows I'm Hurtin'* [L] **MERLE HAGGARD And The Strangers** (all of above)	$7		Capitol 3641
11/24/73	28	11		6 **If We Make It Through December** CW⁴ X:7 *Bobby Wants A Puppy Dog For Christmas* [X] Christmas charts: #7/'73 (2 weeks)	$7		Capitol 3746
10/22/77	58	9		7 **From Graceland To The Promised Land** ...*Are You Lonesome Tonight* Jordanaires (backing vocals); an **Elvis Presley** tribute	$6		MCA 40804

DEBUT	PEAK	WKS	Gold	A-side (Chart Hit)......B-side	$	Sym	Label & Number

HAHN, Joyce — '57

Ballad singer, similar in style to **Margaret Whiting**.

DEBUT	PEAK	WKS	Gold	A-side (Chart Hit)......B-side	$	Sym	Label & Number
6/3/57	84	4		**Gonna Find Me A Bluebird** ......T:84 *I Saw You, I Saw You* **Archie Bleyer** (orch.)	$15		Cadence 1318

HAILEY, K-Ci — see K-CI & JOJO / JODECI

HAIR Soundtrack — see BARNES, Cheryl

HAIRCUT ONE HUNDRED — ROK/BUB/LP '82

Pop-rock group from Beckenham, Kent, England: Nick Heyward (vocals), Graham Jones (guitar), Phil Smith (saxophone), Mark Fox (percussion), Les Nemes (bass) and Blair Cunningham (drums).

DEBUT	PEAK	WKS	Gold	A-side (Chart Hit)......B-side	$	Sym	Label & Number
5/15/82	37	17		**Love Plus One** ......*Favourite Shirts (Boy Meets Girl)* (ROK #50)	$4		Arista 0672

HALEY, Bill, And His Comets ★138★ — MEM/POP/BUB/LP '55

Born on 7/6/25 in Highland Park, Michigan. Died of a heart attack on 2/9/81 (age 55). Began career as a singer with a New England Country band, the Down Homers. Formed the Four Aces of Western Swing in 1948. In 1949 formed the Saddlemen, who recorded on various labels before signing with the Essex label (as Bill Haley and the Saddlemen) in 1952; signed with Decca in 1954. The original Comets band backing Haley on "Rock Around The Clock," recorded on 4/12/54, were Danny Cedrone (lead guitar; died of a heart attack on 7/10/54), Joey D'Ambrose (sax), Billy Williamson (steel guitar), Johnny Grande (piano), Marshall Lytle (bass) and Billy Guesack (session drums; Dick Richards was their live drummer). D'Ambrose, Richards and Lytle left in September 1955 to form the Jodimars. Comets lineup on subsequent recordings included Williamson, Grande, Rudy Pompilli (sax; died on 2/5/76, age 47), Al Rex (bass; born Al Piccarelli), Ralph Jones (drums) and Frank Beecher (lead guitar). They also recorded as **The Kingsmen** in 1958 (see #25 below). Inducted into the Rock and Roll Hall of Fame in 1987. Haley's 1953 hit "Crazy Man, Crazy" was the first rock and roll hit (#12) on the pop charts.

1)Rock Around The Clock 2)See You Later, Alligator 3)Shake, Rattle And Roll 4)Burn That Candle 5)Dim, Dim The Lights

DEBUT	PEAK	WKS	Gold	A-side (Chart Hit)......B-side	$	Sym	Label & Number
8/21/54	7	27	●	1 **Shake, Rattle And Roll** ......S:7 / J:8 / A:9 *A.B.C. Boogie* #1 R&B hit for **Joe Turner** in 1954	$30		Decca 29204
11/20/54+	11	15		2 **Dim, Dim The Lights (I Want Some Atmosphere)** ......S:11 / A:16 / J:16 *Happy Baby*	$30		Decca 29317
3/19/55	17	4		3 **Birth Of The Boogie /** J:17 / S:26			
3/5/55	18	8		4 **Mambo Rock** ......S:18 / J:flip	$30		Decca 29418
5/14/55	❶^{8}	24	●	5 **(We're Gonna) Rock Around The Clock** S:❶^{8} / J:❶^{7} / A:❶^{6} / T:56 *Thirteen Women (And Only One Man In Town)* first released on 5/10/54; featured in the movie *Blackboard Jungle* starring Glenn Ford; original version released by Sonny Dae in 1954 on Arcade 123 ($200); Grammy Hall of Fame Award winner in 1982; also see #28 below	$25		Decca 29124
7/23/55	15	4		6 **Razzle-Dazzle /** S:15			
7/23/55		2		7 **Two Hound Dogs** ......S:flip	$25		Decca 29552
11/12/55+	9	17		8 **Burn That Candle /** J:9 / S:16 / T:20			
11/12/55	23	17		9 **Rock-A-Beatin' Boogie** ......S:23 / T:41 / J:flip first recorded by the Esquire Boys in 1953 on Rainbow 200 ($40)	$25		Decca 29713
1/14/56	6	19	●	10 **See You Later, Alligator** ......S:6 / T:6 / A:6 / J:6 *The Paper Boy (On Main Street, U.S.A.)* #14 R&B hit in 1955 for Bobby Charles as "Later Alligator" on Chess 1609 ($50)	$25		Decca 29791
4/7/56	16	14		11 **R-O-C-K /** J:16 / S:20 / T:29 featured in the movie *Rock Around The Clock* starring Alan Freed			
4/7/56	18	10		12 **The Saints Rock 'N Roll** ......S:18 / T:42 / J:flip rock version of the spiritual "When The Saints Go Marching In"	$25		Decca 29870
6/16/56	60	6		13 **Hot Dog Buddy Buddy /** T:60			
7/14/56	78	3		14 **Rockin' Through The Rye** ......T:78 rock version of a 1796 Scottish tune "Comin' Thro' The Rye"	$25		Decca 29948
8/11/56	25	14		15 **Rip It Up /** S:25 / T:30			
8/25/56	68	5		16 **Teenager's Mother (Are You Right?)** T:68	$25		Decca 30028
11/3/56	34	13		17 **Rudy's Rock** ......T:34 *Blue Comet Blues* [I] named for Haley's saxophonist Rudy Pompilli	$25		Decca 30085
12/15/56	30^{CU}	3		18 **Don't Knock The Rock /** title song from the movie starring Haley			
12/15/56		1		19 **Choo Choo Ch'Boogie** ......CU:flip #1 R&B hit for Louis Jordan in 1946	$25		Decca 30148
4/6/57	70	4		20 **Forty Cups Of Coffee /** T:70 original version by Ella Mae Morse in 1953 on Capitol 2539 ($25)			
3/23/57		1		21 **Hook, Line And Sinker** ......CU:flip	$25		Decca 30214
6/10/57	60	7		22 **(You Hit The Wrong Note) Billy Goat** ......T:60 *Rockin' Rollin' Rover*	$25	■	Decca 30314
4/14/58	22	15		23 **Skinny Minnie** ......T:22 / S:24 *Sway With Me*	$25		Decca 30592
8/11/58	67	1		24 **Lean Jean** ......H:67 *Don't Nobody Move*	$25		Decca 30681
9/1/58	35	3		25 **Week End** ......S:35 / H:84 *Better Believe It* [I] **THE KINGSMEN**	$40		East West 115
10/5/59	46	12		26 **Joey's Song** ......*Ooh! Look-A There, Ain't She Pretty* [I] named for its composer, arranger/conductor **Joe Reisman**	$20		Decca 30956
1/4/60	70	6		27 **Skokiaan (South African Song)** ......*Puerto Rican Peddler* [I] named for a South African Zulu tribal drink; #3 hit for **Ralph Marterie** in 1954	$20		Decca 31030
3/16/74	39	14		28 **(We're Gonna) Rock Around The Clock** ......*Thirteen Women (And Only One Man In Town)* [R] re-popularized due to its use as the original opening theme of TV's *Happy Days*; "Bubbled Under" (#118) in 1968	$6		MCA 60025

HALL, Aaron — R&B/BUB/LP '94

Born on 8/10/64 in Brooklyn, New York. R&B singer. Member of the New York City trio **Guy** which included his younger brother Damion Hall. Also see **Heavy D & The Boyz**.

DEBUT	PEAK	WKS	Gold	A-side (Chart Hit)......B-side	$	Sym	Label & Number
3/14/92	44	16		1 **Don't Be Afraid** ......RB^{2} S:22 / A:72 *(album version)* from the movie *Juice* starring Omar Epps	$4	▮	Soul 54330
5/14/94	14	23	●	2 **I Miss You** ......S:8 / A:20 *(instrumental)*	$4	▮	Silas/MCA 54847

DEBUT	PEAK	WKS	Gold	A-side (Chart Hit)...B-side	$	Sym	Label & Number
				HALL, Aaron — Cont'd			
3/16/96	82	7		3 **Scent Of Attraction** ......S:70 *(remix) / Dip & Fall Back* **PATRA with Aaron Hall** samples "Shadows" by **Tom Scott**	$4	▮	550 Music/Epic 78257
10/17/98	26	16		4 **All The Places (I Will Kiss You)** ......S:12 *Move It Girl*	$4	★	MCA 55473
				HALL, Arsenio — see CHUNKY A			
				HALL, Daryl LP **'86** Born Daryl Franklin Hohl on 10/11/48 in Philadelphia, Pennsylvania. Half of **Hall & Oates** duo.			
8/2/86	5	15		1 **Dreamtime** ......A:4 / S:5 *Let It Out*	$3	■	RCA 14387
10/18/86	33	13		2 **Foolish Pride** ......A:30 / S:37 *What's Gonna Happen To Us*	$3	■	RCA 5038
1/24/87	57	8		3 **Someone Like You** ......*(with sax solo)* Robbie McIntosh (guitar solo)	$3	■	RCA 5105
10/2/93	82	2		4 **I'm In A Philly Mood** ......*Money Changes Everything*	$3	▮V	Epic 77139
				**HALL, Daryl, & John Oates** ★37★ R&B/BUB/AC/LP **'81** **Daryl Hall** (born on 10/11/48) and John Oates (born on 4/7/49 in New York City, New York) met while students at Temple University in 1967. Hall sang backup for many top soul groups before teaming up with Oates in 1972. They passed **The Everly Brothers** as the #1 charting duo of the rock era. Also see **Holly Knight** and **INXS**'s "Original Sin." *1)Maneater 2)Kiss On My List 3)Private Eyes 4)Out Of Touch 5)Rich Girl*			
2/9/74	60	8		1 **She's Gone** ......*I'm Just A Kid (Don't Make Me Feel Like A Man)*	$6		Atlantic 2993
1/31/76	4	28	●	2 **Sara Smile** ......*Soldering* written for Hall's girlfriend Sara Allen	$5		RCA Victor 10530
7/24/76	7	20		3 **She's Gone** ......*I'm Just A Kid (Don't Make Me Feel Like A Man)* [R] same version as #1 above	$5		Atlantic 3332
10/30/76	39	15		4 **Do What You Want, Be What You Are** ......*You'll Never Learn*	$4		RCA 10808
1/22/77	❶[2]	20	●	5 **Rich Girl** ......*London Luck, & Love*	$4	■	RCA 10860
5/7/77	28	10		6 **Back Together Again** ......*Room To Breathe*	$4		RCA 10970
7/30/77	80	3		7 **It's Uncanny** ......*Lilly (Are You Happy)*	$5		Atlantic 3397
10/22/77	73	6		8 **Why Do Lovers (Break Each Other's Heart?)** ......*The Girl Who Used To Be*	$4		RCA 11132
8/26/78	20	14		9 **It's A Laugh** ......*Serious Music*	$4		RCA 11371
12/9/78+	42	10		10 **I Don't Wanna Lose You** ......*August Day*	$4		RCA 11424
10/27/79+	18	19		11 **Wait For Me** ......*No Brain No Pain*	$4		RCA 11747
7/19/80	30	13		12 **How Does It Feel To Be Back** ......*United State*	$4		RCA 12048
9/27/80	12	20		13 **You've Lost That Lovin' Feeling** ......*Diddy Doo Wop (I Hear The Voices)*	$4		RCA 12103
1/24/81	❶[3]	23	●	14 **Kiss On My List** ......*Africa*	$3		RCA 12142
5/2/81	5	21		15 **You Make My Dreams** ......*Gotta Lotta Nerve (Perfect Perfect)* above 4 from the album *Voices*	$3		RCA 12217
8/29/81	❶[2]	23	●	16 **Private Eyes** ......*Tell Me What You Want*	$3		RCA 12296
11/14/81+	❶[1]	21	●	17 **I Can't Go For That (No Can Do)** ......RB[1] *Unguarded Minute*	$3		RCA 12357
3/20/82	9	16		18 **Did It In A Minute** ......*Head Above Water*	$3		RCA 13065
6/19/82	33	11		19 **Your Imagination** ......*Sara Smile* above 4 from the album *Private Eyes*	$3		RCA 13252
10/16/82	❶[4]	23	●	20 **Maneater** *Delayed Reaction*	$3	■	RCA 13354
1/29/83	7	18		21 **One On One** ......*Art Of Heartbreak*	$3	■	RCA 13421
4/30/83	6	16		22 **Family Man** ......*Open All Night*	$3		RCA 13507
				DARYL HALL JOHN OATES:			
10/29/83	2[4]	18		23 **Say It Isn't So** ......*Kiss On My List*	$3	■	RCA 13654
2/18/84	8	17		24 **Adult Education** ......*Maneater*	$3	■	RCA 13714
9/29/84	❶[2]	23		25 **Out Of Touch** ......A:❶[3] / S:3 *Cold, Dark And Yesterday*	$3	■	RCA 13916
12/15/84+	5	19		26 **Method Of Modern Love** ......A:5 / S:7 *Bank On Your Love*	$3	■	RCA 13970
3/16/85	18	13		27 **Some Things Are Better Left Unsaid** ......A:16 / S:17 *All American Girl*	$3	■	RCA 14035
6/1/85	30	12		28 **Possession Obsession** ......A:29 *Dance On Your Knees* above 4 from the album *Big Bam Boom*	$3	■	RCA 14098
8/31/85	20	11		29 **A Nite At The Apollo Live! The Way You Do The Things You Do/My Girl** ......S:21 / A:23 *Everytime You Go Away* [L] **DARYL HALL JOHN OATES with David Ruffin & Eddie Kendrick** recorded at the reopening of New York's Apollo Theatre	$3	■	RCA 14178
4/16/88	3	16		30 **Everything Your Heart Desires** ......S:4 / A:4 *Realove*	$3	■	Arista 9684
7/9/88	29	11		31 **Missed Opportunity** ......S:29 / A:29 *Soul Love*	$3	■	Arista 9727
10/1/88	31	9		32 **Downtown Life** ......A:32 / S:33 *(Urban mix)*	$3	■	Arista 9753
9/29/90	11	19		33 **So Close** ......A:11 / S:14 *(unplugged version)* co-written and co-produced by **Jon Bon Jovi**	$3	▮V	Arista 2085
1/5/91	41	11		34 **Don't Hold Back Your Love** ......A:39 *Change Of Season*	$3	▮V	Arista 2157
				HALL, Jimmie — see WET WILLIE			
				HALL, Lani — see MENDES, Sergio			
				HALL, Larry **'60** Born on 6/30/40 in Hamlett, Ohio. Died of cancer on 9/24/97 (age 57). Teen rock and roll singer.			
11/23/59+	15	15		**Sandy** ......*Lovin' Tree* first released on Hot 1 in 1959 ($60) with a promo picture sleeve; also released on Ever Green 1001 in 1959 ($50)	$25		Strand 25007

DEBUT	PEAK	WKS	Gold	A-side (Chart Hit).....B-side	$	Sym	Label & Number

HALL, Tom T. — C&W/BUB/LP '74

Born on 5/25/36 in Olive Hill, Kentucky. Country music storyteller (charted 54 hits, 1967-86). Wrote "Harper Valley P.T.A." hit for **Jeannie C. Riley** and "Little Bitty" hit for **Alan Jackson**. Hosted *Pop Goes The Country* TV series.

DEBUT	PEAK	WKS	Gold	A-side (Chart Hit).....B-side	$	Sym	Label & Number
8/21/71	42	12		1 **The Year That Clayton Delaney Died**.....CW² *Second Handed Flowers*	$7		Mercury 73221
5/13/72	98	2		2 **Me And Jesus**.....*Coot Marseilles Blues* The Mt. Pisgah United Methodist Church Choir (backing vocals)	$7		Mercury 73278
12/8/73+	12	16		3 **I Love** CW² *Back When We Were Young*	$6		Mercury 73436
6/15/74	63	4		4 **That Song Is Driving Me Crazy**.....*Forget It*	$6		Mercury 73488
3/15/75	55	6		5 **Sneaky Snake**.....*I Care* (C&W #1)	$6		Mercury 73641

HALLORAN, Jack, Singers — BUB '61

Born on 1/10/16 in Rock Rapids, Iowa. Died of a stroke on 1/24/97 (age 81). Conductor/arranger.

DEBUT	PEAK	WKS	Gold	A-side (Chart Hit).....B-side	$	Sym	Label & Number
1/6/62-	96	1		**The Little Drummer Boy**.....*Mary's Little Boy Chile* [X]	$10		Dot 16275

HALLYDAY, David — '91

Born David Smet on 8/14/66 in Boulogne-Billancourt, France; raised in Los Angeles, California. Actor/singer. Son of French superstars, Sylvie Vartan & Johnny Hallyday. Starred in the movie *He's My Girl*. Married to actress/model Estelle LeFebure from 1989-2000.

DEBUT	PEAK	WKS	Gold	A-side (Chart Hit).....B-side	$	Sym	Label & Number
8/29/87	79	6		1 **He's My Girl**.....*Church Of The Poison Spider* title song from the movie starring Hallyday	$3	■	Scotti Brothers 07299
5/25/91	51	10		2 **Ooh La La**.....*Change Of Heart / (3 album snippets)*	$3	▮	Scotti Brothers 5282

HALOS, The — '61

R&B vocal group from Harlem, New York: Harold Johnson, Al Cleveland, Phil Johnson and Arthur Crier. Backing group on **Curtis Lee**'s "Pretty Little Angel Eyes" and **Barry Mann**'s "Who Put The Bomp."

DEBUT	PEAK	WKS	Gold	A-side (Chart Hit).....B-side	$	Sym	Label & Number
7/17/61	25	11		**"Nag"**.....*Copy Cat*	$25		7 Arts 709

HAMBLEN, Stuart — C&W '54

Born Carl Stuart Hamblen on 10/20/08 in Kellyville, Texas. Died on 3/8/89 (age 80). Singer/actor. On radio from age 17. Moved to Hollywood in the early 1930s and appeared in many western movies and on radio with own band. Wrote "It Is No Secret (What God Can Do)," "This Ole House," "Open Up Your Heart (And Let The Sunshine In)," and many others. Ran for president on Prohibition Party ticket in 1952. Also see **The Cowboy Church Sunday School**.

DEBUT	PEAK	WKS	Gold	A-side (Chart Hit).....B-side	$	Sym	Label & Number
11/13/54	26	4		**This Ole House**.....S:26 *When My Lord Picks Up The 'Phone*	$20		RCA Victor 5739

HAMILTON, Bobby — '58

Born Robert Caristo on 10/5/39 in Locust Valley, Long Island, New York. Rock and roll singer/songwriter.

DEBUT	PEAK	WKS	Gold	A-side (Chart Hit).....B-side	$	Sym	Label & Number
8/4/58	40	3		**Crazy Eyes For You**.....H:40 *While Walking Together (Thinking of Love)*	$25		Apt 25002

★582★ HAMILTON, George IV — C&W/BUB/LP '58

Born on 7/19/37 in Winston-Salem, North Carolina. Country-folk-pop singer/songwriter/guitarist. Toured with **Buddy Holly**, **Gene Vincent** and **The Everly Brothers**. Moved to Nashville in 1959 and joined the *Grand Ole Opry*. Own TV series on ABC in 1959, and in Canada in the late 1970s. Charted 40 Country hits, 1960-78. **The Bluenotes** were Hamilton's backing vocalists.

1)A Rose And A Baby Ruth 2)Why Don't They Understand 3)Abilene

DEBUT	PEAK	WKS	Gold	A-side (Chart Hit).....B-side	$	Sym	Label & Number
11/3/56	6	20	●	1 **A Rose And A Baby Ruth** T:6 / S:7 / A:7 / J:8 *If You Don't Know* first released on Colonial 420 in 1956 as George Hamilton IV and The Country Gentlemen ($75)	$30		ABC-Paramount 9765
2/16/57	33	10		2 **Only One Love**.....T:33 *If I Possessed A Printing Press*	$25		ABC-Paramount 9782
8/19/57	80	5		3 **High School Romance**.....T:80 *Everybody's Body*	$25		ABC-Paramount 9838
12/2/57+	10	19		4 **Why Don't They Understand**.....A:10 / T:17 / S:19 *Even Tho'*	$25		ABC-Paramount 9862
3/31/58	25	11		5 **Now And For Always**.....A:25 / S:37 / T:37 *One Heart*	$25		ABC-Paramount 9898
6/9/58	43	8		6 **I Know Where I'm Goin'**.....T:43 / S:45 *Who's Taking You To The Prom* folk song from Scotland	$25		ABC-Paramount 9924
8/25/58	65	4		7 **When Will I Know** / H:65			
9/8/58	72	4		8 **Your Cheatin' Heart**.....H:72 #1 Country hit for Hank Williams in 1953	$25		ABC-Paramount 9946
12/1/58+	29	8		9 **The Teen Commandments**.....*If You Learn To Pray* (**Don Costa** Chorus) [S] **PAUL ANKA-GEO. HAMILTON IV-JOHNNY NASH** Bill Givens (narrative); inspirational talk from the three ABC-Paramount artists	$25		ABC-Paramount 9974
8/3/59	73	7		10 **Gee**.....*I Know Your Sweetheart* written by **Dick Flood**; **Don Costa** (orch., all of above)	$20		ABC-Paramount 10028
6/22/63	15	14		11 **Abilene**.....CW⁴ *Oh So Many Years* produced by **Chet Atkins**; #1 & 11 written by **John D. Loudermilk**	$10		RCA Victor 8181

HAMILTON, Roy — R&B/MEM/BUB '55

Born on 4/16/29 in Leesburg, Georgia. Died of a stroke on 7/20/69 (age 40). R&B ballad singer. Moved to Jersey City at age 14. Sang with the Searchlight Gospel Singers in 1948.

1)Unchained Melody 2)You Can Have Her 3)Don't Let Go

DEBUT	PEAK	WKS	Gold	A-side (Chart Hit).....B-side	$	Sym	Label & Number
4/23/55	6	16		1 **Unchained Melody** RB³ A:6 / J:6 / S:9 *From Here To Eternity* from the movie *Unchained* starring football great Elroy "Crazylegs" Hirsch	$30		Epic 9102
7/23/55	30^CU	3		2 **Forgive This Fool**.....*You Wanted To Change Me*	$25		Epic 9111
11/26/55	77	3		3 **Without A Song**.....T:77 *Cuban Love Song* #6 hit for Paul Whiteman in 1930	$25		Epic 9125
12/24/55+	42	7		4 **Everybody's Got A Home**.....T:42 *Take Me With You* from the Broadway musical *Pipe Dream* starring Helen Traubel; O.B. Masingill (orch., all of above)	$25		Epic 9132
1/13/58	13	16		5 **Don't Let Go**.....T:13 / S:14 / A:16 *The Right To Love* Jesse Stone (orch.)	$20		Epic 9257
11/17/58	45	12		6 **Pledging My Love**.....*My One And Only Love* **Neal Hefti** (orch.)	$20		Epic 9294
4/20/59	62	5		7 **I Need Your Lovin'**.....*Blue Prelude* **Joe Sherman** (orch.)	$20		Epic 9307
8/3/59	84	3		8 **Time Marches On**.....*Take It Easy, Joe* written by **Neil Sedaka**	$20		Epic 9323
1/30/61	12	10		9 **You Can Have Her**.....*Abide With Me*	$15	■	Epic 9434
5/1/61	80	3		10 **You're Gonna Need Magic**.....*To The One I Love* Sammy Lowe (orch., above 2)	$15	■	Epic 9443

DEBUT	PEAK	WKS	Gold	A-side (Chart Hit)..........B-side	$	Sym	Label & Number
				HAMILTON, Russ '57 Born Ronald Hulme in 1934 in Liverpool, England. Pop singer/songwriter.			
6/17/57	4	23	●	Rainbow ....A:4 / S:7 / T:7 *We Will Make Love* Johnny Gregory (orch.)	$20		Kapp 184
				HAMILTON, JOE FRANK & REYNOLDS BUB/LP '75 Pop vocal trio: Dan Hamilton, Joe Frank Carollo and Tommy Reynolds. Trio were members of **The T-Bones**. Reynolds left group in 1972 and was replaced by Alan Dennison. Although Reynolds had left, group still recorded as Hamilton, Joe Frank & Reynolds until July 1976. Hamilton died on 12/23/94 (age 48).			
5/22/71	4	14	●	1 **Don't Pull Your Love** ....*Funk-In-Wagnal*	$5	⊙	Dunhill/ABC 4276
8/28/71	46	7		2 **Annabella** ....*Goin' Down*	$5		Dunhill/ABC 4287
12/4/71+	41	11		3 **Daisy Mae** ....*It Takes The Best*	$5		Dunhill/ABC 4296
6/21/75	❶[1]	17	●	4 **Fallin' In Love** AC[1] *So Good At Lovin' You*	$4		Playboy 6024
11/8/75+	21	15		5 **Winners And Losers** ....*Barroom Blues*	$4		Playboy 6054
4/3/76	62	7		6 **Everyday Without You** ....*Badman*	$4		Playboy 6068
				HAMILTON, JOE FRANK & DENNISON:			
7/17/76	67	5		7 **Light Up The World With Sunshine** ....*Houdini* [I]	$4	■	Playboy 6077
10/30/76	72	8		8 **Don't Fight The Hands (That Need You)** ....*Get On The Bus*	$4	■	Playboy 6088
				HAMLISCH, Marvin LP '74 Born on 6/2/44 in Brooklyn, New York. Pianist/composer/conductor. Won the 1974 Best New Artist Grammy Award.			
3/23/74	3	16	●	**The Entertainer** ....AC[1] *Solace* [I] written in 1902 by Scott Joplin; featured in the movie *The Sting* starring Paul Newman and Robert Redford	$5		MCA 40174
				HAMMEL, Karl Jr. '61 Pop-rockabilly singer. First recorded for Gone in 1958.			
7/31/61	68	8		**Summer Souvenirs** ....*The Magic Of Summer* Chuck Sagle (orch.); co-written by **Paul Evans**	$25		Arliss 1007
				HAMMER — see M.C. HAMMER			
				HAMMER, Jan ROK/AC/LP '85 Born on 4/17/48 in Prague, Czechoslovakia. Jazz-rock keyboard virtuoso. Toured with **Sarah Vaughan** as conductor/keyboardist. Member of Mahavishnu Orchestra until 1973.			
9/7/85	❶[1]	22		**Miami Vice Theme** ....S:❶[3] / A:2 *Evan / The Original Miami Vice Theme* [I] from the *Miami Vice* TV series starring **Don Johnson**	$3	■	MCA 52666
				HAMMOND, Albert LP '72 Born on 5/18/42 in London, England; raised in Gibraltar, Spain. Pop singer/songwriter. Member of the **Magic Lanterns** in 1971.			
7/22/72	91	7		1 **Down By The River** ....*The Last One To Know*	$6		Mums 6009
10/21/72	5	16	●	2 **It Never Rains In Southern California** *Anyone Here In The Audience*	$6		Mums 6011
3/3/73	63	6		3 **If You Gotta Break Another Heart** ....*That Old American Dream*	$6		Mums 6015
4/28/73	48	11		4 **The Free Electric Band** ....*You Taught Me To Sing The Blues*	$6		Mums 6018
9/1/73	80	4		5 **The Peacemaker** ....*Who's For Lunch Today?*	$6		Mums 6021
12/1/73	87	5		6 **Half A Million Miles From Home** ....*I Think I'll Go That Way*	$6		Mums 6024
3/2/74	31	12		7 **I'm A Train** ....*Brand New Day*	$6		Mums 6026
6/29/74	81	4		8 **Air Disaster** ....*Candle Light, Sweet Candle Light*	$6		Mums 6030
4/26/75	91	6		9 **99 Miles From L.A.** ....AC[1] *Rivers Are For Boats*	$6		Mums 6037
				HAMPSHIRE, Keith '73 Born in Canada. Pop singer/songwriter. Worked as a DJ at CKFH.			
12/23/72+	51	9		1 **Daytime Night-Time** ....*Turned The Other Way*	$5		A&M 1403
4/21/73	70	13		2 **First Cut Is The Deepest** ....*You Can't Hear The Song I Sing* written and recorded by **Cat Stevens** on his 1968 album *New Masters*	$5		A&M 1432
12/8/73	81	4		3 **Big Time Operator** ....*You Can't Hear The Song I Sing*	$5		A&M 1486
				HAMPTON THE HAMPSTER '00 Hampton is a cartoon hampster. Created by producers Robert DeBoer and Anthony Grace. Based on a real hampster owned by Deidre LeCarte.			
8/12/00	41[S]	22		**The Hampsterdance Song** ....*(2 versions)* [I-N] samples "Whistle Stop" by **Roger Miller**	$5	★	Koch 8161
				HANCOCK, Herbie R&B/BUB/LP '74 Born on 4/12/40 in Chicago, Illinois. Jazz electronic keyboardist. Pianist with the Miles Davis band, 1963-68. Won an Oscar in 1987 for his *Round Midnight* movie score. Also scored the 1988 movie *Colors*. Wrote **Mongo Santamaria**'s "Watermelon Man."			
3/23/74	42	11		1 **Chameleon** ....*Vein Melter* [I]	$5		Columbia 46002
9/10/83	71	9	●	2 **Rockit** ....*(album version)* [I]	$4		Columbia 04054
				HANDY, John LP '76 Born on 2/3/33 in Dallas, Texas. Jazz saxophonist.			
6/26/76	46	12		**Hard Work** ....*Young Enough To Dream* [I]	$5		ABC Impulse 31005
				HANSON LP '97 Teen pop-rock trio of brothers from Tulsa, Oklahoma: Isaac (age 16 in 1997; guitar), Taylor (age 14; keyboards) and Zac (age 11; drums) Hanson. All share vocals.			
5/3/97	❶[3]	22	▲	1 **MMMBop** ....A:❶[4] / S:❶[3] *(remix) / (3 album snippets)*	$3	▮[V]	Mercury 574261
7/26/97	27[A]	10		2 **Where's The Love** .... "45" issued for above 2 on Mercury 574260		V	album cut
11/29/97	9	20	●	3 **I Will Come To You** ....S:4 / A:43 *Cried* "45": Mercury 568066; B-side: "With You In Your Dreams"; above 3 from the album *Middle Of Nowhere* on Mercury 534615	$3	▮[V]	Mercury 568132 ■
4/22/00	20	7	●	4 **This Time Around** ....S:2 *Love Song* "45": Island 562800; B-side: "If Only"	$4	★[V]	Island 562716

DEBUT	PEAK	WKS	Gold	A-side (Chart Hit)	B-side	$	Sym	Label & Number
				HAPPENINGS, The BUB/LP **'67**				
				Pop vocal group from Paterson, New Jersey: Bob Miranda (lead), Tom Giuliano (tenor), Ralph DiVito (baritone) and Dave Libert (bass). Originally the Four Graduates, recorded for Rust in 1963. Bernie LaPorta replaced DiVito in mid-1967.				
7/9/66	**3**	14		1 **See You In September**	*He Thinks He's A Hero*	$10		B.T. Puppy 520
10/1/66	**12**	9		2 **Go Away Little Girl**	*Tea Time*	$10		B.T. Puppy 522
12/10/66+	**51**	6		3 **Goodnight My Love**	*Lillies By Monet*	$10		B.T. Puppy 523
4/8/67	**3**	13		4 **I Got Rhythm**	*You're In A Bad Way*	$10		B.T. Puppy 527
				written in 1930 by George & Ira Gershwin for the musical *Girl Crazy* starring Ginger Rogers				
7/15/67	**13**	8		5 **My Mammy**	*I Believe In Nothing*	$10	■	B.T. Puppy 530
				Al Jolson's theme song; written in 1920				
9/23/67	**41**	6		6 **Why Do Fools Fall In Love**	*When The Summer Is Through*	$10	■	B.T. Puppy 532
2/17/68	**96**	2		7 **Music Music Music**	*When I Lock My Door*	$10	■	B.T. Puppy 538
				#1 hit for **Teresa Brewer** in 1950				
7/27/68	**67**	5		8 **Breaking Up Is Hard To Do**	*Anyway*	$10		B.T. Puppy 543
				all of above produced by **The Tokens** (on their own label)				
7/12/69	**66**	6		9 **Where Do I Go/Be-In/Hare Krishna**	*New Day Comin'*	$8		Jubilee 5666
				medley from the off-Broadway rock musical *Hair* starring Steve Curry				
				HAPPY MONDAYS ROK/LP **'91**				
				Dance-rock group formed in Manchester, England: brothers Shaun (vocals) and Paul (bass) Ryder, Mark Day (guitar), Paul Davis (keyboards), Mark Berry (percussion) and Gary Whelan (drums).				
3/16/91	**57**	10		**'Step On' Remix '91**	*(instrumental)*	$3	▌	Elektra 64899
				original version "Step On" made the Modern Rock charts (#9) and Dance Club Play charts (#13) in 1990				
				HARDCASTLE, Paul R&B/LP **'85**				
				Born on 12/10/57 in London, England. Contemporary jazz keyboardist/producer.				
1/12/85	**57**	18		1 **Rain Forest**	*Sound Chaser* [I]	$4		Profile 5059
6/1/85	**15**	14		2 **19**	S:12 / A:19 *Fly By Night*	$4	■	Chrysalis 42860
				title refers to the average age of U.S. soldiers in Vietnam				
				HARDEN TRIO, The C&W/LP **'66**				
				Country vocal trio from England, Arkansas: siblings Bobby, Robbie and Arlene Harden.				
3/12/66	**44**	10		**Tippy Toeing**	*Don't Remind Me*	$7		Columbia 43463
				HARDIN, Tim LP **'69**				
				Born on 12/23/41 in Eugene, Oregon. Died of a drug overdose on 12/29/80 (age 39). Folk-blues singer/songwriter. Relative of notorious outlaw John Wesley Hardin.				
8/2/69	**50**	7		**Simple Song Of Freedom**	*Question Of Birth*	$8		Columbia 44920
				written by **Bobby Darin**				
				HARDTIMES, The **'67**				
				Pop-rock group from San Diego, California: Rudy Romero, Bill Richardson, Bob Morris, Lee Kiefer and Paul Wheatbread. Regulars on Dick Clark's daily ABC-TV show *Where The Action Is.* Wheatbread later joined **Gary Puckett & The Union Gap** and **Flash Cadillac & The Continental Kids**.				
12/31/66+	**97**	2		**Fortune Teller**	*Goodby*	$10		World Pacific 77851
				HARDY, Hagood LP **'76**				
				Born in 1937 in Angola, Indiana. Died of cancer on 1/1/97 (age 59). Vibraphonist based in Toronto. Sideman for **Herbie Mann** and George Shearing.				
12/20/75+	**41**	13		**The Homecoming**	*Quorum* [I]	$5		Capitol 4156
				from the made-for-TV pilot movie *The Waltons* starring Richard Thomas				
				HARLEY, Steve, And Cockney Rebel **'76**				
				Born Steven Nice on 2/27/51 in London, England. Ex-journalist turned rock singer. Cockney Rebel: Jim Cregan (guitar), Duncan MacKay (keyboards), George Ford (bass) and Stuart Elliott (drums).				
2/28/76	**96**	3		**Make Me Smile (Come Up And See Me)**	*Another Journey*	$6		EMI 4201
				co-produced by **Alan Parsons**				
				HARMONICATS MEM/POP/LP **'47**				
				Harmonica trio formed in Chicago, Illinois: Jerry Murad (died on 5/11/96, age 80), Al Fiore (died on 10/25/96, age 73) and Don Les (died on 8/25/94, age 79). Hit #1 in 1947 with "Peg O' My Heart."				
12/26/60+	**56**	8		**Cherry Pink And Apple Blossom White**	*Lonely Love* [I]	$8	■	Columbia 41816
				JERRY MURAD'S HARMONICATS				
				French song written in 1950; also issued with a different promotional picture sleeve				
				HARNELL, Joe, And His Orchestra AC/LP **'63**				
				Born on 8/2/24 in the Bronx, New York. "Bossa Nova" conductor/arranger.				
12/29/62+	**14**	13		1 **Fly Me To The Moon - Bossa Nova**	*Harlem Nocturne* [I]	$8		Kapp 497
				first recorded in 1954 by Kaye Ballard as "In Other Words"				
4/20/63	**97**	1		2 **Diane**	*The Walking Song* [I]	$8		Kapp 521
				#2 hit for the Nat Shilkret Orchestra in 1928				
				HARNEN, Jimmy — see SYNCH				
				HARPER, Janice **'57**				
				Born in Flushing, New York. Adult Contemporary singer.				
9/2/57	**46**	14		1 **Bon Voyage**	T:46 *Tell Me That You Love Me*	$15		Prep 111
12/16/57	**84**	4		2 **That's Why I Was Born**	T:84 *Moonlit Sea*	$15	⊙	Prep 123
				Earl Sheldon (orch. and chorus, above 2)				
8/18/58	**82**	3		3 **Devotion**	H:82 *Hands Across The Sea*	$12		Capitol 3984
				Arnold Goland (orch.)				
1/18/60	**91**	3		4 **Cry Me A River**	*Just Say I Love Him*	$10		Capitol 4324
				Stan Applebaum (orch.)				

DEBUT	PEAK	WKS	Gold	A-side (Chart Hit)...B-side	$	Sym	Label & Number
				HARPERS BIZARRE AC/BUB/LP **'67**			
				Adult Contemporary vocal group from Santa Cruz, California: Ted Templeman, Eddie James, Dick Yount, John Petersen and Dick Scoppettone. Petersen was a member of **The Beau Brummels**. Templeman later produced many albums for **The Doobie Brothers** and **Van Halen**.			
2/18/67	**13**	11		1 **The 59th Street Bridge Song (Feelin' Groovy)** *Lost My Love Today*	$8		Warner 5890
				written by **Paul Simon**; arranged by **Leon Russell**			
5/20/67	**37**	7		2 **Come To The Sunshine** ... *The Debutante's Ball*	$7		Warner 7028
8/19/67	**43**	8		3 **Anything Goes** ... *Malibu U.*	$7		Warner 7063
				written in 1934 by Cole Porter for the musical starring Ethel Merman			
11/18/67	**45**	7		4 **Chattanooga Choo Choo** ... AC[2] *Hey, You In The Crowd*	$7		Warner 7090
				#1 hit for Glenn Miller in 1941 (from the movie *Sun Valley Serenade*)			
9/21/68	**95**	2		5 **Battle Of New Orleans** ... *Green Apple Tree*	$6		Warner 7223
				HARPO, Slim BUB/R&B **'66**			
				Born James Moore on 1/11/24 in Lobdell, Louisiana. Died of a heart attack on 1/31/70 (age 46). Blues singer/harmonica player. Also known as Harmonica Slim.			
5/29/61	**34**	8		1 **Rainin' In My Heart** ... *Don't Start Cryin' Now*	$25		Excello 2194
				featuring blues guitarist Lightnin' Slim (Otis Hicks)			
1/29/66	**16**	13		2 **Baby Scratch My Back** ... RB[2] *I'm Gonna Miss You (Like The Devil)* [I]	$20		Excello 2273
				HARPTONES, The MEM **'61**			
				Black doo-wop group from Harlem, New York: Willie Winfield, William James, Jimmie Beckum, Bill Brown and Nicky Clark.			
5/8/61	**96**	2		**What Will I Tell My Heart** ... *Foolish Me*	$100		Companion 103
				#2 hit for Andy Kirk in 1937			
				HARRIET **'91**			
				Born Harriet Roberts in 1966 in Sheffield, Yorkshire, England. Female dance singer.			
2/16/91	**39**	11		**Temple Of Love** ... S:37 / A:38 *(Tuff Stuff edit)*	$3	▮	EastWest 98863
				HARRIS, Betty **'63**			
				Born in 1943 in Orlando, Florida. R&B singer.			
9/21/63	**23**	11		1 **Cry To Me** ... *I'll Be A Liar*	$15		Jubilee 5456
				re-entered the R&B charts (#44) in 1969 on Jubilee 5658			
1/4/64	**89**	4		2 **His Kiss** ... *It's Dark Outside*	$15		Jubilee 5465
7/29/67	**85**	4		3 **Nearer To You** ... *I'm Evil Tonight*	$15		Sansu 466
				HARRIS, Eddie BUB/R&B/LP **'61**			
				Born on 10/20/36 in Chicago, Illinois. Died of cancer on 11/5/96 (age 60). Jazz tenor saxophonist. Wrote much of the music for TV's *The **Bill Cosby** Show* and several books of music theory.			
4/10/61	**36**	11		1 **Exodus** ... *Alicia* [I]	$15		Vee-Jay 378
				jazz version of the main theme from the Otto Preminger movie starring Paul Newman			
6/15/68	**45**	13		2 **Listen Here** ... *Theme In Search Of A Movie* [I]	$7		Atlantic 2487
10/26/68	**88**	2		3 **It's Crazy** ... *Live Right Now* [I]	$7		Atlantic 2561
1/10/70	**85**	4		4 **Compared To What** ... *Cold Duck* (R&B #44)	$6		Atlantic 2694
				LES McCANN & EDDIE HARRIS			
				HARRIS, Emmylou C&W/BUB/AC/LP **'81**			
				Born on 4/2/47 in Birmingham, Alabama. Country singer/guitarist (charted 51 hits, 1975-93). Sang backup with Gram Parsons until his death in 1973. Own band from 1975. Recipient of *Billboard*'s Century Award in 1999.			
8/30/75	**58**	5		1 **If I Could Only Win Your Love** ... *Boulder To Birmingham*	$6		Reprise 1332
				Herb Pedersen (harmony vocal)			
3/13/76	**65**	5		2 **Here, There And Everywhere** ... *Together Again* (C&W #1)	$5		Reprise 1346
				originally recorded by **The Beatles** on their 1966 album *Revolver*			
6/28/80	**55**	8		3 **That Lovin' You Feelin' Again** ... *Lola* (Craig Hundley)	$5		Warner 49262
				ROY ORBISON & EMMYLOU HARRIS			
				from the movie *Roadie* starring **Meat Loaf**			
2/28/81	**37**	13		4 **Mister Sandman** ... *Fools Thin Air*	$4		Warner 49684
				solo version; album version featured harmony vocals by **Dolly Parton** and **Linda Ronstadt**			
				HARRIS, Major R&B/LP **'75**			
				Born on 2/9/47 in Richmond, Virginia. R&B singer. With **The Jarmels** in the early 1960s. With **The Delfonics** from 1971-74.			
3/29/75	**5**	18	●	1 **Love Won't Let Me Wait** ... RB[1] *After Loving You*	$5		Atlantic 3248
4/10/76	**73**	4		2 **Jealousy** ... *Tynisa (Goddess Of Love)*	$5		Atlantic 3321
11/27/76	**91**	4		3 **Laid Back Love** ... *This Is What You Mean To Me*	$5		WMOT 4002
				HARRIS, Richard BUB/LP **'68**			
				Born on 10/1/30 in Limerick, Ireland. Died on 10/25/2002 (age 72). Began prolific acting career in 1958. Portrayed "King Arthur" in the long-running stage production and movie version of *Camelot*. Played "Headmaster Albus Dumbledore" in *Harry Potter and the Sorcerer's Stone*.			
5/11/68	**2[1]**	13		1 **MacArthur Park** ... *Didn't We*	$6	■	Dunhill 4134
11/2/68	**64**	6		2 **The Yard Went On Forever** ... *Lucky Me*	$6	□	Dunhill/ABC 4170
6/7/69	**63**	6		3 **Didn't We** ... *Paper Chase*	$6		Dunhill/ABC 4194
				originally the B-side of #1 above; above 3 written and produced by Jimmy Webb			
11/20/71+	**41**	11		4 **My Boy** ... *Why Did You Leave Me*	$6		Dunhill/ABC 4293
				HARRIS, Rolf BUB/AC/LP **'63**			
				Born on 3/30/30 in Perth, Australia. Played piano from age nine. Moved to England in the mid-1950s. Developed his unique "wobble board sound" out of a sheet of masonite. Own BBC-TV series from 1970.			
3/16/63	**61**	7		1 **Sun Arise** ... *Someone's Pinched My Winkles*	$15		Epic 9567
6/8/63	**3**	11		2 **Tie Me Kangaroo Down, Sport** ... AC[3] *The Big Black Hat* [N]	$15	■	Epic 9596
9/28/63	**95**	1		3 **Nick Teen And Al K. Hall** ... *I Know A Man* [N]	$15	■	Epic 9615
				different versions of above 2 first released on 20th Fox 207 in 1960 ($20)			

DEBUT	PEAK	WKS	Gold	A-side (Chart Hit)..........B-side	$	Sym	Label & Number
				HARRIS, Sam BUB/LP '84			
				Born on 6/4/61 in Cushing, Oklahoma. Pop singer/actor. Winner of TV's *Star Search* male vocalist category in 1984.			
9/15/84	**36**	14		1 **Sugar Don't Bite**..........*You Keep Me Hangin' On*	$3	■	Motown 1743
2/1/86	**52**	9		2 **I'd Do It All Again**..........*The Rescue*	$3	■	Motown 1829
				Lauren Wood (backing vocal)			
				HARRIS, Thurston '57			
				Born on 7/11/31 in Indianapolis, Indiana. Died of a heart attack on 4/14/90 (age 58). Black singer/songwriter. First recorded with the R&B group The Lamplighters in 1953.			
10/21/57	**6**	17		1 **Little Bitty Pretty One**..........S:6 / T:6 / A:12 *I Hope You Won't Hold It Against Me*	$40		Aladdin 3398
				The Sharps (later **The Rivingtons**, backing vocals)			
1/13/58	**57**	8		2 **Do What You Did**..........T:57 *I'm Asking Forgiveness*	$30		Aladdin 3399
8/4/58	**96**	1		3 **Over And Over**..........H:96 *You're Gonna' Need Me*	$30		Aladdin 3430
				HARRIS, Tony '57			
				Male R&B-rock and roll singer.			
9/2/57	**89**	3		**Chicken, Baby, Chicken**..........T:89 *I'll Forever Love You*	$40		Ebb 104
				HARRISON, Don, Band LP '76			
				Rock group: Don Harrison (vocals), Russell DaShiell (guitar), Stu Cook (bass) and Doug Clifford (drums). Cook and Clifford were members of **Creedence Clearwater Revival**.			
4/24/76	**47**	9		**Sixteen Tons**..........*Who I Really Am*	$7		Atlantic 3323
	★221★			**HARRISON, George** ROK/AC/BUB/LP '71			
				Born on 2/24/43 in Wavertree, Liverpool, England. Died of cancer on 11/29/2001 (age 58). Formed his first group, the Rebels, at age 13. Joined **John Lennon** and **Paul McCartney** in The Quarrymen in 1958; group later evolved into **The Beatles**, with Harrison as lead guitarist. Organized the Bangladesh benefit concerts at Madison Square Garden in 1971. Member of the supergroup **Traveling Wilburys**. Recipient of *Billboard*'s Century Award in 1992.			
				1)My Sweet Lord 2)Got My Mind Set On You 3)Give Me Love (Give Me Peace On Earth)			
11/28/70	❶[4]	14	●	1 **My Sweet Lord** /			
				a 1976 court ruling found this tune plagiarized **The Chiffons**' tune "He's So Fine"; also see #17 below			
11/28/70		14		2 **Isn't It A Pity**..........	$10	■	Apple 2995
2/27/71	**10**	9		3 **What Is Life**..........*Apple Scruffs*	$10	■	Apple 1828
8/14/71	**23**	7		4 **Bangla-Desh** /			
9/11/71		3		5 **Deep Blue**..........	$10	■	Apple 1836
				all of above produced by Phil Spector and Harrison			
5/19/73	❶[1]	14		6 **Give Me Love - (Give Me Peace On Earth)**..........*Miss O'Dell*	$10		Apple 1862
11/23/74+	**15**	10		7 **Dark Horse**..........*I Don't Care Anymore*	$10	■	Apple 1877
1/11/75	**36**	6		8 **Ding Dong; Ding Dong**..........*Hari's On Tour (Express)*	$15	■	Apple 1879
9/20/75	**20**	10		9 **You**..........*World Of Stone*	$8	■	Apple 1884
11/20/76+	**25**	11		10 **This Song**..........*Learning How To Love You*	$8	■	Dark Horse 8294
				song refers to the plagiarism case involving "My Sweet Lord" and "He's So Fine" (see #1 above); also issued with a promo sleeve explaining the facts about the suit			
1/29/77	**19**	11		11 **Crackerbox Palace**..........*Learning How To Love You*	$8		Dark Horse 8313
3/3/79	**16**	14		12 **Blow Away**..........*Soft-Hearted Hana*	$8	■	Dark Horse 8763
5/23/81	**2[3]**	16		13 **All Those Years Ago**..........AC[1] *Writing's On The Wall*	$6	■	Dark Horse 49725
				tribute to **John Lennon**; assisted by **Ringo Starr** and **Paul and Linda McCartney**			
11/20/82	**53**	5		14 **Wake Up My Love**..........*Greece* [I]	$8		Dark Horse 29864
10/24/87+	❶[1]	22		15 **Got My Mind Set On You**..........AC[4] S:❶[2] / A:❶[1] *Lay His Head*	$5	■	Dark Horse 28178
				originally recorded by James Ray in 1962 on Dynamic Sound 503 ($40)			
2/6/88	**23**	11		16 **When We Was Fab**..........S:18 / A:31 *Zig Zag*	$5	■	Dark Horse 28131
				above 2 produced by **Jeff Lynne** and Harrison			
2/2/02	**94**	1		17 **My Sweet Lord**..........S:2 *Let It Down / My Sweet Lord (2000)* [R]	$6	★[V]	gn/Capitol 50438
				same version as #1 above; "45": gn/Capitol 15930; B-side: (new 2000 version); all of above (except #15) written by Harrison			
				HARRISON, Harry '65			
				DJ at WMCA in New York City at the time of his hit.			
12/25/65	**26[X]**	1		**May You Always**..........*Auld Lang Syne* [X-S]	$15		Amy 944
				New Years' Eve resolutions featuring the tune "Auld Lang Syne"			
				HARRISON, Noel LP '66			
				Born on 1/29/34 in London, England. Singer/actor. Son of actor Rex Harrison.			
12/4/65+	**51**	8		1 **A Young Girl**..........*The Future Mrs. 'Awkins*	$8		London 9795
10/28/67	**56**	6		2 **Suzanne**..........*Life Is A Dream*	$6		Reprise 0615
				written by singer/poet/vocalist Leonard Cohen			
				HARRISON, Wilbert BUB/LP '59			
				Born on 1/5/29 in Charlotte, North Carolina. Died of a stroke on 10/26/94 (age 65). R&B singer/songwriter.			
4/13/59	❶[2]	16	●	1 **Kansas City**..........RB[7] *Listen, My Darling*	$25		Fury 1023
				first released by Little Willie Littlefield in 1952 as "K.C. Lovin'" on Federal 12110 ($150)			
12/6/69+	**32**	13		2 **Let's Work Together (Part 1)**..........*(Part 2)*	$10		Sue 11
				first released as "Let's Stick Together" on Fury 1059 and Fury 1063 in 1962 ($15 each)			
3/13/71	**98**	2		3 **My Heart Is Yours**..........*Pretty Little Women*	$8		SSS Int'l. 830
				first released on Wet Soul 4 in 1970 ($10)			
				HARRY, Debbie ROK/BUB/LP '81			
				Born on 7/1/45 in Miami, Florida; raised in Hawthorne, New Jersey. Lead singer of **Blondie**. In several movies and in several episodes of TV's *Wiseguy*.			
8/15/81	**43**	10		1 **Backfired**..........*Military Rap*	$5	■	Chrysalis 2526
10/31/81	**82**	3		2 **The Jam Was Moving**..........*Inner City Spillover*	$5		Chrysalis 2554
11/22/86+	**57**	11		3 **French Kissin**..........*Rockbird*	$4	■	Geffen 28546
7/4/87	**70**	7		4 **In Love With Love**..........*Secret Life*	$4	■	Geffen 28476
				HART, Beth LP '99			
				Born in Santa Monica, California. Blues-rock singer/songwriter.			
11/27/99+	**90**	12		**L.A. Song**..........*(original edit)*	$5	★[+]	143/Lava 84547

DEBUT	PEAK	WKS	Gold	A-side (Chart Hit)	B-side	$	Sym	Label & Number
				HART, Bobby — see BOYCE, Tommy				
	★493★			**HART, Corey** LP '85				
				Born on 5/31/62 in Montreal, Quebec, Canada; raised in Malaga, Spain and Mexico City, Mexico. Male pop singer/songwriter/keyboardist.				
				1)Never Surrender 2)Sunglasses At Night 3)It Ain't Enough				
5/26/84	7	23		1 **Sunglasses At Night**	*At The Dance*	$3	■	EMI America 8203
9/29/84	17	19		2 **It Ain't Enough** A:17 / S:18	*Araby (She's Just A Girl)*	$3	■	EMI America 8236
6/8/85	3	20		3 **Never Surrender** S:❶[1] / A:3	*Water From The Moon*	$3	■	EMI America 8268
9/14/85	26	12		4 **Boy In The Box** S:26 / A:26	*Silent Talking*	$3	■	EMI America 8287
11/30/85+	30	15		5 **Everything In My Heart** S:26 / A:30	*Sunny Place-Shady People*	$3	■	EMI America 8300
9/20/86	18	13		6 **I Am By Your Side** S:14 / A:22	*Political Cry*	$3	■	EMI America 8348
12/13/86+	24	14		7 **Can't Help Falling In Love** S:18 / A:34	*Broken Arrow*	$3	■	EMI America 8368
				#3 & 7: picture sleeves are foldout posters				
3/28/87	88	3		8 **Dancin' With My Mirror**	*(instrumental mix)*	$3		EMI America 8385
6/11/88	38	10		9 **In Your Soul** A:39	*Chippin' Away*	$3	■	EMI-Manhattan 50134
3/17/90	37	11		10 **A Little Love** A:35 / S:39	*Kisses On The Train*	$3	▮	EMI 50239
				all of above (except #7) written by Hart				
				HART, Freddie C&W/LP '71				
				Born Fred Segrest on 12/21/26 in Lochapoka, Alabama. Country singer/songwriter/guitarist (charted 48 hits, 1959-87).				
8/21/71	17	17	●	**Easy Loving** CW[3]	*Brother Bluebird*	$6		Capitol 3115
				HART, Rod '77				
				Born in Beulah, Michigan. Acted in the movie *Junior Bonner*.				
12/25/76+	67	7		**C.B. Savage**	*Better Off Gone* [N]	$5	⊙	Plantation 144
				"gay" answer to **C.W. McCall**'s hit "Convoy"				
				HARTMAN, Dan BUB/AC/LP '84				
				Born on 12/8/50 in Harrisburg, Pennsylvania. Died of a brain tumor on 3/22/94 (age 43). Singer/songwriter/multi-instrumentalist/producer. Member of the **Edgar Winter Group** from 1972-76. Writer/producer of several disco club anthems in the late '70s. Own studio, the Schoolhouse, in Westport, Connecticut.				
10/14/78+	29	17	●	1 **Instant Replay**	*Instant Replay (Replayed)*	$4		Blue Sky 2772
2/24/79	91	3		2 **This Is It**	*Countdown*	$4		Blue Sky 2775
4/11/81	86	5		3 **Heaven In Your Arms**	*Hello Again*	$4		Blue Sky 70053
6/27/81	72	5		4 **It Hurts To Be In Love**	*Pick It Up*	$4		Blue Sky 02115
5/5/84	6	25		5 **I Can Dream About You**	*Blue Shadows* (The Blasters)	$3	■	MCA 52378
				from the movie *Streets Of Fire* starring Michael Pare				
10/6/84	25	17		6 **We Are The Young** S:21	*I'm Not A Rolling Stone*	$3	■	MCA 52471
2/9/85	39	12		7 **Second Nature**	*I Can't Get Enough*	$3	■	MCA 52519
				HARVEY, PJ ROK/LP '95				
				Born Polly Jean Harvey on 10/9/69 in Yeovil, England. Female singer/guitarist. Had own trio, also named PJ Harvey, which included bassist Stephen Vaughan and drummer Rob Ellis.				
2/25/95	48[A]	9		**Down By The Water**				album cut
				from the album *To Bring You My Love* on Island 524085				
				HARVEY & THE MOONGLOWS — see MOONGLOWS				
				HARVEY BOYS, The '57				
				Pop vocal group, similar in style to the **Four Aces**.				
3/9/57	84	3		**Nothing Is Too Good For You** T:84	*Marina Girl*	$15		Cadence 1306
				Archie Bleyer (orch.)				
				HARVEY DANGER ROK/LP '98				
				Rock group from Seattle, Washington: Sean Nelson (vocals), Jeff Lin (guitar), Aaron Huffman (bass) and Evan Sult (drums).				
5/2/98	38[A]	22		**Flagpole Sitta**			V	album cut
				from the album *Where Have All The Merrrymakers Gone?* on Slash 556000; "45": Slash 570290; B-side: "Private Helicopter" by Carlotta Valdez				
				HATFIELD, Bobby — see RIGHTEOUS BROTHERS, The				
				HATFIELD, Juliana ROK/BUB/LP '95				
				Born on 7/2/67 in Wiscasset, Maine. Female rock singer/guitarist. Originally recorded as The Juliana Hatfield 3. Attended Berklee College of Music where she was a member of the Blake Babies. Also played bass with **The Lemonheads**.				
11/19/94	97	2		1 **Spin The Bottle**	*I'm Nuthin'* (Ethan Hawke)	$3	▮	RCA 64207
				from the movie *Reality Bites* starring Winona Ryder; originally recorded in 1993				
4/22/95	84	6		2 **Universal Heart-Beat**	*Where Would I Be Without You*	$3	▮	Mammoth 98179
	★593★			**HATHAWAY, Donny** R&B/BUB/LP '72				
				Born on 10/1/45 in Chicago, Illinois; raised in St. Louis, Missouri. Committed suicide by jumping from the 15th floor of New York City's Essex House hotel on 1/13/79 (age 33). R&B singer/songwriter/keyboardist/producer/arranger. Gospel singer since age three. Attended Washington DC's Howard University on a fine arts scholarship; classmate of **Roberta Flack**. Sang the theme of TV show *Maude*. His wife Eulalah was a classical singer. Their daughter Lalah Hathaway began her solo recording career in 1990.				
				1)The Closer I Get To You 2)Where Is The Love 3)You've Got A Friend				
1/17/70	87	8		1 **The Ghetto-Part 1**	*Part 2*	$7		Atco 6719
6/12/71	29	12		2 **You've Got A Friend**	*Gone Away*	$7		Atlantic 2808
10/23/71	71	6		3 **You've Lost That Lovin' Feelin'**	*Be Real Black For Me*	$7		Atlantic 2837
				ROBERTA FLACK & DONNY HATHAWAY (above 2)				
5/13/72	81	5		4 **Giving Up**	*Jealous Guy*	$7		Atco 6884
5/27/72	94	5		5 **I Thank You**	*Just Another Reason*	$7		Curtom 1971
				DONNY HATHAWAY AND JUNE CONQUEST				
				written and produced by **Curtis Mayfield**				
6/10/72	5	13	●	6 **Where Is The Love** RB[1] / AC[1]	*Mood*	$5		Atlantic 2879
				ROBERTA FLACK & DONNY HATHAWAY				
10/21/72	60	6		7 **I Love You More Than You'll Ever Know**	*Lord Help Me*	$7		Atco 6903

DEBUT	PEAK	WKS	Gold	A-side (Chart Hit)...B-side	$	Sym	Label & Number
				HATHAWAY, Donny — Cont'd			
12/23/72	11^{X}	1		8 **This Christmas** ... *Be There* [X]	$7		Atco 6799
				first released in 1970			
7/7/73	44	9		9 **Love, Love, Love** ... *Someday We'll All Be Free*	$7		Atco 6928
2/18/78	2^{2}	20	●	10 **The Closer I Get To You** RB^{2} *Love Is The Healing* (Flack)	$5		Atlantic 3463
2/16/80	47	11		11 **You Are My Heaven** ... *I'll Love You Forever And Ever* (Flack)	$5		Atlantic 3627
				co-written by **Stevie Wonder**			
5/17/80	56	8		12 **Back Together Again** ... *God Don't Like Ugly* (Flack)	$5		Atlantic 3661
				ROBERTA FLACK with DONNY HATHAWAY (above 3)			
				HAVANA '00			
				Born Havana Mena in Miami, Florida. Female R&B singer/rapper.			
9/9/00	72^{S}	1		**How Much You Want Me** ... *(original version)*	$6	★	Heat/Lightyear 54382
				HAVENS, Richie BUB/LP '71			
				Born on 1/21/41 in Brooklyn, New York. Black folk singer/guitarist. Opening act of the 1969 Woodstock concert. Since the '80s, sang commercial jingles for Amtrak, McDonald's and others.			
3/20/71	16	14		**Here Comes The Sun** ... *Younger Men Get Older*	$7		Stormy Forest 656
				written by **George Harrison** (on **The Beatles**' 1969 *Abbey Road* album)			
				HAWKES, Chesney '91			
				Born on 9/22/71 in England. Pop-rock singer. Son of Len "Chip" Hawkes of **The Tremeloes**.			
8/3/91	10	20		**The One And Only** ... A:28 / S:53 *It's Gonna Be Tough*	$3	▮	Chrysalis 23730
				written by **Nik Kershaw**			
				HAWKINS, Dale '57			
				Born Delmar Allen Hawkins on 8/22/38 in Goldmine, Louisiana. Rockabilly singer/guitarist. Toured with R&B package shows. Record production work since 1965. First cousin to **Ronnie Hawkins**. The first white rocker to play at the Apollo Theater.			
6/10/57	27	19		1 **Susie-Q** ... S:27 / T:29 *Don't Treat Me This Way*	$50		Checker 863
				recorded at KWKH radio studio in Shreveport, Louisiana			
9/1/58	32	12		2 **La-Do-Dada** ... H:32 / S:44 *Cross-Ties*	$30		Checker 900
11/10/58	88	5		3 **A House, A Car And A Wedding Ring** ... *My Babe*	$30		Checker 906
3/16/59	52	6		4 **Yea - Yea (Class Cutter)** ... *Lonely Nights*	$30		Checker 916
				first pressings show title only as "Class Cutter" ($30); B-side features narration by **The Moonglow**'s **Harvey Fuqua**			
				HAWKINS, Edwin, Singers R&B/BUB/LP '69			
				Born in August 1943 in Oakland, California. Formed gospel group with Betty Watson in 1967 as the Northern California State Youth Choir. Consisted of 46 black men and women. **Dorothy Morrison** (see #2 & 4 below) was lead singer and **Odia Coates** was a member.			
4/26/69	4	10	●	1 **Oh Happy Day** ... *Jesus, Lover Of My Soul*	$8		Pavilion 20001
				THE EDWIN HAWKINS' SINGERS Featuring Dorothy Combs Morrison			
				recorded by the Northern California State Youth Choir in a Church of God; Pavilion reissued it from their original master tape			
10/11/69	95	1		2 **All God's Children Got Soul** ... *Put A Little Love In Your Heart*	$8	■	Elektra 45671
				DOROTHY MORRISON			
4/25/70	6	17		3 **Lay Down (Candles In The Rain)** ... *Candles In The Rain* (Melanie)	$8	■	Buddah 167
				MELANIE with The Edwin Hawkins Singers			
10/31/70	99	2		4 **Spirit In The Sky** ... *Black California*	$8		Buddah 196
				DOROTHY MORRISON			
				HAWKINS, Hawkshaw C&W/BUB/POP '52			
				Born Harold Hawkins on 12/22/21 in Huntington, West Virginia. Killed in the plane crash with **Patsy Cline** and **Cowboy Copas** on 3/5/63 (age 41). Country singer. Married **Jean Shepard**. Hit #1 on the Country charts in 1963 with "Lonesome 7-7203."			
8/3/59	87	2		**Soldier's Joy** ... *Big Red Benson*	$20		Columbia 41419
				HAWKINS, Jennell R&B '62			
				Born Jennell Grimes on 4/8/38 in Los Angeles, California. Black singer/keyboardist.			
3/24/62	50	8		**Moments** ... *Can I*	$15		Amazon 1003
				first released as "Moments To Remember" on Titanic 1001 ($25) and also on Amazon 1003			
				HAWKINS, Ronnie BUB '59			
				Born on 1/10/35 in Huntsville, Arkansas. Rock and roll singer/songwriter. Formed The Hawks in 1952. To Canada in 1958. Assembled group later known as **The Band**. First cousin to **Dale Hawkins**.			
6/8/59	45	8		1 **Forty Days** ... *One Of These Days*	$30		Roulette 4154
				#2 R&B hit for Chuck Berry in 1955 as "Thirty Days" on Chess 1610 ($50)			
8/17/59	26	16		2 **Mary Lou** ... *Need Your Lovin' (Oh So Bad)*	$30		Roulette 4177
				RONNIE HAWKINS and The Hawks			
				original version by Young Jessie in 1955 on Modern 961 ($75)			
1/31/70	75	5		3 **Down In The Alley** ... *Matchbox*	$8		Cotillion 44060
				HAWKINS, Sophie B. AC/LP '95			
				Born Sophie Ballantine Hawkins on 11/1/67 in Manhattan, New York. Adult Contemporary singer/songwriter.			
4/18/92	5	21		1 **Damn I Wish I Was Your Lover** ... S:6 / A:6 *Don't Stop Swaying*	$3	▮ V	Columbia 74164
8/20/94	56	13		2 **Right Beside You** ... A:59 *The Ballad Of Sleeping Beauty*	$3	▮	Columbia 77537
6/3/95	6	44		3 **As I Lay Me Down** ... AC^{6} A:4 / S:25 *I Need Nothing Else*	$3	▮	Columbia 77801
3/2/96	49	11		4 **Only Love (The Ballad Of Sleeping Beauty)** ... A:37 *Did We Not Choose Each Other*	$3	▮	Columbia 78177
				HAWKS ROK '81			
				Rock group from Otho, Iowa: Dave Hearn (vocals), Kirk Kaufman and Dave Steen (guitars), Frank Wiewel (bass), and Larry Adams (drums).			
3/14/81	63	7		**Right Away** ... *Need Your Love*	$5		Columbia 60500
				HAWLEY, Deane '60			
				Born William Dean Hawley in Los Angeles, California. Pop singer.			
6/20/60	29	11		1 **Look For A Star** ... *Bossman*	$20		Dore 554
				from the British movie *Circus Of Horrors* starring Donald Pleasence			
10/2/61	93	1		2 **Pocketful Of Rainbows** ... *That Dream Could Never Be*	$20		Liberty 55359
				recorded by **Elvis Presley** on his 1960 album *G.I. Blues*			
				HAY, Colin James — see MEN AT WORK			

DEBUT	PEAK	WKS	Gold	A-side (Chart Hit)	B-side	$	Sym	Label & Number

HAYES, Bill — '55

Born on 6/5/26 in Harvey, Illinois. Hayes was a regular on Sid Caesar's TV series *Your Show of Shows.* Played "Doug Williams" on the TV soap opera *Days Of Our Lives.*

DEBUT	PEAK	WKS	Gold	A-side (Chart Hit)	B-side	$	Sym	Label & Number
2/26/55	❶ 5	20	●	1 **The Ballad Of Davy Crockett** ....S:❶ 5 / A:❶ 3 / J:❶ 3 **Archie Bleyer** (orch.); from the ABC-TV *Disneyland* series which featured 3 "Davy Crockett" segments (Dec. 1954-Feb. 1955); picture sleeve issued on Cadence Children's Series (CCS-1)	*Farewell*	$20		Cadence 1256
1/26/57	33	12		2 **Wringle, Wrangle** ....T:33 **Don Costa** (orch.); from the Disney movie *Westward Ho, The Wagons* starring **Fess Parker**	*Westward Ho, The Wagons*	$15	■	ABC-Paramount 9785

HAYES, Darren — see SAVAGE GARDEN

HAYES, Isaac — R&B/BUB/LP '71

★410★

Born on 8/20/42 in Covington, Tennessee. R&B singer/songwriter/keyboardist/actor. Session musician for **Otis Redding** and other artists on the Stax label. Teamed with songwriter David Porter to compose "Soul Man," "Hold On! I'm A Comin'" and many others. Composed movie scores for *Shaft, Tough Guys, Truck Turner* and *Robin Hood: Men In Tights.* Acted in the movie *Flipper.* Supplies the voice for "Chef" on the animated TV series *South Park.* Inducted into the Rock and Roll Hall of Fame in 2002.

1)Theme From Shaft 2)Don't Let Go 3)Never Can Say Goodbye

DEBUT	PEAK	WKS	Gold	A-side (Chart Hit)	B-side	$	Sym	Label & Number
8/23/69	30	12		1 **Walk On By /**				
8/30/69	37	8		2 **By The Time I Get To Phoenix**		$6	□	Enterprise 9003
12/20/69+	5^X	3		3 **The Mistletoe And Me** X: 8/'69; 5/'73	*Winter Snow* [X]	$6		Enterprise 9006
8/29/70	42	9		4 **I Stand Accused**	*I Just Don't Know What To Do With Myself*	$6		Enterprise 9017
2/13/71	79	5		5 **The Look Of Love**	*Ike's Mood I*	$6		Enterprise 9028
5/15/71	22	9		6 **Never Can Say Goodbye**	*I Can't Help It (If I'm Still In Love With You)*	$6		Enterprise 9031
10/16/71	❶ 2	13	●	7 **Theme From Shaft** the **Bar-Kays** (instrumental backing); from the movie *Shaft* starring Richard Roundtree	*Cafe Regio's*	$6		Enterprise 9038
2/26/72	30	11		8 **Do Your Thing**	*Ellie's Love Theme* [I]	$6		Enterprise 9042
4/1/72	48	7		9 **Let's Stay Together**	*Soulsville* [I]	$6		Enterprise 9045
5/13/72	86	4		10 **Ain't That Loving You (For More Reasons Than One)** **ISAAC HAYES & DAVID PORTER**	*Baby I'm-A Want You*	$6		Enterprise 9049
10/21/72	38	9		11 **Theme From The Men** from the ABC-TV series *The Men* starring Robert Conrad	*Type Thang* [I]	$5		Enterprise 9058
12/22/73+	30	9		12 **"Joy" Pt. I**	*Pt. II*	$5		Enterprise 9085
5/4/74	71	8		13 **Wonderful**	*Someone Made You For Me*	$5		Enterprise 9095
8/23/75	92	2		14 **Chocolate Chip**	*(instrumental)*	$5		HBS/ABC 12118
10/27/79+	18	21		15 **Don't Let Go**	*You Can't Hold Your Woman*	$4		Polydor 2011

HAYES, Peter Lind, & Mary Healy — POP '55

Husband-and-wife vocal duo. Hayes was born on 6/25/15 in San Francisco, California; died on 4/21/98 (age 82). Healy was born on 4/14/18 in New Orleans, Louisiana. Married in 1940.

DEBUT	PEAK	WKS	Gold	A-side (Chart Hit)	B-side	$	Sym	Label & Number
11/12/55	57	3		**Rememb'ring** ....T:57 Norman Leyden (orch.); written and popularized (#4 hit) in 1924 by the Duncan Sisters	*I Wish I Was A Car*	$10		Columbia 40547

HAYES, Wade — C&W/BUB/LP '98

Born on 4/20/69 in Bethel Acres, Oklahoma. Country singer/songwriter/guitarist.

DEBUT	PEAK	WKS	Gold	A-side (Chart Hit)	B-side	$	Sym	Label & Number
2/14/98	86	5		1 **The Day That She Left Tulsa (In A Chevy)** S:70	*Wichita Lineman*	$4	▮	Columbia 78745
12/5/98	67	3		2 **How Do You Sleep At Night** ....A:53 from the album *When The Wrong One Loves You Right* on Columbia 68037				album cut

HAYMAN, Richard — MEM/POP '53

Born on 3/27/20 in Cambridge, Massachusetts. Conductor/arranger/harmonica soloist. Long-time associate conductor of the **Boston Pops Orchestra**. "Ruby" by Hayman hit #3 in 1953.

DEBUT	PEAK	WKS	Gold	A-side (Chart Hit)	B-side	$	Sym	Label & Number
2/4/56	11	15		1 **A Theme from "The Three Penny Opera" (Moritat)** ....A:11 / T:12 / S:13 / J:13 **RICHARD HAYMAN and JAN AUGUST** (August died on 1/17/76)	*I'll Be With You In Apple Blossom Time* [I]	$15		Mercury 70781
9/18/61	80	1		2 **Night Train** #1 R&B hit for Jimmy Forest in 1952 (riff borrowed from Duke Ellington's 1946 tune "Happy-Go-Lucky Local")	*Moon River* [I]	$10		Mercury 71869

HAYMES, Dick — MEM/POP '45

Born on 9/13/16 in Buenos Aires, Argentina (of British parents); raised in Paris, France, and in New Jersey. Died on 3/28/80 (age 63). Ballad singer with Harry James, **Benny Goodman** and **Tommy Dorsey** in the early '40s. Appeared in various movies from 1944-51. Charted 45 pop hits, 1943-46. Married briefly to actress Rita Hayworth. His daughter Stephanie Haymes (with his fifth wife, singer Fran Jeffries) married rock songwriter Bernie Taupin in 1993.

DEBUT	PEAK	WKS	Gold	A-side (Chart Hit)	B-side	$	Sym	Label & Number
12/29/56	80	2		**Two Different Worlds** ....T:80 Ian Bernard (orch.)	*Never Leave Me*	$12		Capitol 3565

HAYSI FANTAYZEE — '83

Pop vocal duo from England: Kate Garner and Jeremiah Healy.

DEBUT	PEAK	WKS	Gold	A-side (Chart Hit)	B-side	$	Sym	Label & Number
7/23/83	74	5		**Shiny Shiny**	*Shiny Shiny (Bon temps)*	$4	■	RCA 13534

HAYWARD, Justin — see MOODY BLUES, The

HAYWOOD, Leon — R&B/BUB/LP '75

Born on 2/11/42 in Houston, Texas. R&B singer/songwriter/keyboardist.

DEBUT	PEAK	WKS	Gold	A-side (Chart Hit)	B-side	$	Sym	Label & Number
11/20/65	92	3		1 **She's With Her Other Love** **LEON HAYWARD**	*Pain In My Heart*	$15		Imperial 66123
8/12/67	63	11		2 **It's Got To Be Mellow**	*Cornbread And Buttermilk*	$10		Decca 32164
12/30/67+	92	3		3 **Mellow Moonlight**	*Tennessee Waltz*	$10		Decca 32230
3/23/74	50	9		4 **Keep It In The Family**	*Long As There's You (I Got Love)* (R&B #63)	$6		20th Century 2065
2/8/75	94	2		5 **Believe Half Of What You See (And None Of What You Hear)**	*The Day I Laid Eyes On You*	$6		20th Century 2146
7/12/75	83	3		6 **Come An' Get Yourself Some**	*Who You Been Giving It Up To*	$6		20th Century 2191
9/6/75	15	17		7 **I Want'a Do Something Freaky To You**	*I Know What Love Is*	$6		20th Century 2228
4/5/80	49	11		8 **Don't Push It Don't Force It**	*Who You Been Giving It Up To?*	$4		20th Century 2443

DEBUT	PEAK	WKS	Gold	A-side (Chart Hit)	B-side	$	Sym	Label & Number

HAZARD, Robert — BUB/LP '83

Born in Philadelphia, Pennsylvania. Rock singer/songwriter. Wrote **Cyndi Lauper**'s "Girls Just Want To Have Fun."

DEBUT	PEAK	WKS	Gold	A-side (Chart Hit)	B-side	$	Sym	Label & Number
3/5/83	58	9		**Escalator Of Life**	*Say Yo*	$4		RCA 13449

HAZLEWOOD, Lee — see SINATRA, Nancy

HEAD, Murray — '85

Born on 3/5/46 in London, England. Pop singer/actor. Appeared on the 1970 rock concept album *Jesus Christ Superstar*. Played juvenile lead in the 1971 movie *Sunday, Bloody Sunday*.

DEBUT	PEAK	WKS	Gold	A-side (Chart Hit)	B-side	$	Sym	Label & Number
1/31/70	74	7		1 **Superstar** — from *Jesus Christ Superstar-A Rock Opera*	*John Nineteen Forty-One* (The Andrew Lloyd Webber Orchestra)	$6	■	Decca 32603
1/2/71	14	24		2 **Superstar** — **MURRAY HEAD With The Trinidad Singers** (above 2); above 2 are the same version and were issued with 3 different picture sleeves	*John Nineteen Forty-One* (The Andrew Lloyd Webber Orchestra) [R]	$6	■	Decca 32603
2/23/85	3	20		3 **One Night In Bangkok** — from the Tim Rice and **Abba** members Benny Andersson and Bjorn Ulvaeus musical project *Chess*	S:2 / A:4 *Merano*	$4	■	RCA 13988

HEAD, Roy — C&W/BUB/LP '65

Born on 9/1/41 in Three Rivers, Texas. Rock-country singer/guitarist. Charted 24 Country hits, 1974-85. Head's backing band, **The Traits** (see #7 below), included **Johnny Winter**.

DEBUT	PEAK	WKS	Gold	A-side (Chart Hit)	B-side	$	Sym	Label & Number
9/4/65	2^2	11		1 **Treat Her Right**	*So Long, My Love*	$15		Back Beat 546
10/30/65	39	7		2 **Just A Little Bit**	*Treat Me Right*	$12		Scepter 12116
11/20/65	32	8		3 **Apple Of My Eye**	*I Pass The Day*	$12		Back Beat 555
1/15/66	88	2		4 **Get Back** — written by **Jimmy McCracklin**	*(instrumental)*	$12		Scepter 12124
3/12/66	99	1		5 **My Babe** — **ROY HEAD And The Traits** (#1, 3 & 5); #1 R&B hit for Little Walter in 1955	*Pain*	$12		Back Beat 560
9/17/66	95	2		6 **To Make A Big Man Cry**	*Don't Cry No More*	$12		Back Beat 571
11/12/66	94	2		7 **Harlem Shuffle** — **THE TRAITS**; originally released on Universal 30494 in 1966 ($15)	*Somewhere*	$12		Scepter 12169
6/26/71	96	1		8 **Puff Of Smoke**	*Lord Take A Bow*	$7		TMI 9000

HEADBOYS, The — LP '79

Rock group from Edinburgh, Scotland: Lou Lewis (guitar), Calum Malcolm (keyboards), George Boyter (bass) and Davy Ross (drums). All share vocals.

DEBUT	PEAK	WKS	Gold	A-side (Chart Hit)	B-side	$	Sym	Label & Number
11/10/79	67	5		**The Shape Of Things To Come**	*The Mood I'm In*	$6		RSO 1005

HEAD EAST — BUB/LP '78

Rock group from St. Louis, Missouri: John Schlitt (vocals), Michael Somerville (guitar), Roger Boyd (keyboards), Dan Birney (bass) and Steve Huston (drums).

DEBUT	PEAK	WKS	Gold	A-side (Chart Hit)	B-side	$	Sym	Label & Number
10/18/75	68	9		1 **Never Been Any Reason**	*One Against The Other*	$6		A&M 1718
2/7/76	54	6		2 **Love Me Tonight**	*Fly By Night Lady*	$6		A&M 1784
4/15/78	46	8		3 **Since You Been Gone**	*Pictures*	$6	■	A&M 2026

HEADLEY, Heather — LP '02

Born on 10/5/74 in Barataria, Trinidad; raised in Fort Wayne, Indiana. R&B singer/actress. Starred in the Broadway musical *Aida*.

DEBUT	PEAK	WKS	Gold	A-side (Chart Hit)	B-side	$	Sym	Label & Number
10/26/02+	90	13		**He Is**	*(2 versions)*	$6	T	RCA 60635

HEADPINS — LP '84

Rock group from Canada: Darby Mills (female vocals), Brian MacLeod (guitar), Ab Bryant (bass) and Bernie Aubin (drums). MacLeod and Bryant were with **Chilliwack**. Bryant was also with **Prism**. MacLeod died of cancer on 4/25/92.

DEBUT	PEAK	WKS	Gold	A-side (Chart Hit)	B-side	$	Sym	Label & Number
12/24/83+	70	9		**Just One More Time**	*I've Heard It All Before*	$6	■	SGR 90001

HEALEY, Jeff, Band — ROK/LP '89

Born on 3/25/66 in Toronto, Ontario, Canada. Blues-rock singer/guitarist. Blind since age one. Formed own group with Joe Rockman (bass) and Tom Stephen (drums). Group appeared in the 1989 movie *Road House*.

DEBUT	PEAK	WKS	Gold	A-side (Chart Hit)	B-side	$	Sym	Label & Number
6/17/89	5	22		1 **Angel Eyes**	S:4 / A:7 *Don't Let Your Chance Go By*	$3	■	Arista 9808
5/8/93	91	3		2 **Lost In Your Eyes** — written by **Tom Petty**	*Cruel Little Number* (ROK #2)	$4	▮	Arista 12521

HEAP, Jimmy — C&W '56

Born on 3/3/22 in Taylor, Texas. Died on 12/4/77 (age 55). Perk Williams was lead singer of Heap's country band, The Melody Masters. Hit #5 on the Country charts in 1954 with "Release Me."

DEBUT	PEAK	WKS	Gold	A-side (Chart Hit)	B-side	$	Sym	Label & Number
3/10/56	93	1		**Butternut** — **JIMMY HEAP And THE MELODY MASTERS with PERK WILLIAMS**	T:93 *It Takes A Heap Of Lovin'* [I]	$25		Capitol 3333

HEART ★61★ — ROK/BUB/AC/LP '87

Rock group formed in Seattle, Washington: sisters **Ann Wilson** (vocals; born on 6/19/50) (see #17, 23 & 28 below) and Nancy Wilson (guitar, keyboards; born on 3/16/54), brothers Roger (born on 2/14/50) and Mike Fisher (guitars), Steve Fossen (bass; born on 11/15/49) and Mike DeRosier (drums; born on 8/24/51). The Fishers left in 1979. Howard Leese (guitar) joined in 1980. Fossen and DeRosier left by 1982, replaced by Mark Andes (of **Spirit**, **Jo Jo Gunne** and **Firefall**) and Denny Carmassi (of **Gamma**). In 1990, former members Fossen, DeRosier and Roger Fisher joined **Alias**. Andes left by 1993. Carmassi left in 1994 to join **Whitesnake**. Nancy married movie director Cameron Crowe on 7/27/86. Ann and Nancy's brother, Karl Wilson, played guitar for **Merrilee Rush**.

1)Alone 2)These Dreams 3)All I Wanna Do Is Make Love To You 4)Never 5)Surrender To Me

DEBUT	PEAK	WKS	Gold	A-side (Chart Hit)	B-side	$	Sym	Label & Number
4/17/76	35	13		1 **Crazy On You** — also see re-entry at #7 below	*Dreamboat Annie*	$6		Mushroom 7021
7/17/76	9	23		2 **Magic Man**	*How Deep It Goes*	$6		Mushroom 7011
12/18/76+	42	10		3 **Dreamboat Annie** — originally released as the B-side of #1 above	*Sing Child*	$6		Mushroom 7023
5/28/77	11	20		4 **Barracuda**	*Cry To Me*	$5		Portrait 70004
9/17/77	62	6		5 **Little Queen**	*Treat Me Well*	$5		Portrait 70008

DEBUT	PEAK	WKS	Gold	A-side (Chart Hit)...B-side	$	Sym	Label & Number
				HEART — Cont'd			
11/26/77	79	3		6 **Kick It Out** ...*Go On Cry*	$5		Portrait 70010
1/7/78	62	6		7 **Crazy On You**...*Dreamboat Annie* [R]	$6		Mushroom 7021
4/8/78	24	15		8 **Heartless**...*Just The Wine*	$6		Mushroom 7031
				above 2 recorded in 1976			
9/23/78	15	18		9 **Straight On**...*Lighter Touch*	$5		Portrait 70020
2/3/79	34	10		10 **Dog & Butterfly**...*Mistral Wind*	$5		Portrait 70025
2/9/80	33	12		11 **Even It Up**...*Pilot*	$4		Epic 50847
				all of above produced by Mike Flicker			
11/22/80+	8	16		12 **Tell It Like It Is**...*Strange Euphoria*	$4		Epic 50950
3/28/81	83	3		13 **Unchained Melody**...*Mistral Wind* [L]	$4		Epic 51010
				recorded at McNichols Arena in Denver			
5/15/82	33	13		14 **This Man Is Mine**...*America*	$4	■	Epic 02925
8/13/83	44	11		15 **How Can I Refuse**...AR[1] *Johnny Moon*	$4	■	Epic 04047
10/29/83	83	4		16 **Allies**...*Together Now*	$4	■	Epic 04184
5/12/84	7	20		17 **Almost Paradise...Love Theme From Footloose**...AC[1] *Strike Zone* (**Loverboy** - ROK #23)	$3	■	Columbia 04418
				MIKE RENO and ANN WILSON			
				co-written by **Eric Carmen**; from the movie *Footloose* starring Kevin Bacon and Lori Singer			
6/1/85	10	21		18 **What About Love?**...S:8 / A:14 *Heart Of Darkness*	$3	■	Capitol 5481
9/14/85	4	24		19 **Never**...S:3 / A:5 *Shell Shock*	$3	■	Capitol 5512
1/18/86	❶[1]	20		20 **These Dreams**...AC[3] S:❶[1] / A:❶[1] *Shell Shock*	$3	■	Capitol 5541
4/19/86	10	16		21 **Nothin' At All**...S:9 / A:10 *The Wolf*	$3	■	Capitol 5572
7/19/86	54	9		22 **If Looks Could Kill**...*What He Don't Know*	$3	■	Capitol 5605
				above 5 from the album *Heart*			
11/29/86+	61	12		23 **The Best Man In The World**...*(instrumental)*	$3	■	Capitol 5654
				ANN WILSON			
				from the movie *The Golden Child* starring **Eddie Murphy**			
5/16/87	❶[3]	21		24 **Alone** S:❶[2] / A:❶[2] *Barracuda (live)*	$3	■	Capitol 44002
				originally recorded by i-Ten in 1983 on their album *Taking A Cold Look*			
8/15/87	7	22		25 **Who Will You Run To**...S:6 / A:6 *Magic Man (live)*	$3	■	Capitol 44040
11/7/87+	12	19		26 **There's The Girl**...S:10 / A:14 *Bad Animals*	$3	■	Capitol 44089
2/20/88	49	9		27 **I Want You So Bad**...*Easy Target*	$3		Capitol 44116
				above 4 from the album *Bad Animals*			
12/24/88+	6	19		28 **Surrender To Me**...S:5 / A:8 *Tequila Dreams* (**Dave Grusin** w/**Lee Ritenour**)	$3	■	Capitol 44288
				ANN WILSON AND ROBIN ZANDER			
				co-written by **Richard Marx**; love theme from the movie *Tequila Sunrise* starring Mel Gibson and Michelle Pfeiffer			
3/31/90	2[2]	20	●	29 **All I Wanna Do Is Make Love To You**...S:3 / A:3 *Call Of The Wild*	$3	▮V	Capitol 44507
6/23/90	23	14		30 **I Didn't Want To Need You**...S:24 / A:25 *The Night*	$3	▮V	Capitol 44553
9/22/90	13	22		31 **Stranded**...A:8 / S:19 *Under The Sky*	$3	▮	Capitol 44621
2/2/91	64	8		32 **Secret**...*I Love You*	$3	▮	Capitol 44614
				above 4 from the album *Brigade*			
12/25/93+	39	18		33 **Will You Be There (In The Morning)**...A:42 / S:63 *Risin' Suspicion*	$3	▮V	Capitol 58041
				"45": Capitol 17799; B-side: "Back To Avalon"			
				HEART AND SOUL ORCHESTRA, The '77			
				Disco studio group assembled by DJ/VJ Frankie Crocker.			
2/26/77	46	7		**Love In 'C' Minor**...*Poinciana* [I]	$5		Casablanca 876
				HEARTBEATS, The '57			
				R&B vocal group from Queens, New York: James "Shep" Sheppard, Wally Roker, Walter Crump, Robbie Adams and Vernon Walker. Group disbanded in 1960. Sheppard formed **Shep & The Limelites** in 1961; was murdered on 1/24/70 (age 34).			
12/22/56+	53	16		1 **A Thousand Miles Away**...T:53 *Oh Baby Don't*	$80		Rama 216
				first released on Hull 720 in 1956 ($200)			
7/15/57	78	3		2 **Everybody's Somebody's Fool**...T:78 *I Want To Know*	$80		Rama 231
11/7/60	96	1		3 **A Thousand Miles Away**...*Oh Baby Don't* [R]	$80		Rama 216
				HEARTS, The R&B '63			
				Female R&B vocal group from Harlem, New York: Joyce James, Joyce Peterson, **Jeanette "Baby" Washington** and Zell Sanders. Sanders, the mother of Johnnylouise Richardson of **Johnnie & Joe**, produced group's records. Not to be confused with Lee Andrews's male group of the same name. Also see **The Jaynetts**.			
10/19/63	94	3		**Dear Abby**...*(instrumental)*	$15		Tuff 370
				HEARTSFIELD LP '74			
				Rock band from Chicago, Illinois: J.C. Heartsfield (vocals), Fred Dobbs, Perry Cordell and Phil Lucafo (guitars), Greg Biela (bass), and Artie Baldacci (drums).			
3/2/74	95	5		**Music Eyes**...*Gypsy Rider*	$5		Mercury 73449
				HEATH, Ted, And His Music LP '56			
				Born Edward Heath on 3/30/1900 in London, England. Died on 11/18/69 (age 69). Trombonist/bandleader.			
10/13/56	52	8		**The Faithful Hussar**...T:52 *Have You Met Miss Jones* [I]	$12		London 1675
				HEATHER B. R&B/BUB '98			
				Born Heather Gardener on 11/13/70 in Jersey City, New Jersey. Female rapper. One of the first-season cast members of MTV's *The Real World* in 1992.			
8/1/98	89	2		**Do You**...S:66 *(TV track remix)*	$4	▮	MCA 55452
				HEATHERLY, Eric C&W/LP '00			
				Born on 2/2/70 in Chattanooga, Tennessee. Country-rockabilly singer/songwriter/guitarist.			
4/29/00	50	20		**Flowers On The Wall**...A:45 / S:48 *Someone Else's Cadillac*	$5	★+V	Mercury 170128
				"45": Mercury 172152			

DEBUT	PEAK	WKS	Gold	A-side (Chart Hit)......B-side	$	Sym	Label & Number

HEATHERTON, Joey — LP '72

Born Johanna Heatherton on 9/14/44 in Rockville Centre, Long Island, New York. Movie/TV actress.

DEBUT	PEAK	WKS	Gold	A-side (Chart Hit)......B-side	$	Sym	Label & Number
5/27/72	24	15		1 **Gone** ......*The Road I Took To You (Pieces)*	$7	■	MGM 14387
				also released with "Someone To Watch Over Me" as the B-side			
11/25/72+	87	9		2 **I'm Sorry** ......*Crazy*	$7		MGM 14434

HEATWAVE — R&B/BUB/LP '77

Multi-national, interracial dance group formed in Germany. Core members: brothers Johnnie and Keith Wilder (vocals), Eric Johns and William Jones (guitars), Rod Temperton and Calvin Duke (keyboards), Derek Bramblz (bass), and Ernest Berger (drums). Johnnie Wilder became a paraplegic due to a car accident in 1979 but continued singing with the group. Temperton left in late 1978 and went on to become a prolific songwriter ("Rock With You," "Baby Come To Me," among others).

DEBUT	PEAK	WKS	Gold	A-side (Chart Hit)......B-side	$	Sym	Label & Number
7/23/77	2^{2}	27	▲	1 **Boogie Nights** ......*All You Do Is Dial*	$5		Epic 50370
1/7/78	18	20	▲	2 **Always And Forever** ......*Super Soul Sister*	$5		Epic 50490
5/6/78	7	17	▲	3 **The Groove Line** ......*Happiness Togetherness*	$5		Epic 50524

HEAVEN BOUND with Tony Scotti — BUB '71

Pop producer/backing vocalist Scotti with Joan Medora (lead vocals), Eddie Medora, Tommy Oliver and Michael Lloyd. Tony appeared in the movie *Valley Of The Dolls*.

DEBUT	PEAK	WKS	Gold	A-side (Chart Hit)......B-side	$	Sym	Label & Number
9/4/71	83	5		1 **He'd Rather Have The Rain** ......*Come Run With Me*	$6		MGM 14284
				single also issued with a hard cover picture sleeve promoting the B-side, which was featured in a Toyota car commercial			
12/11/71+	79	9		2 **Five Hundred Miles** ......*I Will*	$6		MGM 14314
				traditional folk ballad written by Hedy West as "500 Miles"			

HEAVEN 17 — BUB/LP '83

Electro-pop-dance trio from England: Glenn Gregory (vocals) and former **Human League** co-founders/synthesists Martyn Ware and Ian Craig Marsh.

DEBUT	PEAK	WKS	Gold	A-side (Chart Hit)......B-side	$	Sym	Label & Number
3/12/83	74	5		**Let Me Go** ......*I'm Your Money*	$4		Arista/Virgin 1050

HEAVY D & THE BOYZ — R&B/BUB/LP '91

Born Dwight Meyers on 5/24/67 in Queens, New York; raised in Mt. Vernon, New York. Male rapper. Former president of Uptown Records. Played "Peaches" in the movie *The Cider House Rules*. The Boyz consisted of Glen Parrish, Troy Dixon and Edward Ferrell. Dixon died on 7/15/90 (age 22) from an accidental fall in Indianapolis. Also see **Michael Jackson**'s hit "Jam."

DEBUT	PEAK	WKS	Gold	A-side (Chart Hit)......B-side	$	Sym	Label & Number
6/29/91	11	22	●	1 **Now That We Found Love** S:5 / A:12 *(instrumental)*	$3	▮	Uptown/MCA 54090
				Aaron Hall (backing vocal)			
11/23/91+	32	20		2 **Is It Good To You** ......A:27 / S:28 *(instrumental)*	$3	▮V	Uptown/MCA 54200
1/23/93	56^{S}	7		3 **Who's The Man?** ......BUB:106 *(instrumental)*	$3	▮	Uptown/MCA 54543
3/26/94	20	20		4 **Got Me Waiting** ......S:11 / A:28 *(same version)*	$3	▮	Uptown/MCA 54815
				samples "Don't You Know That" by **Luther Vandross**			
7/2/94	40	20		5 **Nuttin' But Love** ......S:28 / A:40 *(album instrumental)*	$3	▮	Uptown/MCA 54865
11/5/94+	57	15		6 **Black Coffee** ......S:37 *Spend A Little Time On Top*	$3	▮	Uptown/MCA 54931
				samples "The Payback" by **James Brown**			
3/8/97	18	19	●	7 **Big Daddy** ......S:10 / A:70 *(2 versions)*	$3	▮	Uptown/Universal 56039
9/6/97	70	5		8 **Need Your Love** ......S:50 *(2 versions) / (4 album snippets)*	$3	▮	Kedar/Universal 56129
				BIG BUB featuring Queen Latifah & Heavy D			
				samples "I Want Your Love" by **Chic**			

HEBB, Bobby — R&B/LP '66

Born on 7/26/41 in Nashville, Tennessee. Black singer/songwriter/multi-instrumentalist. Featured on the *Grand Ole Opry* at age 12. His brother Hal was a member of The Marigolds.

DEBUT	PEAK	WKS	Gold	A-side (Chart Hit)......B-side	$	Sym	Label & Number
6/25/66	2^{2}	15	●	1 **Sunny** ......*Bread*	$10		Philips 40365
				written by Hebb after his brother Hal was killed in a mugging			
10/8/66	39	6		2 **A Satisfied Mind** ......*Love Love Love*	$10	■	Philips 40400
				picture sleeve issued with back of sleeve blank or with text; #1 Country hit for **Porter Wagoner** in 1955			
12/31/66+	84	3		3 **Love Me** ......*Crazy Baby*	$10		Philips 40421

HEDGEHOPPERS ANONYMOUS — BUB '66

Rock group from England: Mick Tinsley, Ray Honeyball, Leslie Dash, Alan Laud and John Stewart. Produced by **Jonathan King**.

DEBUT	PEAK	WKS	Gold	A-side (Chart Hit)......B-side	$	Sym	Label & Number
12/4/65+	48	10		**It's Good News Week** ......*Afraid Of Love*	$12		Parrot 9800

HEFTI, Neal — AC/LP '66

Born on 10/29/22 in Hastings, Nebraska. Conductor/trumpeter. Gained fame as arranger for **Woody Herman** (1944-46), Harry James and **Count Basie**, then as composer of TV themes.

DEBUT	PEAK	WKS	Gold	A-side (Chart Hit)......B-side	$	Sym	Label & Number
2/12/66	35	8		**Batman Theme** ......*Batman Chase* [I]	$7	■	RCA Victor 8755
				original theme from the *Batman* TV series starring Adam West and Burt Ward			

HEIGHT, Ronnie — '59

Born on 3/2/37 in Seattle, Washington. Pop singer. Started career as lead first tenor of vocal group the Five Checks.

DEBUT	PEAK	WKS	Gold	A-side (Chart Hit)......B-side	$	Sym	Label & Number
3/23/59	45	6		**Come Softly To Me** ......*So Young, So Wise*	$20		Dore 516

HEIGHTS, The — BUB/LP '92

Band made up of cast members from the Fox network prime time TV show of the same name: **Jamie Walters** (born on 6/13/69 in Boston, Massachusetts) (see #2 below) and Shawn Thompson (vocals), Alex Desert, Ken Garito, Cheryl Pollack, Charlotte Ross, Zachary Throne and Tarisa Valenza. Show is based on fictional adventures featuring the band.

DEBUT	PEAK	WKS	Gold	A-side (Chart Hit)......B-side	$	Sym	Label & Number
10/3/92	❶^{2}	20	●	1 **How Do You Talk To An Angel** ......S:3 / A:3 *Walkin' Nerve*	$3	▮V	Capitol 44890
				"45": Capitol 56783			
1/28/95	16	27		2 **Hold On** ......A:12 / S:34 *I Know The Game*	$3	▮V	Atlantic 87240
				JAMIE WALTERS			
				"45": Atlantic 87159; B-side: "Why"			

HELLO PEOPLE — BUB/LP '75

White-faced, mime-rock group: Greg Geddes, Robert Sedita, N.D. Smart and Laurence Tasse.

DEBUT	PEAK	WKS	Gold	A-side (Chart Hit)......B-side	$	Sym	Label & Number
1/18/75	71	7		**Future Shock** ......*Destiny*	$6		ABC/Dunhill 15023

DEBUT	PEAK	WKS	Gold	A-side (Chart Hit)..........B-side	$	Sym	Label & Number
				HELMS, Bobby C&W/BUB/AC **'57**			
				Born on 8/15/35 in Bloomington, Indiana. Died of emphysema on 6/19/97 (age 61). Country singer/guitarist. Appeared on father's local TV show.			
				1)Jingle Bell Rock 2)My Special Angel 3)Fraulein			
7/15/57	**36**	27		1 **Fraulein** ....CW[4] T:36 / S:46 *(Got A) Heartsick Feeling*	$25	■	Decca 30194
				made *Billboard's* Country charts for 52 weeks; a new version "Bubbled Under" (#127) in 1963 on Columbia 42801; picture sleeve has a center-cut hole and introduces Helms as a "New Singing Sensation"			
10/14/57	**7**	23	●	2 **My Special Angel** ....CW[4] S:7 / T:7 / A:8 *Standing At The End Of My World*	$25		Decca 30423
12/23/57	**6**	6	●	3 **Jingle Bell Rock** T:6 / S:7 / A:11 *Captain Santa Claus (And His Reindeer Space Patrol)* [X]	$20	■	Decca 30513
5/12/58	**63**	8		4 **Jacqueline** ....T:63 *Living In The Shadow Of The Past*	$20		Decca 30619
				from the movie *The Case Against Brooklyn* starring Darren McGavin; **The Anita Kerr Singers** (backing vocals, #2 & 4)			
8/18/58	**60**	2		5 **Borrowed Dreams** ....H:60 *Schoolboy Crush*	$20		Decca 30682
12/8/58+	**75**	6		6 **The Fool And The Angel**..........*A Hundred Hearts*	$20		Decca 30749
12/22/58	**35**	4		7 **Jingle Bell Rock** ....*Captain Santa Claus (And His Reindeer Space Patrol)* [X-R]	$20		Decca 30513
12/12/60	**36**	3		8 **Jingle Bell Rock** ....*Captain Santa Claus (And His Reindeer Space Patrol)* [X-R]	$12		Decca 30513
12/11/61	**41**	4		9 **Jingle Bell Rock** ....*Captain Santa Claus (And His Reindeer Space Patrol)* [X-R]	$12		Decca 30513
12/8/62	**56**	4		10 **Jingle Bell Rock** ....X:❶[2] *Captain Santa Claus (And His Reindeer Space Patrol)* [X-R]	$12		Decca 30513
				above 3 Decca reissues are on a multi-color Decca label; Christmas charts: [#1[2]-36 weeks] 3/'63; 13/'64; 4/'65; 2/'66; 5/'67 (Decca and 1967 remake on Little Darlin' 0038); 16/'68; 1/'69 (Decca and 1965 remake on Kapp 719); 5/'70 (Decca, Kapp and 1970 remake on Certron 10021 with a color picture sleeve); 7/'72 (Kapp Winners Circle 85 - also in '73); 4/'73; 6/'83 (Decca reissue on MCA 65026 - also in '84 & '85); 3/'84; 4/'85; same version on #11 below			
1/4/97	**73[A]**	1		11 **Jingle Bell Rock**.......... [X-R]			album cut
				from the movie *Jingle All The Way* starring Arnold Schwarzenegger (reissued on soundtrack on TVT 8070)			
				HELTAH SKELTAH R&B/BUB/LP **'96**			
				Male rap duo from Brooklyn, New York: Tawl Sean (a.k.a. Ruck or Sparsky) and Da Rockness Monsta (a.k.a. Rock or Dutch).			
2/3/96	**75**	8		1 **LeFlaur LeFlah Eshkoshka** ....S:66 *Blah* (#103)	$3	▮	Priority 53223
				THE FABULOUS FIVE Featuring Heltah Skeltah and Originoo Gunn Clappaz			
				contains elements from "Uzuri" by The Catalysts; Eshkoshka: an ancient warrior yell			
10/3/98	**80**	7		2 **I Ain't Havin' That**..........S:62 *Worldwide*	$3	▮	Duck Down 53324
				HELTAH SKELTAH feat. Starang Wondah of O.G.C. & Doc Holiday			
				samples "Hot Sex" by **A Tribe Called Quest** and "Pick It Up" by **Redman**			
				HENDERSON, Joe BUB/R&B/LP **'62**			
				Born in 1937 in Como, Mississippi; raised in Gary, Indiana. Died on 10/24/64 (age 27). R&B singer.			
5/19/62	**8**	12		1 **Snap Your Fingers**..........*If You See Me Cry*	$15		Todd 1072
9/8/62	**74**	4		2 **Big Love** ....*After Loving You*	$12		Todd 1077
11/24/62	**94**	1		3 **The Searching Is Over**..........*Three Steps*	$12		Todd 1079
				Cliff Parman (orch., all of above)			
				HENDERSON, Michael — see CONNORS, Norman			
				HENDERSON, Willie R&B **'74**			
				Born on 8/9/41 in Pensacola, Florida. Black producer/music director for Brunswick/Dakar in Chicago, Illinois.			
3/21/70	**91**	2		1 **Funky Chicken (Part 1)**..........*(Part 2)* [I]	$8		Brunswick 55429
				WILLIE HENDERSON AND THE SOUL EXPLOSIONS			
7/6/74	**73**	5		2 **Dance Master Pt. 1**..........*Pt. 2* [I]	$5		Playboy 50057
				HENDRICKS, Bobby **'58**			
				Born on 2/22/38 in Columbus, Ohio. R&B singer. Lead singer with **The Swallows** in 1958. First recorded with the Flyers for Atco in 1957. With **The Drifters** in 1958 (sang lead on "Drip Drop").			
8/4/58	**25**	14		1 **Itchy Twitchy Feeling** ....H:25 / S:35 *A Thousand Dreams*	$30		Sue 706
				The Coasters (backing vocals); Jimmy Oliver (orch.); also see **The Swallows**' version with Hendricks			
11/7/60	**73**	4		2 **Psycho** ....*Too Good To Be True* [N]	$20		Sue 732
				duet with New York DJ Dr. Jive (as the psychiatrist); co-written by **Clyde McPhatter**			
				HENDRIX, Jimi BUB/LP **'68**			
				Born on 11/27/42 in Seattle, Washington. Died of a drug overdose on 9/18/70 (age 27). Legendary psychedelic-blues guitarist. Began career as a studio guitarist. Played with **Joey Dee & The Starliters**. In 1965, formed own band, Jimmy James & The Blue Flames. In 1966, discovered by **The Animals**' bassist Chas Chandler at New York City's Cafe Wha?, who invited Hendrix to London, where he created The Jimi Hendrix Experience with Noel Redding (bass; died on 5/11/2003, age 57) and Mitch Mitchell (drums). Formed new group in 1969, Band of Gypsys, with **Buddy Miles** (drums) and Billy Cox (bass). The Jimi Hendrix Experience was inducted into the Rock and Roll Hall of Fame in 1992. Won Grammy's Lifetime Achievement Award in 1992.			
8/26/67	**65**	8		1 **Purple Haze**..........*The Wind Cries Mary*	$25		Reprise 0597
12/23/67+	**67**	4		2 **Foxey Lady** ....*Hey Joe*	$25		Reprise 0641
3/16/68	**82**	4		3 **Up From The Skies** ....*One Rainy Wish*	$25		Reprise 0665
9/21/68	**20**	9		4 **All Along The Watchtower** *Burning Of The Midnight Lamp*	$20		Reprise 0767
				written by **Bob Dylan** (from his 1968 album *John Wesley Harding*)			
11/30/68	**52**	8		5 **Crosstown Traffic** ....*Gypsy Eyes*	$20		Reprise 0792
				THE JIMI HENDRIX EXPERIENCE (#1 & 3-5)			
4/3/71	**59**	8		6 **Freedom**..........*Angel*	$15		Reprise 1000
10/23/71	**74**	7		7 **Dolly Dagger**..........*Star Spangled Banner*	$15		Reprise 1044
				from the Hendrix concert movie *Rainbow Bridge*			
				HENDRYX, Nona R&B/LP **'87**			
				Born on 8/18/45 in Trenton, New Jersey. Member of **Patti LaBelle & The Blue-Belles** from 1961-77.			
6/4/83	**91**	3		1 **Keep It Confidential**..........*Dummy Up*	$3		RCA 13437
5/23/87	**58**	9		2 **Why Should I Cry?**..........*Funkyland*	$3	■	EMI America 8382
				HENHOUSE FIVE PLUS TOO — see STEVENS, Ray			

HENLEY, Don

★216★ ROK/AC/C&W/LP '85

Born on 7/22/47 in Gilmer, Texas. Soft-rock singer/songwriter/drummer. Own band, Shiloh, in the early 1970s. Worked with **Glenn Frey** in **Linda Ronstadt**'s backup band, then the two formed the **Eagles** with **Randy Meisner** and Bernie Leadon. Went solo in 1982. Married model Sharon Summerall on 5/20/95.

1)Dirty Laundry 2)The Boys Of Summer 3)The End Of The Innocence

DEBUT	PEAK	WKS	Gold	A-side (Chart Hit)...B-side	$	Sym	Label & Number
10/24/81+	6	19		1 **Leather And Lace**...*Bella Donna* (Nicks) **STEVIE NICKS (with DON HENLEY)** written for **Waylon Jennings** and **Jessi Colter**	$4	■	Modern 7341
8/21/82	42	11		2 **Johnny Can't Read**...*Long Way Home* **Andrew Gold** (keyboards)	$4	■	Asylum 69971
10/30/82+	3	19	●	3 **Dirty Laundry** AR[3] *Lilah* **Joe Walsh** and Steve Lukather (**Toto**) (guitar solos)	$4	■	Asylum 69894
1/15/83	48	11		4 **I Can't Stand Still**...*Them And Us*	$4		Asylum 69931
11/10/84+	5	22		5 **The Boys Of Summer**...AR[5] A:5 / S:7 *A Month Of Sundays*	$3	■	Geffen 29141
2/23/85	9	19		6 **All She Wants To Do Is Dance**...AR[2] A:8 / S:12 *Building The Perfect Beast* **Martha Davis** of **The Motels** and **Patty Smyth** (harmony vocals)	$3	■	Geffen 29065
5/25/85	34	17		7 **Not Enough Love In The World**...A:30 *Man With A Mission*	$3	■	Geffen 29012
8/31/85	22	14		8 **Sunset Grill**...A:15 / S:27 *Man With A Mission* **Patty Smyth** (harmony vocal); above 4 from the album *Building The Perfect Beast*	$3		Geffen 28906
6/24/89	8	18		9 **The End Of The Innocence**...AR[4] A:7 / S:9 *If Dirt Were Dollars* (ROK #8) co-written and co-produced by **Bruce Hornsby** (also on piano)	$3	■	Geffen 22925
10/7/89	21	18		10 **The Last Worthless Evening**...S:19 / A:22 *Gimme What You Got*	$3	■	Geffen 22771
2/17/90	21	21		11 **The Heart Of The Matter**...A:20 / S:21 *Little Tin God*	$3	▮	Geffen 19898
7/7/90	48	12		12 **How Bad Do You Want It?**...A:39 *New York Minute*	$3	▮	Geffen 19699
11/10/90	48	16		13 **New York Minute**...*The Heart Of The Matter (acoustic version)* above 5 from the album *The End Of The Innocence*	$3	▮V	Geffen 19660
8/15/92	2^6	24	●	14 **Sometimes Love Just Ain't Enough**...AC[4] S:3 / A:3 *Out There* (Smyth) **PATTY SMYTH with Don Henley**	$3	▮V	MCA 54403
10/9/93	46[A]	20		15 **Sit Down You're Rockin' The Boat**... from the movie *Leap Of Faith* starring **Steve Martin** (soundtrack on MCA 10671)			album cut
6/24/00	58	20		16 **Taking You Home**...AC[4] A:53 from the album *Inside Job* on Warner 47083			album cut

HENRY, Clarence

BUB '61

Born on 3/19/37 in Algiers, Louisiana. R&B vocalist/pianist/songwriter. With Bobby Mitchell's R&B band from 1953-55. Nicknamed "Frog Man" because of his frog sounds in his hit "Ain't Got No Home."

DEBUT	PEAK	WKS	Gold	A-side (Chart Hit)...B-side	$	Sym	Label & Number
12/15/56+	20	16		1 **Ain't Got No Home**...S:20 / T:30 *Troubles, Troubles* [N] **CLARENCE HENRY "FROG MAN"**	$30		Argo 5259
2/20/61	4	16		2 **But I Do** *Just My Baby And Me* some pressings show title as "I Don't Know Why" (both are the same song)	$20		Argo 5378
5/15/61	12	10		3 **You Always Hurt The One You Love**...*Little Suzy* #1 hit in 1944 for **The Mills Brothers**	$20		Argo 5388
8/7/61	57	6		4 **Lonely Street**...*Why Can't You*	$20		Argo 5395
10/30/61	64	5		5 **On Bended Knees**...*Standing In The Need Of Love* (#109)	$15		Argo 5401
1/13/62	77	5		6 **A Little Too Much**...*I Wish I Could Say The Same*	$15		Argo 5408

HENSON, Jim

'70

Born on 9/24/36 in Greenville, Mississippi. Died of a sudden virus on 5/16/90 (age 53). Creator of The Muppets, that famous crew of puppets starring in TV's *Sesame Street* and *The Muppet Show*, also in the movies *The Muppet Movie* and *The Great Muppet Caper*. Henson was the voice for both Ernie and Kermit.

DEBUT	PEAK	WKS	Gold	A-side (Chart Hit)...B-side	$	Sym	Label & Number
8/15/70	16	9		1 **Rubber Duckie**...*Sesame Street* (The Kids) [N] **ERNIE (JIM HENSON)**	$6		Columbia 45207
9/15/79	25	17		2 **Rainbow Connection**...*I Hope That Somethin' Better Comes Along* (Kermit & Rowlf) **KERMIT (JIM HENSON)** from the original soundtrack of *The Muppet Movie*	$5		Atlantic 3610

HERMAN, Keith

'79

Pop-rock singer/songwriter/guitarist.

DEBUT	PEAK	WKS	Gold	A-side (Chart Hit)...B-side	$	Sym	Label & Number
10/20/79	87	4		**She's Got A Whole Number**...*High School Q.T.*	$5		Radio 418

HERMAN, Woody, And His Orchestra

MEM/POP/R&B/LP '45

Born on 5/16/13 in Milwaukee, Wisconsin. Died of heart failure on 10/29/87 (age 74). Saxophonist/clarinetist of dance bands beginning in 1929. Formed own band in 1936. Charted 53 pop hits, 1937-52. Won Grammy's Lifetime Achievement Award in 1987. One of the most innovative and contemporary of all big band leaders. Hit #1 in 1942 with "Blues In The Night."

DEBUT	PEAK	WKS	Gold	A-side (Chart Hit)...B-side	$	Sym	Label & Number
11/12/55	79	6		1 **Love Is A Many-Splendored Thing**...T:79 *House Of Bamboo* [I] title song from the movie starring William Holden and Jennifer Jones	$12		Capitol 3202
8/18/56	75	5		2 **I Don't Want Nobody (To Have My Love But You)**...T:75 *To Love Again* Woody Herman (vocal); #14 R&B hit for **Buddy Johnson** in 1956	$12		Capitol 3488

HERMAN'S HERMITS

★128★ BUB/LP '65

Teen pop-rock group from Manchester, England: Peter "Herman" Noone (vocals; born on 11/5/47), Derek Leckenby (born on 5/14/45) and Keith Hopwood (guitars; born on 10/26/46), Karl Green (bass; born on 7/31/47), and Barry Whitwam (drums; born on 7/21/46). Group name derived from cartoon character Sherman of TV's *The Bullwinkle Show*. Noone left in 1972 for a solo career; formed Los Angeles-based group The Tremblers in late '70s. Noone hosted own show on music video TV channel VH-1. Leckenby died of cancer on 6/4/94 (age 48).

1)Mrs. Brown You've Got A Lovely Daughter 2)I'm Henry VIII, I Am 3)Can't You Hear My Heartbeat 4)Listen People 5)There's A Kind Of Hush

DEBUT	PEAK	WKS	Gold	A-side (Chart Hit)...B-side	$	Sym	Label & Number
10/17/64	13	13		1 **I'm Into Something Good**...*Your Hand In Mine*	$10		MGM 13280
1/30/65	2^2	15		2 **Can't You Hear My Heartbeat**...*I Know Why*	$8	■	MGM 13310
4/3/65	5	13		3 **Silhouettes**...*Walkin' With My Angel*	$8		MGM 13332
4/17/65	1^3	11	●	4 **Mrs. Brown You've Got A Lovely Daughter** *I Gotta Dream On*	$8	■	MGM 13341

DEBUT	PEAK	WKS	Gold	A-side (Chart Hit)..................B-side	$	Sym	Label & Number
				HERMAN'S HERMITS — Cont'd			
5/29/65	4	10		5 **Wonderful World** .... *Traveling Light*	$8	■	MGM 13354
7/3/65	1[1]	10	●	6 **I'm Henry VIII, I Am** .... *The End Of The World*	$8	■	MGM 13367
				written in 1911; popularized in England by Harry Champion			
9/18/65	7	10		7 **Just A Little Bit Better** .... *Sea Cruise*	$8	■	MGM 13398
12/25/65+	8	9		8 **A Must To Avoid** .... *The Man With The Cigar*	$8		MGM 13437
2/19/66	3	9		9 **Listen People** .... *Got A Feeling*	$8		MGM 13462
				from the movie *When The Boys Meet The Girls* starring **Connie Francis**			
4/9/66	9	8		10 **Leaning On The Lamp Post** .... *Hold On!*	$8	□	MGM 13500
				front of picture sleeve promotes the soundtrack "Hold On" and back of sleeve promotes mod shirts; #8 & 10: from the movie *Hold On!* starring Herman's Hermits			
7/9/66	12	8		11 **This Door Swings Both Ways** .... *For Love*	$8		MGM 13548
10/1/66	5	11		12 **Dandy** .... *My Reservation's Been Confirmed*	$8	■	MGM 13603
				written by Ray Davies of **The Kinks**			
12/3/66	27	8		13 **East West** .... *What Is Wrong What Is Right*	$8		MGM 13639
2/11/67	4	12	●	14 **There's A Kind Of Hush** /			
2/18/67	35	10		15 **No Milk Today**	$8	■	MGM 13681
6/24/67	18	7		16 **Don't Go Out Into The Rain (You're Going To Melt)** .... *Moonshine Man*	$8	■	MGM 13761
8/26/67	39	6		17 **Museum** .... *Last Bus Home*	$8	■	MGM 13787
				written by **Donovan**			
1/13/68	22	11		18 **I Can Take Or Leave Your Loving** .... *Marcel's*	$8		MGM 13885
5/11/68	61	6		19 **Sleepy Joe** .... *Just One Girl*	$8		MGM 13934
				all of above produced by Mickie Most			

HERNANDEZ, Patrick — LP '79

Born on 4/6/49 in Paris, France. Disco singer/songwriter.

DEBUT	PEAK	WKS	Gold	A-side (Chart Hit)..................B-side	$	Sym	Label & Number
6/23/79	16	19	●	**Born To Be Alive** .... *Too Many People*	$4		Columbia 10986

HERNDON, Ty — C&W/LP '98

Born Boyd Tyrone Herndon on 5/2/62 in Meridian, Mississippi; raised in Butler, Alabama. Country singer/songwriter/guitarist.

DEBUT	PEAK	WKS	Gold	A-side (Chart Hit)..................B-side	$	Sym	Label & Number
5/20/95	90	3		1 **What Mattered Most** .... S:59 *You Don't Mess Around With Jim*	$4	▮V	Epic 77843
6/6/98	81	10		2 **A Man Holdin' On (To A Woman Lettin' Go)** .... S:53 *Just Enough To Get To Memphis*	$4	▮V	Epic 78904
12/5/98	38	10		3 **It Must Be Love** CW[1] A:28		V	album cut
				"45" issued for above 2 on Epic 79049			
3/20/99	47	14		4 **Hands Of A Working Man** A:33			album cut
				above 3 from the album *Big Hopes* on Epic 68167			
10/16/99	83	12		5 **Steam** .... S:41 *Lookin' For The Good Life*	$4	★V	Epic 79269
3/18/00	92	8		6 **No Mercy** .... S:42 *Tears In God's Eyes*	$4	★V	Epic 79345
				"45" issued for above 2 on Epic 79345			

HESITATIONS, The — R&B/BUB/LP '68

R&B vocal group from Cleveland, Ohio: brothers George "King" and Charles Scott, Fred Deal, Robert Sheppard, Arthur Blakely, Phillip Dorroh and Leonard Veal. George Scott was accidentally shot to death in February 1968 (age 38).

DEBUT	PEAK	WKS	Gold	A-side (Chart Hit)..................B-side	$	Sym	Label & Number
1/6/68	38	10		1 **Born Free** .... *Love Is Everywhere*	$15		Kapp 878
				title song from the movie starring Virginia McKenna			
3/16/68	42	8		2 **The Impossible Dream** .... *Nobody Knows You When You're Down And Out*	$15		Kapp 899
				from the Broadway musical *Man Of La Mancha* starring Richard Kiley			
5/25/68	90	3		3 **Climb Every Mountain** .... *My World*	$15		Kapp 911
				from the Rodgers & Hammerstein musical *The Sound of Music*			
11/9/68	100	2		4 **A Whiter Shade Of Pale** .... *With Pen In Hand*	$15		Kapp 948
				melody based on the Bach cantata *Sleepers Awake*			

HEWETT, Howard — R&B/AC/LP '90

Born on 10/1/57 in Akron, Ohio. Lead vocalist of **Shalamar**, 1979-85. Married to **Nia Peeples** from 1989-93.

DEBUT	PEAK	WKS	Gold	A-side (Chart Hit)..................B-side	$	Sym	Label & Number
11/8/86	90	3		1 **I'm For Real** .... *Eye On You*	$3	■	Elektra 69527
				George Duke, **Stanley Clark** and Wilton Felder (backing musicians)			
5/26/90	62	7		2 **Show Me** .... *Natural Love*	$3	▮	Elektra 64978
10/26/96	6	20	▲	3 **This Is For The Lover In You** .... S:3 / A:37 *(remix)*	$3	▮V	Epic 78443
				BABYFACE Featuring LL Cool J, Howard Hewett, Jody Watley and Jeffrey Daniels			
				#17 R&B hit for **Shalamar** in 1981 (Hewett, Watley and Daniels were members of **Shalamar**)			

HEWITT, Jennifer Love — BUB '99

Born on 2/21/79 in Waco, Texas. Pop singer/actress. Starred on TV's *Party Of Five* and in such movies as *I Know What You Did Last Summer*, *Can't Hardly Wait*, *Heartbreakers* and *The Tuxedo*.

DEBUT	PEAK	WKS	Gold	A-side (Chart Hit)..................B-side	$	Sym	Label & Number
2/6/99	59	8		**How Do I Deal** .... S:15 *Try To Say Goodbye* (Jory Eve)	$5	★V	Warner 17105
				from the movie *I Still Know What You Did Last Summer* starring Hewitt			

HEYETTES, The — '76

Female novelty-pop vocal trio: Julia Tillman, Maxine Willard and Jessica Smith.

DEBUT	PEAK	WKS	Gold	A-side (Chart Hit)..................B-side	$	Sym	Label & Number
4/10/76	91	6		**The Fonz Song** .... *(instrumental)* [N]	$5		London 232
				inspired by the Henry Winkler character "Fonzie" of TV's *Happy Days*			

HEYWOOD, Eddie — MEM/POP/LP '56

Born on 12/4/15 in Atlanta, Georgia. Died on 1/2/89 (age 73). Black jazz pianist/composer/arranger. Played professionally by age 14. Own band in New York City in 1941. Worked with Billie Holiday. To the West Coast in 1947, with own trio. Hit #11 in 1947 with "Guilty" featuring **Ella Fitzgerald**.

DEBUT	PEAK	WKS	Gold	A-side (Chart Hit)..................B-side	$	Sym	Label & Number
6/23/56	2[2]	31	●	1 **Canadian Sunset** .... A:2 / T:2 / S:3 / J:3 *This Is Real (We're In Love, We're In Love, We're In Love)* [I]	$15		RCA Victor 6537
				HUGO WINTERHALTER and his Orchestra with EDDIE HEYWOOD			
6/30/56	11	25		2 **Soft Summer Breeze** .... S:11 / T:12 / J:13 / A:14 *Heywood's Bounce* [I]	$12		Mercury 70863

HEYWOODS — see DONALDSON, Bo

DEBUT	PEAK	WKS	Gold	A-side (Chart Hit)..............................B-side	$	Sym	Label & Number
				HIBBLER, Al R&B/LP **'55**			
				Born on 8/16/15 in Tyro, Mississippi. Died on 4/24/2001 (age 85). Black vocalist. Blind since birth, studied voice at Little Rock's Conservatory for the Blind. First recorded with Jay McShann for Decca in 1942. With Duke Ellington, 1943-51. Also recorded with Harry Carney, **Tab Smith**, Mercer Ellington and Billy Strayhorn.			
4/9/55	3	19		1 **Unchained Melody** RB[1] A:3 / J:3 / S:5 *Daybreak*	$20		Decca 29441
				from the movie *Unchained* starring football great Elroy "Crazylegs" Hirsch			
10/15/55	4	22		2 **He** ....S:4 / T:7 / A:7 / J:8 *Breeze (Blow My Baby Back To Me)*	$20		Decca 29660
2/4/56	21	16		3 **11th Hour Melody** ....T:21 *Let's Try Again*	$15		Decca 29789
6/16/56	22	7		4 **Never Turn Back /** A:22 / T:48			
8/18/56	77	2		5 **Away All Boats** T:77	$15		Decca 29950
				title song from the movie starring Jeff Chandler			
8/4/56	10	20		6 **After The Lights Go Down Low** ....A:10 / J:14 / T:15 / S:20 *I Was Telling Her About You*	$15		Decca 29982
				earlier version released in 1955 on Original 1006 ($30)			
2/2/57	92	1		7 **Trees** ....T:92 *The Town Crier*	$12		Decca 30176
				Hibbler's original version was a #2 R&B hit in 1948 on Miracle 501; #12 hit for Donald Novis in 1933; **Jack Pleis** (orch., all of above)			
				HI-C LP **'91**			
				Born in 1972 in Louisiana; raised in California. Male rapper.			
8/17/91	63	13		**I'm Not Your Puppet** ....S:36 *(radio mix)*	$5	▮	Hollywood 64849
				samples **James & Bobby Purify**'s "I'm Your Puppet"			
				HICKEY, Ersel **'58**			
				Born on 6/27/34 in Brighton, New York. Rockabilly singer/guitarist.			
4/28/58	75	6		**Bluebirds Over The Mountain** ....T:75 *Hangin' Around*	$40		Epic 9263
				HICKS, Erik **'93**			
				R&B singer/songwriter.			
6/26/93	74[A]	1		**Let's Get Into Something Sexy** ....BUB:115 *(original version)*	$4	▮	Riot/RCA 62573
				HI-FI FOUR, The **'56**			
				White pop vocal group from Toronto, Ontario, Canada: Jack McNicol, Don Wainman, Doug Harman and John Van Evera.			
2/18/56	93	1		**Band Of Gold** ....T:93 *Davy, You Upset My Life*	$40		King 4856
				HI-FIVE R&B/LP **'91**			
				R&B vocal group from Waco, Texas: **Tony Thompson** (see #8 below), Roderick Clark, Russell Neal, Marcus Sanders and Toriano Easley. Treston Irby replaced Easley in late 1991.			
2/23/91	❶[1]	23	●	1 **I Like The Way (The Kissing Game)** RB[2] S:❶[2] / A:4 *Sweetheart*	$3	▮	Jive 1424
6/22/91	8	21		2 **I Can't Wait Another Minute** ....RB[1] A:4 / S:15 *I Know Love*	$3	▮	Jive 1445
11/23/91	88	8		3 **Just Another Girlfriend** ....*I Can't Wait Another Minute (live)*	$3	▮	Jive 42009
8/1/92	5	20		4 **She's Playing Hard To Get** ....A:6 / S:8 *Whenever You Say*	$3	▮	Jive 42067
12/5/92+	38	17		5 **Quality Time** ....S:18 / A:54 *Let's Get It Started (Keep It Goin' On)*	$3	▮	Jive 42109
				written, produced and backing vocal by **R. Kelly**			
7/17/93	92	4		6 **Unconditional Love** ....*She Said*	$3	▮	Jive 42144
				from the movie *Menace II Society* starring Tyrin Turner			
10/16/93	30	20		7 **Never Should've Let You Go** ....S:27 / A:40 *Whenever You Say*	$3	▮	Jive 42178
				from the movie *Sister Act II: Back In The Habit* starring Whoopi Goldberg			
5/27/95	59	16		8 **I Wanna Love Like That** ....S:42 *(rap mix)*	$3	▮	Giant 17871
				TONY THOMPSON			
				HIGGINS, Bertie C&W/AC/LP **'82**			
				Born Elbert Higgins on 12/8/44 in Tarpon Springs, Florida. Soft-rock singer/songwriter. First recorded for ABC in 1964. Worked as a drummer with **Tommy Roe**, 1964-66.			
11/14/81+	8	29	●	1 **Key Largo** ....AC[2] *White Line Fever*	$5		Kat Family 02524
				inspired by the movie starring Humphrey Bogart and Lauren Bacall			
5/1/82	46	10		2 **Just Another Day In Paradise** ....*She's Gone To Live On The Mountain*	$5		Kat Family 02839
				HIGH & MIGHTY, The LP **'99**			
				Rap duo from Philadelphia, Pennsylvania: Mighty Mi and Mr. Eon. Members of **Smut Peddlers**.			
8/7/99	48[S]	7		**B-Boy Document 99** ....*(instrumental) / Weed*	$4	★	Rawkus 53498
				THE HIGH & MIGHTY Featuring Mos Def & Mad Skillz			
				samples "Polarizer" by Joe Thomas; clean version released on Rawkus 53499			
				HIGH INERGY R&B/BUB/LP **'77**			
				Female R&B vocal group from Pasadena, California: sisters Vernessa and **Barbara Mitchell** (see #4 below), Linda Howard and Michelle Rumph. Vernessa left in 1978; group continued as a trio.			
9/17/77	12	22		1 **You Can't Turn Me Off (In The Middle Of Turning Me On)** ....*Save It For A Rainy Day*	$5		Gordy 7155
				also issued with "Let Me Get Close To You" as the B-side			
3/4/78	89	5		2 **Love Is All You Need** ....*Some Kinda Magic*	$5		Gordy 7157
5/21/83	82	5		3 **He's A Pretender** ....*Don't Let Up On The Groove*	$4		Gordy 1662
7/2/83	48	12		4 **Blame It On Love** ....*Even Tho'* (Robinson)	$4		Tamla 1684
				SMOKEY ROBINSON And BARBARA MITCHELL			
				some pressings credit artist as: **SMOKEY ROBINSON with High Energy**			
				HIGH KEYES, The **'63**			
				R&B vocal group: **Troy Keyes** (lead singer), Jimmy Williams, Bobby Haggard and Cliff Rice.			
7/27/63	47	9		**Que Sera, Sera (Whatever Will Be, Will Be)** ....*Daddy, Ooh Long Legs*	$20		Atco 6268
				from the 1956 movie *The Man Who Knew Too Much* starring **Doris Day** and James Stewart			

DEBUT	PEAK	WKS	Gold	A-side (Chart Hit)	B-side	$	Sym	Label & Number

HIGHLIGHTS, The '56

White vocal group from Chicago, Illinois: **Frank Pizani** (lead; born on 1/24/35) (see #3 below), brothers Frank and Tony Calzaretta, Bill Melshimer, and Jerry Oleski.

DEBUT	PEAK	WKS	Gold	A-side (Chart Hit)	B-side	$	Sym	Label & Number
10/20/56	19	18		1 City Of Angels ... S:19 / T:30	*Listen, My Love*	$25		Bally 1016
4/20/57	84	1		2 To Be With You ... T:84	*Will I Ever Know?*	$25		Bally 1027
				THE HIGHLIGHTS Featuring Frank Pisani				
9/16/57	70	3		3 Angry ... T:70	*Every Time*	$20		Bally 1040
				FRANK PIZANI				
				#6 hit for Art Gillham in 1925; Lew Douglas (orch., above 3)				

HIGHWAYMEN, The LP '61

Folk group formed in Middletown, Connecticut: Dave Fisher, Bob Burnett, Chan Daniels, Steve Trott and Steve Butts. Daniels died of pneumonia on 8/2/75 (age 35).

DEBUT	PEAK	WKS	Gold	A-side (Chart Hit)	B-side	$	Sym	Label & Number
7/10/61	1[2]	17	●	1 Michael AC[5]	*Santiano*	$15		United Artists 258
				19th-century folk song ("Michael Row The Boat Ashore")				
11/27/61+	13	18		2 Cotton Fields /				
				traditional American ballad, copyrighted in 1850				
11/6/61	42	10		3 The Gypsy Rover ...		$12		United Artists 370
4/14/62	90	1		4 I'm On My Way ...	*Whiskey In The Jar*	$12		United Artists 439
7/14/62	64	6		5 The Bird Man ...	*Cindy Oh Cindy*	$12		United Artists 475
				Burt Lancaster (narration); inspired by the movie *The Bird Man of Alcatraz* starring Lancaster				

HILL, Bunker '62

Born David Walker on 5/5/41 in Washington DC. R&B singer. Member of **Mighty Clouds Of Joy**.

DEBUT	PEAK	WKS	Gold	A-side (Chart Hit)	B-side	$	Sym	Label & Number
8/25/62	33	13		Hide & Go Seek, Part I ...	*Part II*	$20		Mala 451

HILL, Dan AC/LP '78

Born on 6/3/54 in Toronto, Ontario, Canada. Adult Contemporary singer/songwriter.

DEBUT	PEAK	WKS	Gold	A-side (Chart Hit)	B-side	$	Sym	Label & Number
1/24/76	67	6		1 Growin' Up ...	*People*	$5		20th Century 2254
11/26/77+	3	22	●	2 Sometimes When We Touch	*Still Not Used To*	$4		20th Century 2355
8/12/78	41	9		3 All I See Is Your Face ...	*Longer Fuse*	$4		20th Century 2378
11/25/78	91	3		4 Let The Song Last Forever ...	*Indian Woman*	$4	■	20th Century 2392
6/6/87	6	24		5 Can't We Try ... S:4 / A:9	*Pleasure Centre*	$3		Columbia 07050
				DAN HILL (with Vonda Sheppard)				
12/12/87+	43	20		6 Never Thought (That I Could Love) ... A:37	*Blood In My Veins*	$3		Columbia 07618

HILL, David '59

Born David Hess on 9/19/36 in Brooklyn, New York. Pop singer. Starred in the movie *Last House On The Left.*

DEBUT	PEAK	WKS	Gold	A-side (Chart Hit)	B-side	$	Sym	Label & Number
4/20/59	90	2		1 Two Brothers ...	*Deep Goes My Love*	$20		Kapp 266
10/19/59	92	2		2 Living Doll ...	*Keep The Miracle Going*	$20		Kapp 293

HILL, Faith ★271★ C&W/BUB/LP '00

Born on 9/21/67 in Jackson, Mississippi. Country singer. Adopted at less than a week old and raised as Audrey Faith Perry in Star, Mississippi. Married **Tim McGraw** on 10/6/96. Charted 32 Country hits, 1993-2003.

1)Breathe 2)The Way You Love Me 3)This Kiss

DEBUT	PEAK	WKS	Gold	A-side (Chart Hit)	B-side	$	Sym	Label & Number
12/23/95+	74	16		1 It Matters To Me ... CW[3] S:36	*Keep Walkin' On* (w/**Shelby Lynne**)	$4	▮V	Warner 17718
5/17/97	7	20	▲	2 It's Your Love ... CW[6] S:3	*She Never Lets It Go To Her Heart* (McGraw - C&W #1)	$4	▮V	Curb 73019
				TIM McGRAW with Faith Hill				
3/21/98	7	48	▲	3 This Kiss ... CW[3] A:12 / S:13	*Better Days*	$4	★V	Warner 17247
				a cassette single is available in both a radio and album version				
5/30/98	56	20		4 One Heart At A Time ... S:33	*(same version)*	$4	▮	Atlantic 84117
				GARTH BROOKS, BILLY DEAN, FAITH HILL, OLIVIA NEWTON-JOHN, NEAL McCOY, MICHAEL McDONALD, VICTORIA SHAW, BRYAN WHITE				
12/5/98	33	10		5 Let Me Let Go ... CW[1] A:24				album cut
3/6/99	68	8		6 Love Ain't Like That ... A:54				album cut
6/26/99	46	18		7 The Secret Of Life ... A:34				album cut
				#3 & 5-7: from the album *Faith* on Warner 46790				
11/6/99+	2[5]	53	●	8 Breathe CW[6] / AC[17] A:2 / S:3	*It All Comes Down To Love*	$4	★V	Warner 16884
3/11/00+	6	56		9 The Way You Love Me ... CW[4] S:6 / A:9	*Never Gonna Be Your Lady*	$4	★V	Warner 16818
8/12/00	54	14		10 Let's Make Love ... A:50			V	album cut
				FAITH HILL with TIM McGRAW				
				"45": Warner/Curb 16792; B-side: "There Will Come A Day" (Hill - C&W #59)				
1/6/01-	65	1		11 Where Are You Christmas? ... A:57 [X]				album cut
				written by **Mariah Carey**; from the movie *Dr. Seuss' How The Grinch Stole Christmas* starring Jim Carrey				
2/3/01	39	18		12 If My Heart Had Wings ... A:29			V	album cut
				"45": Warner 16773; B-side: "It Will Be Me"; #8-10 & 12: from the album *Breathe* on Warner 47373				
5/26/01	10	20		13 There You'll Be ... AC[12] A:8			V	album cut
				from the soundtrack of the movie *Pearl Harbor* starring Ben Affleck on Hollywood 48113; "45": Warner 16739; B-side: "Breathe"				
8/31/02	33	26		14 Cry ... A:31			V	album cut
				from the album *Cry* on Warner 48001; "45": Warner 16688; B-side: "Wicked"				

HILL, Jessie '60

Born on 12/9/32 in New Orleans, Louisiana. Died of heart failure on 9/17/96 (age 63). R&B singer/drummer/pianist. With **Huey (Piano) Smith** to 1958.

DEBUT	PEAK	WKS	Gold	A-side (Chart Hit)	B-side	$	Sym	Label & Number
3/28/60	28	16		1 Ooh Poo Pah Doo Part II ...	*Part I* [I]	$20		Minit 607
7/25/60	91	1		2 Whip It On Me ...	*I Need Your Love*	$20		Minit 611

DEBUT	PEAK	WKS	Gold	A-side (Chart Hit)......B-side	$	Sym	Label & Number
				HILL, Jordan AC **'96**			
				Born on 4/17/78 in Knoxville, Tennessee. White female teen pop singer.			
7/8/95	**80**	10		1 **Remember Me This Way**......*(album version)*	$3	▮	MCA Soundtracks 55046
				from the movie *Casper* starring Christina Ricci			
6/8/96	**66**	8		2 **For The Love Of You**......S:66 *(dance remix edit)*	$3	▮	143/Atlantic 87061
				HILL, Lauryn R&B/BUB/LP **'98**			
				Born on 5/25/75 in South Orange, New Jersey. Black singer/actress. Member of **The Fugees**. Acted on TV's *As The World Turns* and in the movie *Sister Act 2*. Also see **Nas**'s "If I Ruled The World."			
3/9/96	**2^{3A}**	35		1 **Killing Me Softly**......RB^{5A}			album cut
				FUGEES (feat. Lauryn Hill)			
5/10/97	**61^{A}**	2		2 **The Sweetest Thing**......			album cut
				REFUGEE CAMP ALL-STARS Featuring Lauryn Hill			
				from the movie *Love Jones* starring Larenz Tate (soundtrack on Columbia 67917)			
6/13/98	**35^{A}**	24		3 **Can't Take My Eyes Off Of You**......			album cut
				from the movie *Conspiracy Theory* starring Mel Gibson			
11/14/98	**❶^{2}**	21	●	4 **Doo Wop (That Thing)** S:❶^{1} / A:2 *Lost Ones (remix)*	$4	★^{V}	Rufhouse 78868 ■
				Hot 100 Airplay debut: 9/5/98			
1/9/99	**21**	22		5 **Ex-Factor**......A:11		V	album cut
				samples "Can It All Be So Simple" by **Wu-Tang Clan**; "45": Ruffhouse 79077; B-side: "When It Hurts So Bad"			
6/19/99	**35**	18	●	6 **Everything Is Everything**......S:18 / A:50 *Ex-Factor (remix)*	$4	★^{V}	Ruffhouse 79206
				above 4 from the album *The Miseducation Of Lauryn Hill* on Ruffhouse 69035			
				HILL, Warren — see RESTLESS HEART			
				HILL, Z.Z. R&B/BUB/LP **'71**			
				Born Arzel Hill on 9/30/35 in Naples, Texas. Died of a heart attack on 4/27/84 (age 48). Blues singer/guitarist. Formed Hill Records in 1970.			
3/7/64	**100**	1		1 **You Were Wrong**......*Tomble Weed*	$15		M.H. 200
2/27/71	**62**	5		2 **Don't Make Me Pay For His Mistakes**......*Think People*	$10		Hill 222
6/19/71	**86**	3		3 **I Need Someone (To Love Me)**......*Oh Darling*	$10		Kent 4547
				recorded in 1964			
				HILLSIDE SINGERS, The AC/LP **'72**			
				Adult Contemporary vocal group: Lori Ham, Mary Mayo, Joelle Marino, Bill Marino, Frank Marino, Laura Marino, Rick Shaw, Ron Shaw and Susan Wiedinman. The Marinos are siblings. Mary Mayo was the wife of producer Al Ham; Lori Ham is their daughter. Rick and Ron Shaw are brothers; Ron went on to a country music career.			
11/27/71+	**13**	12		1 **I'd Like To Teach The World To Sing (In Perfect Harmony)**......*I Believed It All*	$5		Metromedia 231
				adapted from a Coca-Cola jingle			
2/26/72	**100**	1		2 **We're Together**......*Day By Day*	$5		Metromedia 241
				adapted from a McDonald's jingle			
				HILLTOPPERS, The MEM/POP **'53**			
				White vocal group formed in Bowling Green, Kentucky: Jimmy Sacca, Don McGuire, Seymour Spiegelman and **Billy Vaughn**. Vaughn left for own conducting career in 1955; replaced by Chuck Schrouder. Spiegelman died on 2/13/87 (age 56). Vaughn died of cancer on 9/26/91 (age 72). Group charted 7 Top 10 hits, 1952-54.			
				1)Marianne 2)Only You (And You Alone) 3)The Kentuckian Song			
				THE HILLTOPPERS Featuring Jimmy Sacca:			
7/30/55	**20**	4		1 **The Kentuckian Song**......S:20 *I Must Be Dreaming*	$15		Dot 15375
				from the movie *The Kentuckian* starring Burt Lancaster			
11/12/55	**8**	19		2 **Only You (And You Alone)**......A:8 / T:9 / J:10 / S:15 *Until The Real Thing Comes Along*	$15		Dot 15423
11/12/55	**81**	2		3 **Searching**......T:81 *All I Need Is You*	$15		Dot 15415
12/31/55+	**31**	7		4 **My Treasure**......T:31 *The Last Word In Love*	$15		Dot 15437
9/15/56	**38**	10		5 **Ka-Ding-Dong**......T:38 *Into Each Life Some Rain Must Fall*	$15		Dot 15489
				THE HILLTOPPERS Featuring Chuck Schrouder			
2/9/57	**3**	16		6 **Marianne** J:3 / A:6 / T:8 / S:12 *You're Wasting Your Time*	$12		Dot 15537
				adapted from a Bahamian folk song			
4/29/57	**74**	1		7 **I'm Serious /** T:74			
				original version recorded by Bobby Chandler in 1957 on OJ 1000 ($40)			
4/27/57	**75**	4		8 **I Love My Girl**......T:75	$12		Dot 15560
7/15/57	**58**	10		9 **A Fallen Star**......T:58 *Footsteps*	$12		Dot 15594
11/25/57	**22**	13		10 **The Joker (That's What They Call Me)**......A:22 / S:34 / T:37 *Chicken Chicken*	$12		Dot 15662
				HINE, Eric **'81**			
				Born in England. Pop-rock singer/songwriter/keyboardist.			
8/22/81	**73**	5		**Not Fade Away**......*After Dark*	$5		Montage 1200
				Buddy Holly song first recorded by **The Crickets** in 1957 (B-side of "Oh, Boy!")			
				HINES, Gregory — see VANDROSS, Luther			
				HINES GIRLS **'02**			
				Studio group from Ft. Lauderdale, Florida. Formed to cover the **Las Ketchup** hit.			
11/23/02	**30^{S}**	1		**The Ketchup Song "Asereje"**......*(3 versions)* [F]	$8	★*	Artemis 872411
				HINTON, Joe BUB/R&B **'64**			
				Born on 11/15/29 in Evansville, Indiana. Died of cancer on 8/13/68 (age 38). R&B singer. With the Chosen Gospel Singers. Lead singer of the Spirit Of Memphis (gospel group).			
6/1/63	**88**	3		1 **You Know It Ain't Right**......*Love Sick Blues*	$15		Back Beat 537
10/12/63	**89**	1		2 **Better To Give Than Receive**......*There's No In Between*	$15		Back Beat 539
8/15/64	**13**	12		3 **Funny**......*You Gotta Have Love*	$15		Back Beat 541
				written by **Willie Nelson**			
				HIP HOP FOR RESPECT **'00**			
				All-star rap group: **Talib Kweli**, **Kool G. Rap**, Rah Digga, **Sporty Thievz**, **Mos Def**, Shabaam Sahdeeq, **Common**, **Pharoahe Monch** and Posdnous.			
5/13/00	**31^{S}**	9		**One Four Love Pt. 1**......*(Pt. 2) / Protective Custody / A Tree Never Grown*	$8	★*	Rawkus 38712

DEBUT	PEAK	WKS	Gold	A-side (Chart Hit)...B-side	$	Sym	Label & Number
				HIPPIES, The (Formerly The Tams) '63			
				White doo-wop group. Not to be confused with the Atlanta R&B group, The Tams.			
4/13/63	63	5		**Memory Lane** ...*A Lonely Piano* (Reggie Harrison)	$20		Parkway 863
				first released on Mink 22 as by The Stereos ($75) and then on Mink 22 as by The Tams; B-side: "Teenage Kiss" ($50) (both in 1959); also released on Parkway 863 as by The Tams in 1963 ($25)			
				HIPSWAY LP '87			
				Pop group from Scotland: Graham Skinner (vocals), Pim Jones (guitar), John McElhone (bass) and Harry Travers (drums). McElhone later joined **Texas**.			
1/24/87	19	15		**The Honeythief** ...S:16 / A:21 *Forbidden*	$3	■	Columbia 06579
				HIRT, Al AC/BUB/LP '64			
				Born Alois Maxwell Hirt on 11/7/22 in New Orleans, Louisiana. Died of liver failure on 4/27/99 (age 76). Trumpet virtuoso. Toured with **Jimmy** and **Tommy Dorsey**, Ray McKinley and Horace Heidt. Formed own Dixieland combo (with **Pete Fountain**) in the late 1950s.			
1/4/64	4	16		1 **Java** AC[4] *I Can't Get Started* [I]	$8		RCA Victor 8280
4/11/64	15	12		2 **Cotton Candy** ...*Walkin'* (#103) [I]	$8		RCA Victor 8346
7/11/64	30	7		3 **Sugar Lips** ...*Poupee Brisee (Broken Doll)* [I]	$8		RCA Victor 8391
10/10/64	85	5		4 **Up Above My Head (I Hear Music In The Air)** ...*September Song*	$7		RCA Victor 8439
				#6 R&B hit for Sister Rosetta Tharpe in 1949			
12/5/64	6[X]	4		5 **Hooray For Santa Claus** ...*White Christmas* [X]	$10	■	RCA Victor 8478
				from the movie *Santa Claus Conquers the Martians* starring **Pia Zadora**			
1/16/65	47	7		6 **Fancy Pants** ...*Star Dust* [I]	$7		RCA Victor 8487
				#28 hit for **Floyd Cramer** in 1954 on Fabor 146 ($20)			
4/17/65	57	7		7 **Al's Place** ...*Mister Sandman* [I]	$7		RCA Victor 8542
				all of above produced by **Chet Atkins**; all of above (except #2) shown as **Al (He's the King) Hirt**			
9/11/65	96	2		8 **The Silence (Il Silenzio)** ...*Love Theme From "The Sandpiper"* [I]	$7		RCA Victor 8653
1/27/68	100	1		9 **Keep The Ball Rollin'** ...*Manhattan Safari*	$7		RCA Victor 9417
				HI-TEK — see KWELI, Talib			
				HI TEK 3 Featuring Ya Kid K '90			
				Dance trio from Belgium: Kovali, El Sati and Yosev. Ya Kid K is the female rapper of **Technotronic**.			
4/14/90	69	7		**Spin That Wheel** ...*Turtle Rhapsody* (Orchestra On The Half-Shell)	$3	▮[V]	SBK 07320
				from the movie *Teenage Mutant Ninja Turtles* starring Elias Koteas			
				HI-TOWN DJ'S '98			
				Rap group from Florida: Kalo, Derrick Rahming, Matt Young, Teeze, JP and Chyna Doll.			
5/2/98	56	19		**Ding-A-Ling** ...S:37 *(remix)*	$4	▮	Restless 72961
				HIVES, The LP '02			
				Rock group from Fagersta, Sweden: brothers Pelle (vocals) and Niklas (guitar) Almqvist, Vigilante Carlstroem (guitar), Dr. Matt Destruction (bass) and Chris Dangerous (drums).			
7/20/02	86	11		**Hate To Say I Told You So** ...*Die, All Right! / The Hives Are Law, You Are Crime*	$8	★*[V]	Gearhead 024 ■
				"45" issued on either black, clear or yellow vinyl (all with same picture sleeve); B-side: "Die, All Right!"			
				HO, Don, and The Aliis LP '67			
				Born on 8/13/30 in Kakaako, Oahu, Hawaii. Adult Contemporary singer/actor. Father of **Hoku**.			
11/26/66+	57	17		**Tiny Bubbles** ...*Born Free*	$8		Reprise 0507
				HODGE, Chris '72			
				Born in England. Pop-rock singer/songwriter.			
6/3/72	44	8		**We're On Our Way** ...*Supersoul*	$8	■	Apple 1850
				HODGES, Eddie BUB '61			
				Born on 3/5/47 in Hattiesburg, Mississippi. Pop singer/actor. Appeared in many movies and TV shows.			
6/19/61	12	13		1 **I'm Gonna Knock On Your Door** ...*Ain't Gonna Wash For A Week*	$15	■	Cadence 1397
				originally recorded by **The Isley Brothers** on RCA Victor 7537 in 1959 ($30); a promotional insert was also issued featuring photos of Hodges in his movie roles			
1/27/62	65	6		2 **Bandit Of My Dreams** ...*Mugmates*	$15		Cadence 1410
6/23/62	14	11		3 **(Girls, Girls, Girls) Made To Love** ...*I Make Believe It's You*	$15		Cadence 1421
				written and recorded by **The Everly Brothers** on their 1960 album *A Date With The Everly Brothers*			
7/3/65	44	9		4 **New Orleans** ...*Hard Times For Young Lovers*	$12		Aurora 153
				HODGES, JAMES AND SMITH R&B '77			
				Female R&B vocal trio from Detroit, Michigan: Pat Hodges, Denita James and Jessica Smith.			
7/9/77	96	6		**Since I Fell For You/I'm Falling In Love** ...*Off*	$6		London 256
				HODGSON, Roger — see SUPERTRAMP			
				HOFFS, Susanna — see BANGLES			
				HOG HEAVEN — see JAMES, Tommy			
				HOKU LP '00			
				Born Hoku Ho on 6/10/81 in Oahu, Hawaii. Teen pop-rock singer. Daughter of singer/actor **Don Ho**.			
2/19/00	27	14		**Another Dumb Blonde** ...S:5 *(remix)*	$4	★	Geffen 497246
				from the movie *Snow Day* starring Chris Elliott			
				HOLDEN, Ron BUB/R&B '60			
				Born on 8/7/39 in Seattle, Washington. Died of a heart attack on 1/22/97 (age 57). R&B singer.			
4/4/60	7	19		**Love You So** ...*My Babe*	$30		Donna 1315
				RON HOLDEN with The Thunderbirds			

DEBUT	PEAK	WKS	Gold	A-side (Chart Hit)...B-side	$	Sym	Label & Number
				HOLE ROK/LP '95			
				Rock group formed in Los Angeles, California: Courtney Love (vocals, guitar), Eric Erlandson (guitar), Kristen Pfaff (bass) and Patty Schemel (drums). Love acted in the movies *Sid & Nancy*, *Straight To Hell*, *Feeling Minnesota* and *The People Vs. Larry Flynt*. Love was married to Kurt Cobain (**Nirvana**) from 2/24/92 until his death on 4/8/94. Pfaff was found dead in her bathtub on 6/16/94 (age 27). Melissa Auf Der Maur replaced Pfaff.			
12/10/94+	**58**	12		1 **Doll Parts**...A:39 *Plump (live)*	$4	▮V	DGC 19379
9/12/98	**56**[A]	12		2 **Celebrity Skin** ...MR[4] HOT:85(9 wks)		V	album cut
2/27/99	**81**	3		3 **Malibu**...A:69		V	album cut
				above 2 from the album *Celebrity Skin* on DGC 25164; "45" issued for above 2 on DGC 97087			
				HOLIDAY, Chico '59			
				Born Ralph Vergolino on 8/24/34 in Waukesha, Wisconsin. Rock and roll singer.			
5/4/59	**74**	6		**Young Ideas**...*Cuckoo Girl*	$12		RCA Victor 7499
				Billy Mure (orch.); written by **Sonny James**			
				HOLIDAY, Jimmy BUB/R&B '63			
				Born on 7/24/34 in Durant, Mississippi; raised in Waterloo, Iowa. Died of heart failure on 2/15/87 (age 52). R&B singer/songwriter.			
3/16/63	**57**	9		1 **How Can I Forget**...*Janet*	$15		Everest 2022
9/3/66	**98**	1		2 **Baby I Love You**...*You Won't Get Away*	$12		Minit 32002
				HOLIDAY, Tasha R&B '97			
				Born in Atlantic City, New Jersey. Female R&B singer.			
4/19/97	**93**	5		**Just The Way You Like It**...*(instrumental)*	$3	▮	MCA 55090
				samples "School Boy Crush" by **Average White Band**			
				HOLIDAYS, The '66			
				R&B vocal trio from Detroit, Michigan: **Edwin Starr**, **J.J. Barnes** and Steve Mancha. Each recorded solo.			
5/7/66	**63**	9		**I'll Love You Forever**...*Makin' Up Time*	$25		Golden World 36
				HOLIEN, Danny '72			
				Born on 1/29/49 in Red Wing, Minnesota. Folk-rock singer/songwriter/guitarist.			
9/9/72	**66**	8		**Colorado**...*Red Wing*	$7		Tumbleweed 1004
				HOLLAND, Amy BUB/LP '80			
				Pop singer. Daughter of country singer Esmereldy and opera singer Harry Boersma. Married **Michael McDonald** in 1983.			
8/9/80	**22**	16		1 **How Do I Survive**...*Don't Kid Yourself*	$4	■	Capitol 4884
				produced by **Michael McDonald**			
8/28/82	**88**	3		2 **Ain't Nothing Like The Real Thing/You're All I Need To Get By**...*Houston* (Christian)	$4		Boardwalk 149
				CHRIS CHRISTIAN (with Amy Holland)			
				HOLLAND-DOZIER-HOLLAND R&B/BUB/LP '74			
				One of the most successful songwriting teams of all-time. All were born in Detroit, Michigan. **Eddie Holland** was born on 10/30/39; **Lamont Dozier** was born on 6/16/41; Brian Holland was born on 2/15/41. Most of their songs were written for other Motown artists. Trio left Motown in 1968 and formed own Invictus/Hot Wax label. Trio inducted into the Rock and Roll Hall of Fame in 1990.			
				EDDIE HOLLAND:			
1/20/62	**30**	13		1 **Jamie**...*Take A Chance On Me*	$25		Motown 1021
2/8/64	**76**	5		2 **Leaving Here**...*Brenda*	$20		Motown 1052
5/23/64	**54**	7		3 **Just Ain't Enough Love**...*Last Night I Had A Vision*	$20		Motown 1058
8/29/64	**58**	6		4 **Candy To Me**...*If You Don't Want My Love*	$20		Motown 1063
9/30/72	**57**	10		5 **Why Can't We Be Lovers**...*Don't Leave Me* [I]	$7		Invictus 9125
				HOLLAND-DOZIER featuring LAMONT DOZIER			
1/6/73	**52**	6		6 **Don't Leave Me Starvin' For Your Love (Part 1)**...*(Part 2)*	$7		Invictus 9133
				HOLLAND-DOZIER featuring BRIAN HOLLAND			
				LAMONT DOZIER:			
12/22/73+	**15**	18		7 **Trying To Hold On To My Woman**...*We Don't Want Nobody To Come Between Us*	$5		ABC 11407
6/15/74	**26**	12		8 **Fish Ain't Bitin'**...*Breaking Out All Over*	$5		ABC 11438
				also released on ABC 12012 in 1974			
1/4/75	**87**	5		9 **Let Me Start Tonite**...*I Wanna Be With You*	$5		ABC 12044
				HOLLIDAY, Jennifer R&B/BUB/LP '82			
				Born on 10/19/60 in Riverside, Texas. R&B singer/actress. Appeared in several Broadway musicals. Also see **Foreigner**'s "I Want To Know What Love Is."			
7/3/82	**22**	14		1 **And I Am Telling You I'm Not Going**...RB[4] *Fake Your Way To The Top* (Cleavant Derricks/Loretta Devine/Jennifer Holliday/Sheryl Lee Ralph)	$4		Geffen 29983
				from the original Broadway cast *Dreamgirls* starring Holliday; first pressings listed artist as "**Dreamgirls**"; also see #5 below			
10/22/83	**49**	11		2 **I Am Love**...*Heartstrings*	$4		Geffen 29525
9/21/85	**69**	7		3 **Hard Times For Lovers**...*He's A Pretender*	$3	■	Geffen 28958
2/8/86	**87**	3		4 **No Frills Love**...*I Rest My Case*	$3	■	Geffen 28845
				#1 Dance Club Play hit in 1986 and 1996			
11/24/01	**66**[S]	1		5 **And I Am Telling You I'm Not Going**...*(5 versions)* [R]	$8	★*	Tommy Boy Silver 2251
				ROSABEL with JENNIFER HOLLIDAY			

DEBUT	PEAK	WKS	Gold	A-side (Chart Hit)	B-side	$	Sym	Label & Number

HOLLIES, The ★173★ BUB/LP '67

Pop-rock group from Manchester, England: **Allan Clarke** (vocals; born on 4/15/42) (see #23 & 24 below), **Graham Nash** (born on 2/2/42) and Tony Hicks (guitars; born on 12/16/43), Eric Haydock (bass; born on 2/3/43), and Bobby Elliott (drums; born on 12/8/42). Haydock left in 1966; replaced by Bernie Calvert (first heard on "Bus Stop"). Nash left in December 1968 to join **David Crosby** and **Stephen Stills** in new trio; replaced by Terry Sylvester, formerly in **The Swinging Blue Jeans**. Shuffling personnel since then. Clarke, Nash, Hicks and Elliott regrouped briefly in 1983.

1)Long Cool Woman (In A Black Dress) 2)Bus Stop 3)The Air That I Breathe 4)He Ain't Heavy, He's My Brother 5)Stop Stop Stop

DEBUT	PEAK	WKS	Gold	A-side (Chart Hit)	B-side	$	Sym	Label & Number
5/16/64	98	1		1 **Just One Look** — also see #9 below	*Keep Off That Friend Of Mine*	$20		Imperial 66026
11/20/65+	32	12		2 **Look Through Any Window**	*So Lonely*	$15		Imperial 66134
3/19/66	42	10		3 **I Can't Let Go**	*I've Got A Way Of My Own*	$15		Imperial 66158
7/23/66	5	14		4 **Bus Stop**	*Don't Run And Hide*	$12		Imperial 66186
10/29/66	7	10		5 **Stop Stop Stop**	*It's You*	$12		Imperial 66214
3/18/67	11	14		6 **On A Carousel**	*All The World Is Love*	$12	■	Imperial 66231
6/3/67	28	7		7 **Pay You Back With Interest**	*Whatcha Gonna Do 'Bout It*	$12		Imperial 66240
6/17/67	9	13		8 **Carrie-Anne** — written for **Marianne Faithfull**; promo picture sleeve also issued with **The Tremeloes**' "Silence Is Golden" on the flip side	*Signs That Will Never Change*	$8	■	Epic 10180
9/30/67	44	7		9 **Just One Look** — same version as #1 above	*Running Through The Night* [R]	$12		Imperial 66258
10/7/67	51	5		10 **King Midas In Reverse**	*Water On The Brain*	$8	■	Epic 10234
12/2/67	50	8		11 **Dear Eloise**	*When Your Lights Turned On*	$8	■	Epic 10251
3/16/68	40	11		12 **Jennifer Eccles**	*Try It*	$8		Epic 10298
9/14/68	93	1		13 **Do The Best You Can**	*Elevated Observations*	$8		Epic 10361
4/19/69	56	8		14 **Sorry Suzanne**	*Not That Way At All*	$8		Epic 10454
12/20/69+	7	18		15 **He Ain't Heavy, He's My Brother** — famous slogan of Father Flanagan's Boys Town in Nebraska	*Cos You Like To Love Me*	$6		Epic 10532
5/30/70	82	4		16 **I Can't Tell The Bottom From The Top**	*Mad Professor Blyth*	$6		Epic 10613
6/24/72	2[2]	15	▲	17 **Long Cool Woman (In A Black Dress)**	*Look What We've Got*	$6		Epic 10871
11/4/72	26	11		18 **Long Dark Road**	*Indian Girl*	$6		Epic 10920
2/10/73	60	8		19 **Magic Woman Touch**	*Blue In The Morning*	$6		Epic 10951
4/20/74	6	21	●	20 **The Air That I Breathe** — originally recorded by **Albert Hammond** in 1972 on his album *It Never Rains In Southern California*	*No More Riders*	$6		Epic 11100
4/12/75	85	2		21 **Sandy** — written by **Bruce Springsteen**	*Second Hand Hangups*	$6		Epic 50086
6/28/75	71	3		22 **Another Night** — all of above produced by Ron Richards	*Time Machine Jive*	$6		Epic 50110
3/25/78	41	10		23 **(I Will Be Your) Shadow In The Street**	*The Passenger*	$4	⊙	Atlantic 3459
5/24/80	70	4		24 **Slipstream** — **ALLAN CLARKE** (above 2)	*Imagination's Child*	$4		Elektra 46617
6/4/83	29	12		25 **Stop In The Name Of Love**	*Musical Pictures*	$4	■	Atlantic 89819

HOLLISTER, Dave R&B/LP '99

Born in Chicago, Illinois. R&B/hip-hop singer/songwriter. Former member of **BLACKstreet**.

DEBUT	PEAK	WKS	Gold	A-side (Chart Hit)	B-side	$	Sym	Label & Number
4/10/99	39	17		1 **My Favorite Girl**	S:9 *(3 versions)*	$4	★	Def Squad 59019
3/25/00	84	4		2 **Can't Stay** — above 2 from the album *Ghetto Hymns* on Def Squad 50047	A:75			album cut
12/9/00+	44	20		3 **One Woman Man** — song is sampled on #4 below; from the album *Chicago '85...The Movie* on Def Squad 50278	A:35			album cut
1/12/02	5[S]	17		4 **That Was Then** — **ROY JONES JR. feat. Dave Hollister, Perion & Hahz The Rippa**	*(3 versions) / Unfaithful*	$4	★	Body Head/EMI 74767

HOLLOWAY, Brenda BUB '64

Born on 6/21/46 in Atascadero, California. R&B singer/songwriter. Later a backup singer for **Joe Cocker**.

DEBUT	PEAK	WKS	Gold	A-side (Chart Hit)	B-side	$	Sym	Label & Number
5/2/64	13	10		1 **Every Little Bit Hurts**	*Land Of A Thousand Boys*	$20		Tamla 54094
8/8/64	60	5		2 **I'll Always Love You**	*Sad Song*	$20		Tamla 54099
3/6/65	25	9		3 **When I'm Gone**	*I've Been Good To You*	$20	■	Tamla 54111
6/5/65	78	5		4 **Operator** — above 2 written and produced by **Smokey Robinson**	*I'll Be Available*	$20		Tamla 54115
4/22/67	69	5		5 **Just Look What You've Done**	*Starting The Hurt All Over Again*	$20		Tamla 54148
9/9/67	39	10		6 **You've Made Me So Very Happy**	*I've Got To Find It*	$20		Tamla 54155

HOLLOWAY, Loleatta R&B/LP '75

Born on 11/11/46 in Chicago, Illinois. Female disco singer.

DEBUT	PEAK	WKS	Gold	A-side (Chart Hit)	B-side	$	Sym	Label & Number
3/15/75	68	6		1 **Cry To Me**	*So Can I*	$6		Aware 047
2/5/77	72	9		2 **Dreamin**	*Worn Out Broken Heart* (R&B #25)	$5		Gold Mind 4000
11/4/78	87	5		3 **Only You** — **LOLEATTA HOLLOWAY AND BUNNY SIGLER**	*Good Good Feeling*	$5		Gold Mind 4012
7/20/91	❶[1]	20	●	4 **Good Vibrations** — **MARKY MARK And The Funky Bunch Featuring Loleatta Holloway**; samples Holloway's 1980 #1 disco hit "Love Sensation"	S:2 / A:6 *So What Chu Sayin*	$3	▮[V]	Interscope 98764

DEBUT	PEAK	WKS	Gold	A-side (Chart Hit)...B-side	$	Sym	Label & Number
	★417★			**HOLLY, Buddy/The Crickets** BUB/LP '57			

Born Charles Hardin Holley on 9/7/36 in Lubbock, Texas. One of rock and roll's most original and innovative performers. Began recording western and pop demos with Bob Montgomery in 1954. Signed to Decca label in January 1956 and recorded in Nashville as Buddy Holly & The Three Tunes (Sonny Curtis, lead guitar; Don Guess, bass; and Jerry **Ivan** Allison, drums) (see #9 below). In February 1957, Holly assembled his backing group, **The Crickets** (Allison; Niki Sullivan, rhythm guitar; and Joe B. Mauldin, bass), for recordings at **Norman Petty**'s studio in Clovis, New Mexico. Signed to Brunswick and Coral labels (subsidiaries of Decca Records). Because of contract arrangements, all Brunswick records were released as The Crickets, and all Coral records were released as Buddy Holly. Holly split from The Crickets in the fall of 1958. Holly (age 22), **Ritchie Valens** and the **Big Bopper** were killed in a plane crash near Mason City, Iowa, on 2/3/59. Gary Busey starred in the 1978 biographical movie *The Buddy Holly Story*. Holly was inducted into the Rock and Roll Hall of Fame in 1986. Won Grammy's Lifetime Achievement Award in 1997.

1)That'll Be The Day 2)Peggy Sue 3)Oh, Boy!

DEBUT	PEAK	WKS	Gold	A-side (Chart Hit)...B-side	$	Sym	Label & Number
8/12/57	❶^1	22	●	1 That'll Be The Day *[THE CRICKETS]* S:❶^1 / T:3 / A:3 *I'm Lookin' For Someone To Love*	$60		Brunswick 55009
				different version released on Decca 30434 in September 1957 as by Buddy Holly And The Three Tunes (recorded July 1956) ($300)			
11/11/57	3	22	●	2 Peggy Sue ...T:3 / S:3 / A:3 *Everyday*	$50		Coral 61885
				first written as "Cindy Lou"; renamed for Allison's girlfriend, Peggy Sue Gerrow, later his wife			
11/25/57+	10	20		3 Oh, Boy! *[THE CRICKETS]*...T:10 / S:11 / A:20 *Not Fade Away*	$50		Brunswick 55035
3/3/58	17	14		4 Maybe Baby *[THE CRICKETS]*...A:17 / S:18 / T:18 *Tell Me How*	$50		Brunswick 55053
5/26/58	37	10		5 Rave On...T:37 / S:41 *Take Your Time*	$50		Coral 61985
7/21/58	27	9		6 Think It Over *[THE CRICKETS]* / H:27 / S:38			
8/4/58	58	1		7 Fool's Paradise *[THE CRICKETS]*...H:58	$50		Brunswick 55072
				The Crickets non-charted classic "It's So Easy" was released on Brunswick 55094 ($50) in 1958			
8/4/58	32	7		8 Early In The Morning...H:32 / S:45 *Now We're One*	$50		Coral 62006
				The Helen Way Singers (backing vocals); written by **Bobby Darin**			
9/22/58	68	5		9 Real Wild Child...H:68 *Oh You Beautiful Doll*	$200		Coral 62017
				IVAN (Jerry Ivan Allison) **Buddy Holly** (lead guitar); The Roses (backing vocals)			
12/29/58+	82	4		10 Heartbeat...*Well....All Right*	$50		Coral 62051
2/23/59	13	14		11 It Doesn't Matter Anymore /			
				written by **Paul Anka**			
3/30/59	88	2		12 Raining In My Heart...	$50		Coral 62074
				Dick Jacobs (orch.: #8, 11 & 12); other non-charted classic Holly tunes include: "Words Of Love" on Coral 61852 ($300), "I'm Gonna Love You, Too" on Coral 61947 ($50) and "True Love Ways" on Coral 62210 ($50)			
9/22/62	99	2		13 Someday (When I'm Gone From You)...	$20	■	Liberty 55479
				BOBBY VEE and THE CRICKETS			

HOLLYRIDGE STRINGS, The BUB/LP '64

Arranged and conducted by Stu Phillips, later of the Golden Gate Strings.

DEBUT	PEAK	WKS	Gold	A-side (Chart Hit)...B-side	$	Sym	Label & Number
7/4/64	93	1		All My Loving...*Love Me Do* (#134) [I]	$10		Capitol 5207
				written by **John Lennon** and **Paul McCartney**			

HOLLYWOOD ARGYLES '60

Gary Paxton recorded "Alley-Oop" as a solo artist; since he was still under contract to Brent Records, where he recorded as Flip of "**Skip & Flip**," he made up the name Hollywood Argyles after street signs at Hollywood & Argyle. After the song was a hit, Paxton assembled a Hollywood Argyles group. Formed Garpax Records. Paxton is now a gospel artist.

DEBUT	PEAK	WKS	Gold	A-side (Chart Hit)...B-side	$	Sym	Label & Number
5/30/60	❶^1	15	●	Alley-Oop...*Sho' Know A Lot About Love* [N]	$25		Lute 5905
				written by **Dallas Frazier**; based on the comic strip character; reissued on Wham 7037 with a picture sleeve			

HOLLYWOOD FLAMES R&B '58

R&B vocal group from Los Angeles, California: Earl Nelson and **Bobby Day** (both of **Bob & Earl**), David Ford, Clyde Tillis and Curtis Williams (former member of **The Penguins**). Day died on 7/15/90 (age 60).

DEBUT	PEAK	WKS	Gold	A-side (Chart Hit)...B-side	$	Sym	Label & Number
11/25/57+	11	17		1 Buzz-Buzz-Buzz / T:11 / S:12			
12/16/57		1		2 Crazy...S:flip	$40		Ebb 119

HOLLYWOOD STARS, The '77

Rock group from Los Angeles, California: Mark Anthony (vocals), Rueben De Fuentes and Steve DeLacy (guitars), Michael Rummans (bass), and Bobby Drier (drums).

DEBUT	PEAK	WKS	Gold	A-side (Chart Hit)...B-side	$	Sym	Label & Number
5/14/77	94	4		All The Kids On The Street...*All For Love*	$6	□	Arista 0241
				promo sleeve and record issued with The Kinks' "Sleepwalker" as the B-side			

HOLM, Michael '75

Born Lothar Walter on 7/29/43 in Stettin, Germany. Adult Contemporary singer/songwriter/producer.

DEBUT	PEAK	WKS	Gold	A-side (Chart Hit)...B-side	$	Sym	Label & Number
12/14/74	53	7		When A Child Is Born...*Other Way Round* [X]	$6		Mercury 73642

HOLMAN, Eddie R&B/BUB/LP '70

Born on 6/3/46 in Norfolk, Virginia. R&B singer/songwriter. Recorded for Leopard in the early 1960s.

DEBUT	PEAK	WKS	Gold	A-side (Chart Hit)...B-side	$	Sym	Label & Number
1/15/66	57	11		1 This Can't Be True...*A Free Country*	$20		Parkway 960
12/27/69+	2^1	14	●	2 Hey There Lonely Girl *It's All In The Game*	$10		ABC 11240
				recorded in 1963 by **Ruby & The Romantics** as "Hey There Lonely Boy"			
4/4/70	48	8		3 Don't Stop Now /			
				originally "Bubbled Under" (#104) on 4/23/66 on Parkway 981			
5/9/70		2		4 Since I Don't Have You...	$10		ABC 11261
6/25/77	90	2		5 This Will Be A Night To Remember...*Time Will Tell*	$5		Salsoul 2026

HOLMES, Clint BUB/AC/LP '73

Born on 5/9/46 in Bournemouth, England; raised in Farnham, New York. Adult Contemporary singer.

DEBUT	PEAK	WKS	Gold	A-side (Chart Hit)...B-side	$	Sym	Label & Number
3/24/73	2^2	23	●	Playground In My Mind...*There's No Future In My Future*	$5		Epic 10891
				child's vocal is by producer and songwriter **Paul Vance**'s son, Philip			

HOLMES, Jake LP '70

Born on 12/28/39 in San Francisco, California. Folk-rock singer/songwriter.

DEBUT	PEAK	WKS	Gold	A-side (Chart Hit)...B-side	$	Sym	Label & Number
10/3/70	49	11		So Close...*Django & Friend*	$6		Polydor 14041

DEBUT	PEAK	WKS	Gold	A-side (Chart Hit)..............B-side	$	Sym	Label & Number
				HOLMES, LeRoy, And His Orchestra MEM/POP/LP **'54**			
				Born Alvin Holmes on 9/22/13 in Pittsburgh, Pennsylvania. Died on 7/27/86 (age 72). Orchestra conductor/arranger. Hit #9 on the pop charts in 1954 with "The High And The Mighty."			
8/11/56	95	1		1 **Theme From "The Proud Ones"**..............T:95 *Wouldn't It Be Loverly* [I]	$12		MGM 12275
				with Whistlin' Jones; title song from the movie *The Proud Ones* starring Robert Ryan			
9/8/56	59	7		2 **When The White Lilacs Bloom Again**..............T:59 *The Last Wagon* [I]	$10		MGM 12317
				HOLMES, Richard "Groove" BUB/LP **'66**			
				Born on 5/2/31 in Camden, New Jersey. Died of cancer on 6/29/91 (age 60). Black jazz organist. Discovered by **Les McCann**. Recorded with Joe Pass, Gene Ammons and Clifford Scott.			
6/25/66	44	11		1 **Misty** *["GROOVE" HOLMES]*..............*Groove's Groove* [I]	$8		Prestige 401
				original version by the Erroll Garner Trio in 1954 on Mercury 70442 ($20)			
10/1/66	96	3		2 **What Now My Love** *["GROOVE" HOLMES]*..............*Living Soul*	$8		Prestige 427
				written in France in 1962 by Gilbert Becaud as "Et Maintenant"			
10/1/66	99	2		3 **Secret Love**..............*Hallelujah, I Love Her So* [I]	$8		Pacific Jazz 88130
				#1 hit for **Doris Day** in 1954			
				HOLMES, Rupert BUB/AC/LP **'79**			
				Born on 2/24/47 in Northwich, Cheshire, England; raised in Manhattan, New York. Pop singer/songwriter. Member of **Street People**. Wrote the Broadway musical *Drood*. Created the TV show *Remember WENN* for American Movie Classics cable channel.			
9/2/78	72	6		1 **Let's Get Crazy Tonight**..............*The Long Way Home*	$5		Private Stock 45,199
10/20/79	1[3]	21	●	2 **Escape (The Pina Colada Song)**..............*Drop It*	$4	⊙	Infinity 50,035
				also released on MCA 50035			
1/19/80	6	17		3 **Him**..............*Get Outta Yourself*	$4		MCA 41173
5/3/80	32	11		4 **Answering Machine**..............*Lunch Hour*	$4		MCA 41235
11/8/80	68	7		5 **Morning Man**..............*The Mask*	$4		MCA 51019
4/4/81	56	7		6 **I Don't Need You**..............*Cold*	$4		MCA 51092
				HOLY, Steve C&W/BUB/LP **'02**			
				Born on 2/23/72 in Dallas, Texas. Country singer/songwriter.			
12/1/01+	29	20		**Good Morning Beautiful**..............CW[5] A:27			album cut
				from the album *Blue Moon* on Curb 77972; from the movie *Angel Eyes* starring **Jennifer Lopez**			
				HOMBRES, The BUB/LP **'67**			
				Rock group from Mephis, Tennessee: B.B. Cunningham (vocals, organ), Gary McEwen (guitar), Jerry Masters (bass) and Johnny Hunter (drums). Hunter committed suicide in February 1976 (age 34). Cunningham's brother, Bill, was a member of **The Box Tops**.			
9/16/67	12	13		**Let It Out (Let It All Hang Out)**..............*Go Girl, Go*	$12		Verve Forecast 5058
				first pressings issued as "Let It All Hang Out"; spoken opening copied from Red Ingle's 1948 novelty hit "Cigareetes, Whuskey, And Wild, Wild Women"			
				HOMER AND JETHRO C&W/BUB/POP **'59**			
				Country comedy duo from Knoxville, Tennessee. Henry "Homer" Haynes (guitar; born on 7/29/17; died on 8/7/71, age 54) and Kenneth "Jethro" Burns (mandolin; born on 3/10/23; died on 2/4/89, age 65). Country music's foremost comedy duo from the 1940s until Homer's death. Jethro went on to work with popular folk singer Steve Goodman. Hit #17 in 1953 with "(How Much Is) That Hound Dog In The Window."			
9/7/59	14	10		**The Battle Of Kookamonga**..............*Waterloo* [N]	$15		RCA Victor 7585
				a parody of "The Battle Of New Orleans"; produced by **Chet Atkins**			
				HOME TEAM **'92**			
				Rap duo from Brooklyn, New York; later relocated to Miami, Florida: brothers Debonaire and Drugzie.			
12/26/92	90	2		**Pick It Up Pick It Up**..............A:74 *(2 versions)*	$6	▮*	Luke 454
				HONDELLS, The BUB/LP **'64**			
				Producer Gary Usher recorded various studio musicians in Southern California under different group names. "Little Honda" featured Usher, Chuck Girard (**The Castells**; vocals), **Glen Campbell** and Richie Podolor (**Richie Allen**; guitars), Hal Blaine (drums) and Ritchie Burns (backing vocals). Usher (**Sagittarius**; died of cancer on 5/25/90, age 51) later formed touring group with Burns (lead vocals), Wayne Edwards (drums) and varying members. Randy Thomas sang lead on "Younger Girl."			
9/12/64	9	12		1 **Little Honda**..............*Hot Rod High*	$20		Mercury 72324
12/12/64+	87	4		2 **My Buddy Seat**..............*You're Gonna' Ride With Me*	$20	■	Mercury 72366
				above 2 written by **Brian Wilson** of **The Beach Boys**			
5/28/66	52	9		3 **Younger Girl**..............*All American Girl*	$20		Mercury 72563
				first recorded by **The Lovin' Spoonful** on their 1965 debut album			
				HONEYCOMBS, The LP **'64**			
				Rock and roll band from London, England: Dennis D'ell (vocals), Allan Ward and Martin Murray (guitars), John Lantree (bass) and his sister Ann "Honey" Lantree (drums).			
9/19/64	5	13		1 **Have I The Right?**..............*Please Don't Pretend Again*	$12		Interphon 7707
12/19/64+	48	7		2 **I Can't Stop**..............*I'll Cry Tomorrow*	$12	■	Interphon 7713
				HONEY CONE, The R&B/BUB/LP **'71**			
				Female R&B vocal trio from Los Angeles, California: Carolyn Willis (member of **The Girlfriends** and **Bob B. Soxx & The Blue Jeans**), Edna Wright (sister of **Darlene Love**) and Shellie Clark (former **Ikette** and regular on the TV series *The Jim Nabors Hour* from 1969-70). Willis left in 1973; replaced by Denise Mills.			
6/28/69	62	8		1 **While You're Out Looking For Sugar?**..............*The Feeling's Gone*	$8		Hot Wax 6901
11/8/69	68	6		2 **Girls It Ain't Easy**..............*The Feeling's Gone*	$8		Hot Wax 6903
4/10/71	1[1]	16	●	3 **Want Ads**..............RB[3] *We Belong Together*	$8		Hot Wax 7011
8/7/71	11	12	●	4 **Stick-Up**..............RB[2] *V.I.P.*	$8		Hot Wax 7106
11/20/71+	15	11		5 **One Monkey Don't Stop No Show Part I**..............*Part II*	$8		Hot Wax 7110
2/19/72	23	11		6 **The Day I Found Myself**..............*When Will It End*	$8		Hot Wax 7113
7/29/72	96	4		7 **Sittin' On A Time Bomb (Waitin' For The Hurt To Come)**..............*It's Better To Have Loved And Lost*	$8		Hot Wax 7205

DEBUT	PEAK	WKS	Gold	A-side (Chart Hit)..................B-side	$	Sym	Label & Number
				HONEYCONES, The '58			
				Five-man rock and roll band.			
7/28/58	**69**	2		**Op**..................H:69 *Vision Of You* [N]	$25		Ember 1036
				"Op" (rhymes with "bop") was a popular expression used on TV's *American Bandstand*			
				HONEYDRIPPERS, The LP '85			
				A rock superstar gathering: vocalist **Robert Plant** (**Led Zeppelin**), with guitarists Jimmy Page (**The Yardbirds**, Led Zeppelin, **The Firm**), **Jeff Beck** (The Yardbirds) and **Nile Rodgers** (**Chic**).			
10/13/84+	**3**	20		1 **Sea Of Love**..................AC[1] A:3 / S:4 *I Get A Thrill*	$4	■	Es Paranza 99701
				first issued with "Rockin' At Midnight" as the B-side			
1/5/85	**25**	11		2 **Rockin' At Midnight**..................A:25 / S:27 *Young Boy Blues*	$4	■	Es Paranza 99686
				#2 R&B hit for **Roy Brown** in 1949			
				HONEYMOON SUITE ROK/LP '86			
				Rock group from Toronto, Ontario, Canada: Johnnie Dee (vocals), Dermot Grehan (guitar), Ray Coburn (keyboards), Garry Lalonde (bass) and Dave Betts (drums). Rob Preuss replaced Coburn in 1987.			
9/8/84	**57**	7		1 **New Girl Now**..................*It's Your Heart*	$3	■	Warner 29208
3/8/86	**34**	16		2 **Feel It Again**..................A:30 *Wounded*	$3	■	Warner 28779
7/12/86	**52**	16		3 **What Does It Take**..................*Words In The Wind*	$3	■	Warner 28670
				from the movie *One Crazy Summer* starring Demi Moore and John Cusack			
4/30/88	**91**	2		4 **Love Changes Everything**..................*Fast Company*	$3	■	Warner 27935
				HOOBASTANK ROK/LP '02			
				Hard-rock group from Agoura Hills, California: Doug Robb (vocals), Dan Estrin (guitar), Markku Lappalainen (bass) and Chris Hesse (drums).			
3/2/02	**68**	19		1 **Crawling In The Dark**..................A:66			album cut
7/6/02	**44**	20		2 **Running Away**..................A:46			album cut
				above 2 from the album *Hoobastank* on Island 586435			
				HOOKER, John Lee R&B/LP '62			
				Born on 8/22/17 in Clarksdale, Mississippi. Died on 6/21/2001 (age 83). Legendary blues singer/guitarist. Featured in the movie *The Blues Brothers*. Inducted into the Rock and Roll Hall of Fame in 1991. Won Grammy's Lifetime Achievement Award in 2000. Had 2 #1 R&B hits: "Boogie Chillen'" and "I'm In The Mood."			
5/26/62	**60**	10		**Boom Boom**..................*Drug Store Woman*	$25		Vee-Jay 438
				HOOTERS ROK/LP '85			
				Pop-rock group from Philadelphia, Pennsylvania: Eric Bazilian (vocals, guitar), Rob Hyman (vocals, keyboards), John Lilley (guitar), Andy King (bass) and David Uosikkinen (drums). Fran Smith Jr. replaced King in early 1989. Bazilian and Hyman were arrangers/musicians/backing vocalists on **Cyndi Lauper**'s album *She's So Unusual*. Hooter: nickname of Hyman's keyboard-harmonica.			
5/18/85	**58**	11		1 **All You Zombies**..................*Nervous Night*	$4		Columbia 04854
8/10/85	**21**	20		2 **And We Danced**..................S:19 / A:23 *Blood From A Stone*	$3	■	Columbia 05568
12/14/85+	**18**	18		3 **Day By Day** S:15 / A:36 *South Ferry Road*	$3	■	Columbia 05730
4/5/86	**38**	12		4 **Where Do The Children Go**..................A:36 *Nervous Night*	$3	■	Columbia 05854
				Patty Smyth (backing vocal); all of above from the album *Nervous Night*			
7/18/87	**61**	11		5 **Johnny B**..................*Lucy In The Sky With Diamonds*	$3	■	Columbia 07241
10/3/87	**61**	8		6 **Satellite**..................*One Way Home*	$3	■	Columbia 07607
12/9/89	**97**	5		7 **500 Miles**..................*The House Of Wolfgang*	$3		Columbia 73013
				Peter, Paul & Mary (harmony vocals); traditional folk ballad written by Hedy West			
	★472★			**HOOTIE & THE BLOWFISH** ROK/AC/LP '95			
				Pop-rock group formed in South Carolina: Darius Rucker (vocals; born on 5/13/66), Mark Bryan (guitar; born on 5/6/67), Dean Felber (bass; born on 6/9/67) and Jim Sonefeld (drums; born on 10/20/64). Won the 1995 Best New Artist Grammy Award. Also see **Edwin McCain**'s "Solitude."			
10/8/94+	**10**	44		1 **Hold My Hand**..................A:2 / S:41 *I Go Blind*	$3	■V	Atlantic 87230
				David Crosby (backing vocal)			
3/11/95	**9**	35		2 **Let Her Cry**..................A:5 / S:32 *(album version)*	$3	■V	Atlantic 87231
				"45" issued for above 2 on Atlantic 87231			
8/5/95	**6**	32		3 **Only Wanna Be With You** A:2 / S:38 *Where Were You*	$3	■V	Atlantic 87132
11/11/95+	**14**	26		4 **Time**..................A:4 *Goodbye (live)*	$3	■V	Atlantic 87095
				"45" issued for above 2 on Atlantic 87095; all of above from the album *Cracked Rear View*			
4/27/96	**13**	20		5 **Old Man & Me (When I Get To Heaven)**..................A:7 / S:57 *Before The Heartache Rolls In*	$3	■V	Atlantic 87074 ■
				"45" has a small hole with a color photo of the group on the label; regular "45" also issued on Atlantic 87057			
7/13/96	**38**	20		6 **Tucker's Town**..................A:23 *Araby*	$3	■V	Atlantic 87051
9/7/96	**13**[A]	39		7 **I Go Blind**..................			album cut
				from the TV soundtrack album *Friends* on Reprise 46008; first issued as the B-side of #1 above			
11/23/96	**74**[A]	1		8 **Sad Caper**..................			album cut
				#5, 6 & 8: from the album *Fairweather Johnson* on Atlantic 82886			
8/29/98	**18**[A]	14		9 **I Will Wait**..................		V	album cut
				from the album *Musical Chairs* on Atlantic 83136; "45": Atlantic 84411; B-side: "Wishing"			
				HOPKIN, Mary BUB/LP '68			
				Born on 5/3/50 in Pontardawe, Wales. Discovered by the model Twiggy. Recorded with the group Hobby Horse in 1972 for Bell Records. Married to producer Tony Visconti (worked with **David Bowie**) from 1971-81.			
9/28/68	**2**[3]	14	●	1 **Those Were The Days** AC[6] *Turn, Turn, Turn*	$10		Apple 1801
				melody based on the traditional Russian folk song "Dear For Me"			
4/19/69	**13**	9		2 **Goodbye**..................*Sparrow*	$10	■	Apple 1806
				written by **John Lennon** and **Paul McCartney**			
2/21/70	**39**	8		3 **Temma Harbour**..................*Lontano Dagli Occhi*	$8	■	Apple 1816
7/11/70	**77**	5		4 **Que Sera, Sera (Whatever Will Be, Will Be)**..................*Fields Of St. Etienne*	$8		Apple 1823
				from the 1956 movie *The Man Who Knew Too Much* starring **Doris Day** and James Stewart; #1, 2 & 4: produced by **Paul McCartney**			
11/21/70	**87**	4		5 **Think About Your Children**..................*Heritage*	$8	■	Apple 1825
12/9/72	**92**	4		6 **Knock Knock Who's There**..................*International*	$8		Apple 1855
				HOPKINS, Linda — see WILSON, Jackie			

DEBUT	PEAK	WKS	Gold	A-side (Chart Hit)..........B-side	$	Sym	Label & Number
				HORNE, Jimmy "Bo" R&B/BUB/LP '78			
				Born on 9/28/49 in West Palm Beach, Florida. R&B-disco singer.			
4/1/78	38	18		**Dance Across The Floor**..........*It's Your Sweet Love*	$5		Sunshine Sound 1003
				written and produced by H.W. Casey (of **KC And The Sunshine Band**)			
				HORNE, Lena MEM/BUB/LP '55			
				Born on 6/30/17 in Brooklyn, New York. Singer/actress. Starred in several movies and Broadway shows. Won Grammy's Lifetime Achievement Award in 1989.			
7/9/55	19	1		1 **Love Me Or Leave Me**..........T:19 / A:19 *I Love To Love*	$12		RCA Victor 6073
				Lennie Hayton (orch.); #2 hit in 1929 for Ruth Etting, and title song of Etting's 1955 biopic starring **Doris Day**			
11/23/63	92	2		2 **Now!**..........*Silent Spring*	$10		20th Century 449
				Ray Ellis (orch.); a civil rights plea set to the tune of "Hava Nagila"			
				HORNER, James '98			
				Born on 8/14/53 in London, England. Scored several movies including the 1997 blockbuster *Titanic*.			
3/21/98	55^A	3		**Southampton**.......... [I]			album cut
				from the movie *Titanic* starring Leonardo DiCaprio (soundtrack on Sony Classical 63213)			
	★501★			**HORNSBY, Bruce, And The Range** AC/BUB/ROK/LP '86			
				Born on 11/23/54 in Williamsburg, Virginia. Adult Contemporary singer/songwriter/pianist. The Range: George Marinelli and David Mansfield (guitars), Joe Puerta (bass) and John Molo (drums). Puerta was a member of **Ambrosia**. Hornsby later toured as a member of the **Grateful Dead** and The Other Ones. Won the 1986 Best New Artist Grammy Award.			
				1)The Way It Is 2)Mandolin Rain 3)The Valley Road			
7/26/86	72	9		1 **Every Little Kiss**..........*The Red Plains*	$3		RCA 14361
				also see #4 below			
9/20/86	❶[1]	22		2 **The Way It Is** AC[2] A:❶[2] / S:2 *The Wild Frontier*	$3		RCA 5023
1/17/87	4	18		3 **Mandolin Rain**..........AC[3] A:2 / S:5 *The Red Plains (live)*	$3	■	RCA 5087
5/16/87	14	15		4 **Every Little Kiss**..........A:12 / S:15 *Mandolin Rain (live)* [R]	$3		RCA 5165
				remix of #1 above; all of above from the album *The Way It Is*			
4/30/88	5	16		5 **The Valley Road**..........AC[1] / AR[3] S:5 / A:6 *The Long Race*	$3	■	RCA 7645
7/23/88	35	12		6 **Look Out Any Window**..........S:34 / A:38 *The Way It Is (live)*	$3	■	RCA 8678
6/23/90	18	16		7 **Across The River**..........AR[1] A:17 / S:23 *Fire On The Cross* (ROK #50)	$3	▮V	RCA 2621
				Jerry Garcia (of the **Grateful Dead**; guitar)			
10/27/90	84	3		8 **Lost Soul**..........*Stander On The Mountain*	$3	▮V	RCA 2704
				Shawn Colvin (female vocal)			
				BRUCE HORNSBY:			
10/9/93	69	11		9 **Fields Of Gray**..........A:59 *Song A*	$3	▮	RCA 62618
8/26/95	54	9		10 **Walk In The Sun**..........A:48 *Cruise Control*	$3	▮V	RCA 64382
				all of above written by Hornsby			
				HORTON, Jamie '60			
				Born Gayla Peevey on 3/8/43 in Oklahoma City, Oklahoma. Teen female pop singer. Recorded the novelty song "I Want A Hippopotamus For Christmas" under her real name in 1953.			
1/25/60	84	3		**My Little Marine**..........*Missin'*	$15		Joy 234
				Joe Sherman (orch.)			
				HORTON, Johnny C&W/BUB/LP '59			
				Born on 4/30/25 in Los Angeles, California; raised in Tyler, Texas. Died in a car crash on 11/5/60 (age 35). Singer/songwriter/guitarist. Known as "The Singing Fisherman." Married to Billie Jean Horton, widow of Hank Williams, from 1953 until his death.			
4/27/59	❶[6]	21	●	1 **The Battle Of New Orleans** CW[10] *All For The Love Of A Girl*	$15	■	Columbia 41339
				original melody written in celebration of the final battle of the War of 1812; a promotional 4-page foldout picture sleeve was also issued			
8/24/59	54	8		2 **Johnny Reb /**			
8/17/59	81	7		3 **Sal's Got A Sugar Lip**..........	$15		Columbia 41437
3/7/60	3	18		4 **Sink The Bismarck**..........*The Same Old Tale The Crow Told Me*	$15	■	Columbia 41568
				inspired by the movie starring Kenneth More, which is based on the sinking of the German battleship in World War II on 5/27/41			
7/4/60	69	4		5 **Johnny Freedom**..........*Comanche (The Brave Horse)*	$15	■	Columbia 41685
				inspired by the "Freedomland, U.S.A." park in New York City			
9/19/60	4	23		6 **North To Alaska**..........CW[5] *The Mansion You Stole*	$15	■	Columbia 41782
				title song from the movie starring John Wayne			
3/27/61	54	7		7 **Sleepy-Eyed John**..........*They'll Never Take Her Love From Me*	$15	■	Columbia 41963
				picture sleeve issued with Johnny's name in red or black print			
3/31/62	96	2		8 **Honky-Tonk Man**..........*Words*	$15	■	Columbia 42302
				new version of Horton's first charted Country single (#9) on Columbia 21504 in 1956			
				HOT LP '77			
				Interracial female vocal trio from Los Angeles, California: Gwen Owens, Cathy Carson and Juanita Curiel.			
2/19/77	6	27	●	1 **Angel In Your Arms**..........*Just 'Cause I'm Guilty*	$5		Big Tree 16085
8/27/77	65	5		2 **The Right Feeling At The Wrong Time**..........*Why Don't You Believe In Your Man*	$5		Big Tree 16099
2/4/78	71	5		3 **You Brought The Woman Out Of Me**..........*If You Don't Love Her (When You Gonna Leave Her?)*	$5		Big Tree 16108
				HOT BOY$ R&B/LP '00			
				All-star rap group from New Orleans, Louisiana: **B.G.**, **Juvenile**, **Lil Wayne** and Young Turk.			
2/19/00	65	13		**I Need A Hot Girl**..........A:55			album cut
				from the album *Guerrilla Warfare* on Cash Money 53264			
				HOT BUTTER BUB/AC/LP '72			
				Group is actually Stan Free (Moog synthesizer player).			
7/8/72	9	18		**Popcorn**..........*At The Movies* [I]	$6		Musicor 1458

DEBUT	PEAK	WKS	Gold	A-side (Chart Hit)..........B-side	$	Sym	Label & Number
				HOT CHOCOLATE LP **'75**			
				Interracial rock-soul group formed in London, England: Errol Brown (vocals), Harvey Hinsley (guitar), Larry Ferguson (keyboards), Patrick Olive (bass) and Tony Connor (drums).			
2/8/75	**8**	14		1 **Emma**..........*A Love Like Yours*	$5		Big Tree 16031
5/31/75	**28**	11		2 **Disco Queen**..........*Makin' Music*	$5		Big Tree 16038
11/1/75+	**3**	21	●	3 **You Sexy Thing** *Amazing Skin Song*	$5		Big Tree 16047
4/17/76	**42**	6		4 **Don't Stop It Now**..........*Beautiful Lady*	$5		Big Tree 16060
7/16/77	**31**	11		5 **So You Win Again**..........*A Part Of Being With You*	$5		Big Tree 16096
11/11/78+	**6**	18	●	6 **Every 1's A Winner**..........*Power Of Love*	$5		Infinity 50,002
7/14/79	**53**	6		7 **Going Through The Motions**..........*Don't Turn It Off*	$5		Infinity 50,016
12/18/82+	**65**	7		8 **Are You Getting Enough Happiness**..........*One Night's Not Enough*	$4		EMI America 8143
				all of above produced by Mickie Most			
				HOTEL **'79**			
				Pop-rock group from Birmingham, Alabama: Marc Phillips (vocals, keyboards), Tommy Colton and Mike Reid (guitars), Lee Bargeron (keyboards), George Creasman (bass) and Michael Cadenhead (drums).			
3/11/78	**71**	7		1 **You'll Love Again**..........*Take A Chance*	$5		Mercury 73979
7/14/79	**54**	8		2 **You've Got Another Thing Coming**..........*One Time Too Many*	$4	⊙	MCA 41050
9/22/79	**80**	4		3 **Hold On To The Night**..........*Losing My Mind*	$4		MCA 41113
7/12/80	**72**	7		4 **Half Moon Silver**..........*I Can't Believe*	$4		MCA 41277
				HOTLEGS **'70**			
				Pop-rock trio from Manchester, England: Eric Stewart (of **The Mindbenders**), Kevin Godley and Lol Creme. Group evolved into **10cc**. **Godley & Creme** later recorded as a duo.			
8/22/70	**22**	9		**Neanderthal Man**..........*You Didn't Like It, Because You Didn't Think Of It*	$10		Capitol 2886
				HOT SAUCE R&B **'72**			
				R&B vocal trio from Detroit, Michigan: Ronda Washington, Glynton Ashley and William Callaway. Washington also recorded solo as Hot Sauce.			
5/20/72	**96**	3		**Bring It Home (And Give It To Me)**..........*Echoes From The Past*	$10		Volt 4076
				HOT-TODDYS — see REBELS			
				HOUSE OF LORDS ROK/LP **'89**			
				Hard-rock group: James Christian (vocals), Lanny Cordola (guitar), Gregg Giuffria (keyboards), Chuck Wright (bass) and Ken Mary (drums). Cordola was with **Ozzy Osbourne**. Giuffria and Wright were both with **Giuffria**; Wright was also with **Quiet Riot**. Mary was with **Alice Cooper**. Michael Guy replaced Cordola in 1990.			
1/7/89	**58**	7		1 **I Wanna Be Loved**..........*Call My Name*	$4	■	RCA/Simmons 8805
1/5/91	**72**	9		2 **Remember My Name**..........*Sahara*	$4	▮	RCA/Simmons 2736
				HOUSE OF PAIN LP **'92**			
				White hip-hop group from Los Angeles, California: Erik "**Everlast**" Schrody (born on 8/18/69), "Danny Boy" O'Connor and Leor "DJ Lethal" DiMant. Both Schrody and O'Connor were born in the U.S. of Irish parentage. DiMant was born in Latvia.			
6/27/92	**3**	30	▲	1 **Jump Around**..........S:2 / A:29 *(same version)*	$3	▮V	Tommy Boy 7526
				samples "Harlem Shuffle" by **Bob & Earl** and the chorus line from "Jump" by **Kris Kross**; "45": Tommy Boy/Collectables 526			
12/12/92+	**65**	10		2 **Shamrocks And Shenanigans (Boom Shalock Lock Boom)**..........S:47 / A:74 *(4 versions) / Put Your Head Out*	$5	▮*V	Tommy Boy 543
				samples "I Come To You Baby" by **John Lee Hooker**; "45": Tommy Boy/Collectables 543; B-side: (Butch Vig mix)			
5/29/93	**96**	2		3 **Who's The Man?**..........S:66 *(instrumental) / Put On Your Shit Kickers*	$5	▮*V	Tommy Boy 556
				title song from the movie starring **Doctor Dre and Ed Lover**; "45" B-side: "Kick Some"			
7/30/94	**85**	5		4 **On Point**..........S:66 *(3 remixes) / Word Is Bond*	$5	▮*	Tommy Boy 623
				samples "Inside Straight" by **Cannonball Adderley**, "Rivers Invitation" by **Freddy Robinson** and "Death Becomes You" by **Pete Rock & C.L. Smooth**			
				HOUSTON, Cissy R&B/BUB **'71**			
				Born Emily Houston on 9/30/33 in Newark, New Jersey. R&B singer. Lead singer of **The Sweet Inspirations** from 1967-70. Mother of **Whitney Houston**.			
4/24/71	**92**	2		**Be My Baby**..........*I'll Be There*	$7		Janus 145
				HOUSTON, David C&W/BUB/LP **'66**			
				Born on 12/9/38 in Bossier City, Louisiana. Died of an aneurysm on 11/30/93 (age 54). Country singer/songwriter/guitarist. Charted 61 hits, 1963-89.			
7/16/66	**24**	15		1 **Almost Persuaded**..........CW[9] *We Got Love*	$10	□	Epic 10025
7/8/67	**89**	5		2 **My Elusive Dreams**..........CW[2] *Marriage On The Rocks*	$10		Epic 10194
				DAVID HOUSTON and TAMMY WYNETTE			
10/7/67	**75**	7		3 **You Mean The World To Me**..........CW[2] *Don't Mention Tomorrow*	$10	■	Epic 10224
3/9/68	**98**	2		4 **Have A Little Faith**..........CW[1] *Too Far Gone*	$8	■	Epic 10291
				HOUSTON, Thelma R&B/LP **'77**			
				Born on 5/7/46 in Leland, Mississippi. R&B-dance singer/actress.			
1/31/70	**74**	3		1 **Save The Country**..........*I Just Can't Stay Away*	$8		Dunhill/ABC 4222
				written by **Laura Nyro**			
12/18/76+	❶[1]	24		2 **Don't Leave Me This Way**..........RB[1] *Today Will Soon Be Yesterday*	$5		Tamla 54278
6/4/77	**47**	11		3 **If It's The Last Thing I Do**..........*If You Won't Let Me Walk On The Water*	$5		Tamla 54283
				#4 hit for **Tommy Dorsey** in 1937			
3/24/79	**34**	13		4 **Saturday Night, Sunday Morning**..........*Come To Me*	$5		Tamla 54297

DEBUT	PEAK	WKS	Gold	A-side (Chart Hit).....B-side	$	Sym	Label & Number

HOUSTON, Whitney ★16★ R&B/LP **'87**

Born on 8/9/63 in Newark, New Jersey. R&B singer/actress. Daughter of **Cissy Houston** and cousin of **Dionne Warwick** and **Dee Dee Warwick**. Began singing career at age 11 with the gospel group New Hope Baptist Junior Choir. As a teen, worked as a backing vocalist for **Chaka Khan** and **Lou Rawls**. Pursued modeling career in 1981, appearing in *Glamour* magazine and on the cover of *Seventeen.* Married **Bobby Brown** on 7/18/92. Starred in the movies *The Bodyguard*, *Waiting To Exhale* and *The Preacher's Wife*.

1)I Will Always Love You 2)Greatest Love Of All 3)I Wanna Dance With Somebody 4)All The Man That I Need 5)Didn't We Almost Have It All

DEBUT	PEAK	WKS	Gold	A-side (Chart Hit).....B-side	$	Sym	Label & Number
6/9/84	46	18		1 **Hold Me**.....*Love* (Pendergrass) **TEDDY PENDERGRASS (with Whitney Houston)**	$4	■	Asylum 69720
5/11/85	3	21	●	2 **You Give Good Love**.....RB[1] S:2 / A:5 *Greatest Love Of All* B-side charted at #5 below	$3	■	Arista 9274
8/17/85	❶[1]	22	●	3 **Saving All My Love For You**.....RB[1] / AC[3] S:❶[2] / A:3 *All At Once*	$3	■	Arista 9381
12/7/85+	❶[2]	23	●	4 **How Will I Know**.....RB[1] / AC[1] A:❶[2] / S:❶[1] *Someone For Me* **Cissy Houston** (Whitney's mother, backing vocal)	$3	■	Arista 9434
3/29/86	❶[3]	18	●	5 **Greatest Love Of All**.....AC[5] A:❶[2] / S:❶[1] *Thinking About You* B-side made the R&B charts (#10) in 1985 on Arista 9412; all of above from the album *Whitney Houston*	$3	■	Arista 9466
5/16/87	❶[2]	18	▲	6 **I Wanna Dance With Somebody (Who Loves Me)**..AC[3] A:❶[3] / S:❶[2] *Moment Of Truth*	$3	■	Arista 9598
8/1/87	❶[2]	17		7 **Didn't We Almost Have It All**.....AC[3] S:❶[2] / A:❶[1] *Shock Me* (w/**Jermaine Jackson**)	$3	■	Arista 9616
10/31/87+	❶[1]	19	●	8 **So Emotional**.....S:❶[2] / A:2 *For The Love Of You*	$3	■	Arista 9642
2/27/88	❶[2]	18		9 **Where Do Broken Hearts Go**.....AC[3] S:❶[2] / A:❶[1] *Where You Are*	$3	■	Arista 9674
7/2/88	9	16		10 **Love Will Save The Day**.....S:8 / A:9 *How Will I Know* above 5 from the album *Whitney*	$3	■	Arista 9720
9/10/88	5	17		11 **One Moment In Time**.....AC[2] S:3 / A:7 *Love Is A Contact Sport* tune used by NBC-TV for the 1988 Summer Olympics	$3	■	Arista 9743
7/1/89	41	8		12 **It Isn't, It Wasn't, It Ain't Never Gonna Be**.....S:35 *If Ever A Love There Was* (Franklin) **ARETHA FRANKLIN AND WHITNEY HOUSTON**	$3	■	Arista 9850
10/20/90	❶[1]	19	●	13 **I'm Your Baby Tonight**.....RB[2] A:❶[1] / S:3 *I'm Knockin'*	$3	▮[V]	Arista 2108
12/22/90+	❶[2]	23	●	14 **All The Man That I Need**.....RB[2] / AC[4] S:❶[1] / A:❶[1] *Dancin' On The Smooth Edge* **Kenny G** (sax solo); recorded in 1982 by **Sister Sledge**	$3	▮[V]	Arista 2156
3/9/91	20	11	●	15 **The Star Spangled Banner**.....S:3 *America The Beautiful* [L] recorded at Super Bowl XXV (1/27/91); also see #39 below	$3	▮[V]	Arista 2207
4/13/91	9	14		16 **Miracle**.....S:8 / A:13 *After We Make Love*	$3	▮[V]	Arista 2222
7/27/91	20	10		17 **My Name Is Not Susan**.....A:33 / S:44 *(U.K. mix)* #13, 14, 16 & 17: from the album *I'm Your Baby Tonight*	$3	▮[V]	Arista 12259
11/14/92	❶[14]	26	▲[4]	18 **I Will Always Love You** RB[11] / AC[5] S:❶[14] / A:❶[11] *Jesus Loves Me* written by **Dolly Parton** in 1974; 1993 Grammy winner: Record of the Year	$3	▮[V]	Arista 12490
1/9/93	4	23	●	19 **I'm Every Woman**.....A:2 / S:11 *Who Do You Love* written by **Ashford & Simpson**	$3	▮[V]	Arista 12519
2/27/93	4	20	●	20 **I Have Nothing**.....AC[2] A:❶[6] / S:7 *Where You Are*	$3	▮[V]	Arista 12527
6/26/93	31	20		21 **Run To You**.....A:26 / S:41 *After We Make Love*	$3	▮[V]	Arista 12570
11/20/93	32[A]	9		22 **Something In Common**..... **BOBBY BROWN With WHITNEY HOUSTON** from Brown's album *Remixes N The Key Of B* on MCA 10974			album cut
11/27/93+	36[A]	20		23 **Queen Of The Night**..... #18-21 & 23: from the movie *The Bodyguard* starring Houston and Kevin Costner (soundtrack on Arista 18699)			album cut
3/12/94	68[A]	2		24 **Look Into Your Heart**..... from the album *A Tribute To Curtis Mayfield* on Warner 45500			album cut
11/25/95	❶[1]	21	▲	25 **Exhale (Shoop Shoop)**.....RB[8] S:❶[1] / A:4 *Dancin' On The Smooth Edge*	$3	▮[V]	Arista 12885
3/23/96	8	20	●	26 **Count On Me**.....S:5 / A:29 *One Moment In Time* (Houston) **WHITNEY HOUSTON & CECE WINANS**	$3	▮[V]	Arista 12976
8/3/96	26	20		27 **Why Does It Hurt So Bad**.....S:19 / A:69 *I Wanna Dance With Somebody (Who Loves Me)* "45" B-side: (live version); above 3 from the movie *Waiting To Exhale* starring Houston	$3	▮[V]	Arista 13213
12/28/96+	4	20	▲	28 **I Believe In You And Me**.....S:3 / A:29 *Somebody Bigger Than You And I* (R&B flip) originally recorded by the **Four Tops** in 1982 on the album *One More Mountain*; "45" B-side: "Step By Step"	$3	▮[V]	Arista 13293
3/15/97	15	17	●	29 **Step By Step**.....S:16 / A:39 *(teddy riley remix)* written by **Annie Lennox**	$3	▮[V]	Arista 13312
7/5/97	77	4		30 **My Heart Is Calling**.....S:57 *I Go To The Rock* above 3 from the movie *The Preacher's Wife* starring Houston and Denzel Washington	$3	▮	Arista 13362
12/5/98+	15	17	●	31 **When You Believe**.....S:7 / A:38 *(instrumental)* **WHITNEY HOUSTON and MARIAH CAREY** from the animated movie *The Prince Of Egypt*	$4	★	DreamWorks 59022
12/26/98+	2[3]	28	▲	32 **Heartbreak Hotel**.....RB[7] S:2 / A:5 *(dance mix) / It's Not Right But It's Okay* (Houston - #4) **WHITNEY HOUSTON (Feat. Faith Evans & Kelly Price)**	$4	★	Arista 13619
5/8/99	4	20	●	33 **It's Not Right But It's Okay**.....S:4 / A:13 *(2 versions)* charted its first 5 weeks as the B-side of "Heartbreak Hotel"; also see #38 below	$4	★	Arista 13681
9/4/99+	4	28	▲	34 **My Love Is Your Love**.....S:3 / A:8 *(2 versions)* Family Friends Community Choir (backing vocals); co-written and co-produced by **Wyclef Jean**	$4	★	Arista 13730
2/19/00	27	11		35 **I Learned From The Best**.....S:8 / A:71 *(2 remixes)* Sue Ann Carwell (backing vocal); above 5 from the album *My Love Is Your Love* on Arista 19037	$4	★	Arista 13790
6/17/00	52	19		36 **Could I Have This Kiss Forever**.....A:48 **WHITNEY HOUSTON & ENRIQUE IGLESIAS**			album cut
6/17/00	70	9		37 **Same Script, Different Cast**.....A:64 *(4 remixes)* **WHITNEY HOUSTON & DEBORAH COX** 12" single released as a 2-disc set; above 2 from the album *The Greatest Hits* on Arista 14626	$6	T	Arista 13860
4/28/01	63[S]	2		38 **It's Not Right But It's Okay**.....*(6 remixes) / I Will Always Love You (Club Mix)* [R] remixed reissue of #33 above on Arista's "Maximum Hits" series	$8	★*	Arista 13680
9/29/01	6	16	▲	39 **The Star Spangled Banner**.....S:❶[6] / A:45 *America The Beautiful* [L-R] also see #15 above; re-charted due to the 9/11/01 terrorist attack in the United States	$4	★[V]	Arista 15054

DEBUT	PEAK	WKS	Gold	A-side (Chart Hit)..........B-side	$	Sym	Label & Number
				HOUSTON, Whitney — Cont'd			
8/24/02	**96**	3		40 **Whatchulookinat** ....S:71 *(3 versions)*	$6	T	Arista 15170
11/16/02+	**72**	19		41 **One Of Those Days** ....A:72 *(3 versions)*	$6	T[V]	Arista 15197
				samples "Between The Sheets" by **The Isley Brothers**; "45": Arista 50978; B-side: My Love (with **Bobby Brown**)			
				HOWARD, Adina R&B/LP **'95**			
				Born on 11/14/74 in Grand Rapids, Michigan. Female R&B singer.			
2/11/95	**2**[2]	30	▲	1 **Freak Like Me** ....S:2 / A:9 *(remix w/o rap) / (3 album snippets)*	$3	▮	EastWest 64484
				samples "I'd Rather Be With You" by Bootsy Collins			
7/15/95	**68**	10		2 **My Up And Down** ....S:54 *Freak Like Me (remix)*	$4	▮	EastWest 64412
9/21/96	**32**	19		3 **What's Love Got To Do With It** ....S:15 *(instrumental)*	$4	▮	Interscope 97008
				WARREN G featuring Adina Howard			
				from the movie *Supercop* starring Jackie Chan			
7/26/97	**70**	7		4 **[Freak] And U Know It** ....S:57 *Swerve On* (w/Menajahtwa)	$4	▮	EastWest 64161
				HOWARD, Eddy, and His Orchestra MEM/POP **'47**			
				Born on 9/12/14 in Woodland, California. Died on 5/23/63 (age 48). Singer with the Dick Jurgens band from 1934-40. Composer of "My Last Goodbye" and "Careless." Charted 41 pop hits, 1946-54, including the #1 hits "To Each His Own" and "Sin."			
12/17/55	**90**	3		**The Teen-Ager's Waltz** ....T:90 *Choo-Choo Cha-Cha*	$12		Mercury 70700
				HOWARD, Miki R&B/AC/LP **'92**			
				Born in 1962 in Chicago, Illinois. Black female session singer/songwriter. Former lead singer of Side Effect. Portrayed Billie Holiday in the movie *Malcolm X*.			
11/21/92	**84**	4		**Ain't Nobody Like You** ....RB[1] A:68 *(instrumental)*	$3	▮	Giant 18849
				HOWARD, Rebecca Lynn C&W/LP **'02**			
				Born on 4/24/79 in Salyersville, Kentucky. Country singer/songwriter.			
11/9/02	**71**	5		**Forgive** A:69		V	album cut
				from the album *Forgive* on MCA 170288: "45": MCA 172242; B-side: "Pink Flamingo Kind Of Love"			
				HOWELL, Reuben **'74**			
				Pop singer/songwriter.			
7/20/74	**86**	3		**Rings** ....*I'll Be Your Brother*	$6		Motown 1305
				H-TOWN R&B/LP **'93**			
				R&B vocal trio from Houston, Texas: brothers Shazam and Keven "Dino" Conner, with Darryl Jackson. Keven Conner died in a car crash on 1/28/2003 (age 28).			
4/10/93	**3**	25	▲	1 **Knockin' Da Boots** RB[4] S:❶[2] / A:5 *(instrumental)*	$3	▮	Luke 161
7/31/93	**67**	11		2 **Lick U Up** ....S:48 *(instrumental)*	$4	▮	Luke 163
4/16/94	**57**	16		3 **Part Time Lover** ....S:40 / A:65 *I'm Still In Love With You* (**Al B. Sure!** - flip)	$4	▮	Death Row 98283
				from the movie *Above The Rim* starring **2Pac**; "Part Time Lover" and "I'm Still In Love With You" by **Al B. Sure!** were issued on the same cassette single and were listed together at one chart position each week ("Part Time Lover" was always listed first)			
4/22/95	**51**	15		4 **Emotions** ....S:24 *(instrumental)*	$4	▮	Luke 185
2/17/96	**37**	20	●	5 **A Thin Line Between Love & Hate** ....S:19 *(instrumental)*	$3	▮	Jac-Mac/Warner 17699
				Shirley Murdock (female vocal); title song from the movie starring Martin Lawrence			
10/11/97	**35**	20		6 **They Like It Slow** ....S:20 *Jezebel*	$3	▮	Relativity 1642
				Roger (talk box, above 2)			
				HUDSON, David LP **'80**			
				Born in Miami, Florida. R&B singer.			
6/28/80	**59**	11		**Honey, Honey** ....*Come On Back Baby*	$5		Alston 3750
				HUDSON, "Pookie" **'63**			
				Born James Hudson in Gary, Indiana. Lead singer of **The Spaniels**.			
5/25/63	**96**	1		**I Know I Know** ....*Jealous Heart*	$20		Double-L 711
				HUDSON AND LANDRY LP **'71**			
				Comedy duo of DJs Bob Hudson and Ron Landry from Los Angeles, California. Split up in 1976. Hudson died on 9/20/97 (age 66). Landry died on 9/16/2002 (age 64).			
4/24/71	**43**	14		1 **Ajax Liquor Store** ....*The Hippie & The Redneck* [C]	$10		Dore 855
1/15/72	**68**	6		2 **Ajax Airlines** ....*Bruiser La Rue* [C]	$10		Dore 868
				HUDSON BROTHERS BUB/LP **'75**			
				Pop vocal trio from Portland, Oregon: Bill, Brett and Mark Hudson. Hosted own TV variety show during the summer of 1974; also hosted kiddie TV show *The Hudson Brothers Razzle Dazzle Comedy Show*. Bill was married to actress Goldie Hawn from 1976-79 (their daughter is actress Kate Hudson).			
9/21/74	**21**	14		1 **So You Are A Star** ....*Ma Ma Ma Baby*	$5		Casablanca 0108
6/21/75	**26**	12		2 **Rendezvous** ....*Medley: These Things We Do/Home/Out Of The Rainbow/Find Me A Woman/Little Brown Box/One And The Same*	$5		Rocket 40417
11/22/75	**57**	5		3 **Lonely School Year** ....*If You Really Need Me*	$5	■	Rocket 40464
11/6/76	**70**	5		4 **Help Wanted** ....*The Last Time I Looked*	$4		Arista 0208
				HUES CORPORATION, The LP **'74**			
				R&B-disco vocal trio formed in Los Angeles, California: St. Clair Lee, Fleming Williams (died in 1992) and Ann Kelley. Williams replaced by Tommy Brown after "Rock The Boat." Brown replaced by Karl Russell in 1976. Group named after Howard Hughes.			
8/11/73	**63**	8		1 **Freedom For The Stallion** ....*Off My Cloud*	$5		RCA Victor 0900
5/25/74	❶[1]	18	●	2 **Rock The Boat** *All Goin' Down Together*	$5		RCA Victor 0232
10/12/74	**18**	12		3 **Rockin' Soul** ....*Go To The Poet*	$5		RCA Victor 10066
2/22/75	**62**	6		4 **Love Corporation** ....*He's My Home*	$5		RCA Victor 10200
4/30/77	**92**	2		5 **I Caught Your Act** ....*Natural Find*	$5		Warner/Curb 8334
				HUGH, Grayson LP **'89**			
				Born in Connecticut. Blue-eyed soul singer/songwriter/pianist.			
6/24/89	**19**	18		1 **Talk It Over** ....S:15 / A:24 *Empty As The Wind*	$3	■	RCA 8802
10/28/89	**87**	4		2 **Bring It All Back** ....*Who Are You And How Are You? (live)*	$3	■	RCA 9093
3/31/90	**67**	7		3 **How 'Bout Us** ....*Finally Found A Friend* (Hugh)	$3	▮[V]	RCA 9163
				GRAYSON HUGH and BETTY WRIGHT			
				from the movie *True Love* starring Annabella Sciorra			

DEBUT	PEAK	WKS	Gold	A-side (Chart Hit)...B-side	$	Sym	Label & Number

HUGHES, Fred — R&B '65

Born in Arkansas. R&B singer/songwriter.

DEBUT	PEAK	WKS	Gold	A-side (Chart Hit)...B-side	$	Sym	Label & Number
5/29/65	23	10		1 Oo Wee Baby, I Love You ... *Love Me Baby*	$15		Vee-Jay 684
9/25/65	96	3		2 You Can't Take It Away ... *My Heart Cries Oh*	$15		Vee-Jay 703
7/6/68	94	6		3 Send My Baby Back ... *Where's My Baby* FREDDIE HUGHES	$15		Wand 1182

HUGHES, Jimmy — R&B/BUB '64

Born in Florence, Alabama. Died of cancer on 4/1/97 (age 62). R&B singer. Cousin of **Percy Sledge**.

DEBUT	PEAK	WKS	Gold	A-side (Chart Hit)...B-side	$	Sym	Label & Number
6/20/64	17	12		1 Steal Away ... *Lolly Pops, Lace And Lipstick*	$15		Fame 6401
9/26/64	65	4		2 Try Me ... *Lovely Ladies*	$15		Fame 6403
6/4/66	65	6		3 Neighbor, Neighbor ... *It's A Good Thing*	$15		Fame 1003
3/18/67	90	2		4 Why Not Tonight ... *I'm A Man Of Action*	$15		Fame 1011

HUGHES/THRALL — ROK '83

Rock duo of singer/bassist Glenn Hughes (Trapeze, **Deep Purple**) and guitarist Pat Thrall (**Automatic Man**, **Asia**, **Pat Travers Band**).

DEBUT	PEAK	WKS	Gold	A-side (Chart Hit)...B-side	$	Sym	Label & Number
12/18/82+	79	5		Beg, Borrow Or Steal ... *Who Will You Run To*	$4		Boulevard 03355

HUGO & LUIGI — LP '60

Producers/songwriters/label executives Hugo Peretti (born on 12/6/16; died on 5/1/86, age 69) and Luigi Creatore (born on 12/21/20). Owned record labels Roulette and Avco/Embassy.

DEBUT	PEAK	WKS	Gold	A-side (Chart Hit)...B-side	$	Sym	Label & Number
12/10/55	90	1		1 Young Abe Lincoln ... T:90 *Two Thirds Of The Tennessee River* **HUGO AND LUIGI with Their Family Singers** melody based on "Battle Hymn of The Republic"	$15		Mercury 70721
6/8/59	86	5		2 La Plume De Ma Tante ... *Honolulu Lu* vocals by a children's chorus; French song translation: "The Pen of My Aunt" (sung in French and in English)	$8		RCA Victor 7518
12/14/59+	35	9		3 Just Come Home ... *Lonesome Stranger* vocals by a large chorus; written by French songstress **Edith Piaf** as "C'est L'Amour"	$8		RCA Victor 7639

HULIN, T.K. — '63

Born Alton James Hulin on 8/16/43 in St. Martinville, Louisiana. Pop singer.

DEBUT	PEAK	WKS	Gold	A-side (Chart Hit)...B-side	$	Sym	Label & Number
8/17/63	92	2		I'm Not A Fool Anymore ... *Teardrops, More Teardrops* first released on L.K. 1112 in 1963 ($25)	$12		Smash 1830

HULLABALLOOS, The — BUB '65

Bleached-blond rock and roll group from England: Ricky Knight, Harry Dunn, Andy Woonton and Geoff Mortimer.

DEBUT	PEAK	WKS	Gold	A-side (Chart Hit)...B-side	$	Sym	Label & Number
11/28/64+	56	9		1 I'm Gonna Love You Too ... *Party Doll* first recorded by **Buddy Holly** in 1958 on Coral 61947 ($50)	$20	■	Roulette 4587
2/13/65	74	6		2 Did You Ever ... *Beware*	$20	■	Roulette 4593

HUM — ROK/LP '95

Rock group from Champaign, Illinois: Matt Talbott (vocals), Tim Lash (guitar), Jeff Dimpsey (bass) and Bryan St. Pere (drums).

DEBUT	PEAK	WKS	Gold	A-side (Chart Hit)...B-side	$	Sym	Label & Number
7/15/95	72[A]	1		Stars ... from the album *You'd Prefer An Astronaut* on RCA 66577			album cut

HUMAN BEINZ, The — LP '68

Rock group from Youngstown, Ohio: Dick Belly (vocals, guitar), Joe Markulin (guitar), Mel Pachuta (bass) and Mike Tateman (drums).

DEBUT	PEAK	WKS	Gold	A-side (Chart Hit)...B-side	$	Sym	Label & Number
12/9/67+	8	15		1 Nobody But Me ... *Sueno* originally recorded (and written) by **The Isley Brothers** in 1962 on Wand 131 ($15)	$12		Capitol 5990
3/9/68	80	5		2 Turn On Your Love Light ... *It's Fun To Be Clean*	$10	■	Capitol 2119

HUMAN LEAGUE, The — LP '82 ★521★

Electro-pop trio from Sheffield, Yorkshire, England: lead singer/synthesist Philip Oakey (born on 10/2/55), with female vocalists Joanne Catherall (born on 9/18/62) and Susanne Sulley (born on 3/22/63). Early members Martyn Ware and Ian Craig Marsh left to form **Heaven 17**.

DEBUT	PEAK	WKS	Gold	A-side (Chart Hit)...B-side	$	Sym	Label & Number
3/6/82	❶[3]	28	●	1 Don't You Want Me ... *Seconds*	$3	■	A&M/Virgin 2397
5/28/83	8	20		2 (Keep Feeling) Fascination ... *Total Panic*	$3	■	A&M/Virgin 2547
10/1/83	30	12		3 Mirror Man ... *Non-Stop*	$3	■	A&M/Virgin 2587
6/9/84	64	5		4 The Lebanon ... *Thirteen*	$3	■	A&M/Virgin 2641
9/13/86	❶[1]	20		5 Human ... S:❶[1] / A:❶[1] *(instrumental)*	$3	■	A&M/Virgin 2861
12/6/86+	44	11		6 I Need Your Loving ... A:40 *Are You Ever Coming Back?*	$3	■	A&M/Virgin 2893
9/22/90	32	11		7 Heart Like A Wheel ... A:31 / S:35 *Rebound*	$3	▮	A&M/Virgin 1520
3/25/95	31	12		8 Tell Me When ... A:29 / S:75 *Kimi Ni Mune Kyum*	$3	▮[V]	EastWest 64443

HUMBLE PIE — BUB/ROK/LP '72

Hard-rock group formed in Essex, England: **Peter Frampton** (guitar, vocals; The Herd), Steve Marriott (vocals, guitar; **Small Faces**; died on 4/20/91, age 44), Greg Ridley (bass; Spooky Tooth) and Jerry Shirley (drums). Frampton left in October 1971, replaced by Clem Clempson (Rough Diamond). Disbanded in 1975. Reunited from 1980-81 with Marriott, Shirley, Bobby Tench (guitar) and Anthony Jones (bass).

DEBUT	PEAK	WKS	Gold	A-side (Chart Hit)...B-side	$	Sym	Label & Number
9/25/71	73	8		1 I Don't Need No Doctor ... *A Song For Jenny* [L] recorded at the Fillmore East; written by **Ashford & Simpson**	$7	■	A&M 1282
5/6/72	52	8		2 Hot 'N' Nasty ... *You're So Good For Me*	$7	■	A&M 1349
4/26/80	52	7		3 Fool For A Pretty Face (Hurt By Love) ... *You Soppy Pratt* early pressings show title only as "Fool For A Pretty Face"	$4		Atco 7216

HUMPERDINCK, Engelbert — AC/BUB/LP '67 ★267★

Born Arnold Dorsey on 5/2/36 in Madras, India; raised in Leicester, England. First recorded for Decca in 1958. Met **Tom Jones**'s manager, Gordon Mills, in 1965, who suggested his name change to Engelbert Humperdinck (a famous German opera composer). Starred in his own musical variety TV series in 1970. Had 11 consecutive Top 10 Adult Contemporary hits, 1967-71.

1)Release Me (And Let Me Love Again) 2)After The Lovin' 3)Winter World Of Love 4)Am I That Easy To Forget 5)A Man Without Love

DEBUT	PEAK	WKS	Gold	A-side (Chart Hit)...B-side	$	Sym	Label & Number
4/8/67	4	14		1 Release Me (And Let Me Love Again) ... *Ten Guitars* dance version made the Club Play charts (#10) in 1998; #5 Country hit for **Jimmy Heap** in 1954	$7		Parrot 40011
6/24/67	20	7		2 There Goes My Everything ... *You Love*	$7		Parrot 40015

DEBUT	PEAK	WKS	Gold	A-side (Chart Hit)...B-side	$	Sym	Label & Number
				HUMPERDINCK, Engelbert — Cont'd			
9/23/67	**25**	9		3 **The Last Waltz** ... *That Promise*	$7	■	Parrot 40019
12/16/67+	**18**	10		4 **Am I That Easy To Forget** ... AC[1] *Pretty Ribbons* #9 Country hit for Carl Belew in 1959	$7	■	Parrot 40023
5/11/68	**19**	9		5 **A Man Without Love (Quando M'innamoro)** ... *Call On Me* **The Sandpipers**' Italian version "Bubbled Under" (#124) in 1968	$7		Parrot 40027
10/19/68	**31**	9		6 **Les Bicyclettes De Belsize** ... *Three Little Words*	$7	■	Parrot 40032
3/1/69	**42**	11		7 **The Way It Used To Be** ... *A Good Thing Going*	$6	■	Parrot 40036
8/23/69	**38**	7		8 **I'm A Better Man** ... *Cafe*	$6		Parrot 40040
12/6/69+	**16**	12		9 **Winter World Of Love** ... *Take My Heart*	$6	■	Parrot 40044
6/27/70	**43**	8		10 **My Marie** ... *Our Song (La Paloma)*	$6	■	Parrot 40049
9/26/70	**47**	11		11 **Sweetheart** ... *Born To Be Wanted* written by Maurice and **Barry Gibb**; all of above produced by Peter Sullivan	$6	■	Parrot 40054
3/6/71	**45**	7		12 **When There's No You** ... AC[1] *Stranger Step Into My World (Romantico Blues)*	$6	■	Parrot 40059
8/21/71	**43**	8		13 **Another Time, Another Place** ... *You're The Window Of My World (Frin, Frin, Frin)*	$6		Parrot 40065
4/29/72	**86**	3		14 **Too Beautiful To Last** ... *A Hundred Times A Day* theme from the movie *Nicholas and Alexandra* starring Michael Jayston and Janet Suzman	$6		Parrot 40069
8/5/72	**69**	8		15 **In Time** ... *How Does It Feel*	$6		Parrot 40071
12/30/72+	**61**	7		16 **I Never Said Goodbye** ... *Time After Time*	$6		Parrot 40072
6/2/73	**99**	1		17 **I'm Leavin' You** ... *My Summer Song*	$6		Parrot 40073
9/29/73	**91**	3		18 **Love Is All** ... *Lady Of The Night* #12-18: produced by Gordon Mills	$6		Parrot 40076
10/23/76+	**8**	19	●	19 **After The Lovin'** ... AC[2] *Let's Remember The Good Times*	$5		Epic/MAM 50270
7/9/77	**97**	3		20 **Goodbye My Friend** ...	$5		Epic/MAM 50365
12/23/78+	**58**	6		21 **This Moment In Time** ... AC[2] *And The Day Begins*	$5		Epic/MAM 50632
3/15/80	**83**	2		22 **Love's Only Love** *[ENGELBERT]* ... *Burning Embers*	$4		Epic 50844
7/16/83	**77**	5		23 **Til You And Your Lover Are Lovers Again** ... *What Will I Write*	$4		Epic 03817
				HUMPHREY, Della '68 Female R&B singer.			
11/30/68	**79**	4		**Don't Make The Good Girls Go Bad** ... *Your Love Is All I Need*	$8		Arctic 144
				HUMPHREY, Paul BUB/R&B/LP '71 Born on 10/12/35 in Detroit, Michigan. Black jazz session drummer. Member of **Afrique**. The Cool Aid Chemists were Clarence MacDonald, David T. Walker (also in Afrique) and Bill Upchurch.			
3/13/71	**29**	16		**Cool Aid** ... *Detroit* [I] **PAUL HUMPHREY & HIS COOL AID CHEMISTS**	$7		Lizard 21006
				HUNT, Tommy BUB/R&B '61 Born Charles Hunt on 6/18/33 in Pittsburgh, Pennsylvania. R&B singer. With The Five Echoes, 1952-53. First recorded for Sabre in 1953. In **The Flamingos**, 1956-61. Moved to Wales in 1970.			
9/4/61	**48**	10		1 **Human** ... *The Parade Of Broken Hearts*	$15		Scepter 1219
1/27/62	**92**	1		2 **The Door Is Open** ... *I'm Wondering*	$15		Scepter 1226
11/9/63	**71**	5		3 **I Am A Witness** ... *I'm With You*	$15		Scepter 1261
				HUNTER, Alfonzo '96 Born in Chicago, Illinois. R&B singer/saxophonist.			
11/2/96	**85**	8		1 **Just The Way (Playas Play)** ... S:55 *(3 versions)* "45": EMI 19337; B-side: "Slow Motion"	$3	▮V	EMI 58579
3/15/97	**90**	5		2 **Weekend Thang** ... S:65 *Quiet Time* "45": EMI 19487; above 2 co-written and produced by **Erick Sermon**	$3	▮V	EMI 58615
				HUNTER, Ian — see MOTT THE HOOPLE			
				HUNTER, Ivory Joe R&B '56 Born on 10/10/14 in Kirbyville, Texas. Died of cancer on 11/8/74 (age 60). R&B singer/songwriter/pianist. First recorded in 1933 (a cylinder record for the Library Of Congress). Own radio shows, KFDM-Beaumont, Texas, early 1940s. Own record labels, Ivory and Pacific, 1944. Signed by King Records, 1947; MGM, 1950. Charted 14 Top 10 R&B hits from 1945-50.			
11/17/56	**12**	22	●	1 **Since I Met You Baby** .. RB[3] S:12 / T:12 / A:14 / J:14 *You Can't Stop This Rocking And Rolling*	$30		Atlantic 1111
4/13/57	**43**	16		2 **Empty Arms** ... T:43 *Love's A Hurting Game* (R&B #7) **Ray Ellis** (orch., above 2)	$30		Atlantic 1128
9/8/58	**94**	1		3 **Yes I Want You** ... H:94 *You Flip Me Baby*	$30		Atlantic 1191
3/2/59	**92**	2		4 **City Lights** ... *Stolen Moments* Milton Rogers (orch.); #1 Country hit for **Ray Price** in 1958 and for **Mickey Gilley** in 1975	$25		Dot 15880
				HUNTER, John LP '85 Born in Chicago, Illinois. Rock singer/keyboardist/songwriter.			
12/8/84+	**39**	16		**Tragedy** ... *Aphrodisia Here*	$4		Private I 04643
				HUNTER, Tab '57 Born Arthur Gelien on 7/11/31 in Brooklyn, New York. Singer/actor. Starred in several movies.			
1/12/57	❶[6]	21	●	1 **Young Love /** T:❶[6] / A:❶[6] / J:❶[5] / S:❶[4]			
2/2/57	**57**	9		2 **Red Sails In The Sunset** ... T:57 / S:flip #1 hit for both **Bing Crosby** and Guy Lombardo in 1935	$25		Dot 15533
3/23/57	**11**	14		3 **Ninety-Nine Ways /** T:11 / A:11 / S:12 / J:17 written by **Charlie Gracie**			
3/30/57	**74**	3		4 **Don't Get Around Much Anymore** ... T:74 there were 3 Top 10 versions of this Duke Ellington song in 1943; **Billy Vaughn** (orch., all of above)	$25		Dot 15548
10/20/58	**62**	10		5 **Jealous Heart** ... *Lonesome Road* Marty Wilson (orch.); insert features a full-color photo of Tab's first Warner album; #2 Country hit for **Tex Ritter** in 1945; #4 hit for Al Morgan in 1949	$20	⊙	Warner 5008
2/2/59	**31**	11		6 **I'll Be With You In Apple Blossom Time** ... *(What Can I Give) My Only Love* #2 hit for Charles Harrison in 1920	$20		Warner 5032
4/27/59	**68**	5		7 **There's No Fool Like A Young Fool** ... *I'll Never Smile Again* **Don Ralke** (orch., above 2)	$20	■	Warner 5051

RARE PICTURE SLEEVES

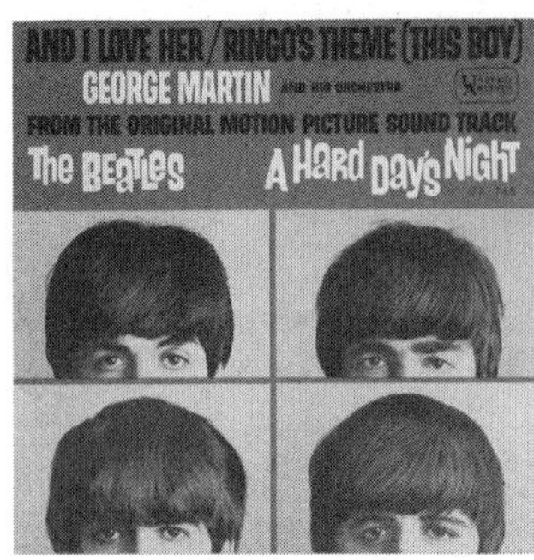

The Beatles
And I Love Her

The Bee Gees
If Only I Had My Mind On Something Else

The Blue Belles
I Sold My Heart To The Junkman

The Byrds
Mr. Tambourine Man

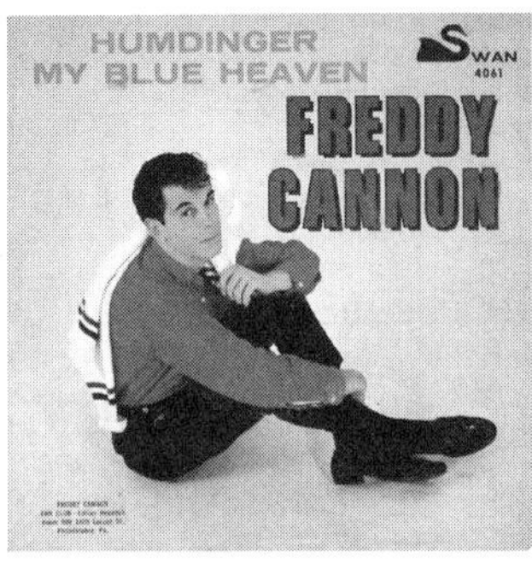

Freddy Cannon
Humdinger

Nat "King" Cole
The Song Of Raintree County

Dick & Dee Dee
Thou Shalt Not Steal

The Five Keys
Out Of Sight, Out Of Mind

Stan Freberg
Wun'erful, Wun'erful!

Herman's Hermits
Hold On!

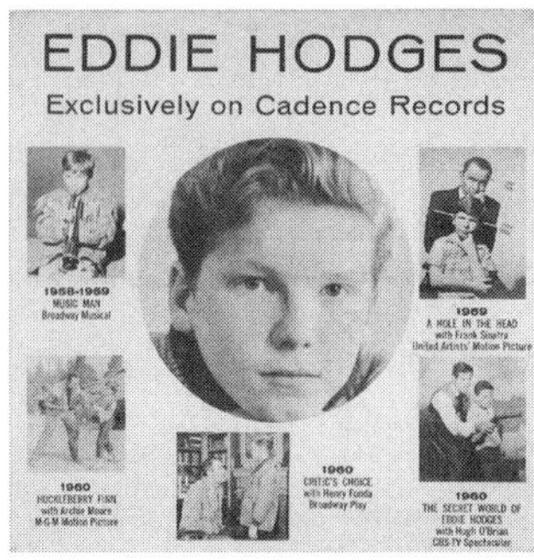

Eddie Hodges
I'm Gonna Knock On Your Door

Brian Hyland
That's How Much

RARE PICTURE SLEEVES

Steve Lawrence
My Claire De Lune

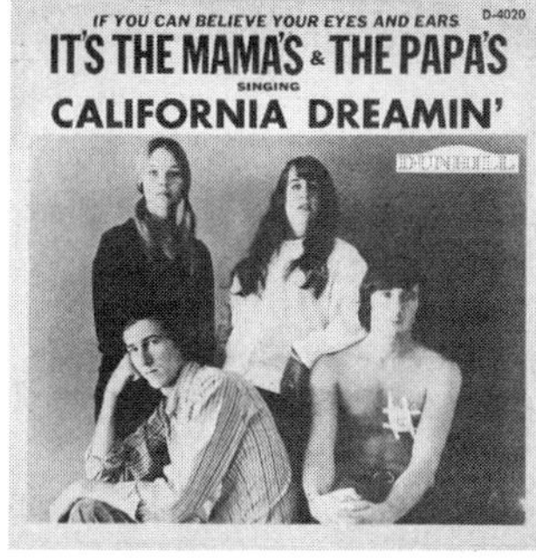

The Mama's & The Papa's
California Dreamin'

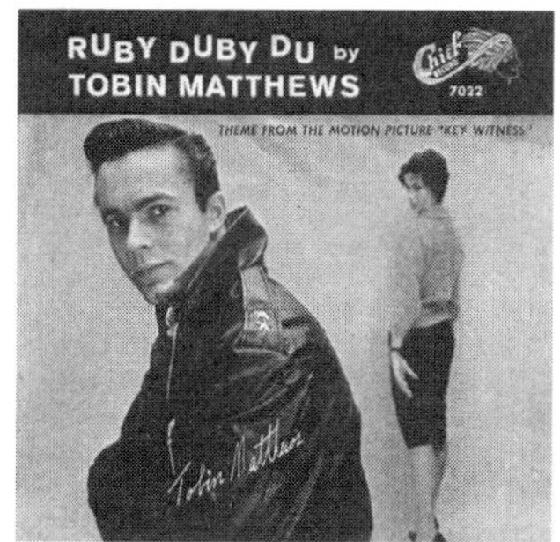

Tobin Matthews
Ruby Duby Du

Jack Nitzsche
The Lonely Surfer

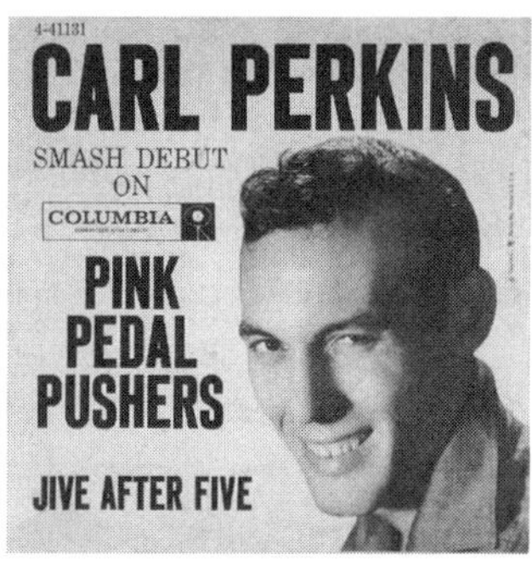

Carl Perkins
Pink Pedal Pushers

Paul Petersen
My Dad

Nelson Riddle
Lisbon Antigua

Jack Scott
Is There Something On Your Mind

The Slades
You Cheated

The Betty Smith Group
Bewitched

Ray Stevens
Harry, the Hairy Ape

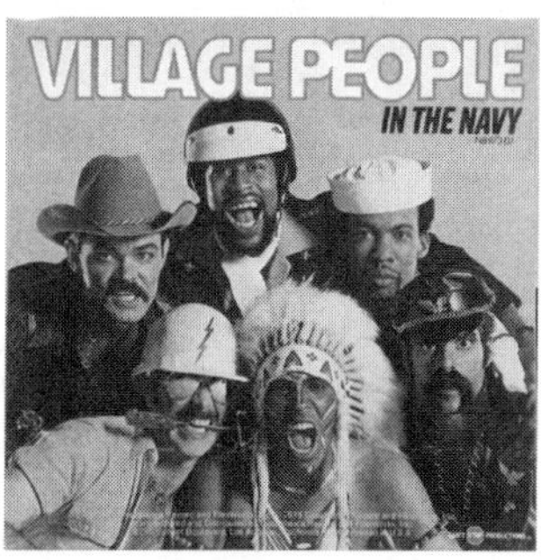

Village People
In The Navy

DEBUT	PEAK	WKS	Gold	A-side (Chart Hit)...B-side	$	Sym	Label & Number
				HURRICANE G — see PUFF DADDY			
				HURT, Jim '80			
				Pop-dance singer.			
10/11/80	**90**	4		**I Love Women** ... *Someone To Put Out The Fire*	$4		Scotti Brothers 605
				HUSKY, Ferlin C&W/MEM/POP '57			
				Born on 12/3/25 in Flat River, Missouri. Country singer/songwriter/guitarist. Charted 51 Country hits, 1953-75. Recorded as Terry Preston in the early 1950s; also did humorous recordings as Simon Crum. Hit #4 on the pop charts in 1953 with "A Dear John Letter' (with **Jean Shepard**).			
3/2/57	**4**	27		1 **Gone** ... CW[10] A:4 / J:4 / T:4 / S:5 *Missing Persons*	$20		Capitol 3628
				originally recorded by Husky in 1952 as by Terry Preston on Capitol 2298 ($30)			
7/8/57	**47**	15		2 **A Fallen Star** ... T:47 *Prize Possession*	$20		Capitol 3742
11/28/60+	**12**	18		3 **Wings Of A Dove** ... CW[10] *Next To Jimmy*	$15		Capitol 4406
1/6/62	**94**	1		4 **The Waltz You Saved For Me** ... *Out Of A Clear Blue Sky*	$12	■	Capitol 4650
				Smiley and Kitty Wilson (backing vocals); Wayne King's theme song			
				HUTCH, Willie R&B/LP '73			
				Born Willie Hutchinson in 1946 in Los Angeles, California; raised in Dallas, Texas. R&B singer/producer/songwriter.			
5/19/73	**67**	10		1 **Brother's Gonna Work It Out** ... *I Choose You*	$5		Motown 1222
8/11/73	**65**	6		2 **Slick** ... *Mother's Theme (Mama)*	$5	■	Motown 1252
				above 2 from the movie *The Mack* starring Richard Pryor			
11/1/75	**41**	6		3 **Love Power** ... *Talk To Me*	$5		Motown 1360
				HUTTON, Danny BUB '65			
				Born on 9/10/42 in Buncrana, Ireland; raised in Los Angeles, California. Member of **Three Dog Night**.			
10/16/65	**73**	6		**Roses And Rainbows** ... *Monster Shindig*	$15	■	HBR 447
				HYDE, Paul, And The Payola$ ROK/LP '87			
				Pop-rock group from Canada: Paul Hyde (vocals), Bob Rock (guitar), Alex Boynton (bass) and Chris Taylor (drums). Hyde and Rock later recorded as the duo **Rock and Hyde** (see #2 below).			
5/18/85	**84**	4		1 **You're The Only Love** ... *Eyes Of A Stranger* (ROK #22/'82)	$3	■	A&M 2733
4/25/87	**61**	10		2 **Dirty Water** ... *There's Always Someone Tougher*	$3	■	Capitol 5691
				ROCK AND HYDE			
	★280★			**HYLAND, Brian** BUB/LP '62			
				Born on 11/12/43 in Queens, New York. Teen pop singer. Own group, the Delphis, at age 12. In production company with **Del Shannon** in 1970.			
				1)Itsy Bitsy Teenie Weenie Yellow Polkadot Bikini 2)Gypsy Woman 3)Sealed With A Kiss 4)The Joker Went Wild 5)Let Me Belong To You			
7/4/60	**1**[1]	15	●	1 **Itsy Bitsy Teenie Weenie Yellow Polkadot Bikini** *Don't Dilly Dally, Sally* [N]	$30	■	Leader 805
				Trudy Packer (female spoken voice); first 7 weeks (including #1 peak) charted on Leader; remaining weeks on Kapp 342 ($15); picture sleeve is on Kapp			
10/10/60	**73**	3		2 **The Clickity Clack Song Four Little Heels /**			
10/24/60	**74**	4		3 **That's How Much** ...	$15	■	Kapp 352
				promotional picture sleeve also issued crediting Hyland as "The Bikini Boy"			
8/7/61	**20**	11		4 **Let Me Belong To You** ... *Let It Die!*	$12		ABC-Paramount 10236
11/27/61	**83**	1		5 **I'll Never Stop Wanting You** ... *The Night I Cried*	$12	■	ABC-Paramount 10262
3/10/62	**21**	11		6 **Ginny Come Lately** ... *I Should Be Gettin' Better*	$12	■	ABC-Paramount 10294
6/9/62	**3**	14		7 **Sealed With A Kiss** ... *Summer Job*	$12	■	ABC-Paramount 10336
				first recorded by **The Four Voices** in 1960 on Columbia 41699			
9/22/62	**25**	8		8 **Warmed Over Kisses (Left Over Love)** ... *Walk A Lonely Mile*	$12	■	ABC-Paramount 10359
11/24/62+	**69**	7		9 **I May Not Live To See Tomorrow** ... *It Ain't That Way At All*	$12	■	ABC-Paramount 10374
3/2/63	**88**	2		10 **If Mary's There** ... *Remember Me*	$12	■	ABC-Paramount 10400
				Stan Applebaum (orch.: #4-10)			
6/29/63	**63**	8		11 **I'm Afraid To Go Home** ... *Save Your Heart For Me*	$12		ABC-Paramount 10452
				B-side is Hyland's original version of **Gary Lewis & The Playboys**' 1965 hit			
4/16/66	**99**	1		12 **3000 Miles** ... *Sometimes They Do, Sometimes They Don't*	$10		Philips 40354
7/16/66	**20**	11		13 **The Joker Went Wild** ... *I Can Hear The Rain*	$8		Philips 40377
10/22/66	**25**	9		14 **Run, Run, Look And See** ... *Why Did You Do It*	$8		Philips 40405
2/18/67	**58**	5		15 **Hung Up In Your Eyes** ... *Why Mine*	$8	■	Philips 40424
5/27/67	**94**	3		16 **Holiday For Clowns** ... *Yesterday I Had A Girl*	$8		Philips 40444
8/12/67	**91**	2		17 **Get The Message** ... *Kinda Groovy*	$8		Philips 40472
1/11/69	**56**	10		18 **Tragedy** ... *You'd Better Stop - And Think It Over*	$7		Dot 17176
4/5/69	**90**	5		19 **A Million To One** ... *It Could All Begin Again (In You)*	$7		Dot 17222
7/12/69	**82**	3		20 **Stay And Love Me All Summer** ... *Rainy April Morning*	$7		Dot 17258
9/5/70	**3**	20	●	21 **Gypsy Woman** ... *You And Me (#2)*	$6		Uni 55240
2/13/71	**54**	8		22 **Lonely Teardrops** ... *Lorrayne*	$6		Uni 55272
				above 2 produced by **Del Shannon**			
				HYMAN, Dick BUB/MEM/LP '56			
				Born on 3/8/27 in Manhattan, New York. Pianist/composer/conductor/arranger. Toured Europe with **Benny Goodman** in 1950. Staff pianist at WMCA and WNBC-New York from 1951-57. Music director of *Arthur Godfrey And His Friends* from 1958-62.			
1/21/56	**8**	20	●	1 **Moritat A Theme from "The Three Penny Opera"** ... A:8 / T:9 / S:10 / J:14 *Baubles, Bangles And Beads* [I]	$15	■	MGM 12149
				THE "UNFORGETTABLE" SOUND OF THE DICK HYMAN TRIO			
				written in 1928; known later as "Mack The Knife"			
4/21/56	**78**	5		2 **Hi-Lili, Hi-Lo** ... T:78 *Junglero* [I]	$12		MGM 12207
				DICK HYMAN TRIO			
				from the 1953 movie *Lili* starring Leslie Caron			
5/31/69	**38**	8		3 **The Minotaur** ... *Topless Dancers Of Corfu* [I]	$10		Command 4126
				DICK HYMAN & HIS ELECTRIC ECLECTICS			
				HYNDE, Chrissie — see PRETENDERS, The / UB40			

DEBUT	PEAK	WKS	Gold	A-side (Chart Hit)....B-side	$	Sym	Label & Number

I

IAN, Janis

AC/BUB/LP **'75**

Born Janis Eddy Fink on 4/7/51 in Brooklyn, New York. Contemporary-folk singer/songwriter/pianist/guitarist.

DEBUT	PEAK	WKS	Gold	A-side (Chart Hit)....B-side	$	Sym	Label & Number
5/27/67	14	12		1 **Society's Child (Baby I've Been Thinking)** ....*Letter To Jon* written in 1965 by Ian (at age 14) about interracial romance; also released on Verve Folkways 5027 in 1967 ($10)	$10		Verve 5027
6/14/75	3	20		2 **At Seventeen** ....AC[2] *Stars*	$5	■	Columbia 10154
7/11/81	71	4		3 **Under The Covers** ....*Sugar Mountain*	$4		Columbia 02176

IAN VAN DAHL

'01

Female electronica-dance trio from Belgium: Marsha Theeuwen, Diana Dander and Jeanine Tiemissen. Annemie Coenen replaced Theeuwen in early 2002.

DEBUT	PEAK	WKS	Gold	A-side (Chart Hit)....B-side	$	Sym	Label & Number
8/4/01	91	10		1 **Castles In The Sky** ....*(6 remixes)* **IAN VAN DAHL Featuring Marsha**	$8	★*	Robbins 72046
2/23/02	55^{S}	8		2 **Will I?** ....*(9 versions)*	$8	★*	Robbins 72055
10/12/02	58^{S}	3		3 **Reason** ....*(6 extended mixes)*	$8	★*	Robbins 72070

ICE CUBE

★449★ R&B/BUB/LP **'93**

Born O'Shea Jackson on 6/15/69 in Los Angeles, California. Male rapper/actor. Former member of **N.W.A.** Acted in the movies *Boyz N The Hood, Trespass, Higher Learning, Friday* and *Anaconda.* Also see **Westside Connection** and **Yo-Yo**.

1)It Was A Good Day 2)Check Yo Self 3)Bop Gun (One Nation)

DEBUT	PEAK	WKS	Gold	A-side (Chart Hit)....B-side	$	Sym	Label & Number
5/25/91	36	12		1 **You Can't Play With My Yo-Yo** ....S:17 *Sisterland* **YO-YO Featuring Ice Cube**	$5	▮	EastWest 98831
2/1/92	67^{S}	3		2 **Steady Mobbin'** ....*Us* samples "Reach Out" by **Average White Band**	$5	▮	Priority 7247
11/21/92	55	10	●	3 **Wicked** ....S:24 *(2 versions) / U Ain't Gonna Take My Life* samples "Funky Worm" by the **Ohio Players**, "Welcome To The Terrordome" and "Can't Truss It" by **Public Enemy**, and "Loosey's" by **DAS EFX**	$6	▮*	Priority 53813
3/6/93	15	20	●	4 **It Was A Good Day** S:7 / A:32 *(instrumental)* samples "Sexy Mama" by **The Moments** and "Footsteps In The Dark" by **The Isley Brothers**	$3	▮	Priority 53817
7/31/93	20	20	▲	5 **Check Yo Self** ....RB[1] S:9 / A:47 *(instrumental) / It Was A Good Day / 24 With a L* **ICE CUBE featuring DAS EFX** samples "The Message" by **Grandmaster Flash & The Furious Five**	$5	▮*	Priority 53830
7/31/93	72	12		6 **The Bonnie And Clyde Theme** ....S:56 **YO YO (Featuring Ice Cube)** samples "Master Rocker" by Bernard Wright	$5		EastWest 98394
12/11/93	54	9		7 **Really Doe** ....S:25 *(instrumental) / My Skin Is My Sin*	$4	▮	Priority 53843
2/12/94	30	20		8 **You Know How We Do It** ....S:20 / A:46 *2 n The Morning* samples "The Show Is Over" by **Evelyn "Champagne" King**	$4	▮	Priority 53847
7/30/94	23	20	●	9 **Bop Gun (One Nation)** ....S:12 / A:34 *Down For Whatever* **ICE CUBE featuring George Clinton** rap version of **Funkadelic**'s "One Nation Under A Groove"; "Bop Gun" by **Parliament** "Bubbled Under" (#102) in 1977	$3	▮	Priority 53155
3/11/95	74	7		10 **People Don't Believe (a.k.a. Hand Of The Dead Body)** ....S:39 *(5 remixes) / Mind Playin' Tricks* **SCARFACE featuring Ice Cube** samples "Hung Up On My Baby" by **Isaac Hayes**	$4	▮	Rap-A-Lot 38469
9/30/95	88	10		11 **West Up!** ....*(instrumental)* **WC AND THE MAAD CIRCLE Featuring Ice Cube and Mack 10** samples "Reach For It" by **George Duke**	$4	▮	Payday 850258
9/13/97	82	7		12 **Men Of Steel** ....S:59 *(instrumental)* **SHAQUILLE O'NEAL, ICE CUBE, B REAL, PETER GUNZ & KRS-ONE** inspired by the movie *Steel* starring Shaquille O'Neal	$3	▮	Qwest 17305
2/21/98	56^{A}	16		13 **We Be Clubbin'** .... from the movie *The Players Club* starring Ice Cube (soundtrack on A&M 540886)			album cut
10/31/98+	26	19	●	14 **Pushin' Weight** ....S:13 *(instrumental) / Ghetto Vet* **ICE CUBE Featuring Mr. Short Khop** clean version available on Best Side/Priority 53458	$4	★	Priority 53456
12/4/99+	35	12		15 **You Can Do It** ....S:7 *(instrumental) / Money Stretch* (**Lil' Zane**) **ICE CUBE Feat. Mack 10** Ms. Toi (female vocal); samples "Planet Rock" by **Afrika Bambaataa**; from the movie *Next Friday* starring Ice Cube	$4	★	Priority 53562

ICEHOUSE

ROK/LP **'88**

Rock group formed in Sydney, Australia: Iva Davies (vocals, guitar), Anthony Smith (keyboards), Keith Welsh (bass) and John Lloyd (drums). Numerous personnel changes through the 1980s, with Davies the only constant. Group name is Australian slang for an insane asylum.

DEBUT	PEAK	WKS	Gold	A-side (Chart Hit)....B-side	$	Sym	Label & Number
8/1/81	62	7		1 **We Can Get Together** ....*Not My Kind*	$4	■	Chrysalis 2530
7/5/86	79	9		2 **No Promises** ....*Into The Wild*	$3	■	Chrysalis 42978
10/17/87+	14	21		3 **Crazy** ....S:11 / A:21 *No Promises (live)*	$3	■	Chrysalis 43156
2/13/88	7	21		4 **Electric Blue** S:5 / A:10 *Over My Head* co-written by John Oates (of **Hall & Oates**)	$3	■	Chrysalis 43201
7/9/88	88	4		5 **My Obsession** ....*Your Confession*	$3	■	Chrysalis 43240
10/7/89	84	4		6 **Touch The Fire** ....*Great Southern Land*	$3		Chrysalis 23414

ICE-T

R&B/BUB/LP **'91**

Born Tracy Morrow on 2/16/58 in Newark, New Jersey. Male rapper/actor. In the movies *Breakin', Breakin' II, New Jack City, Who's The Man?, Trespass* and *Tank Girl.* Formed own Rhyme Syndicate label in 1988. Formed controversial speed-metal band, Body Count, in 1992. Star of the TV series *Players.*

DEBUT	PEAK	WKS	Gold	A-side (Chart Hit)....B-side	$	Sym	Label & Number
6/11/88	70	7		1 **Colors** ....*Squeeze The Trigger* title song from the movie starring Sean Penn and Robert Duvall	$4	■	Sire/Warner 27902
4/27/91	67	8		2 **New Jack Hustler (Nino's Theme)** ....S:35 *(instrumental)* from the movie *New Jack City* starring Wesley Snipes and Ice-T	$4	▮	Giant/Sire 19442
12/19/98	74^{S}	1		3 **The Real One** ....BUB:103 *(clean version) / Shake Your Pants* **THE 2 LIVE CREW Featuring Ice-T**	$6	▮	Lil' Joe 899

DEBUT	PEAK	WKS	Gold	A-side (Chart Hit)..........B-side	$	Sym	Label & Number
				ICICLE WORKS ROK/LP **'84**			
				Rock trio from Liverpool, England: Robert Ian McNabb (vocals, guitar), Chris Layhe (bass) and Chris Sharrock (drums).			
4/21/84	**37**	12		**Whisper To A Scream (Birds Fly)**..........*In The Dance The Shaman Led*	$4		Arista 9155
				ICONZ LP **'01**			
				Rap group from Miami, Florida: Luc Duc, Stage McCloud, Bull Dog, Chapter, Tony Manshino, Screwface and Supastar.			
2/17/01	**93**	5		**Get Crunked Up**..........*(4 versions)*	$6	T	Slip-N-Slide 67154
				ICY BLU **'91**			
				Born Laurel Urchick on 6/1/74 in Austin, Texas. White female rapper.			
7/6/91	**78**	5		1 **Pump It (Nice An' Hard)**..........*(club mix)*	$3	▮	Giant 19377
				samples **Salt-N-Pepa**'s "Push It"			
11/2/91+	**46**	20		2 **I Wanna Be Your Girl**..........A:35 / S:41 *(album version)*	$3	▮	Giant 19170
				IDEAL R&B/LP **'99**			
				R&B vocal group from Houston, Texas: J-Dante, Maverick, PZ and Swab.			
8/21/99	**13**	22		1 **Get Gone**..........S:9 / A:35 *(2 versions)*	$4	★V	Noontime 38666
6/10/00	**47**	18		2 **Whatever**..........A:39 *(3 versions) / Get Gone*	$6	TV	Virgin 38713
				IDEAL Featuring Lil' Mo			
				"45" issued for above 2 on Virgin 38730			
				IDES OF MARCH, The BUB/LP **'70**			
				Rock group from Chicago, Illinois: Jim Peterik (vocals, guitar), Ray Herr (guitar), Larry Millas (keyboards), John Larson and Chuck Soumar (horns), Bob Bergland (bass), and Mike Borch (drums). Group named after a line in Shakespeare's *Julius Caesar*. Peterik later played keyboards for **Survivor**.			
6/25/66	**42**	7		1 **You Wouldn't Listen** *[THE I'DES OF MARCH]*..........*I'll Keep Searching*	$10		Parrot 304
9/10/66	**92**	1		2 **Roller Coaster**..........*Things Aren't Always What They Seem*	$10		Parrot 310
3/28/70	**2**[1]	12		3 **Vehicle**..........*Lead Me Home, Gently*	$7		Warner 7378
7/4/70	**64**	5		4 **Superman**..........*Home*	$7		Warner 7403
3/13/71	**73**	9		5 **L.A. Goodbye**..........*Mrs. Grayson's Farm*	$7		Warner 7466
	★308★			**IDOL, Billy** ROK/BUB/LP **'87**			
				Born William Broad on 11/30/55 in Stanmore, Middlesex, England. Leader of the London punk band Generation X from 1977-81. Suffered serious leg injuries in a motorcycle crash on 2/6/90. Appeared in the movies ***The Doors*** and *The Wedding Singer*.			
				1)Mony Mony "Live" 2)Cradle Of Love 3)Eyes Without A Face			
7/3/82	**23**	17		1 **Hot In The City**..........*Hole In The Wall*	$5	■	Chrysalis 2605
				also see #11 below			
5/21/83	**36**	13		2 **White Wedding**..........*Dead On Arrival*	$4		Chrysalis 42697
				originally "Bubbled Under" (#108) on 11/27/82 on Chrysalis 2648			
1/28/84	**46**	14		3 **Rebel Yell**..........*Crank Call*	$4	■	Chrysalis 42762
5/5/84	**4**	22		4 **Eyes Without A Face**..........*Blue Highway*	$3	■	Chrysalis 42786
8/25/84	**29**	12		5 **Flesh For Fantasy**..........A:29 *The Dead Next Door*	$3	■	Chrysalis 42809
11/3/84	**50**	11		6 **Catch My Fall**..........*Daytime Drama*	$3		Chrysalis 42840
				above 4 from the album *Rebel Yell*			
10/4/86	**6**	18		7 **To Be A Lover**..........S:5 / A:9 *All Summer Single*	$3	■	Chrysalis 43024
				#45 hit for **William Bell** in 1969 as "I Forgot To Be Your Lover"			
1/24/87	**37**	9		8 **Don't Need A Gun**..........S:32 / A:34 *Fatal Charm*	$3	■	Chrysalis 43087
4/25/87	**20**	14		9 **Sweet Sixteen**..........S:16 / A:25 *Beyond Belief*	$3	■	Chrysalis 43114
9/5/87	**❶**[1]	22		10 **Mony Mony "Live"**..........S:❶[1] / A:2 *Shakin' All Over "Live"* [L]	$3	■	Chrysalis 43161
				studio version "Bubbled Under" (#107) on 9/26/81 on Chrysalis 2543			
12/12/87+	**48**	10		11 **Hot In The City**..........*Catch My Fall (remix)* [R]	$3	■	Chrysalis 43203
				same version as #1 above			
5/5/90	**2**[1]	24	●	12 **Cradle Of Love**..........AR[2] S:2 / A:5 *311 Man*	$3	▮V	Chrysalis 23509
				from the movie *The Adventures Of Ford Fairlane* starring Andrew Dice Clay			
9/8/90	**52**	9		13 **L.A. Woman**..........*License To Thrill*	$3	▮V	Chrysalis 23571
				first recorded by **The Doors** on their 1971 album of the same title; all of above produced by Keith Forsey			
				IFIELD, Frank BUB/C&W/LP **'62**			
				Born on 11/30/37 in Coventry, Warwickshire, England; raised in New South Wales, Australia. Pop singer.			
9/8/62	**5**	11		1 **I Remember You**..........AC[1] *I Listen To My Heart*	$12		Vee-Jay 457
				early pressings credited as **Farnk Ifield**; #9 hit for **Jimmy Dorsey** in 1942			
12/22/62+	**44**	7		2 **Lovesick Blues**..........*Anytime*	$12		Vee-Jay 477
				written in 1922; #1 Country hit for Hank Williams in 1949			
9/7/63	**58**	7		3 **I'm Confessin' (That I Love You)**..........*Waltzing Matilda*	$10	⊙	Capitol 5032
				Guy Lombardo and Rudy Vallee both had Top 5 versions in 1930; first released on Vee-Jay 553 in 1963			
12/14/63+	**71**	6		4 **Please**..........*Mule Train*	$10		Capitol 5089
				#1 hit for **Bing Crosby** in 1932			
	★536★			**IGLESIAS, Enrique** BUB/LP **'00**			
				Born on 5/8/75 in Madrid, Spain; raised in Miami, Florida. Latin singer. Son of **Julio Iglesias**. Younger brother of **Julio Iglesias Jr.**			
7/10/99	**❶**[2]	20		1 **Bailamos**..........S:2 / A:6 *(Latin radio mix)*	$4	★	Overbrook 97122
				from the movie *Wild Wild West* starring **Will Smith**; title is Spanish for "we dance"			
12/4/99+	**32**	17		2 **Rhythm Divine**..........A:25 *(3 remixes)*	$6	T	Interscope 497226
4/1/00	**❶**[3]	20		3 **Be With You**..........S:❶[3] / A:3 *(Spanish version: "Solo Me Importas Tu")*	$4	★	Interscope 490366
6/17/00	**52**	19		4 **Could I Have This Kiss Forever**..........A:48			album cut
				WHITNEY HOUSTON & ENRIQUE IGLESIAS			
				from the album *The Greatest Hits* on Arista 14626			
9/29/01	**3**	34		5 **Hero**..........AC[15] A:3			album cut
2/23/02	**12**	20		6 **Escape**..........A:10			album cut
				above 2 from the album *Escape* on Interscope 493148			

DEBUT	PEAK	WKS	Gold	A-side (Chart Hit)..........B-side	$	Sym	Label & Number
				IGLESIAS, Julio BUB/AC/C&W/LP **'84**			
				Born on 9/23/43 in Madrid, Spain. Latin singer, immensely popular worldwide. Soccer goalie for the pro Real Madrid team until temporary paralysis from a car crash. Father of **Julio Iglesias Jr.** and **Enrique Iglesias**.			
3/3/84	5	21	▲	1 **To All The Girls I've Loved Before** ....CW^2 *I Don't Want To Wake You* (Iglesias) — **JULIO IGLESIAS & WILLIE NELSON**	$4	■	Columbia 04217
7/7/84	19	16		2 **All Of You**..........*The Last Time* (Iglesias) — **JULIO IGLESIAS & DIANA ROSS**	$3	■	Columbia 04507
5/21/88	80	5		3 **My Love**..........*My Love* (Iglesias) — **JULIO IGLESIAS FEATURING STEVIE WONDER**	$3	■	Columbia 07781
				IGLESIAS, Julio Jr. **'99**			
				Born on 2/25/73 in Madrid, Spain; raised in Miami, Florida. Son of **Julio Iglesias**. Older brother of **Enrique Iglesias**.			
10/2/99	31^S	19		**One More Chance**..........*(remix) / I Don't Know Why*	$4	★	Epic 79230
				IIO **'02**			
				Electronic-dance duo from New York: female singer Nadia Ali and male producer Markus Moser.			
2/16/02	46	15		**Rapture (Tastes So Sweet)**..........S:12 / A:52 *(3 remixes)*	$8	★*	Universal 015672
				IKETTES, The R&B/BUB **'62**			
				Female R&B trio formed for the **Ike & Tina Turner** Revue. Atco group consisted of Delores Johnson (lead), Eloise Hester and "Joshie" Jo Armstead. Modern group consisted of Vanetta Fields, Robbie Montgomery and Jessie Smith; later known as **The Mirettes**.			
1/13/62	19	12		1 **I'm Blue (The Gong-Gong Song)**..........*Find My Baby* — **Tina Turner** (backing vocal); first released as "So Blue Over You" on Innis 6667	$15		Atco 6212
3/13/65	36	8		2 **Peaches "N" Cream**..........*The Biggest Players*	$10		Modern 1005
10/9/65	74	7		3 **I'm So Thankful**..........*Don't Feel Sorry For Me*	$10		Modern 1011
2/17/68	45	7		4 **In The Midnight Hour**..........*To Love Somebody* — **THE MIRETTES**	$10		Revue 11004
				ILL AL SKRATCH R&B/BUB/LP **'94**			
				Male rap duo from Brooklyn, New York: ILL (I Lyrical Lord) and Al Skratch.			
7/16/94	59^S	6		1 **Where My Homiez? (Come Around My Way)**..........BUB:103 *(instrumental)* — **ILL Featuring AL SKRATCH**	$3	▮	Mercury 858462
9/24/94	62	14		2 **I'll Take Her**..........S:42 *The Brooklyn Uptown Connection* — **ILL AL SKRATCH Featuring Brian McKnight**	$3	▮	Mercury 856124
				ILLEGAL R&B/LP **'93**			
				Male rap duo of Malik Edwards and Jamal Phillips. Discovered by Lisa Lopes of **TLC**.			
10/23/93	95	2		**We Getz Buzy**..........S:63 *(instrumental)* — co-written and produced by **Erick Sermon**	$4	▮	Rowdy 35024
				ILLICIT BIZNEZ **'02**			
				Rap group.			
7/20/02	14^S	12		**Throw It Up**..........*(2 versions)* — **ILLICIT BIZNEZ Feat. Coo Coo Cal**	$5	★	Felonious 80012
				ILLUSION, The BUB/LP **'69**			
				Rock group from Long Island, New York: John Vinci (vocals), Richie Cerniglia (guitar), Mike Maniscalco (keyboards), Chuck Adler (bass) and Mike Ricciardella (drums).			
7/5/69	32	13		1 **Did You See Her Eyes**..........*Falling In Love* — a slightly different version was issued on Steed 712 in 1969	$7		Steed 718
12/20/69+	80	4		2 **Together**..........*Don't Push It*	$7		Steed 722
6/27/70	98	2		3 **Let's Make Each Other Happy**..........*Beside You (B-Side-U)*	$7		Steed 726
				IMAJIN R&B **'98**			
				Male R&B vocal group: Jamal Hampton, Talib Kareem, Olamide Faison and John Fitch.			
5/30/98	25	20		1 **Shorty (You Keep Playin' With My Mind)**..S:18 *(remix w/***Mr. Cheeks** *of* **The Lost Boyz***)* — **IMAJIN Featuring Keith Murray** — samples "Dance With Me" by **Peter Brown**	$4	▮	Jive 42525
1/9/99	56^S	6		2 **No Doubt**..........*(5 album snippets)* — samples "It's A Natural Affair" by the **Spinners**	$5	★+	Jive 42551
				IMBRUGLIA, Natalie LP **'98**			
				Born on 2/4/75 in Sydney, Australia. Alternative pop-rock singer/songwriter.			
2/14/98	❶ ^{11A}	44		1 **Torn** HOT:42(2 wks)			album cut
7/4/98	25^A	18		2 **Wishing I Was There**.......... — above 2 from the album *Left Of The Middle* on RCA 67634			album cut
1/19/02	72^S	1		3 **Torn /** [R]			
1/19/02		1		4 **Wishing I Was There**.......... [R] — above 2 reissued on RCA's "Double-Play CD Single"	$5	★	RCA 60508
3/2/02	64	8		5 **Wrong Impression**..........A:67 — from the album *White Lillies Island* on RCA 68082			album cut
				IMMATURE R&B/BUB/LP **'94**			
				Teen male R&B vocal trio from Los Angeles, California: Marques Houston (born on 8/4/81), Jerome Jones and Kelton Kessee. Houston acted on TV's *Sister, Sister*. Group later shortened name to **IMx**.			
				1)Never Lie 2)Constantly 3)Stay The Night			
7/30/94	5	26	●	1 **Never Lie** S:2 / A:13 *(padapella version)*	$3	▮	MCA 54850
11/26/94+	16	20	●	2 **Constantly**..........S:8 / A:40 *Never Lie (remix)*	$3	▮	MCA 54948
5/20/95	95	2		3 **I Don't Mind**..........S:74 *Constantly (R&B mix)*	$3	▮	MCA 55015
9/23/95	46	13		4 **Feel The Funk**..........S:22 / A:69 *(same version)* — samples "Love Changes" by **Mother's Finest**; from the movie *Dangerous Minds* starring Michelle Pfeiffer	$3	▮	MCA 55130
12/9/95+	37	20		5 **We Got It**..........S:18 *(instrumental)* — **Smooth** (rap); samples "Girl Callin'" by **Chocolate Milk**	$3	▮	MCA 55148
5/4/96	36	13		6 **Please Don't Go**..........S:17 *We Got It (flava remix)*	$3	▮	MCA 55158
10/12/96	64^S	2		7 **Lover's Groove**..........BUB:102 *(remix w/***Shyheim***)*	$3	▮	MCA 55234

DEBUT	PEAK	WKS	Gold	A-side (Chart Hit)..........B-side	$	Sym	Label & Number

IMMATURE — Cont'd

DEBUT	PEAK	WKS	Gold	A-side (Chart Hit)..........B-side	$	Sym	Label & Number
2/1/97	32	14		8 Watch Me Do My Thing .... S:19 **IMMATURE Featuring Smooth and Ed From Good Burger** from the Nickelodeon TV show *All That*	$3	▮	Loud/RCA 64737
9/13/97	69	8		9 I'm Not A Fool .... S:44 *(instrumental)*	$3	▮	MCA 55367
10/9/99+	23	20		10 Stay The Night *[IMx]* .... S:9 *(instrumental)*	$4	★	MCA 155630

IMPACT R&B/BUB **'76**

R&B group from Baltimore, Maryland: Damon Otis Harris (vocals), John Simms, Charles Timmons and Donald Tilghman. Harris was a member of **The Temptations** from 1971-75.

DEBUT	PEAK	WKS	Gold	A-side (Chart Hit)..........B-side	$	Sym	Label & Number
6/19/76	94	2		Happy Man (Pt. I) .... *(Pt. II)*	$6		Atco/WMOT 7049

IMPALAS, The **'59**

Doo-wop group from Brooklyn, New York: Joe "Speedo" Frazier, Richard Wagner, Lenny Renda and Tony Carlucci. All members, except black lead singer Frazier, are white.

DEBUT	PEAK	WKS	Gold	A-side (Chart Hit)..........B-side	$	Sym	Label & Number
3/16/59	2^2	18	●	1 Sorry (I Ran All the Way Home) .... *Fool, Fool, Fool* early pressings issued as "I Ran All The Way Home" ($75)	$25		Cub 9022
6/22/59	86	5		2 Oh, What A Fool .... *Sandy Went Away*	$25		Cub 9033

IMPRESSIONS, The ★98★ R&B/BUB/LP **'64**

R&B group formed in Chicago, Illinois: **Jerry Butler** (born on 12/8/39), **Curtis Mayfield** (born on 6/3/42), Sam Gooden (born on 9/2/39) and brothers Arthur and Richard Brooks. Originally known as The Roosters. Butler left for a solo career in 1958; replaced by Fred Cash (born on 10/8/40). The Brooks brothers left in 1962, leaving Mayfield as the trio's leader. Mayfield left in 1970 for a solo career; replaced by Leroy Hutson. In 1973, Hutson was replaced by Reggie Torian and Ralph Johnson. Johnson joined Mystique in 1976. Group did movie soundtrack for *Three The Hard Way* (1974). Butler, Mayfield, Gooden and Cash reunited for a tour in 1983. Mayfield died on 12/26/99 (age 57). Group inducted into the Rock and Roll Hall of Fame in 1991.

1)It's All Right 2)Amen 3)Keep On Pushing 4)For Your Precious Love 5)Talking About My Baby

DEBUT	PEAK	WKS	Gold	A-side (Chart Hit)..........B-side	$	Sym	Label & Number
6/16/58	11	12		1 For Your Precious Love .... S:11 / T:11 / A:25 *Sweet Was The Wine* **JERRY BUTLER and The Impressions** originally released on Vee-Jay 280 ($6000), then on Falcon 1013 ($50) and then on Abner 1013	$50		Abner 1013
10/16/61	20	15		2 Gypsy Woman .... *As Long As You Love Me*	$20		ABC-Paramount 10241
2/17/62	99	1		3 Grow Closer Together .... *Can't You See*	$20		ABC-Paramount 10289
7/28/62	96	1		4 Little Young Lover .... *Never Let Me Go*	$20		ABC-Paramount 10328
2/9/63	73	6		5 I'm The One Who Loves You .... *I Need Your Love*	$15		ABC-Paramount 10386
5/25/63	84	4		6 Sad, Sad Girl And Boy .... *Twist And Limbo*	$15		ABC-Paramount 10431
9/28/63	4	14		7 It's All Right RB[2] *You'll Want Me Back* above 6 from the album *The Impressions*	$15		ABC-Paramount 10487
1/18/64	12	9		8 Talking About My Baby .... *Never Too Much Love*	$15		ABC-Paramount 10511
4/4/64	14	11		9 I'm So Proud .... *I Made A Mistake*	$15		ABC-Paramount 10544
6/6/64	10	13		10 Keep On Pushing .... *I Love You (Yeah)*	$15		ABC-Paramount 10554
9/5/64	15	10		11 You Must Believe Me .... *See The Real Me*	$15		ABC-Paramount 10581
11/21/64+	7	11		12 Amen .... *Long, Long Winter* (R&B #35) [X] featured in the 1963 movie *Lilies Of The Field* starring Sidney Poitier; re-make "Bubbled Under" (#110) on 12/20/69 on Curtom 1948	$15		ABC-Paramount 10602
2/13/65	14	8		13 People Get Ready .... *I've Been Trying* (#133)	$15		ABC-Paramount 10622
4/3/65	29	7		14 Woman's Got Soul .... *Get Up And Move*	$15		ABC-Paramount 10647
6/5/65	48	8		15 Meeting Over Yonder .... *I've Found That I've Lost*	$12		ABC-Paramount 10670
8/14/65	64	7		16 I Need You .... *Never Could You Be* (R&B #35)	$12		ABC-Paramount 10710
10/2/65	76	5		17 Just One Kiss From You .... *Twilight Time*	$12		ABC-Paramount 10725
11/20/65+	33	9		18 You've Been Cheatin' .... *Man Oh Man*	$12		ABC-Paramount 10750
2/5/66	90	2		19 Since I Lost The One I Love .... *Falling In Love With You*	$12		ABC-Paramount 10761
4/2/66	91	3		20 Too Slow .... *No One Else*	$12		ABC-Paramount 10789
9/3/66	65	7		21 Can't Satisfy .... *This Must End*	$10		ABC 10831
3/4/67	96	2		22 You Always Hurt Me .... *Little Girl*	$8		ABC 10900
9/2/67	80	4		23 I Can't Stay Away From You .... *You Ought To Be In Heaven*	$8		ABC 10964
12/30/67+	14	13		24 We're A Winner .... RB[1] *It's All Over*	$8		ABC 11022
4/20/68	59	7		25 We're Rolling On (Part I) .... *(Part II)*	$8		ABC 11071
7/20/68	61	8		26 I Loved And I Lost .... *Up Up And Away* **Johnny Pate** (orch.: #8-26)	$8		ABC 11103
9/7/68	22	12		27 Fool For You .... *I'm Loving Nothing*	$6	■	Curtom 1932
11/23/68	71	4		28 Don't Cry My Love .... *Sometimes I Wonder*	$8		ABC 11135
11/30/68+	25	10		29 This Is My Country .... *My Woman's Love*	$6		Curtom 1934
4/26/69	84	4		30 Seven Years .... *The Girl I Find*	$6		Curtom 1940
6/28/69	21	11		31 Choice Of Colors .... RB[1] *Mighty Mighty Spade & Whitey*	$6		Curtom 1943
10/18/69	58	9		32 Say You Love Me .... *You'll Be Always Mine*	$6		Curtom 1946
5/16/70	28	12		33 Check Out Your Mind .... *Can't You See*	$6		Curtom 1951
9/5/70	56	8		34 (Baby) Turn On To Me .... *Soulful Love*	$6		Curtom 1954
2/27/71	53	6		35 Ain't Got Time .... *I'm So Proud*	$6		Curtom 1957
7/31/71	94	3		36 Love Me .... *Do You Wanna Win* all of above (except #1 & 12) written by **Curtis Mayfield**	$6		Curtom 1959
5/4/74	17	18		37 Finally Got Myself Together (I'm A Changed Man) .... RB[2] *I'll Always Be Here*	$5		Curtom 1997
7/5/75	68	8		38 Sooner Or Later .... *Miracle Woman*	$5		Curtom 0103
11/1/75	75	4		39 Same Thing It Took .... *I'm So Glad*	$5		Curtom 0106

IMx — see IMMATURE

INC., The R&B/LP **'02**

All-star rap group assembled by producer Irv Gotti. Featuring **Ja Rule**, **Ashanti**, **Charli Baltimore** and Vita.

DEBUT	PEAK	WKS	Gold	A-side (Chart Hit)..........B-side	$	Sym	Label & Number
6/22/02	6	20		Down 4 U .... A:6 **IRV GOTTI PRESENTS THE INC. Featuring Ja Rule, Ashanti, Charli Balitimore & Vita** from the album *Irv Gotti Presents The Inc.* on Murder Inc. 062033			album cut

DEBUT	PEAK	WKS	Gold	A-side (Chart Hit)...B-side	$	Sym	Label & Number
				INCREDIBLE BONGO BAND, The R&B/BUB/LP **'73**			
				Instrumental studio band assembled in Canada by producer Michael Viner.			
7/21/73	**57**	7		**Bongo Rock**...*Bongolia* [I]	$6		MGM 14588
				first released on Pride 1015 in 1973 ($8)			
				IN CROWD, The **'66**			
				White vocal trio of Ron Hicklin, Stan Farber and Al Capps. Hicklin and Farber were member of The Eligibles (charted on *Bubbling Under* in 1959).			
12/10/66	**92**	2		**Questions And Answers**...*Happiness In My Heart*	$8		Viva 604
				INCUBUS ROK/BUB/LP **'01**			
				Hard-rock group from Calabasas, California: Brandon Boyd (vocals), Mike Einziger (guitar), Chris Kilmore (DJ), Alex Katunich (bass) and Jose Pasillas (drums).			
2/17/01	**9**	39		1 **Drive**...MR[8] A:7		V	album cut
				"45": Epic 79627; B-side: (same); from the album *Make Yourself* on Epic/Immortal 63652			
9/22/01	**60**	20		2 **Wish You Were Here**...A:59		V	album cut
				"45": Epic 76655; B-side: (same); from the album *Morning View* on Epic/Immortal 85227			
				INDECENT OBSESSION LP **'90**			
				Pop group from Brisbane, Australia: David Dixon (vocals), Andrew Coyne (guitar), Michael Szumowski (keyboards) and Darryl Simms (drums). Band's name taken from a Colleen McCullough novel.			
7/28/90	**31**	12		**Tell Me Something**...S:28 / A:32 *(no B-side)*	$3	▮V	MCA 53830
				"45": MCA 79029; B-side: "Take Me Higher"			
				INDEPENDENTS, The R&B/BUB/LP **'73**			
				R&B vocal group: Chuck Jackson, Maurice Jackson, Helen Curry and Eric Thomas. Chuck (no relation to Maurice) and Marvin Yancey, Jr. were producers/writers for the group; later teamed in production work, especially for **Natalie Cole**, to whom Yancey was once married. Chuck Jackson, not to be confused with the same-named solo singer, is the brother of civil rights leader the Rev. Jesse Jackson.			
5/13/72	**84**	5		1 **Just As Long As You Need Me, Part I**...*Part II*	$7		Wand 11245
4/7/73	**21**	13	●	2 **Leaving Me** RB[1] *I Love You, Yes I Do*	$7		Wand 11252
7/21/73	**41**	8		3 **Baby I've Been Missing You**...*Couldn't Hear Nobody Say (I Love You Like You Do)*	$7		Wand 11258
11/17/73	**65**	4		4 **It's All Over**...*Sara Lee*	$7		Wand 11263
11/16/74	**88**	4		5 **Let This Be A Lesson To You**...*No Wind, No Rain*	$7		Wand 11279
				INDIA.ARIE R&B/BUB/LP **'01**			
				Born India Arie Simpson on 10/3/76 in Denver, Colorado; raised in Atlanta, Georgia. Female contemporary R&B singer/songwriter/guitarist.			
3/31/01	**47**	17		1 **Video**...A:40			album cut
10/6/01	**56^S**	4		2 **Brown Skin**...BUB:109 *(5 mixes)*	$8	★*	Motown 015315
3/9/02	**59**	14		3 **Video**...A:63 [R]			album cut
				above 3 from the album *Acoustic Soul* on Motown 013770			
9/28/02	**89**	13		4 **Little Things**...*(2 versions)*	$4	★	Motown 019440
				samples "Hollywood" by **Rufus Feat. Chaka Khan**			
				INDIGO GIRLS ROK/AC/LP **'89**			
				Folk-rock duo from Decatur, Georgia: singers/songwriters/guitarists Amy Ray (born on 4/12/64) and Emily Saliers (born on 7/22/63).			
7/22/89	**52**	9		1 **Closer To Fine**...*Cold As Ice*	$5		Epic 68912
				Peter O'Toole (of Hothouse Flowers; backing vocals, mandolin)			
8/8/92	**89**	2		2 **Galileo**...*(4 album snippets)*	$3	▮	Epic 74326
5/31/97	**42^A**	14		3 **Shame On You**...			album cut
				from the album *Shaming Of The Sun* on Epic 67891			
				INDUSTRY **'83**			
				Rock group from Long Island, New York: Jon Carin (vocals), Brian Unger (guitar), Rudy Perrone (bass) and Mercury Caronia (drums).			
11/19/83	**81**	8		**State Of The Nation**...*Communication*	$4		Capitol 5268
				INFAMOUS SYNDICATE **'99**			
				Female rap duo from Chicago, Illinois: Rashawnna Guy and Lateefa Harland.			
3/6/99	**60^S**	6		**Here I Go**...*(3 album snippets) / Clock Strikes 12* (w/Fatal)	$4	★	Relativity 1771
				INFINITY - THA GHETTO CHILD **'02**			
				Born Antwon Buie in Charleston, South Carolina. Male rapper.			
10/5/02	**65^S**	1		**In Tha Ghetto**...*Throw Ya Fingaz Up*	$5	★	MCA 155912
				INFORMATION SOCIETY BUB/LP **'88**			
				Techno-dance group from Minneapolis, Minnesota: Kurt Valaquen and Paul Robb (vocals), Amanda Kramer (keyboards) and James Cassidy (bass). Reduced to a trio in 1990 with departure of Kramer.			
7/16/88	**3**	25	●	1 **What's On Your Mind (Pure Energy)** S:4 / A:4 *(club radio edit)*	$3	■	Tommy Boy 27826
11/26/88+	**9**	19		2 **Walking Away**...A:7 / S:10 *Make It Funkier*	$3	■	Tommy Boy 27736
4/1/89	**76**	6		3 **Repetition**...*Something In The Air*	$3		Tommy Boy 27659
8/12/89	**83**	8		4 **Lay All Your Love On Me**...*Funky At 45*	$3		Tommy Boy 27534
				original version is by **Abba** on their 1980 album *Super Trouper;* all of above from the album *Information Society*			
10/6/90	**28**	16		5 **Think**...S:24 / A:30 *(radio edit)*	$3	▮V	Tommy Boy 19591
				INGMANN, Jorgen, & His Guitar **'61**			
				Born Jorgen Ingmann-Pedersen on 4/26/25 in Copenhagen, Denmark. Male guitarist.			
1/23/61	**2^2**	17		1 **Apache**...*Echo Boogie* [I]	$15		Atco 6184
5/22/61	**54**	6		2 **Anna**...*Cherokee* [I]	$12		Atco 6195
				#5 hit in 1953 for Silvana Mangano (star of the movie *Anna*)			

DEBUT	PEAK	WKS	Gold	A-side (Chart Hit)...B-side	$	Sym	Label & Number
	★327★			**INGRAM, James** R&B/AC/BUB/LP **'90**			
				Born on 2/16/56 in Akron, Ohio. R&B singer/songwriter/pianist.			
				1)I Don't Have The Heart 2)Baby, Come To Me 3)Somewhere Out There			
8/15/81	17	23		1 **Just Once** ... *The Dude*	$4		A&M 2357
12/19/81+	14	21		2 **One Hundred Ways** ... *Velas*	$4		A&M 2387
				QUINCY JONES Featuring JAMES INGRAM (above 2)			
4/24/82+	❶[2]	32	●	3 **Baby, Come To Me** ... AC[3] *Solero*	$3		Qwest 50036
				originally charted for 4 weeks at #73; re-entered on 10/16/82			
				PATTI AUSTIN (with James Ingram)			
5/14/83	45	17		4 **How Do You Keep The Music Playing** ... *(long version)*	$3		Qwest 29618
				JAMES INGRAM AND PATTI AUSTIN			
				theme from the movie *Best Friends* starring **Burt Reynolds** and Goldie Hawn			
12/10/83+	19	18		5 **Yah Mo B There** ... *Come A Da Machine (To Take A My Place)* (Ingram)	$3		Qwest 29394
				JAMES INGRAM (with Michael McDonald)			
4/7/84	58	10		6 **There's No Easy Way** ... *Come A Da Machine (To Take A My Place)*	$3	■	Qwest 29316
9/15/84	15	19		7 **What About Me?** ... AC[2] A:14 / S:16 *The Rest Of Last Night* (Rogers)	$3	■	RCA 13899
				KENNY ROGERS with KIM CARNES and JAMES INGRAM			
12/20/86+	2[1]	22	●	8 **Somewhere Out There** ... S:❶[2] / A:7 *(instrumental)*	$3	■	MCA 52973
				LINDA RONSTADT AND JAMES INGRAM			
				from the animated movie *An American Tail*			
3/10/90	31	13	●	9 **The Secret Garden (Sweet Seduction Suite)** ... RB[1] S:20 *(instrumental)*	$3	▮V	Qwest 19992 ■
				QUINCY JONES/Al B. Sure!/James Ingram/El DeBarge/Barry White			
8/4/90	❶[1]	26		10 **I Don't Have The Heart** A:❶[2] / S:2 *Baby Be Mine*	$3	▮V	Warner 19911
4/11/98	66[A]	11		11 **Give Me Forever (I Do)** ...			album cut
				JOHN TESH Featuring James Ingram			
				from the Tesh album *Grand Passion* on GTSP 539804			
				INGRAM, Luther R&B/BUB/LP **'72**			
				Born on 11/30/44 in Jackson, Tennessee. R&B singer/songwriter.			
1/10/70	55	7		1 **My Honey And Me** ... *I Can't Stop*	$10		KoKo 2104
5/23/70	45	9		2 **Ain't That Loving You (For More Reasons Than One)** .. *Home Don't Seem Like Home*	$10		KoKo 2105
5/1/71	97	2		3 **Be Good To Me Baby** ... *Since You Don't Want Me*	$8		KoKo 2107
4/8/72	93	3		4 **You Were Made For Me** ... *Missing You* (#108)	$8		KoKo 2110
				all of above from the album *I've Been Here All The Time*			
6/3/72	3	16		5 **(If Loving You Is Wrong) I Don't Want To Be Right** RB[4] *Puttin' Game Down*	$8		KoKo 2111
12/2/72+	40	11		6 **I'll Be Your Shelter (In Time Of Storm)** ... *I Can't Stop*	$8		KoKo 2113
4/7/73	64	5		7 **Always** ... *Help Me Love*	$8		KoKo 2115
				INMAN, Autry C&W **'68**			
				Born Robert Autry Inman on 1/6/29 in Florence, Alabama. Died on 9/6/88 (age 59). Country singer/songwriter.			
11/16/68	48	7		**Ballad Of Two Brothers** ... *Don't Call Me (I'll Call You)*	$8		Epic 10389
				patriotic-styled narrative, featuring strains of "Battle Hymn Of The Republic"			
				INMATES, The BUB/LP **'80**			
				Rock group from England: Bill Hurley (vocals), Peter "Gunn" Staines and Tony Oliver (guitars), Ben Donnelly (bass) and Jim Russell (drums).			
12/8/79+	51	10		**Dirty Water** ... *I Can't Sleep*	$5		Polydor 2032
				INNER CIRCLE LP **'93**			
				Reggae group formed in Kingston, Jamaica: Calton Coffie (vocals), Touter Harvey, Lancelot Hall, brothers Ian and Roger Lewis, and Lester Adderly (left by mid-1994).			
5/1/93	8	20	●	1 **Bad Boys** S:6 / A:15 *(dub mix)*	$3	▮V	Big Beat 98426
				theme from the Fox TV series *Cops*			
8/7/93	16	25		2 **Sweat (A La La La La Long)** ... S:16 / A:17 *(edit)*	$3	▮V	Big Beat 98429
				"45" issued for above 2 on Big Beat 98426			
12/18/93	98	2		3 **Rock With You** ... *(remix edit)*	$3	▮	Big Beat 98351
9/3/94	84	5		4 **Games People Play** ... *(dancehall version)*	$3	▮	Big Beat 98235
8/1/98	92	6		5 **Not About Romance** ... *(dance mix)*	$3	▮	SoundBwoy 56200
				originally released on SoundBwoy 119 in 1997			
				INNER CITY R&B/LP **'89**			
				Techno-funk-dance group led by producer/songwriter/mixer Kevin Saunderson (from Detroit, Michigan) and female vocalist Paris Grey (from Glencove, Illinois).			
3/4/89	73	11		1 **Good Life** ... *(7" mix)*	$3	■	Virgin 99236
3/3/90	76	6		2 **Whatcha Gonna Do With My Lovin'** ... *Set Your Body Free*	$3	▮V	Virgin 98999
				INNERLUDE **'98**			
				Male R&B vocal trio from San Jose, California: brothers James and Eric Visperas, with Cyrus Mallare.			
5/16/98	95	2		**I Don't Wanna Go On** ... *(instrumental)*	$6	★	Straight Hits 001
				INNOCENCE, The — see TRADE WINDS, The			
				INNOCENTS, The — see YOUNG, Kathy			
				INNOSENSE **'00**			
				Female teen pop vocal group: Mandy Ashford, Nikki DeLoach, Danay Ferrer, Veronica Finn and Jenny Morris.			
7/15/00	20[S]	18		**Say No More** ... *You Can't Touch Me Now*	$4	★V	RCA 60257
				"45": RCA 60257; B-side: "This Is It"			
				INOJ **'98**			
				Born Ayanna Porter on 11/27/76 in Madison, Wisconsin. Female R&B singer. Given pet name of Joni, spelled backwards is Inoj. Pronounced: i-no-jay.			
2/7/98	25	20		1 **Love You Down** ... A:26 / S:30 *Freak It* (Lathun)	$3	▮	So So Def 78801
8/22/98	6	16	●	2 **Time After Time** ... S:11 / A:29 *(instrumental) / (3 album snippets)*	$4	★	So So Def 79016
6/26/99	45[S]	12		3 **Ring My Bell** ... *(3 album snippets)*	$4	★	So So Def 79154

DEBUT	PEAK	WKS	Gold	A-side (Chart Hit)...B-side	$	Sym	Label & Number

INSANE CLOWN POSSE — BUB/LP '99

White rap duo from Detroit, Michigan Joe "Violent J" Bruce and Joe "Shaggy 2 Dope" Utsler. Both wear clown makeup.

DEBUT	PEAK	WKS	Gold	A-side (Chart Hit)...B-side	$	Sym	Label & Number
12/27/97	67	5		1 **Santa's A Fat Bitch** ...S:40 *Red Christmas* [X-N]	$6	▮	Island 572192
5/8/99	29^S	10		2 **Mad Professor** ...BUB:118 *(3 album snippets)* [N]	$4	★	Island 572604

INSPEKTAH DECK — see GZA/GENIUS

INSTANT FUNK — R&B/BUB/LP '79

Dance-funk group from Philadelphia, Pennsylvania: James Carmichael (vocals), brothers Kim (guitar) and Scotty (drums) Miller, George Bell (guitar), Dennis Richardson (keyboards), Charles Williams (percussion), Larry Davis (trumpet), Johnny Onderline (sax) and Raymond Earl (bass). Former backup band for **Bunny Sigler**.

DEBUT	PEAK	WKS	Gold	A-side (Chart Hit)...B-side	$	Sym	Label & Number
2/17/79	20	18	●	**I Got My Mind Made Up (You Can Get It Girl)** ...RB^3 *Wide World Of Sports*	$5		Salsoul 2078

INTONATION featuring JOEE — '95

Pop group fronted by Toronto, Ontario, Canada, native Joee. In 1988, Joee appeared on TV's *Star Search*.

DEBUT	PEAK	WKS	Gold	A-side (Chart Hit)...B-side	$	Sym	Label & Number
7/8/95	86	7		**Died In Your Arms** ...*(pop radio mix)*	$5	▮	Ti Amo/Metropolitan 907

INTRIGUES, The — R&B '69

R&B vocal group from Philadelphia, Pennsylvania: Alfred Brown, Ronald Hamilton, James Harris and James Lee.

DEBUT	PEAK	WKS	Gold	A-side (Chart Hit)...B-side	$	Sym	Label & Number
8/2/69	31	14		1 **In A Moment**...*Scotchman Rock*	$12		Yew 1001
12/20/69+	86	3		2 **I'm Gonna Love You** ...*I Gotta Find Out For Myself*	$10		Yew 1002
6/19/71	100	1		3 **The Language Of Love** ...*I Got Love*	$10		Yew 1012

INTRO — R&B/BUB/LP '93

R&B vocal trio from New York: Kenny Greene, Clinton Wike and Jeff Sanders. Greene wrote **Mary J. Blige**'s "Reminisce" and **Father MC**'s "Close To You" (which featured Intro). Intro stands for Innovative New Talent Reaching Out.

DEBUT	PEAK	WKS	Gold	A-side (Chart Hit)...B-side	$	Sym	Label & Number
9/4/93	33	20		1 **Come Inside** ...S:21 / A:38 *(remix)* Sebrina Morrison (female voice)	$3	▮	Atlantic 87317
3/19/94	72^S	2		2 **Ribbon In The Sky** ...BUB:105 *(album version)*	$3	▮	Atlantic 87269
11/25/95	90	3		3 **Funny How Time Flies** ...*(instrumental)*	$3	▮	Atlantic 87093

INTRUDERS — '59

Instrumental rock and roll trio from Hammonton, New Jersey: guitarists/brothers George and Augie Mitchell, with drummer Joe Rebardo.

DEBUT	PEAK	WKS	Gold	A-side (Chart Hit)...B-side	$	Sym	Label & Number
3/23/59	73	3		**Fried Eggs** ...*Jefferie's Rock* [I]	$30		Fame 101

★600★ INTRUDERS, The — R&B/BUB/LP '68

R&B vocal group from Philadelphia, Pennsylvania: Sam "Little Sonny" Brown, Eugene "Bird" Daughtry (born on 10/29/39; died on 12/25/94, age 55), Phil Terry (born on 11/1/43) and Robert "Big Sonny" Edwards (born on 2/22/42). First recorded for Gowen in 1961.

1)Cowboys To Girls 2)(Love Is Like A) Baseball Game 3)I'll Always Love My Mama

DEBUT	PEAK	WKS	Gold	A-side (Chart Hit)...B-side	$	Sym	Label & Number
7/16/66	78	6		1 **(We'll Be) United** ...*Up And Down The Ladder*	$10		Gamble 201
4/29/67	48	9		2 **Together**...*Up And Down The Ladder*	$10		Gamble 205
9/16/67	70	5		3 **Baby I'm Lonely** /			
12/2/67	82	3		4 **A Love That's Real**...	$10		Gamble 209
3/23/68	6	14	●	5 **Cowboys To Girls** RB^1 *Turn The Hands Of Time*	$10		Gamble 214
7/6/68	26	9		6 **(Love Is Like A) Baseball Game** ...*Friends No More*	$10		Gamble 217
11/9/68	54	7		7 **Slow Drag** ...*So Glad I'm Yours*	$10		Gamble 221
8/30/69	47	9		8 **Sad Girl**...*Let's Go Downtown*	$10		Gamble 235
6/20/70	45	8		9 **When We Get Married**...*(Love Doctor) Doctor, Doctor*	$10		Gamble 4004
11/14/70	85	4		10 **This Is My Love Song**...*Let Me In Your Mind*	$10		Gamble 4007
3/20/71	88	4		11 **I'm Girl Scoutin'** ...*Wonder What Kind Of Bag She's In*	$10		Gamble 4009
10/30/71	92	4		12 **I Bet He Don't Love You (Like I Love You)** ...*Do You Remember Yesterday*	$10		Gamble 4016
6/2/73	36	12		13 **I'll Always Love My Mama (Part I)** ...*(Part II)*	$10		Gamble 2506
10/27/73	60	13		14 **I Wanna Know Your Name** ...*Hang On In There* all of above written (except #8 & 9) and produced by Kenny Gamble and Leon Huff	$10		Gamble 2508

INVISIBLE MAN'S BAND, The — see FIVE STAIRSTEPS

★211★ INXS — ROK/BUB/LP '88

Rock group from Sydney, Australia: Michael Hutchence (vocals; born on 1/22/60), Kirk Pengilly (guitar, saxophone; born on 7/4/58), Garry Beers (bass, born on 6/22/57) and brothers Tim (guitar; born on 8/16/57), Andy (keyboards, guitar; born on 3/27/59) and Jon (drums; born on 8/10/61) Farriss. Hutchence starred in the movies *Dogs In Space* and *Frankenstein Unbound*; formed the group Max Q. Jon Farriss was married to actress Leslie Bega (TV's *Head Of The Class*) from 1992-97. Hutchence committed suicide on 11/22/97 (age 37).

1)Need You Tonight 2)Devil Inside 3)New Sensation

DEBUT	PEAK	WKS	Gold	A-side (Chart Hit)...B-side	$	Sym	Label & Number
3/26/83	30	14		1 **The One Thing**...*Phantim Of The Opera*	$5	■	Atco 99905
7/16/83	80	4		2 **Don't Change**...*Long In Tooth*	$5	■	Atco 99874
4/28/84	58	7		3 **Original Sin** ...*Stay Young* **Daryl Hall** (backing vocal)	$5	■	Atco 99766
7/21/84	77	7		4 **I Send A Message** ...*Mechanical*	$5	■	Atco 99731
11/16/85	81	6		5 **This Time**...*I'm Over You*	$4	■	Atlantic 89497
1/18/86	5	20		6 **What You Need**...A:3 / S:7 *Sweet As Sin*	$4	■	Atlantic 89460
5/10/86	54	9		7 **Listen Like Thieves** ...*Begotten*	$4	■	Atlantic 89429
6/20/87	47	13		8 **Good Times** ...*Laying Down The Law* **INXS AND JIMMY BARNES** from the movie *The Lost Boys* starring Kiefer Sutherland	$3	■	Atlantic 89237
10/24/87+	❶^1	25		9 **Need You Tonight** S:❶^1 / A:❶^1 *I'm Coming (Home)*	$3	■	Atlantic 89188
2/13/88	2^2	17		10 **Devil Inside**...S:2 / A:2 *On The Rocks*	$3	■	Atlantic 89144
5/14/88	3	17		11 **New Sensation**...S:2 / A:4 *Guns In The Sky*	$3	■	Atlantic 89080
8/13/88	7	23		12 **Never Tear Us Apart**...A:6 / S:8 *Different World* above 4 from the album *Kick*	$3	■	Atlantic 89038
9/8/90	9	13	●	13 **Suicide Blonde** ...AR^4 / MR^1 A:9 / S:12 *Everybody Wants U Tonight*	$3	▮^{V}	Atlantic 87860
11/24/90+	8	20		14 **Disappear**...A:9 / S:11 *Middle Beast*	$3	▮^{V}	Atlantic 87784

DEBUT	PEAK	WKS	Gold	A-side (Chart Hit)...B-side	$	Sym	Label & Number
				INXS — Cont'd			
4/6/91	**46**	10		15 **Bitter Tears** ...A:39 *The Other Side*	$3	▮	Atlantic 87760
				#5-7 & 9-15: produced by Chris Thomas			
8/22/92	**28**	15		16 **Not Enough Time**...A:34 / S:52 *Deepest Red*	$3	▮	Atlantic 87437
2/20/93	**46**	12		17 **Beautiful Girl** ...A:44 *Strange Desire*	$3	▮	Atlantic 87383
3/29/97	**27**[A]	11		18 **Elegantly Wasted**...			album cut
				from the album *Elegantly Wasted* on Mercury 534531			
				IRBY, Joyce "Fenderella" — see KLYMAXX			
				IRIS, Donnie ROK/LP **'82**			
				Born Dominic Ierace on 2/28/47 in Beaver Falls, Pennsylvania. Rock singer/songwriter/guitarist. Former member of **The Jaggerz**. Toured briefly with **Wild Cherry**.			
12/13/80+	**29**	18		1 **Ah! Leah!**...*Joking*	$5		MCA/Carousel 51025
				originally issued on Midwest National 6006 in 1980			
10/31/81	**80**	6		2 **Sweet Merilee** ...*Back On The Streets*	$4		MCA/Carousel 51198
12/19/81+	**37**	14		3 **Love Is Like A Rock** ...*Agnes*	$4		MCA/Carousel 51223
3/27/82	**25**	14		4 **My Girl** *The Last To Know*	$4		MCA/Carousel 52031
10/23/82	**57**	6		5 **Tough World** ...*You're Gonna Miss Me*	$4	■	MCA/Carousel 52127
7/2/83	**64**	7		6 **Do You Compute?**...*I Belong*	$4	■	MCA/Carousel 52230
3/23/85	**91**	2		7 **Injured In The Game Of Love** ...*I Want You Back*	$3	■	HME 04734
				IRISH ROVERS, The AC/BUB/C&W/LP **'68**			
				Irish-born folk group formed in Calgary, Alberta, Canada: brothers Will (vocals, drums) and George (guitar) Millar, their cousin Joe Millar (bass), Jimmy Ferguson (vocals) and Wilcil McDowell (accordian). Ferguson died in October 1997 (age 57).			
3/23/68	**7**	12		1 **The Unicorn**...*Black Velvet Band*	$8		Decca 32254
6/22/68	**75**	7		2 **(The Puppet Song) Whiskey On A Sunday** ...*The Orange And The Green*	$8		Decca 32333
9/14/68	**91**	5		3 **The Biplane, Ever More** ...*Liverpool Lou*	$8		Decca 32371
2/21/81	**37**	17		4 **Wasn't That A Party** ...*Matchstalk Men And Matchstalk Cats And Dogs*	$5		Epic 51007
				THE ROVERS			
				IRON BUTTERFLY BUB/LP **'68**			
				Hard-rock group from San Diego, California: Doug Ingle (vocals, keyboards), Erik Braunn (guitar), Lee Dorman (bass) and Ron Bushy (drums). Braunn left in late 1969; replaced by **Mike Pinera** (leader of **Blues Image**) and Larry Reinhardt. Split in mid-1971. Braunn and Bushy regrouped in early 1975 with Phil Kramer (bass) and Howard Reitzes (keyboards). Kramer, who later earned a physics degree and became a multimedia executive, mysteriously disappeared on 2/12/95; his remains were found at the bottom of a Malibu canyon on 5/29/99. Braunn died of heart failure on 7/25/2003 (age 52).			
8/24/68	**30**	12		1 **In-A-Gadda-Da-Vida** *Iron Butterfly Theme*	$8		Atco 6606
				7" version edited down from original 17-minute album cut; also see re-entry at #3 below			
2/22/69	**75**	5		2 **Soul Experience**...*In The Crowds*	$8		Atco 6647
5/17/69	**68**	5		3 **In-A-Gadda-Da-Vida**...*Iron Butterfly Theme* [R]	$8		Atco 6606
7/12/69	**96**	2		4 **In The Time Of Our Lives** ...*It Must Be Love*	$8		Atco 6676
10/24/70	**66**	6		5 **Easy Rider (Let The Wind Pay The Way)**...*Soldier In Our Town*	$8		Atco 6782
				IRONHORSE LP **'79**			
				Rock group: Randy Bachman (vocals, guitar; **The Guess Who**, **Bachman-Turner Overdrive**), Tom Sparks (guitar), John Pierce (bass) and Mike Baird (drums).			
3/17/79	**36**	10		1 **Sweet Lui-Louise** ...*Watch Me Fly*	$5		Scotti Brothers 406
4/26/80	**89**	6		2 **What's Your Hurry Darlin'** ...*Try A Little Harder*	$5		Scotti Brothers 512
				IRWIN, Big Dee BUB **'63**			
				Born Difosco Erwin on 8/4/39 in Harlem, New York. Died of heart failure on 8/27/95 (age 56). R&B singer. Former lead singer of **The Pastels**.			
5/25/63	**38**	10		**Swinging On A Star**...*Another Night With The Boys* (Irwin)	$25		Dimension 1010
				BIG DEE IRWIN (with Little Eva)			
				#1 hit for **Bing Crosby** in 1944			
				IRWIN, Russ **'91**			
				Born in 1968 in Huntington Hills, Long Island, New York. Pop-rock singer/songwriter.			
9/14/91	**28**	13		**My Heart Belongs To You**...S:74 *That's What Love Should Be*	$3	▮	SBK 07363
				ISAAK, Chris BUB/ROK/AC/LP **'91**			
				Born on 6/26/56 in Stockton, California. Rockabilly singer/songwriter/guitarist. Attended college in Japan. Acted in several movies; starred in own TV show.			
12/1/90+	**6**	24	●	1 **Wicked Game**...S:3 / A:17 *(instrumental)*	$4	▮[V]	Reprise 19704
				featured in the movie *Wild at Heart* starring Laura Dern and Nicolas Cage			
6/10/95	**45**	20		2 **Somebody's Crying** ...A:42 *Changed Your Mind*	$4	▮[V]	Reprise 17872
				ISLANDERS, The **'59**			
				Pop instrumental duo of **Randy Starr** (guitar) and Frank Metis (accordion).			
9/28/59	**15**	13		**The Enchanted Sea** ...*Pollyanna* [I]	$15		Mayflower 16
				ISLE OF MAN LP **'86**			
				Multi-ethnic pop group (members are from France, Nicaragua, Italy and U.S.): Robere Parlez (vocals), Raun (guitar), Jamie Roberto (bass) and Ronnie Lee Sage (drums).			
8/9/86	**90**	4		**Am I Forgiven** ...*Afraid Of Heights*	$4	■	Pasha 05900

DEBUT	PEAK	WKS	Gold	A-side (Chart Hit)...B-side	$	Sym	Label & Number

ISLEY BROTHERS, The ★69★ R&B/BUB/ROK/LP '69

R&B vocal trio of brothers from Cincinnati, Ohio: O'Kelly, Ronald and Rudolph Isley. Moved to New York in 1957 and first recorded for Teenage Records. Trio added their younger brothers Ernie (guitar, drums) and Marvin (bass, percussion) Isley and brother-in-law Chris Jasper (keyboards) in September 1969. Formed own T-Neck label the same year. Charted 80 R&B hits, 1962-02. Ernie, Marvin and Chris began recording as the trio **Isley, Jasper, Isley** in 1984. O'Kelly died of a heart attack on 3/31/86 (age 48); Ronald and Rudolph continued on as The Isley Brothers through 1990. Ronald, Ernie and Marvin reunited as The Isley Brothers in 1991. Ronald became the featured member beginning in 1989; he married **Angela Winbush** on 6/26/93. Group inducted into the Rock and Roll Hall of Fame in 1992.

1)It's Your Thing 2)Fight The Power 3)That Lady 4)This Old Heart Of Mine (Is Weak For You) 5)Twist And Shout

DEBUT	PEAK	WKS	Gold	A-side (Chart Hit)...B-side	$	Sym	Label & Number
9/21/59	47	9		1 **Shout - Part 1** ... *Part 2*	$30		RCA Victor 47-7588
3/24/62	94	3		2 **Shout - Part 1** ... *Part 2* [R]	$25		RCA Victor 447-0589
				above 2 are the same version			
6/2/62	17	16		3 **Twist And Shout** ... *Spanish Twist* [I]	$20		Wand 124
				song first recorded by the Top Notes in 1961 on Atlantic 2115 ($30)			
9/22/62	54	9		4 **Twistin' With Linda** ... *You Better Come Home*	$20		Wand 127
2/19/66	12	12		5 **This Old Heart Of Mine (Is Weak For You)** ... *There's No Love Left*	$15		Tamla 54128
				also see #39 below			
5/28/66	66	4		6 **Take Some Time Out For Love** ... *Who Could Ever Doubt My Love*	$15		Tamla 54133
7/16/66	61	7		7 **I Guess I'll Always Love You** ... *I Hear A Symphony*	$15		Tamla 54135
5/6/67	93	2		8 **Got To Have You Back** ... *Just Ain't Enough Love*	$15		Tamla 54146
3/15/69	2[1]	14	●	9 **It's Your Thing** RB[4] *Don't Give It Away*	$7		T-Neck 901
5/31/69	23	10		10 **I Turned You On** ... *I Know Who You Been Socking It To*	$7		T-Neck 902
8/30/69	79	4		11 **Black Berries - Pt 1** ... *Pt 2*	$7		T-Neck 906
9/27/69	83	5		12 **Was It Good To You** ... *I Got To Get Myself Together*	$7		T-Neck 908
2/14/70	75	5		13 **Keep On Doin'** ... *Save Me*	$7		T-Neck 914
7/25/70	75	2		14 **Girls Will Be Girls, Boys Will Be Boys** ... *Get Down Off Of The Train*	$7		T-Neck 921
10/17/70	89	3		15 **Get Into Something** ... *Get Into Something Part II*	$7		T-Neck 924
1/23/71	72	5		16 **Freedom** ... *I Need You So*	$7		T-Neck 927
6/19/71	18	11		17 **Love The One You're With** ... *He's Got Your Love*	$7		T-Neck 930
10/2/71	49	6		18 **Spill The Wine** ... *Take Inventory*	$7		T-Neck 932
12/4/71+	71	5		19 **Lay Lady Lay** ... *Vacuum Cleaner*	$7		T-Neck 933
4/1/72	54	9		20 **Lay-Away** ... *Feel Like The World*	$7		T-Neck 934
7/1/72	24	15		21 **Pop That Thang** ... *I Got To Find Me One*	$7		T-Neck 935
10/28/72	51	8		22 **Work To Do** ... *Beautiful*	$7		T-Neck 936
7/14/73	6	20	●	23 **That Lady (Part 1)** ... *(Part 2)*	$6		T-Neck 2251
				originally recorded and released by The Isley Brothers as "Who's That Lady" in 1964 on United Artists 714			
12/29/73+	55	11		24 **What It Comes Down To** ... *The Highways Of My Life*	$6		T-Neck 2252
3/23/74	60	7		25 **Summer Breeze (Part 1)** ... *(Part 2)*	$6		T-Neck 2253
7/27/74	52	16		26 **Live It Up Part 1** ... *Part 2*	$6		T-Neck 2254
1/4/75	73	5		27 **Midnight Sky (Part 1)** ... *(Part 2)*	$6		T-Neck 2255
6/21/75	4	18	●	28 **Fight The Power Part 1** ... RB[3] *Part 2*	$5		T-Neck 2256
11/15/75	22	12		29 **For The Love Of You (Part 1&2)** ... *You Walk Your Way*	$5		T-Neck 2259
5/29/76	47	7		30 **Who Loves You Better - Part 1** ... *Part 2*	$5		T-Neck 2260
8/21/76	63	11		31 **Harvest For The World** ... *(instrumental)*	$5		T-Neck 2261
5/7/77	63	7		32 **The Pride (Part I)** ... RB[1] *(Part II)*	$5		T-Neck 2262
6/25/77	40	8		33 **Livin' In The Life** ... *Go For Your Guns*	$5		T-Neck 2264
10/20/79	90	2		34 **It's A Disco Night (Rock Don't Stop)** ... *Ain't Givin' Up No Love*	$5		T-Neck 2287
4/19/80	39	9		35 **Don't Say Goodnight (It's Time For Love) (Parts 1 & 2)** ... RB[4] *(instrumental)*	$5		T-Neck 2290
4/18/81	58	7		36 **Hurry Up And Wait** ... *(instrumental)*	$5		T-Neck 02033
2/16/85	63	7		37 **Kiss And Tell** ... *(instrumental)*	$4		CBS Associated 04741
12/7/85+	51	14		38 **Caravan Of Love** ... RB[3] *I Can't Get Over Losin' You*	$4		CBS Associated 05611
				ISLEY, JASPER, ISLEY (above 2)			
3/24/90	10	16		39 **This Old Heart Of Mine (1989 Version)** ... AC[5] A:7 / S:15 *You're In My Heart*	$3	▮[V]	Warner 19983
				ROD STEWART (with Ronald Isley)			
				also see #5 above			
3/2/96	4	20	▲	40 **Down Low (Nobody Has To Know)** ... RB[7] S:2 / A:32 *(3 mixes)*	$3	▮[V]	Jive 42373
				R. KELLY (featuring Ronald Isley and Ernie Isley)			
5/18/96	93	5		41 **Let's Lay Together** ... S:58 *(instrumental)*	$4	▮	Island 854586
				from the movie *Don't Be A Menace* starring Marlon Wayans; written and produced by **R. Kelly**			
9/28/96	47	18		42 **Floatin' On Your Love** ... S:30 *(3 remixes w/***Lil' Kim** *&* **112***)*	$4	▮	Island 854738
				THE ISLEY BROTHERS featuring Ronald Isley and Angela Winbush			
1/11/97	55	11		43 **Tears** ... S:25 *(album version)*	$4	▮	Island 854862
				THE ISLEY BROTHERS featuring Ronald Isley			
6/14/97	68	11		44 **Come With Me** ... S:45 *Just A Touch*	$4	▮	Elektra 64175
				KEITH SWEAT Featuring Ronald Isley			
6/21/97	35	14		45 **Smokin' Me Out** ... S:21 *We Brings Heat*	$4	▮	Def Jam 571024
				WARREN G Featuring Ronald Isley			
				contains an interpolation of "Coolin' Me Out" by **The Isley Brothers**			
7/14/01	19	19		46 **Contagious** ... A:16			album cut
				THE ISLEY BROTHERS Featuring RONALD ISLEY aka MR. BIGGS			
				written and produced by **R. Kelly**; additional vocals by **Chanté Moore**; from the album *Eternal* on DreamWorks 50291			

ISYSS LP '02

Female R&B vocal group from Los Angeles, California: Lamyia Good, Letecia Harrison, Ardena Clark and Quierra Davis-Martin.

DEBUT	PEAK	WKS	Gold	A-side (Chart Hit)...B-side	$	Sym	Label & Number
6/8/02	98	4		1 **Day + Night** ... S:3 *(4 album snippets)*	$4	★	Arista 15132
				Jadakiss (rap)			
10/26/02	71	12		2 **Single For The Rest Of My Life** ... A:70 *(instrumental)*	$6	T	Arista 15166

ITALIAN ASPHALT & PAVEMENT COMPANY — see DUPREES, The

DEBUT	PEAK	WKS	Gold	A-side (Chart Hit)	B-side	$	Sym	Label & Number

I TO I — '94

Dance trio from Amsterdam, Netherlands: producers Edward Smidt and Ewart van Horst with vocalist Susan (toured as vocalist with **Candy Dulfer**).

DEBUT	PEAK	WKS	Gold	A-side (Chart Hit)	B-side	$	Sym	Label & Number
4/16/94	81	8		**The Right Time** A:60 from the movie *Four Weddings And A Funeral* starring Andie MacDowell	*(radio version)*	$3	▮	Next Plateau 127010

IVAN — see HOLLY, Buddy / VEE, Bobby

IVES, Burl — MEM/BUB/POP/AC/C&W/LP '62

Born on 6/14/09 in Huntington Township, Illinois. Died on 4/14/95 (age 85). Actor/author/folk singer. Played semi-pro football. Began Broadway career in the late 1930s. Worked in *This Is The Army* service show during World War II. Own CBS radio show *The Wayfaring Stranger* in 1944. Appeared in many movies, including *Our Man In Havana, East Of Eden, Cat On A Hot Tin Roof* and *The Big Country.* Narrated the animated TV classic *Rudolph The Red-Nosed Reindeer.* Worked on the TV series *The Bold Ones* in the early 1970s.

1)A Little Bitty Tear 2)Funny Way Of Laughin' 3)Call Me Mr. In-Between

DEBUT	PEAK	WKS	Gold	A-side (Chart Hit)	B-side	$	Sym	Label & Number
3/2/57	84	5		1 **Marianne** T:84 **BURL IVES With The Trinidaddies** Tony Mottola (orch.); adapted from a Bahamian folk song	*Pretty Girl*	$15		Decca 30217
12/18/61+	9	14		2 **A Little Bitty Tear** AC[1]	*Shanghied*	$10		Decca 31330
4/7/62	10	11		3 **Funny Way Of Laughin'**	*Mother Wouldn't Do That*	$10		Decca 31371
7/21/62	19	9		4 **Call Me Mr. In-Between**	*What You Gonna Do, Leroy?*	$10		Decca 31405
11/3/62	39	7		5 **Mary Ann Regrets**	*How Do You Fall Out Of Love*	$10		Decca 31433
1/26/63	91	2		6 **The Same Old Hurt** #2, 3 & 6: written by country singer/songwriter Hank Cochran	*Curry Road*	$8		Decca 31453
8/3/63	67	5		7 **This Is All I Ask** [S] written in 1958 by band leader **Gordon Jenkins**	*There Goes Another Pal Of Mine*	$8		Decca 31518
12/28/63+	66	6		8 **True Love Goes On And On** **Gordon Jenkins** (orch. and chorus); same version released by Ives in 1954 on Decca 29088	*I Wonder What's Become Of Sally*	$8		Decca 31571
9/12/64	60	6		9 **Pearly Shells (Popo O Ewa)** song charted earlier in 1964 with different lyrics as "The First Night Of The Full Moon" by **Jack Jones**	*What Little Tears Are Made Of*	$8		Decca 31659
12/19/64	13[X]	3		10 **A Holly Jolly Christmas** [X] X: 13/'64; 29/'68; featured in the animated TV show *Rudolph The Red-Nosed Reindeer*	*Snow For Johnny*	$10	■	Decca 31695

IVEYS, The — see BADFINGER

IVORY — '97

Born in Brooklyn, New York. Male R&B-funk singer.

DEBUT	PEAK	WKS	Gold	A-side (Chart Hit)	B-side	$	Sym	Label & Number
8/16/97	88	5		**Relax & Party**	*(instrumental)*	$4	▮	Loud/RCA 64860

IVY LEAGUE, The — '65

British songwriting team of John Carter and Ken Lewis. Wrote "Little Bit O' Soul" and "Can't You Hear My Heartbeat."

DEBUT	PEAK	WKS	Gold	A-side (Chart Hit)	B-side	$	Sym	Label & Number
9/18/65	83	5		**Tossing & Turning**	*Graduation Day*	$15	■	Cameo 377

IVY THREE, The — '60

Pop vocal trio formed in Long Island, New York: Charles Koppelman (lead), Art Berkowitz and Don Rubin. Koppelman and Rubin did production work for **The Turtles** and **The Lovin' Spoonful**. Label executive Koppelman founded SBK Records in 1989, with Rubin as senior vice president. Koppelman became CEO of EMI Records Group, North America in 1991.

DEBUT	PEAK	WKS	Gold	A-side (Chart Hit)	B-side	$	Sym	Label & Number
8/8/60	8	10		**Yogi** [N] inspired by the Yogi Bear character from TV's animated *Huckleberry Hound* show	*Was Judy There*	$20		Shell 720

J

JACKS, Susan & Terry — see POPPY FAMILY, The

JACKS, The — see CADETS, The

JACKSON, Alan — C&W/BUB/LP '02

★366★

Born on 10/17/58 in Newnan, Georgia. Country singer/songwriter/guitarist. Former car salesman and construction worker. Formed own band, Dixie Steel. Signed to **Glen Campbell**'s publishing company in 1985. Charted 63 Country hits (20 #1s), 1989-02.

1)Where Were You (When The World Stopped Turning) 2)Drive (For Daddy Gene) 3)Where I Come From

DEBUT	PEAK	WKS	Gold	A-side (Chart Hit)	B-side	$	Sym	Label & Number
7/10/93	46	20	●	1 **Chattahoochee** CW[4] S:19 "45": Arista 12560; B-side: "I Don't Need The Booze (To Get A Buzz On)"	*(club mix)*	$4	▮V	Arista 12573
8/6/94	60[S]	3		2 **Summertime Blues** CW[3] BUB:104	*Hole In The Wall*	$4	▮V	Arista 12697
10/15/94	54[S]	8		3 **Livin' On Love** CW[3] BUB:101	*Let's Get Back To Me And You*	$4	▮V	Arista 12745
6/29/96	66	10		4 **Redneck Games** S:34 [L-N] **JEFF FOXWORTHY with ALAN JACKSON**	*NASA & Alabama & Fishing Shows* (Foxworthy)	$4	▮V	Warner 17648
11/16/96+	58	10		5 **Little Bitty** CW[3] S:36 written by **Tom T. Hall**	*Must've Had A Ball*	$4	▮V	Arista 13048
12/5/98+	43	12		6 **Right On The Money** CW[1] A:32 "45": Arista 13136; B-side: "A Woman's Love"			V	album cut
3/13/99	43	13		7 **Gone Crazy** A:29 "45": Arista 13155; B-side: "Amarillo"			V	album cut
7/10/99	39	17		8 **Little Man** A:29 "45": Arista 13145; B-side: "Hurtin' Comes Easy"; above 3 from the album *High Mileage* on Arista 18864			V	album cut
11/13/99+	43	17		9 **Pop A Top** A:36 #3 Country hit for **Jim Ed Brown** in 1967; "45": Arista 13183; B-side: "Revenooer Man"			V	album cut
6/24/00	37	20		10 **It Must Be Love** CW[1] A:28 #1 Country hit for **Don Williams** in 1979; above 2 from the album *Under The Influence* on Arista 18892				album cut
11/4/00	45	15		11 **www.memory** A:39 "45": Arista 69020; B-side: "It's Alright To Be A Redneck" (C&W #53/'01)			V	album cut
4/28/01	52	17		12 **When Somebody Loves You** A:43 "45": Arista 69049; B-side: "Meat And Potato Man"			V	album cut
8/25/01	34	20		13 **Where I Come From** CW[3] A:29 "45": Arista 69102; B-side: "A Love Like That"; above 3 from the album *When Somebody Loves You* on Arista 69335			V	album cut

DEBUT	PEAK	WKS	Gold	A-side (Chart Hit)...B-side	$	Sym	Label & Number
				JACKSON, Alan — Cont'd			
11/24/01+	**28**	20		14 **Where Were You (When The World Stopped Turning)** CW[5] A:26		V	album cut
				written by Jackson after the 9/11 attacks			
3/16/02	**28**	20		15 **Drive (For Daddy Gene)**...CW[4] A:27		V	album cut
				"45" issued for above 2 on Arista 69129			
8/24/02	**35**	19		16 **Work In Progress**...A:32			album cut
				above 3 from the album *Drive* on Arista 67039			
				JACKSON, Bull Moose R&B/POP '48			
				Born Benjamin Jackson on 4/22/19 in Cleveland, Ohio. Died of cancer on 7/31/89 (age 70). R&B singer/saxophonist. Joined Lucky Millinder in 1943 as a replacement for Wynonie Harris. Own band with Millinder sidemen in 1947. One of the first major stars of R&B.			
9/11/61	**98**	2		**I Love You Yes I Do**...*Aw Shucks Baby*	$30		7 Arts 705
				new version of his 78 rpm #1 R&B hit (and #24 pop hit) in 1948 on King 4181 ($40)			
	★476★			**JACKSON, Chuck** BUB/R&B '62			
				Born on 7/22/37 in Latta, South Carolina; raised in Pittsburgh, Pennsylvania. R&B singer. Cousin of singer Ann Sexton. Left college in 1957 to work with the Raspberry Singers gospel group. With **The Dell-Vikings** from 1957-59. First recorded solo as Charles Jackson for Clock in 1959.			
				1)Any Day Now 2)I Don't Want To Cry 3)Tell Him I'm Not Home 4)Beg Me 5)If I Didn't Love You			
2/20/61	**36**	7		1 **I Don't Want To Cry**...*Just Once*	$20		Wand 106
				arranged by **Carole King**			
4/10/61	**46**	7		2 **(It Never Happens) In Real Life**...*The Same Old Story*	$20		Wand 108
4/10/61	**91**	1		3 **Mr. Pride**...*Hula Lula*	$25		Beltone 1005
8/21/61	**59**	8		4 **I Wake Up Crying**...*Everybody Needs Love*	$15		Wand 110
4/28/62	**23**	12		5 **Any Day Now (My Wild Beautiful Bird)** *The Prophet*	$15		Wand 122
9/1/62	**55**	7		6 **I Keep Forgettin'**...*Who's Gonna Pick Up The Pieces (#119)*	$15		Wand 126
11/17/62	**88**	4		7 **Getting Ready For The Heartbreak**...*In Between Tears*	$15		Wand 128
2/2/63	**42**	10		8 **Tell Him I'm Not Home**...*Lonely Am I*	$15	■	Wand 132
7/6/63	**85**	2		9 **Tears Of Joy**...*I Will Never Turn My Back On You (#110, R&B #29)*	$15		Wand 138
11/2/63	**81**	5		10 **Any Other Way**...*Big New York*	$15		Wand 141
3/28/64	**92**	3		11 **Hand It Over**...*Look Over Your Shoulder*	$15		Wand 149
5/23/64	**45**	10		12 **Beg Me**...*This Broken Heart That You Gave Me*	$15		Wand 154
10/3/64	**93**	2		13 **Somebody New**...*Stand By Me*	$15		Wand 161
11/14/64	**47**	8		14 **Since I Don't Have You**...*Hand It Over*	$15		Wand 169
4/24/65	**55**	9		15 **Something You Got**...*Baby Take Me*	$15		Wand 181
				CHUCK JACKSON & MAXINE BROWN			
4/24/65	**75**	4		16 **I Need You**...*Soul Brother's Twist*	$15		Wand 179
8/7/65	**46**	7		17 **If I Didn't Love You**...*Just A Little Bit Of Your Soul*	$15		Wand 188
8/21/65	**91**	4		18 **Can't Let You Out Of My Sight**...*Don't Go*	$15		Wand 191
10/23/65	**98**	1		19 **I Need You So**...*'Cause We're In Love*	$15		Wand 198
				written by **Ivory Joe Hunter**			
2/18/67	**91**	4		20 **Hold On I'm Coming**...*Never Had It So Good*	$15		Wand 1148
5/6/67	**91**	1		21 **Daddy's Home**...*Don't Go*	$15		Wand 1155
				CHUCK JACKSON & MAXINE BROWN (above 4)			
10/14/67	**76**	9		22 **Shame On Me**...*Candy*	$15		Wand 1166
3/9/68	**94**	1		23 **(You Can't Let The Boy Overpower) The Man In You**...*Girls, Girls, Girls*	$12		Motown 1118
				written and produced by **Smokey Robinson** (also see his **Miracles** version)			
				JACKSON, Deon BUB '66			
				Born on 1/26/46 in Ann Arbor, Michigan. R&B singer/clarinetist/drummer.			
1/22/66	**11**	14		1 **Love Makes The World Go Round**...*You Said You Loved Me*	$15		Carla 2526
4/30/66	**77**	5		2 **Love Takes A Long Time Growing**...*Hush Little Baby*	$15		Carla 2527
11/18/67	**65**	6		3 **Ooh Baby**...*All On A Sunny Day*	$15		Carla 2537
				JACKSON, Earnest '73			
				R&B singer/guitarist.			
6/2/73	**58**	6		**Love And Happiness**...*Hogwash*	$8		Stone 200
				co-written by **Al Green**			
				JACKSON, Freddie R&B/AC/LP '85			
				Born on 10/2/56 in Harlem, New York. R&B singer/songwriter. Backup singer for **Melba Moore**, **Evelyn King** and others. Member of R&B group Mystic Merlin.			
5/25/85	**18**	19		1 **Rock Me Tonight (For Old Times Sake)**...RB[6] S:18 / A:20 *(groove version)*	$3	■	Capitol 5459
9/7/85	**12**	20		2 **You Are My Lady** RB[2] S:7 / A:12 *I Wanna Say I Love You*	$3	■	Capitol 5495
12/14/85+	**25**	15		3 **He'll Never Love You (Like I Do)**...S:23 / A:28 *I Wanna Say I Love You*	$3	■	Capitol 5535
11/8/86	**41**	12		4 **Tasty Love**...RB[4] S:29 *I Wanna Say I Love You*	$3	■	Capitol 5616
2/7/87	**69**	9		5 **Have You Ever Loved Somebody**...RB[2] *Tasty Love [I]*	$3	■	Capitol 5661
6/27/87	**32**	13		6 **Jam Tonight**...RB[1] S:25 / A:38 *Have You Ever Loved Somebody (w/Najee)*	$3		Capitol 44037
7/23/88	**61**	12		7 **Nice 'N' Slow**...RB[3] *You Are My Love*	$3	■	Capitol 44171
				JACKSON, J.J. R&B/BUB '66			
				Born Jerome Louis Jackson on 4/8/41 in Brooklyn, New York. R&B singer/songwriter. Became permanent resident of England in 1969. Not to be confused with the former MTV DJ.			
10/1/66	**22**	13		1 **But It's Alright**...*Boogaloo Baby*	$12		Calla 119
12/31/66+	**83**	3		2 **I Dig Girls**...*That Ain't Right*	$10		Calla 125
5/24/69	**45**	10		3 **But It's Alright**...*Ain't Too Proud To Beg* [R]	$8		Warner 7276
				same version as #1 above			

DEBUT	PEAK	WKS	Gold	A-side (Chart Hit)..........B-side	$	Sym	Label & Number

JACKSON, Janet ★9★ R&B/BUB/LP '90

Born on 5/16/66 in Gary, Indiana. R&B singer/actress. Sister of **The Jacksons** (youngest of nine children). Regular on TV's *Good Times*, *Diff'rent Strokes* and *Fame*. Co-starred in the movies *Poetic Justice* and *Nutty Professor 2: The Klumps*. Married to James DeBarge (of **DeBarge**) from 1984-85. Secretly married to producer Rene Elizondo from 1991-2000.

1)That's The Way Love Goes 2)All For You 3)Miss You Much 4)Doesn't Really Matter 5)Escapade

DEBUT	PEAK	WKS	Gold	A-side (Chart Hit)..........B-side	$	Sym	Label & Number
12/18/82+	64	6		1 **Young Love** .... *The Magic Is Working*	$5	■	A&M 2440
2/5/83	58	9		2 **Come Give Your Love To Me**....... *Forever Yours*	$5	■	A&M 2522
2/22/86	4	21	●	3 **What Have You Done For Me Lately** ....RB[2] S:3 / A:8 *He Doesn't Know I'm Alive*	$3	■	A&M 2812
5/17/86	3	19	●	4 **Nasty** ....RB[2] S:❶[1] / A:5 *You'll Never Find (A Love Like Mine)*	$3	■	A&M 2830
8/9/86	❶[2]	19	●	5 **When I Think Of You**.......A:❶[2] / S:2 *Pretty Boy*	$3	■	A&M 2855
11/1/86+	5	18	●	6 **Control** ....RB[1] S:4 / A:4 *Fast Girls*	$3	■	A&M 2877
1/17/87	2[1]	19		7 **Let's Wait Awhile**.......RB[1] S:3 / A:4 *Pretty Boy*	$3	■	A&M 2906
4/11/87	5	19		8 **Diamonds**.......RB[2] S:5 / A:7 *African Flame*	$3	■	A&M 2929
				HERB ALPERT (with Janet Jackson)			
				Lisa Keith (backing vocal)			
5/23/87	14	18		9 **The Pleasure Principle** ....RB[1] A:13 / S:17 *Fast Girls*	$3	■	A&M 2927
				#3-7 & 9: from the album *Control*			
9/2/89	❶[4]	20	▲	10 **Miss You Much**.......RB[2] S:❶[3] / A:❶[3] *You Need Me*	$3		A&M 1445
11/11/89+	2[2]	17	●	11 **Rhythm Nation**.......RB[1] S:2 / A:2 *(instrumental)*	$3	▮V	A&M 1455
1/20/90	❶[3]	17	●	12 **Escapade** ....RB[1] A:❶[4] / S:❶[2] *(instrumental)*	$3	▮V	A&M 1490
4/7/90	4	16	●	13 **Alright**.......A:2 / S:8 *(7" remix)*	$3	▮V	A&M 1479
6/30/90	2[2]	17		14 **Come Back To Me** ....AC[3] A:❶[2] / S:7 *Vuelve A Mi (Come Back To Me)*	$3	▮V	A&M 1475
9/15/90	❶[1]	16	●	15 **Black Cat**.......S:2 / A:2 *(remix)*	$3	▮V	A&M 1477
				Vernon Reid (of **Living Colour**; lead guitar)			
11/17/90+	❶[1]	22	●	16 **Love Will Never Do (Without You)**.......A:❶[3] / S:6 *(7" version)*	$3	▮V	A&M 1538
2/16/91	5[A]	13		17 **State Of The World**			album cut
				#10-17: from the album *Janet Jackson's Rhythm Nation 1814* on A&M 3920			
5/30/92	10	20		18 **The Best Things In Life Are Free** ....RB[1] A:5 / S:16 *(3 album snippets)*	$3	▮V	Perspective 0010
				LUTHER VANDROSS and JANET JACKSON with BBD and Ralph Tresvant			
				from the movie *Mo' Money* starring Damon Wayans; "45" B-side: (edit-no rap)			
5/1/93	❶[8]	23	▲	19 **That's The Way Love Goes** A:❶[10] / S:❶[5] *(instrumental)*	$3	▮V	Virgin 12650
				samples "Papa Don't Take No Mess" by **James Brown**; "45": Virgin 17332 (red vinyl)			
6/5/93	30[A]	37		20 **Where Are You Now**			album cut
6/12/93	66[A]	1		21 **Throb**		V	album cut
				see #25 below for issuance of "45"			
7/24/93	4	27	●	22 **If** ....A:3 / S:5 *One More Chance*	$3	▮V	Virgin 12676
				samples "Someday We'll Be Together" by **Diana Ross & The Supremes**; "45": Virgin 17446			
10/23/93	❶[2]	23	▲	23 **Again** ....A:❶[4] / S:2 *(piano/vocal version)*	$3	▮V	Virgin 38404
				from the movie *Poetic Justice* starring Jackson and **2 Pac**; "45": Virgin 17582 (issued on yellow or black vinyl)			
1/29/94	10	20		24 **Because Of Love**.......A:6 / S:29 *Funky Big Band*	$3	▮V	Virgin 38422
				"45": Virgin 17807			
5/28/94	2[1]	20	●	25 **Any Time, Any Place** / RB[10] A:3 / S:5		V	
				"45" issued for #21 and above A-side on Virgin 18095			
5/28/94		20		26 **And On And On** A:38	$3	▮	Virgin 38435
				samples "Family Affair" by **Sly & The Family Stone**			
10/22/94	8	22	●	27 **You Want This** / A:9 / S:12		V	
				MC Lyte (rap); "45": Virgin 18307; B-side: "New Agenda"; #19-25 & 27: from the album *janet.* on Virgin 87825			
11/5/94		17		28 **70's Love Groove**	$3	▮	Virgin 38455
				#26 & 28: previously unreleased bonus tracks			
6/17/95	5	17	▲	29 **Scream** ....S:3 / A:12 *Childhood* (Michael Jackson - flip)	$3	▮V	Epic 78000
				MICHAEL JACKSON & JANET JACKSON			
9/16/95	3	24	●	30 **Runaway**.......S:3 / A:3 *When I Think Of You (house mix)*	$3	▮V	A&M 1194 ■
				JANET:			
9/13/97	36[A]	8		31 **Got 'Til It's Gone**		V	album cut
				JANET Featuring Q-Tip and Joni Mitchell			
				samples "Big Yellow Taxi" by **Joni Mitchell**			
12/20/97+	❶[2]	46	●	32 **Together Again** ....S:3 / A:8 *(2 versions) / Got 'Til It's Gone*	$3	▮V	Virgin 38623 ■
				"45" (33-1/3 rpm) issued for above 2 on Virgin 38623			
5/23/98	3	20	●	33 **I Get Lonely**.......RB[2] S:2 / A:24 *(2 edits)*	$3	▮V	Virgin 38631
				JANET (Featuring BLACKstreet)			
				"45" B-side: (radio edit)			
6/27/98	28[A]	22		34 **Go Deep**.......			album cut
				above 4 from the album *The Velvet Rope* on Virgin 44762			
12/19/98	76	17		35 **Luv Me, Luv Me**.......A:54			album cut
				SHAGGY Featuring Janet			
				samples "Impeach The President" by The Honey Drippers; from the movie *How Stella Got Her Groove Back* starring Angela Bassett (soundtrack on Flyte Tyme 11806)			
3/13/99	3	20	●	36 **What's It Gonna Be?!** ....RB[1] S:2 / A:9 *Tear Da Roof Off*	$5	★+	Elektra 64051
				BUSTA RHYMES Featuring Janet			
				Antoinette Roberson (backing vocal)			
3/13/99	47	11		37 **Girlfriend/Boyfriend**.......A:28 *(2 versions) / Take Me There*	$6	T	Interscope 95043
				BLACKSTREET With Janet			
				Ja Rule and **Eve** (rap vocals)			
6/17/00	❶[3]	24	●	38 **Doesn't Really Matter**.......S:❶[2] / A:2 *(3 mixes)*	$3	★V	Def Jam 562846
				from the movie *Nutty Professor II: The Klumps* starring **Eddie Murphy** and **Janet Jackson**; "45": Def Jam 562913; B-side: (same)			
3/17/01	❶[7]	22		39 **All For You** ....RB[2] S:❶[4] / A:❶[2] *(video mix)*	$3	★V	Virgin 97522
				samples "The Glow Of Love" by **Change**			

DEBUT	PEAK	WKS	Gold	A-side (Chart Hit)...B-side	$	Sym	Label & Number

JACKSON, Janet — Cont'd

DEBUT	PEAK	WKS	Gold	A-side (Chart Hit)...B-side	$	Sym	Label & Number
6/23/01	3	20		40 **Someone To Call My Lover** ...S:❶[3] / A:9 *(remix)* samples "Ventura Highway" by **America**; "45" issued for above 2 on Virgin 38800	$3	★[V]	Virgin 38799
11/24/01	28	12		41 **Son Of A Gun (I Betcha Think This Song Is About You)** ...A:26 *(3 versions)* **JANET Featuring Missy Elliott and P. Diddy with Carly Simon** samples "You're So Vain" by **Carly Simon**; above 4 from the album *All For You*; all of above (except #1, 2, 9, 15, 36 & 37) produced and/or co-written by Jimmy Jam & Terry Lewis	$6	T	Virgin 46171
8/3/02	28	12		42 **Feel It Boy** ...S:12 / A:30 *(3 remixes)* **BEENIE MAN feat. JANET**	$4	★	Virgin 38846

★322★ **JACKSON, Jermaine** R&B/LP **'80**

Born on 12/11/54 in Gary, Indiana. Fourth eldest of **The Jacksons**. Vocalist/bassist of **The Jackson 5** until group left Motown in 1976. Married Hazel Joy Gordy, daughter of Berry Gordy, Jr., on 12/15/73; divorced in 1987. Rejoined The Jacksons in 1984 for the group's *Victory* album and tour.

1)Let's Get Serious 2)Daddy's Home 3)Do What You Do

DEBUT	PEAK	WKS	Gold	A-side (Chart Hit)...B-side	$	Sym	Label & Number
9/16/72	46	11		1 **That's How Love Goes** ...*I Lost My Love In The Big City*	$5		Motown 1201
12/9/72+	9	18		2 **Daddy's Home** ...*Take Me In Your Arms (Rock Me For A Little While)*	$5		Motown 1216
10/20/73	79	5		3 **You're In Good Hands** ...*Does Your Mama Know About Me*	$5		Motown 1244
9/18/76	55	13		4 **Let's Be Young Tonight** ...*Bass Odyssey*	$4		Motown 1401
3/29/80	9	23		5 **Let's Get Serious** RB[6] *Je Vous Aime Beaucoup (I Love You)*	$4		Motown 1469
7/12/80	34	13		6 **You're Supposed To Keep Your Love For Me** ...*Let It Ride* above 2 written, produced and arranged by **Stevie Wonder**	$4		Motown 1490
4/18/81	50	9		7 **You Like Me Don't You** ...*(instrumental)*	$4		Motown 1503
10/31/81	60	8		8 **I'm Just Too Shy** ...*All Because Of You*	$4		Motown 1525
7/24/82	18	15		9 **Let Me Tickle Your Fancy** ...*Maybe Next Time* **Devo** (backing vocals)	$4		Motown 1628
7/21/84	15	17		10 **Dynamite** ...*Tell Me I'm Not Dreamin'* [I]	$3	■	Arista 9190
10/27/84+	13	20		11 **Do What You Do** ...AC[3] A:12 / S:14 *Tell Me I'm Not Dreamin'* (w/**Michael Jackson**)	$3		Arista 9279
2/2/85	54	11		12 **When The Rain Begins To Fall** ...*Substitute* (Zadora) **JERMAINE JACKSON/PIA ZADORA** from the movie *Voyage of the Rock Aliens* starring **Pia Zadora**	$3	■	Curb/MCA 52521
6/8/85	67	7		13 **(Closest Thing To) Perfect** ...*(instrumental)* from the movie *Perfect* starring **John Travolta** and Jamie Lee Curtis	$3	■	Arista 9356
2/22/86	16	15		14 **I Think It's Love** ...S:16 / A:16 *Voices In The Dark*	$3	■	Arista 9444
7/5/86	71	5		15 **Do You Remember Me?** ...*Whatcha Doin'*	$3	■	Arista 9502
12/2/89+	64	11		16 **Don't Take It Personal** ...RB[1] *Clean Up Your Act*	$3	■[V]	Arista 9875
11/30/91	78	2		17 **Word To The Badd!!** ...A:56 *(3 album snippets)* a message of concern to Jermaine's brother **Michael Jackson**	$3	▮	LaFace 24011

JACKSON, Joe ROK/BUB/LP **'82**

Born on 8/11/55 in Burton-on-Trent, England. Singer/songwriter/pianist, featuring an ever-changing music style. Moved to New York City in 1982.

DEBUT	PEAK	WKS	Gold	A-side (Chart Hit)...B-side	$	Sym	Label & Number
6/9/79	21	15		1 **Is She Really Going Out With Him?** ...*(Do The) Instant Mash*	$5	■	A&M 2132
8/21/82	6	27		2 **Steppin' Out** *Chinatown*	$4	■	A&M 2428
1/15/83	18	16		3 **Breaking Us In Two** ...*Target*	$4	■	A&M 2510
11/26/83	85	4		4 **Memphis** ...*Breakdown* from the movie *Mike's Murder* starring Debra Winger	$4	■	A&M 2601
4/21/84	15	16		5 **You Can't Get What You Want (Till You Know What You Want)** ...*Cha Cha Loco*	$4	■	A&M 2628
7/14/84	57	8		6 **Happy Ending** ...*Loisaida* Elaine Caswell (female vocal)	$4	■	A&M 2635

JACKSON, LaToya R&B/BUB/LP **'84**

Born on 5/29/56 in Gary, Indiana. Sister of **The Jacksons**. The fifth of nine children.

DEBUT	PEAK	WKS	Gold	A-side (Chart Hit)...B-side	$	Sym	Label & Number
5/5/84	56	8		**Heart Don't Lie** ...*Without You*	$4	■	Private I 04439

JACKSON, Mahalia MEM/BUB/LP **'58**

Born on 10/26/11 in New Orleans, Louisiana. Died of heart failure on 1/27/72 (age 60). Began recording for Apollo Records in the mid-1940s. One of the world's greatest gospel singers. Won Grammy's Lifetime Achievement Award in 1972. Inducted into the Rock and Roll Hall of Fame in 1997 as an Early Influence.

DEBUT	PEAK	WKS	Gold	A-side (Chart Hit)...B-side	$	Sym	Label & Number
4/28/58	69	6		1 **He's Got The Whole World In His Hands** ...T:69 *Didn't It Rain*	$12		Columbia 41150
12/29/62	99	1		2 **Silent Night, Holy Night** ...X:5 *Lord's Prayer* [X] Christmas charts: [#5-11 weeks] 22/'64; 5/'67; 13/'68; 7/'69; 9/'73; first released on Apollo 235 in 1941; new version released on Apollo 750 in 1962; same version released and charted on Kenwood 750, 1967-73; same picture sleeve issued for both Apollo and Kenwood	$12	■	Apollo 750

JACKSON, Michael ★7★ R&B/BUB/LP **'83**

Born on 8/29/58 in Gary, Indiana. The seventh of nine children. Became lead singer of his brothers' group, **The Jackson 5** (later known as **The Jacksons**), at age five. Played "The Scarecrow" in the 1978 movie musical *The Wiz*. His 1982 *Thriller* album, with sales of over 40 million copies, is the best-selling album in history. Starred in the 15-minute movie *Captain EO*, which was shown exclusively at Disneyland and Disneyworld. His 1988 autobiography, *Moonwalker*, became a movie the same year. Awarded Grammy's Living Legends Award in 1993. Signed a $1 billion multimedia contract with Sony Software on 3/20/91. On 1/25/94, settled out of court after child sexual molestation allegations were made against him. Married **Elvis Presley**'s daughter, Lisa Marie, on 5/26/94; divorced in 1996. Inducted into the Rock and Roll Hall of Fame in 2001.

1)Billie Jean 2)Black Or White 3)Say Say Say 4)Rock With You 5)Beat It

DEBUT	PEAK	WKS	Gold	A-side (Chart Hit)...B-side	$	Sym	Label & Number
10/30/71	4	14		1 **Got To Be There** ...*Maria (You Were The Only One)*	$5		Motown 1191
3/11/72	2[2]	13		2 **Rockin' Robin** ...*Love Is Here And Now You're Gone*	$5		Motown 1197
5/27/72	16	11		3 **I Wanna Be Where You Are** ...*We've Got A Good Thing Going*	$5	■	Motown 1202
8/5/72	❶[1]	16		4 **Ben** ...*You Can Cry On My Shoulder* title song from the sequel to the movie *Willard* starring Lee Harcourt Montgomery	$5		Motown 1207
5/5/73	50	7		5 **With A Child's Heart** ...*Morning Glow*	$5		Motown 1218
3/1/75	54	8		6 **We're Almost There** ...*Take Me Back*	$5		Motown 1341
6/7/75	23	12		7 **Just A Little Bit Of You** ...*Dear Michael*	$5		Motown 1349

DEBUT	PEAK	WKS	Gold	A-side (Chart Hit)	B-side	$	Sym	Label & Number
				JACKSON, Michael — Cont'd				
9/9/78	41	9		8 **Ease On Down The Road**	*Poppy Girls* (**Quincy Jones**)	$5	■	MCA 40947
				DIANA ROSS MICHAEL JACKSON				
				from the movie *The Wiz* starring Ross and Jackson				
2/24/79	81	3		9 **You Can't Win** (Part 1)	*(Part 2)*	$6		Epic 50654
7/28/79	❶[1]	21	▲	10 **Don't Stop 'Til You Get Enough** RB[5]	*I Can't Help It*	$4		Epic 50742
11/3/79+	❶[4]	24	▲	11 **Rock With You** RB[6]	*Working Day And Night*	$4		Epic 50797
2/16/80	10	17	●	12 **Off The Wall**	*Get On The Floor*	$4		Epic 50838
4/19/80	10	16	●	13 **She's Out Of My Life**	*Get On The Floor*	$4		Epic 50871
				above 4 from the album *Off The Wall*				
4/18/81	55	7		14 **One Day In Your Life**	*Take Me Back*	$4		Motown 1512
				first released on his 1975 album *Forever, Michael*				
11/6/82+	2[3]	18	●	15 **The Girl Is Mine** RB[3] / AC[4]	*Can't Get Outta The Rain* (Jackson)	$4	■	Epic 03288
				MICHAEL JACKSON/PAUL McCARTNEY				
1/22/83	❶[7]	24	▲	16 **Billie Jean** RB[9]	*Can't Get Outta The Rain*	$4		Epic 03509
2/26/83	❶[3]	25	▲	17 **Beat It** RB[1]	*Get On The Floor*	$4		Epic 03759
				Eddie **Van Halen** (lead guitar); 1983 Grammy winner: Record of the Year				
5/28/83	5	15		18 **Wanna Be Startin' Somethin'**	*(instrumental)*	$4	■	Epic 03914
7/23/83	7	14		19 **Human Nature**	*Baby Be Mine*	$4	■	Epic 04026
				also see "Right Here/Human Nature" by **SWV**				
10/8/83	10	16		20 **P.Y.T. (Pretty Young Thing)**	*Working Day And Night* (**Jacksons**)	$4	■	Epic 04165
10/15/83	❶[6]	22	▲	21 **Say Say Say**	*Ode To A Koala Bear* (McCartney)	$4	■	Columbia 04168
				PAUL McCARTNEY AND MICHAEL JACKSON				
2/11/84	4	14	▲	22 **Thriller**	*Can't Get Outta The Rain*	$4		Epic 04364
				#15-20 & 22: from the #1 best-selling album in history, *Thriller*				
5/26/84	38	12		23 **Farewell My Summer Love**	*Call On Me*	$4	■	Motown 1739
				remix of a recording from 8/31/73				
8/8/87	❶[1]	14	●	24 **I Just Can't Stop Loving You** RB[1] / AC[3] S:❶[1] / A:❶[1]	*Baby Be Mine*	$3	■	Epic 07253
				Siedah Garrett (backing vocal)				
9/19/87	❶[2]	14		25 **Bad** RB[3] S:❶[2] / A:❶[2]	*I Can't Help It*	$3	■	Epic 07418
				Jimmy Smith (organ solo)				
11/21/87+	❶[1]	18		26 **The Way You Make Me Feel** RB[1] S:2 / A:3	*(instrumental)*	$3	■	Epic 07645
2/6/88	❶[2]	17		27 **Man In The Mirror** RB[1] A:❶[3] / S:❶[2]	*(instrumental)*	$3	■	Epic 07668
				Siedah Garrett, Winans and Andrae Crouch Choir (backing vocals)				
5/7/88	❶[1]	14		28 **Dirty Diana** S:❶[1] / A:3	*(instrumental)*	$3	■	Epic 07739
				featuring Steve Stevens (**Billy Idol**'s guitarist)				
5/7/88	80	6		29 **Get It**	*(instrumental)*	$3	■	Motown 1930
				STEVIE WONDER & MICHAEL JACKSON				
7/23/88	11	13		30 **Another Part Of Me** RB[1] S:8 / A:10	*(instrumental)*	$3	■	Epic 07962
11/12/88+	7	15		31 **Smooth Criminal** S:5 / A:9	*(instrumental)*	$3	■	Epic 08044
				#24-28, 30 & 31: from the album *Bad*; all of above Epic recordings produced by **Quincy Jones**				
11/23/91	❶[7]	20	▲	32 **Black Or White** S:❶[4] / A:❶[4]	*(instrumental)*	$3	■V	Epic 74100
				Bill Bottrell (rap); Slash (of **Guns N' Roses**; guitar)				
1/25/92	3	20	●	33 **Remember The Time** RB[2] A:❶[2] / S:5	*Black Or White (Clivilles & Cole mix)*	$3	■V	Epic 74200
4/25/92	6	20	●	34 **In The Closet** RB[1] A:5 / S:15	*(radio edit)*	$3	■V	Epic 74266
				features the "Mystery Girl" vocal (Princess Stephanie of Monaco)				
7/11/92	26	14		35 **Jam** S:19 / A:21	*Rock With You (remix)*	$3	■V	Epic 74333
				Heavy D (rap)				
12/12/92+	27	20		36 **Heal The World** S:18 / A:24	*She Drives Me Wild*	$3	■V	Epic 74708
4/10/93	14	18		37 **Who Is It** A:14 / S:26	*(Oprah Winfrey intro)*	$3	■V	Epic 74406
				"45" B-side: "Wanna Be Startin' Somethin'" (remix)				
7/17/93	7	20	●	38 **Will You Be There** A:6 / S:12	*(instrumental)*	$3	■V	Epic 77060
				from the movie *Free Willy* starring Jason James Richter; #32-38: from the album *Dangerous*				
6/17/95	5	17	▲	39 **Scream** / S:3 / A:12				
				MICHAEL JACKSON & JANET JACKSON				
6/17/95		17		40 **Childhood** S:flip		$3	■V	Epic 78000
				theme from the movie *Free Willy 2* starring Jason James Richter				
9/2/95	❶[1]	20	▲	41 **You Are Not Alone** RB[4] S:2 / A:2	*Scream Louder (remix -w/***Janet Jackson***)*	$3	■V	Epic 78002
				written and produced by **R. Kelly**				
6/8/96	30	13		42 **They Don't Care About Us** S:12	*(remix) / Earth Song / Rock With You (remix)*	$3	■V	Epic 78264
				above 4 from the album *HIStory: Past, Present And Future - Book I*				
5/10/97	42	11		43 **Blood On The Dance Floor** S:30 / A:69	*(remix by* **Wyclef Jean***) / Dangerous (edit)*	$3	■V	Epic 78007
8/23/97	91	2		44 **Stranger In Moscow** S:75	*Off The Wall / (remix)*	$3	■V	Epic 78012
9/8/01	10	20		45 **You Rock My World** A:9			V	album cut ■
				"45": Epic 79656; B-side: (same)				
11/17/01+	14	20		46 **Butterflies** A:14				album cut
				above 2 from the album *Invincible* on Epic 69400				
				JACKSON, Mick '78				
				Born in England. R&B singer. Later based in Germany.				
8/12/78	61	5		**Blame It On The Boogie**	*All Night Boppin'*	$5		Atco 7091
				JACKSON, Millie R&B/BUB/LP '72				
				Born on 7/15/44 in Thomson, Georgia. R&B singer/songwriter (charted 39 hits, 1971-88). To Newark, New Jersey, in 1958. Worked as a model in New York City. Professional singing debut at Club Zanzibar in Hoboken, New Jersey, in 1964. First recorded for MGM in 1970. Founded and produced the trio **Facts Of Life**.				
3/25/72	27	14		1 **Ask Me What You Want**	*I Just Can't Stand It*	$6		Spring 123
8/5/72	42	10		2 **My Man, A Sweet Man**	*I Gotta Get Away (From My Own Self)*	$6		Spring 127
12/9/72+	95	4		3 **I Miss You Baby**	*I Ain't Giving Up*	$6		Spring 131
9/8/73	24	12		4 **Hurts So Good**	*Love Doctor*	$5		Spring 139
				from the movie *Cleopatra Jones* starring Tamara Dobson				
6/8/74	77	7		5 **How Do You Feel The Morning After**	*In The Wash*	$5		Spring 147

DEBUT	PEAK	WKS	Gold	A-side (Chart Hit)...B-side	$	Sym	Label & Number

JACKSON, Millie — Cont'd

DEBUT	PEAK	WKS	Gold	A-side (Chart Hit)...B-side	$	Sym	Label & Number
1/25/75	42	7		6 If Loving You Is Wrong I Don't Want To Be Right ... *The Rap* (R&B #42)	$5		Spring 155
9/27/75	87	2		7 Leftovers ... *Loving Arms* (R&B #45)	$5		Spring 161
11/19/77+	43	11		8 If You're Not Back In Love By Monday ... *A Little Taste Of Outside Love*	$5		Spring 175
				#2 Country hit for **Merle Haggard** in 1977 as "If We're Not Back In Love By Monday"			

JACKSON, Rebbie

R&B/LP '84

Born Maureen Jackson on 5/29/50 in Gary, Indiana. Eldest of the nine-sibling Jackson family. Worked with **The Jacksons** from 1974-77, then went solo.

DEBUT	PEAK	WKS	Gold	A-side (Chart Hit)...B-side	$	Sym	Label & Number
10/6/84	24	19	●	Centipede ... S:22 *(instrumental)*	$4	■	Columbia 04547
				written and produced by **Michael Jackson**			

JACKSON, Stonewall

C&W '59

His real name. Born on 11/6/32 in Emerson, North Carolina. Country singer/guitarist/pianist (charted 44 hits, 1958-73). Descended from General Thomas Jonathan "Stonewall" Jackson.

DEBUT	PEAK	WKS	Gold	A-side (Chart Hit)...B-side	$	Sym	Label & Number
5/25/59	4	16		1 Waterloo ... CW[5] *Smoke Along The Track* (C&W #24)	$15	■	Columbia 41393
10/19/59	95	2		2 Igmoo (The Pride Of South Central High) ... *Uncle Sam And Big John Bull*	$15		Columbia 41488
12/28/59+	41	7		3 Mary Don't You Weep ... *Run*	$15		Columbia 41533
				adapted from a traditional black American spiritual			
3/28/60	83	3		4 Why I'm Walkin' ... *Life Of A Poor Boy* (C&W #15)	$15		Columbia 41591

JACKSON, Walter

R&B/BUB/LP '64

Born on 3/19/38 in Pensacola, Florida; raised in Detroit, Michigan. Died of a cerebral hemorrhage on 6/20/83 (age 45). R&B singer. Contracted polio at an early age; performed on crutches.

DEBUT	PEAK	WKS	Gold	A-side (Chart Hit)...B-side	$	Sym	Label & Number
11/21/64	67	6		1 It's All Over ... *Lee Cross*	$12		Okeh 7204
				a new version by Jackson made the R&B charts (#75) in 1977 on Chi-Sound 1044			
2/13/65	96	1		2 Suddenly I'm All Alone ... *Special Love*	$10		Okeh 7215
6/12/65	95	2		3 Welcome Home ... *Blowin' In The Wind*	$10		Okeh 7219
				above 3 co-produced by **Curtis Mayfield**			
6/4/66	88	5		4 It's An Uphill Climb To The Bottom ... *Tear For Tear*	$10	■	Okeh 7247
11/5/66	83	4		5 A Corner In The Sun ... *Not You*	$10		Okeh 7260
4/15/67	89	2		6 Speak Her Name ... *They Don't Give Medals (To Yesterday's Heroes)*	$10	■	Okeh 7272
12/25/76+	93	4		7 Feelings ... *Words (Are Impossible)*	$6		Chi-Sound 908

JACKSON, Wanda

C&W/BUB '61

Born on 10/20/37 in Maud, Oklahoma. Country-rockabilly singer/songwriter/guitarist. First recorded for Decca in 1954. Charted 30 Country hits, 1954-74. Toured with **Elvis Presley** from 1955-56.

DEBUT	PEAK	WKS	Gold	A-side (Chart Hit)...B-side	$	Sym	Label & Number
8/29/60	37	10		1 Let's Have A Party ... *Cool Love*	$40		Capitol 4397
				Gene Vincent's Blue Caps (backing); introduced by **Elvis Presley** as "Party" in his 1957 movie *Loving You*			
6/5/61	29	11		2 Right Or Wrong ... *Funnel Of Love*	$25		Capitol 4553
10/16/61	27	10		3 In The Middle Of A Heartache ... *I'd Be Ashamed*	$25		Capitol 4635
1/20/62	84	3		4 A Little Bitty Tear ... *I Don't Wanta Go*	$25		Capitol 4681
4/21/62	58	8		5 If I Cried Every Time You Hurt Me ... *Let My Love Walk In*	$25	■	Capitol 4723

JACKSON 5, The ★55★

R&B/LP '70

R&B group of brothers from Gary, Indiana: **Michael Jackson** (born on 8/29/58), **Jermaine Jackson** (born on 12/11/54), Marlon Jackson (born on 3/12/57), Tito Jackson (born on 10/15/53) and Jackie Jackson (born on 5/4/51). First recorded for Steeltown in 1968. Known as The Jackson 5 from 1968-75, then changed name to The Jacksons. Jermaine replaced by Randy (born on 10/29/61) in 1976. Jermaine rejoined the group for 1984's highly publicized *Victory* album and tour. Marlon left for a solo career in 1987. Their sisters **Rebbie Jackson**, **LaToya Jackson** and **Janet Jackson** backed the group; each had solo hits. Michael and Janet emerged with superstar solo careers in the 1980s. Group lineup in 1989: Jackie, Tito, Jermaine and Randy Jackson. Group inducted into the Rock and Roll Hall of Fame in 1997. **Boyz II Men** appeared in the 1992 TV mini-series *The Jacksons: An American Dream.* Also see **Stevie Wonder**'s "You Haven't Done Nothin" and **3T**.

1)I'll Be There 2)ABC 3)The Love You Save 4)I Want You Back 5)Never Can Say Goodbye

DEBUT	PEAK	WKS	Gold	A-side (Chart Hit)...B-side	$	Sym	Label & Number
11/15/69+	❶[1]	19	▲	1 I Want You Back ... RB[4] *Who's Lovin You* (R&B flip)	$8		Motown 1157
3/14/70	❶[2]	13		2 ABC ... RB[4] *The Young Folks*	$8	□	Motown 1163
				a promotional re-service sleeve was issued several weeks after its chart debut			
5/30/70	❶[2]	13		3 The Love You Save / RB[6]			
8/1/70		4		4 I Found That Girl ...	$8		Motown 1166
9/19/70	❶[5]	16		5 I'll Be There ... RB[6] *One More Chance*	$8		Motown 1171
12/19/70	❶[2X]	5		6 Santa Claus Is Comin' To Town / [X]			
				X: 1/'70; 1/'71; 9/'73			
12/26/70		1		7 Christmas Won't Be The Same This Year ... [X]	$12		Motown 1174
1/30/71	2[2]	10		8 Mama's Pearl ... *Darling Dear*	$7	■	Motown 1177
4/3/71	2[3]	12		9 Never Can Say Goodbye ... RB[3] *She's Good*	$7		Motown 1179
7/10/71	20	9		10 Maybe Tomorrow ... *I Will Find A Way*	$6		Motown 1186
12/11/71+	10	10		11 Sugar Daddy ... *I'm So Happy*	$6		Motown 1194
4/22/72	13	9		12 Little Bitty Pretty One ... *If I Have To Move A Mountain*	$6		Motown 1199
7/15/72	16	10		13 Lookin' Through The Windows ... *Love Song*	$6		Motown 1205
10/28/72	18	12		14 Corner Of The Sky ... *To Know*	$6		Motown 1214
				from the Broadway musical *Pippin* starring Ben Vereen			
3/17/73	28	10		15 Hallelujah Day ... *You Made Me What I Am*	$6		Motown 1224
9/1/73	28	13		16 Get It Together ... *Touch*	$6		Motown 1277
3/16/74	2[2]	22		17 Dancing Machine ... RB[1] *It's Too Late To Change The Time*	$6		Motown 1286
10/26/74	38	11		18 Whatever You Got, I Want ... *I Can't Quit Your Love*	$6		Motown 1308
1/18/75	15	14		19 I Am Love (Parts I & II) ...	$6		Motown 1310
7/5/75	60	9		20 Forever Came Today ... *All I Do Is Think Of You* (R&B #50)	$6		Motown 1356
				THE JACKSONS:			
11/13/76+	6	21	▲	21 Enjoy Yourself ... *Style Of Life*	$5		Epic/Phil. Int. 50289
4/9/77	28	10		22 Show You The Way To Go ... *Blues Away*	$5		Epic/Phil. Int. 50350

DEBUT	PEAK	WKS	Gold	A-side (Chart Hit)	B-side	$	Sym	Label & Number
				JACKSONS, The — Cont'd				
10/8/77	52	7		23 Goin' Places	*Do What You Wanna*	$5		Epic/Phil. Int. 50454
11/4/78	54	6		24 Blame It On The Boogie	*Do What You Wanna*	$4		Epic 50595
2/17/79	7	22	▲	25 Shake Your Body (Down To The Ground)	*That's What You Get (For Being Polite)*	$4		Epic 50656
9/27/80	12	18		26 Lovely One	*Bless His Soul*	$4		Epic 50938
12/6/80+	22	16		27 Heartbreak Hotel	*Things I Do For You*	$4		Epic 50959
5/2/81	77	5		28 Can You Feel It	*Everybody*	$4		Epic 01032
6/27/81	73	4		29 Walk Right Now above 4 from the album *Triumph*	*Your Ways*	$4		Epic 02132
6/30/84	3	15	●	30 State Of Shock **Mick Jagger** (guest vocalist)	*Your Ways*	$4	■	Epic 04503
8/18/84	17	12		31 Torture	*(instrumental)*	$4	■	Epic 04575
10/27/84	47	7		32 Body	*(instrumental)*	$4	■	Epic 04673
6/3/89	77	7		33 Nothin (That Compares 2 U)	*Alright With Me*	$3		Epic 68688
				JACOBS, Debbie BUB/R&B/LP **'80** Born in Baltimore, Maryland. Black disco singer.				
3/15/80	70	4		High On Your Love	*I Can Never Forget A Friend*	$4		MCA 41167
				JACOBS, Dick, And His Orchestra BUB **'56** Born on 3/29/18 in Brooklyn, New York. Died of cancer on 5/20/88 (age 70). Music director of TV's *Your Hit Parade* from 1957-58. A&R director for Coral and Brunswick Records. Author of *Who Wrote That Song.*				
3/24/56	22	14		1 "Main Title" And "Molly-O" from the Otto Preminger movie *The Man With The Golden Arm* starring **Frank Sinatra**	A:22 / T:26 *Butternut*	$12		Coral 61606
7/7/56	70	4		2 Te Amo	T:70 *The Golden Baton*	$10		Coral 61653
10/6/56	73	1		3 Theme From "East Of Eden" from the movie *East Of Eden* starring James Dean	T:73 *The Seven Wonders Of The World* [I]	$10		Coral 61692
10/27/56	16	13		4 Petticoats Of Portugal	A:16 / T:20 / J:20 / S:23 *Song Of The Vagabonds/Only A Rose*	$10		Coral 61724
3/9/57	73	6		5 Tower's Trot (And Then You Do That Step) / dance tune co-written by comedian Sid Caesar and featured on his NBC-TV series	T:73			
3/16/57	87	3		6 The Big Beat	T:87 [I]	$10		Coral 61794
9/2/57	17	11		7 Fascination from the movie *Love In The Afternoon* starring Gary Cooper and Audrey Hepburn	A:17 / T:52 *Summertime In Venice*	$10		Coral 61864
				JACOBS, Hank **'64** Born in 1946 in Los Angeles, California. R&B organist.				
1/18/64	91	3		So Far Away	*Monkey Hips And Rice* [I]	$12		Sue 795
				JADAKISS R&B/BUB/LP **'00** Born Jayson Phillips in Yonkers, New York. Male rapper. Member of **The Lox**.				
4/15/00	50	17		1 Best Of Me **MÝA Featuring Jadakiss** from the album *Fear Of Flying* on University 490640	A:44			album cut
7/15/00	88	5		2 Got It All **EVE & JADAKISS**	*(3 versions)*	$6	T	Ruff Ryders 497360
9/1/01	69^S	1		3 We Gonna Make It **JADAKISS Featuring Styles of the Lox**	*(2 versions)*	$6	T	Ruff Ryders 497598
10/12/02	3	20		4 Jenny From The Block **JENNIFER LOPEZ Featuring Jadakiss & Styles** samples "South Bronx" by Boogie Down Productions and "Hijack" by **Herbie Mann**	A:3 / S:16 *(4 versions)*	$6	T	Epic 79825
11/2/02	67^S	1		5 Up & Down (In & Out) **DEBORAH COX (feat. Jadakiss)**	*(5 versions)*	$6	T	J Records 21204
				JADE R&B/LP **'93** Female R&B vocal trio: Joi Marshall and Tonya Kelly (both born in Chicago, Illinois), with Di Reed (born in Houston, Texas).				
7/11/92	16	21		1 I Wanna Love You from the movie *Class Act* starring **Kid 'N Play**	A:10 / S:27 *(dub mix)*	$3	▮^V	Giant 18950
12/19/92+	4	35	●	2 Don't Walk Away	A:2 / S:10 *(instrumental)*	$3	▮^V	Giant 18686
6/5/93	22	20		3 One Woman	A:17 / S:37 *(instrumental)*	$3	▮	Giant 18606
11/6/93	69	14		4 Looking For Mr. Do Right all of above from the album *Jade To The Max*	S:47 *(live version)*	$3	▮	Giant 18429
9/24/94	72	13		5 5-4-3-2 (Yo! Time Is Up)	S:42 *(album version) / When Will I See You*	$3	▮	Giant 18066
11/26/94+	20	22		6 Every Day Of The Week	A:20 / S:30 *If The Mood Is Right*	$3	▮	Giant 17988
				J.A.G. **'01** Born in Brooklyn, New York. Male rapper.				
4/28/01	64^S	5		Bomb Bomb Girl **J.A.G. featuring Cameo and Raa'k**	*(2 mixes) / Introducing Cameo (snippet)*	$4	★	Blakcity 10022
	★406★			**JAGGED EDGE** R&B/BUB/LP **'01** Male R&B vocal group from Atlanta, Georgia: identical twin brothers Brian and Brandon Casey, with Richard Wingo and Kyle Norman. Also see **Usher**'s "Nice & Slow." *1)Where The Party At 2)Promise 3)Let's Get Married*				
9/20/97	65	9		1 The Way That You Talk **JAGGED EDGE featuring Da Brat & JD**	S:59 *(4 album snippets)*	$3	▮	So So Def 78639
8/15/98	23	16		2 Gotta Be	S:16 *(3 album snippets)*	$3	▮	So So Def 79010
12/11/99+	15	20	●	3 He Can't Love U	S:4 / A:43 *(4 album snippets)*	$4	★	So So Def 79146
5/6/00	11	24		4 Let's Get Married	RB³ S:8 / A:15 *(5 remixes)*	$8	★*	So So Def 79437
12/23/00+	9	21		5 Promise samples "I Need Love" by **LL Cool J**	RB² S:6 / A:11 *(4 remixes)*	$8	★*	So So Def 79545
4/14/01	75	7		6 Puppy Love **LIL BOW WOW Featuring Jagged Edge** samples "Kanday" by **LL Cool J**; "45": So So Def 79556; B-side: "Bow Wow (That's My Name)"; from the album *Beware Of Dog* on So So Def/Columbia 69981	A:66		V	album cut

DEBUT	PEAK	WKS	Gold	A-side (Chart Hit)...B-side	$	Sym	Label & Number
				JAGGED EDGE — Cont'd			
6/2/01	3	29		7 **Where The Party At** RB[3] S:❶[3] / A:4 *Let's Get Married* (w/Run of **Run-DMC**)	$4	★	So So Def 79626
				JAGGED EDGE featuring Nelly			
11/17/01	58	15		8 **Goodbye**...A:62			album cut
				from the album *Jagged Little Thrill* on So So Def 85646			
1/5/02	93	5		9 **Thank You**...*(4 versions)*	$6	T	So So Def 79685
				LIL BOW WOW Featuring Jagged Edge And Fundisha			
				samples "I'm Not The One" by **The Cars**			
5/11/02	42[S]	3		10 **I Got It 2**...BUB:103 *(3 versions)*	$6	T	So So Def 79739
				JAGGED EDGE featuring Nas			
				#7, 8 & 10: from the album *Jagged Little Thrill* on So So Def 85646			
8/10/02	8	36		11 **Don't Mess With My Man**...S:❶[1] / A:8 *(version 2)*	$4	★	Jive 40041
				NIVEA Featuring Brian & Brandon Casey Of Jagged Edge			
8/17/02	20	18		12 **Trade It All (Part 2)**...A:13			album cut
				FABOLOUS featuring P. DIDDY & JAGGED EDGE			
				from the movie *Barbershop* starring **Ice Cube** (soundtrack on Epic 86575)			
				JAGGER, Mick ROK/LP '85			
				Born Michael Phillip Jagger on 7/26/43 in Dartford, Kent, England. Lead singer of **The Rolling Stones**. Appeared in the movies *Ned Kelly* and *Freejack*. Married to model Bianca Jagger from 1971-80. Married actress/model Jerry Hall from 1990-99. Also see **The Jacksons**' "State Of Shock," **Carly Simon**'s "You're So Vain" and **Peter Frampton**'s "Tried To Love."			
11/4/78	81	5		1 **(You Got To Walk And) Don't Look Back**...*Soon Come*	$6	■	Rolling Stones 19308
				PETER TOSH with Mick Jagger			
2/9/85	12	14		2 **Just Another Night**...AR[2] A:9 / S:12 *Turn The Girl Loose*	$4	■	Columbia 04743
4/27/85	38	11		3 **Lucky In Love**...*Running Out Of Luck*	$4	■	Columbia 04893
8/31/85	7	14		4 **Dancing In The Street** S:5 / A:8 *(instrumental)*	$4	■	EMI America 8288
				MICK JAGGER/DAVID BOWIE			
				from the Live-Aid project for Africa			
8/2/86	51	8		5 **Ruthless People**...S:38 *I'm Ringing*	$3	■	Epic 06211
				title song from the movie starring **Bette Midler** and Danny DeVito			
9/12/87	39	9		6 **Let's Work**...S:37 / A:39 *Catch As Catch Can*	$3	■	Columbia 07306
11/28/87	67	9		7 **Throwaway**...*Peace For The Wicked*	$3	■	Columbia 07653
2/13/93	84	5		8 **Sweet Thing**...*Wandering Spirit*	$3	▮[V]	Atlantic 87410
				JAGGERZ, The LP '70			
				Pop-rock group from Pittsburgh, Pennsylvania: **Donnie Iris** (vocals, trumpet), Jimmy Ross (vocals, trombone), Billy Maybray (vocals, bass), Benny Faiella (guitar), Thom Davis (organ) and Jim Pugliano (drums). Also see **Q**.			
1/31/70	2[1]	13	●	1 **The Rapper**...*Born Poor*	$7		Kama Sutra 502
5/9/70	75	3		2 **I Call My Baby Candy**...*Will She Believe Me?*	$6		Kama Sutra 509
8/22/70	88	2		3 **What A Bummer**...*Memoirs Of The Traveler*	$6		Kama Sutra 513
				JAGS, The '80			
				Rock group from Scarborough, England: Nick Watkinson (vocals, guitar), John Alder (guitar), Steve Prudence (bass) and Alex Baird (drums).			
6/7/80	84	2		**Back Of My Hand (I've Got Your Number)**...*Single Vision/BWM*	$5		Island 49202
				remixed by **The Buggles**			
				JAHARI '00			
				Born in Brooklyn, New York. Male rapper.			
9/9/00	51[S]	12		**Come Ride With Me**...*(3 versions) / I Ain't F#ckin' Witcha*	$8	★*	Success 54392
				JAHEIM LP '02			
				Born Jaheim Hoagland in 1979 in New Brunswick, New Jersey. Male rapper.			
12/16/00+	26	20		1 **Could It Be**...S:4 *(4 album snippets)*	$4	★	Warner 16791
6/30/01	52	20		2 **Just In Case**...A:48 *(2 versions) / Lil' Nigga Ain't Mine (w/Castro, DUNGANZ & Precise)*	$6	T	Warner 42381
2/23/02	28	20		3 **Anything**...A:25			album cut
				JAHEIM Featuring Next			
				above 3 from the album *Ghetto Love* on Warner 47452			
11/16/02+	28	20		4 **Fabulous**...A:26			album cut
				JAHEIM Featuring Tha Rayne			
				samples "Wake Up Everybody" by **Harold Melvin & The Blue Notes**; from the album *Still Ghetto* on Warner 48214			
				JA-KKI '76			
				Interracial R&B-disco group from Flint, Michigan. Named after lead singer Jacqueline (sole female member).			
9/11/76	96	3		**Sun...Sun...Sun...Pt. I**...*Pt. II*	$6		Pyramid 8004
				JAMES ROK/BUB/LP '94			
				Rock group from Manchester, England: Tim Booth (vocals), James Gott (guitar), Mark Hunter (keyboards), Saul Davies (violin), Andy Diagram (trumpet), Jim Glennie (bass) and David Baynton-Power (drums).			
2/5/94	61	13		**Laid**...A:61 *(3 album snippets)*	$3	▮	Fontana 858217
				JAMES, Bob BUB/LP '74			
				Born on 12/25/39 in Marshall, Missouri. Jazz-fusion keyboardist.			
11/9/74	88	2		**Feel Like Making Love**...*Soulero* [I]	$5		CTI 24
	★263★			**JAMES, Etta** R&B/BUB/LP '61			
				Born Jamesetta Hawkins on 1/25/38 in Los Angeles, California. R&B pioneer. Nicknamed "Miss Peaches." First recorded for Modern in 1954 (had #1 R&B hit "The Wallflower"). Recorded duets with **Harvey Fuqua** of **The Moonglows** as Etta & Harvey. Frequent bouts with heroin addiction; finally cured in the late 1970s. Inducted into the Rock and Roll Hall of Fame in 1993. Won Grammy's Lifetime Achievement Award in 2003.			
				1)Tell Mama 2)Pushover 3)Trust In Me 4)All I Could Do Was Cry 5)My Dearest Darling			
5/2/60	33	15		1 **All I Could Do Was Cry**...*Girl (Boy) Of My Dreams*	$15		Argo 5359
8/1/60	52	12		2 **If I Can't Have You**...*My Heart Cries*	$25		Chess 1760
				ETTA & HARVEY			
9/19/60	34	13		3 **My Dearest Darling**...*Tough Mary*	$15		Argo 5368
12/26/60	78	3		4 **Spoonful**...*It's a Crying Shame*	$25		Chess 1771
				ETTA AND HARVEY			

DEBUT	PEAK	WKS	Gold	A-side (Chart Hit)	B-side	$	Sym	Label & Number
				JAMES, Etta — Cont'd				
1/16/61	**47**	8		5 **At Last** #14 hit for Glenn Miller in 1942	*I Just Want To Make Love To You*	$15		Argo 5380
3/13/61	**30**	9		6 **Trust In Me** #4 hit for Mildred Bailey in 1937	*Anything To Say You're Mine*	$15		Argo 5385
6/12/61	**50**	6		7 **Fool That I Am /**				
6/26/61	**55**	3		8 **Dream** there were 5 Top 20 versions of this Johnny Mercer tune in 1945		$15		Argo 5390
8/7/61	**39**	7		9 **Don't Cry, Baby**	*Sunday Kind Of Love*	$15		Argo 5393
11/6/61	**54**	7		10 **It's Too Soon To Know /** #1 R&B hit for The Orioles in 1948				
12/18/61	**95**	1		11 **Seven Day Fool**		$15		Argo 5402
2/24/62	**37**	12		12 **Something's Got A Hold On Me**	*Waiting For Charlie To Come Home*	$12		Argo 5409
7/28/62	**34**	9		13 **Stop The Wedding**	*Street Of Tears*	$12		Argo 5418
10/13/62	**71**	7		14 **Next Door To The Blues /**				
10/13/62	**87**	4		15 **Fools Rush In** #3 hit for Glenn Miller in 1940		$12		Argo 5424
1/12/63	**64**	7		16 **Would It Make Any Difference To You**	*How Do You Talk To An Angel* (#109)	$12		Argo 5430
4/20/63	**25**	10		17 **Pushover**	*I Can't Hold It In Any More*	$12		Argo 5437
8/10/63	**78**	6		18 **Pay Back**	*Be Honest With Me*	$12		Argo 5445
10/5/63	**63**	4		19 **Two Sides (To Every Story)**	*I Worry Bout You* (#118)	$12		Argo 5452
2/1/64	**82**	3		20 **Baby What You Want Me To Do**	*What I Say*	$12		Argo 5459
4/18/64	**65**	6		21 **Loving You More Every Day**	*Look Who's Blue*	$12		Argo 5465
12/18/65	**96**	1		22 **Do I Make Myself Clear**	*Somewhere Down The Line*	$12		Cadet 5519
8/13/66	**97**	2		23 **In The Basement - Part 1** **ETTA JAMES & SUGAR PIE DeSANTO** (above 2)	*Part 2* (DeSanto)	$12		Cadet 5539
11/11/67+	**23**	14		24 **Tell Mama** written by **Clarence Carter**	*I'd Rather Go Blind*	$8		Cadet 5578
3/2/68	**35**	10		25 **Security** written by **Otis Redding**	*I'm Gonna Take What He's Got*	$8		Cadet 5594
5/18/68	**69**	7		26 **I Got You Babe**	*I Worship The Ground You Walk On*	$8		Cadet 5606
1/18/69	**79**	5		27 **Almost Persuaded**	*Steal Away*	$8		Cadet 5630
10/17/70	**94**	3		28 **Losers Weepers - Part I**	*Weepers*	$8		Cadet 5676
				JAMES, Jesse R&B/BUB **'67** Born James McClelland on 3/1/43 in Eldorado, Arkansas. R&B singer/record producer. Also see **The Fantastic Johnny C** and **Cliff Nobles & Co.**				
10/21/67	**92**	1		**Believe In Me Baby - Part I**	*Part II*	$10		20th Century 6684
				JAMES, Jesse — see JAYMES, Jesse				
				JAMES, Jimmy, & The Vagabonds BUB/LP **'68** Born on 9/15/40 in Jamaica. The Vagabonds: Count Prince Miller (vocals), Wallace Wilson (guitar), Carl Noel (keyboards), Matt Fredericks and Milton James (horns), Phil Chen (bass) and Rupert Balgobin (drums).				
3/23/68	**76**	3		1 **Come To Me Softly**	*Hi-Diddly Dee Dum Dum (It's A Good Feelin')*	$10		Atco 6551
2/21/76	**94**	3		2 **I Am Somebody**	*Chains Of Love*	$6		Pye 71057
	★452★			**JAMES, Joni** MEM/POP/BUB/LP **'53** Born Giavanna Carmello Babbo on 9/22/30 in Chicago, Illinois. Worked as a dancer from age 12; model during high school. Toured Canada as a dancer in the late 1940s. First recorded for Sharp in 1952. Charted 8 Top 20 pop hits, 1952-53, including her #1 hit "Why Don't You Believe Me." Married her orchestral arranger/conductor (1958-61) Tony Acquaviva (died on 9/27/86, age 61). *1)How Important Can It Be? 2)You Are My Love 3)There Goes My Heart*				
2/19/55	**2^1**	16	●	1 **How Important Can It Be?** **Ray Charles Singers** (backing vocals)	A:2 / J:6 / S:8 *This Is My Confession*	$20		MGM 11919
10/22/55	**6**	15		2 **You Are My Love**	A:6 / T:15 / S:18 *I Lay Me Down To Sleep*	$20		MGM 12066
12/10/55+	**49**	13		3 **My Believing Heart**	T:49 *You Never Fall In Love Again*	$20		MGM 12126
3/10/56	**83**	1		4 **Don't Tell Me Not To Love You**	T:83 *Somewhere Someone Is Lonely*	$20		MGM 12175
4/28/56	**72**	7		5 **I Woke Up Crying**	T:72 *The Maverick Queen*	$20		MGM 12213
8/4/56	**30**	11		6 **Give Us This Day /**	T:30			
7/21/56	**70**	8		7 **How Lucky You Are** #22 hit for The Andrews Sisters in 1947	T:70	$20		MGM 12288
7/15/57	**97**	1		8 **Summer Love** David Terry (orch., all of above; Tony Acquaviva on all below)	T:97 *I'm Sorry For You, My Friend*	$20		MGM 12480
9/15/58	**19**	16		9 **There Goes My Heart** #13 hit for Enric Madriguera in 1934; promo picture sleeve mentions "MGM Records is First! with a Single Stereo disc"	H:19 / S:45 *Funny*	$15	□	MGM 12706
1/19/59	**33**	12		10 **There Must Be A Way** #9 hit for both Johnnie Johnston and Charlie Spivak in 1945	*Sorry For Myself?*	$15		MGM 12746
4/13/59	**51**	7		11 **I Still Get A Thrill (Thinking Of You)** there were 4 Top 20 versions of this tune in 1930	*Perhaps*	$15	■	MGM 12779
7/13/59	**63**	6		12 **I Still Get Jealous** from the 1947 Broadway musical *High Button Shoes* starring Phil Silvers	*My Prayer Of Love*	$15		MGM 12807
12/28/59+	**35**	9		13 **Little Things Mean A Lot** #1 hit for **Kitty Kallen** in 1954	*I Laughed At Love* (#108)	$12		MGM 12849
3/28/60	**98**	1		14 **I Need You Now** **100 Strings and JONI (Choir of 40 Voices)**	*You Belong To Me* (#101)	$12		MGM 12885
12/19/60+	**38**	7		15 **My Last Date (With You)** lyric version of **Floyd Cramer**'s "Last Date"	*I Can't Give You Anything But Love*	$12	■	MGM 12933

DEBUT	PEAK	WKS	Gold	A-side (Chart Hit)	B-side	$	Sym	Label & Number

JAMES, Rick ★546★ R&B/BUB/LP '81

Born James Johnson on 2/1/48 in Buffalo, New York. Funk-rock singer/songwriter/guitarist. In Mynah Birds band with **Neil Young** in the late 1960s. To London; formed the band Main Line. Returned to the U.S. and formed Stone City Band; produced **Teena Marie**, **Mary Jane Girls**, **Eddie Murphy** and others. In mid-1994, sentenced to five years in prison for assaults on two women; released from prison in August 1996.

1)You And I 2)Super Freak 3)17

DEBUT	PEAK	WKS	Gold	A-side (Chart Hit)	B-side	$	Sym	Label & Number
7/1/78	13	17		1 **You And I** RB²	*Hollywood*	$5		Gordy 7156
11/4/78+	41	12		2 **Mary Jane**	*Dream Maker*	$5		Gordy 7162
4/7/79	72	6		3 **High On Your Love Suite**	*Stone City Band, Hi!*	$5	■	Gordy 7164
5/12/79	71	6		4 **Bustin' Out**	*Sexy Lady*	$5		Gordy 7167
5/30/81	40	14		5 **Give It To Me Baby** RB⁵	*Don't Give Up On Love*	$5		Gordy 7197
8/8/81	16	24		6 **Super Freak (Part I)** **The Temptations** (backing vocals); music used for **M.C. Hammer**'s 1990 hit "U Can't Touch This"	*(Part II)*	$5		Gordy 7205
5/8/82	66	8		7 **Standing On The Top-Part 1** **THE TEMPTATIONS FEATURING RICK JAMES**	*Part 2*	$4		Gordy 1616
5/29/82	64	9		8 **Dance Wit' Me - Part 1**	*Part 2*	$4	■	Gordy 1619
7/30/83	40	12		9 **Cold Blooded** RB⁶	*(instrumental)*	$4		Gordy 1687
12/10/83+	43	11		10 **Ebony Eyes** **RICK JAMES Featuring SMOKEY ROBINSON** early pressings credit artist as: RICK JAMES AND FRIEND	*1,2,3 (You Her And Me)* (James)	$4		Gordy 1714
7/14/84	36	14		11 **17**	*(instrumental)*	$4		Gordy 1730
3/30/85	50	8		12 **Can't Stop**	*Oh What A Night (4 Luv)*	$4	■	Gordy 1776

JAMES, Sonny C&W/BUB/LP '57

Born James Loden on 5/1/29 in Hackleburg, Alabama. Country singer/songwriter/guitarist. Nicknamed "The Southern Gentleman." Brought to Capitol Records in Nashville by **Chet Atkins**. Charted 72 Country hits (21 #1s), 1953-83. In the movies *Second Fiddle To A Steel Guitar*, *Nashville Rebel*, *Las Vegas Hillbillies* and *Hillbillys In A Haunted House*.

1)Young Love 2)First Date, First Kiss, First Love 3)Since I Met You, Baby

DEBUT	PEAK	WKS	Gold	A-side (Chart Hit)	B-side	$	Sym	Label & Number
12/29/56+	❶¹	21	●	1 **Young Love** CW⁹ A:❶¹ / S:2 / T:2 / J:4	*You're The Reason I'm In Love* (C&W #6)	$20		Capitol 3602
3/30/57	25	11		2 **First Date, First Kiss, First Love** A:25 / T:39	*Speak To Me*	$20		Capitol 3674
12/30/57	92	1		3 **Uh-Huh--mm** T:92	*Why Can't They Remember?*	$20		Capitol 3840
9/22/58	94	2		4 **You Got That Touch** H:94	*I Can See It In Your Eyes*	$20		Capitol 4020
5/4/59	85	5		5 **Talk Of The School** The Eligibles (backing vocals)	*The Table*	$20		Capitol 4178
1/18/60	80	3		6 **I Forgot More Than You'll Ever Know** #1 Country hit for The Davis Sisters in 1953	*'Till Tomorrow*	$15		Capitol 4307
4/11/60	67	6		7 **Jenny Lou**	*Passin' Through*	$25	■	NRC 050
3/6/61	87	2		8 **Apache**	*Magnetism*	$20		RCA Victor 7858
8/10/63	95	1		9 **The Minute You're Gone**	*Gold And Silver*	$12	□	Capitol 4969
11/28/64	91	6		10 **You're The Only World I Know** CW⁴	*Tying The Pieces Together*	$12	■	Capitol 5280
12/10/66	9ˣ	6		11 **Barefoot Santa Claus** X: 9/'66; 12/'68; children's chorus (backing vocals)	*My Christmas Dream* [X]	$15	■	Capitol 5733
7/22/67	97	3		12 **I'll Never Find Another You** CW⁴	*Goodbye, Maggie, Goodbye*	$12	■	Capitol 5914
11/23/68	81	4		13 **Born To Be With You** CW¹	*In Waikiki*	$10	■	Capitol 2271
2/8/69	92	4		14 **Only The Lonely** CW³	*The Journey*	$10	■	Capitol 2370
5/31/69	94	2		15 **Running Bear** CW³	*A Midnight Mood*	$10	■	Capitol 2486
9/20/69	65	7		16 **Since I Met You, Baby** CW³	*Clinging To A Hope*	$10	■	Capitol 2595
1/24/70	87	4		17 **It's Just A Matter Of Time** CW⁴	*This World Of Ours*	$8	■	Capitol 2700
4/10/71	93	3		18 **Empty Arms** CW⁴	*Everything Begins And Ends With You*	$8	■	Capitol 3015
7/17/71	91	3		19 **Bright Lights, Big City** CW¹	*True Love Lasts Forever*	$8	■	Capitol 3114

JAMES, Tommy, And The Shondells ★83★ BUB/LP '69

Born Thomas Jackson on 4/29/47 in Dayton, Ohio; raised in Niles, Michigan. Formed pop group The Shondells at age 12. Recorded "Hanky Panky" on the Snap label in 1963. James relocated to Pittsburgh in 1965 after a DJ there popularized "Hanky Panky." Original master was sold to Roulette, whereupon James recruited Pittsburgh group The Raconteurs to become the official Shondells. Consisted of Eddie Gray (guitar), Ronnie Rosman (organ), Mike Vale (bass) and Pete Lucia (drums). Group split from James in 1970; recorded as **Hog Heaven** (see #23 below).

1)Crimson And Clover 2)Hanky Panky 3)Crystal Blue Persuasion 4)Mony Mony 5)I Think We're Alone Now

DEBUT	PEAK	WKS	Gold	A-side (Chart Hit)	B-side	$	Sym	Label & Number
6/4/66	❶²	12	●	1 **Hanky Panky** first released on Snap 102 in 1963 ($75), then on Red Fox 110 in 1965 ($40) (both by The Shondells)	*Thunderbolt*	$12		Roulette 4686
8/6/66	21	8		2 **Say I Am (What I Am)**	*Lots Of Pretty Girls*	$10	■	Roulette 4695
11/5/66	31	9		3 **It's Only Love** melody based partially on "This Old Man" ("The Children's Marching Song")	*Don't Let My Love Pass You By*	$10		Roulette 4710
2/11/67	4	17		4 **I Think We're Alone Now**	*Gone, Gone, Gone*	$10	■	Roulette 4720
4/29/67	10	10		5 **Mirage**	*Run, Run, Baby, Run*	$10	■	Roulette 4736
7/1/67	25	7		6 **I Like The Way**	*(Baby) Baby I Can't Take It No More*	$10		Roulette 4756
8/26/67	18	8		7 **Gettin' Together**	*Real Girl*	$10	■	Roulette 4762
10/28/67	43	6		8 **Out Of The Blue**	*Love's Closin' In On Me*	$10		Roulette 4775
1/27/68	48	7		9 **Get Out Now**	*Wish It Were You*	$10		Roulette 7000
4/6/68	3	17		10 **Mony Mony** inspired by a sign for Mutual Of New York; #3-10: produced by Bo Gentry and Ritchie Cordell	*One Two Three And I Fell*	$10		Roulette 7008
7/27/68	53	5		11 **Somebody Cares**	*Do Unto Me*	$10		Roulette 7016
10/12/68	38	9		12 **Do Something To Me**	*Ginger Bread Man*	$10		Roulette 7024
12/14/68+	❶²	16		13 **Crimson And Clover**	*Some Kind Of Love*	$8		Roulette 7028
3/22/69	7	10		14 **Sweet Cherry Wine**	*Breakaway*	$8		Roulette 7039

DEBUT	PEAK	WKS	Gold	A-side (Chart Hit)...B-side	$	Sym	Label & Number
				JAMES, Tommy, And The Shondells — Cont'd			
6/7/69	2^3	15		15 **Crystal Blue Persuasion**...*I'm Alive*	$8		Roulette 7050
10/4/69	19	8		16 **Ball Of Fire**...*Makin' Good Time*	$8		Roulette 7060
12/13/69+	23	8		17 **She**...*Loved One*	$8		Roulette 7066
2/21/70	45	8		18 **Gotta Get Back To You**...*Red Rover*	$8		Roulette 7071
5/16/70	47	8		19 **Come To Me**...*Talkin' And Signifyin'*	$8		Roulette 7076
				TOMMY JAMES:			
8/1/70	57	7		20 **Ball And Chain**...*Candy Maker*	$8		Roulette 7084
12/19/70+	62	7		21 **Church Street Soul Revival**...*Draggin' The Line*	$8		Roulette 7093
3/20/71	93	3		22 **Adrienne**...*Light Of Day*	$8		Roulette 7100
4/24/71	98	2		23 **Happy**...*Prayer*	$8		Roulette 7101
				HOG HEAVEN			
6/12/71	4	13		24 **Draggin' The Line**...*Bits & Pieces* first released as the B-side of #21 above	$6		Roulette 7103
9/25/71	40	7		25 **I'm Comin' Home**...*Sing, Sing, Sing* The Stephentown Singers (backing vocals)	$6		Roulette 7110
11/27/71	41	9		26 **Nothing To Hide**...*Walk A Country Mile*	$6		Roulette 7114
2/19/72	89	4		27 **Tell 'Em Willie Boy 'S A'Comin'**...*Forty Days And Forty Nights*	$6		Roulette 7119
6/17/72	90	4		28 **Cat's Eye In The Window**...*Dark Is The Night*	$6		Roulette 7126
8/19/72	67	6		29 **Love Song**...*Kingston Highway*	$6		Roulette 7130
11/4/72	95	3		30 **Celebration**...*The Last One To Know*	$6		Roulette 7135
2/17/73	70	6		31 **Boo, Boo, Don't 'Cha Be Blue**...*Rings And Things*	$6		Roulette 7140
1/26/80	19	16		32 **Three Times In Love**...AC^1 *I Just Wanna Play The Music*	$5		Millennium 11785
5/9/81	58	7		33 **You're So Easy To Love**...*Halfway To Heaven*	$5		Millennium 11802
				JAMES BOYS, The — see MFSB			
				JAMES GANG, The BUB/LP '71 Rock group from Cleveland, Ohio: **Joe Walsh** (vocals, guitar, keyboards), Dale Peters (bass) and Jim Fox (drums). Walsh (later in the **Eagles**) left in late 1971; replaced by Dominic Troiano and Roy Kenner. Troiano joined the **Guess Who** in 1973; replaced by Tommy Bolin (died on 12/4/76, age 25). Many personnel changes from 1974 until group disbanded in 1976.			
8/29/70	59	10		1 **Funk # 49**...*Thanks* a different version, "Funk No. 48," "Bubbled Under" (#126) in 1969 on BluesWay 61030	$7		ABC 11272
5/29/71	51	10		2 **Walk Away**...*Yadig?* **Walsh**'s "live" solo version "Bubbled Under" (#105) in 1976 on ABC 12187	$6		ABC 11301
10/9/71	80	4		3 **Midnight Man**...*White Man/Black Man*	$6		ABC 11312
2/2/74	54	11		4 **Must Be Love**...*Got No Time For Trouble*	$6		Atco 6953
				JAMESON, Cody '77 Born in Manhattan, New York. Female pop singer.			
4/9/77	74	4		**Brooklyn**...*That Little Bit Of Us*	$5		Atco 7073
				JAMESON, Nick '86 Born in Missouri. Pop-rock singer/bassist. Former member of **Foghat**.			
8/23/86	95	2		**Weatherman**...*Casco Bay* [I]	$4		Motown 1853
				JAMESTOWN MASSACRE '72 Rock group from Chicago, Illinois: Dave Bickler (vocals), Len Fogerty (guitar), Mark Ayers (keyboards), Gary Manata (bass) and Jim Smith (drums). Bickler later joined **Survivor**.			
8/12/72	90	5		**Summer Sun**...*Words And Rhymes*	$8		Warner 7603
				JAMIES, The '58 Pop vocal group from Dorchester, Massachusetts: Tom Jameson, his sister Serena Jameson, Jeannie Roy and Arthur Blair.			
8/18/58	26	11		1 **Summertime, Summertime**...H:26 / S:28 *Searching For You*	$12		Epic 9281
6/23/62	38	8		2 **Summertime, Summertime**...*Searching For You* [R] above 2 are the same version	$12	■	Epic 9281
				JAMIROQUAI ROK/LP '00 Interracial alternative dance group led by singer/songwriter Jason Kay (born on 12/30/69 in Stretford, Manchester, England).			
10/11/97	78	8		1 **Alright**...*Tee's In House* samples "It's Alright Now" by **Eddie Harris**	$3	▮	Work 78703
6/12/99	58^S	6		2 **Canned Heat**...*Wolf In Sheep's Clothing*	$4	★^{V}	Work 79189 ■
12/11/99+	29^S	11		3 **Supersonic**...*(2 remixes)*	$4	★	Work 79320
				JAMUL '70 Rock group from San Diego, California: Steve Williams (vocals), Bob Desnoyers (guitar), John Fergus (bass) and Ron Armstrong (drums).			
5/9/70	93	2		**Tobacco Road**...*Sunrise Over Jamul*	$7		Lizard 21001
				JAN & DEAN ★162★ BUB/LP '64 Influential surf-rock male vocal duo from Los Angeles, California. Jan Berry (born on 4/3/41) and Dean Torrence (born on 3/10/40) formed group called the Barons while attending high school in Los Angeles. Jan & Dean and Barons' member Arnie Ginsburg recorded "Jennie Lee" in Jan's garage. Dean left for a six-month Army Reserve stint, whereupon Jan signed with Arwin (label owned by **Doris Day**'s husband, Marty Melcher) and released the record as by **Jan & Arnie**. Upon Dean's return from the service, Arnie (not to be confused with the famed DJ of the same name) joined the Navy, and Jan & Dean signed with the Dore label. Dean sang lead on **The Beach Boys**'s 1966 hit "Barbara Ann." Jan was critically injured in an auto accident on 4/12/66. Duo made a comeback in 1978, after their biographical movie *Dead Man's Curve* aired on TV. *1)Surf City 2)The Little Old Lady (From Pasadena) 3)Dead Man's Curve 4)Jennie Lee 5)Drag City*			
5/19/58	8	13		1 **Jennie Lee** *[JAN & ARNIE]*...S:8 / T:8 / A:17 *Gotta Getta Date* **Don Ralke** (orch.)	$50		Arwin 108
8/18/58	81	2		2 **Gas Money** *[JAN & ARNIE]*...H:81 *Bonnie Lou* Adam Ross (orch.)	$50		Arwin 111

DEBUT	PEAK	WKS	Gold	A-side (Chart Hit)	B-side	$	Sym	Label & Number
				JAN & DEAN — Cont'd				
8/3/59	10	12		3 **Baby Talk**	*Jeanette, Get Your Hair Done*	$30		Dore 522
				promotional pressings issued as by **Jan & Arnie** on Dore 522 ($1000)				
10/26/59	97	3		4 **There's A Girl**	*My Heart Sings*	$30		Dore 531
2/8/60	65	6		5 **Clementine**	*You're On My Mind*	$30		Dore 539
				folk tune written in 1884				
8/1/60	53	7		6 **We Go Together**	*Rosie Lane*	$30	■	Dore 555
				#9 R&B hit for **The Moonglows** in 1956				
11/14/60	81	5		7 **Gee**	*Such A Good Night For Dreaming*	$35	■	Dore 576
				#2 R&B hit for The Crows in 1954; #3-7: co-produced by **Herb Alpert**				
6/26/61	25	7		8 **Heart And Soul**	*Those Words*	$40		Challenge 9111
				Larry Clinton hit #1 in 1938 with this Hoagy Carmichael tune				
1/20/62	95	1		9 **A Sunday Kind Of Love**	*Poor Little Puppet*	$25		Liberty 55397
				co-written by **Louis Prima**; #15 hit for **Jo Stafford** in 1947				
5/26/62	69	7		10 **Tennessee**	*Your Heart Has Changed Its Mind*	$25		Liberty 55454
2/23/63	28	13		11 **Linda**	*When I Learn How To Cry*	$25		Liberty 55531
				#1 hit in 1947 for Buddy Clark with Ray Noble's orch.; written for then four-year-old Linda Eastman (**Paul McCartney**'s late wife)				
6/15/63	❶[2]	13		12 **Surf City**	*She's My Summer Girl*	$20	■	Liberty 55580
				Brian Wilson (backing vocal)				
9/7/63	11	10		13 **Honolulu Lulu**	*Someday (You'll Go Walking By)*	$15	■	Liberty 55613
12/7/63+	10	11		14 **Drag City**	*Schlock Rod (Part 1)*	$15	■	Liberty 55641
3/7/64	8	14		15 **Dead Man's Curve** /				
3/21/64	37	8		16 **The New Girl In School**		$15	■	Liberty 55672
				Dean overdubbed his vocal to this track and released it in 1973 as "Gonna Hustle You" by The Legendary Masked Surfers on United Artists 50958 ($100)				
6/27/64	3	11		17 **The Little Old Lady (From Pasadena)**	*My Mighty G.T.O.*	$15	■	Liberty 55704
9/19/64	16	8		18 **Ride The Wild Surf** /				
				title song from the movie starring **Tab Hunter** and **Fabian**				
10/3/64	77	3		19 **The Anaheim, Azusa & Cucamonga Sewing Circle, Book Review And Timing Association**		$15	■	Liberty 55724
10/31/64	25	8		20 **Sidewalk Surfin'**	*When It's Over*	$15	■	Liberty 55727
				a version with newly recorded vocals "Bubbled Under" (#107) on 7/24/76 on United Artists 670; new lyrics to **The Beach Boys**' 1963 recording "Catch A Wave"; #12, 14-16, 18 & 20: co-written by **Brian Wilson** (**The Beach Boys**)				
3/13/65	56	5		21 (Here They Come) **From All Over The World**	*Freeway Flyer* [L]	$15	■	Liberty 55766
				from the Santa Monica teen-rock concert movie *The T.A.M.I. Show*				
5/22/65	27	9		22 **You Really Know How To Hurt A Guy**	*It's As Easy As 1, 2, 3*	$15	■	Liberty 55792
10/16/65	30	7		23 **I Found A Girl**	*It's A Shame To Say Goodbye*	$15		Liberty 55833
2/12/66	66	5		24 **Batman**	*Bucket "T"* [N]	$25		Liberty 55860
				inspired by the popular *Batman* TV series starring Adam West and Burt Ward				
6/4/66	21	9		25 **Popsicle**	*Norwegian Wood (This Bird Has Flown)*	$12		Liberty 55886
				remix of a track from the 1963 album *Drag City* ("Popsicle Truck")				
9/3/66	93	4		26 **Fiddle Around**	*A Surfer's Dream*	$12		Liberty 55905
				previously unreleased 1962 recording				
				JAN AND KJELD '60				
				Duo of brothers from Copenhagen, Denmark: Jan (born on 7/27/46) and Kjeld (born on 2/3/44) Wennick.				
6/6/60	58	7		**Banjo Boy**	*Don't Raise A Storm* [F]	$12	■	Kapp 335
				JANIS, Johnny '57				
				Born on 3/20/20 in Chicago, Illinois. Pop singer.				
4/29/57	63	3		**Pledge Of Love**	T:63 *I Played The Field*	$20		ABC-Paramount 9800
				Don Costa (orch.)				
				JANKOWSKI, Horst AC/LP '65				
				Born on 1/30/36 in Berlin, Germany. Died of cancer on 6/29/98 (age 62). Jazz pianist.				
5/8/65	12	13		1 **A Walk In The Black Forest**	AC[2] *Nola* [I]	$8		Mercury 72425
9/4/65	91	1		2 **Simpel Gimpel**	*Charming Vienna* [I]	$6	■	Mercury 72465
				JARMELS, The '61				
				R&B vocal group from Richmond, Virginia: Nathaniel Ruff, Ray Smith, Paul Burnett, Earl Christian and Tom Eldridge. Named for a street in Harlem. **Major Harris** was later a member. Eldridge died on 6/19/2000 (age 59). Burnett died on 3/21/2001 (age 55).				
7/31/61	12	10		**A Little Bit Of Soap**	*The Way You Look Tonight*	$20		Laurie 3098
				JARREAU, Al R&B/AC/BUB/LP '83				
				Born on 3/12/40 in Milwaukee, Wisconsin. R&B/jazz-styled singer. Has master's degree in psychology from the University of Iowa. Worked clubs in San Francisco with **George Duke**.				
8/1/81	15	24		1 **We're In This Love Together**	*Alonzo*	$4		Warner 49746
12/5/81+	43	10		2 **Breakin' Away**	*(Round, Round, Round) Blue Rondo A La Turk*	$4		Warner 49842
4/3/82	70	7		3 **Teach Me Tonight**	*Easy*	$4		Warner 50032
3/19/83	21	15		4 **Mornin'** *[JARREAU]*	*Not Like This*	$4	■	Warner 29720
6/18/83	77	6		5 **Boogie Down** *[JARREAU]*	*Our Love*	$4		Warner 29624
9/10/83	63	7		6 **Trouble In Paradise** *[JARREAU]*	*Step By Step*	$4	■	Warner 29501
10/13/84	69	9		7 **After All**	*I Keep Callin'*	$4	■	Warner 29262
5/30/87	23	13		8 **Moonlighting** (Theme)	AC[1] S:13 / A:37 *(dub version)*	$3	■	MCA 53124
				theme from the TV series starring **Bruce Willis** and Cybill Shepherd				
				JARS OF CLAY ROK/LP '96				
				Christian pop group formed in Illinois: Dan Haseltine (vocals), Steve Mason and Matt Odmark (guitars), and Charlie Lowell (keyboards).				
5/18/96	37	19		**Flood**	A:32 / S:48 *Sinking*	$4	▮	Silvertone 42375
				produced by **Adrian Belew**				

DEBUT	PEAK	WKS	Gold	A-side (Chart Hit)..........B-side	$	Sym	Label & Number

JA RULE ★199★ R&B/LP '02

Born Jeffrey Atkins on 2/29/76 in Queens, New York. Male rapper/actor. Appeared in the movies *The Fast And The Furious* and *Half Past Dead.* Also see **BLACKstreet**'s "Girlfriend/Boyfriend" and **Dru Hill**'s "You Are Everything."

1)Always On Time 2)Livin' It Up 3)Put It On Me

DEBUT	PEAK	WKS	Gold	A-side (Chart Hit)..........B-side	$	Sym	Label & Number
4/3/99	35	20		1 **Holla Holla** ....S:13 / A:46 *(instrumental) / It*s Murda* (w/**DMX** & **Jay-Z**) */ Kill *Em All* (w/**Jay-Z**)	$8	★*	Def Jam 566959
11/6/99	35^{S}	10		2 **Damn (Should've Treated U Right)**..........*(3 versions)* **SO PLUSH Featuring Ja Rule**	$5	★	Darkchild/Epic 79283
9/16/00	11	20		3 **Between Me And You** ....A:7 *(3 versions) / Die* (w/Tah Murdah, Black Child & Dave Bing) **JA RULE (Featuring Christina Milian)**	$6	T	Def Jam 562890
12/23/00+	8	27		4 **Put It On Me** ....A:4 / S:62 *(2 versions) / Love Me, Hate Me* **JA RULE (feat. Lil' Mo and Vita)**	$6	T	Def Jam 572751
5/5/01	40	14		5 **I Cry** ....A:34 *(2 versions) / Rule Won't Die* **JA RULE (Feat. Lil' Mo)** samples "Cry Together" by **The O'Jays**	$6	T	Def Jam 572856
7/7/01	❶^{5}	31		6 **I'm Real** ....A:❶^{6} / S:31 *(3 versions)* **JENNIFER LOPEZ featuring Ja Rule** samples "All Night Long" by the **Mary Jane Girls**; "45": Epic 79662; B-side: "Love Don't Cost A Thing"	$6	T^{V}	Epic 79639
9/1/01	6	25		7 **Livin' It Up**..........A:6 / S:29 *(2 versions) / The Inc.* (w/Caddillac Tah & Black Child) **JA RULE (feat. Case)** samples "Do I Do" by **Stevie Wonder**	$6	T	Def Jam 588741
11/17/01+	❶^{2}	27		8 **Always On Time** RB^{8} A:❶^{2} / S:27 *(2 versions) / Worldwide Gangsta* **JA RULE (feat. Ashanti)**	$6	T	Def Jam 588795
12/29/01+	❶^{6}	27		9 **Ain't It Funny** ....A:❶^{6} **JENNIFER LOPEZ featuring Ja Rule** samples "Flava In Ya Ear" by **Craig Mack**; from the album *J.Lo* on Epic 85965			album cut
3/30/02	12	20		10 **Rainy Dayz**..........A:10 / S:60 *(3 versions)* **MARY J. BLIGE Featuring Ja Rule**	$6	T	MCA 155972
4/13/02	21	19		11 **Down A** Chick**..........A:20 / S:63 *Smokin And Ridin* (w/Jodi Mack & 0-1) **JA RULE feat. Charli "Chuck" Baltimore**	$4	★	Def Jam 063946
6/22/02	6	20		12 **Down 4 U** ....A:6 **IRV GOTTI PRESENTS THE INC. Featuring Ja Rule, Ashanti, Charli Baltimore & Vita** from the album *Irv Gotti Presents The Inc.* on Murder Inc. 062033			album cut
11/23/02	42	10		13 **Thug Lovin'**..........S:24 / A:42 *(3 versions)* **JA RULE feat. Bobby Brown** contains an interpolation of "Knocks Me Off My Feet" by **Stevie Wonder**	$6	T	Murder Inc. 063838
12/28/02+	2^{1}	20		14 **Mesmerize**..........A:2 / S:23 *(2 versions) / Pop N****s* **JA RULE feat. Ashanti** samples "Stop, Look, Listen" by **The Stylistics**	$6	T	Murder Inc. 063773

JARVIS, Carol '57

Teen pop singer. Daughter of Los Angeles DJ Al Jarvis (died in 1970).

DEBUT	PEAK	WKS	Gold	A-side (Chart Hit)..........B-side	$	Sym	Label & Number
9/2/57	48	16		**Rebel**..........T:48 *Whirlpool Of Love*	$15		Dot 15586

JASON — see J'SON / J-SHIN

JAY, Morty, And The Surferin' Cats '63

Studio duo of Morty Jay (arranger from New York) and Mack Wolfson (songwriter). Wolfson was later the head of Golden Crest Records. Also see **Johnny Kaye**.

DEBUT	PEAK	WKS	Gold	A-side (Chart Hit)..........B-side	$	Sym	Label & Number
11/9/63	93	1		**Saltwater Taffy** ....*What Is Surfin' All About* (Jerry Norell & The Beach Girls) [I]	$25	■	Legend 124

JAYA '90

Born Maria Louise Ramsey in 1970 in Manila, Philippines. To California in 1985. Discovered by **Stevie B.**

DEBUT	PEAK	WKS	Gold	A-side (Chart Hit)..........B-side	$	Sym	Label & Number
10/14/89+	44	26		**If You Leave Me Now** ....A:40 *(instrumental)* **Stevie B** (writer, producer, backing vocal); "45": LMR 77000	$3	▮^{V}	LMR 87000

JAY & THE AMERICANS ★277★ BUB/LP '65

Pop-rock vocal group formed in New York: John "Jay" Traynor (an early member of **The Mystics**), Sandy Yaguda (born on 1/30/43), Kenny Vance (born on 12/9/43; later a Hollywood musical director) and Howie Kane (born on 6/6/42). Guitarist Marty Sanders (born on 2/28/41) joined during production of their first album in 1961. Traynor left after their first hit and was replaced by lead singer **Jay Black** (born David Blatt on 11/2/41) in 1962.

1)Come A Little Bit Closer 2)Cara, Mia 3)She Cried

DEBUT	PEAK	WKS	Gold	A-side (Chart Hit)..........B-side	$	Sym	Label & Number
3/17/62	5	14		1 **She Cried**..........*Dawning*	$15		United Artists 415
8/17/63	25	11		2 **Only In America** ....*My Clair De Lune*	$12		United Artists 626
11/30/63	76	8		3 **Come Dance With Me**..........*Look In My Eyes Maria*	$12		United Artists 669
9/12/64	3	15		4 **Come A Little Bit Closer** *Goodbye Boys Goodbye*	$12		United Artists 759
12/26/64+	11	10		5 **Let's Lock The Door (And Throw Away The Key)**..........*I'll Remember You*	$12		United Artists 805
3/27/65	57	8		6 **Think Of The Good Times**..........*If You Were Mine, Girl*	$12		United Artists 845
6/5/65	4	13		7 **Cara, Mia** ....*When It's All Over* (#129)	$12		United Artists 881
9/4/65	13	10		8 **Some Enchanted Evening** ....*Girl* there were 6 Top 10 versions of this *South Pacific* Broadway musical song in 1949	$10	■	United Artists 919
11/20/65	18	8		9 **Sunday And Me**..........*Through This Doorway* **Neil Diamond**'s first major hit as a songwriter; back of sleeve promotes Paris belts	$10	■	United Artists 948
2/19/66	63	6		10 **Why Can't You Bring Me Home**..........*Baby Stop Your Cryin'*	$10		United Artists 992
5/28/66	25	6		11 **Crying**..........*I Don't Need A Friend*	$10	■	United Artists 50016
7/30/66	76	5		12 **Livin' Above Your Head**..........*Look At Me - What Do You See* #7-12: produced by **Gerry Granahan** of **Dicky Doo & The Don'ts**	$10	■	United Artists 50046
11/26/66	90	4		13 **(He's) Raining In My Sunshine**..........*The Reason For Living (For You My Darling)*	$10		United Artists 50094

DEBUT	PEAK	WKS	Gold	A-side (Chart Hit)........B-side	$	Sym	Label & Number
				JAY & THE AMERICANS — Cont'd			
12/28/68+	6	14	●	14 **This Magic Moment** .... *Since I Don't Have You*	$10		United Artists 50475
4/5/69	70	5		15 **When You Dance** .... *No, I Don't Know Her*	$8		United Artists 50510
5/31/69	62	7		16 **Hushabye** .... *Gypsy Woman*	$8		United Artists 50535
11/22/69+	19	15		17 **Walkin' In The Rain** .... *(I'd Kill) For The Love Of A Lady*	$8		United Artists 50605
3/28/70	57	6		18 **Capture The Moment** .... *Do You Ever Think Of Me?*	$8		United Artists 50654
9/20/80	98	4		19 **The Part Of Me That Needs You Most** .... *You Stole The Music* **JAY BLACK**	$5		Midsong 72012
				JAY AND THE TECHNIQUES BUB/R&B/LP **'67** Interracial R&B-rock group from Allentown, Pennsylvania: Jay Proctor (lead singer; born on 10/28/40), Karl Landis, Ronnie Goosly, John Walsh, George Lloyd, Chuck Crowl and Dante Dancho.			
7/15/67	6	17		1 **Apples, Peaches, Pumpkin Pie** .... *Stronger Than Dirt*	$10		Smash 2086
10/21/67	14	12		2 **Keep The Ball Rollin'** .... *Here We Go Again*	$10	■	Smash 2124
1/20/68	39	6		3 **Strawberry Shortcake** .... *Still (In Love With You)*	$10	■	Smash 2142
4/13/68	64	8		4 **Baby Make Your Own Sweet Music** .... *Help Yourself To All My Lovin'*	$10	■	Smash 2154
				JAYE, Jerry C&W/BUB/LP **'67** Born Gerald Jaye Hatley on 10/19/37 in Manila, Arkansas. Rockabilly singer.			
4/15/67	29	9		**My Girl Josephine** .... *Five Miles From Home* originally released as "Hello Josephine" on Connie Records ($30)	$15		Hi 2120
				JAYHAWKS, The — see VIBRATIONS, The			
				JAYMES, Jesse **'91** Born in Roslyn, New York. White male rapper.			
7/6/91	74	5		**Shake It (Like A White Girl)** .... *(groove version)*	$4	▮	Delicious Vinyl 868214
				JAYNETTS, The BUB **'63** Female R&B group from the Bronx, New York. Formed by producer/composer/owner of J&S Records Zelma "Zell" Sanders. Consisted of Ethel Davis, Mary Sue Wells, Yvonne Bushnell and Ada Ray. Johnnie Louise Richardson (ex-**Johnnie & Joe**) was Sanders's daughter and a touring member of the group; died from a stroke on 10/25/88. Also see **The Hearts**.			
8/31/63	2^2	12		**Sally, Go 'Round The Roses** .... *(instrumental)* first released on Soultown 505 in 1962 ($25)	$15		Tuff 369
				**JAY-Z** ★95★ R&B/BUB/LP **'02** Born Shawn Carter on 12/4/69 in Brooklyn, New York. Male rapper/songwriter. Founded the Roc-A-Fella record label. Appeared in the movie *State Property*. *1)'03 Bonnie & Clyde 2)Izzo (H.O.V.A.) 3)I Just Wanna Love U (Give It 2 Me) 4)Hard Knock Life (Ghetto Anthem) 5)Girls, Girls, Girls*			
4/6/96	50	20	●	1 **Ain't No Nigga /** S:37 **Foxy Brown** (guest rapper); incorporates the tune "Ain't No Woman (Like The One I've Got)"			
4/13/96		19		2 **Dead Presidents**	$6	▮*	Roc-A-Fella 53233
9/14/96	73	14		3 **Can't Knock The Hustle** .... S:58 *(clean version)* **Mary J. Blige** (backing vocal); samples "Much Too Much" by Marcus Miller	$5	▮	Roc-A-Fella 53242
2/15/97	7	20	●	4 **I'll Be** .... S:2 / A:52 *La Familia* **FOXY BROWN Featuring Jay-Z** samples "I'll Be Good" by **Rene & Angela**	$3	▮	Violator 574028
5/3/97	79	9		5 **Feelin' It** .... S:73 *(2 versions) / Friend Or Foe* #1-3 & 5: from the album *Reasonable Doubt*	$4	▮	Roc-A-Fella 53272
6/7/97	84	4		6 **Who You Wit** .... *(3 versions)* from the movie *Sprung* starring Tisha Campbell	$6	T	Qwest 43883
10/25/97	95	2		7 **Sunshine** .... *(2 versions)* **JAY-Z featuring Babyface and Foxy Brown**	$6	T	Roc-A-Fella 574923
11/8/97	65	12		8 **All Of My Days** .... S:54 *(instrumental)* **CHANGING FACES (Featuring Jay-Z)** written and produced by **R. Kelly**; from the movie *Space Jam* starring Michael Jordan	$3	▮	Big Beat 98000
1/31/98	52	20		9 **The City Is Mine** .... S:32 *(TV track) / A Million And One Questions* (Jay-Z) **JAY-Z (Featuring BlackStreet)** samples "You Belong To The City" by **Glenn Frey** and "You Gonna Make Me Love Somebody Else" by **The Jones Girls**	$3	▮	Roc-A-Fella 568592
7/4/98	52	20		10 **Money Ain't A Thang** .... A:62 *(3 versions)* **JD Featuring JAY-Z**	$6	T	So So Def 78864
8/1/98	86	3		11 **Love For Free** .... S:59 *(TV track remix)* **RELL (featuring Jay-Z)** samples "Do It ('Til You're Satisfied)" by **B.T. Express**	$3	▮	Roc-A-Fella 568842
8/8/98	61	12		12 **It's Alright** .... S:51 *The Doe* **MEMPHIS BLEEK & JAY-Z** samples "Once In A Lifetime" by **Talking Heads**; above 2 from the movie *Streets Is Watching* starring Jay-Z	$3	▮	Roc-A-Fella 566210
10/3/98+	19	37		13 **Can I Get A...** ......A:9 *Bitch Betta Have My Money* (**Ja Rule**) */ And You Don't Stop* (**Wu-Tang Clan**) **JAY-Z (featuring Amil of Major Coinz) and Ja** from the movie *Rush Hour* starring Jackie Chan	$6	T	Def Jam 567683
11/7/98+	15	22	●	14 **Hard Knock Life (Ghetto Anthem)** ...S:5 / A:23 *(remix) / Money, Cash, Hoes* (w/**Beanie Sigel, Memphis Bleek** & **DMX** - R&B #36) samples "Hard Knock Life" by The Original Broadway Cast of *Annie*	$5	★	Roc-A-Fella 566977
5/8/99	84	3		15 **Jigga What?** .... A:68 *Nigga What, Nigga Who / Money, Cash, Hoes*	$7	T	Roc-A-Fella 566893
6/26/99	28	20		16 **Jigga My Nigga** .... S:10 / A:47 *Memphis Bleek Is...* (**Memphis Bleek**) */ When Will U See* (**Rell** w/Amil) */ What A Thug About* (**Beanie Sigel**)	$5	★	Roc-A-Fella 562201
8/28/99	52	13		17 **Girls' Best Friend** .... A:44 from the movie *Blue Streak* starring Martin Lawrence (soundtrack on Epic 63615)			album cut

DEBUT	PEAK	WKS	Gold	A-side (Chart Hit)..........B-side	$	Sym	Label & Number
				JAY-Z — Cont'd			
9/4/99	❶^2	20	●	18 **Heartbreaker** RB^2 S:❶^2 / A:8 *(remix* w/**Da Brat & Missy Elliott**)	$4	★^{V}	Columbia 79260
				MARIAH CAREY (Featuring Jay-Z)			
				samples "Attack Of The Name Game" by **Stacy Lattisaw**			
1/15/00	65	9		19 **Do It Again (Put Ya Hands Up)**..........A:55 / S:68 *(2 versions) / So Ghetto*	$6	T	Roc-A-Fella 562575
				JAY-Z Featuring Beanie Sigel & Amil			
4/22/00	18	20		20 **Big Pimpin'** / A:13			
				JAY-Z (featuring UGK)			
2/26/00	55	8		21 **Anything**..........A:48 / S:71	$6	T	Roc-A-Fella 562670
				samples "I'd Do Anything" from the 1968 soundtrack album *Oliver!*			
8/12/00	76	15		22 **Hey Papi**..........A:70 *(3 versions)*	$6	T	Def Jam 562862
				JAY-Z (Featuring Memphis Bleek & Amil)			
				from the movie *Nutty Professor II: The Klumps* starring **Eddie Murphy** and **Janet Jackson**			
10/28/00	11	21		23 **I Just Wanna Love U (Give It 2 Me)**....RB^3 A:7 / S:34 *(2 versions) / Parking Lot Pimpin'* (w/**Beanie Sigel** & **Memphis Bleek**)	$6	T	Roc-A-Fella 572666
				samples "Give It To Me Baby" by **Rick James** and "The World Is Filled..." by **The Notorious B.I.G.**			
12/16/00+	68	13		24 **Is That Your Chick**..........S:55 / A:62 *(2 versions) / All Types Of S****	$6	T	Roc-A-Fella 562865
				MEMPHIS BLEEK (feat. Jay-Z and Missy Elliott)			
2/3/01	86	14		25 **Change The Game**..........S:68 *(2 versions) / You, Me, Him And Her* (Dynasty)	$6	T	Roc-A-Fella 572761
				JAY-Z, BEANIE SIGEL and MEMPHIS BLEEK			
3/31/01	6	21		26 **Fiesta Remix**..........RB^5 S:4 / A:12 *(clean version) / Fiesta / True Baller*	$8	★*	Jive 42904
				R. KELLY (Featuring Jay-Z and Boo & Gotti)			
4/7/01	82	8		27 **Guilty Until Proven Innocent**..........S:58 *(2 versions) / 1-900-Hustler* (w/**Beanie Sigel, Memphis Bleek** & **Freeway**)	$6	T	Roc-A-Fella 572809
				JAY-Z (feat. R. Kelly)			
7/28/01	8	20		28 **Izzo (H.O.V.A.)**..........A:7 / S:19 *(2 versions) / You Don't Know*	$6	T	Roc-A-Fella 588701
				samples "I Want You Back" by **The Jackson 5**			
10/13/01	17	17		29 **Girls, Girls, Girls**..........A:15 / S:32 *(2 versions) / Takeover*	$6	T	Roc-A-Fella 588793
				Q-Tip, Slick Rick and **Biz Markie** (backing vocals); samples "I Love You More And More Every Time" performed by Tom Brock			
1/26/02	66	9		30 **Jigga**..........S:27 / A:64 *Renegade* (w/**Eminem**)	$6	T	Roc-A-Fella 588930
				above 3 from the album *The Blueprint* on Roc-A-Fella 586396			
3/30/02	81	8		31 **Take You Home With Me A.K.A. Body** S:16 *(2 versions) / Get This Money* (#115/R&B #37)	$6	T	Roc-A-Fella 588988
				R. KELLY & JAY-Z			
5/18/02	79	8		32 **Guess Who's Back**..........S:21 *(2 versions) / My Block* (R&B #46)	$6	T	Def Jam 582865
				SCARFACE (featuring Jay-Z & Beanie Sigel)			
				samples "Sunrise" by **The Originals**			
6/29/02	35^S	6		33 **Welcome To New York City**..........*(3 versions)*	$6	T	Roc-A-Fella 582970
				CAM'RON feat. Jay-Z and Juelz Santana			
10/26/02	4	23		34 **'03 Bonnie & Clyde**..........A:4 / S:15 *(3 versions)*	$6	T	Roc-A-Fella 063843
				JAY-Z Featuring Beyoncé Knowles			
				samples "If I Was Your Girlfriend" by **Prince**			
12/7/02	36^S	3		35 **Hovi Baby**..........*(2 versions) / U Don't Know* (w/**M.O.P.**)	$6	T	Roc-A-Fella 063819
				samples "Diggin' On You" by **TLC**			
				JAZZ CRUSADERS — see CRUSADERS			
				JAZZY JEFF — see D.J. JAZZY JEFF			
				JB's, The R&B/BUB/LP **'73**			
				James Brown's super-funk backup band led by **Fred Wesley**, also of **Parliament/Funkadelic**. Also recorded as **Nat Kendrick And The Swans** and **Maceo And The Macks**.			
2/15/60	84	2		1 **(Do The) Mashed Potatoes (Part 1)**..........*(Part 2)*	$20		Dade 1804
				NAT KENDRICK AND THE SWANS			
				Miami DJ "King" Coleman (vocal shouts); **James Brown** (piano); also see **The Dartells**' "Hot Pastrami"			
1/22/72	67	8		2 **Gimme Some More**..........*The Rabbit Got The Gun* [I]	$8		People 602
5/27/72	95	2		3 **Pass The Peas**..........*Hot Pants Road* [I]	$8		People 607
6/2/73	22	11	●	4 **Doing It To Death** RB^2 *Everybody Got Soul*	$8		People 621
				FRED WESLEY & THE J.B's			
9/1/73	71	5		5 **Parrty - Part I**..........*Part II* [I]	$8		People 624
				MACEO AND THE MACKS			
				above 4 written, produced and arranged by **James Brown**			
				JD — see DUPRI, Jermaine			
	★596★			**JEAN, Wyclef** R&B/LP **'98**			
				Born on 10/17/72 in Croix Des Bouquets, Haiti; raised in Brooklyn, New York. Hip-hop singer/songwriter/guitarist/producer. Member of **The Fugees**.			
				1)Gone Till November 2)Two Wrongs 3)911			
6/14/97	45	12		1 **We Trying To Stay Alive**..........S:34 *Anything Can Happen / (3 album snippets)*	$6	▮*	Ruffhouse 78602
				samples "Stayin' Alive" by the **Bee Gees** and "Top Billin'" by Audio Two			
9/6/97	62^A	7		2 **Guantanamera**..........			album cut
				WYCLEF JEAN Featuring Refugee Allstars (above 2)			
11/29/97+	3	35	▲	3 **No, No, No Part 2**..........RB^1 S:❶^1 / A:22 *(Part 1)*	$3	▮	Columbia 78618
				DESTINY'S CHILD (featuring Wyclef Jean)			
2/7/98	7	20	▲	4 **Gone Till November** S:4 / A:48 *(remix* w/**Canibus**)	$4	▮	Ruffhouse 78752
				R. Kelly (backing vocal)			
8/8/98	61	1		5 **What's Clef** / S:46			
				Naomi Campbell (female vocal); samples "What's Love Got To Do With It" by **Tina Turner**			
8/15/98	69	2		6 **Chickenhead** /			
				WYCLEF JEAN Featuring Spragga Benz			
				samples "Sister Christian" by **Night Ranger** and the theme from TV's *Knight Rider*			
8/22/98	74	5		7 **Cheated (To All The Girls)**..........	$6	▮*	Ruffhouse 78993
				WYCLEF JEAN featuring Queen Pen & The Product			
				samples "To All The Girls I've Loved Before" by **Julio Iglesias** & **Willie Nelson**; above 3 all charted from the same maxi-cassette; #1, 2, 4 & 7: from the album *Wyclef Jean Presents The Carnival* on Ruffhouse 67974			
10/2/99	41^S	7		8 **New Day**..........*(clean version* w/**Refugee Camp** & guests)	$5	★	Ruffhouse 79274
				WYCLEF JEAN Featuring BONO			

DEBUT	PEAK	WKS	Gold	A-side (Chart Hit)	B-side	$	Sym	Label & Number
				JEAN, Wyclef — Cont'd				
10/7/00	38	19		9 **911** ... A:30 / S:61	*(5 versions)*	$6	T	Columbia 79460
				WYCLEF JEAN Featuring Mary J. Blige samples "The Payback" by **James Brown** and "What I Am" by **Edie Brickell & New Bohemians**				
7/14/01	18^{S}	17		10 **Cluck Cluck**	*(Henhouse Mix) / Freak Freak* (w/**Lil' Kim**)	$4	★^{V}	YClef/J Records 21068
				THE PRODUCT G&B Feat. Wyclef from the movie *Dr. Dolittle 2* starring **Eddie Murphy**; "45": J Records 21049				
7/13/02	28	20		11 **Two Wrongs** ... S:❸ / A:46	*(instrumental)*	$4	★	Columbia 79776
				WYCLEF JEAN feat. Claudette Ortiz of City High				

JEAN & THE DARLINGS '67

R&B trio of sisters from Arkansas: Jeanne, Phefe and Dee Dolphus. First recorded as The Dolphus Singers.

DEBUT	PEAK	WKS	Gold	A-side (Chart Hit)	B-side	$	Sym	Label & Number
8/26/67	96	1		**How Can You Mistreat The One You Love**	*That Man Of Mine*	$10		Volt 151
				written and produced by **Isaac Hayes** and **David Porter**				

JEFFERSON '70

Born Geoff Turton on 3/11/44 in Birmingham, England. Male singer.

DEBUT	PEAK	WKS	Gold	A-side (Chart Hit)	B-side	$	Sym	Label & Number
8/16/69	68	9		1 **The Colour Of My Love**	*Look No Further*	$8		Decca 32501
12/20/69+	23	12		2 **Baby Take Me In Your Arms**	*I Fell Flat On My Face*	$8		Janus 106

JEFFERSON AIRPLANE/STARSHIP ★68★ ROK/BUB/AC/LP '67

Rock group formed as **Jefferson Airplane** in San Francisco, California: **Marty Balin** (born on 1/30/42) and **Grace Slick** (see #20 below) (vocals; born on 10/30/39), Paul Kantner (vocals, guitar; born on 3/17/41), Jorma Kaukonen (guitar; born on 12/23/40), Jack Casady (bass; born on 4/13/44) and Spencer Dryden (drums; born on 4/7/43). Original drummer Skip Spence formed **Moby Grape**. Dryden left in 1970 to join **New Riders Of The Purple Sage**; replaced by Joey Covington. Casady and Kaukonen left by 1974 to go full time with Hot Tuna. Balin left in 1971, rejoined in 1975, by which time group was renamed **Jefferson Starship** and consisted of Slick, Kantner, Papa John Creach (violin; died on 2/22/94, age 76), David Freiberg (bass), Craig Chaquico (guitar), Pete Sears (bass) and John Barbata (drums). Slick left group from June 1978 to January 1981. In 1979, singer Mickey Thomas joined (replaced Balin), along with Aynsley Dunbar (**John Mayall**'s Bluesbreakers, Mothers Of Invention, **Journey**) who replaced Barbata. Don Baldwin (formerly with **Snail**) replaced Dunbar (later with **Whitesnake**) in 1982. Kantner left in 1984, and, due to legal difficulties, band's name was shortened to **Starship**, whose lineup included Slick, Thomas, Sears, Chaquico and Baldwin. Slick left in early 1988. Kantner, Balin and Casady formed the **KBC Band** (see #31 below) in 1986. In 1989, the original 1966 lineup of Balin, Slick, Kantner, Kaukonen and Casady reunited as Jefferson Airplane with Kenny Aronoff (from **John Cougar Mellencamp**'s band) replacing Dryden. Continuing as Starship were Thomas, Chaquico, Baldwin, Brett Bloomfield (bass) and Mark Morgan (keyboards). Starship disbanded in 1990. Jefferson Airplane was inducted into the Rock and Roll Hall of Fame in 1996.

1)Nothing's Gonna Stop Us Now 2)We Built This City 3)Sara 4)Miracles 5)Somebody To Love

DEBUT	PEAK	WKS	Gold	A-side (Chart Hit)	B-side	$	Sym	Label & Number
				JEFFERSON AIRPLANE:				
4/1/67	5	15		1 **Somebody To Love**	*She Has Funny Cars*	$12		RCA Victor 9140
				originally released by the Great Society on North Beach 1001 in 1966, entitled "Someone To Love" ($300)				
6/24/67	8	10		2 **White Rabbit**	*Plastic Fantastic Lover*	$12		RCA Victor 9248
9/2/67	42	6		3 **Ballad Of You & Me & Pooneil**	*Two Heads* (#124)	$12		RCA Victor 9297
12/16/67	61	4		4 **Watch Her Ride**	*Martha*	$12		RCA Victor 9389
4/20/68	98	3		5 **Greasy Heart**	*Share alittle Joke (With the World)*	$12		RCA Victor 9496
11/2/68	64	6		6 **Crown Of Creation**	*Lather*	$12	■	RCA Victor 9644
11/8/69	65	10		7 **Volunteers**	*We Can Be Together*	$12	■	RCA Victor 0245
11/20/71+	60	10		8 **Pretty As You Feel**	*Wild Turkey*	$8	■	Grunt 0500
				JEFFERSON STARSHIP:				
11/16/74	84	5		9 **Ride The Tiger**	*Devils Den*	$6		Grunt 10080
8/23/75	3	17		10 **Miracles**	*Ai Garimasu (There Is Love)*	$5		Grunt 10367
12/13/75+	49	6		11 **Play On Love**	*I Want To See Another World*	$5		Grunt 10456
7/24/76	12	17		12 **With Your Love**	*Switchblade*	$5		Grunt 10746
12/4/76	64	5		13 **St. Charles**	*Love Lovely Love*	$5		Grunt 10791
3/11/78	8	14		14 **Count On Me**	*Show Yourself*	$5	■	Grunt 11196
5/27/78	12	16		15 **Runaway**	*Hot Water*	$5	■	Grunt 11274
9/9/78	54	6		16 **Crazy Feelin'**	*Love Too Good*	$5	■	Grunt 11374
12/2/78	66	6		17 **Light The Sky On Fire**	*Hyperdrive*	$5	■	Grunt 11426
				promo sleeve issued with a slightly different message than the commercial sleeve				
11/3/79+	14	15		18 **Jane**	*Freedom At Point Zero*	$5	■	Grunt 11750
2/23/80	55	6		19 **Girl With The Hungry Eyes**	*Just The Same*	$5	■	Grunt 11921
4/19/80	95	2		20 **Seasons**	*Angel Of Night*	$5	■	RCA 11939
				GRACE SLICK				
4/4/81	29	13		21 **Find Your Way Back**	*Modern Times*	$5		Grunt 12211
7/11/81	48	11		22 **Stranger**	*Free*	$5		Grunt 12275
10/9/82	28	16		23 **Be My Lady**	*Out Of Control*	$4		Grunt 13350
1/29/83	38	11		24 **Winds Of Change**	*Black Widow*	$4		Grunt 13439
5/12/84	23	16		25 **No Way Out** ... AR^{1}	*Rose Goes To Yale*	$4		Grunt 13811
9/8/84	66	6		26 **Layin' It On The Line**	*Showdown*	$4	■	Grunt 13872
				STARSHIP:				
9/7/85	❶^{2}	24	●	27 **We Built This City** ... AR^{1} A:❶^{2} / S:2	*Private Room* [I]	$3	■	Grunt 14170
				San Francisco veteran DJ Les Garland (DJ voice)				
12/28/85+	❶^{1}	20		28 **Sara** ... AC^{3} S:❶^{1} / A:❶^{1}	*Hearts Of The World (Will Understand)*	$3	■	Grunt 14253
4/5/86	26	13		29 **Tomorrow Doesn't Matter Tonight** ... A:25 / S:27	*Love Rusts*	$3	■	Grunt 14332
7/5/86	68	7		30 **Before I Go**	*Cut You Down To Size*	$3	■	Grunt 14393
				above 4 from the album *Knee Deep In The Hoopla*				
11/29/86	89	4		31 **It's Not You, It's Not Me**	*Dream Motorcycle*	$3	■	Arista 9526
				KBC BAND				
1/31/87	❶^{2}	22	●	32 **Nothing's Gonna Stop Us Now** AC^{2} A:❶^{3} / S:❶^{2}	*Layin' It On The Line (live)*	$3	■	Grunt 5109
				from the movie *Mannequin* starring Andrew McCarthy; picture sleeve features Andrew McCarthy on a motorcycle; also issued with a "Special Holiday Re-service" sleeve featuring a color photo of the group				

DEBUT	PEAK	WKS	Gold	A-side (Chart Hit)...B-side	$	Sym	Label & Number
				STARSHIP — Cont'd			
6/27/87	9	16		33 **It's Not Over ('Til It's Over)**...S:9 / A:13 *Babylon*	$3	■	RCA/Grunt 5225
9/26/87	46	10		34 **Beat Patrol**...*Girls Like You*	$3	■	RCA/Grunt 5308
12/17/88+	73	8		35 **Wild Again**...*Laying It On The Line (live)* from the movie *Cocktail* starring Tom Cruise	$3	■	Elektra 69349
8/5/89	12	16		36 **It's Not Enough**...A:11 / S:15 *Love Among The Cannibals*	$3	■	RCA 9032
11/25/89	75	8		37 **I Didn't Mean To Stay All Night**...*We Dream In Color*	$3	▮	RCA 9109
4/27/91	81	4		38 **Good Heart**...*(3 album snippets)*	$3	▮	RCA 2796
				JEFFREY, Joe, Group BUB **'69** Born in Buffalo, New York. R&B singer/guitarist.			
6/7/69	14	12		**My Pledge Of Love**...*Margie*	$10		Wand 11200
				JEFFREYS, Garland BUB/ROK/LP **'81** Born on 6/29/43 in Brooklyn, New York. Black rock singer.			
3/14/81	66	7		**96 Tears**...*Escape Goat Dub*	$4		Epic 51008
				JELLEESTONE **'01** Born David Carty in Brooklyn, New York. Male rapper.			
8/18/01	75[S]	1		**Money (Part 1)**...*Inner City Pressure*	$5	★[V]	Warner 16745
				JELLYBEAN **'87** Born John Benitez on 11/7/57 in the Bronx, New York. Renowned dance club DJ/remixer/producer. Remixing career took off with his "Flashdance" and "Maniac" remixes, later to include many of **Madonna**'s hits.			
11/16/85+	18	18		1 **Sidewalk Talk**...S:15 / A:19 *The Mexican* Catherine Buchanan (lead vocal); written and background vocal by **Madonna**	$5		EMI America 8297
7/11/87	16	15		2 **Who Found Who**...A:13 / S:14 *The Real Thing Part II* (w/Steven Dante) **JELLYBEAN/Elisa Fiorillo**	$3	■	Chrysalis 43120
11/7/87	82	6		3 **The Real Thing**...*Am I Dreaming* [I] **JELLYBEAN Featuring Steven Dante**	$3	■	Chrysalis 43167
2/9/91	90	5		4 **What's It Gonna Be**...*(dub version)* **JELLYBEAN Featuring Niki Haris**	$3	▮	Atlantic 87782
				JELLY BEANS, The **'64** R&B vocal group from Jersey City, New Jersey: sisters Elyse and Maxine Herbert, Alma Brewer, Diane Taylor and Charles Thomas.			
6/20/64	9	12		1 **I Wanna Love Him So Bad**...*So Long*	$20		Red Bird 10-003
9/26/64	51	7		2 **Baby Be Mine**...*The Kind Of Boy You Can't Forget*	$20		Red Bird 10-011
				JELLYFISH ROK/LP **'91** Rock group from San Francisco, California: Andy Sturmer (vocals, drums), Jason Falkner (guitar), and brothers Chris (bass) and Roger (keyboards) Manning.			
3/9/91	62	8		**Baby's Coming Back**...*The King Is Half Undressed* (ROK #19)	$3	▮	Charisma 98837
				JENKINS, Donald, & The Delighters **'63** R&B trio from Chicago, Illinois: Jenkins, Walter Granger and Ronnie Strong. Also recorded as Donald & The Daylighters (& The Delighters).			
9/14/63	64	8		**(Native Girl) Elephant Walk**...*Wang Dang Dula* some pressings label artist as: DONALD & The Delighters	$25		Cortland 109
				JENKINS, Gordon, And His Orchestra MEM/POP/LP **'50** Born on 5/12/10 in Webster Groves, Missouri. Died of ALS (Lou Gehrig's disease) on 5/1/84 (age 73). Pianist/arranger/composer ("This Is All I Ask," "P.S. I Love You") in the early 1930s with Isham Jones, **Benny Goodman** and others. Musical director/conductor for Decca Records beginning in 1945. Hit #1 for 13 weeks in 1950 with "Goodnight Irene" (with The Weavers).			
9/3/55	30[CU]	2		1 **Goodnight, Sweet Dreams**...*Young Ideas*	$15		"X" 0159
11/3/56	29	11		2 **Blueberry Hill**...T:29 *That Lucky Old Sun* (#19/'49) **LOUIS ARMSTRONG And GORDON JENKINS And His Orchestra and Chorus** first released in 1949 on Decca 24752; #2 hit for Glenn Miller in 1940	$20		Decca 30091
				JENKINS, Gus — see JINKINS, Gus			
				JENNINGS, Waylon C&W/BUB/LP **'80** Born on 6/15/37 in Littlefield, Texas. Died of diabetes on 2/13/2002 (age 64). While working as a DJ in Lubbock, Texas, Jennings befriended **Buddy Holly**. Holly produced Jennings's first record "Jole Blon" in 1958. Jennings then joined with Holly's backing band as bass guitarist on the fateful "Winter Dance Party" tour in 1959. Established himself in the mid-1970s as a leader of the "outlaw" movement in Country music. Charted 96 Country hits, 1965-91. Married **Jessi Colter** on 10/26/69. In the movies *Nashville Rebel* and *MacKintosh And T.J.* Narrator for TV's *The Dukes Of Hazzard*. *1)Theme From The Dukes Of Hazzard 2)Luckenbach, Texas 3)Good Hearted Woman*			
9/6/69	93	2		1 **MacArthur Park**...*But You Know I Love You* **WAYLON JENNINGS AND THE KIMBERLYS**	$8		RCA Victor 0210
10/17/70	94	1		2 **The Taker**...*Shadow Of The Gallows* written by **Kris Kristofferson** and Shel Silverstein	$8		RCA Victor 9885
9/7/74	75	7		3 **I'm A Ramblin' Man**...CW[1] *Got A Lot Going For Me*	$6		RCA Victor 10020
9/20/75	60	9		4 **Are You Sure Hank Done It This Way**...CW[1] *Bob Wills Is Still The King* (C&W flip) issued with a plain white sleeve with a center-cut hole and the heading "Waylon"	$6	■	RCA Victor 10379
2/7/76	25	12		5 **Good Hearted Woman**...CW[3] *Heaven Or Hell* [L] **WAYLON & WILLIE** Jennings' solo version made the Country charts (#3) on RCA Victor 0615 in 1972	$6		RCA Victor 10529
10/9/76	97	1		6 **Can't You See**...*I'll Go Back To Her* (C&W flip)	$6		RCA Victor 10721
5/7/77	25	16		7 **Luckenbach, Texas (Back to the Basics of Love)**...CW[6] *Belle Of The Ball* **Willie Nelson** (ending vocal)	$5		RCA 10924
2/11/78	42	10		8 **Mammas Don't Let Your Babies Grow Up To Be Cowboys**...CW[4] *I Can Get Off On You* (C&W flip) **WAYLON & WILLIE**	$5		RCA 11198
6/9/79	54	7		9 **Amanda** *[WAYLON]*...CW[3] *Lonesome, On'ry And Mean*	$4	■	RCA 11596

DEBUT	PEAK	WKS	Gold	A-side (Chart Hit)..........B-side	$	Sym	Label & Number
				JENNINGS, Waylon — Cont'd			
9/13/80	21	23	●	10 **Theme From The Dukes Of Hazzard (Good Ol' Boys)** CW[1] *It's Alright*	$4	■	RCA 12067
				WAYLON from *The Dukes Of Hazzard* TV series starring **John Schneider** and Tom Wopat			
4/3/82	52	9		11 **Just To Satisfy You**..........CW[2] *Get Naked With Me* (Waylon)	$4		RCA 13073
				WAYLON & WILLIE			
				JENSEN, Kris BUB **'62**			
				Born Peter Jensen on 4/4/42 in New Haven, Connecticut. Pop singer/guitarist.			
9/1/62	20	14		**Torture**..........*Let's Sit Down*	$15		Hickory 1173
				written by **John D. Loudermilk**			
				JERRYO — see TOM & JERRIO			
				JERU THE DAMAJA R&B/BUB/LP **'94**			
				Born Kendrick Jeru Davis in Brooklyn, New York. Male rapper.			
1/29/94	88	4		**Come Clean**..........S:71 *(radio mix)*	$4	▮	Payday 127000
				side 1 billed as "D. Original Dirty Rotten Scoundrel" mix			
				JESSICA **'00**			
				Born Jessica Betts in 1981 in Chicago, Illinois. Female R&B singer.			
8/19/00	42[S]	10		**Get Up**..........*(2 versions)*	$4	★	G-Funk 73741
				JESTERS, The BUB **'58**			
				R&B vocal group formed in Harlem, New York: Adam Jackson and Lenny McKay (co-lead singers), Noel Grant (bass), Leo Vincent (baritone) and Jimmy Smith (2nd tenor). Both chart hits arranged by **Dave "Baby" Cortez**.			
7/15/57	100	1		1 **So Strange**..........T:100 *Love No One But You*	$60		Winley 218
3/3/58	74	2		2 **The Plea**..........T:74 *Oh Baby*	$60		Winley 225
				JESUS & MARY CHAIN, The ROK/LP **'94**			
				Alternative pop-rock group from Glasgow, Scotland. Led by brothers William and Jim Reid.			
10/15/94	96	2		**Sometimes Always**..........*Drop*	$3	▮	American 18078
				JESUS JONES ROK/LP **'91**			
				Alternative pop-rock group formed in London, England: Mike Edwards (vocals, guitar), Jerry DeBorg (guitar), Iain Baker (keyboards), Al Jaworski (bass) and Simon Matthews (drums).			
4/13/91	2[1]	25		1 **Right Here, Right Now**..........MR[5] A:3 / S:9 *(album version) / Move Me*	$3	▮	SBK/Food 07345
8/24/91	4	20		2 **Real, Real, Real**..........A:30 / S:67 *Maryland*	$3	▮	SBK/Food 07364
				JETHRO TULL ROK/BUB/LP **'73**			
				Progressive-rock group formed in Blackpool, England. Led by Ian Anderson (vocals, flute) and Martin Barre (guitar). Band named after 18th-century agriculturist/inventor of seed drill. Lineups from 1971 through 1977 included Anderson, Barre, John Evan (piano), Clive Bunker (drums; replaced by Barriemore Barlow by 1972) and Jeffrey Hammond-Hammond (bass; replaced in 1976 by John Glascock who died in 1979). Charted 25 pop albums, 1969-95.			
8/14/71	91	2		1 **Hymn 43**..........*Mother Goose*	$8		Reprise 1024
11/4/72+	11	14		2 **Living In The Past** *Christmas Song*	$6		Chrysalis 2006
5/19/73	80	5		3 **A Passion Play (Edit #8)**..........*A Passion Play (Edit #9)*	$6		Chrysalis 2012
				"A Passion Play (Edit #10)" "Bubbled Under" (#105) in 1973 on Chrysalis 2017			
11/2/74+	12	16		4 **Bungle In The Jungle**..........*Back-Door Angels*	$5	■	Chrysalis 2101
				album title *War Child* is shown on the front side of the picture sleeve			
10/11/75	79	4		5 **Minstrel In The Gallery**..........*Summer Day Sand*	$5		Chrysalis 2106
2/14/76	62	8		6 **Locomotive Breath**..........*Fat Man*	$5		Chrysalis 2110
				first released in 1971 on Reprise 1054			
4/9/77	59	6		7 **The Whistler**..........*Strip Cartoon*	$5		Chrysalis 2135
	★473★			**JETS, The** R&B/AC/LP **'87**			
				Family group from Minneapolis, Minnesota (eight brothers and sisters): Leroy (born on 7/19/65), Eddie (born on 8/14/66), Eugene (born on 9/24/67), Haini (born on 1/25/68), Rudy (born on 3/1/69), Kathi (born on 9/6/70), Elizabeth (born on 8/19/72) and Moana Wolfgramm (born on 10/13/73). Their parents are from the South Pacific country of Tonga. All members play at least two instruments. Eugene left group and formed duo **Boys Club** in 1988.			
				1)Crush On You 2)You Got It All 3)Make It Real			
4/12/86	3	20		1 **Crush On You** S:3 / A:4 *Right Before My Eyes*	$3	■	MCA 52774
8/9/86	47	11		2 **Private Number**..........S:40 *Look, No Strings*	$3	■	MCA 52846
11/15/86+	3	26		3 **You Got It All**..........AC[2] S:3 / A:3 *Burn The Candle*	$3		MCA 52968
6/6/87	7	16		4 **Cross My Broken Heart**..........S:7 / A:8 *Bad Guys* (The Heat)	$3	■	MCA 53123
				from the movie *Beverly Hills Cop II* starring **Eddie Murphy**			
10/17/87	20	15		5 **I Do You**..........S:15 / A:21 *Cross The Line*	$3	■	MCA 53193
1/23/88	6	22		6 **Rocket 2 U**..........S:4 / A:7 *Our Only Chance*	$3	■	MCA 53254
4/16/88	4	20		7 **Make It Real**..........AC[3] S:2 / A:4 *Alla Tu/Make It Real*	$3	■	MCA 53311
8/13/88	88	4		8 **Sendin' All My Love**..........*Today It's Your Birthday*	$3	■	MCA 53380
				above 5 from the album *Magic*			
7/29/89	59	7		9 **You Better Dance**..........*Do You Remember*	$3		MCA 53673
10/21/89	87	6		10 **The Same Love**..........*Can't Get Over You*	$3		MCA 53734
	★426★			**JETT, Joan, & The Blackhearts** ROK/BUB/LP **'82**			
				Born Joan Larkin on 9/22/58 in Philadelphia, Pennsylvania. Rock singer/guitarist. Member of The Runaways from 1975-78. The Blackhearts: Ricky Byrd (guitar), Gary Ryan (bass) and Lee Crystal (drums). Ryan and Crystal left in 1987; replaced by Kasim Sulton (bass; **Utopia**) and Thommy Price (drums). Jett starred in the 1987 movie *Light Of Day* as the leader of a rock band called **The Barbusters**.			
				1)I Love Rock 'N Roll 2)Crimson And Clover 3)I Hate Myself For Loving You			
2/6/82	1[7]	20	▲	1 **I Love Rock 'N Roll** AR[5] *You Don't Know What You've Got*	$5	■	Boardwalk 135
5/1/82	7	15		2 **Crimson And Clover**..........*Oh Woe Is Me*	$5	■	Boardwalk 144
7/31/82	20	14		3 **Do You Wanna Touch Me (Oh Yeah)**..........*Victim Of Circumstance*	$5	■	Boardwalk 150
7/9/83	35	10		4 **Fake Friends**..........*Nitetime*	$4	■	Blackheart/MCA 52240
				also released on Blackheart/MCA 52256 in 1983 (B-side: "Handyman")			
9/10/83	37	9		5 **Everyday People**..........*Why Can't We Be Happy*	$4	■	Blackheart/MCA 52272

DEBUT	PEAK	WKS	Gold	A-side (Chart Hit)...B-side	$	Sym	Label & Number
				JETT, Joan, & The Blackhearts — Cont'd			
10/11/86	**83**	6		6 **Good Music**...*Fantasy* The Beach Boys (backing vocals)	$4	■	Blackheart 06336
2/21/87	**33**	11		7 **Light Of Day**...S:25 *Roadrunner (Radio On)* (Jett - ROK #46) **THE BARBUSTERS (JOAN JETT AND THE BLACKHEARTS)** written by **Bruce Springsteen**; title song from the movie starring Michael J. Fox and Michael McKean	$3	■	Blackheart 06692
6/25/88	**8**	26		8 **I Hate Myself For Loving You**...S:4 / A:11 *Love Is Pain (live)*	$3	■	Blackheart 07919
10/29/88+	**19**	20		9 **Little Liar**...S:15 / A:17 *What Can I Do For You*	$3	■	Blackheart 08095
1/27/90	**36**	10		10 **Dirty Deeds** *[JOAN JETT]*...A:37 / S:39 *Let It Bleed* recorded by **AC/DC** in 1981 as "Dirty Deeds Done Dirt Cheap"; "45": Blackheart 73267	$3	▮V	Blackheart 73215
	★583★			**JEWEL** LP **'97** Born Jewel Kilcher on 5/23/74 in Payson, Utah; raised in Homer, Alaska. Adult Alternative singer/songwriter/guitarist. Wrote own book of poetry. Played "Sue Lee Shelley" in the movie *Ride With The Devil*.			
6/1/96	**11**	30		1 **Who Will Save Your Soul**...A:4 / S:17 *Near You Always*	$3	▮	Atlantic 87151
11/30/96+	**2²**	65	▲	2 **You Were Meant For Me /** AC¹ A:❶⁹ / S:6			
9/13/97	**7**	24		3 **Foolish Games**...A:❶³ / S:39 from the movie *Batman & Robin* starring George Clooney	$3	▮	Atlantic 87021
12/5/98+	**6**	16		4 **Hands**...A:3			album cut
4/17/99	**59**	6		5 **Down So Long**...A:47			album cut
9/4/99	**51ˢ**	4		6 **Jupiter (Swallow The Moon)**...*Deep Water (live) / Emily* above 3 from the album *Spirit* on Atlantic 82950	$7	★*	Atlantic 84515
11/17/01+	**25**	20		7 **Standing Still**...A:29 from the album *This Way* on Atlantic 83519; "45": Atlantic 85185; B-side: "Grey Matter (live)"		V	album cut
10/12/02	**36ˢ**	5		8 **Serve The Ego**...*(7 extended mixes)*	$7	★*	Atlantic 85398
				JEWELL **'95** Born in Los Angeles, California. Female rapper. Discovered and produced by **Dr. Dre**.			
1/28/95	**72**	9		**Woman To Woman**...S:31 *Natural Born Killaz* (**Dr. Dre** & **Ice Cube**-R&B flip) from the 18-minute, long-form video *Murder Was The Case* starring **Snoop Doggy Dogg**	$4	▮	Death Row 98185
				JEWELS, The BUB **'64** Female R&B vocal group from Washington DC: Sandra Bears, Grace Ruffin, Margie Clark and Martha Harvin. Ruffin is the first cousin of **Billy Stewart**.			
10/10/64	**64**	10		**Opportunity**...*Gotta Find A Way*	$20		Dimension 1034
				JIGSAW LP **'75** Pop group from England: Des Dyer (vocals, drums), Tony Campbell (guitar), Clive Scott (keyboards) and Barrie Bernard (bass).			
8/30/75	**3**	21		1 **Sky High**...*Brand New Love Affair* from the movie *The Dragon Flies* starring George Lazenby	$5		Chelsea 3022
2/7/76	**30**	11		2 **Love Fire**...*Mystic Harmony*	$5		Chelsea 3037
8/21/76	**66**	7		3 **Brand New Love Affair**...*Have You Heard The News* originally on the B-side of #1 above (this is the exact same recording, with live effects dubbed in)	$5		Chelsea 3043
8/27/77	**93**	4		4 **If I Have To Go Away**...*One More Time For Love*	$4		20th Century 2347
				JIM & JEAN BUB **'68** Husband-and-wife pop duo: Jim and Jean Glover.			
2/3/68	**94**	3		**People World**...*Time Goes Backwards*	$10		Verve Forecast 5073
				JIM and MONICA **'64** Pop vocal duo. **Jimmy Gilmer** of **The Fireballs** is not the "Jim."			
1/18/64	**96**	2		**Slipin' And Slidin'**...*(instrumental)*	$15		Betty 1207
				JIM CROW R&B **'02** Male rap trio from Atlanta, Georgia: Ricardo "Cutty Cartel" Lewis, Mr. Mo and Polow Freaché.			
7/6/02	**65ˢ**	4		**Holla At A Playa**...*(2 album snippets) / (2 remixes* w/**Too $hort**) **JIM CROW featuring Sean Paul and Jazze Pha**	$5	★	Interscope 497699
				JIMENEZ, Jose LP **'61** Born William Szathmary on 10/5/24 in Quincy, Massachusetts. Became known as Bill Dana. Head comedy writer for **Steve Allen**'s TV show. Star of own TV series from 1963-65. Created the Latin American comic character Jose Jimenez for Steve Allen's TV series.			
7/10/61	**19**	11		**The Astronaut (Parts 1 & 2)**... [C-L] interviewed by Don Hinckley	$15	■	Kapp 409
				JIMMY EAT WORLD ROK/LP **'02** Rock group from Mesa, Arizona: Jim Adkins (vocals), Tom Linton (guitar), Rick Burch (bass) and Zach Lind (drums).			
3/16/02	**5**	33		1 **The Middle**...MR⁴ A:5			album cut
8/3/02	**75**	14		2 **Sweetness**...A:74 above 2 from the album *Jimmy Eat World* (originally titled *Bleed American*) on DreamWorks 450334			album cut
				JINKINS, Gus, And Orchestra BUB **'56** Born Gus Jenkins on 3/24/31 in Birmingham, Alabama. Black singer/pianist. Also known as "Little Temple." First own recording in 1952 for Combo.			
12/1/56	**79**	1		**Tricky**...T:79 *You Told Me* [I]	$30		Flash 115
				JINNY **'91** Born in Italy. Female dance singer.			
9/14/91	**97**	2		**Keep Warm**...A:56 *(4 versions)*	$6	▮*	Next Plateau 50168
				JIVE BOMBERS, The **'57** R&B vocal group from Harlem, New York: Clarence Palmer, Earl Johnson, Al Tinney and William "Pee Wee" Tinney. Al Tinney died of cancer on 12/11/2002 (age 81).			
2/2/57	**36**	14		**Bad Boy**...T:36 *When Your Hair Has Turned To Silver* written and recorded by Lil Armstrong as "Brown Gal" in 1936 on Decca 1092 ($50)	$30		Savoy 1508

DEBUT	PEAK	WKS	Gold	A-side (Chart Hit)...B-side	$	Sym	Label & Number
				JIVE BUNNY AND THE MASTERMIXERS LP **'90**			
				Dance group from England: DJ Les Hemstock and mixers John Pickles, his son Andy Pickles and Ian Morgan.			
10/28/89+	**11**	20	●	1 **Swing The Mood**...S:2 / A:27 *Glenn Miller Medley*	$4	■V	Music Fac./Atco 99140
				samples: Let's Twist Again (**Chubby Checker**)/In The Mood (Glenn Miller)/Rock Around The Clock (**Bill Haley**)/Rock-A-Beatin' Boogie (**Haley**)/Tutti-Frutti (**Little Richard**)/Wake Up Little Susie (**Everly Brothers**)/C'mon Everybody (**Eddie Cochran**)/ Hound Dog (**Elvis**)/Shake, Rattle And Roll (**Haley**)/All Shook Up (**Elvis**)/Jailhouse Rock (**Elvis**)/At The Hop (**Danny & The Juniors**); Elvis samplings are by impersonator Pete Willcox			
2/3/90	**69**	5		2 **That's What I Like**...*Pretty Blue Eyes*	$4	▮V	Music Fac./Atco 99122
				samples: Hawaii 5-O (**Ventures**)/Let's Twist Again (**Chubby Checker**)/Let's Dance (**Chris Montez**)/Wipe Out (**Surfaris**)/ Great Balls Of Fire (**Jerry Lee Lewis**)/Johnny B. Goode (**Chuck Berry**)/Good Golly Miss Molly (**Little Richard**)/The Twist (**Checker**)/Summertime Blues (**Eddie Cochran**)/Razzle Dazzle (**Bill Haley**)/Runaround Sue (**Dion**)/Chantilly Lace (**Big Bopper**)			
				JIVE FIVE, The BUB/R&B **'61**			
				R&B vocal group from Brooklyn, New York: Eugene Pitt (lead singer; born on 11/6/37), Jerome Hanna and Billy Prophet (tenors), Richard Harris (baritone) and Norman Johnson (bass). After Johnson's death in 1970, group name changed to Jyve Fyve.			
7/3/61	**3**	19		1 **My True Story**...RB^{3} *When I Was Single*	$30		Beltone 1006
11/13/61	**74**	6		2 **Never, Never**...*People From Another World*	$25		Beltone 1014
				Joe Rene (orch., above 2)			
9/15/62	**67**	5		3 **What Time Is It?**...*Beggin' You Please*	$25		Beltone 2024
8/14/65	**36**	8		4 **I'm A Happy Man**...*Kiss, Kiss, Kiss*	$20		United Artists 853
				JIVE FIVE (featuring Eugene Pitt) (above 2)			
				JIVIN' GENE And The Jokers BUB **'59**			
				Born Gene Bourgeois in Port Arthur, Texas. Rock and roll singer/songwriter/guitarist.			
9/7/59	**69**	4		**Breaking Up Is Hard To Do**...*My Need For Love*	$20		Mercury 71485
				originally released on JIN 116 in 1959 ($40)			
				J.J. FAD LP **'88**			
				Female rap trio from Los Angeles, California: Juana Burns, Dania Birks and Michelle Franklin. J.J. FAD stands for Just Jammin' Fresh And Def.			
4/23/88	**30**	22	●	1 **Supersonic**...S:20 *(instrumental)*	$3	■	Ruthless 99328
9/17/88	**61**	9		2 **Way Out**...*Now Really*	$3	■	Ruthless 99285
12/10/88	**92**	5		3 **Is It Love**...*My Dope Intro*	$3	■	Ruthless 99257
				above 3 co-produced by **Dr. Dre** and **Eazy-E**			
				JO — see DAMITA JO / MARCY JOE / SAMI JO			
				JO ANN & TROY — see CAMPBELL, Jo Ann			
				JoBOXERS LP **'83**			
				Pop group formed in London, England: Dig Wayne (vocals), Rob Marche (guitar), Dave Collard (keyboards), Chris Bostock (bass) and Sean McLusky (drums).			
9/10/83	**36**	15		**Just Got Lucky**...*Forget Me Love*	$4		RCA 13601
	★422★			**JODECI** R&B/BUB/LP **'93**			
				Two pairs of brothers/R&B singers from Charlotte, North Carolina: Cedric "K-Ci" (born on 9/2/69) and Joel "JoJo" (born on 6/10/71) Hailey, with Dalvin (born on 7/23/71) and Donald "DeVante Swing" (born on 9/29/69) DeGrate. The Haileys are cousins of **Dave Hollister** (**BLACKstreet**). **K-Ci & JoJo** began as a successful duo in 1996. Also see **Tony Terry**'s "Everlasting Love." Group name pronounced: joe-deh-see.			
				1)Lately 2)Come & Talk To Me 3)Freek 'n You			
10/26/91	**25**	20		1 **Forever My Lady**...RB^{2} S:12 / A:29 *(4 album snippets)*	$3	▮	Uptown/MCA 54197
1/4/92	**41**	18		2 **Stay**...RB^{2} S:18 / A:54 *(instrumental)*	$3	▮	Uptown/MCA 54285
4/4/92	**11**	28	●	3 **Come & Talk To Me**...RB^{2} S:9 / A:10 *(hip hop version)*	$3	▮V	Uptown/MCA 54175
10/31/92	**85**	7		4 **I'm Still Waiting**...A:73 *(jazz version)*	$3	▮V	Uptown/MCA 54451
				all of above co-produced by **Al B. Sure!** and from the album *Forever My Lady*			
4/24/93	**65**	12		5 **Let's Go Through The Motions**...S:27 / A:51 *(instrumental)*	$3	▮V	Uptown/MCA 54602
				from the movie *Who's The Man?* starring **Doctor Dre & Ed Lover**			
6/12/93	**4**	24	●	6 **Lately** RB^{4} S:4 / A:9 *(album version)* [L]	$3	▮V	Uptown/MCA 54652
				from MTV's *Unplugged* series; written by **Stevie Wonder**			
11/27/93+	**15**	20	●	7 **Cry For You**...RB^{4} S:9 / A:23 *(instrumental)*	$3	▮	Uptown/MCA 54723
3/12/94	**25**	20		8 **Feenin'**...S:19 / A:37 *(instrumental)*	$3	▮	Uptown/MCA 54798
				contains elements of **EPMD**'s "Get Off My Bandwagon"			
8/13/94	**74**^{S}	2		9 **What About Us**...BUB:101 *(instrumental)*	$3	▮	Uptown/MCA 54861
				samples "Computer Love" by **Zapp**			
6/17/95	**14**	20	●	10 **Freek 'n You**...S:5 / A:56 *(radio edit)*	$3	▮	Uptown/MCA 55023
11/4/95+	**31**	20		11 **Love U 4 Life**...S:17 / A:59 *(instrumental)*	$3	▮	Uptown/MCA 55133
				all of above (except #6) written by Donald DeGrate			
5/18/96	**22**	18		12 **Get On Up**...S:12 / A:62 *Freek 'n You* (w/**Raekwon** & **Ghostface Killah**)	$3	▮	MCA 55123
				samples "Velas" by **Quincy Jones**			
	★321★			**JOE** R&B/LP **'01**			
				Born Joseph Thomas in 1972 in Cuthbert, Georgia. R&B singer/songwriter/guitarist. Also see **Brandy**'s "Angel In Disguise."			
				1)Stutter 2)I Wanna Know 3)Faded Pictures			
8/28/93	**64**	13		1 **I'm In Luv**...S:42 *(4 versions)*	$3	▮	Mercury 862462
2/10/96	**11**	20	●	2 **All The Things (Your Man Won't Do)**...S:6 / A:49 *(radio edit)*	$3	▮V	Island 854530
				from the movie *Don't Be A Menace* starring Marlon Wayans; "45": Island 854552; B-side: "Can't Be Wasting My Time" by **Mona Lisa featuring Lost Boyz** (#65)			
5/3/97	**21**	20	●	3 **Don't Wanna Be A Player**...S:13 *(3 album snippets)*	$3	▮	Jive 42450
				from the movie *Booty Call* starring Jamie Foxx; also see #5 below			
9/6/97	**65**^{A}	1		4 **The Love Scene**...			album cut
				above 3 from the album *All That I Am* on Jive 41603			
6/13/98	**24**	23		5 **Still Not A Player**...A:23 *(instrumental) / Twinz (Deep Cover 98)*	$6	T	Loud/RCA 65478
				BIG PUNISHER (Featuring Joe)			
				combines **Big Punisher**'s 1997 hit (#57) "I'm Not A Player" with the chorus from Joe's 1997 hit "Don't Wanna Be A Player"			

DEBUT	PEAK	WKS	Gold	A-side (Chart Hit)..........B-side	$	Sym	Label & Number
				JOE — Cont'd			
12/26/98+	10	20		6 **Faded Pictures** ....S:8 / A:56 *(TV track) / (5 album snippets - Case)* **CASE & JOE** from the movie *Rush Hour* starring Jackie Chan	$4	★	Def Jam 566494
12/11/99+	❶[1]	20	●	7 **Thank God I Found You** ....RB[1] S:❶[3] / A:15 *(remix)* **MARIAH With Joe & 98°** **Trey Lorenz** (backing vocal); remix versions with **Nas** and **Joe** issued on Columbia 79339	$4	★[V]	Columbia 79338
1/1/00	4	44		8 **I Wanna Know** ....A:2 from the movie *The Wood* starring Taye Diggs (soundtrack on Jive 41686)			album cut
8/5/00	63	17		9 **Treat Her Like A Lady** A:56			album cut
1/6/01	❶[4]	26	●	10 **Stutter** RB[5] S:❶[5] / A:5 *(2 versions)* **JOE (featuring Mystikal)** samples "Passin' Me By" by **The Pharcyde**; from the movie *Double Take* starring Eddie Griffin; above 4 from the album *My Name Is Joe* on Jive 41703	$4	★	Jive 42870
12/22/01	68	12		11 **Let's Stay Home Tonight** ....A:68 *(remix w/***Petey Pablo***)*	$6	T	Jive 42995
5/11/02	63	16		12 **What If A Woman** ....A:61 above 2 from the album *Better Days* on Jive 41786			album cut

JOEL, Billy ★34★

ROK/AC/LP **'80**

Born William Martin Joel on 5/9/49 in the Bronx, New York; raised in Hicksville, Long Island, New York. Pop-rock singer/songwriter/pianist. Member of The Hassles in the late 1960s. Involved in a serious motorcycle accident in Long Island in 1982. Married to supermodel Christie Brinkley from 1985-94. Recipient of Grammy's Living Legends Award in 1990 and *Billboard's* Century Award in 1994. Inducted into the Rock and Roll Hall of Fame in 1999.

1)It's Still Rock And Roll To Me 2)We Didn't Start The Fire 3)Tell Her About It 4)Uptown Girl 5)My Life

DEBUT	PEAK	WKS	Gold	A-side (Chart Hit)..........B-side	$	Sym	Label & Number
2/23/74	25	14		1 **Piano Man**..........*You're My Home*	$8		Columbia 45963
6/29/74	80	4		2 **Worse Comes To Worst** ....*Somewhere Along The Line*	$8		Columbia 46055
8/17/74	77	4		3 **Travelin' Prayer** ....*Ain't No Crime*	$8		Columbia 10015
11/30/74+	34	10		4 **The Entertainer**..........*The Mexican Connection* all of above produced by Michael Stewart	$7		Columbia 10064
11/12/77+	3	27	●	5 **Just The Way You Are**..........AC[4] *Get It Right The First Time* 1978 Grammy winner: Record of the Year	$5		Columbia 10646
3/18/78	17	14		6 **Movin' Out (Anthony's Song)** ....*Everybody Has A Dream*	$5		Columbia 10708
5/13/78	24	13		7 **Only The Good Die Young**..........*Get It Right The First Time*	$5		Columbia 10750
8/12/78	17	15		8 **She's Always A Woman** ....*Vienna* #6 & 8: first released on Columbia 10624 in 1977; above 4 from the album *The Stranger*	$5		Columbia 10788
11/4/78+	3	19	▲	9 **My Life** ....*52nd Street* **Peter Cetera** (backing vocal); later used as the theme song to TV's *Bosom Buddies* starring Tom Hanks	$5		Columbia 10853
2/10/79	14	11		10 **Big Shot**..........*Root Beer Rag*	$5		Columbia 10913
4/21/79	24	11		11 **Honesty** ....*The Mexican Connection*	$5		Columbia 10959
3/15/80	7	15		12 **You May Be Right** ....*Close To The Borderline* later used as the theme song to the CBS-TV sitcom *Dave's World* starring Harry Anderson	$4	■	Columbia 11231
5/24/80	❶[2]	21	▲	13 **It's Still Rock And Roll To Me** *Through The Long Night*	$4	■	Columbia 11276
8/2/80	19	15		14 **Don't Ask Me Why**..........AC[2] *C'etait Toi (You Were The One)*	$4	■	Columbia 11331
10/11/80	36	9		15 **Sometimes A Fantasy** ....*All For Leyna* above 4 from the album *Glass Houses*	$4	■	Columbia 11379
9/12/81	17	15		16 **Say Goodbye To Hollywood** ....*Summer, Highland Falls (live)* **[L]** written for **Ronnie Spector** (**The Ronettes**); studio version released on Columbia 10562 in 1977	$4	■	Columbia 02518
11/21/81+	23	14		17 **She's Got A Way** ....*The Ballad Of Billy The Kid (live)* **[L]** recorded at the Paradise Club in Boston; studio version released on Family 0900 in 1971 ($20)	$4	■	Columbia 02628
9/25/82	20	17		18 **Pressure**..........*Laura*	$4	■	Columbia 03244
11/27/82+	17	22		19 **Allentown** ....*Elvis Presley Blvd.*	$4	■	Columbia 03413
3/19/83	56	7		20 **Goodnight Saigon**..........*A Room Of Our Own* (ROK #27)	$4	■	Columbia 03780
7/30/83	❶[1]	18	●	21 **Tell Her About It** ....AC[2] *Easy Money*	$3	■	Columbia 04012
9/24/83	3	22	●	22 **Uptown Girl**..........*Careless Talk*	$3	■	Columbia 04149
12/17/83+	10	18		23 **An Innocent Man** ....AC[1] *I'll Cry Instead*	$3	■	Columbia 04259
3/24/84	14	18		24 **The Longest Time**..........AC[2] *Christie Lee*	$3	■	Columbia 04400
7/7/84	27	15		25 **Leave A Tender Moment Alone** ....AC[2] *This Night*	$3	■	Columbia 04514
1/26/85	18	16		26 **Keeping The Faith**..........A:14 / S:21 *She's Right On Time* #21-26: from the album *An Innocent Man*	$3	■	Columbia 04681
7/13/85	9	16		27 **You're Only Human (Second Wind)** ....S:8 / A:9 *Surprises*	$3	■	Columbia 05417
10/5/85	34	10		28 **The Night Is Still Young**..........*Summer, Highland Falls (live)* also issued with a special promotional picture sleeve	$3	■	Columbia 05657
6/7/86	10	15		29 **Modern Woman** ....S:10 / A:10 *Sleeping With The Television On* from the movie *Ruthless People* starring Danny DeVito and **Bette Midler**	$3	■	Epic 06118
8/9/86	10	18		30 **A Matter Of Trust** ....S:9 / A:17 *Getting Closer*	$3		Columbia 06108
11/15/86+	18	17		31 **This Is The Time**..........AC[3] S:14 / A:23 *Code Of Silence* (w/**Cyndi Lauper**)	$3	■	Columbia 06526
4/4/87	75	7		32 **Baby Grand** ....*Big Man On Mulberry Street* (Joel) **BILLY JOEL Featuring Ray Charles** above 4 from the album *The Bridge*; #5-32: produced by Phil Ramone	$3	■	Columbia 06994
10/14/89	❶[2]	19	●	33 **We Didn't Start The Fire**..........S:❶[3] / A:❶[1] *House Of Blue Light*	$3		Columbia 73021
1/13/90	6	16		34 **I Go To Extremes**..........A:6 / S:8 *When In Rome*	$3	▮[V]	Columbia 73091
5/5/90	57	8		35 **The Downeaster "Alexa"** ....*And So It Goes*	$3	▮	Columbia 73333
8/4/90	77	6		36 **That's Not Her Style** ....*And So It Goes* **Richard Marx** (backing vocal)	$3	▮[V]	Columbia 73442
10/20/90	37	12		37 **And So It Goes**..........A:32 / S:36 *(3 album snippets)* "45": B-side of above 2; above 5 produced by Mick Jones (**Foreigner**) and Billy Joel and from the album *Storm Front*	$3	▮[V]	Columbia 73602
8/22/92	92	3		38 **All Shook Up**..........*Wear My Ring Around Your Neck* (Ricky Van Shelton) from the movie *Honeymoon In Vegas* starring Nicolas Cage	$3	▮[V]	Epic Soundtrax 74422

DEBUT	PEAK	WKS	Gold	A-side (Chart Hit)..........B-side	$	Sym	Label & Number
				JOEL, Billy — Cont'd			
7/31/93	3	27		39 The River Of Dreams..........AC[12] A:2 / S:7 *No Man's Land* (ROK #18)	$3	▮V	Columbia 77086
11/6/93	29	20		40 All About Soul..........A:24 *You Picked A Real Bad Time* **Color Me Badd** (guest vocals)	$3	▮V	Columbia 77254
3/26/94	77	8		41 Lullabye (Goodnight, My Angel)..........A:75 *Two Thousand Years* all of above (except #38) written by Joel	$3	▮V	Columbia 77363
8/16/97	50	9		42 To Make You Feel My Love..........S:53 / A:68 *Intro/Summer, Highland Falls / Summer, Highland Falls* written by **Bob Dylan**	$3	▮V	Columbia 78641
				JOE PUBLIC R&B/LP **'92** R&B vocal group from Buffalo, New York: Kevin Scott, Joe Carter, Joe Sayles and Dwight Wyatt.			
3/14/92	4	21		1 Live And Learn..........A:3 / S:9 *(dub version)*	$3	▮	Columbia 74012
7/4/92	55	13		2 I Miss You..........S:46 / A:51 *(album version)*	$3	▮	Columbia 74321
10/17/92	98	3		3 Do You Everynite..........A:69 *I've Been Watchin'* (R&B #54)	$3	▮	Columbia 74467
				JOHN, Elton ★3★ ROK/AC/BUB/LP **'75** Born Reginald Kenneth Dwight on 3/25/47 in Pinner, Middlesex, England. Pop-rock singer/songwriter/pianist. Formed his first group Bluesology. Took the name of Elton John from the first names of Bluesology members Elton Dean and **Long John Baldry**. Teamed up with lyricist Bernie Taupin beginning in 1967. Formed Rocket Records in 1973. Played the "Pinball Wizard" in the movie version of *Tommy*. Elton was the #1 pop artist of the 1970s. Inducted into the Rock and Roll Hall of Fame in 1994. Also see **Neil Sedaka**'s "Bad Blood." *1)Candle In The Wind 1997 2)Don't Go Breaking My Heart 3)Crocodile Rock 4)Island Girl 5)Philadelphia Freedom*			
8/15/70	92	5		1 Border Song..........*Bad Side Of The Moon* first released on Congress 6022 in 1970 ($50)	$10		Uni 55246
11/28/70+	8	14		2 Your Song..........*Take Me To The Pilot*	$8		Uni 55265
3/20/71	34	9		3 Friends..........*Honey Roll* title song from the British movie starring Sean Bury	$8		Uni 55277
12/18/71+	24	10		4 Levon..........*Goodbye*	$8		Uni 55314
3/4/72	41	7		5 Tiny Dancer..........*Razor Face*	$8		Uni 55318
5/6/72	6	15		6 Rocket Man..........*Suzie (Dramas)*	$8		Uni 55328
8/12/72	8	10		7 Honky Cat..........*Slave*	$8		Uni 55343
12/9/72+	❶ ^{3}	17	▲	8 Crocodile Rock..........*Elderberry Wine*	$6		MCA 40000
4/7/73	2^{1}	15	●	9 Daniel..........AC[2] *Skyline Pigeon*	$6		MCA 40046
8/4/73	12	12		10 Saturday Night's Alright For Fighting..........*Jack Rabbit / Whenever You're Ready*	$6		MCA 40105
10/27/73	2^{3}	17	▲	11 Goodbye Yellow Brick Road..........*Young Man's Blues*	$6		MCA 40148
12/8/73	❶ ^{1X}	3		12 Step Into Christmas..........*Ho Ho Ho (Who'd Be A Turkey At Christmas)* [X]	$6		MCA 65018
2/16/74	❶ ^{1}	18	▲	13 Bennie And The Jets..........*Harmony*	$6		MCA 40198
6/22/74	2^{2}	15	●	14 Don't Let The Sun Go Down On Me..........*Sick City* **Carl Wilson** and Bruce Johnston of **The Beach Boys** and Toni Tennille of **Captain & Tennille** (backing vocals); also see #54 below	$6		MCA 40259
9/7/74	4	14	●	15 The Bitch Is Back..........*Cold Highway* **Dusty Springfield** (backing vocal)	$6		MCA 40297
11/30/74+	❶ ^{2}	14	●	16 Lucy In The Sky With Diamonds..........*One Day At A Time* with the Reggae guitars of Dr. Winston O'Boogie (**John Lennon**); **Beatles**' song introduced on their 1967 album *Sgt. Pepper's Lonely Hearts Club Band*; also see "live" version on the "45" B-side of #63 below	$6	■	MCA 40344
3/8/75	❶ ^{2}	21	▲	17 Philadelphia Freedom..........*I Saw Her Standing There* (w/**John Lennon**) **THE ELTON JOHN BAND** tribute to tennis star Billie Jean King and her team, the Philadelphia Freedoms; a special souvenir picture sleeve was issued by WFIL Radio in Philadelphia	$6	■	MCA 40364
7/5/75	4	13	●	18 Someone Saved My Life Tonight..........*House Of Cards* original pressings have custom "Captain Fantastic" label	$6		MCA 40421
10/11/75	❶ ^{3}	15	▲	19 Island Girl..........*Sugar On The Floor*	$6		MCA 40461
1/24/76	14	11		20 Grow Some Funk Of Your Own /			
1/24/76	14	11		21 I Feel Like A Bullet (In The Gun Of Robert Ford).......... Ford: the man who shot outlaw Jesse James	$6		MCA 40505
7/4/76	❶ ^{4}	20	●	22 Don't Go Breaking My Heart..........AC[1] *Snow Queen* **ELTON JOHN and KIKI DEE** also see #59 below	$5	■	Rocket 40585
11/13/76	6	14	●	23 Sorry Seems To Be The Hardest Word..........AC[1] *Shoulder Holster*	$5		MCA/Rocket 40645
2/12/77	28	6		24 Bite Your Lip (Get up and dance!)..........*Chameleon*	$5		MCA/Rocket 40677
4/15/78	34	8		25 Ego..........*Flinstone Boy*	$5	■	MCA 40892
11/11/78	22	10		26 Part-Time Love..........*I Cry At Night*	$5	■	MCA 40973
6/9/79	9	18	●	27 Mama Can't Buy You Love..........AC[1] *Three Way Love Affair*	$5	■	MCA 41042
9/29/79	31	10		28 Victim Of Love..........*Strangers*	$5		MCA 41126
5/3/80	3	21	●	29 Little Jeannie..........AC[2] *Conquer The Sun*	$5	■	MCA 41236
8/9/80	39	12		30 (Sartorial Eloquence) Don't Ya Wanna Play This Game No More?..........*Cartier / White Man Danger*	$5		MCA 41293
5/9/81	21	13		31 Nobody Wins..........*Fools In Fashion*	$4	■	Geffen 49722
7/25/81	34	13		32 Chloe..........*Tortured*	$4		Geffen 49788
3/20/82	13	17		33 Empty Garden (Hey Hey Johnny)..........*Take Me Down To The Ocean* tribute to **John Lennon**	$4	■	Geffen 50049
7/10/82	12	18		34 Blue Eyes..........AC[2] *Hey Papa Legba*	$4	■	Geffen 29954
5/7/83	12	16		35 I'm Still Standing..........*Love So Cold*	$4	■	Geffen 29639
8/6/83	25	12		36 Kiss The Bride..........*Choc Ice Goes Mental*	$4	■	Geffen 29568
10/29/83+	4	23		37 I Guess That's Why They Call It The Blues..........*The Retreat* **Stevie Wonder** (harmonica solo)	$4	■	Geffen 29460
6/9/84	5	19		38 Sad Songs (Say So Much)..........*A Simple Man*	$4		Geffen 29292

JOHN, Elton — Cont'd

DEBUT	PEAK	WKS	Gold	A-side (Chart Hit)...B-side	$	Sym	Label & Number
9/8/84	16	14		39 **Who Wears These Shoes?** ...A:10 / S:27 *Lonely Boy*	$4	■	Geffen 29189
12/1/84+	38	13		40 **In Neon** ...*Tactics*	$4		Geffen 29111
10/26/85	20	14		41 **Wrap Her Up** ...A:16 / S:27 *The Man Who Never Died*	$3	■	Geffen 28873
11/9/85+	❶[4]	23	●	42 **That's What Friends Are For** ...RB[3] / AC[2] S:❶[5] / A:❶[3] *Two Ships Passing In The Night* (Warwick)	$3	■	Arista 9422
				DIONNE & FRIENDS: Elton John, Gladys Knight and Stevie Wonder			
				song introduced by **Rod Stewart** on the 1982 movie soundtrack of *Night Shift*			
1/18/86	7	18		43 **Nikita** ...A:6 / S:8 *Restless* (ROK #16/'84)	$3	■	Geffen 28800
				George Michael (backing vocal, #41 & 43)			
10/18/86	55	8		44 **Heartache All Over The World** ...*Highlander*	$3	■	Geffen 28578
5/16/87	36	13		45 **Flames Of Paradise** ...S:32 / A:34 *Call My Name* (Rush)	$3	■	Epic 07119
				JENNIFER RUSH (with Elton John)			
11/7/87+	6	21		46 **Candle In The Wind** ...S:6 / A:7 *Sorry Seems To Be The Hardest Word (live)* [L]	$3	■	MCA 53196
				recorded with The Melbourne Symphony Orchestra; tribute to Marilyn Monroe; first recorded for Elton's *Goodbye Yellow Brick Road* album in 1973; picture sleeve issued with either a yellow or ivory background; also see #66 below; #1-24, 41, 43, 44 & 46: produced by Gus Dudgeon			
6/18/88	2[1]	18		47 **I Don't Wanna Go On With You Like That** ...AC[1] S:2 / A:3 *Rope Around A Fool*	$3	■	MCA 53345
9/17/88	19	13		48 **A Word In Spanish** ...S:15 / A:27 *Heavy Traffic*	$3	■	MCA 53408
4/15/89	16	11		49 **Through The Storm** ...S:13 / A:19 *Come To Me* (Franklin)	$3	■	Arista 9809
				ARETHA FRANKLIN AND ELTON JOHN			
8/26/89	13	15		50 **Healing Hands** ...AC[1] S:8 / A:20 *Dancing In The End Zone*	$3		MCA 53692
1/13/90	18	17		51 **Sacrifice** ...S:14 / A:25 *Love Is A Cannibal*	$3	▮[V]	MCA 53750
4/28/90	28	16		52 **Club At The End Of The Street** ...S:26 / A:34 *(no B-side)*	$3	▮[V]	MCA 53818
				"45": MCA 79026; B-side: "Sacrifice"			
11/24/90+	43	13		53 **You Gotta Love Someone** ...AC[5] S:36 *(no B-side)*	$3	▮	MCA 53953
12/7/91+	❶[1]	20	●	54 **Don't Let The Sun Go Down On Me** ...AC[2] S:4 / A:4 *I Believe (When I Fall In Love It Will Be Forever)* (Michael) [L-R]	$3	▮[V]	Columbia 74086
				GEORGE MICHAEL/ELTON JOHN			
				recorded in London, March 1991; also see #14 above			
6/27/92	9	22		55 **The One** ...AC[6] A:8 / S:17 *Suit Of Wolves*	$3	▮[V]	MCA 54423
10/31/92	23	20		56 **The Last Song** ...A:27 / S:30 *The Man Who Never Died / Song For Guy*	$3	▮	MCA 54510
2/27/93	30	16		57 **Simple Life** ...AC[3] A:26 / S:69 *The North*	$3	▮[V]	MCA 54581
11/27/93	56	12		58 **True Love** ...S:54 *Runaway Train* (**Elton John** & **Eric Clapton** - ROK #10)	$3	▮[V]	MCA 54762
				ELTON JOHN & KIKI DEE			
				written by Cole Porter in 1956 for the movie *High Society* starring **Bing Crosby** and **Frank Sinatra**			
3/26/94	92	2		59 **Don't Go Breaking My Heart** ...S:66 *(12" remix)* [R]	$3	▮	MCA 54813
				ELTON JOHN & RuPAUL			
				also see #22 above			
5/21/94	4	26	●	60 **Can You Feel The Love Tonight** ...AC[8] A:2 / S:6 *(same version)*	$3	▮	Hollywood 64543
				Kiki Dee and **Rick Astley** (backing vocals)			
8/27/94	18	20		61 **Circle Of Life** ...A:15 / S:34 *(same version)*	$3	▮	Hollywood 64516
				above 2 from the Disney animated movie *The Lion King*			
3/11/95	13	20		62 **Believe** ...AC[2] A:14 / S:19 *The One (live)*	$3	▮[V]	Rocket 856014
7/15/95	52	10		63 **Made In England** ...A:43 *(edited version)*	$3	▮[V]	Rocket 852092
				"45": Rocket 852172; B-side: "Lucy In The Sky With Diamonds" (live w/**John Lennon**)			
11/4/95	34	20		64 **Blessed** ...A:31 / S:46 *Latitude*	$3	▮[V]	Rocket 852394
10/26/96	70	17		65 **You Can Make History (Young Again)** ...A:63 *Song For Guy*	$3	▮	MCA 55222
10/11/97	❶[14]	42	▲[11]	66 **Candle In The Wind 1997 /** S:❶[14] / A:21 [R]			
				produced by **George Martin**; song was originally written about Marilyn Monroe (see #46 above); this is a new version with new lyrics honoring Princess Diana who died in a car crash in France on 8/31/97 (age 36); the biggest-selling record of all time			
10/11/97		42		67 **Something About The Way You Look Tonight** ...AC[10] A:18	$3	▮[V]	Rocket 568108
				Billboard's policy states that whichever side of a single has the most airplay will be listed first – "Candle In The Wind 1997" was shown as the A-side for the first three weeks, then "Something About The Way You Look Tonight" was shown as the A-side for the remaining weeks on the chart; due to the special nature and record sales of "Candle In The Wind 1997," we are showing it as the A-side for the entire chart run			
4/18/98	55	20		68 **Recover Your Soul** ...A:65 *I Know Why I'm In Love*	$3	▮	Rocket 568762
				#1-15, 17-25, 33, 35-41, 43, 44, 46-48, 50-57, 59 & 62-68: written by Elton John & Bernie Taupin; #31, 33-40, 47, 48, 50-52, 55-57, 60, 61, 65, 67 & 68: produced by Chris Thomas			
3/13/99	29	10	●	69 **Written In The Stars** ...S:13 *(alternate version) / (3 album snippets)*	$4	★	Rocket/Curb 566918
				ELTON JOHN & LEANN RIMES			
				from Elton John and Tim Rice's musical interpretation of the stage show *Aida*			
4/22/00	49	15		70 **Someday Out Of The Blue (Theme From El Dorado)** ...S:15 / A:71 *Cheldorado* (Hans Zimmer)	$3	★	DreamWorks 59039
				from the animated movie *The Road To El Dorado*			

★592★

JOHN, Little Willie

R&B/BUB **'60**

Born William Edgar John on 11/15/37 in Cullendale, Arkansas; raised in Detroit, Michigan. Died of a heart attack in Washington State Prison on 5/26/68 (age 30). R&B singer. Brother of **Mable John** (of **The Raeletts**). Convicted of manslaughter in 1966. Inducted into the Rock and Roll Hall of Fame in 1996.

1)Sleep 2)Talk To Me, Talk To Me 3)Fever

DEBUT	PEAK	WKS	Gold	A-side (Chart Hit)...B-side	$	Sym	Label & Number
7/7/56	24	15		1 **Fever** ...RB[5] S:24 / T:27 *Letter From My Darling* (R&B #10)	$30		King 4935
4/7/58	20	17		2 **Talk To Me, Talk To Me** ...T:20 / S:22 *Spasms*	$25		King 5108
8/11/58	66	4		3 **You're A Sweetheart** ...H:66 *Let's Rock While The Rockin's Good*	$25		King 5142
				#1 hit for Dolly Dawn in 1938			
8/3/59	60	9		4 **Leave My Kitten Alone** ...*Let Nobody Love You* (#108)	$25		King 5219
				also see #10 below			
2/22/60	100	1		5 **Let Them Talk** ...*Right There*	$25		King 5274
5/9/60	63	6		6 **A Cottage For Sale** ...*I'm Shakin'*	$25		King 5342
				#4 hit for Guy Lombardo in 1930			
5/30/60	38	12		7 **Heartbreak (It's Hurtin' Me)** ...*Do You Love Me*	$20		King 5356
9/5/60	13	16		8 **Sleep** *There's A Difference*	$20		King 5394
				#1 hit for Fred Waring's Pennsylvanians in 1924			

DEBUT	PEAK	WKS	Gold	A-side (Chart Hit)......B-side	$	Sym	Label & Number
				JOHN, Little Willie — Cont'd			
11/28/60	48	8		9 **Walk Slow** ...... *You Hurt Me*	$20		King 5428
1/23/61	60	6		10 **Leave My Kitten Alone** ...... *I'll Never Go Back On My Word* [R] same version as #4 above	$20		King 5452
3/13/61	61	6		11 **The Very Thought Of You** ...... *I'm Sorry* #1 hit for Ray Noble in 1934	$15		King 5458
5/15/61	71	5		12 **(I've Got) Spring Fever** ...... *Flamingo* (R&B #17)	$15		King 5503
7/17/61	93	3		13 **Now You Know /**			
9/18/61	87	1		14 **Take My Love (I Want To Give It All To You)**	$15		King 5516
				JOHN, Mable '66 Born on 11/3/30 in Bastrop, Louisiana. R&B singer. Member of **The Raeletts**. Sister of **Little Willie John**.			
8/6/66	95	2		**Your Good Thing (Is About To End)** ...... *It's Catching*	$20		Stax 192
				JOHN, Robert BUB/AC/LP '79 Born Robert John Pedrick on 1/3/46 in Brooklyn, New York. Pop singer. First recorded at age 12 for Big Top Records. In 1963 recorded as lead singer with Bobby & The Consoles. *1)Sad Eyes 2)The Lion Sleeps Tonight 3)Hey There Lonely Girl*			
11/10/58	74	4		1 **White Bucks And Saddle Shoes** ...... *Stranded* **BOBBY PEDRICK, Jr.**	$40		Big Top 3004
4/13/68	49	12		2 **If You Don't Want My Love** ...... *Don't* (w/Michael Gately)	$10		Columbia 44435
11/28/70	71	5		3 **When The Party Is Over** ...... *Raindrops, Love And Sunshine*	$6		A&M 1210
1/1/72	3	17	●	4 **The Lion Sleeps Tonight** ...... *Janet* #14 hit for The Weavers in 1952 (as "Wimoweh"); originally recorded in 1939 as "Mbube" by the South African Zulu group Solomon Linda & The Evening Birds	$6		Atlantic 2846
6/24/72	99	2		5 **Hushabye** ...... *To Touch, To Feel*	$6		Atlantic 2884
5/19/79	1[1]	27	●	6 **Sad Eyes** *Am I Ever Gonna Hold You Again*	$4		EMI America 8015
12/8/79+	41	11		7 **Lonely Eyes** ...... *Dance The Night Away*	$4		EMI America 8030
7/19/80	31	13		8 **Hey There Lonely Girl** ...... *You Could Have Told Me*	$4		EMI America 8049
10/25/80	70	5		9 **Sherry** ...... *On My Own*	$4		EMI America 8061
2/12/83	68	4		10 **Bread And Butter** ...... *If You Don't Want My Love*	$5		Motown 1664
				JOHN & ERNEST R&B '73 R&B novelty duo: John Free and Ernest Smith.			
4/14/73	31	11		**Super Fly Meets Shaft** ...... *Part Two* [N] "break-in" record; written and produced by **Dickie Goodman**; also released with "Problems" as the B-side	$8		Rainy Wednesday 201
				JOHNNIE & JOE R&B '57 R&B duo from the Bronx, New York: Johnnie Louise Richardson (died of a stroke on 10/25/88) and Joe Rivers. Johnnie was the daughter of the late J&S Records owner Zelma "Zell" Sanders and a touring member of **The Jaynetts**.			
5/13/57	8	22		1 **Over The Mountain; Across The Sea** ..T:8 / S:9 / J:17 *My Baby's Gone, On, On* (R&B #15) first released on J&S 1664 in 1957 ($75)	$35		Chess 1654
9/26/60	89	2		2 **Over The Mountain; Across The Sea** ...... *My Baby's Gone, On, On* [R] #1: silver & blue label; #2: blue label	$20		Chess 1654
				JOHNNY and THE EXPRESSIONS '66 R&B group led by Johnny Matthews.			
1/22/66	79	5		**Something I Want To Tell You** ...... *Where Is The Party*	$12		Josie 946
				JOHNNY AND THE HURRICANES BUB/LP '59 Rock and roll instrumental group from Toledo, Ohio: leader Johnny "Paris" Pocisk (saxophone), Paul Tesluk (organ), Dave Yorko (guitar), Lionel "Butch" Mattice (bass) and Tony Kaye (drums; replaced in late 1959 by Bo Savich). First recorded for Twirl in 1958. Paris had own Attila label from 1965-70. Savich died of cancer on 1/4/2002 (age 62).			
4/27/59	23	14		1 **Crossfire** ...... *Lazy* [I] first released on Twirl 1001 in 1958 ($50)	$30		Warwick 502
8/3/59	5	17		2 **Red River Rock** *Buckeye* [I] rock version of "Red River Valley"	$30		Warwick 509
11/2/59	25	13		3 **Reveille Rock** ...... *Time Bomb* [I] rock version of the Army bugle call "Reveille"	$30		Warwick 513
2/15/60	15	13		4 **Beatnik Fly** ...... *Sand Storm* [I] rock version of "Blue Tail Fly"	$25	■	Warwick 520
5/30/60	48	9		5 **Down Yonder** ...... *Sheba* [I] there were 10 charted versions of this tune between 1921 and 1951	$20	■	Big Top 3036
9/5/60	60	6		6 **Rocking Goose /** [I]			
8/29/60	97	1		7 **Revival** ...... [I] rock version of "When The Saints Go Marching In"	$20	■	Big Top 3051
12/5/60	91	1		8 **You Are My Sunshine** ...... *Molly-O* [I] written in 1940 by former Louisiana governor Jimmie Davis	$20	■	Big Top 3056
2/27/61	86	2		9 **Ja-Da** ...... *Mr. Lonely* [I] #4 hit for Arthur Fields in 1919	$20	■	Big Top 3063
				JOHNNY HATES JAZZ AC/LP '88 Pop trio formed in England: Clark Datcher (vocals), Calvin Hayes (keyboards, drums) and Mike Nocito (guitar, bass). Hayes is the son of producer Mickie Most.			
3/19/88	2[3]	19		1 **Shattered Dreams** ......AC[1] A:2 / S:3 *My Secret Garden*	$3	■	Virgin 99383
7/9/88	31	12		2 **I Don't Want To Be A Hero** ......A:28 / S:33 *The Cage*	$3	■	Virgin 99304
				JOHNNY O. '90 Born Johnny Ortiz in the Bronx, New York. Dance singer.			
9/1/90	53	15		1 **Dream Boy-Dream Girl** ...... *(4 versions)* **CYNTHIA & JOHNNY 'O'**	$6	■*	MicMac 2539
1/29/94	87	5		2 **Runaway Love** ...... *(3 remixes)*	$6	■*	Ex-It 198

DEBUT	PEAK	WKS	Gold	A-side (Chart Hit)...B-side	$	Sym	Label & Number
				JOHNNY T. ANGEL '74			
				Born in Canada. Pop singer.			
6/8/74	**94**	4		**Tell Laura I Love Her** ... *The Way I Feel Tonite*	$6		Bell 45,472
				first released on Yorksville 45090 in 1974 ($10)			
				JOHNS, Sammy AC/BUB/C&W/LP '75			
				Born on 2/7/46 in Charlotte, North Carolina. Pop singer/songwriter/guitarist.			
10/12/74	**68**	8		1 **Early Morning Love** ... *Holy Mother, Aging Father*	$6		GRC 2021
2/1/75	**5**	17	●	2 **Chevy Van** ... *Hang My Head And Moan*	$5		GRC 2046
				a new version by Johns made the country charts (#80) in 1988 on MCA 53398			
5/31/75	**52**	8		3 **Rag Doll** ... *Friends Of Mine*	$5		GRC 2062
				JOHNSON — see BROTHERS JOHNSON			
				JOHNSON, Betty BUB/MEM '57			
				Born on 3/16/29 in Burlington, North Carolina. Pop singer. Married to musical conductor **Charles Randolph Grean**. Regular on Don McNeill's daily *Breakfast Club* radio show, and on NBC-TV's *Tonight Show* starring Jack Parr.			
3/3/56	**94**	1		1 **I'll Wait** ... T:94 *Please Tell Me Why*	$20		Bally 1000
8/18/56	**72**	4		2 **Clay Idol** ... T:72 *Why Do You Cry?*	$20		Bally 1013
11/24/56+	**9**	22		3 **I Dreamed** A:9 / T:12 / J:15 / S:22 *If It's Wrong To Love You*	$20		Bally 1020
				featured on an episode of NBC-TV's *Modern Romances;* Lew Douglas (orch., above 3)			
4/29/57	**25**	9		4 **Little White Lies /** A:25 / T:40			
				#1 hit for Fred Waring's Pennsylvanians in 1930			
5/6/57	**70**	6		5 **1492** ... T:70	$20		Bally 1033
2/24/58	**17**	16		6 **The Little Blue Man** ... A:17 / T:19 / S:20 *Winter In Miami* [N]	$15		Atlantic 1169
				voice of the Little Blue Man: Fred Ebb (the song's co-writer)			
6/16/58	**19**	7		7 **Dream** ... A:19 / T:58 *How Much*	$15		Atlantic 1186
				#1 hit for the Pied Pipers in 1945			
10/6/58	**56**	5		8 **Hoopa Hoola** ... H:56 *One More Time*	$15		Atlantic 2002
1/12/59	**99**	1		9 **You Can't Get To Heaven On Roller Skates** ... *I Want A Good Home For My Cat*	$15		Atlantic 2009
				Charles Randolph Grean (orch.: #4-9)			
				JOHNSON, Bubber '55			
				R&B singer/pianist/songwriter Robert Johnson.			
11/12/55	**92**	1		**Come Home** ... T:92 *There'll Be No One*	$30		King 4822
				JOHNSON, Buddy, And His Orchestra R&B/POP/C&W '49			
				Born Woodrow Wilson Johnson on 1/10/15 in Darlington, South Carolina. Died of a brain tumor on 2/9/77 (age 62). Black orchestra leader/pianist. Charted 14 R&B hits from 1943-57.			
11/12/55	**94**	1		1 **It's Obdacious** ... T:94 *Save Your Love For Me*	$20		Mercury 70695
				Buddy Johnson and Gil Askey (vocals)			
12/31/60+	**78**	3		2 **I Don't Want Nobody (To Have My Love But You)** ... *I'm Just Your Fool*	$12		Mercury 71723
				ELLA JOHNSON with BUDDY JOHNSON And His Orchestra			
				same version was a #14 R&B hit in 1956 on both Mercury 70775 ($20) and Wing 90064 ($25)			
				JOHNSON, Carolyn Dawn C&W/LP '01			
				Born on 4/30/71 in Grand Prairie, Alberta, Canada. Country singer/songwriter/guitarist.			
1/27/01	**98**	5		1 **Georgia** ... S:52 *Love Is Always Worth The Ache*	$4	★V	Arista 69010
				Martina McBride (backing vocal)			
9/8/01	**59**	17		2 **Complicated** ... A:54		V	album cut
				"45": Arista 69050; B-side: "Georgia"			
5/11/02	**54**	10		3 **I Don't Want You To Go** ... A:52		V	album cut
				above 3 from the album *Room With A View* on Arista 69336; "45": Arista 69133; B-side: "Room With A View"			
				JOHNSON, Don LP '86			
				Born on 12/15/49 in Flatt Creek, Missouri. Actor/singer. Played "Sonny Crockett" on TV's *Miami Vice* and title role on TV's *Nash Bridges*. Starred in several movies. Twice married to and divorced from actress Melanie Griffith.			
8/23/86	**5**	15		1 **Heartbeat** ... S:3 / A:6 *Can't Take Your Memory*	$3	■	Epic 06285
				issued with 2 different picture sleeves			
11/22/86	**56**	11		2 **Heartache Away** ... *Love Roulette*	$3	■	Epic 06426
10/22/88	**25**	12		3 **Till I Loved You** ... S:22 / A:32 *Two People (Theme From "Nuts")* (Streisand)	$3	■	Columbia 08062
				BARBRA STREISAND AND DON JOHNSON			
				love theme from the Broadway musical *Goya*			
				JOHNSON, Ella — see JOHNSON, Buddy			
				JOHNSON, Holly '89			
				Born William Johnson on 2/19/60 in Rio de Janeiro, Brazil; raised in Liverpool, England. Male singer. At age 16, joined Big In Japan as bassist. Lead singer of **Frankie Goes To Hollywood**, 1980-87.			
6/17/89	**65**	6		**Love Train** ... *Murder In Paradise*	$3		Uni 50023
				JOHNSON, Jack ROK/LP '02			
				Born in Hawaii. Adult Alternative pop-rock singer/songwriter/guitarist. Professional surfer.			
8/3/02	**73**	17		**Flake** ... A:68		V	album cut
				from the album *Brushfire Fairytales* on Enjoy 860994; "live" version issued on "45": Enjoy 060086; B-side: "Inaudible Melodies" (live)			
				JOHNSON, Jesse R&B/BUB/LP '86			
				Born on 5/29/60 in Rock Island, Illinois. Lead guitarist of **The Time**.			
3/16/85	**61**	11		1 **Be Your Man** ... *Special Love*	$3	■	A&M 2702
7/20/85	**76**	8		2 **I Want My Girl** ... *Fast Girls*	$3	■	A&M 2749
				JESSE JOHNSON'S REVUE (above 2)			
10/25/86	**53**	16		3 **Crazay** ... *Drive Yo Cadillac* (Johnson)	$3	■	A&M 2878
				JESSE JOHNSON (Featuring Sly Stone)			
4/23/88	**78**	8		4 **Love Struck** ... *Do Yourself A Favor*	$3	■	A&M 3020
				JOHNSON, Kevin '73			
				Born in Australia. Pop singer/songwriter/guitarist.			
11/10/73	**73**	4		**Rock 'N Roll (I Gave You The Best Years of My Life)** ... *There's Nothing I'd Rather Do*	$6		Mainstream 5548

DEBUT	PEAK	WKS	Gold	A-side (Chart Hit)..........B-side	$	Sym	Label & Number
				JOHNSON, Lou BUB **'64**			
				Born in 1941 in Harlem, New York. R&B singer.			
10/19/63	**74**	8		1 **Reach Out For Me**..........*Magic Potion*	$15		Big Top 3153
8/22/64	**49**	7		2 **(There's) Always Something There To Remind Me**..........*Magic Potion*	$15		Big Hill 552
11/13/65	**59**	9		3 **A Time To Love-A Time To Cry (Petite Fleur)**..........*Unsatisfied*	$15		Big Top 101
				JOHNSON, Marv R&B **'60**			
				Born on 10/15/38 in Detroit, Michigan. Died on 5/16/93 (age 54). R&B singer/songwriter/pianist. With the Serenaders vocal group, mid-1950s. First recorded for Kudo in 1958. Worked in sales and promotion for Motown in the early 1970s. Recognized as a co-creator of the Motown sound with Berry Gordy.			
3/16/59	**30**	15		1 **Come To Me**..........*Whisper*	$25		United Artists 160
				released regionally on Tamla 101 ($300); Berry Gordy's first release			
7/13/59	**82**	4		2 **I'm Coming Home**..........*River Of Tears*	$25		United Artists 175
11/2/59+	**10**	22		3 **You Got What It Takes**..........*Don't Leave Me*	$20		United Artists 185
3/7/60	**9**	13		4 **I Love The Way You Love** *Let Me Love You*	$20		United Artists 208
6/13/60	**63**	6		5 **All The Love I've Got /**			
5/30/60	**74**	7		6 **Ain't Gonna Be That Way**..........	$20		United Artists 226
				The Rayber Voices (female backing singers, all of above)			
9/5/60	**20**	11		7 **(You've Got To) Move Two Mountains**..........*I Need You*	$20		United Artists 241
12/12/60+	**58**	7		8 **Happy Days**..........*Baby, Baby*	$20		United Artists 273
3/13/61	**61**	6		9 **Merry-Go-Round**..........*Tell Me That You Love Me*	$20		United Artists 294
				JOHNSON, Michael C&W/AC/BUB/LP **'78**			
				Born on 8/8/44 in Alamosa, Colorado; raised in Denver, Colorado. Adult Contemporary singer. Studied classical guitar in 1966 in Spain. In the **Chad Mitchell Trio** with **John Denver** in 1968.			
4/22/78	**12**	16		1 **Bluer Than Blue**..........AC^3 *Two In Love*	$4		EMI America 8001
8/12/78	**32**	12		2 **Almost Like Being In Love**..........*Ridin' In The Sky*	$4	■	EMI America 8004
				recorded by **Frank Sinatra** in 1947 on Columbia 37382 (from the musical *Brigadoon*)			
8/4/79	**19**	20		3 **This Night Won't Last Forever**..........*I Just Can't Say No To You*	$4		EMI America 8019
8/23/80	**86**	3		4 **You Can Call Me Blue**..........*Don't Ask Why*	$4		EMI America 8054
				JOHNSON, Puff R&B/BUB **'96**			
				Born in 1973 in Detroit, Michigan; raised in Los Angeles, California. Female R&B singer.			
5/18/96	**63**	13		**Forever More**..........S:54 *(album version)*	$3	▮	Work 78297
				JOHNSON, Rozetta R&B **'70**			
				Born in Tuscaloosa, Alabama. Female R&B singer.			
12/12/70	**94**	1		**A Womans' Way**..........*Mine Was Real*	$8		Clintone 001
				JOHNSON, Syl R&B/BUB **'75**			
				Born Syl Thompson on 7/1/39 in Holly Springs, Mississippi; raised in Chicago, Illinois. R&B singer/songwriter/guitarist. Recorded for Federal Records, 1959-62. Father of **Syleena Johnson**.			
8/19/67	**97**	3		1 **Come On Sock It To Me**..........*Try Me*	$10		Twilight 100
10/14/67	**95**	2		2 **Different Strokes**..........*Sorry Bout Dat*	$10		Twilight 103
12/13/69+	**68**	6		3 **Is It Because I'm Black**..........*Let Them Hang High*	$10		Twinight 125
2/24/73	**95**	3		4 **We Did It**..........*Any Way The Wind Blows*	$6		Hi 2229
10/27/73	**72**	6		5 **Back For A Taste Of Your Love**..........*Wind, Blow Her Back My Way*	$6		Hi 2250
6/14/75	**48**	7		6 **Take Me To The River** *Could I Be Falling In Love*	$6		Hi 2285
				JOHNSON, Syleena R&B/LP **'02**			
				Born in 1976 in Chicago, Illinois. Female R&B singer. Daughter of singer **Syl Johnson**.			
8/31/02	**53^S**	9		**Tonight I'm Gonna Let Go**..........*(5 versions)*	$6	T	Jive 40042
				SYLEENA JOHNSON Featuring Busta Rhymes, Rampage, Sham & Spliff Star			
				samples "Put Your Hands Where My Eyes Can See" by **Busta Rhymes** and "Sweet Green Fields" by **Seals & Crofts**			
				JOHNSTON, Freedy AC/LP **'95**			
				Born in 1961 in Kinsley, Kansas. Male Adult Alternative pop-rock singer/songwriter.			
12/24/94+	**54**	12		**Bad Reputation**..........A:73 *Disappointed Man*	$3	▮	Elektra 64495
				JOHNSTON, Sabrina **'91**			
				Born in New Jersey. Female dance singer.			
11/9/91	**75^A**	1		**Peace (In The Valley)**..........*(2 mixes)*	$6	▮	JBR/Atco 98675
				JOHNSTON, Tom — see DOOBIE BROTHERS, The			
				JOINER, ARKANSAS JUNIOR HIGH SCHOOL BAND **'60**			
				There never was a junior high school in Joiner, Arkansas. Group is actually a band of studio musicians led by **Ernie Freeman**. Joiner is the hometown of Liberty Records president Al Bennett. Also see **Sir Chauncey**.			
5/16/60	**53**	8		**National City**..........*Big Ben* [I]	$15		Liberty 55244
				rock version of the 1906 march "National Emblem"			
				JO JO GUNNE LP **'72**			
				Rock group from Los Angeles, California: **Jay Ferguson** (vocals, keyboards), brothers Matthew (guitar) and Mark (bass) Andes, and Curly Smith (drums). Both Ferguson and Mark Andes had been in **Spirit**. Group named after the 1958 **Chuck Berry** hit. Mark Andes was later with **Firefall** and **Heart**.			
3/18/72	**27**	11		**Run Run Run**..........*Take It Easy*	$6		Asylum 11003
				JOLI, France BUB/LP **'79**			
				Born in 1963 in Montreal, Quebec, Canada. Female dance singer.			
9/1/79	**15**	16		**Come To Me**..........*Let Go*	$5		Prelude 8001
				JOMANDA BUB **'91**			
				Female R&B-dance vocal trio from New Jersey: Joanne Thomas, Cheri Williams and Renee Washington.			
7/6/91	**40**	15		1 **Got A Love For You**..........A:26 / S:54 *(dub mix)*	$4	▮	Big Beat 5031
7/10/93	**83**	6		2 **I Like It**..........A:59 *(remix edit)*	$4	▮	Big Beat 98413
				written by Randy and **El DeBarge**			

DEBUT	PEAK	WKS	Gold	A-side (Chart Hit)....B-side	$	Sym	Label & Number
				JON & ROBIN and The In Crowd BUB **'67**			
				Duo of Jon Abnor and Javonne "Robin" Braga (who married James Wright of **The Five Americans** in 1970).			
5/6/67	18	10		1 **Do It Again A Little Bit Slower** ....*If I Need Someone—It's You*	$10		Abnak 119
8/19/67	100	2		2 **Drums** *[JON & ROBIN]* ....*You Don't Care* above 2 produced by **Dale Hawkins**	$10		Abnak 122
3/16/68	87	4		3 **Dr. Jon (The Medicine Man)** ....*Love Me Baby*	$8		Abnak 127
				JON & VANGELIS ROK/LP **'82**			
				Duo of Jon Anderson (lead singer of **Yes**) and Greek keyboardist Evangelos (**Vangelis**) Papathanassiou.			
8/16/80	58	6		1 **I Hear You Now** ....*Thunder*	$5		Polydor 2098
5/22/82	51	9		2 **I'll Find My Way Home** ....*I Hear You Now*	$5		Polydor 2205
				JON B R&B/BUB/LP **'98**			
				Born Jonathan Buck on 11/11/74 in Rhode Island. R&B singer/songwriter.			
4/29/95	10	30	●	1 **Someone To Love** ....S:9 / A:16 *(3 album snippets)* **JON b featuring BABYFACE** from the movie *Bad Boys* starring Martin Lawrence and **Will Smith**; "45" B-side: "Pretty Girl"	$3	▮V	Yab Yum 77895
9/2/95	25	20		2 **Pretty Girl** ....S:27 / A:39 *(remix) / Someone To Love (remix)*	$3	▮V	Yab Yum 77813
8/30/97	68	15		3 **Don't Say** ....S:52 *Let U Shine*	$3	▮V	Yab Yum 78614
5/23/98	7	15	▲	4 **They Don't Know /** S:5 / A:54			
1/31/98	29	16		5 **Are U Still Down** .... co-written and produced by **2Pac**	$3	▮	Yab Yum 78793
10/17/98	64	7		6 **Better Days** ....S:36 *(instrumental) / Cheddar* (w/**Mack 10** & **Ice Cube**) **WC Featuring Jon B** samples "We Are One" by **Maze Featuring Frankie Beverly**	$4	▮	Payday 570258
2/17/01	58	14		7 **Don't Talk** ....A:54 / S:73 *(3 versions)*	$6	T	Epic/Edmonds 570258
				JONELL R&B **'02**			
				Born in Queens, New York. Female R&B singer/rapper.			
12/15/01+	62	17		**Round and Round Remix** ....S:2 *(original version) / (instrumental)* **JONELL (Featuring Method Man)** original version made the R&B charts earlier in 2001 (#55) as by **Hi-Tek** featuring Jonell; from the movie *How High* starring **Method Man** and **Redman**	$4	★	Def Soul 588852
				JONES, Davy BUB/LP **'71**			
				Born on 12/30/45 in Manchester, England. Member of **The Monkees**. Played "The Artful Dodger" in Broadway's *Oliver.*			
8/14/65	93	3		1 **What Are We Going To Do?** *[DAVID JONES]* ....*This Bouquet*	$20	■	Colpix 784
6/19/71	52	9		2 **Rainy Jane** ....*Welcome To My Love* co-written by **Neil Sedaka**	$15		Bell 45,111
				JONES, Donell R&B/LP **'99**			
				Born on 5/22/73 in Chicago, Illinois. R&B singer/songwriter.			
7/6/96	79	8		1 **In The Hood** ....S:53 *(instrumental) / (4 album snippets)*	$3	▮	LaFace 24127
11/2/96+	49	20		2 **Knocks Me Off My Feet** ....S:25 *You Should Know* written by **Stevie Wonder** (on his 1976 album *Songs In The Key Of Life*)	$3	▮V	LaFace 24210
9/25/99	7	24	●	3 **U Know What's Up** RB[8] S:7 / A:12 *(5 album snippets)*	$4	★	Untouchables 24420
4/22/00	29	20		4 **Where I Wanna Be** ....A:23 *(3 remixes)*	$6	T	Untouchables 24481
4/22/00	75	15		5 **It's So Hard** ....A:63 *(3 versions) / Leatherface* **BIG PUN Featuring Donell Jones** Tony Sunshine (backing vocal)	$6	T	Loud 79350
4/27/02	54	20		6 **You Know That I Love You** ....A:54 / S:67 *(2 versions)*	$6	T	Arista 15112
9/14/02	98	3		7 **Put Me Down** ....S:50 *(5 versions w/***Styles** *& Lady May)*	$6	T	Arista 15165
				JONES, Etta BUB **'60**			
				Born on 11/25/28 in Aiken, South Carolina. Died of cancer on 10/16/2001 (age 72). Jazz singer with Earl Hines's orchestra from 1949-52.			
11/7/60	36	7		1 **Don't Go To Strangers** ....*If I Had You* written in 1954 and introduced by **Al Martino** on Capitol 2899	$12		Prestige 180
1/16/61	65	8		2 **When I Fall In Love** ....*People Will Say We're In Love* #20 hit for **Doris Day** in 1952	$12		King 5424
3/13/61	91	1		3 **Canadian Sunset** ....*That's All There Is To That*	$12		Prestige 191
				JONES, George C&W/BUB/LP **'59**			
				Born on 9/12/31 in Saratoga, Texas. Ranks as the #2 Country artist, according to *Joel Whitburn's Top Country Singles* book. Charted 166 Country hits, 1955-02. First recorded for Starday in 1954. Married to **Tammy Wynette** from 1969-75. Recorded rockabilly music under pseudonyms Hank Smith and Thumper Jones.			
5/4/59	73	5		1 **White Lightning** CW[5] *Long Time To Forget* written by the **Big Bopper** (J.P. Richardson)	$20		Mercury 71406
7/27/59	93	3		2 **Who Shot Sam** ....*Into My Arms Again*	$20		Mercury 71464
7/3/61	76	4		3 **Tender Years** ....CW[7] *Battle Of Love*	$15	■	Mercury 71804
1/23/65	96	1		4 **The Race Is On** ....*She's Lonesome Again*	$12		United Artists 751
4/17/65	99	1		5 **I've Got Five Dollars And It's Saturday Night** ....*Wreck On The Highway* **GEORGE & GENE George Jones & Gene Pitney** #4 Country hit for **Faron Young** in 1956	$15		Musicor 1066
12/25/65	23[X]	1		6 **My Mom And Santa Claus** ....*Lonely Christmas Call* [X-N] **GEORGE JONES & The Jones Boys** "twist" tune similar to "I Saw Mommy Kissing Santa Claus"; first released in 1962	$20		United Artists 530
1/1/00	75	3		7 **A Country Boy Can Survive (Y2K Version)** ....S:25 *Going The Distance* **CHAD BROCK (With Hank Williams, Jr. & George Jones)** #2 Country hit for **Hank Williams, Jr.** in 1982	$4	★V	Warner 16895
				JONES, Glenn R&B/AC/LP **'87**			
				Born in 1961 in Jacksonville, Florida. R&B singer/songwriter.			
10/31/87	66	14		**We've Only Just Begun (The Romance Is Not Over)** ....*(instrumental)*	$3	■	Jive 1049

DEBUT	PEAK	WKS	Gold	A-side (Chart Hit)...B-side	$	Sym	Label & Number

JONES, Grace

R&B/BUB/LP **'77**

Born Grace Mendoza on 5/19/52 in Spanishtown, Jamaica; raised in Syracuse, New York. Dance singer/actress/model. Acted in several movies. Also see **Arcadia**'s "Election Day."

DEBUT	PEAK	WKS	Gold	A-side (Chart Hit)...B-side	$	Sym	Label & Number
1/22/77	71	7		1 **Sorry /**			
1/22/77		7		2 **That's The Trouble**	$8		Beam Junction 102
<u>5/7/77</u>	83	6		3 **I Need A Man** ... *(instrumental)*	$8		Beam Junction 104
11/29/86+	69	9		4 **I'm Not Perfect (But I'm Perfect For You)** ... *Scary But Fun*	$3	■	Manhattan 50052

JONES, Hannah

'98

Black female dance singer.

DEBUT	PEAK	WKS	Gold	A-side (Chart Hit)...B-side	$	Sym	Label & Number
6/13/98	65	20		**You Only Have To Say You Love Me** ... *(remix)*	$4	▮	Ariola Dance 54443

JONES, Howard

★431★

BUB/ROK/LP **'86**

Born on 2/23/55 in Southampton, Hampshire, England. Pop singer/songwriter/keyboardist.

1)No One Is To Blame 2)Things Can Only Get Better 3)Everlasting Love

DEBUT	PEAK	WKS	Gold	A-side (Chart Hit)...B-side	$	Sym	Label & Number
1/21/84	27	15		1 **New Song** ... *Conditioning*	$4	■	Elektra 69766
4/21/84	33	13		2 **What Is Love?** ... *It Just Doesn't Matter*	$4	■	Elektra 69737
3/23/85	5	23		3 **Things Can Only Get Better** ... A:4 / S:8 *Why Look For The Key*	$3	■	Elektra 69651
7/6/85	19	16		4 **Life In One Day** ... A:16 / S:20 *Learning How To Love*	$3	■	Elektra 69631
9/28/85	49	9		5 **Like To Get To Know You Well** ... *Equality*	$3		Elektra 69598
4/12/86	4	23		6 **No One Is To Blame** AC[1] A:2 / S:6 *The Chase*	$3	■	Elektra 69549
				Phil Collins (drums, backing vocal, producer)			
10/18/86	17	16		7 **You Know I Love You...Don't You?** ... A:12 / S:20 *Roll Right Up*	$3	■	Elektra 69512
1/24/87	76	5		8 **All I Want** ... *Dig This Well Deep*	$3	■	Elektra 69494
3/18/89	12	19		9 **Everlasting Love** ... AC[2] A:10 / S:12 *The Brutality of Fact*	$3	■	Elektra 69308
7/1/89	30	13		10 **The Prisoner** ... A:28 / S:34 *Rubber Morals*	$3		Elektra 69288
4/11/92	32	15		11 **Lift Me Up** ... A:26 *I.G.Y. (live)*	$3	▮	Elektra 64779

JONES, Jack

★446★

AC/BUB/LP **'65**

Born on 1/14/38 in Los Angeles, California. One of the top Adult Contemporary singers of the 1960s. Son of actress Irene Hervey and actor/singer Allan Jones, who had the #8 Pop hit "The Donkey Serenade" the year Jack was born. First recorded for Capitol in 1959. Performed the theme for the *Love Boat* TV series. Married to actress Jill St. John from 1967-69.

1)Wives And Lovers 2)The Race Is On 3)Dear Heart 4)The Impossible Dream 5)Lady

DEBUT	PEAK	WKS	Gold	A-side (Chart Hit)...B-side	$	Sym	Label & Number
3/3/62	66	8		1 **Lollipops And Roses** ... *This Was My Love*	$8	□	Kapp 435
				two special picture sleeves were issued: one for the 1962 Confectionary Exposition and one as a special Juke Box Record (KJB-13)			
5/4/63	75	4		2 **Call Me Irresponsible** ... *Love Song From "Mutiny On The Bounty"*	$8		Kapp 516
				from the movie *Papa's Delicate Condition* starring **Jackie Gleason**			
11/2/63+	14	14		3 **Wives And Lovers /**			
				inspired by the movie starring Janet Leigh			
10/5/63	92	1		4 **Toys In The Attic**	$8	■	Kapp 551
				title song from the movie starring **Dean Martin**			
2/15/64	62	8		5 **Love With The Proper Stranger** ... *The Mood I'm In*	$8	■	Kapp 571
				title song from the movie starring Natalie Wood			
5/30/64	59	9		6 **The First Night Of The Full Moon** ... *Far Away*	$8	■	Kapp 589
				also see "Pearly Shells" by **Burl Ives**			
8/15/64	62	6		7 **Where Love Has Gone** ... *The Lorelei*	$8	■	Kapp 608
				title song from the movie starring Bette Davis and Susan Hayward			
11/28/64+	30	11		8 **Dear Heart** ... *Emily*	$8	■	Kapp 635
				title song from the movie starring Glenn Ford; a promotional text-only sleeve was also issued			
2/27/65	15	11		9 **The Race Is On** ... AC[1] *I Can't Believe I'm Losing You*	$7	■	Kapp 651
6/12/65	46	9		10 **Seein' The Right Love Go Wrong** ... *Travellin' On (#132)*	$7		Kapp 672
10/9/65	73	5		11 **Just Yesterday** ... *The True Picture (#134)*	$7		Kapp 699
12/11/65+	71	6		12 **Love Bug** ... *And I Love Her*	$7	■	Kapp 722
				#6 Country hit for **George Jones** in 1965 and #8 Country hit for **George Strait** in 1994			
6/4/66	35	10		13 **The Impossible Dream (The Quest)** ... AC[1] *Strangers In The Night*	$7		Kapp 755
				from the musical *Man Of La Mancha* starring Richard Kiley			
10/29/66	62	8		14 **A Day In The Life Of A Fool** ... *The Shining Sea*	$7	■	Kapp 781
				lyric version of a theme from the French movie *Black Orpheus* starring Breno Mello			
1/21/67	39	11		15 **Lady** ... AC[4] *Afraid To Love*	$7		Kapp 800
				co-written by **Bert Kaempfert**			
4/15/67	81	5		16 **I'm Indestructible** ... *Afterthoughts (AC #19)*	$7		Kapp 818
6/10/67	73	6		17 **Now I Know** ... *More And More*	$7		Kapp 833
9/9/67	92	2		18 **Our Song** ... *Michelle*	$7		Kapp 847
12/2/67	99	2		19 **Live For Life** ... *That Tiny World*	$6		RCA Victor 9365
				title song from the movie starring Yves Montand			
2/17/68	92	2		20 **If You Ever Leave Me** ... *Pretty*	$6		RCA Victor 9441
				Jones's musical conductors and arrangers: Ralph Carmichael (#14, 15, 17, 18), **Don Costa** (#8, 9, 11, 12), Jack Elliott (#10), Bob Florence (#16), Pete King (#1-7, 13) and Marty Paich (#19, 20)			

JONES, Jimmy

BUB **'60**

Born on 6/2/37 in Birmingham, Alabama. R&B singer.

DEBUT	PEAK	WKS	Gold	A-side (Chart Hit)...B-side	$	Sym	Label & Number
12/28/59+	2[1]	18	●	1 **Handy Man** ... *The Search Is Over*	$25		Cub 9049
4/18/60	3	15	●	2 **Good Timin'** ... *My Precious Angel*	$25		Cub 9067
7/11/60	83	5		3 **That's When I Cried** ... *I Just Go For You*	$20	■	Cub 9072
3/27/61	85	3		4 **I Told You So** ... *You Got It*	$20		Cub 9085

JONES, Joe

'60

Born on 8/12/26 in New Orleans, Louisiana. R&B singer/songwriter. Pianist/valet for **B.B. King** in the early 1950s. First recorded for Capitol in 1954. Produced and managed **The Dixie Cups** and **Alvin Robinson**.

DEBUT	PEAK	WKS	Gold	A-side (Chart Hit)...B-side	$	Sym	Label & Number
9/19/60	3	13		1 **You Talk Too Much** ... *I Love You Still*	$20		Roulette 4304
				first 3 weeks charted on RIC 972 ($25); remaining weeks on Roulette			
4/3/61	89	3		2 **California Sun** ... *Please Don't Talk About Me When I'm Gone*	$20		Roulette 4344

DEBUT	PEAK	WKS	Gold	A-side (Chart Hit)........B-side	$	Sym	Label & Number
				JONES, Kay Cee '56			
				Born Ruthie Reece on 12/20/29 in Childress, Texas. White female singer. Appeared in the movie *Gentlemen From Arizona*. Once married to songwriter/movie historian Eddie Brandt.			
12/3/55+	52	7		**The Japanese Farewell Song** ....T:52 *I Wore Dark Glasses (At Your Wedding)*	$25		Marquee 1031
				Lou Raderman (orch.); label displays a picture of Kay Cee			
				JONES, Linda R&B/BUB '67			
				Born on 1/14/44 in Newark, New Jersey. Died of diabetes on 3/14/72 (age 28). Soul singer. First recorded for MGM/Cub as Linda Lane in 1963.			
6/24/67	21	12		1 **Hypnotized**..........*I Can't Stop Lovin' My Baby*	$10		Loma 2070
9/30/67	61	6		2 **What've I Done (To Make You Mad)** ....*Make Me Surrender (Baby, Baby Please)*	$10		Loma 2077
1/20/68	93	3		3 **Give My Love A Try** ....*I Can't Stand It*	$10		Loma 2085
2/26/72	74	9		4 **Your Precious Love** ....*Don't Go (I can't bear to be alone)*	$8		Turbo 021
				JONES, Miss — see MISSJONES			
				JONES, Norah LP '02			
				Born on 3/30/79 in Manhattan, New York; raised in Dallas, Texas. Jazz-styled singer/pianist. Daughter of legendary sitar player Ravi Shankar. Won the 2002 Best New Artist Grammy Award.			
9/28/02+	30	31		**Don't Know Why**..........A:29			album cut
				from the album *Come Away With Me* on Blue Note 32088; 2002 Grammy winner: Record of the Year			
				JONES, Oran "Juice" R&B/LP '86			
				Born on 3/28/57 in Houston, Texas; raised in Harlem, New York. R&B singer/rapper.			
9/13/86	9	19	●	**The Rain** ....RB[2] S:8 / A:10 *Your Song*	$3		Def Jam 06209
	★513★			**JONES, Quincy** R&B/BUB/AC/LP '81			
				Born Quincy Delight Jones on 3/14/33 in Chicago, Illinois; raised in Seattle, Washington. Composer/producer/conductor/arranger. Began as a jazz trumpeter with Lionel Hampton, 1950-53. Music director for Mercury Records in 1961, then vice president in 1964. Wrote scores for many movies, 1965-73. Scored TV series *Roots* in 1977. Arranger/producer for hundreds of successful singers and orchestras. Produced **Michael Jackson**'s mega-albums *Off The Wall*, *Thriller* and *Bad*. Established own Qwest label in 1981. Line producer for the movie *The Color Purple*. Married to actress Peggy Lipton (TV's *Mod Squad*) from 1974-89. Won the Grammy's Trustees Award in 1989. Won Grammy's Living Legends Award in 1990. His biographical movie *Listen Up: The Lives Of Quincy Jones* was released in 1990.			
				1)One Hundred Ways 2)Just Once 3)I'll Be Good To You			
5/16/70	74	3		1 **Killer Joe** ....*Maybe Tomorrow*	$6		A&M 1163
3/11/72	57	8		2 **Money Runner**..........*Money Is* (**Little Richard**) [I]	$6		Reprise 1062
				from the movie *"$"* starring Warren Beatty			
10/11/75	70	10		3 **Is It Love That We're Missin'** ....*Cry Baby*	$5	■	A&M 1743
				QUINCY JONES (featuring The Brothers Johnson)			
3/5/77	57	7		4 **"Roots" Medley** ....*Many Rains Ago (Oluwa)* [I]	$5	■	A&M 1909
				themes from the #1 ABC-TV mini-series *Roots*: Motherland/ Theme From "Roots" (Roots Mural Theme); Bill Summers (bata drums)			
6/10/78	21	16		5 **Stuff Like That**..........RB[1] *There's A Train Leavin'*	$5	■	A&M 2043
				Ashford & Simpson and **Chaka Khan** (vocals)			
4/11/81	28	12		6 **Ai No Corrida (I-No-Ko-ree-da)**..........*There's A Train Leavin'*	$4		A&M 2309
				Dune (vocals); originally recorded by Chas Jankel on his 1980 album *Chas Jankel*			
8/15/81	17	23		7 **Just Once**..........*The Dude*	$4		A&M 2357
12/19/81+	14	21		8 **One Hundred Ways** ....*Velas*	$4		A&M 2387
				QUINCY JONES Featuring JAMES INGRAM (above 2)			
11/18/89+	18	16		9 **I'll Be Good To You** ....RB[2] S:13 / A:26 *(instrumental)*	$3	■V	Qwest 22697
				QUINCY JONES Featuring Ray Charles and Chaka Khan			
3/10/90	31	13	●	10 **The Secret Garden (Sweet Seduction Suite)**..........RB[1] S:20 *(instrumental)*	$3	▮V	Qwest 19992 ■
				QUINCY JONES/Al B. Sure!/James Ingram/El DeBarge/Barry White			
5/26/90	75	5		11 **Tomorrow (A Better You, Better Me)**..........RB[1] *(instrumental)*	$4	▮V	Qwest 19881
				QUINCY JONES Featuring Tevin Campbell			
12/30/95	98	4		12 **You Put A Move On My Heart** ....S:72 *The Secret Garden (instrumental)*	$3	▮V	Qwest 17751
				QUINCY JONES introducing TAMIA			
4/20/96	68	9		13 **Slow Jams** ....S:43 *(remix)*	$3	▮V	Qwest 17673
				QUINCY JONES Featuring Babyface and Tamia with Portrait and Barry White			
				JONES, Rickie Lee ROK/LP '79			
				Born on 11/8/54 in Chicago, Illinois. Female jazz-styled singer/songwriter. Moved to Los Angeles in 1977. Won the 1979 Best New Artist Grammy Award.			
4/28/79	4	15		1 **Chuck E.'s In Love**..........*On Saturday Afternoons In 1963*	$5		Warner 8825
				Chuck E. is Chuck E. Weiss, a friend that Jones met in Los Angeles			
7/28/79	40	9		2 **Young Blood** ....*Coolsville*	$4		Warner 49018
10/3/81	64	7		3 **A Lucky Guy** ....*Skeletons*	$4		Warner 49816
9/29/84	83	4		4 **The Real End**..........*Woody And Dutch On The Slow Train To Peking* (ROK #31)	$4	■	Warner 29191
				JONES, Roy Jr. '02			
				Born on 1/16/69 in Pensacola, Florida. R&B singer/rapper/songwriter. Won boxing's WBA heavyweight championship on 3/2/2003. Owner of Body Head Records.			
1/12/02	5S	17		**That Was Then**..........*(3 versions) / Unfaithful*	$4	★	Body Head/EMI 74767
				ROY JONES JR. feat. Dave Hollister, Perion & Hahz The Rippa			
				samples "One Woman Man" by **Dave Hollister**			
				JONES, Shae '99			
				Born on 7/27/78 in Kansas City, Missouri. Female R&B singer.			
1/2/99	88	9		**Talk Show Shhh!** ....S:28 *(instrumental)*	$3	★	M3/Universal 56216
				written and produced by **Montell Jordan**			
				JONES, Shirley — see PARTRIDGE FAMILY, The			

DEBUT	PEAK	WKS	Gold	A-side (Chart Hit)...B-side	$	Sym	Label & Number

JONES, Tamiko

R&B '75

Born Barbara Tamiko Ferguson in 1945 in Kyle, West Virginia; raised in Detroit, Michigan. First recorded for Atlantic in 1966. Moved to London; married to John Abbey (publisher of *Blues & Soul* magazine). **Smokey Robinson**'s manager in 1991.

DEBUT	PEAK	WKS	Gold	A-side (Chart Hit)...B-side	$	Sym	Label & Number
11/12/66	88	2		1 **A Man And A Woman**...*Sidewinder* **TAMIKO JONES with HERBIE MANN** title song from the French movie starring Anouk Aimee	$8		Atlantic 2362
4/5/75	60	10		2 **Touch Me Baby (Reaching Out For Your Love)**...*Creepin' (In My Dreams)*	$5		Arista 0110

JONES, Tom ★97★

C&W/AC/BUB/LP '65

Born Thomas Jones Woodward on 6/7/40 in Pontypridd, South Wales. Worked local clubs as Tommy Scott; formed own trio The Senators in 1963. Began solo career in London in 1964. Won the 1965 Best New Artist Grammy Award. Host of own TV musical variety series from 1969-71.

1)She's A Lady 2)What's New Pussycat? 3)Without Love 4)I'll Never Fall In Love Again 5)It's Not Unusual

DEBUT	PEAK	WKS	Gold	A-side (Chart Hit)...B-side	$	Sym	Label & Number
4/10/65	10	12		1 **It's Not Unusual**...*To Wait For Love (Is To Waste Your Life Away)*	$10		Parrot 9737
5/29/65	42	9		2 **Little Lonely One**...*That's What We'll All Do*	$15		Tower 126
6/19/65	3	12		3 **What's New Pussycat?**...*Once Upon A Time* title song from the movie starring Peter Sellers and Peter O'Toole	$10	■	Parrot 9765
8/28/65	27	8		4 **With These Hands**...*Some Other Guy* #7 hit for **Eddie Fisher** in 1953	$8	■	Parrot 9787
12/11/65+	25	9		5 **Thunderball**...*Key To My Heart* title song from the James Bond movie starring Sean Connery	$8	■	Parrot 9801
2/19/66	74	4		6 **Promise Her Anything**...*A Little You* title song from the movie starring Warren Beatty	$8		Parrot 9809
6/18/66	58	6		7 **Not Responsible**...*Once There Was A Time*	$8		Parrot 40006
12/24/66+	11	12		8 **Green, Green Grass Of Home**...*If I Had You* #4 Country hit for **Porter Wagoner** in 1965	$8		Parrot 40009
3/11/67	27	8		9 **Detroit City**...*Ten Guitars*	$8		Parrot 40012
5/20/67	49	6		10 **Funny Familiar Forgotten Feelings**...*I'll Never Let You Go* #8 Country hit for **Don Gibson** in 1967	$8		Parrot 40014
8/12/67	68	4		11 **Sixteen Tons**...*Things I Wanna Do*	$8		Parrot 40016
9/9/67	49	7		12 **I'll Never Fall In Love Again**...*Once Upon A Time* also see #18 below	$7		Parrot 40018
12/30/67+	57	5		13 **I'm Coming Home**...*The Lonely One*	$7		Parrot 40024
3/16/68	15	15		14 **Delilah**...*Smile Away Your Blues*	$7		Parrot 40025
8/31/68	35	8		15 **Help Yourself**...*Day By Day*	$7		Parrot 40029
12/21/68+	48	10		16 **A Minute Of Your Time**...*Looking Out My Window*	$7		Parrot 40035
5/24/69	13	11		17 **Love Me Tonight**...*Hide And Seek*	$7	■	Parrot 40038
7/26/69	6	16	●	18 **I'll Never Fall In Love Again**...AC[1] *Once Upon A Time* [R] same melody as **Sammy Kaye**'s #11 hit "Wanderin'" in 1950; also see #12 above	$7		Parrot 40018
12/27/69+	5	11	●	19 **Without Love (There Is Nothing)**...AC[1] *The Man Who Knows Too Much*	$6	■	Parrot 40045
5/2/70	13	9		20 **Daughter Of Darkness**...AC[1] *Tupelo Mississippi Flash*	$6	■	Parrot 40048
8/22/70	14	8		21 **I (Who Have Nothing)**...*Stop Breaking My Heart*	$6	■	Parrot 40051
11/21/70	25	8		22 **Can't Stop Loving You**...*Never Give Away Love* all of above produced by Peter Sullivan	$6	■	Parrot 40056
2/6/71	2[1]	14	●	23 **She's A Lady** *My Way* written by **Paul Anka**	$6	■	Parrot 40058
5/22/71	26	10		24 **Puppet Man** / co-written by **Neil Sedaka**; first 6 weeks charted on Parrot 40062 (with a picture sleeve and a different B-side-"Every Mile"); remaining weeks on Parrot 40064			
7/3/71	38	5		25 **Resurrection Shuffle**...	$6		Parrot 40064
10/30/71	41	7		26 **Till**...*One Day Soon*	$6		Parrot 40067
4/29/72	80	7		27 **The Young New Mexican Puppeteer**...*All That I Need Is Some Time*	$6		Parrot 40070
5/12/73	60	8		28 **Letter To Lucille**...*Thank The Lord*	$6		Parrot 40074
1/8/77	15	16		29 **Say You'll Stay Until Tomorrow**...CW[1] *Lady Lay* #23-29: produced by Gordon Mills	$5		Epic/MAM 50308
12/3/88+	31	11		30 **Kiss**...S:23 / A:35 *E.F.L.* (Art Of Noise) **THE ART OF NOISE Featuring Tom Jones**	$5	■	China 871038

JONESES, The

R&B '75

R&B-disco group from Pittsburgh, Pennsylvania: Glenn Dorsey, Harold Taylor, Cy Brooks and Ernest Holt.

DEBUT	PEAK	WKS	Gold	A-side (Chart Hit)...B-side	$	Sym	Label & Number
10/5/74+	47	16		**Sugar Pie Guy Pt. 1**...*Pt. 2*	$6		Mercury 73614

JONES GIRLS, The

R&B/AC/LP '79

Female R&B vocal trio from Detroit, Michigan: sisters Shirley, Brenda and Valorie Jones. Backup singers for **Lou Rawls**, **Teddy Pendergrass** and **Aretha Franklin**. With **Diana Ross** from 1975-78. Valorie died on 12/2/2001 (age 45).

DEBUT	PEAK	WKS	Gold	A-side (Chart Hit)...B-side	$	Sym	Label & Number
6/23/79	38	11	●	**You Gonna Make Me Love Somebody Else**...*Who Can I Run To*	$5		Philadelphia I. 3680

JOOSE

'97

Male R&B vocal group from Oklahoma: Leonardo Pettis, Rocky McKaufman, Trell Lewis and Jay Farmer.

DEBUT	PEAK	WKS	Gold	A-side (Chart Hit)...B-side	$	Sym	Label & Number
3/22/97	51	17		**If Tomorrow Never Comes**...S:64 / A:65 *(2 remixes)* #1 Country hit for **Garth Brooks** in 1989	$5	▮	Flavor Unit 64195

DEBUT	PEAK	WKS	Gold	A-side (Chart Hit)...B-side	$	Sym	Label & Number

JOPLIN, Janis — BUB/ROK/LP '71

Born on 1/19/43 in Port Arthur, Texas. Died of a heroin overdose on 10/4/70 (age 27). White blues-rock singer. Nicknamed "Pearl." To San Francisco in 1966; joined **Big Brother & The Holding Company**. Left band to go solo in 1968. The **Bette Midler** movie *The Rose* was inspired by Joplin's life. Inducted into the Rock and Roll Hall of Fame in 1995.

DEBUT	PEAK	WKS	Gold	A-side (Chart Hit)...B-side	$	Sym	Label & Number
				BIG BROTHER & THE HOLDING COMPANY:			
8/31/68	12	12		1 **Piece Of My Heart** ... *Turtle Blues*	$12		Columbia 44626
8/31/68	43	8		2 **Down On Me** ... *Call On Me*	$15		Mainstream 662
				also see #8 below			
11/23/68	84	3		3 **Coo Coo** ... *The Last Time*	$15		Mainstream 678
				JANIS JOPLIN:			
11/8/69	41	9		4 **Kozmic Blues** ... *Little Girl Blue*	$8		Columbia 45023
1/30/71	❶[2]	15		5 **Me And Bobby McGee** ... *Half Moon*	$7		Columbia 45314
				#12 Country hit for **Roger Miller** in 1969			
5/15/71	42	6		6 **Cry Baby** ... *Mercedes Benz*	$7		Columbia 45379
9/11/71	78	2		7 **Get It While You Can** ... *Move Over*	$7		Columbia 45433
7/15/72	91	4		8 **Down On Me** ... *Bye Bye Baby* [L]	$7		Columbia 45630
				studio version on #2 above			

JORDAN, Jeremy — LP '93

Born Don Henson on 9/19/73 in Hammond, Indiana; raised in Calumet City, Illinois. Teen pop singer. Relative of **Tobin Mathews**.

DEBUT	PEAK	WKS	Gold	A-side (Chart Hit)...B-side	$	Sym	Label & Number
12/12/92+	14	25		1 **The Right Kind Of Love** ... A:11 / S:20 *(instrumental)*	$3	▮[V]	Giant 18718
				co-written and co-produced by **Robbie Nevil**; from the TV soundtrack album *Beverly Hills, 90210*			
5/1/93	28	14		2 **Wannagirl** ... A:20 *(instrumental)*	$3	▮[V]	Giant 18548

JORDAN, Montell — ★372★ — R&B/BUB/LP '95

Born on 12/3/68 in Los Angeles, California. R&B singer/songwriter. Also see **Deborah Cox**'s "We Can't Be Friends."

DEBUT	PEAK	WKS	Gold	A-side (Chart Hit)...B-side	$	Sym	Label & Number
2/25/95	❶[7]	29	▲	1 **This Is How We Do It** RB[7] S:❶[8] / A:5 *I Wanna*	$3	▮[V]	PMP/RAL 851468
				samples "Children's Story" by **Slick Rick**			
8/12/95	21	15	●	2 **Somethin' 4 Da Honeyz** ... S:12 / A:63 *This Is How We Do It (remix)*	$3	▮[V]	PMP/RAL 856962
				samples "Summer Madness" by **Kool & The Gang**; "45" issued for above 2 on PMP/RAL 579580			
6/29/96	28	20		3 **I Like** ... S:14 *Come Around* (Dos Of Soul)	$3	▮	Def Jam/RAL 575046
				MONTELL JORDAN FEATURING SLICK RICK			
				samples "I Get Lifted" by **KC & The Sunshine Band**; from the movie *The Nutty Professor* starring **Eddie Murphy**			
10/5/96	18	20	●	4 **Falling** ... S:12 *I Like (remix w/rap)*	$3	▮	Def Jam 575648
				contains an interpolation of "Streiht Up Menace" by **MC Eiht**			
2/15/97	21	20	●	5 **What's On Tonight** ... S:14 *Superlover Man*	$3	▮	Def Jam 574032
3/7/98	2[2]	21	▲	6 **Let's Ride** ... RB[3] S:❶[1] / A:55 *(instrumental)*	$3	▮	Def Jam 568475
				MONTELL JORDAN Featuring Master P & Silkk "The Shocker"			
8/15/98	14	18	●	7 **I Can Do That** ... S:2 *Let's Ride* (w/Shaunta) / *Let's Ride* (w/**Master P** & **Silkk The Shocker**)	$4	★	Def Jam 566106
10/23/99+	4	32		8 **Get It On...Tonite** ... RB[3] S:2 / A:12 *(remix w/***LL Cool J***)* / *Once Upon A Time* (R&B #35)	$4	★	Def Soul 562622
				samples "Love For The Sake Of Love" by **Claudja Barry**			
5/13/00	91	4		9 **Love Sets You Free** ... S:18 *It's Gonna Rain* (Price)	$4	★	Def Soul 562683
				KELLY PRICE & FRIENDS (Dru Hill, Montell Jordan, Case, Playa, Kandice Love, Lovher)			
				from the movie *The Hurricane* starring Denzel Washington			

JORDAN, Sass — ROK/LP '94

Born in 1962 in Montreal, Quebec, Canada. Female rock singer.

DEBUT	PEAK	WKS	Gold	A-side (Chart Hit)...B-side	$	Sym	Label & Number
11/19/94	86	3		**Sun's Gonna Rise** ... *I'm Not*	$3	▮	Impact/MCA 54970

JORDY — '93

Born Jordy Lemoine on 1/14/88 in Paris, France. Age 5 in 1993. His father, Claude, is a record producer.

DEBUT	PEAK	WKS	Gold	A-side (Chart Hit)...B-side	$	Sym	Label & Number
6/19/93	58	9		**Dur Dur D'Etre Bébé! (It's Tough To Be A Baby!)** ... S:37 / A:70 *(French single mix)*	$4	▮	Columbia 74987
				song combines French and English lyrics			

JOSEPH, Margie — R&B/BUB/LP '74

Born in 1950 in Gautier, Mississippi. R&B singer.

DEBUT	PEAK	WKS	Gold	A-side (Chart Hit)...B-side	$	Sym	Label & Number
4/3/71	96	3		1 **Stop! In The Name Of Love** ... *Make Me Believe You'll Stay*	$7		Volt 4056
8/10/74	69	4		2 **My Love** ... *Sweet Surrender*	$6		Atlantic 3032
12/21/74+	91	4		3 **Words (Are Impossible)** ... *(Strange) I Still Love You*	$6		Atlantic 3220

JOURNEY — ★112★ — ROK/AC/LP '81

Rock group formed in San Francisco, California: Neal Schon (born on 2/27/54) and George Tickner (guitars), Gregg Rolie (keyboards, vocals; born on 6/17/47), Ross Valory (bass; born on 2/2/49) and Aynsley Dunbar (drums; born on 1/10/46; **John Mayall**, Mothers Of Invention). Schon and Rolie had been in **Santana**. Tickner left in 1975. **Steve Perry** (lead vocals; born on 1/22/49) added by 1978. In 1979, Steve Smith replaced Dunbar, who later joined **Jefferson Starship**, then **Whitesnake**. **Jonathan Cain** (ex-keyboardist of **The Babys**) added in 1981, replacing Rolie. In 1986 group pared down to a three-man core: Perry, Schon and Cain. The latter two hooked up with **Bad English** in 1989. Smith, Valory and Rolie joined **The Storm** in 1991. Schon with Hardline in 1992. Reunion in 1996 of Perry, Schon, Cain, Valory and Smith. Steve Augeri replaced Perry in 2001.

1)Open Arms 2)Who's Crying Now 3)Separate Ways (Worlds Apart) 4)Don't Stop Believin' 5)Only The Young

DEBUT	PEAK	WKS	Gold	A-side (Chart Hit)...B-side	$	Sym	Label & Number
4/8/78	57	8		1 **Wheel In The Sky** ... *Can Do*	$5		Columbia 10700
7/1/78	83	4		2 **Anytime** ... *Can Do*	$5		Columbia 10757
8/19/78	68	10		3 **Lights** ... *Somethin' To Hide*	$5		Columbia 10800
				also see #25 below			
4/7/79	58	8		4 **Just The Same Way** ... *Somethin' To Hide*	$5		Columbia 10928
7/21/79	16	20	●	5 **Lovin', Touchin', Squeezin'** ... *Daydream*	$5		Columbia 11036
1/12/80	70	4		6 **Too Late** ... *Do You Recall*	$5		Columbia 11143
				all of above produced by Roy Thomas Baker			
3/1/80	23	15		7 **Any Way You Want It** ... *When You're Alone (It Ain't Easy)*	$5		Columbia 11213
5/24/80	32	13		8 **Walks Like A Lady** ... *People And Places*	$5		Columbia 11275
8/23/80	55	8		9 **Good Morning Girl/Stay Awhile** ... *Line Of Fire*	$5		Columbia 11339

DEBUT	PEAK	WKS	Gold	A-side (Chart Hit)...B-side	$	Sym	Label & Number
				JOURNEY — Cont'd			
2/28/81	34	13		10 **The Party's Over (Hopelessly In Love)**...*Just The Same Way (live)*	$5		Columbia 60505
7/18/81	4	21	●	11 **Who's Crying Now**...*Mother, Father*	$4	■	Columbia 02241
10/31/81	9	16	●	12 **Don't Stop Believin'**...*Natural Thing*	$4	■	Columbia 02567
1/16/82	2^{6}	18	●	13 **Open Arms** *Little Girl*	$4	■	Columbia 02687
5/22/82	19	14		14 **Still They Ride**...*La Raza Del Sol*	$4	■	Columbia 02883
				above 4 from the album *Escape*			
2/5/83	8	17		15 **Separate Ways (Worlds Apart)**...AR^{4} *Frontiers*	$4	■	Columbia 03513
4/16/83	12	16		16 **Faithfully**...*Frontiers*	$4		Columbia 03840
7/9/83	23	12		17 **After The Fall**...*Only Solutions* (ROK #22)	$4		Columbia 04004
9/24/83	23	15		18 **Send Her My Love**...*Chain Reaction*	$4		Columbia 04151
				above 4 from the album *Frontiers*			
1/26/85	9	16		19 **Only The Young**...A:6 / S:20 *I'll Fall In Love Again* (**Sammy Hagar**)	$3	■	Geffen 29090
				from the movie *Vision Quest* starring Matthew Modine; #11-19: produced by Mike Stone			
4/12/86	9	15		20 **Be Good To Yourself**...S:7 / A:10 *Only The Young*	$3	■	Columbia 05869
6/21/86	17	13		21 **Suzanne**...S:16 / A:19 *Ask The Lonely* (ROK #3/'84)	$3	■	Columbia 06134
8/30/86	17	14		22 **Girl Can't Help It**...S:17 / A:17 *It Could Have Been You*	$3	■	Columbia 06302
12/6/86+	14	21		23 **I'll Be Alright Without You**...A:11 / S:12 *The Eyes Of A Woman*	$3	■	Columbia 06301
4/25/87	60	12		24 **Why Can't This Night Go On Forever**...*Positive Touch*	$3	■	Columbia 07043
				above 5 from the album *Raised On Radio*			
1/16/93	74	7		25 **Lights**...A:64 *(6 album snippets)* [L-R]	$3	▮	Columbia 74842
				recorded in 1980; also see studio version (#3 above)			
10/26/96	12	22	●	26 **When You Love A Woman**...AC^{3} A:9 / S:17 *Open Arms / Message Of Love* (ROK #18)	$3	▮^{V}	Columbia 78428
				JOY, Roddie '65			
				Female R&B singer.			
3/20/65	86	5		**Come Back Baby**...*Love Hit Me With A Wallop*	$20		Red Bird 10-021
				JOY OF COOKING LP '71			
				Country-rock group from Berkeley, California: Terry Garthwaite (vocals), Toni Brown (vocals, keyboards), Ron Wilson (percussion), Jeff Neighbor (bass) and Fritz Kasten (drums).			
4/24/71	66	8		**Brownsville**...*Only Time Will Tell Me*	$7		Capitol 3075
				J-SHIN R&B/LP '00			
				Born in Miami, Florida. Male R&B singer.			
12/25/99+	34	17		**One Night Stand**...S:9 / A:75 *(instrumental)*	$4	★	Slip n Slide 84489
				J-SHIN Featuring LaTocha Scott Of Xscape			
				J'SON '96			
				Born J'son Tyrel Thomas on 5/14/80 in Los Angeles, California. R&B singer.			
2/24/96	74	12		1 **Take A Look**...S:71 *(2 mixes)*	$3	▮	Hollywood 64003
				Terri Robinson (backing vocal)			
5/25/96	62	16		2 **I'll Never Stop Loving You**...S:44 *(R&B mix)*	$3	▮	Hollywood 64008
				Joey Diggs (backing vocal)			
9/5/98	72	13		3 **I Should Cheat On You**...S:48 *Where Would I Be* (w/Derek & Tina)	$3	▮	Hollywood 64021
				JT MONEY — see MONEY, JT			
				JUDAS PRIEST ROK/LP '82			
				Hard-rock group formed in Birmingham, England: Rob Halford (vocals), K.K. Downing and Glenn Tipton (guitars), Ian Hill (bass), and Dave Holland (drums). Halford left band in mid-1992 to form the rock group Fight.			
11/6/82	67	7		**You've Got Another Thing Comin'**...*Diamonds And Rust (live)*	$5		Columbia 03168
				JUDD, Cledus T. C&W/LP '00			
				Born Barry Poole on 12/18/64 in Crowe Springs, Georgia. Country novelty-parody singer/songwriter.			
9/30/00	26^{S}	21		**My Cellmate Thinks I'm Sexy**...*(dance mix)* [N]	$4	★^{V}	Monument 79495
				parody of "She Thinks My Tractor's Sexy" by **Kenny Chesney**			
				JUDD, Wynonna — see WYNONNA			
				JUDE, Patrick — see BURTON, Jenny			
				JULIE '76			
				Born Julie Budd in Manhattan, New York. Singer/actress. Played "Stella Summers" in the movie *The Devil And Max Devlin.*			
1/17/76	93	4		**One Fine Day**...*Mama Joan*	$6		Tom Cat 10454
				JUMP 5 LP '01			
				Teen pop vocal group from Nashville, Tennessee: siblings Brandon and Brittany Hargest, with Lesley Moore, Libby Hodges and Christopher Fedun.			
11/24/01	18^{S}	15		**God Bless The U.S.A.**...*(instrumental) / Start Jumpin'*	$4	★	Sparrow 51912
				JUMP 'N THE SADDLE '84			
				Country-pop group from Chicago, Illinois: Peter Quinn (vocals, harmonica), T.C. Furlong and Barney Schwartz (guitars), Tom Trinka (sax), Rick Gorley (bass) and Vincent Dee (drums).			
12/3/83+	15	14		**The Curly Shuffle**...*Jump For Joy* [N]	$4	■	Atlantic 89718
				a Three Stooges tribute; first released on Acme 416 in 1983 ($6) with a different picture sleeve			
				JUNGKLAS, Rob ROK/LP '87			
				Born in Boston, Massachusetts. Rock singer/songwriter/guitarist.			
2/7/87	86	3		**Make It Mean Something**...*Memphis Thing*	$3	■	Manhattan 50054
				JUNIOR R&B/BUB/LP '82			
				Born Norman Giscombe on 11/10/61 in London, England. R&B singer/songwriter.			
2/13/82	30	13		**Mama Used To Say**...*(instrumental)*	$4		Mercury 76132

DEBUT	PEAK	WKS	Gold	A-side (Chart Hit)..........B-side	$	Sym	Label & Number
				JUNIOR M.A.F.I.A. R&B/BUB/LP **'95**			
				Gathering of four rap acts: **Lil' Kim**, Klepto, Snakes (Trife & Larceny) and The Sixes (Little Caesar, Chico & Nino Brown). Proteges of **The Notorious B.I.G.** M.A.F.I.A.: Masters At Finding Intelligent Attitudes. Also see **Skindeep**.			
7/22/95	13	20	●	1 **Player's Anthem** ....S:7 / A:47 *(radio remix)* samples "Ladi Dadi" by Doug E. Fresh	$3	▮	Undeas/Big Beat 98149
12/16/95	60^{S}	2		2 **I Need You Tonight** ....BUB:103 *Realms Of Junior M.A.F.I.A. (Part II)* **JUNIOR M.A.F.I.A. Featuring Aaliyah** **Lil' Kim**, Trife and Klepto (rap); samples "I Wonder If I Take You Home" by **Lisa Lisa and Cult Jam**	$4	▮	Undeas/Big Beat 98097
2/10/96	17	20	▲	3 **Get Money** ....S:9 / A:57 *I Need You Tonight* **The Notorious B.I.G.** (guest rapper); samples "You Can't Turn Me Away" by Sylvia Striplin	$3	▮	Undeas/Big Beat 98087
				JURASSIC 5 LP **'02**			
				Interracial rap group from Los Angeles, California: rappers Chali2NA, Zaakir, Akil and Marc 7, with DJs Cut Chemist and Nu-Mark.			
6/10/00	74^{S}	2		1 **Quality Control** ....*(2 versions) / Twelve*	$6	T	Interscope 497330
12/2/00	59^{S}	4		2 **W.O.E. Is Me (World Of Entertainment)**.......*(2 versions) / Long Road To Glory / Monkey Bars*	$6	T	Rawkus 284
5/25/02	54^{S}	2		3 **Hard Times** ....*Verbal Murder* (Ras Kass) **PHARCYDE/JURASSIC 5**	$6	T	Avatar 10104
10/19/02	43^{S}	4		4 **What's Golden?**..........*(2 versions) / High Fidelity* samples "Prophets Of Rage" by **Public Enemy**	$6	T	Interscope 497801
				JUSTIS, Bill BUB/LP **'57**			
				Born on 10/14/26 in Birmingham, Alabama. Died on 7/15/82 (age 55). Session saxophonist/arranger/producer. Led house band for Sun Records.			
11/18/57	2^{1}	20	●	1 **Raunchy** ....RB^{1} S:2 / T:3 / A:5 *The Midnite Man* [I] Bill Justis (sax); Sid Manker (guitar)	$30		Phillips 3519
3/10/58	42	8		2 **College Man**..........S:42 / T:42 *The Stranger* [I] 15 seconds of vocal at end of song	$20		Phillips 3522
				JUST US BUB **'66**			
				Pop duo of New York City producers Chip Taylor and Al Gorgoni.			
3/12/66	34	11		**I Can't Grow Peaches On A Cherry Tree** ....*I Can Save You* first released on Minuteman 203 in 1965 ($15); #120 hit for **The Browns** in 1965	$10		Colpix 803
				JUVENILE R&B/LP **'99**			
				Born Terius Gray in 1975 in New Orleans, Louisiana. Male rapper. Also see **Hot Boy$**.			
2/6/99	68	10		1 **"Ha"** ....A:55 *(6 versions)* 12" dirty and clean remix versions by **Jay-Z**	$6	T	Cash Money 56234
7/10/99	19	30		2 **Back That Azz Up** A:9 / S:64 *(4 versions)* **JUVENILE Feat. Mannie Fresh and Lil' Wayne**	$6	T	Cash Money 156482
9/18/99	36	19		3 **Bling Bling**..........A:25 / S:72 *(3 versions)* **B.G. Feat. Baby, Turk, Mannie Fresh, Juvenile and Lil Wayne**	$6	T	Cash Money 156483
12/4/99+	72	11		4 **Tha Block Is Hot** ....A:57 *(3 versions)* **LIL WAYNE (featuring Juvenile and B.G.)**	$6	T	Cash Money 156546
2/5/00	83	6		5 **U Understand**..........A:71 from the album *Tha G-Code* on Cash Money 542179			album cut
8/11/01	65	15		6 **Set It Off** ....A:60 / S:72 *(4 versions)* samples the opening riff of "Dragnet"	$6	T	Cash Money 860956
11/10/01+	65	15		7 **From Her Mama (Mama Got A**)**..........A:61 *(2 versions) / Set It Off (remix w/***Lil Wayne***)*	$6	T	Cash Money 860962
3/9/02	29^{S}	9		8 **Put Yo Sets Up** ....*(6 versions)* **REDD EYEZZ featuring Juvenile & slanted eyezz**	$8	★*	Z-Bo 2503
				JXL — see PRESLEY, Elvis			

K

DEBUT	PEAK	WKS	Gold	A-side (Chart Hit)..........B-side	$	Sym	Label & Number
				KACI **'01**			
				Born Kaci Battaglia on 10/3/87 in Clearwater, Florida. Female teen pop singer.			
7/7/01	50^{S}	15		**Paradise** ....*(2 versions)*	$4	★	Curb 73124
				KADISON, Joshua LP **'94**			
				Born on 2/8/63 in Los Angeles, California. Adult Contemporary singer/songwriter/pianist.			
10/9/93+	26	22		1 **Jessie** ....A:21 / S:30 *When A Woman Cries*	$3	▮V	SBK 50429
4/16/94	19	21		2 **Beautiful In My Eyes** ....A:22 / S:26 *All I'll Ever Ask / Jessie (original demo)*	$3	▮	SBK 58099
11/12/94	84	9		3 **Picture Postcards From L.A.** ....*(live version) / Invisible Man (live)* "45" issued for #1 & 3 on SBK 18130 (yellow vinyl); above 3 produced by Peter Van Hooke (**Mike + The Mechanics**) and Rod Argent (**Zombies/Argent**)	$3	▮V	SBK 58238
	★544★			**KAEMPFERT, Bert, And His Orchestra** AC/BUB/LP **'61**			
				Born on 10/16/23 in Hamburg, Germany. Died on 6/21/80 (age 56). Multi-instrumentalist/bandleader/producer/arranger for Polydor Records in Germany. Composed "Strangers In The Night" and "Spanish Eyes" among others. Produced first **Beatles** recording session in Hamburg ("Cry For A Shadow"/"Ain't She Sweet"). *1)Wonderland By Night 2)Red Roses For A Blue Lady 3)Tenderly*			
11/14/60+	❶^{3}	17	●	1 **Wonderland By Night** *Dreaming The Blues* [I] Charly Tabor plays trumpet on #1 & 3; Fred Moch on others	$10		Decca 31141
2/6/61	73	6		2 **Cerveza** ....*Catalania* [I]	$8		Decca 30866
3/27/61	31	7		3 **Tenderly**..........*Without Your Love* [I] #17 hit for **Rosemary Clooney** in 1952	$8		Decca 31236
7/31/61	48	7		4 **Now And Forever**..........*Only Those In Love* [I]	$8		Decca 31279
1/20/62	42	10		5 **Afrikaan Beat**..........*Echo In The Night* (#108) [I]	$8		Decca 31350
5/19/62	67	6		6 **That Happy Feeling**..........*Take Me* [I] written in 1956 as "Eyi Wala Dong"	$8		Decca 31388
12/7/63	8^{X}	5		7 **Jingo Jango** ....*The Little Drummer Boy* [X-I] X: 8/'63; 25/'65	$10		Decca 31560

DEBUT	PEAK	WKS	Gold	A-side (Chart Hit)..........B-side	$	Sym	Label & Number
				KAEMPFERT, Bert, And His Orchestra — Cont'd			
1/23/65	**11**	13		8 **Red Roses For A Blue Lady** ....*Lonely Nightingale* [I] #3 hit for **Vaughn Monroe** in 1949	$7		Decca 31722
5/1/65	**33**	8		9 **Three O'Clock In The Morning** ....*Nothing's New* [I] there were 6 Top 10 versions of this tune from 1921-30	$7		Decca 31778
7/10/65	**59**	10		10 **Moon Over Naples** ....*The Moon Is Making Eyes* [I] tune later known as "Spanish Eyes"	$7		Decca 31812
1/22/66	**54**	7		11 **Bye Bye Blues**..........*Remember When* [I] #5 hit in 1930 for Bert Lown's orchestra (their theme song)	$7		Decca 31882
10/15/66	**100**	1		12 **I Can't Give You Anything But Love**..........*Milica* [I] there were 6 Top 20 versions of this tune from 1928-29	$7		Decca 32008
				KAGE '02 Born Mezeio Jackson on 1/30/70 in Atlanta, Georgia. Male rapper/songwriter.			
8/31/02	**55^{S}**	3		**Big Big**..........*(3 album snippets)* **KAGE feat. Tempest**	$5	★	RocWilda 90428
				KAI '98 Male R&B vocal group from San Francisco, California: Andrey Silva, Errol Viray, Andrew Gapuz, A.C. Lorenzo and Leo Chan.			
12/20/97+	**59**	19		**Say You'll Stay**..........S:46 *(2 versions) / Last To Know* first issued in 1997 on HB 41211 ($5)	$3	▌	Tidal Wave/Geffen 19419
				KAJAGOOGOO LP '83 Pop-synth group formed in London, England: Chris "**Limahl**" Hamill (vocals; left in late 1983), Steve Askew (guitar), Stuart Neale (keyboards), Nick Beggs (bass) and Jez Strode (drums).			
4/23/83	**5**	19		1 **Too Shy**..........*Take Another View*	$4	■	EMI America 8161
8/27/83	**78**	4		2 **Hang On Now**..........*Kajagoogoo*	$4	■	EMI America 8171
				KALIN TWINS BUB '58 Pop duo of twins Herbert and Harold Kalin. Born on 2/16/34 in Port Jervis, New York.			
6/23/58	**5**	15	●	1 **When**..........RB[1] H:5 / S:7 / A:8 *Three O'Clock Thrill* co-written by **Paul Evans**	$25		Decca 30642
9/29/58	**12**	15		2 **Forget Me Not**..........H:12 *Dream Of Me*	$20		Decca 30745
1/12/59	**42**	10		3 **It's Only The Beginning**..........*Oh! My Goodness* **Jack Pleis** (orch., all of above)	$20		Decca 30807
7/6/59	**97**	1		4 **Sweet Sugar Lips**..........*Moody*	$20		Decca 30911
				KALLEN, Kitty MEM/POP/BUB '54 Born on 5/25/22 in Philadelphia, Pennsylvania. Big band singer with Jack Teagarden, **Jimmy Dorsey**, Harry James and Artie Shaw. Her 1954 smash hit "Little Things Mean A Lot" was #1 for 9 weeks.			
11/12/55	**76**	3		1 **Sweet Kentucky Rose**..........T:76 *How Lonely Can I Get?*	$15		Decca 29708
1/7/56	**39**	9		2 **Go On With The Wedding**..........T:39 *The Second Greatest Sex* **KITTY KALLEN and GEORGIE SHAW** **Jack Pleis** (orch., above 2)	$15		Decca 29776
10/5/59	**34**	12		3 **If I Give My Heart To You**..........*The Door That Won't Open* there were 3 Top 10 versions of this tune in 1954	$12		Columbia 41473
2/1/60	**55**	5		4 **That Old Feeling**..........*Need Me* #1 hit for Shep Fields in 1937; Milton De Lugg (orch., above 2)	$12		Columbia 41546
12/22/62+	**18**	10		5 **My Coloring Book**..........*Here's To Us* **Ray Ellis** (orch.)	$10		RCA Victor 8124
				KALLMANN, Gunter, Chorus AC/LP '67 Born on 11/19/30 in Berlin, Germany. Choral director.			
12/24/66+	**63**	8		**Wish Me A Rainbow**..........*The Day The Rains Came* from the movie *This Property Is Condemned* starring Robert Redford	$6		4 Corners 138
				KAMON, Karen '84 Female pop singer. Married to producer Phil Ramone, who worked with **Billy Joel** and many others.			
7/28/84	**88**	2		**Loverboy**..........*You Can Do Better Than That*	$4	■	Columbia 04474
				KAMOZE, Ini '94 Born on 10/9/57 in Jamaica. Male dancehall reggae singer/author. Name means "mountain of the true God."			
9/17/94	**❶^{2}**	30	▲	1 **Here Comes The Hotstepper**..........S:❶[8] / A:3 *(remix)* samples "Hot Pants-I'm Coming" by **Bobby Byrd** and "Heartbeat" by Taana Gardner; incorporates "Land Of 1000 Dances"; recorded in 1992; later included in the movie *Ready To Wear (Pret-A-Porter)* starring Julia Roberts; "45": Collectables 4679	$3	▌V	Columbia 77614
7/29/95	**88**	5		2 **Listen Me Tic (Woyoi)**..........S:64 *(album version)* samples "I Get Lifted" by **KC And The Sunshine Band** and "School Boy Crush" by **Average White Band**	$3	▌	EastWest 64414
				KANDI LP '00 Born Kandi Burruss on 5/17/76 in Atlanta, Georgia. Female R&B singer/songwriter. Former member of **Xscape**. Also see **P!nk**.			
8/5/00	**24**	24		1 **Don't Think I'm Not**..........S:23 / A:25 *(4 versions)* samples "Ike's Mood" by **Isaac Hayes**	$7	★*	Columbia 79450
2/17/01	**59^{S}**	2		2 **Cheatin' On Me**..........*(4 remixes)*	$7	★*	Columbia 79529
12/8/01+	**6^{S}**	37		3 **It's The Weekend**..........*(instrumental)* **LIL' J featuring Kandi**	$5	★+	Hollywood 64060
9/7/02	**41^{S}**	7		4 **Crew Deep**..........*(2 versions) / Imagine* **SKILLZ feat. Missy "Misdemeanor" Elliott and Kandi** samples "Rapper's Delight" by **Sugarhill Gang**	$6	T	Rawkus 113991
				KANE, Big Daddy R&B/BUB/LP '93 Born Antonio Hardy on 9/10/68 in Brooklyn, New York. Rap singer/lyricist for Cold Chillin' Records. Wrote songs for Roxanne Shante and **Biz Markie**. Toured as Shante's DJ in 1985. Kane is an acronym for King Asiatic Nobody's Equal. Appeared in the movies *The Meteor Man* and *Posse*.			
7/10/93	**31**	20		**Very Special**..........S:30 / A:31 *Stop Shammin'* Spinderella, Laree Williams and Karen Anderson (vocals and rap)	$3	▌	Cold Chillin' 18437
				KANE, Madleen '82 Born in Sweden. Female disco singer produced by **Giorgio Moroder**.			
2/6/82	**77**	5		**You Can**..........*Mon Amour*	$5		Chalet 1225

DEBUT	PEAK	WKS	Gold	A-side (Chart Hit)..........B-side	$	Sym	Label & Number
				KANE & ABEL LP **'00**			
				Male rap duo from Oakland, California: twin brothers David and Daniel Garcia.			
9/16/00	53S	10		**Shake It Like A Dog** ....*(clean version) / Get It Right*	$6	★	Most Wanted 0002
				KANE & ABEL Featuring PNC and 5th Ward Weebie			
				KANE GANG, The LP **'87**			
				Soul-styled pop trio formed in England: vocalists Martin Brammer and Paul Woods with guitarist David Brewis. Band's name derived from the movie *Citizen Kane*.			
10/17/87	36	16		1 **Motortown**..........S:32 / A:40 *Spend*	$3	■	Capitol 44062
2/6/88	64	8		2 **Don't Look Any Further** ....*A Finer Place*	$3		Capitol 44115
				KANO R&B/LP **'82**			
				Disco group from Italy: Rosanna Casale, Lella Esposito, Piero Cairo, Bruno Gergonzi, Luciano Nenzatti and Stefano Pulga.			
12/26/81+	89	5		**Can't Hold Back (Your Loving)** ....*She's A Star*	$4		Mirage 3878
	★450★			**KANSAS** ROK/LP **'78**			
				Pop-rock group from Topeka, Kansas: Steve Walsh (vocals, keyboards; born on 6/15/51), Kerry Livgren (guitar, keyboards; born on 9/18/49), Rich Williams (guitar), Robby Steinhardt (violin), Dave Hope (bass; born on 10/7/49) and Phil Ehart (drums). Walsh left in 1981 and formed **Streets**; replaced by John Elefante (later a prolific Christian rock producer/artist). Livgren became a popular Contemporary Christian artist in the 1980s. Revised lineup in 1986: Walsh, Ehart, Williams, Steve Morse (guitarist from The Dregs) and Billy Greer (bass).			
				1)Dust In The Wind 2)Carry On Wayward Son 3)Play The Game Tonight			
12/25/76+	11	20	●	1 **Carry On Wayward Son** ....*Questions Of My Childhood*	$6		Kirshner 4267
11/12/77+	28	14		2 **Point Of Know Return** ....*Closet Chronicles*	$5		Kirshner 4273
1/28/78	6	20	●	3 **Dust In The Wind** *Paradox*	$5		Kirshner 4274
6/10/78	64	6		4 **Portrait (He Knew)** ....*Lightning's Hand*	$5		Kirshner 4276
1/20/79	60	5		5 **Lonely Wind** ....*Song For America* [L]	$5		Kirshner 4280
				studio version released on Kirshner 4256 in 1974			
6/2/79	23	12		6 **People Of The South Wind**..........*Stay Out Of Trouble*	$5		Kirshner 4284
9/8/79	52	8		7 **Reason To Be** ....*How My Soul Cries Out For You*	$5		Kirshner 4285
9/20/80	40	11		8 **Hold On** ....*Don't Open Your Eyes*	$5		Kirshner 4291
12/27/80+	76	5		9 **Got To Rock On**..........*No Room For A Stranger*	$5		Kirshner 4292
5/8/82	17	15		10 **Play The Game Tonight** ....*Play On*	$5		Kirshner 02903
8/21/82	73	6		11 **Right Away**..........*Windows*	$5	■	Kirshner 03084
9/3/83	58	7		12 **Fight Fire With Fire** ....*Incident On A Bridge*	$4	■	CBS Associated 04057
11/1/86+	19	18		13 **All I Wanted** ....S:18 / A:21 *We're Not Alone Anymore*	$3	■	MCA 52958
2/14/87	84	4		14 **Power**..........*Tomb 19*	$3	■	MCA 53027
				KAOMA LP **'90**			
				Multi-national group of singers, musicians and dancers based in Paris, France. Fronted by keyboardist/arranger Jean-Claude Bonaventure.			
3/3/90	46	12		**Lambada** ....S:34 *(instrumental)* [F]	$4	■V	Epic 73090
				title refers to an erotic Brazilian dance craze			
				KAPLAN, Gabriel **'77**			
				Born on 3/31/45 in Brooklyn, New York. Comedian/actor. Star of TV's *Welcome Back Kotter*.			
1/22/77	91	3		**Up Your Nose** ....*Bye Centennial Minutes* [N]	$6	■	Elektra 45369
				KAREN, Kenny **'73**			
				Born in Toronto, Ontario, Canada. Pop singer/songwriter/actor. Played "David Miller" in the 1978 movie *If Ever I See You Again*.			
9/8/73	82	4		**That's Why You Remember** ....*A Nice Place To Live*	$6		Big Tree 16007
				adapted from a Faygo soda jingle			
				KARL, Frankie, & The Dreams **'68**			
				R&B vocal group led by Frankie Karl Springs.			
12/14/68	93	1		**Don't Be Afraid (Do As I Say)** ....*I'm So Glad*	$15		D.C. 180
				KaSANDRA LP **'68**			
				Born John W. Anderson on 7/30/36 in Panama City, Florida. R&B singer/songwriter.			
12/14/68	91	2		**Don't Pat Me On The Back And Call Me Brother**..........*Just Look In My Face* [S]	$8		Capitol 2342
				JOHN W. ANDERSON presents KASANDRA			
				KASENETZ-KATZ SINGING ORCHESTRAL CIRCUS BUB **'68**			
				Bubblegum rock group assembled by producers Jerry Kasenetz and Jeff Katz. Features members from **The 1910 Fruitgum Co./The Ohio Express/The Music Explosion**.			
10/5/68	25	11		**Quick Joey Small (Run Joey Run)** ....*(Poor Old) Mr. Jensen*	$8		Buddah 64
				Joey Levine (lead singer; **Ohio Express**, **Reunion**)			
				KASHIF — see WARWICK, Dionne			
				KATALINA **'96**			
				Born in Chicago, Illinois; raised in California. Female dance singer.			
9/14/96	86	11		**DJ Girl** ....S:74 *(same version)*	$5	▮	Thump 2227
				KATFISH **'75**			
				Rock group from Lewiston, Maine.			
9/27/75	62	6		**Dear Prudence** ....*Street Walkin'*	$6		Big Tree 16045
				written by **John Lennon** and **Paul McCartney** (on **The Beatles**' 1968 *"White Album"*)			
				KATRINA AND THE WAVES LP **'85**			
				Pop-rock group formed in London, England: Katrina Leskanich (vocals; born in Topeka, Kansas), Kimberley Rew (guitar), Vince Dela Cruz (bass) and Alex Cooper (drums).			
3/23/85	9	21		1 **Walking On Sunshine** S:4 / A:10 *Going Down To Liverpool*	$3	■	Capitol 5466
7/27/85	37	10		2 **Do You Want Crying** ....*The Sun Won't Shine Without You*	$3	■	Capitol 5450
10/12/85	71	6		3 **Que Te Quiero**..........*He's A Charmer*	$3	■	Capitol 5528
4/5/86	70	8		4 **Is That It?**..........*I Really Taught Me To Watusi*	$3	■	Capitol 5566
7/22/89	16	12		5 **That's The Way** ....S:14 / A:26 *Love Calculator*	$3	■	SBK 07303

DEBUT	PEAK	WKS	Gold	A-side (Chart Hit)..........B-side	$	Sym	Label & Number

KAY, John — see STEPPENWOLF

KAYAK LP **'78**

Rock group from Holland: **Max Werner** (vocals), Johan Slager (guitar), Ton Scherpenzeel (keyboards), Theo DeJong (bass) and Charles Schouten (drums).

DEBUT	PEAK	WKS	Gold	A-side (Chart Hit)..........B-side	$	Sym	Label & Number
5/13/78	55	6		**I Want You To Be Mine** ....*Irene*	$5		Janus 274

KAYE, Johnny **'63**

Born John Kaminsky in Chicago, Illinois. Adult Contemporary singer; similar in style to **Perry Como**.

DEBUT	PEAK	WKS	Gold	A-side (Chart Hit)..........B-side	$	Sym	Label & Number
12/28/63	20^{X}	1		**A Christmas Love**..........*Christmas In Paree* [X] **Morty Jay** (orch.)	$25		Legend 127

KAYE, Mary, Trio MEM **'59**

Adult Contemporary vocal trio: Mary, her brother Norman, and Frankie Ross (died on 5/9/95, age 70).

DEBUT	PEAK	WKS	Gold	A-side (Chart Hit)..........B-side	$	Sym	Label & Number
4/13/59	75	3		**You Can't Be True Dear**..........*Because Of You* **Big Sound of Don Ralke** (orch.); #1 hit for Ken Grififn in 1948	$10		Warner 5050

KAYE, Sammy, And His Orchestra MEM/POP/LP **'46**

Born on 3/13/10 in Rocky River, Ohio. Died of cancer on 6/2/87 (age 77). Leader of popular "sweet" dance band with the slogan "Swing and Sway with Sammy Kaye." Also played clarinet and alto sax. Charted 103 pop hits (1937-53), including several big #1 hits: "Love Walked In," "Daddy," "Chickery Chick," "The Old Lamp-Lighter" and "Harbor Lights."

DEBUT	PEAK	WKS	Gold	A-side (Chart Hit)..........B-side	$	Sym	Label & Number
4/3/61	68	3		1 **Welcome Home**..........*What's New At The Zoo* The Kaydets (vocals); Johnny Amoroso (trumpet solo)	$7		Decca 31204
4/4/64	36	7		2 **Charade**..........*Maria Elena* [I] title song from the movie starring Cary Grant and Audrey Hepburn	$7		Decca 31589

KAYLE, Kortney C&W **'02**

Born on 2/8/79 in Ayr, Ontario, Canada. Country singer.

DEBUT	PEAK	WKS	Gold	A-side (Chart Hit)..........B-side	$	Sym	Label & Number
8/3/02	73^{S}	1		**Unbroken By You**..........*Don't Let Me Down*	$5	★	Lyric Street 64048

KAYLI, Bob **'58**

Born Robert Gordy on 7/15/31 in Detroit, Michigan. Brother of Motown founder Berry Gordy, Jr. Executive with Motown's music publishing firm, Jobete, from 1961-85. Appeared in the 1972 movie *Lady Sings The Blues*.

DEBUT	PEAK	WKS	Gold	A-side (Chart Hit)..........B-side	$	Sym	Label & Number
11/17/58	96	2		**Everyone Was There**..........*I Took A Dare* [N]	$30		Carlton 482

KBC BAND — see JEFFERSON AIRPLANE

KC AND THE SUNSHINE BAND ★144★ R&B/BUB/AC/LP **'75**

Disco group from Hialeah, Florida. Formed by Harry Wayne "KC" Casey (vocals, keyboards; born on 1/31/51) and Richard Finch (bass; born on 1/25/54). Other members included Jerome Smith (guitar), Fermin Coytisolo (congas), Robert Johnson (drums), and Ronnie Smith, Denvil Liptrot, James Weaver and Charles Williams (horn section). Jerome Smith died in a construction accident on 7/28/2000 (age 47).

1)That's The Way (I Like It) 2)Please Don't Go 3)(Shake, Shake, Shake) Shake Your Booty

DEBUT	PEAK	WKS	Gold	A-side (Chart Hit)..........B-side	$	Sym	Label & Number
7/12/75	❶^{1}	15		1 **Get Down Tonight**..........RB^{1} *You Don't Know*	$5		T.K. 1009
9/6/75	88	2		2 **Shotgun Shuffle** *[THE SUNSHINE BAND]*..........*Hey J* [I]	$5		T.K. 1010
10/25/75	❶^{2}	16		3 **That's The Way (I Like It)** RB^{1} *What Makes You Happy*	$5		T.K. 1015
3/13/76	66	5		4 **Queen Of Clubs**..........*Do It Good* first released in 1974	$5		T.K. 1005
7/10/76	❶^{1}	21		5 **(Shake, Shake, Shake) Shake Your Booty**..........RB^{4} *Boogie Shoes*	$5		T.K. 1019
12/4/76+	37	12		6 **I Like To Do It**..........*Come On In*	$5		T.K. 1020
2/26/77	❶^{1}	23		7 **I'm Your Boogie Man** /			
12/3/77+	48	7		8 **Wrap Your Arms Around Me**..........	$5		T.K. 1022
7/30/77	2^{3}	20		9 **Keep It Comin' Love**..........RB^{1} *Baby I Love You* above 5 from the album *Part 3*	$5	■	T.K. 1023
2/11/78	35	10		10 **Boogie Shoes**..........*I Get Lifted* originally released as the B-side of #5 above; re-released due to inclusion on the *Saturday Night Fever* soundtrack	$5	■	T.K. 1025
5/13/78	35	10		11 **It's The Same Old Song**..........*Let's Go Party*	$5	■	T.K. 1028
10/7/78	63	5		12 **Do You Feel All Right**..........*I Will Love You Tomorrow*	$5	■	T.K. 1030
12/16/78+	68	8		13 **Who Do Ya Love**..........*Sho-Nuff*	$5	■	T.K. 1031
5/19/79	50	10		14 **Do You Wanna Go Party**..........*Come To My Island*	$5		T.K. 1033
8/25/79+	❶^{1}	26		15 **Please Don't Go**..........*I Betcha Didn't Know That* (R&B #25) all of above (except #11) written by Harry Casey and Richard Finch	$5		T.K. 1035
11/17/79+	2^{2}	23	●	16 **Yes, I'm Ready**..........AC^{2} *With Your Love* (DeSario)	$4		Casablanca 2227
6/28/80	66	6		17 **Dancin' In The Streets**..........*Moonlight Madness* (DeSario) **TERI DeSARIO with K.C.** (above 2)	$4		Casablanca 2278
12/24/83+	18	21		18 **Give It Up** *[KC]*..........*Uptight*	$4		Meca 1001

★317★ **K-CI & JOJO** R&B/LP **'98**

Brothers Cedric "K-Ci" and Joel "JoJo" Hailey from Charlotte, North Carolina. K-Ci was born on 9/2/69; JoJo was born on 6/10/71. Both were founding members of the R&B vocal group **Jodeci**. Also see **Milestone**.

1)All My Life 2)Tell Me It's Real 3)Crazy

DEBUT	PEAK	WKS	Gold	A-side (Chart Hit)..........B-side	$	Sym	Label & Number
2/18/95	17	16		1 **If You Think You're Lonely Now**..........S:7 / A:33 *(studio version)* **K-Ci HAILEY of Jodeci** from the movie *Jason's Lyric* starring Forest Whitaker	$4	▮	Mercury 856572
6/15/96	❶^{2}	24	▲^{2}	2 **How Do U Want It**..RB^{3} S:❶^{4} / A:68 *California Love* (**2 PAC w/Dr. Dre & Roger Troutman** - #6) **2 PAC (featuring KC and JoJo)** samples "Body Heat" by **Quincy Jones**	$3	▮	Death Row 854652
11/16/96	53	15		3 **How Could You**..........S:30 *(radio mix)* **K-Ci and JoJo of Jodeci** from the movie *Bulletproof* starring Damon Wayans	$3	▮	MCA Soundtracks 55279

DEBUT	PEAK	WKS	Gold	A-side (Chart Hit)..........B-side	$	Sym	Label & Number
				K-CI & JOJO — Cont'd			
2/1/97	flip	14		4 **Rappers' Ball**..........*Things'll Never Change* (**E-40** - #29)	$4	▮	Sick Wid' It/Jive 42436
				E-40 Featuring Too $hort and K-Ci			
				samples "Playboy $hort" by **Too $hort**			
6/14/97	26	20		5 **You Bring Me Up**..........S:16 *(remix)*	$3	▮	MCA 55346
10/4/97	46	20		6 **Last Night's Letter**..........S:25 *Baby Come Back*	$3	▮	MCA 55380
3/28/98	❶[3]	36		7 **All My Life** RB[2] S:❶[2] / A:3 *Don't Rush (Take Love Slowly)*	$3	▮V	MCA 55420
				also see reissue on the B-side of #12 below			
3/20/99	60	17		8 **Life**..........A:43			album cut
				written and produced by **R. Kelly**; from the movie *Life* starring **Eddie Murphy** (soundtrack album on Rock Land 90314)			
5/29/99	2[1]	20		9 **Tell Me It's Real**..........S:2 / A:12 *(remix)*	$4	★V	MCA 55551
				also see reissue at #12 below; "45" issued for #7 & 9 on MCA 55604			
10/30/99	25	13		10 **Will 2K**..........A:20 *(2 versions)*	$6	TV	Columbia 79287
				WILL SMITH (Featuring K-Ci)			
				samples "Rock The Casbah" by **The Clash**; "45": Columbia 79286; B-side: (instrumental)			
12/9/00+	11	25		11 **Crazy**..........A:8			album cut
				from the album *X* on MCA 112398			
10/27/01+	47[S]	11		12 **Tell Me It's Real**..........*All My Life* [R]	$8	★**	MCA 155868
				reissue of #9 & 7 above			
				K-DOE, Ernie R&B/BUB **'61**			
				Born Ernest Kador on 2/22/36 in New Orleans, Louisiana. Died on 7/5/2001 (age 65). R&B singer/songwriter. Recorded with the Blue Diamonds on Savoy in 1954. First solo recording for Specialty in 1955.			
3/27/61	❶[1]	14		1 **Mother-In-Law** RB[5] *Wanted, $10,000.00 Reward*	$25		Minit 623
				Benny Spellman (bass vocal)			
6/26/61	53	5		2 **Te-Ta-Te-Ta-Ta**..........*Real Man*	$15		Minit 627
11/6/61	69	5		3 **I Cried My Last Tear /**			
11/13/61	71	4		4 **A Certain Girl**..........	$15		Minit 634
2/24/62	99	1		5 **Popeye Joe**..........*Come On Home*	$15		Minit 641
				KEANE BROTHERS, The **'76**			
				Pop duo: brothers Tom (piano; born on 3/13/64) and John (drums; born on 4/26/65) Keane. Sons of label owner Bob Keane. Duo hosted own summer replacement variety show on CBS-TV in 1977.			
11/13/76	84	5		**Sherry**..........*God Loves Little Girls*	$6		20th Century 2302
				KEATING, Ronan **'02**			
				Born on 3/3/77 in Dublin, Ireland. Pop singer. Former member of Boyzone.			
6/23/01+	38[S]	16		**Lovin' Each Day**..........*When You Say Nothing At All*	$4	★	A&M 71272
				KEEDY **'91**			
				Born Kelly Keedy on 7/26/65 in Abilene, Texas. Female dance singer.			
3/16/91	15	15		1 **Save Some Love**..........S:13 / A:15 *Lazy Day*	$3	▮V	Arista 2153
8/17/91	86	4		2 **Wishing On The Same Star**..........*Gettin' Around*	$3	▮V	Arista 2255
				KEITH BUB/LP **'67**			
				Born James Barry Keefer on 5/7/49 in Philadelphia, Pennsylvania. Pop singer/songwriter.			
9/17/66	39	10		1 **Ain't Gonna Lie**..........*Our Love Started All Over Again*	$8		Mercury 72596
12/10/66+	7	14		2 **98.6**..........*The Teeny Bopper Song*	$8	■	Mercury 72639
				The Tokens (backing vocals, above 2)			
3/18/67	37	6		3 **Tell Me To My Face**..........*Pretty Little Shy One*	$8	■	Mercury 72652
				first recorded by **The Hollies** on their 1967 album *Stop! Stop! Stop!*			
6/17/67	79	4		4 **Daylight Savin' Time**..........*Happy Walking Around*	$8	■	Mercury 72695
				KEITH, Lisa **'93**			
				Born in Minneapolis, Minnesota. Adult Contemporary singer/songwriter. Vocalist on **Herb Alpert**'s "Keep Your Eye On Me," "Diamonds" and "Making Love In The Rain."			
8/21/93	36	20		1 **Better Than You**..........A:33 *True To You*	$3	▮	Perspective 7430
1/22/94	84	3		2 **I'm In Love**..........*(radio remix) / True To You*	$3	▮	Perspective 7436
	★574★			**KEITH, Toby** C&W/BUB/LP **'97**			
				Born Toby Keith Covel on 7/8/61 in Clinton, Oklahoma; raised in Moore, Oklahoma. Country singer/songwriter/guitarist. Former rodeo hand, oil field worker and semi-pro football player.			
				1)Who's Your Daddy 2)Courtesy Of The Red, White And Blue (The Angry American) 3)My List			
6/26/93	93	2		1 **Should've Been A Cowboy**..........CW[2] S:58 *(3 album snippets)*	$4	▮V	Mercury 864990
				"45" B-side: "Some Kinda Good Kinda Hold On Me"			
9/10/94	50[S]	8		2 **Who's That Man**..........CW[1] BUB:102 *(3 album snippets)*	$4	▮V	Polydor 853358
				"45" B-side: "You Ain't Much Fun"			
12/6/97	84	5		3 **I'm So Happy I Can't Stop Crying**..........S:67 *Jacky Don Tucker (Play By The Rules Miss All The Fun)*	$4	▮V	Mercury 568114
				TOBY KEITH with Sting			
				also see **Sting**'s 1996 solo version (#94)			
1/29/00	31	20		4 **How Do You Like Me Now?!**..........CW[5] A:24 / S:29 *(2 versions)*	$4	★V	DreamWorks 50932
				"45": DreamWorks 459041; B-side: "When Love Fades"			
8/5/00	54	15		5 **Country Comes To Town**..........A:47		V	album cut
				"45": DreamWorks 459033; B-side: "When Love Fades"			
12/30/00+	32	20		6 **You Shouldn't Kiss Me Like This**..........CW[3] A:25			album cut
				above 3 from the album *How Do You Like Me Now?!* on DreamWorks 50209			
6/16/01	27	20		7 **I'm Just Talkin' About Tonight**..........CW[1] A:24		V	album cut
10/13/01	28	20		8 **I Wanna Talk About Me**..........CW[5] A:26		V	album cut
				"45" issued for above 2 on DreamWorks 450874			
2/16/02	26	20		9 **My List**..........CW[5] A:26			album cut
				above 3 from the album *Pull My Chain* on DreamWorks 450297			
6/8/02	25	20		10 **Courtesy Of The Red, White And Blue (The Angry American)**....CW[1] A:24		V	album cut
10/5/02	22	20		11 **Who's Your Daddy?** CW[1] A:20		V	album cut
				above 2 from the album *Unleashed* on DreamWorks 450254; "45" issued for above 2 on DreamWorks 450815			

DEBUT	PEAK	WKS	Gold	A-side (Chart Hit)...B-side	$	Sym	Label & Number

KELIS — R&B/LP '99

Born Kelis Rogers in Harlem, New York. Female R&B singer.

DEBUT	PEAK	WKS	Gold	A-side (Chart Hit)...B-side	$	Sym	Label & Number
10/23/99	33	20		1 **Got Your Money** ...A:20 / S:26 *(2 versions) / I Can't Wait / Cold Blooded* **OL' DIRTY BASTARD featuring Kelis**	$8	★*	Elektra 67022
12/4/99+	54	12		2 **Caught Out There** ...S:12 *(3 versions)*	$4	★	Virgin 38677
9/8/01	59[S]	2		3 **Candy** ...BUB:124 *(2 versions) / 730* **FOXY BROWN Featuring Kelis** a limited edition 12" single issued on pink vinyl ($20)	$6	T	Def Jam 588738

KELLEM, Manny, His Orchestra And Voices — LP '68

Born on 11/1/16 in Philadelphia, Pennsylvania. Prolific record producer.

DEBUT	PEAK	WKS	Gold	A-side (Chart Hit)...B-side	$	Sym	Label & Number
2/24/68	96	2		**Love Is Blue (L'Amour Est Bleu)** ...*Claudine*	$6		Epic 10282

KELLER, Jerry — BUB '59

Born on 6/20/37 in Fort Smith, Arkansas; raised in Tulsa, Oklahoma. Pop singer/songwriter.

DEBUT	PEAK	WKS	Gold	A-side (Chart Hit)...B-side	$	Sym	Label & Number
6/29/59	14	13		**Here Comes Summer** ...*Time Has A Way*	$15	■	Kapp 277

KELLUM, Murry — C&W '63

Born in Jackson, Tennessee and raised in Plain, Texas. Died in a plane crash on 9/30/90 (age 47). Novelty country singer/songwriter.

DEBUT	PEAK	WKS	Gold	A-side (Chart Hit)...B-side	$	Sym	Label & Number
11/9/63	51	11		**Long Tall Texan** ...*I Gotta Leave This Town* (**Glenn Sutton**)	$15		M.O.C. 653

KELLY, Casey — BUB '72

Born Daniel Cohen in Baton Rouge, Louisiana. Pop singer/songwriter/pianist/guitarist.

DEBUT	PEAK	WKS	Gold	A-side (Chart Hit)...B-side	$	Sym	Label & Number
9/23/72	52	9		**Poor Boy** ...*You'll Never Leave My Mind*	$6		Elektra 45804

KELLY, Grace — see CROSBY, Bing

KELLY, Monty, And His Orchestra — MEM/POP '60

Born on 6/8/10 in Modesto, California. Died on 3/15/71 (age 60). Conductor/arranger. Trumpeter with Paul Whiteman in the early 1940s.

DEBUT	PEAK	WKS	Gold	A-side (Chart Hit)...B-side	$	Sym	Label & Number
2/29/60	30	11		**Summer Set** ...*Amalia* [I] written by **Mr. Acker Bilk**	$10		Carlton 527

KELLY, Paul — R&B/BUB '70

Born on 6/19/40 in Miami, Florida. R&B singer/songwriter. Member of **The Valadiers**.

DEBUT	PEAK	WKS	Gold	A-side (Chart Hit)...B-side	$	Sym	Label & Number
7/4/70	49	9		1 **Stealing In The Name Of The Lord** ...*The Day After Forever*	$8		Happy Tiger 541
1/27/73	79	5		2 **Don't Burn Me** ...*Love Me Now*	$6		Warner 7657

KELLY, R. ★63★ — R&B/BUB/LP '96

Born Robert Kelly on 1/8/67 in Chicago, Illinois. R&B singer/songwriter/producer/multi-instrumentalist. Married **Aaliyah** on 7/31/94 (marriage later annulled). **Public Announcement** was his assembly of backing singers and dancers.

1)I'm Your Angel 2)Bump N' Grind 3)Ignition 4)I Believe I Can Fly 5)Down Low (Nobody Has To Know)

DEBUT	PEAK	WKS	Gold	A-side (Chart Hit)...B-side	$	Sym	Label & Number
				R. KELLY and Public Announcement:			
3/14/92	59	12		1 **She's Got That Vibe** ...A:41 / S:74 *(4 album snippets)*	$4	▮	Jive 42026
5/23/92	39	19		2 **Honey Love** ...RB[2] S:30 / A:42 *(2 remixes)*	$4	▮	Jive 42031
8/22/92	43	19		3 **Slow Dance (Hey Mr. DJ)** ...RB[1] S:26 / A:48 *After The Party's Over*	$4	▮	Jive 42092
2/27/93	31	20		4 **Dedicated** ...A:18 / S:55 *Hangin' Out* above 4 from the album *Born Into The '90's*	$4	▮	Jive 42115
				R. KELLY:			
10/30/93	20	19	●	5 **Sex Me (Parts I & II)** ...S:9 / A:55 *Born Into The 90's*	$3	▮	Jive 42161
2/5/94	❶[4]	25	▲	6 **Bump N' Grind** ...RB[12] S:❶[10] / A:7 *(2 remixes) / Definition Of A Hotti*	$3	▮	Jive 42207
5/14/94	13	20	●	7 **Your Body's Callin'** ...S:6 / A:17 *(2 versions)*	$3	▮	Jive 42220
8/20/94	55	7		8 **Summer Bunnies** ...S:41 / A:62 *(2 remixes) / Freak Dat Body* samples "Outstanding" by **The Gap Band**	$3	▮	Jive 42238
11/26/94	59[A]	3		9 **It Seems Like You're Ready** ... above 5 from the album *12 Play* on Jive 41527			album cut
11/18/95	4	20	▲	10 **You Remind Me Of Something** ...RB[1] S:2 / A:47 *Homie, Lover, Friend*	$3	▮	Jive 42344
3/2/96	4	20	▲	11 **Down Low (Nobody Has To Know)** ...RB[7] S:2 / A:32 *(3 mixes)* **R. KELLY (featuring Ronald Isley and Ernie Isley)**	$3	▮[V]	Jive 42373
7/13/96	5	20	▲	12 **I Can't Sleep Baby (If I)** ...RB[2] S:4 / A:14 *(remix) / Animation Soundtrack medley* "45" issued for above 2 on Jive 42373	$3	▮[V]	Jive 42377
12/14/96	2[4]	34	▲	13 **I Believe I Can Fly** ...RB[6] S:❶[7] / A:9 *Religious Love* from the movie *Space Jam* starring Michael Jordan	$3	▮[V]	Jive 42422
7/19/97	9	20	●	14 **Gotham City** ...S:5 / A:37 *(acappella version)* from the movie *Batman & Robin* starring George Clooney	$3	▮[V]	Jive 42473
5/9/98	32[A]	16		15 **Be Careful** ...RB[6A] **SPARKLE featuring R. Kelly** from the album *Sparkle* on Rock Land 90149			album cut
12/5/98	❶[6]	18	▲	16 **I'm Your Angel** AC[12] S:❶[6] / A:22 *(no B-side)* **R. KELLY & CELINE DION**	$4	★[V]	Jive 42557
12/5/98	65	16		17 **Home Alone** ...A:53 **R. KELLY featuring Keith Murray** **Kelly Price** (backing vocal)			album cut
12/5/98	79	5		18 **Lean On Me** ...A:67 **KIRK FRANKLIN featuring Mery J. Blige, Bono, R. Kelly, Crystal Lewis and The Family** from the album *The Nu Nation Project* on Gospo Centric 90178			album cut
12/26/98+	22	20		19 **When A Woman's Fed Up** ...A:12			album cut
5/29/99	27	16		20 **Did You Ever Think** ...S:16 / A:40 *(3 versions) / Home Alone* (w/**Keith Murray**) **R. KELLY (featuring Nas)**	$8	★*	Jive 42604

DEBUT	PEAK	WKS	Gold	A-side (Chart Hit)...B-side	$	Sym	Label & Number
				KELLY, R. — Cont'd			
8/28/99	12	17	●	21 **If I Could Turn Back The Hands Of Time**............S:4 / A:46 *Dancing With A Rich Man* **Sparkle** and Bruce Kelly (backing vocals); #13, 16, 17 & 19-21: from the album *R.* on Jive 41625	$4	★^{V}	Jive 42623
9/25/99	2^3	20	●	22 **Satisfy You**..........RB^2 S:❶^3 / A:13 *(instrumental)* **PUFF DADDY (Featuring R. KELLY)** samples "Why You Treat Me So Bad" by **Club Nouveau**	$4	★	Bad Boy 79283
9/30/00+	14	22		23 **I Wish**..........RB^2 A:10 *(radio edit) / Homie, Lover, Friend* "45": Jive 42744; B side: (same)	$6	T^V	Jive 42740
3/31/01	6	21		24 **Fiesta Remix**..........RB^5 S:4 / A:12 *(clean version) / Fiesta / True Baller* **R. KELLY (Featuring Jay-Z and Boo & Gotti)** remix version received more airplay points than Kelly's solo version	$8	★*	Jive 42904
4/7/01	82	8		25 **Guilty Until Proven Innocent**..........S:58 *(2 versions) / 1-900-Hustler* (w/**Beanie Sigel**, **Memphis Bleek** & **Freeway**) **JAY-Z (feat. R. Kelly)**	$6	T	Roc-A-Fella 572809
8/25/01	36	19		26 **Feelin' On Yo Booty**..........A:35 *(4 versions)*	$6	T	Jive 42946
10/27/01+	15	20		27 **We Thuggin**..........A:15 / S:39 *(2 versions) / My Lifestyle* (R&B #94) **FAT JOE (Featuring R. Kelly)**	$6	T	Atlantic 85174
12/29/01+	34	18		28 **The World's Greatest**..........A:38 from the movie *Ali* starring **Will Smith** (soundtrack on Interscope 493172)			album cut
3/30/02	81	8		29 **Take You Home With Me A.K.A. Body**..S:16 *(2 versions) / Get This Money* (#115/R&B #37) **R. KELLY & JAY-Z**	$6	T	Roc-A-Fella 588988
11/9/02+	2^5	40↑		30 **Ignition**..........S:2 / A:2 *(instrumental) / (3 album snippets)*	$4	★	Jive 40065
				KEMI '02 Born in Nigeria. Female R&B singer.			
6/15/02	10^S	16		**Crawl To Me**..........*It's My World / Raw*	$5	★	Mack Dawg 8271
				KEMP, Johnny R&B/LP '88 Born in Nassau, Bahamas; raised in Harlem, New York. R&B singer/songwriter/actor/dancer.			
5/14/88	10	21	●	1 **Just Got Paid**..........RB^2 S:9 / A:12 *(instrumental)*	$3		Columbia 07744
2/25/89	36	14		2 **Birthday Suit**..........A:33 / S:36 *(instrumental)* from the movie *Sing* starring Lorraine Bracco	$3		Columbia 68569
				KEMP, Tara LP '91 Born on 5/11/64 in San Francisco, California. R&B singer/songwriter/pianist.			
1/19/91	3	22	●	1 **Hold You Tight**..........A:3 / S:7 *(extended mix)*	$3	▮^{V}	Giant 19458
5/11/91	7	18		2 **Piece Of My Heart**..........A:9 / S:48 *(remix)*	$3	▮	Giant 19364
10/26/91	95	2		3 **Too Much**..........*Be My Lover*	$3	▮	Giant 19168
				KENDALLS, The C&W '77 Father-and-daughter country duo from St. Louis, Missouri: Royce and Jeannie Kendall. Royce died on 5/22/98 (age 63). Charted 37 Country hits, 1970-89.			
11/5/77	69	7		**Heaven's Just A Sin Away**..........CW^4 *Live And Let Live*	$6		Ovation 1103
				KENDALL SISTERS, The '58 Rock and roll duo from Ohio: sisters Polly and Dolly Kendall.			
3/24/58	73	2		**Yea, Yea**..........T:73 *Won't You Be My Baby* also released on Checker 889 in 1958 ($20)	$25		Argo 5291
				KENDRICK, Nat, And The Swans — see JB's, The			
	★370★			**KENDRICKS, Eddie** R&B/BUB/AC/LP '74 Born on 12/17/39 in Union Springs, Alabama; raised in Birmingham, Alabama. Died of cancer on 10/5/92 (age 52). Joined the R&B group the Primes in Detroit in the late 1950s. Group later evolved into **The Temptations**; Kendricks sang lead from 1960-71. Kendricks later dropped the letter "s" from his last name. *1)Keep On Truckin' 2)Boogie Down 3)Shoeshine Boy*			
5/29/71	88	3		1 **It's So Hard For Me To Say Good-Bye**..........*This Used To Be The Home Of Johnnie Mae*	$6		Tamla 54203
6/10/72	77	8		2 **Eddie's Love**..........*Let Me Run Into Your Lonely Heart*	$6		Tamla 54218
10/7/72	66	8		3 **If You Let Me**..........*Just Memories*	$6		Tamla 54222
2/24/73	87	3		4 **Girl You Need A Change Of Mind (Part 1)**..........*(Part 2)*	$6		Tamla 54230
7/14/73	67	5		5 **Darling Come Back Home**..........*Loving You The Second Time Around*	$6		Tamla 54236
8/25/73	❶^2	19		6 **Keep On Truckin' (Part 1)**..........RB^2 *(Part 2)*	$5		Tamla 54238
1/5/74	2^2	18		7 **Boogie Down**..........RB^3 *Can't Help What I Am*	$5		Tamla 54243
5/11/74	28	8		8 **Son Of Sagittarius**..........*Trust Your Heart*	$5		Tamla 54247
8/10/74	50	10		9 **Tell Her Love Has Felt The Need**..........*Loving You The Second Time Around*	$5		Tamla 54249
12/7/74	71	8		10 **One Tear**..........*The Thin Man*	$5		Tamla 54255
2/15/75	18	18		11 **Shoeshine Boy**..........RB^1 *Hooked On Your Love*	$5		Tamla 54257
7/12/75	50	8		12 **Get The Cream Off The Top**..........*Honey Brown*	$5		Tamla 54260
10/11/75	66	13		13 **Happy**..........*Deep And Quiet Love*	$5		Tamla 54263
2/14/76	36	12		14 **He's A Friend**..........*All Of My Love*	$5		Tamla 54266
8/31/85	20	11		15 **A Nite At The Apollo Live! The Way You Do The Things You Do/My Girl**..........S:21 / A:23 *Everytime You Go Away* [L] **DARYL HALL JOHN OATES with David Ruffin & Eddie Kendrick** recorded at the reopening of New York's Apollo Theatre	$3	■	RCA 14178
				KENNEDY, Joyce — see OSBORNE, Jeffrey			
				KENNEDY, Mike '72 Born Michael Kogel on 4/25/45 in Berlin, Germany. Lead singer of **Los Bravos**.			
3/4/72	62	7		**Louisianna**..........*The Lover (Of The Lost Face Of The Moon)*	$5		ABC 11309
				KENNEDY, Ray BUB '80 Pop-rock singer/songwriter. Member of KGB (Kennedy, Rick Grech, Mike Bloomfield).			
5/3/80	82	3		**Just For The Moment**..........*Isn't It Time?*	$4	■	ARC 11242

DEBUT	PEAK	WKS	Gold	A-side (Chart Hit)..................B-side	$	Sym	Label & Number
				KENNER, Chris R&B/BUB **'61**			
				Born on 12/25/29 in Kenner, Louisiana. Died of a heart attack on 1/28/76 (age 46). Male R&B singer/songwriter. First recorded for Baton in 1956.			
5/29/61	2^{3}	17		1 **I Like It Like That, Part 1**..................*Part 2*	$20		Instant 3229
				first released on Valiant 3229 in 1961 ($40)			
6/29/63	77	7		2 **Land Of 1000 Dances**..................*That's My Girl*	$15		Instant 3252
	★392★			**KENNY G** AC/R&B/BUB/LP **'87**			
				Born Kenny Gorelick on 7/6/56 in Seattle, Washington. Fusion saxophonist. Joined **Barry White**'s **Love Unlimited Orchestra** at age 17. Graduated Phi Beta Kappa and Magna Cum Laude from the University of Washington with an accounting degree. The #1 instrumentalist of the '90s. Also see **Babyface**'s "Every Time I Close My Eyes."			
				1)Songbird 2)Auld Lang Syne (The Millennium Mix) 3)Silhouette			
4/4/87	4	22		1 **Songbird** S:4 / A:5 *Midnight Motion* [I]	$3	■	Arista 9588
				charted first 4 weeks on Arista 9573 (issued with a promo picture sleeve)			
8/29/87	15	19		2 **Don't Make Me Wait For Love**..................S:14 / A:18 *Midnight Motion*	$3	■	Arista 9625
				Lenny Williams (**Tower Of Power**; vocal); originally made the R&B charts (#77) on 12/13/86 on Arista 9544			
10/29/88+	13	17		3 **Silhouette**..................S:10 / A:17 *Home* [I]	$3	■	Arista 9751
2/4/89	47	9		4 **We've Saved The Best For Last**..................*Silhouette*	$3	■	Arista 9785
				KENNY G (with Smokey Robinson)			
1/6/90	56	7		5 **Going Home**..................*Sade (live)* [I-L]	$3	▮	Arista 9913
1/25/92	12	20		6 **Missing You Now**..................AC[3] A:10 / S:33 *It's Only My Heart* (Bolton)	$3	▮V	Columbia 74184
				MICHAEL BOLTON Featuring Kenny G			
12/19/92+	18	23		7 **Forever In Love**..................AC[2] A:13 / S:21 *End Of The Night* [I]	$3	▮	Arista 12482
5/22/93	25	20		8 **By The Time This Night Is Over**..................AC[2] A:24 / S:57 *Homeland* (Kenny G)	$3	▮	Arista 12565
				KENNY G with Peabo Bryson			
12/11/93	72	10		9 **Sentimental**..................*Alone* [I]	$3	▮V	Arista 12618
				"45": Arista 12674; B-side: "Even If My Heart Would Break" with **Aaron Neville** (#122)			
11/16/96	63	14		10 **The Moment**..................S:46 *Remember* [I]	$3	▮	Arista 13260
3/8/97	66	19		11 **Havana**..................*(2 versions)* [I]	$3	▮	Arista 13326
8/14/99	53^{S}	15		12 **What A Wonderful World**..................*Desafinado* (Kenny G)	$4	★	Arista 13710
				LOUIS ARMSTRONG With KENNY G			
				Armstrong's vocal track was a #32 hit in 1988			
12/25/99+	7	5		13 **Auld Lang Syne (The Millennium Mix)**..................S:4 / A:31 *(2 versions)* [I-S]	$4	★	Arista 13769
11/23/02+	2^{1S}	14		14 **Auld Lang Syne (Freedom Mix)**..................*(4 album snippets)* [I-S-R]	$4	★	Arista 15215
				new mix of #13 above; the highest charted *Hot 100 Sales* hit that never made the *Hot 100*; above 2 contain different audioclips from dozens of historical events			
				KENT, Al **'67**			
				Born Al Hamilton in 1937 in Detroit, Michigan. R&B singer/guitarist/producer. In the mid-1950s, member of group The Nitecaps with his brother **Ronnie Savoy**.			
8/19/67	49	9		**You've Got To Pay The Price**..................*Where Do I Go From Here* [I]	$20		Ric-Tic 127
				Dennis Coffey (guitar); A-side artist shown as: **INSTRUMENTAL**; also see **Gloria Taylor**'s 1969 hit version			
				KENTON, Stan MEM/POP/AC/LP **'45**			
				Born on 2/19/12 in Wichita, Kansas. Died of a stroke on 8/25/79 (age 67). Progressive-jazz bandleader/pianist/composer. Organized his first jazz band in 1941. Third person named to the Jazz Hall of Fame. Had a #2 hit in 1945 with "Tampico."			
8/1/60	47	8		1 **My Love**..................*Steady*	$12		Capitol 4393
				NAT KING COLE-STAN KENTON			
10/13/62	32	9		2 **Mama Sang A Song**..................*Whispering Hope* [S]	$8		Capitol 4847
				Ralph Carmichael (orch.)			
				KERMIT — see HENSON, Jim			
				KERR, Anita — see ANITA & TH' SO-AND-SO'S / LITTLE DIPPERS			
				KERSH, David C&W/BUB/LP **'98**			
				Born on 12/9/70 in Humble, Texas. Country singer/songwriter.			
2/14/98	67	16		**If I Never Stop Loving You**..................S:51 *The Need*	$4	▮V	Curb 73045
				KERSHAW, Nik BUB/LP **'84**			
				Born on 3/1/58 in Bristol, Somerset, England. Pop singer/songwriter/multi-instrumentalist.			
3/31/84	46	13		**Wouldn't It Be Good**..................*Monkey Business*	$4	■	MCA 52371
				KERSHAW, Sammy C&W/BUB/LP **'98**			
				Born on 2/24/58 in Abbeville, Louisiana; raised in Kaplan, Louisiana. Country singer. Married **Lorrie Morgan** on 9/29/2001.			
11/5/94	66^{S}	2		1 **Third Rate Romance**..................BUB:105 *Paradise From Nine To One*	$4	▮V	Mercury 858922
12/27/97+	85	5		2 **Love Of My Life**..................S:73 *Roamin' Love*	$4	▮V	Mercury 568140
5/15/99	86	5		3 **Maybe Not Tonight**..................A:73		V	album cut
				SAMMY KERSHAW & LORRIE MORGAN			
				from Kershaw's album *Maybe Not Tonight* on Mercury 538889 and Morgan's album *My Heart* on BNA 67763; "45": BNA 65729; B-side: "Go Away" (Morgan - C&W #3/'97)			
				KESSEL, Barney — see NELSON, Ricky			
				KEYES, Troy **'68**			
				R&B singer. Lead singer with **The High Keyes**.			
2/17/68	92	3		**Love Explosion**..................*I'm Crying (Inside)*	$10		ABC 11027
				KEYS, Alicia R&B/LP **'01**			
				Born Alicia Cook on 1/25/81 in Manhattan, New York. R&B singer/songwriter/keyboardist. Won the 2001 Best New Artist Grammy Award.			
6/16/01	❶^{6}	34		1 **Fallin'**..................RB[4] A:❶^{6} / S:34 *Girlfriend* (R&B #82)	$6	TV	J Records 21041
				"45": J Records 21101; B-side: (remix)			
10/27/01+	7	20		2 **A Woman's Worth**..................A:6 / S:72 *(instrumental)*	$6	T	J Records 21112

DEBUT	PEAK	WKS	Gold	A-side (Chart Hit)...B-side	$	Sym	Label & Number
				KEYS, Alicia — Cont'd			
4/6/02	59	9		3 **How Come You Don't Call Me** ...A:58			album cut
				written and first recorded by **Prince**; above 3 from the album *Songs In A Minor* on J Records 20002			
7/13/02	2^4	22		4 **Gangsta Lovin'** ...A:2 / S:6 *(4 album snippets)*	$4	★	Ruff Ryders 497817
				EVE Feat. Alicia Keys			
				samples "Don't Stop The Music" by **Yarbrough & Peoples**			
				K5 '97			
				Dance group assembled by producer Kevin "KJ" Shiver: vocalists Tammy Wright and Tessa Nollenberger with instrumentalists Mark Hibbard and Christian Orshal.			
2/8/97	98	3		**Passion** ...*(euro mix)*	$4	▮	Robbins 72009
				KHAN, Chaka/RUFUS ★137★ R&B/BUB/LP '74			
				Born Yvette Marie Stevens on 3/23/53 in Great Lakes, Illinois. Became lead singer of **Rufus** in 1972. Rufus members Andre Fischer and Kevin Murphy were with **The American Breed**. Recorded solo and with Rufus since 1978. Sister of vocalists **Taka Boom** and Mark Stevens (Jamaica Boys). Khan's daughter Milini is a member of **Pretty In Pink**.			
				1)I Feel For You 2)Tell Me Something Good 3)Sweet Thing 4)Once You Get Started 5)You Got The Love			
				RUFUS:			
6/15/74	3	17	●	1 **Tell Me Something Good** ...*Smokin' Room*	$6		ABC 11427
				written by **Stevie Wonder**; also released on ABC 12010 in 1974			
				RUFUS Featuring CHAKA KHAN:			
10/12/74	11	16		2 **You Got The Love** ...*Rags To Rufus* [I]	$5		ABC 12032
2/15/75	10	13		3 **Once You Get Started** ...*Rufusized*	$5		ABC 12066
5/31/75	48	6		4 **Please Pardon Me (You Remind Me Of A Friend)** ...*Somebody's Watching You*	$5		ABC 12099
1/3/76	5	21	●	5 **Sweet Thing** ...*Circles*	$5		ABC 12149
5/1/76	39	8		6 **Dance Wit Me** ...*Everybody's Got An Aura*	$5		ABC 12179
2/12/77	30	12		7 **At Midnight (My Love Will Lift You Up)** ...*Better Days*	$5		ABC 12239
5/7/77	32	8		8 **Hollywood** ...*Earth Song*	$5		ABC 12269
4/8/78	38	11		9 **Stay** *[RUFUS/CHAKA KHAN]* ...*Change Your Ways*	$5		ABC 12349
10/7/78	21	16		10 **I'm Every Woman** *[CHAKA KHAN]* ...RB^3 *A Woman In A Man's World*	$4	■	Warner 8683
				written by **Ashford & Simpson**			
11/24/79+	30	15		11 **Do You Love What You Feel** *[RUFUS AND CHAKA]* ...*Dancin' Mood* (Rufus)	$4		MCA 41131
5/16/81	53	9		12 **What Cha' Gonna Do For Me** *[CHAKA KHAN]* ...RB^2 *Lover's Touch*	$4		Warner 49692
12/5/81	91	5		13 **Sharing The Love** *[RUFUS WITH CHAKA KHAN]* ...*We Got The Way* (Rufus)	$4		MCA 51203
1/8/83	67	7		14 **Got To Be There** *[CHAKA KHAN]* ...*Pass It On, A Sure Thing*	$4		Warner 29881
10/1/83	22	19		15 **Ain't Nobody** *[RUFUS AND CHAKA KHAN]* ...*Sweet Thing (live)*	$4		Warner 29555
				CHAKA KHAN:			
9/8/84	3	26	●	16 **I Feel For You** RB^3 S:2 / A:2 *Chinatown*	$4	■	Warner 29195
				with **Grandmaster Melle Mel** (rap) and **Stevie Wonder** (harmonica); written by **Prince**			
1/19/85	60	9		17 **This Is My Night** ...*Caught In The Act*	$3	■	Warner 29097
4/27/85	60	19		18 **Through The Fire** ...*La Flamme*	$3		Warner 29025
12/21/85+	57	9		19 **Own The Night** ...*(instrumental)*	$3	■	MCA 52730
				from the TV series *Miami Vice* starring **Don Johnson**			
7/12/86	53	12		20 **Love Of A Lifetime** ...*Coltrane Dreams*	$3	■	Warner 28671
11/18/89+	18	16		21 **I'll Be Good To You** ...RB^2 S:13 / A:26 *(instrumental)*	$3	■V	Qwest 22697
				QUINCY JONES Featuring Ray Charles and Chaka Khan			
4/25/92	68	9		22 **Love You All My Lifetime** ...A:54 *Keep Givin' Me Lovin'*	$3	▮	Warner 18987
1/23/93	71	8		23 **Feels Like Heaven** ...A:70 *World Falling Down* (Cetera)	$3	▮V	Warner 18651
				PETER CETERA with Chaka Khan			
8/24/96	25	20		24 **Missing You** ...S:15 *(acappella version) / So Right, For Life* (Michael Speaks)	$3	▮V	EastWest 64262
				BRANDY, TAMIA, GLADYS KNIGHT & CHAKA KHAN			
				from the movie *Set It Off* starring Jada Pinkett and **Queen Latifah**			
				KHIA LP '02			
				Born Khia Chambers in Philadelphia, Pennsylvania; raised in Tampa, Florida. Female rapper.			
5/25/02	42	18		1 **My Neck, My Back (Lick It)** ...A:41 / S:61 *(4 versions) / The K-Wang*	$6	T	Dirty Down 751136
				KHIA Featuring: DSD			
11/23/02	13^S	14		2 **Play Wit It** ...*(4 versions)*	$8	★*	Dirty Down 316
				DSD (The Dirty South Divas) featuring Khia			
				KIARA R&B '89			
				R&B duo from Detroit, Michigan: Gregory Charley (vocals, bass) and John Winston (guitar, backing vocals). Kiara (pronounced: kee-air-a) is Swahili for change.			
2/25/89	78	5		**This Time** ...*Wait So Long*	$3	■	Arista 9772
				KIARA (with Shanice Wilson)			
				KID, Joey '90			
				Born in the Bronx, New York. Dance singer. Cousin of **George LaMond**. Also see **Trilogy**.			
5/5/90	70	12		**Counting The Days** ...*(house mix)*	$3	▮	Atlantic 87898
				KID CREOLE & THE COCONUTS — see MANILOW, Barry			
				KID FROST — see FROST			
				KID 'N PLAY R&B/LP '92			
				Rap duo: Christopher "Kid" Reid (born in Bronx, New York) and Christopher "Play" Martin (born in Queens, New York). Starred in the *House Party* movies and *Class Act*. Starred in own Saturday morning cartoon show.			
11/16/91+	51	19		**Ain't Gonna Hurt Nobody** ...S:34 / A:59 *(hip hop mix)*	$4	▮	Select 64847

DEBUT	PEAK	WKS	Gold	A-side (Chart Hit)...B-side	$	Sym	Label & Number
				KID ROCK ROK/BUB/LP **'03**			
				Born Robert Ritchie on 1/17/71 in Romeo, Michigan. White hip-hop/rock singer.			
10/30/99	82	5		1 **Cowboy** ...A:70		V	album cut
				"45": Lava/Atlantic 84705; B-side: "Bawitdaba" (ROK #10)			
2/19/00	19	20		2 **Only God Knows Why** ...A:18		V	album cut
				"45": Lava/Atlantic 84708; B-side: "American Bad Ass" (ROK #20); above 2 from the album *Devil Without A Cause* on Lava/Atlantic 83119			
11/30/02+	4	34	●	3 **Picture** ...S:❶12 / A:6 *(2 versions)*	$4	★	Universal South 172274
				KID ROCK Featuring ALLISON MOORER or SHERYL CROW			
				commerical single features Moorer; the vast majority of radio stations played the original album version featuring Crow			
				KIDS NEXT DOOR, The **'65**			
				Pop vocal group featuring Mary Sinclair.			
10/23/65	84	3		**Inky Dinky Spider (The Spider Song)** ...*Goodbye, Don't Cry (Fare Thee Well)* [N]	$8	■	4 Corners 129
				KIHN, Greg, Band ROK/BUB/LP **'83**			
				Born on 7/10/50 in Baltimore, Maryland. Rock singer/songwriter/guitarist. His band consisted of Dave Carpender (guitar), Gary Phillips (keyboards), Steve Wright (bass) and Larry Lynch (drums). Greg Douglass replaced Carpender in late 1982. Kihn went solo in late 1984.			
5/23/81	15	23		1 **The Breakup Song (They Don't Write 'Em)** ...*When The Music Starts*	$5	■	Beserkley 47149
5/22/82	62	7		2 **Happy Man** ...*Trouble In Paradise*	$5	■	Beserkley 47463
7/17/82	82	2		3 **Every Love Song** ...*Trouble In Paradise*	$5		Beserkley 47441
1/29/83	2[1]	22		4 **Jeopardy** *Fascination*	$5		Beserkley 69847
6/4/83	59	6		5 **Love Never Fails** ...*Talkin' To Myself*	$5		Beserkley 69820
				GREG KIHN:			
2/16/85	30	12		6 **Lucky** ...S:25 *Sad Situation*	$4	■	EMI America 8255
3/29/86	92	5		7 **Love And Rock And Roll** ...*Paint You A Picture*	$4		EMI America 8306
				KILGORE, Theola BUB **'63**			
				Born in Shreveport, Louisiana; raised in Oakland, California. Female gospel-blues singer.			
4/20/63	21	12		1 **The Love Of My Man** ...*I Know That He Loves Me*	$15		Serock 2004
8/10/63	60	9		2 **This Is My Prayer** ...*As Long As You Need Me (Want Me, Love Me)*	$15		Serock 2006
				above 2 written and produced by **Ed Townsend**			
				KILLARMY LP **'97**			
				Male rap group from Staten Island, New York: Killa Sin, Shogun Assassin, Ninth Prince, Baretta Nine, Islord and Dom Pachino.			
5/31/97	69[S]	1		**Wu-Renegades** ...BUB:101 *(same version)*	$5	▮	Wu-Tang/Priority 53267
				produced by Robert Diggs ("**RZA**") of **Wu-Tang Clan**			
	★517★			**KIM, Andy** BUB/LP **'74**			
				Born Androwis Jovakim on 12/5/52 in Montreal, Quebec, Canada. His parents were from Lebanon. Pop singer/songwriter. Recorded briefly in the early 1980s as Baron Longfellow on Ice Records. Teamed with Jeff Barry to write "Sugar, Sugar."			
				1)Rock Me Gently 2)Baby, I Love You 3)Be My Baby			
5/4/68	21	12		1 **How'd We Ever Get This Way** ...*Are You Ever Coming Home*	$8		Steed 707
9/7/68	31	10		2 **Shoot'em Up, Baby** ...*Ordinary Kind Of Girl*	$8		Steed 710
12/21/68+	49	7		3 **Rainbow Ride** ...*Resurrection*	$8		Steed 711
5/24/69	9	16	●	4 **Baby, I Love You** ...*Gee Girl*	$7		Steed 716
9/27/69	36	9		5 **So Good Together** ...*I Got To Know*	$7	■	Steed 720
2/14/70	90	2		6 **A Friend In The City** ...*You*	$7	■	Steed 723
7/25/70	85	4		7 **It's Your Life** ...*To Be Continued*	$7		Steed 727
11/7/70	17	11		8 **Be My Baby** ...*Love That Little Woman*	$7		Steed 729
3/27/71	62	6		9 **I Wish I Were** ...*Walkin' My La De Da*	$7		Steed 731
7/10/71	97	3		10 **I Been Moved** ...*If I Had You Here*	$7	■	Steed 734
				all of above produced and co-written by Jeff Barry			
6/22/74	❶[1]	18	●	11 **Rock Me Gently** *Rock Me Gently Part II*	$5		Capitol 3895
10/26/74	28	9		12 **Fire, Baby I'm On Fire** ...*Here Comes The Mornin'*	$5	■	Capitol 3962
				KIMBERLY, Adrian **'61**			
				Artist is actually a Don Everly (**Everly Brothers**) production, recorded on Don's own label.			
6/26/61	34	5		**The Graduation Song... Pomp And Circumstance** ...*Black Mountain Stomp* [I]	$40		Calliope 6501
				written in 1902 for the coronation of King Edward VII; song also known as "Land Of Hope And Glory"			
				KIMBERLYS, The LP **'71**			
				Country vocal group from Oklahoma: brothers Harold and Carl Kimberly, with their spouses, sisters Verna and Vera Kimberly.			
9/6/69	93	2		1 **MacArthur Park** ...*But You Know I Love You*	$8		RCA Victor 0210
				WAYLON JENNINGS AND THE KIMBERLYS			
3/20/71	99	1		2 **I Don't Know How To Love Him/Everything's Alright** ...*Hello And Happy Birthday*	$7		Happy Tiger 572
				medley from the rock opera *Jesus Christ Superstar*			
				KIMMEL, Tom LP **'87**			
				Born in Memphis, Tennessee. Rock singer/songwriter.			
6/20/87	64	8		**That's Freedom** ...*No Tech*	$3	■	Mercury 888571
				KINA **'00**			
				Born Kina Cosper on 1/25/69 in Detroit, Michigan. Female R&B singer. Former member of **Brownstone**.			
6/24/00	28[S]	15		**Girl From The Gutter** ...*Stop*	$4	★	DreamWorks 59035
				KING LP **'85**			
				Pop-rock group from Coventry, England: Paul King (vocals), Jim Lantsbery (guitar), Mick Roberts (keyboards), Tony Wall (bass) and Adrian Lillywhite (drums).			
7/20/85	55	11		**Love & Pride** ...*Don't Stop*	$3	■	Epic 04917

DEBUT	PEAK	WKS	Gold	A-side (Chart Hit)...B-side	$	Sym	Label & Number

KING, Albert — R&B/BUB/LP '68

Born Albert Nelson on 4/25/23 in Indianola, Mississippi. Died of a heart attack on 12/21/92 (age 69). Noted blues singer/guitarist/drummer.

DEBUT	PEAK	WKS	Gold	A-side (Chart Hit)...B-side	$	Sym	Label & Number
2/3/68	67	4		1 **Cold Feet**...*You Sure Drive A Hard Bargain* [I-S]	$10		Stax 241
2/17/73	91	2		2 **Breaking Up Somebody's Home**...*Little Brother (Make A Way)*	$8		Stax 0147

KING, Anna — '64

Born Anna Williams on 12/9/37 in Philadelphi, Pennsylvania. Died on 10/21/2002 (age 64). Former female vocalist with the **James Brown** Revue.

DEBUT	PEAK	WKS	Gold	A-side (Chart Hit)...B-side	$	Sym	Label & Number
1/4/64	67	6		1 **If Somebody Told You**...*Come And Get These Memories*	$20		Smash 1858
4/4/64	52	6		2 **Baby Baby Baby**...*(instrumental - Sammy Lowe)* **ANNA KING-BOBBY BYRD** above 2 produced by **James Brown**	$20		Smash 1884

★244★ KING, B.B. — R&B/BUB/ROK/LP '70

Born Riley King on 9/16/25 in Itta Bena, Mississippi. The most famous blues singer/guitarist in the world today. Moved to Memphis in 1946. Own radio show on WDIA-Memphis, 1949-50, where he was dubbed "The Beale Street Blues Boy," later shortened to "Blues Boy," then simply "B.B." First recorded for Bullet in 1949. Charted 75 R&B hits, 1951-92. Inducted into the Rock and Roll Hall of Fame in 1987. Won Grammy's Lifetime Achievement Award in 1987. Appeared in the movies *Into The Night* (1985) and *Amazon Women On The Moon* (1987).

1)The Thrill Is Gone 2)I Like To Live The Love 3)Rock Me Baby 4)To Know You Is To Love You 5)Paying The Cost To Be The Boss

DEBUT	PEAK	WKS	Gold	A-side (Chart Hit)...B-side	$	Sym	Label & Number
7/22/57	95	1		1 **Be Careful With A Fool**...T:95 *Quit My Baby*	$30		RPM 494
11/18/57	85	1		2 **I Need You So Bad**...T:85 *I Wonder* **B.B. "BLUES BOY" KING and his Orchestra** (above 2)	$30		RPM 498
3/28/64	97	2		3 **How Blue Can You Get**...*Please Accept My Love*	$15		ABC-Paramount 10527
5/9/64	34	8		4 **Rock Me Baby**...*I Can't Lose*	$15		Kent 393
6/27/64	98	2		5 **Help The Poor**...*I Wouldn't Have It Any Other Way* also see #26 below	$15		ABC-Paramount 10552
11/7/64	82	3		6 **Beautician Blues**...*I Can Hear My Name*	$15		Kent 403
11/7/64	90	3		7 **Never Trust A Woman**...*Worryin' Blues* written by **Bill Doggett** and Louis Jordan	$15		ABC-Paramount 10599
12/26/64	17X	2		8 **Christmas Celebration**...*Easy Listening* [X] X: 25/'64; 17/'67; first released on Kent 387 in 1963	$15		Kent 412
7/3/65	97	1		9 **Blue Shadows**...*And Like That* #1 R&B hit for **Lowell Fulson** in 1950	$15		Kent 426
10/22/66	72	9		10 **Don't Answer The Door - Part 1**...*Part 2*	$12		ABC 10856
4/1/67	94	2		11 **The Jungle**...*Long Gone Baby*	$12		Kent 462
4/20/68	39	7		12 **Paying The Cost To Be The Boss**...*Having My Say*	$10		BluesWay 61015
7/27/68	74	5		13 **I'm Gonna Do What They Do To Me**...*Losing Faith In You*	$10		BluesWay 61018
8/24/68	94	3		14 **The Woman I Love**...*Blues For Me*	$10		Kent 492
10/5/68	82	5		15 **You Put It On Me** /			
9/28/68	98	1		16 **The B.B. Jones**... above 2 from the movie *For Love Of Ivy* starring Sidney Poitier; above 2 produced and conducted by **Quincy Jones**	$8		BluesWay 61019
5/17/69	61	10		17 **Why I Sing The Blues**...*Friends*	$8		BluesWay 61024
8/30/69	74	8		18 **Get Off My Back Woman**...*I Want You So Bad (#127)*	$8		BluesWay 61026
10/18/69	76	5		19 **Just A Little Love**...*My Mood*	$8		BluesWay 61029
12/27/69+	15	14		20 **The Thrill Is Gone**...*You're Mean* #6 R&B hit for Roy Hawkins in 1951	$8	■	BluesWay 61032
4/11/70	54	6		21 **So Excited**...*Confessin' The Blues*	$8		BluesWay 61035
7/25/70	48	7		22 **Hummingbird**...*Ask Me No Questions* written by **Leon Russell** for his then-girlfriend **Rita Coolidge**	$7		ABC 11268
10/31/70	45	8		23 **Chains And Things**...*King's Special*	$7		ABC 11280
2/13/71	40	10		24 **Ask Me No Questions**...*Nobody Loves Me But My Mother*	$7		ABC 11290
4/24/71	97	2		25 **That Evil Child**...*Tell Me Baby* all Kent label recordings are from 1958-62	$7		Kent 4542
6/12/71	90	2		26 **Help The Poor**...*Lucille's Granny* [I-R] instrumental version of #5 above	$6		ABC 11302
9/11/71	68	5		27 **Ghetto Woman**...*The Seven Minutes*	$6		ABC 11310
11/13/71+	46	12		28 **Ain't Nobody Home**...*Alexis' Boogie*	$6		ABC 11316
3/4/72	93	3		29 **Sweet Sixteen**...*(I Believe) I've Been Blue Too Long* new version of King's #2 R&B hit in 1960 (Kent 330)	$6		ABC 11319
5/6/72	92	6		30 **I Got Some Help I Don't Need**...*Lucille's Granny*	$6		ABC 11321
8/19/72	62	11		31 **Guess Who**...*Better Lovin' Man*	$6		ABC 11330
8/4/73	38	14		32 **To Know You Is To Love You**...*I Can't Leave* co-written by **Stevie Wonder**	$6		ABC 11373
12/8/73+	28	16		33 **I Like To Live The Love**...*Love*	$5		ABC 11406
6/8/74	78	3		34 **Who Are You**...*Oh To Me*	$5		ABC 11433
11/30/74+	64	7		35 **Philadelphia**...*Up At 5 AM* [I]	$5		ABC 12029
4/1/89	68	7		36 **When Love Comes To Town**...*Dancing Barefoot (U2 - ROK #14)* **U2 WITH B.B. KING**	$3	■	Island 99225

★303★ KING, Ben E. — R&B/BUB/LP '61

Born Benjamin Earl Nelson on 9/23/38 in Henderson, North Carolina; raised in Harlem, New York. Worked with **The Moonglows** for six months while still in high school. Joined the Five Crowns in 1957, which became the new **Drifters** in 1959. Wrote lyrics to "There Goes My Baby," his first lead performance with The Drifters. Went solo in May 1960. Also see **The Soul Clan**.

1)Stand By Me 2)Supernatural Thing 3)Spanish Harlem 4)Don't Play That Song (You Lied) 5)Amor

DEBUT	PEAK	WKS	Gold	A-side (Chart Hit)...B-side	$	Sym	Label & Number
12/31/60+	10	16		1 **Spanish Harlem** /			
12/31/60+	53	7		2 **First Taste Of Love**...	$20		Atco 6185
5/8/61	4	14		3 **Stand By Me** RB[4] *On The Horizon* based on the spiritual "Lord Stand By Me"; also see #22 below	$20		Atco 6194

DEBUT	PEAK	WKS	Gold	A-side (Chart Hit)...B-side	$	Sym	Label & Number
				KING, Ben E. — Cont'd			
7/31/61	18	10		4 **Amor** ... *Souvenir Of Mexico*	$15		Atco 6203
				there were 3 Top 10 versions of this Mexican song in 1944			
10/16/61	66	6		5 **Young Boy Blues /**			
10/9/61	81	2		6 **Here Comes The Night** ...	$15		Atco 6207
2/3/62	56	6		7 **Ecstasy** ... *Yes*	$15		Atco 6215
4/21/62	11	12		8 **Don't Play That Song (You Lied)** ... *The Hermit Of Misty Mountain*	$15		Atco 6222
8/11/62	88	2		9 **Too Bad** ... *My Heart Cries For You*	$15		Atco 6231
3/16/63	85	4		10 **How Can I Forget** ... *Gloria Gloria*	$15		Atco 6256
6/29/63	29	12		11 **I (Who Have Nothing)** ... *The Beginning Of Time*	$12		Atco 6267
11/2/63	72	4		12 **I Could Have Danced All Night** ... *Gypsy*	$12		Atco 6275
				from the Lerner-Loewe musical *My Fair Lady*; #1-7, 11 & 12: produced by Leiber & Stoller			
4/4/64	63	7		13 **That's When It Hurts** ... *Around The Corner* (#125)	$12		Atco 6288
9/12/64	72	5		14 **It's All Over** ... *Let The Water Run Down*	$12		Atco 6315
12/19/64+	45	7		15 **Seven Letters** ... *River Of Tears*	$12		Atco 6328
4/3/65	84	3		16 **The Record (Baby I Love You)** ... *The Way You Shake It*	$12		Atco 6343
1/8/66	91	3		17 **Goodnight My Love** ... *I Can't Break The News To Myself*	$12		Atco 6390
				#7 R&B hit for **Jesse Belvin** in 1956			
5/21/66	96	2		18 **So Much Love** ... *Don't Drive Me Away*	$10		Atco 6413
4/22/67	93	2		19 **Tears, Tears, Tears** ... *A Man Without A Dream*	$10		Atco 6472
2/8/75	5	14		20 **Supernatural Thing - Part I** ... RB[1] *Part II*	$6		Atlantic 3241
6/7/75	60	4		21 **Do It In The Name Of Love** ... *Imagination*	$6		Atlantic 3274
10/4/86	9	21		22 **Stand By Me** ... S:7 / A:12 *Yakety Yak* (**The Coasters**) [R]	$3	■	Atlantic 89361
				title song from the movie starring Will Wheaton and River Phoenix; same version as #3 above; King's musical arrangers and conductors: Stan Applebaum (#1-7, 22), Seymour Barab (#13), Artie Butler (#17), Bert DeCoteaux (#20, 21), **Ray Ellis** (#14, 15), Bob Gallo (#19), Jimmie Haskell (#8), Bert Keyes (#16), Claus Ogermann (#9, 10) and Garry Sherman (#12)			
	★254★			**KING, Carole** AC/BUB/LP '71			
				Born Carole Klein on 2/9/42 in Brooklyn, New York. Singer/songwriter/pianist. **Neil Sedaka** wrote his 1959 hit "Oh! Carol" about her. Married lyricist Gerry Goffin in 1958; team wrote four #1 hits: "Will You Love Me Tomorrow," "Go Away Little Girl," "Take Good Care Of My Baby" and "The Loco-Motion." Divorced Goffin in 1968. In 1971, won four Grammys. King and Goffin's daughter, **Louise Goffin**, began a solo career in 1979. One of the most successful female songwriters of the rock era. King and Goffin were inducted as a songwriting team into the Rock and Roll Hall of Fame in 1990.			
				1)It's Too Late 2)Jazzman 3)Nightingale			
8/25/62	22	9		1 **It Might As Well Rain Until September** ... *Nobody's Perfect*	$20		Dimension 2000
				first released on Companion 2000 in 1962 ($300)			
4/27/63	94	3		2 **He's A Bad Boy** ... *We Grew Up Together*	$25		Dimension 1009
5/8/71	1[5]	17	●	3 **It's Too Late /** AC[5]			
				1971 Grammy winner: Record of the Year			
6/12/71		12		4 **I Feel The Earth Move** ...	$5	■	Ode 66015
8/28/71	14	10		5 **So Far Away /**			
				James Taylor (acoustic guitar)			
9/4/71		9		6 **Smackwater Jack** ...	$5	■	Ode 66019
				above 4 from the album *Tapestry*			
1/29/72	9	10		7 **Sweet Seasons** ... *Pocket Money*	$5	■	Ode 66022
11/25/72+	24	10		8 **Been To Canaan** ... AC[1] *Bitter With The Sweet*	$5	■	Ode 66031
7/14/73	28	9		9 **Believe In Humanity /**			
7/14/73	67	9		10 **You Light Up My Life** ...	$5	■	Ode 66035
10/27/73	37	10		11 **Corazón** ... *That's How Things Go Down* [F]	$5		Ode 66039
8/31/74	2[1]	16		12 **Jazzman** ... *You Go Your Way, I'll Go Mine*	$5	■	Ode 66101
				Tom Scott (sax solo); first released on Ode 66047 in 1974			
1/4/75	9	12		13 **Nightingale** ... AC[1] *You're Something New*	$5		Ode 66106
2/14/76	28	11		14 **Only Love Is Real** ... AC[1] *Still Here Thinking Of You*	$5		Ode 66119
5/22/76	76	3		15 **High Out Of Time** ... *I'd Like To Know You Better*	$5		Ode 66123
				#3-15: produced by Lou Adler			
7/23/77	30	11		16 **Hard Rock Cafe** ... *To Know That I Love You*	$4	■	Capitol 4455
5/17/80	12	17		17 **One Fine Day** ... *Rulers Of This World*	$4	■	Capitol 4864
3/27/82	45	10		18 **One To One** ... *Goat Annie*	$4	■	Atlantic 4026
				KING, Claude C&W/BUB/LP '62			
				Born on 2/5/33 in Shreveport, Louisiana. Country singer/songwriter/guitarist (charted 30 hits, 1961-77). Acted in the TV mini-series *The Blue And The Gray* in 1982.			
7/17/61	82	5		1 **Big River, Big Man** ... *Sweet Lovin'*	$12		Columbia 42043
11/13/61	71	7		2 **The Comancheros** ... *I Can't Get Over The Way You Got Over Me*	$12	■	Columbia 42196
				inspired by the movie starring John Wayne			
5/26/62	6	16	●	3 **Wolverton Mountain** ... CW[9] *Little Bitty Heart*	$12	■	Columbia 42352
				title is an actual place in Arkansas where Clifton Clowers lived (died on 8/15/94, age 102)			
10/6/62	53	6		4 **The Burning Of Atlanta** ... *Don't That Moon Look Lonesome*	$10	■	Columbia 42581
				KING, Diana R&B/LP '95			
				Born on 11/8/70 in St. Catherine, Jamaica. Reggae-dancehall singer/songwriter.			
4/1/95	13	29	●	1 **Shy Guy** ... S:10 / A:22 *(remix)*	$3	▮	Work 77678
				from the movie *Bad Boys* starring Martin Lawrence and **Will Smith**			
3/16/96	94	4		2 **Ain't Nobody** ... *(remix)*	$3	▮	Work 78228
7/19/97	38	20		3 **I Say A Little Prayer** ... S:48 / A:53 *Tumble Down*	$3	▮	Work 78596
				from the movie *My Best Friend's Wedding* starring Julia Roberts			
11/22/97	71	15		4 **L-L-Lies** ... *By Hook Or By Crook*	$3	▮	Work 78698

DEBUT	PEAK	WKS	Gold	A-side (Chart Hit)....B-side	$	Sym	Label & Number
				KING, Evelyn "Champagne" R&B/BUB/AC/LP **'78**			
				Born on 6/29/60 in the Bronx, New York; raised in Philadelphia, Pennsylvania. Disco singer. Employed as a cleaning woman at Sigma Sound Studios when discovered. Originally nicknamed "Bubbles;" then "Champagne."			
6/17/78	**9**	19	●	1 **Shame** *Dancin', Dancin', Dancin'*	$4		RCA 11122
1/6/79	**23**	16	●	2 **I Don't Know If It's Right** .... *We're Going To A Party*	$4	■	RCA 11386
5/26/79	**75**	6		3 **Music Box** .... *It's OK*	$4		RCA 11586
7/25/81	**40**	14		4 **I'm In Love** .... RB[1] *The Other Side Of Love* picture sleeve is a 4-page black & white sleeve	$4	■	RCA 12243
8/28/82	**17**	16		5 **Love Come Down** .... RB[5] *(instrumental)*	$4		RCA 13273
1/15/83	**49**	11		6 **Betcha She Don't Love You** .... *Get Up Off Your Love* **EVELYN KING** (above 3)	$4		RCA 13380
1/7/84	**75**	7		7 **Action** .... *Let's Get Crazy*	$4		RCA 13682
1/11/86	**86**	4		8 **Your Personal Touch** .... *Talking In My Sleep*	$3	■	RCA 14201
				KING, Freddy R&B/BUB/LP **'61**			
				Born Freddie Christian on 9/3/34 in Gilmer, Texas. Died of a heart attack on 12/28/76 (age 42). Blues singer/guitarist. Moved to Chicago in 1950. Released albums as Freddie King.			
1/9/61	**93**	2		1 **You've Got To Love Her With A Feeling** .... *Have You Ever Loved A Woman*	$35		Federal 12384
3/6/61	**29**	10		2 **Hide Away** *I Love The Woman* [I] titled after Mel's Hide Away Lounge in Chicago	$30		Federal 12401
5/22/61	**88**	4		3 **Lonesome Whistle Blues** .... *It's Too Bad Things Are Going So Tough*	$30		Federal 12415
8/7/61	**47**	5		4 **San-Ho-Zay** .... *See See Baby* (R&B #21) [I]	$30		Federal 12428
12/12/64	**12**[X]	3		5 **Christmas Tears** .... *I Hear Jingle Bells* [X] X: 12/'64; 21/'66; #26 R&B hit in 1961	$30		Federal 12439
				KING, Jonathan BUB/AC **'65**			
				Born Kenneth King on 12/6/44 in London, England. Pop singer/songwriter/producer. Formed U.K. Records in 1972. Produced **Hedgehoppers Anonymous**. Also see **Blue Swede**'s "Hooked On A Feeling."			
9/25/65	**17**	11		1 **Everyone's Gone To The Moon** .... *Summer's Coming*	$8		Parrot 9774
1/15/66	**97**	2		2 **Where The Sun Has Never Shone** .... *Green Is The Grass*	$8		Parrot 9804
				KING, Peggy **'55**			
				Born on 2/16/30 in Greensburg, Pennsylvania. Adult Contemporary singer. Regular on TV's *The George Gobel Show*, 1954-56. In the 1957 movie *Zero Hour*.			
2/5/55	**30**	1		1 **Make Yourself Comfortable** .... T:30 / S:30 *The Gentleman In The Next Apartment* **Percy Faith** (orch.)	$10		Columbia 40363
11/12/55	**61**	5		2 **Learning To Love** .... T:61 *Song Of Seventeen* also released on Columbia 40614 in 1956	$10		Columbia 40562
4/7/56	**81**	2		3 **Angel Pie (Postillon!)** / T:81			
3/3/56	**88**	2		4 **Kiss And Run** .... T:88 Jimmy Carroll (orch., above 3)	$10		Columbia 40638
				KING, Rev. Martin Luther LP **'68**			
				Born on 1/15/29 in Atlanta, Georgia. Assassinated on 4/4/68 (age 39) in Memphis, Tennessee. America's civil rights leader. Nobel prize winner in 1964. The third Monday in January is a principal U.S. holiday: Martin Luther King Day.			
5/4/68	**88**	4		**I Have A Dream** .... *We Shall Overcome* (Liz Lands) [S] excerpt from King's famous speech on 8/28/63 at the March on Washington civil rights rally	$8		Gordy 7023
				KING, Sleepy **'62**			
				Male R&B singer/organist.			
12/18/61+	**92**	3		**Pushin' Your Luck** .... *The King Steps Out* Mort Garson (orch.)	$15		Joy 257
				KING, Teddi **'56**			
				Born Theodora King on 9/18/29 in Boston, Massachusetts. Died on 11/18/77 (age 48). Female jazz-styled singer.			
2/18/56	**18**	12		1 **Mr. Wonderful** .... A:18 / T:32 *Are You Slipping Thru My Fingers* from the Broadway musical starring **Sammy Davis Jr.**; picture sleeve is a "This Is Her Life" comic strip-styled sleeve	$12	□	RCA Victor 6392
11/10/56	**75**	4		2 **Married I Can Always Get** .... T:75 *Traveling Down A Lonely Road* from the **Gordon Jenkins** musical score *Manhattan Tower*; **Hugo Winterhalter** (orch., above 2)	$12		RCA Victor 6660
5/6/57	**98**	1		3 **Say It Isn't So** .... T:98 *There's So Much More* Jackie Kane (orch.); George Olsen's version of this Irving Berlin tune hit #1 in 1932	$12		RCA Victor 6866
				KINGBEES, The LP **'80**			
				Rock trio from Los Angeles, California: Jamie James (vocals, guitar), Michael Rummons (bass) and Rex Roberts (drums).			
6/28/80	**81**	8		**My Mistake** .... *Once Is Not Enough*	$5		RSO 1032
				KING CRIMSON ROK/LP **'70**			
				Progressive-rock group formed in England by eccentric guitarist Robert Fripp. Group featured an ever-changing lineup of top British artists. 1970 lineup: Fripp (guitar, keyboards), **Greg Lake** (vocals, bass; **Emerson, Lake & Palmer**), Ian McDonald (flute; **Foreigner**) and Mike Giles (drums).			
1/31/70	**80**	3		**The Court Of The Crimson King-Part 1** .... *Part 2*	$10		Atlantic 2703
				KING CURTIS BUB/R&B/LP **'62**			
				Born Curtis Ousley on 2/7/34 in Fort Worth, Texas. Stabbed to death on 8/13/71 (age 37). R&B saxophonist. With Lionel Hampton in 1950. Moved to New York City; did session work. First own recording on Gem in 1953. Also recorded solo as the Rinky Dinks in 1962 on Enjoy and as The Ramrods in 1963 on R&H. Played on sessions for **Bobby Darin**, **Aretha Franklin**, **Brook Benton**, **Nat King Cole**, **McGuire Sisters**, **Andy Williams**, **The Coasters**, **The Shirelles** and hundreds of others. Also see **Pat and the Satellites**. *1)Soul Twist 2)Ode To Billie Joe 3)Memphis Soul Stew*			
2/17/62	**17**	13		1 **Soul Twist** RB[2] *Twisting Time* [I]	$15		Enjoy 1000
7/21/62	**60**	9		2 **Beach Party** .... *Turn 'Em On* [I] **KING CURTIS and THE NOBLE KNIGHTS** (above 2)	$10		Capitol 4788
8/24/63	**92**	2		3 **Do The Monkey** .... *Feel All Right* co-written by **Bobby Darin**	$10		Capitol 4998
3/7/64	**51**	12		4 **Soul Serenade** .... *More Soul* [I]	$10		Capitol 5109
12/25/65+	**89**	5		5 **Spanish Harlem** .... *Boss* [I]	$8		Atco 6387

DEBUT	PEAK	WKS	Gold	A-side (Chart Hit)...B-side	$	Sym	Label & Number
				KING CURTIS — Cont'd			
5/13/67	63	6		6 **Jump Back** ... *When Something Is Wrong With My Baby* [I]	$8		Atco 6476
8/26/67	33	9		7 **Memphis Soul Stew** ... *Blue Nocturne* [I]	$8		Atco 6511
9/23/67	28	6		8 **Ode To Billie Joe** ... *In The Pocket* [I]	$8		Atco 6516
				THE KINGPINS			
				KING CURTIS & THE KINGPINS:			
11/25/67	87	4		9 **For What It's Worth** ... *Cook - Out* [I]	$8		Atco 6534
12/30/67+	76	6		10 **I Was Made To Love Her** ... *I Never Loved A Man (The Way I Love You)* [I]	$8		Atco 6547
				above 4 from the album *King Size Soul*			
3/9/68	84	5		11 **(Sittin' On) The Dock Of The Bay** ... *This Is Soul* [I]	$8		Atco 6562
6/15/68	83	2		12 **Valley Of The Dolls** ... *8th Wonder* [I]	$8		Atco 6582
8/10/68	83	3		13 **I Heard It Thru The Grapevine** ... *A Whiter Shade Of Pale* [I]	$8		Atco 6598
10/12/68	93	2		14 **Harper Valley P.T.A.** ... *Makin' Hey* [I]	$8		Atco 6613
1/23/71	64	6		15 **Whole Lotta Love** ... *Floatin'* [I]	$8		Atco 6779
				KINGDOM COME ROK/LP **'88**			
				Hard-rock group formed in America: Lenny Wolf (vocals; from Hamburg, Germany), Danny Stag and Rick Steier (guitars), Johnny Frank (bass) and James Kottak (drums).			
4/2/88	69	6		**Get It On** ... *17*	$3	■	Polydor 887436
				KING HARVEST LP **'73**			
				Pop-rock group from Olcott, New York: Ron Altback (vocals, piano), Eddie Tuleja (guitar), Rod Novack (sax), Dave Robinson (trombone), Tony Cahill (bass) and David Montgomery (drums). Altback and Robinson later joined **Celebration featuring Mike Love**.			
10/28/72+	13	22		1 **Dancing In The Moonlight** ... *Marty And The Captain*	$6		Perception 515
5/5/73	91	4		2 **A Little Bit Like Magic** ... *Elmore Bacon*	$6		Perception 527
				KING JUST BUB **'94**			
				Born Adrian Angevin in Staten Island, New York. Male rapper.			
7/2/94	96	5		**Warrior's Drum (Hay-Ya Hay-Ya Hay-Ya Ho!)** ... *(clean version) / Move On 'Em Stomp*	$4	▮	Black Fist/Select 27491
				KINGOFTHEHILL ROK/LP **'91**			
				Rock-funk group from St. Louis, Missouri: Frankie Muriel (vocals), Jimmy Griffin (guitar), George Potsos (bass) and Vito Bono (drums).			
8/10/91	63	6		**If I Say** ... *Pieces Of The Hill*	$3	▮	SBK 07358
				KING PINS, The R&B **'63**			
				R&B vocal group from Clarksdale, Mississippi: brothers Andrew, Curtis and Robert Kelly with Charles Lee and Offe Reece.			
8/17/63	89	2		**It Won't Be This Way (Always)** ... *How Long Will It Last*	$25		Federal 12484
				KINGPINS, The — see KING CURTIS			
				KINGS, The BUB/LP **'80**			
				Rock group from Toronto, Ontario, Canada: David Diamond (vocals, bass), Aryan Zero (guitar), Sonny Keyes (keyboards) and Max Styles (drums).			
8/23/80	43	23		1 **Switchin' To Glide /**			
				first 13 weeks charted on Elektra 47006 (with a different B-side: "My Habit"); remaining weeks on Elektra 47052			
11/22/80		10		2 **This Beat Goes On** ...	$5		Elektra 47052
				KINGSMEN, The — see HALEY, Bill			
				KINGSMEN, The BUB/LP **'63**			
				Rock group from Portland, Oregon: Jack Ely (vocals, guitar), Mike Mitchell (guitar), Don Gallucci (piano), Bob Nordby (bass) and Lynn Easton (drums). After release of "Louie Louie" (featuring lead vocal by Ely), Easton took over leadership of band and replaced Ely as lead singer. One of America's premier 1960s garage rock bands. Gallucci later formed **Don And The Goodtimes**.			
11/9/63	2^6	16		1 **Louie Louie** *Haunted Castle*	$20		Wand 143
				originally written and recorded as a Jamaican love song in 1957 by Richard Berry (died on 1/23/97) & The Pharaohs on Flip 321 ($75); originally released by The Kingsmen on Jerden 712 in 1963 ($60); also see #9 below			
3/14/64	16	11		2 **Money** ... *Bent Scepter*	$15		Wand 150
7/11/64	46	9		3 **Little Latin Lupe Lu** ... *David's Mood*	$15		Wand 157
9/12/64	42	9		4 **Death Of An Angel** ... *Searching For Love*	$15		Wand 164
1/9/65	4	12		5 **The Jolly Green Giant** ... *Long Green*	$15		Wand 172
				same tune (different lyrics) as **The Olympics**' "Big Boy Pete"; lyrics inspired by the "Green Giant" vegetable commercials			
5/8/65	65	6		6 **The Climb** ... *The Waiting*	$15		Wand 183
8/7/65	47	8		7 **Annie Fanny** ... *Give Her Lovin'*	$15		Wand 189
				lyrics inspired by the Playboy cartoon character, Little Annie Fanny; same melody as the **Hollywood Argyles**' "Alley-Oop"			
4/2/66	77	4		8 **Killer Joe** ... *Little Green Thing*	$15		Wand 1115
5/14/66	97	2		9 **Louie Louie** ... *Haunted Castle* [R]	$20		Wand 143
				reissue of #1 above (reissue has larger and bolder print for title and artist)			
				KINGS OF THE SUN ROK/LP **'88**			
				Hard-rock group from Sydney, Australia: brothers Jeffrey (vocals) and Clifford (drums) Hoad, Glen Morris (guitar), and Anthony Ragg (bass).			
7/30/88	98	2		**Black Leather** ... *Bad Love*	$4	■	RCA 8646
	★339★			**KINGSTON TRIO, The** BUB/AC/LP **'58**			
				Folk trio formed in San Francisco, California: Dave Guard (banjo), Bob Shane and Nick Reynolds (guitars). Five of the trio's first six albums hit #1 for a total of 46 weeks. Big break came at San Francisco's Purple Onion, where the group stayed for eight months. Guard left in 1961 to form the Whiskeyhill Singers; **John Stewart** replaced him. Disbanded in 1968, Shane formed New Kingston Trio. Guard died of cancer on 3/22/91 (age 56). Current trio consists of Shane, Reynolds and George Grove (joined group in 1972). Originators of the folk music craze of the 1960s.			
				1)Tom Dooley 2)Reverend Mr. Black 3)The Tijuana Jail			
9/29/58	❶[1]	21	●	1 **Tom Dooley** H:❶[1] / S:22 *Ruby Red*	$20		Capitol 4049
				traditional American folk song written in 1868 as "Tom Dula"			
1/12/59	70	8		2 **Raspberries, Strawberries** ... *Sally*	$15		Capitol 4114
3/23/59	12	13		3 **The Tijuana Jail** ... *Oh Cindy*	$15		Capitol 4167

DEBUT	PEAK	WKS	Gold	A-side (Chart Hit)...B-side	$	Sym	Label & Number
				KINGSTON TRIO, The — Cont'd			
6/15/59	15	11		4 **M.T.A.** ...*All My Sorrows*	$15		Capitol 4221
				M.T.A.: Metropolitan Transit Authority; protest song written in 1948; melody based on the traditional folk song "The Wreck Of The Old 97"			
9/14/59	20	11		5 **A Worried Man** ...*San Miguel*	$15		Capitol 4271
				adapted from the traditional American folk song "Worried Man Blues" (#14 hit for the Carter Family in 1930)			
12/14/59	98	1		6 **CooCoo-U** ...*Green Grasses*	$15		Capitol 4303
2/22/60	32	11		7 **El Matador** ...*Home From The Hill (#102)*	$15		Capitol 4338
6/20/60	37	10		8 **Bad Man Blunder** ...*The Escape Of Old John Webb* [N]	$15	□	Capitol 4379
				promo picture sleeve shows the artist as "Rowdy Reynolds/Shoot 'Em Up Shane/Gunman Guard"			
10/10/60	60	5		9 **Everglades** ...*This Mornin', This Evenin', So Soon*	$15		Capitol 4441
1/20/62	21	14		10 **Where Have All The Flowers Gone** ...*O Ken Karanga*	$15		Capitol 4671
				written by folk legend **Pete Seeger**			
4/28/62	81	7		11 **Scotch And Soda /**			
				originally released on the 1958 debut album *The Kingston Trio*; a new version "Bubbled Under" (#124) in 1969 on Tetragrammaton 1526			
5/19/62	93	1		12 **Jane, Jane, Jane** ...	$15	■	Capitol 4740
10/27/62	97	2		13 **One More Town** ...*She Was Too Good To Me*	$15	□	Capitol 4842
1/26/63	21	11		14 **Greenback Dollar** ...*The New Frontier*	$15		Capitol 4898
4/6/63	8	11		15 **Reverend Mr. Black** ...*One More Round*	$15		Capitol 4951
				chorus is from the traditional folk song "Lonesome Valley" (#15 hit for the Carter Family in 1931)			
8/3/63	33	8		16 **Desert Pete** ...*Ballad Of The Thresher*	$12		Capitol 5005
11/23/63	61	7		17 **Ally Ally Oxen Free** ...*Marcelle Vahine*	$12		Capitol 5078
	★204★			**KINKS, The** ROK/BUB/LP **'65**			
				Rock group formed in London, England: Ray Davies (lead vocals, guitar; born on 6/21/44) and his brother Dave Davies (lead guitar, vocals; born on 2/3/47). Original lineup also included Peter Quaife (bass; born on 12/27/43) and Mick Avory (drums; born on 2/15/44). Numerous personnel changes during the 1970s. Ray appeared in the 1986 movie *Absolute Beginners*. Longtime members included the Davies brothers, Ian Gibbons (keyboards; 1979-88, 1996), Jim Rodford (bass; from 1978) and Bob Henrit (drums; from 1984; **Charlie**). Henrit and Rodford were members of **Argent**. Inducted into the Rock and Roll Hall of Fame in 1990.			
				1)Come Dancing 2)Tired Of Waiting For You 3)You Really Got Me 4)All Day And All Of The Night 5)Lola			
9/26/64	7	15		1 **You Really Got Me** ...*It's All Right*	$20		Reprise 0306
12/26/64+	7	12		2 **All Day And All Of The Night** ...*I Gotta Move*	$20		Reprise 0334
3/13/65	6	11		3 **Tired Of Waiting For You** ...*Come On Now*	$20		Reprise 0347
6/12/65	23	8		4 **Set Me Free** ...*I Need You*	$15		Reprise 0379
8/14/65	34	7		5 **Who'll Be The Next In Line** ...*Ev'rybody's Gonna Be Happy*	$15		Reprise 0366
12/4/65+	13	14		6 **A Well Respected Man** ...*Such A Shame*	$15		Reprise 0420
3/26/66	50	8		7 **Till The End Of The Day** ...*Where Have All The Good Times Gone*	$15		Reprise 0454
5/21/66	36	6		8 **Dedicated Follower Of Fashion** ...*Sittin' On My Sofa*	$15		Reprise 0471
8/6/66	14	11		9 **Sunny Afternoon** ...*I'm Not Like Everybody Else*	$15		Reprise 0497
1/7/67	73	4		10 **Deadend Street** ...*Big Black Smoke*	$30		Reprise 0540
7/1/67	80	4		11 **Mr. Pleasant** ...*Harry Rag*	$30		Reprise 0587
				all of above produced by Shel Talmy			
1/31/70	62	9		12 **Victoria** ...*Brainwashed*	$15		Reprise 0863
8/29/70	9	14		13 **Lola** ...*Mindless Child Of Motherhood*	$15		Reprise 0930
				also see #18 below			
1/2/71	45	9		14 **Apeman** ...*Rats*	$12		Reprise 0979
4/2/77	48	7		15 **Sleepwalker** ...*Full Moon*	$6	□	Arista 0240
				promo sleeve and record issued with The Hollywood Stars "All The Kids On The Street" on the B-Side			
7/22/78	30	11		16 **A Rock 'N' Roll Fantasy** ...*Live Life*	$6		Arista 0342
4/28/79	41	12		17 **(Wish I Could Fly Like) Superman** ...*Low Budget*	$6		Arista 0409
8/30/80	81	6		18 **Lola** ...*Celluloid Heroes (live)* [L-R]	$6	■	Arista 0541
				studio version on #13 above			
10/31/81	85	4		19 **Destroyer** ...*Back To Front*	$5		Arista 0619
				borrows guitar riff from #2 above			
11/28/81+	92	8		20 **Better Things** ...*Yo-Yo*	$5		Arista 0649
5/7/83	6	17		21 **Come Dancing** ...*Noise*	$4	■	Arista 1054
				also released on Arista 9016 in 1983			
8/20/83	29	10		22 **Don't Forget To Dance** ...*Young Conservatives*	$4		Arista 9075
12/22/84+	41	10		23 **Do It Again** ...*Guilty*	$4	■	Arista 9309
				all of above written by Ray Davies			
				KINLEYS, The C&W/BUB/LP **'99**			
				Country vocal duo of identical twin sisters Heather and Jennifer Kinley (born on 11/5/70 in Philadelphia, Pennsylvania).			
10/4/97	67	12		1 **Please** ...S:46 *(3 album snippets)*	$4	▮V	Epic 78656
1/23/99	64	9		2 **Somebody's Out There Watching** ...S:40 / A:66 *Just Between You And Me* (C&W #12/'98)	$3	★V	Epic 79064
				from the TV show *Touched By An Angel* starring Roma Downey; "45": Epic 79071; B-side: "Please"			
5/27/00	61S	11		3 **She Ain't The Girl For You** ...*Somebody's Out There Watching*	$4	★	Epic 79380
11/25/00	66S	6		4 **I'm In** ...*I Need You Now*	$4	★	Epic 79496
				KINNEY, Fern **'79**			
				Born in Jackson, Mississippi. Female R&B-dance singer.			
8/18/79	54	8		**Groove Me** ...*Let's Keep It Right There*	$5		Malaco 1058
				KINSU **'98**			
				Born in Brooklyn, New York. Male hardcore rapper.			
1/24/98	88	8		**Tha Hop** ...*(remix)*	$4	▮	Blunt 4417
				KIRBY, Kathy **'65**			
				Born on 10/20/40 in Ilford, Essex, England. Pop singer.			
9/18/65	88	3		**The Way Of Love** ...*Oh Darling How I Miss You*	$12		Parrot 9775

DEBUT	PEAK	WKS	Gold	A-side (Chart Hit)...B-side	$	Sym	Label & Number

KIRK, Jim, And The TM Singers — '80

Kirk was vice president of TM Communications, a radio syndication organization. Wrote the original moog synthesizer theme music for radio's *American Top 40.*

DEBUT	PEAK	WKS	Gold	A-side (Chart Hit)...B-side	$	Sym	Label & Number
2/16/80	71	3		**Voice Of Freedom**...*Star Spangled Banner*	$4	■	Capitol 4834

KISS ★148★ — ROK/BUB/LP '76

Hard-rock group formed in New York City, New York: **Gene Simmons** (bass; born on 8/25/49) (see #16 below), **Paul Stanley** (guitar; born on 1/20/50) (see #15 below), **Ace Frehley** (lead guitar; born on 4/27/51) (see #14 below) and Peter Criss (drums; born on 12/20/47). All shared vocals. Noted for elaborate makeup and highly theatrical stage shows; Simmons was made up as "The Bat Lizard," Stanley as "Star Child," Frehley as "Space Man" and Criss as "The Cat." Criss replaced by Eric Carr in 1981. Frehley replaced by Vinnie Vincent in 1982. Group appeared without makeup for the first time in 1983 on album cover *Lick It Up.* Mark St. John replaced Vincent in 1984. Bruce Kulick, brother of Bob Kulick of **Balance**, replaced St. John in 1985. Carr died of cancer on 11/25/91 (age 41). Drummer Eric Singer joined in 1991. Original members reunited in 1996.

1)Beth 2)Forever 3)I Was Made For Lovin' You 4)Rock And Roll All Nite 5)Hard Luck Woman

DEBUT	PEAK	WKS	Gold	A-side (Chart Hit)...B-side	$	Sym	Label & Number
5/25/74	83	5		1 **Kissin' Time**...*Nothin' To Lose*	$15		Casablanca 0011
5/17/75	68	6		2 **Rock And Roll All Nite**...*Getaway*	$15		Casablanca 829
11/15/75+	12	14		3 **Rock And Roll All Nite**...*(studio version)* [L-R] an *MTV Unplugged* "live" version made the Album Rock Tracks chart in 1996 (#13)	$12		Casablanca 850
3/20/76	31	10		4 **Shout It Out Loud**...*Sweet Pain* also see #12 below	$10		Casablanca 854
6/5/76	74	3		5 **Flaming Youth**...*God Of Thunder*	$10	■	Casablanca 858
9/4/76	7	21	●	6 **Beth** /			
9/4/76		3		7 **Detroit Rock City**... above 4 from the album *Destroyer*	$6		Casablanca 863
12/18/76+	15	13		8 **Hard Luck Woman**...*Mr. Speed*	$6		Casablanca 873
3/19/77	16	14		9 **Calling Dr. Love**...*Take Me*	$6		Casablanca 880
7/16/77	25	12		10 **Christine Sixteen**...*Shock Me*	$6		Casablanca 889
9/24/77	61	7		11 **Love Gun**...*Hooligan*	$6		Casablanca 895
1/21/78	54	5		12 **Shout It Out Loud**...*Nothin' To Lose* [L-R] studio version on #4 above	$6		Casablanca 906
2/25/78	39	10		13 **Rocket Ride**...*Tomorrow And Tonight*	$6		Casablanca 915
10/14/78+	13	21		14 **New York Groove**...*Snow Blind* **ACE FREHLEY** first recorded by the British group Hello in 1975 (hit #9 on the UK singles chart)	$6		Casablanca 941
11/4/78	46	12		15 **Hold Me, Touch Me**...*Goodbye* **PAUL STANLEY**	$6		Casablanca 940
12/2/78+	47	8		16 **Radioactive**...*See You In Your Dreams* **GENE SIMMONS**	$6		Casablanca 951
5/26/79	11	16	●	17 **I Was Made For Lovin' You**...*Hard Times*	$6		Casablanca 983
9/1/79	47	11		18 **Sure Know Something**...*Dirty Livin'*	$6		Casablanca 2205
6/21/80	47	10		19 **Shandi**...*She's So European*	$6		Casablanca 2282
12/12/81+	56	9		20 **A World Without Heroes**...*Dark Light*	$6		Casablanca 2343
11/12/83	66	11		21 **Lick It Up**...*Dance All Over Your Face*	$4		Mercury 814671
10/13/84	49	10		22 **Heaven's On Fire**...*Lonely Is The Hunter*	$4		Mercury 880205
10/19/85	51	13		23 **Tears Are Falling**...*Any Way You Slice It*	$4	■	Mercury 884141
9/26/87	65	7		24 **Crazy Crazy Nights**...*No No No*	$3	■	Mercury 888796
12/5/87+	64	12		25 **Reason To Live**...*Thief In The Night*	$3	■	Mercury 870022
1/14/89	97	2		26 **Let's Put The X In Sex**...*Calling Dr. Love*	$3	■	Mercury 872246
11/25/89	66	10		27 **Hide Your Heart**...*Betrayed*	$3	■	Mercury 876146
2/3/90	8	17		28 **Forever**...S:5 / A:9 *The Street Giveth And The Street Taketh Away* co-written by **Michael Bolton**	$3	▮V	Mercury 876716
6/9/90	81	6		29 **Rise To It**...*Silver Spoon*	$3	▮	Mercury 875098

KISSING THE PINK — '83

Synth-pop-dance group from England. Featuring singer/guitarist Nick Whitecross. Shortened name to KTP in 1985.

DEBUT	PEAK	WKS	Gold	A-side (Chart Hit)...B-side	$	Sym	Label & Number
8/6/83	87	5		1 **Maybe This Day**...*Garden Party*	$3		Atlantic 89796
6/13/87	97	4		2 **Certain Things Are Likely** *[KTP]*...*(longer version)*	$3	■	Mercury 885727

KISSOON, Mac And Katie — '71

Brother-and-sister pop duo from Port-of-Spain, Trinidad. Mac was born Gerald Farthing on 11/11/43. Katie was born Kathleen Farthing on 11/3/51. Moved to England in the late 1950s.

DEBUT	PEAK	WKS	Gold	A-side (Chart Hit)...B-side	$	Sym	Label & Number
7/24/71	20	15		**Chirpy Chirpy Cheep Cheep**...*Walking Around* B-side on some pressings spells last name: Kisson	$6		ABC 11306

KIX — ROK/BUB/LP '89

Hard-rock group from Hagerstown, Maryland: Steve Whiteman (vocals), Ronnie Younkins and Brian Forsythe (guitars), Donnie Purnell (bass), and Jimmy Chalfant (drums).

DEBUT	PEAK	WKS	Gold	A-side (Chart Hit)...B-side	$	Sym	Label & Number
9/9/89	11	23	●	**Don't Close Your Eyes**...S:8 / A:14 *Get It While It's Hot*	$3	■	Atlantic 88902

KLAATU — LP '77

Rock trio from Toronto, Ontario, Canada: Dee Long (vocals, guitar), Terry Draper (keyboards) and John Woloschuck (drums). Anonymous first release led to speculation that they were **The Beatles**. Name taken from alien character in the classic 1951 sci-fi movie *The Day The Earth Stood Still.*

DEBUT	PEAK	WKS	Gold	A-side (Chart Hit)...B-side	$	Sym	Label & Number
4/2/77	62	6		1 **Sub-Rosa Subway** /			
4/2/77		6		2 **Calling Occupants**...	$6		Capitol 4412

DEBUT	PEAK	WKS	Gold	A-side (Chart Hit)...B-side	$	Sym	Label & Number
				KLF, The LP **'91**			
				Pop-electronica-dance duo formed in England. Previously known as **The Timelords**: Bill Drummond (founding member of Big In Japan; former manager of Echo & The Bunnymen and Teardrop Explodes) and Jimmy Cauty (formerly with Zodiac Mindwarp). KLF stands for Kopyright Liberation Front.			
12/17/88+	66	13		1 **Doctorin' The Tardis** ... *Gary in The Tardis*	$6	■	TVT 4025
				THE TIMELORDS			
				song combines the music of **Gary Glitter**'s "Rock And Roll Part 2" with the TV theme of the BBC's *Dr. Who*			
6/22/91	5	19	●	2 **3 A.M. Eternal** ... S:5 / A:28 *(Guns of Mu Mu version)*	$4	■V	Arista 2230
10/26/91	57	12		3 **What Time Is Love?** ... *Build A Fire*	$4	■V	Arista 2365
				samples "Kick Out The Jams" by **MC5**; "45": Arista 12365			
2/1/92	11	18	●	4 **Justified & Ancient** ... S:10 / A:12 *(album version w/o Wynette)*	$4	■V	Arista 8657
				THE KLF (Featuring Tammy Wynette)			
				KLINT, Pete, Quintet **'67**			
				Rock and roll band from Mason City, Iowa: Pete Klint, Jamie Wornson, John Peterson, Mike Hesselink and Bill Morisky.			
10/7/67	98	3		**Walkin' Proud** ... *Shake*	$12		Mercury 72709
				KLIQUE R&B/LP **'83**			
				R&B vocal trio: Howard Huntsberry, Isaac Suthers and his sister Deborah Hunter. Huntsberry portrayed **Jackie Wilson** in the movie *La Bamba*.			
10/8/83	50	9		**Stop Doggin' Me Around** ... *Burning Hot*	$5		MCA 52250
				remake of **Jackie Wilson**'s "Doggin' Around" hit from 1960			
				KLOWNS, The LP **'70**			
				Four-man, two-woman group produced by Jeff Barry. Actor Barry Bostwick was a member. Group hosted own ABC-TV special on 11/15/70.			
12/5/70	95	2		**Lady Love** ... *If You Can't Be A Clown*	$5	■	RCA Victor 0393
				KLYMAXX R&B/BUB/LP **'85**			
				Female R&B group from Los Angeles, California: Lorena Porter (vocals), Cheryl Cooley (guitar), Lynn Malsby and Robbin Grider (keyboards), **Joyce "Fenderella" Irby** (bass, vocals) (see #6 below), and Bernadette Cooper (drums, vocals).			
5/11/85	59	11		1 **Meeting In The Ladies Room** ... *Ask Me No Questions*	$3	■	Constellation 52545
9/14/85	5	29		2 **I Miss You** S:3 / A:6 *Video Kid*	$3		Constellation 52606
2/15/86	80	8		3 **The Men All Pause** ... *Don't Hide Your Love* [R]	$3	■	Constellation 52486
				originally made the R&B charts (#5) on 11/10/84; also "Bubbled Under" (#105) on 2/2/85			
7/5/86	15	15		4 **Man Size Love** ... S:12 / A:19 *(remix)*	$3	■	MCA 52841
				from the movie *Running Scared* starring **Gregory Hines** and **Billy Crystal**			
5/2/87	18	20		5 **I'd Still Say Yes** ... S:14 / A:19 *Ask Me No Questions*	$3	■	Constellation 53028
2/17/90	70	7		6 **I'll Be There** ... *(instrumental)*	$3	■V	Motown 2032
				JOYCE "FENDERELLA" IRBY			
				K.M.C. KRU R&B **'91**			
				Rap duo from Lansing, Michigan: Tracy "T The Sarge" Edmond and Ken "The Butcher" White.			
8/31/91	46	14		**The Devil Came Up To Michigan** ... S:47 / A:72 *(house mix) / T The Sarge*	$4	▮	Curb 76884
				rap version of **Charlie Daniels**' "The Devil Went Down To Georgia"			
				KNACK, The ROK/LP **'79**			
				Rock group formed in Los Angeles, California: Doug Fieger (vocals, guitar), Berton Averre (guitar), Prescott Niles (bass) and Bruce Gary (drums). Disbanded in 1982. All members but Gary reunited in 1986, replaced by drummer Billy Ward. Fieger was a member of the Detroit rock trio Sky.			
6/23/79	❶6	22	●	1 **My Sharona** *Let Me Out*	$5	■	Capitol 4731
				also see #6 below			
9/1/79	11	16		2 **Good Girls Don't** ... *Frustrated*	$5	■	Capitol 4771
2/9/80	38	8		3 **Baby Talks Dirty** ... *End Of The Game*	$5	■	Capitol 4822
4/5/80	62	6		4 **Can't Put A Price On Love** ... *(Havin' a) Rave Up*	$5		Capitol 4853
10/31/81	67	5		5 **Pay The Devil (Ooo, Baby, Ooo)** ... *Lil' Cals Big Mistake*	$5	■	Capitol 5054
4/16/94	91	4		6 **My Sharona** ... *Tempted (94)* (**Squeeze**) [R]	$4	■V	RCA 62800
				remix of #1 above; from the movie *Reality Bites* starring Winona Ryder			
				KNICKERBOCKERS, The BUB/LP **'66**			
				Rock group from Bergenfield, New Jersey: Buddy Randell (vocals, sax; **The Royal Teens**), brothers Beau (guitar) and Johnny (bass) Charles, and Jimmy Walker (drums). Walker replaced **Bill Medley**, for a time, in **The Righteous Brothers**. Band named after Knickerbocker Avenue in their hometown.			
12/4/65+	20	13		1 **Lies** ... *The Coming Generation*	$15		Challenge 59321
3/19/66	46	7		2 **One Track Mind** ... *I Must Be Doing Something Right*	$15		Challenge 59326
7/2/66	94	3		3 **High On Love** ... *Stick With Me*	$15		Challenge 59332
				KNIGHT, Frederick R&B/BUB **'72**			
				Born on 8/15/44 in Alabama. R&B singer/producer.			
4/22/72	27	14		**I've Been Lonely For So Long** ... *Lean On Me*	$7		Stax 0117
				KNIGHT, Gladys, & The Pips ★42★ R&B/BUB/AC/LP **'73**			
				R&B family group from Atlanta, Georgia: Gladys Knight (born on 5/28/44), her brother Merald "Bubba" Knight and sister Brenda, and cousins William and Eleanor Guest. Named "Pips" for their manager, cousin James "Pip" Woods. First recorded for Brunswick in 1958. Brenda and Eleanor replaced by cousins Edward Patten and Langston George in 1959. Langston left group in 1962 and group has remained a quartet with the same members ever since. Due to legal problems, Gladys could not record with the Pips from 1977-80. Gladys played "Diana Richmond" on the 1985 TV series *Charlie & Co.* Group inducted into the Rock and Roll Hall of Fame in 1996.			
				1)Midnight Train To Georgia 2)I Heard It Through the Grapevine 3)Neither One Of Us 4)Best Thing That Ever Happened To Me 5)I've Got To Use My Imagination			
5/15/61	6	13		1 **Every Beat Of My Heart** *[PIPS]* ... RB[1] *Room In Your Heart*	$25		Vee-Jay 386
5/15/61	45	7		2 **Every Beat Of My Heart** ... *Room In Your Heart* [R]	$30		Fury 1050
				written by **Johnny Otis**; song first released in 1961 on Huntom 2510 ($500); re-recorded for Fury; Huntom master sold to Vee-Jay and released as by the Pips			

DEBUT	PEAK	WKS	Gold	A-side (Chart Hit)...B-side	$	Sym	Label & Number
				KNIGHT, Gladys, & The Pips — Cont'd			
12/11/61+	19	12		3 **Letter Full Of Tears** ... *You Broke Your Promise*	$20		Fury 1054
				written by **Don Covay**			
4/14/62	97	2		4 **Operator** ... *I'll Trust In You*	$20		Fury 1064
5/9/64	38	10		5 **Giving Up** ... *Maybe Maybe Baby*	$20		Maxx 326
8/22/64	89	5		6 **Lovers Always Forgive** ... *Another Love*	$20		Maxx 329
5/6/67	98	2		7 **Take Me In Your Arms And Love Me** ... *Do You Love Me Just A Little, Honey*	$12		Soul 35033
7/8/67	39	9		8 **Everybody Needs Love** ... *Stepping Closer To Your Heart*	$12		Soul 35034
10/21/67	2^{3}	17		9 **I Heard It Through The Grapevine** ... RB^{6} *It's Time To Go Now*	$12		Soul 35039
2/10/68	15	10		10 **The End Of Our Road** ... *Don't Let Her Take Your Love From Me*	$12		Soul 35042
6/8/68	40	8		11 **It Should Have Been Me** ... *You Don't Love Me No More*	$12		Soul 35045
8/24/68	41	10		12 **I Wish It Would Rain** ... *It's Summer*	$12		Soul 35047
3/8/69	63	7		13 **Didn't You Know (You'd Have To Cry Sometime)** ... *Keep An Eye*	$12		Soul 35057
7/19/69	19	11		14 **The Nitty Gritty** ... *Got Myself A Good Man*	$10		Soul 35063
10/25/69	17	14		15 **Friendship Train** ... *Cloud Nine*	$10		Soul 35068
3/21/70	25	8		16 **You Need Love Like I Do (Don't You)** ... *You're My Everything*	$10		Soul 35071
				#7-12 & 14-16: produced by Norman Whitfield			
11/28/70+	9	15		17 **If I Were Your Woman** ... RB^{1} *The Tracks Of My Tears*	$8		Soul 35078
6/5/71	17	11		18 **I Don't Want To Do Wrong** ... *Is There A Place (In His Heart For Me)*	$8		Soul 35083
12/18/71+	27	10		19 **Make Me The Woman That You Go Home To** ... *It's All Over But The Shoutin'*	$8		Soul 35091
3/25/72	33	8		20 **Help Me Make It Through The Night** ... *If You Gonna Leave (Just Leave)*	$8		Soul 35094
1/27/73	2^{2}	16		21 **Neither One Of Us (Wants To Be The First To Say Goodbye)** ... RB^{4} *Can't Give It Up No More*	$7		Soul 35098
4/28/73	19	15		22 **Daddy Could Swear, I Declare** ... *For Once In My Life*	$7		Soul 35105
6/16/73	28	11		23 **Where Peaceful Waters Flow** ... *Perfect Love*	$6	■	Buddah 363
8/11/73	61	7		24 **All I Need Is Time** ... *The Only Time You Love Me Is When You're Losing Me*	$7		Soul 35107
9/1/73	❶^{2}	19	●	25 **Midnight Train To Georgia** RB^{4} *Window Raising Granny*	$6		Buddah 383
11/24/73+	4	16	●	26 **I've Got To Use My Imagination** ... RB^{1} *I Can See Clearly Now*	$6		Buddah 393
2/16/74	3	17	●	27 **Best Thing That Ever Happened To Me** ... RB^{2} *Once In A Lifetime Thing*	$6		Buddah 403
				#23 & 25-27: from the album *Imagination*			
5/25/74	5	17	●	28 **On And On** ... *The Makings Of You*	$6	■	Buddah 423
				written and produced by **Curtis Mayfield**; from the movie *Claudine* starring Diahann Carroll			
6/29/74	57	9		29 **Between Her Goodbye And My Hello** ... *This Child Needs Its Father*	$7		Soul 35111
10/12/74	21	17		30 **I Feel A Song (In My Heart)** / RB^{2}			
1/25/75		2		31 **Don't Burn Down The Bridge** ...	$5		Buddah 433
2/22/75	47	8		32 **Love Finds It's Own Way** ... *Better You Go Your Way*	$5		Buddah 453
				#21, 23, 25, 27, 29 & 32: written by **Jim Weatherly**			
4/26/75	11	17		33 **The Way We Were/Try To Remember** ... *The Need To Be*	$5		Buddah 463
				above 4 from the album *I Feel A Song*			
8/30/75	50	7		34 **Money** ... *Street Brothers*	$5		Buddah 487
11/8/75	22	11		35 **Part Time Love** ... *Where Do I Put His Memory*	$5		Buddah 513
10/9/76	47	8		36 **So Sad The Song** ... *(instrumental)*	$5		Buddah 544
				from the movie *Pipe Dreams* starring Gladys Knight			
6/11/77	52	11		37 **Baby Don't Change Your Mind** ... *I Love To Feel That Feeling*	$5		Buddah 569
6/14/80	46	9		38 **Landlord** ... *We Need Hearts*	$4		Columbia 11239
				#13 & 38: written and produced by **Ashford & Simpson**			
5/21/83	66	10		39 **Save The Overtime (For Me)** ... RB^{1} *Ain't No Greater Love*	$4		Columbia 03761
11/9/85+	❶^{4}	23	●	40 **That's What Friends Are For** ... RB^{3} / AC^{2} S:❶^{5} / A:❶^{3} *Two Ships Passing In The Night* (Warwick)	$3	■	Arista 9422
				DIONNE & FRIENDS: Elton John, Gladys Knight and Stevie Wonder			
				song introduced by **Rod Stewart** on the 1982 movie soundtrack of *Night Shift*			
1/9/88	13	14		41 **Love Overboard** ... RB^{1} S:11 / A:20 *(instrumental)*	$3	■	MCA 53210
8/24/96	25	20		42 **Missing You** ... S:15 *(acappella version) / So Right, For Life* (Michael Speaks)	$3	■^{V}	EastWest 64262
				BRANDY, TAMIA, GLADYS KNIGHT & CHAKA KHAN			
				from the movie *Set It Off* starring Jada Pinkett and **Queen Latifah**			
				KNIGHT, Holly '88			
				Female singer/songwriter. Former member of the rock groups **Spider** and **Device**. Wrote **Tina Turner**'s "Better Be Good To Me," **Heart**'s "Never," **Aerosmith**'s "Rag Doll," **Animotion**'s "Obsession" and others.			
9/3/88	59	9		**Heart Don't Fail Me Now** ... *Howling At The Moon*	$3	■	Columbia 07932
				Daryl Hall (backing vocal)			
				KNIGHT, Jean R&B/LP '71			
				Born on 1/26/43 in New Orleans, Louisiana. Female R&B singer.			
5/29/71	2^{2}	16	▲^{2}	1 **Mr. Big Stuff** ... RB^{5} *Why I Keep Living These Memories*	$8		Stax 0088
10/16/71	57	5		2 **You Think You're Hot Stuff** ... *Don't Talk About Jody*	$8		Stax 0105
5/4/85	50	15		3 **My Toot Toot** ... *My Heart Is Willing (And My Body Is Too)*	$4	■	Mirage 99643
				KNIGHT, Jordan — see NEW KIDS ON THE BLOCK			
				KNIGHT, Robert LP '67			
				Born on 4/21/45 in Franklin, Tennessee. R&B singer. Recorded for Dot in 1960.			
9/30/67	13	12		1 **Everlasting Love** ... *Somebody's Baby*	$10		Rising Sons 705
1/20/68	97	2		2 **Blessed Are The Lonely** ... *It's Been Worth It All*	$8		Rising Sons 707
				above 2 co-written and co-produced by Buzz Cason (**Garry Miles**)			
10/19/68	97	2		3 **Isn't It Lonely Together** ... *We'd Better Stop*	$8		Elf 90,019
				written by **Ray Stevens**			

DEBUT	PEAK	WKS	Gold	A-side (Chart Hit)...B-side	$	Sym	Label & Number
				KNIGHT, Sonny '56 Born Joseph Smith on 5/17/34 in Maywood, Illinois. Died on 9/5/98 (age 64). R&B singer/songwriter/pianist. Wrote the book *The Day The Music Died* in 1981 under his real name.			
11/17/56	17	13		1 **Confidential** ...J:17 / S:19 / T:20 *Jail Bird* Jack Collier (orch.); first released on Vita 137 in 1956 ($50)	$25		Dot 15507
10/10/64	71	9		2 **If You Want This Love** ...*I Just Called To Say Hello*	$15		Aura 403
2/6/65	100	1		3 **Love Me As Though There Were No Tomorrow** ...*A Fool Like Me*	$15	■	Aura 4505
				KNIGHT, Terry, and The Pack — see GRAND FUNK RAILROAD			
				KNIGHT BROS, The '65 R&B duo from Washington DC: Richard Dunbar and Jerry Diggs.			
6/12/65	70	5		**Temptation 'Bout To Get Me** ...*Sinking Low*	$20		Checker 1107
				KNIGHTSBRIDGE STRINGS, The '59 Ensemble of 34 strings conducted by British conductor-arrangers **Reg Owen** and Malcolm Lockyer (died on 6/28/76, age 53). Also see **The Cambridge Strings And Singers**.			
7/20/59	53	7		1 **Cry** ...*My Prayer* [I] #1 hit for **Johnnie Ray** in 1951	$10		Top Rank 2006
11/2/59	88	3		2 **Wheel Of Fortune** ...*Cow Cow Boogie* [I] #1 hit for **Kay Starr** in 1952	$10		Top Rank 2014
				KNOBLOCK, Fred C&W/AC/BUB/LP '80 Born J. Fred Knobloch on 4/28/53 in Jackson, Mississippi. Member of the country trios Schuyler, Knobloch & Overstreet (SKO) and Schuyler, Knobloch & Bickhardt (SKB).			
6/28/80	18	14		1 **Why Not Me** ...AC[2] *Can I Get A Wish* also released on Scotti Brothers 600 in 1980	$4		Scotti Brothers 518
11/22/80+	28	18		2 **Killin' Time** ...*Love Is No Friend To A Fool* (Anton) **FRED KNOBLOCK AND SUSAN ANTON** (Anton is an actress/model)	$4		Scotti Brothers 609
				KNOCKOUTS, The '60 Rock and roll group from Lyndhust, New Jersey: Bob D'Andrea (vocals), Eddie Parenti (guitar), Bob Collada (piano) and Harry Venuta (drums).			
12/28/59+	46	11		**Darling Lorraine** ...*Riot In Room 3C*	$25		Shad 5013
				KNOC-TURN'AL LP '02 Born in Los Angeles, California. Male rapper. Protege of **Dr. Dre**.			
3/9/02	98	3		**Knoc** ...S:39 *(4 versions)* **KNOC-TURN'AL w/ Dr. Dre and Missy "Misdemeanor" Elliott**	$6	T	LA Confidential 67290
				KNOWLES, Beyoncé — see JAY-Z			
				KNOX, Buddy BUB/C&W '57 Born Buddy Wayne Knox on 7/20/33 in Happy, Texas. Died of cancer on 2/14/99 (age 65). Formed the rock and roll band The Rhythm Orchids at West Texas State University: Knox (guitar), **Jimmy Bowen** (bass), Don Lanier (guitar) and Dave "**Dicky Doo**" Alldred (drums). Formed own record label, Triple-D, named after KDDD radio in Dumas, Texas. *1)Party Doll 2)Hula Love 3)Rock Your Little Baby To Sleep*			
				BUDDY KNOX With The Rhythm Orchids:			
2/23/57	❶[1]	23	●	1 **Party Doll** S:❶[1] / J:2 / T:2 / A:5 *My Baby's Gone* originally released on Triple-D 798 in 1956; flip side was "I'm Stickin' With You" by **Jimmy Bowen** ($900)	$50		Roulette 4002
5/13/57	17	16		2 **Rock Your Little Baby To Sleep** ...A:17 / S:23 / T:23 *Don't Make Me Cry* **Lieutenant BUDDY KNOX With The Rhythm Orchids**	$40		Roulette 4009
9/2/57	9	23		3 **Hula Love** ...A:9 / T:12 / S:13 *Devil Woman* featured in the movie *Jamboree!* starring Kay Medford; song originated in 1911 as "My Hula Hula Love"	$25		Roulette 4018
2/10/58	80	6		4 **Swingin' Daddy** ...T:80 *Whenever I'm Lonely*	$25		Roulette 4042
8/4/58	22	14		5 **Somebody Touched Me** ...H:22 / S:32 *C'mon Baby* first recorded in 1954 by **Ruth Brown** on Atlantic 1044 ($30)	$25		Roulette 4082
				BUDDY KNOX:			
1/19/59	85	2		6 **Teasable, Pleasable You /**			
1/5/59	88	2		7 **That's Why I Cry** ...	$25		Roulette 4120
4/13/59	55	6		8 **I Think I'm Gonna Kill Myself** ...*To Be With You*	$25		Roulette 4140
12/19/60+	25	9		9 **Lovey Dovey** ...*I Got You* #2 R&B hit for **The Clovers** in 1954	$15		Liberty 55290
3/6/61	65	7		10 **Ling-Ting-Tong** ...*The Kisses (They're All Mine)*	$15	■	Liberty 55305
				KNUCKLES, Frankie R&B '91 Born on 1/18/55 in the Bronx, New York. Record mixer. Moved to Chicago, Illinois, in 1977. Worked at Chicago's Warehouse club and remixed hits by **Chaka Khan** and **Pet Shop Boys**. Dubbed the "Godfather of House" music.			
9/7/91	67[A]	5		1 **The Whistle Song** ...*Workout*	$4	▮	Virgin 98762
6/20/92	68[A]	2		2 **Rain Falls** ...*Workout* **FRANKIE KNUCKLES Featuring Lisa Michaelis**	$4	▮	Virgin 98543
				KODA '01 Born Koda Kumi on 11/13/75 in Japan. Female dance club singer.			
12/1/01	19[S]	11		**Trust Your Love** ...*(5 remixes)*	$4	★	Orpheus 70595
				KOFFEE BROWN R&B/LP '01 Male/female R&B duo from Minneapolis, Minnesota: Fonz and Vee. Also see **Next**.			
1/13/01	44	20		**After Party** ...A:40 / S:70 *(2 versions)* **Next** (backing vocals)	$6	T	Arista 13924
				KOFFMAN, Moe, Quartette BUB '58 Born Morris Koffman on 12/28/28 in Toronto, Ontario, Canada. Died of cancer on 3/28/2001 (age 72). Saxophonist with several U.S. big bands from 1950-55. Other members of his quartette: Ed Bickert (guitar), Hugh Currie (bass) and Ron Rully (drums).			
2/3/58	23	13		1 **The Swingin' Shepherd Blues** ...A:23 / S:36 / T:36 *Hambourg Bound* [I] a twist version "Bubbled Under" (#110) in 1962 on Ascot 2100	$12		Jubilee 5311
6/23/58	72	3		2 **Little Pixie** ...T:72 *Koko-Mamey* [I]	$12		Jubilee 5324

DEBUT	PEAK	WKS	Gold	A-side (Chart Hit)..........B-side	$	Sym	Label & Number

KOKOMO '61

Born Jimmy Wisner on 12/8/31 in Philadelphia, Pennsylvania. Record producer/pianist.

DEBUT	PEAK	WKS	Gold	A-side (Chart Hit)..........B-side	$	Sym	Label & Number
2/20/61	8	14		**Asia Minor** ....*Roy's Tune* [I] adapted from Grieg's *Piano Concerto in A minor*	$12	■	Felsted 8612

KOLBY, Diane '70

White singer/songwriter/guitarist.

DEBUT	PEAK	WKS	Gold	A-side (Chart Hit)..........B-side	$	Sym	Label & Number
9/19/70	67	6		**Holy Man** ....*Hallelujah, Baby*	$6		Columbia 45169

KONGAS LP '78

Disco studio group assembled by **Cerrone**.

DEBUT	PEAK	WKS	Gold	A-side (Chart Hit)..........B-side	$	Sym	Label & Number
4/8/78	84	7		**Africanism/Gimme Some Lovin'** ....*Tatoo Woman*	$5		Polydor 14461

KONGOS, John BUB '71

Born on 9/6/45 in Johannesburg, South Africa. Pop-rock singer/songwriter.

DEBUT	PEAK	WKS	Gold	A-side (Chart Hit)..........B-side	$	Sym	Label & Number
7/10/71	70	7		**He's Gonna Step On You Again** ....*Sometimes It's Not Enough*	$6	■	Elektra 45729

KON KAN '89

Dance duo from Toronto, Ontario, Canada: Barry Harris (piano, guitar) and Kevin Wynne (vocals). Became a one-man band when Wynne left in 1989. Name derived from the opposite of Can Con, as in Canadian Content.

DEBUT	PEAK	WKS	Gold	A-side (Chart Hit)..........B-side	$	Sym	Label & Number
12/24/88+	15	18		1 **I Beg Your Pardon** ....S:12 / A:16 *(instrumental)* includes several lines from **Lynn Anderson**'s "Rose Garden"; samples "Disco Nights (Rock-Freak)" by **GQ**	$4		Atlantic 88969
9/2/89	58	8		2 **Puss N' Boots/These Boots (Are Made For Walkin')** ....*Harry Houdini* tune uses sound-alike clips from **Led Zeppelin**'s "Immigrant Song" and **Nancy Sinatra**'s "These Boots Are Made For Walkin'"	$4		Atlantic 88828

KOOL & THE GANG ★70★ R&B/BUB/LP '85

R&B-funk group formed in Jersey City, New Jersey: Robert "Kool" Bell (bass; born on 10/8/50), his brother Ronald Bell (sax; born on 11/1/51), Claydes Smith (guitar; born on 9/6/48), Rick Westfield (keyboards), Dennis Thomas (sax; born on 2/9/51), Robert Mickens (trumpet) and George Brown (drums; born on 1/5/49). All shared vocals. Added lead singer James "J.T." Taylor in 1978. Earl Toon replaced Westfield in 1978. Taylor left in 1988.

1)Celebration 2)Cherish 3)Joanna 4)Jungle Boogie 5)Too Hot

DEBUT	PEAK	WKS	Gold	A-side (Chart Hit)..........B-side	$	Sym	Label & Number
9/13/69	59	12		1 **Kool And The Gang** ....*Raw Hamburgers* [I]	$8		De-Lite 519
12/27/69+	85	5		2 **The Gangs Back Again**..........*Kools Back Again* (R&B flip) [I]	$8		De-Lite 523
7/4/70	78	6		3 **Let The Music Take Your Mind** ....*Chocolate Buttermilk*	$6		De-Lite 529
9/26/70	87	4		4 **Funky Man** *1-2-3-4-5-6-7-8*	$6		De-Lite 534
9/8/73	29	12		5 **Funky Stuff** ....*More Funky Stuff*	$6		De-Lite 557
12/8/73+	4	22	●	6 **Jungle Boogie**..........*North, East, South, West*	$5		De-Lite 559
4/20/74	6	19	●	7 **Hollywood Swinging** ....RB[1] *Dujii*	$5		De-Lite 561
9/7/74	37	8		8 **Higher Plane** ....RB[1] *Wild Is Love*	$5		De-Lite 1562
1/4/75	63	8		9 **Rhyme Tyme People**..........*Father Father*	$5		De-Lite 1563
4/5/75	35	17		10 **Spirit Of The Boogie** / RB[1]			
6/21/75		6		11 **Summer Madness** .... [I]	$5		De-Lite 1567
11/8/75	55	7		12 **Caribbean Festival** ....*(disco version)* [I]	$5		De-Lite 1573
3/20/76	77	8		13 **Love And Understanding (Come Together)** ....*Sunshine And Love*	$5		De-Lite 1579
11/6/76+	55	13		14 **Open Sesame - Part 1** ....*Part 2* [I]	$5		De-Lite 1586
10/6/79+	8	24	●	15 **Ladies Night**..........RB[3] *If You Feel Like Dancin'*	$4		De-Lite 801
1/19/80	5	18	●	16 **Too Hot**..........*Tonight's The Night* also released as the B-side of "Ladies Night" (on some pressings)	$4		De-Lite 802
10/25/80+	❶[2]	30	▲	17 **Celebration** RB[6] *Morning Star*	$4		De-Lite 807
5/16/81	39	11		18 **Jones Vs. Jones**..........*Night People*	$4		De-Lite 813
10/17/81	17	17		19 **Take My Heart (You Can Have It If You Want It)**..........RB[1] *Just Friends* some pressings show title only as "Take My Heart"	$4		De-Lite 815
2/13/82	89	2		20 **Steppin' Out** ....*Love Festival*	$4		De-Lite 816
2/27/82	10	17	●	21 **Get Down On It**..........*Steppin' Out*	$4		De-Lite 818
8/28/82	21	11		22 **Big Fun**..........*No Show*	$4		De-Lite 822
10/30/82+	30	15		23 **Let's Go Dancin' (Ooh La, La, La)**..........*Be My Lady* #15-23: produced by Eumir **Deodato**	$4		De-Lite 824
11/5/83+	2[1]	24	●	24 **Joanna**..........RB[2] *Place For Us*	$4		De-Lite 829
2/25/84	13	18		25 **Tonight**..........*Home Is Where The Heart Is*	$4		De-Lite 830
11/24/84+	10	24		26 **Misled**..........S:8 / A:10 *Rollin'*	$3		De-Lite 880431
3/23/85	9	19		27 **Fresh** ....RB[1] S:6 / A:12 *In The Heart*	$3	■	De-Lite 880623
7/6/85	2[3]	25	●	28 **Cherish** ....RB[1] / AC[6] S:❶[1] / A:2 *(instrumental)*	$3	■	De-Lite 880869
10/26/85	18	16		29 **Emergency** ....S:17 / A:19 *You Are The One* above 4 from the album *Emergency*	$3		De-Lite 884199
11/1/86+	10	18		30 **Victory**..........S:6 / A:13 *Bad Woman*	$3	■	Mercury 888074
2/7/87	10	18		31 **Stone Love**..........S:8 / A:16 *Dance Champion*	$3	■	Mercury 888292
6/27/87	66	7		32 **Holiday** ....*(jam mix)*	$3	■	Mercury 888712
10/17/87	72	14		33 **Special Way** ....*God's Country* above 4 from the album *Forever*	$3	■	Mercury 888867

KOOL G RAP R&B/BUB/LP '95

Born Nathaniel Wilson on 7/20/68 in Elmhurst, Queens, New York. Name is short for Kool Genius of Rap. Also see **T.C.F.**

DEBUT	PEAK	WKS	Gold	A-side (Chart Hit)..........B-side	$	Sym	Label & Number
12/2/95	74	12		1 **Fast Life**..........S:71 *(2 versions) / It's A Shame* **Nas** (additional rap); samples "Happy" by **Surface**	$5	▌	Cold Chillin' 78081
10/20/01	41[S]	7		2 **My Life**..........*(2 versions) / Nobody Can't Eat* **KOOL G RAP feat. G Wise**	$6	T	Rawkus 351

DEBUT	PEAK	WKS	Gold	A-side (Chart Hit)...B-side	$	Sym	Label & Number
				KOOL MOE DEE R&B/LP **'88**			
				Born Mohanndas DeWese on 8/8/67 in Harlem, New York. Male rapper. Formerly with the Treacherous Three.			
4/18/87	89	5		1 **Go See The Doctor**...*(instrumental)*	$5		Jive/Rooftop 1041
4/30/88	62	11		2 **Wild, Wild West**...*(instrumental)* also see #4 below	$5		Jive 1086
6/8/91	58[S]	3		3 **Rise 'N' Shine**...*(instrumental)* **KOOL MOE DEE Featuring KRS-One and Chuck D.**	$4	■	Jive/RCA 1454
5/22/99	❶[1]	17	●	4 **Wild Wild West**...S:❶[1] / A:2 *Y'All Know* (Smith) [R] **WILL SMITH featuring Dru Hill and Kool Mo Dee** samples "Wild, Wild West" by **Kool Moe Dee** and "I Wish" by **Stevie Wonder**; title song from the movie starring Smith and Kevin Kline	$4	★	Overbrook 79157
				KORGIS, The LP **'80**			
				Pop trio formed in England: James Warren and Andy Davis (both formerly with Stackridge), with Stuart Gordon.			
10/11/80	18	19		**Everybody's Got To Learn Sometime**...*Perfect Hostess*	$4		Asylum 47055
				KORN ROK/BUB/LP **'02**			
				Hard-rock group from Huntington Beach, California: Jonathan Davis (vocals), Brian Welch and James Munkey (guitars), Reggie Fieldy Arvizu (bass) and David Silveria (drums).			
5/25/02	72	12		**Here To Stay**...A:71 from the album *Untouchables* on Immortal 61488			album cut
				KORONA **'80**			
				Born Bruce Blackman in Greenville, Mississippi. Leader of **Eternity's Children** and **Starbuck**.			
3/22/80	43	8		**Let Me Be**...*I'm In Love With You*	$4		United Artists 1341
				K.P. & ENVYI **'98**			
				Female rap duo: Kia "K.P." Philips and Susan "Envyi" Hedgepeth.			
12/27/97+	6	20	●	**Swing My Way**...S:5 / A:34 *Bass Is Lo* (Zae')	$4	■	EastWest 64135
				KRAFTWERK BUB/R&B/LP **'75**			
				Progressive-rock group formed in Dusseldorf, Germany: Ralf Hutter (keyboards), Florian Schneider (woodwinds), Klaus Roeder (guitar) and Wolfgang Flur (drums).			
3/15/75	25	10		1 **Autobahn**...*Morganspaziergang (Morning Walk)* [I]	$7		Vertigo 203
6/10/78	67	7		2 **Trans-Europe Express**...*Franz Schubert* [I]	$5		Capitol 4460
				KRAMER, Billy J., With The Dakotas LP **'64**			
				Born William Ashton on 8/19/43 in Bootle, Merseyside, England. Pop singer. The Dakotas consisted of Michael Maxfield and Robin MacDonald (guitars), Ray Jones (bass) and Tony Mansfield (drums).			
4/18/64	7	15		1 **Little Children** /			
5/30/64	9	10		2 **Bad To Me**... first released on Liberty 55626 with "I Call Your Name" as the B-side ($30) and then on Liberty 55667 with "Do You Want To Know A Secret" as the B-side ($30)	$12		Imperial 66027
7/25/64	30	7		3 **I'll Keep You Satisfied**...*I Know* first released on Liberty 55643 in 1964 ($30)	$12		Imperial 66048
8/22/64	23	10		4 **From A Window**...*I'll Be On My Way* above 3 written by **John Lennon** and **Paul McCartney**	$12	■	Imperial 66051
2/6/65	67	5		5 **It's Gotta Last Forever**...*They Remind Me Of You*	$12		Imperial 66085
6/26/65	47	7		6 **Trains And Boats And Planes**...*I'll Be On My Way* also released with "That's The Way I Feel" as the B-side	$12		Imperial 66115
				KRAUSS, Alison, & Union Station C&W/AC/LP **'95**			
				Born on 7/23/71 in Champaign, Illinois. Country singer/bluegrass fiddler. Union Station is her backing band: Dan Tyminski (guitar), Ron Block (banjo), Adam Steffey (mandolin) and Barry Bales (bass).			
5/13/95	53	18		1 **When You Say Nothing At All**...S:19 *A Voice Still Rings True* (Various Artists) #1 Country hit for Keith Whitley in 1988; "45": BNA 64277; B-side: "Charlotte's In North Carolina" by Keith Whitley	$4	■V	BNA 64329
3/11/00	40	20		2 **Buy Me A Rose**...CW[1] A:34 **KENNY ROGERS With Alison Krauss & Billy Dean** from Rogers' album *She Rides Wild Horses* on DreamCatcher 004			album cut
	★484★			**KRAVITZ, Lenny** ROK/R&B/BUB/LP **'01**			
				Born on 5/26/64 in Brooklyn, New York. R&B-rock singer/songwriter/guitarist. Married to actress Lisa Bonet (played "Denise Huxtable" on TV's *The Cosby Show*) from 1987-93. Son of actress Roxie Roker (played "Helen Willis" on TV's *The Jeffersons*). *1)It Ain't Over 'Til It's Over 2)Again 3)Fly Away*			
1/27/90	89	4		1 **Let Love Rule**...*Empty Hands*	$4	■	Virgin 99166
6/8/91	2[1]	19		2 **It Ain't Over 'Til It's Over** A:8 / S:16 *I'll Be Around*	$3	■	Virgin 98795
10/19/91	76	8		3 **Stand By My Woman**...*Light Skin Girl From London*	$3	■	Virgin 98736
7/3/93	60	17		4 **Believe**...S:62 / A:73 *For The First Time* "45": Virgin 17445	$3	■V	Virgin 12662
3/5/94	80	3		5 **Heaven Help** /			
3/5/94		3		6 **Spinning Around Over You**... from the movie *Reality Bites* starring Winona Ryder; "45" issued for above 2 on Virgin 17711	$3	■V	Virgin 38412
10/14/95	75	2		7 **Rock And Roll Is Dead**...A:63 *Another Life / Are You Gonna Go My Way (live)*	$3	■	Virgin 38514
3/23/96	62	20		8 **Can't Get You Off My Mind**...A:67 *Empty Hands / Stand By My Woman*	$3	■	Virgin 38535
12/5/98+	12	32		9 **Fly Away**...AR[3] / MR[2] A:10		V	album cut
7/17/99	49	21		10 **American Woman**...A:44 from the movie *Austin Powers: The Spy Who Shagged Me* starring Mike Myers (soundtrack on Maverick 47348); "45" issued for above 2 on Virgin 38668		V	album cut
3/25/00	71	9		11 **I Belong To You**...A:65 above 3 from the album *5* on Virgin 45605			album cut
11/18/00+	4	32		12 **Again**...A:2 from the album *Greatest Hits* on Virgin 50316; "45": Virgin 38782; B-side: "Black Velveteen"		V	album cut
10/13/01	31	20		13 **Dig In**...A:31 from the album *Lenny* on Virgin 11233; "45": Virgin 38816; B-side: "Stillness Of Heart" (ROK #38)		V	album cut

DEBUT	PEAK	WKS	Gold	A-side (Chart Hit)...B-side	$	Sym	Label & Number
				KREVIAZUK, Chantal '98			
				Born on 5/18/73 in Winnipeg, Manitoba, Canada. Female Adult Alternative singer/pianist.			
1/31/98	74^A	1		**Surrounded**			album cut
				from the album *Under These Rocks And Stones* on Columbia 67926			
				KRIS KROSS R&B/BUB/LP '92			
				Male teen rap duo from Atlanta, Georgia: Chris "Mack Daddy" Kelly (born on 5/1/78) and Chris "Daddy Mack" Smith (born on 1/10/79). Appeared in the movie *Who's The Man?*			
4/4/92	❶⁸	21	▲²	1 **Jump** S:❶⁹ / A:4 *Lil Boys In Da Hood*	$3	▮ᵛ	Ruffhouse 74197
				also see #8 below			
6/6/92	13	20	●	2 **Warm It Up** S:4 / A:28 *(album version)*	$3	▮ᵛ	Ruffhouse 74376
10/3/92	63	15		3 **I Missed The Bus** S:36 *(remix)*	$3	▮	Ruffhouse 74498
7/31/93	19	19	●	4 **Alright** S:9 / A:36 *D.J. Nabs Break*	$3	▮ᵛ	Ruffhouse 77103
				Super Cat (guest vocal); samples "Just A Touch Of Love" by **Slave**			
11/20/93	84	6		5 **I'm Real** S:50 *Sound Of My Hood*	$3	▮ᵛ	Ruffhouse 77236
				samples "Mary Jane" by **Rick James**			
12/9/95+	12	20	●	6 **Tonite's Tha Night** S:4 / A:50 *(TV track version)*	$3	▮	Ruffhouse 78092
				Trey Lorenz (backing vocal)			
4/27/96	72	10		7 **Live And Die For Hip Hop** S:36 *(remix)*	$3	▮	Ruffhouse 78270
				Aaliyah, **Da Brat** and Mr. Black (guest vocals); samples "Baby Come To Me" by **Regina Belle**			
3/23/02	64^S	4		8 **Jump** *Lil Boys In Da Hood* [R]	$4	★	Ruffhouse 79695
				reissue of #1 above on Columbia's "Platinum Hits" series; all of above written and produced by **Jermaine Dupri**			
				KRISTINE W '96			
				Born Kristine Weitz on 6/8/62 in Pasco, Washington. Dance singer/songwriter.			
6/1/96	78	15		1 **One More Try** *(remix)*	$4	▮	RCA 64533
8/12/00	65^S	1		2 **Stronger** *(3 mixes)*	$8	★*	RCA 60281
2/3/01	47^S	2		3 **Lovin' You** *(6 mixes)*	$8	★*	RCA 60400
				KRISTOFFERSON, Kris C&W/AC/LP '73			
				Born on 6/22/36 in Brownsville, Texas. Singer/songwriter/actor. Attended England's Oxford University on a Rhodes scholarship. Married to **Rita Coolidge** from 1973-80. Wrote "Me And Bobby McGee," "For The Good Times" and "Help Me Make It Through The Night." Has starred in many movies since 1972.			
8/21/71	26	13		1 **Loving Her Was Easier (Than Anything I'll Ever Do Again)** *Epitaph (Black And Blue)*	$6		Monument 8525
3/11/72	63	8		2 **Josie** *Border Lord*	$6		Monument 8536
12/30/72	91	3		3 **Jesus Was A Capricorn** *Enough For You*	$6		Monument 8558
				music is the same as John Prine's "Grandpa Was A Carpenter"			
4/7/73	16	38	●	4 **Why Me** CW¹ *Help Me*	$6		Monument 8571
11/17/73	49	10		5 **A Song I'd Like To Sing** *From The Bottle To The Bottom*	$5	■	A&M 1475
				all of above written by Kristofferson			
3/23/74	86	5		6 **Loving Arms** *I'm Down (But I Keep Falling)*	$5		A&M 1498
				KRIS KRISTOFFERSON & RITA COOLIDGE (above 2)			
5/21/77	52	6		7 **Watch Closely Now** *Crippled Crow*	$4	■	Columbia 10525
				from the movie *A Star Is Born* starring Kristofferson and **Barbra Streisand**			
				KROEGER, Chad '02			
				Born on 11/15/74 in Hanna, Alberta, Canada. Lead singer of **Nickelback**.			
5/18/02	3	22		**Hero** AR² / MR³ A:3			album cut
				CHAD KROEGER Featuring Josey Scott			
				from the movie *Spider-Man* starring Tobey Maguire and Kirsten Dunst (soundtrack on Columbia 86402)			
				KROKUS ROK/LP '86			
				Hard-rock group from Zurich, Switzerland: Marc Storace (vocals), Fernando Von Arb and Mark Kohler (guitars), Chris Von Rohr (bass) and Steve Pace (drums). Pace was replaced by Jeff Klaven in 1984. Von Rohr left in 1984.			
9/15/84	71	6		1 **Midnite Maniac** *Ready To Rock*	$4	■	Arista 9248
6/7/86	67	7		2 **School's Out** *Screaming In The Night* (ROK #21/'83)	$4	■	Arista 9468
				KRS-ONE R&B/BUB/LP '95			
				Born Lawrence Parker on 8/20/65 in Harlem, New York. Co-founder of Boogie Down Productions. Brother-in-law of female rapper Harmony.			
6/8/91	58^S	3		1 **Rise 'N' Shine** *(instrumental)*	$4	▮	Jive/RCA 1454
				KOOL MOE DEE Featuring KRS-One and Chuck D.			
2/5/94	89	6		2 **Sound Of Da Police** *(remix) / Hip Hop VS Rap / Black Cop*	$3	▮	Jive 42192
				samples "Inside Looking Out" by **Grand Funk Railroad**			
9/9/95	57	11		3 **MC's Act Like They Don't Know** S:34 *Represent The Real Hip Hop* (w/**DAS EFX**)	$3	▮	Jive 42319
4/5/97	70	13		4 **Step Into A World (Rapture's Delight)** *(instrumental) / (album version)*	$6	T	Jive 42442
				Keva (female vocal); samples "Rapture" by **Blondie** and "The Champ" by The Mohawks			
9/13/97	82	7		5 **Men Of Steel** S:59 *(instrumental)*	$3	▮	Qwest 17305
				SHAQUILLE O'NEAL, ICE CUBE, B REAL, PETER GUNZ & KRS-ONE			
				inspired by the movie *Steel* starring **Shaquille O'Neal**			
				KRUMB SNATCHA R&B '02			
				Born in Boston, Massachusetts. Male rapper.			
11/30/02	45^S	2		**Oxygen** *(2 versions) / Strike Back (Closer to God Pt. II)*	$8	T	D&D 641250
				KRUMB SNATCHA Featuring Boogie			
				K'S CHOICE ROK/LP '97			
				Rock group from Belgium: Sarah Bettens (vocals), her brother Gert Bettens (vocals, keyboards), Jan Van Sichem (guitar) and Bart Van Der Zeeuw (drums).			
5/3/97	56^A	10		**Not An Addict**			album cut
				from the album *Paradise In Me* on 550 Music/Epic 67720			

DEBUT	PEAK	WKS	Gold	A-side (Chart Hit)...B-side	$	Sym	Label & Number
				K7 BUB/LP **'93**			
				Born Louis Sharpe on 8/25/69 in Harlem, New York. Male rapper/dancer. Former member of **TKA**.			
9/4/93	18	21	●	1 **Come Baby Come** ...S:17 / A:30 *I'll Make You Feel Good*	$3	▮V	Tommy Boy 7572
				"45": Tommy Boy/Collectables 572; B-side: (instrumental)			
1/29/94	61	15		2 **Zunga Zeng** / S:56 / A:72		V	
				"45": Tommy Boy/Collectables 599; B-side: (same)			
2/26/94		5		3 **Body Rock** ...S:flip	$3	▮	Tommy Boy 7599
2/11/95	54	20		4 **Move It Like This** ...A:52 *(Ragga edit)*	$3	▮	Tommy Boy 7633
				all of above from the album *Swing Batta Swing*			
				KTP — see KISSING THE PINK			
				KUBAN, Bob, And The In-Men LP **'66**			
				Pop-rock group from St. Louis, Missouri: Bob Kuban (drums), Walter Scott (vocals), Ray Schulte (guitar), Greg Hoeltzel (keyboards), Pat Hixton (trumpet), Harry Simon (sax), Skip Weisser (trombone) and Mike Krenski (bass). Scott disappeared on 12/27/83; his ex-wife and her husband were charged with Scott's murder after his body was found three years later with a gunshot wound to the back.			
1/29/66	12	11		1 **The Cheater** ...*Try Me Baby*	$12		Musicland 20,001
4/30/66	70	3		2 **The Teaser** ...*All I Want*	$10		Musicland 20,006
7/16/66	93	3		3 **Drive My Car** ...*The Pretzel*	$10		Musicland 20,007
				written by **John Lennon** and **Paul McCartney** (from **The Beatles**' 1966 album *Yesterday...And Today*)			
				KUF-LINX **'58**			
				Black vocal quintet: John Jennings, George McFadden, Leo Manley, Gaines Steele and Zena Aya. Jennings and McFadden were with the gospel group The Jubilaires.			
3/3/58	76	6		**So Tough** ...T:76 *What 'Cha Gonna Do?*	$30		Challenge 1013
				The Champs (instrumental backing)			
				KULA SHAKER ROK/LP **'96**			
				Rock group from London, England: Crispian Mills (vocals, guitar), Jay Darlington (keyboards), Alonza Bevan (bass) and Paul Winter-Hart (drums). Mills is the son of actress/singer **Hayley Mills**.			
11/23/96	63A	5		**Tattva** ...			album cut
				from the album *K* on Columbia 67822			
				KULIS, Charlie **'75**			
				Born in New York City, New York. Pop singer/guitarist.			
3/15/75	46	8		**Runaway** ...*When I See Her*	$5		Playboy 6023
				KUMBIA KINGS LP **'00**			
				Latin group: Jason Cano, Roy Ramirez and Andrew Maes (vocals), Jorge Pena (percussion), Alex Ramirez and Cruz Martinez (keyboards), A.B. Quintanilla (bass) and Robert Del Moral (drums). Quintanilla is the brother of **Selena**.			
3/4/00	62	10		**U Don't Love Me** ...S:16 *Reggae Kumbia*	$5	★	EMI Latin 58831
				KUMBIA KINGS featuring A.B. Quintanilla			
				KURUPT R&B/BUB/LP **'00**			
				Born Ricardo Brown in Los Angeles, California. Male rapper. Member of **Tha Dogg Pound**.			
4/3/99	70S	1		1 **Gangsta! Gangsta! (How U Do It)** ...*(4 versions)*	$10	★	Humility 54317
				C. WEBB Featuring Kurupt			
				samples "White Horse" by **Laid Back** and "Put Your Hands Where My Eyes Can See" by **Busta Rhymes**			
11/13/99	70S	1		2 **A Whole Lot Of Gangstas Die** ...*(instrumental)*	$6	★	Shanty Town 1005
				FLEXX G. featuring Kurupt and Alkatraz			
11/11/00	95	5		3 **Where I Wanna Be** ...S:28 *(3 album snippets)*	$6	★	Baby Ree 35058
				SHADE SHEIST Featuring Nate Dogg & Kurupt			
				samples "Waiting For Your Love" by **Toto**			
				KUT KLOSE R&B/LP **'95**			
				Female R&B vocal trio from Atlanta, Georgia: **Athena Cage**, Tabitha Duncan and LaVonn Battle. Also see **Keith Sweat**.			
4/15/95	34	20		**I Like** ...S:18 / A:60 *(remix)*	$3	▮	Keia/Elektra 64486
				KWELI, Talib, & Hi-Tek R&B/LP **'00**			
				Born Talib Kweli Greene in Brooklyn, New York. Male rapper. Member of **Black Star**. DJ Hi-Tek was born in Cincinnati, Ohio.			
8/22/98	60	10		1 **Definition** ...S:45 *(2 versions) / Twice Inna Lifetime*	$4	▮	Rawkus 173
				MOS DEF & KWELI are BLACK STAR			
3/13/99	50S	9		2 **Respiration** ...*(4 versions)*	$5	★	Rawkus 53473
				MOS DEF & TALIB KWELI ARE BLACK STAR			
2/26/00	66S	1		3 **The Express** ...*(2 versions) / Some Kind Of Wonderful*	$6	T	Rawkus 222
9/30/00	26S	15		4 **Move Somethin'** *(instrumental) / Good Mourning*	$4	★	Rawkus 38703
2/3/01	36S	9		5 **The Blast** ...*(2 versions) / Down For The Count / Train Of Thought*	$6	T	Rawkus 294
				TALIB KWELI & HI-TEK featuring Vinia Mojica			
6/23/01	50S	7		6 **The Sun God** ...*(3 versions) / Get Back Pt. 2* (w/**Talib Kweli** & DCQ)	$6	T	Rawkus 320
				HI-TEK feat. Common & Vinia Mojica			
7/20/02	44S	5		7 **Good To You** *[KWELI]* ...*(2 versions) / Put It In The Air*	$6	T	Rawkus 155987
				samples "Simply Beautiful" by **Al Green**			
10/5/02	39S	7		8 **Waitin' For The DJ** ...*(2 versions) / Guerrilla Monsoon Rap* (w/Black Thought, **Pharoahe Monch** & Kanye West)	$6	T	Rawkus 113974
				TALIB KWELI Featuring Bilal			
				K.W.S. LP **'92**			
				Dance trio from Nottingham, England: Chris King, Winnie Williams and "Mystic Meg" St. Joseph.			
6/20/92	6	26	●	**Please Don't Go** ...A:4 / S:15 *(same version)*	$4	▮	Next Plateau 339
				KYA-PI **'02**			
				Born in St. Andrews, Jamaica. Male reggae singer.			
9/14/02	22S	11		**Me U Want** ...*(5 versions) / (5 album snippets)*	$5	★*	Caribbean Gold 723
				KYA-PI Feat. Lil Genius			
				KYPER LP **'90**			
				Born Randall Kyper in Baton Rouge, Louisiana. Male rapper.			
6/30/90	14	25	●	**Tic-Tac-Toe** ...S:7 / A:31 *(Short Game)*	$4	▮	Atlantic 87910
				borrows guitar riffs from "Owner Of A Lonely Heart" by **Yes**			

L

DEBUT	PEAK	WKS	Gold	A-side (Chart Hit)....B-side	$	Sym	Label & Number
				LABAN '86			
				Pop-dance duo from Denmark: vocalists Lecia Jonsson and Ivan Pedersen.			
11/8/86	88	4		**Love In Siberia** ....*Radio*	$4	■	Critique 725
				picture sleeve made in Canada and distributed in the U.S.			
	★288★			**LaBELLE, Patti** R&B/BUB/AC/LP '86			
				Born Patricia Holt on 5/24/44 in Philadelphia, Pennsylvania. R&B-dance singer. Began singing career as leader of the Ordettes which evolved into **The Blue Belles**. The quartet, formed in Philadelphia in 1962, included **Nona Hendryx**, **Sarah Dash** and Cindy Birdsong. Birdsong left in 1967 to join **The Supremes**. Group continued as a trio. In 1971, group shortened its name to **LaBelle**. In 1977, group disbanded and Patti recorded solo. Charted 47 R&B hits, 1962-98.			
				1)On My Own 2)Lady Marmalade 3)New Attitude			
				THE BLUE-BELLES:			
4/21/62	15	11		1 **I Sold My Heart To The Junkman** ....*Itty Bitty Twist*	$25		Newtown 5000
				vocal group is actually **The Starlets**; reissued on Peak 7042 with a picture sleeve			
				PATTI LaBELLE And Her Blue Belles:			
9/14/63	37	13		2 **Down The Aisle (Wedding Song)** ....*C'est La Vie (So Goes Life)*	$25		Newtown 5777
1/4/64	34	8		3 **You'll Never Walk Alone** ....*Decatur Street*	$20	■	Parkway 896
				first released on Nicetown 5020 in 1963 ($20); from the Rodgers & Hammerstein musical *Carousel*			
12/19/64+	76	4		4 **Danny Boy** ....*I Believe*	$20		Parkway 935
				based on the traditional Irish tune "Londonderry Air" written in 1855			
12/4/65+	68	6		5 **All Or Nothing** ....*You Forgot How To Love*	$15		Atlantic 2311
12/31/66+	89	2		6 **Take Me For A Little While** ....*I Don't Want To Go On Without You*	$15		Atlantic 2373
				LaBELLE:			
1/4/75	❶[1]	18	●	7 **Lady Marmalade** ....RB[1] *Space Children*	$6		Epic 50048
5/10/75	48	6		8 **What Can I Do For You?** ....*Nightbird*	$6		Epic 50097
				PATTI LaBELLE:			
1/7/84	46	13		9 **If Only You Knew** ....RB[4] *I'll Never, Never Give Up*	$5		Philadelphia I. 04248
3/24/84	88	5		10 **Love Has Finally Come At Last** ....*American Dream* (Womack)	$5		Beverly Glen 2012
				BOBBY WOMACK and PATTI LaBELLE			
2/16/85	17	21		11 **New Attitude** ....S:13 / A:24 *Shoot Out* (**Harold Faltermeyer**)	$3	■	MCA 52517
6/15/85	41	14		12 **Stir It Up**....S:25 *The Discovery* (**Harold Faltermeyer**)	$3	■	MCA 52610
				above 2 from the movie *Beverly Hills Cop* starring **Eddie Murphy**			
3/22/86	❶[3]	23	●	13 **On My Own** RB[4] S:❶[5] / A:❶[2] *Stir It Up* (LaBelle)	$3	■	MCA 52770
				PATTI LaBELLE AND MICHAEL McDONALD			
7/19/86	29	12		14 **Oh, People**....S:26 *Love Attack*	$3	■	MCA 52877
10/7/89	79	5		15 **If You Asked Me To**....*(instrumental)*	$3		MCA 53358
				from the James Bond movie *Licence To Kill* starring Timothy Dalton			
2/29/92	57[S]	9		16 **Somebody Loves You Baby (You Know Who It Is)**....*(instrumental)*	$3	▮[V]	MCA 54315
				"45": MCA/Collectables 90170; B-side: "Feels Like Another One" (w/**Big Daddy Kane**)			
7/2/94	61	16		17 **The Right Kinda Lover**....S:38 *(instrumental)*	$3	▮[V]	MCA 54673
7/19/97	56	12		18 **When You Talk About Love** ....S:36 *(remix)*	$3	▮	MCA 55357
				samples "Love And Happiness" by **Al Green**			
				LA BOUCHE BUB/LP '96			
				Black male/female dance duo: Lane McCray and Melanie Thornton. Thornton died in a plane crash on 11/24/2001 (age 34); replaced by Kayo Shekoni. La Bouche is French for "mouth."			
11/11/95+	6	38	●	1 **Be My Lover**....S:6 / A:9 *(radio edit 2)*	$3	▮[V]	RCA 64446
3/30/96	13	32		2 **Sweet Dreams** ....A:15 / S:22 *(radio edit 2)*	$3	▮[V]	RCA 64505
				"45" issued for above 2 on RCA 64446			
10/19/96	35[A]	11		3 **Fallin' In Love**....*(club mix)*	$3	▮	Logic 59018
				originally a Dance Club hit in 1986; "Bubbled Under" (#111) on 7/22/95; re-entered the Bubbling chart (#114) on 3/15/97 (both on Logic 59018)			
6/6/98	48	20		4 **You Won't Forget Me** ....S:35 *(edit)*	$3	▮	RCA 65428
				LaBOUNTY, Bill AC/BUB '78			
				Born on 5/3/50 in Los Angeles, California. Pop singer/songwriter/pianist.			
5/27/78	65	9		**This Night Won't Last Forever**....*I Hope You'll Be Very Unhappy Without Me*	$4		Warner/Curb 8529
				LABRADO, Darrell '01			
				Born in 1985 in Honolulu, Hawaii. Teen hip-hop/pop singer.			
12/15/01	71[S]	1		**Master Blaster (Jammin')**....*(4 versions)*	$8	★*	Monkeypod 81244
				inspired by **Bob Marley**'s classic reggae tune "Jamming"			
				LACHEY, Nick — see SIMPSON, Jessica			
				L.A.D. Featuring Darvy Traylor '96			
				Creation of Los Angeles-based producer Richard "Rikko" Preuss. Group features singers/rappers Darvy Traylor, Derrick Wilson, Larry Goldsmith and Reggie Smith.			
11/18/95+	47	20		**Ridin' Low** ....S:36 / A:59 *(2 versions)*	$3	▮	Hollywood 64004
				contains an interpolation of "My Girl"			
				LADD, Cheryl LP '78			
				Born Cheryl Stoppelmoor on 7/2/51 in Huron, South Dakota. Singer/actress. Starred in several movies and TV shows. Married to David Ladd (son of actor Alan Ladd) from 1974-80. Married producer/songwriter Brian Russell (Brian & Brenda) in 1981.			
7/22/78	34	11		**Think It Over** ....*Here Is A Song*	$5	■	Capitol 4599
				LADY FLASH '76			
				Female R&B vocal trio: Lorraine Mazzola (lead), Monica Burruss and Debra Byrd. Backing vocal group for **Barry Manilow**. Mazzola was in **Reparata And The Delrons** from 1966-73.			
7/17/76	27	12		**Street Singin'** ....*Hypnotizin'*	$5		RSO 852
				written, produced and arranged by **Barry Manilow**			

DEBUT	PEAK	WKS	Gold	A-side (Chart Hit)...B-side	$	Sym	Label & Number
				LADY OF RAGE, The LP **'94**			
				Born Robin Allen in Farmville, Virginia. Female rapper.			
8/13/94	57	11		**Afro Puffs** ...S:28 *(instrumental)*	$4	▮	Death Row 98233
				Snoop Doggy Dogg (backing vocal); co-produced by **Dr. Dre**; from the movie *Above The Rim* starring **2 Pac** and Duane Martin			
				LAFAYETTES, The **'62**			
				Pop-rock group from Bethesda, Maryland. Led by singer Frank Bonarrigo.			
7/21/62	87	3		**Life's Too Short** ...*Nobody But You*	$25		RCA Victor 8044
				LAFLAMME, David LP **'77**			
				Born on 4/5/41 in Salt Lake City, Utah. Rock singer/electric violinist. Leader of the San Francisco "flower-rock" group It's A Beautiful Day.			
12/11/76+	89	7		**White Bird** ...*Spirit Of America*	$5	■	Amherst 717
				original version by LaFlamme's group, It's A Beautiful Day, "Bubbled Under" (#118) in 1969			
				LA FLAVOUR R&B **'80**			
				Pop-disco assemblage featuring lead singer Craig DeBock.			
6/14/80	91	2		**Only The Lonely (Have A Reason To Be Sad)** ...*Can't Kill the Beat*	$5		Sweet City 7377
				LaFORGE, Jack, His Piano and Orchestra **'65**			
				Born on 8/8/24 in Manhattan, New York. Pianist/composer/conductor.			
1/30/65	96	5		**Goldfinger** ...*Zelda's Theme* [I]	$15		Regina 1323
				title song from the James Bond movie starring Sean Connery			
				L.A. GUNS ROK/LP **'90**			
				Hard-rock group from Los Angeles, California: Philip Lewis (vocals), Tracii Guns and Mick Cripps (guitars), Kelly Nickels (bass), and Steve Riley (drums).			
4/7/90	33	22		1 **The Ballad of Jayne** ...S:22 *I Wanna Be Your Man*	$4	▮	Vertigo 876984
3/14/92	62	11		2 **It's Over Now** ...S:68 *(3 album snippets)*	$4	▮	Polydor 865494
				LAI, Francis, And His Orchestra **'71**			
				Born on 4/26/32 in Nice, France. Male composer/conductor.			
1/30/71	31	9		**Theme From Love Story** ...*Skating In Central Park* [I]	$6	■	Paramount 0064
				Georges Pludermacher (piano solo); theme from the movie *Love Story* starring Ali McGraw and Ryan O'Neal			
				LAID BACK LP **'84**			
				Synth-pop duo from Denmark: Tim Stahl (keyboards) and John Guldberg (guitar).			
2/25/84	26	18		**White Horse** ...*So Wie So*	$4		Sire 29346
	★460★			**LAINE, Frankie** MEM/POP/AC/BUB/LP **'49**			
				Born Frank Paul LoVecchio on 3/30/13 in Chicago, Illinois. First recorded for Exclusive in 1945. Signed to the Mercury label in 1947. Charted 44 pop hits, 1947-54, including 3 #1 hits: "That Lucky Old Sun," "Mule Train" and "The Cry Of The Wild Goose." Dynamic singer whose popularity lasted well into the rock era.			
				1)Moonlight Gambler 2)Love Is A Golden Ring 3)Humming Bird			
9/3/55	17	3		1 **Humming Bird** ...J:17 *My Little One*	$15		Columbia 40526
				Jimmy Carroll (orch.)			
11/12/55	73	4		2 **Hawk-Eye** ...T:73 *Your Love*	$15		Columbia 40558
11/26/55	19	17		3 **A Woman In Love** ...S:19 / T:24 *Walking The Night Away*	$15		Columbia 40583
				Percy Faith (orch.); from the movie *Guys And Dolls* starring Marlon Brando			
7/7/56	83	2		4 **Don't Cry** ...T:83 *Ticky Ticky Tick (I'm Gonna Tell On You)*	$15		Columbia 40693
				FRANKIE LAINE with PAUL WESTON and his MUSIC FROM HOLLYWOOD & The Mellomen			
				from the Broadway musical *The Most Happy Fella* starring Robert Weede; charted for 1 week on 7/7/56 (#99) and 1 week on 9/22/56			
12/1/56+	3	22	●	5 **Moonlight Gambler** T:3 / J:3 / A:4 / S:5 *Lotus Land*	$15	■	Columbia 40780
				Ray Conniff (orch.: #2 & 5)			
3/30/57	10	14		6 **Love Is A Golden Ring** ...A:10 / S:22 / T:23 *There's Not A Moment To Spare*	$15		Columbia 40856
				FRANKIE LAINE with The Easy Riders			
5/11/63	51	7		7 **Don't Make My Baby Blue** ...*The Moment Of Truth*	$10		Columbia 42767
				Jack Nitzsche (orch.)			
1/21/67	39	9		8 **I'll Take Care Of Your Cares** ...*Ev'ry Street's A Boulevard (In Old New York)*	$6		ABC 10891
				song first recorded in 1927 by Franklyn Baur on Victor 20504			
4/8/67	35	8		9 **Making Memories** ...*The Moment Of Truth*	$6		ABC 10924
6/17/67	48	7		10 **You Wanted Someone To Play With (I Wanted Someone To Love)** ...*The Real True Meaning Of Love*	$6		ABC 10946
				song first recorded in 1929 by Johnny Marvin on Victor 21839			
8/12/67	66	6		11 **Laura, What's He Got That I Ain't Got** ...*Sometimes (I Just Can't Stand You)*	$6		ABC 10967
10/7/67	83	3		12 **You, No One But You** ...*Somewhere There's Someone*	$6		ABC 10983
1/20/68	82	6		13 **To Each His Own** ...*I'm Happy To Hear You're Sorry*	$6		ABC 11032
				there were 3 #1 versions of this tune in 1946; Peter DeAngelis (orch.: #8-13)			
2/8/69	24	11		14 **You Gave Me A Mountain** ...AC[2] *The Secret Of Happiness*	$6		ABC 11174
				written by **Marty Robbins**; **Jimmy Bowen** (orch. and chorus)			
6/14/69	86	3		15 **Dammit Isn't God's Last Name** ...*Fresh Out Of Tears*	$6		ABC 11224
				LAISSEZ FAIRE **'92**			
				Female dance trio from New York: Marlo Falcone, Gina Cardinale and Jennifer Castiello.			
12/7/91+	64	17		**In Paradise** ...A:43 *(4 versions)*	$6	▮*	Metropolitan 4475
				L.A. JETS **'77**			
				Rock group from Los Angeles, California: Karen Lawrence (vocals), Harlin McNees (guitar), Ron Cindrich (bass) and John DeSautels (drums).			
12/25/76+	86	5		**Prisoner (Captured By Your Eyes)** ...*I'll Get Along Somehow*	$5		RCA 10826
				charted by **Barbra Streisand** in 1978 as "Love Theme From 'Eyes Of Laura Mars' (Prisoner)"			
				LAKE LP **'77**			
				Progressive-rock group from Hamburg, Germany: James Hopkins-Harrison (vocals), Alex Conti (guitar), Geoffrey Peacey (keyboards), Martin Tiefensee (bass) and Dieter Ahrendt (drums). Hopkins-Harrison died of a drug overdose on 5/16/91 (age 41).			
10/22/77	83	3		**Time Bomb** ...*Chasing Colours*	$5		Columbia 10614
				LAKE, Greg — see EMERSON, LAKE & PALMER			

DEBUT	PEAK	WKS	Gold	A-side (Chart Hit)..........B-side	$	Sym	Label & Number

LAKESIDE — R&B/BUB/LP '81

R&B-funk group from Dayton, Ohio: Tiemeyer McCain, Thomas Shelby, Otis Stokes and Mark Wood (vocals), Steve Shockley (guitar), Norman Beavers (keyboards), Fred Lewis (percussion), Marvin Craig (bass) and Fred Alexander (drums).

DEBUT	PEAK	WKS	Gold	A-side (Chart Hit)..........B-side	$	Sym	Label & Number
1/31/81	55	8		**Fantastic Voyage** ....RB^{2} *I Can't Get You Out Of My Head* also see **Coolio**'s rap version #3 hit in 1994	$5		Solar 12129

LAMAS, Lorenzo — '85

Born on 1/20/58 in San Francisco, California. Son of actress Arlene Dahl and actor Fernando Lamas (died on 10/9/82). Played "Lance" on TV's *Falcon Crest* and starred in *Renegade*. Also see **Billy Crystal**.

DEBUT	PEAK	WKS	Gold	A-side (Chart Hit)..........B-side	$	Sym	Label & Number
12/22/84+	85	5		**Fools Like Me** ....*Smooth Talker*	$4	■	Scotti Brothers 04686

LAMB, Becky — '67

Five years old in 1967.

DEBUT	PEAK	WKS	Gold	A-side (Chart Hit)..........B-side	$	Sym	Label & Number
12/16/67	2^{1X}	3		**Little Becky's Christmas Wish** ....*Go To Sleep Little Lambs* (Bill Lamb) [X] Becky lost her brother Tommy to the Vietnam War	$12		Warner 7154

LAMB, Kevin — '78

Rock singer/guitarist/keyboardist. Session work for the British group Rare Bird, 1970-76.

DEBUT	PEAK	WKS	Gold	A-side (Chart Hit)..........B-side	$	Sym	Label & Number
6/24/78	82	4		**On The Wrong Track** ....*When My Love*	$5		Arista 0316

LaMOND, George — BUB/LP '90

Born George Garcia on 2/25/67 in Washington DC; raised in the Bronx, New York. Dance singer. Cousin of **Joey Kid**.

DEBUT	PEAK	WKS	Gold	A-side (Chart Hit)..........B-side	$	Sym	Label & Number
5/12/90	25	17		1 **Bad Of The Heart** A:23 / S:25 *(1990 club remix)*	$3	▮V	Columbia 73339
8/18/90	63	13		2 **Look Into My Eyes** ....*What Could've Been*	$3	▮	Columbia 73486
12/1/90+	49	16		3 **No Matter What** ....*Without You* (LaMond) **GEORGE LaMOND With BRENDA K. STARR**	$3	▮	Columbia 73603
8/8/92	59	20		4 **Where Does That Leave Love** ....A:40 *My One And Only Love*	$3	▮	Columbia 74425
12/5/92	66	7		5 **Baby, I Believe In You** ....A:53 *(head boppin' mix)* samples "(They Long To Be) Close To You" by the **Carpenters**	$3	▮V	Columbia 74756

LANCE, Herb, & The Classics — R&B '61

R&B singer. Charted 3 Top 10 R&B hits in 1949, including the #4 hit "Close Your Eyes." **The Classics** are an Italian-American doo-wop quartet.

DEBUT	PEAK	WKS	Gold	A-side (Chart Hit)..........B-side	$	Sym	Label & Number
3/6/61	50	5		**Blue Moon** ....*Little Boy Lost* (Lance) there were 3 Top 10 versions of this Rodgers & Hart tune in 1935	$40		Promo 1010

LANCE, Major — R&B/BUB/LP '64

★580★

Born on 4/4/42 in Chicago, Illinois. Died of heart disease on 9/3/94 (age 52). R&B singer. First recorded for Mercury in 1959. Lived in Britain, 1972-74. Had own Osiris label with Al Jackson of **Booker T. & The MG's** in 1975. In prison for selling cocaine, 1978-81.

1)Um, Um, Um, Um, Um, Um 2)The Monkey Time 3)Hey Little Girl

DEBUT	PEAK	WKS	Gold	A-side (Chart Hit)..........B-side	$	Sym	Label & Number
7/13/63	8	15		1 **The Monkey Time** ....*Mama Didn't Know*	$15		Okeh 7175
10/19/63	13	10		2 **Hey Little Girl** ....*Crying In The Rain* also released on Okeh 7180 with "Um, Um, Um, Um, Um, Um" on the B-side	$15		Okeh 7181
1/4/64	5	11		3 **Um, Um, Um, Um, Um, Um** *Sweet Music* a disco version by Lance made the R&B charts (#59) in 1974 on Playboy 6017	$15	■	Okeh 7187
3/28/64	20	8		4 **The Matador** ....*Gonna Get Married*	$15		Okeh 7191
6/6/64	68	8		5 **It Ain't No Use /**			
6/27/64	68	6		6 **Girls**	$15		Okeh 7197
8/22/64	24	10		7 **Rhythm** ....*Please Don't Say No More*	$15	■	Okeh 7203
12/5/64	64	8		8 **Sometimes I Wonder** ....*I'm So Lost*	$15		Okeh 7209
3/6/65	40	7		9 **Come See** ....*You Belong To Me My Love*	$15	■	Okeh 7216
6/5/65	91	3		10 **Ain't It A Shame** ....*Gotta Get Away*	$15		Okeh 7223
8/28/65	93	3		11 **Too Hot To Hold** ....*Dark And Lonely*	$15		Okeh 7226
8/22/70	67	7		12 **Stay Away From Me (I Love You Too Much)** ....*Gypsy Woman* all of above (except #4 & 11) written by **Curtis Mayfield**	$7		Curtom 1953

LANCERS, The — see BREWER, Teresa

LANDIS, Jerry — see SIMON, Paul

LANE, Mark — '02

Born in Tennessee. Male rapper.

DEBUT	PEAK	WKS	Gold	A-side (Chart Hit)..........B-side	$	Sym	Label & Number
10/12/02	16^{S}	14		**Run 4 Us** ....*(2 versions) / Shorty Can Get It*	$6	★*	Intelligent 670841

LANE, Mickey Lee — '64

Born Mickey Lee Schreiber in 1945 in Rochester, New York. Rock and roll singer/songwriter.

DEBUT	PEAK	WKS	Gold	A-side (Chart Hit)..........B-side	$	Sym	Label & Number
10/10/64	38	9		**Shaggy Dog** ....*Oo-Oo*	$15		Swan 4183

LANE, Robin, & The Chartbusters — ROK/LP '80

Rock band formed in Boston, Massachusetts, by female singer Lane, with Asa Brebner (guitar), Leroy Radcliffe (keyboards), Scott Baerenwald (bass) and Tim Jackson (drums). Lane is the daughter of **Dean Martin**'s pianist, Ken Lane.

DEBUT	PEAK	WKS	Gold	A-side (Chart Hit)..........B-side	$	Sym	Label & Number
7/12/80	87	3		**When Things Go Wrong** ....*Many Years Ago* first released on Deli Platters 1 in 1979 with a picture sleeve	$4	■	Warner 49246

LANE BROTHERS, The — C&W '57

Pop vocal trio from Brooklyn, New York: brothers Pete, Frank and Art Loconto.

DEBUT	PEAK	WKS	Gold	A-side (Chart Hit)..........B-side	$	Sym	Label & Number
3/9/57	64	4		**Marianne** ....T:64 *Sogno D'Oro* **Joe Reisman** (orch. and chorus); adapted from a Bahamian folk song; a new version by The Lane Brothers made the Country charts (#83) in 1981 on FXL 0026	$20		RCA Victor 6810

lang, k.d. — C&W/AC/BUB/LP '92

Born Kathryn Dawn Lang on 11/2/61 in Consort, Alberta, Canada. Eclectic singer/songwriter. Charted 5 Country hits, 1987-89.

DEBUT	PEAK	WKS	Gold	A-side (Chart Hit)..........B-side	$	Sym	Label & Number
8/1/92	38	19		**Constant Craving** ....A:33 / S:65 *Season Of Hollow Soul*	$3	▮V	Sire 18942

LANIER & CO. — R&B '83

R&B singer Farris Lanier, Jr.

DEBUT	PEAK	WKS	Gold	A-side (Chart Hit)..........B-side	$	Sym	Label & Number
12/4/82+	48	13		**After I Cry Tonight** ....*Living For My Music*	$4		Larc 81010

DEBUT	PEAK	WKS	Gold	A-side (Chart Hit)..........B-side	$	Sym	Label & Number
				LANSON, Snooky POP **'55**			
				Born Roy Landman on 3/27/14 in Memphis, Tennessee. Died of cancer on 7/2/90 (age 76). Star of TV's *Your Hit Parade* (1950-57). Hit #12 on the pop charts in 1950 with "The Old Master Painter."			
8/20/55	30^{CU}	2		1 **Why Don't You Write Me**..........*Last Minute Love*	$15		Dot 15385
11/12/55	20	16		2 **It's Almost Tomorrow**..........T:20 / A:20 / J:20 *Stop (Let Me Off The Bus)*	$15		Dot 15424
				LANZA, Mario MEM/POP/LP **'51**			
				Born Alfredo Cocozza on 1/31/21 in Philadelphia, Pennsylvania. Died of a heart attack on 10/7/59 (age 38). Became the most popular operatic tenor since Caruso, with his voice featured in seven movies, though no theatrical operas. Hit #1 in 1951 with "Be My Love."			
9/15/56	53	8		1 **Earthbound**..........T:53 *This Land*	$12		RCA Victor 6644
				Jeff Alexander Choir (backing vocals); **Henri Rene** (orch.)			
5/26/58	97	1		2 **Arrivederci Roma**..........T:97 *Younger Than Springtime*	$12		RCA Victor 7164
				featured in the movie *Seven Hills of Rome* starring Lanza (different version is on the soundtrack album)			
				LA RISSA **'00**			
				Born in Miami, Florida. Female dance singer.			
3/25/00	58^{S}	10		**I Do Both Jay & Jane**..........*(8 mixes)*	$8	★*	Aureus 431
				LARKS, The **'61**			
				R&B vocal group from Philadelphia, Pennsylvania: Jackie Marsh (lead), Calvin Nichols (tenor), Earl Oxeindine (baritone) and Weldon McDougal III (bass). Named for the Lark cigarette. Backed **Barbara Mason** on several of her recordings.			
3/6/61	69	3		**It's Unbelievable**..........*I Can't Believe It*	$40		Sheryl 334
				LARKS, The BUB/LP **'64**			
				R&B vocal group from Los Angeles, California. Originally named Don Julian & The Meadowlarks: Don Julian, Ted Walters and Charles Morrison. Julian died of pneumonia on 11/6/98 (age 61).			
11/14/64+	7	13		**The Jerk**..........*Forget Me*	$20		Money 106
				LaROSA, Julius MEM/POP/AC **'53**			
				Born on 1/2/30 in Brooklyn, New York. Regular singer on *Arthur Godfrey And His Friends* TV show until he was fired on the air on 10/19/53. Popular DJ in New York (WNEW) for many years. Had 2 top 5 hits in 1953: "Anywhere I Wander" and "Eh, Cumpari."			
7/23/55	13	7		1 **Domani (Tomorrow)** S:13 / J:13 / A:15 *Mama Rosa*	$12		Cadence 1265
10/8/55	20	9		2 **Suddenly There's A Valley**..........A:20 / S:22 / T:29 *Everytime That I Kiss Carrie*	$12		Cadence 1270
				Archie Bleyer (orch., above 2)			
2/11/56	15	12		3 **Lipstick And Candy And Rubbersole Shoes**..........A:15 / T:21 *Winter In New England*	$12	□	RCA Victor 6416
				picture sleeve is a "This Is His Life" comic strip-styled sleeve			
6/30/56	93	1		4 **I've Got Love**..........T:93 *Augustine*	$10		RCA Victor 6499
7/14/56	89	4		5 **Get Me To The Church On Time**..........T:89 *I've Grown Accustomed To Her Face*	$10		RCA Victor 6567
				from the Broadway musical *My Fair Lady* starring **Julie Andrews**; **Joe Reisman** (orch., above 3)			
4/27/57	98	1		6 **Mama Guitar**..........T:98 *Man To Man*	$10		RCA Victor 6878
				Hugo Winterhalter (orch. and chorus); from the movie *A Face In The Crowd* starring **Andy Griffith**			
6/16/58	21	1		7 **Torero**..........A:21 *Milano*	$10		RCA Victor 7227
				Nick Perito (orch. and chorus)			
				LARRIEUX, Amel R&B/LP **'00**			
				Born in Manhattan, New York. Female R&B singer/songwriter. Former member of **Groove Theory**.			
3/4/00	97	3		**Get Up**..........S:47 *(instrumental)*	$3	★	550 Music 79280
				LARSEN-FEITEN BAND LP **'80**			
				Top session musicians Neil Larsen (keyboards) and Buzz Feiten (guitar). Feiten, a former member of the Paul Butterfield Blues Band, **The Rascals** and **Stevie Wonder**'s band, joined **Mr. Mister** in 1989.			
8/16/80	29	14		**Who'll Be The Fool Tonight**..........*Further Notice*	$4		Warner 49282
				LARSON, Nicolette C&W/BUB/AC/LP **'79**			
				Born on 7/17/52 in Helena, Montana; raised in Kansas City, Missouri. Died of a cerebral edema on on 12/16/97 (age 45). Session vocalist with **Neil Young**, **Emmylou Harris**, **Linda Ronstadt**, **Van Halen** and many others. Married session drummer Russ Kunkel. Also see **Nitty Gritty Dirt Band** and **Christopher Cross**.			
11/25/78+	8	19		1 **Lotta Love**..........AC^{1} *Angels Rejoiced*	$5		Warner 8664
				written by **Neil Young**			
3/31/79	47	9		2 **Rhumba Girl**..........*Last In Love*	$5		Warner 8795
				written by **Jesse Winchester**			
1/12/80	35	11		3 **Let Me Go, Love**..........*Trouble*	$4	■	Warner 49130
				duet with **Michael McDonald**			
8/7/82	53	9		4 **I Only Want To Be With You**..........*How Can We Go On*	$4		Warner 29948
				LaRUE, D.C. LP **'76**			
				Born David Charles L'Heureux on 4/26/48 in Meriden, Connecticut. Disco singer/songwriter.			
11/6/76	94	2		**Cathedrals**..........*Deep, Dark, Delicious Night*	$6		Pyramid 8007
				LA'S, The ROK/LP **'91**			
				Rock group from Liverpool, England: brothers Lee (vocals) and Neil (drums) Mavers, with Peter Camell (guitar), and John Power (bass). Group name is slang for lads.			
7/20/91	49	10		**There She Goes**..........*All By Myself / (3 album snippets)*	$4	▌	London 869370
				LaSALLE, Denise R&B/BUB/LP **'71**			
				Born Denise Craig on 7/16/39 in LeFlore County, Mississippi. R&B singer/songwriter. Moved to Chicago in the early 1950s. First recorded for Tarpen (Chess) in 1967. Had own Crajon Productions with husband Bill Jones from 1969.			
8/21/71	13	14	●	1 **Trapped By A Thing Called Love**..........RB^{1} *Keep It Coming*	$7		Westbound 182
2/5/72	46	11		2 **Now Run And Tell That**..........*The Deeper I Go (The Better It Gets)*	$7		Westbound 201
10/7/72	55	9		3 **Man Sized Job**..........*I'm Over You*	$7		Westbound 206
				some pressings show title as "A Man Size Job"			
1/14/78	80	10		4 **Love Me Right**..........*Fool Me Good*	$5		ABC 12312
				LASGO **'03**			
				Dance trio from Belgium: Evi Griffin, Peter Luts and David Vervoort.			
11/2/02+	35	20		**Something**..........A:40 / S:47 *(4 versions)*	$8	★*	Robbins 72056

DEBUT	PEAK	WKS	Gold	A-side (Chart Hit)..........B-side	$	Sym	Label & Number
				LAS KETCHUP '02			
				Female pop vocal trio from Cordoba, Argentina: sisters Lola, Lucía and Pilar Muñoz.			
10/12/02	54	9		**The Ketchup Song (Hey Hah)**..........A:51 *(3 versions)* [F]	$6	T	Sony Discos 79822
				melody loosely based on "Rapper's Delight" by **Sugarhill Gang**			
				LASLEY, David '82			
				Born on 8/20/47 in Sault St. Marie, Michigan. Singer/songwriter.			
3/13/82	36	10		**If I Had My Wish Tonight**..........*There's Got To Be Somebody (Back On The Street Again)*	$4		EMI America 8111
				LASSIES, The '56			
				Female pop vocal trio.			
6/23/56	66	1		**I Look At You**..........T:66 *Sleepy Head*	$20		Decca 29868
				Ray Charles Singers (backing vocals); **Jack Pleis** (orch.)			
				LAST, James AC/BUB/LP '80			
				Born on 4/17/29 in Bremen, Germany. Producer/arranger/conductor.			
1/15/72	84	4		1 **Music From Across The Way**..........*Endless Joureny*	$5	■	Polydor 15028
3/29/80	28	13		2 **The Seduction (Love Theme)** *[JAMES LAST BAND]*..........*Night Drive* [I]	$4		Polydor 2071
				from the movie *American Gigolo* starring Richard Gere			
				LAST WORD, The BUB '67			
				Rock group from Miami, Florida: Johnny Lombardo (vocals), Mike Byrnes (guitar), Steve Sechak (keyboards) and Ricky Cook (drums).			
10/21/67	78	5		**Can't Stop Loving You**..........*Don't Fight It*	$8		Atco 6498
				L.A. STYLE BUB '92			
				Techno-rave creation of Dutch producer/musician Denzil Slemming.			
4/11/92	59	20	●	**James Brown Is Dead**..........S:46 / A:65 *(4 remixes)* [I]	$7	▮*	Arista 12387
				LaTANYA R&B '98			
				Born in Chicago, Illinois. Female R&B singer.			
6/13/98	85	7		1 **Whatuon**..........S:58 *(instrumental)*	$5	▮	TVT 4402
				LaTANYA featuring Twista			
1/22/00	50^S	6		2 **Keys**..........*(3 versions)*	$4	★	TVT 4405
				LATIMORE R&B/BUB/LP '74			
				Born Benjamin Latimore on 9/7/39 in Charleston, Tennessee. R&B singer/songwriter.			
10/26/74	31	12		1 **Let's Straighten It Out**..........RB^2 *Ain't Nobody Gonna Make Me Change My Mind*	$6		Glades 1722
2/5/77	37	10		2 **Somethin' 'Bout 'Cha**..........*Sweet Vibrations*	$6		Glades 1739
				above 2 produced by **Steve Alaimo**			
				LATIN ALLIANCE Featuring War LP '91			
				All-star rap trio: **Kid Frost**, **Mellow Man Ace** and **A.L.T.**			
8/10/91	54	11		**Lowrider (On The Boulevard)**..........S:28 *Smooth Roughness* (Latin Alliance)	$4	▮	Virgin 98751
				samples **War**'s "Low Rider" and **Santana**'s "Evil Ways"			
				LATIN LOU & THE MAMBO ALL-STARS '99			
				Studio group from Miami, Florida.			
10/16/99	33^S	18		**Mambo #5**..........	$4	★	Groove 5105
				cover version of **Lou Bega**'s #3 hit			
				LaTOUR LP '91			
				Born William LaTour in Chicago, Illinois. Techno-dance artist.			
4/6/91	35	11		**People Are Still Having Sex**..........S:25 / A:38 *(remix)*	$4	▮	Smash 879666
				LATTIMORE, Kenny R&B/LP '97			
				Born on 4/10/70 in Washington DC. R&B singer. Married **Chanté Moore** on 1/1/2002. Also see **Ray J**.			
7/20/96	89	4		1 **Never Too Busy**..........S:61 *(4 album snippets)*	$3	▮	Columbia 78245
3/29/97	33	20		2 **For You**..........S:20 *(Spanish version)*	$3	▮	Columbia 78456
				LATTISAW, Stacy R&B/BUB/LP '80			
				Born on 11/25/66 in Washington DC. Female R&B singer. Recorded her first album at age 12. Charted 22 R&B hits, 1979-89. Childhood friend of **Johnny Gill**. Her younger brother Jerry is a member of Me-2-U.			
8/9/80	21	24		1 **Let Me Be Your Angel** *You Don't Love Me Anymore*	$5		Cotillion 46001
6/20/81	26	17		2 **Love On A Two Way Street**..........*Baby I Love You*	$5		Cotillion 46015
10/16/82	70	6		3 **Attack Of The Name Game**..........*I Could Love You So Divine* [N]	$5		Cotillion 99968
8/13/83	40	16		4 **Miracles**..........*Black Pumps And Pink Lipstick*	$5		Cotillion 99855
3/10/84	75	9		5 **Perfect Combination**..........*Heartbreak Look*	$4		Cotillion 99785
				STACY LATTISAW & JOHNNY GILL			
				all of above produced by **Narada Michael Walden**			
10/18/86	48	13		6 **Nail It To The Wall**..........*(instrumental)*	$3	■	Motown 1859
	★231★			**LAUPER, Cyndi** BUB/AC/LP '84			
				Born on 6/20/53 in Queens, New York. Recorded an album for Polydor Records in 1980 with the group Blue Angel. Supported by the **Hooters**, 1983-84. Won the 1984 Best New Artist Grammy Award. In the movies *Vibes* and *Life With Mikey*. Married actor David Thornton on 11/24/91.			
				1)Time After Time 2)True Colors 3)Girls Just Want To Have Fun			
12/17/83+	2^2	25	▲	1 **Girls Just Want To Have Fun**..........*Right Track Wrong Train*	$3	■	Portrait 04120
				also see #14 below			
4/14/84	❶^2	20	●	2 **Time After Time** AC^3 *I'll Kiss You*	$3		Portrait 04432
7/21/84	3	18	●	3 **She Bop**..........S:16 / A:24 *Witness*	$3	■	Portrait 04516
10/6/84	5	19		4 **All Through The Night**..........A:4 / S:9 *Witness*	$3	■	Portrait 04639
				written by **Jules Shear** (backing vocal)			
12/22/84+	27	13		5 **Money Changes Everything**..........A:23 / S:28 *(live version)*	$3	■	Portrait 04737
				all of above from the album *She's So Unusual*			
5/18/85	10	15		6 **The Goonies 'R' Good Enough**..........S:10 / A:10 *What A Thrill*	$3	■	Portrait 04918
				from the movie *The Goonies* starring Sean Astin			

DEBUT	PEAK	WKS	Gold	A-side (Chart Hit)...B-side	$	Sym	Label & Number
				LAUPER, Cyndi — Cont'd			
8/30/86	❶²	20		7 **True Colors** ...A:❶² / S:2 *Heading For The Moon*	$3	■	Portrait 06247
11/29/86+	3	17		8 **Change Of Heart** ...S:2 / A:5 *Witness* **The Bangles** (guest vocals)	$3	■	Portrait 06431
3/14/87	12	13		9 **What's Going On** ...S:10 / A:12 *One Track Mind*	$3	■	Portrait 06970
6/13/87	71	4		10 **Boy Blue** ...*The Faraway Nearby* above 4 from the album *True Colors*	$3	■	Portrait 07181
7/9/88	54	8		11 **Hole In My Heart (All The Way To China)** ...*Boy Blue (live)* from the movie *Vibes* starring Lauper	$3	■	Epic 07940
5/6/89	6	15		12 **I Drove All Night** ...S:5 / A:7 *Maybe He'll Know*	$3		Epic 68759
8/5/89	62	6		13 **My First Night Without You** ...*Unabbreviated Love*	$3		Epic 68945
9/9/95	87	5		14 **Hey Now (Girls Just Want To Have Fun)** ...*Who Let In The Rain* (AC #33/'93) [R] new version of #1 above and **Redbone**'s "Come And Get Your Love"; from the movie *To Wong Foo* starring Wesley Snipes	$3	▮	Epic 77967
				LAUREN, Rod '60 Born on 3/26/40 in Fresno, California. Lauren was groomed by RCA in 1960 to be a hot new teen idol.			
12/21/59+	31	10		**If I Had A Girl** ...*No Wonder* Shorty Rogers (orch. and chorus)	$15	■	RCA Victor 7645
				LAURIE, Annie R&B/BUB '57 Born in Atlanta, Georgia. R&B singer. Joined **Paul Gayten**'s band in 1947.			
7/8/57	61	6		**It Hurts To Be In Love** ...T:61 *Hand In Hand*	$25		DeLuxe 6107
				LAURIE, Linda '59 Born Linda Gertz in Brooklyn, New York. Novelty-pop singer/songwriter. Wrote **Helen Reddy**'s "Delta Dawn" and "Leave Me Alone (Ruby Red Dress)."			
1/26/59	52	9		**Ambrose (Part Five)** ...*Ooh, What A Lover!* [N]	$20		Glory 290
				LAURIE SISTERS, The '55 Vocal group; similar in style to The Andrews Sisters.			
4/16/55	30	1		**Dixie Danny** ...S:30 *No Chance* Hugo Peretti (of **Hugo & Luigi**; orch.)	$15		Mercury 70548
				LAURNEÁ R&B/BUB '97 Born Laurneá Wilkinson in Omaha, Nebraska; raised in Los Angeles, California. Female R&B singer.			
6/28/97	55	15		**Can't Let Go** ...S:47 *(2 remixes) / Today*	$4	▮	Yab Yum 78565
				LaVERNE & SHIRLEY '76 Duo of Penny Marshall and Cindy Williams; stars of the TV series *LaVerne & Shirley.* Marshall was born on 10/15/42 in the Bronx, New York. Directed many movies including *Big*, *Awakenings* and *A League Of Their Own.* Married to actor/director Rob Reiner from 1971-79. Williams was born on 8/22/47 in Van Nuys, California. Played Ron Howard's girlfriend in the movie *American Graffiti.* Also see **Cyndi Grecco**.			
11/27/76	65	4		**Sixteen Reasons** ...*Chapel Of Love*	$6	■	Atlantic 3367
				LAVIGNE, Avril LP '02 Born on 9/30/84 in Napanee, Ontario, Canada. Teen pop-rock female singer/songwriter.			
6/1/02	2²	31		1 **Complicated** ...A:2 / S:25 *(remix)* "45": Arista 50982; B-side: (The Matrix Mix)	$4	★ᵛ	Arista 15185
12/7/02+	4	27	●	2 **I'm With You** / A:5 / S:11			
9/14/02	10	20		3 **Sk8er Boi** ...A:10 "45" issued for above 2 on Arista 50972	$8	▶ᵛ	Arista 51024
				LAWRENCE, Billy '97 Born in St. Louis, Missouri. Female singer/songwriter.			
7/30/94	87	4		1 **Happiness** ...*(3 album snippets)*	$3	▮	EastWest 98264
4/12/97	44	19		2 **Come On** ...S:33 *When Alone* **BILLY LAWRENCE Featuring MC Lyte**	$3	▮	EastWest 64239
7/19/97	34	17		3 **Take It To The Streets** ...S:21 *Wild For The Night* (w/**Busta Rhymes**) **RAMPAGE Featuring Billy Lawrence** samples "I Hear Music In The Streets" by Unlimited Touch	$3	▮	Violator 64171
12/13/97	92	7		4 **Up & Down** ...*Footsteps* samples "The Glow Of Love" by **Change**	$3	▮	EastWest 64138
				LAWRENCE, Eddie '56 Born Lawrence Eisler on 3/2/19 in Brooklyn, New York. Comedian/actor/author/playwright.			
8/11/56	34	9		**The Old Philosopher** ...T:34 *King Arthur's Mines* [C] The Sentimental Four (musical accompaniment); background music: "Beautiful Dreamer"	$20		Coral 61671
				LAWRENCE, Joey LP '93 Born on 4/20/76 in Montgomery, Pennsylvania. Teen actor/singer. Acted on TV's *Gimme A Break*, *Blossom* and *Brotherly Love.*			
3/6/93	19	20		1 **Nothin' My Love Can't Fix** ...S:20 / A:22 *(3 album snippets)*	$3	▮ᵛ	Impact/MCA 54562
7/17/93	52	12		2 **Stay Forever** ...S:57 *(remix)* "45" B-sides of above 2 feature alternate mixes of the A-sides	$3	▮ᵛ	Impact/MCA 54653
				LAWRENCE, Steve ★198★ AC/BUB/MEM/POP/LP '63 Born Sidney Leibowitz on 7/8/35 in Brooklyn, New York. Regular performer on **Steve Allen**'s *Tonight Show* for five years. First recorded for King in 1952. Married singer **Eydie Gorme** on 12/29/57; they recorded as Parker & Penny in 1979. **Steve and Eydie** remain a popular nightclub act. Steve first hit the pop charts in 1952 with "Poinciana" (#21). *1)Go Away Little Girl 2)Party Doll 3)Footsteps 4)Pretty Blue Eyes 5)Portrait Of My Love*			
1/12/57	18	14		1 **The Banana Boat Song** ...A:18 / T:30 *Long Before I Knew You*	$20		Coral 61761
2/23/57	5	20		2 **Party Doll** / A:5 / T:10 / J:11 / S:12			
3/16/57	45	7		3 **(The Bad Donkey) Pum-Pa-Lum** ...T:45 / S:flip	$20		Coral 61792

DEBUT	PEAK	WKS	Gold	A-side (Chart Hit)......B-side	$	Sym	Label & Number
				LAWRENCE, Steve — Cont'd			
5/27/57	42	11		4 **Can't Wait For Summer /** T:42			
5/27/57	71	7		5 **Fabulous** T:71	$20		Coral 61834
10/28/57	54	8		6 **Fraulein**....T:54 *Blue Rememberin' You*	$15		Coral 61876
				Dick Jacobs (orch., all of above)			
3/17/58	73	2		7 **Uh-Huh, Oh Yeah**....T:73 *Lover In The House*	$15		Coral 61950
				from the Broadway musical *The Body Beautiful* starring **Mindy Carson**			
9/22/58	97	2		8 **Many A Time**....H:97 *All About Love*	$15		Coral 62025
				Jack Kane (orch., above 2)			
5/18/59	62	4		9 **(I Don't Care) Only Love Me**....HOT:62(0 wks) *Loving Is A Way Of Living*	$12		ABC-Paramount 10005
11/23/59+	9	18		10 **Pretty Blue Eyes**....*You're Nearer*	$12		ABC-Paramount 10058
3/7/60	7	13		11 **Footsteps**....*You Don't Know*	$12		ABC-Paramount 10085
3/6/61	9	16		12 **Portrait Of My Love**....*Oh How You Lied*	$10		United Artists 291
7/17/61	68	5		13 **My Claire De Lune /**			
				adapted from Debussy's *Suite Bergamesque*			
8/14/61	94	1		14 **In Time**....	$10	■	United Artists 335
				adapted from Tchaikovsky's *Pathetique Symphony*			
10/23/61	67	5		15 **Somewhere Along The Way**....*While There's Still Time*	$10		United Artists 364
				#8 hit for **Nat King Cole** in 1952; **Don Costa** (orch.: #9-15)			
11/10/62+	❶[2]	17	●	16 **Go Away Little Girl** AC[6] *If You Love Her Tell Her So*	$10	■	Columbia 42601
				issued with 2 different picture sleeves			
3/9/63	26	9		17 **Don't Be Afraid, Little Darlin'**....*Don't Come Running Back*	$8	□	Columbia 42699
5/25/63	27	8		18 **Poor Little Rich Girl**....*More (Theme from "Mondo Cane") (#117)*	$8		Columbia 42795
7/20/63	28	11		19 **I Want To Stay Here**....*Ain't Love*	$8	□	Columbia 42815
				STEVE And EYDIE			
10/19/63	26	9		20 **Walking Proud**....*All The Way Home*	$8	■	Columbia 42865
				also issued with a promo sleeve			
12/21/63+	35	9		21 **I Can't Stop Talking About You**....*To The Movies We Go*	$8		Columbia 42932
				STEVE And EYDIE			
				Marion Evans (orch.: #16-21); above 6 (except #17) written by **Carole King** and Gerry Goffin			
5/30/64	72	5		22 **Everybody Knows**....*One Love Too Late*	$8		Columbia 43047
8/29/64	77	6		23 **Yet...I Know (Et Pourtant)**....*Put Away Your Teardrops*	$8		Columbia 43095
				Robert Mersey (orch., above 2)			
9/16/72	68	10		24 **We Can Make It Together**....*E Fini* (Steve & Eydie)	$6	■	MGM 14383
				STEVE & EYDIE featuring The Osmonds			
				LAWRENCE, Tracy C&W/BUB/LP **'00**			
				Born on 1/27/68 in Atlanta, Texas; raised in Foreman, Arkansas. Male country singer. In May 1991, he was shot four times in an attempted holdup in Nashville; fully recovered.			
4/17/93	72	12		1 **Alibis**....CW[2] S:33 *(3 album snippets)*	$4	■ V	Atlantic 87372
				"45" B-side: "Somebody Paints The Wall" (C&W #8)			
11/5/94	84	9		2 **I See It Now**....S:44 *(3 album snippets)*	$4	■ V	Atlantic 87199
				"45" B-side: "God Made Woman On A Good Day"			
1/29/00	40	20		3 **Lessons Learned**....A:32			album cut
				from the album *Lessons Learned* on Atlantic 83269			
				LAWRENCE, Vicki AC/LP **'73**			
				Born on 5/26/49 in Inglewood, California. Regular on Carol Burnett's CBS-TV series from 1967-78. Also starred in TV's *Mama's Family* from 1982-87. Married to songwriter/singer **Bobby Russell** from 1972-74.			
2/10/73	❶[2]	20	●	1 **The Night The Lights Went Out In Georgia**....*Dime A Dance*	$5		Bell 45,303
				written by Lawrence's husband, **Bobby Russell**; song inspired the 1981 movie starring **Kristy McNichol**			
6/23/73	75	7		2 **He Did With Me**....*Mr. Allison*	$5		Bell 45,362
10/18/75	81	3		3 **The Other Woman**....*Cameo*	$4		Private Stock 45,036
				LAWS, Debra R&B/LP **'81**			
				Born on 9/10/56 in Houston, Texas. R&B singer. Sister of **Eloise Laws** and **Ronnie Laws**.			
8/15/81	90	5		**Very Special**....*All The Things I Love*	$4		Elektra 47142
				Debra's brother, **Ronnie Laws** (male vocal)			
				LAWS, Eloise R&B/LP **'78**			
				Born Lavern Eloise Laws on 11/6/43 in Houston, Texas. R&B singer. Sister of **Debra Laws** and **Ronnie Laws**.			
1/14/78	91	6		1 **1,000 Laughs**....*You're Incredible*	$4		ABC 12313
3/18/78	97	2		2 **Number One**....*Forever Now*	$4		ABC 12341
				LAWS, Ronnie R&B/LP **'81**			
				Born on 10/3/50 in Houston, Texas. R&B-jazz saxophonist. Brother of **Debra Laws** and **Eloise Laws**. With **Earth, Wind & Fire** from 1972-73.			
9/12/81	60	9		**Stay Awake**....*Summer Fool*	$4		Liberty 1424
				LAYNE, Joy **'57**			
				Born in 1941 in Chicago, Illinois. Teen female pop singer.			
2/16/57	20	7		**Your Wild Heart**....J:20 / T:30 *Dum-Dum*	$15		Mercury 71038
				Carl Stevens (orch.)			
				LAZY RACER **'79**			
				Pop-rock group: Tim Renwick and Kelly Harland (vocals), Bill Lamb (guitar), Tim Gorman (keyboards), Dave Markee (bass) and Henry Spinetti (drums).			
7/7/79	81	4		**Keep On Running Away**....*Every Other Day*	$5		A&M 2152
				L.B.C. CREW **'96**			
				Rap group from Long Beach, California: Tray Dee, South Sentrell, Lil' Style, LT, Soopafly and Technique. Assembled by **Snoop Dogg**. Tray Dee later joined **Tha Eastsidaz**.			
12/16/95+	75	20		**Beware Of My Crew**....S:58 *(album version)*	$4	▮	Jac-Mac/Warner 17722
				L.B.C. CREW featuring Tray D & South Sentrell			
				co-written and co-produced by **Snoop Doggy Dogg**; samples "Heartbreaker" by **Zapp**; from the movie *A Thin Line Between Love And Hate* starring Martin Lawrence			

DEBUT	PEAK	WKS	Gold	A-side (Chart Hit)...B-side	$	Sym	Label & Number

LEACH, Billy — '57

Born William Leech on 1/9/11 in Pittsburgh, Pennsylvania. Died on 11/11/97 (age 86). Began singing career at age 14 on Pittsburgh's KDKA radio. Worked with Art Kassel, Raymond Scott and Guy Lombardo. On Chicago's WBBM radio for 21 years.

DEBUT	PEAK	WKS	Gold	A-side (Chart Hit)...B-side	$	Sym	Label & Number
9/16/57	86	3		**Song Of The Barefoot Mailman** ....T:86 *Lil's Grill* Lee Armentrout (orch.)	$20		Bally 1039

LEAPY LEE — C&W/LP '68

Born Lee Graham on 7/2/42 in Eastbourne, England. Acted on stage and TV in England.

DEBUT	PEAK	WKS	Gold	A-side (Chart Hit)...B-side	$	Sym	Label & Number
10/12/68	16	14		**Little Arrows** ....*Time Will Tell*	$8		Decca 32380

LEAVES, The — LP '66

Garage-rock band from Northridge, California: Robert Arlin (vocals), John Beck and Robert Lee Reiner (guitars), Jim Pons (bass), and Tom Ray (drums). Pons was later a brief member of **The Turtles**.

DEBUT	PEAK	WKS	Gold	A-side (Chart Hit)...B-side	$	Sym	Label & Number
5/21/66	31	9		**Hey Joe** ....*Funny Little World* released in 1965 as "Hey Joe, Where You Gonna Go?" on Mira 207 ($75); Mira 222 also issued with "Girl From The East" as the B-side	$40		Mira 222

LEAVILL, Otis — BUB/R&B '70

Born Otis Leavill Cobb on 2/8/37 in Dewey Rose, Georgia. Died of a heart attack on 7/17/2002 (age 65). R&B singer/songwriter.

DEBUT	PEAK	WKS	Gold	A-side (Chart Hit)...B-side	$	Sym	Label & Number
11/29/69+	63	9		1 **I Love You** ....*I Need You*	$10		Dakar 614
9/19/70	72	7		2 **Love Uprising** *[OTIS LEAVILLE]* ....*I Need You*	$10		Dakar 620

LeBLANC, Lenny — LP '77

Born on 6/17/51 in Leominster, Massachusetts. In duo with Pete Carr (born in 4/22/50 in Daytona Beach, Florida). Lenny (bass) and Pete (lead guitar) were both session musicians at Muscle Shoals, Alabama. Lenny later recorded Contemporary Christian music.

DEBUT	PEAK	WKS	Gold	A-side (Chart Hit)...B-side	$	Sym	Label & Number
7/2/77	48	6		1 **Something About You** ....*Coming And Going* **LeBLANC & CARR**	$5		Big Tree 16092
9/3/77	58	5		2 **Hound Dog Man (Play It Again)** ....*Sharing The Night Together*	$6		Big Tree 16062
10/15/77+	13	28		3 **Falling** *I Believe That We*	$5		Big Tree 16100
6/3/78	91	4		4 **Midnight Light** ....*How Does It Feel (To Be In Love)* **LeBLANC & CARR** (above 2)	$5		Big Tree 16114
3/28/81	55	7		5 **Somebody Send My Baby Home** ....*You Can't Run*	$4		Capitol/MSS 4979

LE CLICK — '97

Male/female techno-dance duo: Robert Haynes and Kayo Shekoni.

DEBUT	PEAK	WKS	Gold	A-side (Chart Hit)...B-side	$	Sym	Label & Number
7/22/95	89	6		1 **Tonight Is The Night** ....*(fluid mix)*	$3	▮	Logic 59011
10/19/96+	68	14		2 **Tonight Is The Night** ....A:69 *(fluid mix)* [R] above 2 are the same version	$3	▮	Logic 59011
3/8/97	35	25		3 **Call Me** ....S:36 / A:44 *(remix)*	$3	▮	Logic 45726
9/27/97	62	19		4 **Don't Go** ....S:67 *Love Is A Wonderful Thing* **LE CLICK Featuring Kayo**	$3	▮	Logic 64975

LED ZEPPELIN — ★597★ — ROK/LP '70

Hard-rock group formed in England: **Robert Plant** (vocals; born on 8/20/48), **Jimmy Page** (guitar; born on 1/9/44), John Paul Jones (bass, keyboards; born on 1/3/46) and John Bonham (drums; born on 5/31/48). First known as the New Yardbirds. Page had been in **The Yardbirds**, 1966-68. Plant and Bonham had been in a group called Band Of Joy. Led Zeppelin's U.S. tour in 1973 broke many box office records. Formed own Swan Song label in 1974. In concert movie *The Song Remains The Same* in 1976. Bonham died of asphyxiation on 9/25/80 (age 33). Group disbanded in December 1980. Plant and Page formed **The Honeydrippers** in 1984. Page also with **The Firm** (1984-86). "**Bonham**" is the name of group formed by Jason Bonham, John's son, in 1989. Led Zeppelin's most famous recording, "Stairway To Heaven" (on album *Led Zeppelin IV*), was never released as a commercial single. Their first 9 albums sold over 88 million copies in the U.S. Group inducted into the Rock and Roll Hall of Fame in 1995.

1)Whole Lotta Love 2)Black Dog 3)Immigrant Song

DEBUT	PEAK	WKS	Gold	A-side (Chart Hit)...B-side	$	Sym	Label & Number
3/29/69	80	4		1 **Good Times Bad Times** ....*Communication Breakdown*	$25		Atlantic 2613
11/22/69+	4	15	●	2 **Whole Lotta Love /** issued with times of 5:33 or 3:12			
3/14/70	65	5		3 **Living Loving Maid (She's Just A Woman)**....	$15		Atlantic 2690
11/21/70+	16	13		4 **Immigrant Song** ....*Hey, Hey, What Can I Do*	$15		Atlantic 2777
12/25/71+	15	12		5 **Black Dog** ....*Misty Mountain Hop*	$10		Atlantic 2849
3/18/72	47	7		6 **Rock And Roll** ....*Four Sticks* 1972: "Stairway To Heaven" issued as a promotional release with a special sleeve on Atlantic PR-175 ($100) and again in 1973 on PR-269 ($50)	$10		Atlantic 2865
6/23/73	51	8		7 **Over The Hills And Far Away** ....*Dancing Days*	$10		Atlantic 2970
10/20/73	20	16		8 **D'yer Mak'er** ....*The Crunge*	$10		Atlantic 2986
4/19/75	38	7		9 **Trampled Under Foot** ....*Black Country Woman*	$6		Swan Song 70102
12/22/79+	21	13		10 **Fool In The Rain** ....*Hot Dog*	$6		Swan Song 71003

LEE, Brenda ★33★ — C&W/BUB/LP '60

Born Brenda Mae Tarpley on 12/11/44 in Lithonia, Georgia. Pop singer. Professional singer since age six. Signed to Decca Records in 1956. Became known as "Little Miss Dynamite." Successful country singer from 1971-85. Lee ranks as the #1 female singer of the 1960s. Inducted into the Country Music Hall of Fame in 1997 and the Rock and Roll Hall of Fame in 2002.

1)I'm Sorry 2)I Want To Be Wanted 3)All Alone Am I 4)Fool #1 5)Dum Dum

DEBUT	PEAK	WKS	Gold	A-side (Chart Hit)...B-side	$	Sym	Label & Number
3/2/57	43	11		1 **One Step At A Time** ....T:43 *Fairyland* **Jack Pleis** (orch.)	$25		Decca 30198
7/15/57	72	7		2 **Dynamite** ....T:72 *Love You 'Till I Die* The Anita Kerr Singers (backing vocals)	$25		Decca 30333
12/21/59+	4	24		3 **Sweet Nothin's** ....*Weep No More My Baby*	$20	■	Decca 30967

DEBUT	PEAK	WKS	Gold	A-side (Chart Hit)..................B-side	$	Sym	Label & Number
				LEE, Brenda — Cont'd			
5/30/60	1 [3]	23	●	4 **I'm Sorry /**			
6/6/60	6	14		5 **That's All You Gotta Do**........................	$15	■	Decca 31093
				written by **Jerry Reed**			
9/12/60	1 [1]	15		6 **I Want To Be Wanted /**			
				Italian song: "Per Tutta La Vita"			
10/3/60	40	5		7 **Just A Little**........................	$15	■	Decca 31149
12/12/60	14	4	●	8 **Rockin' Around The Christmas Tree**..................*Papa Noël* [X]	$15	■	Decca 30776
				first released in 1958 (original on black label; reissues on multi-color label from 1960-on); picture sleeve issued in 1960; a new picture sleeve (same Decca number) issued in 1964			
12/31/60+	7	12		9 **Emotions /**			
1/30/61	33	4		10 **I'm Learning About Love**........................	$15	■	Decca 31195
3/27/61	6	12		11 **You Can Depend On Me**..................*It's Never Too Late* (#101)	$15	■	Decca 31231
				#4 hit for **Louis Armstrong** in 1932			
6/19/61	4	12		12 **Dum Dum /**			
7/3/61	56	3		13 **Eventually**........................	$15		Decca 31272
10/2/61	3	14		14 **Fool #1 /**			
10/2/61	31	9		15 **Anybody But Me**........................	$15	■	Decca 31309
12/11/61	50	4	●	16 **Rockin' Around The Christmas Tree**..................*Papa Noël* [X-R]	$15	■	Decca 30776
1/13/62	4	13		17 **Break It To Me Gently /**			
1/13/62	52	4		18 **So Deep**........................	$15	■	Decca 31348
4/14/62	6	11		19 **Everybody Loves Me But You /**			
4/28/62	89	3		20 **Here Comes That Feelin'**........................	$15		Decca 31379
				co-written by **Dorsey Burnette**			
7/7/62	15	10		21 **Heart In Hand /**			
6/30/62	29	8		22 **It Started All Over Again**........................	$15		Decca 31407
9/29/62	3	15		23 **All Alone Am I /** AC[5]			
9/22/62	53	6		24 **Save All Your Lovin' For Me**........................	$15	■	Decca 31424
12/15/62	59	3	●	25 **Rockin' Around The Christmas Tree**..................X:3 *Papa Noël* [X-R]	$15	■	Decca 30776
				Christmas charts: [#3-25 weeks] 12/'63; 4/'64; 3/'65; 4/'66; 8/'67; 14/'68; 4/'69; 16/'73; 9/'83; 5/'84; also made the Adult Contemporary chart (#16) and Country chart (#62) during the 1997 Christmas season on MCA 54292			
1/26/63	32	7		26 **Your Used To Be /**			
1/26/63	47	6		27 **She'll Never Know**........................	$15	■	Decca 31454
4/6/63	6	13		28 **Losing You /**			
4/13/63	73	3		29 **He's So Heavenly**........................	$15	■	Decca 31478
7/6/63	24	9		30 **My Whole World Is Falling Down /**			
				melody based on the traditional children's song "London Bridge Is Falling Down"			
7/13/63	25	8		31 **I Wonder**........................	$12	■	Decca 31510
				#1 R&B hit in 1945 for both Pvt. Cecil Gant and Roosevelt Sykes			
9/28/63	17	8		32 **The Grass Is Greener /**			
9/28/63	70	5		33 **Sweet Impossible You**........................	$12	■	Decca 31539
				#3, 4, 13, 15, 19 & 33: written by **Ronnie Self**			
12/14/63+	12	11		34 **As Usual**..................*Lonely Lonely Lonely Me*	$12		Decca 31570
3/7/64	25	9		35 **Think**..................*The Waiting Game* (#101)	$12	■	Decca 31599
6/13/64	48	6		36 **Alone With You /**			
				#12, 18, 21, 29 & 36: written by **Jackie DeShannon**			
6/6/64	85	3		37 **My Dreams**........................	$12	■	Decca 31628
8/8/64	47	7		38 **When You Loved Me**..................*He's Sure To Remember Me* (#135)	$12	■	Decca 31654
10/17/64	17	9		39 **Is It True**..................*Just Behind The Rainbow*	$12	■	Decca 31690
12/19/64	8[X]	5		40 **Jingle Bell Rock**..................*Winter Wonderland* [X]	$15	■	Decca 31687
				X: 10/'64; 8/'67			
12/19/64	12[X]	2		41 **This Time Of The Year /** [X]			
12/26/64	24[X]	1		42 **Christmas Will Be Just Another Lonely Day**.................. [X]	$15	■	Decca 31688
1/16/65	45	7		43 **Thanks A Lot /**			
				#3 Country hit for Ernest Tubb in 1963			
1/9/65	87	4		44 **The Crying Game**........................	$10		Decca 31728
4/3/65	54	6		45 **Truly, Truly, True**..................*I Still Miss Someone*	$10	■	Decca 31762
5/29/65	13	13		46 **Too Many Rivers /**			
5/29/65	98	1		47 **No One**........................	$10		Decca 31792
10/9/65	33	9		48 **Rusty Bells**..................*If You Don't (Not Like You)*	$10		Decca 31849
7/2/66	77	4		49 **Ain't Gonna Cry No More**..................*It Takes One To Know One*	$10		Decca 31970
				written by **David Gates** (**Bread**)			
10/1/66	11	13		50 **Coming On Strong**..................*You Keep Coming Back To Me*	$10		Decca 32018
1/14/67	37	7		51 **Ride, Ride, Ride**..................*Lonely People Do Foolish Things*	$10		Decca 32079
				#36 Country hit for **Lynn Anderson** in 1966			
2/8/69	41	11		52 **Johnny One Time**..................*I Must Have Been Out Of My Mind*	$8	■	Decca 32428
				#36 Country hit for **Willie Nelson** in 1968			
5/17/69	84	3		53 **You Don't Need Me For Anything Anymore**..................*Bring Me Sunshine*	$7		Decca 32491
				some pressings released as "You Don't Need Me Anymore"			
5/30/70	97	2		54 **I Think I Love You Again**..................*Hello Love*	$7		Decca 32675
3/31/73	70	5		55 **Nobody Wins**..................*We Had A Good Thing Going*	$6		MCA 40003
				written by **Kris Kristofferson**			
				LEE, Curtis BUB **'61**			
				Born on 10/28/41 in Yuma, Arizona. Pop singer/songwriter.			
7/3/61	7	11		1 **Pretty Little Angel Eyes**..................*Gee How I Wish You Were Here*	$25		Dunes 2007
				The Halos (backing vocals)			
10/16/61	46	7		2 **Under The Moon Of Love**..................*Beverly Jean*	$25		Dunes 2008
				above 2 produced by Phil Spector			

LEE, Dick — '61

Born Richard Lee Beurer on 2/20/33 in Philadelphia, Pennsylvania. Pop ballad singer. Nicknamed "The Golden Boy." Featured vocalist for eight months on the *Ted Mack Matinee.*

DEBUT	PEAK	WKS	Gold	A-side (Chart Hit)	B-side	$	Sym	Label & Number
3/13/61	94	1		**Oh Mein Papa** Richard Rome (orch.); #1 hit for **Eddie Fisher** in 1954 as "Oh! My Pa-Pa"	*There's No Forgetting You*	$20		Blue Bell 503

LEE, Dickey — C&W/BUB/LP '62

Born Dickey Lipscomb on 9/21/36 in Memphis, Tennessee. Pop-country singer/songwriter. First recorded for Tampa Bay Records and then Sun Records in 1957. Charted 29 Country hits, 1971-82.

DEBUT	PEAK	WKS	Gold	A-side (Chart Hit)	B-side	$	Sym	Label & Number
8/25/62	6	14		1 **Patches** first recorded by Jimmy Isle in 1960 on Everest 19383	*More Or Less*	$15		Smash 1758
12/8/62+	14	12		2 **I Saw Linda Yesterday**	*The Girl I Can't Forget*	$15		Smash 1791
3/16/63	68	5		3 **Don't Wanna Think About Paula**	*Just A Friend*	$15		Smash 1808
5/15/65	14	13		4 **Laurie (Strange Things Happen)** inspired by a ghost story written by 15-year-old Cathie Harmon	*Party Doll*	$12		TCF Hall 102
9/4/65	73	6		5 **The Girl From Peyton Place** above 2 produced by **Ray Stevens**	*A Girl I Used To Know*	$10		TCF Hall 111
11/20/76+	52	10		6 **9,999,999 Tears**	*I Never Will Get Over You*	$5		RCA 10764

LEE, Jackie — POP '54

Born in May 1932 in Philadelphia, Pennsylvania. Nicknamed "Mr. Hot Piano." Hit #17 on the pop charts in 1954 with "Isle Of Capri."

DEBUT	PEAK	WKS	Gold	A-side (Chart Hit)	B-side	$	Sym	Label & Number
6/29/59	95	2		**Happy Vacation** Pep Lattanzi (orch.); organ instrumental styled after **Dave "Baby" Cortez**'s "The Happy Organ"	*The Hucklebuck* [I]	$15		Swan 4034

LEE, Jackie — BUB/R&B/LP '66

Born on 9/8/28 in Lake Charles, Louisiana. Earl Nelson of **Bob & Earl**. Took name from his wife's middle name, Jackie, and his middle name, Lee. Sang lead on the **Hollywood Flames**' "Buzz-Buzz-Buzz."

DEBUT	PEAK	WKS	Gold	A-side (Chart Hit)	B-side	$	Sym	Label & Number
11/20/65+	14	14		**The Duck**	*Let Your Conscience Be Your Guide*	$15		Mirwood 5502

LEE, Jaimie — '02

Born Jaimie Lee Hoffmann in 1990 in San Diego, California. Female dance singer.

DEBUT	PEAK	WKS	Gold	A-side (Chart Hit)	B-side	$	Sym	Label & Number
12/7/02	14^S	24		**Dance With Me** **JAIMIE LEE Featuring AJ and Young Blaze**	*(4 versions)*	$6	★	Ripe 17002

LEE, Johnny — C&W/BUB/LP '80

Born John Lee Ham on 7/3/46 in Texas City, Texas; raised in Alta Loma, Texas. Country singer/songwriter (charted 31 hits, 1975-89). Married to actress Charlene Tilton from 1982-84.

DEBUT	PEAK	WKS	Gold	A-side (Chart Hit)	B-side	$	Sym	Label & Number
7/12/80	5	21	●	1 **Lookin' For Love** CW^3 from the movie *Urban Cowboy* starring **John Travolta** and Debra Winger	*Lyin' Eyes* (**Eagles**)	$4	■	Full Moon/Asylum 47004
10/10/81	54	9		2 **Bet Your Heart On Me** CW^1	*Highways Run On Forever*	$4		Full Moon/Asylum 47215

LEE, Larry — see OZARK MOUNTAIN DAREDEVILS

LEE, Laura — R&B/BUB/LP '71

Born Laura Lee Rundless on 3/9/45 in Chicago, Illinois. R&B singer/songwriter.

DEBUT	PEAK	WKS	Gold	A-side (Chart Hit)	B-side	$	Sym	Label & Number
9/23/67	68	7		1 **Dirty Man**	*It's Mighty Hard*	$15		Chess 2013
12/2/67	84	2		2 **Wanted: Lover, No Experience Necessary /**				
12/23/67+	93	6		3 **Up Tight, Good Man**		$15		Chess 2030
9/4/71	36	11		4 **Women's Love Rights**	*Her Picture Matches Mine*	$8		Hot Wax 7105
1/22/72	94	1		5 **Love And Liberty**	*I Don't Want Nothing Old "But Money"*	$8		Hot Wax 7111
3/4/72	76	5		6 **Since I Fell For You** #3 R&B hit for **Annie Laurie & Paul Gayten** in 1947	*I Don't Want Nothing Old (But Money)*	$8		Hot Wax 7201
6/10/72	68	11		7 **Rip Off**	*Two Lovely Pillows*	$8		Hot Wax 7204
9/30/72	65	8		8 **If You Can Beat Me Rockin' (You Can Have My Chair)**	*If I'm Good Enough To Love (I'm Good Enough To Marry)*	$8		Hot Wax 7207

LEE, Leapy — see LEAPY LEE

LEE, Michele — AC '68

Born Michele Dusick on 6/24/42 in Los Angeles, California. Actress/singer. Played "Karen MacKenzie" on TV's *Knots Landing.*

DEBUT	PEAK	WKS	Gold	A-side (Chart Hit)	B-side	$	Sym	Label & Number
3/2/68	52	11		**L. David Sloane**	*Everybody Loves My Baby (But My Baby Don't Love Nobody But Me)*	$8		Columbia 44413

LEE, Peggy — MEM/POP/AC/BUB/LP '48

Born Norma Jean Egstrom on 5/26/20 in Jamestown, North Dakota. Died of a heart attack on 1/21/2002 (age 81). Jazz singer with Jack Wardlow band (1936-40), Will Osborne (1940-41) and **Benny Goodman** (1941-43). Went solo in March 1943. In movies *Mister Music* (1950), *The Jazz Singer* (1953) and *Pete Kelly's Blues* (1955). Co-wrote many songs with husband Dave Barbour (married, 1943-52). Charted 23 hits, 1945-52, including "Mañana" which was #1 for 9 weeks in 1948. Awarded nearly $4 million in court for her singing in the animated movie *Lady And The Tramp.* Won Grammy's Lifetime Achievement Award in 1995.

1)Fever 2)Is That All There Is 3)Mr. Wonderful

DEBUT	PEAK	WKS	Gold	A-side (Chart Hit)	B-side	$	Sym	Label & Number
3/3/56	14	20		1 **Mr. Wonderful** A:14 / T:23 / S:25 from the Broadway musical starring **Sammy Davis Jr.**	*Crazy In The Heart*	$15		Decca 29834
5/5/56	76	6		2 **Joey, Joey, Joey** T:76 from the Broadway musical *The Most Happy Fella* starring Robert Weede; Sy Oliver (orch., above 2)	*They Can't Take That Away From Me*	$12		Decca 29877
7/14/58	8	15		3 **Fever** H:8 / S:9 / A:10	*You Don't Know*	$12		Capitol 3998
11/3/58	63	6		4 **Light Of Love /** Ev. Freeman Singers (backing vocals)				
11/24/58	98	2		5 **Sweetheart**		$12		Capitol 4071
1/26/59	68	6		6 **Alright, Okay, You Win /** first popularized in 1955 by **Count Basie** and Joe Williams (Clef 89152)				
1/19/59	81	6		7 **My Man** #1 hit for Fanny Brice in 1922		$12		Capitol 4115
5/18/59	77	2		8 **Hallelujah, I Love Him So** #5 R&B hit for **Ray Charles** in 1956 as "Hallelujah, I Love Her So"; Jack Marshall (orch.: #3-8)	*I'm Lookin' Out The Window*	$12		Capitol 4189
1/5/63	54	9		9 **I'm A Woman** Benny Carter (orch.)	*Big Bad Bill (Is Sweet William Now)*	$10		Capitol 4888

DEBUT	PEAK	WKS	Gold	A-side (Chart Hit)	B-side	$	Sym	Label & Number
				LEE, Peggy — Cont'd				
2/27/65	93	3		10 **Pass Me By** Lou Levy (orch.); main theme from the movie *Father Goose* starring Cary Grant	*That's What It Takes*	$8		Capitol 5346
9/27/69	11	10		11 **Is That All There Is** AC[2] arranged and conducted by **Randy Newman**	*Me And My Shadow*	$6		Capitol 2602
				LEE, Tracey LP **'97** Born in Philadelphia, Pennsylvania. Male rapper.				
2/15/97	55	18		**The Theme (It's Party Time)** samples "Mt. Airy Groove" by Pieces Of A Dream	S:40 *(2 versions) / Repent*	$3	■	Universal 56114
				LEE and PAUL **'66** Songwriters Lee Pockriss (born on 1/20/27 in Brooklyn, New York) and **Paul Vance** (born on 11/4/29 in Brooklyn, New York). Wrote "Calcutta," "Itsy Bitsy Teenie Weenie Yellow Polkadot Bikini" and many other hits. Also see **Salvage**.				
3/30/59	100	1		1 **The Chick**	*Valentina, My Valentina* [N]	$15		Columbia 41337
10/8/66	97	2		2 **Dommage, Dommage (Too Bad, Too Bad)** **PAUL VANCE**	*Sexy*	$8		Scepter 12164
				LEFEVRE, Raymond, and His Orchestra BUB/AC/LP **'58** Born in 1922 in Paris, France. Conductor/pianist/flutist.				
10/27/58	30	9		1 **The Day The Rains Came**	*Butter Fingers* [I]	$10		Kapp 231
2/24/68	37	12		2 **Ame Caline (Soul Coaxing)** some pressings show title as "Soul Coaxing (Ame Caline)"	*If I Were A Carpenter* [I]	$6		4 Corners 147
				LEFT BANKE, The BUB/LP **'66** Rock group from Brooklyn, New York: Steve Martin (vocals), Rick Brand (guitar), Michael Brown (piano; **Stories**), Tom Finn (bass) and George Cameron (drums).				
9/10/66	5	13		1 **Walk Away Renee**	*I Haven't Got The Nerve*	$12		Smash 2041
1/7/67	15	10		2 **Pretty Ballerina**	*Lazy Day*	$12		Smash 2074
10/28/67	98	2		3 **Desiree'**	*I've Got Something On My Mind*	$12	■	Smash 2119
				LEFT EYE — see LIL' KIM				
				LEGACY OF SOUND featuring Meja **'93** Dance group from Sweden. Featuring producers Bag and Snowman, with female singer Meja.				
7/24/93	68	12		**Happy**	A:52 *(radio version)*	$4	■	RCA 62538
				LeGRAND, Michel LP **'72** Born on 2/24/32 in Paris, France. Conductor/arranger/pianist.				
1/29/72	56	8		**Brian's Song** from the TV movie *Brian's Song* starring Billy Dee Williams and James Caan (as Chicago Bears' Brian Piccolo, who died 6/16/70); lyrical version entitled "The Hands Of Time")	*Theme From "The Go-Between"* [I]	$5		Bell 45,171
				LEILA K with Rob 'n' Raz **'90** Born Leila Khalifi in Stockholm, Sweden, of Moroccan descent. Female rapper/dancer.				
2/17/90	48	11		**Got To Get**	S:37 *(remix)*	$4	■	Arista 9931
				LEKAKIS, Paul **'87** Born on 10/22/65 in Yonkers, New York. Disco singer/model/dancer.				
3/7/87	43	13		**Boom Boom (Let's Go Back To My Room)**	S:37 *Instrumental Room*	$5		ZYX 1266
				LEMMONS, Billy **'77** Born in Atlanta, Georgia. Country singer/songwriter. Record promotion man with several different companies.				
3/26/77	93	1		**Six Packs A Day**	*I Found A Him For Her* [N]	$6		Ariola America 7661
				LEMONHEADS, The ROK/BUB/LP **'93** Rock group formed in Boston, Massachusetts, by Evan Dando (vocals, guitar; born on 3/4/67). Numerous personnel changes with Dando the only constant.				
11/13/93	67	14		**Into Your Arms** MR[9]	A:63 *Miss Otis Regrets*	$4	■	Atlantic 87294
				LEMON PIPERS, The BUB/LP **'68** Psychedelic/bubblegum rock group from Oxford, Ohio: Ivan Browne (vocals, guitar), Bill Bartlett (guitar; **Ram Jam**), R.G. Nave (organ), Steve Walmsley (bass) and Bill Albaugh (drums). Albaugh died on 1/20/99 (age 53).				
12/16/67+	1[1]	13	●	1 **Green Tambourine**	*No Help From Me*	$10		Buddah 23
3/9/68	46	7		2 **Rice Is Nice**	*Blueberry Blue*	$10	■	Buddah 31
5/18/68	51	5		3 **Jelly Jungle (Of Orange Marmalade)**	*Shoeshine Boy*	$10		Buddah 41
				LEN LP **'99** Rock group from Toronto, Ontario, Canada: Marc Costanzo (vocals), his sister Sharon Costanzo, D. Rock, DJ Moves, Planet Pea and Drunkness Monster.				
8/14/99	9	25		**Steal My Sunshine** samples "More More More" by **Andrea True Connection**; from the movie *Go* starring Katie Holmes (soundtrack on Work 69851)	A:5			album cut
				LENNON, John ★134★ ROK/BUB/LP **'71** Born on 10/9/40 in Woolton, Liverpool, England. Shot to death on 12/8/80 in Manhattan, New York (age 40). Founding member of **The Beatles**. Married to Cynthia Powell from 8/23/62 to 11/8/68; their son is **Julian Lennon**. Met **Yoko Ono** (see #15 below) in 1966; married her on 3/20/69. Formed **Plastic Ono Band** in 1969. To New York City in 1971. Fought deportation from the U.S., 1972-76, until he was granted a permanent visa. Won Grammy's Lifetime Achievement Award in 1991. Inducted into the Rock and Roll Hall of Fame in 1994. *1)(Just Like) Starting Over 2)Whatever Gets You Thru The Night 3)Woman 4)Instant Karma 5)Imagine*				
7/26/69	14	9		1 **Give Peace A Chance** recorded in a hotel suite in Montreal; new version by **Peace Choir** (featuring son Sean) charted in 1991	*Remember Love*	$10	■	Apple 1809
11/15/69+	30	12		2 **Cold Turkey** **PLASTIC ONO BAND** (above 2) **Eric Clapton** (guitar)	*Don't Worry Kyoko (Mummy's Only Looking For A Hand In The Snow)*	$10	■	Apple 1813

DEBUT	PEAK	WKS	Gold	A-side (Chart Hit)...B-side	$	Sym	Label & Number
				LENNON, John — Cont'd			
2/28/70	3	13	●	3 **Instant Karma (We All Shine On)** ...*Who Has Seen The Wind?* (**Yoko Ono** Lennon)	$10	■	Apple 1818
				George Harrison (guitar) and **Billy Preston** (keyboards)			
1/9/71	43	6		4 **Mother** ...*Why*	$10	■	Apple 1827
4/3/71	11	9		5 **Power To The People** ...*Touch Me*	$10	■	Apple 1830
				JOHN LENNON/PLASTIC ONO BAND YOKO ONO/PLASTIC ONO BAND (above 2)			
10/23/71	3	9		6 **Imagine** ...*It's So Hard*	$10		Apple 1840
				JOHN LENNON PLASTIC ONO BAND			
12/25/71	3^X	10		7 **Happy Xmas (War Is Over)** ...*Listen, The Snow Is Falling* (Yoko Ono) [X]	$10	■	Apple 1842
				JOHN & YOKO and the PLASTIC ONO BAND with THE HARLEM COMMUNITY CHOIR			
				X: 3/'71; 6/'72; 6/'83; 6/'84; 5/'85; reissued on Capitol 1842 in 1980; #32 Adult Contemporary hit, Christmas 1995			
5/20/72	57	5		8 **Woman Is The Nigger Of The World** ...*Sisters O Sisters* (Yoko Ono/Plastic Ono Band)	$10	■	Apple 1848
				JOHN LENNON/PLASTIC ONO BAND With Elephants Memory and The Invisible Strings			
11/10/73	18	13		9 **Mind Games** ...*Meat City*	$8	■	Apple 1868
9/28/74	❶^1	15		10 **Whatever Gets You Thru The Night** ...*Beef Jerky*	$8		Apple 1874
				JOHN LENNON With The PLASTIC ONO NUCLEAR BAND			
				Elton John (backing vocal)			
12/21/74+	9	12		11 **#9 Dream** ...*What You Got*	$8		Apple 1878
3/15/75	20	9		12 **Stand By Me** ...*Move Over Ms. L*	$8		Apple 1881
11/1/80	❶^5	22	●	13 **(Just Like) Starting Over** *Kiss Kiss Kiss* (**Yoko Ono**)	$5	■	Geffen 49604
1/17/81	2^3	20	●	14 **Woman** ...*Beautiful Boys* (**Yoko Ono**)	$5	■	Geffen 49644
3/7/81	58	10		15 **Walking On Thin Ice** ...*It Happened*	$5	■	Geffen 49683
				YOKO ONO			
				picture sleeve included an insert with the song's lyrics			
3/28/81	10	17		16 **Watching The Wheels** ...*Yes, I'm Your Angel* (**Yoko Ono**)	$5	■	Geffen 49695
1/21/84	5	14		17 **Nobody Told Me** ...*O' Sanity* (**Yoko Ono**)	$5	■	Polydor 817254
3/31/84	55	6		18 **I'm Stepping Out** ...*Sleepless Night* (**Yoko Ono**)	$5	■	Polydor 821107
				#13-18: recorded in 1980; John and Yoko were remixing #15 the day he was killed			
10/15/88	80	4		19 **Jealous Guy** ...*Give Peace A Chance* (Plastic Ono Band)	$4	■	Capitol/EMI 44230
				JOHN LENNON AND THE PLASTIC ONO BAND (with The Flux Fiddlers)			
				from the movie documentary *Imagine: John Lennon*; originally released on John's *Imagine* album in 1971			
				LENNON, Julian ROK/LP '85			
				Born John Charles Julian Lennon on 4/8/63 in Liverpool, England. Pop-rock singer/songwriter/keyboardist. Son of Cynthia and **John Lennon**. First child to be born to any of **The Beatles**.			
10/20/84+	9	19		1 **Valotte** ...S:7 / A:7 *Well I Don't Know*	$4	■	Atlantic 89609
1/26/85	5	17		2 **Too Late For Goodbyes** AC^2 A:4 / S:7 *Let Me Be*	$4	■	Atlantic 89589
4/20/85	21	12		3 **Say You're Wrong** ...A:18 / S:27 *Big Mama*	$4	■	Atlantic 89567
8/3/85	54	6		4 **Jesse** ...*Bebop*	$4	■	Atlantic 89529
				all of above from the album *Valotte*			
3/22/86	32	13		5 **Stick Around** ...AR^3 *Always Think Twice*	$4	■	Atlantic 89437
5/13/89	93	4		6 **Now You're In Heaven** ...AR^1 *Second Time*	$4	■	Atlantic 88925
				LENNON SISTERS, The LP '56			
				Vocal group of sisters from Venice, California: Dianne, Peggy, Kathy and Janet Lennon. TV debut on **Lawrence Welk**'s Christmas Eve show in 1955. Left Welk in 1968.			
9/22/56	15	13		1 **Tonight You Belong To Me** ...T:15 / S:16 / A:16 / J:17 *When The White Lilacs Bloom Again* (Welk - #70)	$10		Coral 61701
				LAWRENCE WELK And His Sparkling Strings (with The Lennon Sisters and The Sparklers)			
9/25/61	56	7		2 **Sad Movies (Make Me Cry)** ...*I Don't Know Why*	$8		Dot 16255
				Billy Vaughn (orch.)			
				LENNOX, Annie ROK/BUB/LP '92			
				Born on 12/25/54 in Aberdeen, Scotland. Member of **The Tourists**. Lead singer of the **Eurythmics**. Appeared in the movie *Edward II* and TV movie *The Room*. Married to movie director Uri Fruchtman from 1988-2000. Recipient of *Billboard's Century Award in 2002*.			
11/5/88+	9	17		1 **Put A Little Love In Your Heart** A:8 / S:11 *A Great Big Piece Of Love* (The Spheres Of Celestial Influence)	$3	■	A&M 1255
				ANNIE LENNOX & AL GREEN			
				from the movie *Scrooged* starring Bill Murray; picture sleeve has a center-cut hole and pictures of Bill Murray			
5/16/92	34	20		2 **Why** ...A:38 / S:52 *Primitive*	$3	▮	Arista 12419
9/5/92	14	25		3 **Walking On Broken Glass** ...A:12 / S:24 *Don't Let Me Down*	$3	▮	Arista 12452
1/23/93	49	12		4 **Little Bird** ...S:53 / A:62 *Love Song For A Vampire* (ROK #24)	$3	▮	Arista 12508
3/11/95	23	21		5 **No More "I Love You's"** ...S:22 / A:25 *Ladies Of The Canyon*	$3	▮^{V}	Arista 12804
				originally recorded by The Lover Speaks			
8/19/95	66^S	2		6 **A Whiter Shade Of Pale** ...BUB:101 *No More "I Love You's" (remix)*	$4	▮	Arista 12850
				LEONETTI, Tommy AC/MEM/BUB '56			
				Born on 9/10/29 in Bergen, New Jersey. Died of cancer on 9/15/79 (age 50). Vocalist with Charlie Spivak and other big bands. Featured singer on TV's *Your Hit Parade*, 1957-58.			
12/10/55	99	1		1 **Heartless** ...T:99 *Sometime*	$15		Capitol 3274
				Dennis Farnon (orch.)			
6/9/56	23	10		2 **Free** ...A:23 / T:40 *It's Wild*	$15		Capitol 3442
				Neal Hefti (orch. and chorus)			
1/18/69	54	9		3 **Kum Ba Yah** ...*Cheatin' On Me*	$8		Decca 32421
				Bill Justis (orch.); based on a traditional Afro-American slave song			
				LE PAMPLEMOUSSE R&B/LP '78			
				Disco studio group led by producers Laurin Rinder and W. Michael Lewis. Group name is French for "The Grapefruit."			
11/26/77+	58	15		**Le Spank** ...*Monkey See, Monkey Do* (R&B #76) [I]	$5		AVI 153

LE ROUX
ROK/BUB/LP **'82**

Rock group from Louisiana: Jeff Pollard (vocals), Tony Haseldon (guitar), Rod Roddy (piano), Bobby Campo (horns), Leon Medica (bass) and David Peters (drums).

DEBUT	PEAK	WKS	Gold	A-side (Chart Hit)	B-side	$	Sym	Label & Number
6/24/78	59	14		1 **New Orleans Ladies** *[LOUISIANA'S LE ROUX]*	*Love Abductor*	$5		Capitol 4586
2/13/82	18	13		2 **Nobody Said It Was Easy (Lookin' For The Lights)**	*Can't You See It In My Eyes*	$4		RCA 13059
5/29/82	77	5		3 **The Last Safe Place On Earth**	*Make Believe*	$4		RCA 13224
3/19/83	81	4		4 **Carrie's Gone**	*Look Out*	$4		RCA 13456
				written about Carol Burnett's daughter, Carrie				

LESCHEA
'97

Born in Brooklyn, New York. Female singer. Pronounced: la-SHAY.

DEBUT	PEAK	WKS	Gold	A-side (Chart Hit)	B-side	$	Sym	Label & Number
6/14/97	90	2		**Fulton St.**	*How We Stay*	$3	▮	Warner 17572
				samples "New Generation" by Classical Too				

LES COMPAGNONS DE LA CHANSON
POP **'52**

"The Companions Of Song." Vocal group from France: Fred Mella, Jean-Pierre Calvert, Jacob Jaubert, Guy Bourguignon, Jo Frachon and Marc Herrand. Sometimes accompanied **Edith Piaf**. Hit #14 in 1952 with "The Three Bells."

DEBUT	PEAK	WKS	Gold	A-side (Chart Hit)	B-side	$	Sym	Label & Number
3/7/60	60	8		**Down By The Riverside**	*Margoton* [F]	$10		Capitol 4342
				traditional black American spiritual; #17 hit for **The Four Lads** in 1953				

LESTER, Ketty
BUB/LP **'62**

Born Revoyda Frierson on 8/16/34 in Hope, Arkansas. R&B singer/actress. Acted in several movies and TV shows.

DEBUT	PEAK	WKS	Gold	A-side (Chart Hit)	B-side	$	Sym	Label & Number
2/24/62	5	14		1 **Love Letters**	*I'm A Fool To Want You*	$15		Era 3068
				#11 hit for **Dick Haymes** in 1945 (title song from the movie starring Jennifer Jones)				
6/23/62	41	7		2 **But Not For Me**	*Once Upon A Time*	$12		Era 3080
				from the 1930 Gershwin musical *Girl Crazy* starring Ethel Merman				
10/13/62	90	1		3 **You Can't Lie To A Liar**	*River Of Salt*	$12		Era 3088
12/1/62	97	1		4 **This Land Is Your Land**	*Love Is For Everyone*	$12		Era 3094
				the Woody Guthrie folk classic				

LETTERMEN, The
★330★ AC/BUB/LP **'62**

Vocal group formed in 1958 in Los Angeles, California: Tony Butala (born on 11/20/38), Jim Pike (born on 11/6/36) and Bob Engemann (born on 2/19/36). Played the part of Paul Whiteman's Rhythm Boys in the Las Vegas review *Newcomers Of 1928*. First recorded for Warner Bros. in 1960. Engemann replaced by Gary Pike (Jim's brother) in 1968. The #1 Adult Contemporary vocal group of the 1960s. Tony sang with the Mitchell Boys Choir in the 1951 movie *On Moonlight Bay* and the 1954 movie *White Christmas*. Tony also sang with **Connie Stevens** in the group The Fourmost in 1954. Tony still performs with a touring Lettermen group today. Bob's nephew and niece recorded as **Christopher Paul And Shawn**.

1)Goin' Out Of My Head/Can't Take My Eyes Off You 2)When I Fall In Love 3)Hurt So Bad 4)The Way You Look Tonight 5)Theme From "A Summer Place"

DEBUT	PEAK	WKS	Gold	A-side (Chart Hit)	B-side	$	Sym	Label & Number
9/4/61	13	13		1 **The Way You Look Tonight**	*That's My Desire*	$12	■	Capitol 4586
				#1 hit for Fred Astaire in 1936 (from the movie *Swing Time*)				
11/20/61+	7	14		2 **When I Fall In Love** AC[1]	*Smile*	$12	■	Capitol 4658
				#20 hit for **Doris Day** in 1952				
2/17/62	17	11		3 **Come Back Silly Girl**	*A Song For Young Love*	$10	■	Capitol 4699
				first recorded by **Steve Lawrence** in 1960 on ABC-Paramount 10146 ($12)				
5/12/62	42	8		4 **How Is Julie?**	*Turn Around, Look At Me* (#105)	$10	■	Capitol 4746
8/18/62	81	4		5 **Silly Boy (She Doesn't Love You)**	*I Told The Stars*	$10	■	Capitol 4810
12/28/63+	98	2		6 **Where Or When**	*Be My Girl*	$8		Capitol 5091
				#1 hit for Hal Kemp in 1937				
6/26/65	16	9		7 **Theme From "A Summer Place"**	*Sealed With A Kiss*	$8		Capitol 5437
				from the 1959 movie *A Summer Place* starring Sandra Dee and Troy Donahue				
10/2/65	64	6		8 **Secretly**	*The Things We Did Last Summer*	$7	■	Capitol 5499
6/18/66	72	6		9 **I Only Have Eyes For You**	*Love Letters*	$7	■	Capitol 5649
				#2 hit for Ben Selvin in 1934 (from the movie musical *Dames* starring Joan Blondell); Jimmie Haskell (orch., all of above)				
1/28/67	72	4		10 **Our Winter Love**	*Warm*	$7		Capitol 5813
12/9/67+	7	15		11 **Goin' Out Of My Head/Can't Take My Eyes Off You**	*I Believe*	$7		Capitol 2054
3/23/68	52	8		12 **Sherry Don't Go**	*Never My Love*	$6		Capitol 2132
11/16/68	44	8		13 **Put Your Head On My Shoulder**	*Mary's Rainbow*	$6		Capitol 2324
5/31/69	12	21		14 **Hurt So Bad**	*Catch The Wind*	$6		Capitol 2482
10/18/69	64	5		15 **Shangri-La**	*When Summer Ends*	$6		Capitol 2643
12/27/69+	47	8		16 **Traces/Memories Medley**	*For Once In A Lifetime*	$6		Capitol 2697
4/4/70	93	2		17 **Hang On Sloopy**	*For Love*	$6		Capitol 2774
6/6/70	73	7		18 **She Cried**	*For Love*	$6		Capitol 2820
1/30/71	74	7		19 **Everything Is Good About You**	*It's Over*	$6		Capitol 3020
				#13-19: produced by **Al DeLory**				
10/9/71	42	10		20 **Love**	*Maybe Tomorrow*	$6	■	Capitol 3192
				written by **John Lennon**				

LETTERS TO CLEO
LP **'95**

Pop-rock group from Boston, Massachusetts: Kay Hanley (vocals), Michael Eisenstein and Greg McKenna (guitars), Scott Riebling (bass), and Stacy Jones (drums; **American Hi-Fi**).

DEBUT	PEAK	WKS	Gold	A-side (Chart Hit)	B-side	$	Sym	Label & Number
3/25/95	56	13		1 **Here & Now** S:69 / A:72	*Big Star*	$4	▮V	Giant 17913
9/9/95	88	3		2 **Awake**	*Acid Jed*	$4	▮V	Giant 17823
				"45" pressed in gold vinyl and issued in a clear plastic sleeve				

LEVEL 42
AC/LP **'86**

Pop-rock-dance group formed in Manchester, England: Mark King (vocals, bass), brothers Boon (guitar) and Phil (drums) Gould, and Mike Lindup (keyboards). The Goulds left in October 1987; replaced by Alan Murphy (guitar) and Gary Husband (drums). Murphy died of AIDS on 10/19/89.

DEBUT	PEAK	WKS	Gold	A-side (Chart Hit)	B-side	$	Sym	Label & Number
2/15/86	7	27		1 **Something About You** S:4 / A:8	*Coup D'etat*	$3		Polydor 883362
7/26/86	87	4		2 **Hot Water**	*Dream Crazy*	$3	■	Polydor 885155
4/4/87	12	18		3 **Lessons In Love** S:7 / A:13	*Hot Water (live)*	$3	■	Polydor 883956
8/8/87	83	4		4 **Running In The Family**	*Fashion Fever*	$3	■	Polydor 885957
				also released on Mercury 885957 in 1987				

DEBUT	PEAK	WKS	Gold	A-side (Chart Hit)..........B-side	$	Sym	Label & Number
	★528★			**LEVERT, Gerald/LEVERT** R&B/BUB/LP **'98** Born on 7/13/66 in Cleveland, Ohio. Lead singer of R&B trio **Levert** (with his brother Sean Levert and Marc Gordon). Son of **The O'Jays' Eddie Levert, Sr.** Discovered the R&B group **Troop**. Also see **LSG**. *1)Casanova 2)Taking Everything 3)Thinkin' Bout It*			
8/15/87	5	18	●	1 **Casanova** *[LEVERT]* S:5 / A:6 *Throwdown*	$3	■	Atlantic 89217
2/15/92	37	20		2 **Baby Hold On To Me**..........RB[1] S:20 / A:60 *Shootin' The Breeze* **GERALD LEVERT (with Eddie Levert)** "45": EastWest 98577; B-side: "School Me"	$3	▮V	EastWest 98639
3/20/93	78	11		3 **Good Ol' Days** *[LEVERT]*..........S:50 *(remix)*	$3	▮V	Atlantic 87379
6/5/93	46	17		4 **abc-123** *[LEVERT]*..........S:27 / A:60 *(album version)*	$3	▮V	Atlantic 87366
8/6/94	28	20		5 **I'd Give Anything**..........S:16 / A:42 *(3 album snippets)* #4 Country hit for Boy Howdy in 1994 as "She'd Give Anything"	$3	▮	EastWest 98244
11/26/94	98	5		6 **Can't Help Myself**..........*(album edit)*	$3	▮	EastWest 98208
3/18/95	65[S]	5		7 **Answering Service**..........BUB:105 *Nice & Wet*	$3	▮	EastWest 64458
10/21/95	75	10		8 **Already Missing You**..........S:40 *The Apple Don't Fall* **GERALD & EDDIE LEVERT, SR.**	$3	▮	EastWest 64374
3/9/96	71[S]	2		9 **Wind Beneath My Wings**..........BUB:103 *Get Your Thing Off* **GERALD LEVERT & EDDIE LEVERT, SR.**	$3	▮	EastWest 64306
9/5/98	12	16	●	10 **Thinkin' Bout It**..........S:2 *(remix w/Rah Digga)*	$4	★	EastWest 64091
11/7/98	54	4		11 **Money's Just A Touch Away**..........S:29 *(instrumental) / (acappella)* **MACK 10 featuring Gerald Levert** samples "Love Is Just A Touch Away" by **Freddie Jackson**	$3	▮	Hoo Bangin' 53327
1/30/99	11	12	●	12 **Taking Everything**..........S:4 *(remix w/Antoinette Roberson)*	$4	★	EastWest 64061
3/18/00	76	8		13 **Mr. Too Damn Good**..........A:66			album cut
8/19/00	89	5		14 **Baby U Are**..........S:18 *Spill A Little Love* above 2 from the album *G* on EastWest 62417	$4	★	EastWest 67066
				LEVINE, Hank, And Orchestra **'61** Born on 6/9/32 in Pittsburgh, Pennsylvania. Conductor/producer/arranger. Assembled the studio band **The Miniature Men.**			
10/9/61	98	1		**Image - Part 1**..........*Part 2* [I] originally released on Vogue International 112 in 1961 ($20)	$12		ABC-Paramount 10256
				LEVY, Marcy — see GIBB, Robin			
				LEWIS, Aaron — see STAIND			
				LEWIS, Barbara BUB/LP **'63** Born on 2/9/43 in South Lyon, Michigan. R&B singer/songwriter. *1)Hello Stranger 2)Baby, I'm Yours 3)Make Me Your Baby*			
5/4/63	3	14		1 **Hello Stranger** RB[2] *Think A Little Sugar* **The Dells** (backing vocals)	$20		Atlantic 2184
8/17/63	43	7		2 **Straighten Up Your Heart**..........*If You Love Her (#131)*	$15		Atlantic 2200
1/11/64	38	12		3 **Puppy Love /**			
12/28/63+	71	5		4 **Snap Your Fingers**..........	$15		Atlantic 2214
6/19/65	11	14		5 **Baby, I'm Yours**..........*I Say Love*	$15		Atlantic 2283
9/11/65	11	12		6 **Make Me Your Baby**..........*Love To Be Loved*	$15		Atlantic 2300
1/29/66	91	3		7 **Don't Forget About Me**..........*It's Magic*	$12		Atlantic 2316
7/23/66	28	8		8 **Make Me Belong To You**..........*Girls Need Loving Care*	$12		Atlantic 2346
10/29/66	74	6		9 **Baby What Do You Want Me To Do**..........*I Remember The Feeling*	$12		Atlantic 2361
4/22/67	72	5		10 **I'll Make Him Love Me**..........*Love Makes The World Go Round*	$12		Atlantic 2400
				LEWIS, Bobby BUB **'61** Born on 2/17/33 in Indianapolis, Indiana; raised in Detroit, Michigan. R&B singer/songwriter.			
4/24/61	❶[7]	23		1 **Tossin' And Turnin'**..........RB[10] *Oh Yes, I Love You*	$25		Beltone 1002
8/28/61	9	10		2 **One Track Mind**..........*Are You Ready*	$25		Beltone 1012
11/20/61	77	3		3 **What A Walk**..........*Cry No More* Joe Rene (orch., above 3)	$20		Beltone 1015
7/28/62	98	1		4 **I'm Tossin' And Turnin' Again**..........*Nothin' But The Blues*	$20		Beltone 2023
				LEWIS, Crystal — see FRANKLIN, Kirk			
				LEWIS, Donna LP **'96** Born in Cardiff, Wales. White Adult Contemporary singer/songwriter.			
6/22/96	2[9]	41	●	1 **I Love You Always Forever**..........A:❶[13] / S:4 *(remix) / Simone* inspired by the H.E. Bates novel *Love For Lydia*	$3	▮	Atlantic 87072
12/14/96+	41	15		2 **Without Love**..........A:57 / S:71 *Silent World*	$3	▮	Atlantic 87028
11/8/97+	45	20		3 **At The Beginning**..........S:60 / A:60 *(instrumental)* **DONNA LEWIS & RICHARD MARX** from the animated movie *Anastasia*	$3	▮	Atlantic 84037
				LEWIS, Ephraim R&B **'92** Born in 1968 in Birmingham, England (Jamaican parents). Committed suicide on 3/18/94 (age 26). Male R&B singer.			
9/12/92	72	9		**Drowning In Your Eyes**..........A:66 *Dreams From The Trees*	$3	▮	Elektra 64710
	★234★			**LEWIS, Gary, And The Playboys** BUB/LP **'65** Born Gary Levitch on 7/31/45 in Brooklyn, New York. Pop singer/drummer. Son of comedian **Jerry Lewis**. The Playboys consisted of Al Ramsey and John West (guitars), David Walker (keyboards) and David Costell (bass). *1)This Diamond Ring 2)Count Me In 3)Save Your Heart For Me*			
1/16/65	❶[2]	12	●	1 **This Diamond Ring** *Tijuana Wedding* also issued with "Hard To Find" as the B-side	$10		Liberty 55756
4/3/65	2[2]	11		2 **Count Me In**..........*Little Miss Go-Go*	$10		Liberty 55778
7/3/65	2[1]	11		3 **Save Your Heart For Me**..........AC[3] *Without A Word Of Warning* first recorded by **Brian Hyland** (B-side of his 1963 hit "I'm Afraid To Go Home")	$10		Liberty 55809
9/25/65	4	11		4 **Everybody Loves A Clown**..........*Time Stands Still*	$10	■	Liberty 55818

DEBUT	PEAK	WKS	Gold	A-side (Chart Hit)...B-side	$	Sym	Label & Number
				LEWIS, Gary, And The Playboys — Cont'd			
12/11/65+	3	12		5 She's Just My Style...*I Won't Make That Mistake Again*	$10	■	Liberty 55846
3/5/66	9	9		6 Sure Gonna Miss Her...*I Don't Wanna Say Goodnight*	$10	■	Liberty 55865
5/14/66	8	8		7 Green Grass...*I Can Read Between The Lines*	$10	■	Liberty 55880
7/30/66	13	7		8 My Heart's Symphony...*Tina (I Held You In My Arms)*	$10	■	Liberty 55898
10/8/66	15	8		9 (You Don't Have To) Paint Me A Picture...*Looking For The Stars*	$10	■	Liberty 55914
12/17/66+	21	9		10 Where Will The Words Come From...*May The Best Man Win*	$10		Liberty 55933
3/11/67	43	6		11 The Loser (With A Broken Heart)...*Ice Melts In The Sun (#121)* all of above arranged by **Leon Russell**	$8	■	Liberty 55949
5/13/67	39	6		12 Girls In Love...*Let's Be More Than Friends*	$8		Liberty 55971
8/12/67	52	7		13 Jill...*New In Town*	$8		Liberty 55985
6/22/68	19	14		14 Sealed With A Kiss...*Sara Jane* first recorded by **The Four Voices** in 1960 on Columbia 41699	$8		Liberty 56037
4/5/69	63	12		15 Rhythm Of The Rain...*Mister Memory* all of above (except #7 & 11-13) produced by Snuff Garrett	$8		Liberty 56093
				LEWIS, Glenn R&B/LP **'02** Born in Toronto, Ontario, Canada. R&B singer/songwriter.			
12/1/01+	30	20		Don't You Forget It...A:28 *(2 versions)*	$6	T	Red Star/Epic 79649
				LEWIS, Huey, and The News ★96★ ROK/AC/BUB/LP **'84** Born Hugh Cregg III on 7/5/50 in New York; raised in Danville, California. Joined the country-rock group Clover in the late 1970s. Formed the News in San Francisco: Lewis (vocals, harmonica), Chris Hayes (guitar), Johnny Colla (sax, guitar), Sean Hopper (keyboards), Mario Cipollina (bass; brother of **Quicksilver Messenger Service** guitarist John Cipollina) and Bill Gibson (drums). Lewis acted in the movie *Short Cuts* and had a cameo appearance in *Back To The Future*. *1)Stuck With You 2)The Power Of Love 3)Jacob's Ladder 4)Hip To Be Square 5)Perfect World*			
2/6/82	7	17		1 Do You Believe In Love...*Is It Me*	$4	□	Chrysalis 2589
5/15/82	36	11		2 Hope You Love Me Like You Say You Do...*Whatever Happened To True Love*	$4	■	Chrysalis 2604
8/14/82	41	9		3 Workin' For A Livin'...*(live version)*	$4		Chrysalis 2630
9/10/83	8	21		4 Heart And Soul...AR[1] *You Crack Me Up* originally "Bubbled Under" (#102) in 1981 by **Exile**	$3	■	Chrysalis 42726
1/14/84	6	19	●	5 I Want A New Drug...*Finally Found A Home* (ROK #41)	$3	■	Chrysalis 42766
4/21/84	6	20		6 The Heart Of Rock & Roll...*Workin' For A Livin' (live)*	$3	■	Chrysalis 42782
7/21/84	6	17		7 If This Is It...S:20 *Change Of Heart*	$3	■	Chrysalis 42803
10/20/84	18	15		8 Walking On A Thin Line...A:12 / S:28 *The Only One* above 5 from the album *Sports*	$3	■	Chrysalis 42825
6/29/85	❶[2]	19	●	9 The Power Of Love...AR[2] A:❶[3] / S:❶[1] *Bad Is Bad* from the movie *Back To The Future* starring Michael J. Fox; some pressings titled as "Power Of Love"	$3	■	Chrysalis 42876
8/2/86	❶[3]	19		10 Stuck With You AC[3] A:❶[3] / S:❷[2] *Don't Ever Tell Me That You Love Me*	$3	■	Chrysalis 43019
10/18/86	3	16		11 Hip To Be Square...AR[1] S:❶[1] / A:3 *Some Of My Lies Are True*	$3	■	Chrysalis 43065
1/17/87	❶[1]	15		12 Jacob's Ladder...A:❶[1] / S:2 *The Heart Of Rock & Roll (live)* written by **Bruce Hornsby**	$3	■	Chrysalis 43097
4/4/87	9	14		13 I Know What I Like...S:10 / A:10 *Forest For The Trees* members of the 1985 San Francisco 49'ers football team (backing vocals: #11 & 13)	$3	■	Chrysalis 43108
7/18/87	6	16		14 Doing It All For My Baby...A:5 / S:9 *Naturally* above 5 from the album *Fore!*	$3	■	Chrysalis 43143
7/16/88	3	15		15 Perfect World...A:❶[1] / S:3 *Slammin'*	$3	■	Chrysalis 43265
10/8/88	25	11		16 Small World...S:25 / A:26 *Small World (Part One & Two)*	$3	■	Chrysalis 43306
1/21/89	47	8		17 Give Me The Keys (And I'll Drive You Crazy)...S:40 *It's All Right (live)*	$3	■	Chrysalis 43335
4/27/91	11	13		18 Couple Days Off...A:16 / S:25 *Time Ain't Money* "45": Collectables 6318; B-side: "I Want A New Drug"	$3	▌V	EMI 50346
7/20/91	21	13		19 It Hit Me Like A Hammer...A:37 *Do You Love Me, Or What?* "45": Collectables 6316; B-side: Do You Believe In Love"	$3	▌V	EMI 50364
7/31/93	37[A]	16		20 It's Alright... from the album *People Get Ready: A Tribute To Curtis Mayfield* on Shanachie 9004; see B-side of #17 above for "live" version			album cut
5/14/94	44	12		21 (She's) Some Kind Of Wonderful...A:35 *Good Morning Little School Girl*	$3	▌V	Elektra 64542
8/27/94	54	20		22 But It's Alright...A:38 *Flip Flop & Fly* #20 is a remake of **The Impressions** 1963 hit; #22 is a remake of the **J.J. Jackson** 1966 hit	$3	▌	Elektra 64524
				LEWIS, Jerry POP/LP **'56** Born Joseph Levitch on 3/16/25 in Newark, New Jersey. Comedian/actor. Father of **Gary Lewis**. Formed comedy duo with **Dean Martin** in 1946. Starred in several movies.			
11/24/56	10	19	●	1 Rock-A-Bye Your Baby With A Dixie Melody...S:10 / T:12 / J:13 / A:17 *Come Rain Or Come Shine* Buddy Bregman (orch.); #1 hit for Al Jolson in 1918	$15		Decca 30124
4/27/57	68	1		2 It All Depends On You...T:68 *Let Me Sing And I'm Happy* **Jack Pleis** (orch.); #2 hit for Paul Whiteman in 1927	$15		Decca 30263
	★411★			**LEWIS, Jerry Lee** C&W/BUB/R&B/LP **'57** Born on 9/29/35 in Ferriday, Louisiana. Played piano since age nine, professionally since age 15. First recorded for Sun in 1956. Appeared in the movie *Jamboree!* in 1957. Career waned in 1958 after marriage to 13-year-old cousin, Myra Gale Brown, daughter of his bass player. Made comeback in Country music beginning in 1968. Charted 65 Country hits, 1957-89. Nicknamed "The Killer," Lewis has been surrounded by personal tragedies in the past two decades, survived several serious illnesses. Cousin to Country singer **Mickey Gilley** and former TV evangelist Jimmy Swaggart. Inducted into the Rock and Roll Hall of Fame in 1986. Jerry's early career is documented in the 1989 movie *Great Balls Of Fire* starring Dennis Quaid. *1)Great Balls Of Fire 2)Whole Lot Of Shakin' Going On 3)Breathless*			
6/24/57	3	29	●	1 Whole Lot Of Shakin' Going On...RB[2] / CW[2] S:3 / T:3 / A:9 *It'll Be Me* the first song played on the national edition of *American Bandstand*; first recorded by **Big Maybelle** in 1955 on Okeh 7060 ($50)	$40		Sun 267

DEBUT	PEAK	WKS	Gold	A-side (Chart Hit)....B-side	$	Sym	Label & Number
				LEWIS, Jerry Lee — Cont'd			
11/25/57+	2^{4}	21	●	2 **Great Balls Of Fire** / CW^{2} T:2 / S:2 / A:9			
1/20/58	95	1		3 **You Win Again** ....T:95 / S:flip	$40	■	Sun 281
				the Hank Williams penned tune hit #13 in 1952 for **Tommy Edwards**			
3/3/58	7	15		4 **Breathless** ....T:7 / S:9 / A:23 *Down The Line*	$40		Sun 288
6/2/58	21	11		5 **High School Confidential** ....T:21 / S:22 *Fools Like Me* (R&B #11)	$30	■	Sun 296
				title song from the movie starring Russ Tamblyn (song introduced by Lewis in the movie)			
9/15/58	52	5		6 **Break-Up** / H:52			
9/8/58	85	1		7 **I'll Make It All Up To You**....H:85	$30		Sun 303
				above 2 written by **Charlie Rich**			
1/19/59	93	1		8 **I'll Sail My Ship Alone** ....*It Hurt Me So*	$30		Sun 312
				#1 Country hit for Moon Mullican in 1950			
4/3/61	30	8		9 **What'd I Say** ....*Livin' Lovin' Wreck*	$25		Sun 356
				JERRY LEE LEWIS And His Pumping Piano (all of above - except #1)			
9/15/62	95	3		10 **Sweet Little Sixteen** ....*How's My Ex Treating You* (#114)	$25		Sun 379
4/11/64	98	1		11 **I'm On Fire**....*Bread And Butter Man*	$35		Smash 1886
11/21/64	91	1		12 **High Heel Sneakers** ....*You Went Back On Your Word*	$15		Smash 1930
3/30/68	97	2		13 **Another Place Another Time**....*Walking The Floor Over You*	$10		Smash 2146
7/6/68	94	3		14 **What's Made Milwaukee Famous (Has Made A Loser Out Of Me)** ....*All The Good Is Gone*	$10		Smash 2164
11/27/71+	40	10		15 **Me And Bobby McGee**....*Would You Take Another Chance On Me* (C&W #1)	$8		Mercury 73248
3/4/72	43	10		16 **Chantilly Lace**....CW^{3} *Think About It Darlin'* (C&W flip)	$8		Mercury 73273
7/22/72	95	3		17 **Turn On Your Love Light** ....*Lonely Weekends* (C&W #11)	$8		Mercury 73296
4/7/73	41	10		18 **Drinking Wine Spo-Dee O'Dee** ....*Rock & Roll Medley*	$8		Mercury 73374
				#2 R&B hit for Stick McGhee in 1949			
				LEWIS, Jimmy — see CHARLES, Ray			
	★440★			**LEWIS, Ramsey** R&B/BUB/AC/LP '65			
				Born on 5/27/35 in Chicago, Illinois. R&B-jazz pianist. His trio included Eldee Young (bass) and Isaac "Red" Holt (drums). Disbanded in 1965. Young and Holt then formed **The Young-Holt Trio**. Lewis re-formed his trio with Cleveland Eaton (bass) and **Maurice White** (drums). White later formed **Earth, Wind & Fire**.			
				1)The "In" Crowd 2)Hang On Sloopy 3)Wade In The Water			
				RAMSEY LEWIS TRIO:			
10/10/64	63	6		1 **Something You Got**....*My Babe* [I-L]	$10		Argo 5481
				written by **Chris Kenner**			
7/31/65	5	16		2 **The "In" Crowd** *Since I Fell For You* [I-L]	$10		Argo 5506
11/20/65	11	8		3 **Hang On Sloopy**....*Movin' Easy* [I-L]	$10		Cadet 5522
12/25/65	21^{X}	1		4 **Jingle Bells**....*Egg Nog* [X-I-L]	$10		Cadet 5488
				originally released in 1964 on Argo 5488 ($10)			
1/22/66	29	6		5 **A Hard Day's Night**....*All My Love Belongs To You* [I-L]	$8		Cadet 5525
3/26/66	70	5		6 **Hi Heel Sneakers - Pt. 1** ....*Pt. 2* [I-L]	$8		Cadet 5531
				RAMSEY LEWIS:			
7/9/66	19	13		7 **Wade In The Water**....*Ain't That Peculiar* (#129) [I]	$8		Cadet 5541
10/15/66	49	5		8 **Up Tight**....*Money In The Pocket* [I]	$8		Cadet 5547
12/17/66	23^{X}	2		9 **Winter Wonderland** *[RAMSEY LEWIS TRIO]*....*Santa Claus Is Coming To Town* [X-I]	$10		Cadet 5377
				originally released in 1960 on Argo 5377 ($12)			
12/24/66+	74	4		10 **Day Tripper** ....*Rudolph The Red-Nosed Reindeer* [I]	$7		Cadet 5553
2/11/67	67	6		11 **One, Two, Three**....*Down By The Riverside* [I]	$7		Cadet 5556
9/23/67	84	4		12 **Dancing In The Street**....*Girl Talk* [I-L]	$7		Cadet 5573
11/11/67	49	6		13 **Soul Man** ....*Struttin' Lightly* [I]	$7		Cadet 5583
8/31/68	98	2		14 **Since You've Been Gone**....*Les Fleur* [I]	$7		Cadet 5609
9/27/69	76	8		15 **Julia** ....*Do What You Wanna* [I]	$7		Cadet 5640
				written by **John Lennon** (on **The Beatles**' 1968 *White Album*)			
3/17/73	93	3		16 **Kufanya Mapenzi (Making Love)** ....*What It Is!* [I]	$5		Columbia 45766
1/18/75	50	6		17 **Hot Dawgit**....*Tambura* (Lewis) [I]	$5		Columbia 10056
3/22/75	44	7		18 **Sun Goddess**....*Jungle Strut* (Lewis) [I]	$5		Columbia 10103
				RAMSEY LEWIS and EARTH, WIND & FIRE (above 2)			
1/24/76	69	4		19 **What's The Name Of This Funk (Spider Man)**....*Juaacklyn*	$5		Columbia 10235
				LEWIS, Shirley '89			
				Born in London, England. Black dance singer. Worked with **Elton John**, mid-1980s. Sister of singer Linda Lewis.			
10/28/89	84	6		**Realistic** ....*Life After Love*	$3		Vendetta 1448
				LEWIS & CLARKE EXPEDITION, The BUB '67			
				Folk duo: Travis Lewis (**Michael Martin Murphey**) and Owen "Boomer" Clarke (**Boomer Castleman**).			
8/26/67	64	4		1 **I Feel Good (I Feel Bad)** ....*Blue Revelations*	$10	■	Colgems 1006
5/3/75	33	8		2 **Judy Mae**....*Three Feet High And Growin'*	$6		Mums 6038
				BOOMER CASTLEMAN			
				LFO BUB/LP '99			
				White pop vocal trio from Orlando, Florida: Rich Cronin, David Brian and Brad Young. Brian and Young left in 1999; replaced by Brad Fischetti and Devin Lima.			
11/7/98	70	4		1 **If I Can't Have You** ....S:31 *(talk intro)*	$3	▌	Logic 62166
				L.F.O. (Lyte Funkie Ones) (featuring Kayo)			
				samples "The Glow Of Love" by **Change**; rap version of **Yvonne Elliman**'s #1 hit in 1978			
7/17/99	3	17	▲	2 **Summer Girls** S:❶^{6} / A:71 *(instrumental) / Can't Have You*	$4	★	Logic/Arista 13692
				B-side "Can't Have You" is the same version as #1 above			
11/20/99	10	17	●	3 **Girl On TV**....S:2 *(instrumental) / All I Need To Know*	$4	★	Logic/Arista 13756
4/15/00	61	5		4 **I Don't Wanna Kiss You Goodnight** ....S:10 *(remix) / Girl On TV (remix)*	$4	★	Arista 13824
8/5/00	84	4		5 **West Side Story** ....S:6 *(remix) / Summer Girls 2000 (remix)*	$4	★	Arista 13858
				above 4 from the album *LFO*			

DEBUT	PEAK	WKS	Gold	A-side (Chart Hit)..........B-side	$	Sym	Label & Number
				LFO — Cont'd			
8/25/01	44	18		6 **Every Other Time**..........A:49		V	album cut
2/9/02	40^S	5		7 **Life Is Good**..........*(remix w/***M.O.P.***) / Dandelion*	$4	★^{V}	J Records 21153
				above 2 from the album *Life Is Good* on J Records 20006; 45" issued for above 2 on J Records 21091			
				LIA, Orsa '79 Born in Virginia. Female pop singer. Sang several TV jingles in the mid-1970s.			
3/31/79	84	5		**I Never Said I Love You**..........AC^1 *No Walls, No Ceilings, No Floors*	$5		Infinity 50,004
				LIBERTY CITY Fla. '00 R&B vocal group from Liberty City, Florida: City, KB, TJ and Dream.			
8/14/99	68^S	3		1 **24-7**..........*(remix) / (5 album snippets)*	$4	★	Harrell/Jive 42592
10/21/00	60^S	5		2 **Who's She Lovin' Now?**..........*Come On Back*	$4	★	Harrell/Jive 42728
3/31/01	68^S	1		3 **I Met Her In Miami**..........*(radio mix)*	$4	★	Harrell/Jive 42881
				LIFEHOUSE ROK/BUB/LP '01 Rock trio from Malibu, California: Jason Wade (vocals, guitar), Sergio Andrade (bass) and Rick Woolstenhulme (drums).			
2/10/01	2^4	54		1 **Hanging By A Moment**..........MR^3 A:$❶^1$			album cut
				from the album *No Name Face* on DreamWorks 50231			
11/16/02	71	14		2 **Spin**..........*What's Wrong With That*	$4	★	DreamWorks 450803
				LIFER'S '02 Rap group produced by **Keith Murray**.			
4/27/02	41^S	10		**Beat Your Chest!!**..........*Big Thangz Poppin!! / Sheeese!! / All My Niggas!!*	$8	★*	All Out 46332
				LIGHT, Enoch, & The Light Brigade MEM/AC/LP '58 Born on 8/18/07 in Canton, Ohio. Died on 7/31/78 (age 70). Conductor of own orchestra, The Light Brigade, since 1935. Pioneer in stereo recording. President of Grand Award label and managing director for Command Records. Charted 25 albums, 1959-71.			
11/10/58	48	7		1 **I Want To Be Happy Cha Cha**..........*Cara Mia Cha Cha (Ciribiribin)* [I]	$12		Grand Award 1020
				arrangement styled after **Perez Prado**'s "Patricia"; #2 hit for Vincent Lopez in 1925			
6/15/59	99	1		2 **With My Eyes Wide Open I'm Dreaming**..........*I Cried For You* [I]	$12		Grand Award 1032
				#3 hit for Leo Reisman in 1934			
				LIGHTER SHADE OF BROWN, A BUB/LP '92 Hispanic rap duo from Riverside, California: Robert Gutierrez and Bobby Ramirez.			
7/20/91	59	12		1 **Latin Active**..........A:72 *(extended club mix)*	$4	▌	Pump 15168
				featuring Teardrop & Shiro			
11/30/91+	39	20		2 **On A Sunday Afternoon**..........S:24 / A:39 *(remix)*	$4	▌	Pump 15186
				featuring Shiro and Huggy Boy; basslines and samples from "Groovin'," "Crystal Blue Persuasion" and "Just My Imagination"			
12/12/92+	57	19		3 **Homies**..........S:34 / A:52 *Low Rider Madness*	$4	▌	Pump 19134
				samples "The Tracks Of My Tears" by **The Miracles**			
2/19/94	43	18		4 **Hey D.J.**..........S:36 / A:42 *(remix)*	$3	▌	Mercury 858402
				from the movie *Mi Vida Loca* starring Angel Aviles and Seidy Lopez			
	★459★			**LIGHTFOOT, Gordon** AC/BUB/C&W/LP '74 Born on 11/17/38 in Orillia, Ontario, Canada. Adult Contemporary-folk singer/songwriter/guitarist. Worked on *Country Hoedown*, CBC-TV series. Teamed with Jim Whalen as the Two Tones in the mid-1960s. Wrote hit "Early Mornin' Rain" for **Peter, Paul and Mary**. First recorded for Chateau in 1962. *1)Sundown 2)The Wreck Of The Edmund Fitzgerald 3)If You Could Read My Mind*			
12/26/70+	5	15		1 **If You Could Read My Mind**..........AC^1 *Poor Little Allison*	$6		Reprise 0974
6/19/71	64	7		2 **Talking In Your Sleep**..........*Nous Vivons Ensemble*	$6		Reprise 1020
9/11/71	98	2		3 **Summer Side Of Life**..........*Love & Maple Syrup*	$6		Reprise 1035
5/27/72	58	11		4 **Beautiful**..........*Don Quixote*	$6		Reprise 1088
4/13/74	$❶^1$	18	●	5 **Sundown**..........AC^2 *Too Late For Prayin'*	$5		Reprise 1194
8/31/74	10	14		6 **Carefree Highway**..........AC^1 *Seven Island Suite*	$5		Reprise 1309
3/29/75	26	11		7 **Rainy Day People**..........AC^1 *Cherokee Bend*	$5		Reprise 1328
8/28/76	2^2	21		8 **The Wreck Of The Edmund Fitzgerald**..........*The House You Live In*	$5		Reprise 1369
				true story of an ore vessel, named after a Milwaukee civic leader, that sank in Lake Superior on 11/10/75			
2/19/77	65	4		9 **Race Among The Ruins**..........*Protocol*	$5		Reprise 1380
2/11/78	33	12		10 **The Circle Is Small (I Can See It In Your Eyes)**..........*Sweet Guinevere*	$4		Warner 8518
				first pressings show title simply as "The Circle Is Small"			
4/3/82	50	8		11 **Baby Step Back**..........*Thank You For The Promises*	$4		Warner 50012
				all of above written by Lightfoot			
				LIGHTHOUSE BUB/LP '71 Rock group from Toronto, Ontario, Canada. Featured a fluctuating lineup of at least 10 members. Core members: Bob McBride (vocals), Skip Prokop (vocals, drums; The Paupers), Ralph Cole (guitar), Paul Hoffert (keyboards), Howard Shore (sax), Louie Yacknin (bass), Don Dinovo (viola) and Dick Armin (cello). Shore went on to become the original musical director of TV's *Saturday Night Live*. McBride died on 2/20/98 (age 51).			
9/11/71	24	12		1 **One Fine Morning**..........*Little Kind Words*	$6		Evolution 1048
12/11/71+	64	7		2 **Take It Slow (Out In The Country)**..........*Sweet Lullabye*	$6		Evolution 1052
4/29/72	93	2		3 **I Just Wanna Be Your Friend**..........*1849*	$6		Evolution 1058
10/7/72	34	12		4 **Sunny Days**..........*Lonely Places*	$6		Evolution 1069
11/3/73	53	8		5 **Pretty Lady**..........*Bright Side*	$5		Polydor 14198
				LIGHTNING SEEDS, The ROK/LP '90 Group is actually singer/producer Ian Broudie (born on 8/4/58 in Liverpool, England).			
5/19/90	31	15		1 **Pure**..........S:24 / A:38 *(no B-side)*	$3	▌	MCA 53816
4/25/92	98	2		2 **The Life Of Riley**..........*(3 album snippets)*	$3	▌	MCA 54195
				LIL — also see LITTLE			

DEBUT	PEAK	WKS	Gold	A-side (Chart Hit)...B-side	$	Sym	Label & Number
				LIL BOW WOW R&B/LP **'00** Born Shad Moss on 3/9/87 in Columbus, Ohio. Teen male rapper. Starred in the movie *Like Mike*.			
8/19/00	20	20		1 **Bounce With Me** RB[1] S:7 / A:29 *(4 versions w/***Lil Mo** & **R.O.C.***)* **LIL BOW WOW (featuring Xscape)** from the movie *Big Momma's House* starring Martin Lawrence	$7	★*	So So Def 79476
11/25/00+	21	20		2 **Bow Wow (That's My Name)**......S:2 / A:26 *Ghetto Girls*	$4	★V	So So Def 79556
4/14/01	75	7		3 **Puppy Love**......A:66 **LIL BOW WOW Featuring Jagged Edge** samples "Kanday" by **LL Cool J**; "45" issued for above 2 on So So Def 79556		V	album cut
8/18/01	91	4		4 **Ghetto Girls**......S:50 *(2 versions) / Puppy Love* (w/Tigah) samples "Covert Action" by **The Crusaders**; first released as the B-side of #2 above; above 4 from the album *Beware Of Dog* on So So Def/Columbia 69981	$7	★*	So So Def 79612
1/5/02	93	5		5 **Thank You**......*(4 versions)* **LIL BOW WOW Featuring Jagged Edge And Fundisha** samples "I'm Not The One" by **The Cars**	$6	T	So So Def 79685
4/13/02	72	7		6 **Take Ya Home**......S:47 / A:68 *Thank You* Fundisha (female vocal)	$8	◗	So So Def 79727
				LIL' CEASE LP **'99** Born James Lloyd in 1977 in Brooklyn, New York. Male rapper.			
3/29/97	52^A	8		1 **Crush On You**...... **LIL' KIM Featuring Lil' Cease** samples "Rain Dance" by **Jeff Lorber**; from **Lil' Kim**'s album *Hard Core* on Undeas 92733			album cut
8/28/99	41^S	6		2 **Play Around**......*(instrumental)* **LIL' CEASE Featuring Lil' Kim, Mr. Bristal and Joe Hooker** samples "One More Chance" by **The Notorious B.I.G.**	$5	★	Queen Bee/Undeas 84482
				LIL' J LP **'02** Born Jonathan McDaniel in 1985 in Long Beach, California. Teen male rapper.			
12/8/01+	6^S	37		**It's The Weekend**......*(instrumental)* **LIL' J featuring Kandi**	$5	★+	Hollywood 64060
				LIL JON & the East Side Boyz R&B/LP **'00** Black hip-hop group led by Jonathan "Lil Jon" Smith. The East Side Boyz are: Lil Bo, Big Sam and Playa Poncho.			
4/8/00	35^S	28		1 **I Like Dem Girlz**......*(2 versions) / Just A Bit*h* (w/**Too $hort** & Chyna)	$7	★*	BME 7777
8/25/01	94	3		2 **Bia' Bia'**......*(2 versions)* **LIL JON & the East Side Boyz featuring Ludacris, Big Kap, Too $hort & Chyna**	$6	T	BME 7780
				LIL' KEKE LP **'98** Born Marcus Edwards in Houston, Texas. Male rapper.			
4/25/98	71^S	2		**Southside**......BUB:101 *(instrumental)* samples "Friends" by **Whodini**	$5	▮	Jam Down 482000
	★375★			**LIL' KIM** R&B/LP **'97** Born Kimberly Jones on 7/11/75 in Brooklyn, New York. Female rapper. Member of **Junior M.A.F.I.A.** *1)Lady Marmalade 2)Not Tonight 3)No Time*			
4/27/96	92	5		1 **No More Games**......*(album version)* **SKINDEEP Featuring Li'l Kim of Junior M.A.F.I.A.** samples "In All My Wildest Dreams" by Joe Sample	$4	▮	Loose Cannon 852706
11/9/96+	18	20	●	2 **No Time**......S:7 *(instrumental)* **LIL' KIM Featuring Puff Daddy** samples "Take Me Just As I Am" by **Lyn Collins**	$4	▮	Undeas/Big Beat 98044
3/29/97	52^A	8		3 **Crush On You**...... **LIL' KIM Featuring Lil' Cease** samples "Rain Dance" by **Jeff Lorber**; above 2 from the album *Hard Core* on Undeas 92733			album cut
5/10/97	90	3		4 **Call Me**......*(radio version)* **TOO $HORT & LIL' KIM** from the movie *Booty Call* starring Jamie Foxx	$6	T	Jive 42447
7/12/97	6	21	▲	5 **Not Tonight**......S:3 / A:39 *(instrumental)* **LIL' KIM Featuring Da Brat, Left Eye, Missy "Misdemenaor" Elliott and Angie Martinez** samples "Ladies Night" by **Kool & The Gang**; from the movie *Nothing To Lose* starring Martin Lawrence	$3	▮	Undeas/Big Beat 98019
12/6/97+	2^2	6	▲	6 **It's All About The Benjamins**......S:2 / A:62 *Been Around The World* (**Puff Daddy** - #4) **PUFF DADDY & THE FAMILY Feat. The Notorious B.I.G., Lil' Kim, The Lox, Dave Grohl, Perfect, FuzzBubble & Rob Zombie** samples "I Did It For Love" by **Love Unlimited Orchestra**	$3	▮	Bad Boy 79130
4/4/98	17	20	●	7 **Money, Power & Respect**......S:10 / A:65 *(instrumental)* **THE LOX [Feat. DMX & Lil' Kim]** samples "New Beginning" by Dexter Wansel	$4	▮	Bad Boy 79156
8/28/99	41^S	6		8 **Play Around**......*(instrumental)* **LIL' CEASE Featuring Lil' Kim, Mr. Bristal and Joe Hooker** samples "One More Chance" by **The Notorious B.I.G.**	$5	★	Queen Bee/Undeas 84482
12/11/99	82	7		9 **Notorious B.I.G.**......A:61 **THE NOTORIOUS B.I.G. featuring Puff Daddy & Lil' Kim** samples "Notorious" by **Duran Duran**; from **The Notorious B.I.G.** album *Born Again* on Bad Boy 73023			album cut
7/15/00	60	10		10 **No Matter What They Say**......A:59 / S:73 *(3 versions)* samples "Esto Es El Guaguanco" by **Jose Feliciano**, "I Know I Got Soul" by **Eric B. & Rakim**, "I Got It Made" by **Special Ed** and "Rappers Delight" by **Sugarhill Gang**; "45": Queen Bee/Undeas 84770; B-side: "Single Black Female" (w/**Mario Winans**)	$6	TV	Queen Bee/Undeas 84703
11/25/00	75	9		11 **How Many Licks?**......A:69 *(3 versions)* **LIL' KIM (featuring Sisqó)**	$6	T	Queen Bee/Undeas 85032
4/14/01	❶5	20		12 **Lady Marmalade** A:❶6 *(3 mixes)* **CHRISTINA AGUILERA, LIL' KIM, MÝA and P!NK** co-produced by **Missy "Misdemeanor" Elliott**; from the movie *Moulin Rouge* starring Nicole Kidman and Ewan McGregor	$6	T	Interscope 497066
5/26/01	30	17		13 **Wait A Minute**......A:27 / S:55 *(3 versions)* **RAY-J Featuring Lil' Kim** "45": Atlantic 85077; B-side: "Keep Your Head Up"	$6	TV	Atlantic 85066

DEBUT	PEAK	WKS	Gold	A-side (Chart Hit)...B-side	$	Sym	Label & Number
				LIL' KIM — Cont'd			
10/6/01	**84**	16		14 **Do U Wanna Roll** ...S:12 *(2 versions) / Lookin' For Love* (w/**Next**) **R.L., SNOOP DOGG and LIL' KIM** samples "Doo Wa Ditty (Blow That Thing)" by **Zapp**; from the movie *Dr. Dolittle 2* starring **Eddie Murphy**	$4	★	J Records 21132
5/18/02	**50^S**	3		15 **Fresh From Yard** ...*(2 versions) / Bossman* (w/**Lady Saw** & **Sean Paul**) **BEENIE MAN & LIL' KIM** samples "Flex" by **Mad Cobra** and "Roots & Culture" by **Shabba Ranks**	$6	T	Shocking Vibes 38827
				LIL LOUIS '89 Born Louis Burns in Chicago, Illinois. Noted DJ of Chicago dance club scene. Son of blues guitarist Bobby Sims.			
10/21/89	**50**	13		**French Kiss** ...*(instrumental)* **Shawn Christopher** (vocal)	$4	▮	Epic 73007
				LIL' MO R&B/LP '01 Born Cynthia Loving on 3/10/76 in Long Island, New York. Female R&B singer. Also see **Next**.			
6/10/00	**47**	18		1 **Whatever** ...A:39 *(3 versions) / Get Gone* **IDEAL Featuring Lil' Mo** "45": Virgin 38730	$6	T^V	Virgin 38713
8/12/00	**95**	7		2 **Ta Da** ...S:19 *(3 album snippets)*	$4	★	EastWest 67019
12/23/00+	**8**	27		3 **Put It On Me** ...A:4 / S:62 *(2 versions) / Love Me, Hate Me* **JA RULE (feat. Lil' Mo and Vita)**	$6	T	Def Jam 572751
3/31/01	**11**	22		4 **Superwoman Pt. II** S:2 / A:22 *Superwoman* **LIL' MO (Featuring Fabolous)** charted first 7 weeks as "Superwoman" (the B-side)	$4	★	EastWest 67171
5/5/01	**40**	14		5 **I Cry** ...A:34 *(2 versions) / Rule Won't Die* **JA RULE (Feat. Lil' Mo)** samples "Cry Together" by **The O'Jays**	$6	T	Def Jam 572856
6/22/02	**15**	26		6 **If I Could Go!** ...A:14 / S:55 *(3 versions)* **ANGIE MARTINEZ (Featuring Lil' Mo & Sacario)**	$6	T	Elektra 67311
				LIL' ROMEO R&B/LP '01 Born Percy Romeo Miller on 8/19/89 in New Orleans, Louisiana. Pre-teen male rapper. Son of **Master P**.			
5/19/01	**3**	14		1 **My Baby** ...RB^1 S:❶^6 / A:52 *(3 versions) / (5 album snippets)* an adaptation of "I Want You Back" by **The Jackson 5**; Ms. Peaches (female vocal); "45": Soulja/Priority 79849; B-side: "The Girlies" (R&B #62)	$4	★^{V}	Soulja 50202
1/26/02	**63**	13		2 **Hush Lil' Lady** ...S:2 *(2 versions) / (5 album snippets)* **COREY featuring Lil' Romeo** contains an interpolation of the folk song "Hush Little Baby"	$5	★	Motown 015474
				LIL RU '02 Male rapper.			
4/6/02	**23^S**	8		1 **Will Destroy** ...*(5 versions)*	$7	★	How You Love That 10121
4/6/02	**43^S**	7		2 **Shawty** ...*(5 versions)* **P-LO featuring Lil Ru & T. Supreme (of the Filthy Boys)**	$7	★	How You Love That 10123
				LIL SUZY BUB '95 Born Suzanne Casale in 1980 in the Bronx, New York. Dance singer. Appeared on TV's *Star Search*.			
7/4/92	**67**	19		1 **Take Me In Your Arms** ...S:56 / A:57 *(2 versions) / Love Can't Wait*	$6	▮*	High Power 109
12/24/94+	**62**	18		2 **Promise Me** ...S:72 *(original mix)*	$3	▮	Empire/Metro. 301
8/2/97	**79**	10		3 **Can't Get You Out Of My Mind** ...*(3 versions)*	$3	▮	Metropolitan 307
11/28/98	**94**	1		4 **I Still Love You** ...*(3 versions)*	$4	▮	Metropolitan 4529
				LIL' TROY LP '99 Born Troy Carter in Philadelphia, Pennsylvania. Male rapper. Former member of 2 Too Many.			
8/14/99	**70**	12		**Wanna Be A Baller** ...A:61 *(3 versions)* features Yungstar, **Fat Pat**, Lil' Will, Hawk, Big T	$6	T	Short Stop 156495
				LIL' TYKES '02 Teen rap group from Dayton, Ohio: Playa, Nappy, Lil' Jay and Shay.			
7/6/02	**27^S**	20		**Who U Rollin' Wit** ...*Mid West Funk*	$6	★	Mamas Boy 1930
				LIL WAYNE R&B/LP '02 Born Wayne Carter on 9/27/83 in New Orleans, Louisiana. Male rapper. Also see **Hot Boy$**.			
7/10/99	**19**	30		1 **Back That Azz Up** ...A:9 / S:64 *(4 versions)* **JUVENILE Feat. Mannie Fresh and Lil' Wayne**	$6	T	Cash Money 156482
9/18/99	**36**	19		2 **Bling Bling** ...A:25 / S:72 *(3 versions)* **B.G. Feat. Baby, Turk, Mannie Fresh, Juvenile and Lil Wayne**	$6	T	Cash Money 156483
12/4/99+	**72**	11		3 **Tha Block Is Hot** ...A:57 *(3 versions)* **LIL WAYNE (featuring Juvenile and B.G.)**	$6	T	Cash Money 156546
9/22/01	**96**	3		4 **Shine** ...*(5 versions)* **LIL WAYNE Feat. Baby and Mac-10**	$6	T	Cash Money 860941
7/6/02	**71**	12		5 **Way Of Life** S:34 / A:71 *(same version)* samples "Don't Look Any Further" by **Dennis Edwards**	$4	★	Cash Money 060074
				LIL' ZANE R&B/LP '00 Born Zane Copeland Jr. on 7/11/82 in Yonkers, New York; raised in Atlanta, Georgia. Male rapper.			
3/20/99	**15**	25		1 **Anywhere** ...A:7 *(5 versions)* **112 Featuring Lil' Z**	$6	T	Bad Boy 79214
7/29/00	**21**	13		2 **Callin' Me** ...S:3 *(2 versions)* **LIL' ZANE Feat. 112**	$4	★	Priority 53582
6/16/01	**16^S**	21		3 **None Tonight** ...*(2 remixes) / (4 album snippets)*	$4	★	Priority 50200
				LIMAHL LP '85 Born Christopher Hamill on 12/19/58 in England. Former lead singer of **Kajagoogoo**.			
3/23/85	**17**	19		1 **Never Ending Story** ...S:14 / A:19 *Ivory Tower* (**Giorgio Moroder**) from the movie *The Never Ending Story* starring Barret Oliver	$3	■	EMI America 8230
7/20/85	**51**	7		2 **Only For Love** ...*The Waiting Game*	$3	■	EMI America 8277

DEBUT	PEAK	WKS	Gold	A-side (Chart Hit)..........B-side	$	Sym	Label & Number
				LIMELITERS, The LP **'61**			
				Folk trio formed in Hollywood, California: **Glenn Yarbrough**, Lou Gottlieb and Alex Hassilev. Yarbrough went solo in 1963; replaced by Ernie Sheldon. Gottlieb died of cancer on 7/11/96 (age 72).			
4/24/61	60	3		**A Dollar Down** ....*When Twice The Moon Has Come And Gone* [N]	$8	■	RCA Victor 7859
				LIMITED WARRANTY **'86**			
				Pop-rock group from Minneapolis, Minnesota: Dale Goulett (vocals, guitar), Greg Sotebeer (vocals, bass), Erik Newman (guitar), Paul Hartwig (keyboards) and Jerry Brunskill (drums).			
6/28/86	79	8		**Victory Line**..........*Yesterday's News*	$3	■	Atco 99541
				LIMMIE & FAMILY COOKIN' **'73**			
				Pop family trio from Canton, Ohio: sisters Martha Stewart and Jimmy Thomas, and brother Limmie Snell.			
11/18/72+	84	10		**You Can Do Magic**..........*Spider*	$6		Avco 4602
				LIMP BIZKIT ROK/BUB/LP **'00**			
				Hard-rock/hip-hop group from Jacksonville, Florida: **Fred Durst** (vocals), Wes Borland (guitar), Sam Rivers (bass) and John Otto (drums). Also see **Staind**.			
7/31/99	80	11		1 **Nookie** A:74			album cut
12/4/99+	73	11		2 **n 2 gether now**..........A:63 *(2 versions)* **LIMP BIZKIT (featuring Method Man)**	$6	T	Flip/Interscope 497183
12/4/99+	88	18		3 **Re-Arranged**..........MR[1] A:71 samples "I Know You Got Soul" by **Eric B. & Rakim**; above 3 from the album *Significant Other* on Flip/Interscope 90335			album cut
11/11/00	65	17		4 **Rollin' (Urban Assault Vehicle)** A:60 **DMX**, **Redman** and **Method Man** (guest rappers)			album cut
1/27/01	56	19		5 **Outside**..........A:54 [L] **AARON LEWIS from Staind (with Fred Durst from Limp Bizkit)** from the album *The Family Values Tour 1999* on Flawless 490641; Staind's original version "Bubbled Under" (#111 in 2001)			album cut
4/28/01	75	14		6 **My Way**..........A:70 above 2 from the album *Chocolate Starfish And The Hot Dog Flavored Water* on Flip 490759			album cut
				LIND, Bob BUB/LP **'66**			
				Born on 11/25/44 in Baltimore, Maryland. Folk-rock singer/songwriter.			
1/22/66	5	13		1 **Elusive Butterfly** ....*Cheryl's Goin Home*	$10		World Pacific 77808
4/23/66	64	5		2 **Remember The Rain** /			
5/7/66	65	5		3 **Truly Julie's Blues** (I'll Be There)..........	$10		World Pacific 77822
				LINDEN, Kathy **'58**			
				Born in Moorestown, New Jersey. Female pop singer.			
3/17/58	7	17		1 **Billy**..........A:7 / T:12 / S:14 *If I Could Hold You In My Arms* introduced by the American Quartet in 1911 on Victor 16965	$15		Felsted 8510
6/9/58	50	8		2 **You'd Be Surprised**..........T:50 *Why Oh Why* written by Irving Berlin; Wee Bonnie Baker of Orrin Tucker's band had Top 10 hits of above 2 in 1939; #3 hit for Eddie Cantor in 1920	$15		Felsted 8521
4/13/59	11	14		3 **Goodbye Jimmy, Goodbye**..........*Heartaches At Sweet Sixteen*	$15		Felsted 8571
7/27/59	92	3		4 **You Don't Know Girls** ....*So Close To My Heart* **Joe Leahy** (orch., all of above)	$15		Felsted 8587
				LINDISFARNE **'78**			
				Folk-rock group from England: Alan Hull (vocals), Ray Jackson (guitar), Simon Crowe (mandolin), Rod Clements (bass) and Ray Laidlaw (drums). Group's name is an island off of Northumberland, U.K. Hull died of a heart attack on 11/18/95 (age 50).			
9/2/72	82	5		1 **Lady Eleanor** ....*Down*	$6		Elektra 45799
9/30/78	33	14		2 **Run For Home** ....*Stick Together*	$5		Atco 7093
				LINDSAY, Mark AC/LP **'70**			
				Born on 3/9/42 in Eugene, Oregon. Lead singer/saxophonist of **Paul Revere & The Raiders**. Also recorded with Raider, Keith Allison, and **Steve Alaimo** as **The Unknowns**.			
7/26/69	81	4		1 **First Hymn From Grand Terrace**..........*The Old Man At The Fair*	$7		Columbia 44875
12/6/69+	10	16	●	2 **Arizona** *Man From Houston*	$6		Columbia 45037
4/4/70	44	8		3 **Miss America** ....*Small Town Woman*	$6		Columbia 45125
6/13/70	25	10		4 **Silver Bird** ....*So Hard To Leave You*	$6		Columbia 45180
9/19/70	44	12		5 **And The Grass Won't Pay No Mind** ....*Funny How Little Men Care* written by **Neil Diamond**	$6		Columbia 45229
1/9/71	80	4		6 **Problem Child**..........*Bookends*	$6		Columbia 45286
6/12/71	98	1		7 **Been Too Long On The Road**..........*All I Really See Is You* all of above produced by **Jerry Fuller**	$6		Columbia 45385
10/16/71	87	3		8 **Are You Old Enough** ....*Don't You Know*	$6		Columbia 45462
				LINEAR LP **'90**			
				Pop trio from Miami, Florida: Charlie Pennachio (vocals), Wyatt Pauley (guitar) and Joey Restivo (percussion).			
2/17/90	5	27	●	1 **Sending All My Love** ....S:6 / A:7 *(instrumental)*	$3	▮V	Atlantic 87961
7/14/90	70	7		2 **Don't You Come Cryin'** ....*(instrumental)*	$3	▮	Atlantic 87877
5/9/92	30	13		3 **T.L.C.** ....A:20 / S:65 *I Just Can't Stop Loving You*	$3	▮	Atlantic 87484
				LINER **'79**			
				Pop trio: brothers Tom (vocals, bass) and Dave (drums) Farmer, with Eddie Golga (guitar).			
3/17/79	92	2		**You And Me** ....*Ship On The Ocean*	$5		Atco 7097
				LINES, Aaron C&W/LP **'03**			
				Born in 1978 in Fort McMurray, Alberta, Canada. Country singer/songwriter/guitarist.			
12/28/02+	38	17		**You Can't Hide Beautiful** ....A:35 from the album *Living Out Loud* on RCA 67057			album cut
				LINK R&B/LP **'98**			
				Born Lincoln Browder on 10/12/64 in Dallas, Texas. Male rapper.			
6/6/98	23	19		1 **Whatcha Gone Do?**..........S:22 *(instrumental) / (Sex Down Snippet)*	$3	▮	Relativity 1691
5/15/99	25^{S}	15		2 **I Don't Wanna See**..........*(clean version)*	$4	★	Relativity 1789

DEBUT	PEAK	WKS	Gold	A-side (Chart Hit)...B-side	$	Sym	Label & Number
				LINKIN PARK ROK/R&B/LP '01			
				Alternative hard-rock/hip-hop group from Los Angeles, California: Chester Bennington (vocals), **Mike Shinoda** (rap vocals), Joseph "**Mr. Hahn**" (DJ), Brad Delson (guitar), Phoenix (bass) and Rob Bourdon (drums).			
2/10/01	75	17		1 **One Step Closer** ...A:68			album cut
				featured in the movie *Dracula 2000* starring Christopher Plummer			
8/11/01	79	20		2 **Crawling** ...A:75			album cut
11/3/01+	2[1]	38		3 **In The End** ...MR[5] A:2			album cut
				above 3 from the album *Hybrid Theory* on Warner 47755			
3/9/02	85	11		4 **It's Goin' Down** ...*(2 versions) / X-Ecutioners (Theme) Song*	$7	T	Loud 9133
				X-ECUTIONERS Featuring Mike Shinoda and Mr. Hahn of Linkin Park			
				LINKLETTER, Art LP '69			
				Born Arthur Kelly on 7/17/12 in Moose Jaw, Saskatchewan, Canada. Popular radio and TV personality. Hosted own shows *Art Linkletter's House Party* (later known as *The Linkletter Show*) and several others.			
11/1/69	42	6		**We Love You, Call Collect** ...*Dear Mom And Dad* [S]	$7	■	Capitol 2678
				B-side is a response by Art's daughter, Diane, who committed suicide on 10/4/69; picture sleeve has a cut-out hole in the middle and a drug abuse message			
				LIPPS, INC. R&B/LP '80			
				Funk-dance project from Minneapolis, Minnesota. Formed by white producer/songwriter/multi-instrumentalist Steven Greenberg. Vocals by black singer Cynthia Johnson. Pronounced: lip-synch.			
3/29/80	❶[4]	23	▲	1 **Funkytown** ...*All Night Dancing*	$4		Casablanca 2233
8/2/80	64	7		2 **Rock It** ...*Power*	$4		Casablanca 2281
				LIQUID GOLD '79			
				Disco group from England: Ellie Hope (vocals), Syd Twynham (guitar), Ray Knott (bass) and Wally Rothe (drums).			
4/28/79	45	9		1 **My Baby's Baby** ...*(instrumental)*	$5		Parachute 524
9/3/83	86	4		2 **What's She Got** ...*Coming Down*	$5		Critique 701
				LIQUID SMOKE '70			
				White R&B-rock group from North Carolina: Sandy Pantaleo (vocals), Vince Fersak (guitar), Benny Ninmann (keyboards), Mike Archeleta (bass) and Chas Kimbrell (drums).			
4/18/70	82	3		**I Who Have Nothing** ...*Warm Touch*	$8		Avco Embassy 4522
	★532★			**LISA LISA AND CULT JAM** R&B/BUB/LP '87			
				R&B-dance trio from Harlem, New York: Lisa Velez (vocals; born on 1/15/67), Alex "Spanador" Moseley (guitar) and Mike Hughes (drums). Assembled and produced by Full Force.			
6/8/85	34	21	●	1 **I Wonder If I Take You Home** ...S:27 *If I Take You Home Tonight*	$3		Columbia 04886
11/16/85	69	20		2 **Can You Feel The Beat** ...*Beat The Feel You Can*	$3	■	Columbia 05669
				LISA LISA and CULT JAM with FULL FORCE (above 2)			
7/26/86	8	26	●	3 **All Cried Out** ...S:8 / A:8 *Behind My Eyes*	$3		Columbia 05844
				LISA LISA AND CULT JAM WITH FULL FORCE FEATURING PAUL ANTHONY & BOW LEGGED LOU			
4/11/87	❶[1]	20	●	4 **Head To Toe** RB[2] S:❶[1] / A:❶[1] *You'll Never Change*	$3	■	Columbia 07008
8/1/87	❶[1]	20	●	5 **Lost In Emotion** ...RB[1] S:❶[1] / A:❶[1] *Motion Is Lost*	$3	■	Columbia 07267
11/14/87	78	10		6 **Someone To Love Me For Me** ...*Spanish Fly*	$3	■	Columbia 07619
				LISA LISA AND CULT JAM FEATURING FULL FORCE			
4/15/89	29	11		7 **Little Jackie Wants To Be A Star** ...S:25 / A:36 *Star*	$3	■	Columbia 68674
6/22/91	37	16	●	8 **Let The Beat Hit 'Em** ...RB[1] S:19 / A:38 *(house version)*	$3	▮[V]	Columbia 73847
				LIT ROK/BUB/LP '99			
				Rock group from Los Angeles, California: brothers A.J. (vocals) and Jeremy (bass) Popoff, Kevin Blades (bass) and Allen Shellenberger (drums).			
4/24/99	51	20		**My Own Worst Enemy** ...MR[11] A:45			album cut
				from the album *A Place In The Sun* on RCA 67775			
				LITTLE — also see LIL			
	★394★			**LITTLE ANTHONY AND THE IMPERIALS** BUB/R&B/LP '58			
				R&B vocal group from Brooklyn, New York: Anthony Gourdine (born on 1/8/40), Ernest Wright, Tracy Lord, Glouster Rogers and Clarence Collins. Gourdine first recorded on Winley in 1955 with The DuPonts. Formed The Chesters in 1957, then changed name to The Imperials in 1958. Sammy Strain, who joined group in 1964, left in 1975 to join **The O'Jays**. Gourdine became an Inspirational artist in 1980.			
				1)Tears On My Pillow 2)Goin' Out Of My Head 3)Hurt So Bad			
8/11/58	4	19		1 **Tears On My Pillow** H:4 / S:5 *Two People In The World*	$30		End 1027
				first released on End 1027 as by **The Imperials** ($40)			
12/22/58	87	2		2 **So Much** ...*Oh Yeah*	$25		End 1036
3/23/59	79	2		3 **Wishful Thinking** ...*When You Wish Upon A Star*	$25		End 1039
6/15/59	81	4		4 **A Prayer And A Juke Box** ...*River Path*	$25		End 1047
12/7/59+	24	16		5 **Shimmy, Shimmy, Ko-Ko-Bop** ...*I'm Still In Love With You*	$30		End 1060
4/18/60	86	2		6 **My Empty Room** ...*Bayou, Bayou, Baby*	$25		End 1067
8/22/64	15	10		7 **I'm On The Outside (Looking In)** ...*Please Go*	$15		DCP 1104
11/7/64	6	14		8 **Goin' Out Of My Head** ...*Make It Easy On Yourself*	$15		DCP 1119
2/6/65	10	9		9 **Hurt So Bad** ...*Reputation*	$15	■	DCP 1128
6/26/65	16	11		10 **Take Me Back** ...*Our Song*	$15		DCP 1136
10/2/65	34	7		11 **I Miss You So** ...*Get Out Of My Life*	$15		DCP 1149
				The 101 Strings (orchestral backing); #20 hit for The Cats and the Fiddle in 1940			
1/1/66	51	6		12 **Hurt** ...*Never Again*	$15		DCP 1154
				#8 R&B hit for **Roy Hamilton** in 1955			
5/14/66	54	7		13 **Better Use Your Head** ...*The Wonder Of It All*	$15	■	Veep 1228
11/12/66	92	2		14 **It's Not The Same** *[ANTHONY AND THE IMPERIALS]* ...*Down On Love*	$12		Veep 1248
2/17/68	98	1		15 **I'm Hypnotized** *[ANTHONY AND THE IMPERIALS]* ...*Hungry Heart*	$12		Veep 1278
				#7-15: written (except #11 & 12) and produced by **Teddy Randazzo**			
7/26/69	52	9		16 **Out Of Sight, Out Of Mind** ...*Summer's Comin' In*	$8		United Artists 50552

DEBUT	PEAK	WKS	Gold	A-side (Chart Hit)..........B-side	$	Sym	Label & Number
				LITTLE ANTHONY AND THE IMPERIALS — Cont'd			
11/8/69	**82**	4		17 **The Ten Commandments Of Love** ....*Let The Sunshine In*	$8		United Artists 50598
11/21/70	**92**	4		18 **Help Me Find A Way (To Say I Love You)** ....*If I Love You*	$8		United Artists 50720
6/15/74	**86**	4		19 **I'm Falling In Love With You** ....*What Good Am I Without You*	$7		Avco 4635
				LITTLE BILL and The Bluenotes '59			
				Pop group from Tacoma, Washington: "Little Bill" Engelhart (vocals), Lassie Aanes, Frank Dutra, Tom Geving, Buck Mann and Buck Ormsby.			
6/22/59	**66**	6		**I Love An Angel** ....*Bye Bye Baby*	$25		Dolton 4
				produced by **Bonnie Guitar**			
				LITTLE CAESAR LP '91			
				Hard-rock group formed in Los Angeles, California: Ron Young (vocals), Apache and Louren Molinare (guitars), Fidel Paniagua (bass), and Tom Morris (drums). Group named after a 1930 gangster movie. Young had cameo in movie *Terminator 2: Judgment Day*.			
6/16/90	**88**	4		1 **Chain Of Fools** ....*Rock-N-Roll State Of Mind*	$3	▮	DGC 19693
3/2/91	**79**	5		2 **In Your Arms** ....*Wrong Side Of The Tracks*	$3	▮	DGC 19003
				LITTLE CAESAR And The Consuls '65			
				Five-man garage-rock band from Canada led by saxophonist Norm Sherratt. Also included Tommy Wilson (bass) and Gary Wright (drums).			
8/14/65	**50**	8		**(My Girl) Sloopy** ....*Poison Ivy*	$15		Mala 512
				LITTLE CAESAR and The Romans BUB '61			
				R&B vocal group from Los Angeles, California: Carl "Little Caesar" Burnett, David Johnson, Early Harris, Leroy Sanders and Johnny Simmons.			
5/1/61	**9**	13		1 **Those Oldies But Goodies (Remind Me Of You)** ....*She Don't Wanna Dance (No More)* (The Romans)	$30		Del-Fi 4158
8/7/61	**54**	4		2 **Hully Gully Again** ....*Frankie And Johnnie*	$30		Del-Fi 4164
				LITTLE DIPPERS, The '60			
				One-time studio session recording produced by Buddy Killen; featuring **Floyd Cramer** (piano), **Bob Moore** (bass), Hank Garland (lead guitar), Kelso Herston (rhythm guitar), Buddy Harmon (drums) and the Anita Kerr Singers (vocals). Killen later formed a quartet to lip-synch the song on the Dick Clark show.			
1/25/60	**9**	14		**Forever** ....*Two By Four*	$15		University 210
				LITTLE EVA BUB/LP '62			
				Born Eva Narcissus Boyd on 6/29/45 in Belhaven, North Carolina. Died of cancer on 4/10/2003 (age 57). Discovered by songwriters **Carole King** and Gerry Goffin while Eva was babysitting their daughter **Louise Goffin**.			
6/30/62	**❶**[1]	16	●	1 **The Loco-Motion** RB[3] *He Is The Boy*	$25		Dimension 1000
				Carole King (backing vocal)			
11/3/62	**12**	12		2 **Keep Your Hands Off My Baby** ....*Where Do I Go?*	$20		Dimension 1003
2/2/63	**20**	10		3 **Let's Turkey Trot** ....*Down Home*	$20		Dimension 1006
				same melody as **The Cleftones**' 1956 hit "Little Girl Of Mine"			
5/25/63	**38**	10		4 **Swinging On A Star** ....*Another Night With The Boys* (Irwin)	$25		Dimension 1010
				BIG DEE IRWIN (with Little Eva)			
				#1 hit for **Bing Crosby** in 1944			
6/1/63	**48**	6		5 **Old Smokey Locomotion** ....*Just A Little Girl*	$20		Dimension 1011
				new version of the traditional folk song "On Top Of Old Smokey"			
				LITTLE JO ANN '62			
				Born Jo Ann Morse (age seven in 1962). Female singer.			
7/7/62	**67**	5		**My Daddy Is President** ....*Macaroni (Caroline's Pony)* (Harmony Jones Orchestra) [N]	$15		Kapp 467
				Harmony Jones (orch.)			
				LITTLE JOE & THE THRILLERS '57			
				R&B vocal group from Harlem, New York: Joe Cook, Farris Hill, Richard Frazier, Donald Burnett and Harry Pascle.			
9/30/57	**22**	15		**Peanuts** ....S:22 / T:23 *Lilly Lou*	$30		Okeh 7088
				Leroy Kirkland (orch.)			
				LITTLE JOEY And The Flips '62			
				R&B vocal group from Philadelphia, Pennsylvania: Joey Hall, James Meagher, John Smith, Jeff Leonard and Fred Gerace. Hall died in 1972.			
6/16/62	**33**	10		**Bongo Stomp** ....*Lost Love*	$15		Joy 262
				LITTLE MILTON R&B/BUB/LP '65			
				Born James Milton Campbell on 9/7/34 in Inverness, Mississippi. Blues singer/guitarist. Charted 29 R&B hits, 1962-83. Recorded with **Ike Turner** at Sun Records, 1953-54. In concert movie *Wattstax*. Also see **Herbie Mann**'s "It's A Funky Thing-Right On."			
				1)We're Gonna Make It 2)Who's Cheating Who? 3)That's What Love Will Make You Do			
1/2/65	**86**	4		1 **Blind Man** ....*Blues In The Night*	$15		Checker 1096
3/27/65	**25**	11		2 **We're Gonna Make It** RB[3] *Can't Hold Back The Tears*	$15		Checker 1105
6/12/65	**43**	7		3 **Who's Cheating Who?** ....*Ain't No Big Deal On You*	$15		Checker 1113
2/12/66	**100**	1		4 **We Got The Winning Hand** ....*Sometimey*	$15		Checker 1132
2/4/67	**91**	3		5 **Feel So Bad** ....*You Colored My Blues Bright*	$15		Checker 1162
				#8 R&B hit for **Chuck Willis** in 1954			
2/1/69	**73**	5		6 **Grits Ain't Groceries (All Around The World)** ....*I Can't Quit You Baby*	$12		Checker 1212
				#5 R&B hit in 1955 for **Little Willie John** as "All Around The World"			
5/10/69	**97**	2		7 **Just A Little Bit** ....*Spring*	$12		Checker 1217
1/17/70	**71**	5		8 **If Walls Could Talk** ....*Loving You*	$12		Checker 1226
5/9/70	**82**	3		9 **Baby I Love You** ....*Don't Talk Back*	$12		Checker 1227
2/12/72	**59**	6		10 **That's What Love Will Make You Do** ....*I'm Living Off The Love You Give*	$7		Stax 0111

DEBUT	PEAK	WKS	Gold	A-side (Chart Hit)...B-side	$	Sym	Label & Number

★255★ **LITTLE RICHARD** R&B/BUB/LP **'57**

Born Richard Wayne Penniman on 12/5/32 in Macon, Georgia. R&B-rock and roll singer/pianist. Talent contest win led to first recordings for RCA Victor in 1951. Worked with the Tempo Toppers, 1953-55. Appeared in three early rock and roll movies: *Don't Knock The Rock*, *The Girl Can't Help It* and *Mister Rock 'n' Roll* and the 1986 comedy *Down And Out In Beverly Hills*. Earned theology degree in 1961 and was ordained a minister. Left R&B for gospel music, 1959-62, and again in the mid-1970s. One of the key figures in the transition from R&B to rock and roll. Inducted into the Rock and Roll Hall of Fame in 1986. Won Grammy's Lifetime Achievement Award in 1993. Also see **Canned Heat**'s "Rockin' With The King."

1)Long Tall Sally 2)Keep A Knockin' 3)Jenny, Jenny 4)Good Golly, Miss Molly 5)Tutti-Frutti

DEBUT	PEAK	WKS	Gold	A-side (Chart Hit)...B-side	$	Sym	Label & Number
1/14/56	17	12		1 **Tutti-Frutti** J:17 / S:18 / T:21 *I'm Just A Lonely Guy*	$50		Specialty 561
4/7/56	6	19	●	2 **Long Tall Sally** / RB[8] S:6 / T:13 / J:14 / A:16			
4/21/56	33	14		3 **Slippin' And Slidin' (Peepin' And Hidin')** T:33 / S:flip	$40		Specialty 572
7/7/56	17	18		4 **Rip It Up** / RB[2] S:17 / T:27			
7/7/56	44	8		5 **Ready Teddy** T:44 / S:flip	$40		Specialty 579
1/26/57	49	8		6 **The Girl Can't Help It** T:49 *All Around The World* (R&B #13) title song from the movie starring Jayne Mansfield	$40		Specialty 591
3/23/57	21	21		7 **Lucille** / CW[2] S:21 / T:27			
4/6/57	54	12		8 **Send Me Some Lovin'** T:54 / S:flip **LITTLE RICHARD And His Band** (all of above)	$40		Specialty 598
6/17/57	10	20		9 **Jenny, Jenny** / S:10 / T:14			
6/24/57	56	10		10 **Miss Ann** T:56 / S:flip	$35	■	Specialty 606
9/30/57	8	18		11 **Keep A Knockin'** T:8 / S:9 / A:24 *Can't Believe You Wanna Leave* from the movie *Mister Rock 'n' Roll* starring Alan Freed	$35	■	Specialty 611
2/17/58	10	15		12 **Good Golly, Miss Molly** T:10 / S:13 *Hey-Hey-Hey-Hey* piano intro inspired by Jackie Brenston's early rock & roll #1 R&B hit from 1951, "Rocket '88'"	$35	■	Specialty 624
6/9/58	31	8		13 **Ooh! My Soul** / S:31 / T:35 recorded by **Ritchie Valens** in 1958 on his debut album as "Ooh! My Head"			
6/30/58	68	3		14 **True, Fine Mama** T:68 / S:flip	$30	■	Specialty 633
9/15/58	41	10		15 **Baby Face** H:41 / S:50 *I'll Never Let You Go* there were 4 Top 10 versions of this tune in 1926; #3 hit for **Art Mooney** in 1948; Little Richard's only non-charted record in his above string of hits on Specialty was #584: "Heebie-Jeebies"/"She's Got It"	$25		Specialty 645
5/11/59	95	2		16 **Kansas City** *Lonesome And Blue*	$25		Specialty 664
7/18/64	82	4		17 **Bama Lama Bama Loo** *Annie Is Back*	$20		Specialty 692
11/27/65	92	1		18 **I Don't Know What You've Got But It's Got Me - Part I** *Part II* written by **Don Covay**	$20		Vee-Jay 698
5/23/70	47	9		19 **Freedom Blues** *Dew Drop Inn*	$10		Reprise 0907
9/5/70	85	5		20 **Greenwood Mississippi** *I Saw Her Standing There*	$10		Reprise 0942
3/8/86	42	10		21 **Great Gosh A'Mighty! (It's A Matter Of Time)** *The Ride* (Charlie Midnight) theme song from the movie *Down And Out In Beverly Hills* starring Nick Nolte	$4	■	MCA 52780

★208★ **LITTLE RIVER BAND** AC/LP **'79**

Pop-rock group formed in Australia: **Glenn Shorrock** (vocals; born on 6/30/44) (see #16 below), Rick Formosa (born on 9/1/54), Beeb Birtles (born on 11/28/48) and Graham Goble (born on 5/15/47; guitars), Roger McLachlan (bass), and Derek Pellicci (drums; born on 2/18/53). McLachlan replaced by George McArdle in 1977 and Formosa replaced by David Briggs in 1978. In 1983, Shorrock replaced by **John Farnham** (born on 7/1/49) (see #18 below) and Briggs replaced by Steve Housden. By 1985, Pellicci replaced by Steven Prestwich, and Birtles had left and keyboardist David Hirschfelder joined. Pellicci and Shorrock returned in 1987. By 1992, Goble had left and Peter Beckett, ex-leader of **Player**, had joined. Band named after a resort town near Melbourne.

1)Reminiscing 2)The Night Owls 3)Lonesome Loser

DEBUT	PEAK	WKS	Gold	A-side (Chart Hit)...B-side	$	Sym	Label & Number
9/18/76	28	16		1 **It's A Long Way There** *Meanwhile...*	$5		Harvest 4318
2/5/77	62	5		2 **I'll Always Call Your Name** *The Man In Black*	$5		Harvest 4380
8/6/77	14	22		3 **Help Is On Its Way** *The Inner Light*	$5		Harvest 4428
12/17/77+	16	18		4 **Happy Anniversary** *Changed And Different*	$5		Harvest 4524
7/29/78	3	20		5 **Reminiscing** *So Many Paths*	$5		Harvest 4605
1/6/79	10	20		6 **Lady** *Take Me Home*	$5	■	Harvest 4667
7/21/79	6	18		7 **Lonesome Loser** *Shut Down Turn Off*	$4		Capitol 4748
10/20/79+	10	18		8 **Cool Change** *Middle Man*	$4		Capitol 4789
5/3/80	51	6		9 **It's Not A Wonder** *Man On The Run* [L]	$4		Capitol 4862
8/22/81	6	21		10 **The Night Owls** *Suicide Boulevard*	$4		Capitol 5033
12/5/81+	10	19		11 **Take It Easy On Me** *Orbit Zero*	$4	■	Capitol 5057
4/3/82	14	16		12 **Man On Your Mind** *Orbit Zero*	$4	■	Capitol 5061
11/20/82+	11	18		13 **The Other Guy** *No More Tears*	$4	■	Capitol 5185
5/7/83	22	12		14 **We Two** *Falling*	$3		Capitol 5231
7/23/83	35	11		15 **You're Driving Me Out Of My Mind** *Mr. Socialite*	$3	■	Capitol 5256
9/24/83	69	6		16 **Don't Girls Get Lonely** *Do It Anyway* **GLENN SHORROCK**	$3	■	Capitol 5267
1/26/85	60	8		17 **Playing To Win** *[LRB]* *Through Her Eyes*	$3	■	Capitol 5411
2/10/90	82	8		18 **You're The Voice** *(long version)* **JOHN FARNHAM**	$3	▮	RCA 9086

LITTLE SISTER R&B **'70**

Female R&B vocal trio formed by **Sly Stone**: Vanetta Stewart (Sly's sister), Mary Rand and Elva Melton.

DEBUT	PEAK	WKS	Gold	A-side (Chart Hit)...B-side	$	Sym	Label & Number
2/28/70	22	11		1 **You're The One-Part I** *Part II*	$10		Stone Flower 9000
12/12/70+	32	13		2 **Somebody's Watching You** *Stanga* (R&B #44)	$10		Stone Flower 9001

LITTLE STEVEN AND THE DISCIPLES OF SOUL ROK/LP **'83**

Born Steven Van Zandt on 11/22/50 in Boston, Massachusetts; raised in New Jersey. Formed **Southside Johnny & The Jukes** with co-lead singer Johnny Lyon in 1974. Joined **Bruce Springsteen**'s E Street Band in 1975. Organized **Artists United Against Apartheid**. Plays "Silvio Dante" on TV's *The Sopranos*. Also see **Jean Beauvoir**.

DEBUT	PEAK	WKS	Gold	A-side (Chart Hit)...B-side	$	Sym	Label & Number
12/25/82+	63	9		**Forever** *Caravan*	$4	■	EMI America 8144

DEBUT	PEAK	WKS	Gold	A-side (Chart Hit)..........B-side	$	Sym	Label & Number

LITTLE STINKERS, The '02

Children's chorus assembled by husband-and-wife Anthony S. (piano; music) and Gina (lyrics) Beltrami: their daughter Mary Beltrami (lead vocal), with their son Anthony P. Beltrami, and siblings Hannah & Emily Hartman and Olivia & Lauren Albright.

DEBUT	PEAK	WKS	Gold	A-side (Chart Hit)..........B-side	$	Sym	Label & Number
12/28/02+	38^S	3		**I Farted On Santa's Lap (Now Christmas Is Gonna Stink For Me)** ..*(no B-side)* [X-N] first released in 1998	$12	★	Beltrami 01

LITTLE TEXAS C&W/BUB/LP '94

Country group from Arlington, Texas: **Tim Rushlow** (vocals) (see #7 below), Porter Howell and Dwayne O'Brien (guitars), **Brady Seals** (keyboards) (see #6 below), Duane Propes (bass) and Del Gray (drums). Seals is the cousin of Jim [**Seals & Crofts**] and "England" **Dan Seals** and nephew of Troy Seals [**Jo Ann & Troy**]) Seals was replaced by Jeff Huskins in 1995.

DEBUT	PEAK	WKS	Gold	A-side (Chart Hit)..........B-side	$	Sym	Label & Number
8/7/93+	74	20		1 **What Might Have Been** ....S:46 / A:61 *Stop On A Dime* originally charted for 12 weeks (#79); re-entered on 2/12/94	$4	■^{V}	Warner 18516
11/13/93+	55	12		2 **God Blessed Texas** S:32 *Cutoff Jeans*	$4	■^{V}	Warner 18385
2/26/94	83	10		3 **My Love** ....CW^2 S:44 *Only Thing I'm Sure Of*	$4	■^{V}	Warner 18295
11/12/94	68^S	1		4 **Kick A Little** ....*Hit Country Song*	$4	■^{V}	Warner 18103
8/19/95	60^S	5		5 **Party All Night** ....BUB:101 *Southern Accent* (Foxworthy) [L-N] **JEFF FOXWORTHY With Little Texas and Scott Rouse**	$4	■^{V}	Warner 17806
1/25/97	91	4		6 **Another You, Another Me** ....S:65 *You Can Have Your Way With Me* **BRADY SEALS**	$4	■^{V}	Reprise 17615
3/17/01	59	11		7 **She Misses Him** ....A:49 **TIM RUSHLOW** from the album *Tim Rushlow* on Atlantic 83326			album cut

LIVE ROK/LP '95

Rock group from York, Pennsylvania: Edward Kowalczyk (vocals), Chad Taylor (guitar), Patrick Dahlheimer (bass) and Chad Gracey (drums).

DEBUT	PEAK	WKS	Gold	A-side (Chart Hit)..........B-side	$	Sym	Label & Number
6/4/94	43	19		1 **Selling The Drama** ....MR^3 A:42 *Lightning Crashes*	$5	■	Radioactive 54816
10/29/94+	38^A	21		2 **I Alone**			album cut
2/4/95	12^A	31		3 **Lightning Crashes** AR^{10} / MR^9 also see the B-side of #1 above			album cut
5/13/95	33^A	25		4 **All Over You**			album cut
8/19/95	71^A	1		5 **White, Discussion** .... all of above from the album *Throwing Copper* on Radioactive 10997 (produced by Jerry Harrison of **Talking Heads**)			album cut
1/25/97	35^A	14		6 **Lakini's Juice** ....MR^1			album cut
5/10/97	73^A	2		7 **Freaks**			album cut
6/21/97	45^A	16		8 **Turn My Head** .... above 3 from the album *Secret Samadhi* on Radioactive 11590			album cut
10/16/99	78	10		9 **The Dolphin's Cry** ....A:65 from the album *The Distance To Here* on Radioactive 111966; "45": Radioactive 155689; B-side: "Run To The Water" (ROK #14)		V	album cut

LIVERPOOL FIVE '66

Rock group formed in Liverpool, England; later based in Spokane, Washington: Steve Laine (vocals), Ken Cox (guitar), Ron Henley (keyboards), Dave "Burgess" McKuminskey (bass) and Jimmy May (drums).

DEBUT	PEAK	WKS	Gold	A-side (Chart Hit)..........B-side	$	Sym	Label & Number
12/24/66	98	1		**Any Way That You Want Me** ....*The Snake*	$12		RCA Victor 8968

LiVIGNI, John — see VALENTI, John

LIVING COLOUR ROK/LP '89

Black rock group from Brooklyn, New York: Corey Glover (vocals), Vernnon Reid (guitar), Muzz Skillings (bass) and William Calhoun (drums). Glover played "Francis" in the movie *Platoon*.

DEBUT	PEAK	WKS	Gold	A-side (Chart Hit)..........B-side	$	Sym	Label & Number
3/11/89	13	15		1 **Cult Of Personality** ....S:7 / A:17 *Funny Vibe*	$3		Epic 68611
7/8/89	82	5		2 **Open Letter (To A Landlord)** ....*Talkin' Bout A Revolution (live)*	$3		Epic 68934
8/26/89	31	13		3 **Glamour Boys** ....A:28 / S:32 *Cult Of Personality (live)* **Mick Jagger** (producer; backing vocal)	$3		Epic 68548

LIVING IN A BOX LP '87

Soul-styled pop-dance trio from Sheffield, Yorkshire, England: Richard Darbyshire (vocals), Marcus Vere (keyboards) and Anthony Critchlow (drums).

DEBUT	PEAK	WKS	Gold	A-side (Chart Hit)..........B-side	$	Sym	Label & Number
6/20/87	17	15		1 **Living In A Box** ....S:13 / A:20 *(edited dance mix)*	$3	■	Chrysalis 43104
10/17/87	81	4		2 **So The Story Goes** ....*The Liam McCoy*	$3	■	Chrysalis 43162

LIVIN' JOY '97

Italian techno-dance group featuring American lead singer Janice Robinson (left group in April 1995). New lead singer Tameka Star joined in 1996.

DEBUT	PEAK	WKS	Gold	A-side (Chart Hit)..........B-side	$	Sym	Label & Number
1/28/95	72	17		1 **Dreamer** ....*(radio mix)*	$3	■	MCA 55017
6/15/96	95	2		2 **Dreamer** ....A:73 *(radio mix)* [R] above 2 are the same version	$3	■	MCA 55017
1/25/97	67	20		3 **Don't Stop Movin'** ....A:68 *(3 versions)*	$3	■	MCA 55300

LL COOL J ★172★ R&B/BUB/LP '96

Born James Todd Smith on 8/16/68 in Queens, New York. Male rapper/actor. Stage name is abbreviation for Ladies Love Cool James. Appeared in several movies and TV shows.

1)Hey Lover 2)Loungin 3)Luv U Better 4)Around The Way Girl 5)Doin It

DEBUT	PEAK	WKS	Gold	A-side (Chart Hit)..........B-side	$	Sym	Label & Number
7/11/87	84	4		1 **I'm Bad** ....*Get Down*	$4		Def Jam 07120
8/1/87	14	13		2 **I Need Love** ....RB^1 S:11 / A:13 *My Rhyme Ain't Done*	$3		Def Jam 07350
2/20/88	31	14	●	3 **Going Back To Cali** ....S:26 / A:32 *Jack The Ripper* from the movie *Less Than Zero* starring Robert Downey, Jr.	$3	■	Def Jam 07679
6/10/89	15	16	●	4 **I'm That Type Of Guy** ....S:9 / A:28 *It Gets No Rougher*	$3		Def Jam 68902
9/29/90	48	11		5 **The Boomin' System** ....S:27 *(underground mix)*	$3	■	Def Jam 73457

DEBUT	PEAK	WKS	Gold	A-side (Chart Hit)...B-side	$	Sym	Label & Number
				LL COOL J — Cont'd			
12/1/90+	9	23	●	6 **Around The Way Girl** ...S:5 / A:19 *(remix)*	$3	▮V	Def Jam 73609
4/13/91	17	16	●	7 **Mama Said Knock You Out** ...S:5 / A:47 *(hot mix)*	$3	▮V	Def Jam 73706
				"45" issued for above 2 on Def Jam 73609			
9/14/91	95	2		8 **6 Minutes Of Pleasure** ...S:55 *Eat Em Up L Chill*	$3	▮	Def Jam 73820
				above 4 from the album *Mama Said Knock You Out*			
4/3/93	57	9		9 **How I'm Comin'** ...S:26 *(remix) / Buckin' Em Down*	$3	▮	Def Jam 74811
				samples "Hot Pants - I'm Coming, I'm Coming, I'm Coming" by **Bobby Byrd**			
6/19/93	42	13		10 **Back Seat (Of My Jeep) /** S:28 / A:54			
6/19/93	96	10		11 **Pink Cookies In A Plastic Bag Getting Crushed By Buildings** ...S:29	$3	▮	Def Jam 74984
				samples "Blind Alley" by **The Emotions**			
11/18/95	3	21	▲	12 **Hey Lover** S:2 / A:17 *(instrumental)*	$3	▮V	Def Jam 577494
				Boyz II Men (backing vocals); based on the song "The Lady In My Life" by **Michael Jackson**; "45" B-side: (radio edit)			
3/9/96	9	20	●	13 **Doin It** ...S:6 / A:46 *(album version)*	$3	▮V	Def Jam 576120
				LeShaun Williams (guest vocal); samples "My Jamaican Guy" by **Grace Jones**; "45" B-side: "Hey Lover" w/**Boyz II Men**			
7/6/96	3	29	▲	14 **Loungin** ...S:2 / A:24 *Summer Luv*	$3	▮	Def Jam 575062
				Total (guest vocals); samples "Who Do You Love" by Bernard Wright			
10/26/96	6	20	▲	15 **This Is For The Lover In You** ...S:3 / A:37 *(remix)*	$3	▮V	Epic 78443
				BABYFACE Featuring LL Cool J, Howard Hewett, Jody Watley and Jeffrey Daniels			
				#17 R&B hit for **Shalamar** in 1981 (Hewett, Watley and Daniels were members of **Shalamar**)			
12/28/96+	46	11		16 **Ain't Nobody** ...S:25 *Pimp'n Ain't EZ* (Madd Head)	$3	▮	Geffen 19410
				from the animated movie *Beavis And Butt-Head Do America*			
11/1/97	55	9		17 **Phenomenon** ...A:49 *(5 versions)*	$6	T	Def Jam 568081
				samples "Who Is He And What Is He To You" by **Creative Source**			
12/27/97	75	12		18 **4, 3, 2, 1** ...*(5 versions)*	$6	T	Def Jam 568321
				LL COOL J Featuring Method Man, Redman, DMX, Canibus and Master P			
				samples "Fight For Your Right" by **Beastie Boys**, "Rock The Bells" by LL Cool J and "Shut 'Em Down" by **Public Enemy**			
1/31/98	18	16		19 **Father** ...S:7 *4, 3, 2, 1* (same version as #18 above)	$3	▮	Def Jam 568332
				samples "Father Figure" by **George Michael**			
8/12/00	98	2		20 **Imagine That** ...*(2 versions) / LL Cool J*	$6	T	Def Jam 562827
				LeShaun Williams (backing vocal)			
11/3/01	87	14		21 **Fatty Girl** ...S:50 *(4 versions)*	$6	T	Universal 15283
				LUDACRIS, LL COOL J, KEITH MURRAY			
8/24/02	4	22		22 **Luv U Better** ...RB4 A:3 / S:14 *(2 versions) / Fa Ha*	$6	T	Def Jam 063956
				Marc Dorsey (additional vocals); all of above (except #15) written or co-written by LL Cool J			
12/14/02+	36	15		23 **Paradise** ...S:33 / A:36 *(2 versions) / After School* (w/**P. Diddy**)	$6	T	Def Jam 063820
				LL COOL J feat. Amerie			
				samples "Rising To The Top" by Keni Burke			
12/28/02+	❶4	21		24 **All I Have** ...A:❶4			album cut
				JENNIFER LOPEZ Featuring LL Cool J			
				from the album *This Is Me...Then* on Epic 86231			
				LLOYD, Ian — see STORIES			
				LMNT '01			
				Pop vocal group from Orlando, Florida: Bryan Chan, Mike Miller, Ikaika Kahoano and Jonas Persch. Formed for the ABC-TV series *Making The Band.*			
12/8/01	40S	11		**Juliet** ...*Greatest Gift*	$5	★+	Atlantic 85199
	★358★			**LOBO** C&W/AC/LP '72			
				Born Roland Kent Lavoie on 7/31/43 in Tallahassee, Florida. Pop singer/songwriter/guitarist. Played with the Legends in Tampa in 1961. The Legends included **Jim Stafford**, Gerald Chambers, Gram Parsons and Jon Corneal. Lobo is Spanish for wolf. Lavoie formed own publishing company, Boo Publishing, in 1974.			
				1)I'd Love You To Want Me 2)Me And You And A Dog Named Boo 3)Don't Expect Me To Be Your Friend			
4/3/71	5	13		1 **Me And You And A Dog Named Boo** ...AC2 *Walk Away From It All*	$6		Big Tree 112
6/26/71	46	9		2 **She Didn't Do Magic /**			
6/26/71		9		3 **I'm The Only One** ...	$6		Big Tree 116
9/4/71	72	3		4 **California Kid And Reemo** ...*A Little Different*	$6		Big Tree 119
7/8/72	56	9		5 **A Simple Man** ...*Don't Expect Me To Be Your Friend*	$6		Big Tree 141
9/23/72	22	14	●	6 **I'd Love You To Want Me** AC1 *Am I True To Myself*	$5		Big Tree 147
12/30/72+	8	13		7 **Don't Expect Me To Be Your Friend** ...AC2 *A Big Red Kite*	$5		Big Tree 158
				first issued as the B-side of #5 above			
4/7/73	27	11		8 **It Sure Took A Long, Long Time** ...*Running Deer*	$5		Big Tree 16001
6/23/73	22	12		9 **How Can I Tell Her** ...*Hope You're Proud Of Me Girl*	$5		Big Tree 16004
11/3/73	68	7		10 **There Ain't No Way /**			
				#5-7 & 10: from the album *Of A Simple Man*			
12/8/73	86	2		11 **Love Me For What I Am** ...	$5		Big Tree 16012
4/13/74	37	7		12 **Standing At The End Of The Line** ...*Stoney*	$5		Big Tree 15001
				#8, 9, 11 & 12: from the album *Calumet*			
7/20/74	43	9		13 **Rings** ...*I'm Only Sleeping*	$5		Big Tree 15008
3/29/75	27	9		14 **Don't Tell Me Goodnight** ...*My Momma Had Soul*	$5		Big Tree 16033
				all of above (except #4 & 13) written by Lobo; all of above produced by Phil Gernhard			
7/28/79	23	17		15 **Where Were You When I Was Falling In Love** ...AC2 *I Don't Wanna Make Love Anymore*	$4		MCA/Curb 41065
12/22/79+	75	8		16 **Holdin' On For Dear Love** ...*Gus, The Dancing Dog*	$4		MCA/Curb 41152
				LOCAL H ROK/LP '96			
				Rock duo from Zion, Illinois: Scott Lucas (vocals, guitar, bass) and Joe Daniels (drums).			
11/16/96	46A	13		**Bound For The Floor** ...			album cut
				from the album *As Good As Dead* on Island 524202			

DEBUT	PEAK	WKS	Gold	A-side (Chart Hit)	B-side	$	Sym	Label & Number

LOCKLIN, Hank

C&W/BUB '60

Born Lawrence Hankins Locklin on 2/15/18 in McLellan, Florida. Country singer/songwriter/guitarist. Charted 33 Country hits, 1949-71. Elected mayor of McLellan in the early 1960s. Own TV series in Houston and Dallas in the 1970s.

DEBUT	PEAK	WKS	Gold	A-side (Chart Hit)	B-side	$	Sym	Label & Number
12/30/57+	66	11		1 **Geisha Girl** ...T:66	*Livin' Alone*	$20		RCA Victor 6984
6/2/58	77	2		2 **Send Me The Pillow You Dream On** ...T:77	*Why Don't You Haul Off And Love Me*	$15		RCA Victor 7127
5/23/60	8	22		3 **Please Help Me, I'm Falling** ...CW[14]	*My Old Home Town*	$15		RCA Victor 7692

LODGE, John — see MOODY BLUES, The

LOEB, Lisa

BUB/LP '94

Born on 3/11/68 in Bethesda, Maryland; raised in Dallas, Texas. Adult Alternative pop-rock singer/songwriter/guitarist. Nine Stories consisted of Tim Bright (guitar), Joe Quigley (bass) and Jonathan Feinberg (drums).

DEBUT	PEAK	WKS	Gold	A-side (Chart Hit)	B-side	$	Sym	Label & Number
5/7/94	❶[3]	30	●	1 **Stay (I Missed You)** A:❶[4] / S:2	*(remix)*	$3	▮	RCA 62870
				from the movie *Reality Bites* starring Winona Ryder; Loeb was not under contract to a record label during this hit				
9/23/95	18	20		2 **Do You Sleep?** ...A:23 / S:24	*When All The Stars Were Falling*	$3	▮[V]	Geffen 19388
7/20/96	83	5		3 **Waiting For Wednesday** ...	*Stay (live)*	$3	▮	Geffen 19400
				LISA LOEB & Nine Stories (above 3)				
11/1/97+	17	22		4 **I Do** ...A:13 / S:34	*Jake*	$3	▮	Geffen 19416
5/2/98	71	7		5 **Let's Forget About It** ...	*I Do (remix)*	$3	▮	Geffen 19424

LOGGINS, Dave

AC/LP '74

Born on 11/10/47 in Mountain City, Tennessee. Pop-country singer/songwriter. Cousin of **Kenny Loggins**.

DEBUT	PEAK	WKS	Gold	A-side (Chart Hit)	B-side	$	Sym	Label & Number
6/1/74	5	18		1 **Please Come To Boston** ...AC[1]	*Let Me Go Now*	$5		Epic 11115
11/16/74	57	5		2 **Someday** ...	*Girl From Knoxville*	$5		Epic 50035

LOGGINS, Kenny ★135★

AC/LP '84

Born on 1/7/48 in Everett, Washington; raised in Alhambra, California. Pop-rock singer/songwriter/guitarist. Cousin of **Dave Loggins**. In band Gator Creek with producer Michael Omartian (later with **Rhythm Heritage**), later in Second Helping. Worked as a songwriter for Wingate Music; wrote **Nitty Gritty Dirt Band**'s "House At Pooh Corner." Signed as a solo artist with Columbia in 1971 where he met and recorded with Jim Messina from 1972-76 (as **Loggins & Messina**).

1)Footloose 2)Danger Zone 3)Whenever I Call You "Friend" 4)I'm Alright 5)Nobody's Fool

DEBUT	PEAK	WKS	Gold	A-side (Chart Hit)	B-side	$	Sym	Label & Number
7/30/77	66	11		1 **I Believe In Love** ...	*Enter My Dream*	$5		Columbia 10569
7/29/78	5	20		2 **Whenever I Call You "Friend"** ...	*Angelique*	$5		Columbia 10794
				Stevie Nicks (harmony vocal)				
12/2/78+	60	8		3 **Easy Driver** ...	*Somebody Knows*	$5		Columbia 10866
10/20/79+	11	23		4 **This Is It** ...	*Will It Last*	$4		Columbia 11109
2/23/80	36	13		5 **Keep The Fire** ...	*Now And Then*	$4		Columbia 11215
7/12/80	7	22		6 **I'm Alright** ...	*Lead The Way*	$4		Columbia 11317
				Eddie Money (backing vocal); theme from the movie *Caddyshack* starring Ted Knight and **Rodney Dangerfield**				
8/28/82	17	12		7 **Don't Fight It** ...	*The More We Try (Loggins)*	$3	■	Columbia 03192
				KENNY LOGGINS with Steve Perry				
11/27/82+	15	17		8 **Heart To Heart** ...	*The More We Try*	$3		Columbia 03377
				Michael McDonald (backing vocal, #4 & 8)				
3/12/83	24	14		9 **Welcome To Heartlight** ...	*Only A Miracle*	$3	■	Columbia 03555
				inspired by the writings of children from Heartlight School				
1/28/84	❶[3]	23	▲	10 **Footloose**	*Swear Your Love*	$3	■	Columbia 04310
6/16/84	22	14		11 **I'm Free (Heaven Helps The Man)** ...	*Welcome To Heartlight*	$3	■	Columbia 04452
				above 2 from the movie *Footloose* starring Kevin Bacon				
3/23/85	29	10		12 **Vox Humana** ...A:25	*Love Will Follow*	$3	■	Columbia 04849
5/25/85	40	22		13 **Forever** ...	*At Last*	$3	■	Columbia 04931
10/12/85	88	2		14 **I'll Be There** ...	*No Lookin' Back*	$3		Columbia 05625
5/10/86	2[1]	21		15 **Danger Zone** ...S:❶[1] / A:3	*I'm Gonna Do It Right*	$3	■	Columbia 05893
8/16/86	60	12		16 **Playing With The Boys** ...	*Love Will Follow*	$3	■	Columbia 05902
				above 2 from the movie *Top Gun* starring Tom Cruise				
3/7/87	11	25		17 **Meet Me Half Way** ...A:10 / S:11	*Semifinal* (**Giorgio Moroder**)	$3	■	Columbia 06690
				from the movie *Over The Top* starring Sylvester Stallone				
7/9/88	8	18		18 **Nobody's Fool** ...A:6 / S:10	*I'm Gonna Do It Right*	$3	■	Columbia 07971
				theme from the movie *Caddyshack II* starring Jackie Mason and Chevy Chase				
11/12/88	82	5		19 **I'm Gonna Miss You** ...	*Isabella's Eyes*	$3	■	Columbia 08091
				Mickey Thomas (backing vocal)				
2/4/89	76	8		20 **Tell Her** ...	*Hope For The Runaway*	$3		Columbia 68531
				remake of **The Exciters**' 1963 hit "Tell Him"; above 4 from the album *Back To Avalon*				
10/26/91	65	13		21 **Conviction Of The Heart** ...A:75	*My Father's House*	$3	▮[V]	Columbia 74029
4/5/97	60[A]	15		22 **For The First Time** ...AC[2]				album cut
				from the album *Yesterday, Today, Tomorrow - The Greatest Hits Of Kenny Loggins* on Columbia 67986				

LOGGINS & MESSINA

C&W/LP '73

Duo of **Kenny Loggins** (see above bio) and Jim Messina (born on 12/5/47 in Maywood, California; raised in Harlingen, Texas). Messina was a member of **Buffalo Springfield** and **Poco**.

1)Your Mama Don't Dance 2)My Music 3)Thinking Of You

DEBUT	PEAK	WKS	Gold	A-side (Chart Hit)	B-side	$	Sym	Label & Number
4/15/72	84	5		1 **Vahevala** ...	*Same Old Wine*	$6		Columbia 45550
				early pressings show title as "Vahevella" (pronounced va-hee-va-la)				
6/10/72	86	2		2 **Nobody But You** ...	*Danny's Song*	$6		Columbia 45617
				B-side was a #7 hit for **Anne Murray** in 1973				
11/11/72+	4	16	●	3 **Your Mama Don't Dance**	*Golden Ribbons*	$5		Columbia 45719
				KENNY LOGGINS AND JIM MESSINA (above 3)				
3/31/73	18	13		4 **Thinking Of You** ...	*Till The Ends Meet*	$5		Columbia 45815
11/3/73	16	13		5 **My Music** ...	*A Love Song*	$5		Columbia 45952

DEBUT	PEAK	WKS	Gold	A-side (Chart Hit)	B-side	$	Sym	Label & Number
				LOGGINS & MESSINA — Cont'd				
3/2/74	71	6		6 **Watching The River Run**	*Travelin' Blues*	$5		Columbia 46010
2/8/75	84	2		7 **Changes**	*Get A Hold*	$5		Columbia 10077
4/5/75	52	7		8 **Growin'**	*Keep Me In Mind*	$5		Columbia 10118
8/30/75	84	2		9 **I Like It Like That**	*Angry Eyes*	$5		Columbia 10188
10/18/75	89	2		10 **A Lover's Question**	*Angry Eyes*	$5		Columbia 10222
				later pressings have "Oh, Lonesome Me" as the B-side (#92 Country hit); all of above produced by Jim Messina				
				LO-KEY? R&B/LP '93				
				Funk group from Minneapolis, Minnesota: Prof T. and Dre (vocals), Lance Alexander (keyboards), T-Bone (bass) and "D" (drums).				
11/14/92+	27	20		1 **I Got A Thang 4 Ya!** RB[1] S:20 / A:31	*(album version) / (3 album snippets)*	$4	▮	Perspective 0008
4/24/93	91	2		2 **Sweet On U**	*(remix)*	$4	▮	Perspective 7418
				LOLITA BUB '60				
				Born Ditta Zuza Einzinger on 1/17/31 in St. Poelten, Austria. Female singer.				
10/24/60	5	18		1 **Sailor (Your Home Is The Sea)**	*La Luna (Quando La Luna)* [F]	$12	■	Kapp 349
2/6/61	94	3		2 **Cowboy Jimmy Joe (Die Sterne Der Prarie)**	*Theme From "A Summer Place"* (#112) [F]	$12	■	Kapp 370
				LONDON, Julie BUB/LP '55				
				Born Julie Peck on 9/26/26 in Santa Rosa, California. Died of a stroke on 10/18/2000 (age 74). Singer/actress. Played "Dixie McCall" on TV's *Emergency.* Married to Jack Webb from 1945-53.				
11/12/55	9	20	●	**Cry Me A River** A:9 / T:13 / J:14 / S:23	*S'Wonderful*	$15		Liberty 55006
				Barney Kessel (guitar); Ray Leatherwood (bass)				
				LONDON, Laurie '58				
				Born on 1/19/44 in London, England. Teen male singer.				
3/24/58	❶[4]	19	●	**He's Got The Whole World (In His Hands)** A:❶[4] / S:2 / T:2	*Handed Down*	$15		Capitol 3891
				Geoff Love (orch.); traditional Afro-American gospel song				
				LONDONBEAT LP '91				
				R&B-dance vocal trio of Americans Jimmy Helms and George Chandler, with Trinidad native Jimmy Chambers. Backed by British producer/multi-instrumentalist Willy M.				
2/9/91	❶[1]	19	●	1 **I've Been Thinking About You** A:❶[2] / S:❶[1]	*(3 album snippets)*	$3	▮	Radioactive 54005
5/11/91	18	15		2 **A Better Love** A:31	*(3 album snippets)*	$3	▮	Radioactive 54101
4/15/95	62	5		3 **Come Back** A:39	*Be There For Me*	$3	▮	Radioactive 54956
				LONDON QUIREBOYS, The ROK/LP '90				
				Hard-rock group formed in London, England: Spike (vocals), Guy Bailey and Guy Griffin (guitars), Chris Johnstone (keyboards), Nigel Mogg (bass) and Ian Wallace (drums).				
9/22/90	76	9		**I Don't Love You Anymore**	*Mayfair*	$4	▮	Capitol 44588
				LONDON SYMPHONY ORCHESTRA — see WILLIAMS, John				
				LONE JUSTICE LP '87				
				Country-rock group from Los Angeles, California: Maria McKee (vocals), Ryan Hedgecock (guitar), Marvin Etzioni (bass) and Dan Heffington (drums). Etzioni and Heffington left in early 1986; Shane Fontayne (guitar), Bruce Brody (keyboards), Gregg Sutton (bass) and Rudy Richman (drums) joined.				
5/11/85	71	6		1 **Ways To Be Wicked**	*Cactus Rose*	$3	■	Geffen 29023
				co-written by **Tom Petty**				
7/27/85	73	5		2 **Sweet, Sweet Baby (I'm Falling)**	*Don't Toss Us Away*	$3	■	Geffen 28965
1/10/87	47	12		3 **Shelter**	*Belfry*	$3	■	Geffen 28520
	★578★			**LONESTAR** C&W/BUB/LP '00				
				Country group from Nashville, Tennessee: Richie McDonald (vocals, guitar), John Rich (vocals, bass), Michael Britt (guitar), Dean Sams (keyboards) and Keech Rainwater (drums). Rich left in January 1998.				
11/22/97	93	4		1 **You Walked In** S:71	*Keys To My Heart*	$4	▮[V]	BNA 64942
12/5/98	95	2		2 **Everything's Changed**				album cut
				above 2 from the album *Crazy Nights* on BNA 67422				
6/5/99+	❶[2]	55	●	3 **Amazed** CW[8] S:3 / A:5	*(AC mix)*	$4	★[V]	BNA 65957
				charted 20 weeks (#24); re-entered on 12/25/99; "45": BNA 65755; B-side: "Tell Her"				
12/18/99+	39	20		4 **Smile** CW[1] A:32			V	album cut
				"45": BNA 65906; B-side: "Amazed"				
6/10/00	30	20		5 **What About Now** CW[4] A:23			V	album cut
				"45": BNA 60212; B-side: "Smile"				
11/18/00+	39	20		6 **Tell Her** CW[2] A:33			V	album cut
				above 4 from the album *Lonely Grill* on BNA 67762				
5/5/01	24	20		7 **I'm Already There** CW[6] A:19			V	album cut
				"45" issued for above 2 on BNA 69083				
10/27/01	63	15		8 **With Me** A:62			V	album cut
				"45": BNA 69105; B-side: "Out Go The Lights"				
5/11/02	36	17		9 **Not A Day Goes By** A:35			V	album cut
				"45": BNA 69134; B-side: "Unusually Unusual"; above 3 from the album *I'm Already There* on BNA 67011				
				LONG, Shorty BUB '68				
				Born Frederick Earl Long on 5/20/40 in Birmingham, Alabama. Drowned in a boating accident on the Detroit River on 6/29/69 (age 29). R&B singer/songwriter. Moved to Detroit in 1959. First recorded for Tri-Phi in 1962.				
9/24/66	97	1		1 **Function At The Junction**	*Call On Me*	$15		Soul 35021
2/17/68	75	4		2 **Night Fo' Last**	*(instrumental)*	$15		Soul 35040
6/1/68	8	11		3 **Here Comes The Judge**	*Sing What You Wanna* [N]	$15		Soul 35044
				title inspired by a recurrent gag line on TV's *Rowan & Martin's Laugh-In*; Judge: Pervis Jackson of the **Spinners**				
				LONGET, Claudine AC/BUB/LP '68				
				Born on 1/29/42 in Paris, France. Singer/actress. Married to **Andy Williams** from 1962-67. Charged but later acquitted of fatally shooting her boyfriend, skier Spider Sabich.				
11/5/66	98	2		1 **Meditation (Meditacao)**	*Sunrise, Sunset*	$7		A&M 817
5/27/67	91	1		2 **Hello, Hello**	*Wanderlove*	$7		A&M 846

DEBUT	PEAK	WKS	Gold	A-side (Chart Hit)..........B-side	$	Sym	Label & Number
				LONGET, Claudine — Cont'd			
8/5/67	100	2		3 **Good Day Sunshine**..........*The Look Of Love*	$7		A&M 864
				written by **John Lennon** and **Paul McCartney** (on **The Beatles**' 1966 album *Revolver*)			
12/23/67	30[X]	2		4 **Snow**..........*I Don't Intend To Spend Christmas Without You* [X]	$7		A&M 895
				written by **Randy Newman**			
2/24/68	71	9		5 **Love Is Blue (L'Amour Est Bleu)** *Think Of Rain* [F]	$6		A&M 909
				LOOKING GLASS AC/BUB/LP **'72**			
				Pop-rock group formed in New Jersey: Elliot Lurie (vocals, guitar), Larry Gonsky (keyboards), Piet Sweval (bass; **Starz**) and Jeff Grob (drums). Sweval died on 1/23/90 (age 51).			
6/17/72	❶[1]	16	●	1 **Brandy (You're A Fine Girl)**..........*One By One*	$6		Epic 10874
7/21/73	33	15		2 **Jimmy Loves Mary-Anne**..........*Wooly Eyes*	$6		Epic 11001
				LOON **'02**			
				Born in Harlem, New York. Male rapper.			
3/16/02	2[4]	23		1 **I Need A Girl (Part One)**..........A:2 / S:23 *(3 versions)*	$6	T	Bad Boy 79436
				P. DIDDY Featuring Usher & Loon			
6/8/02	4	26		2 **I Need A Girl (Part Two)**..........A:4 / S:17 *(instrumental) / So Complete*	$6	T	Bad Boy 79441
				P. DIDDY AND GINUWINE Featuring Loon, Mario Winans & Tammy Ruggeri			
8/3/02	58	14		3 **I Do (Wanna Get Close To You)**..........S:41 / A:59 *(4 versions)*	$6	T	Epic 79769
				3LW Featuring P. Diddy & Loon			
				LOOSE ENDS R&B/LP **'85**			
				R&B-dance trio formed in London, England: Carl McIntosh (vocals, guitar), Steve Nichol and Jane Eugene.			
7/20/85	43	10		**Hangin' On A String (Contemplating)**..........RB[1] S:27 *A Little Spice*	$3	■	MCA/Virgin 52570
				LOPEZ, Denise LP **'88**			
				Born in Queens, New York. Female dance singer.			
6/11/88	31	17		1 **Sayin' Sorry (Don't Make It Right)**..........S:22 *(Latin dub)*	$3	■	Vendetta 7200
11/12/88	94	3		2 **If You Feel It**..........*(instrumental)*	$3		Vendetta 7213
11/3/90	86	3		3 **Don't You Wanna Be Mine**..........*(**Clivilles & Cole** club edit)*	$3	▮	A&M 1526
				LOPEZ, Jennifer ★253★ AC/LP **'02**			
				Born on 7/24/70 in the Bronx, New York (of Puerto Rican parents). Singer/actress/dancer. In 1990 was a "Fly Girl" dancer on TV's *In Living Color*. Movie break came as the star of ***Selena*** in 1997; others movies include *Out Of Sight*, *The Cell*, *The Wedding Planner*, *Enough* and *Maid In Manhattan*. Married to professional dancer Cris Judd briefly in 2001. Engaged to actor Ben Affleck in October 2002.			
				1)Ain't It Funny 2)I'm Real 3)If You Had My Love			
5/15/99	❶[5]	25	▲	1 **If You Had My Love**..........S:❶[5] / A:3 *No Me Ames* (w/**Marc Anthony**)	$4	★[V]	Epic/Work 79163 ■
10/16/99	8	20		2 **Waiting For Tonight**..........A:4 *(3 versions)*	$6	T	Epic/Work 79292
				12" single contains special extended versions			
2/19/00	51	17		3 **Feelin' So Good**..........S:7 / A:48 *(album version)*	$4	★[V]	Epic/Work 79387 ■
				JENNIFER LOPEZ (Featuring Big Pun & Fat Joe)			
				samples "Set It Off" by Strafe			
12/9/00+	3	21		4 **Love Don't Cost A Thing**..........A:❶[2] / S:10 *(3 mixes) / Let's Get Loud*	$8	★[*V]	Epic 79547
				"45": Epic 79560; B-side: (same)			
4/7/01	18	20		5 **Play**..........A:15			album cut
				Christina Milian (backing vocal)			
7/7/01	❶[5]	31		6 **I'm Real**..........A:❶[6] / S:31 *(3 versions)*	$6	T[V]	Epic 79639
				JENNIFER LOPEZ featuring Ja Rule			
				samples "All Night Long" by the **Mary Jane Girls**; "45": Epic 79662; B-side: "Love Don't Cost A Thing"			
12/29/01+	❶[6]	27		7 **Ain't It Funny** A:❶[6]			album cut
				JENNIFER LOPEZ featuring Ja Rule			
				samples "Flava In Ya Ear" by **Craig Mack**			
4/27/02	10	23		8 **I'm Gonna Be Alright**..........S:7 / A:10 *(2 versions) / Alive* (Lopez - AC #18)	$8	★[*]	Epic 79759
				JENNIFER LOPEZ Featuring Nas			
				samples "Why You Treat Me So Bad" by **Club Nouveau**; above 5 from the album *J.Lo* on Epic 63786			
10/12/02	3	20		9 **Jenny From The Block**..........A:3 / S:16 *(4 versions)*	$6	T	Epic 79825
				JENNIFER LOPEZ Featuring Jadakiss & Styles			
				samples "South Bronx" by Boogie Down Productions and "Hijack" by **Herbie Mann**			
12/28/02+	❶[4]	21		10 **All I Have**..........A:❶[4]			album cut
				JENNIFER LOPEZ Featuring LL Cool J			
				above 2 from the album *This Is Me...Then* on Epic 86231			
				LOPEZ, Trini AC/BUB/LP **'63**			
				Born Trinidad Lopez on 5/15/37 in Dallas, Texas. Pop-folk singer/guitarist. Discovered by **Don Costa** while performing at PJs nightclub in Los Angeles. Played "Pedro Jiminez" in the movie *The Dirty Dozen*.			
				1)If I Had A Hammer 2)Lemon Tree 3)Kansas City			
7/27/63	3	14		1 **If I Had A Hammer** *Unchain My Heart* [L]	$10		Reprise 20,198
				written as "The Hammer Song" by **Pete Seeger** & Lee Hays of The Weavers in 1958			
11/16/63+	23	10		2 **Kansas City**..........*Lonesome Traveler* [L]	$10		Reprise 20,236
3/21/64	94	2		3 **Jailer, Bring Me Water**..........*You Can't Say Good-Bye* [L]	$10		Reprise 0260
				adaptation by **Bobby Darin**; based on the folk song "Go Tell Aunt Rhody"			
5/9/64	43	13		4 **What Have I Got Of My Own**..........*Ya Ya* [L]	$10		Reprise 0276
8/22/64	42	8		5 **Michael**..........*San Francisco De Assisi*	$10		Reprise 0300
1/23/65	20	7		6 **Lemon Tree**..........*Pretty Eyes*	$10	■	Reprise 0336
5/1/65	94	1		7 **Sad Tomorrows**..........*I've Lost My Love For You*	$8	■	Reprise 0328
6/12/65	85	3		8 **Are You Sincere**..........*You'll Be Sorry*	$8		Reprise 0376
10/16/65	54	9		9 **Sinner Man**..........*Double Trouble*	$8	■	Reprise 0405
				from the movie *Marriage On The Rocks* starring **Frank Sinatra**			

DEBUT	PEAK	WKS	Gold	A-side (Chart Hit)...B-side	$	Sym	Label & Number
				LOPEZ, Trini — Cont'd			
4/9/66	**39**	7		10 **I'm Comin' Home, Cindy** ... *The 32nd Of May*	$8		Reprise 0455
6/25/66	**86**	5		11 **La Bamba - Part I** ... *Trini's Tune* [F-L]	$8		Reprise 0480
				originally released on Reprise 20,190 in 1963			
2/18/67	**93**	3		12 **Gonna Get Along Without Ya' Now** ... *Love Letters*	$7		Reprise 0547
				#25 hit for **Teresa Brewer** in 1952			
3/2/68	**99**	2		13 **Sally Was A Good Old Girl** ... *It's A Great Life*	$7		Reprise 0659
				#20 Country hit for Hank Cochran in 1962; all of above arranged and produced by **Don Costa**			
				LORAIN, A'Me '90			
				Born in Simi Valley, California. White female pop-dance singer.			
1/20/90	**9**	20		1 **Whole Wide World** ... S:9 / A:11 *Stop Twistin' My Arm* (Barrence Whitfield & The Savages)	$3	■V	RCA 9099
				from the movie *True Love* starring Annabella Sciorra; "45": RCA 9098 and issued with 2 different picture sleeves			
6/16/90	**72**	6		2 **Follow My Heartbeat** ... *Whole Wide World (12" remix)*	$3	■V	RCA 2620
				LORBER, Jeff BUB/LP '87			
				Born on 11/4/52 in Philadelphia, Pennsylvania. Jazz fusion keyboardist.			
12/6/86+	**27**	16		**Facts Of Love** ... A:27 / S:29 *Sand Castles* (Lorber)	$3	■	Warner 28588
				JEFF LORBER Featuring Karyn White			
				LORD ROCKINGHAM'S XI '58			
				Studio rock and roll band led by Harry Robinson (born in Scotland). Included Cherry Wainer (organ), Benny Green and Red Price (saxophones), and Rory Blackwell (drums). Green died on 6/22/98 (age 71).			
10/6/58	**96**	1		**Fried Onions** ... H:96 *The Squelch* [I]	$20		London 1810
				LORDS OF THE UNDERGROUND R&B/BUB/LP '93			
				Black rap trio from Newark, New Jersey: Al "Mr. Funkyman" Wardrick, Dupre "Do It All" Kelly and Bruce "Lord Jazz" Colston.			
3/27/93	**74**	11		1 **Funky Child** ... S:49 *(instrumental)*	$4	■	Pendulum 64672
7/10/93	**55**	20		2 **Chief Rocka** ... S:41 / A:61 *(instrumental)*	$4	■	Pendulum 64631
12/18/93	**93**	6		3 **Here Come The Lords** ... *(7" version)*	$4	■	Pendulum 58065
10/29/94+	**73**	15		4 **Tic Toc** ... *(TV mix)*	$4	■	Pendulum 58246
				samples "La Di Da Di" by Doug E. Fresh			
				LORD TARIQ & PETER GUNZ R&B/LP '98			
				Black rap duo from Brooklyn, New York: Sean Hamilton ("Lord Tariq") and Peter Panky ("Peter Gunz").			
11/15/97+	**9**	28	▲	**Deja Vu (Uptown Baby)** ... S:5 / A:42 *(remix) / Marmalade*	$3	■	Columbia 78755
				samples "Black Cow" by **Steely Dan**			
				LORELEIS, The '55			
				Female pop vocal duo from Wyandotte, Michigan: Peggy Reinagle and Gail Menafee.			
11/12/55	**91**	1		**You're So Nice To Be Near** ... T:91 *Wildsville*	$40		Spotlight 390
				George Annis (orch.)			
				LORENZ, Trey R&B/BUB/LP '92			
				Born on 1/19/69 in Florence, South Carolina. Male R&B singer. Also see **Mariah Carey**'s "I'll Be There."			
10/3/92	**19**	20		1 **Someone To Hold** ... S:21 / A:27 *Find A Way*	$3	■V	Epic 74482
				co-written and co-produced by **Mariah Carey**			
3/23/02	**54^S**	3		2 **I'll Be There** ... *So Blessed* [L]	$4	★	Columbia 79698
				MARIAH CAREY Featuring Trey Lorenz			
				LORENZO '93			
				Born Lorenzo Smith on 5/23/72 in Miami, Florida. Male R&B singer.			
1/23/93	**57^S**	4		**Make Love 2 Me** ... BUB:103 *(3 versions)*	$4	■	Alpha Int'l. 787001
				LORING, Gloria LP '86			
				Born on 12/10/46 in Manhattan, New York. Played "Liz Curtis" on the TV soap *Days Of Our Lives.* Married to actor Alan Thicke from 1970-83. Mother of singer Robin **Thicke**.			
7/5/86	**2^2**	21		**Friends And Lovers** ... AC² S:❶¹ / A:2 *You Always Knew* (Loring)	$3	■	USA Carrere 06122
				GLORIA LORING & CARL ANDERSON			
				popularized due to exposure on TV's *Days Of Our Lives*			
				LOS BRAVOS LP '66			
				Rock group formed in Spain: Mike Kogel (vocals; born in Germany), Tony Martinez (guitar), Manuel Fernandez (organ), Miguel Danus (bass) and Pablo Gomez (drums). Kogel also recorded as **Mike Kennedy**.			
8/13/66	**4**	12		1 **Black Is Black** ... *I Want A Name*	$15		Press 60002
12/17/66	**91**	2		2 **Going Nowhere** ... *Brand New Baby*	$12		Press 60003
5/25/68	**51**	7		3 **Bring A Little Lovin'** ... *Make It Last*	$12		Parrot 3020
				from the Spanish movie *Bravos II*			
				LOS DEL MAR '96			
				Studio group from Canada featuring lead singer Wil Veloz. Formed to 'cover' the **Los Del Rio** version below.			
6/22/96	**71**	15		**Macarena** ... S:44 *(same version)* [F]	$4	■	Critique 15558
				LOS DEL RIO LP '96			
				Flamenco guitar duo from Seville, Spain: Antonio Romero Monge and Rafael Ruiz Perdigones. Formed duo in the 1960s. In 1993, they wrote and recorded "Macarena," which became a worldwide dance craze after it was remixed by the Miami production team of the Bayside Boys.			
9/2/95+	**❶[14]**	60	▲[4]	1 **Macarena (bayside boys mix)** ... S:❶[13] / A:7 *Can You Feel It* (Matrix) [F]	$3	■V	RCA 64407
				above is a U.S. remix by the Bayside Boys (Carlos A. de Yarza and Mike Triay) of #2 below; female vocal sung in English, male chorus sung in Spanish; originally charted for 20 weeks (#45); re-charted on 5/11/96; "45": RCA 64415; B-side: "Scatman" by **Scatman John** (#60)			
7/6/96	**23**	21		2 **Macarena (non stop)** ... S:13 *Pura Carroceria / La Niña* [F]	$3	■	BMG/U.S. Latin 39227
				the original Spanish version; The Bass Bumper Remixes released on BMG/U.S. Latin 41143			
12/21/96	**57**	4		3 **Macarena Christmas** ... S:43 *(club version) / Macarena (2 mixes)* [X]	$4	■	BMG/U.S. Latin 44124
				"Macarena" mixed with a medley of holiday tunes including "Joy To The World," "Jingle Bells," "Silent Night," "Rudolph The Red-Nosed Reindeer," "White Christmas" and "Auld Lang Syne"			

DEBUT	PEAK	WKS	Gold	A-side (Chart Hit)..................B-side	$	Sym	Label & Number
				LOS INDIOS TABAJARAS LP **'63**			
				Indian guitar instrumental duo from Ceara, Brazil: brothers Natalicio (born Musiperi) and Antenor (born Herundy) Lima.			
9/21/63	6	14		1 **Maria Elena**..................*Jungle Dream* [I]	$8		RCA Victor 8216
				recorded in 1958; #1 hit in 1941 for **Jimmy Dorsey & His Orchestra**			
3/14/64	82	2		2 **Always In My Heart**..................*Moonlight And Shadows* [I]	$8		RCA Victor 8313
				#10 hit in 1942 for Glenn Miller & His Orchestra (title song from the movie starring Kay Francis)			
				LOS LOBOS ROK/C&W/LP **'87**			
				Hispanic-American rock group from East Los Angeles, California: David Hildago (vocals), Cesar Rosas (guitar), Steve Berlin (saxophone), Conrad Lozano (bass) and Louie Perez (drums).			
3/23/85	78	5		1 **Will The Wolf Survive?**..................*The Breakdown*	$4	■	Slash 29093
6/27/87	❶[3]	21		2 **La Bamba**..................S:❶[3] / A:❶[3] *Charlena* [F]	$4	■	Slash 28336
9/12/87	21	14		3 **Come On, Let's Go**..................A:18 / S:24 *Ooh! My Head*	$4		Slash 28186
				above 2 from the **Ritchie Valens**' biographical movie *La Bamba* starring Lou Diamond Phillips			
				LOS POP TOPS **'71**			
				Pop vocal group based in Spain. Lead singer Phil Trim is from the West Indies.			
9/28/68	78	4		1 **Oh Lord, Why Lord**..................*The Voice Of The Dying Man*	$8	■	Calla 154
				melody based on Pachelbel's *Canon in D Major*			
10/9/71	57	10		2 **Mammy Blue** *[POP-TOPS]*..................*Road To Freedom*	$6		ABC 11311
				LOST BOYZ LP **'96**			
				Rap group from Queens, New York: Spigg Nice, **Mr. Cheeks**, Freekie Tah and Pretty Lou. Freekie Tah (born Raymond Rogers) was shot to death on 3/29/99 (age 28). Also see **Imagin**, **Joe** and **112**.			
5/13/95	91	6		1 **LifestyLes Of The Rich And ShameLess**.........S:69 *Jeeps, Lex Coups, Bimaz & Benz*	$4	▮	Uptown/MCA 55006
				samples "Jealousy" by **Club Nouveau**			
9/9/95	67	11		2 **Jeeps, Lex Coups, Bimaz & Benz**..................S:58 *Keep It Real*	$4	▮	Uptown/MCA 55062
2/17/96	65	13		3 **Can't Be Wasting My Time**..................S:55 *(w/o rap)*	$3	▮[V]	Island 854538
				MONA LISA featuring Lost Boyz			
				samples "MC's Act Like They Don't Know" by **KRS-One**; "45": Island 854552; B-side: "All The Things" by **Joe** (#11)			
3/23/96	33	18	●	4 **Renee** S:16 / A:72 *(remix)*	$3	▮	Island 854584
				above 2 from the movie *Don't Be A Menace* starring Marlon Wayans			
10/5/96	51	16		5 **Music Makes Me High**..................S:36 *(album version)*	$3	▮	Universal 56022
				LOST BOYZ (featuring Tha Dogg Pound)			
				samples "Bounce, Rock, Skate, Roll" by **Vaughan Mason & Crew**			
1/4/97	60	17		6 **Get Up**..................S:53 *(3 versions)*	$3	▮	Universal 56032
				samples "What Cha Gonna Do With My Lovin'" by **Stephanie Mills**			
9/20/97	52	10		7 **Me And My Crazy World**..................S:39 *(remix) / Summer Time*	$3	▮	Universal 56131
				LOST GENERATION, The R&B/BUB **'70**			
				R&B vocal group from Chicago, Illinois: brothers Lowrell (lead) and Fred Simon, Larry Brownlee (of **The C.O.D.'s**; died in 1978) and Jesse Dean. Disbanded in 1974. Lowrell began recording solo (as Lowrell) in 1978.			
6/6/70	30	14		**The Sly, Slick, And The Wicked**..................*You're So Young But You're So True*	$10		Brunswick 55436
				LOS UMBRELLOS **'97**			
				Dance trio from Denmark. Male singer Al Agami is originally from the African nation of Lado. The female singers are Grith Hojfeldt and Mai-Britt.			
8/30/97	42	27		**No Tengo Dinero**..................S:40 / A:54 *(remix) / Theme From Los Umbrellos*	$3	▮[V]	Flex/EMI 58663
				melody is from the 1960 movie and song hit "Never On Sunday"; "45": Flex/Virgin 19731; B-side: "Hasta La Fuego"			
				LOU, Bonnie — see BONNIE LOU			
				LOUCHIE LOU & MICHIE ONE **'02**			
				Female dancehall-reggae vocal duo from London, England: Louchie Gold and Michie Charles.			
4/6/02	20[S]	4		**10 Out Of 10**..................*Dynamite*	$5	★	Interscope 97413
				melody is from Mozart Symphony No. 40, 1st Movement			
				LOUDERMILK, John D. C&W/BUB **'61**			
				Born on 3/31/34 in Durham, North Carolina. Pop-country singer/songwriter/multi-instrumentalist. Wrote "Waterloo," "Tobacco Road," "Indian Reservation" and many others. Recorded as **Johnny Dee** and Ebe Sneezer in 1957.			
3/16/57	38	11		1 **Sittin' In The Balcony**..................T:38 *A-Plus In Love*	$40	□	Colonial 430
				JOHNNY DEE			
				Joe Tanner (guitar); a promotional sleeve including a 4-page booklet insert was issued to introduce Johnny Dee			
11/6/61	32	9		2 **Language Of Love** *Darling Jane*	$12		RCA Victor 7938
4/7/62	73	5		3 **Thou Shalt Not Steal**..................*Mister Jones*	$12		RCA Victor 7993
7/28/62	83	3		4 **Callin' Doctor Casey**..................*Oh How Sad*	$12		RCA Victor 8054
12/1/62	65	4		5 **Road Hog**..................*Angela Jones*	$12	■	RCA Victor 8101
				same melody as **The Browns**' "Ground Hog"			
				LOUIE LOUIE LP **'90**			
				Born Louis Cordero in Los Angeles, California. Dance singer/songwriter. Played **Madonna**'s boyfriend in her "Borderline" video.			
4/28/90	19	16		1 **Sittin' In The Lap Of Luxury**..................A:15 / S:18 *(remix)*	$3	▮[V]	WTG 73266
				"45": WTG 73432			
8/18/90	69	7		2 **I Wanna Get Back With You**..................*Mata Hari*	$3	▮	WTG 73472
				LOUISIANA'S LE ROUX — see LE ROUX			
				LOVE BUB/LP **'66**			
				Rock group from Los Angeles, California. Core members from 1966-68: Arthur Lee (vocals), John Echols and Bryan MacLean (guitars), and Ken Forssi (bass). Forssi died of cancer on 1/5/98 (age 63). MacLean died of a heart attack on 12/25/98 (age 52).			
4/30/66	52	11		1 **My Little Red Book**..................*A Message To Pretty*	$10		Elektra 45603
				"Bubbled Under" (#124) for **Manfred Mann**; from the 1965 movie *What's New Pussycat* starring Peter Sellers			
7/30/66	33	10		2 **7 And 7 Is**..................*No. Fourteen*	$10		Elektra 45605
9/12/70	99	3		3 **Alone Again Or**..................*Good Times*	$8		Elektra 45700
				originally "Bubbled Under" (#123) on 5/4/68 on Elektra 45629			

DEBUT	PEAK	WKS	Gold	A-side (Chart Hit)...B-side	$	Sym	Label & Number

LOVE, Darlene '63

Born Darlene Wright on 7/26/38 in Los Angeles, California. Lead singer of backing group **The Blossoms**. Sang lead on two songs by **The Crystals** and with **Bob B. Soxx & The Blue Jeans**. Phil Spector suggested that she change her name to Darlene Love. Her sister, Edna Wright, was a member of **The Honey Cone**. Starred in the off-Broadway show *Leader of The Pack*. Played Danny Glover's wife in all three *Lethal Weapon* movies.

DEBUT	PEAK	WKS	Gold	A-side (Chart Hit)...B-side	$	Sym	Label & Number
4/6/63	39	8		1 **(Today I Met) The Boy I'm Gonna Marry** ... *Playing For Keeps*	$20		Philles 111
7/20/63	26	10		2 **Wait Til' My Bobby Gets Home** ... *Take It From Me*	$20		Philles 114
10/19/63	53	6		3 **A Fine Fine Boy** ... *Nino & Sonny (Big Trouble)* all of above produced by Phil Spector	$20		Philles 117
1/2/93-	83	3		4 **All Alone On Christmas** ... A:52 *(instrumental)* [X] written and produced by **Little Steven**; from the movie *Home Alone 2: Lost In New York* starring Macauley Culkin	$6	▮	Fox 10003

LOVE, Mike — see CELEBRATION

LOVE, Monie R&B/LP '91

Born Simone Johnson on 7/2/70 in London, England; raised in Brooklyn, New York. Black dance club singer/songwriter.

DEBUT	PEAK	WKS	Gold	A-side (Chart Hit)...B-side	$	Sym	Label & Number
3/16/91	26	16		1 **It's A Shame (My Sister)** ... S:21 / A:31 *(remix)* rap version of the **Spinners**' 1970 hit "It's A Shame"	$3	▮	Warner 19515
8/8/92	96	1		2 **Full Term Love** ... *(Monie's mix)* from the movie *Class Act* starring **Kid 'N Play**	$3	▮	Giant 18954
3/13/93	89	6		3 **Born 2 B.R.E.E.D.** ... A:63 *(Paisley Park version)* B.R.E.E.D.: Build Relationships where Education and Enlightenment Dominate; produced and co-written by **Prince**	$3	▮	Warner 18691

LOVE, Ronnie, And His Orchestra '61

R&B singer.

DEBUT	PEAK	WKS	Gold	A-side (Chart Hit)...B-side	$	Sym	Label & Number
1/9/61	72	4		**Chills And Fever** ... *No Use Pledging My Love* first released on Startime 5001 in 1960 as by Johnny Love ($50)	$20		Dot 16144

LOVE AND KISSES LP '78

Disco studio group assembled by European producer Alec Costandinos. Consisted of singers Don Daniels, Elaine Hill, Dianne Brooks and Jean Graham.

DEBUT	PEAK	WKS	Gold	A-side (Chart Hit)...B-side	$	Sym	Label & Number
5/6/78	22	16		**Thank God It's Friday** ... *You're The Most Precious Thing In My Life* title song from the movie starring Jeff Goldblum	$5		Casablanca 925

LOVE AND MONEY LP '89

Pop trio from Scotland: James Grant (vocals, guitar), Bobby Paterson (bass) and Paul McGeechan (keyboards).

DEBUT	PEAK	WKS	Gold	A-side (Chart Hit)...B-side	$	Sym	Label & Number
2/18/89	75	7		**Halleluiah Man** ... *Love Is A Million Miles Away*	$3	■	Mercury 870596

LOVE AND ROCKETS ROK/LP '89

Pop-rock trio formed in England: Daniel Ash (vocals, guitar), David J (bass) and Kevin Haskins (drums).

DEBUT	PEAK	WKS	Gold	A-side (Chart Hit)...B-side	$	Sym	Label & Number
5/20/89	3	20		1 **So Alive** ... MR[5] S:3 / A:5 *Dreamtime*	$3	■	RCA 8956
9/23/89	82	4		2 **No Big Deal** ... *No Words No More*	$3		Big Time 9045
4/6/96	66[A]	3		3 **Sweet Lover Hangover** ... from the album *Sweet F.A.* on American 43058			album cut

LOVE CHILDS AFRO CUBAN BLUES BAND LP '75

Disco studio group assembled by **Michael Zager**.

DEBUT	PEAK	WKS	Gold	A-side (Chart Hit)...B-side	$	Sym	Label & Number
7/19/75	90	3		**Life And Death In G&A** ... *Bang Bang* [I] written by **Sly Stone**	$6		Roulette 7172

LOVE GENERATION, The '67

Pop group formed in Los Angeles, California: brothers Tom and John Bahler, Mitch Gordon, Jim Wasson, Marilyn Miller and Ann White.

DEBUT	PEAK	WKS	Gold	A-side (Chart Hit)...B-side	$	Sym	Label & Number
6/24/67	74	7		1 **Groovy Summertime** ... *Playin' On The Strings Of The Wind*	$8		Imperial 66243
8/3/68	86	3		2 **Montage From How Sweet It Is (I Know That You Know)** ... *Consciousness Expansion* from the movie *How Sweet It Is* starring James Garner and **Debbie Reynolds**	$8		Imperial 66310

LOVELESS, Patty C&W/BUB/LP '00

Born Patricia Ramey on 1/4/57 in Pikeville, Kentucky. Country singer/songwriter/guitarist.

DEBUT	PEAK	WKS	Gold	A-side (Chart Hit)...B-side	$	Sym	Label & Number
4/17/99	96	4		1 **Can't Get Enough** ... A:75 from the album *Classics* on Epic 69808			album cut
9/16/00	71	14		2 **That's The Kind Of Mood I'm In** ... A:67 / S:73 *You Don't Get No More*	$4	★	Epic 79447

LOVELITES, The R&B '70

Female R&B vocal trio from Chicago, Illinois: sisters Patti Hamilton and Rozena Petty, with Ardell McDaniel.

DEBUT	PEAK	WKS	Gold	A-side (Chart Hit)...B-side	$	Sym	Label & Number
1/10/70	60	10		**How Can I Tell My Mom & Dad** ... *Hey! Stars Of Tomorrow* [I] first released on Lock 723 in 1969 ($10)	$8		Uni 55181

LOVERBOY ROK/BUB/LP '86

★346★

Rock group formed in Canada: **Mike Reno** (vocals; born on 1/8/55) (see #7 below), Paul Dean (guitar; born on 2/19/46), Scott Smith (bass; born on 2/13/55), Matt Frenette (drums; born on 3/7/54) and Doug Johnson (keyboards; left by 1989). Smith drowned on 11/30/2000 (age 45).

1)Lovin' Every Minute Of It 2)This Could Be The Night 3)Hot Girls In Love

DEBUT	PEAK	WKS	Gold	A-side (Chart Hit)...B-side	$	Sym	Label & Number
1/31/81	35	17		1 **Turn Me Loose** ... *Prissy Prissy*	$4		Columbia 11421
6/20/81	55	7		2 **The Kid Is Hot Tonite** ... *Teenage Overdose*	$4	■	Columbia 02068
11/14/81+	29	20		3 **Working For The Weekend** ... *Emotional*	$3	■	Columbia 02589
4/10/82	26	15		4 **When It's Over** ... *It's Your Life* Nancy Nash (backing vocal)	$3	■	Columbia 02814
6/11/83	11	16		5 **Hot Girls In Love** ... *Meltdown*	$3	■	Columbia 03941
9/17/83	34	12		6 **Queen Of The Broken Hearts** ... *Chance Of A Lifetime*	$3	■	Columbia 04096
5/12/84	7	20		7 **Almost Paradise...Love Theme From Footloose** ... AC[1] *Strike Zone* **(Loverboy** - ROK #23) **MIKE RENO and ANN WILSON** from the movie *Footloose* starring Kevin Bacon and Lori Singer	$3	■	Columbia 04418
8/24/85	9	21		8 **Lovin' Every Minute Of It** S:8 / A:11 *Bullet In The Chamber*	$3	■	Columbia 05569
11/16/85	65	9		9 **Dangerous** ... *Too Much Too Soon* co-written by **Bryan Adams**	$3	■	Columbia 05711

DEBUT	PEAK	WKS	Gold	A-side (Chart Hit)................B-side	$	Sym	Label & Number
				LOVERBOY — Cont'd			
1/18/86	**10**	18		10 **This Could Be The Night** ....A:9 / S:13 *It's Your Life*	$3	■	Columbia 05765
4/26/86	**68**	7		11 **Lead A Double Life** ....*Steal The Thunder*	$3	■	Columbia 05867
				above 4 from the album *Lovin' Every Minute Of It*			
8/2/86	**12**	17		12 **Heaven In Your Eyes** ....A:10 / S:13 *Friday Night*	$3	■	Columbia 06178
				from the movie *Top Gun* starring Tom Cruise			
8/22/87	**38**	14		13 **Notorious** ....A:33 *Wildside*	$3	■	Columbia 07324
				co-written by **Jon Bon Jovi**			
12/23/89+	**84**	5		14 **Too Hot** ....*When It's Over*	$3	▮	Columbia 73066
				LOVERS, The R&B **'57**			
				Husband-and-wife R&B duo: Alden "Tarheel Slim" Bunn (born on 9/24/24 in Bailey, North Carolina; died of pneumonia on 8/21/77, age 52) and Anna "Little Ann" Sandford.			
8/19/57	**48**	9		**Darling It's Wonderful** ....T:48 *Gotta Whole Lot Of Lovin' To Do*	$50		Lamp 2005
				Ray Ellis (orch.); reissued on Post 10007 in 1963			
				LOVERS, The **'77**			
				Disco studio group from Philadelphia, Pennsylvania.			
5/14/77	**100**	2		**Discomania** ....*(same version)* [N]	$5		Marlin 3313
				LOVE SPIT LOVE ROK/LP **'94**			
				Rock group featuring brothers/former **Psychedelic Furs** Richard (vocals) and Tim (bass) Butler, with Richard Fortus (guitar) and Frank Ferrer (drums).			
9/10/94	**83**	10		**Am I Wrong** ....*Codeine*	$3	▮	Imago 25073
				LOVE TRIBE **'97**			
				Dance studio group assembled by producers Dewey Bullock, Latanza Waters and Victor Mitchell.			
1/25/97	**89**	5		**Stand Up** ....*(alcatraz robs the edit)*	$3	▮	DV8/A&M 7057
				samples "There But For The Grace Of God Go I" by **Machine**			
				LOVETTE, Eddie **'69**			
				Born in Jamaica. Reggae singer/songwriter.			
5/24/69	**95**	3		**Too Experienced** ....*You're My Girl*	$10		Steady 124
				LOVE UNLIMITED R&B/BUB/LP **'72**			
				Female R&B vocal trio from San Pedro, California: sisters Glodean and Linda James, with Diane Taylor. **Barry White**, who was married to Glodean from 1974-88, was their manager and producer.			
4/1/72	**14**	14	●	1 **Walkin' In The Rain With The One I Love** ....*I Should Have Known*	$6		Uni 55319
				featuring **Barry White**'s voice on the telephone			
12/15/73	**83**	4		2 **It May Be Winter Outside, (But In My Heart It's Spring)** ....*It's Winter Again* [I]	$5		20th Century 2062
3/30/74	**76**	8		3 **Under The Influence Of Love** ....*(instrumental)*	$5		20th Century 2082
11/30/74+	**27**	15		4 **I Belong To You** ....RB[1] *And Only You*	$5		20th Century 2141
				all of above written and produced by **Barry White**			
				LOVE UNLIMITED ORCHESTRA R&B/BUB/LP **'74**			
				Disco studio orchestra conducted and arranged by **Barry White**. Formed to back **Love Unlimited**; also heard on some of White's solo hits. **Kenny G** was a member at age 17.			
12/1/73+	**1**[1]	22	●	1 **Love's Theme** AC[2] *Sweet Moments* [I]	$5		20th Century 2069
4/27/74	**63**	8		2 **Rhapsody In White** ....*Barry's Theme* [I]	$5		20th Century 2090
2/8/75	**22**	12		3 **Satin Soul** ....*Just Living It Up* [I]	$5		20th Century 2162
9/11/76	**48**	11		4 **My Sweet Summer Suite** ....*Just Living It Up* [I]	$5		20th Century 2301
1/22/77	**68**	7		5 **Theme From King Kong (Pt. I)** ....*(Pt. II)* [I]	$5		20th Century 2325
				from the Dino De Laurentiis movie *King Kong* starring Jeff Bridges and Jessica Lange			
	★294★			**LOVIN' SPOONFUL, The** BUB/LP **'66**			
				Jug-band rock group formed in New York: **John Sebastian** (lead vocals, songwriter, guitarist, harmonica; born on 3/17/44), Zal Yanovsky (lead guitar; born on 12/19/44; died of a heart attack on 12/13/2002, age 57), Steve Boone (bass; born on 9/23/43) and Joe Butler (drums; born on 1/19/43). Sebastian had been with the Even Dozen Jug Band; did session work at Elektra. Yanovsky and Sebastian were members of the Mugwumps with **Mama Cass Elliot** and Denny Doherty (later with **The Mamas & The Papas**). Yanovsky replaced by Jerry Yester (keyboards) in 1967. Disbanded in 1968. Group inducted into the Rock and Roll Hall of Fame in 2000.			
				1)Summer In The City 2)Daydream 3)Did You Ever Have To Make Up Your Mind?			
8/21/65	**9**	13		1 **Do You Believe In Magic** ....*On The Road Again*	$10		Kama Sutra 201
11/27/65+	**10**	12		2 **You Didn't Have To Be So Nice** ....*My Gal*	$10	■	Kama Sutra 205
2/26/66	**2**[2]	12		3 **Daydream** ....*Night Owl Blues*	$10	■	Kama Sutra 208
5/7/66	**2**[2]	11		4 **Did You Ever Have To Make Up Your Mind?** ....*Didn't Want To Have To Do It*	$10	■	Kama Sutra 209
7/16/66	**1**[3]	11	●	5 **Summer In The City** *Butchie's Tune*	$10	■	Kama Sutra 211
10/15/66	**10**	10		6 **Rain On The Roof** ....*Pow (Theme From "What's Up, Tiger Lily?")*	$10	■	Kama Sutra 216
12/17/66+	**8**	10		7 **Nashville Cats** /			
				full-color promo picture sleeve also issued with "A Word from **Buck Owens**" on the back			
1/7/67	**87**	3		8 **Full Measure**	$10	■	Kama Sutra 219
				above 4 from the album *Hums Of The Lovin' Spoonful*			
2/11/67	**15**	8		9 **Darling Be Home Soon** ....*Darlin' Companion*	$10	■	Kama Sutra 220
				from the Francis Ford Coppola movie *You're A Big Boy Now* starring Peter Kastner			
4/29/67	**18**	8		10 **Six O'Clock** ....*You're A Big Boy Now (the Finale)*	$10	■	Kama Sutra 225
				all of above produced by Erik Jacobsen			
10/28/67	**27**	6		11 **She Is Still A Mystery** ....*Only Pretty, What A Pity*	$10	■	Kama Sutra 239
1/6/68	**48**	6		12 **Money** ....*Close Your Eyes*	$8		Kama Sutra 241
7/27/68	**73**	5		13 **Never Going Back** ....*Forever*	$8		Kama Sutra 250
2/8/69	**91**	2		14 **Me About You** ....*Amazing Air*	$8		Kama Sutra 255
				LOW, Andy Fairweather **'75**			
				Born on 8/8/50 in Ystrad Mynach, Wales. Rock singer/guitarist.			
4/12/75	**87**	3		**Spider Jiving** ....*The Light Is Within*	$6		A&M 1649

DEBUT	PEAK	WKS	Gold	A-side (Chart Hit)....B-side	$	Sym	Label & Number
				LOWE, Bernie, Orchestra '58			
				Born on 11/22/17 in Philadelphia, Pennsylvania. Founder/chief producer of Cameo-Parkway Records. Wrote #1 hits "Teddy Bear" and "Butterfly."			
11/24/58	46	7		1 **Sing Sing Sing /** [I]			
				Jerry Gilgor (drums); written by **Louis Prima** in 1936; #7 hit for **Benny Goodman** (with Gene Krupa) in 1938			
11/24/58	61	4		2 **Intermission Riff** [I]	$12		Cameo 153
				revival of **Stan Kenton**'s 1946 recording			
				LOWE, Jim MEM/BUB/R&B '56			
				Born on 5/7/27 in Springfield, Missouri. DJ/vocalist/composer. DJ in New York City when he recorded "The Green Door" in 1956.			
7/23/55	27[CU]	3		1 **Close The Door** ....*Nuevo Laredo* [N]	$15		Dot 15381
				Norman Leyden (orch.)			
9/22/56	❶[3]	26	●	2 **The Green Door** T:❶[3] / J:❶[3] / S:2 / A:2 *(The Story of) The Little Man In Chinatown*	$20		Dot 15486
				High Fives (backing vocals); Bob **Hutch Davie** (piano)			
1/5/57	43	10		3 **By You, By You, By You /** T:43			
				based on the same familiar one-finger piano melody as "Down At Papa Joe's"			
1/19/57	84	3		4 **I Feel The Beat** T:84	$15		Dot 15525
5/6/57	15	18		5 **Four Walls /** J:15 / A:16 / S:19 / T:20			
5/6/57	15	12		6 **Talkin' To The Blues** ....J:15 / A:20 / T:21 / S:flip	$15		Dot 15569
				from the TV production *Modern Romances*; Bob **Hutch Davie** (orch.: #2-6)			
				LOWE, Nick ROK/BUB/LP '79			
				Born on 3/25/49 in Walton, Surrey, England. Pop-rock singer/songwriter/guitarist. With Brinsley Schwarz (1970-75) and **Rockpile**. Married to **Carlene Carter** from 1979-90. Produced albums for **Elvis Costello**, **Graham Parker** and others.			
7/28/79	12	15		1 **Cruel To Be Kind** ....*Endless Grey Ribbon*	$5		Columbia 11018
11/30/85+	77	9		2 **I Knew The Bride (When She Use To Rock And Roll)** ....*Long Walk Back*	$5		Columbia 05570
				NICK LOWE AND HIS COWBOY OUTFIT			
				produced by **Huey Lewis**; the Cowboy Outfit included **Paul Carrack**			
				LOX, The R&B/LP '98			
				Rap trio from Yonkers, New York: David **Styles**, Shawn "Sheek" Jacobs and Jayson "**Jadakiss**" Phillips. Group name is short for Living Off Xperience. Also see **DMX**'s "Get At Me Dog".			
12/6/97+	2[2]	6	▲	1 **It's All About The Benjamins** ....S:2 / A:62 *Been Around The World* (**Puff Daddy** - #4)	$3	▮	Bad Boy 79130
				PUFF DADDY & THE FAMILY Feat. The Notorious B.I.G., Lil' Kim, The Lox, Dave Grohl, Perfect, FuzzBubble & Rob Zombie			
				samples "I Did It For Love" by **Love Unlimited Orchestra**			
2/7/98	30	13		2 **If You Think I'm Jiggy** ....S:16 *(remix) / (instrumental)*	$4	▮	Bad Boy 79115
				samples "Da Ya Think I'm Sexy?" by **Rod Stewart**			
4/4/98	17	20	●	3 **Money, Power & Respect** ....S:10 / A:65 *(instrumental)*	$4	▮	Bad Boy 79156
				THE LOX [Feat. DMX & Lil' Kim]			
				samples "New Beginning" by Dexter Wansel			
3/18/00	73	7		4 **Ryde Or Die, Chick** A:65			album cut
				LOX Featuring Timbaland and Eve			
				from the album *We Are The Streets* on Ruff Ryders 490599			
				LSG R&B/LP '97			
				All-star R&B trio: **Gerald Levert**, **Keith Sweat** and **Johnny Gill**.			
11/1/97	4	20	▲	**My Body** ....RB[7] S:2 / A:36 *The Check Is In The Mail*	$3	▮	EastWest 64132
				L.T.D. R&B/BUB/LP '77			
				R&B-funk group from Greensboro, North Carolina: **Jeffrey Osborne** (vocals, drums), John McGhee (guitar), Abraham Miller, Lorenzo Carnegie, Carle Vickers and Jake Riley (horns), Billy Osborne and Jimmy Davis (keyboards), Henry Davis (bass), and Alvino Bennett (drums). The Osborne brothers left after "Shine On." L.T.D. stands for Love, Togetherness and Devotion.			
10/2/76	20	18		1 **Love Ballad** ....RB[2] *Let The Music Keep Playing*	$5	■	A&M 1847
1/29/77	91	3		2 **Love To The World** ....*Get Your It Together*	$5		A&M 1897
10/15/77	4	19	●	3 **(Every Time I Turn Around) Back In Love Again** RB[2] *Material Things*	$5	■	A&M 1974
3/11/78	56	7		4 **Never Get Enough Of Your Love** ....*Make Someone Smile, Today!*	$5	■	A&M 2005
8/19/78	49	10		5 **Holding On (When Love Is Gone)** ....RB[2] *Together Forever*	$5		A&M 2057
11/15/80+	40	16		6 **Shine On** ....*Love Is What You Need*	$5		A&M 2283
				L'TRIMM R&B/LP '88			
				Female rap duo: Tigra (from New York) and Bunny D. (from Chicago, Illinois).			
9/24/88	54	15		**Cars With The Boom** ....*Don't Come To My House*	$3	■	Atlantic 89005
				LUCAS LP '94			
				Born Lucas Secon in 1970 in Copenhagen, Denmark. Male rapper/producer.			
10/1/94	29	19		**Lucas With The Lid Off** ....S:22 / A:46 *(remix)*	$3	▮	Big Beat 98219
				Junior Dangerous (ragga vocal)			
				LUCAS, Carrie R&B/LP '77			
				Born in Los Angeles, California. R&B-disco singer.			
4/30/77	64	8		1 **I Gotta Keep Dancin'** *[CARRIE]*....*What's The Question*	$5		Soul Train 10891
5/12/79	70	7		2 **Dance With You** ....*Simpler Days*	$5		Solar 11482
				LUCAS, Frank R&B '77			
				Born in Louisiana; later based in San Bernardino, California. R&B singer.			
6/25/77	92	3		**Good Thing Man** ....*I Want My Mule Back*	$7		ICA 001
				LUCAS, Matt '63			
				Born on 7/19/35 in Memphis, Tennessee. "Blue-eyed soul" singer/drummer.			
5/4/63	56	9		**I'm Movin' On** ....*My Heavenly Angel*	$10		Smash 1813
				originally released on Renay 304 in 1963 ($20); #1 Country hit for **Hank Snow** in 1950			

DEBUT	PEAK	WKS	Gold	A-side (Chart Hit)...B-side	$	Sym	Label & Number
				LUCY PEARL R&B/LP **'00**			
				All-star R&B trio: Raphael Saadiq (of **Tony Toni Toné**), **Dawn Robinson** (of **En Vogue**) and Ali Shaheed Muhammad (of **A Tribe Called Quest**). Joi replaced Robinson in 2001.			
5/20/00	36	19		1 **Dance Tonight** ...A:30 from the movie *Love & Basketball* starring Omar Epps (soundtrack on Pookie/Beyond 9001)			album cut
10/14/00	42S	10		2 **Don't Mess With My Man** ...*Can't Stand Your Mother*	$5	★	Pookie/Beyond 78153
	★465★			**LUDACRIS** R&B/LP **'02**			
				Born Christopher Bridges on 9/11/78 in Atlanta, Georgia. Male rapper. *1)Move B***h 2)Rollout (My Business) 3)What's Your Fantasy*			
9/30/00	21	22		1 **What's Your Fantasy** ...A:17 / S:73 *(2 versions) / Get Off Me* (w/**Pastor Troy**) **LUDACRIS (Featuring Shawna)**	$6	T	Def Jam 562944
1/20/01	23	20		2 **Southern Hospitality** ...A:17 / S:50 *(2 versions) / Catch Up*	$6	T	Def Jam 572749
7/14/01	15	21		3 **One Minute Man**...A:13 **MISSY "MISDEMEANOR" ELLIOTT (featuring Ludacris)** from the album *Miss E...So Addictive* on Goldmind 62639			album cut
7/14/01	24	17		4 **Area Codes** ...A:21 / S:55 *(3 versions)* **LUDACRIS (Feat. Nate Dogg)** samples "Do It ('Til You're Satisfied)" by **B.T. Express**; from the movie *Rush Hour 2* starring Jackie Chan	$6	T	Def Jam 588671
8/25/01	94	3		5 **Bia' Bia'** ...*(2 versions)* **LIL JON & the East Side Boyz featuring Ludacris, Big Kap, Too $hort & Chyna**	$6	T	BME 7780
11/3/01	87	14		6 **Fatty Girl**...S:50 *(4 versions)* **LUDACRIS, LL COOL J, KEITH MURRAY**	$6	T	Universal 15283
11/10/01+	17	21		7 **Rollout (My Business)**...A:17 / S:60 *(2 versions) / Go To Sleep*	$6	T	Def Jam 588792
12/29/01+	35	20		8 **Welcome To Atlanta** ...A:36 **JERMAINE DUPRI • LUDACRIS** from the Dupri album *Instructions* on So So Def 85830 and the Ludacris album *Word Of Mouf* on Def Jam 586446			album cut
2/16/02	22	20		9 **Saturday (Oooh! Ooooh!)** ...A:22 / S:34 *(2 versions) / She Said* **LUDACRIS (featuring Sleepy Brown)**	$6	T	Def Jam 588875
6/8/02	10	23		10 **Move B***h** A:9 / S:20 *Keep It On The Hush* **LUDACRIS feat. Mystikal and Infamous 2.0**	$4	★	Def Jam 063949
6/8/02	23	19		11 **Why Don't We Fall In Love** ...S:17 / A:22 *(6 versions)* **AMERIE (featuring Ludacris)**	$6	T	Rise/Columbia 79774
12/28/02+	8	20		12 **Gossip Folks** ...A:6 / S:11 *(4 versions)* **MISSY ELLIOTT Featuring Ludacris** samples "Double Dutch Bus" by **Frankie Smith**	$6	T	Goldmind 67356
				LUGO, Richard **'01**			
				Born in 1985 in Queens, New York; raised in Hialeah, Florida. Latin teen pop singer.			
2/17/01	60S	6		**Boom** ...*(3 album snippets)* samples "Esa Morena" by DJ Laz; CD package includes a pull-out sticker	$4	★	EastWest 67155
				LUHRMANN, Baz LP **'99**			
				Born Bazmark Luhrmann on 9/17/62 in New South Wales, Australia. Produced and directed the movies *Romeo & Juliet* (1996) and *Moulin Rouge* (2001).			
3/27/99	45	7		**everybody's free (to wear Sunscreen) The Speech Song** ...A:24 *I'm Losing You* (Lani) [S] speech taken from a *Chicago Tribune* commentary written by Mary Schmich and spoken by actor Lee Perry; song "Everybody's Free (To Feel Good)" sung by Quindon Tarver from the 1996 movie *Romeo & Juliet* starring Leonardo DiCaprio	$4	★	Capitol 58764
				LUKE, Robin **'58**			
				Born on 3/19/42 in Los Angeles, California. Male teen rock and roll singer/songwriter.			
8/11/58	5	17	●	**Susie Darlin'** ...H:5 / S:6 *Living's Loving You* first released on International 206 in 1958 ($60) with a picture sleeve	$25		Dot 15781
				LUKE — see 2 LIVE CREW			
				LULU BUB/AC/LP **'67**			
				Born Marie Lawrie on 11/3/48 in Glasgow, Scotland. Pop singer/actress. Married to Maurice Gibb (of the **Bee Gees**) from 1969-73. Appeared in the 1967 movie *To Sir With Love*. Hosted own U.K. TV show in 1968. *1)To Sir With Love 2)I Could Never Miss You (More Than I Do) 3)Oh Me Oh My (I'm A Fool For You Baby)*			
8/1/64	94	3		1 **Shout** *[LULU AND THE LUVERS]*...*Forget Me Baby*	$20		Parrot 9678
9/9/67	①5	17	●	2 **To Sir With Love** *The Boat That I Row* (#115) title song from the movie starring Sidney Poitier	$10		Epic 10187
12/9/67	96	3		3 **Shout** ...*When He Touches Me* [R] same version as #1 above, but 12 seconds longer	$15		Parrot 40021
12/16/67+	32	10		4 **Best Of Both Worlds** ...*Love Loves To Love Love*	$8	■	Epic 10260
3/23/68	53	7		5 **Me, The Peaceful Heart**...*Look Out*	$8	■	Epic 10302
8/10/68	52	8		6 **Morning Dew**...*You And I*	$8		Epic 10367
12/27/69+	22	14		7 **Oh Me Oh My I'm A Fool For You Baby** ...*Sweep Around Your Own Back Door*	$8		Atco 6722
4/25/70	54	6		8 **Hum A Song (From Your Heart)** *[LULU with The Dixie Flyers]*...*Where's Eddie*	$8		Atco 6749
8/1/81	18	18		9 **I Could Never Miss You (More Than I Do)**...*Dance To The Feeling In Your Heart* 2 different picture sleeves were issued	$5	■	Alfa 7006
11/21/81+	44	11		10 **If I Were You**...*You Win, I Lose*	$5	■	Alfa 7011
				LUMAN, Bob C&W/BUB **'60**			
				Born on 4/15/37 in Nacogdoches, Texas. Died on 12/27/78 (age 41). Country-rockabilly singer/songwriter/guitarist. First recorded for Imperial in 1957. Charted 39 Country hits, 1960-78.			
9/5/60	7	14		**Let's Think About Living**...*You've Got Everything* [N] a jibe at the "death-song" fad of 1960	$20	■	Warner 5172
				LUNAR FUNK **'72**			
				R&B-funk instrumental band.			
2/5/72	63	8		**Mr. Penguin-Pt. I** ...*Pt. II* [I]	$6		Bell 45,172

DEBUT	PEAK	WKS	Gold	A-side (Chart Hit)...B-side	$	Sym	Label & Number
				LUND, Art MEM/POP **'47**			
				Born on 4/1/15 in Salt Lake City, Utah. Died on 5/31/90 (age 75). Baritone with **Benny Goodman** during the 1940s as both Art Lund and Art London. Starred in the classic 1956 Broadway musical *The Most Happy Fella.* #1 hit in 1947: "Mam'selle."			
12/15/58	89	3		**Philadelphia U.S.A.** .... *Mam'selle*	$10		Coral 62054
				Dick Jacobs (orch.); B-side is a new version of Lund's #1 hit in 1947			
				LUNDBERG, Victor **'67**			
				Born on 9/2/23 in Grand Rapids, Michigan. Died on 2/14/90 (age 66). News reader at WMAX in Grand Rapids.			
11/11/67	10	6		**An Open Letter To My Teenage Son** .... *My Buddy Carl* [S]	$6		Liberty 55996
				LUNDI, Pat R&B **'75**			
				Dance singer/actress. Appeared in the Broadway musical *Don't Bother Me, I Can't Cope.*			
9/6/75	78	5		**Party Music** .... *(instrumental)*	$5		Vigor 1723
				co-written by **Melissa Manchester**			
				LUNIZ R&B/BUB/LP **'95**			
				Rap duo from Oakland, California: Jerold "Yukmouth" Ellis and Garrick "Knumskull" Husband.			
6/10/95	8	25	▲	1 **I Got 5 On It** .... S:4 / A:36 *(instrumental) / So Much Drama*	$3	▮	Noo Trybe 38474
				samples material by **Kool & The Gang**			
11/11/95	65^{S}	4		2 **Playa Hata** .... BUB:102 *(2 versions) / Pimps, Playas & Hustlas*	$3	▮	Noo Trybe 38517
				LUNIZ Featuring Teddy			
				LUSCIOUS JACKSON ROK/LP **'97**			
				Female pop-rock group from Manhattan, New York: Jill Cunniff (vocals, bass), Gabrielle Glaser (vocals, guitar), Vivian Trimble (keyboards) and Kate Schellenbach (drums). Named after the former pro basketball player.			
12/21/96+	36	26		**Naked Eye** .... A:31 / S:44 *(2 mixes)*	$4	▮^{V}	Grand Royal 58619
				"45": Grand Royal/Capitol 19333; B-side: "Don't Look Back"			
				LV R&B **'95**			
				Born Larry Sanders in Los Angeles, California. R&B singer/songwriter. Former member of **South Central Cartel**. L.V. stands for Large Variety.			
8/19/95	❶^{3}	38	▲^{3}	1 **Gangsta's Paradise** .... S:❶^{7} / A:7 *(instrumental)*	$3	▮^{V}	MCA Soundtracks 55104
				COOLIO featuring L.V.			
				rap version of "Pastime Paradise" by **Stevie Wonder**; from the movie *Dangerous Minds* starring Michelle Pfeiffer; also see #3 below			
11/18/95+	63	16		2 **Throw Your Hands Up /** A:69 / S:70			
				L.V. (Featuring Treach)			
				samples "Bounce, Rock, Skate, Roll" by **Vaughan Mason And Crew**			
11/18/95		15		3 **Gangsta's Paradise** .... [R]	$4	▮	Tommy Boy 7699
				background vocals and music same as #1 above (without rap by **Coolio**)			
4/8/00	26^{S}	11		4 **How Long** .... *(remix)*	$5	★	Loud 79349
				LV Featuring Shari Watson			
				LY - DELLS, The **'61**			
				White male doo-wop trio from Philadelphia, Pennsylvania: Gary Young, Chuck Hatfield and Paul O'Lone.			
8/21/61	54	6		**Wizard Of Love** .... *Let This Night Last*	$75		Master 251
				LYMAN, Arthur, Group BUB/LP **'61**			
				Born on 2/2/32 in Kauai, Hawaii. Died of cancer on 2/24/2002 (age 70). Played vibraphone, guitar, piano and drums. Formerly with **Martin Denny**.			
6/15/59	55	6		1 **Taboo** *[ARTHUR LYMAN]* .... *Dahil Sayo* [I]	$10		Hi Fi 550
				written by Margarita Lecuona (niece of famed Cuban composer Ernesto Lecuona)			
5/29/61	4	12		2 **Yellow Bird** .... *Havah Nagilah* [I]	$12		Hi Fi 5024
				adapted from a West Indian folk song			
2/2/63	43	11		3 **Love For Sale** .... *Love* [I]	$10		Hi Fi 5066
				Libby Holman's version of the Cole Porter tune hit #5 in 1931			
				LYME & CYBELLE **'66**			
				Male/female pop-rock duo: **Warren Zevon** and Victoria Santangelo (later acted on Broadway as Laura Kenyon).			
3/19/66	65	6		**Follow Me** .... *Like The Seasons*	$10		White Whale 228
				LYMON, Frankie, and The Teenagers R&B/LP **'56**			
				R&B vocal group from the Bronx, New York. Lead singer Lymon was born on 9/30/42; died of a drug overdose on 2/28/68 (age 25). Other members included Herman Santiago and Jimmy Merchant (tenors), Joe Negroni (baritone; died on 9/5/78, age 37) and Sherman Garnes (bass; died on 2/26/77, age 36). Group appeared in the movies *Rock, Rock, Rock* and *Mister Rock 'n' Roll.* Group inducted into the Rock and Roll Hall of Fame in 1993.			
2/11/56	6	21	●	1 **Why Do Fools Fall In Love** RB^{5} S:6 / T:7 / J:8 / A:9 *Please Be Mine*	$50		Gee 1002
				THE TEENAGERS Featuring FRANKIE LYMON			
4/28/56	13	15		2 **I Want You To Be My Girl** .... S:13 / T:17 / J:20 / A:25 *I'm Not A Know It All*	$50		Gee 1012
				reissued on Big Kat 7008 with a picture sleeve in 1968			
7/28/56	57	7		3 **I Promise To Remember /** T:57			
7/21/56		1		4 **Who Can Explain?** .... CU:flip	$40		Gee 1018
10/20/56	77	2		5 **The ABC's Of Love** .... T:77 *Share*	$40		Gee 1022
7/22/57	20	17		6 **Goody Goody** .... S:20 / A:21 / T:22 *Creation Of Love*	$40		Gee 1039
				#1 hit for **Benny Goodman** in 1936; Jimmy Wright (orch., all of above)			
8/8/60	58	4		7 **Little Bitty Pretty One** *[FRANKIE LYMON]* .... *Creation Of Love*	$20		Roulette 4257
				Rudy Traylor (orch.)			
				LYNN, Barbara BUB/R&B **'62**			
				Born Barbara Lynn Ozen on 1/16/42 in Beaumont, Texas. R&B singer/songwriter/guitarist.			
6/16/62	8	13		1 **You'll Lose A Good Thing** RB^{3} *Lonely Heartache*	$20		Jamie 1220
9/22/62	63	8		2 **Second Fiddle Girl** .... *Letter To Mommy And Daddy*	$15		Jamie 1233
12/15/62+	65	6		3 **You're Gonna Need Me** .... *I'm Sorry I Met You*	$15		Jamie 1240
2/23/63	93	4		4 **Don't Be Cruel** .... *You Can't Be Satisfied*	$15		Jamie 1244
8/10/63	68	8		5 **(I Cried at) Laura's Wedding** .... *You Better Stop*	$15		Jamie 1260
6/20/64	69	8		6 **Oh! Baby (We Got A Good Thing Goin')** .... *Unfair*	$15		Jamie 1277
10/3/64	93	3		7 **Don't Spread It Around** .... *Let Her Knock Herself Out*	$15		Jamie 1286

DEBUT	PEAK	WKS	Gold	A-side (Chart Hit)	B-side	$	Sym	Label & Number
				LYNN, Barbara — Cont'd				
1/9/65	95	2		8 **It's Better To Have It**	*People Gonna Talk*	$15		Jamie 1292
2/17/68	65	2		9 **This Is The Thanks I Get**	*Ring Telephone Ring*	$8		Atlantic 2450
				all of above produced by Huey P. Meaux in New Orleans				
				LYNN, Cheryl R&B/BUB/AC/LP '79				
				Born on 3/11/57 in Los Angeles, California. R&B-disco singer. Discovered on TV's *Gong Show*. Also see **Toto**'s "Georgy Porgy."				
12/2/78+	12	18	▲	1 **Got To Be Real** RB[1]	*Come In From The Rain*	$5		Columbia 10808
4/14/79	62	10		2 **Star Love**	*You're The One*	$5		Columbia 10907
8/8/81	70	7		3 **Shake It Up Tonight**	*Baby*	$4		Columbia 02102
				produced by **Ray Parker, Jr.**				
2/11/84	69	8		4 **Encore** RB[1]	*Free*	$4		Columbia 04256
				LYNN, Donna BUB '64				
				Teen pop singer.				
2/22/64	83	4		**My Boyfriend Got A Beatle Haircut**	*That Winter Weekend* [N]	$20		Capitol 5127
				LYNN, Loretta C&W/BUB/LP '71				
				Born Loretta Webb on 4/14/35 in Butcher Holler, Kentucky. Country singer/songwriter/guitarist (charted 78 hits, 1960-00). Sister of **Crystal Gayle** and country singers Jay Lee Webb and Peggy Sue; distant cousin of country singer **Patty Loveless**. The 1980 movie *Coal Miner's Daughter* was based on Loretta's autobiography.				
12/5/70	83	4		1 **Coal Miner's Daughter** CW[1]	*The Man Of The House*	$8	■	Decca 32749
2/27/71	56	6		2 **After The Fire Is Gone** CW[2]	*The One I Can't Live Without*	$7		Decca 32776
				CONWAY TWITTY/LORETTA LYNN				
4/24/71	94	2		3 **I Wanna Be Free**	*If I Never Love Again (It'll Be Too Soon)*	$7		Decca 32796
3/1/75	70	7		4 **The Pill**	*Will You Be There*	$6		MCA 40358
				LYNN, Vera MEM/POP/AC '52				
				Born Vera Margaret Welsh on 3/20/17 in London. England's most popular female singer during World War II. Her 1952 hit "Auf Wiederseh'n Sweetheart" was #1 for 9 weeks.				
3/3/56	96	1		1 **Such A Day**	T:96 *Unfaithful You*	$12		London 1642
				Roland Shaw (orch.)				
5/6/57	55	8		2 **Don't Cry My Love (The Faithful Hussar)**	T:55 *By The Fountains Of Rome*	$12		London 1729
				Glen Somers (orch.)				
				LYNNE, Gloria BUB/LP '64				
				Born Gloria Alleyne on 11/23/31 in Harlem, New York. Black jazz-styled vocalist.				
9/11/61	95	4		1 **Impossible**	*This Little Boy Of Mine*	$12		Everest 19418
12/18/61	100	1		2 **You Don't Have To Be A Tower Of Strength**	*I Will Follow You*	$12		Everest 19428
				answer song to **Gene McDaniel**'s hit "Tower Of Strength"				
1/11/64	28	12		3 **I Wish You Love**	*Through A Long And Sleepless Night*	$10		Everest 2036
				French song written and recorded by Charles Trenet in 1943				
4/4/64	64	5		4 **I Should Care**	*Indian Love Call*	$10		Everest 2042
				there were 4 Top 20 versions of this song in 1945				
4/4/64	88	4		5 **Be Anything (But Be Mine)**	*Soul Serenade*	$10	■	Fontana 1890
				#7 hit for **Eddy Howard** in 1952				
7/4/64	76	3		6 **Don't Take Your Love From Me**	*You Don't Know What Love Is*	$10		Everest 2044
				#21 hit for Glen Gray in 1944				
6/26/65	62	5		7 **Watermelon Man**	*All Alone*	$10		Fontana 1511
				LYNNE, Jeff — see ELECTRIC LIGHT ORCHESTRA				
				LYNYRD SKYNYRD ROK/BUB/LP '74				
				Southern-rock group formed by Ronnie Van Zant (lead singer; born on 1/15/49), Gary Rossington (guitar) and Allen Collins (guitar) while they were in junior high in Jacksonville, Florida. Named after their gym teacher Leonard Skinner. Changing lineup featured drummers Bob Burns, Rickey Medlocke (later of **Blackfoot**) and Artimus Pyle; bassists Larry Junstrom (later of **38 Special**), Greg Walker (later of Blackfoot), Leon Wilkeson and Ed King (**Strawberry Alarm Clock**); pianist Billy Powell; and guitarist Steve Gaines. Plane crash on 10/20/77 in Gillsburg, Mississippi, killed Van Zant and members Steve and his sister Cassie Gaines (vocals). Gary and Allen formed the **Rossington Collins Band** (see #8 below) in 1980 with Wilkeson and Powell; split in 1982. Rossington and vocalist Johnny Van Zant (the younger brother of Ronnie and Donnie [lead singer of 38 Special] Van Zant) regrouped with old and new band members for the 1987 Lynyrd Skynyrd Tribute Tour. Collins (paralyzed in a car accident in 1986) died of pneumonia on 1/23/90 (age 37). Rossington, Van Zant, Pyle, Wilkeson, King and Powell regrouped in 1991 with Randall Hall (guitar) and Custer (drums). Pyle left by 1993; replaced by Mike Estes. Custer left by 1994 and Owen Hale joined. Wilkeson died on 7/27/2001 (age 49).				
7/27/74	8	17		1 **Sweet Home Alabama**	*Take Your Time*	$7		MCA 40258
				answer song to **Neil Young**'s "Alabama" and "Southern Man"; released on MCA's "Sounds Of The South" label				
11/23/74+	19	12		2 **Free Bird**	*Down South Jukin'*	$6		MCA 40328
				tribute to Duane Allman of **The Allman Brothers Band**; also see #5 below				
6/14/75	27	9		3 **Saturday Night Special**	*Made In The Shade*	$5		MCA 40416
3/20/76	80	3		4 **Double Trouble**	*Roll Gypsy Roll*	$5		MCA 40532
12/4/76+	38	8		5 **Free Bird**	*Searching (live)* [L-R]	$5		MCA 40665
				studio version on #2 above				
12/3/77+	13	18		6 **What's Your Name**	*I Know A Little*	$5		MCA 40819
4/15/78	69	4		7 **You Got That Right**	*Ain't No Good Life*	$5		MCA 40888
7/26/80	55	9		8 **Don't Misunderstand Me**	*Winners And Losers*	$4		MCA 41284
				ROSSINGTON COLLINS BAND				
				LYSETTE '98				
				Born Lysette Titi in Washington DC. Female R&B singer.				
1/10/98	75	10		**Young, Sad And Blue**	S:54 *(instrumental)*	$4	▮	Freeworld 34277
				LYTLE, Johnny LP '66				
				Born on 10/13/32 in Springfield, Ohio. Died of kidney failure on 12/15/95 (age 63). Jazz vibraphonist. Worked with jazz greats **Louis Armstrong**, Miles Davis and Lionel Hampton, among others.				
1/22/66	80	5		**The Loop**	*Hot Sauce* [I]	$12		Tuba 2004

M

M — LP '79
Born Robin Scott on 4/1/47 in England. Male new-wave singer.

DEBUT	PEAK	WKS	Gold	A-side (Chart Hit)...B-side	$	Sym	Label & Number
8/11/79	❶[1]	24	●	Pop Muzik ...M Factor	$4	■	Sire 49033

MABLEY, Moms — LP '69
Born Loretta Mary Aiken on 3/19/1894 in Brevard, North Carolina. Died on 5/23/75 (age 81). Bawdy comedienne/actress. Adopted the name Jackie Mabley from her first boyfriend. Charted 13 comedy albums on *Billboard's* Top Pop Albums charts. In the movies *Boarding House Blues*, *Emperor Jones* and *Amazing Grace*.

DEBUT	PEAK	WKS	Gold	A-side (Chart Hit)...B-side	$	Sym	Label & Number
6/28/69	35	6		**Abraham, Martin And John** ...*Sunny* a tribute to Abraham Lincoln, **Martin Luther King**, and John and Robert Kennedy	$8		Mercury 72935

MacARTHUR, James — '63
Born on 12/8/37 in Los Angeles, California. Movie/TV actor; adopted son of actress Helen Hayes. Played "Danny Williams" on TV's *Hawaii Five-O*. Appeared in such movies as *Swiss Family Robinson*, *Kidnapped* and others.

DEBUT	PEAK	WKS	Gold	A-side (Chart Hit)...B-side	$	Sym	Label & Number
6/22/63	94	2		**The Ten Commandments Of Love** ...*Padre* [S] produced by Bill Buchanan (of **Buchanan & Goodman**)	$12		Scepter 1250

MacDONALD, Kathi — see BALDRY, Long John

MacDONALD, Ralph — R&B/LP '84
Born in 1944 in Harlem, New York. Black session percussionist/bandleader.

DEBUT	PEAK	WKS	Gold	A-side (Chart Hit)...B-side	$	Sym	Label & Number
9/1/84	58	10		**In The Name Of Love** ...*Play Pen* (MacDonald) **RALPH MacDONALD (with Bill Withers)**	$4		Polydor 881221

MACEO AND THE MACKS — see JB's, The

MacGREGOR, Byron — '74
Born Gary Mack in 1948 in Calgary, Alberta, Canada. Died on 1/3/95 (age 46). News director at CKLW-Detroit when he did the narration for "Americans." Narration was originally written and delivered as an editorial by **Gordon Sinclair** for CFRB-Toronto on 6/5/73.

DEBUT	PEAK	WKS	Gold	A-side (Chart Hit)...B-side	$	Sym	Label & Number
1/5/74	4	12	●	Americans ...*America The Beautiful* (The Westbound Strings) [S] background music: "America The Beautiful"	$5		Westbound 222

MacGREGOR, Mary — AC/LP '77
Born on 5/6/48 in St. Paul, Minnesota. Adult Contemporary singer/songwriter.

DEBUT	PEAK	WKS	Gold	A-side (Chart Hit)...B-side	$	Sym	Label & Number
11/20/76+	❶[2]	22	●	1 Torn Between Two Lovers AC[2] *I Just Want To Love You*	$5		Ariola America 7638
4/23/77	46	8		2 **This Girl (Has Turned Into A Woman)** ...*Good Together*	$5		Ariola America 7662
8/6/77	90	4		3 **For A While** ...*The Lady I Am* above 3 written and produced by **Peter Yarrow** (**Peter, Paul & Mary**)	$5		Ariola America 7667
11/25/78	81	4		4 **The Wedding Song (There Is Love)** ...*Benjamin* written by **Paul Stookey** (**Peter, Paul & Mary**)	$5		Ariola America 7726
8/11/79	39	12		5 **Good Friend** ...*Rudy And Tripper* [I] from the movie *Meatballs* starring Bill Murray	$4		RSO 938
5/17/80	72	4		6 **Dancin' Like Lovers** ...*I Can't Hold On*	$4		RSO 1025

MACHINE — '79
Disco group consisting of Jay Stovall (vocals, lead guitar), Kevin Nance (keyboards), Melvin Lee (bass), Lonnie Ferguson (drums) and Clare Bathe (vocals).

DEBUT	PEAK	WKS	Gold	A-side (Chart Hit)...B-side	$	Sym	Label & Number
3/17/79	77	10		**There But For The Grace Of God Go I** ...*Get Your Body Ready*	$5		RCA 11456

MACK, Craig — R&B/BUB/LP '94
Born in Long Island, New York. Male rapper. Was a roadie for **EPMD**. Discovered by producer Sean "**Puff Daddy**" Combs.

DEBUT	PEAK	WKS	Gold	A-side (Chart Hit)...B-side	$	Sym	Label & Number
8/13/94	9	25	▲	1 Flava In Ya Ear ...S:3 / A:44 *Shinika* remix versions available on Bad Boy 79010	$4	▮	Bad Boy 79001
12/31/94+	38	20	●	2 **Get Down** ...S:15 *Flava In Ya Ear (remix* w/**Notorious B.I.G. & LL Cool J**) remix versions available on Bad Boy 79021; "45": Bad Boy 79021; B-side: (**Q-Tip** remix)	$4	▮[V]	Bad Boy 79012
5/31/97	66	13		3 **No One But You** ...S:63 *(remix)* **VERONICA Featuring Craig Mack** from the movie *BAPS* starring Halle Berry	$4	▮	H.O.L.A. 341014
5/31/97	70[S]	2		4 **Spirit** ...BUB:102 *(remix)* **SOUNDS OF BLACKNESS Featuring Craig Mack**	$4	▮	Perspective 7574

MACK, Kelli — '01
Born in Los Angeles, California. Female R&B singer.

DEBUT	PEAK	WKS	Gold	A-side (Chart Hit)...B-side	$	Sym	Label & Number
5/26/01	17[S]	23		**Keep It Real** ...*(4 album snippets)* samples "Free" by **Deniece Williams**	$4	★	Rising High 30003

MACK, Lonnie — BUB/LP '63
Born Lonnie McIntosh on 7/18/41 in Aurora, Indiana. Rockabilly guitarist/R&B-styled singer. Own Country band in 1954. Lead guitarist of band for country singer Troy Seals (**Jo Ann & Troy**) in the early 1960s. Rediscovered in 1968. Session work with **James Brown**, **The Doors** and **Freddy King**. Retired from music, 1971-85.

DEBUT	PEAK	WKS	Gold	A-side (Chart Hit)...B-side	$	Sym	Label & Number
6/8/63	5	13		1 Memphis ...*Down In The Dumps* [I] written and recorded in 1959 by **Chuck Berry** as "Memphis, Tennessee" on Chess 1729 ($30); originally released on Buccaneer 3001 in 1963 ($50)	$20		Fraternity 906
8/24/63	24	9		2 **Wham!** ...*Suzie-Q* [I]	$15		Fraternity 912
11/30/63	93	1		3 **Baby, What's Wrong** ...*Where There's A Will* (#113) written and recorded in 1962 by **Jimmy Reed** on Vee-Jay 425 ($15)	$15		Fraternity 918
10/30/65	78	5		4 **Honky Tonk '65** ...*Chicken' Pickin'* [I]	$15		Fraternity 951

MACK, Warner — C&W '57
Born Warner MacPherson on 4/2/35 in Nashville, Tennesee; raised in Mississippi. Country singer/guitarist (charted 23 hits, 1957-77).

DEBUT	PEAK	WKS	Gold	A-side (Chart Hit)...B-side	$	Sym	Label & Number
7/29/57	61	5		1 **Is It Wrong (For Loving You)** ...T:61 *Baby Squeeze Me*	$25		Decca 30301
1/20/58	74	3		2 **Roc-A-Chicka** ...T:74 *Since I Lost You* Anita Kerr Quartet (backing vocals); picture sleeve has a center-cut hole and the words "The Exciting Warner Mack"	$30	■	Decca 30471

DEBUT	PEAK	WKS	Gold	A-side (Chart Hit)...B-side	$	Sym	Label & Number
				MACK 10 R&B/BUB/LP **'99**			
				Born Dedrick Rolison on 8/9/71 in Inglewood, California. Male rapper. Discovered by **Ice Cube**. Married **T-Boz** on 8/19/2000. Also see **Westside Connection**.			
6/24/95	**71**	11		1 **Foe Life**...S:50 *(radio version)*	$4	▮	Priority 53192
				co-written and produced by **Ice Cube**			
9/30/95	**88**	10		2 **West Up!**...*(instrumental)*	$4	▮	Payday 850258
				WC AND THE MAAD CIRCLE Featuring Ice Cube and Mack 10			
				samples "Reach For It" by **George Duke**			
12/14/96+	**38**	20		3 **Nothin' But The Cavi Hit**...S:22 *Is There A Heaven 4 A Gangsta?* (**Master P**)	$3	▮	Priority 53263
				MACK 10 & THA DOGG POUND			
				from the rap documentary movie *Rhyme & Reason*			
8/30/97	**37**	20		4 **Backyard Boogie** S:25 *Only In California* (w/**Ice Cube** & **Snoop Dogg**)	$3	▮	Priority 53282
				original cassette single repeated the A-side and did not have "Only In California" as the B-side			
11/7/98	**54**	4		5 **Money's Just A Touch Away**...S:29 *(instrumental) / (acappella)*	$3	▮	Hoo Bangin' 53327
				MACK 10 featuring Gerald Levert			
				samples "Love Is Just A Touch Away" by **Freddie Jackson**			
9/18/99	**23**	15	●	6 **I Want It All**...S:7 *(3 versions)*	$4	★	G-Funk 73721
				WARREN G Featuring Mack 10			
				samples "I Like It" by **DeBarge**			
12/4/99+	**35**	12		7 **You Can Do It**...S:7 *(instrumental) / Money Stretch* (**Lil' Zane**)	$4	★	Priority 53562
				ICE CUBE Feat. Mack 10			
				Ms. Toi (female vocal); samples "Planet Rock" by **Afrika Bambaataa**; from the movie *Next Friday* starring **Ice Cube**			
				MacKENZIE, Gisele MEM/POP **'55**			
				Born Gisele LaFleche on 1/10/27 in Winnipeg, Manitoba, Canada. Star of TV's *Your Hit Parade* from 1953-57.			
6/4/55	**4**	19		1 **Hard To Get**...A:4 / J:5 / S:5 / T:84 *Boston Fancy*	$15	■	"X" 0137
				introduced by MacKenzie on a 5/12/55 episode of the NBC-TV drama series *Justice*			
11/19/55	**60**	4		2 **Pepper Hot Baby**...T:60 *That's The Chance I've Got To Take*	$15		"X" 0172
11/10/56	**42**	12		3 **The Star You Wished Upon Last Night**...T:42 *It's Delightful To Be Married*	$12		Vik 0233
				Richard Maltby (orch., all of above)			
				MacRAE, Gordon MEM/POP **'49**			
				Born on 3/12/21 in East Orange, New Jersey. Died of cancer on 1/24/86 (age 64). Sang with Horace Heidt (1942-43) and recorded numerous duets with **Jo Stafford**, including the #1 hit "My Darling, My Darling" in 1949. Starred in the movie musicals *Oklahoma!* and *Carousel*. Actresses Sheila and Meredith were his wife and daughter, respectively.			
5/12/56	**96**	3		1 **I've Grown Accustomed To Your Face**...T:96 *Who Are We*	$10		Capitol 3384
				from the Broadway musical *My Fair Lady* starring **Julie Andrews**			
9/15/58	**18**	13		2 **The Secret**...H:18 *A Man Once Said*	$10	□	Capitol 4033
				promo sleeve came with an insert featuring a photo of MacRae; Van Alexander (orch., above 2)			
				MAD COBRA BUB/LP **'93**			
				Born Ewart Everton Brown on 3/31/68 in Kingston; raised in St. Mary's, Jamaica. Reggae rapper.			
10/17/92+	**13**	19	●	**Flex**...S:9 / A:38 *(straight mix)*	$3	▮	Columbia 74373
				MADDOX, Johnny MEM/POP **'55**			
				Born on 8/4/29 in Gallatin, Tennessee. Honky-tonk pianist. Hit #15 in 1953 with "Dipsy Doodle."			
2/5/55	**2**[7]	20	●	1 **The Crazy Otto**...J:2 / S:2 / A:7 *Humoresque* [I]	$15		Dot 15325
				original version released in 1954 in Germany on Polydor 22009 by Der Schrage Otto as a 2-sided medley: "Die Beschwipste Drahtkommode"			
10/6/56	**57**	4		2 **Heart And Soul**...T:57 *Dixieland Band* [I]	$12		Dot 15488
				JOHNNY MADDOX and The Rhythmasters (above 2)			
				#1 hit for Larry Clinton in 1938			
1/27/58	**87**	6		3 **Yellow Dog Blues**...T:87 *Sugar Train* [I]	$10		Dot 15683
				written in 1928 by legendary composer W.C. Handy			
				MADIGAN, Betty MEM/POP **'54**			
				Born in Washington DC. Adult Contemporary singer. Hit #12 on the pop charts in 1954 with "Joey."			
11/19/55	**54**	11		1 **There Should Be Rules (Protecting Fools Who Fall In Love)**...T:54 *Strangers*	$12		MGM 12094
				Norman Leyden (orch.)			
4/20/57	**78**	3		2 **True Love Gone (Come On Home)**...T:78 *A Lovely Night*	$10		Coral 61812
8/18/58	**31**	9		3 **Dance Everyone Dance**...S:31 / H:34 *My Symphony Of Love*	$10		Coral 62007
				based on the Israeli harvest song "Hava Nagila"; **Dick Jacobs** (orch., above 2)			
				MADISON AVENUE **'00**			
				Male/female dance duo from Melbourne, Australia: producer Andy Van Dorsselaer and singer Cheyne Coates.			
7/8/00	**88**	20		**Don't Call Me Baby**...S:45 *(4 mixes)*	$8	★*	C2/Columbia 79371
				samples "Ma Quale Idea" by Pino D'Angio			
				MAD LADS, The R&B/LP **'66**			
				R&B vocal group from Detroit, Michigan: John Gary Williams, Julius Green, William Brown and Robert Phillips. Williams and Brown replaced by Sam Nelson and Quincy Clifton Billops, Jr. (later with **Ollie & The Nightingales** and **The Ovations**) from 1966-69. Brown's brother Bertrand was a member of **The Newcomers** (later known as Kwick).			
10/23/65	**93**	5		1 **Don't Have To Shop Around**...*Tear-Maker*	$15		Volt 127
3/5/66	**74**	6		2 **I Want Someone**...*Nothing Can Break Through*	$15		Volt 131
8/2/69	**84**	2		3 **By The Time I Get To Phoenix**...*No Strings Attached*	$10		Volt 4016
				MAD LION BUB/R&B/LP **'94**			
				Born Oswald Preist in London, England; raised in Jamaica. Male dancehall rapper. Based in Brooklyn. Also see **Born Jamericans**.			
7/30/94	**69**	20		1 **Take It Easy**...S:47 *(instrumental)*	$4	▮	Weeded 20094
				produced and mixed by **KRS-One**			
8/31/02	**22**[S]	9		2 **Give It To Me**...*(2 versions)*	$6	★	Killah Pride 90429
				MAD LION featuring Total			

DEBUT	PEAK	WKS	Gold	A-side (Chart Hit)	B-side	$	Sym	Label & Number
				MADNESS LP '83				
				Ska-rock group formed in London, England: Graham McPherson (vocals), Chris Foreman (guitar), Mike Barson (keyboards), Carl Smyth (trumpet), Lee Thompson (sax), Mark Bedford (bass) and Dan Woodgate (drums).				
5/7/83	7	19		1 Our House	*Cardiac Arrest*	$4	■	Geffen 29668
8/20/83	33	12		2 It Must Be Love	*Calling Cards*	$4	■	Geffen 29562
3/3/84	72	5		3 The Sun And The Rain	*Time For Tea*	$4	■	Geffen 29350

DEBUT	PEAK	WKS	Gold	A-side (Chart Hit)	B-side	$	Sym	Label & Number
				MADONNA ★4★ BUB/R&B/LP '87				
				Born Madonna Louise Ciccone on 8/16/58 in Bay City, Michigan. To New York in 1977; performed with the Alvin Ailey dance troupe. Member of the **Breakfast Club** in 1979. Formed her own band, Emmy, in 1980. Married to actor Sean Penn from 1985-89. Acted in the movies *Desperately Seeking Susan*, *Dick Tracy*, *A League Of Their Own*, *Body Of Evidence*, *Evita* and *Swept Away*, among others. Appeared in Broadway's *Speed-The-Plow*. Released concert tour documentary movie *Truth Or Dare* in 1991. Released her graphic and erotic book *Sex* in 1992. Married British movie director Guy Ritchie on 12/22/2000. Madonna is the #1 female vocalist of the entire rock era. Also see **Jellybean**'s "Sidewalk Talk."				
				1)Take A Bow 2)Like A Virgin 3)Music 4)Vogue 5)Like A Prayer				
10/29/83+	16	21		1 Holiday	*I Know It*	$5		Sire 29478
				Madonna's first and only non-*Hot 100* "45": "Everybody"/(Part 2) "Bubbled Under" (#107) in 1982 on Sire 29841 ($20)				
3/10/84	10	30	●	2 Borderline	*Think Of Me*	$4	■	Sire 29354
				picture sleeve is a foldout poster				
8/25/84	4	16		3 Lucky Star	A:3 / S:6 *I Know It*	$4		Sire 29177
11/17/84	❶[6]	19	●	4 Like A Virgin	A:❶[5] / S:❶[4] *Stay*	$3	■	Sire 29210
2/9/85	2[2]	17		5 Material Girl	A:2 / S:3 *Pretender*	$3	■	Sire 29083
3/2/85	❶[1]	21	●	6 Crazy For You	A:❶[1] / S:2 *No More Words* (**Berlin**)	$3	■	Geffen 29051
				from the movie *Vision Quest* starring Matthew Modine				
4/27/85	5	17		7 Angel	A:4 / S:9 *(dance mix edit)*	$3	■	Sire 29008
				"Into The Groove" (Dance Club Play #1/R&B #19/from the movie *Desperately Seeking Susan*) was released only as the B-side of a special 12" extended dance mix of "Angel" on Sire 20335. This 12" single, although it did not chart on the *Hot 100*, was certified gold				
8/17/85	5	16		8 Dress You Up	A:3 / S:12 *Shoo-Bee-Doo*	$3	■	Sire 28919
				#4, 5, 7 & 8: from the album *Like A Virgin*				
4/12/86	❶[1]	18		9 Live To Tell AC[3]	A:❶[3] / S:2 *(instrumental)*	$3	■	Sire 28717
				from the movie *At Close Range* starring Sean Penn				
6/28/86	❶[2]	18	●	10 Papa Don't Preach	S:❶[3] / A:❶[2] *Pretender*	$3	■	Sire 28660
10/4/86	3	16	●	11 True Blue	A:3 / S:4 *Ain't No Big Deal*	$3	■	Sire 28591
				issued on blue vinyl				
12/6/86+	❶[1]	18		12 Open Your Heart	A:❶[2] / S:2 *White Heat*	$3	■	Sire 28508
3/21/87	4	17		13 La Isla Bonita AC[1]	S:3 / A:3 *(instrumental remix)*	$3	■	Sire 28425
				above 5 from the album *True Blue*				
7/11/87	❶[1]	16		14 Who's That Girl	A:❶[2] / S:❶[1] *White Heat*	$3	■	Sire 28341
9/12/87	2[3]	18		15 Causing A Commotion	S:2 / A:2 *Jimmy, Jimmy*	$3	■	Sire 28224
				above 2 from the movie *Who's That Girl* starring Madonna				
1/16/88	32[A]	5		16 Spotlight				album cut
				from the extended remix album *You Can Dance* on Sire 25535				
3/18/89	❶[3]	16	▲	17 Like A Prayer	S:❶[3] / A:❶[3] *Act Of Contrition*	$3	■	Sire 27539
6/3/89	2[2]	16	●	18 Express Yourself	S:2 / A:3 *The Look Of Love*	$3	■	Sire 22948
8/19/89	2[2]	15		19 Cherish AC[2]	S:2 / A:2 *Supernatural*	$3	■	Sire 22883
11/11/89+	20	13		20 Oh Father	S:16 / A:22 *Pray For Spanish Eyes*	$4	▮[V]	Sire 22723
2/3/90	8	13	●	21 Keep It Together	S:7 / A:7 *(instrumental)*	$3	▮[V]	Sire 19986 ■
				above 5 from the album *Like A Prayer*				
4/14/90	❶[3]	24	▲[2]	22 Vogue	A:❶[3] / S:❶[2] *(Bette Davis dub)*	$3	▮[V]	Sire 19863
6/30/90	10	11	●	23 Hanky Panky	A:11 / S:13 *More*	$3	▮[V]	Sire 19789
				music inspired by the movie *Dick Tracy* starring Madonna and Warren Beatty				
11/17/90+	❶[2]	16	▲	24 Justify My Love	S:❶[5] / A:2 *Express Yourself (1990 remix)*	$3	▮[V]	Sire 19485
				co-written and produced by **Lenny Kravitz**				
3/2/91	9	8	●	25 Rescue Me	A:5 / S:11 *(alternate single mix)*	$3	▮[V]	Sire 19490
7/4/92	❶[1]	20	●	26 This Used To Be My Playground	A:2 / S:3 *(long version)*	$3	▮[V]	Sire 18822
				from the movie *A League Of Their Own* starring Madonna and Tom Hanks (not on soundtrack album)				
10/17/92	3	18	●	27 Erotica	A:2 / S:4 *(instrumental)*	$3	▮[V]	Maverick/Sire 18782
				contains a sample of "Jungle Boogie" by **Kool & The Gang**				
12/5/92+	7	17		28 Deeper And Deeper	A:8 / S:15 *(instrumental)*	$3	▮[V]	Maverick/Sire 18639
2/20/93	36	11		29 Bad Girl	S:36 / A:44 *Fever*	$4	▮[V]	Maverick/Sire 18650
7/24/93	14	20		30 Rain	A:11 / S:31 *Waiting*	$3	▮[V]	Maverick/Sire 18505
				above 4 from the album *Erotica*				
4/2/94	2[4]	26	●	31 I'll Remember AC[4]	S:2 / A:2 *Secret Garden*	$3	▮[V]	Maverick/Sire 18247
				theme from the movie *With Honors* starring Joe Pesci				
10/8/94	3	22	●	32 Secret	A:3 / S:11 *(instrumental)*	$3	▮[V]	Maverick/Sire 18035
12/17/94+	❶[7]	30	●	33 Take A Bow AC[9]	A:❶[9] / S:4 *(InDaSoul mix)*	$3	▮[V]	Maverick/Sire 18000
				Babyface (backing vocal, co-writer and co-producer)				
4/22/95	42	7		34 Bedtime Story	S:27 / A:68 *Survival*	$4	▮[V]	Maverick/Sire 17924
6/24/95	46	15		35 Human Nature	S:35 / A:58 *Sanctuary*	$4	▮[V]	Maverick/Sire 17882
				samples "What You Need" by Main Source; above 4 from the album *Bedtime Stories*				
12/9/95	6	20	●	36 You'll See	S:6 / A:10 *(instrumental) / Live To Tell (live)*	$3	▮[V]	Maverick/Sire 17719
4/20/96	78	8		37 Love Don't Live Here Anymore	*(album remix)*	$4	▮[V]	Maverick/Sire 17714
				first released by Madonna on her 1984 album *Like A Virgin*				
11/16/96	18	20	●	38 You Must Love Me	S:14 / A:25 *Rainbow High*	$3	▮[V]	Warner 17495
2/22/97	8	16		39 Don't Cry For Me Argentina	A:5 / S:11 *(5 versions)*	$8	★*	Warner 43809
				above 2 from the movie *Evita* starring Madonna				
3/21/98	2[1]	20	●	40 Frozen	A:7 / S:10 *Shanti/Ashtangi*	$3	▮[V]	Maverick 17244

DEBUT	PEAK	WKS	Gold	A-side (Chart Hit)..................B-side	$	Sym	Label & Number
				MADONNA — Cont'd			
7/11/98	5	20	●	41 **Ray Of Light** ....S:5 / A:26 *Has To Be*	$3	■V	Maverick 17206
10/17/98	11	19		42 **The Power Of Good-Bye** ....S:13 / A:26 *Mer Girl*	$3	★V	Maverick 17160
5/1/99	93	2		43 **Nothing Really Matters** ....S:27 *To Have And Not To Hold*	$5	★V	Maverick 17102
				above 4 from the album *Ray Of Light*			
6/12/99	19	19		44 **Beautiful Stranger** A:11			album cut
				from the movie *Austin Powers: The Spy Who Shagged Me* starring Mike Myers (soundtrack on Maverick 47348)			
2/19/00	29	9		45 **American Pie** A:23			album cut
				from the movie *The Next Best Thing* starring Madonna (soundtrack on Maverick 47595)			
8/12/00	❶4	24	▲	46 **Music** ....S:❶4 / A:3 *Cyberraga*	$4	★V	Maverick 16826
12/9/00+	4	21	●	47 **Don't Tell Me** ....S:❶1 / A:10 *(Thunderpuss' Hands In The Air Radio version)*	$4	★V	Maverick 16825
5/5/01	23	10		48 **What It Feels Like For A Girl** ....S:9 / A:36 *(8 remixes)*	$8	★*	Maverick 42372
10/19/02	8	17		49 **Die Another Day** ....S:❶11 / A:15 *(5 remixes)*	$8	★*V	Warner 42492
				title song from the James Bond movie starring Pierce Brosnan; "45": Warner 16684; B-side: (album version); #1, 3-5, 7, 12, 15, 17, 18, 21, 22, 24, 27, 28, 32, 34, 39-41 & 43-49: #1 Dance hits; Madonna wrote or co-wrote all of above (except #1, 2, 4-6, 8, 34, 37-39 & 45)			
				MAESTRO, Johnny — see CRESTS, The			
				MAGAZINE 60 '86			
				Electro-pop group from France.			
5/10/86	56	11		**Don Quichotte** ....*(bonus beats version)* [F]	$5		Baja 001
				MAGGARD, Cledus, And The Citizen's Band C&W/LP '76			
				Born Jay Huguely in Quick Sand, Kentucky. Former actor. Worked at Leslie Advertising in Greenville, South Carolina, when he recorded "The White Knight." Later worked as a story editor for TV's *Magnum P.I.*			
12/27/75+	19	15		1 **The White Knight** ....CW[1] *(long version)* [N]	$5		Mercury 73751
				jargon-laced CB radio conversation			
4/24/76	85	4		2 **Kentucky Moonrunner** ....*Dad I Gotta Go* [N]	$5		Mercury 73789
				MAGIC LANTERNS BUB '68			
				Rock group from Manchester, England: Jimmy Bilsbury (vocals), Peter Shoesmith (guitar), Ian Moncur (bass) and Allan Wilson (drums). The latter three left in 1969, replaced by Alistair Beveridge and Paul Garner (guitars), Mike Osbourne (bass) and Paul Ward (drums).			
10/26/68	29	12		1 **Shame, Shame** ....*Baby, I Gotta Go Now*	$10		Atlantic 2560
1/9/71	74	6		2 **One Night Stand** ....*Frisco Annie*	$7		Big Tree 109
				also released on Atlantic 2715 in 1970 ($8)			
7/8/72	88	4		3 **Country Woman** *[THE MAGIC LANTERN]* ....*Pa Bradley*	$7		Charisma 100
				all of above produced by Steve Rowland			
				MAGIC MUSHROOMS, The '66			
				Hard-rock group from Philadelphia, Pennsylvania: Stewart Freeman, Edward Cahill, Joseph Genetti, Joseph Lacavera, David Rice and Christopher Barbieri. One of the first hard-rock groups.			
11/12/66	93	1		**It's-A-Happening** ....*Never More*	$15		A&M 815
				MAGISTRATES, The — see DOVELLS, The			
				MAGNIFICENT BASTARDS, The '95			
				Side project of Scott Weiland, leader of **Stone Temple Pilots**. Group consists of Weiland (vocals), Zander Schloss (Thelonious Monster, **Red Hot Chili Peppers**) and Jeff Nolan (guitars), and Bob Thomson (bass).			
5/6/95	66A	4		**Mockingbird Girl**			album cut
				from the movie *Tank Girl* starring Lori Petty (soundtrack on Elektra 61760)			
				MAGNIFICENT MEN, The BUB/LP '67			
				White R&B-styled group from Harrisburg, Pennsylvania: David Bupp (vocals), Terry Crousore (guitar), Tommy Hoover (organ), Tom Pane (saxophone), Buddy King (trumpet), Jimmy Seville (bass) and Bob "Puff" Angelucci (drums).			
7/15/67	93	1		1 **I Could Be So Happy** ....*You Changed My Life*	$8		Capitol 5905
9/9/67	90	2		2 **Sweet Soul Medley - Part 1** ....*Part 2*	$8		Capitol 5976
				Sweet Soul Music/Ain't Too Proud To Beg/Ooh Baby Baby/ I Can't Help Myself			
				MAGOO — see TIMBALAND			
				MAG 7 '98			
				R&B pre-teen vocal group. Features lead singers Antuan and Ray Ray.			
10/31/98	93	5		**The Street Mix** ....S:62 *(instrumental)*	$4	■	Biv 10 860850
				samples "Dancing Machine" by **The Jackson 5**			
				MAHARIS, George BUB/LP '62			
				Born on 9/1/28 in Astoria, New York. Actor/singer. Played "Buz Murdock" on TV's *Route 66*.			
4/21/62	25	11		1 **Teach Me Tonight** *After The Lights Go Down Low (#104)*	$8	■	Epic 9504
8/4/62	54	6		2 **Love Me As I Love You** ....*They Knew About You (#111)*	$8	■	Epic 9522
11/17/62	62	5		3 **Baby Has Gone Bye Bye** ....*After One Kiss*	$8	■	Epic 9555
2/23/63	93	2		4 **Don't Fence Me In** ....*Alright, Okay, You Win*	$8	■	Epic 9569
				#1 hit for **Bing Crosby** & The Andrews Sisters in 1944; Robert Mersey (orch., all of above)			
9/21/63	88	3		5 **That's How It Goes** ....*It Isn't There*	$8	■	Epic 9613
				Don Costa (orch.); arrangement similar to **Johnny Cash**'s "I Walk The Line"			
				MAIN INGREDIENT, The R&B/BUB/LP '72			
				R&B vocal trio from the Bronx, New York: Donald McPherson, Luther Simmons and Tony Sylvester. McPherson died of leukemia on 7/4/71; replaced by Cuba Gooding. Gooding's son, Cuba Jr., is a prominent movie actor.			
				1)Everybody Plays The Fool 2)Just Don't Want To Be Lonely 3)Happiness Is Just Around The Bend			
6/27/70	64	9		1 **You've Been My Inspiration** ....*Life Won't Be The Same (Without You)*	$6		RCA Victor 0340
10/10/70	91	2		2 **I'm Better Off Without You** ....*Need Her Love (Mr. Bugler)*	$6		RCA Victor 0382
12/12/70+	49	13		3 **I'm So Proud** ....*Brotherly Love*	$6		RCA Victor 0401
5/8/71	52	9		4 **Spinning Around (I Must Be Falling In Love)** ....*Magic Shoes*	$6		RCA Victor 0456
9/11/71	97	3		5 **Black Seeds Keep On Growing** ....*Baby Change Your Mind*	$6	■	RCA Victor 0517
7/15/72	3	18	●	6 **Everybody Plays The Fool** *Who Can I Turn To (When Nobody Needs Me)*	$6		RCA Victor 0731

DEBUT	PEAK	WKS	Gold	A-side (Chart Hit)......B-side	$	Sym	Label & Number
				MAIN INGREDIENT, The — Cont'd			
12/23/72+	46	9		7 **You've Got To Take It (If You Want It)**......*Traveling*	$6		RCA Victor 0856
2/2/74	10	20	●	8 **Just Don't Want To Be Lonely**......*Goodbye My Love*	$5		RCA Victor 0205
6/29/74	35	12		9 **Happiness Is Just Around The Bend**......*Why Can't We All Unite*	$5		RCA Victor 0305
11/16/74	75	3		10 **California My Way**......*Looks Like Rain*	$5		RCA Victor 10095
5/24/75	92	3		11 **Rolling Down A Mountainside**......*Family Man*	$5		RCA Victor 10224
				MAI TAI R&B/BUB **'86**			
				Female black dance trio from Amsterdam, Netherlands: Jettie Wells, Carolien De Windt and Mildred Douglas.			
5/24/86	71	7		**Female Intuition**......*You Control Me*	$4	■	Critique 722
				picture sleeve made in Holland and distributed in the U.S.			
				MAJOR FIGGAS LP **'00**			
				Rap group from Philadelphia, Pennsylvania: female Bianca Jones with males Far'd Nasir, Maurice Brown, Michael Allen, Antonio Walker, Asa Burbage and Rennard East.			
7/29/00	26^{S}	17		**Yeah That's Us**......*(clean version)*	$5	★	Ruff Nation 16854
				MAJORS, The BUB **'62**			
				R&B vocal group from Philadelphia, Pennsylvania: Ricky Cordo (lead), Eugene Glass, Frank Troutt, Ronald Gathers and Idella Morris.			
8/11/62	22	11		1 **A Wonderful Dream**......*Time Will Tell*	$20		Imperial 5855
11/17/62	63	6		2 **A Little Bit Now (A Little Bit Later)** /			
11/24/62	83	3		3 **She's A Troublemaker**......	$20		Imperial 5879
				MAKEBA, Miriam BUB/LP **'67**			
				Born Zensi Miriam Makeba on 3/4/32 in Johannesburg, South Africa. Black folk singer. Married to **Hugh Masekela** (1964-66) and black-power activist Stokeley Carmichael (1968-78).			
2/25/56	45	9		1 **Lovely Lies**......T:45 *Kilimanjaro* (Manhattan Brothers)	$15		London 1610
				MANHATTAN BROTHERS AND MIRIAM MAKEBA			
10/7/67	12	11		2 **Pata Pata**......*The Ballad Of The Sad Young Men* [F]	$10		Reprise 0606
1/27/68	85	3		3 **Malayisha**......*Ring Bell, Ring Bell* [F]	$10		Reprise 0654
				MALAIKA **'92**			
				Born in Seattle, Washington. Black female dance singer.			
10/31/92	55^{A}	7		1 **So Much Love**......BUB:102 *(radio mix)*	$4	▮	A&M 0071
6/12/93	74^{A}	1		2 **Gotta Know (Your Name)**......BUB:120 *("CD" mix)*	$4	▮	A&M 0254
				MALKMUS, Stephen LP **'01**			
				Born on 5/30/66 in Santa Monica, California. Rock singer/songwriter/guitarist. Former member of Pavement.			
2/3/01	40^{S}	2		1 **Discretion Grove**......*Leisurely Poison / Sin Taxi*	$5	★V	Matador 494 ■
4/28/01	75^{S}	1		2 **Jenny & The Ess-Dog**......*Keep The Faith / That's What Mama Said / Alien Boy*	$8	★*	Matador 495
				MALLOY, Mitch **'92**			
				Born in Dickinson, North Dakota. Rock singer/songwriter.			
5/2/92	49	9		1 **Anything At All**......A:68 *(3 album snippets)*	$3	▮V	RCA 62196
				"45" B-side: "Mirror, Mirror"			
8/8/92	66	8		2 **Nobody Wins In This War**......A:72 *(3 album snippets)*	$3	▮	RCA 62270
				MALMKVIST, Siw - Umberto Marcato **'64**			
				Female singer Malmkvist was born on 12/31/36 in Landskrona, Sweden. Male singer Umberto was born in Italy.			
7/18/64	58	5		**Sole Sole Sole**......*Sabato Sera* [F]	$8		Jubilee 5479
				MALO BUB/LP **'72**			
				Latin-rock group from San Francisco, California. Core members: Arcelio Garcia (vocals), Jorge Santana (guitar; brother of Carlos **Santana**), Richard Kermode (keyboards) and Pablo Tellez (bass). Malo is Spanish for "Bad."			
3/4/72	18	12		**Suavecito**......*Nena*	$7	□	Warner 7559
				MALTBY, Richard, and his Orchestra MEM/POP **'56**			
				Born on 6/26/14 in Chicago, Illinois. Died on 8/19/91 (age 77). Trumpeter/composer/bandleader. Hit #21 on the pop charts in 1954 with "St. Louis Blues Mambo."			
3/17/56	14	16		**Themes From "The Man With The Golden Arm"**......T:14 / S:15 / J:19 / A:20 *Heart Of Paris* [I]	$15	■	Vik 0196
				title song from the movie *The Man With The Golden Arm* starring **Frank Sinatra**			
				MAMA CASS BUB/AC/LP **'68**			
				Born Ellen Naomi Cohen on 9/19/41 in Baltimore, Maryland. Died of a heart attack (despite rumors, she did not choke to death on a ham sandwich) on 7/29/74 (age 32). Member of **The Mamas & The Papas**. Her sister Leah Kunkel is a member of **The Coyote Sisters**.			
7/6/68	12	11		1 **Dream A Little Dream Of Me** *Midnight Voyage*	$8		Dunhill 4145
				MAMA CASS with The Mamas & The Papas			
				#1 hit for Wayne King in 1931			
11/2/68	67	5		2 **California Earthquake**......*Talkin' To Your Toothbrush*	$8		Dunhill/ABC 4166
3/15/69	58	6		3 **Move In A Little Closer, Baby**......*All For Me*	$8		Dunhill/ABC 4184
6/7/69	30	19		4 **It's Getting Better**......*Who's To Blame*	$8		Dunhill/ABC 4195
				MAMA CASS ELLIOT:			
10/18/69	36	9		5 **Make Your Own Kind Of Music**......*Lady Love*	$7		Dunhill/ABC 4214
1/31/70	42	7		6 **New World Coming**......*Blow Me A Kiss*	$7		Dunhill/ABC 4225
8/1/70	99	2		7 **A Song That Never Comes**......*I Can Dream, Can't I*	$7		Dunhill/ABC 4244

DEBUT	PEAK	WKS	Gold	A-side (Chart Hit)...B-side	$	Sym	Label & Number
	★252★			**MAMAS & THE PAPAS, The** BUB/LP '66			

Folk-pop group formed in Los Angeles, California: **John Phillips** (born on 8/30/35 in Paris Island, South Carolina) (see #16 below); Michelle Phillips (born on 6/4/45 in Long Beach, California); Denny Doherty (born on 11/29/41 in Halifax, Nova Scotia, Canada) and Cass Elliot (see **Mama Cass** above). Disbanded in 1968, reunited briefly in 1971. John and Michelle were married from 1962-70; their daughter is Chynna Phillips of the **Wilson Phillips** trio. John is also the father of actress MacKenzie Phillips. Michelle Phillips later became a successful actress; briefly married to Dennis Hopper in 1970. Mama Cass died of a heart attack on 7/29/74 (age 32). John Phillips died of heart failure on 3/18/2001 (age 65). Group inducted into the Rock and Roll Hall of Fame in 1998.

1)Monday, Monday 2)Dedicated To The One I Love 3)California Dreamin'

DEBUT	PEAK	WKS	Gold	A-side (Chart Hit)...B-side	$	Sym	Label & Number
1/8/66	4	17	●	1 **California Dreamin'** ...*Somebody Groovy*	$10	□	Dunhill 4020
4/9/66	1[3]	12	●	2 **Monday, Monday** *Got A Feelin'*	$10		Dunhill 4026
				an unreleased issue of Dunhill 4026 came with a black-and-white picture sleeve ($600), with "I Call Your Name" as the B-side			
7/2/66	5	9		3 **I Saw Her Again**...*Even If I Could*	$10		Dunhill 4031
10/22/66	24	7		4 **Look Through My Window** ...*Once Was A Time I Thought*	$10		Dunhill 4050
12/3/66+	5	12		5 **Words Of Love** /			
12/17/66+	73	6		6 **Dancing In The Street**...	$10		Dunhill 4057
2/25/67	2[3]	10		7 **Dedicated To The One I Love**...*Free Advice*	$10		Dunhill 4077
4/29/67	5	9		8 **Creeque Alley** ...*Did You Ever Want To Cry*	$10	□	Dunhill 4083
				name of the street on which the group lived in the Virgin Islands; a musical biography of the group members			
8/26/67	20	6		9 **Twelve Thirty (Young Girls Are Coming To The Canyon)**...*Straight Shooter (#130)*	$10		Dunhill 4099
10/28/67	26	7		10 **Glad To Be Unhappy**...*Hey Girl (#134)*	$10		Dunhill 4107
				from the 1936 Rodgers & Hart musical *On Your Toes* starring Ray Bolger			
12/9/67+	51	7		11 **Dancing Bear**...*John's Music Box*	$8	■	Dunhill 4113
6/8/68	53	6		12 **Safe In My Garden** ...*Too Late*	$8		Dunhill 4125
7/6/68	12	11		13 **Dream A Little Dream Of Me**...*Midnight Voyage*	$8		Dunhill 4145
				MAMA CASS with The Mamas & The Papas			
				#1 hit for Wayne King in 1931			
9/14/68	81	5		14 **For The Love Of Ivy**...*Strange Young Girls*	$8		Dunhill/ABC 4150
				inspired by the 1968 Sidney Poitier movie *For Love Of Ivy*			
11/23/68	76	5		15 **Do You Wanna Dance** ...*My Girl*	$8		Dunhill/ABC 4171
				all of above (except #13) produced by Lou Adler			
5/16/70	32	12		16 **Mississippi** ...*April Anne*	$7		Dunhill/ABC 4236
				JOHN PHILLIPS			
2/12/72	81	3		17 **Step Out** ...*Shooting Star*	$7		Dunhill/ABC 4301

MANASSAS — see STILLS, Stephen

DEBUT	PEAK	WKS	Gold	A-side (Chart Hit)...B-side	$	Sym	Label & Number
	★425★			**MANCHESTER, Melissa** AC/BUB/LP '75			

Born on 2/15/51 in the Bronx, New York. Adult Contemporary singer/pianist/composer. Father was a bassoon player with the New York Metropolitan Opera Orchestra. She studied songwriting under **Paul Simon** at the University School of the Arts in the early 1970s. Former backup singer for **Bette Midler**. Also see **National Lampoon**.

1)You Should Hear How She Talks About You 2)Midnight Blue 3)Don't Cry Out Loud

DEBUT	PEAK	WKS	Gold	A-side (Chart Hit)...B-side	$	Sym	Label & Number
5/10/75	6	17		1 **Midnight Blue** ...AC[2] *I Got Eyes*	$4		Arista 0116
9/20/75	30	12		2 **Just Too Many People** ...*This Lady's Not Home*	$4		Arista 0146
2/7/76	27	9		3 **Just You And I**...*My Sweet Thing*	$4		Arista 0168
5/1/76	71	5		4 **Better Days** ...*Sing, Sing, Sing*	$4		Arista 0183
8/7/76	78	3		5 **Rescue Me** ...*Happy Endings* (AC #33)	$4		Arista 0196
11/18/78+	10	23		6 **Don't Cry Out Loud** ...*We Had This Time*	$4		Arista 0373
				#79 R&B hit for **The Moments** as "We Don't Cry Out Loud" in 1977			
5/5/79	76	4		7 **Theme From Ice Castles (Through The Eyes Of Love)**...*Such A Morning*	$4		Arista 0405
				theme song from the movie *Ice Castles* starring Lynn-Holly Johnson			
10/13/79	39	10		8 **Pretty Girls** ...*It's All In The Sky Above*	$4		Arista 0456
2/23/80	32	13		9 **Fire In The Morning**...*Lights Of Dawn*	$4		Arista 0485
2/28/81	54	9		10 **Lovers After All** ...*Happier Than I've Ever Been* (Manchester)	$4		Arista 0587
				MELISSA MANCHESTER AND PEABO BRYSON			
5/22/82	5	25		11 **You Should Hear How She Talks About You** *Long Goodbyes*	$4		Arista 0676
2/5/83	42	11		12 **Nice Girls** ...*Hey Ricky (You're A Low-Down Heel)*	$4		Arista 1045
10/29/83	78	4		13 **No One Can Love You More Than Me** ...*White Rose*	$4		Arista 9087
11/24/84	86	6		14 **Thief Of Hearts** ...*(instrumental)*	$3		Casablanca 880308
				title song from the movie starring Steven Bauer			
4/27/85	74	5		15 **Mathematics** ...*So Full Of Yourself*	$3	■	MCA 52575
	★475★			**MANCINI, Henry, And His Orchestra** AC/BUB/LP '69			

Born on 4/16/24 in Cleveland, Ohio; raised in Aliquippa, Pennsylvania. Died of cancer on 6/14/94 (age 70). Leading movie and TV composer/arranger/conductor. Staff composer for Universal Pictures, 1952-58. Winner of four Oscars and 20 Grammys, plus Grammy's Lifetime Achievement Award (1995). Married Ginny O'Connor, an original member of **Mel Torme**'s Mel-Tones.

1)Love Theme From Romeo & Juliet 2)Moon River 3)(Theme From) Love Story

DEBUT	PEAK	WKS	Gold	A-side (Chart Hit)...B-side	$	Sym	Label & Number
4/4/60	21	13		1 **Mr. Lucky**...*Floating Pad* [I]	$12		RCA Victor 7705
				title song from the TV series starring John Vivyan			
4/3/61	90	1		2 **Theme from The Great Imposter** ...*Love Music* [I]	$10	■	RCA Victor 7830
				from the movie *The Great Impostor* starring Tony Curtis			
10/9/61	11	26		3 **Moon River**...*Breakfast At Tiffany's*	$10	■	RCA Victor 7916
				from the movie *Breakfast At Tiffany's* starring Audrey Hepburn; originally charted for 20 weeks; re-entered on 5/5/62 (#32); 1961 Grammy winner: Record of the Year			
7/14/62	95	4		4 **Theme From "Hatari!"** ...*Your Father's Feathers* [I]	$8	■	RCA Victor 8037
				from the movie *Hatari!* starring John Wayne			
1/26/63	33	18		5 **Days Of Wine And Roses** ...*Seventy Six Trombones*	$8	■	RCA Victor 8120
				title song from the movie starring Jack Lemmon and Lee Remick; 1963 Grammy winner: Record of the Year			
6/22/63	93	1		6 **Banzai Pipeline** ...*Rhapsody In Blue* [I]	$15	■	RCA Victor 8184
12/7/63+	36	11		7 **Charade**...*Orange Tamouré*	$8	■	RCA Victor 8256
				title song from the movie starring Cary Grant and Audrey Hepburn			

DEBUT	PEAK	WKS	Gold	A-side (Chart Hit)..........B-side	$	Sym	Label & Number
				MANCINI, Henry, And His Orchestra — Cont'd			
4/4/64	31	8		8 **The Pink Panther Theme** ....*It Had Better Be Tonight* [I]	$8	■	RCA Victor 8286
				Johnny Beecher (sax); from the first of the *Pink Panther* movies starring Peter Sellers			
7/18/64	97	2		9 **A Shot In The Dark**.......*The Shadows Of Paris* [I]	$8	■	RCA Victor 8381
				second in the series of *Pink Panther* movies starring Peter Sellers			
12/12/64+	77	7		10 **Dear Heart**.......*How Soon*	$8	■	RCA Victor 8458
				title song from the movie starring Glenn Ford and Angela Lansbury; all of above composed by Mancini			
5/10/69	1[2]	14	●	11 **Love Theme From Romeo & Juliet** AC[8] *The Windmills Of Your Mind* [I]	$8		RCA Victor 0131
				from the 1968 movie *Romeo & Juliet* starring Leonard Whiting and Olivia Hussey			
9/6/69	87	4		12 **Moonlight Sonata**.......*Natalie* [I]	$7		RCA Victor 0212
				written by Beethoven in 1802			
1/16/71	13	11		13 **Theme From Love Story**.......*Phone Call To The Past* [I]	$7		RCA Victor 9927
				from the movie *Love Story* starring Ali McGraw and Ryan O'Neal			
4/1/72	92	3		14 **All His Children**.......*You'll Still Be The One* (Pride)	$7		RCA Victor 0624
				CHARLEY PRIDE with HENRY MANCINI			
				from the movie *Sometimes A Great Notion* starring Paul Newman and Henry Fonda			
3/19/77	45	9		15 **Theme from Charlie's Angels**.......*Bumper's Theme* [I]	$5		RCA 10888
				from the TV series *Charlie's Angels* starring Farrah Fawcett, Kate Jackson and Jaclyn Smith			
				M+M — see MARTHA & THE MUFFINS			
				MANDRELL, Barbara C&W/BUB/AC/LP **'79**			
				Born on 12/25/48 in Houston, Texas; raised in Oceanside, California. Country singer. Moved to Nashville in 1971. Host of own TV variety series *Barbara Mandrell & The Mandrell Sisters*, 1980-82. Suffered severe injuries in an auto accident in 1984, from which she fully recovered. Acted on TV's *Sunset Beach* in 1997. Charted 55 Country hits, 1969-89.			
3/4/78	92	5		1 **Woman To Woman**.......*Let The Rain Out*	$6		ABC/Dot 17736
3/17/79	31	16		2 **(If Loving You Is Wrong) I Don't Want To Be Right**....CW[1] *I Feel The Hurt Coming On*	$5		MCA 12451
				also released on ABC 12451 in 1979 (charted its first 4 weeks on ABC)			
10/6/79	89	5		3 **Fooled By A Feeling**.......*Love Takes A Long Time To Die*	$4		MCA 41077
				MANDRILL R&B/BUB/LP **'73**			
				Latin jazz-rock-funk group from Brooklyn, New York: brothers Louis "Sweet Lou" (trumpet), Richard "Dr. Ric" (sax) and Carlos "Mad Dog" (flute) Wilson, Omar Mesa (guitar), Claude "Coffee" Cave (keyboards), Fudgie Kae (bass) and Charlie Pardo (drums).			
6/5/71	94	3		1 **Mandrill**.......*Warning Blues* [I]	$6		Polydor 14070
4/14/73	52	10		2 **Fencewalk**.......*Hágalo*	$5		Polydor 14163
8/11/73	83	7		3 **Hang Loose**.......*Polk Street Carnival* [I]	$5		Polydor 14187
	★441★			**MANFRED MANN** BUB/ROK/LP **'64**			
				Born Michael Lubowitz on 10/21/40 in Johannesburg, South Africa. Formed pop-rock group in England: Mann (keyboards), Paul Jones (vocals; born on 2/24/42), Michael Vickers (guitar; born on 4/18/41), Tom McGuinness (bass; born on 12/2/41) and Mike Hugg (drums; born on 8/11/42). Mike D'Abo replaced Jones in 1967. McGuinness left to form **McGuinness Flint** in 1970. Manfred Mann formed his new Earth Band in 1971: Mann, Mick Rogers (vocals), Colin Pattenden (bass) and Chris Slade (drums). Rogers replaced by Chris Thompson (vocals, guitar) in 1976. Pattenden replaced by Pat King in June 1977. Thompson also recorded with own group **Night** in 1979. Lineup in 1979: Mann, Thompson, King, Steve Waller (guitar, vocals) and Geoff Britton (drums). King replaced by Matt Irving in 1981. Earth Band dissolved in 1986.			
				1)Do Wah Diddy Diddy 2)Blinded By The Light 3)Mighty Quinn (Quinn The Eskimo)			
9/5/64	1[2]	13		1 **Do Wah Diddy Diddy** *What You Gonna Do?*	$15		Ascot 2157
11/14/64+	12	12		2 **Sha La La**.......*John Hardy*	$12	■	Ascot 2165
2/20/65	50	6		3 **Come Tomorrow**.......*What Did I Do Wrong*	$12	■	Ascot 2170
7/2/66	29	8		4 **Pretty Flamingo**.......*You're Standing By*	$10		United Artists 50040
3/2/68	10	11		5 **Mighty Quinn (Quinn The Eskimo)**.......*By Request - Edwin Garvey*	$10		Mercury 72770
				written by **Bob Dylan**; early pressings show title only as "Quinn The Eskimo"			
1/18/69	97	2		6 **Fox On The Run**.......*Too Many People*	$10		Mercury 72879
				MANFRED MANN'S EARTH BAND:			
2/26/72	69	7		7 **Living Without You**.......*Tribute*	$7		Polydor 14113
4/3/76	97	3		8 **Spirit In The Night**.......*As Above So Below*	$6		Warner 8176
				first released on Warner 8152 in 1975 (Mick Rogers, vocal); also see #10 below			
11/20/76+	1[1]	20	●	9 **Blinded By The Light**.......*Starbird No. 2*	$5	■	Warner 8252
				picture sleeve features the song's lyrics; above 2 written by **Bruce Springsteen**			
4/30/77	40	8		10 **Spirit In The Night**.......*Questions* [R]	$5		Warner 8355
				new recording of #8 above (**Chris Thompson**, vocal)			
6/16/79	58	7		11 **You Angel You**.......*"Belle" Of The Earth*	$5		Warner 8850
				written by **Bob Dylan**			
1/21/84	22	15		12 **Runner**.......*Where Do They Send Them*	$4		Arista 9143
				MANGIONE, Chuck AC/BUB/R&B/LP **'78**			
				Born on 11/29/40 in Rochester, New York. Flugelhorn player/bandleader/composer. Recorded with older brother Gaspare ("Gap") as The Jazz Brothers for Riverside in 1960. To New York City in 1965; played with **Maynard Ferguson**, **Kai Winding**, and Art Blakey's Jazz Messengers.			
7/3/71	76	6		1 **Hill Where The Lord Hides**.......*Friends & Love* [I-L]	$8		Mercury 73208
				with the Rochester Philharmonic Orchestra; Gary Niewood (flute); recorded in Rochester, New York			
7/19/75	96	4		2 **Chase The Clouds Away**.......*Soft* (w/Esther Satterfield) [I]	$5		A&M 1707
6/11/77	86	3		3 **Land Of Make Believe**.......*As Long As We're Together* [L]	$5		Mercury 73920
				with The Hamilton Philharmonic Orchestra; Esther Satterfield (vocal); recorded at Massey Hall in Toronto in 1973; originally released on Mercury 73432 in 1973 ($6)			
2/11/78	4	25		4 **Feels So Good** AC[1] *Maui-Waui* [I]	$4	■	A&M 2001
1/19/80	18	16		5 **Give It All You Got**.......AC[3] *B'bye* [I]	$4	■	A&M 2211
				featured song by ABC Sports for the 1980 Winter Olympics			

MANHATTAN BROTHERS '56

Vocal group from Johannesburg, South Africa: Nathan Mdledle, Joseph Mogotsi, Rufus Khoza and Ronnie Sehume. **Miriam Makeba** was a member from 1954 to late 1956.

DEBUT	PEAK	WKS	Gold	A-side (Chart Hit)	B-side	$	Sym	Label & Number
2/25/56	45	9		**Lovely Lies** T:45 **MANHATTAN BROTHERS AND MIRIAM MAKEBA**	*Kilimanjaro* (Manhattan Brothers)	$15		London 1610

MANHATTANS, The ★512★ R&B/BUB/LP '76

R&B vocal group from Jersey City, New Jersey: George "Smitty" Smith (lead vocals), Winfred "Blue" Lovett (bass; born on 11/16/43), Edward "Sonny" Bivins (born on 1/15/42) and Kenneth "Wally" Kelly (tenors; born on 1/9/43) and Richard Taylor (baritone). Smith replaced by Gerald Alston in 1971. First recorded for Piney in 1962. Taylor (aka Abdul Rashid Talhah) left in 1976. Charted 44 R&B hits, 1965-90. Smith died of spinal meningitis on 12/16/70. Taylor died following a lengthy illness on 12/7/87 (age 47). Featured female vocalist **Regina Belle** began solo career in 1987. Alston went solo in 1988.

1)Kiss And Say Goodbye 2)Shining Star 3)Don't Take Your Love

DEBUT	PEAK	WKS	Gold	A-side (Chart Hit)	B-side	$	Sym	Label & Number
1/16/65	68	8		1 **I Wanna Be (Your Everything)**	*What's It Gonna Be*	$15		Carnival 507
1/1/66	92	2		2 **Follow Your Heart**	*The Boston Monkey*	$15		Carnival 512
3/19/66	96	2		3 **Baby I Need You**	*Teach Me (The "Philly" Dog)*	$15		Carnival 514
12/23/67+	96	3		4 **I Call It Love**	*Manhattan Stomp*	$15		Carnival 533
6/20/70	98	1		5 **If My Heart Could Speak**	*Loneliness*	$12		Deluxe 122
6/9/73	43	11		6 **There's No Me Without You**	*I'm Not A Run Around*	$6		Columbia 45838
9/22/73	77	8		7 **You'd Better Believe It**	*Soul Train*	$6		Columbia 45927
1/4/75	37	10		8 **Don't Take Your Love**	*The Day The Robin Sang To Me*	$6		Columbia 10045
5/31/75	97	2		9 **Hurt** #8 R&B hit for **Roy Hamilton** in 1955	*Nursery Rhymes*	$6		Columbia 10140
4/17/76	❶[2]	26	▲	10 **Kiss And Say Goodbye** RB[1]	*Wonderful World Of Love*	$5		Columbia 10310
10/30/76	46	8		11 **I Kinda Miss You**	*Gypsy Man*	$5		Columbia 10430
3/26/77	66	18		12 **It Feels So Good To Be Loved So Bad**	*Up On The Street (Where I Live)*	$5		Columbia 10495
10/29/77	93	2		13 **We Never Danced To A Love Song**	*Let's Start It All Over Again*	$5		Columbia 10586
4/26/80	5	25	▲	14 **Shining Star**	*I'll Never Run Away From Love Again*	$5		Columbia 11222
7/30/83	72	6		15 **Crazy**	*Love Is Gonna Find You*	$4		Columbia 03939
3/2/85	81	5		16 **You Send Me**	*You're Gonna Love Being Loved By Me*	$4	■	Columbia 04754

MANHATTAN TRANSFER, The AC/BUB/LP '81

Versatile vocal harmony group formed in Manhattan, New York: Tim Hauser, Alan Paul, Janis Siegel and Laurel Masse. Cheryl Bentyne replaced Masse in 1979. Group hosted own TV variety show on CBS in 1975.

DEBUT	PEAK	WKS	Gold	A-side (Chart Hit)	B-side	$	Sym	Label & Number
9/20/75	22	12		1 **Operator**	*Tuxedo Junction*	$5		Atlantic 3292
4/19/80	30	12		2 **Twilight Zone/Twilight Tone** "Twilight Zone" was the theme from the Rod Serling TV series	*Body And Soul*	$5		Atlantic 3649
11/29/80	73	8		3 **Trickle Trickle** originally recorded in 1958 by the doo-wop group The Videos on Casino 102 ($40)	*Foreign Affair*	$10		Atlantic 3772
5/23/81	7	21		4 **Boy From New York City**	*(The Word Of) Confirmation*	$4		Atlantic 3816
5/29/82	78	5		5 **Route 66** featured in the movie *Sharky's Machine* starring **Burt Reynolds**; #11 hit for **Nat "King" Cole** in 1946	*On The Boulevard*	$4		Atlantic 4034
9/10/83	40	13		6 **Spice Of Life**	*The Night That Monk Returned To Heaven*	$4	■	Atlantic 89786
2/2/85	83	3		7 **Baby Come Back To Me (The Morse Code Of Love)** doo-wop tune dedicated to **The Capris**	*That's The Way It Goes*	$10		Atlantic 89594

MANILOW, Barry ★71★ AC/LP '75

Born Barry Alan Pincus on 6/17/46 in Brooklyn, New York. Pop singer/pianist/composer. Studied at New York's Juilliard School. Music director for the WCBS-TV series *Callback*. Worked at New York's Continental Baths bathhouse/nightclub in New York as **Bette Midler**'s accompanist in 1972; later produced her first two albums. First recorded solo as Featherbed. Wrote jingles for Dr. Pepper, Pepsi, State Farm Insurance, Band-Aids and McDonald's ("You Deserve A Break Today," which he also sang). One of the all-time top Adult Contemporary vocalists. Also see **Lady Flash**.

1)I Write The Songs 2)Looks Like We Made It 3)Mandy 4)Can't Smile Without You 5)Could It Be Magic

DEBUT	PEAK	WKS	Gold	A-side (Chart Hit)	B-side	$	Sym	Label & Number
11/16/74+	❶[1]	16	●	1 **Mandy** AC[2] written and charted by **Scott English** in 1972 as "Brandy"	*Something's Comin' Up*	$5		Bell 45,613
3/1/75	12	13		2 **It's A Miracle** AC[1]	*One Of These Days*	$5		Arista 0108
6/28/75	6	18		3 **Could It Be Magic** new version of song first released on Bell 45,133 in 1971 as by **Featherbed Featuring Barry Manilow** ($25), and then on Bell 45,422 in 1973 by Manilow ($6); inspired by Chopin's *Prelude in C Minor*	*I Am Your Child*	$5		Arista 0126
11/15/75+	❶[1]	20	●	4 **I Write The Songs** AC[2] written by **The Beach Boys**' Bruce Johnston (**Bruce & Terry**)	*A Nice Boy Like Me*	$5		Arista 0157
3/20/76	10	15		5 **Tryin' To Get The Feeling Again** AC[1]	*Beautiful Music*	$4		Arista 0172
9/18/76	29	10		6 **This One's For You** AC[1]	*Riders To The Stars*	$4		Arista 0206
11/27/76+	10	19		7 **Weekend In New England** AC[1]	*Say The Words*	$4		Arista 0212
5/7/77	❶[1]	19	●	8 **Looks Like We Made It** AC[3]	*New York City Rhythm*	$4		Arista 0244
10/1/77	23	10		9 **Daybreak** "live" recording of tune from his 1976 album *This One's For You*	*Jump Shout Boogie* [L]	$4		Arista 0273
2/4/78	3	19	●	10 **Can't Smile Without You** AC[2]	*Sunrise*	$4		Arista 0305
5/6/78	19	13		11 **Even Now** AC[3]	*I Was A Fool (To Let You Go)*	$4	■	Arista 0330
6/10/78	8	16	●	12 **Copacabana (At The Copa)**	*(long version)*	$4		Arista 0339
9/16/78	11	16		13 **Ready To Take A Chance Again** above 2 from the movie *Foul Play* starring Goldie Hawn and Chevy Chase	*Sweet Life*	$4	□	Arista 0357
12/16/78+	9	15		14 **Somewhere In The Night** #10-12 & 14: from the album *Even Now*	*Leavin' In The Morning*	$4		Arista 0382
10/13/79	9	14		15 **Ships** first recorded by **Ian Hunter** on his 1979 *You're Never Alone With A Schizophrenic* album	*They Gave In To The Blues*	$4		Arista 0464
12/15/79+	20	16		16 **When I Wanted You** AC[1]	*Bobbie Lee (What's The Difference, I Gotta Live)*	$4		Arista 0481

DEBUT	PEAK	WKS	Gold	A-side (Chart Hit)..........B-side	$	Sym	Label & Number
				MANILOW, Barry — Cont'd			
4/12/80	36	11		17 **I Don't Want To Walk Without You**..........*One Voice*	$4		Arista 0501
				#2 hit for Harry James in 1942 (from the movie *Sweater Girl* starring Eddie Bracken)			
11/22/80+	10	16		18 **I Made It Through The Rain**..........*Only In Chicago*	$4		Arista 0566
				all of above produced by Manilow and Ron Dante (**The Archies, The Detergents, The Cuff Links**)			
3/14/81	45	10		19 **Lonely Together**..........*The Last Duet* (w/Lily Tomlin)	$4		Arista 0596
10/10/81	15	16		20 **The Old Songs**..........AC[3] *Don't Fall In Love With Me*	$4		Arista 0633
12/19/81+	21	15		21 **Somewhere Down The Road**..........AC[2] *Let's Take All Night (To Say Goodbye)*	$3		Arista 0658
3/20/82	32	10		22 **Let's Hang On**..........*No Other Love*	$3		Arista 0675
7/31/82	38	11		23 **Oh Julie**..........*Break Down The Door*	$3		Arista 0698
11/20/82+	39	14		24 **Memory**..........*Heart Of Steel*	$3		Arista 1025
				theme from Andrew Lloyd Webber's musical *Cats* starring Betty Buckley			
2/26/83	26	16		25 **Some Kind Of Friend**..........*Heaven*	$3		Arista 1046
				also released on Arista 9003 in 1983			
11/19/83+	18	14		26 **Read 'Em And Weep**..........AC[6] *One Voice*	$3		Arista 9101
7/12/86	86	5		27 **I'm Your Man**..........*(dub mix)*	$3	■	RCA 14397
3/19/88	90	2		28 **Hey Mambo**..........*When October Goes* (Manilow)	$3	■	Arista 9666
				BARRY MANILOW With Kid Creole And The Coconuts			
				MANN, Aimee — see 'TIL TUESDAY			
				MANN, Barry BUB/AC **'61**			
				Born Barry Iberman on 2/9/39 in Brooklyn, New York. One of pop music's most prolific songwriters in a partnership with wife Cynthia Weil, including "You've Lost That Lovin' Feelin'," "(You're My) Soul & Inspiration," "Kicks," "Hungry," "We Gotta Get Out Of This Place," and many others. Established own publishing company, Dyad Music.			
8/7/61	7	12		1 **Who Put The Bomp (In The Bomp, Bomp, Bomp)**..........*Love, True Love* [N]	$25		ABC-Paramount 10237
12/5/64	94	2		2 **Talk To Me Baby**..........*Amy*	$15		Red Bird 10-015
5/30/70	93	3		3 **Feelings**..........*Let Me Stay With You*	$7		Scepter 12281
				from the movie *Getting Straight* starring Elliott Gould and Candice Bergen			
8/14/76	78	6		4 **The Princess And The Punk**..........*Jennifer*	$5		Arista 0194
				MANN, Carl C&W **'59**			
				Born on 8/24/42 in Huntingdon, Tennessee. Rockabilly singer/pianist.			
6/1/59	25	16		1 **Mona Lisa**..........*Foolish One*	$30		Phillips 3539
				#1 hit for **Nat "King" Cole** in 1950			
10/26/59	57	7		2 **Pretend**..........*Rockin' Love*	$25		Phillips 3546
				#2 hit for **Nat "King" Cole** in 1953			
				MANN, Gloria **'55**			
				Pop-rock and roll singer. Her son, Bob Rosenberg, is the leader of **Will To Power**.			
2/12/55	18	2		1 **Earth Angel Will You Be Mine**..........J:18 / S:24 *I Love You, Yes I Do*	$30		Sound 109
12/10/55+	19	13		2 **Teen Age Prayer**..........S:19 / T:21 *Gypsy Lady*	$30		Sound 126
				Sid Bass (orch.)			
3/10/56	59	5		3 **Why Do Fools Fall In Love?**..........T:59 *Partners For Life*	$20		Decca 29832
				Sonny Burke (orch.)			
				MANN, Herbie BUB/R&B/AC/LP **'75**			
				Born Herbert Jay Solomon on 4/16/30 in Brooklyn, New York. Died of cancer on 7/1/2003 (age 73). Renowned jazz flutist. First recorded with Mat Mathews Quintet for Brunswick in 1953. First recorded as a solo for Bethlehem in 1954.			
10/1/66	93	1		1 **Philly Dog**..........*Frere Jacques* [I]	$8		Atlantic 5074
				King Curtis (sax)			
11/12/66	88	2		2 **A Man And A Woman**..........*Sidewinder*	$8		Atlantic 2362
				TAMIKO JONES with HERBIE MANN			
				title song from the French movie starring Anouk Aimee			
10/21/67	93	1		3 **To Sir, With Love**..........*Hold Back (Just A Little)* [I]	$8		Atlantic 2444
				title song from the movie starring Sidney Poitier			
2/17/68	81	2		4 **Unchain My Heart**..........*Glory Of Love* [I]	$7		A&M 896
				Eric Gale (guitar solo)			
5/24/69	44	10		5 **Memphis Underground**..........*New Orleans* [I]	$6		Atlantic 2621
11/22/69	95	2		6 **It's A Funky Thing-Right On (Part 1)**..........*(Part 2)* [N]	$6		Atlantic 2671
				novelty vocal version of "Memphis Underground" (**Little Milton**, Swee-Tee, and Percy - vocals)			
2/8/75	14	15		7 **Hijack** *The Orient Express*	$5		Atlantic 3246
1/13/79	26	18		8 **Superman**..........*Etagui*	$5	■	Atlantic 3547
				MANN, Johnny, Singers AC/BUB/LP **'67**			
				Born on 8/30/28 in Baltimore, Maryland. Musical director for Joey Bishop's TV talk show.			
6/24/67	91	3		**Up-Up And Away**..........*Joey Is The Name*	$6		Liberty 55972
				MANN, Manfred — see MANFRED MANN			
				MANONE, Wingy, And His Orchestra MEM **'36**			
				Born Joseph Mannone on 2/13/04 in New Orleans, Louisiana. Died on 7/9/82 (age 78). Trumpeter/bandleader. Lost right arm at age eight in streetcar accident. Composed "Tar Paper Stomp" which Glenn Miller later made famous in revised form as "In The Mood."			
3/30/57	56	7		**Party Doll**..........T:56 *Real Gone*	$20		Decca 30211
				MANTLE, Mickey — see BREWER, Teresa			
				MANTOVANI And His Orchestra MEM/POP/AC/BUB/LP **'35**			
				Born Annunzio Paolo Mantovani on 11/15/05 in Venice, Italy. Died on 3/29/80 (age 74). Played classical violin in England before forming his own orchestra in the early 1930s. Had first U.S. chart hit in 1935, "Red Sails In The Sunset" (#2). Achieved international fame 20 years later with his 40-piece orchestra and distinctive "cascading strings" sound. Charted 53 pop albums, 1952-72.			
8/14/54	10	18	●	1 **Cara Mia** S:10 / A:17 *How, When Or Where*	$20		London 1486
2/4/56	62	8		2 **When You Lose The One You Love**..........T:62 *Angelus*	$15		London 1617
				DAVID WHITFIELD with MANTOVANI and his Orchestra and Chorus (above 2)			

DEBUT	PEAK	WKS	Gold	A-side (Chart Hit)..........B-side	$	Sym	Label & Number
				MANTOVANI And His Orchestra — Cont'd			
6/10/57	12	32		3 **Around The World** ....A:12 / S:23 / T:25 *The Road To Ballingarry* [I]	$10	■	London 1746
				Stan Newsome (trumpet solo); from the movie *Around The World In 80 Days* starring David Niven			
11/7/60	93	1		4 **Theme From The Sundowners**..........*Mine Alone* [I]	$8		London 1946
				from the movie *The Sundowners* starring Deborah Kerr and **Robert Mitchum**			
11/21/60+	31	13		5 **Main Theme from Exodus (Ari's Theme)**..........*Karen* [I]	$8	■	London 1953
				from the movie *Exodus* starring Paul Newman and Eva Marie Saint			
				MANTRONIX (Featuring Wondress) R&B/LP **'90**			
				Hip-hop/dance duo from Brooklyn, New York: Curtis "Mantronik" Kahleel and M.C. Tee. Bryce Wilson replaced Tee in 1989. Wilson later formed **Groove Theory**.			
2/24/90	82	4		**Got To Have Your Love** ....*(2 versions)*	$4	▮	Capitol 44466
				MARA, Tommy MEM **'58**			
				Born in Waterbury, Connecticut. Adult Contemporary singer; similar in style to **Steve Lawrence**.			
8/18/58	76	4		**Where The Blue Of The Night** ....H:76 *What Makes You So Lovely*	$15		Felsted 8532
				Joe Leahy (orch.); **Bing Crosby**'s radio theme song			
				MARATHONS, The **'61**			
				The Olympics' Arvee label needed a new single, but since The Olympics were on tour, the label brought in **The Vibrations**, who were under contract with the Chess/Checker label. The Vibrations recorded "Peanut Butter," and Arvee released it as by **The Marathons**. Chess discovered the fraud and stopped the Arvee release and then released a re-recorded version on their subsidiary label, Argo. Arvee followed up with a new song by The Marathons, recorded by an unknown non-Vibrations group.			
4/24/61	20	12		**Peanut Butter** ....*Talkin' Trash*	$25		Arvee 5027
				same tune (different lyrics) as **The Olympics**' 1960 hit "(Baby) Hully Gully"; re-recorded on Argo 5389 in 1961 and labeled as: **"Vibrations Named by Others As MARATHONS"** ($20) and as **"Vibrations Recorded as MARATHONS"** ($20)			
				MARCELS, The BUB **'61**			
				R&B doo-wop group from Pittsburgh, Pennsylvania: Cornelius "Nini" Harp (lead singer), Ronald "Bingo" Mundy and Gene Bricker (tenors), Richard Knauss (baritone) and Fred Johnson (bass). Knauss replaced by Fred's brother, Allen Johnson (died on 9/28/95), and Bricker replaced by Walt Maddox, mid-1961. Mundy left in late 1961.			
3/6/61	❶[3]	14		1 **Blue Moon** ....RB[2] *Goodbye To Love*	$30	■	Colpix 186
				there were 3 Top 10 versions of this Rodgers & Hart tune in 1935			
5/29/61	78	3		2 **Summertime**..........*Teeter Totter Love*	$30		Colpix 196
				#12 hit in 1936 for Billie Holiday; from George Gershwin's 1935 folk opera *Porgy And Bess*			
10/9/61	7	12		3 **Heartaches**..........*My Love For You*	$30	■	Colpix 612
				#12 hit for Guy Lombardo in 1931; #1 hit for Ted Weems in 1947			
2/3/62	58	5		4 **My Melancholy Baby**..........*Really Need Your Love*	$30		Colpix 624
				this song charted in 6 separate decades from 1915-1962			
				MARCH, Little Peggy LP **'63**			
				Born Margaret Battivio on 3/8/48 in Lansdale, Pennsylvania. Lived in Germany from 1969-81. Youngest female singer to have a #1 single on the pop charts.			
3/23/63	❶[3]	14		1 **I Will Follow Him** RB[1] *Wind-Up Doll*	$20		RCA Victor 8139
				adapted from the French song "Chariot"			
6/1/63	32	7		2 **I Wish I Were A Princess** ....*My Teenage Castle (Is Tumblin' Down)*	$15	■	RCA Victor 8189
9/7/63	26	9		3 **Hello Heartache, Goodbye Love**..........*Boy Crazy*	$15	■	RCA Victor 8221
11/23/63	57	6		4 **The Impossible Happened**..........*Waterfall*	$15		RCA Victor 8267
2/1/64	84	3		5 **(I'm Watching) Every Little Move You Make**..........*After You*	$15		RCA Victor 8302
				written by **Paul Anka**; Sammy Lowe (orch., all of above)			
				MARCHAN, Bobby BUB/R&B **'60**			
				Born Oscar James Gibson on 4/30/30 in Youngstown, Ohio. Died on 12/5/99 (age 69). Lead singer with **Huey "Piano" Smith & The Clowns**.			
6/13/60	31	11		**There's Something On Your Mind Part 2**..........RB[1] *Part 1* [N]	$25		Fire 1022
				MARCY JOE BUB **'61**			
				Born Marcy Rae Sockel on 1/4/44 in Pittsburgh, Pennsylvania. Teen pop singer.			
5/22/61	81	3		**Ronnie**..........*My First Mistake*	$20		Robbee 110
				MARCY PLAYGROUND ROK/LP **'98**			
				Rock trio from Manhattan, New York: John Wozniak (vocals, guitar), Dylan Keefe (bass) and Dan Reiser (drums).			
4/11/98	8	28		**Sex and Candy** ....MR[15] A:4 / S:21 *The Angel Of The Forever Sleep / Memphis*	$3	▮[V]	Capitol 58695
				"45": Capitol 19864; B-side: "Ancient Walls Of Flowers"			
				MARDONES, Benny AC/BUB/LP **'80**			
				Born on 11/9/48 in Cleveland, Ohio. Pop singer/songwriter.			
<u>6/14/80</u>	11	20		1 **Into The Night**..........*She's So French*	$4		Polydor 2091
5/6/89	20	17		2 **Into The Night**..........S:17 / A:25 *She's So French* [R]	$3		Polydor 889368
				above 2 are the same version; a new non-charted version was released on Curb 10549 in 1989			
				MARESCA, Ernie **'62**			
				Born on 4/21/39 in the Bronx, New York. Rock and roll singer/songwriter. Wrote "Runaround Sue" and "The Wanderer" for **Dion**.			
3/31/62	6	14		**Shout! Shout! (Knock Yourself Out)**..........*Crying Like A Baby Over You*	$20		Seville 117
				Del Satins (backing vocals); **Billy Mure** (orch.)			
				MARIE, Teena R&B/BUB/LP **'85**			
				Born Mary Christine Brockert on 3/5/56 in Santa Monica, California; raised in Venice, California. White funk singer/songwriter.			
11/22/80+	37	14		1 **I Need Your Lovin'** ....*Irons In The Fire*	$4		Gordy 7189
7/25/81	50	13		2 **Square Biz**..........*Opus III (Does Anybody Care)*	$4		Gordy 7202
12/15/84+	4	24		3 **Lovergirl** A:4 / S:5 *(instrumental)*	$3	■	Epic 04619
4/27/85	81	3		4 **Jammin** ....*(instrumental)*	$3	■	Epic 04738
3/12/88	85	5		5 **Ooo La La La**..........RB[1] *Sing One To Your Love* [I]	$3	■	Epic 07708
				MARIE & REX **'59**			
				R&B duo: Marie Knight and Rex Garvin. Marie teamed with Sister Rosetta Tharpe from 1947-54.			
3/9/59	94	2		**I Can't Sit Down** ....*Miracles* (Marie Knight)	$15		Carlton 502

DEBUT	PEAK	WKS	Gold	A-side (Chart Hit)..........B-side	$	Sym	Label & Number
				MARILLION ROK/LP **'85**			
				Rock group from Aylesbury, England: Derek "Fish" Dick (vocals), Steve Rothery (guitar), Mark Kelly (keyboards), Pete Trewavas (bass) and Ian Mosley (drums).			
10/5/85	74	8		**Kayleigh** ....*Heart of Lothian*	$4	■	Capitol 5493
				MARIMBA CHIAPAS **'56**			
				Marimba band from Mexico. Led by brothers Francisco and Ricardo Sanchez.			
7/14/56	82	4		**Marimba Charleston** ....T:82 *La Marimba* [I]	$10		Capitol 3447
				MARIO LP **'02**			
				Born Mario Barrett in 1987 in Baltimore, Maryland; raised in Teaneck, New Jersey. Teen R&B singer/rapper.			
5/25/02	4	21		1 **Just A Friend 2002** ....A:5 / S:22 *(remix w/***Biz Markie***) / Girl In The Picture*	$6	★V	J Records 21219
				based on "Just A Friend" by **Biz Markie**; samples "Sucker MC's" by **Run-D.M.C.**; "45": J Records 21212; B-side: (**Biz Markie** version)			
10/12/02	74	8		2 **Braid My Hair** A:68			album cut
				above 2 from the album *Mario* on J Records 20026			
				MARK-ALMOND AC/LP **'72**			
				Pop-rock duo from England: Jon Mark and Johnny Almond.			
2/19/72	94	2		**One Way Sunday** ....*The Bay*	$6		Blue Thumb 206
				MARKETTS, The AC/LP **'64**			
				Surf-rock instrumental group formed in Hollywood, California: Ben Benay (guitar), Mike Henderson (sax), Richard Hobriaco (keyboards), Ray Pohlman (bass) and Gene Pello (drums).			
1/13/62	31	9		1 **Surfer's Stomp** *[THE MAR-KETS]* ....*Start* [I]	$20		Liberty 55401
				first released on Union 501 in 1961 ($40)			
4/28/62	48	10		2 **Balboa Blue** ....*Stompede* [I]	$20		Liberty 55443
				first released on Union 504 in 1961 ($40)			
12/7/63+	3	14		3 **Out Of Limits** *Bella Dalena* [I]	$15		Warner 5391
				opening riff is similar to *The Twilight Zone* TV series theme song (not from the *Outer Limits* TV series, although first pressings issued as "Outer Limits"-$30)			
3/28/64	90	4		4 **Vanishing Point** ....*Borealis* [I]	$15		Warner 5423
2/5/66	17	9		5 **Batman Theme** ....*Richie's Theme* [I]	$12		Warner 5696
				from the hit TV series starring Adam West and Burt Ward			
				MAR-KEYS BUB/LP **'61**			
				White instrumental group formed in Memphis, Tennessee: Charles Axton (tenor sax), Wayne Jackson (trumpet), **Don Nix** (baritone sax), Jerry Lee "Smoochie" Smith (keyboards), Steve Cropper (guitar), Donald "Duck" Dunn (bass) and Terry Johnson (drums). Staff musicians at Stax/Volt. Cropper and Dunn later joined **Booker T. & The MG's**; also backing work for the **Blues Brothers**. Axton died in January 1974 (age 32). Also see the **Bar-Kays** and **The Parkays**.			
7/3/61	3	14		1 **Last Night** ....*Night Before* [I]	$30		Satellite 107
10/9/61	60	6		2 **Morning After** ....*Diana* [I]	$15		Stax 112
3/31/62	94	1		3 **Pop-Eye Stroll** ....*Po-Dunk* [I]	$15		Stax 121
3/5/66	89	5		4 **Philly Dog** ....*Honey Pot* [I]	$15		Stax 185
				MARKHAM, Pigmeat BUB/LP **'68**			
				Born Dewey Markham on 4/18/04 in Durham, North Carolina. Died of a stroke on 12/13/81 (age 77). Black comedian. Regular on TV's *Laugh-In* (1968-69).			
6/15/68	19	8		**Here Comes The Judge** ....*The Trial* [N]	$10		Chess 2049
				title inspired by a recurrent gag line originated by Markham on TV's *Rowan & Martin's Laugh-In*			
				MARK II, The **'60**			
				Pop-rock and roll instrumental duo: Wayne Cogswell and Ray Peterson.			
10/17/60	75	7		**Night Theme** ....*Confusion* [I]	$15		Wye 1001
				MARK IV, The **'59**			
				Pop-rock and roll group from Chicago, Illinois.			
3/24/58	69	3		1 **(Make With) The Shake** ....T:69 *45 R.P.M.*	$20		Cosmic 704
1/26/59	24	12		2 **I Got A Wife** ....*Ah-ooo-gah* [N]	$15		Mercury 71403
				written by **Eddie & Dutch**			
				MARKS, Guy **'68**			
				Born Mario Scarpa in 1923 in Philadelphia, Pennsylvania. Died on 11/28/87 (age 64). Comedian-impressionist/TV actor. Regular on TV's *The Joey Bishop Show, The John Forsythe Show, Rango* and *You Again.*			
4/13/68	51	6		**Loving You Has Made Me Bananas** ....*Forgive Me My Love* [N]	$8		ABC 11055
				Peter DeAngelis (orch.); parody of the dance band remote broadcasts of the swing era			
				MARKY MARK And The Funky Bunch BUB/LP **'91**			
				Born Mark Wahlberg on 6/5/71 in Dorchester, Massachusetts. Singer/rapper/actor. Starred in movies since 1994. Younger brother of **Donnie Wahlberg** of **New Kids On The Block**. The Funky Bunch is DJ Terry Yancey and three male and two female dancers.			
7/20/91	❶[1]	20	●	1 **Good Vibrations** S:2 / A:6 *So What Chu Sayin*	$3	▮V	Interscope 98764
				MARKY MARK And The Funky Bunch Featuring Loleatta Holloway			
				samples **Loleatta Holloway**'s 1980 #1 disco hit "Love Sensation"			
11/9/91	10	20	●	2 **Wildside** ....S:5 / A:30 *On The House Tip*	$3	▮V	Interscope 98673
				samples **Lou Reed**'s "Walk On The Wild Side"; "45" issued for above 2 on Atlantic Oldies Series 94939			
2/15/92	61	7		3 **I Need Money** ....A:59 / S:62 *(album version)*	$3	▮	Interscope 98614
				samples **The O'Jays**' "For The Love Of Money"			
9/26/92	49	10		4 **You Gotta Believe** ....S:27 / A:45 *Super Cool Mack Daddy*	$3	▮	Interscope 98492
12/5/92	72[A]	2		5 **Gonna Have A Good Time** ....BUB:104 *Don't Ya Sleep*	$4	▮	Interscope 98493
				all of above co-written and produced by **Donnie Wahlberg** (**New Kids On The Block**)			

DEBUT	PEAK	WKS	Gold	A-side (Chart Hit)	B-side	$	Sym	Label & Number

MARLEY, Bob, & The Wailers — R&B/BUB/ROK/LP '76

Born on 2/6/45 in Rhoden Hall, Jamaica. Died of cancer on 5/11/81 (age 36). Legendary reggae singer/songwriter/guitarist. The Wailers included **Peter Tosh** and Bunny Wailer; both left in 1974. Wrote **Eric Clapton**'s hit "I Shot The Sheriff." Father of **Ziggy Marley**. In 1990, Marley's birthday proclaimed a national holiday in Jamaica. Inducted into the Rock and Roll Hall of Fame in 1994. Won Grammy's Lifetime Achievement Award in 2001.

DEBUT	PEAK	WKS	Gold	A-side	B-side	$	Sym	Label & Number
7/4/76	51	6		1 **Roots, Rock, Reggae**	*Cry To Me*	$8		Island 060
4/22/00	75 S	1		2 **Sun Is Shining** — BOB MARLEY VS. FUNKSTAR DE LUXE; dance remix of a recording which first appeared on Marley's 1978 album *Kaya*	*(4 mixes)*	$8	★	Edel America 58802

MARLEY, Ziggy, And The Melody Makers — ROK/R&B/BUB/LP '88

Family reggae group from Kingston, Jamaica. Children of the late reggae master **Bob Marley**: David "Ziggy" (vocals, guitar), Stephen, Sharon and Cedella Marley.

DEBUT	PEAK	WKS	Gold	A-side	B-side	$	Sym	Label & Number
5/14/88	39	13		1 **Tomorrow People** S:37 / A:40 — Jerry Harrison (of **Talking Heads**; organ)	*We A Guh Some Weh*	$3	■	Virgin 99347
9/21/91	85	5		2 **Good Time**	*Herbs An' Spices*	$4	▮	Virgin 98735

MARLO, Micki — '57

Female pop singer. Former magazine pin-up model. First recorded for Capitol in 1954. Appeared in the 1957 Broadway musical *Follies*.

DEBUT	PEAK	WKS	Gold	A-side	B-side	$	Sym	Label & Number
2/16/57	55	4		**Little By Little** T:55 — **Don Costa** (orch. and chorus)	*It All Started With Your Kiss*	$20		ABC-Paramount 9762

MARLOWE, Marion — MEM '55

Born on 3/7/29 in St. Louis, Missouri. Featured singer on *Arthur Godfrey And His Friends* from 1950-55.

DEBUT	PEAK	WKS	Gold	A-side	B-side	$	Sym	Label & Number
7/16/55	14	2		**The Man In The Raincoat** A:14 / J:18 — **Archie Bleyer** (orch.)	*Heartbeat*	$20		Cadence 1266

MARMALADE, The — AC/BUB/LP '70

Pop group from Scotland: Thomas "Dean Ford" McAleese (vocals), Junior Campbell (guitar), Patrick Fairley (piano), Graham Knight (bass) and Alan Whitehead (drums).

DEBUT	PEAK	WKS	Gold	A-side	B-side	$	Sym	Label & Number
3/14/70	10	15		1 **Reflections Of My Life**	*Rollin' My Thing*	$6		London 20058
8/8/70	51	8		2 **Rainbow**	*The Ballad Of Cherry Flavar*	$6		London 20059
3/27/76	49	9		3 **Falling Apart At The Seams**	*Fly, Fly, Fly*	$4		Ariola America 7619

M/A/R/R/S — '88

Electro-funk group from England featuring two pairs of brothers: Martyn and Steve Young, with Alex and Rudi Kane. Includes mixers: Chris "CJ" Mackintosh and DJ Dave Dorrell.

DEBUT	PEAK	WKS	Gold	A-side	B-side	$	Sym	Label & Number
11/28/87+	13	23	●	**Pump Up The Volume** S:11 / A:13	*Anitina*	$4	■	4th & B'way 7452

MARSHALL, Amanda — LP '96

Born in 1972 in Toronto, Ontario, Canada. Adult Alternative singer/songwriter.

DEBUT	PEAK	WKS	Gold	A-side	B-side	$	Sym	Label & Number
9/28/96	43	20		**Birmingham** A:28	*Let's Get Lost*	$3	▮	Epic 78385

MARSHALL HAIN — '79

Pop-rock duo from England: Julian Marshall and Kit Hain. Marshall later formed the duo **Eye To Eye**.

DEBUT	PEAK	WKS	Gold	A-side	B-side	$	Sym	Label & Number
12/9/78+	43	11		**Dancing In The City**	*Take My Number*	$5		Harvest 4648

MARSHALL TUCKER BAND, The — C&W/BUB/ROK/LP '77

Southern-rock group from South Carolina: Doug Gray (vocals), brothers Toy (guitar) and Tommy Caldwell (bass), George McCorkle (guitar), Jerry Eubanks (sax, flute) and Paul Riddle (drums). Tommy died in a car crash on 4/28/80 (age 30); replaced by Franklin Wilkie. Toy left band in 1984; died of respiratory failure on 2/25/93 (age 45). Marshall Tucker was the owner of the band's rehearsal hall.

DEBUT	PEAK	WKS	Gold	A-side	B-side	$	Sym	Label & Number
4/26/75	78	4		1 **This Ol' Cowboy**	*Try One More Time*	$5		Capricorn 0228
10/18/75	38	13		2 **Fire On The Mountain** — **Charlie Daniels** (fiddle)	*Bob Away My Blues*	$5		Capricorn 0244
3/12/77	14	21		3 **Heard It In A Love Song**	*Life In A Song*	$5		Capricorn 0270
8/20/77	75	6		4 **Can't You See** — studio version "Bubbled Under" (#108) on 9/1/73 on Capricorn 0021	*Fly Like An Eagle* [L]	$5		Capricorn 0278
6/24/78	75	4		5 **Dream Lover**	*Change Is Gonna Come*	$5		Capricorn 0300
6/30/79	42	8		6 **Last Of The Singing Cowboys**	*Pass It On*	$4	■	Warner 8841
4/26/80	79	3		7 **It Takes Time**	*Jimi*	$4		Warner 49215

MARTERIE, Ralph, And His Orchestra — MEM/POP/BUB '53

Born on 12/24/14 in Naples, Italy; raised in Chicago, Illinois. Died on 10/8/78 (age 63). Very popular early 1950s band leader; played trumpet in the 1940s for Enric Madriguera and other bands. Had 2 gold records in 1953: "Pretend" and "Caravan." Hit #3 in 1954 with "Skokiaan."

DEBUT	PEAK	WKS	Gold	A-side	B-side	$	Sym	Label & Number
2/19/55	14 HR	10		1 **Blue Mirage (Don't Go)**	*Remember Me* [I]	$12		Mercury 70535
5/19/56	64	7		2 **Theme from Picnic** T:64 — Gus Bivona (alto sax solo); from the movie *Picnic* starring William Holden and Kim Novak	*Rock And Roll The Barrel* [I]	$12		Mercury 70836
3/9/57	25	11		3 **Tricky** A:25 / T:37	*Travel At Your Own Risk* [I]	$10		Mercury 71050
4/29/57	10	16		4 **Shish-Kebab** A:10 / T:29 — same tune as **Armenian Jazz Sextet**'s "Harem Dance"	*Bop A Doo - Bop A Doo* [I]	$10		Mercury 71092

MARTHA & THE MUFFINS — LP '84

Rock group from Toronto, Ontario, Canada: led by Martha Johnson (vocal) and Mark Gane (guitars). Numerous personnel changes. Member Jocelyn Lanois is the sister of Daniel Lanois, noted producer of **U2** and **Peter Gabriel**.

DEBUT	PEAK	WKS	Gold	A-side	B-side	$	Sym	Label & Number
6/30/84	63	7		**Black Stations/White Stations** *[M+M]*	*Xoa Oho*	$4		RCA 13824

DEBUT	PEAK	WKS	Gold	A-side (Chart Hit)...B-side	$	Sym	Label & Number

MARTHA & THE VANDELLAS ★187★ R&B/BUB/LP '64

Female R&B vocal trio from Detroit, Michigan: **Martha Reeves** (born on 7/18/41), Annette Beard and Rosalind Ashford (born on 9/2/43). Reeves had been in The Del-Phis, recorded for Checkmate. Worked at Motown as an A&R secretary and sang backup. Vandellas sang backup on several of **Marvin Gaye**'s hits. Beard left group in 1963; replaced by Betty Kelly (born on 9/16/44; formerly with **The Velvelettes**). Group disbanded from 1969-71; re-formed with Martha and sister Lois Reeves, and Sandra Tilley in 1971. Martha Reeves went solo in late 1972. Group inducted into the Rock and Roll Hall of Fame in 1995.

1)Dancing In The Street 2)Heat Wave 3)Nowhere To Run 4)Quicksand 5)I'm Ready For Love

DEBUT	PEAK	WKS	Gold	A-side (Chart Hit)	B-side	$	Sym	Label & Number
4/6/63	29	16		1 Come And Get These Memories	*Jealous Lover*	$20		Gordy 7014
8/3/63	4	14		2 Heat Wave RB^4	*A Love Like Yours (Don't Come Knocking Everyday)*	$15		Gordy 7022
11/23/63+	8	12		3 Quicksand	*Darling, I Hum Our Song*	$15		Gordy 7025
2/8/64	42	7		4 Live Wire	*Old Love (Let's Try It Again)*	$15		Gordy 7027
4/11/64	44	6		5 In My Lonely Room	*A Tear For The Girl*	$15		Gordy 7031
8/22/64	2^2	14	●	6 Dancing In The Street	*There He Is (At My Door)*	$15	■	Gordy 7033
12/5/64+	34	7		7 Wild One	*Dancing Slow*	$15		Gordy 7036
2/27/65	8	11		8 Nowhere To Run	*Motoring*	$15		Gordy 7039
8/14/65	36	7		9 You've Been In Love Too Long /				
12/11/65+	70	7		10 Love (Makes Me Do Foolish Things)		$12		Gordy 7045
1/22/66	22	11		11 My Baby Loves Me	*Never Leave Your Baby's Side*	$12		Gordy 7048
6/11/66	71	5		12 What Am I Going To Do Without Your Love	*Go Ahead And Laugh*	$12		Gordy 7053
10/29/66	9	10		13 I'm Ready For Love	*He Doesn't Love Her Anymore*	$12		Gordy 7056
2/25/67	10	14		14 Jimmy Mack RB^1	*Third Finger, Left Hand*	$12		Gordy 7058
8/19/67	25	9		15 Love Bug Leave My Heart Alone	*One Way Out*	$12		Gordy 7062
				MARTHA REEVES & THE VANDELLAS:				
11/18/67	11	12		16 Honey Chile	*Show Me The Way*	$10		Gordy 7067
4/20/68	62	7		17 I Promise To Wait My Love /				
6/15/68	93	3		18 Forget Me Not		$10		Gordy 7070
8/10/68	42	8		19 I Can't Dance To That Music You're Playin'	*I Tried*	$10		Gordy 7075
11/2/68	80	5		20 Sweet Darlin'	*Without You*	$10		Gordy 7080
4/19/69	56	6		21 (We've Got) Honey Love	*I'm In Love (And I Know It)*	$10		Gordy 7085
				#15-18 & 21: from the album *Ridin' High*				
11/7/70	93	3		22 I Gotta Let You Go	*You're The Loser Now*	$10		Gordy 7103
10/16/71	53	6		23 Bless You	*Hope I Don't Get My Heart Broke*	$10		Gordy 7110
3/30/74	76	5		24 Power Of Love *[MARTHA REEVES]*	*Stand By Me*	$6		MCA 40194

MARTIKA LP '89

Born Marta Marrero on 5/18/69 in Whittier, California. Latin singer/actress. Starred on TV's *Kids, Incorporated.* Appeared in the 1982 movie musical *Annie.*

DEBUT	PEAK	WKS	Gold	A-side (Chart Hit)	B-side	$	Sym	Label & Number
12/24/88+	18	20		1 More Than You Know S:17 / A:18	*Alibis*	$3	■	Columbia 08103
5/20/89	❶^2	20	●	2 Toy Soldiers A:❶^1 / S:2	*Exchange Of Hearts*	$3		Columbia 68747
9/2/89	25	11		3 I Feel The Earth Move S:27 / A:27	*More Than You Know (Spanish version)*	$3		Columbia 68996
8/10/91	10	15		4 Love...Thy Will Be Done S:24 / A:31	*Mi Tierra*	$3	▮^{V}	Columbia 73853
1/4/92	93	2		5 Martika's Kitchen	*Broken Heart*	$3	▮	Columbia 74094
				above 2 written by **Prince**				

MARTIN, Andrea R&B '98

Born in 1975 in New York City, New York. R&B singer/songwriter.

DEBUT	PEAK	WKS	Gold	A-side (Chart Hit)	B-side	$	Sym	Label & Number
10/31/98	82	5		Let Me Return The Favor S:48	*Baby Can I Hold You*	$3	▮	Arista 13541

MARTIN, Billie Ray '96

Born in Hamburg, Germany. Female dance singer.

DEBUT	PEAK	WKS	Gold	A-side (Chart Hit)	B-side	$	Sym	Label & Number
4/1/95	87	10		1 Your Loving Arms	*(extended mix)*	$3	▮	Sire 64450
4/20/96	46	13		2 Your Loving Arms A:32	*(extended mix)* [R]	$3	▮	Sire 64450
				above 2 are the same version				

MARTIN, Bobbi AC/BUB/C&W/LP '65

Born Barbara Martin on 11/29/38 in Brooklyn, New York; raised in Baltimore, Maryland. Died of cancer on 5/2/2000 (age 61). Adult Contemporary singer/songwriter.

DEBUT	PEAK	WKS	Gold	A-side (Chart Hit)	B-side	$	Sym	Label & Number
11/28/64+	19	12		1 Don't Forget I Still Love You	*On The Outside (Looking In)*	$7		Coral 62426
3/13/65	46	8		2 I Can't Stop Thinking Of You	*A Million Thanks To You*	$7		Coral 62447
5/29/65	70	7		3 I Love You So	*When Will The Torch Go Out*	$7	■	Coral 62452
3/14/70	13	14		4 For The Love Of Him AC^2	*I Think Of You*	$6		United Artists 50602
7/11/70	97	1		5 Give A Woman Love	*Goin' South*	$6		United Artists 50687

DEBUT	PEAK	WKS	Gold	A-side (Chart Hit)......B-side	$	Sym	Label & Number

MARTIN, Dean ★109★ MEM/POP/AC/BUB/C&W/LP '56

Born Dino Crocetti on 6/7/17 in Steubenville, Ohio. Died of respiratory failure on 12/25/95 (age 78). Pop singer/actor. To California in 1937; worked local clubs. Teamed with comedian **Jerry Lewis** in Atlantic City in 1946. First movie, *My Friend Irma*, in 1949. Team broke up after 16th movie, *Hollywood Or Bust*, in 1956. Appeared in many movies since then. Own TV series from 1965-74. Hit #2 in 1953 with "That's Amore." His son Dino (killed in a military jet crash in 1987) was in **Dino, Desi & Billy**.

1)Memories Are Made Of This 2)Everybody Loves Somebody 3)Return To Me 4)The Door Is Still Open To My Heart 5)I Will

DEBUT	PEAK	WKS	Gold	A-side (Chart Hit)......B-side	$	Sym	Label & Number
12/3/55+	❶[6]	24	●	1 **Memories Are Made Of This** A:❶[6] / S:❶[5] / T:❶[5] / J:❶[4] *Change Of Heart* **The Easy Riders** (backing vocals)	$15		Capitol 3295
3/10/56	27	12		2 **Innamorata**......T:27 *The Lady With The Big Umbrella* from the movie *Artists and Models* starring Martin and **Jerry Lewis**	$12		Capitol 3352
5/19/56	22	15		3 **Standing On The Corner /** A:22 / T:29 from the Broadway musical *The Most Happy Fella* starring Robert Weede			
6/2/56	83	2		4 **Watching The World Go By**......T:83	$12		Capitol 3414
4/7/58	4	21		5 **Return To Me**......A:4 / S:4 / T:4 *Forgetting You*	$12		Capitol 3894
7/14/58	30	9		6 **Angel Baby**......H:30 / S:43 *I'll Gladly Make The Same Mistake Again*	$12		Capitol 3988
8/4/58	12	13		7 **Volare (Nel Blu Dipinto Di Blu)**......S:12 / H:15 *Outta My Mind*	$12	■	Capitol 4028
7/13/59	59	13		8 **On An Evening In Roma**......*You Can't Love 'Em All*	$12	■	Capitol 4222
12/1/62+	91	6		9 **From The Bottom Of My Heart (Dammi, Dammi, Dammi)** ......*In A Little Spanish Town* also released with "Who's Got The Action?" as the B-side	$12	■	Reprise 20,116
12/22/62	94	3		10 **Sam's Song**......*Me And My Shadow* (**Frank Sinatra & Sammy Davis Jr.**-#64) [N] **DEAN MARTIN and SAMMY DAVIS JR.** #3 hit for Gary & **Bing Crosby** in 1950	$15	■	Reprise 20,128
6/27/64	❶[1]	15	●	11 **Everybody Loves Somebody**......AC[8] *A Little Voice* first recorded by **Frank Sinatra** in 1948 on Columbia 38225	$10		Reprise 0281
9/26/64	6	11		12 **The Door Is Still Open To My Heart**......AC[1] *Every Minute Every Hour* (#123) #4 R&B hit for The Cardinals in 1955	$8		Reprise 0307
12/12/64+	25	9		13 **You're Nobody Till Somebody Loves You /** AC[1] #14 hit for **Russ Morgan** in 1946			
12/26/64+	64	5		14 **You'll Always Be The One I Love**...... first recorded by **Dinah Shore** in 1946 on Columbia 37188	$8		Reprise 0333
2/20/65	22	9		15 **Send Me The Pillow You Dream On**......*I'll Be Seeing You*	$8		Reprise 0344
5/22/65	32	7		16 **(Remember Me) I'm The One Who Loves You**......*Born To Lose* #2 Country hit for Stuart Hamblen in 1950	$8		Reprise 0369
8/7/65	21	9		17 **Houston**......*Bumming Around*	$8		Reprise 0393
10/30/65	10	10		18 **I Will**......*You're The Reason I'm In Love*	$8		Reprise 0415
2/12/66	32	8		19 **Somewhere There's A Someone**......*That Old Clock On The Wall*	$8		Reprise 0443
5/7/66	35	7		20 **Come Running Back**......*Bouquet Of Roses*	$8		Reprise 0466
7/23/66	41	7		21 **A Million And One**......*Shades* #2 Country hit for **Billy Walker** in 1966	$7		Reprise 0500
10/8/66	60	6		22 **Nobody's Baby Again**......*It Just Happened That Way*	$7		Reprise 0516
12/17/66+	55	6		23 **(Open Up The Door) Let The Good Times In**......*I'm Not The Marrying Kind (Matt Helm's Theme)*	$7		Reprise 0538
4/29/67	55	5		24 **Lay Some Happiness On Me**......*Think About Me*	$7		Reprise 0571
7/8/67	25	7		25 **In The Chapel In The Moonlight**......AC[3] *Welcome To My World* #1 hit for Shep Fields in 1936	$7		Reprise 0601
8/19/67	38	6		26 **Little Ole Wine Drinker, Me**......*I Can't Help Remembering You*	$7		Reprise 0608
12/2/67	46	7		27 **In The Misty Moonlight**......AC[2] *Wallpaper Roses*	$7		Reprise 0640
3/23/68	60	7		28 **You've Still Got A Place In My Heart**......*Old Yellow Line*	$6		Reprise 0672
11/2/68	43	9		29 **Not Enough Indians**......*Rainbows Are Back In Style*	$6		Reprise 0780
8/9/69	75	4		30 **I Take A Lot Of Pride In What I Am**......*Drowning In My Tears* written by **Merle Haggard**; #11-30: produced by **Jimmy Bowen**; Martin's musical arrangers and conductors: **Ernie Freeman** (#11-16, 19, 22, 24-27, 29), Glen D. Hardin (#28, 30), **Bill Justis** (#17, 18, 21, 23), Gus Levene (#5-8), **Billy May** (#10), Chuck Sagle (#9), Dick Stabile (#1-4) and **Billy Strange** (#20)	$6		Reprise 0841

MARTIN, Derek '65

Soul singer formerly with the Pearls (Five Pearls).

DEBUT	PEAK	WKS	Gold	A-side (Chart Hit)......B-side	$	Sym	Label & Number
7/31/65	78	6		**You Better Go**......*You Know* written and produced by **Teddy Randazzo**	$12		Roulette 4631

MARTIN, Eric — see MR. BIG

MARTIN, George — see BEATLES, The

MARTIN, Janis '56

Born on 3/27/40 in Sutherlin, Virginia. Dubbed as "the female **Elvis Presley**" by RCA Records.

DEBUT	PEAK	WKS	Gold	A-side (Chart Hit)......B-side	$	Sym	Label & Number
5/5/56	35[CU]	1		**Will You, Willyum**......*Drugstore Rock And Roll*	$40		RCA Victor 6491

MARTIN, Keith '95

Born in Washington DC. R&B singer. Toured as a background vocalist with **Johnny Gill** and **M.C. Hammer**.

DEBUT	PEAK	WKS	Gold	A-side (Chart Hit)......B-side	$	Sym	Label & Number
3/4/95	53	16		**Never Find Someone Like You**......S:55 / A:63 *Think Of You All The Time* from the movie *Bad Boys* starring Martin Lawrence and **Will Smith**	$3	■[V]	Ruffhouse 77817

MARTIN, Marilyn AC/LP '85

Born in Louisville, Kentucky. Adult Contemporary singer/songwriter. Former session singer.

DEBUT	PEAK	WKS	Gold	A-side (Chart Hit)......B-side	$	Sym	Label & Number
10/5/85	❶[1]	21		1 **Separate Lives**......AC[3] A:❶[2] / S:2 *I Don't Wanna Know* (Collins - ROK #42) **PHIL COLLINS and MARILYN MARTIN** love theme from the movie *White Nights* starring Mikhail Baryshnikov; issued with 2 different picture sleeves	$3	■	Atlantic 89498
1/18/86	28	18		2 **Night Moves**......A:21 *Wildest Dreams*	$3	■	Atlantic 89465

DEBUT	PEAK	WKS	Gold	A-side (Chart Hit)........B-side	$	Sym	Label & Number
				MARTIN, Moon BUB/LP **'79**			
				Born John Martin in 1950 in Oklahoma. Rock and roll singer/songwriter/guitarist. Wrote **Robert Palmer**'s hit "Bad Case Of Loving You." Moved to Los Angeles in 1968. Lead guitarist of group Southwind. **Jude Cole** was a member of Martin's band.			
8/18/79	**30**	11		1 **Rolene**........*Dangerous*	$4		Capitol 4765
11/3/79	**50**	7		2 **No Chance**........*Gun Shy*	$4		Capitol 4794
	★454★			**MARTIN, Ricky** LP **'99**			
				Born Enrique Martin Morales on 12/24/71 in San Juan, Puerto Rico. Latin singer/actor. Member of **Menudo** from 1984-89. Acted on the TV soap *General Hospital* and on Broadway in *Les Miserables*.			
				1)Livin' La Vida Loca 2)She's All I Ever Had 3)She Bangs			
7/20/96	**88**	14		1 **Maria**........*(Spanish radio edit)*	$3	▮	Columbia 78351
6/27/98	**60**	16		2 **The Cup Of Life**........S:38 *Maria (remix)*	$3	▮	Columbia 78931
				the official song of the World Cup, France '98; also see #4 below			
4/17/99	1^5	20	▲	3 **Livin' La Vida Loca** S:1^4 / A:1^4 *(Spanish version)*	$3	★V	C2/Columbia 79124
				also see #11 below			
6/12/99	**45**	18		4 **The Cup Of Life**........A:31 / S:47 *María (remix)* [R]	$3	★	Columbia 78931
				same version as #2 above			
8/7/99	2^2	20	●	5 **She's All I Ever Had**........S:2 / A:7 *Bella (She's All I Ever Had)*	$3	★V	C2/Columbia 79259
				co-written and co-produced by **Jon Secada**			
11/20/99+	**22**	18		6 **Shake Your Bon-Bon**........S:6 / A:31 *Almost A Love Song (Casi Un Bolero)*	$3	★	C2/Columbia 79333
3/11/00	**67**	5		7 **Private Emotion**........A:68			album cut
				RICKY MARTIN Featuring Meja			
				all of above from the album *Ricky Martin* on Columbia 69891			
10/7/00	**12**	18		8 **She Bangs**........A:8		V	album cut
				"45": Columbia 79514; B-side: (Spanish edit)			
1/27/01	**13**	20		9 **Nobody Wants To Be Lonely**........A:10		V	album cut
				RICKY MARTIN with CHRISTINA AGUILERA			
				"45": Columbia 79573; B-side: "Solo Quiero Amarte (Nobody Wants To Be Lonely)"			
6/16/01	**97**	2		10 **Loaded**........S:54 *(4 mixes)*	$8	★*	Columbia 79596
				above 3 from the album *Sound Loaded* on Columbia 61394			
3/30/02	70^S	2		11 **Livin' La Vida Loca**........*(Spanish version)* [R]	$4	★	C2/Columbia 79703
				reissue of #3 above on Columbia's "Platinum Hits" series			
				MARTIN, Steve LP **'78**			
				Born on 6/8/45 in Waco, Texas; raised in California. Popular TV and movie comedian/actor. Comedy writer for the ***Smothers Brothers*** *Comedy Hour* TV show and others; frequent appearances on *Saturday Night Live*. Starred in numerous movies. Married to actress Victoria Tennant from 1986-94.			
12/3/77	**72**	3		1 **Grandmother's Song**........*Let's Get Small* [C]	$5	■	Warner 8503
5/27/78	**17**	15	●	2 **King Tut**........*Sally Goodin/Hoedown At Alice's* [N]	$4	■	Warner 8577
				STEVE MARTIN and the Toot Uncommons			
				Toot Uncommons is actually **The Dirt Band**; Tut: ancient Egyptian King Tutankhamen (1355 B.C.)			
11/24/79	**91**	4		3 **Cruel Shoes**........*Drop Thumb Medley* [C]	$4		Warner 49122
				MARTIN, Tony MEM/POP/BUB/AC **'51**			
				Born Alvin Morris on 12/25/12 in San Francisco, California. Singer/actor. Starred in over 30 movies from 1936-56. Hosted own TV show from 1954-56. Married actress/dancer Cyd Charisse in 1948. Charted 30 hits, 1940-54, including "There's No Tomorrow" ('50), "I Get Ideas" ('51) and "Here" ('54).			
4/21/56	**10**	20		1 **Walk Hand In Hand**........T:10 / A:13 / J:16 / S:21 *Flamenco Love*	$15		RCA Victor 6493
9/1/56	**60**	2		2 **It's Better In The Dark**........T:60 *Your Place In The Sun*	$12		RCA Victor 6597
				Hugo Winterhalter (orch. and chorus, above 2)			
4/20/57	**82**	5		3 **Do I Love You (Because You're Beautiful)**........T:82 *Ten Minutes Ago*	$12		RCA Victor 6863
				Henri Rene (orch.); from the Rodgers & Hammerstein TV musical *Cinderella* starring **Julie Andrews**			
				MARTIN, Trade BUB **'62**			
				Born on 11/19/43 in Union City, New Jersey. Teen pop singer. Also see **The Epic Splendor**.			
10/20/62	**28**	8		**That Stranger Used To Be My Girl**........*We'll Be Dancin' On The Moon*	$15		Coed 570
				MARTIN, Vince **'56**			
				Born on 3/17/37 in New York City, New York. Teen folk singer. Recorded as a folk duo with Fred Neil in 1964.			
10/13/56	**9**	19		**Cindy, Oh Cindy**........J:9 / S:12 / T:12 / A:12 *Only If You Praise The Lord*	$25		Glory 247
				VINCE MARTIN With The Tarriers			
				adapted from a sailor's sea chantey			
				MARTINDALE, Wink BUB **'59**			
				Born Winston Martindale on 12/4/33 in Jackson, Tennessee. DJ since 1950. Own TV shows starting with *Teenage Dance Party*. Host of *Tic Tac Dough*, *Gambit*, *Debt* and other TV game shows.			
9/14/59	**7**	17	●	1 **Deck Of Cards**........*Love's Old Sweet Song* [S]	$12	■	Dot 15968
				picture sleeve and first issue of record released with "Now You Know How It Feels" as the B-side; #2 Country hit for T. Texas Tyler in 1948			
8/21/61	**85**	2		2 **Black Land Farmer**........*Make Him Happy*	$8		Dot 16243
				Milt Rogers (orch., above 2)			
				MARTINE, Layng C&W **'71**			
				Born on 3/24/42 in Greenwich, Connecticut. Male pop singer/songwriter.			
10/2/71	**65**	8		**Rub It In**........*Live On The Sunshine*	$6		Barnaby 2041
				produced by **Ray Stevens**			
				MARTINEZ, Angie R&B/LP **'02**			
				Born in the Bronx, New York (of Puerto Rican parents). Female rapper. Radio personality at Hot 97 in New York City.			
7/12/97	**6**	21	▲	1 **Not Tonight**........S:3 / A:39 *(instrumental)*	$3	▮	Undeas/Big Beat 98019
				LIL' KIM Featuring Da Brat, Left Eye, Missy "Misdemenaor" Elliott and Angie Martinez			
				samples "Ladies Night" by **Kool & The Gang**; from the movie *Nothing To Lose* starring Martin Lawrence			
6/22/02	**15**	26		2 **If I Could Go!**........A:14 / S:55 *(3 versions)*	$6	T	Elektra 67311
				ANGIE MARTINEZ (Featuring Lil' Mo & Sacario)			
8/3/02	48^S	1		3 **Live Big**........*(3 versions)*	$6	T	Elektra 67319
				SACARIO Featuring Angie Martinez & Fat Joe			

DEBUT	PEAK	WKS	Gold	A-side (Chart Hit)	B-side	$	Sym	Label & Number
				MARTINEZ, Nancy LP **'86**				
				Born on 8/26/60 in Quebec City, Quebec, Canada. Dance singer/actress.				
10/4/86	32	21		**For Tonight** S:29	*(Central Park version)*	$3	■	Atlantic 89371
				MARTINEZ, Rosco **'94**				
				Born in Oriente Holguin, Cuba; raised in Plantation, Florida. Latin pop singer/songwriter.				
4/2/94	57	10		**Neon Moonlight** A:50	*Capturame*	$3	■	Zoo 14121

MARTINO, Al ★127★ MEM/POP/AC/BUB/LP **'63**

Born Alfred Cini on 10/7/27 in Philadelphia, Pennsylvania. Adult Contemporary singer. Encouraged by success of boyhood friend **Mario Lanza**. Winner on *Arthur Godfrey's Talent Scouts* in 1952. Played singer "Johnny Fontane" in the 1972 movie *The Godfather*.

1)I Love You Because 2)I Love You More And More Every Day 3)Spanish Eyes 4)Painted, Tainted Rose 5)To The Door Of The Sun (Alle Porte Del Sole)

DEBUT	PEAK	WKS	Gold	A-side (Chart Hit)	B-side	$	Sym	Label & Number
5/18/59	44	9		1 **I Can't Get You Out Of My Heart** also see #10 below	*Two Hearts Are Better Than One*	$15		20th Fox 132
9/28/59	63	6		2 **Darling, I Love You**	*The Memory Of You*	$15		20th Fox 153
7/24/61	86	4		3 **Here In My Heart** Martino's original gold record version hit #1 in 1952 on BBS 101 ($25)	*Granada*	$10		Capitol 4593
4/6/63	3	16		4 **I Love You Because** AC^2 #1 Country hit for Leon Payne in 1950	*Merry-Go-Round*	$8		Capitol 4930
7/27/63	15	12		5 **Painted, Tainted Rose**	*That's The Way It's Got To Be*	$8		Capitol 5000
10/26/63	22	10		6 **Living A Lie**	*I Love You Truly*	$8		Capitol 5060
2/1/64	9	11		7 **I Love You More And More Every Day**	*I'm Living My Heaven With You*	$8		Capitol 5108
5/16/64	20	8		8 **Tears And Roses**	*A Year Ago Tonight*	$8		Capitol 5183
8/15/64	33	8		9 **Always Together**	*Thank You For Loving Me* (#118)	$8		Capitol 5239
8/15/64	99	2		10 **I Can't Get You Out Of My Heart** same version as #1 above	*Come Back To Me* [R]	$12		20th Fox 530
11/7/64	41	6		11 **We Could**	*Sunrise To Sunrise*	$8		Capitol 5293
12/5/64	6^X	12		12 **Silver Bells** X: 6/'64; 22/'65; 8/'66; 17/'67	*You're All I Want For Christmas* [X]	$8		Capitol 5311
1/16/65	52	7		13 **My Heart Would Know** written by Hank Williams	*Hush... Hush, Sweet Charlotte*	$7	■	Capitol 5341
3/27/65	53	6		14 **Somebody Else Is Taking My Place** #5 hit for **Benny Goodman** in 1942	*With All My Heart* (#122)	$7		Capitol 5384
6/12/65	88	3		15 **My Cherie**	*Ramona*	$7		Capitol 5434
10/16/65	61	6		16 **Forgive Me** #1 hit for **Gene Austin** in 1927; #7 hit for **Eddie Fisher** in 1952	*What Now, My Love*	$7		Capitol 5506
12/4/65+	15	12		17 **Spanish Eyes** AC^4 melody written by **Bert Kaempfert** in 1965 as "Moon Over Naples"	*Melody Of Love*	$7		Capitol 5542
3/12/66	30	8		18 **Think I'll Go Somewhere And Cry Myself To Sleep** written by **Bill Anderson**; #26 Country hit for Charlie Louvin in 1965	*Hello Memory*	$7		Capitol 5598
5/28/66	57	4		19 **Wiederseh'n**	*The Minute You're Gone*	$7	■	Capitol 5652
8/6/66	77	4		20 **Just Yesterday**	*By The River Of Roses*	$7		Capitol 5702
10/15/66	59	8		21 **The Wheel Of Hurt**	*Somewhere In This World*	$7		Capitol 5741
1/28/67	42	9		22 **Daddy's Little Girl** #5 hit for **The Mills Brothers** in 1950	*Devotion*	$7		Capitol 5825
5/27/67	27	8		23 **Mary In The Morning** AC^2	*I Love You And You Love Me*	$7		Capitol 5904
9/23/67	54	6		24 **More Than The Eye Can See** AC^2	*Red Is Red*	$7		Capitol 5989
12/9/67+	80	6		25 **A Voice In The Choir**	*The Glory Of Love*	$7		Capitol 2053
2/10/68	57	7		26 **Love Is Blue**	*I'm Carryin' The World On My Shoulders*	$7		Capitol 2102
4/27/68	87	7		27 **Lili Marlene** song usually identified with Marlene Dietrich; #13 hit for **Perry Como** in 1944	*Georgia*	$7		Capitol 2158
12/28/68+	97	3		28 **I Can't Help It (If I'm Still In Love With You)** #2 Country hit for Hank Williams in 1951	*I Can See Only You*	$6		Capitol 2355
5/17/69	99	3		29 **Sausalito**	*Take My Hand For A While*	$6		Capitol 2468
12/6/69+	86	5		30 **I Started Loving You Again** written by **Merle Haggard**	*Let Me Stay Awhile With You*	$6		Capitol 2674
2/7/70	51	8		31 **Can't Help Falling In Love** from the **Elvis Presley** movie *Blue Hawaii*	*You're All The Woman That I Need*	$6		Capitol 2746
4/29/72	80	4		32 **Speak Softly Love** love theme from the movie *The Godfather* starring Marlon Brando	*I Have But One Heart*	$6		Capitol 3313
12/21/74+	17	16		33 **To The Door Of The Sun (Alle Porte Del Sole)**	*Mary Go Lightly*	$5		Capitol 3987
11/1/75	33	10		34 **Volare**	*You Belong To Me*	$5		Capitol 4134
12/10/77+	49	9		35 **The Next Hundred Years**	*After The Lovin'*	$4		Capitol 4508

Martino's musical arrangers and conductors: Charles Calello (#27), Al Capps (#34), Michel Columbia (#31), Peter DeAngelis (#5-7, 9, 11-18, 20-25, 32, 33), **Al DeLory** (#29), Jimmie Haskell (#30); Belford Hendricks (#4, 8, 19), **Monty Kelly** (#3), Pete King (#26), Aldo Provenzano (#1, 2, 10), John Tartaglia (#28) and Harold Wheeler (#35)

DEBUT	PEAK	WKS	Gold		A-side (Chart Hit)	B-side	$	Sym	Label & Number

MARVELETTES, The

★201★ R&B/BUB/LP **'61**

Female R&B vocal group from Inkster, Michigan: Gladys Horton, Georgeanna Marie Tillman Gordon (married Billy Gordon of **The Contours**), Wanda Young (married Bobby Rogers of **The Miracles**), Katherine Anderson and Juanita Cowart. Young and Horton both sang lead. Cowart left in 1962. Gordon left in 1965; died of lupus on 1/6/80 (age 35). Horton left in 1967; replaced by Anne Bogan (later a member of Love, Peace & Happiness and **New Birth**). Disbanded in 1969. Also recorded as The Darnells.

1)Please Mr. Postman 2)Playboy 3)Don't Mess With Bill 4)The Hunter Gets Captured By The Game 5)My Baby Must Be A Magician

DEBUT	PEAK	WKS	Gold		A-side (Chart Hit)	B-side	$	Sym	Label & Number
9/4/61	❶[1]	23	●	1	**Please Mr. Postman** RB[7] first #1 pop hit on a Motown label	*So Long Baby*	$25	■	Tamla 54046
1/27/62	34	9		2	**Twistin' Postman**	*I Want A Guy*	$20	■	Tamla 54054
5/5/62	7	15		3	**Playboy**	*All The Love I've Got*	$20		Tamla 54060
8/11/62	17	11		4	**Beechwood 4-5789**	*Someday, Someway* (R&B #8)	$20		Tamla 54065
12/1/62+	49	14		5	**Strange I Know**	*Too Strong To Be Strung Along*	$15		Tamla 54072
3/23/63	44	9		6	**Locking Up My Heart /**				
5/4/63	78	6		7	**Forever**		$15		Tamla 54077
8/3/63	67	6		8	**My Daddy Knows Best**	*Tie A String Around Your Finger*	$15		Tamla 54082
11/9/63	47	13		9	**As Long As I Know He's Mine**	*Little Girl Blue*	$12		Tamla 54088
2/22/64	55	7		10	**He's A Good Guy (Yes He Is)**	*Goddess Of Love*	$12		Tamla 54091
7/4/64	48	7		11	**You're My Remedy**	*A Little Bit Of Sympathy, A Little Bit Of Love*	$12	■	Tamla 54097
11/7/64+	25	12		12	**Too Many Fish In The Sea**	*A Need For Love*	$12		Tamla 54105
5/29/65	34	7		13	**I'll Keep Holding On**	*No Time For Tears*	$12		Tamla 54116
8/14/65	61	8		14	**Danger Heartbreak Dead Ahead**	*Your Cheating Ways*	$12		Tamla 54120
1/1/66	7	12		15	**Don't Mess With Bill**	*Anything You Wanna Do*	$12		Tamla 54126
4/23/66	48	6		16	**You're The One**	*Paper Boy*	$12		Tamla 54131
1/21/67	13	11		17	**The Hunter Gets Captured By The Game**	*I Think I Can Change You*	$12		Tamla 54143
4/22/67	23	10		18	**When You're Young And In Love**	*The Day You Take One, You Have To Take The Other*	$12		Tamla 54150
12/16/67+	17	11		19	**My Baby Must Be A Magician** opening male voice: Melvin Franklin of **The Temptations**	*I Need Someone*	$12		Tamla 54158
6/8/68	44	9		20	**Here I Am Baby** #9-11, 15-17, 19 & 20: written and produced by **Smokey Robinson**	*Keep Off, No Trespassing*	$12		Tamla 54166
10/5/68	63	5		21	**Destination: Anywhere**	*What's Easy For Two Is Hard For One* (#114)	$12		Tamla 54171
1/18/69	76	3		22	**I'm Gonna Hold On Long As I Can**	*Don't Make Hurting Me A Habit*	$12		Tamla 54177
11/8/69	97	1		23	**That's How Heartaches Are Made**	*Rainy Mourning*	$12		Tamla 54186

MARVELOWS, The

R&B/BUB **'65**

R&B vocal group from Chicago, Illinois: Melvin Mason, Willie Stevenson, Frank Paden, Johnny Paden and Jesse Smith.

DEBUT	PEAK	WKS	Gold		A-side (Chart Hit)	B-side	$	Sym	Label & Number
5/15/65	37	9			**I Do** **Johnny Pate** (orch.)	*My Heart*	$15		ABC-Paramount 10629

MARX, Richard

★120★ ROK/AC/LP **'89**

Born on 9/16/63 in Chicago, Illinois. Pop-rock singer/songwriter. Married Cynthia Rhodes (of **Animotion**) on 1/8/89. Professional jingle singer since age five. Backing singer for **Lionel Richie**.

1)Right Here Waiting 2)Hold On To The Nights 3)Satisfied

DEBUT	PEAK	WKS	Gold		A-side (Chart Hit)	B-side	$	Sym	Label & Number
6/13/87	3	21		1	**Don't Mean Nothing** AR[1] S:4 / A:4	*The Flame Of Love*	$3	■	Manhattan 50079
9/26/87	3	21		2	**Should've Known Better** S:3 / A:4 Fee Waybill (of **The Tubes**) and **Timothy B. Schmit** (backing vocals)	*Rhythm Of Life*	$3	■	Manhattan 50083
1/23/88	2[2]	21		3	**Endless Summer Nights** S:2 / A:2	*Have Mercy (live)*	$3	■	EMI-Manhattan 50113
5/21/88	❶[1]	21		4	**Hold On To The Nights** S:❶[1] / A:❶[1] above 4 from the album *Richard Marx*	*Lonely Heart*	$3	■	EMI-Manhattan 50106
5/6/89	❶[1]	15		5	**Satisfied** A:❶[2] / S:3 picture sleeve is a foldout poster	*Should've Known Better (live)*	$3	■	EMI 50189
7/8/89	❶[3]	21	▲	6	**Right Here Waiting** AC[6] A:❶[5] / S:❶[1]	*Wait For The Sunrise*	$3		EMI 50219
10/7/89	4	17		7	**Angelia** S:4 / A:4	*Endless Summer Nights (live)*	$3		EMI 50218
1/20/90	12	13		8	**Too Late To Say Goodbye** A:10 / S:14	*Real World*	$3	■V	EMI 50234
4/28/90	13	15		9	**Children Of The Night** A:8 / S:17 tribute to the Los Angeles organization helping child prostitutes; above 5 from the album *Repeat Offender*	*Real World (live)*	$3	■V	EMI 50288
11/2/91	12	20		10	**Keep Coming Back** AC[4] A:10 / S:43 "45" B-side: "I Get No Sleep"	*(3 album snippets)*	$3	■V	Capitol 44753
2/15/92	9	20		11	**Hazard** AC[1] S:10 / A:11 "45": Capitol 57701; B-side: "Thunder And Lightning"	*Big Boy Now*	$3	■V	Capitol 44796
6/13/92	20	20		12	**Take This Heart** A:14 / S:42 "45": Capitol 57731	*I Get No Sleep*	$3	■V	Capitol 44782
10/24/92	44	13		13	**Chains Around My Heart** A:45 "45": Capitol 57880; above 4 from the album *Rush Street*	*Don't Mean Nothing*	$3	■V	Capitol 44848
1/22/94	7	27		14	**Now and Forever** AC[11] A:5 / S:10 "45": Capitol 17705	*Hazard (live)*	$3	■V	Capitol 58005
7/16/94	20	19		15	**The Way She Loves Me** A:20 / S:30 includes bonus cassette of "Hold On To The Nights" and "Take It To The Limit" (live) on Capitol 79378; "45": Capitol 18040 (white vinyl); price includes the bonus cassette	*Now And Forever (live)*	$6	■V	Capitol 58167
2/18/95	74[A]	2		16	**Nothing Left Behind Us** "45": Capitol 18479; B-side: "Nothing To Hide"; above 3 from the album *Paid Vacation* on Capitol 81232			V	album cut

DEBUT	PEAK	WKS	Gold	A-side (Chart Hit)...B-side	$	Sym	Label & Number
				MARX, Richard — Cont'd			
4/19/97	42	20		17 **Until I Find You Again** ...S:41 / A:57 *Silent Scream / Right Here Waiting* "45": Capitol 19507; B-side: (live version); all of above written or co-written by Marx	$3	▮[V]	Capitol 58633
11/8/97+	45	20		18 **At The Beginning** ...S:60 / A:60 *(instrumental)* **DONNA LEWIS & RICHARD MARX** from the animated movie *Anastasia*	$3	▮	Atlantic 84037
				MARY JANE GIRLS R&B/BUB/LP **'85** Black female funk-dance group: Joanne McDuffie, Candice Ghant, Kim Wuletich and Yvette Marina. Formed and produced by **Rick James**. Marina is the daughter of disco singer Pattie Brooks.			
3/9/85	7	22		1 **In My House** ...S:5 / A:9 *(instrumental)*	$3	■	Gordy 1741
7/20/85	42	10		2 **Wild And Crazy Love** ...*(instrumental)*	$3	■	Gordy 1798
7/12/86	41	10		3 **Walk Like A Man** ...S:38 *Shadow Lover* from the movie *A Fine Mess* starring Ted Danson and Howie Mandel; also released on Gordy 1851 in 1986	$3	■	Motown 1851
				MARYMARY R&B/LP **'00** Black female gospel vocal duo from Inglewood, California: sisters Erica and Tina Atkins.			
3/25/00	28	20		**Shackles (Praise You)** ...S:6 / A:58 *(4 album snippets)*	$3	★	C2/Columbia 79303
				MAS, Carolyne LP **'79** Born in the Bronx, New York. Rock singer/guitarist.			
9/8/79	71	5		**Stillsane** ...*Baby Please*	$5		Mercury 76004
				MASCOLO, Tony BUB **'98** Born in Long Island, New York. Pop singer.			
12/5/98	68[S]	1		**Night Wind** ...*(3 versions)*	$7	★	Modern Voices 007
	★275★			**MASE** R&B/BUB/LP **'97** Born Mason Betha on 3/24/70 in Jacksonville, Florida; raised in Harlem, New York. Male rapper. In 2000 became a pastor and leader of Sane Ministries in Atlanta, Georgia. *1)Feel So Good 2)What You Want 3)Lookin' At Me*			
1/25/97	❶[6]	28	▲[2]	1 **Can't Nobody Hold Me Down** ...RB[6] S:❶[7] / A:25 *(instrumental) / (club mix)* **PUFF DADDY Featuring Mase** samples "The Message" by **Grandmaster Flash** and "Break My Stride" by **Matthew Wilder**	$3	▮	Bad Boy 79083
8/2/97	❶[2]	30	▲	2 **Mo Money Mo Problems** ...S:❶[4] / A:12 *(instrumental)* **THE NOTORIOUS B.I.G. Featuring Puff Daddy & Mase** **Kelly Price** (female vocal); samples "I'm Coming Out" by **Diana Ross**; also see #12 below	$3	▮	Bad Boy 79100
9/6/97	17	20		3 **You Should Be Mine (Don't Waste Your Time)** ...S:9 / A:69 *(remix)* **BRIAN McKNIGHT Featuring Mase** samples "I Got Ants In My Pants" by **James Brown**	$3	▮	Mercury 574760
11/1/97	5	20	▲	4 **Feel So Good** S:3 / A:25 *(instrumental)* samples "Hollywood Swinging" by **Kool & The Gang** and "Bad Boy" by **Miami Sound Machine**; from the movie *Money Talks* starring Chris Tucker; **Kelly Price** (female vocal, above 3)	$3	▮	Bad Boy 79122
1/17/98	4	15	▲	5 **Been Around The World** ...S:❷[2] / A:58 *It's All About The Benjamins* (**Puff Daddy** - #2) **PUFF DADDY & THE FAMILY Featuring The Notorious B.I.G. & Mase** samples "Let's Dance" by **David Bowie** and "All Around The World" by **Lisa Stansfield**	$3	▮	Bad Boy 79130
1/31/98	6	24	●	6 **What You Want** ...S:6 / A:26 *Will They Die 4 You?* (w/**Puff Daddy** & **Lil' Kim**) **MASE (FEATURING TOTAL)** samples "Right On For The Darkness" by **Curtis Mayfield**	$3	▮	Bad Boy 79141
7/4/98	44[A]	16		7 **Top Of The World** ... **BRANDY (Featuring Mase)** from the Brandy album *Never S-a-y Never* on Atlantic 83039			album cut
7/18/98	41	17		8 **Horse & Carriage** ...A:46 *(4 versions) / F**k You* **CAM'RON featuring Mase**	$6	T	Untertainment 78938
7/25/98	8	19	●	9 **Lookin' At Me** ...S:5 / A:69 *24 Hrs. To Live* (w/**The Lox**, **Black Rob** & **DMX**) **MA$E Featuring Puff Daddy**	$3	▮	Bad Boy 79176
10/24/98	17	16	●	10 **Love Me** ...S:8 *(instrumental)* **112 featuring MA$E** samples "Don't You Know That?" by **Luther Vandross**	$4	★	Bad Boy 79184
12/5/98+	14	17		11 **Take Me There** ...A:8 **BLACKSTREET & MÝA featuring MA$E & BLINKY BLINK** samples "I Want You Back" by **The Jackson 5**; from the animated movie *The RugRats Movie*;			album cut
6/9/01	63[S]	2		12 **Mo Money Mo Problems** ...*(3 versions) / Lovin' You Tonight* (w/**R. Kelly**) [R] **THE NOTORIOUS B.I.G. Featuring Puff Daddy & Mase** reissue of #2 above on Bad Boy/Arista's "Maximum Hits" series	$8	★*	Bad Boy 79109
				MASEKELA, Hugh R&B/BUB/LP **'68** Born on 4/4/39 in Wilbank, South Africa. Trumpeter/bandleader/arranger. Married to **Miriam Makeba** from 1964-66.			
12/9/67+	71	8		1 **Up-Up And Away** ...*Son Of Ice Bag* [I]	$6		Uni 55037
6/8/68	❶[2]	12	●	2 **Grazing In The Grass** ...RB[4] *Bajabula Bonke (The Healing Song)* [I]	$6		Uni 55066
9/28/68	71	5		3 **Puffin' On Down The Track** ...*Do Me So La So So* [I]	$6		Uni 55085
1/11/69	55	8		4 **Riot** ...*Mace And Grenades* [I]	$6		Uni 55102
				MASHMAKHAN **'70** Rock group from Montreal, Quebec, Canada: Pierre Senecal (vocals, keyboards), Rayburn Blake (guitar), Brian Edwards (bass) and Jerry Mercer (drums). Mercer later joined **April Wine**.			
8/22/70	31	18		**As The Years Go By** ...*Days When We Are Free*	$7		Epic 10634
				MASKMAN & THE AGENTS, The **'69** R&B novelty vocal group: Harmon "Maskman" Bethea, Tyrone Gray, Paul Williams and Johnny Hood.			
3/29/69	95	1		1 **One Eye Open** ...*Yaw'll* [N]	$12		Dynamo 125
5/17/69	91	2		2 **My Wife, My Dog, My Cat** ...*Love Bandito* [N] Billy Clark (orch., above 2)	$12		Dynamo 131

DEBUT	PEAK	WKS	Gold	A-side (Chart Hit)...B-side	$	Sym	Label & Number
				MASON, Barbara R&B/BUB/LP '65			
				Born on 8/9/47 in Philadelphia, Pennsylvania. R&B singer/songwriter. *1)Yes, I'm Ready 2)Sad, Sad Girl 3)From His Woman To You*			
5/15/65	5	14		1 **Yes, I'm Ready** *Keep Him*	$20		Arctic 105
				a new version by Mason "Bubbled Under" (#125) in 1973 on Buddah 355			
8/7/65	27	9		2 **Sad, Sad Girl** ...*Come To Me*	$15		Arctic 108
11/6/65	85	3		3 **If You Don't (Love Me, Tell Me So)** ...*You Got What It Takes*	$12		Arctic 112
1/29/66	97	2		4 **Is It Me?** ...*Don't Ever Want To Lose Your Love*	$12		Arctic 116
6/11/66	98	2		5 **I Need Love** ...*Bobby, Is My Baby*	$12		Arctic 120
12/23/67+	59	9		6 **Oh, How It Hurts** ...*Ain't Got Nobody*	$12		Arctic 137
9/14/68	97	1		7 **(I Can Feel Your Love) Slipping Away** ...*Half A Love*	$12		Arctic 142
6/10/72	70	6		8 **Bed And Board** ...*Yes, It's You*	$6		Buddah 296
1/13/73	31	12		9 **Give Me Your Love**...*You Can Be With The One You Don't Love*	$6		Buddah 331
				written and produced by **Curtis Mayfield**			
11/30/74+	28	10		10 **From His Woman To You**...*When You Wake Up In Georgia*	$6		Buddah 441
4/19/75	91	4		11 **Shackin' Up** ...*(There's) One Man Between Us*	$6		Buddah 459
				MASON, Dave AC/BUB/ROK/LP '77			
				Born on 5/10/46 in Worcester, England. Soft-rock singer/songwriter/guitarist. Original member of **Traffic**. Joined **Delaney & Bonnie** for a short time in 1970. Joined **Fleetwood Mac** for a short time in 1993.			
8/1/70	42	10		1 **Only You Know And I Know**...*Sad And Deep As You*	$7		Blue Thumb 114
12/12/70	97	2		2 **Satin Red And Black Velvet Woman**...*Shouldn't Have Took More Than You Gave*	$7		Blue Thumb 117
5/28/77	89	3		3 **So High (Rock Me Baby And Roll Me Away)**...*You Just Have To Wait Now*	$5		Columbia 10509
9/3/77	12	19		4 **We Just Disagree** *Mystic Traveler*	$5		Columbia 10575
1/21/78	45	8		5 **Let It Go, Let It Flow** ...*Takin' The Time To Find*	$5		Columbia 10662
6/3/78	39	12		6 **Will You Still Love Me Tomorrow** ...*Mystic Traveler*	$5		Columbia 10749
7/12/80	71	3		7 **Save Me** ...*Tryin' To Get Back To You*	$4		Columbia 11289
				MASON, Vaughan, And Crew R&B '80			
				Disco-funk group from Brooklyn, New York. Led by multi-instrumentalist Mason, former manager of **The 21st Century** and engineer for **B.T. Express**. Mason formed Raze in 1988. Lead singer of the Crew was Jerome Bell.			
3/22/80	81	3		**Bounce, Rock, Skate, Roll** Pt. 1 ...*Pt. 2*	$8	T^V	Brunswick 211
				available commercially only as a 12" single; promotional "45" available on Brunswick 55548 ($10)			
				MASQUERADERS, The R&B/BUB '68			
				R&B group from Texas: Lee Hatim, Robert Wrightsil, David Sanders, Harold Thomas and Sammy Hutchinson.			
9/28/68	57	5		**I Ain't Got To Love Nobody Else** ...*I Got It*	$12		Bell 733
				MASSEY, Wayne C&W '80			
				Born in Glendale, California. Singer/actor. Played "Johnny Drummond" on TV's *One Life To Live* (1980-84). Married country singer Charly McClain in July 1984.			
10/11/80	92	2		**One Life To Live**...*(Theme from) One Life To Live* [I]	$4		Polydor 2112
				from the TV soap opera starring Massey			
				MASS PRODUCTION R&B/LP '79			
				Disco-funk group from Richmond, Virginia: Agnes "Tiny" Kelly (female vocals), Larry Marshall (male vocals), LeCoy Bryant (guitar), James "Otiste" Drumgole (trumpet), Gregory McCoy (sax), Tyrone Williams (keyboards), Emanual Redding (percussion), Kevin Douglas (bass) and Ricardo Williams (drums).			
2/19/77	68	4		1 **Welcome To Our World (Of Merry Music)**...*Just A Song*	$5		Cotillion 44213
8/4/79	43	10		2 **Firecracker** ...*With Pleasure*	$5		Cotillion 44254
				MASTA ACE INCORPORATED R&B/LP '94			
				Masta Ace is rapper Duval Clear from Brownsville, New York. Member of **The Crooklyn Dodgers**. His posse includes Lord Digga and rap trio Eyceurokk (Master Eyce, Uneek and Diesalrokk).			
3/12/94	23	20		1 **Born To Roll** ...S:21 / A:35 *(instrumental)*	$3	▌	Delicious Vinyl 98315
4/29/95	69	16		2 **The INC Ride** ...S:58 *(2 mixes)*	$3	▌	Delicious Vinyl 58376
				samples "For The Love Of You" by **The Isley Brothers**			
9/16/95	84	8		3 **Sittin' On Chrome**...S:69 *(3 remixes)*	$3	▌	Delicious Vinyl 58452
	★382★			**MASTER P** R&B/BUB/LP '98			
				Born Percy Miller on 4/29/70 in New Orleans, Louisiana. Male rapper/producer. Member of **504 Boyz** and **Tru**. Founder of the No Limit record label. Played professional basketball for the CBA's Fort Wayne Fury in 1998. Brother of **Silkk The Shocker**. Father of **Lil' Romeo**. *1)Make Em' Say Uhh! 2)I Got The Hook Up! 3)I Miss My Homies*			
4/27/96	90	9		1 **Mr. Ice Cream Man** ...S:61 *(video version) / It Ain't All Good / I Got That Yaho*	$4	▌	No Limit 53218
				begins with the children's song "Pop Goes The Weasel"			
5/17/97	60	15		2 **If I Could Change**...S:36 *(2 versions) / Down To Do Whatever* (w/**Mia X** & **Mo B. Dick**)	$4	▌	No Limit 53273
				MASTER P Featuring Steady Mobb'n with Mo B. Dick and O'Dell			
9/6/97	25	20	●	3 **I Miss My Homies** ...S:15 *(2 versions) / Here We Go* (w/**Mystikal** & Fiend)	$3	▌	No Limit 53290
				MASTER P Featuring Pimp C, The Shocker, Mo B. Dick, O'Dell, Sons of Funk and Mercedes			
10/25/97	97	2		4 **Pushin' Inside You** ...*(2 versions) / How Ya Do Dat* (w/Young Bleed & C-Loc - R&B #29)	$4	▌	No Limit 53284
				SONS OF FUNK Featuring Master P, The Shocker, Young Bleed & C-Loc			
				#2 & 4: from the movie *I'm Bout It* starring Master P			
12/27/97	75	12		5 **4, 3, 2, 1** ...*(5 versions)*	$6	T	Def Jam 568321
				LL COOL J Featuring Method Man, Redman, DMX, Canibus and Master P			
				samples "Fight For Your Right" by **Beastie Boys**, "Rock The Bells" by **LL Cool J** and "Shut 'Em Down" by **Public Enemy**			
1/31/98	16	27	▲	6 **Make Em' Say Uhh!** S:9 *(2 versions) / Weed And Hennesey* (w/C-Murder & **Silkk The Shocker**)	$3	▌	No Limit 53302
				MASTER P Featuring Fiend, Silkk (The Shocker), Mia X and Mystikal			
				clean version available on No Limit 53303			
3/7/98	2^2	21	▲	7 **Let's Ride** ...RB^3 S:❶[1] / A:55 *(instrumental)*	$3	▌	Def Jam 568475
				MONTELL JORDAN Featuring Master P & Silkk "The Shocker"			
3/21/98	57	16		8 **Just Be Straight With Me**...S:40 *(instrumental)*	$5	▌	No Limit 53305
				SILKK the SHOCKER Featuring Master P, Destiny's Child, O'Dell, Mo B. Dick			
				rap version with new lyrics of "Just Be Good To Me" by **The S.O.S. Band**; clean version available on No Limit 53313			

DEBUT	PEAK	WKS	Gold	A-side (Chart Hit)..........B-side	$	Sym	Label & Number

MASTER P — Cont'd

DEBUT	PEAK	WKS	Gold	A-side (Chart Hit)..........B-side	$	Sym	Label & Number
4/11/98	16	20	●	9 **I Got The Hook Up!**..........S:11 *(2 versions) / From What I Was Told* (Soulja Slim) **MASTER P Featuring: Sons Of Funk** title song from the movie starring Master P	$3	▮	No Limit 53311
8/15/98	27	16		10 **Goodbye To My Homies**..........S:17 *(2 versions) / Homie Ride* (w/C-Murder) **MASTER P Featuring Silkk the Shocker, Sons of Funk and Mo B. Dick** samples "It's So Hard To Say Goodbye To Yesterday" by **Boyz II Men**; clean version available on No Limit 53451	$3	▮	No Limit 53326
7/31/99	96	4		11 **It's Your Thing**..........S:25 *(2 versions) / N's Ain't S**t* **MERCEDES Featuring Master P** clean version available on No Limit 53566	$4	★	No Limit 53565
11/13/99	88	3		12 **Step To This**..........S:20 *(radio version) / (instrumental)* **MASTER P Featuring D.I.G.** clean version available on No Limit 38681	$4	★	No Limit 38680
9/23/00	20^{S}	28		13 **He Did That**..........*(3 versions)* **SILKK THE SHOCKER feat. Master P and Mac**	$4	★	No Limit 38736
11/18/00	98	1		14 **Souljas**..........S:14 *(2 versions) / Trick or Treat Whodi*	$5	★	No Limit 38747
3/24/01	50	19		15 **Lay Low**..........A:44 / S:53 *Wrong Idea* (w/**Bad Azz**, Kokane & Lil Half Dead - R&B #75) **SNOOP DOGG (featuring Master P, Nate Dogg, Butch Cassidy & Tha Eastsidaz)**	$6	T	No Limit 50174
12/29/01	63	11		16 **Ooohhhwee**..........A:62 **MASTER P (Featuring Weebie)** from the album *Game Face* on No Limit 860977			album cut
10/19/02	54^{S}	1		17 **Bout It Bout It... Part III**....*(2 versions) / I'm Ready* (w/**Cam'ron**, Jimmy Jones & **Juelz Santana**) **THE DIPLOMATS Feat. Master P** samples "Bout It Bout It II" by **Master P** (from his 1996 album *Ice Cream Man*)	$6	T	Roc-A-Fella 063918

MASTERS, Sammy — '60

Born Samuel Lawmaster on 7/18/30 in Saskawa, Oklahoma. Rock and roll singer. Moved to Los Angeles, California, in 1947. Appeared on *Cal's Corral* TV show from 1959-72.

DEBUT	PEAK	WKS	Gold	A-side (Chart Hit)..........B-side	$	Sym	Label & Number
4/4/60	64	5		**Rockin' Red Wing**..........*Lonely Weekend* adaptation of "Red Wing," popularized in 1907 by Frank Stanley and Henry Burr	$25		Lode 108

★362★

MATCHBOX TWENTY — ROK/BUB/LP '00

Pop-rock group from Orlando, Florida: **Rob Thomas** (vocals; born on 2/14/72), Kyle Cook (born on 8/29/75) and Adam Gaynor (guitars; born on 11/26/63), Brian Yale (bass; born on 10/24/68) and Paul Doucette (drums; born on 8/22/72). Also see **Santana**'s "Smooth."

DEBUT	PEAK	WKS	Gold	A-side (Chart Hit)..........B-side	$	Sym	Label & Number
6/7/97	5^{A}	52		1 **Push**..........MR[1]		V	album cut
10/25/97+	3^{A}	58		2 **3 AM**..........			album cut
4/11/98	9^{A}	36		3 **Real World**..........HOT:38(2 wks)			album cut
12/26/98+	24	28		4 **Back 2 Good**..........A:15 **MATCHBOX 20** (above 4) "45" issued for #1 & 4 on Lava/Atlantic 84410; all of above from the album *Yourself Or Someone Like You* on Lava/Atlantic 92721		V	album cut
4/29/00	❶[1]	39	●	5 **Bent** S:❶[1] / A:2 *Push (acoustic)*	$4	★V	Lava/Atlantic 84704
10/21/00+	5	42		6 **If You're Gone**..........AC[2] A:4			album cut
5/5/01	48	20		7 **Mad Season**..........A:49 above 3 from the album *Mad Season* on Lava/Atlantic 83339			album cut
10/19/02	29	20		8 **Disease**..........A:30 written by **Mick Jagger** and **Rob Thomas**; from the album *More Than You Think You Are* on Atlantic 83612			album cut

MATHEWS, Tobin, & Co. — '60

Born Willy Henson in Calumet City, Illinois. Rock and roll singer/guitarist. Relative of **Jeremy Jordan**. Last name also spelled: Matthews.

DEBUT	PEAK	WKS	Gold	A-side (Chart Hit)..........B-side	$	Sym	Label & Number
10/31/60	30	8		**Ruby Duby Du**..........*Leatherjacket Cowboy* [I] from the movie *Key Witness* starring Jeffrey Hunter	$20	■	Chief 7022

MATHIESON, Muir — LP '56

Born on 1/24/11 in Stirling, Scotland. Died on 8/2/75 (age 64). Conductor/arranger.

DEBUT	PEAK	WKS	Gold	A-side (Chart Hit)..........B-side	$	Sym	Label & Number
8/4/56	67	5		**Lola's Theme**..........T:67 *Mike And Lola's Love Theme* [I] from the movie *Trapeze* starring Burt Lancaster and Tony Curtis	$15		Columbia 40725

MATHIS, Johnny ★59★ — AC/BUB/R&B/LP '57

Born on 9/30/35 in San Francisco, California. Studied opera from age 13. Track scholarship at the San Francisco State College. Invited to Olympic tryouts; chose singing career instead. Discovered by George Avakian of Columbia Records. To New York City in 1956. Initially recorded as a jazz-styled singer. Columbia A&R executive **Mitch Miller** switched him to singing pop ballads. One of the top album artists of the rock era, Mathis has charted over 70 entries on *Billboard's* Top Pop Albums charts. Won Grammy's Lifetime Achievement Award in 2003.

1)Chances Are 2)Too Much, Too Little, Too Late 3)It's Not For Me To Say 4)Gina 5)What Will Mary Say

DEBUT	PEAK	WKS	Gold	A-side (Chart Hit)..........B-side	$	Sym	Label & Number
2/9/57	14	39		1 **Wonderful! Wonderful!**..........A:14 / T:17 / S:18 *When Sunny Gets Blue*	$15		Columbia 40784
4/29/57	5	34	●	2 **It's Not For Me To Say**..........T:5 / A:5 / S:6 *Warm And Tender* performed by Mathis in the movie *Lizzie* starring Eleanor Parker; promo sleeve issued for above 2 with a foldout cover and the heading "Take 2"	$15	□	Columbia 40851
9/16/57	❶[1]	28	●	3 **Chances Are /** A:❶[1] / S:4 / T:5			
10/14/57	9	17		4 **The Twelfth Of Never**..........A:9 / T:51 / S:flip adapted from a folk song known as both "The Riddle Song" and "I Gave My Love A Cherry"	$15	■	Columbia 40993
12/16/57+	21	10		5 **No Love (But Your Love) /** A:21 / S:37 / T:48			
12/16/57	22	18		6 **Wild Is The Wind**..........A:22 / S:30 / T:37 title song from the movie starring Anthony Quinn	$12	■	Columbia 41060
2/10/58	22	13		7 **Come To Me**..........A:22 / S:40 / T:43 *When I Am With You* from the 12/4/57 Kraft TV Theater production of *Come To Me*	$12		Columbia 41082
4/21/58	21	14		8 **All The Time /** A:21 / S:30 / T:42 from the Broadway musical *Oh Captain!* starring Tony Randall			
5/5/58	21	11		9 **Teacher, Teacher**..........A:21 / S:30 / T:43	$12		Columbia 41152

DEBUT	PEAK	WKS	Gold	A-side (Chart Hit)...B-side	$	Sym	Label & Number
				MATHIS, Johnny — Cont'd			
6/30/58	**14**	14		10 **A Certain Smile**...A:14 / T:19 / S:21 *Let It Rain*	$12	■	Columbia 41193
				title song from the movie starring Joan Fontaine			
9/29/58	**21**	15		11 **Call Me**...H:21 *Stairway To The Sea*	$12	■	Columbia 41253
1/5/59	**44**	9		12 **Let's Love /**			
1/5/59	**60**	6		13 **You Are Beautiful**...	$12		Columbia 41304
				from the Broadway musical *Flower Drum Song* starring Keye Luke			
3/23/59	**35**	13		14 **Someone**...*Very Much In Love*	$12		Columbia 41355
6/15/59	**20**	15		15 **Small World**...*You Are Everything To Me* (#109)	$12		Columbia 41410
				from the Broadway musical *Gypsy* starring Ethel Merman			
10/5/59	**12**	17		16 **Misty /**			
				introduced by the Erroll Garner Trio in 1954 on Mercury 70442 ($15)			
10/12/59	**93**	2		17 **The Story Of Our Love**...	$12	■	Columbia 41483
11/16/59	**62**	5		18 **The Best Of Everything**...*Cherie*	$10	■	Columbia 41491
				title song from the movie starring Hope Lange			
2/29/60	**25**	11		19 **Starbright**...*All Is Well*	$10	■	Columbia 41583
5/30/60	**78**	4		20 **Maria**...*Hey Love*	$10		Columbia 41684
				from the Broadway musical *West Side Story* starring Carol Lawrence (Maria); also see #24 below			
8/29/60	**47**	11		21 **My Love For You**...*Oh That Feeling*	$10		Columbia 41764
12/26/60	**64**	3		22 **How To Handle A Woman**...*While You're Young*	$10	■	Columbia 41866
				from the Broadway musical *Camelot* starring Richard Burton			
10/23/61	**89**	1		23 **Wasn't The Summer Short?**...*There You Are*	$10	■	Columbia 42156
12/11/61+	**88**	3		24 **Maria**...*Hey Love* [R]	$10		Columbia 41684
				same version as #20 above			
3/17/62	**99**	2		25 **Sweet Thursday**...*One Look*	$10	■	Columbia 42261
6/16/62	**86**	1		26 **Marianna**...*Unaccustomed As I Am*	$10	■	Columbia 42420
				from the movie *The Counterfeit Traitor* starring William Holden			
9/22/62	**6**	12		27 **Gina**...*I Love Her That's Why*	$8	■	Columbia 42582
1/26/63	**9**	12		28 **What Will Mary Say**...*Quiet Girl*	$8	■	Columbia 42666
				above 2 were also issued with promotional text sleeves			
5/25/63	**30**	7		29 **Every Step Of The Way**...*No Man Can Stand Alone*	$8	■	Columbia 42799
9/7/63	**84**	3		30 **Sooner Or Later**...*In Wisconsin*	$8		Columbia 42836
10/12/63	**61**	6		31 **Come Back /**			
10/12/63	**68**	7		32 **Your Teenage Dreams**...	$8	■	Mercury 72184
12/14/63	**90**	4		33 **I'll Search My Heart**...*All The Sad Young Men*	$8		Columbia 42916
12/28/63	**11**[X]	2		34 **The Little Drummer Boy**...*Have Reindeer, Will Travel* [X]	$10	■	Mercury 72217
				X: 21/'63; 11/'64			
2/1/64	**53**	7		35 **Bye Bye Barbara**...*A Great Night For Crying*	$8	■	Mercury 72229
6/20/64	**87**	3		36 **Taste Of Tears**...*White Roses From A Blue Valentine*	$8		Mercury 72287
10/24/64	**62**	8		37 **Listen Lonely Girl**...*All I Wanted*	$7	■	Mercury 72339
12/18/65	**98**	2		38 **On A Clear Day You Can See Forever**...*Come Back To Me*	$7		Mercury 72493
				title song from the Broadway musical starring Barbara Harris			
7/26/69	**96**	3		39 **Love Theme From "Romeo And Juliet" (A Time For Us)**...*The World I Threw Away*	$6		Columbia 44915
				from the 1968 movie *Romeo And Juliet* starring Leonard Whiting and Olivia Hussey			
9/22/73	**75**	10		40 **I'm Coming Home**...AC[1] *Stop Look And Listen To Your Heart*	$5		Columbia 45908
12/29/73+	**54**	12		41 **Life Is A Song Worth Singing**...*I Just Wanted To Be Me*	$5		Columbia 45975
4/1/78	**1**[1]	18	●	42 **Too Much, Too Little, Too Late**...RB[4] / AC[1] *Emotion*	$5		Columbia 10693
7/29/78	**47**	8		43 **You're All I Need To Get By**...*You're A Special Part Of My Life*	$5		Columbia 10772
				JOHNNY MATHIS/DENIECE WILLIAMS (above 2)			
4/17/82	**38**	13		44 **Friends In Love**...*What Is This* (Warwick)	$4		Arista 0673
				DIONNE WARWICK AND JOHNNY MATHIS			
6/23/84	**81**	8		45 **Simple**...*Lead Me To Your Love*	$4		Columbia 04468
				Mathis's musical arrangers and conductors: Thom Bell (#40, 41), Michel Colombier (#45), **Ray Conniff** (#1-5), **Don Costa** (#27, 28, 30-36), **Ray Ellis** (#6-14, 23, 24), **Percy Faith** (#22), **Ernie Freeman** (#39), Jay Graydon (#44), Pete King (#26); Claus Ogermann (#37), Glenn Osser (#15-21, 29, 38) and Gene Page (#42, 43)			
	★570★			**MATTHEWS, Dave, Band** ROK/BUB/LP '97			
				Born on 1/9/67 in Johannesburg, South Africa; raised in New York. Adult Alternative rock singer/guitarist/songwriter. His band: Leroi Moore (sax), Boyd Tinsley (violin), Stefan Lessard (bass) and Carter Beauford (drums).			
				1)Crash Into Me 2)Ants Marching 3)The Space Between			
4/1/95	**22**[A]	21		1 **What Would You Say**...BUB:115			album cut
8/5/95	**21**[A]	22		2 **Ants Marching**...			album cut
12/30/95+	**55**[A]	15		3 **Satellite**...			album cut
				above 3 from the album *Under The Table And Dreaming* on RCA 66449			
4/13/96	**39**[A]	12		4 **Too Much**...			album cut
7/20/96	**48**[A]	11		5 **So Much To Say**...			album cut
1/4/97	**19**[A]	52		6 **Crash Into Me**			album cut
				above 3 from the album *Crash* on RCA 66904			
4/11/98	**50**[A]	12		7 **Don't Drink The Water**...			album cut
7/11/98	**44**[A]	12		8 **Stay (Wasting Time)**...			album cut
2/13/99	**75**	16		9 **Crush**...A:57			album cut
				above 3 from the album *Before These Crowded Streets* on RCA 67660			
1/27/01	**71**	11		10 **I Did It**...A:65		V	album cut
5/19/01	**22**	23		11 **The Space Between**...A:20		V	album cut
				above 2 from the album *Everyday* on RCA 67988; "45" issued for above 2 on RCA 60458			
6/15/02	**39**	20		12 **Where Are You Going**...A:38			album cut
				from the movie **Mr. Deeds** starring **Adam Sandler** (soundtrack on RCA 68118)			

DEBUT	PEAK	WKS	Gold	A-side (Chart Hit)...B-side	$	Sym	Label & Number
				MATTHEWS, Ian AC/LP '79			
				Born Ian Matthews MacDonald on 6/16/46 in Scunthorpe, Lincolnshire, England. Founder of Fairport Convention and **Matthews' Southern Comfort**. From 1984-87, in A&R for Island and Windham Hill record labels.			
3/6/71	23	16		1 **Woodstock**...*Ballad Of Obray Ramsey*	$6		Decca 32774
				written by **Joni Mitchell** about the legendary 1969 rock festival			
7/24/71	96	2		2 **Mare, Take Me Home**...*The Brand New Tennessee Waltz*	$6		Decca 32845
10/16/71	98	2		3 **Tell Me Why**...*To Love*	$6		Decca 32874
				MATTHEWS' SOUTHERN COMFORT (above 3)			
				written by **Neil Young**			
2/19/72	96	3		4 **Da Doo Ron Ron (When He Walked Me Home)**...*House Of Unamerican Blues Activity Dream*	$6		Vertigo 103
11/18/78+	13	19		5 **Shake It** *Stealin' Home*	$5		Mushroom 7039
4/7/79	67	5		6 **Give Me An Inch**...*Let There Be Blues*	$5		Mushroom 7040
				written by **Robert Palmer**			
				MATYS BROS., The MEM '63			
				Polka band from Chester, Pennsylvania. Led by Emil Matys on saxophone.			
1/19/63	55	9		**Who Stole The Keeshka?**...*Portki*	$10		Select 719
				Keeshka is slang for a type of Polish sausage			
				MAUDS, The BUB '68			
				Pop group from Chicago, Illinois: Jimmy Rogers (vocals), Fuzzy Fuscaldo (guitar), Timmy Coniglio (trumpet), Billy Winter (bass) and Phil Weinberg (drums).			
10/19/68	85	4		**Soul Drippin'**...*Forever Gone*	$8		Mercury 72832
				MAURIAT, Paul, and His Orchestra AC/BUB/LP '68			
				Born on 3/4/25 in Marseilles, France. Orchestra leader.			
1/6/68	❶[5]	18	●	1 **Love Is Blue**...AC[11] *Alone In The World* [I]	$6		Philips 40495
				French song "L'Amour Est Bleu"			
5/11/68	60	6		2 **Love In Every Room**...*The English Nightingale* [I]	$6	■	Philips 40530
11/23/68+	76	8		3 **Chitty Chitty Bang Bang**...*Comme Un Garcon (What A Guy)* [I]	$6		Philips 40574
				title song from the movie starring **Dick Van Dyke**			
				MAX, Christopher R&B '89			
				Born in Seattle, Washington. R&B singer.			
12/2/89	75	8		**Serious Kinda Girl**...*(instrumental)*	$3	▮	EMI 50229
				MAX-A-MILLION '95			
				Techno-funk trio from Chicago, Illinois: A'Lisa B (female vocals), Duran Estevez and Tommye.			
2/4/95	69	20		1 **Fat Boy**...A:73 *(20 Fingers urban mix)*	$3	▮	SOS/Zoo 14215
7/8/95	64	12		2 **Take Your Time (Do It Right)**...*(J.J.'s Club Mix)*	$3	▮	SOS/Zoo 14229
11/4/95	60	20		3 **Sexual Healing**...A:68 / S:73 *Run Tings*	$3	▮	SOS/Zoo 14248
				all of above produced by **20 Fingers**			
				MAXWELL R&B/BUB/LP '99			
				Born Maxwell Musze on 5/23/73 in Brooklyn, New York. R&B singer/songwriter/producer.			
8/17/96	36	18	●	1 **Ascension (Don't Ever Wonder)**...S:24 *Lock You Up N' Love Fa Days*	$3	▮	Columbia 78372
4/10/99	4	25	●	2 **Fortunate**...RB[8] S:2 / A:14 *Submerge: Til We We Become The Sun*	$4	★	Rock Land 79135
				from the movie *Life* starring **Eddie Murphy**; written, produced and arranged by **R. Kelly**			
9/8/01	22	20		3 **Lifetime**...S:11 / A:21 *(4 versions)*	$7	★*	Columbia 79640
3/16/02	58	15		4 **This Woman's Work**...A:56			album cut
				first recorded by **Kate Bush** in 1988; above 2 from the album *Now* on Columbia 67136;			
				MAXWELL, Diane '59			
				Born on 5/24/42 in Los Angeles, California. Teen pop singer.			
3/23/59	95	1		**Jimmy Kiss And Run**...*Date Bait*	$20		Challenge 59039
				MAXWELL, Robert, His Harp And Orchestra POP/LP '64			
				Born on 4/19/21 in Brooklyn, New York. Jazz harpist/composer. With NBC Symphony under Toscanini at age 17. Also recorded as **Mickey Mozart** and Harmony Jones. Hit #24 in 1952 with "Chinatown My Chinatown." Also see **Little Jo Ann**.			
5/11/59	30	10		1 **Little Dipper**...*Mexican Hop* [I]	$12		Roulette 4148
				THE MICKEY MOZART QUINTET			
				a new version (as by Robert Maxwell) is on the B-side of #3 below			
3/21/64	15	12		2 **Shangri-La**...*That Old Black Magic* [I]	$7		Decca 25622
				co-written by Maxwell in 1946			
6/20/64	64	6		3 **Peg O' My Heart**...*Little Dipper* [I]	$7		Decca 25637
				there were 4 #1 versions of this tune from 1913-1947			
				MAY, Billy, and His Orchestra POP/AC/LP '52			
				Born on 11/10/16 in Pittsburgh, Pennsylvania. Arranger/conductor/sideman for many of the big bands. After leading his own band in the early 1950s, Billy went on to arrange/conduct for **Frank Sinatra** and compose movie scores. Hit #8 in 1952 with "Walkin' My Baby Back Home."			
3/24/56	49	14		**Main Title From "The Man With The Golden Arm"**...T:49 *The Phonograph Song (Our Melody)* [I]	$15		Capitol 3372
				from the Otto Preminger movie starring **Frank Sinatra**			
				MAYALL, John BUB/LP '69			
				Born on 11/29/33 in Macclesfield, Cheshire, England. Blues-rock singer. His band spawned many of Britain's leading rock musicians.			
10/11/69	81	3		**Don't Waste My Time**...*Don't Pick A Flower*	$7		Polydor 14004
				MAYER, John LP '02			
				Born on 10/16/77 in Fairfield, Connecticut; later based in Atlanta, Georgia. Adult Alternative pop-rock singer/songwriter/guitarist.			
6/1/02	13	24		1 **No Such Thing**...A:12			album cut
11/2/02+	18	29		2 **Your Body Is A Wonderland**...A:20			album cut
				above 2 from the album *Room For Squares* on Aware 85293			

DEBUT	PEAK	WKS	Gold	A-side (Chart Hit)..............................B-side	$	Sym	Label & Number
				MAYER, Nathaniel '62			
				Born on 2/10/44 in Detroit, Michigan. R&B singer/songwriter.			
4/28/62	22	12		**Village Of Love** .... *I Want A Woman* **NATHANIEL MAYER And The Fabulous Twilights**	$25		Fortune 449
				MAYFIELD, Curtis R&B/BUB/LP '72			
				Born on 6/3/42 in Chicago, Illinois. Died on 12/26/99 (age 57). R&B singer/songwriter/producer. Leader of **The Impressions** from 1957-70. Started own Curtom record label in 1968. Played "Pappy" in the movie *Short Eyes.* Charted 32 R&B hits, 1970-97. Paralyzed from the chest down when a stage lighting tower fell on him before a concert on 8/13/90. Won Grammy's Lifetime Achievement Award in 1995. Inducted into the Rock and Roll Hall of Fame in 1999.			
11/21/70+	29	12		1 **(Don't Worry) If There's A Hell Below We're All Going To Go** .... *The Makings Of You*	$6		Curtom 1955
11/13/71	69	7		2 **Get Down** .... *We're A Winner (live)*	$6		Curtom 1966
8/19/72	4	16	●	3 **Freddie's Dead (Theme From "Superfly")** *Underground*	$6		Curtom 1975
11/18/72+	8	15	●	4 **Superfly** .... *Underground* above 2 from the movie *Superfly* starring Ron O'Neal	$6	■	Curtom 1978
7/21/73	39	10		5 **Future Shock** .... *The Other Side Of Town*	$6		Curtom 1987
10/20/73	71	4		6 **If I Were Only A Child Again** .... *Think* [I]	$6		Curtom 1991
12/29/73+	88	5		7 **Can't Say Nothin'** .... *Future Song (Love A Good Woman, Love A Good Man)*	$6		Curtom 1993
6/22/74	40	13		8 **Kung Fu** .... *Right On For The Darkness*	$6	■	Curtom 1999
9/27/75	67	7		9 **So In Love** .... *Hard Times*	$5		Curtom 0105
				MAYFIELD, Percy R&B '63			
				Born on 8/12/20 in Minden, Louisiana. Died of a heart attack on 8/11/84 (age 64). R&B singer/songwriter/pianist. Wrote the classic "Hit The Road Jack." Charted 7 Top 10 R&B hits, 1950-52.			
6/1/63	99	1		**River's Invitation** .... *Baby Please*	$15		Tangerine 931
				MAZE Featuring Frankie Beverly R&B/BUB/LP '79			
				R&B group formed in Philadelphia, Pennsylvania: Frankie Beverly (vocals), Wayne Thomas (guitar), Sam Porter (keyboards), Ronald Lowry (percussion), Robin Duhe (bass) and McKinley Williams (drums). Charted 29 R&B hits, 1977-94.			
5/28/77	89	11		1 **While I'm Alone** .... *Color Blind*	$4		Capitol 4392
6/16/79	67	5		2 **Feel That You're Feelin'** .... *Welcome Home*	$4		Capitol 4686
6/4/83	80	5		3 **Love Is The Key** .... *Lady Of Magic*	$3	■	Capitol 5221
3/16/85	88	6		4 **Back In Stride** .... RB[2] *Joy And Pain*	$3	■	Capitol 5431
				MAZELLE, Kym — see RAPINATION			
				MAZZY STAR ROK/LP '94			
				Alternative rock duo from California: songwriter/guitarist David Roback and vocalist Hope Sandoval. Roback was a member of Rain Parade and Opal.			
9/3/94	44	20		**Fade Into You** .... A:38 / S:72 *Halah* (ROK #19) "45": Capitol 18300; B-side: "She's My Baby"	$4	▮V	Capitol 58286

MC/M.C.:

DEBUT	PEAK	WKS	Gold	A-side (Chart Hit)..............................B-side	$	Sym	Label & Number
				MC BRAINS LP '92			
				Born James Davis in 1975 in Cleveland, Ohio. Male rapper.			
1/18/92	21	18	●	1 **Oochie Coochie** .... S:6 / A:66 *(instrumental)*	$4	▮	Motown 2146
7/4/92	69	9		2 **Brainstorming** .... S:56 / A:62 *G-String* **Boyz II Men** (backing vocals)	$4	▮	Motown 2170
				MC BREED R&B/LP '92			
				Born Eric Breed in Flint, Michigan. Male rapper.			
9/14/91+	66	20		1 **Ain't No Future In Yo' Frontin'** .... S:23 *Just Kickin' It* **M.C. BREED & DFC**	$4	▮	SDEG/Ichiban 91-062
8/21/93	96	2		2 **Gotta Get Mine** .... S:75 *(album version)* **2 Pac** (guest rapper)	$4	▮	WRAP/Ichiban 93-154
				MC EIHT R&B/LP '93			
				Born Aaron Tyler in Los Angeles, California. Male rapper. Leader of **Compton's Most Wanted**. Played "A-Wax" in the movie *Menace II Society.* EIHT stands for "Experienced In Hardcore-Thumpin'."			
7/27/91	62[S]	5		1 **Growin' Up In The Hood** .... **COMPTON'S MOST WANTED** from the movie *Boyz N The Hood* starring **Ice Cube**	$4	▮	Qwest 19243
8/14/93	72	8		2 **Streiht Up Menace** .... S:50 *(street remix)* from the movie *Menace II Society* starring Tyrin Turner	$4	▮	Jive 42154
5/22/99	53[S]	5		3 **Automatic** .... *(2 versions) / Tha Hood Still Got Me Under*	$4	★	Hoo-Bangin' 53480
				MC5 LP '69			
				Hard-rock group from Detroit, Michigan: Rob Tyner (vocals), Wayne Kramer and Fred "Sonic" Smith (guitars), Michael Davis (bass) and Dennis Thompson (drums). Tyner died of a heart attack on 9/17/91 (age 46). Smith married **Patti Smith** in 1980; died of a heart attack on 11/4/94 (age 45). MC5 is short for Motor City Five.			
3/15/69	82	4		**Kick Out The Jams** .... *Motor City Is Burning*	$25		Elektra 45648
	★434★			**M.C. HAMMER** R&B/BUB/LP '90			
				Born Stanley Kirk Burrell on 3/30/63 in Oakland, California. Rapper/producer/founder/leader of The Posse, an eight-member group of dancers, DJs and singers. Burrell was an Oakland A's batboy in the 1970s; his nickname "The Little Hammer" stemmed from his resemblance to baseball great "Hammerin'" Hank Aaron. **Oaktown's 3-5-7** and Ace Juice are members of The Posse. Dropped the M.C. from his name in mid-1991; re-added it in 1995. Also see **Special Generation**. *1)Pray 2)Have You Seen Her 3)2 Legit 2 Quit*			
4/28/90	8	17		1 **U Can't Touch This** .... RB[1] A:2 / S:18 *(2 versions) / Dancin' Machine* music is from **Rick James**'s "Super Freak"; "45" promo: Capitol 79072; B-side: (same version)	$6	TV	Capitol 15571
6/30/90	4	20	●	2 **Have You Seen Her** .... A:4 / S:5 *(instrumental)* "45" promo: Capitol 79150: B-side: (same version)	$3	▮V	Capitol 44573
9/29/90	2[2]	18	●	3 **Pray** S:3 / A:5 *(instrumental)* rhythm track is from **Prince**'s "When Doves Cry"; "45" promo: Capitol 79284; B-side: (album version)	$3	▮V	Capitol 44609

DEBUT	PEAK	WKS	Gold	A-side (Chart Hit)...B-side	$	Sym	Label & Number
				M.C. HAMMER — Cont'd			
1/5/91	**54**	14		4 **Here Comes The Hammer**...S:37 *(instrumental) / Uh-Oh Here Comes The Hammer '91*	$4	▮	Capitol 44572
				samples **James Brown**'s 1970 hit "Super Bad"; above 4 from the album *Please Hammer Don't Hurt 'Em*			
				HAMMER:			
11/9/91+	**5**	20	▲	5 **2 Legit 2 Quit**...S:❶[3] / A:37 *(remix)*	$3	▮V	Capitol 44785
				Sonja "Saja" Moore (female vocal); "45": Capitol 57700; B-side: (short version)			
12/7/91+	**7**	20	●	6 **Addams Groove**...S:3 / A:36 *(instrumental)*	$3	▮V	Capitol 44794
				from the movie *The Addams Family* starring Anjelica Huston; incorporates "The Addams Family Theme"			
3/14/92	**62**	8		7 **Do Not Pass Me By**...S:38 / A:59 *(instrumental)*	$4	▮V	Capitol 44797
				traditional hymn features gospel singer Tramaine Hawkins; "45": Capitol 57730; B-side: "Gaining Momentum"			
5/23/92	**86**	3		8 **This Is The Way We Roll**...S:59 *(2 versions)*	$4	▮	Capitol 44786
				above 4 from the cassette version of the album *Too Legit To Quit* ("Addams Groove" not available on the CD)			
2/12/94	**46**	19		9 **It's All Good**...S:17 *(instrumental)*	$4	▮V	Giant 18271
				samples "Dusic" by **Brick**			
3/26/94	**26**	20	●	10 **Pumps And A Bump**...S:11 / A:74 *(album mix)*	$3	▮V	Giant 18218
				samples "Atomic Dog" by **George Clinton**			
				M.C. HAMMER:			
9/2/95	**64**[S]	5		11 **Sultry Funk**...BUB:102 *I Need That Number*	$4	▮	Giant 17791
				M.C. HAMMER Featuring VMF			
2/3/96	**70**[S]	3		12 **Goin' Up Yonder**...BUB:101 *Keep On*	$4	▮	Giant 17717
				featuring Angel Burgess and the San Jose Community Choir			
				M.C. LUCIOUS '92			
				Born in Fort Lauderdale, Florida. Female rapper/dance singer.			
2/8/92	**61**	20		1 **Boom! I Got Your Boyfriend**...S:26 *(club mix)*	$4	▮V	Avenue 7203
				"45": Collectables 3942; B-side: (X-rated version)			
6/14/97	**82**	4		2 **Da' Dip**...S:56 *(remix) / Bass Check*	$4	▮	Big Beat 98022
				MC LUSCIOUS			
				MC LYTE R&B/BUB/LP '96			
				Born Lana Moorer on 10/11/71 in Queens; raised in Brooklyn, New York. Female rapper.			
3/7/92	**83**	5		1 **Poor Georgie**...S:44 *Search 4 The Lyte*	$4	▮	First Priority 98638
				samples **Toto**'s "Georgy Porgy" and **The Supremes**' "My World Is Empty Without You"			
7/17/93	**35**	20	●	2 **RuffNeck**...S:24 / A:45 *Brooklyn*	$3	▮	First Priority 98401
3/16/96	**10**	20	●	3 **Keep On, Keepin' On** S:4 / A:42 *(instrumental)*	$3	▮	Flavor Unit 64302
				MC LYTE Featuring Xscape			
				samples "Liberian Girl" by **Michael Jackson**; from the movie *Sunset Park* starring Rhea Perlman			
4/13/96	**56**	11		4 **Can't Hang**...S:52 *Do You Want To* (Xscape - #50)	$4	▮	So So Def 78263
				XSCAPE Featuring MC Lyte			
11/30/96+	**11**	20	●	5 **Cold Rock A Party**...S:6 / A:53 *Have U Ever*	$3	▮	EastWest 64212
				samples "Upside Down" by **Diana Ross**			
4/12/97	**44**	19		6 **Come On**...S:33 *When Alone*	$3	▮	EastWest 64239
				BILLY LAWRENCE Featuring MC Lyte			
				MC NAS-D & DJ FRED R&B '93			
				Rap-bass music duo from Tampa, Florida: Darnell Williams (born on 8/15/71) and Frederick Gray (born on 7/28/67).			
9/19/92	**96**	2		1 **It's My Cadillac (Got That Bass)**...S:71 *(2 mixes)*	$7	▮*	Pandisc 079
5/29/93	**91**	4		2 **Gold Diggin' Girls** *[MC NAS-D & DJ FREAKY FRED]*...A:60 *(5 versions)*	$7	▮*	Pandisc 088
				samples "No Parking (On The Dance Floor)" by **Midnight Star**			
				MC REN R&B/BUB/LP '93			
				Born Lorenzo Patterson in Los Angeles, California. Male rapper. Former member of N.W.A.			
12/4/93	**90**	4		**Same Ol' Shit**...S:56 *(radio version)*	$4	▮	Ruthless 5510
				samples "La Di Da Di" by Doug E. Fresh, "Let's Get It On" by **Marvin Gaye** and "Stoned To The Bone" by **James Brown**			
				MC SERCH R&B/LP '92			
				Born Michael Berrin in Queens, New York. White rapper. Former member of **3rd Bass**.			
10/17/92	**71**	10		**Here It Comes**...S:55 *Back To The Grill* (R&B flip)	$4	▮	Def Jam/Chaos 74414
				MC SKAT KAT And The Stray Mob LP '91			
				MC Skat Kat is an animated character featured in **Paula Abdul**'s "Opposites Attract" video. Created by Michael Patterson and Candace Reckinger. The Stray Mob are Fatz, Taboo, Leo, Micetro, Katleen and Silk.			
10/12/91	**80**	4		**Skat Strut**...S:67 *(club mix) / Get A Grip*	$4	▮	Virgin 98770
				samples **Earth, Wind & Fire**'s "Let's Groove"			

Mc:

DEBUT	PEAK	WKS	Gold	A-side (Chart Hit)...B-side	$	Sym	Label & Number
				McANALLY, Mac AC/C&W '77			
				Born Lyman McAnally on 7/15/57 in Red Bay, Alabama. Singer/songwriter/guitarist.			
7/9/77	**37**	9		1 **It's A Crazy World**...*We Can Be Strong*	$5		Ariola America 7665
3/5/83	**41**	12		2 **Minimum Love**...*Like Your Mother*	$4		Geffen 29736
				McAULEY SCHENKER GROUP ROK/LP '90			
				Hard-rock group led by Irish vocalist Robin McAuley (former leader of **Far Corporation**) and West German-born guitarist Michael Schenker (brother Rudolf is a member of **Scorpions**). Schenker was also a member of Contraband in 1991.			
2/17/90	**69**	10		**Anytime**...*There Has To Be Another Way (instrumental)*	$4	▮	Capitol 44471
				McBRIDE, Martina C&W/AC/BUB/LP '99			
				Born Martina Schiff on 7/29/66 in Medicine Lodge, Kansas; raised in Sharon, Kansas. Country singer.			
				1)I Love You 2)Blessed 3)Wrong Again			
11/1/97	**50**	16		1 **Valentine /** S:36 / A:65			
				MARTINA McBRIDE with Jim Brickman			
10/4/97	**61**	4		2 **A Broken Wing**...CW[1]	$4	▮V	RCA 64963
12/5/98+	**36**	9		3 **Wrong Again**...CW[1] A:26 *Happy Girl*	$4	★V	RCA 65456
5/1/99	**37**	20		4 **Whatever You Say**...A:26		V	album cut
				"45": RCA 65730; B-side: "Be That Way"; all of above from the album *Evolution* on RCA 67516			

DEBUT	PEAK	WKS	Gold	A-side (Chart Hit)......B-side	$	Sym	Label & Number
				McBRIDE, Martina — Cont'd			
8/28/99	24	20		5 **I Love You** CW[5] A:15		V	album cut
				from the movie *Runaway Bride* starring Julia Roberts and Richard Gere; "45": RCA 65896; B-side: "Whatever You Say"			
2/5/00	42	20		6 **Love's The Only House**......A:34		V	album cut
				"45": RCA 65933; B-side: "I Love You"			
9/9/00	60	13		7 **There You Are**......A:55		V	album cut
				"45": RCA 60214; B-side: "Do What You Do"; above 3 from the album *Emotion* on RCA 67824			
9/15/01	64	10		8 **When God-Fearin' Women Get The Blues**......A:61		V	album cut
1/12/02	31	20		9 **Blessed**......CW[2] A:28		V	album cut
				"45" issued for above 2 on RCA 69135			
9/7/02	45	16		10 **Where Would You Be**......A:44		V	album cut
				"45": RCA 69173; B-side: "Concrete Angel"; above 3 from the album *Greatest Hits* on RCA 67012			
				McCAIN, Edwin AC/LP '98			
				Born on 1/20/70 in Greenville, South Carolina. Adult Alternative pop-rock singer/songwriter/guitarist.			
10/7/95	72	20		1 **Solitude**......*Jesters, Dreamers & Thieves / (3 album snippets)*	$4	▮V	Lava/Atlantic 98141
				Darius Rucker of **Hootie & The Blowfish** (guest vocal); "45" B-side: "Alive"			
9/26/98	5	24		2 **I'll Be**......A:4 / S:27 *Grind Me In The Gears*	$5	★+V	Lava/Atlantic 84191
				Hot 100 Airplay debut: 2/28/98			
6/26/99	37	20		3 **I Could Not Ask For More**......A:31			album cut
				from the album *Messenger* on Lava/Atlantic 83197			
				McCALL, C.W. C&W/BUB/LP '76			
				Born William Fries on 11/15/28 in Audubon, Iowa. The character "C.W. McCall" was created for the Mertz Bread Company. Fries was its advertising man. Elected mayor of Ouray, Colorado in the early '80s.			
6/29/74	54	7		1 **Old Home Filler-Up An' Keep On-A-Truckin' Cafe**......*Old 30* [N]	$6		MGM 14738
				first released on American Gramaphone 351 in 1974 ($15)			
2/1/75	40	11		2 **Wolf Creek Pass**......*Sloan* [N]	$6		MGM 14764
12/6/75+	❶[1]	16	●	3 **Convoy**......CW[6] *Long Lonesome Road* [N]	$6		MGM 14839
				jargon-laced CB radio conversation			
3/27/76	73	4		4 **There Won't Be No Country Music (There Won't Be No Rock 'N' Roll)**......*Green River* [S]	$5		Polydor 14310
				McCALL, Toussaint '67			
				Born in 1934 in Monroe, Louisiana. R&B singer/songwriter/organist.			
3/25/67	52	11		1 **Nothing Takes The Place Of You**......*Shimmy*	$10		Ronn 3
7/1/67	77	4		2 **I'll Do It For You**......*The Toussaint Shuffle*	$10		Ronn 9
				McCANN, Les BUB/LP '70			
				Born on 9/23/35 in Lexington, Kentucky. Jazz keyboardist/vocalist.			
1/10/70	85	4		**Compared To What**......*Cold Duck* (R&B #44)	$6		Atlantic 2694
				LES McCANN & EDDIE HARRIS			
				McCANN, Lila C&W/LP '99			
				Born on 12/4/81 in Steilacoom, Washington. Country singer.			
4/3/99	41	19		1 **With You**......S:37 / A:39 *When You Walked Into My Life*	$4	★	Asylum 64052
6/23/01	53[S]	5		2 **Come A Little Closer**......*Lost In Your Love*	$4	★V	Warner 16762
				McCANN, Peter LP '77			
				Born in Connecticut. Pop singer/songwriter.			
4/23/77	5	22	●	**Do You Wanna Make Love**......*Right Time Of The Night*	$5		20th Century 2335
				McCARTNEY, Paul/Wings ★19★ ROK/AC/BUB/LP '73			
				Born James Paul McCartney on 6/18/42 in Allerton, Liverpool, England. Founding member/bass guitarist of **The Beatles**. Writer of over 50 Top 10 singles. Married Linda Eastman on 3/12/69. First solo album in 1970. Formed group **Wings** in 1971 with Linda (keyboards, backing vocals), Denny Laine (guitar; **Moody Blues**) and Denny Seiwell (drums). Henry McCullough (guitar) joined in 1972. Seiwell and McCullough left in 1973. In 1975, Joe English (drums) and **Thunderclap Newman** guitarist Jimmy McCulloch (died of heart failure on 9/27/79, age 26) joined; both left in 1977. Wings officially disbanded in April 1981. McCartney starred in own movie *Give My Regards To Broad Street* (1984). Won Grammy's Lifetime Achievement Award in 1990. Knighted by Queen Elizabeth II in 1997. Inducted into the Rock and Roll Hall of Fame in 1999. Linda died of cancer on 4/17/98 (age 56).			
				1)Ebony And Ivory 2)Say Say Say 3)Silly Love Songs 4)My Love 5)Coming Up			
3/6/71	5	12		1 **Another Day** *[PAUL McCARTNEY]* /			
3/27/71	9			2 **Oh Woman Oh Why** *[PAUL McCARTNEY]*......	$12		Apple 1829
8/14/71	❶[1]	13	●	3 **Uncle Albert/Admiral Halsey** *[PAUL & LINDA McCARTNEY]*......*Too Many People*	$12		Apple 1837
				WINGS:			
3/11/72	21	8		4 **Give Ireland Back To The Irish**......*(instrumental version)*	$12	■	Apple 1847
				picture sleeve has a center-cut hole and features the song's controversial lyrics			
6/17/72	28	7		5 **Mary Had A Little Lamb** /			
6/24/72		6		6 **Little Woman Love**......	$12	■	Apple 1851
12/16/72+	10	11		7 **Hi, Hi, Hi**......*C Moon*	$10		Apple 1857
				PAUL McCARTNEY & WINGS:			
4/14/73	❶[4]	18	●	8 **My Love**......AC[3] *The Mess*	$8		Apple 1861
7/7/73	2[3]	14	●	9 **Live And Let Die** *[WINGS]*......*I Lie Around*	$8		Apple 1863
				title song from the James Bond movie starring Roger Moore			
11/24/73+	10	13		10 **Helen Wheels**......*Country Dreamer*	$8		Apple 1869
2/9/74	7	14		11 **Jet**......*Mamunia*	$8		Apple 1871
				also released with "Let Me Roll It" as the B-side			
4/20/74	❶[1]	18	●	12 **Band On The Run**......*Nineteen Hundred And Eighty Five*	$8		Apple 1873
11/9/74+	3	12		13 **Junior's Farm** /			
12/14/74+	17	12		14 **Sally G**......	$8		Apple 1875
				WINGS:			
5/31/75	❶[1]	14	●	15 **Listen To What The Man Said**......*Love In Song*	$6	■	Capitol 4091

DEBUT	PEAK	WKS	Gold	A-side (Chart Hit)...B-side	$	Sym	Label & Number
				McCARTNEY, Paul/Wings — Cont'd			
10/4/75	39	6		16 **Letting Go** ... *You Gave Me The Answer*	$6		Capitol 4145
11/1/75	12	9		17 **Venus And Mars Rock Show** ... *Magneto And Titanium Man*	$6		Capitol 4175
4/10/76	1^{5}	19	●	18 **Silly Love Songs** ... AC^{1} *Cook Of The House*	$6		Capitol 4256
7/4/76	3	16	●	19 **Let 'Em In** ... AC^{1} *Beware My Love*	$6		Capitol 4293
2/12/77	10	13		20 **Maybe I'm Amazed** ... *Soily* [L]	$6		Capitol 4385
				"live" version of song from McCartney's first solo album in 1970			
6/18/77	59	5		21 **Seaside Woman** ... *B-Side To Seaside*	$10		Epic 50403
				SUZY AND THE RED STRIPES (Linda McCartney and Wings)			
11/19/77+	33	11		22 **Girls' School** ... *Mull Of Kintyre* (AC #45)	$6	■	Capitol 4504
				B-side was a #1 hit for 9 weeks in England			
3/25/78	1^{2}	18		23 **With A Little Luck** ... *Backwards Traveller/Cuff Link*	$6		Capitol 4559
6/17/78	25	11		24 **I've Had Enough** ... *Deliver Your Children*	$6		Capitol 4594
9/9/78	39	8		25 **London Town** ... *I'm Carrying*	$6		Capitol 4625
3/31/79	5	16	●	26 **Goodnight Tonight** ... *Daytime Nightime Suffering*	$5		Columbia 10939
6/16/79	20	10		27 **Getting Closer** ... *Spin It On*	$5	■	Columbia 11020
				picture sleeve has a center-cut hole and lists only the artist and titles			
8/25/79	29	10		28 **Arrow Through Me** ... *Old Siam, Sir*	$5		Columbia 11070
4/26/80	1^{3}	21	●	29 **Coming Up (Live At Glasgow)** ... *Coming Up* (McCartney) / *Lunch Box/Odd Sox* [L]	$5	■	Columbia 11263
				PAUL McCARTNEY & WINGS			
				recorded on 12/17/79 at the Glasgow Apollo in Scotland; the B-side studio version charted first; however, airplay and sales quickly favored the "live" version			
				PAUL McCARTNEY:			
4/10/82	1^{7}	19	●	30 **Ebony And Ivory** AC^{5} *Rainclouds* (McCartney)	$4	■	Columbia 02860
				PAUL McCARTNEY (with Stevie Wonder)			
7/10/82	10	16		31 **Take It Away** ... *I'll Give You A Ring*	$4	■	Columbia 03018
10/2/82	53	8		32 **Tug Of War** ... *Get It*	$4		Columbia 03235
11/6/82+	2^{3}	18	●	33 **The Girl Is Mine** ... RB^{3} / AC^{4} *Can't Get Outta The Rain* (Jackson)	$4	■	Epic 03288
				MICHAEL JACKSON/PAUL McCARTNEY			
10/15/83	1^{6}	22	▲	34 **Say Say Say** ... *Ode To A Koala Bear* (McCartney)	$4	■	Columbia 04168
				PAUL McCARTNEY AND MICHAEL JACKSON			
12/24/83+	23	14		35 **So Bad** ... *Pipes Of Peace*	$4	■	Columbia 04296
10/13/84	6	18		36 **No More Lonely Nights** ... A:5 / S:9 *(playout version)*	$4	■	Columbia 04581
				also released with (Special Dance Version) as the B-side; from the movie *Give My Regards To Broad Street* starring McCartney			
12/15/84	10^{X}	2		37 **Wonderful Christmastime** ... *Rudolph The Red-Nosed Reggae* [X]	$30		Columbia 04127
				first released in 1979 on Columbia 11162 ($10) with a picture sleeve (reissue above is scarce)			
11/23/85+	7	17		38 **Spies Like Us** ... S:6 / A:8 *My Carnival* (**& Wings**)	$4	■	Capitol 5537
				title song from the movie starring Chevy Chase and Dan Aykroyd			
8/2/86	21	11		39 **Press** ... S:17 / A:32 *It's Not True*	$4	■	Capitol 5597
11/15/86	81	6		40 **Stranglehold** ... *Angry* (ROK #44)	$4	■	Capitol 5636
5/27/89	25	10		41 **My Brave Face** ... S:20 / A:33 *Flying To My Home*	$4	■	Capitol 44367
				co-written by **Elvis Costello**			
9/9/89	94	3		42 **This One** ... *The First Stone*	$5	▮^{V}	Capitol 44438
				"45" promo: Capitol 79700			
1/13/90	92	5		43 **Figure Of Eight** ... *Ou Est Le Soleil?* (Dance #10)	$5	▮^{V}	Capitol 44489
				"45" promo: Capitol 79889 (both sides of label are blank)			
2/20/93	83	6		44 **Hope Of Deliverance** ... *Long Leather Coat*	$5	▮^{V}	Capitol 44904
				"45": Capitol 56946			
5/24/97	64	10		45 **The World Tonight** ... S:52 *Looking For You*	$4	▮	Capitol 58650
				Jeff Lynne (harmony vocal); from the movie *Father's Day* starring Billy Crystal and Robin Williams			
11/17/01	56^{S}	2		46 **From A Lover To A Friend** ... *(2 remixes)*	$4	★^{V}	MPL/Capitol 77671
				also released as the B-side of #47 below			
12/15/01	97	2		47 **Freedom** ... S:14 *From A Lover To A Friend*	$4	★^{V}	MPL/Capitol 50291
				Eric Clapton (guitar); "45" issued for above 2 on MPL/Capitol 50291; all of above (except #33) written or co-written by McCartney			
				McCLAIN, Alton, & Destiny R&B/LP **'79**			
				Female R&B vocal trio: Alton McClain, Delores Warren and Robyrda Stiger. Warren died in a car crash on 2/22/85 (age 32).			
4/7/79	32	12		**It Must Be Love** ... *Taking My Love For Granted*	$4		Polydor 14532
				McCLINTON, Delbert C&W/BUB/ROK/LP **'81**			
				Born on 11/4/40 in Lubbock, Texas. Played harmonica on **Bruce Channel**'s hit "Hey Baby." Leader of **The Ron-Dels**. Recorded as a duo with Glen Clark (see #1 below).			
12/2/72	90	3		1 **I Received A Letter** ... *I Feel The Burden (Being Lifted Off My Shoulders)*	$6		Clean 60003
				DELBERT & GLEN			
12/6/80+	8	19		2 **Giving It Up For Your Love** ... *My Sweet Baby*	$4		MSS/Capitol 4948
3/28/81	70	6		3 **Shotgun Rider** ... *Baby Ruth*	$4		MSS/Capitol 4984
				McCLOUD, Nicole J. **'02**			
				Born in South Africa; later based in Miami, Florida. Black dance singer.			
2/9/02	47^{S}	5		**One Good Reason** ... *(7 mixes)*	$8	★*	24/7 872471
				McCLURE, Bobby **'65**			
				Born on 4/21/42 in Chicago, Illinois; raised in St. Louis, Missouri. Died on 11/13/92 (age 50). R&B singer.			
2/6/65	33	11		1 **Don't Mess Up A Good Thing** ... *Jerk Loose* (Oliver Sain)	$12		Checker 1097
5/29/65	91	2		2 **You'll Miss Me (When I'm Gone)** ... *Don't Jump*	$12		Checker 1111
				FONTELLA BASS & BOBBY McCLURE (above 2)			
12/10/66	97	2		3 **Peak Of Love** ... *You Got Me Baby*	$10		Checker 1152
				McCOMAS, Brian C&W **'02**			
				Born on 5/23/72 in Harrison, Arkansas. Country singer/songwriter.			
9/7/02	61^{S}	1		**Night Disappear With You** ... *I Could Never Love You Enough* (C&W #46)	$5	★+	Lyric Street 64062
				made the Country charts on 8/25/01 on Lyric Street 64050			

DEBUT	PEAK	WKS	Gold	A-side (Chart Hit)...B-side	$	Sym	Label & Number
				McCOO, Marilyn, & Billy Davis, Jr. R&B/AC/LP '77			
				Husband-and-wife vocal duo. McCoo was born on 9/30/43 in Jersey City, New Jersey. Davis was born on 6/26/39 in St. Louis, Missouri. Both were members of **The 5th Dimension**. Married on 7/26/69. Duo hosted own summer variety TV series in 1977. McCoo co-hosted TV's *Solid Gold* from 1981-84.			
3/27/76	91	8		1 **I Hope We Get To Love In Time**...*There's Got To Be A Happy Ending* originally charted for 5 weeks (#92); re-entered on 6/26/76	$5		ABC 12170
9/11/76+	❶[1]	26	●	2 **You Don't Have To Be A Star (To Be In My Show)** ...RB[1] *We've Got To Get It On Again*	$5		ABC 12208
3/19/77	15	11		3 **Your Love**...*My Love For You (Will always be the same)*	$5		ABC 12262
8/20/77	51	7		4 **Look What You've Done To My Heart**...*In My Lifetime*	$5		ABC 12298
				McCOOL — see M'COOL, Shamus			
				McCORMICK, Gayle AC/LP '71			
				Born in 1949 in St. Louis, Missouri. Former lead singer of **Smith**.			
7/10/71	84	5		1 **Gonna Be Alright Now**...*Save Me*	$5		Dunhill/ABC 4281
9/18/71	44	12		2 **It's A Cryin' Shame**...*If Only You Believe*	$5		Dunhill/ABC 4288
1/22/72	98	1		3 **You Really Got A Hold On Me**...*C'est La Vie*	$5		Dunhill/ABC 4298
				McCOY, Charlie C&W/BUB/LP '61			
				Born on 3/28/41 in Oak Hill, West Virginia. Country harmonica player.			
2/27/61	99	1		**Cherry Berry Wine**...*My Little Woman*	$10		Cadence 1390
				McCOY, Freddie '67			
				R&B-jazz vibraphonist/songwriter.			
10/7/67	92	2		**Peas 'N' Rice**...*Summer In The City* [I]	$8		Prestige 450
				McCOY, Neal C&W/BUB/LP '94			
				Born Hubert Neal McGauhey on 7/30/58 in Jacksonville, Texas. Country singer.			
4/2/94	75	5		1 **No Doubt About It**...CW[2] S:39 *(3 album snippets)* "45" B-side: "The City Put The Country Back In Me" (C&W #5)	$4	▮[V]	Atlantic 87287
7/16/94	91	4		2 **Wink**...CW[4] S:46 *(3 album snippets)* "45" B-side: "No Doubt About It"	$4	▮[V]	Atlantic 87247
2/18/95	60[S]	7		3 **For A Change**...BUB:108 *(3 album snippets)* "45" B-side: "You're Backin' Up"	$4	▮[V]	Atlantic 87176
5/30/98	56	20		4 **One Heart At A Time**...S:33 *(same version)* **GARTH BROOKS, BILLY DEAN, FAITH HILL, OLIVIA NEWTON-JOHN, NEAL McCOY, MICHAEL McDONALD, VICTORIA SHAW, BRYAN WHITE**	$4	▮	Atlantic 84117
				McCOY, Van R&B/AC/BUB/LP '75			
				Born on 1/6/40 in Washington DC. Died of a heart attack on 7/6/79 (age 39). Disco songwriter/producer.			
4/19/75	❶[1]	19	●	1 **The Hustle**...RB[1] *Hey Girl, Come And Get It* [I] The Soul City Symphony (orch.)	$5		Avco 4653
10/11/75	46	8		2 **Change With The Times**...*Good Night, Baby*	$5		Avco 4660
5/29/76	96	2		3 **Night Walk**...*Love Child* [I]	$5		H&L 4667
8/14/76	69	5		4 **Party**...*The Disco Kid*	$5		H&L 4670
				McCOYS, The LP '65			
				Pop-rock group from Union City, Indiana: brothers Rick (vocals, guitar) and Randy (drums) Zehringer, Randy Hobbs (bass) and Ronnie Brandon (keyboards). Rick later recorded as **Rick Derringer**. Hobbs died on 8/5/93 (age 45).			
8/14/65	❶[1]	14		1 **Hang On Sloopy**...*I Can't Explain It*	$15		Bang 506
11/13/65	7	11		2 **Fever**...*Sorrow*	$12		Bang 511
2/12/66	46	6		3 **Up And Down**...*If You Tell A Lie*	$10		Bang 516
4/23/66	22	9		4 **Come On Let's Go**...*Little People*	$10		Bang 522
7/30/66	53	4		5 **(You Make Me Feel) So Good**...*Runaway*	$10		Bang 527
10/1/66	67	5		6 **Don't Worry Mother, Your Son's Heart Is Pure**...*Ko-Ko*	$10		Bang 532
1/7/67	69	5		7 **I Got To Go Back (And Watch That Little Girl Dance)**...*Dynamite*	$10		Bang 538
5/13/67	92	2		8 **Beat The Clock**...*Like You Do To Me*	$15		Bang 543
10/26/68	98	2		9 **Jesse Brady**...*Resurrection*	$12		Mercury 72843
				McCRACKLIN, Jimmy R&B/BUB '58			
				Born James David Walker on 8/13/21 in Helena, Arkansas. Blues singer/harmonica player/songwriter. Professional boxer in the mid-1940s. First recorded for Globe in 1945. Own band, the Blues Blasters, in 1949.			
2/24/58	7	16		1 **The Walk** *[JIMMY McCRACKLIN And his Band]* T:7 / S:11 / A:23 *I'm To Blame*	$25		Checker 885
12/11/61+	64	7		2 **Just Got To Know**...*The Drag*	$20		Art-tone 825
4/10/65	91	1		3 **Every Night, Every Day**...*Can't Raise Me*	$12		Imperial 66094
10/23/65	95	2		4 **Think**...*Steppin' Up In Class*	$12		Imperial 66129
1/29/66	92	1		5 **My Answer**...*Beulah*	$12		Imperial 66147
				McCRAE, George R&B/BUB/LP '74			
				Born on 10/19/44 in West Palm Beach, Florida. Disco singer. Married to **Gwen McCrae** from 1967-77.			
6/1/74	❶[2]	17		1 **Rock Your Baby** RB[2] *pt. 2*	$5		T.K. 1004
1/25/75	37	9		2 **I Get Lifted /**			
10/12/74	50	6		3 **I Can't Leave You Alone**...	$5		T.K. 1007
5/17/75	95	1		4 **Look At You**...*I Need Somebody Like You*	$5		T.K. 1011
1/10/76	65	5		5 **Honey I**...*Sing A Happy Song* all of above written and produced by Harry Wayne Casey and Richard Finch of **KC & The Sunshine Band**	$5		T.K. 1016
				McCRAE, Gwen R&B/BUB/LP '75			
				Born on 12/21/43 in Pensacola, Florida. Disco singer. Married to **George McCrae** from 1967-77.			
5/17/75	9	14		1 **Rockin' Chair**...RB[1] *It Keeps On Raining* **George McCrae** (backing vocal)	$5		Cat 1996
7/15/00	74[S]	2		2 **Gittin' What I Want**...*Make Me Yours* produced by Jo Jo Benson (**Peggy Scott & Jo Jo Benson**)	$7	★	Alpine 3003

DEBUT	PEAK	WKS	Gold	A-side (Chart Hit)...B-side	$	Sym	Label & Number
				McCRARYS, The R&B/LP **'78**			
				R&B vocal group: siblings Linda, Charity, Alfred and Sam McCrary.			
8/19/78	45	8		**You**...*Looking Ahead*	$5		Portrait 70014
				McCREADY, Mindy C&W/BUB/LP **'96**			
				Born on 11/30/75 in Fort Myers, Florida. Country singer.			
8/31/96	72	9		1 **Guys Do It All The Time**...CW[1] S:41 *(dance mix)*	$4	▮V	BNA 64575
11/8/97	72^S	2		2 **What If I Do**...BUB:102 *If I Don't Stay The Night*	$4	▮V	BNA 64990
				McCURN, George **'63**			
				Adult Contemporary singer.			
3/2/63	55	8		**I'm Just A Country Boy**...*In My Little Corner Of The World*	$10		A&M 705
				arranged and conducted by **Herb Alpert**; #1 Country hit for **Don Williams** in 1977			
				McDANIEL, Donna **'77**			
				Disco singer.			
7/2/77	90	5		**Save Me**...*I Must Be Doing Something Right*	$4		Midsong Int'l. 11005
				McDANIELS, Gene **'61**			
				Born on 2/12/35 in Kansas City, Missouri; raised in Omaha, Nebraska. R&B-pop singer. Appeared in the 1962 movie *It's Trad, Dad.* Recorded and "Bubbled Under" as Universal Jones in 1972.			
3/20/61	3	15		1 **A Hundred Pounds Of Clay** *Take A Chance On Love*	$15		Liberty 55308
7/3/61	31	8		2 **A Tear**...*She's Come Back*	$15		Liberty 55344
10/2/61	5	13		3 **Tower Of Strength**...*The Secret*	$15		Liberty 55371
1/20/62	10	11		4 **Chip Chip**...*Another Tear Falls*	$15		Liberty 55405
4/21/62	99	1		5 **Funny**...*Chapel Of Tears*	$15		Liberty 55444
8/4/62	21	10		6 **Point Of No Return**...*Warmer Than A Whisper*	$15		Liberty 55480
11/10/62	31	9		7 **Spanish Lace**...*Somebody's Waiting*	$15		Liberty 55510
				The Johnny Mann Singers (backing vocals, all of above)			
8/10/63	64	7		8 **It's A Lonely Town (Lonely Without You)**...*False Friends*	$12		Liberty 55597
				McDEVITT, Chas., Skiffle Group **'57**			
				Born on 12/4/34 in Glasgow, Scotland. Singer/guitarist. Chas plays guitar and still performs 'skiffle' music today.			
5/27/57	40	5		**Freight Train**...T:40 *The Cotton Song*	$25		Chic 1008
				Nancy Whiskey (vocal); folk song composed in the early 1900s			
				McDONALD, Country Joe — see COUNTRY JOE			
	★575★			**McDONALD, Michael** AC/ROK/BUB/LP **'86**			
				Born on 2/12/52 in St. Louis, Missouri. Pop-rock singer/songwriter/keyboardist. First recorded for RCA in 1972. Formerly with **Steely Dan** and **The Doobie Brothers**. Married **Amy Holland** in 1983. Also see **Nicolette Larson**, **Christopher Cross** and **Lauren Wood**.			
8/7/82	4	19		1 **I Keep Forgettin' (Every Time You're Near)**...*Losin' End*	$4	■	Warner 29933
				first pressings show title only as "I Keep Forgettin'"			
11/13/82	44	11		2 **I Gotta Try**...*Believe In It*	$4	■	Warner 29862
12/10/83+	19	18		3 **Yah Mo B There**...*Come A Da Machine (To Take A My Place)* (Ingram)	$3		Qwest 29394
				JAMES INGRAM (with Michael McDonald)			
7/27/85	34	12		4 **No Lookin' Back**...A:30 *Don't Let Me Down*	$3	■	Warner 28960
				#2 & 4: co-written and backing vocal by **Kenny Loggins**			
3/22/86	❶^3	23	●	5 **On My Own** RB[4] S:❶[5] / A:❶[2] *Stir It Up* (LaBelle)	$3	■	MCA 52770
				PATTI LaBELLE AND MICHAEL McDONALD			
6/14/86	7	20		6 **Sweet Freedom**...S:6 / A:7 *The Freedom Eights*	$3	■	MCA 52857
				theme from the movie *Running Scared* starring **Billy Crystal** and **Gregory Hines**			
6/9/90	98	2		7 **Take It To Heart**...*Plain Of Jars*	$3	▮	Reprise 19828
5/30/98	56	20		8 **One Heart At A Time**...S:33 *(same version)*	$4	▮	Atlantic 84117
				GARTH BROOKS, BILLY DEAN, FAITH HILL, OLIVIA NEWTON-JOHN, NEAL McCOY, MICHAEL McDONALD, VICTORIA SHAW, BRYAN WHITE			
				McDOWELL, Ronnie C&W **'77**			
				Born on 3/26/50 in Portland, Tennessee. Country singer/songwriter. Charted 37 Country hits, 1977-90.			
9/10/77	13	12	●	1 **The King Is Gone**...*Walking Through Georgia In The Rain*	$7		Scorpion 135
				a tribute to **Elvis Presley** after his death on 8/16/77			
3/18/78	81	4		2 **I Love You, I Love You, I Love You**...*Fallin'*	$7		Scorpion 149
				McDUFF, Brother Jack BUB/R&B/LP **'69**			
				Born Eugene McDuffy on 9/17/26 in Champaign, Illinois. Died of a heart attack on 1/23/2001 (age 74). R&B/jazz-styled organist.			
12/27/69	95	2		**Theme From Electric Surfboard**...*Down Home Style* [I]	$8		Blue Note 1953
				McENTIRE, Reba C&W/BUB/LP **'99**			
				Born on 3/28/54 in Chockie, Oklahoma. Country singer/actress. Appeared in several movies and TV shows. Played "Heather Gummer" in the movie *Temors.* Starred in own TV sitcom *Reba.* Charted 83 Country hits, 1976-02.			
5/7/94	50^S	11		1 **Why Haven't I Heard From You**...BUB:101 *If I Had Only Known* (C&W #72)	$4	▮V	MCA 54823
8/27/94	65^S	12		2 **She Thinks His Name Was John**...BUB:101 *I Wish That I Could Tell You*	$4	▮V	MCA 54899
12/17/94+	78	10		3 **Till You Love Me**...S:43 *I Wouldn't Wanna Be You*	$4	▮V	MCA 54888
12/13/97+	50	15		4 **What If**...S:31 *(same version)*	$4	▮V	MCA 72026
				all royalties donated to The Salvation Army			
12/12/98+	52	13		5 **Wrong Night**...A:41		V	album cut
				"45": MCA 72075; B-side: "Up And Flying"			
5/29/99	54	10		6 **One Honest Heart**...A:42		V	album cut
				"45": MCA 72094; B-side: "I'll Give You Something To Miss"; above 2 from the album *If You See Him* on MCA 70019			
10/30/99+	31	20		7 **What Do You Say** A:25		V	album cut
				"45": MCA 72131; B-side: "Nobody Dies From A Broken Heart"			

DEBUT	PEAK	WKS	Gold	A-side (Chart Hit)...B-side	$	Sym	Label & Number
				McENTIRE, Reba — Cont'd			
5/13/00	51	20		8 **I'll Be** ...A:42		V	album cut
				"45": MCA 72143; B-side: "When You're Not Trying To"; above 2 from the album *So Good Together* on MCA 170119			
9/15/01	49	19		9 **I'm A Survivor** ...A:48		V	album cut
				from the album *Greatest Hits Volume III - I'm A Survivor* on MCA 170202; "45": MCA 72212; B-side: "'Til I Said It To You" (C&W #70/'99)			
				McFADDEN, Bob, And Dor '59			
				Born on 1/19/23 in East Liverpool, Ohio. Died on 1/7/2000 (age 76). Began career in 1950 as a singing emcee for a special Navy show called *The Bob McFadden Show*. Appeared on the comedy albums *The First Family* and *You Don't Have To Be Jewish*. Dor is poet/singer/songwriter/actor **Rod McKuen**.			
8/24/59	39	8		**The Mummy** ...*The Beat Generation* [N]	$25	■	Brunswick 55140
				Jack Hansen (orch.); inspired by the 1959 movie of the same title starring Peter Cushing; picture sleeve features a photo of "The Mummy" as seen in the movie			
				McFADDEN & WHITEHEAD R&B/LP '79			
				R&B duo from Philadelphia, Pennsylvania: Gene McFadden and John Whitehead. Wrote songs for many Philadelphia soul acts; defined "The Sound Of Philadelphia." Whitehead recorded solo in 1988. John's sons, Kenny & Johnny, charted as the **Whitehead Bros.**			
4/28/79	13	18	▲	**Ain't No Stoppin' Us Now** ...RB[1] *I Got The Love*	$5		Philadelphia I. 3681
				McFERRIN, Bobby LP '88			
				Born on 3/11/50 in Manhattan, New York. Unaccompanied, jazz-styled improvisation vocalist. Sang the 1987 *Cosby Show* theme and the Levi's 501 Blues jingle. Father was a baritone with the New York Metropolitan Opera.			
7/30/88	❶[2]	26	●	**Don't Worry Be Happy** ...S:❶[3] / A:2 *Simple Pleasures*	$3	■	EMI-Manhattan 50146
				featured in the movie *Cocktail* starring Tom Cruise; 1988 Grammy winner: Record of the Year			
				McGEE, Parker '77			
				Born in Mississippi. Pop singer/songwriter.			
1/22/77	42	7		**I Just Can't Say No To You** ...*Talkin' 'Bout Loving You*	$5		Big Tree 16082
				McGHEE, Jacci R&B/BUB '88			
				Born in the Bronx, New York. Female R&B singer.			
7/23/88	59	11		1 **Make It Last Forever** ...*(vocal beat version)*	$3		Vintertainment 69386
				KEITH SWEAT (with Jacci McGhee)			
3/20/93	70[S]	1		2 **It Hurts Me** ...BUB:109 *The Other Woman*	$4	▌	MCA 54528
				McGILPIN, Bob '78			
				Born in Fort Dix, New Jersey. Disco singer/songwriter.			
9/23/78	91	5		**When You Feel Love** ...*Moon Dancin'*	$5		Butterfly 1211
				McGOVERN, Maureen AC/BUB/LP '73			
				Born on 7/27/49 in Youngstown, Ohio. Adult Contemporary singer. Sang theme of TV show *Angie*. Cameo roles in *The Towering Inferno* and *Airplane* (as Sister Angelina). Starred in Broadway's *Pirates Of Penzance* for 14 months.			
6/23/73	❶[2]	15	●	1 **The Morning After** *Midnight Storm*	$5		20th Century 2010
				love theme from the movie *The Poseidon Adventure* starring Gene Hackman			
10/13/73	89	5		2 **I Won't Last A Day Without You** ...*Darlene*	$5		20th Century 2051
10/19/74	71	7		3 **Give Me A Reason To Be Gone** ...*Love Knots*	$5		20th Century 2109
1/25/75	83	4		4 **We May Never Love Like This Again** ...*Wherever Love Takes Me*	$5		20th Century 2158
				from the movie *The Towering Inferno* starring Paul Newman and Steve McQueen			
2/24/79	52	9		5 **Can You Read My Mind** ...*You Love Me Too Late*	$5		Warner/Curb 8750
				love theme from the movie *Superman* starring Christopher Reeve			
7/7/79	18	16		6 **Different Worlds** ...AC[2] *Carolina Moon*	$4		Warner/Curb 8835
				theme from the TV series *Angie* starring Donna Pescow			
				McGRAW, Tim ★194★ C&W/BUB/LP '99			
				Born on 5/1/67 in Delhi, Louisiana. Country singer. Son of ex-professional baseball player Tug McGraw. Attended Northeast Louisiana University on several sports scholarships. Married **Faith Hill** on 10/6/96. Charted 44 Country hits, 1992-2003.			
				1)It's Your Love 2)Please Remember Me 3)Indian Outlaw 4)Don't Take The Girl 5)Grown Men Don't Cry			
3/5/94	15	20	●	1 **Indian Outlaw** ...S:4 *(dance mix)*	$5	▌V	Curb 76920
				includes a verse from the 1971 #1 hit "Indian Reservation"			
5/21/94	17	20	●	2 **Don't Take The Girl** ...CW[2] S:3 *Welcome To The Club* (C&W #47/'92)	$5	▌V	Curb 76925
				"45" issued for above 2 on Curb 76923			
4/1/95	69[S]	1		3 **Refried Dreams** ...BUB:106 *Not A Moment Too Soon* (C&W #1)	$5	▌V	Curb 76931
8/26/95	25	20	●	4 **I Like It, I Love It** ...CW[5] S:8 *(dance mix)*	$5	▌V	Curb 76961
				"45" title: "I Like It, I Love It, I Want Some More Of It"; B-side: (club mix)			
1/6/96	87	5		5 **Can't Be Really Gone** ...S:56 *That's Just Me*	$5	▌V	Curb 76971
5/17/97	7	20	▲	6 **It's Your Love** CW[6] S:3 *She Never Lets It Go To Her Heart* (McGraw - C&W #1)	$4	▌V	Curb 73019
				TIM McGRAW with Faith Hill			
5/2/98	74	10		7 **One Of These Days** ...S:57 *Just To See You Smile* (C&W #1)	$4	▌V	Curb 73056
12/5/98	79	4		8 **Where The Green Grass Grows** ...CW[4] A:67			album cut
12/5/98+	37	15		9 **For A Little While** ...A:24		V	album cut
				above 4 from the album *Everywhere* on Curb 77886			
4/3/99	10	20		10 **Please Remember Me** ...CW[5] S:15 / A:17 *For A Little While*	$4	★V	Curb 73080
				Patty Loveless (backing vocals); "45" issued for above 2 on Curb 73080			
8/14/99	28	20		11 **Something Like That** ...CW[5] A:20			album cut
11/27/99+	29	21		12 **My Best Friend** ...CW[2] A:23			album cut
5/13/00	58	14		13 **Some Things Never Change** ...A:50			album cut

DEBUT	PEAK	WKS	Gold	A-side (Chart Hit)	B-side	$	Sym	Label & Number
				McGRAW, Tim — Cont'd				
8/12/00	54	14		14 **Let's Make Love**	A:50		V	album cut
				FAITH HILL with TIM McGRAW				
				from Hill's album *Breathe* on Warner 47373; "45": Warner/Curb 16792; B-side: "There Will Come A Day" (Hill - C&W #59)				
10/21/00	27	20		15 **My Next Thirty Years**	CW^5 A:21			album cut
				#10-13 & 15: from the album *A Place In The Sun* on Curb 77942				
3/31/01	25	20		16 **Grown Men Don't Cry**	CW^1 A:17			album cut
8/18/01	38	20		17 **Angry All The Time**	CW^2 A:31			album cut
12/8/01+	36	20		18 **Bring On The Rain**	CW^1 A:34			album cut
				JO DEE MESSINA with Tim McGraw				
				from Messina's album *Burn* on Curb 77977				
1/12/02	33	20		19 **The Cowboy In Me**	CW^1 A:30			album cut
7/6/02	26	20		20 **Unbroken**	CW^1 A:24			album cut
				#16, 17, 19 & 20: from the album *Set This Circus Down* on Curb 78711				
10/12/02	40	20		21 **Red Rag Top**	A:38			album cut
				from the album *Tim McGraw and the Dancehall Doctors* on Curb 78746				
				McGRIFF, Jimmy BUB/LP **'62**				
				Born on 4/3/36 in Philadelphia, Pennsylvania. Jazz-R&B organist/multi-instrumentalist/songwriter.				
10/13/62	20	9		1 **I've Got A Woman Part I**	*Part II* [I]	$10		Sue 770
				#1 R&B hit for **Ray Charles** in 1955				
1/5/63	50	11		2 **All About My Girl /**	[I]			
2/2/63	95	3		3 **M.G. Blues**	[I]	$10		Sue 777
5/25/63	99	1		4 **The Last Minute Pt. I**	*Pt. II* [I]	$10		Sue 786
5/16/64	79	4		5 **Kiko**	*Jumpin' At The Woodside* [I]	$10		Sue 10-001
12/14/68	97	1		6 **The Worm**	*Keep Loose* [I]	$8		Solid State 2524
				McGUFFEY LANE C&W/LP **'81**				
				Country-rock group from Columbus, Ohio: Bob McNelley (vocals), Terry Efaw and John Schwab (guitars), Stephen Douglass (keyboards), Stephen Reis (bass) and Dave Rangeler (drums). Group name taken from a street in Athens, Ohio. Douglass died in a car accident on 1/12/84 (age 33). McNelley died from a self-inflicted gunshot wound on 1/7/87 (age 36).				
1/17/81	85	7		1 **Long Time Lovin' You**	*People Like You*	$5		Atco 7319
2/6/82	97	3		2 **Start It All Over**	*Don't You Think About Me (When I'm Gone)*	$5		Atco 7345
				McGUINN, Mark C&W/LP **'01**				
				Born in 1969 in Greensboro, North Carolina. Country singer/songwriter/guitarist.				
3/24/01	44	15		**Mrs. Steven Rudy**	S:12 / A:51 *That's A Plan* (C&W #25)	$5	★+	VFR 734758
				McGUINN, CLARK & HILLMAN BUB/AC/LP **'79**				
				Pop-rock trio: Roger McGuinn (vocals, guitar; born on 7/13/42), Gene Clark (guitar; born on 11/17/44; died on 5/24/91, age 46) and Chris Hillman (bass; born on 6/4/42). All were founding members of **The Byrds**.				
3/17/79	33	11		**Don't You Write Her Off**	*Sad Boy*	$5		Capitol 4693
				McGUINNESS FLINT LP **'71**				
				Rock group formed in England: Tom McGuinness (guitar; **Manfred Mann**), Hughie Flint (drums), Dennis Coulson (vocals), Graham Lyle (guitar) and Benny Gallagher (bass). Also see **Gallagher & Lyle**.				
1/9/71	47	9		**When I'm Dead And Gone**	*Lazy Afternoon*	$6		Capitol 3014
				McGUIRE, Barry BUB/LP **'65**				
				Born on 10/15/37 in Oklahoma City, Oklahoma. Folk-rock singer. Member of **The New Christy Minstrels** from 1962-65.				
8/21/65	❶^{1}	11		1 **Eve Of Destruction**	*What Exactly's The Matter With Me*	$12		Dunhill 4009
				backing by the original members of **The Grass Roots**				
11/6/65	72	4		2 **Child Of Our Times**	*Upon A Painted Ocean* (#117)	$10	■	Dunhill 4014
5/21/66	62	7		3 **Cloudy Summer Afternoon (Raindrops)**	*I'd Have To Be Outta My Mind*	$10		Dunhill 4028
				first recorded in 1960 by **Bud & Travis** on Liberty 55235 ($12)				
				McGUIRE SISTERS, The ★124★ MEM/POP/BUB/AC/LP **'55**				
				Vocal trio from Middletown, Ohio: sisters Phyllis (born on 2/14/31) (see #31 below), Christine (born on 7/30/29) and Dorothy (born on 2/13/26) McGuire. Replaced **The Chordettes** on *Arthur Godfrey And His Friends* show in 1953. Phyllis went solo in 1964. Reunited in 1986. First charted in 1954 at #7 with "Goodnight, Sweetheart, Goodnight."				
				1)Sincerely 2)Sugartime 3)Something's Gotta Give 4)He 5)May You Always				
1/8/55	❶^{10}	21	●	1 **Sincerely /**	A:❶^{10} / J:❶^{7} / S:❶^{6}			
				written by legendary DJ Alan Freed and Harvey Fuqua (of **The Moonglows**)				
1/29/55	17	6		2 **No More**	A:17 / J:17 / S:23	$15		Coral 61323
3/26/55	11	7		3 **It May Sound Silly /**	A:11 / J:14 / S:23			
				#14 R&B hit for **Ivory Joe Hunter** in 1955				
4/16/55		2		4 **Doesn't Anybody Love Me?**	J:flip	$12		Coral 61369
6/4/55	5	14		5 **Something's Gotta Give /**	A:5 / S:6 / J:6			
				from the movie *Daddy Long Legs* starring Fred Astaire				
6/25/55		2		6 **Rhythm 'N' Blues (Mama's Got The Rhythm - Papa's Got The Blues)**	S:flip / J:flip	$12		Coral 61423
10/29/55	10	19		7 **He**	J:10 / S:12 / T:12 / A:16 *If You Believe*	$12		Coral 61501
11/12/55	95	1		8 **Give Me Love**	T:95 *Sweet Song Of India*	$10		Coral 61494
1/7/56	32^{CU}	4		9 **My Baby's Got Such Lovin' Ways /**				
1/7/56	34^{CU}	4		10 **(Baby, Baby) Be Good To Me**		$10		Coral 61532
3/10/56	44	6		11 **Missing**	T:44 *Tell Me Now*	$10		Coral 61587
5/5/56	13	20		12 **Picnic /**	T:13 / A:14 / S:15 / J:18			
				based on the theme from the movie starring William Holden; lyrics written by **Steve Allen**				
5/5/56	37	11		13 **Delilah Jones**	T:37 / S:flip	$10		Coral 61627
				based on the "Main Title" theme from the movie *The Man With The Golden Arm* starring **Frank Sinatra**				

DEBUT	PEAK	WKS	Gold	A-side (Chart Hit)..........B-side	$	Sym	Label & Number
				McGUIRE SISTERS, The — Cont'd			
7/28/56	32	8		14 **Weary Blues /** T:32 **THE McGUIRE SISTERS and LAWRENCE WELK And His Champagne Music** traditional tune first recorded in 1923 by The New Orleans Rhythm Kings			
8/4/56	63	5		15 **In The Alps** ....T:63 **LAWRENCE WELK AND HIS CHAMPAGNE MUSIC and THE McGUIRE SISTERS**	$10	■	Coral 61670
9/22/56	37	12		16 **Ev'ry Day Of My Life /** T:37			
9/22/56	52	8		17 **Endless** T:52	$10		Coral 61703
12/8/56+	32	9		18 **Goodnight My Love, Pleasant Dreams** ....T:32 *Mommy* #7 R&B hit for **Jesse Belvin** in 1956	$10		Coral 61748
8/19/57	73	6		19 **Around The World In Eighty Days** ....T:73 *Interlude* Skip Martin (orch.); title song from the movie starring David Niven	$10		Coral 61856
12/30/57+	❶[4]	23	●	20 **Sugartime** ....A:❶[4] / T:5 / S:7 *Banana Split* a twist version "Bubbled Under" (#107) in 1962 on Coral 62305	$10		Coral 61924
6/9/58	25	6		21 **Ding Dong** ....A:25 / T:43 / S:44 *Since You Went Away To School*	$10		Coral 61991
9/1/58	80	1		22 **Volare (Nel Blu, Dipinto Di Blu)** ....H:80 *Do You Love Me Like You Kiss Me* **Neal Hefti** (orch.: #4 & 20-22)	$10		Coral 62021
1/5/59	11	16		23 **May You Always** ....*Achoo--Cha Cha (Gesundheit)*	$10		Coral 62059
4/27/59	55	7		24 **Summer Dreams /** melody based on a 1914 European song "Estrellita (Little Star)"			
5/4/59	85	3		25 **Peace**	$10		Coral 62106
1/25/60	97	1		26 **Livin' Dangerously** ....*Lovers Lullaby*	$8	■	Coral 62162
8/15/60	99	1		27 **The Last Dance** ....*Nine O'Clock*	$8		Coral 62216
3/13/61	20	14		28 **Just For Old Time's Sake** ....*Really Neat*	$8	■	Coral 62249
7/24/61	59	5		29 **Tears On My Pillow** ....*(Will There Be Space In A) Space Ship* written and recorded in 1941 by **Gene Autry** on Okeh 6239 ($20)	$8	■	Coral 62276
11/6/61	99	1		30 **Just Because** ....*I Do, I Do, I Do* **Dick Jacobs** (orch.: #1-3, 5, 13, 16-18 & 23-30)	$8		Coral 62288
12/5/64	79	3		31 **I Don't Want To Walk Without You** ....*That's Life* **PHYLLIS McGUIRE** #2 hit for Harry James in 1942 (from the movie *Sweater Girl* starring Eddie Bracken)	$7		Reprise 0310
				McIAN, Peter '80 Born in California. Pop singer/songwriter. Wrote music for TV's *Starsky And Hutch* and *The Love Boat*.			
4/5/80	52	7		**Solitaire** ....*Listen To Your Heart*	$4		ARC 11214
				McINTYRE, Joey — see NEW KIDS ON THE BLOCK			
				McKENNITT, Loreena LP '98 Born on 2/17/57 in Morden, Manitoba, Canada. Adult Alternative singer/harpist/songwriter.			
3/7/98	18	20		**The Mummers' Dance** ....A:11 / S:36 *(album version) / The Mystic's Dream*	$3	▮V	Warner 17241
				McKENZIE, Bob & Doug LP '82 The McKenzie brothers are actually Canadian comedians Rick "Bob" Moranis (born on 4/18/54) and Dave "Doug" Thomas (born on 5/20/49) of *SCTV*. Both featured (as the McKenzie brothers) in the movie *Strange Brew*. Thomas is the brother of **Ian Thomas**.			
1/30/82	16	14		**Take Off** ....*Elron McKenzie* [N] Geddy Lee (of **Rush**; vocal)	$6	■	Mercury 76134
				McKENZIE, Scott BUB/LP '67 Born Philip Blondheim on 1/10/39 in Jacksonville, Florida; raised in Virginia. Sang with **John Phillips** (**The Mamas & The Papas**) in the folk group The Journeymen. Co-wrote **The Beach Boys**' 1988 #1 hit "Kokomo."			
5/27/67	4	12		1 **San Francisco (Be Sure To Wear Flowers In Your Hair)** ....*What's The Difference*	$8		Ode 103
10/21/67	24	7		2 **Like An Old Time Movie** ....*What's The Difference - Chapter II* above 2 written and produced by **John Phillips**	$8		Ode 105
	★318★			**McKNIGHT, Brian** R&B/BUB/AC/LP '99 Born on 6/5/69 in Buffalo, New York. R&B singer/composer. His older brother is Claude McKnight of Take 6. *1)Back At One 2)Love Is 3)Anytime*			
1/23/93	3	28		1 **Love Is** ....AC[3] A:2 / S:13 *(instrumental)* **VANESSA WILLIAMS and BRIAN McKNIGHT** from the album *Beverly Hills, 90210 - The Soundtrack*	$3	▮V	Giant 18630
6/12/93	13	22		2 **One Last Cry** ....A:12 / S:18 *(2 album snippets)* "45": Collectables 4938; B-side: "The Way Love Goes" (R&B #11/'92)	$3	▮V	Mercury 862404
9/24/94	62	14		3 **I'll Take Her** ....S:42 *The Brooklyn Uptown Connection* **ILL AL SKRATCH Featuring Brian McKnight**	$3	▮	Mercury 856124
4/15/95	45	20		4 **Crazy Love** ....S:23 *U Will Know / (2 album snippets)* from the movie *Jason's Lyric* starring Forest Whitaker; written by **Van Morrison** (from his 1970 album *Moondance*)	$3	▮	Mercury 856730
8/19/95	73	9		5 **On The Down Low** ....S:37 *(3 album snippets)*	$3	▮	Mercury 852082
9/6/97	17	20		6 **You Should Be Mine (Don't Waste Your Time)** ....S:9 / A:69 *(remix)* **BRIAN McKNIGHT Featuring Mase** **Kelly Price** (female vocal); samples "I Got Ants In My Pants" by **James Brown**	$3	▮	Mercury 574760
2/7/98	6[A]	40		7 **Anytime** ....RB[4A]		V	album cut
6/13/98	60[A]	14		8 **The Only One For Me** .... "45" issued for above 2 on Motown 860768		V	album cut
12/5/98+	35	12		9 **Hold Me** ....S:9 *(2 versions)* **BRIAN McKNIGHT (featuring Tone & Kobe Bryant)** Bryant is a pro basketball player with the L.A. Lakers; samples "Sugar Free" by Juicy; above 4 from the album *Anytime* on Mercury 5362154	$4	★	Motown 860885
8/28/99	2[8]	37		10 **Back At One** A:❶[6] *(3 remixes)* "45": Motown 156402; B-side: "Anytime"	$6	T[V]	Motown 156501
2/26/00	76	8		11 **Stay Or Let It Go** ....A:69 *(3 versions)*	$6	T	Motown 156248
12/23/00+	21[S]	31		12 **Win** ....*Stay* from the movie *Men Of Honor* starring Robert DeNiro and Cuba Gooding, Jr.	$4	★	Motown 158549

DEBUT	PEAK	WKS	Gold	A-side (Chart Hit)..........B-side	$	Sym	Label & Number
				McKNIGHT, Brian — Cont'd			
9/15/01	51	20		13 **Love Of My Life**..........A:46			album cut
4/20/02	91	5		14 **Tell Me What's It Gonna Be**..........S:65 *(3 versions)* **BRIAN McKNIGHT Featuring Jermaine Dupri** samples "Hydra" by **Grover Washington, Jr.**; above 2 from the album *Superhero* on Motown 014743	$6	T	Motown 015880
				McKUEN, Rod LP **'62** Born on 4/29/33 in Oakland, California. Poet/singer/songwriter/actor. Wrote songs for 20th Century-Fox and Universal movies in the 1950s and 1960s. Co-wrote (with **Anita Kerr**) and narrated a popular late 1960s series of concept albums beginning with *The Sea*. Also see **Bob McFadden And Dor**.			
1/20/62	76	6		**Oliver Twist**..........*Celebrity Twist*	$15		Spiral 1407
	★555★			**McLACHLAN, Sarah** ROK/LP **'98** Born on 1/28/68 in Halifax, Nova Scotia, Canada. Adult Alternative folk-pop singer/songwriter/guitarist.			
5/7/94	73	19		1 **Possession**..........A:62 *Black (live)*	$4	▮	Arista 12662
10/8/94	77	10		2 **Good Enough**..........*Blue*	$4	▮	Arista 12690
11/11/95+	65	20		3 **I Will Remember You**..........S:50 *Ice Cream* theme from the movie *The Brothers McMullen* starring Jack Mulcahy; also see #8 below	$4	▮	Arista 12893
9/6/97	13	22		4 **Building A Mystery**..........A:9 / S:27 *I Will Remember You*	$3	▮	Arista 13395
2/14/98	28	14		5 **Sweet Surrender**..........A:22 / S:46 *(2 versions)*	$3	▮	Arista 13453
5/30/98	3	27	●	6 **Adia** S:5 / A:13 *Angel / I Will Remember You*	$3	▮	Arista 13497
11/14/98+	4	31		7 **Angel**..........AC[12] A:2 / S:5 *Ice Cream (Live) / I Will Not Forget You (Live)* from the movie *City Of Angels* starring Nicolas Cage; charted on 11/14/98 as "Adia/Angel"; then for 2 weeks as "Angel/Adia"; then debuted solely as "Angel" on 12/5/98, after which the single was cut out by the label; finally released on its own on 2/20/99; above 4 from the album *Surfacing*	$4	★	Arista 13621
5/22/99	14	20		8 **I Will Remember You**..........A:7 [L-R] studio version on #3 above; from the album *Mirrorball* on Arista 19049			album cut
1/20/01	58[S]	17		9 **Silence**..........*(3 remixes) / Aria* **DELERIUM Featuring Sarah McLachlan** recorded in 1997; featured in the movies *Breakdown Palace* starring Claire Daines and *Bounce* starring Ben Affleck	$8	★*	Nettwerk 33111
				McLAIN, Tommy **'66** Born on 3/15/40 in Jonesville, Louisiana. White "swamp-pop" singer/songwriter.			
6/25/66	15	11		**Sweet Dreams**..........*I Need You So* first released on Jin 197 in 1966 ($20)	$12		MSL 197
	★567★			**McLEAN, Don** C&W/AC/BUB/LP **'72** Born on 10/2/45 in New Rochelle, New York. Adult Contemporary singer/songwriter/guitarist. The hit "Killing Me Softly With His Song" was inspired by a McLean performance. *1)American Pie - Parts I & II 2)Crying 3)Vincent*			
11/27/71+	❶[4]	19	●	1 **American Pie - Parts I & II** AC[3] inspired by the death of **Buddy Holly**	$6	■	United Artists 50856
3/18/72	12	12		2 **Vincent /** a tribute to artist Vincent Van Gogh			
4/22/72		7		3 **Castles In The Air**.......... first made the Adult Contemporary charts (#40) on 2/27/71 on Mediarts 108 ($7); also released on United Artists 50796 in 1971; also see #10 below	$6	■	United Artists 50887
12/23/72+	21	12		4 **Dreidel**..........*Bronco Bill's Lament*	$5		United Artists 51100
3/31/73	58	7		5 **If We Try**..........*The More You Pay (The More It's Worth)*	$5		United Artists 206
6/14/75	93	3		6 **Wonderful Baby**..........AC[1] *Birthday Song* written as a tribute to Fred Astaire	$5		United Artists 614
1/24/81	5	18		7 **Crying**..........*Genesis (In The Beginning)*	$4		Millennium 11799
4/11/81	23	14		8 **Since I Don't Have You**..........*Your Cheating Heart*	$4		Millennium 11804
8/8/81	83	2		9 **It's Just The Sun**..........*Words And Music*	$4		Millennium 11809
10/31/81	36	14		10 **Castles In The Air**..........*Crazy Eyes* [R] new version of #3 above	$4		Millennium 11819
				McLEAN, Penny BUB **'76** Born on 11/4/48 in Klagenfurt, Austria. Disco singer. Member of **Silver Convention**.			
1/3/76	48	10		**Lady Bump**..........*The Lady Bumps On*	$5		Atco 7038
				McLEAN, Phil **'62** Born in Detroit, Michigan. Veteran DJ on Cleveland's WERE radio station.			
12/4/61+	21	10		**Small Sad Sam**..........*Chicken* [N-S] a parody of "Big Bad John"	$10		Versatile 107
				McLOLLIE, Oscar, and Jeanette Baker **'58** Black orchestra leader/baritone singer McLollie first recorded for Mercury in 1950. Baker was a member of the female vocal group The Dots on the Caddy label.			
8/4/58	61	5		**Hey Girl - Hey Boy**..........H:61 *Let Me Know Let Me Know* (McLollie) **Googie Rene** (orch.)	$25		Class 228
				McMAHON, Gerard BUB **'83** Born in Wichita, Kansas. Rock singer/songwriter/guitarist. "Bubbled Under" in 1976 as Gerard.			
4/9/83	85	3		**Count On Me**..........*Nickel Charm Jack*	$4		Full Moon 29699
				McNALLY, Larry John **'81** Born in Bangor, Maine. Pop singer/songwriter. Wrote "The Motown Song" by **Rod Stewart**.			
8/8/81	86	2		**Just Like Paradise**..........*Lose Myself*	$4		ARC 02200
				McNAMARA, Robin **'70** Born in Boston, Massachusetts. Male pop singer. One of the original cast members of *Hair*.			
5/30/70	11	15		1 **Lay A Little Lovin' On Me**..........*I'll Tell You Tomorrow*	$7		Steed 724
10/3/70	80	5		2 **Got To Believe In Love**..........*Aren't You Thinking Of Me* cast of *Hair* (backing vocals, above 2)	$7		Steed 728

DEBUT	PEAK	WKS	Gold	A-side (Chart Hit)..........B-side	$	Sym	Label & Number
				McNEAL, Lutricia '98			
				Born in Oklahoma City, Oklahoma. Female R&B singer.			
1/3/98	63	16		**Ain't That Just The Way**........*Always*	$3	▌	Crave 78764
				written by Glen Larson and Bruce Belland of **The Four Preps**.			
				McNEELY, Big Jay, and Band R&B '59			
				Born Cecil James McNeely on 4/29/27 in Los Angeles, California. R&B tenor saxophonist/bandleader. Originator of the acrobatic, wild honking sax style. Active into the 1980s.			
5/25/59	44	16		**There Is Something On Your Mind**........*Back...Shack...Track*	$25		Swingin' 614
				Haywood "Little Sonny" Warner (vocal)			
				McNICHOL, Kristy & Jimmy LP '78			
				TV/movie stars born in Los Angeles, California: Kristy (born on 9/11/62), a cast member of TV's *Family* and *Empty Nest*, and her brother Jimmy (born on 7/2/61). Each starred in several movies.			
7/22/78	70	8		**He's So Fine**........*He's A Dancer*	$5	■	RCA 11271
				M'COOL, Shamus '81			
				Stand-up comedian Richard Doyle; hosted his own cable TV show *Comic Talk* in Los Angeles.			
12/22/73	11^X	1		1 **Santa's Little Helper, Dingo**........[X-N]	$75		Perspective 6002
				reissued in 1976 on Perspective 777 ($75)			
7/4/81	80	3		2 **American Memories**........*American Humor*	$75		Perspective 107
	★290★			**McPHATTER, Clyde** BUB/R&B '59			
				Born Clyde Lensley McPhatter on 11/15/32 in Durham, North Carolina. Died of a heart attack on 6/13/72 (age 39). Signed by **Billy Ward** for The Dominoes in 1950. Left The Dominoes in June 1953 to form own group, **The Drifters** (originally billed as **CLYDE McPHATTER & THE DRIFTERS**). Drafted in 1954, returned to sing solo. One of the most influential and distinctive male voices of the R&B era. Inducted into the Rock and Roll Hall of Fame in 1987.			
				1)A Lover's Question 2)Lover Please 3)Treasure Of Love 4)Without Love (There Is Nothing) 5)Ta Ta			
2/4/56	44	5		1 **Seven Days**........T:44 *I'm Not Worthy Of You*	$40		Atlantic 1081
5/26/56	16	17		2 **Treasure Of Love**........RB^1 S:16 / J:18 / T:22 *When You're Sincere*	$40		Atlantic 1092
2/2/57	19	11		3 **Without Love (There Is Nothing)**........A:19 / T:38 *I Make Believe*	$30		Atlantic 1117
5/20/57	26	11		4 **Just To Hold My Hand**........S:26 / T:30 *No Matter What*	$25		Atlantic 1133
8/12/57	49	13		5 **Long Lonely Nights**........RB^1 T:49 *Heartaches*	$25		Atlantic 1149
12/2/57	93	1		6 **Rock And Cry**........T:93 *You'll Be There*	$25		Atlantic 1158
				from the movie *Mr. Rock 'n' Roll* starring Alan Freed			
5/12/58	43	15		7 **Come What May**........H:43 / S:47 *Let Me Know*	$25		Atlantic 1185
10/6/58+	6	24	●	8 **A Lover's Question**........RB^1 H:6 *I Can't Stand Up Alone*	$25		Atlantic 1199
4/6/59	49	8		9 **Lovey Dovey**........*My Island Of Dreams*	$20		Atlantic 2018
				#2 R&B hit for **The Clovers** in 1954			
4/20/59	70	5		10 **I Told Myself A Lie**........*(I'm Afraid) The Masquerade Is Over*	$20		MGM 12780
6/15/59	38	13		11 **Since You've Been Gone**........*Try Try Baby*	$20		Atlantic 2028
				written by **Neil Sedaka**			
8/24/59	91	2		12 **Twice As Nice**........*Where Did I Make My Mistake*	$20		MGM 12816
11/2/59	72	3		13 **You Went Back On Your Word**........*There You Go*	$20		Atlantic 2038
				#8 & 13: written by **Brook Benton**			
12/21/59+	48	8		14 **Let's Try Again**........*Bless You*	$20		MGM 12843
2/29/60	96	2		15 **Just Give Me A Ring**........*Don't Dog Me*	$20		Atlantic 2049
4/4/60	66	6		16 **Think Me A Kiss**........*When The Right Time Comes Along*	$20		MGM 12877
7/18/60	23	14		17 **Ta Ta**........*I Ain't Givin' Up Nothin' (If I Can't Get Somethin' From You)*	$15		Mercury 71660
7/24/61	56	5		18 **I Never Knew**........*Happiness*	$15	■	Mercury 71841
3/3/62	7	14		19 **Lover Please**........*Let's Forget About The Past*	$15	■	Mercury 71941
				written by **Billy Swan**			
6/16/62	25	8		20 **Little Bitty Pretty One**........*Next To Me*	$15	■	Mercury 71987
				The Merry Melody Singers (backing vocals)			
1/4/64	90	5		21 **Deep In The Heart Of Harlem**........*Happy Good Times*	$15	■	Mercury 72220
				McPhatter's musical arrangers and conductors: Stan Applebaum (#19), Howard Biggs (#7, 8), **Ray Ellis** (#3, 4, 6, 10, 12, 14, 16), Budd Johnson (#5), Jerry Kennedy (#20), Alan Lorber (#21) and Chuck Sagle (#18)			
				McPHERSON, Wyatt (Earp) '61			
				Male R&B singer/songwriter.			
5/15/61	97	2		**Here's My Confession**........*That's Why I Love My Baby*	$25		Savoy 1599
				McRAE, Carmen AC/BUB/LP '56			
				Born on 4/8/22 in Harlem, New York. Died of a stroke on 11/10/94 (age 72). Jazz singer/pianist.			
2/4/56	75	2		1 **The Next Time It Happens**........T:75 *Come On, Come In*	$12		Decca 29749
				from the Broadway musical *Pipe Dream* starring Helen Traubel			
3/2/57	92	1		2 **Skyliner**........T:92 *If You Should Leave Me*	$12		Decca 30004
				introduced by Charlie Barnet's Orchestra in 1945; **Jack Pleis** (orch., above 2)			
				McVIE, Christine ROK/LP '84			
				Born Christine Perfect on 7/12/43 in Birmingham, England. Vocalist/keyboardist with **Fleetwood Mac** since 1970. Married to Fleetwood Mac bassist John McVie, 1968-77.			
1/28/84	10	16		1 **Got A Hold On Me**........AC^4 / AR^2 *Who's Dreaming This Dream*	$4	■	Warner 29372
				Steve Winwood (synthesizer)			
4/28/84	30	10		2 **Love Will Show Us How**........*The Challenge*	$4	■	Warner 29313
				MEAD, Sister Janet '74			
				Born in 1938 in Adelaide, Australia. Nun at the Sisters of Mercy convent. Gained prominence through her weekly cathedral rock masses and weekly radio programs.			
2/23/74	4	13	●	**The Lord's Prayer**........*Brother Sun And Sister Moon*	$5		A&M 1491
				Les Sands (orch.); Biblical text with new music by Arnold Strals			

DEBUT	PEAK	WKS	Gold	A-side (Chart Hit)...B-side	$	Sym	Label & Number
	★500★			**MEAT LOAF** ROK/LP '93			
				Born Marvin Lee Aday on 9/27/47 in Dallas, Texas. Pop-rock singer. Sang lead vocals on **Ted Nugent**'s 1976 *Free-For-All* album. Played "Eddie" in the Los Angeles production and movie of *The Rocky Horror Picture Show.* Appeared in several other movies.			
				1)I'd Do Anything For Love (But I Won't Do That) 2)Two Out Of Three Ain't Bad 3)I'd Lie For You (And That's The Truth)			
5/22/71	71	6		1 **What You See Is What You Get** ...*Lady Be Mine* — **STONEY & MEATLOAF** (Stoney is Cheryl Murphy from Detroit)	$7		Rare Earth 5027
3/18/78	11	23	●	2 **Two Out Of Three Ain't Bad** ...*For Crying Out Loud*	$5		Cleveland I./Epic 50513
8/12/78	39	10		3 **Paradise By The Dashboard Light** ...*"Bat" Overture* [N] — **Ellen Foley** (female vocal); Phil Rizzuto (baseball announcer)	$5		Cleveland I./Epic 50588
11/11/78+	39	13		4 **You Took The Words Right Out Of My Mouth** ...*Paradise By The Dashboard Light* — first released on Epic 50467 in 1977; above 3 produced by **Todd Rundgren**	$5		Cleveland I./Epic 50634
9/19/81	84	3		5 **I'm Gonna Love Her For Both Of Us** ...*Peel Out*	$4		Cleveland I./Epic 02490
9/18/93	❶[5]	22	▲	6 **I'd Do Anything For Love** (But I Won't Do That) S:❶[7] / A:4 *(edit)* — Patti Russo (female vocal)	$3	▮[V]	MCA 54626
1/29/94	13	20		7 **Rock And Roll Dreams Come Through** ...S:11 / A:24 *I'd Do Anything For Love (But I Won't Do That) (live)*	$3	▮[V]	MCA 54757
5/14/94	38	11		8 **Objects In The Rear View Mirror May Appear Closer Than They Are** ...S:31 / A:67 *Two Out Of Three Ain't Bad (live)* — all of above (except #1) written and produced by **Jim Steinman**	$3	▮[V]	MCA 54848
10/21/95	13	20	●	9 **I'd Lie For You** (And That's The **Truth**) ...S:6 / A:43 *I'd Do Anything For Love (But I Won't Do That) (live)*	$3	▮	MCA 55134
2/17/96	82	4		10 **Not A Dry Eye In The House** ...S:71 *I'd Lie For You (And That's The Truth) (live)*	$3	▮	MCA 55174
				MEAT PUPPETS ROK/LP '94			
				Rock trio from Phoenix, Arizona: brothers Curt (vocals, guitar) and Cris (bass) Kirkwood with Derrick Bostrom (drums).			
6/11/94	47	20		**Backwater** ...A:42 *Open Wide / Animal / Up On the Sun / White Sport Coat*	$8	★*	London 857553
				MECO BUB/AC/LP '77			
				Born Domenico Monardo on 11/29/39 in Johnsonburg, Pennsylvania. Disco producer. Played trombone in Cadet Band at West Point. Later moved to New York and became a session musician and arranger. Co-produced **Gloria Gaynor**'s hit "Never Can Say Goodbye."			
8/6/77	❶[2]	20	▲	1 **Star Wars Theme/Cantina Band** ...*Funk* [I]	$5		Millennium 604
1/7/78	25	10		2 **Theme From Close Encounters** ...*Roman Nights* [I]	$5		Millennium 608
9/9/78	35	10		3 **Themes From The Wizard Of Oz** ...*Fantasy* [N]	$5		Millennium 620
6/14/80	18	14		4 **Empire Strikes Back (Medley)** ...*The Force Theme* [I] — Darth Vader/Yoda's Theme; all of above inspired by movie themes	$5		RSO 1038
10/11/80	70	4		5 **Love Theme From Shogun** (Mariko's Theme) ...*The Main Theme From Shogun* [I] — from the TV mini-series *Shogun* starring **Richard Chamberlain**	$5		RSO 1052
12/13/80	69	6		6 **What Can You Get A Wookiee For Christmas (When He Already Owns A Comb?)** ...*R2D2 We Wish You A Merry Christmas* (Original Star Wars Cast) [X-N] — **THE STAR WARS INTERGALACTIC DROID CHOIR & CHORALE** — featuring Star Wars' Chewbacca; also issued with a promotional insert	$5	■	RSO 1058
7/25/81	81	3		7 **Summer '81 medley** ...*Out In California* — **THE CANTINA BAND (featuring Lou Christie)** — **Beach Boys**' medley: Surfer Girl/Fun, Fun, Fun/409/I Get Around/ Dance, Dance, Dance/California Girls/ Wouldn't It Be Nice/Help Me, Rhonda/Good Vibrations	$8		Millennium 11818
2/13/82	35	11		8 **Pop Goes The Movies** Part I ...*Part II* [I] — medley: 20th Century Fox Trademark/Tara's Theme/The Magnificent Seven/The James Bond Theme/Goldfinger/ The Good, The Bad And The Ugly/Theme From The Apartment/Theme From The High & The Mighty	$4		Arista 0660
7/2/83	60	8		9 **Ewok Celebration** ...*Lapti Nek* [N] — Duke Bootee (guest rapper); inspired by the movie *Return Of The Jedi* starring Harrison Ford	$4		Arista 9045
				MEDEIROS, Glenn LP '90			
				Born on 6/24/70 in Lihue, Kauai, Hawaii (of Portugese parents). Pop singer.			
2/14/87	12	25		1 **Nothing's Gonna Change My Love For You** ...S:6 / A:17 *(instrumental)*	$3	■	Amherst 311
8/1/87	80	8		2 **Watching Over You** ...*You Left The Loneliest Heart*	$3	■	Amherst 314
12/19/87+	67	11		3 **Lonely Won't Leave Me Alone** ...*You Left The Loneliest Heart*	$3	■	Amherst 317
8/13/88	68	10		4 **Long And Lasting Love (Once In A Lifetime)** ...*You're My Woman, You're My Lady*	$3	■	Amherst 324
5/19/90	❶[2]	18	●	5 **She Ain't Worth It** A:❶[3] / S:4 *(no B-side)* — **GLENN MEDEIROS Featuring Bobby Brown** — "45": MCA 79047; B-side: "Victim Of Love" (Medeiros)	$3	▮[V]	MCA 53831
8/18/90	32	13		6 **All I'm Missing Is You** ...S:29 / A:29 *Let Me Show You What Love Is* — **GLENN MEDEIROS Featuring Ray Parker Jr.**	$3	▮	MCA 53886
11/10/90	78	4		7 **Me - U = Blue** ...*Remember* — **The Stylistics** (backing vocals)	$3	▮	MCA 53945
				MEDLEY, Bill C&W/AC/BUB/LP '87			
				Born on 9/19/40 in Santa Ana, California. Baritone of **The Righteous Brothers** duo. Co-owner of a Las Vegas nightclub named Kicks with **Paul Revere** of **The Raiders**.			
5/18/68	95	2		1 **I Can't Make It Alone** ...*One Day Girl*	$8		MGM 13931
8/3/68	43	11		2 **Brown Eyed Woman** ...*Let The Good Times Roll*	$8		MGM 13959
10/26/68	48	7		3 **Peace Brother Peace** ...*Winter Won't Come This Year*	$8		MGM 14000
3/28/81	88	4		4 **Don't Know Much** ...*Woman* — #77 hit for **Bette Midler** in 1983 as "All I Need To Know"	$4		Liberty 1402
10/2/82	58	8		5 **Right Here And Now** ...*The Best Of My Life*	$4		Planet 13317
9/26/87	❶[1]	21	●	6 **(I've Had) The Time Of My Life** AC[4] A:❷[2] / S:❶[1] *Love Is Strange* (**Mickey & Sylvia**) — **BILL MEDLEY AND JENNIFER WARNES** — love theme from the movie *Dirty Dancing* starring **Patrick Swayze** and Jennifer Grey	$3	■	RCA 5224
				MEDLIN, Joe '59			
				Born on 4/1/19 in Norfolk, Virginia. Died on 12/12/95 (age 76). Black vocalist. Sang with **Buddy Johnson**'s band at age 19.			
3/9/59	85	4		**I Kneel At Your Throne** ...*Out Of Sight-Out Of Mind*	$15		Mercury 71415

DEBUT	PEAK	WKS	Gold	A-side (Chart Hit)...B-side	$	Sym	Label & Number
				MEGADETH ROK/LP '92			
				Hard-rock group formed in Los Angeles, California: Dave Mustaine (vocals, guitar), Marty Friedman (guitar), Dave Ellefson (bass) and Nick Menza (drums). Mustaine was an early guitarist with **Metallica**.			
10/17/92	71	15		**Symphony Of Destruction**...S:36 *(edited version) / Skin O' My Teeth (live)*	$4	▮V	Capitol 44886
				"45": Capitol 57798; B-side: "Breakpoint"			
				MEGATONS, The '62			
				Rock and roll group led by **Billy Lee Riley** (guitar/harmonica) with Jimmy Wilson (piano), Martin Willis (sax), Pat O'Neil (bass) and James Van Eaton (drums).			
1/27/62	88	4		**Shimmy, Shimmy Walk, Part 1**...*Part 2* [I]	$20		Checker 1005
				first released on Dodge 808 in 1961 ($25)			
				MEGATRONS, The '59			
				Rock and roll group of studio musicians led by John Summers.			
6/1/59	51	9		**Velvet Waters**...*The Merry Piper* [I]	$30		Acousticon 101
				Heywood Henry (clarinet solo); also released on Audicon 101 in 1959 ($30)			
				MEISNER, Randy BUB/LP '81			
				Born on 3/8/46 in Scottsbluff, Nebraska. Pop-rock singer/bassist. Member of **Poco** (1968-69), **Rick Nelson**'s Stone Canyon Band (1969-71) and the **Eagles** (1977-77).			
10/18/80	22	16		1 **Deep Inside My Heart**...*I Need You Bad*	$4		Epic 50939
				Kim Carnes (backing vocal)			
1/24/81	19	15		2 **Hearts On Fire**...*Anyway Bye Bye*	$4		Epic 50964
7/31/82	28	11		3 **Never Been In Love**...*Nothing Is Said ('Til The Artist Is Dead)*	$4		Epic 03032
				MEJA — see MARTIN, Ricky			
				MEL & KIM '87			
				Dance duo from London, England: sisters Melanie and Kim Appleby. Mel was born on 7/11/66; died of cancer on 1/19/90 (age 23). Kim was born on 8/28/61.			
2/21/87	78	7		**Showing Out (Get Fresh at the Weekend)**...*System*	$3	■	Atlantic 89329
				MEL AND TIM R&B/BUB/LP '69			
				R&B vocal duo from Holly Springs, Mississippi: cousins Mel Hardin and Tim McPherson.			
10/18/69	10	14	●	1 **Backfield In Motion**...*Do Right Baby*	$8		Bamboo 107
2/7/70	45	7		2 **Good Guys Only Win In The Movies**...*I Found That I Was Wrong*	$8		Bamboo 109
				above 2 produced by **Gene Chandler**			
7/8/72	19	20		3 **Starting All Over Again**...*It Hurts To Want It So Bad*	$6		Stax 0127
				MELANIE BUB/LP '71			
				Born Melanie Safka on 2/3/47 in Queens, New York. Folk-pop singer/songwriter. Neighborhood Records formed by Melanie and her husband/producer Peter Schekeryk. Wrote **The New Seekers**' hit "Look What They've Done To My Song Ma."			
4/25/70	6	17		1 **Lay Down (Candles In The Rain)**...*Candles In The Rain* (Melanie)	$8	■	Buddah 167
				MELANIE with The Edwin Hawkins Singers			
8/22/70	32	7		2 **Peace Will Come (According To Plan)**...*Close To It All*	$8	■	Buddah 186
				also released with the B-side "Stop! I Don't Wanna Hear It Anymore" which "Bubbled Under" (#112) on 10/17/70			
12/5/70+	52	7		3 **Ruby Tuesday**...*Merry Christmas*	$8		Buddah 202
10/30/71	❶3	18	●	4 **Brand New Key** *Some Say (I Got Devil)*	$6		Neighborhood 4201
1/22/72	35	10		5 **The Nickel Song**...*What Have They Done To My Song Ma*	$6	■	Buddah 268
				also issued on Buddah were promotional blue sleeves and red sleeves with "Melanie" printed repetitively			
1/29/72	31	9		6 **Ring The Living Bell**...*Railroad*	$6	■	Neighborhood 4202
10/21/72	86	4		7 **Together Alone**...*Center Of The Circle*	$6	■	Neighborhood 4207
				also issued was a special replacement disc jockey sleeve on 9/14/72			
2/17/73	36	10		8 **Bitter Bad**...*Do You Believe* (#115)	$6	■	Neighborhood 4210
				all of above (except #3) written by Melanie			
12/15/73	82	4		9 **Will You Love Me Tomorrow?**...*Here I Am*	$6	■	Neighborhood 4213
				MELANIE C — see SPICE GIRLS			
				MELENDEZ, Lisette BUB '91			
				Born in Harlem, New York. Female dance singer.			
2/2/91	35	19		1 **Together Forever**...A:21 / S:33 *(new school dub)*	$3	▮	Fever/RAL 73629
9/28/91	49	20		2 **A Day In My Life (Without You)**...A:35 / S:52 *(new school club)*	$3	▮	Fever/RAL 73787
12/11/93+	53	15		3 **Goody Goody**...A:40 *I Know That You Know*	$3	▮	Fever/RAL 77158
				Greg Nice (guest rapper)			
				MELLENCAMP, John Cougar ★64★ ROK/BUB/AC/LP '82			
				Born on 10/7/51 in Seymour, Indiana. Rock singer/songwriter/guitarist. Worked outside of music until 1975. Given name Johnny Cougar by **David Bowie**'s manager, Tony DeFries. First recorded for MCA in 1976. Directed and starred in the 1992 movie *Falling from Grace*; leader of the Buzzin' Cousins group that appeared in the movie. Married model Elaine Irwin on 9/5/92. Recipient of *Billboard's Century Award in 2001.*			
				1)Jack & Diane 2)Hurts So Good 3)R.O.C.K. In The U.S.A. 4)Wild Night 5)Small Town			
				JOHN COUGAR:			
10/13/79	28	14		1 **I Need A Lover**...*Welcome To Chinatown*	$6	■	Riva 202
2/16/80	87	3		2 **Small Paradise**...*Sugar Marie*	$6		Riva 203
9/27/80	27	17		3 **This Time**...*Don't Misunderstand Me*	$5		Riva 205
1/31/81	17	21		4 **Ain't Even Done With The Night**...*Make Me Feel*	$5		Riva 207
4/24/82	2[4]	28	●	5 **Hurts So Good**...AR[1] *Close Enough*	$5	■	Riva 209
7/24/82	❶4	22	●	6 **Jack & Diane** *Can You Take It*	$5		Riva 210
11/6/82+	19	18		7 **Hand To Hold On To**...*Small Paradise*	$5		Riva 211
				JOHN COUGAR MELLENCAMP:			
10/15/83	9	16		8 **Crumblin' Down**...*Golden Gates*	$5	■	Riva 214

DEBUT	PEAK	WKS	Gold	A-side (Chart Hit)...B-side	$	Sym	Label & Number
				MELLENCAMP, John Cougar — Cont'd			
12/10/83+	8	16		9 **Pink Houses** ...*Serious Business* (ROK #34)	$5	■	Riva 215
3/17/84	15	15		10 **Authority Song** ...*Pink Houses (acoustic version)*	$5	■	Riva 216
8/24/85	6	20		11 **Lonely Ol' Night** ...AR[5] S:5 / A:5 *The Kind Of Fella I Am*	$4	■	Riva 880984
11/2/85	6	18		12 **Small Town** ...A:4 / S:6 *(acoustic version)*	$4	■	Riva 884202
2/1/86	2[1]	17		13 **R.O.C.K. In The U.S.A. (A Salute To 60's Rock)**...A:2 / S:3 *Under The Boardwalk* (ROK #19)	$4	■	Riva 884455
4/26/86	21	12		14 **Rain On The Scarecrow** ...S:18 / A:26 *Pretty Ballerina*	$4	■	Riva 884635
6/28/86	28	13		15 **Rumbleseat** ...S:23 / A:36 *Cold Sweat*	$4	■	Riva 884856
				above 5 from the album *Scarecrow*			
8/15/87	9	16		16 **Paper In Fire** ...AR[5] S:9 / A:9 *Never Too Old*	$3	■	Mercury 888763
10/24/87+	8	21		17 **Cherry Bomb**...AR[1] S:6 / A:13 *Shama Lama Ding Dong*	$3	■	Mercury 888934
2/6/88	14	15		18 **Check It Out**...S:14 / A:14 *We Are The People*	$3	■	Mercury 870126
5/14/88	61	8		19 **Rooty Toot Toot** ...*Check It Out (live)*	$3	■	Mercury 870327
				above 4 from the album *The Lonesome Jubilee*			
4/29/89	15	12		20 **Pop Singer**...S:12 / A:22 *J.M.'s Question*	$3	■	Mercury 874012
7/15/89	48	8		21 **Jackie Brown**...S:38 *(acoustic version)*	$3	■	Mercury 874644
				JOHN MELLENCAMP:			
10/5/91	14	15		22 **Get A Leg Up** ...AR[3] A:58 / S:75 *Whenever We Wanted*	$3	■[V]	Mercury 867890
2/1/92	36	13		23 **Again Tonight** ...AR[2] A:40 *Get A Leg Up (live)*	$3	■[V]	Mercury 866414
9/18/93	48	14		24 **Human Wheels** ...A:67 *(edit)*	$3	■[V]	Mercury 862702
5/28/94	3	42		25 **Wild Night**...AC[8] A:3 / S:6 *Brothers (live)* (Mellencamp)	$3	■[V]	Mercury 858738
				JOHN MELLENCAMP ME'SHELL NDEGÉOCELLO			
10/29/94	41	17		26 **Dance Naked** ...A:58 / S:60 *R.O.C.K. In The U.S.A.*	$6	■[V]	Mercury 856346
				includes bonus cassette with "live" versions of "Human Wheels" and "Pink Houses"; "45": Mercury 856258			
8/31/96	14	24		27 **Key West Intermezzo (I Saw You First)** ...A:15 / S:23 *Like A Rolling Stone*	$3	■[V]	Mercury 578398
2/22/97	46	20		28 **Just Another Day** ...A:43 / S:67 *Jerry*	$3	■[V]	Mercury 578816
				"45" issued for above 2 on Mercury 574244			
9/19/98	62[A]	6		29 **Your Life Is Now** ...			album cut
				from the album *John Mellencamp* on Columbia 69602; all of above (except #25) written by Mellencamp			
				MELLO-KINGS '57			
				White teen doo-wop group from Mount Vernon, New York: Bob Scholl (lead; died on 8/27/75, age 30), Jerry Scholl and Eddie Quinn (tenors), Neil Arena (baritone) and Larry Esposito (bass). Originally known as The Mellotones; changed their name to the Mello-Kings since another Mello-Tones group recorded on Gee (see below).			
8/19/57	77	10		1 **Tonite, Tonite**...T:77 *Do Baby Do*	$60		Herald 502
				Al Caiola (guitar); written by **Billy Myles**; first pressings released as by The Mellotones ($500)			
1/23/61	95	1		2 **Tonite, Tonite**...*Do Baby Do* [R]	$40		Herald 502
				above 2 are the same version; reissue has Herald in block print, versus script print for the original			
				MELLO-TONES, The '57			
				R&B vocal group from Detroit, Michigan, featuring lead singer Jerry Carr (composed "Rosie Lee").			
5/13/57	24	7		**Rosie Lee** ...S:24 / T:60 *I'll Never Fall In Love Again*	$60		Gee 1037
				Hank Ivory (orch.); first released on Fascination 1001 in 1957 ($300)			
				MELLOW MAN ACE R&B/LP '90			
				Born Ulpiano Sergio Reyes on 4/12/67 in Cuba; raised in Southgate, California. Black Hispanic rapper. His brother Senan is a member of **Cypress Hill**.			
5/12/90	14	24	●	**Mentirosa** ...S:5 / A:28 *Welcome To My Groove*	$3	▮	Capitol 44533
				samples **Santana**'s "Evil Ways" and "No One To Depend On"			
				MELODEERS, The '60			
				White male doo-wop trio from Brooklyn, New York: Robert Rogers, Phil Seminara and Joe Toscano.			
12/19/60	71	2		**Rudolph The Red Nosed Reindeer**...*Wishing Is For Fools* [X]	$40	■	Studio 9908
				Vince Catalano (orch.); doo-wop version of the Johnny Marks classic Christmas tune			
	★541★			**MELVIN, Harold, And The Blue Notes** R&B/BUB/LP '72			
				Born on 6/25/39 in Philadelphia, Pennsylvania. Died of a stroke on 3/24/97 (age 57). R&B singer. **The Blue Notes** in 1960: Bernard Williams, Jesse Gillis, Franklin Peaker and Roosevelt Brodie. Numerous personnel changes. Hit lineup from 1972-76: **Teddy Pendergrass**, Lawrence Brown, Lloyd Parks (replaced by Jerry Cummings in 1974) and Bernard Wilson. David Ebo replaced Pendergrass in late 1976.			
				1)If You Don't Know Me By Now 2)The Love I Lost 3)Wake Up Everybody			
10/3/60	78	4		1 **My Hero** *[THE BLUE NOTES]* ...*A Good Woman*	$75		Val-ue 213
				#2 hit for Lucy Isabelle Marsh in 1910 (from Broadway's *The Chocolate Soldier* starring Ida Brooks)			
7/1/72	58	9		2 **I Miss You (Part I)** ...*(Part II)*	$5		Philadelphia I. 3516
9/30/72	3	17	●	3 **If You Don't Know Me By Now** RB[2] *Let Me Into Your World*	$5		Philadelphia I. 3520
3/3/73	63	7		4 **Yesterday I Had The Blues**...*Ebony Woman*	$5	■	Philadelphia I. 3525
9/29/73	7	18	●	5 **The Love I Lost (Part 1)**...RB[2] *(Part 2)*	$5		Philadelphia I. 3533
4/6/74	58	10		6 **Satisfaction Guaranteed (Or Take Your Love Back)**...*I'm Weak For You* (R&B #87)	$5		Philadelphia I. 3543
11/9/74	80	6		7 **Where Are All My Friends** ...*Let It Be You*	$5		Philadelphia I. 3552
3/22/75	15	17		8 **Bad Luck (Part 1)** ...*(Part 2)*	$5		Philadelphia I. 3562
7/5/75	42	10		9 **Hope That We Can Be Together Soon**...RB[1] *Be For Real* (Blue Notes)	$5		Philadelphia I. 3569
				SHARON PAIGE and Harold Melvin And The Blue Notes			
11/22/75+	12	17		10 **Wake Up Everybody (Part 1)**...RB[2] *(Part 2)*	$5		Philadelphia I. 3579
4/17/76	94	2		11 **Tell The World How I Feel About 'Cha Baby** ...*You Know How To Make Me Feel So Good*	$5		Philadelphia I. 3588
2/12/77	74	4		12 **Reaching For The World**...*Stay Together*	$5		ABC 12240

DEBUT	PEAK	WKS	Gold	A-side (Chart Hit)..........B-side	$	Sym	Label & Number
				MEMPHIS BLEEK R&B/LP **'01**			
				Born Malik Cox on 6/23/80 in Brooklyn, New York. Male rapper.			
8/8/98	61	12		1 **It's Alright** ....S:51 *The Doe*	$3	▌	Roc-A-Fella 566210
				MEMPHIS BLEEK & JAY-Z			
				samples "Once In A Lifetime" by **Talking Heads**; from the movie *Streets Is Watching* starring **Jay-Z**			
8/12/00	76	15		2 **Hey Papi** ....A:70 *(3 versions)*	$6	T	Def Jam 562862
				JAY-Z (Featuring Memphis Bleek & Amil)			
				from the movie *Nutty Professor II: The Klumps* starring **Eddie Murphy** and **Janet Jackson**			
12/16/00+	68	13		3 **Is That Your Chick** ....S:55 / A:62 *(2 versions) / All Types Of S****	$6	T	Roc-A-Fella 562865
				MEMPHIS BLEEK (feat. Jay-Z and Missy Elliott)			
2/3/01	86	14		4 **Change The Game** ....S:68 *(2 versions) / You, Me, Him And Her* (Dynasty)	$6	T	Roc-A-Fella 572761
				JAY-Z, BEANIE SIGEL and MEMPHIS BLEEK			
				MEN AT LARGE R&B/BUB/LP **'93**			
				R&B vocal duo from Cleveland, Ohio: David Tolliver and Jason Champion.			
2/20/93	31	20		**So Alone** ....S:25 / A:37 *You Me*	$3	▌	EastWest 98459
				co-written and co-produced by **Gerald Levert**			
	★543★			**MEN AT WORK** ROK/LP **'82**			
				Pop-rock group from Melbourne, Australia: **Colin James Hay** (lead singer, guitar; born on 6/29/53) (see #7 below), Ron Strykert (lead guitar; born on 8/18/57), Greg Ham (sax, keyboards; born on 9/27/53), John Rees (bass) and Jerry Speiser (drums). Won the 1982 Best New Artist Grammy Award. Speiser and Rees left in 1984.			
7/10/82	❶[1]	27		1 **Who Can It Be Now?** ....*Anyone For Tennis*	$4		Columbia 02888
11/6/82+	❶[4]	25	▲	2 **Down Under** AR[5] *Crazy*	$4		Columbia 03303
4/9/83	3	16		3 **Overkill** ....*Till The Money Runs Out*	$4	■	Columbia 03795
				a full-color promotional picture sleeve was also issued			
7/2/83	6	15		4 **It's A Mistake** ....*Shintaro*	$4	■	Columbia 03959
9/17/83	28	11		5 **Dr. Heckyll & Mr. Jive** ....*I Like To (live)*	$4	■	Columbia 04111
5/25/85	47	9		6 **Everything I Need** ....*Sail To You*	$4	■	Columbia 04929
3/7/87	99	1		7 **Hold Me** ....*Home Sweet Home*	$3	■	Columbia 06580
				COLIN JAMES HAY			
	★477★			**MENDES, Sergio, & Brasil '66** AC/R&B/BUB/LP **'68**			
				Born on 2/11/41 in Niteroi, Brazil. Pianist/bandleader. Brasil '66 consisted of **Lani Hall** (see #11 below) and Janis Hensen (vocals), Joses Soares (percussion), Bob Matthews (bass) and Jao Palma (drums). Hall married **Herb Alpert**.			
				1)Never Gonna Let You Go 2)The Look Of Love 3)The Fool On The Hill			
9/24/66	47	8		1 **Mas Que Nada** ....*The Joker* [F]	$6		A&M 807
12/24/66+	71	6		2 **Constant Rain (Chove Chuva)** ....*Slow Hot Wind*	$6		A&M 825
4/1/67	98	2		3 **For Me** ....*Gente (99 Lollipops)*	$6		A&M 836
6/3/67	82	5		4 **Night And Day** ....*Cinnamon And Clove*	$6		A&M 853
				#1 hit for Fred Astaire; all of above produced by **Herb Alpert**			
5/11/68	4	14		5 **The Look Of Love** ....*Like A Lover*	$6	■	A&M 924
				from the movie *Casino Royale* starring David Niven and Peter Sellers			
8/10/68	6	12		6 **The Fool On The Hill** ....AC[6] *So Many Stars*	$6	■	A&M 961
				written by **John Lennon** and **Paul McCartney** (from **The Beatles**' 1967 album *Magical Mystery Tour*)			
11/16/68	16	9		7 **Scarborough Fair** ....*Canto Triste*	$6	■	A&M 986
5/3/69	62	6		8 **Pretty World** ....*Festa*	$6	■	A&M 1049
6/28/69	66	5		9 **(Sittin' On) The Dock Of The Bay** ....*Song Of No Regrets*	$6	■	A&M 1073
11/29/69	95	2		10 **Wichita Lineman** ....*Ye-Me-Le*	$6		A&M 1132
3/21/81	88	3		11 **Where's Your Angel?** ....*Only You*	$4		A&M 2305
				LANI HALL			
				SERGIO MENDES:			
4/16/83	4	23		12 **Never Gonna Let You Go** AC[4] *Carnaval*	$4		A&M 2540
				Joe Pizzulo and Leza Miller (**Lise Miller**) (vocals)			
8/13/83	52	8		13 **Rainbow's End** ....*Carnaval*	$4		A&M 2563
				Dan Sembello (vocal)			
4/7/84	58	7		14 **Olympia** ....*Carnaval*	$4	■	A&M 2623
5/26/84	29	19		15 **Alibis** ....*Confetti*	$4		A&M 2639
				Joe Pizzulo (vocal, above 2)			
				MEN OF VIZION R&B/LP **'96**			
				R&B vocal group from Brooklyn, New York: George Spencer, Corley Randolph, Prathan "Spanky" Williams, Brian Deramus and Desmond Greggs.			
6/1/96	67	11		1 **House Keeper** ....S:42 *(same version)*	$3	▌	MJJ Music 78274
1/23/99	44[S]	9		2 **Do You Feel Me? (...Freak You)** ....*All Night Long*	$4	★	MJJ Music 78862
				Mr. Cheeks (rap)			
				MENUDO BUB/R&B/LP **'85**			
				Teen vocal group from Puerto Rico. The superstar group of Latin America. Many personnel changes due to a rule that members must retire at age 16. **Ricky Martin** was a member from 1984-89.			
5/11/85	62	11		**Hold Me** ....*When I Dance With You*	$3	■	RCA 14087
				MEN WITHOUT HATS LP **'83**			
				Techno-rock/dance group from Montreal, Quebec, Canada: brothers Ivan (vocals, songwriter), Stefan (guitar) and Colin (keyboards) Dodoschuk, with Allan McCarthy (drums).			
6/25/83	3	24		1 **The Safety Dance** ....*Living In China*	$4	■	Backstreet 52232
11/12/83	84	3		2 **I Like** ....*Things In My Life*	$4	■	MCA 52293
10/31/87+	20	21		3 **Pop Goes The World** ....S:16 / A:25 *The End Of The World*	$4	■	Mercury 888859
				ME PHI ME R&B **'92**			
				Born Laron Wilburn in Flint, Michigan. Male rapper. Me Phi Me is Greek for Fraternity Of One.			
8/29/92	83	4		**Sad New Day** ....A:70 *(remix) / ...and I Believe (the CREDO)*	$4	▌	RCA 62307

DEBUT	PEAK	WKS	Gold	A-side (Chart Hit)..........B-side	$	Sym	Label & Number
				MERCEDES LP **'97**			
				Born Raquel Miller in 1978 in Detroit, Michigan. Female rapper.			
9/6/97	**25**	20	●	1 **I Miss My Homies** ....S:15 *(2 versions) / Here We Go* (w/**Mystikal** & Fiend)	$3	▮	No Limit 53290
				MASTER P Featuring Pimp C, The Shocker, Mo B. Dick, O'Dell, Sons of Funk and Mercedes			
7/31/99	**96**	4		2 **It's Your Thing**..........S:25 *(2 versions) / N's Ain't S**t*	$4	★	No Limit 53565
				MERCEDES Featuring Master P			
				clean version available on No Limit 53566			
				MERCHANT, Natalie ROK/LP **'95**			
				Born on 10/26/63 in Jamestown, New York. Alternative-rock singer/songwriter. Lead singer of **10,000 Maniacs** from 1981-93.			
8/5/95	**10**	31		1 **Carnival** ....A:6 / S:54 *I May Know The Word*	$3	▮	Elektra 64413
12/9/95+	**20**	38		2 **Wonder**..........A:7 / S:62 *Baby I Love You*	$3	▮	Elektra 64376
6/15/96	**23**	20		3 **Jealousy**..........A:12 *Sympathy For The Devil (live)*	$3	▮	Elektra 64301
5/9/98	**18^A**	24		4 **Kind & Generous**			album cut
				from the album *Ophelia* on Elektra 62196			
				MERCURY, Freddie — see QUEEN			
				MERCY LP **'69**			
				Adult Contemporary group from Florida: James Marvell, Ronnie Caudill, Roger Fuentes, Buddy Good, Debbie Lewis and Brenda McNish.			
4/12/69	**2^2**	13	●	1 **Love (Can Make You Happy)** ....*Fire Ball*	$8		Sundi 6811
6/28/69	**79**	5		2 **Forever** ....*The Mornings Come*	$6		Warner 7297
				MERRY-GO-ROUND, The LP **'67**			
				Pop-rock group from Los Angeles, California: **Emitt Rhodes** (vocals), Gary Kato (guitar), Bill Rinehart (bass; **The Leaves**) and Joel Larson (drums; **The Grass Roots**).			
4/29/67	**63**	4		1 **Live** ....*Time Will Show The Wiser*	$10		A&M 834
9/9/67	**94**	3		2 **You're A Very Lovely Woman**..........*Where Have You Been All My Life*	$10		A&M 863
				recorded by **Linda Ronstadt** in 1971 as "She's A Very Lovely Woman"			
				MESA **'77**			
				Pop group from Los Angeles, California: Ed Rekers (vocals, guitar), Jeff Des Enfants (percussion), Roger Paglia (bass) and Carmine Notaro (drums).			
2/26/77	**55**	9		**Sailing Ships** ....*City Lights*	$6		Ariola America 7654
				MESSENGERS BUB **'71**			
				Rock group from Milwaukee, Wisconsin: Jeff Taylor (vocals), Pete Barans (guitar), Michael Morgan (organ), Greg Jeresek (bass) and Augie Jurishica (drums).			
9/11/71	**62**	9		**That's The Way A Woman Is** ....*In The Jungle*	$8		Rare Earth 5032
				MESSINA, Jim — see LOGGINS & MESSINA			
				MESSINA, Jo Dee C&W/BUB/LP **'99**			
				Born on 8/25/70 in Framingham, Massachusetts; raised in Holliston, Massachusetts. Country singer.			
3/14/98	**43**	20	●	1 **Bye Bye** / CW^2 S:25			
8/15/98	**43**	4		2 **I'm Alright**..........CW^3	$4	▮V	Curb 73034
12/12/98+	**34**	20		3 **Stand Beside Me** ....CW^3 A:20			album cut
6/5/99	**28**	20		4 **Lesson In Leavin'** A:15			album cut
1/29/00	**53**	13		5 **Because You Love Me** A:47			album cut
				all of above from the album *I'm Alright* on Curb 77904			
6/24/00	**25**	20		6 **That's The Way** CW^4 S:21 / A:25 *Even God Must Get The Blues*	$4	★	Curb 73106
12/2/00+	**42**	20		7 **Burn**..........A:39			album cut
6/16/01	**46**	15		8 **Downtime** A:45			album cut
12/8/01+	**36**	20		9 **Bring On The Rain** ....CW^1 A:34			album cut
				JO DEE MESSINA with Tim McGraw			
				above 4 from the album *Burn* on Curb 77977; all of above co-produced by **Tim McGraw**			
	★504★			**METALLICA** ROK/BUB/LP **'96**			
				Hard-rock group formed in Los Angeles: James Hetfield (vocals, guitar; born on 8/3/63), Kirk Hammett (guitar; born on 11/18/62), Jason Newsted (bass; born on 3/4/63) and Lars Ulrich (drums; born on 12/26/63). Original guitarist Dave Mustaine left in 1982 to form **Megadeth**. Original bassist Cliff Burton was killed in a bus crash on 9/27/86 (age 24). Newsted left the group in January 2001; replaced by Rob Trujillo.			
				1)Until It Sleeps 2)Enter Sandman 3)The Memory Remains			
2/18/89	**35**	15	●	1 **One** ....S:18 *The Prince*	$5	■	Elektra 69329
8/24/91	**16**	20	●	2 **Enter Sandman**..........S:3 *Stone Cold Crazy*	$4	▮	Elektra 64857
12/7/91+	**35**	17		3 **The Unforgiven** ....S:16 *Killing Time*	$4	▮	Elektra 64814
				also see #11 below			
3/28/92	**34**	15		4 **Nothing Else Matters** ....S:18 *Enter Sandman (live)*	$4	▮	Elektra 64770
7/18/92	**82**	7		5 **Wherever I May Roam**..........S:49 *Fade To Black (live)*	$4	▮	Elektra 64741
10/31/92	**98**	1		6 **Sad But True**..........S:56 *So What*	$4	▮	Elektra 64696
				above 5 from the album *Metallica*			
6/8/96	**10**	20	●	7 **Until It Sleeps** AR^8 S:3 *Overkill*	$3	▮	Elektra 64276
11/9/96+	**60**	18		8 **Hero Of The Day**..........AR^3 S:49 *Kill/Ride Medley (live)*	$3	▮	Elektra 64248
3/1/97	**90**	8		9 **King Nothing** ....*Ain't My Bitch (live)*	$3	▮	Elektra 64197
11/29/97	**28**	19		10 **The Memory Remains** ....S:16 *For Whom The Bell Tolls*	$3	▮	Elektra 64126
				Marianne Faithfull (guest vocal)			
4/4/98	**59**	15		11 **The Unforgiven II**..........S:44 *The Thing That Should Not Be (Live)*	$3	▮	Elektra 64114
				new version of #3 above			
2/12/00	**74**	10		12 **No Leaf Clover** ....AR^7 A:64 [L]			album cut
				METALLICA with Michael Kamen conducting The San Francisco Symphony Orchestra			
				from the album *S&M* on Elektra 62504			
5/13/00	**76**	20		13 **I Disappear** ....AR^7 A:72			album cut
				from the movie *Mission: Impossible 2* starring Tom Cruise (soundtrack on Hollywood 62244)			

DEBUT	PEAK	WKS	Gold	A-side (Chart Hit)..........B-side	$	Sym	Label & Number

METERS, The R&B/LP **'69**

R&B instrumental group formed in New Orleans, Louisiana: Arthur Neville (keyboards; brother of **Aaron Neville**), Leo Nocentelli (guitar), George Porter (bass) and Joseph Modeliste (drums). Group disbanded in 1977, when Art, Aaron, and brothers Charles and Cyril formed The Neville Brothers.

DEBUT	PEAK	WKS	Gold	A-side (Chart Hit)..........B-side	$	Sym	Label & Number
2/8/69	34	8		1 **Sophisticated Cissy** .... *Sehorns Farms* [I]	$10		Josie 1001
4/12/69	23	11		2 **Cissy Strut** *Here Comes The Meter Man* [I]	$10		Josie 1005
7/26/69	61	6		3 **Ease Back** .... *Ann* [I]	$10		Josie 1008
12/6/69+	56	10		4 **Look-Ka Py Py** .... *This Is My Last Affair* [I]	$10		Josie 1015
4/4/70	50	8		5 **Chicken Strut** .... *Hey! Last Minute* [I]	$10		Josie 1018
7/4/70	89	4		6 **Hand Clapping Song** .... *Joog*	$10		Josie 1021
10/1/77	78	2		7 **Be My Lady** .... *No More Okey Doke*	$5		Warner 8434

METHENY, Pat, Group — see BOWIE, David

METHOD MAN ★526★ R&B/BUB/LP **'95**

Born Clifford Smith on 4/1/71 in Staten Island, New York. Male rapper. Member of **Wu-Tang Clan**. Also known as Johnny Blaze or Meth-Tical or The Ticalion Stallion. Starred in the 2001 movie *How High*. Also see **Raekwon**'s "Ice Cream."

1)I'll Be There For You/You're All I Need To Get By 2)How High 3)Bring The Pain

DEBUT	PEAK	WKS	Gold	A-side (Chart Hit)..........B-side	$	Sym	Label & Number
11/12/94	45	20		1 **Bring The Pain** .... S:28 / A:73 *(radio edit)*	$4	▮	Def Jam 853964
2/25/95	54S	4		2 **No Hook** .... BUB:103 *(2 remixes) / (So U Wanna Be) Hardcore* **SHAQUILLE O'NEAL (featuring Prince Rakeem The RZA and Method Man)**	$4	▮	Jive 42284
3/18/95	98	1		3 **Release Yo' Delf** .... *(4 versions) / Bring The Pain (remix)* Blue Raspberry (female backing vocals)	$6	T	Def Jam 854185
5/6/95	3	20	▲	4 **I'll Be There For You/You're All I Need To Get By** RB[3] S:❶[1] / A:33 *(**Puff Daddy** mix)* **METHOD MAN featuring Mary J. Blige** medley of 2 songs written by **Ashford & Simpson**	$3	▮	Def Jam 851878
7/22/95	flip	3		5 **The What** .... S:flip *One More Chance/Stay With Me* (Notorious B.I.G. - #2) **THE NOTORIOUS B.I.G. and METHOD MAN**	$3	▮	Bad Boy 79031
8/26/95	13	15	●	6 **How High** .... S:7 / A:64 *(remix)* **REDMAN/METHOD MAN** samples "I Am Woman" by **The Cover Girls**; from the rap concert movie *The Show!*	$3	▮	Def Jam 579924
10/28/95	79	10		7 **Wings Of The Morning** .... S:57 *(album version)* **CAPLETON (Featuring Method Man)** contains an interpolation of **Otis Redding**'s "Hard To Handle"	$6	▮	African Star 577198
11/11/95	56	11		8 **The Riddler** .... S:15 *(Riddler Hide-Out remix)* from the movie *Batman Forever* starring Val Kilmer	$4	▮	Atlantic 87100
4/6/96	67	13		9 **Shadowboxin'** .... S:56 *(instrumental) / 4th Chamber* **GENIUS/GZA Featuring Method Man**	$4	▮	Geffen 19396
8/17/96	60	12		10 **Wu Wear: The Garment Renaissance** .... S:34 *Get Down For Mine* (Real Live) **RZA featuring METHOD MAN & CAPPADONNA** from the movie *High School High* starring Jon Lovitz	$4	▮	Big Beat 98045
12/27/97	75	12		11 **4, 3, 2, 1** .... *(5 versions)* **LL COOL J Featuring Method Man, Redman, DMX, Canibus and Master P** samples "Fight For Your Right" by **Beastie Boys**, "Rock The Bells" by **LL Cool J** and "Shut 'Em Down" by **Public Enemy**	$6	T	Def Jam 568321
2/27/99	98	2		12 **Break Ups 2 Make Ups** .... *(2 versions) / Suspect Chin Music* (w/Streetlife) **METHOD MAN featuring D'Angelo**	$6	T	Def Jam 563405
12/4/99+	73	11		13 **n 2 gether now** .... A:63 *(2 versions)* **LIMP BIZKIT (featuring Method Man)**	$6	T	Flip/Interscope 497183
12/11/99+	70	5		14 **Left & Right** .... S:20 *(w/o rap version)* **D'ANGELO featuring Method Man and Redman** "45": Virgin 58836; B-side: "Untitled (How Does It Feel)" (**D'Angelo** - #25)	$4	★V	Virgin 38678
12/15/01+	62	17		15 **Round and Round Remix** .... S:2 *(original version) / (instrumental)* **JONELL (Featuring Method Man)**	$4	★	Def Soul 588852
12/22/01+	72	12		16 **Part II** .... S:35 / A:75 *(3 versions)* **METHOD MAN AND REDMAN** samples "You're Makin' Me High" by **Toni Braxton**; above 2 from the movie *How High* starring Method Man and **Redman**	$6	T	Def Jam 588891

METROS, The **'67**

Black male vocal group: James Buckman, Gordon Dunn, Arthur Mitchell, Robert Suttles and Paul Williams.

DEBUT	PEAK	WKS	Gold	A-side (Chart Hit)..........B-side	$	Sym	Label & Number
1/14/67	88	4		**Sweetest One** .... *Time Changes Things*	$15		RCA Victor 8994

MFSB R&B/LP **'74**

Group of studio musicians based at Philadelphia Sigma Sound Studios owned by writer/producers Kenny Gamble and Leon Huff for their own label, Philadelphia International. Recorded earlier as **The Music Makers** (see #1 below), **The James Boys** (see #2 below) and Family. Name stands for "Mother, Father, Sister, Brother." Also see **The Atlanta Disco Band**.

DEBUT	PEAK	WKS	Gold	A-side (Chart Hit)..........B-side	$	Sym	Label & Number
12/30/67+	78	7		1 **United (Part 1)** .... *(Part 2)* [I] **THE MUSIC MAKERS** instrumental version of **The Intruders**' "(We'll Be) United"	$10		Gamble 210
8/31/68	82	4		2 **The Mule** .... *The Horse* (R&B #49) [I] **THE JAMES BOYS**	$10		Phil-L.A. of Soul 316
3/2/74	❶[2]	18	●	3 **TSOP (The Sound Of Philadelphia)** RB[1] / AC[2] *Something For Nothing* [I] theme from the TV show *Soul Train*	$6		Philadelphia I. 3540
7/6/74	85	4		4 **Love Is The Message** .... *My One And Only Love* **MFSB featuring The Three Degrees** (above 2)	$6		Philadelphia I. 3547
6/21/75	42	7		5 **Sexy** .... *Human Machine* [I]	$5		Philadelphia I. 3567
11/29/75	91	6		6 **The Zip** .... *My Mood* [I]	$5		Philadelphia I. 3578

M:G BUB **'98**

Born Maribel Gonzalez in San Francisco, California. Female dance singer.

DEBUT	PEAK	WKS	Gold	A-side (Chart Hit)..........B-side	$	Sym	Label & Number
5/2/98	91	5		**Sweet Honesty** .... *(remix)*	$5	▮	Classified 7249

MIAMI SOUND MACHINE — see ESTEFAN, Gloria

DEBUT	PEAK	WKS	Gold	A-side (Chart Hit)...B-side	$	Sym	Label & Number

MIA X

R&B/LP **'98**

Born Mia Young in New Orleans, Louisiana; moved to Queens, New York. Female rapper. Member of **Tru**.

DEBUT	PEAK	WKS	Gold	A-side (Chart Hit)...B-side	$	Sym	Label & Number
1/31/98	16	27	▲	1 **Make Em' Say Uhh!** ..S:9 *(2 versions) / Weed And Hennesey* (w/C-Murder & **Silkk The Shocker**) **MASTER P Featuring Fiend, Silkk (The Shocker), Mia X and Mystikal** clean version available on No Limit 53303	$3	▮	No Limit 53302
10/31/98	41	7		2 **Whatcha Wanna Do?** ....S:20 *(instrumental) / I Can't Take The Heat* (w/**Snoop Dogg**) **MIA X Featuring Charlie Wilson** clean version available on No Limit 53460; above 2 produced by **Master P**	$3	▮	No Limit 53459

MICHAEL, George/Wham! ★39★

R&B/BUB/LP **'88**

Born Georgios Kyriacos Panayiotou on 6/25/63 in Bushey, England. **Wham!**, formed in early 1980s, centered around Michael's vocals and songwriting, and included **Andrew Ridgeley** (born on 1/26/63 in Bushey, England) (see #18 below) on guitar. Their association ended in 1986. Ridgeley pursued race car driving, then solo career in 1990.

1)Faith 2)Careless Whisper 3)Wake Me Up Before You Go-Go 4)One More Try 5)I Knew You Were Waiting (For Me)

DEBUT	PEAK	WKS	Gold	A-side (Chart Hit)...B-side	$	Sym	Label & Number
				WHAM!:			
8/20/83	60	9		1 **Bad Boys** *[WHAM! U.K.]*...*(instrumental)* early pressings shown only as WHAM!	$5		Columbia 03932
9/8/84	1[3]	24	▲	2 **Wake Me Up Before You Go-Go** ...S:1[3] / A:1[3] *(instrumental)*	$3	■	Columbia 04552
12/22/84+	1[3]	21	▲	3 **Careless Whisper** ...AC[5] S:1[3] / A:1[3] *(instrumental)* **WHAM! Featuring George Michael** originally released as a solo single by George Michael; issued with 2 different picture sleeves: full color and black & white	$3	■	Columbia 04691
3/23/85	1[2]	20	●	4 **Everything She Wants**...S:1[2] / A:1[2] *Like A Baby*	$3	■	Columbia 04840
7/27/85	3	18		5 **Freedom** ...S:3 / A:5 *Heartbeat* also see #20 below; above 4 from the album *Make It Big*	$3	■	Columbia 05409
11/30/85+	3	18		6 **I'm Your Man** ...S:3 / A:3 *Do It Right* [I] also see the '96 version on the B-side of #28 below	$3	■	Columbia 05721
4/26/86	7	16		7 **A Different Corner** *[GEORGE MICHAEL]* ...S:5 / A:8 *(instrumental)*	$3	■	Columbia 05888
7/5/86	10	13		8 **The Edge Of Heaven** ...S:8 / A:10 *Blue (live in China)*	$3	■	Columbia 06182
10/11/86	50	8		9 **Where Did Your Heart Go?**...*Wham! Rap '86* above 4 and #29 below from the album *Music From The Edge Of Heaven*	$3	■	Columbia 06294
				GEORGE MICHAEL:			
2/21/87	1[2]	17		10 **I Knew You Were Waiting (For Me)** ...S:1[2] / A:1[1] *(instrumental)* **ARETHA FRANKLIN AND GEORGE MICHAEL**	$3	■	Arista 9559
6/6/87	2[1]	20	▲	11 **I Want Your Sex** ...S:1[2] / A:5 *(Rhythm 2 Brass In Love version)* from the movie *Beverly Hills Cop II* starring **Eddie Murphy**	$3	■	Columbia 07164
10/24/87	1[4]	20	●	12 **Faith** A:1[5] / S:1[1] *Hand To Mouth*	$3	■	Columbia 07623
1/16/88	1[2]	17		13 **Father Figure**...A:1[4] / S:1[1] *(instrumental)* also see **PM Dawn**'s "Looking Through Patient Eyes"	$3	■	Columbia 07682
4/16/88	1[3]	18	●	14 **One More Try**...RB[1] / AC[3] A:1[4] / S:1[3] *Look At Your Hands* also see the live gospel version on the B-side of #27 below	$3	■	Columbia 07773
7/9/88	1[2]	16		15 **Monkey** ...S:1[2] / A:1[2] *(acappella version)*	$3	■	Columbia 07941
10/8/88	5	15		16 **Kissing A Fool** ...AC[1] S:3 / A:6 *(instrumental)* above 6 from the album *Faith*	$3	■	Columbia 08050
2/25/89	5	16		17 **Heaven Help Me** ...S:4 / A:6 *It's A Party* **DEON ESTUS (with George Michael)**	$3	■	Mika 871538
5/12/90	77	6		18 **Shake** ...*Hangin'* **ANDREW RIDGELEY**	$3	▮	Columbia 73337
9/1/90	1[1]	14		19 **Praying For Time** ...A:1[2] / S:3 *If You Were My Woman*	$3	▮V	Columbia 73512
10/27/90	8	16	●	20 **Freedom** ...S:7 / A:9 *Fantasy* different tune from #5 above; also see "Voice Of Freedom" by **Freedom Williams**	$3	▮V	Columbia 73559
1/19/91	27	10		21 **Waiting For That Day** / A:24 / S:28 includes the title line from "You Can't Always Get What You Want" by **The Rolling Stones**			
2/2/91	46	9		22 **Mother's Pride** ...A:38 above 4 from the album *Listen Without Prejudice*	$3	▮V	Columbia 73663
12/7/91+	1[1]	20	●	23 **Don't Let The Sun Go Down On Me** ....AC[2] S:4 / A:4 *I Believe (When I Fall In Love It Will Be Forever)* (Michael) [L] **GEORGE MICHAEL/ELTON JOHN** recorded in London, March 1991	$3	▮V	Columbia 74086
6/13/92	10	20	●	24 **Too Funky** ...A:6 / S:17 *Crazyman Dance* from the AIDS benefit album *Red, Hot & Dance*	$3	▮V	Columbia 74353
5/15/93	30	9		25 **Somebody To Love** ...A:25 / S:72 *Love Of My Life* (Queen) [L] **GEORGE MICHAEL And QUEEN**	$3	▮	Hollywood 64647
7/3/93	69	7		26 **Killer/Papa Was A Rollin' Stone** ....A:67 *(**P.M. Dawn** remix - extended version)* [L] above 2 recorded at Wembley Stadium for the **Freddie Mercury** Tribute Concert	$3	▮	Hollywood 64626
2/24/96	7	14	●	27 **Jesus To A Child** ...S:3 / A:40 *One More Try (live gospel version)*	$3	▮V	DreamWorks 59000
5/11/96	8	19	●	28 **Fastlove** ...S:7 / A:18 *I'm Your Man '96* contains an interpolation of "Forget Me Nots" by **Patrice Rushen**	$3	▮V	DreamWorks 59001
1/3/98-	58[A]	2		29 **Last Christmas** *[WHAM!]* ... [X] recorded in 1985; from the Australian import album *Christmas Wishes* on Dino 147 (also see "Do They Know It's Christmas?" by **Band Aid**); all of above (except #9, 10, 18, 23, 25 & 26) written by Michael			album cut

MICHAELS, Lee

BUB/LP **'71**

Born on 11/24/45 in Los Angeles, California. Rock singer/songwriter/keyboardist.

DEBUT	PEAK	WKS	Gold	A-side (Chart Hit)...B-side	$	Sym	Label & Number
7/31/71	6	17		1 **Do You Know What I Mean** ...*Keep The Circle Turning*	$6	■	A&M 1262
11/20/71	39	9		2 **Can I Get A Witness** ...*You Are What You Do*	$6	■	A&M 1303

DEBUT	PEAK	WKS	Gold	A-side (Chart Hit)...B-side	$	Sym	Label & Number
				MICHEL, Pras R&B/LP **'98**			
				Born Prakazrel Michael on 10/19/72 in Harlem, New York. Member of **The Fugees**. Also see **Queen Latifah**'s "Paper."			
9/20/97	35	14		1 **Avenues**...S:24 *Back In You Again* (**Rick James** w/**Lil Cease**)	$4	▮	Arista 13411
				REFUGEE CAMP ALL-STARS Featuring Pras (With Ky-Mani)			
				rap version of **Eddy Grant**'s "Electric Avenue"; from the movie *Money Talks* starring Chris Tucker			
12/27/97+	59	13		2 **Roxanne '97 - Puff Daddy Remix**...S:34 *(2 versions) / Voices Inside My Head*	$6	▮*	A&M 2449
				STING & THE POLICE Featuring Pras			
				Full Force (backing vocals); samples "Roxanne, Roxanne" by **UTFO** and "Kools Back Again" by **Kool & The Gang**			
6/27/98	15	21		3 **Ghetto Supastar (That Is What You Are)**...A:11 *(3 versions)*	$6	T	Interscope 95021
				PRAS MICHEL featuring OL' DIRTY BASTARD & introducing MÝA			
				samples "Get Up, Get Into It, Get Involved" by **James Brown** and contains an interpolation of "Islands In The Stream"; from the movie *Bulworth* starring Warren Beatty			
7/14/01	85	6		4 **Miss California**...S:22 *(rap remix)*	$5	★	Rat Pack 67157
				DANTE THOMAS Featuring Pras			
				MICHELE, Yvette **'97**			
				Born in Brooklyn, New York. Female singer/rapper.			
2/3/96	60	10		1 **EveryDay & EveryNight**...S:55 / A:71 *(2 versions)*	$3	▮	Loud/RCA 64489
2/22/97	44	14		2 **I'm Not Feeling You**...S:31 *(radio version)*	$3	▮	Loud/RCA 64790
				samples "Was It Something I Said" by **Sylvester**			
8/16/97	81	3		3 **Far From Yours**...*My World*	$4	▮	Payday 850916
				O.C. featuring Yvette Michelle			
				samples "Tomorrow" by **The Brothers Johnson** and "(Beat) For The Listeners" by **Eric B. & Rakim**			
11/15/97	84	7		4 **DJ Keep Playin' (Get Your Music On)**...*(instrumental) / The First Time*	$3	▮	Loud/RCA 64985
				samples "Super Sporm" by Captain Sky			
				MICHEL'LE R&B/LP **'90**			
				Born Michel'le (pronounced: mee-shell-LAY) Toussant in Los Angeles, California. R&B-dance singer. Former vocalist with **The World Class Wreckin Cru**.			
11/18/89+	7	29	●	1 **No More Lies**...S:4 / A:14 *Never Been In Love*	$3	▮V	Ruthless 99149
4/14/90	29	16		2 **Nicety**...S:21 / A:35 *Special Thanks*	$3	▮V	Ruthless 98980
1/12/91	31	22		3 **Something In My Heart**...S:23 / A:61 *Just Not Ready To Love You*	$3	▮V	Ruthless 98885
				"45" issued for #1 & 3 on Atlantic Oldies Series 94947; above 3 produced by **Dr. Dre** and **Eazy-E**			
1/6/96	45	16		4 **Let's Play House**...S:18 *(instrumental)*	$3	▮	Death Row 53230
				THA DOGG POUND Featuring Michel'le			
				MICKEY and SYLVIA **'57**			
				R&B-rock and roll duo: McHouston "Mickey" Baker and Sylvia Vanderpool. Baker (born on 10/15/25 in Louisville, Kentucky) was a prolific session guitarist. Sylvia (born on 5/29/36 in Queens, New York) began solo career in 1973, recorded as **Sylvia**. Their son Joey was leader of **West Street Mob**.			
1/5/57	11	18		1 **Love Is Strange** RB[2] S:11 / A:11 / T:13 / J:17 *I'm Going Home*	$40		Groove 0175
				also released on Vik 0252 in 1957 ($30)			
4/20/57	47	5		2 **There Oughta Be A Law** / T:47			
7/1/57	85	2		3 **Dearest**...T:85	$25		Vik 0267
				co-written by **Bo Diddley**			
6/16/58	57	5		4 **Bewildered**...T:57 *Rock And Stroll Room*	$25		Vik 0324
				#1 R&B hit for both Amos Milburn and the Red Miller Trio in 1948			
12/31/60+	46	9		5 **What Would I Do** /			
				first recorded as "That's What I'll Do" by **Shirley & Lee** in 1955 on Aladdin 3313 ($40)			
12/31/60	100	1		6 **This Is My Story**...	$20		RCA Victor 7811
				#8 R&B hit for **Gene & Eunice** in 1955			
8/21/61	52	6		7 **Baby You're So Fine** /			
				song "Bubbled Under" in 1960 by Joe & Ann as "Gee Baby"			
8/7/61	97	1		8 **Lovedrops**...	$20		Willow 23000
				MIDI MAXI & EFTI **'92**			
				Female pop trio of 16-year-olds (in 1992) formed in Sweden: twin sisters Midi and Maxi (from Ethiopia) with Efti (from the warring Ethiopian province of Eritrea).			
5/30/92	98	3		**Bad Bad Boys**...A:66 *Culture Of Youth*	$4	▮	Columbia 74215
	★268★			**MIDLER, Bette** AC/LP **'80**			
				Born on 12/1/45 in Paterson, New Jersey; raised in Honolulu, Hawaii. Adult Contemporary singer/actress. In the Broadway show *Fiddler On The Roof* for three years. Won the 1973 Best New Artist Grammy Award. **Barry Manilow** was her arranger/accompanist in early years. Nominated for an Oscar for her performance in *The Rose* (1979). Also in movies *Down And Out In Beverly Hills*, *Ruthless People*, *Beaches*, *For The Boys* and others. Married commodities trader/performance artist Martin von Haselberg on 12/14/84.			
				1)Wind Beneath My Wings 2)From A Distance 3)The Rose			
12/23/72+	17	16		1 **Do You Want To Dance?**...*Superstar*	$5		Atlantic 2928
5/12/73	8	16		2 **Boogie Woogie Bugle Boy**...AC[2] *Delta Dawn*	$5		Atlantic 2964
				#15 hit for The Andrews Sisters in 1941 (introduced in the movie *Buck Privates* starring Abbott & Costello)			
9/29/73	40	10		3 **Friends** /			
11/24/73		2		4 **Chapel Of Love**...	$5		Atlantic 2980
				above 4 from the album *The Divine Miss M*			
1/26/74	51	7		5 **In The Mood**...*Drinking Again*	$5		Atlantic 3004
				#1 hit for Glenn Miller in 1940; above 4 produced by **Barry Manilow**			
4/9/77	42	14		6 **You're Movin' Out Today**...*Let Me Just Follow Behind*	$4		Atlantic 3379
1/14/78	57	10		7 **Storybook Children (Daybreak)**...*Empty Bed Blues*	$4		Atlantic 3431
6/2/79	40	9		8 **Married Men**...*Bang, You're Dead*	$4		Atlantic 3582
1/19/80	35	10		9 **When A Man Loves A Woman**...*Love Me With A Feeling* [L]	$4		Atlantic 3643
3/22/80	3	25	●	10 **The Rose**...AC[5] *Stay With Me*	$4	■	Atlantic 3656
				above 2 from the movie *The Rose* starring Midler			
11/22/80+	39	13		11 **My Mother's Eyes**...*Chapel Of Love (live)* [L]	$4		Atlantic 3771
				from the Bette Midler concert movie *Divine Madness*; #8 hit for George Jessel in 1929			
9/3/83	77	4		12 **All I Need To Know**...*My Eye On You*	$3	■	Atlantic 89789
				#2 hit in 1989 for **Linda Ronstadt & Aaron Neville** as "Don't Know Much"			

DEBUT	PEAK	WKS	Gold	A-side (Chart Hit)	B-side	$	Sym	Label & Number
				MIDLER, Bette — Cont'd				
10/22/83	78	4		13 **Favorite Waste Of Time**	*My Eye On You*	$3		Atlantic 89761
				written by **Marshall Crenshaw**				
2/11/84	71	6		14 **Beast Of Burden**	*Come Back Jimmy Dean*	$3		Atlantic 89712
3/4/89	❶^{1}	29	▲	15 **Wind Beneath My Wings** S:❶^{1} / A:2	*Oh Industry*	$3	■	Atlantic 88972
				from the movie *Beaches* starring Midler; song also known as "Hero"; 1989 Grammy winner: Record of the Year				
10/6/90	2^{1}	26	▲	16 **From A Distance** AC^{6} S:❶^{1} / A:3	*One More Round*	$3	▮^{V}	Atlantic 87820
1/26/91	62	7		17 **Night And Day**	*The Girl Is On To You*	$3	▮^{V}	Atlantic 87825
12/21/91+	78	6		18 **Every Road Leads Back To You**	*I Remember You/Dixie's Dream*	$3	▮^{V}	Atlantic 87572
				from the movie *For The Boys* starring Midler				
2/13/99	60^{S}	2		19 **I'm Beautiful**	*(7 versions)*	$8	★*	Warner 44586
				MIDNIGHTERS, The — see BALLARD, Hank				
				MIDNIGHT OIL ROK/BUB/LP **'88**				
				Rock group formed in Sydney, Australia: Peter Garrett (vocals), Martin Rotsey (guitar), James Moginie (keyboards), Dwayne Hillman (bass) and Rob Hirst (drums).				
4/2/88	17	22		1 **Beds Are Burning** S:11 / A:22	*Bullroarer*	$3		Columbia 07433
8/6/88	53	10		2 **The Dead Heart**	*Kosciusko*	$3	■	Columbia 07964
				written for the movie *Uluru - An Anangu Story*				
2/17/90	47	10		3 **Blue Sky Mine** AR^{1} / MR^{1} S:39	*Wedding Cake Island*	$3	▮	Columbia 73250
				MIDNIGHT STAR R&B/BUB/LP **'85**				
				R&B-dance group from Louisville, Kentucky: Belinda Lipscomb (vocals), brothers Reggie and Vince Calloway (horns), Jeff Cooper (guitar), Ken Gant (keyboards), Melvin Gentry (bass) and Bill Simmons (drums). The Calloway brothers later formed **Calloway** (see #8 & 9 below).				
8/20/83	66	8		1 **Freak-A-Zoid**	*Move Me*	$4		Solar 69828
11/26/83+	61	11		2 **Wet My Whistle**	*You Can't Stop Me*	$4		Solar 69790
3/3/84	81	8		3 **No Parking (On The Dance Floor)**	*Feels So Good*	$4		Solar 69753
12/1/84+	18	17		4 **Operator** RB^{5} A:17 / S:18	*Playmates*	$3		Solar 69684
3/2/85	80	7		5 **Scientific Love**	*Make Time (To Fall In Love)*	$3		Solar 69659
6/14/86	69	7		6 **Headlines**	*(instrumental)*	$3	■	Solar 69547
9/20/86	42	14		7 **Midas Touch** S:40	*Searching For Love*	$3		Solar 69525
				CALLOWAY:				
2/10/90	2^{1}	23	●	8 **I Wanna Be Rich** S:2 / A:2	*(instrumental)*	$3	▮^{V}	Solar 74005
7/21/90	63	7		9 **All The Way**	*(one way dub)*	$3	▮^{V}	Solar 74516
				all of above produced by Reggie Calloway				
				MIDWEST MAFIA **'00**				
				Rap group from Detroit, Michigan.				
6/17/00	44^{S}	10		**So Flossy**	*Marchin' and Mobbin' / Fo Sho*	$6	★	Buchanan 41111
				MIDWEST MAFIA featuring Phatty Banks				
				MIGHTY CLOUDS OF JOY R&B/BUB/LP **'76**				
				Gospel group from Los Angeles, California: Willie Joe Ligon, Johnny Martin, Elmo Franklin, Richard Wallace, Leon Polk and David Walker (**Bunker Hill**). Martin died in 1987.				
2/21/76	69	10		**Mighty High**	*Touch My Soul*	$5		ABC 12164
				MIGHTY DUB KATS, The **'95**				
				Studio dance group assembled by producer Norman "**Fatboy Slim**" Cook.				
10/14/95	58	20		**Magic Carpet Ride** A:57	*(no comprende edit)* [I]	$3	▮	Sm:)e 9014
				MIGHTY MIGHTY BOSSTONES, The ROK/LP **'97**				
				Ska-rock group from Boston, Massachusetts: Dicky Barrett (vocals), Nate Albert (guitar), Ben Carr (dancer), Kevin Lenear, Tim Burton and Dennis Brockenborough (horns), Joe Gittleman (bass) and Joe Sirois (drums).				
4/12/97	23^{A}	36		1 **The Impression That I Get** MR^{1}				album cut
9/13/97	68^{A}	6		2 **The Rascal King**			V	album cut ■
				"45" issued on Big Rig (no number) on light blue opaque vinyl (small hole) and with a picture sleeve; B-side: "Is It"; above 2 from the album *Let's Face It* on Big Rig/Mercury 534472				
				MIGUEL, Luis LP **'99**				
				Born on 4/19/70 in Veracruz, Mexico. Latin singer/actor.				
8/21/99	67^{S}	2		**Sol, Arena y Mar**	*(3 remixes)* [F]	$5	★	WEA 29289
				title is Spanish for "Sun, Sand and Sea"				
				MIKAILA **'01**				
				Born Mikaila Enriquez on 12/15/86 in Edmond, Oklahoma; raised in Dallas, Texas. Female teen pop singer.				
11/25/00+	25	16		**So In Love With Two** S:4	*(club mix) / The Art Of Letting Go*	$4	★^{V}	Island 572664
				"45": Island 572769				
				MIKE + THE MECHANICS AC/LP **'89**				
				Pop-rock group formed in England: Mike Rutherford (bass; **Genesis**), **Paul Carrack** and Paul Young (vocals; **Sad Café**), Adrian Lee (keyboards) and Peter Van Hooke (drums). Young, not to be confused with the same-named solo singer, died of a heart attack on 7/17/2000 (age 53).				
11/23/85+	6	24		1 **Silent Running (On Dangerous Ground)** AR^{5} A:5 / S:7	*Par Avion*	$3	■	Atlantic 89488
				promotional copies issued with a text insert				
3/22/86	5	19		2 **All I Need Is A Miracle** A:5 / S:8	*You Are The One*	$3	■	Atlantic 89450
6/28/86	32	15		3 **Taken In** A:24 / S:37	*A Call To Arms*	$3	■	Atlantic 89404
11/5/88	63	11		4 **Nobody's Perfect**	*Nobody Knows*	$3	■	Atlantic 88990
1/7/89	❶^{1}	20		5 **The Living Years** AC^{4} S:❶^{2} / A:❶^{1}	*Too Many Friends*	$3	■	Atlantic 88964
4/22/89	62	6		6 **Seeing Is Believing**	*Don't*	$3	■	Atlantic 88921
4/6/91	78	6		7 **Word Of Mouth**	*Let's Pretend It Didn't Happen*	$3	▮	Atlantic 87714

DEBUT	PEAK	WKS	Gold	A-side (Chart Hit)	B-side	$	Sym	Label & Number
				MILES, Buddy R&B/BUB/LP **'71**				
				Born George Miles on 9/5/46 in Omaha, Nebraska. R&B singer/drummer. Prominent session musician. Lead singer of **The Fidelity's** in 1958. Worked as sideman in the Dick Clark Revue, 1963-64. With **Wilson Pickett**, 1965-66. In Michael Bloomfield's Electric Flag, 1967. In **Jimi Hendrix**'s Band Of Gypsys, 1969-70. Was the voice of **The California Raisins**, the claymation TV ad characters.				
				1)Them Changes 2)Down By The River 3)Wholesale Love				
8/23/69	**100**	1		1 **Memphis Train** *[BUDDY MILES EXPRESS]*	*My Chant*	$7		Mercury 72945
5/2/70	**81**	6		2 **Them Changes** *[BUDDY MILES & THE FREEDOM EXPRESS]*	*Spot On The Wall*	$7		Mercury 73008
				also see #7 & 9 below				
7/18/70	**68**	7		3 **Down By The River**	*Heart's Delight*	$6		Mercury 73086
				written by **Neil Young**				
10/10/70	**86**	3		4 **Dreams**	*Your Feeling Is Mine*	$6		Mercury 73119
				introduced on **The Allman Brothers Band** 1970 debut album; above 4 from the album *Them Changes*				
12/12/70+	**86**	6		5 **We Got To Live Together - Part I**	*Part II*	$6		Mercury 73159
5/15/71	**71**	6		6 **Wholesale Love**	*That's The Way Life Is*	$6		Mercury 73205
				written by **Otis Redding**				
7/17/71	**62**	11		7 **Them Changes**	*The Way I Feel Tonight* [R]	$6		Mercury 73228
				same version as #2 above (#9 below is different)				
9/9/72	**84**	5		8 **Evil Ways /**	[L]			
9/16/72		1		9 **Them Changes**	[L-R]	$6		Columbia 45666
				CARLOS SANTANA & BUDDY MILES (above 2)				
9/20/75	**91**	3		10 **Rockin' And Rollin' On The Streets Of Hollywood**	*Livin' In The Right Space*	$5		Casablanca 839
				MILES, Garry **'60**				
				Born James Cason on 11/27/39 in Nashville, Tennessee. Lead singer of **The Statues** and **Brenda Lee**'s backing group, The Casuals. Also recorded as Buzz Cason. Also see **Garry Mills**, who is a different artist with the original version of "Look For A Star."				
6/20/60	**16**	13		**Look For A Star**	*Afraid Of Love*	$15	■	Liberty 55261
				from the British movie *Circus Of Horrors* starring Donald Pleasence				
				MILES, John LP **'77**				
				Born on 4/23/49 in Jarrow, England. Rock vocalist/guitarist/keyboardist. Guest vocalist with the **Alan Parsons Project**.				
2/14/76	**68**	10		1 **Highfly**	*There's A Man Behind The Guitar*	$5		London 20084
				originally charted for 7 weeks; re-entered on 8/14/76 (#69)				
5/15/76	**88**	3		2 **Music**	*When You Lose Someone So Young*	$5		London 20086
				above 2 produced by **Alan Parsons**				
3/26/77	**34**	14		3 **Slowdown**	*Stand Up (And Give Me A Reason)*	$5		London 20092
				MILES, Lenny **'61**				
				Born on 12/22/34 in Fort Worth, Texas. Died of cancer in the early 1960s. R&B singer.				
12/31/60+	**41**	7		1 **Don't Believe Him, Donna**	*Invisible*	$20		Scepter 1212
5/8/61	**84**	2		2 **In Between Tears**	*I Know Love*	$20		Scepter 1218
				MILES, Robert LP **'96**				
				Born Roberto Concina on 11/3/69 in Venice, Italy. DJ/dance musician.				
5/11/96	**21**	20		1 **Children**	S:20 / A:25 *(full length version)* [I]	$3	▮V	Arista 13006
10/5/96	**54**	19		2 **One And One**	S:44 *(3 album snippets)*	$3	▮V	Arista 13247
				Maria Nayler (vocal); "45" issued for above 2 on Arista 13247				
				MILESTONE **'97**				
				All-star R&B group: brothers Kenneth (**Babyface**), Melvin and **Kevon Edmonds** (both from **After 7**), with **K-Ci & JoJo**.				
8/30/97	**23**	20	●	**I Care 'Bout You**	S:13 *(instrumental)*	$3	▮	LaFace 24264
				from the movie *Soul Food* starring **Vanessa Williams**				
				MILIAN, Christina **'00**				
				Born in New Jersey; raised in Waldorf, Maryland. R&B singer/songwriter. Also see **Jennifer Lopez**'s "Play."				
9/16/00	**11**	20		1 **Between Me And You**	A:7 *(3 versions) / Die* (w/Tah Murdah, Black Child & Dave Bing)	$6	T	Def Jam 562890
				JA RULE (Featuring Christina Milian)				
8/25/01	**27**	20		2 **AM To PM**	S:❶[1] / A:70 *(5 album snippets) / Between Me And You* (w/**Ja Rule**)	$5	★+	Def Soul 588775
				MILITIA **'98**				
				Duo of rap producers Emanuel Dean and Shawn Billups. Featuring rappers Diz and Devious.				
1/10/98	**52**	20		**Burn**	S:40 *(radio edit)*	$4	▮	Red Ant 119006
				MILLER, Chuck **'55**				
				Born in California. Rock and roll singer/pianist.				
6/18/55	**9**	14		1 **The House Of Blue Lights**	S:9 / A:18 / J:19 *Can't Help Wonderin'*	$25		Mercury 70627
				#8 hit for Freddie Slack in 1946				
12/22/56	**59**	9		2 **The Auctioneer**	T:59 *Baby Doll* [N]	$20		Mercury 71001
				Hugo Peretti (of **Hugo & Luigi**, orch.)				
				MILLER, Clint **'58**				
				Born Isaac Clinton Miller on 5/24/39 in Ferguson, North Carolina. Teen rockabilly singer.				
1/27/58	**79**	7		**Bertha Lou**	T:79 *Doggone It Baby, I'm In Love*	$40		ABC-Paramount 9878
				Don Costa (orch.)				
				MILLER, Frankie C&W **'61**				
				Born on 12/17/30 in Victoria, Texas. Country singer/songwriter. Appeared on *Jubilee USA* on ABC-TV.				
7/10/61	**82**	4		**Black Land Farmer**	*True Blue*	$15		Starday 424
				this same version by Miller first made the Country charts (#5) on 4/13/59				
				MILLER, Frankie BUB/LP **'82**				
				Born on 11/2/49 in Glasgow, Scotland. Blues-tinged rock singer/songwriter.				
6/25/77	**71**	5		1 **The Doodle Song**	*(I'll Never) Live In Vain*	$5		Chrysalis 2145
6/19/82	**62**	6		2 **To Dream The Dream**	*Don't Stop*	$4	■	MSS/Capitol 5131

DEBUT	PEAK	WKS	Gold	A-side (Chart Hit)..........B-side	$	Sym	Label & Number
				MILLER, Jody C&W/AC/BUB/LP **'65**			
				Born Myrna Joy Brooks on 11/29/41 in Phoenix, Arizona; raised in Blanchard, Oklahoma. Country singer. Charted 27 Country hits, 1965-79.			
2/8/64	66	6		1 **He Walks Like A Man** ....*Looking At The World Through A Tear*	$10		Capitol 5090
4/24/65	12	9		2 **Queen Of The House** *The Greatest Actor*	$10		Capitol 5402
				answer song to **Roger Miller**'s "King Of The Road"			
6/26/65	54	6		3 **Silver Threads And Golden Needles** ....*Melody For Robin*	$10	■	Capitol 5429
8/28/65	25	9		4 **Home Of The Brave**..........*This Is The Life*	$10	■	Capitol 5483
6/26/71	53	9		5 **He's So Fine** ....*You Number Two*	$8		Epic 10734
				arrangement similar to **George Harrison**'s 1970 hit "My Sweet Lord"			
10/9/71	91	4		6 **Baby, I'm Yours** ....*Good Lovin' (Makes It Right)*	$8		Epic 10785
				MILLER, Lise **'67**			
				Female pop singer. Sang with **Sergio Mendes** in 1983 as Leza Miller.			
12/23/67	20[X]	2		**Love Is** ....*Loneliest Christmas Tree* [X]	$20		Canterbury 519
	★447★			**MILLER, Mitch, & his Orch. and Chorus** MEM/POP/BUB/LP **'55**			
				Born on 7/4/11 in Rochester, New York. Producer/conductor/arranger. A&R executive for both Columbia and Mercury Records. Best known for his sing-along albums and TV show (1961-64). Won Grammy's Lifetime Achievement Award in 2000. Hit #3 in 1950 with "Tzena Tzena Tzena."			
				1)The Yellow Rose Of Texas 2)Theme Song (from "Song For A Summer Night") 3)The Children's Marching Song			
8/6/55	❶[6]	19	●	1 **The Yellow Rose Of Texas** S:❶[6] / A:❶[6] / J:❶[6] / T:4 *Blackberry Winter*	$15		Columbia 40540
				adaptation of a Civil War campfire song			
11/12/55	41	14		2 **Autumn Leaves**..........T:41 *Under Paris Skies*	$12		Columbia 50033
				label is Columbia's "Hall Of Fame Series"; originally released by Mitch in 1950 on Columbia 38971			
11/12/55	51	4		3 **The Bonnie Blue Gal**..........T:51 *Bel Sante*	$12		Columbia 40575
				adapted from the Civil War song "The Bonnie Blue Flag"			
2/4/56	19	13		4 **Lisbon Antigua (In Old Lisbon)**..........A:19 / T:30 *Willy Can* [I]	$12		Columbia 40635
3/10/56	50	7		5 **Madeira** ....T:50 *Bolero Gaucho* [I]	$12		Columbia 40655
				originally released by Mitch in 1953 as "Tira Lira Madeira" on Columbia 39982; B-side released by Mitch in 1952 as "Without My Lover" on Columbia 39901			
7/21/56	88	2		6 **The President On The Dollar** ....T:88 *Trapeze*	$12		Columbia 40715
8/4/56	8	17		7 **Theme Song From "Song For A Summer Night" (Parts I & II)** ..A:8 / S:9 / T:10 / J:10 [I]	$12		Columbia 40730
				Part I: instrumental version; Part II: vocal version; from the 7/8/56 *Studio One* TV production "Song For A Summer Night"			
12/1/56	94	1		8 **Theme from Song Of The Sparrow** ....T:94 *(vocal version)* [I]	$10		Columbia 40772
				from the *Studio One* TV production "A Man's World"			
3/2/57	94	1		9 **A Very Special Love (Song for The Ninth Day)**..........T:94 *Song For The Ninth Day* [I]	$10		Columbia 40831
				from the *Playhouse 90* TV production "The Ninth Day"			
1/13/58	20	29		10 **March From The River Kwai and Colonel Bogey** ....A:20 / S:21 / T:21 *Hey Little Baby* [I]	$10		Columbia 41066
				from the movie *The Bridge On The River Kwai* starring Alec Guinness and William Holden; "March" written for the movie; "Bogey" is a 1916 traditional march			
10/13/58	94	1		11 **Bluebell**..........H:94 *It Seems Like Only Yesterday*	$10		Columbia 41235
1/12/59	16	14		12 **The Children's Marching Song (Nick Nack Paddy Whack)**....*Carolina In The Morning*	$10	■	Columbia 41317
				based on the traditional nursery song "This Old Man"; from the movie *The Inn Of The Sixth Happiness* starring Ingrid Bergman; with the children from the Broadway musical *Flower Drum Song*			
12/14/59	70	4		13 **Do-Re-Mi**..........*Alouette March*	$8	■	Columbia 41499
				with the children from the Broadway musical *The Sound Of Music* starring Mary Martin			
2/27/61	88	2		14 **Tunes Of Glory**..........*Shlub-A-Dubba-Dub (Tango Bombastico)* [I]	$8	■	Columbia 41941
				title song from the movie starring Alec Guinness; charted in 1955 by **The Ames Brothers** as "My Bonnie Lassie" (adapted from "Scotland The Brave")			
				MILLER, Mrs. LP **'66**			
				Born Elva Miller on 10/5/07 in Dodge City, Kansas. Died on 6/28/97 (age 89). Tone-deaf singer. As a joke, Capitol released her first album as *Mrs. Miller's Greatest Hits.*			
4/30/66	82	4		1 **Downtown** / [N]			
5/7/66	95	2		2 **A Lover's Concerto**.......... [N]	$10		Capitol 5640
				MILLER, Ned C&W/BUB/LP **'63**			
				Born Henry Ned Miller on 4/12/25 in Rains, Utah. Country singer/songwriter. To California in 1956. Signed with Fabor in 1956. Wrote the **Gale Storm** and **Bonnie Guitar** hit "Dark Moon."			
12/29/62+	6	13		1 **From A Jack To A King** ....*Parade Of Broken Hearts*	$15		Fabor 114
				original version released on Dot 15601 in 1957 ($40)			
12/26/64+	52	9		2 **Do What You Do Do Well**..........*Dusty Guitar*	$12		Fabor 137
	★340★			**MILLER, Roger** C&W/AC/BUB/LP **'65**			
				Born on 1/2/36 in Fort Worth, Texas; raised in Erick, Oklahoma. Died of cancer on 10/25/92 (age 56). Country singer/songwriter/guitarist. To Nashville in the mid-1950s, began songwriting career. Charted 42 Country hits, 1960-86. With **Faron Young** as writer/drummer in 1962. Won six Grammys in 1965. Own TV show in 1966. Songwriter of 1985's Broadway musical *Big River.*			
				1)King Of The Road 2)Dang Me 3)Engine Engine #9			
6/13/64	7	11		1 **Dang Me** ....CW[6] *Got 2 Again* [N]	$10	■	Smash 1881
				issued with 3 different picture sleeves			
9/5/64	9	13		2 **Chug-A-Lug**..........*Reincarnation* [N]	$10		Smash 1926
11/28/64+	31	8		3 **Do-Wacka-Do**..........*Love Is Not For Me* [N]	$10	■	Smash 1947
1/30/65	4	13	●	4 **King Of The Road** CW[5] / AC[10] *Atta Boy Girl*	$10		Smash 1965
5/8/65	7	9		5 **Engine Engine #9** ....*The Last Word In Lonesome Is Me*	$10		Smash 1983
7/10/65	34	7		6 **One Dyin' And A Buryin'**..........*It Happened Just That Way (#105)*	$10	■	Smash 1994
9/11/65	31	7		7 **Kansas City Star**..........*Guess I'll Pick Up My Heart (And Go Home)* [N]	$10		Smash 1998
11/6/65	8	11		8 **England Swings**..........AC[1] *Good Old Days*	$10		Smash 2010
2/19/66	26	7		9 **Husbands And Wives** ....*I've Been A Long Time Leavin' (#103)*	$10		Smash 2024
6/25/66	40	6		10 **You Can't Roller Skate In A Buffalo Herd** ....*Train Of Life* [N]	$8		Smash 2043
9/17/66	58	5		11 **My Uncle Used To Love Me But She Died** ....*You're My Kingdom* [N]	$8		Smash 2055

DEBUT	PEAK	WKS	Gold	A-side (Chart Hit)...B-side	$	Sym	Label & Number
				MILLER, Roger — Cont'd			
11/5/66	84	4		12 **Heartbreak Hotel** ... *Less And Less*	$8		Smash 2066
3/25/67	37	7		13 **Walkin' In The Sunshine** ... *Home*	$8		Smash 2081
12/16/67	13[X]	3		14 **Old Toy Trains** ... *Silent Night* [X]	$10	■	Smash 2130
				all of above (except #12) written by Miller			
3/2/68	39	9		15 **Little Green Apples** ... *Our Little Love*	$8	■	Smash 2148
12/7/68	80	6		16 **Vance** ... *Little Children Run And Play*	$8		Smash 2197
				above 2 written by **Bobby Russell**; all of above produced by Jerry Kennedy			

MILLER, Steve, Band ★196★ ROK/BUB/LP '77

Born on 10/5/43 in Milwaukee, Wisconsin; raised in Dallas, Texas. Rock singer/songwriter/guitarist. Formed band in high school, The Marksmen, which included **Boz Scaggs**. While at the University of Wisconsin-Madison, Miller led the blues-rock band the Ardells, later known as the Fabulous Night Trains, featuring Scaggs. After graduating, studied literature at the University of Copenhagen. To San Francisco in 1966; formed the Steve Miller Band, which featured a fluctuating lineup.

1)Abracadabra 2)The Joker 3)Rock'n Me 4)Fly Like An Eagle 5)Jet Airliner

DEBUT	PEAK	WKS	Gold	A-side (Chart Hit)...B-side	$	Sym	Label & Number
11/23/68	94	2		1 **Living In The U.S.A.** ... *Quicksilver Girl*	$10		Capitol 2287
				also see #5 below			
8/15/70	69	6		2 **Going To The Country** ... *Never Kill Another Man*	$8		Capitol 2878
10/20/73+	❶[1]	20	●	3 **The Joker** ... *Something To Believe In*	$6		Capitol 3732
3/2/74	51	7		4 **Your Cash Ain't Nothin' But Trash** ... *Evil*	$6		Capitol 3837
				#6 R&B hit for **The Clovers** in 1954			
5/18/74	49	7		5 **Living In The U.S.A.** ... *Kow Kow Calqulator* [R]	$6		Capitol 3884
				same version as #1 above			
5/8/76	11	16		6 **Take The Money And Run** *[STEVE MILLER]* ... *Sweet Maree*	$5		Capitol 4260
8/14/76	❶[1]	18		7 **Rock'n Me** *[STEVE MILLER]* ... *Shu Ba Da Du Ma Ma Ma Ma*	$5		Capitol 4323
				also released with "Living In The U.S.A." as the B-side			
12/18/76+	2[2]	20	●	8 **Fly Like An Eagle** *[STEVE MILLER]* ... *Lovin' Cup*	$5		Capitol 4372
4/30/77	8	18		9 **Jet Airliner** ... *Babes In The Wood*	$5		Capitol 4424
8/6/77	23	14		10 **Jungle Love** ... *Wish Upon A Star*	$5		Capitol 4466
10/15/77	17	15		11 **Swingtown** ... *Winter Time*	$5		Capitol 4496
10/31/81	24	14		12 **Heart Like A Wheel** ... *True Fine Love*	$4	■	Capitol 5068
1/23/82	55	7		13 **Circle Of Love** ... *(instrumental)*	$4		Capitol 5086
5/29/82	❶[2]	25	●	14 **Abracadabra** *Give It Up*	$4	■	Capitol 5126
				also released with "Baby Wanna Dance" as the B-side			
10/16/82	57	8		15 **Cool Magic** ... *Young Girl's Heart*	$4	■	Capitol 5162
12/11/82+	60	9		16 **Give It Up** ... *Heart Like A Wheel*	$4	■	Capitol 5194
10/6/84	57	6		17 **Shangri-La** ... *Circle Of Love*	$3	■	Capitol 5407
2/16/85	84	3		18 **Bongo Bongo** ... *Get On Home*	$3	■	Capitol 5442
11/15/86	97	3		19 **I Want To Make The World Turn Around** ... AR[6] *Slinky*	$3	■	Capitol 5646
7/10/93	64	8		20 **Wide River** ... A:74 *Stranger Blues*	$4	▌	Sailor 859194
				all of above written or co-written (except #4, 9, 10 & 15) and produced by Steve Miller			

MILLIONS LIKE US LP '87

Pop-rock duo from England: John O'Kane (vocals) and Jeep MacNichol (guitar, keyboards).

DEBUT	PEAK	WKS	Gold	A-side (Chart Hit)...B-side	$	Sym	Label & Number
11/14/87	69	6		**Guaranteed For Life** ... *Heaven Help The Child*	$3	■	Virgin 99412

★518★ **MILLI VANILLI** LP '89

Europop act formed in Germany by producer Frank Farian (created **Boney M** and **Far Corporation**). Milli Vanilli is Turkish for positive energy. Originally thought to be Rob Pilatus (born on 6/8/65 in Germany) and Fabrice Morvan (born on 5/14/66 in France). Duo was stripped of its 1989 Best New Artist Grammy Award when it was revealed that they didn't sing on their debut album. Actual vocalists are Charles Shaw, John Davis and Brad Howe. Pilatus died of a drug overdose on 4/2/98 (age 32).

DEBUT	PEAK	WKS	Gold	A-side (Chart Hit)...B-side	$	Sym	Label & Number
1/7/89	2[1]	26	▲	1 **Girl You Know It's True** ... S:❷[2] / A:4 *Magic Touch*	$3	■	Arista 9781
4/29/89	❶[1]	21	●	2 **Baby Don't Forget My Number** ... S:❶[1] / A:2 *Too Much Monkey Business*	$3	■	Arista 9832
8/5/89	❶[2]	22	●	3 **Girl I'm Gonna Miss You** ... A:❶[3] / S:❶[1] *All Or Nothing (remix)*	$3	■	Arista 9870
10/7/89	❶[2]	23	▲	4 **Blame It On The Rain** A:❶[2] / S:❶[1] *Dance With A Devil*	$3	■	Arista 9904
1/6/90	4	14		5 **All Or Nothing** ... A:4 / S:6 *Dreams To Remember*	$3	▌	Arista 9923
				also see the B-side of #3 above; all of above from the album *Girl You Know It's True*			

MILLS, Frank AC/BUB/LP '79

Born on 6/27/42 in Toronto, Ontario, Canada. Pianist/composer/producer/arranger.

DEBUT	PEAK	WKS	Gold	A-side (Chart Hit)...B-side	$	Sym	Label & Number
1/29/72	46	9		1 **Love Me, Love Me Love** ... *Windsong*	$5		Sunflower 118
1/27/79	3	20	●	2 **Music Box Dancer** ... *The Poet And I* [I]	$4		Polydor 14517
11/3/79	48	9		3 **Peter Piper** ... *Interlude* [I]	$4		Polydor 2002

MILLS, Garry '60

Born on 10/13/41 in West Wickham, Kent, England. Pop singer. Also see **Garry Miles**.

DEBUT	PEAK	WKS	Gold	A-side (Chart Hit)...B-side	$	Sym	Label & Number
6/20/60	26	11		**Look For A Star - Part I** ... *Part II*	$15		Imperial 5674
				original version of song from the British movie *Circus Of Horrors* starring Donald Pleasence			

MILLS, Hayley BUB '61

Born on 4/18/46 in London, England. Daughter of English actor John Mills. Disney teen movie star of *Pollyanna*, *The Parent Trap*, *In Search Of The Castaways* and others. Her son, Crispian Mills, is lead singer of **Kula Shaker**.

DEBUT	PEAK	WKS	Gold	A-side (Chart Hit)...B-side	$	Sym	Label & Number
9/4/61	8	14		1 **Let's Get Together** *[HAYLEY MILLS and HAYLEY MILLS]* ... *Cobbler Cobbler*	$15	■	Buena Vista 385
				from the movie *The Parent Trap* starring Mills			
3/17/62	21	11		2 **Johnny Jingo** ... *Jeepers Creepers*	$15	■	Buena Vista 395

DEBUT	PEAK	WKS	Gold	A-side (Chart Hit)..........B-side	$	Sym	Label & Number

MILLS, Stephanie — R&B/BUB/LP '80

Born on 3/26/56 in Brooklyn, New York. R&B singer/actress. Played "Dorothy" in Broadway's *The Wiz*. Briefly married to **Jeffrey Daniels** of **Shalamar** in 1980. Charted 29 R&B hits, 1979-93.

DEBUT	PEAK	WKS	Gold	A-side (Chart Hit)..........B-side	$	Sym	Label & Number
7/21/79	22	14		1 **What Cha Gonna Do With My Lovin'** .... *Starlight*	$5		20th Century 2403
6/14/80	52	6		2 **Sweet Sensation** .... *Wish That You Were Mine*	$5	■	20th Century 2449
8/9/80	6	25	●	3 **Never Knew Love Like This Before** *Still Mine*	$5		20th Century 2460
5/16/81	40	13		4 **Two Hearts** .... *I Just Wanna Say* (Mills) **STEPHANIE MILLS Featuring Teddy Pendergrass**	$5		20th Century 2492
10/13/84	65	6		5 **The Medicine Song** .... *(instrumental)*	$4		Casablanca 880180
7/6/85	78	6		6 **Bit By Bit** .... *Exotic Skates* theme from the movie *Fletch* starring Chevy Chase	$3	■	MCA 52617
10/10/87	85	2		7 **(You're Puttin') A Rush On Me** .... RB^{1} *(instrumental)*	$3	■	MCA 53151

MILLS BROTHERS, The — MEM/POP/R&B/AC/C&W/LP '32

Legendary black family vocal group from Piqua, Ohio: father John Mills (died on 12/8/67, age 78), with sons Herbert (died on 4/12/89, age 67), Harry (died on 6/28/82, age 68) and Donald (died on 11/13/99, age 84) Mills. Charted 61 pop hits, 1931-54 (including 5 #1s: "Tiger Rag," "Dinah" (w/**Bing Crosby**), "Paper Doll," "You Always Hurt The One You Love" and "The Glow-Worm"). Won Grammy's Lifetime Achievement Award in 1998.

DEBUT	PEAK	WKS	Gold	A-side (Chart Hit)..........B-side	$	Sym	Label & Number
11/12/55	45	9		1 **Suddenly There's A Valley** .... T:45 *Gum Drop*	$15		Decca 29686
1/28/56	63	2		2 **All The Way 'Round The World** .... T:63 *I've Changed My Mind A Thousand Times*	$15		Decca 29781
5/26/56	57	10		3 **Standing On The Corner** .... T:57 *King Porter Stomp* Sonny Burke (orch.); from the Broadway musical *The Most Happy Fella* starring Robert Weede	$15		Decca 29897
5/27/57	39	8		4 **Queen Of The Senior Prom** .... T:39 *My Troubled Mind*	$15		Decca 30299
3/3/58	21	2		5 **Get A Job** A:21 *I Found A Million Dollar Baby In A Five And Ten Cent Store* Milton Rodgers (orch.)	$15		Dot 15695
1/5/59	70	5		6 **Yellow Bird** .... *Baby Clementine* Milton DeLugg (orch.); adapted from a West Indian folk song	$10		Dot 15858
1/27/68	23	15		7 **Cab Driver** .... *Fortuosity* Sy Oliver (orch.: #1, 2, 4 & 7)	$7		Dot 17041
5/18/68	73	7		8 **My Shy Violet** .... *The Flower Road*	$7		Dot 17096
11/23/68	83	2		9 **The Ol' Race Track** .... *But For Love* George Tipton (orch., above 2)	$7		Dot 17162

★467★ MILSAP, Ronnie — C&W/BUB/AC/R&B/LP '81

Born on 1/16/43 in Robbinsville, North Carolina. Country singer/pianist/guitarist. Blind since birth; multi-instrumentalist by age 12. With **J.J. Cale** band; own band from 1965. First charted (Bubbling Under) in 1965 on Scepter Records. Charted 63 Country hits, 1973-00.

1)(There's) No Gettin' Over Me 2)Any Day Now 3)It Was Almost Like A Song

DEBUT	PEAK	WKS	Gold	A-side (Chart Hit)..........B-side	$	Sym	Label & Number
9/12/70	87	3		1 **Loving You Is A Natural Thing** .... *So Hung Up On Sylvia*	$10		Chips 2889
9/14/74	95	2		2 **Please Don't Tell Me How The Story Ends** .... CW^{2} *Streets Of Gold* written by **Kris Kristofferson**	$6		RCA Victor 0313
6/18/77	16	22		3 **It Was Almost Like A Song** .... CW^{3} *It Don't Hurt To Dream*	$5		RCA 10976
12/24/77+	80	5		4 **What A Difference You've Made In My Life** .... CW^{1} *Selfish*	$5		RCA 11146
7/1/78	63	6		5 **Only One Love In My Life** .... CW^{3} *Back On My Mind Again* Lea Jane Singers (backing vocals, above 3)	$5		RCA 11270
10/6/79	43	11		6 **Get It Up** .... *In No Time At All* (C&W #6)	$5		RCA 11695
11/29/80+	24	21		7 **Smoky Mountain Rain** .... CW^{1} / AC^{1} *Crystal Fallin' Rain*	$4		RCA 12084
6/27/81	5	20		8 **(There's) No Gettin' Over Me** CW^{2} *I Live My Whole Life At Night*	$4		RCA 12264
10/24/81+	20	17		9 **I Wouldn't Have Missed It For The World** .. CW^{1} *It Happens Every Time (I Think of You)*	$4		RCA 12342
5/1/82	14	16		10 **Any Day Now** .... CW^{1} / AC^{5} *It's Just A Room*	$4		RCA 13216
8/21/82	59	7		11 **He Got You** .... CW^{1} *I Love New Orleans Music*	$4		RCA 13286
3/26/83	23	16		12 **Stranger In My House** .... *Is It Over*	$4		RCA 13470
8/13/83	58	7		13 **Don't You Know How Much I Love You** .... CW^{1} *Feelings Change*	$4		RCA 13564
8/4/84	84	4		14 **She Loves My Car** .... *Prisoner Of The Highway* (C&W #6)	$4		RCA 13847

MIMMS, Garnet, & The Enchanters — BUB/R&B/LP '63

Born Garrett Mimms on 11/16/33 in Ashland, Kentucky. Sang in gospel groups the Evening Stars, Norfolk Four, Harmonizing Four. Formed group The Gainors in 1958. **The Enchanters** (see #7 below) consisting of Zola Pearnell, Sam Bell and Charles Boyer was formed in 1961.

1)Cry Baby 2)For Your Precious Love 3)Baby Don't You Weep

DEBUT	PEAK	WKS	Gold	A-side (Chart Hit)..........B-side	$	Sym	Label & Number
8/17/63	4	14		1 **Cry Baby** RB^{3} *Don't Change Your Heart*	$15		United Artists 629
11/23/63+	26	9		2 **For Your Precious Love /**			
11/16/63	30	9		3 **Baby Don't You Weep**	$15	■	United Artists 658
				GARNET MIMMS:			
2/15/64	69	7		4 **Tell Me Baby** .... *Anytime You Want Me*	$15		United Artists 694
5/16/64	67	4		5 **One Girl /**			
7/18/64	78	7		6 **A Quiet Place** *[GARNET MIMMS & THE ENCHANTERS]*	$15		United Artists 715
9/5/64	91	3		7 **I Wanna Thank You** .... *I'm A Good Man* **THE ENCHANTERS**	$15		Warner 5460
10/17/64	73	5		8 **Look Away** .... *One Woman Man*	$15		United Artists 773
1/2/65	95	1		9 **A Little Bit Of Soap** .... *I'll Make It Up To You*	$15		United Artists 796
3/26/66	30	9		10 **I'll Take Good Care Of You** .... *Prove It To Me*	$15		United Artists 995

MINA — '61

Born Anna Mazzini on 3/25/40 in Cremona, Italy.

DEBUT	PEAK	WKS	Gold	A-side (Chart Hit)..........B-side	$	Sym	Label & Number
5/8/61	90	1		**This World We Love In (Il Cielo In Una Stanza)** .... *You're Tired Of Me (Mi Vuoi Lasciar)* [F]	$10		Time 1030

DEBUT	PEAK	WKS	Gold	A-side (Chart Hit)..........B-side	$	Sym	Label & Number
				MINDBENDERS, The LP **'65**			
				Rock and roll band from Manchester, England: Wayne Fontana (lead singer; born Glyn Geoffrey Ellis on 10/28/45), Eric Stewart (lead guitar, vocals), Bob Lang (bass) and Ric Rothwell (drums). Fontana left in October 1965. Graham Gouldman joined in 1968. Stewart and Gouldman were later members of **Hotlegs** and **10cc**.			
3/20/65	❶[1]	11		1 **Game Of Love** ....*One More Time*	$12		Fontana 1509
				first released on Fontana 1503 in 1964 ($15)			
6/12/65	45	8		2 **It's Just A Little Bit Too Late** ....*Long Time Comin'*	$12		Fontana 1514
				WAYNE FONTANA & THE MINDBENDERS (above 2)			
4/16/66	2[2]	13		3 **A Groovy Kind Of Love**..........*Love Is Good*	$12		Fontana 1541
8/13/66	55	6		4 **Ashes To Ashes**..........*You Don't Know About Love*	$12		Fontana 1555
				MINEO, Sal **'57**			
				Born Salvatore Mineo on 1/10/39 in the Bronx, New York. Stabbed to death on 2/12/76 (age 37). Singer/actor. Starred in several movies and Broadway shows.			
5/20/57	9	19		1 **Start Movin' (In My Direction)** / S:9 / T:10 / A:16 / J:18			
				introduced by Mineo on the 5/1/57 Kraft TV Theater production of *Drummer Man*			
6/24/57		5		2 **Love Affair** ....S:flip	$25	■	Epic 9216
				Ray Ellis (orch., above 2)			
9/9/57	27	10		3 **Lasting Love** / S:27 / T:35			
9/30/57		1		4 **You Shouldn't Do That** ....S:flip	$25	■	Epic 9227
				Mark Ellis (orch., above 2)			
11/11/57	45	7		5 **Party Time** ....S:45 / T:47 *The Words That I Whisper*	$25	■	Epic 9246
1/27/58	45	8		6 **Little Pigeon** ....S:45 / T:47 *Cuttin' In*	$25		Epic 9260
				Mark Jeffrey (orch., above 2)			
				MINIATURE MEN, The **'62**			
				Studio band under the direction of **Hank Levine**.			
6/9/62	87	4		**Baby Elephant Walk**..........*Bool-Ya-Base* [I]	$20		Dolton 57
				written by **Henry Mancini**; from the movie *Hatari!* starring John Wayne			
				MINK DeVILLE LP **'84**			
				Rock trio formed in London, England: Willy DeVille (vocals, guitar), Ruben Siguenza (bass) and Thomas Allen (drums).			
2/11/84	89	4		**Each Word's A Beat Of My Heart**..........*River Of Tears*	$4		Atlantic 89750
				MINOGUE, Kylie LP **'88**			
				Born on 5/28/68 in Melbourne, Australia. Dance singer/actress. Regular on the Australian soap opera *Neighbours*.			
5/7/88	28	14		1 **I Should Be So Lucky**..........S:27 / A:32 *(instrumental)*	$3	■	Geffen 27922
8/27/88	3	27	●	2 **The Loco-Motion** S:❶[1] / A:4 *I'll Still Be Loving You*	$3	■	Geffen 27752
12/10/88+	37	13		3 **It's No Secret**..........S:35 / A:37 *Made In Heaven*	$3	■	Geffen 27651
1/26/02	7	20		4 **Can't Get You Out Of My Head** ....A:8 / S:72 *(3 remixes)*	$6	T[V]	Capitol 77685
				"45": Capitol 77697; B-side: "Boy"			
6/29/02	23	16		5 **Love At First Sight**..........A:26 *(5 remixes)*	$7	T	Capitol 77724
				12" single contains 2 discs			
12/14/02+	91	8		6 **Come Into My World**..........*(3 remixes)*	$6	T	Capitol 77829
				MINOR, Shane C&W/BUB **'99**			
				Born on 5/3/68 in Modesto, California. Male country singer.			
6/19/99	82	7		**Slave To The Habit**..........A:75 *(alternate version)*	$4	★[+V]	Mercury 870818
				co-written by **Toby Keith**; "45" B-side: "Tell Me Now"			
				MINOR DETAIL LP **'83**			
				Pop duo from Ireland: brothers John and Willie Hughes.			
9/24/83	92	2		**Canvas Of Life**..........*I'll Always Love You*	$4	■	Polydor 815329
				MINOTT **'01**			
				Born in Kingston, Jamaica. Reggae singer. Began singing career at age 12. Not to be confused with reggae singer Sugar Minott.			
11/17/01	61[S]	4		**Playa Playa (playing the game right)** ....*(3 versions) / Wham Bam*	$8	★[*]	World Beat 412
				MINOTT Featuring: Mydus			
				MINT CONDITION R&B/BUB/LP **'92**			
				R&B group from Minneapolis, Minnesota: Stokley Williams (vocals, drums), Homer O'Dell (guitar), Larry Waddell and Keri Lewis (keyboards), Jeff Allen (sax) and Ricky Kinchen (bass). Lewis married **Toni Braxton** on 4/21/2001.			
1/4/92	6	24	●	1 **Breakin' My Heart (Pretty Brown Eyes)** A:6 / S:9 *(Brown Eyed edit)*	$3	▮	Perspective 0004
6/20/92	81	8		2 **Forever In Your Eyes**..........*(2 versions) / (3 album snippets)*	$3	▮	Perspective 0009
1/22/94	33	16		3 **U Send Me Swingin'**..........S:26 / A:47 *(3 versions)*	$3	▮	Perspective 7439
9/7/96	17	24	●	4 **What Kind Of Man Would I Be**..........S:12 / A:46 *(3 album snippets)*	$3	▮[V]	Perspective 7558
3/29/97	32	16		5 **You Don't Have To Hurt No More**..........S:22 *Change Your Mind*	$3	▮[V]	Perspective 7564
				"45" issued for above 2 on Perspective 7564			
11/6/99	30	20		6 **If You Love Me**..........S:9 / A:68 *(Spanish version)*	$3	★	Elektra 64027
				MIRACLE LP **'00**			
				Born Peter Evans in Augusta, Georgia. Male rapper			
2/12/00	37[S]	23		**Bounce**..........*(4 versions)*	$8	★[*]	Sound Of Atlanta 0001

DEBUT	PEAK	WKS	Gold	A-side (Chart Hit)	B-side	$	Sym	Label & Number

MIRACLES, The ★44★ R&B/BUB/LP '63

R&B vocal group from Detroit, Michigan: **Smokey Robinson** (born on 2/19/40), Claudette Rogers (born in 1942), Bobby Rogers (born on 2/19/40), Ronnie White (born on 4/5/39) and Warren Moore (born on 11/19/39). Claudette Rogers retired in 1964; married to Robinson from 1958-86. Bobby Rogers married Wanda Young of **The Marvelettes**. Robinson wrote many hit songs for the group and other Motown artists. Robinson went solo in 1972; replaced by Billy Griffin. White died of leukemia on 8/26/95 (age 56).

1)The Tears Of A Clown 2)Love Machine 3)Shop Around 4)Second That Emotion 5)You've Really Got A Hold On Me

DEBUT	PEAK	WKS	Gold	A-side (Chart Hit)	B-side	$	Sym	Label & Number
10/5/59	93	2		1 **Bad Girl**	*I Love Your Baby*	$75		Chess 1734
				test pressings released on Motown G-1 ($2000) and Motown 2207 ($2000) in 1959				
12/12/60+	2[1]	16		2 **Shop Around** RB[8]	*Who's Lovin You*	$30		Tamla 54034
				THE MIRACLES (featuring Bill "Smokey" Robinson)				
				early pressings feature a different, slower version [hit version master no. 45-LI(3)]				
3/27/61	49	6		3 **Ain't It, Baby**	*The Only One I Love*	$100		Tamla 54036
7/10/61	51	6		4 **Mighty Good Lovin'** /				
7/3/61	97	1		5 **Broken Hearted**		$50	■	Tamla 54044
10/23/61	52	8		6 **Everybody's Gotta Pay Some Dues**	*I Can't Believe*	$50	■	Tamla 54048
1/13/62	35	10		7 **What's So Good About Good-by**	*I've Been Good To You (#103)*	$30	■	Tamla 54053
5/12/62	39	10		8 **I'll Try Something New**	*You Never Miss A Good Thing*	$20	■	Tamla 54059
9/15/62	94	3		9 **Way Over There**	*If Your Mother Only Knew*	$20		Tamla 54069
				first released on Tamla 54028 in 1960 ($75) with "Depend On Me" as the B-side				
12/8/62+	8	16		10 **You've Really Got A Hold On Me** RB[1]	*Happy Landing*	$20		Tamla 54073
3/30/63	31	9		11 **A Love She Can Count On**	*I Can Take A Hint (#107)*	$20		Tamla 54078
8/17/63	8	12		12 **Mickey's Monkey**	*Whatever Makes You Happy*	$20		Tamla 54083
11/23/63+	35	10		13 **I Gotta Dance To Keep From Crying**	*Such Is Love, Such Is Life*	$15		Tamla 54089
3/7/64	59	5		14 (You Can't Let The Boy Overpower) **The Man In You**	*Heartbreak Road*	$15		Tamla 54092
6/27/64	27	9		15 **I Like It Like That**	*You're So Fine And Sweet*	$15	■	Tamla 54098
9/19/64	35	6		16 **That's What Love Is Made Of**	*Would I Love You*	$15		Tamla 54102
12/12/64+	50	8		17 **Come On Do The Jerk**	*Baby Don't You Go*	$15		Tamla 54109
3/27/65	16	11		18 **Ooo Baby Baby**	*All That's Good*	$12		Tamla 54113
7/17/65	16	12		19 **The Tracks Of My Tears**	*A Fork In The Road*	$12		Tamla 54118
10/9/65	14	10		20 **My Girl Has Gone**	*Since You Won My Heart*	$12		Tamla 54123
12/25/65+	11	12		21 **Going To A Go-Go**	*Choosey Beggar* (R&B #35)	$12	■	Tamla 54127
				above 4 from the album *Going To A Go-Go*				
6/18/66	46	8		22 **Whole Lot Of Shakin' In My Heart (Since I Met You)**	*Oh Be My Love*	$12		Tamla 54134
11/5/66	17	9		23 (Come 'Round Here) **I'm The One You Need**	*Save Me*	$12	■	Tamla 54140
				SMOKEY ROBINSON & THE MIRACLES:				
2/18/67	20	10		24 **The Love I Saw In You Was Just A Mirage**	*Come Spy With Me*	$10		Tamla 54145
				also see #37 below				
6/17/67	23	11		25 **More Love**	*Swept For You Baby*	$10		Tamla 54152
11/4/67	4	15		26 **I Second That Emotion** RB[1]	*You Must Be Love*	$10		Tamla 54159
2/24/68	11	12		27 **If You Can Want**	*When The Words From Your Heart Get Caught Up In Your Throat*	$10		Tamla 54162
6/1/68	31	8		28 **Yester Love**	*Much Better Off*	$10		Tamla 54167
8/17/68	26	9		29 **Special Occasion**	*Give Her Up*	$10		Tamla 54172
1/4/69	8	14		30 **Baby, Baby Don't Cry**	*Your Mother's Only Daughter*	$10		Tamla 54178
6/21/69	32	8		31 **Doggone Right** /				
8/23/69	37	9		32 **Here I Go Again**		$10		Tamla 54183
7/5/69	33	6		33 **Abraham, Martin And John**	*Much Better Off*	$10		Tamla 54184
				a tribute to Abraham Lincoln, **Martin Luther King**, and John and Robert Kennedy; above 4 from the album *Time Out*				
12/13/69+	37	8		34 **Point It Out** /				
5/2/70	100	1		35 **Darling Dear**		$10		Tamla 54189
5/23/70	46	7		36 **Who's Gonna Take The Blame**	*I Gotta Thing For You*	$10		Tamla 54194
10/17/70	❶[2]	16		37 **The Tears Of A Clown** RB[3]	*Promise Me*	$8		Tamla 54199
				originally released on The Miracles' 1967 album *Make It Happen*; also issued with "The Love I Saw In You Was Just A Mirage" as the B-side				
3/20/71	18	12		38 **I Don't Blame You At All**	*That Girl*	$8		Tamla 54205
7/3/71	56	7		39 **Crazy About The La La La**	*Oh Baby Baby I Love You*	$8		Tamla 54206
11/20/71+	49	9		40 **Satisfaction**	*Flower Girl*	$8		Tamla 54211
				all of above (except #12, 13, 22, 23, 33, 35 & 36) written or co-written by Robinson				
6/24/72	46	10		41 **We've Come Too Far To End It Now**	*When Sundown Comes*	$8		Tamla 54220
12/16/72+	45	8		42 **I Can't Stand To See You Cry**	*With Your Love Came*	$8		Tamla 54225
				THE MIRACLES:				
8/4/73	56	8		43 **Don't Let It End ('Til You Let It Begin)**	*Wigs And Lashes*	$6		Tamla 54237
8/24/74	13	15		44 **Do It Baby**	*I Wanna Be With You*	$6		Tamla 54248
12/21/74+	78	4		45 **Don't Cha Love It**	*Up Again*	$6		Tamla 54256
10/25/75+	❶[1]	28		46 **Love Machine** (Part 1)	*(Part 2)*	$6		Tamla 54262

MIRANDA BUB '94

Born in 1976 in Burbank, California. Female techno-dance singer/songwriter.

DEBUT	PEAK	WKS	Gold	A-side (Chart Hit)	B-side	$	Sym	Label & Number
6/18/94	66	14		**Your Love Is So Divine** S:51	*(So Divine dub)*	$4	▮	Sunshine 822

MIRETTES, The — see IKETTES, The

DEBUT	PEAK	WKS	Gold	A-side (Chart Hit)...B-side	$	Sym	Label & Number

MISSING PERSONS — LP '82

New-wave group formed in Los Angeles, California: Dale Bozzio (vocals), her then-husband Terry Bozzio (drums), Warren Cuccurullo (guitar), Patrick O'Hearn (bass, synthesizer) and Chuck Wild (keyboards). All but Wild were with **Frank Zappa**'s band. Disbanded in 1986. Terry Bozzio worked with **Jeff Beck** in 1989. Cuccurullo joined **Duran Duran** in 1990.

DEBUT	PEAK	WKS	Gold	A-side (Chart Hit)...B-side	$	Sym	Label & Number
7/3/82	42	11		1 **Words**...*Hello, I Love You*	$4	■	Capitol 5127
10/2/82	42	14		2 **Destination Unknown** *No Way Out*	$4	■	Capitol 5161
1/15/83	63	8		3 **Windows**...*Rock And Roll Suspension*	$4	■	Capitol 5200
3/12/83	70	6		4 **Walking In L.A.**...*Mental Hopscotch*	$4		Capitol 5212
3/17/84	67	6		5 **Give**...*Clandestine People*	$4	■	Capitol 5326

MISSJONES — R&B '98

Born Tarsha Jones in Brooklyn, New York. Female hip-hop singer/songwriter. Also see **AZ**.

DEBUT	PEAK	WKS	Gold	A-side (Chart Hit)...B-side	$	Sym	Label & Number
2/11/95	79	7		1 **Where I Wanna Be Boy**...*(remix) / In Debt To You*	$4	▮	StepSun 7144
7/4/98	62	13		2 **2 Way Street**...S:41 *(instrumental)* **Mario Winans** (backing vocal)	$3	▮	Motown 860788

MISTA — R&B/LP '96

R&B vocal group: Darryl Allen, Bobby Wilson, Brandon Brown and Byron Reeder.

DEBUT	PEAK	WKS	Gold	A-side (Chart Hit)...B-side	$	Sym	Label & Number
6/29/96	53	18		1 **Blackberry Molasses**...S:30 *(3 album snippets)*	$3	▮	EastWest 64299
1/4/97	90	3		2 **Lady**...S:75 *Blackberry Molasses (hotlanta remix)*	$3	▮	EastWest 64222

MISTA GRIMM — R&B '93

Born Rojai Trawick on 8/21/73 in West Covina, California. Male rapper.

DEBUT	PEAK	WKS	Gold	A-side (Chart Hit)...B-side	$	Sym	Label & Number
9/25/93	56	20		**Indo Smoke**...S:40 / A:68 *(radio edit)* from the movie *Poetic Justice* starring **Janet Jackson** and **2 Pac**	$3	▮	Epic Soundtrax 77256

MR. BIG — '77

Pop-disco group from Oxford, England: Jeff Dicken (vocals), Ed Carter (guitar), Robert Hirschman (bass) and Vince Chalk (drums).

DEBUT	PEAK	WKS	Gold	A-side (Chart Hit)...B-side	$	Sym	Label & Number
3/5/77	87	7		**Romeo**...*Ain't Bin A Man*	$4		Arista 0229

MR. BIG — ROK/LP '92

Rock group from San Francisco, California: **Eric Martin** (vocals) (see #1 below), Paul Gilbert (guitar), Billy Sheehan (bass) and Pat Torpey (drums).

DEBUT	PEAK	WKS	Gold	A-side (Chart Hit)...B-side	$	Sym	Label & Number
8/24/85	87	2		1 **Information**...*I Can't Stop The Fire* **ERIC MARTIN**	$3	■	Capitol 5502
12/21/91+	❶^{3}	24	●	2 **To Be With You** S:2 / A:3 *Green-Tinted Sixties Mind* (ROK #33)	$3	▮^{V}	Atlantic 87580
4/11/92	16	20		3 **Just Take My Heart**...A:25 / S:26 *Road To Ruin*	$3	▮^{V}	Atlantic 87509
10/9/93	27	20		4 **Wild World**...S:35 / A:36 *Temperamental*	$3	▮	Atlantic 87308
2/26/94	83	6		5 **Ain't Seen Love Like That**...*What's It Gonna Be*	$3	▮	Atlantic 87278

MR. CHEEKS

Born John Kelly in New York City. Male rapper. Former member of **Lost Boyz**.

DEBUT	PEAK	WKS	Gold	A-side (Chart Hit)...B-side	$	Sym	Label & Number
10/13/01+	14	30		1 **Lights, Camera, Action!**..RB^{1} S:❷^{2} / A:22 *(remix w/***Missy Elliott**, **P. Diddy** & **Petey Pablo**) samples "Keep On Truckin'" by **Eddie Kendricks**	$4	★	Universal 156257
6/1/02	52^{S}	1		2 **Friday Night**...*(3 versions)* **MR. CHEEKS featuring Horace Brown** samples "Fly Robin Fly" by **Silver Convention**	$6	T	Universal 015975

MR. C THE SLIDE MAN — LP '01

Born William Perry in Brooklyn, New York. R&B singer/rapper.

DEBUT	PEAK	WKS	Gold	A-side (Chart Hit)...B-side	$	Sym	Label & Number
1/6/01	83	10		1 **Cha-Cha Slide**...*(3 versions)* "45": Universal 158332; B-side: (album version)	$6	T^{V}	MOB/Universal 158378
6/8/02	74^{S}	2		2 **The Cha Cha Slide Pt. III: Roll Like This**...*(2 versions)*	$6	T	MOB/Orpheus 90410

MR. MISTER — LP '86

Pop-rock group formed in Los Angeles, California: Richard Page (vocals, bass), Steve Farris (guitar), Steve George (keyboards) and Pat Mastelotto (drums). Also see **Pages** and **Larsen-Feiten Band**.

DEBUT	PEAK	WKS	Gold	A-side (Chart Hit)...B-side	$	Sym	Label & Number
3/17/84	57	8		1 **Hunters Of The Night**...*I Get Lost Sometimes*	$4		RCA 13741
9/21/85	❶^{2}	22		2 **Broken Wings** S:❶^{2} / A:❶^{1} *Uniform Of Youth*	$3		RCA 14136
12/21/85+	❶^{2}	20		3 **Kyrie**...AR^{1} S:❶^{2} / A:❶^{2} *Run To Her*	$3	■	RCA 14258
3/29/86	8	17		4 **Is It Love**...A:7 / S:14 *32*	$3	■	RCA 14313
8/22/87	29	11		5 **Something Real (Inside Me/Inside You)**...S:25 / A:30 *Bare My Soul*	$3	■	RCA 5273

MR. PRESIDENT — '97

Dance group consisting of German-born singers T-Seven and Lady Danii with British-born rapper DJ Lazy Dee.

DEBUT	PEAK	WKS	Gold	A-side (Chart Hit)...B-side	$	Sym	Label & Number
8/2/97	21	20		**Coco Jamboo**...S:26 / A:36 *(R&B mix)*	$3	▮^{V}	Warner 17331

MR. SHORT KHOP — LP '01

Born in Los Angeles, California. Male rapper. Discovered by **Ice Cube**.

DEBUT	PEAK	WKS	Gold	A-side (Chart Hit)...B-side	$	Sym	Label & Number
2/10/01	34^{S}	12		**Dollaz, Drank & Dank**...*(3 versions) / M.V.P.'s* (w/**Shaquille O'Neal**) **MR. SHORT KHOP featuring Kokane**	$5	★	TVT 2152

MR. VEGAS — see PAUL, Sean

MISTRESS — LP '79

Rock group from Georgia: Charlie Williams (vocals), Kenny Hopkins and Danny Chauncey (guitars), David Brown (bass) and Chris Paulsen (drums).

DEBUT	PEAK	WKS	Gold	A-side (Chart Hit)...B-side	$	Sym	Label & Number
11/10/79	49	9		**Mistrusted Love**...*You Got The Love*	$5		RSO 1009

MITCHELL, Barbara — see ROBINSON, Smokey

DEBUT	PEAK	WKS	Gold	A-side (Chart Hit)...B-side	$	Sym	Label & Number
				MITCHELL, Chad, Trio LP **'62**			
				Born in 1939 in Spokane, Washington. Folk singer. His trio included Mike Koluk and Joe Frazier. Mitchell left in 1964. **John Denver** joined and group was renamed The Mitchell Trio.			
1/27/62	44	8		1 **Lizzie Borden**...*Super Skier* [C-L]	$12	■	Kapp 439
				originally from the musical revue *New Faces of 1952* starring Eartha Kitt; title refers to the infamous Boston murderess			
5/19/62	99	1		2 **The John Birch Society**...*Golden Vanity* [L-N]	$10	■	Kapp 457
				Jim (Roger) McGuinn of **The Byrds** (banjo and guitar, above 2)			
11/30/63+	43	9		3 **The Marvelous Toy**...*The Bonny Streets Of Fyve-Io* [N]	$8	■	Mercury 72197
	★397★			**MITCHELL, Guy** MEM/POP/BUB/C&W **'56**			
				Born Al Cernik on 2/27/27 in Detroit, Michigan. Died on 7/1/99 (age 72). Sang briefly with Carmen Cavallaro's orchestra in the late '40s. Appearances in several TV series. In the movies *Those Redheads From Seattle* and *Red Garters*. Married Playboy Playmate Elsa Sorenson (aka Dane Arden). Had 2 #2 hits in 1951: "My Heart Cries For You" and "Truly, Truly Fair."			
				1)Singing The Blues 2)Heartaches By The Number 3)Rock-A-Billy			
1/21/56	23	11		1 **Ninety Nine Years (Dead Or Alive)**...T:23 *Perfume, Candy And Flowers*	$20		Columbia 40631
10/27/56	❶[10]	26	●	2 **Singing The Blues /** J:❶[10] / S:❶[9] / T:❶[9] / A:❶[9]			
11/10/56	53	14		3 **Crazy With Love**...T:53	$15	■	Columbia 40769
1/19/57	16	12		4 **Knee Deep In The Blues /** T:16 / J:16 / A:17 / S:21			
2/2/57	47	7		5 **Take Me Back Baby**...T:47 / S:flip	$15	■	Columbia 40820
				Ray Conniff (orch.: #2-5)			
4/6/57	10	17		6 **Rock-A-Billy**...S:10 / T:13 / J:14 / A:15 *Hoot Owl*	$15	■	Columbia 40877
6/17/57	83	1		7 **Sweet Stuff**...T:83 *In The Middle Of A Dark, Dark Night*	$15		Columbia 40940
				Jimmy Carroll (orch.: #1, 6 & 7)			
10/5/59	❶[2]	20		8 **Heartaches By The Number**...*Two*	$15	■	Columbia 41476
2/29/60	51	6		9 **The Same Old Me**...*Build My Gallows High (The Clock In The Tower)*	$10		Columbia 41576
				Joe Sherman (orch., above 2)			
7/11/60	45	10		10 **My Shoes Keep Walking Back To You**...*Silver Moon Upon The Golden Sands*	$10		Columbia 41725
				Monty Kelly (orch.); above 3 were originally Country hits for **Ray Price** in the late '50s			
				MITCHELL, Joni BUB/ROK/LP **'74**			
				Born Roberta Joan Anderson on 11/7/43 in Fort McLeod, Alberta, Canada; raised in Saskatoon, Saskatchewan, Canada. Singer/songwriter/guitarist/pianist. Moved to New York in 1966. Wrote the hits "Both Sides Now" and "Woodstock." Married to her producer/bassist, Larry Klein, from 1982-94. Recipient of *Billboard*'s Century Award in 1995. Inducted into the Rock and Roll Hall of Fame in 1997. Won Grammy's Lifetime Achievement Award in 2002. Also see **James Taylor**.			
				1)Help Me 2)Free Man In Paris 3)Big Yellow Taxi ("live")			
7/25/70	67	6		1 **Big Yellow Taxi**...*Woodstock*	$8		Reprise 0906
				also see #7 & 11 below; B-side is Mitchell's original version of the **Crosby, Stills, Nash & Young** hit			
9/4/71	93	1		2 **Carey**...*This Flight Tonight*	$8		Reprise 1029
11/11/72+	25	16		3 **You Turn Me On, I'm A Radio**...*Urge For Going*	$5		Asylum 11010
				Graham Nash (harmonica)			
12/22/73+	65	8		4 **Raised On Robbery**...*Court And Spark*	$5		Asylum 11029
				Robbie Robertson of **The Band** (guitar)			
3/16/74	7	19		5 **Help Me** AC[1] *Just Like This Train*	$5		Asylum 11034
7/27/74	22	14		6 **Free Man In Paris**...*People's Parties*	$5		Asylum 11041
				David Crosby and **Graham Nash** (backing vocals); **Larry Carlton** and **Jose Feliciano** (guitars)			
12/28/74+	24	10		7 **Big Yellow Taxi**...*Rainy Night House* [L-R]	$5		Asylum 45221
				studio version on #1 above; also see #11 below			
2/7/76	66	4		8 **In France They Kiss On Main Street**...*The Boho Dance*	$5		Asylum 45296
11/20/82	47	9		9 **(You're So Square) Baby, I Don't Care**...*Love*	$4	■	Geffen 29849
				first recorded by **Elvis Presley** for his 1957 movie *Jailhouse Rock*			
12/28/85+	85	3		10 **Good Friends**...*Smokin' (Empty, Try Another)*	$3	■	Geffen 28840
9/13/97	36[A]	8		11 **Got 'Til It's Gone**...		V	album cut
				JANET Featuring Q-Tip and Joni Mitchell			
				samples #1 above; from **Janet Jackson**'s album *The Velvet Rope* on Virgin 44762; "45" (33-1/3 rpm): Virgin 38623; B-side: "Together Again" (Jackson)			
				MITCHELL, Kim ROK/LP **'85**			
				Born on 7/10/52 in Sarnia, Ontario, Canada. Male rock singer/guitarist.			
5/18/85	86	9		**Go For Soda**...*Called Off*	$5		Bronze 99652
				MITCHELL, Willie BUB/R&B/LP **'68**			
				Born on 1/3/28 in Ashland, Mississippi; raised in Memphis, Tennessee. R&B keyboardist/arranger/producer. Led house band and later became president of Hi Records.			
8/29/64	31	10		1 **20-75**...*Secret Home* [I]	$8		Hi 2075
				title refers to the record's label number			
12/19/64+	85	3		2 **Percolatin'**...*Empty Rooms* [I]	$8		Hi 2066
7/17/65	96	2		3 **Buster Browne**...*Woodchopper's Ball* [I]	$8		Hi 2091
5/7/66	92	1		4 **Bad Eye**...*Sugar T* [I]	$8		Hi 2103
7/22/67	96	2		5 **Slippin' & Slidin'**...*Aw Shucks* [I]	$8		Hi 2125
3/9/68	23	15		6 **Soul Serenade** *Mercy Mercy Mercy* [I]	$8		Hi 2140
7/13/68	45	7		7 **Prayer Meetin'**...*Bum Daddy* [I]	$8		Hi 2147
10/5/68	91	4		8 **Up-Hard**...*Beale Street Mood* [I]	$8	■	Hi 2151
2/1/69	69	5		9 **30-60-90**...*Take Five* [I]	$8		Hi 2154
				MITCHUM, Robert C&W **'58**			
				Born on 8/6/17 in Bridgeport, Connecticut. Died of cancer on 7/1/97 (age 79). Legendary actor. Father of actor Chris Mitchum.			
9/8/58	62	11		1 **The Ballad Of Thunder Road**...H:62 *My Honey's Lovin' Arms*	$15		Capitol 3986
				Jack Marshall (orch.); from the movie *Thunder Road* starring Mitchum			
2/24/62	65	10		2 **The Ballad Of Thunder Road**...*My Honey's Lovin' Arms* [R]	$10		Capitol 3986
				#1 on purple label; #2 on yellow/orange label			
8/12/67	96	2		3 **Little Old Wine Drinker Me**...*Walker's Woods*	$8		Monument 1006

DEBUT	PEAK	WKS	Gold	A-side (Chart Hit)...B-side	$	Sym	Label & Number
				MIXTURES, The '71			
				Pop group from Melbourne, Australia: Peter Williams (vocals), Fred Wieland (guitar), Chris Spooner (bass) and Don Lebler (drums).			
3/6/71	44	11		**Pushbike Song**...*Who Loves Ya*	$6		Sire 350
				MOB, The '71			
				Pop group from Chicago, Illinois: Artie Herrera (vocals), Al Herrera, Jimmy "Ford" Franz, Mike "Paris" Sistak, Tony "Roman" Nedza, Gary "Stevens" Beisber, Bobby Raffino and Jimmy "Soul" Holvay. Holvay and Beisber wrote several hits for **The Buckinghams**.			
1/23/71	83	3		1 **I Dig Everything About You**...*Love Has Got A Hold On Me*	$6		Colossus 130
3/13/71	71	4		2 **Give It To Me**...*I'd Like To See More Of You*	$6	■	Colossus 134
				MOBB DEEP R&B/BUB/LP '95			
				Rap duo formed in Queensbridge, New York: Havoc and Prodigy. Both are members of **QB Finest**.			
2/25/95	59	10		1 **Shook Ones Pt. II**...S:31 *Pt. I*	$3	▮	Loud/RCA 64294
6/17/95	69	12		2 **Survival Of The Fittest**...S:45 *(2 remixes)*	$3	▮	Loud/RCA 64356
2/17/96	86	3		3 **Microphone Master**...S:48 *(album version)* **DAS EFX featuring Mobb Deep** samples "Come Clean" by **Jeru The Damaja** and "Neva Go Back" by **Special Ed**	$3	▮	EastWest 64309
5/3/97	72^S	2		4 **G.O.D. Pt. III**...BUB:101 *The After Hours G.O.D. Pt. III* samples "Play This Only At Night" by Doug E. Fresh	$3	▮	Loud/RCA 64833
10/10/98	79	7		5 **Deadly Zone**...S:66 *(instrumental)* **BOUNTY KILLER Featuring Mobb Deep & Rappin' Noyd** from the movie *Blade* starring Wesley Snipes	$5	▮	TVT Soundtrax 8215
1/19/02	99	2		6 **Burn**...*(2 versions)* Vita (female vocal)	$6	T	Loud/Columbia 79669
1/26/02	58	15		7 **Hey Luv (Anything) /** A:57 **MOBB DEEP (Featuring 112)**			
6/15/02	48^S	2		8 **Get Away**... samples "Taking Me Higher" by Barclay James Harvest	$6	T	Loud/Columbia 79753
				MO B. DICK LP '97			
				Born in Morgan City, Louisiana. Male rapper. Cousin of **Master P**. Member of **Tru**.			
5/17/97	60	15		1 **If I Could Change**...S:36 *(2 versions) / Down To Do Whatever* (w/**Mia X** & **Mo B. Dick**) **MASTER P Featuring Steady Mobb'n with Mo B. Dick and O'Dell**	$4	▮	No Limit 53273
9/6/97	25	20	●	2 **I Miss My Homies**...S:15 *(2 versions) / Here We Go* (w/**Mystikal** & Fiend) **MASTER P Featuring Pimp C, The Shocker, Mo B. Dick, O'Dell, Sons of Funk and Mercedes**	$3	▮	No Limit 53290
3/21/98	57	16		3 **Just Be Straight With Me**...S:40 *(instrumental)* **SILKK the SHOCKER Featuring Master P, Destiny's Child, O'Dell, Mo B. Dick** rap version with new lyrics of "Just Be Good To Me" by **The S.O.S. Band**; clean version available on No Limit 53313	$5	▮	No Limit 53305
8/15/98	27	16		4 **Goodbye To My Homies**...S:17 *(2 versions) / Homie Ride* (w/C-Murder) **MASTER P Featuring Silkk the Shocker, Sons of Funk and Mo B. Dick** samples "It's So Hard To Say Goodbye To Yesterday" by **Boyz II Men**; clean version available on No Limit 53451	$3	▮	No Limit 53326
				MOBY ROK/LP '01			
				Born Richard Melville Hall on 9/11/65 in Harlem, New York; raised mostly in Connecticut. Techno-dance artist.			
4/8/00	75^S	1		1 **Natural Blues**...*(3 versions) / Whispering Wind* samples "Trouble So Hard" by Vera Hall	$7	★	V2 27639
12/2/00+	14	32		2 **South Side**...S:7 / A:15 *(album version)* **MOBY Featuring Gwen Stefani**	$5	★	V2 27665
				MOBY GRAPE BUB/LP '67			
				Rock group from San Francisco, California: Alexander "Skip" Spence (vocals, guitar), Jerry Miller and Peter Lewis (guitars), Bob Mosley (bass) and Don Stevenson (drums). Spence, former drummer with **Jefferson Airplane**, left in 1968. Lewis is the son of actress Loretta Young. Spence died of cancer on 4/16/99 (age 52).			
7/8/67	88	3		**Omaha**...*Someday* one in a series of 5 Moby Grape singles released simultaneously	$10	■	Columbia 44173
				MOCEDADES AC/LP '74			
				Vocal group from Bilbao, Spain: siblings Amaya, Izaskum and Roberto Amezaga, with Jose Urien, Carlos Uribarri and Javier Barrenechea.			
1/12/74	9	17		**Eres Tu (Touch The Wind)**...*Touch The Wind (Eres Tu)* [F]	$5		Tara 100
				MODELS ROK/LP '86			
				Pop-rock group formed in Melbourne, Australia: Sean Kelly (vocals, guitar), Roger Mason (keyboards), James Valentine (saxophone), James Freud (bass) and Barton Price (drums).			
4/26/86	37	13		**Out Of Mind Out Of Sight**...A:34 / S:36 *Down In The Garden*	$3	■	Geffen 28762
				MODERNAIRES, The MEM/POP '46			
				Vocal group from Buffalo, New York: husband-and-wife Hal Dickinson and Paula Kelly, Chuck Goldstein, Bill Conway and Ralph Brewster. Dickinson died on 11/18/70 (age 59). Kelly died on 4/2/92 (age 72). Hit #3 in 1946 with "To Each His Own."			
3/31/56	97	1		**April In Paris**...T:97 *Hi-Diddlee-I-Di* Skip Martin (orch.)	$12		Coral 61599
				MODERN ENGLISH LP '90			
				New wave band formed in 1978 in Colchester, England: Robbie Grey (vocals), Gary McDowell (guitar), Stephen Walker (keyboards), Michael Conroy (bass) and Richard Brown (drums).			
4/2/83	78	7		1 **I Melt With You**...*After The Snow* also see #3 below	$5		Sire 29775
4/7/84	91	3		2 **Hands Across The Sea**...*Reflection*	$4		Sire 29339
6/23/90	76	10		3 **I Melt With You**...*Beautiful People* [R] new recording of #1 above	$4	▮	TVT 2812
				MODJO '01			
				Dance duo from France: Yann Destagnol and Romain Branchart.			
1/6/01	81	19		**Lady (hear me tonight)**...S:22 *(3 versions)* samples "Soup For One" by **Chic**	$6	★+	Barclay/MCA 587900

DEBUT	PEAK	WKS	Gold	A-side (Chart Hit)...B-side	$	Sym	Label & Number
				MODUGNO, Domenico LP **'58**			
				Born on 1/9/28 in Polignano a Mare, Italy. Died of a heart attack on 8/6/94 (age 66). Singer/actor.			
8/4/58	❶[5]	16	●	1 **Nel Blu Dipinto Di Blu (Volaré)** ....S:❶[5] / H:❶[5] *Mariti In Citta* [F]	$12		Decca 30677
				title is Italian for "In The Blue Sky Painted Blue (To Fly)"; 1958 Grammy winner: Record of the Year			
3/9/59	97	1		2 **Piove (Ciao, Ciao Bambina)** ....*Farfalle* [F]	$10		Decca 30845
				Piove is Italian for "It Rains"; Fonit (orch., above 2)			
				MOFFATTS, The LP **'99**			
				Family pop vocal group from Canada: Scott (born on 3/30/84) with his triplet brothers, Dave, Bob and Clint (born on 3/8/85) Moffatt.			
5/22/99	75[S]	2		**Until You Loved Me** ....*Let's Party / (3 album snippets)*	$4	★[V]	Capitol 58769
				"45": Capitol 58779; B-side: "Say'n I Love You"			
				MOJO MEN, The **'67**			
				Rock group from San Francisco, California: Jimmy Alaimo (vocals, guitar), Paul Curcio (guitar), Don Metchick (organ) and Dennis DeCarr (drums). Jimmy, cousin of **Steve Alaimo**, died of heart failure on 6/30/92 (age 53).			
10/30/65	61	6		1 **Dance With Me** ....*Loneliest Boy In Town*	$15		Autumn 19
				produced by **Sly Stone**			
2/4/67	36	11		2 **Sit Down, I Think I Love You** ....*Don't Leave Me Crying Like Before*	$10		Reprise 0539
				written by **Stephen Stills**			
5/27/67	83	3		3 **Me About You** ....*When You're In Love*	$10		Reprise 0580
				MOKENSTEF R&B/BUB/LP **'95**			
				Black female vocal trio from Los Angeles, California: Monifa, Kenya and Stephanie. All three were cheerleaders at Morningside High School in Inglewood, California.			
6/17/95	7	23	●	**He's Mine** ....S:5 / A:19 *(instrumental)*	$3	▮	OutBurst 851704
				contains interpolations of "Be Alright" by **Zapp** and "Do Me Baby" by **Prince**			
				MOLLY HATCHET ROK/BUB/LP **'80**			
				Southern-rock group from Jacksonville, Florida: Danny Joe Brown (vocals), Dave Hlubek, Duane Roland and Steve Holland (guitars), Banner Thomas (bass) and Bruce Crump (drums). Jimmy Farrar replaced Brown in 1980; Brown returned and replaced Farrar in 1983. Holland and Thomas left in 1983; John Galvin (keyboards) and Riff West (bass) joined.			
1/5/80	42	10		1 **Flirtin' With Disaster** ....*Gunsmoke*	$5		Epic 50822
3/7/81	91	3		2 **The Rambler** ....*Get Her Back*	$5		Epic 50965
2/6/82	96	2		3 **Power Play** ....*Bloody Reunion* (ROK #31)	$5		Epic 02680
10/20/84	81	5		4 **Satisfied Man** ....*Straight Shooter*	$5		Epic 04648
				MOMENTS, The **'63**			
				Folk singing group put together by producer **Lee Hazlewood**.			
1/12/63	82	5		**Walk Right In** ....*(instrumental)*	$10		Era 3099
	★503★			**MOMENTS, The** R&B/BUB/LP **'70**			
				R&B trio from Hackensack, New Jersey, featuring Mark Greene (falsetto lead). Greene left after first record; replaced by William Brown (lead; born on 6/30/46) and Al Goodman (born on 3/31/47). Harry Ray (born on 12/15/46) joined after "Love On A Two-Way Street" in 1970. Became **Ray, Goodman & Brown** in 1978. Ray died of a stroke on 10/1/92 (age 45).			
				1)Love On A Two-Way Street 2)Special Lady 3)Sexy Mama			
12/28/68+	57	7		1 **Not On The Outside** ....*Understanding*	$8		Stang 5000
5/10/69	90	3		2 **Sunday** ....*Somebody Loves You Baby*	$8		Stang 5003
8/16/69	62	6		3 **I Do** ....*Pocketful of Heartbreaks*	$8		Stang 5005
4/11/70	3	15	●	4 **Love On A Two-Way Street** RB[5] *I Won't Do Anything*	$8		Stang 5012
8/22/70	44	8		5 **If I Didn't Care** ....*You Make Me Feel Good*	$7		Stang 5016
				#2 hit for the Ink Spots in 1939; Willie & The Mighty Magnificents (backing band, above 3)			
11/21/70+	56	9		6 **All I Have** ....*Hurts On Me, Baby*	$7		Stang 5017
8/21/71	98	2		7 **Lucky Me** ....*I Lost One Bird In The Hand (Reaching For Two In The Bush)*	$7		Stang 5031
				all of above co-produced by **Sylvia** (Robinson)			
9/22/73	68	8		8 **Gotta Find A Way** ....*Sweeter As The Days Go By*	$6		Stang 5050
1/12/74	17	13		9 **Sexy Mama** ....*Where Can I Find Her*	$6		Stang 5052
6/8/74	80	4		10 **Sho Nuff Boogie (Part I)** ....*(Part II)*	$5		All Platinum 2350
				SYLVIA & THE MOMENTS			
7/5/75	39	8		11 **Look At Me (I'm In Love)** ....RB[1] *You've Come A Long Way*	$5		Stang 5060
				RAY, GOODMAN & BROWN:			
1/26/80	5	18	●	12 **Special Lady** ....RB[1] *Deja Vu*	$4		Polydor 2033
5/10/80	76	4		13 **Inside Of You** ....*Treat Her Right*	$4		Polydor 2077
8/23/80	47	10		14 **My Prayer** ....*The Way It Should Be*	$4		Polydor 2116
				MONACO **'97**			
				Rock duo from England: Peter Hook (of **New Order**) and David Potts.			
8/16/97	61[A]	4		**What Do You Want From Me?**			album cut
				from the album *Music For Pleasure* on Polydor 537629			
				MONA LISA R&B/BUB **'96**			
				Born on 11/20/79 in Brooklyn, New York. Female hip-hop singer.			
2/17/96	65	13		1 **Can't Be Wasting My Time** ....S:55 *(w/o rap)*	$3	▮[V]	Island 854538
				MONA LISA featuring Lost Boyz			
				samples "MC's Act Like They Don't Know" by **KRS-One**; from the movie *Don't Be A Menace* starring Marlon Wayans; "45": Island 854552; B-side: "All The Things" by **Joe** (#11)			
6/22/96	83	5		2 **You Said** ....S:66 *(instrumental) / You Can't Be Wasting My Time (remix)*	$3	▮	Island 854630
				MONARCHS, The **'64**			
				Pop group from Louisville, Kentucky: Mike Gibson (lead vocals), cousins Bob and Lou Lange, Don Leffler, Leon Middleton, Dusty Miller, Paul Schuler, Butch Snyder and Jimmy Wells. Bob Lange died on 9/26/94 (age 51).			
2/22/64	47	13		**Look Homeward Angel** ....*What Made You Change Your Mind*	$15		Sound Stage 7 2516

MONCH, Pharoahe — see PHAROAHE MONCH

DEBUT	PEAK	WKS	Gold	A-side (Chart Hit)...B-side	$	Sym	Label & Number
				MONDAY, Julie '66			
				Pop singer; similar in style to **Petula Clark**.			
8/20/66	**96**	2		**Come Share The Good Times With Me** .... *Time Is Running Out For Me*	$12		Rainbow 100
				MONDO ROCK '87			
				Rock group formed in Australia: Ross Wilson (vocals), Eric McCusker (guitar), Duncan Veall (keyboards), Andrew Ross (sax), James Gillard (bass) and J.J. Hackett (drums).			
5/23/87	**71**	6		**Primitive Love Rites** .... *Under Lights*	$4		Columbia 06981
				MONEY, Eddie ★190★ ROK/BUB/LP '86			
				Born Edward Mahoney on 3/2/49 in Brooklyn, New York. Rock singer/songwriter. Discovered and subsequently managed by the late West Coast promoter Bill Graham. Formerly an officer with the New York Police Department. Also see **Kenny Loggins**' "I'm Alright."			
				1)Take Me Home Tonight 2)Walk On Water 3)Baby Hold On 4)Peace In Our Time 5)I Wanna Go Back			
2/25/78	**11**	20		1 **Baby Hold On** .... *Save A Little Room In Your Heart For Me*	$5		Columbia 10663
6/24/78	**22**	14		2 **Two Tickets To Paradise** .... *Don't Worry*	$5		Columbia 10765
11/25/78+	**72**	8		3 **You've Really Got A Hold On Me** .... *Jealousys*	$5		Columbia 10842
1/27/79	**22**	13		4 **Maybe I'm A Fool** .... *Life For The Taking*	$5		Columbia 10900
5/12/79	**63**	5		5 **Can't Keep A Good Man Down** .... *Nightmare*	$5		Columbia 10981
8/25/79	**46**	8		6 **Get A Move On** .... *Don't You Ever Say No* (Zane Buzby) from the movie *Americathon* starring John Ritter	$5		Columbia 11064
9/13/80	**78**	4		7 **Running Back** .... *The Wish*	$4		Columbia 11325
10/18/80	**65**	6		8 **Let's Be Lovers Again** .... *Million Dollar Girl* (Money) **EDDIE MONEY (with Valerie Carter)**	$4		Columbia 11377
7/3/82	**16**	17		9 **Think I'm In Love** .... AR^{3} *Drivin' Me Crazy*	$4	■	Columbia 02964
10/9/82	**63**	9		10 **Shakin'** .... *My Friends, My Friends*	$4		Columbia 03252
11/19/83+	**54**	11		11 **The Big Crash** .... *Backtrack*	$4	■	Columbia 04199
2/25/84	**66**	7		12 **Club Michelle** .... *Back On The Road*	$4	■	Columbia 04376
8/16/86	**4**	23		13 **Take Me Home Tonight** AR^{2} A:4 / S:5 *Calm Before The Storm* **Ronnie Spector** (**The Ronettes**) sings the lead line from "Be My Baby"	$4	□	Columbia 06231
12/20/86+	**14**	21		14 **I Wanna Go Back** .... A:10 / S:17 *Broken Down Chevy*	$3	■	Columbia 06569
4/11/87	**21**	19		15 **Endless Nights** .... S:19 / A:20 *Bring On The Rain*	$3	■	Columbia 07035
9/19/87	**90**	3		16 **We Should Be Sleeping** .... *I Can't Hold Back* above 4 from the album *Can't Hold Back*	$3	■	Columbia 07359
10/1/88	**9**	21		17 **Walk On Water** .... A:8 / S:10 *Dancing With Mr. Jitters*	$3	■	Columbia 08060
1/14/89	**24**	18		18 **The Love In Your Eyes** .... AR^{1} A:20 / S:27 *Bad Boy*	$3		Columbia 68532
4/22/89	**60**	7		19 **Let Me In** .... *Forget About Love* (ROK #36)	$3		Columbia 68739
12/2/89+	**11**	15		20 **Peace In Our Time** .... S:9 / A:9 *Where's The Party? (live)*	$3	▮V	Columbia 73047
9/14/91	**58**	8		21 **Heaven In The Back Seat** .... *Fire And Water*	$3	▮V	Columbia 73976
12/21/91+	**21**	20		22 **I'll Get By** .... A:23 / S:39 *Think Twice*	$3	▮	Columbia 74109
5/16/92	**54**	11		23 **Fall In Love Again** .... A:54 *(acoustic version)*	$3	▮	Columbia 74262
				MONEY, JT R&B/LP '99			
				Born Jeff Tompkins in Florida. Male rapper. Former leader of the rap duo Poison Clan.			
4/24/99	**5**	20	●	1 **Who Dat** .... S:2 / A:47 *(2 versions)* **JT MONEY Featuring Solé**	$4	★	Tony Mercedes 53469
10/30/99	**21**	16	●	2 **4,5,6** .... S:7 *(clean version) / Da Story* **SOLÉ Featuring J.T. Money and Kandi**	$4	★	DreamWorks 59029
	★222★			**MONICA** R&B/BUB/LP '98			
				Born Monica Arnold on 10/24/80 in Atlanta, Georgia. R&B singer.			
				1)The Boy Is Mine 2)The First Night 3)Angel Of Mine			
4/29/95	**2**^{3}	29	▲	1 **Don't Take It Personal (just one of dem days)** .... RB^{2} S:❶^{1} / A:9 *(2 versions)* samples "Back Seat (Of My Jeep)" by **L.L. Cool J**; "45" B-side: (instrumental)	$3	▮V	Rowdy 35040
10/21/95	**7**	28	▲	2 **Before You Walk Out Of My Life** / RB^{2} S:5 / A:28			
10/21/95		28		3 **Like This And Like That** .... Mr. Malik (guest rapper); samples "Spoonin' Rap" by **Sugarhill Gang**	$3	▮	Rowdy 35052
6/8/96	**9**	20	●	4 **Why I Love You So Much** / S:5 / A:46 all of above from the album *Miss Thang*			
6/15/96		19		5 **Ain't Nobody** .... features **Naughty By Nature**; contains portions of "Poverty's Paradise" by 24 Karat Black	$3	▮V	Rowdy 35072
3/15/97	**4**	32	▲	6 **For You I Will** .... A:4 / S:5 *(instrumental)* from the movie *Space Jam* starring Michael Jordan	$3	▮	Warner Sunset 87003
5/30/98	❶^{13}	27	▲^{2}	7 **The Boy Is Mine** RB^{8} S:❶^{9} / A:2 *(instrumental)* **BRANDY & MONICA**	$3	▮V	Atlantic 84089
8/15/98	❶^{5}	23	▲	8 **The First Night** .... RB^{6} S:❶^{6} / A:18 *Cross The Room* samples "Love Hangover" by **Diana Ross**	$4	★	Arista 13522
12/5/98+	❶^{4}	30	▲	9 **Angel Of Mine** .... S:❶^{4} / A:❶^{2} *The First Night (remix w/***Jermaine Dupri** *& R.O.C.)*	$4	★	Arista 13590
2/24/01	**64**	13		10 **Just Another Girl** .... A:61 from the movie *Down To Earth* starring Chris Rock (soundtrack on Epic 61599)			album cut
8/10/02	**69**	7		11 **All Eyez On Me** .... S:50 / A:67 *(3 versions)* samples "P.Y.T. (Pretty Young Thing)" by **Michael Jackson**	$6	T	J Records 21181

DEBUT	PEAK	WKS	Gold	A-side (Chart Hit)....B-side	$	Sym	Label & Number

MONIFAH R&B/BUB/LP **'98**

Born Monifah Carter on 1/28/68 in Harlem, New York. Female R&B singer/actress. Sang backup for **Maxi Priest**.

DEBUT	PEAK	WKS	Gold	A-side (Chart Hit)....B-side	$	Sym	Label & Number
10/28/95+	56	20		1 **I Miss You (Come Back Home)** *[MONIFA]*....S:39 *(instrumental)*	$3	▮	Uptown/MCA 55107
				from the TV series *New York Undercover* starring Michael DeLorenzo			
5/11/96	32	19	●	2 **You**....S:14 *I Miss You (Come Back Home) (remix)*	$3	▮	Uptown/Universal 56001
				above 2 written and produced by **Heavy D**			
1/4/97	82	9		3 **You Don't Have To Love Me**....S:56 *Nobody's Body* (R&B #71A)	$3	▮	Uptown/Universal 56026
8/8/98	9	26		4 **Touch It** S:11 / A:22 *(album version) / (3 album snippets)*	$4	★	Uptown/Universal 56207
				samples "White Horse" by **Laid Back**			
4/10/99	68[S]	3		5 **Suga Suga**....*(album version) / Bad Girl*	$4	★	Uptown/Universal 56237

MONITORS, The R&B/BUB **'66**

R&B vocal group: Sandra and John "Maurice" Fagin, Warren Harris and Richard Street. Street, formerly with the Distants, joined **The Temptations** in 1971. Also recorded as The Majestics.

DEBUT	PEAK	WKS	Gold	A-side (Chart Hit)....B-side	$	Sym	Label & Number
4/16/66	100	1		**Greetings (This Is Uncle Sam)**....*Number One In Your Heart*	$20		V.I.P. 25032

MONK, T.S. R&B/LP **'81**

Born Thelonious Sphere Monk on 12/27/49 in Harlem, New York. R&B singer/drummer. Son of legendary jazz pianist Thelonious Monk.

DEBUT	PEAK	WKS	Gold	A-side (Chart Hit)....B-side	$	Sym	Label & Number
2/21/81	63	8		**Bon Bon Vie (Gimme The Good Life)**....*Stay Free Of His Love*	$4	⊙	Mirage 3780

MONKEES, The ★152★ BUB/LP **'67**

Pop group formed in 1965 in Los Angeles, California. Members chosen from over 400 applicants for new Columbia TV series. Consisted of **Davy Jones** (vocals; born on 12/30/45 in Manchester, England), **Michael Nesmith** (guitar, vocals; born on 12/30/42 in Houston, Texas), Peter Tork (bass, vocals; born on 2/13/44 in Washington DC) and **Micky Dolenz** (drums, vocals; born on 3/8/45 in Tarzana, California). Jones had been a racehorse jockey, and appeared in London musicals *Oliver* and *Pickwick*. Nesmith had done session work for Stax/Volt. Tork had been in the Phoenix Singers. Dolenz had appeared in the TV series *Circus Boy*, using the name Mickey Braddock in 1956. Group starred in the movie *Head* (1968) and 58 episodes of *The Monkees* TV show, 1966-68. Tork left in 1968. Group disbanded in 1969. Re-formed (minus Nesmith) in 1986 and again (with Nesmith) in 1996.

1)I'm A Believer 2)Daydream Believer 3)Last Train To Clarksville 4)A Little Bit Me, A Little Bit You 5)Pleasant Valley Sunday

DEBUT	PEAK	WKS	Gold	A-side (Chart Hit)....B-side	$	Sym	Label & Number
9/10/66	❶[1]	15	●	1 **Last Train To Clarksville**....*Take A Giant Step*	$15	■	Colgems 1001
				picture sleeve issued with either a full-color or a black-and-white photo of the group			
12/10/66	❶[7]	15	●	2 **I'm A Believer /**			
12/17/66+	20	8		3 **(I'm Not Your) Steppin' Stone**....	$15	■	Colgems 1002
				first recorded by **Paul Revere & The Raiders** on their 1966 album *Midnight Ride*			
3/25/67	2[1]	10	●	4 **A Little Bit Me, A Little Bit You /**			
				an early unreleased issue on Colgems 1003 (B-side: "She Hangs Out") featured the same color picture sleeve ($800) used for #6 below; #2 & 4: written by **Neil Diamond**			
3/25/67	39	5		5 **The Girl I Knew Somewhere**....	$15		Colgems 1004
7/22/67	3	10	●	6 **Pleasant Valley Sunday /**			
7/22/67	11	9		7 **Words**....	$15	■	Colgems 1007
11/18/67	❶[4]	12	●	8 **Daydream Believer**....*Goin' Down (#104)*	$15	■	Colgems 1012
				also see #20 below			
3/9/68	3	10	●	9 **Valleri /**			
3/9/68	34	6		10 **Tapioca Tundra**....	$12		Colgems 1019
6/15/68	19	7		11 **D. W. Washburn /**			
6/15/68	51	7		12 **It's Nice To Be With You**....	$12	■	Colgems 1023
10/12/68	62	6		13 **Porpoise Song**....*As We Go Along (#106)*	$20	■	Colgems 1031
				from the movie *Head* starring The Monkees			
2/22/69	56	7		14 **Tear Drop City**....*A Man Without A Dream*	$20	■	Colgems 5000
				#1, 3, 7, 9 & 14: written by **Tommy Boyce & Bobby Hart**			
6/7/69	63	8		15 **Listen To The Band /**			
5/10/69	81	2		16 **Someday Man**....	$20	■	Colgems 5004
9/20/69	82	5		17 **Good Clean Fun**....*Mommy And Daddy (#109)*	$30	■	Colgems 5005
6/6/70	98	2		18 **Oh My My**....*I Love You Better*	$30	■	Colgems 5011
7/5/86	20	14		19 **That Was Then, This Is Now**....S:16 / A:28 *(Theme From) The Monkees*	$5	■	Arista 9505
				second pressings labeled as: **MICKY DOLENZ AND PETER TORK (OF THE MONKEES)** ($5)			
11/1/86	79	4		20 **Daydream Believer**....*Randy Scouse Git* [R]	$5	■	Arista 9532
				remix of #8 above			
9/26/87	87	4		21 **Heart and Soul**....*MGBGT (live)*	$4	■	Rhino 74408

MONO LP **'98**

Dance duo from England: Siobahn DeMare (female vocals) and Martin Virgo (instruments).

DEBUT	PEAK	WKS	Gold	A-side (Chart Hit)....B-side	$	Sym	Label & Number
2/14/98	70	15		**Life In Mono**....*(5 versions)*	$8	★*	Echo/Mercury 568285
				samples "The Ipcress File" by **John Barry**; from the movie *Great Expectations* starring Gwyneth Paltrow			

MONOTONES, The **'58**

R&B vocal group from Newark, New Jersey: Charles Patrick (lead), Warren Davis (1st tenor), George Malone (2nd tenor), Warren Ryanes (baritone), Frank Smith (bass) and John Ryanes (bass). John Ryanes died on 5/30/72 (age 31). Warren Ryanes died in June 1982 (age 45). Smith died of cancer on 11/26/2000 (age 61).

DEBUT	PEAK	WKS	Gold	A-side (Chart Hit)....B-side	$	Sym	Label & Number
3/24/58	5	18		**Book Of Love**....T:5 / S:6 / A:9 *You Never Loved Me*	$40		Argo 5290
				first released on Mascot 124 in 1957 ($700)			

MONRO, Matt BUB/AC/LP **'61**

Born Terrence Parsons on 12/1/32 in London, England. Died of cancer on 2/7/85 (age 52). Sang with **Cyril Stapleton's Orchestra** before going solo.

DEBUT	PEAK	WKS	Gold	A-side (Chart Hit)....B-side	$	Sym	Label & Number
5/29/61	18	14		1 **My Kind Of Girl**....*This Time*	$12		Warwick 636
10/16/61	92	3		2 **Why Not Now**....*Love Is The Same Anywhere*	$12		Warwick 669
				melody is from the 1927 tune "Ay, Ay, Ay"			
11/28/64+	23	9		3 **Walk Away**....*April Fool*	$10		Liberty 55745
				Johnnie Spence (orch., all of above)			

DEBUT	PEAK	WKS	Gold	A-side (Chart Hit).....B-side	$	Sym	Label & Number

MONROE, Vaughn — MEM/POP/BUB '49

Born on 10/7/11 in Akron, Ohio. Died on 5/21/73 (age 61). Big-voiced baritone/trumpeter/bandleader. Very popular on radio, and featured in several movies. Charted 52 pop hits, 1940-54 (including 5 #1s: "There! I've Said It Again," "Let It Snow! Let It Snow! Let It Snow!," "Ballerina," "(Ghost) Riders In The Sky" and "Someday").

DEBUT	PEAK	WKS	Gold	A-side (Chart Hit).....B-side	$	Sym	Label & Number
11/12/55	38	4		1 **Black Denim Trousers And Motorcycle Boots** .....T:38 *All By Myself*	$12		RCA Victor 6260
1/21/56	38	7		2 **Don't Go To Strangers** .....T:38 *Steel Guitar* first recorded by **Al Martino** in 1954 on Capitol 2899 ($12)	$12		RCA Victor 6358
9/1/56	11	13		3 **In The Middle Of The House** .....A:11 / T:21 *Rollin' Heart* [N] **Joe Reisman** (orch.)	$12		RCA Victor 6619
5/25/59	87	2		4 **The Battle Of New Orleans** .....*Hercules* Norman Leyden (orch. and chorus); promo picture sleeve issued for the B-side movie theme *Hercules*	$10	□	RCA Victor 7495

MONROES, The — LP '82

Pop-rock group from San Diego, California: Jesus Ortiz (vocals), Rusty Jones (guitar), Eric Denton (keyboards), Bob "Monroe" Davis (bass) and Jonnie Gilstrap (drums).

DEBUT	PEAK	WKS	Gold	A-side (Chart Hit).....B-side	$	Sym	Label & Number
5/29/82	59	8		**What Do All The People Know** .....*Yamarock*	$5		Alfa 7119

MONTANAS, The — BUB '68

Pop-rock group from England.

DEBUT	PEAK	WKS	Gold	A-side (Chart Hit).....B-side	$	Sym	Label & Number
3/2/68	58	7		**You've Got To Be Loved** .....*Difference Of Opinion*	$10		Independence 83

MONTE, Lou — BUB/MEM/POP/LP '63

Born on 4/2/17 in Lyndhurst, New Jersey. Died on 6/12/89 (age 72). Italian-styled novelty singer/guitarist. Hit #7 on the pop charts in 1954 with "Darktown Strutters Ball."

DEBUT	PEAK	WKS	Gold	A-side (Chart Hit).....B-side	$	Sym	Label & Number
3/10/58	12	18		1 **Lazy Mary (Luna Mezzo Mare)** .....S:12 / T:12 / A:22 *Angelique* [F] Italian song also known as "The Butcher Boy"; #5 hit for Rudy Vallee in 1938	$10		RCA Victor 7160
6/30/58	54	5		2 **The Sheik Of Araby (Italian Style)** .....T:54 *Eh, Marie! Eh, Marie!* [F] Italian version of popular song written in 1921; above 2 sung in Italian and English	$10		RCA Victor 7265
12/8/62+	5	10	●	3 **Pepino The Italian Mouse** ...*What Did Washington Say (When He Crossed the Delaware)* [N]	$10	■	Reprise 20,106
3/9/63	78	3		4 **Pepino's Friend Pasqual (The Italian Pussy-Cat)** .....*I Like You, You Like Me, Eh Paisan* [N] **Joe Reisman** (orch., all of above)	$10	■	Reprise 20,146

MONTENEGRO, Hugo, His Orchestra And Chorus — BUB/AC/LP '68

Born on 9/2/25 in Brooklyn, New York. Died of emphysema on 2/6/81 (age 55). Conductor/composer/arranger.

DEBUT	PEAK	WKS	Gold	A-side (Chart Hit).....B-side	$	Sym	Label & Number
2/17/68	2^1	22		1 **The Good, The Bad And The Ugly** .....AC^3 *March With Hope* [I]	$8		RCA Victor 9423
6/29/68	82	5		2 **Hang 'Em High** .....*Tomorrow's Love* [I] above 2 are title songs from movies starring **Clint Eastwood**	$7		RCA Victor 9554

MONTENEGRO, Pilar — '02

Born Maria Lopez in Mexico. Latin singer/actress.

DEBUT	PEAK	WKS	Gold	A-side (Chart Hit).....B-side	$	Sym	Label & Number
5/25/02	74	13		**Quítame Ese Hombre** .....A:72 [F] title is Spanish for "Remembering That Man"; from the album *Deshago* on Univision 310026			album cut

MONTEZ, Chris — BUB/AC/LP '62

Born Ezekiel Christopher Montanez on 1/17/43 in Los Angeles, California. Protege of **Ritchie Valens**. Began career as a rock and roll singer, then switched to an Adult Contemporary-style under the tutelage of **Herb Alpert**.

DEBUT	PEAK	WKS	Gold	A-side (Chart Hit).....B-side	$	Sym	Label & Number
8/4/62	4	14		1 **Let's Dance** *You're The One*	$20		Monogram 505
12/8/62+	43	9		2 **Some Kinda Fun** .....*Tell Me (It's Not Over)*	$15		Monogram 507
1/8/66	22	10		3 **Call Me** .....*Go Head On*	$8		A&M 780
4/16/66	16	14		4 **The More I See You** .....*You, I Love You* #7 hit for **Dick Haymes** in 1945 (from the movie *Billy Rose's Diamond Horseshoe* starring Betty Grable)	$8		A&M 796
8/13/66	33	8		5 **There Will Never Be Another You** .....*You Can Hurt The One You Love* #19 hit for **Sammy Kaye** in 1943 (from the movie *Iceland* starring Sonja Henie)	$8		A&M 810
10/29/66	36	8		6 **Time After Time** .....*Keep Talkin'* #16 hit for **Frank Sinatra** in 1947 (from the movie *It Happened In Brooklyn*)	$8		A&M 822
3/4/67	71	5		7 **Because Of You** .....*Elena* #1 hit for **Tony Bennett** in 1951; written in 1940; #3, 4, 6 & 7: produced by **Herb Alpert**	$8		A&M 839

MONTGOMERY, John Michael — C&W/BUB/LP '99

Born on 1/20/65 in Danville, Kentucky. Country singer/guitarist. Charted 30 Country hits, 1992-02. Younger brother of Eddie of **Montgomery Gentry**.

1)Hold On To Me 2)The Little Girl 3)I Swear

DEBUT	PEAK	WKS	Gold	A-side (Chart Hit).....B-side	$	Sym	Label & Number
5/8/93	60	13		1 **I Love The Way You Love Me** .....CW^3 S:30 *(3 album snippets)* "45" B-side: "Life's A Dance" (C&W #4)	$4	▮V	Atlantic 87371
2/12/94	42	20	●	2 **I Swear** .....CW^4 S:12 *(3 album snippets)* "45" B-side: "Dream On Texas Ladies"	$4	▮V	Atlantic 87288
5/14/94	63^S	4		3 **Rope The Moon** .....BUB:115 *(3 album snippets)* "45" B-side: "Friday At Five"	$4	▮V	Atlantic 87248
8/6/94	73	10		4 **Be My Baby Tonight** .....CW^2 S:32 *(3 album snippets)* "45" B-side: "Full-Time Love"	$4	▮V	Atlantic 87236
12/28/96+	69	12		5 **Friends** .....S:45 *(3 album snippets)* "45" B-side: "A Few Cents Short"	$4	▮V	Atlantic 87019
8/1/98	91	9		6 **Cover You In Kisses** .....S:65 *(3 album excerpts)* "45" B-side: "Little Cowboy's Cry"	$4	▮V	Atlantic 84157
12/5/98+	33	19		7 **Hold On To Me** A:32 / S:46 *(3 album excerpts)* "45" B-side: "This One's Gonna 'Leave A Mark'"	$4	★V	Atlantic 84197
6/5/99	71	6		8 **Hello L.O.V.E.** A:61			album cut
10/2/99	45	20		9 **Home To You** .....A:31 above 2 from the album *Home To You* on Atlantic 83185			album cut
9/9/00	35	20		10 **The Little Girl** .....CW^3 A:22 from the album *Brand New Me* on Atlantic 83378; "45": Atlantic 85006; B-side: "Brand New Me"		V	album cut

DEBUT	PEAK	WKS	Gold	A-side (Chart Hit)...B-side	$	Sym	Label & Number
				MONTGOMERY, Melba C&W '74			
				Born on 10/14/38 in Iron City, Tennessee; raised in Florence, Alabama. Country singer/guitarist/fiddler. Charted 30 Country hits, 1963-86.			
4/13/74	39	10		**No Charge**...CW[1] *I Love Him Because He's That Way*	$6		Elektra 45883
				MONTGOMERY, Tammy — see TERRELL, Tammi			
				MONTGOMERY, Wes BUB/AC/LP '67			
				Born John Leslie Montgomery on 3/6/25 in Indianapolis, Indiana. Died on 6/15/68 (age 43). Jazz guitarist.			
11/25/67	44	11		1 **Windy**...*Watch What Happens* [I]	$8		A&M/CTI 883
7/6/68	91	3		2 **Georgia On My Mind**...*I Say A Little Prayer For You* [I]	$8		A&M/CTI 940
				MONTGOMERY GENTRY C&W/LP '99			
				Country vocal duo of Eddie Montgomery and Troy Gentry. Montgomery is the older brother of **John Michael Montgomery**.			
3/27/99	62	11		1 **Hillbilly Shoes**...S:50 / A:56 *All Night Long*	$4	★V	Columbia 79115
7/31/99	46	19		2 **Lonely And Gone**...A:41 / S:62 *I've Loved A Lot More Than I've Hurt* "45" B-side: "Hillbilly Shoes"	$4	★V	Columbia 79210
3/4/00	79	6		3 **Daddy Won't Sell The Farm**...A:68			album cut
11/11/00+	47[S]	9		4 **All Night Long**...*Merry Christmas From The Family* (C&W #38) **MONTGOMERY GENTRY Featuring Charlie Daniels** all of above from the album *Tattoos & Scars* on Columbia 69156	$4	★V	Columbia 79515
4/7/01	37	21		5 **She Couldn't Change Me** S:28 / A:29 *Hillbilly Shoes (acoustic version)*	$4	★V	Columbia 79540
9/28/02	40	20		6 **My Town**...A:36 from the album *My Town* on Columbia 86520; "45": Columbia 79786; B-side: "Hell Yeah"		V	album cut
				**MOODY BLUES, The** ★186★ ROK/BUB/AC/LP '72			
				Art-rock group formed in Birmingham, England: Denny Laine (guitar, vocals; born on 10/29/44), Ray Thomas (flute, vocals; born on 12/29/41), Mike Pinder (keyboards, vocals; born on 12/27/41), Clint Warwick (bass; born on 6/25/39) and Graeme Edge (drums; born on 3/30/41). Laine and Warwick left in the summer of 1966; replaced by **Justin Hayward** (lead vocals, lead guitar; born on 10/14/46) (see #12, 13 & 15 below) **& John Lodge** (vocals, bass; born on 7/20/45). Laine joined **Paul McCartney**'s **Wings** in 1971. Switzerland-born Patrick Moraz (born on 6/24/48; former keyboardist of **Yes**) replaced Pinder in 1978; left group in early 1992.			
				1)Nights In White Satin 2)Your Wildest Dreams 3)Go Now! 4)I'm Just A Singer (In A Rock And Roll Band) 5)Gemini Dream			
2/20/65	10	14		1 **Go Now!**...*Lose Your Money* song introduced in 1964 by Bessie Banks on Tiger 102 ($20)	$15		London 9726
6/5/65	93	3		2 **From The Bottom Of My Heart (I Love You)**...*And My Baby's Gone*	$15		London 9764
4/2/66	98	1		3 **Stop!**...*Bye Bye Bird* Denny Laine (of **Wings**, lead singer on above 3)	$15		London 9810
7/20/68	24	11		4 **Tuesday Afternoon (Forever Afternoon)**...*Another Morning*	$10		Deram 85028
10/12/68	61	5		5 **Ride My See-Saw**...*Voices In The Sky*	$10		Deram 85033
6/28/69	91	4		6 **Never Comes The Day**...*So Deep Within You*	$10		Deram 85044
5/2/70	21	12		7 **Question**...*Candle Of Life*	$7		Threshold 67004
8/7/71	23	11		8 **The Story In Your Eyes**...*Melancholy Man*	$7	■	Threshold 67006
4/22/72	29	10		9 **Isn't Life Strange**...*After You Came*	$7		Threshold 67009
8/5/72	2[2]	18	●	10 **Nights In White Satin** *Cities* with the London Festival Orchestra; originally "Bubbled Under" (#103) on 2/10/68	$8		Deram 85023
2/3/73	12	10		11 **I'm Just A Singer (In A Rock And Roll Band)**...*For My Lady*	$7		Threshold 67012
5/17/75	47	7		12 **I Dreamed Last Night**...*Remember Me, My Friend*	$6		Threshold 67019
12/13/75+	94	5		13 **Blue Guitar**...*When You Wake Up* **JUSTIN HAYWARD & JOHN LODGE** (above 2)	$6	■	Threshold 67021
7/29/78	39	8		14 **Steppin' In A Slide Zone**...*I'll Be Level With You*	$6		London 270
10/7/78	47	13		15 **Forever Autumn**...*The Fighting Machine* (The Fighting Machine) **JUSTIN HAYWARD** from the musical album version of H.G. Wells' *War Of The Worlds*	$6		Columbia 10799
11/4/78	59	7		16 **Driftwood**...*I'm Your Man* #4-14 & 16: produced by Tony Clarke	$6		London 273
6/6/81	12	15		17 **Gemini Dream**...*Painted Smile*	$5		Threshold 601
8/8/81	15	17		18 **The Voice**...AR[4] *22,000 Days* (ROK #38)	$5	■	Threshold 602
11/7/81	65	7		19 **Talking Out Of Turn**...*Veteran Cosmic Rocker*	$5		Threshold 603
9/3/83	27	10		20 **Sitting At The Wheel**...*Going Nowhere*	$4	■	Threshold 604
11/12/83	62	6		21 **Blue World**...*Sorry*	$4		Threshold 605
4/19/86	9	21		22 **Your Wildest Dreams**...AC[2] S:8 / A:13 *Talkin' Talkin'*	$3	■	Polydor 883906
8/16/86	58	9		23 **The Other Side Of Life**...*The Spirit* also released on Polydor 885212 in 1986 (with an updated tour schedule on back of sleeve)	$3	■	Polydor 885201
6/4/88	30	16		24 **I Know You're Out There Somewhere**...S:27 / A:36 *Miracle* all of above (except #1-3 & 15) written by Hayward and/or Lodge	$3	■	Polydor 887600
				MOONEY, Art, And His Orchestra MEM/POP/BUB '48			
				Born on 1/26/13 in Lowell, Massachusetts. Died on 9/9/93 (age 80). Orchestra leader. Hit #1 in 1948 with "I'm Looking Over A Four Leaf Clover."			
4/23/55	6	17	●	1 **Honey-Babe** S:6 / J:6 / A:10 *No Regrets* adaptation of a traditional army marching chant, as featured in the movie *Battle Cry* starring Aldo Ray and **Tab Hunter**	$15		MGM 11900
12/17/55	6	4	●	2 **Nuttin' For Christmas**...S:6 / T:7 / J:9 / A:10 *Santa Claus Looks Just Like Daddy* [X-N] **ART MOONEY And His ORCHESTRA with Barry Gordon** verse melody based on traditional 19th century French song "Vive La Companie"; picture sleeve issued Christmas, 1956	$20	■	MGM 12092
7/7/56	73	2		3 **Daydreams**...T:73 *Somebody Stole My Muchacha (Cha-Cha-Cha)* The Cloverleafs (backing vocals); charted for 1 week on 7/7/56 and 1 week on 9/8/56 (#94)	$10		MGM 12277
11/3/56	77	2		4 **Giant**...T:77 *Rock And Roll Tumbleweed* title song from the movie starring Elizabeth Taylor, Rock Hudson and James Dean	$10		MGM 12320

DEBUT	PEAK	WKS	Gold	A-side (Chart Hit)...B-side	$	Sym	Label & Number
				MOONEY, Art, And His Orchestra — Cont'd			
2/24/58	**88**	2		5 **The River Kwai March and Colonel Bogey** ...T:88 *Bullfight* [I]	$10		MGM 12590
				from the movie *The Bridge On The River Kwai* starring Alec Guinness and William Holden; "March" written for the movie; "Bogey" is a 1916 traditional march			
6/13/60	**100**	2		6 **Banjo Boy** ...*Captain Buffalo*	$8		MGM 12908
				The Ivys (vocals)			
				MOONGLOWS, The R&B/LP **'55**			
				R&B group from Louisville, Kentucky: lead singers Bobby Lester (died of cancer on 10/15/80, age 50) and **Harvey Fuqua**, with Alexander "Pete" Graves (tenor), Prentiss Barnes (bass) and Billy Johnson (guitar; died on 4/29/87). Group inducted into the Rock and Roll Hall of Fame in 2000.			
3/26/55	**20**	1		1 **Sincerely** ...RB[2] J:20 *Tempting*	$60		Chess 1581
				Bobby Lester (lead vocal); legendary DJ Alan Freed listed as co-writer			
9/1/56	**25**	14		2 **See Saw** ...S:25 / T:28 *When I'm With You* (R&B #15)	$50		Chess 1629
7/8/57	**73**	6		3 **Please Send Me Someone To Love** ...T:73 *Mr. Engineer (Bring Her Back To Me)*	$50		Chess 1661
				#1 R&B hit in 1950 for **Percy Mayfield**			
9/15/58	**22**	16		4 **Ten Commandments Of Love** ...H:22 / S:39 *Mean Old Blues*	$30		Chess 1705
				HARVEY and The Moonglows			
				Marvin Gaye (member on #4); Harvey Fuqua (lead vocal, above 3)			
				MOONLION **'76**			
				Studio instrumental disco group assembled by producers Rick Bleiweiss and Bill Stahl.			
1/10/76-	**95**	1		**The Little Drummer Boy** ...*Laid Back* [X-I]	$7		P.I.P. 6513
				MOORE, Abra **'97**			
				Born on 6/8/69 in San Diego, California; raised in Puna, Hawaii. Female alternative pop-rock singer/songwriter/guitarist/actress.			
7/19/97	**63**	13		**Four Leaf Clover** ...A:73 *Guitar Song*	$4	▮V	Arista/Austin 13097
				"45": Arista/Austin 13082; B-side: (alternate version)			
				MOORE, Bob, and His Orch. BUB/LP **'61**			
				Born on 11/30/32 in Nashville, Tennessee. Top session bass player. Member of the **Owen Bradley Quintet**. Led the band on **Roy Orbison**'s sessions for Monument Records. Also worked as sideman for **Elvis Presley**, **Brenda Lee**, **Pat Boone** and others.			
8/14/61	**7**	15		**Mexico** ...AC[1] *Hot Spot* [I]	$15		Monument 446
				MOORE, Bobby R&B **'75**			
				R&B-disco singer/bassist. Session work for **J.J. Cale**, **Bob Dylan** and **Moby Grape**.			
8/9/75	**99**	2		**(Call Me Your) Anything Man** ...*(disco version)*	$6		Scepter 12405
				MOORE, Bobby, & The Rhythm Aces R&B **'66**			
				R&B group from Montgomery, Alabama: Bobby Moore (tenor sax), Chico Jenkins (vocals), Larry Moore, Joe Frank, Clifford Laws, Marion Sledge and John Baldwin, Jr.			
6/25/66	**27**	10		1 **Searching For My Love** ...*Hey, Mr. D.J.*	$15		Checker 1129
12/17/66	**97**	2		2 **Try My Love Again** ...*Go Ahead And Burn*	$12		Checker 1156
				BOBBY MOORE'S RHYTHM ACES featuring Chico			
				MOORE, Chanté R&B/BUB/AC/LP **'99**			
				Born on 2/17/67 in San Francisco, California. Female R&B-dance singer. Married to actor Kadeem Hardison from 1996-2000. Married **Kenny Lattimore** on 1/1/2002.			
12/26/92+	**86**	11		1 **Love's Taken Over** ...S:69 *(4 album snippets)*	$3	▮	Silas/MCA 54321
5/15/99	**10**	18	●	2 **Chanté's Got A Man** ...S:6 / A:25 *Your Home Is In My Heart* (w/**Boyz II Men**)	$4	★	Silas/MCA 55544
				samples "One Bad Apple" by **The Osmonds**			
10/28/00	**83**	9		3 **Straight Up** ...*(3 versions)*	$6	T	Silas/MCA 155775
				MOORE, Dorothy R&B/BUB/LP **'76**			
				Born on 10/13/47 in Jackson, Mississippi. R&B singer. Lead singer of **The Poppies**.			
3/20/76	**3**	22		1 **Misty Blue** ...*Here It Is*	$7		Malaco 1029
				#4 Country hit for Wilma Burgess in 1966			
7/24/76	**58**	11		2 **Funny How Time Slips Away** ...*Ain't That A Mother's Luck*	$6		Malaco 1033
				written by **Willie Nelson**			
8/6/77	**27**	15		3 **I Believe You** ...*Love Me*	$6		Malaco 1042
				written by **The Addrisi Brothers**			
				MOORE, Gary ROK/BUB/LP **'91**			
				Born on 4/4/52 in Belfast, Ireland. Rock guitarist with **Thin Lizzy** (1974, 1978-79) and BBM.			
2/16/91	**97**	3		**Still Got The Blues** ...*Oh Pretty Woman* (ROK #15)	$4	▮	Charisma 98854
				MOORE, Jackie R&B/BUB **'71**			
				Born in 1946 in Jacksonville, Florida. Female R&B singer.			
12/5/70+	**30**	15	●	1 **Precious, Precious** ...*Willpower*	$6		Atlantic 2681
7/7/73	**42**	12		2 **Sweet Charlie Babe** ...*If*	$6		Atlantic 2956
				MOORE, Mandy BUB/LP **'00**			
				Born Amanda Moore on 4/10/84 in Nashua, New Hampshire. Pop singer/actress. Played "Jamie Sullivan" in the movie *A Walk To Remember.*			
9/11/99	**41**	20		1 **Candy** ...S:8 *(instrumental) / (4 album snippets)*	$4	★+V	550 Music 79240
				"45" B-side: (same version)			
6/17/00	**24**	17		2 **I Wanna Be With You** ...A:23			album cut
				from the movie *Center Stage* starring Amanda Schull (soundtrack on Epic 63969)			
				MOORE, Melba R&B/BUB/LP **'79**			
				Born Melba Hill on 10/29/45 in Harlem, New York. R&B-disco singer/actress. Charted 32 R&B hits, 1975-90. Appeared in several movies and Broadway shows.			
4/24/76	**91**	5		1 **This Is It** ...*Stay Awhile*	$5	■	Buddah 519
1/20/79	**47**	7		2 **You Stepped Into My Life** ...*There's No Other Like You*	$4		Epic 50600
				written by the **Bee Gees**; produced by **McFadden & Whitehead**			

DEBUT	PEAK	WKS	Gold	A-side (Chart Hit)...B-side	$	Sym	Label & Number
				MOORE, Tim LP '74			
				Born in Manhattan, New York. Pop singer/songwriter/guitarist/keyboardist.			
4/14/73	93	3		1 **Fool Like You** ... *Thinking About You*	$5		Dunhill/ABC 4337
9/21/74	58	5		2 **Second Avenue** ... *Aviation Man*	$4		Asylum 45208
				first released on 'a small record company' 0601 in 1974 ($10)			
2/8/75	91	3		3 **Charmer** ... *I'll Be Your Time*	$4	■	Asylum 45214
				text sleeve states "1974 Grand Prize winner best song first annual American Song Festival"			
7/16/77	75	3		4 **In The Middle** ... *To Cry For Love*	$4		Asylum 45394
				MOORER, Allison — see KID ROCK			
				M.O.P. R&B/LP '01			
				Rap duo from Brooklyn, New York: Lil' Fame and Billy Danzenie. M.O.P.: Mashed Out Posse.			
3/17/01	63S	1		1 **Ante Up (Remix)** ... *(2 versions) / Cold As Ice*	$7	T	Loud 1984
				M.O.P. (feat. Busta Rhymes, Tephlon, and Remy Martin)			
5/26/01	40S	10		2 **Torture** ... *Turn It Up*	$5	★	Hydra 9111
				SCREWBALL Feat. M.O.P.			
				MORALES, Michael LP '89			
				Born on 4/25/63 in San Antonio, Texas. Pop singer/songwriter.			
4/29/89	15	19		1 **Who Do You Give Your Love To?** ... A:14 / S:16 *Won't You Come Home*	$3	■	Wing 887743
8/12/89	28	13		2 **What I Like About You** ... A:21 / S:30 *Won't You Come Home*	$3	▮	Wing 889678
12/9/89	81	6		3 **I Don't Know** ... *Hey Lori!*	$3	▮V	Wing 873282
7/27/91	73	4		4 **I Don't Wanna See You** ... *What Will I Do? / (3 album snippets)*	$3	▮	Wing 867396
				MORGAN, Debelah R&B '00			
				Born in Detroit, Michigan. Female R&B singer.			
9/19/98	56	11		1 **Yesterday** ... S:36 *Whatever*	$3	▮	Motown 860800
7/29/00+	8	29	●	2 **Dance With Me** ... S:3 / A:20 *(2 remixes)*	$5	★+V	Atlantic 84783
				melody is from "Hernando's Hideaway" by **Archie Bleyer** (#2 hit in 1954); "45" B-side: (Soul Central mix)			
				MORGAN, Jane AC/BUB/C&W/LP '57			
				Born Jane Currier in 1920 in Boston, Massachusetts; raised in Florida. Pop singer.			
11/10/56	41	12		1 **Two Different Worlds** ... T:41 *Nights In Verona* (Williams)	$12		Kapp 161
				ROGER WILLIAMS and JANE MORGAN			
8/26/57	7	29	●	2 **Fascination** A:7 / T:11 / S:12 *(whistling instrumental w/The Troubadors)*	$12	■	Kapp 191
				JANE MORGAN and The Troubadors			
				from the movie *Love In The Afternoon* starring Gary Cooper and Audrey Hepburn; French melody composed in 1904 as "Valse Tzigane"			
9/22/58	21	15		3 **The Day The Rains Came** ... H:21 *Le Jour Ou La Pluie Viendra*	$12		Kapp 235
				Vic Schoen (orch.); above 2 reissued in 1962 on Kapp 14 "Special Juke Box Record" with a text sleeve			
7/27/59	39	11		4 **With Open Arms** ... *I Can't Begin To Tell You* (#113)	$12	■	Kapp 284
11/9/59+	57	9		5 **Happy Anniversary** ... *C'est La Vie, C'est L'Amour*	$10	■	Kapp 305
				title song from the movie starring David Niven; Frank Hunter (orch., above 2)			
	★360★			**MORGAN, Jaye P.** MEM/AC/BUB '55			
				Born Mary Margaret Morgan on 12/3/31 in Mancos, Colorado. Sang with **Frank DeVol**'s band from 1950-53. Regular on TV's *The Gong Show*. Sister of recording group **The Morgan Brothers**.			
				1)That's All I Want From You 2)The Longest Walk 3)Danger! Heartbreak Ahead 4)Chee Chee-oo-Chee 5)If You Don't Want My Love			
11/27/54+	3	21		1 **That's All I Want From You** A:3 / S:5 / J:5 *Dawn*	$15		RCA Victor 5896
3/12/55	12	8		2 **Danger! Heartbreak Ahead** / A:12 / J:13 / S:18			
4/9/55	12	1		3 **Softly, Softly** ... S:flip	$15		RCA Victor 6016
6/11/55	12	5		4 **Chee Chee-oo Chee (Sang the Little Bird)** / A:12 / J:14 / S:24			
6/25/55	18	1		5 **Two Lost Souls** ... A:18 / S:flip	$15		RCA Victor 6137
				PERRY COMO and JAYE P. MORGAN (above 2)			
				from the Broadway musical *Damn Yankees* starring Gwen Verdon; Mitchell Ayres (orch., above 2)			
8/20/55	6	14		6 **The Longest Walk** / A:6 / J:7 / S:13 / T:19			
10/8/55	6	1		7 **Swanee** ... J:flip	$15		RCA Victor 6182
				#1 hit for Al Jolson in 1920			
11/12/55	12	10		8 **If You Don't Want My Love** / J:12 / T:40			
11/12/55+	14	13		9 **Pepper-Hot Baby** ... J:14 / T:21	$15		RCA Victor 6282
				Joe Thomas (orch.)			
12/24/55+	48	8		10 **Not One Goodbye** ... T:48 *My Bewildered Heart*	$15		RCA Victor 6329
3/31/56	83	2		11 **Get Up! Get Up! (You Sleepyhead)** / T:83			
3/24/56	85	3		12 **Sweet Lips** ... T:85	$15		RCA Victor 6441
5/26/56	69	5		13 **Lost In The Shuffle** / T:69			
5/26/56	79	4		14 **Play For Keeps** ... T:79	$15		RCA Victor 6505
7/21/56	81	1		15 **Johnny Casanova** ... T:81 *The West Point Dress Parade*	$15		RCA Victor 6565
10/27/56	97	1		16 **Just Love Me** ... T:97 *The Call Of The Wild*	$15		RCA Victor 6653
				Hugo Winterhalter (orch., all of above - except #4, 5 & 9)			
12/1/56	47	9		17 **Mutual Admiration Society** ... T:47 *If'n*	$20		RCA Victor 6708
				EDDY ARNOLD and JAYE P. MORGAN			
				from the musical *Happy Hunting* starring Ethel Merman			
2/9/59	65	6		18 **Are You Lonesome Tonight** /			
				#4 hit for Vaughn Deleath in 1927			
2/16/59	78	5		19 **Miss You** ...	$10		MGM 12752
				#8 hit for **Dinah Shore** in 1942 (written in 1929); **Ray Ellis** (orch., above 2)			
8/29/60	66	6		20 **I Walk The Line** ... *Wondering Where You Are*	$10		MGM 12924
				MORGAN, Lee LP '65			
				Born on 7/10/38 in Philadelphia, Pennsylvania. Fatally shot on 2/19/72 (age 33). Jazz trumpeter.			
12/19/64+	81	4		**The Sidewinder, Part 1** ... *Part 2* [I]	$8		Blue Note 1911

DEBUT	PEAK	WKS	Gold	A-side (Chart Hit)..................B-side	$	Sym	Label & Number
				MORGAN, Lorrie C&W/BUB/LP **'97**			
				Born Loretta Lynn Morgan on 6/27/59 in Nashville, Tennessee. Country singer. Married to Keith Whitley from 1986 until his death in 1989. Married to Jon Randall from 1996-99. Married **Sammy Kershaw** on 9/29/2001.			
10/4/97	85	6		1 **Go Away** ....S:65 *I've Enjoyed As Much Of This As I Can Stand*	$4	▮V	BNA 64914
5/15/99	86	5		2 **Maybe Not Tonight** A:73		V	album cut
				LORRIE MORGAN & SAMMY KERSHAW			
				from Kershaw's album *Maybe Not Tonight* on Mercury 538889 and Morgan's album *My Heart* on BNA 67763; "45": BNA 65729; B-side: "Go Away" (Morgan - C&W #3/'97)			
				MORGAN, Meli'sa R&B/LP **'86**			
				Born in Queens, New York. Female R&B singer.			
1/25/86	46	14		**Do Me Baby** ....RB^{3} *(interlude version)*	$3	■	Capitol 5523
				written by **Prince**			
				MORGAN, Russ, And His Orchestra MEM/POP **'49**			
				Born on 4/29/04 in Scranton, Pennsylvania. Died on 8/8/69 (age 65). Trombonist/pianist/vocalist/bandleader. Hit #1 in 1949 with "Cruising Down The River" and "Forever And Ever." His trademark: "Music In The Morgan Manner."			
11/12/55	30	8		1 **Dogface Soldier** ....T:30 *Don't Cry Sweetheart*	$12		Decca 29703
				from the movie *To Hell And Back* starring Audie Murphy; tune originally written in 1942			
3/3/56	19	15		2 **The Poor People Of Paris** ....J:19 / A:23 / T:26 *Annabelle* [I]	$12		Decca 29835
				MORGAN BROTHERS, The **'59**			
				Vocal trio from Mancos, Colorado: Dick, Duke and Charley Morgan. Brothers of **Jaye P. Morgan**.			
2/9/59	50	8		**Nola** ....*Guiding Star*	$12		MGM 12747
				LeRoy Holmes (orch.); #3 instrumental hit for bandleader Vincent Lopez in 1922			
				MORISETTE, Johnnie **'62**			
				Born in 1935 in Montu Island, South Pacific. Died on 8/1/2000 (age 65). Sang with the R&B group The Medallions as "Johnny Twovoice."			
4/14/62	63	9		**Meet Me At The Twistin' Place** ....*Anytime, Anyplace, Anywhere*	$15		SAR 126
				written by **Sam Cooke**			
	★357★			**MORISSETTE, Alanis** ROK/LP **'96**			
				Born on 6/1/74 in Ottawa, Ontario, Canada. Adult Alternative rock singer/songwriter. At age 12, she acted on the Nickelodeon cable-TV kids series *You Can't Do That On Television.* Played God in the 1999 movie *Dogma.*			
				1)Ironic 2)You Learn 3)Thank U			
6/17/95	13^{A}	32		1 **You Oughta Know** ....MR^{5}			album cut
				also see #6 below			
8/19/95	15^{A}	28		2 **Hand In My Pocket** ....MR^{1}			album cut
11/18/95	65^{A}	6		3 **All I Really Want**			album cut
3/16/96	4	32	●	4 **Ironic** MR^{3} A:2 / S:10 *Not The Doctor (live) / Forgiven (live)*	$3	▮V	Maverick/Sire 17698
7/27/96	6	30		5 **You Learn** / A:❶^{5} / S:30			
7/27/96		30		6 **You Oughta Know** ....S:flip [L-R]	$3	▮V	Maverick/Sire 17644
				recorded at the Grammy Awards in Los Angeles on 2/28/96; also see #1 above			
8/10/96	3^{A}	47		7 **Head Over Feet**			album cut
				all of above (except #6) from the album *Jagged Little Pill* on Maverick/Sire 45901			
3/28/98	4^{A}	29		8 **Uninvited**			album cut
				from the movie *City Of Angels* starring Nicolas Cage (soundtrack on Warner Sunset 46867)			
10/3/98	2^{1A}	18		9 **Thank U** ....HOT:17(11 wks)			album cut
2/6/99	58	6		10 **Unsent** A:50			album cut
				above 2 from the album *Supposed Former Infatuation Junkie* on Maverick 47094			
2/2/02	23	20		11 **Hands Clean** A:24			album cut
				from the album *Under Rug Swept* on Maverick 47988			
				MORLEY, Cozy **'57**			
				Born in Philadelphia, Pennsylvania. Teen pop singer.			
5/6/57	62	3		**I Love My Girl** ....T:62 *Why Don't You Fall In Love?*	$20		ABC-Paramount 9811
				Peter DeAngelis (orch. and chorus)			
				MORMON TABERNACLE CHOIR, The LP **'59**			
				Popular 375-voice choir directed by Richard Condie (died on 12/22/85).			
9/7/59	13	16		**Battle Hymn Of The Republic** ....*The Lord's Prayer*	$10	■	Columbia 41459
				with the Philadelphia Orchestra, Eugene Ormandy, conductor; written in 1862; #1 hit for The Columbia Stellar Quartet in 1918			
				MORNING MIST — see CASHMAN & WEST			
				MORODER, Giorgio BUB/LP **'79**			
				Born on 4/26/40 in Ortisel, Italy. Disco-electronica composer/conductor/producer for numerous soundtracks. Produced seven of **Donna Summer**'s albums.			
3/4/72	46	8		1 **Son Of My Father** *[GIORGIO]* ....*Underdog*	$6		Dunhill/ABC 4304
1/20/79	33	12		2 **Chase** ....*Love's Theme* [I]	$5		Casablanca 956
				from the movie *Midnight Express* starring Brad Davis			
7/21/84	81	4		3 **Reach Out** ....*(instrumental)*	$4	■	Columbia 04511
				GIORGIO MORODER (Featuring Paul Engemann)			
				Track Theme from the Official Music of the XXIIIrd Olympiad in Los Angeles, 1984			
				MORRIS, Marlowe, Quintet **'62**			
				Born on 5/16/15 in Harlem, New York. Died in May 1978 (age 63). Black jazz pianist.			
3/31/62	95	1		**Play The Thing** ....*Bad Business Baby* (John "Mr. Soul" McArthur) [I]	$10	□	Columbia 42218
				MORRIS, Nathan — see BOYZ II MEN			
				MORRISON, Dorothy — see HAWKINS, Edwin, Singers			
				MORRISON, Mark R&B/BUB/LP **'97**			
				Born on 5/12/74 in Hanover, Germany; raised in Leicester, England. R&B singer.			
3/1/97	2^{1}	40	▲	1 **Return Of The Mack** ....S:5 / A:5 *(remix)*	$3	▮	Atlantic 84868
				samples "N.T." by **Kool & The Gang**			
4/18/98	76	7		2 **Moan & Groan** ....S:59 *Return Of The Mack (remix)*	$3	▮	Atlantic 84038

DEBUT	PEAK	WKS	Gold	A-side (Chart Hit).......B-side	$	Sym	Label & Number

MORRISON, Van — ROK/BUB/AC/LP '71

Born George Ivan on 8/31/45 in Belfast, Ireland. "Blue-eyed soul"-rock singer/songwriter. Leader of **Them**. Wrote the classic rock hit "Gloria." Inducted into the Rock and Roll Hall of Fame in 1993.

1)Domino 2)Brown Eyed Girl 3)Blue Money

DEBUT	PEAK	WKS	Gold	A-side (Chart Hit).......B-side	$	Sym	Label & Number
7/15/67	10	16		1 **Brown Eyed Girl** ....*Goodbye Baby (Baby Goodbye)*	$12		Bang 545
4/4/70	39	8		2 **Come Running** ....*Crazy Love*	$6		Warner 7383
11/14/70+	9	12		3 **Domino** *Sweet Jannie*	$6		Warner 7434
2/6/71	23	12		4 **Blue Money** ....*Sweet Thing*	$6		Warner 7462
6/5/71	95	2		5 **Call Me Up In Dreamland** ....*Street Choir*	$6		Warner 7488
10/9/71	28	11		6 **Wild Night** ....*When That Evening Sun Goes Down*	$6		Warner 7518
1/1/72	47	8		7 **Tupelo Honey** ....*Starting A New Life*	$6		Warner 7543
8/19/72	61	6		8 **Jackie Wilson Said (I'm In Heaven When You Smile)** ....*You've Got The Power*	$6		Warner 7616
10/28/72	98	2		9 **Redwood Tree** ....*Saint Dominic's Preview*	$6		Warner 7638
11/19/77	92	4		10 **Moondance** ....*Cold Wind In August* title cut from his 1970 album	$5		Warner 8450
9/16/78	42	11		11 **Wavelength** ....*Checkin' It Out* all of above written by Morrison	$5		Warner 8661

MORRISSEY — ROK/BUB/LP '94

Born Steven Patrick Morrissey on 5/22/59 in Davyhulme, Manchester, England. Alternative-rock singer/songwriter. Former lead singer/songwriter of The Smiths.

DEBUT	PEAK	WKS	Gold	A-side (Chart Hit).......B-side	$	Sym	Label & Number
3/19/94	46	15		**The More You Ignore Me, The Closer I Get**......MR^7 A:33 *Used To Be A Sweet Boy*	$4	▮	Sire/Reprise 18207

MORROW, Buddy, and His Orchestra — MEM/POP '51

Born Muni Zudecoff on 2/8/19 in New Haven, Connecticut. Trombone star for many top big bands. His own swing band was a hit in the early 1950s. Later played with the *Tonight Show* band and conducted the **Tommy Dorsey Orchestra**. Hit #8 in 1951 with "Rose, Rose, I Love You."

DEBUT	PEAK	WKS	Gold	A-side (Chart Hit).......B-side	$	Sym	Label & Number
4/21/56	82	4		**Main Title From "The Man With The Golden Arm"** ....T:82 *I Should Care* [I] title song from the movie starring **Frank Sinatra**	$15		Wing 90063

MOS DEF — LP '01

Born in Brooklyn, New York. Male rapper. Member of the rap duo **Black Star** and the rap trio **Urban Renewal Program**.

DEBUT	PEAK	WKS	Gold	A-side (Chart Hit).......B-side	$	Sym	Label & Number
8/22/98	60	10		1 **Definition** ....S:45 *(2 versions) / Twice Inna Lifetime* **MOS DEF & KWELI are BLACK STAR**	$4	▮	Rawkus 173
3/13/99	50^S	9		2 **Respiration** ....*(4 versions)* **MOS DEF & TALIB KWELI ARE BLACK STAR**	$5	★	Rawkus 53473
12/23/00+	83	12		3 **Oh No** ....S:33 *(2 versions) / Battle* (**Erick Sermon** w/Sy Scott) **MOS DEF & PHAROAHE MONCH Featuring Nate Dogg**	$6	T	Rawkus 289
10/13/01	50^S	5		4 **Jam On It** *(3 versions)* [N]	$5	★	MIC 470102
9/7/02	55^S	3		5 **Brown Sugar (Extra Sweet)** ....*(5 versions)* **MOS DEF Featuring Faith Evans** from the movie *Brown Sugar* starring Taye Diggs	$6	T	Fox/MCA 113986
11/2/02	10^S	6		6 **Six Days** ....*(2 versions) / 100 Metre Dash* **DJ SHADOW featuring Mos Def** samples "Six Day War" by Colonel Bagshot and "I Cry In The Morning" by Dennis Olivieri	$8	★$^{++}$	MCA 063874

MOSLEY, Lou — '02

Born in Compton, California. R&B singer/songwriter/guitarist.

DEBUT	PEAK	WKS	Gold	A-side (Chart Hit).......B-side	$	Sym	Label & Number
4/20/02	13^S	29		**Slow Dance** ....*(2 versions) / It's Your Love*	$5	★	Jenstar 1380

MOSS-SCOTT, Brandy — '02

Born in Los Angeles, California. Female R&B singer.

DEBUT	PEAK	WKS	Gold	A-side (Chart Hit).......B-side	$	Sym	Label & Number
12/16/00	61^S	1		1 **Tears Of A Clown** ....*(2 versions)* **BRANDY MOSS-SCOTT (featuring Coolio)**	$6	★	Heavenly 2000
9/15/01	15^S	20		2 **Bye-Bye Baby** ....*(instrumental)*	$6	★	Heavenly 2002
6/22/02	5^S	27		3 **I Don't Really Know** ....*(no B-side)*	$6	★	Heavenly 2004

MOST, Donny — '76

Born on 8/8/53 in Brooklyn, New York. Actor/singer. Played "Ralph Malph" on TV's *Happy Days*.

DEBUT	PEAK	WKS	Gold	A-side (Chart Hit).......B-side	$	Sym	Label & Number
12/4/76	97	3		**All Roads (Lead Back To You)** ....*Better To Forget Him*	$5	■	United Artists 871

MOTELS, The — ROK/BUB/LP '82

Pop-rock group formed in Los Angeles, California: **Martha Davis** (vocals) (see #8 below), Guy Perry (guitar), Marty Jourard (keyboards), Michael Goodroe (bass) and Brian Glascock (drums). Guitarist Scott Thurston joined in 1983. Group disbanded in 1987.

DEBUT	PEAK	WKS	Gold	A-side (Chart Hit).......B-side	$	Sym	Label & Number
4/24/82	9	23		1 **Only The Lonely** *Change My Mind*	$4	■	Capitol 5114
9/4/82	52	9		2 **Take The L.** ....*Mission Of Mercy* (ROK #23)	$4	■	Capitol 5149
11/13/82	60	8		3 **Forever Mine** ....*So L.A.*	$4	■	Capitol 5182
9/3/83	9	20		4 **Suddenly Last Summer** ....AR^2 *Some Things Never Change*	$3	■	Capitol 5271
12/3/83+	36	12		5 **Remember The Nights** ....*Killing Time*	$3	■	Capitol 5246
7/20/85	21	13		6 **Shame** ....S:22 / A:22 *Save The Last Dance For Love*	$3	■	Capitol 5497
10/26/85	84	3		7 **Shock** ....*In The Jungle (Concrete Jungle)*	$3	■	Capitol 5529
11/21/87	80	8		8 **Don't Tell Me The Time** ....*Lust* **MARTHA DAVIS**	$3	■	Capitol 44057

MOTEN, Wendy — R&B '93

Born in Memphis, Tennessee. R&B singer/actress. Starred in the musical *Mama I Want To Sing*.

DEBUT	PEAK	WKS	Gold	A-side (Chart Hit).......B-side	$	Sym	Label & Number
2/20/93	55	15		**Come In Out Of The Rain** ....A:44 *Magic Touch* "45": EMI 17322; B-side: "A Matter Of Fact"	$3	▮^{V}	EMI 50417

MOTHERLODE — BUB/LP '69

Pop-rock group from Canada: William Smith (vocals, keyboards), Ken Marco (guitar), Steve Kennedy (sax) and Wayne Stone (drums). Smith died of a heart attack on 12/1/97 (age 53).

DEBUT	PEAK	WKS	Gold	A-side (Chart Hit).......B-side	$	Sym	Label & Number
8/9/69	18	13		**When I Die** ....*Hard Life*	$8		Buddah 131

DEBUT	PEAK	WKS	Gold	A-side (Chart Hit)...B-side	$	Sym	Label & Number
				MOTHER'S FINEST R&B/LP **'77**			
				R&B group from Dayton, Ohio: husband-and-wife Glenn Murdoch and **Joyce Kennedy** (vocals), Gary Moore (guitar), Michael Keck (keyboards), Jerry Seay (bass) and Barry Borden (drums).			
9/4/76	93	2		1 **Fire** ... *Dontcha Wanna Love Me*	$5		Epic 50269
9/10/77	58	6		2 **Baby Love** ... *Hard Rock Lover*	$5		Epic 50407
				MO THUGS FAMILY — see BONE THUGS-N-HARMONY			
	★482★			**MÖTLEY CRÜE** ROK/LP **'90**			
				Hard-rock group from Los Angeles: Vince Neil (vocals; born Vince Wharton on 2/8/61), Mick Mars (guitar; born Bob Deal on 4/3/56), Nikki Sixx (bass; born Frank Ferranno on 12/11/58) and Tommy Lee (drums; born Thomas Bass on 10/3/62). Sixx married actress Donna D'Errico on 12/23/96. Lee was married to actress Heather Locklear from 1986-93; married to actress Pamela Anderson from 1995-98.			
				1)Dr. Feelgood 2)Without You 3)Girls, Girls, Girls			
2/4/84	54	10		1 **Looks That Kill** ... *Piece Of Your Action*	$5	■	Elektra 69756
6/16/84	90	2		2 **Too Young To Fall In Love** ... *Take Me To The Top*	$5	■	Elektra 69732
7/13/85	16	15		3 **Smokin' In The Boys Room** ... S:15 / A:15 *Use It Or Lose It*	$4	■	Elektra 69625
10/26/85	89	6		4 **Home Sweet Home** ... *Red Hot*	$4		Elektra 69591
				also see #13 below			
5/30/87	12	15		5 **Girls, Girls, Girls** ... S:9 / A:14 *Sumthin' For Nuthin'*	$3	■	Elektra 69465
11/28/87	83	8		6 **You're All I Need** ... *All In The Name*	$3		Elektra 69429
				first pressings titled only as "All I Need"			
9/2/89	6	16	●	7 **Dr. Feelgood** S:5 / A:12 *Sticky Sweet*	$3	■	Elektra 69271
11/25/89+	27	16		8 **Kickstart My Heart** ... S:19 / A:31 *She Goes Down*	$3	▮V	Elektra 69248
2/24/90	8	17		9 **Without You** ... S:6 / A:9 *Slice Of Your Pie*	$3	▮V	Elektra 64985
6/2/90	19	16		10 **Don't Go Away Mad (Just Go Away)** ... A:16 / S:18 *Rattlesnake Shake*	$3	▮	Elektra 64962
9/8/90	78	9		11 **Same Ol' Situation (S.O.S.)** ... *Wild Side*	$3	▮	Elektra 64942
				above 5 from the album *Dr. Feelgood*			
9/21/91	63	5		12 **Primal Scream** ... S:27 *Dancing On Glass*	$3	▮	Elektra 64848
11/9/91+	37	17		13 **Home Sweet Home '91** ... S:42 / A:61 *You're All I Need* [R]	$3	▮	Elektra 64818
				remix of #4 above			
				MOTORS, The LP **'80**			
				Pop-rock duo from England: Andy McMaster and Nick Garvey. Peter Bramall (later of **Bram Tchaikovsky**) was an early group member through 1978.			
5/17/80	78	5		**Love And Loneliness** ... *Time For Make-Up*	$5	■	Virgin 67007
				MOTT THE HOOPLE ROK/BUB/LP **'72**			
				Glitter-rock group formed in England: **Ian Hunter** (vocals; born on 6/3/46) (see #4 below), Mick Ralphs (guitar), Pete Watts (bass) and Dale Griffin (drums). Group name taken from a Willard Manus novel. Ralphs left in 1973 to join **Bad Company**; guitarists Morgan Fisher and Ariel Bender joined. Hunter left in 1976; Fisher, Watts and Griffin formed the **British Lions**.			
9/23/72	37	11		1 **All The Young Dudes** ... *One Of The Boys*	$8	■	Columbia 45673
				David Bowie (rhythm guitar and backing vocal)			
1/27/73	96	1		2 **One Of The Boys** ... *Sucker*	$7		Columbia 45754
				above 2 produced by **David Bowie**			
6/8/74	96	2		3 **The Golden Age Of Rock 'N' Roll** ... *Rest In Peace*	$7		Columbia 46035
8/11/79	68	6		4 **Just Another Night** ... *Cleveland Rocks*	$5		Chrysalis 2352
				IAN HUNTER			
				MOUNTAIN BUB/LP **'70**			
				Power-rock group led by Leslie West (born Leslie Weinstein on 10/22/45 in New York City, New York) and Felix Pappalardi (born in 1939 in the Bronx, New York; fatally shot on 4/17/83, age 44). Group formed after Pappalardi produced West's solo album *Mountain*. Numerous personnel changes with regular members Steve Knight (keyboards) and Corky Laing (drums).			
4/4/70	21	17		1 **Mississippi Queen** ... *The Laird*	$7		Windfall 532
3/27/71	76	7		2 **The Animal Trainer And The Toad** ... *Tired Angels (For J.M.H.)*	$7		Windfall 534
				MOUTH & MACNEAL LP **'72**			
				Pop vocal duo from Holland: Willem "Mouth" Duyn and Maggie MacNeal (born Sjoukje Van't Spijker).			
4/29/72	8	19	●	1 **How Do You Do?** ... *Land Of Milk And Honey*	$6		Philips 40715
10/21/72	87	3		2 **Hey, You Love** ... *Why Did You, Why?*	$6		Philips 40717
				MOVE, The — see ELECTRIC LIGHT ORCHESTRA			
				MOVEMENT, The **'92**			
				Techno-dance trio from Los Angeles, California: AJ Mora (synthesizers), Richard "Humpty" Vission (drums) and Hazze (rapper).			
8/8/92	53	20		**Jump!** ... S:32 / A:49 *(Hipno mix w/rap)*	$3	▮	Arista 12474
				MOVING PICTURES LP **'83**			
				Pop group from Sydney, Australia: Alex Smith (vocals), Garry Frost (guitar), Andrew Thompson (sax), Charlie Cole (keyboards), Ian Lees (bass) and Paul Freeland (drums). Frost later formed **1927**.			
9/18/82+	29	26		1 **What About Me** ... *Joni And The Romeo*	$4	■	Network 69952
8/12/89	46	17		2 **What About Me** ... *Joni And The Romeo* [R]	$3		Geffen 22859
				above 2 are the same version			
				MOYET, Alison ROK/LP **'85**			
				Born Genevieve Alison-Jane Moyet on 6/18/61 in Basildon, Essex, England. Female vocalist of synth pop duo **Yaz**.			
3/9/85	31	17		1 **Invisible** ... A:28 *Hitch Hike (w/the Darts)*	$4	■	Columbia 04781
7/20/85	82	4		2 **Love Resurrection** ... *Baby I Do*	$3	■	Columbia 05411
				MOZART, Mickey — see MAXWELL, Robert			
				M PEOPLE BUB **'94**			
				Dance trio of Michael Pickering (from Manchester, England), Heather Small and Paul Heard (both from London, England). Charted 4 #1 Dance hits, 1994-95.			
5/7/94	34	16		**Moving On Up** ... A:30 / S:75 *(gospel revival edit)*	$3	▮V	Epic 77392
				"45": Epic 77884; B-side: "Open Your Heart" (#125)			

DEBUT	PEAK	WKS	Gold	A-side (Chart Hit)...B-side	$	Sym	Label & Number
				MPRESS '01			
				Teen female pop vocal trio from Orlando, Florida: Lauren Hart, Marissa Clark and Zoraida Rosario.			
10/6/01	9^S	18		Maybe ...*(no B-side)*	$4	★	Big 3 6747
				Paul Anka (executive producer)			
				MS. ADVENTURES '90			
				Dance vocal trio of sisters Charity (age 13 in 1990), Kindra (17) and Amy (20) Morriss from Texas.			
9/1/90	73	9		**Undeniable** ...*All Dressed Up*	$3	▮	Atco 98938
				MS. JADE R&B/BUB '02			
				Born Chevon Young on 8/3/79 in Philadelphia, Pennsylvania. Female rapper.			
3/30/02	92	4		1 **Feel The Girl** ...*(3 versions) / Dream*	$7	T	Beat Club 497687
				MS. JADE Featuring Tweet			
10/5/02	96	5		2 **Are We Cuttin'** ...S:68 *(radio edit)*	$4	★	Universal 019327
				PASTOR TROY featuring Ms. Jade			
12/7/02	46^S	2		3 **Ching Ching** ...BUB:114 *(2 versions) / Jade's The Champ*	$7	T	Beat Club 497820
				MS. JADE Featuring Timbaland & Nelly Furtado			
				MTUME R&B/BUB/LP '83			
				Funk group formed in Philadelphia, Pennsylvania: James Mtume (male vocals, drums), Tawatha Agee (female vocals), Reggie Lucas (guitar), Phil Fields (keyboards) and Ray Johnson (bass).			
6/18/83	45	12	●	1 **Juicy Fruit** ...RB8 *Part II (reprise)*	$4		Epic 03578
9/15/84	83	5		2 **You, Me And He** ...*(instrumental rap)*	$4		Epic 04504
				M2M LP '00			
				Female pop vocal duo from Lorenskog, Norway: Marion Ravn and Marit Larsen.			
11/20/99+	21	12	●	1 **Don't Say You Love Me** ...S:5 *Mewtwo Strikes Back Suite*	$5	★+	Atlantic 84551
				from the animated movie *Pokémon - The First Movie*			
4/1/00	62	18	●	2 **Mirror Mirror** ...S:4 *Don't Say You Love Me (acoustic version)*	$4	★V	Atlantic 84658
				MUDVAYNE ROK/LP '01			
				Hard-rock group from Peoria, Illinois: Chad Gray (vocals), Greg Tribbett (guitar), Ryan Martinie (bass) and Matt McDonough (drums).			
4/28/01	42^S	6		**Dig** ...	$8	◗	No Name/Epic 79548
				DVD video features include photo gallery, Dolby digital surround sound and interactive menus			
				MUHAMMAD, Idris R&B/BUB/LP '77			
				Born Leo Morris in 1939 in New Orleans, Louisiana. R&B drummer.			
10/1/77	76	2		**Could Heaven Ever Be Like This (Part 1)** ...*(Part 2)*	$5		Kudu 939
				MULBERRY LANE '02			
				Pop vocal group from Omaha, Nebraska: sisters Jaymie, Rachel, Allie and Heather Suiter.			
5/8/99	99	3		1 **Harmless** ...S:56 *(group interview w/3 album snippets)*	$4	★	Refuge/MCA 55531
6/1/02	35^S	1		2 **Yo-Yo** ...*U Decide*	$4	★	Refuge/MCA 155709
				MULDAUR, Maria AC/LP '74			
				Born Maria D'Amato on 9/12/43 in the Bronx, New York. Female jazz-styled singer.			
2/23/74	6	24		1 Midnight At The Oasis ...*Any Old Time*	$5		Reprise 1183
12/28/74+	12	14		2 **I'm A Woman** ...*Cool River*	$5		Reprise 1319
				MULL, Martin, and Orchestra LP '73			
				Born on 8/18/43 in Chicago, Illinois. Comedian/actor. Acted in several movies and TV shows.			
5/5/73	92	3		**Dueling Tubas** ...*2001 Polkas* [I-N]	$8		Capricorn 0019
				parody of "Dueling Banjos" from the movie *Deliverance* ("Belligerence") starring **Burt Reynolds**			
				MULLEN, Larry — see U2			
				MULLINS, Shawn LP '99			
				Born on 3/8/68 in Atlanta, Georgia. Male Adult Alternative pop-rock singer/songwriter/guitarist.			
12/5/98+	7	18		Lullaby ...A:❶2		V	album cut
				Hot 100 Airplay debut: 9/19/98; from the album *Soul's Core* on Columbia 69637; "45": Columbia 79080; B-side: "The Gulf Of Mexico"			
				MUMBA, Samantha LP '00			
				Born on 1/18/83 in Dublin, Ireland. R&B singer.			
9/9/00	4	22		1 Gotta Tell You ...S:❶1 / A:16 *(dub version)*	$4	★	Wild Card 497408
5/12/01	49	17		2 **Baby, Come Over (This Is Our Night)** ...A:51			album cut
				samples "Ladies Night" by **Kool & The Gang**; above 2 from the album *Gotta Tell You* on A&M 549799			
9/29/01	20^S	29		3 **Don't Need You To (Tell Me I'm Pretty)** ...*The Boy* (w/Will.I.Am of **Black Eyed Peas**)	$4	★	A&M 87195
				from the movie *Legally Blonde* starring Reese Witherspoon			
				MUNGO JERRY LP '70			
				Skiffle group formed in England: Ray Dorset (lead vocals), Colin Earl, Paul King and Mike Cole.			
7/11/70	3	13	●	In The Summertime ...*Mighty Man*	$7		Janus 125
				MURAD, Jerry — see HARMONICATS			
				MURDOCK, Shirley R&B/BUB/LP '87			
				Born in Toledo, Ohio. Female R&B singer.			
1/17/87	23	18		**As We Lay** ...S:17 / A:34 *Danger Zone*	$3		Elektra 69518
				MURE, Billy — see TRUMPETEERS, The			
				MURMAIDS, The BUB '64			
				Teen "girl group" from Los Angeles, California: sisters Carol and Terry Fischer, with Sally Gordon.			
11/23/63+	3	14		Popsicles And Icicles ...*Huntington Flats*	$15		Chattahoochee 628
				written by **David Gates** of **Bread**; also released with 3 other B-sides: "Blue Dress" ($20), "Bunny Stomp" ($15) and "Comedy and Tragedy" ($15)			
				MURMURS, The '94			
				Female rock duo from Manhattan, New York: singers/guitarists Heather Grody and Leisha Hailey.			
12/17/94	89	7		**You Suck** ...*Mission*	$4	▮	MCA 54979

DEBUT	PEAK	WKS	Gold	A-side (Chart Hit)	B-side	$	Sym	Label & Number

MURPHEY, Michael — C&W/AC/BUB/LP '75

Born on 3/14/45 in Oak Cliff, Texas. Country-pop singer/songwriter. Recorded as Travis Lewis of **The Lewis & Clarke Expedition** in 1967. Worked as a staff writer for Screen Gems. Appeared in the movies *Take This Job And Shove It* and *Hard Country*. In 1984, changed his artist billing to Michael Martin Murphey. Charted 29 Country hits, 1976-91.

DEBUT	PEAK	WKS	Gold	A-side (Chart Hit)	B-side	$	Sym	Label & Number
8/5/72	37	13		1 **Geronimo's Cadillac**	*Boy From The Country*	$6	■	A&M 1368
3/29/75	3	19	▲	2 **Wildfire** AC[1]	*Night Thunder*	$5		Epic 50084
8/16/75	21	13		3 **Carolina In The Pines**	*Without My Lady There*	$5		Epic 50131
				a new version by Murphey hit #9 on the Country charts in 1985				
1/24/76	39	7		4 **Renegade**	*A Mansion On The Hill* (C&W #36)	$5		Epic 50184
7/24/82	19	20		5 **What's Forever For** CW[1]	*Crystal*	$4		Liberty 1466
1/8/83	76	7		6 **Still Taking Chances**	*Lost River*	$4		Liberty 1486

MURPHY, Eddie — R&B/BUB/LP '85

Born on 4/3/61 in Hempstead, New York. Comedian/actor. Former cast member of TV's *Saturday Night Live*. Starred in several movies. Married model Nicole Mitchell on 3/18/93.

DEBUT	PEAK	WKS	Gold	A-side (Chart Hit)	B-side	$	Sym	Label & Number
10/5/85	2[3]	22	▲	1 **Party All The Time** S:2 / A:2	*(instrumental)*	$3	■	Columbia 05609
				written, produced and arranged by **Rick James**				
7/29/89	27	13		2 **Put Your Mouth On Me** S:23 / A:40	*With All I Know*	$3		Columbia 68897

MURPHY, Peter — ROK/LP '90

Born on 7/11/57 in Northampton, England. Rock singer/songwriter. Lead singer of the goth-rock band Bauhaus.

DEBUT	PEAK	WKS	Gold	A-side (Chart Hit)	B-side	$	Sym	Label & Number
3/24/90	55	9		**Cuts You Up** MR[7]	*Roll Call*	$3	▮	Beggars Banquet 9140

MURPHY, Walter — AC/BUB/LP '76

Born on 12/19/52 in Manhattan, New York. Studied classical and jazz piano at Manhattan School of Music. Former arranger for Doc Severinsen and *The Tonight Show* orchestra.

DEBUT	PEAK	WKS	Gold	A-side (Chart Hit)	B-side	$	Sym	Label & Number
5/29/76	1[1]	28	●	1 **A Fifth Of Beethoven** *[WALTER MURPHY & THE BIG APPLE BAND]*	*California Strut* [I]	$5		Private Stock 45,073
				based on Beethoven's *Fifth Symphony*				
11/13/76	44	10		2 **Flight '76** *[THE WALTER MURPHY BAND]*	*(Part 2)* [I]	$5		Private Stock 45,123
				based on Rimsky-Korsakov's *Flight Of The Bumble Bee*; "Part 2" is the theme from the NBC-TV movie *Attack Of The Killer Bees*				
7/31/82	47	9		3 **Themes From E.T. (The Extra-Terrestrial)**	*Your Planet Or Mine?* [I]	$4	■	MCA 52099
				from the Steven Spielberg movie *E.T.* starring Henry Thomas; text sleeve issued either in full color or in purple and black				

MURRAY, Anne ★157★ — C&W/AC/BUB/LP '78

Born Morna Anne Murray on 6/20/45 in Springhill, Nova Scotia, Canada. High school teacher for one year after college. With CBC-TV show *Sing Along Jubilee*. First recorded for Arc in 1968. Regular on **Glen Campbell**'s *Goodtime Hour* TV series. Charted 54 Country hits, 1970-91 and 41 Adult Contemporary hits, 1970-87.

1)You Needed Me 2)Danny's Song 3)You Won't See Me 4)Snowbird 5)Daydream Believer

DEBUT	PEAK	WKS	Gold	A-side (Chart Hit)	B-side	$	Sym	Label & Number
7/18/70	8	16	●	1 **Snowbird** AC[6]	*Just Bidin' My Time*	$6		Capitol 2738
12/5/70+	83	5		2 **Sing High - Sing Low**	*Days Of The Looking Glass*	$6		Capitol 2988
9/11/71	57	7		3 **Talk It Over In The Morning**	*Head Above The Water*	$6		Capitol 3159
10/23/71	81	5		4 **I Say A Little Prayer/By The Time I Get To Phoenix**	*All Through The Night*	$6		Capitol 3200
				GLEN CAMPBELL/ANNE MURRAY				
4/1/72	71	5		5 **Cotton Jenny**	*Destiny*	$6		Capitol 3260
				written by **Gordon Lightfoot**				
1/6/73	7	18		6 **Danny's Song** AC[2]	*Drown Me*	$5		Capitol 3481
				written by **Kenny Loggins** for his nephew (also co-wrote #9)				
5/26/73	64	8		7 **What About Me**	*Let Sunshine Have Its Day*	$5		Capitol 3600
8/18/73	72	7		8 **Send A Little Love My Way**	*Head Above The Water*	$5		Capitol 3648
				written by **Henry Mancini**; from the movie *Oklahoma Crude* starring George C. Scott				
12/15/73+	12	17		9 **Love Song** AC[1]	*You Can't Go Back*	$5		Capitol 3776
4/20/74	8	20		10 **You Won't See Me** AC[2]	*He Thinks I Still Care* (C&W #1)	$5		Capitol 3867
11/9/74	86	2		11 **Just One Look**	*Son Of A Rotten Gambler* (C&W #5)	$5		Capitol 3955
12/21/74+	59	6		12 **Day Tripper**	*Lullaby*	$5		Capitol 4000
				all of above produced by Brian Ahern				
11/29/75	98	2		13 **Sunday Sunrise**	*Out On The Road Again*	$5		Capitol 4142
2/21/76	91	5		14 **The Call**	*Lady Bug*	$5		Capitol 4207
10/30/76	89	3		15 **Things**	*Caress Me Pretty Music*	$5		Capitol 4329
7/15/78	1[1]	26	●	16 **You Needed Me**	*I Still Wish The Very Best For You*	$4		Capitol 4574
1/27/79	12	16		17 **I Just Fall In Love Again** CW[3] / AC[4]	*Just To Feel This Love From You*	$4	■	Capitol 4675
5/26/79	25	12		18 **Shadows In The Moonlight** CW[1] / AC[3]	*Yucatan Cafe*	$4		Capitol 4716
9/22/79	12	17		19 **Broken Hearted Me** CW[1] / AC[5]	*Why Don't You Stick Around*	$4		Capitol 4773
12/22/79+	12	17		20 **Daydream Believer** AC[1]	*Do You Think Of Me*	$4		Capitol 4813
4/5/80	42	8		21 **Lucky Me**	*Somebody's Waiting*	$4		Capitol 4848
6/14/80	64	6		22 **I'm Happy Just To Dance With You**	*What's Forever For*	$4		Capitol 4878
				#10, 12 & 22: written by **John Lennon** & **Paul McCartney**				
9/6/80	33	14		23 **Could I Have This Dance** CW[1]	*Somebody's Waiting*	$4	■	Capitol 4920
				from the movie *Urban Cowboy* starring **John Travolta** and Debra Winger				
3/28/81	34	13		24 **Blessed Are The Believers** CW[1]	*Only Love*	$4	■	Capitol 4987
9/26/81	53	9		25 **It's All I Can Do**	*If A Heart Must Be Broken*	$4		Capitol 5023
1/30/82	44	9		26 **Another Sleepless Night**	*It Should Have Been Easy*	$4		Capitol 5083
9/17/83	74	9		27 **A Little Good News** CW[1]	*I'm Not Afraid Anymore*	$4	■	Capitol 5264
				#16-27: produced by Jim Ed Norman				
3/1/86	92	6		28 **Now And Forever (You And Me)** CW[1]	*I Don't Wanna Spend Another Night Without You*	$4	■	Capitol 5547

DEBUT	PEAK	WKS	Gold	A-side (Chart Hit)..........B-side	$	Sym	Label & Number
				MURRAY, Keith R&B/BUB/LP **'98** Born in 1972 in Long Island, New York. Male rapper/songwriter.			
10/22/94	50	18		1 **The Most Beautifullest Thing In This World** S:26 *(remix) / Herb Is Pumpin'* samples "Between The Sheets" by **The Isley Brothers**, "Bootsy Gets Live" by Bootsy Collins and "Slow Down" by **Brand Nubian**	$4	▮	Jive 42249
3/4/95	71	10		2 **Get Lifted** ....S:43 *(**Erick Sermon**'s remix) / Pay Per View* samples "I Get Lifted" by **George McCrae**; **Erick Sermon** (backing vocal/producer, above 2)	$4	▮	Jive 42282
12/20/97+	51^{A}	12		3 **Rapper's Delight** .... **ERICK SERMON, KEITH MURRAY & REDMAN** from the album *In Tha Beginning...There Was Rap* on Priority 50639			album cut
5/30/98	25	20		4 **Shorty (You Keep Playin' With My Mind)** ..S:18 *(remix w/**Mr. Cheeks** of **The Lost Boyz**)* **IMAJIN Featuring Keith Murray** samples "Dance With Me" by **Peter Brown**	$4	▮	Jive 42525
12/5/98	65	16		5 **Home Alone** ....A:53 **R. KELLY featuring Keith Murray** **Kelly Price** (backing vocal); from Kelly's album *R.* on Jive 41625			album cut
11/3/01	87	14		6 **Fatty Girl**..........S:50 *(4 versions)* **LUDACRIS, LL COOL J, KEITH MURRAY**	$6	T	Universal 15283
				MURRAY, Mickey **'67** Soul singer/songwriter.			
10/7/67	54	8		**Shout Bamalama** ....*Lonely Room* written by **Otis Redding**	$10		SSS Int'l. 715
				MUSICAL YOUTH R&B/LP **'83** Pop-reggae group from Birmingham, England: Dennis Seaton (vocals), with brothers Kelvin (guitar) and Michael (keyboards) Grant, and Patrick (bass) and Junior Waite (drums). Patrick Waite died on 2/18/93 (age 24). Also see **Donna Summer**'s "Unconditional Love."			
12/11/82+	10	18		1 **Pass The Dutchie** ....*Give Love A Chance* clean version of the Jamaican hit "Pass The Kouchie," which means "pass the joint"; a dutchie is a Jamaican cooking pot	$4	■	MCA 52149
1/14/84	65	7		2 **She's Trouble**..........*Yard Stylee*	$4	■	MCA 52312
				MUSIC EXPLOSION, The BUB/LP **'67** Rock and roll band from Mansfield, Ohio: James Lyons (vocals), Don Atkins and Richard Nesta (guitars), Burton Stahl (bass) and Bob Avery (drums).			
5/13/67	2^{2}	16	●	1 **Little Bit O' Soul** ....*I See The Light*	$12		Laurie 3380
9/9/67	63	5		2 **Sunshine Games**..........*Can't Stop Now*	$12		Laurie 3400
				MUSIC MACHINE, The BUB/LP **'67** Rock group from Los Angeles, California: Sean Bonniwell (vocals, guitar), Mark Landon (guitar), Doug Rhodes (organ), Keith Olsen (bass) and Ron Edgar (drums). Olsen became a top record producer in the 1980s.			
11/12/66+	15	12		1 **Talk Talk** ....*Come On In*	$12		Original Sound 61
1/28/67	66	8		2 **The People In Me** ....*Masculine Intuition* picture sleeve issued with a center-cut hole and photos of the group members	$12	■	Original Sound 67
				MUSIC MAKERS, The — see MFSB			
				MUSIQ LP **'02** Born Taalib Johnson in Philadelphia, Pennsylvania. Male R&B singer/songwriter. Also recorded as **Musiq Soulchild**.			
10/14/00	31	20		1 **Just Friends (Sunny)** ....A:27 *(2 versions) / Even If* (**Method Man**) samples "Sunny" by **Bobby Hebb**; from the movie *Nutty Professor II: The Klumps* starring **Eddie Murphy** and **Janet Jackson**	$6	T	Def Jam 562902
2/17/01	24	21		2 **Love** *[MUSIQ Soulchild]*..........A:18			album cut
8/25/01	85	8		3 **Girl Next Door** ....*(2 versions) / Seventeen* **MUSIQ Soulchild (Feat. Ayana Of Aaries)** above 3 from the album *AIJUSWANASEING (I Just Want To Sing)* on Def Soul 548289	$6	T	Def Soul 572835
3/23/02	16	25		4 **halfcrazy** A:14 / S:70 *(2 versions) / caughtup* samples "Live For Life" by **Francis Lai**	$6	T	Def Soul 588989
9/7/02	17	26		5 **dontchange** ....A:13 *(2 versions)*	$6	T	Def Soul 063790
				MUSIQUE R&B/LP **'78** Disco trio: Christine Wiltshire, Gina Tharps and Mary Seymour.			
10/21/78	58	13		**In The Bush**..........*(short version)* controversial disco song banned on many radio stations	$6		Prelude 71110
				MUSTANGS, The **'64** Rock and roll instrumental band.			
10/3/64	92	3		**The Dartell Stomp** ....*Lazy Love* [I] song first recorded by **The Dartells** in 1962 (B-side of "Hot Pastrami")	$20		Providence 401
				MUSTO & BONES **'91** Dance duo of Tommy Musto and Frankie Bones.			
6/8/91	59^{A}	7		**Dangerous On The Dancefloor**..........*(7" version)*	$4	▮	CityBeat/RCA 2798
	★352★			**MÝA** R&B/LP **'98** Born Mýa Harrison on 10/10/79 in Washington DC. Female R&B singer/songwriter/dancer. *1)Lady Marmalade 2)Case Of The Ex (Whatcha Gonna Do) 3)It's All About Me*			
3/14/98	6	20	●	1 **It's All About Me** ....S:5 / A:50 *(album version)* **MÝA With Special Guest SISQO** samples "Moments In Love" by **The Art Of Noise**; reissue of cassette box shows artist as **MÝA & SISQO**	$3	▮	University 97024
6/27/98	15	21		2 **Ghetto Supastar (That Is What You Are)** ....A:11 *(3 versions)* **PRAS MICHEL featuring OL' DIRTY BASTARD & introducing MÝA** samples "Get Up, Get Into It, Get Involved" by **James Brown** and contains an interpolation of "Islands In The Stream"; from the movie *Bulworth* starring Warren Beatty	$6	T	Interscope 95021
8/8/98	34	20		3 **Movin' On** ....A:38 *(3 versions)* **MÝA featuring Silkk the Shocker**	$6	T	University 95032
12/5/98+	14	17		4 **Take Me There**..........A:8 **BLACKSTREET & MÝA featuring MA$E & BLINKY BLINK** samples "I Want You Back" by **The Jackson 5**; from the animated movie *The RugRats Movie*			album cut

DEBUT	PEAK	WKS	Gold	A-side (Chart Hit)......B-side	$	Sym	Label & Number
				MÝA — Cont'd			
3/20/99	28	14		5 **My First Night With You** ......S:14 *Baby It's Yours* "45": University 97088	$4	★^{V}	University 97049
4/15/00	50	17		6 **Best Of Me**......A:44 **MÝA Featuring Jadakiss**			album cut
8/19/00	2^{3}	30		7 **Case Of The Ex (Whatcha Gonna Do)** ......S:❶^{3} / A:5 *(2 versions)*	$4	★	University 97457
10/21/00	54	15		8 **Girls Dem Sugar** ......A:54 **BEENIE MAN Featuring Mýa** from the Beenie Man album *Art And Life* on Virgin 49093; "45" B-side: (instrumental)		V	album cut
2/3/01	42	16		9 **Free**......A:41 featured in the movie *Bait* starring Jamie Foxx; #6, 7 & 9: from the album *Fear Of Flying* on University 490853			album cut
4/14/01	❶^{5}	20		10 **Lady Marmalade** A:❶^{6} *(3 mixes)* **CHRISTINA AGUILERA, LIL' KIM, MÝA and P!NK** co-produced by **Missy "Misdemeanor" Elliott**; from the movie *Moulin Rouge* starring Nicole Kidman and Ewan McGregor	$6	T	Interscope 497066
				MYERS, Billie LP **'98** Born on 6/14/70 in Coventry, England. Female Adult Alternative pop-rock singer.			
11/8/97+	15	31		**Kiss The Rain**......A:12 / S:29 *The Shark And The Mermaid* produced by **Desmond Child**; "45": Universal 56192; B-side: "Tell Me"	$3	▮^{V}	Universal 56140
				MYLES, Alannah LP **'90** Born on 12/25/55 in Toronto, Ontario, Canada; raised in Buckhorn, Ontario, Canada. Female pop-rock singer.			
1/6/90	❶^{2}	24	●	1 **Black Velvet** ......AR^{2} S:❶^{3} / A:2 *If You Want To*	$3	▮^{V}	Atlantic 88742
5/5/90	36	13		2 **Love Is** ......A:28 *Rock This Joint* first released as a "45" in 1989 on Atlantic 88918 with a picture sleeve	$3	▮^{V}	Atlantic 87945
				MYLES, Billy **'57** Born in Harlem, New York. R&B singer/songwriter. Wrote the **Mello-Kings**' doo-wop hit "Tonite, Tonite" and **Hank Ballard**'s "The Hoochi Coochi Coo."			
11/18/57	25	14		**The Joker (That's What They Call Me)**......S:25 / T:30 *Honey Bee*	$30		Ember 1026
				MYRON R&B/BUB/LP **'98** Born Myron Davis in Cleveland, Ohio. R&B singer/songwriter.			
9/6/97	75	8		1 **We Can Get Down** ......S:52 *(no rap version)* Dee Dee "Spinderella" Roper of **Salt-N-Pepa** (guest rapper)	$3	▮	Island 572064
7/18/98	47	13		2 **Destiny** ......S:29 *(instrumental) / (3 album snippets)* samples "Come Running To Me" by **Herbie Hancock**	$3	▮	Island 572334
				MYSTIC MOODS, The AC/BUB/R&B/LP **'73** Instrumental studio group produced by Brad Miller. Had a dozen "mood music" charted albums.			
4/21/73	83	6		1 **Cosmic Sea**......*The Awakening* [I]	$5		Warner 7686
7/12/75	98	6		2 **Honey Trippin'** ......*Midnight Snack* [I]	$5		Sound Bird 5002
				MYSTICS, The BUB **'59** White doo-wop group from Brooklyn, New York: Phil Cracolici (lead), Bob Ferrante & George Galfo (tenors), Albee Cracolici (baritone) and Allie Contrera (bass). John Traynor of **Jay & The Americans** was an early member.			
5/25/59	20	15		1 **Hushabye** ......*Adam And Eve*	$30		Laurie 3028
10/19/59	98	2		2 **Don't Take The Stars** ......*So Tenderly*	$25		Laurie 3038
	★480★			**MYSTIKAL** R&B/BUB/LP **'00** Born Michael Tyler on 9/22/75 in New Orleans, Louisiana. Male rapper/songwriter.			
1/31/98	16	27	▲	1 **Make Em' Say Uhh!** ..S:9 *(2 versions) / Weed And Hennesey* (w/C-Murder & **Silkk The Shocker**) **MASTER P Featuring Fiend, Silkk The Shocker, Mia X and Mystikal** clean version available on No Limit 53303	$3	▮	No Limit 53302
1/30/99	62	12		2 **Woof** ......S:14 *(instrumental) / It's All On A *** **SNOOP DOGG Featuring Mystikal and Fiend** clean version available on No Limit 53463	$4	★	No Limit 53462
3/6/99	18	18		3 **It Ain't My Fault 2** ......S:8 *Somebody Like Me* (w/**Mýa** - R&B #43) **SILKK THE SHOCKER And Mystikal** *Billboard* combined the Airplay points of above title with Silkk The Shocker's original solo version of "It Ain't My Fault" (R&B #20^{A}); clean version available on No Limit 53471	$4	★	No Limit 53470
8/12/00	13	20		4 **Shake Ya Ass** A:6 / S:60 *(3 versions)*	$6	T	Jive 42721
12/16/00+	14	20		5 **Danger (Been So Long)** ......RB^{1} A:11 / S:50 *(3 versions)* **MYSTIKAL Featuring Nivea**	$6	T	Jive 42860
1/6/01	❶^{4}	26	●	6 **Stutter** ......RB^{5} S:❶^{5} / A:5 *(2 versions)* **JOE (featuring Mystikal)** samples "Passin' Me By" by **The Pharcyde**; from the movie *Double Take* starring Eddie Griffin	$4	★	Jive 42870
12/15/01+	37	20		7 **Bouncin' Back (Bumpin' Me Against The Wall)** .....A:35 / S:42 *(instrumental) / P***y Crook*	$6	T	Jive 42992
4/6/02	75^{S}	1		8 **Tarantula** ......*(2 versions) / If It Ain't Live, It Ain't Me* **MYSTIKAL Featuring Butch Cassidy**	$6	T	Jive 42999
6/8/02	10	23		9 **Move B***h** ......A:9 / S:20 *Keep It On The Hush* **LUDACRIS feat. Mystikal and Infamous 2.0**	$4	★	Def Jam 063949
				MYTOWN **'00** Male teen pop vocal group from Dublin, Ireland: Terry Daly, Danny O'Donoghue, Marc Sheehan and Paul Walker.			
4/22/00	55^{S}	3		**Now That I Found You** ......*(2 album snippets)*	$5	★	Cherry 156703

SELECTED CASSETTE SINGLES

Fiona Apple
Criminal

Aqua
Barbie Girl

The Black Crowes
Jealous Again

Blind Melon
No Rain

David Cassidy
Lyin' To Myself

Crash Test Dummies
Mmm Mmm Mmm Mmm

Deadeye Dick
New Age Girl

ESPN Presents
The Jock Jam

Gloria Estefan
Everlasting Love

Fleetwood Mac
Save Me

Jeff Foxworthy
Redneck Stomp

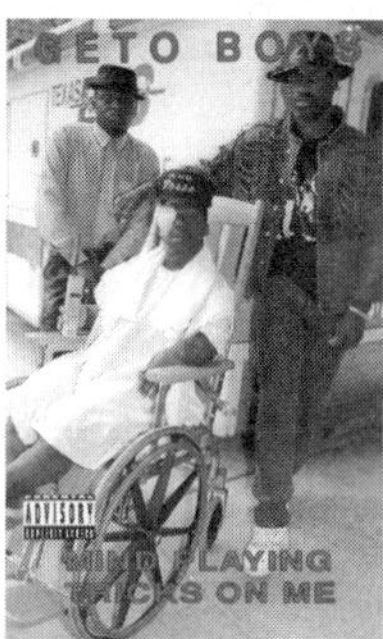

Geto Boys — *Mind Playing Tricks On Me*

Green Jellö
Three Little Pigs

Haddaway
Life

INXS
Beautiful Girl

Jay-Z
The City Is Mine

Jive Bunny
That's What I Like

Elton John
Recover Your Soul

Jordy
Dur Dur D'Etre Bébé!

The KLF
Justified & Ancient

SELECTED CASSETTE SINGLES

Letters To Cleo
Here & Now

Los Del Rio
Macarena Christmas

Aimee Mann
That's Just What You Are

Method Man
The Riddler

Next
Butta Love

Shaquille O'Neal
I'm Outstanding

Iggy Pop
Candy

The Presidents Of The United States Of America — *Peaches*

The Puppies
Funky Y-2-C

Quad City DJ's — *C'Mon N' Ride It (The Train)*

Queen Latifah
U.N.I.T.Y.

Righteous Brothers
Unchained Melody

Smokey Robinson
Double Good Everything

The Simpsons
Deep, Deep Trouble

Tag Team
Whoomp! (There It Went)

TLC
Waterfalls

Voices
Yeah! Yeah! Yeah!

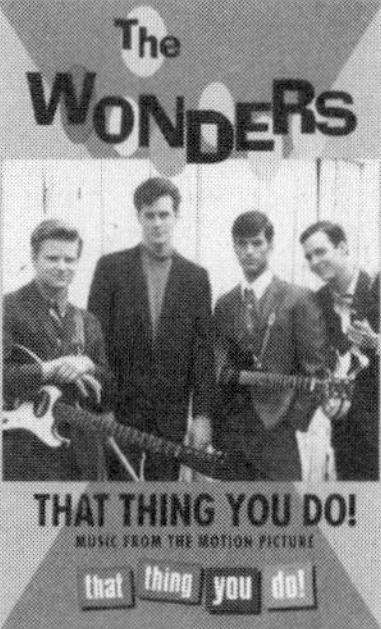

The Wonders
That Thing You Do!

"Weird Al" Yankovic
Gump

ZZ Top
Give It Up

DEBUT	PEAK	WKS	Gold	A-side (Chart Hit)..................B-side	$	Sym	Label & Number

N

NADA SURF — LP '96

Rock trio from Los Angeles, California: Matthew Caws (vocals, guitar), Daniel Lorca (bass) and Ira Elliot (drums).

DEBUT	PEAK	WKS	Gold	A-side (Chart Hit)..................B-side	$	Sym	Label & Number
7/13/96	51^A	8		**Popular** .... from the album *High/Low* on Elektra 61913			album cut

NAKED EYES — LP '83

Synth-pop duo from England: Pete Byrne (vocals) and Rob Fisher (keyboards, synthesizer). Split in 1984. Fisher later in duo **Climie Fisher**. Fisher died on 8/25/99 (age 39).

DEBUT	PEAK	WKS	Gold	A-side (Chart Hit)..................B-side	$	Sym	Label & Number
3/12/83	8	22		1 **Always Something There To Remind Me** .... *The Time Is Now*	$4		EMI America 8155
7/16/83	11	20		2 **Promises, Promises** .... *A Very Hard Act To Follow*	$4	■	EMI America 8170
10/22/83	37	14		3 **When The Lights Go Out** .... *Low Life*	$4		EMI America 8183
8/11/84	39	12		4 **(What) In The Name Of Love** .... *Two Heads Together*	$4	■	EMI America 8219

NAPOLEON XIV — '66

Born Jerry Samuels in 1938 in Brooklyn, New York. Novelty singer/songwriter.

DEBUT	PEAK	WKS	Gold	A-side (Chart Hit)..................B-side	$	Sym	Label & Number
7/23/66	3	6		1 **They're Coming To Take Me Away, Ha-Haaa!** .... *Yawa Em Ekat Ot Gnimoc Er'yeht! Aaah-Ah* [N]	$12		Warner 5831
9/1/73	87	4		2 **They're Coming To Take Me Away, Ha-Haa!** .... *!Aah-Ah, Yawa Em Ekat Ot Gnimoc Er'yeht* [N-R] above 2 are the same version	$8		Warner 7726

NAPPY ROOTS — R&B/LP '02

Rap group formed in Bowling Green, Kentucky: Brian "B. Stille" Scott, Melvin "Scales" Adams, William "Skinny DeVille" Hughes, Vito "Big V" Tisdale, Ken "R. Prophet" Anthony and Ron "Clutch" Wilson.

DEBUT	PEAK	WKS	Gold	A-side (Chart Hit)..................B-side	$	Sym	Label & Number
3/9/02	51	20		1 **Awnaw** .... A:51 *(3 versions) / Set It Out*	$6	T	Atlantic 85222
7/20/02	21	23		2 **Po' Folks** .... A:20 *(2 versions) / Headz Up* — **NAPPY ROOTS Featuring Anthony Hamilton**	$6	T	Atlantic 85323

NARÁE — '02

Female R&B singer.

DEBUT	PEAK	WKS	Gold	A-side (Chart Hit)..................B-side	$	Sym	Label & Number
11/2/02	18^S	13		**Truly Yours** .... *(instrumental)*	$5	★	Kirv 0001

★428★ NAS — R&B/BUB/LP '99

Born Nasir Jones on 9/14/73 in Long Island, New York. Male rapper. Also known as Nasty Nas and Nas Escobar. Also see **Kool G Rap & D.J. Polo**.

1)Street Dreams 2)Hot Boyz 3)I'm Gonna Be Alright

DEBUT	PEAK	WKS	Gold	A-side (Chart Hit)..................B-side	$	Sym	Label & Number
4/16/94	91	8		1 **It Ain't Hard To Tell** .... S:55 *(instrumental)* — samples "Human Nature" by **Michael Jackson** and "N.T." by **Kool & The Gang**	$4	▮	Columbia 77385
6/22/96	53	20		2 **If I Ruled The World** .... A:33 *(3 versions)* — **Lauryn Hill** (female vocal); samples "Friends" by **Whodini** and "If I Ruled The World" by **Kurtis Blow**	$6	T	Columbia 78327
11/9/96+	22	17	●	3 **Street Dreams** .... S:15 *Affirmative Action* (R&B #75^A) — contains an interpolation of "Sweet Dreams" by **Eurythmics**; samples "Never Gonna Stop" by **Linda Clifford**	$3	▮	Columbia 78409
3/15/97	35	15		4 **Head Over Heels** .... S:32 / A:61 *(3 versions)* — **ALLURE featuring Nas**; samples "The Bridge" by MC Shan; co-produced by **Mariah Carey**	$3	▮	Crave 78522
3/20/99	86	4		5 **Nas Is Like** .... S:27 *(2 versions) / Dr. Knockboots*	$4	★^V	Columbia 79113
4/24/99	62	8		6 **Hate Me Now** .... A:48 / S:62 *(3 versions) / Blaze A 50 / Natures Shine* — **NAS (featuring Puff Daddy)**; "45" issued for above 2 on Columbia 79150	$6	T^V	Columbia 79070
5/29/99	27	16		7 **Did You Ever Think** .... S:16 / A:40 *(3 versions) / Home Alone* (w/**Keith Murray**) — **R. KELLY (featuring Nas)**	$8	★*	Jive 42604
11/27/99+	5	21	▲	8 **Hot Boyz** .... RB^6 S:2 / A:24 *U Can't Resist* (w/**Juvenile** & **B.G.**) — **MISSY "MISDEMEANOR" ELLIOTT [featuring NAS, EVE & Q-TIP]**; **Lil' Mo** (vocal ad libs)	$4	★	The Gold Mind 64029
11/27/99	92	6		9 **Nastradamus** .... S:28 *(2 versions) / Shoot 'em Up* — samples "(It's Not The Express) It's The J.B.'s Monorail (Pts. 1 & 2)" by The JB Horns	$8	★*	Columbia 79299
3/25/00	59	16		10 **You Owe Me** .... A:49 — **NAS (featuring Ginuwine)**; above 2 from the album *Nastradamus* on Columbia 63930			album cut
3/3/01	26	20		11 **Oochie Wally** .... S:13 / A:19 *(2 versions) / Find Ya Wealth* — **QB FINEST Featuring NAS And Bravehearts**; Shelene Thomas (female vocal)	$8	★*	Columbia 79586
12/15/01+	87	19		12 **Got Ur Self A...** .... S:30 *(2 versions) / You're Da Man* — samples "Woke Up This Morning" by Alabama 3	$6	T	Columbia 79676
4/20/02	43	13		13 **One Mic** .... S:23 / A:42 *Got Ur Self A... (video)*	$8	◗	Columbia 79710
4/27/02	10	23		14 **I'm Gonna Be Alright** .... S:7 / A:10 *(2 versions) / Alive* (Lopez - AC #18) — **JENNIFER LOPEZ Featuring Nas**; samples "Why You Treat Me So Bad" by **Club Nouveau**	$8	★*	Epic 79759
5/11/02	42^S	3		15 **I Got It 2** .... BUB:103 *(3 versions)* — **JAGGED EDGE featuring Nas**	$6	T	So So Def 79739
12/21/02+	32	13		16 **Made You Look** .... A:31 — from the album *God's Son* on Columbia 86930			album cut

NASH, Graham — BUB/AC/LP '72

Born on 2/2/42 in Blackpool, Lancashire, England. Pop-rock singer/songwriter/guitarist. Former member of **The Hollies**. Formed **Crosby, Stills & Nash** in 1968.

DEBUT	PEAK	WKS	Gold	A-side (Chart Hit)..................B-side	$	Sym	Label & Number
6/5/71	35	11		1 **Chicago** .... *Simple Man*	$6		Atlantic 2804
9/4/71	73	6		2 **Military Madness** .... *Sleep Song*	$6		Atlantic 2827
5/6/72	36	9		3 **Immigration Man** .... *Whole Cloth* — **GRAHAM NASH & DAVID CROSBY**	$6		Atlantic 2873
7/1/72	61	6		4 **War Song** .... *The Needle And The Damage Done* (Young) — **NEIL YOUNG and GRAHAM NASH**	$6	⊙	Reprise 1099
8/12/72	99	2		5 **Southbound Train** .... *The Wall Song*	$6		Atlantic 2892

DEBUT	PEAK	WKS	Gold	A-side (Chart Hit)...B-side	$	Sym	Label & Number
				NASH, Graham — Cont'd			
11/15/75	52	6		6 **Carry Me** ... *Mama Lion*	$5		ABC 12140
8/7/76	89	3		7 **Out Of The Darkness** ... *Broken Bird* **GRAHAM NASH & DAVID CROSBY** (above 3)	$5		ABC 12199
4/26/86	84	7		8 **Innocent Eyes** ... *I Got A Rock* **Kenny Loggins** (backing vocal)	$3	■	Atlantic 89434
	★481★			**NASH, Johnny** BUB/R&B/AC/LP '72 Born on 8/19/40 in Houston, Texas. Black singer/guitarist/actor. Appeared on local TV from age 13. With Arthur Godfrey's TV and radio shows from 1956-63. In the movie *Take A Giant Step* in 1959. Own JoDa label in 1965. Began recording in Jamaica in the late 1960s. *1)I Can See Clearly Now 2)Hold Me Tight 3)Stir It Up*			
12/30/57+	23	10		1 **A Very Special Love** ... A:23 / S:45 / T:46 *Won't You Let Me Share My Love With You*	$20		ABC-Paramount 9874
11/10/58	78	4		2 **Almost In Your Arms** ... *Midnight Moonlight* love song from the movie *Houseboat* starring Cary Grant and Sophia Loren	$20		ABC-Paramount 9960
12/1/58+	29	8		3 **The Teen Commandments** ... *If You Learn To Pray* (**Don Costa** Chorus) [S] **PAUL ANKA-GEO. HAMILTON IV-JOHNNY NASH** Bill Givens (narrative); inspirational talk from the three ABC-Paramount artists	$25		ABC-Paramount 9974
3/16/59	43	11		4 **As Time Goes By** ... *The Voice Of Love* from the 1942 movie *Casablanca* starring Humphrey Bogart; written in 1931; **Don Costa** (orch., all of above)	$20	■	ABC-Paramount 9996
9/25/65	88	7		5 **Let's Move & Groove (Together)** ... *Understanding*	$10		JoDa 102
9/14/68	5	15		6 **Hold Me Tight** ... *Cupid*	$10		JAD 207
12/14/68+	58	7		7 **You Got Soul** ... *Don't Cry*	$10		JAD 209
11/1/69+	39	14		8 **Cupid** ... *People In Love* first issued as the B-side of #6 above	$10		JAD 220
9/9/72	$❶^{4}$	20	●	9 **I Can See Clearly Now** AC^4 *How Good It Is* **Bob Marley**'s Wailers (backing band)	$6		Epic 10902
2/10/73	12	14		10 **Stir It Up** ... *Ooh Baby You've Been Good To Me* written by **Bob Marley**	$6		Epic 10949
6/30/73	77	5		11 **My Merry-Go-Round** ... *(Oh Jesus) We're Trying To Get Back To You*	$6		Epic 11003
4/13/74	91	3		12 **Loving You** ... *Gonna Open Up My Heart Again*	$6		Epic 11070
				NASHVILLE TEENS, The BUB '64 Rock group from Weybridge, Surrey, England: Arthur Sharp (vocals), John Allen (guitar), Ramon "Ray" Phillips (harmonica), John Hawkes (keyboards), Pete Shannon (bass) and Barry Jenkins (drums; joined **The Animals** in 1966).			
9/12/64	14	11		1 **Tobacco Road** ... *I Like It Like That*	$15		London 9689
3/13/65	98	2		2 **Find My Way Back Home** ... *Devil-In-Law*	$12		London 9736
				NASTYBOY KLICK R&B/BUB '98 Latin hip-hop group from Phoenix, Arizona: Marco "MC Magic" Cardenas and his son Li'l Mischief, with Sly, Zig Zag, and Dos. Changed name to **NB-Ridaz** in 2001.			
8/9/97	69	17		1 **Down For Yours** ... S:60 *(original version) / Lost In Love* **NASTYBOY KLICK Featuring Roger Troutman**	$4	▮	Mercury 574748
10/3/98	53	9		2 **Lost In Love** ... S:62 *(remix)*	$4	▮	Upstairs 0137
1/19/02	97	4		3 **Runaway** *[NB-RIDAZ]* ... *Party In Arizona*	$6	★	Nastyboy 2001
				NATÉ, Ultra BUB '97 Born in Baltimore, Maryland. Black female dance singer.			
8/23/97	75	19		1 **Free** ... *(remix)*	$4	▮	Strictly Rhythm 12512
8/29/98	52	15		2 **If You Could Read My Mind** ... S:55 *(instrumental)* **STARS ON 54: ULTRA NATÉ, AMBER, JOCELYN ENRIQUEZ** from the movie *54* starring Ryan Phillippe; originally charted its first 5 weeks as a CD maxi-single on Tommy Boy 497, then charted 9 more weeks as a cassette single; re-entered *Hot 100* on 2/27/99 at #99 for 1 more week as a regular CD single	$4	★	Tommy Boy 7497
	★566★			**NATE DOGG** R&B/BUB/LP '94 Born Nathan Hale in Los Angeles, California. Male rapper. Former partner of **Warren G**. Cousin of **Snoop Doggy Dogg**. *1)Regulate 2)Nobody Does It Better 3)Never Leave Me Alone*			
4/23/94	2^3	20	▲	1 **Regulate** S:❶^2 / A:15 *(same version)* **WARREN G. & NATE DOGG** samples "I Keep Forgettin'" by **Michael McDonald**; from the movie *Above The Rim* starring **2Pac** and Duane Martin	$4	▮	Death Row 98280
11/9/96	33	19		2 **Never Leave Me Alone** ... S:23 *(instrumental)* **NATE DOGG featuring Snoop Doggy Dogg** Val Young (female vocal); samples "Where Is The Love" by **Roberta Flack & Donny Hathaway**	$4	▮	Death Row 97012
7/11/98	18	18		3 **Nobody Does It Better** ... S:10 *(instrumental)* **NATE DOGG featuring WARREN G** samples "Let's Get Closer" by **Atlantic Starr**	$4	▮	Breakaway 4000
10/9/99	77	9		4 **B-Please** ... A:62 **SNOOP DOGG Featuring Xzibit and Nate Dogg** produced by **Dr. Dre**; from Snoop Dogg's album *No Limit Top Dogg* on No Limit 50052			album cut
11/11/00	95	5		5 **Where I Wanna Be** ... S:28 *(3 album snippets)* **SHADE SHEIST Featuring Nate Dogg & Kurupt** samples "Waiting For Your Love" by **Toto**	$6	★	Baby Ree 35058
12/23/00+	83	12		6 **Oh No** ... S:33 *(2 versions) / Battle* (**Erick Sermon** w/Sy Scott) **MOS DEF & PHAROAHE MONCH Featuring Nate Dogg**	$6	T	Rawkus 289
3/24/01	50	19		7 **Lay Low** ... A:44 / S:53 *Wrong Idea* (w/**Bad Azz**, Kokane & Lil Half Dead - R&B #75) **SNOOP DOGG (featuring Master P, Nate Dogg, Butch Cassidy & Tha Eastsidaz)**	$6	T	No Limit 50174
7/14/01	24	17		8 **Area Codes** ... A:21 / S:55 *(3 versions)* **LUDACRIS (Feat. Nate Dogg)** samples "Do It ('Til You're Satisfied)" by **B.T. Express**; from the movie *Rush Hour 2* starring Jackie Chan	$6	T	Def Jam 588671
7/21/01	25	20		9 **Can't Deny It** ... A:24 *(4 versions)* **FABOLOUS featuring Nate Dogg** **Lil' Mo** (background vocal); samples "Ambitionz Az A Ridah" by **2Pac**	$6	T	Desert Storm 67231
10/20/01	95	5		10 **Ballin' Out Of Control** ... S:53 *(3 versions) / Hate Blood* (w/**Jadakiss** & **Freeway**) **JERMAINE DUPRI featuring Nate Dogg**	$6	T	So So Def 79590

DEBUT	PEAK	WKS	Gold	A-side (Chart Hit)..........B-side	$	Sym	Label & Number
				NATE DOGG — Cont'd			
12/1/01	69^{S}	1		11 **I Got Love** ....BUB:118 *(3 versions) / (remix w/***Fabolous**, B.R.E.T.T. & **Kurupt***)*	$6	T	Elektra 67270
9/28/02	81	13		12 **The Streets** ....*(2 versions) / Wanna Ride (w/***Ice Cube** & **MC Ren***)* **WC (feat. Nate Dogg)**	$6	T	Def Jam 063974
				NATIONAL LAMPOON LP **'72** Comedy troupe spawned from the magazine of the same name.			
10/14/72	91	4		**Deteriorata** ....*Those Fabulous Sixties* [N] Norman Rose (narration); **Melissa Manchester** (vocal); parody of **Les Crane**'s 1971 hit "Desiderata"	$8		Banana 218
				NATURAL **'01** Teen "boy band" from Orlando, Florida: Patrick King (guitar), Josh Horn (keyboards), Marc Terenzi (sax), Ben Bledsoe (bass) and Michael Johnson (drums). All share vocals.			
10/6/01	8^{S}	21	●	**Put Your Arms Around Me** ....*(2 album snippets)* originally available exclusively at Claire's accessory stores and certified gold on Trans Continental 70050	$4	★	Trans Continental 00712
				NATURAL FOUR R&B/LP **'74** R&B vocal group from San Francisco, California: Delmos Whitley, Ollan Christopher James, Darryl Cannady and Steve Striplin.			
1/5/74	31	10		1 **Can This Be Real** ....*Try Love Again*	$6		Curtom 1990
5/25/74	98	2		2 **Love That Really Counts** ....*Love's Society*	$6		Curtom 1995
				NATURAL SELECTION **'91** Black funk duo from Minneapolis, Minnesota: Elliott Erickson (keyboards) and Frederick Thomas (vocals).			
8/10/91	2^{2}	21		1 **Do Anything** ....A:3 / S:5 *(raw mix)* **NATURAL SELECTION featuring Niki Haris**	$3	▮	EastWest 98724
12/7/91+	28	14		2 **Hearts Don't Think (They Feel)!** ....A:32 *(radio remix)*	$3	▮	EastWest 98652
				NATURE'S DIVINE LP **'79** R&B group from Detroit, Michigan: Lynn Smith (female vocals), Robert Carter (male vocals), Duane Mitchell (guitar), Charles Woods and Marvin Jones (keyboards), Charles Green and Opelton Parker (horns), Robert Johnson (percussion), Keith Fondren (bass) and Mark Mitchell (drums).			
11/3/79	65	7		**I Just Can't Control Myself** ....*Love Is You*	$5		Infinity 50,027
				NAUGHTON, David **'79** Born on 2/13/52 in Hartford, Connecticut. Pop singer/dancer/actor. Starred in the 1981 movie *An American Werewolf In London* and TV shows *Makin' It* and *My Sister Sam*.			
3/31/79	5	24	●	**Makin' It** ....*Still Makin' It* from the movie *Meatballs* starring Bill Murray	$5	■	RSO 916
	★573★			**NAUGHTY BY NATURE** R&B/BUB/LP **'93** Black hip-hop trio from East Orange, New Jersey: Anthony "**Treach**" Criss (born on 12/2/70; **The Flavor Unit Mcs**), Vincent Brown and Kier Gist (born on 9/15/69). Appeared in the movies *The Meteor Man* and *Who's The Man*. Treach married Sandra "Pepa" Denton (of **Salt-N-Pepa**) on 7/24/99. Also see **L.V.** and **Monica**'s "Ain't Nobody." *1)O.P.P. 2)Hip Hop Hooray 3)Jamboree*			
9/7/91	6	21	▲^{2}	1 **O.P.P.** S:❶[1] / A:24 *(instrumental) / Wickedest Man Alive* O.P.P.: Other People's Property; samples "ABC" by **The Jackson 5**	$5	▮*V	Tommy Boy 988
2/8/92	53	20		2 **Everything's Gonna Be Alright** ....A:35 / S:41 *(3 versions) / O.P.P. (live)* samples "No Woman, No Cry" by **Boney M**; "45" issued for above 2 on Tommy Boy/Collectables 512	$5	▮*V	Tommy Boy 999
6/20/92	65^{S}	2		3 **Uptown Anthem** ....*(2 versions) / Guard Your Grill* from the movie *Juice* starring **2Pac** and Omar Epps	$5	▮*	Tommy Boy 519
1/30/93	8	22	▲	4 **Hip Hop Hooray** ....RB[1] S:2 / A:11 *(2 versions) / The Hood Comes First* "45": Tommy Boy/Collectables 554; B-side: (album version)	$5	▮*V	Tommy Boy 554
6/26/93	74	12		5 **It's On** ....S:64 *(3 versions) / Hip Hop Hooray (***Pete Rock** *remix)* "45": Tommy Boy/Collectables 569; B-side: (same version)	$5	▮*V	Tommy Boy 569
10/16/93	93	3		6 **Written On Ya Kitten** ....*(3 versions) / Klickow-Klickow*	$5	▮*	Tommy Boy 583
4/15/95	51	10		7 **Craziest** ....S:24 *(2 versions) / Holdin' Fort* samples "That's All That Matters Baby" by **Charles Wright**; "45": Tommy Boy/Collectables 670; B-side: (same version)	$5	▮*V	Tommy Boy 670
6/10/95	17	20	●	8 **Feel Me Flow** ....S:8 / A:40 *Hang Out And Hustle* samples "Find Yourself" by **The Meters**; "45": Tommy Boy/Collectables 682; B-side: (original mix)	$3	▮V	Tommy Boy 7682
11/15/97	51	12		9 **Mourn You Til I Join You** ....S:26 *Nothing To Lose (Naughty Live)*	$3	▮	Tommy Boy 7427
7/3/99	10	17	●	10 **Jamboree** ....S:4 / A:58 *On The Run* **NAUGHTY BY NATURE (Feat. Zhané)** samples "I'm Always Dancin' To The Music" by Benny Golson	$4	★	Arista 13712
3/30/02	53	20		11 **Feels Good (Don't Worry Bout A Thing)** ....S:3 / A:64 *(3 remixes) / Rah Rah* **NAUGHTY BY NATURE Featuring 3LW** contains an interpolation of "Feels Good" by **Tony! Toni! Toné!**	$4	★	TVT 2344
				NAYLOR, Jerry C&W **'70** Born on 3/6/39 in Stephenville, Texas. Replaced Joe B. Mauldin in **The Crickets** in 1961.			
3/28/70	69	4		**But For Love** ....*Angeline* a new version by Naylor was a #54 Country hit in 1979 on Warner/Curb 8767	$7		Columbia 45106
				NAZARETH BUB/ROK/LP **'76** Hard-rock group formed in Dumerferline, Scotland: Dan McCafferty (vocals), Manny Charlton (guitar), Pete Agnew (bass) and Darrell Sweet (drums). **Billy Rankin** (guitar) (see #3 below) and John Locke (keyboards) added in 1981. Sweet died of a heart attack on 4/30/99 (age 51).			
11/22/75+	8	23	●	1 **Love Hurts** ....*Hair Of The Dog* first released in 1960 on **The Everly Brothers**' album *A Date With The Everly Brothers*	$5	■	A&M 1671
3/29/80	87	3		2 **Holiday** ....*Ship Of Dreams*	$4		A&M 2219
3/10/84	52	11		3 **Baby Come Back** ....*Part Of The Scenery* **BILLY RANKIN**	$4		A&M 2613

DEBUT	PEAK	WKS	Gold	A-side (Chart Hit)...B-side	$	Sym	Label & Number
				NAZZ BUB/LP '70 Rock group from Philadelphia, Pennsylvania: **Todd Rundgren** (guitar), Robert "Stewkey" Antoni (vocals), Carson Van Osten (bass) and Thom Mooney (drums).			
2/15/69	**71**	7		1 **Hello It's Me**...*Open My Eyes* (#112) also see **Todd Rundgren**'s 1973 solo version	$12	■	SGC 001
1/17/70	**66**	6		2 **Hello It's Me**...*Open My Eyes* [R] above 2 are the same version (#1: yellow label; #2: yellow and green label)	$12	■	SGC 001
				NB-RIDAZ — see NASTYBOY KLICK			
				NDEGÉOCELLO, Me'Shell R&B/BUB/LP '94 Born Michelle Johnson on 8/29/69 in Berlin, Maryland; raised in Oxon Hill, Maryland. Black female R&B-dance singer/bassist. Last name (pronounced: Nuh-DAY-gay-O-CHEL-lo) means "free like a bird" in Swahili.			
2/5/94	**73**	6		**If That's Your Boyfriend (He Wasn't Last Night)**...A:70 *Two Lonely Hearts (On The Subway)*	$3	I[V]	Maverick/Sire 18326
				N'DOUR, Youssou ROK '94 Born on 10/1/59 in Dakar, Senegal, Africa. Popular singer in his native country. Often sings in his native language of Wolof. Backing vocalist on **Peter Gabriel**'s "In Your Eyes." Pronounced: YOU-sue en-DURE.			
10/8/94	**98**	4		**7 Seconds**...*Mame Bamba* (N'Dour) **YOUSSOU N'DOUR & NENEH CHERRY** Cherry sings in English; N'Dour sings in French and Wolof	$3	I	Chaos/Columbia 77483
				NEELY, Sam C&W/BUB/LP '72 Born on 8/22/48 in Cuero, Texas. Pop-country singer/songwriter/guitarist.			
9/2/72	**29**	12		1 **Loving You Just Crossed My Mind** *Every Day Is The Same As Today*	$6		Capitol 3381
1/27/73	**43**	8		2 **Rosalie**...*Try To Reason Why*	$6		Capitol 3510
9/21/74	**34**	11		3 **You Can Have Her**...*It's A Fine Morning*	$6		A&M 1612
2/1/75	**54**	7		4 **I Fought The Law**...*Guitar Man*	$6		A&M 1651
8/27/77	**84**	4		5 **Sail Away**...*My Lover And My Friend*	$5		Elektra 45419
				NEIGHBORHOOD, The BUB '70 Seven-man, two-woman pop vocal group.			
6/27/70	**29**	11		**Big Yellow Taxi**...*You Could Be Born Again*	$8		Big Tree 102
				NEKTAR LP '75 Art-rock group formed in England: Roye Albrighton (vocals, guitar), Allan Freeman (keyboards), Derek Moore (bass) and Ron Howden (drums).			
5/10/75	**91**	5		**Astral Man**...*Nelly The Elephant*	$7		Passport 7904
				NELLY ★276★ R&B/LP '02 Born Cornell Haynes on 11/2/74 in Travis, Texas; raised in St. Louis, Missouri. Male rapper. Member of **St. Lunatics**. Played "Prolifik" in the movie *Snipes*. Started own Vokal Clothing line in 2002. *1)Dilemma 2)Hot In Herre 3)Ride Wit Me*			
4/29/00	**7**	34		1 **(Hot S**t) Country Grammar**...S:2 / A:3 *(dirty edit) / (3 album snippets)*	$4	★	Fo' Reel/Universal 156800
10/7/00+	**15**	20		2 **E.I.**...A:10			album cut
2/24/01	**3**	29		3 **Ride Wit Me**...A:3 **NELLY (Featuring City Spud)** samples "I Like It" by **DeBarge**; above 3 from the album *Country Grammar* on Fo' Reel/Universal 157743			album cut
6/2/01	**3**	29		4 **Where The Party At**...RB[3] S:❶[3] / A:4 *Let's Get Married* (w/Run of **Run-DMC**) **JAGGED EDGE featuring Nelly**	$4	★	So So Def 79626
10/20/01	**22**	20		5 **#1**...A:20 from the movie *Training Day* starring Denzel Washington (soundtrack on Priority 50213)			album cut
2/9/02	**5**	20		6 **Girlfriend**...S:❶[14] / A:9 *(album version) / Gone* ***NSYNC featuring Nelly** "45": Jive 40017; B-side: (same version)	$8	★*+V	Jive 40013
5/4/02	**❶[7]**	26		7 **Hot In Herre**...RB[6] A:❶[7] / S:5 *(clean album version)* samples "Bustin' Loose" by **Chuck Brown & The Soul Searchers**	$4	★	Fo' Reel/Universal 019279
7/13/02	**❶[10]**	29		8 **Dilemma** / RB[9] A:❶[12] / S:17 **NELLY Featuring Kelly Rowland** samples "Love, Need And Want You" by **Patti LaBelle**			
11/9/02+	**3**	20		9 **Air Force Ones**...A:3 **NELLY Featuring Kyjuan, Ali and Murphy Lee**	$6	T	Fo' Reel/Universal 019509
				NELSON BUB/LP '90 Pop-rock duo from Los Angeles, California: Gunnar (vocals, bass) and Matthew (vocals, guitar) Nelson. The identical twin sons (born on 9/20/67) of **Ricky Nelson**.			
7/7/90	**❶[1]**	26	●	1 **(Can't Live Without Your) Love And Affection**...S:❶[1] / A:4 *Will You Love Me?*	$3	I[V]	DGC 19689
11/3/90+	**6**	22		2 **After The Rain**...S:4 / A:6 *Fill You Up*	$3	I[V]	DGC 19667
3/9/91	**14**	17		3 **More Than Ever**...A:12 / S:14 *Keep One Heart (live)*	$3	I[V]	DGC 19002
6/22/91	**28**	14		4 **Only Time Will Tell**...A:42 / S:51 *(Can't Live Without Your) Love And Affection (acoustic version)* all of above from the album *After The Rain*	$3	I[V]	DGC 19014
				NELSON, Karen, And Billy T '77 Nelson was born in Kansas City, Kansas; served three years as backup singer/pianist for **Paul Anka**. Billy T (Tragesser) is from Pittsburgh, Pennsylvania.			
9/10/77	**79**	4		**Love Me One More Time (Just For Old Times Sake)**...*It's A Long Way From Kansas City*	$8		Amherst 724

DEBUT	PEAK	WKS	Gold	A-side (Chart Hit)..........B-side	$	Sym	Label & Number

NELSON, Marc — R&B '99

Born in Philadelphia, Pennsylvania. R&B singer/songwriter. Son of **Phyllis Nelson**.

DEBUT	PEAK	WKS	Gold	A-side (Chart Hit)..........B-side	$	Sym	Label & Number
10/2/99	27	16		**15 Minutes** ....S:10 *(3 album snippets)* co-written by **Sam Salter**	$4	★	Columbia 79220

NELSON, Phyllis — '86

Born in Philadelphia, Pennsylvania. Dance singer. Mother of **Marc Nelson**.

DEBUT	PEAK	WKS	Gold	A-side (Chart Hit)..........B-side	$	Sym	Label & Number
2/8/86	61	11		**I Like You** ....*Reachin'* originally released in 1985 on Carrere 05583 with a picture sleeve	$3		USA Carrere 05719

NELSON, Ricky ★26★ — BUB/AC/C&W/LP '58

Born Eric Hilliard Nelson on 5/8/40 in Teaneck, New Jersey. Died in a plane crash in DeKalb, Texas, on 12/31/85 (age 45). Son of bandleader Ozzie Nelson and vocalist Harriet Hilliard. Rick and brother David appeared on Nelson's radio show from March 1949, later on TV, 1952-66. Formed own Stone Canyon Band in 1969. In movies *Rio Bravo*, *The Wackiest Ship In The Army* and *Love And Kisses*. Married Kristin Harmon (sister of actor Mark Harmon) in 1963; divorced in 1982. Their daughter Tracy is a movie/TV actress. Their twin sons began recording as **Nelson** in 1990. Ricky was one of the first teen idols of the rock era. Inducted into the Rock and Roll Hall of Fame in 1987.

1)Poor Little Fool 2)Travelin' Man 3)Stood Up 4)A Teenager's Romance 5)Be-Bop Baby

DEBUT	PEAK	WKS	Gold	A-side (Chart Hit)..........B-side	$	Sym	Label & Number
5/13/57	2[1]	19	●	1 **A Teenager's Romance /** S:2 / T:8 / A:8 / J:12			
5/6/57	4	17		2 **I'm Walking** ....S:4 / J:16 / T:17	$40		Verve 10047
8/26/57	14	12		3 **You're My One And Only Love /** S:14 / T:16 Gloria Wood (female vocal)			
9/16/57		5		4 **Honey Rock** ....S:flip [I] **BARNEY KESSEL** (Nelson not credited on B-side) Barney Kessel (orch., all of above)	$40		Verve 10070
10/7/57	3	20	●	5 **Be-Bop Baby /** S:3 / T:5 / A:10			
10/7/57	29	9		6 **Have I Told You Lately That I Love You?** ....T:29 / S:flip #24 hit for **Bing Crosby** & The Andrews Sisters in 1950	$25	■	Imperial 5463
12/30/57+	2[3]	18	●	7 **Stood Up /** S:2 / T:5 / A:5			
12/30/57+	18	14		8 **Waitin' In School** ....T:18 / A:24 / S:flip	$25	■	Imperial 5483
4/7/58	4	12	●	9 **Believe What You Say /** S:4 / T:8 / A:20			
3/31/58	12	12		10 **My Bucket's Got A Hole In It** ....S:12 / T:18 / A:25 #2 Country hit for Hank Williams in 1949	$25	■	Imperial 5503
7/7/58	❶[2]	15	●	11 **Poor Little Fool** S:❶[2] / H:❶[2] / A:2 *Don't Leave Me This Way* the #1 hit on *Billboard's* first "Hot 100" chart (8/4/58)	$25		Imperial 5528
10/20/58	7	18	●	12 **Lonesome Town /**			
10/13/58	10	17		13 **I Got A Feeling** H:10	$25	■	Imperial 5545
2/23/59	6	16	●	14 **Never Be Anyone Else But You /**			
3/2/59	9	13		15 **It's Late**	$25	■	Imperial 5565
6/29/59	9	13		16 **Just A Little Too Much /** #8, 9, 15 & 16: written by **Johnny** and/or **Dorsey Burnette** (also #42 below)			
7/6/59	9	12		17 **Sweeter Than You**	$25	■	Imperial 5595
11/30/59	20	11		18 **I Wanna Be Loved /**			
11/30/59	38	9		19 **Mighty Good**	$20	■	Imperial 5614
4/25/60	12	13		20 **Young Emotions /**			
5/2/60	59	6		21 **Right By My Side**	$20	■	Imperial 5663
9/5/60	27	8		22 **I'm Not Afraid /**			
9/12/60	34	6		23 **Yes Sir, That's My Baby** .... #1 hit for **Gene Austin** in 1925	$20	■	Imperial 5685
12/26/60+	25	8		24 **You Are The Only One /**			
12/31/60+	79	3		25 **Milk Cow Blues** .... originally recorded by the song's writer, Kokomo Arnold, in 1935	$20	■	Imperial 5707
4/24/61	❶[2]	16	●	26 **Travelin' Man /**			
5/1/61	9	15		27 **Hello Mary Lou**	$20	■	Imperial 5741
				RICK NELSON:			
10/2/61	11	11		28 **A Wonder Like You /**			
10/2/61	16	10		29 **Everlovin'**	$20	■	Imperial 5770
3/3/62	5	13		30 **Young World /**			
3/10/62	89	2		31 **Summertime** .... from Gershwin's folk opera *Porgy And Bess*; #12 hit for Billie Holiday in 1936	$20	■	Imperial 5805
8/11/62	5	11		32 **Teen Age Idol** ....*I've Got My Eyes On You (And I Like What I See)* (#105)	$20	■	Imperial 5864
12/15/62+	6	12		33 **It's Up To You /** #26-28, 30 & 33: written by **Jerry Fuller** (also #46 below)			
12/22/62+	83	4		34 **I Need You** .... #12-14, 17-19, 21, 24 & 34: written by Baker Knight	$20	■	Imperial 5901
3/2/63	48	6		35 **That's All /** from his 1959 album *Songs By Ricky* (tune written in 1952)			
2/23/63	67	6		36 **I'm In Love Again** .... from his 1958 album *Ricky Nelson*	$20		Imperial 5910
3/9/63	47	7		37 **You Don't Love Me Anymore (And I Can Tell) /**			
3/16/63	49	6		38 **I Got A Woman** .... #1 R&B hit for **Ray Charles** in 1955	$15	■	Decca 31475
5/4/63	94	3		39 **Old Enough To Love** *[RICKY NELSON]* **/** from his 1959 album *Ricky Sings Again*			
4/20/63	100	1		40 **If You Can't Rock Me** *[RICKY NELSON]* .... from his 1957 debut album *Ricky*	$20	■	Imperial 5935

DEBUT	PEAK	WKS	Gold	A-side (Chart Hit)..........B-side	$	Sym	Label & Number
				NELSON, Ricky — Cont'd			
5/25/63	**25**	9		41 **String Along** /			
5/18/63	**62**	9		42 **Gypsy Woman**	$15	■	Decca 31495
				#37, 38, 41 & 42: from his 1963 album *For Your Sweet Love*			
9/14/63	**12**	13		43 **Fools Rush In**..........*Down Home* (#126)	$15	■	Decca 31533
				#3 hit for Glenn Miller in 1940			
11/30/63+	**54**	9		44 **Today's Teardrops**..........*Thank You Darlin'*	$15	■	Imperial 66004
				#27 & 44: written by **Gene Pitney**			
12/28/63+	**6**	11		45 **For You**..........AC² *That's All She Wrote*	$15	■	Decca 31574
				first popularized by Glen Gray in 1933 on Brunswick 6606			
3/14/64	**63**	5		46 **Congratulations**..........*One Minute To One*	$15		Imperial 66017
				#44 & 46: from his 1962 *Album Seven By Rick*; #26, 28, 30, 33 & 46: written by **Jerry Fuller**			
4/25/64	**26**	7		47 **The Very Thought Of You**..........*I Wonder (If Your Love Will Ever Belong To Me)*	$12	■	Decca 31612
				#1 hit for Ray Noble in 1934			
8/22/64	**47**	6		48 **There's Nothing I Can Say**..........*Lonely Corner* (#113)	$12	■	Decca 31656
11/28/64	**82**	4		49 **A Happy Guy**..........*Don't Breathe A Word*	$12	■	Decca 31703
3/20/65	**96**	2		50 **Mean Old World**..........*When The Chips Are Down*	$12	■	Decca 31756
				written by **Billy Vera** of **Billy & The Beaters**			
				RICK NELSON & THE STONE CANYON BAND:			
10/11/69+	**33**	18		51 **She Belongs To Me**..........*Promises*	$10		Decca 32550
				written by **Bob Dylan** (from his 1965 album *Bringing It All Back Home*)			
3/7/70	**48**	6		52 **Easy To Be Free** *[RICK NELSON]*..........*Come On In*	$10	■	Decca 32635
7/29/72	**6**	19	●	53 **Garden Party**..........AC² *So Long Mama*	$10		Decca 32980
				inspired by Nelson's experience during a Madison Square Garden concert			
2/3/73	**65**	5		54 **Palace Guard**..........*A Flower Opens Gently By*	$8		MCA 40001
				NELSON, Sandy BUB/LP **'59**			
				Born Sander Nelson on 12/1/38 in Santa Monica, California. Rock and roll drummer. Became prominent studio musician. Heard on "Alley Oop," "To Know Him Is To Love Him," "A Thousand Stars" and many others. Lost portion of right leg in a motorcycle accident in 1963. Returned to performing in 1964.			
9/7/59	**4**	16		1 **Teen Beat**..........*Big Jump* [I]	$25		Original Sound 5
				also see #9 below			
10/30/61	**7**	16		2 **Let There Be Drums**..........*Quite A Beat!* [I]	$15		Imperial 5775
				"live" version "Bubbled Under" (#120) on 5/22/65 on Imperial 66107			
2/10/62	**29**	7		3 **Drums Are My Beat** / [I]			
2/24/62	**75**	1		4 **The Birth Of The Beat** [I]	$12		Imperial 5809
4/28/62	**67**	8		5 **Drummin' Up A Storm** / [I]			
5/26/62	**86**	3		6 **Drum Stomp** [I]	$12		Imperial 5829
7/14/62	**75**	3		7 **All Night Long**..........*Rompin' & Stompin'* [I]	$12		Imperial 5860
9/22/62	**65**	4		8 **...And Then There Were Drums**..........*Live It Up* (#101) [I]	$12		Imperial 5870
9/19/64	**44**	10		9 **Teen Beat '65**..........*Kitty's Theme* [I-L-R]	$10		Imperial 66060
				studio version on #1 above			
	★498★			**NELSON, Willie** C&W/AC/BUB/LP **'82**			
				Born on 4/30/33 in Abbott, Texas. Prolific country singer/songwriter (writer of the classic "Funny How Time Slips Away," **Patsy Cline**'s "Crazy" and **Faron Young**'s "Hello Walls"). Played bass for **Ray Price**. Moved to Nashville in 1960. Moved back to Texas in 1970. Pioneered the "outlaw" Country movement. Charted 117 Country hits, 1962-02. Appeared in several movies including *The Electric Horseman*, *Honeysuckle Rose* and *Barbarosa*. Elected to the Country Music Hall of Fame in 1993. Won Grammy's Lifetime Achievement Award in 2000. Also see **Waylon Jennings**'s "Luckenbach, Texas."			
				1)Always On My Mind 2)To All The Girls I've Loved Before 3)On The Road Again			
8/30/75	**21**	18		1 **Blue Eyes Crying In The Rain**..........CW² *Bandera*	$7		Columbia 10176
				written in 1945 by Fred Rose			
1/10/76	**67**	8		2 **Remember Me**..........*Time Of The Preacher*	$7		Columbia 10275
2/7/76	**25**	12		3 **Good Hearted Woman**..........CW³ *Heaven Or Hell* [L]	$6		RCA Victor 10529
				#3 Country hit for **Waylon Jennings** in 1972			
2/11/78	**42**	10		4 **Mammas Don't Let Your Babies Grow Up To Be Cowboys**..........CW⁴ *I Can Get Off On You* (C&W flip)	$5		RCA 11198
				WAYLON & WILLIE (above 2)			
5/27/78	**84**	6		5 **Georgia On My Mind**..........CW¹ *On The Sunny Side Of The Street*	$5		Columbia 10704
				written in 1930 by Hoagy Carmichael			
2/9/80	**44**	10		6 **My Heroes Have Always Been Cowboys**..........CW² *Rising Star (Love Theme)*	$4		Columbia 11186
				from the movie *The Electric Horseman* starring Nelson, Robert Redford and Jane Fonda			
9/6/80	**20**	20		7 **On The Road Again**..........CW¹ *Jumpin' Cotton Eyed Joe* (Johnny Gimble)	$4		Columbia 11351
				from the movie *Honeysuckle Rose* starring Nelson and Dyan Cannon			
3/6/82	**5**	23	▲	8 **Always On My Mind**..........CW² *The Party's Over*	$4		Columbia 02741
				#45 Country hit for **Brenda Lee** in 1972			
4/3/82	**52**	9		9 **Just To Satisfy You**..........CW² *Get Naked With Me* (Waylon)	$4		RCA 13073
				WAYLON & WILLIE			
8/7/82	**40**	12		10 **Let It Be Me**..........*Permanently Lonely*	$4		Columbia 03073
3/3/84	**5**	21	▲	11 **To All The Girls I've Loved Before**..........CW² *I Don't Want To Wake You* (Iglesias)	$4	■	Columbia 04217
				JULIO IGLESIAS & WILLIE NELSON			
				NENA BUB/LP **'84**			
				Rock group formed in Berlin, Germany: Gabriele "Nena" Kerner (vocals), Carlo Karges (guitar), Uwe Fahrenkrog-Petersen (keyboards), Jurgen Demel (bass) and Rolf Brendel (drums). Karges died of liver failure on 1/30/2002 (age 50).			
12/10/83+	**2¹**	23	●	**99 Luftballons**..........*99 Red Ballons* [F]	$5		Epic 04108
				NEON PHILHARMONIC, The BUB/AC **'69**			
				Chamber-sized orchestra of Nashville Symphony Orchestra musicians. Project headed by Tupper Saussy (composer) and Don Gant (vocals). Gant died on 3/6/87 (age 44).			
4/5/69	**17**	12		1 **Morning Girl**..........*Brilliant Colors*	$8		Warner 7261
5/30/70	**94**	2		2 **Heighdy-Ho Princess**..........*Don't Know My Way Around My Soul*	$6		Warner 7380
				NEPTUNES, The — see PUFF DADDY			

DEBUT	PEAK	WKS	Gold	A-side (Chart Hit)	B-side	$	Sym	Label & Number

NERO, Peter — AC/BUB/LP '71

Born Bernard Nierow on 5/22/34 in Brooklyn, New York. Pop-jazz-classical pianist. Won the 1961 Best New Artist Grammy Award.

DEBUT	PEAK	WKS	Gold	A-side (Chart Hit)	B-side	$	Sym	Label & Number
10/16/71	21	13		**Theme From "Summer Of '42"** title song from the movie starring Jennifer O'Neill	*Theme From "Jesus Christ, Superstar"* [I]	$5		Columbia 45399

NERVOUS NORVUS — '56

Born James Drake on 5/13/12 in Nashville, Tennessee. Died of liver failure on 7/24/68 (age 56). Novelty singer/songwriter.

DEBUT	PEAK	WKS	Gold	A-side (Chart Hit)	B-side	$	Sym	Label & Number
6/2/56	8	14		1 **Transfusion** originally released in early 1956 by the Four Jokers (Nervous Norvus a member) on Diamond 3004 ($50)	S:8 / T:13 / A:14 / J:18 *Dig* [N]	$30		Dot 15470
7/28/56	24	10		2 **Ape Call** Red Blanchard (ape calls)	S:24 / T:28 *Wild Dog Of Kentucky* [N]	$30		Dot 15485

NESMITH, Michael, & The First National Band — LP '70

Born on 12/30/42 in Houston, Texas. Pop-rock singer/songwriter/guitarist. Was a professional musician before joining **The Monkees**; had done session work for Stax/Volt. Wrote **Linda Ronstadt**'s hit "Different Drum." Formed own video production company, Pacific Arts, in 1977; produced movies *Elephant Parts*, *Repo Man* and others.

DEBUT	PEAK	WKS	Gold	A-side (Chart Hit)	B-side	$	Sym	Label & Number
8/8/70	21	12		1 **Joanne**	*One Rose*	$12		RCA Victor 0368
11/28/70+	42	9		2 **Silver Moon**	*Lady Of The Valley*	$10		RCA Victor 0399
4/17/71	70	4		3 **Nevada Fighter**	*Here I Am*	$10	■	RCA Victor 0453

NETTO, Loz — see SNIFF 'N THE TEARS

NEVIL, Robbie — LP '87

Born on 10/2/60 in Los Angeles, California. Pop singer/songwriter/guitarist.

DEBUT	PEAK	WKS	Gold	A-side (Chart Hit)	B-side	$	Sym	Label & Number
10/11/86+	2^2	23		1 **C'est La Vie** title is French for "That's Life"	S:❶^1 / A:3 *Time Waits For No One*	$3	■	Manhattan 50047
2/14/87	14	16		2 **Dominoes**	A:13 / S:14 *Neighbors*	$3	■	Manhattan 50053
5/30/87	10	16		3 **Wot's It To Ya**	S:8 / A:16 *(remix)*	$3	■	Manhattan 50075
11/12/88+	34	14		4 **Back On Holiday**	S:31 / A:32 *Too Soon*	$3	■	EMI-Manhattan 50152
3/18/89	63	11		5 **Somebody Like You**	*Can I Count On You*	$3		EMI 50176
7/6/91	25	14		6 **Just Like You**	A:43 *(power mix) / Paradise*	$3	▮	EMI 50356
10/26/91	86	4		7 **For Your Mind**	*(remix) / Sensual*	$3	▮	EMI 50367

NEVILLE, Aaron — AC/R&B/BUB/C&W/LP '67

Born on 1/24/41 in New Orleans, Louisiana. Member of the R&B family group, The Neville Brothers. Brother Art was keyboardist of **The Meters**. Bassist/singer **Ivan Neville** is Aaron's son.

DEBUT	PEAK	WKS	Gold	A-side (Chart Hit)	B-side	$	Sym	Label & Number
12/3/66+	2^1	14		1 **Tell It Like It Is**	RB^5 *Why Worry*	$20		Par-Lo 101
3/25/67	92	4		2 **She Took You For A Ride**	*Space Man*	$15		Par-Lo 103
9/30/89	2^2	26	●	3 **Don't Know Much** AC^5 #77 hit for **Bette Midler** in 1983 as "All I Need To Know"	S:❷^2 / A:4 *Cry Like A Rainstorm* (Ronstadt)	$3		Elektra 69261
2/10/90	11	15		4 **All My Life** AC^3	S:10 / A:14 *Shattered* (Ronstadt)	$3	▮^{V}	Elektra 64987
5/12/90	78	6		5 **When Something Is Wrong With My Baby** **LINDA RONSTADT (featuring Aaron Neville)** (above 3)	*Try Me Again* (Ronstadt)	$3	▮	Elektra 64968
7/20/91	8	20		6 **Everybody Plays The Fool** AC^1	A:19 / S:47 *House On A Hill*	$3	▮^{V}	A&M 1563
5/22/93	56	20		7 **Don't Take Away My Heaven**	A:37 *(album version) / The Roadie Song*	$3	▮^{V}	A&M 0240
10/9/93	90	5		8 **The Grand Tour** #1 Country hit for **George Jones** in 1974; "45" issued for above 2 on A&M 0312	S:56 *The Roadie Song*	$3	▮^{V}	A&M 0312
7/29/95	99	1		9 **Can't Stop My Heart From Loving You (The Rain Song)**	*In Your Eyes*	$3	▮	A&M 1038

NEVILLE, Ivan — LP '88

Born on 7/23/65 in New Orleans, Louisiana. Rock singer/bassist. Played on **The Rolling Stones**' *Dirty Work* album. Son of **Aaron Neville**.

DEBUT	PEAK	WKS	Gold	A-side (Chart Hit)	B-side	$	Sym	Label & Number
10/8/88	26	19		1 **Not Just Another Girl**	S:27 / A:28 *Up To You*	$3	■	Polydor 887814
2/25/89	91	3		2 **Falling Out Of Love**	*Sun*	$3	■	Polydor 871484

NEWBEATS, The — BUB/LP '64

Pop trio: Larry Henley (lead singer; born on 6/30/41 in Arp, Texas) with brothers **Dean And Marc** Mathis (born on 3/17/39 and on 2/9/42, respectively, in Hahira, Georgia) (see #1 below). Henley co-wrote "Wind Beneath My Wings."

DEBUT	PEAK	WKS	Gold	A-side (Chart Hit)	B-side	$	Sym	Label & Number
3/23/59	42	8		1 **Tell Him No** **DEAN AND MARC**	*Change Of Heart*	$40		Bullseye 1025
8/15/64	2^2	12		2 **Bread And Butter**	*Tough Little Buggy*	$15		Hickory 1269
10/24/64	16	9		3 **Everything's Alright**	*Pink Dally Rue*	$12		Hickory 1282
1/23/65	40	7		4 **Break Away (From That Boy)**	*Hey-O-Daddy-O* (#118)	$10		Hickory 1290
4/3/65	50	7		5 **(The Bees Are For The Birds) The Birds Are For The Bees**	*Better Watch Your Step*	$10		Hickory 1305
10/2/65	12	13		6 **Run, Baby Run (Back Into My Arms)**	*Mean Woolly Willie*	$10		Hickory 1332
2/26/66	92	3		7 **Shake Hands (And Come Out Crying)**	*Too Sweet To Be Forgotten*	$10		Hickory 1366
12/20/69+	82	5		8 **Groovin' (Out On Life)**	*Bread And Butter*	$10		Hickory 1552

NEW BIRTH, The — R&B/LP '73

R&B group formed in Louisville, Kentucky, by **Harvey Fuqua** and Tony Churchill as **The Nite-Liters** (see #1 & 3 below). Expanded to 17 members with two vocal groups (**The New Birth** and Love, Peace & Happiness) and a band (The Nite-Liters). Renamed New Birth, Inc. Band consisted of Churchill, Austin Lander, James Baker, Robert "Lurch" Jackson, Leroy Taylor and Robin Russell. Vocal groups consisted of Ann Bogan, Melvin Wilson, Leslie Wilson, Bobby Downs, Londee Loren, and Alan Frye. Bogan was a former member of **The Marvelettes**.

1)I Can Understand It 2)Dream Merchant 3)K-Jee

DEBUT	PEAK	WKS	Gold	A-side (Chart Hit)	B-side	$	Sym	Label & Number
7/3/71	39	16		1 **K-Jee** *[THE NITE-LITERS]*	*Tanga Boo Gonk* [I]	$6		RCA Victor 0461
10/9/71	52	9		2 **It's Impossible**	*Honeybee*	$6		RCA Victor 0520
2/26/72	49	8		3 **Afro-Strut** *[THE NITE-LITERS]*	*(We've Got To) Pull Together* (R&B #27) [I]	$6		RCA Victor 0591
3/24/73	35	13		4 **I Can Understand It**	*Oh, Baby, I Love The Way*	$6		RCA Victor 0912
8/25/73	97	3		5 **Until It's Time For You To Go**	*You Are What I'm All About*	$6		RCA Victor 0003
2/16/74	66	6		6 **It's Been A Long Time**	*Keep On Doin' It*	$6		RCA Victor 0185

DEBUT	PEAK	WKS	Gold	A-side (Chart Hit)...B-side	$	Sym	Label & Number
				NEW BIRTH, The — Cont'd			
5/11/74	45	9		7 **Wildflower**...*Got To Get A Knutt*	$6		RCA Victor 0265
10/12/74	88	3		8 **I Wash My Hands Of The Whole Damn Deal, Part I**...*Part II*	$6		RCA Victor 10017
5/24/75	95	3		9 **Granddaddy (Part 1)**...*(Part 2)*	$5		Buddah 464
7/5/75	36	11		10 **Dream Merchant**...RB[1] *Why Did I*	$5		Buddah 470
				NEW BORN '93			
				Born Sammy Sanford in Philadelphia, Pennsylvania (nine years old in 1993). Male rapper.			
6/19/93	97	2		**Falling In Love**...A:75 *(2 versions)*	$4	▮	Relativity 1174
				rap version of **Hamilton, Joe Frank & Reynolds**'s "Fallin' In Love"			
				NEWBURY, Mickey C&W/BUB/LP '72			
				Born Milton Newbury on 5/19/40 in Houston, Texas. Died on 9/28/2002 (age 62). Pop-country singer/songwriter/guitarist.			
11/6/71+	26	11		1 **An American Trilogy**...*San Francisco Mabel Joy*	$8		Elektra 45750
				Dixie/Battle Hymn Of The Republic/All My Trials; a new version made the Country charts (#93) in 1988 on Airborne 10005			
7/21/73	87	3		2 **Sunshine**...*Song For Susan*	$5		Elektra 45853
				NEW CHRISTY MINSTRELS, The BUB/AC/LP '63			
				Folk-balladeer troupe named after the Christy Minstrels (formed in 1842 by Edwin "Pop" Christy). Group founded and led by Randy Sparks, and featured **Barry McGuire** (1963), **Kenny Rogers** (1966) and **Kim Carnes** (1968).			
12/1/62	93	1		1 **This Land Is Your Land**...*Don't Cry, Suzanne* (Randy Sparks)	$10	■	Columbia 42592
				the Woody Guthrie folk classic written in 1956; first picture sleeve pressings show New Cristy Minstrels			
6/29/63	14	12		2 **Green, Green** *The Banjo*	$8		Columbia 42805
				Barry McGuire (lead vocal)			
10/26/63	29	7		3 **Saturday Night**...*The Wheeler Dealers*	$8		Columbia 42887
4/18/64	17	13		4 **Today**...*Miss Katy Cruel*	$7		Columbia 43000
				from the movie *Advance To The Rear* starring Glenn Ford			
8/8/64	92	2		5 **Silly Ol' Summertime**...*The Far Side Of The Hill*	$6		Columbia 43092
4/24/65	81	5		6 **Chim, Chim, Cheree**...*They Gotta Quit Kickin' My Dog Around*	$6		Columbia 43215
				from the movie *Mary Poppins* starring **Julie Andrews** and **Dick Van Dyke**			
				NEWCITY ROCKERS '87			
				Rock group from Boston, Massachusetts: Ken Kozdra (vocals), Cliff Goodwin (guitar), Mitch Chakour (bass) and Bob Rivers (drums).			
4/18/87	80	6		1 **Black Dog**...*Gun Shy*	$4		Critique 99451
9/12/87	86	4		2 **Rev It Up**...*Break A Heart*	$4	■	Critique 99437
				NEWCLEUS R&B/LP '84			
				Rap-dance group from Brooklyn, New York: brother-and-sister Ben "Cozmo D" and Yvette Cenad, with brother-and-sister Bob "Chilly B" and Monique Crafton.			
6/2/84	56	15		**Jam On It**...*(instrumental)* [N]	$4		Sunnyview 3010
				NEW COLONY SIX, The BUB/LP '69			
				Soft-rock group from Chicago, Illinois: Raymond Graffia (vocals), Patrick McBride (harmonica), Gerald Van Kollenburg (guitar), cousins Craig (organ) and Walter (bass) Kemp and Chic James (drums). Craig Kemp left in mid-1966, replaced by Ronnie Rice. Walter Kemp left in mid-1967, replaced by Ellery Temple. Temple left in late 1967, replaced by Les Kummel. James left in 1969, replaced by Billy Herman (vocals, drums). Graffia left in late 1969, replaced by Bruce Gordon (guitar) and Chuck Jobes (keyboards). Kummel and McBride left in 1970. Kummel died in a car crash on 12/18/78 (age 33).			
				1)Things I'd Like To Say 2)I Will Always Think About You 3)I Could Never Lie To You			
2/19/66	80	4		1 **I Confess**...*Dawn Is Breaking*	$15		Centaur 1201
2/18/67	61	6		2 **Love You So Much**...*Let Me Love You*	$15		Sentar 1205
3/30/68	22	13		3 **I Will Always Think About You**...*Hold Me With Your Eyes*	$10		Mercury 72775
6/15/68	52	8		4 **Can't You See Me Cry**...*Summertime's Another Name For Love*	$10	■	Mercury 72817
12/28/68+	16	16		5 **Things I'd Like To Say** *Come And Give Your Love To Me*	$10		Mercury 72858
5/3/69	50	8		6 **I Could Never Lie To You**...*Just Feel Worse*	$10		Mercury 72920
8/30/69	65	6		7 **I Want You To Know**...*Free*	$10		Mercury 72961
1/10/70	78	5		8 **Barbara, I Love You**...*Prairie Grey*	$10		Mercury 73004
8/21/71	56	9		9 **Roll On**...*If You Could See*	$6		Sunlight 1001
12/11/71+	93	4		10 **Long Time To Be Alone**...*Never Be Lonely*	$6		Sunlight 1004
				NEWCOMERS, The R&B '71			
				R&B trio from Memphis, Tennessee: Terry Bartlett, William Somlin and Bertrand Brown. Changed name to Kwick in 1980.			
9/11/71	74	5		**Pin The Tail On The Donkey**...*Mannish Boy*	$8		Stax 0099
				Bar-Kays (instrumental backing)			
				NEW DIRECTION R&B '99			
				Contemporary gospel group from Chicago, Illinois.			
5/29/99	67[S]	2		**Lighthouse**...*(remix)*	$4	★	Word/Epic 79161
	★315★			**NEW EDITION** R&B/BUB/LP '85			
				R&B teen vocal group from Boston, Massachusetts: **Ralph Tresvant** (born on 5/16/68), Ronald DeVoe (born on 11/17/67), Michael Bivins (born on 8/10/68), Ricky Bell (born on 9/18/67) and **Bobby Brown** (born on 2/5/69). Formed in 1982 by future **New Kids On The Block** and **Perfect Gentlemen** producer, Maurice Starr. Brown left for solo career in 1986; replaced by **Johnny Gill** in 1988. Bell, Bivins and DeVoe recorded as **Bell Biv DeVoe** in 1990. Tresvant and Gill recorded solo in the 1990s. All six members reunited in 1996.			
				1)Hit Me Off 2)Cool It Now 3)I'm Still In Love With You			
5/7/83	46	11		1 **Candy Girl**...RB[1] *(sing-a-long version)*	$8		StreetWise 1108
10/15/83	85	4		2 **Is This The End**...*(same version)*	$8		StreetWise 1111
9/22/84+	4	25	●	3 **Cool It Now**...RB[1] S:❶[1] / A:9 *(sing along version)*	$4	■	MCA 52455
12/22/84+	12	16		4 **Mr. Telephone Man**...RB[3] S:7 / A:13 *(instrumental)*	$4	■	MCA 52484
				written and produced by **Ray Parker, Jr.**			
3/30/85	35	14		5 **Lost In Love**...S:26 *Gold Mine*	$4	■	MCA 52553
11/2/85	51	15		6 **Count Me Out**...*Good Boys*	$4	■	MCA 52703
2/22/86	38	15		7 **A Little Bit Of Love (Is All It Takes)**...S:26 *Sneakin' Around*	$4	■	MCA 52768
6/14/86	51	11		8 **With You All The Way**...*All For Love*	$4	■	MCA 52829

DEBUT	PEAK	WKS	Gold	A-side (Chart Hit) ... B-side	$	Sym	Label & Number
				NEW EDITION — Cont'd			
8/23/86	21	14		9 **Earth Angel** ... S:18 / A:32 *With You All The Way* featured in the movie *The Karate Kid Part II* starring Ralph Macchio	$4		MCA 52905
7/2/88	7	21		10 **If It Isn't Love** ... S:5 / A:8 *(instrumental)*	$3	■	MCA 53264
11/12/88	95	4		11 **You're Not My Kind Of Girl** ... *(instrumental)*	$3	■	MCA 53405
2/11/89	44	13		12 **Can You Stand The Rain** ... RB^2 S:37 *(instrumental)*	$3	■	MCA 53464
<u>10/19/91</u>	42^S	3		13 **Boys To Men** ... *(3 album snippets)* above 4 from the album *Heart Break*	$3	▮	MCA 54204
8/31/96	3	20	●	14 **Hit Me Off** RB^3 S:2 / A:44 *(instrumental)* samples "I Got Cha Opin" by **Black Moon** and "Storm King" by **Bob James**	$3	▮	MCA 55210
11/9/96+	7	20	●	15 **I'm Still In Love With You** ... S:7 / A:17 *You Don't Have To Worry* (R&B #10)	$3	▮	MCA 55264
6/7/97	61	10		16 **One More Day** ... S:53 *Something About You (remix)*	$3	▮	MCA 55350
				NEW ENGLAND LP **'79** Rock group formed in New York: John Fannon (vocals, guitar), Jimmy Waldo (keyboards), Gary Shea (bass) and Hirsh Gardner (drums).			
5/5/79	40	12		1 **Don't Ever Wanna Lose Ya** ... *Shoot*	$5		Infinity 50,013
9/1/79	69	5		2 **Hello, Hello, Hello** ... *Encore*	$5		Infinity 50,021
				NEW ESTABLISHMENT, The AC **'69** Pop vocal group: Vicki Lemon, Arnold Rollins, Rick Ward, Lenny Mathieson, Ron Wilson, Mike Alley and Kenny Johnson. Wilson (of **The Surfaris**) died of an aneurysm in May 1989.			
11/29/69	92	2		**(One Of These Days) Sunday's Gonna' Come On Tuesday** ... *Baby The Rain Must Fall*	$8		Colgems 5006
				NEW FOUND GLORY ROK/LP **'02** Rock group from Coral Springs, Florida: Jordan Pundik (vocals), Chad Gilbert and Steve Klein (guitars), Ian Grushka (bass) and Cyrus Bolooki (drums).			
9/7/02	85	6		**My Friends Over You** ... *It's Been A Summer*	$5	★	Drive-Thru/MCA 113995
				NEW HOPE, The **'70** Pop group from New Hope, Pennsylvania, led by Carl Hausman. Originally known as The Kit Kats ("Bubbled Under" in 1966 and 1967). Drummer Carson Stewart died on 7/2/2001 (age 61).			
1/3/70	57	9		**Won't Find Better (Than Me)** ... *They Call It Love*	$10		Jamie 1381
				**NEW KIDS ON THE BLOCK** ★169★ R&B/LP **'89** Teen vocal group from Boston, Massachusetts: **Joey McIntyre** (born on 12/3/72) (see #14 & 16 below), **Donnie Wahlberg** (born on 8/17/69), Danny Wood (born on 5/14/69), and brothers Jon (born on 11/29/68) and **Jordan Knight** (born on 5/17/70) (see #15 below). Formed in the summer of 1984 by **New Edition**'s founder/producer, Maurice Starr. Shortened group name to **NKOTB** in 1992. McIntyre plays teacher "Colin Flynn" on TV's *Boston Public*. Also see **Tommy Page**'s "I'll Be Your Everything." *1)Step By Step 2)I'll Be Loving You (Forever) 3)Hangin' Tough*			
6/25/88	10	28		1 **Please Don't Go Girl** ... S:9 / A:13 *Whatcha Gonna Do About It*	$3	■	Columbia 07700
11/19/88+	3	26	●	2 **You Got It (The Right Stuff)** ... S:2 / A:5 *(long version)*	$3	■	Columbia 08092
4/1/89	❶^1	21	●	3 **I'll Be Loving You (Forever)** ... A:❶^2 / S:❶^1 *(instrumental)*	$3		Columbia 68671
7/15/89	❶^1	17	▲	4 **Hangin' Tough** / S:❶^1 / A:3			
9/16/89	8	19		5 **Didn't I (Blow Your Mind)** ... S:8 / A:8 from the group's 1987 debut album *New Kids On The Block*	$3		Columbia 68960
9/16/89	2^1	18	●	6 **Cover Girl** ... S:2 / A:3 *Merry, Merry Christmas* #1-4 & 6: from the album *Hangin' Tough*	$3		Columbia 69088
11/11/89	7	16	●	7 **This One's For The Children** ... S:6 / A:12 *Funky, Funky, Xmas* [X]	$3	▮^{V}	Columbia 73064
5/26/90	❶^3	15	▲	8 **Step By Step** S:❶^3 / A:❶^1 *Valentine Girl*	$3	▮^{V}	Columbia 73343
8/4/90	7	12		9 **Tonight** ... S:6 / A:8 *Hold On*	$3	▮^{V}	Columbia 73461
10/6/90	53	8		10 **Let's Try It Again** ... *Popsicle* all of above written (except #5) and produced by Maurice Starr	$3	▮^{V}	Columbia 73443
				NKOTB:			
1/26/91	58^A	5		11 **Games** ... from the album *No More Games/The Remix Album* on Columbia 46959			album cut
2/22/92	16	13		12 **If You Go Away** ... S:8 / A:22 *Games (The Kids Get Hard mix)*	$3	▮^{V}	Columbia 74255
<u>1/22/94</u>	66	6		13 **Dirty Dawg** ... S:60 *(remix)* **Nice & Smooth** (rap); samples "Papa Don't Take No Mess" by **James Brown**; "45": Columbia 77410; B-side: "Never Let You Go"	$3	▮^{V}	Columbia 77293
2/27/99	10	14	●	14 **Stay The Same** ... S:8 / A:62 *(3 album excerpts)* **JOEY McINTYRE** issued with 2 different CD picture covers	$4	★	C2/Columbia 79103
4/3/99	10	20	●	15 **Give It To You** ... S:3 / A:54 *(no B-side)* **JORDAN KNIGHT** "45": Interscope 97089; B-side: "A Different Party"	$4	★^{V}	Interscope 97048
9/4/99	54	6		16 **I Love You Came Too Late** ... S:9 *Stay The Same (remix)* **JOEY McINTYRE**	$4	★	C2/Columbia 79244
				NEWLEY, Anthony AC/BUB **'60** Born on 9/24/31 in London, England. Died of cancer on 4/14/99 (age 67). Adult Contemporary singer/actor/composer/comedian.			
7/18/60	91	2		1 **Do You Mind?** ... *Girls Were Made To Love And Kiss* from the British movie *Let's Get Married* starring Newley	$10		London 1918
10/10/60	67	5		2 **If She Should Come To You (La Montana)** ... *Lifetime Of Happiness*	$10		London 1929
12/4/61+	85	4		3 **Pop Goes The Weasel** ... *Gone With The Wind* [N] hip version of a traditional English tune from 1853	$10		London 9501
9/22/62	85	4		4 **What Kind Of Fool Am I** ... *Gonna Build A Mountain* from the Broadway musical *Stop The World-I Want To Get Off* starring Newley	$10		London 9546

DEBUT	PEAK	WKS	Gold	A-side (Chart Hit)..........B-side	$	Sym	Label & Number
				NEWMAN, Jimmy C&W **'57**			
				Born on 8/27/27 in High Point, Louisiana. Cajun-country singer/guitarist (charted 33 hits, 1954-70).			
6/10/57	23	16		**A Fallen Star**..........A:23 / T:42 *I Can't Go On This Way*	$15		Dot 15574
				also released on Dot 1289 (Country series)			
				NEWMAN, Lionel, & his Orch. **'56**			
				Born on 1/4/16 in New Haven, Connecticut. Died of heart failure on 2/3/89 (age 73). Top movie composer/conductor with 20th Century Fox for 45 years; responsible for 250+ movie scores. Received 10 Oscar nominations and won an Oscar in 1969 for *Hello Dolly*. Uncle of **Randy Newman** and brother of composers Alfred and Emil Newman.			
8/4/56	72	1		**Theme From "The Proud Ones"**..........T:72 *Who Gave You The Roses?* [I]	$15		Columbia 40717
				Muzzy Marcellino (whistler); theme song from the movie starring Robert Ryan			
				NEWMAN, Randy BUB/C&W/LP **'78**			
				Born on 11/28/43 in New Orleans, Louisiana. Singer/composer/pianist. Nephew of composers Alfred, Emil and **Lionel Newman**. Scored the movies *Ragtime, The Natural* and *Avalon*. Won *Billboard's* Century Award in 2000.			
11/12/77+	2^{3}	20	●	1 **Short People**..........*Old Man On The Farm* [N]	$5		Warner 8492
				Glenn Frey, **J.D. Souther** and **Timothy B. Schmit** (backing vocals)			
1/22/83	51	8		2 **The Blues**..........*Same Girl* (Newman)	$4	■	Warner 29803
				RANDY NEWMAN AND PAUL SIMON			
11/5/88	60	12		3 **It's Money That Matters**..........AR^{2} *Roll With The Punches*	$3	■	Reprise 27709
				Mark Knopfler (of **Dire Straits**; guitar and producer)			
				NEWMAN, Ted **'57**			
				Born on 5/6/39 in Custer, South Dakota. Teen pop singer. Later worked as a teacher in Phoenix, Arizona.			
9/30/57	45	9		**Plaything**..........T:45 *Unlucky Me*	$20		Rev 3505
				NEWMAN, Thunderclap — see THUNDERCLAP NEWMAN			
				NEWMAN, Troy **'91**			
				Born on 10/12/64 in Perth, Australia. Rock singer/guitarist.			
6/15/91	92	4		**Love Gets Rough**..........*Gypsy Girl*	$4	▮	EastWest 98801
				NEW ORDER ROK/BUB/R&B/LP **'93**			
				Techno-dance group formed in Manchester, England: Bernard Sumner (vocals, guitar), Gillian Gilbert (keyboards), Peter Hook (bass) and Stephen Morris (drums). Hook also recorded with **Monaco**. Sumner also recorded with **Electronic**.			
10/24/87	32	18		1 **True Faith**..........A:28 / S:35 *1963*	$4	■	Qwest 28271
4/30/88	68	10		2 **Blue Monday 1988**..........*Touched By The Hand Of God*	$4	■	Qwest 27979
				original version by New Order made the Disco charts (#5) in 1983			
4/22/89	64	9		3 **Round & round**..........*Best and Marsh*	$4	■	Qwest 27524
5/1/93	28	19		4 **Regret** MR^{6} A:21 / S:73 *(The New Order mix)*	$4	$▮^{V}$	Qwest 18586
9/11/93	92	4		5 **World (The Price Of Love)**..........*Ruined In A Day* (ROK #30)	$4	▮	Qwest 18432
				above 4: #1 Dance Club Play hits			
7/22/95	98	2		6 **Bizarre Love Triangle**..........*(2 remixes) / State Of The Nation*	$8	★*	Qwest 20546
				originally released in 1986 on Qwest 28421			
9/1/01	19^{S}	12		7 **Crystal**..........*(7 mixes) / Behind Closed Doors*	$8	★*	Reprise 42397
				NEW RADICALS LP **'99**			
				Group is actually solo rock singer/musician Gregg Alexander.			
12/5/98+	36	20		**You Get What You Give**..........A:30			album cut
				from the album *Maybe You've Been Brainwashed Too* on MCA 11858			
				NEW RIDERS OF THE PURPLE SAGE BUB/LP **'72**			
				Country-rock group formed in San Francisco, California: John Dawson (vocals, guitar), David Nelson (guitar), Dave Torbert (bass) and Spencer Dryden (drums; **Jefferson Airplane**).			
6/10/72	81	5		**I Don't Need No Doctor**..........*Runnin' Back To You*	$6		Columbia 45607
				written by **Ashford & Simpson**			
				NEW SEEKERS, The AC/LP **'72**			
				British-Australian pop group formed by Keith Potger after disbandment of **The Seekers** in 1969. Consisted of Eve Graham, Lyn Paul, Peter Doyle, Marty Kristian and Paul Layton. Doyle died cancer on 10/13/2001 (age 52).			
9/5/70	14	12		1 **Look What They've Done To My Song Ma**..........*It's A Beautiful Day*	$6		Elektra 45699
1/9/71	67	7		2 **Beautiful People**..........*When There's No Love Left* (AC #33)	$6		Elektra 45710
3/20/71	81	5		3 **Nickel Song**..........*Cincinnati*	$6		Elektra 45719
				THE NEW SEEKERS featuring Eve Graham (above 3)			
				above 3 written by **Melanie**			
12/4/71+	7	11	●	4 **I'd Like To Teach The World To Sing (In Perfect Harmony)** *Boom-Town*	$6		Elektra 45762
				adapted from a Coca-Cola jingle			
4/22/72	81	4		5 **Beg, Steal Or Borrow**..........*Mystic Queen*	$5		Elektra 45780
7/15/72	87	5		6 **Circles**..........*I Can Say You're Beautiful*	$5		Elektra 45787
				written by **Harry Chapin**			
9/23/72	84	5		7 **Dance, Dance, Dance**..........*I Can Say You're Beautiful*	$5		Elektra 45805
				written by **Neil Young**			
1/27/73	95	3		8 **Come Softly To Me**..........*Unwithered Rose*	$5	■	MGM/Verve 10698
				THE NEW SEEKERS featuring MARTY KRISTIAN			
2/24/73	29	13		9 **Pinball Wizard/See Me, Feel Me**..........*Come Softly To Me*	$5		MGM/Verve 10709
				from the rock opera *Tommy*; also released with "Time Limit" as the B-side			
				NEWSONG LP **'00**			
				Christian pop group formed in Kennesaw, Georgia: Eddie Carswell (vocals), Billy Goodwin and Leonard Ahlstrom (guitars), Scotty Wilbanks (sax, keyboards), Mark Clay (bass) and Jack Pumphrey (drums).			
12/30/00+	42	2		**The Christmas Shoes**..........AC^{1} A:33 [X]			album cut
				from the album *Sheltering Tree* on Benson 83327			

DEBUT	PEAK	WKS	Gold	A-side (Chart Hit)...B-side	$	Sym	Label & Number

★443★ NEWTON, Juice — C&W/LP '81

Born Judy Kay Newton on 2/18/52 in Lakehurst, New Jersey; raised in Virginia Beach, Virginia. Pop-country singer/guitarist. Performed folk music from age 13. Moved to Los Angeles with own Silver Spur band in 1974; recorded for RCA in 1975; group disbanded in 1978. Newton is an accomplished equestrienne.

1)Queen Of Hearts 2)Angel Of The Morning 3)The Sweetest Thing (I've Ever Known)

DEBUT	PEAK	WKS	Gold	A-side (Chart Hit)	B-side	$	Sym	Label & Number
4/8/78	86	3		1 **It's A Heartache**	*Wouldn't Mind The Rain*	$6		Capitol 4552
2/21/81	4	22	●	2 **Angel Of The Morning** AC[3]	*Headin' For A Heartache*	$4	■	Capitol 4976
5/30/81	2[2]	27	●	3 **Queen Of Hearts**	*River Of Love*	$4	■	Capitol 4997
10/17/81+	7	24		4 **The Sweetest Thing (I've Ever Known)** CW[1] / AC[1]	*Ride 'Em Cowboy*	$4	■	Capitol 5046
5/8/82	7	17		5 **Love's Been A Little Bit Hard On Me** **Andrew Gold** (guitar)	*Ever True*	$4	■	Capitol 5120
8/21/82	11	17		6 **Break It To Me Gently** AC[2]	*Adios Mi Corazon*	$4	■	Capitol 5148
11/27/82+	25	16		7 **Heart Of The Night**	*Love Sail Away*	$4	■	Capitol 5192
8/13/83	27	11		8 **Tell Her No**	*Stranger At My Door* (C&W #45)	$4	■	Capitol 5265
11/5/83	90	3		9 **Dirty Looks**	*Twenty Years Ago*	$4	■	Capitol 5289
6/2/84	44	10		10 **A Little Love**	*Waiting For The Sun*	$4	■	RCA 13823
8/11/84	66	6		11 **Can't Wait All Night** written by **Bryan Adams**; #2-11: produced by Richard Landis	*Restless Heart* (C&W #57)	$4	■	RCA 13863

★486★ NEWTON, Wayne — AC/BUB/C&W/LP '72

Born on 4/3/42 in Roanoke, Virginia. Singer/multi-instrumentalist. Top Las Vegas entertainer. Began singing career with regular appearances on **Jackie Gleason**'s TV variety series in 1962. Appeared in the movies *License To Kill*, *The Adventures Of Ford Fairlane* and *Vegas Vacation*.

1)Daddy Don't You Walk So Fast 2)Danke Schoen 3)Red Roses For A Blue Lady

DEBUT	PEAK	WKS	Gold	A-side (Chart Hit)	B-side	$	Sym	Label & Number
4/27/63	82	4		1 **Heart! (I Hear You Beating)**	*So Long Lucy*	$10		Capitol 4920
7/13/63	13	12		2 **Danke Schoen**	*Better Now Than Later*	$10		Capitol 4989
10/26/63	58	7		3 **Shirl Girl** **WAYNE NEWTON and The Newton Brothers** (above 3) written by **Bobby Darin**	*Someone's Ahead Of You*	$10		Capitol 5058
5/2/64	99	2		4 **The Little White Cloud That Cried** #2 hit for **Johnnie Ray** in 1952	*Born When You Kissed Me*	$12		Challenge 59238
1/30/65	65	5		5 **Comin' On Too Strong** **Bruce & Terry** (backing vocals)	*Looking Through A Tear*	$20		Capitol 5338
2/27/65	23	9		6 **Red Roses For A Blue Lady** #3 hit for **Vaughn Monroe** in 1949	*One More Memory*	$8		Capitol 5366
5/22/65	52	6		7 **I'll Be With You In Apple Blossom Time** #2 hit for Charles Harrison in 1920	*Laura Lee*	$8		Capitol 5419
8/7/65	78	4		8 **Summer Wind**	*I'll Be Standing By*	$8		Capitol 5470
10/16/65	69	4		9 **Remember When** #2 & 9: written by **Bert Kaempfert**	*Keep The Lovin' Feelin'*	$8		Capitol 5514
10/22/66	86	6		10 **Games That Lovers Play**	*Half A World Away*	$8		Capitol 5754
6/29/68	60	7		11 **Dreams Of The Everyday Housewife**	*The Tip Of My Fingers*	$6		MGM 13955
4/22/72	4	20	●	12 **Daddy Don't You Walk So Fast**	*Echo Valley 2-6809*	$5		Chelsea 0100
9/23/72	48	8		13 **Can't You Hear The Song?**	*You Don't Have To Ask*	$5		Chelsea 0105
12/23/72+	65	5		14 **Anthem**	*Fool*	$5		Chelsea 0109
5/29/76	82	4		15 **The Hungry Years** written by **Neil Sedaka**	*In Dreams*	$5		Chelsea 3041
9/15/79	90	8		16 **You Stepped Into My Life** written by the **Bee Gees**	*She Believes In Me*	$4		Aries II 101
2/2/80	35	13		17 **Years**	*Rhythm Rhapsody*	$4		Aries II 108

Newton's musical arrangers and conductors: **Perry Botkin, Jr.** (#10), Tom Collins (#17), Robert Cullen (#16), Jimmie Haskell (#1, 2, 7-9), Bert Keyes (#3), Terry Melcher (#5), Mike Melvoin (#12-14), Don Peake (#11), **Don Ralke** (#4), Don Vincent (#15) and Richard Wess (#6)

NEWTON-JOHN, Olivia ★32★ — AC/BUB/LP '78

Born on 9/26/48 in Cambridge, England; raised in Melbourne, Australia. At age 16, won talent contest trip to England; sang with Pat Carroll as Pat & Olivia. With the group Toomorrow in a British movie of the same name. Granddaughter of Nobel Prize-winning German physicist Max Born. In movies *Grease*, *Xanadu* and *Two Of A Kind*. Married to actor Matt Lattanzi from 1984-96. Opened own chain of clothing boutiques (Koala Blue) in 1984.

1)Physical 2)Magic 3)I Honestly Love You 4)You're The One That I Want 5)Have You Never Been Mellow

DEBUT	PEAK	WKS	Gold	A-side (Chart Hit)	B-side	$	Sym	Label & Number
5/29/71	25	17		1 **If Not For You** AC[3] written by **Bob Dylan** (from his 1970 album *New Morning*)	*The Biggest Clown*	$10		Uni 55281
10/16/71	94	4		2 **Banks Of The Ohio** Country song recorded in 1936 by the Blue Sky Boys on Bluebird 6480	*It's So Hard To Say Goodbye*	$10		Uni 55304
11/17/73+	6	19	●	3 **Let Me Be There**	*Maybe Then I'll Think Of You*	$6		MCA 40101
4/13/74	5	20	●	4 **If You Love Me (Let Me Know)**	*Brotherly Love*	$6		MCA 40209
8/17/74	❶[2]	15	●	5 **I Honestly Love You** AC[3] 1974 Grammy winner: Record of the Year; also see #16 & 41 below	*Home Ain't Home Anymore*	$5		MCA 40280
1/25/75	❶[1]	16	●	6 **Have You Never Been Mellow** AC[1]	*Water Under The Bridge*	$5		MCA 40349
6/7/75	3	15	●	7 **Please Mr. Please** AC[3]	*And In The Morning*	$5	■	MCA 40418
9/20/75	13	11		8 **Something Better To Do** AC[3]	*He's My Rock*	$5	■	MCA 40459
12/6/75+	30	9		9 **Let It Shine /** AC[2]				
12/6/75		9		10 **He Ain't Heavy...He's My Brother** famous slogan of Father Flanagan's Boys Town in Nebraska		$5		MCA 40495
3/13/76	23	12		11 **Come On Over** AC[1] written by **Barry** and **Robin Gibb**	*Small Talk And Pride*	$5		MCA 40525
8/7/76	33	9		12 **Don't Stop Believin'** AC[1]	*Greensleeves*	$5	■	MCA 40600

DEBUT	PEAK	WKS	Gold	A-side (Chart Hit)....................B-side	$	Sym	Label & Number
				NEWTON-JOHN, Olivia — Cont'd			
11/6/76	55	9		13 **Every Face Tells A Story** ....*Love You Hold The Key*	$5		MCA 40642
1/29/77	20	13		14 **Sam** ....AC[2] *I'll Bet You A Kangaroo*	$5		MCA 40670
6/18/77	87	4		15 **Making A Good Thing Better** ....*I Think I'll Say Goodbye*	$5		MCA 40737
11/5/77	48	9		16 **I Honestly Love You**....................*Don't Cry For Me Argentina* [R]	$5	■	MCA 40811
				same version as #5 above; #41 below is a different version			
4/1/78	❶[1]	24	▲	17 **You're The One That I Want** ....*Alone At A Drive-In Movie* [I]	$5	■	RSO 891
				JOHN TRAVOLTA AND OLIVIA NEWTON-JOHN			
7/8/78	3	19	●	18 **Hopelessly Devoted To You**....................*Love Is A Many Splendored Thing* [I]	$5		RSO 903
8/5/78	5	16	●	19 **Summer Nights** ....*Rock 'N' Roll Party Queen* (Louis St. Louis)	$5		RSO 906
				JOHN TRAVOLTA, OLIVIA NEWTON-JOHN & CAST			
				above 3 from the movie *Grease* starring Newton-John and Travolta (also see #39 below)			
11/25/78+	3	20	●	20 **A Little More Love** ....*Borrowed Time*	$4	■	MCA 40975
4/14/79	11	13		21 **Deeper Than The Night** ....*Please Don't Keep Me Waiting*	$4		MCA 41009
7/28/79	52	6		22 **Totally Hot /**			
9/22/79	82	2		23 **Dancin' 'Round And 'Round**	$4	■	MCA 41074
				above 4 from the album *Totally Hot*			
3/29/80	12	13		24 **I Can't Help It**....................*Someone I Ain't* (Gibb)	$4		RSO 1026
				ANDY GIBB AND OLIVIA NEWTON-JOHN			
5/24/80	❶[4]	23	●	25 **Magic** ....AC[5] *Fool Country*	$4	■	MCA 41247
8/9/80	8	17		26 **Xanadu**....................*Whenever You're Away From Me* (Newton-John & Gene Kelly)	$4		MCA 41285
				OLIVIA NEWTON-JOHN/ELECTRIC LIGHT ORCHESTRA			
10/25/80+	20	19		27 **Suddenly** ....*You Made Me Love You* (Newton-John)	$4	■	MCA 51007
				OLIVIA NEWTON-JOHN AND CLIFF RICHARD			
				above 3 from the movie *Xanadu* starring Newton-John			
10/3/81	❶[10]	26	▲	28 **Physical** *The Promise (The Dolphin Song)*	$4	■	MCA 51182
2/13/82	5	14	●	29 **Make A Move On Me** ....*Falling*	$4	■	MCA 52000
6/12/82	52	8		30 **Landslide**....................*Recovery*	$4		MCA 52069
				originally released on MCA 51155 in 1981 with a picture sleeve			
9/4/82	3	21		31 **Heart Attack**....................*Stranger's Touch*	$4	■	MCA 52100
1/15/83	38	11		32 **Tied Up**....................*Silvery Rain*	$4	■	MCA 52155
11/5/83+	5	18		33 **Twist Of Fate** ....*Take A Chance* (w/**John Travolta**-AC #3)	$4	■	MCA 52284
2/11/84	31	10		34 **Livin' In Desperate Times** ....*Landslide*	$4	■	MCA 52341
				above 2 from the movie *Two Of A Kind* starring Newton-John and Travolta			
10/5/85	20	15		35 **Soul Kiss**....................S:12 / A:25 *Electric*	$4	■	MCA 52686
				all of above (except #19, 24, 26, 33 & 34) produced by John Farrar			
6/14/86	80	8		36 **The Best Of Me**....................*Sajé* (Foster)	$3	■	Atlantic 89420
				DAVID FOSTER AND OLIVIA NEWTON-JOHN			
8/20/88	62	6		37 **The Rumour**....................S:39 *Winter Angel*	$3	■	MCA 53294
				written and produced by **Elton John**			
7/11/92	96	2		38 **I Need Love** ....*Warm And Tender*	$3	▮	Geffen 19128
				produced by **Giorgio Moroder**			
11/9/96	25[A]	16		39 **The Grease Megamix**....................			album cut
				JOHN TRAVOLTA & OLIVIA NEWTON-JOHN			
				from the album *Pure Disco* on Polydor 535877; medley of songs ("Greased Lightnin'" and #17 & 19 above) from the 1978 movie *Grease*			
5/30/98	56	20		40 **One Heart At A Time**....................S:33 *(same version)*	$4	▮	Atlantic 84117
				GARTH BROOKS, BILLY DEAN, FAITH HILL, OLIVIA NEWTON-JOHN, NEAL McCOY, MICHAEL McDONALD, VICTORIA SHAW, BRYAN WHITE			
5/30/98	67	12		41 **I Honestly Love You**....................*(remix)* [R]	$3	▮[V]	MCA Nashville 72053
				Babyface (backing vocal); new version of #5 & 16 above			
				NEW VAUDEVILLE BAND, The BUB/AC/LP **'66**			
				Studio creation of British songwriter/record producer Geoff Stephens (born on 10/1/34 in London, England). Arrangements similar to Rudy Vallee's hits during the 1930s.			
10/29/66	❶[3]	15	●	1 **Winchester Cathedral**....................AC[4] *Wait For Me Baby*	$8		Fontana 1562
2/18/67	72	4		2 **Peek-A-Boo** ....*Amy*	$7		Fontana 1573
				NEW YORK CITY R&B/BUB/LP **'73**			
				R&B vocal group from Harlem, New York: Tim McQueen, John Brown, Ed Shell and Claude Johnston.			
3/3/73	17	20		1 **I'm Doin' Fine Now**....................*Ain't It So*	$5		Chelsea 0113
9/1/73	93	5		2 **Make Me Twice The Man** ....*Uncle James*	$5		Chelsea 0025
2/2/74	79	7		3 **Quick, Fast, In A Hurry** ....*Set The Record Straight*	$5		Chelsea 0150
				NEW YORKERS, The **'61**			
				R&B group led by Fred Parris of **The Five Satins**.			
5/15/61	69	5		**Miss Fine**....................*(At Night) Dream A Little Dream*	$30		Wall 547
				NEXT R&B/LP **'98**			
				R&B vocal trio from Minneapolis, Minnesota: **R.L.**, Tweety and T-Low. Also see **Deborah Cox**'s "We Can't Be Friends," **3rd Storee**'s "Party Tonight" and **Koffee Brown**.			
9/6/97	16	23	●	1 **Butta Love**....................S:8 *Problems*	$3	▮	Arista 13407
2/14/98	❶[5]	53	▲	2 **Too Close** RB[3] S:❶[4] / A:4 *Butta Love (remix w/***Naughty By Nature** *& Castro)*	$4	★	Arista 13456
				Koffee Brown (vocals); samples "X-mas Rappin'" by **Kurtis Blow**; also see #5 below			
8/8/98	14	20	●	3 **I Still Love You**....................S:7 / A:63 *Penetration* (w/**Naughty By Nature**)	$4	★	Arista 13509
				contains resung elements of "Two Occasions" by **The Deele**			
5/27/00	7	21		4 **Wifey** ....RB[1] S:5 / A:13 *(instrumental)*	$4	★	Arista 13881
				Lil' Mo (female vocal); re-entered the R&B Sales chart on 3/2/02 (#65)			
5/19/01	69[S]	1		5 **Too Close**....................*(2 versions) / Butta Love* [R]	$8	★*	Arista 13457
				reissue of #2 above on Arista's "Maximum Hits" series			
2/23/02	28	20		6 **Anything**....................A:25			album cut
				JAHEIM Featuring Next			
				from the album *Ghetto Love* on Divine Mill 47452			

DEBUT	PEAK	WKS	Gold	A-side (Chart Hit)..................B-side	$	Sym	Label & Number
				NICE & SMOOTH R&B/LP **'92**			
				Rap duo from Brooklyn, New York: Gregg "Nice" Mays and Darryl "Smooth" Barnes.			
11/16/91	61^S	4		1 **Hip Hop Junkies** ....*(remix)* samples **The Partridge Family**'s "I Think I Love You"	$3	▮	RAL/Columbia 73784
5/9/92	44	18		2 **Sometimes I Rhyme Slow**..................S:16 *(album version)* rap to **Tracy Chapman**'s "Fast Car" melody	$3	▮	RAL/Columbia 74167
7/2/94	59	7		3 **Old To The New**..................S:44 *Blunts* samples "Easy To Be Hard" by **Three Dog Night** and the theme of **The Monkees** TV show	$3	▮	RAL/Polygram 853238
				NICHOLAS, Paul **'77**			
				Born Paul Beuselinck on 12/3/45 in Peterborough, Cambridgeshire, England. Singer/actor. Played "Dougie Shears" in the 1978 movie *Sgt. Pepper's Lonely Hearts Club Band.*			
8/20/77	6	23	●	1 **Heaven On The 7th Floor** ....*Do You Want My Love*	$5		RSO 878
7/29/78	67	5		2 **On The Strip**..................*Beauty Queen*	$5		RSO 887
				NICHOLS, Joe C&W/LP **'02**			
				Born in Rogers, Arkansas. Country singer/songwriter.			
6/1/02	29	21		**The Impossible**..................S:11 / A:29 *Can't Hold A Halo To You* "45" B-side: "Brokenheartsville"; also released in 2003 as a CD single on Universal South 000792 (with "Everything's A Thing" as the B-side)	$4	★^{V}	Universal South 172241
				NICKELBACK ROK/BUB/LP **'01**			
				Rock group from Vancouver, British Columbia, Canada: brothers **Chad Kroeger** (vocals, guitar) and Mike Kroeger (bass), with Ryan Peake (guitar) and Ryan Vikedal (drums).			
9/8/01	❶^4	49		1 **How You Remind Me** ....AR^{13} / MR^{13} S:❶^3 / A:2 *Leader Of Men (acoustic)*	$4	★	Roadrunner 612053
3/16/02	42	20		2 **Too Bad** ....AR^3 A:43 above 2 from the album *Silver Side Up* on Roadrunner 618485			album cut
	★282★			**NICKS, Stevie** ROK/AC/LP **'81**			
				Born Stephanie Nicks on 5/26/48 in Phoenix, Arizona; raised in San Francisco, California. Became vocalist of Bay-area group Fritz and subsequently met guitarist **Lindsey Buckingham**. Teamed up and recorded album *Buckingham-Nicks* in 1973. Joined **Fleetwood Mac** in January 1975 as vocalist. Quit touring with band after 1990; left in January 1993. Reunited with Fleetwood Mac in 1997. Also see **Robbie Patton**.			
				1)Stop Draggin' My Heart Around 2)Talk To Me 3)Stand Back			
7/25/81	3	21		1 **Stop Draggin' My Heart Around** *Kind Of Woman* (Nicks) **STEVIE NICKS (with Tom Petty and The Heartbreakers)**	$4	■	Modern 7336
10/24/81+	6	19		2 **Leather And Lace**..................*Bella Donna* (Nicks) **STEVIE NICKS (with DON HENLEY)** written for **Waylon Jennings** and **Jessi Colter**	$4	■	Modern 7341
2/20/82	11	14		3 **Edge Of Seventeen (Just Like The White Winged Dove)**..................*(live version)*	$4	■	Modern 7401
5/15/82	32	11		4 **After The Glitter Fades**..................*Think About It* all of above from the album *Bella Donna*	$4	■	Modern 7405
6/4/83	5	19		5 **Stand Back**..................*Garbo*	$3	■	Modern 99863
9/10/83	14	14		6 **If Anyone Falls**..................*Wild Heart*	$3	■	Modern 99832
12/17/83+	33	12		7 **Nightbird**..................*Gate And Garden* (Nicks) **STEVIE NICKS (with Sandy Stewart)**	$3	■	Modern 99799
11/16/85+	4	18		8 **Talk To Me**..................AR^2 A:4 / S:5 *One More Big Time Rock And Roll Star*	$3	■	Modern 99582
2/1/86	37	9		9 **Needles And Pins** ....*Spike (live)* (Petty) [L] **TOM PETTY and the HEARTBREAKERS with STEVIE NICKS** recorded at LA's Wiltern Theater; written by **Sonny** Bono and **Jack Nitzsche**	$3	■	MCA 52772
2/22/86	16	13		10 **I Can't Wait**..................A:14 / S:21 *The Nightmare* a promotional text sleeve was also issued; all of above produced by Jimmy Iovine	$3	■	Modern 99565
5/17/86	60	6		11 **Has Anyone Ever Written Anything For You**..................*Imperial Hotel*	$3	■	Modern 99532
5/6/89	16	14		12 **Rooms On Fire**..................AR^1 S:14 / A:18 *Alice*	$3	■	Modern 99216
9/7/91	56	8		13 **Sometimes It's A Bitch**..................*Desert Angel* written by **Billy Falcon** and **Jon Bon Jovi** (also on guitar)	$3	▮	Modern 98758
6/18/94	57	10		14 **Maybe Love Will Change Your Mind** ....A:57 *Inspiration*	$3	▮	Modern 98270
7/21/01	36^S	5		15 **Planets Of The Universe**..................*(5 mixes)*	$8	★*	Reprise 42385
				NICOLE R&B/LP **'98**			
				Born Nicole Wray in Salinas, California; raised in Portsmouth, Virginia. R&B-dance singer.			
6/27/98	5	23	●	1 **Make It Hot** ....S:2 / A:39 *(2 versions)* **NICOLE Featuring Missy "Misdemeanor" Elliott and Mocha**	$3	▮	The Gold Mind 64110
7/24/99	64	14		2 **All N My Grill**..................A:54 **MISSY "MISDEMEANOR" ELLIOTT (Featuring Big Boi of Outkast & Nicole)** from Elliott's album *Da Real World* on The Gold Mind 62232			album cut
				NIELSEN/PEARSON BUB **'80**			
				Pop duo from Sacramento, California: singer/guitarists Reed Nielsen and Mark Pearson.			
9/13/80	38	14		1 **If You Should Sail**..................*Don't Forget*	$4		Capitol 4910
8/8/81	56	8		2 **The Sun Ain't Gonna Shine Anymore** ....*Don't Let Me Go*	$4		Capitol 5032
				NIGHT LP **'79**			
				Pop-rock group: Stevie Lange (female vocals), Chris Thompson (male vocals, guitar; **Manfred Mann's Earth Band**), Robbie McIntosh (guitar), Nicky Hopkins (piano), Billy Kristian (bass) and Rick Marotta (drums). McIntosh later joined **The Pretenders** and **Paul McCartney**'s backing band.			
6/23/79	18	15		1 **Hot Summer Nights** ....*Party Shuffle* written by **Walter Egan**	$5	■	Planet 45903
8/25/79	17	19		2 **If You Remember Me**..................*Theme From "The Champ"* (Dave Grusin) **CHRIS THOMPSON & NIGHT** first pressings credit only **CHRIS THOMPSON** as the artist; also released on Planet 45909 with "You Ain't Pretty Enough" by **Night** as the B-side	$5		Planet 45904
2/21/81	87	3		3 **Love On The Airwaves** ....*Day After Day*	$4	■	Planet 47921

DEBUT	PEAK	WKS	Gold	A-side (Chart Hit)	B-side	$	Sym	Label & Number
				NIGHTCRAWLERS '93				
				Studio dance project from Glasgow, Scotland; spearheaded by vocalist/DJ Jon Reed.				
10/2/93	80	15		**Push The Feeling On** A:65	*(2 versions)*	$6	▮*	Great Jones 530620
				NIGHTCRAWLERS, The '67				
				Garage-rock band from Daytona Beach, Florida: Chuck Conlon (vocals, bass), Robbie Rouse (vocals), Sylvan Wells (guitar), Pete Thomason (guitar) and Tom Ruger (drums).				
1/21/67	85	4		**The Little Black Egg**	*You're Running Wild*	$15		Kapp 709
				first released on Lee 1012 in 1965 ($50); "Bubbled Under" (#135) on 12/18/65				
				NIGHTINGALE, Maxine R&B/LP '76				
				Born on 11/2/52 in Wembly, England. R&B-disco singer. First recorded in 1968. In productions of *Hair*, *Jesus Christ Superstar*, *Godspell* and *Savages*.				
2/14/76	2^2	20	●	1 **Right Back Where We Started From**	*Believe In What You Do*	$5		United Artists 752
7/17/76	53	8		2 **Gotta Be The One**	*One Last Ride*	$5		United Artists 820
5/26/79	5	23	●	3 **Lead Me On** AC^7	*Love Me Like You Mean It*	$5		Windsong 11530
11/3/79	73	5		4 **(Bringing Out) The Girl In Me**	*Hideaway*	$5	■	Windsong 11729
				written and co-produced by **Ray Parker Jr.**				
	★522★			**NIGHT RANGER** ROK/BUB/LP '84				
				Rock group formed in San Francisco, California: Jack Blades (vocals, bass; born on 4/24/54), Kelly Keagy (vocals, drums; born on 9/15/52), Jeff Watson (guitar; born on 11/4/56), Brad Gillis (guitar; born on 6/15/57), and Alan Fitzgerald (keyboards; born on 6/16/54). Blades and Gillis were members of **Rubicon**. Fitzgerald left in 1988; band split up in early 1989. Blades joined supergroup **Damn Yankees** and formed duo with **Tommy Shaw**. Night Ranger reunited with original lineup in 1997.				
				1)Sister Christian 2)Sentimental Street 3)When You Close Your Eyes				
1/15/83	40	11		1 **Don't Tell Me You Love Me**	*Night Ranger*	$5		Boardwalk 171
4/9/83	54	9		2 **Sing Me Away**	*Play Rough*	$5		Boardwalk 175
12/3/83+	51	12		3 **(You Can Still) Rock In America**	*Let Him Run*	$4	□	MCA/Camel 52305
				promo sleeve states "For Recurrent Airplay Only"				
3/10/84	5	24		4 **Sister Christian**	*Chippin' Away*	$3		MCA/Camel 52350
7/14/84	14	17		5 **When You Close Your Eyes** S:26	*Why Does Love Have To Change*	$3	■	MCA/Camel 52420
5/25/85	8	17		6 **Sentimental Street** S:5 / A:9	*Night Machine*	$3	■	MCA/Camel 52591
8/24/85	19	13		7 **Four In The Morning (I Can't Take Any More)** S:20 / A:23	*This Boy Needs To Rock*	$3	■	MCA/Camel 52661
11/9/85+	17	18		8 **Goodbye** S:14 / A:23	*Seven Wishes*	$3	■	MCA/Camel 52729
				all of above produced by Pat Glasser				
3/28/87	64	8		9 **The Secret Of My Success**	*Carry On*	$3	■	MCA/Camel 53013
				title song from the movie starring Michael J. Fox				
7/4/87	90	3		10 **Hearts Away**	*Better Let It Go*	$3		MCA/Camel 53131
10/1/88	75	5		11 **I Did It For Love**	*Woman In Love*	$3	■	MCA/Camel 53364
				NIKKI '90				
				Born Nikki Lee in Okinawa, Japan; raised in Dayton, Ohio. American male singer/multi-instrumentalist. Backing member of the soul-funk group **Sun**. Jingle writer of TV commercials.				
4/28/90	21	15		**Notice Me** A:19 / S:23	*Come On Over*	$3	▮	Geffen 19946
				NIKKI D '91				
				Born Nichelle Strong on 9/10/68 in Los Angeles, California. Female rapper/songwriter.				
6/8/91	48^S	4		**Daddy's Little Girl**	*(dub version)*	$3	▮	Def Jam 73696
				samples "Tom's Diner" by **D.N.A. Featuring Suzanne Vega**				
	★495★			**NILSSON** BUB/AC/LP '72				
				Born Harry Nelson on 6/15/41 in Brooklyn, New York. Died of a heart attack on 1/15/94 (age 52). Pop singer/songwriter. Wrote **Three Dog Night**'s hit "One"; scored the movie *Skidoo*, the animated TV movie *The Point*, and TV's *The Courtship Of Eddie's Father*.				
				1)Without You 2)Everybody's Talkin' 3)Coconut				
8/16/69	6	12		1 **Everybody's Talkin'**	*Rainmaker*	$10		RCA Victor 0161
				theme song from the movie *Midnight Cowboy* starring Dustin Hoffman and Jon Voight; originally "Bubbled Under" (#113) on 8/10/68 on RCA Victor 9544				
11/1/69	34	7		2 **I Guess The Lord Must Be In New York City**	*Maybe*	$8		RCA Victor 0261
				written for, but not included in, the movie *Midnight Cowboy*; exact same recording reissued in 1972 as by Buck Earl (Jon Voight's character in *Midnight Cowboy* was Joe Buck) on RCA Victor 0755 ($20)				
3/20/71	34	15		3 **Me And My Arrow**	*Are You Sleeping?*	$8		RCA Victor 0443
				from Nilsson's animated TV special *The Point*				
12/18/71+	❶^4	19	●	4 **Without You** AC^5	*Gotta Get Up*	$7		RCA Victor 0604
				Gary Wright (piano); written by **Badfinger**'s Pete Ham and Tom Evans				
3/18/72	27	9		5 **Jump Into The Fire**	*The Moonbeam Song*	$7		RCA Victor 0673
6/10/72	8	14		6 **Coconut**	*Down*	$7		RCA Victor 0718
9/16/72	23	10		7 **Spaceman**	*Turn On Your Radio*	$7		RCA Victor 0788
				Peter Frampton (guitar)				
12/23/72+	53	6		8 **Remember (Christmas)**	*The Lottery Song*	$6		RCA Victor 0855
9/1/73	86	5		9 **As Time Goes By**	*Lullaby In Ragtime*	$6		RCA Victor 0039
				Gordon Jenkins (orch.); #2 hit for Rudy Vallee in 1943; written in 1931				
4/13/74	39	9		10 **Daybreak**	*Down*	$6	■	RCA Victor 0246
				from the movie *Son Of Dracula* starring Nilsson and **Ringo Starr** (drums); **Peter Frampton** (guitar); **George Harrison** (cowbell); picture sleeve issued with 2 slightly different photos of Nilsson and Ringo Starr				
				NINE R&B/BUB/LP '95				
				Born on 9/19/69 in Queens, New York. Male rapper.				
12/24/94+	50	17		**Whutcha Want?** S:23	*Redrum*	$3	▮	Profile 5426

DEBUT	PEAK	WKS	Gold	A-side (Chart Hit)...B-side	$	Sym	Label & Number
				NINEDAYS LP **'00**			
				Rock group from New York: John Hampson (vocals, guitar), Brian Desveaux (vocals, guitar), Jeremy Dean (keyboards), Nick Dimichino (bass) and Vincent Tattanelli (drums).			
5/6/00	6	27		1 **Absolutely (Story Of A Girl)** ...A:5			album cut
12/2/00	68	5		2 **If I Am** ...A:74			album cut
				above 2 from the album *The Madding Crowd* on 550 Music 63634; "45" issued for above 2 on 550 Music 79532			
				NINE INCH NAILS ROK/BUB/LP **'99**			
				Group is actually industrial rock musician Trent Reznor (born on 5/17/65 in Mercer, Pennsylvania).			
3/12/94	59	3		1 **March Of The Pigs** ...S:25 *Reptilian / All The Pigs, All Lined Up / A Violet Fluid / Underneath The Skin*	$8	★*	Nothing/TVT 95938
6/11/94	41	22		2 **Closer** ...S:26 / A:51 *March Of The Pigs (live)*	$4	▮	Nothing/TVT 98263
4/29/95	54^{A}	8		3 **Hurt** ...			album cut
				all of above from the album *The Downward Spiral* on Nothing/TVT 92346			
5/31/97	46	9		4 **The Perfect Drug** ...S:23 / A:63 *(4 versions)*	$8	★*	Nothing 95007
				from the movie *Lost Highway* starring Bill Pullman			
8/7/99	17	5		5 **The Day The World Went Away** S:5 *(quiet version) / Starfuckers, Inc.* (ROK #39)	$4	★	Nothing/Interscope 97026
				9.9 R&B/LP **'85**			
				R&B vocal trio from Boston, Massachusetts: Margo Thunder, Leslie Jones and Wanda Perry.			
8/24/85	51	13		**All Of Me For All Of You** ...*Little Bitty Woman*	$3	■	RCA 14082
				1910 FRUITGUM CO. BUB/LP **'68**			
				Bubblegum group from New Jersey: Mark Gutkowski (vocals), Floyd Marcus, Pat Karwan, Steve Mortkowitz and Frank Jeckell. Quintet recorded first 2 hits, then producers Jerry **Kasenetz** and Jeff **Katz** used a revolving-door studio-based membership centered around lead singer Gutkowski.			
1/27/68	4	14	●	1 **Simon Says** *Reflections From The Looking Glass*	$8		Buddah 24
4/20/68	63	8		2 **May I Take A Giant Step (Into Your Heart)** ...*(Poor Old) Mr. Jensen*	$8		Buddah 39
7/27/68	5	13	●	3 **1, 2, 3, Red Light** ...*Sticky, Sticky*	$8		Buddah 54
				The Trade Winds (backing vocals)			
10/26/68	37	9		4 **Goody Goody Gumdrops** ...*Candy Kisses*	$8		Buddah 71
				Billy Carl (lead vocal)			
1/25/69	5	13	●	5 **Indian Giver** ...*Pow Wow*	$8		Buddah 91
5/10/69	38	9		6 **Special Delivery** ...*No Good Annie*	$8		Buddah 114
8/23/69	57	10		7 **The Train** ...*Eternal Light*	$8		Buddah 130
				1927 **'89**			
				Soft-rock group from Australia: Eric Weideman (vocals, guitar), brothers Garry (keyboards) and Bill (bass) Frost, and James Barton (drums). Garry Frost was also a member of **Moving Pictures**.			
8/26/89	100	1		**That's When I Think Of You** ...*Alright*	$3	■	Atlantic 88878
				NINE20 **'02**			
				R&B vocal trio from Atlanta, Georgia: Byrd, Miz and Antonio.			
2/23/02	65^{S}	4		**What Would You Do?** ...*(instrumental)*	$5	★	MCA 155919
	★432★			**98°** LP **'00**			
				White teen pop vocal group from Cincinnati, Ohio: brothers Drew (born on 8/8/76) and **Nick Lachey** (born on 11/9/73) and with Jeff Timmons (born on 4/30/73) and Justin Jeffre (born on 2/25/73). Nick Lachey married **Jessica Simpson** on 10/26/2002.			
7/12/97	12	28	●	1 **Invisible Man** ...S:12 / A:23 *(instrumental)*	$3	▮V	Motown 860650
				"45": Motown 860674			
10/3/98	3	20	▲	2 **Because Of You** ...S:4 / A:38 *True To Your Heart* (w/**Stevie Wonder**)	$4	★	Motown 860830
3/27/99	5	24	●	3 **The Hardest Thing** ...S:5 / A:12 *(edit) / Because Of You (dance mix) / Invisible Man*	$4	★	Universal 156246
8/7/99	13	20		4 **I Do (Cherish You)** ...A:9		V	album cut
				see #7 below for "45" issue; above 3 from the album *98° And Rising* on Motown 530956			
12/11/99+	❶^{1}	20	●	5 **Thank God I Found You** RB^{1} S:❶^{3} / A:15 *(remix)*	$4	★V	Columbia 79338
				MARIAH With Joe & 98°			
				Trey Lorenz (backing vocal); remix versions with **Nas** and **Joe** issued on Columbia 79339			
1/1/00-	49	3		6 **This Gift** ...A:39 [X]			album cut
				from the album *This Christmas* on Universal 153918			
8/19/00	2^{2}	20	●	7 **Give Me Just One Night (Una Noche)** ...S:2 / A:14 *(Spanish version)*	$4	★V	Universal 153296
				Deetah (female vocal); "45" issued for #4 & 7 on Universal 158224			
12/9/00+	34	20		8 **My Everything** ...A:34			album cut
				above 2 from the album *Revelation* on Universal 159354			
				95 SOUTH R&B/BUB/LP **'93**			
				Hip-hop/bass group from Miami, Florida: Church's, Black, C.C. Lemonhead, Bootyman and K-Knock. Group named after the interstate highway. By 1995, group reduced to a duo of A.B. and Black. Lemonhead later joined the **Quad City DJ's**.			
5/1/93	11	25	▲	1 **Whoot, There It Is** ...S:5 / A:44 *(ultimix radio)*	$3	▮V	Wrap/Toy 162
				samples **Afrika Bambaataa**'s "Looking For The Perfect Beat"; "45": Wrap/Toy 286 on either an orange or a green label			
2/11/95	77	18		2 **Rodeo** ...S:43 *(album sampler)*	$3	▮	Rip-It 9511
				NINO & the EBB TIDES **'61**			
				White doo-wop group from the Bronx, New York: Antonio "Nino" Aiello (lead), Tony DiBari (tenor), Tony Imbimbo (baritone) and Vinnie Drago (bass).			
9/4/61	57	5		**Juke Box Saturday Night** ...*(Someday) I'll Fall In Love*	$40		Madison 166
				song features "Book Of Love" and "Get A Job"; update of Glenn Miller's #7 hit in 1942			
				NIRVANA ROK/LP **'92**			
				Grunge-rock trio from Aberdeen, Washington: Kurt Cobain (vocals), Krist "Chris" Novoselic (bass) and Dave Grohl (drums). Cobain married Courtney Love (lead singer of **Hole**) on 2/24/92. Cobain died of a self-inflicted gunshot wound on 4/8/94 (age 27). Grohl formed **Foo Fighters** in 1995. Also see **For Squirrels**.			
12/7/91+	6	20	▲	1 **Smells Like Teen Spirit** MR^{1} S:❶^{2} / A:41 *Even In His Youth*	$4	▮V	DGC 19050
3/21/92	32	18		2 **Come As You Are** ...S:27 / A:62 *Drain You (live)*	$4	▮V	DGC 19120
8/8/92	64	9		3 **Lithium** ...S:31 *Been A Son (live)*	$5	▮	DGC 19134
				special package - includes lyrics to every song on their album *Nevermind*			

DEBUT	PEAK	WKS	Gold	A-side (Chart Hit)..........B-side	$	Sym	Label & Number
				NIRVANA — Cont'd			
1/15/94	45^{A}	22		4 **All Apologies**..........			album cut
				from the album *In Utero* on DGC 24607			
10/15/94	22^{A}	16		5 **About A Girl**..........MR[1] [L]			album cut
2/4/95	39^{A}	12		6 **The Man Who Sold The World**.......... [L]			album cut
				written and recorded by **David Bowie** in 1970; above 2 from the album *MTV Unplugged In New York* on DGC 24727			
9/28/96	63^{A}	8		7 **Aneurysm**.......... [L]			album cut
				from the album *From The Muddy Banks Of The Wishkah* on DGC 25105; recorded on 12/28/91 at Del Mar Fairgrounds, California			
10/19/02	45	20		8 **You Know You're Right**..........AR[4] / MR[4] A:43			album cut
				recorded on 1/30/94; from the album *Nirvana* on DGC 493507			
				NITE-LITERS, The — see NEW BIRTH, The			
				NITEFLYTE R&B '79			
				R&B/disco group led by Howard Johnson and Sandy Torano.			
9/15/79	37	13		**If You Want It**..........*I Wonder (If I'm Falling In Love Again)*	$5		Ariola America 7747
				NITTY GRITTY DIRT BAND C&W/BUB/LP '71			
				Country-folk-rock group from Long Beach, California. Led by Jeff Hanna (vocals, guitar; born on 7/11/47) and John McEuen (banjo, mandolin; born on 12/19/45). Changed name to **Dirt Band** in 1976. Resumed using Nitty Gritty Dirt Band name in 1982. Various members included ex-**Eagle** Bernie Leadon, who replaced McEuen briefly in early 1987. Revamped quartet since late 1987: Hanna, Jimmy Ibbotson, Bob Carpenter and Jimmie Fadden. In the movies *For Singles Only* and *Paint Your Wagon*. Hanna married country singer/songwriter Matraca Berg. Also see **Steve Martin**'s "King Tut."			
				1)Mr. Bojangles 2)An American Dream 3)Make A Little Magic			
4/8/67	45	7		1 **Buy For Me The Rain**..........*Candy Man*	$10		Liberty 55948
11/21/70+	9	19		2 **Mr. Bojangles** *Uncle Charlie Interview #2/Spanish Fandango*	$8	□	Liberty 56197
				prologue: Uncle Charlie And His Dog Teddy; promo sleeve issued featuring an interview with the band			
4/24/71	53	13		3 **House At Pooh Corner**..........*Travelin' Mood*	$6	■	United Artists 50769
				written by **Kenny Loggins**; title taken from the same-named book by A.A. Milne			
9/11/71	64	8		4 **Some Of Shelly's Blues**..........*The Cure*	$6		United Artists 50817
				written by **Michael Nesmith** (**The Monkees**); originally "Bubbled Under" (#106) on 10/18/69 on Liberty 56134			
4/1/72	84	3		5 **Jambalaya (On The Bayou)**..........*Hoping To Say*	$6	■	United Artists 50890
				#1 Country hit for Hank Williams in 1952			
10/12/74	72	4		6 **Battle Of New Orleans**..........*The Mountain Whippoorwill (Or, How Hillbilly Jim Won The Great Fiddler's Prize)*	$5	■	United Artists 544
8/30/75	66	6		7 **(All I Have To Do Is) Dream**..........*Raleigh-Durham Reel*	$5		United Artists 655
				THE DIRT BAND:			
9/2/78	86	3		8 **In For The Night**..........*Wild Nights*	$4		United Artists 1228
12/8/79+	13	19		9 **An American Dream**..........*Take Me Back*	$4		United Artists 1330
				Linda Ronstadt (harmony vocal)			
6/21/80	25	16		10 **Make A Little Magic**..........*Jas' Moon*	$4		United Artists 1356
				Nicolette Larson (backing vocal)			
10/3/81	76	4		11 **Fire In The Sky**..........*Easy Slow*	$4		Liberty 1429
				NITZSCHE, Jack BUB '63			
				Born Bernard Nitzsche on 4/22/37 in Chicago, Illinois. Died of heart failure on 8/25/2000 (age 63). Arranger/producer/composer/keyboardist. Arranger for many of Phil Spector's productions. Co-wrote "Needles And Pins" and scored the movies *One Flew Over The Cuckoo's Nest* and *An Officer And A Gentleman*. His wife, Grazia, sang on several of **The Blossoms**' recordings.			
8/10/63	39	8		1 **The Lonely Surfer**..........*Song For A Summer Night* [I]	$30	■	Reprise 20,202
11/23/63	91	2		2 **Rumble**..........*Theme For A Broken Heart* [I]	$20		Reprise 20,225
				above 2 produced by **Jimmy Bowen**			
				NIVEA LP '02			
				Born Nivea Hamilton in 1981 in Atlanta, Georgia. Female R&B singer.			
8/18/01	90	3		1 **Don't Mess With The Radio**..........S:8 *(instrumental) / (6 album snippets)*	$4	★	Jive 42902
8/10/02	8	36		2 **Don't Mess With My Man**..........S:❶[1] / A:8 *(version 2)*	$4	★	Jive 40041
				NIVEA Featuring Brian & Brandon Casey Of Jagged Edge			
				NIX, Don LP '71			
				Born on 9/27/41 in Memphis, Tennessee. White soul-rock singer/guitarist/saxophonist. Formerly in the **Mar-Keys**.			
10/9/71	94	3		**Olena**..........*Riding The Blinds*	$6		Elektra 45746
				NIXONS, The ROK/LP '96			
				Rock group from Dallas, Texas: Zac Maloy (vocals, guitar), Jesse Davis (guitar), Ricky Brooks (bass) and John Humphrey (drums).			
4/20/96	48^{A}	20		**Sister**..........			album cut
				from the album *Foma* on MCA 11209			
				NKOTB — see NEW KIDS ON THE BLOCK			
				NO ANGELS '02			
				Interracial female vocal group formed for the German version of the TV series *PopStars*: Vanessa Petruo, Lucy Diakovska, Sandy Moelling, Nadja Benaissa and Jessica Wahls.			
6/1/02	36^{S}	1		**Daylight In Your Eyes**..........*(extended version)*	$5	★	MCA/Polydor 561732
				NO AUTHORITY BUB '00			
				Teen pop vocal group from California: Ricky Felix, Danny Zavatsky, Josh Keaton and Eric Stretch.			
7/17/99	56^{S}	10		1 **What I Wanna Do**..........*Girlfriend*	$4	★	MJJ Music/Work 79196
7/8/00	35^{S}	29		2 **Can I Get Your Number**..........	$4	★	Maverick 16853
				NOBLE, Nick C&W/AC '57			
				Born Nicholas Valkan on 6/21/36 in Chicago, Illinois. Adult Contemporary singer. Attended Loyola University.			
8/20/55	22	4		1 **The Bible Tells Me So**..........S:22 / T:61 *Army Of The Lord*	$15		Wing 90003
				Lew Douglas (orch.); written by **Roy Rogers**'s wife, Dale Evans			
2/25/56	27	16		2 **To You, My Love**..........T:27 *You Are My Only Love*	$12		Mercury 70821
				charted its first 2 weeks on Wing 90045; French song "Je Ne Sais Pas"; **Jack Halloran** Choir (backing vocals, above 2)			

DEBUT	PEAK	WKS	Gold	A-side (Chart Hit)..........B-side	$	Sym	Label & Number
				NOBLE, Nick — Cont'd			
7/15/57	20	1		3 **A Fallen Star** ....A:20 *Let Me Hold You In My Arms*	$10		Mercury 71124
				Dick Noel Singers (backing vocals); first released on Mercury 71117 in 1957			
9/9/57	37	8		4 **Moonlight Swim** ....T:37 *Lucy Lou*	$10		Mercury 71169
				Carl Stevens (orch., above 3)			
				NOBLES, Cliff, & Co. R&B/LP '68			
				Born in 1944 in Mobile, Alabama. R&B bandleader/singer.			
5/25/68	2^3	14	●	1 **The Horse** ....*Love Is All Right* [I]	$10		Phil-L.A. 313
9/14/68	68	5		2 **Horse Fever** ....*Judge Baby, I'm Back* [I]	$8		Phil-L.A. 318
2/15/69	93	3		3 **Switch It On** ....*Burning Desire* [I]	$8		Phil-L.A. 324
				all of above written and produced by **Jesse James**			
				NOBODY'S ANGEL LP '00			
				Interracial female teen pop-dance vocal group from Los Angeles, California: Amy Harding, Sarah Smith, Stacey Harper and Ali Navarro.			
1/15/00	25^S	12		**If You Wanna Dance** ....*(radio mix) / Wishing On You*	$4	★	Hollywood 64034
				samples "Spirit Of The Boogie" and "Get Down On It" by **Kool & The Gang**			
				NOCERA R&B '87			
				Born Maria Nocera in Italy. Female dance singer.			
1/17/87	84	7		**Summertime, Summertime** ....*(club mix)*	$5		Sleeping Bag 22
	★420★			**NO DOUBT** ROK/BUB/LP '96			
				New wave-ska band from Orange County, California: Gwen Stefani (vocals), Tom Dumont (guitar), Tony Kanal (bass) and Adrian Young (drums). Stefani married Gavin Rossdale (lead singer of **Bush**) on 9/14/2002.			
12/16/95+	23	29		1 **Just A Girl** ....S:21 / A:32 *Different People*	$4	▮	Trauma 98116
5/18/96	18^A	39		2 **Spiderwebs**			album cut
10/19/96	❶^{16A}	63		3 **Don't Speak**			album cut
				the first album cut to hit #1 on the *Hot 100 Airplay* chart; all of above from the album *Tragic Kingdom* on Trauma 92580 (produced by **Matthew Wilder**)			
7/1/00	38	13		4 **Simple Kind Of Life** ....S:5 / A:73 *Full Circle / Beauty Contest*	$4	★^{V}	Trauma 490365
				"45": Trauma 497403; B-side: "Ex-Girlfriend" (ROK #2/BUB #111)			
12/8/01+	5	20		5 **Hey Baby** A:5			album cut
				NO DOUBT Featuring Bounty Killer			
4/20/02	13	20		6 **Hella Good** A:14			album cut
8/31/02	3	30		7 **Underneath It All** ....A:4 / S:64 *Hella Good / Hey Baby*	$4	★	Interscope 497768
				NO DOUBT featuring Lady Saw			
				above 3 from the album *Rock Steady* on Interscope 493158			
				NOEL LP '87			
				Born Noel Pagan in the Bronx, New York. Latin-disco singer.			
8/22/87	47	22		1 **Silent Morning** ....*(percapella mix)*	$3	■	4th & B'way 7439
4/9/88	67	8		2 **Like A Child** ....*(heartthrob dub)*	$3	■	4th & B'way 7458
				NO GOOD '02			
				Male rap duo from Miami, Florida: Derrick Hill and Tracy Lattimer.			
3/23/02	3^S	23		**Ballin' Boy** ....*(3 versions)*	$5	★	Artistdirect 01022
				NOGUEZ, Jacky, And His Orchestra '59			
				Born in Paris, France. Male orchestra leader.			
6/22/59	24	12		1 **Ciao, Ciao Bambina (Chiow, Chiow, Bambeena)** ....*De Serait Dommage* [I]	$12		Jamie 1127
				original Italian title: "Piove"			
11/16/59	87	3		2 **Marina** ....*Adonis* [I]	$12		Jamie 1137
1/18/60	63	6		3 **Amapola** ....*Mahzel* [I]	$12	■	Jamie 1148
				#1 hit in 1941 for **Jimmy Dorsey**			
				NOKIO — see EVE			
				NOLAN — see PORTER, Nolan			
				NOLAN, Kenny LP '77			
				Born in Los Angeles, California. Pop singer/songwriter. Wrote "My Eyes Adored You," "Lady Marmalade" and "Get Dancin'." Fronted studio group **The Eleventh Hour** and **Firefly**.			
11/6/76+	3	27	●	1 **I Like Dreamin'** ....*Time Ain't Time Enough*	$5		20th Century 2287
4/2/77	20	18		2 **Love's Grown Deep** ....*Today I Met The Girl I'm Gonna Marry*	$5		20th Century 2331
10/15/77	97	3		3 **My Eyes Get Blurry** ....*Monette*	$5		20th Century 2352
2/2/80	44	8		4 **Us And Love (We Go Together)** ....*You're So Beautiful Tonight*	$5		Casablanca 2234
				NOLEN, Gabbie '02			
				Born on 7/7/82 in La Grange, Texas. Female country singer.			
11/16/02	27^S	1		**Almost There** ....*Little Did She Know (She'd Kiss A Hero)*	$6	★	Republic 015736
				NOMAD '91			
				Dance duo of Damon Rocheforte and Steve McCutcheon.			
6/22/91	66^A	6		**(i wanna give you) Devotion** ....*(2 remixes)*	$5	▮	Rumour/Capitol 44723
				NO MERCY LP '96			
				Male techno-dance trio: brothers Ariel and Gabriel Hernandez from Miami, Florida, with Marty Cintron from New York.			
7/6/96	5	39	●	1 **Where Do You Go** ....A:3 / S:10 *(remix)*	$3	▮^{V}	Arista 13225
2/8/97	21	18		2 **Please Don't Go** ....S:21 / A:41 *Do You Want Me*	$3	▮^{V}	Arista 13304
				"45" B-side: "Where Do You Go"			
6/7/97	41	20		3 **When I Die** ....S:35 / A:66 *Bonita*	$3	▮	Arista 13367
11/15/97	80	3		4 **Kiss You All Over** ....*(remix)*	$3	▮	Arista 13429

DEBUT	PEAK	WKS	Gold	A-side (Chart Hit)..........B-side	$	Sym	Label & Number
				NONCHALANT R&B/LP '96			
				Born Tanya Pointer in Washington DC. Female singer/rapper/songwriter.			
3/2/96	24	20	●	1 **5 O'Clock**..........S:14 *(instrumental)*	$3	▮	MCA 55075
9/29/01	14^{S}	9		2 **How We Do**..........*(4 versions)*	$15	★	Col-Beast 22172
				BIG LEW Betta Known As "POPEYE REDS" Featuring: Nonchalant			
				NO QUESTION LP '00			
				R&B vocal group from Philadelphia, Pennsylvania: Damon Core, Nicholas Johnson, Thomas Blackwell and Dante Massey.			
10/16/99	73^{S}	1		1 **I Don't Care**..........*(2 versions) / This Weekend*	$4	★	Philadelphia I. 16842
8/5/00	28^{S}	18		2 **I Don't Care**..........*(remix)* [R]	$4	★	RuffNation 16842
				above 2 are the same version			
				N.O.R.E. (Noreaga) R&B/BUB/LP '02			
				Born Victor Santiago in Queens, New York. Male rapper. Half of **Capone**-N-Noreaga duo.			
9/12/98	36	13		1 **SuperThug (What What)** *[NOREAGA]*..........S:27 *(album version)*	$5	★	Penalty 0237
				Tammy Lucas and The Neptunes (backing vocals); samples "Heart Of Glass" by **Blondie**			
5/25/02	10	24		2 **Nothin'** *[N.O.R.E.]*..........A:8 / S:12 *(instrumental) / Nahmeanuheard*	$6	T	Def Jam 582914
11/30/02	67^{S}	1		3 **Full Mode**..........*(3 versions)*	$6	T	Def Jam 063826
				N.O.R.E. featuring Musaliny-N-Maze			
				from the movie *I Spy* starring **Eddie Murphy**			
				NORMAN, Chris — see QUATRO, Suzi / SMOKIE			
				NORMAN, Jimmy R&B '62			
				Born on 8/12/37 in Nashville, Tennessee. R&B singer. Member of **The Chargers** and **The Dyna-Sores**.			
6/16/62	47	8		**I Don't Love You No More (I Don't Care About You)**..........*Tell Her For Me*	$15		Little Star 113
				NORTH, Freddie R&B/BUB/LP '71			
				Born on 5/28/39 in Nashville, Tennessee. R&B singer/songwriter/guitarist.			
10/2/71	39	12		**She's All I Got**..........*Ain't Nothing In The News (But The Blues)*	$8		Mankind 12004
				NORTHCOTT, Tom BUB '68			
				Born in 1943 in Canada. Folk singer. Hosted own TV show.			
3/16/68	88	2		**1941**..........*Other Times*	$8		Warner 7160
				written by Harry **Nilsson**; arranged and produced by **Leon Russell**			
				NORTHERN LIGHT '75			
				Pop-rock group from Minneapolis, Minnesota: Dave Sandler, Spence Peterson, Bud Phillips, Don Beckwith and Steve Hough.			
5/3/75	88	6		**Minnesota**..........*Theme From Minnesota* [I]	$6		Columbia 10136
				originally released on Glacier 4501 in 1975 ($10)			
				NORTHERN PIKES, The ROK '92			
				Rock group from Saskatoon, Saskatchewan, Canada: Jay Semko (vocals, bass), Merl Bryck (vocals, guitar), Bryan Potvin (guitar) and Don Schmid (drums).			
1/4/92	86	5		**She Ain't Pretty**..........*Isn't It Lovely*	$4	▮	Scotti Brothers 75287
				NORWOOD, Dorothy R&B '74			
				Gospel singer; formerly with the Caravans. Own group, the Dorothy Norwood Singers.			
2/23/74	88	4		**There's Got To Be Rain In Your Life (To Appreciate The Sunshine)**..........*Get Aboard The Soul Train*	$6		GRC 1011
				NO SECRETS LP '02			
				Female teen pop vocal group from Florida: Angel Faith, Jessica Fried, Erin Tanner, Jade Gaspar and Carly Lewis.			
7/6/02	7^{S}	26		**That's What Girls Do**..........*Comes Back / (3 album snippets)*	$5	★+	Jive 40035
				NOTORIOUS '90			
				Rock duo from England: **Robin George** (guitar) and Sean Harris (vocals).			
12/15/90	90	5		**The Swalk**..........*Eyes Of The World*	$4	▮	Geffen 19698
				NOTORIOUS B.I.G., The ★166★ R&B/BUB/LP '97			
				Born Christopher Wallace on 5/21/72 in Brooklyn, New York. Shot to death on 3/9/97 (age 24). Male rapper. Also recorded as Biggy Smallz. Married to **Faith Evans** from 1994-97. Arrested on 6/18/95 on robbery and assault charges and on 3/23/96 for assault and weapon offenses. Discovered **Junior M.A.F.I.A.** Also see "I'll Be Missing You" by **Puff Daddy & Faith Evans**.			
				1)Hypnotize 2)Mo Money Mo Problems 3)One More Chance/Stay With Me 4)Big Poppa 5)Going Back To Cali			
8/27/94	27	20	●	1 **Juicy** / S:13 / A:50			
9/17/94		17		2 **Unbelievable**..........	$5	▮	Bad Boy 79004
1/14/95	6	24	▲	3 **Big Poppa** / S:2 / A:37			
				samples "Between The Sheets" by **The Isley Brothers**; remix issued with the B-side "Who Shot Ya?" on Bad Boy 79019 (v)			
1/14/95		24		4 **Warning**..........S:flip	$4	▮V	Bad Boy 79015
				samples "Walk On By" by **Isaac Hayes**; above 2 issued as radio edits on Bad Boy 79024 (v); also see #18 & 19 below			
4/8/95	13	20	●	5 **Can't You See**..........S:9 / A:28 *(instrumental)*	$3	▮V	Tommy Boy 7676
				TOTAL featuring The Notorious B.I.G.			
				samples "The Payback" by **James Brown**; from the movie *New Jersey Drive* starring Sharron Corley; "45": Tommy Boy/Collectables 676			
6/24/95	2^{3}	20	▲	6 **One More Chance/Stay With Me** / RB^{9} S:❶^{5} / A:24			
				Faith Evans (backing vocal); samples "Stay With Me" by **DeBarge**; also see #20 below			
7/22/95		3		7 **The What**..........S:flip	$3	▮	Bad Boy 79031
				THE NOTORIOUS B.I.G. and METHOD MAN			
				all of above (except #5) from the album *Ready To Die*			
2/1/97	81	14		8 **Runnin'**..........S:57 *Is It A Dream*	$5	▮	Mergela/Solar 70134
				2PAC, NOTORIOUS B.I.G., Radio, Dramacydal & Stretch			

DEBUT	PEAK	WKS	Gold	A-side (Chart Hit).....B-side	$	Sym	Label & Number
				NOTORIOUS B.I.G., The — Cont'd			
4/26/97	❶^{3}	20	▲	9 **Hypnotize** RB^{3} S:❶^{3} / A:23 *I Got A Story To Tell*	$3	▮	Bad Boy 79092
				Pam Long (female vocal); samples "La Di Da Di" by **Slick Rick** and "Rise" by **Herb Alpert**			
4/26/97	77	7		10 **Stop The Gunfight** .....S:55 *(R&B version) / When I Come Down*	$5	▮	Deff Trapp 9269
				TRAPP · 2PAC · NOTORIOUS B.I.G.			
				recorded in 1993; released after 2Pac and Biggy were shot to death within 6 months of each other			
8/2/97	❶^{2}	30	▲	11 **Mo Money Mo Problems** .....S:❶^{4} / A:12 *(instrumental)*	$3	▮	Bad Boy 79100
				THE NOTORIOUS B.I.G. Featuring Puff Daddy & Mase			
				Kelly Price (female vocal); samples "I'm Coming Out" by **Diana Ross**; also see #21 below			
12/6/97+	2^{2}	6	▲	12 **It's All About The Benjamins** / S:2 / A:62			
				PUFF DADDY & THE FAMILY Feat. The Notorious B.I.G., Lil' Kim, The Lox, Dave Grohl, Perfect, FuzzBubble & Rob Zombie			
				samples "I Did It For Love" by **Love Unlimited Orchestra**			
1/17/98	4	15	▲	13 **Been Around The World**.....S:❷^{2} / A:58	$3	▮	Bad Boy 79130
				PUFF DADDY & THE FAMILY Featuring The Notorious B.I.G. & Mase			
				samples "Let's Dance" by **David Bowie** and "All Around The World" by **Lisa Stansfield**			
12/13/97+	26	18	▲	14 **Going Back To Cali** / S:19			
12/6/97	60	1		15 **Sky's The Limit**	$3	▮	Bad Boy 79131
				THE NOTORIOUS B.I.G. (Featuring 112)			
				samples "My Flame" by **Bobby Caldwell**; #9, 11, 14 & 15: from the album *Life After Death*			
3/21/98	19	20	●	16 **Victory** .....S:11 *(remix) / Bad Boy's Been Around The World Remix* (w/**Mase**)	$3	▮	Bad Boy 79155
				PUFF DADDY & THE FAMILY Featuring The Notorious B.I.G. & Busta Rhymes			
				samples "Alone In The Ring" (from the movie *Rocky*) by **Bill Conti**			
12/11/99	82	7		17 **Notorious B.I.G.** A:61			album cut
				THE NOTORIOUS B.I.G. featuring Puff Daddy & Lil' Kim			
				samples "Notorious" by **Duran Duran**; from the album *Born Again* on Bad Boy 73023			
4/21/01	38^{S}	44		18 **Big Poppa** / [R]			
4/21/01		44		19 **Warning**.....*(4 remixes) / Who Shot Ya?* [R]	$8	★*	Bad Boy 79377
5/26/01	35^{S}	34		20 **One More Chance/Stay With Me**.....*(3 edits) / The What* (w/**Method Man**) [R]	$8	★*	Bad Boy 79380
6/9/01	63^{S}	2		21 **Mo Money Mo Problems**.....*(3 versions) / Lovin' You Tonight* (w/**R. Kelly**) [R]	$8	★*	Bad Boy 79109
				THE NOTORIOUS B.I.G. Featuring Puff Daddy & Mase			
				above 4 reissued on Bad Boy/Arista's "Maximum Hits" series			
				NOVA, Aldo ROK/BUB/LP **'82**			
				Born Aldo Scarporuscio in Montreal, Quebec, Canada. Rock singer/songwriter/guitarist.			
3/27/82	23	16		1 **Fantasy** .....*Under The Gun*	$4	■	Portrait 02799
7/17/82	65	6		2 **Foolin' Yourself**.....*See The Light*	$4		Portrait 03001
				NOVA, Heather LP **'95**			
				Born on 7/6/68 on an island in the Bermuda Sound. Adult Alternative pop-rock singer/songwriter. Raised on a 40-foot sailboat in the Caribbean. Later settled in London, England.			
10/7/95	63^{A}	7		**Walk This World**			album cut
				from the album *Oyster* on Big Cat/Work 67113			
				NOVAS, The **'65**			
				Garage-rock band from Edina, Minnesota: Bob Nolan (vocals), John Eckley and Jim Ronald (guitars), Jim Owens (bass) and Jeff Raymond (drums).			
1/9/65	88	3		**The Crusher** .....*Take 7* [N]	$80		Parrot 45005
				vocal is an impersonation of former pro wrestler Reggie "The Crusher" Lisowski from Milwaukee			
				NRBQ BUB/LP **'74**			
				Blues-rock group formed in Miami, Florida. Numerous personnel changes. 1974 lineup: brothers Terry (vocals) and Donn (trombone) Adams, Al Anderson (guitar; **Clean Living**, **The Wildweeds**), Keith Spring (sax), Joey Spampinato (bass) and Tom Ardolino (drums). Spampinato was married to **Skeeter Davis** from 1983-96.			
2/2/74	70	6		**Get That Gasoline Blues**.....*Mona*	$7		Kama Sutra 586
	★220★			***NSYNC** AC/BUB/LP **'00**			
				Male teen vocal group formed in Orlando, Florida: Chris Kirkpatrick (born on 10/17/71), Josh ("JC") Chasez (born on 8/8/76), Joey Fatone (born on 1/28/77), **Justin Timberlake** (born on 1/31/81) and Lance Bass (born on 5/4/79). Timberlake and Chasez were regulars on TV's *The Mickey Mouse Club*. Fatone appeared in the 2002 movie *My Big Fat Greek Wedding*.			
				1)It's Gonna Be Me 2)Music Of My Heart 3)Bye Bye Bye			
3/7/98	13	24	●	1 **I Want You Back**.....S:15 / A:20 *Giddy Up*	$3	▮V	RCA 65348
7/11/98	15^{A}	22		2 **Tearin' Up My Heart** .....HOT:59(1 wk)		V	album cut
				"45" issued for above 2 on RCA 65469			
12/5/98+	8	22		3 **(God Must Have Spent) A Little More Time On You** .....S:9 / A:12 *(remix) / Sailing (live)*	$12	★+V	RCA 65685
4/24/99	67	12		4 **I Drive Myself Crazy** A:60		V	album cut
				"45" issued for above 2 on RCA 65721; all of above from the album **NSYNC*			
5/29/99	29	20		5 **God Must Have Spent A Little More Time On You**.....A:22 / S:23 *Sad Lookin' Moon* (Alabama)	$4	★V	RCA 65759
				ALABAMA (featuring *NSYNC)			
9/4/99	2^{1}	20		6 **Music Of My Heart** .....S:❶^{1} / A:26 *(remix)*	$4	★	Miramax/Epic 79245
				***NSYNC and GLORIA ESTEFAN**			
				from the movie *Music Of The Heart* starring Meryl Streep			
10/23/99+	5	29		7 **Bring It All To Me** A:4			album cut
				BLAQUE Featuring *NSYNC			
				from the album *Blaque* on Track Masters 68987			
1/29/00	4	23		8 **Bye Bye Bye** .....A:❶^{5} *(5 remixes)*	$6	TV	Jive 42681
				"45": Jive 42694; B-side: (same version)			
5/6/00	❶^{2}	25	●	9 **It's Gonna Be Me** S:❶^{1} / A:3 *(remix)*	$6	★V	Jive 42664
				"45": Jive 42695; B-side: (same version)			
9/30/00	5	26		10 **This I Promise You** .....AC^{13} A:4 *(3 versions)*	$6	TV	Jive 42746
				written and produced by **Richard Marx**; "45": Jive 42747; B-side: (Spanish version)			
6/2/01	19	15		11 **Pop** .....A:17 *(3 remixes)*	$6	T	Jive 42933

DEBUT	PEAK	WKS	Gold	A-side (Chart Hit)	B-side	$	Sym	Label & Number
				***NSYNC — Cont'd**				
9/22/01	**11**	24		12 **Gone**	A:11			album cut
2/9/02	**5**	20		13 **Girlfriend**	S:❶[14] / A:9 *(album version) / Gone*	$8	★*+V	Jive 40013
				***NSYNC Featuring Nelly** "45": Jive 40017; B-side: (same version); above 3 from the album *Celebrity* on Jive 41758				
				N-TOON — '00				
				Pre-teen R&B vocal group from Atlanta, Georgia: Lloyd Polite, Chuckie Reynolds, Justin Clark and Everett Hall.				
3/18/00	**45**[S]	15		**Ready**	*(2 versions) / (3 album snippets)*	$5	★	DreamWorks 59036
				N-TRANCE — '96				
				Electronic dance group from England: Ricardo Da Force (rapper), Gillian Wisdom, Dale Longworth, Lee Limer and Kevin O'Toole.				
1/20/96	**62**	17		**Stayin' Alive**	S:35 *(long version)*	$5	▮	Radikal/Critique 15562
				N2DEEP — LP '93				
				White rap duo from Vallejo, California: Jay Trujillo and T.L. Lyon.				
7/11/92+	**14**	30	●	1 **Back To The Hotel**	S:5 / A:44 *(remix)*	$3	▮V	Profile 5367
2/13/93	**92**	3		2 **Toss-Up**	S:68 *(remix)*	$3	▮V	Profile 5383
				"45" issued for above 2 on Profile 5383				
				NIIU — R&B '95				
				Male R&B vocal group from New Jersey: Chuckie Howard, Chris Herbert, Don Carlis and Craig Hill.				
12/3/94+	**22**	20		**I Miss You**	S:16 / A:44 *Right Now*	$3	▮	Arista 12768
				NU FLAVOR — '98				
				Teen pop-R&B vocal group from Long Beach, California: Jacob Ceniceros, Anthony Dacosta, Rico Luna and Frank Pangelinan.				
4/19/97	**62**	20		1 **Sweet Sexy Thing**	*(album edit) / (English/Spanish edit)*	$3	▮V	Reprise 17402
				NU FLAVOR Featuring Roger				
10/11/97+	**27**	24		2 **Heaven**	S:32 / A:32 *Havin' A Party*	$3	▮V	Reprise 17408
6/13/98	**83**	7		3 **Baby Be There**	S:75 *(Hot Sauce mix) / (G&G Groove mix)*	$3	▮V	Reprise 17410
6/3/00	**89**	9		4 **3 Little Words**	S:20 *(3 album snippets)*	$4	★V	Reprise 16868
				NUGENT, Ted — ROK/BUB/LP '77				
				Born on 12/13/48 in Detroit, Michigan. Hard-rock guitarist/songwriter. Moved to Chicago in 1965 and formed **The Amboy Dukes**. Moved back to Detroit in 1967. Joined the supergroup **Damn Yankees** in 1989. An avid game hunter and an active supporter of the National Rifle Association.				
3/27/76	**72**	5		1 **Hey Baby**	*Stormtroopin'*	$5		Epic 50197
11/27/76	**91**	2		2 **Dog Eat Dog**	*Light My Way*	$5		Epic 50301
8/13/77	**30**	11		3 **Cat Scratch Fever**	*Wang Dang Sweet Poontang*	$5		Epic 50425
2/4/78	**70**	4		4 **Home Bound**	*Death By Misadventure* [I]	$5		Epic 50493
4/1/78	**58**	7		5 **Yank Me, Crank Me**	*Cat Scratch Fever (live)* [L]	$5		Epic 50533
1/6/79	**84**	2		6 **Need You Bad**	*I Got The Feelin'*	$5		Epic 50648
7/26/80	**86**	4		7 **Wango Tango**	*Scream Dream*	$5		Epic 50907
				NUMAN, Gary — BUB/LP '80				
				Born Gary Webb on 3/8/58 in Hammersmith, England. Synth-techno-rock artist.				
2/16/80	**9**	25		**Cars**	*Metal*	$5		Atco 7211
				NU SHOOZ — LP '86				
				R&B-dance vocal group from Portland, Oregon, centered around husband-and-wife team of guitarist/songwriter John Smith and lead singer Valerie Day.				
3/8/86	**3**	23	●	1 **I Can't Wait**	S:3 / A:3 *Make Your Mind Up*	$3	■	Atlantic 89446
7/5/86	**28**	22		2 **Point Of No Return**	S:21 / A:39 *Goin' Thru The Motions*	$3	■	Atlantic 89392
				above 2: #1 Dance Club Play hits				
4/16/88	**41**	16		3 **Should I Say Yes?**	A:37 *Montecarlo Nite*	$3	■	Atlantic 89108
				NU TORNADOS, The — '58				
				String band from Philadelphia, Pennsylvania: Eddie Dono (leader), Phil Dale, Tom Dell, Mike Perna and Louie Mann.				
11/17/58	**26**	12		**Philadelphia U.S.A.**	*Magic Record*	$20		Carlton 492
				NUTTA BUTTA — '98				
				Born in 1973 in Harlem, New York. Male rapper.				
6/20/98	**63**	11		1 **Freak Out**	S:46 *(2 versions)*	$4	▮	Lil' Man 97028
				NUTTA BUTTA Featuring Teddy Riley and Anonymous samples "Le Freak" by **Chic**				
6/20/98	**74**	4		2 **Party Ain't A Party**	A:51 *(2 versions)*	$6	T	Lil' Man 95024
				QUEEN PEN Featuring Teddy Riley, Nutta Butta, Markell & Jesse West samples "On Your Face" by **Earth, Wind & Fire**				
				NUTTIN' NYCE — R&B '95				
				Female rap-R&B trio from California: Eboni Foster, Onnie Ponder and Teece Wallace.				
8/14/93	**83**	6		1 **In My Nature**	A:74 *(3 versions)*	$4	▮	Pocketown 42150
1/14/95	**92**	4		2 **Down 4 Whateva**	*(remix) / Behind Closed Doors*	$3	▮	Jive 42261
				samples "Back To Life" by **Soul II Soul**; from the movie *A Low Down Dirty Shame* starring Keenan Wayans				
5/27/95	**63**	13		3 **Froggy Style**	S:39 *Proof Is In The Pudding*	$3	▮	Jive 42296
				samples "Don't Stop The Music" by **Yarbrough & Peoples**, "Atomic Dog" by **George Clinton** and "Shake" by **The Gap Band**				
				NUTTY SQUIRRELS, The — '59				
				Creators and voices: Don Elliot (from Sommerville, New Jersey) and Alexander "Sascha" Burland (from Brooklyn, New York). Also see **Shirley & Squirrely**.				
11/9/59	**14**	12		1 **Uh! Oh! Part 2** /	[N]			
12/7/59	**45**	6		2 **Uh! Oh! Part 1**	[N]	$25	■	Hanover 4540
				NYASIA — '92				
				Born Blanca Iris Battista on 7/31/67 in Nantana, Florida; raised in Brooklyn, New York. Female dance singer.				
7/11/92	**95**	6		**Who's Got Your Love**	A:54 *(4 remixes)*	$6	▮*	MicMac 2572

DEBUT	PEAK	WKS	Gold	A-side (Chart Hit)..........B-side	$	Sym	Label & Number
				NYLONS, The LP **'87**			
				Acappella group formed in Toronto, Ontario, Canada: Marc Connors, Paul Cooper, Claude Morrison and Arnold Robinson. Connors died on 3/25/91 (age 41).			
5/16/87	**12**	17		1 **Kiss Him Goodbye** ....S:10 / A:12 *It's What They Call Magic*	$4	■	Open Air 0022
				same tune as **Steam**'s 1969 hit "Na Na Hey Hey Kiss Him Goodbye"			
8/29/87	**75**	7		2 **Happy Together** ....*Face In The Crowd*	$4	■	Open Air 0024
				NYRO, Laura BUB/LP **'70**			
				Born Laura Nigro on 10/18/47 in the Bronx, New York. Died of cancer on 4/8/97 (age 49). White soul-gospel singer/songwriter. Wrote "Stoned Soul Picnic," "Eli's Coming," "Wedding Bell Blues," "And When I Die," "Stoney End" and others.			
10/10/70	**92**	2		**Up On The Roof** ....*Captain Saint Lucifer*	$8		Columbia 45230

O

DEBUT	PEAK	WKS	Gold	A-side (Chart Hit)..........B-side	$	Sym	Label & Number
				O **'99**			
				Born in Los Angeles, California. Male rapper.			
11/20/99	**65**[S]	1		**In The Game** ....*(album version) / (5 album snippets)*	$6	★+	Hollywood 64031
				OAK BUB **'80**			
				Pop-rock group from Maine: Rick Pinette (vocals), Scott Weatherspoon (guitar), David Stone (keyboards), John Foster (bass) and Daniel Caron (drums).			
7/21/79	**58**	7		1 **This Is Love** ....*Goin' Nowhere Fast*	$4		Mercury 74076
5/10/80	**36**	14		2 **King Of The Hill** ....*Listen To Your Heart*	$4		Mercury 76049
				RICK PINETTE AND OAK			
12/13/80+	**71**	6		3 **Set The Night On Fire** ....*She's An "11"*	$4		Mercury 76087
				OAKENFOLD LP **'02**			
				Born Paul Oakenfold on 8/30/63 in London, England. Dance DJ/remixer.			
10/19/02	**41**	8		**Starry Eyed Surprise** A:49			album cut
				vocals by Shifty Shellshock (of **Crazy Town**); from the album *Bunkka* on Maverick 48204			
				OAK RIDGE BOYS C&W/AC/BUB/LP **'81**			
				Country vocal group formed in Oak Ridge, Tennessee: Duane Allen, Joe Bonsall, Richard Sterban and William Lee Golden. Charted 48 Country hits, 1973-99.			
5/16/81	**5**	22	▲	1 **Elvira** ....CW[1] *A Woman Like You*	$4		MCA 51084
1/16/82	**12**	14		2 **Bobbie Sue** ....CW[1] *Live In Love*	$4		MCA 51231
6/12/82	**76**	4		3 **So Fine** ....*I Wish You Were Here (Oh My Darlin')*	$4		MCA 52065
3/19/83	**72**	5		4 **American Made** ....CW[1] *The Cure For My Broken Heart*	$4		MCA 52179
				OAKTOWN'S 3.5.7 R&B/LP **'91**			
				Female rap group from Oakland, California: Djuana "Sweet L.D." Johnican, Tabatha "Terrible T" King, Vicious C and Sweet Pea (former Oakland Raiders cheerleader). By 1991, reduced to a duo of Johnican and King, who were dancers with **M.C. Hammer**'s touring posse.			
8/3/91	**66**	6		**Turn It Up** ....A:57 / S:66 *(dub version)*	$3	▮	Bust It/Capitol 44717
				Tata Vega (guest vocal)			
				OASIS ROK/LP **'96**			
				Rock group from Manchester, England: brothers Liam (vocals) and Noel (guitar) Gallagher, Paul Arthurs (guitar), Paul McGuigan (bass) and Tony McCarroll (drums). Alan White replaced McCarroll in 1995. Liam was married Patsy Kensit of **Eighth Wonder** from 1997-2000. Also see **The Chemical Brothers**.			
1/14/95	**39**[A]	18		1 **Live Forever**			album cut
				from the album *Definitely Maybe* on Epic 66431			
1/27/96	**8**	20		2 **Wonderwall** MR[10] A:8 / S:13 *Talk Tonight / Round Are Way*	$3	▮V	Epic 78216
2/24/96	**20**[A]	31		3 **Champagne Supernova** ....MR[5]			album cut
8/17/96	**55**	14		4 **Don't Look Back In Anger** ....A:41 / S:69 *Cum On Feel The Noize*	$3	▮	Epic 78356
				above 3 from the album *(What's The Story) Morning Glory?* on Epic 67351			
7/19/97	**49**[A]	10		5 **D'You Know What I Mean?**			album cut
9/27/97	**35**[A]	12		6 **Don't Go Away**			album cut
				above 2 from the album *Be Here Now* on Epic 68530			
				O'BANION, John LP **'81**			
				Born on 4/28/56 in Kokomo, Indiana. Pop singer.			
3/28/81	**24**	13		**Love You Like I Never Loved Before** ....*She's Not For You*	$4		Elektra 47125
				O'BRYAN R&B/BUB/LP **'82**			
				Born O'Bryan Burnett in 1961 in Sneads Ferry, North Carolina. Male R&B singer.			
3/27/82	**57**	9		**The Gigolo** ....*Can't Live Without Your Love*	$4		Capitol 5067
				OBSCURE, The **'99**			
				Studio group from Minneapolis, Minnesota. Assembled to offer a commercial single of the airplay hit by **The Offspring**.			
3/13/99	**68**[S]	4		**Pretty Fly (For A White Guy)** ....*(3 versions)*	$5	★	Twin Sounds 4261
				O.C. R&B/LP **'97**			
				Born Omar Credle on 5/13/71 in Brooklyn, New York. Male rapper.			
8/16/97	**81**	3		**Far From Yours** ....*My World*	$4	▮	Payday 850916
				O.C. featuring Yvette Michelle			
				samples "Tomorrow" by **The Brothers Johnson** and "(Beat) For The Listeners" by **Eric B. & Rakim**			
				OCASEK, Ric — see CARS, The			

DEBUT	PEAK	WKS	Gold	A-side (Chart Hit)..........B-side	$	Sym	Label & Number
				OCEAN LP '71			
				Pop group from London, Ontario, Canada: Janice Morgan (vocals), David Tamblyn (guitar), Greg Brown (keyboards), Jeff Jones (bass) and Charles Slater (drums).			
3/13/71	2^{1}	14	●	1 **Put Your Hand In The Hand** ....*Tear Down The Fences*	$6		Kama Sutra 519
6/26/71	73	4		2 **Deep Enough For Me**..........*No Other Woman*	$5		Kama Sutra 525
8/7/71	82	5		3 **We Got A Dream**..........*Will The Circle Be Unbroken*	$5		Kama Sutra 529
9/23/72	76	4		4 **One More Chance**..........*Will The Circle Be Unbroken*	$5		Kama Sutra 556
	★225★			**OCEAN, Billy** R&B/BUB/AC/LP '86			
				Born Leslie Sebastian Charles on 1/21/50 in Trinidad, West Indies; raised in England. R&B-pop singer.			
				1)Caribbean Queen 2)Get Outta My Dreams, Get Into My Car 3)There'll Be Sad Songs			
4/3/76	22	11		1 **Love Really Hurts Without You**..........*You're Running Outa Fools*	$6		Ariola America 7621
8/11/84	❶^{2}	26	●	2 **Caribbean Queen (No More Love On The Run)** RB^{4} S:❶^{2} / A:2 *(instrumental)*	$3		Jive 9199
				same song "African Queen" is on the B-side of #5 below			
12/1/84+	2^{1}	21		3 **Loverboy**..........S:2 / A:4 *(dub mix)*	$3	■	Jive 9284
3/23/85	4	22		4 **Suddenly**..........AC^{2} S:3 / A:3 *Lucky Man*	$3	■	Jive 9323
7/6/85	24	15		5 **Mystery Lady**..........S:19 / A:21 *African Queen (No More Love On The Run)*	$3	■	Jive 9374
				above 4 from the album *Suddenly*			
11/30/85+	2^{1}	23		6 **When The Going Gets Tough, The Tough Get Going**......S:2 / A:2 *(instrumental)*	$3	■	Jive 9432
				from the movie *The Jewel of the Nile* starring Michael Douglas and Kathleen Turner			
4/19/86	❶^{1}	21		7 **There'll Be Sad Songs (To Make You Cry)** ..RB^{2} / AC^{1} S:❶^{1} / A:❶^{1} *If I Should Lose You*	$3	■	Jive 9465
7/26/86	10	16		8 **Love Zone**..........RB^{1} S:9 / A:11 *(instrumental)*	$3	■	Jive 9510
10/25/86	16	16		9 **Love Is Forever**..........AC^{3} S:13 / A:18 *Dancefloor*	$3	■	Jive 9540
				above 4 from the album *Love Zone*			
2/13/88	❶^{2}	20		10 **Get Outta My Dreams, Get Into My Car**..........RB^{1} S:❶^{2} / A:❶^{2} *Showdown*	$3	■	Jive 9678
5/28/88	17	16		11 **The Colour Of Love**..........S:13 / A:17 *It's Never Too Late To Try*	$3	■	Jive 9707
10/7/89	32	9		12 **Licence To Chill**..........S:26 / A:38 *Pleasure*	$3	■	Jive 1283
				O'CONNOR, Carroll, And Jean Stapleton LP '72			
				"Archie and Edith Bunker" of TV's *All In The Family.* Veteran actors. O'Connor was born on 8/2/24 in Manhattan, New York; died of a heart attack on 6/21/01 (age 76). Stapleton was born Jean Murray on 1/19/23 in Manhattan, New York.			
12/11/71+	43	9		**Those Were The Days**..........*(long version)* [N]	$5	■	Atlantic 2847
				theme song from TV's *All In The Family*			
				O'CONNOR, Sinéad ROK/LP '90			
				Born on 12/8/66 in Dublin, Ireland. Female singer/songwriter. Gained notoriety in her various protests.			
3/17/90	❶^{4}	21	▲	1 **Nothing Compares 2 U**..........MR^{1} A:❶^{4} / S:❶^{3} *Jump In The River* (ROK #17/'88)	$4	▮V	Ensign/Chrysalis 23488
				written by **Prince**; first recorded by the Minneapolis group **The Family** in 1985			
6/23/90	60	9		2 **The Emperor's New Clothes**..........MR^{1} *What Do You Want?*	$3	▮V	Ensign/Chrysalis 23528
				O'DAY, Alan LP '77			
				Born on 10/3/40 in Hollywood, California. Pop singer/songwriter/pianist.			
4/2/77	❶^{1}	25	●	1 **Undercover Angel**..........*Just You*	$5		Pacific 001
10/1/77	73	6		2 **Started Out Dancing, Ended Up Making Love**..........*Angie Baby*	$5		Pacific 002
				ODDS & ENDS R&B '71			
				Two-man, one-woman R&B vocal group from Philadelphia, Pennsylvania.			
3/13/71	83	6		**Love Makes The World Go Round**..........*Yesterday My Love*	$6		Today 1003
				O'DELL — see MASTER P			
				O'DELL, Brooks '64			
				Born in Philadolphia, Pennsylvania. Male R&B singer. Sang lead with The Commanders and with own group, The Majestics.			
12/14/63+	58	9		**Watch Your Step**..........*Walk On By*	$15		Gold 214
				O'DELL, Kenny C&W/BUB '67			
				Born Kenneth Gist in 1942 in Oklamhoma. Pop singer/songwriter/guitarist. Worked with **Duane Eddy** and own band, Guys And Dolls. Moved to Nashville in 1969. Wrote **Charlie Rich**'s "Behind Closed Doors."			
11/18/67	38	7		1 **Beautiful People**..........*Flower Girl*	$8		Vegas 718
2/24/68	94	2		2 **Springfield Plane**..........*I'm Gonna Take It*	$8		Vegas 722
				ODYSSEY R&B/BUB/LP '78			
				Disco vocal trio from the Bronx, New York: Manila-born Tony Reynolds, and sisters Lillian and Louise Lopez, originally from the Virgin Islands.			
11/12/77+	21	19		1 **Native New Yorker**..........*Ever Lovin' Sam*	$4		RCA 11129
5/6/78	57	7		2 **Weekend Lover**..........*Golden Hands*	$4		RCA 11245
				OFARIM, Esther & Abi '68			
				Wife and husband from Israel. Esther was born Esther Zaled on 6/13/43; Abi was born Abraham Reichstadt on 10/5/39.			
3/30/68	68	6		**Cinderella Rockefella**..........*Your Heart Is Free Just Like The Wind*	$6		Philips 40526
				OFF BROADWAY USA LP '80			
				Rock group from Oak Park, Illinois: Cliff Johnson (vocals), Rob Harding and John Ivan (guitars), John Pazdan (bass) and Ken Harck (drums).			
3/22/80	51	7		**Stay In Time**..........*Full Moon Turn My Head Around*	$4		Atlantic 3647
				OFFITT, Lillian '57			
				Born on 11/4/38 in Nashville, Tennessee. Female R&B singer.			
7/29/57	66	10		**Miss You So**..........T:66 *If You Only Knew*	$30		Excello 2104

DEBUT	PEAK	WKS	Gold	A-side (Chart Hit)...B-side	$	Sym	Label & Number

OFFSPRING, The — ROK/BUB/LP '94

Punk-rock group from California: Brian "Dexter" Holland (vocals), Kevin "Noodles" Wasserman (guitar), Greg Kriesel (bass) and Ron Welty (drums).

1)Pretty Fly (For A White Guy) 2)Come Out And Play 3)Self Esteem

DEBUT	PEAK	WKS	Gold	A-side (Chart Hit)...B-side	$	Sym	Label & Number
6/25/94	38^{A}	18		1 **Come Out And Play** ... MR[2]			album cut
9/3/94	45^{A}	31		2 **Self Esteem**			album cut
1/7/95	58^{A}	4		3 **Gotta Get Away**			album cut
				above 3 from the album *Smash* on Epitaph 86432			
7/1/95	47^{A}	7		4 **Smash It Up**			album cut
				from the movie soundtrack album *Batman Forever* on Atlantic 82759			
1/18/97	65^{A}	4		5 **All I Want**			album cut
3/22/97	50^{A}	12		6 **Gone Away** ... AR[2]			album cut
				above 2 from the album *Ixnay On The Hombre* on Columbia 67810			
12/5/98+	53	16		7 **Pretty Fly (For A White Guy)** ... A:43		V	album cut
				intro samples "Rock Of Ages" by **Def Leppard**; "45": Columbia 79081; B-side: (Geek mix)			
4/10/99	74	15		8 **Why Don't You Get A Job?** ... A:62			album cut
				above 2 from the album *Americana* on Columbia 69661			
11/25/00	70	9		9 **Original Prankster** ... A:66			album cut
				Redman (guest vocal); samples "Low Rider" by **War**; from the album *Conspiracy Of One* on Columbia 61419			
1/5/02	77	11		10 **Defy You** ... A:72			album cut
				from the movie *Orange County* starring Jack Black (soundtrack on Columbia 85933)			

O'HENRY, Lenny — '64

Born Daniel Cannon. R&B singer. Popular "beach music" performer.

DEBUT	PEAK	WKS	Gold	A-side (Chart Hit)...B-side	$	Sym	Label & Number
5/30/64	98	1		**Across The Street** ... *Saturday Angel*	$15		Atco 6291

OHIO EXPRESS — BUB/LP '68

Bubblegum-rock group from Mansfield, Ohio. Produced by Jerry **Kasenetz** and Jeff **Katz** (worked with **The Music Explosion** and **1910 Fruitgum Co.**). Joey Levine (born on 5/29/47; later with **Reunion** and several Kasenetz-Katz productions) was lead singer on most of the hits. Other members: Dale Powers and Doug Grassel (guitars), Jim Pflayer (keyboards), Dean Krastan (bass) and Tiim Corwin (drums). Also see **The Third Rail** and **U.S. 1**.

DEBUT	PEAK	WKS	Gold	A-side (Chart Hit)...B-side	$	Sym	Label & Number
10/7/67	29	12		1 **Beg, Borrow And Steal** ... *Maybe*	$12		Cameo 483
				record is actually a reissue of a release by The Rare Breed on Attack 1401 in 1966 ($30)			
2/3/68	83	2		2 **Try It** ... *Soul Struttin'*	$12		Cameo 2001
				originally released by **The Standells** in 1967 on Tower 310 ($20)			
5/4/68	4	14	●	3 **Yummy Yummy Yummy** ... *Zig Zag*	$8		Buddah 38
8/3/68	33	9		4 **Down At Lulu's** ... *She's Not Comin' Home*	$8		Buddah 56
10/19/68	15	13	●	5 **Chewy Chewy** ... *Firebird*	$8		Buddah 70
3/1/69	96	1		6 **Sweeter Than Sugar** ... *Bitter Lemon*	$8		Buddah 92
3/29/69	30	8		7 **Mercy** ... *Roll It Up*	$8		Buddah 102
				#2-7: sung and written by Joey Levine			
6/21/69	99	2		8 **Pinch Me (Baby, Convince Me)** ... *Peanuts*	$8		Buddah 117
				Buddy Bengert, lead singer			
9/6/69	86	2		9 **Sausalito (Is The Place To Go)** ... *Make Love Not War*	$8		Buddah 129
				Graham Gouldman (of **10cc**), lead singer			

★337★ OHIO PLAYERS — R&B/BUB/LP '75

R&B-funk group from Dayton, Ohio: Clarence Satchell (vocals, sax; born on 4/15/40), Leroy Bonner (vocals, guitar), Billy Beck (keyboards), Marvin Pierce and Ralph Middlebrook (trumpets; born on 8/20/39), Marshall Jones (bass; born on 10/4/42) and Jimmy Williams (drums). Jones died on 8/18/84 (age 41). Satchell died of a brain aneurysm on 12/30/95 (age 55). Group started as the Ohio Untouchables (backing band for **The Falcons**).

1)Love Rollercoaster 2)Fire 3)Skin Tight

DEBUT	PEAK	WKS	Gold	A-side (Chart Hit)...B-side	$	Sym	Label & Number
12/25/71+	64	8		1 **Pain (Part I)** ... *(Part II)*	$6		Westbound 188
2/24/73	15	19	●	2 **Funky Worm** ... RB[1] *Paint Me* [N]	$6		Westbound 214
8/11/73	31	15		3 **Ecstasy** ... *Not So Sad And Lonely*	$6		Westbound 216
6/15/74	47	11		4 **Jive Turkey (Part 1)** ... *Streakin' Cheek To Cheek*	$5		Mercury 73480
9/7/74	13	11	●	5 **Skin Tight** ... *Heaven Must Be Like This*	$5		Mercury 73609
12/14/74+	❶[1]	17	●	6 **Fire** ... RB[2] *Together*	$5		Mercury 73643
4/12/75	44	7		7 **I Want To Be Free** ... *Smoke*	$5		Mercury 73675
9/20/75	33	8		8 **Sweet Sticky Thing** ... RB[1] *Alone*	$5		Mercury 73713
11/15/75+	❶[1]	16	●	9 **Love Rollercoaster** ... RB[1] *It's All Over*	$5		Mercury 73734
2/21/76	30	11		10 **Fopp** ... *Let's Love*	$5		Mercury 73775
2/21/76	90	4		11 **Rattlesnake** ... *Gone Forever* [I]	$6		Westbound 5018
6/26/76	18	17		12 **Who'd She Coo?** ... RB[1] *Bi-Centennial*	$5		Mercury 73814
1/29/77	61	5		13 **Feel The Beat (Everybody Disco)** ... *Contradiction*	$5		Mercury 73881
7/23/77	45	12		14 **O-H-I-O** ... *Can You Still Love Me* [I]	$5		Mercury 73932

OINGO BOINGO — ROK/LP '85

New wave rock group formed in Los Angeles, California: Danny Elfman (vocals), Steve Bartek (guitar), John Avila (bass) and Johnny Hernandez (drums). Group appeared in the 1986 movie *Back To School*. Among several movies, Elfman scored *Beetlejuice*, *Batman*, *Dick Tracy*, and *The Simpsons* TV theme, with Bartek as orchestrator. Band name shortened to Boingo in 1994.

DEBUT	PEAK	WKS	Gold	A-side (Chart Hit)...B-side	$	Sym	Label & Number
8/31/85	45	12		1 **Weird Science** ... *Weird Mama* (Ira & The Geeks)	$4	■	MCA 52633
				title song from the movie starring Anthony Michael Hall			
1/25/86	85	4		2 **Just Another Day** ... *Dead Man's Party*	$4	■	MCA 52726

DEBUT	PEAK	WKS	Gold	A-side (Chart Hit)..........B-side	$	Sym	Label & Number

O'JAYS, The ★146★ R&B/BUB/LP '73

R&B vocal group from Canton, Ohio: **Eddie Levert** (born on 6/16/42), Walter Williams (born on 8/25/42), William Powell (born on 12/9/41), Bobby Massey and Bill Isles. First known as the Triumphs. Recorded as the Mascots for the King label in 1961. Renamed by Cleveland disc jockey Eddie O'Jay. Isles left in 1965. Massey left to become a record producer in 1971; Levert, Williams and Powell continued as a trio. Powell retired from touring due to illness in late 1975 (died on 5/26/77, age 35); replaced by Sammy Strain, formerly with **Little Anthony & The Imperials**. Strain (married to **Yvonne Fair**) returned to his former group by 1993; replaced by Nathaniel Best. Levert's sons **Gerald** and Sean are members of the trio **Levert**. Gerald also charted duets with Eddie.

1)Love Train 2)Back Stabbers 3)Use Ta Be My Girl 4)I Love Music 5)For The Love Of Money

DEBUT	PEAK	WKS	Gold	A-side (Chart Hit)..........B-side	$	Sym	Label & Number
9/14/63	93	3		1 **Lonely Drifter**..........*That's Enough*	$15		Imperial 5976
5/8/65	48	7		2 **Lipstick Traces (On A Cigarette)**..........*Think It Over, Baby*	$15		Imperial 66102
8/7/65	94	2		3 **I've Cried My Last Tear**..........*Whip It On Me Baby*	$15		Imperial 66121
10/22/66	95	3		4 **Stand In For Love**..........*Friday Night*	$15		Imperial 66197
11/25/67+	66	9		5 **I'll Be Sweeter Tomorrow (Than I Was Today)**..........*I Dig Your Act*	$10		Bell 691
6/29/68	89	5		6 **Look Over Your Shoulder**..........*I'm So Glad I Found You*	$10		Bell 704
9/21/68	94	3		7 **The Choice**..........*Going Going Gone*	$10		Bell 737
8/9/69	68	6		8 **One Night Affair**..........*There's Someone (Waiting Back Home)*	$10		Neptune 12
4/4/70	64	7		9 **Deeper (In Love With You)**..........*I've Got The Groove*	$10		Neptune 22
9/5/70	98	2		10 **Looky Looky (Look At Me Girl)**..........*Let Me In Your World*	$10		Neptune 31
7/22/72	3	15	●	11 **Back Stabbers**..........RB[1] *Sunshine*	$6		Philadelphia I. 3517
11/11/72	57	8		12 **992 Arguments**..........*Listen To The Clock On The Wall*	$6		Philadelphia I. 3522
1/20/73	1[1]	14	●	13 **Love Train** RB[4] *Who Am I*	$6		Philadelphia I. 3524
5/19/73	33	12		14 **Time To Get Down**..........*Shiftless, Shady, Jealous Kind Of People* above 4 from the album *Back Stabbers*	$6		Philadelphia I. 3531
12/22/73+	10	16		15 **Put Your Hands Together**..........*You Got Your Hooks In Me*	$5		Philadelphia I. 3535
4/13/74	9	16	●	16 **For The Love Of Money**..........*People Keep Tellin' Me*	$5		Philadelphia I. 3544
12/14/74+	48	6		17 **Sunshine Part II**..........*Part I* [L] studio version is on the B-side of #11 above	$5		Philadelphia I. 3558
5/3/75	45	9		18 **Give The People What They Want**..........RB[1] *What Am I Waiting For*	$5		Philadelphia I. 3565
7/26/75	75	3		19 **Let Me Make Love To You**..........*Survival* (R&B flip)	$5		Philadelphia I. 3573
11/1/75+	5	17	●	20 **I Love Music (Part 1)**..........RB[1] *(Part II)*	$5		Philadelphia I. 3577
3/6/76	20	12		21 **Livin' For The Weekend**..........RB[2] *Stairway To Heaven* (R&B flip)	$5		Philadelphia I. 3587
9/11/76	49	9		22 **Message In Our Music**..........RB[1] *She's Only A Woman*	$5		Philadelphia I. 3601
1/22/77	72	4		23 **Darlin' Darlin' Baby (Sweet, Tender, Love)**..........RB[1] *A Prayer*	$5		Philadelphia I. 3610
4/29/78	4	19	●	24 **Use Ta Be My Girl**..........RB[5] *This Time Baby*	$5		Philadelphia I. 3642
9/23/78	79	3		25 **Brandy**..........*Take Me To The Stars*	$5		Philadelphia I. 3652
11/24/79+	28	13		26 **Forever Mine**..........*Get On Out And Party*	$5		Philadelphia I. 3727
8/23/80	55	11		27 **Girl, Don't Let It Get You Down**..........*You're The Girl Of My Dreams (Sho Nuff Real)* #8-16, 18-24, 26 & 27: produced by Kenny Gamble and Leon Huff	$5		TSOP 4790
3/16/96	79	8		28 **Stairway To Heaven**..........S:56 *(love version)* **PURE SOUL featuring The O'Jays** also see the B-side of #21 above (written by Kenny Gamble and Leon Huff)	$5	▮	StepSun/Interscope 98086
7/5/97	73	11		29 **What's Stopping You**..........S:49 *(3 remixes)*	$5	▮	Global Soul 34273
11/8/97	76	7		30 **Baby You Know**..........S:56 *(3 versions)*	$5	▮	Global Soul 34278

O'KAYSIONS, The LP '68

White pop-rock band from Wilson, North Carolina: Donny Weaver (vocals, organ), Wayne Pittman (guitar), Ron Turner (trumpet), Jim Speidel (sax), Jimmy Hennant (bass) and Bruce Joyner (drums).

DEBUT	PEAK	WKS	Gold	A-side (Chart Hit)..........B-side	$	Sym	Label & Number
8/17/68	5	14	●	1 **Girl Watcher**..........*Deal Me In* first released on North State 1001 in 1968 ($30) with a picture sleeve	$8		ABC 11094
11/23/68	76	6		2 **Love Machine**..........*Dedicated To The One I Love*	$8		ABC 11153

O'KEEFE, Danny BUB/LP '72

Born in 1943 in Wenatchee, Washington. Pop singer/songwriter.

DEBUT	PEAK	WKS	Gold	A-side (Chart Hit)..........B-side	$	Sym	Label & Number
9/2/72	9	13		**Good Time Charlie's Got The Blues**..........*The Valentine Pieces*	$7		Signpost 70006

OLA & THE JANGLERS '69

Pop-rock group from Sweden; led by male vocalist Ola Hakansson.

DEBUT	PEAK	WKS	Gold	A-side (Chart Hit)..........B-side	$	Sym	Label & Number
5/24/69	92	3		**Let's Dance**..........*Strolling Along*	$8		GNP Crescendo 423

OLDFIELD, Mike ROK/LP '74

Born on 5/15/53 in Reading, England. Classical-rock, multi-instrumentalist/composer.

DEBUT	PEAK	WKS	Gold	A-side (Chart Hit)..........B-side	$	Sym	Label & Number
2/23/74	7	16		**Tubular Bells**..........*(long version)* [I] theme from the movie *The Exorcist* starring Linda Blair; edited version of the 49-minute album version	$8		Virgin 55100

OL DIRTY BASTARD R&B/BUB/LP '98

Born Russell Jones on 11/15/68 in Brooklyn, New York. Member of **Wu-Tang Clan**. Also known as Dirt Megirt, Unique Ason, Osirus or Big Baby Jesus.

DEBUT	PEAK	WKS	Gold	A-side (Chart Hit)..........B-side	$	Sym	Label & Number
2/25/95	54	16		1 **Brooklyn Zoo**..........S:24 *(remix)*	$4	▮	Elektra 64477
5/20/95	62	15		2 **Shimmy Shimmy Ya**..........S:47 *(album version)*	$4	▮	Elektra 64419
6/28/97	66	9		3 **Hip Hop Drunkies**..........S:49 *(remix)* **THA ALKAHOLIKS Featuring Ol Dirty Bastard**	$4	▮	Loud/RCA 64882
8/2/97	58	10		4 **Fix**..........S:49 *(5 mixes) / Man Behind The Music* (**Queen Pen**) **BLACKstreet Featuring Ol Dirty Bastard and Slash**	$8	★*	Interscope 95011
6/27/98	15	21		5 **Ghetto Supastar (That Is What You Are)** A:11 *(3 versions)* **PRAS MICHEL featuring OL' DIRTY BASTARD & introducing MÝA** samples "Get Up, Get Into It, Get Involved" by **James Brown** and contains an interpolation of "Islands In The Stream"; from the movie *Bulworth* starring Warren Beatty	$6	T	Interscope 95021
10/23/99	33	20		6 **Got Your Money**..........A:20 / S:26 *(2 versions) / I Can't Wait / Cold Blooded* **OL' DIRTY BASTARD featuring Kelis**	$8	★*	Elektra 67022

DEBUT	PEAK	WKS	Gold	A-side (Chart Hit)...B-side	$	Sym	Label & Number
				OLEANDER ROK/LP **'01**			
				Pop-rock group from Sacramento, California: Thomas Flowers (vocals), Ric Ivanisevich (guitar), Doug Eldridge (bass) and Fred Nelson (drums).			
11/3/01	16[S]	10		**Champion** ...*(no B-side)*	$4	★	Republic 015459
				all proceeds donated to the September 11th Fund			
				OLIVE **'97**			
				Electro-pop/dance group from England: Ruth-Ann Boyle (vocals) and producers Robin Taylor-Firth and Tim Kellett.			
10/25/97	56	20		1 **You're Not Alone** ...S:64 *(remix)*	$4	▮	RCA 64999
7/15/00	60[S]	3		2 **I'm Not In Love** ...*(radio mix)*	$5	★	Maverick 16859
				OLIVER AC/BUB/LP **'69**			
				Born William Oliver Swofford on 2/22/45 in North Wilkesboro, North Carolina. Died of cancer on 2/12/2000 (age 54). Adult Contemporary singer.			
5/24/69	3	13		1 **Good Morning Starshine** ...*Can't You See*	$8		Jubilee 5659
				from the off-Broadway musical *Hair* starring Steve Curry			
8/16/69	2[2]	14	●	2 **Jean** ...AC[4] *The Arrangement*	$8	■	Crewe 334
				written by **Rod McKuen**; from the movie *The Prime Of Miss Jean Brodie* starring Maggie Smith			
11/22/69	35	9		3 **Sunday Mornin'** ...*Letmekissyouwithadream*	$6		Crewe 337
4/11/70	97	3		4 **Angelica** ...*Anna*	$6		Crewe 341
				all of above produced by **Bob Crewe**			
				OLIVIA LP **'01**			
				Born Olivia Longott in 1980 in Brooklyn, New York; raised in Queens, New York. R&B singer/rapper.			
3/17/01	15	14		**Bizounce** ...S:2 / A:73 *(PG-13 version) / (2 album snippets)*	$4	★	J Records 21026
				OLIVOR, Jane AC/BUB/LP **'78**			
				Born in 1947 in Manhattan, New York. Adult Contemporary singer.			
9/10/77	91	3		1 **Some Enchanted Evening** ...*One More Ride On The Merry-Go-Round*	$4		Columbia 10527
				from the Rodgers & Hammerstein musical *South Pacific*			
5/20/78	77	9		2 **He's So Fine** ...*Turn Away*	$4		Columbia 10724
				OLLIE & JERRY R&B **'84**			
				Dance duo of Ollie Brown and Jerry Knight (former member of **Raydio**).			
6/2/84	9	18		**Breakin'...There's No Stopping Us** ...*Showdown*	$4		Polydor 821708
				from the movie *Breakin'* starring break-dancers Adolfo Quinones and Michael Chambers			
				OLLIE & THE NIGHTINGALES R&B/BUB **'68**			
				Formed as the gospel group The Dixie Nightingales in 1950. Consisted of Ollie Nightingale (Ollie Hoskins), Quincy Clifton Billops Jr., Bill Davis, Nelson Lesure and Rochester Neal. Hoskins died on 10/26/97 (age 61). Also see **The Ovations**.			
4/6/68	73	9		**I Got A Sure Thing** ...*Girl, You Have My Heart Singing*	$8		Stax 245
				OL SKOOL R&B/LP **'98**			
				R&B group from St. Louis, Missouri: Pookie (vocals), Tony Love (guitar), Curtis Jefferson (bass) and Bobby Crawford (drums).			
2/7/98	31	13		**Am I Dreaming** ...S:16 *(2 versions) / (3 album snippets)*	$4	▮	Universal 56163
				OL SKOOL [Featuring Keith Sweat and Xscape]			
				OLSON, Rocky **'59**			
				Rockabilly singer.			
5/4/59	60	4		**Kansas City** ...*Jet Tone Boogie* (Jet Tones)	$25		Chess 1723
				B-side is a rock and roll instrumental by the Jet Tones			
				OLSSON, Nigel BUB/LP **'79**			
				Born on 2/10/49 in Merseyside, England. Drummer for **Elton John**'s band from 1971-76.			
3/1/75	91	6		1 **Only One Woman** ...*In Good Time*	$6		Rocket 40337
				written by the **Bee Gees**			
12/16/78+	18	16		2 **Dancin' Shoes** ...*Living In A Fantasy*	$5		Bang 740
4/14/79	34	12		3 **Little Bit Of Soap** ...*Thinking Of You*	$5		Bang 4800
				OLYMPICS, The **'58**			
				R&B vocal group from Compton, California: Walter Ward (lead), Eddie Lewis (tenor), Charles Fizer (baritone) and Walter Hammond (baritone; **The 3 Friends**). Recorded as The Challengers for Melatone in 1956. Melvin King replaced Fizer in 1958; remained in group as replacement for Hammond when Fizer returned in 1959. Fizer was killed on 8/14/65 (during the Watts rioting, age 25); replaced by Julian McMichael ("Mack Starr"), former lead of **The Paragons**. King left in 1966. Kenny Sinclair, formerly of **The Six Teens**, joined in 1970. McMichael died in a motorcycle accident in June 1981 (age 45). Sinclair died of cancer on 3/16/2003 (age 63). Also see **The Marathons**.			
				1)Western Movies 2)The Bounce 3)Shimmy Like Kate			
7/21/58	8	14		1 **Western Movies** H:8 / S:11 *Well!* [N]	$30		Demon 1508
				reissued on Titan 1801 with a picture sleeve in 1962; also see the B-side of #14 below			
12/8/58+	71	5		2 **(I Wanna) Dance With The Teacher** ...*Ev'rybody Needs Love*	$30		Demon 1512
2/1/60	72	7		3 **(Baby) Hully Gully /**			
				same melody as "Peanut Butter" by **The Marathons**			
9/14/59	95	1		4 **Private Eye** ... [N]	$25		Arvee 562
5/23/60	50	14		5 **Big Boy Pete** ...*The Slop*	$25		Arvee 595
				same melody as "The Jolly Green Giant" by **The Kingsmen**; also see "Surfer Street" by **The Allisons**			
9/12/60	42	11		6 **Shimmy Like Kate** ...*Workin' Hard*	$20		Arvee 5006
				adapted from the 1923 hit "I Wish I Could Shimmy Like My Sister Kate"			
12/5/60	47	11		7 **Dance By The Light Of The Moon** ...*Dodge City*	$20		Arvee 5020
				adapted from the 1844 song "Buffalo Gals" and the 1944 hit "Dance With A Dolly"			
3/27/61	76	4		8 **Little Pedro** ...*Bull Fight* (Cappy Lewis)	$20		Arvee 5023
6/19/61	94	1		9 **Dooley** ...*Stay Where You Are*	$40		Arvee 5031
4/27/63	40	10		10 **The Bounce** ...*Fireworks*	$15		Tri Disc 106
7/6/63	86	6		11 **Dancin' Holiday** ...*Do The Slauson Shuffle*	$15		Tri Disc 107
				melody adapted from Liszt's *Hungarian Rhapsody No. 2*			
5/1/65	81	5		12 **Good Lovin'** ...*Olympic Shuffle*	$12		Loma 2013

DEBUT	PEAK	WKS	Gold	A-side (Chart Hit)........B-side	$	Sym	Label & Number
				OLYMPICS, The — Cont'd			
4/30/66	**99**	2		13 **Mine Exclusively**........*Secret Agents*	$10		Mirwood 5513
10/1/66	**63**	6		14 **Baby, Do The Philly Dog**........*Western Movies*	$10		Mirwood 5523
				B-side is a new version of #1 above			
				O'MALLEY, Lenore '80			
				Female disco singer.			
7/26/80	**53**	8		**First...Be A Woman**........*Put A Rainbow In Your Heart*	$4		Polydor 2055
				OMC LP '97			
				Born Pauly Fuemana on 2/8/69 in Otara, New Zealand. Singer/songwriter. OMC stands for Otara Millionaires Club.			
4/26/97	**4**[A]	51		**How Bizarre**........			album cut
				from the album *How Bizarre* on Mercury 533435			
				O'NEAL, Alexander R&B/BUB/LP '87			
				Born on 11/15/53 in Natchez, Mississippi. Minneapolis-based R&B vocalist. Own band, Alexander, in the late 1970s. Lead singer of Flyte Tyme which included Jimmy "Jam" Harris, Terry Lewis and Monte Moir and later evolved into **The Time**. Went solo in 1980.			
2/15/86	**26**	17		1 **Saturday Love**........S:19 *Will You Satisfy?* (Cherrelle)	$3	■	Tabu 05767
				CHERRELLE with ALEXANDER O'NEAL			
7/25/87	**25**	15		2 **Fake** RB[2] S:24 / A:27 *A Broken Heart Can Mend*	$3	■	Tabu 07100
11/14/87	**70**	11		3 **Criticize**........*A Broken Heart Can Mend*	$3	■	Tabu 07600
1/23/88	**28**	14		4 **Never Knew Love Like This**........A:26 / S:28 *What's Missing* (O'Neal)	$3	■	Tabu 07646
				ALEXANDER O'NEAL featuring Cherrelle			
2/23/91	**43**	11		5 **All True Man**........A:39 *(instrumental)*	$3	▮V	Tabu 73627
				O'NEAL, Jamie C&W/LP '01			
				Born Jamie Murphy on 6/3/68 in Sydney, Australia; raised in Hawaii and Nevada. Female country singer.			
12/23/00+	**40**	20		1 **There Is No Arizona**........CW[1] A:33		V	album cut
				"45": Mercury 172177; B-side: "Frantic" (C&W #41/'02)			
6/9/01	**35**	20		2 **When I Think About Angels**........CW[1] A:26		V	album cut
				"45": Mercury 172202; B-side: "The Only Thing Wrong"; above 2 from the album *Shiver* on Mercury 170132			
				O'NEAL, Shaquille R&B/BUB/LP '93			
				Born on 3/6/72 in Newark, New Jersey. Male rapper/actor. Professional basketball player with the NBA's Orlando Magic and Los Angeles Lakers. Starred in the movies *Blue Chips*, *Kazaam* and *Steel*.			
7/3/93	**39**	17	●	1 **What's Up Doc? (Can We Rock?)**........S:21 / A:66 *(instrumental)*	$4	▮	Jive 42164
				FU-SCHNICKENS with Shaquille O'Neal (Shaq-Fu)			
10/23/93	**35**	20	●	2 **(I Know I Got) Skillz** S:15 *(remix)*	$4	▮	Jive 42177
				samples "Snake Eyes" by Main Source			
2/26/94	**47**	11		3 **I'm Outstanding**........S:18 *(remix)*	$4	▮	Jive 42201
				produced by **Erick Sermon**; samples "Outstanding" by **The Gap Band**, "The Payback" by **James Brown**, "Don't Stop The Music" by **Yarbrough & Peoples**, "Eric B. Is President" by **Eric B. & Rakim** and "Funkin' For Jamaica (N.Y.)" by Tom Browne			
11/26/94+	**78**	11		4 **Biological Didn't Bother**........S:46 *(original flow version)*	$4	▮	Jive 42267
				samples "They Reminisce Over You (T.R.O.Y.)" by **Pete Rock & C.L. Smooth**			
2/25/95	**54**[S]	4		5 **No Hook**........BUB:103 *(2 remixes) / (So U Wanna Be) Hardcore*	$4	▮	Jive 42284
				SHAQUILLE O'NEAL (featuring Prince Rakeem The RZA and Method Man)			
4/19/97	**72**[A]	1		6 **Strait Playin'**........			album cut
				from the album *You Can't Stop The Reign* on Trauma 90087			
9/13/97	**82**	7		7 **Men Of Steel**........S:59 *(instrumental)*	$3	▮	Qwest 17305
				SHAQUILLE O'NEAL, ICE CUBE, B REAL, PETER GUNZ & KRS-ONE			
				inspired by the movie *Steel* starring O'Neal			
				100 PROOF AGED IN SOUL R&B/BUB/LP '70			
				R&B vocal trio from Detroit, Michigan: Clyde Wilson ("Steve Mancha"), lead; Joe Stubbs and Eddie Anderson ("Eddie Holiday"). Stubbs, brother of Levi Stubbs of the **Four Tops**, had been in **The Contours** and **The Falcons**.			
12/20/69	**94**	2		1 **Too Many Cooks (Spoil The Soup)**........*Not Enough Love To Satisfy*	$8		Hot Wax 6904
				first pressings released as by: **AGED IN SOUL** ($12)			
9/5/70	**8**	14	●	2 **Somebody's Been Sleeping**........*I've Come To Save You*	$8		Hot Wax 7004
2/27/71	**96**	2		3 **One Man's Leftovers (Is Another Man's Feast)**..*If I Could See The Light In The Window*	$8		Hot Wax 7009
4/1/72	**45**	11		4 **Everything Good Is Bad**........*I'd Rather Fight Than Switch*	$8		Hot Wax 7202
				1 OF THE GIRLS '93			
				Black female teen vocal group from Cleveland, Ohio: Le'Shawn Sykes, Nina Creque, Ra-Deon Kirkland and Marvelous Ray Miles. Discovered and produced by **Gerald Levert**.			
6/26/93	**74**	4		**Do Da What**........A:42 *(3 album snippets)*	$3	▮	EastWest 98419
				samples "You Can Have Watergate" by **The JB's**, "Get Up And Dance" by Freedom, and "What" by **A Tribe Called Quest**			
				ONE 2 MANY AC '89			
				Pop trio from Norway: Camilla Griehsel (vocals), Jan Gisle Ytterdal (guitar) and Dag Kolsrud (keyboards). Kolsrud was **A-Ha**'s world tour musical director.			
3/25/89	**37**	13		**Downtown**........A:31 *Welcome To My City*	$3	■	A&M 1272
				ONE TO ONE '86			
				Male/female pop duo from Canada: Leslie Howe (keyboards) and Louise Reny (vocals).			
8/23/86	**92**	4		1 **Angel In My Pocket**........*Where's The Answer*	$3	■	Warner 28739
3/7/92	**95**	2		2 **Peace Of Mind (Love Goes On)** *[ONE 2 ONE]*........*(3 album snippets)*	$3	▮	A&M 1591
	★207★			**112** R&B/BUB/LP '01			
				R&B group from Atlanta, Georgia: Daron Jones (keyboards; born on 12/27/76), Michael Keith (strings; born on 12/18/76), Marvin Scandrick (keyboards; born on 9/25/74) and Quinnes Parker (drums; born on 3/24/76). All share lead vocals. Also see **Total**'s "When Boy Meets Girl."			
				1)Peaches & Cream 2)It's Over Now 3)Only You			
6/1/96	**13**	28	●	1 **Only You**........S:8 / A:32 *(remix w/***Notorious B.I.G.***) / (instrumental)*	$3	▮V	Bad Boy 79060
				samples "I Get Lifted" by **KC & The Sunshine Band**			
11/9/96+	**33**	20		2 **Come See Me**........S:22 *(instrumental)*	$3	▮	Bad Boy 79073
				Mr. Cheeks of **Lost Boyz** (rap)			

DEBUT	PEAK	WKS	Gold	A-side (Chart Hit)..........B-side	$	Sym	Label & Number
				112 — Cont'd			
3/1/97	13	28	▲	3 **Cupid** ....S:10 / A:33 *This Is Your Day* "45" issued for #1 & 3 on Bad Boy 79087	$3	▮^{V}	Bad Boy 79087
6/14/97	❶^{11}	33	▲^{3}	4 **I'll Be Missing You** .....RB^8 S:❶^9 / A:4 *We'll Always Love Big Poppa* (**The Lox**) / *Cry On* (112) **PUFF DADDY & FAITH EVANS (Featuring 112)** "tribute to **The Notorious B.I.G.**"; melody is from "Every Breath You Take" by **The Police**; also see #12 below	$6	▮*	Bad Boy 79097
8/30/97	4	25	●	5 **All Cried Out** ....S:6 / A:8 *Head Over Heels* (w/Tone & **AZ**) **ALLURE featuring 112** co-produced by **Mariah Carey** (on her own label, Crave)	$3	▮	Crave 78678
12/6/97	60	1		6 **Sky's The Limit** ....*Going Back To Cali* (Notorious B.I.G. - #26) **THE NOTORIOUS B.I.G. (Featuring 112)** samples "My Flame" by **Bobby Caldwell**	$3	▮	Bad Boy 79131
10/24/98	17	16	●	7 **Love Me** ....S:8 *(instrumental)* **112 featuring MA$E** samples "Don't You Know That?" by **Luther Vandross**	$4	★	Bad Boy 79184
3/20/99	15	25		8 **Anywhere** ....A:7 *(5 versions)* **112 [Feat. Lil' Z]**	$6	T	Bad Boy 79214
7/29/00	21	13		9 **Callin' Me** ....S:3 *(2 versions)* **LIL' ZANE feat. 112**	$4	★	Priority 53582
12/9/00+	6	20		10 **It's Over Now** ....RB^2 S:❶^2 / A:31 *(remix* w/**G. Dep** & **Shyne**) contains an interpolation of "White Lines" by **Grandmaster & Melle Mel**; also see #15 below	$4	★	Bad Boy 79366
4/14/01	4	29		11 **Peaches & Cream** A:2 / S:58 *(2 mixes) / Dance With Me* 12" single features remixes with **Ludacris** and **P. Diddy**; also see #16 below	$6	T	Bad Boy 79387
6/2/01	56^S	8		12 **I'll Be Missing You** ....*We'll Always Love Big Poppa* (**The Lox**) / Cry On (112) [R] **PUFF DADDY & FAITH EVANS (Featuring 112)** reissue of #4 above on Bad Boy/Arista's "Maximum Hits" series	$8	★*	Bad Boy 79097
9/15/01	39	20		13 **Dance With Me** ....A:34 *(3 versions)*	$6	T	Bad Boy 79413
1/26/02	58	15		14 **Hey Luv (Anything)** ....A:57 *(2 versions) / Get Away* (Mobb Deep #48^S) **MOBB DEEP (Featuring 112)**	$6	T	Loud/Columbia 79753
2/16/02	55^S	2		15 **It's Over Now** ....*(3 versions)* [R] reissue of #10 above on Bad Boy/Arista's "Maximum Hits" series	$8	★*	Bad Boy 79432
2/23/02	38^S	11		16 **Peaches & Cream** ....*(3 versions) / Dance With Me* [R] reissue of #11 above on Bad Boy/Arista's "Maximum Hits" series	$8	★	Bad Boy 79431
				ONE WAY R&B/BUB/LP **'82** R&B group from Detroit, Michigan: Al Hudson (vocals), Dave Robertson (guitar), Kevin McCord (bass) and Gregory Green (drums). Recorded from 1976-79 as Al Hudson & The Soul Partners. Signed with MCA in 1979; name changed to One Way.			
5/29/82	61	10		**Cutie Pie** ....*Give Me One More Chance*	$4		MCA 52049
				ONO, Yoko — see LENNON, John			
				ONYX R&B/BUB/LP **'93** Rap group from Jamaica, New York: Sticky Fingaz, Big D.S., Fredro Star and Suave Sonny Caesar. Big D.S. left in 1995. Star acted in the movie *Sunset Park*.			
4/3/93	81	3		1 **Throw Ya Gunz** ....S:52 *(2 versions) / Blac Vagina Finda*	$6	▮*	JMJ/RAL 74766
5/29/93	4	20	▲	2 **Slam** S:3 / A:23 *(instrumental)*	$3	▮	JMJ/RAL 77053
10/16/93	92	3		3 **Shifftee** ....*(5 versions) / Bichasniguz*	$6	▮*	JMJ/RAL 74982
8/5/95	65^S	3		4 **Live!!!** ....BUB:102 *Kill Dem All* (Kali Ranks) samples "Wherever You Are" by **Isaac Hayes**; from the rap concert movie *The Show!*	$4	▮	Def Jam 579620
11/11/95	89	5		5 **Last Dayz** ....S:56 *All We Got Iz Us (Evil Streets) / Walk In New York* samples "Love Lips" by Earl Klugh and **Bob James**	$4	▮	JMJ/RAL 577114
				OPERA TRANCE **'01** Studio production by Jean-Patrick Capdevielle from France.			
1/20/01	63^S	3		**Spente Le Stelle** ....*(2 remixes) / Cuor Senza Sangue* [F] **OPERA TRANCE featuring Emma Shapplin** operatic electronic dance tune written in 14th Century Italian style	$8	★*	Radikal 99050
				OPUS LP **'86** Pop-rock group from Austria: Herwig Rudisser (vocals), Ewald Pfleger (guitar), Kurt Rene Plisnier (keyboards), Niki Gruber (bass) and Gunter Grasmuck (drums).			
1/25/86	32	16		**Live Is Life** ....S:23 *She Loves You* [L]	$4		Polydor 883730
				ORBISON, Roy ★74★ BUB/AC/C&W/ROK/LP **'61** Born on 4/23/36 in Vernon, Texas. Died of a heart attack on 12/6/88 (age 52). Pop-rock singer/songwriter/guitarist. Had own band, the Wink Westerners, in 1952. Attended North Texas State University with **Pat Boone**. First recorded for Je-Wel in early 1956 as leader of The Teen Kings. Toured with Sun Records shows to 1958. Toured with **The Beatles** in 1963. Wife Claudette killed in a motorcycle accident on 6/7/66; two sons died in a fire in 1968. Member of the supergroup **Traveling Wilburys** in 1988. Inducted into the Rock and Roll Hall of Fame in 1987. Won Grammy's Lifetime Achievement Award in 1998. *1)Oh, Pretty Woman 2)Running Scared 3)Only The Lonely 4)Crying 5)Dream Baby*			
6/16/56	59	8		1 **Ooby Dooby** ....T:59 *Go! Go! Go!* **ROY ORBISON and Teen Kings** different version released on Je-Wel 101 as by The Teen Kings in 1956 ($3000)	$100		Sun 242
1/18/60	72	6		2 **Up Town** ....*Pretty One*	$30		Monument 412
6/6/60	2^1	21		3 **Only The Lonely (Know How I Feel)** ....*Here Comes That Song Again*	$25		Monument 421
9/19/60	9	14		4 **Blue Angel** ....*Today's Teardrops* B-side is Orbison's original version of **Rick Nelson**'s 1964 hit (written by **Gene Pitney**)	$25		Monument 425
12/12/60+	27	8		5 **I'm Hurtin'** ....*I Can't Stop Loving You*	$25	■	Monument 433
4/10/61	❶^1	17		6 **Running Scared** ....*Love Hurts* B-side first released in 1960 on **The Everly Brothers**' album *A Date With The Everly Brothers*	$20	■	Monument 438

DEBUT	PEAK	WKS	Gold	A-side (Chart Hit)...B-side	$	Sym	Label & Number
				ORBISON, Roy — Cont'd			
8/14/61	2[1]	16		7 **Crying** /			
				new version with **k.d. lang** made the Adult Contemporary charts in 1987 (#28) and 1993 (#40)			
8/7/61	25	14		8 **Candy Man**	$20	■	Monument 447
2/17/62	4	12		9 **Dream Baby (How Long Must I Dream)** ... *The Actress*	$20	■	Monument 456
6/2/62	26	10		10 **The Crowd** ... *Mama*	$20	■	Monument 461
10/6/62	25	10		11 **Léah** /			
9/22/62	33	11		12 **Workin' For The Man**	$20	■	Monument 467
				Bob Moore (orch.: #2-12)			
2/9/63	7	13		13 **In Dreams** ... *Shahdaroba*	$20	■	Monument 806
				a new version (#75 Country hit in 1987) was featured in the 1986 movie *Blue Velvet* starring Dennis Hopper			
6/8/63	22	8		14 **Falling** ... *Distant Drums*	$20	■	Monument 815
				B-side is Orbison's original version of **Jim Reeves**' 1966 #1 Country hit; also see the B-side of #24 below			
9/7/63	5	13		15 **Mean Woman Blues** /			
				#11 R&B and Country hit for **Elvis Presley** in 1957 (from the Elvis movie *Loving You*)			
9/14/63	29	10		16 **Blue Bayou**	$20		Monument 824
12/14/63	15	7		17 **Pretty Paper** ... X:27 *Beautiful Dreamer* [X]	$20		Monument 830
				written by **Willie Nelson**; Christmas charts: #27/'64 (1 week)			
4/11/64	9	11		18 **It's Over** ... *Indian Wedding*	$20	■	Monument 837
8/29/64	❶[3]	15	●	19 **Oh, Pretty Woman** ***[ROY ORBISON And The Candy Men]*** *Yo Te Amo Maria*	$20		Monument 851
				"live" version made the Adult Contemporary (#48) and Country (#89) charts in 1989			
2/13/65	21	7		20 **Goodnight** ... *Only With You*	$15		Monument 873
7/10/65	39	7		21 **(Say) You're My Girl** ... *Sleepy Hollow*	$15		Monument 891
8/21/65	25	10		22 **Ride Away** ... *Wondering*	$12	■	MGM 13386
11/6/65	46	7		23 **Crawling Back** ... *If You Can't Say Something Nice*	$12	■	MGM 13410
11/13/65	81	3		24 **Let The Good Times Roll** ... *Distant Drums*	$15		Monument 906
1/22/66	31	8		25 **Breakin' Up Is Breakin' My Heart** ... *Wait*	$12	■	MGM 13446
4/30/66	39	6		26 **Twinkle Toes** ... *Where Is Tomorrow*	$12	■	MGM 13498
8/6/66	68	5		27 **Too Soon To Know** ... *You'll Never Be Sixteen Again*	$12	■	MGM 13549
				written and recorded by **Don Gibson** in 1957 on RCA 7010 ($15)			
12/10/66+	60	7		28 **Communication Breakdown** ... *Going Back To Gloria*	$12		MGM 13634
7/29/67	52	6		29 **Cry Softly Lonely One** ... *Pistolero*	$12	■	MGM 13764
6/28/80	55	8		30 **That Lovin' You Feelin' Again** ... *Lola* (Craig Hundley)	$5		Warner 49262
				ROY ORBISON & EMMYLOU HARRIS			
				from the movie *Roadie* starring **Meat Loaf**; all of above (except #1, 8, 9, 15, 17, 24, 27 & 29) written by Orbison			
1/21/89	9	18		31 **You Got It** ... AC[2] S:6 / A:15 *The Only One*	$4	■	Virgin 99245
				written by Orbison, **Jeff Lynne** and **Tom Petty**; first released with "Crying" as the B-side			
6/20/92	74[S]	1		32 **I Drove All Night** ... *(2 album snippets)*	$6	▮	MCA 54287
				recorded in 1988; **Celine Dion**'s version charted in 2003			
				ORCHESTRAL MANOEUVRES IN THE DARK ROK/BUB/LP **'86**			
				Electro-pop group formed in England: keyboardists/vocalists Andrew McCluskey and Paul Humphreys, multi-instrumentalist Martin Cooper and drummer Malcolm Holmes. Humphreys left in 1989.			
8/31/85	26	17		1 **So In Love** ... S:23 / A:23 *Concrete Hands*	$3	■	A&M 2746
12/14/85+	63	13		2 **Secret** ... *Firegun*	$3	■	A&M 2794
3/8/86	4	20		3 **If You Leave** A:3 / S:5 *La Femme Accident*	$3	■	A&M 2811
				from the movie *Pretty In Pink* starring Molly Ringwald			
9/27/86	19	17		4 **(Forever) Live And Die** ... S:18 / A:23 *This Town*	$3	■	A&M 2872
3/12/88	16	17		5 **Dreaming** ... S:15 / A:15 *Satellite*	$3	■	A&M 3002
7/17/93	75[A]	1		6 **Stand Above Me** ... BUB:111 *Can I Believe You*	$4	▮	Virgin 12666
				ORGY ROK/LP **'99**			
				Electronic alternative-metal rock group from Los Angeles, California: Jay Gordon (vocals), Ryan Shuck (guitar), Amir Derakh (keyboards), Paige Haley (bass) and Bobby Hewitt (drums).			
2/27/99	56	20		1 **Blue Monday** ... S:30 *(5 versions) / Stitches* (ROK #18)	$8	★**	Elementree 44555
				from the movie *I Still Know What You Did Last Summer* starring **Jennifer Love Hewitt**			
4/7/01	56[S]	5		2 **Opticon** ... *(4 mixes) / Fiction (Dreams In Digital)* (ROK #6)	$8	★**	Elementree 44976
				from the movie *Valentine* starring David Boreanaz			
				ORIGINAL, The **'96**			
				Born Everett Bradley in Indiana. Dance singer/songwriter/instrumentalist. Directed and performed in the off-Broadway musical *Stomp*.			
10/19/96	66	16		**I Luv U Baby** ... A:62 *(same version)*	$5	▮	Next Plateau 1436
				ORIGINAL CASTE, The BUB **'70**			
				Pop group from Canada: Dixie Lee Innes (lead vocals), Bruce Innes, Graham Bruce, Joseph Cavender and Bliss Mackie.			
11/15/69+	34	17		**One Tin Soldier** ... *Live For Tomorrow*	$12	■	T-A 186
				version by **Coven** became the theme for the 1971 movie *Billy Jack* starring Tom Laughlin			
				ORIGINAL CASUALS, The **'58**			
				Rock and roll vocal trio from Dallas, Texas: Frederick "Gary" Mears (lead), Jay Joe Adams and Paul Kearney.			
2/24/58	42	12		**So Tough** ... S:42 / T:42 *I Love My Darling*	$25		Back Beat 503
				Alex Sample (orch.); first pressings shown only as: **THE CASUALS** ($40)			
				ORIGINAL P **'01**			
				R&B-rap-funk group consisting of former **Parliament** members: Raymond Davis, Calvin Simon, Clarence "Fuzzy" Haskins and Grady Thomas.			
9/29/01+	29[S]	25		**Jump Up In The Air** ... *(2 versions) / Atomic Dawg 2001*	$5	★	Westbound 555
				ORIGINAL P Introducing Hyped Up Westbound Soljaz			

DEBUT	PEAK	WKS	Gold	A-side (Chart Hit)......B-side	$	Sym	Label & Number

ORIGINALS, The — R&B/BUB/LP '70

R&B vocal group from Detroit, Michigan: Freddie Gorman (bass), Crathman Spencer and Henry Dixon (tenors) and Walter Gaines (baritone). Spencer replaced by Ty Hunter (of **The Glass House**) in 1971.

DEBUT	PEAK	WKS	Gold	A-side (Chart Hit)......B-side	$	Sym	Label & Number
9/27/69	14	16		1 **Baby, I'm For Real**......RB[5] *Moment Of Truth*	$10		Soul 35066
2/7/70	12	14		2 **The Bells** *I'll Wait For You*	$10		Soul 35069
8/22/70	74	6		3 **We Can Make It Baby**......*I Like Your Style* (R&B flip) first pressings show title as "We Can Make It"; above 3 written and produced by **Marvin Gaye**	$10		Soul 35074
12/19/70+	53	12		4 **God Bless Whoever Sent You**......*Desperate Young Man*	$10		Soul 35079
10/23/76	47	9		5 **Down To Love Town**......*Just To Be Closer To You*	$7		Soul 35119

ORION THE HUNTER — LP '84

Rock group formed in Boston, Massachusetts: Fran Cosmo (vocals), Barry Goudreau (guitar), Bruce Smith (bass) and Michael DeRosier (drums). Goudreau was a member of **Boston** and later with **RTZ**. Cosmo joined Boston in 1994.

DEBUT	PEAK	WKS	Gold	A-side (Chart Hit)......B-side	$	Sym	Label & Number
6/2/84	58	8		**So You Ran**......*Fast Talk*	$5		Portrait 04483

ORLANDO, Tony (& DAWN) ★115★ — BUB/AC/LP '73

Born Michael Anthony Orlando Cassavitis on 4/3/44 in Manhattan, New York (of Greek/Puerto Rican parents). At age 16 was discovered by producer Don Kirshner. In 1967, became manager of April-Blackwood Music publishing company. Lead singer of New York studio group **Wind** in 1969. In 1970, formed Dawn which featured studio vocalists Toni Wine and **Ellie Greenwich**; then in 1971, teamed with session singers Telma Hopkins (from Louisville) and Joyce Vincent (from Detroit) to form a permanent Dawn. All of their hits were produced by Hank Medress (**The Tokens**) and Dave Appell (**The Applejacks**). Trio hosted weekly TV variety show *Tony Orlando & Dawn* from 1974-76. Group split in 1977. Orlando continued solo career. Hopkins acted on TV's *Bosom Buddies, Gimme A Break* and *Family Matters*. Orlando opened the Tony Orlando Yellow Ribbon Music Theater in Branson, Missouri, in the early 1990s.

1)Tie A Yellow Ribbon Round The Ole Oak Tree 2)Knock Three Times 3)He Don't Love You (Like I Love You) 4)Candida 5)Say, Has Anybody Seen My Sweet Gypsy Rose

DEBUT	PEAK	WKS	Gold	A-side (Chart Hit)......B-side	$	Sym	Label & Number
				TONY ORLANDO:			
5/1/61	39	8		1 **Halfway To Paradise**......*Lonely Tomorrows* picture sleeve also issued with a promotional text insert	$15	■	Epic 9441
8/14/61	15	12		2 **Bless You**......*Am I The Guy* also issued with a promotional text sleeve	$15	■	Epic 9452
11/27/61	82	3		3 **Happy Times (Are Here To Stay)**......*Lonely Am I* all of above arranged by **Carole King**	$15	■	Epic 9476
9/6/69	28	9		4 **Make Believe** *[WIND]*......*Groovin With Mr. Bloe* B-side charted in 1970 as by **Cool Heat** (#89)	$7		Life 200
				DAWN:			
7/25/70	3	18	●	5 **Candida**......*Look At...*	$6		Bell 903
11/21/70+	1[3]	18	●	6 **Knock Three Times**......*Home* **Tony Orlando** with Toni Wine and **Ellie Greenwich** (vocals, above 2)	$6		Bell 938
3/27/71	25	8		7 **I Play And Sing**......*Get Out From Where We Are*	$5		Bell 970
6/19/71	33	10		8 **Summer Sand**......*The Sweet Soft Sounds Of Love*	$5		Bell 45,107
				DAWN Featuring Tony Orlando:			
10/2/71	39	9		9 **What Are You Doing Sunday**......*The Sweet Soft Sounds Of Love*	$5		Bell 45,141
1/29/72	79	4		10 **Runaway/Happy Together**......*Don't Act Like A Baby*	$5		Bell 45,175
6/24/72	95	3		11 **Vaya Con Dios**......*I Can't Believe How Much I Love You* #1 hit for **Les Paul & Mary Ford** in 1953	$5		Bell 45,225
11/25/72+	70	8		12 **You're A Lady**......*In The Park*	$5		Bell 45,285
2/17/73	1[4]	23	●	13 **Tie A Yellow Ribbon Round The Ole Oak Tree** AC[2] *I Can't Believe How Much I Love You*	$5		Bell 45,318
7/14/73	3	16	●	14 **Say, Has Anybody Seen My Sweet Gypsy Rose** ..AC[3] *The Spark Of Love Is Kindlin'*	$5		Bell 45,374
				TONY ORLANDO & DAWN:			
11/10/73	27	12		15 **Who's In The Strawberry Patch With Sally**......*Ukulele Man*	$5		Bell 45,424
3/30/74	81	5		16 **It Only Hurts When I Try To Smile**......*Sweet Summer Days Of My Life*	$5		Bell 45,450
8/24/74	7	13		17 **Steppin' Out (Gonna Boogie Tonight)**......*She Can't Hold A Candle To You*	$5		Bell 45,601
12/21/74+	11	12		18 **Look In My Eyes Pretty Woman**......*My Love Has No Pride*	$5		Bell 45,620
3/15/75	1[3]	14	●	19 **He Don't Love You (Like I Love You)**......AC[1] *Pick It Up*	$4		Elektra 45240
6/21/75	14	10		20 **Mornin' Beautiful**......*Dance, Rosie, Dance*	$4		Elektra 45260
8/30/75	34	7		21 **You're All I Need To Get By**......*I Know You Like A Book*	$4		Elektra 45275
11/1/75	49	5		22 **Skybird**......*That's The Way A Wallflower Grows*	$4		Arista 0156
2/7/76	22	9		23 **Cupid**......*(You're) Growin' On Me*	$4		Elektra 45302
4/2/77	58	4		24 **Sing**......*Sweet On Candy*	$4		Elektra 45387
7/7/79	54	6		25 **Sweets For My Sweet** *[TONY ORLANDO]*......*High Steppin'*	$4		Casablanca 991

ORLEANS — BUB/AC/C&W/LP '75

Pop-rock group formed in New York: **John Hall** (vocals, guitar; born on 10/25/47) (see #6 & 7 below), brothers Lawrence (vocals, guitar) and Lance (bass) Hoppen, Jerry Marotta (keyboards), and Wells Kelly (drums). Hall and Marotta left in 1977; replaced by Bob Leinback (keyboards) and R.A. Martin (horns). Kelly died on 10/29/84 (age 35).

DEBUT	PEAK	WKS	Gold	A-side (Chart Hit)......B-side	$	Sym	Label & Number
4/26/75	55	7		1 **Let There Be Music**......*Give One Heart*	$5		Asylum 45243
7/19/75	6	18	●	2 **Dance With Me**......*Ending Of A Song*	$5		Asylum 45261
7/31/76	5	18	●	3 **Still The One** *Siam Sam*	$5		Asylum 45336
1/29/77	51	8		4 **Reach**......*Sweet Destiny*	$5		Asylum 45375
3/24/79	11	15		5 **Love Takes Time**......*Isn't It Easy*	$4		Infinity 50,006
				THE JOHN HALL BAND:			
12/26/81+	42	11		6 **Crazy (Keep On Falling)**......*Can't Stand To See You Go*	$4		EMI America 8096
1/22/83	64	10		7 **Love Me Again**......*Nobody Knows*	$4		EMI America 8151

DEBUT	PEAK	WKS	Gold	A-side (Chart Hit)..........B-side	$	Sym	Label & Number
	★576★			**ORLONS, The** BUB/LP **'62** R&B group from Philadelphia, Pennsylvania: Rosetta Hightower (lead; born on 6/23/44), Marlena Davis (born on 10/4/44), Steve Caldwell (born on 11/22/42) and Shirley Brickley (born on 12/9/44). Davis and Caldwell left in 1964; replaced by Audrey Brickley. Disbanded in 1968. Shirley Brickley was shot to death on 10/13/77 (age 32).			
6/9/62	2[2]	14		1 **The Wah Watusi** *Holiday Hill*	$20		Cameo 218
10/13/62	4	15		2 **Don't Hang Up**..........*The Conservative*	$20	■	Cameo 231
2/16/63	3	13		3 **South Street**..........*Them Terrible Boots*	$20	■	Cameo 243
6/15/63	12	10		4 **Not Me**..........*My Best Friend* written and charted ("Bubbled Under" #116 in 1961) by **Gary (U.S.) Bonds**	$20	■	Cameo 257
9/28/63	19	9		5 **Cross Fire!**..........*It's No Big Thing* some pressings show title as "Crossfire!"	$20	■	Cameo 273
12/14/63+	55	6		6 **Bon-Doo-Wah**..........*Don't Throw Your Love Away* calypso song recorded in 1958 by **The Kingston Trio** as "Banua"	$15	■	Cameo 287
2/1/64	66	5		7 **Shimmy Shimmy**..........*Everything Nice*	$15	■	Cameo 295
5/16/64	66	6		8 **Rules Of Love**..........*Heartbreak Hotel* all of above (except #4 & 7) written by Dave Appell (**The Applejacks**) and Kal Mann	$15	■	Cameo 319
8/29/64	64	6		9 **Knock! Knock! (Who's There?)**..........*Goin' Places*	$15	■	Cameo 332
				OR-N-MORE **'91** Dance duo from New York: female singer Orfeh and producer Mike More.			
8/31/91	46	8		**Everyotherday**..........A:50 *(2 versions)* **Father MC** (rap)	$3	▮	EMI 50359
				ORPHEUS LP **'69** Soft-rock group from Boston, Massachusetts: Bruce Arnold (vocals, guitar), Jack McKenes (guitar), John Eric Gulliksen (bass) and Harry Sandler (drums).			
5/31/69	91	3		1 **Brown Arms In Houston**..........*I Can Make The Sun Rise*	$7	■	MGM 14022
8/23/69	80	7		2 **Can't Find The Time**..........*Lesley's World* originally "Bubbled Under" (#111) on 3/9/68	$7		MGM 13882
				ORR, Benjamin — see CARS, The			
				ORRALL, Robert Ellis C&W/LP **'83** Born on 5/4/55 in Winthrop, Massachusetts. Country-pop singer/songwriter/pianist.			
3/26/83	32	12		**I Couldn't Say No**..........*The Message* (Orrall) **ROBERT ELLIS ORRALL WITH CARLENE CARTER**	$4		RCA 13431
	★461★			**OSBORNE, Jeffrey** R&B/AC/LP **'87** Born on 3/9/48 in Providence, Rhode Island. R&B singer/songwriter/drummer. Lead singer of **L.T.D.** until 1980. *1)Love Power 2)You Should Be Mine (The Woo Woo Song) 3)Don't You Get So Mad*			
6/5/82	39	15		1 **I Really Don't Need No Light**..........*One Million Kisses*	$4		A&M 2410
9/25/82	29	18		2 **On The Wings Of Love**..........*I'm Beggin'*	$4	■	A&M 2434
3/19/83	76	5		3 **Eenie Meenie**..........*New Love*	$4		A&M 2530
7/16/83	25	14		4 **Don't You Get So Mad**..........*So Much Love*	$4		A&M 2561
10/15/83+	30	21		5 **Stay With Me Tonight**..........*Baby*	$4		A&M 2591
2/25/84	48	12		6 **We're Going All The Way**..........*Two Wrongs Don't Make A Right*	$4	■	A&M 2618
8/18/84	40	12		7 **The Last Time I Made Love**..........*Different Now* (Kennedy) **JOYCE KENNEDY & JEFFREY OSBORNE**	$4		A&M 2656
10/13/84	44	15		8 **Don't Stop**..........*Forever Mine*	$4	■	A&M 2687
1/19/85	38	11		9 **The Borderlines**..........*I'll Make Believe* all of above (except #7) produced by **George Duke**	$4		A&M 2695
5/24/86	13	19		10 **You Should Be Mine (The Woo Woo Song)**..........S:13 / A:16 *Who Would Have Guessed* (w/Portia Griffin)	$4	■	A&M 2814
7/11/87	12	14		11 **Love Power** AC[1] S:7 / A:14 *In A World Such As This* (Warwick) **DIONNE WARWICK & JEFFREY OSBORNE**	$3	■	Arista 9567
8/20/88	48	11		12 **She's On The Left**..........RB[1] *A Second Chance*	$3	■	A&M 1227
				OSBORNE, Joan LP **'96** Born on 7/8/62 in Anchorage, Kentucky. Adult Alternative singer/songwriter/guitarist.			
12/9/95+	4	22	●	**One Of Us**..........S:5 / A:5 *Dracula Moon* written by Eric Bazilian (**Hooters**); contains an introduction of "The Airplane Ride" by Nell Hampton	$3	▮	Blue Gorilla 852368
				OSBORNE BROTHERS, The LP **'02** Bluegrass duo of brothers from Hyden, Kentucky: Bobby (mandolin; born on 12/7/31) and Sonny (banjo; born on 10/29/37) Osborne. Charted 19 Country hits, 1958-96.			
9/14/02	62[S]	3		**Rocky Top**..........*(3 versions)* original version made the Country charts (#33) in 1968; above version made the Country Sales charts as "Rocky Top '96" in 1996; popularized due to play at the Tennessee Volunteers football games; "45": MCA 53587; B-side: "Up This Hill And Down" (C&W #41/'66)	$5	★[V]	Decca 55274
				OSBOURNE, Kelly **'02** Born on 10/27/84 in London, England. Daughter of **Ozzy Osbourne**.			
7/13/02	74	2		**Papa Don't Preach**..........S:4 / A:73 *(karaoke/instrumental version)*	$5	★[+]	Epic 79794
				OSBOURNE, Ozzy ROK/BUB/LP **'92** Born John Michael Osbourne on 12/3/48 in Birmingham, England. Hard-rock singer; former lead singer of **Black Sabbath** (1967-79, periodic reunions since). Controversial in his concert antics. Married his manager Sharon Arden on 7/4/82. Appeared in the 1986 movie *Trick Or Treat*. MTV began airing *The Osbournes*, a reality show based on his family's home life, in 2002.			
3/22/86	68	9		1 **Shot In The Dark**..........*You Said It All*	$5	■	CBS Associated 05810
3/4/89	8	25	●	2 **Close My Eyes Forever**..........S:4 / A:13 *Under The Gun* (Ford) **LITA FORD (with Ozzy Osbourne)**	$3	■	RCA 8899
11/30/91+	71	9		3 **No More Tears**..........S:40 *(edited version)* "45": CBS Associated 73973; B-side: "S.I.N."	$3	▮[V]	Epic Associated 73973
2/15/92	28	17		4 **Mama, I'm Coming Home**..........S:17 / A:75 *Don't Blame Me*	$3	▮[V]	Epic Associated 74093
				OSKAR, Lee — see WAR			

DEBUT	PEAK	WKS	Gold	A-side (Chart Hit)..................B-side	$	Sym	Label & Number

OSMOND, Donny ★176★ BUB/AC/LP '71

Born on 12/9/57 in Ogden, Utah. Seventh son of George and Olive Osmond. Became a member of **The Osmonds** in 1963. Co-hosted both the musical/variety series *Donny & Marie* with his sister **Marie Osmond** and later the daytime talk show of the same name. Owned production company Night Star. In the 1990s, starred in the long-running stage production of *Joseph and the Amazing Technicolor Dreamcoat.*

1)Go Away Little Girl 2)Soldier Of Love 3)Puppy Love 4)Sweet And Innocent 5)The Twelfth Of Never

DEBUT	PEAK	WKS	Gold	A-side (Chart Hit)..................B-side	$	Sym	Label & Number
3/27/71	7	16	●	1 **Sweet And Innocent** *[DONNY OSMOND of The Osmonds]* .... *Flirtin'* original version recorded in 1958 by **Roy Orbison** on RCA Victor 7381 ($40)	$7	■	MGM 14227
8/7/71	❶[3]	15	●	2 **Go Away Little Girl** *The Wild Rover (Time To Ride)*	$6		MGM 14285
11/27/71+	9	10	●	3 **Hey Girl** /			
11/27/71		10		4 **I Knew You When**	$6		MGM 14322
2/26/72	3	12	●	5 **Puppy Love** .... *Let My People Go*	$6		MGM 14367
6/10/72	13	9		6 **Too Young** .... *Love Me* #1 hit for **Nat "King" Cole** in 1951	$6		MGM 14407
8/26/72	13	12		7 **Why** /			
9/16/72		9		8 **Lonely Boy**	$5		MGM/Kolob 14424
3/3/73	8	13	●	9 **The Twelfth Of Never** .... *Life Is Just What You Make It*	$5	■	MGM/Kolob 14503
7/28/73	23	9		10 **A Million To One** /			
7/14/73	25	11		11 **Young Love**	$5		MGM/Kolob 14583
11/24/73+	14	13		12 **Are You Lonesome Tonight** / #4 hit for Vaughn Deleath in 1927			
11/24/73	55	13		13 **When I Fall In Love** .... #20 hit for **Doris Day** in 1952	$5		MGM/Kolob 14677
2/15/75	50	7		14 **I Have A Dream** .... *I'm Dyin'* #5-14: produced by **Mike Curb** and **Don Costa**	$5		MGM/Kolob 14781
6/5/76	38	11		15 **C'mon Marianne** .... *Old Man Auctioneer*	$5		Polydor/Kolob 14320
3/25/89	2[1]	18		16 **Soldier Of Love** .... S:❶[1] / A:4 *My Secret Touch*	$3	■	Capitol 44369
6/17/89	13	16		17 **Sacred Emotion** .... A:11 / S:15 *Groove*	$3	■	Capitol 44379
9/30/89	73	7		18 **Hold On** .... *Only Heaven Knows*	$3		Capitol 44423
10/13/90	21	16		19 **My Love Is A Fire** .... A:18 / S:28 *(remix) / Eyes Don't Lie*	$3	▮	Capitol 44634
1/19/91	54	12		20 **Sure Lookin'** .... *(remix) / Take Another Try (At Love)*	$3	▮	Capitol 44670

OSMOND, Donny And Marie LP '74

Brother-and-sister co-hosts of own musical/variety TV series and later of own daytime talk show. Starred in the movie *Goin' Coconuts.*

DEBUT	PEAK	WKS	Gold	A-side (Chart Hit)..................B-side	$	Sym	Label & Number
7/6/74	4	15	●	1 **I'm Leaving It (All) Up To You** AC[1] *The Umbrella Song* first recorded by Don & Dewey in 1957 on Specialty 610 ($30)	$5		MGM/Kolob 14735
11/16/74+	8	16		2 **Morning Side Of The Mountain** .... AC[1] *One Of These Days* #16 hit for Paul Weston in 1951	$5		MGM/Kolob 14765
6/7/75	44	6		3 **Make The World Go Away** .... *Living On My Suspicion*	$5		MGM/Kolob 14807
12/13/75+	14	23		4 **Deep Purple** .... *Take Me Back Again* #1 hit for Larry Clinton in 1939	$5		MGM/Kolob 14840
				DONNY & MARIE:			
11/27/76+	21	13		5 **Ain't Nothing Like The Real Thing** .... *Sing*	$5		Polydor/Kolob 14363
11/19/77+	38	11		6 **(You're My) Soul And Inspiration** .... *Now We're Together*	$5		Polydor/Kolob 14439
10/7/78	38	10		7 **On The Shelf** .... *Certified Honey* all of above produced by **Mike Curb**	$5		Polydor/Kolob 14510

OSMOND, Little Jimmy BUB/LP '72

Born on 4/16/63 in Canoga Park, California. Youngest member of **The Osmonds**.

DEBUT	PEAK	WKS	Gold	A-side (Chart Hit)..................B-side	$	Sym	Label & Number
4/22/72	38	10		1 **Long Haired Lover From Liverpool** .... *Mother Of Mine* (#101) **LITTLE JIMMY OSMOND with The Mike Curb Congregation** first released in 1970 by **The Mike Curb Congregation** on MGM 14140	$5		MGM 14376
1/13/73	59	6		2 **Tweedlee Dee** .... *Mama'd Know What To Do*	$5		MGM/Kolob 14468

OSMOND, Marie C&W/BUB/LP '73

Born Olive Marie Osmond on 10/13/59 in Ogden, Utah. Began performing in concert with her brothers at age 14. Co-hosted both the musical/variety series *Donny & Marie* with her brother **Donny Osmond** and later the daytime talk show of the same name. Hosted own musical/variety series *Marie.* Co-hosted the TV series *Ripley's Believe It Or Not.* Emerged as a top country artist in the 1980s. Starred in the 1995 sitcom *Maybe This Time.*

DEBUT	PEAK	WKS	Gold	A-side (Chart Hit)..................B-side	$	Sym	Label & Number
9/15/73	5	16	●	1 **Paper Roses** .... CW[2] / AC[1] *Least Of All You*	$5	■	MGM/Kolob 14609
3/8/75	40	6		2 **Who's Sorry Now** .... *This I Promise You* #3 hit for Isham Jones in 1923; above 2 produced by **Sonny James**	$5		MGM/Kolob 14786
4/23/77	39	8		3 **This Is The Way That I Feel** .... *Play The Music Loud*	$5	■	Polydor/Kolob 14385

★319★ OSMONDS, The C&W/AC/LP '71

Family group from Ogden, Utah. Alan (born on 6/22/49), Wayne (born on 8/28/51), Merrill (born on 4/30/53), Jay (born on 3/2/55) and **Donny Osmond** (born on 12/9/57). Began as a quartet in 1959, singing religious and barbershop-quartet songs. Regulars on **Andy Williams'** TV show from 1962-67. Alan, Wayne, Merrill and Jay turned to country music as The Osmond Brothers in the early 1980s.

1)One Bad Apple 2)Yo-Yo 3)Down By The Lazy River

DEBUT	PEAK	WKS	Gold	A-side (Chart Hit)..................B-side	$	Sym	Label & Number
1/2/71	❶[5]	15	●	1 **One Bad Apple** *He Ain't Heavy...He's My Brother* an early picture sleeve release credits "Osmond Brothers"	$7	■	MGM 14193
3/13/71	96	1		2 **I Can't Stop** *[THE OSMOND BROTHERS]* .... *Flower Music* originally released on Uni 55015 in 1967 ($15)	$10		Uni 55276
5/15/71	14	9		3 **Double Lovin'** .... *Chilly Winds*	$6		MGM 14259

DEBUT	PEAK	WKS	Gold	A-side (Chart Hit)..........B-side	$	Sym	Label & Number
				OSMONDS, The — Cont'd			
9/11/71	3	13	●	4 **Yo-Yo** ....*Keep On My Side*	$6		MGM 14295
				written by **Joe South**; "Bubbled Under" (#117) for **Billy Joe Royal** in 1966			
1/22/72	4	14	●	5 **Down By The Lazy River** ....*He's The Light Of The World*	$6		MGM 14324
7/1/72	14	9		6 **Hold Her Tight**..........*Love Is*	$6		MGM 14405
9/16/72	68	10		7 **We Can Make It Together**..........*E Fini* (Steve & Eydie)	$6	■	MGM 14383
				STEVE & EYDIE featuring The Osmonds			
10/21/72	14	12		8 **Crazy Horses**..........*That's My Girl*	$5		MGM/Kolob 14450
6/16/73	36	8		9 **Goin' Home** ....*Are You Up There?*	$5		MGM/Kolob 14562
9/8/73	36	10		10 **Let Me In**..........*One Way Ticket To Anywhere*	$5	■	MGM/Kolob 14617
8/31/74	10	13		11 **Love Me For A Reason** ....*Fever*	$5		MGM/Kolob 14746
7/26/75	22	11		12 **The Proud One**..........AC[1] *The Last Day Is Coming*	$5		MGM/Kolob 14791
10/2/76	46	9		13 **I Can't Live A Dream** ....*Check It Out*	$5		Polydor/Kolob 14348
				O'SULLIVAN, Gilbert AC/BUB/LP **'72**			
				Born Raymond O'Sullivan on 12/1/46 in Waterford, Ireland. Adult Contemporary singer/songwriter.			
6/17/72	❶[6]	18	●	1 **Alone Again (Naturally)** AC[6] *Save It*	$6		MAM 3619
10/28/72	2[2]	16	●	2 **Clair**..........AC[3] *Ooh-Wakka-Doo-Wakka-Day*	$6	■	MAM 3626
3/3/73	17	15		3 **Out Of The Question**..........*Everybody Knows*	$6		MAM 3628
6/23/73	7	15	●	4 **Get Down**..........*A Very Extraordinary Sort Of Girl*	$6		MAM 3629
10/13/73	25	10		5 **Ooh Baby**..........*Good Company*	$6		MAM 3633
3/23/74	62	7		6 **Happiness Is Me And You** ....*Breakfast Dinner And Tea*	$6		MAM 3636
				all of above written by O'Sullivan and produced by Gordon Mills			
				OTHER ONES, The LP **'87**			
				Pop-rock group consisting of Australian siblings Jayney (vocals), Alf (vocals) and Johnny (bass) Klimek, and Germans Andreas Schwarz-Ruszczynski (guitar), Stephen Gottwald (keyboards) and Uwe Hoffmann (drums).			
4/18/87	53	9		1 **We Are What We Are**..........*Islands*	$4	■	Virgin 99473
8/1/87	29	17		2 **Holiday** ....A:28 / S:32 *Dark Ages*	$4	■	Virgin 99428
				OTIS, Johnny, Show R&B **'58**			
				Born John Veliotes on 12/8/21 in Vallejo, California (of Greek parentage). R&B bandleader/composer. Wrote "Every Beat Of My Heart." Johnny's R&B Caravan featured the top R&B artists of the 1950s. Inducted into the Rock and Roll Hall of Fame in 1994.			
6/23/58	9	16		1 **Willie And The Hand Jive** ....H:9 / S:14 / A:17 *Ring-A-Ling*	$30		Capitol 3966
11/10/58	87	4		2 **Crazy Country Hop** ....*Willie Did The Cha Cha*	$25		Capitol 4060
4/27/59	52	5		3 **Castin' My Spell** ....*Telephone Baby*	$25		Capitol 4168
				Marci Lee (female vocal)			
2/15/60	80	2		4 **Mumblin' Mosie** ....*Hey Baby, Don't You Know?*	$20		Capitol 4326
				OTIS & CARLA — see REDDING, Otis / THOMAS, Carla			
				O-TOWN BUB/LP **'01**			
				Male teen pop vocal group from Orlando, Florida: Trevor Penick, Jacob Underwood, Ashley Parker Angel, Erik-Michael Estrada and Dan Miller. Group was put together while auditioning for the TV series *Making The Band*.			
12/23/00+	10	12	●	1 **Liquid Dreams** ....S:❶[1] *(matrix remix) / All For Love*	$4	★[V]	J Records 21001
				"45": J Records 21006; CD package includes 1 of 5 artist trading cards; the first #1 *Hot 100 Sales* hit that did not make the *Hot 100 Airplay* chart			
6/9/01	3	20		2 **All Or Nothing** ....S:4 / A:10 *(2 mixes) / Liquid Dreams (remix) / Take Me Under (live) / We Fit Together* (#104)	$8	★*[V]	J Records 21056
				"45": J Records 21060; B-side: (radio mix)			
12/7/02	64	5		3 **These Are The Days**..........A:68		V	album cut
				from the album *O2* on J Records 20033; "45": J Records 21174; B-side: "I Showed Her"			
				OUR LADY PEACE ROK/LP **'02**			
				Rock group from Toronto, Ontario, Canada: Raine Maida (vocals), Mike Turner (guitar), Duncan Coutts (bass) and Jeremy Taggart (drums).			
10/4/97	74[A]	2		1 **Superman's Dead**			album cut
12/27/97+	59[A]	16		2 **Clumsy**..........			album cut
				from the movie *I Know What You Did Last Summer* starring Jennifer Love Hewitt; above 2 from the album *Clumsy* on Columbia 67940			
8/24/02	44	20		3 **Somewhere Out There** A:46			album cut
				from the album *Gravity* on Columbia 86585			
				OUTFIELD, The ROK/LP **'86**			
				Pop-rock trio formed in London, England: Tony Lewis (vocals, bass), John Spinks (guitar, songwriter) and Alan Jackman (drums). Jackman left by 1990; Lewis and Spinks continued as a duo.			
2/15/86	6	22		1 **Your Love** S:6 / A:6 *61 Seconds*	$3	■	Columbia 05796
6/7/86	19	16		2 **All The Love In The World**..........A:17 / S:21 *Taking My Chances*	$3	■	Columbia 05894
9/20/86	66	10		3 **Everytime You Cry** ....*Tiny Lights*	$3	■	Columbia 06295
6/13/87	31	15		4 **Since You've Been Gone** ....A:31 / S:32 *Better Than Nothing*	$3	■	Columbia 07170
3/25/89	25	14		5 **Voices Of Babylon**..........S:23 / A:25 *Inside Your Skin*	$3		Columbia 68601
7/22/89	72	6		6 **My Paradise**..........*Somewhere In America '89*	$3		Columbia 68943
11/3/90+	21	18		7 **For You**..........S:21 / A:22 *(3 album snippets)*	$3	▮	MCA 53935
5/16/92	43	11		8 **Closer To Me** ....A:50 *(3 album snippets)*	$3	▮	MCA 54378
				OUTHERE BROTHERS, The **'95**			
				Male rap-dance duo from Chicago, Illinois: Malik and Hula.			
9/30/95	65	20		**Boom Boom Boom** ....A:66 *(club mix)*	$6	▮	Aureus 1100
	★462★			**OUTKAST** R&B/BUB/LP **'01**			
				Male rap duo from Atlanta, Georgia: Andre "Dre" Benjamin (born on 5/27/75) and Antoine "Big Boi" Patton (born on 2/1/75). Also see **Missy "Misdemeanor" Elliott**'s "All N My Grill."			
				1)Ms. Jackson 2)Elevators (me & you) 3)The Whole World			
2/26/94	37	20	●	1 **Player's Ball**..........S:15 *(instrumental)*	$4	▮	LaFace 24060
7/16/94	74	10		2 **Southernplayalisticadillacmuzik**..........S:38 *(instrumental)*	$4	▮	LaFace 24070
11/19/94	75[S]	1		3 **Git Up, Git Out** ....BUB:109 *(instrumental)*	$4	▮	LaFace 24085
				OutKast (featuring The Goodie Mob)			

DEBUT	PEAK	WKS	Gold	A-side (Chart Hit)...B-side	$	Sym	Label & Number
				OUTKAST — Cont'd			
7/27/96	**12**	20	●	4 **Elevators (me & you)** ...S:5 *(instrumental)* Debra Killins and Sleepy Brown (background vocals)	$3	▌	LaFace 24177
11/30/96+	**35**	17		5 **ATLiens** ...S:23 *Wheelz Of Steel* (R&B flip)	$3	▌	LaFace 24196
4/12/97	**52**	14		6 **Jazzy Belle** ...S:35 *(album version)*	$3	▌	LaFace 24224
6/27/98	**50**	15		7 **Black Ice (Sky High)** ...S:31 *(**Goodie Mob** version) / (instrumental)* **GOODIE MOB featuring Outkast** clean version available on LaFace 24332	$3	▌	LaFace 24337
12/5/98+	**55**	17		8 **Rosa Parks** ...A:37 from the album *Aquemini* on LaFace 26053			album cut
1/30/99	**73**	10		9 **Watch For The Hook** ...S:20 *(instrumental)* **COOL BREEZE Featuring OutKast, Goodie Mob & Witchdoctor** samples **Neil Young**'s "Southern Man" performed by **Merry Clayton**	$4	★	Organized Noize 97046
11/11/00+	❶[1]	23		10 **Ms. Jackson** RB[2] S:2 / A:3 *(instrumental) / Sole Sunday* (w/**Goodie Mob**)	$8	★*	LaFace 24525
3/3/01	**30**	20		11 **So Fresh, So Clean** ...A:24 / S:64 *(2 versions) / Gangsta Sh*t* (w/**Slimm Calhoun**, *C-Bone & T-Mo Goodie*)	$6	T	LaFace 24537
12/22/01+	**19**	20		12 **The Whole World** ...A:17 / S:46 *(3 versions)* **OUTKAST Featuring Killer Mike & Joi**	$6	T	LaFace 24550
				OUTLAWS BUB/LP **'81** Rock group formed in Tampa, Florida: **Henry Paul** (vocals, guitar), Hughie Thomasson and Billy Jones (guitars), Frank O'Keefe (bass) and Monte Yoho (drums). By 1981, Freddie Salem, Rick Cua and David Dix had replaced Paul, O'Keefe and Yoho. Paul was a member of the country trio **Blackhawk** by 1993. Jones died on 2/7/95 (age 45). O'Keefe died of a drug overdose on 2/26/95 (age 44).			
9/6/75	**34**	10		1 **There Goes Another Love Song** ...*Keep Prayin'*	$6		Arista 0150
7/4/76	**94**	2		2 **Breaker - Breaker** ...*South Carolina*	$6		Arista 0188
7/30/77	**60**	5		3 **Hurry Sundown** ...*So Afraid*	$6		Arista 0258
12/27/80+	**31**	15		4 **(Ghost) Riders In The Sky** ...*Devil's Road* #1 hit for **Vaughn Monroe** in 1949	$6		Arista 0582
				OUTLAWZ — see 2PAC			
				OUTSIDERS, The BUB/LP **'66** Rock group from Cleveland, Ohio: Sonny Geraci (lead singer), Tom King (guitar), Bill Bruno (lead guitar), Mert Madsen (bass) and Rick Baker (drums). Geraci later led the group **Climax**.			
2/19/66	**5**	15		1 **Time Won't Let Me** ...*Was It Really Real*	$12		Capitol 5573
5/14/66	**21**	9		2 **Girl In Love** ...*What Makes You So Bad You Weren't Brought Up That Way*	$12	■	Capitol 5646
8/6/66	**15**	8		3 **Respectable** ...*Lost In My World* written by **The Isley Brothers**	$12		Capitol 5701
10/29/66	**37**	10		4 **Help Me Girl** ...*You Gotta Look*	$10	■	Capitol 5759
				OUTSIDERZ 4 LIFE **'01** White male pop vocal group from Newport News, Virginia: Todd White, Alan Healy, Dave Smith, Jimmy Marble and Jason Dowty.			
2/10/01	**18**[S]	11		**[Not Enough]** ...*(album version) / Sex On The Beach*	$4	★	Blackground 38763
				OVATIONS, The R&B/BUB **'73** R&B group led by Louis Williams. Re-formed in 1972 with former members of **Ollie & The Nightingales**: Rochester Neal, Bill Davis and Quincy Billops (**The Mad Lads**). Williams died on 10/13/2002 (age 61).			
5/22/65	**61**	6		1 **It's Wonderful To Be In Love** ...*Dance Party* **THE OVATIONS (featuring Louis Williams)**	$15		Goldwax 113
10/13/73	**56**	9		2 **"Having A Party" medley** ...*Just Too Good To Be True* remake of **Sam Cooke**'s hit infused with a line or 2 of other top R&B hits	$8		MGM 14623
				OVERLANDERS, The **'64** Male pop group from England: Paul Arnold, Laurie Mason, Pete Bartholomew, Terry Widlake and David Walsh.			
5/23/64	**75**	7		**Yesterday's Gone** ...*Gone The Rainbow*	$15		Hickory 1258
				OVIS **'94** Born in New Orleans, Louisiana. Male singer/songwriter. As a sound engineer, worked with **The B-52s**, **Green Jelly** and **Tiffany**.			
4/23/94	**72**	13		**Regular Thang** ...A:56 *Too Beautiful People*	$4	▌	Restless 72760
				OWEN, Reg, And His Orchestra **'59** Born in 1928 in England. Orchestra leader. Also see **The Knightsbridge Strings**.			
12/8/58+	**10**	16		**Manhattan Spiritual** ...*Ritual Blues* [I]	$15		Palette 5005
				OWEN B. **'70** Rock group from Columbus, Ohio; led by Robert L. Ross.			
3/7/70	**97**	2		**Mississippi Mama** ...*Nowhere To Run*	$8		Janus 107
				OWENS, Buck C&W/BUB/LP **'65** Born Alvis Edgar Owens on 8/12/29 in Sherman, Texas; raised in Mesa, Arizona. Country singer/guitarist/songwriter (charted 21 #1 hits, 1963-88). Moved to Bakersfield, California, in 1951. Owens and **Roy Clark** hosted TV's *Hee Haw*, 1969-86. Backing group: The Buckaroos. *1)I've Got A Tiger By The Tail 2)Waitin' In Your Welfare Line 3)Buckaroo*			
7/4/64	**94**	2		1 **My Heart Skips A Beat** ...CW[7] *Together Again* (C&W #1)	$12		Capitol 5136
8/22/64	**92**	3		2 **I Don't Care (Just as Long as You Love Me)** ...CW[6] *Don't Let Her Know* (#130/C&W #33)	$12		Capitol 5240
1/23/65	**25**	9		3 **I've Got A Tiger By The Tail** CW[5] *Cryin' Time*	$12	■	Capitol 5336
5/15/65	**83**	2		4 **Before You Go** ...CW[6] *(I Want) No One But You*	$12	■	Capitol 5410
11/13/65	**60**	9		5 **Buckaroo** *[BUCK OWENS & His Buckaroos]* ...CW[2] *If You Want A Love* (C&W #24) [I]	$12	■	Capitol 5517
12/11/65	**2**[2X]	6		6 **Santa Looked A Lot Like Daddy** ...*All I Want For Christmas Dear Is You* [X] X: 2/'65; 18/'67	$15	■	Capitol 5537
1/29/66	**57**	7		7 **Waitin' In Your Welfare Line** ...CW[7] *In The Palm Of Your Hand* (C&W #43)	$10		Capitol 5566
				BUCK OWENS And The Buckaroos:			
5/28/66	**74**	5		8 **Think Of Me** ...CW[6] *Heart Of Glass*	$10	■	Capitol 5647

DEBUT	PEAK	WKS	Gold	A-side (Chart Hit)...B-side	$	Sym	Label & Number
				OWENS, Buck — Cont'd			
4/15/67	**92**	2		9 **Sam's Place** ...CW^{3} *Don't Ever Tell Me Goodbye*	$10	■	Capitol 5865
12/7/68	**5^{X}**	4		10 **Christmas Shopping** ...*One Of Everything You Got* [X]	$8	■	Capitol 2328
12/13/69	**100**	1		11 **Big In Vegas** ...*White Satin Bed*	$8	■	Capitol 2646
				OWENS, Donnie '58			
				Born on 10/30/38 in Pennsylvania. Accidentally shot to death on 10/27/94 (age 55). Pop singer/guitarist. Played guitar for **Duane Eddy**'s Rebels.			
10/6/58	**25**	15		**Need You** ...H:25 *If I'm Wrong*	$25		Guyden 2001
				The Ben Denton Singers (backing vocals); **Duane Eddy** (acoustic guitar)			
				OXO LP '83			
				Pop-rock group from Miami, Florida: Ish "Angel" Ledesma (vocals; **Foxy**, **Company B**), Orlando (guitar), Frank Garcia (bass) and Freddy Alwag (drums).			
2/19/83	**28**	14		**Whirly Girl** ...*In The Stars*	$4	■	Geffen 29765
				OZARK MOUNTAIN DAREDEVILS BUB/C&W/LP '75			
				Country-rock group from Springfield, Missouri: **Larry Lee** (vocals, drums) (see #6 below), John Dillon (guitar), Steve Cash (harmonica) and Michael Granda (bass).			
4/20/74	**25**	16		1 **If You Wanna Get To Heaven** ...*Spaceship Orion*	$6		A&M 1515
2/8/75	**3**	21		2 **Jackie Blue** *Better Days*	$6	■	A&M 1654
1/17/76	**65**	7		3 **If I Only Knew** ...*Dreams*	$5	■	A&M 1772
1/22/77	**74**	12		4 **You Know Like I Know** ...*Arroyo*	$5	■	A&M 1888
5/24/80	**67**	5		5 **Take You Tonight** ...*Runnin' Out*	$4		Columbia 11247
6/26/82	**81**	2		6 **Don't Talk** ...*Hang On*	$4		Columbia 02740
				LARRY LEE			
				OZO '76			
				British-based, pop-reggae group (eight members hail from seven different countries).			
8/14/76	**96**	3		**Listen To The Buddha** ...*Kites*	$6		DJM 1012

P

DEBUT	PEAK	WKS	Gold	A-side (Chart Hit)...B-side	$	Sym	Label & Number
				PABLO, Petey R&B/LP '01			
				Born Moses Barrett in Greenville, North Carolina. Male rapper/songwriter.			
8/11/01	**25**	21		1 **Raise Up** ...S:3 / A:24 *(2 versions) / 911 / (3 album snippets)*	$8	★*	Jive 42937
5/4/02	**94**	3		2 **I Told Y'all** ...*(3 versions)*	$6	T	Jive 40006
12/21/02	**75^{S}**	1		3 **Club Banger** ...*(3 versions)*	$6	T	Jive 40072
				from the movie *Drumline* starring Orlando Jones			
				PABLO CRUISE BUB/LP '78			
				Pop-rock group formed in San Francisco, California: Dave Jenkins (vocals, guitar), Bud Cockrell (bass, vocals; It's A Beautiful Day), Cory Lerios (keyboards, vocals) and Stephen Price (drums). Cockrell replaced by Bruce Day in 1977. John Pierce replaced Day, and guitarist Angelo Rossi joined in 1980.			
4/16/77	**6**	26		1 **Whatcha Gonna Do?** *Atlanta June*	$5	■	A&M 1920
9/17/77	**42**	9		2 **A Place In The Sun** ...*El Verano*	$5		A&M 1976
1/28/78	**87**	4		3 **Never Had A Love** ...*Atlanta June*	$5		A&M 1999
6/3/78	**6**	18		4 **Love Will Find A Way** ...*Always Be Together*	$5	■	A&M 2048
9/16/78	**21**	16		5 **Don't Want To Live Without It** ...*Raging Fire*	$5		A&M 2076
1/13/79	**46**	8		6 **I Go To Rio** ...*Raging Fire*	$5		A&M 2112
10/13/79	**19**	16		7 **I Want You Tonight** ...*Family Man*	$5		A&M 2195
7/4/81	**13**	17		8 **Cool Love** ...*Jenny*	$4		A&M 2349
10/17/81	**75**	5		9 **Slip Away** ...*That's When*	$4	■	A&M 2373
				PACIFIC GAS & ELECTRIC LP '70			
				Blues-rock group from California: Charles Allen (vocals), Glenn Schwartz and Tom Marshall (guitars), Brent Block (bass) and Frank Cook (drums). Allen spearheaded a new lineup in 1971; group name shortened to PG&E. Allen died on 5/7/90 (age 48).			
5/30/70	**14**	12		1 **Are You Ready?** ...*Staggolee*	$7		Columbia 45158
				The Blackberries (backing vocals)			
10/10/70	**93**	3		2 **Father Come On Home** ...*Elvira*	$6		Columbia 45221
3/18/72	**97**	2		3 **Thank God For You Baby** *[PG&E]*...*See The Monkey Run*	$6		Columbia 45519
				PACK, David — see AMBROSIA			
				PACKERS, The '65			
				R&B band formed by Charles "Packy" Axton (tenor sax). Axton, son of Estelle Axton, co-owner of Stax/Volt, had been in the **Mar-Keys**. Axton died in January 1974 (age 32).			
11/13/65	**43**	11		**Hole In The Wall** ...*Go 'Head On* [I]	$20		Pure Soul 1107
				PAGAN, Ralfi — see SYLVIA			
				PAGANO, Lindsay '01			
				Born in 1986 in Philadelphia, Pennsylvania. Teen female pop singer/songwriter.			
9/15/01	**8^{S}**	42		**Everything U R**...*(remix) / Burning In Me*	$4	★^{V}	Warner 16737
				PAGE, Jimmy — see PUFF DADDY			
				PAGE, Martin LP '95			
				Born on 9/23/59 in Southampton, England. Pop singer/songwriter. Wrote the hits "We Built This City," "These Dreams" and "King Of Wishful Thinking." Former member of the techno-dance duo **Q-Feel**.			
12/17/94+	**14**	35		1 **In The House Of Stone And Light** ...AC^{4} A:4 / S:55 *The Door*	$3	▮	Mercury 858940
8/19/95	**83**	7		2 **Keeper Of The Flame** ...*Broken Stairway*	$3	▮	Mercury 856862

DEBUT	PEAK	WKS	Gold	A-side (Chart Hit)......B-side	$	Sym	Label & Number

PAGE, Patti ★84★ MEM/POP/BUB/C&W/AC/LP '50

Born Clara Ann Fowler on 11/8/27 in Muskogee, Oklahoma; raised in Tulsa, Oklahoma. One of 11 children. On radio KTUL with Al Klauser & His Oklahomans, as Ann Fowler, late 1940s. Another singer was billed as "Patti Page" for the Page Milk Company show on KTUL. When she left, Fowler took her place and name. With the Jimmy Joy band in 1947. On *Breakfast Club*, Chicago radio in 1947; signed by Mercury Records. Used multi-voice effect on her recordings. Charted 39 pop hits, 1948-54, including 4 #1s: "All My Love," "The Tennessee Waltz," "I Went To Your Wedding" and "The Doggie In The Window." Own TV series *The Patti Page Show*, 1955 58, and *The Big Record*, 1957-58. In the 1960 movie *Elmer Gantry*.

1)Allegheny Moon 2)Old Cape Cod 3)Hush, Hush, Sweet Charlotte 4)Let Me Go, Lover! 5)Left Right Out Of Your Heart

DEBUT	PEAK	WKS	Gold	A-side (Chart Hit)......B-side	$	Sym	Label & Number
12/18/54	8	7		1 **Let Me Go, Lover!** ......A:8 / J:12 / S:24 *Hocus-Pocus*	$15		Mercury 70511
7/30/55	32^{CU}	1		2 **Piddily Patter Patter**......*Every Day*	$12		Mercury 70657
				#10 R&B hit in 1955 as "Pitter Patter" by **Nappy Brown**			
11/12/55	16	13		3 **Croce Di Oro (Cross Of Gold)**......T:16 / J:16 / A:17 / S:20 *Search My Heart*	$12		Mercury 70713
1/7/56	11	13		4 **Go On With The Wedding**......T:11 / J:12 / A:16 / S:17 *The Voice Inside*	$12		Mercury 70766
4/14/56	73	3		5 **Too Young To Go Steady** / T:73			
				from the musical *Strip For Action*			
3/31/56	80	4		6 **My First Formal Gown**......T:80	$12		Mercury 70820
6/16/56	2^2	27	●	7 **Allegheny Moon** / J:2 / T:2 / A:2 / S:5			
7/7/56	93	1		8 **The Strangest Romance**......T:93	$12		Mercury 70878
10/27/56	11	17		9 **Mama From The Train** / T:11 / A:12 / J:12 / S:17			
11/24/56	87	1		10 **Every Time (I Feel His Spirit)**......T:87	$12		Mercury 70971
				traditional Afro-American spiritual			
2/2/57	53	5		11 **Repeat After Me**......T:53 *Learnin' My Latin*	$12		Mercury 71015
3/2/57	14	12		12 **A Poor Man's Roses (Or A Rich Man's Gold)** / A:14 / T:27			
				a new version by Page made the Country charts (#66) in 1981			
3/16/57	43	6		13 **The Wall**......T:43	$12		Mercury 71059
5/20/57	3	23		14 **Old Cape Cod** / A:3 / T:7 / S:8			
5/20/57	12	6		15 **Wondering**......A:12 / T:35 / S:flip	$12		Mercury 71101
10/28/57	23	14		16 **I'll Remember Today**......A:23 / S:31 / T:32 *My How The Time Goes By*	$12		Mercury 71189
2/3/58	13	13		17 **Belonging To Someone**......A:13 / S:32 / T:34 *Bring Us Together*	$10		Mercury 71247
5/5/58	20	3		18 **Another Time, Another Place**......A:20 / T:81 *These Worldly Wonders*	$10		Mercury 71294
				title song from the movie starring Lana Turner			
6/30/58	9	12		19 **Left Right Out Of Your Heart (Hi Lee Hi Lo Hi Lup Up Up)**......A:9 / H:13 / S:14 *Longing To Hold You Again*	$10		Mercury 71331
9/22/58	39	9		20 **Fibbin'**......H:39 *You Will Find Your Love (In Paris)*	$10	■	Mercury 71355
1/12/59	43	9		21 **Trust In Me**......*Under The Sun Valley Moon*	$10		Mercury 71400
				#4 hit for Mildred Bailey in 1937			
4/13/59	77	4		22 **The Walls Have Ears**......*My Promise*	$10		Mercury 71428
6/15/59	59	7		23 **With My Eyes Wide Open I'm Dreaming**......*My Mother's Eyes* [R]	$10		Mercury 71469
				Page's original version charted in 1950 (#11) on Mercury 5344; #3 hit for Leo Reisman in 1934			
10/12/59	90	3		24 **Goodbye Charlie**......*Because Him Is A Baby*	$10		Mercury 71510
12/28/59+	90	3		25 **The Sound Of Music**......*Little Donkey*	$10		Mercury 71555
				title song from the Rodgers & Hammerstein musical			
4/25/60	67	2		26 **Two Thousand, Two Hundred, Twenty-Three Miles**......*Promise Me Thomas*	$10		Mercury 71597
6/6/60	31	14		27 **One Of Us (Will Weep Tonight)**......*What Will My Future Be*	$10	■	Mercury 71639
				issued with 2 different but similar picture sleeves			
10/3/60	52	7		28 **I Wish I'd Never Been Born**......*I Need You*	$10	■	Mercury 71695
12/31/60+	65	4		29 **Don't Read The Letter**......*That's All I Need To Know*	$10	■	Mercury 71745
				issued with 2 different but similar picture sleeves			
4/10/61	90	1		30 **A City Girl Stole My Country Boy**......*Dondi*	$10	■	Mercury 71792
6/26/61	46	6		31 **You'll Answer To Me** /			
6/12/61	58	6		32 **Mom And Dad's Waltz**......	$10	■	Mercury 71823
				#2 Country hit for **Lefty Frizzell** in 1951			
10/2/61	91	4		33 **Broken Heart And A Pillow Filled With Tears**......*Dark Moon*	$10	■	Mercury 71870
				written by **Paul Anka**; The Mike Stewart Singers (backing vocals: #30, 31 & 33)			
12/25/61+	42	8		34 **Go On Home**......*Too Late To Cry*	$10	■	Mercury 71906
4/21/62	27	8		35 **Most People Get Married**......*You Don't Know Me*	$8	■	Mercury 71950
8/4/62	49	9		36 **The Boys' Night Out**......*Three Fools*	$8	■	Mercury 72013
				The Merry Melody Singers (backing vocals); title song from the movie starring James Garner			
3/9/63	98	1		37 **Pretty Boy Lonely**......*Just A Simple Melody* (#114)	$8	□	Columbia 42671
6/1/63	81	7		38 **Say Wonderful Things**......*I Knew I Would See Him Again*	$8		Columbia 42791
4/24/65	8	14		39 **Hush, Hush, Sweet Charlotte**......*Longing To Hold You Again*	$8		Columbia 43251
				title song from the movie starring Bette Davis			
9/11/65	94	2		40 **You Can't Be True, Dear**......*Who's Gonna Shoe My Pretty Little Feet*	$7		Columbia 43345
				there were 8 Top 20 versions of this tune in 1948			
12/16/67	15^X	3		41 **Happy Birthday, Jesus (A Child's Prayer)**......*Christmas Bells* [X-S]	$8	■	Columbia 43447
				backing music: "Silent Night"; issued with 2 different picture sleeves			
2/10/68	66	16		42 **Gentle On My Mind**......*Excuse Me*	$6		Columbia 44353
7/6/68	96	2		43 **Little Green Apples**......*This House*	$6		Columbia 44556

Page's musical arrangers and conductors: **Don Costa** (#42, 43), **Ray Ellis** (#30, 33), Jimmie Haskell (#28, 29), Belford Hendricks (#25, 26), Jerry Kennedy (#36), Robert Mersey (#37-40), Cliff Parman (#32), Jack Rael (#1-6), Pete Rugolo (#24), Vic Schoen (#7-23) and **Hugo Winterhalter** (#31)

PAGE, Tommy LP '90

Born on 5/24/69 in West Caldwell, New Jersey. Pop singer/songwriter.

DEBUT	PEAK	WKS	Gold	A-side (Chart Hit)......B-side	$	Sym	Label & Number
2/11/89	29	20		1 **A Shoulder To Cry On**......A:27 / S:30 *Christmas Without You*	$3	■	Sire 27645
2/17/90	❶^1	18	●	2 **I'll Be Your Everything**......S:❶^1 / A:2 *I'm Falling In Love*	$3	■^{V}	Sire 19959
				backing vocals by 3 members of **New Kids On The Block**			
5/12/90	42	10		3 **When I Dream Of You**......A:32 *You're The Best Thing (That Ever Happened To Me)*	$3	■^{V}	Sire 19839

DEBUT	PEAK	WKS	Gold	A-side (Chart Hit)..........B-side	$	Sym	Label & Number
				PAGES '79			
				Rock group from Los Angeles, California: Richard Page, Steve George, Charles Johnson, Jerry Manfredi and George Lawrence. Page and George later formed **Mr. Mister**.			
12/1/79	84	3		**I Do Believe In You**..........*Two People*	$4		Epic 50769
				PAIGE, Jennifer LP '98			
				Born on 9/3/75 in Marietta, Georgia. Pop singer.			
7/4/98	3	25	●	1 **Crush**..........S:3 / A:4 *(dance mix/instrumental)*	$4	★	Edel America 64024
				originally available on Edel America 3871			
8/21/99	31^{S}	9		2 **Always You**..........*(3 album snippets)*	$4	★	Edel America 64030
				PAIGE, Kevin LP '89			
				Born on 10/10/66 in Memphis, Tennessee. Pop singer/songwriter.			
8/19/89	18	24		1 **Don't Shut Me Out**..........S:15 / A:20 *(dance mix edit)*	$3	■	Chrysalis 23389
1/20/90	29	12		2 **Anything I Want**..........A:28 / S:31 *(remix) / Don't Shut Me Out*	$3	▮	Chrysalis 23444
				PAIGE, Sharon — see MELVIN, Harold			
				PAINTER '73			
				Rock group from Canada: Doran Beattie (vocals), Barry Allen and Dan Lowe (guitars), Royden Morice (bass) and Bob Ego (drums).			
9/29/73	79	5		**West Coast Woman**..........*Space Truck*	$5		Elektra 45862
				PAISLEY, Brad C&W/LP '02			
				Born on 10/28/72 in Glen Dale, West Virginia. Country singer/songwriter/guitarist. Married actress Kimberly Williams on 3/15/2003.			
6/19/99	65	13		1 **Who Needs Pictures**..........A:57 *It Never Woulda Worked Out Anyway*	$4	★V	Arista 13156
10/23/99	30	20		2 **He Didn't Have To Be**..........CW^{1} A:20		V	album cut
				"45": Arista 13176; B-side: "I've Been Better"			
5/13/00	85	4		3 **Me Neither**..........A:74		V	album cut
				"45": Arista 13172; B-side: "Don't Breathe"			
10/14/00	29	20		4 **We Danced**..........CW^{2} A:25		V	album cut
				"45" issued for above 2 on Arista 69009; above 4 from the album *Who Needs Pictures* on Arista 18871			
4/28/01	51	18		5 **Two People Fell In Love**..........A:43		V	album cut
				"45": Arista 69051; B-side: "Me Neither"			
11/17/01+	35	20		6 **Wrapped Around**..........A:31		V	album cut
				"45": Arista 69103; B-side: "All You Really Need Is Love"			
5/4/02	29	20		7 **I'm Gonna Miss Her (The Fishin' Song)** CW^{2} A:26 [N]		V	album cut
				"45": Arista 69152; B-side: "I Wish You'd Stay"; above 3 from the album *Part II* on Arista 67008			
				PAJAMA PARTY '89			
				Female dance-pop vocal trio from New York: Daphne Rubin-Vega, Jennifer McQuilkin and Susan Ranta. Lynn Critelli and Marialisa Costanzo replaced the latter two by 1991. Rubin-Vega acted in the Broadway show *Rent*.			
5/20/89	75	10		1 **Yo No Se'**..........*(dub version)*	$3		Atlantic 88984
11/11/89	59	14		2 **Over And Over**..........*(alternative vocal version)*	$3		Atlantic 88799
3/10/90	73	10		3 **Hide And Seek**..........*(club version)*	$3	▮	Atlantic 87973
4/13/91	70^{A}	3		4 **Got My Eye On You**..........			album cut
				from the album *Can't Live Without It* on Atlantic 82207			
	★295★			**PALMER, Robert** ROK/BUB/AC/LP '86			
				Born Alan Palmer on 1/19/49 in Batley, Yorkshire, England; raised on the Mediterranean island of Malta. Formed first band Mandrake Paddle Steamer in 1969. Lead singer of short-lived supergroup **The Power Station**.			
				1)Addicted To Love 2)Simply Irresistible 3)I Didn't Mean To Turn You On			
12/4/76+	63	7		1 **Man Smart, Woman Smarter**..........*Keep In Touch*	$5		Island 075
3/25/78	16	18		2 **Every Kinda People**..........*How Much Fun*	$5		Island 100
				a new version by Palmer made the Adult Contemporary charts (#8) in 1992			
7/21/79	14	15		3 **Bad Case Of Loving You (Doctor, Doctor)**..........*Love Can Run Faster*	$5		Island 49016
12/22/79+	52	9		4 **Can We Still Be Friends**..........*Remember To Remember*	$5		Island 49137
				written and recorded by **Todd Rundgren** in 1978			
6/18/83	78	6		5 **You Are In My System**..........*Deadline*	$4	■	Island 99866
11/16/85	82	5		6 **Discipline Of Love (Why Did You Do It)**..........*Dance For Me*	$4	■	Island 99597
2/8/86	❶^{1}	22	●	7 **Addicted To Love** AR^{2} S:❶^{2} / A:2 *Let's Fall In Love Tonight*	$3	■	Island 99570
				2 different picture sleeves were issued			
6/7/86	33	12		8 **Hyperactive**..........S:29 / A:36 *Woke Up Laughing*	$3		Island 99545
8/16/86	2^{1}	22		9 **I Didn't Mean To Turn You On**..........S:2 / A:2 *Get It Through Your Heart*	$3	■	Island 99537
				above 4 produced by Bernard Edwards (**Chic**) and from the album *Riptide*			
3/26/88	94	2		10 **Sweet Lies**..........*Want You More*	$3	■	Island 99377
				title song from the movie starring Treat Williams			
7/2/88	2^{2}	20		11 **Simply Irresistible**..........AR^{3} S:2 / A:2 *Nova*	$3	■	EMI-Manhattan 50133
10/22/88	19	15		12 **Early In The Morning**..........A:18 / S:19 *Disturbing Behavior*	$3	■	EMI-Manhattan 50157
7/1/89	60	8		13 **Tell Me I'm Not Dreaming**..........*(2 versions) / More Than Ever*	$3	▮	EMI 50206
				B.J. Nelson (female vocal); song first recorded by **Jermaine** and **Michael Jackson** for 1984's *Jermaine Jackson* album			
11/17/90+	28	13		14 **You're Amazing**..........S:21 / A:36 *So Emboldened*	$3	▮	EMI 50338
2/16/91	16	17		15 **Mercy Mercy Me (The Ecology)/I Want You**..........A:10 / S:21 *(2 edits)*	$3	▮	EMI 50344
				medley of 2 **Marvin Gaye** hits			
				PALMER, Suzanne '01			
				Born in Chicago, Illinois. Electronica-dance singer/songwriter/pianist. Lead vocalist for **Club 69**.			
12/15/01	68^{S}	1		**Hide U**..........*(4 versions - orange cover)*	$8	★	Star 69 12182
				a second CD single featuring 4 additional remixes issued on Star 69 12262 (purple cover)			
				PANTHER Soundtrack R&B/BUB/LP '95			
				Featured on the soundtrack from the movie *Panther* starring Kadeem Hardison.			
4/22/95	45	13		**Freedom (Theme from Panther)**..........S:24 *(rap version)*	$5	▮	Mercury 856800
				over 60 female R&B and rap artists pay tribute to the empowerment of women			

DEBUT	PEAK	WKS	Gold	A-side (Chart Hit)..........B-side	$	Sym	Label & Number
				PAONE, Nicola '59			
				Born in Spangler, Pennsylvania; raised in Sicily until coming to New York at age 15. Male vocalist/songwriter.			
2/9/59	57	7		**Blah, Blah, Blah** ....*Ciao, Belleza (So Long, Beautiful)* [N]	$10		ABC-Paramount 9993
				PAPA ROACH ROK/LP '00			
				Hard-rock group from Vacaville, California: Coby Dick (vocals), Jerry Horton (guitar), Tobin Esperance (bass) and Dave Buckner (drums).			
7/29/00	57	20		1 **Last Resort**..........MR[7] A:56			album cut
				from the album *Infest* on DreamWorks 450223			
7/20/02	76	12		2 **She Loves Me Not** A:73			album cut
				from the album *Lovehatetragedy* on DreamWorks 450381			
				PAPERBOY R&B/BUB/LP '93			
				Born in Los Angeles, California. Male rapper.			
12/19/92+	10	30	▲	**Ditty**..........S:4 / A:21 *(divine street mix)*	$3	■	Next Plateau 357012
				samples "Doo Wa Ditty (Blow That Thing)" by **Zapp** (**Roger**)			
				PAPER LACE LP '74			
				Pop-rock group formed in England: Phil Wright (vocals, drums), Michael Vaughan and Chris Morris (guitars), and Cliff Fish (bass).			
4/27/74	96	3		1 **Billy - Don't Be A Hero**..........*Celia*	$6		Mercury 73479
6/15/74	❶[1]	17	●	2 **The Night Chicago Died** ....*Can You Get It When You Want It*	$6		Mercury 73492
10/12/74	41	9		3 **The Black-Eyed Boys** ....*Jean*	$5		Mercury 73620
				PARADE, The BUB '67			
				Pop-rock trio from Los Angeles, California: Jerry Riopelle, Murray MacLeod and Smokey Roberds.			
4/15/67	20	8		**Sunshine Girl**..........*This Old Melody*	$10		A&M 841
				PARADONS, The '60			
				R&B vocal group from Bakersfield, California: West Tyler, Chuck Weldon, Billy Myers and William Powers.			
8/22/60	18	16		**Diamonds And Pearls**..........*I Want Love*	$30		Milestone 2003
				PARAGONS, The BUB '61			
				R&B vocal group from Brooklyn, New York: Julian McMichael, Ben Frazier, Donald Travis, Ricky Jackson and Al Brown. McMichael later joined **The Olympics**. McMichael died in a motorcycle accident in June 1981 (age 45).			
7/17/61	82	5		**If** ....*Hey Baby*	$50		Tap 500
				there were 8 Top 30 versions of this tune in 1951			
				PARIS, Mica R&B/LP '89			
				Born Michelle Wallen on 4/27/69 in London, England. R&B-dance singer.			
6/24/89	97	4		**My One Temptation**..........*Wicked*	$3	■	Island 99252
				PARIS, Sarina LP '01			
				Born in Canada. Female dance-pop singer.			
2/24/01	59	20		**Look At Us** ....S:9 / A:72 *(2 versions)*	$5	★	Playland 38721
				PARIS SISTERS, The '61			
				White "girl group" from San Francisco, California: Albeth, Priscilla and Sherrell Paris. First recorded for Decca in 1954.			
4/24/61	56	5		1 **Be My Boy**..........*I'll Be Crying Tomorrow*	$25		Gregmark 2
9/4/61	5	15		2 **I Love How You Love Me** *All Through The Night*	$25		Gregmark 6
1/27/62	34	10		3 **He Knows I Love Him Too Much** ....*A Lonely Girl's Prayer*	$25		Gregmark 10
5/12/62	87	5		4 **Let Me Be The One**..........*What Am I To Do*	$25		Gregmark 12
				all of above produced by Phil Spector			
6/13/64	91	4		5 **Dream Lover** ....*Lonely Girl*	$15	■	MGM 13236
				PARKAYS, The '61			
				Staff musicians at Stax Records in Memphis, Tennessee: Gilbert Caple, Fred "David E." Ford and Walter Maynard, Jr. Session work for the **Bar-Kays** and the **Mar-Keys**.			
10/9/61	89	2		**Late Date** ....*Get It* [I]	$20		ABC-Paramount 10242
				first released on Safire 101 in 1961 ($40)			
				PARKER, Bobby '61			
				Born on 8/31/37 in Lafayette, Louisiana. Blues singer/guitarist. Guitarist with **The Charms**, **Bo Diddley** and Paul "Hucklebuck" Williams.			
6/12/61	51	6		**Watch Your Step**..........*Steal Your Heart Away*	$20		V-Tone 223
				PARKER, Fess '55			
				Born on 8/16/27 in Fort Worth, Texas. Actor; starred in the movie *Davy Crockett* and TV's *Daniel Boone* (1964-70).			
3/12/55	5	17		1 **Ballad Of Davy Crockett** ....S:5 / A:10 *I Gave My Love (Riddle Song)*	$15		Columbia 40449
				introduced by Parker in the 12/15/54 *Disneyland* TV episode "Davy Crockett Indian Fighter"; picture sleeve issued on Columbia Children's Series (J4-242)			
1/26/57	12	10		2 **Wringle Wrangle**..........S:12 / T:21 *The Ballad Of John Colter*	$12	■	Disneyland 43
				Camarata (orch.); from the movie *Westward Ho The Wagons* starring Parker			
				PARKER, Graham ROK/BUB/LP '85			
				Born on 11/18/50 in London, England. Pop-rock singer/songwriter/guitarist. The Rumour: Brinsley Schwarz and Martin Belmont (guitars), Bob Andrews (keyboards), Andrew Bodnar (bass) and Stephen Goulding (drums).			
4/9/77	58	8		1 **Hold Back The Night**......*(Let Me Get) Sweet On You (#107) / White Honey / Soul Shoes* [EP]	$8	■	Mercury 74000
				GRAHAM PARKER AND THE RUMOUR			
				4-track pink vinyl EP; picture sleeve titled "The Pink Parker"			
9/24/83	94	2		2 **Life Gets Better**..........*Beyond A Joke*	$4		Arista 9065
5/4/85	39	12		3 **Wake Up (Next To You)**..........*Bricks And Mortar*	$3	■	Elektra 69654
				GRAHAM PARKER AND THE SHOT			

DEBUT	PEAK	WKS	Gold	A-side (Chart Hit)......B-side	$	Sym	Label & Number

PARKER, Little Junior — R&B/BUB '62

Born Herman Parker, Jr. on 3/3/27 in West Memphis, Arkansas. Died of a brain tumor on 11/8/71 (age 44). Blues singer/harmonica player. Formed own combo, Little Junior's Blue Flames, in 1951. First recorded for Modern Records in l952. Wrote and recorded a future **Elvis Presley** classic "Mystery Train" on Sun 192 in 1953 ($300).

DEBUT	PEAK	WKS	Gold	A-side (Chart Hit)......B-side	$	Sym	Label & Number
7/8/57	74	6		1 **Next Time You See Me**......T:74 *My Dolly Bee* Bill Harvey's Band	$40		Duke 164
1/27/58	78	3		2 **That's Alright** *[LITTLE JUNIOR PARKER and His Combo]*......T:78 *Pretty Baby* charted for 1 week (#97) on 1/27/58; re-entered on 3/31/58	$30		Duke 168
5/22/61	85	2		3 **Driving Wheel** *[JUNIOR PARKER]*......*Seven Days*	$25		Duke 335
3/10/62	51	8		4 **Annie Get Your Yo-Yo**......*Mary Jo*	$15		Duke 345
1/12/63	95	1		5 **Someone Somewhere** *[JUNIOR PARKER]*......*Foxy Devil*	$15		Duke 357
2/8/64	99	2		6 **Strange Things Happening**......*I'm Gonna Stop*	$15		Duke 371

★251★ PARKER, Ray Jr./Raydio — R&B/BUB/AC/LP '84

Born on 5/1/54 in Detroit, Michigan. R&B singer/songwriter/guitarist. Prominent session guitarist in California; worked with **Stevie Wonder**, **Barry White** and others. Formed and led the band **Raydio** in 1977 with Arnell Carmichael, Jerry Knight, Larry Tolbert, Darren Carmichael and Charles Fearing. Parker went solo in 1982. Knight later recorded in duo **Ollie & Jerry**.

1)Ghostbusters 2)The Other Woman 3)A Woman Needs Love (Just Like You Do)

DEBUT	PEAK	WKS	Gold	A-side (Chart Hit)......B-side	$	Sym	Label & Number
				RAYDIO:			
1/14/78	8	21	●	1 **Jack And Jill**......*Get Down*	$5	■	Arista 0283
4/28/79	9	22		2 **You Can't Change That**......*Rock On*	$5		Arista 0399
				RAY PARKER JR. & RAYDIO:			
4/19/80	30	14		3 **Two Places At The Same Time**......*Everybody Makes Mistakes*	$4		Arista 0494
3/7/81	4	27		4 **A Woman Needs Love (Just Like You Do)**......RB[2] *So Into You*	$4		Arista 0592
7/11/81	21	15		5 **That Old Song**......*Old Pro*	$4	■	Arista 0616
				RAY PARKER JR.:			
3/20/82	4	21		6 **The Other Woman**......*Stay The Night*	$4		Arista 0669
7/17/82	38	9		7 **Let Me Go**......*Stop, Look Before You Love*	$4		Arista 0695
12/4/82+	35	12		8 **Bad Boy**......*Let's Get Off*	$4		Arista 1030
11/12/83+	12	19		9 **I Still Can't Get Over Loving You**......*She Still Feels The Need*	$4		Arista 9116
6/16/84	❶[3]	21	●	10 **Ghostbusters**......RB[2] *(instrumental)* from 1984's #1 box-office movie *Ghostbusters* starring Bill Murray	$3		Arista 9212
11/17/84+	14	17		11 **Jamie**......A:11 / S:18 *Christmas Time Is Here*	$3		Arista 9293
10/5/85	34	15		12 **Girls Are More Fun**......*I'm In Love*	$3	■	Arista 9352
2/15/86	96	3		13 **One Sunny Day/Dueling Bikes From Quicksilver**......*How Long* (The Motor Band) **RAY PARKER, JR. AND HELEN TERRY** from the movie *Quicksilver* starring Kevin Bacon	$3	■	Atlantic 89456
8/29/87	68	7		14 **I Don't Think That Man Should Sleep Alone**......*After Midnite*	$3	■	Geffen 28417
8/18/90	32	13		15 **All I'm Missing Is You**......S:29 / A:29 *Let Me Show You What Love Is* **GLENN MEDEIROS Featuring Ray Parker Jr.**	$3	▌	MCA 53886

PARKER, Robert — BUB '66

Born on 10/14/30 in Crescent City, Louisiana. Black saxophonist/vocalist/bandleader. In Professor Longhair's (Roy Byrd) band from 1949. Led house band at Club Tijuana, New Orleans. Prolific session work.

DEBUT	PEAK	WKS	Gold	A-side (Chart Hit)......B-side	$	Sym	Label & Number
4/23/66	7	14		1 **Barefootin'**......*Let's Go Baby (Where The Action Is)*	$20		Nola 721
1/21/67	83	3		2 **Tip Toe**......*Soul Kind Of Loving*	$15		Nola 729

PARKS, Michael — BUB/LP '70

Born on 4/4/38 in Corona, California. Singer/actor. Appeared in several movies. Played "Jim Bronson" in the 1969 TV series *Then Came Bronson.*

DEBUT	PEAK	WKS	Gold	A-side (Chart Hit)......B-side	$	Sym	Label & Number
2/28/70	20	12		**Long Lonesome Highway**......*Mountain High* introduced by Parks on 10/29/69 on his TV series *Then Came Bronson*	$6		MGM 14104

★529★ PARLIAMENT/FUNKADELIC — R&B/BUB/LP '78

Highly influential and prolific funk aggregation of nearly 40 musicians spearheaded by **George Clinton** (born on 7/22/40; producer/songwriter/lead singer). Clinton founded doo-wop group **The Parliaments** in 1955 in Newark, New Jersey. First recorded for Hull in 1958. By 1967, evolved into a soul group with lineup of vocalists Clinton, Raymond Davis, Calvin Simon, Clarence "Fuzzy" Haskins and Grady Thomas. In 1967, relocated to Detroit and added rhythm section. In 1968, Clinton formed **Funkadelic** with rhythm section of The Parliaments, recruited keyboardist Bernie Worrell and changed The Parliaments name to **Parliament**. Although on different labels, Parliament and Funkadelic shared the same personnel which included former members of **The JB's**: brothers Phelps "Catfish" (guitar) and William "Bootsy" Collins (bass), Frank "Kash" Waddy (drums) and horn players Maceo Parker (**Maceo And The Macks**) and **Fred Wesley**. Known as "A Parliafunkadelicament Thang," this funk corporation included various offshoots: Bootsy's Rubber Band, The Horny Horns, The Brides Of Funkenstein, Parlet and Xavion, among others. Concert tours featured elaborate staging and characters. Parliament/Funkadelic were inducted into the Rock and Roll Hall of Fame in 1997. Also see **Original P**.

1)Tear The Roof Off The Sucker 2)Flash Light 3)(I Wanna) Testify

DEBUT	PEAK	WKS	Gold	A-side (Chart Hit)......B-side	$	Sym	Label & Number
				THE PARLIAMENTS:			
7/1/67	20	13		1 **(I Wanna) Testify**......*I Can Feel The Ice Melting* first released on Trans World 1677 in 1967 ($40)	$20		Revilot 207
10/14/67	80	7		2 **All Your Goodies Are Gone (The Loser's Seat)**......*Don't Be Sore At Me*	$20		Revilot 211
				FUNKADELIC:			
10/4/69	63	7		3 **I'll Bet You**......*Open Our Eyes*	$10		Westbound 150
3/21/70	80	6		4 **I Got A Thing, You Got A Thing, Everybody's Got A Thing**...*Fish, Chips & Sweat*	$8		Westbound 158
8/22/70	81	4		5 **I Wanna Know If It's Good To You?**......*(instrumental)*	$8		Westbound 167
4/10/71	91	2		6 **You And Your Folks, Me And My Folks**......*Funky Dollar Bill*	$8		Westbound 175
9/11/71+	93	3		7 **Can You Get To That**......*Back In Our Minds*	$8		Westbound 185
				PARLIAMENT:			
8/31/74	63	9		8 **Up For The Down Stroke**......*Presence Of A Brain* also released on Casablanca 803 and 0104 in 1974	$7		Casablanca 0013
6/14/75	94	3		9 **Chocolate City**......*(long version)* [S]	$7		Casablanca 831
11/1/75	99	3		10 **Better By The Pound** *[FUNKADELIC]*......*Stuffs & Things*	$8		Westbound 5014

DEBUT	PEAK	WKS	Gold	A-side (Chart Hit)...B-side	$	Sym	Label & Number
				PARLIAMENT/FUNKADELIC — Cont'd			
5/15/76	15	17	●	11 **Tear The Roof Off The Sucker (Give Up The Funk)** *P. Funk*	$6		Casablanca 856
2/11/78	16	16	●	12 **Flash Light** ....RB[3] *Swing Down, Sweet Chariot*	$6		Casablanca 909
9/16/78	28	14	●	13 **One Nation Under A Groove - Part I** *[FUNKADELIC]*....RB[6] *Part II* also see #16 below	$6	■	Warner 8618
2/24/79	89	2		14 **Aqua Boogie (A Psychoalphadiscobetabio-aquadoloop)**....RB[4] *(You're A Fish And I'm A) Water Sign*	$6	■	Casablanca 950
10/27/79	77	4		15 **(not just) Knee Deep - Part 1** *[FUNKADELIC]*....RB[3] *Part 2* all of above produced by **George Clinton**	$6		Warner 49040
7/30/94	23	20	●	16 **Bop Gun (One Nation)**....S:12 / A:34 *Down For Whatever* **ICE CUBE featuring George Clinton** rap version of #13 above	$3	▮	Priority 53155
8/24/96	68	10		17 **Gettin' It**....S:54 *(remix) / Never Talk Down* (w/**Rappin' 4-Tay** & **M.C. Breed**) **TOO $HORT featuring Parliament Funkadelic** samples "I'd Rather Be With You" by Bootsy's Rubber Band and "Inner City Blues" by **Marvin Gaye**; all of above (except #4) written or co-written by Clinton	$3	▮	Jive 42409
				PARR, John LP **'85** Born on 11/18/54 in Nottingham, Nottinghamshire, England. Pop-rock singer/songwriter.			
12/15/84+	23	20		1 **Naughty Naughty**....A:22 / S:25 *Revenge*	$3		Atlantic 89612
4/6/85	73	5		2 **Magical**....*Treat Me Like An Animal*	$3	■	Atlantic 89568
6/22/85	❶[2]	22		3 **St. Elmo's Fire (Man In Motion)** S:❶[2] / A:❶[1] *One Love* (**David Foster**) from the movie *St. Elmo's Fire* starring Emilio Estevez and Rob Lowe	$3	■	Atlantic 89541
11/16/85	89	2		4 **Love Grammar**....*Treat Me Like An Animal*	$3	■	Atlantic 89484
12/13/86	88	6		5 **Blame It On The Radio**....*Two Hearts (American Anthem)*	$3	■	Atlantic 89333
				PARRIS, Fred — see FIVE SATINS, The			
				PARRISH, Dean **'66** Born Phil Anastasi in 1942 in Brooklyn, New York. White R&B-styled vocalist.			
7/16/66	97	2		**Tell Her**....*Fall On Me* Roy Glover (orch.)	$20		Boom 60,012
	★345★			**PARSONS, Alan, Project** ROK/BUB/AC/LP **'82** Born on 12/20/49 in London, England. Guitarist/keyboardist/producer. Engineered *Abbey Road* by **The Beatles** and *Dark Side Of The Moon* by **Pink Floyd**. Project features various musicians and vocalists. Eric Woolfson (vocals, keyboards) contributes most of the lyrics. *1)Eye In The Sky 2)Time 3)Don't Answer Me*			
7/24/76	37	10		1 **(The System Of) Doctor Tarr And Professor Fether**....*A Dream Within A Dream* **John Miles** (vocal)	$5		20th Century 2297
10/16/76	80	4		2 **The Raven**....*Prelude To The Fall Of The House Of Usher*	$5		20th Century 2308
8/20/77	36	13		3 **I Wouldn't Want To Be Like You** *[ALAN PARSONS]*....*Nucleus*	$4		Arista 0260
12/17/77+	92	4		4 **Don't Let It Show**....*I Robot*	$4		Arista 0288
9/23/78	87	3		5 **What Goes Up**....*In The Lap Of The Gods*	$4		Arista 0352
9/29/79	27	17		6 **Damned If I Do**....*If I Could Change Your Mind*	$4		Arista 0454
12/6/80+	16	23		7 **Games People Play**....*The Ace Of Swords* Lenny Zakatek (vocal, above 3)	$4		Arista 0573
4/18/81	15	23		8 **Time**....*The Gold Bug*	$4		Arista 0598
10/17/81	67	5		9 **Snake Eyes**....*I Don't Wanna Go Home*	$4		Arista 0635
7/3/82	3	25		10 **Eye In The Sky** *Gemini*	$4		Arista 0696
11/27/82	57	10		11 **Psychobabble**....*Children Of The Moon*	$4		Arista 1029
11/19/83	54	10		12 **You Don't Believe**....*Lucifer*	$4		Arista 9108
3/3/84	15	15		13 **Don't Answer Me**....*Don't Let It Show*	$4	■	Arista 9160
5/19/84	34	11		14 **Prime Time**....*The Gold Bug*	$4		Arista 9208
2/16/85	56	10		15 **Let's Talk About Me**....*Hawkeye*	$4	■	Arista 9282
4/27/85	71	5		16 **Days Are Numbers (The Traveller)**....*Somebody Out There*	$4		Arista 9349
2/15/86	82	4		17 **Stereotomy**....*Urbania* **John Miles** (vocal); all of above produced by Parsons and written by Parsons and Woolfson	$4		Arista 9443
				PARSONS, Bill — see BARE, Bobby			
				PARTLAND BROTHERS LP **'87** Rock duo from Colgan, Ontario, Canada: Chris (vocals, guitars) and G.P. (vocals, percussion) Partland.			
5/2/87	27	13		**Soul City**....S:26 / A:27 *Outside The City*	$3	■	Manhattan 50065
				PARTNERS IN KRYME **'90** Hip-hop duo formed in Syracuse, New York: DJ James Alpern and rapper Richard Usher. KRYME: Keeping Rhythm Your Motivating Energy.			
4/21/90	13	16	●	**Turtle Power!**....S:12 / A:17 *Splinter's Tale I & Splinter's Tale II* from the movie *Teenage Mutant Ninja Turtles* starring Elias Koteas	$3	▮V	SBK 07325
	★256★			**PARTON, Dolly** C&W/BUB/AC/LP **'81** Born on 1/19/46 in Locust Ridge, Tennessee. Country singer/songwriter/actress. Regular on **Porter Wagoner**'s TV show (1967-74). Starred in the movies *9 To 5, The Best Little Whorehouse In Texas, Steel Magnolias* and *Straight Talk*. In 1986, opened Dollywood theme park in the Smoky Mountains. Hosted own TV variety show in 1987. Charted 106 Country hits, 1967-98. *1)9 To 5 2)Islands In The Stream 3)Here You Come Again 4)Two Doors Down 5)Baby I'm Burnin'*			
1/26/74	60	8		1 **Jolene**....CW[1] *Love, You're So Beautiful Tonight*	$7		RCA Victor 0145
6/18/77	87	5		2 **Light Of A Clear Blue Morning**....*There*	$6		RCA 10935
10/15/77+	3	19	●	3 **Here You Come Again**....CW[5] *Me And Little Andy*	$5		RCA 11123
3/18/78	19	12		4 **Two Doors Down**....*It's All Wrong, But It's All Right* (C&W #1)	$5		RCA 11240
8/26/78	37	10		5 **Heartbreaker**....CW[3] *Sure Thing*	$5		RCA 11296
12/9/78+	25	14		6 **Baby I'm Burnin'**....*I Really Got The Feeling* (C&W #1)	$5		RCA 11420
6/30/79	59	6		7 **You're The Only One**....CW[2] *Down*	$5		RCA 11577

DEBUT	PEAK	WKS	Gold	A-side (Chart Hit)..........B-side	$	Sym	Label & Number
				PARTON, Dolly — Cont'd			
9/29/79	77	3		8 **Sweet Summer Lovin'**..........*Great Balls Of Fire* (C&W flip)	$5		RCA 11705
3/29/80	36	10		9 **Starting Over Again**..........CW[1] *Sweet Agony* written by **Donna Summer** and her husband Bruce Sudano	$5		RCA 11926
11/29/80+	1[2]	26	●	10 **9 To 5** CW[1] / AC[2] *Sing For The Common Man* title song from the movie starring Parton and Jane Fonda	$4	■	RCA 12133
4/4/81	41	10		11 **But You Know I Love You**..........CW[1] *Poor Folks Town*	$4		RCA 12200
9/19/81	77	4		12 **The House Of The Rising Sun**..........*Working Girl* (C&W flip)	$4		RCA 12282
7/31/82	53	14		13 **I Will Always Love You**..........CW[1] *Do I Ever Cross Your Mind* (C&W flip) Parton's original version hit #1 on the Country charts on 6/8/74 on RCA Victor 0234; from the movie *The Best Little Whorehouse In Texas* starring Parton and **Burt Reynolds**	$4	■	RCA 13260
8/27/83	1[2]	25	▲	14 **Islands In The Stream**..........CW[2] / AC[4] *I Will Always Love You* (Rogers) **KENNY ROGERS with Dolly Parton** written by the **Bee Gees**	$4	■	RCA 13615
12/10/83+	45	12		15 **Save The Last Dance For Me**..........*Elusive Butterfly* **DOLLY PARTON (with The Jordanaires)**	$4		RCA 13703
4/14/84	80	4		16 **Downtown**..........*The Great Pretender*	$4	■	RCA 13756
12/22/84	6[X]	1		17 **Medley: Winter Wonderland/Sleigh Ride**....*The Christmas Song* (**Kenny Rogers**) [X]	$4		RCA 13944
12/22/84	81	4		18 **The Greatest Gift Of All**..........*White Christmas* (Parton) [X] **KENNY ROGERS & DOLLY PARTON** above 2 from their Christmas TV special *Once Upon A Christmas*	$4		RCA 13945
6/8/85	91	3		19 **Real Love**..........CW[1] *I Can't Be True* (Parton) **DOLLY PARTON (with Kenny Rogers)**	$4	■	RCA 14058
3/13/93	50	14		20 **Romeo**..........S:23 *High And Mighty* (Parton) **DOLLY PARTON AND FRIENDS** (**Billy Ray Cyrus**, **Tanya Tucker**, Kathy Mattea, **Mary Chapin Carpenter** and Pam Tillis)	$4	▮V	Columbia 74876
	★553★			**PARTRIDGE FAMILY, The** LP '70 Popularized through *The Partridge Family* TV series, broadcast from 1970-74. Recordings by series stars **David Cassidy** (lead singer) and real-life stepmother Shirley Jones (backing vocals). David, son of actor Jack Cassidy, was born on 4/12/50 in New York City; raised in California. Shirley, born on 3/31/34 in Smithton, Pennsylvania, starred in the movie musicals *Oklahoma* and *The Music Man*; married David's father in 1956.			
				THE PARTRIDGE FAMILY Starring Shirley Jones Featuring David Cassidy:			
10/10/70	1[3]	19	●	1 **I Think I Love You** *Somebody Wants To Love You* David's daughter, Katie Cassidy (age 15), recorded this song in 2002 on Artemis Records	$6	■	Bell 910
2/13/71	6	12	●	2 **Doesn't Somebody Want To Be Wanted**..........*You Are Always On My Mind*	$6	■	Bell 963
5/8/71	9	9		3 **I'll Meet You Halfway**..........*Morning Rider On The Road*	$6		Bell 996
8/14/71	13	11		4 **I Woke Up In Love This Morning**..........*Twenty Four Hours A Day*	$6		Bell 45,130
12/18/71+	20	8		5 **It's One Of Those Nights (Yes Love)**..........*One Night Stand*	$6		Bell 45,160
4/1/72	59	7		6 **Am I Losing You**..........*If You Ever Go*	$6		Bell 45,200
7/1/72	28	10		7 **Breaking Up Is Hard To Do**..........*I'm Here, You're Here*	$6		Bell 45,235
12/16/72+	39	8		8 **Looking Through The Eyes Of Love**..........*Storybook Love*	$6		Bell 45,301
4/14/73	99	2		9 **Friend And A Lover**..........*Something's Wrong*	$6		Bell 45,336
				PARTY, The LP '91 Pop-dance group from Florida: Tiffini Hale, Albert Fields, Chase Hampton, Damon Pampolina and Deedee Magno. All were cast members of TV's *The Mickey Mouse Club* in 1988.			
7/21/90	72	9		1 **Summer Vacation**..........*(2 versions)* also see #4 below (same version)	$3	▮	Hollywood 64945
11/3/90	79	11		2 **I Found Love**..........*(Besame mix)*	$3	▮	Hollywood 64931
3/2/91	55	12		3 **That's Why**..........*(power mix) / Adult Decision*	$3	▮	Hollywood 64903
6/15/91	86	5		4 **Summer Vacation**..........A:51 *(2 versions)* [R]	$3	▮	Hollywood 64945
11/16/91+	34	18		5 **In My Dreams** A:30 / S:54 *I Gotcha*	$3	▮	Hollywood 64832
				PASADENAS, The R&B/LP '89 R&B-dance vocal group from England: brothers Aaron, David and Michael Milliner, with John Banfield and Hammish Seelochan.			
2/25/89	52	10		**Tribute (Right On)**..........*I Believe*	$4		Columbia 68575
				PASSIONS, The BUB '59 White doo-wop group from Brooklyn, New York: Jimmy Gallagher (lead), Tony Armato, Albee Galione and Vinnie Acierno.			
10/5/59	69	10		**Just To Be With You**..........*Oh Melancholy Me* Paul Swain (orch.)	$40		Audicon 102
				PASTELS, The '58 R&B vocal group formed at the U.S. Air Force base in Narsarssuak, Greenland: **Big Dee Irwin** (lead), Richard Travis, Tony Thomas and Jimmy Willingham. Irwin died on 8/27/95 (age 63).			
3/3/58	24	16		**Been So Long**..........T:24 / S:25 *My One And Only Dream* originally released on Mascot 123 in 1957 ($300)	$30		Argo 5287
				PASTEL SIX, The '63 Pop group from California: Bob Toten (lead vocals), Tony Stealman, Rick Rodriguez, Erick Fickert, Lynn Hamm, Bill Myers, Dave Cadison. Ages 18-21 in 1962. Headlined at the Cinnamon Cinder club in North Hollywood.			
12/29/62+	25	10		**The Cinnamon Cinder (It's A Very Nice Dance)**..........*Bandido*	$25		Zen 102
				PASTOR TROY LP '02 Born Micah LeVar Troy in Augusta, Georgia. Male rapper.			
10/5/02	96	5		**Are We Cuttin'**..........S:68 *(radio edit)* **PASTOR TROY featuring Ms. Jade**	$4	★	Universal 019327
				PAT & MICK '91 DJs Pat Sharp and Mick Brown from London, England. Backing vocals by Mae McKenna, Mirian Stockley and Mike Stock (of the prolific production trio of Stock, Aitken and Waterman).			
12/15/90+	81	7		**Use It Up And Wear It Out**..........*Star Teaser* proceeds donated to the London charity "Help A London Child"	$4	▮	Charisma 98870

DEBUT	PEAK	WKS	Gold	A-side (Chart Hit)...B-side	$	Sym	Label & Number
				PAT and the SATELLITES '59			
				Rock and roll band of studio musicians featuring Pat Otts (from Olean, New York), **King Curtis** and Wayne Lips.			
2/9/59	**81**	4		**Jupiter-C** ...*Oh! Oh! Darlin'* [I]	$20		Atco 6131
				PATE, Johnny, Quintet '58			
				Born on 12/5/23 in Chicago Heights, Illinois. Black bassist/bandleader/arranger. Conductor for many of **The Impressions** hits.			
1/27/58	**43**	12		**Swinging Shepherd Blues** ...S:43 / T:44 *The Elder* [I]	$20		Federal 12312
				Lennie Druss (flute)			
				PATIENCE & PRUDENCE '56			
				White vocal duo from Los Angeles, California: sisters Patience and Prudence McIntyre (ages 14 & 11 in 1956).			
8/4/56	**4**	25	●	1 **Tonight You Belong To Me** ...S:4 / J:4 / A:5 / T:6 *A Smile And A Ribbon* (Prudence)	$25		Liberty 55022
				#1 hit for **Gene Austin** in 1927			
12/1/56	**11**	16		2 **Gonna Get Along Without Ya Now** / A:11 / S:12 / T:12 / J:16			
				#25 hit for **Teresa Brewer** in 1952			
12/8/56+	**73**	9		3 **The Money Tree** ...T:73	$20		Liberty 55040
				all of above with the orchestra of their father, Mark McIntyre			
				PATRA LP '94			
				Born Dorothy Smith on 11/22/72 in Kingston, Jamaica. Female dance-reggae singer.			
2/19/94	**84**	2		1 **Family Affair** ...S:51 *(dub mix)*	$4	▮	Atlas 855232
				SHABBA RANKS featuring Patra and Terri & Monica			
				from the movie *Addams Family Values* starring Raul Julia and Angelica Huston			
4/30/94	**53**	16		2 **Worker Man** S:41 / A:60 *(Salaam's mix)*	$4	▮V	Epic 77289
				"45": Collectables 4688; B-side: "I Can See Clearly Now" by **Jimmy Cliff** (#18)			
8/13/94	**55**	16		3 **Romantic Call** ...S:36 / A:66 *Love All The Men* (Patra)	$4	▮	Epic 77624
				PATRA Featuring Yo-Yo			
				samples "Bitches Brew" by Miles Davis			
8/5/95	**60**	10		4 **Pull Up To The Bumper** ...S:43 *(2 versions) / Whining Skill*	$4	▮	550 Music/Epic 77931
				#5 R&B hit for **Grace Jones** in 1981			
3/16/96	**82**	7		5 **Scent Of Attraction** ...S:70 *(remix) / Dip & Fall Back*	$4	▮	550 Music/Epic 78257
				PATRA with Aaron Hall			
				samples "Shadows" by **Tom Scott**			
				PATTERSON, Kellee R&B '78			
				Born in Gary, Indiana. Soul singer/actress. Crowned Miss Indiana in 1971.			
12/17/77+	**75**	8		**If It Don't Fit, Don't Force It** ...*Be Happy*	$6		Shady Brook 1041
				PATTON, Robbie LP '81			
				Born in England. Pop-rock singer/songwriter.			
7/11/81	**26**	13		1 **Don't Give It Up** ...*When Love Disappears*	$4		Liberty 1420
				co-produced by **Christine McVie** (of **Fleetwood Mac**)			
3/12/83	**52**	12		2 **Smiling Islands** ...*Look Away*	$4		Atlantic 89955
				Stevie Nicks (backing vocal)			
				PATTY & THE EMBLEMS '64			
				R&B vocal group from Camden, New Jersey: Patty Russell (lead), Eddie Watts (1st tenor), Vance Walker (2nd tenor) and Alexander Wilde (baritone). Patty died of leukemia on 9/5/98 (age 56). Wilde died of kidney failure on 11/13/98 (age 60).			
6/20/64	**37**	11		**Mixed-Up, Shook-Up, Girl** ...*Ordinary Guy*	$20		Herald 590
				PAUL, Billy R&B/LP '72			
				Born Paul Williams on 12/1/34 in Philadelphia, Pennsylvania. R&B singer. Also see the **Philadelphia International All Stars**.			
11/4/72	**1**[3]	16	●	1 **Me And Mrs. Jones** ...RB[4] *Your Song*	$5		Philadelphia I. 3521
4/7/73	**79**	5		2 **Am I Black Enough For You** ...*I'm Gonna Make It This Time*	$5		Philadelphia I. 3526
1/26/74	**37**	17		3 **Thanks For Saving My Life** ...*I Was Married*	$5		Philadelphia I. 3538
4/10/76	**83**	4		4 **Let's Make A Baby** ...*My Head's On Straight*	$5		Philadelphia I. 3584
				PAUL, Christopher, And Shawn AC '75			
				Brother-and-sister teen pop vocal duo from Salt Lake City, Utah: Christopher and Shawn Engemann. Shawn later known as Shawn Southwick (married TV talk show host Larry King on 9/5/97). Their father, Carl Engemann, was vice president of A&R for Capitol Records and once managed **The Osmonds**. Their uncle, Bob Engemann, was a member of **The Lettermen**.			
8/2/75	**91**	5		**For Your Love** ...*My Love's Never Gonna Burn Out, Baby*	$6		Casablanca 838
				PAUL, Henry, Band BUB/LP '82			
				Born on 8/25/49 in Kingston, New York. Southern-rock singer/guitarist. Member of the **Outlaws** and **BlackHawk**. His band: Dave Fiester and Billy Crain (guitars), Wally Dentz (bass) and Bill Hoffman (drums).			
12/12/81+	**50**	10		**Keeping Our Love Alive** ...*Hollywood Paradise*	$5		Atlantic 3883
				PAUL, Les, and Mary Ford MEM/POP/BUB/LP '51			
				Paul was born Lester Polsfuss on 6/9/15 in Waukesha, Wisconsin. Ford was born Colleen Summers on 7/7/24 in Pasadena, California; died on 9/30/77 (age 53). Les Paul was an innovator in electric guitar and multi-track recordings. Married to vocalist Mary Ford from 1949-63. Charted 33 hits, 1945-54, including 2 #1 hits: "How High The Moon" and "Vaya Con Dios." Les Paul won the Grammy's Trustees Award in 1983 and was inducted into the Rock and Roll Hall of Fame in 1988.			
7/9/55	**7**	13		1 **Hummingbird** J:7 / S:8 / A:8 *Goodbye, My Love*	$15		Capitol 3165
11/12/55	**38**	9		2 **Amukiriki (The Lord Willing)** / T:38			
11/12/55	**96**	2		3 **Magic Melody** ...T:96 [I]	$12		Capitol 3248
				charted for 1 week on 11/12/55 and 1 week on 2/4/56 (#98)			
1/28/56	**91**	2		4 **Texas Lady** ...T:91 *Alabamy Bound*	$12		Capitol 3301
				title song from the movie starring Claudette Colbert			
2/11/56	**49**	12		5 **Moritat (Theme From "Three Penny Opera")** *[LES PAUL]* / T:49 [I]			
2/18/56	**91**	1		6 **Nuevo Laredo** ...T:91	$12		Capitol 3329
1/12/57	**35**	14		7 **Cinco Robles (Five Oaks)** ...T:35 *Ro-Ro-Robinson* (Paul)	$12		Capitol 3612
8/18/58	**32**	10		8 **Put A Ring On My Finger** ...H:32 / S:44 *Fantasy*	$10	■	Columbia 41222
4/24/61	**37**	10		9 **Jura (I Swear I Love You)** ...*It's Been A Long, Long Time* (#105)	$8	■	Columbia 41994

DEBUT	PEAK	WKS	Gold	A-side (Chart Hit)..................B-side	$	Sym	Label & Number

PAUL, Sean
R&B/LP **'02**

Born Sean Paul Henriquez on 1/8/75 in Kingston, Jamaica. Reggae singer.

DEBUT	PEAK	WKS	Gold	A-side (Chart Hit)..................B-side	$	Sym	Label & Number
6/24/00	60^{S}	2		1 **Hot Gal Today (Haffi Get De Gal Yah)** ...*(2 remixes)* **SEAN PAUL & MR. VEGAS**	$6	★	VP 6349
5/4/02	7	39		2 **Gimme The Light** S:5 / A:7 *(instrumental) / Can You Do The Work* also see #5 below; "45": Black Shadow 030 (as "Give Me The Light"); B-side: (instrumental)	$4	$★^{V}$	VP 6400
7/6/02	65^{S}	4		3 **Holla At A Playa** ...*(2 album snippets) / (2 remixes w/***Too $hort***)* **JIM CROW featuring Sean Paul and Jazze Pha**	$5	★	Interscope 497699
11/16/02	59^{S}	1		4 **Hey Sexy Lady** ...*(6 versions)* **SHAGGY w/ Sean Paul feat. Brian & Tony Gold**	$8	T	Big Yard/MCA 113958
12/14/02	17^{S}	7		5 **Gimme The Light (Remix)** ...*(2 versions)* [R] **SEAN PAUL Featuring Busta Rhymes** remix of #2 above; "45": VP/Atlantic 8809; B-side: (clean radio edit)	$6	T^{V}	Atlantic 85422

PAUL & PAULA
BUB/LP **'63**

Pop vocal duo. Ray "Paul" Hildebrand was born on 12/21/40 in Joshua, Texas. Jill "Paula" Jackson was born on 5/20/42 in McCaney, Texas.

DEBUT	PEAK	WKS	Gold	A-side (Chart Hit)..................B-side	$	Sym	Label & Number
12/29/62+	$❶^{3}$	15	●	1 **Hey Paula** RB² *Bobby Is The One* first released on LeCam 979 as by Jill & Ray in 1962 ($50)	$15		Philips 40084
3/16/63	6	10		2 **Young Lovers** ...*Ba-Hey-Be*	$15	■	Philips 40096
6/1/63	27	8		3 **First Quarrel** ...*School Is Thru*	$12	■	Philips 40114
8/24/63	77	5		4 **Something Old, Something New** ...*Flipped Over You (#108)*	$12		Philips 40130
10/5/63	60	4		5 **First Day Back At School** ...*A Perfect Pair (#105)*	$12	⊙	Philips 40142
12/28/63	19^{X}	1		6 **Holiday Hootenanny** ...*Holiday For Teens* [X] "surf-hootenanny" version of "Jingle Bells"; #2, 3, 5 & 6: promo records issued with a foldout insert; #2 featured a photo of Paul & Paula	$15	⊙	Philips 40158

PAULETTE SISTERS
'55

Pop vocal group: sisters Barbara, Jane, Gloria and Betty Paulette.

DEBUT	PEAK	WKS	Gold	A-side (Chart Hit)..................B-side	$	Sym	Label & Number
11/19/55	92	2		**You Win Again** ...T:92 *Mama, El Baion* Dave Cavanaugh (orch.); #10 Country hit for Hank Williams in 1952	$15		Capitol 3186

PAUSINI, Laura
'02

Born in 1974 in Italy. Dance singer.

DEBUT	PEAK	WKS	Gold	A-side (Chart Hit)..................B-side	$	Sym	Label & Number
11/23/02	43^{S}	3		**Surrender** ...*(6 remixes)*	$8	★*	Atlantic 49446

PAVONE, Rita
BUB/LP **'64**

Born on 8/23/45 in Turin, Italy. Pop singer.

DEBUT	PEAK	WKS	Gold	A-side (Chart Hit)..................B-side	$	Sym	Label & Number
6/6/64	26	9		**Remember Me** ...*Just Once More (#123)* Teacho Wiltshire (orch.); picture sleeve issued with name and title in green or black ink	$8	■	RCA Victor 8365

PAYCHECK, Johnny
C&W/LP **'71**

Born Donald Eugene Lytle on 5/31/38 in Greenfield, Ohio. Died of emphysema on 2/18/2003 (age 64). Country singer/songwriter/guitarist (charted 60 hits, 1965-89).

DEBUT	PEAK	WKS	Gold	A-side (Chart Hit)..................B-side	$	Sym	Label & Number
12/18/71	91	2		**She's All I Got** ...*You Touched My Life* co-written by **Gary (U.S.) Bonds**	$7		Epic 10783

PAYNE, Freda
R&B/LP **'70**

Born on 9/19/45 in Detroit, Michigan. R&B singer. Sister of Scherrie Payne (of **The Supremes**). Formerly married to **Gregory Abbott**.

DEBUT	PEAK	WKS	Gold	A-side (Chart Hit)..................B-side	$	Sym	Label & Number
4/25/70	3	20	●	1 **Band Of Gold** *The Easiest Way To Fall*	$7		Invictus 9075
9/12/70	24	12		2 **Deeper & Deeper** ...*Unhooked Generation*	$7		Invictus 9080
2/13/71	44	8		3 **Cherish What Is Dear To You (While It's Near to You)** ...*The World Don't Owe You A Thing*	$7	■	Invictus 9085
6/5/71	12	13	●	4 **Bring The Boys Home** ...*I Shall Not Be Moved*	$7		Invictus 9092
10/2/71	52	8		5 **You Brought The Joy** ...*Suddenly It's Yesterday*	$7		Invictus 9100
1/8/72	100	2		6 **The Road We Didn't Take** ...*I'm Not Getting Any Better* above 4 from the album *Contact*	$7		Invictus 9109

PC QUEST
'91

Teen pop vocal group from Shawnee, Oklahoma: Kim Whipkey, Drew Nichols, and brothers Chad and Steve Petree.

DEBUT	PEAK	WKS	Gold	A-side (Chart Hit)..................B-side	$	Sym	Label & Number
5/4/91	58	15		1 **Can I Call You My Girl?** ...*Ready, Aim, Dance!* originally released on Headliner 5649 in 1991	$4	▮	Headliner 62018
8/17/91	41	11		2 **After The Summer's Gone** ...*Can I Call You My Girl?*	$4	▮	Headliner 62051

PEACE CHOIR
'91

All-star choir assembled by **Yoko Ono**, Sean Ono Lennon and **Lenny Kravitz**. Comprised of Amina, **Adam Ant**, Sebastian Bach (**Skid Row**), **Bros**, **Felix Cavaliere** (**The Rascals**), **Terence Trent D'Arby**, John Frusciante and Flea (both of **The Red Hot Chili Peppers**), **Peter Gabriel**, Kadeem Hardison (TV actor), Ofra Haza, Joe Higgs, **Bruce Hornsby**, Lee Jaffe, **Al Jarreau**, Jazzie B (**Soul II Soul**), Davey Johnstone, **Cyndi Lauper**, **Little Richard**, **L.L. Cool J**, **M.C. Hammer**, **Michael McDonald**, Duff McKagan (**Guns N' Roses**), **Alannah Myles**, New Voices Of Freedom, **Randy Newman**, **Tom Petty**, **Iggy Pop**, **Q-Tip**, **Bonnie Raitt**, Run (**Run-DMC**), **Dave Stewart**, **Teena Marie**, **Little Steven** Van Zandt, Don Was [**Was (Not Was)**], **Wendy & Lisa**, and Ahmet, Dweezil and Moon Zappa.

DEBUT	PEAK	WKS	Gold	A-side (Chart Hit)..................B-side	$	Sym	Label & Number
3/9/91	54	4		**Give Peace A Chance** ...S:29 *(video version)* #14 hit for **John Lennon**'s **Plastic Ono Band** in 1969; Sean Ono Lennon (son of **John Lennon** and **Yoko Ono**) and **Lenny Kravitz** (producer of song) wrote new lyrics	$6	▮	Virgin 98839

PEACHES & HERB
★310★ R&B/BUB/LP **'79**

R&B vocal duo from Washington DC: Francine "Peaches" Barker (born Francine Hurd in 1947) and Herb Fame (born Herbert Feemster on 10/1/42). Marlene Mack filled in for Francine from 1968-69. Re-formed with Fame and Linda "Peaches" Green in 1977.

1)Reunited 2)Shake Your Groove Thing 3)Close Your Eyes

DEBUT	PEAK	WKS	Gold	A-side (Chart Hit)..................B-side	$	Sym	Label & Number
12/31/66+	21	12		1 **Let's Fall In Love** ...*We're In This Thing Together* #1 hit for Eddy Duchin in 1934	$10	□	Date 1523
3/25/67	8	12		2 **Close Your Eyes** ...*I Will Watch Over You* written by **Chuck Willis**; #5 R&B hit for **The Five Keys** in 1955	$10	■	Date 1549
6/24/67	20	8		3 **For Your Love** ...*I Need Your Love So Desperately*	$10	■	Date 1563

DEBUT	PEAK	WKS	Gold	A-side (Chart Hit)..........B-side	$	Sym	Label & Number
				PEACHES & HERB — Cont'd			
9/30/67	13	9		4 **Love Is Strange**..........*It's True I Love You*	$10	■	Date 1574
12/16/67+	31	8		5 **Two Little Kids**..........*We've Got To Love One Another* co-written by **Barbara Acklin**	$10		Date 1586
2/24/68	55	5		6 **The Ten Commandments Of Love**..........*What A Lovely Way (To Say Goodnight)*	$10		Date 1592
5/18/68	46	8		7 **United**..........*Thank You* see sequel at #13 below	$10	■	Date 1603
11/9/68	75	4		8 **Let's Make A Promise**..........*Me And You*	$10	■	Date 1623
3/1/69	49	7		9 **When He Touches Me (Nothing Else Matters)**..........*Thank You*	$10		Date 1637
8/16/69	74	4		10 **Let Me Be The One**..........*I Need Your Love So Desperately*	$10		Date 1649
6/26/71	100	2		11 **The Sound Of Silence**..........*The Two Of Us*	$7		Columbia 45386
12/16/78+	5	22	●	12 **Shake Your Groove Thing**..........*All Your Love (Give It Here)*	$5		Polydor/MVP 14514
3/17/79	❶^4	23	▲	13 **Reunited** RB^4 *Easy As Pie*	$5		Polydor/MVP 14547
6/30/79	44	8		14 **We've Got Love**..........*Four's A Traffic Jam*	$5		Polydor/MVP 14577
11/24/79	66	4		15 **Roller-Skatin' Mate (Part I)**..........*(Part II)*	$5		Polydor/MVP 2031
1/19/80	19	19		16 **I Pledge My Love**..........*(I Want Us) Back Together*	$5		Polydor/MVP 2053

PEACH UNION '97

Pop trio from England: Lisa Lamb, Pascal Gabriel and Paul Statham.

DEBUT	PEAK	WKS	Gold	A-side	$	Sym	Label & Number
9/20/97	39	13		**On My Own**..........A:39 / S:73 *(remix) / Higher Ground*	$3	▌	Mute/Epic 78666

PEANUT BUTTER CONSPIRACY, The BUB/LP '67

Psychedelic rock group from California: Sandi Robinson (vocals), Lance Fent and John Merrill (guitars), Al Brackett (bass) and Jim Voight (drums). Robinson died on 4/22/88 (age 43).

DEBUT	PEAK	WKS	Gold	A-side	$	Sym	Label & Number
3/11/67	93	3		**It's A Happening Thing**..........*Twice Is Life*	$12	□	Columbia 43985

PEARL, Leslie '82

Born on 7/26/52 in Pennsylvania. Pop singer/songwriter.

DEBUT	PEAK	WKS	Gold	A-side	$	Sym	Label & Number
5/22/82	28	16		**If The Love Fits Wear It**..........*Anything But Yes Is Still A No*	$5		RCA 13235

PEARL, Lucy — see LUCY PEARL

PEARLETTES '62

R&B vocal group from Los Angeles, California: sisters Lynda and Sheila Galloway with Mary Meade and Priscilla Kennedy.

DEBUT	PEAK	WKS	Gold	A-side	$	Sym	Label & Number
3/10/62	96	2		**Duchess Of Earl**..........*Everyday* answer song to **Gene Chandler**'s "Duke Of Earl"	$20		Vee-Jay 435

★377★ **PEARL JAM** ROK/BUB/LP '95

Rock group formed in Seattle, Washington: Eddie Vedder (vocals; born on 12/23/64), Stone Gossard (guitar; born on 7/20/66), Mike McCready (guitar; born on 4/5/66), Jeff Ament (bass; born on 3/10/63) and Dave Krusen (drums; born on 3/10/66). Dave Abbruzzese (born on 5/17/68) replaced Krusen in 1993. Gossard and Ament were members of Mother Love Bone. All except Krusen recorded with Temple Of The Dog. Band acted in the movie *Singles* as Matt Dillon's band, Citizen Dick. Abbruzzese left band in August 1994. Drummer Jack Irons (of the **Red Hot Chili Peppers**; born on 7/18/62) joined in late 1994. McCready also put together Mad Season in 1994. Matt Cameron (born on 11/28/62) replaced Irons in 1999.

1)Last Kiss 2)I Got Id 3)Better Man

DEBUT	PEAK	WKS	Gold	A-side	$	Sym	Label & Number
11/19/94	18	6		1 **Tremor Christ** / S:13 / A:69			
11/19/94	58	6		2 **Spin The Black Circle**..........A:60	$8	★^{V}	Epic 77771 ■
12/10/94+	13^A	36		3 **Better Man**..........AR^8			album cut
12/10/94+	53^A	23		4 **Corduroy**.......... all of above from the album *Vitalogy* on Epic 66900			album cut
8/12/95	79	9		5 **Jeremy** / S:58 / A:70 charted in 1992 at #5 on both the Album Rock and Modern Rock charts; originally released briefly in 1991 as a "45" on Epic/Associated 74745; B-side: "Alive" (ROK #16)			
8/12/95		9		6 **Yellow Ledbetter**.......... first charted in 1994 on both the Album Rock and Modern Rock charts; also see #10 below	$8	★*	Epic 77935
12/23/95	7	20	●	7 **I Got Id** / S:5 / A:34		V	
12/23/95		20		8 **Long Road**.......... recorded during the sessions for **Neil Young**'s *Mirror Ball* album; "Merkinball" and "Mirror Ball" CD packaging are almost identical; above 2 from the group's CD single titled "Merkinball"	$7	★^{V}	Epic 78199 ■
2/3/96	97	2		9 **Daughter** / AR^8 / MR^1 A:33 first charted in 1993 on both the Album Rock and Modern Rock charts			
2/3/96		2		10 **Yellow Ledbetter**.......... [L-R] recorded on 11/6/93 in Mesa, Arizona; also see studio version on #6 above; #6-8 & 10: issued as CD singles only	$7	★	Epic 77938
8/17/96	31	9		11 **Who You Are**..........MR^1 A:27 / S:29 *Habit*	$5	▌^{V}	Epic 78389 ■
10/12/96	69^A	5		12 **Hail, Hail**.......... above 2 from the album *No Code* on Epic 67500			album cut
1/24/98	21	16		13 **Given To Fly**..........AR^6 S:19 / A:46 *Pilate / Leatherman*	$5	▌^{V}	Epic 78797 ■
5/23/98	47	20		14 **Wishlist**..........S:47 / A:52 *U / Brain Of J*	$6	★^{V}	Epic 78896 ■
5/29/99	2^1	21		15 **Last Kiss** S:❶^1 / A:7 *Soldier Of Love* first issued as the B-side of a "45" promo (Christmas 1998) on Epic 41700 with a picture sleeve	$5	★^{V}	Epic 79197 □
5/13/00	49	6		16 **Nothing As It Seems**..........S:12 *Insignificance*	$5	★	Epic 79416
8/5/00	42^S	5		17 **Light Years**..........*Grievance (live) / Soon Forget (live)*	$5	★	Epic 79452
10/12/02	43	8		18 **I Am Mine**..........S:2 / A:69 *Down* "45" B-side: "Undone"; all of above (except #15 & 16) written or co-written by Vedder	$5	★^{V}	Epic 79809

PEBBLES R&B/LP '88

Born Perri McKissack on 8/29/65 in Oakland, California. R&B-dance singer. Nicknamed "Pebbles" by her family for her resemblance to cartoon character Pebbles Flintstone. Formerly married to L.A. Reid (of **The Deele**). Cousin of **Cherrelle**. Assembled/managed **TLC**.

DEBUT	PEAK	WKS	Gold	A-side	$	Sym	Label & Number
1/30/88	5	20		1 **Girlfriend**..........RB^2 S:4 / A:6 *(instrumental)*	$3	■	MCA 53185
5/7/88	2^2	18		2 **Mercedes Boy** RB^1 S:❶^1 / A:3 *(instrumental)*	$3	■	MCA 53279
8/18/90	4	22		3 **Giving You The Benefit**..........RB^3 S:5 / A:5 *(no B-side)* "45": MCA 79079; B-side: (instrumental)	$3	▌^{V}	MCA 53891

DEBUT	PEAK	WKS	Gold	A-side (Chart Hit)...B-side	$	Label & Number
				PEBBLES — Cont'd		
12/1/90+	13	19		4 **Love Makes Things Happen** RB^2 S:7 / A:26 *(no B-side)*	$3	MCA 53973
				Babyface (backing vocal)		
4/13/91	73	7		5 **Backyard** *(no B-side)*	$3	MCA 53982
				PEBBLES With Salt-N-Pepa		
				PEDICIN, Mike, Quintet '58		
				Rock and roll band from Philadelphia, Pennsylvania; led by white saxophonist Pedicin. Includes Sam Cooke (not to be confused with the same-named soul singer), Lou DeFrancis, Johnny Jones and Al Mauro.		
3/17/56	79	1		1 **The Large Large House** T:79 *Hotter Than A Pistol*	$25	RCA Victor 6369
2/10/58	71	2		2 **Shake A Hand** T:71 *The Dickie Doo*	$25	Cameo 125
				#1 R&B hit for Faye Adams in 1953		
				PEDRICK, Bobby Jr. — see JOHN, Robert		
				PEEBLES, Ann R&B/BUB/LP '73		
				Born on 4/27/47 in St. Louis, Missouri. R&B singer/songwriter.		
10/3/70	45	11		1 **Part Time Love** *I Still Love You*	$7	Hi 2178
3/6/71	85	4		2 **I Pity The Fool** *Heartaches, Heartaches*	$7	Hi 2186
9/1/73	38	21		3 **I Can't Stand The Rain** *I've Been There Before*	$7	Hi 2248
				all of above produced by **Willie Mitchell**		
				PEEK, Dan — see AMERICA		
				PEEK, Paul '61		
				Born on 6/23/37 in High Point, North Carolina. Died of liver failure on 4/3/2001 (age 63). Rock and roll singer/guitarist. Joined **Gene Vincent**'s Blue Caps as a rhythm guitarist in 1956. Left for a solo career in 1958.		
5/15/61	84	3		1 **Brother-In-Law (He's A Moocher)** *Through The Teenage Years*	$20	Fairlane 702
4/16/66	91	5		2 **Pin The Tail On The Donkey** *Rockin' Pneumonia And Boogie Woogie Flu*	$15	Columbia 43527
				PEELS, The '66		
				Novelty-pop studio production by Tash Howard.		
3/12/66	59	6		**Juanita Banana** *Fun* [N]	$15	Karate 522
				melody adapted from "Caro Nome" from Verdi's opera *Rigoletto*		
				PEEPLES, Nia LP '91		
				Born on 12/10/61 in Hollywood, California. R&B singer/actress. Played "Nicole Chapman" on TV's *Fame*. Hosted *Top Of The Pops* TV show and own syndicated music video dance TV program, *Party Machine*. Married to **Howard Hewett** from 1989-93.		
5/14/88	35	15		1 **Trouble** S:29 *(instrumental)*	$3	Mercury 870154
10/12/91	12	20		2 **Street Of Dreams** A:11 / S:65 *(edit)*	$3	Charisma 98690
2/22/92	76	5		3 **Kissing The Wind** A:70 *Men And Boys*	$3	Charisma 98633
6/27/92	88	4		4 **Faces Of Love** A:65 *Street Of Dreams*	$3	Charisma 98568
				Howard Hewett (guest vocal)		
				PENDERGRASS, Teddy R&B/AC/BUB/LP '78		
				Born on 3/26/50 in Philadelphia, Pennsylvania. Male R&B singer. Lead singer of **Harold Melvin & The Blue Notes** from 1970-76. Went solo in 1976. Acted in the 1982 movie *Soup For One*. Auto accident on 3/18/82 left him partially paralyzed. Also see **Philadelphia International All Stars**.		
				1)Close The Door 2)Two Hearts 3)I Don't Love You Anymore		
5/21/77	41	14		1 **I Don't Love You Anymore** *Somebody Told Me*	$5	Philadelphia I. 3622
7/8/78	25	13	●	2 **Close The Door** RB^2 *Get Up, Get Down, Get Funky, Get Loose*	$5	Philadelphia I. 3648
7/21/79	48	6		3 **Turn Off The Lights** *If You Know Like I Know*	$5	Philadelphia I. 3696
8/30/80	52	12		4 **Can't We Try** *This Gift Of Life*	$5	Philadelphia I. 3107
				from the movie *Roadie* starring **Meat Loaf**; B-side made the R&B charts in 1982 on Philadelphia International 02856		
11/29/80+	44	13		5 **Love T.K.O.** *I Just Called To Say*	$5	Philadelphia I. 3116
5/16/81	40	13		6 **Two Hearts** *I Just Wanna Say* (Mills)	$5	20th Century 2492
				STEPHANIE MILLS Featuring Teddy Pendergrass		
1/9/82	43	11		7 **You're My Latest, My Greatest Inspiration** *Keep On Lovin' Me*	$5	Philadelphia I. 02619
6/9/84	46	18		8 **Hold Me** *Love* (Pendergrass)	$4	Asylum 69720
				TEDDY PENDERGRASS (with Whitney Houston)		
6/18/88	77	6		9 **Joy** RB^2 *Let Me Be Closer*	$3	Asylum 69401
3/26/94	58^S	7		10 **Believe In Love** BUB:105 *Say It*	$3	Elektra 64574
4/19/97	90	6		11 **Don't Keep Wastin' My Time** S:70 *Slow Ride To Heaven*	$3	Surefire 18002
				PENDULUM AC '80		
				Techno-rock/dance trio: David Barrow, James Paul Kenny and David Quintana. All share vocals.		
11/29/80	89	7		**Gypsy Spirit** *Movin' Day*	$5	Venture 131
				PENGUINS, The R&B/BUB '55		
				R&B vocal group from Los Angeles, California: Cleveland Duncan (lead), Dexter Tisby (tenor), Bruce Tate (baritone) and Curtis Williams (bass). The second R&B/doo-wop group to make the Top 10 on the pop charts, after The Chords hit #5 in the summer of 1954 with "Sh-Boom."		
12/25/54+	8	15	●	**Earth Angel (Will You Be Mine)** RB^3 S:8 / J:10 / A:13 *Hey Senorita*	$150	DooTone 348
				written by **Jesse Belvin** and Curtis Williams; "Bubbled Under" (#101) on 12/28/59; first pressings on shiny red labels; reissued on Power 7023 with a picture sleeve		
				PENISTON, Ce Ce R&B/BUB/LP '92		
				Born on 9/6/69 in Dayton, Ohio; raised in Phoenix, Arizona. R&B-dance singer/songwriter.		
9/28/91+	5	33	●	1 **Finally** A:4 / S:9 *(7" choice mix)*	$3	A&M 1586
				MC Lethal (rap)		
2/1/92	20	20		2 **We Got A Love Thang** A:11 / S:37 *(album version)*	$3	A&M 1594
				Kym Sims (backing vocal); "45" issued for above 2 on A&M 1594		
5/23/92	15	21		3 **Keep On Walkin'** A:9 / S:18 *(2 versions) / (2 album snippets)*	$3	A&M 1598
10/10/92	94	3		4 **Inside That I Cried** A:75 *(album version)*	$3	A&M 0059
12/26/92	97	2		5 **Crazy Love** A:55 *(hard radio mix)*	$3	A&M 0034
				all of above from the album *Finally*		

DEBUT	PEAK	WKS	Gold	A-side (Chart Hit)...B-side	$	Sym	Label & Number
				PENISTON, Ce Ce — Cont'd			
1/1/94	**32**	20		6 **I'm In The Mood** ...A:27 / S:44 *(2 remixes)*	$3	▮V	A&M 0460
				"45" issued for #3 & 5 on A&M 0498			
6/18/94	**41**	14		7 **I'm Not Over You** ...S:33 / A:72 *(3 remixes)*	$3	▮	A&M 0574
11/5/94	**90**	3		8 **Hit By Love** ...*(3 remixes)*	$3	▮	A&M 0768
				#1-3, 6 & 8: #1 Dance Club Play hits			
8/24/96	**83**	7		9 **Movin' On** ...S:53 *(edit)*	$3	▮	A&M 1656
				PENN, Dawn '94			
				Born in 1952 in Kingston, Jamaica. Reggae singer/songwriter.			
2/26/94	**58**	12		**You Don't Love Me (No, No, No)** ...A:45 / S:60 *(remix edit)*	$4	▮	Big Beat 98311
				PENN, Michael ROK/LP '90			
				Born on 8/1/58 in Manhattan, New York. Pop-rock singer/songwriter/guitarist. Brother of actors Sean and Christopher Penn. Son of actor/director Leo Penn and actress Eileen Ryan. Married **Aimee Mann** on 12/29/97.			
1/6/90	**13**	16		1 **No Myth** ...S:10 / A:18 *Big House*	$3	▮V	RCA 9111 ■
4/28/90	**53**	8		2 **This & That** ...*No Myth (acoustic version)*	$3	▮V	RCA 2512
				PENTAGONS, The '61			
				Doo-wop group from San Bernardino, California: Josephus Jones (lead), his half-brother Otis Munson and brothers Ken and Ted Goodloe. Herb Reed of **The Platters** married the Goodloe's sister, Pauline. Ken Goodloe died of a heart attack on 8/4/91.			
2/20/61	**48**	10		1 **To Be Loved (Forever)** ...*Down At The Beach*	$30		Donna 1337
				first released on Fleetwood International 100 in 1960 ($125)			
10/30/61	**84**	5		2 **I Wonder (If Your Love Will Ever Belong To Me)** ...*She's Mine*	$25		Jamie 1201
				PEOPLE BUB/LP '68			
				Pop-rock group from San Jose, California: Gene Mason and Larry Norman (vocals), Jeoff Levin (guitar), Albert Ribisi (keyboards), Robb Levin (bass) and Denny Friedkin (drums).			
4/6/68	**14**	18		**I Love You** ...*Somebody Tell Me My Name*	$12		Capitol 2078
				PEOPLE'S CHOICE R&B/LP '75			
				R&B-dance group from Philadelphia, Pennsylvania: Frankie Brunson (vocals), Guy Fiske and Leon Lee (guitars), Roger Andrews (bass) and Dave Thompson (drums). Darnell Jordan replaced Lee in 1973.			
7/24/71	**38**	10		1 **I Likes To Do It** ...*Big Ladies Man* [I]	$7		Phil-L.A. 349
8/23/75	**11**	16	●	2 **Do It Any Way You Wanna** ...RB[1] *The Big Hurt* [I]	$5		TSOP 4769
2/7/76	**93**	3		3 **Nursery Rhymes (Part I)** ...*(Part II)*	$5		TSOP 4773
				PEPPERMINT, Danny, and the Jumping Jacks '61			
				Rock and roll band led by Peppermint (born Daniel Lamego) who was electrocuted on stage.			
12/4/61	**54**	4		**The Peppermint Twist** ...*Somebody Else Is Taking My Place*	$20		Carlton 565
				different song than **Joey Dee**'s "Peppermint Twist"			
				PEPPERMINT RAINBOW, The LP '69			
				Pop group from Baltimore, Maryland: sisters Bonnie and Pat Lamdin (vocals), Doug Lewis (guitar), Skip Harris (bass) and Tony Corey (drums). Discovered by producer Paul Leka (**Steam**).			
1/18/69	**32**	14		1 **Will You Be Staying After Sunday** ...*And I'll Be There*	$8		Decca 32410
6/14/69	**54**	9		2 **Don't Wake Me Up In The Morning, Michael** ...*Rosemary*	$8	■	Decca 32498
				PEPPERMINT TROLLEY COMPANY, The '68			
				Rock group from Redlands, California: brothers Danny (keyboards) and Jimmy (bass) Faragher (**Faragher Bros.**), Greg Tornquist (guitar) and Casey Cunningham (drums). All share vocals. Group later recorded as **Bones**.			
6/8/68	**59**	10		1 **Baby You Come Rollin' Across My Mind** ...*9 O'Clock Business Man*	$12		Acta 815
11/4/72	**94**	2		2 **Roberta** ...*The Bust Song*	$6		Signpost 70008
				BONES			
				co-written by **Huey (Piano) Smith**			
				PEPPERS, The R&B '74			
				Pop instrumental studio duo from Paris, France: Mat Camison (synthesizer) and Pierre Dahan (drums).			
3/9/74	**76**	7		**Pepper Box** ...*Pinch Of Salt* [I]	$6		Event 213
				PEPSI AND SHIRLIE LP '88			
				Female R&B-dance vocal duo from England: Lawrie "Pepsi" DeMacque (born on 12/10/58) and Shirlie Holliman (born on 4/18/62).			
8/15/87	**78**	8		1 **Heartache** ...*Surrender*	$3	■	Polydor 885470
2/20/88	**66**	6		2 **All Right Now** ...*Feels Like The First Time*	$3	■	Polydor 887277
				PERCELLS, The '63			
				R&B "girl group."			
3/30/63	**53**	6		**What Are Boys Made Of** ...*Cheek To Cheek*	$20		ABC-Paramount 10401
				PEREZ, Amanda '02			
				Born in Fort Wayne, Indiana. R&B-dance singer/songwriter.			
2/16/02	**79**	16		**Never** ...S:8 *(2 versions)*	$4	★	Universal 015542
				PERFECT GENTLEMEN R&B/LP '90			
				Pre-teen R&B trio from Boston, Massachusetts: Corey Blakely, Tyrone Sutton and Maurice Starr Jr. All were between the ages of 11-12 in 1990. Produced by **New Edition** and **New Kids On The Block** producer, Maurice Starr Sr.			
4/14/90	**10**	16		**Ooh La La (I Can't Get Over You)** ...S:11 / A:11 *Rated PG*	$4	▮V	Columbia 73211
				"45": Columbia 73379			
				PERFECT STRANGER C&W/LP '95			
				Country group from Carthage, Texas: Steve Murray (vocals), Richard Raines (guitar), Shayne Morrison (bass) and Andy Ginn (drums).			
8/5/95	**61**	10		**You Have The Right To Remain Silent** ...S:33 *It's Up To You*	$4	▮V	Curb 76956
				PERICOLI, Emilio '62			
				Born on 1/7/28 in Cesenatico, Italy. Adult Contemporary singer/actor.			
5/19/62	**6**	14		**Al Di La'** ...*Sassi* (Gino Paoli) [F]	$8		Warner 5259
				Giampiero Boneschi (orch.); from the movie soundtrack *Rome Adventure* starring Troy Donahue			

DEBUT	PEAK	WKS	Gold	A-side (Chart Hit)...B-side	$	Sym	Label & Number
				PERKINS, Carl C&W/LP **'56**			
				Born on 4/9/32 in Tiptonville, Tennessee. Died of a stroke on 1/19/98 (age 65). Rockabilly singer/songwriter/guitarist. Formed family band consisting of Carl (guitar), brothers Jay B. (guitar) and Clayton (bass), and W.B. Holland (drums). Signed with Flip Records in 1954; recorded "Movie Magg" (Flip 501-$1000). Member of **Johnny Cash**'s touring troupe from 1965-75. In the movie *Into The Night* (1985). Inducted into the Rock and Roll Hall of Fame in 1987.			
3/3/56	2[4]	21		1 **Blue Suede Shoes** CW[3] J:2 / S:3 / T:4 / A:5 *Honey, Don't!*	$60		Sun 234
				Grammy Hall of Fame Award winner in 1986; the B-sides of #1 & 3 were recorded by **The Beatles** in 1964			
7/14/56	70	4		2 **Boppin' The Blues**...T:70 *All Mama's Children*	$50		Sun 243
3/23/57	67	7		3 **Your True Love**...T:67 *Matchbox*	$50		Sun 261
5/26/58	91	1		4 **Pink Pedal Pushers**...T:91 *Jive After Five*	$40	■	Columbia 41131
				a promotional orange-colored picture sleeve also issued: "Carl Perkins now on Columbia Records"			
6/1/59	93	2		5 **Pointed Toe Shoes**...*Highway Of Love*	$30		Columbia 41379
				PERKINS, George, & The Silver Stars **'70**			
				R&B group from Shreveport, Louisiana. Led by singer George Perkins.			
4/4/70	61	6		**Cryin' In The Streets (Part 1)**...*(Part 2)*	$10		Silver Fox 18
				PERKINS, Joe **'63**			
				Novelty "eefin-style" vocalist. Produced by **Bob Moore**.			
9/28/63	76	5		**Little Eeefin Annie**...*Uncle Eeef* [N]	$12		Sound Stage 7 2511
				PERKINS, Tony **'57**			
				Born on 4/14/32 in Manhattan, New York. Died of AIDS on 9/12/92 (age 60). Actor/singer. Starred in several movies.			
10/7/57	24	11		**Moon-Light Swim**...A:24 / T:43 *First Romance*	$12		RCA Victor 7020
				Frank DeVol (orch.); re-issued in 1958 on RCA Victor 7295 ($10)			
				PERRY, Steve ROK/LP **'84**			
				Born on 1/22/49 in Hanford, California. Lead singer of **Journey**.			
8/28/82	17	12		1 **Don't Fight It**...*The More We Try* (Loggins)	$3	■	Columbia 03192
				KENNY LOGGINS with Steve Perry			
4/7/84	3	20		2 **Oh Sherrie** AR[2] *Don't Tell Me Why You're Leaving*	$3	■	Columbia 04391
6/30/84	21	13		3 **She's Mine**...*You Should Be Happy*	$3	■	Columbia 04496
9/8/84	40	13		4 **Strung Out**...*Captured By The Moment*	$3		Columbia 04598
11/24/84+	18	19		5 **Foolish Heart**...A:12 / S:16 *It's Only Love*	$3		Columbia 04693
				above 4 from the album *Street Talk*			
7/16/94	29	16		6 **You Better Wait**...A:25 *Stand Up (Before It's Too Late)*	$3	▮	Columbia 77580
12/3/94	74	6		7 **Missing You**...A:73 *What Was*	$3	▮	Columbia 77760
				PERSON, Houston R&B **'76**			
				Born on 11/10/34 in Florence, South Carolina. Black jazz tenor saxophonist.			
1/17/76	91	4		1 **Disco Sax /** [I]			
1/17/76		4		2 **For The Love Of You**... [I]	$5		Westbound 5015
				PERSUADERS, The R&B/BUB/LP **'71**			
				R&B vocal group formed in Harlem, New York: Doug Scott, Willie Holland, James Barnes and Charles Stodghill.			
8/28/71	15	12	●	1 **Thin Line Between Love & Hate**...RB[2] *Thigh Spy*	$10		Atco 6822
12/25/71+	64	10		2 **Love Gonna Pack Up (And Walk Out)**...*You Must Have Put Something In Your Love*	$10		Win Or Lose 220
11/3/73	39	11		3 **Some Guys Have All The Luck**...*Love Attack*	$8		Atco 6943
3/2/74	85	6		4 **Best Thing That Ever Happened To Me**...*That's The Way She Is*	$8		Atco 6956
	★368★			**PETER AND GORDON** BUB **'64**			
				Pop vocal duo formed in London, England: Peter Asher (born on 6/22/44 in London, England) and Gordon Waller (born on 6/4/45 in Braemar, Scotland). Asher later went into production and management, including work with **Linda Ronstadt**, **James Taylor** and **10,000 Maniacs**.			
				1)A World Without Love 2)Lady Godiva 3)I Go To Pieces			
5/9/64	❶[1]	12		1 **A World Without Love** *If I Were You*	$12		Capitol 5175
6/27/64	12	9		2 **Nobody I Know**...*You Don't Have To Tell Me*	$12	■	Capitol 5211
10/3/64	16	9		3 **I Don't Want To See You Again**...*I Would Buy You Presents*	$12	■	Capitol 5272
1/9/65	9	11		4 **I Go To Pieces**...*Love Me, Baby*	$12	■	Capitol 5335
				written by **Del Shannon**			
4/17/65	14	11		5 **True Love Ways**...*If You Wish*	$12	■	Capitol 5406
				written by **Buddy Holly** and **Norman Petty**			
7/10/65	24	7		6 **To Know You Is To Love You**...*I Told You So*	$12	■	Capitol 5461
				same song as **The Teddy Bears**' "To Know Him, Is To Love Him"			
11/6/65	83	4		7 **Don't Pity Me**...*Crying In The Rain*	$10		Capitol 5532
2/12/66	14	12		8 **Woman**...*Wrong From The Start*	$10		Capitol 5579
				#1-3 & 8: written by **Paul McCartney**			
5/7/66	50	7		9 **There's No Living Without Your Loving**...*Stranger With A Black Dove* (#130)	$10	■	Capitol 5650
7/30/66	98	2		10 **To Show I Love You**...*Start Trying Someone Else*	$10	■	Capitol 5684
10/8/66	6	14		11 **Lady Godiva**...*The Town I Live In*	$10		Capitol 5740
				also released with "Morning's Calling" as the B-side			
12/24/66+	15	9		12 **Knight In Rusty Armour**...*The Flower Lady*	$10	■	Capitol 5808
3/25/67	31	6		13 **Sunday For Tea**...*Hurtin' Is Lovin'*	$10	■	Capitol 5864
				promotional copies issued with a special "Rush Release" text insert			
6/24/67	97	1		14 **The Jokers**...*Red, Cream And Velvet*	$10		Capitol 5919
				title song from the movie starring Michael Crawford			

DEBUT	PEAK	WKS	Gold	A-side (Chart Hit)...B-side	$	Sym	Label & Number
	★214★			**PETER, PAUL & MARY** BUB/AC/LP **'63**			
				Folk trio formed in New York: **Peter Yarrow** (born on 5/31/38 in Brooklyn, New York) (see #23 below), **Paul Stookey** (born on 12/30/37 in Baltimore, Maryland) (see #22 below) and **Mary Travers** (born on 11/7/37 in Louisville, Kentucky) (see #21 below).			
				1)Leaving On A Jet Plane 2)Blowin' In The Wind 3)Puff (The Magic Dragon) 4)I Dig Rock And Roll Music 5)Don't Think Twice, It's All Right			
5/5/62	35	8		1 **Lemon Tree** ... *Early In The Morning*	$10		Warner 5274
8/18/62	10	12		2 **If I Had A Hammer (The Hammer Song)** ... *Gone The Rainbow*	$10		Warner 5296
				written as "The Hammer Song" by **Pete Seeger** & Lee Hays of The Weavers in 1958			
12/15/62+	93	2		3 **Big Boat** ... *Tiny Sparrow*	$10	■	Warner 5325
1/19/63	56	6		4 **Settle Down (Goin' Down That Highway)** ... *500 Miles*	$10		Warner 5334
3/16/63	2^{1}	14		5 **Puff The Magic Dragon** ... AC^{2} *Pretty Mary*	$10		Warner 5348
				some pressings show title only as "Puff"			
6/29/63	2^{1}	15		6 **Blowin' In The Wind** ... AC^{5} *Flora*	$10		Warner 5368
9/14/63	9	10		7 **Don't Think Twice, It's All Right** ... *Autumn To May*	$10		Warner 5385
				above 2 written and recorded by **Bob Dylan** in 1963 (A & B sides of a 7" single) on Columbia 42856 ($500)			
11/30/63	35	7		8 **Stewball** ... *The Cruel War*	$10		Warner 5399
				based on the 1822 ballad "Skewbald"			
12/28/63	15^{X}	1		9 **A'Soalin'** ... *Hush-A-Bye* [X]	$12	■	Warner 5402
3/7/64	33	7		10 **Tell It On The Mountain** ... *Old Coat*	$10		Warner 5418
				adapted from the Christmas spiritual "Go Tell It On The Mountain"; #6-8 & 10: from the album *In The Wind*			
6/27/64	93	3		11 **Oh, Rock My Soul (Part I)** ... *(Part II)* [L]	$10		Warner 5442
				based on the spiritual "Bosom Of Abraham" (also known as "So High, So Low")			
1/23/65	30	7		12 **For Lovin' Me** ... *Monday Morning*	$8		Warner 5496
5/15/65	91	3		13 **When The Ship Comes In** ... *The Times They Are A Changin'*	$8		Warner 5625
10/9/65	91	3		14 **Early Morning Rain** ... *The Rising Of The Moon*	$8		Warner 5659
				#12 & 14: written by **Gordon Lightfoot**			
4/23/66	52	5		15 **The Cruel War** ... *Mon Vrai Destin*	$8		Warner 5809
				a different version is on the B-side of #8 above			
9/24/66	100	1		16 **The Other Side Of This Life** ... *Sometime Lovin'*	$8		Warner 5849
8/19/67	9	11		17 **I Dig Rock And Roll Music** ... *The Great Mandella (The Wheel Of Life)*	$8		Warner 7067
11/25/67	35	7		18 **Too Much Of Nothing** ... *The House Song*	$8		Warner 7092
				#6, 7, 13 & 18: written by **Bob Dylan**			
4/26/69	21	10		19 **Day Is Done** ... *Make Believe Town*	$7		Warner 7279
10/25/69	①^{1}	17	●	20 **Leaving On A Jet Plane** AC^{3} *The House Song*	$7		Warner 7340
				from the trio's 1967 *Album 1700*			
5/22/71	56	11		21 **Follow Me** ... *I Guess He'd Rather Be In Colorado*	$6		Warner 7481
				MARY TRAVERS			
				above 2 written by **John Denver**			
7/31/71	24	14		22 **Wedding Song (There Is Love)** ... *Give A Damn*	$6		Warner 7511
				PAUL STOOKEY			
4/8/72	100	2		23 **Don't Ever Take Away My Freedom** ... *Greenwood*	$6		Warner 7567
				PETER YARROW			
				PETERS, Bernadette LP **'80**			
				Born Bernadette Lazzara on 2/28/44 in Queens, New York. Actress/singer. Appeared in several movies and TV shows.			
3/29/80	31	13		1 **Gee Whiz** ... *I Never Thought I'd Break*	$4	■	MCA 41210
8/8/81	65	8		2 **Dedicated To The One I Love** ... *Broadway Baby*	$4	■	MCA 51152
				PETERSEN, Paul LP **'62**			
				Born on 9/23/45 in Glendale, California. Pop singer/actor. Member of Disney's "Mouseketeers" and played "Jeff Stone" on TV's *Donna Reed Show* (1958-66).			
3/3/62	19	12		1 **She Can't Find Her Keys** ... *Very Unlikely* (w/**Shelley Fabares**)	$20	■	Colpix 620
6/9/62	58	6		2 **Keep Your Love Locked (Deep In Your Heart)** ... *Be Everything To Anyone You Love*	$20	■	Colpix 632
8/25/62	54	7		3 **Lollipops And Roses** ... *Please Mr. Sun*	$20		Colpix 649
11/17/62+	6	16		4 **My Dad** *Little Boy Sad*	$20	■	Colpix 663
3/30/63	65	4		5 **Amy** ... *Goody Goody*	$15		Colpix 676
				also released with "I Only Have Eyes For You" as the B-side			
11/30/63+	78	7		6 **The Cheer Leader** ... *Polka Dots And Moonbeams*	$15		Colpix 707
				all of above produced by Stu Phillips			
				PETERSON, Bobby, Quintet **'59**			
				R&B-jazz band from Chester, Pennsylvania: Bobby Peterson (vocals, piano), Joe Pyatt (tenor sax), Chico Green (bass), David Butler (drums) and **Jamo Thomas** (conga drums, bongos).			
10/26/59	71	7		1 **The Hunch** ... *Love You Pretty Baby* [I]	$20		V-Tone 205
10/31/60	96	1		2 **Irresistable You** *[BOBBY PETERSON]* ... *Piano Rock*	$20		V-Tone 214
				PETERSON, Michael C&W/BUB/LP **'97**			
				Born on 8/7/59 in Tucson, Arizona. Country singer/songwriter/guitarist.			
8/9/97	86	7		**Drink, Swear, Steal & Lie** ... S:71 *For A Song*	$4	■^{V}	Reprise 17379
				PETERSON, Ray BUB **'60**			
				Born on 4/23/39 in Denton, Texas. Rock and roll singer. Started singing in his early teens while being treated for polio at a Texas hospital. Formed own Dunes label in 1960.			
5/18/59	25	16		1 **The Wonder Of You** ... *I'm Gone*	$20		RCA Victor 7513
				Shorty Rogers (orch.); also see #9 below			
11/16/59	64	6		2 **Goodnight My Love (Pleasant Dreams)** ... *Till Then*	$20	■	RCA Victor 7635
				#7 R&B hit for **Jesse Belvin** in 1956; also see the B-side of #9 below			
6/13/60	7	14		3 **Tell Laura I Love Her** *Wedding Day*	$20		RCA Victor 7745
11/21/60+	9	15		4 **Corinna, Corinna** ... *Be My Girl*	$20	■	Dunes 2002
				#18 hit for Red Nichols jazz band in 1931 (as "Corrine Corrina"); #2 R&B hit for **Joe Turner** in 1956			
4/3/61	100	1		5 **Sweet Little Kathy** ... *You Didn't Care*	$20		Dunes 2004
7/31/61	29	15		6 **Missing You** ... *You Thrill Me*	$20		Dunes 2006
				#7 Country hit for **Webb Pierce** in 1957			

DEBUT	PEAK	WKS	Gold	A-side (Chart Hit)..........B-side	$	Sym	Label & Number
				PETERSON, Ray — Cont'd			
12/18/61+	57	8		7 **I Could Have Loved You So Well** .... *Why Don't You Write Me*	$20		Dunes 2009
				#4 & 7: produced by Phil Spector			
6/1/63	70	6		8 **Give Us Your Blessing** .... *Without Love (There Is Nothing)*	$20		Dunes 2025
4/25/64	70	3		9 **The Wonder Of You** .... *Goodnight My Love (Pleasant Dreams)* [R]	$15		RCA Victor 8333
				same version as #1 above			

PETS, The '58

Session group formed by Joe Lubin; included Plas Johnson (sax) and Earl Palmer (drums). Touring group was put together featuring Richard Podolor (**Richie Allen**, **The Hondells**), who later became a top producer, working with **Three Dog Night** and **Steppenwolf**, among others.

DEBUT	PEAK	WKS	Gold	A-side (Chart Hit)..........B-side	$	Sym	Label & Number
6/2/58	34	8		**Cha-Hua-Hua** .... T:34 / S:38 *Cha-Kow-Ski* [I]	$15		Arwin 109

PET SHOP BOYS ★402★ BUB/ROK/LP '86

Synth-pop/dance duo formed in England: Neil Tennant (vocals; born on 7/10/54) and Chris Lowe (keyboards; born on 10/4/59). Tennant was a writer for the British fan magazine *Smash Hits.* Tennant also recorded with the group **Electronic**.

1)West End Girls 2)What Have I Done To Deserve This? 3)Always On My Mind

DEBUT	PEAK	WKS	Gold	A-side (Chart Hit)..........B-side	$	Sym	Label & Number
3/1/86	❶[1]	20		1 **West End Girls** S:❶[2] / A:❶[2] *A Man Could Get Arrested*	$3	■	EMI America 8307
5/31/86	10	16		2 **Opportunities (Let's Make Lots Of Money)** .... S:10 / A:11 *Was That What It Was*	$3	■	EMI America 8330
				first 5 chart weeks on EMI America 8321			
8/30/86	62	8		3 **Love Comes Quickly** .... *That's My Impression*	$3	■	EMI America 8338
12/6/86+	70	10		4 **Suburbia** .... *Jack The Lad*	$3	■	EMI America 8355
				all of above from the album *Please*			
9/5/87	9	19		5 **It's A Sin** .... S:5 / A:10 *You Know Where You Went Wrong*	$3	■	EMI America 43027
12/12/87+	2[2]	18		6 **What Have I Done To Deserve This?** .... S:❶[1] / A:4 *A New Life* (Pet Shop Boys)	$3	■	EMI-Manhattan 50107
				PET SHOP BOYS (and Dusty Springfield)			
				also released on EMI America 50107 in 1987			
3/26/88	4	15		7 **Always On My Mind** .... S:2 / A:6 *Do I Have To?*	$3		EMI-Manhattan 50123
10/8/88	18	14		8 **Domino Dancing** .... S:15 / A:23 *Don Juan*	$3	■	EMI-Manhattan 50161
				The Voice In Fashion (backing vocals)			
1/28/89	84	3		9 **Left To My Own Devices** .... *The Sound Of The Atom Splitting*	$3	■	EMI-Manhattan 50171
10/20/90	62	8		10 **So Hard** .... *It Must Be Obvious*	$3	▮	EMI 50329
2/16/91	93	3		11 **How Can You Expect To Be Taken Seriously?** .. *What Have I Done To Deserve This?*	$3	▮	EMI 50343
5/25/91	72	7		12 **Where The Streets Have No Name (I Can't Take My Eyes Off You)** .... A:68 / S:70 *Bet She's Not Your Girlfriend*	$3	▮	EMI 50351
				medley of **U2**'s #13 hit in 1987 and **Frankie Valli**'s #2 hit in 1967			
11/27/99	53[S]	7		13 **New York City Boy** .... *(8 mixes)*	$8	★*	Parlophone 35013
6/17/00	66[S]	1		14 **I Don't Know What You Want But I Can't Give It Any More** .... *(6 mixes)*	$8	★*	Sire 35022
12/15/01	51[S]	1		15 **Break 4 Love** .... *(7 versions - white cover)*	$8	★*	Star 69 12172
				PETER RAUHOFER + THE PET SHOP BOYS = THE COLLABORATION			
				written by **Vaughan Mason** and recorded by Raze in 1988 on Columbia 07890; "Break 4 Love, Part 2" (featuring 6 additional remixes) issued on Star 69 12192 (black cover)			

PETTY, Norman, Trio MEM/POP '54

Born on 5/25/27 in Clovis, New Mexico. Died on 8/15/84 (age 57). His trio: Petty (piano), wife Violet Ann (piano) and Jack Vaughn (guitar). Later produced **Buddy Holly** and **The Fireballs**. Hit #14 on the pop charts in 1954 with "Mood Indigo."

DEBUT	PEAK	WKS	Gold	A-side (Chart Hit)..........B-side	$	Sym	Label & Number
2/23/57	56	13		1 **Almost Paradise** .... T:56 *It's Been A Long Long Time* [I]	$15		ABC-Paramount 9787
8/12/57	81	5		2 **The First Kiss** .... T:81 *The First Kiss* (vocal by Vi Petty) [I]	$15		Columbia 40929

PETTY, Tom, And The Heartbreakers ★126★ ROK/BUB/LP '89

Born on 10/20/50 in Gainesville, Florida. Rock singer/songwriter/guitarist. Formed The Heartbreakers in Los Angeles, California: Mike Campbell (guitar; born on 2/1/54), Benmont Tench (keyboards; born on 9/7/54) Ron Blair (bass; born on 9/16/52) and Stan Lynch (drums; born on 5/21/55). Howie Epstein (born on 7/21/55; died of a drug overdose on 2/23/2003, age 47) replaced Blair in 1982. Blair returned in 2002, replacing Epstein. Steve Ferrone replaced Lynch in 1995. Petty appeared in the movies *FM* and *Made In Heaven.* Member of the **Traveling Wilburys**. Group inducted into the Rock and Roll Hall of Fame in 2002.

1)Free Fallin' 2)Don't Do Me Like That 3)Stop Draggin' My Heart Around 4)I Won't Back Down 5)You Don't Know How It Feels

DEBUT	PEAK	WKS	Gold	A-side (Chart Hit)..........B-side	$	Sym	Label & Number
11/5/77+	40	17		1 **Breakdown** .... *Fooled Again (I Don't Like It)*	$7		Shelter 62008
				originally released on Shelter 62006 in 1977 ($10)			
6/17/78	41	10		2 **I Need To Know** .... *No Second Thoughts*	$7		Shelter 62010
9/23/78	59	6		3 **Listen To Her Heart** *[TOM PETTY]* .... *I Don't Know What To Say To You*	$7	■	Shelter 62011
11/17/79+	10	18		4 **Don't Do Me Like That** .... *Casa Dega*	$5	■	Backstreet 41138
1/26/80	15	14		5 **Refugee** .... *It's Rainin' Again*	$5	■	Backstreet 41169
4/26/80	59	7		6 **Here Comes My Girl** .... *Louisiana Rain*	$5	■	Backstreet 41227
5/2/81	19	13		7 **The Waiting** .... AR[6] *Nightwatchman* (ROK #21)	$4	■	Backstreet 51100
7/25/81	3	21		8 **Stop Draggin' My Heart Around** .... *Kind Of Woman* (Nicks)	$4	■	Modern 7336
				STEVIE NICKS (with Tom Petty and The Heartbreakers)			
8/1/81	79	6		9 **A Woman In Love (It's Not Me)** .... *Gator On The Lawn*	$4	■	Backstreet 51136
11/13/82+	20	18		10 **You Got Lucky** .... AR[3] *Between Two Worlds* (ROK #35)	$4	■	Backstreet 52144
2/26/83	21	11		11 **Change Of Heart** .... *Heartbreakers Beach Party*	$4	■	Backstreet 52181
				also issued with a red vinyl record in a clear plastic sleeve with a sticker			
3/16/85	13	14		12 **Don't Come Around Here No More** .... S:8 / A:21 *Trailer*	$4	■	MCA 52496
6/8/85	54	8		13 **Make It Better (Forget About Me)** .... *Cracking Up*	$3	■	MCA 52605
8/17/85	74	5		14 **Rebels** .... *Southern Accents*	$3	■	MCA 52658
2/1/86	37	9		15 **Needles And Pins** .... *Spike (live)* (Petty) [L]	$3	■	MCA 52772
				TOM PETTY and the HEARTBREAKERS with STEVIE NICKS			
				written by **Sonny** Bono and **Jack Nitzsche**; recorded at LA's Wiltern Theater			
4/25/87	18	12		16 **Jammin' Me** .... AR[4] S:16 / A:23 *Make That Connection*	$3	■	MCA 53065
				co-written by **Bob Dylan**			
4/29/89	12	15		17 **I Won't Back Down** *[TOM PETTY]* .... AR[5] S:8 / A:19 *The Apartment Song*	$4		MCA 53369
				George Harrison (backing vocal, guitar)			

DEBUT	PEAK	WKS	Gold	A-side (Chart Hit)..................B-side	$	Sym	Label & Number
				PETTY, Tom, And The Heartbreakers — Cont'd			
7/29/89	**23**	14		18 **Runnin' Down A Dream** *[TOM PETTY]* ....AR[1] S:11 / A:31 *Alright For Now*	$3		MCA 53682
11/4/89+	**7**	21		19 **Free Fallin'** *[TOM PETTY]* AR[1] S:3 / A:9 *Down The Line*	$3	▮V	MCA 53748
3/3/90	**46**	8		20 **A Face In The Crowd** *[TOM PETTY]*..........S:35 *A Mind With A Heart Of Its Own* above 4 from the album *Full Moon Fever*	$3	▮V	MCA 53781
6/29/91	**28**	14		21 **Learning To Fly**..........AR[6] A:63 *Too Good To Be True*	$3	▮V	MCA 54124
11/16/91	**92**	5		22 **Into The Great Wide Open** ....*Makin' Some Noise* (ROK #30) above 6 co-produced by **Jeff Lynne**	$3	▮V	MCA 54131
12/25/93+	**14**	20		23 **Mary Jane's Last Dance**..........AR[2] S:15 / A:31 *The Waiting*	$3	▮V	MCA 54732
12/3/94+	**13**	22		24 **You Don't Know How It Feels** *[TOM PETTY]* ....AR[1] S:12 / A:19 *Girl On LSD*	$3	▮V	Warner 18030
4/29/95	**68**	8		25 **It's Good To Be King** *[TOM PETTY]* ....*Cabin Down Below (acoustic version)*	$3	▮V	Warner 17925
9/28/96	**69**	4		26 **Walls**..........A:57 *(No. 3 version)* from the movie *She's The One* starring Jennifer Aniston; "45" shows title as "Walls (Circus)'; all of above (except #15) written or co-written by Petty	$3	▮V	Warner 17593
				PG&E — see PACIFIC GAS & ELECTRIC			
				PHAIR, Liz ROK/LP **'94** Born on 4/17/67 in New Haven, Connecticut. Rock singer/songwriter.			
10/15/94	**78**	14		**Supernova**..........A:68 *Combo Platter* "45": Matador 103 (issued on blue vinyl and with a picture sleeve)	$4	▮V	Matador 98206 ■
				PHAJJA R&B/BUB **'98** R&B vocal trio from Chicago, Illinois: sisters Kena and Nakia Epps, with Karen Johnson.			
2/21/98	**87**	5		**So Long (Well, Well, Well)**..........S:75 *(remix)*	$3	▮	Warner 17308
				PHARCYDE, The R&B/LP **'93** Male rap group from Los Angeles, California: Trevant Hardson, Imani Wilcox, Romye Robinson and Derrick Stewart.			
5/1/93	**52**	17		1 **Passin' Me By**..........S:30 / A:52 *Pork* samples "Summer In The City" by **Quincy Jones**	$4	▮	Delicious Vinyl 98434
10/21/95	**55**	15		2 **Runnin'** / S:34 samples "Saudade Ven Correndo" by **Stan Getz** and "Rock Box" by **Run-DMC**			
4/13/96	**93**	3		3 **Drop**..........	$4	▮	Delicious Vinyl 58483
5/25/02	**54**[S]	2		4 **Hard Times**..........*Verbal Murder* (Ras Kass) **PHARCYDE/JURASSIC 5**	$6	T	Avatar 10104
				PHAROAHE MONCH R&B/LP **'01** Born Troy Jamerson in Queens, New York. Male rapper. Former member of Organized Konfusion. Also see **Sway & King Tech**.			
10/23/99	**97**	5		1 **Simon Says**..........S:32 *(instrumental) / Behind Closed Doors*	$4	★	Rawkus 53567
9/9/00	**52**[S]	8		2 **Connect**..........*(2 versions) / The Life* (w/**Kool G Rap**) **DJ HURRICANE w/Xzibit, Big Gipp & Pharoahe Monch**	$5	★	TVT 6451
12/23/00+	**83**	12		3 **Oh No**..........S:33 *(2 versions) / Battle* (**Erick Sermon** w/Sy Scott) **MOS DEF & PHAROAHE MONCH Featuring Nate Dogg**	$6	T	Rawkus 289
				PHELPS, James **'65** Born in Shreveport, Louisiana. Gospel singer. Member of The Soul Stirrers from 1964-65.			
5/8/65	**66**	7		**Love Is A 5-Letter Word**..........*I'll Do The Best I Can* 5-Letter Word: Money	$10		Argo 5499
				PHENOMENON **'01** Male rap duo from Brooklyn, New York: David Shepard and Dannie Longmire.			
3/10/01	**45**[S]	7		**Tha' Rodeo**..........*(2 versions) / Ghetto Life*	$5	★*	King B 3001
				PHIFE DAWG — see TRIBE CALLED QUEST			
				PHILADELPHIA INTERNATIONAL ALL STARS **'77** Supergroup of Philadelphia International artists: **Lou Rawls**, **Billy Paul**, **Teddy Pendergrass**, **The O'Jays**, **Archie Bell** and **Dee Dee Sharp** Gamble.			
8/13/77	**91**	4		**Let's Clean Up The Ghetto**..........*(instrumental* by **MFSB**) all profits were committed to a 5-year charity project	$6		Philadelphia I. 3627
				PHILARMONICS, The **'77** Studio group assembled by British conductor/arranger Steve Gray.			
3/12/77	**100**	2		**For Elise**..........*A La Turka* [I] a disco adaptation of Beethoven's *Fur Elise*	$5		Capricorn 0268
				PHILLIPS, Esther R&B/BUB/AC/LP **'62** Born Esther Mae Jones on 12/23/35 in Galveston, Texas. Died of liver failure on 8/7/84 (age 48). R&B singer. One of the first female superstars of R&B. Recorded and toured with The **Johnny Otis** Orchestra as "Little Esther," 1948-54; scored seven Top 10 hits on the R&B charts in 1950. Bouts with drug addiction frequently interrupted her career and eventually led to her death.			
10/27/62	**8**	14		1 **Release Me** RB[3] *Don't Feel Rained On* **ESTHER PHILLIPS "Little Esther"** #5 Country hit for **Jimmy Heap** in 1954; also see #6 below	$25		Lenox 5555
2/9/63	**61**	5		2 **I Really Don't Want To Know** ....*Am I That Easy To Forget* (#112) **"LITTLE ESTHER" PHILLIPS** #11 hit for **Les Paul & Mary Ford** in 1954	$20		Lenox 5560
4/27/63	**73**	2		3 **You Never Miss Your Water (Till The Well Runs Dry)**..*If You Want It (I've Got It)* (#129) **"LITTLE ESTHER" PHILLIPS & "BIG AL" DOWNING**	$15		Lenox 5565
5/8/65	**54**	9		4 **And I Love Him**..........*Shangri-La* female version of **The Beatles**' "And I Love Her"	$12		Atlantic 2281
6/4/66	**73**	5		5 **When A Woman Loves A Man**..........*Ups And Downs* female version of **Percy Sledge**'s "When A Man Loves A Woman"	$12		Atlantic 2335
6/3/67	**93**	2		6 **Release Me**..........*Don't Feel Rained On* [R] same version as #1 above	$12		Atlantic 2411
8/16/75	**20**	16		7 **What A Diff'rence A Day Makes**..........*Turn Around, Look At Me* #5 hit for the Dorsey Brothers Orchestra in 1934	$6		Kudu 925
				PHILLIPS, John — see MAMAS AND THE PAPAS, The			

DEBUT	PEAK	WKS	Gold	A-side (Chart Hit)..........B-side	$	Sym	Label & Number
				PHILLIPS, Phil, With The Twilights BUB '59			
				Born John Phillip Baptiste on 3/14/31 in Lake Charles, Louisiana. Black vocalist.			
7/6/59	2^2	18	●	Sea Of Love..........RB[1] *Juella*	$25		Mercury 71465
				first released on Khoury's 711 in 1959 ($1000)			
				PHILLIPS, Shawn BUB/LP '73			
				Born on 2/3/43 in Fort Worth, Texas. Male Adult Contemporary singer/songwriter/guitarist.			
1/13/73	89	3		1 **We**..........*'L' Ballade*	$7		A&M 1402
2/10/73	63	6		2 **Lost Horizon**..........*Landscape*	$7	■	A&M 1405
				title song from the movie starring Peter Finch and Liv Ullmann			
				PHILLY CREAM R&B '79			
				Soul session band from Philadelphia, Pennsylvania. Featured vocalists Valarie Lipford and Samuel Tompkins.			
6/30/79	67	5		**Motown Review**..........*Join The Army*	$5		Fantasy/WMOT 862
				PHILLY DEVOTIONS R&B/BUB '75			
				R&B-dance group from Philadelphia, Pennsylvania: Ellis "Butch" Hill, Ernest "Chucky" Gibson, Morris Taylor and Matthew Cogington.			
2/8/75	95	2		**I Just Can't Say Goodbye**..........*(instrumental)*	$5		Columbia 10076
				PHILLY'S MOST WANTED R&B/LP '01			
				Male rap duo from Philadelphia, Pennsylvania: Al "Boobonic" Holly and Joel "Mr. Man" Witherspoon.			
7/8/00	75^S	1		1 **Y'all Can't Never Hurt Us**..........*What Makes Me*	$5	★+	Atlantic 84699
3/3/01	98	5		2 **Cross The Border**..........S:21 *Suckas Pt. 2 (For Da' Gangsta's)* (w/**Beanie Sigel**)	$4	★	Atlantic 85008
				PHOTOGLO, Jim AC/BUB/LP '81			
				Born in Los Angeles, California. Pop singer/songwriter.			
3/29/80	31	14		1 **We Were Meant To Be Lovers** *[PHOTOGLO]*..........*Beg, Borrow Or Steal*	$4		20th Century 2446
4/18/81	25	16		2 **Fool In Love With You**..........*Ruled By My Heart*	$4		20th Century 2487
				PIAF, Edith POP/BUB '50			
				Born Edith Giovanna Gassion on 12/19/15 in Belleville, Paris. Died on 10/11/63 (age 47). Legendary French chanteuse. As a teen, sang for pennies in Paris streets; eventually became an international music hall/cabaret star. Hit #23 in 1950 with "La Vie En Rose."			
3/6/61	88	3		**Milord**..........*Milord* (**Franck Pourcel** - #112) [F]	$12		Capitol 4493
				Robert Chauvigny (orch.); French vocal, recorded in 1959			
				PICKETT, Bobby "Boris", And The Crypt-Kickers BUB/LP '62			
				Born on 2/11/40 in Somerville, Massachusetts. Began recording career in Hollywood while aspiring to be an actor. A member of **The Stompers** in early 1962. **Leon Russell**, Johnny McCrae (**Ronny & The Daytonas**), Rickie Page (**The Bermudas**) and Gary Paxton (**Hollywood Argyles**) were The Crypt-Kickers.			
9/8/62	❶²	14	●	1 **Monster Mash** *Monsters' Mash Party* [N]	$25	■	Garpax 44167
				also see #4 & 5 below; first released on Garpax 1 in 1962 ($25)			
12/8/62	30	6		2 **Monsters' Holiday**..........*Monster Motion* [X-N]	$25	■	Garpax 44171
6/22/63	88	2		3 **Graduation Day** *[BOBBY PICKETT]*..........*The Humpty Dumpty*	$25	■	Garpax 44175
8/29/70	91	3		4 **Monster Mash**..........*Monsters' Mash Party* [N-R]	$10		Parrot 348
5/5/73	10	20	●	5 **Monster Mash**..........*Monsters' Mash Party* [N-R]	$10		Parrot 348
				#1, 4 & 5: all the same version; all of above produced by Gary Paxton			

DEBUT	PEAK	WKS	Gold	A-side (Chart Hit)..........B-side	$	Sym	Label & Number
				PICKETT, Wilson ★100★ R&B/BUB/LP '66			
				Born on 3/18/41 in Prattville, Alabama. R&B singer/songwriter. Nicknamed the "Wicked Pickett." Sang in local gospel groups. To Detroit in 1955. With **The Falcons**, 1961-63. Career took off after recording in Memphis with guitarist/producer Steve Cropper. Inducted into the Rock and Roll Hall of Fame in 1991.			
				1)Land Of 1000 Dances 2)Funky Broadway 3)634-5789 4)Don't Knock My Love 5)Engine Number 9			
5/4/63	64	6		1 **If You Need Me**..........*Baby Call On Me*	$20		Double-L 713
7/27/63	49	10		2 **It's Too Late**..........*I'm Gonna Love You*	$20		Double-L 717
11/9/63	95	4		3 **I'm Down To My Last Heartbreak**..........*I Can't Stop*	$20		Double-L 724
7/10/65	21	12		4 **In The Midnight Hour**..........RB[1] *I'm Not Tired*	$12		Atlantic 2289
11/6/65	53	10		5 **Don't Fight It**..........*It's All Over*	$12		Atlantic 2306
2/12/66	13	11		6 **634-5789 (Soulsville, U.S.A.)**..........RB[7] *That's A Man's Way*	$12		Atlantic 2320
5/28/66	53	8		7 **Ninety-Nine And A Half (Won't Do)**..........*Danger Zone*	$12		Atlantic 2334
7/30/66	6	11		8 **Land Of 1000 Dances** RB[1] *You're So Fine*	$12		Atlantic 2348
11/26/66	23	9		9 **Mustang Sally**..........*Three Time Loser*	$12		Atlantic 2365
				#15 R&B hit for Sir Mack Rice in 1965			
2/4/67	29	7		10 **Everybody Needs Somebody To Love**..........*Nothing You Can Do*	$12		Atlantic 2381
4/1/67	32	6		11 **I Found A Love - Part 1**..........*Part II*	$12		Atlantic 2394
				also see version by **The Falcons** featuring Wilson Pickett			
6/17/67	55	5		12 **Soul Dance Number Three** /			
5/27/67	70	5		13 **You Can't Stand Alone**..........	$12		Atlantic 2412
8/5/67	8	12		14 **Funky Broadway**..........RB[1] *I'm Sorry About That*	$12		Atlantic 2430
11/4/67	22	6		15 **Stag-O-Lee** /			
				adapted from the traditional folk song "Stack-O-Lee"			
12/2/67	45	10		16 **I'm In Love**..........	$10		Atlantic 2448
2/17/68	50	5		17 **Jealous Love**..........*I've Come A Long Way* (#101)	$10		Atlantic 2484
4/13/68	15	10		18 **She's Lookin' Good**..........*We've Got To Have Love*	$10		Atlantic 2504
				original version by Rodger Collins "Bubbled Under" (#101) in 1967; above 4 from the album *I'm In Love*			
6/22/68	24	7		19 **I'm A Midnight Mover**..........*Deborah*	$10		Atlantic 2528

DEBUT	PEAK	WKS	Gold	A-side (Chart Hit)...B-side	$	Sym	Label & Number
				PICKETT, Wilson — Cont'd			
9/21/68	42	7		20 **I Found A True Love** ... *For Better Or Worse*	$10		Atlantic 2558
				#16, 17, 19 & 20: written by **Bobby Womack**			
11/16/68	42	6		21 **A Man And A Half** ... *People Make The World (What It Is)*	$10		Atlantic 2575
12/21/68+	23	9		22 **Hey Jude** ... *Search Your Heart*	$10		Atlantic 2591
				Duane **Allman** (guitar solo)			
3/29/69	50	6		23 **Mini-Skirt Minnie** ... *Back In Your Arms*	$10		Atlantic 2611
5/10/69	64	4		24 **Born To Be Wild** ... *Toe Hold*	$10		Atlantic 2631
7/12/69	59	6		25 **Hey Joe** ... *Night Owl*	$10		Atlantic 2648
11/29/69	92	3		26 **You Keep Me Hanging On** ... *Now You See Me, Now You Don't*	$10		Atlantic 2682
5/2/70	25	12		27 **Sugar Sugar** /			
4/4/70	91	5		28 **Cole, Cooke & Redding** ...	$8		Atlantic 2722
				tribute to Nat, Sam & Otis using the "Abraham, Martin And John" melody			
8/22/70	68	5		29 **She Said Yes** ... *It's Still Good*	$8		Atlantic 2753
				#25-27 & 29: from the album *Right On*			
9/26/70	14	13		30 **Engine Number 9** ... *International Playboy*	$8		Atlantic 2765
1/16/71	17	11	●	31 **Don't Let The Green Grass Fool You** ... *Ain't No Doubt About It*	$8		Atlantic 2781
4/24/71	13	12	●	32 **Don't Knock My Love - Pt. 1** ... RB[1] *Pt. II*	$8		Atlantic 2797
8/28/71	52	7		33 **Call My Name, I'll Be There** ... *Woman Let Me Be Down Home*	$8		Atlantic 2824
12/25/71+	24	11		34 **Fire And Water** ... *Pledging My Love*	$8		Atlantic 2852
5/27/72	58	8		35 **Funk Factory** ... *One Step Away*	$8		Atlantic 2878
11/11/72	99	2		36 **Mama Told Me Not To Come** ... *Covering The Same Old Ground*	$8		Atlantic 2909
				#32-34 & 36: from the album *Don't Knock My Love*			
4/14/73	98	1		37 **Mr. Magic Man** ... *I Sho' Love You*	$6		RCA Victor 0898
9/29/73	90	5		38 **Take A Closer Look At The Woman You're With** ... *Two Women And A Wife*	$6		RCA Victor 0049
				PICKETTYWITCH '70			
				Pop group from London, England. Led by female singers **Polly Brown** and Maggie Farran. Polly later became lead singer of **Sweet Dreams**.			
5/16/70	67	12		**That Same Old Feeling** ... *Maybe We've Been Loving Too Long*	$7		Janus 118
				PIECES OF EIGHT '67			
				Pop-rock duo: Brent Forston and Steven Caldwell of the **Swingin' Medallions**. Caldwell died of cancer on 1/28/2002 (age 54).			
6/24/67	59	8		**Lonely Drifter** ... *Who's Afraid Of Virginia Woolf*	$10		A&M 854
				PIERCE, Webb C&W/BUB/MEM '59			
				Born on 8/8/21 in West Monroe, Louisiana. Died of heart failure on 2/24/91 (age 69). Country singer/songwriter/guitarist. Acted in the movies *Buffalo Guns*, *Music City USA* and *Road To Nashville*. Charted 96 Country hits, 1952-82.			
6/3/57	73	9		1 **Bye Bye, Love** ... T:73 *Missing You* (C&W #7)	$20		Decca 30321
8/10/59	24	14		2 **I Ain't Never** ... *Shanghied*	$15		Decca 30923
12/28/59+	54	9		3 **No Love Have I** ... *Whirlpool Of Love*	$15		Decca 31021
				above 2 written by Mel Tillis			
5/2/60	69	3		4 **Is It Wrong (For Loving You)** /			
4/25/60	93	2		5 **(Doin' The) Lovers Leap** ...	$12		Decca 31058
11/21/60	99	1		6 **Fallen Angel** ... *Truck Driver's Blues*	$12		Decca 31165
				PILOT LP '75			
				Pop-rock trio from Edinburgh, Scotland: David Paton (vocals, guitar), Bill Lyall (keyboards) and Stuart Tosh (drums). Lyall died of AIDS in December 1989 (age 36).			
4/5/75	5	20	●	1 **Magic** ... *Just Let Me Be*	$5		EMI 3992
10/11/75	90	5		2 **Just A Smile** ... *Don't Speak Loudly*	$5		EMI 4135
1/31/76	87	6		3 **January** ... *Do Me Good*	$5		EMI 4202
				all of above produced by **Alan Parsons**			
				PILTDOWN MEN, The '60			
				Rock and roll band. Members Eddie Cobb and Lincoln Mayorga recorded as the Link-Eddy Combo (R&B charts, 1961).			
9/12/60	75	3		**Brontosaurus Stomp** ... *McDonald's Cave* [I]	$20		Capitol 4414
				Tommy Tedesco (guitar)			
				PINERA, Mike '80			
				Born on 9/29/48 in Tampa, Florida. Rock singer/songwriter/guitarist. Member of **Iron Butterfly** and **Blues Image**.			
1/5/80	70	8		**Goodnight My Love** ... *Looking For The Light*	$6		Spector 00003
	★439★			**P!NK** LP '01			
				Born Alecia Moore on 9/8/79 in Doylestown, Pennsylvania. Female pop-dance singer/songwriter.			
				1)Lady Marmalade 2)Get The Party Started 3)Most Girls			
3/4/00	7	32	●	1 **There You Go** ... S:2 / A:6 *(instrumental)*	$4	★	LaFace 24456
				Kandi (backing vocal)			
8/12/00	4	27		2 **Most Girls** ... A:3 / S:15 *(3 versions) / There You Go (remix)*	$8	★*	LaFace 24490
1/6/01	33	19		3 **You Make Me Sick** ... A:31 *(3 mixes)*	$6	T	LaFace 24533
				also see #6 below			
4/14/01	❶5	20		4 **Lady Marmalade** ... A:❶6 *(3 mixes)*	$6	T	Interscope 497066
				CHRISTINA AGUILERA, LIL' KIM, MÝA and P!NK			
				co-produced by **Missy "Misdemeanor" Elliott**; from the movie *Moulin Rouge* starring Nicole Kidman and Ewan McGregor			
10/27/01	4	24		5 **Get The Party Started** ... A:4 *(5 remixes)*	$8	T	Arista 15074
				12" single issued with 2 discs (6 total versions)			
3/2/02	45S	5		6 **You Make Me Sick** ... *(4 versions)* [R]	$8	★*	LaFace 24556
				reissue of #3 above on Arista's "Maximum Hits" series			
3/9/02	8	21		7 **Don't Let Me Get Me** ... A:8 / S:29 *Get The Party Started*	$8	▶V	Arista 15133
				see #9 below for the "45" issue			
7/6/02	8	20		8 **Just Like A Pill** ... A:8 / S:32 *(instrumental) / Don't Let Me Get Me (remix)*	$4	★	Arista 15186
11/16/02+	20	20	●	9 **Family Portrait** ... A:21 / S:30 *(live version) / Don't Let Me Get Me / Numb*	$8	▶V	Arista 51158
				"45" issued for #7 & 9 on Arista 50977; above 5 (except #6) from the album *M!ssundaztood*			

DEBUT	PEAK	WKS	Gold	A-side (Chart Hit)...B-side	$	Sym	Label & Number

PINK FLOYD — ROK/BUB/LP '80

Progressive-rock group formed in England: **David Gilmour** (vocals, guitar; born on 3/6/47; replaced Syd Barrett in 1968) (see #4 below), Roger Waters (vocals, bass), Rick Wright (keyboards) and Nick Mason (drums). Wright left in early 1982. Waters went solo in 1984. Band inactive, 1984-86. Gilmour, Mason and Wright regrouped in 1987. Charted 5 #1 albums, 1973-95. Inducted into the Rock and Roll Hall of Fame in 1996. Group name taken from Georgia bluesmen Pink Anderson and Floyd Council.

DEBUT	PEAK	WKS	Gold	A-side (Chart Hit)...B-side	$	Sym	Label & Number
5/19/73	13	15		1 **Money**...*Any Colour You Like* from the album *The Dark Side Of The Moon* which charted for a record 741 weeks (plus over 600 weeks on the *Top Pop Catalog* charts)	$15	⊙	Harvest 3609
1/19/80	❶[4]	25	▲	2 **Another Brick In The Wall Part II** *One Of My Turns* some pressings issued with a custom "wall" label	$5	■	Columbia 11187
5/10/80	53	6		3 **Run Like Hell**...*Don't Leave Me Now*	$4		Columbia 11265
4/7/84	62	7		4 **Blue Light**...*Cruise* **DAVID GILMOUR**	$4	■	Columbia 04378
10/10/87	70	8		5 **Learning To Fly**...AR[3] *Terminal Frost*	$4	■	Columbia 07363
6/18/94	73	7		6 **Take It Back**...S:71 *Astronomy Domine (live)*	$4	■[V]	Columbia 77493

PINK LADY — '79

Female disco duo from Japan: Mie Nemoto and Kei Masuda. Hosted own summer TV variety show in U.S., 1979.

DEBUT	PEAK	WKS	Gold	A-side (Chart Hit)...B-side	$	Sym	Label & Number
6/2/79	37	11		**Kiss In The Dark**...*Walk Away Renee*	$4	■	Elektra/Curb 46040

PIPKINS, The — LP '70

Pop vocal duo formed in England: Roger Greenaway and **Tony Burrows** (low voice). Worked together in studio group **White Plains**.

DEBUT	PEAK	WKS	Gold	A-side (Chart Hit)...B-side	$	Sym	Label & Number
5/23/70	9	12		**Gimme Dat Ding**...*To Love You* [N] featured in the British children's TV show *Oliver & The Overlord*	$7		Capitol 2819

PIPS — see KNIGHT, Gladys

PITNEY, Gene ★161★ — BUB/C&W/LP '62

Born on 2/17/41 in Hartford, Connecticut; raised in Rockville, Connecticut. Own band at Rockville High School. Recorded for Decca in 1959 with **Ginny Arnell** as Jamie & Jane. Recorded for Blaze in 1960 as Billy Bryan. First recorded under own name for Festival in 1960. Wrote "Hello Mary Lou," "He's A Rebel" and "Rubber Ball." Inducted into the Rock and Roll Hall of Fame in 2002.

1)Only Love Can Break A Heart 2)(The Man Who Shot) Liberty Valance 3)It Hurts To Be In Love 4)I'm Gonna Be Strong 5)Mecca

DEBUT	PEAK	WKS	Gold	A-side (Chart Hit)...B-side	$	Sym	Label & Number
1/30/61	39	8		1 **(I Wanna) Love My Life Away**...*I Laughed So Hard I Cried* picture sleeve issued with titles in aqua blue or dark blue ink	$20	■	Musicor 1002
8/7/61	42	8		2 **Every Breath I Take**...*Mr. Moon, Mr. Cupid And I* produced by Phil Spector; picture sleeve issued with titles in 2 different type styles	$20	■	Musicor 1011
10/30/61+	13	19		3 **Town Without Pity**...*Air Mail Special Delivery* title song from the movie starring Kirk Douglas	$15		Musicor 1009
4/28/62	4	13		4 **(The Man Who Shot) Liberty Valance**...*Take It Like A Man* recorded for but not included in the movie starring John Wayne and Jimmy Stewart	$15		Musicor 1020
9/15/62	2[1]	14		5 **Only Love Can Break A Heart** / AC[2]			
9/1/62	58	7		6 **If I Didn't Have A Dime (To Play The Jukebox)**...	$15		Musicor 1022
12/15/62+	12	12		7 **Half Heaven - Half Heartache**...*Tower-Tall*	$15		Musicor 1026
3/23/63	12	11		8 **Mecca**...*Teardrop By Teardrop (#130)*	$15	■	Musicor 1028
7/6/63	21	11		9 **True Love Never Runs Smooth**...*Donna Means Heartbreak* #4-7 & 9: from the album *Only Love Can Break A Heart*	$15		Musicor 1032
10/19/63	17	11		10 **Twenty Four Hours From Tulsa**...*Lonely Night Dreams (Of Far Away Arms)* #4, 5, 9 & 10: written by **Burt Bacharach** and Hal David	$15	■	Musicor 1034
1/18/64	49	7		11 **That Girl Belongs To Yesterday**...*Who Needs It (#131)* written by **Mick Jagger** and Keith Richards	$15	■	Musicor 1036
5/9/64	64	5		12 **Yesterday's Hero**...*Cornflower Blue*	$15		Musicor 1038
7/18/64	7	16		13 **It Hurts To Be In Love**...*Hawaii*	$15	■	Musicor 1040
10/24/64	9	12		14 **I'm Gonna Be Strong**...*E Se Domani (If Tomorrow)*	$15	■	Musicor 1045
2/27/65	31	7		15 **I Must Be Seeing Things**...*Marianne*	$15	■	Musicor 1070
4/17/65	99	1		16 **I've Got Five Dollars And It's Saturday Night**...*Wreck On The Highway* **GEORGE & GENE George Jones & Gene Pitney** #4 Country hit for **Faron Young** in 1956	$15		Musicor 1066
5/8/65	13	10		17 **Last Chance To Turn Around**...*Save Your Love*	$12		Musicor 1093
7/24/65	28	8		18 **Looking Through The Eyes Of Love**...*There's No Livin' Without Your Lovin'*	$12		Musicor 1103
11/20/65	37	8		19 **Princess In Rags**...*Amore Mio*	$12		Musicor 1130
4/23/66	25	8		20 **Backstage**...*Blue Color*	$12	■	Musicor 1171
12/24/66+	64	6		21 **Just One Smile**...*Innamorato*	$12		Musicor 1219
5/11/68	16	13		22 **She's A Heartbreaker**...*Conquistador*	$10		Musicor 1306
11/2/68	92	3		23 **Billy You're My Friend**...*Lonely Drifter*	$10	■	Musicor 1331
12/13/69+	89	5		24 **She Lets Her Hair Down (Early In The Morning)**...*I Remember* tune originated as a TV jingle for a shampoo	$10		Musicor 1384

PIXIES THREE, The — BUB '63

White teen female trio (ages 14-16 in 1963) from Hanover, Pennsylvania: Midge Bollinger (lead), Debbie Swisher and Kaye McColl. Bonnie Long replaced Bollinger in 1964. Swisher replaced Peggy Santiglia as lead singer of **The Angels**, 1967-68.

DEBUT	PEAK	WKS	Gold	A-side (Chart Hit)...B-side	$	Sym	Label & Number
8/17/63	40	9		1 **Birthday Party**...*Our Love*	$15	■	Mercury 72130
1/18/64	56	7		2 **442 Glenwood Avenue** /			
12/14/63+	79	5		3 **Cold Cold Winter**...	$15	■	Mercury 72208
4/18/64	87	3		4 **Gee**...*After The Party* #2 R&B hit for The Crows in 1954	$15	■	Mercury 72250

PIZANI, Frank — see HIGHLIGHTS, The

DEBUT	PEAK	WKS	Gold	A-side (Chart Hit)..........B-side	$	Sym	Label & Number
				PJ HARVEY — see HARVEY, PJ			
				PLACE, Mary Kay C&W **'76** Born on 8/23/47 in Tulsa, Oklahoma. Singer/composer/comedienne. Script writer for many TV comedy shows. Played "Loretta Haggers" on TV's *Mary Hartman, Mary Hartman.*			
10/30/76	60	13		**Baby Boy**..........*Streets Of This Town (Ode To Fernwood)* **MARY KAY PLACE as LORETTA HAGGERS**	$5		Columbia 10422
				PLANET P ROK/LP **'83** Studio group assembled by German producer Peter Hauke. **Tony Carey** was lead singer.			
4/16/83	64	9		**Why Me?**..........*Only You And Me*	$4	■	Geffen 29705
				PLANET SOUL LP **'96** Dance duo from Miami, Florida: producer George Costa and singer Nadine Renee. Brenda Dee replaced Renee in early 1996.			
10/21/95+	26	26	●	1 **Set U Free**..........S:25 / A:25 *(same version)*	$3	▮	Strictly Rhythm 12362
4/27/96	73	10		2 **Feel The Music** *[PLANET SOUL Featuring Brenda Dee]*..........S:69 *(same version)*	$3	▮	Strictly Rhythm 12430
				PLANT, Robert ROK/BUB/LP **'83** Born on 8/20/48 in West Bromwich, England. Lead singer of **Led Zeppelin** and **The Honeydrippers**. Studied accounting before becoming lead singer of such British blues groups as Black Snake Moan, The Banned and The Crawling King Snakes. Also with the groups Listen and Band Of Joy. Fully recovered from a serious auto accident in Greece on 8/4/75.			
9/11/82	64	6		1 **Burning Down One Side**..........*Moonlight In Samosa*	$5	■	Swan Song 99979
11/13/82	74	5		2 **Pledge Pin**..........*Fat Lip*	$5	■	Swan Song 99952
8/6/83	20	16		3 **Big Log** *Far Post* (ROK #12)	$4	■	Es Paranza 99844
11/19/83+	39	12		4 **In The Mood**..........*Horizontal Departure* (ROK #44)	$4	■	Es Paranza 99820
5/18/85	36	11		5 **Little By Little**..........AR[2] *Trouble Your Money*	$4	■	Es Paranza 99644
4/16/88	25	18		6 **Tall Cool One**..........AR[4] S:18 / A:27 *White, Clean And Neat* Jimmy Page (guitar solo); features brief guitar riffs from **Led Zeppelin**'s "Whole Lotta Love," "Dazed And Confused," "Custard Pie," "Black Dog" and "The Ocean"	$4	■	Es Paranza 99348
8/27/88	84	4		7 **Ship Of Fools**..........*Billy's Revenge*	$3	■	Es Paranza 99333
3/24/90	46	10		8 **Hurting Kind (I've Got My Eyes On You)**..........AR[6] *I Cried* (ROK #39)	$3	▮	Es Paranza 98985
				PLASTIC ONO BAND — see LENNON, John			
				PLATINUM BLONDE **'86** Rock group from Canada: Mark Holmes (vocals), Sergio Galli, Kenny MacLean and Chris Steffler.			
4/12/86	82	5		**Somebody Somewhere**..........*Red Light*	$4		Epic 05804
				PLATT, Eddie, And His Orchestra **'58** Born Eddie Platakis on 12/8/21 in Cleveland, Ohio; raised in Rossford, Ohio. Saxophonist/bandleader.			
3/3/58	20	10		1 **Tequila**..........A:20 / S:35 / T:35 *Popcorn* [I]	$20		ABC-Paramount 9899
6/9/58	74	5		2 **Cha-Hua-Hua**..........T:74 *Vodka* [I]	$20		Gone 5031
				PLATTERS, The ★51★ BUB/LP **'56** R&B group formed in Los Angeles, California: Tony Williams (lead; born on 4/16/28), David Lynch (tenor; born on 7/3/29), Paul Robi (baritone; born on 8/20/31), Herb Reed (bass; born on 8/7/28) and Zola Taylor. Group first recorded for Federal in 1954, with Alex Hodge instead of Robi, and without Zola Taylor. Hit "Only You" was written by manager Buck Ram (died on 1/1/91, age 83) and first recorded for Federal. To Mercury in 1955, re-recorded "Only You." Williams left to go solo, replaced by Sonny Turner in 1961. Taylor replaced by Sandra Dawn; Robi replaced by Nate Nelson (formerly in **The Flamingos**) in 1966. In 1976, Turner replaced by Monroe Powell. Lynch died of cancer on 1/2/81 (age 61). Nelson died of a heart attack on 6/1/84 (age 52). Robi died of cancer on 2/1/89 (age 57). Williams died of diabetes and emphysema on 8/14/92 (age 64). Group inducted into the Rock and Roll Hall of Fame in 1990. Reed is the only original member still performing; billed as Herb Reed & The Platters. The #1 vocal group of the 1950s. *1)My Prayer 2)Smoke Gets In Your Eyes 3)The Great Pretender 4)Twilight Time 5)The Magic Touch*			
10/1/55	5	22	●	1 **Only You (And You Alone)**..........RB[7] J:5 / S:5 / T:5 / A:5 *Bark, Battle And Ball* different version released on Federal 12244 in 1954 ($200); reissued on Power 7012 with a picture sleeve	$40		Mercury 70633
12/17/55+	❶[2]	24	●	2 **The Great Pretender** / RB[11] T:❶[2] / A:❶[2] / J:❶[1] / S:2			
2/11/56	87	1		3 **I'm Just A Dancing Partner**..........T:87	$40		Mercury 70753
3/24/56	4	20		4 **(You've Got) The Magic Touch** / J:4 / T:4 / A:5 / S:5			
4/7/56	50	9		5 **Winner Take All**..........T:50 / J:flip	$40		Mercury 70819
7/7/56	❶[5]	23	●	6 **My Prayer** / RB[2] T:❶[5] / A:❶[3] / S:❶[2] / J:❶[1] #3 hit for the Ink Spots in 1939			
7/14/56	39	14		7 **Heaven On Earth**..........T:39 / S:flip / J:flip	$40		Mercury 70893
9/29/56	11	18		8 **You'll Never Never Know** / J:11 / T:14 / S:15 / A:18			
9/29/56	13	15		9 **It Isn't Right**..........S:13 / J:13 / T:23	$30		Mercury 70948
12/29/56+	20	14		10 **On My Word Of Honor** / J:20 / S:23 / T:27			
12/22/56+	20	12		11 **One In A Million**..........S:20 / T:31	$30		Mercury 71011
3/23/57	11	14		12 **I'm Sorry** / J:11 / S:14 / T:19 recorded by Bobby Wayne in 1952 on Mercury 5847 ($25)			
4/6/57	16	23		13 **He's Mine**..........S:16 / J:18 / T:23 / A:24	$25		Mercury 71032
5/27/57	24	14		14 **My Dream** / S:24 / T:26			
7/15/57		2		15 **I Wanna**..........S:flip	$25		Mercury 71093
10/28/57	65	8		16 **Only Because**..........T:65 *The Mystery Of You*	$25		Mercury 71184
2/3/58	56	8		17 **Helpless**..........T:56 *Indiff'rent*	$25		Mercury 71246
4/7/58	❶[1]	17	●	18 **Twilight Time**..........RB[3] S:❶[1] / T:❶[1] / A:❶[1] *Out Of My Mind* #8 hit for The Three Suns in 1944	$25		Mercury 71289
6/30/58	50	8		19 **You're Making A Mistake**..........S:50 / T:51 *My Old Flame*	$25		Mercury 71320
9/15/58	42	10		20 **I Wish** / H:42 / S:46			
10/6/58	93	2		21 **It's Raining Outside**..........H:93	$25		Mercury 71353
11/17/58+	❶[3]	19	●	22 **Smoke Gets In Your Eyes**..........*No Matter What You Are* #1 hit for Paul Whiteman's Orchestra in 1934 (from the 1933 musical *Roberta* starring Bob Hope)	$25		Mercury 71383
3/23/59	12	15		23 **Enchanted**..........*The Sound And The Fury*	$20		Mercury 71427

DEBUT	PEAK	WKS	Gold	A-side (Chart Hit)	B-side	$	Sym	Label & Number
				PLATTERS, The — Cont'd				
6/22/59	**41**	9		24 **Remember When**	*Love Of A Lifetime*	$20		Mercury 71467
				written in 1945 by former *Billboard* employee Mickey Addy				
9/7/59	**44**	9		25 **Where** /				
				adaptation of Tchaikovsky's *Pathetique Symphony*				
9/14/59	**61**	7		26 **Wish It Were Me**		$20		Mercury 71502
				from the movie *Girls' Town* starring Mamie Van Doren; #1, 2, 4, 7, 12, 14, 15, 17, 18, 20, 21, 23, 24 & 26: written or co-written by Buck Ram				
1/25/60	**8**	16		27 **Harbor Lights** /				
				#1 hit for **Sammy Kaye** in 1950				
2/22/60	**65**	5		28 **Sleepy Lagoon**		$20	■	Mercury 71563
				#1 hit in 1942 for Harry James				
5/16/60	**56**	6		29 **Ebb Tide**	*(I'll Be With You In) Apple Blossom Time* (#102)	$15		Mercury 71624
				#2 hit for **Frank Chacksfield** in 1953				
8/1/60	**36**	8		30 **Red Sails In The Sunset**	*Sad River*	$15	■	Mercury 71656
				THE PLATTERS Featuring TONY WILLIAMS (above 2)				
				#1 hit for both **Bing Crosby** and Guy Lombardo in 1935				
10/10/60	**21**	11		31 **To Each His Own**	*Down The River Of Golden Dreams*	$15	■	Mercury 71697
				there were 3 #1 versions of this tune in 1946				
1/9/61	**30**	8		32 **If I Didn't Care**	*True Lover*	$15	■	Mercury 71749
				#2 hit for the Ink Spots in 1939				
4/3/61	**62**	4		33 **Trees**	*Immortal Love*	$15	■	Mercury 71791
				words are from Joyce Kilmer's famous poem				
7/31/61	**25**	8		34 **I'll Never Smile Again**	*You Don't Say*	$15	■	Mercury 71847
				#1 hit for **Tommy Dorsey** in 1940; issued with 2 different picture sleeves				
2/17/62	**91**	2		35 **It's Magic**	*Reaching For A Star*	$15	■	Mercury 71921
				there were 3 Top 10 versions of this tune in 1948; **David Carroll** (orch.: #27-35)				
4/30/66	**31**	14		36 **I Love You 1000 Times**	*Don't Hear, Speak, See No Evil*	$10		Musicor 1166
12/3/66	**97**	2		37 **I'll Be Home**	*(You've Got) The Magic Touch*	$10		Musicor 1211
				#5 R&B hit for **The Flamingos** in 1956				
2/25/67	**14**	12		38 **With This Ring**	*If I Had A Love*	$10		Musicor 1229
7/1/67	**56**	8		39 **Washed Ashore (On A Lonely Island In The Sea)**	*What Name Shall I Give You My Love*	$10		Musicor 1251
10/21/67	**70**	7		40 **Sweet, Sweet Lovin'**	*Sonata*	$10		Musicor 1275
				PLAY LP **'01**				
				Female teen vocal group from Stockholm, Sweden: Anna Sundstrand, Anais Lameche (sister of **Amanda**), Rosie Munter and Faye Hamlin.				
9/29/01+	**10**[S]	65		**Us Against The World**	*(4 album snippets)*	$4	★	Columbia 79632
				PLAYA LP **'98**				
				R&B vocal trio from Louisville, Kentucky: Ben Bush, John Peacock and Stephen Garrett. Also see **Ginuwine**'s "So Anxious."				
11/15/97	**73**	15		1 **Don't Stop The Music**	S:56 *(6 album snippets)*	$3	▮	Def Jam 571680
				samples "Thank You" by **Sly & The Family Stone**				
3/28/98	**38**	20		2 **Cheers 2 U**	S:20 *(instrumental)*	$3	▮	Def Jam 568214
5/13/00	**91**	4		3 **Love Sets You Free**	S:18 *It's Gonna Rain* (Price)	$4	★	Def Soul 562683
				KELLY PRICE & FRIENDS (Dru Hill, Montell Jordan, Case, Playa, Kandice Love, Lovher)				
				from the movie *The Hurricane* starring Denzel Washington				
				PLAYBOYS, The **'58**				
				Rock and roll group from Philadelphia, Pennsylvania: Sammy Vale (vocals), Irv Mellman (piano), Ray D'Agostino (saxophone), Joe Franzosa (bass) and Lou Mauro (drums). D'Agostino died on 3/22/95 (age 64).				
9/1/58	**62**	6		**Over The Weekend**	H:62 *Double Talk*	$25		Cameo 142
				originally released on Martinique 101 in 1958 ($50)				
				PLAYER BUB/LP **'78**				
				Pop-rock group formed in Los Angeles, California: Peter Beckett (vocals, guitar), John Crowley (vocals, guitar), Wayne Cooke (keyboards), Ronn Moss (bass) and John Friesen (drums). Moss played "Ridge Forrester" on the TV soap *The Bold & The Beautiful*.				
10/1/77+	**1**[3]	32	●	1 **Baby Come Back**	*Love Is Where You Find It*	$5		RSO 879
3/11/78	**10**	17		2 **This Time I'm In It For Love**	*Every Which Way*	$4		RSO 890
9/9/78	**27**	11		3 **Prisoner Of Your Love**	*Join In The Dance*	$4		RSO 908
12/16/78+	**62**	6		4 **Silver Lining**	*Forever*	$4		RSO 914
6/7/80	**46**	8		5 **It's For You**	*Tip Of The Iceberg*	$4		Casablanca 2265
1/23/82	**48**	9		6 **If Looks Could Kill**	*Born To Be With You*	$4		RCA 13006
				PLAYMATES, The **'58**				
				Pop vocal trio from Waterbury, Connecticut: Donny Conn, Morey Carr and Chic Hetti.				
				1)Beep Beep 2)What Is Love? 3)Jo-Ann				
1/20/58	**19**	13		1 **Jo-Ann**	S:19 / T:20 *You Can't Stop Me From Dreaming*	$25		Roulette 4037
				originally recorded by The Twin-Tones on their RCA Victor EP 4107				
4/21/58	**87**	2		2 **Let's Be Lovers**	T:87 *Give Me Another Chance*	$20		Roulette 4056
6/9/58	**22**	9		3 **Don't Go Home**	A:22 / T:36 / S:38 *Can't You Get It Through Your Head*	$20		Roulette 4072
9/29/58	**81**	2		4 **The Day I Died**	H:81 *While The Record Goes Around*	$20		Roulette 4100
11/3/58	**4**	15	●	5 **Beep Beep**	*Your Love* [N]	$20		Roulette 4115
3/30/59	**75**	4		6 **Star Love**	*The Thing-A-Ma-Jig*	$15		Roulette 4136
				Hugo Peretti (of **Hugo & Luigi** - orch., all of above)				
7/6/59	**15**	13		7 **What Is Love?**	*I Am*	$15		Roulette 4160
10/24/60	**37**	8		8 **Wait For Me**	*Eyes Of An Angel*	$15		Roulette 4276
3/6/61	**70**	5		9 **Little Miss Stuck-Up**	*Real Life*	$15		Roulette 4322
				Joe Reisman (orch., above 3)				
7/14/62	**88**	2		10 **Keep Your Hands In Your Pockets**	*The Cop On The Beat*	$12		Roulette 4432

DEBUT	PEAK	WKS	Gold	A-side (Chart Hit)..........B-side	$	Sym	Label & Number
				PLEASURE R&B/LP **'80** R&B group from Portland, Oregon. Core members: Sherman Davis (vocals), Marlon McClain (guitar), brothers Donald and Michael Hepburn (keyboards), Bruce Smith (percussion), Dennis Springer (sax), Nathaniel Phillips (bass) and Bruce Carter (drums).			
12/8/79+	55	10		**Glide**..........*Thoughts Of Old Flames*	$5		Fantasy 874
				PLEIS, Jack, And His Orchestra **'56** Born on 5/11/17 in Philadelphia, Pennsylvania. Died on 12/6/90 (age 73). Conducted the studio orchestra and chorus behind many of Decca's pop vocalists during the 1950s. Piano soloist on **Teresa Brewer**'s 1950 #1 hit "Music! Music! Music!"			
10/20/56	91	2		1 **Giant**..........T:91 *Lonesome Without You* Ralph Young (vocal); title song from the movie starring Elizabeth Taylor, Rock Hudson and James Dean; charted for 1 week on 10/20/56 (#93) and 1 week on 12/29/56	$12		Decca 30055
12/8/56	65	1		2 **I'll Always Be In Love With You**..........T:65 *The Waltz Of Tears* [I] originally recorded by Pleis in 1951; #3 hit for Fred Waring's Pennsylvanians in 1929	$12		Decca 30086
6/17/57	69	1		3 **(But As They Say) That's Life**..........T:69 *Goodnight Waltz* [I]	$12		Decca 30303
				PLIMSOULS, The ROK/LP **'83** Rock group from Los Angeles, California: Peter Case (vocals), Eddie Munoz (guitar), Dave Pahoa (bass) and Lou Ramirez (drums). Group appeared in the 1983 movie *Valley Girl*. Group name is British slang for gym shoes.			
7/30/83	82	3		**A Million Miles Away**..........*Play The Breaks* originally hit the Album Rock charts (#11) on 5/1/82 on Shaky City 134 ($8) with a picture sleeve	$5	■	Geffen 29600
				P-LO **'02** Born in Stone Mountain, Georgia. Male rapper.			
4/6/02	43^S	7		**Shawty**..........*(5 versions)* **P-LO featuring Lil Ru and T. Supreme (of the Filthy Boys)**	$7	★	How You Love That 10123
	★577★			**PM DAWN** BUB/LP **'92** Black dance-rap duo from Jersey City, New Jersey: brothers Attrell (born on 5/15/70) and Jarrett (born on 7/17/71) Cordes—nicknamed "**Prince Be**" (see #8 below) and "DJ Minutemix." PM Dawn means "from the darkest hour comes the light."			
10/19/91	❶^1	20	●	1 **Set Adrift On Memory Bliss** S:❶^3 / A:2 *A Watcher's Point Of View (Don't 'Cha Think)* samples **Spandau Ballet**'s "True"	$3	▮	Gee Street 866094
1/18/92	28	12		2 **Paper Doll**..........A:20 / S:46 *For The Love of Peace*	$3	▮	Gee Street 866374
9/12/92	3	28	●	3 **I'd Die Without You**..........A:❶^2 / S:5 *On A Clear Day* from the movie *Boomerang* starring **Eddie Murphy**	$3	▮	Gee Street/LaFace 24034
3/20/93	6	21		4 **Looking Through Patient Eyes**..........A:4 / S:20 *(album version)* **Cathy Dennis** (backing vocal); samples "Father Figure" by **George Michael**	$3	▮V	Gee Street 862024
7/24/93	54	11		5 **The Ways Of The Wind**..........A:52 *(2 versions)* samples "I Had A King" by **Joni Mitchell**; "45" issued for above 2 on Gee Street 862024	$3	▮V	Gee Street 862475
9/23/95	48	8		6 **Downtown Venus**..........A:45 *She Dreams Persistent Maybes* samples "Hush" by **Deep Purple**	$3	▮V	Gee Street 854408
12/23/95	95	5		7 **Sometimes I Miss You So Much (dedicated to the christ-consciousness)**..........*(Dallas Austin remix)* samples "Nite And Day" by **Al B. Sure!**	$3	▮V	Gee Street 854476
3/28/98	90	5		8 **Gotta Be...Movin' On Up**..........*(instrumental)* **PRINCE BE featuring Ky-Mani** samples "Just An Illusion" by Imagination; from the movie *Senseless* starring David Spade	$3	▮	Gee Street 33513
9/26/98	44	10		9 **I Had No Right**..........S:49 *As Disappointing As Your Mercy Is*	$3	▮	Gee Street 33535
				P-NUT GALLERY **'71** Studio group featuring lead singer Tommy Nolan. Early pressings credit artist as: **CIRCA '58 and the Peanut Gallery**.			
6/12/71	62	7		**Do You Know What Time It Is?**..........*Welcome Back To Dootieville* [N] inspired by TV's *Howdy Doody* show	$6		Buddah 239
				POCKETS R&B/BUB/LP **'78** R&B group from Baltimore, Maryland: Larry Jacobs (vocals), Jacob Sheffer (guitar), Albert McKinney (keyboards), Charles Williams (trumpet), Irving Madison (sax), Kevin Barnes (trombone), Gary Grainger (bass) and George Gray (drums).			
1/7/78	84	9		**Come Go With Me**..........*Wizzard Wuzzit*	$5		Columbia 10632
	★572★			**POCO** ROK/BUB/AC/LP **'79** Country-rock band formed in Los Angeles, California: Rusty Young (pedal steel guitar; born on 2/23/46) and **Buffalo Springfield** members **Richie Furay** (rhythm guitar; born on 5/9/44) and **Jim Messina** (lead guitar; born on 12/5/47). **Randy Meisner** (born on 3/8/46; later of the **Eagles**) left in 1969; replaced by bassist **Timothy B. Schmit** (born on 10/30/47). As of 1970, group consisted of Furay, Messina, Young, Schmit and George Grantham (drums; born on 1/20/47). Messina left in 1970; replaced by Paul Cotton. Furay left in 1973. Grantham and Schmit (joined Eagles) left in 1977; replacements: Charlie Harrison, Kim Bullard and Steve Chapman. Disbanded in 1984. In 1989, Young, Furay, Messina, Grantham and Meisner reunited. *1)Crazy Love 2)Call It Love 3)Heart Of The Night*			
10/3/70	72	8		1 **You Better Think Twice**..........*Anyway Bye Bye*	$7		Epic 10636
3/27/71	69	7		2 **C'mon**..........*I Guess You Made It*	$7		Epic 10714
9/20/75	50	9		3 **Keep On Tryin'**..........*Georgia, Bind My Ties*	$5		ABC 12126
8/14/76	94	1		4 **Rose Of Cimarron**..........*Tulsa Turnaround*	$5		ABC 12204
8/6/77	50	8		5 **Indian Summer**..........*Me And You*	$5		ABC 12295
1/20/79	17	14		6 **Crazy Love** AC^7 *Barbados*	$5		ABC 12439
5/12/79	20	14		7 **Heart Of The Night**..........*The Last Goodbye*	$5		MCA 41023
7/19/80	48	10		8 **Under The Gun**..........*Reputation*	$4	■	MCA 41269
10/11/80	74	4		9 **Midnight Rain**..........*A Fool's Paradise*	$4		MCA 41326
12/18/82+	50	13		10 **Shoot For The Moon**..........*The Midnight Rodeo (In The Lead Tonight)*	$4		Atlantic 89919
4/28/84	80	5		11 **Days Gone By**..........*Daylight*	$4		Atlantic 89674
8/26/89	18	16		12 **Call It Love**..........S:16 / A:21 *Lovin' You Every Minute*	$3	■	RCA 9038
12/2/89+	39	12		13 **Nothin' To Hide**..........S:32 *If It Wasn't For You* co-written and produced by **Richard Marx**	$3	■	RCA 9131

DEBUT	PEAK	WKS	Gold	A-side (Chart Hit)...B-side	$	Sym	Label & Number

P.O.D. — ROK/BUB/LP '02

Christian hard-rock group from San Diego, California: Sonny (vocals), Marcos (guitar), Traa (bass) and Wuv (drums). P.O.D.: Payable On Death.

DEBUT	PEAK	WKS	Gold	A-side (Chart Hit)...B-side	$	Sym	Label & Number
11/3/01+	41	20		1 **Alive** ... A:38		V	album cut
2/9/02	28	19		2 **Youth Of The Nation** ... MR^2 A:27		V	album cut
				above 2 from the album *Satellite* on Atlantic 83475; "45" issued for above 2 on Atlantic 85301			

POE — ROK/BUB/LP '96

Born Annie Danielewski in Manhattan, New York. Female rock-dance singer/songwriter.

DEBUT	PEAK	WKS	Gold	A-side (Chart Hit)...B-side	$	Sym	Label & Number
8/3/96	60^A	11		1 **Angry Johnny** ...			album cut
12/28/96+	65^A	4		2 **Hello** ... BUB:104 *(album version)*	$3	▌	Modern 98028
				above 2 from the album *Hello* on Modern 92605			

POETS, The — '66

R&B vocal group: Ronnie Lewis, Melvin Bradford, Paul Fulton and Johnny James.

DEBUT	PEAK	WKS	Gold	A-side (Chart Hit)...B-side	$	Sym	Label & Number
3/19/66	45	10		**She Blew A Good Thing** ... *Out To Lunch*	$15		Symbol 214

POINDEXTER, Buster — AC/LP '88

Born David Johansen on 1/9/50 in Staten Island, New York. Founder and lead singer of the pre-punk group the New York Dolls, 1971-75. Assumed the Buster Poindexter persona in 1987. Appeared in the movies *Married To The Mob*, *Let It Ride*, *Tales From The Darkside*, *Freejack* and others.

DEBUT	PEAK	WKS	Gold	A-side (Chart Hit)...B-side	$	Sym	Label & Number
12/12/87+	45	13		**Hot Hot Hot** ... S:36 *Cannibal*	$3	■	RCA 5357
				BUSTER POINDEXTER AND HIS BANSHEES OF BLUE			

POINT BLANK — ROK/BUB/LP '81

Rock group from Texas: Bubba Keith (vocals), Rusty Burns and Kim Davis (guitars), Mike Hamilton (keyboards), Bill Randolph (bass) and Buzzy Gruen (drums). Randolph died of a heart attack on 6/19/2001 (age 50).

DEBUT	PEAK	WKS	Gold	A-side (Chart Hit)...B-side	$	Sym	Label & Number
6/27/81	39	14		**Nicole** ... *Restless*	$4		MCA 51132

POINTER, Bonnie — R&B/LP '79

Born on 7/11/50 in Oakland, California. Member of the **Pointer Sisters** from 1971-78.

DEBUT	PEAK	WKS	Gold	A-side (Chart Hit)...B-side	$	Sym	Label & Number
11/18/78+	58	14		1 **Free Me From My Freedom/Tie Me To A Tree (Handcuff Me)** ... *(instrumental)*	$4	■	Motown 1451
6/16/79	11	23		2 **Heaven Must Have Sent You** ... *(album version)*	$4		Motown 1459
12/22/79+	40	13		3 **I Can't Help Myself (Sugar Pie, Honey Bunch)** ... *I Wanna Make It (In Your World)*	$4		Motown 1478

POINTER SISTERS ★91★ — R&B/BUB/AC/LP '84

R&B vocal group from Oakland, California: sisters Ruth (born on 3/19/46), Anita (born on 1/23/48), June (born on 11/30/54) and **Bonnie Pointer**. Sang in nostalgic 1940s style from 1973-77. Appeared as the "Wilson Sisters" in the 1976 movie *Car Wash*. Bonnie went solo in 1978, group continued as a trio in a more contemporary style.

1)Slow Hand 2)Fire 3)He's So Shy 4)Jump (For My Love) 5)Automatic

DEBUT	PEAK	WKS	Gold	A-side (Chart Hit)...B-side	$	Sym	Label & Number
8/18/73	11	16		1 **Yes We Can Can** ... *Jada*	$6		Blue Thumb 229
				#46 R&B hit for **Lee Dorsey** in 1970			
12/22/73+	61	8		2 **Wang Dang Doodle** ... *Cloudburst*	$6		Blue Thumb 243
				#4 R&B hit for Ko Ko Taylor in 1966			
10/5/74	13	16		3 **Fairytale** ... *Love In Them There Hills*	$6		ABC/Blue Thumb 254
3/8/75	89	5		4 **Live Your Life Before You Die** ... *Shaky Flat Blues*	$6		ABC/Blue Thumb 262
7/19/75	20	15		5 **How Long (Betcha' Got A Chick On The Side)** ... RB^2 *Easy Days*	$6		ABC/Blue Thumb 265
11/22/75	61	7		6 **Going Down Slowly** ... *Sleeping Alone*	$6		ABC/Blue Thumb 268
				all of above produced by David Rubinson			
11/11/78+	2^2	23	●	7 **Fire** ... *Love Is Like A Rolling Stone*	$5	■	Planet 45901
				written by **Bruce Springsteen**			
3/17/79	30	10		8 **Happiness** ... *Lay It On The Line*	$5		Planet 45902
7/26/80	3	26	●	9 **He's So Shy** ... *Movin' On*	$4		Planet 47916
11/8/80	52	11		10 **Could I Be Dreaming** ... *Evil*	$4		Planet 47920
5/30/81	2^3	24	●	11 **Slow Hand** *Holdin' Out For Love*	$4		Planet 47929
1/23/82	13	16		12 **Should I Do It** ... *We're Gonna Make It*	$4		Planet 47960
6/26/82	16	14		13 **American Music** ... *I Want To Do It With You*	$4		Planet 13254
9/18/82	30	16		14 **I'm So Excited** ... *Nothin' But A Heartache*	$4		Planet 13327
				also see #19 below			
3/26/83	67	5		15 **If You Wanna Get Back Your Lady** ... *All Of You*	$4		Planet 13430
10/8/83	48	15		16 **I Need You** ... *Operator*	$4		Planet 13639
1/28/84	5	20		17 **Automatic** ... *Nightline*	$4		Planet 13730
4/28/84	3	24		18 **Jump (For My Love)** ... *Heart Beat*	$4		Planet 13780
8/4/84	9	24		19 **I'm So Excited** ... S:7 / A:12 *Dance Electric* [R]	$4		Planet 13857
				slightly different mix from #14 above			
11/24/84+	6	23		20 **Neutron Dance** ... S:5 / A:5 *Telegraph Your Love*	$4		Planet 13951
				from the movie *Beverly Hills Cop* starring **Eddie Murphy**			
3/23/85	44	11		21 **Baby Come And Get It** ... *Operator*	$4	■	Planet 14041
				#16-21: from the album *Break Out*			
7/13/85	11	18		22 **Dare Me** ... S:8 / A:13 *I'll Be There*	$3	■	RCA 14126
11/2/85	59	11		23 **Freedom** ... *Telegraph Your Love*	$3	■	RCA 14224
3/1/86	83	5		24 **Twist My Arm** ... *Easy Persuasion*	$3	■	RCA 14197
11/1/86	33	13		25 **Goldmine** ... S:33 / A:34 *Sexual Power*	$3	■	RCA 5062
2/21/87	93	2		26 **All I Know Is The Way I Feel** ... *Translation*	$3		RCA 5112
				#7-26: produced by Richard Perry			
8/8/87	42	9		27 **Be There** ... S:33 *(dub version)*	$3	■	MCA 53120
				from the movie *Beverly Hills Cop II* starring **Eddie Murphy**			

DEBUT	PEAK	WKS	Gold	A-side (Chart Hit)..........B-side	$	Sym	Label & Number
	★292★			**POISON** BUB/LP **'88**			
				Hard-rock group formed in Harrisburg, Pennsylvania: Bret Michaels (vocals; born on 3/15/63), C.C. DeVille (guitar; born on 5/14/62), Bobby Dall (bass; born on 11/2/63) and Rikki Rockett (drums; born on 8/8/61). Richie Kotzen (born on 3/5/60) replaced DeVille from 1992-97.			
				1)Every Rose Has Its Thorn 2)Unskinny Bop 3)Something To Believe In			
3/14/87	9	16		1 **Talk Dirty To Me**..........S:6 / A:11 *Want Some, Need Some*	$3	■	Capitol 5686
6/13/87	50	10		2 **I Want Action**..........S:37 *Play Dirty*	$3	■	Enigma 44004
				picture sleeve issued as a foldout poster			
9/5/87	13	21		3 **I Won't Forget You**..........S:12 / A:12 *Blame It On You*	$3	■	Enigma 44038
4/23/88	6	19		4 **Nothin' But A Good Time**..........S:3 / A:11 *Look But You Can't Touch*	$3	■	Enigma 44145
7/30/88	12	16		5 **Fallen Angel**..........S:10 / A:15 *Bad To Be Good*	$3	■	Enigma 44191
10/29/88	❶^3	21	●	6 **Every Rose Has Its Thorn** S:❶^3 / A:❶^3 *Livin' For The Minute*	$3	■	Enigma 44203
2/18/89	10	14		7 **Your Mama Don't Dance**..........S:9 / A:11 *Look What The Cat Dragged In*	$3	■	Enigma 44293
				above 4 from the album *Open Up And Say...Ahh!*			
7/7/90	3	19	●	8 **Unskinny Bop**..........S:3 / A:3 *Swampjuice (Soul-O) / Valley Of Lost Souls*	$3	▮^{V}	Enigma 44584
10/6/90	4	21	●	9 **Something To Believe In**..........S:4 / A:5 *Ball And Chain*	$3	▮	Enigma 44617
2/2/91	38	12		10 **Ride The Wind**..........S:38 / A:39 *Come Hell Or High Water*	$3	▮	Enigma 44616
5/4/91	35	13		11 **Life Goes On**..........S:47 / A:73 *Something To Believe In (acoustic version)*	$3	▮	Capitol 44705
				above 4 from the album *Flesh & Blood*			
1/30/93	50	10		12 **Stand**..........S:51 / A:66 *Native Tongue/The Scream*	$3	▮^{V}	Capitol 44905
				"45": Capitol 56969 (blue vinyl); B-side: "Until You Suffer Some (Fire And Ice)"			
				POKÉMON LP **'99**			
				Studio rock band production for the animated movie *Pokémon - The First Movie.*			
11/27/99+	62^S	7		**Pokémon Theme**..........*(2 versions)*	$6	★*	Robbins 72038
				Billy Crawford (vocal)			
	★266★			**POLICE, The** ROK/LP **'83**			
				Pop-rock trio formed in England: Gordon "**Sting**" Sumner (vocals, bass; born on 10/2/51), Andy Summers (guitar; born on 12/31/42) and Stewart Copeland (drums; born on 7/16/52). First guitarist was Henri Padovani, replaced by Summers in 1977. Copeland had been with Curved Air. Inactive as a group since appearance at "Amnesty '86." Sting began recording solo in 1985. Copeland formed group Animal Logic in 1989. Group inducted into the Rock and Roll Hall of Fame in 2003.			
				1)Every Breath You Take 2)King Of Pain 3)Every Little Thing She Does Is Magic			
2/24/79	32	13		1 **Roxanne**..........*Dead End Job*	$6		A&M 2096
				also see #13 below			
11/24/79	74	7		2 **Message In A Bottle**..........*Landlord*	$6	■	A&M 2190
				issued with either a regular picture sleeve or a foldout poster sleeve			
10/25/80+	10	21		3 **De Do Do Do, De Da Da Da**..........*Friends*	$5	■	A&M 2275
				picture sleeve has a center-cut hole and shows only the artist name and title			
2/7/81	10	18		4 **Don't Stand So Close To Me**..........*A Sermon*	$5	■	A&M 2301
				also see #12 below			
9/26/81	3	19		5 **Every Little Thing She Does Is Magic**..........AR^2 *Shambelle*	$4	■	A&M 2371
1/16/82	11	13		6 **Spirits In The Material World**..........*Flexible Strategies*	$4	■	A&M 2390
4/10/82	46	8		7 **Secret Journey**..........*Darkness*	$4	■	A&M 2408
6/4/83	❶^8	22	●	8 **Every Breath You Take** AR^9 *Murder By Numbers*	$4	■	A&M 2542
8/27/83	3	16		9 **King Of Pain**..........AR^5 *Someone To Talk To*	$4	■	A&M 2569
11/5/83	16	14		10 **Synchronicity II**..........*Once Upon A Daydream*	$4	■	A&M 2571
1/7/84	8	16		11 **Wrapped Around Your Finger**..........*Tea In The Sahara (live)*	$4	■	A&M 2614
				above 4 from the album *Synchronicity*			
10/25/86	46	9		12 **Don't Stand So Close To Me '86**..........S:35 *(live version)* [R]	$4	■	A&M 2879
				new version of #4 above; all of above written by **Sting**			
12/27/97+	59	13		13 **Roxanne '97 - Puff Daddy Remix**..........S:34 *(2 versions) / Voices Inside My Head* [R]	$6	▮*	A&M 2449
				STING & THE POLICE Featuring Pras			
				Full Force (backing vocals); samples "Roxanne, Roxanne" by **UTFO** and "Kools Back Again" by **Kool & The Gang**			
				POLNAREFF, Michel LP **'76**			
				Born in France. Pop singer/guitarist/keyboardist.			
2/21/76	48	7		1 **If You Only Believe (Jesus For Tonite)**..........*Since I Saw You*	$4		Atlantic 3314
5/29/76	61	7		2 **Lipstick**..........*Part II* [I]	$4		Atlantic 3330
				title song from the movie starring Margaux Hemingway			
				PONDEROSA TWINS + ONE R&B/BUB **'71**			
				Teen R&B group from Cleveland, Ohio: twins Alvin & Alfred Pelham and twins Keith & Kirk Gardner, plus Ricky Spencer. Produced by Bobby Massey of **The O'Jays**.			
9/25/71	78	7		**You Send Me**..........*Hey Girl*	$10		Horoscope 102
				PONI-TAILS **'58**			
				Pop female vocal trio from Lyndhurst, Ohio: Toni Cistone (lead), LaVerne Novak (high harmony) and Patti McCabe (died on 1/17/89).			
7/21/58	7	16		1 **Born Too Late**..........H:7 / S:11 *Come On Joey Dance With Me*	$25		ABC-Paramount 9934
12/1/58	85	3		2 **Seven Minutes In Heaven**..........*Close Friends*	$20		ABC-Paramount 9969
				Don Costa (orch.)			
10/26/59	87	3		3 **I'll Be Seeing You**..........*I'll Keep Tryin'*	$20		ABC-Paramount 10047
				#1 hit for **Bing Crosby** in 1944; O.B. Masingill (orch.: #1 & 3)			
				POOLE, Brian — see TREMELOES, The			
				POP, Iggy ROK/LP **'91**			
				Born James Jewel Osterberg on 4/21/47 in Muskegon, Michigan. Punk-rock pioneer. Leader of The Stooges from 1969-74. Acted in the movies *Cry Baby, Hardware* and *The Crow: City Of Angels.* Adopted nickname "Iggy" from his first band, The Iguanas.			
11/24/90+	28	15		**Candy**..........S:23 / A:38 *Neon Forest*	$4	▮	Virgin 98900
				Kate Pierson (of **The B-52's**, female vocal)			
				POP-TOPS — see LOS POP TOPS			

DEBUT	PEAK	WKS	Gold	A-side (Chart Hit)...B-side	$	Sym	Label & Number
				POPPIES, The BUB **'66**			
				Black vocal trio: **Dorothy Moore** (lead), Petsye McCune and Rosemary Taylor. Formed at Jackson State University.			
3/5/66	**56**	6		**Lullaby Of Love** ... *I Wonder Why*	$10		Epic 9893
				Bill Justis (orch.); melody adapted from Brahms' *Lullaby*			
				POPPY FAMILY, The AC/BUB/LP **'70**			
				Pop group from Canada: **Susan Jacks** (vocals) (see #9 below), her husband **Terry Jacks** (born on 3/29/44) (see #6-8 below), Craig MacCaw (guitar) and Satwan Singh (percussion). Group and marriage broke up in 1973; Susan and Terry began solo careers.			
3/28/70	**2**^{2}	17	●	1 **Which Way You Goin' Billy?** ... *Endless Sleep*	$5		London 129
8/8/70	**29**	13		2 **That's Where I Went Wrong** ... *Shadows On My Wall*	$5		London 139
				THE POPPY FAMILY (Featuring Susan Jacks) (above 2)			
7/31/71	**45**	12		3 **Where Evil Grows** /			
4/3/71	**100**	2		4 **I Was Wondering** ...	$5		London 148
12/11/71	**84**	4		5 **No Good To Cry** ... *I'll See You There*	$5		London 164
				TERRY JACKS:			
1/12/74	**❶**^{3}	21	●	6 **Seasons In The Sun** AC^1 *Put The Bone In*	$5		Bell 45,432
				recorded by **The Kingston Trio** in 1963 on Capitol 5166			
6/8/74	**68**	5		7 **If You Go Away** ... *Me And You*	$5		Bell 45,467
				above 2 are French songs written by Jacques Brel, with English lyrics by **Rod McKuen**			
12/7/74	**97**	1		8 **Rock 'N' Roll (I Gave You The Best Years Of My Life)** ... *The Love Game*	$5		Bell 45,606
				SUSAN JACKS:			
3/8/75	**90**	5		9 **You're A Part Of Me** ... *I'd Rather Know You*	$5		Mercury 73649
				PORNO FOR PYROS ROK/LP **'96**			
				Rock group formed by former Jane's Addiction members Perry Farrell (vocals) and Stephen Perkins (drums). Includes Peter DiStefano (guitar) and Martyn LeNoble (bass). Mike Watt replaced LeNoble in 1995.			
7/10/93	**67**	10		1 **Pets** ... MR^5 A:67 / S:74 *Tonight*	$4	▮	Warner 18480
5/25/96	**46**^{A}	15		2 **Tahitian Moon** ...			album cut
				from the album *Good God's Urge* on Warner 46126			
				PORTER, David — see HAYES, Isaac			
				PORTER, Nolan **'71**			
				Born in 1949 in Los Angeles, California. R&B singer. Also recorded as **Nolan** and **N.F. Porter**. Produced by Gabriel Mekler.			
9/18/71	**70**	8		1 **I Like What You Give** *[NOLAN]* ... *Somebody's Cryin'*	$6		Lizard 1008
12/18/71+	**77**	6		2 **Keep On Keeping On** *[N.F. PORTER]* ... *Don't Make Me Color My Black Face Blue*	$6		Lizard 1010
3/31/73	**89**	4		3 **If I Could Only Be Sure** ... *Work It Out In The Morning*	$5		ABC 11343
				PORTISHEAD LP **'95**			
				Modern rock duo from Bristol, England: multi-instrumentalist Geoff Barrow and vocalist Beth Gibbons. Duo named after a coastal shipping town near Bristol.			
2/11/95	**53**	9		**Sour Times (Nobody Loves Me)** ... A:50 *Airbus Reconstruction*	$4	▮	Go! Discs 857816
				samples "Danube Incident" by **Lalo Schifrin**			
				PORTNOY, Gary **'83**			
				Born on 6/8/56 in Valley Stream, New York. Pop singer/songwriter.			
4/30/83	**83**	4		**Where Everybody Knows Your Name (The Theme From "Cheers")** ... *Jenny*	$5		Applause 106
				first released on Earthtone 7004 ($6) in 1982 with a picture sleeve; originally titled "(Theme From The T.V. Show) 'Cheers'"			
				PORTRAIT R&B/BUB/LP **'93**			
				Male R&B vocal group: Eric Kirkland and Michael Angelo Saulsberry (both from Los Angeles, California), Irving Washington III (from Providence, Rhode Island) and Phillip Johnson (from Tulsa, Oklahoma). In 1995, Johnson was replaced by Kurt Jackson (from Aurora, Colorado).			
11/14/92+	**11**	23		1 **Here We Go Again!** ... A:8 / S:17 *(2 versions)*	$3	▮^{V}	Capitol 44865
4/17/93	**71**^{S}	4		2 **Honey Dip** ... BUB:102 *(2 mixes) / (3 album snippets)*	$3	▮^{V}	Capitol 44870
				"45" issued for above 2 on Capitol 56947			
7/15/95	**93**	5		3 **How Deep Is Your Love** ... S:74 *Me Oh My*	$3	▮^{V}	Capitol 58421
				"45": Capitol 18126; B-side: "I Can Call You" (#119)			
4/20/96	**68**	9		4 **Slow Jams** ... S:43 *(remix)*	$3	▮^{V}	Qwest 17673
				QUINCY JONES Featuring Babyface and Tamia with Portrait and Barry White			
				POSEY, Sandy C&W/BUB/LP **'66**			
				Born on 6/18/44 in Jasper, Alabama; raised in West Memphis, Arkansas. Pop singer.			
7/23/66	**12**	14		1 **Born A Woman** ... *Caution To The Wind*	$8		MGM 13501
11/19/66	**12**	12		2 **Single Girl** *Blue Is My Best Color*	$8	■	MGM 13612
3/11/67	**31**	7		3 **What A Woman In Love Won't Do** ... *Shattered*	$8		MGM 13702
6/10/67	**12**	12		4 **I Take It Back** ... *The Boy I Love*	$8	■	MGM 13744
10/21/67	**59**	5		5 **Are You Never Coming Home** ... *I Can Show You How To Live*	$8		MGM 13824
				POSITIVE K R&B/BUB/LP **'93**			
				Born Darryl Gibson in the Bronx, New York. Male rapper.			
12/19/92+	**14**	22	●	**I Got A Man** ... S:5 / A:19 *Night Shift* (#101/R&B flip) */ (3 album snippets)*	$3	▮	Island 864305
				samples "Rescue Me" by **A Taste Of Honey**			
				POST, Mike AC **'75**			
				Born on 9/29/44 in Los Angeles, California. Composer/producer.			
5/17/75	**10**	16		1 **The Rockford Files** ... *Dixie Lullabye* [I]	$5		MGM 14772
				theme from the TV series starring James Garner			
9/27/75	**56**	7		2 **Manhattan Spiritual** ... *Lay Back Lafayette* [I]	$5		MGM 14829
8/22/81	**10**	22		3 **The Theme From Hill Street Blues** ... *Aaron's Tune* [I]	$4	■	Elektra 47186
				MIKE POST featuring Larry Carlton			
				theme from the TV series starring Daniel J. Travanti			
2/6/82	**25**	17		4 **Theme From Magnum P.I.** ... *Gumbus Red* [I]	$4	■	Elektra 47400
				theme from the TV series starring Tom Selleck			

DEBUT	PEAK	WKS	Gold	A-side (Chart Hit)......B-side	$	Sym	Label & Number
				POTLIQUOR LP **'72**			
				Rock group from Baton Rouge, Louisiana: George Ratzlaff (vocals), Les Wallace (guitar), Guy Schaeffer (bass) and Jerry Amoroso (drums).			
2/5/72	**65**	11		**Cheer**......*Chattanooga*	$7		Janus 179
				POURCEL('S), Franck, French Fiddles AC/BUB **'59**			
				Born on 1/1/15 in Marseilles, France. String orchestra leader/composer/arranger/violinist.			
4/6/59	**9**	16		**Only You**......*Rainy Night In Paris* [I]	$10		Capitol 4165
				POUSETTE-DART BAND LP **'79**			
				Pop group from Canada: Jon Pousette-Dart (vocals), John Curtis (guitar), John Troy (bass) and Michael Dawe (drums).			
9/8/79	**83**	4		**For Love**......*She Found Out*	$5		Capitol 4764
				POWELL, Bobby R&B/BUB **'66**			
				Born in Baton Rouge, Louisiana. R&B singer. Blind since birth.			
12/4/65+	**76**	7		1 **C.C. Rider**......*That Little Girl Of Mine*	$15		Whit 714
				#14 hit for Ma Rainey in 1925 (as "See See Rider Blues")			
6/17/67	**91**	3		2 **Why (Am I Treated So Bad)**......*Thank You*	$12		Whit 730
				POWELL, Cozy **'74**			
				Born Colin Powell on 12/29/47 in Cirencester, Glouchester, England. Died in a car crash on 4/5/98 (age 50). Rock drummer. Member of **Jeff Beck**'s group (1971-72), **Rainbow** (1976-80), **Whitesnake** (1984), **Emerson, Lake & Powell** (1986) and **Black Sabbath** (1990).			
3/16/74	**49**	9		**Dance With The Devil**......*And Then There Was Skin* [I]	$6		Chrysalis 2029
				POWELL, Jane **'56**			
				Born Suzanne Burce on 4/1/29 in Portland, Oregon. Star of many movie musicals, 1944-58.			
8/25/56	**15**	25		**True Love**......S:15 / T:24 *Mind If I Make Love To You*	$15		Verve 2018
				Buddy Bregman (orch.); Cole Porter song from the movie *High Society* starring **Bing Crosby** and **Frank Sinatra**			
				POWELL, Jesse R&B/BUB/LP **'99**			
				Born in Gary, Indiana. R&B singer/songwriter. Brother of **Trina & Tamara**.			
8/22/98	**85**	9		1 **I Wasn't With It**......S:56 *(3 album snippets)*	$3	▮	Silas/MCA 55457
2/20/99	**10**	20		2 **You**......S:8 / A:17 *(darkchild remix* w/**Trina & Tamara**)	$4	★V	Silas/MCA 55500
				"45": Silas/MCA 55580; B-side: "'Bout It, 'Bout It"			
				POWERS, Joey **'63**			
				Born in 1939 in Canonsburg, Pennsylvania. Pop singer.			
11/9/63+	**10**	13		**Midnight Mary**......*Where Do You Want The World Delivered*	$12		Amy 892
				POWERS, Tom **'77**			
				Born in 1948 in Washington DC. Pop singer/songwriter.			
10/8/77	**92**	5		**It Ain't Love**......*Live And Learn*	$5		Big Tree 16103
				POWERSOURCE **'88**			
				A 21-member evangelical youth chorus from Bedford, Texas, featuring 6-year-old Sharon Batts.			
12/19/87+	**61**	7		**Dear Mr. Jesus**......*Love, Sharon*	$25		PowerVision 8603
				recorded in 1985; popularized due to the killing of 6-year-old Sharon Steinberg in New York City by her adoptive father, lawyer Joel Steinberg			
				POWER STATION, The LP **'85**			
				All-star rock group: **Robert Palmer** (vocals), **Andy Taylor** (guitar), **John Taylor** (bass) and Tony Thompson (drums). The Taylors were members of **Duran Duran**. Thompson was a member of **Chic**.			
3/16/85	**6**	18		1 **Some Like It Hot**......S:6 / A:8 *The Heat Is On* [I]	$3	■	Capitol 5444
6/8/85	**9**	15		2 **Get It On**......S:8 / A:10 *Go To Zero*	$3	■	Capitol 5479
				revival of 1972's "Bang A Gong" by **T. Rex** (Marc Bolan)			
9/7/85	**34**	10		3 **Communication**......*Murderess*	$3	■	Capitol 5511
				PO' WHITE TRASH **'01**			
				Born in Houston, Texas. White male rapper.			
9/1/01	**25**S	20		**Po' Punch**......*(3 versions)*	$5	★	Pocket Change 2121
				PO' WHITE TRASH AND THE TRAILER PARK SYMPHONY			
				POWW BROS., The **'03**			
				R&B vocal duo from Detroit, Michigan: brothers John and Shawn Powe (former members of **UNV**).			
12/21/02+	**25**S	9		**Faithful To**......*(remix) / Clap Ya Hands*	$6	★	Powwer Moves 90457
				POZO-SECO SINGERS BUB/LP **'66**			
				Folk-rock trio from Texas: **Don Williams**, Susan Taylor and Lofton Kline. Williams later became a major country star.			
2/26/66	**47**	7		1 **Time**......*Down The Road I Go*	$8	□	Columbia 43437
				first released on Edmark 10017 in 1965 ($20)			
6/18/66	**92**	2		2 **I'll Be Gone**......*It Ain't Worth The Lonely Road Back*	$8		Columbia 43646
9/10/66	**32**	11		3 **I Can Make It With You** *Come A Little Bit Closer*	$8		Columbia 43784
12/17/66+	**32**	9		4 **Look What You've Done**......*Almost Persuaded*	$8		Columbia 43927
5/6/67	**96**	1		5 **I Believed It All**......*Excuse Me Dear Martha (#102)*	$8		Columbia 44041
9/16/67	**97**	3		6 **Louisiana Man**......*Tomorrow Proper*	$8		Columbia 44263

DEBUT	PEAK	WKS	Gold	A-side (Chart Hit)..........B-side	$	Sym	Label & Number
				PRADO, Perez, And His Orchestra MEM/LP '55			
				Born Damaso Perez Prado on 12/11/16 in Mantanzas, Cuba. Died of a stroke on 9/14/89 (age 72). Bandleader/organist. Known as "The King of The Mambo." Appeared in the movie *Underwater!*			
3/5/55	❶[10]	26	●	1 **Cherry Pink And Apple Blossom White** S:❶[10] / J:❶[8] / A:❶[6] *Rhythm Sticks* [I]	$20		RCA Victor 5965
				Billy Regis (trumpet solo); from the movie *Underwater!* starring Jane Russell; French song written in 1950			
6/16/58	❶[1]	21	●	2 **Patricia** ....RB[2] T:❶[1] / A:❶[1] / S:2 *Why Wait* [I]	$15		RCA Victor 7245
				also see #5 below			
10/13/58	**53**	9		3 **Guaglione /** H:53 [I]			
				Italian song included in the movie *Ten Thousand Bedrooms* starring **Dean Martin**			
10/20/58	**95**	1		4 **Paris** .... [I]	$12		RCA Victor 7337
4/7/62	**65**	5		5 **Patricia - Twist**..........*Ti-Pi-Tin - Twist* [I-R]	$10		RCA Victor 8006
				new version of #2 above			
				PRAS — see MICHEL, Pras			
				PRATT, Andy LP '73			
				Born on 1/25/47 in Boston, Massachusetts. Soft-rock singer/songwriter/keyboardist/guitarist.			
4/28/73	**78**	10		**Avenging Annie** ....*So Fine (It's Frightening)*	$5		Columbia 45804
				PRATT & McCLAIN LP '76			
				Pop vocal duo: Truett Pratt (from San Antonio, Texas) and Jerry McClain (from Pasadena, California).			
4/3/76	**5**	14		1 **Happy Days** ....*Cruisin' With The Fonz*	$5		Reprise 1351
				theme from the TV series starring Ron Howard and Henry Winkler			
7/17/76	**71**	4		2 **Devil With A Blue Dress** ....*Tonight We're Gonna Fall In Love*	$5		Reprise 1361
				Shorty Long's original version "Bubbled Under" (#125) in 1964			
				PRECISIONS, The R&B '67			
				R&B vocal group led by Bobby Brooks.			
10/7/67	**60**	6		**If This Is Love (I'd Rather Be Lonely)** ....*You'll Soon Be Gone*	$25		Drew 1003
				PRELUDE AC/LP '74			
				Folk trio formed in England: husband-and-wife Irene (vocals) and Brian (vocals, guitar) Hume, with Ian Vardy (guitar).			
10/5/74	**22**	13		1 **After The Goldrush** ....*Johnson Boy*	$6		Island 002
				written by **Neil Young** in 1970			
11/29/75+	**63**	8		2 **For A Dancer** ....*Best Of A Bad Time* (AC #42)	$5		Pye 71045
				written by **Jackson Browne** in 1974			
				PRELUDES FIVE, The '61			
				Black male doo-wop group. Also known as The Chessmen on the Mirasonic label.			
8/14/61	**80**	5		**Starlight** ....*Don't You Know Love*	$30		Pik 231
				some pressings credit artist as: **THE PRELUDES**			
				PREMIERS, The '64			
				Latin-rock group from San Gabriel, California: George Delgado (vocals), Larry Perez (guitar), Phil Ruiz and Joe Urzua (horns), Frank Zuniga (bass) and Johnny Perez (drums).			
6/20/64	**19**	9		**Farmer John** ....*Duffy's Blues*	$15		Warner 5443
				first released on Faro 615 in 1964 ($30); label claims record was recorded "live" at The Rhythm Room in Fullerton, California (actually recorded in the studio in front of some of the band's friends)			
				PRESIDENTS, The R&B/LP '70			
				R&B vocal trio from Washington DC: Archie Powell, Bill Shorter and Tony Boyd. Also recorded as **Anacostia** (see #3 below).			
10/3/70	**11**	15		1 **5-10-15-20 (25-30 Years Of Love)** ....*I'm Still Dancing*	$8		Sussex 207
1/30/71	**68**	7		2 **Triangle Of Love (Hey Diddle Diddle)** ....*Sweet Magic*	$7		Sussex 212
1/6/73	**90**	4		3 **On And Off (Part 1)** ....*(Part 2)*	$5		Columbia 45685
				ANACOSTIA			
				PRESIDENTS OF THE UNITED STATES OF AMERICA, The LP '96			
				Rock trio from Seattle, Washington: Chris Ballew (vocals), Dave Dederer (guitar) and Jason Finn (drums).			
8/19/95	**21**[A]	22		1 **Lump** ....MR[1]			album cut
12/16/95	**67**[A]	2		2 **Kitty**			album cut
3/9/96	**29**	14		3 **Peaches** ....S:22 / A:37 *Candy Cigarette*	$4	▮[V]	Columbia 78254 ■
				"45": Dry Hump 018 (yellow vinyl); B-side: "Video Killed The Radio Star"; issued with a hard cover picture sleeve; all of above from the album *The Presidents of The United States of America* on Columbia 67291			
11/16/96	**68**[A]	5		4 **Mach 5**			album cut
				from the album *II* on Columbia 67577			

DEBUT	PEAK	WKS	Gold		A-side (Chart Hit)..........B-side	$	Sym	Label & Number

PRESLEY, Elvis ★1★ — C&W/BUB/AC/R&B/LP '56

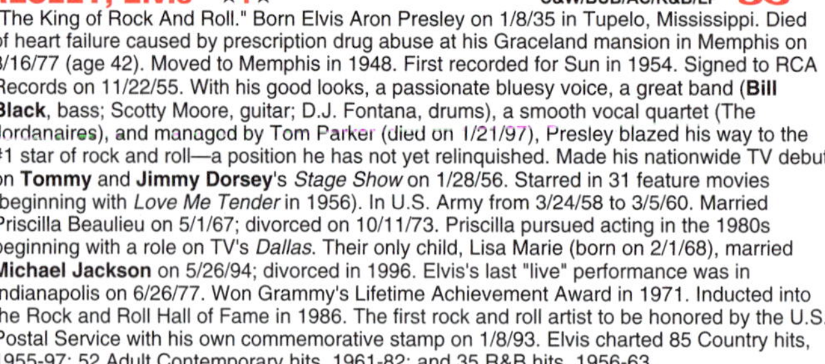

"The King of Rock And Roll." Born Elvis Aron Presley on 1/8/35 in Tupelo, Mississippi. Died of heart failure caused by prescription drug abuse at his Graceland mansion in Memphis on 8/16/77 (age 42). Moved to Memphis in 1948. First recorded for Sun in 1954. Signed to RCA Records on 11/22/55. With his good looks, a passionate bluesy voice, a great band (**Bill Black**, bass; Scotty Moore, guitar; D.J. Fontana, drums), a smooth vocal quartet (The Jordanaires), and managed by Tom Parker (died on 1/21/97), Presley blazed his way to the #1 star of rock and roll—a position he has not yet relinquished. Made his nationwide TV debut on **Tommy** and **Jimmy Dorsey**'s *Stage Show* on 1/28/56. Starred in 31 feature movies (beginning with *Love Me Tender* in 1956). In U.S. Army from 3/24/58 to 3/5/60. Married Priscilla Beaulieu on 5/1/67; divorced on 10/11/73. Priscilla pursued acting in the 1980s beginning with a role on TV's *Dallas*. Their only child, Lisa Marie (born on 2/1/68), married **Michael Jackson** on 5/26/94; divorced in 1996. Elvis's last "live" performance was in Indianapolis on 6/26/77. Won Grammy's Lifetime Achievement Award in 1971. Inducted into the Rock and Roll Hall of Fame in 1986. The first rock and roll artist to be honored by the U.S. Postal Service with his own commemorative stamp on 1/8/93. Elvis charted 85 Country hits, 1955-97; 52 Adult Contemporary hits, 1961-82; and 35 R&B hits, 1956-63.

Here, in chronological order, are Presley's singles released in the U.S. prior to 1956:
1)July 1954: That's All Right/Blue Moon Of Kentucky...Sun 209 ($6000)
2)Sep. 1954: Good Rockin' Tonight/I Don't Care If The Sun Don't Shine...Sun 210 ($3500)
3)Jan. 1955: You're A Heartbreaker/Milkcow Blues Boogie...Sun 215 ($5000)
4)Apr. 1955: Baby Let's Play House (C&W #5)/I'm Left, You're Right, She's Gone (C&W flip)...Sun 217 ($3000)
5)Sep. 1955: Mystery Train (C&W #11)/I Forgot To Remember To Forget (C&W #1)...Sun 223 ($2500)

After signing with RCA Victor (November 1955) the above five singles were released on RCA Victor 6380, 6381 (see #10 below), 6382, 6383 and 6357 respectively ($60 each). "Mystery Train" issued with a "This Is His Life" comic strip-styled promo picture sleeve ($2000).

1)Don't Be Cruel 2)Hound Dog 3)All Shook Up 4)Heartbreak Hotel 5)Jailhouse Rock 6)(Let Me Be Your) Teddy Bear 7)Are You Lonesome To-night? 8)Love Me Tender 9)It's Now Or Never 10)Don't

DEBUT	PEAK	WKS	Gold		A-side (Chart Hit)..........B-side	$	Sym	Label & Number
3/3/56	❶[8]	27	▲[2]	1	**Heartbreak Hotel** / CW[17] S:❶[8] / J:❶[8] / T:❶[7] / A:❶[3]			
3/10/56	19	16		2	**I Was The One**.....A:19 / T:23 / S:flip / J:flip	$50		RCA Victor 47-6420
4/7/56	20	12	●	3	**Blue Suede Shoes**.....S:20 / T:24 / A:24 *Tutti Frutti / I Got A Woman / Just Because* [EP] from the EP *Elvis Presley* (promo EP issued with a paper sleeve featuring "Blue Suede Shoes"); single released on 9/8/56 on RCA Victor 47-6636 ($80); all EP prices include the EP cover	$125	■	RCA Victor EPA-747
5/12/56	76	5		4	**Money Honey**....T:76 *I Forgot To Remember To Forget / Heartbreak Hotel / I Was The One* [EP] from the EP *Heartbreak Hotel*; single released on 9/8/56 on RCA Victor 47-6641 ($60); #1 R&B hit for **The Drifters** in 1953	$125	■	RCA Victor EPA-821
5/26/56	❶[1]	24	▲	5	**I Want You, I Need You, I Love You** / CW[2] S:❶[1] / T:3 / J:3 / A:6			
5/26/56	31	14		6	**My Baby Left Me**.....T:31 / S:flip / J:flip written and recorded on RCA Victor 50-0109 by Arthur "Big Boy" Crudup in 1951 ($150)	$50		RCA Victor 47-6540
8/11/56	❶[11]	27	▲[4]	7	**Don't Be Cruel** / RB[6] / CW[10] S:❶[11] / J:❶[11] / A:❶[8] / T:❶[7] *Billboard's* Best Sellers and Juke Box charts combined "Don't Be Cruel" and "Hound Dog" as one listing; "Don't Be Cruel" had more #1 weeks as the top side on both charts			
8/4/56	❶[11]	28		8	**Hound Dog** RB[6] / CW[10] S:❶[11] / J:❶[11] / T:2 / A:4 Grammy Hall of Fame winner (1988); #1 R&B hit for Big Mama Thornton in 1953	$40	■	RCA Victor 47-6604
9/29/56	55	17		9	**Blue Moon**.....T:55 *Just Because* reissue of a Sun recording from 1954; #1 hit for the Glen Gray Orchestra in 1935	$60		RCA Victor 47-6640
10/13/56	74	6		10	**I Don't Care If The Sun Don't Shine**.....T:74 *Good Rockin' Tonight* originally released on Sun 210 in 1954; #8 hit for **Patti Page** in 1950	$60		RCA Victor 47-6381
10/20/56	❶[5]	23	▲[3]	11	**Love Me Tender** / S:❶[5] / A:❶[5] / T:❶[4] / J:❶[1] title song from Presley's first movie (also see #17 below); adapted from the 1861 tune "Aura Lee"			
11/3/56	20	10		12	**Anyway You Want Me (That's How I Will Be)**.....A:20 / T:27 / S:flip / J:flip picture sleeve issued with four color variations: black & white, green, light pink and dark pink	$40	■	RCA Victor 47-6643
11/17/56+	2[2]	19		13	**Love Me** / A:2 / T:6 / S:7 / J:8 first issued by Willie & Ruth in 1954 on Spark 105 ($75)			
12/1/56	19	15		14	**When My Blue Moon Turns To Gold Again** / A:19 / T:27 country song introduced in 1941 by Wiley Walker and Gene Sullivan on Okeh 6374 ($30)			
12/29/56+	59	7		15	**Paralyzed**.....T:59 *Rip It Up* [EP] above 3 from the EP *Elvis, Volume 1*	$100	■	RCA Victor EPA-992
12/29/56	47	2		16	**Old Shep**.....T:47 *So Glad You're Mine / Ready Teddy / Anyplace Is Paradise* [EP] written in 1933 by Red Foley; from the EP *Elvis, Volume II*; above 4 from the album *Elvis*	$100	■	RCA Victor EPA-993
12/29/56+	24	11		17	**Poor Boy**.....A:24 / T:35 *We're Gonna Move / Love Me Tender / Let Me* [EP] from the Presley movie and EP *Love Me Tender*	$100	■	RCA Victor EPA-4006
1/26/57	❶[3]	17	▲	18	**Too Much** / S:❶[3] / J:❶[1] / T:2 / A:2 first issued by Bernard Hardison in 1955 on Republic 7111 ($75)			
2/2/57	21	9		19	**Playing For Keeps**.....A:21 / T:34 / S:flip / J:flip	$40	■	RCA Victor 47-6800
4/6/57	❶[9]	30	▲[2]	20	**All Shook Up** / RB[4] / CW[1] J:❶[9] / S:❶[8] / T:❶[8] / A:❶[7]			
4/13/57	58	7		21	**That's When Your Heartaches Begin**.....T:58 written in 1937; recorded in 1941 by the Ink Spots; picture sleeves issued with RCA's "Gold Standard Series" (447) for Sun 209 (0601) and #1 & 2 (0605), #7 & 8 (0608), #10 (0602) and #20 & 21 (0618)	$40	■	RCA Victor 47-6870
4/13/57	25	10		22	**(There'll Be) Peace In The Valley (For Me)**.....S:25 / T:39 *It Is No Secret / I Believe / Take My Hand, Precious Lord* [EP] from the EP *Peace In The Valley*; #5 Country hit for Red Foley in 1951	$100	■	RCA Victor EPA-4054
6/24/57	❶[7]	25	▲[2]	23	**Let Me Be Your Teddy Bear** / RB[1] / CW[1] S:❶[7] / T:❶[7] / A:❶[3]			
6/24/57	20	22		24	**Loving You**.....A:20 / T:28 / S:flip above 2 from the Presley movie and album *Loving You*	$40	■	RCA Victor 47-7000
10/14/57	❶[7]	27	▲[2]	25	**Jailhouse Rock** / RB[5] / CW[1] S:❶[7] / T:❶[6] / A:❶[2]			
10/14/57	18	10		26	**Treat Me Nice**.....A:18 / T:27 / S:flip above 2 from the Presley movie *Jailhouse Rock*	$40	■	RCA Victor 47-7035
1/27/58	❶[5]	20	▲	27	**Don't** / S:❶[5] / T:❶[1] / A:❶[1] not counting EPs and the 2 Sun recordings, the above string of 10 consecutive #1 hits is the longest in *Billboard's* pop chart history; #8, 13 & 24-27: written by Leiber & Stoller (also #50, 57, 58 & 65 below)			
1/27/58	8	12		28	**I Beg Of You**.....T:8 / A:11 / S:flip	$30	■	RCA Victor 47-7150

DEBUT	PEAK	WKS	Gold		A-side (Chart Hit)..................B-side	$	Sym	Label & Number
					PRESLEY, Elvis — Cont'd			
4/21/58	2^1	15	▲	29	Wear My Ring Around Your Neck / RB^3 S:2 / T:3 / A:3			
					#27 & 29: reissued in 1960 as a promo single with a special sleeve ("Extra! Extra!") on RCA Victor SP45-76 ($1000)			
4/21/58	15	6		30	Doncha' Think It's Time ....A:15 / T:21 / S:flip	$30	■	RCA Victor 47-7240
6/30/58	❶^2	16	▲	31	Hard Headed Woman / S:❶^2 / A:❶^1 / T:2			
7/7/58	25	9		32	Don't Ask Me Why ....A:25 / T:28 / S:flip	$30	■	RCA Victor 47-7280
					above 2 from the Presley movie and album *King Creole*			
11/10/58	4	17	▲	33	One Night /			
					#11 R&B hit for Smiley Lewis in 1956 on Imperial 5380 ($80); originally written as "One Night (Of Sin)"			
11/3/58	8	16		34	I Got Stung	$25	■	RCA Victor 47-7410
3/23/59	2^1	15	▲	35	(Now and Then There's) A Fool Such As I /			
					#4 Country hit for **Hank Snow** in 1953			
3/30/59	4	13		36	I Need Your Love Tonight	$25	■	RCA Victor 47-7506
7/6/59	❶^2	14	●	37	A Big Hunk O' Love /			
7/13/59	12	11		38	My Wish Came True	$25	■	RCA Victor 47-7600
					recorded by Presley in 1957; written by **Ivory Joe Hunter**			
4/4/60	❶^4	16	▲	39	Stuck On You /			
4/11/60	17	10		40	Fame And Fortune	$20	■	RCA Victor 47-7740
					above 2 recorded 15 days after Presley's Army discharge; picture sleeve has a center-cut hole and states: "Elvis' 1st New Recording For His 50,000,000 Fans All Over The World"; above 2 also issued on 61-7740: "Living Stereo" ($500)			
7/18/60	❶^5	20	▲	41	It's Now Or Never /			
					adapted from the Italian song "O Sole Mio" of 1899			
7/25/60	32	11		42	A Mess Of Blues	$20	■	RCA Victor 47-7777
					above 2 also issued on 61-7777: "Living Stereo" ($750)			
11/14/60	❶^6	16	▲^{2}	43	Are You Lonesome To-night? /			
					#4 hit for Vaughn Deleath in 1927			
11/14/60	20	11		44	I Gotta Know	$20	■	RCA Victor 47-7810
					above 2 also issued on 61-7810: "Living Stereo" ($750)			
2/20/61	❶^2	12	▲	45	Surrender /			
					adapted from the Italian song "Torna A Surriento"			
2/27/61	32	5		46	Lonely Man	$20	■	RCA Victor 47-7850
					from the Presley movie *Wild In The Country*; above 2 also issued on 61-7850: "Living Stereo" ($1200); 37-7850: "Compact 33 Single" ($700); 68-7850: "Living Stereo Compact 33 Single" ($1500)			
4/17/61	14	7		47	Flaming Star ....*Summer Kisses, Winter Tears / Are You Lonesome To-night? / It's Now Or Never* [EP]	$80	■	RCA Victor LPC-128
					title song from the movie starring Presley; from the "Compact 33 Double" EP *Elvis By Request*			
5/15/61	5	9	●	48	I Feel So Bad /			
					#8 R&B hit for **Chuck Willis** in 1954 on Okeh 7029 ($50)			
6/5/61	26	5		49	Wild In The Country	$20	■	RCA Victor 47-7880
					title song from the movie starring Presley; above 2 also issued on 37-7880: "Compact 33 Single" ($1500)			
8/28/61	4	11	●	50	Marie's the Name His Latest Flame /			
8/21/61	5	13		51	Little Sister	$20	■	RCA Victor 47-7908
					above 2 also issued on 37-7908: "Compact 33 Single" ($6000)			
12/4/61+	2^1	14	▲	52	Can't Help Falling In Love / AC^6			
					inspired by the French melody "Plasir d'Amour"			
12/4/61+	23	9		53	Rock-A-Hula Baby ("Twist" Special)	$20	■	RCA Victor 47-7968
					above 2 from the Presley movie and album *Blue Hawaii*; above 2 also issued on 37-7968: "Compact 33 Single" ($8000)			
3/17/62	❶^2	13	▲	54	Good Luck Charm /			
3/17/62	31	8		55	Anything That's Part Of You	$20	■	RCA Victor 47-7992
					above 2 also issued on 37-7992: "Compact 33 Single" ($10,000)			
5/12/62	15	10	▲	56	Follow That Dream ....*Angel / What A Wonderful Life / I'm Not The Marrying Kind* [EP]	$75	■	RCA Victor EPA-4368
					title song from the Presley movie and EP			
8/4/62	5	10	●	57	She's Not You /			
8/11/62	55	5		58	Just Tell Her Jim Said Hello	$20	■	RCA Victor 47-8041
9/22/62	30	7		59	King Of The Whole Wide World ....*This Is Living / Riding The Rainbow Home Is Where The Heart Is / I Got Lucky / A Whistling Tune* [EP]	$75	■	RCA Victor EPA-4371
					from the Presley movie and EP *Kid Galahad*; also issued with a "DJ Preview Special" sleeve (SP 45-118/$250)			
10/20/62	2^5	16	▲	60	Return To Sender /			
10/27/62	99	1		61	Where Do You Come From	$20	■	RCA Victor 47-8100
					above 2 from the Presley movie and album *Girls! Girls! Girls!*; at least one side of each of Presley's first 24 regular RCA releases peaked in the Top 5			
2/16/63	11	9	●	62	One Broken Heart For Sale /			
2/23/63	53	4		63	They Remind Me Too Much Of You	$15	■	RCA Victor 47-8134
					ELVIS PRESLEY with The Mellow Men (above 2)			
					above 2 from the Presley movie and album *It Happened At The World's Fair*			
6/29/63	3	11	●	64	(You're the) Devil In Disguise ....*Please Don't Drag That String Around*	$15	■	RCA Victor 47-8188
					the first of Presley's regular RCA releases which did not chart both the A- & B-sides			
10/19/63	8	10	●	65	Bossa Nova Baby /			
					from the Presley movie and album *Fun In Acapulco*; first issued by Tippie & The Clovers in 1962 on Tiger 201 ($50)			
10/19/63	32	7		66	Witchcraft	$15	■	RCA Victor 47-8243
					#5 R&B hit for The Spiders in 1956 on Imperial 5366 ($100)			
2/22/64	12	9	●	67	Kissin' Cousins /			
					from the Presley movie and album *Kissin' Cousins*			
2/29/64	29	7		68	It Hurts Me	$15	■	RCA Victor 47-8307
5/2/64	34	6		69	Kiss Me Quick ....*Suspicion* (#103)	$15	■	RCA Victor 447-0639
					issued on RCA's "Gold Standard Series" (from Presley's 1962 album *Pot Luck*)			
5/23/64	21	6	●	70	What'd I Say /			
					ELVIS PRESLEY with the Jubilee Four and Carole Lombard Quartet			
5/9/64	29	7		71	Viva Las Vegas	$15	■	RCA Victor 47-8360
7/4/64	92	1		72	Viva Las Vegas (EP)	$100	■	RCA Victor EPA-4382
					EP includes 4 songs: "C'mon Everybody"/ "Today, Tomorrow And Forever"/ "If You Think I Don't Need You"/"I Need Somebody To Lean On"; above 3 from the Presley movie *Viva Las Vegas*			
7/25/64	16	8		73	Such A Night ....*Never Ending* (#111)	$15	■	RCA Victor 47-8400
					from Presley's 1960 album *Elvis Is Back!*; #2 R&B hit for **Clyde McPhatter & The Drifters** in 1954			

DEBUT	PEAK	WKS	Gold		A-side (Chart Hit)	B-side	$	Sym	Label & Number
					PRESLEY, Elvis — Cont'd				
10/10/64	12	12	●	74	**Ask Me** /				
					adapted from the Italian song "Io" written by **Domenico Modugno**				
10/10/64	16	10		75	**Ain't That Loving You Baby**		$15	■	RCA Victor 47-8440
					co-written by **Ivory Joe Hunter**; recorded on 6/10/58				
12/5/64	❶ 2X	34	▲	76	**Blue Christmas**	*Wooden Heart* (#107) [X]	$20	■	RCA Victor 447-0720
					X: 1/'64; 4/'65; 12/'66; 5/'67; 8/'68; 2/'69; 4/'70; 2/'72; 1/'73; 3/'83; 4/'84; 3/'85; issued on RCA's "Gold Standard Series" (from the 1957 *Elvis' Christmas Album*); reissued on RCA Victor 447-0647 from 1965-on (with a new picture sleeve; different sleeve also issued in 1977) (B-side "Santa Claus Is Back In Town"); #55 Country hit in 1997 on RCA 62403 (B-side: "Love Me Tender")				
2/27/65	21	8		77	**Do The Clam**	*You'll Be Gone* (#121)	$12	■	RCA Victor 47-8500
					ELVIS PRESLEY With The Jordanaires, Jubilee Four & Carol Lombard Trio				
					from the Presley movie and album *Girl Happy* (also see #83 below)				
4/24/65	3	14	▲	78	**Crying In The Chapel** AC[7]	*I Believe In The Man In The Sky*	$12	■	RCA Victor 447-0643
					issued on RCA's "Gold Standard Series" (recorded on 10/31/60); there were 5 Top 20 versions of this song in 1953				
6/19/65	11	8		79	**(Such An) Easy Question** / AC[2]				
					from Presley's 1962 album *Pot Luck*				
6/19/65	55	6		80	**It Feels So Right**		$12	■	RCA Victor 47-8585
					from Presley's 1960 album *Elvis Is Back!*				
7/10/65	70	7		81	**Tickle Me (EP)**		$70	■	RCA Victor EPA-4383
					EP includes 5 songs: "I Feel That I've Known You Forever"/"Slowly But Surely"/"Night Rider"/"Put The Blame On Me"/ "Dirty, Dirty Feeling"; above 3 from the Presley movie *Tickle Me*				
8/28/65	11	11	●	82	**I'm Yours** AC[3]	*(It's A) Long Lonely Highway* (#112)	$12	■	RCA Victor 47-8657
					from Presley's 1962 album *Pot Luck*				
11/13/65	14	10	●	83	**Puppet On A String**	*Wooden Heart* (#110)	$12	■	RCA Victor 447-0650
					issued on RCA's "Gold Standard Series"; from the Presley movie and album *Girl Happy* (also see #77 above)				
1/1/66	33	7	●	84	**Tell Me Why** /				
					written by **Titus Turner**; recorded on 1/12/57				
1/1/66	95	1		85	**Blue River**		$12	■	RCA Victor 47-8740
					written by **Paul Evans**; recorded on 5/27/63				
3/19/66	25	8	●	86	**Frankie And Johnny** /				
					version of mid-19th century traditional folk song				
3/19/66	45	8		87	**Please Don't Stop Loving Me**		$12	■	RCA Victor 47-8780
					above 2 from the Presley movie and album *Frankie And Johnny*				
7/2/66	19	7		88	**Love Letters**	*Come What May* (#109)	$12	■	RCA Victor 47-8870
					#11 hit for **Dick Haymes** in 1945 (title song from the movie starring Jennifer Jones)				
10/8/66	40	7		89	**Spinout** /				
10/8/66	41	8		90	**All That I Am**		$12	■	RCA Victor 47-8941
					above 2 from the Presley movie and album *Spinout*				
12/3/66	2 1X	8		91	**If Every Day Was Like Christmas**	*How Would You Like To Be* [X]	$20	■	RCA Victor 47-8950
					X: 2/'66; 12/'67				
1/28/67	33	8		92	**Indescribably Blue**	*Fools Fall In Love* (#102)	$12	■	RCA Victor 47-9056
					ELVIS PRESLEY with The Jordanaires and The Imperials Quartet (above 2)				
5/20/67	63	5		93	**Long Legged Girl (With The Short Dress On)** /				
					from the Presley movie and album *Double Trouble* (#85 above on album as a bonus song)				
5/27/67	92	1		94	**That's Someone You Never Forget**		$12	■	RCA Victor 47-9115
					from Presley's 1962 album *Pot Luck*				
8/26/67	56	6		95	**There's Always Me** /				
9/9/67	78	5		96	**Judy**		$15	■	RCA Victor 47-9287
					above 2 from Presley's 1961 album *Something For Everybody*				
10/14/67	38	6		97	**Big Boss Man** /				
10/14/67	44	6		98	**You Don't Know Me**		$12	■	RCA Victor 47-9341
1/27/68	43	6		99	**Guitar Man**	*High Heel Sneakers*	$12	■	RCA Victor 47-9425
					also see #150 below; above 3 from Presley's movie and album *Clambake*				
3/23/68	28	9		100	**U.S. Male** /				
					above 2 written and originally recorded by **Jerry Reed**				
3/16/68	67	5		101	**Stay Away**		$12	■	RCA Victor 47-9465
					melody is "Greensleeves"; from the Presley movie *Stay Away, Joe* (title tune is a different song than "Stay Away")				
4/20/68	90	2		102	**You'll Never Walk Alone**	*We Call On Him* (#106)	$20	■	RCA Victor 47-9600
					from the Rodgers & Hammerstein musical *Carousel*				
6/15/68	71	5		103	**Let Yourself Go** /				
6/22/68	72	7		104	**Your Time Hasn't Come Yet, Baby**		$12	■	RCA Victor 47-9547
					above 2 from the Presley movie and album *Speedway*				
10/12/68	69	4		105	**A Little Less Conversation** /				
					also see a remix version on #153 below				
9/28/68	95	2		106	**Almost In Love**		$12	■	RCA Victor 47-9610
					ELVIS PRESLEY with The Jordanaires (#18-24, 27-32, 35-47, 49, 52-55, 57-61, 64-69, 71, 73, 74, 78-81, 83, 84, 89, 90, 93-95, 98 & 100-106)				
					above 2 from the Presley movie *Live A Little, Love A Little*				
11/30/68+	12	13	●	107	**If I Can Dream**	*Edge Of Reality* (#112)	$10	■	RCA Victor 47-9670
					reissued as the B-side of #152 below				
3/22/69	35	7		108	**Memories**	*Charro*	$10	■	RCA Victor 47-9731
					above 2 from the NBC-TV special and album *Elvis* (#107 is not the actual TV show version)				
5/3/69	3	13	▲	109	**In The Ghetto**	*Any Day Now*	$10	■	RCA Victor 47-9741
7/5/69	35	8	●	110	**Clean Up Your Own Back Yard**	*The Fair Is Moving On*	$10	■	RCA Victor 47-9747
					from the Presley movie *The Trouble With Girls (and how to get into it)*				
9/13/69	❶ 1	15	▲	111	**Suspicious Minds**	*You'll Think Of Me*	$10	■	RCA Victor 47-9764
					first issued by its writer Mark James in 1968 on Scepter 12221 ($25)				
11/29/69+	6	13	▲	112	**Don't Cry Daddy** /				
					#105, 108-110 & 112: written by **Mac Davis**				
11/29/69		13		113	**Rubberneckin'**		$10	■	RCA Victor 47-9768
					from Presley's last feature movie *Change Of Habit*				
2/14/70	16	9	●	114	**Kentucky Rain**	*My Little Friend*	$8	■	RCA Victor 47-9791
5/16/70	9	12	●	115	**The Wonder Of You** / AC[1] [L]				
5/16/70		12		116	**Mama Liked The Roses**		$8	■	RCA Victor 47-9835

DEBUT	PEAK	WKS	Gold		A-side (Chart Hit)	B-side	$	Sym	Label & Number
					PRESLEY, Elvis — Cont'd				
8/1/70	32	9	●	117	**I've Lost You /**				
8/1/70		9		118	**The Next Step Is Love**		$8	■	RCA Victor 47-9873
10/24/70	11	10	●	119	**You Don't Have To Say You Love Me /** AC[1]				
10/24/70		10		120	**Patch It Up**		$8	■	RCA Victor 47-9916
					#114 & 120: written by **Eddie Rabbitt**; above 4 from the soundtrack album *Elvis-That's The Way It Is*				
12/26/70+	21	9	●	121	**I Really Don't Want To Know /**				
					#11 hit for **Les Paul & Mary Ford** in 1954				
12/26/70		9		122	**There Goes My Everything**		$7	■	RCA Victor 47-9960
3/13/71	33	7		123	**Where Did They Go, Lord /**				
3/13/71		7		124	**Rags To Riches**		$7	■	RCA Victor 47-9980
					#1 hit for **Tony Bennett** in 1953				
5/15/71	53	7		125	**Life /**				
5/15/71		7		126	**Only Believe**		$7	■	RCA Victor 47-9985
7/10/71	36	9		127	**I'm Leavin'**	*Heart Of Rome*	$7	■	RCA Victor 47-9998
10/9/71	51	6		128	**It's Only Love**	*The Sound Of Your Cry* (AC flip)	$7	■	RCA Victor 48-1017
1/29/72	40	9		129	**Until It's Time For You To Go**	*We Can Make The Morning* (AC flip)	$7	■	RCA Victor 74-0619
					first issued by its writer **Buffy Sainte-Marie** in 1970 on Vanguard 35116 ($7)				
5/6/72	66	6		130	**An American Trilogy**	*The First Time Ever I Saw Your Face* [L]	$20	■	RCA Victor 74-0672
					Dixie / Battle Hymn Of The Republic / All My Trials				
8/19/72	2[1]	15	▲	131	**Burning Love**	*It's A Matter Of Time* (C&W #36/AC #9)	$7	■	RCA Victor 74-0769
12/2/72+	20	12	●	132	**Separate Ways**	*Always On My Mind* (C&W #16)	$7	■	RCA Victor 74-0815
					featured in the movie *Elvis on Tour*				
4/14/73	17	12		133	**Steamroller Blues /** [L]				
					first issued by its writer **James Taylor** in 1970 on his *Sweet Baby James* album; from the TV special and album *Aloha from Hawaii via Satellite*				
4/14/73		12		134	**Fool**		$7	■	RCA Victor 74-0910
9/22/73	41	9		135	**Raised On Rock /**				
9/22/73		9		136	**For Ol' Times Sake**		$6	■	RCA Victor APBO-0088
2/9/74	39	12		137	**I've Got A Thing About You Baby /**				
					above 2 written by **Tony Joe White**				
3/16/74		7		138	**Take Good Care Of Her**		$6	■	RCA Victor APBO-0196
6/8/74	17	13		139	**If You Talk In Your Sleep**	*Help Me* (C&W #6)	$6	■	RCA Victor APBO-0280
10/26/74	14	13		140	**Promised Land**	*It's Midnight* (C&W #9/AC #8)	$6	■	RCA Victor PB-10074
					written by **Chuck Berry**				
1/25/75	20	11		141	**My Boy** AC[1]	*Thinking About You*	$6	■	RCA Victor PB-10191
5/10/75	35	9		142	**T-R-O-U-B-L-E**	*Mr. Songman*	$6	■	RCA Victor PB-10278
10/25/75	65	5		143	**Bringing It Back**	*Pieces Of My Life* (C&W #33)	$6	■	RCA Victor PB-10401
3/27/76	28	11		144	**Hurt /**				
					#8 R&B hit for **Roy Hamilton** in 1955				
4/3/76		10		145	**For The Heart**		$6	■	RCA Victor PB-10601
12/25/76+	31	13		146	**Moody Blue /** CW[1]				
12/25/76		13		147	**She Thinks I Still Care**		$6	■	RCA PB-10857
					written by **Dickey Lee**; #1 Country hit for **George Jones** in 1962				
6/25/77	18	21	▲	148	**Way Down** CW[1]	*Pledging My Love* (C&W flip)	$6	■	RCA PB-10998
					Presley's last chart hit while still alive				
11/12/77	22	12	●	149	**My Way**	*America* [L]	$6	■	RCA PB-11165
					co-written in 1969 by **Paul Anka**; based on the French standard "Comme d'Habitude"; from the CBS-TV special and album *Elvis In Concert*; some records and picture sleeves show the B-side as "America The Beautiful" (see #152 below)				
1/24/81	28	14		150	**Guitar Man** CW[1]	*Faded Love* [R]	$5	■	RCA PB-12158
					Jerry Reed (guitar); remix by Felton Jarvis (died on 1/3/81) of #99 above				
11/27/82	71	7		151	**The Elvis Medley**	*Always On My Mind* (#105/C&W flip)	$5	■	RCA PB-13351
					Jailhouse Rock/(Let Me Be Your) Teddy Bear/Hound Dog/Don't Be Cruel (To A Heart That's True)/Burning Love/Suspicious Minds				
11/3/01	6[S]	46		152	**America The Beautiful**	*If I Can Dream / Amazing Grace* [L]	$5	★[+]	RCA 60501
					re-issue of the B-side of #149 above; recorded at the Las Vegas Hilton on 12/6/75; all proceeds donated to the American Red Cross Liberty Disaster Relief Fund				
7/13/02	50	9		153	**A Little Less Conversation**	S:❶[3] *(2 versions)* [R]	$5	★[V]	RCA 60555
					ELVIS vs JXL				
					remix of #105 above; used in a Nike shoe commercial; "45": RCA 60575; B-side: (original 1968 version)				

9/8/56: 7 Presley RCA Victor releases: "Blue Suede Shoes"/ "Tutti Frutti" (6636-see #3 above); "I Got A Woman"/ "I'm Counting On You" (6637); I'll Never Let You Go (Little Darlin')"/"I'm Gonna Sit Right Down And Cry (Over You)" (6638); "Tryin' To Get To You"/ "I Love You Because" (6639); 6640 (see #9 above); "Money Honey"/ "One-Sided Love Affair" (6641-see #4 above); "Lawdy Miss Clawdy"/ "Shake, Rattle And Roll" (6642)

Presley's non-charted RCA Victor Christmas singles (both with picture sleeves):
1) Nov. 1971: Merry Christmas Baby/O Come All Ye Faithful...74-0572
2) Nov. 1985: Merry Christmas Baby/Santa Claus Is Back In Town...PB-14237

Presley's non-charted RCA Victor Easter singles (all with picture sleeves):
1) Mar. 1966: Joshua Fit The Battle/Known Only To Him...447-0651
2) Mar. 1966: Milky White Way/Swing Down Sweet Chariot...447-0652
3) Mar. 1967: How Great Thou Art/So High...45-162 (promo only)
4) Mar. 1969: How Great Thou Art (#101)/His Hand In Mine... 74-0130
5) Mar. 1972: He Touched Me/Bosom Of Abraham...74-0651
6) Mar. 1982: You'll Never Walk Alone (C&W #73)/There Goes My Everything (C&W flip)...PB-13058

DEBUT	PEAK	WKS	Gold	A-side (Chart Hit)	B-side	$	Sym	Label & Number

PRESLEY, Elvis — Cont'd

> Presley's non-charted regular commercial RCA "45" releases (all, except #5 & 12-14, with picture sleeves):
> 1) Apr. 1978: Softly, As I Leave You (#109/C&W flip)/Unchained Melody (C&W #6)...PB-11212
> 2) Aug. 1978: (Let Me Be Your) Teddy Bear (#105/C&W flip)/Puppet On A String (C&W #78)...PB-11320
> 3) Apr. 1979: Are You Sincere (C&W #10)/Solitaire (C&W flip)...PB 11533
> 4) Aug. 1979: There's A Honky Tonk Angel (Who Will Take Me Back In) (C&W #6)/I Got A Feelin' In My Body (C&W flip)...PB-11679
> 5) Apr. 1981: Lovin' Arms (C&W #8)/You Asked Me To (C&W flip)...PB-12205
> 6) Apr. 1983: I Was The One (C&W #92)/Wear My Ring Around Your Neck (C&W flip)...PB-13500
> 7) June 1983: Little Sister/Paralyzed...PB-13547
> 8) Aug. 1984: Baby, Let's Play House/Hound Dog...PB-13875
> 9) Dec. 1984: Blue Suede Shoes/Promised Land...PB-13929
> 10) June 1985: Always On My Mind/My Boy...PB-14090
> 11) Sep. 1988: Heartbreak Hotel/Heartbreak Hotel (David Keith & Charlie Schlatter with Zulu Time)...RCA 8760 (promo picture sleeve issued with RCA executive Butch Waugh posing as Elvis)
> 12) Sep. 1992: Don't Be Cruel/Ain't That Lovin' You Baby...RCA 62402
> 13) Sep. 1992: Blue Christmas/Love Me Tender...RCA 62403 (above 2 issued with a generic white sleeve and an "ELVIS The King Of Rock 'N' Roll" sticker)
> 14) Jan. 1993: Heartbreak Hotel/Hound Dog...RCA 62449
> 15) Jan. 1996: Heartbreak Hotel/I Was The One...RCA 64476

PRESSHA — '98

Born David Jones in Atlanta, Georgia. Male R&B singer.

DEBUT	PEAK	WKS	Gold	A-side (Chart Hit)	B-side	$	Sym	Label & Number
9/5/98	27	14		**Splackavellie**	S:15 *(instrumental)*	$4	★	Tony Mercedes 24302

★297★ PRESTON, Billy — R&B/BUB/LP '73

Born on 9/9/46 in Houston, Texas; raised in Los Angeles, California. R&B vocalist/keyboardist. With **Mahalia Jackson** in 1956. Played piano in movie *St. Louis Blues*, 1958. Regular on *Shindig* TV show. Recorded with **The Beatles** on "Get Back" and "Don't Let Me Down"; worked Concert For Bangladesh in 1969. Prominent session man, played on **Sly & The Family Stone** hits. With **The Rolling Stones** U.S. tour in 1975.

1)Will It Go Round In Circles 2)Nothing From Nothing 3)Outa-Space

DEBUT	PEAK	WKS	Gold	A-side (Chart Hit)	B-side	$	Sym	Label & Number
8/2/69	62	6		1 **That's The Way God Planned It** — also see #5 below	*What About You?*	$12	■	Apple 1808
2/13/71	90	3		2 **My Sweet Lord** — above 2 produced by **George Harrison**	*Little Girl*	$12		Apple 1826
4/22/72	2^1	17	●	3 **Outa-Space** / RB^1 [I]				
1/22/72	77	5		4 **I Wrote A Simple Song**		$6		A&M 1320
7/8/72	65	10		5 **That's The Way God Planned It** — same version as #1 above	*What About You?* [R]	$12	■	Apple 1808
9/9/72	50	8		6 **Slaughter** — title song from the movie starring football great Jim Brown	*God Loves You*	$6	■	A&M 1380
3/31/73	❶^2	22	●	7 **Will It Go Round In Circles**	*Blackbird*	$6		A&M 1411
9/22/73	4	18	●	8 **Space Race** RB^1	*We're Gonna Make It* [I]	$6	■	A&M 1463
1/5/74	48	8		9 **You're So Unique**	*How Long Has The Train Been Gone*	$5		A&M 1492
7/13/74	❶^1	18	●	10 **Nothing From Nothing**	*My Soul Is A Witness*	$5	■	A&M 1544
12/14/74+	22	10		11 **Struttin'**	*You Are So Beautiful* [I]	$5		A&M 1644
10/4/75	71	4		12 **Fancy Lady**	*Song Of Joy*	$5	■	A&M 1735
10/28/78	86	2		13 **Get Back** — from the movie *Sgt. Pepper's Lonely Hearts Club Band* starring **Peter Frampton** and the **Bee Gees**	*Space Race*	$5		A&M 2071
12/8/79+	4	29		14 **With You I'm Born Again** — from the movie *Fast Break* starring **Gabe Kaplan**; also on Motown 1460 with "Go For It" as the B-side	*All I Wanted Was You* (Preston)	$5		Motown 1477
6/14/80	52	10		15 **One More Time For Love** — **BILLY PRESTON & SYREETA** (above 2); Syreeta (Wright) was married to **Stevie Wonder** from 1970-72	*Dance For Me Children* (Syreeta)	$5		Tamla 54312
9/25/82	88	3		16 **I'm Never Gonna Say Goodbye**	*I Love You So*	$5		Motown 1625

PRESTON, Johnny — BUB '60

Born John Preston Courville on 8/18/39 in Port Arthur, Texas. Discovered by J.P. "**Big Bopper**" Richardson at the Twilight Club in Port Neches, Texas.

DEBUT	PEAK	WKS	Gold	A-side (Chart Hit)	B-side	$	Sym	Label & Number
10/12/59+	❶^3	27	●	1 **Running Bear** — Indian sounds by the **Big Bopper** and **George Jones**; written and backing vocal by the Big Bopper	*My Heart Knows*	$25		Mercury 71474
3/28/60	7	15		2 **Cradle Of Love**	*City Of Tears*	$20	■	Mercury 71598
6/20/60	14	14		3 **Feel So Fine** — **Shirley & Lee**'s version "Feel So Good" was a #2 R&B hit in 1955	*I'm Starting To Go Steady*	$15	■	Mercury 71651
1/30/61	73	5		4 **Leave My Kitten Alone**	*Token Of Love*	$15	■	Mercury 71761
12/25/61	97	1		5 **Free Me** — all of above picture sleeves feature the same photo of Preston	*Kissin' Tree*	$15	■	Mercury 71908

PRESTON, Mike — '58

Born Jack Davis on 5/14/34 in London, England. Pop singer.

DEBUT	PEAK	WKS	Gold	A-side (Chart Hit)	B-side	$	Sym	Label & Number
12/1/58	93	1		**A House, A Car And A Wedding Ring** — Harry Robinson (orch.)	*My Lucky Love*	$20		London 1834

★489★ PRETENDERS, The — ROK/BUB/AC/LP '83

Pop-rock group formed in England: **Chrissie Hynde** (vocals, guitar; born on 9/7/51 in Akron, Ohio) (see #7 below), James Honeyman-Scott (guitar; born on 11/4/57), Pete Farndon (bass; born on 6/2/52) and Martin Chambers (drums; born on 9/4/51). Honeyman-Scott died of a drug overdose on 6/16/82 (age 24); replaced by Robbie McIntosh (of **Night**). Farndon died of a drug overdose on 4/14/83 (age 30); replaced by Malcolm Foster. Hynde was married to Jim Kerr of **Simple Minds** from 1984-90. Lineup in 1994: Hynde, Chambers, Adam Seymour (guitar) and Andy Hobson (bass).

1)Back On The Chain Gang 2)Don't Get Me Wrong 3)Brass In Pocket (I'm Special)

DEBUT	PEAK	WKS	Gold	A-side (Chart Hit)	B-side	$	Sym	Label & Number
2/16/80	14	22		1 **Brass In Pocket (I'm Special)**	*Space Invader*	$6		Sire 49181
6/21/80	65	5		2 **Stop Your Sobbing** — originally recorded by **The Kinks** on their 1964 album *You Really Got Me*	*The Phone Call*	$6	■	Sire 49506
12/11/82+	5	24		3 **Back On The Chain Gang** — from the movie *The King Of Comedy* starring Robert DeNiro and **Jerry Lewis**	*My City Was Gone* (ROK #11)	$4	■	Sire 29840
12/17/83+	19	14		4 **Middle Of The Road**	*2000 Miles*	$4	■	Sire 29444

DEBUT	PEAK	WKS	Gold	A-side (Chart Hit)....B-side	$	Sym	Label & Number
				PRETENDERS, The — Cont'd			
3/17/84	28	13		5 **Show Me**....*Fast Or Slow (The Law's The Law)*	$4	■	Sire 29317
6/30/84	83	5		6 **Thin Line Between Love And Hate**....*Time The Avenger (live)*	$4	■	Sire 29249
				Paul Carrack (piano, backing vocal); above 4 from the album *Learning To Crawl*			
7/27/85	28	14		7 **I Got You Babe**....S:24 *Nkomo A Go Go* (UB40)	$4	■	A&M 2758
				UB40 WITH CHRISSIE HYNDE			
				picture sleeve issued with either a green or a brown background			
10/11/86	10	18		8 **Don't Get Me Wrong**....AR^{3} A:7 / S:11 *Dance!*	$3	■	Sire 28630
2/7/87	64	7		9 **My Baby**....AR^{2} *Room Full Of Mirrors* (ROK #28)	$3	■	Sire 28496
5/21/94	71	8		10 **Night In My Veins**....A:60 *Angel Of The Morning*	$3	▮^{V}	Sire 18163
8/13/94	16	30		11 **I'll Stand By You**....A:11 / S:39 *Rebel Rock Me*	$3	▮^{V}	Sire 18160
				above 2 produced by Ian Stanley (**Tears For Fears**); all of above (except #2, 6 & 7) written or co-written by Hynde			
				PRETTY IN PINK '91			
				Female teen vocal group: Milini Khan (the 17-year-old daughter of **Chaka Khan**), Tameika Chaney, Shey Sperry, Maurissa Tancharoen and Taniya Robinson.			
9/21/91	96	3		**All About You**....*(house mix)*	$4	▮	Motown 2087
				PRETTY POISON R&B/LP '87			
				Dance group from Philadelphia, Pennsylvania: Jade Starling (vocals), Whey Cooler (keyboards), Louie Franco (guitar) and Bobby Corea (drums).			
9/26/87	8	23	●	1 **Catch Me (I'm Falling)**....S:8 / A:9 *(Spanish mix)*	$3	■	Virgin 99416
				from the movie *Hiding Out* starring Jon Cryer; issued with 2 different picture sleeves			
4/2/88	36	12		2 **Nightime**....A:33 / S:35 *(Spanish mix)*	$3	■	Virgin 99350
				original version hit #82 on the R&B charts in 1984 on Svengali 8403			
				PRETTY WILLIE '02			
				Born William Woods in St. Louis, Missouri. R&B singer/rapper/songwriter.			
1/5/02	23^{S}	24		**Roll Wit Me**....*(3 album snippets)*	$4	★	Republic 015545
				PREVIN, Andre BUB/LP '59			
				Born on 4/6/29 in Berlin, Germany. Pianist/conductor/arranger/composer. Became musical director for MGM movies by the age of 21. Composed and arranged background music for *Gigi* and many other movies. In the 1970s, served as resident conductor of the **London Symphony Orchestra**. Married to actress Mia Farrow from 1970-79.			
6/1/59	46	12		**Like Young**....*Young Man's Lament* [I]	$10		MGM 12792
				The Piano Magic of ANDRE PREVIN Combined With The Lush Strings of DAVID ROSE			
				PRICE, Alan, Set LP '66			
				Born on 4/19/42 in Fairfield, Durham, England. Organist with the original **Animals**; left in 1965; rejoined group in 1983.			
7/30/66	80	3		**I Put A Spell On You**....*Iechyd-Da*	$10		Parrot 3001
				written and recorded by Screamin' Jay Hawkins (died on 2/12/2000) in 1956 on Okeh 7072 ($50)			
				PRICE, Kelly R&B/BUB/LP '98			
				Born on 4/4/73 in Queens, New York. Female R&B singer/songwriter. Backing vocalist on several **Mariah Carey** albums. Also see **The Notorious B.I.G.**'s "Mo Money Mo Problems" and **Mase**'s "Feel So Good."			
7/18/98	12	20	●	1 **Friend of Mine**....RB^{5} S:7 / A:74 *(instrumental) / (3 album snippets)*	$3	▮^{V}	Island 572330
				samples "Summer Breeze" by **Seals & Crofts**; "45" B-side: "Soul Of A Woman"			
12/26/98+	2^{3}	28	▲	2 **Heartbreak Hotel**....RB^{7} S:2 / A:5 *(dance mix) / It's Not Right But It's Okay* (Houston - #4)	$4	★	Arista 13619
				WHITNEY HOUSTON (Feat. Faith Evans & Kelly Price)			
5/13/00	91	4		3 **Love Sets You Free**....S:18 *It's Gonna Rain* (Price)	$4	★	Def Soul 562683
				KELLY PRICE & FRIENDS (Dru Hill, Montell Jordan, Case, Playa, Kandice Love, Lovher)			
				from the movie *The Hurricane* starring Denzel Washington			
7/15/00	65	8		4 **As We Lay**....A:55			album cut
9/23/00	64	20		5 **You Should've Told Me**....A:62 *(instrumental) / Like You Do* (w/**Method Man**)	$6	T	Def Soul 562864
				above 3 from the album *Mirror Mirror* on Def Soul 542472			
	★272★			**PRICE, Lloyd** R&B/BUB '59			
				Born on 3/9/33 in Kenner, Louisiana. R&B vocalist/pianist/composer. First recording was the #1 R&B hit "Lawdy Miss Clawdy" on Specialty in 1952. In U.S. Army, 1953-56. Formed own record company, KRC, in 1956; leased "Just Because" to ABC Records. Signed to ABC in 1957. Formed Double-L label in 1963 and Turntable Records in 1969. In later years has continued in music, production, and booking agency work. Inducted into the Rock and Roll Hall of Fame in 1998.			
				1)Stagger Lee 2)Personality 3)I'm Gonna Get Married			
3/2/57	29	20		1 **Just Because**....T:29 *Why*	$25		ABC-Paramount 9792
				first released on KRC 587 in 1956 ($75); melody adapted from "Caro Nome" from Verdi's opera *Rigoletto*			
9/30/57	88	1		2 **Lonely Chair**....T:88 *The Chicken And The Bop*	$50		KRC 301
12/8/58+	1^{4}	21	●	3 **Stagger Lee**....RB^{4} *You Need Love*	$20		ABC-Paramount 9972
				adapted from the traditional folk song "Stack-O-Lee"			
3/2/59	23	11		4 **Where Were You (On Our Wedding Day)?**....*Is It Really Love?*	$20		ABC-Paramount 9997
4/27/59	2^{3}	19	●	5 **Personality**....RB^{4} *Have You Ever Had The Blues*	$20		ABC-Paramount 10018
8/10/59	3	14		6 **I'm Gonna Get Married**....RB^{3} *Three Little Pigs* (R&B #15)	$20		ABC-Paramount 10032
				Don Costa (orch., above 4)			
10/26/59	20	14		7 **Come Into My Heart** /			
11/9/59	43	10		8 **Wont'cha Come Home**....	$20		ABC-Paramount 10062
2/1/60	14	13		9 **Lady Luck** /			
3/7/60	82	3		10 **Never Let Me Go**....	$20		ABC-Paramount 10075
4/25/60	40	7		11 **No If's - No And's** /			
5/2/60	43	6		12 **For Love**....	$20		ABC-Paramount 10102
6/27/60	19	11		13 **Question**....*If I Look A Little Blue*	$20		ABC-Paramount 10123
9/12/60	79	4		14 **Just Call Me (And I'll Understand)**....*Who Coulda' Told You (They Lied)* (#103)	$15		ABC-Paramount 10139
12/5/60	90	2		15 **(You Better) Know What You're Doin'**....*That's Why Tears Come And Go*	$15		ABC-Paramount 10162
				Sid Feller (orch.: #7-15)			
10/5/63	21	9		16 **Misty**....*Cry On*	$15		Double-L 722
				introduced by the Erroll Garner Trio in 1954 on Mercury 70442 ($15)			
1/11/64	84	3		17 **Billie Baby**....*Try A Little Bit Of Tenderness*	$15	■	Double-L 729
				re-make of the standard "Won't You Come Home Bill Bailey"; all of above (except #10 & 16) written or co-written by Price			

DEBUT	PEAK	WKS	Gold	A-side (Chart Hit)..........B-side	$	Sym	Label & Number

PRICE, Ray
C&W/BUB/LP **'70**

Born on 1/12/26 in Perryville, Texas; raised in Dallas, Texas. Country singer. Known as "The Cherokee Cowboy." Charted 109 Country hits, 1952-89.

1)For The Good Times 2)I Won't Mention It Again 3)Danny Boy

DEBUT	PEAK	WKS	Gold	A-side (Chart Hit)..........B-side	$	Sym	Label & Number
12/29/56	27[HR]	1		1 **Crazy Arms**..........CW[20] *You Done Me Wrong* (C&W #7)	$20		Columbia 21510
10/14/57	63	5		2 **My Shoes Keep Walking Back To You**..........CW[4] T:63 *Don't Do This To Me*	$15		Columbia 40951
8/25/58	71	3		3 **City Lights /** CW[13] H:71			
9/8/58	92	1		4 **Invitation To The Blues**..........H:92	$15		Columbia 41191
8/31/63	100	1		5 **Make The World Go Away**..........*Night Life* (C&W #28)	$12	□	Columbia 42827
3/25/67	60	8		6 **Danny Boy**..........*I Let My Mind Wander* based on the traditional Irish song "Londonderry Air" written in 1855	$8	■	Columbia 44042
8/29/70+	11	24		7 **For The Good Times** CW[1] *Grazin' In Greener Pastures* (C&W flip)	$6		Columbia 45178
3/20/71	42	14		8 **I Won't Mention It Again**..........CW[3] *Kiss The World Goodbye*	$6		Columbia 45329
8/14/71	70	6		9 **I'd Rather Be Sorry**..........*When I Loved Her* #7 & 9: written by **Kris Kristofferson**	$6		Columbia 45425
1/6/73	93	4		10 **She's Got To Be A Saint**..........CW[3] *Oh, Lonesome Me*	$6		Columbia 45724
8/25/73	82	9		11 **You're The Best Thing That Ever Happened To Me**..........CW[1] *What Kind Of Love Is This*	$6		Columbia 45889

PRIDE, Charley
C&W/BUB/LP **'72**

Born on 3/18/38 in Sledge, Mississippi. The most successful black country performer (29 #1 singles). Discovered by **Red Sovine** in 1963.

1)Kiss An Angel Good Mornin' 2)Mississippi Cotton Picking Delta Town 3)Is Anybody Goin' To San Antone

DEBUT	PEAK	WKS	Gold	A-side (Chart Hit)..........B-side	$	Sym	Label & Number
8/23/69	91	5		1 **All I Have To Offer You (Is Me)**..........CW[1] *A Brand New Bed Of Roses*	$7		RCA Victor 0167
11/8/69	74	6		2 **(I'm So) Afraid Of Losing You Again**..........CW[3] *A Good Chance Of Tear-Fall Tonight*	$7		RCA Victor 0265
3/14/70	70	7		3 **Is Anybody Goin' To San Antone**..........CW[2] *Things Are Looking Up*	$7		RCA Victor 9806
7/4/70	87	3		4 **Wonder Could I Live There Anymore**..........CW[2] *Piroque Joe*	$7		RCA Victor 9855
10/24/70	71	6		5 **I Can't Believe That You've Stopped Loving Me**..........CW[2] *Time (You're Not A Friend of Mine)*	$7		RCA Victor 9902
12/19/70	11[X]	2		6 **Christmas In My Home Town**..........*Santa And The Kids* [X]	$8		RCA Victor 9933
3/13/71	79	3		7 **I'd Rather Love You**..........CW[3] *(In My World) You Don't Belong*	$7		RCA Victor 9952
8/21/71	94	2		8 **I'm Just Me**..........CW[4] *A Place For The Lonesome*	$7		RCA Victor 9996
11/20/71+	21	16	●	9 **Kiss An Angel Good Mornin'** CW[5] *No One Could Ever Take Me From You*	$7		RCA Victor 0550
4/1/72	92	3		10 **All His Children**..........*You'll Still Be The One* (Pride) **CHARLEY PRIDE with HENRY MANCINI** from the movie *Sometimes A Great Notion* starring Paul Newman and Henry Fonda	$7		RCA Victor 0624
11/16/74	70	4		11 **Mississippi Cotton Picking Delta Town**..........*Mary Go Round* The Jordanaires (backing vocals); all of above produced by Jack Clement	$6		RCA Victor 10030

PRIEST, Maxi
R&B/BUB/LP **'90**

Born Max Elliott on 6/10/60 in London, England (of Jamaican parents). Dancehall reggae singer.

DEBUT	PEAK	WKS	Gold	A-side (Chart Hit)..........B-side	$	Sym	Label & Number
10/29/88+	25	18		1 **Wild World**..........S:24 / A:24 *On And On*	$4	■	Virgin 99269
6/30/90	❶[1]	30	●	2 **Close To You** S:❶[1] / A:3 *I Know Love* "45": Virgin 56977; B-side: "One More Chance" (R&B #77)	$3	▌	Charisma 98951
12/8/90+	62	11		3 **Just A Little Bit Longer**..........*Not On My Own*	$4	▌	Charisma 98883
9/21/91	6	20		4 **Set The Night To Music**..........A:23 / S:25 *Natural Thing* (Flack) **ROBERTA FLACK with Maxi Priest**	$3	▌[V]	Atlantic 87607
10/26/91	37	15		5 **Housecall (Your Body Can't Lie To Me)**..........S:32 / A:39 *(Ragga mix)* **SHABBA RANKS (Featuring Maxi Priest)**	$4	▌	Epic 73928
10/31/92	63	8		6 **Groovin' In The Midnight**..........A:53 *Dreaming*	$4	▌[V]	Charisma 12617
6/29/96	20	20		7 **That Girl**..........S:16 / A:41 *(2 versions) / Heartbreak Lover* (w/Beres Hammond & Buju Banton) **MAXI PRIEST FEATURING SHAGGY** samples "Green Onions" by **Booker T. & The MG's**; "45": Virgin 19173	$3	▌[V]	Virgin 38550

PRIMA, Louis, And Keely Smith
MEM/POP/R&B/BUB/LP **'35**

Prima was born on 12/7/11 in New Orleans, Louisiana. Died on 8/24/78 (age 66). Jazz trumpeter/singer/composer/bandleader. Smith was born on 3/9/32 in Norfolk, Virginia. Female singer. They were married from 1952-61.

DEBUT	PEAK	WKS	Gold	A-side (Chart Hit)..........B-side	$	Sym	Label & Number
11/3/58	18	13		1 **That Old Black Magic**..........*You Are My Love* (Smith) performed by Prima & Smith in the movie *Senior Prom*; #1 hit for Glenn Miller in 1943	$12	□	Capitol 4063
2/23/59	95	2		2 **I've Got You Under My Skin**..........*Don't Take Your Love From Me* (Smith) written by Cole Porter; #3 hit for Ray Noble in 1936; Sam Butera and The Witnesses (backing combo, above 2)	$12		Capitol 4140
7/6/59	69	6		3 **Bei Mir Bist Du Schön**..........*I Don't Know Why* #1 hit for The Andrews Sisters in 1938	$10		Dot 15956
11/14/60+	15	14		4 **Wonderland By Night** *[LOUIS PRIMA]*..........*Ol' Man Mose* [I]	$10		Dot 16151

PRIMITIVE RADIO GODS
LP **'96**

Group is actually solo alternative-rock artist Chris O'Connor. Touring group includes Luke McAuliffe (guitar), Jeff Sparks (bass) and Tim Lauteiro (drums).

DEBUT	PEAK	WKS	Gold	A-side (Chart Hit)..........B-side	$	Sym	Label & Number
6/8/96	10[A]	23		**Standing Outside A Broken Phone Booth With Money In My Hand**....MR[6] samples "How Blue Can You Get" by **B.B. King**; from the album *Rocket* on Ergo/Columbia 67600			album cut

PRIMUS
ROK/LP **'95**

Thrash-jazz-rock trio from San Francisco, California: Les Claypool (vocals, bass), Larry LaLonde (guitar) and Tim Alexander (drums).

DEBUT	PEAK	WKS	Gold	A-side (Chart Hit)..........B-side	$	Sym	Label & Number
7/15/95	62[A]	4		**Wynona's Big Brown Beaver**.......... from the album *Tales From The Punchbowl* on Interscope 92553			album cut

DEBUT	PEAK	WKS	Gold		A-side (Chart Hit)	B-side	$	Sym	Label & Number

PRINCE ★20★

R&B/BUB/LP **'84**

Born Prince Roger Nelson on 6/7/58 in Minneapolis, Minnesota. Vocalist/multi-instrumentalist/composer/producer. Named for the Prince Roger Trio, led by his father. Self-taught musician; own band, Grand Central, in junior high school. Self-produced first album in 1978. Starred in the movies *Purple Rain, Under The Cherry Moon, Sign 'O' The Times* and *Graffiti Bridge*. Founded own label, Paisley Park. The Revolution featured Lisa Coleman (keyboards), Wendy Melvoin (guitar), Bobby Z (percussion), Matt "Dr." Fink (keyboards), Eric Leeds (saxophone) and Andre Cymone (bass; replaced by Brownmark in 1981). Coleman and Melvoin formed duo **Wendy & Lisa** in 1987. **Sheila E.** (drums) joined Prince's band in 1986. Prince formed new band, New Power Generation (named for the oldest Prince fan club in Britain) in 1990, featuring Levi Seacer, Jr. (guitar), Sonny T. (bass), Tommy Barbarella (keyboards), dancer/percussionists Kirk Johnson and Damon Dickson, Michael Bland (drums), rapper Tony M. and Rosie Gaines (keyboards, vocals; replaced by Mayte [pronounced: my-tie] Garcia by 1992). Prince announced that he would no longer record on 4/27/93. Changed his name on 6/7/93 to a combination male/female symbol. His music was featured in The Joffrey's 1993 rock ballet titled *Billboards*. By 1994 referred to as "The Artist Formerly Known As Prince" or "The Artist." Married to Mayte from 1996-99. Announced in May 2000 that he would once again be called "Prince." Also see **Apollonia 6** and **Vanity**.

1)When Doves Cry 2)Let's Go Crazy 3)Cream 4)Kiss 5)Batdance

DEBUT	PEAK	WKS	Gold	#	A-side (Chart Hit)	B-side	$	Sym	Label & Number
11/4/78	92	4		1	**Soft And Wet**	*So Blue*	$30		Warner 8619
11/24/79+	11	16	●	2	**I Wanna Be Your Lover** RB[2]	*My Love Is Forever*	$15		Warner 49050
10/24/81	70	11		3	**Controversy**	*When You Were Mine*	$15		Warner 49808
10/30/82+	12	27		4	****1999****	*How Come U Don't Call Me Anymore?*	$7	■	Warner 29896
					originally charted for 12 weeks (#44); re-entered on 6/4/83; also see #50 & 52 below				
2/26/83	6	22		5	**Little Red Corvette**	*All The Critics Love U In New York*	$6		Warner 29746
9/3/83	8	18		6	**Delirious**	*Horny Toad*	$6	■	Warner 29503
					picture sleeve is a foldout poster				
12/17/83+	52	10		7	**Let's Pretend We're Married** /				
					above 4 from the album **1999**				
12/17/83		10		8	**Irresistible Bitch**		$6	■	Warner 29548
6/2/84	❶[5]	21	▲	9	**When Doves Cry** RB[8]	*17 Days (the rain will come down, then U will have 2 choose. If U believe, look 2 the dawn and U shall never lose.)*	$5	■	Warner 29286
					PRINCE and The Revolution:				
8/4/84	❶[2]	19	●	10	**Let's Go Crazy** RB[1] S:4 / A:5	*Erotic City*	$5	■	Warner 29216
10/6/84	2[2]	16	●	11	**Purple Rain** S:2 / A:2	*God*	$5	■	Warner 29174
12/15/84+	8	15		12	**I Would Die 4 U** / A:8 / S:14				
					above 2 recorded at the First Avenue nightclub in Minneapolis				
12/22/84	5[X]	1		13	**Another Lonely Christmas** [X]		$5	■	Warner 29121
2/9/85	25	12		14	**Take Me With U** A:20	*Baby I'm A Star*	$5	■	Warner 29079
					Apollonia (female vocal); #9-12 & 14: from the Prince movie and album *Purple Rain*				
5/18/85	2[1]	17		15	**Raspberry Beret** A:❶[1] / S:2	*She's Always In My Hair*	$4	■	Paisley Park 28972
7/27/85	7	14		16	**Pop Life** A:7 / S:11	*Hello*	$4	■	Paisley Park 28998
10/19/85	46	7		17	**America**	*Girl*	$4	■	Paisley Park 28999
2/22/86	❶[2]	18	●	18	**Kiss** RB[4] A:❶[2] / S:❶[1]	*Love Or $*	$4	■	Paisley Park 28751
5/24/86	23	11		19	**Mountains** S:21 / A:23	*Alexa De Paris*	$4	■	Paisley Park 28711
7/19/86	63	10		20	**Anotherloverholenyohead**	*Girls & Boys*	$4	■	Paisley Park 28620
					above 3 from the Prince movie *Under The Cherry Moon* (and from the album *Parade*)				
					PRINCE:				
3/7/87	3	14		21	**Sign 'O' The Times** RB[3] S:3 / A:5	*La, La, La, He, He, Hee*	$3	■	Paisley Park 28399
5/30/87	67	6		22	**If I Was Your Girlfriend**	*Shockadelica*	$3	■	Paisley Park 28334
8/1/87	2[1]	25		23	**U Got The Look** S:2 / A:3	*Housequake*	$3	■	Paisley Park 28289
					Sheena Easton (backing vocal)				
11/14/87+	10	17		24	**I Could Never Take The Place Of Your Man** / S:9 / A:10				
2/6/88	63	9		25	**Hot Thing**		$3	■	Paisley Park 28288
					above 5 from the album *Sign 'O' The Times*				
4/30/88	8	13		26	**Alphabet St.** S:7 / A:11	*Alphabet St. (cont.)*	$3	■	Paisley Park 27900
					picture sleeve is a clear heavy plastic sleeve with an oval sticker				
6/17/89	❶[1]	18	▲	27	**Batdance** RB[1] S:❶[3] / A:2	*200 Balloons*	$3	■	Warner 22924
8/26/89	18	10	●	28	**Partyman** S:14 / A:19	*Feel U Up*	$3	■	Warner 22814
10/21/89	36	14		29	**The Arms Of Orion** A:35 / S:37	*I Love U In Me* (Prince)	$3	■	Warner 22757
					PRINCE with Sheena Easton				
					above 3 from the Prince soundtrack album and movie *Batman* starring Michael Keaton				
8/4/90	6	13	●	30	**Thieves In The Temple** RB[1] A:5 / S:6	*Part II*	$3	■V	Paisley Park 19751
11/3/90	64	5		31	**New Power Generation**	*(Pt. II)*	$3	■V	Paisley Park 19525
					Tevin Campbell and **Mavis Staples** (backing vocals); above 2 from the movie *Graffiti Bridge* starring Prince				
					PRINCE AND THE NEW POWER GENERATION:				
8/17/91	21	14	●	32	**Gett Off** S:8 / A:56	*Horny Pony*	$3	■V	Paisley Park 19225
9/28/91	❶[2]	20	●	33	**Cream** A:5 / S:10	*Horny Pony*	$3	■V	Paisley Park 19175
12/7/91+	3	21		34	**Diamonds And Pearls** RB[1] A:2 / S:10	*(7 album snippets)*	$3	■V	Paisley Park 19083
12/14/91+	77	7		35	**Insatiable** S:52	*I Love U In Me*	$3	■V	Paisley Park 19090
3/28/92	23	13		36	**Money Don't Matter 2 Night** A:24 / S:69	*Call The Law*	$3	■V	Paisley Park 19020
					above 5 from the album *Diamonds And Pearls*				
7/25/92	66	4		37	**Sexy M.F.** S:34	*Strollin'*	$3	■V	Paisley Park 18817
					edited "clean" version is on the B-side of #38 below				
10/10/92	36	11		38	**My Name Is Prince** S:22 / A:37	*Sexy Mutha*	$3	■V	Paisley Park 18707
11/28/92+	7	23	●	39	**7** A:12 / S:13	*(acoustic version)*	$3	■V	Paisley Park 18824
					samples "Tramp" by **Lowell Fulsom**				
4/3/93	44	11		40	**The Morning Papers** A:37	*Live 4 Love*	$3	■V	Paisley Park 18583
					above 4 from the album ⚥				
9/18/93	50	9		41	**Pink Cashmere** *[PRINCE]* A:45 / S:46	*Soft And Wet (remix)*	$3	■V	Paisley Park 18371

DEBUT	PEAK	WKS	Gold	A-side (Chart Hit)	B-side	$	Sym	Label & Number
				PRINCE — Cont'd				
				[Prince symbol]:				
3/5/94	3	26	●	42 **The Most Beautiful Girl In The World**	A:3 / S:5 *Beautiful*	$3	▮	NPG/Bellmark 72514
8/6/94	72^{A}	1		43 **Love Sign**				album cut
				NONA GAYE & [Prince symbol]				
				from the various artists album *1-800-New-Funk* on NPG 71006				
8/20/94	31	14		44 **Letitgo** *[PRINCE]*	S:32 / A:36 *Solo*	$3	▮V	Warner 18074
4/1/95	84	2		45 **Purple Medley** *[PRINCE]*	S:40 *(Kirk J's B Sides remix)*	$4	▮V	Warner 17903
				Batdance/Kiss/Erotic City/Darling Nikki/1999/Baby I'm A Star/Diamonds And Pearls/Purple Rain/Let's Go Crazy				
9/23/95	12	10		46 **I Hate U**	S:6 / A:46 *(remix)*	$3	▮V	NPG/Warner 17811
12/23/95	88	2		47 **Gold**	*Rock 'N' Roll Is Alive! (and it lives in Minneapolis)*	$4	▮V	NPG/Warner 17715
11/30/96	31^{A}	8		48 **Betcha By Golly Wow!**				album cut
2/8/97	58^{A}	5		49 **The Holy River**				album cut
				above 2 from the album *Emancipation* on NPG 54982				
1/16/99	40	1		50 **1999** *[PRINCE]*	A:33 / S:61 *Little Red Corvette* [R]	$6	★V	Warner 21881
				same version as #4 above; reissue is on Warner's cdBACKtrax label; "45": Warner "Back To Back Hits" 0468				
10/23/99	63	13		51 **The Greatest Romance Ever Sold**	S:19 *(remix w/***Eve***)*	$5	★	NPG/Arista 13749
1/15/00	56^{S}	3		52 **1999** *[PRINCE]*	[R]	$6	★V	Warner 21881
				same version as #4 & 50 above				
5/5/01	59^{S}	5		53 **U Make My Sun Shine**	*When Will We B Paid?*	$5	★	NPG 05052
				PRINCE With ANGIE STONE				
				CD single released simultaneously on Wingspan 00102; all of above (except #48) written by Prince				
				PRINCE BE — see PM DAWN				
				PRINCE BUSTER '67				
				Born Cecil Bustamente Campbell on 5/24/38 in Kingston, Jamaica. Owned 10 record stores in the Caribbean. Influential artist/producer of Jamaican ska music.				
2/4/67	81	4		**Ten Commandments**	*Don't Make Me To Cry* [S]	$15		Philips 40427
				PRINCE EP '03				
				Male rapper.				
12/28/02+	22^{S}	8		**Can I**	*(4 versions)*	$6	★	AVS/Lightyear 54580
				PRINCE MARKIE DEE — see FAT BOYS				
				PRINCIPAL, Victoria — see GIBB, Andy				
				PRISM ROK/LP '82				
				Rock group from Canada: Ron Tabak (vocals), Lindsay Mitchell and Tom Lavin (guitars), John Hall (keyboards), Ab Bryant (bass; **Chilliwack**, **Headpins**), Rodney Higgs (drums). Bryant and Higgs left in 1978, replaced by Allen Harlow and Rocket Norton. Tabak left by 1982, replaced by Henry Small. Tabak died in a car crash in 1984.				
10/22/77	82	4		1 **Spaceship Superstar**	*Julie*	$5		Ariola America 7672
1/7/78	59	7		2 **Take Me To The Kaptin**	*I Ain't Lookin' Anymore*	$5		Ariola America 7678
7/22/78	53	8		3 **Flyin'**	*Crime Wave*	$5		Ariola America 7714
1/30/82	39	10		4 **Don't Let Him Know**	AR^{1} *Wings Of Your Love*	$4	■	Capitol 5082
				co-written by **Bryan Adams**				
4/17/82	64	7		5 **Turn On Your Radar**	*When Love Goes Wrong (You're Not Alone)*	$4		Capitol 5106
				PROBY, P.J. BUB '67				
				Born James Marcus Smith on 11/6/38 in Houston, Texas. Rock and roll singer/songwriter.				
9/5/64	70	4		1 **Hold Me**	*The Tip Of My Fingers*	$15		London 9688
				#3 hit for the Hotel Commodore Orchestra in 1933; originally released on London 9648 in 1964				
2/13/65	91	2		2 **Somewhere**	*Just Like Him*	$12		Liberty 55757
				from the Broadway musical *West Side Story* starring Carol Lawrence				
1/28/67	23	10		3 **Niki Hoeky**	*Good Things Are Coming My Way*	$12		Liberty 55936
				a different song "Neki-Hokey" was recorded by **The Cleftones** in 1956 on Gee 1016 ($60)				
				PROCLAIMERS, The LP '93				
				Pop-rock duo from Edinburgh, Scotland: identical twin brothers Craig and Charlie Reid (born on 3/5/62).				
6/12/93	3	20	●	**I'm Gonna Be (500 Miles)**	S:4 / A:11 *Better Days*	$3	▮V	Chrysalis 24846
				featured in the movie *Benny & Joon* starring Johnny Depp; first released in 1988 on Chrysalis 43283 with a picture sleeve; produced by **Pete Wingfield**; #21 Modern Rock hit in 1989; "45": Chrysalis 17493 (green vinyl)				
				PROCOL HARUM ROK/BUB/LP '67				
				Pop-rock group formed in England: Gary Brooker (vocals, piano), Keith Reid (lyrics), Ray Royer (guitar), Matthew Fisher (organ), Dave Knights (bass) and Bobby Harrison (drums). Numerous personnel changes. **Robin Trower** was lead guitarist from 1968-71.				
6/24/67	5	12		1 **A Whiter Shade Of Pale**	*Lime Street Blues*	$15		Deram 7507
				melody based on the Bach cantata *Sleepers Awake*				
10/28/67	34	5		2 **Homburg**	*Good Captain Clack*	$10		A&M 885
5/27/72	16	13		3 **Conquistador**	*A Salty Dog* [L]	$8	■	A&M 1347
				featuring the Edmonton Symphony Orchestra; studio version on their 1967 album *Procol Harum*				
				PRODIGY ROK/LP '97				
				Techno-rave-dance group from England: Maxim Reality and Keith Flint (vocals), Liam Howlett (instruments) and Leeroy Thornhill (dancer).				
1/18/97	30	20	●	1 **Firestarter**	S:20 *(instrumental)*	$3	▮	Maverick 17387
				samples "SOS" by **The Breeders** and "Close (To The Edit)" by **The Art Of Noise**				
12/20/97+	89	7		2 **Smack My Bitch Up**	*No Man Army / Mindfields / (remix)*	$6	★	Maverick 43946
				samples "Give The Drummer Some" by Ultramagnetic M.C.'s				
8/3/02	21^{S}	11		3 **Baby's Got A Temper**	*(3 versions)*	$8	★++	Maverick 42456
				PRODUCERS, The ROK/BUB/LP '81				
				Pop-rock group formed in Atlanta, Georgia: Van Temple (vocals, guitar), Wayne Famous (keyboards), Kyle Henderson (bass) and Bryan Holmes (drums).				
6/13/81	61	6		**What She Does To Me (The Diana Song)**	*Here's To You*	$4		Portrait 02092

DEBUT	PEAK	WKS	Gold	A-side (Chart Hit)..........B-side	$	Sym	Label & Number
				PRODUCT G&B, The '01 Rap duo from Hempstead, Long Island, New York: David McRae and Marvin Moore-Hough. G&B: Ghetto & Blues.			
8/22/98	72	14		1 **Here We Go**..........*(instrumental)* **FUNKMASTER FLEX Presents Kadejia featuring Product** co-written and produced by **Wyclef Jean**	$6	T	Loud/RCA 65542
8/22/98	74	5		2 **Cheated (To All The Girls)**..........*What's Clef* (#61) / *Chickenhead* (#69 - both Jean) **WYCLEF JEAN featuring Queen Pen & The Product** samples "To All The Girls I've Loved Before" by **Julio Iglesias** & **Willie Nelson**	$6	▮*	Ruffhouse 78993
2/12/00	❶[10]	26	▲	3 **Maria Maria** RB[3] S:❶[5] / A:❶[1] *(remix) / Migra* **SANTANA Featuring The Product G&B**	$4	★[V]	Arista 13773
5/12/01	59[S]	3		4 **Maria Maria**..........*(4 remixes) / Migra* [R] **SANTANA Featuring The Product G&B** reissue of #2 above on Arista's "Maximum Hits" series	$8	★*	Arista 13774
7/14/01	18[S]	17		5 **Cluck Cluck**..........*(Henhouse Mix) / Freak Freak* (w/**Lil' Kim**) **THE PRODUCT G&B Feat. Wyclef** from the movie *Dr. Dolittle 2* starring **Eddie Murphy**; "45": J Records 21049; B-side (instrumental)	$4	★[V]	YClef/J Records 21068
				PROFESSOR MORRISON'S LOLLIPOP '68 Bubblegum-rock group from Lincoln, Nebraska: Jeff Travis (vocals, guitar), Frank Elia (guitar), Kelly Kotera (keyboards), Craig Perkins (bass) and Bruce Watson (drums). Previously recorded as The Coachmen ("Bubbled Under" in 1966). Perkins died on 5/5/2000 (age 52).			
10/5/68	88	3		**You Got The Love**..........*Gypsy Lady*	$10		White Whale 275
				PROFYLE R&B/LP '00 Male R&B vocal group from Shreveport, Louisiana: Baby Boy, Face, Hershey and L Jai.			
8/21/99	71[S]	1		1 **I Ain't The One**..........*(edit w/rap) / (5 album snippets)*	$4	★	Motown 156315
2/26/00	55[S]	8		2 **Whispers In The Dark**..........*(2 versions) / (5 album snippets)*	$4	★	Motown 156409
9/16/00	14	20		3 **Liar**..........RB[1] S:4 / A:37 *(instrumental) / (6 album snippets)*	$4	★	Motown 158262
				PROJECT PAT R&B/LP '01 Born Patrick Houston in 1974 in Memphis, Tennessee. Male rapper. Brother of Three 6 Mafia member Juicy J.			
3/3/01	87	12		**Chickenhead**..........*(2 versions)* La Chat (of Three 6 Mafia, female vocal)	$7	T	Loud 1973
				PROOF '02 Born DeShaun Holton in Detroit, Michigan. Hardcore male rapper. Member of **Eminem**'s **D12** posse.			
10/26/02	61[S]	1		**The Remedy**..........*Can U Stop? / Kentucky Niggaz / No More* (w/Naya)	$8	★*	Intelligent 606
				PROTHEROE, Brian '75 Born in 1944 in Salisbury, Wiltshire, England. Pop-rock singer/composer/actor/guitarist.			
3/29/75	60	7		**Pinball**..........*Money Love*	$6		Chrysalis 2104
				PRUETT, Jeanne C&W/LP '73 Born Norma Jean Bowman on 1/30/37 in Pell City, Alabama. Country singer/songwriter.			
5/12/73	28	15		**Satin Sheets**..........CW[3] *Sweet Sweetheart*	$6		MCA 40015
				PRYMARY COLORZ '02 Interracial Contemporary Christian vocal group: Marcus Dilley, Jonathan Thomas, Raj Nichols and Josh Royals.			
9/14/02	4[S]	8		**If You Only Knew**..........*(2 versions* w/Rah Digga)	$5	★	Big 3 838277
				PRYSOCK, Arthur R&B/BUB/AC/C&W/LP '65 Born on 1/2/29 in Spartanburg, South Carolina. Died on 6/14/97 (age 68). R&B singer.			
7/17/65	56	8		1 **It's Too Late, Baby Too Late**..........*Who Can I Turn To*	$10		Old Town 1183
1/6/68	74	6		2 **A Working Man's Prayer**..........*No More In Life* #59 Country hit for **Tex Ritter** in 1967	$8		Verve 10574
12/25/76+	64	9		3 **When Love Is New**..........*All I Need Is You Tonight* **John Davis & Monster Orchestra** (backing band)	$5		Old Town 1000
				PSEUDO ECHO LP '87 Pop-rock-dance group formed in Melbourne, Australia: Brian Canham (vocals, guitar), James Leigh (keyboards), Pierre Gigliotti (bass) and Vince Leigh (drums).			
3/28/87	57	9		1 **Living In A Dream**..........*Don't Go*	$3		RCA 5125
5/16/87	6	15		2 **Funky Town**..........S:6 / A:8 *Lies Are Nothing*	$3		RCA 5217
				PSYCHEDELIC FURS ROK/LP '87 Techno-rock group formed in England: brothers Richard (vocals) and Tim (bass) Butler, John Ashton (guitar), and Vince Ely (drums). Ely left in 1983; returned briefly in 1989. The Butlers formed **Love Spit Love** in 1994.			
3/5/83	44	10		1 **Love My Way**..........*I Don't Want To Be Your Shadow* produced by **Todd Rundgren**	$4		Columbia 03340
5/12/84	59	9		2 **The Ghost In You**..........*Heartbeat (remix)*	$4	■	Columbia 04416
4/12/86	41	11		3 **Pretty In Pink**..........S:45 *(dub version)* title song from the movie starring Molly Ringwald; new version of a cut from the group's 1981 album *Talk Talk Talk*	$3	■	A&M 2826
3/14/87	26	14		4 **Heartbreak Beat**..........S:23 / A:28 *New Dream*	$3	■	Columbia 06420
				PUBLIC ANNOUNCEMENT R&B/BUB/LP '98 R&B vocal group from Chicago, Illinois: Earl Robinson, Felony Davis, Euclid Gray and Glen Wright. Former backing group for **R. Kelly**.			
2/21/98	5	22	▲	1 **Body Bumpin' Yippie-Yi-Yo**..........S:3 / A:45 *(acappella version)*	$3	▮	A&M 582444
12/23/00+	39	8		2 **Mamacita**..........S:4 *Step On part II*	$4	★	RCA 60342
9/29/01	95	3		3 **John Doe**..........*(4 versions) / Mamacity* (w/**Big Daddy Kane**) **PUBLIC ANNOUNCEMENT Featuring MZ Lelee**	$6	T	RCA 60485

DEBUT	PEAK	WKS	Gold	A-side (Chart Hit)...B-side	$	Sym	Label & Number

PUBLIC ENEMY R&B/BUB/LP '94

Highly influential rap group from Long Island, New York: Carlton Ridenhour ("Chuck D"), William Drayton ("Flavor Flav"), Norman Rogers ("Terminator X") and William Griffin ("Professor Griff"). Griffin left in 1989.

DEBUT	PEAK	WKS	Gold	A-side (Chart Hit)...B-side	$	Sym	Label & Number
6/9/90	34^S	3		1 **911 Is A Joke**...*Revolutionary Generation* the first *Hot 100 Sales*-only chart hit	$6	▮	Def Jam 73309
10/19/91	50	15	●	2 **Can't Truss It**...S:16 *(radio mix)*	$4	▮	Def Jam 73870
7/16/94	33	14		3 **Give It Up**...S:14 / A:70 *Bedlam* samples "Opus De Soul" by **Albert King**, Steve Cropper & Pop **Staples**	$4	▮	Def Jam 853316

PUCKETT, Gary, And The Union Gap ★487★ AC/LP '68

Born on 10/17/42 in Hibbing, Minnesota; raised in Yakima, Washington. Soft-rock singer/guitarist. Formed The Union Gap in San Diego, California: Gary Withem (keyboards; born on 8/22/46), Dwight Bement (sax; born on 12/28/45), **Kerry Chater** (bass; born on 8/7/44) (see #10 below) and Paul Wheatbread (drums; born on 2/8/46). Wheatbread was a member of **The Hardtimes**. Bement and Wheatbread later joined **Flash Cadillac & The Continental Kids**.

1)Young Girl 2)Lady Willpower 3)Woman, Woman

DEBUT	PEAK	WKS	Gold	A-side (Chart Hit)...B-side	$	Sym	Label & Number
				THE UNION GAP Featuring Gary Puckett:			
11/18/67+	4	17	●	1 **Woman, Woman**...*Don't Make Promises*	$7	■	Columbia 44297
3/2/68	2^3	15	●	2 **Young Girl** *I'm Losing You*	$7	■	Columbia 44450
				GARY PUCKETT AND THE UNION GAP:			
6/8/68	2^2	13	●	3 **Lady Willpower**...*Daylight Stranger*	$7	■	Columbia 44547
9/21/68	7	11	●	4 **Over You**...*If The Day Would Come*	$6	■	Columbia 44644
3/15/69	15	9		5 **Don't Give In To Him**...*Could I* all of above produced by and #2-4 written by **Jerry Fuller**	$6		Columbia 44788
8/23/69	9	11		6 **This Girl Is A Woman Now**...*His Other Woman*	$6		Columbia 44967
3/7/70	41	7		7 **Let's Give Adam And Eve Another Chance**...*The Beggar*	$6	■	Columbia 45097
				GARY PUCKETT:			
10/31/70	61	4		8 **I Just Don't Know What To Do With Myself**...*All That Matters*	$5		Columbia 45249
2/6/71	71	5		9 **Keep The Customer Satisfied**...*No One Really Knows* first recorded by **Simon & Garfunkel** on their 1970 album *Bridge Over Troubled Water*	$5		Columbia 45303
3/26/77	97	2		10 **Part Time Love**...*No Love On The Black Keys* **KERRY CHATER**	$5		Warner 8310

PUDDLE OF MUDD ROK/LP '02

Hard-rock group formed in Los Angeles, California: Wes Scantlin (vocals, guitar), Paul Phillips (guitar), Doug Ardito (bass) and Greg Upchurch (drums). Group records on Fred Durst's (**Limp Bizkit**) Flawless record label.

DEBUT	PEAK	WKS	Gold	A-side (Chart Hit)...B-side	$	Sym	Label & Number
10/13/01	68	20		1 **Control**...A:63			album cut
12/22/01+	5	38		2 **Blurry**...AR^{10} / MR^9 A:5			album cut
5/25/02	61	20		3 **Drift & Die**...AR^6 A:60			album cut
10/12/02	13	23		4 **She Hates Me**...AR^1 A:13 all of above from the album *Come Clean* on Flawless 493074			album cut

PUFF DADDY ★66★ R&B/BUB/LP '97

Born Sean Combs on 11/4/69 in Harlem, New York. Rapper/songwriter/producer/entrepreneur. Founder of Bad Boy Entertainment in 1993. Changed performing name to **P. Diddy** in 2001. Played "Lawrence Musgrove" in the movie *Monster's Ball*. The most successful hip-hop artist of all time.

1)I'll Be Missing You 2)Can't Nobody Hold Me Down 3)Bump, Bump, Bump 4)I Need A Girl (Part One) 5)Satisfy You

DEBUT	PEAK	WKS	Gold	A-side (Chart Hit)...B-side	$	Sym	Label & Number
11/9/96+	18	20	●	1 **No Time**...S:7 *(instrumental)* **LIL' KIM Featuring Puff Daddy** samples "Take Me Just As I Am" by **Lyn Collins**	$4	▮	Undeas/Big Beat 98044
1/25/97	$❶^6$	28	$▲^2$	2 **Can't Nobody Hold Me Down**...RB^6 S:$❶^7$ / A:25 *(instrumental) / (club mix)* **PUFF DADDY Featuring Mase** samples "The Message" by **Grandmaster Flash** and "Break My Stride" by **Matthew Wilder**	$3	▮	Bad Boy 79083
6/14/97	$❶^{11}$	33	$▲^3$	3 **I'll Be Missing You** RB^8 S:$❶^9$ / A:4 *We'll Always Love Big Poppa* (**The Lox**) / *Cry On* (112) **PUFF DADDY & FAITH EVANS (Featuring 112)** "tribute to **The Notorious B.I.G.**"; melody is from "Every Breath You Take" by **The Police**; also see #18 below	$6	▮*	Bad Boy 79097
7/26/97	19	20	●	4 **Someone**...S:10 *Love Like This* **SWV (Featuring Puff Daddy)** samples "Ten Crack Commandments" and "The World Is Filled" by **The Notorious B.I.G.**	$3	▮	RCA 64926
8/2/97	$❶^2$	30	▲	5 **Mo Money Mo Problems**...S:$❶^4$ / A:12 *(instrumental)* **THE NOTORIOUS B.I.G. Featuring Puff Daddy & Mase** **Kelly Price** (female vocal); samples "I'm Coming Out" by **Diana Ross**; also see #19 below	$3	▮	Bad Boy 79100
12/6/97+	2^2	6	▲	6 **It's All About The Benjamins** / S:2 / A:62 **PUFF DADDY & THE FAMILY Feat. The Notorious B.I.G., Lil' Kim, The Lox, Dave Grohl, Perfect, FuzzBubble & Rob Zombie** samples "I Did It For Love" by **Love Unlimited Orchestra**			
1/17/98	4	15	▲	7 **Been Around The World**...S:$❶^2$ / A:58 **PUFF DADDY & THE FAMILY Featuring The Notorious B.I.G. & Mase** samples "Let's Dance" by **David Bowie** and "All Around The World" by **Lisa Stansfield**	$3	▮	Bad Boy 79130
3/21/98	19	20	●	8 **Victory**...S:11 *(remix) / Bad Boy's Been Around The World Remix* (w/**Mase**) **PUFF DADDY & THE FAMILY Featuring The Notorious B.I.G. & Busta Rhymes** samples "Alone In The Ring" (from the movie *Rocky*) by **Bill Conti**; #2, 3 & 6-8: from the album *No Way Out*	$3	▮	Bad Boy 79155
6/27/98	4	20	▲	9 **Come With Me**...S:2 *(radio version II)* **PUFF DADDY featuring Jimmy Page** melody is from Led Zeppelin's "Kashmir"; from the movie *Godzilla* starring Matthew Broderick	$3	▮	Epic 78954
7/25/98	8	19	●	10 **Lookin' At Me**...S:5 / A:69 *24 Hrs. To Live* (w/**The Lox**, **Black Rob** & **DMX**) **MA$E Featuring Puff Daddy**	$3	▮	Bad Boy 79176
2/6/99	9	19		11 **All Night Long**...S:9 / A:29 *Life Will Pass You By* **FAITH EVANS (feat. Puff Daddy)** samples "I Hear Music In The Streets" by Unlimited Touch	$4	★	Bad Boy 79203

DEBUT	PEAK	WKS	Gold	A-side (Chart Hit)......B-side	$	Sym	Label & Number
				PUFF DADDY — Cont'd			
4/24/99	62	8		12 **Hate Me Now**......A:48 / S:62 *(3 versions) / Blaze A 50 / Natures Shine* **NAS (featuring Puff Daddy)** "45": Columbia 79150; B-side: "Nas Is Like" (Nas - #86)	$6	T^V	Columbia 79070
9/25/99	2^3	20	●	13 **Satisfy You**......RB[2] S:❶[3] / A:13 *(instrumental)* **PUFF DADDY (Featuring R. KELLY)** samples "Why You Treat Me So Bad" by **Club Nouveau**	$4	★	Bad Boy 79283
10/16/99	46^S	6		14 **P.E. 2000**......*(4 versions)* **PUFF DADDY (featuring Hurricane G)**	$4	★	Bad Boy 79276
12/11/99	82	7		15 **Notorious B.I.G.**......A:61 **THE NOTORIOUS B.I.G. featuring Puff Daddy & Lil' Kim** samples "Notorious" by **Duran Duran**; from The Notorious B.I.G. album *Born Again* on Bad Boy 73023			album cut
2/12/00	59	5		16 **Best Friend**......S:8 *(instrumental)* **PUFF DADDY Featuring Mario Winans & Hezekiah Walker & The Love Fellowship Crusade Choir** samples "Sailing" by **Christopher Cross**	$5	★	Bad Boy 79318
5/26/01	80	9		17 **Let's Get It**......S:58 / A:74 *(3 versions)* **THREE THE... G. Dep, P. Diddy & Black Rob** samples "Love & Happiness" by **Al Green**	$6	T	Bad Boy 79383
6/2/01	56^S	8		18 **I'll Be Missing You**......*We'll Always Love Big Poppa* (**The Lox**) / Cry On (112) [R] **PUFF DADDY & FAITH EVANS (Featuring 112)** reissue of #3 above on Bad Boy/Arista's "Maximum Hits" series	$8	★*	Bad Boy 79097
6/9/01	63^S	2		19 **Mo Money Mo Problems**......*(3 versions) / Lovin' You Tonight* (w/**R. Kelly**) [R] **THE NOTORIOUS B.I.G. Featuring Puff Daddy & Mase** reissue of #5 above on Bad Boy/Arista's "Maximum Hits" series	$8	★*	Bad Boy 79109
				P. DIDDY:			
7/28/01	33	12		20 **Bad Boy For Life**......A:30 / S:49 *(3 versions)* **P. DIDDY, BLACK ROB & MARK CURRY**	$6	T	Bad Boy 79400
10/27/01	66	9		21 **Diddy**......S:65 / A:65 *(2 versions) / On Top* (w/**Loon** & Marsha) **P. DIDDY Featuring The Neptunes** samples "Paid In Full" by **Eric B. & Rakim** and "Jimmy" by Boogie Down Productions	$6	T	Bad Boy 79408
11/24/01	28	12		22 **Son Of A Gun (I Betcha Think This Song Is About You)**......A:26 *(3 versions)* **JANET Featuring Missy Elliott and P. Diddy with Carly Simon** samples "You're So Vain" by **Carly Simon**	$6	T	Virgin 46171
3/2/02	11	20		23 **Pass The Courvoisier Part II**......A:10 / S:14 *(5 versions)* **BUSTA RHYMES featuring P. Diddy & Pharrell**	$6	T	J Records 21154
3/16/02	2^4	23		24 **I Need A Girl (Part One)**......A:2 / S:23 *(3 versions)* **P. DIDDY Featuring Usher & Loon**	$6	T	Bad Boy 79436
6/8/02	4	26		25 **I Need A Girl (Part Two)**......A:4 / S:17 *(instrumental) / So Complete* **P. DIDDY AND GINUWINE Featuring Loon, Mario Winans & Tammy Ruggeri**	$6	T	Bad Boy 79441
8/3/02	58	14		26 **I Do (Wanna Get Close To You)**......S:41 / A:59 *(4 versions)* **3LW Featuring P. Diddy & Loon**	$6	T	Epic 79769
8/17/02	20	18		27 **Trade It All (Part 2)**......A:13 **FABOLOUS featuring P. DIDDY & JAGGED EDGE** from the movie *Barbershop* starring **Ice Cube** (soundtrack on Epic 86575)			album cut
11/16/02+	33	20		28 **Do That...**......S:22 / A:33 *(3 versions)* **BABY (AKA DA #1 STUNNA) Featuring P. Diddy**	$6	T	Cash Money 060079
11/30/02+	❶[1]	22		29 **Bump, Bump, Bump**......A:❶[2] / S:24 *(instrumental)* **B2K & P. DIDDY** produced and co-written by **R. Kelly**	$4	★	Epic 79842
				PULLINS, Leroy '66 Born Carl Leroy Pullins on 11/12/40 in Elgin, Illinois. Country singer/songwriter; similar in style to **Roger Miller**.			
6/25/66	57	6		**I'm A Nut**......*Knee Deep* [N]	$8		Kapp 758
				PUPPIES, The '94 Rap duo from Miami, Florida: brother-and-sister Calvin and Tamara Mills. Produced by their father, Calvin Mills II.			
7/2/94	40	17		**Funky Y-2-C**......S:22 *(instrumental)*	$4	▌	Chaos/Columbia 77461
				PURDIE, Pretty R&B '67 Born Bernard Purdie on 6/11/39 in Elkton, Maryland. Highly regarded R&B session drummer.			
9/23/67	87	3		**Funky Donkey**......*Caravan* [I]	$10		Date 1568
				PURE PRAIRIE LEAGUE BUB/C&W/LP '80 Country-rock group formed in Cincinnati, Ohio. Core members: Craig Fuller (vocals, guitar; **American Flyer**), George Ed Powell and Larry Goshorn (guitars), Michael Connor (keyboards), **Mike Reilly** (bass) and Billy Hinds (drums). Fuller left after "Amie," Powell and Reilly took over lead vocals. **Vince Gill** joined as lead singer in 1979. Group disbanded in 1983.			
3/1/75	27	13		1 **Amie**......*Memories*	$5		RCA Victor 10184
6/28/75	97	1		2 **Two Lane Highway**......*Sister's Keeper*	$5		RCA Victor 10302
5/10/80	10	17		3 **Let Me Love You Tonight** AC[3] *Janny Lou*	$4		Casablanca 2266
8/23/80	34	13		4 **I'm Almost Ready**......*You're My True Love*	$4		Casablanca 2294
12/6/80	77	6		5 **I Can't Stop The Feelin'**......*Lifetime Of Nighttime*	$4		Casablanca 2319
4/18/81	28	14		6 **Still Right Here In My Heart**......*Don't Keep Me Hangin'*	$4		Casablanca 2332
7/25/81	68	5		7 **You're Mine Tonight**......*Do You Love Me Truly, Julie*	$4		Casablanca 2337
				PURE SOUL R&B/BUB/LP '95 Female R&B vocal quartet from Washington DC: Shawn Allen, Heather Perkins, Keitha Shepherd and Kirstin Hall.			
8/5/95	65	11		1 **We Must Be In Love**......S:36 *(extended version)*	$5	▌	StepSun/Interscope 98137
3/16/96	79	8		2 **Stairway To Heaven**......S:56 *(love version)* **PURE SOUL featuring The O'Jays** charted as a "tag-along" B-side to "Livin' For The Weekend" on the R&B charts for **The O'Jays** in 1976	$5	▌	StepSun/Interscope 98086
				PURE SUGAR '98 Dance trio from Los Angeles, California: Jennifer Starr (lead vocals), Pete Lorimer and Richard "Humpty" Vission.			
8/8/98	66	12		**Delicious**......S:73 *(2 versions) / No More Words* samples "Boogie Oogie Oogie" by **A Taste Of Honey**	$3	▌	Geffen 19422

DEBUT	PEAK	WKS	Gold	A-side (Chart Hit)......B-side	$	Sym	Label & Number
				PURIFY, James & Bobby R&B/BUB **'66**			
				R&B vocal duo: cousins James Purify (born on 5/12/44 in Pensacola, Florida) and Robert Lee Dickey (born on 9/2/39 in Tallahassee, Florida).			
9/24/66	**6**	14		1 **I'm Your Puppet** *So Many Reasons*	$12		Bell 648
1/28/67	**38**	6		2 **Wish You Didn't Have To Go** *You Can't Keep A Good Man Down*	$10		Bell 660
4/15/67	**25**	9		3 **Shake A Tail Feather** *Goodness Gracious*	$10		Bell 669
7/15/67	**41**	6		4 **I Take What I Want** *Sixteen Tons*	$8		Bell 680
9/9/67	**23**	9		5 **Let Love Come Between Us** *I Don't Want To Have To Wait*	$8		Bell 685
1/13/68	**73**	6		6 **Do Unto Me** *Everybody Needs Somebody*	$8		Bell 700
4/27/68	**51**	6		7 **I Can Remember** *I Was Born To Lose Out*	$8		Bell 721
8/31/68	**94**	3		8 **Help Yourself (To All Of My Lovin')** *Last Piece Of Love*	$8		Bell 735
				PURPLE REIGN **'75**			
				Pop studio group formed in Philadelphia, Pennsylvania. Led by producer Mike Natale.			
11/22/75	**48**	8		**This Old Man** *(instrumental)*	$5		Private Stock 45,052
				traditional nursery song (also known as "The Children's Marching Song")			
				PURSELL, Bill BUB/LP **'63**			
				Born in Oakland, California; raised in Tulare, California. Session pianist.			
2/2/63	**9**	14		**Our Winter Love** *A Wound Time Can't Erase* [I]	$10		Columbia 42619
				PYRAMIDS, The LP **'64**			
				Surf-rock and roll band from Long Beach, California: Skip Mercer, Willie Glover, Steve Leonard, Ron McMullen and Tom Pittman. Performed with shaved heads. Appeared in the movie *Bikini Beach*.			
2/1/64	**18**	10		**Penetration** *Here Comes Marsha* [I]	$20	■	Best 13002
				first released on Best 102 in 1963 ($30); picture sleeve issued in either red & white or black & white colors			
				PYT **'01**			
				Female teen pop vocal group from Tampa, Florida: Lydia Bell, Lauren Mayhew, Ashley Niven and Tracy Williams. PYT: Prove Yourself True.			
4/7/01	**33^S**	21		**Same Ol' Same Ol'** *(4 album snippets)*	$4	★	Epic 79554
				PYTHON LEE JACKSON LP **'72**			
				Rock group from Australia: David Bently (keyboards), Mick Liber and Gary Boyle (guitars), Tony Cahill (bass) and David Montgomery (drums).			
5/27/72	**56**	10		**In A Broken Dream** *Doin Fine*	$8		GNP Crescendo 449
				Rod Stewart (vocal; hired as a session singer, not a group member); also released with "Turn The Music Down" as the B-side			
				Q			
				Q BUB/LP **'77**			
				Pop group from Beaver Falls, Pennsylvania: Don Garvin (guitar), Robert Peckman (bass), Bill Thomas (keyboards) and Bill Vogel (drums). All share vocals. Garvin and Peckman were members of **The Jaggerz**.			
3/12/77	**23**	13		**Dancin' Man** *Love Pollution*	$5		Epic/Sweet City 50335
				QB FINEST LP **'01**			
				All-star rap group: **Nas**, **Capone**, **Mobb Deep**, **Tragedy**, MC Shan, Marley Marl, Nature, Cormega and Millennium Thug. QB: Queens Bridge.			
3/3/01	**26**	20		**Oochie Wally** S:13 / A:19 *(2 versions) / Find Ya Wealth*	$8	★*	Columbia 79586
				QB FINEST Featuring NAS And Bravehearts			
				Shelene Thomas (female vocal)			
				Q-FEEL **'89**			
				Techno-dance duo from England: **Martin Page** and Brian Fairweather.			
6/17/89	**75**	7		**Dancing In Heaven (Orbital Be-Bop)** *At The Top (All The Way To St. Tropez)*	$3	■	Jive 1220
				originally "Bubbled Under" (#110) on 3/26/83 on Jive 2001			
				QKUMBA ZOO **'96**			
				Dance group from Johannesburg, South Africa: Levannah (female vocals), Owl (all instruments) and Tziki (dancer).			
10/12/96	**69**	7		**The Child (Inside)** S:67 *(3 album snippets) / (remix)*	$4	▮^{V}	Arista 13259
				QT **'97**			
				Born Quentin Bush in Nashville, Tennessee. Male R&B singer.			
2/1/97	**94**	4		**My Baby Mama** S:72 *(instrumental)*	$4	▮	Rowdy/Arista 35093
				Q-TIP R&B/BUB/LP **'99**			
				Born Jonathan Davis on 11/20/70 in Queens, New York. Male rapper. Member of **A Tribe Called Quest**. Also see **Deee-Lite**.			
9/13/97	**36^A**	8		1 **Got 'Til It's Gone**		V	album cut
				JANET Featuring Q-Tip and Joni Mitchell			
				samples "Big Yellow Taxi" by **Joni Mitchell**; "45" (33-1/3 rmp): Virgin 38623; B-side: "Together Again" (Jackson - #1)			
4/3/99	**67**	8		2 **Get Involved** A:50 *(instrumental) / What I Am* (Sy Smith)	$6	T	Hollywood 66009
				RAPHAEL SAADIQ & Q-TIP			
				samples "I'll Always Love My Mama" by **The Intruders**; from the animated TV series *The PJs*			
7/17/99	**26**	20		3 **Vivrant Thing** A:16 / S:67 *Do What Playas Do* (w/Mysonne, **Mase** & Eightball) */ You Know Why* (w/**LL Cool J**)	$6	T	Violator 562170
				12" remix featuring **Missy Elliott** & **Busta Rhymes** on Violator 562441			
11/27/99+	**5**	21	▲	4 **Hot Boyz** RB^6 S:2 / A:24 *U Can't Resist* (w/**Juvenile** & **B.G.**)	$4	★	The Gold Mind 64029
				MISSY "MISDEMEANOR" ELLIOTT [featuring NAS, EVE & Q-TIP]			
				Lil' Mo (vocal ad libs)			
1/22/00	**71**	5		5 **Breathe And Stop** A:57			album cut
				samples "N.T." by **Kool & The Gang**; from the album *Amplified* on Arista 14619			

DEBUT	PEAK	WKS	Gold	A-side (Chart Hit)......B-side	$	Sym	Label & Number

QUAD CITY DJ'S — R&B/BUB/LP '96

Studio rap-bass group from Orlando, Florida: Nathaniel "C.C. Lemonhead" Orange, Johnny "Jay Ski" McGowan and Lana. Orange was a member of **95 South**.

DEBUT	PEAK	WKS	Gold	A-side (Chart Hit)......B-side	$	Sym	Label & Number
3/16/96	**3**	42	▲	1 **C'Mon N' Ride It (The Train)**......S:4 / A:6 *(instrumental)* samples "Theme From Together Brothers" by **Love Unlimited Orchestra**	$3	▮	Big Beat 98083
5/18/96	**95**	3		2 **Hoop N Yo Face**......S:72 *(remix)* **69 BOYZ featuring Quad City DJ's** from the movie *Sunset Park* starring Rhea Perlman	$4	▮	Flavor Unit 64312
12/21/96+	**37**	20		3 **Space Jam**......S:26 *Get On Up And Dance* title song from the movie starring Michael Jordan	$4	▮	Warner Sunset 87018

QUAITE, Christine — '64

Born in 1950 in England. Pop singer.

DEBUT	PEAK	WKS	Gold	A-side (Chart Hit)......B-side	$	Sym	Label & Number
5/23/64	**85**	2		**Tell Me Mamma**......*In The Middle Of The Floor* **Frank Barber** (orch.); written by **Gerry Granahan**	$15		World Artists 1022

QUAKER CITY BOYS — '59

String band from Philadelphia, Pennsylvania. Led by Tommy Reilly.

DEBUT	PEAK	WKS	Gold	A-side (Chart Hit)......B-side	$	Sym	Label & Number
12/22/58+	**39**	9		**Teasin'**......*Won't Y' Come Out, Mary Ann*	$15		Swan 4023

QUARTERFLASH — LP '82

Pop-rock group from Portland, Oregon: husband-and-wife Marv (guitar) and Rindy (vocals, saxophone) Ross, with Jack Charles (guitar), Rick DiGiallonardo (keyboards), Rich Gooch (bass) and Brian David Willis (drums). Group originally known as Seafood Mama.

DEBUT	PEAK	WKS	Gold	A-side (Chart Hit)......B-side	$	Sym	Label & Number
10/17/81+	**3**	24	●	1 **Harden My Heart** AR[3] *Don't Be Lonely* originally released as by Seafood Mama on Whitefire in 1980 with a picture sleeve	$4		Geffen 49824
2/13/82	**16**	13		2 **Find Another Fool**......*Cruisin' With The Deuce*	$4	■	Geffen 50006
5/29/82	**56**	8		3 **Right Kind Of Love**......*You're Holding Me Back*	$4	■	Geffen 29994
8/14/82	**60**	8		4 **Night Shift**......*Love Should Be So Kind* title song from the movie starring Michael Keaton and Henry Winkler	$4		Warner 29932
6/18/83	**14**	16		5 **Take Me To Heart**......*Nowhere Left To Hide*	$4	■	Geffen 29603
10/1/83	**58**	6		6 **Take Another Picture**......*One More Round To Go*	$4	■	Geffen 29523
10/19/85	**83**	6		7 **Talk To Me**......*Grace Under Fire*	$3	■	Geffen 28908

QUARTER NOTES, The — '59

Instrumental rock and roll group from Buffalo, New York. Led by Anthony Sperry.

DEBUT	PEAK	WKS	Gold	A-side (Chart Hit)......B-side	$	Sym	Label & Number
3/23/59	**82**	1		**Record Hop Blues**......*Suki-Yaki-Rocki* [I]	$25		Wizz 715

QUATEMAN, Bill — LP '73

Born on 11/4/47 in Chicago, Illinois. Pop singer/songwriter/guitarist.

DEBUT	PEAK	WKS	Gold	A-side (Chart Hit)......B-side	$	Sym	Label & Number
4/7/73	**86**	5		**Only Love**......*Keep Dreaming*	$5	■	Columbia 45792

QUATRO, Suzi — LP '79

Born on 6/3/50 in Detroit, Michigan. Rock singer/songwriter/guitarist. Played "Leather Tuscadero" on TV's *Happy Days* in 1977. Her sister Patti was a member of **Fanny**.

DEBUT	PEAK	WKS	Gold	A-side (Chart Hit)......B-side	$	Sym	Label & Number
9/14/74	**85**	3		1 **All Shook Up**......*Glycerine Queen*	$6		Bell 45,477
2/7/76	**56**	4		2 **Can The Can**......*Don't Mess Around*	$6		Big Tree 16053
1/27/79	**4**	22	●	3 **Stumblin' In** *A Stranger To Paradise* **SUZI QUATRO AND CHRIS NORMAN**	$4		RSO 917
5/26/79	**45**	8		4 **If You Can't Give Me Love**......*Non-Citizen*	$4		RSO 929
9/8/79	**44**	8		5 **I've Never Been In Love**......*Space Cadets*	$4		RSO 1001
11/24/79+	**41**	11		6 **She's In Love With You**......*Starlight Lady*	$4		RSO 1014
1/24/81	**51**	9		7 **Lipstick**......*Woman Cry* all of above produced by Mike Chapman	$4		Dreamland 107

QUE BO GOLD — '02

Born in Atlanta, Georgia. Male Latin rapper.

DEBUT	PEAK	WKS	Gold	A-side (Chart Hit)......B-side	$	Sym	Label & Number
8/3/02	**43**[S]	1		**Lil Buddy**......*(album version) / (3 album snippets) / Her* (w/Kilo) **QUE BO GOLD (featuring Polo, Akon and Rasheeda)** samples "Bad To The Bone" by **George Thorogood**	$6	★	Universal 015143

QUEEN ★93★ — ROK/BUB/R&B/LP '80

Rock group formed in England: **Freddie Mercury** (vocals; born Frederick Bulsara on 9/5/46 in Zanzibar, Tanzania) (see #22 & 23 below), Brian May (guitar; born on 7/19/47), John Deacon (bass; born on 8/19/51) and Roger Taylor (drums; born on 7/26/49). May and Taylor had been in the group Smile. Mercury had recorded as Larry Lurex. Wrote soundtrack for the movie *Flash Gordon* in 1980. Mercury died of AIDS on 11/24/91 (age 45). Group inducted into the Rock and Roll Hall of Fame in 2001.

1)Crazy Little Thing Called Love 2)Another One Bites The Dust 3)Bohemian Rhapsody 4)We Will Rock You/We Are The Champions 5)Body Language

DEBUT	PEAK	WKS	Gold	A-side (Chart Hit)......B-side	$	Sym	Label & Number
2/8/75	**12**	19		1 **Killer Queen**......*Flick Of The Wrist*	$7		Elektra 45226
1/3/76	**9**	24	●	2 **Bohemian Rhapsody**......*I'm In Love With My Car* same version re-charted in 1992 (see #27 below)	$7		Elektra 45297
5/22/76	**16**	16		3 **You're My Best Friend**......*'39*	$6		Elektra 45318
11/27/76+	**13**	15		4 **Somebody To Love**......*White Man* also see "live" version (#29 below)	$6		Elektra 45362
3/19/77	**49**	6		5 **Tie Your Mother Down**......*Drowse*	$6		Elektra 45385
10/22/77+	**4**	27	▲	6 **We Will Rock You/We Are The Champions**...... "We Will Rock You" did not chart; however, it received extensive airplay as both sides were segued together on the album *News Of The World*; both sides charted together on #28 below	$6	■	Elektra 45441
5/13/78	**74**	5		7 **It's Late**......*Sheer Heart Attack*	$6	■	Elektra 45478
11/11/78+	**24**	12		8 **Bicycle Race** /			
11/11/78		12		9 **Fat Bottomed Girls**......	$6	■	Elektra 45541

DEBUT	PEAK	WKS	Gold	A-side (Chart Hit)...B-side	$	Sym	Label & Number
				QUEEN — Cont'd			
2/17/79	86	4		10 **Don't Stop Me Now** ... *More Of That Jazz*	$6		Elektra 46008
12/22/79+	❶[4]	22	●	11 **Crazy Little Thing Called Love** *Spread Your Wings*	$5		Elektra 46579
6/28/80	42	9		12 **Play The Game** ... *A Human Body*	$5	■	Elektra 46652
8/16/80	❶[3]	31	▲	13 **Another One Bites The Dust** ... *Don't Try Suicide*	$5		Elektra 47031
11/29/80	44	11		14 **Need Your Loving Tonight** ... *Rock It (Prime Jive)* above 4 from the album *The Game*	$5		Elektra 47086
1/17/81	42	10		15 **Flash's Theme aka Flash** ... *Football Fight* from the movie *Flash Gordon* starring Sam Jones	$5	■	Elektra 47092
11/7/81+	29	15		16 **Under Pressure** ... *Soul Brother* (Queen) **QUEEN & DAVID BOWIE** also see "Ice Ice Baby" by **Vanilla Ice**	$5	■	Elektra 47235
5/1/82	11	14		17 **Body Language** ... *Life Is Real (Song For Lennon)* (ROK #57) issued with either a sexually suggestive sleeve or a plain white sleeve	$5	■	Elektra 47452
7/31/82	60	6		18 **Calling All Girls** ... *Put Out The Fire* (ROK #15)	$5	■	Elektra 69981
2/18/84	16	13		19 **Radio Ga-Ga** ... *I Go Crazy*	$4	■	Capitol 5317
4/28/84	45	8		20 **I Want To Break Free** ... *Machines (or "Back To Humans")* 4 different picture sleeves issued, each featuring a photo of a group member	$4	■	Capitol 5350
7/28/84	72	4		21 **It's A Hard Life** ... *Is This The World We Created...?*	$4	■	Capitol 5372
9/29/84	69	6		22 **Love Kills** ... *Rotwang's Party (Robot Dance)* (**Giorgio Moroder**) from the movie *Metropolis* starring Brigitte Helm (restored from the 1926 original silent movie)	$4	■	Columbia 04606
4/27/85	76	4		23 **I Was Born To Love You** ... *Stop All The Fighting* **FREDDIE MERCURY** (above 2)	$4	■	Columbia 04869
12/7/85+	61	10		24 **One Vision** ... *Blurred Vision* from the movie *Iron Eagle* starring Louis Gossett, Jr.	$4	■	Capitol 5530
6/21/86	42	11		25 **A Kind Of Magic** ... S:34 *Gimme The Prize (Kurgan's Theme)*	$4	■	Capitol 5590
5/13/89	50	10		26 **I Want It All** ... S:35 *Hang On In There*	$4	■	Capitol 44372
3/21/92	2[1]	17		27 **Bohemian Rhapsody** ... S:2 / A:9 *The Show Must Go On* (ROK #40) [R] featured in the movie *Wayne's World* starring Mike Myers and Dana Carvey; also see #2 above	$3	▮V	Hollywood 64794
7/11/92	52	14		28 **We Will Rock You/We Are The Champions** ... S:28 *These Are The Days Of Our Lives* [R] "45" A-side: "We Are The Champions"; B-side: "The Days Of Our Lives"; also see #6 above	$5	▮V	Hollywood 64725
5/15/93	30	9		29 **Somebody To Love** ... A:25 / S:72 *Love Of My Life* (Queen) [L-R] **GEORGE MICHAEL And QUEEN** recorded at Wembley Stadium for the **Freddie Mercury** Tribute Concert; also see #4 above	$3	▮	Hollywood 64647
				QUEEN LATIFAH R&B/BUB/LP **'94** Born Dana Owens on 3/18/70 in Newark, New Jersey. Female rapper/actress. Appeared in the movies *Jungle Fever*, *Set It Off*, *The Bone Collector*, *Chicago* and *Bringing Down The House*. Cast member of Fox TV series *Living Single*. CEO of Flavor Unit Records. Latifah is Arabic for delicate and sensitive.			
11/27/93+	23	20		1 **U.N.I.T.Y.** S:16 / A:24 *(instrumental) / 4 The D.J.'s* samples "Message From The Inner City" by **The Crusaders**	$4	▮	Motown 2225
3/12/94	54	11		2 **Just Another Day...** ... S:41 / A:54 *(4 album snippets)*	$3	▮	Motown 2233
7/23/94	70	13		3 **Weekend Love** ... S:62 *Black Hand Side* Tony Rebel (reggae vocal)	$3	▮	Motown 2249
9/6/97	70	5		4 **Need Your Love** ... S:50 *(2 versions) / (4 album snippets)* **BIG BUB featuring Queen Latifah & Heavy D** samples "I Want Your Love" by **Chic**	$3	▮	Kedar/Universal 56129
9/13/97	76	4		5 **It's Alright** ... *(remix)* samples "I Want To Thank You" by Alicia Myers; from the movie *Nothing To Lose* starring Martin Lawrence	$3	▮	Tommy Boy 7402
8/15/98	50	10		6 **Paper** ... S:30 *Bananas [Who You Gonna Call?]* (w/**Apache**) **Pras Michel** (rap); new lyrics to the tune of "I Heard It Through The Grapevine"	$3	▮	Motown 860814
				QUEEN PEN R&B/BUB/LP **'98** Born Lynise Walters in Harlem, New York. Female rapper. Also see **BLACKstreet**'s "No Diggity."			
12/13/97+	84	9		1 **Man Behind The Music** ... S:69 *(instrumental)* **QUEEN PEN Featuring Teddy Riley** contains interpolations of "Your Love" and "I Know You Got Soul" by **Eric B. & Rakim**	$4	▮	Lil' Man 97020
2/7/98	28	15		2 **All My Love** ... S:23 / A:51 *No Diggity* (**BLACKstreet w/Queen Pen**) **QUEEN PEN Featuring Eric Williams of BLACKstreet** samples "Never Too Much" by **Luther Vandross**; B-side is a remix of **BLACKstreet**'s 1996 #1 hit	$4	▮	Lil' Man 97023
6/20/98	74	4		3 **Party Ain't A Party** ... A:51 *(2 versions)* **QUEEN PEN Featuring Teddy Riley, Nutta Butta, Markell & Jesse West** samples "On Your Face" by **Earth, Wind & Fire**	$6	T	Lil' Man 95024
8/22/98	74	5		4 **Cheated (To All The Girls)** ... *What's Clef* (#61) / *Chickenhead* (#69 - both Jean) **WYCLEF JEAN featuring Queen Pen & The Product** samples "To All The Girls I've Loved Before" by **Julio Iglesias** & **Willie Nelson**	$6	▮*	Ruffhouse 78993
				QUEENS OF THE STONE AGE ROK/BUB/LP **'03** Rock duo from Seattle, Washington: Josh Homme and Nick Oliveri.			
12/28/02+	51	20		**No One Knows** ... A:51 from the album *Songs For The Deaf* on Interscope 493425			album cut
				QUEENSRŸCHE ROK/BUB/LP **'91** Hard-rock group from Bellevue, Washington: Geoff Tate (vocals), Chris DeGarmo and Michael Wilton (guitars), Eddie Jackson (bass), and Scott Rockenfield (drums).			
3/23/91	9	17		**Silent Lucidity** ... AR[1] S:4 / A:15 *The Mission (live)* "45": EMI 57752; B-side: "Anybody Listening?"	$3	▮V	EMI 50345

DEBUT	PEAK	WKS	Gold	A-side (Chart Hit)...B-side	$	Sym	Label & Number
				? (QUESTION MARK) & THE MYSTERIANS BUB/LP '66			
				Garage-rock band formed in Texas: Mexican-born Rudy "?" Martinez (vocals), Bobby Balderrama (guitar), Frank Rodriguez (organ), Frank Lugo (bass) and Eddie Serrato (drums).			
9/3/66	❶[1]	15	●	1 **96 Tears** ...*Midnight Hour*	$15		Cameo 428
				first released on Pa-Go-Go 102 in 1966 ($500)			
				? & THE MYSTERIANS:			
11/19/66	**22**	10		2 **I Need Somebody** ...*"8" Teen*	$15		Cameo 441
3/25/67	**56**	6		3 **Can't Get Enough Of You, Baby** ...*Smokes*	$15		Cameo 467
6/10/67	**98**	2		4 **Girl (You Captivate Me)** ...*Got To*	$15		Cameo 479
				QUICKSILVER MESSENGER SERVICE BUB/LP '70			
				Rock group from San Francisco, California: Gary Duncan (vocals, guitar), John Cipollina (guitar), David Freiberg (bass) and Greg Elmore (drums). Dino Valenti joined as lead singer in 1970. Freiberg left in 1973 to join **Jefferson Starship**. Cipollina, brother of **Huey Lewis & The News**' bassist Mario Cipollina, died on 5/29/89 (age 45). Valenti died on 11/16/94 (age 57).			
8/9/69	**91**	3		1 **Who Do You Love** ...*Which Do You Love*	$12		Capitol 2557
				written and introduced by **Bo Diddley** in 1956 on Checker 842 ($50)			
10/3/70	**49**	9		2 **Fresh Air** ...*Freeway Flyer*	$10		Capitol 2920
3/6/71	**100**	2		3 **What About Me** ...*Good Old Rock And Roll*	$8		Capitol 3046
				QUIET RIOT ROK/LP '83			
				Hard-rock group formed in Los Angeles, California: Kevin DuBrow (vocals), Carlos Cavazo (guitar), Rudy Sarzo (bass) and Frankie Banali (drums). Sarzo later joined **Whitesnake**.			
9/17/83	**5**	21	●	1 **Cum On Feel The Noize** ...*Run For Cover*	$4		Pasha 04005
1/7/84	**31**	12		2 **Bang Your Head (Metal Health)** ...*(live version)*	$4	■	Pasha 04267
7/7/84	**51**	12		3 **Mama Weer All Crazee Now** ...*Bad Boy*	$4	■	Pasha 04505
				QUIN-TONES, The '58			
				Black doo-wop group from York, Pennsylvania: Roberta Haymon (lead), Phyllis Carr, Carolyn Holmes, Kenny Sexton, Jeannie Crist and Ronnie Scott (pianist). Holmes died in 1995; Haymon died in 1996.			
8/18/58	**18**	12		**Down The Aisle Of Love** ...S:18 / H:20 *Please Dear*	$40		Hunt 321
				first released on Red Top 108 in 1958 ($100)			

R

DEBUT	PEAK	WKS	Gold	A-side (Chart Hit)...B-side	$	Sym	Label & Number
				RAab R&B '93			
				Male R&B singer from Florida.			
10/16/93	**74**	11		**Foreplay** ...S:48 *(3 versions)*	$5	▌	Rip-It 1001
	★328★			**RABBITT, Eddie** C&W/AC/LP '81			
				Born Edward Thomas Rabbitt on 11/27/41 in Brooklyn, New York; raised in East Orange, New Jersey. Died of cancer on 5/7/98 (age 56). Country singer/songwriter/guitarist (charted 43 hits, 1974-91). First recorded for 20th Century in 1964. Moved to Nashville in 1968. Became established after **Elvis Presley** recorded his song "Kentucky Rain" in 1970.			
				1)I Love A Rainy Night 2)Step By Step 3)Drivin' My Life Away			
7/24/76	**76**	8		1 **Rocky Mountain Music** ...*Do You Right Tonight* (C&W flip)	$5		Elektra 45315
6/25/77	**77**	9		2 **I Can't Help Myself** ...*She Loves Me Like She Means It*	$5		Elektra 45390
6/24/78	**53**	7		3 **You Don't Love Me Anymore** ...CW[1] *Caroline*	$5		Elektra 45488
1/20/79	**30**	11		4 **Every Which Way But Loose** ...CW[3] *Under The Double Eagle* [I]	$5		Elektra 45554
				title song from the movie starring **Clint Eastwood**			
6/9/79	**13**	17		5 **Suspicions** ...CW[1] *I Don't Wanna Make Love (With Anyone Else But You)*	$5		Elektra 46053
5/3/80	**82**	4		6 **Gone Too Far** ...CW[1] *Loveline*	$4		Elektra 46613
6/21/80	**5**	25	●	7 **Drivin' My Life Away** ...CW[1] *Pretty Lady*	$4		Elektra 46656
				from the movie *Roadie* starring **Meat Loaf**			
11/8/80+	❶[2]	28	●	8 **I Love A Rainy Night** CW[1] / AC[3] *Short Road To Love*	$4		Elektra 47066
7/25/81	**5**	22		9 **Step By Step** ...CW[1] *My Only Wish*	$4	■	Elektra 47174
11/14/81+	**15**	15		10 **Someone Could Lose A Heart Tonight** ...CW[1] *Nobody Loves Me Like My Baby*	$4		Elektra 47239
4/10/82	**35**	13		11 **I Don't Know Where To Start** ...*Skip-A-Beat*	$4		Elektra 47435
10/9/82+	**7**	29		12 **You And I** ...CW[1] *All My Life, All My Love* (Rabbitt)	$4		Elektra 69936
				EDDIE RABBITT with CRYSTAL GAYLE			
4/23/83	**55**	8		13 **You Can't Run From Love** ...CW[1] *You Got Me Now*	$4		Warner 29712
9/10/83	**81**	5		14 **You Put The Beat In My Heart** ...*Our Love Will Survive*	$4		Warner 29512
				all of above (except #4) produced by David Malloy			
				RACKET CITY '02			
				Rap group from Atlanta, Georgia.			
10/26/02+	**45**[S]	11		**Throw Up** ...*(2 versions) / Ryders*	$8	★*	447/Landspeed 1122
				RADIANTS, The BUB/R&B '65			
				R&B vocal group from Chicago, Illinois: Maurice McAlister (lead), Jerome Brookes and Green "Mac" McLaurin (tenors), Wallace Sampson (baritone) and Elzie Butler (bass).			
11/3/62	**100**	1		1 **Father Knows Best** ...*One Day I'll Show You (I Really Love You)*	$15		Chess 1832
12/26/64+	**51**	9		2 **Voice Your Choice** ...*If I Only Had You*	$12		Chess 1904
5/8/65	**91**	3		3 **It Ain't No Big Thing** ...*I Got A Girl*	$12		Chess 1925
5/25/68	**68**	9		4 **Hold On** ...*I'm Glad I'm The Loser*	$12		Chess 2037
				RADIOHEAD ROK/LP '93			
				Alternative-rock group from Oxford, England: Thom Yorke (vocals), brothers Jon (guitar) and Colin (bass) Greenwood, Ed O'Brien (guitar) and Phil Selway (drums).			
6/26/93	**34**	20		1 **Creep** S:23 *Faithless, The Wonder Boy*	$4	▌[V]	Capitol 44932
				"45": Capitol 17591 (green vinyl); B-side: "Anyone Can Play Guitar"			
5/20/95	**65**[A]	4		2 **Fake Plastic Trees** ...		V	album cut
				"45": Capitol 18728; B-side: "The Bends"			

DEBUT	PEAK	WKS	Gold	A-side (Chart Hit)...B-side	$	Sym	Label & Number
				RADIOHEAD — Cont'd			
3/16/96	78	8		3 **High & Dry** ...A:73 *Fake Plastic Trees*	$4	▮V	Capitol 58537
				"45": Capitol 19017; B-side: "Black Star"; above 2 from the album *The Bends* on Capitol 29626			
2/28/98	69A	1		4 **Karma Police** ...		V	album cut
				from the album *OK Computer* on Capitol 55229; "45": Capitol 19624; B-side: "Let Down" (ROK #29)			
9/15/01	20S	8		5 **Knives Out** ...*Cuttooth / Life In A Glasshouse*	$6	★+	Capitol 77668
				RAEKWON R&B/LP '95			
				Born Corey Woods on 1/12/70 in Staten Island, New York. Male rapper. Member of **Wu-Tang Clan**. Also known as **Chef Raekwon** or Lou Diamonds. Also see **Fat Joe**'s "Firewater."			
7/15/95	43	9		1 **Glaciers Of Ice /** S:22			
				Ghostface Killah and Masta Killa (guest rappers)			
7/22/95		8		2 **Criminology** ...S:flip	$5	▮	Loud/RCA 64375
				Ghostface Killah (guest rapper); samples "I Keep Asking You Questions" by Black Ivory			
				CHEF RAEKWON:			
10/14/95	37	18		3 **Ice Cream /** S:19 / A:74			
				Ghostface Killah, **Method Man** and Cappachino (guest rappers)			
12/9/95+	71	10		4 **Incarcerated Scarfaces** ...S:flip	$5	▮	Loud/RCA 64426
				all of above from the album *Only Built 4 Cuban Linx*			
				RAELETTS, The R&B/BUB '71			
				Female vocal group formed as a backup group for **Ray Charles** in 1958. Initial lineup: Margie Hendrix and Ethel "Darlene" McCrea of **The Cookies** with Pat Moseley and Gwendolyn Berry. Lineup from 1967-69: Berry, **Merry Clayton** (lead), Alexandra Brown and Clydie King (also recorded as **Brown Sugar**). Lineup in 1970: **Mable John**, Susaye Green, Vernita Moss and Estella Yarbrough.			
4/15/67	76	6		1 **One Hurt Deserves Another** ...*One Room Paradise*	$10		Tangerine 972
5/16/70	96	2		2 **I Want To (Do Everything For You)** ...*Keep It To Yourself*	$10		Tangerine 1006
3/13/71	58	13		3 **Bad Water** ...*That Goes To Show You*	$10		Tangerine 1014
				co-written by **Jackie DeShannon**			
				RAES, The LP '79			
				Husband-and-wife disco duo: Robbie (born in Resloven, Wales) and Cherrill (born in Carlisle, Wales) Rae.			
12/16/78+	61	9		**A Little Lovin' (Keeps The Doctor Away)** ...*To Love Somebody*	$5		A&M 2091
				RAFFERTY, Gerry LP '78			
				Born on 4/16/47 in Paisley, Scotland. Adult Contemporary singer/songwriter/guitarist. Co-leader of **Stealers Wheel**.			
4/22/78	2⁶	20	●	1 **Baker Street** *Big Change In The Weather*	$4		United Artists 1192
				Raphael Ravenscroft (sax solo); also released on Liberty 1192			
8/12/78	12	15		2 **Right Down The Line** ...AC4 *Waiting For The Day*	$4	■	United Artists 1233
12/2/78+	28	13		3 **Home And Dry** ...*Mattie's Rag*	$4		United Artists 1266
6/2/79	17	10		4 **Days Gone Down (Still Got The Light In Your Eyes)** ...*Why Won't You Talk To Me?*	$4		United Artists 1298
8/11/79	21	13		5 **Get It Right Next Time** ...*It's Gonna Be A Long Night*	$4		United Artists 1316
7/19/80	54	8		6 **The Royal Mile (Sweet Darlin')** ...*In Transit*	$4		United Artists 1366
				all of above written and co-produced by Rafferty			
				RAG DOLLS, The '65			
				"Girl group" headed by Sarasota, Florida native Jean Thomas with Mikie Harris and Susan Lewis. **Tracey Dey** was the actual voice on the recordings.			
9/12/64	91	3		1 **Society Girl** ...*Ragen (Society Girl Bossa Nova)* (The Caliente Combo)	$15		Parkway 921
				answer song to **The 4 Seasons**' "Rag Doll"			
1/23/65	55	6		2 **Dusty** ...*Hey, Hoagy*	$15		Mala 493
				RAGE AGAINST THE MACHINE ROK/BUB/LP '99			
				Alternative hard-rock group formed in Los Angeles, California: Zack DeLa Rocha (vocals), Tom Morello (guitar), Tim Bob (bass) and Brad Wilk (drums). DeLa Rocha left in October 2000; the other three recorded with Chris Cornell as **Audioslave**.			
5/11/96	62A	7		1 **Bulls On Parade** ...		V	album cut ■
				from the album *Evil Empire* on Epic 57523; 7" 33-1/3 rpm single issued on Epic 663152 on red vinyl with a picture sleeve; B-side: "Hadda Be Playing On The Jukebox"			
10/30/99	69	20		2 **Guerrilla Radio** ...S:21 *Without A Face (live)*	$4	★V	Epic 79270 ■
				"45" issued with a picture sleeve			
				RAHEEM R&B/BUB '98			
				Born Oscar Seres on 7/6/71 in Houston, Texas. Male rapper. Early member of **The Geto Boys**.			
4/5/97	51	20		1 **That's Right** ...S:40 *(2 versions)*	$4	▮	Breakaway/EMI 58641
				DJ TAZ Featuring Raheem The Dream			
				samples "Tonight" by **Ready For The World**			
7/4/98	70S	3		2 **The Most Beautiful Girl** ...BUB:101 *(instrumental)*	$5	▮	Tight 2 Def 482001
				samples "Sally" by the Gucci Crew			
				RAHZEL LP '99			
				Born Rahzel Brown in Brooklyn, New York. Male singer/rapper/songwriter.			
7/10/99	52S	7		1 **All I Know** ...*(instrumental)*	$5	★+	MCA 55597
8/28/99	76	6		2 **Southern Gul** ...S:16 *(2 versions)*	$4	★	Motown 56360
				ERYKAH BADU featuring Rahzel			
				RAIDERS — see REVERE, Paul			
				RAINBOW ROK/BUB/LP '82			
				Hard-rock band led by British guitarist Ritchie Blackmore and bassist Roger Glover, both members of **Deep Purple**. Fluctuating lineup included vocalists Ronnie James Dio (**Black Sabbath**), Graham Bonnet (Michael Schenker Group, Alcatrazz) and Joe Lynn Turner, keyboardist **Tony Carey** and drummer **Cozy Powell** (**Emerson, Lake & Powell**). Group split up upon re-formation of Deep Purple in 1984. In 1990 Turner joined Deep Purple, and Powell joined **Black Sabbath**. Powell died in a car crash on 4/5/98 (age 50).			
11/17/79	57	8		1 **Since You Been Gone** ...*Bad Girls*	$5		Polydor 2014
4/24/82	40	12		2 **Stone Cold** ...AR1 *Rock Fever*	$4	■	Mercury 76146
11/5/83	60	10		3 **Street Of Dreams** ...*Anybody There*	$4	■	Mercury 815660

DEBUT	PEAK	WKS	Gold	A-side (Chart Hit)...B-side	$	Sym	Label & Number

RAINDROPS, The — BUB '63

Songwriting team of **Ellie Greenwich** (born on 10/23/40) (see #7 below) and husband Jeff Barry (born on 4/3/38). Divorced in 1965, but continued to work together. Barry wrote "Tell Laura I Love Her"; team wrote "Be My Baby," "Da Doo Ron Ron," "Chapel Of Love," "River Deep-Mountain High," "Hanky Panky," "Leader Of The Pack" and many more. Barry produced such mega-hits as "Sugar Sugar" (**The Archies**) and "I'm A Believer" (**The Monkees**). Their song hits were celebrated in the 1985 Broadway musical *Leader Of The Pack*. Ellie recorded as **The Butterflys** (see #5 below). Also see **Tony Orlando & Dawn**'s "Candida" and "Knock Three Times."

DEBUT	PEAK	WKS	Gold	A-side (Chart Hit)...B-side	$	Sym	Label & Number
4/27/63	41	8		1 **What A Guy**...*It's So Wonderful*	$20		Jubilee 5444
8/10/63	17	11		2 **The Kind Of Boy You Can't Forget** *Even Though You Can't Dance*	$20		Jubilee 5455
11/30/63+	64	8		3 **That Boy John**...*Hanky Panky* B-side is the original version of "Hanky Panky"	$20		Jubilee 5466
3/14/64	62	7		4 **Book Of Love**...*I Won't Cry*	$20		Jubilee 5469
9/12/64	51	7		5 **Good Night Baby**...*The Swim* **THE BUTTERFLYS**	$25		Red Bird 009
9/12/64	97	1		6 **One More Tear**...*Another Boy Like Mine*	$20		Jubilee 5487
5/6/67	83	3		7 **I Want You To Be My Baby**...*Goodnight, Goodnight (What's So Good About It?)* **ELLIE GREENWICH**	$15		United Artists 50151

RAINES, Rita — '56

Adult Contemporary singer.

DEBUT	PEAK	WKS	Gold	A-side (Chart Hit)...B-side	$	Sym	Label & Number
2/18/56	89	1		**Such A Day (So Ein Tag)**...T:89 *Ol' Devil Moon* Paul Jordan (orch.)	$20		Deed 1010

RAINWATER, Marvin — C&W/BUB '57

Born Marvin Percy on 7/2/25 in Wichita, Kansas. Country singer/songwriter/guitarist.

DEBUT	PEAK	WKS	Gold	A-side (Chart Hit)...B-side	$	Sym	Label & Number
5/20/57	18	22	●	1 **Gonna Find Me A Bluebird**....J:18 / S:19 / T:22 *So You Think You've Got Troubles* (C&W flip)	$25		MGM 12412
12/2/57	93	1		2 **The Majesty Of Love**...T:93 *You, My Darlin', You* **MARVIN RAINWATER and CONNIE FRANCIS**	$25		MGM 12555
3/31/58	60	2		3 **Whole Lotta Woman**...T:60 *Baby, Don't Go*	$20		MGM 12609
7/27/59	66	7		4 **Half-Breed**...*A Song Of Love*	$20		MGM 12803

RAINY DAZE, The — '67

Pop-rock group from Denver, Colorado: brothers Tim (vocals, guitar) and Kip (drums) Gilbert, with Mac Ferris (guitar), Bob Heckendorf (keyboards) and Sam Fuller (bass).

DEBUT	PEAK	WKS	Gold	A-side (Chart Hit)...B-side	$	Sym	Label & Number
3/11/67	70	4		**That Acapulco Gold**...*In My Mind Lives A Forest* first released on IP 100 in 1966 ($30) and on Chicory 404 in 1967 ($15)	$10		Uni 55002

RAITT, Bonnie — ROK/AC/BUB/C&W/LP '91

Born on 11/8/49 in Burbank, California. White blues-rock singer/guitarist. Daughter of Broadway actor/singer John Raitt. Married to actor Michael O'Keefe from 1991-99. Inducted into the Rock and Roll Hall of Fame in 2000.

1)Something To Talk About 2)I Can't Make You Love Me 3)Love Sneakin' Up On You

DEBUT	PEAK	WKS	Gold	A-side (Chart Hit)...B-side	$	Sym	Label & Number
5/21/77	57	12		1 **Runaway**...*Louise* **Michael McDonald** (backing vocal)	$5		Warner 8382
12/8/79+	73	6		2 **You're Gonna Get What's Coming**...*The Glow* written by **Robert Palmer**	$4	■	Warner 49116
3/10/90	49	9		3 **Have A Heart**...*The Road's My Middle Name* theme from the movie *Heart Condition* starring Denzel Washington and Bob Hoskins; "45": Capitol 79940 (promo only)	$3	▮V	Capitol 44501
5/19/90	92	3		4 **Nick Of Time**...*The Road's My Middle Name* originally made the Adult Contemporary charts (#10) on 9/16/89	$3	▮V	Capitol 44364
7/20/91	5	20		5 **Something To Talk About** S:14 / A:19 *One Part Be My Lover* "45": Capitol 57741; B-side: "I Can't Make You Love Me"	$3	▮V	Capitol 44724
11/23/91+	18	20		6 **I Can't Make You Love Me**...S:23 / A:25 *Come To Me*	$3	▮V	Capitol 44729
4/18/92	34	17		7 **Not The Only One**...A:35 *Come To Me* "45": Capitol 57698; B-side: "All At Once"	$3	▮V	Capitol 44764
3/12/94	19	20		8 **Love Sneakin' Up On You**...A:14 *Hell To Pay* "45": Capitol 17816	$3	▮V	Capitol 58125
8/6/94	92	7		9 **You**...*Feeling Of Falling* "45": Capitol 18039 (red vinyl)	$3	▮V	Capitol 58195
2/18/95	33	17		10 **You Got It**...A:36 / S:42 *Feeling Of Falling* written by **Roy Orbison**, **Tom Petty** and **Jeff Lynne**; from the movie *Boys On The Side* starring Whoopi Goldberg	$3	▮V	Arista 12795
11/25/95	73	4		11 **Rock Steady**...*Come To Me* (Raitt) [L] **BONNIE RAITT BRYAN ADAMS**	$3	▮	Capitol 58500

RALEIGH, Kevin — '89

Born in Cleveland, Ohio. Rock singer/songwriter/keyboardist. Member of the **Michael Stanley Band** from 1978-86.

DEBUT	PEAK	WKS	Gold	A-side (Chart Hit)...B-side	$	Sym	Label & Number
5/20/89	60	9		**Moonlight On Water**...*The Art Of War*	$3	■	Atlantic 88962

RALKE, Don — '59

Born on 7/13/20 in Battle Creek, Michigan. Died on 1/26/2000 (age 79). Conductor/composer/arranger.

DEBUT	PEAK	WKS	Gold	A-side (Chart Hit)...B-side	$	Sym	Label & Number
4/6/59	69	5		**77 Sunset Strip** *[THE BIG SOUND OF DON RALKE]*...*Sebastian* [I] theme from the TV series starring Efrem Zimbalist Jr., **Roger Smith** and **Edward Byrnes**	$12		Warner 5025

RAMBEAU, Eddie — BUB/AC/LP '65

Born Edward Flurie on 6/30/43 in Hazleton, Pennsylvania. Pop singer/songwriter.

DEBUT	PEAK	WKS	Gold	A-side (Chart Hit)...B-side	$	Sym	Label & Number
5/1/65	35	9		**Concrete And Clay**...*Don't Believe Him*	$10		DynoVoice 204

RAMBLERS, The — '60

Instrumental rock and roll group from Westport, Connecticut: Kip Martin, Michael Burke, Mike Anthony, Chuck Kenney and Vince Rissolo.

DEBUT	PEAK	WKS	Gold	A-side (Chart Hit)...B-side	$	Sym	Label & Number
12/5/60	73	4		**Rambling**...*Devil Train* [I]	$30		Addit 1257

RAMBLERS, The — '64

Pop singer/songwriter/guitar duo from New York: John Herbert and Sal Nastasi.

DEBUT	PEAK	WKS	Gold	A-side (Chart Hit)...B-side	$	Sym	Label & Number
8/8/64	86	4		**Father Sebastian**...*Barbara (I Love You)*	$25		Almont 311

DEBUT	PEAK	WKS	Gold	A-side (Chart Hit)....B-side	$	Sym	Label & Number
				RAM JAM LP **'77**			
				Rock group formed in Long Island, New York: Myke Scavone (vocals), Bill Bartlett (guitar; **The Lemon Pipers**), Howie Blauvelt (bass) and Peter Charles (drums). Blauvelt died of a heart attack on 10/25/93 (age 44).			
6/11/77	18	17		**Black Betty** ....*I Should Have Known*	$5		Epic 50357
				written by legendary black folksinger Hudie Ledbetter (Leadbelly); a remix hit #13 on the Dance charts in 1990			
				RAMONES ROK/LP **'78**			
				Highly influential punk-rock group formed in Brooklyn, New York. All members have taken Ramone as their last name: Joey (Jeffrey Hyman; vocals), Johnny (John Cummings; guitar), Dee Dee (Douglas Colvin; bass) and Tommy (Tom Erdelyi; drums). Group appeared in the 1979 movie *Rock 'n' Roll High School*. Joey Ramone died of cancer on 4/15/2001 (age 49). Dee Dee Ramone died of a drug overdose on 6/5/2002 (age 49). Group inducted into the Rock and Roll Hall of Fame in 2002.			
7/2/77	81	13		1 **Sheena Is A Punk Rocker**....*I Don't Care*	$15	■	Sire 746
				also released on Sire 1006 (with same picture sleeve) in 1977			
12/3/77+	66	14		2 **Rockaway Beach** ....*Locket Love*	$12	■	Sire 1008
4/15/78	86	5		3 **Do You Wanna Dance** ....*Babysitter*	$12	■	Sire 1017
				RAMPAGE R&B/BUB/LP **'97**			
				Born in Brooklyn, New York. Male rapper. Childhood friend of **Busta Rhymes**. Member of the Flipmode Squad.			
7/19/97	34	17		1 **Take It To The Streets** ....S:21 *Wild For The Night* (w/**Busta Rhymes**)	$3	▮	Violator 64171
				RAMPAGE Featuring Billy Lawrence			
				samples "I Hear Music In The Streets" by Unlimited Touch			
6/19/99	57^S	9		2 **Come Get It**....*(instrumental) / For The Thugs* (**Trick Daddy**)	$5	★	TVT 8311
				DJ HURRICANE featuring Flipmode Squad's Rah Digga, Rampage and Lord Have Mercy			
8/31/02	53^S	9		3 **Tonight I'm Gonna Let Go** ....*(5 versions)*	$6	T	Jive 40042
				SYLEENA JOHNSON Featuring Busta Rhymes, Rampage, Sham & Spliff Star			
				samples "Put Your Hands Where My Eyes Can See" by **Busta Rhymes** and "Sweet Green Fields" by **Seals & Crofts**			
				RAMRODS **'61**			
				Instrumental rock and roll group from Connecticut: Vincent Bell Lee (lead guitar; not to be confused with Vincent Bell [Gambella]), his cousin Eugene Moore (since deceased), Richard Lane and his sister Claire.			
1/9/61	30	9		**(Ghost) Riders In The Sky** ....*Zig Zag* [I]	$25		Amy 813
				#1 hit for **Vaughn Monroe** in 1949			
				RAM SQUAD **'00**			
				Rap group from Philadelphia, Pennsylvania: Tommy Hill, Boy Backs, 6-Nine and Suave.			
10/14/00	60^S	2		**Ballers (Up In Here)**....*(2 remixes* w/**Nelly**)	$5	★	Universal 156249
				RAM-Z **'01**			
				Male R&B vocal trio from Cincinnati, Ohio: Zach Adams, Robert Lee and Michael Smith.			
9/9/00	72^S	7		1 **Let Me Be The One**....*(4 versions)*	$4	★	TVT 6473
				RAM-Z (Featuring Drag-On)			
				samples "Rockin' Chair" by **Gwen McCrae**			
4/21/01	45^S	6		2 **Trickin'**....*(3 versions)*	$4	★	TVT 6475
				RANCID ROK/LP **'95**			
				Punk-rock group from Berkeley, California: Tim Armstrong (vocals, guitar), Lars Frederiksen (vocals, guitar), Matt Freeman (bass) and Brett Reed (drums).			
9/9/95	48^A	12		1 **Time Bomb**....		V	album cut ■
				"45": Epitaph 86455; B-side: "The Wars End"/"Blast 'Em"			
12/30/95+	63^A	6		2 **Ruby Soho**....		V	album cut ■
				"45": Epitaph 86464; B-side: "That's Entertainment/Disorder And Disarray"; above 2 from the album *...And Out Come The Wolves* on Epitaph 86444			
				RANDAZZO, Teddy BUB/AC **'60**			
				Born on 5/20/37 in Brooklyn, New York. Member of **The Three Chuckles**. Appeared in vintage rock 'n roll movies *Rock Rock Rock* (1956) and *Mr. Rock & Roll* (1957). Produced and wrote several hits for **Little Anthony & The Imperials** from 1964-68.			
7/21/58	66	2		1 **Little Serenade (Piccolissima Serenata)**....T:66 *Be My Kitten Little Chicken*	$15		Vik 0330
				Henri Rene (orch. and chorus)			
4/18/60	44	9		2 **The Way Of A Clown**....*Cherie*	$12		ABC-Paramount 10088
				Sid Feller (orch.); based on "Vesti La Giubba" from the opera *I Pagliacci*			
1/26/63	51	8		3 **Big Wide World** ....*Be Sure My Love*	$12		Colpix 662
				RAN-DELLS, The **'63**			
				Rock and roll trio from Villas, New Jersey: brothers Steve and Robert Rappaport, with cousin John Spirt (**Sidekicks**).			
8/3/63	16	13		**Martian Hop** ....*Forgive Me Darling (I Have Lied)* [N]	$20	■	Chairman 4403
				RANDOLPH, Boots AC/BUB/LP **'63**			
				Born Homer Randolph on 6/3/27 in Paducah, Kentucky. Session saxophonist.			
2/23/63	35	9		1 **Yakety Sax** ....*I Really Don't Want To Know* [I]	$10	□	Monument 804
				inspired by the sax solo by **King Curtis** in **The Coasters**' 1958 #1 hit "Yakety Yak"; original version released in 1958 as by Randy Randolph on RCA 7395 ($12); promo text sleeve states "Dance 'The Lorenzo Stomp' To Yakety Sax"			
4/4/64	77	6		2 **Hey, Mr. Sax Man** ....*Baby, Go To Sleep*	$8		Monument 835
12/24/66+	93	3		3 **The Shadow Of Your Smile** ....*I'll Just Walk Away*	$7		Monument 976
				from the movie *The Sandpiper* starring Elizabeth Taylor and **Richard Burton**			
7/8/67	93	1		4 **Temptation**....*You've Lost That Lovin' Feelin'* [I]	$7		Monument 1009
				#3 hit for **Bing Crosby** in 1934			
				RANDY & THE RAINBOWS BUB **'63**			
				White doo-wop group from Queens, New York: Dominick "Randy" Safuto (lead) and brother Frank Safuto, brothers Mike and Sal Zero, and Ken Arcipowski. Originally called Jr. And The Counts.			
6/15/63	10	17		1 **Denise**....*Come Back*	$20		Rust 5059
12/14/63	97	2		2 **Why Do Kids Grow Up**....*She's My Angel*	$15		Rust 5073
				RANKIN, Billy — see NAZARETH			

DEBUT	PEAK	WKS	Gold	A-side (Chart Hit).....B-side	$	Sym	Label & Number

RANKS, Shabba — R&B/LP '92

Born Rawlston Gordon on 1/17/66 in Sturgetown, Jamaica. Male reggae singer.

DEBUT	PEAK	WKS	Gold	A-side (Chart Hit).....B-side	$	Sym	Label & Number
10/26/91	37	15		1 **Housecall (Your Body Can't Lie To Me)** .....S:32 / A:39 *(Ragga mix)* **SHABBA RANKS (Featuring Maxi Priest)**	$4	▮	Epic 73928
6/13/92	40	19		2 **Mr. Loverman** .....S:23 / A:55 *(remix)* Chevelle Franklin (female vocal); from the movie *Deep Cover* starring Larry Fishburne	$4	▮	Epic 74257
10/24/92+	33	19	●	3 **Slow And Sexy** S:14 / A:63 *Ting-A-Ling* (Ranks) **SHABBA RANKS (featuring Johnny Gill)**	$3	▮	Epic 74741
2/19/94	84	2		4 **Family Affair** .....S:51 *(dub mix)* **SHABBA RANKS featuring Patra and Terri & Monica** from the movie *Addams Family Values* starring Raul Julia and Anjelica Huston	$4	▮	Atlas 855232
3/11/95	81	9		5 **Let's Get It On** .....S:58 *(album version) / Original Woman*	$3	▮V	Epic 77833

RAPINATION and KYM MAZELLE — '93

Rapination is the Rapino Brothers, two Italian producers. Mazelle is a London-based dance singer from Gary, Indiana (childhood neighbor of **The Jacksons**). Studied opera at Chicago's Mundelein College of Music.

DEBUT	PEAK	WKS	Gold	A-side (Chart Hit).....B-side	$	Sym	Label & Number
3/20/93	97	4		**Love Me The Right Way** .....A:50 *(12" mix)*	$4	▮	Logic/RCA 62492

RAPPIN' 4-TAY — R&B/BUB/LP '94

Born Anthony Forté in 1969 in San Francisco, California. Male rapper.

DEBUT	PEAK	WKS	Gold	A-side (Chart Hit).....B-side	$	Sym	Label & Number
9/24/94	36	21		1 **Playaz Club** .....S:26 / A:49 *(album version)*	$3	▮	Chrysalis/EMI 58267
3/25/95	39	16		2 **I'll Be Around** .....S:26 / A:63 *Playaz Club (remix)* **RAPPIN' 4-TAY Featuring The Spinners** Rappin' 4-Tay raps new verse over the **Spinners**' 1972 hit, with its original music and chorus	$3	▮	Chrysalis/EMI 58331
3/2/96	73	11		3 **Ain't No Playa Like...** .....S:58 *(remix)* Passion (female vocal) and Lil' Fly (rap); rap version of the **Four Tops** 1973 hit "Ain't No Woman (Like The One I've Got)"; "45": Chrysalis/EMI 19103; B-side: "Off Parole"	$3	▮V	Chrysalis/EMI 58528
5/8/99	90	16		4 **Players Holiday** .....S:37 *(2 versions)* **T.W.D.Y. featuring Too Short, Ant Banks, Rappin 4-Tay, Captain Save Em, Mac Mall** samples "Lovely Day" by **Bill Withers**	$4	★	Thump Street 2265

RARE EARTH — BUB/R&B/LP '70

Rock group from Detroit, Michigan: Pete Rivera (vocals, drums), Rod Richards (guitar), Kenny James (keyboards), Gil Bridges (sax), Ed Guzman (percussion) and John Persh (bass). In 1971, Ray Monette replaced Richards and Mark Olson replaced James. Mike Urso replaced Persh in 1972. Persh died of a staph virus in January 1981 (age 38). Olson died of alcohol-related complications in 1982. Guzman died on 7/29/93 (age 49). One of the first white acts signed to a Motown label.

DEBUT	PEAK	WKS	Gold	A-side (Chart Hit).....B-side	$	Sym	Label & Number
3/14/70	4	20	●	1 **Get Ready** *Magic Key*	$6		Rare Earth 5012
8/1/70	7	14		2 **(I Know) I'm Losing You** .....*When Joanie Smiles*	$6		Rare Earth 5017
12/12/70+	17	11		3 **Born To Wander** .....*Here Comes The Night*	$6		Rare Earth 5021
7/17/71	7	13		4 **I Just Want To Celebrate** .....*The Seed*	$6	■	Rare Earth 5031
11/27/71+	19	10		5 **Hey Big Brother** .....*Under God's Light*	$6		Rare Earth 5038
4/8/72	61	5		6 **What'd I Say** .....*Nice To Be With You*	$6		Rare Earth 5043
11/4/72	67	8		7 **Good Time Sally** .....*Love Shines Down*	$6		Rare Earth 5048
1/27/73	93	3		8 **We're Gonna Have A Good Time** .....*Would You Like To Come Along*	$6		Rare Earth 5052
4/29/78	39	11		9 **Warm Ride** .....*Would You Like To Come Along* written by the **Bee Gees**	$5		Prodigal 0640

RASCAL FLATTS — C&W/LP '02

Country vocal trio formed in Columbus, Ohio: Jay DeMarcus, Gary LeVox and Joe Don Rooney.

DEBUT	PEAK	WKS	Gold	A-side (Chart Hit).....B-side	$	Sym	Label & Number
5/6/00	38	20		1 **Prayin' For Daylight** .....A:33 / S:42 *Long Slow Beautiful Dance* (C&W #73)	$4	★	Lyric Street 164039
12/23/00+	56	14		2 **This Everyday Love** A:52			album cut
6/30/01	60	12		3 **While You Loved Me** A:53			album cut
2/2/02	41	19		4 **I'm Movin' On** .....A:37 above 4 from the album *Rascal Flatts* on Lyric Street 65011			album cut
10/5/02	23	20		5 **These Days** CW[3] A:22 from the album *Melt* on Lyric Street 65031			album cut

RASCALS, The ★164★ — BUB/LP '67

"Blue-eyed soul" pop-rock group formed in New York: **Felix Cavaliere** (vocals, organ; born on 11/29/44) (see #19 below), Gene Cornish (vocals, guitar; born on 5/14/45), Eddie Brigati (vocals, percussion; born on 10/22/46) and Dino Danelli (drums; born on 7/23/45). All except Danelli had been in **Joey Dee's Starliters**. Brigati and Cornish left in 1971; replaced by Robert Popwell (bass), Buzz Feiten (guitar; **Larsen-Feiten Band**) and Ann Sutton (vocals). Group disbanded in 1972. Cavaliere, Cornish and Danelli reunited in June 1988. Original group inducted into the Rock and Roll Hall of Fame in 1997. Also see **Bulldog** and **Fotomaker**.

1)People Got To Be Free 2)Groovin' 3)Good Lovin'

DEBUT	PEAK	WKS	Gold	A-side (Chart Hit).....B-side	$	Sym	Label & Number
				THE YOUNG RASCALS:			
12/25/65+	52	9		1 **I Ain't Gonna Eat Out My Heart Anymore** .....*Slow Down*	$15		Atlantic 2312
3/12/66	❶[1]	14		2 **Good Lovin'** .....*Mustang Sally*	$12		Atlantic 2321
6/18/66	20	7		3 **You Better Run** .....*Love Is A Beautiful Thing*	$12	■	Atlantic 2338
9/24/66	43	7		4 **Come On Up** .....*What Is The Reason*	$12		Atlantic 2353
1/28/67	16	14		5 **I've Been Lonely Too Long** .....*If You Knew*	$10	■	Atlantic 2377
4/22/67	❶[4]	13	●	6 **Groovin'** .....*Sueno*	$10	■	Atlantic 2401
7/15/67	10	9		7 **A Girl Like You** .....*It's Love*	$8	■	Atlantic 2424
9/9/67	4	11		8 **How Can I Be Sure** .....*I'm So Happy Now*	$8		Atlantic 2438
12/9/67+	20	7		9 **It's Wonderful** .....*Of Course*	$8		Atlantic 2463
				THE RASCALS:			
4/13/68	3	13	●	10 **A Beautiful Morning** .....*Rainy Day*	$8	■	Atlantic 2493
7/20/68	❶[5]	14	●	11 **People Got To Be Free** *My World*	$8	■	Atlantic 2537
12/7/68+	24	8		12 **A Ray Of Hope** .....*Any Dance'll Do!*	$8	■	Atlantic 2584
2/8/69	39	6		13 **Heaven** .....*Baby I'm Blue*	$8		Atlantic 2599

DEBUT	PEAK	WKS	Gold	A-side (Chart Hit)......B-side	$	Sym	Label & Number
				RASCALS, The — Cont'd			
5/24/69	27	8		14 **See** ......*Away Away*	$8	■	Atlantic 2634
9/6/69	26	8		15 **Carry Me Back** ......*Real Thing*	$8	■	Atlantic 2664
1/3/70	51	7		16 **Hold On** ......*I Believe*	$7	■	Atlantic 2695
7/25/70	58	6		17 **Glory Glory** ......*You Don't Know* **The Sweet Inspirations** (backing vocals)	$7	■	Atlantic 2743
6/26/71	95	4		18 **Love Me** ......*Happy Song*	$6		Columbia 45400
3/1/80	36	11		19 **Only A Lonely Heart Sees** ......*You Turned Me Around* **FELIX CAVALIERE**	$5		Epic 50829
				RASHEEDA R&B **'02** Born in Atlanta, Georgia. Female rapper.			
8/3/02	43^S	1		**Lil Buddy** ......*(album version) / (3 album snippets) / Her (w/Kilo)*	$6	★	Universal 015143
				RASPBERRIES LP **'72** Pop-rock group formed in Mentor, Ohio: **Eric Carmen** (vocals, guitar), Wally Bryson (guitar), David Smalley (bass) and Jim Bonfanti (drums). Smalley and Bonfanti replaced by Scott McCarl and Michael McBride in 1974. Carmen went solo in 1975. Also see **The Choir** and **Fotomaker**.			
5/13/72	86	2		1 **Don't Want To Say Goodbye** ......*Rock & Roll Mama*	$8	■	Capitol 3280
7/1/72	5	18	●	2 **Go All The Way** *With You In My Life*	$7		Capitol 3348
11/25/72+	16	11		3 **I Wanna Be With You** ......*Goin' Nowhere Tonight*	$7		Capitol 3473
3/24/73	35	16		4 **Let's Pretend** ......*Every Way I Can* picture sleeve features a contest to win a customized Volkswagen	$7	■	Capitol 3546
9/1/73	69	7		5 **Tonight** ......*Hard To Get Over A Heartbreak*	$6		Capitol 3610
12/8/73	94	3		6 **I'm A Rocker** ......*Money Down*	$6		Capitol 3765
9/14/74	18	12		7 **Overnight Sensation (Hit Record)** ......*Hands On You* all of above written by **Eric Carmen** and produced by Jimmy Ienner	$6		Capitol 3946
				RATIONALS, The **'66** Garage-rock band from Ann Arbor, Michigan: Scott Morgan (vocals, guitar), Steve Correl (guitar), Terry Trabandt (bass) and Bill Figg (drums).			
11/12/66	92	3		**Respect** ......*Feelin' Lost* first released on A-Square 104 in 1966 ($30)	$15		Cameo 437
				RATT ROK/LP **'84** Hard-rock group formed in Los Angeles, California: Stephen Pearcy (vocals), Warren DeMartini and Robbin Crosby (guitars), Juan Croucier (bass) and Bobby Blotzer (drums). Crosby died of AIDS on 6/6/2002 (age 42).			
6/16/84	12	18		1 **Round And Round** *The Morning After*	$4	■	Atlantic 89693
10/6/84	87	3		2 **Wanted Man** ......*She Wants Money*	$4	■	Atlantic 89618
7/6/85	40	11		3 **Lay It Down** ......*Got Me On The Line*	$3	■	Atlantic 89546
10/12/85	89	2		4 **You're In Love** ......*Between The Eyes*	$3		Atlantic 89502
2/21/87	59	9		5 **Dance** ......*Take A Chance*	$3	■	Atlantic 89354
1/7/89	75	7		6 **Way Cool Jr.** ......*Chain Reaction*	$3	■	Atlantic 88985
				RATTLES, The **'70** Rock group from Germany: Edna Bejarano (vocals), Frank Mille (guitar), Zappo Lüngen (bass) and Herbert Bornhold (drums).			
6/27/70	79	5		**The Witch** ......*Geraldine* an earlier version was recorded in 1968 by lineup of Lüngen and 3 other members	$8		Probe/ABC 480
				RAUHOFER, Peter — see PET SHOP BOYS			
				RAVAN, Genya — see TEN WHEEL DRIVE			
				RAVEN-SYMONÉ **'93** Born Raven-Symoné Pearman on 12/10/85 in Los Angeles, California. Singer/actress (7 years old in 1993). Played "Olivia Kendall" on TV's *The Cosby Show*.			
8/7/93	68	8		**That's What Little Girls Are Made Of** ......S:64 / A:70 *(album dub version)* **Missy "Misdemeanor" Elliott** (guest rapper)	$4	▮	MCA 54625
				RAWLO BOYS, The **'02** Rap group from Atlanta, Georgia.			
12/1/01+	21^S	16		**Ain't Nobody (We Got It Locked!)** ......*(2 versions) / I Got A Dollar* **THE RAWLO BOYS featuring T.O.R.O. and Lil' Smoke** CD single issued with 2 different picture inserts and different B-sides ("We Don't Give A ****" w/**Pastor Troy**)	$5	★	House of Fire 91285
	★354★			**RAWLS, Lou** R&B/BUB/AC/LP **'76** Born on 12/1/35 in Chicago, Illinois. R&B singer known for his very deep voice. Hosted own TV variety show with The Golddiggers in 1969. Appeared in the movies *Angel Angel*, *Down We Go* and *Believe In Me*. Voice of many Budweiser beer ads and featured singer in the *Garfield* TV specials. Also see **Philadelphia International All Stars**. *1)You'll Never Find Another Love Like Mine 2)Love Is A Hurtin' Thing 3)A Natural Man*			
6/5/65	83	1		1 **Three O'Clock In The Morning** ......*Nothing Really Feels The Same* #1 hit for Paul Whiteman in 1922	$10		Capitol 5424
9/10/66	13	14		2 **Love Is A Hurtin' Thing** ......RB[1] *Memory Lane*	$10		Capitol 5709
11/26/66+	55	8		3 **You Can Bring Me All Your Heartaches** ......*A Woman Who's A Woman*	$10		Capitol 5790
1/28/67	92	3		4 **Trouble Down Here Below** ......*The Life That I Lead*	$10	■	Capitol 5824
3/25/67	29	11		5 **Dead End Street Monologue/Dead End Street** ......*Yes It Hurts - Doesn't It* the first 1:27 of this tune is a monologue by Rawls	$10		Capitol 5869
7/1/67	45	7		6 **Show Business** ......*When Love Goes Wrong*	$10		Capitol 5941
12/2/67	2^2X	7		7 **Little Drummer Boy** ......*A Child With A Toy* [X] X: 2/'67; 5/'69	$10		Capitol 2026
8/31/68	69	5		8 **Down Here On The Ground** ......*I'm Satisfied (The Duffy Theme)* from the movie *Cool Hand Luke* starring Paul Newman	$8		Capitol 2252
7/19/69	18	14		9 **Your Good Thing (Is About To End)** ......*Season Of The Witch*	$8		Capitol 2550
11/1/69	63	7		10 **I Can't Make It Alone** ......*Make The World Go Away*	$8		Capitol 2668
3/14/70	95	3		11 **You've Made Me So Very Happy** ......*Let's Burn Down The Cornfield*	$8		Capitol 2734

DEBUT	PEAK	WKS	Gold	A-side (Chart Hit)...B-side	$	Sym	Label & Number
				RAWLS, Lou — Cont'd			
8/1/70	**96**	5		12 **Bring It On Home** ... *Can You Dig It/Take Me For What I Am*	$8		Capitol 2856
				also see **Sam Cooke**'s 1962 version featuring backing vocals by Rawls; all of above produced by David Axelrod			
8/28/71	**17**	18		13 **A Natural Man** ... *You Can't Hold On*	$6		MGM 14262
				also released with "Believe In Me" as the B-side			
6/5/76	**2^2**	21	●	14 **You'll Never Find Another Love Like Mine** RB^2 / AC^1 *Let's Fall In Love All Over Again*	$5		Philadelphia I. 3592
10/16/76	**64**	5		15 **Groovy People** ... *This Song Will Last Forever* (R&B #74)	$5		Philadelphia I. 3604
7/23/77	**66**	7		16 **See You When I Git There** ... *Spring Again*	$5		Philadelphia I. 3623
1/21/78	**24**	17		17 **Lady Love** ... *Not The Staying Kind*	$5		Philadelphia I. 3634
4/26/80	**77**	3		18 **You're My Blessing** ... *Heartaches (Just When You Think You're Loved)*	$5		Philadelphia I. 3750
3/26/83	**65**	6		19 **Wind Beneath My Wings** ... *Midnight Sunshine*	$4		Epic 03758
				RAY, Diane '63			
				Born on 9/1/42 in Gastonia, North Carolina. Pop singer.			
8/3/63	**31**	9		**Please Don't Talk To The Lifeguard** ... *That's All I Want From You*	$15	■	Mercury 72117
				first recorded by **Andrea Carroll** in 1961 on Epic 9450 ($20)			
				RAY, Don LP '78			
				Born in Germany. Disco producer/arranger/composer.			
9/23/78	**44**	16		**Got To Have Loving** ... *My Desire*	$5		Polydor 14489
				RAY, James '62			
				Born James Ray Raymond in 1941 in Washington DC. R&B singer.			
11/20/61+	**22**	14		1 **If You Gotta Make A Fool Of Somebody** ... *It's Been A Drag*	$30		Caprice 110
4/7/62	**41**	10		2 **Itty Bitty Pieces** ... *You Remember The Face*	$25		Caprice 114
				Hutch Davie (orch., above 2)			
				RAY, Jimmy LP '98			
				Born on 10/3/75 in Walthamstow, East London, England. Pop-rock singer.			
2/21/98	**13**	18	●	**Are You Jimmy Ray?** ... S:10 / A:29 *(remix)*	$3	▮	Epic 78816
				RAY, Johnnie MEM/POP/LP '51			
				Born on 1/10/27 in Dallas, Oregon. Died of liver failure on 2/25/90 (age 63). Wore hearing aid since age 14. First recorded for Okeh in 1951. Famous for emotion-packed delivery with R&B influences. Appeared in three movies. His debut single in 1951, "Cry," was #1 for 11 weeks.			
11/12/55	**100**	1		1 **Johnnie's Comin' Home** ... T:100 *Love, Love, Love*	$15		Columbia 40578
				Paul Weston (orch.); the #100 entry on *Billboard's* first *Top 100* chart			
9/1/56	**2^1**	28	●	2 **Just Walking In The Rain** T:2 / J:2 / A:3 / S:3 *In The Candlelight*	$15		Columbia 40729
				first recorded by The Prisonaires in 1953 on Sun 186 ($500)			
1/12/57	**10**	12		3 **You Don't Owe Me A Thing /** S:10 / T:10 / A:10 / J:12			
				written by **Marty Robbins**			
1/26/57	**36**	9		4 **Look Homeward, Angel** ... T:36 / S:flip	$15	■	Columbia 40803
4/20/57	**12**	13		5 **Yes Tonight, Josephine** ... A:12 / T:18 *No Wedding Today*	$15		Columbia 40893
7/22/57	**58**	9		6 **Build Your Love (On A Strong Foundation)** ... T:58 *Street Of Memories*	$15		Columbia 40942
				Ray Conniff (orch. and chorus, above 5)			
9/1/58	**81**	3		7 **Up Until Now** ... H:81 *No Regrets*	$12		Columbia 41213
9/14/59	**75**	6		8 **I'll Never Fall In Love Again** ... *You're All That I Live For*	$10		Columbia 41438
				Richard Maltby (orch.)			
				RAY, Ricardo '68			
				Born Ricardo Maldonado on 2/15/45 in Brooklyn, New York (of Puerto Rican parents). Bandleader; known as the "king of salsa."			
10/5/68	**90**	3		**Nitty Gritty** ... *Ya Ya*	$10		Alegre 4024
				Hutch Davie (orch.)			
				RAY AND BOB '62			
				Pop-rock duo from Los Angeles, California: Ray Swayne and Bob Appleberry.			
6/23/62	**99**	1		**Air Travel** ... *Palms Of Paradise*	$20		Ledo 1151
				RAYBON BROS. C&W '97			
				Country vocal duo from Greenville, Alabama: brothers Tim and Marty Raybon (Shenandoah).			
6/14/97	**22**	17	●	**Butterfly Kisses** ... S:11 *(instrumental)*	$4	▮V	MCA 72016
				RAYBURN, Margie '57			
				Born in 1924 in Madera, California. Died of a heart attack on 6/14/2000 (age 76). Member of **The Sunnysiders**. Married Norman Milkin of The Sunnysiders.			
10/28/57	**9**	19		**I'm Available** ... A:9 / S:15 / T:16 *If You Were*	$15		Liberty 55102
				written by Dave Burgess (**The Champs**)			
				RAYDIO — see PARKER, Ray Jr.			
				RAYE, Collin C&W/BUB/AC/LP '99			
				Born on 8/22/59 in DeQueen, Arkansas. Country singer (charted 33 hits, 1991-01).			
9/16/95	**87**	7		1 **One Boy, One Girl** ... S:49 *I Love Being Wrong*	$4	▮V	Epic 77973
12/27/97+	**65^A**	7		2 **The Gift** ... [X]			album cut
				COLLIN RAYE with Jim Brickman			
				from the album *The Best Of Collin Raye - Direct Hits* on Epic 67893			
11/21/98	**37**	14		3 **Someone You Used To Know** ... A:35 / S:62 *Make Sure You've Got It All*	$4	★	Epic 79011
3/13/99	**37**	20		4 **Anyone Else** A:29			album cut
				above 2 from the album *The Walls Came Down* on Epic 68876			
3/18/00	**43**	20		5 **Couldn't Last A Moment** ... S:34 / A:37 *You Still Take Me There* (C&W #57)	$4	★V	Epic 79353
				RAYE, Susan C&W/LP '71			
				Born on 10/18/44 in Eugene, Oregon. Country singer (charted 29 hits, 1970-86). Regular on TV's *Hee-Haw.*			
4/17/71	**54**	9		**L.A. International Airport** ... *Merry-Go-Round Of Love*	$7		Capitol 3035
				RAY, GOODMAN & BROWN — see MOMENTS, The			

DEBUT	PEAK	WKS	Gold	A-side (Chart Hit)...B-side	$	Sym	Label & Number

RAY J — LP '97

Born Willie Ray Norwood on 1/17/81 in McComb, Mississippi; raised in California. Male rapper. Brother of **Brandy**. Acted on TV's *The Sinbad Show* and in the movie *Steel.*

DEBUT	PEAK	WKS	Gold	A-side (Chart Hit)...B-side	$	Sym	Label & Number
3/8/97	25	20		1 **Let It Go**.....S:15 *Days Of Our Livez* (**Bone thugs-n-harmony** - #39[A]) from the movie *Set It Off* starring Jada Pinkett and **Queen Latifah**	$3	▮	EastWest 64206
7/12/97	83	6		2 **Everything You Want**.....S:56 *(3 album snippets)* **Kenny Lattimore** (backing vocal)	$3	▮	EastWest 64209
5/26/01	30	17		3 **Wait A Minute**.....A:27 / S:55 *(3 versions)* **RAY-J Featuring Lil' Kim** "45": Atlantic 85077; B-side: "Keep Your Head Up"	$6	T[V]	Atlantic 85066
11/24/01	71[S]	1		4 **Formal Invite**.....*(5 remixes)* **RAY J (Featuring Brandy, Teddy Riley & Shorty Mack)**	$6	T	Atlantic 85182

RAYS, The — '57

Black doo-wop group formed in Harlem, New York: Harold Miller (lead), Walter Ford and David Jones (tenors) and Harry James (baritone). First recorded for Chess in 1955.

DEBUT	PEAK	WKS	Gold	A-side (Chart Hit)...B-side	$	Sym	Label & Number
10/14/57	3	20	●	1 **Silhouettes** / T:3 / S:4 / A:5 first released on XYZ 102 in 1957 ($75)			
1/20/58		4		2 **Daddy Cool**.....S:flip	$30		Cameo 117
1/25/60	95	2		3 **Mediterranean Moon**.....*It's A Cryin' Shame*	$40		XYZ 605
8/14/61	49	8		4 **Magic Moon (Clair De Lune)**.....*Louie Hoo Hoo* adaptation of Debussy's *Suite Bergamesque*; **Frank Slay** (orch., all of above)	$40		XYZ 607

RAYVON — '01

Born Bruce Brewster in Barbados. Male R&B-reggae singer/songwriter.

DEBUT	PEAK	WKS	Gold	A-side (Chart Hit)...B-side	$	Sym	Label & Number
8/6/94	94	4		1 **No Guns, No Murder**.....*(instrumental)*	$5	▮	V.P. 7399
7/29/95	flip	19		2 **Summer Time**.....S:flip *Gal Yu A Pepper* **SHAGGY (featuring Rayvon)** #3 hit for **Mungo Jerry** in 1970 as "In The Summertime"; "45": Virgin 18586	$3	▮[V]	Virgin 38482
12/30/00+	❶[1]	28		3 **Angel** A:❶[5] / S:10 *(3 versions)* **SHAGGY Featuring Rayvon** samples "The Joker" by **Steve Miller** and "Angel Of The Morning" by **Merrilee Rush**; "45": MCA 155820; B-side: "Chica Bonita"	$8	★*[V]	MCA 155811
12/22/01+	41[S]	6		4 **2-Way**.....*(instrumental)* **RAYVON featuring Shaggy, Ricardo "Rik Rok" Ducent, Brian & Tony Gold**	$5	★	Big Yard/MCA 155891
6/1/02	34[S]	12		5 **My Bad**.....*2-Way*	$5	★	Big Yard/MCA 155905

RAZOR'S EDGE, The — '66

Pop-rock group from West Palm Beach, Florida: Bill Ande (guitar), Tom Condra (rhythm guitar), Vic Gray (bass) and Dave Allen Hieronymus (drums). All shared vocals. Took name from the 1946 movie. Hit "Bubbling Under" chart in 1963 as The Ardells. Recorded as The American Beetles in 1964.

DEBUT	PEAK	WKS	Gold	A-side (Chart Hit)...B-side	$	Sym	Label & Number
7/30/66	77	7		**Let's Call It A Day Girl**.....*Avril (April)*	$15		Pow! 101

RAZZY — see BAILEY, Razzy

RCR — BUB/R&B '80

Pop vocal trio: sisters Donna and Sandra Rhodes and Charles Chalmers. Backed **Frank Sinatra** on his 1975 hit "Anytime." Also see **Candi Staton**.

DEBUT	PEAK	WKS	Gold	A-side (Chart Hit)...B-side	$	Sym	Label & Number
4/5/80	94	2		**Scandal**.....*Moments Of Magic*	$4		Radio 711

REA, Chris — ROK/AC/LP '78

Born on 3/4/51 in Middlesborough, Cleveland, England. Soft-rock singer/songwriter.

DEBUT	PEAK	WKS	Gold	A-side (Chart Hit)...B-side	$	Sym	Label & Number
7/8/78	12	15		1 **Fool (If You Think It's Over)** AC[3] *Midnight Love*	$4	■	United Artists 1198
11/11/78	71	4		2 **Whatever Happened To Benny Santini?**.....*Three Angels*	$4		United Artists 1252
4/7/79	44	8		3 **Diamonds**.....*Cleveland Calling*	$4		United Artists 1285
4/10/82	88	3		4 **Loving You**.....*Let Me Be The One*	$4		Columbia 02727
8/29/87	81	5		5 **Let's Dance**.....*I Don't Care Anymore*	$3	■	Motown 1900
3/25/89	73	7		6 **Working On It**.....AR[1] *Loving You Again*	$3	■	Geffen 27535

READ, John Dawson — '75

Born in England. Adult Contemporary singer/songwriter/guitarist.

DEBUT	PEAK	WKS	Gold	A-side (Chart Hit)...B-side	$	Sym	Label & Number
8/30/75	72	4		**A Friend Of Mine Is Going Blind**.....*Superficial Things*	$5		Chrysalis 2105

READY FOR THE WORLD — R&B/BUB/LP '85

R&B-funk-dance group from Flint, Michigan: Melvin Riley (vocals), Gordon Strozier (guitar), Gregory Potts (keyboards), Willie Triplett (percussion), John Eaton (bass) and Gerald Valentine (drums).

DEBUT	PEAK	WKS	Gold	A-side (Chart Hit)...B-side	$	Sym	Label & Number
8/3/85	❶[1]	21		1 **Oh Sheila**.....RB[2] S:❶[1] / A:3 *I'm The One Who Loves You*	$3	■	MCA 52636
12/7/85+	21	18		2 **Digital Display**.....S:14 *I'm The One Who Loves You*	$3	■	MCA 52734
11/29/86+	9	19		3 **Love You Down**.....RB[2] S:9 / A:12 *Human Toy*	$3	■	MCA 52947

REALITY — '93

Dance duo from Chicago, Illinois: Essential Rudolph and Bad Boy Bill.

DEBUT	PEAK	WKS	Gold	A-side (Chart Hit)...B-side	$	Sym	Label & Number
10/30/93	72	10		**Yolanda**.....A:45 *(5 remixes)*	$6		Strictly Rhythm 12172

REAL LIFE — ROK/LP '84

Pop-rock group from Melbourne, Australia: David Sterry (vocals, guitar), Richard Zatorski (keyboards), Allan Johnson (bass) and Danny Simcic (drums).

DEBUT	PEAK	WKS	Gold	A-side (Chart Hit)...B-side	$	Sym	Label & Number
11/12/83+	29	19		1 **Send Me An Angel**.....*Like A Gun* also see #3 below	$4		Curb/MCA 52287
3/24/84	40	11		2 **Catch Me I'm Falling**.....*Exploding Bullets*	$4	■	Curb/MCA 52362
5/13/89	26	16		3 **Send Me An Angel '89**.....A:22 / S:28 *Always* [R] new recording of #1 above	$3		Curb/MCA 10531

REAL McCOY — BUB/LP '95

Techno-dance trio: German rapper/songwriter Olaf "O-Jay" Jeglitza with American singers Vanessa Mason and Lisa Cork.

DEBUT	PEAK	WKS	Gold	A-side (Chart Hit)...B-side	$	Sym	Label & Number
8/27/94	3	45	▲	1 **Another Night** S:2 / A:2 *(house mix)*	$3	▮	Arista 12724
3/11/95	3	20	●	2 **Run Away**.....A:4 / S:6 *I Want You*	$3	▮[V]	Arista 12808
6/10/95	19	20		3 **Come And Get Your Love**.....S:21 / A:29 *Megablast*	$3	▮[V]	Arista 12834

DEBUT	PEAK	WKS	Gold	A-side (Chart Hit)...B-side	$	Sym	Label & Number

REAL McCOY — Cont'd

DEBUT	PEAK	WKS	Gold	A-side (Chart Hit)...B-side	$	Sym	Label & Number
10/21/95	52	19		4 **Automatic Lover (Call For Love)** ...S:64 / A:67 *(house mix)* all of above from the album *Another Night*	$3	▮	Arista 12876
3/29/97	27	20		5 **One More Time** ...A:25 / S:29 *Love Is A Stranger*	$3	▮	Arista 13328

REAL THING, The '76

R&B vocal group from Liverpool, England: Chris Amoo, Ray Lake, Dave Smith and Eddie Amoo. Group appeared in the movie *The Stud.*

DEBUT	PEAK	WKS	Gold	A-side (Chart Hit)...B-side	$	Sym	Label & Number
7/17/76	64	8		**You To Me Are Everything** ...*Keep An Eye (On Your Best Friend)*	$5		United Artists 833

REBEKAH '98

Born Rebecca Johnson in 1973 in Cleveland, Ohio. R&B singer/songwriter.

DEBUT	PEAK	WKS	Gold	A-side (Chart Hit)...B-side	$	Sym	Label & Number
6/20/98	80	6		**Sin So Well** ...*Little Black Girl*	$3	▮	Elektra 64153

REBEL PEBBLES, The '91

Female pop group from Los Angeles, California: Rachel Murray (vocals), Karen Blankfeld (guitar), Robin Fox (bass) and Cheryl Bullock (drums).

DEBUT	PEAK	WKS	Gold	A-side (Chart Hit)...B-side	$	Sym	Label & Number
4/20/91	42	10		**Dream Lover** ...S:39 *Elephant's Revenge*	$3	▮	I.R.S. 13821

REBELS, The LP '63

Buffalo DJ Tom Shannon and producer Phil Todaro (Shan-Todd label) produced the **Hot-Toddys featuring Bill Pennell** on sax, a group from Port Colborne, Canada. In 1960 they brought in the Buffalo group, **The Rebels**, to record Shannon's theme song, "Wild Weekend." After the song's success in 1963, they re-released the original Hot-Toddys' single as by the **Rockin' Rebels**.

DEBUT	PEAK	WKS	Gold	A-side (Chart Hit)...B-side	$	Sym	Label & Number
3/30/59	57	11		1 **Rockin' Crickets** ...*Shakin' And Stompin'* [I] **HOT - TODDYS featuring Bill Pennell** also see #3 below	$40		Shan-Todd 0056
12/29/62+	8	17		2 **Wild Weekend** ...*Wild Weekend Cha-Cha* [I] first released on Mar-Lee 0094 in 1960 ($100); later pressings on Swan 4125 show artist as **Rockin' Rebels**	$30		Swan 4125
4/27/63	87	4		3 **Rockin' Crickets** ***[ROCKIN' REBELS]*** ...*Hully Gully Rock* [I-R] same recording as #1 above	$25		Swan 4140

RECORDS, The LP '79

Rock group from England: Huw Gower (vocals), John Wicks (guitar), Phil Brown (bass) and Will Birch (drums). **Jude Cole** replaced Gower in late 1979, left in 1981.

DEBUT	PEAK	WKS	Gold	A-side (Chart Hit)...B-side	$	Sym	Label & Number
9/29/79	56	6		**Starry Eyes** ...*Paint Her Face*	$5	■	Virgin 67000

REDBONE BUB/LP '74

Native American "swamp-rock" group formed in Los Angeles, California: brothers Lolly (vocals, guitar) and Pat (vocals, bass) Vegas, Anthony Bellamy (guitar) and Peter De Poe (drums). The Vegas brothers had been session musicians and worked the *Shindig* TV show.

DEBUT	PEAK	WKS	Gold	A-side (Chart Hit)...B-side	$	Sym	Label & Number
12/5/70+	45	17		1 **Maggie** ...*New Blue Sermonette* originally charted for 5 weeks (#80); re-entered on 7/10/71	$6		Epic 10670
11/20/71+	21	17		2 **The Witch Queen Of New Orleans** ...*Chant: 13th Hour*	$6		Epic 10749
1/12/74	5	23	●	3 **Come And Get Your Love** ...*Day To Day Life*	$5		Epic 11035

REDBONE, Leon LP '81

Born on 10/29/29 in Brooklyn, New York. White blues singer. Rose to fame in the mid-1970s with appearances on TV's *Saturday Night Live.* Baritone voice of several TV commercials.

DEBUT	PEAK	WKS	Gold	A-side (Chart Hit)...B-side	$	Sym	Label & Number
4/11/81	72	6		**Seduced** ...*(Mama's Got A Baby Named) Te Na Na*	$8		Emerald City 7326

REDD EYEZZ '02

Born James Pierre in Miami, Florida. Male rapper.

DEBUT	PEAK	WKS	Gold	A-side (Chart Hit)...B-side	$	Sym	Label & Number
3/9/02	29S	9		**Put Yo Sets Up** ...*(6 versions)* **REDD EYEZZ featuring Juvenile & Slanted Eyezz**	$8	★*	Z-Bo 2503

REDDING, Gene R&B '74

Born in 1945 in Anderson, Indiana. R&B singer. No relation to Otis Redding.

DEBUT	PEAK	WKS	Gold	A-side (Chart Hit)...B-side	$	Sym	Label & Number
5/4/74	24	16		**This Heart** ...*What Do I Do On Sunday Morning?*	$5		Haven 7000

REDDING, Otis ★168★ R&B/BUB/LP '68

Born on 9/9/41 in Dawson, Georgia. Killed in a plane crash on 12/10/67 (age 26) in Lake Monona in Madison, Wisconsin. Soul singer/songwriter/producer/pianist. First recorded with Johnny Jenkins & The Pinetoppers on Confederate in 1960. Own label, Jotis. Plane crash also killed four members of the **Bar-Kays**. Otis's sons formed **The Reddings**. Inducted into the Rock and Roll Hall of Fame in 1989. Won Grammy's Lifetime Achievement Award in 1999.

1)(Sittin' On) The Dock Of The Bay 2)I've Been Loving You Too Long 3)Papa's Got A Brand New Bag 4)Try A Little Tenderness 5)The Happy Song (Dum-Dum)

DEBUT	PEAK	WKS	Gold	A-side (Chart Hit)...B-side	$	Sym	Label & Number
5/25/63	85	3		1 **These Arms Of Mine** ...*Hey Hey Baby*	$20		Volt 103
11/23/63+	61	11		2 **Pain In My Heart** ...*Something Is Worrying Me*	$20		Volt 112
3/21/64	69	7		3 **Come To Me** ...*Don't Leave Me This Way*	$20		Volt 116
5/23/64	97	1		4 **Security** ...*I Want To Thank You*	$20		Volt 117
10/24/64	70	7		5 **Chained And Bound** ...*Your One And Only Man*	$20		Volt 121
2/20/65	41	9		6 **Mr. Pitiful /**			
1/30/65	74	4		7 **That's How Strong My Love Is** ... #3 & 5-7: from the album *The Great Otis Redding Sings Soul Ballads*	$20		Volt 124
5/15/65	21	11		8 **I've Been Loving You Too Long (To Stop Now)** ...*I'm Depending On You* a "live" version "Bubbled Under" (#110) on 2/6/71 on Atco 6802	$15		Volt 126
9/4/65	35	11		9 **Respect** ...*Ole Man Trouble*	$15		Volt 128
12/4/65	85	5		10 **Just One More Day** ...*I Can't Turn You Loose* (R&B #11)	$15		Volt 130
3/5/66	31	8		11 **Satisfaction** ...*Any Ole Way*	$15		Volt 132
6/4/66	61	7		12 **My Lover's Prayer** ...*Don't Mess With Cupid*	$15		Volt 136
10/1/66	29	8		13 **Fa-Fa-Fa-Fa-Fa (Sad Song)** ...*Good To Me*	$15		Volt 138
12/3/66+	25	10		14 **Try A Little Tenderness** ...*I'm Sick Y'all* #6 hit for Ted Lewis in 1933	$15		Volt 141

DEBUT	PEAK	WKS	Gold	A-side (Chart Hit)...B-side	$	Sym	Label & Number
				REDDING, Otis — Cont'd			
4/8/67	**78**	3		15 **I Love You More Than Words Can Say** ... *Let Me Come On Home*	$15		Volt 146
5/6/67	**26**	9		16 **Tramp** ... *Tell It Like It Is*	$12		Stax 216
				OTIS & CARLA			
5/20/67	**47**	6		17 **Shake** ... *You Don't Miss Your Water* [L]	$12		Volt 149
7/29/67	**60**	4		18 **Glory Of Love** ... *I'm Coming Home*	$12		Volt 152
				#1 hit for **Benny Goodman** in 1936; theme from the 1967 movie *Guess Who's Coming To Dinner*			
8/12/67	**30**	9		19 **Knock On Wood** ... *Let Me Be Good To You*	$12		Stax 228
				OTIS & CARLA			
1/27/68	❶[4]	16	●	20 **(Sittin' On) The Dock Of The Bay** RB[3] *Sweet Lorene*	$12		Volt 157
				recorded on 11/22/67			
2/10/68	**60**	6		21 **Lovey Dovey** ... *New Year's Resolution*	$12		Stax 244
				OTIS & CARLA			
				#2 R&B hit for **The Clovers** in 1954			
4/27/68	**25**	8		22 **The Happy Song (Dum-Dum)** ... *Open The Door*	$10		Volt 163
7/6/68	**36**	5		23 **Amen** /			
7/13/68	**51**	7		24 **Hard To Handle** ...	$10		Atco 6592
9/28/68	**41**	7		25 **I've Got Dreams To Remember** ... *Nobody's Fault But Mine*	$10		Atco 6612
				above 4 from the album *The Immortal Otis Redding*			
11/30/68+	**21**	9		26 **Papa's Got A Brand New Bag** ... *Direct Me* [L]	$10		Atco 6636
				recorded at the Whisky A Go-Go			
12/28/68	**9**[X]	1		27 **Merry Christmas, Baby** / [X]			
12/21/68	**12**[X]	2		28 **White Christmas** ... [X]	$12		Atco 6631
3/1/69	**48**	6		29 **A Lover's Question** ... *You Made A Man Out Of Me*	$10		Atco 6654
5/24/69	**72**	5		30 **Love Man** ... *Can't Turn You Loose*	$10		Atco 6677

REDDINGS, The

R&B/LP **'82**

R&B trio formed in Atlanta, Georgia: **Otis Redding**'s sons Dexter (vocals, bass) and Otis III (guitar), with cousin Mark Locket (vocals, drums, keyboards).

DEBUT	PEAK	WKS	Gold	A-side (Chart Hit)...B-side	$	Sym	Label & Number
11/15/80	**89**	13		1 **Remote Control** ... *The Awakening*	$4		Believe 5600
6/12/82	**55**	9		2 **(Sittin' On) The Dock Of The Bay** ... *Time Won't Wait*	$4		Believe 02836

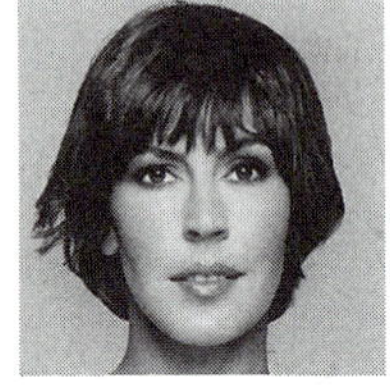

REDDY, Helen ★140★

AC/C&W/LP **'73**

Born on 10/25/41 in Melbourne, Australia. Adult Contemporary singer. Family was in show business; Helen made stage debut at age four. Own TV series in the early 1960s. Migrated to U.S. in 1966. Acted in the movies *Airport 1975*, *Pete's Dragon* and *Sgt. Pepper's Lonely Hearts Club Band*.

1)I Am Woman 2)Delta Dawn 3)Angie Baby 4)Leave Me Alone (Ruby Red Dress) 5)Ain't No Way To Treat A Lady

DEBUT	PEAK	WKS	Gold	A-side (Chart Hit)...B-side	$	Sym	Label & Number
2/20/71	**13**	20		1 **I Don't Know How To Love Him** ... *I Believe In Music*	$6		Capitol 3027
				from the rock opera *Jesus Christ Superstar*			
8/7/71	**51**	9		2 **Crazy Love** ... *Best Friend*	$6		Capitol 3138
				written by **Van Morrison**			
12/4/71+	**62**	8		3 **No Sad Song** ... *More Than You Could Take*	$6		Capitol 3231
6/24/72	❶[1]	22	●	4 **I Am Woman** *More Than You Could Take*	$5		Capitol 3350
				originally charted for 3 weeks (#97); re-entered on 9/16/72; from the movie *Stand Up And Be Counted* starring Stella Stevens; a different version was included on Reddy's 1971 album *I Don't Know How To Love Him*			
2/3/73	**12**	17		5 **Peaceful** ... *What Would They Say*	$5		Capitol 3527
6/23/73	❶[1]	20	●	6 **Delta Dawn** ... AC[2] *If We Could Still Be Friends*	$5		Capitol 3645
11/3/73	**3**	16	●	7 **Leave Me Alone (Ruby Red Dress)** ... AC[4] *The Old Fashioned Way*	$5		Capitol 3768
3/9/74	**15**	13		8 **Keep On Singing** ... AC[2] *You're My Home*	$5		Capitol 3845
6/15/74	**9**	20		9 **You And Me Against The World** ... AC[1] *Love Song For Jeffrey*	$5		Capitol 3897
				includes a brief spoken dialogue with Reddy's daughter, Tracy			
10/19/74	❶[1]	17	●	10 **Angie Baby** ... AC[1] *I Think I'll Write A Song*	$5		Capitol 3972
2/8/75	**22**	9		11 **Emotion** ... AC[1] *I've Been Wanting You So Long*	$5		Capitol 4021
7/5/75	**35**	6		12 **Bluebird** ... *You Don't Need A Reason*	$5		Capitol 4108
				written by **Leon Russell**			
8/9/75	**8**	16		13 **Ain't No Way To Treat A Lady** ... AC[1] *Long Time Looking*	$5		Capitol 4128
12/6/75+	**19**	14		14 **Somewhere In The Night** ... *Ten To Eight*	$5		Capitol 4192
8/7/76	**29**	9		15 **I Can't Hear You No More** / AC[1]			
				charted by **Betty Everett** in 1964 as "I Can't Hear You"			
8/28/76		6		16 **Music Is My Life** ...	$5		Capitol 4312
4/30/77	**18**	22		17 **You're My World** ... *Thank You*	$5		Capitol 4418
10/8/77	**57**	7		18 **The Happy Girls** ... *Laissez Les Bontemps Rouler* (C&W #98)	$5		Capitol 4487
7/15/78	**73**	5		19 **Ready Or Not** ... *If I Ever Had To Say Goodbye To You*	$5		Capitol 4582
5/19/79	**60**	10		20 **Make Love To Me** ... *More Than You Could Take*	$5		Capitol 4712
5/23/81	**88**	3		21 **I Can't Say Goodbye To You** ... *Let's Just Stay Home Tonight*	$4		MCA 51106

REDEYE

'71

Rock group formed in Los Angeles, California: Douglas "Red" Mark (vocals), Dave Hodgkins (guitar), Bill Kirkham (bass) and Bob Bereman (drums). Mark was a member of **The Sunshine Company**.

DEBUT	PEAK	WKS	Gold	A-side (Chart Hit)...B-side	$	Sym	Label & Number
11/7/70+	**27**	14		1 **Games** ... *Collections Of Yesterday And Now*	$6		Pentagram 204
4/24/71	**78**	6		2 **Red Eye Blues** ... *The Making Of A Hero*	$6		Pentagram 206

REDHEAD KINGPIN AND THE FBI

R&B/LP **'92**

Born David Guppy in Englewood, New Jersey. Black rap-dance artist. Members of backing outfit, The FBI, included D.J. Wildstyle, Bo Roc, Lt. Squeak, Buzz and Poochie.

DEBUT	PEAK	WKS	Gold	A-side (Chart Hit)...B-side	$	Sym	Label & Number
3/28/92	**52**	15		**3-2-1 Pump** ... A:45 / S:47 *(remix) / Harlem Brown*	$3	▌	Virgin 98592
				samples "Let's Groove" by **Earth, Wind & Fire**			

DEBUT	PEAK	WKS	Gold	A-side (Chart Hit)...B-side	$	Sym	Label & Number

★430★ RED HOT CHILI PEPPERS

ROK/BUB/LP **'92**

Rock group formed in Los Angeles, California: Anthony Kiedis (vocals; born on 11/1/62), Hillel Slovak (guitar; born on 4/13/62), Michael "Flea" Balzary (bass; born on 10/16/62) and Jack Irons (drums; born on 7/18/62). Slovak died of a drug overdose on 6/25/88 (age 26); replaced by John Frusciante (born on 3/5/70. Irons left in 1988 and later joined Eleven, then **Pearl Jam**; replaced by Chad Smith (born on 10/25/62). Frusciante left in May 1992; replaced by Zander Schloss (Thelonious Monster, **The Magnificent Bastards**), then by Arik Marshall, then by Jesse Tobias and finally by Dave Navarro (Jane's Addiction) in September 1993. Frusciante returned in 1998, replacing Navarro. Kiedis appeared in the movie *Point Break*. Flea and Kiedes appeared in the movie *The Chase*.

1)Under The Bridge 2)Scar Tissue 3)Otherside

DEBUT	PEAK	WKS	Gold	A-side (Chart Hit)...B-side	$	Sym	Label & Number
12/21/91+	73	15		1 **Give It Away**....MR^2 S:48 *Search And Destroy* charted for 6 weeks (#76); re-entered on 7/25/92; "45": Warner 15993; B-side: "Under The Bridge"	$4	▮V	Warner 19147
4/4/92	2^1	26	●	2 **Under The Bridge** S:2 / A:3 *The Righteous & The Wicked*	$3	▮V	Warner 18978
8/28/93	22	20		3 **Soul To Squeeze**....MR^5 S:10 / A:43 *Nobody Weird Like Me* from the movie *Coneheads* starring Dan Aykroyd and Jane Curtin	$3	▮V	Warner 18401
9/2/95	41^A	9		4 **Warped**....			album cut
9/30/95	27^A	18		5 **My Friends**....AR^4 / MR^4			album cut
2/3/96	49^A	17		6 **Aeroplane**.... above 3 from the album *One Hot Minute* on Warner 45733			album cut
11/23/96+	40^A	14		7 **Love Rollercoaster**.... from the movie soundtrack album *Beavis And Butt-Head Do America* on Geffen 25002			album cut
6/5/99	9	29		8 **Scar Tissue**....AR^{10} / MR^{16} A:8 / S:13 *Instrumental #1 / Gong Li*	$4	★V	Warner 16913
2/12/00	14	22		9 **Otherside**....MR^{13} S:9 / A:21 *How Strong*	$4	★V	Warner 16875
7/29/00	69	19		10 **Californication**....AR^2 / MR^1 A:64 above 3 from the album *Californication* on Warner 47386			album cut
6/15/02	34	20		11 **By The Way**....AR^7 / MR^{14} A:33 / S:74 *(video)*	$8	◗	Warner 38574
11/9/02	49	14		12 **The Zephyr Song**....A:50 above 2 from the album *By The Way* on Warner 48140			album cut

REDJACKS, The

'58

Rock and roll group. Led by singer Harold Jackson.

DEBUT	PEAK	WKS	Gold	A-side (Chart Hit)...B-side	$	Sym	Label & Number
9/15/58	84	2		**Big Brown Eyes**....H:84 *To Make You Mine* Sandy Block (orch.); "Ling-Ting-Tong" melody; first released on Oklahoma 5005 in 1958 ($50)	$25		Apt 25006

★569★ REDMAN

R&B/BUB/LP **'98**

Born Reggie Noble on 4/17/70 in Newark, New Jersey. Male rapper. Discovered by **Erick Sermon**. Starred in the 2001 movie *How High*.

1)How Deep Is Your Love 2)How High 3)Whateva Man

DEBUT	PEAK	WKS	Gold	A-side (Chart Hit)...B-side	$	Sym	Label & Number
11/19/94	67^S	1		1 **Rockafella**....BUB:105 *(remix)* samples "I Want'a Do Something Freaky To You" by **Leon Haywood** and "Flash Light" by **Parliament**	$5	▮	RAL 853966
2/25/95	94	4		2 **Can't Wait**....S:61 *(instrumental)* samples "All Night Long" by the **Mary Jane Girls** and "Just Rhymin' With Biz" by **Big Daddy Kane**	$5	▮	RAL 851466
8/26/95	13	15	●	3 **How High**....S:7 / A:64 *(remix)* **REDMAN/METHOD MAN** samples "I Am Woman" by **The Cover Girls**; from the rap concert movie *The Show!*	$3	▮	Def Jam 579924
3/23/96	81	4		4 **Funkorama**....S:57 *Up Jump The Boogie* (The Wixtons) samples "Midnight" by **A Tribe Called Quest** and "Stick 'Em" by **Fat Boys**	$3	▮	Interscope 98084
12/28/96	95	2		5 **It's Like That (My Big Brother)**....*(3 versions) / That's How It Is (It's Like That)* K-Solo (guest rapper); samples "Cold Getting Dumb" by Just Ice	$6	T	Def Squad 573201
2/1/97	42	15		6 **Whateva Man**....S:22 *It's Like That (My Big Brother)* **Erick Sermon** (featured vocalist)	$3	▮	Def Jam 574026
12/20/97+	51^A	12		7 **Rapper's Delight**.... **ERICK SERMON, KEITH MURRAY & REDMAN** from the album *In Tha Beginning...There Was Rap* on Priority 50639			album cut
12/27/97	75	12		8 **4, 3, 2, 1**....*(5 versions)* **LL COOL J Featuring Method Man, Redman, DMX, Canibus and Master P** samples "Fight For Your Right" by **Beastie Boys**, "Rock The Bells" by **LL Cool J** and "Shut 'Em Down" by **Public Enemy**	$6	T	Def Jam 568321
10/10/98	3	20	●	9 **How Deep Is Your Love** RB^3 S:❶² / A:16 *(w/o rap) / (3 album snippets)* **DRU HILL Featuring REDMAN**	$4	★	Island 572424
3/20/99	56^S	4		10 **Soopaman Lover**....*(2 versions) / Superman/Virgin* (R&B #97) **CHICO DeBARGE Featuring Erick Sermon & Redman** samples "Superman Lover" by **Johnny "Guitar" Watson**	$8	★*	Motown 56233
12/11/99+	70	5		11 **Left & Right**....S:20 *(w/o rap version)* **D'ANGELO featuring Method Man and Redman** "45": Virgin 58836; B-side: "Untitled (How Does It Feel)" (**D'Angelo** - #25)	$4	★V	Virgin 38678
7/22/00	68^S	4		12 **Oooh.**....BUB:125 *(2 versions) / Foolin* **DE LA SOUL Feat: Redman** samples "Enter The Dragon" by **Chubb Rock**	$6	T	Tommy Boy 2118
10/7/00	69^S	3		13 **And You Know That**....*(2 versions) / Blazin* (w/Govna-Mattic) **D-DON (Featuring Redman)** samples "Catch The Beat" by Ski Valley	$6	★	Lock Down 54398
5/19/01	97	2		14 **Let's Get Dirty (I Can't Get In Da Club)**....S:48 *(3 versions)* **REDMAN Feat. DJ Kool**	$6	T	Def Jam 572917
12/22/01+	72	12		15 **Part II**....S:35 / A:75 *(3 versions)* **METHOD MAN AND REDMAN** samples "You're Makin' Me High" by **Toni Braxton**; from the movie *How High* starring **Method Man** and Redman	$6	T	Def Jam 588891
9/21/02	48	20		16 **Dirrty**....S:2 / A:49 *Make Over* **CHRISTINA AGUILERA Featuring Redman**	$4	★	RCA 60669
10/19/02	36	16		17 **React**....S:7 / A:34 *(3 versions)* **ERICK SERMON Featuring Redman**	$6	T	J Records 21221

REDNEX

LP **'95**

Euro-dance group from Sweden. Core members: Goran Danielsson, Annika Ljungberg, Cool James and Pat Reiniz (vocals), Bosse Nilsson (fiddle), General Custer (banjo) and Animal (drums).

DEBUT	PEAK	WKS	Gold	A-side (Chart Hit)...B-side	$	Sym	Label & Number
3/11/95	25	20	●	**Cotton Eye Joe**....S:8 / A:75 *(dosey-doe mix) / (madcow mix)* techno-dance version of traditional bluegrass song; "45" B-side: (slide to the side mix)	$4	▮V	Battery 46501

DEBUT	PEAK	WKS	Gold	A-side (Chart Hit)	B-side	$	Sym	Label & Number

REDNOW, Eivets — see WONDER, Stevie

RED RIDER — see COCHRANE, Tom

RED RIVER DAVE '60

Born David McEnery on 12/15/14 in San Antonio, Texas. Died on 1/15/2002 (age 87). In singing cowboy movies, late 1940s.

DEBUT	PEAK	WKS	Gold	A-side (Chart Hit)	B-side	$	Sym	Label & Number
6/27/60	64	6		**There's A Star Spangled Banner Waving #2 (The Ballad Of Francis Powers)**	*The Pony Express*	$15		Savoy 3020
				original version was a #17 hit in 1942 for Elton Britt; Francis Powers: U.S. "U-2" pilot shot down in Russia on 5/1/60				

RED ROCKERS ROK/LP '83

Rock group from Algiers, Louisiana: John Griffith (vocals), James Singletary (guitar), Darren Hill (bass) and Jim Reilly (drums).

DEBUT	PEAK	WKS	Gold	A-side (Chart Hit)	B-side	$	Sym	Label & Number
6/4/83	53	10		**China**	*Voice Of America*	$4		Columbia 03786

REDWAY, Michael '73

Born in England. Pop singer/songwriter.

DEBUT	PEAK	WKS	Gold	A-side (Chart Hit)	B-side	$	Sym	Label & Number
2/10/73	85	4		**Good Morning**	*Shobhan (Shevawn)*	$5		Philips 40720

REED, Dan, Network LP '88

Multi-racial funk-rock group from Portland, Oregon: Dan Reed (vocals), Brion James (guitar), Blake Sakomoto (keyboards), Melvin Brannon (bass) and Daniel Pred (drums).

DEBUT	PEAK	WKS	Gold	A-side (Chart Hit)	B-side	$	Sym	Label & Number
3/12/88	38	11		**Ritual**	S:27 *Forgot To Make Her Mine*	$4	■	Mercury 870183

REED, Dean '59

Born in 1939 in Denver, Colorado. Pop vocalist/actor. Moved to East Germany in 1972; very popular in the former Soviet Bloc countries. Drowned in an East German lake, under mysterious circumstances, on 6/17/86.

DEBUT	PEAK	WKS	Gold	A-side (Chart Hit)	B-side	$	Sym	Label & Number
3/2/59	96	1		**The Search**	*Annabelle*	$20		Capitol 4121

REED, Denny '60

Born on 9/25/41 in East St. Louis, Illinois; raised in Cahokia, Illinois. Teen pop singer.

DEBUT	PEAK	WKS	Gold	A-side (Chart Hit)	B-side	$	Sym	Label & Number
8/29/60	94	3		**A Teenager Feels It Too**	*Hot Water*	$25		3 Trey 3007
				first released on MCI 1024 in 1960 ($50)				

REED, Jerry C&W/BUB/LP '71

Born Jerry Reed Hubbard on 3/20/37 in Atlanta, Georgia. Country singer/guitarist/songwriter/actor (charted 57 hits, 1967-83). Among his many movies, co-starred in *Gator* and *Smokey & The Bandit I & II*. Own TV series *Concrete Cowboys*. **Elvis Presley** recorded two of Reed's songs: "U.S. Male" and "Guitar Man."

1)Amos Moses 2)When You're Hot, You're Hot 3)Ko-Ko Joe

DEBUT	PEAK	WKS	Gold	A-side (Chart Hit)	B-side	$	Sym	Label & Number
6/30/62	79	5		1 **Goodnight, Irene**	*I'm Movin' On*	$12		Columbia 42417
				written in 1933 by Leadbelly; #1 hit for The Weavers in 1950				
10/13/62	99	1		2 **Hully Gully Guitar**	*Twist-A-Roo* [I]	$12	■	Columbia 42533
				JERRY REED and The Hully Girlies (above 2)				
10/31/70+	8	24	●	3 **Amos Moses**	*The Preacher And The Bear* (C&W flip) [N]	$6		RCA Victor 9904
5/8/71	9	12		4 **When You're Hot, You're Hot**	CW[5] *You've Been Cryin' Again* [N]	$6		RCA Victor 9976
9/4/71	51	6		5 **Ko-Ko Joe**	*I Feel For You*	$6		RCA Victor 1011
1/8/72	65	5		6 **Another Puff**	*Love Man* [N]	$6		RCA Victor 0613
7/15/72	62	8		7 **Alabama Wild Man**	*Take It Easy (In Your Mind)*	$6	■	RCA Victor 0738
				different version by Reed made the Country charts (#48) in 1968 on RCA 9623				
7/7/73	68	7		8 **Lord, Mr. Ford**	CW[1] *Two-Timin'* [N]	$6		RCA Victor 0960
2/16/74	91	5		9 **The Crude Oil Blues**	*Pickie, Pickie, Pickie* [N]	$6		RCA Victor 0224
7/24/82	57	9		10 **She Got The Goldmine (I Got The Shaft)**	CW[2] *"44"* [N]	$5		RCA 13268

REED, Jimmy R&B/BUB/LP '57

Born Mathis James Reed on 9/6/25 in Dunleith, Mississippi. Died from an epileptic seizure on 8/29/76 (age 50). Distinctive, influential blues singer/guitarist/harmonica player/songwriter; active until his death. Afflicted with epilepsy since 1957. Inducted into the Rock and Roll Hall of Fame in 1991.

1)Honest I Do 2)Baby What You Want Me To Do 3)Shame, Shame, Shame

DEBUT	PEAK	WKS	Gold	A-side (Chart Hit)	B-side	$	Sym	Label & Number
7/8/57	65	5		1 **The Sun Is Shining**	T:65 *Baby, What's On Your Mind?*	$30		Vee-Jay 248
9/30/57	32	15		2 **Honest I Do**	T:32 / S:36 *Signals Of Love*	$30		Vee-Jay 253
8/11/58	93	2		3 **Down In Virginia**	H:93 *I Know It's A Sin*	$30		Vee-Jay 287
2/15/60	37	14		4 **Baby What You Want Me To Do**	*Caress Me Baby*	$30		Vee-Jay 333
5/23/60	88	3		5 **Found Love**	*Where Can You Be*	$30		Vee-Jay 347
10/10/60	75	2		6 **Hush-Hush**	*Going By The River (Part II)* (#104)	$25		Vee-Jay 357
1/30/61	68	4		7 **Close Together**	*Laughing At The Blues*	$25		Vee-Jay 373
5/29/61	78	3		8 **Big Boss Man**	*I'm A Love You*	$25		Vee-Jay 380
9/18/61	58	9		9 **Bright Lights Big City**	*I'm Mr. Luck*	$25		Vee-Jay 398
1/27/62	93	5		10 **Aw Shucks, Hush Your Mouth**	*Baby, What's Wrong*	$20		Vee-Jay 425
6/23/62	77	4		11 **Good Lover**	*Tell Me You Love Me*	$20		Vee-Jay 449
4/13/63	52	8		12 **Shame, Shame, Shame**	*There'll Be A Day*	$20		Vee-Jay 509
				all of above (except #8) written by Reed				

REED, Lou ROK/BUB/LP '73

Born Lewis Alan Reed on 3/2/42 in Freeport, Long Island, New York. Lead singer/songwriter of the New York seminal rock band Velvet Underground; regarded as the godfather of punk rock. Appeared in the movie *One Trick Pony*.

DEBUT	PEAK	WKS	Gold	A-side (Chart Hit)	B-side	$	Sym	Label & Number
2/17/73	16	14		**Walk On The Wild Side**	*Perfect Day*	$7		RCA Victor 0887
				produced by **David Bowie** and Mick Ronson				

REEL BIG FISH LP '97

Ska-punk group from Huntington Beach, California: Aaron Barrett (vocals, guitar), Scott Klopfenstein (vocals, trumpet), Tavis Werts (trumpet), Grant Barry and Dan Regan (trombones), Matt Wong (bass) and Andrew Gonzales (drums).

DEBUT	PEAK	WKS	Gold	A-side (Chart Hit)	B-side	$	Sym	Label & Number
8/30/97	69[A]	4		**Sell Out**				album cut
				from the album *Turn The Radio Off* on Mojo/Universal 53013				

DEBUT	PEAK	WKS	Gold	A-side (Chart Hit)..........B-side	$	Sym	Label & Number
				REEL TIGHT BUB/LP **'99**			
				R&B vocal group from Chattanooga, Tennessee: Reggie Long, Danny Johnson, Bobby Rice and Bobby Torrence.			
11/28/98	80	1		1 **(Do You) Wanna Ride**..........S:29 *(4 versions)*	$4	▮	G-Funk/Restless 72980
4/17/99	39^{S}	14		2 **I Want U**..........BUB:121 *(2 versions)*	$5	★	G-Funk/Restless 73509
				REEL 2 REAL **'94**			
				Reggae-rap-dance duo: producer/composer Erick Morillo (born in New York and raised in Union City, New Jersey) and rapper Mark "The Mad Stuntman" Quashie (a native of Trinidad).			
3/12/94	89	6		**I Like To Move It**..........*(3 remixes)* **REEL 2 REAL Featuring The Mad Stuntman**	$7	▮*	Strictly Rhythm 12192
				REESE, Della BUB/LP **'59**			
				Born Delloreese Patricia Early on 7/6/31 in Detroit, Michigan. With **Mahalia Jackson** gospel troupe from 1945-49; with Erskine Hawkins in the early '50s. First recorded for Great Lakes in 1954. Solo since 1957. Actress/singer on many TV shows. Appeared in the 1958 movie *Let's Rock* and the 1989 movie *Harlem Nights*. Regular on TV's *Della*, *Chico & The Man*, *The Royal Family* and *Touched By An Angel*.			
				1)Don't You Know 2)And That Reminds Me 3)Not One Minute More			
8/26/57	12	18		1 **And That Reminds Me**..........A:12 / S:23 / T:29 *I Cried For You* — Honey Dreamers (backing vocals); lyric version of the Italian instrumental "Autumn Concerto"; reissued in 1965 on ABC 10721 with a picture sleeve	$15		Jubilee 5292
1/5/59	99	1		2 **Sermonette**..........*Dreams End At Dawn* — Billy Rock (orch., above 2)	$15		Jubilee 5345
9/21/59	2^{1}	18		3 **Don't You Know** RB² *Soldier, Won't You Marry Me?* — same melody as **Sammy Kaye**'s 1952 hit "You"; adapted from "Musetta's Waltz" from the Puccini opera *La Boheme*	$12		RCA Victor 7591
12/14/59+	16	11		4 **Not One Minute More**..........*You're My Love*	$12		RCA Victor 7644
3/21/60	56	7		5 **Someday (You'll Want Me to Want You)**..........*Faraway Boy* — **Neal Hefti** (orch.); #5 hit for the **Mills Brothers** in 1949	$10		RCA Victor 7706
9/5/60	69	5		6 **And Now**..........*There's Nothin' Like A Boy*	$10	■	RCA Victor 7784
2/6/61	67	5		7 **The Most Beautiful Words**..........*You Mean All The World To Me* — Glenn Osser (orch.: #3, 4, 6 & 7)	$10		RCA Victor 7833
4/24/61	98	1		8 **Won'cha Come Home, Bill Bailey**..........*The Touch Of Your Lips* — Duke Ellington's son, Mercer (orch.); #1 hit for Arthur Collins in 1902	$10		RCA Victor 7867
7/31/65	95	2		9 **After Loving You**..........*How Do You Keep From Cryin'* — Peter DeAngelis (orch.)	$8		ABC-Paramount 10691
9/10/66	99	2		10 **It Was A Very Good Year**..........*Solitary Woman* — Bobby Bryant Quintet (backing band); song introduced in 1961 by **The Kingston Trio** on the album *Goin' Places*	$8		ABC 10841
				REEVES, Del C&W **'65**			
				Born Franklin Delano Reeves on 7/14/33 in Sparta, North Carolina. Country singer/songwriter/guitarist (charted 55 hits, 1961-86).			
6/26/65	96	1		**Girl On The Billboard**..........CW² *Eyes Don't Come Crying To Me* [N]	$8		United Artists 824
	★385★			**REEVES, Jim** C&W/BUB/MEM/LP **'60**			
				Born on 8/20/23 in Panola County, Texas. Died in a plane crash in Nashville on 7/31/64 (age 40). Charted 80 Country hits, 1953-84. Aspirations of a professional baseball career cut short by an ankle injury. DJ at KWKH-Shreveport, Louisiana, home of the *Louisiana Hayride*, early '50s. First recorded for Macy's in 1950. Joined *Hayride* cast in 1953. Joined the *Grand Ole Opry* in 1955. In the 1963 movie *Kimberley Jim*. Elected to the Country Music Hall of Fame in 1967.			
				1)He'll Have To Go 2)Four Walls 3)Am I Losing You 4)I'm Gettin' Better 5)I Missed Me			
4/29/57	11	22		1 **Four Walls**..........CW⁸ A:11 / T:12 / J:13 / S:14 *I Know And You Know*	$15		RCA Victor 6874
2/3/58	93	1		2 **Anna Marie**..........T:93 *Everywhere You Go*	$15		RCA Victor 7070
8/4/58	45	6		3 **Blue Boy**..........H:45 *Theme Of Love (I Love to Say, "I Love You")*	$15		RCA Victor 7266
12/8/58	95	1		4 **Billy Bayou**..........CW⁵ *I'd Like To Be* (C&W #18) — written by **Roger Miller**	$15		RCA Victor 7380
12/28/59+	2^{3}	23	●	5 **He'll Have To Go** CW¹⁴ *In A Mansion Stands My Love*	$12		RCA Victor 7643
6/20/60	37	10		6 **I'm Gettin' Better** /			
7/25/60	82	2		7 **I Know One**..........	$12	■	RCA Victor 7756
10/24/60	31	11		8 **Am I Losing You** / — a different version by Reeves made the Country charts (#3) in 1957 on RCA Victor 6749			
11/14/60	44	6		9 **I Missed Me**..........	$12	■	RCA Victor 7800
3/20/61	62	4		10 **The Blizzard**..........*Danny Boy*	$10		RCA Victor 7855
7/10/61	73	5		11 **What Would You Do?**..........*Stand At Your Window* (C&W #16)	$10		RCA Victor 7905
11/6/61	89	3		12 **Losing Your Love** / — #9 & 12: written by **Bill Anderson**			
12/4/61	92	2		13 **(How Can I Write On Paper) What I Feel In My Heart**..........	$10		RCA Victor 7950
5/5/62	90	6		14 **Adios Amigo**..........*A Letter To My Heart* (C&W #20)	$10		RCA Victor 8019
10/13/62	95	2		15 **I'm Gonna Change Everything**..........*Pride Goes Before A Fall* (C&W #18)	$10	■	RCA Victor 8080
6/29/63	91	2		16 **Guilty**..........*Little Ole You* (C&W #11)	$10	■	RCA Victor 8193
8/22/64	82	5		17 **I Guess I'm Crazy**..........CW⁷ *Not Until The Next Time* — #13 Country hit for Tommy Collins in 1955	$10		RCA Victor 8383
11/21/64	93	3		18 **I Won't Forget You**..........*Highway To Nowhere*	$10		RCA Victor 8461
3/13/65	88	1		19 **This Is It**..........CW³ *There's That Smile Again*	$10		RCA Victor 8508
8/14/65	79	6		20 **Is It Really Over?**..........CW³ *Rosa Rio*	$8	■	RCA Victor 8625
1/15/66	66	6		21 **Snow Flake**..........*Take My Hand Precious Lord* — written by **Ned Miller**	$8		RCA Victor 8719
4/9/66	45	7		22 **Distant Drums**..........CW⁴ *Old Tige*	$8		RCA Victor 8789
8/27/66	59	8		23 **Blue Side Of Lonesome**..........CW¹ *It Hurts So Much (To See You Go)* — all of above produced by **Chet Atkins**	$8		RCA Victor 8902

REEVES, Martha — see MARTHA & THE VANDELLAS

DEBUT	PEAK	WKS	Gold	A-side (Chart Hit)...B-side	$	Sym	Label & Number

REFLECTIONS, The
BUB '64

Rock and roll vocal group from Detroit, Michigan: Tony Micale, Danny Bennie, Phil Castrodale, Johnny Dean and Ray Steinberg.

DEBUT	PEAK	WKS	Gold	A-side (Chart Hit)...B-side	$	Sym	Label & Number
4/11/64	6	12		1 (Just Like) Romeo & Juliet ... *Can't You Tell By The Look In My Eyes*	$20		Golden World 9
7/11/64	96	1		2 Like Columbus Did ... *Lonely Girl*	$15		Golden World 12
3/13/65	55	5		3 Poor Man's Son ... *Comin' At You*	$15		Golden World 20

REFLECTIONS, The
R&B '75

R&B vocal group from Harlem, New York: Herman Edwards, Josh Pridgen, Edmund "Butch" Simmons and John Simmons (died on 3/16/89, age 45). Toured as backup group with **Melba Moore** in 1972.

DEBUT	PEAK	WKS	Gold	A-side (Chart Hit)...B-side	$	Sym	Label & Number
7/12/75	94	4		Three Steps From True Love ... *How Could We Let The Love Get Away*	$7		Capitol 4078

RE-FLEX
LP '84

Techno-rock/dance group formed in London, England: Baxter (vocals, guitar), Paul Fishman (keyboards), Nigel Ross-Scott (bass) and Roland Kerridge (drums).

DEBUT	PEAK	WKS	Gold	A-side (Chart Hit)...B-side	$	Sym	Label & Number
11/26/83+	24	21		1 The Politics Of Dancing ... *Flex It!*	$4	■	Capitol 5301
5/5/84	82	4		2 Hurt ... *Cruel World*	$4	■	Capitol 5348

REFRESHMENTS, The
ROK/LP '96

Rock group from Tempe, Arizona: Roger Clyne (vocals, guitar), Brian Blush (guitar), Buddy Edwards (bass) and P.H. Naffah (drums).

DEBUT	PEAK	WKS	Gold	A-side (Chart Hit)...B-side	$	Sym	Label & Number
7/13/96	71[A]	2		Banditos ... from the album *Fizzy Fuzzy Big & Buzzy* on Mercury 528999; title is Spanish for "Bandits"			album cut

REFUGEE CAMP — see FUGEES

REGAN, Joan
MEM '55

Born on 1/19/28 in Romford, Essex, England. Adult Contemporary singer.

DEBUT	PEAK	WKS	Gold	A-side (Chart Hit)...B-side	$	Sym	Label & Number
11/12/55	55	8		Croce Di Oro ... T:55 *Evermore* Johnny Douglas (orch.)	$15		London 1605

REGENTS, The
'61

Italian-American doo-wop group from the Bronx, New York: Guy Villari (lead), Sal Cuomo, Chuck Fassert, Don Jacobucci and Tony "Hot Rod" Gravagna. Formed as the Desires in 1958. "Barbara-Ann," written for Fassert's sister, was first recorded as a demo in 1958. Group had disbanded by the time "Barbara-Ann" was released.

DEBUT	PEAK	WKS	Gold	A-side (Chart Hit)...B-side	$	Sym	Label & Number
5/15/61	13	10		1 Barbara-Ann ... *I'm So Lonely* first released on Cousins 1002 in 1961 ($400)	$30		Gee 1065
7/10/61	28	7		2 Runaround ... *Laura My Darling*	$30		Gee 1071

REGINA
LP '86

Born Regina Richards in Brooklyn, New York. Female dance singer.

DEBUT	PEAK	WKS	Gold	A-side (Chart Hit)...B-side	$	Sym	Label & Number
6/21/86	10	20		Baby Love ... S:10 / A:11 *(dub mix)*	$3	■	Atlantic 89417

REID, Clarence
R&B/BUB '69

Born on 2/14/45 in Cochran, Georgia. R&B singer/songwriter. Also recorded X-rated party records as Blowfly.

DEBUT	PEAK	WKS	Gold	A-side (Chart Hit)...B-side	$	Sym	Label & Number
8/2/69	40	10		1 Nobody But You Babe ... *Send Me Back My Money* answer song to **The Isley Brothers**' "It's Your Thing"	$8		Alston 4574
8/10/74	99	1		2 Funky Party ... *Winter Man*	$6		Alston 4621

REILLY, Mike
'71

Born in Long Island, New York. Pop singer/songwriter/bassist. Later joined **Pure Prairie League**.

DEBUT	PEAK	WKS	Gold	A-side (Chart Hit)...B-side	$	Sym	Label & Number
3/13/71	88	6		1927 Kansas City ... *Early Bird*	$6		Paramount 0053

REISMAN, Joe, and his Orchestra
'56

Born on 9/16/24 in Dallas, Texas. Died of a heart attack on 9/25/87 (age 63). Conductor/composer/arranger for TV, Broadway and movies. Musical conductor at RCA Victor during the 1950s. Headed RCA's A&R department in Los Angeles from 1962-77.

DEBUT	PEAK	WKS	Gold	A-side (Chart Hit)...B-side	$	Sym	Label & Number
12/8/56	46	10		1 Armen's Theme ... T:46 *I'll Take You Dancing* [I] Tony Mottola (guitar solo); written by **David Seville**	$15		RCA Victor 6740
3/23/57	55	5		2 Pamela Throws A Party ... T:55 *Navajo Nocturne*	$15		RCA Victor 6826
7/3/61	74	6		3 The Guns Of Navarone ... *Yassu* [I] title song from the movie starring Gregory Peck and David Niven	$15		Landa 674

REISS
'98

Born Michael Reiss in Brooklyn, New York. Pop-rock singer/songwriter.

DEBUT	PEAK	WKS	Gold	A-side (Chart Hit)...B-side	$	Sym	Label & Number
8/1/98	90	2		Boom Bye Yae ... S:68 *(remix)* **REISS Featuring Michie Mee** samples "Die Young Stay Pretty" by **Blondie**	$4	▮	Mercury 566076

REJOICE!
AC/BUB '68

Husband-and-wife pop duo from Sausalito, California: Tom and Nancy Brown.

DEBUT	PEAK	WKS	Gold	A-side (Chart Hit)...B-side	$	Sym	Label & Number
10/26/68	96	1		Golden Gate Park ... *Sonora*	$7		Dunhill/ABC 4158

RELL
R&B '98

Born in Harlem, New York. Male rapper.

DEBUT	PEAK	WKS	Gold	A-side (Chart Hit)...B-side	$	Sym	Label & Number
8/1/98	86	3		Love For Free ... S:59 *(TV track remix)* **RELL (featuring Jay-Z)** samples "Do It ('Til You're Satisfied)" by **B.T. Express**; from the movie *Streets Is Watching* starring **Jay-Z**	$3	▮	Roc-A-Fella 568842

R.E.M.
★248★ ROK/BUB/LP '91

Alternative-rock group formed in Athens, Georgia: Michael Stipe (vocals; born on 1/4/60), Peter Buck (guitar; born on 12/6/56), Mike Mills (bass; born on 12/17/58) and Bill Berry (drums; born on 7/31/58). Developed huge following with college audiences in the early 1980s as one of the first alternative-rock bands. Buck, Mills and Berry also recorded with **Warren Zevon** as the Hindu Love Gods in 1990. Berry fully recovered from a brain aneurysm suffered on stage in Lausanne, Switzerland, on 3/1/95; announced he was leaving the group in October 1997. R.E.M. is abbreviation for Rapid Eye Movement, the dream stage of sleep.

1)Losing My Religion 2)Stand 3)The One I Love 4)Shiny Happy People 5)Bang And Blame

DEBUT	PEAK	WKS	Gold	A-side (Chart Hit)...B-side	$	Sym	Label & Number
7/23/83	78	5		1 Radio Free Europe ... *There She Goes Again* first released on Hib-Tone 0001 in 1981 ($75) with a picture sleeve	$10	■	I.R.S. 9916
6/23/84	85	6		2 so. Central Rain (I'm Sorry) ... *King Of The Road*	$8	■	I.R.S. 9927
10/4/86	94	3		3 Fall On Me ... *Rotary Ten*	$8	■	I.R.S. 52883

DEBUT	PEAK	WKS	Gold	A-side (Chart Hit)...B-side	$	Sym	Label & Number
				R.E.M. — Cont'd			
9/19/87	9	20		4 **The One I Love** ....S:5 / A:13 *Maps And Legends (live)*	$6	■	I.R.S. 53171
1/30/88	69	9		5 **Its The End Of The World As We Know It (And I Feel Fine)**....*Last Date*	$6	■	I.R.S. 53220
				the B-sides of #2 & 5 are re-makes of classic hits by **Roger Miller** and **Floyd Cramer**, respectively			
1/21/89	6	19		6 **Stand** ....AR^{1} / MR^{2} S:4 / A:5 *Memphis Train Blues*	$4	■	Warner 27688
				became the theme for TV's *Get A Life* starring Chris Elliott			
6/10/89	86	4		7 **Pop Song 89** ....*(acoustic version)*	$4	■	Warner 27640
4/6/91	4	21	●	8 **Losing My Religion** AR^{3} / MR^{8} S:5 / A:8 *Rotary Eleven*	$3	▮^{V}	Warner 19392
7/27/91	10	15		9 **Shiny Happy People** ....A:25 / S:38 *Forty Second Song*	$3	▮^{V}	Warner 19242
				Kate Pierson of **The B-52's** (backing vocals)			
10/31/92	28	15		10 **Drive** ....MR^{5} S:32 / A:34 *Winged Mammal Theme*	$3	▮^{V}	Warner 18729
2/6/93	30	15		11 **Man On The Moon** ....A:26 / S:56 *New Orleans Instrumental No. 2*	$3	▮^{V}	Warner 18642
				tribute to the late comedian Andy Kaufman (also the title of the 1999 movie starring Jim Carrey - see #21 below)			
9/11/93	29	20		12 **Everybody Hurts** ....S:34 / A:38 *Mandolin Strum*	$3	▮^{V}	Warner 18638
9/24/94	21	20		13 **What's The Frequency, Kenneth?** ....MR^{5} A:14 / S:31 *(instrumental)*	$3	▮^{V}	Warner 18050
1/21/95	19	14		14 **Bang And Blame** ....MR^{3} A:17 / S:52 *(instrumental)*	$3	▮^{V}	Warner 17994
3/18/95	74^{A}	1		15 **Star 69**			album cut
4/29/95	47	15		16 **Strange Currencies** ....A:45 *(instrumental)*	$3	▮^{V}	Warner 17900
				above 4 from the album *Monster* on Warner 45740			
9/7/96	49	9		17 **E-Bow The Letter** ....A:45 / S:59 *Tricycle*	$3	▮^{V}	Warner 17529
				Patti Smith (female vocal); an e-bow is an electronic gadget that produces a tone when held over an electric guitar's strings			
11/16/96	46	12		18 **Bittersweet Me** ....A:36 *Undertow (live)*	$3	▮^{V}	Warner 17490
2/22/97	96	2		19 **Electrolite** ....*The Wake-Up Bomb (live)*	$3	▮^{V}	Warner 17446
11/14/98	57	3		20 **Daysleeper** ....*Emphysema*	$3	▮^{V}	Warner 17129
12/25/99+	57	14		21 **The Great Beyond** ....S:25 / A:50 *Man On The Moon (live)*	$3	★^{V}	Jersey/Warner 16888
				from the movie *Man On The Moon* starring Jim Carrey			
5/26/01	83	5		22 **Imitation Of Life** ....S:29 *The Lifting / Beat A Drum / 2JN*	$8	★$^{++}$	Warner 42363
				REMBRANDTS, The ROK/LP **'95**			
				Pop-rock duo from Los Angeles, California: Danny Wilde and Phil Solem.			
2/9/91	14	19		1 **Just The Way It Is, Baby** A:15 / S:18 *New King*	$3	▮	Atco 98874
5/25/91	78	10		2 **Someone** ....*Just The Way It Is, Baby (acoustic version)*	$3	▮	Atco 98786
10/31/92	54	8		3 **Johnny Have You Seen Her?** ....A:54 *In The Back Of Your Mind*	$3	▮	Atco 98504
9/30/95	17	20		4 **I'll Be There For You (Theme from "Friends")** / AC^{7} A:❶^{8} / S:35		V	
				Hot 100 Airplay debut: 5/20/95; theme from the *Friends* TV series; "45": EastWest 64429; B-side: (6 album snippets)			
9/30/95		20		5 **This House Is Not A Home** ....S:flip	$4	▮	EastWest 64384
				released as the A-side of the cassettte single (as a follow-up to #4 which had not been available on cassette)			
				REMEDY **'93**			
				Multi-ethnic R&B trio from San Jose, California: Sean Daniel Alaura, Jesse Rodriguez Aguirre and Darryl Lamont Sherman.			
3/27/93	66	6		**Closer** ....A:43 / S:75 *(same version)*	$3	▮	Hollywood 64645
				REN **'02**			
				Born Joseph Postell in Chicago, Illinois. Male rapper.			
4/13/02	31^{S}	6		**Calling My Name** ....*(2 versions)*	$7	★	MusicMind/Orpheus 90404
				REN with Christina Sanchez introducing "Rhyme"			
				RENAY, Diane BUB/LP **'64**			
				Born Renee Diane Kushner in Philadelphia, Pennsylvania. Teen pop singer.			
1/25/64	6	12		1 **Navy Blue** ....AC^{1} *Unbelievable Guy*	$15		20th Century 456
4/4/64	29	8		2 **Kiss Me Sailor** ....*Soft-Spoken Guy*	$15		20th Century 477
				RENE, Googie, Combo R&B/BUB **'66**			
				Born Raphael Rene in Chicago, Illinois. Bandleader/keyboardist. Son of songwriter/producer Leon Rene.			
2/26/66	77	3		**Smokey Joe's La La** ....*Needing You* [I]	$15		Class 1517
				RENÉ, Henri, and his Orchestra MEM/POP **'54**			
				Born on 12/29/06 in Germany. Died on 4/25/93 (age 86). Bandleader/arranger/conductor. Began long career with Victor in 1936 as director of their international branch. Arranger/conductor for **Perry Como**, **Dinah Shore**, Eartha Kitt, **Mindy Carson**, and many other singers. Hit #6 in 1951 with "I'm In Love Again."			
12/8/56	44	8		**Love Me Tender** ....T:44 *The Little White Horse* [I]	$12		RCA Victor 6728
				adapted from the 1861 tune "Aura Lee"; title song from the movie starring **Elvis Presley**			
				RENÉ AND ANGELA R&B/BUB/LP **'85**			
				R&B vocal duo from Los Angeles, California: René Moore and **Angela Winbush**. Winbush married **Ronald Isley** on 6/26/93.			
9/28/85	47	10		1 **I'll Be Good** ....*(instrumental)*	$3	■	Mercury 884009
3/22/86	62	6		2 **Your Smile** ....RB^{1} *(instrumental)*	$3		Mercury 884271
6/21/86	75	7		3 **You Don't Have To Cry** ....*(instrumental)*	$3	■	Mercury 884587
				RENÉ AND RAY **'62**			
				Hispanic duo: Paul Venezuela (René; born in Puerto Rico) and Ray Quinones (born on 1/31/41 in Manhattan, New York); both sang with The Velveteens.			
6/9/62	79	3		**Queen Of My Heart** ....*Do What You Feel*	$25		Donna 1360
				The Velveteens (backing vocals)			
				RENE & RENE BUB/LP **'69**			
				Mexican-American duo from Laredo, Texas: Rene Ornelas (born on 8/26/36) and Rene Herrera (born on 10/2/35).			
7/11/64	43	8		1 **Angelito** ....*Write Me Soon*	$10	□	Columbia 43045
				first released on Jox 017 in 1964 ($20)			
11/23/68+	14	12		2 **Lo Mucho Que Te Quiero (The More I Love You)** ....*Mornin'*	$6		White Whale 287
				first released on ARV International 5011 in 1968 ($15)			
				RENÉE, Nicole **'98**			
				Born in 1975 in Philadelphia, Pennsylvania. R&B singer/songwriter.			
11/21/98	83	2		**Strawberry** ....S:60 *Yea, Yea, Yea*	$3	▮^{V}	Atlantic 84161
				samples "Paradise" by **Grover Washington, Jr.**; "45" B-side: (instrumental)			

DEBUT	PEAK	WKS	Gold	A-side (Chart Hit)....B-side	$	Sym	Label & Number

RENO, Mike — see LOVERBOY

RENTALS, The — '95

Pop-rock group from Los Angeles, California: Matt Sharp (vocals, bass), Cherielynn Westrich (vocals), Petra Haden (violin), Rod Cervera (guitar), Tom Gaimley (synthesizer) and Pat Wilson (drums). Sharp and Wilson are also members of **Weezer**.

DEBUT	PEAK	WKS	Gold	A-side (Chart Hit)....B-side	$	Sym	Label & Number
12/9/95	82	3		**Friends Of P.** ....A:49 *So Soon*	$3	▮V	Maverick/Reprise 17720

REO SPEEDWAGON ★184★ — ROK/BUB/LP '81

Rock group from Champaign, Illinois: Mike Murphy (vocals), Gary Richrath (guitar; born on 10/18/49), Neal Doughty (keyboards; born on 7/29/46), Gregg Philbin (bass) and Alan Gratzer (drums; born on 11/9/48). Murphy left by 1976; replaced by Kevin Cronin (born on 10/6/51). Philbin left in 1978; replaced by Bruce Hall (born on 5/3/53). Gratzer left in 1988; replaced by former **Santana** drummer Graham Lear. Lineup in 1990: Cronin, Doughty and Hall, joined by new members Dave Amato (guitar), Jesse Harms (keyboards; left by 1991) and Bryan Hitt (drums). Group named after a 1911 fire truck.

1)Can't Fight This Feeling 2)Keep On Loving You 3)Take It On The Run

DEBUT	PEAK	WKS	Gold	A-side (Chart Hit)....B-side	$	Sym	Label & Number
5/28/77	94	3		1 **Ridin' The Storm Out** ....*Being Kind (Can Hurt Someone Sometimes)* [L] "live" version of REO's 1974 album title song	$6		Epic 50367
5/13/78	58	11		2 **Roll With The Changes** ....*The Unidentified Flying Tuna Trot*	$5		Epic 50545
7/22/78	56	7		3 **Time For Me To Fly** ....*Runnin' Blind*	$5		Epic 50582
5/31/80	77	6		4 **Time For Me To Fly** ....*Lightning* [R] longer album version (3:39) than #3 above (2:58)	$5		Epic 50858
11/29/80+	❶[1]	28	▲	5 **Keep On Loving You** ....*Follow My Heart*	$4		Epic 50953
3/21/81	5	20	●	6 **Take It On The Run** ....*Someone Tonight*	$4		Epic 01054
6/13/81	24	14		7 **Don't Let Him Go** ....*I Wish You Were There*	$4	■	Epic 02127
8/8/81	20	13		8 **In Your Letter** ....*Shakin' It Loose* above 4 from the album *Hi Infidelity*	$4		Epic 02457
6/12/82	7	16		9 **Keep The Fire Burnin'** ....*I'll Follow You*	$4		Epic 02967
8/28/82	26	14		10 **Sweet Time** ....*Stillness Of The Night*	$4	■	Epic 03175
10/27/84	29	13		11 **I Do'wanna Know** ....A:27 *Rock 'N Roll Star*	$3	■	Epic 04659
1/19/85	❶[3]	18	●	12 **Can't Fight This Feeling** A:❶[3] / S:❶[2] *Break His Spell*	$3	■	Epic 04713
3/30/85	19	16		13 **One Lonely Night** ....A:19 / S:21 *Wheels Are Turnin'*	$3	■	Epic 04848
7/13/85	34	11		14 **Live Every Moment** ....*Gotta Feel More* above 4 from the album *Wheels Are Turnin'*	$3		Epic 05412
1/31/87	16	14		15 **That Ain't Love** ....S:16 / A:17 *Accidents Can Happen*	$3	■	Epic 06656
5/9/87	60	9		16 **Variety Tonight** ....*Tired Of Gettin Nowhere*	$3	■	Epic 07055
7/18/87	19	30		17 **In My Dreams** ....A:17 / S:18 *Over The Edge*	$3	■	Epic 07255
6/25/88	20	19		18 **Here With Me** ....A:19 / S:23 *Wherever You're Goin' (It's Alright)*	$3	■	Epic 07901
10/13/90	65	6		19 **Love Is A Rock** ....*Go For Broke*	$3	▮V	Epic 73540

REPARATA AND THE DELRONS — BUB '65

"Girl group" from Brooklyn, New York: Mary "Reparata" Aiese, Sheila Reillie and Carol Drobnicki. First recorded for Laurie in 1964. Lorraine Mazzola, member from 1966-73, later was leader of **Lady Flash** under the name "Reparata." Mary Aiese recorded "Shoes" solo as **Reparata**.

DEBUT	PEAK	WKS	Gold	A-side (Chart Hit)....B-side	$	Sym	Label & Number
1/9/65	60	9		1 **Whenever A Teenager Cries** ....*He's My Guy*	$12		World Artists 1036
5/8/65	92	3		2 **Tommy** ....*Mama Don't Allow* Hash Brown (orch., above 2)	$12		World Artists 1051
7/5/75	92	3		3 **Shoes** *[REPARATA]*....*A Song For All*	$6		Polydor 14271

REPLACEMENTS, The — ROK/LP '89

Rock group from Minneapolis, Minnesota: Paul Westerberg (vocals, guitar, piano), Slim Dunlap (guitar), Tommy Stinson (bass) and Chris Mars (drums).

DEBUT	PEAK	WKS	Gold	A-side (Chart Hit)....B-side	$	Sym	Label & Number
4/8/89	51	10		**I'll Be You** ....AR[3] / MR[1] *Date To Church*	$4	■	Sire 22992

REPUBLICA — ROK/LP '96

Rock group from London, England: Saffron Sprackling (female vocals), Jonny Male (guitar), Tim Dorney and Andy Todd (keyboards) and Dave Barbarossa (drums).

DEBUT	PEAK	WKS	Gold	A-side (Chart Hit)....B-side	$	Sym	Label & Number
8/10/96	56	20		1 **Ready To Go** ....A:56 / S:75 *(original mix)*	$4	▮V	dc/RCA 64540
2/15/97	93	3		2 **Drop Dead Gorgeous** ....*(riprock's runway mix)* "45" issued for above 2 on dc/RCA 64771	$4	▮V	dc/RCA 64767

RES — LP '02

Born in Philadelphia, Pennsylvania. Female R&B-dance singer. Pronounced: reese.

DEBUT	PEAK	WKS	Gold	A-side (Chart Hit)....B-side	$	Sym	Label & Number
6/29/02	37[S]	5		**They-Say Vision** ....BUB:119 *(4 remixes)*	$8	★*	MCA 155961

RESTIVO, Johnny — '59

Born in the Bronx, New York. Pop singer (15 years old in 1959).

DEBUT	PEAK	WKS	Gold	A-side (Chart Hit)....B-side	$	Sym	Label & Number
9/7/59	80	3		**The Shape I'm In** ....*Ya Ya*	$20	■	RCA Victor 7559

RESTLESS HEART — C&W/AC/LP '93

Country group formed in Nashville, Tennessee: Larry Stewart (vocals), Greg Jennings (guitar), David Innis (keyboards), Paul Gregg (bass) and John Dittrich (drums). Charted 6 consecutive #1 Country hits, 1986-88. Stewart went solo in early 1992. Keyboardist Innis left in early 1993. Remaining three continued on with two backing musicians. Group disbanded in 1996.

DEBUT	PEAK	WKS	Gold	A-side (Chart Hit)....B-side	$	Sym	Label & Number
4/11/87	33	18		1 **I'll Still Be Loving You** ....CW[1] S:29 / A:40 *Victim Of The Game*	$4		RCA 5065
11/14/92+	11	20		2 **When She Cries** ....A:12 / S:22 *(3 album snippets)* "45": RCA 62334; B-side: "Just In Time"	$4	▮V	RCA 62412
3/27/93	43	13		3 **Tell Me What You Dream** ....AC[2] A:45 *Mending Fences* (C&W #13) **RESTLESS HEART featuring Warren Hill** (saxophone) first recorded in 1984 by **Timothy B. Schmit** on his album *Playin' It Cool*	$4	▮V	RCA 62468

REUNION — BUB/AC '74

Pop group formed in New York: Joey Levine (lead vocals; **Ohio Express**), Marc Bellack, Paul DiFranco and Norman Dolph.

DEBUT	PEAK	WKS	Gold	A-side (Chart Hit)....B-side	$	Sym	Label & Number
9/7/74	8	15		**Life Is A Rock (But The Radio Rolled Me)** ....*Are You Ready To Believe* [N]	$5		RCA Victor 10056

DEBUT	PEAK	WKS	Gold	A-side (Chart Hit)	B-side	$	Sym	Label & Number

REVELATION
R&B '76

R&B-disco group: Phillip Ballou, Benny Diggs, Arthur Freeman and Arnold McCuller.

DEBUT	PEAK	WKS	Gold	A-side (Chart Hit)	B-side	$	Sym	Label & Number
7/31/76	98	2		**You To Me Are Everything, Part I**	*Part II*	$5		RSO 854

REVELS, The
'59

Black vocal group from Philadelphia, Pennsylvania: John Kelly, John Grant, Henry Colclough, John Jones and Bill Jackson.

DEBUT	PEAK	WKS	Gold	A-side (Chart Hit)	B-side	$	Sym	Label & Number
10/19/59	35	10		**Midnight Stroll** Harold Karr (orch.); originally released as "Dead Man's Stroll" on Norgolde 103 ($125)	*Talking To My Heart*	$30		Norgolde 103

REVERE, Paul, And The Raiders ★145★
BUB/LP '66

Born on 1/7/38 in Harvard, Nebraska. Rock and roll keyboardist. Formed The Raiders in Boise, Idaho. Group had numerous personnel changes through the years. Core members: **Mark Lindsay** (vocals; born on 3/9/42), Freddy Weller (guitar), Keith Allison (bass) and Michael Smith (drums). On daily ABC-TV show *Where The Action Is*. Own TV show *Happening* in 1968. Lindsay and Allison recorded with **Steve Alaimo** as **The Unknowns** in 1966. Weller went on to become a prolific country singer. Smith died on 3/6/2001 (age 58).

1)Indian Reservation 2)Good Thing 3)Kicks 4)Him Or Me - What's It Gonna Be? 5)Hungry

DEBUT	PEAK	WKS	Gold	A-side (Chart Hit)	B-side	$	Sym	Label & Number
3/27/61	38	6		1 **Like, Long Hair** based on Rachmaninoff's "Prelude In C-Sharp Minor"; arranged by Gary "Alley Oop" Paxton	*Sharon* [I]	$30		Gardena 116
9/18/65	46	9		2 **Steppin' Out**	*Blue Fox*	$12		Columbia 43375
				PAUL REVERE AND THE RAIDERS Featuring Mark Lindsay:				
12/4/65+	11	15		3 **Just Like Me**	*B.F.D.R.F. Blues*	$10		Columbia 43461
3/19/66	4	14		4 **Kicks** the first major hit with an anti-drug message	*Shake It Up*	$10		Columbia 43556
6/18/66	6	11		5 **Hungry**	*There She Goes*	$10	■	Columbia 43678
10/1/66	20	8		6 **The Great Airplane Strike**	*In My Community*	$10	■	Columbia 43810
12/3/66+	4	12		7 **Good Thing**	*Undecided Man*	$10	■	Columbia 43907
2/18/67	22	8		8 **Ups And Downs**	*Leslie*	$10	■	Columbia 44018
4/29/67	5	9		9 **Him Or Me - What's It Gonna Be?**	*Legend Of Paul Revere*	$10	■	Columbia 44094
				PAUL REVERE AND THE RAIDERS (above 2)				
8/19/67	17	9		10 **I Had A Dream**	*Upon Your Leaving*	$10	■	Columbia 44227
11/18/67	42	6		11 **Peace Of Mind** all of above Columbia records produced by Terry Melcher (of **Bruce & Terry**)	*Do Unto Others* (#102)	$10	■	Columbia 44335
2/10/68	19	8		12 **Too Much Talk**	*Happening '68*	$8	■	Columbia 44444
6/22/68	27	9		13 **Don't Take It So Hard**	*Observation From Flight 285 (in 3/4 time)*	$8	■	Columbia 44553
10/12/68	58	6		14 **Cinderella Sunshine**	*It's Happening*	$8		Columbia 44655
2/15/69	18	12		15 **Mr. Sun, Mr. Moon**	*Without You*	$8	■	Columbia 44744
5/17/69	20	12	●	16 **Let Me**	*I Don't Know*	$8		Columbia 44854
9/6/69	50	7		17 **We Gotta All Get Together**	*Frankfort Side Street*	$8		Columbia 44970
				RAIDERS:				
2/21/70	82	3		18 **Just Seventeen**	*Sorceress With Blue Eyes*	$7		Columbia 45082
4/10/71	❶[1]	22	▲	19 **Indian Reservation (The Lament Of The Cherokee Reservation Indian)**	*Terry's Tune*	$6		Columbia 45332
9/11/71	23	10		20 **Birds Of A Feather**	*The Turkey*	$6		Columbia 45453
1/29/72	51	6		21 **Country Wine**	*It's So Hard Getting Up Today*	$6		Columbia 45535
5/20/72	54	8		22 **Powder Blue Mercedes Queen**	*Golden Girls Sometimes*	$6		Columbia 45601
10/21/72	96	3		23 **Song Seller**	*A Simple Song*	$6		Columbia 45688
2/3/73	97	5		24 **Love Music**	*Goodbye, No. 9*	$6		Columbia 45759

REYNOLDS, Burt
'80

Born on 2/11/36 in Waycross, Georgia. Became a movie box-office superstar in the mid-1970s.

DEBUT	PEAK	WKS	Gold	A-side (Chart Hit)	B-side	$	Sym	Label & Number
10/18/80	88	5		**Let's Do Something Cheap And Superficial** from the movie *Smokey & The Bandit 2* starring Reynolds	*Pickin' Lone Star Style* (The Bandit Band)	$4	■	MCA 51004

REYNOLDS, Debbie
POP/LP '57

Born Mary Reynolds on 4/1/32 in El Paso, Texas. Actress/singer. Starred in several movies. Married to **Eddie Fisher** from 1955-59. Mother of actress/author Carrie Fisher. Hit #3 in 1951 with "Aba Daba Honeymoon" (w/Carleton Carpenter).

DEBUT	PEAK	WKS	Gold	A-side (Chart Hit)	B-side	$	Sym	Label & Number
7/22/57	❶[5]	31	●	1 **Tammy** T:❶[5] / A:❶[5] / S:❶[3] Joseph Gershenson (orch.); from the movie soundtrack *Tammy And The Bachelor* starring Reynolds	*French Heels*	$15		Coral 61851
1/20/58	20	3		2 **A Very Special Love** A:20 / T:83 **George Cates** (orch.)	*I Saw A Country Boy*	$12		Coral 61897
1/18/60	25	17		3 **Am I That Easy To Forget** #9 Country hit for Carl Belew in 1959	*Ask Me To Go Steady*	$10	■	Dot 15985
5/2/60	55	4		4 **City Lights** #1 Country hit for **Ray Price** in 1958 and for **Mickey Gilley** in 1975; **Billy Vaughn** (orch., above 2)	*Just For A Touch Of Your Love*	$10	■	Dot 16071

REYNOLDS, Jody
'58

Born on 12/3/38 in Denver, Colorado; raised in Oklahoma. Male rockabilly singer/guitarist.

DEBUT	PEAK	WKS	Gold	A-side (Chart Hit)	B-side	$	Sym	Label & Number
5/19/58	5	17		1 **Endless Sleep** T:5 / S:5 / A:7 **Al Casey** (guitar); reissued on Titan 1801 with a picture sleeve in 1962	*Tight Capris* (w/The Storms)	$30		Demon 1507
8/18/58	66	5		2 **Fire Of Love** H:66	*Daisy Mae*	$25		Demon 1509

REYNOLDS, Lawrence
'69

Born in Mobile, Alabama. White folk-pop-country singer.

DEBUT	PEAK	WKS	Gold	A-side (Chart Hit)	B-side	$	Sym	Label & Number
9/20/69	28	10		**Jesus Is A Soul Man**	*I Know A Good Girl (When I Hold One)*	$8		Warner 7322

RHINOCEROS
BUB/LP '69

Rock group from Los Angeles, California: John Finley (vocals), Danny Weis and Doug Hastings (guitars), Michael Fonfara (organ), Alan Gerber (piano), Jerry Penrod (bass) and Billy Mundi (drums).

DEBUT	PEAK	WKS	Gold	A-side (Chart Hit)	B-side	$	Sym	Label & Number
2/22/69	46	10		**Apricot Brandy**	*When You Say You're Sorry* [I]	$8		Elektra 45647

DEBUT	PEAK	WKS	Gold		A-side (Chart Hit)	B-side	$	Sym	Label & Number
					RHODES, Emitt LP **'71**				
					Born on 2/25/50 in Hawthorne, California. Pop singer/songwriter. Lead singer of **The Merry-Go-Round**.				
1/9/71	54	9			**Fresh As A Daisy**	*You Take The Dark Out Of The Night*	$6		Dunhill/ABC 4267
					RHYTHM HERITAGE R&B/BUB/AC/LP **'76**				
					Studio group assembled by producers Steve Barri and Michael Omartian (keyboards). Vocals by Oren and Luther Waters. Omartian was in the band Gator Creek with **Kenny Loggins**.				
11/15/75+	①^{1}	24	●	1	**Theme From S.W.A.T.**	*I Wouldn't Treat A Dog (The Way You Treated Me)* [I]	$5		ABC 12135
					from the ABC-TV series *S.W.A.T.* starring Steve Forrest				
4/10/76	20	13		2	**Baretta's Theme ("Keep Your Eye On The Sparrow")**	*My Cherie Amour*	$5		ABC 12177
					from the TV series *Baretta* starring Robert Blake				
2/26/77	94	3		3	**Theme From Rocky (Gonna Fly Now)**	*Last Night On Earth* [I]	$5		ABC 12243
					from the movie *Rocky* starring Sylvester Stallone				
					RHYTHM SYNDICATE **'91**				
					R&B group from Connecticut: Evan Rogers (vocals), Carl Sturken (guitar), John Nevin (keyboards), Rob Mingrino (bass) and Kevin Cloud (drums). Rogers and Sturken produced **Donny Osmond**'s "Soldier Of Love" and "Sacred Emotion." Changed spelling of name from Rythm Syndicate to Rhythm Syndicate after first album.				
6/1/91	2^{2}	17		1	**P.A.S.S.I.O.N**	A:5 / S:19 *(3 album snippets)*	$3	▮V	Impact 54046
9/7/91	13	14		2	**Hey Donna**	A:29 *(3 album snippets)*	$3	▮V	Impact 54208
					"45" issued for above 2 on Collectables/MCA 90194				
1/18/92	76	6		3	**Blinded By Love**	*(3 album snippets)*	$3	▮	Impact 54275
					RYTHM SYNDICATE (above 3)				
9/12/92	73	8		4	**I Wanna Make Love To You**	A:68 *P.A.S.S.I.O.N*	$3	▮	Impact 54458
					from the movie *Innocent Blood* starring Anne Parillaud				
					RIBBONS, The **'63**				
					Female R&B vocal group from Los Angeles, California: Vessie Simmons, Aretha Gibson, Evelyn Doty and Lovie.				
2/2/63	81	4			**Ain't Gonna Kiss Ya**	*My Baby Said*	$20		Marsh 202
	★376★				**RICH, Charlie** C&W/BUB/AC/LP **'73**				
					Born on 12/14/32 in Colt, Arkansas. Died of an acute blood clot on 7/25/95 (age 62). Rockabilly-country singer/pianist/songwriter (charted 45 hits, 1968-81). First played jazz and blues. Own jazz group, the Velvetones, mid-1950s, while in U.S. Air Force. Session work with Sun Records in 1958. Known as "The Silver Fox."				
					1)The Most Beautiful Girl 2)A Very Special Love Song 3)Behind Closed Doors				
3/14/60	22	21		1	**Lonely Weekends**	*Everything I Do Is Wrong*	$30		Phillips 3552
					The Gene Lowery Chorus (backing vocals)				
8/28/65	21	11		2	**Mohair Sam**	*I Washed My Hands In Muddy Water*	$20		Smash 1993
3/28/70	85	4		3	**July 12, 1939**	*I'm Flying To Nashville Tonight*	$7		Epic 10585
4/28/73	15	19	▲	4	**Behind Closed Doors**	CW^{2} *A Sunday Kind Of Woman*	$5		Epic 10950
9/29/73	①^{2}	22	●	5	**The Most Beautiful Girl**	CW^{3} / AC^{3} *I Feel Like Going Home*	$5		Epic 11040
1/26/74	18	15		6	**There Won't Be Anymore**	CW^{2} *It's All Over Now*	$5		RCA Victor 0195
					originally released on RCA Victor 8536 in 1965 ($8)				
2/23/74	11	14		7	**A Very Special Love Song**	CW^{3} / AC^{2} *I Can't Even Drink It Away*	$5		Epic 11091
5/4/74	47	6		8	**I Don't See Me In Your Eyes Anymore**	CW^{1} *No Room To Dance*	$5		RCA Victor 0260
					#5 hit for The Stardusters in 1949				
8/3/74	24	13		9	**I Love My Friend**	CW^{1} / AC^{1} *Why, Oh Why*	$5		Epic 20006
9/28/74	47	7		10	**She Called Me Baby**	CW^{1} *Ten Dollars And A Clean White Shirt*	$5		RCA Victor 10062
					The Jordanaires (backing vocals); all RCA Victor titles were recorded 1963-65				
2/1/75	49	6		11	**My Elusive Dreams**	*Whatever Happened*	$5		Epic 50064
5/31/75	19	12		12	**Every Time You Touch Me (I Get High)**	AC^{1} *Pass On By*	$5		Epic 50103
1/24/76	71	6		13	**Since I Fell For You**	*She*	$5		Epic 50182
					#3 R&B hit for **Annie Laurie** & **Paul Gayten** in 1947; all Epic hits produced by Billy Sherrill				
					RICH, Tony, Project LP **'96**				
					Born Anthony Jeffries on 11/19/71 in Detroit, Michigan. R&B singer/songwriter/keyboardist.				
12/16/95+	2^{2}	47	▲	1	**Nobody Knows**	S:3 / A:4 *(instrumental)*	$3	▮	LaFace 24115
7/27/96	41	15		2	**Like A Woman**	S:32 / A:68 *(instrumental)*	$3	▮V	LaFace 24175
12/7/96+	88	8		3	**Leavin'**	S:64 *(instrumental)*	$3	▮	LaFace 24204
	★309★				**RICHARD, Cliff** BUB/AC/LP **'80**				
					Born Harry Rodger Webb on 10/14/40 in Lucknow, India (of British parentage). Rock and roll-pop singer/guitarist/actor. To England in 1948. Worked in skiffle groups, mid-1950s. Backing band: The Drifters (later: The Shadows). Richard also recorded Inspirational music since 1967. The Shadows disbanded in 1969. Superstar in England, with over 125 charted hits, including 14 #1 singles. British movies *Expresso Bongo*, *The Young Ones*, *Summer Holiday* and *Wonderful Life*. Knighted by Queen Elizabeth II in 1995.				
					1)Devil Woman 2)We Don't Talk Anymore 3)Dreaming				
9/28/59	30	13		1	**Living Doll**	*Apron Strings*	$25		ABC-Paramount 10042
					CLIFF RICHARD and The Drifters				
					from the movie *Serious Charge* starring Anthony Quayle				
8/3/63	62	8		2	**Lucky Lips**	*The Next Time*	$20	■	Epic 9597
12/7/63+	25	13		3	**It's All In The Game**	*I'm Looking Out Of The Window*	$20		Epic 9633
4/18/64	92	2		4	**I'm The Lonely One**	*I Only Have Eyes For You (#109)*	$20	■	Epic 9670
8/1/64	99	1		5	**Bachelor Boy**	*True True Lovin'*	$20		Epic 9691
					CLIFF RICHARD And The Shadows				
6/8/68	99	3		6	**Congratulations**	*High 'N' Dry*	$10		Uni 55069
7/4/76	6	22	●	7	**Devil Woman**	*Love On (Shine On)*	$5		Rocket 40574
12/18/76	80	4		8	**I Can't Ask For Anymore Than You**	*Junior Cowboy*	$5		Rocket 40652
6/4/77	57	7		9	**Don't Turn The Light Out**	*Nothing Left For Me To Say*	$5		Rocket 40724
10/20/79+	7	20		10	**We Don't Talk Anymore**	*Count Me Out*	$4		EMI America 8025
2/23/80	34	11		11	**Carrie**	*Language Of Love*	$4		EMI America 8035
9/13/80	10	22		12	**Dreaming**	*Dynamite*	$4		EMI America 8057

DEBUT	PEAK	WKS	Gold	A-side (Chart Hit)...B-side	$	Sym	Label & Number
				RICHARD, Cliff — Cont'd			
10/25/80+	20	19		13 **Suddenly** ... *You Made Me Love You* (Newton-John) **OLIVIA NEWTON-JOHN AND CLIFF RICHARD** from the movie *Xanadu* starring Newton-John	$4	■	MCA 51007
12/13/80+	17	22		14 **A Little In Love** ... *Everyman*	$4		EMI America 8068
4/25/81	41	11		15 **Give A Little Bit More** ... *Keep On Lookin'*	$4	■	EMI America 8076
10/10/81	71	4		16 **Wired For Sound** ... *Hold On*	$4		EMI America 8095
1/16/82	23	13		17 **Daddy's Home** ... *Summer Rain* [L]	$4		EMI America 8103
10/9/82	64	7		18 **The Only Way Out** ... *Be In My Heart*	$4		EMI America 8135
10/8/83	73	7		19 **Never Say Die (Give A Little Bit More)** ... *Front Page* #15 and 19 are different songs	$4		EMI America 8180
				RICHARD and THE YOUNG LIONS '66 Psychedelic garage-rock band from Newark, New Jersey: Howie "Richard" Tepp (vocals), Lou Vlahakes and Bob Freeman (guitars), Freddy Randle (bass) and Mark Greenberg (drums). Previously known as The Emeralds and The Original Kounts.			
9/24/66	99	1		**Open Up Your Door** ... *Once Upon Your Smile*	$20	■	Philips 40381
				RICHARDS, Carol — see CROSBY, Bing			
				RICHARDS, Turley '80 Born in 1941 in Charleston, West Virginia. White soft-rock singer/guitarist. Went blind at age 28.			
4/4/70	84	3		1 **Love Minus Zero-No Limit** ... *Gone From Yesterday* written by **Bob Dylan** (from his 1965 album *Bring It All Back Home*)	$8		Warner 7376
6/20/70	99	3		2 **I Heard The Voice Of Jesus** ... *Then I'll Go Away*	$8		Warner 7397
1/26/80	54	7		3 **You Might Need Somebody** ... *It's All Up To You*	$5		Atlantic 3645

RICHIE, Lionel ★86★ AC/R&B/BUB/LP '84

Born on 6/20/49 in Tuskegee, Alabama. R&B-Adult Contemporary singer/songwriter. Grew up on the campus of Tuskegee Institute where his grandfather worked. Former lead singer of the **Commodores**. Appeared in the movie *Thank God It's Friday*. Had 11 #1 Adult Contemporary hits.

1)Endless Love 2)All Night Long (All Night) 3)Say You, Say Me

DEBUT	PEAK	WKS	Gold	A-side (Chart Hit)...B-side	$	Sym	Label & Number
7/11/81	❶[9]	27	▲	1 **Endless Love** RB[7] / AC[3] *(instrumental)* **DIANA ROSS & LIONEL RICHIE** title song from the movie starring Brooke Shields	$4		Motown 1519
10/9/82	❶[2]	18	●	2 **Truly** ... AC[4] *Just Put Some Love In Your Heart*	$4		Motown 1644
1/15/83	4	18		3 **You Are** ... AC[6] *You Mean More To Me*	$4	■	Motown 1657
4/9/83	5	16		4 **My Love** ... AC[4] *Round And Round*	$4	■	Motown 1677
9/17/83	❶[4]	24	●	5 **All Night Long (All Night)** ... RB[7] / AC[4] *Wandering Stranger*	$4		Motown 1698
11/26/83+	7	19		6 **Running With The Night** ... *Serves You Right*	$4		Motown 1710
2/25/84	❶[2]	24	●	7 **Hello** ... RB[3] / AC[6] *You Mean More To Me*	$4		Motown 1722
6/23/84	3	19		8 **Stuck On You** ... AC[5] *Round And Round*	$4	■	Motown 1746
10/6/84	8	18		9 **Penny Lover** ... AC[4] A:5 / S:13 *Tell Me* above 5 from the album *Can't Slow Down*	$4	■	Motown 1762
11/9/85	❶[4]	20	●	10 **Say You, Say Me** ... RB[2] / AC[5] A:❶[5] / S:❶[3] *Can't Slow Down* from the movie *White Nights* starring Mikhail Baryshnikov; issued with 2 different picture sleeves and a promotional "This Dub's For You" sleeve	$3	■	Motown 1819
7/19/86	2[2]	17		11 **Dancing On The Ceiling** ... A:❶[1] / S:3 *Love Will Find A Way*	$3	■	Motown 1843
10/4/86	9	18		12 **Love Will Conquer All** ... AC[2] S:8 / A:8 *The Only One*	$3	■	Motown 1866
12/6/86+	7	18		13 **Ballerina Girl** / AC[4] S:5 / A:8			
1/17/87	71	8		14 **Deep River Woman** ... **LIONEL RICHIE with Alabama**	$3	■	Motown 1873
3/28/87	20	13		15 **Se La** ... S:17 / A:23 *Serves You Right* #10-15: from the album *Dancing On The Ceiling*	$3	■	Motown 1883
5/2/92	21	20		16 **Do It To Me** ... RB[1] S:23 / A:31 *(instrumental)*	$3	▮[V]	Motown 2160
4/13/96	39	15		17 **Don't Wanna Lose You** ... S:26 / A:59 *(talk version) / (album version)* "45": Mercury 852856	$3	▮[V]	Mercury 852857
5/5/01	70	18		18 **Angel** ... A:65 *(4 versions)* all of above written or co-written by Richie	$6	T	Island 572831
				RICHIE RICH R&B/LP '97 Born Richard Serrell on 6/25/67 in Oakland, California. Male rapper. Member of group 415. Influenced such rappers as **Snoop Doggy Dogg** and **Warren G**.			
11/30/96+	67	13		1 **Let's Ride** ... S:53 *Funk* samples "(not just) Knee Deep" by **Funkadelic**	$4	▮	Def Jam 575774
3/1/97	57	15		2 **Do G's Get To Go To Heaven?** ... S:35 dedicated to **2 Pac** who died on 9/13/96	$4	▮	Def Jam 574030
				RICK And The Keens '61 Rock and roll band from Wichita Falls, Texas, consisting of 4 men and 1 woman.			
7/3/61	60	8		**Peanuts** ... *I'll Be Home* first released on Austin 303 ($50) and Le Cam 721 ($50) in 1961	$20		Smash 1705
				RICKS, Jimmy — see BAKER, LaVern			

DEBUT	PEAK	WKS	Gold	A-side (Chart Hit)........B-side	$	Sym	Label & Number

RIDDLE, Nelson, and His Orchestra
MEM/BUB/AC/LP **'56**

Born on 6/1/21 in Oradell, New Jersey. Died on 10/6/85 (age 64). Trombonist/arranger with Charlie Spivak and **Tommy Dorsey** in the 1940s. One of the most in-demand of all arranger/conductors for many top artists, including **Frank Sinatra** (several classic 1950s albums), **Nat King Cole**, Ella Mae Morse, and more recently, **Linda Ronstadt**; also arranger/musical director for many movies.

DEBUT	PEAK	WKS	Gold	A-side (Chart Hit)........B-side	$	Sym	Label & Number
12/10/55+	❶ (4)	29	●	1 **Lisbon Antigua** S:❶ (4) / A:❷ (2) / T:2 / J:2 *Robin Hood* [I] from a 1937 Portuguese song "Lisboa Antigua"; a promo booklet-type sleeve issued in 1956 because of the song's incorporation in the musical score of the movie *Lisbon* starring Ray Milland	$15	□	Capitol 3287
3/24/56	20	14		2 **Port Au Prince**........A:20 / T:32 *Midnight Blues* [I]	$12		Capitol 3374
7/14/56	39	10		3 **Theme From "The Proud Ones"**........T:39 *The Love Of Genevieve* [I] title song from the movie *The Proud Ones* starring Robert Ryan	$12		Capitol 3472
6/2/62	30	12		4 **Route 66 Theme**........*Lolita Ya Ya* [I] from the CBS-TV series starring **George Maharis** and Martin Milner	$10		Capitol 4741
10/29/83	53	14		5 **What's New**........*Crazy He Calls Me* **LINDA RONSTADT & THE NELSON RIDDLE ORCHESTRA** first written as the instrumental "I'm Free"; #2 hit for **Bing Crosby** in 1939	$4		Asylum 69780

RIDGELEY, Andrew — see MICHAEL, George

RIFF
R&B/LP **'91**

R&B vocal group from Paterson, New Jersey: Ken Kelly, Steven Capers, Anthony Fuller, Dwayne Jones and Michael Best.

DEBUT	PEAK	WKS	Gold	A-side (Chart Hit)........B-side	$	Sym	Label & Number
2/23/91	52	7		1 **I Love You**........S:66 *Stop That Train* **VANILLA ICE Introducing Riff**	$4	▮	SBK 07346
3/23/91	25	14		2 **My Heart Is Failing Me**........S:24 / A:29 *Temporary Insanity*	$3	▮	SBK 07342
9/14/91	88	5		3 **If You're Serious**........*All Or Nothing*	$3	▮	SBK 07361
5/2/92	90	4		4 **White Men Can't Jump**........S:45 *(instrumental)* title song from the movie starring Wesley Snipes and Woody Harrelson	$3	▮	SBK 07384

RIGHTEOUS BROTHERS, The ★147★
BUB/AC/LP **'65**

"Blue-eyed soul" duo: **Bill Medley** (baritone; born on 9/19/40 in Santa Ana, California) and **Bobby Hatfield** (tenor; born on 8/10/40 in Beaver Dam, Wisconsin) (see #19 below). Formed duo in 1962. First recorded as the Paramours for Smash in 1962. On *Hullabaloo* and *Shindig* TV shows. Split up from 1968-74. Medley went solo, replaced by Jimmy Walker (**The Knickerbockers**); rejoined Hatfield in 1974. Inducted into the Rock and Roll Hall of Fame in 2003.

1)(You're My) Soul And Inspiration 2)You've Lost That Lovin' Feelin' 3)Rock And Roll Heaven 4)Unchained Melody 5)Ebb Tide

DEBUT	PEAK	WKS	Gold	A-side (Chart Hit)........B-side	$	Sym	Label & Number
5/11/63	49	7		1 **Little Latin Lupe Lu**........*I'm So Lonely*	$20		Moonglow 215
9/7/63	75	7		2 **My Babe**........*Fee-Fi-Fidily-I-Oh (Dinah Blow Your Horn)* "Bubbled Under" (#101) on 2/6/65	$20		Moonglow 223
12/12/64+	❶ (2)	16		3 **You've Lost That Lovin' Feelin'**........*There's A Woman* the first 8-million performance song according to BMI	$15		Philles 124
1/30/65	83	3		4 **Bring Your Love To Me**........*Fannie Mae (#117)*	$15		Moonglow 238
4/10/65	9	11		5 **Just Once In My Life**........*The Blues*	$15	■	Philles 127
5/8/65	67	5		6 **You Can Have Her**........*Love Or Magic*	$15		Moonglow 239
7/3/65	85	3		7 **Justine**........*In That Great Gettin' Up Mornin'* from the movie *A Swingin' Summer* starring Raquel Welch (movie debut)	$15		Moonglow 242
7/17/65	4	13		8 **Unchained Melody** / also see #23 & 24 below			
7/17/65	47	7		9 **Hung On You**........	$15		Philles 129
12/4/65+	5	9		10 **Ebb Tide**........*(I Love You) For Sentimental Reasons* picture sleeve issued with titles in blue or black ink; #2 hit for **Frank Chacksfield** in 1953; all Phillies hits produced by Phil Spector	$15	■	Philles 130
2/5/66	62	5		11 **Georgia On My Mind**........*My Tears Will Go Away* #10 hit for Frankie Trumbauer in 1931	$15		Moonglow 244
3/5/66	❶ (3)	13	●	12 **(You're My) Soul And Inspiration** *B Side Blues*	$15	■	Verve 10383
6/4/66	18	8		13 **He** /			
6/4/66	91	1		14 **He Will Break Your Heart**........	$12	■	Verve 10406
8/6/66	30	6		15 **Go Ahead And Cry**........*Things Didn't Go Your Way*	$12	■	Verve 10430
10/29/66	47	6		16 **On This Side Of Goodbye**........*A Man Without A Dream*	$10		Verve 10449
4/22/67	43	6		17 **Melancholy Music Man**........*Don't Give Up On Me*	$10		Verve 10507
9/30/67	72	4		18 **Stranded In The Middle Of Noplace**........*Been So Nice (#128)*	$10	■	Verve 10551
3/8/69	95	4		19 **Only You (And You Alone)**........*The Wonder Of You* **BOBBY HATFIELD**	$10		Verve 10634
5/25/74	3	17		20 **Rock And Roll Heaven**........*I Just Wanna Be Me*	$6		Haven 7002
9/7/74	20	9		21 **Give It To The People**........*Love Is Not A Dirty Word*	$6		Haven 7004
11/9/74	32	8		22 **Dream On**........*Dr. Rock And Roll*	$6		Haven 7006
8/25/90	13	19		23 **Unchained Melody**........AC (2) A:3 *Hung On You* [R] same version as #8 above; featured in the movie *Ghost* starring **Patrick Swayze** and Demi Moore	$5	V	Verve Forecast 871882
10/6/90	19	25	▲	24 **Unchained Melody**........S:4 *American Rock And Roll* [R] newly recorded 1990 version; #23: "45" 7" vinyl only; #24: cassette only	$4	▮	Curb 76842

RIGHT SAID FRED (R*S*F)
LP **'92**

Pop-dance-novelty trio from England: brothers Fred (guitar) and Richard (vocals) Fairbrass with Rob Manzoli (guitar).

DEBUT	PEAK	WKS	Gold	A-side (Chart Hit)........B-side	$	Sym	Label & Number
12/21/91+	❶ (3)	21	▲	1 **I'm Too Sexy**........S:❶ (7) / A:8 *(Spanish version)*	$3	▮V	Charisma 98671
4/18/92	76	7		2 **Don't Talk Just Kiss**........A:49 *(7" dance mix)*	$3	▮V	Charisma 98595

RILEY, Billy Lee
'72

Born on 10/5/33 in Pocahontas, Arkansas. White session musician in Memphis, Tennessee; one of the lesser-known Sun rockabilly artists from 1956-59. Led **The Megatons** and wrote their 1962 hit "Shimmy, Shimmy Walk."

DEBUT	PEAK	WKS	Gold	A-side (Chart Hit)........B-side	$	Sym	Label & Number
11/4/72	93	2		**I Got A Thing About You Baby**........*You Don't Love Me*	$6		Entrance 7508

DEBUT	PEAK	WKS	Gold	A-side (Chart Hit)..........B-side	$	Sym	Label & Number
				RILEY, Cheryl Pepsii R&B/LP **'88**			
				Born in Brooklyn, New York. R&B singer. Discovered by the group **Full Force**.			
10/29/88	32	13		**Thanks For My Child** ....RB[1] S:31 / A:31 *Child (The Confrontation mix)*	$3	■	Columbia 07996
				written, produced and arranged by **Full Force**			
				RILEY, Jeannie C. C&W/BUB/LP **'68**			
				Born Jeannie Carolyn Stephenson on 10/19/45 in Anson, Texas. Country singer (charted 23 hits, 1968-76).			
8/24/68	❶[1]	13	●	1 **Harper Valley P.T.A.** CW[3] *Yesterday All Day Long Today*	$6		Plantation 3
				written by **Tom T. Hall**; reissued for same-titled movie in 1978 on Plantation 173 (with a picture sleeve)			
12/7/68	55	6		2 **The Girl Most Likely** ....*My Scrapbook*	$6		Plantation 7
3/29/69	77	4		3 **There Never Was A Time** ....*Back To School*	$6		Plantation 16
4/3/71	74	6		4 **Oh, Singer** ....*I'll Take What's Left Of You*	$6		Plantation 72
7/31/71	97	4		5 **Good Enough To Be Your Wife** ....*Light Your Light (And Let It Shine)*	$6		Plantation 75
				RILEY, Teddy R&B **'98**			
				Born on 10/8/66 in Harlem, New York. R&B singer/songwriter/producer. Member of Kids At Work, **Guy** and **BLACKstreet**. Brother of Markell Riley of **Wreckx-N-Effect**.			
9/23/89	62	6		1 **My Fantasy** RB[1] *(instrumental)*	$3		Motown 1968
				TEDDY RILEY FEATURING GUY			
				from the movie *Do The Right Thing* starring Spike Lee			
12/13/97+	84	9		2 **Man Behind The Music** ....S:69 *(instrumental)*	$4	▮	Lil' Man 97020
				QUEEN PEN Featuring Teddy Riley			
				contains interpolations of "Your Love" and "I Know You Got Soul" by **Eric B. & Rakim**			
6/20/98	63	11		3 **Freak Out** ....S:46 *(2 versions)*	$4	▮	Lil' Man 97028
				NUTTA BUTTA Featuring Teddy Riley and Anonymous			
				samples "Le Freak" by **Chic**			
6/20/98	74	4		4 **Party Ain't A Party** ....A:51 *(2 versions)*	$6	T	Lil' Man 95024
				QUEEN PEN Featuring Teddy Riley, Nutta Butta, Markell & Jesse West			
				samples "On Your Face" by **Earth, Wind & Fire**			
11/24/01	71[S]	1		5 **Formal Invite** ....*(5 remixes)*	$6	T	Atlantic 85182
				RAY J (Featuring Brandy, Teddy Riley & Shorty Mack)			
	★393★			**RIMES, LeAnn** C&W/AC/BUB/LP **'97**			
				Born Margaret LeAnn Rimes on 8/28/82 in Jackson, Mississippi; raised in Garland, Texas. Country singer. Married actor Dean Sheremet on 2/23/2002. Won the 1996 Best New Artist Grammy Award.			
				1)How Do I Live 2)Can't Fight The Moonlight (2001) 3)I Need You			
6/22/96	26	20	●	1 **Blue** ....S:11 *The Light In Your Eyes*	$4	▮[V]	Curb 76959
				song originally written for, but not recorded by, **Patsy Cline**			
6/21/97	2[4]	69	▲[3]	2 **How Do I Live** AC[11] S:2 / A:3 *(extended mix)*	$3	▮[V]	Curb 73022
				from the movie *Con Air* starring Nicolas Cage			
9/13/97	34	20	●	3 **You Light Up My Life** ....S:20 *I Believe*	$3	▮[V]	Curb 73027
4/18/98	18	24	●	4 **Looking Through Your Eyes** ....S:13 / A:70 *Commitment* (C&W #4)	$3	▮[V]	Curb 73055
				from the animated movie *Quest For Camelot*			
3/13/99	29	10	●	5 **Written In The Stars** ....S:13 *(alternate version) / (3 album snippets)*	$4	★	Rocket/Curb 566918
				ELTON JOHN & LEANN RIMES			
				from Elton John and Tim Rice's musical interpretation of the stage show *Aida*			
10/16/99+	23	20		6 **Big Deal** ....S:18 / A:39 *Leaving's Not Leaving*	$4	★[V]	Curb 73086
5/27/00	11	25		7 **I Need You** ....S:3 / A:23 *Spirit In The Sky* (**dc Talk**)	$4	★[V]	Curb/Capitol 58863
				from the TV movie *Jesus* starring Jeremy Sisto; "45": Capitol 88644; B-side: "Jesus, Theme" (Patrick Williams)			
9/9/00	71	20	●	8 **Can't Fight The Moonlight** ....S:5 *But I Do Love You*	$4	★	Curb 73116
				theme from the movie *Coyote Ugly* starring Piper Perabo; also see #10 below			
11/3/01	12[S]	15		9 **God Bless America** ....*Put A Little Holiday In Your Heart*	$4	★	Curb 73127
12/8/01+	11	22	●	10 **Can't Fight The Moonlight** ....S:4 / A:15 / BUB:103 *But I Do Love You* (C&W #18) [R]	$4	★	Curb 73116
				same version as #8 above; CD packaging: #8: cardboard case; #10: jewel box case			
				RINGS, The LP **'81**			
				Rock group from Boston, Massachusetts: Mark Sutton (vocals, guitar), Mike Baker (keyboards), Bob Gifford (bass) and Matt Thurber (drums).			
3/7/81	75	5		**Let Me Go** ....*Third Generation*	$5		MCA 51069
				RINKY-DINKS, The — see DARIN, Bobby			
				RIOS, Augie **'58**			
				Child singer/actor. Appeared in the Broadway musical *Jamaica*.			
12/15/58	47	4		**¿Dònde Està Santa Claus? (Where Is Santa Claus?)** ....*Ol' Fatso* [X-N]	$40		Metro 20010
				Mark Jeffrey (orch.)			
				RIOS, Miguel LP **'70**			
				Born on 6/7/44 in Granada, Spain. Adult Contemporary singer.			
6/13/70	14	9		**A Song Of Joy (Himno A La Alegria)** ....AC[2] *El Rio*	$6	■	A&M 1193
				Waldo de los Rios (conductor); based on the last movement of Beethoven's Ninth Symphony			
				RIOS, Waldo De Los LP **'71**			
				Born in 1934 in Buenos Aires, Argentina. Committed suicide on 3/28/77 (age 42). Composer/conductor.			
6/19/71	67	8		**Mozart Symphony No. 40 In G Minor K.550, 1st Movement** .....*Ode To Joy* [I]	$5		United Artists 50772
				RIP CHORDS, The BUB/LP **'64**			
				Rock and roll group formed in California. Featuring the duo of **Bruce And Terry** (see #4 & 6 below): Terry Melcher (**Doris Day**'s son — produced **The Byrds**, **Paul Revere & The Raiders**) and Bruce Johnston (**Beach Boys**). Other members: Ernie Bringas, Phil Stewart, Richard Rotkin and Arnie Marcus. Touring group included Phil, Richard and Arnie who also appeared in the Raquel Welch beach movie *A Swingin' Summer*.			
3/30/63	51	8		1 **Here I Stand** ....*Karen*	$15	□	Columbia 42687
8/17/63	88	4		2 **Gone** ....*She Thinks I Still Care*	$15	□	Columbia 42812
12/14/63+	4	14		3 **Hey Little Cobra** *The Queen*	$20		Columbia 42921
2/22/64	85	3		4 **Custom Machine** ....*Makaha At Midnight*	$20		Columbia 42956
				BRUCE AND TERRY			
				written by **Brian Wilson** of **The Beach Boys**			

DEBUT	PEAK	WKS	Gold	A-side (Chart Hit)	B-side	$	Sym	Label & Number
				RIP CHORDS, The — Cont'd				
4/25/64	28	9		5 **Three Window Coupe** co-written by Jan Berry (**Jan & Dean**)	*Hot Rod U.S.A.*	$20		Columbia 43035
7/25/64	72	5		6 **Summer Means Fun** **BRUCE AND TERRY**	*Yeah!*	$20		Columbia 43055
8/8/64	96	1		7 **One Piece Topless Bathing Suit**	*Wah-Wahini*	$15		Columbia 43093
				RIPERTON, Minnie R&B/AC/LP **'75** Born on 11/8/47 in Chicago, Illinois. Died of cancer on 7/12/79 (age 31). R&B singer. Member of **Rotary Connection** from 1967-70. Her daughter Maya Rudolph is a cast member of TV's *Saturday Night Live*.				
1/18/75	❶^{1}	18	●	1 **Lovin' You**	*The Edge Of A Dream*	$5		Epic 50057
8/9/75	76	4		2 **Inside My Love**	*Don't Let Anyone Bring You Down*	$5		Epic 50128
				RIPPLE R&B/BUB **'73** Interracial progressive soul group from Kalamazoo, Michigan: Dave Ferguson, Bill Hull, Keith "Doc" Samuels, Curtis Reynolds, Ken Carter, Walter Carter and Brian Sherrer.				
11/3/73	67	6		**I Don't Know What It Is, But It Sure Is Funky**	*Dance Lady Dance*	$6		GRC 1004
				RISING SON **'01** Born Archie Blaine in Cleveland, Ohio. Male rapper.				
7/14/01	37^{S}	18		**Make It Vibrate**	*(3 versions) / Rising Son*	$8	★*	Darkside 003
				RITCHIE FAMILY, The R&B/BUB/LP **'75** Female disco trio from Philadelphia, Pennsylvania: Cheryl Jackson, Cassandra Wooten and Gwen Oliver. Named for producer Ritchie Rome.				
8/2/75	11	18		1 **Brazil** disco version of the #2 hit for Xavier Cugat in 1943	*Hot Trip* [I]	$5		20th Century 2218
12/6/75	84	4		2 **I Want To Dance With You (Dance With Me)**	*Lady Champagne*	$5		20th Century 2252
8/28/76	17	20		3 **The Best Disco In Town**	*(long version)*	$5		Marlin 3306
				RITENOUR, Lee R&B/LP **'81** Born on 1/11/52 in Los Angeles, California. Guitarist/composer/arranger. Top session guitarist. Has appeared on more than 200 albums. Nicknamed "Captain Fingers." Member of jazz outfits Brass Fever and Fourplay.				
4/25/81	15	16		1 **Is It You**	*Countdown (Captain Fingers)*	$4		Elektra 47124
12/4/82	69	7		2 **Cross My Heart** Eric Tagg (vocal, above 2)	*Road Runner*	$4		Elektra 69892
				RITTER, Tex C&W/MEM/POP **'61** Born Maurice Ritter on 1/12/05 in Murvaul, Texas. Died of a heart attack on 1/3/74 (age 68). Country singer/guitarist/actor. Starred in several western movies. Father of actor John Ritter.				
6/30/56	28	13		1 **The Wayward Wind** T:28 Harry Geller (orch.)	*The Searchers (Ride Away)*	$20		Capitol 3430
7/3/61	20	12		2 **I Dreamed Of A Hill-Billy Heaven** Ralph Carmichael (orch.); #10 Country hit for Eddie Dean in 1955	*The Wind And The Tree* [S]	$12		Capitol 4567
2/9/74	90	3		3 **The Americans (A Canadian's Opinion)** originally broadcast on radio by **Gordon Sinclair** in 1973 in Toronto	*He Who Is Without Sin (Let Him Judge Me)* [S]	$6		Capitol 3814
				RIVERS, Johnny ★107★ BUB/C&W/LP **'66** Born John Ramistella on 11/7/42 in Brooklyn, New York; raised in Baton Rouge, Louisiana. Rock and roll singer/guitarist/songwriter/producer. Recorded with the Spades for Suede in 1957. Named Johnny Rivers by DJ Alan Freed in 1958. To Los Angeles in 1961. Recorded for 12 different labels (1958-64) before his smash debut on Imperial. Began own Soul City label in 1966. Recorded Christian music in the early 1980s. *1)Poor Side Of Town 2)Memphis 3)Baby I Need Your Lovin' 4)Secret Agent Man 5)Rockin' Pneumonia - Boogie Woogie Flu*				
5/30/64	2^{2}	12		1 **Memphis** first recorded by **Chuck Berry** in 1959 as "Memphis, Tennessee" on Chess 1729 ($30)	*It Wouldn't Happen With Me* [L]	$12		Imperial 66032
8/15/64	12	9		2 **Maybelline** above 2 written by **Chuck Berry**	*Walk Myself On Home* [L]	$12	■	Imperial 66056
10/31/64	9	11		3 **Mountain Of Love**	*Moody River*	$10		Imperial 66075
2/6/65	20	8		4 **Midnight Special /** written by Leadbelly, whose first recorded version was released in 1941 on Victor 27266 ($20)	[L]			
2/20/65	76	4		5 **Cupid**		$10		Imperial 66087
6/5/65	7	11		6 **Seventh Son** written by blues great, Willie Dixon; first recorded by Willie Mabon in 1955 on Chess 1608 ($60)	*Un-Square Dance* [L]	$10	■	Imperial 66112
10/2/65	26	9		7 **Where Have All The Flowers Gone**	*Love Me While You Can*	$10		Imperial 66133
12/18/65+	35	8		8 **Under Your Spell Again** #4 Country hit for **Buck Owens** in 1959	*Long Time Man*	$10	■	Imperial 66144
3/19/66	3	11		9 **Secret Agent Man** theme from the TV series *Secret Agent* starring Patrick McGoohan	*You Dig*	$10	■	Imperial 66159
6/11/66	19	8		10 **(I Washed My Hands In) Muddy Water** #8 Country hit for **Stonewall Jackson** in 1965; #1, 2, 4, 6 & 10: recorded at the Whisky A Go-Go	*Roogalator* [L]	$10		Imperial 66175
9/17/66	❶^{1}	15		11 **Poor Side Of Town**	*A Man Can Cry*	$10	■	Imperial 66205
2/4/67	3	11		12 **Baby I Need Your Lovin'**	*Gettin' Ready For Tomorrow*	$10	■	Imperial 66227
6/3/67	10	9		13 **The Tracks Of My Tears**	*Rewind Medley*	$10	■	Imperial 66244
11/18/67+	14	10		14 **Summer Rain**	*Memory Of The Coming Good*	$10		Imperial 66267
4/6/68	49	7		15 **Look To Your Soul**	*Something Strange*	$8	■	Imperial 66286
11/23/68	61	3		16 **Right Relations**	*A Better Life*	$8	■	Imperial 66335
2/22/69	55	6		17 **These Are Not My People** written by **Joe South**	*Going Back To Big Sur*	$8		Imperial 66360
6/28/69	41	11		18 **Muddy River**	*Resurrection*	$8	■	Imperial 66386
10/25/69	89	4		19 **One Woman**	*Ode To John Lee*	$8		Imperial 66418

DEBUT	PEAK	WKS	Gold	A-side (Chart Hit)...B-side	$	Sym	Label & Number
				RIVERS, Johnny — Cont'd			
5/9/70	**51**	8		20 **Into The Mystic** ...*Jesus Is A Soul Man* written by **Van Morrison**; #1-13, 19 & 20: produced by Lou Adler	$8		Imperial 66448
9/5/70	**94**	2		21 **Fire And Rain**...*Apple Tree* **JOHNNY RIVERS & Friends**	$8		Imperial 66453
5/8/71	**84**	4		22 **Sea Cruise** ...*Our Lady Of The Well*	$6	■	United Artists 50778
8/28/71	**65**	6		23 **Think His Name** ...*Permanent Change* The Guru Ram Das Ashram Singers (backing vocals)	$6		United Artists 50822
10/7/72+	**6**	19	●	24 **Rockin' Pneumonia - Boogie Woogie Flu** ...*Come Home America*	$6		United Artists 50960
3/17/73	**38**	10		25 **Blue Suede Shoes**...*Stories To A Child*	$6		United Artists 198
7/12/75	**22**	10		26 **Help Me Rhonda**...*New Lovers And Old Friends* **Brian Wilson** of **The Beach Boys** (backing vocal)	$6	■	Soul City/Epic 50121
2/5/77	**96**	4		27 **Ashes And Sand** ...*Outside Help*	$6		Soul City 007
6/25/77	**10**	24	●	28 **Swayin' To The Music (Slow Dancin')**...*Outside Help* also released on Soul City 008 as "Slow Dancin'" ($6)	$5		Big Tree 16094
12/24/77+	**41**	10		29 **Curious Mind (Um, Um, Um, Um, Um, Um)** ...*Ashes And Sand*	$5		Big Tree 16106
				RIVIERAS, The BUB **'59** R&B vocal group from New Jersey: Homer Dunn, Charles Allen, Ronald Cook and Andrew Jones.			
8/25/58	**73**	4		1 **Count Every Star**...H:73 *True Love Is Hard To Find* #4 hit for **Ray Anthony** in 1950	$40		Coed 503
2/9/59	**47**	11		2 **Moonlight Serenade** ...*Neither Rain Nor Snow* #3 hit for Glenn Miller in 1939 (Miller's theme song)	$40		Coed 508
1/18/60	**93**	3		3 **Since I Made You Cry**...*11th Hour Melody*	$35		Coed 522
				RIVIERAS, The LP **'64** Teen rock and roll band from South Bend, Indiana: Bill Dobslaw (vocals), Jim Boal and Willie Gout (guitars), Otto Nuss (organ), Doug Gean (bass) and Paul Dennert (drums). Marty Fortson was lead singer on "California Sun."			
1/25/64	**5**	10		1 **California Sun**...*H B Goose Step* also issued with "Played On" as the B-side ($40)	$20		Riviera 1401
5/2/64	**93**	3		2 **Little Donna** /			
5/30/64	**99**	1		3 **Let's Have A Party** ...	$20		Riviera 1402
9/5/64	**96**	3		4 **Rockin' Robin** ...*Battle Line*	$20		Riviera 1403
				RIVINGTONS, The BUB **'62** R&B vocal group from Los Angeles, California: Carl White (lead; died on 1/7/80, age 47), Sonny Harris, Rocky Wilson and Al Frazier. Backup on **Paul Anka**'s first recording, **Duane Eddy**'s "Rebel Rouser", and "Little Bitty Pretty One" by **Thurston Harris**. Known then as The Sharps. Also see **The Trashmen**.			
8/18/62	**48**	8		1 **Papa-Oom-Mow-Mow**...*Deep Water* a sequel ("Mama-Oom-Mow-Mow") "Bubbled Under" (#106) in 1963	$25		Liberty 55427
3/30/63	**52**	7		2 **The Bird's The Word** ...*I'm Losing My Grip*	$20	■	Liberty 55553
				RJD2 R&B **'02** Born on 5/27/76 in Eugene, Oregon; raised in Columbus, Ohio. Male hip-hop DJ/producer.			
8/17/02	**63^{S}**	1		**Let The Good Times Roll Pt. 1** ...*Pt. 2 / Bus Stop Bitties / Counseling*	$10	T	Definitive Jux 34
				R.L. R&B/LP **'00** Born Robert L. Huggar in Minneapolis, Minnesota. R&B singer/songwriter. Member of **Next**.			
1/8/00	**77**	12		1 **The Best Man I Can Be**...A:67 **GINUWINE, R.L., TYRESE, CASE** from the movie *The Best Man* starring Taye Diggs (soundtrack on Columbia 69924)			album cut
10/6/01	**84**	16		2 **Do U Wanna Roll**...S:12 *(2 versions) / Lookin' For Love* (w/**Next**) **R.L., SNOOP DOGG and LIL' KIM** samples "Doo Wa Ditty (Blow That Thing)" by **Zapp**; from the movie *Dr. Dolittle 2* starring **Eddie Murphy**	$4	★	J Records 21132
				ROACHFORD LP **'89** R&B-rock group formed in England: Andrew Roachford (vocals, keyboards; born on 1/22/65), Hawi Gondwe (guitar), Derrick Taylor (bass) and Chris Taylor (drums).			
4/15/89	**25**	14		**Cuddly Toy (Feel For Me)** ...S:25 / A:26 *Lying Again*	$5		Epic 68549
				ROAD APPLES, The BUB **'75** Pop group from Boston, Massachusetts. Led by singer/guitarist David Finnerty.			
9/27/75+	**35**	14		**Let's Live Together**...*(instrumental)* first released in 1975 on Mums 6039	$6		Polydor 14285
				ROB BASE & D.J. E-Z ROCK R&B/LP **'88** Rap-dance duo from Harlem, New York: Robert Ginyard with DJ Rodney "Skip" Bryce.			
8/20/88	**36**	16	▲	1 **It Takes Two**...S:23 *(instrumental)* samples **Lyn Collins**' 1972 hit "Think (About It)"	$4		Profile 5186
5/27/89	**58**	13		2 **Joy And Pain**...S:39 *Times Are Gettin' Ill* samples the same-named tune (from 1980) by **Maze Featuring Frankie Beverly**	$4	■	Profile 5247
				ROBBINS, Marty ★156★ C&W/BUB/LP **'60** Born Martin David Robinson on 9/26/25 in Glendale, Arizona. Died of a heart attack on 12/8/82 (age 57). Country singer/guitarist/songwriter (charted 94 hits, 1952-83). Own radio show with K-Bar Cowboys, late 1940s. Own TV show, *Western Caravan*, KPHO-Phoenix, 1951. First recorded for Columbia in 1952. Regular on the *Grand Ole Opry* since 1953. Own Robbins label in 1958. Raced stock cars. Movies: *Road To Nashville* and *Guns Of A Stranger*. Robbins, **Eddy Arnold**, **Jim Reeves** and **Johnny Cash** were the first major country stars to have a big impact on the pop charts. *1)El Paso 2)A White Sport Coat (And A Pink Carnation) 3)Don't Worry 4)The Story Of My Life 5)Devil Woman*			
11/3/56	**17**	18		1 **Singing The Blues** ...CW^{13} J:17 / T:26 *I Can't Quit (I've Gone Too Far)* (C&W #7) first released on Columbia 21508 in 1956 ($40)	$40		Columbia 21545
4/13/57	**2^{1}**	26	●	2 **A White Sport Coat (And A Pink Carnation)** ...CW^{5} S:2 / T:3 / A:4 / J:4 *Grown-Up Tears*	$25	■	Columbia 40864
11/11/57+	**15**	24		3 **The Story Of My Life**...CW^{4} A:15 / T:30 / S:31 *Once-A-Week Date* the first hit record of a **Burt Bacharach** song	$25	■	Columbia 41013

DEBUT	PEAK	WKS	Gold	A-side (Chart Hit)..........B-side	$	Sym	Label & Number
				ROBBINS, Marty — Cont'd			
4/14/58	**26**	16		4 **Just Married /** CW[2] S:26 / T:35			
4/28/58	**68**	4		5 **Stairway Of Love** ....T:68 / S:flip	$20		Columbia 41143
8/4/58	**27**	13		6 **She Was Only Seventeen (He Was One Year More)** ....H:27 *Sittin' In A Tree House*	$20	■	Columbia 41208
2/2/59	**38**	13		7 **The Hanging Tree**..........*The Blues Country Style* title song from the movie starring Gary Cooper; **Ray Conniff** (orch., above 6)	$20	■	Columbia 41325
6/15/59	**45**	6		8 **Cap And Gown**..........*Last Night About This Time*	$15		Columbia 41408
11/9/59+	❶[2]	22		9 **El Paso** CW[7] *Running Gun* also issued with a special promotional red and white sleeve	$15	■	Columbia 41511
3/14/60	**26**	10		10 **Big Iron**..........*Saddle Tramp*	$15	■	Columbia 41589
6/20/60	**31**	12		11 **Is There Any Chance** ....*I Told My Heart*	$15		Columbia 41686
9/12/60	**74**	4		12 **Five Brothers** ....*Ride, Cowboy Ride*	$15		Columbia 41771
10/17/60	**34**	13		13 **Ballad Of The Alamo** ....*A Time And A Place For Everything* from the movie *The Alamo* starring John Wayne	$15	■	Columbia 41809
1/30/61	**3**	15		14 **Don't Worry** ....CW[10] *Like All The Other Times* song is famous for its "fuzztone" bass guitar solo by Grady Martin	$15	■	Columbia 41922
5/29/61	**51**	5		15 **Jimmy Martinez**..........*Ghost Train*	$12	■	Columbia 42008
9/11/61	**51**	9		16 **It's Your World**..........*You Told Me So*	$12	■	Columbia 42065
12/25/61+	**81**	4		17 **I Told The Brook** ....*Sometimes I'm Tempted* (#109)	$12	■	Columbia 42246
4/28/62	**69**	6		18 **Love Can't Wait**..........*Too Far Gone*	$12	■	Columbia 42375
7/28/62	**16**	11		19 **Devil Woman**..........CW[8] *April Fool's Day*	$12	■	Columbia 42486
11/17/62	**18**	10		20 **Ruby Ann** ....CW[1] *Won't You Forgive*	$12	■	Columbia 42614
3/16/63	**93**	2		21 **Cigarettes And Coffee Blues**..........*Teenager's Dad* #13 Country hit for **Lefty Frizzell** in 1958; above 3 each issued with 2 different picture sleeves	$12	■	Columbia 42701
11/30/63	**74**	5		22 **Begging To You**..........CW[3] *Over High Mountain*	$12		Columbia 42890
10/26/68	**65**	8		23 **I Walk Alone**..........CW[2] *Lily Of The Valley* song first recorded by **Eddy Arnold** in 1945 on Bluebird 0535 ($25)	$7		Columbia 44633
3/14/70	**42**	8		24 **My Woman, My Woman, My Wife**..........CW[1] *Martha Ellen Jenkins* all of above (except #1, 3-5, 7, 8, 12, 13, 20 & 23) written by Robbins	$6		Columbia 45091
				ROBBINS, Rockie R&B/LP **'80** Born Edward Robbins in Minneapolis, Minnesota. R&B singer/songwriter.			
7/19/80	**80**	4		**You And Me**..........*Together*	$4	■	A&M 2231
				ROBERT & JOHNNY **'58** R&B duo from the Bronx, New York: Robert Carr (died on 5/18/93) and Johnny Mitchell.			
2/24/58	**32**	22		1 **We Belong Together** ....S:32 / T:33 *Walking In The Rain* "Bubbled Under" (#104) in 1961 on Old Town 1086	$40		Old Town 1047
8/4/58	**93**	2		2 **I Believe In You** ....H:93 *Marry Me*	$30		Old Town 1052
				ROBERTS, Austin BUB **'75** Born on 9/19/45 in Newport News, Virginia. Writer of several country songs. Collaborator on the cartoon series *Scooby Doo* and *Josie & The Pussycats*. Replaced Gene Pistilli in **Buchanan Brothers**/**Cashman**, Pistilli **&** **West** trio in 1972, and was a member of **Arkade**.			
10/14/72	**12**	15		1 **Something's Wrong With Me**..........*My Song*	$5		Chelsea 0101
2/3/73	**50**	8		2 **Keep On Singing** ....*Take Away The Sunshine*	$5		Chelsea 0110
7/19/75	**9**	17		3 **Rocky** ....*You Got The Power*	$5		Private Stock 45,020
				ROBERTS, Derrik BUB **'65** Pop singer.			
12/18/65	**8**[X]	2		**There Won't Be Any Snow (Christmas In The Jungle)**..........*A World Without Sunshine* [X-S] "Bubbled Under" (#105) in 1966	$20	■	Roulette 4656
				ROBERTS, John **'67** Born on 11/28/41 in Houston, Texas. R&B singer/songwriter. Former school teacher.			
12/2/67	**71**	4		**Sockin' 1-2-3-4**..........*Sophisticated Funk*	$10		Duke 425
				ROBERTS, Juliet **'94** Born in London, England (West Indian parents). Black dance singer.			
3/19/94	**44**	14		**I Want You**..........A:39 *Force Of Nature*	$3	▮	Reprise 18222
				ROBERTS, Kane **'91** Born in Boston, Massachusetts. Rock singer/guitarist. Guitar work with **Alice Cooper**, **Rod Stewart** and **Berlin**.			
4/27/91	**38**	13		**Does Anybody Really Fall In Love Anymore?**..........*I'm Not Lookin' For An Angel* first recorded by **Cher** in 1989 on her *Heart Of Stone* album; songwriters include **Jon Bon Jovi** and **Richie Sambora**	$4	▮	DGC 19009
				ROBERTS, Lea R&B/BUB **'75** Born Leatha Roberta Hicks on 4/15/46 in Dayton, Ohio. R&B singer.			
4/12/75	**92**	3		**All Right Now**..........*All Over Again*	$5		United Artists 626
				ROBERTSON, Don BUB **'56** Born on 12/5/22 in Peking, China; raised in Chicago, Illinois. Pianist/composer. Created the Nashville piano style. Wrote "Born To Be With You," "Hummingbird," "Please Help Me I'm Falling" and "Ringo." Also wrote several of **Elvis Presley**'s hits.			
4/28/56	**6**	20		**The Happy Whistler** ....A:6 / S:9 / T:9 / J:12 *You're Free To Go* (w/Lou Dinning) [I]	$12		Capitol 3391
				ROBEY **'85** Born Louise Robey on 3/14/60 in Montreal, Quebec, Canada. Dance singer/actress/model. Played "Micki Foster" on *Friday the 13th - The TV Series* (1987-90).			
3/2/85	**77**	3		**One Night In Bangkok**..........*Bored & Beautiful* from the Tim Rice and **Abba** members Benny Andersson and Bjorn Ulvaeus musical project *Chess*	$4		Silver Blue 04774

ROBIC, Ivo — '59

Born on 1/29/26 in Bjelovar, Yugoslavia. Died of cancer on 3/10/2000 (age 74). Male singer. Pronounced: eevo robish.

DEBUT	PEAK	WKS	Gold	A-side (Chart Hit)...B-side	$	Sym	Label & Number
8/17/59	13	17		1 **Morgen** ...*Ay, Ay, Ay Paloma* [F] **IVO ROBIC and The Song-Masters** German song also known as "One More Sunrise"; "Morgen": Tomorrow	$12		Laurie 3033
1/18/60	58	6		2 **The Happy Muleteer** ...*Rhondaly*	$10		Laurie 3045

ROBIN, Tina — '61

Pop singer. Regular on TV's *Sing Along* in 1958, hosted by **Jim Lowe**.

DEBUT	PEAK	WKS	Gold	A-side (Chart Hit)...B-side	$	Sym	Label & Number
9/18/61	95	1		**Dear Mr. D.J. Play It Again** ...*Nothing Is Impossible* [N] Tina sings bits of classic R&B hits	$25		Mercury 71852

ROBIN S — BUB/R&B/LP '93

Born Robin Stone in Queens, New York. Female dance singer.

DEBUT	PEAK	WKS	Gold	A-side (Chart Hit)...B-side	$	Sym	Label & Number
4/3/93	5	28	●	1 **Show Me Love** ...A:3 / S:10 *(remix)*	$3	▮V	Big Beat 10118
8/21/93	53	19		2 **Love For Love** ...A:49 / S:66 *(dubstrumental edit)* "45" issued for above 2 on Big Beat 98363	$3	▮V	Big Beat 98382
5/17/97	91	5		3 **It Must Be Love** ...*(instrumental)* above 3: #1 Dance Club Play hits	$3	▮	Big Beat 98023

ROBINS, The — see COASTERS, The

ROBINSON, Alvin — BUB '64

Born on 12/22/37 in New Orleans, Louisiana. Died of a heart attack on 1/24/89 (age 51). R&B session guitarist/vocalist. Worked with **Joe Jones** and **Dr. John**.

DEBUT	PEAK	WKS	Gold	A-side (Chart Hit)...B-side	$	Sym	Label & Number
6/6/64	52	8		**Something You Got** ...*Searchin'* written by **Chris Kenner**; produced by **Joe Jones**	$20		Tiger 104

ROBINSON, Dawn — see EN VOGUE

ROBINSON, Floyd — '59

Born in 1937 in Nashville, Tennessee. Rock and roll singer/guitarist/composer. Worked on local radio with his high school band, the Eagle Rangers, at age 12. Own programs on WLAC and WSM-Nashville.

DEBUT	PEAK	WKS	Gold	A-side (Chart Hit)...B-side	$	Sym	Label & Number
7/20/59	20	18		**Makin' Love** ...*My Girl* produced by **Chet Atkins**	$20		RCA Victor 7529

ROBINSON, Freddy — LP '70

Born on 2/24/39 in Memphis, Tennessee. Black jazz-rock guitarist. With Little Walter's Band, Howling Wolf and **John Mayall**.

DEBUT	PEAK	WKS	Gold	A-side (Chart Hit)...B-side	$	Sym	Label & Number
7/25/70	56	9		**Black Fox** ...*The Oogum Boogum Song* [I]	$8		World Pacific Jazz 88155

ROBINSON, Rosco — R&B/BUB '66

Born on 5/22/28 in Dumont, Arkansas. R&B singer/producer.

DEBUT	PEAK	WKS	Gold	A-side (Chart Hit)...B-side	$	Sym	Label & Number
8/6/66	62	8		**That's Enough** ...*One More Time*	$12		Wand 1125

ROBINSON, Smokey ★175★ — R&B/BUB/AC/LP '81

Born William Robinson on 2/19/40 in Detroit, Michigan. Formed **The Miracles** (then called the Matadors) at Northern High School in 1955. First recorded for End in 1958. Married to Miracles' member Claudette Rogers from 1958-86. Left The Miracles on 1/29/72. Wrote dozens of hit songs for Motown artists. Vice President of Motown Records, 1985-88. Inducted into the Rock and Roll Hall of Fame in 1987. Won Grammy's Lifetime Achievement Award in 1999.

1)Being With You 2)Cruisin' 3)Just To See Her 4)One Heartbeat 5)Baby That's Backatcha

DEBUT	PEAK	WKS	Gold	A-side (Chart Hit)...B-side	$	Sym	Label & Number
7/7/73	48	13		1 **Sweet Harmony** ...*Want To Know My Mind*	$5		Tamla 54233
11/17/73+	27	16		2 **Baby Come Close** ...*A Silent Partner In A Three-Way Love Affair*	$5		Tamla 54239
5/25/74	82	5		3 **It's Her Turn To Live** ...*Just My Soul Responding*	$5		Tamla 54246
9/28/74	56	7		4 **Virgin Man** ...*Fulfill Your Need*	$5		Tamla 54250
12/14/74+	56	9		5 **I Am I Am** ...*The Family Song*	$5		Tamla 54251
4/26/75	26	11		6 **Baby That's Backatcha** ...RB[1] *Just Passing Through*	$5		Tamla 54258
9/6/75	36	12		7 **The Agony And The Ecstasy** ...*Wedding Song*	$5		Tamla 54261
1/17/76	61	7		8 **Quiet Storm** ...*Asleep On My Love*	$5		Tamla 54265
5/8/76	81	9		9 **Open** ...*Coincidentally*	$5		Tamla 54267
2/19/77	42	11		10 **There Will Come A Day (I'm Gonna Happen To You)** ...*The Humming Song (Lost For Words)*	$5		Tamla 54279
6/10/78	75	8		11 **Daylight And Darkness** ...*Why You Wanna See My Bad Side* (R&B #52)	$5		Tamla 54293
1/20/79	59	8		12 **Pops, We Love You (A Tribute To Father)** ...*(instrumental)* **DIANA ROSS, MARVIN GAYE, SMOKEY ROBINSON & STEVIE WONDER** song commemorates Berry Gordy Sr.'s death at age 90	$5		Motown 1455
10/6/79+	4	25		13 **Cruisin'** ...*Ever Had A Dream*	$4		Tamla 54306
3/15/80	31	14		14 **Let Me Be The Clock** ...*Travelin' Through*	$4		Tamla 54311
2/14/81	2^3	25	●	15 **Being With You** RB[5] *What's In Your Life For Me*	$4		Tamla 54321
6/20/81	59	7		16 **You Are Forever** ...*I Hear The Children Singing*	$4		Tamla 54327
1/16/82	33	12		17 **Tell Me Tomorrow - Part I** ...*Part II*	$4		Tamla 1601
4/17/82	60	9		18 **Old Fashioned Love** ...*Destiny*	$4		Tamla 1615
7/2/83	48	12		19 **Blame It On Love** ...*Even Tho'* (Robinson) **SMOKEY ROBINSON And BARBARA MITCHELL** some pressings credit artist as: **SMOKEY ROBINSON with High Inergy**	$4		Tamla 1684
12/10/83+	43	11		20 **Ebony Eyes** ...*1,2,3 (You Her And Me)* (James) **RICK JAMES Featuring SMOKEY ROBINSON** early pressings credit artist as: **RICK JAMES AND FRIEND**	$4		Gordy 1714
3/28/87	8	21		21 **Just To See Her** ...AC[1] S:8 / A:8 *I'm Gonna Love You Like There's No Tomorrow*	$3	■	Motown 1877
7/18/87	10	19		22 **One Heartbeat** ...A:10 / S:11 *Love Will Set You Free*	$3	■	Motown 1897
11/14/87	79	10		23 **What's Too Much** ...*I've Made Love To You A Thousand Times*	$3	■	Motown 1911

DEBUT	PEAK	WKS	Gold	A-side (Chart Hit)..........B-side	$	Sym	Label & Number
				ROBINSON, Smokey — Cont'd			
2/4/89	47	9		24 **We've Saved The Best For Last**..........*Silhouette*	$3	■	Arista 9785
				KENNY G (with Smokey Robinson)			
11/9/91	91	3		25 **Double Good Everything**..........*Guess What I Got For You*	$3	▮V	SBK 07370
				all of above (except #10, 12, 17-22 & 24) written or co-written by Robinson			
				ROBINSON, Stan '59			
				Rock and roll singer. Father of Chris and Rich Robinson of **The Black Crowes**. Member of the folk group **The Appalachians**.			
3/30/59	83	4		**Boom-A-Dip-Dip**..........*My Heart Beats*	$15		Monument 402
				ROBINSON, Vicki Sue BUB/LP '76			
				Born on 5/31/54 in Philadelphia, Pennsylvania. Died of cancer on 4/27/2000 (age 45). Disco singer. Appeared in the original Broadway productions of *Hair* and *Jesus Christ Superstar*.			
4/10/76	10	25	●	1 **Turn The Beat Around**..........*Lack Of Respect*	$5		RCA Victor 10562
10/2/76	63	7		2 **Daylight**..........*Never Gonna Let You Go*	$5		RCA 10775
8/6/77	67	9		3 **Hold Tight**..........*Falling In Love*	$5		RCA 11028
				written by **David Gates** (of **Bread**)			
				ROBYN LP '97			
				Born Robyn Carlsson on 6/12/79 in Stockholm, Sweden. Female dance singer.			
5/31/97	7	28	●	1 **Do You Know (What It Takes)**..........S:13 / A:13 *(2 versions)*	$3	▮V	RCA 64865
11/15/97	7	24	●	2 **Show Me Love**..........A:9 / S:11 *(remix)*	$3	▮V	RCA 64970
				"45" issued for above 2 on RCA 65300			
3/14/98	32[A]	12		3 **Do You Really Want Me (Show Respect)**..........		V	album cut
				from the album *Robyn Is Here* on RCA 67477; "45": RCA 65468; B-side: (QDIII mix)			
				ROCHELL AND THE CANDLES '61			
				R&B vocal group from Los Angeles, California: Johnny Wyatt (1st tenor; born in 1938; died in December 1983, age 45), Rochell Henderson (tenor), Melvin Sasso (baritone) and T.C. Henderson (bass).			
2/6/61	26	13		**Once Upon A Time**..........*When My Baby Is Gone*	$25		Swingin' 623
				ROCHELL AND THE CANDLES with Johnny Wyatt			
				ROCK, Pete, & C.L. Smooth R&B/BUB/LP '92			
				Hip-hop duo from Mt. Vernon, New York: producer/DJ Peter "Pete Rock" Phillips and rapper Corey "C.L. Smooth" Penn.			
6/27/92	58	15		1 **They Reminisce Over You (T.R.O.Y.)**..........S:39 / A:59 *Creator (Slide To The Side)*	$3	▮	Elektra 64773
2/4/95	76	5		2 **Take You There**..........*(remix)*	$3	▮	Elektra 64496
				Crystal Johnson (female vocal); samples "Risin' To The Top" by Keni Burke			
				ROCK AND HYDE — see HYDE, Paul			
				ROCK AND ROLL DUBBLE BUBBLE '69			
				Studio creation by producers Bob Feldman and Jerry Goldstein (**The Sheep/The Strangeloves**).			
1/18/69	74	4		**Bubble Gum Music**..........*On A Summer Night* [N]	$8		Buddah 78
				THE ROCK AND ROLL DUBBLE BUBBLE TRADING CARD CO. OF PHILADELPHIA-19141			
				ROCK-A-TEENS '59			
				Rock and roll teen group from Richmond, Virginia: Vic Mizell (leader), Bobby "Boo" Walker, Bill Cook, Paul Evans, Eddie Robertson and Bill Smith.			
10/5/59	16	12		**Woo-Hoo**..........*Untrue* [I]	$30		Roulette 4192
				first released on Doran 3515 in 1959 ($125)			
				ROCKELL '98			
				Born Rachel Mercaldo on 3/4/77 in Long Island, New York. Female techno-dance singer.			
11/9/96+	61	18		1 **I Fell In Love**..........A:62 *(instrumental)*	$4	▮	Robbins 72007
9/6/97+	72	20		2 **In A Dream**..........*(remix)*	$4	▮V	Robbins 72012
7/4/98	59	20		3 **Can't We Try**..........S:62 *(remix)*	$5	▮V	Robbins 72025
				ROCKELL (With Collage)			
				"45" issued for above 2 on Robbins 72025			
				ROCKETS ROK/LP '79			
				Rock group from Detroit, Michigan: David Gilbert (vocals), Jim McCarty and Dennis Robbins (guitars), Donnie Backus (keyboards), Bobby Neil Haralson (bass) and John Badanjek (drums). McCarty and Badanjek were members of **Mitch Ryder & The Detroit Wheels**. Gilbert died of cancer on 8/1/2001 (age 49).			
4/21/79	51	9		1 **Can't Sleep**..........*Something Ain't Right*	$4		RSO 926
7/7/79	30	13		2 **Oh Well**..........*Love Me Once Again*	$4		RSO 935
2/16/80	70	6		3 **Desire**..........*Troublemaker*	$4		RSO 1022
				ROCK FLOWERS '72			
				Female pop vocal trio: Rindy Dunn, Ardie Tillman and Debbie Clinger.			
2/12/72	95	2		**Number Wonderful**..........*Mother You, Smother You*	$8	■	Wheel 0032
				ROCKINGHAM, David, Trio BUB '63			
				R&B organist Rockingham with guitarist/producer R.C. "Bobby" Robinson and drummer Shante Hamilton.			
11/9/63	62	8		**Dawn**..........*That's All* [I]	$10		Josie 913
				first released on Dee Dee 1000 ($20) in 1963; sequel "Midnight" by Rockingham "Bubbled Under" (#119) on 3/7/64 on Josie 917			
				ROCKIN' REBELS — see REBELS, The			
				ROCKIN R'S, The '59			
				Instrumental rock and roll trio from Metamora, Illinois: Ron Volz and Ron Wernsman (guitars) and Ted Minar (drums).			
3/23/59	57	8		**The Beat**..........*Crazy Baby* [I]	$40		Tempus 7541
				ROCKPILE ROK/LP '81			
				Rock and roll group formed in London, England: **Dave Edmunds** (vocals, guitar), **Nick Lowe** (vocals, bass), Billy Bremner (guitar) and Terry Williams (drums).			
11/22/80+	51	12		**Teacher Teacher**..........*Fool Too Long*	$5	⊙	Columbia 11388

DEBUT	PEAK	WKS	Gold	A-side (Chart Hit)....B-side	$	Sym	Label & Number

ROCKWELL — R&B/BUB/LP '84

Born Kennedy Gordy on 3/15/64 in Detroit, Michigan. R&B singer/songwriter. Son of Motown chairman, Berry Gordy, Jr.

DEBUT	PEAK	WKS	Gold	A-side (Chart Hit)....B-side	$	Sym	Label & Number
1/28/84	2^3	19	●	1 **Somebody's Watching Me**....RB^5 *(instrumental)* Michael Jackson (backing vocal)	$4		Motown 1702
5/5/84	35	14		2 **Obscene Phone Caller**....*(instrumental)*	$4	■	Motown 1731

ROCKY FELLERS, The — '63

Rock and roll family group from Manila, Philippines: Pop Feller and his four sons (Eddie, Albert, Tony and Junior Feller).

DEBUT	PEAK	WKS	Gold	A-side (Chart Hit)....B-side	$	Sym	Label & Number
3/23/63	16	13		1 **Killer Joe**....*Lonely Teardrops*	$15		Scepter 1246
6/29/63	55	5		2 **Like The Big Guys Do**....*Great Big World*	$12	■	Scepter 1254

RODGERS, Eileen — '56

Born in 1933 in Pittsburgh, Pennsylvania. Adult Contemporary singer. Featured vocalist in Charlie Spivak's band, 1954-56.

DEBUT	PEAK	WKS	Gold	A-side (Chart Hit)....B-side	$	Sym	Label & Number
8/18/56	18	17		1 **Miracle Of Love** A:18 / T:19 / S:23 *Unwanted Heart*	$15		Columbia 40708
12/15/56+	61	8		2 **Give Me**....T:61 *I Wish I Didn't Have To Dream So Far*	$10		Columbia 40791
4/6/57	62	2		3 **The Wall**....T:62 *This Day* Jimmy Carroll (orch.)	$10		Columbia 40850
6/3/57	83	2		4 **Don't Call Me Sweetie (Cause I'm Bitter)**....T:83 *Everything But Love*	$10		Columbia 40908
9/16/57	82	2		5 **Third Finger - Left Hand**....T:82 *Crazy Dream* **Ray Conniff** (orch. and chorus: #1, 2, 4 & 5)	$10		Columbia 40956
8/25/58	26	15		6 **Treasure Of Your Love**....H:26 *A Little Bit Bluer*	$15		Columbia 41214

RODGERS, Jimmie ★131★ — AC/BUB/C&W/LP '58

Born on 9/18/33 in Camas, Washington. Pop-folk singer/guitarist. Hosted own TV variety series in 1959. Career hampered following mysterious assault on the San Diego Freeway on 12/1/67, which left him with a fractured skull. Returned to performing a year later. Starred in movies *The Little Shepherd of Kingdom Come* and *Back Door To Hell.* Not to be confused with the country music pioneer of the same name.

1)Honeycomb 2)Kisses Sweeter Than Wine 3)Secretly 4)Oh-Oh, I'm Falling In Love Again 5)Are You Really Mine

DEBUT	PEAK	WKS	Gold	A-side (Chart Hit)....B-side	$	Sym	Label & Number
8/12/57	❶^4	28	●	1 **Honeycomb** RB^2 A:❶^4 / S:❶^2 / T:❶^2 *Their Hearts Were Full Of Spring* introduced by **Georgie Shaw** in 1954 on Decca 28937	$20		Roulette 4015
11/18/57	3	21	●	2 **Kisses Sweeter Than Wine**....A:3 / T:7 / S:8 *Better Loved You'll Never Be* adapted from an Irish folk song; #19 hit for The Weavers in 1951	$20		Roulette 4031
2/17/58	7	15	●	3 **Oh-Oh, I'm Falling In Love Again** / A:7 / T:22 / S:23			
5/5/58	77	9		4 **The Long Hot Summer**....T:77 title song from the movie starring Paul Newman and Joanne Woodward	$20		Roulette 4045
5/5/58	3	17	●	5 **Secretly** / A:3 / S:3 / T:4 a new version by Rodgers made the Adult Contemporary charts (#46) in 1978 on Scrimshaw 1318			
5/19/58	16	9		6 **Make Me A Miracle**....A:16 / T:54 / S:flip	$15	■	Roulette 4070
8/4/58	10	13		7 **Are You Really Mine** / H:10 / S:10 a promo insert (in letter form) was also issued with the picture sleeve			
8/11/58	45	7		8 **The Wizard**....H:45 / S:flip	$15	■	Roulette 4090
11/10/58	11	16		9 **Bimbombey**....*You Understand Me*	$15		Roulette 4116
2/23/59	36	11		10 **I'm Never Gonna Tell** /			
3/9/59	62	5		11 **Because You're Young**.... Hugo Peretti (of **Hugo & Luigi**; orch., all of above)	$15		Roulette 4129
6/1/59	32	8		12 **Ring-A-Ling-A-Lario** /			
6/15/59	40	7		13 **Wonderful You**....	$15	■	Roulette 4158
9/21/59	32	9		14 **Tucumcari**....*The Night You Became Seventeen*	$15		Roulette 4191
1/11/60	24	10		15 **T.L.C. Tender Love And Care** / reissued on Peak 7011 with a picture sleeve			
1/18/60	41	8		16 **Waltzing Matilda**.... famous Australian Army march tune featured in the movie *On The Beach* starring Gregory Peck; different version issued on Rodgers' 1958 album *Sings Folk Songs*	$15		Roulette 4218
4/11/60	44	9		17 **Just A Closer Walk With Thee**....*Joshua Fit The Battle O' Jericho* traditional hymn; #9 Country hit for Red Foley in 1950	$15		Roulette 4234
8/1/60	64	9		18 **The Wreck Of The "John B"**....*Four Little Girls In Boston* 1927 West Indies folk song recorded in 1966 by **The Beach Boys** as "Sloop John B"; **Joe Reisman** (orch.: #12-18)	$15		Roulette 4260
9/4/61	71	4		19 **A Little Dog Cried**....*English Country Garden* [S]	$15		Roulette 4384
9/1/62	43	11		20 **No One Will Ever Know**....*Because* first recorded in 1946 by Roy Acuff on Columbia 36891	$10	■	Dot 16378
11/24/62	62	7		21 **Rainbow At Midnight**....*Rhumba Boogie* #1 Country hit for Ernest Tubb in 1947	$10		Dot 16407
10/12/63	78	7		22 **Two-Ten, Six-Eighteen (Doesn't Anybody Know My Name)**....*The Banana Boat Song*	$10		Dot 16527
5/30/64	51	9		23 **The World I Used To Know**....*I Forgot More Than You'll Ever Know* above 2 written by poet **Rod McKuen**	$10		Dot 16595
5/14/66	37	7		24 **It's Over**....*Anita, You're Dreaming*	$10		Dot 16861
9/23/67	31	8		25 **Child Of Clay**....*Turnaround*	$8		A&M 871

RODGERS, Nile — see CHIC

RODNEY O & JOE COOLEY — R&B/BUB/LP '93

Rap trio from Los Angeles, California: Rodney Oliver, Joe Cooley and Jeff Page.

DEBUT	PEAK	WKS	Gold	A-side (Chart Hit)....B-side	$	Sym	Label & Number
6/19/93	84	7		1 **Humps For The Blvd.**....A:48 *(album ban) / California Cruiser*	$6	■*	Psychotic 1203
7/3/93	93	5		2 **U Don't Hear Me Tho'**....A:58 *(2 versions) / Chase The Bass* samples "Flash Light" by **Parliament**	$6	■*	Psychotic 1201

DEBUT	PEAK	WKS	Gold	A-side (Chart Hit)	B-side	$	Sym	Label & Number
				RODRIGUEZ, Daniel LP **'01**				
				Born in Brooklyn, New York. Operatic tenor. Member of the New York City Police Department; was on duty during the 9/11 terrorist attacks. Known as "The Singing Policeman."				
12/29/01	99	2		**God Bless America** S:8	*We Will Go On*	$5	★	Manhattan 77684
				spoken introduction by New York City Mayor Rudolph Giuliani; Irving Berlin classic song, popularized by Kate Smith in 1939				
				RODRIGUEZ, Johnny C&W/LP **'73**				
				Born Juan Rodriguez on 12/10/51 in Sabinal, Texas. Country singer/songwriter/guitarist (charted 45 hits, 1972-89).				
6/23/73	86	4		1 **You Always Come Back (To Hurting Me)** CW[1]	*I Wonder Where You Are Tonight*	$6		Mercury 73368
9/29/73	70	5		2 **Ridin' My Thumb To Mexico** CW[2]	*Release Me*	$6		Mercury 73416
5/4/74	85	4		3 **Something**	*Born To Lose*	$6		Mercury 73471
				RODWAY **'82**				
				Born Steve Rodway in Kent, England. Electro-pop singer/songwriter.				
12/11/82	83	5		**Don't Stop Trying**	*Living On An Island*	$4		Millennium 13111

DEBUT	PEAK	WKS	Gold	A-side (Chart Hit)	B-side	$	Sym	Label & Number
				ROE, Tommy ★200★ C&W/BUB/LP **'69**				
				Born on 5/9/42 in Atlanta, Georgia. Pop-rock and roll singer/guitarist/composer. Formed band The Satins at Brown High School, worked local dances in the late 1950s. Group recorded for Judd in 1960. Moved to Britain in the mid-1960s, returned in 1969.				
				1)Dizzy 2)Sheila 3)Everybody 4)Hooray For Hazel 5)Sweet Pea				
7/28/62	❶[2]	14	●	1 **Sheila**	*Save Your Kisses*	$15		ABC-Paramount 10329
				different version first released on Judd 1022 in 1962 ($75)				
10/6/62	35	8		2 **Susie Darlin'**	*Piddle de Pat (#108)*	$12	■	ABC-Paramount 10362
5/4/63	84	3		3 **The Folk Singer**	*Count On Me*	$12		ABC-Paramount 10423
10/12/63	3	14		4 **Everybody**	*Sorry I'm Late, Lisa*	$12		ABC-Paramount 10478
1/18/64	36	8		5 **Come On**	*There Will Be Better Years*	$12		ABC-Paramount 10515
4/25/64	61	6		6 **Carol**	*Be A Good Little Girl*	$12		ABC-Paramount 10543
12/5/64	85	3		7 **Party Girl**	*Oh How I Could Love You*	$12		ABC-Paramount 10604
				all of above produced by Felton Jarvis				
6/11/66	8	14	●	8 **Sweet Pea**	*Much More Love*	$10		ABC 10762
				also released on ABC-Paramount 10762 in 1966 ($20)				
9/17/66	6	13		9 **Hooray For Hazel**	*Need Your Love*	$10		ABC 10852
12/24/66+	23	11		10 **It's Now Winters Day**	*Kick Me Charlie*	$8	■	ABC 10888
4/8/67	91	1		11 **Sing Along With Me**	*Nightime*	$8		ABC 10908
6/10/67	99	1		12 **Little Miss Sunshine**	*The You I Need*	$8		ABC 10945
2/1/69	❶[4]	15	●	13 **Dizzy**	*The You I Need*	$8	⊙	ABC 11164
				foldout insert features a charcoal portrait of Roe				
4/26/69	29	8		14 **Heather Honey**	*Money Is My Pay*	$8		ABC 11211
7/19/69	53	13		15 **Jack And Jill**	*Tip Toe Tina*	$8		ABC 11229
11/15/69+	8	14	●	16 **Jam Up Jelly Tight**	*Moontalk*	$8	■	ABC 11247
2/28/70	50	6		17 **Stir It Up And Serve It**	*Firefly*	$8		ABC 11258
6/20/70	50	9		18 **Pearl**	*Dollars Worth Of Pennies*	$8		ABC 11266
				#13 & 15-18: co-written by Freddy Weller (**Paul Revere & The Raiders**)				
9/12/70	49	6		19 **We Can Make Music**	*Gotta Keep Rolling Along*	$8	■	ABC 11273
8/21/71	25	12		20 **Stagger Lee**	*Back Streets And Alleys*	$8		ABC 11307
				adapted from the traditional folk song "Stack-O-Lee"; #13-20: produced by Steve Barri				
9/23/72	92	3		21 **Mean Little Woman, Rosalie**	*Skyline*	$6		MGM South 7001
5/5/73	97	4		22 **Working Class Hero**	*Sun In My Eyes*	$6		MGM South 7013
				all of above (except #2, 3, 5-7 & 19-21) written or co-written by Roe				
				ROGER/ZAPP R&B/BUB/LP **'88**				
				Born Roger Troutman on 11/29/51 in Hamilton, Ohio. Shot to death by his brother Larry in a murder-suicide on 4/25/99. Roger was age 47 and Larry was age 54. Roger was the leader of the family electro-funk group **Zapp** (Roger, Lester, Larry and Tony). Worked with **Sly Stone** and **George Clinton**. Father of male singer Lynch. Also see **H-Town**.				
				1)I Want To Be Your Man 2)California Love 3)Slow And Easy				
10/4/80	86	7		1 **More Bounce To The Ounce Part I** *[ZAPP]*	*Part II*	$4		Warner 49534
11/7/81	79	7		2 **I Heard It Through The Grapevine** (Part 1) *[ROGER]* RB[2]	*(Part II)*	$4		Warner 49786
11/14/87+	3	21		3 **I Want To Be Your Man** *[ROGER]* RB[1] S:3 / A:5	*I Really Want To Be Your Man*	$3	■	Reprise 28229
6/18/88	53	11		4 **Boom! There She Was**	*A World Come Back To Life*	$3	■	Warner 27976
				SCRITTI POLITTI Featuring Roger				
8/7/93	54	15		5 **Mega Medley** *[ZAPP & ROGER]* S:42 / A:62	*I Want To Be Your Man*	$3	▮	Reprise 18420
				medley of 9 **Zapp** and **Roger** recordings: More Bounce To The Ounce/Do It Roger/Heartbreaker (Part I, Part II)/ Playin' Kinda Ruff/So Ruff, So Tuff/Dance Floor (Part I)/ I Can Make You Dance (Part I)/ Do Wah Ditty (Blow That Thing)/I Heard It Through The Grapevine				
10/30/93+	43	20		6 **Slow And Easy** *[ZAPP & ROGER]* A:36 / S:46	*A Chunk Of Sugar*	$3	▮	Reprise 18315
6/15/96	6	24		7 **California Love** S:3 / A:19	*How Do U Want It* (**2 PAC w/KC & JoJo** - #1)	$3	▮	Death Row 854652
				2 PAC (featuring Dr. Dre and Roger Troutman)				
				samples "So Ruff So Tuff" by **Roger** and "Woman To Woman" by **Joe Cocker**				
12/14/96+	43	19		8 **It's Your Body** S:16	*(instrumental)*	$3	▮	Motown 0462
				JOHNNY GILL Featuring Roger Troutman				
4/19/97	62	20		9 **Sweet Sexy Thing**	*(album edit) / (English/Spanish edit)*	$3	▮[V]	Reprise 17402
				NU FLAVOR Featuring Roger				
8/9/97	69	17		10 **Down For Yours** S:60	*(original version) / Lost In Love*	$4	▮	Mercury 574748
				NASTYBOY KLICK Featuring Roger Troutman				

DEBUT	PEAK	WKS	Gold	A-side (Chart Hit)...B-side	$	Sym	Label & Number
				ROGERS, D.J. R&B/LP **'76**			
				Born DeWayne Julius Rogers in Los Angeles, California. R&B singer/songwriter/keyboardist.			
7/4/76	98	2		**Say You Love Me** ...*(It's Alright Now) Think I'll Make It Anyhow*	$5		RCA Victor 10568
				ROGERS, Dann AC/C&W **'80**			
				Adult Contemporary/country singer. Nephew of **Kenny Rogers**.			
12/15/79+	41	11		**Looks Like Love Again** ...*Lucy*	$5		ia 500
				ROGERS, Julie **'65**			
				Born Julie Rolls on 4/6/43 in London, England. Adult Contemporary singer.			
11/21/64+	10	11		1 **The Wedding** ...AC[3] *Without Your Love*	$10		Mercury 72332
				Argentinian hit "La Novia" introduced in the U.S. in 1961 by **Anita Bryant** on Columbia 42148			
2/13/65	67	5		2 **Like A Child** ...*The Love Of A Boy*	$8	■	Mercury 72380
				Johnny Arthey (orch., above 2)			

				ROGERS, Kenny/First Edition ★40★ C&W/AC/BUB/LP **'80**			
				Born on 8/21/38 in Houston, Texas. Country singer/songwriter/guitarist/actor. With high school band the Scholars in 1958. Bass player of jazz group the Bobby Doyle Trio, recorded for Columbia. First recorded for Carlton in 1958. In **Kirby Stone Four** and **The New Christy Minstrels**, mid-1960s. Formed and fronted **The First Edition** in 1967. Original lineup included Thelma Camacho, Mike Settle, Terry Williams and Mickey Jones. All but Jones were members of The New Christy Minstrels. Group hosted own syndicated TV variety show *Rollin* in 1972. Rogers split from group in 1973. Starred in movie *Six Pack* and several TV movies including *The Gambler I, II & III* miniseries, *Coward Of The County*, *Wild Horses* and *Rio Diablo*. Married to actress Marianne Gordon from 1977-93. Later started the Kenny Rogers Roasters restaurant chain.			
				1)Lady 2)Islands In The Stream 3)Coward Of The County 4)I Don't Need You 5)Don't Fall In Love With A Dreamer			
				THE FIRST EDITION:			
2/10/68	5	10		1 **Just Dropped In (To See What Condition My Condition Was In)** ...*Shadow In The Corner Of Your Mind*	$10		Reprise 0655
1/18/69	19	11		2 **But You Know I Love You** ...*Homemade Lies*	$8		Reprise 0799
				KENNY ROGERS AND THE FIRST EDITION:			
6/7/69	6	13		3 **Ruby, Don't Take Your Love To Town** ...*Girl Get Ahold Of Yourself*	$8		Reprise 0829
				written by Mel Tillis			
9/27/69	26	12		4 **Ruben James** ...*Sunshine*	$8		Reprise 0854
				some pressings show title as "Reuben James"			
2/14/70	11	16		5 **Something's Burning** ...*Momma's Waiting*	$8		Reprise 0888
				written by **Mac Davis**			
7/4/70	17	11		6 **Tell It All Brother** ...*Just Remember You're My Sunshine*	$7		Reprise 0923
10/17/70	33	10		7 **Heed The Call** ...*A Stranger In My Place*	$7		Reprise 0953
3/27/71	51	7		8 **Someone Who Cares** ...*Mission Of San Nohero*	$7		Reprise 0999
				love theme from the movie *Fools* starring Jason Robards			
6/26/71	91	2		9 **Take My Hand** ...*All God's Lonely Children*	$6		Reprise 1018
4/1/72	91	4		10 **School Teacher** ...*Trigger Happy Kid*	$6		Reprise 1069
				Kin Vassy (lead vocal)			
				KENNY ROGERS:			
3/13/76	97	3		11 **Love Lifted Me** ...*Home-Made Love*	$5		United Artists 746
3/26/77	5	19	●	12 **Lucille** ...*Till I Get It Right*	$5		United Artists 929
8/6/77	28	12		13 **Daytime Friends** ...CW[1] *We Don't Make Love Anymore*	$5		United Artists 1027
12/17/77+	44	8		14 **Sweet Music Man** ...*Lying Again*	$5		United Artists 1095
6/3/78	32	12		15 **Love Or Something Like It** ...CW[1] *Starting Again*	$5		United Artists 1210
11/4/78+	16	22		16 **The Gambler** ...CW[3] *Momma's Waiting*	$5		United Artists 1250
4/28/79	5	16	●	17 **She Believes In Me** ...CW[2] / AC[2] *Morgana Jones*	$5	■	United Artists 1273
9/8/79	7	18		18 **You Decorated My Life** ...CW[2] *One Man's Woman*	$5	■	United Artists 1315
11/17/79+	3	19	●	19 **Coward Of The County** ...CW[3] *I Want To Make You Smile*	$5		United Artists 1327
3/29/80	4	19		20 **Don't Fall In Love With A Dreamer** ...*Goin' Home To The Rock/Gideon Tanner* (Rogers)	$5	■	United Artists 1345
				KENNY ROGERS with Kim Carnes			
6/21/80	14	12		21 **Love The World Away** ...*Sayin' Goodbye/Requiem: Goin' Home To The Rock*	$5		United Artists 1359
				from the movie *Urban Cowboy* starring **John Travolta** and Debra Winger; #11-21: produced by Larry Butler			
10/4/80	❶[6]	25	●	22 **Lady** CW[1] / AC[4] *Sweet Music Man*	$4	■	Liberty 1380
				written by **Lionel Richie**			
3/28/81	14	20		23 **What Are We Doin' In Love** ...CW[1] *Choosin' Means Losin'* (West)	$4		Liberty 1404
				DOTTIE WEST (with Kenny Rogers)			
6/13/81	3	18		24 **I Don't Need You** ...CW[2] / AC[6] *Without You In My Life*	$4	■	Liberty 1415
9/5/81	14	15		25 **Share Your Love With Me** ...AC[2] *Greybeard*	$4	■	Liberty 1430
				Gladys Knight & The Pips and **Lionel Richie** (backing vocals)			
11/21/81	66	9		26 **Blaze Of Glory** ...*The Good Life*	$4		Liberty 1441
12/26/81+	13	15		27 **Through The Years** ...AC[2] *So In Love With You*	$4		Liberty 1444
				above 4 from the album *Share Your Love*; #22 & 24-27: produced by **Lionel Richie**			
7/3/82	13	17		28 **Love Will Turn You Around** ...CW[1] / AC[2] *I Want A Son*	$4	■	Liberty 1471
				from the movie *Six Pack* starring Rogers			
10/16/82	47	10		29 **A Love Song** ...*The Fool In Me*	$4		Liberty 1485
				written by **Lee Greenwood**			
1/29/83	6	18		30 **We've Got Tonight** ...CW[1] *You Are So Beautiful* (Rogers)	$4	■	Liberty 1492
				KENNY ROGERS and SHEENA EASTON			
4/30/83	37	11		31 **All My Life** ...*Farther I Go*	$4	■	Liberty 1495
8/20/83	94	2		32 **Scarlet Fever** ...*What I Learned From Loving You*	$4		Liberty 1503
8/27/83	❶[2]	25	▲	33 **Islands In The Stream** ...CW[2] / AC[4] *I Will Always Love You* (Rogers)	$4	■	RCA 13615
				KENNY ROGERS with Dolly Parton			
1/14/84	23	13		34 **This Woman** ...*Buried Treasure* (C&W #3)	$4	■	RCA 13710
4/28/84	79	5		35 **Eyes That See In The Dark** ...*Hold Me*	$4		RCA 13774
				above 3 feature writing and production work by the **Bee Gees**			

DEBUT	PEAK	WKS	Gold	A-side (Chart Hit)...B-side	$	Sym	Label & Number
				ROGERS, Kenny — Cont'd			
9/15/84	15	19		36 **What About Me?**...AC[2] A:14 / S:16 *The Rest Of Last Night* (Rogers) **KENNY ROGERS with KIM CARNES and JAMES INGRAM**	$3	■	RCA 13899
12/22/84	81	4		37 **The Greatest Gift Of All**...*White Christmas* (Parton) [X] **KENNY ROGERS & DOLLY PARTON** from their Christmas TV special *Once Upon A Christmas*	$4		RCA 13945
1/26/85	79	8		38 **Crazy**...CW[1] *The Stranger* #36 & 38: co-written by **Richard Marx**	$4	■	RCA 13975
6/8/85	91	3		39 **Real Love**...CW[1] *I Can't Be True* (Parton) **DOLLY PARTON (with Kenny Rogers)**	$4	■	RCA 14058
11/23/85	72	9		40 **Morning Desire**...CW[1] *People In Love* written by **Dave Loggins**; picture sleeve is a foldout poster	$4	■	RCA 14194
3/11/00	40	20		41 **Buy Me A Rose**...CW[1] A:34 **KENNY ROGERS With Alison Krauss & Billy Dean** from the album *She Rides Wild Horses* on DreamCatcher 004			album cut
				ROGERS, Roy C&W/MEM/LP **'38** Born Leonard Franklin Slye on 11/5/11 in Cincinnati, Ohio. Died of heart failure on 7/6/98 (age 86). Popular "singing cowboy" who starred in several movies. Original member of the famous western group Sons Of The Pioneers. Starred in close to 100 movie Westerns, then in a popular radio and TV series with his wife Dale Evans (died of heart failure on 2/7/2001, age 88).			
12/21/74+	65	7		**Hoppy, Gene And Me**...*Good News, Bad News* [N] tribute to Hopalong Cassidy, **Gene Autry** and Rogers	$6		20th Century 2154
				ROGERS, Shorty — see BROWN, Boots			
				ROGERS, Timmie "Oh Yeah!" **'57** Born on 7/4/15 in Detroit, Michigan. Black vaudeville and nightclub comedian.			
10/7/57	36	15		**Back To School Again**...T:36 / S:37 *I've Got A Dog Who Loves Me* **Bernie Lowe** (orch.)	$30		Cameo 116
				ROLLERS, The **'61** R&B vocal group from San Bernardino, California: Johnny Torrence (lead), Don Sampson, Willie Willingham, and brothers Eddie and **Al Wilson**.			
4/10/61	80	3		**The Continental Walk**...*I Want You So*	$20		Liberty 55320
				ROLLIN, Dana **'66** Born in New York. Female pop singer.			
11/5/66	71	6		**Winchester Cathedral**...*Patty's Pad*	$8		Tower 283

ROLLING STONES, The ★8★ ROK/BUB/LP **'65**

Blues-influenced rock group formed in London, England: **Mick Jagger** (vocals; born on 7/26/43), Keith Richards (lead guitar; born on 12/18/43), Brian Jones (guitar; born on 2/28/42; died on 7/3/69, age 27), **Bill Wyman** (bass; born on 10/24/36) (see #20 below) and Charlie Watts (drums; born on 6/2/41). Jagger was the lead singer of Blues, Inc. The Stones took its name from the 1950 Muddy Waters song "Rollin' Stone." Promoted as the bad boys in contrast to **The Beatles**. First U.K. tour with **The Ronettes** in 1964. Jones left group shortly before drowning; replaced by Mick Taylor (born on 1/17/48). In 1975, **Ron Wood** (ex-**Jeff Beck Group**, ex-**Faces**) replaced Taylor. Movie *Gimme Shelter* is a documentary of the Stones's controversial Altamont concert on 12/6/69 at which a concertgoer was murdered by a member of the Hell's Angels. Won Grammy's Lifetime Achievement Award in 1986. Group inducted into the Rock and Roll Hall of Fame in 1989. Wyman left band in late 1992. Bassist Darryl Jones (billed as a "side musician") played on the 1994 *Voodoo Lounge* album and tour. Considered by many as the world's all-time greatest rock and roll band.

1)(I Can't Get No) Satisfaction 2)Honky Tonk Women 3)Brown Sugar 4)Paint It, Black 5)Get Off Of My Cloud

DEBUT	PEAK	WKS	Gold	A-side (Chart Hit)...B-side	$	Sym	Label & Number
5/2/64	48	13		1 **Not Fade Away**...*I Wanna Be Your Man* **Buddy Holly** song first recorded by **The Crickets** in 1957 (B-side of "Oh Boy!"); B-side written and recorded by **The Beatles**	$40	■	London 9657
7/4/64	24	10		2 **Tell Me (You're Coming Back)**...*I Just Want To Make Love To You*	$40	■	London 9682
7/25/64	26	10		3 **It's All Over Now**...*Good Times Bad Times*	$40	■	London 9687
10/17/64	6	13		4 **Time Is On My Side**...*Congratulations* first recorded by **Irma Thomas** in 1964 (B-side of her R&B chart hit "Anyone Who Knows What Love Is")	$30	■	London 9708
1/9/65	19	9		5 **Heart Of Stone**...*What A Shame* (#124)	$30	■	London 9725
3/27/65	9	10		6 **The Last Time** /			
5/22/65	96	1		7 **Play With Fire**... Phil Spector (guitar)	$25	■	London 9741
6/12/65	❶[4]	14	●	8 **(I Can't Get No) Satisfaction** *The Under Assistant West Coast Promotion Man*	$20	■	London 9766
10/9/65	❶[2]	12		9 **Get Off Of My Cloud**...*I'm Free*	$20	■	London 9792
12/25/65+	6	9		10 **As Tears Go By**...*Gotta Get Away*	$15	■	London 9808
2/26/66	2[3]	10		11 **19th Nervous Breakdown**...*Sad Day*	$15	■	London 9823
5/14/66	❶[2]	11		12 **Paint It, Black**...*Stupid Girl*	$15	■	London 901
7/9/66	8	9		13 **Mothers Little Helper** /			
7/23/66	24	6		14 **Lady Jane**...	$15	■	London 902
10/8/66	9	7		15 **Have You Seen Your Mother, Baby, Standing In The Shadow?**...*Who's Driving My Plane*	$15	■	London 903
1/21/67	❶[1]	12	●	16 **Ruby Tuesday** /			
1/21/67	55	8		17 **Let's Spend The Night Together**...	$15	■	London 904
9/9/67	14	8		18 **Dandelion** /			
9/16/67	50	6		19 **We Love You**... **John Lennon** (backing vocal); all of above (and #35) produced by Andrew Loog Oldham	$20	■	London 905
12/16/67+	87	5		20 **In Another Land**...*The Lantern* (**Rolling Stones**) **BILL WYMAN**	$20	■	London 907
12/30/67+	25	7		21 **She's A Rainbow**...*2,000 Light Years From Home*	$15	■	London 906
6/8/68	3	12		22 **Jumpin' Jack Flash**...*Child Of The Moon*	$15	■	London 908
9/7/68	48	6		23 **Street Fighting Man**...*No Expectations* picture sleeve is extremely rare ($10,000)	$15	■	London 909
7/19/69	❶[4]	15	●	24 **Honky Tonk Women**...*You Can't Always Get What You Want* (#42/'73) also see #29 below	$15	■	London 910

DEBUT	PEAK	WKS	Gold	A-side (Chart Hit)..........B-side	$	Sym	Label & Number
				ROLLING STONES, The — Cont'd			
5/1/71	1^{2}	12		25 **Brown Sugar**......*Bitch*	$6		Rolling Stones 19100
				Rolling Stones Records issued sleeves featuring their logo with a die-cut hole in the mouth			
6/19/71	28	8		26 **Wild Horses**......*Sway*	$6		Rolling Stones 19101
4/29/72	7	10		27 **Tumbling Dice**......*Sweet Black Angel*	$6		Rolling Stones 19103
7/15/72	22	8		28 **Happy**......*All Down The Line*	$6		Rolling Stones 19104
				lead vocal by Keith Richards			
4/28/73	42	8		29 **You Can't Always Get What You Want**......*Honky Tonk Women* (#1/'69)	$15	■	London 910
				London Bach Choir (chorus); Al Kooper of **Blood, Sweat & Tears** (keyboards, french horn); B-side of #24 above			
9/8/73	1^{1}	16	●	30 **Angie**......*Silver Train*	$6		Rolling Stones 19105
				Angie is Angie Barnett, **David Bowie**'s wife from 1970-80			
1/12/74	15	11		31 **Doo Doo Doo Doo Doo (Heartbreaker)**......*Dancing With Mr. D.*	$6		Rolling Stones 19109
8/3/74	16	10		32 **It's Only Rock 'N Roll (But I Like It)**......*Through The Lonely Nights*	$6		Rolling Stones 19301
11/9/74	17	10		33 **Ain't Too Proud To Beg**......*Dance Little Sister*	$6		Rolling Stones 19302
6/14/75	42	6		34 **I Don't Know Why**......*Try A Little Harder*	$10		Abkco 4701
				previously unreleased 1968 recording; #22-31 & 34: produced by Jimmy Miller			
8/23/75	81	3		35 **Out Of Time**......*Jiving Sister Fanny*	$10		Abkco 4702
				different version released on the 1967 album *Flowers*; song "Bubbled Under" (#122) in 1966 for Chris Farlowe			
4/24/76	10	15		36 **Fool To Cry** /			
6/26/76	49	6		37 **Hot Stuff**	$5		Rolling Stones 19304
5/27/78	1^{1}	20	●	38 **Miss You**......*Far Away Eyes*	$5	■	Rolling Stones 19307
9/9/78	8	13		39 **Beast Of Burden**......*When The Whip Comes Down*	$5	■	Rolling Stones 19309
12/16/78+	31	10		40 **Shattered**......*Everything Is Turning To Gold*	$5	■	Rolling Stones 19310
7/5/80	3	19		41 **Emotional Rescue**......*Down In The Hole*	$4	■	Rolling Stones 20001
9/27/80	26	13		42 **She's So Cold**......*Send It To Me*	$4	■	Rolling Stones 21001
8/22/81	2^{3}	24		43 **Start Me Up**......AR^{13} *No Use In Crying*	$4	■	Rolling Stones 21003
12/5/81+	13	15		44 **Waiting On A Friend**......*Little T & A* (ROK #5)	$4	■	Rolling Stones 21004
3/20/82	20	11		45 **Hang Fire**......*Neighbours*	$4		Rolling Stones 21300
6/12/82	25	11		46 **Going To A Go-Go**......*Beast Of Burden (live)* [L]	$4	■	Rolling Stones 21301
11/12/83	9	14		47 **Undercover Of The Night**......*All The Way Down*	$4	■	Rolling Stones 99813
2/4/84	44	9		48 **She Was Hot**......*Think I'm Going Mad* (ROK #50)	$4	■	Rolling Stones 99788
3/15/86	5	13		49 **Harlem Shuffle**......S:5 / A:7 *Had It With You*	$4	■	Rolling Stones 05802
5/17/86	28	11		50 **One Hit (To The Body)**......S:23 / A:36 *Fight*	$4	■	Rolling Stones 05906
9/2/89	5	12		51 **Mixed Emotions**......AR^{5} S:4 / A:11 *Fancy Man Blues*	$3		Rolling Stones 69008
11/4/89	23	14		52 **Rock And A Hard Place**......AR^{5} S:19 / A:23 *Cook Cook Blues*	$3		Rolling Stones 73057
2/10/90	50	9		53 **Almost Hear You Sigh**......AR^{1} *Break The Spell*	$3	▮V	Rolling Stones 73093
3/9/91	57	7		54 **Highwire**......AR^{3} *2000 Light Years From Home*	$3	▮V	Rolling Stones 73742
8/13/94	91	5		55 **Love Is Strong**......S:63 *(remix) / The Storm*	$3	▮V	Virgin 38446 ■
10/15/94	60	15		56 **Out Of Tears**......S:47 *(remix) / I'm Gonna Drive*	$3	▮V	Virgin 38459 ■
3/7/98	94	4		57 **Saint Of Me**......*Anyway You Look At It*	$3	▮V	Virgin 38626 ■
				all of above (except #1, 3, 4, 20, 33, 34, 46 & 49) written by Jagger and Richards			

ROMAN, Dick — '62

Born Ricardo DeGiacomo in 1937 in Brooklyn, New York. Died of a heart attack on 10/21/76 (age 39). Regular on TV's *The Liberace Show*, 1958-59.

DEBUT	PEAK	WKS	Gold	A-side (Chart Hit)..........B-side	$	Sym	Label & Number
8/4/62	64	7		**Theme from A Summer Place**......*Butterfly*	$15		Harmon 1004
				lyric version of theme from the movie starring Troy Donahue and Sandra Dee			

ROMAN HOLLIDAY — LP '83

Pop-rock group from London, England: Steve Lambert (vocals), Brian Bonhomme (guitar), Adrian York (keyboards), John Eacott (trumpet), Rob Lambert (saxophone), Jon Durno (bass) and Simon Cohen (drums). Group named after the 1953 movie starring Audrey Hepburn.

DEBUT	PEAK	WKS	Gold	A-side (Chart Hit)..........B-side	$	Sym	Label & Number
6/18/83	54	9		1 **Stand By**......*Round And Round*	$4		Jive 9036
10/1/83	68	6		2 **Don't Try To Stop It**......*Beat My Time*	$4		Jive 9092
2/9/85	76	5		3 **One Foot Back In Your Door**......*Far Away Now*	$4		Jive 9287
				from the movie *Teachers* starring Nick Nolte and JoBeth Williams			

ROMANTICS, The — ROK/LP '84

Pop-rock group from Detroit, Michigan: Wally Palmar (vocals, guitar), Coz Canler (guitar), Mike Skill (bass) and Jimmy Marinos (drums). David Petratos replaced Marinos in early 1985.

DEBUT	PEAK	WKS	Gold	A-side (Chart Hit)..........B-side	$	Sym	Label & Number
2/16/80	49	8		1 **What I Like About You**......*First In Line*	$5	■	Nemperor 7527
10/8/83+	3	26		2 **Talking In Your Sleep**......*I'm Hip*	$4		Nemperor 04135
2/25/84	37	12		3 **One In A Million**......*Do Me Anyway You Wanna*	$4	■	Nemperor 04373
8/31/85	71	6		4 **Test Of Time**......*Better Make A Move*	$4	■	Nemperor 05587

ROME — R&B/BUB/LP '97

Born Jerome Woods on 3/5/70 in Benton Harbor, Michigan. Male R&B singer.

DEBUT	PEAK	WKS	Gold	A-side (Chart Hit)..........B-side	$	Sym	Label & Number
3/15/97	6	26	▲	1 **I Belong To You (Every Time I See Your Face)**...S:3 / A:26 *Crazy Love / Do You Like This*	$3	▮V	RCA 64759
8/2/97	31	20		2 **Do You Like This**......S:19 *Heaven*	$3	▮V	RCA 64874
				"45" issued for above 2 on RCA 64759			

ROMEO & JULIET SOUNDTRACK — LP '69

Artist credited on label as: **JULIET: OLIVIA HUSSEY; ROMEO: LEONARD WHITING; NURSE: PAT HEYWOOD.**

DEBUT	PEAK	WKS	Gold	A-side (Chart Hit)..........B-side	$	Sym	Label & Number
8/9/69	86	4		**Farewell Love Scene**......*What Is A Youth* (Glen Weston) [S]	$7	■	Capitol 2502
				actual dialogue from the 1968 *Romeo & Juliet* movie soundtrack; musical background composed and conducted by **Nino Rota**			

ROMEOS, The — '67

R&B group from Philadelphia, Pennsylvania: producers Kenny Gamble, Leon Huff and Thom Bell, with brothers Karl and Roland Chambers, and Winnie Walford. Karl Chambers died of cancer on 2/24/2002 (age 55). Roland Chambers died of heart failure on 5/8/2002 (age 58).

DEBUT	PEAK	WKS	Gold	A-side (Chart Hit)..........B-side	$	Sym	Label & Number
4/1/67	67	7		**Precious Memories**......*Juicy Lucy* [I]	$15		Mark II 101

DEBUT	PEAK	WKS	Gold	A-side (Chart Hit)	B-side	$	Sym	Label & Number

ROMEO'S DAUGHTER — LP '88

Rock trio from England: Leigh Matty (vocals), Craig Joiner (guitars, vocals) and Tony Mitman (keyboards).

DEBUT	PEAK	WKS	Gold	A-side (Chart Hit)	B-side	$	Sym	Label & Number
10/15/88	73	7		**Don't Break My Heart**	*Wild Child*	$4	■	Jive 1140

ROMEO VOID — ROK/LP '84

Pop-rock-dance group from San Francisco, California: Debora Iyall (vocals), Peter Woods (guitar), Ben Bossi (sax), Frank Zincavage (bass) and Aaron Smith (drums).

DEBUT	PEAK	WKS	Gold	A-side (Chart Hit)	B-side	$	Sym	Label & Number
9/1/84	35	13		**A Girl In Trouble (Is A Temporary Thing)**	*Going To Neon*	$4		Columbia 04534

RONALD AND RUBY — '58

Teen pop duo: Ronald Gumbs and Beverly "Ruby" Ross (born in 1939). The New Jersey-born Ross wrote "Dim, Dim The Lights," "Lollipop," "Judy's Turn To Cry" and **Roy Orbison**'s "Candy Man."

DEBUT	PEAK	WKS	Gold	A-side (Chart Hit)	B-side	$	Sym	Label & Number
3/17/58	20	7		**Lollipop** A:20 / T:39 / S:40	*Fickle Baby*	$15		RCA Victor 7174

RON AND THE D.C. CREW — '87

Ficticious rap group — features Miami D.J. Mark Moseley.

DEBUT	PEAK	WKS	Gold	A-side (Chart Hit)	B-side	$	Sym	Label & Number
1/24/87	93	4		**Ronnies Rapp** [N] novelty rap song featuring an impersonation of President Ronald Reagan	*(instrumental)*	$6		Profile 5130

RONDELS, The — '61

Rock and roll band from Boston, Massachusetts: Leonard Petze and cousin James Petze (died of cancer on 9/12/93, age 48) with Raymond Pizzi and Leonard Collins. Leonard Petze is a former VP of A&R for Epic Records.

DEBUT	PEAK	WKS	Gold	A-side (Chart Hit)	B-side	$	Sym	Label & Number
8/14/61	66	4		**Back Beat No. 1** [I]	*Shades Of Green*	$25		Amy 825

RON-DELS, The — '65

Pop duo: **Delbert McClinton** and Ronnie Kelly (died in May 1993, age 49).

DEBUT	PEAK	WKS	Gold	A-side (Chart Hit)	B-side	$	Sym	Label & Number
7/24/65	97	1		**If You Really Want Me To, I'll Go** first released on Brownfield 18 in 1965 ($25)	*Walk About*	$15		Smash 1986

RONDO, Don — '57

Born in Springfield, Massachusetts. Adult Contemporary baritone singer. Sang on TV/radio commercials.

DEBUT	PEAK	WKS	Gold	A-side (Chart Hit)	B-side	$	Sym	Label & Number
10/27/56	11	18		1 **Two Different Worlds** A:11 / T:19 / S:23 Dave Terry (orch.)	*He Made You Mine*	$15		Jubilee 5256
7/15/57	7	19		2 **White Silver Sands** A:7 / S:9 / T:10 Billy Rock (orch.)	*Stars Fell On Alabama*	$15		Jubilee 5288
10/28/57	77	2		3 **There's Only You** T:77 Morty Palitz (orch.)	*Forsaking All Others*	$12		Jubilee 5297

RONETTES, The — BUB/LP '63

R&B-rock and roll "girl group" from New York: Veronica Bennett (**Ronnie Spector**) (see #9 below), sister Estelle Bennett Vann and cousin Nedra Talley Ross. Formed as the Darling Sisters in 1958. Sang professionally since junior high school. Backup work for Phil Spector in 1962. Veronica married to Phil Spector, 1968-74. Also see **Billy Joel**'s "Say Goodbye To Hollywood" and **Eddie Money**'s "Take Me Home Tonight."

DEBUT	PEAK	WKS	Gold	A-side (Chart Hit)	B-side	$	Sym	Label & Number
8/31/63	2^{3}	13		1 **Be My Baby**	*Tedesco And Pitman*	$30		Philles 116
12/21/63+	24	9		2 **Baby, I Love You**	*Miss Joan And Mr. Sam*	$30		Philles 118
4/4/64	39	8		3 **(The Best Part Of) Breakin' Up**	*Big Red*	$30		Philles 120
6/20/64	34	9		4 **Do I Love You?**	*Bebe And Susu*	$30		Philles 121
10/24/64	23	11		5 **Walking In The Rain**	*How Does It Feel?*	$40	■	Philles 123
				THE RONETTES Featuring Veronica:				
2/6/65	52	6		6 **Born To Be Together**	*Blues For Baby*	$25	■	Philles 126
5/29/65	75	4		7 **Is This What I Get For Loving You?** all of above produced by Phil Spector	*Oh, I Love You*	$25	■	Philles 128
10/29/66	100	1		8 **I Can Hear Music**	*When I Saw You*	$25		Philles 133
5/8/71	77	4		9 **Try Some, Buy Some** **RONNIE SPECTOR** written by **George Harrison**; produced by Harrison and Phil Spector	*Tandoori Chicken*	$15	■	Apple 1832

RONNIE and THE HI-LITES — BUB '62

Doo-wop group from Jersey City, New Jersey: Ronnie Goodson (lead singer; 12 years old in 1962), Sonny Caldwell and John Whitney (tenors), Stanley Brown (baritone) and Kenny Overby (bass). Originally called The Cascades. Goodson died of a brain tumor on 11/4/80 (age 31).

DEBUT	PEAK	WKS	Gold	A-side (Chart Hit)	B-side	$	Sym	Label & Number
3/31/62	16	12		**I Wish That We Were Married**	*Twistin' And Kissin'*	$30		Joy 260

RONNY & THE DAYTONAS — BUB/LP '64

Pop-rock group: Ronny is John "Bucky" Wilkin (vocals; born on 4/26/46 in Tulsa, Oklahoma; son of country songwriter Marijohn Wilkin). Backed on recordings by well-known sessionmen **Bobby Russell** (wrote "Little Green Apples"), Chips Moman (prolific producer) and Johnny McCrae (member of **Bobby "Boris" Pickett And The Crypt-Kickers**), among others. The touring group, which featured an entirely different lineup, later charted as **The Hombres**.

DEBUT	PEAK	WKS	Gold	A-side (Chart Hit)	B-side	$	Sym	Label & Number
8/1/64	4	13		1 **G.T.O.**	*Hot Rod Baby*	$25		Mala 481
11/7/64	72	5		2 **California Bound**	*Hey Little Girl*	$20		Mala 490
12/19/64+	54	7		3 **Bucket "T"** co-written by Jan Berry (of **Jan & Dean**)	*Little Rail Job*	$20		Mala 492
12/4/65+	27	11		4 **Sandy** all of above produced by **Bill Justis**	*(instrumental)*	$20		Mala 513
9/3/66	69	5		5 **Dianne, Dianne**	*All American Girl*	$15	■	RCA Victor 8896

DEBUT	PEAK	WKS	Gold	A-side (Chart Hit)..........B-side	$	Sym	Label & Number

RONSTADT, Linda ★62★ C&W/AC/BUB/LP '75

Born on 7/15/46 in Tucson, Arizona. While in high school formed folk trio The Three Ronstadts (with sister and brother). To Los Angeles in 1964. Formed the **Stone Poneys** with Bobby Kimmel (guitar) and Ken Edwards (keyboards); recorded for Sidewalk in 1966. Went solo in 1968. In 1971 formed backing band with **Glenn Frey**, **Don Henley**, **Randy Meisner** and Bernie Leadon (later became the **Eagles**). Appeared in the 1978 movie *FM.* In *Pirates Of Penzance* operetta in New York City in 1980, also in the movie version in 1983. Also see **Nitty Gritty Dirt Band**'s "An American Dream."

1)You're No Good 2)Don't Know Much 3)When Will I Be Loved 4)Somewhere Out There 5)Blue Bayou

DEBUT	PEAK	WKS	Gold	A-side (Chart Hit)	B-side	$	Sym	Label & Number
11/11/67+	13	17		1 **Different Drum**	*I've Got To Know*	$15		Capitol 2004
				STONE PONEYS Featuring Linda Ronstadt written by **Michael Nesmith**				
3/30/68	93	2		2 **Up To My Neck In High Muddy Water**	*Carnival Bear*	$10	■	Capitol 2110
				LINDA RONSTADT And The Stone Poneys				
8/15/70	25	12		3 **Long Long Time**	*Nobodys*	$7		Capitol 2846
1/23/71	70	5		4 **(She's A) Very Lovely Woman** /				
				recorded by **The Merry-Go-Round** in 1967 as "You're A Very Lovely Woman"				
1/23/71		5		5 **The Long Way Around**		$7		Capitol 3021
3/4/72	85	3		6 **Rock Me On The Water**	*Crazy Arms*	$7		Capitol 3273
				Glenn Frey, **Don Henley** and **Randy Meisner** (backing vocals)				
12/1/73+	51	11		7 **Love Has No Pride**	*I Can Almost See It*	$5		Asylum 11026
4/6/74	67	7		8 **Silver Threads And Golden Needles**	*Don't Cry Now*	$5		Asylum 11032
12/7/74+	❶[1]	16		9 **You're No Good**	*I Can't Help It (If I'm Still In Love With You)* (C&W #2)	$5		Capitol 3990
				Andrew Gold (guitar solo)				
4/12/75	2[2]	19		10 **When Will I Be Loved** /	CW[1]			
7/26/75	47	4		11 **It Doesn't Matter Anymore**		$5		Capitol 4050
9/20/75	5	13		12 **Heat Wave** /				
9/6/75	63	15		13 **Love Is A Rose**		$5		Asylum 45282
				written by **Neil Young**; originally released on Asylum 45271 with "Silver Blue" as the B-side				
12/20/75+	25	13		14 **Tracks Of My Tears**	*The Sweetest Gift* (w/**Emmylou Harris** - C&W #12)	$5		Asylum 45295
8/21/76	11	16		15 **That'll Be The Day**	*Try Me Again*	$5		Asylum 45340
12/4/76+	42	11		16 **Someone To Lay Down Beside Me**	*Crazy* (C&W #6)	$5		Asylum 45361
6/4/77	76	5		17 **Lose Again**	*Lo Siento Mi Vida*	$5		Asylum 45402
				above 2 written by **Karla Bonoff** (also #34 below)				
9/10/77	3	23	▲	18 **Blue Bayou**	*Old Paint*	$5		Asylum 45431
10/8/77	5	18		19 **It's So Easy**	*Lo Siento Mi Vida*	$5		Asylum 45438
				Buddy Holly song first recorded by his group **The Crickets** in 1958 on Brunswick 55094				
1/28/78	31	9		20 **Poor Poor Pitiful Me**	*Simple Man, Simple Dream*	$5		Asylum 45462
				written by **Warren Zevon**				
4/22/78	32	8		21 **Tumbling Dice**	*I Never Will Marry* (C&W #8)	$5		Asylum 45479
				above 4 from the album *Simple Dreams*				
8/19/78	16	13		22 **Back In The U.S.A.**	*White Rhythm & Blues*	$5	■	Asylum 45519
11/11/78+	7	16		23 **Ooh Baby Baby**	*Blowing Away*	$5		Asylum 45546
				David Sanborn (sax solo)				
2/10/79	44	8		24 **Just One Look**	*Love Me Tender* (C&W #59)	$5		Asylum 46011
2/2/80	10	16		25 **How Do I Make You**	*Rambler Gambler* (C&W #42)	$4	■	Asylum 46602
4/12/80	8	14		26 **Hurt So Bad**	*Justine*	$4		Asylum 46624
6/28/80	31	12		27 **I Can't Let Go**	*Look Out For My Love*	$4		Asylum 46654
10/2/82	29	12		28 **Get Closer**	*Sometimes You Just Can't Win* (w/**J.D. Souther** - C&W #27)	$4	■	Asylum 69948
12/11/82+	37	12		29 **I Knew You When**	*Talk To Me Of Mendocino*	$4	■	Asylum 69853
4/23/83	54	10		30 **Easy For You To Say**	*Mr. Radio*	$4		Asylum 69838
10/29/83	53	14		31 **What's New**	*Crazy He Calls Me*	$4		Asylum 69780
				LINDA RONSTADT & THE NELSON RIDDLE ORCHESTRA first written as the instrumental "I'm Free"; #2 hit for **Bing Crosby** in 1939				
12/20/86+	2[1]	22	●	32 **Somewhere Out There**	S:❶[2] / A:7 *(instrumental)*	$3	■	MCA 52973
				LINDA RONSTADT AND JAMES INGRAM from the animated movie *An American Tail*				
9/30/89	2[2]	26	●	33 **Don't Know Much** AC[5]	S:❶[2] / A:4 *Cry Like A Rainstorm* (Ronstadt)	$3		Elektra 69261
				song also known as "All I Need To Know"				
2/10/90	11	15		34 **All My Life** AC[3]	S:10 / A:14 *Shattered* (Ronstadt)	$3	▮[V]	Elektra 64987
5/12/90	78	6		35 **When Something Is Wrong With My Baby**	*Try Me Again* (Ronstadt)	$3	▮	Elektra 64968
				LINDA RONSTADT (featuring Aaron Neville) (above 3) #9-35: produced by Peter Asher (**Peter & Gordon**)				
10/21/95	60[S]	2		36 **A Dream Is A Wish Your Heart Makes**	BUB:101 *Un Precioso Sueño*	$3	▮	Walt Disney 60344
				from the Disney animated movie *Cinderella*				

ROOFTOP SINGERS, The LP '63

Folk trio from New York: Erik Darling, Willard Svanoe and Lynne Taylor (died in 1982). Disbanded in 1967. Darling was a member of **The Tarriers** in 1956 and The Weavers, 1958-62. Taylor was a vocalist with **Benny Goodman** and Buddy Rich.

DEBUT	PEAK	WKS	Gold	A-side (Chart Hit)	B-side	$	Sym	Label & Number
1/5/63	❶[2]	13	●	1 **Walk Right In** AC[5]	*Cool Water*	$12	□	Vanguard 35017
				originally recorded in 1929 by Gus Cannon's Jug Stompers				
3/23/63	20	10		2 **Tom Cat**	*Shoes*	$8	■	Vanguard 35019
7/20/63	55	7		3 **Mama Don't Allow**	*It Don't Mean A Thing*	$8	■	Vanguard 35020
				revival of the 1936 song "Mama Don't Allow It"				

ROOMMATES, The — see CATHY JEAN and THE ROOMMATES

DEBUT	PEAK	WKS	Gold	A-side (Chart Hit)...B-side	$	Sym	Label & Number

ROOTS, The — R&B/BUB/LP '97

Hip-hop group from Philadelphia, Pennsylvania: Tariq Trotter, Ahmir-Khalib Thompson, Malik Abdul-Basit and Leonard Hubbard. Also see **Tracie Spencer**'s "It's All About You."

DEBUT	PEAK	WKS	Gold	A-side (Chart Hit)...B-side	$	Sym	Label & Number
8/3/96	72^S	1		1 **Clones** ...BUB:101 *(instrumental) / Section*	$3	▮	DGC 19402
1/11/97	34	15		2 **What They Do** ...S:17 *(instrumental) / Respond/React*	$3	▮	DGC 19407
2/13/99	39	14		3 **You Got Me** ...A:24 *(5 versions)* **THE ROOTS featuring Erykah Badu** co-written and backing vocals by **Jill Scott**	$6	T	MCA 55539

ROS, Edmundo, and His Orchestra — POP/LP '50

Born on 12/7/10 in Trinidad. Bandleader/drummer based in London, England. Hit #16 in 1950 with "The Wedding Samba."

DEBUT	PEAK	WKS	Gold	A-side (Chart Hit)...B-side	$	Sym	Label & Number
2/10/58	75	6		1 **Colonel Bogey**...T:75 *Spanish Gypsy Dance* [I] from the movie *The Bridge On The River Kwai* starring Alec Guinness and William Holden; "Bogey" is a 1916 traditional march	$10		London 1779
1/5/59	77	4		2 **I Talk To The Trees** ...*I Whistle A Happy Tune* [I] from the Broadway musical *Paint Your Wagon* starring James Barton	$10		London 1831

ROSABEL — '01

Remixing duo: Chicago-based DJ/producer Ralphi Rosario and Miami-based DJ/producer Abel Aguilera.

DEBUT	PEAK	WKS	Gold	A-side (Chart Hit)...B-side	$	Sym	Label & Number
11/24/01	66^S	1		**And I Am Telling You I'm Not Going**...*(5 versions)* **ROSABEL with JENNIFER HOLLIDAY** re-recording of Holliday's 1982 hit	$8	★*	Tommy Boy Silver 2251

ROSE, Andy — '58

Teen pop singer.

DEBUT	PEAK	WKS	Gold	A-side (Chart Hit)...B-side	$	Sym	Label & Number
10/6/58	69	7		**Just Young**...H:69 *Lov-A Lov-A Love*	$30		Aamco 100

ROSE, David, and His Orchestra — POP/LP '62

Born on 6/15/10 in London, England; raised in Chicago, Illinois. Died of heart failure on 8/23/90 (age 80). Conductor/composer/arranger for numerous movies. Scored many TV series, such as *The Red Skelton Show*, *Bonanza* and *Little House On The Prairie*. Married to Martha Raye (1938-41) and Judy Garland (1941-43). Hit #2 in 1944 with "Holiday For Strings."

DEBUT	PEAK	WKS	Gold	A-side (Chart Hit)...B-side	$	Sym	Label & Number
11/12/55	54	10		1 **Love Is A Many-Splendored Thing** ...T:54 *You And You Alone (Gelsomina)* [I] title song from the movie starring William Holden and Jennifer Jones	$12		MGM 30883
2/2/57	84	2		2 **Holiday For Trombones** ...T:84 *Midnight On The Cliffs (Theme From "Julie")* [I] similar to Rose's 1944 hit "Holiday For Strings"	$12		MGM 12376
3/23/57	42	12		3 **Calypso Melody** ...T:42 *Theme From "The Wings Of Eagles"* [I] composed by swing-era bandleader Larry Clinton in 1951	$12		MGM 12430
2/24/58	47	9		4 **Swinging Shepherd Blues**...S:47 / T:50 *Rock Fiddle* [I]	$12		MGM 12608
6/1/59	46	12		5 **Like Young** ...*Young Man's Lament* [I] **The Piano Magic of ANDRE PREVIN Combined With The Lush Strings of DAVID ROSE**	$10		MGM 12792
5/12/62	1^1	17	●	6 **The Stripper** AC^2 *Ebb Tide* [I]	$10		MGM 13064

ROSE COLORED GLASS — '71

Pop vocal group from Dallas, Texas: Mary Owens, Larry Meletio, Bob Caldwell and Bill Tillman (**Blood, Sweat & Tears**).

DEBUT	PEAK	WKS	Gold	A-side (Chart Hit)...B-side	$	Sym	Label & Number
4/10/71	54	14		1 **Can't Find The Time** ...*Mystic Touch*	$6		Bang 584
10/23/71	95	4		2 **If It's Alright With You** ...*You're Good For Me*	$6		Bang 588

ROSE GARDEN, The — LP '67

Pop group formed in Parkersburg, West Virginia: Diana Di Rose (vocals), John Noreen and James Groshong (guitars), William Fleming (bass, piano) and Bruce Boudin (drums).

DEBUT	PEAK	WKS	Gold	A-side (Chart Hit)...B-side	$	Sym	Label & Number
10/21/67	17	14		**Next Plane To London** ...*Flower Town*	$10		Atco 6510

ROSELLI, Jimmy — AC/BUB/LP '67

Born in 1926 in Hoboken, New Jersey. Italian-American Adult Contemporary singer.

DEBUT	PEAK	WKS	Gold	A-side (Chart Hit)...B-side	$	Sym	Label & Number
8/12/67	93	2		**There Must Be A Way**...*I'm Yours To Command* #9 hit for both Johnnie Johnston and Charlie Spivak in 1945	$6		United Artists 50179

ROSE ROYCE — R&B/BUB/LP '77

R&B-dance group from Los Angeles, California: Gwen "Rose" Dickey (vocals), Kenji Brown (guitar), Kenny Copeland and Freddie Dunn (trumpets), Michael Moore (sax), Terral Santiel (percussion), Victor Nix (keyboards), Lequeint "Duke" Jobe (bass) and Henry Garner (drums). Dickey left after first album, replaced by Rose Norwalt. Dickey then returned from 1978 until she was replaced by Richee McKinney in 1980. Group backed **Edwin Starr** as Total Concept Unlimited in 1973. Backed **The Temptations**, became regular band for **Undisputed Truth**. Name changed to Rose Royce in 1976. Did soundtrack for the movie *Car Wash*.

DEBUT	PEAK	WKS	Gold	A-side (Chart Hit)...B-side	$	Sym	Label & Number
10/23/76+	1^1	23	▲	1 **Car Wash** RB^2 *Water*	$5		MCA 40615
2/26/77	10	17		2 **I Wanna Get Next To You** ...*Sunrise*	$5		MCA 40662
6/4/77	70	7		3 **I'm Going Down** ...*Yo Yo* above 3 from the movie *Car Wash* starring Richard Pryor and Franklin Ajaye	$5		MCA 40721
9/17/77	39	8		4 **Do Your Dance - Part 1**...*Part 2*	$5		Whitfield 8440
11/26/77+	72	11		5 **Ooh Boy** ...*You Can't Please Everybody*	$5		Whitfield 8491
12/9/78+	32	11		6 **Love Don't Live Here Anymore**...*That's What's Wrong With Me* all of above produced and arranged by Norman Whitfield	$5		Whitfield 8712

ROSIE And The Originals — '61

Pop group from San Diego, California. Rosie was born Rosalie Hamlin on 7/21/45 in Klamath Falls, Oregon; raised in Anchorage, Alaska. The Originals: David Ponci and Noah Tafolla (guitars), Tony Gomez (sax) and Carl Von Goodat (drums).

DEBUT	PEAK	WKS	Gold	A-side (Chart Hit)...B-side	$	Sym	Label & Number
12/12/60+	5	13		1 **Angel Baby** ...*Give Me Love*	$30		Highland 1011
3/13/61	66	4		2 **Lonely Blue Nights**...*We'll Have A Chance* **ROSIE formerly with The Originals** **Dick Jacobs** (orch.); different version released later on Highland 1032 as by Rosie & The Originals ($30)	$25		Brunswick 55205

ROSS, Charlie — C&W '76

Born in Greenville, Mississippi. Pop/country singer. Bassist for **Eternity's Children**.

DEBUT	PEAK	WKS	Gold	A-side (Chart Hit)...B-side	$	Sym	Label & Number
1/18/75	61	5		1 **Thanks For The Smiles** ...*Can't Live With You, Can't Live Without You*	$6		Big Tree 16025
2/28/76	42	7		2 **Without Your Love (Mr. Jordan)**...*Sneaking Round Corners*	$6		Big Tree 16056

DEBUT	PEAK	WKS	Gold	A-side (Chart Hit)...B-side	$	Sym	Label & Number

ROSS, Diana ★35★ R&B/AC/BUB/LP '76

Born Diane Ernestine Ross on 3/26/44 in Detroit, Michigan. R&B singer/actress. In vocal group The Primettes, first recorded for LuPine in 1960. Lead singer of **The Supremes** from 1961-69. Went solo in late 1969. Oscar nominee for the 1972 movie *Lady Sings The Blues*. Also appeared in the movies *Mahogany* and *The Wiz*. Own Broadway show *An Evening With Diana Ross*, 1976. Married to Norwegian shipping magnate Arne Naess from 1986-2000. Ross would rank among the Top 5 artists of the rock era if her solo and Supremes' hits were combined.

1)Endless Love 2)Upside Down 3)Ain't No Mountain High Enough 4)Love Hangover 5)Touch Me In The Morning

DEBUT	PEAK	WKS	Gold	A-side (Chart Hit)...B-side	$	Sym	Label & Number
4/25/70	20	9		1 **Reach Out And Touch (Somebody's Hand)**...*Dark Side Of The World*	$6	■	Motown 1165
8/8/70	1[3]	14		2 **Ain't No Mountain High Enough**...RB[1] *Can't It Wait Until Tomorrow*	$6	■	Motown 1169
12/26/70+	16	10		3 **Remember Me**...*How About You*	$6	■	Motown 1176
5/1/71	29	7		4 **Reach Out I'll Be There**...*(They Long To Be) Close To You*	$6		Motown 1184
8/14/71	38	8		5 **Surrender**...*I'm A Winner*	$6		Motown 1188
				all of above written (except #4) and produced by **Ashford & Simpson**			
11/6/71	63	5		6 **I'm Still Waiting**...*A Simple Thing Like Cry*	$6		Motown 1192
1/13/73	34	13		7 **Good Morning Heartache**...*God Bless The Child*	$6	■	Motown 1211
				from the movie *Lady Sings The Blues* starring Ross (inspired by Billie Holiday's 1946 recording on Decca 23676-$25)			
6/2/73	1[1]	21		8 **Touch Me In The Morning**...AC[1] *I Won't Last A Day Without You*	$6		Motown 1239
10/6/73	12	12		9 **You're A Special Part Of Me**...*I'm Falling In Love With You*	$6		Motown 1280
				DIANA ROSS & MARVIN GAYE			
1/5/74	14	14		10 **Last Time I Saw Him**...AC[3] *Save The Children*	$6		Motown 1278
2/23/74	19	16		11 **My Mistake (Was To Love You)**...*Include Me In Your Life*	$6		Motown 1269
				DIANA ROSS & MARVIN GAYE			
5/11/74	70	5		12 **Sleepin'**...*You*	$6		Motown 1295
7/13/74	46	9		13 **Don't Knock My Love**...*Just Say, Just Say*	$6		Motown 1296
				DIANA ROSS & MARVIN GAYE			
11/1/75+	1[1]	17		14 **Theme From Mahogany (Do You Know Where You're Going To)**...AC[1] *No One's Gonna Be A Fool Forever*	$5	■	Motown 1377
				from the movie *Mahogany* starring Ross			
3/20/76	47	7		15 **I Thought It Took A Little Time (But Today I Fell In Love)**...*After You*	$5	■	Motown 1387
4/3/76	1[2]	18		16 **Love Hangover**...RB[1] *Kiss Me Now*	$5		Motown 1392
8/7/76	25	12		17 **One Love In My Lifetime**...*Smile*	$5		Motown 1398
				above 4 from the album *Diana Ross* on Motown 861			
11/5/77+	27	13		18 **Gettin' Ready For Love**...*Confide In Me*	$5		Motown 1427
3/4/78	49	7		19 **Your Love Is So Good For Me**...*Baby It's Me*	$5		Motown 1436
5/6/78	49	7		20 **You Got It**...*Too Shy To Say*	$5		Motown 1442
9/9/78	41	9		21 **Ease On Down The Road**...*Poppy Girls* (**Quincy Jones**)	$5	■	MCA 40947
				DIANA ROSS MICHAEL JACKSON			
				from the movie *The Wiz* starring Ross and Jackson			
1/20/79	59	8		22 **Pops, We Love You (A Tribute To Father)**...*(instrumental)*	$5		Motown 1455
				DIANA ROSS, MARVIN GAYE, SMOKEY ROBINSON & STEVIE WONDER			
				song commemorates Berry Gordy Sr.'s death at age 90			
7/14/79	19	16		23 **The Boss**...*I'm In The World*	$4		Motown 1462
7/12/80	1[4]	29	●	24 **Upside Down**...RB[4] *Friend To Friend*	$4		Motown 1494
9/6/80	5	23		25 **I'm Coming Out**...*Friend To Friend*	$4		Motown 1491
				also released with "Give Up" as the B-side			
10/25/80+	9	21		26 **It's My Turn**...*Together*	$4	■	Motown 1496
				title song from the movie starring Jill Clayburgh and Michael Douglas			
4/11/81	79	5		27 **One More Chance**...*After You*	$4		Motown 1508
7/11/81	1[9]	27	▲	28 **Endless Love** RB[7] / AC[3] *(instrumental)*	$4		Motown 1519
				DIANA ROSS & LIONEL RICHIE			
				title song from the movie starring Brooke Shields			
10/17/81	7	20		29 **Why Do Fools Fall In Love**...*Think I'm In Love*	$4		RCA 12349
1/9/82	8	14		30 **Mirror, Mirror**...*Sweet Nothings*	$4		RCA 13021
4/10/82	44	7		31 **Work That Body**...*Two Can Make It*	$4		RCA 13201
10/2/82	10	17		32 **Muscles**...*I Am Me*	$4	■	RCA 13348
				written and produced by **Michael Jackson**			
2/5/83	40	10		33 **So Close**...*Fool For Your Love*	$4		RCA 13424
6/25/83	31	10		34 **Pieces Of Ice**...*Still In Love*	$4	■	RCA 13549
12/17/83+	77	6		35 **Let's Go Up**...*Girls*	$4		RCA 13671
				written and produced by **Ray Parker Jr.**			
7/7/84	19	16		36 **All Of You**...*The Last Time* (Iglesias)	$3	■	Columbia 04507
				JULIO IGLESIAS & DIANA ROSS			
9/1/84	19	14		37 **Swept Away**...S:17 / A:18 *Fight For It*	$3	■	RCA 13864
				written and produced by **Daryl Hall**			
12/1/84+	10	27		38 **Missing You**...RB[3] S:5 / A:13 *We Are The Children Of The World*	$3	■	RCA 13966
				dedicated to **Marvin Gaye**; written and produced by **Lionel Richie**			
9/21/85	77	7		39 **Eaten Alive**...*(different mix)*	$3	■	RCA 14181
				Michael Jackson (backing vocal; also co-writer and co-producer)			
11/30/85	95	3		40 **Chain Reaction**...*More And More*	$3	■	RCA 14244
5/3/86	66	8		41 **Chain Reaction**...*More And More* [R]	$3		RCA 14244
				"Special New Mix" of previous hit (with same label number); above 3 co-produced by **Barry Gibb**			

ROSS, Jack '62

Born in Los Angeles, California. Died on 12/16/82 (age 66). Comedian.

DEBUT	PEAK	WKS	Gold	A-side (Chart Hit)...B-side	$	Sym	Label & Number
1/13/62	57	6		1 **Happy Jose (Ching-Ching)**...*Sweet Georgia Brown* [I-N]	$12		Dot 16302
3/17/62	16	9		2 **Cinderella**...*Margarita* [C-L]	$12		Dot 16333

DEBUT	PEAK	WKS	Gold	A-side (Chart Hit)...B-side	$	Sym	Label & Number
				ROSS, Jackie BUB '64			
				Born on 1/30/46 in St. Louis, Missouri; raised in Chicago, Illinois. Female R&B singer.			
8/1/64	11	10		1 **Selfish One** ... *Everything But Love*	$10		Chess 1903
11/14/64	89	2		2 **I've Got The Skill** ... *Change Your Ways*	$10		Chess 1913
1/30/65	85	4		3 **Jerk And Twine** ... *New Lover*	$10		Chess 1920
				ROSS, Spencer '60			
				Born Robert Mersey in Manhattan, New York. Conductor/arranger.			
1/4/60	13	14		**Tracy's Theme** ... *Thanksgiving Day Parade* [I]	$12		Columbia 41532
				Jimmy Abato (sax); from the 12/7/59 TV drama special *Philadelphia Story*			
				ROSSINGTON COLLINS BAND — see LYNYRD SKYNYRD			
				ROTA, Nino — see ROMEO & JULIET SOUNDTRACK / SAVINA, Carlo			
				ROTARY CONNECTION BUB/LP '70			
				Multi-racial rock/R&B group formed in Chicago, Illinois: **Minnie Riperton**, Judy Huff and Sid Barnes (vocals), Bobby Simms (guitar), Charles Stepney (keyboards), Mitch Aliotta (bass) and Kenny Venegas (drums).			
1/3/70	96	2		**Want You To Know** ... *Memory Band*	$10		Cadet Concept 7018
				ROTH, David Lee ROK/LP '85			
				Born on 10/10/55 in Bloomington, Indiana. Lead singer of **Van Halen** from 1973-1985. Rejoined Van Halen briefly in 1996 to record two new songs.			
1/19/85	3	16		1 **California Girls** A:3 / S:4 *(remix)*	$3	■	Warner 29102
				Carl Wilson (backing vocal)			
3/23/85	12	17		2 **Just A Gigolo/I Ain't Got Nobody** ... A:11 / S:16 *(remix)*	$3	■	Warner 29040
				"Just A Gigolo": #1 hit for Ted Lewis in 1931; "I Ain't Got Nobody": #3 hit for Marion Harris in 1921; arrangement copied from a **Louis Prima** recording on Capitol in 1956			
7/5/86	16	15		3 **Yankee Rose** ... S:15 / A:22 *Shyboy*	$3	■	Warner 28656
9/27/86	66	7		4 **Goin' Crazy!** ... *(Spanish version)*	$3	■	Warner 28584
11/22/86	85	4		5 **That's Life** ... *Bump And Grind*	$3	■	Warner 28511
1/16/88	6	16		6 **Just Like Paradise** ... AR[4] S:4 / A:8 *The Bottom Line*	$3	■	Warner 28119
4/16/88	64	8		7 **Stand Up** ... *Knucklebones* (ROK #45)	$3	■	Warner 28108
				ROTHBERG, Patti '96			
				Born in 1973 in Scarsdale, New York. Alternative-rock singer/songwriter/multi-instrumentalist.			
7/20/96	71[A]	3		**Inside** ...		V	album cut
				from the album *Between The 1 And The 9* on EMI 36834; "45": EMI 19334; B-side: "Treat Me Like Dirt"			
				ROUGH TRADE '83			
				Rock group from Toronto, Ontario, Canada: Carole Pope (vocals), Kevan Staples (guitar), Dave McMorrow (keyboards), Terry Wilkins (bass) and Bucky Berger (drums).			
12/18/82+	58	7		**All Touch** ... *The Sacred And The Profane*	$4		Boardwalk 167
				ROULA '95			
				Born in Chicago, Illinois. Female dance singer. Produced by **20 Fingers**.			
3/25/95	72	15		**Lick It** ... S:60 *(club mix)*	$3	▮	SOS/Zoo 14214
				ROUND ROBIN BUB '64			
				Pop singer; similar in style to **Chubby Checker**.			
5/30/64	61	8		**Kick That Little Foot Sally Ann** ... *Slauson Party*	$12		Domain 1404
				song introduced on **Harry Belafonte**'s 1964 album *Belafonte At The Greek Theatre* ("Shake That Little Foot")			
				ROUSSOS, Demis LP '78			
				Born on 6/15/47 in Alexandria, Egypt (Greek parents). Male singer.			
6/3/78	47	11		**That Once In A Lifetime** ... *This Song*	$5	■	Mercury 73992
				ROUTERS, The BUB/LP '62			
				Rock and roll instrumental group formed in Los Angeles, California: Mike Gordon, Al Kait, Bill Moody and Lynn Frazier. Produced by Joe Saraceno (**The T-Bones**).			
11/3/62	19	13		1 **Let's Go** (pony) ... *Mashy* [I]	$15		Warner 5283
4/27/63	50	10		2 **Sting Ray** ... *Snap Happy* [I]	$15		Warner 5349
				ROVER BOYS, The '56			
				Pop vocal group formed in Toronto, Ontario, Canada: Bill Albert, Doug Wells, Larry Amato and Al Osten.			
5/12/56	16	11		1 **Graduation Day** ... A:16 / S:19 / T:20 *I Hear Music*	$20		ABC-Paramount 9700
				THE ROVER BOYS featuring Billy Albert			
9/22/56	79	3		2 **From A School Ring To A Wedding Ring** ... T:79 *Young Love*	$20		ABC-Paramount 9732
				Don Costa (orch., above 2)			
				ROVERS, The — see IRISH ROVERS			
				ROWANS, The BUB '76			
				Pop-rock trio from Boston, Massachusetts: brothers Peter (vocals, guitar), Lorin (guitar) and Chris (keyboards) Rowan. Peter was a member of **Earth Opera** and **Seatrain**.			
10/16/76	74	4		**If I Only Could** ... *Tired Hands*	$5		Asylum 45347
				ROWLAND, Kelly LP '02			
				Born on 2/11/81 in Atlanta, Georgia. Female R&B singer. Member of **Destiny's Child**.			
7/13/02	❶[10]	29		1 **Dilemma** ... RB[9] A:❶[12] / S:17 *Air Force Ones* (Nelly - #3)	$6	T	Fo' Reel/Universal 019509
				NELLY Featuring Kelly Rowland			
				samples "Love, Need And Want You" by **Patti LaBelle**			
9/28/02	27	20		2 **Stole** ... A:27 *(5 remixes)*	$6	T[V]	Columbia 79820
				"45": Columbia 79818; B-side: (urban edit)			
				ROWLES, John LP '71			
				Born on 3/26/47 in Whakatane, New Zealand. Pop singer/songwriter.			
1/2/71	64	8		**Cheryl Moana Marie** ... *The Love I Had With You*	$6		Kapp 2102

DEBUT	PEAK	WKS	Gold	A-side (Chart Hit)	B-side	$	Sym	Label & Number
				ROXANNE '88				
				Rock group from Riverside, California: Jamie Brown (vocals), John Butler (guitar), Joey Infante (bass) and Dave Landry (drums).				
3/12/88	63	7		**Play That Funky Music**	*Over You*	$4		Scotti Brothers 07724
	★259★			**ROXETTE** AC/LP '89				
				Pop-rock duo from Sweden: Marie Fredriksson (born on 5/30/58 in Ostra Ljungby, Sweden) and Per Gessle (born on 6/12/59 in Halmstad, Sweden). *1)It Must Have Been Love 2)The Look 3)Listen To Your Heart*				
2/11/89	❶^{1}	19	●	1 **The Look** A:❷^{2} / S:2	*Silver Blue*	$3		EMI 50190
				popularized after American student Dean Cushman brought the record back from Sweden and gave it to Minneapolis radio station KDWB				
5/27/89	14	18		2 **Dressed For Success** S:12 / A:18	*The Look (album version)*	$3		EMI 50204
8/26/89	❶^{1}	22		3 **Listen To Your Heart** A:❶^{1} / S:3	*Half A Woman, Half A Shadow*	$3	▮V	EMI 50223
12/16/89+	2^{2}	21		4 **Dangerous** S:2 / A:3	*(12" version)*	$3	▮V	EMI 50233
				above 4 from the album *Look Sharp!*				
4/7/90	❶^{2}	25	●	5 **It Must Have Been Love** A:❶^{3} / S:2	*Chances*	$3	▮V	EMI 50283
				from the movie *Pretty Woman* starring Richard Gere and Julia Roberts; above 3 "45s" released September 1990				
3/2/91	❶^{1}	19		6 **Joyride** S:❶^{1} / A:2	*(remix) / Come Back (Before You Leave)*	$3	▮V	EMI 50342
				"45": Collectables 6242; B-side: "The Look"				
6/15/91	2^{1}	18		7 **Fading Like A Flower (Every Time You Leave)** A:11 / S:23	*I Remember You*	$3	▮V	EMI 50355
				"45": Collectables 6239; B-side: "Dangerous"				
10/26/91+	32	20		8 **Spending My Time** A:32 / S:49	*The Sweet Hello, The Sad Goodbye*	$3	▮	EMI 50366
2/29/92	36	11		9 **Church Of Your Heart** A:34	*I Call Your Name*	$3	▮V	EMI 50380
				"45": EMI 57697; above 4 from the album *Joyride*				
10/17/92	58	8		10 **How Do You Do!** A:70	*(U.S. edit) / Fading Like A Flower (live)*	$3	▮V	EMI 50410
				"45": EMI 57991				
6/19/93	94	2		11 **Almost Unreal**	*The Heart Shaped Sea*	$3	▮V	Capitol 44942
				from the movie *Super Mario Bros.* starring Bob Hoskins; "45": Capitol 17400				
7/2/94	50	8		12 **Sleeping In My Car** A:60	*The Look (unplugged version)*	$3	▮V	EMI 58143
				"45": EMI 18044 (yellow vinyl); all of above written by Gessle and produced by Clarence Ofwerman				
				ROXY MUSIC ROK/BUB/LP '76				
				Art-rock group from England: **Bryan Ferry** (vocals, keyboards), Phil Manzanera (guitar), Andy MacKay (horns) and Paul Thompson (drums).				
12/27/75+	30	14		1 **Love Is The Drug**	*Both Ends Burning*	$6		Atco 7042
4/28/79	44	9		2 **Dance Away**	*Trash 2*	$5		Atco 7100
8/9/80	80	4		3 **Over You**	*My Only Love*	$5		Atco 7301
				ROYAL, Billy Joe C&W/BUB/LP '65				
				Born on 4/3/42 in Valdosta, Georgia; raised in Marietta, Georgia. Country-rock singer/guitarist.				
7/3/65	9	13		1 **Down In The Boondocks**	*Oh, What A Night*	$10		Columbia 43305
9/18/65	14	11		2 **I Knew You When**	*Steal Away*	$8		Columbia 43390
				first recorded by **Wade Flemons** in 1964 on Vee Jay 614				
12/4/65+	38	8		3 **I've Got To Be Somebody**	*You Make Me Feel Like A Man*	$8		Columbia 43465
5/21/66	88	3		4 **Heart's Desire**	*Deep Inside Me*	$8		Columbia 43622
9/3/66	91	2		5 **Campfire Girls**	*Should I Come Back*	$8		Columbia 43740
9/30/67	52	8		6 **Hush**	*Watching From The Bandstand*	$8		Columbia 44277
				all of above written (except #5) and produced by **Joe South**				
10/4/69	15	15		7 **Cherry Hill Park**	*Helping Hand*	$8		Columbia 44902
2/20/71	86	3		8 **Tulsa**	*Pick Up The Pieces*	$6		Columbia 45289
6/3/78	82	4		9 **Under The Boardwalk**	*Precious Time*	$5		Private Stock 45,192
				ROYALETTES, The BUB '65				
				R&B vocal group from Baltimore, Maryland: sisters Anita and Sheila Ross, with Terry Jones and Ronnie Brown.				
7/17/65	41	11		1 **It's Gonna Take A Miracle**	*Out Of Sight, Out Of Mind*	$15		MGM 13366
11/6/65	72	6		2 **I Want To Meet Him**	*Never Again*	$15		MGM 13405
				above 2 written and produced by **Teddy Randazzo**				
				ROYAL GUARDSMEN, The BUB/LP '67				
				Novelty-pop group from Ocala, Florida: Barry Winslow (vocals, guitar), Chris Nunley (vocals), Tom Richards (lead guitar), Bill Balough (bass) and Billy Taylor (organ). "Snoopy" songs inspired by Snoopy the Beagle in the "Peanuts" comic strip.				
12/17/66	2^{4}	12	●	1 **Snoopy Vs. The Red Baron**	*I Needed You* [N]	$12		Laurie 3366
				original Canadian version (also on Laurie 3366) released as "Squeaky Vs. The Black Knight"				
2/25/67	15	7		2 **The Return Of The Red Baron**	*Sweetmeats Slide* [N]	$12		Laurie 3379
6/17/67	46	6		3 **Airplane Song (My Airplane)**	*Om*	$8		Laurie 3391
				written by **Michael Murphey** and **Boomer Castleman**				
9/9/67	97	2		4 **Wednesday**	*So Right (To Be In Love)*	$8		Laurie 3397
12/2/67	❶^{5X}	7		5 **Snoopy's Christmas**	*It Kinda Looks Like Christmas* [X-N]	$12	■	Laurie 3416
				X: 1/'67; 15/'68; 11/'69				
2/17/68	72	4		6 **I Say Love**	*I'm Not Gonna Stay*	$8		Laurie 3428
7/13/68	85	2		7 **Snoopy For President**	*Down Behind The Lines* [N]	$12		Laurie 3451
				a slightly different and shorter version issued on Laurie 3451 (A)				
11/16/68+	35	13		8 **Baby Let's Wait**	*Biplane "Evermore"*	$10		Laurie 3461
				first released on Laurie 3359 in 1966; also released on Laurie 3461 with "So Right (To Be In Love)" on the B-side; all of above produced by Phil Gernhard				
				ROYAL JOKERS, The '55				
				R&B vocal group from Detroit, Michigan: Norman Thrasher (bass), Noah Howell (tenor), Thearon Hill (tenor), Willie Jones (tenor) and Albert Green (baritone).				
12/10/55	77	1		**You Tickle Me Baby** T:77	*Stay Here*	$60		Atco 6052

DEBUT	PEAK	WKS	Gold	A-side (Chart Hit)......B-side	$	Sym	Label & Number
				ROYAL PHILHARMONIC ORCHESTRA LP **'82**			
				Orchestra based in London, England. Conducted by Louis Clark. Founded in 1946 by Sir Thomas Beecham.			
10/31/81+	10	20		**Hooked On Classics** ...... *Hooked On Classics (different medley)* [I]	$6		RCA 12304
				LOUIS CLARK CONDUCTING THE ROYAL PHILHARMONIC ORCHESTRA			
				Tchaikovsky Piano Concerto No. 1/Flight of the Bumble Bee/ Mozart Symphony No. 40 in G Minor/Rhapsody In Blue/Karelia Suite/ The Marriage of Figaro/Romeo & Juliet/Trumpet Voluntary/Hallelujah Chorus/Grieg Piano Concerto in A Minor/March of the Toreadors/ 1812 Overture			
				ROYAL SCOTS DRAGOON GUARDS LP **'72**			
				The military band of Scotland's armored regiment. Led by bagpipe soloist Major Tony Crease.			
5/20/72	11	9		**Amazing Grace** ...... *Cornet Carillon* [I]	$7		RCA Victor 0709
				THE PIPES AND DRUMS AND THE MILITARY BAND OF THE ROYAL SCOTS DRAGOON GUARDS			
				Rev. John Newton wrote the words in 1779; William Walker composed the melody in 1844			
				ROYAL TEENS **'58**			
				Rock and roll group from Fort Lee, New Jersey: Bob Gaudio, Bill Crandall, Billy Dalton and Tom Austin. Crandall was replaced by Larry Qualiano, and Joseph "Joe Villa" Francavilla joined as vocalist in late 1958. In 1960, Gaudio joined **The 4 Seasons**. Al Kooper joined the group for a short time in 1959.			
1/27/58	3	16		1 **Short Shorts** ...... T:3 / S:4 / A:6 *Planet Rock*	$30		ABC-Paramount 9882
				first released on Power 215 in 1957 ($125)			
8/11/58	78	2		2 **Harvey's Got A Girl Friend** ...... H:78 *Hangin' Around*	$30		ABC-Paramount 9945
10/26/59	26	15		3 **Believe Me** ...... *Little Cricket*	$30		Capitol 4261
				ROYALTONES, The BUB **'58**			
				Rock and roll instrumental band from Dearborn, Michigan: David Sanderson (guitar), George Katsakis (sax), brothers Mike (piano) and Greg (drums) Popoff and Kenny Anderson (bass). Sanderson died of a heart attack on 6/25/94 (age 59).			
10/20/58	17	17		1 **Poor Boy** ...... *Wail!* [I]	$25		Jubilee 5338
1/16/61	82	3		2 **Flamingo Express** ...... *Tacos* [I]	$20		Goldisc 3011
				also released with "Secret Love" as the B-side			
				ROZALLA BUB **'92**			
				Born Rozalla Miller on 3/18/64 in Ndola, Zambia. Dance singer.			
6/27/92	37	20		1 **Everybody's Free (To Feel Good)** ...... A:26 / S:50 *(remix)*	$4	▮	Epic 74388
				also see "everybody's free (to wear Sunscreen)" by **Baz Luhrmann**			
12/12/92	63^{A}	1		2 **Are You Ready To Fly?** ...... BUB:106 *(rave mix)*	$4	▮	Epic 74728
12/25/93+	76	7		3 **I Love Music** ...... *(radio version)*	$3	▮	Epic Soundtrax 77286
				from the movie *Carlito's Way* starring Al Pacino and Sean Penn; above 3: #1 Dance Club Play hits			
				ROZELLY PRESENTS DA FAM **'02**			
				Male rap trio from Los Angeles, California: Rozelly, Skubie Tha Ciko and Unique.			
5/4/02	8^{S}	12		**Bang My Hit** ...... *Bang My Shit / What U Fucin Wit / Daily Bread*	$8	★*	Brainstorm 20020
				ROZELLY PRESENTS DA FAM f/Skubie Tha Ciko and Unique			
				R*S*F — see RIGHT SAID FRED			
				RTZ ROK/LP **'92**			
				Rock group formed in Boston, Massachusetts: Brad Delp (vocals), Barry Goudreau (guitar), Brian Maes (keyboards), Tim Archibald (bass) and David Stefanelli (drums). Delp and Goudreau were members of **Boston**. Goudreau was also with **Orion The Hunter**. RTZ: Return To Zero.			
8/17/91	49	10		1 **Face The Music** ...... *Return To Zero*	$3	▮	Giant 19273
1/18/92	26	18		2 **Until Your Love Comes Back Around** ...... A:30 / S:71 *Every Door Is Open*	$3	▮^{V}	Giant 19051
6/6/92	56	8		3 **All You've Got** ...... A:61 *Livin' For The Rock 'N' Roll*	$3	▮	Giant 19112
				RUBBER RODEO **'84**			
				Pop-rock group from Rhode Island: Trish Milliken (vocals), Bob Holmes (guitar), Mark Tomeo (steel guitar), Gary Leib (keyboards), John Doelp (bass) and Barc Holmes (drums).			
8/25/84	86	5		**Anywhere With You** ...... *Slow Me Down*	$4		Mercury 880175
				RUBETTES, The **'74**			
				Pop-rock group from London, England: Alan Wilkins (vocals), Tony Thorpe (guitar), Peter Arnisson and Bill Herd (keyboards), Mickey Clarke (bass), and John Richardson (drums).			
7/20/74	37	10		**Sugar Baby Love** ...... *You Could Have Told Me*	$6		Polydor 15089
				RUBICON LP **'78**			
				Pop-rock group from San Francisco, California: Greg Eckler (vocals, drums), Brad Gillis (guitar), Jerry Martini (**Sly & The Family Stone**), Max Haskett and Dennis Marcellino (horns), Jim Pugh (keyboards), and Jack Blades (bass). Gillis and Blades later formed **Night Ranger**.			
2/25/78	28	11		**I'm Gonna Take Care Of Everything** ...... *That's The Way Things Are*	$5		20th Century 2362
				RUBINOOS, The **'77**			
				Pop group formed in Berkeley, California: John Rubin (vocals), Tom Dunbar (guitar), Royse Ader (bass) and Donn Spindt (drums).			
3/5/77	45	12		**I Think We're Alone Now** ...... *As Long As I'm With You*	$5	■	Beserkley 5741
				RUBIO, Paulina LP **'02**			
				Born on 6/17/71 in Mexico City, Mexico. Latin pop-dance singer.			
5/4/02	41	16		1 **Don't Say Goodbye** ...... A:47 *(3 versions)*	$6	T	Universal 015860
10/26/02	97	3		2 **The One You Love** ...... *(no B-side)*	$4	★	Universal 019280
				RUBY AND THE ROMANTICS BUB/LP **'63**			
				R&B vocal group from Akron, Ohio: Ruby Nash Curtis (lead; born on 11/12/39 in New York), Ed Roberts (died of cancer on 8/10/93, age 57) and George Lee (tenors), Ronald Mosley (baritone) and Leroy Fann (bass; died in 1973).			
2/9/63	❶^{1}	13		1 **Our Day Will Come** RB^{2} *Moonlight And Music*	$15		Kapp 501
5/18/63	16	11		2 **My Summer Love** ...... *Sweet Love And Sweet Forgiveness*	$12		Kapp 525
8/10/63	27	9		3 **Hey There Lonely Boy** ...... *Not A Moment Too Soon*	$12	■	Kapp 544
				recorded later by both **Eddie Holman** and **Robert John** as "Hey There Lonely Girl"			
10/26/63	47	8		4 **Young Wings Can Fly (Higher Than You Know)** ...... *Day Dreaming*	$12	■	Kapp 557
3/21/64	64	6		5 **Our Everlasting Love** ...... *Much Better Off Than I've Ever Been*	$12		Kapp 578
7/18/64	75	4		6 **Baby Come Home** ...... *Every Day's A Holiday*	$12		Kapp 601

DEBUT	PEAK	WKS	Gold	A-side (Chart Hit)...B-side	$	Sym	Label & Number
				RUBY AND THE ROMANTICS — Cont'd			
10/3/64	**48**	8		7 **When You're Young And In Love** ... *I Cry Alone* all of above produced by Allen Stanton	$12		Kapp 615
2/20/65	**87**	3		8 **Does He Really Care For Me** ... *Nevertheless (I'm In Love With You)*	$12		Kapp 646
				RUDE BOYS R&B/LP **'91** R&B vocal group from Cleveland, Ohio: Larry Marcus, Melvin Sephus, and brothers Edward Lee "Buddy" Banks and J. Little. Marcus is the cousin of **B.B. King**. Group discovered by **Levert**.			
3/9/91	**16**	18		**Written All Over Your Face** ... RB[1] S:11 / A:22 *Fool For You* "45": Atlantic Oldies Series 84874; B-side: "Are You Lonely For Me" (R&B #1/'91)	$4	▮[V]	Atlantic 87805
				RUFF ENDZ R&B/LP **'00** R&B vocal duo from Baltimore, Maryland: David Chance and Dante Jordan.			
7/1/00	**5**	26		1 **No More** ... RB[1] S:3 / A:12 *(remix) / Are U Messing Around / (3 album snippets)*	$4	★	Epic 79400
5/11/02	**49**	20		2 **Someone To Love You** ... A:43 from the album *Someone To Love* on Epic 85691			album cut
8/3/02	**58[S]**	1		3 **Baller** ... *(instrumental)* **RICHARD BURTON Featuring Ruff Endz**	$5	★	MCA 155855
				RUFFIN, David R&B/BUB/AC/LP **'76** Born on 1/18/41 in Meridian, Mississippi. Died of a drug overdose on 6/1/91 (age 50). R&B singer. Brother of **Jimmy Ruffin**. Co-lead singer of **The Temptations** from 1963-68.			
2/15/69	**9**	10		1 **My Whole World Ended (The Moment You Left Me)** ... *I've Got To Find Myself A Brand New Baby*	$7		Motown 1140
7/19/69	**58**	5		2 **I've Lost Everything I've Ever Loved** ... *We'll Have A Good Thing Going On*	$7		Motown 1149
12/20/69+	**53**	7		3 **I'm So Glad I Fell For You** ... *I Pray Everyday You Won't Regret Loving Me* The Hal Davis Singers (gospel-styled backing vocals)	$7		Motown 1158
10/24/70	**61**	7		4 **Stand By Me** ... *Your Love Was Worth Waiting For* **DAVID & JIMMY RUFFIN**	$7		Soul 35076
11/8/75+	**9**	15		5 **Walk Away From Love** RB[1] *Love Can Be Hazardous To Your Health*	$6		Motown 1376
3/20/76	**47**	7		6 **Heavy Love** ... *Love Can Be Hazardous To Your Health*	$5		Motown 1388
6/12/76	**49**	9		7 **Everything's Coming Up Love** ... *No Matter Where*	$5		Motown 1393
8/31/85	**20**	11		8 **A Nite At The Apollo Live! The Way You Do The Things You Do/My Girl** ... S:21 / A:23 *Everytime You Go Away* [L] **DARYL HALL JOHN OATES with David Ruffin & Eddie Kendrick** recorded at the reopening of New York's Apollo Theatre	$3	■	RCA 14178
				RUFFIN, Jimmy BUB/R&B/LP **'66** Born on 5/7/39 in Collinsville, Mississippi. R&B singer. Brother of **David Ruffin**.			
8/20/66	**7**	17		1 **What Becomes Of The Brokenhearted** *Baby I've Got It*	$12		Soul 35022
12/3/66+	**17**	11		2 **I've Passed This Way Before** ... *Tomorrow's Tears*	$12		Soul 35027
3/18/67	**29**	7		3 **Gonna Give Her All The Love I've Got** ... *World So Wide, Nowhere To Hide (From Your Heart)*	$8		Soul 35032
7/22/67	**68**	5		4 **Don't You Miss Me A Little Bit Baby** ... *I Want Her Love*	$8		Soul 35035
3/9/68	**77**	5		5 **I'll Say Forever My Love** ... *Everybody Needs Love*	$8		Soul 35043
10/24/70	**61**	7		6 **Stand By Me** ... *Your Love Was Worth Waiting For* **DAVID & JIMMY RUFFIN**	$7		Soul 35076
2/13/71	**97**	2		7 **Maria (You Were The Only One)** ... *Living In A World I Created For Myself*	$7		Soul 35077
3/1/80	**10**	14		8 **Hold On To My Love** ... *(instrumental)* co-written and produced by **Robin Gibb**	$5		RSO 1021
				RUFFNECK featuring YAVAHN **'96** Dance group consisting of New Jersey-based producers Dwayne Richardson, Derek Jenkins and Stephen Wilson. Featured vocalist is Joanne "Yavahn" Thomas.			
1/27/96	**82**	7		**Everybody Be Somebody** ... *(2 versions)* samples "Bostich" by **Yello**; #1 Dance Club Play hit for 3 weeks in 1995	$5	▮	MAW 0004
				RUFUS — see KHAN, Chaka			
				RUFUS & CARLA — see THOMAS, Rufus / THOMAS, Carla			
				RUGBYS, The **'69** Rock group from Nashville, Tennessee: Steve McNicol (vocals, guitar), Ed Vernon (keyboards), Mike Mornei (bass) and Glenn Howerton (drums).			
8/23/69	**24**	11		**You, I** ... *Stay With Me*	$8		Amazon 1
				RUMBLERS, The **'63** Instrumental rock and roll band from Norwalk, California: Bob Jones (sax), Johnny Kirkland and Mike Kelishes (guitars), Wayne Matteson (bass) and Adrian Lloyd (drums).			
2/16/63	**87**	2		**Boss** ... *I Don't Need You No More* [I] first released on Downey 103 in 1962 ($30)	$15		Dot 16421
				RUNDGREN, Todd ROK/BUB/LP **'73** Born on 6/22/48 in Upper Darby, Pennsylvania. Virtuoso rock musician/songwriter/producer/engineer. Leader of groups **Nazz** and **Utopia**. Produced **Meat Loaf**'s *Bat Out Of Hell* album and albums for **Badfinger**, **Grand Funk Railroad**, **The Tubes**, **XTC**, **Patti Smith** and many others. *1)Hello It's Me 2)I Saw The Light 3)We Gotta Get You A Woman*			
11/14/70+	**20**	17		1 **We Gotta Get You A Woman** .. *Baby Let's Swing/The Last Thing You Said/Don't Tie My Hands* **RUNT**	$10		Ampex 31001
4/24/71	**71**	5		2 **Be Nice To Me** ... *Broke Down And Busted*	$8		Bearsville 31002
9/4/71	**92**	2		3 **A Long Time, A Long Way To Go** ... *Parole* **RUNT-TODD RUNDGREN** (above 2)	$8		Bearsville 31004
4/8/72	**16**	14		4 **I Saw The Light** ... *Marlene* most pressings available on blue vinyl	$10		Bearsville 0003
7/29/72	**93**	2		5 **Couldn't I Just Tell You** ... *Wolfman Jack* B-side "Bubbled Under" (#105) in 1975 on Bearsville 0301	$7		Bearsville 0007

DEBUT	PEAK	WKS	Gold	A-side (Chart Hit)...B-side	$	Sym	Label & Number
				RUNDGREN, Todd — Cont'd			
10/6/73	**5**	20		6 **Hello It's Me** ... *Cold Morning Light*	$7		Bearsville 0009
				original version by Rundgren's group **Nazz** charted in 1969 and 1970			
4/6/74	**69**	6		7 **A Dream Goes On Forever** ... *Heavy Metal Kids*	$6		Bearsville 0020
4/26/75	**83**	3		8 **Real Man** ... *Prana (from Cosmic Fire)*	$6		Bearsville 0304
6/5/76	**34**	8		9 **Good Vibrations** ... *When I Pray*	$6		Bearsville 0309
5/27/78	**29**	15		10 **Can We Still Be Friends** ... *Determination*	$6		Bearsville 0324
5/7/83	**63**	5		11 **Bang The Drum All Day** ... *Chant*	$6		Bearsville 29686
				all of above written (except #9) and produced by Rundgren			
				RUN-D.M.C. R&B/BUB/LP '86			
				Highly influential rap trio from Queens, New York: rappers Joseph Simmons (Run) and Darryl McDaniels (DMC) with DJ Jason Mizell (Jam Master Jay). In movies *Krush Groove* and *Tougher Than Leather.* Jam Master Jay was shot to death on 10/30/2002 (age 37).			
7/26/86	**4**	16	●	1 **Walk This Way** S:2 / A:7 *King Of Rock*	$4	■	Profile 5112
				with **Aerosmith**'s Steve Tyler (vocals) and Joe Perry (guitar)			
10/25/86	**29**	18		2 **You Be Illin'** ... S:26 / A:36 *Hit It Run*	$4	■	Profile 5119
2/28/87	**57**	10		3 **It's Tricky** ... S:39 *Proud To Be Black*	$4	■	Profile 5131
7/30/88	**75**	6		4 **Mary, Mary** ... *Rock Box*	$4	■	Profile 5211
				originally recorded by **The Monkees** on their 1967 album *More Of The Monkees*			
3/20/93	**21**	17	●	5 **Down With The King** ... S:7 / A:46 *(instrumental)*	$4	▮	Profile 5391
				samples "Where Do I Go" by the original off-Broadway cast of *Hair*			
				RUNT — see RUNDGREN, Todd			
				RuPAUL BUB/LP '93			
				Born RuPaul Andre Charles on 11/17/60 in San Diego, California. Black male dance singer/transvestite. Appeared in the movies *Crooklyn* and *The Brady Bunch Movie.* Hosted own talk show on VH-1.			
2/13/93	**45**	20		1 **Supermodel (You Better Work)** ... S:29 / A:55 *House Of Love*	$4	▮V	Tommy Boy 7542
				"45": Tommy Boy/Collectables 542			
3/26/94	**92**	2		2 **Don't Go Breaking My Heart** ... S:66 *(12" remix)*	$3	▮	MCA 54813
				ELTON JOHN & RuPAUL			
11/2/96	**95**	5		3 **Snapshot** ... *(radio edit)*	$3	▮	Rhino 74454
				RUSH ROK/BUB/LP '82			
				Hard-rock trio formed in Toronto, Ontario, Canada: Geddy Lee (vocals, bass; born on 7/29/53), Alex Lifeson (guitar; born on 8/27/53) and Neil Peart (drums; born on 9/12/52). Peart writes most of the group's lyrics. Also see **Bob & Doug McKenzie**.			
1/8/77	**88**	4		1 **Fly By Night/In The Mood** ... *Something For Nothing* [L]	$10		Mercury 73873
11/26/77	**76**	4		2 **Closer To The Heart** ... *Madrigal*	$10		Mercury 73958
				also see #6 below			
2/23/80	**51**	8		3 **The Spirit Of Radio** ... *Circumstances*	$8		Mercury 76044
3/14/81	**55**	9		4 **Limelight** ... *YYZ*	$8		Mercury 76095
6/6/81	**44**	13		5 **Tom Sawyer** ... *Witch Hunt*	$8	■	Mercury 76109
12/12/81+	**69**	7		6 **Closer To The Heart** ... *Freewill* [L-R]	$8		Mercury 76124
				studio version on #2 above			
9/18/82	**21**	12		7 **New World Man** AR[2] *Vital Signs (live)*	$8	■	Mercury 76179
11/9/85+	**45**	14		8 **The Big Money** ... *Red Sector A (live)*	$7	■	Mercury 884191
				all of above written by Lee, Lifeson and Peart			
				RUSH, Jennifer LP '87			
				Born Heidi Stern on 9/29/69 in Queens, New York. Pop singer/songwriter.			
2/8/86	**57**	13		1 **The Power Of Love** ... *I See A Shadow (Not A Fantasy)*	$3		Epic 05754
5/16/87	**36**	13		2 **Flames Of Paradise** ... S:32 / A:34 *Call My Name* (Rush)	$3	■	Epic 07119
				JENNIFER RUSH (with Elton John)			
				RUSH, Merrilee BUB/LP '68			
				Born in Seattle, Washington. Female pop singer. The Turnabouts: her brother Neil Rush (sax), Karl Wilson (guitar; brother of Nancy and **Ann Wilson** of **Heart**), Terry Craig (bass) and Pete Sack (drums).			
5/4/68	**7**	16		1 **Angel Of The Morning** ... *Reap What You Sow*	$8		Bell 705
8/31/68	**76**	6		2 **That Kind Of Woman** ... *Sunshine & Roses*	$8		Bell 738
				MERRILEE RUSH & THE TURNABOUTS (above 2)			
12/7/68	**79**	4		3 **Reach Out** ... *Love Street*	$8		AGP 107
6/11/77	**54**	7		4 **Save Me** ... *Easy, Soft And Slow*	$5		United Artists 993
				RUSHEN, Patrice R&B/BUB/LP '82			
				Born on 9/30/54 in Los Angeles, California. Jazz-soul-dance singer/songwriter/keyboardist.			
1/26/80	**42**	9		1 **Haven't You Heard** ... *Keepin' Faith In Love*	$4		Elektra 46551
5/1/82	**23**	16		2 **Forget Me Nots** ... *(She Will) Take You Down To Love*	$4	■	Elektra 47427
6/30/84	**78**	6		3 **Feels So Real (Won't Let Go)** ... *(instrumental)*	$4		Elektra 69742
				RUSHLOW, Tim — see LITTLE TEXAS			
				RUSS, Lonnie '63			
				Born Gerald Lionel Russ in 1943 in San Francisco, California. R&B singer/songwriter.			
12/8/62+	**57**	8		**My Wife Can't Cook** ... *Something Old, Something New*	$15		4J 501
				RUSSELL, Bobby C&W/AC/BUB/LP '71			
				Born on 4/19/41 in Nashville, Tennessee. Died of a heart attack on 11/19/92 (age 51). Singer/songwriter. Married to **Vicki Lawrence** from 1972-74.			
10/26/68	**36**	7		1 **1432 Franklin Pike Circle Hero** ... *Let's Talk About Them*	$7		Elf 90,020
7/10/71	**28**	14		2 **Saturday Morning Confusion** ... *Little Ole Song About Love* [N]	$6		United Artists 50788
				RUSSELL, Brenda AC/R&B/LP '88			
				Born Brenda Gordon in Brooklyn, New York. R&B singer/songwriter/pianist.			
8/18/79	**30**	17		1 **So Good, So Right** ... *You're Free*	$4		Horizon 123
2/20/88	**6**	25		2 **Piano In The Dark** ... S:6 / A:11 *This Time I Need You*	$3	■	A&M 3003
				Joe Esposito (of **Brooklyn Dreams**, backing vocal)			

DEBUT	PEAK	WKS	Gold	A-side (Chart Hit)........B-side	$	Sym	Label & Number
				RUSSELL, Leon C&W/BUB/ROK/LP **'72**			
				Born Claude Russell Bridges on 4/2/42 in Lawton, Oklahoma. Pop-rock singer/songwriter/multi-instrumentalist sessionman. Regular with Phil Spector's "Wall of Sound" session group. Formed Shelter Records with British producer Denny Cordell in 1970. Recorded as **Hank Wilson** (see #4 & 5 below) in 1973. Married Mary McCreary (vocalist with **Little Sister**, part of **Sly Stone**'s "family") in 1976. Formed Paradise label in 1976. Wrote "Superstar" and "This Masquerade." Also see **Joe Cocker**'s "Delta Lady" and "The Letter."			
8/26/72	**11**	12		1 **Tight Rope** *This Masquerade*	$8		Shelter 7325
				B-side was a Top 10 hit for **George Benson** in 1976			
12/16/72	**4**[X]	2		2 **Slipping Into Christmas** ....*Christmas In Chicago* [X]	$8		Shelter 7328
9/15/73	**89**	2		3 **Queen Of The Roller Derby** ....*Roll Away The Stone* [L]	$8		Shelter 7337
10/6/73	**78**	5		4 **Roll In My Sweet Baby's Arms** /			
				written by bluegrass legend **Lester Flatt**			
10/6/73		5		5 **I'm So Lonesome I Could Cry**	$7		Shelter 7336
				HANK WILSON (above 2)			
				written in 1949 by Hank Williams			
4/20/74	**73**	5		6 **If I Were A Carpenter...** ....*Wild Horses*	$6	■	Shelter 40210
8/2/75	**14**	19		7 **Lady Blue** ....*Laying Right Here In Heaven*	$6		Shelter 40378
				written for Russell's daughter Blue			
1/3/76	**53**	5		8 **Back To The Island** ....*Little Hideaway*	$6		Shelter 40483
				The MG's of **Booker T. & The MG's** (backing band)			
6/19/76	**52**	12		9 **Rainbow In Your Eyes** ....*Love's Supposed To Be That Way*	$5		Paradise 8208
				LEON & MARY RUSSELL			
				RUSSO, Charlie **'63**			
				Pop-jazz clarinetist/saxophonist.			
3/30/63	**92**	5		**Preacherman** ....*Teresa* [I]	$10		Diamond 131
				RUSTED ROOT LP **'95**			
				Rock group from Pittsburgh, Pennsylvania: Mike Glabicki (vocals, guitar), John Buynak, Liz Berlin, Jenn Wertz and Jim DiSpirito (percussion), Patrick Norman (bass) and Jim Donovan (drums).			
9/2/95	**72**	7		**Send Me On My Way** ....A:75 *Laugh As The Sun*	$4	▮	Mercury 856568
				RYAN, Barry **'69**			
				Born Barry Sapherson on 10/24/48 in Leeds, England. Pop singer. Recorded with twin brother Paul in the mid-1960s.			
12/28/68+	**86**	4		**Eloise** ....*Love, I Almost Found You*	$8		MGM 14010
				RYAN, Charlie, and the Timberline Riders **'60**			
				Born on 12/19/15 in Graceville, Minnesota; raised in Montana. Country singer/songwriter.			
5/9/60	**33**	19		1 **Hot Rod Lincoln** ....*Thru The Mill* [N-S]	$20		4 Star 1733
				originally released on Souvenir 101 in 1955 ($40); original version by Tiny Hill ("Hot Rod Race") charted in 1951 (#29)			
10/17/60	**84**	6		2 **Side Car Cycle** ....*Steel Rock* [N-S]	$20		4 Star 1745
				RYDELL, Bobby ★113★ BUB/LP **'60**			
				Born Robert Ridarelli on 4/26/42 in Philadelphia, Pennsylvania. Pop singer. Regular on Paul Whiteman's amateur TV show, 1951-54. Drummer with Rocco & His Saints, which included **Frankie Avalon** on trumpet in 1956. First recorded for Veko in 1957. In the movies *Bye Bye Birdie* and *That Lady From Peking*. Rydell, **Fabian**, **Frankie Avalon** and **Chubby Checker** were Philadelphia-based teen idols of the late 1950s-early 1960s.			
				1)Wild One 2)Forget Him 3)Volare 4)Swingin' School 5)We Got Love			
6/29/59	**11**	17		1 **Kissin' Time** ....*You'll Never Tame Me*	$20	■	Cameo 167
				Georgie Young And The Rockin' Bocs (backing group)			
10/12/59	**6**	17		2 **We Got Love** /			
10/12/59	**46**	6		3 **I Dig Girls**	$20	■	Cameo 169
				picture sleeve issued with either a red background or a blue background			
2/1/60	**2**[1]	16	●	4 **Wild One** /			
2/1/60	**19**	15		5 **Little Bitty Girl**	$20	■	Cameo 171
5/9/60	**5**	12		6 **Swingin' School** /			
				from the movie *Because They're Young* starring **James Darren** and Tuesday Weld			
5/9/60	**18**	11		7 **Ding-A-Ling**	$20	■	Cameo 175
				Cameo 175 issued with 2 different picture sleeves			
7/18/60	**4**	15		8 **Volare** ....*I'd Do It Again*	$15	■	Cameo 179
11/7/60	**14**	11		9 **Sway** /			
				#15 hit for **Dean Martin** in 1954			
12/5/60	**70**	2		10 **Groovy Tonight**	$15	■	Cameo 182
1/23/61	**11**	11		11 **Good Time Baby** /			
2/13/61	**54**	4		12 **Cherié**	$15	■	Cameo 186
5/1/61	**21**	8		13 **That Old Black Magic** ....*Don't Be Afraid (To Fall In Love)*	$15	■	Cameo 190
				#1 hit for Glenn Miller in 1943 (from the movie *Star-Spangled Rhythm* starring **Bing Crosby**)			
7/3/61	**25**	7		14 **The Fish** ....*The Third House (In From The Right)*	$15	■	Cameo 192
				melody is similar to **The Shirelles**' "Mama Said"			
10/16/61	**21**	9		15 **I Wanna Thank You** /			
10/9/61	**85**	2		16 **The Door To Paradise**	$15	■	Cameo 201
12/11/61	**21**	5		17 **Jingle Bell Rock** ....*Jingle Bells Imitations* [X]	$15	■	Cameo 205
				BOBBY RYDELL CHUBBY CHECKER			
2/17/62	**18**	11		18 **I've Got Bonnie** /			
2/17/62	**69**	4		19 **Lose Her**	$15	■	Cameo 209
6/2/62	**14**	12		20 **I'll Never Dance Again** ....*Gee, It's Wonderful* (#109)	$15	■	Cameo 217
10/13/62	**10**	11		21 **The Cha-Cha-Cha** ....*The Best Man Cried*	$15	■	Cameo 228
				melody and arrangement are similar to "Rinky Dink" by **Dave "Baby" Cortez**			

DEBUT	PEAK	WKS	Gold	A-side (Chart Hit)...B-side	$	Sym	Label & Number
				RYDELL, Bobby — Cont'd			
12/15/62	92	2		22 **Jingle Bell Rock** .... *Jingle Bell Imitations* [X-R]	$15	■	Cameo 205
				BOBBY RYDELL CHUBBY CHECKER			
2/9/63	23	9		23 **Butterfly Baby** .... *Love Is Blind*	$15	■	Cameo 242
5/11/63	17	9		24 **Wildwood Days** .... *Will You Be My Baby* (#114)	$15	■	Cameo 252
				#1, 2, 4, 6, 7, 10-12, 15, 16, 19, 21, 23 & 24: written by Kal Mann, **Bernie Lowe** and Dave Appell			
9/28/63	98	2		25 **Let's Make Love Tonight** .... *Childhood Sweetheart*	$12	■	Cameo 272
11/9/63+	4	16		26 **Forget Him** .... *Love, Love Go Away*	$12	■	Cameo 280
3/28/64	43	6		27 **Make Me Forget** .... *Little Girl You've Had A Busy Day*	$12	■	Cameo 309
5/9/64	80	6		28 **A World Without Love** .... *Our Faded Love*	$15	■	Cameo 320
12/19/64	94	1		29 **I Just Can't Say Goodbye** .... *Two Is The Loneliest Number*	$10	■	Capitol 5305
2/13/65	98	1		30 **Diana** .... *Stranger In The World*	$10		Capitol 5352
				RYDER, John & Anne AC '69			
				Husband-and-wife Adult Contemporary duo from Sheffield, England.			
10/25/69	70	5		**I Still Believe In Tomorrow** .... *Daffodil Rain*	$8		Decca 32506
	★590★			**RYDER, Mitch, And The Detroit Wheels** BUB/LP '66			
				Born William Levise on 2/26/45 in Detroit, Michigan. White rock and roll/R&B singer. The Detroit Wheels: Jim McCarty and Joe Cubert (guitars), Earl Elliott (bass) and John Badanjek (drums). McCarty and Badanjek later joined the **Rockets**.			
				1)Devil With A Blue Dress On & Good Golly Miss Molly 2)Sock It To Me-Baby! 3)Jenny Take A Ride!			
12/11/65+	10	12		1 **Jenny Take A Ride!** .... *Baby Jane (Mo-Mo Jane)*	$12		New Voice 806
				medley: **Little Richard**'s "Jenny, Jenny" and **Chuck Willis**'s "C.C. Rider"			
3/5/66	17	9		2 **Little Latin Lupe Lu** .... *I Hope*	$10		New Voice 808
5/28/66	62	5		3 **Break Out** .... *I Need Help*	$10		New Voice 811
7/30/66	100	1		4 **Takin' All I Can Get** .... *You Get Your Kicks*	$10		New Voice 814
10/8/66	4	16		5 **Devil With A Blue Dress On & Good Golly Miss Molly** *I Had It Made*	$12		New Voice 817
				Shorty Long's original version "Devil With The Blue Dress" "Bubbled Under" (#125) in 1964			
2/4/67	6	11		6 **Sock It To Me-Baby!** .... *I Never Had It Better*	$10	■	New Voice 820
				picture sleeve issued with either a colored or a black & white title strip across the top of the sleeve			
4/29/67	24	6		7 **Too Many Fish In The Sea & Three Little Fishes** .... *One Grain Of Sand*	$10	■	New Voice 822
				"Three Little Fishes" was a #1 hit for Kay Kyser in 1939			
				MITCH RYDER:			
7/1/67	41	6		8 **Joy** .... *I'd Rather Go To Jail*	$8		New Voice 824
9/9/67	30	7		9 **What Now My Love** .... *Blessing In Disguise*	$8		DynoVoice 901
				written in France in 1962 by Gilbert Becaud as "Et Maintenant"			
10/28/67	88	3		10 **You Are My Sunshine** .... *Wild Child* (w/Detroit Wheels)	$8		New Voice 826
				classic Country song written in 1940 by Jimmie Davis			
2/3/68	87	4		11 (You've Got) **Personality And Chantilly Lace** .... *I Make A Fool Of Myself*	$8		DynoVoice 905
				all of above produced by **Bob Crewe**			
7/16/83	87	4		12 **When You Were Mine** .... *Stand*	$5		Riva 213
				written by **Prince**; produced by **John Cougar Mellencamp**			
				RYLES, John Wesley, I C&W '69			
				Born on 12/2/50 in Bastrop, Louisiana. Country singer/songwriter/guitarist.			
12/28/68+	83	5		**Kay** .... *Come On Home*	$7		Columbia 44682
				a new version by Ryles made the Country charts (#50) in 1978			
				RYSER, Jimmy '90			
				Born on 1/31/65 in Cleveland, Ohio; raised in Columbus, Indiana. Pop-rock singer/guitarist.			
7/14/90	78	7		**Same Old Look** .... *Climbing Out*	$4	▮V	Arista 2039
				RYTHM SYNDICATE — see RHYTHM SYNDICATE			
				RZA R&B/BUB/LP '96			
				Born Robert Diggs in Staten Island, New York. Rapper/producer. Member of **Wu-Tang Clan** and **Gravediggaz**. Pronounced: riz-ah.			
2/25/95	54S	4		1 **No Hook** .... BUB:103 *(2 remixes) / (So U Wanna Be) Hardcore*	$4	▮	Jive 42284
				SHAQUILLE O'NEAL (featuring Prince Rakeem The RZA and Method Man)			
8/17/96	60	12		2 **Wu-Wear: The Garment Renaissance** .... S:34 *Get Down For Mine* (Real Live)	$4	▮	Big Beat 98045
				RZA featuring METHOD MAN & CAPPADONNA			
				from the movie *High School High* starring Jon Lovitz			

S

DEBUT	PEAK	WKS	Gold	A-side (Chart Hit)...B-side	$	Sym	Label & Number
				SAADIQ, Raphael R&B/BUB '95			
				Born Raphael Wiggins on 5/14/66 in Oakland, California. R&B singer. Member of **Tony! Toni! Tone!** and **Lucy Pearl**.			
3/25/95	19	20		1 **Ask Of You** .... S:10 / A:30 *Situation: Grimm* (**Mista Grimm**)	$3	▮	550 Music/Epic 77862
				RAPHAEL SAADIQ (of Tony! Toni! Toné!)			
				contains the melody of "Sukiyaki"; from the movie *Higher Learing* starring Laurence Fishburne			
11/7/98	49	10		2 **Can't Get Enough** S:22 *24*	$4	★	Motown 860848
				WILLIE MAX Featuring Raphael Saadiq			
4/3/99	67	8		3 **Get Involved** .... A:50 *(instrumental) / What I Am* (Sy Smith)	$6	T	Hollywood 66009
				RAPHAEL SAADIQ & Q-TIP			
				samples "I'll Always Love My Mama" by **The Intruders**; from the animated TV series *The PJs*			
4/27/02	99	2		4 **Be Here** .... S:72 *(3 versions)*	$6	T	Universal 015788
				RAPHAEL SAADIQ f/ D'Angelo			
				SABLE, Sweet — see SWEET SABLE			

DEBUT	PEAK	WKS	Gold	A-side (Chart Hit)...B-side	$	Sym	Label & Number
				SACARIO '02			
				Born on 1/16/80 in Brooklyn, New York. Male rapper.			
6/22/02	15	26		1 **If I Could Go!** ...A:14 / S:55 *(3 versions)*	$6	T	Elektra 67311
				ANGIE MARTINEZ (Featuring Lil' Mo & Sacario)			
8/3/02	48S	1		2 **Live Big** ...*(3 versions)*	$6	T	Elektra 67319
				SACARIO Featuring Angie Martinez & Fat Joe			
				SADAT X R&B/BUB/LP '96			
				Born Derek Murphy on 12/29/68 in New Rochelle, New York. Male rapper. Former member of the rap group **Brand Nubian**.			
7/27/96	98	2		1 **Hang 'Em High** ...*Stages & Lights*	$4	▮	Loud/RCA 64561
				featuring DV alias Christ; samples "The Good, The Bad & The Ugly"			
4/17/99	35S	10		2 **One-Nine-Nine-Nine** ...BUB:110 *(instrumental) / Like They Used To Say*	$5	★	Rawkus 53474
				COMMON feat. Sadat X			
				clean version available on Rawkus 53475			
				SAD CAFÉ BUB/LP '79			
				Pop-rock group formed in Manchester, England: Paul Young (vocals; **Mike + The Mechanics**), Ashley Mulford and Ian Wilson (guitars), Vic Emerson (keyboards), John Stimpson (bass) and Dave Irving (drums). Young died of a heart attack on 7/17/2000 (age 53).			
1/13/79	71	9		1 **Run Home Girl** ...*Feel Like Dying*	$4		A&M 2111
8/15/81	78	4		2 **La-Di-Da** ...*Love Today*	$4	■	Swan Song 72002
				SADE R&B/AC/BUB/LP '85			
				Born Helen Folasade Adu on 1/16/59 in Ibadan, Nigeria, Africa (of Nigerian/English parents); raised in London, England. Jazz-styled R&B singer/fashion designer/model. Appeared in the 1986 movie *Absolute Beginners*. Won the 1985 Best New Artist Grammy Award. Pronounced: shah-day.			
3/2/85	5	20		1 **Smooth Operator** AC2 A:4 / S:6 *Spirit*	$3	■	Portrait 04807
6/22/85	54	11		2 **Your Love Is King** ...*Love Affair With Life*	$3		Portrait 05408
				released later in 1985 on Portrait 05437 with a picture sleeve			
11/23/85+	5	22		3 **The Sweetest Taboo** ...AC1 S:6 / A:6 *You're Not The Man*	$3	■	Portrait 05713
3/29/86	20	12		4 **Never As Good As The First Time** ...S:20 / A:20 *Keep Hanging On (live instrumental)*	$3	■	Portrait 05846
5/14/88	16	15		5 **Paradise** ...RB1 S:15 / A:21 *Super Bien Total*	$3	■	Epic 07904
11/7/92+	28	27		6 **No Ordinary Love** ...S:32 / A:33 *Paradise (remix)*	$3	▮V	Epic 74734
				included in the movie *Indecent Proposal* starring Robert Redford and Demi Moore (not on the soundtrack album)			
3/20/93	78	11		7 **Kiss Of Life** ...A:65 *Room 55*	$3	▮V	Epic 74848
1/20/01	75	11		8 **By Your Side** ...S:18 / A:73 *(3 remixes)*	$8	★*V	Epic 79544
				"45": Epic 79508; B-side: (same version)			
				SADLER, SSgt Barry LP '66			
				Born on 11/1/40 in Carlsbad, New Mexico. Died of heart failure on 11/5/89 (age 49). Staff Sergeant of U.S. Army Special Forces (a.k.a. the Green Berets). Served in Vietnam until injuring his leg in a booby trap. Shot in the head during a 1988 robbery attempt at his Guatemala home; suffered brain damage.			
2/5/66	❶5	13	●	1 **The Ballad Of The Green Berets** ...AC5 *Letter From Vietnam*	$7	■	RCA Victor 8739
4/23/66	28	7		2 **The "A" Team** ...*An Empty Glass*	$7	■	RCA Victor 8804
				Sid Bass (orch., above 2)			
				SAFARIS '60			
				White vocal group from Los Angeles, California: Jim Stephens, Richard Clasky, Sheldon Briar and Marvin Rosenberg. Briar died on 12/24/99 (age 57).			
6/6/60	6	18		1 **Image Of A Girl** ...*4 Steps To Love*	$25		Eldo 101
10/17/60	85	3		2 **The Girl With The Story In Her Eyes** ...*Summer Nights*	$25		Eldo 105
				above 2 with The Phantom's Band			
				SA-FIRE LP '89			
				Born Wilma Cosme in the Bronx, New York. Latin American dance singer.			
9/24/88	48	16		1 **Boy, I've Been Told** ...S:39 *(club edit)*	$3	■	Cutting 870514
2/4/89	12	24		2 **Thinking Of You** A:9 / S:14 *Let Me Be The One*	$3	■	Cutting 872502
6/24/89	71	7		3 **Gonna Make It** ...*(club edit)*	$3	■	Cutting 874278
				SAFIRE:			
12/16/89+	53	11		4 **I Will Survive** ...*(rap version)*	$3	▮	Mercury 876368
				from the movie *She-Devil* starring Meryl Streep and Roseanne Barr			
3/2/91	82	6		5 **Made Up My Mind** ...*(remix) / (3 album snippets)*	$3	▮	Mercury 878784
				George LaMond and **Cynthia** (backing vocals)			
				SAGA ROK/LP '83			
				Rock group formed in Toronto, Ontario, Canada: Michael Sadler (vocals), brothers Ian (guitar) and Jim (bass) Crichton, Jim Gilmour (keyboards) and Steve Negus (drums).			
12/4/82+	26	18		1 **On The Loose** ...*Framed*	$4		Portrait 03359
4/2/83	64	8		2 **Wind Him Up** ...*Amnesia*	$4		Portrait 03791
11/26/83	79	3		3 **The Flyer** ...*The Sound Of Strangers*	$4	■	Portrait 04178
				SAGAT '94			
				Born in Baltimore, Maryland. Male club dance singer/rapper. Also produced under the name Chico Jump Slamm. Pronounced: say-GOT.			
1/1/94	63	17		**(Funk Dat)** ...S:52 / A:71 *(2 versions)* [N]	$5	▮	Maxi 101
				originally released as a cassette maxi-single "Why Is It? (Fuk Dat)" on Maxi 2014			
				SAGER, Carole Bayer LP '81			
				Born on 3/8/46 in Manhattan, New York. Pop singer/prolific songwriter. Married to **Burt Bacharach** from 1982-91.			
10/15/77	69	7		1 **You're Moving Out Today** ...*Shy As A Violet*	$4		Elektra 45422
				co-written by **Bette Midler**			
5/16/81	30	13		2 **Stronger Than Before** ...*Somebody's Been Lying*	$4	■	Boardwalk 02054

DEBUT	PEAK	WKS	Gold	A-side (Chart Hit)...B-side	$	Sym	Label & Number
				SAGITTARIUS BUB **'67**			
				Pop studio band. Included at various times Bruce Johnston and Terry Melcher (**Bruce And Terry**), Gary Usher (died of cancer on 5/25/90, age 51), Kurt Boettcher (died in 1987) and **Glen Campbell**. The latter three also recorded in **The Hondells**.			
6/24/67	70	5		1 **My World Fell Down**...*Libra*	$12		Columbia 44163
8/2/69	86	2		2 **In My Room**...*Navajo Girl*	$12		Together 105
				SAIGON KICK ROK/BUB/LP **'92**			
				Hard-rock group formed in Miami, Florida: Matt Kramer (vocals), Jason Bieler (guitar), Tom DeFile (bass) and Phil Varone (drums).			
9/5/92	12	22	●	**Love Is On The Way**...S:12 / A:20 *Sleep*	$4	▮V	Third Stone 98530
				"45" B-side: "All I Want" (ROK #15 / BUB #111/'93)			
				SAILCAT BUB/LP **'72**			
				Pop duo from Alabama: Court Pickett (vocals) and John Wyker (vocals, guitar).			
6/10/72	12	15		**Motorcycle Mama**...*Rainbow Road*	$6		Elektra 45782
				SAINTE-MARIE, Buffy BUB/LP **'72**			
				Born on 2/20/41 in Saskatchewan, Canada. Folk singer/songwriter.			
11/27/71	98	3		1 **I'm Gonna Be A Country Girl Again**...*The Piney Wood Hills*	$8		Vanguard 35143
4/1/72	38	8		2 **Mister Can't You See**...*Moonshot*	$8		Vanguard 35151
8/19/72	98	2		3 **He's An Indian Cowboy In The Rodeo**...*Not The Lovin' Kind*	$8		Vanguard 35156
				ST. ETIENNE **'92**			
				Dance trio formed in London, England, by keyboardists Bob Stanley and Peter Wiggs. Moira Lambert was vocalist in 1990 for recording "Only Love Can Break Your Heart." Sarah Cracknell joined as permanent vocalist in 1991. Group took its name from a French soccer club. Saint Etienne is also a city in France.			
3/7/92	97	2		1 **Only Love Can Break Your Heart**...A:70 *Stoned To Say The Least*	$4	▮	Warner 19078
				written by **Neil Young**			
5/27/00	72^S	1		2 **Tell Me Why (The Riddle)**...*(5 mixes)*	$8	★*	Mute 9129
				PAUL VAN DYK feat. Saint Etienne			
				ST. LUNATICS LP **'01**			
				Rap group from St. Louis, Missouri: **Nelly**, Ali, City Spud, Kyjuan and Murphy Lee.			
6/30/01	88	5		1 **Midwest Swing**...*(2 versions) / Dis Iz Da Life*	$7	T	Fo' Reel/Universal 158815
11/9/02+	3	20		2 **Air Force Ones**...A:3 *Dilemma* (Nelly - #1)	$6	T	Fo' Reel/Universal 019509
				NELLY Featuring Kyjuan, Ali and Murphy Lee			
				ST. PAUL R&B **'90**			
				Born Paul Peterson in Minneapolis, Minnesota. R&B singer/bassist. Member of **The Time** and **The Family**.			
7/7/90	52	11		**Stranger To Love**...A:40 *Heart To Heart*	$3	▮	Atlantic 87899
				ST. PETERS, Crispian BUB **'66**			
				Born Peter Smith on 4/5/44 in Swanley, Kent, England. Pop singer/guitarist.			
6/11/66	4	12		1 **The Pied Piper**...*Sweet Dawn My True Love*	$12		Jamie 1320
9/17/66	57	7		2 **Changes**...*My Little Brown Eyes*	$10		Jamie 1324
7/1/67	36	6		3 **You Were On My Mind**...*What I'm Gonna Be*	$10		Jamie 1310
				ST. ROMAIN, Kirby **'63**			
				Born on 10/12/42 in Alexandria, Louisiana. Pop singer/songwriter.			
6/15/63	49	7		**Summer's Comin'**...*Miss You So*	$12		Inette 103
				SAINT TROPEZ R&B/BUB/LP **'79**			
				Female disco trio: Teresa Burton, Kathy Deckard and Phyllis Rhodes. Pronounced: san tro-pay.			
4/14/79	49	11		**One More Minute**...*Belle De Jour*	$5		Butterfly 41080
				SAKAMOTO, Kyu LP **'63**			
				Born in 1941 in Kawasaki, Japan. Died in a plane crash on 8/12/85 (age 43). Male singer.			
5/11/63	❶^3	14	●	1 **Sukiyaki**...AC^5 *Anoko No Namaewa Nantenkana* [F]	$10		Capitol 4945
				released in Japan as "Ue O Muite Aruko" (I Look Up When I Walk)			
8/24/63	58	6		2 **China Nights (Shina No Yoru)**...*Benkyo No Cha Cha Cha* [F]	$8		Capitol 5016
				SALES, Soupy LP **'65**			
				Born Milton Supman on 1/8/26 in Franklinton, North Carolina. Slapstick comedian. Own ABC-TV series, 1959-60; syndicated show, 1966-68. His sons, Hunt and Tony, were members of the group Tin Machine.			
4/24/65	76	6		**The Mouse**...*Pachalafaka*	$12		ABC-Paramount 10646
				SALIVA ROK/BUB/LP **'03**			
				Hard-rock group from Memphis, Tennessee: Josey Scott (vocals), Wayne Swinny (guitar), Dave Novotny (bass) and Paul Crosby (drums). Also see **Chad Kroeger**.			
12/14/02+	51	20		**Always**...A:49		V	album cut
				from the album *Back Into Your System* on Island 063153; "45": Island 063863; B-side: (same version)			
				SALSOUL ORCHESTRA BUB/R&B/LP **'76**			
				Disco orchestra conducted by Philadelphia producer/arranger Vincent Montana, Jr. Vocalists included Phyllis Rhodes, Ronni Tyson, Carl Helm, Philip Hurt and **Jocelyn Brown**.			
9/13/75	76	6		1 **Salsoul Hustle**...*(disco version)* [I]	$5		Salsoul 2002
1/24/76	18	13		2 **Tangerine** *Salsoul Hustle* [I]	$5		Salsoul 2004
				#1 hit for **Jimmy Dorsey** in 1942 (from the movie *The Fleet's In* starring Dorothy Lamour)			
5/29/76	88	5		3 **You're Just The Right Size**...*Chicago Bus Stop (Ooh, I Love It)*	$5		Salsoul 2007
9/18/76	30	14		4 **Nice 'N' Naasty**...*Nightcrawler*	$5		Salsoul 2011
				some pressings show title as "Nice 'N' Nasty"			
2/26/77	99	1		5 **Ritzy Mambo**...*Salsoul: 3001*	$5		Salsoul 2018
				SALTER, Sam R&B/LP **'97**			
				Born on 2/16/75 in Los Angeles, California. R&B singer/songwriter.			
8/23/97	51	16		1 **After 12, Before 6**...S:29 *(instrumental) / (4 album snippets)*	$3	▮	LaFace 24253
6/20/98	57	12		2 **There You Are**...S:35 *It's On Tonight* (R&B #50^A)	$3	▮	LaFace 24321

★365★ SALT-N-PEPA — R&B/LP '94

Female hip-hop trio from Queens, New York: Cheryl "Salt" James (born on 3/8/64), Sandra "Pepa" Denton (born on 11/9/61 in Kingston, Jamaica) and Dee Dee "Spinderella" Roper (born on 8/3/62). Appeared in the movie *Who's The Man?* Pepa married Treach (of **Naughty By Nature**) on 7/24/99. Also see **Myron**.

1)Whatta Man 2)Shoop 3)Let's Talk About Sex

DEBUT	PEAK	WKS	Gold	A-side (Chart Hit)	B-side	$	Sym	Label & Number
11/21/87+	19	25	▲	1 **Push It**	S:18 / A:21 *(same version)*	$4		Next Plateau 315
3/10/90	26	21	▲	2 **Expression**	S:17 *(remix)*	$4	▮V	Next Plateau 329
3/23/91	21	26	●	3 **Do You Want Me** — Herby "Hurby Luv Bug" Azor (male vocal)	S:8 / A:10 *(remix)*	$4	▮	Next Plateau 331
4/13/91	73	7		4 **Backyard** — **PEBBLES With Salt-N-Pepa**	*(no B-side)*	$3	▮	MCA 53982
8/24/91	13	20	●	5 **Let's Talk About Sex**	S:9 / A:17 *(original version)*	$4	▮	Next Plateau 333
2/1/92	47	20		6 **You Showed Me** — #2, 3, 5 & 6: from the album *Black's Magic*	A:24 *(3 versions)*	$6	▮*	Next Plateau 50165
10/9/93	4	25	●	7 **Shoop** — samples "I'm Blue" by **The Sweet Inspirations** and "Super Sporm" by Captain Sky	S:2 / A:2 *(remix) / Emphatically No*	$3	▮V	Next Plateau 857314
1/22/94	3	29	▲	8 **Whatta Man** — **SALT 'N' PEPA with En Vogue** — samples "What A Man" by Linda Lyndell (#50 R&B hit in 1968); "45" issued for above 2 on Next Plateau/London 857356	S:2 / A:4 *(7" edit)*	$3	▮V	Next Plateau 857390
7/23/94	32	22		9 **None Of Your Business** / — originally released on Next Plateau 857578 with "Heaven 'N Hell" as the A-side	S:19 / A:74			
8/6/94		4		10 **Heaven 'N Hell** — samples "Heaven And Hell Is On Earth" and "Think About It" by Odell Brown; above 4 from the album *Very Necessary*		$3	▮	Next Plateau 857776
10/21/95	38	15		11 **Ain't Nuthin' But A She Thing** — samples "What Becomes Of The Brokenhearted" by **Jimmy Ruffin**	S:17 *(remix)*	$3	▮V	London 850346
10/18/97	61^A	5		12 **R U Ready**				album cut
3/28/98	50	14		13 **Gitty Up** — samples "Give It To Me Baby" by **Rick James**; above 2 from the album *Brand New* on Red Ant/London 828959	S:31 *(2 versions)*	$4	▮	Red Ant 570100

SALVAGE — '71

Pop studio group assembled by producers **Paul Vance** and Lee Pockriss.

DEBUT	PEAK	WKS	Gold	A-side (Chart Hit)	B-side	$	Sym	Label & Number
3/13/71	54	7		**Hot Pants**	*Foundation Of Love*	$7		Odax 420

SALVO, Sammy — '58

Born on 1/20/39 in Birmingham, Alabama. Pop singer.

DEBUT	PEAK	WKS	Gold	A-side (Chart Hit)	B-side	$	Sym	Label & Number
2/10/58	23	4		**Oh Julie**	A:23 / T:78 *Say Yeah*	$20		RCA Victor 7097

SAM & BILL — '65

R&B vocal duo: Sam Gary and Bill Johnson.

DEBUT	PEAK	WKS	Gold	A-side (Chart Hit)	B-side	$	Sym	Label & Number
9/18/65	95	3		1 **For Your Love**	*Beautiful Baby*	$12		JoDa 100
1/29/66	98	1		2 **Fly Me To The Moon** — first recorded in 1954 by Kaye Ballard as "In Other Words"; above 2 produced by **Johnny Nash**	*Treat Me Right*	$12		JoDa 104

★547★ SAM & DAVE — R&B/BUB/LP '67

R&B vocal duo: Sam Moore (born on 10/12/35 in Miami, Florida) and Dave Prater (born on 5/9/37 in Ocilla, Georgia). Prater was killed in a car crash on 4/9/88 (age 50). Duo inducted into the Rock and Roll Hall of Fame in 1992.

1)Soul Man 2)I Thank You 3)Hold On! I'm A Comin'

DEBUT	PEAK	WKS	Gold	A-side (Chart Hit)	B-side	$	Sym	Label & Number
1/15/66	90	2		1 **You Don't Know Like I Know**	*Blame Me (Don't Blame My Heart)*	$12		Stax 180
4/23/66	21	13	●	2 **Hold On! I'm A Comin'**	RB[1] *I Got Everything I Need*	$12		Stax 189
9/10/66	64	6		3 **Said I Wasn't Gonna Tell Nobody**	*If You Got The Loving (I Got The Time)*	$10		Stax 198
12/3/66+	77	6		4 **You Got Me Hummin'**	*Sleep Good Tonight*	$10		Stax 204
2/25/67	42	8		5 **When Something Is Wrong With My Baby**	*A Small Portion Of Your Love*	$10		Stax 210
6/17/67	56	7		6 **Soothe Me** — written by **Sam Cooke**	*I Can't Stand Up For Falling Down* [L]	$10		Stax 218
9/9/67	2^3	15	●	7 **Soul Man**	RB[7] *May I Baby*	$10		Stax 231
1/27/68	9	13		8 **I Thank You**	*Wrap It Up*	$10		Stax 242
5/25/68	48	8		9 **You Don't Know What You Mean To Me**	*This Is Your World*	$8		Atlantic 2517
8/3/68	54	6		10 **Can't You Find Another Way (Of Doing It)**	*Still Is The Night*	$8		Atlantic 2540
11/2/68	73	3		11 **Everybody Got To Believe In Somebody**	*If I Didn't Have A Girl Like You*	$8		Atlantic 2568
12/21/68+	41	9		12 **Soul Sister, Brown Sugar**	*Come On In*	$8		Atlantic 2590
3/22/69	92	3		13 **Born Again**	*Get It*	$8		Atlantic 2608

SAMBORA, Richie — see BON JOVI

SAMI JO — C&W '74

Born Sami Jo Cole in Batesville, Arkansas. Female country singer.

DEBUT	PEAK	WKS	Gold	A-side (Chart Hit)	B-side	$	Sym	Label & Number
2/9/74	21	14		1 **Tell Me A Lie**	*Stay Where You Are*	$5		MGM South 7029
7/13/74	46	13		2 **It Could Have Been Me**	*Look At Us*	$5		MGM South 7034

SAMMIE — R&B/BUB/LP '00

Born Sammie Bush on 3/1/87 in Boynton Beach, Florida. Pre-teen male R&B singer.

DEBUT	PEAK	WKS	Gold	A-side (Chart Hit)	B-side	$	Sym	Label & Number
1/29/00	24	20	●	**I Like It** — "45": Capitol/Freeworld 58826	S:4 *(instrumental) / The Bottom* (w/**J.T. Money**)	$4	★V	Freeworld 58776

SAM THE SHAM AND THE PHARAOHS — BUB/LP '65

Born Domingo Samudio on 3/6/39 in Dallas, Texas. Leader of rock and roll group The Pharaohs: Ray Stinnet (guitar), Butch Gibson (sax), David Martin (bass) and Jerry Patterson (drums). Martin died of a heart attack on 8/2/87 (age 50).

DEBUT	PEAK	WKS	Gold	A-side (Chart Hit)	B-side	$	Sym	Label & Number
4/3/65	2^2	18	●	1 **Wooly Bully** — originally released on XL 906 in 1964 ($300)	*Ain't Gonna Move*	$15		MGM 13322
7/31/65	26	7		2 **Ju Ju Hand**	*Big City Lights*	$12	■	MGM 13364
10/9/65	33	9		3 **Ring Dang Doo**	*Don't Try It*	$12	■	MGM 13397
2/5/66	82	5		4 **Red Hot** — rockabilly song originally recorded in 1955 by Billy "The Kid" Emerson on Sun 219 ($100)	*A Long Long Way*	$12		MGM 13452
6/11/66	2^2	14	●	5 **Lil' Red Riding Hood**	*Love Me Like Before*	$12		MGM 13506

DEBUT	PEAK	WKS	Gold	A-side (Chart Hit)...B-side	$	Sym	Label & Number
				SAM THE SHAM AND THE PHARAOHS — Cont'd			
10/1/66	22	8		6 **The Hair On My Chinny Chin Chin** ...*(I'm In With) The Out Crowd*	$12	■	MGM 13581
12/24/66+	27	8		7 **How Do You Catch A Girl** ...*The Love You Left Behind*	$12	■	MGM 13649
3/18/67	54	6		8 **Oh That's Good, No That's Bad** ...*Take What You Can Get*	$10		MGM 13713
6/17/67	68	6		9 **Black Sheep** ...*My Day's Gonna Come*	$10		MGM 13747
				all of above produced by Stan Kesler			
				SANBORN, David R&B/BUB/AC/LP **'92**			
				Born on 7/30/45 in Tampa, Florida; raised in St. Louis, Missouri. Saxophonist/flutist. Stricken with polio as a child. Played with Paul Butterfield from 1967-71; **Stevie Wonder** from 1972-73. Formed own group in 1975.			
8/29/92	53	11		**Bang Bang** ...A:54 / S:70 *Ramblin'*	$3	▮	Elektra 64735
				SANDÉE R&B **'91**			
				Born Sandra Casanas in New York; raised in Florida. Dance singer. Early member of **Exposé**. Pronounced: sahn-day.			
6/1/91	49	11		**Love Desire** ...A:38 / S:63 *(Urban radio mix)*	$3	▮	Fever/RAL 73755
				SANDERS, Felicia **'55**			
				Born in Manhattan, New York; raised in California. Died on 2/7/75. Vocalist on **Percy Faith**'s 1953 #1 hit "Song From Moulin Rouge."			
5/28/55	29	3		**Blue Star (The "Medic" Theme)** ...S:29 *My Love's A Gentle Man*	$12		Columbia 40508
				Norman Leyden (orch.); theme from the TV series starring Richard Boone			
				SANDERS, Kim **'98**			
				Female dance singer.			
1/31/98	89	10		**Jealousy** ...*(remix) / Feel Like It* (Mera)	$4	▮	Dancin' Music 572158
				SANDLER, Adam BUB/ROK/LP **'95**			
				Born on 9/9/66 in Brooklyn, New York. Actor/comedian. Cast member of TV's *Saturday Night Live* (1990-95). Starred in several movies.			
12/30/95	10[A]	2		1 **The Chanukah Song** [X-C-L]			album cut
12/14/96	67[A]	1		2 **The Thanksgiving Song** ...[C-L]			album cut
				from the "live" album *They're All Gonna Laugh At You!* on Warner 45393; "Bubbled Under" (#107) in 1998 and (#109) in 1999			
12/21/96	46[A]	3		3 **The Chanukah Song**... [X-C-L-R]			album cut
12/27/97	25[A]	3		4 **The Chanukah Song**... [X-C-L-R]			album cut
1/2/99-	80	2		5 **The Chanukah Song** ...A:61 [X-C-L-R]			album cut
				#1 & 3-5: from the album *What The Hell Happened To Me?* on Warner 46151; recorded at UC Santa Barbara on 11/1/95			
				SANDMAN **'02**			
				Born in Detroit, Michigan. Male rapper.			
11/23/02	20[S]	10		**Ahh!! Dee!! Ahh!!** ...*(3 versions) / Baby I'm Down*	$8	★*	Lo-End 03
				SANDPEBBLES, The BUB/R&B **'68**			
				R&B vocal trio: Calvin White, Andrea Bolden and Lonzine Wright.			
9/9/67	81	3		1 **Forget It** ...*Psychedelic Technicolor Dream*	$10		Calla 134
11/25/67+	22	12		2 **Love Power** ...*Because Of Love*	$10		Calla 141
10/19/68	98	2		3 **Never My Love** ...*Who Knows What Will Be Tomorrow*	$10		Calla 155
				SANDPIPERS, The AC/BUB/LP **'66**			
				Adult Contemporary trio from Los Angeles, California: Jim Brady (born on 8/24/44), Michael Piano (born on 10/26/44) and Richard Shoff (born on 4/30/44). Met while in the Mitchell Boys Choir.			
7/30/66	9	11		1 **Guantanamera** ...*What Makes You Dream, Pretty Girl* [F]	$7		A&M 806
				Pete Seeger adapted this song from a poem by Cuban writer Jose Marti			
10/22/66	30	7		2 **Louie, Louie** ...*Things We Said Today* [F]	$7		A&M 819
12/20/69+	17	20		3 **Come Saturday Morning** ...*Pretty Flamingo*	$6		A&M 1185
				from the movie *The Sterile Cuckoo* starring Liza Minnelli; originally charted for 8 weeks (#83) on A&M 1134; re-entered on 4/11/70			
12/5/70	94	4		4 **Free To Carry On**...*(He's Got The) Whole World In His Hands*	$6		A&M 1227
				SANDS, Evie BUB/AC **'75**			
				Born in Brooklyn, New York. Female singer.			
8/16/69	53	17		1 **Any Way That You Want Me** ...*I'll Never Be Alone Again*	$8		A&M 1090
3/29/75	50	8		2 **You Brought The Woman Out Of Me** ...*Early Morning Sunshine*	$5		Haven 7010
8/2/75	50	10		3 **I Love Makin' Love To You** ...*One Thing On My Mind*	$5		Haven 7013
				SANDS, Jodie **'57**			
				Born in Philadelphia, Pennsylvania. Teen pop singer.			
5/27/57	15	18		1 **With All My Heart** ...A:15 / T:20 / S:21 *(Can't We Be) More Than Only Friends*	$20		Chancellor 1003
10/27/58	95	1		2 **Someday (You'll Want Me To Want You)**...*Always In My Heart*	$20		Chancellor 1023
				#5 hit for the **Mills Brothers** in 1949; Peter DeAngelis (orch., above 2)			
				SANDS, Tommy LP **'57**			
				Born on 8/27/37 in Chicago, Illinois. Teen idol/pop-rock and roll singer/actor. Mother was a vocalist with Art Kassel's band. Married to **Nancy Sinatra** from 1960-65. In the movies *Sing Boy Sing, Mardi Gras, Babes In Toyland* and *The Longest Day*.			
				1)Teen-Age Crush 2)Goin' Steady 3)Sing Boy Sing			
2/23/57	2[2]	17	●	1 **Teen-Age Crush** S:2 / T:3 / A:4 / J:7 *Hep Dee Hootie (Cutie Wootie)*	$25		Capitol 3639
				introduced by Sands on the 1/30/57 Kraft TV production of *The Singin' Idol*			
4/20/57	50	5		2 **Ring-A-Ding-A-Ding** / T:50			
4/27/57	62	7		3 **My Love Song** ...T:62	$20		Capitol 3690
5/20/57	16	13		4 **Goin' Steady** / A:16 / S:18 / T:19			
				#2 Country hit for **Faron Young** in 1953			
6/24/57		2		5 **Ring My Phone** ...S:flip	$20		Capitol 3723
				from the Kraft NBC-TV show *Flesh and Blood*			
2/17/58	24	11		6 **Sing Boy Sing** ...A:24 / S:46 / T:46 *Crazy 'Cause I Love You*	$20		Capitol 3867
				title song from the movie starring Sands			
5/19/58	81	2		7 **Teen-Age Doll**...T:81 *Hawaiian Rock*	$20		Capitol 3953
				Bob Bain (orch., all of above)			

DEBUT	PEAK	WKS	Gold	A-side (Chart Hit)	B-side	$	Sym	Label & Number
				SANDS, Tommy — Cont'd				
9/1/58	50	11		8 **Blue Ribbon Baby**	H:50 *I Love You Because*	$20		Capitol 4036
				TOMMY SANDS And The Raiders				
12/29/58+	69	9		9 **The Worryin' Kind**	*Bigger Than Texas*	$15		Capitol 4082
9/28/59	51	5		10 **I'll Be Seeing You**	*That's The Way I Am*	$15	■	Capitol 4259
				Nelson Riddle (orch.); from the 1938 Broadway musical *Right This Way*; #1 hit for **Bing Crosby** in 1944				
8/22/60	73	4		11 **The Old Oaken Bucket**	*These Are The Things You Are*	$12		Capitol 4405
				Jimmie Haskell (orch.); hip version of a tune written in 1843				
				SANFORD/TOWNSEND BAND, The LP '77				
				Pop-rock duo from Los Angeles, California: singers/keyboardists Ed Sanford and John Townsend.				
6/18/77	9	18		**Smoke From A Distant Fire**	*Lou*	$5		Warner 8370
				SANG, Samantha LP '78				
				Born Cheryl Gray on 8/5/53 in Melbourne, Australia. Pop singer.				
11/19/77+	3	27	▲	1 **Emotion**	*When Love Is Gone*	$5		Private Stock 45,178
				Barry Gibb (backing vocal); written by **Barry** and **Robin Gibb**				
5/6/78	56	7		2 **You Keep Me Dancing**	*Change Of Heart*	$4		Private Stock 45,188
7/28/79	88	2		3 **In The Midnight Hour**	*Now*	$4		United Artists 1313
				SAN REMO GOLDEN STRINGS '65				
				R&B instrumental studio band produced by **Al Kent** and Bob Hamilton (aka Rob Reeco; brother of **Ronnie Savoy**).				
9/11/65	27	10		1 **Hungry For Love**	*All Turned On* (Bob Wilson & The San Remo Quartet) [I]	$12		Ric-Tic 104
11/27/65	89	4		2 **I'm Satisfied**	*Blueberry Hill* [I]	$12		Ric-Tic 108
				SANS, Billie BUB '71				
				Male pop singer.				
9/11/71	91	4		**Solo**	*I Don't Want To Lose A Good Thing*	$6		Invictus 9102
				SANTA ESMERALDA LP '78				
				Spanish-flavored disco studio project produced by Nicolas Skorsky and Jean-Manuel de Scarano.				
11/5/77+	15	19		1 **Don't Let Me Be Misunderstood**	*You're My Everything*	$5		Casablanca 902
				SANTA ESMERALDA Starring Leroy Gomez				
4/1/78	78	3		2 **The House Of The Rising Sun**	*Nothing Else Matters*	$5		Casablanca 913
				SANTAMARIA, Mongo R&B/BUB/LP '63				
				Born Ramon Santamaria on 4/7/22 in Havana, Cuba. Died on 2/1/2003 (age 80). Conga player.				
3/16/63	10	11		1 **Watermelon Man**	*Don't Bother Me No More* [I]	$10		Battle 45909
				written by **Herbie Hancock**				
6/22/63	92	1		2 **Yeh-Yeh!**	*Get The Money* [I]	$10		Battle 45917
3/6/65	97	3		3 **El Pussy Cat**	*Black-Eyed Peas* [I]	$8	□	Columbia 43171
				text only sleeve states "It's A Hit!"				
2/1/69	32	8		4 **Cloud Nine**	*Son-Of-A-Preacher Man* [I]	$8		Columbia 44740
11/29/69	96	2		5 **Feeling Alright**	*I Can't Get Next To You* [I]	$6		Atlantic 2689
				SANTANA ★117★ ROK/BUB/AC/LP '99				
				Born Carlos Santana on 7/20/47 in Autlan de Navarro, Mexico. Latin-rock guitarist. Formed his group in San Francisco, California. Various members over the years include Alex Ligertwood (vocals), Gregg Rolie (keyboards, vocals), Neal Schon (guitar), David Brown (bass) and Michael Shrieve (drums). Rolie and Schon formed **Journey**. Shrieve formed **Automatic Man**. Santana's brother Jorge was a member of **Malo**. Inducted into the Rock and Roll Hall of Fame in 1998.				
				1)Smooth 2)Maria Maria 3)Black Magic Woman 4)The Game Of Love 5)Evil Ways				
10/25/69	56	8		1 **Jingo**	*Persuasion* [I]	$8		Columbia 45010
				some pressing show title as "Jin-Go-Lo-Ba"				
1/24/70	9	13		2 **Evil Ways**	*Waiting*	$7		Columbia 45069
				written in 1957 and first recorded by Willie Bobo in 1967 on Verve 10550 ($10); also see #7 below				
11/14/70+	4	13		3 **Black Magic Woman**	*Hope You're Feeling Better*	$7	■	Columbia 45270
				originally recorded by **Fleetwood Mac** in 1968 for their album *English Rose*				
2/20/71	13	10		4 **Oye Como Va**	*Samba Pa Ti* [F]	$7	■	Columbia 45330
10/16/71	12	10		5 **Everybody's Everything**	*Guajira*	$7		Columbia 45472
2/12/72	36	9		6 **No One To Depend On**	*Taboo*	$7	■	Columbia 45552
9/9/72	84	5		7 **Evil Ways** /	[L-R]			
				studio version on #2 above				
9/16/72		1		8 **Them Changes**	[L]	$6		Columbia 45666
				CARLOS SANTANA & BUDDY MILES (above 2)				
				also see **Buddy Miles**' 1970-71 solo version				
5/22/76	77	3		9 **Let It Shine**	*Tell Me Are You Tired*	$5		Columbia 10336
10/8/77	27	14		10 **She's Not There**	*Zulu*	$5		Columbia 10616
11/11/78	69	8		11 **Well All Right**	*Wham!*	$5		Columbia 10839
				originally recorded by **Buddy Holly** in 1958 (B-side of "Heartbeat")				
1/6/79	32	10		12 **Stormy**	*Move On*	$5		Columbia 10873
4/14/79	59	8		13 **One Chain (Don't Make No Prison)**	*Life Is A Lady/Holiday*	$5		Columbia 10938
11/24/79+	35	13		14 **You Know That I Love You**	*Aqua Marine*	$5		Columbia 11144
4/11/81	17	18		15 **Winning**	*Brightest Star*	$4		Columbia 01050
8/1/81	56	8		16 **The Sensitive Kind**	*American Gypsy*	$4	■	Columbia 02178
				written by **J.J. Cale**				
8/14/82	15	14		17 **Hold On**	*Oxun (Oshun)*	$4		Columbia 03160
11/27/82	66	8		18 **Nowhere To Run**	*Nueva York*	$4		Columbia 03376
2/23/85	46	11		19 **Say It Again**	*Touchdown Raiders* [I]	$4	■	Columbia 04758

DEBUT	PEAK	WKS	Gold	A-side (Chart Hit)............B-side	$	Sym	Label & Number
				SANTANA — Cont'd			
7/31/99	❶[12]	58	▲	20 **Smooth** A:❶[5] / S:❶[2] *El Farol*	$4	★[V]	Arista 13718
				SANTANA Feat. Rob Thomas (of **Matchbox 20**) 1999 Grammy winner: Record of the Year			
2/12/00	❶[10]	26	▲	21 **Maria Maria** ....RB[3] S:❶[5] / A:❶[1] *(remix) / Migra*	$4	★[V]	Arista 13773
				SANTANA Featuring The Product G&B "45" issued for above 2 on Arista 13773			
5/12/01	59[S]	3		22 **Maria Maria** ....*(4 remixes) / Migra* [R]	$8	★*	Arista 13774
				SANTANA Featuring The Product G&B reissue of #21 above on Arista's "Maximum Hits" series			
10/5/02	5	37		23 **The Game Of Love** ....A:5 / S:19 *(instrumental)*	$4	★[V]	Arista 15203
				SANTANA featuring Michelle Branch "45": Arista 50980; B-side: "Nothing At All" (featuring **Musiq**)			
				SANTIAGO, Lina '96			
				Born on 9/5/78 in Los Angeles, California. Female dance singer.			
1/27/96	35	20		1 **Feels So Good (Show Me Your Love)** ....A:28 / S:38 *(remix)*	$3	▮	Universal 56004
8/10/96	78	8		2 **Just Because I Love You** ....S:60 *(Spanish version)*	$3	▮	Universal 56012
				SANTO & JOHNNY BUB/LP '59			
				Guitar duo from Brooklyn, New York (of Filipino ancestry): brothers Santo (steel guitar; born on 10/24/37) and Johnny (rhythm guitar; born on 4/30/41) Farina. Mother Ann Farina helped with songwriting.			
7/27/59	❶[2]	18	●	1 **Sleep Walk** *All Night Diner* [I]	$25		Canadian American 103
11/30/59	23	11		2 **Tear Drop** ....*The Long Walk Home* [I]	$20		Canadian American 107
3/14/60	48	8		3 **Caravan** ....*Summertime* [I]	$15		Canadian American 111
				#4 hit for Duke Ellington in 1937			
12/19/60	49	3		4 **Twistin' Bells** ....*Bullseye!* [X-I]	$15	■	Canadian American 120
				"twist-rock" version of "Jingle Bells"			
4/17/61	90	2		5 **Hop Scotch** ....*Sea Shells* [I]	$15		Canadian American 124
1/18/64	58	7		6 **I'll Remember (In The Still Of The Night)** ....*Song For Rosemary* [I]	$12	■	Canadian American 164
				SANTOS, Larry BUB/AC '76			
				Born on 6/2/41 in Oneonta, New York. Pop singer/songwriter.			
2/14/76	36	10		**We Can't Hide It Anymore** ....*Can't Get You Off My Mind*	$5		Casablanca 844
				SAPPHIRES, The BUB '64			
				R&B vocal trio from Philadelphia, Pennsylvania: Carol Jackson, George Garner and Joe Livingston.			
1/11/64	25	12		1 **Who Do You Love** ....*Oh So Soon*	$20		Swan 4162
5/1/65	77	5		2 **Gotta Have Your Love** ....*Gee I'm Sorry Baby*	$15		ABC-Paramount 10639
				SARAYA ROK/LP '89			
				Rock group from New Jersey: Sandi Saraya (vocals), Tony Rey (guitar), Gregg Munier (keyboards), Gary Taylor (bass) and Chuck Bonfante (drums). Rey, Munier and Taylor left in 1990; Tony Bruno (guitar) and Barry Dunaway (bass) joined.			
7/8/89	64	9		1 **Love Has Taken Its Toll** ....*Runnin' Out Of Time*	$3	■	Polydor 889292
11/11/89	63	9		2 **Back To The Bullet** ....*Fire To Burn*	$3	▮	Polydor 889976
1/13/90	85	5		3 **Timeless Love** ....*Shocker* (The Dudes Of Wrath)	$3	▮	SBK 07316
				written and produced by **Desmond Child**; from the Wes Craven movie *Shocker* starring Peter Berg			
				SARIDIS, Saverio '62			
				Born on 6/16/33 in Brooklyn, New York. Operatic tenor. Worked as a New York City policeman.			
1/27/62	86	5		**Love Is The Sweetest Thing** ....*Here's Where I Belong*	$8	■	Warner 5243
				#1 hit for Ray Noble in 1933			
				SARSTEDT, Peter BUB '69			
				Born on 12/10/42 in New Delhi, India; raised in England. Pop-folk singer/songwriter.			
4/5/69	70	6		**Where Do You Go To (My Lovely)** ....*Morning Mountain*	$8		World Pacific 77911
				SATISFACTIONS, The '70			
				R&B vocal group from Washington DC: James Isom, Lorenzo Hines, Earl Jones and Fletcher Lee.			
6/20/70	96	3		1 **This Bitter Earth** ....*Ol' Man River*	$12		Lionel 3201
10/31/70	94	2		2 **One Light Two Lights** ....*Turn Back The Tears*	$12		Lionel 3205
				SAVAGE, Chantay R&B/BUB/LP '96			
				Born on 7/16/67 in Chicago, Illinois. Female dance singer/songwriter. Also see **Malaika** and **Tené Williams**.			
12/18/93+	70	14		1 **Betcha'll Never Find** ....A:74 / S:75 *(Old Skool version)*	$3	▮	ID/RCA 62652
2/17/96	24	20	●	2 **I Will Survive** ....S:14 *(extended remix)*	$3	▮[V]	RCA 64492
	★386★			**SAVAGE GARDEN** LP '99			
				Adult Alternative-pop duo from Brisbane, Queensland, Australia: **Darren Hayes** (born on 5/8/72) (see #8 below) and Daniel Jones (born on 7/22/73). Duo split up in 2001.			
3/1/97	4	33	●	1 **I Want You** ....A:3 / S:8 *Tears Of Pearls*	$3	▮	Columbia 78503
7/26/97	37	20		2 **To The Moon And Back** ....S:40 / A:48 *Memories Are Designed To Fade*	$3	▮[V]	Columbia 78576
				also see #4 below			
12/6/97+	❶[2]	52		3 **Truly Madly Deeply** ....AC[11] A:❶[5] / S:5 *I'll Bet He Was Cool*	$3	▮[V]	Columbia 78723
				also see #9 below			
7/11/98	24	13		4 **To The Moon And Back** ....A:26 *Memories Are Designed To Fade* [R]	$3	▮[V]	Columbia 78576
				same version and release as #2 above; above 4 from the album *Savage Garden*			
3/13/99	19	10		5 **The Animal Song** ....S:15 / A:48 *Santa Monica*	$4	★	Hollywood 79112
				from the movie *The Other Sister* starring Juliette Lewis			
10/23/99+	❶[4]	33	●	6 **I Knew I Loved You** AC[17] A:❶[6] / S:❶[2] *(remix)*	$4	★[V]	Columbia 79236
				#3 & 6 charted for a total of 247 weeks on the Adult Contemporary charts			
4/8/00	24	20		7 **Crash And Burn** A:26			album cut
				above 3 from the album *Affirmation* on Columbia 63711			
3/2/02	77	7		8 **Insatiable** ....*(3 versions)*	$6	T	Columbia 79708
				DARREN HAYES			
3/23/02	29[S]	19		9 **Truly Madly Deeply** ....*I'll Bet He Was Cool* [R]	$4	★	Columbia 79701
				reissue of #3 above on Columbia's "Platinum Hits" series			

DEBUT	PEAK	WKS	Gold	A-side (Chart Hit)..........B-side	$	Sym	Label & Number
				SAVATAGE — see TRANS-SIBERIAN ORCHESTRA			
				SAVINA, Carlo LP '72			
				Born on 8/2/19 in Turin, Italy. Died of heart failure on 6/23/2002 (age 82). Conductor/arranger. The composer of *The Godfather*, Nino Rota, died on 4/10/79 (age 68).			
4/22/72	**66**	9		**Love Theme From "The Godfather"**..........*The Godfather Waltz (Main Title)* [I]	$6	■	Paramount 0152
				title song from the movie *The Godfather* starring Marlon Brando			
				SAVOY, Ronnie '61			
				Born Eugene Hamilton on 10/10/39 in Detroit, Michigan. R&B singer. With his brothers Al and Bob Hamilton and Freddie Price in The Nitecaps. Al recorded later as **Al Kent**.			
1/9/61	**84**	2		**And The Heavens Cried**..........*The Big Chain*	$20		MGM 12950
				Cliff Parman (orch.)			
				SAVOY BROWN BUB/LP '81			
				Blues-rock group formed in England: Chris Youlden (vocals), Lonesome Dave Peverett (vocals, guitar), Kim Simmonds (guitar), Tony Stevens (bass) and Roger Earl (drums). Youlden left in mid-1970. Peverett, Stevens and Earl left in 1971 to form **Foghat**. Many personnel changes thereafter, with Simmonds the only constant member. Peverett died of cancer on 2/7/2000 (age 57).			
11/29/69	**74**	5		1 **I'm Tired**..........*Stay With Me Baby*	$6		Parrot 40042
11/6/71	**83**	6		2 **Tell Mama**..........*Rock And Roll On The Radio*	$6		Parrot 40066
10/10/81	**68**	5		3 **Run To Me**..........*Georgie*	$5		Town House 1055
				SAWYER, Ray — see DR. HOOK			
				SAWYER BROWN C&W/BUB/LP '99			
				Country group formed in Nashville, Tennessee: Mark Miller (vocals), Duncan Cameron (guitar), Gregg Hubbard (keyboards), Jim Scholten (bass) and Joe Smyth (drums). Charted 48 Country hits, 1984-2002.			
2/27/99	**44**	14		**Drive Me Wild**..........A:31 / S:69 *We're Everything To Me*	$4	★V	Curb 73075
	★399★			**SAYER, Leo** BUB/LP '77			
				Born Gerard Sayer on 5/21/48 in Shoreham, Sussex, England. Pop singer/songwriter.			
				1)You Make Me Feel Like Dancing 2)When I Need You 3)More Than I Can Say			
2/22/75	**9**	15		1 **Long Tall Glasses (I Can Dance)**..........*In My Life*	$5		Warner 8043
				first pressings issued only as "Long Tall Glasses"			
6/28/75	**96**	1		2 **One Man Band**..........*Telepath*	$5		Warner 8097
				originally "Bubbled Under" (#103) on 7/13/74 on Warner 7824			
10/23/76+	**1^{1}**	21	●	3 **You Make Me Feel Like Dancing** *Magdalena*	$5		Warner 8283
2/26/77	**1^{1}**	20	●	4 **When I Need You**..........AC^{1} *I Think We Fell In Love Too Fast*	$5		Warner 8332
				originally recorded by **Albert Hammond** in 1976 on his album *When I Need You*			
7/9/77	**17**	15		5 **How Much Love**..........*I Hear The Laughter*	$5		Warner 8319
10/8/77	**38**	9		6 **Thunder In My Heart**..........*Get The Girl*	$5		Warner 8465
12/10/77+	**36**	10		7 **Easy To Love**..........*Haunting Me*	$5		Warner 8502
9/30/78	**47**	7		8 **Raining In My Heart**..........*No Looking Back*	$5		Warner 8682
9/27/80	**2^{5}**	23	●	9 **More Than I Can Say**..........AC^{3} *Millionaire*	$4		Warner 49565
1/24/81	**23**	12		10 **Living In A Fantasy**..........*Only Foolin'*	$4		Warner 49657
				SCAFFOLD, The '68			
				Pop-rock vocal trio from England: Mike McGear (**Paul McCartney**'s brother), John Gorman and Roger McGough.			
2/10/68	**69**	5		**Thank U Very Much**..........*Ide B The First*	$15		Bell 701
	★373★			**SCAGGS, Boz** BUB/AC/LP '76			
				Born William Scaggs on 6/8/44 in Canton, Ohio; raised in Dallas, Texas. Eclectic singer/songwriter. Recorded in several different styles (pop, rock, soul and jazz). Played in various groups with **Steve Miller** during the 1960s. Based in San Francisco since the early 1970s; owned a restaurant there from 1983-87.			
				1)Lowdown 2)Lido Shuffle 3)Look What You've Done To Me			
4/17/71	**61**	6		1 **We Were Always Sweethearts**..........*Painted Bells*	$7		Columbia 45353
7/3/71	**96**	2		2 **Near You**..........*Downright Women*	$7		Columbia 45408
9/30/72	**86**	4		3 **Dinah Flo**..........*He's A Fool For You*	$7		Columbia 45670
4/10/76	**38**	10		4 **It's Over**..........*Harbor Lights*	$6		Columbia 10319
7/4/76	**3**	22	●	5 **Lowdown** *Harbor Lights*	$6	□	Columbia 10367
				promotional record and picture sleeve issued on Columbia 71100			
11/20/76	**42**	14		6 **What Can I Say**..........*We're All Alone*	$6		Columbia 10440
3/12/77	**11**	17		7 **Lido Shuffle**..........*We're All Alone*	$6		Columbia 10491
				B-side (written by Scaggs) was a Top 10 hit for **Rita Coolidge**; above 4 from the album *Silk Degrees*			
10/15/77	**58**	6		8 **Hard Times**..........*We're Waiting*	$5	■	Columbia 10606
2/4/78	**49**	10		9 **Hollywood**..........*A Clue*	$5		Columbia 10679
3/29/80	**15**	14		10 **Breakdown Dead Ahead**..........*Isn't It Time*	$4		Columbia 11241
6/14/80	**17**	17		11 **JoJo**..........*Do Like You Do In New York*	$4		Columbia 11281
				Ray Parker Jr. (guitar, above 2)			
8/23/80	**14**	17		12 **Look What You've Done To Me**..........*Simone*	$4		Columbia 11349
				Glenn Frey, **Don Henley** and **Timothy B. Schmit** (backing vocals); from the movie *Urban Cowboy* starring **John Travolta**			
11/29/80+	**14**	17		13 **Miss Sun**..........*Dinah Flo*	$4		Columbia 11406
				Lisa Dal Bello (backing vocal); all of above written or co-written by Scaggs			
4/30/88	**35**	14		14 **Heart Of Mine**..........A:33 / S:34 *You'll Never Know*	$3	■	Columbia 07780
				written and recorded by **Bobby Caldwell** in 1987			
				SCALES, Harvey, & The Seven Sounds '67			
				R&B group from Milwaukee, Wisconsin: Scales (lead; born in 1943), Monny Smith, Bill Purdie, Rudy Jacobs, Al Vance, Bill Stonewall and Ray Armstead. Scales was formerly with **The Esquires**.			
10/14/67	**79**	6		**Get Down**..........*Love Itis*	$15		Magic Touch 2007

DEBUT	PEAK	WKS	Gold	A-side (Chart Hit)....B-side	$	Sym	Label & Number
	★599★			**SCANDAL/PATTY SMYTH** ROK/BUB/AC/LP **'92**			
				Rock group formed in New York: **Patty Smyth** (vocals; born on 6/26/57), Zack Smith and Keith Mack (guitars), Ivan Elias (bass) and Thommy Price (drums). Smyth was married to punk rocker Richard Hell (Television) in the 1980s; married pro tennis player John McEnroe in 1997. Not to be confused with Patti Smith. Also see the **Hooters**' "Where Do The Children Go."			
				1)Sometimes Love Just Ain't Enough 2)The Warrior 3)No Mistakes			
				SCANDAL:			
11/13/82	65	11		1 **Goodbye To You**....*All My Life*	$4		Columbia 03234
4/2/83	59	13		2 **Love's Got A Line On You**....*Another Bad Love*	$4	■	Columbia 03615
				SCANDAL FEATURING PATTY SMYTH:			
6/30/84	7	21		3 **The Warrior**....AR^{2} S:19 / A:26 *Less Than Half*	$4	■	Columbia 04424
10/20/84	41	13		4 **Hands Tied**....*Maybe We Went Too Far*	$4	■	Columbia 04650
1/26/85	41	14		5 **Beat Of A Heart**....*Tonight*	$4	■	Columbia 04750
				PATTY SMYTH:			
2/28/87	61	11		6 **Never Enough**....*Heartache Heard Round The World*	$3	■	Columbia 06643
6/13/87	95	2		7 **Downtown Train**....*Tough Love*	$3	■	Columbia 07112
8/15/92	2^{6}	24	●	8 **Sometimes Love Just Ain't Enough** AC^{4} S:3 / A:3 *Out There* (Smyth)	$3	▮V	MCA 54403
				PATTY SMYTH with Don Henley			
12/26/92+	33	16		9 **No Mistakes**....A:33 *River Of Love*	$3	▮V	MCA 54554
6/19/93	86	4		10 **I Should Be Laughing**....*Drive You Away*	$3	▮V	MCA 54627
				SCARBURY, Joey AC/C&W/LP **'81**			
				Born on 6/7/55 in Ontario, California. Adult Contemporary session singer for producer **Mike Post**.			
1/16/71	73	4		1 **Mixed Up Guy**....*Loved You Darlin' From The Very Start*	$5		Lionel 3208
5/9/81	2^{2}	26	●	2 **Theme From "Greatest American Hero" (Believe It or Not)**....*That Little Bit Of Us*	$4	■	Elektra 47147
				from the *Greatest American Hero* TV series starring William Katt			
10/10/81	49	9		3 **When She Dances**....*Everything But Love*	$4		Elektra 47201
				SCARFACE R&B/BUB/LP **'97**			
				Born Brad Jordan on 11/9/69 in Houston, Texas. Member of the rap group **The Geto Boys**.			
8/7/93	87	4		1 **Let Me Roll**....S:60 *(instrumental)*	$4	▮	Rap-A-Lot 53831
11/19/94+	37	17		2 **I Never Seen A Man Cry (aka I Seen A Man Die)**....S:19 *(instrumental) / G's*	$4	▮	Rap-A-Lot 38461
3/11/95	74	7		3 **People Don't Believe (a.k.a. Hand Of The Dead Body)**....S:39 *(5 remixes) / Mind Playin' Tricks*	$4	▮	Rap-A-Lot 38469
				SCARFACE featuring Ice Cube			
				samples "Hung Up On My Baby" by **Isaac Hayes**			
6/21/97	12	19	●	4 **Smile** S:4 / A:62 *(instrumental) / Untouchable*	$4	▮	Rap-A-Lot 38581
				SCARFACE Featuring 2 Pac & Johnny P			
5/18/02	79	8		5 **Guess Who's Back**....S:21 *(2 versions) / My Block* (R&B #46)	$6	T	Def Jam 582865
				SCARFACE (featuring Jay-Z & Beanie Sigel)			
				samples "Sunrise" by **The Originals**			
				SCARLETT & BLACK LP **'88**			
				Electro-pop duo from England: Robin Hild and Sue West.			
1/30/88	20	18		**You Don't Know**....S:19 / A:21 *Japan*	$3	■	Virgin 99405
				SCATMAN JOHN **'95**			
				Born John Larkin on 3/13/42 in El Monte, California. Died of cancer on 12/3/99 (age 57). Dance singer/pianist.			
8/19/95	60	13		**Scatman (Ski-Ba-Bop-Ba-Dop-Bop)**....S:47 *(radio edit)*	$4	▮V	RCA 64380
				"45": RCA 64415; B-side: "Macarena" by **Los Del Rio** (#1)			
				SCHIFRIN, Lalo LP **'68**			
				Born Boris Schifrin on 6/21/32 in Buenos Aires, Argentina. Pianist/conductor/composer. Scored several movies.			
1/6/68	41	14		**Mission-Impossible**....*Jim On The Move* [I]	$10		Dot 17059
				theme from the TV series starring Peter Graves and Greg Morris			
				SCHILLING, Peter LP **'83**			
				Born on 1/28/56 in Stuttgart, Germany. Pop singer/songwriter.			
9/24/83	14	22		1 **Major Tom (Coming Home)**....*(German version)*	$4		Elektra 69811
				inspired by **David Bowie**'s 1973 hit "Space Oddity"			
3/25/89	61	10		2 **The Different Story (World Of Lust And Crime)**....*(instrumental)*	$3	■	Elektra 69307
				SCHMIT, Timothy B. BUB/AC/ROK/LP **'87**			
				Born on 10/30/47 in Sacramento, California. Singer/songwriter/bassist. Member of **Poco** and the **Eagles**.			
10/2/82	59	8		1 **So Much In Love**....*She's My Baby (And She's Outta Control)* (Palmer/Jost)	$4	■	Full Moon 69939
				from the movie *Fast Times At Ridgemont High* starring Sean Penn and Phoebe Cates			
9/19/87	25	13		2 **Boys Night Out**....S:21 / A:30 *Into The Night*	$3	■	MCA 53137
				SCHNEIDER, Fred — see B-52's, The			
				SCHNEIDER, John C&W/LP **'81**			
				Born on 4/8/60 in Mount Kisco, New York. Country singer/actor. Played "Bo Duke" on TV's *The Dukes Of Hazzard.* Appeared in many TV movies.			
5/30/81	14	19		1 **It's Now Or Never**....*Stay*	$4	■	Scotti Brothers 02105
9/26/81	69	5		2 **Still**....*Them Good Ol' Boys Are Bad* (C&W #13)	$4	■	Scotti Brothers 02489
5/15/82	45	8		3 **Dreamin'**....*Let Me Love You*	$4		Scotti Brothers 02889
8/14/82	72	6		4 **In The Driver's Seat**....*They Got Nothin' On Him*	$4		Scotti Brothers 03062
				SCHOOLBOYS, The R&B **'57**			
				R&B vocal group from Harlem, New York: Leslie Martin (lead), James Edwards (1st tenor), Roger Hayes (2nd tenor), James McKay (baritone) and Renaldo Gamble (bass). Similar in style to **Frankie Lymon & The Teenagers**.			
2/16/57	91	2		**Shirley**....T:91 *Please Say You Want Me* (R&B #13)	$30		Okeh 7076
				Leroy Kirkland (orch.)			

DEBUT	PEAK	WKS	Gold	A-side (Chart Hit)..................B-side	$	Sym	Label & Number

SCHUMANN, Walter, The Voices of — MEM '55

Born on 10/8/13 in Brooklyn, New York. Died on 8/21/58 (age 44). Leader of own choral group. Composer of the theme for TV's *Dragnet*.

DEBUT	PEAK	WKS	Gold	A-side (Chart Hit)..................B-side	$	Sym	Label & Number
4/9/55	14	6		**The Ballad Of Davy Crockett**.....A:14 / S:29 *Let's Make Up* from the ABC-TV *Disneyland* series which featured 3 "Davy Crockett" segments (Dec. 1954 - Feb. 1955)	$10		RCA Victor 6041

SCHWARTZ, Eddie — ROK/LP '82

Born in 1949 in Toronto, Ontario, Canada. Pop-rock singer/songwriter/producer.

DEBUT	PEAK	WKS	Gold	A-side (Chart Hit)..................B-side	$	Sym	Label & Number
12/12/81+	28	15		1 **All Our Tomorrows**..... *Tonight*	$4		Atco 7342
3/20/82	91	5		2 **Over The Line**..... *Auction Block*	$4		Atco 7402

S CLUB 7 — LP '01

Teen multi-racial pop vocal group formed in England: Tina Barrett, Paul Cattermole, Jon Lee, Bradley McIntosh, Jo O'Meara, Hannah Spearritt and Rachel Stevens. Group starred in its own TV series on the Fox Family Channel.

DEBUT	PEAK	WKS	Gold	A-side (Chart Hit)..................B-side	$	Sym	Label & Number
1/8/00	22^{S}	15		1 **Bring It All Back**..... *(club mix)*	$4	★	Interscope 7158
3/25/00	19^{S}	16		2 **Two In A Million**..... *(club mix) / (2 album snippets)*	$4	★	Interscope 7064
10/28/00	15^{S}	26		3 **Natural**..... *(4 album snippets)*	$4	★	Interscope 7797
3/3/01	10	20		4 **Never Had A Dream Come True**.....S:2 / A:21 *Spiritual Love* above 3 co-written by **Cathy Dennis**	$4	★	A&M 7074

SCORPIONS — ROK/LP '91

Hard-rock group from Germany: Klaus Meine (vocals), Rudolf Schenker and Matthias Jabs (guitars), Francis Buchholz (bass) and Herman Rarebell (drums). Schenker is the brother of Michael Schenker (**McAuley Schenker Group**).

DEBUT	PEAK	WKS	Gold	A-side (Chart Hit)..................B-side	$	Sym	Label & Number
6/19/82	65	7		1 **No One Like You**.....AR^{1} *Now!*	$4		Mercury 76153
3/24/84	25	16		2 **Rock You Like A Hurricane**..... *Coming Home*	$4	■	Mercury 818440
7/7/84	64	6		3 **Still Loving You**..... *Bad Boys Running Wild*	$4		Mercury 880082
6/4/88	75	6		4 **Rhythm Of Love**..... *We Let It Rock...You Let It Roll*	$3	■	Mercury 870323
6/1/91	4	25	●	5 **Wind Of Change** S:5 / A:9 *Money And Fame*	$3	■V	Mercury 868180
11/9/91+	44	18		6 **Send Me An Angel**.....A:59 *Restless Nights* "45": Mercury 866236; B-side: "Wind Of Change (Russian version)"	$3	■V	Mercury 868956

SCOTT, Billy — '58

Born in Philadelphia, Pennsylvania. R&B-Adult Contemporary singer.

DEBUT	PEAK	WKS	Gold	A-side (Chart Hit)..................B-side	$	Sym	Label & Number
1/13/58	73	5		**You're The Greatest**.....T:73 *That's Why I Was Born* O.B. Masingill (orch.)	$25		Cameo 121

SCOTT, Bobby — '56

Born on 1/29/37 in Mount Pleasant, New York. Died of cancer on 11/5/90 (age 53). White pop-jazz singer/pianist.

DEBUT	PEAK	WKS	Gold	A-side (Chart Hit)..................B-side	$	Sym	Label & Number
1/14/56	13	13		**Chain Gang**.....A:13 / J:13 / T:15 / S:17 *Shadrach* **Don Costa** (orch.)	$20		ABC-Paramount 9658

SCOTT, Freddie — R&B/BUB '63

Born on 4/24/33 in Providence, Rhode Island. R&B singer/songwriter.

DEBUT	PEAK	WKS	Gold	A-side (Chart Hit)..................B-side	$	Sym	Label & Number
7/27/63	10	12		1 **Hey, Girl** *The Slide*	$15		Colpix 692
11/2/63	48	7		2 **I Got A Woman**..... *Brand New World* #1 R&B hit for **Ray Charles** in 1955	$15		Colpix 709
3/14/64	82	7		3 **Where Does Love Go**..... *Where Have All The Flowers Gone*	$15		Colpix 724
12/24/66+	39	12		4 **Are You Lonely For Me**.....RB^{4} *Where Were You*	$10		Shout 207
3/25/67	70	5		5 **Cry To Me**..... *No One Could Ever Love You*	$10		Shout 211
5/13/67	71	5		6 **Am I Grooving You**..... *Never You Mind*	$10		Shout 212
11/11/67	100	1		7 **He Ain't Give You None**..... *Run Joe* written by **Van Morrison**	$10		Shout 220

SCOTT, Jack — ★329★ — C&W '60

Born Jack Scafone, Jr. on 1/28/36 in Windsor, Ontario, Canada. Rock and roll-ballad singer/songwriter/guitarist. Moved to Hazel Park, Michigan, in 1946. First recorded for ABC-Paramount in 1957.

1)Burning Bridges 2)My True Love 3)What In The World's Come Over You

DEBUT	PEAK	WKS	Gold	A-side (Chart Hit)..................B-side	$	Sym	Label & Number
6/30/58	3	19	●	1 **My True Love** / H:3 / S:7 / A:13			
6/9/58	11	18		2 **Leroy**.....S:11 / T:25	$25		Carlton 462
9/29/58	28	10		3 **With Your Love** / H:28			
10/13/58	96	1		4 **Geraldine**.....H:96	$25	■	Carlton 483
12/15/58+	8	16		5 **Goodbye Baby** /			
12/29/58+	73	3		6 **Save My Soul**.....	$25	■	Carlton 493
4/6/59	78	4		7 **I Never Felt Like This**..... *Bella*	$25		Carlton 504
6/29/59	35	14		8 **The Way I Walk**..... *Midgie*	$25		Carlton 514
10/12/59	71	5		9 **There Comes A Time**..... *Baby Marie*	$25		Carlton 519
1/11/60	5	16	●	10 **What In The World's Come Over You**..... *Baby, Baby*	$25		Top Rank 2028
4/18/60	3	17		11 **Burning Bridges** /			
5/2/60	34	7		12 **Oh, Little One**.....	$25	■	Top Rank 2041
8/1/60	38	9		13 **It Only Happened Yesterday** /			
7/25/60	85	3		14 **Cool Water**..... western tune written in 1936 by Bob Nolan (Sons of The Pioneers)	$20		Top Rank 2055
10/17/60	65	4		15 **Patsy**..... *Old Time Religion*	$20		Top Rank 2075
1/9/61	89	1		16 **Is There Something On Your Mind**..... *Found A Woman*	$20	■	Top Rank 2093
5/29/61	91	2		17 **A Little Feeling (Called Love)**..... *Now That I*	$25	■	Capitol 4554
8/28/61	83	4		18 **My Dream Come True**..... *Strange Desire*	$20	■	Capitol 4597
11/6/61	86	3		19 **Steps 1 And 2**..... *One Of These Days* The Chantones (backing vocals, all of above); all of above (except #11, 14, & 15) written by Scott	$20	■	Capitol 4637

DEBUT	PEAK	WKS	Gold	A-side (Chart Hit)....B-side	$	Sym	Label & Number
				SCOTT, Jill R&B/BUB/LP **'01**			
				Born in 1972 in Philadelphia, Pennsylvania. R&B singer/songwriter.			
2/10/01	**43**	19		1 **A Long Walk** ....A:36 *(3 remixes)*	$6	T	Hidden Beach 79557
7/7/01	**60**	20		2 **The Way**....A:53			album cut
				above 2 from the album *Who Is Jill Scott? Words And Sounds Vol. 1* on Hidden Beach 62137			
				SCOTT, Judy **'57**			
				Teen pop singer.			
5/20/57	**76**	1		**With All My Heart** ....T:76 *The Game Of Love (A-One And A-Two)*	$15		Decca 30324
				Jack Pleis (orch.)			
				SCOTT, Kimberly **'98**			
				Born in 1985 in Baltimore, Maryland. R&B singer.			
12/13/97+	**58**	14		**Tuck Me In** ....S:36 *(3 album snippets)*	$4	▮	Columbia 78686
				SCOTT, Linda BUB **'61**			
				Born Linda Joy Sampson on 6/1/45 in Queens, New York. Moved to Teaneck, New Jersey at age 11. Vocalist on Arthur Godfrey's CBS radio show, late 1950s. Co-host of TV's *Where The Action Is.* Joined the U.S. Army, 1970-72. Later earned a degree in Theology and became a music teacher/director at the Christian Academy in New York.			
				1)I've Told Every Little Star 2)Don't Bet Money Honey 3)I Don't Know Why			
3/13/61	**3**	14		1 **I've Told Every Little Star** *Three Guesses*	$20		Canadian American 123
				#10 hit for Jack Denny in 1933 (from the Broadway musical *Music In The Air* starring Walter Slezak)			
7/3/61	**9**	14		2 **Don't Bet Money Honey** /			
7/17/61	**44**	7		3 **Starlight, Starbright**....	$20		Canadian American 127
10/30/61	**12**	14		4 **I Don't Know Why** /			
				#2 hit for Wayne King in 1931			
11/13/61	**50**	8		5 **It's All Because**	$20		Canadian American 129
2/10/62	**60**	7		6 **Yessiree** ....*Town Crier (#116)*	$20		Congress 101
2/10/62	**70**	6		7 **Bermuda**....*Lonely For You*	$20		Canadian American 134
4/7/62	**41**	10		8 **Count Every Star**....*Land Of Stars*	$20		Canadian American 133
				3 versions of this tune made the Top 10 in 1950			
6/16/62	**56**	9		9 **Never In A Million Years** ....*Through The Summer*	$20		Congress 103
				#2 hit for **Bing Crosby** in 1937			
9/22/62	**74**	8		10 **I Left My Heart In The Balcony**....*Lopsided Love Affair*	$20		Congress 106
				Hutch Davie (orch., all of above)			
1/25/64	**100**	1		11 **Who's Been Sleeping In My Bed?**....*My Heart*	$20		Congress 204
				inspired by the movie of the same title starring **Dean Martin**			
				SCOTT, Marilyn R&B/AC/LP **'78**			
				Born on 12/21/49 in Alta Dena, California. Adult Contemporary-dance singer.			
12/10/77+	**61**	9		**God Only Knows** ....*Lay Back Daddy*	$5		Big Tree 16105
				SCOTT, Neil **'61**			
				Born Neil Bogart on 2/3/42 in Brooklyn, New York. Died on 5/10/82 (age 40). Pop singer-turned-producer/promotion man for Cameo/Parkway. President of Buddah; formed Casablanca in 1974; formed Boardwalk in 1980.			
6/12/61	**58**	8		**Bobby**....*I Haven't Found It With Another*	$15		Portrait 102
				Clint Ballard, Jr. (orch.)			
				SCOTT, Peggy, & Jo Jo Benson BUB/R&B/LP **'68**			
				R&B vocal duo. Scott was born Peggy Stoutmeyer on 6/25/48 in Opp, Alabama; raised in Pensacola, Florida. Benson was born in 1940 in Columbia, Ohio.			
6/8/68	**31**	12		1 **Lover's Holiday** ....*Here With Me*	$8		SSS International 736
10/19/68	**27**	10		2 **Pickin' Wild Mountain Berries** *Pure Love And Pleasure*	$8		SSS International 748
2/1/69	**37**	6		3 **Soulshake** ....*We Were Made For Each Other*	$8		SSS International 761
5/3/69	**81**	4		4 **I Want To Love You Baby** ....*We Got Our Bag*	$8		SSS International 769
3/29/97	**87**	4		5 **Bill** ....S:65 *(same version)*	$5	▮V	Miss Butch 2208
				PEGGY SCOTT-ADAMS			
				"45": Miss Butch 209; B-side: "Help Yourself" (R&B #76)			
				SCOTT, Tom R&B/AC/LP **'76**			
				Born on 5/19/48 in Los Angeles, California. Pop-jazz-fusion saxophonist. Session work for **Joni Mitchell**, **Steely Dan**, **Carole King** and others. Composer of movie and TV scores. Led the house band for TV's *Pat Sajak Show.* Son of Nathan Scott, a composer of TV scores for *Dragnet*, *Wagon Train*, *My Three Sons*, and others.			
3/6/76	**80**	3		**Uptown & Country** ....*Appolonia (Foxtrata)* [I]	$5		Ode 66118
				SCOTTI, Tony — see HEAVEN BOUND			
				SCREAMING TREES ROK/LP **'96**			
				Hard-rock group from Ellensburg, Washington: brothers Van (bass) and Gary Lee (guitar) Conner with Mark Lanegan (vocals) and Barrett Martin (drums).			
7/6/96	**62^{A}**	7		**All I Know**			album cut
				from the album *Dust* on Epic 64178			
				SCREWBALL R&B/LP **'01**			
				Rap group from Queensbridge, New York: Poet, KL, Solo and Hostyle.			
5/26/01	**40^{S}**	10		**Torture**....*Turn It Up*	$5	★	Hydra 9111
				SCREWBALL Feat. M.O.P.			
				SCRITTI POLITTI LP **'85**			
				Pop-dance trio formed in England: Green Gartside (vocals), David Gamson (keyboards) and Fred Maher (drums).			
9/7/85	**11**	25		1 **Perfect Way** ....A:10 / S:11 *(edited version)*	$3	■	Warner 28949
2/8/86	**91**	4		2 **Wood Beez (pray like aretha franklin)**....*(longer version)*	$3	■	Warner 28811
6/18/88	**53**	11		3 **Boom! There She Was**....*A World Come Back To Life*	$3	■	Warner 27976
				SCRITTI POLITTI Featuring Roger			

DEBUT	PEAK	WKS	Gold	A-side (Chart Hit)...B-side	$	Sym	Label & Number
				SEA, Johnny C&W/BUB/LP '66			
				Born John Seay on 7/15/40 in Gulfport, Mississippi. Country singer/songwriter/guitarist.			
6/11/66	35	6		**Day For Decision** ...*Mary Rocks Him To Sleep* [S]	$7		Warner 5820
				featuring a chorus singing the patriotic song "America"			
				SEAL BUB/ROK/AC/LP '95			
				Born Sealhenry Samuel on 2/19/63 in Paddington, England (of Nigerian/Brazilian parents). Male singer/songwriter.			
6/22/91	7	19		1 **Crazy** ...S:17 / A:19 *Sparkle*	$3	▮V	ZTT/Sire 19298
3/28/92	100	2		2 **Killer** ...*Hey Joe*	$3	▮	ZTT/Sire 19119
6/11/94	21	20		3 **Prayer For The Dying** ...A:16 / S:56 *Dreaming In Metaphors*	$3	▮V	ZTT/Sire 18138
6/24/95	❶[1]	36	●	4 **Kiss From A Rose** AC[12] A:❶[10] / S:5 *I'm Alive*	$3	▮V	ZTT/Sire 17896
				from the movie *Batman Forever* starring Val Kilmer; 1995 Grammy winner: Record of the Year			
2/17/96	33	20		5 **Don't Cry** ...A:17 *Fast Changes*	$3	▮V	ZTT/Warner 17708
12/21/96+	10	20		6 **Fly Like An Eagle** ...A:12 / S:13 *(instrumental)*	$3	▮	Warner Sunset 87046
				from the movie *Space Jam* starring Michael Jordan			
				SEA LEVEL — see ALLMAN BROTHERS BAND			
				SEALS, Brady — see LITTLE TEXAS			
				SEALS, Dan — see ENGLAND DAN & JOHN FORD COLEY			
	★433★			**SEALS & CROFTS** AC/BUB/LP '73			
				Pop duo: Jim Seals (born on 10/17/41 in Sidney, Texas) and Dash Crofts (born on 8/14/40 in Cisco, Texas). With **The Champs** from 1958-65. Own group, the Dawnbreakers, in the late 1960s; entire band converted to Baha'i faith in 1969. Jim is the brother of "**England" Dan Seals** and the cousin of country singers Troy Seals (**Jo Ann & Troy**), **Brady Seals** (**Little Texas**) and Johnny Duncan.			
				1)Get Closer 2)Summer Breeze 3)Diamond Girl			
9/9/72	6	18		1 **Summer Breeze** ...*East Of Ginger Trees*	$6		Warner 7606
1/20/73	20	13		2 **Hummingbird** ...*Say*	$6		Warner 7671
5/12/73	6	18		3 **Diamond Girl** ...*Wisdom*	$5		Warner 7708
9/22/73	21	12		4 **We May Never Pass This Way (Again)** ...*Jessica*	$5		Warner 7740
3/2/74	66	8		5 **Unborn Child** ...*Ledges*	$5		Warner 7771
5/25/74	60	6		6 **King Of Nothing** ...*Follow Me*	$5		Warner 7810
4/5/75	18	15		7 **I'll Play For You** ...*Truth Is But A Woman*	$4		Warner 8075
4/17/76	6	26		8 **Get Closer** *Don't Fail*	$4	■	Warner 8190
				SEALS & CROFTS (Featuring Carolyn Willis)			
11/20/76	58	7		9 **Baby, I'll Give It To You** ...*Advance Guards*	$4		Warner 8277
9/3/77	28	15		10 **My Fair Share** ...*East Of Ginger Trees*	$4	■	Warner 8405
				love theme from the movie *One On One* starring Robby Benson			
4/15/78	18	16		11 **You're The Love** ...*Midnight Blue*	$4		Warner 8551
9/2/78	79	3		12 **Takin' It Easy** ...*Magnolia Moon*	$4		Warner 8639
				all of above produced by Louie Shelton			
	★497★			**SEARCHERS, The** LP '64			
				Rock and roll band from Liverpool, England: Mike Pender (vocals, guitar; born on 3/3/42), John McNally (vocals, guitar; born on 8/30/41), Tony Jackson (vocals, bass; born on 7/16/40) and Chris Curtis (drums; born on 8/26/42). Frank Allen replaced Jackson in 1965. John Blunt replaced Curtis in 1966. Billy Adamson replaced Blunt in 1969.			
				1)Love Potion Number Nine 2)Needles And Pins 3)Don't Throw Your Love Away			
3/7/64	13	10		1 **Needles And Pins** ...*Ain't That Just Like Me*	$12	■	Kapp 577
				written by **Sonny** Bono and **Jack Nitzsche**; originally released with "Saturday Night Out" as the B-side; 2 different promotional sleeves were also issued with "Ain't That Just Like Me" as the B-side			
4/18/64	61	6		2 **Ain't That Just Like Me** ...*Ain't Gonna Kiss Ya*	$12	□	Kapp 584
				issued with 2 slightly different promo text ("Western Union") sleeves			
5/2/64	44	8		3 **Sugar And Spice** ...*Saints And Searchers*	$15		Liberty 55689
				first released on Liberty 55646 in 1963 ($25)			
5/30/64	16	11		4 **Don't Throw Your Love Away** ...*I Pretend I'm With You*	$12		Kapp 593
8/15/64	34	8		5 **Some Day We're Gonna Love Again** ...*No-One Else Could Love Me*	$12	■	Kapp 609
10/17/64	35	7		6 **When You Walk In The Room** ...*I'll Be Missing You*	$12		Kapp 618
				written by **Jackie DeShannon**			
11/28/64+	3	14		7 **Love Potion Number Nine** *Hi-Heel Sneakers*	$12		Kapp 27
1/30/65	29	7		8 **What Have They Done To The Rain** ...*This Feeling Inside*	$12		Kapp 644
3/20/65	21	8		9 **Bumble Bee** ...*Everything You Do*	$12		Kapp 49
				#7 & 9: released on Kapp's "Winners Circle Series" label			
4/3/65	52	7		10 **Goodbye My Lover Goodbye** ...*'Till I Met You*	$10		Kapp 658
7/31/65	79	3		11 **He's Got No Love** ...*So Far Away*	$10		Kapp 686
1/29/66	76	7		12 **Take Me For What I'm Worth** ...*Too Many Miles*	$10		Kapp 729
11/26/66	94	3		13 **Have You Ever Loved Somebody** ...*It's Just The Way (Love Will Come And Go)*	$10		Kapp 783
9/4/71	94	2		14 **Desdemona** ...*The World Is Waiting For Tomorrow*	$7		RCA Victor 0484
				SEATRAIN BUB/LP '71			
				Fusion-rock group from Marin County, California: John Gregory (vocals, guitar), Jim Roberts (lyricist), Richard Greene (violin), Donald Kretmar (sax), Andy Kulberg (bass) and Roy Blumenfeld (drums). Greene, Kulberg and Blumenfeld were members of **The Blues Project**. Kulberg died of cancer on 1/28/2002 (age 57). Roberts died of cancer on 10/29/2002 (age 59).			
4/3/71	49	12		**13 Questions** ...*Oh My Love/Sally Goodin'*	$7		Capitol 3067
				SEBASTIAN, John LP '76			
				Born on 3/17/44 in Brooklyn, New York. Pop-rock singer/songwriter/guitarist. Lead singer of **The Lovin' Spoonful**.			
1/4/69	84	4		1 **She's A Lady** ...*The Room Nobody Lives In*	$8	■	Kama Sutra 254
3/27/76	❶[1]	14	●	2 **Welcome Back** ...AC[2] *Warm Baby*	$5		Reprise 1349
				also released as "Welcome Back Kotter"; from the TV series *Welcome Back Kotter* starring **Gabriel Kaplan**			
7/31/76	95	2		3 **Hideaway** ...*One Step Forward, Two Steps Back*	$4		Reprise 1355

DEBUT	PEAK	WKS	Gold	A-side (Chart Hit)..................B-side	$	Sym	Label & Number
	★535★			**SECADA, Jon** BUB/AC/LP **'92**			
				Born Juan Secada on 10/4/63 in Havana, Cuba; raised in Hialeah, Florida. Singer/songwriter.			
4/18/92	5	37	●	1 **Just Another Day** A:3 / S:8 *(Spanish version)*	$3	■V	SBK 07383
				Gloria Estefan (backing vocal); "45": SBK 57881			
9/26/92	13	30		2 **Do You Believe In Us**..................A:12 / S:29 *Misunderstood*	$3	■V	SBK 50408
				"45": SBK 57990			
1/30/93	18	22		3 **Angel**..................A:10 / S:33 *(Spanish version)*	$3	■V	SBK 50406
				"45": SBK 56950			
6/26/93	27	20		4 **I'm Free**..................A:15 *(Spanish version) / Time Heals*	$3	■V	SBK 50434
				"45": SBK 17439; B-side: "Do You Really Want Me"; all of above from the album *Jon Secada*			
5/7/94	10	31		5 **If You Go**..................A:6 / S:15 *(Si Te Vas - Spanish version)*	$3	■V	SBK 58156
				"45": SBK 17914			
9/17/94	65	9		6 **Whipped**..................A:74 *(4 versions)*	$3	■V	SBK 58237
				"45": SBK 18127 (red vinyl); B-side: "Quiero Mas (Spanish mix)"			
11/26/94+	29	20		7 **Mental Picture**..................A:28 *Just Another Day (live)*	$3	■V	SBK 58272
				from the movie *The Specialist* starring Sylvester Stallone; "45": SBK 18480; B-side: "Fat Chance"			
3/15/97	41	18		8 **Too Late, Too Soon**..................A:39 / S:52 *Amandolo (Spanish version)*	$3	■V	SBK/EMI 58628
				"45": SBK 19485; all of above co-written by Secada			
				2ND II NONE R&B/LP **'92**			
				Male rap duo from Compton, California: cousins Deon "Tha D" Barnett and Kelton "KK" McDonald. Attended high school with their producer **DJ Quik**.			
1/11/92	78	2		1 **Be True To Yourself**..................S:60 *(album version)*	$3	■	Profile 5343
4/4/92	64	16		2 **If You Want It**..................S:34 / A:75 *(remix)*	$3	■	Profile 5361
				SECRETS, The **'63**			
				White "girl group" from Cleveland, Ohio: Karen Gray, Jackie Allen, Carole Raymont and Pat Miller.			
11/9/63	18	10		**The Boy Next Door**..................*Learnin' To Forget*	$15		Philips 40146
				SECRET TIES **'86**			
				Electro-dance trio from San Diego, California.			
12/13/86	91	5		**Dancin In My Sleep**..................*Do You Wanna Love*	$5		Night Wave 9201
				**SEDAKA, Neil** ★80★ BUB/AC/LP **'62**			
				Born on 3/13/39 in Brooklyn, New York. Pop singer/songwriter/pianist. Studied piano since elementary school. Formed songwriting team with lyricist Howard Greenfield while attending Lincoln High School (partnership lasted over 20 years). Recorded with **The Tokens** on Melba in 1956. Attended Juilliard School for classical piano. Prolific hit songwriter. Career revived in 1974 after signing with **Elton John**'s new Rocket label. Also see **Willows**.			
				1)Bad Blood 2)Breaking Up Is Hard To Do 3)Laughter In The Rain 4)Calendar Girl 5)Next Door To An Angel			
12/8/58+	14	15		1 **The Diary**..................*No Vacancy*	$20		RCA Victor 7408
3/9/59	42	8		2 **I Go Ape**..................*Moon Of Gold*	$25		RCA Victor 7473
10/12/59	9	18		3 **Oh! Carol**..................*One Way Ticket (To the Blues)*	$20		RCA Victor 7595
				written for singer/songwriter **Carole King**			
3/28/60	9	15		4 **Stairway To Heaven**..................*Forty Winks Away*	$20		RCA Victor 7709
8/8/60	17	13		5 **You Mean Everything To Me /**			
8/8/60	28	11		6 **Run Samson Run**..................	$15	■	RCA Victor 7781
12/19/60+	4	15		7 **Calendar Girl**..................*The Same Old Fool*	$15	■	RCA Victor 7829
5/1/61	11	9		8 **Little Devil**..................*I Must Be Dreaming*	$15	■	RCA Victor 7874
8/28/61	59	7		9 **Sweet Little You**..................*I Found My World In You*	$15	■	RCA Victor 7922
11/13/61+	6	14		10 **Happy Birthday, Sweet Sixteen**..................*Don't Lead Me On*	$15		RCA Victor 7957
3/31/62	45	9		11 **King Of Clowns**..................*Walk With Me*	$15	■	RCA Victor 8007
6/30/62	1 (2)	14		12 **Breaking Up Is Hard To Do**..................*As Long As I Live*	$15	■	RCA Victor 8046
				also see #25 below			
10/6/62	5	11		13 **Next Door To An Angel**..................*I Belong To You*	$15	■	RCA Victor 8086
2/2/63	17	10		14 **Alice In Wonderland**..................*Circulate*	$15	■	RCA Victor 8137
4/27/63	26	9		15 **Let's Go Steady Again**..................*Waiting For Never*	$15	■	RCA Victor 8169
7/27/63	47	7		16 **The Dreamer**..................*Look Inside Your Heart*	$12	■	RCA Victor 8209
11/16/63	33	8		17 **Bad Girl**..................*Wait 'Til You See My Baby*	$12		RCA Victor 8254
				all of above produced by Al Nevins and Don Kirshner			
7/25/64	86	3		18 **Sunny**..................*She'll Never Be You*	$12		RCA Victor 8382
8/28/65	76	9		19 **The World Through A Tear**..................*High On A Mountain (Deep In A Valley)*	$10	■	RCA Victor 8637
2/5/66	89	4		20 **The Answer To My Prayer**..................*Blue Boy*	$10		RCA Victor 8737
10/19/74+	1 (1)	20		21 **Laughter In The Rain**..................AC[2] *Endlessly*	$5		Rocket 40313
3/29/75	22	10		22 **The Immigrant**..................AC[1] *Hey Mister Sunshine*	$5		Rocket 40370
				dedicated to **John Lennon** (because of his immigration difficulties)			
6/28/75	27	10		23 **That's When The Music Takes Me**..................*Standing On The Inside*	$5		Rocket 40426
9/13/75	1 (3)	14	●	24 **Bad Blood** *Your Favorite Entertainer*	$5		Rocket 40460
				Elton John (backing vocal)			
12/13/75+	8	14		25 **Breaking Up Is Hard To Do**..................AC[1] *Nana's Song* [R]	$5		Rocket 40500
				slow version of #12 above			
4/10/76	16	11		26 **Love In The Shadows**..................*(Baby) Don't Let It Mess Your Mind*	$5		Rocket 40543
6/26/76	36	9		27 **Steppin' Out**..................*I Let You Walk Away*	$5		Rocket 40582
				Elton John (backing vocal)			
9/25/76	53	5		28 **You Gotta Make Your Own Sunshine**..................*Perfect Strangers*	$5		Rocket 40614

DEBUT	PEAK	WKS	Gold	A-side (Chart Hit)...B-side	$	Sym	Label & Number

SEDAKA, Neil — Cont'd

DEBUT	PEAK	WKS	Gold	A-side (Chart Hit)...B-side	$	Sym	Label & Number
5/28/77	44	7		29 **Amarillo** ... *The Leaving Game* originally "Bubbled Under" (#121) by Tony Christie in 1972	$4		Elektra 45406
3/29/80	19	19		30 **Should've Never Let You Go** ... *You're So Good For Me* (Neil) **NEIL SEDAKA and DARA SEDAKA** (Neil's daughter) all of above (except #9, 16, 19 & 20) written or co-written by Sedaka	$4		Elektra 46615

SEDUCTION — LP '90

Female dance trio from New York: Idalis Leon (born on 6/15/66), April Harris (born on 3/25/67) and **Michelle Visage** (born on 9/20/68). Leon left in 1990; replaced by Sinoa Loren (born on 12/6/66). Leon became a VJ for MTV.

DEBUT	PEAK	WKS	Gold	A-side (Chart Hit)...B-side	$	Sym	Label & Number
7/8/89	23	21		1 **You're My One And Only (True Love)** ... S:21 / A:24 *(instrumental)* **Martha Wash** (of **The Weather Girls**; uncredited lead vocal)	$3		Vendetta 1433
11/11/89+	2[2]	23	●	2 **Two To Make It Right** S:2 / A:2 *(Cole/Clivilles club mix)* samples **The Art Of Noise/Tom Jones**'s version of "Kiss"	$3	▮V	Vendetta 1464
2/24/90	13	16		3 **Heartbeat** ... S:12 / A:15 *(Cole/Clivilles album version)*	$3	▮V	Vendetta 1473
6/9/90	11	18		4 **Could This Be Love** ... A:7 / S:15 *(radio edit)*	$3	▮	Vendetta 1509
10/6/90	82	4		5 **Breakdown** ... *(R&B radio mix)* all of above from the album *Nothing Matters Without Love*	$3	▮	Vendetta 1503

SEEDS, The — LP '67

Garage-rock band from Los Angeles, California: Richard "Sky Saxon" Marsh (vocals, bass), Jan Savage (guitar), Daryl Hooper (keyboards) and Rick Aldridge (drums).

DEBUT	PEAK	WKS	Gold	A-side (Chart Hit)...B-side	$	Sym	Label & Number
12/24/66+	36	11		1 **Pushin' Too Hard** ... *Try To Understand*	$12		GNP Crescendo 372
3/11/67	86	2		2 **Mr. Farmer** ... *No Escape*	$12	■	GNP Crescendo 383
4/29/67	41	7		3 **Can't Seem To Make You Mine** ... *I Tell Myself* originally released in 1965 with "Daisy Mae" on the B-side	$10	■	GNP Crescendo 354
7/15/67	72	4		4 **A Thousand Shadows** ... *March Of The Flower Children*	$10	■	GNP Crescendo 394

SEEGER, Pete — LP '64

Born on 5/3/19 in Manhattan, New York. Legendary folk singer/songwriter. Formed the Almanac Singers with Woody Guthrie in 1940, and then The Weavers in 1948. Wrote "If I Had A Hammer," "Turn! Turn! Turn!" and "Where Have All The Flowers Gone." Won Grammy's Lifetime Achievement Award in 1993. Inducted into the Rock and Roll Hall of Fame in 1996 as an Early Influence.

DEBUT	PEAK	WKS	Gold	A-side (Chart Hit)...B-side	$	Sym	Label & Number
1/11/64	70	8		**Little Boxes** ... *Mail Myself To You* [L] recorded at Carnegie Hall on 6/8/63	$10		Columbia 42940

SEEKERS, The — BUB/AC/LP '65

Pop-folk group formed in Australia: Judith Durham (vocals), Keith Potger and Bruce Woodley (guitars), and Athol Guy (bass). Potger formed **The New Seekers** in 1970.

DEBUT	PEAK	WKS	Gold	A-side (Chart Hit)...B-side	$	Sym	Label & Number
3/27/65	4	13		1 **I'll Never Find Another You** ... *Open Up Them Pearly Gates*	$12		Capitol 5383
5/29/65	19	10		2 **A World Of Our Own** ... *Sinner Man*	$12	■	Capitol 5430
12/3/66+	2[2]	16	●	3 **Georgy Girl** ... *When The Stars Begin To Fall* title song from the movie starring Lynn Redgrave and James Mason	$10		Capitol 5756
2/18/67	44	7		4 **Morningtown Ride** ... *Walk With Me* all of above produced by Tom Springfield (**The Springfields**)	$10		Capitol 5787

SEELY, Jeannie — C&W '66

Born Marilyn Jeanne Seely on 7/6/40 in Titusville, Pennsylvania; raised in Townville, Pennsylvania. Country singer/songwriter (charted 27 hits, 1966-78). Formerly married to Hank Cochran.

DEBUT	PEAK	WKS	Gold	A-side (Chart Hit)...B-side	$	Sym	Label & Number
5/28/66	85	5		**Don't Touch Me** ... *You Tied Tin Cans To My Heart*	$7		Monument 933

SEETHER — ROK/BUB/LP '03

Hard-rock trio from South Africa: Shaun Morgan (vocals, guitar), Dale Stewart (bass) and Nick Oshiro (drums).

DEBUT	PEAK	WKS	Gold	A-side (Chart Hit)...B-side	$	Sym	Label & Number
12/28/02+	61	20		**Fine Again** ... A:60 from the album *Disclaimer* on Wind-Up 13068			album cut

SEGER, Bob ★78★ — ROK/BUB/AC/LP '80

Born on 5/6/45 in Dearborn, Michigan; raised in Detroit, Michigan. Rock singer/songwriter/guitarist. First recorded in 1966, formed the System in 1968. Left music to attend college in 1969; returned in 1970. Formed own backing band, The Silver Bullet Band, in 1976: Alto Reed (horns), Robyn Robbins (keyboards), Drew Abbott (guitar), Chris Campbell (bass) and Charlie Allen Martin (drums). Various personnel changes since then.

1)Shakedown 2)Shame On The Moon 3)Night Moves 4)Still The Same 5)Against The Wind

DEBUT	PEAK	WKS	Gold	A-side (Chart Hit)...B-side	$	Sym	Label & Number
12/21/68+	17	14		1 **Ramblin' Gamblin' Man** ... *Tales Of Lucy Blue*	$10		Capitol 2297
5/10/69	97	1		2 **Ivory** ... *The Last Song (Love Needs To Be Loved)*	$8		Capitol 2480
4/4/70	84	6		3 **Lucifer** ... *Big River* **BOB SEGER SYSTEM** (above 3)	$8		Capitol 2748
11/20/71	96	2		4 **Lookin' Back** ... *Highway Child*	$8		Capitol 3187
7/1/72	76	9		5 **If I Were A Carpenter** ... *Jesse James*	$10		Palladium 1079
7/27/74	80	4		6 **Get Out Of Denver** ... *Long Song Comin'*	$10		Palladium 1205
8/9/75	43	11		7 **Katmandu** ... *Black Night*	$6		Capitol 4116
6/5/76	69	4		8 **Nutbush City Limits** ... *Lookin' Back (live)* [L] recorded at Cobo Hall in Detroit, Michigan	$6		Capitol 4269
12/11/76+	4	21		9 **Night Moves** ... *Ship Of Fools*	$5		Capitol 4369
4/23/77	24	10		10 **Mainstreet** ... *Jody Girl*	$5		Capitol 4422
7/9/77	41	8		11 **Rock And Roll Never Forgets** ... *The Fire Down Below*	$5		Capitol 4449
5/13/78	4	18		12 **Still The Same** ... *Feel Like A Number*	$4		Capitol 4581
8/12/78	12	13		13 **Hollywood Nights** ... *Brave Strangers*	$4		Capitol 4618
10/28/78+	13	17		14 **We've Got Tonite** ... *Ain't Got No Money*	$4	■	Capitol 4653
4/7/79	28	11		15 **Old Time Rock & Roll** ... *Sunspot Baby* above 4 from the album *Stranger In Town*; also see #25 below	$4	■	Capitol 4702

DEBUT	PEAK	WKS	Gold	A-side (Chart Hit)...B-side	$	Sym	Label & Number
				SEGER, Bob — Cont'd			
2/23/80	6	16		16 **Fire Lake** .... *Long Twin Silver Line*	$4	■	Capitol 4836
				Glenn Frey, **Don Henley** and **Timothy B. Schmit** (backing vocals)			
5/3/80	5	17		17 **Against The Wind** .... *No Man's Land*	$4	■	Capitol 4863
7/26/80	14	16		18 **You'll Accomp'ny Me** .... *Betty Lou's Gettin' Out Tonight*	$4	■	Capitol 4904
11/8/80	42	12		19 **The Horizontal Bop** .... *Her Strut*	$4	■	Capitol 4951
				above 4 from the album *Against The Wind*			
9/12/81	5	19		20 **Tryin' To Live My Life Without You** .... *Brave Strangers (live)* [L]	$4	■	Capitol 5042
				recorded at Boston Garden on 10/6/80			
12/19/81+	48	8		21 **Feel Like A Number** .... *Hollywood Nights (live)* [L]	$4	■	Capitol 5077
				recorded at Cobo Hall in Detroit on 6/19/80; studio version is on the B-side of #12 above			
12/18/82+	2^{4}	21		22 **Shame On The Moon** .... AC^{2} *House Behind A House* (ROK #29)	$4	■	Capitol 5187
				Glenn Frey (backing vocal); written by **Rodney Crowell**			
3/12/83	12	12		23 **Even Now** .... *Little Victories*	$4	■	Capitol 5213
5/28/83	27	10		24 **Roll Me Away** .... *Boomtown Blues* (ROK #11)	$3	■	Capitol 5235
9/17/83	48	11		25 **Old Time Rock & Roll** .... *Till It Shines* [R]	$3	■	Capitol 5276
				featured in the movie *Risky Business* starring Tom Cruise; same version as #15 above			
11/10/84+	17	15		26 **Understanding** .... S:16 / A:19 *East L.A.*	$3	■	Capitol 5413
				from the movie *Teachers* starring Nick Nolte and JoBeth Williams			
3/15/86	13	14		27 **American Storm** .... S:9 / A:18 *Fortunate Son (live - ROK #9)*	$3	■	Capitol 5532
5/24/86	12	13		28 **Like A Rock** .... AR^{2} S:9 / A:19 *Livin' Inside My Heart*	$3	■	Capitol 5592
8/16/86	52	9		29 **It's You** .... *The Aftermath* (ROK #9)	$3	■	Capitol 5623
11/15/86	70	9		30 **Miami** .... *Somewhere Tonight*	$3	■	Capitol 5658
				Don Henley and **Timothy B. Schmit** (backing vocals); above 4 from the album *Like A Rock*			
5/23/87	❶^{1}	18		31 **Shakedown** AR^{4} S:❶^{2} / A:❶^{1} *The Aftermath*	$3	■	MCA 53094
				from the movie *Beverly Hills Cop II* starring **Eddie Murphy**; issued with 2 different picture sleeves			
8/24/91	24	11		32 **The Real Love** .... S:54 / A:62 *The Mountain*	$3	▮V	Capitol 44743
				BOB SEGER & THE SILVER BULLET BAND (#12-15, 21-30 & 32)			
				Patty Smyth and **J.D. Souther** (backing vocals); "45": Capitol 44761; B-side: "Roll Me Away"; all of above (except #5, 8, 15, 20, 22 & 25) written by Seger			
				SEIKO and DONNIE WAHLBERG '90			
				Seiko is a Japanese superstar singer; married to popular Japanese actor Masaki Kanda. Wahlberg, older brother of Mark Wahlberg (**Marky Mark**), was a member of **New Kids On The Block**.			
6/16/90	54	13		**The Right Combination** .... *Goodbye My Baby* (Seiko)	$3	▮	Columbia 73417
				SELENA AC/BUB/LP '95			
				Born Selena Quintanilla on 4/16/71 in Corpus Christi, Texas. Shot to death by Yolanda Saldivar (founder of Selena's fan club) on 3/31/95 (age 23). Latin singer. Married her guitarist, Chris Perez. **Jennifer Lopez** starred in the 1997 biographical movie *Selena*.			
7/8/95	8^{A}	23		1 **I Could Fall In Love**		V	album cut
				"45": EMI Latin 18742; B-side: "Tu Solo Tu"			
10/28/95	22	20		2 **Dreaming Of You** .... S:16 / A:25 *Techno Cumbia*	$4	▮V	EMI Latin 58490
				"45": EMI Latin 18849; above 2 from the album *Dreaming Of You* on EMI Latin 34123			
				SELF '00			
				Born Eddie "Whispers" Shuford in Washington DC. Rapper/producer.			
10/21/00	70^{S}	1		**Fire It Up** .... *(2 versions)*	$5	★	Lethal 54407
				SELF, Ronnie '58			
				Born on 7/5/38 in Tin Town, Missouri. Died on 8/28/81 (age 43). Rockabilly singer/songwriter/guitarist. Wrote **Brenda Lee**'s "I'm Sorry" and "Sweet Nothin's."			
3/10/58	63	7		**Bop-A-Lena** .... T:63 *I Ain't Goin' Nowhere*	$40		Columbia 41101
				written by country singers Mel Tillis and **Webb Pierce**			
				SELLARS, Marilyn C&W '74			
				Born on 12/31/50 in Northfield, Minnesota. Country singer. Worked as an airline stewardess.			
8/24/74	37	10		**One Day At A Time** .... *California*	$5		Mega 1205
				SELLERS, Shane '01			
				Born in Erath, Louisiana. Country singer. Former horse racing jockey.			
4/28/01	52^{S}	3		**Matthew, Mark, Luke and Earnhardt** .... *Tears Don't Lie*	$5	★	DreamWorks 50327
				a tribute to Dale Earnhardt, who was killed while racing at the Daytona 500 on February 18, 2001			
				SEMBELLO, Michael AC/R&B/LP '83			
				Born on 4/17/54 in Philadelphia, Pennsylvania. Pop-rock session guitarist/producer/composer/arranger/vocalist. Guitarist on **Stevie Wonder**'s albums from 1974-79.			
6/4/83	❶^{2}	22		1 **Maniac** .... *(instrumental)*	$4		Casablanca 812516
				from the movie *Flashdance* starring Jennifer Beals			
9/24/83	34	10		2 **Automatic Man** .... *Summer Lovers*	$4		Warner 29485
				SEMISONIC ROK/LP '98			
				Rock trio from Minneapolis, Minnesota: Dan Wilson (vocals, guitar), John Munson (bass) and Jacob Slichter (drums).			
3/21/98	11^{A}	37		**Closing Time** .... MR^{5}			album cut
				from the album *Feeling Strangely Fine* on MCA 11733			
				SENATOR BOBBY BUB '67			
				Senator Bobby is Bill Minkin of a comedy troupe called The Hardly-Worthit Players. Another of the members is talkshow host Dennis Wholey. Records feature voice impressions of Senator Robert Kennedy and **Senator Everett McKinley Dirksen**.			
1/7/67	20	7		1 **Wild Thing** .... *Wild Thing* (Senator Everett McKinley) [C]	$10		Parkway 127
3/11/67	99	1		2 **Mellow Yellow** .... *White Christmas (3 O'Clock Weather Report)* (Bobby The Poet) [C]	$10		Parkway 137
				SENATOR BOBBY & SENATOR McKINLEY			

DEBUT	PEAK	WKS	Gold	A-side (Chart Hit)...B-side	$	Sym	Label & Number

SENSATIONS, The — R&B '62
R&B vocal group from Philadelphia, Pennsylvania: Yvonne Mills Baker (lead), Sam Armstrong (baritone), Richard Curtain (tenor) and Alphonso Howell (bass). Howell died on 5/7/98 (age 61).

DEBUT	PEAK	WKS	Gold	A-side (Chart Hit)...B-side	$	Sym	Label & Number
8/14/61	54	8		1 **Music, Music, Music** *[THE SENSATIONS Featuring Yvonne]*...*A Part Of Me* #1 hit for **Teresa Brewer** in 1950; melody based in part on Liszt's "Hungarian Rhapsody No. 2"	$20		Argo 5391
1/6/62	4	18		2 **Let Me In**...*Oh Yes, I'll Be True*	$20		Argo 5405
4/28/62	69	6		3 **That's My Desire** *[YVONNE BAKER and the SENSATIONS]*...*Eyes* #4 hit for **Frankie Laine** in 1947 (written in 1931)	$15		Argo 5412

SERENDIPITY SINGERS, The — BUB/LP '64
Pop-folk group formed in Denver, Colorado: Jon Arbenz, Mike Brovsky, Diane Decker, Brooks Hatch, John Madden, Bryan Sennett, Tom Tiemann, Lynn Weintraub and Bob Young.

DEBUT	PEAK	WKS	Gold	A-side (Chart Hit)...B-side	$	Sym	Label & Number
2/29/64	6	14		1 **Don't Let The Rain Come Down (Crooked Little Man)**...*Freedom's Star* some pressings show title only as "Crooked Little Man"	$10		Philips 40175
5/23/64	30	8		2 **Beans In My Ears**...*Sailin' Away* [N]	$8		Philips 40198

SERMON, Erick/EPMD — R&B/BUB/LP '01
Born on 11/25/68 in Bayshore, New York. Male rapper. One-half of **EPMD** duo with Parrish Smith (born on 5/13/68). EPMD: Erick and Parrish Making Dollars. Duo split in 1992 and reunited in 1997. Also see **Redman**'s "Whateva Man."

1)Music 2)React 3)Crossover

DEBUT	PEAK	WKS	Gold	A-side (Chart Hit)...B-side	$	Sym	Label & Number
7/25/92	42	20	●	1 **Crossover** *[EPMD]*...S:20 / A:65 *Brothers From Brentwood L.I.* samples "You Should Be Mine" by **Roger**	$3	▮	Def Jam/RAL 74173
10/2/93	92	10		2 **Stay Real**...S:62 *Safe Sex* samples "Dance Floor" by **Zapp**	$3	▮	Def Jam/RAL 77140
9/10/94	89	3		3 **I Saw It Cummin'** *[PMD]*...S:62 *Steppin' Thru Hardcore* samples "Funky Worm" by the **Ohio Players**	$3	▮	PMD/RCA 62952
10/28/95	84	6		4 **Bomdigi**...S:58 *(remix)* samples "All Night Long" by **Mary Jane Girls**	$3	▮	Def Jam/RAL 77196
11/8/97	94	3		5 **The Joint** *[EPMD]*...*(2 versions) / You Gots 2 Chill '97* samples "Shake Your Rump" by **Beastie Boys** and "Think" by **Aretha Franklin**	$6	T	Def Jam 571679
12/20/97+	51[A]	12		6 **Rapper's Delight**... **ERICK SERMON, KEITH MURRAY & REDMAN** from the album *In Tha Beginning...There Was Rap* on Priority 50639			album cut
3/20/99	56[S]	4		7 **Soopaman Lover**...*(2 versions) / Superman/Virgin* (R&B #97) **CHICO DeBARGE Featuring Erick Sermon & Redman** samples "Superman Lover" by **Johnny "Guitar" Watson**	$8	★*	Motown 56233
6/2/01	22	20		8 **Music** A:17 / S:31 *(3 versions) / Stick 'Em* (Cha Cha) **ERICK SERMON featuring MARVIN GAYE** samples **Marvin Gaye**'s "Turn On Some Music" from his 1982 *Midnight Love* album; from the movie *What's The Worst That Could Happen?* starring Martin Lawrence	$6	T	NY.LA 497578
10/20/01	47[S]	4		9 **I'm Hot**...*(2 versions) / Do-Re-Mi* (w/**LL Cool J** & **Scarface**) samples "Sexual Healing" by **Marvin Gaye** and "Get Down" by **Craig Mack**	$6	T	J Records 21089
10/19/02	36	16		10 **React**...S:7 / A:34 *(3 versions)* **ERICK SERMON Featuring Redman**	$6	T	J Records 21221

SETZER, Brian — ROK/LP '98
Born on 4/10/60 in Long Island, New York. Lead singer/guitarist of the **Stray Cats**. Played **Eddie Cochran** in the 1987 movie *La Bamba*. Formed own 16-piece swing orchestra in 1994.

DEBUT	PEAK	WKS	Gold	A-side (Chart Hit)...B-side	$	Sym	Label & Number
8/1/98	23[A]	18		**Jump Jive An' Wail** *[THE BRIAN SETZER ORCHESTRA]*...HOT:94(3 wks) from the album *The Dirty Boogie* on Interscope 90183; written and first recorded by **Louis Prima** in 1956			album cut

SEV — '02
Rock group from Seattle, Washington: Danny and Phil (vocals), Max (guitar), Chris (bass) and Dennis (drums).

DEBUT	PEAK	WKS	Gold	A-side (Chart Hit)...B-side	$	Sym	Label & Number
11/9/02	25[S]	14		**Same Old Song**...*(monk remix)*	$4	★	Geffen 497810

SEVELLE, Taja — R&B '87
Born on 3/18/62 in Minneapolis, Minnesota. Black female dance singer.

DEBUT	PEAK	WKS	Gold	A-side (Chart Hit)...B-side	$	Sym	Label & Number
9/12/87	62	10		**Love Is Contagious**...*Mama 16* produced by **Prince**	$3	■	Reprise 28257

7L & ESOTERIC — '01
White hip-hop duo from Boston, Massachusetts: 7L (DJ) and Esoteric (male rapper).

DEBUT	PEAK	WKS	Gold	A-side (Chart Hit)...B-side	$	Sym	Label & Number
6/9/01	44[S]	7		**Call Me E.S.**...*The Soul Purpose*	$6	★	Direct 1224

SEVEN MARY THREE — ROK/LP '96
Rock group from Virginia: Jason Ross (vocals), Jason Pollock (guitar), Casey Daniel (bass) and Giti Khalsa (drums).

DEBUT	PEAK	WKS	Gold	A-side (Chart Hit)...B-side	$	Sym	Label & Number
1/20/96	39	20		**Cumbersome**...AR[4] S:33 / A:45 *(acoustic version)*	$5	▮	Mammoth 98111

7 MILE — R&B/BUB '98
Male R&B vocal group from Detroit, Michigan: Deion Lucas, Seantezz Robinson, Luther Jackson and Glynis Martin.

DEBUT	PEAK	WKS	Gold	A-side (Chart Hit)...B-side	$	Sym	Label & Number
4/25/98	50	19		**Do Your Thing**...S:31 *(same version)*	$4	▮	Crave 78886

702 — R&B/LP '99
Female R&B vocal trio from Las Vegas, Nevada: Kameelah Williams and sisters Irish and Lemisha Grinstead. Group named after the Las Vegas area code.

DEBUT	PEAK	WKS	Gold	A-side (Chart Hit)...B-side	$	Sym	Label & Number
2/4/95	15	20	●	1 **This Lil' Game We Play**...S:7 / A:25 *(4 album snippets)* **SUBWAY featuring 702**	$3	▮	Biv 10 0252
9/14/96	32	20	●	2 **Steelo**...S:20 *(4 album snippets)* **Missy Elliott** (rap); samples "Voices In My Head" by **The Police**	$3	▮V	Biv 10 0530
2/15/97	10	20	●	3 **Get It Together**...S:4 / A:46 *Steelo* written and produced by **Donell Jones**; "45" issued for above 2 on Biv 10 860648	$3	▮V	Biv 10/Motown 0612
8/16/97	35	12		4 **All I Want**...S:21 *Get It Together* (w/Doug Lazy) samples "It's Great To Be Here" by **The Jackson 5**; from the movie *Good Burger* starring Kenan Thompson and Kel Mitchell	$3	▮	Biv 10/Motown 0676
5/1/99	4	42	●	5 **Where My Girls At?** S:2 / A:3 *(instrumental) / (4 album snippets)* co-written and produced by **Missy Elliott**	$4	★	Motown 860891
12/28/02+	13[S]	23		6 **Star**...*(instrumental) / (3 album snippets) / (3 album snippets - Latif)* **702 Featuring Clipse**	$4	★	Motown 019583

DEBUT	PEAK	WKS	Gold	A-side (Chart Hit)..........B-side	$	Sym	Label & Number

707 LP '80

Rock group from Detroit, Michigan: Kevin Russell (vocals, guitar), Phil Bryant (bass) and Jim McClarty (drums). Kevin Chalfant (vocals) and Tod Howarth (keyboards) added in 1982. Chalfant, a backing singer for **Kim Carnes** and **Night Ranger**, co-founded **The Storm** in 1991.

DEBUT	PEAK	WKS	Gold	A-side (Chart Hit)..........B-side	$	Sym	Label & Number
10/11/80	52	9		1 **I Could Be Good For You**..........*Let Me Live My Life*	$5		Casablanca 2280
7/10/82	62	6		2 **Mega Force**..........*Hell Or High Water*	$5		Boardwalk 146

SEVILLE, David/THE CHIPMUNKS BUB/C&W/LP '58

★238★

Born Ross Bagdasarian on 1/27/19 in Fresno, California. Died on 1/16/72 (age 52). To Los Angeles in 1950. Appeared in the movies *Viva Zapata*, *Stalag 17* and *Rear Window*. Wrote "Come On-a My House." Creator of **The Chipmunks**, cartoon characters Seville named Alvin, Simon and Theodore after Liberty executives Alvin Bennett, Simon Waronker and Theodore Keep. The Chipmunks starred in own prime-time animated TV show in the early 1960s and a Saturday morning cartoon series in the mid-1980s. His son, Ross Jr., resurrected the act in 1980. Also see **Canned Heat**'s "Christmas Blues."

1)The Chipmunk Song 2)Witch Doctor 3)Alvin's Harmonica 4)Ragtime Cowboy Joe 5)Rudolph The Red Nosed Reindeer

DEBUT	PEAK	WKS	Gold	A-side (Chart Hit)..........B-side	$	Sym	Label & Number
1/28/56	44	6		1 **The Trouble With Harry** *[ALFI AND HARRY]*..........T:44 *A Little Beauty* [N] inspired by the Alfred Hitchcock movie starring John Forsythe and Shirley MacLaine	$20		Liberty 55008
				THE MUSIC OF DAVID SEVILLE:			
12/15/56+	42	8		2 **Armen's Theme**..........T:42 *Carousel In Rome* [I] named for Seville's wife Armen	$20		Liberty 55041
9/9/57	77	4		3 **Gotta Get To Your House**..........T:77 *Camel Rock* [N]	$20	■	Liberty 55079
4/14/58	❶3	19	●	4 **Witch Doctor**..........RB[1] T:❶3 / S:❷2 / A:2 *Don't Whistle At Me Baby* [N]	$25		Liberty 55132
7/7/58	34	5		5 **The Bird On My Head**..........S:34 / T:36 *Hey There Moon* [N]	$20		Liberty 55140
8/25/58	78	2		6 **Little Brass Band**..........H:78 *Take Five*	$20		Liberty 55153
5/18/59	86	1		7 **Judy**..........*Maria From Madrid* [I-S]	$20		Liberty 55193
				DAVID SEVILLE AND THE CHIPMUNKS:			
12/1/58	❶4	13	●	8 **The Chipmunk Song** *Almost Good* (Seville) [X-N]	$15		Liberty 55168
2/16/59	3	12	●	9 **Alvin's Harmonica**..........*Mediocre* (Seville) [N]	$15		Liberty 55179
7/6/59	16	9		10 **Ragtime Cowboy Joe**..........*Flip Side* (Seville) [N] #1 hit for Bob Roberts in 1912	$15	■	Liberty 55200
12/14/59	41	5		11 **The Chipmunk Song (Christmas Don't Be Late)**..........*Alvin's Harmonica* [X-N-R]	$15	■	Liberty 55250
2/22/60	33	5		12 **Alvin's Orchestra**..........*Copyright 1960* (Seville) [N] all of above on green label; all below on multi-colored label	$15	■	Liberty 55233
9/5/60	95	2		13 **Alvin For President**..........*Sack Time* (Seville) [N]	$15	■	Liberty 55277
12/12/60	45	3		14 **The Chipmunk Song (Christmas Don't Be Late)**..........*Alvin's Harmonica* [X-N-R]	$10	■	Liberty 55250
12/19/60	21	2		15 **Rudolph The Red Nosed Reindeer**..........*Spain* [X-N]	$10	■	Liberty 55289
12/18/61	47	3		16 **Rudolph The Red Nosed Reindeer**..........*Spain* [X-N-R] different picture sleeve issued than the one for #15 above	$10	■	Liberty 55289
12/18/61	39	3		17 **The Chipmunk Song (Christmas Don't Be Late)** / [X-N-R]			
12/25/61	73	2		18 **Alvin's Harmonica**.......... [X-N-R] a different picture sleeve than #11 & 14 issued in 1961	$10	■	Liberty 55250
3/3/62	40	8		19 **The Alvin Twist**..........*I Wish I Could Speak French* [N]	$15		Liberty 55424
12/8/62	40	4		20 **The Chipmunk Song (Christmas Don't Be Late)** / X:5 [X-N-R] Christmas charts: [#5-7 weeks] 5/'63; 6/'64			
12/22/62	87	1		21 **Alvin's Harmonica**.......... [X-N-R]	$10	■	Liberty 55250
12/15/62	77	3		22 **Rudolph The Red Nosed Reindeer**..........X:7 *Spain* [X-N-R] Christmas charts: [#7-7 weeks] 7/'63; 29/'64; 25/'66; all of above (except #1, 3, 10, 15, 16 & 22) written by Seville	$10	■	Liberty 55289

SEVILLE, Papa '01

Born in Houston, Texas. Male rapper.

DEBUT	PEAK	WKS	Gold	A-side (Chart Hit)..........B-side	$	Sym	Label & Number
2/10/01	38[S]	10		**The Wood**..........*(instrumental) / Lost Years*	$8	★*	KMJ 0003

SEVILLES, The '61

Male R&B vocal group from Los Angeles, California: Manny Chavez, Ernest Hamilton, James Spencer and Charles Wright.

DEBUT	PEAK	WKS	Gold	A-side (Chart Hit)..........B-side	$	Sym	Label & Number
1/23/61	84	5		**Charlena**..........*Loving You (Is My Desire)*	$40		J.C. 116

S-EXPRESS '88

Dance-pop duo from England: DJ Mark Moore and vocalist **Sonique**.

DEBUT	PEAK	WKS	Gold	A-side (Chart Hit)..........B-side	$	Sym	Label & Number
6/18/88	91	6		**Theme From S-Express**..........*The Trip*	$4	■	Capitol 44181

SEXTON, Charlie ROK/LP '86

Born on 8/11/68 in San Antonio, Texas. Rock singer/guitarist. Lead guitarist for Joe Ely's band. Co-founder of the Arc Angels. Appeared in the movie *Thelma & Louise*.

DEBUT	PEAK	WKS	Gold	A-side (Chart Hit)..........B-side	$	Sym	Label & Number
12/14/85+	17	20		**Beat's So Lonely**..........S:9 / A:30 *Attractions*	$4	■	MCA 52715

SEYMOUR, Phil BUB/LP '81

Born on 5/15/52 in Tulsa, Oklahoma. Died of cancer on 8/17/93 (age 41). Pop-rock singer/drummer/bassist. Formerly with the **Dwight Twilley Band**.

DEBUT	PEAK	WKS	Gold	A-side (Chart Hit)..........B-side	$	Sym	Label & Number
1/24/81	22	16		**Precious To Me**..........*Baby It's You*	$5	■	Boardwalk 5703

SF SPANISH FLY BUB '95

Pop vocal duo based in San Francisco, California: John "Milo" Pro and Octaviano Silva.

DEBUT	PEAK	WKS	Gold	A-side (Chart Hit)..........B-side	$	Sym	Label & Number
6/10/95	89	6		**Crimson And Clover**..........*Young Love*	$4	▌	Upstairs/Warner 17867

SGH MOCCA SOUL R&B '92

Dance project of producer Ron St. Louis, featuring lead vocals by Joy Rose. St. Louis was a staffwriter with Jobette Music. SGH: Soul Goes House.

DEBUT	PEAK	WKS	Gold	A-side (Chart Hit)..........B-side	$	Sym	Label & Number
5/16/92	99	2		**Losing You**..........A:63 *(hip hop edit)*	$4	▌	Savage 54391

SHACKLEFORDS, The BUB '63

Folk-country singing group put together by producers **Lee Hazlewood** and Marty Cooper. Named after Lee's first wife, Naomi Shackleford.

DEBUT	PEAK	WKS	Gold	A-side (Chart Hit)..........B-side	$	Sym	Label & Number
5/11/63	70	6		**A Stranger In Your Town**..........*Big River*	$12		Mercury 72112

DEBUT	PEAK	WKS	Gold	A-side (Chart Hit)...B-side	$	Sym	Label & Number

SHADES '96

Female R&B vocal group from Boston, Massachusetts: Monique Peoples, Tiffanie Cardwell, Shannon Walker-Williams and Danielle Andrews.

DEBUT	PEAK	WKS	Gold	A-side (Chart Hit)...B-side	$	Sym	Label & Number
8/3/96	50	17		1 **Tell Me (I'll Be Around)**...S:35 / A:70 *(instrumental)* samples "Who Do You Love" by Bernard Wright	$3	▮	Motown 0410
7/5/97	88	7		2 **Serenade**...*(instrumental)* samples "True" by **Spandau Ballet**	$3	▮	Motown 0658

SHADE SHEIST R&B '00

Born in Los Angeles, California. Male rapper/singer.

DEBUT	PEAK	WKS	Gold	A-side (Chart Hit)...B-side	$	Sym	Label & Number
11/11/00	95	5		**Where I Wanna Be**...S:28 *(3 album snippets)* **SHADE SHEIST Featuring Nate Dogg & Kurupt** samples "Waiting For Your Love" by **Toto**	$6	★	Baby Ree 35058

SHADES OF BLUE '66

"Blue-eyed soul" group from Detroit, Michigan: Linda Kerr, Robert Kerr, Ernest Dernai and Nick Marinelli.

DEBUT	PEAK	WKS	Gold	A-side (Chart Hit)...B-side	$	Sym	Label & Number
5/7/66	12	12		1 **Oh How Happy**...*Little Orphan Boy*	$20		Impact 1007
7/30/66	72	6		2 **Lonely Summer**...*With This Ring*	$15		Impact 1014
10/1/66	78	4		3 **Happiness**...*The Night*	$15		Impact 1015

SHADOWS OF KNIGHT, The LP '66

Garage-rock band from Chicago, Illinois: Jim Sohns (vocals), Joe Kelley and Jerry McGeorge (guitars), Warren Rogers (bass) and Tom Schiffour (drums).

DEBUT	PEAK	WKS	Gold	A-side (Chart Hit)...B-side	$	Sym	Label & Number
3/19/66	10	12		1 **Gloria** *Dark Side* written by **Van Morrison**	$20		Dunwich 116
6/4/66	39	6		2 **Oh Yeah**...*Light Bulb Blues* written and recorded by **Bo Diddley** in 1959 on Checker 914 ($30)	$20	■	Dunwich 122
9/10/66	91	2		3 **Bad Little Woman**...*Gospel Zone*	$20	■	Dunwich 128
12/24/66	90	1		4 **I'm Gonna Make You Mine**...*I'll Make You Sorry*	$20		Dunwich 141
10/26/68	46	8		5 **Shake**...*From Way Out To Way Under*	$15		Team 520

SHAFFER, Paul '89

Born on 11/28/49 in Toronto, Ontario, Canada. Keyboardist/arranger. Bandleader for David Letterman's NBC-TV and CBS-TV late night talk shows. Cast member of the 1977 TV sitcom *A Year At The Top.* Piano player on TV's *Saturday Night Live* and for **The Blues Brothers** during the late 1970s.

DEBUT	PEAK	WKS	Gold	A-side (Chart Hit)...B-side	$	Sym	Label & Number
8/12/89	81	8		**When The Radio Is On**...*Metal Beach* **Dion**, **Carole King**, **Johnny Maestro**, **Ellie Greenwich**, Jay Siegel, Ronnie Bright, **The Fresh Prince**, & Ecstasy (backing vocals)	$5	▮	Capitol 44413

SHAFTO, Bobby '64

Rock and roll singer from England.

DEBUT	PEAK	WKS	Gold	A-side (Chart Hit)...B-side	$	Sym	Label & Number
7/18/64	99	1		**She's My Girl**...*Wonderful You*	$12		Rust 5082

★499★

SHAGGY R&B/BUB/LP '01

Born Orville Richard Burrell on 10/22/68 in Kingston, Jamaica. Reggae dancehall vocalist. Moved to Brooklyn at age 18. During his four years as a U.S. Marine, served in Kuwait for Operation Desert Storm.

1)It Wasn't Me 2)Angel 3)Boombastic

DEBUT	PEAK	WKS	Gold	A-side (Chart Hit)...B-side	$	Sym	Label & Number
8/14/93	59	17		1 **Oh Carolina**...S:53 / A:68 *(2 versions) / Love Me Up* samples the **Henry Mancini** tune "Peter Gunn"; from the movie *Sliver* starring Sharon Stone; originally recorded in Jamaica in 1960 by the Folkes Brothers; "45": Virgin 17447	$5	▮V	Virgin 12672
5/20/95	3	29	▲	2 **Boombastic** / RB[1] S:❶[2] / A:27 samples "Baby Let Me Kiss You" by **King Floyd**			
7/29/95		19		3 **Summer Time**...S:flip *Gal Yu A Pepper* **SHAGGY (featuring Rayvon)** #3 hit for **Mungo Jerry** in 1970 as "In The Summertime"; "45": Virgin 18586	$3	▮V	Virgin 38482
6/29/96	20	20		4 **That Girl**...S:16 / A:41 *(2 versions) / Heartbreak Lover* (w/Beres Hammond & Buju Banton) **MAXI PRIEST FEATURING SHAGGY** samples "Green Onions" by **Booker T. & The MG's**; "45": Virgin 19173	$3	▮V	Virgin 38550
8/30/97	72	10		5 **Piece Of My Heart**...S:74 *(urban remix) / One Burner* Marsha (female vocal); samples "Piece Of My Heart" by **Erma Franklin**	$4	▮	Virgin 38601
12/19/98	76	17		6 **Luv Me, Luv Me**...A:54 **SHAGGY Featuring Janet** samples "Impeach The President" by The Honey Drippers; from the movie *How Stella Got Her Groove Back* starring Angela Bassett (soundtrack on Flyte Tyme 11806)			album cut
12/11/99	67^S	3		7 **Hope**...*(remix) / Not Fair* from the movie *For Love Of The Game* starring Kevin Costner	$4	★	MCA 155658
11/4/00+	❶[2]	25		8 **It Wasn't Me** A:❶[5] / S:2 *(3 versions)* **SHAGGY (Featuring Ricardo "RikRok" Ducent)** "45" B-side: (club version)	$8	★*V	MCA 155782
12/30/00+	❶[1]	28		9 **Angel**...A:❶[5] / S:10 *(3 versions)* **SHAGGY Featuring Rayvon** samples "The Joker" by **Steve Miller** and "Angel Of The Morning" by **Merrilee Rush**; "45": MCA 155820; B-side: "Chica Bonita"	$8	★*V	MCA 155811
12/22/01+	41^S	6		10 **2-Way**...*(instrumental)* **RAYVON featuring Shaggy, Ricardo "Rik Rok" Ducent, Brian & Tony Gold**	$5	★	Big Yard/MCA 155891
11/16/02	59^S	1		11 **Hey Sexy Lady**...*(6 versions)* **SHAGGY w/ Sean Paul feat. Brian & Tony Gold**	$8	T	Big Yard/MCA 113958

SHAI R&B/LP '92

R&B vocal group formed in Washington DC: Garfield Bright, Marc Gay, Carl Martin and Darnell Van Rensalier. Pronounced: shy.

DEBUT	PEAK	WKS	Gold	A-side (Chart Hit)...B-side	$	Sym	Label & Number
10/17/92	2^8	27	▲	1 **If I Ever Fall In Love** S:2 / A:2 *(remix)* "45": Collectables/MCA 90175; B-side: "Baby I'm Yours"	$3	▮V	Gasoline Alley 54518
1/23/93	10	24	●	2 **Comforter**...A:8 / S:15 *(3 album snippets)* "45": MCA 54596; B-side: (remix)	$3	▮V	Gasoline Alley 54596
6/5/93	10	25		3 **Baby I'm Yours**...A:5 / S:24 *(remix)* issued with 2 different cassette picture boxes; also see #4 below	$3	▮V	Gasoline Alley 54574
12/11/93+	63	11		4 **Yours**...A:58 *Together Forever* (R&B #89) [R] an acappella remix of #3 above	$4	▮	Gasoline Alley 54770

DEBUT	PEAK	WKS	Gold	A-side (Chart Hit)...B-side	$	Sym	Label & Number
				SHAI — Cont'd			
6/4/94	34	18		5 **The Place Where You Belong** ...S:25 / A:52 *(instrumental)*	$3	▮	MCA 54807
				from the movie *Beverly Hills Cop III* starring **Eddie Murphy**			
9/16/95	43	20		6 **Come With Me** ...S:17 *(remix)*	$3	▮	Gasoline Alley 55081
5/4/96	89	5		7 **I Don't Wanna Be Alone** ...*(remix)*	$3	▮	Gasoline Alley 55178
				SHAKESPEAR'S SISTER ROK/LP '92			
				Female pop-rock duo of British native Siobhan Fahey and Detroit native Marcella Detroit. Fahey, wife of **Dave Stewart** (**Eurythmics**), was a member of **Bananarama**. Detroit is **Marcy Levy** who recorded with **Robin Gibb**, sang backup for **Eric Clapton** and co-wrote "Lay Down Sally." Disbanded in 1993.			
7/4/92	4	20	●	1 **Stay** ...S:4 / A:17 *(3 album snippets) / The Trouble With Andre*	$3	▮	London 869730
11/28/92+	55	12		2 **I Don't Care** ...A:58 / S:74 *Stay (acoustic version)*	$3	▮	London 869946
				SHAKIRA LP '01			
				Born Shakira Isabel Mebarak Ripoll on 2/9/77 in Barranquilla, Colombia. Female Latin-pop singer.			
10/27/01	6	24		1 **Whenever, Wherever** ...A:6		V	album cut
				co-written by **Gloria Estefan**; "45": Epic 79642; B-side: "Suerte (Whenever, Wherever)"			
3/16/02	9	20		2 **Underneath Your Clothes** ...A:9		V	album cut
				"45": Epic 79741; B-side: (same version)			
9/7/02	55	9		3 **Objection (Tango)**...A:59			album cut
				all of above from the album *Laundry Service* on Epic 63900			
				SHALAMAR R&B/BUB/LP '80			
				R&B-dance vocal trio formed in Los Angeles, California: **Jody Watley**, **Jeffrey Daniels** and **Howard Hewett**. Also see **Babyface**'s "This Is For The Lover In You."			
3/12/77	25	17		1 **Uptown Festival (Part 1)**...*(Part 2)*	$6		Soul Train 10885
				Going To A Go-Go/I Can't Help Myself (Sugar Pie, Honey Bunch)/ Uptight (Everything's Alright)/ Stop! In The Name Of Love/It's The Same Old Song; recorded by anonymous session singers prior to formation of actual group			
1/13/79	79	6		2 **Take That To The Bank**...*Shalamar Disco Gardens*	$5		Solar 11379
12/8/79+	8	23	●	3 **The Second Time Around** RB[1] *Leave It All Up To Love*	$5		Solar 11709
12/20/80+	55	12		4 **Full Of Fire** ...*Let's Find The Time For Love*	$5		Solar 12152
4/25/81	60	8		5 **Make That Move**...*Pop Along Kid*	$5		Solar 12192
4/10/82	44	10		6 **A Night To Remember** ...*On Top Of The World*	$4		Solar 48005
6/25/83	22	20		7 **Dead Giveaway**...*I Don't Wanna Be The Last To Know*	$4	■	Solar 69819
3/17/84	17	18		8 **Dancing In The Sheets** ...*(instrumental)*	$4	■	Columbia 04372
				from the movie *Footloose* starring Kevin Bacon and Lori Singer			
11/17/84	73	9		9 **Amnesia**...*You're The One For Me*	$4		Solar 69682
				SHAMEN, The LP '92			
				Techno-rave dance group from Aberdeen, Scotland, formed by Colin "Shamen" Angus and Will "Sin" Sinnott (drowned on 5/23/90, age 31). Features rapper Mr. C.			
12/14/91+	38	17		1 **Move Any Mountain (Progen 91)**...A:36 / S:41 *(edited version)*	$5	▮	Epic 74044
10/24/92	72[A]	1		2 **LSI (Love, Sex, Intelligence)** ...*(edited version)*	$5	▮	Epic 74437
				above 2: #1 Dance Club Play hits			
				SHANA C&W/LP '90			
				Born Shana Petrone on 5/8/72 in Parkridge, Illinois; raised in Ft. Lauderdale, Florida. Dance-disco singer; switched to country in 1998.			
10/7/89+	40	23		1 **I Want You** ...S:35 / A:40 *(house remix)*	$5	▮[V]	Vision 4511
3/24/90	82	5		2 **You Can't Get Away** ...*(radio edit)*	$5	▮	Vision 4515
				SHA NA NA BUB/LP '75			
				Rock and roll group specializing in 1950's-style music. Core members: John "Bowzer" Bauman, Scott Powell, Johnny Contardo, Fred Greene, Don York and Rich Joffe. Group hosted own TV variety show from 1977-81.			
8/7/71	84	3		1 **Top Forty**...*I Wonder Why*	$6	■	Kama Sutra 528
				some pressings show title as "Top Forty Of The Lord"			
4/19/75	55	10		2 **(Just Like) Romeo And Juliet** ...*Circles Of Love*	$5		Kama Sutra 602
				SHAND, Remy LP '02			
				Born in 1979 in Winnipeg, Manitoba, Canada. Male "blue-eyed soul" singer/songwriter/multi-instrumentalist.			
4/27/02	89	6		**Take A Message** ...*(4 versions)*	$6	T	Motown 015625
				SHANGO BUB '69			
				Interracial reggae group.			
3/1/69	57	7		**Day After Day (It's Slippin' Away)** ...*Mescalito*	$8		A&M 1014
				reggae-styled song about the consequences of earthquakes in California			
	★563★			**SHANGRI-LAS, The** BUB/LP '64			
				"Girl group" formed in Queens, New York. Consisted of two sets of sisters: Mary (lead singer) and Betty Weiss, and twins Mary Ann and Marge Ganser. Mary Ann died of encephalitis in 1971; Marge died of cancer on 7/28/96 (age 48).			
				1)Leader Of The Pack 2)Remember (Walkin' in the Sand) 3)I Can Never Go Home Anymore			
8/22/64	5	11		1 **Remember (Walkin' in the Sand)** ...*It's Easier To Cry*	$25		Red Bird 10-008
10/10/64	❶[1]	12		2 **Leader Of The Pack** RB[1] *What Is Love*	$25		Red Bird 10-014
12/26/64+	18	9		3 **Give Him A Great Big Kiss**...*Twist And Shout*	$20		Red Bird 10-018
12/26/64+	91	2		4 **Maybe**...*Shout*	$20		Red Bird 10-019
4/3/65	53	6		5 **Out In The Streets** ...*The Boy*	$20		Red Bird 10-025
5/29/65	29	8		6 **Give Us Your Blessings**...*Heaven Only Knows*	$20		Red Bird 10-030
10/9/65	99	2		7 **Right Now And Not Later** ...*The Train From Kansas City*	$20		Red Bird 10-036
11/6/65	6	11		8 **I Can Never Go Home Anymore**...*Bull Dog*	$20		Red Bird 10-043
				also released with "Sophisticated Boom Boom" as the B-side			
2/5/66	33	6		9 **Long Live Our Love**...*Sophisticated Boom Boom*	$20		Red Bird 10-048
				also released with "Bull Dog" as the B-side			

DEBUT	PEAK	WKS	Gold	A-side (Chart Hit)...B-side	$	Sym	Label & Number
				SHANGRI-LAS, The — Cont'd			
4/9/66	65	6		10 **He Cried** ...*Dressed In Black*	$20		Red Bird 10-053
				female version of "She Cried" by **Jay & The Americans**			
6/25/66	59	6		11 **Past, Present And Future** ...*Love You More Than Yesterday* [S]	$20		Red Bird 10-068
				also released with "Paradise" as the B-side; all of above (except #1 & 7) produced by George "Shadow" Morton			
				SHANICE BUB/R&B/LP **'92**			
				Born Shanice Wilson on 5/14/73 in Pittsburgh, Pennsylvania; raised in Los Angeles, California. Female R&B singer. Also see **Toni Braxton**'s "Un-Break My Heart" and **Kevon Edmonds**' "24/7."			
11/7/87	50	13		1 **(Baby Tell Me) Can You Dance** *[SHANICE WILSON]*...*Summer Love*	$3	■	A&M 2939
2/25/89	78	5		2 **This Time** ...*Wait So Long*	$3	■	Arista 9772
				KIARA (with Shanice Wilson)			
11/23/91+	2[3]	26		3 **I Love Your Smile** RB[4] A:❶[5] / S:6 *(instrumental)*	$3	▮[V]	Motown 2093
				"45": Motown 2163; B-side: "I'm Cryin'"			
4/25/92	31	17		4 **Silent Prayer**...A:29 / S:33 *(instrumental)*	$3	▮[V]	Motown 2165
				SHANICE featuring Johnny Gill			
				"45": Motown 2169; B-side: "Loving You"			
8/22/92	58[A]	6		5 **Don't Wanna Love You**...			album cut
				from the movie *Boomerang* starring **Eddie Murphy** (soundtrack on LaFace 26006)			
10/24/92+	4	24		6 **Saving Forever For You** ...A:4 / S:6 *(instrumental)*	$3	▮	Giant 18719
				from the album *Beverly Hills 90210 (The Soundtrack)*			
7/17/93	57	11		7 **It's For You** ...A:43 *Ain't Nobody Bad Like Meteor Man* (Big Hat Ray Ray)	$3	▮	Motown 2207
				Brett Bouldin (rap); from the movie *The Meteor Man* starring Robert Townsend			
3/27/99	12	10		8 **When I Close My Eyes**...S:9 / A:59 *(4 album snippets) / (instrumental)*	$4	★	LaFace 24365
9/25/99	36[S]	15		9 **You Need A Man**...*(album version) / (instrumental)*	$4	★	LaFace 24428
				co-written and arranged by **Montell Jordan**			
				SHANK, Bud LP **'66**			
				Born Clifford Shank on 5/27/26 in Dayton, Ohio. Jazz saxophonist.			
1/22/66	65	6		**Michelle** ...*Ontem A Note* [I]	$8		World-Pacific 77814
				Bob Florence (orch.); written by **John Lennon** & **Paul McCartney** (from **The Beatles**' *Rubber Soul* album)			
				SHANNON — see WILDE, Marty			
				SHANNON R&B/BUB/LP **'84**			
				Born Brenda Shannon Greene on 5/12/57 in Washington DC. Female dance singer.			
11/12/83+	8	24	●	1 **Let The Music Play** ...*(dub version)*	$4		Mirage 99810
3/31/84	46	13		2 **Give Me Tonight**...*(dub version)*	$4	■	Mirage 99775
4/6/85	49	15		3 **Do You Wanna Get Away**...*(dub version)*	$4	■	Mirage 99655
				all of above: #1 Dance Club Play hits			
	★326★			**SHANNON, Del** BUB/C&W/LP **'61**			
				Born Charles Westover on 12/30/34 in Coopersville, Michigan. Died of a self-inflicted gunshot wound on 2/8/90 (age 55). With U.S. Army *Get Up And Go* radio show in Germany. Discovered by Ann Arbor DJ/producer Ollie McLaughlin. Formed own Berlee label in 1963. Wrote "I Go To Pieces" for **Peter & Gordon**. To Los Angeles in 1966; production work. Inducted into the Rock and Roll Hall of Fame in 1999.			
				1)Runaway 2)Hats Off To Larry 3)Keep Searchin'			
3/6/61	❶[4]	17	●	1 **Runaway** ...*Jody*	$30		Big Top 3067
				electric organ (musitron) solo by co-writer Max Crook; a "live" version by Del "Bubbled Under" (#112) in 1967			
6/5/61	5	13		2 **Hats Off To Larry** ...*Don't Gild The Lily, Lily*	$25		Big Top 3075
9/18/61	28	10		3 **So Long Baby** ...*The Answer To Everything*	$25		Big Top 3083
11/27/61+	38	8		4 **Hey! Little Girl** ...*I Don't Care Anymore*	$25		Big Top 3091
6/30/62	99	1		5 **Cry Myself To Sleep**...*I'm Gonna Move On*	$25		Big Top 3112
9/15/62	64	5		6 **The Swiss Maid**...*You Never Talked About Me*	$25		Big Top 3117
				written by **Roger Miller**			
12/22/62+	12	14		7 **Little Town Flirt** ...*The Wamboo*	$25		Big Top 3131
4/13/63	50	9		8 **Two Kind Of Teardrops** ...*Kelly*	$25		Big Top 3143
6/29/63	77	4		9 **From Me To You** ...*Two Silhouettes*	$50		Big Top 3152
				the first U.S. chart hit of a song written by **John Lennon** and **Paul McCartney**			
11/2/63	71	7		10 **Sue's Gotta Be Mine**...*Now She's Gone*	$20		Berlee 501
7/4/64	22	10		11 **Handy Man**...*Give Her Lots Of Lovin'*	$15		Amy 905
9/19/64	43	7		12 **Do You Want To Dance** ...*This Is All I Have To Give*	$15		Amy 911
11/21/64+	9	14		13 **Keep Searchin' (We'll Follow The Sun)** ...*Broken Promises*	$15		Amy 915
2/27/65	30	6		14 **Stranger In Town** ...*Over You*	$15		Amy 919
5/22/65	95	3		15 **Break Up**...*Why Don't You Tell Him*	$15		Amy 925
				all of above (except #6, 9, 11 & 12) written by Shannon			
5/7/66	94	2		16 **The Big Hurt** ...*I Got It Bad*	$12		Liberty 55866
12/12/81+	33	12		17 **Sea Of Love**...*Midnight Train*	$6		Network 47951
				produced by **Tom Petty**			
				SHAPIRO, Helen **'61**			
				Born on 9/28/46 in London, England. Pop-ballad singer.			
12/4/61	100	1		**Walkin' Back To Happiness**...*Kiss 'N Run*	$12		Capitol 4662
				Norrie Paramor (orch.)			
				SHARISSA R&B/LP **'02**			
				Born Sharissa Dawes on 8/21/75 in Brooklyn, New York. Female R&B singer/songwriter.			
2/9/02	72	14		**Any Other Night**...A:70 *(2 versions) / Henchmen G's*	$6	T	Motown 015378
				SHARKEY, Feargal LP **'86**			
				Born on 8/13/58 in Londonderry, Northern Ireland. Pop-rock singer. Former member of The Undertones.			
3/15/86	74	6		**A Good Heart** ...*Anger Is Holy*	$3	■	A&M/Virgin 2804

DEBUT	PEAK	WKS	Gold	A-side (Chart Hit)....B-side	$	Sym	Label & Number
	★524★			**SHARP, Dee Dee** BUB/R&B/LP '62 Born Dione LaRue on 9/9/45 in Philadelphia, Pennsylvania. R&B singer. Backing vocalist at Cameo Records in 1961. Married record producer Kenny Gamble in 1967, recorded as **Dee Dee Sharp** Gamble. Also see the **Philadelphia International All Stars**. *1)Mashed Potato Time 2)Slow Twistin' 3)Ride!*			
3/3/62	3	14		1 **Slow Twistin'** ....*La Paloma Twist* (Checker - #72) **CHUBBY CHECKER (with Dee Dee Sharp)**	$15	■	Parkway 835
3/3/62	2^2	18	●	2 **Mashed Potato Time** RB^4 *Set My Heart At Ease*	$15		Cameo 212
6/16/62	9	10		3 **Gravy (For My Mashed Potatoes)** ....*Baby Cakes*	$15	■	Cameo 219
10/20/62	5	13		4 **Ride!** ....*The Night*	$15	■	Cameo 230
3/2/63	10	11		5 **Do The Bird**....*Lover Boy*	$15	■	Cameo 244
6/29/63	43	7		6 **Rock Me In The Cradle Of Love**....*You'll Never Be Mine*	$15	■	Cameo 260
10/5/63	33	9		7 **Wild!**....*Why Doncha Ask Me*	$15	■	Cameo 274
2/1/64	82	4		8 **Where Did I Go Wrong /**			
2/29/64	97	1		9 **Willyam, Willyam**	$15	■	Cameo 296
11/6/65	78	7		10 **I Really Love You** ....*Standing In The Need Of Love*	$15	■	Cameo 375
				SHARPE, Mike '67 Born Michael Shapiro on 1/3/40 in Atlanta, Georgia. Pop-jazz alto saxophonist.			
1/28/67	57	7		**Spooky**....*Break Through* [I]	$8		Liberty 55922
				SHARPE, Ray '59 Born on 2/8/38 in Fort Worth, Texas. Rockabilly singer/guitarist.			
7/20/59	46	13		**Linda Lu**....*Red Sails In The Sunset* **Duane Eddy** and **Al Casey** (guitarists)	$20		Jamie 1128
				SHARPEES BUB '66 R&B vocal group from St. Louis, Missouri: Benny Sharp, Herbert Reeves, Vernon Guy and Horise O'Toole. Guy died in a car crash on 9/10/98 (age 53).			
1/15/66	79	3		**Tired Of Being Lonely** ....*Just To Please You*	$15		One-derful! 4839
				SHARPLES, Bob, and His Music LP '56 Born in Bury, Lancashire, England. Bandleader/arranger.			
9/22/56	52	15		**Sadie's Shawl**....T:52 *Hurricane Boogie* [I]	$12		London 1661
				SHAW, Georgie MEM/POP '54 Born in 1930 in Philadelphia, Pennsylvania. Male Adult Contemporary singer. Hit #7 in 1954 with "Till We Two Are One."			
11/12/55	23	12		1 **No Arms Can Ever Hold You (Like These Arms Of Mine)** ....T:23 / S:25 *Look To Your Heart*	$12		Decca 29679
1/7/56	39	9		2 **Go On With The Wedding** ....T:39 *The Second Greatest Sex* **KITTY KALLEN and GEORGIE SHAW**	$15		Decca 29776
4/21/56	70	2		3 **To You, My Love**....T:70 *Fallen Angel (Are You Sorry)*	$12		Decca 29839
12/1/56	54	7		4 **A Faded Summer Love** ....T:54 *No One* The Dave Lambert Singers (backing vocals); #4 hit for Paul Whiteman in 1931; **Jack Pleis** (orch., all of above)	$12		Decca 30078
				SHAW, Marlena R&B/BUB/LP '67 Born Marlena Burgess on 9/22/42 in New Rochelle, New York. Jazz-styled singer. Band vocalist with **Count Basie** from 1967-72.			
3/11/67	58	5		**Mercy, Mercy, Mercy**....*Go Away Little Boy*	$8		Cadet 5557
				SHAW, Sandie BUB/LP '65 Born Sandra Goodrich on 2/26/47 in Dagenham, England. Pop singer. Discovered by **Adam Faith**.			
11/28/64+	52	7		1 **(There's) Always Something There To Remind Me**....*Don't You Know*	$12		Reprise 0320
3/6/65	42	9		2 **Girl Don't Come**....*I'd Be Far Better Off Without You*	$10		Reprise 0342
6/12/65	97	3		3 **Long Live Love**....*I've Heard About Him*	$10		Reprise 0375
				SHAW, Timmy '64 Born in Detroit, Michigan. Died of cancer on 3/29/84. Soul singer.			
1/25/64	41	7		**Gonna Send You Back To Georgia (A City Slick)**....*I'm A Lonely Guy* The Sternphones (backing vocals)	$15		Wand 146
				SHAW, Tommy ROK/BUB/LP '84 Born on 9/11/53 in Montgomery, Alabama. Rock singer/guitarist. Member of **Styx** and **Damn Yankees**.			
9/29/84	33	12		1 **Girls With Guns**....*Heads Up*	$3	■	A&M 2676
12/15/84+	60	9		2 **Lonely School**....*Come In And Explain*	$3		A&M 2696
10/5/85	81	5		3 **Remo's Theme (What If)** ....*Kiss Me Hello* from the movie *Remo Williams: The Adventure Begins* starring Fred Ward	$3	■	A&M 2773
2/13/88	75	9		4 **Ever Since The World Began**....*The Outsider*	$3	■	Atlantic 89138
				SHAW, Victoria — see BROOKS, Garth			
				SHEAR, Jules '85 Born on 3/7/52 in Pittsburgh, Pennsylvania. Leader of **Funky Kings**, Reckless Sleepers and Jules & The Polar Bears.			
4/6/85	57	7		**Steady**....*Still I See You* co-written by **Cyndi Lauper**	$3	■	EMI America 8259
				SHeDAISY C&W/LP '00 Country vocal trio from Magna, Utah: sisters Kristyn, Kelsi and Kassidy Osborn.			
5/8/99	43	20		1 **Little Good-Byes** A:27 / S:63 *Still Holding Out For You* (C&W #27/'01)	$4	★	Lyric Street 64025
12/25/99+	61	3		2 **Deck The Halls** ....S:17 *(edited version)* [X] from the animated movie *Mickey's Once Upon A Christmas*; traditional carol from Wales, written in 1784	$5	★	Lyric Street 64036
2/5/00	57	9		3 **This Woman Needs** A:49			album cut
7/15/00	43	20		4 **I Will...But**....A:33			album cut
3/17/01	79	3		5 **Lucky 4 You (Tonight I'm Just Me)** ....A:73 all of above (except #2) from the album *The Whole SheBang* on Lyric Street 65002			album cut

DEBUT	PEAK	WKS	Gold	A-side (Chart Hit)....B-side	$	Sym	Label & Number

SHEEP, The — BUB '66

Rock group: Jack Rasca, John Shine, Richie Lauro and Joey Richards. Produced by Bob Feldman, Jerry Goldstein and Richard Gottehrer who also charted as **The Strangeloves**.

DEBUT	PEAK	WKS	Gold	A-side (Chart Hit)....B-side	$	Sym	Label & Number
1/29/66	**58**	7		**Hide & Seek** ....*Twelve Months Later*	$20		Boom 60,000

SHEIK, Duncan — BUB/LP '97

Born on 11/18/69 in Montclair, New Jersey; raised in Hilton Head, South Carolina. Alternative pop-rock singer/songwriter/guitarist.

DEBUT	PEAK	WKS	Gold	A-side (Chart Hit)....B-side	$	Sym	Label & Number
11/30/96+	**16**	55		**Barely Breathing** ....A:7 / S:56 *Home* "45": Atlantic 84042; B-side: "Wishful Thinking" (#103/'98)	$4	▮V	Atlantic 87027

SHEILA — R&B '82

Born Annie Chancel on 8/16/46 in Paris, France. White pop singer who also sang disco with a black male trio as Sheila B. Devotion.

DEBUT	PEAK	WKS	Gold	A-side (Chart Hit)....B-side	$	Sym	Label & Number
12/5/81+	**49**	9		**Little Darlin'** ....*Put It In Writing*	$4	■	Carrere 02564

SHEILA E. — R&B/BUB/LP '84

Born Sheila Escovedo on 12/12/59 in San Francisco, California. R&B singer/percussionist. With father Pete Escovedo in the band Azteca in the mid-1970s. Toured with **Lionel Richie**; since 1986, toured and recorded with **Prince**. Member of **The Blackout Allstars**. Her uncle Coke Escovedo is a noted percussionist.

DEBUT	PEAK	WKS	Gold	A-side (Chart Hit)....B-side	$	Sym	Label & Number
6/16/84	**7**	26		1 **The Glamorous Life** ....S:7 / A:14 *Part II*	$4	■	Warner 29285
10/27/84	**34**	15		2 **The Belle Of St. Mark** ....A:26 / S:30 *Too Sexy*	$4	■	Warner 29180
11/16/85+	**11**	23		3 **A Love Bizarre** ....A:10 / S:12 *Part II* **Prince** (backing vocal); from the movie *Krush Groove* starring Sheila E.	$4	■	Paisley Park 28890
2/7/87	**68**	10		4 **Hold Me** ....*The World Is High*	$3	■	Paisley Park 28580

SHELLEY, Peter — '75

Born Peter Southworth in England. Pop singer/songwriter/producer. Began career as a talent scout for Decca in London. Not to be confused with Pete Shelley of The Buzzcocks.

DEBUT	PEAK	WKS	Gold	A-side (Chart Hit)....B-side	$	Sym	Label & Number
12/21/74+	**81**	6		**Gee Baby** ....*I'm In Love Again*	$6		Bell 45,614

SHELLS, The — '61

R&B vocal group from Brooklyn, New York: Nathaniel "Little Nate" Bouknight (lead), Gus Geter (baritone), Bobby Nurse and Shade Alston (tenors) and Danny Small (bass).

DEBUT	PEAK	WKS	Gold	A-side (Chart Hit)....B-side	$	Sym	Label & Number
12/19/60+	**21**	8		**Baby Oh Baby** ....*What's In An Angel's Eyes* originally released in 1957 with the B-side shown as "Angel Eyes" ($50)	$25		Johnson 104

SHELTON, Anne — POP '49

Born Patricia Sibley on 11/10/23 in Dulwich, London, England. Died of a heart attack on 7/31/94 (age 70). Vocalist with the Ambrose Orchestra.

DEBUT	PEAK	WKS	Gold	A-side (Chart Hit)....B-side	$	Sym	Label & Number
9/29/56	**59**	8		**Lay Down Your Arms** ....T:59 *The Madonna In Blue* Wally Stott (orch. and chorus)	$15		Columbia 40759

SHELTON, Blake — C&W/BUB/LP '01

Born on 6/18/76 in Ada, Oklahoma. Country singer/guitarist.

DEBUT	PEAK	WKS	Gold	A-side (Chart Hit)....B-side	$	Sym	Label & Number
5/26/01	**18**	20		1 **Austin** ....CW^{5} S:7 / A:22 *Problems At Home*	$4	★V	Giant 16767
12/7/02+	**28**	20		2 **The Baby** ....A:27 from the album *The Dreamer* on Warner 48237; "45": Warner 16650; B-side: "Heavy Liftin'"		V	album cut

SHE MOVES — '97

Trio of female singers/dancers: Carla, Danielle and Diana. Met while performing as dancers at New York Knicks basketball games.

DEBUT	PEAK	WKS	Gold	A-side (Chart Hit)....B-side	$	Sym	Label & Number
11/8/97	**32**	20		1 **Breaking All The Rules** ....S:29 / A:38 *(3 versions)*	$3	▮	Geffen 19415
3/21/98	**67**	15		2 **It's Your Love** ....S:72 *Every Time You Touch Me (I Get High)*	$3	▮	Geffen 19421

SHEP AND THE LIMELITES — BUB '61

R&B vocal trio from Queens, New York: James "Shep" Sheppard, lead (formerly with **The Heartbeats**) and tenors Clarence Bassett (formerly in The Five Sharps) and Charles Baskerville (formerly in The Videos). Group disbanded after Sheppard's murder on 1/24/70 (age 34).

DEBUT	PEAK	WKS	Gold	A-side (Chart Hit)....B-side	$	Sym	Label & Number
3/27/61	**2^{1}**	14		1 **Daddy's Home** *This I Know* sequel to **The Heartbeats**' "A Thousand Miles Away"	$25		Hull 740
7/10/61	**42**	5		2 **Ready For Your Love** ....*You'll Be Sorry*	$20		Hull 742
10/2/61	**58**	10		3 **Three Steps From The Altar** ....*Oh, What A Feeling*	$20		Hull 747
2/17/62	**59**	8		4 **Our Anniversary** ....*Who Told The Sandman*	$20		Hull 748
6/30/62	**94**	2		5 **What Did Daddy Do** ....*Teach Me, Teach Me How To Twist*	$20		Hull 751
2/9/63	**91**	1		6 **Remember Baby** ....*The Monkey*	$20		Hull 756

SHEPARD, Jean — C&W/MEM/POP '53

Born Ollie Imogene Shepard on 11/21/33 in Pauls Valley, Oklahoma; raised in Visalia, California. Country singer (charted 45 hits, 1953-78). Married **Hawkshaw Hawkins** on 11/26/60. Hit #4 on the pop charts in 1953 with "A Dear John Letter" (with **Ferlin Husky**).

DEBUT	PEAK	WKS	Gold	A-side (Chart Hit)....B-side	$	Sym	Label & Number
9/15/73	**81**	6		**Slippin' Away** ....*Think I'll Go Somewhere And Cry Myself To Sleep* written by **Bill Anderson**	$5		United Artists 248

SHEPARD, Vonda — AC/LP '98

Born on 7/7/63 in Manhattan, New York; raised in Los Angeles, California. Singer/songwriter/keyboardist. Had a recurring role as a singer on TV's *Ally McBeal*.

DEBUT	PEAK	WKS	Gold	A-side (Chart Hit)....B-side	$	Sym	Label & Number
<u>6/6/87</u>	**6**	24		1 **Can't We Try** ....S:4 / A:9 *Pleasure Centre* **DAN HILL (with Vonda Sheppard)**	$3		Columbia 07050
4/25/98	**16^{A}**	16		2 **Searchin' My Soul** .... theme from TV's *Ally McBeal* starring Calista Flockhart (soundtrack on 550 Music/Epic 69365)			album cut

SHEPHERD, Kenny Wayne — ROK/LP '98

Born on 6/12/77 in Shreveport, Louisiana. Blues-rock guitarist/singer/songwriter.

DEBUT	PEAK	WKS	Gold	A-side (Chart Hit)....B-side	$	Sym	Label & Number
5/2/98	**78**	10		**Blue On Black** *[KENNY WAYNE SHEPHERD BAND]*....AR^{6} S:68 *(album version)*	$5	▮V	Revolution 17222

DEBUT	PEAK	WKS	Gold	A-side (Chart Hit)...B-side	$	Sym	Label & Number

SHEPHERD SISTERS '57

Family rock and roll vocal group from Middletown, Ohio: sisters Martha, Mary Lou, Gayle and Judy Shepherd.

DEBUT	PEAK	WKS	Gold	A-side (Chart Hit)...B-side	$	Sym	Label & Number
9/30/57	18	17		1 **Alone (Why Must I Be Alone)** ...S:18 / T:20 / A:22 *Congratulations To Someone*	$25		Lance 125
3/9/63	94	2		2 **Don't Mention My Name** ...*What Makes Little Girls Cry*	$10		Atlantic 2176

SHEPPARD, T.G. C&W/BUB/LP '81

Born William Browder on 7/20/44 in Humbolt, Tennessee. Country singer (charted 42 hits, 1974-91).

DEBUT	PEAK	WKS	Gold	A-side (Chart Hit)...B-side	$	Sym	Label & Number
1/25/75	54	8		1 **Devil In The Bottle** ...CW[1] *Rollin' With The Flow*	$5		Melodyland 6002
5/10/75	95	3		2 **Tryin' To Beat The Morning Home** ...CW[1] *I'll Be Satisfied*	$5		Melodyland 6006
7/24/76	100	1		3 **Solitary Man** ...*Shame*	$5		Hitsville 6032
3/14/81	37	14		4 **I Loved 'Em Every One** CW[1] *I Could Never Dream The Way You Feel*	$4		Warner/Curb 49690
1/30/82	68	8		5 **Only One You** ...CW[1] *We Belong In Love Tonight*	$4		Warner/Curb 49858
4/3/82	58	8		6 **Finally** ...CW[1] *All My Cloudy Days Are Gone*	$4		Warner/Curb 50041
2/18/84	62	6		7 **Make My Day** ...*How Lucky We Are* (Sheppard) [N] **T.G. SHEPPARD WITH CLINT EASTWOOD** inspired by a phrase from the movie *Sudden Impact* starring Eastwood	$4		Warner/Curb 29343

SHERBS ROK/LP '76

Pop-rock group from Australia: **Daryl Braithwaite** (vocals), Harvey James (guitar), Garth Porter (keyboards), Tony Mitchell (bass) and Alan Sandow (drums) Tony Leigh replaced James in early 1981. Group originally known as **Sherbet**.

DEBUT	PEAK	WKS	Gold	A-side (Chart Hit)...B-side	$	Sym	Label & Number
8/21/76	61	8		1 **Howzat** *[SHERBET]* ...*Motor Of Love*	$5		MCA 40610
3/7/81	61	7		2 **I Have The Skill** ...*Into The Heat*	$4		Atco 7325

SHERIDAN, Tony — see BEATLES, The

SHERIFF ROK/LP '89

Pop-rock group from Toronto, Ontario, Canada: Freddy Curci (vocals), Steve DeMarchi (guitar), Arnold Lanni (keyboards), Wolf Hassel (bass) and Rob Elliott (drums). Disbanded in 1983. Hassel and Lanni formed **Frozen Ghost**. Curci and DeMarchi formed **Alias**.

DEBUT	PEAK	WKS	Gold	A-side (Chart Hit)...B-side	$	Sym	Label & Number
5/14/83	61	7		1 **When I'm With You** ...*Crazy Without You*	$5	■	Capitol 5199
11/26/88+	❶[1]	21	●	2 **When I'm With You** ...AC[1] S:❶[1] / A:❶[1] *Give Me Rock 'N' Roll* above 2 are the same version	$3		Capitol 44302

SHERM '01

Born Sherman Redd in San Francisco, California. Male rapper.

DEBUT	PEAK	WKS	Gold	A-side (Chart Hit)...B-side	$	Sym	Label & Number
10/27/01	14[S]	9		**Get Mo** ...*(2 versions) / Fryed Ryde* (w/Daz Dillinger, Tex Mex) **SHERM (feat. Bigga Figgas)**	$8	★	Dean's List 001

SHERMAN, Allan BUB/LP '63

Born Allan Copelon on 11/30/24 in Chicago, Illinois. Died on 11/21/73 (age 48). Novelty singer/songwriter. Creator/producer of TV's *I've Got A Secret*. Began recording career in 1962 with 3 consecutive #1 comedy albums.

DEBUT	PEAK	WKS	Gold	A-side (Chart Hit)...B-side	$	Sym	Label & Number
8/3/63	2[3]	10		1 **Hello Mudduh, Hello Fadduh! (A Letter From Camp)** *Here's To The Crabgrass* [C-L] melody adapted from Ponchielli's *Dance Of The Hours*; **Lou Busch** (orch.); also released with "Rat Fink" as the B-side	$15	■	Warner 5378
12/21/63	5[X]	2		2 **The Twelve Gifts Of Christmas** ...*You Went The Wrong Way, Old King Louie* [X-C-L] comical version of "The Twelve Days Of Christmas"	$20		Warner 5406
7/25/64	59	6		3 **Hello Mudduh, Hello Fadduh! (A Letter From Camp) (New 1964 Version)** ...*(original version)* [C-L] sequel (with the same melody as #1 above); recorded on the Johnny Carson *Tonight Show* on 5/27/64	$12	■	Warner 5449
3/27/65	40	8		4 **Crazy Downtown** ...*The Drop-Outs March* [C-L] parody of **Petula Clark**'s "Downtown"	$10		Warner 5614
12/18/65	98	1		5 **The Drinking Man's Diet** ...*The Laarge Daark Aardvark Song* [C-L] James Joyce Singers (backing vocals)	$10		Warner 5672

SHERMAN, Bobby BUB/AC/LP '70

★531★

Born on 7/22/43 in Santa Monica, California. Teen idol singer/actor. Regular on TV's *Shindig*; played "Jeremy Bolt" on TV's *Here Come The Brides*. First recorded for Starcrest in 1962. Currently involved in TV production.

1)Little Woman 2)Julie, Do Ya Love Me 3)Easy Come, Easy Go

DEBUT	PEAK	WKS	Gold	A-side (Chart Hit)...B-side	$	Sym	Label & Number
8/23/69	3	13	●	1 **Little Woman** *One Too Many Mornings*	$5	■	Metromedia 121
11/22/69+	9	11	●	2 **La La La (If I Had You)** ...*Time*	$5	■	Metromedia 150
2/7/70	9	14	●	3 **Easy Come, Easy Go** ...*Sounds Along The Way* also released with "July Seventeen" as the B-side	$5	■	Metromedia 177
5/16/70	24	9		4 **Hey, Mister Sun** ...*Two Blind Minds*	$5	■	Metromedia 188
8/1/70	5	15	●	5 **Julie, Do Ya Love Me** ...*Spend Some Time Lovin' Me*	$5	■	Metromedia 194
2/13/71	16	9		6 **Cried Like A Baby** ...*Is Anybody There*	$5	■	Metromedia 206
5/1/71	29	8		7 **The Drum** ...*Free Now To Roam*	$5	■	Metromedia 217
8/21/71	54	5		8 **Waiting At The Bus Stop** ...*Run Away*	$5	■	Metromedia 222
10/16/71	60	7		9 **Jennifer** ...*Getting Together*	$5	■	Metromedia 227
2/19/72	91	2		10 **Together Again** ...*Picture A Little Girl*	$5	■	Metromedia 240

SHERMAN, Joe, his Orchestra and Chorus AC '63

Born on 9/25/26 in Manhattan, New York. Prolific producer/conductor.

DEBUT	PEAK	WKS	Gold	A-side (Chart Hit)...B-side	$	Sym	Label & Number
10/5/63	85	2		**Toys In The Attic** ...*Too Much Heartache* title song from the movie starring **Dean Martin** and Geraldine Page	$10		World Artists 1008

SHERRYS, The BUB '62

R&B "girl group" from Philadelphia, Pennsylvania. Formed by Joe Cook, included his daughters Dinell (lead) and Delphine, with Charlotte Butler and Delores "Honey" Wylie. Cook had own hit in 1957, "Peanuts," as **Little Joe & The Thrillers**.

DEBUT	PEAK	WKS	Gold	A-side (Chart Hit)...B-side	$	Sym	Label & Number
10/6/62	35	8		1 **Pop Pop Pop - Pie** ...*Your Hand In Mine*	$20		Guyden 2068
1/12/63	97	1		2 **Slop Time** ...*Let's Stomp Again*	$20		Guyden 2077

SHERWOOD, Roberta '56

Born on 7/1/13 in Long Island, New York. Died of heart failure on 7/5/99 (age 86). Jazz-styled singer.

DEBUT	PEAK	WKS	Gold	A-side (Chart Hit)...B-side	$	Sym	Label & Number
6/9/56	57	4		**Lazy River** ...T:57 *This Train* **Jack Pleis** (orch.); #19 hit for Hoagy Carmichael in 1932	$12		Decca 29911

DEBUT	PEAK	WKS	Gold	A-side (Chart Hit)..........B-side	$	Sym	Label & Number

SHIELDS, The '58

R&B group formed by Los Angeles producer George Motola solely to record "You Cheated." Frankie Ervin (lead), **Jesse Belvin** (falsetto), **Johnny "Guitar" Watson**, Mel Williams and Buster Williams.

DEBUT	PEAK	WKS	Gold	A-side (Chart Hit)..........B-side	$	Sym	Label & Number
8/25/58	12	16		**You Cheated** ....S:12 / H:15 *That's The Way It's Gonna Be* first released on Tender 513 in 1958 ($125)	$25		Dot 15805

SHINAS, Sofia '92

Born in Windsor, Ontario, Canada. Pop-dance singer/songwriter/actress. Appeared in the movies *The Crow*, *Terminal Velocity* and *Hourglass*.

DEBUT	PEAK	WKS	Gold	A-side (Chart Hit)..........B-side	$	Sym	Label & Number
10/3/92	75	7		**The Message** ....A:54 *Let's Go All The Way*	$3	■	Warner 18807

SHINDOGS, The '66

Rock and roll house band for the ABC-TV show *Shindig*: Delaney Bramlett, Joey Cooper, Chuck Blackwell and James Burton. Bramlett later formed **Delaney & Bonnie**.

DEBUT	PEAK	WKS	Gold	A-side (Chart Hit)..........B-side	$	Sym	Label & Number
9/3/66	91	1		**Who Do You Think You Are** ....*Yes, I'm Going Home* produced by **Leon Russell**	$12		Viva 601

SHIRELLES, The ★153★ BUB/LP '61

R&B-pop "girl group" from Passaic, New Jersey: Shirley (Owens) Alston (born on 6/10/41), Beverly Lee (born on 8/3/41), Doris (Coley) Kenner (born on 8/2/41) and Addie "Micki" Harris (born on 1/22/40). Formed in junior high school as the Poquellos. High school classmates of **Joey Dee**. First recorded for Tiara in 1958. Kenner left group in 1968; returned in 1975. Alston left for solo career in 1975, recorded as Lady Rose. Harris died on 6/10/82 (age 42). Kenner died of cancer on 2/4/2000 (age 58). Group inducted into the Rock and Roll Hall of Fame in 1996. The most successful "girl group" of the rock and roll era.

1)Soldier Boy 2)Will You Love Me Tomorrow 3)Dedicated To The One I Love 4)Mama Said 5)Foolish Little Girl

DEBUT	PEAK	WKS	Gold	A-side (Chart Hit)..........B-side	$	Sym	Label & Number
4/21/58	49	10		1 **I Met Him On A Sunday (Ronde-Ronde)**..........S:49 / T:50 *I Want You To Be My Boyfriend* originally released on Tiara 6112 in 1958 ($400)	$25		Decca 30588
7/13/59	83	4		2 **Dedicated To The One I Love** ....*Look A Here Baby* also see #5 below	$20		Scepter 1203
9/12/60	39	12		3 **Tonights The Night** ....*The Dance Is Over*	$20		Scepter 1208
11/21/60+	1[2]	19		4 **Will You Love Me Tomorrow** ....*Boys* first released on Scepter 1211 as simply "Tomorrow" ($25); B-side recorded by **The Beatles** in 1963	$25		Scepter 1211
1/23/61	3	16		5 **Dedicated To The One I Love** ....*Look A Here Baby* [R] same version as #2 above	$20		Scepter 1203
4/17/61	4	11		6 **Mama Said** ....*Blue Holiday*	$20		Scepter 1217
7/10/61	41	8		7 **A Thing Of The Past** /			
7/17/61	54	6		8 **What A Sweet Thing That Was**	$20		Scepter 1220
10/2/61	21	9		9 **Big John** ....*Twenty-One*	$20		Scepter 1223
12/18/61+	8	14		10 **Baby It's You**..........*The Things I Want To Hear (Pretty Words)* (#107)	$20		Scepter 1227
3/24/62	1[3]	14	●	11 **Soldier Boy** *Love Is A Swingin' Thing* (#109)	$20		Scepter 1228
6/23/62	22	8		12 **Welcome Home Baby** ....*Mama, Here Comes The Bride* (#104)	$15		Scepter 1234
9/8/62	36	8		13 **Stop The Music**..........*It's Love That Really Counts* (#102)	$15		Scepter 1237
12/1/62+	19	12		14 **Everybody Loves A Lover** ....*I Don't Think So*	$15		Scepter 1243
3/23/63	4	14		15 **Foolish Little Girl** /			
4/13/63	100	1		16 **Not For All The Money In The World**..........	$15	■	Scepter 1248
6/15/63	26	9		17 **Don't Say Goodnight And Mean Goodbye**..........*I Didn't Mean To Hurt You*	$12	■	Scepter 1255
9/7/63	53	6		18 **What Does A Girl Do?**..........*Don't Let It Happen To Us*	$12		Scepter 1259
10/19/63	92	2		19 **It's A Mad, Mad, Mad, Mad World** /			
11/2/63	97	1		20 **31 Flavors**.......... above 2 from the movie *It's A Mad, Mad, Mad, Mad World* starring Spencer Tracy with an all-star cast	$12		Scepter 1260
1/11/64	57	5		21 **Tonight You're Gonna Fall In Love With Me**..........*20th Century Rock N' Roll*	$12		Scepter 1264
3/21/64	69	4		22 **Sha-La-La** ....*His Lips Get In The Way*	$12		Scepter 1267
7/18/64	63	7		23 **Thank You Baby** ....*Dooms Day* #2-12, 14, 16 & 21-23: produced by Luther Dixon	$12		Scepter 1278
10/31/64	88	2		24 **Maybe Tonight**..........*Lost Love* (#125)	$12		Scepter 1284
12/26/64+	91	4		25 **Are You Still My Baby**..........*I Saw A Tear* written by **Charlie Rich**	$12		Scepter 1292
8/19/67	99	2		26 **Last Minute Miracle**..........*No Doubt About It*	$12		Scepter 12198

SHIRLEY, Don BUB/LP '61

Born on 1/27/27 in Kingston, Jamaica. Black pop-jazz-classical pianist/organist.

DEBUT	PEAK	WKS	Gold	A-side (Chart Hit)..........B-side	$	Sym	Label & Number
7/17/61	40	14		1 **Water Boy** *[DON SHIRLEY TRIO]*..........*Freedom (I'm On My Way)* [I] late 19th century prison work song	$12		Cadence 1392
1/6/62	100	1		2 **Drown In My Own Tears** ....*Lonesome Road* (#116) [I] #1 R&B hit for **Ray Charles** in 1956	$10		Cadence 1408

SHIRLEY (AND COMPANY) R&B/LP '75

Disco group: Shirley Goodman (female vocals), Jesus Alvarez (male vocals), Walter Morris (guitar), Bernadette Randle (keyboards), Seldon Powell (sax), Jonathan Williams (bass) and Clarence Oliver (drums). Goodman was half of **Shirley & Lee** duo.

DEBUT	PEAK	WKS	Gold	A-side (Chart Hit)..........B-side	$	Sym	Label & Number
1/11/75	12	16		1 **Shame, Shame, Shame** ....RB[1] *(instrumental)* #1 Dance Club Play hit for 4 weeks	$5		Vibration 532
6/14/75	91	2		2 **Cry Cry Cry**..........*(instrumental)* above 2 written and produced by **Sylvia** Robinson (**Mickey & Sylvia**)	$5		Vibration 535

SHIRLEY & LEE R&B '56

R&B duo from New Orleans, Louisiana: Shirley Goodman (born on 6/19/36) and Leonard Lee (born on 6/29/36; died on 10/23/76, age 40). First recorded for Aladdin in 1952. Billed as The Sweethearts Of The Blues; recorded together until 1963. Also see **Shirley (And Company)**.

DEBUT	PEAK	WKS	Gold	A-side (Chart Hit)..........B-side	$	Sym	Label & Number
8/11/56	20	19		1 **Let The Good Times Roll** RB[3] S:20 / T:27 *Do You Mean To Hurt Me So* also see #4 below	$50		Aladdin 3325

DEBUT	PEAK	WKS	Gold	A-side (Chart Hit)...B-side	$	Sym	Label & Number
				SHIRLEY & LEE — Cont'd			
12/15/56+	38	8		2 **I Feel Good** ...T:38 *Now That It's Over*	$30		Aladdin 3338
				different song than their 1955 R&B hit "Feel So Good"			
6/27/60	88	6		3 **I've Been Loved Before**...*Like You Used To Do*	$15		Warwick 535
9/5/60	48	5		4 **Let The Good Times Roll** ...*Keep Loving Me* [R]	$15		Warwick 581
				new version of #1 above			
8/7/61	77	6		5 **Well-A, Well-A** ...*Our Kids*	$15		Warwick 664
				SHIRLEY & SQUIRRELY '76			
				Novelty studio production featuring squirrels instead of chipmunks. Conceived by Bob Milsap. Also see **The Nutty Squirrels**.			
7/17/76	48	9		**Hey Shirley (This Is Squirrely)**...*(instrumental)* [N]	$6	■	GRT 054
				SHOCKED, Michelle ROK/LP '89			
				Born Michelle Johnston on 2/24/62 in Dallas, Texas. Folk singer/songwriter.			
12/10/88+	66	8		**Anchorage** ...*(live video version)*	$4	■	Mercury 870611
				SHOCKING BLUE, The BUB/LP '70			
				Rock group from The Hague, Holland: Mariska Veres (vocals), Robbie Leeuwen (guitar), Klaasje Wal (bass) and Cor Beek (drums). Beek died on 4/2/98 (age 49).			
12/13/69+	❶[1]	14	●	1 **Venus** ...*Hot Sand*	$10	■	Colossus 108
3/7/70	43	7		2 **Mighty Joe** ...*I'm A Woman*	$8	■	Colossus 111
6/6/70	75	5		3 **Long And Lonesome Road** ...*Acka Ragh*	$8		Colossus 116
				SHOES LP '79			
				Rock group from Zion, Illinois: Gary Klebe (vocals), brothers Jeff (guitar) and John (bass) Murphy, and Skip Meyer (drums).			
11/3/79	75	5		**Too Late**...*Now And Then*	$4	■	Elektra 46557
				SHONDELL, Troy C&W/BUB '61			
				Born Gary Schelton on 5/14/39 in Fort Wayne, Indiana. Pop-country singer/songwriter.			
9/18/61	6	13		1 **This Time** ...*Girl After Girl*	$20		Liberty 55353
				first released on Goldcrest 161 in 1961 ($25)			
12/25/61+	77	6		2 **Tears From An Angel** /			
				co-written by **Jackie DeShannon**			
1/13/62	92	1		3 **Island In The Sky** ...	$15		Liberty 55398
				SHOOTING STAR ROK/LP '89			
				Rock group from Kansas City, Missouri: Gary West (vocals), Van McLain (guitar, vocals), Bill Guffey (keyboards), Charles Waltz (violin), Ron Verlin (bass) and Steve Thomas (drums).			
4/12/80	76	4		1 **You've Got What I Need** ...*Wild In The Streets*	$5	■	Virgin 67005
3/27/82	70	5		2 **Hollywood**...*Hang On For Your Life* (ROK #52)	$4		Epic/Virgin 02755
11/4/89	67	9		3 **Touch Me Tonight**...*Never Give Up*	$3	▮	Enigma 75054
				SHORE, Dinah MEM/POP/BUB '46			
				Born Frances Rose Shore on 3/1/17 in Winchester, Tennessee. Died of cancer on 2/24/94 (age 76). One of the most popular female vocalists of the 1940s. Charted 62 hits, 1940-54, including four #1s: " I'll Walk Alone," "The Gypsy," "Anniversary Song" and "Buttons And Bows." Sang with Xavier Cugat 1939-40. Hostess of the 15-minute, award-winning early evening TV variety *The Dinah Shore Show* from 1951-57; then hosted the very popular *Dinah Shore Chevy Show* from 1956-63. Own morning talk show *Dinah's Place*, 1970-80. Married to actor George Montgomery from 1943-62.			
5/14/55	12	3		1 **Whatever Lola Wants (Lola Gets)** A:12 / S:28 *Church Twice On Sunday*	$12	□	RCA Victor 6077
				from the Broadway musical *Damn Yankees* starring Gwen Verdon; picture sleeve is a "This Is Her Life" comic strip-styled sleeve			
11/12/55	20	14		2 **Love And Marriage**...A:20 / T:42 *Compare*	$12		RCA Victor 6266
				from the TV production *Our Town* starring **Frank Sinatra**			
2/11/56	73	1		3 **Stolen Love** ...T:73 *That's All There Is To That*	$10		RCA Victor 6360
4/28/56	93	5		4 **I Could Have Danced All Night**...T:93 *What A Heavenly Night*	$10		RCA Victor 6469
				The Skylarks (backing vocals); from the Broadway musical *My Fair Lady* starring **Julie Andrews**; **Henri René** (orch.: #1, 2 & 4)			
2/9/57	19	21		5 **Chantez-Chantez (Shan-Tay, "Sing")** ...A:19 / T:27 *Honky Tonk Heart*	$10		RCA Victor 6792
6/17/57	92	1		6 **The Cattle Call** ...T:92 *Promises, Promises*	$10		RCA Victor 6897
9/9/57	15	7		7 **Fascination** ...A:15 / T:98 *Till*	$10		RCA Victor 6980
				from the movie *Love In The Afternoon* starring Gary Cooper and Audrey Hepburn			
12/2/57	24	1		8 **I'll Never Say "Never Again" Again** ...A:24 *The Kiss That Rocked The World*	$10		RCA Victor 7056
				#4 hit for Ozzie Nelson in 1935; Harry Zimmerman (orch.: #3 & 5-8)			
				SHORR, Mickey, and The Cutups '62			
				Born Mickey Moses on 3/16/26 in Detroit, Michigan. Died on 2/27/88 (age 61). Detroit DJ and owner of a chain of car-stereo stores. Also see **Spencer & Spencer**.			
6/16/62	60	5		**Dr. Ben Basey**...*Roaring 20's Rag* [N]	$15		Tuba 8001
				"break-in" record; parody of TV's *Ben Casey*; co-written by **Dickie Goodman**			
				SHORROCK, Glenn — see LITTLE RIVER BAND			
				SHOT IN THE DARK '81			
				Pop-rock group: Krysia Kristianne (vocals), Adam Yurman (guitar), Bryan Savage (sax), Peter White (keyboards) and Robin Lamble (bass). Former backing band for **Al Stewart**.			
4/4/81	71	5		**Playing With Lightning** ...*Speak My Language*	$4		RSO 1061
				SHOWMEN, The BUB '62			
				R&B vocal group from Norfolk, Virginia: General Norman Johnson (**Chairmen Of The Board**), Milton Wells, brothers Gene and Dorsey Knight, and Leslie Felton.			
11/13/61+	61	12		1 **It Will Stand** ...*Country Fool*	$25		Minit 632
7/4/64	80	3		2 **It Will Stand**...*Country Fool* [R]	$15		Imperial 66033
				above 2 are the same version			
				SHOW STOPPERS, The '68			
				R&B vocal group from Philadelphia, Pennsylvania: brothers Laddie and Alec Burke (**Solomon Burke**'s brothers), and brothers Earl and Timmy Smith.			
6/1/68	87	5		**Ain't Nothin' But A House Party** ...*What Can A Man Do?*	$8		Heritage 800
				originally "Bubbled Under" (#118) on 5/27/67 on Showtime 101			

DEBUT	PEAK	WKS	Gold	A-side (Chart Hit).....B-side	$	Sym	Label & Number
				SHYHEIM R&B/LP **'94**			
				Born Shyheim Franklin in 1980 in Brooklyn, New York. Teen male rapper.			
3/5/94	89	6		**On And On** *[SHYHEIM aka The Rugged Child]*.....*(2 versions) / The B Side*	$3	▮	Virgin 38415
				SHYNE R&B/LP **'00**			
				Born Jamal Barrow in 1978 in Brooklyn, New York. Male rapper. Sentenced to ten years in prison on 6/1/01 for a shooting incident on 12/27/99.			
9/9/00	57	15		**Bad Boyz**.....A:54 / S:74 *(2 versions)*	$6	T	Bad Boy 79324
				SHYNE Featuring Barrington Levy			
				samples "Nightclubbing" by **Grace Jones**			
				SICILIANS, The **'02**			
				Electronica group.			
12/7/02	15^{S}	11		**L'Italiano**.....*(3 remixes)* [F]	$10	★*	Nervous 20527
				THE SICILIANS Featuring Angelo Venuto			
				SIDEKICKS, The BUB **'66**			
				Pop group from Wildwood, New Jersey: brothers Zack (vocals) and Randy (bass) Bocelle, with Mike Burke (guitar) and Jon Spirt (drums; **The Ran-Dells**).			
8/6/66	55	9		**Suspicions**.....*Up On The Roof*	$10		RCA Victor 8864
				SIERRA, Crystal **'00**			
				Born in the Bronx, New York (of Colombian parents). Latin pop-rap singer.			
11/4/00	52^{S}	7		**Playa No More**.....*(3 versions)*	$4	★	Virgin 38735
				SIGEL, Beanie R&B/LP **'02**			
				Born Dwight Grant on 3/6/74 in Philadelphia, Pennsylvania. Male rapper.			
1/15/00	65	9		1 **Do It Again (Put Ya Hands Up)**.....A:55 / S:68 *(2 versions) / So Ghetto*	$6	T	Roc-A-Fella 562575
				JAY-Z Featuring Beanie Sigel & Amil			
2/3/01	86	14		2 **Change The Game**.....S:68 *(2 versions) / You, Me, Him And Her* (Dynasty)	$6	T	Roc-A-Fella 572761
				JAY-Z, BEANIE SIGEL and MEMPHIS BLEEK			
2/23/02	55	19		3 **Roc The Mic**.....A:52			album cut
				BEANIE SIGEL & FREEWAY			
				from the movie *State Property* starring Sigel (soundtrack on Roc-A-Fella 586671); also see the B-side of **Freeway**'s "Line 'Em Up"			
5/18/02	79	8		4 **Guess Who's Back**.....S:21 *(2 versions) / My Block* (R&B #46)	$6	T	Def Jam 582865
				SCARFACE (featuring Jay-Z & Beanie Sigel)			
				samples "Sunrise" by **The Originals**			
				SIGLER, Bunny R&B/BUB/LP **'67**			
				Born Walter Sigler on 3/27/41 in Philadelphia, Pennsylvania. R&B-dance singer/songwriter.			
6/24/67	22	11		1 **Let The Good Times Roll & Feel So Good** *There's No Love Left (In This Old Heart of Mine)*	$12		Parkway 153
				medley of 2 **Shirley & Lee** R&B hits			
10/14/67	86	4		2 **Lovey Dovey/You're So Fine**.....*Sunny Sunday*	$10	■	Parkway 6000
				medley of #2 R&B hits: **The Clovers** (1954) and **The Falcons** (1959)			
2/10/73	97	2		3 **Tossin' And Turnin'**.....*Picture Us*	$8		Philadelphia I. 3523
2/25/78	43	11		4 **Let Me Party With You (Part 1) (Party, Party, Party)**.....*(Part 2)*	$5		Gold Mind 4008
11/4/78	87	5		5 **Only You**.....*Good Good Feeling*	$5		Gold Mind 4012
				LOLEATTA HOLLOWAY AND BUNNY SIGLER			
				SILENCERS, The **'80**			
				Rock group from Pittsburgh, Pennsylvania: Frank Czuri (vocals; **Diamond Reo**), Warren King (guitar), Dennis Takos (keyboards), Michael Pella (bass) and Ronnie Foster (drums).			
7/26/80	81	5		**Shiver And Shake**.....*Illegal*	$5		Precision 9800
				SILENCERS, The ROK/LP **'87**			
				Pop-rock group from Scotland: Jimmie O'Neill (vocals, guitar), Cha Burns (guitar), Joe Donnelly (bass) and Martin Hanlin (drums).			
8/8/87	82	6		**Painted Moon**.....*Here Comes The Train*	$4		RCA 5220
				SILHOUETTES, The **'58**			
				R&B vocal group from Philadelphia, Pennsylvania: William Horton (lead), Richard Lewis (tenor), Earl Beal (baritone) and Raymond Edwards (bass). Horton died on 1/23/95 (age 65). Edwards died of cancer on 3/4/97 (age 74). Beal died on 3/22/2001 (age 76).			
1/20/58	❶ (2)	15	●	**Get A Job**.....RB(6) T:❶(2) / S:2 / A:3 *I Am Lonely*	$40		Ember 1029
				first released on Junior 391 (brown label) in 1957 ($800)			
				SILK R&B/BUB/LP **'93**			
				R&B vocal group from Atlanta, Georgia: Tim Cameron, Jim Gates, John Rasboro, Gary Jenkins and Gary Glenn.			
2/6/93	86	5		1 **Happy Days**.....S:40 *(album version)*	$3	▮V	Keia/Elektra 64701
2/20/93	❶ (2)	24	▲	2 **Freak Me** RB(8) A:❶(3) / S:❶(2) *(2 remixes)*	$3	▮V	Keia/Elektra 64654
				"45" issued for above 2 on Keia/Elektra 64654			
6/19/93	26	20		3 **Girl U For Me** / S:30 / A:38			
7/10/93		17		4 **Lose Control**.....A:48	$3	▮	Keia/Elektra 64643
				above 4 co-written and co-produced by **Keith Sweat** and from the album *Lose Control*			
11/12/94	71	15		5 **I Can Go Deep**.....S:51 *(Low Down remix) / Birthday Girl* (**Hi-Five**)	$3	▮	Hollywood 42264
				from the movie *A Low Down Dirty Shame* starring Keenan Ivory Wayans			
11/4/95	54	18		6 **Hooked On You**.....S:37 *(extended version)*	$3	▮	Keia/Elektra 64359
5/4/96	91	3		7 **Don't Rush**.....*Yes*	$3	▮	Elektra 64324
3/13/99	13	20	●	8 **If You (Lovin' Me)**.....S:7 / A:42 *(remix)*	$4	★	Elektra 64072
8/21/99	62	13		9 **Meeting In My Bedroom**.....A:53			album cut
				above 2 from the album *Tonight* on Elektra 62234			
				SILKIE, The BUB **'65**			
				Folk group formed in Hull, England: Silvia Tatler (vocals), Ivor Aylesbury and Mike Ramsden (guitars), and Kevin Cunningham (bass).			
10/16/65	10	10		**You've Got To Hide Your Love Away**.....*City Winds*	$15		Fontana 1525
				The Beatles contributed musical accompaniment and production assistance; song is from **The Beatles**' movie *Help!*			

DEBUT	PEAK	WKS	Gold	A-side (Chart Hit)..B-side	$	Sym	Label & Number
	★549★			**SILKK THE SHOCKER** R&B/BUB/LP **'99**			
				Born Zyshonne Miller on 2/22/80 in New Orleans, Louisiana. Male rapper. Brother of **Master P** and C-Murder. Member of the group **Tru**.			
9/6/97	25	20	●	1 **I Miss My Homies** ....S:15 *(2 versions) / Here We Go* (w/**Mystikal** & Fiend)	$3	▮	No Limit 53290
				MASTER P Featuring Pimp C, The Shocker, Mo B. Dick, O'Dell, Sons of Funk and Mercedes			
10/25/97	97	2		2 **Pushin' Inside You** ....*(2 versions) / How Ya Do Dat* (w/Young Bleed & C-Loc - R&B #29)	$4	▮	No Limit 53284
				SONS OF FUNK Featuring Master P, The Shocker, Young Bleed & C-Loc			
				from the movie *I'm Bout It* starring **Master P**			
1/31/98	16	27	▲	3 **Make Em' Say Uhh!** ..S:9 *(2 versions) / Weed And Hennesey* (w/C-Murder & **Silkk The Shocker**)	$3	▮	No Limit 53302
				MASTER P Featuring Fiend, Silkk (The Shocker), Mia X and Mystikal			
				clean version available on No Limit 53303			
3/7/98	2^{2}	21	▲	4 **Let's Ride** ....RB^{3} S:❶^{1} / A:55 *(instrumental)*	$3	▮	Def Jam 568475
				MONTELL JORDAN Featuring Master P & Silkk "The Shocker"			
3/21/98	57	16		5 **Just Be Straight With Me** ....S:40 *(instrumental)*	$5	▮	No Limit 53305
				SILKK the SHOCKER Featuring Master P, Destiny's Child, O'Dell, Mo B. Dick			
				rap version with new lyrics of "Just Be Good To Me" by **The S.O.S. Band**; clean version available on No Limit 53313			
8/8/98	34	20		6 **Movin' On** ....A:38 *(3 versions)*	$6	T	University 95032
				MÝA featuring Silkk the Shocker			
8/15/98	27	16		7 **Goodbye To My Homies** ....S:17 *(2 versions) / Homie Ride* (w/C-Murder)	$3	▮	No Limit 53326
				MASTER P Featuring Silkk the Shocker, Sons of Funk and Mo B. Dick			
				samples "It's So Hard To Say Goodbye To Yesterday" by **Boyz II Men**; clean version available on No Limit 53451			
3/6/99	18	18		8 **It Ain't My Fault 2** S:8 *Somebody Like Me* (w/**Mýa** - R&B #43)	$4	★	No Limit 53470
				SILKK THE SHOCKER And Mystikal			
				Billboard combined the Airplay points of above title with Silkk The Shocker's original solo version of "It Ain't My Fault" (R&B #20^{A}); clean version available on No Limit 53471			
9/23/00	20^{S}	28		9 **He Did That** ....*(3 versions)*	$4	★	No Limit 38736
				SILKK THE SHOCKER feat. Master P and Mac			
				SILVA-TONES, The **'57**			
				Rock and roll band from Ayer, Massachusetts. Led by Bob Silva.			
12/16/57	86	2		**That's All I Want From You** ....T:86 *Roses Are Blooming*	$40		Argo 5281
				first released on Monarch 615 in 1957 ($60)			
				SILVER LP **'76**			
				Pop-rock group formed in Los Angeles, California: John Batdorf (vocals, guitar; **Batdorf & Rodney**), Greg Collier (guitar), Brent Mydland (keyboards), Tom Leadon (bass) and Harry Stinson (drums). Mydland later joined the **Grateful Dead**; died of a drug overdose on 7/26/90 (age 37).			
6/19/76	16	21		**Wham Bam** ....*Right On Time*	$5		Arista 0189
				first pressings listed title as "Wham Bam Shang-A-Lang"			
				SILVERADO **'81**			
				Pop-rock musician/songwriting team from Connecticut: Carl Shillo and Buzz Goodwin.			
7/4/81	92	3		**Ready For Love** ....*Slow Down*	$5		Pavillion 02077
				SILVERCHAIR ROK/LP **'95**			
				Rock trio from Newcastle, Australia: Daniel Johns (vocals, guitar), Chris Joannou (bass) and Ben Gillies (drums).			
7/22/95	28^{A}	18		1 **Tomorrow** ....AR^{3} / MR^{3}			album cut
12/16/95	72^{A}	1		2 **Pure Massacre**			album cut
				above 2 from the album *Frogstomp* on Epic 67247			
1/25/97	44^{A}	11		3 **Abuse Me**			album cut
				from the album *Freak Show* on Epic 67905			
				SILVER CONDOR ROK/LP **'81**			
				Rock group from New York: Joe Cerisano (vocals), Earl Slick (guitar), John Corey (keyboards), Jay Davis (bass) and Claude Pepper (drums). Slick joined Phantom, Rocker & Slick in 1985.			
7/25/81	32	13		**You Could Take My Heart Away** ....*Goin' For Broke*	$4	■	Columbia 02268
				SILVER CONVENTION BUB/R&B/LP **'75**			
				Disco studio group from Germany assembled by producer Michael Kunze and writer/arranger Silvester Levay. Female vocal trio formed later in 1976 consisting of **Penny McLean**, Ramona Wolf and Linda Thompson.			
10/11/75	❶^{3}	17	●	1 **Fly, Robin, Fly** ....RB^{1} *Tiger Baby* [I]	$5		Midland Int'l. 10339
3/13/76	2^{3}	21	●	2 **Get Up And Boogie (That's Right)** ....*Son Of A Gun*	$5	■	Midland Int'l. 10571
				issued with times of 4:05 or 2:45			
8/7/76	60	6		3 **No, No, Joe** ....*Another Girl*	$5		Midland Int'l. 10723
				SILVERSPOON, Dooley **'75**			
				Black disco singer. Recorded as Little Dooley on Philadelphia's North Bay label.			
2/15/75	80	6		**Bump Me Baby Part 1** ....*Part 2*	$7		Cotton 636
				SILVETTI **'77**			
				Born Bebu Silvetti in 1944 in Argentina. Died on 7/5/2003 (age 59). Disco producer.			
1/22/77	39	15		**Spring Rain** ....*Travel Check* [I]	$5		Salsoul 2014
				SIMEONE, Harry, Chorale BUB/AC/LP **'58**			
				Born on 5/9/11 in Newark, New Jersey. Arranger/conductor for movies and TV shows. Began career as staff music arranger for CBS radio, followed by 14 years as an arranger for Fred Waring.			
12/22/58	13	9	●	1 **The Little Drummer Boy** *Die Lorelei* (The Voices Of The Junior Chorale) [X]	$7	■	20th Fox 121
				original 1958 picture sleeve is different from the '59-'62 sleeves			
12/14/59	15	7		2 **The Little Drummer Boy** ....*Die Lorelei* [X-R]	$7	■	20th Fox 121
12/12/60	24	4		3 **The Little Drummer Boy** ....*Die Lorelei* [X-R]	$7	■	20th Fox 121
12/11/61	22	4		4 **The Little Drummer Boy** ....*Die Lorelei* [X-R]	$7	■	20th Fox 121
12/8/62	28	4		5 **The Little Drummer Boy** ....X:❶^{10} *Die Lorelei* [X-R]	$7	■	20th Fox 121
				Christmas charts: [#1^{10}-35 weeks] 2/'63; 1/'64; 1/'65; 1/'66 (1963-66: reissue on 20th Century-Fox 429 with a picture sleeve); 2/'67 1/'68; 2/'69; 3/'70 (1967-70: reissue on 20th Century-Fox 6429); 9/'72; 20/'73 (1972-73: 1965 remake on Kapp Winners Circle 86); 10/'83 (1983: Kapp reissue on MCA 65030)			
12/26/64	9^{X}	2		6 **O' Bambino (One Cold And Blessed Winter)** ....*Sing Of A Merry Christmas* [X]	$7	■	Kapp 628
				X: 9/'64; 24/'65; "Bubbled Under" (#105) in 1965			

DEBUT	PEAK	WKS	Gold	A-side (Chart Hit)	B-side	$	Sym	Label & Number

SIMMONS, Gene

C&W/LP **'64**

Born in 1933 in Tupelo, Mississippi. Pop-rock and roll-country singer/songwriter. First recorded for Sun in 1958.

DEBUT	PEAK	WKS	Gold	A-side (Chart Hit)	B-side	$	Sym	Label & Number
8/8/64	11	11		1 **Haunted House**	*Hey, Hey Little Girl* [N]	$15		Hi 2076
11/7/64	83	3		2 **The Dodo** *[JUMPIN' GENE SIMMONS]*	*The Jump* [N]	$12		Hi 2080

SIMMONS, Gene — see KISS

SIMMONS, Patrick — see DOOBIE BROTHERS, The

SIMON, Carly ★129★

AC/BUB/LP **'73**

Born on 6/25/45 in Manhattan, New York. Pop singer/songwriter. Father is co-founder of Simon & Schuster publishing. In folk duo with sister Lucy (born on 5/5/40) as **The Simon Sisters** (see #1 below). Won the 1971 Best New Artist Grammy Award. Married to **James Taylor** from 1972-83. Also see **James Taylor**'s "Shower The People."

1)You're So Vain 2)Nobody Does It Better 3)Mockingbird 4)You Belong To Me 5)That's The Way I've Always Heard It Should Be

DEBUT	PEAK	WKS	Gold	A-side (Chart Hit)	B-side	$	Sym	Label & Number
4/25/64	73	6		1 **Winkin', Blinkin' And Nod** **THE SIMON SISTERS** lyrics are from a favorite children's poem by Eugene Field	*So Glad I'm Here*	$12		Kapp 586
4/17/71	10	17		2 **That's The Way I've Always Heard It Should Be**	*Alone*	$6		Elektra 45724
12/11/71+	13	13		3 **Anticipation**	*The Garden*	$6		Elektra 45759
3/25/72	50	10		4 **Legend In Your Own Time**	*Julie Through The Glass*	$6		Elektra 45774
12/2/72+	1^3	17	●	5 **You're So Vain** AC^2 **Mick Jagger** (backing vocal); also see #25 below	*His Friends Are More Than Fond Of Robin*	$6		Elektra 45824
3/31/73	17	13		6 **The Right Thing To Do**	*We Have No Secrets*	$6		Elektra 45843
2/2/74	5	16	●	7 **Mockingbird** **CARLY SIMON & JAMES TAYLOR** adapted from the same traditional folk lyrics as was the song "Bo Diddley"	*Grownup* (Simon)	$6		Elektra 45880
5/11/74	14	12		8 **Haven't Got Time For The Pain**	*Mind On My Man*	$6		Elektra 45887
5/10/75	21	8		9 **Attitude Dancing** **Carole King** (backing vocal)	*Are You Ticklish*	$6		Elektra 45246
7/26/75	78	3		10 **Waterfall** **James Taylor** (backing vocal)	*After The Storm*	$5		Elektra 45263
10/18/75	94	2		11 **More And More**	*Love Out In The Street*	$5		Elektra 45278
6/19/76	46	8		12 **It Keeps You Runnin'** **The Doobie Brothers** (backing vocals)	*Look Me In The Eyes*	$5		Elektra 45323
7/23/77	2^3	25	●	13 **Nobody Does It Better** AC^7 from the James Bond movie *The Spy Who Loved Me* starring Roger Moore	*After The Storm*	$5		Elektra 45413
4/15/78	6	18		14 **You Belong To Me** **James Taylor** (backing vocal)	*In A Small Moment*	$5	■	Elektra 45477
8/19/78	36	9		15 **Devoted To You** **CARLY SIMON and JAMES TAYLOR**	*Boys In The Trees* (Simon)	$5		Elektra 45506
6/9/79	48	7		16 **Vengeance**	*Love You By Heart*	$5	■	Elektra 46051
8/2/80	11	23	●	17 **Jesse**	*Stardust*	$4	■	Warner 49518
7/17/82	74	6		18 **Why** from the movie *Soup For One* starring Saul Rubinek and Marcia Strassman	*Why* (**Chic**)	$4	■	Mirage 4051
9/24/83	83	4		19 **You Know What To Do**	*Orpheus*	$4	■	Warner 29484
6/29/85	70	5		20 **Tired Of Being Blonde**	*Black Honeymoon*	$3	■	Epic 05419
11/1/86+	18	17		21 **Coming Around Again** S:15 / A:30 from the movie *Heartburn* starring Meryl Streep and Jack Nicholson; issued with 2 different picture sleeves and a black & white promo sleeve with a foldout insert	*Itsy Bitsy Spider*	$3	■	Arista 9525
5/23/87	61	12		22 **Give Me All Night**	*Sleight Of Hand*	$3	■	Arista 9587
1/23/88	54	9		23 **All I Want Is You** **Roberta Flack** (backing vocal)	*Two Hot Girls (On A Hot Summer Night)*	$3	■	Arista 9653
3/4/89	49	10		24 **Let The River Run** S:31 theme from the movie *Working Girl* starring Melanie Griffith and Harrison Ford	*The Turn Of The Tide*	$3	■	Arista 9793
11/24/01	28	12		25 **Son Of A Gun (I Betcha Think This Song Is About You)** A:26 **JANET Featuring Missy Elliott and P. Diddy with Carly Simon** samples "You're So Vain" by Simon; all of above (except #7, 11-13, 15, 18 & 20) written or co-written by Simon	*(3 versions)*	$6	T	Virgin 46171

SIMON, Joe

★203★

R&B/BUB/LP **'72**

Born on 9/2/43 in Simmesport, Louisiana. R&B singer/songwriter. Moved to Oakland in 1959. First recorded with the vocal group the Golden Tones for Hush in 1960.

1)Get Down, Get Down (Get On The Floor) 2)Power Of Love 3)Drowning In The Sea Of Love 4)The Chokin' Kind 5)Theme From Cleopatra Jones

DEBUT	PEAK	WKS	Gold	A-side (Chart Hit)	B-side	$	Sym	Label & Number
6/18/66	66	7		1 **Teenager's Prayer**	*Long Hot Summer*	$8		Sound Stage 7 2564
2/4/67	87	5		2 **My Special Prayer**	*Travelin' Man*	$8		Sound Stage 7 2577
9/23/67	70	9		3 **Nine Pound Steel**	*The Girl's Alright With Me*	$7		Sound Stage 7 2589
1/6/68	49	7		4 **No Sad Songs**	*Come On And Get It*	$7		Sound Stage 7 2602
4/13/68	25	15		5 **(You Keep Me) Hangin' On**	*Long Hot Summer*	$7		Sound Stage 7 2608
9/28/68	75	4		6 **Message From Maria /**				
11/16/68	98	1		7 **I Worry About You**		$7		Sound Stage 7 2617
12/7/68+	70	6		8 **Looking Back**	*Standing In The Safety Zone*	$7		Sound Stage 7 2622
3/22/69	13	12	●	9 **The Chokin' Kind** RB^3	*Come On And Get It*	$7		Sound Stage 7 2628
6/21/69	72	5		10 **Baby, Don't Be Looking In My Mind**	*Don't Let Me Lose The Feeling*	$7		Sound Stage 7 2634
9/27/69	79	3		11 **San Francisco Is A Lonely Town /**				
10/18/69	87	3		12 **It's Hard To Get Along**		$7		Sound Stage 7 2641
1/3/70	54	8		13 **Moon Walk Part 1**	*Part II*	$7		Sound Stage 7 2651
4/18/70	56	8		14 **Farther On Down The Road**	*Wounded Man*	$7		Sound Stage 7 2656

DEBUT	PEAK	WKS	Gold	A-side (Chart Hit)	B-side	$	Sym	Label & Number
				SIMON, Joe — Cont'd				
8/1/70	78	7		15 **Yours Love**	*I Got A Whole Lot Of Lovin'*	$7		Sound Stage 7 2664
				#9, 10 & 15: written by country songwriter Harlan Howard				
10/31/70	93	3		16 **That's The Way I Want Our Love**	*When*	$7		Sound Stage 7 2667
12/19/70+	40	13		17 **Your Time To Cry**	*I Love You More (Than Anything)*	$6		Spring 108
5/15/71	69	4		18 **Help Me Make It Through The Night**	*To Lay Down Beside You* (#117)	$6	■	Spring 113
7/24/71	71	5		19 **You're The One For Me**	*I Ain't Givin' Up*	$6		Spring 115
9/25/71	93	2		20 **All My Hard Times**	*Georgia Blue* (R&B #19)	$6		Spring 118
				written by Joe South; all of above produced by Nashville disc jockey John Richbourg				
11/27/71+	11	13	●	21 **Drowning In The Sea Of Love**	*Let Me Be The One (The One Who Loves You)*	$6		Spring 120
3/25/72	42	8		22 **Pool Of Bad Luck**	*Glad To Be Your Lover*	$6		Spring 124
7/8/72	11	15	●	23 **Power Of Love** RB[2]	*The Mirror Don't Lie*	$6		Spring 128
10/21/72	91	5		24 **Misty Blue**	*That's The Way I Want Our Love*	$6		Sound Stage 7 1508
12/2/72	50	7		25 **Trouble In My Home /**				
11/4/72	78	5		26 **I Found My Dad**		$5		Spring 130
2/17/73	37	12		27 **Step By Step**	*Talk Don't Bother Me*	$5		Spring 133
7/28/73	18	13		28 **Theme From Cleopatra Jones**	*Who Was That Lady*	$5	■	Spring 138
				JOE SIMON featuring The Mainstreeters				
				title song from the movie starring Tamara Dobson				
11/17/73	62	7		29 **River**	*Love Never Hurt Nobody*	$5		Spring 141
				song "Bubbled Under" (#115) in 1972 by **Gene McDaniels** as Universal Jones				
4/5/75	8	17		30 **Get Down, Get Down (Get On The Floor)** RB[2]	*In My Baby's Arms*	$5		Spring 156
8/23/75	92	4		31 **Music In My Bones**	*Fire Burning*	$5		Spring 159

SIMON, Paul ★180★ AC/LP '73

Born on 10/13/41 in Newark, New Jersey; raised in Queens, New York. Singer/composer/guitarist. Met **Art Garfunkel** in high school, recorded together as **Tom & Jerry** in 1957. Recorded as **Jerry Landis** (see #2 below), **Tico And The Triumphs** (see #1 below), Paul Kane, Harrison Gregory and True Taylor in the early 1960s. To England from 1963-64. Returned to the U.S. and recorded first album with Garfunkel in 1964. Went solo in 1971. Married to actress/author Carrie Fisher from 1983-85. Married singer **Edie Brickell** on 5/30/92. In the movies *Annie Hall* and *One-Trick Pony*. Inducted into the Rock and Roll Hall of Fame in 2001.

1)50 Ways To Leave Your Lover 2)Kodachrome 3)Loves Me Like A Rock 4)Mother And Child Reunion 5)Slip Slidin' Away

DEBUT	PEAK	WKS	Gold	A-side (Chart Hit)	B-side	$	Sym	Label & Number
1/6/62	99	1		1 **Motorcycle**	*I Don't Believe Them*	$100		Amy 835
				TICO AND THE TRIUMPHS (Simon, Howie Beck and Mickey Borack)				
				first released on Madison 169 in 1961 ($200)				
1/19/63	97	3		2 **The Lone Teen Ranger**	*Lisa*	$60		Amy 875
				JERRY LANDIS				
2/5/72	4	13		3 **Mother And Child Reunion**	*Paranoia Blues*	$6		Columbia 45547
4/8/72	22	11		4 **Me And Julio Down By The Schoolyard**	*Congratulations*	$6		Columbia 45585
				"live" version by **Simon & Garfunkel** is on the B-side of their 1982 "Wake Up Little Susie" hit				
7/8/72	52	7		5 **Duncan**	*Run That Body Down*	$6		Columbia 45638
5/19/73	2[2]	14		6 **Kodachrome**	*Tenderness*	$5		Columbia 45859
8/4/73	2[1]	16	●	7 **Loves Me Like A Rock** AC[2]	*Learn How To Fall*	$5		Columbia 45907
				PAUL SIMON (with The Dixie Hummingbirds)				
12/1/73+	35	10		8 **American Tune**	*One Man's Ceiling Is Another Man's Floor*	$5	■	Columbia 45900
				based on the classical piece "O Sacred Heart" by Johann Sebastian Bach; reissued as a promo single in 1976 on Columbia 1105 with a sleeve picturing the American flag				
8/16/75	23	10		9 **Gone At Last**	*Take Me To The Mardi Gras* (Simon)	$5		Columbia 10197
				PAUL SIMON/PHOEBE SNOW and The Jessy Dixon Singers				
12/20/75+	❶[3]	17	●	10 **50 Ways To Leave Your Lover** AC[2]	*Some Folks Lives Roll Easy*	$5		Columbia 10270
				Patti Austin, **Phoebe Snow** and **Valerie Simpson** (backing vocals)				
5/1/76	40	7		11 **Still Crazy After All These Years**	*I Do It For Your Love*	$5		Columbia 10332
10/15/77+	5	20	●	12 **Slip Slidin' Away**	*Something So Right*	$5		Columbia 10630
				Oak Ridge Boys (backing vocals)				
1/21/78	17	14		13 **(What A) Wonderful World** AC[5]	*Wooden Planes* (Garfunkel)	$5		Columbia 10676
				ART GARFUNKEL with JAMES TAYLOR & PAUL SIMON				
8/9/80	6	16		14 **Late In The Evening**	*How The Heart Approaches What It Yearns*	$4	■	Warner 49511
10/25/80	40	11		15 **One-Trick Pony**	*Long, Long Day*	$4		Warner 49601
				above 2 from the movie *One-Trick Pony* starring Simon				
1/22/83	51	8		16 **The Blues**	*Same Girl* (Newman)	$4	■	Warner 29803
				RANDY NEWMAN AND PAUL SIMON				
11/5/83	44	10		17 **Allergies**	*Think Too Much*	$4	■	Warner 29453
8/9/86+	23	29		18 **You Can Call Me Al** A:20 / S:27	*Gumboots*	$3	■	Warner 28667
				originally charted for 14 weeks (#44); re-entered on 3/28/87				
12/6/86+	81	7		19 **Graceland**	*Hearts And Bones*	$3	■	Warner 28522
				The Everly Brothers (backing vocals); 1987 Grammy winner: Record of the Year				
3/7/87	86	4		20 **The Boy In The Bubble**	*Crazy Love, Vol. II*	$3	■	Warner 28460
12/15/90+	92	5		21 **The Obvious Child**	*The Rhythm Of The Saints*	$3	▮	Warner 19549
				all of above (except #13 & 16) written by Simon				

DEBUT	PEAK	WKS	Gold	A-side (Chart Hit)...B-side	$	Sym	Label & Number

SIMON & GARFUNKEL ★130★ BUB/LP '66

Folk-rock duo from New York: **Paul Simon** (born on 10/13/41) and **Art Garfunkel** (born on 11/5/41). Recorded as **Tom & Jerry** in 1957. Duo split in 1964; Simon was working solo in England; Garfunkel was in graduate school. They re-formed in 1965 and stayed together until 1971. Reunited briefly in 1981 for a national tour. Duo inducted into the Rock and Roll Hall of Fame in 1990. Won Grammy's Lifetime Achievement Award in 2003.

1)Bridge Over Troubled Water 2)Mrs. Robinson 3)The Sounds Of Silence 4)I Am A Rock 5)Cecelia

DEBUT	PEAK	WKS	Gold	A-side (Chart Hit)...B-side	$	Sym	Label & Number
12/23/57+	49	9		1 **Hey, Schoolgirl** ...S:49 / T:54 *Dancin' Wild* **TOM & JERRY** reissued in 1958 on King 5167 ($75)	$50		Big 613
11/20/65+	❶[2]	14	●	2 **The Sounds Of Silence** ...*We've Got A Groovey Thing Goin'* Simon's "live" solo version made the Adult Contemporary charts (#50) in 1974	$10		Columbia 43396
2/12/66	5	12		3 **Homeward Bound** ...*Leaves That Are Green*	$10		Columbia 43511
5/7/66	3	11		4 **I Am A Rock** ...*Flowers Never Bend With The Rainfall*	$10		Columbia 43617
8/6/66	25	7		5 **The Dangling Conversation** ...*The Big Bright Green Pleasure Machine*	$10	■	Columbia 43728
11/5/66	13	9		6 **A Hazy Shade Of Winter** ...*For Emily, Whenever I May Find Her* a "live" version of the B-side charted on #15 below	$10		Columbia 43873
3/18/67	16	9		7 **At The Zoo** ...*The 59th Street Bridge Song (Feelin' Groovy)* B-side is Simon & Garfunkel's original version of the **Harpers Bizarre** hit	$10	■	Columbia 44046
7/29/67	23	8		8 **Fakin' It**...*You Don't Know Where Your Interest Lies*	$10		Columbia 44232
3/2/68	11	11		9 **Scarborough Fair (/Canticle)**...*April Come She Will* a medieval folk ballad first published in 1673; song also known as "Parsley, Sage, Rosemary And Thyme"	$10		Columbia 44465
4/27/68	❶[3]	13	●	10 **Mrs. Robinson** ...*Old Friends/Bookends* 1968 Grammy winner: Record of the Year; above 2 from the movie *The Graduate* starring Dustin Hoffman and Anne Bancroft (soundtrack versions of "Mrs. Robinson" are different)	$8		Columbia 44511
4/12/69	7	10		11 **The Boxer** ...*Baby Driver* (#101)	$8	■	Columbia 44785
2/7/70	❶[6]	14	●	12 **Bridge Over Troubled Water** AC[6] *Keep The Customer Satisfied* Larry Knechtel (piano); 1970 Grammy winner: Record of the Year	$7	■	Columbia 45079
4/11/70	4	13	●	13 **Cecilia** ...*The Only Living Boy In New York*	$7	■	Columbia 45133
9/12/70	18	11		14 **El Condor Pasa** ...*Why Don't You Write Me* Simon wrote the lyrics to this 18th Century Peruvian folk melody; above 4 from the album *Bridge Over Troubled Water*	$7		Columbia 45237
9/2/72	53	7		15 **For Emily, Whenever I May Find Her** / [L] studio version is on the B-side of #6 above			
11/25/72	97	2		16 **America** ... from the 1968 album *Bookends*	$6		Columbia 45663
10/18/75	9	14		17 **My Little Town**...AC[2] *Rag Doll* (Garfunkel) / *You're Kind* (Simon) all of above written by **Paul Simon**	$5	■	Columbia 10230
4/3/82	27	11		18 **Wake Up Little Susie** ...*Me And Julio Down By The Schoolyard (live)* [L] recorded in New York's Central Park on 9/19/81	$4		Warner 50053

SIMONE, Nina BUB/R&B/LP '59

Born Eunice Waymon on 2/21/33 in Tryon, South Carolina. Died of cancer on 4/21/2003 (age 70). Jazz-styled singer.

DEBUT	PEAK	WKS	Gold	A-side (Chart Hit)...B-side	$	Sym	Label & Number
8/3/59	18	15		1 **I Loves You, Porgy** *Love Me Or Leave Me* from George Gershwin's 1935 folk opera *Porgy And Bess*; some pressings show title as "Porgy"	$15		Bethlehem 11021
9/5/60	93	2		2 **Nobody Knows You When You're Down And Out**...*Black Is The Color Of My True Love's Hair* #15 hit for Bessie Smith in 1929	$12		Colpix 158
1/23/61	92	2		3 **Trouble In Mind**...*Cotton Eyed Joe* blues standard written in 1926	$12		Colpix 175
10/19/68	83	5		4 **Do What You Gotta Do** ...*Peace Of Mind*	$7		RCA Victor 9602
1/4/69	94	4		5 **Ain't Got No; I Got Life**...*Real Real* from the off-Broadway musical *Hair* starring Steve Curry	$7		RCA Victor 9686
12/13/69+	76	7		6 **To Be Young, Gifted And Black** ...*Save Me*	$7		RCA Victor 0269

SIMON F. '87

Born Simon Fellowes on 5/20/61 in Kingston, England. Rock singer; similar in style to **David Bowie**.

DEBUT	PEAK	WKS	Gold	A-side (Chart Hit)...B-side	$	Sym	Label & Number
10/24/87	91	2		**American Dream** ...*Love Bomb*	$4	■	Reprise 28237

SIMON SISTERS, The — see SIMON, Carly

SIMPLĒ E '94

Born Erica Williams in Oakland, California. Female rapper. Produced by Dwayne Wiggins (**Tony! Toni! Toné!**).

DEBUT	PEAK	WKS	Gold	A-side (Chart Hit)...B-side	$	Sym	Label & Number
4/16/94	72	6		**Play My Funk** ...S:59 *(remix edit)* from the movie *Sugar Hill* starring Wesley Snipes	$5	▮	Fox/Beacon 10004

SIMPLE MINDS ROK/LP '85

Pop-rock group formed in Glasgow, Scotland: Jim Kerr (vocals), Charles Burchill (guitar, keyboards), Michael MacNeil (keyboards), John Giblin (bass) and Mel Gaynor (drums). MacNeil and Giblin left in 1989. Kerr was married to **Chrissie Hynde** (**The Pretenders**) (1984-90), then actress Patsy Kensit of **Eighth Wonder** (1992-96).

DEBUT	PEAK	WKS	Gold	A-side (Chart Hit)...B-side	$	Sym	Label & Number
2/23/85	❶[1]	22		1 **Don't You (Forget About Me)** AR[3] S:❶[2] / A:❶[1] *A Brass Band If Africa* from the movie *The Breakfast Club* starring Molly Ringwald and Emilio Estevez; an alternate picture sleeve issued with a color photo of "The Breakfast Club" soundtrack album cover on the front of the sleeve	$3	■	A&M 2703
10/19/85	3	20		2 **Alive & Kicking** ...A:3 / S:5 *Up On The Catwalk (live)*	$3	■	A&M 2783
1/25/86	14	14		3 **Sanctify Yourself**...A:14 / S:16 *(dub version)*	$3	■	A&M 2810
4/5/86	28	13		4 **All The Things She Said** ...A:26 / S:27 *Don't You (Forget About Me) Live*	$3	■	A&M 2828
5/18/91	40	10		5 **See The Lights**...MR[2] A:72 *Goodnight*	$3	▮	A&M 1553
2/18/95	52	9		6 **She's A River**...A:59 *(2 versions)* / E55 "45": Virgin 18402 (blue vinyl); B-side: "Celtic Strings"	$3	▮[V]	Virgin 38467

DEBUT	PEAK	WKS	Gold	A-side (Chart Hit)...B-side	$	Sym	Label & Number

SIMPLY RED
AC/BUB/R&B/LP **'86**

Born Mick Hucknall on 6/8/60 in Denton, Manchester, England. "Blue-eyed soul" singer. Nicknamed "Red" because of his red hair. His backing group included Fritz McIntyre and Tim Kellett (keyboards), Sylvan Richardson (guitar), Tony Bowers (bass) and Chris Joyce (drums).

DEBUT	PEAK	WKS	Gold	A-side (Chart Hit)...B-side	$	Sym	Label & Number
4/5/86	❶[1]	23		1 **Holding Back The Years** ....S:❶[1] / A:3 *I Won't Feel Bad*	$3		Elektra 69564
7/19/86	28	15		2 **Money$ Too Tight (To Mention)** ....A:27 / S:29 *Picture Book (dub)* originally released in 1985 with a picture sleeve on Elektra 69607 with "Open Up The Red Box" on the B-side	$3	■	Elektra 69528
2/28/87	27	15		3 **The Right Thing** ....S:26 / A:26 *There's A Light*	$3	■	Elektra 69487
2/25/89	57	9		4 **It's Only Love** ....*Turn It Up*	$3	■	Elektra 69317
5/6/89	❶[1]	22	●	5 **If You Don't Know Me By Now** AC[6] S:❶[1] / A:❶[1] *Move On Out*	$3	■	Elektra 69297
9/28/91	23	14		6 **Something Got Me Started** ....A:43 *A New Flame*	$3	▮	EastWest 98711
1/25/92	44	14		7 **Stars** ....A:45 *(remix)*	$3	▮	EastWest 98636

SIMPSON, Jessica
'99

Born on 7/10/80 in Dallas, Texas. Pop-dance singer. Began career singing on the Christian Youth Conference circuit which included **Kirk Franklin** and **CeCe Winans**. Married Nick Lachey (of **98°**) on 10/26/2002.

DEBUT	PEAK	WKS	Gold	A-side (Chart Hit)...B-side	$	Sym	Label & Number
10/16/99	3	20	▲	1 **I Wanna Love You Forever** ....S:❶[6] / A:20 *(4 album snippets)*	$4	★	Columbia 79262
4/1/00	62	6		2 **Where You Are** ....S:40 / A:62 *(3 versions) / I Wanna Love You Forever (extended club version)* **JESSICA SIMPSON (Featuring Nick Lachey)** from the movie *Here On Earth* starring Chris Klein	$8	★*	Columbia 79391
7/1/00	21	16		3 **I Think I'm In Love With You** ....A:17 *(4 remixes)* samples "Jack And Diane" by **John Mellencamp**	$8	★*	Columbia 79467
5/19/01	15	20		4 **Irresistible** ....A:13 *(5 versions)* "45": Columbia 79579; B-side: "Irresistible" (w/**Lil Bow Wow**)	$6	T[V]	Columbia 79578

SIMPSON, Valerie — see ASHFORD & SIMPSON

SIMPSONS, The
LP **'91**

The voices of the Fox network's animated TV series. Nancy Cartwright is Bart; Dan Castellaneta is Homer; Julie Kavner is Marge; Yeardley Smith is Lisa; and the show's creator Matt Groening is Maggie.

DEBUT	PEAK	WKS	Gold	A-side (Chart Hit)...B-side	$	Sym	Label & Number
12/15/90+	11[A]	9		1 **Do The Bartman** .... [N]			album cut
3/16/91	69	6		2 **Deep, Deep Trouble** ....S:73 *Sibling Rivalry* [N] **THE SIMPSONS Featuring Bart & Homer** co-written, co-produced and scratches by **D.J. Jazzy Jeff**; above 2 from the album *The Simpsons Sing The Blues* on Geffen 24308	$5	▮[V]	Geffen 19007

SIMS, Kym
'92

Born on 12/28/66 in Chicago, Illinois. Dance singer/songwriter. Former commercial jingle singer (Shasta soft drinks). Also see **CeCe Peniston**'s "We Got A Love Thang."

DEBUT	PEAK	WKS	Gold	A-side (Chart Hit)...B-side	$	Sym	Label & Number
11/16/91+	38	20		1 **Too Blind To See It** ....A:22 *(house mix)*	$3	▮	Atco 98667
5/9/92	86	5		2 **Take My Advice** ....A:52 *Take Me To The Groove*	$3	▮	Atco 98580

SIMS TWINS
'61

R&B vocal duo from Los Angeles, California: brothers Bobby and Kenneth Sims.

DEBUT	PEAK	WKS	Gold	A-side (Chart Hit)...B-side	$	Sym	Label & Number
10/23/61	42	8		**Soothe Me** ....*I'll Never Come Running Back To You* written and produced by **Sam Cooke**; B-side written by Cooke as the sequel to his 1958 hit "I'll Come Running Back To You"	$20		SAR 117

SINATRA, Frank ★28★
MEM/POP/AC/BUB/LP **'46**

Born Francis Albert Sinatra on 12/12/15 in Hoboken, New Jersey. Died of a heart attack on 5/14/98 (age 82). With Harry James from 1939-40 ("All Or Nothing At All"); with **Tommy Dorsey**, 1940-42 ("I'll Never Smile Again"/"Oh! Look At Me Now"/"In The Blue Of Evening"/"There Are Such Things"). Went solo in late 1942 and charted 40 Top 10 pop hits through 1954 (including "Oh! What It Seemed To Be"/"Five Minutes More"/"Mam'selle"/"Young-At-Heart"). Appeared in many movies from 1941. Won an Oscar for the movie *From Here To Eternity* in 1953. Own TV show in 1957. Own Reprise record company in 1961; sold to Warner Bros. in 1963. Won Grammy's Lifetime Achievement Award in 1965. Married to actress Ava Gardner from 1951-57. Married to actress Mia Farrow from 1966-68. Announced his retirement in 1970, but made comeback in 1973. Regarded by many as the greatest popular singer of the 20th century.

1)Somethin' Stupid 2)Learnin' The Blues 3)Strangers In The Night 4)All The Way 5)Hey! Jealous Lover

DEBUT	PEAK	WKS	Gold	A-side (Chart Hit)...B-side	$	Sym	Label & Number
1/22/55	19	4		1 **Melody Of Love** ....A:19 *I'm Gonna Live Till I Die* **FRANK SINATRA and RAY ANTHONY And His Orchestra** music written in 1903; lyrics added in 1954 by **Tom Glazer**	$20		Capitol 3018
5/7/55	❶[2]	21		2 **Learnin' The Blues** ....A:❶[2] / J:2 / S:2 *If I Had Three Wishes*	$20		Capitol 3102
9/24/55	13	5		3 **Same Old Saturday Night /** A:13 / T:65			
9/10/55		5		4 **Fairy Tale** ....CU:flip	$20		Capitol 3218
11/5/55	5	17		5 **Love And Marriage** ....T:5 / A:5 / S:6 / J:7 *The Impatient Years* introduced by Sinatra on TV's *Producer's Showcase* production of *Our Town* (9/19/55); Sinatra's version later used as the theme for the TV series *Married With Children*	$20		Capitol 3260
12/10/55+	7	15		6 **(Love Is) The Tender Trap** ....A:7 / T:23 / S:24 *Weep They Will* from the movie *The Tender Trap* starring Sinatra	$20		Capitol 3290
2/25/56	21	13		7 **Flowers Mean Forgiveness /** A:21 / T:35			
3/3/56	67	5		8 **You'll Get Yours** ....T:67 debuted on *The Top 100* chart at #67, one position higher than **Elvis Presley**'s pop chart debut ("Heartbreak Hotel")	$20		Capitol 3350
5/19/56	13	14		9 **(How Little It Matters) How Little We Know /** A:13 / T:30			
6/2/56	73	3		10 **Five Hundred Guys** T:73	$20		Capitol 3423
7/14/56	52	15		11 **You're Sensational /** T:52 written by Cole Porter (also #13 below)			
7/28/56	75	5		12 **Johnny Concho Theme (Wait For Me)** ....T:75 from the movie *Johnny Concho* starring Sinatra	$20		Capitol 3469
9/22/56	92	2		13 **Well Did You Evah?** ....T:92 *True Love* (**Bing Crosby & Grace Kelly** - #3) [N] **BING CROSBY and FRANK SINATRA** Johnny Green conducts the MGM Studio Orch.; originally from the 1939 Cole Porter Broadway musical starring Ethel Merman; #11 & 13: from the movie *High Society* starring Crosby and Sinatra	$20		Capitol 3507
10/27/56+	3	19		14 **Hey! Jealous Lover** ....A:3 / T:6 / J:7 / S:8 *You Forgot All The Words*	$20		Capitol 3552
1/19/57	15	19		15 **Can I Steal A Little Love /** A:15 / T:20 from the movie *Rock Pretty Baby* starring **Sal Mineo**			
1/19/57	60	8		16 **Your Love For Me** T:60	$20		Capitol 3608

DEBUT	PEAK	WKS	Gold	A-side (Chart Hit)	B-side	$	Sym	Label & Number
				SINATRA, Frank — Cont'd				
4/27/57	60	4		17 **Crazy Love /**	T:60			
4/27/57	74	5		18 **So Long, My Love**	T:74	$15		Capitol 3703
7/22/57	25	1		19 **You're Cheatin' Yourself (If You're Cheatin' On Me)**	A:25 *Something Wonderful Happens In Summer*	$15		Capitol 3744
10/28/57+	2[1]	30		20 **All The Way /**	A:2 / S:15 / T:15			
10/28/57	84	5		21 **Chicago**	T:84 / S:flip	$15		Capitol 3793
				above 2 from the movie *The Joker Is Wild* starring Sinatra ("Chicago" written in 1922)				
1/20/58	6	16		22 **Witchcraft**	A:6 / S:20 / T:20 *Tell Her You Love Her*	$15		Capitol 3859
5/12/58	22	1		23 **How Are Ya' Fixed For Love?**	A:22 / T:97 *Nothing In Common*	$15		Capitol 3952
				FRANK SINATRA and KEELY SMITH				
10/27/58	41	11		24 **Mr. Success**	*Sleep Warm*	$15		Capitol 4070
				the only chart hit showing Sinatra as a co-writer				
3/30/59	61	7		25 **French Foreign Legion**	*Time After Time*	$15		Capitol 4155
6/15/59	30	17		26 **High Hopes**	*All My Tomorrows*	$15	■	Capitol 4214
				FRANK SINATRA "and a bunch of kids" (featuring **Eddie Hodges**) from the movie *A Hole In The Head* starring Sinatra; a special promo record and picture sleeve issued featuring "High Hopes" by Jonah Jones on one side and by Sinatra on the other side				
10/19/59	38	11		27 **Talk To Me**	*They Came To Cordura*	$15		Capitol 4284
5/30/60	82	2		28 **River, Stay 'Way From My Door**	*It's Over, It's Over, It's Over* (#111)	$12		Capitol 4376
				#1 hit for Kate Smith with Guy Lombardo in 1932				
8/29/60	60	6		29 **Nice 'N' Easy**	*This Was My Love*	$12		Capitol 4408
11/7/60	25	9		30 **Ol' Mac Donald**	*You'll Always Be The One I Love*	$12		Capitol 4466
				adaptation of a children's song originating in the early 1700's				
3/6/61	50	7		31 **The Second Time Around**	*Tina*	$20		Reprise 20,001
				the first release on Sinatra's own label; song introduced by **Bing Crosby** in the 1960 movie *High Time*				
7/3/61	64	4		32 **Granada**	*The Curse Of An Aching Heart*	$15	■	Reprise 20,010
				#17 hit for **Frankie Laine** in 1954 as "Grenada" (written in 1932)				
10/16/61	58	7		33 **I'll Be Seeing You**	*The One I Love Belongs To Somebody Else*	$15		Reprise 20,023
				from the 1938 Broadway musical *Right This Way*; Sinatra first recorded this song with **Tommy Dorsey** in 1940 (charted in 1944 - #4)				
12/18/61+	34	8		34 **Pocketful Of Miracles**	*Name It And It's Yours*	$15	■	Reprise 20,040
				title song from the movie starring Bette Davis				
3/17/62	99	1		35 **The Moon Was Yellow**	*I've Heard That Song Before*	$12		Capitol 4677
				#13 hit for **Bing Crosby** in 1934				
3/24/62	98	1		36 **Stardust**	*Come Rain Or Come Shine*	$15		Reprise 20,059
				one of the most recorded, charted, and popular tunes of all-time				
4/7/62	75	2		37 **Ev'rybody's Twistin'**	*Nothing But The Best*	$12	■	Reprise 20,063
12/1/62	64	6		38 **Me And My Shadow**	*Sam's Song* (**Dean Martin & Sammy Davis Jr.**-#94)	$15	■	Reprise 20,128
				FRANK SINATRA and SAMMY DAVIS JR. #1 hit for "Whispering" Jack Smith in 1927				
4/6/63	78	8		39 **Call Me Irresponsible**	*Tina*	$12	■	Reprise 20,151
				from the movie *Papa's Delicate Condition* starring **Jackie Gleason**; originally issued with a picture sleeve with "Come Blow Your Horn" as the B-side; #3, 5, 6, 14, 17, 18, 20, 23, 26, 31, 34 & 39: written by Sammy Cahn (Sinatra's main songwriter)				
1/18/64	81	3		40 **Stay With Me**	*Talk To Me Baby*	$10		Reprise 0249
				from the movie *The Cardinal* starring Tom Tryon				
9/5/64	27	11		41 **Softly, As I Leave You**	*Then Suddenly Love*	$10		Reprise 0301
				song originally "Bubbled Under" (#116) in 1962 for **Matt Monro**; Italian song "Piano" recorded in 1960 by **Mina**				
12/19/64+	32	10		42 **Somewhere In Your Heart**	*Emily*	$10		Reprise 0332
3/13/65	46	6		43 **Anytime At All**	*Available*	$10		Reprise 0350
5/22/65	57	6		44 **Tell Her (You Love Her Every Day)**	*Here's To The Losers*	$10		Reprise 0373
				actual title: "Tell Her (You Love Her Each Day)"; different song than the B-side of #22 above				
6/26/65	78	7		45 **Forget Domani**	*I Can't Believe I'm Losing You*	$10		Reprise 0380
				from the movie *The Yellow Rolls Royce* starring Rex Harrison and Ingrid Bergman				
12/25/65+	28	8		46 **It Was A Very Good Year**	AC[1]	$10	■	Reprise 0429
				song introduced in 1961 by **The Kingston Trio** on the album *Goin' Places*				
5/7/66	❶[1]	15	●	47 **Strangers In The Night**	AC[7] *Oh, You Crazy Moon*	$10		Reprise 0470
				from the movie *A Man Could Get Killed* starring James Garner; 1966 Grammy winner: Record of the Year				
9/3/66	25	7		48 **Summer Wind**	AC[1] *You Make Me Feel So Young* (w/**Count Basie**)	$10		Reprise 0509
11/19/66	4	11		49 **That's Life**	AC[3] *The September Of My Years*	$10	■	Reprise 0531
3/18/67	❶[4]	13	●	50 **Somethin' Stupid**	AC[9] *I Will Wait For You* (Frank)	$10		Reprise 0561
				NANCY SINATRA & FRANK SINATRA				
8/5/67	30	7		51 **The World We Knew (Over And Over)**	AC[5] *You Are There*	$10		Reprise 0610
10/28/67	53	5		52 **This Town**	*This Is My Love*	$10		Reprise 0631
				from the movie *The Cool Ones* starring Roddy McDowall				
4/13/68	60	5		53 **I Can't Believe I'm Losing You**	*How Old Am I?*	$8		Reprise 0677
				originally released as the B-side of #45 above				
10/12/68	23	10		54 **Cycles /**				
8/31/68	64	6		55 **My Way Of Life**		$8		Reprise 0764
				#47, 51 & 55: co-written by **Bert Kaempfert**				
12/14/68	7[X]	3		56 **Whatever Happened To Christmas?**	*I Wouldn't Trade Christmas* (Sinatra Family) [X]	$12		Reprise 0790
1/4/69	62	6		57 **Rain In My Heart**	*Star!*	$8		Reprise 0798
3/29/69	27	8		58 **My Way**	*Blue Lace*	$10		Reprise 0817
				French song ("Comme d'Habitude") with English lyrics by **Paul Anka**				
9/13/69	75	4		59 **Love's Been Good To Me**	*A Man Alone*	$8		Reprise 0852
				written by **Rod McKuen**				
11/29/69	79	4		60 **Goin' Out Of My Head /**				
11/29/69		4		61 **Forget To Remember**		$8		Reprise 0865
				#57, 60 & 61: co-written by **Teddy Randazzo**				
3/21/70	88	3		62 **I Would Be In Love (Anyway)**	*Watertown*	$8		Reprise 0895
11/10/73	63	10		63 **Let Me Try Again (Laisse Moi Le Temps)**	*Send In The Clowns*	$8		Reprise 1181
				French song; English lyrics by **Paul Anka** & Sammy Cahn				
4/6/74	83	7		64 **Bad, Bad Leroy Brown**	*I'm Gonna Make It All The Way*	$8		Reprise 1196

DEBUT	PEAK	WKS	Gold	A-side (Chart Hit)...B-side	$	Sym	Label & Number
				SINATRA, Frank — Cont'd			
8/3/74	**83**	5		65 **You Turned My World Around** ...*Satisfy Me One More Time*	$8		Reprise 1208
				co-written by **Kim Carnes** and **Bert Kaempfert**			
4/19/75	**75**	6		66 **Anytime (I'll Be There)** ...*The Hurt Doesn't Go Away*	$8		Reprise 1327
				RCR (Rhodes, Chalmers & Rhodes - backing vocals); written by **Paul Anka**			
8/2/75	**47**	7		67 **I Believe I'm Gonna Love You** ...*The Only Couple On The Floor*	$8	■	Reprise 1335
5/3/80	**32**	12		68 **Theme From New York, New York** ...*That's What God Looks Like To Me*	$10	■	Reprise 49233
				introduced in the movie musical *New York, New York* by Liza Minnelli (her version "Bubbled Under" at #104 in 1977); Sinatra's musical arrangers and conductors: Al Capps (#67), **Don Costa** (#36, 40, 53-61, 64, 66, 68), **Ernie Freeman** (#41-45, 47, 49, 51), Bob Gaudio (#62), **Neal Hefti** (#37), **Gordon Jenkins** (#46, 63), **Billy May** (#23, 32, 38), Sy Oliver (#33), **Nelson Riddle** (#2-12, 14-22, 24-30, 35, 39, 48), **Felix Slatkin** (#31) and **Billy Strange** (#50, 52)			
	★242★			**SINATRA, Nancy** AC/BUB/LP **'66**			
				Born on 6/8/40 in Jersey City, New Jersey. First child of Nancy and **Frank Sinatra**. Moved to Los Angeles while a child. Made national TV debut with father and **Elvis Presley** in 1959. Married to **Tommy Sands**, 1960-65. Appeared on *Hullabaloo*, *American Bandstand* and own specials in the mid-1960s. In movies *For Those Who Think Young*, *Get Yourself A College Girl*, *The Oscar* and *Speedway* (with Elvis Presley).			
				1)Somethin' Stupid 2)These Boots Are Made For Walkin' 3)Sugar Town 4)How Does That Grab You, Darlin'? 5)Jackson			
10/16/65	**86**	4		1 **So Long Babe**...*If He'd Love Me*	$15		Reprise 0407
1/22/66	**①[1]**	14	●	2 **These Boots Are Made For Walkin'** ...*The City Never Sleeps At Night*	$12		Reprise 0432
				title inspired by a line by **Frank Sinatra** in his 1963 movie *4 For Texas*			
4/23/66	**7**	8		3 **How Does That Grab You, Darlin'?** ...*The Last Of The Secret Agents?*	$10		Reprise 0461
7/9/66	**36**	5		4 **Friday's Child**...*Hutchinson Jail*	$10		Reprise 0491
9/17/66	**46**	6		5 **In Our Time**...*Leave My Dog Alone*	$10		Reprise 0514
11/19/66	**5**	13	●	6 **Sugar Town** / AC[2]			
3/4/67	**49**	9		7 **Summer Wine**...	$10		Reprise 0527
				NANCY SINATRA & LEE HAZLEWOOD			
3/18/67	**①[4]**	13	●	8 **Somethin' Stupid** AC[9] *I Will Wait For You* (Frank)	$10		Reprise 0561
				NANCY SINATRA & FRANK SINATRA			
3/25/67	**15**	8		9 **Love Eyes**...*Coastin'*	$10		Reprise 0559
6/24/67	**14**	9		10 **Jackson** /			
				NANCY SINATRA & LEE HAZLEWOOD			
6/24/67	**44**	9		11 **You Only Live Twice**...	$10		Reprise 0595
				title song from the James Bond movie starring Sean Connery			
9/23/67	**24**	7		12 **Lightning's Girl** ...*Until It's Time For You To Go*	$10	■	Reprise 0620
10/21/67	**20**	6		13 **Lady Bird**...*Sand* (#107)	$10		Reprise 0629
				NANCY SINATRA & LEE HAZLEWOOD			
12/2/67	**83**	3		14 **Tony Rome** ...*This Town*	$10		Reprise 0636
				title song from the movie starring **Frank Sinatra**			
1/6/68	**26**	8		15 **Some Velvet Morning**...*Oh Lonesome Me*	$10		Reprise 0651
				NANCY SINATRA & LEE HAZLEWOOD			
3/23/68	**69**	6		16 **100 Years**...*See The Little Children*	$8		Reprise 0670
7/27/68	**74**	4		17 **Happy** ...*Nice 'n Easy*	$8		Reprise 0756
				all of above produced and written (except #8, 10 & 11) by Lee Hazlewood			
11/30/68	**65**	5		18 **Good Time Girl** ...*Old Devil Moon*	$8		Reprise 0789
3/15/69	**97**	3		19 **God Knows I Love You** ...*Just Being Plain Old Me*	$8		Reprise 0813
				above 2 written by **Mac Davis**			
5/24/69	**98**	2		20 **Here We Go Again**...*Memories*	$8		Reprise 0821
9/20/69	**98**	2		21 **Drummer Man**...*Home*	$8		Reprise 0851
				Hal Blaine (drums); all of above arranged and conducted by **Billy Strange**			
				SINCLAIR, Gordon **'74**			
				Born on 6/3/1900 in Toronto, Ontario, Canada. Died on 5/17/84 (age 83). Broadcaster/author.			
1/12/74	**24**	7		**The Americans (A Canadian's Opinion)**..*A Profile Of Gordon Sinclair* (David Craig) [S]	$5		Avco 4628
				originally broadcast as an editorial on CFRB-Toronto on 6/5/73			
				SINGING BELLES, The **'60**			
				Pop duo from Brooklyn, New York: sisters Anne and Angela Berry.			
4/18/60	**91**	3		**Someone Loves You, Joe** ...*The Empty Mailbox*	$12		Madison 126
				SINGING DOGS, The **'55**			
				Actual recordings of dogs barking, produced by Don Charles in Copenhagen, Denmark.			
12/10/55	**22**	7		1 **Oh! Susanna** ...S:22 / T:37 *Pat-A-Cake/Three Blind Mice/Jingle Bells* [N]	$12	■	RCA Victor 6344
				written in 1848 by Stephen Foster; DJ copies labeled as: "Dolly's Oh! Susanna" (Dogs: Dolly, Pearl, Caesar & King); picture sleeve issued using either red or brown ink			
12/25/71	**①[1X]**	11		2 **Jingle Bells**...*Oh! Susanna* [X-N]	$5		RCA Victor 1020
				Don Charles Presents THE SINGING DOGS (above 2)			
				X: 2/'71; 1/'72; 4/'73; 8/'83; 3/'84; recorded in 1955; re-issued in 1974 on RCA Victor 10129			
				SINGING NUN, The BUB/LP **'63**			
				Born Jeanine Deckers on 10/17/33 in Fichermont, Belgium. Committed suicide on 3/31/85 (age 51). Actual nun; assumed the name Sister Luc-Gabrielle. Recorded under the name Soeur Sourire ("Sister Smile").			
11/9/63	**①[4]**	13		**Dominique** ...AC[4] *Entre Les Etoiles (Among The Stars)* [F]	$8	■	Philips 40152
				also released on Phillips 40163 in 1963			
				SINGLE BULLET THEORY **'83**			
				Pop-rock group from Norfolk, Virginia: Michael Garrett (vocals), Gary Holmes (guitar), Barry Fitzgerald (keyboards), Mick Muller (bass) and Dennis Madigan (drums).			
3/5/83	**78**	4		**Keep It Tight** ...*A Blink Of An Eye*	$5	■	Nemperor 03300
				SINGLETARY, Daryle C&W/LP **'98**			
				Born on 3/10/71 in Cairo, Georgia. Country singer/songwriter.			
2/28/98	**90**	6		**The Note** ...*I Let Her Lie*	$4	▮[V]	Giant 17268

SINITTA — R&B '89

Born on 10/19/64 in Seattle, Washington; raised in England (of Native American descent). Female dance singer. Daughter of singer/dancer Miquel Brown. Niece of **Amii Stewart**. Starred in musicals (*Cats* in London) and TV shows. Appeared in the movies *Shock Treatment* and *Foreign Body*, and a cameo role in *Little Shop of Horrors*.

DEBUT	PEAK	WKS	Gold	A-side (Chart Hit)	B-side	$	Sym	Label & Number
9/23/89	84	4		Right Back Where We Started From	*I Just Can't Help It*	$3		Atlantic 88807

SIOUXSIE AND THE BANSHEES — ROK/BUB/LP '91

Avant-punk group formed by singer Siouxsie Sioux (Susan Dallion) and bassist Steve Severin (Steve Havoc). Fluctuating personnel around group's nucleus: Sioux, Severin and Peter "Budgie" Clark (drums). Husband-and-wife, Sioux and Budgie, also recorded as The Creatures.

DEBUT	PEAK	WKS	Gold	A-side (Chart Hit)	B-side	$	Sym	Label & Number
10/15/88	53	14		1 Peek-A-Boo MR[2]	*False Face*	$3	■	Geffen 27760
8/17/91	23	13		2 Kiss Them For Me MR[5] A:50 / S:58	*Return*	$3	▮	Geffen 19031

SIR CHAUNCEY and his exciting strings — '60

Sir Chauncey is **Ernie Freeman**. Also see **B. Bumble & The Stingers** and **Joiner, Arkansas Junior High School Band**.

DEBUT	PEAK	WKS	Gold	A-side (Chart Hit)	B-side	$	Sym	Label & Number
4/25/60	89	4		Beautiful Obsession	*Tenderfoot* [I]	$10		Warner 5150

SIR DOUGLAS QUINTET — BUB/LP '65

Rock group formed in Houston, Texas: Doug Sahm (vocals, guitar), Augie Myers (organ), Frank Morin (horns), Harvey Regan (bass) and John Perez (drums). Sahm died of heart failure on 11/18/99 (age 58).

DEBUT	PEAK	WKS	Gold	A-side (Chart Hit)	B-side	$	Sym	Label & Number
4/3/65	13	12		1 She's About A Mover	*We'll Take Our Last Walk Tonight*	$12		Tribe 8308
1/29/66	31	11		2 The Rains Came	*Bacon Fat*	$10		Tribe 8314
1/18/69	27	15		3 Mendocino	*I Wanna Be Your Mama Again*	$8		Smash 2191
8/2/69	83	2		4 Dynamite Woman	*Too Many Dociled Minds*	$8		Smash 2233

SIR MIX-A-LOT — R&B/LP '92

Born Anthony Ray on 8/12/63 in Seattle, Washington. Male rapper. Appeared as the host of the anthology TV series *The Watcher*.

DEBUT	PEAK	WKS	Gold	A-side (Chart Hit)	B-side	$	Sym	Label & Number
12/17/88+	70	9		1 Posse' On Broadway	*(video edit)*	$4	■	Nastymix 75555
4/11/92	❶[5]	28	▲[2]	2 Baby Got Back S:❶[9] / A:16	*Cake Boy*	$3	▮[V]	Def American 18947
9/14/96	97	3		3 Jump On It	*(mix 2)*	$3	▮[V]	Rhyme Cartel 17626
				samples **Jorgen Ingmann**'s 1961 hit "Apache"; same rap tune as the **Sugar Hill Gang**'s "Apache"				

SISQÓ — R&B/LP '00

Born Mark Andrews on 11/9/78 in Baltimore, Maryland. R&B singer/songwriter. Member of **Dru Hill**. Appeared as "Dr. Rupert Brooks" in the 2002 movie *Snow Dogs*.

DEBUT	PEAK	WKS	Gold	A-side (Chart Hit)	B-side	$	Sym	Label & Number
3/14/98	6	20	●	1 It's All About Me S:5 / A:50	*(album version)*	$3	▮	University 97024
				MÝA With Special Guest SISQO — samples "Moments In Love" by **The Art Of Noise**; reissue of cassette box shows artist as **MÝA & SISQO**				
11/20/99+	40	20		2 Got To Get It A:33	*(3 versions)*	$6	T[V]	Dragon 562455
				SISQÓ (featuring Make It Hot)				
1/29/00	3	28		3 Thong Song A:❶[7] / S:67	*(2 versions) / Got To Get It*	$6	T[V]	Def Soul 562599
				samples "Livin' La Vida Loca" by **Ricky Martin**; from the movie *Nutty Professor II: The Klumps* starring **Eddie Murphy** and **Janet Jackson**; "45" issued for above 2 on Def Soul 562684				
6/24/00	❶[2]	26	▲	4 Incomplete RB[5] S:❶[4] / A:15	*Thong Song (uncensored w/**Foxy Brown**)*	$4	★[V]	Def Soul 562854
				Shae Jones (backing vocal); "45": Def Soul 562899				
7/1/00	49	20		5 What You Want A:42	*(2 versions) / Fame*	$6	T	Def Jam 562808
				DMX (Featuring Sisqo)				
11/25/00	75	9		6 How Many Licks? A:69	*(3 versions)*	$6	T	Queen Bee/Undeas 85032
				LIL' KIM (featuring Sisqó)				

SISTER HAZEL — LP '97

Pop-rock group formed in Gainesville, Florida: Ken Block (vocals), Ryan Newell and Andrew Copeland (guitars), Jeff Beres (bass) and Mark Trojanowski (drums).

DEBUT	PEAK	WKS	Gold	A-side (Chart Hit)	B-side	$	Sym	Label & Number
7/12/97	11	41		1 All For You A:7 / S:31	*(live version) / Wanted It To Be (live)*	$3	▮[V]	Universal 56135
1/24/98	73[A]	3		2 Happy			V	album cut
				above 2 from the album *...Somewhere More Familiar* on Universal 53030; "45" issued for above 2 on Universal 56190				
7/15/00	59	20		3 Change Your Mind A:66			V	album cut
				from the album *Fortress* on Universal 157883; "45": Universal 158218; B-side: "All For You"				

SISTER 7 — '98

Rock group from Austin, Texas: Patrice Pike (vocals), Wayne Sutton (guitar), Darrell Phillips (bass) and Sean Phillips (drums).

DEBUT	PEAK	WKS	Gold	A-side (Chart Hit)	B-side	$	Sym	Label & Number
5/30/98	76	7		Know What You Mean	*Perfect*	$4	▮	Arista Austin 13095

SISTER SLEDGE — R&B/BUB/LP '79

Dance vocal group from Philadelphia, Pennsylvania: sisters Debra, Joni, Kim and Kathy Sledge. First recorded as Sisters Sledge for Money Back label in 1971. Worked as backup vocalists. Began producing their own albums in 1981.

DEBUT	PEAK	WKS	Gold	A-side (Chart Hit)	B-side	$	Sym	Label & Number
1/4/75	92	4		1 Love Don't You Go Through No Changes On Me	*Don't You Miss Him*	$5		Atco 7008
2/10/79	9	19		2 He's The Greatest Dancer RB[1]	*Somebody Loves Me*	$4		Cotillion 44245
4/28/79	2[2]	19	●	3 We Are Family RB[1]	*Easier To Love*	$4		Cotillion 44251
1/19/80	64	5		4 Got To Love Somebody	*Good Girl Now*	$4		Cotillion 45007
3/21/81	79	5		5 All American Girls	*Happy Feeling*	$4		Cotillion 46007
5/9/81	82	5		6 Next Time You'll Know	*If You Really Want Me*	$4		Cotillion 46012
1/30/82	23	15		7 My Guy	*Il Macquillage Lady*	$4		Cotillion 47000
6/15/85	75	8		8 Frankie	*Peer Pressure*	$3	■	Atlantic 89547

SISTERS WITH VOICES — see SWV

SIXPENCE NONE THE RICHER — LP '99

Alternative Contemporary Christian group from Austin, Texas: **Leigh Nash** (vocals), Matt Slocum and Sean Kelly (guitars), Justin Cary (bass) and Dale Baker (drums).

DEBUT	PEAK	WKS	Gold	A-side (Chart Hit)	B-side	$	Sym	Label & Number
11/28/98+	2[1]	33	●	1 Kiss Me A:2 / S:5	*Love*	$4	★	Squint 79101
				from the movie *She's All That* starring Freddie Prinze, Jr.; charted first week as a CD maxi-single on Squint 85904; re-entered *Hot 100* on 2/13/99 as a regular CD single				
9/11/99	32	20		2 There She Goes A:23				album cut
				above 2 from the album *Sixpence None The Richer* on Squint 7032				

DEBUT	PEAK	WKS	Gold	A-side (Chart Hit)...B-side	$	Sym	Label & Number
				SIXPENCE NONE THE RICHER — Cont'd			
7/7/01	57^S	3		3 **Innocente**...*(4 remixes)*	$8	★*	Nettwerk 33130
				DELERIUM featuring Leigh Nash (of Sixpence None The Richer)			
10/26/02	70^S	1		4 **Breathe Your Name**...*Northern Lights*	$5	★V	Reprise/Squint 886243
				"45": Reprise/Squint 886239; B-side: "Waiting On The Sun"			
				SIX TEENS, The '56			
				Black teen R&B vocal group from Los Angeles, California: Trudy Williams, Ken Sinclair, Darrell Lewis, Beverly Pecot, Ed Wells and Louise Williams. In 1956, members ranged in age from 14 to 17. Wells died on 2/20/2001 (age 63). Sinclair died of cancer on 3/16/2003 (age 63).			
7/14/56	25	13		1 **A Casual Look**...S:25 / T:48 *Teen Age Promise*	$25		Flip 315
7/29/57	80	3		2 **Arrow Of Love**...T:80 *Was It A Dream Of Mine*	$25		Flip 322
				THE SIX TEENS featuring TRUDY WILLIAMS			
				69 BOYZ R&B/LP '94			
				Bass-rap group from Jacksonville, Florida, featuring Albert Bryant and Mike Phillips.			
7/9/94+	8	38	▲	1 **Tootsee Roll** S:3 / A:38 *(album sampler)*	$3	▮	Down Low 6911
				produced by **95 South**; remix version released on Rip-It 6912			
12/10/94+	51	20		2 **Kitty Kitty**...S:26 *(2 versions) / (album sampler)*	$4	▮	Rip-It 6921
5/18/96	95	3		3 **Hoop N Yo Face**...S:72 *(remix)*	$4	▮	Flavor Unit 64312
				69 BOYZ featuring Quad City DJ's			
				from the movie *Sunset Park* starring Rhea Perlman			
7/18/98	31	16		4 **Woof Woof**...S:20 *(instrumental)*	$3	▮	Atlantic 84123
				from the movie *Dr. Dolittle* starring **Eddie Murphy**			
3/11/00	64^S	5		5 **How We Roll**...*(album sampler)*	$5	★	HomeBass 73333
				SKA KINGS, The '64			
				Jamaican group led by Byron Lee. Ska is considered by many to be the original music of Jamaica.			
7/11/64	98	1		**Jamaica Ska**...*Oil In My Lamp*	$12		Atlantic 2232
				SKEE-LO R&B/BUB/LP '95			
				Born Anthony Roundtree on 3/5/75 in Riverside, California. Male rapper.			
4/29/95	13	27	●	**I Wish**...S:7 / A:58 *(street mix)*	$4	▮	Sunshine 78032
				SKELLERN, Peter BUB '73			
				Born on 3/14/47 in Bury, Lancashire, England. Pop singer/songwriter.			
11/25/72+	50	8		**You're A Lady**...*Manifesto*	$6		London 20075
				SKELTON, Red '69			
				Born Richard Skelton on 7/18/13 in Vincennes, Indiana. Died on 9/17/97 (age 84). One of America's most loved and enduring comedians. Own TV variety show from 1951-72.			
3/15/69	44	6		**The Pledge Of Allegiance**...*The Circus* [S]	$8		Columbia 44798
				as reviewed on TV's *Red Skelton Hour* on 1/14/69; musical background: "Red's White and Blue March"			
				SKID ROW ROK/LP '89			
				Hard-rock group formed in New Jersey: Sebastian Bach (vocals), Dave Sabo and Scott Hill (guitars), Rachel Bolan (bass) and Rob Affuso (drums).			
6/10/89	99	2		1 **Youth Gone Wild**...*Sweet Little Sister*	$4	■	Atlantic 88935
7/8/89	4	20	●	2 **18 And Life** S:4 / A:6 *Midnight/Tornado*	$3	■	Atlantic 88883
11/18/89+	6	20		3 **I Remember You**...S:3 / A:13 *Makin' A Mess*	$3	■	Atlantic 88886
6/22/91	65^S	9		4 **Monkey Business**...*Slave To The Grind*	$3	▮	Atlantic 87673
1/4/92	88	3		5 **Wasted Time**...*C'mon And Love Me*	$3	▮	Atlantic 87565
				SKILLZ '02			
				Born in San Francisco, California. Male rapper.			
7/7/01	61^S	2		1 **Y'all Don't Wanna**...*(3 versions) / Do It Real Big*	$6	T	Rawkus 325
9/7/02	41^S	7		2 **Crew Deep**...*(2 versions) / Imagine*	$6	T	Rawkus 113991
				SKILLZ feat. Missy "Misdemeanor" Elliott and Kandi			
				samples "Rapper's Delight" by **Sugarhill Gang**			
				SKINDEEP R&B '96			
				Male R&B vocal trio from Brooklyn, New York: Tracy Hester, Rico Desire and Rick Gilsaint.			
4/27/96	92	5		**No More Games**...*(album version)*	$4	▮	Loose Cannon 852706
				SKINDEEP Featuring Li'l Kim of Junior M.A.F.I.A.			
				samples "In All My Wildest Dreams" by Joe Sample			
				SKIP LP '02			
				Born in New Orleans, Louisiana. Black male rapper.			
2/2/02	72^S	1		**Pimps/Players**...*(2 versions) / Strip B*tch / Black Robin Hood*	$7	T	UTP/Orpheus 90101
				SKIP (Featuring Corey Cee)			
				SKIP & FLIP BUB '59			
				Duo of Gary "Flip" Paxton and Clyde "Skip" Battin. Paxton formed the **Hollywood Argyles** and later started own Garpax record label.			
6/22/59	11	16		1 **It Was I**...*Lunch Hour*	$25		Brent 7002
11/2/59	71	5		2 **Fancy Nancy**...*It Could Be*	$25		Brent 7005
4/4/60	11	15		3 **Cherry Pie**...*(I'll Quit) Cryin' Over You*	$25		Brent 7010
				originally recorded in 1954 by the R&B duo Marvin & Johnny on Modern 933 ($75)			
				SKY LP '81			
				Classical-rock group: John Williams and Kevin Peek (guitars), Francis Monkman (keyboards), Herb Flowers (bass) and Tristan Fly (drums).			
1/10/81	83	2		**Toccata**...*(long version)* [I]	$5		Arista 0568
				written by Johann Sebastian Bach; tune also used in the movie *Rollerball* starring James Caan			
				SKY '99			
				Pop-dance duo from Montreal, Quebec, Canada: Antoine Sicotte and James Renald.			
7/10/99	60^S	7		**Love Song**...*(3 album snippets)*	$4	★	Arista 13684

DEBUT	PEAK	WKS	Gold	A-side (Chart Hit)	B-side	$	Sym	Label & Number
				SKYLARK BUB/AC/R&B/LP **'73**				
				Pop group from Vancouver, British Columbia, Canada: **Donny Gerrard**, **Carl Graves** and Bonnie Jean Cook (vocals), with **David Foster** (keyboards) and Duris Maxwell (drums). Foster was later with **Attitudes**, then a hit producer/songwriter/solo artist.				
2/17/73	9	21		**Wildflower**	*The Writing's On The Wall*	$5		Capitol 3511
				SKYLINERS, The BUB **'59**				
				White doo-wop group from Pittsburgh, Pennsylvania: **Jimmy Beaumont** (lead; born on 10/21/40) (see #5 & 7 below), Janet Vogel and Wally Lester (tenors), Joe VerScharen (baritone) and Jackie Taylor (bass voice, guitarist). The group that recorded on Jubilee (song #6 below) consisted of Jackie Taylor (lead vocals), Thom Davies, Robert Peckman, Jack O'Neil and Elaine Sofocle. Peckman was later a member of **The Jaggerz** and **Q**. Vogel committed suicide on 2/21/80.				
2/16/59	12	19		1 **Since I Don't Have You**	*One Night, One Night*	$50		Calico 103
6/1/59	26	12		2 **This I Swear**	*Tomorrow*	$30		Calico 106
9/28/59	59	8		3 **It Happened Today**	*Lonely Way*	$30		Calico 109
				Lannie Martin (orch., all of above)				
5/9/60	24	13		4 **Pennies From Heaven**	*I'll Be Seeing You*	$30		Calico 117
				#1 hit for **Bing Crosby** in 1936				
12/25/61	100	1		5 **Ev'rybody's Cryin'**	*Camera* [N]	$25		May 112
				JIMMIE BEAUMONT				
7/17/65	72	5		6 **The Loser**	*Everything Is Fine*	$15		Jubilee 5506
3/22/75	100	1		7 **Where Have They Gone**	*I Could Have Loved You So Well*	$25		Capitol 3979
				JIMMY BEAUMONT AND THE SKYLINERS				
				SKYY R&B/BUB/LP **'82**				
				R&B-pop-dance group from Brooklyn, New York: sisters Denise, Delores and Bonnie Dunning (vocals), Solomon Roberts (vocals, guitar), Anibal "Boochie" Sierra (guitar), Wayne Wilentz (keyboards), Gerald LaBon (bass) and Tommy McConnell (drums). Group organized by Randy Muller, former leader of **Brass Construction**.				
1/16/82	26	11		1 **Call Me** RB[2]	*When You Touch Me*	$4		Salsoul 2152
1/20/90	47	12		2 **Real Love** RB[1]	*Feelin' It Now*	$3	▮[V]	Atlantic 88816
				SKYY, Aaron **'99**				
				Born in Los Angeles, California. R&B singer/songwriter.				
8/28/99	42[S]	8		**The One**	*(4 album snippets)*	$4	★	Red Ant 15334
				SLADE BUB/LP **'84**				
				Hard-rock group formed in Wolverhampton, England: Noddy Holder (vocals), David Hill (guitar), Jim Lea (bass, keyboards) and Don Powell (drums).				
9/30/72	97	2		1 **Take Me Bak 'Ome**	*Wonderin' Y*	$10		Polydor 15046
11/18/72+	76	10		2 **Mama Weer All Crazee Now**	*Man Who Speeks Evil*	$10		Polydor 15053
3/10/73	68	6		3 **Gudbuy T' Jane**	*I Won't Let It 'Appen Agen*	$10		Polydor 15060
5/26/73	98	2		4 **Cum On Feel The Noize**	*I'm Mee, I'm Now, An' That's Orl*	$10		Polydor 15069
				all of above produced by Chas Chandler of **The Animals**				
4/7/84	20	17		5 **Run Runaway** AR[2]	*Don't Tame A Hurricane*	$5		CBS Associated 04398
7/7/84	37	11		6 **My Oh My**	*High And Dry*	$5		CBS Associated 04528
5/4/85	86	3		7 **Little Sheila**	*Lock Up Your Daughters*	$5		CBS Associated 04865
				SLADES, The **'58**				
				White doo-wop trio from Austin, Texas: Don Burch (lead), Jimmy Davis and Tommy Kaspar.				
8/4/58	42	12		**You Cheated** H:42	*The Waddle*	$50	⊙	Domino 500
				promo copies issued with an insert featuring photos of the trio and a memo from the president of Domino Records				
				SLATKIN, Felix, Orchestra BUB/LP **'60**				
				Born in 1915 in St. Louis, Missouri. Died on 2/9/63 (age 47). Conductor/composer/arranger.				
10/3/60	70	8		**Theme From The Sundowners**	*Gaythers Gone* [I]	$12		Liberty 55282
				title song from the movie starring **Robert Mitchum** and Deborah Kerr				
				SLAUGHTER ROK/LP **'90**				
				Hard-rock group formed in Las Vegas, Nevada: Mark Slaughter (vocals), Tim Kelly (guitar), Dana Strum (bass) and Blas Elias (drums). Slaughter and Strum were with the Vinnie Vincent Invasion. Kelly died in a car crash on 2/5/98 (age 35).				
4/28/90	27	14		1 **Up All Night** S:15	*Eye To Eye / Stick It To Ya Medley*	$3	▮	Chrysalis 23486
8/18/90	19	18		2 **Fly To The Angels** S:9 / A:35	*Desperately*	$3	▮[V]	Chrysalis 23527
12/22/90+	39	13		3 **Spend My Life** S:27	*She Wants More*	$3	▮	Chrysalis 23605
8/22/92	69	8		4 **Real Love** S:62	*She Wants More (live)*	$3	▮	Chrysalis 50401
				SLAVE R&B/BUB/LP **'77**				
				R&B-funk band from Dayton, Ohio, formed by Steve Washington (trumpet) in 1975. Longtime members of group included Mark "The Hansolor" Adams (bass), Floyd Miller (vocals, horns) and Danny Webster (vocals, guitar). Washington and members Starleana Young and Curt Jones (vocals) and Tom Lockett, Jr. (sax) left to form **Aurra** (see #4 below) in 1979. **Steve Arrington** (drums, vocals) (see #5 below) was a member from 1979-82. Young and Jones later formed **Déja** (see #6 below).				
6/18/77	32	13		1 **Slide** RB[1]	*Son Of Slide* [I]	$5		Cotillion 44218
1/17/81	78	6		2 **Watching You**	*Dreamin'*	$4		Cotillion 46006
10/24/81	91	7		3 **Snap Shot**	*Funken Town*	$4		Cotillion 46022
3/20/82	71	7		4 **Make Up Your Mind**	*(instrumental)*	$4		Salsoul 7017
				AURRA				
8/17/85	68	6		5 **Dancin' In The Key Of Life**	*Brown Baby Boy*	$4		Atlantic 89535
				STEVE ARRINGTON				
11/21/87	54	12		6 **You And Me Tonight**	*Premonition*	$4	■	Virgin 99422
				DÉJA				
				SLAY, Frank, and his Orchestra **'62**				
				Born on 7/8/30 in Dallas, Texas. Head A&R man for Swan, 1961-63. Produced and wrote the majority of **Freddy Cannon**'s hits. Co-writer of "Silhouettes" and "La Dee Dah."				
12/11/61+	45	9		**Flying Circle**	*Cincinnati* [I]	$10		Swan 4085
				adaptation of the traditional Jewish harvest song "Hava Nagila" ("Dance Everyone Dance")				

DEBUT	PEAK	WKS	Gold	A-side (Chart Hit)..........B-side	$	Sym	Label & Number
	★510★			**SLEDGE, Percy** BUB/R&B/LP **'66**			
				Born on 11/25/40 in Leighton, Alabama. R&B singer. Worked local clubs with the Esquires Combo until going solo. Pleaded guilty to tax evasion on 4/7/94. Cousin of **Jimmy Hughes**.			
				1)When A Man Loves A Woman 2)Take Time To Know Her 3)Warm And Tender Love			
4/9/66	1^{2}	13	●	1 **When A Man Loves A Woman** RB^{4} *Love Me Like You Mean It*	$15		Atlantic 2326
				reissued with a picture sleeve in 1987 on Atlantic 89262 as a cut from the movie *Platoon*			
7/23/66	17	9		2 **Warm And Tender Love** ....*Sugar Puddin'*	$10		Atlantic 2342
10/22/66	20	11		3 **It Tears Me Up** ....*Heart Of A Child*	$10		Atlantic 2358
2/18/67	87	5		4 **Baby, Help Me** ....*You've Got That Something Wonderful*	$10		Atlantic 2383
4/8/67	59	7		5 **Out Of Left Field** ....*It Can't Be Stopped*	$10		Atlantic 2396
6/17/67	40	6		6 **Love Me Tender** /			
				adapted from the 1861 tune "Aura Lee"			
7/8/67	91	2		7 **What Am I Living For**	$10		Atlantic 2414
9/2/67	66	4		8 **Just Out Of Reach (Of My Two Empty Arms)** ....*Hard To Believe*	$10		Atlantic 2434
11/25/67+	42	8		9 **Cover Me** ....*Behind Every Great Man There's A Woman*	$10		Atlantic 2453
3/16/68	11	14		10 **Take Time To Know Her** ....*It's All Wrong But It's Alright*	$10		Atlantic 2490
8/3/68	63	5		11 **Sudden Stop** ....*Between These Arms*	$10		Atlantic 2539
2/1/69	93	4		12 **My Special Prayer** ....*Bless Your Little Sweet Soul*	$10		Atlantic 2594
4/12/69	86	4		13 **Any Day Now** ....*The Angels Listened In (#126)*	$10		Atlantic 2616
				all of above produced by Quin Ivy and Marlin Greene			
11/16/74	62	6		14 **I'll Be Your Everything** ....*Blue Water*	$8		Capricorn 0209
				SLICK **'99**			
				Dance-rap studio group from Minneapolis, Minnesota. Formed to "cover" **Will Smith**'s 1999 hit "Miami."			
2/20/99	61^{S}	5		**Miami** ....*(3 versions)*	$5	★	Twin Sounds 4251
				samples "And The Beat Goes On" by **The Whispers**			
				SLICK, Grace — see JEFFERSON AIRPLANE			
				SLICK RICK R&B/BUB/LP **'96**			
				Born Ricky Walters on 1/14/65 in South Wimbledon, London, England (to Jamaican parents). Male rapper. To the U.S. At age 14. Attended New York's High School of Music & Art. Teamed with Doug E. Fresh, 1984-85; known as "M.C. Ricky D." In 1991, sentenced to 3-10 years in prison for a shooting incident. Entered a work-release program in June 1993.			
7/6/91	40^{S}	10		1 **I Shouldn't Have Done It** ....*(instrumental)*	$4	▮	Def Jam 73739
11/26/94	87	3		2 **Behind Bars** ....S:57 *(album version)*	$4	▮	Def Jam 851060
				Warren G (guest rapper); samples "Sometimes I Cry" by **Les McCann**			
3/18/95	54^{S}	4		3 **Sittin' In My Car** ....BUB:101 *(album version)*	$4	▮	Def Jam 853992
				SLICK RICK Featuring Doug E. Fresh On The Beatbox			
				samples "For The Love Of You" by **The Isley Brothers**			
6/29/96	28	20		4 **I Like** S:14 *Come Around* (Dos Of Soul)	$3	▮	Def Jam/RAL 575046
				MONTELL JORDAN FEATURING SLICK RICK			
				samples "I Get Lifted" by **KC & The Sunshine Band**; from the movie *The Nutty Professor* starring **Eddie Murphy**			
7/5/97	68	8		5 **Just Another Case** ....S:58 *(remix) / Pronto*	$4	▮	Violator 573856
				CRU Featuring Slick Rick			
				samples "Mona Lisa" by Slick Rick, "The World Is A Place" by Rhythm and "Everybody Plays The Fool" by **The Main Ingredient**			
				SLOAN, P.F. BUB **'65**			
				Born Phillip "Flip" Sloan in Los Angeles, California. Pop-rock singer/guitarist/songwriter. Recorded for Aladdin in 1959. Wrote "Secret Agent Man," "Eve Of Destruction," "A Must To Avoid" and many others.			
9/25/65	87	2		**The Sins Of A Family** ....*This Mornin'*	$15		Dunhill 4007
				SLUG — see ATMOSPHERE			
				SLUM VILLAGE R&B/LP **'02**			
				Rap trio from Detroit, Michigan: Titus "Baatin" Glover, RL "T3" Altman and Jason "Elzhi" Powers.			
7/20/02	87	11		**Tainted** ....S:40 *(2 versions) / Get Live*	$6	T	Barak/Priority 77750
				SLUM VILLAGE Featuring Dwele			
				SLY & THE FAMILY STONE ★191★ R&B/BUB/LP **'69**			
				Interracial "psychedelic soul" group from San Francisco, California: Sylvester "Sly Stone" Stewart (lead singer, keyboards; born on 3/15/44 in Dallas, Texas). Sly's brother Freddie Stone (guitar), Cynthia Robinson (trumpet), Jerry Martini (saxophone; **Rubicon**), Sly's sister Rosie Stone (piano, vocals), Sly's cousin **Larry Graham** (bass) and Gregg Errico (drums). Sly recorded gospel at age four. Producer and writer for Bobby Freeman, **The Mojo Men**, and **The Beau Brummels**. Formed own groups, The Stoners, in 1966 and The Family Stone and **Abaco Dream** (see #9 below) in 1967. Played Woodstock Festival in 1969. Career waned in the mid-1970s. Worked with George Clinton in 1982. Graham formed **Graham Central Station** in 1973. Group inducted into the Rock and Roll Hall of Fame in 1993. Also see **Little Sister**.			
				1)Everyday People 2)Family Affair 3)Thank You (Falettinme Be Mice Elf Agin) 4)Hot Fun In The Summertime 5)Dance To The Music			
2/10/68	8	15		1 **Dance To The Music** ....*Let Me Hear It From You*	$10		Epic 10256
7/27/68	93	3		2 **Life** /			
8/10/68	93	3		3 **M'Lady**	$10		Epic 10353
11/30/68+	1^{4}	19	●	4 **Everyday People** / RB^{2}			
3/8/69	89	4		5 **Sing A Simple Song**	$10	■	Epic 10407
4/12/69	22	8		6 **Stand!** /			
5/24/69	60	7		7 **I Want To Take You Higher**	$10	■	Epic 10450
				issued with a black-and-white text sleeve; also see #12 below; above 4 from the album *Stand!*			
8/9/69	2^{2}	16		8 **Hot Fun In The Summertime** ....*Fun*	$10		Epic 10497
9/6/69	74	6		9 **Life And Death In G & A** ....*Cat Woman*	$10		A&M 1081
				ABACO DREAM			
				recorded in 1967			
1/3/70	1^{2}	13	●	10 **Thank You Falettinme Be Mice Elf Agin** / RB^{5}			
1/3/70		13		11 **Everybody Is A Star**	$10	■	Epic 10555

DEBUT	PEAK	WKS	Gold	A-side (Chart Hit)......B-side	$	Sym	Label & Number
				SLY & THE FAMILY STONE — Cont'd			
5/23/70	38	9		12 **I Want To Take You Higher** ......*Stand!* [R]	$10	□	Epic 10450
				re-charted due to performance at the Woodstock Festival; promo text sleeve issued (same style as #7 above) except with the additional wording "Special Reservice"			
11/6/71	❶3	14	●	13 **Family Affair** ......RB5 *Luv N' Haight*	$8		Epic 10805
2/5/72	23	10		14 **Runnin' Away** ......*Brave & Strong*	$8		Epic 10829
4/22/72	42	7		15 **Smilin'** ......*Luv N' Haight*	$6		Epic 10850
6/30/73	12	17	●	16 **If You Want Me To Stay** ......*Thankful N' Thoughtful*	$6		Epic 11017
11/24/73	79	2		17 **Frisky** ......*If It Were Left Up To Me* (R&B #57)	$6		Epic 11060
7/6/74	32	12		18 **Time For Livin'** ......*Small Talk*	$6		Epic 11140
10/19/74	84	4		19 **Loose Booty** ......*Can't Strain My Brain*	$6		Epic 50033
9/6/75	52	9		20 **I Get High On You** ......*That's Lovin' You*	$5		Epic 50135
				SLY STONE			
				all of above written and produced by Sly Stone			
10/25/86	53	16		21 **Crazay** ......*Drive Yo Cadillac* (Johnson)	$3	■	A&M 2878
				JESSE JOHNSON (Featuring Sly Stone)			
				SLY FOX LP '86			
				Biracial pop-dance duo: Gary "Mudbone" Cooper (Bootsy's Rubber Band) and Michael Camacho.			
12/28/85+	7	25		1 **Let's Go All The Way** ......S:6 / A:7 *Como Tu Te Llama? (What Is Your Name)*	$3		Capitol 5552
				originally released on Capitol 5463; based on the same groove as The Boogie Boys' "A Fly Girl" ("Bubbled Under" at #102 in 1985)			
6/7/86	94	2		2 **Stay True** ......*If Push Comes To A Shove*	$3	■	Capitol 5581
				SMALL, Millie LP '64			
				Born Millicent Small on 10/6/46 in Jamaica. Reggae-ska singer. Nicknamed "The Blue Beat Girl."			
5/23/64	2¹	12		1 **My Boy Lollipop** ......*Something's Gotta Be Done*	$15		Smash 1893
				originally recorded by Barbie Gaye on DARL 1002 in 1956			
8/8/64	40	7		2 **Sweet William** ......*What Am I Living For*	$12		Smash 1920
				SMALL FACES/FACES BUB/LP '68			
				Rock group formed in England: Steve Marriott (guitar), Ronnie Lane (bass), Ian McLagan (organ) and Kenney Jones (drums). In 1968, Marriott formed **Humble Pie**. In 1969, remaining members formed **Faces** with former **Jeff Beck** Group members **Rod Stewart** (vocals) and **Ronnie Wood** (bass). Lane left in 1973; replaced by Tetsu Yamauchi (**Free**). Disbanded in late 1975. Wood joined **The Rolling Stones** in 1976. Jones joined **The Who** in 1978 and formed The Law in 1991. Marriott died in a fire on 4/20/91 (age 44). Lane died of multiple sclerosis on 6/4/97 (age 51).			
				SMALL FACES:			
11/11/67+	16	17		1 **Itchycoo Park** ......*I'm Only Dreaming*	$15		Immediate 501
3/16/68	73	5		2 **Tin Soldier** ......*I Feel Much Better*	$15	■	Immediate 5003
				picture sleeve issued with either a gold or pink title strip			
				FACES:			
11/20/71	24	9		3 **(I Know) I'm Losing You** *[ROD STEWART With Faces]*......*Mandolin Wind* (Stewart)	$8		Mercury 73244
1/1/72	17	10		4 **Stay With Me** ......*You're So Rude*	$8		Warner 7545
3/10/73	48	9		5 **Cindy Incidentally** ......*Skewiff (Mend The Fuse)*	$8	■	Warner 7681
				Rod Stewart (vocal, above 3)			
				SMART E'S '92			
				Techno-dance trio from Romford, Essex, England: Tom Orton, Chris Howell and Nick Arnold.			
10/10/92	60	16		**Sesame's Treet** ......S:30 *(remix)* [N]	$6	▮	Pyrotech 10083
				based on the theme from the children's PBS-TV show *Sesame Street*			
	★539★			**SMASHING PUMPKINS, The** ROK/BUB/LP '96			
				Rock group formed in Chicago, Illinois: Billy Corgan (vocals, guitar; born on 3/17/67), James Iha (guitar; born on 3/26/68), D'Arcy Wretzky (bass; born on 5/1/68) and Jimmy Chamberlin (drums; born on 6/10/64). Touring keyboardist Jonathan Melvoin, brother of Wendy Melvoin (of **Prince**'s Revolution and **Wendy & Lisa**) died of a drug overdose on 7/12/96 (age 34). Group disbanded in 2001. Corgan and Chamberlain formed Zwan in 2002.			
				1)1979 2)Bullet With Butterfly Wings 3)Landslide			
12/25/93+	69^A	3		1 **Today** BUB:103			album cut
2/19/94	48^A	23		2 **Disarm**			album cut
				above 2 from the album *Siamese Dream* on Virgin 88267			
10/15/94	30^A	14		3 **Landslide**			album cut
				from the album *Pisces Iscariot* on Virgin 39834; recorded by **Fleetwood Mac** on their 1975 self-titled album			
11/11/95+	22	20	●	4 **Bullet With Butterfly Wings** ......S:20 / A:26 ...*Said Sadly*	$3	▮V	Virgin 38522 ■
2/10/96	12	22	●	5 **1979** AR² / MR¹ A:9 / S:24 *Ugly / Believe / Cherry*	$3	▮V	Virgin 38534 ■
				"45" issued for above 2 (with picture sleeve) on Virgin 38522			
3/9/96	49^A	12		6 **Zero**			album cut
				issued as one cut on a special 7-track EP "Zero" on Virgin 38545			
6/29/96	36	20		7 **Tonight, Tonight** ......A:33 / S:44 *Meladori Magpie / Rotten Apples / Medellia Of The Gray Skies*	$4	▮	Virgin 38547
9/28/96	57^A	8		8 **Muzzle**			album cut
11/30/96+	39	20		9 **Thirty-Three** ......A:42 / S:51 *The Last Song / The Aeroplane Flies High / Transformer*	$4	▮	Virgin 38574
				#4-9: from the album *Mellon Collie And The Infinite Sadness* on Virgin 40861			
3/22/97	49^A	11		10 **Eye**			album cut
				from the movie *Lost Highway* starring Bill Pullman (soundtrack on Nothing 90090)			
6/7/97	50^A	8		11 **The End Is The Beginning Is The End**			album cut
				from the movie *Batman & Robin* starring George Clooney (soundtrack on Warner 46620)			
7/4/98	42	20		12 **Ava Adore** ......A:49 / S:59 *Czarina / Once In A While*	$4	▮	Virgin 38647
10/24/98	54	6		13 **Perfect** ......A:53 *Summer / Daphne Descends*	$5	★	Virgin 38650
				all of above (except #3) written by Corgan			

DEBUT	PEAK	WKS	Gold	A-side (Chart Hit)	B-side	$	Sym	Label & Number
				SMASH MOUTH ROK/BUB/LP **'99**				
				Pop-rock group from San Jose, California: Steve Harwell (vocals), Greg Camp (guitar), Paul DeLisle (bass) and Kevin Coleman (drums).				
7/26/97+	2[1A]	60		1 **Walkin' On The Sun** MR[5]				album cut
				from the album *Fush Yu Mang* on Interscope 90142				
7/4/98	27[A]	13		2 **Can't Get Enough Of You Baby**				album cut
				from the movie *Can't Hardly Wait* starring Jennifer Love Hewitt (soundtrack on Elektra 62201)				
5/22/99	4	30		3 **All Star** A:❶[5]			v	album cut
				from the movie *Mystery Men* starring Ben Stiller				
10/30/99+	11	26		4 **Then The Morning Comes** A:8			v	album cut
				above 2 from the album *Astro Lounge* on Interscope 90316; "45" issued for above 2 on Interscope 71007				
7/21/01	25	20		5 **I'm A Believer** A:24				album cut
				from the soundtrack of the animated movie *Shrek* on DreamWorks 450305				
				SMIF-N-WESSUN — see COCOA BROVAZ				
				SMILEZ & SOUTHSTAR LP **'02**				
				Male rap duo from Orlando, Florida.				
6/8/02	8[S]	16		**Who Wants This?**	*(3 versions)*	$6	★	Artist Direct 01042
				SMITH BUB/LP **'69**				
				Pop-rock group from Los Angeles, California: **Gayle McCormick** (vocals), Rick Cliburn and Alan Parker (guitars), Larry Moss (keyboards), Jerry Carter (bass) and Robert Evans (drums).				
9/6/69	5	15		1 **Baby It's You**	*I Don't Believe (I Believe)*	$7	■	Dunhill/ABC 4206
2/21/70	43	7		2 **Take A Look Around**	*Mojalesky Ridge*	$7		Dunhill/ABC 4228
6/6/70	73	4		3 **What Am I Gonna Do**	*Born In Boston*	$7	■	Dunhill/ABC 4238
				SMITH, Betty, Group **'58**				
				British group led by saxophonist Betty Smith.				
6/30/58	50	5		**Bewitched** S:50 / T:51	*Hand Jive* [I]	$20	■	London 1787
				there were 5 Top 10 versions of this tune in 1950 (from the 1941 Rodgers & Hart musical *Pal Joey*; a special foldout picture sleeve was issued by WIL Radio in St. Louis with the heading "Music For Hand Jiving" and instructions on how to do it				
				SMITH, Bro **'76**				
				Born Alan Smith on 4/8/45 in Brooklyn, New York. DJ (under the name of "Brother Love") on WCAO in Baltimore at the time of his hit.				
5/8/76	57	5		**Bigfoot**	*Splish Splash* [N]	$7	■	Big Tree 16061
				SMITH, Cal C&W/LP **'73**				
				Born Calvin Grant Shofner on 4/7/32 in Gans, Oklahoma; raised in Oakland, California. Country singer/guitarist (charted 36 hits, 1967-86). Worked with Ernest Tubb from 1961-67.				
3/10/73	64	8		**The Lord Knows I'm Drinking** AC[1]	*Sweet Things I Remember About You*	$6		Decca 33040
				written by **Bill Anderson**				
				SMITH, Carl C&W/BUB **'59**				
				Born on 3/15/27 in Maynardsville, Tennessee. Country singer/songwriter/guitarist (charted 93 hits, 1951-78). Married to **June Carter** from 1952-56; their daughter is **Carlene Carter**.				
3/24/58	80	2		1 **Your Name Is Beautiful** T:80	*You're So Easy To Love*	$15		Columbia 41092
9/8/58	93	1		2 **Guess I've Been Around Too Long** H:93	*Goodnight Mister Sun*	$15		Columbia 41170
7/6/59	43	9		3 **Ten Thousand Drums**	*The Tall, Tall Gentleman*	$12	■	Columbia 41417
				above 2 co-written by Mel Tillis				
				SMITH, Darden C&W **'93**				
				Born on 3/11/62 in Brenham, Texas. Pop-folk singer/songwriter/guitarist.				
10/2/93	96	2		**Loving Arms**	*Hole In The River*	$3	▮	Chaos/Columbia 77101
				SMITH, Frankie LP **'81**				
				Born in Philadelphia, Pennsylvania. R&B singer/songwriter/producer.				
5/16/81	30	19	●	**Double Dutch Bus** RB[4]	*Double Dutch* [N]	$5		WMOT 5356
				based on the double-dutch jump rope game; certified gold for both the 7" and 12" singles; originally recorded "Double Dutch" in 1972 as Franklin Franklin on Paramount 0227 ($10)				
				SMITH, Huey (Piano), And The Clowns **'58**				
				Born on 1/26/34 in New Orleans, Louisiana. R&B and comical rock and roll band leader/songwriter. With Earl King in the early 1950s. Recorded with Eddie "Guitar Slim" Jones's band from 1951-54. Much session work in New Orleans. Own band, The Clowns, in 1957 with **Bobby Marchan** (vocals). Marchan left in 1960, replaced by Curly Smith. Also see **Frankie Ford**.				
8/12/57	52	13		1 **Rocking Pneumonia And The Boogie Woogie Flu** T:52	*Part 2*	$30		Ace 530
3/24/58	9	13		2 **Don't You Just Know It** T:9 / S:13	*High Blood Pressure*	$30		Ace 545
12/8/58+	56	6		3 **Don't You Know Yockomo**	*Well I'll Be John Brown*	$25		Ace 553
2/17/62	51	8		4 **Pop-Eye** *[HUEY SMITH]*	*Scald-Dog*	$15		Ace 649
				SMITH, Hurricane LP **'73**				
				Born Norman Smith on 2/22/23 in London, England. Pop singer/producer.				
12/2/72+	3	15		1 **Oh, Babe, What Would You Say?**	*Getting To Know You*	$6		Capitol 3383
3/17/73	49	9		2 **Who Was It?**	*Take Suki Home*	$5		Capitol 3455
				SMITH, Jerry, and His Pianos C&W/AC/BUB/LP **'69**				
				Session pianist. Wrote and performed on **The Dixiebelles**' "(Down At) Papa Joe's" as Cornbread & Jerry.				
5/10/69	71	7		**Truck Stop**	*My Happiness* [I]	$7		ABC 11162

DEBUT	PEAK	WKS	Gold	A-side (Chart Hit)..........B-side	$	Sym	Label & Number
				SMITH, Jimmy BUB/LP **'62**			
				Born on 12/8/25 in Norristown, Pennsylvania. Pioneer jazz organist. Won Major Bowes Amateur Show in 1934. With father (James Sr.) in song-and-dance team, 1942. With **Don Gardner** & The Sonotones, recorded for Bruce in 1953. Smith first recorded with own trio for Blue Note in 1956.			
				1)Walk On The Wild Side 2)Got My Mojo Working 3)Back At The Chicken Shack			
3/3/62	69	8		1 **Midnight Special, Part 1**..........*Part 2* [I]	$12		Blue Note 1819
5/12/62	21	13		2 **Walk On The Wild Side Part 1**..........*Part 2* [I] **JIMMY SMITH AND THE BIG BAND** title song from the movie starring Laurence Harvey and Jane Fonda	$12		Verve 10255
9/1/62	82	3		3 **Ol' Man River**..........*Bashin'* [I] from the Hammerstein/Kern musical *Show Boat*	$10		Verve 10262
3/9/63	63	6		4 **Back At The Chicken Shack, Part 1**..........*Part 2* [I] #1 & 4: with Stanley Turrentine (sax), Kenny Burrell (guitar) and Donald Bailey (drums)	$10		Blue Note 1877
5/11/63	69	6		5 **Hobo Flats - Part I**..........*Part II* [I]	$10	■	Verve 10283
11/2/63	96	1		6 **Theme From Any Number Can Win**..........*What'd I Say?* (Smith & **Kenny Burrell** - #113) [I] title song from the French movie starring Jean Gabin	$10		Verve 10299
4/25/64	72	5		7 **Who's Afraid Of Virginia Woolf? (Part I)**..........*(Part II)* [I] from the 1962 Broadway show starring Arthur Hill and Uta Hagen	$10		Verve 10314
9/5/64	67	6		8 **The Cat**..........*Basin Street Blues* [I] from the movie *Joy House* starring Jane Fonda	$10		Verve 10330
10/2/65	92	3		9 **The Organ Grinder's Swing**..........*I'll Close My Eyes* [I] **JIMMY SMITH With KENNY BURRELL And GRADY TATE** #2 hit for Jimmie Lunceford in 1936	$8		Verve 10363
4/2/66	51	7		10 **Got My Mojo Working (Part I)**..........*(Part II)*	$8		Verve 10393
8/27/66	94	2		11 **I'm Your Hoochie Cooche Man (Part 1)**..........*(Part 2)* #3 R&B hit for Muddy Waters in 1954	$8		Verve 10426
4/6/68	100	2		12 **Chain Of Fools (Part 1)**..........*(Part 2)* [I]	$8		Verve 10583
				SMITH, Keely — see PRIMA, Louis / SINATRA, Frank			
				SMITH, Michael W. BUB/AC/LP **'91**			
				Born Michael Whitaker Smith on 10/7/57 in Kenova, West Virginia. Contemporary Christian singer/songwriter/keyboardist. To Nashville in 1978. Wrote Amy Grant's hit "Find A Way." Formed own label, Rocketown, in the mid-1990s.			
5/4/91	6	21		1 **Place In This World** A:17 / S:21 *Seed To Sow* co-written by **Amy Grant**	$3	■V	Reunion 19019
9/14/91	60	11		2 **For You**..........A:68 *(remix)*	$3	■V	Reunion 19103
9/19/92	27	20		3 **I Will Be Here For You**..........AC^{2} A:36 / S:37 *Color Blind*	$3	■	Reunion/Geffen 19139
3/13/93	71	7		4 **Somebody Love Me**..........*Out Of This World*	$3	■	Reunion/RCA 62465
4/25/98	61	5		5 **Love Me Good**..........S:52 *(acoustic version) / Evening Show*	$3	■	Reunion 410010
				SMITH, O.C. R&B/BUB/AC/LP **'68**			
				Born Ocie Lee Smith on 6/21/36 in Mansfield, Louisiana; raised in Los Angeles, California. Died on 11/23/2001 (age 65). Male R&B singer.			
				1)Little Green Apples 2)Daddy's Little Man 3)The Son Of Hickory Holler's Tramp			
2/24/68	40	14		1 **The Son Of Hickory Holler's Tramp**..........*The Best Man*	$8		Columbia 44425
8/17/68	2^{1}	17	●	2 **Little Green Apples** *Long Black Limousine*	$8		Columbia 44616
12/14/68	63	6		3 **Isn't It Lonely Together**..........*I Ain't The Worryin' Kind*	$6		Columbia 44705
2/8/69	44	6		4 **Honey (I Miss You)**..........*Keep On Keepin' On*	$6		Columbia 44751
5/10/69	47	9		5 **Friend, Lover, Woman, Wife**..........*I Taught Her Everything She Knows*	$6		Columbia 44859
8/30/69	34	7		6 **Daddy's Little Man**..........*If I Leave You Know* picture sleeve issued with either a green- or brown-tinted border	$6	■	Columbia 44948
5/30/70	86	3		7 **Primrose Lane**..........*Melodee*	$6		Columbia 45160
8/22/70	52	10		8 **Baby, I Need Your Loving**..........*San Francisco Is A Lonely Town*	$6		Columbia 45206
11/13/71	91	4		9 **Help Me Make It Through The Night**..........*Diamond In The Rough* all of above produced by **Jerry Fuller**	$6		Columbia 45435
9/28/74	62	7		10 **La La Peace Song**..........*When Morning Comes*	$6		Columbia 10031
				SMITH, Patti, Group ROK/LP **'78**			
				Born on 12/31/46 in Chicago, Illinois; raised in New Jersey. Punk-rock singer. Married to Fred "Sonic" Smith of the **MC5** from 1980-94. Her group: Lenny Kaye (guitar), Richard Sohl (keyboards), Ivan Kral (bass) and J.D. Daughtery (drums). Sohl died on 6/3/90 (age 37). Not to be confused with Patty Smyth of Scandal.			
4/8/78	13	18		1 **Because The Night**..........*God Speed* written by Smith and **Bruce Springsteen**	$6	■	Arista 0318
8/18/79	90	3		2 **Frederick**..........*(live version)* produced by **Todd Rundgren**	$5	■	Arista 0427
				SMITH, Ray BUB **'60**			
				Born on 10/31/34 in Melber, Kentucky. Committed suicide on 11/29/79 (age 45). Rockabilly singer/guitarist. Recorded for Sun Records, 1958-62.			
1/4/60	22	16		1 **Rockin' Little Angel**..........*That's All Right* melody adapted from the 1844 tune "Buffalo Gals"	$30		Judd 1016
5/9/60	91	2		2 **Put Your Arms Around Me Honey**..........*Maria Elena* #1 hit for Arthur Collins & Byron Harlan in 1911	$30		Judd 1017
				SMITH, Rex AC/BUB/LP **'79**			
				Born on 9/19/56 in Jacksonville, Florida. Actor/singer. Acted in several movies and Broadway shows. Brother of Michael Lee Smith of **Starz**.			
4/21/79	10	16	●	1 **You Take My Breath Away**..........*You're Never Too Old To Rock & Roll* introduced by Smith on 3/25/79 in the TV movie *Sooner Or Later*; released with 3 different B-sides	$4	■	Columbia 10908
6/27/81	32	13		2 **Everlasting Love**..........*Still Thinking Of You* (Smith) / *Billy And The Gun* (Sweet) **REX SMITH/RACHEL SWEET**	$4	■	Columbia 02169

DEBUT	PEAK	WKS	Gold	A-side (Chart Hit)..........B-side	$	Sym	Label & Number
				SMITH, Roger '59			
				Born on 12/18/32 in South Gate, California. Played "Jeff Spencer" on the TV series *77 Sunset Strip*. Married **Ann-Margret** on 5/8/67.			
6/29/59	64	8		**Beach Time**..........*Cuddle Up A Little Closer*	$12	■	Warner 5068
				SMITH, Sammi C&W/BUB/AC/LP '71			
				Born Jewel Fay Smith on 8/5/43 in Orange, California; raised in Oklahoma. Female country singer (charted 37 hits, 1968-86).			
1/16/71	8	16	●	1 **Help Me Make It Through The Night**..........CW[3] *When Michael Calls*	$6		Mega 0015
8/26/72	77	7		2 **I've Got To Have You**..........*Jimmy's In Georgia*	$6		Mega 0079
				above 2 written by **Kris Kristofferson**			
				SMITH, Somethin', & The Redheads '55			
				Adult Contemporary (1930s-styled) trio from Los Angeles, California: Smith (vocals, guitar), Saul Striks (piano) and Major Short (violin).			
4/2/55	7	23		1 **It's A Sin To Tell A Lie**..........S:7 / J:8 / A:9 *My Baby Just Cares For Me*	$12		Epic 9093
				#1 hit for Fats Waller in 1936			
11/12/55	90	1		2 **When All The Streets Are Dark**..........T:90 *Pretty Baby*	$10		Epic 9119
6/2/56	27	15		3 **In A Shanty In Old Shanty Town**..........T:27 *Coal Dust On The Fiddle*	$10		Epic 9168
				#1 hit for Ted Lewis in 1932			
9/8/56	71	6		4 **Heartaches**..........T:71 *Cecilia*	$10		Epic 9179
				#1 hit for Ted Weems in 1947 (recorded in 1933)			
				SMITH, Tab R&B/POP '51			
				Born Talmadge Smith on 1/11/09 in Kinston, North Carolina. Died on 8/17/71 (age 62). Black jazz alto saxophonist with the Mills Rhythm Band (1936-38), **Count Basie** (1940-42) and Lucky Millinder (1942-44). Hit #20 in 1951 with "Because Of You."			
3/30/57	89	3		**Pretend**..........T:89 *Crazy Walk* [I]	$25		United 205
				TAB SMITH His Fabulous Alto and his Band			
				#2 hit for **Nat "King" Cole** in 1953			
				SMITH, Verdelle '66			
				Born on 8/28/30 in St. Petersburg, Florida. Black female singer.			
2/5/66	62	7		1 **In My Room El Amor**..........*Walk Tall*	$10		Capitol 5567
7/9/66	38	8		2 **Tar And Cement**..........*A Piece Of The Sky*	$10		Capitol 5632
				SMITH, Warren C&W '57			
				Born on 2/7/32 in Humphreys County, Mississippi. Died of a heart attack on 1/30/80 (age 47). Rockabilly singer/songwriter.			
6/10/57	72	2		**So Long I'm Gone**..........T:72 *Miss Froggie*	$50		Sun 268
				written by **Roy Orbison**			
				SMITH, Whistling Jack '67			
				Studio session production conceived by songwriters Roger Greenaway and Roger Cook (**David & Jonathan**) and featuring the Mike Sammes Singers. Billy Moeller (born on 2/2/46 in Liverpool, England) was later hired to tour as Whistling Jack Smith. Not to be confused with the 1920s singer "Whispering" Jack Smith.			
4/29/67	20	7		**I Was Kaiser Bill's Batman**..........*The British Grin And Bear* [I]	$10		Deram 85005
	★456★			**SMITH, Will** LP '98			
				Born on 9/25/68 in Philadelphia, Pennsylvania. Rapper/actor. One-half of **D.J. Jazzy Jeff & The Fresh Prince** (1986-93). Starred on TV's *Fresh Prince of Bel Air* and in such movies as *Bad Boys*, *Independence Day*, *Men In Black* and *Enemy Of The State*. Married actress Jada Pinkett on 12/31/97.			
6/28/97	❶[4A]	25		1 **Men In Black**		V	album cut ■
				from the movie *Men In Black* starring Smith and Tommy Lee Jones (soundtrack on Columbia 68169)			
2/28/98	❶[3]	32	●	2 **Gettin' Jiggy Wit It**..........S:❶[2] / A:8 *Men In Black*	$3	▮[V]	Columbia 78804 ■
				samples "He's The Greatest Dancer" by **Sister Sledge**, "Sang And Dance" by **The Bar-Kays** and "Love Rap" by Spoonie Gee; "45" issued for above 2 on Columbia 78804; also see #8 below			
10/10/98	20	11		3 **Just The Two Of Us**..........A:6 / S:30 *(4 versions)*	$8	★*	Columbia 79038
12/5/98+	17	21		4 **Miami**..........A:8			album cut
				samples "And The Beat Goes On" by **The Whispers**; all of above from the album *Big Willie Style* on Columbia 68683			
5/22/99	❶[1]	17	●	5 **Wild Wild West**..........S:❶[1] / A:2 *Y'All Know* (Smith)	$4	★	Overbrook 79157
				WILL SMITH featuring Dru Hill and Kool Mo Dee			
				samples "Wild, Wild West" by **Kool Moe Dee** and "I Wish" by **Stevie Wonder**; title song from the movie starring Smith and Kevin Kline			
10/30/99	25	13		6 **Will 2K**..........A:20 *(2 versions)*	$6	T[V]	Columbia 79287
				WILL SMITH (Featuring K-Ci)			
				samples "Rock The Casbah" by **The Clash**; "45": Columbia 79286; B-side: (instrumental)			
2/12/00	99	4		7 **Freakin' It**..........S:63 *(3 versions) / Pump Me Up* (**DJ Jazzy Jeff & The Fresh Prince**)	$8	★*	Columbia 79341
				samples "Love Hangover" by **Diana Ross** and "Rapper's Delight" by **Sugarhill Gang**			
3/23/02	30[S]	20		8 **Gettin' Jiggy Wit It**..........*Men In Black (DJ Scratch remix)* [R]	$4	★	Columbia 79702
				reissue of #2 above on Columbia's "Platinum Hits" series			
6/29/02	77	3		9 **Black Suits Comin' (Nod Ya Head)**..........*(5 versions)*	$6	T	Columbia 79768
				WILL SMITH Introducing Tra-Knox			
				from the movie *Men In Black 2* starring Smith and Tommy Lee Jones			
				SMITHEREENS, The ROK/LP '90			
				Power-pop group formed in Carteret, New Jersey: Pat DiNizio (vocals, guitar), Jim Babjak (guitar), Mike Mesaros (bass) and Dennis Diken (drums).			
5/21/88	92	4		1 **Only A Memory**..........AR[1] *The Seeker*	$4	■	Enigma/Capitol 44150
12/9/89+	38	20		2 **A Girl Like You**..........S:34 / A:40 *(Part II) / Like Someone In Love*	$4	▮	Enigma/Capitol 44480
5/5/90	94	2		3 **Blues Before And After**..........*Maria Elena*	$4	▮	Enigma/Capitol 44516
2/8/92	37	14		4 **Too Much Passion**..........A:36 *If You Want The Sun To Shine*	$4	▮	Capitol 44784
				SMOKE RING, The '69			
				Pop group from Norfolk, Nebraska: brothers Joe, Nick and Bob Hupp, Jim Casey, Chuck Asmuss, John Schrad and Gary Benjamin.			
2/15/69	85	4		**No Not Much**..........*How'd You Get To Be So Wonderful*	$8		Buddah 77

DEBUT	PEAK	WKS	Gold	A-side (Chart Hit)...B-side	$	Sym	Label & Number

SMOKIE LP '77

Pop-rock group from Bradford, Yorkshire, England: **Chris Norman** (vocals), Alan Silson (guitar), Terry Utley (bass) and Pete Spencer (drums). Also see **Suzi Quatro**.

DEBUT	PEAK	WKS	Gold	A-side (Chart Hit)...B-side	$	Sym	Label & Number
7/26/75	96	3		1 **If You Think You Know How To Love Me** *[SMOKEY]*... *'Tis Me*	$6		MCA 40429
12/4/76+	25	20		2 **Living Next Door To Alice**... *When My Back Was Against The Wall*	$5		RSO 860
9/17/77	68	5		3 **Needles And Pins**... *No One Could Ever Love You More* written by **Sonny** Bono and **Jack Nitzsche**	$5		RSO 881

SMOOTH R&B/BUB '97

Female rapper. Also see **Immature**'s "We Got It."

DEBUT	PEAK	WKS	Gold	A-side (Chart Hit)...B-side	$	Sym	Label & Number
6/24/95	75	8		1 **Mind Blowin'**... S:54 *Undercover Lover* contains a portion of "Brazillian Rhyme" and samples "For The Love Of You" by **The Isley Brothers**	$4	▮	TNT/Jive 42286
2/1/97	32	14		2 **Watch Me Do My Thing**... S:19 **IMMATURE Featuring Smooth and Ed From Good Burger** from the Nickelodeon TV show *All That*	$3	▮	Loud/RCA 64737
2/21/98	49	17		3 **Strawberries**... S:30 *(instrumental) / (3 album snippets)* samples "Where There Is Love" by **Patrice Rushen**	$3	▮	Perspective 587596

SMOTHERS BROTHERS, The '63

Comedy team from New York: brothers Tom (guitar; born on 2/2/37) and Dick (standup bass; born on 11/20/39) Smothers. Hosted their own TV variety series from 1967-69. Own summer variety series, 1970; 1988-89.

DEBUT	PEAK	WKS	Gold	A-side (Chart Hit)...B-side	$	Sym	Label & Number
9/28/63	84	4		**Jenny Brown**... *You Go Thisaway* [N] **David Carroll** (orch.)	$12		Mercury 72182

SMUT PEDDLERS — see CAGE

SMYTH, Patty — see SCANDAL

SNAIL LP '78

Pop-rock group from Santa Cruz, California: Bob O'Neill (vocals, guitar), Ken Kraft (guitar), Jack Register (bass) and Jim Norris (drums). **Jefferson Starship** drummer Don Baldwin was a member (1979-82).

DEBUT	PEAK	WKS	Gold	A-side (Chart Hit)...B-side	$	Sym	Label & Number
9/23/78	93	2		**The Joker**... *Childhood Dreams*	$5		Cream 7827

SNAP! R&B/LP '90

Techno-dance duo formed in Pittsburgh, Pennsylvania: Turbo B (rap) and his cousin Jackie Harris (vocals). By 1992 Turbo B replaced by Niki Harris; Jackie Harris replaced by Pennye Ford.

DEBUT	PEAK	WKS	Gold	A-side (Chart Hit)...B-side	$	Sym	Label & Number
5/12/90	2^1	22	▲	1 **The Power**... S:❶^3 / A:11 *(remake dub)*	$3	▮^{V}	Arista 2013
9/8/90	35	11	●	2 **Ooops Up**... S:25 *Believe The Hype* samples "I Don't Believe You Want To Get Up And Dance (Oops, Up Side Your Head)" by **The Gap Band**	$3	▮^{V}	Arista 2060
8/15/92+	5	39	●	3 **Rhythm Is A Dancer**... A:4 / S:5 *Who Stole It?*	$3	▮	Arista 12437

SNEAKER LP '82

Pop-rock group formed in Los Angeles, California: Mitch Crane (vocals, guitar), Michael Carey Schneider (vocals, keyboards), Tim Torrance (guitar), Jim King (keyboards), Michael Cottage (bass) and Mike Hughes (drums).

DEBUT	PEAK	WKS	Gold	A-side (Chart Hit)...B-side	$	Sym	Label & Number
10/31/81+	34	15		1 **More Than Just The Two Of Us**... *In Time*	$4	■	Handshake 02557
2/27/82	63	5		2 **Don't Let Me In**... *Looking For Someone Like You* written by Walter Becker and **Donald Fagen** (**Steely Dan**)	$4		Handshake 02714

SNEAKER PIMPS LP '97

Dance-rock trio from Reading, England: Kelli Drayton (vocals), Chris Comer (guitar) and Liam Howe (keyboards).

DEBUT	PEAK	WKS	Gold	A-side (Chart Hit)...B-side	$	Sym	Label & Number
5/3/97	45	22		1 **6 Underground**... A:43 *(2 versions)* samples "Golden Girl" by **John Barry**	$4	▮^{V}	Virgin 38582
10/11/97	87	13		2 **Spin Spin Sugar**... *(remix)* "45" issued for above 2 on Virgin 19565	$4	▮^{V}	Virgin 38590

SNIFF 'N' THE TEARS BUB/LP '79

Rock group formed in London, England: Paul Roberts (vocals), **Loz Netto** (see #2 below) and Mick Dyche (guitars), Alan Fealdman (keyboards), Chris Birkin (bass) and Luigi Salvoni (drums).

DEBUT	PEAK	WKS	Gold	A-side (Chart Hit)...B-side	$	Sym	Label & Number
7/21/79	15	15		1 **Driver's Seat**... *Slide Away*	$5		Atlantic 3604
6/4/83	82	6		2 **Fade Away**... *Show Me* **LOZ NETTO**	$4		21 Records 104

★265★ SNOOP DOGG R&B/BUB/LP '94

Born Calvin Broadus on 10/20/72 in Long Beach, California. Male rapper. Childhood friend of **Dr. Dre** and **Warren G.** Cousin of **Nate Dogg** and Delmar "Dat Nigga Daz" Armaud (**Tha Dogg Pound**). Arrested in connection with a drive-by shooting in Los Angeles on 8/25/93. Acquitted of first-degree murder charges in February 1996. Also see **Lady Of Rage**.

1)What's My Name? 2)Gin & Juice 3)Nuthin' But A "G" Thang 4)Dre Day 5)Still A G Thang

SNOOP DOGGY DOGG:

DEBUT	PEAK	WKS	Gold	A-side (Chart Hit)...B-side	$	Sym	Label & Number
6/6/92	57^S	3		1 **Deep Cover**... *(instrumental)* **DR. DRE Introducing Snoop Doggy Dogg** title song from the movie starring Jeff Goldblum	$6	▮	Solar/Epic 74547
1/30/93	2^1	27	▲	2 **Nuthin' But A "G" Thang**... RB^2 S:❶^1 / A:10 *(instrumental)* "G": Gangsta; samples **Leon Haywood**'s "I Want'a Do Something Freaky To You"; also see #10 below	$3	▮	Death Row 53819
5/15/93	8	20	●	3 **Dre Day**... S:4 / A:17 *(instrumental)* **DR. DRE (featuring Snoop Doggy Dogg)** (above 2)	$3	▮	Death Row 53827
12/4/93+	8	17	●	4 **What's My Name?** S:6 / A:17 *(clean club mix)* also see #19 below	$3	▮	Death Row 98340
1/29/94	8	20	●	5 **Gin & Juice**... S:5 / A:22 *(radio mix)* samples "Watching You" by **Slave**	$3	▮	Death Row 98318
2/12/94	63^A	4		6 **Lodi Dodi**...			album cut
5/14/94	46^A	7		7 **Doggy Dogg World**...			album cut
12/17/94	67^A	1		8 **Murder Was The Case**... from the 18-minute, long-form video *Murder Was The Case* starring Snoop; above 5 from the album *Doggy Style* on Death Row 92279; all of above produced by **Dr. Dre**			album cut
11/9/96	33	19		9 **Never Leave Me Alone**... S:23 *(instrumental)* **NATE DOGG featuring Snoop Doggy Dogg** Val Young (female vocal); samples "Where Is The Love" by **Roberta Flack & Donny Hathaway**	$4	▮	Death Row 97012

DEBUT	PEAK	WKS	Gold	A-side (Chart Hit)......B-side	$	Sym	Label & Number
				SNOOP DOGG:			
9/5/98	**19**	13		10 **Still A G Thang**......S:12 *(remix) / Full Fledged Pimpin' / (instrumental)* clean version available on No Limit 53452; sequel to #2 above	$3	▮	No Limit 53450
10/24/98	**12**	15	●	11 **Come And Get With Me**......S:4 *Yumi* **KEITH SWEAT Featuring Snoop Dogg**	$4	★	Elektra 64080
1/30/99	**62**	12		12 **Woof**......S:14 *(instrumental) / It's All On A* ** **SNOOP DOGG Featuring Mystikal and Fiend** clean version available on No Limit 53463	$4	★	No Limit 53462
3/13/99	**58^{S}**	4		13 **We Be Puttin' It Down**......*(instrumental) / Ghetto Star* **BAD AZZ featuring Snoop Dogg** clean version available on No Limit 53467	$4	★	No Limit 53465
10/9/99	**77**	9		14 **B-Please**......A:62 **SNOOP DOGG Featuring Xzibit and Nate Dogg** produced by **Dr. Dre**; from the album *No Limit Top Dogg* on No Limit 50052			album cut
11/27/99	**93**	5		15 **Still D.R.E.**......S:73 *(3 versions)* **DR. DRE Featuring Snoop Dogg** co-written by **Jay-Z**	$6	T	Aftermath 497192
5/27/00	**23**	20		16 **The Next Episode**......A:16 / S:62 *(3 versions)* **DR. DRE Featuring Snoop Dogg** **Kurupt** (backing vocal)	$6	T	Aftermath 497333
6/24/00	**28**	7		17 **Crybaby**......S:2 *Can't Take That Away / Love Hangover/Heartbreaker* **MARIAH CAREY Featuring Snoop Dogg** samples "Piece Of My Love" by **Guy**; "45" B-side: "Can't Take That Away (Mariah's Theme)"	$4	★V	Columbia 79348
3/24/01	**50**	19		18 **Lay Low /** A:44 / S:53 *Wrong Idea* (w/**Bad Azz**, Kokane & Lil Half Dead - R&B #75) **SNOOP DOGG (featuring Master P, Nate Dogg, Butch Cassidy & Tha Eastsidaz)**			
2/3/01	**77**	5		19 **Snoop Dogg (What's My Name Pt. 2)**......A:69 *(instrumental)* Part 2 of #4 above; samples "Double Dutch Bus" by **Frankie Smith**	$6	T	No Limit 50174
7/14/01	**90**	4		20 **Just A Baby Boy**......*(4 versions)* **SNOOP DOGG feat. Tyrese & Mr. Tan** from the movie *Baby Boy* starring Tyrese	$6	T	Universal 158986
10/6/01	**84**	16		21 **Do U Wanna Roll**......S:12 *(2 versions) / Lookin' For Love* (w/**Next**) **R.L., SNOOP DOGG and LIL' KIM** samples "Doo Wa Ditty (Blow That Thing)" by **Zapp**; from the movie *Dr. Dolittle 2* starring **Eddie Murphy**; all of above (except #11, 13, 15 & 16) written or co-written by Snoop	$4	★	J Records 21132
11/9/02	**77**	10		22 **From Tha Chuuuch To Da Palace**......S:24 / A:73 *(2 versions) / Paper'd Up* (w/Mr. Kane & Traci Nelson)	$6	T	Doggystyle 77843
				SNOW LP **'93** Born Darrin O'Brien on 10/30/69 in Toronto, Ontario, Canada. White male reggae singer.			
1/9/93	**❶7**	25	▲	1 **Informer**......S:❶6 / A:4 *Lonely Monday Morning*	$3	▮V	EastWest 98471
5/15/93	**19**	17		2 **Girl, I've Been Hurt**......A:16 / S:22 *Champion Sound* "45" issued for above 2 on EastWest 98438	$3	▮V	EastWest 98438
				SNOW, Hank C&W/BUB/MEM/LP **'62** Born Clarence Snow on 5/9/14 in Liverpool, Nova Scotia, Canada. Died of heart failure on 12/20/99 (age 85). Country singer/songwriter/guitarist. Nicknamed "The Singing Ranger." Charted 85 Country hits, 1949-80.			
12/5/60	**87**	4		1 **Rockin', Rollin' Ocean**......*Walkin' And Talkin'*	$15		RCA Victor 7702
9/29/62	**68**	8		2 **I've Been Everywhere**......CW2 *Ancient History*	$12		RCA Victor 8072
				SNOW, Phoebe AC/R&B/BUB/LP **'75** Born Phoebe Laub on 7/17/52 in New York; raised in New Jersey. Pop-folk singer/songwriter/guitarist.			
1/4/75	**5**	18		1 **Poetry Man** AC1 *Either Or Both*	$6		Shelter 40353
8/16/75	**23**	10		2 **Gone At Last**......*Take Me To The Mardi Gras* (Simon) **PAUL SIMON/PHOEBE SNOW and The Jessy Dixon Singers**	$5		Columbia 10197
1/22/77	**70**	4		3 **Shakey Ground**......*Don't Sleep With Your Eyes Closed* later used as the theme for the TV series *Shaky Ground* starring Matt Frewer	$4		Columbia 10463
2/21/81	**46**	10		4 **Games**......*Down In The Basement*	$4		Mirage 3800
5/2/81	**52**	8		5 **Mercy, Mercy, Mercy**......*Something Good*	$4		Mirage 3818
				SNUFF C&W **'83** Country-rock group from Virginia: Jim Bowling (vocals), Robbie House and Chuck Larson (guitars), Cecil Hooker (fiddle), C. Scott Trabue (bass) and Michael Johnson (drums).			
8/20/83	**88**	2		**Bad, Bad Billy**......*Defiance*	$4		Warner/Curb 29615
				SO LP **'88** Pop-rock duo from London, England: singer/guitarist Mark Long and multi-instrumentalist Marcus Bell.			
2/20/88	**41**	11		**Are You Sure**......S:32 *Don't Look Back*	$3	■	EMI-Manhattan 50109
				S.O.A.P. **'98** Euro hip-hop vocal duo from Denmark: sisters Heidi and Line (Lee-nah) Sorensen.			
4/18/98	**51**	12		**This Is How We Party**......S:51 / A:62 *(5 album snippets)*	$4	▮	Crave 78876
				SOBER, Errol BUB **'79** Born in Los Angeles, California. Pop session singer.			
3/31/79	**65**	8		**Heart To Heart**......*Somethin's Goin' On*	$5		Number 1 215
				SOBULE, Jill AC **'95** Born on 1/16/59 in Denver, Colorado. Pop-rock singer/songwriter/guitarist.			
5/27/95	**67**	11		**I Kissed A Girl**......A:74 *Resistance Song*	$4	▮	Lava 87169
				SOCA BOYS, The **'00** Latin "soca" dance group featuring lead singer Van B. King.			
11/4/00	**68^{S}**	2		**Follow The Leader**......*(2 versions)*	$5	★	Republic 567471
				SOCCIO, Gino R&B/BUB/LP **'79** Born in 1955 in Montreal, Quebec, Canada. Techno-disco singer/multi-instrumentalist. Producer of **Witch Queen**.			
4/7/79	**48**	6		**Dancer**......*So Lonely*	$5		RFC/Warner 8757

DEBUT	PEAK	WKS	Gold	A-side (Chart Hit).....B-side	$	Sym	Label & Number
				SOCIAL DISTORTION ROK/LP **'96**			
				Punk-rock group formed in Los Angeles, California: Mike Ness (vocals, guitar), Dennis Danell (guitar), John Maurer (bass) and Christopher Reece (drums). Danell died of a brain aneurysm on 2/29/2000 (age 38).			
9/21/96	54^{A}	13		**I Was Wrong**.....			album cut
				from the album *White Light White Heat White Trash* on 550 Music/Epic 64380			
				SOFFICI, Piero **'61**			
				Born in Italy. Orchestra conductor/composer.			
4/24/61	59	7		**That's The Way With Love**.....*Valley Of My Heart* [I]	$12		Kip 224
				similar arrangement to **Percy Faith**'s "The Theme From A Summer Place"			
				SOFT CELL BUB/LP **'82**			
				Techno-pop duo from London, England: Peter **Marc Almond** (vocals; born on 7/9/57 in Southport, England) (see #2 below) and David Ball (synthesizer). Almond began solo career in late 1988.			
1/16/82	8	43		1 **Tainted Love**.....*Memorabilia*	$6	■	Sire 49855
				first recorded in 1964 by Gloria Jones on Champion 14003 ($25); promo copies (Sire 1028) issued as a medley: "Tainted Love/ Where Did Our Love Go" ($12); also see #3 below			
1/21/89	67	8		2 **Tears Run Rings**.....*Everything I Want Love To Be*	$4	■	Capitol 44240
				MARC ALMOND			
2/13/99	59^{S}	2		3 **Tainted Love**.....*(3 versions)* [R]	$6	★	Twisted 55530
				SOFT CELL vs. CLUB 69			
				remix of #1 above by **Club 69**'s producer Peter Rauhofer			
				SOHO LP **'90**			
				Interracial dance trio formed in London, England: identical twin sisters Jackie and Pauline Cuff (vocals), with Timothy Brinkhurst (guitar).			
9/8/90	14	19	●	**Hippychick**.....S:8 / A:22 *Taxi*	$3	▮V	Atco 98908
				samples a riff from The Smiths' "How Soon Is Now"			
				SOLÉ R&B/BUB/LP **'99**			
				Born on 7/17/73 in Kansas City, Missouri. Female rapper.			
4/24/99	5	20	●	1 **Who Dat**.....S:2 / A:47 *(2 versions)*	$4	★	Tony Mercedes 53469
				JT MONEY Featuring Solé			
10/30/99	21	16	●	2 **4,5,6**.....S:7 *(clean version) / Da Story*	$4	★	DreamWorks 59029
				SOLÉ Featuring J.T. Money and Kandi			
				SOLO R&B/BUB/LP **'95**			
				R&B vocal group from Brooklyn, New York: Eunique Mack, Darnell Chavis, Daniele Stokes and Robert Anderson.			
8/12/95	42	20		1 **Heaven**.....S:20 *(2 remixes)*	$4	▮V	Perspective 7498
1/6/96	50	18		2 **Where Do U Want Me To Put It**.....S:21 *A Change Is Gonna Come*	$4	▮V	Perspective 7512
				"45" issued for above 2 on Perspective 7512			
9/12/98	59	12		3 **Touch Me**.....S:37 *(4 album snippets)*	$4	▮	Perspective 7600
				SOLUNA **'02**			
				Female vocal group from Los Angeles, California: Jessica Castellanos, Christina Lopez, America Olivo and Aurora Rodriguez. All hail from Latin parentage.			
6/22/02	72	11		**For All Time**.....S:4 *(radio mix) / Patriotic Medley*	$4	★	DreamWorks 50836
				SOME, Belouis **'85**			
				Born Neville Keighley in England. Techno-dance singer/multi-instrumentalist.			
5/4/85	88	5		1 **Imagination**.....*Walk Away*	$3	■	Capitol 5464
8/3/85	67	6		2 **Some People**.....*Aware Of You*	$3	■	Capitol 5492
				SOMERVILLE, Jimmy LP **'87**			
				Born on 6/22/61 in Glasgow, Scotland. Lead singer/founder of the British dance-pop bands **Bronski Beat** (see #1 below) and **Communards** (see #2 & 3 below).			
12/22/84+	48	16		1 **Smalltown Boy**.....*Memories*	$4	■	MCA 52494
				BRONSKI BEAT			
12/27/86+	40	13		2 **Don't Leave Me This Way**.....S:31 *Sanctified*	$3	■	MCA/London 52928
1/30/88	51	9		3 **Never Can Say Goodbye**.....*'77, The Great Escape*	$3	■	MCA/London 53224
				COMMUNARDS (above 2)			
4/7/90	87	4		4 **You Make Me Feel (Mighty Real)**.....*Not So God Almighty*	$3	▮	London 886973
				SOMETHIN' FOR THE PEOPLE R&B/BUB/LP **'97**			
				R&B vocal trio from Oakland, California: Jeff "Fuzzy" Young, Curtis "Sauce" Wilson and Rochad "Cat Daddy" Holiday.			
8/24/96	98	2		1 **With You**.....S:67 *(album version)*	$4	▮	Warner 17681
8/30/97	4	26	●	2 **My Love Is The Shhh!**.....S:5 / A:17 *(instrumental)*	$3	▮	Warner 17327
				SOMETHIN' FOR THE PEOPLE featuring Trina & Tamara			
2/21/98	47	11		3 **All I Do**.....S:33 *(instrumental)*	$3	▮	Warner 17282
7/8/00	21^{S}	9		4 **Bitch With No Man**.....*(instrumental)*	$4	★	Warner 16877
				SOMMER, Bert **'70**			
				Pop singer/songwriter/actor. Died of liver failure on 7/23/90 (age 42). Played "Claude" in Broadway's *Hair* from 1969-70.			
8/8/70	48	8		**We're All Playing In The Same Band**.....*It's A Beautiful Day*	$7		Eleuthera 470
				SOMMERS, Joanie AC/BUB/LP **'62**			
				Born Joan Drost on 2/24/41 in Buffalo, New York; moved to California in 1954. Sang Pepsi-Cola jingles in the early and mid-1960s. Appeared in the movies *Everything's Ducky* and *The Lively Set*.			
7/4/60	54	9		1 **One Boy**.....*I'll Never Be Free*	$15	□	Warner 5157
				Don Ralke (orch.); from the Broadway musical *Bye Bye Birdie* starring **Dick Van Dyke**; issued with a promo sleeve titled "Sommers' Hot...Sommers' Here!"; also issued with a gold-colored half sleeve showing only Joanie's name and "One Boy"			
5/26/62	7	14		2 **Johnny Get Angry**.....*(Theme From) A Summer Place*	$15		Warner 5275
10/6/62	94	3		3 **When The Boys Get Together**.....*Passing Strangers*	$12		Warner 5308
				Stan Applebaum (orch., above 2)			
				SON BY FOUR BUB/LP **'00**			
				Latin vocal group from Puerto Rico: brothers Javier and George Montes, with cousin Pedro Quiles and friend Angel Lopez.			
4/8/00	26	26		**Purest Of Pain (A Puro Dolor)**.....S:11 / A:35 *(2 versions)*	$4	★	Sony Discos 83942
				sung in English and Spanish			

DEBUT	PEAK	WKS	Gold	A-side (Chart Hit)..................B-side	$	Sym	Label & Number
				SONIQUE LP **'00**			
				Born in England. Black female dance-pop singer. Half of the duo **S-Express**.			
1/22/00	8	24		It Feels So Good..................S:9 / A:9 *(remix)*	$4	★	Caffeine/Republic 156247
	★232★			**SONNY & CHER** BUB/LP **'65**			
				Husband-and-wife duo: **Sonny** Bono (born on 2/16/35 in Detroit, Michigan) and **Cher** (born on 5/20/46). Began career as session singers for Phil Spector. First recorded as Caesar & Cleo for Vault in 1963. Married from 1963-75. In the movies *Good Times* (1967) and *Chastity* (1969). Own CBS-TV variety series from 1971-74, 1976-77. Sonny was mayor of Palm Springs, California, from 1988-92; elected to Congress in 1994. Sonny died in a skiing accident on 1/5/98 (age 62).			
				1)I Got You Babe 2)The Beat Goes On 3)All I Ever Need Is You 4)Baby Don't Go 5)A Cowboys Work Is Never Done			
7/10/65	❶[3]	14	●	1 I Got You Babe *It's Gonna Rain*	$12		Atco 6359
				a new version featuring Cher With Beavis And Butt-Head "Bubbled Under" (#108) in 1993			
8/21/65	10	10		2 Laugh At Me *[SONNY]*..................*Tony* (Sonny's Group)	$12		Atco 6369
8/21/65	8	12		3 Baby Don't Go..................*Walkin' The Quetzal*	$15		Reprise 0392
				originally released in 1964 on Reprise 0309 ($20); 0392 also released with "Love Is Strange" as the B-side			
8/28/65	20	9		4 Just You..................*Sing C'est La Vie*	$12		Atco 6345
10/9/65	15	8		5 But You're Mine..................*Hello*	$12		Atco 6381
10/23/65	75	5		6 The Letter..................*Spring Fever* (Sonny & Orch.)	$15	■	Vault 916
				originally released in 1963 as by Caesar & Cleo on Vault 909 ($30)			
11/27/65	70	4		7 The Revolution Kind *[SONNY]*..................*Georgia And John Quetzal* (Sonny's Group)	$12		Atco 6386
1/29/66	14	8		8 What Now My Love..................*I Look For You*	$12		Atco 6395
				written in France in 1962 by Gilbert Becaud as "Et Maintenant"			
6/4/66	49	6		9 Have I Stayed Too Long..................*Leave Me Be*	$10		Atco 6420
10/1/66	21	7		10 Little Man..................*Monday*	$10		Atco 6440
11/19/66	87	2		11 Living For You..................*Love Don't Come*	$10		Atco 6449
1/14/67	6	11		12 The Beat Goes On..................*Love Don't Come*	$10		Atco 6461
4/29/67	53	5		13 A Beautiful Story..................*Podunk*	$10		Atco 6480
6/10/67	74	3		14 Plastic Man..................*It's The Little Things*	$10		Atco 6486
8/12/67	50	7		15 It's The Little Things..................*Don't Talk To Strangers*	$10		Atco 6507
12/16/67+	56	6		16 Good Combination..................*You And Me*	$10		Atco 6541
10/16/71	7	15		17 All I Ever Need Is You..................AC[5] *I Got You Babe (live)*	$7		Kapp 2151
2/26/72	8	13		18 A Cowboys Work Is Never Done..................*Somebody*	$7		Kapp 2163
7/8/72	32	10		19 When You Say Love..................*Crystal Clear/Muddy Waters*	$7		Kapp 2176
				adapted from a Budweiser jingle			
3/24/73	77	5		20 Mama Was A Rock And Roll Singer, Papa Used To Write All Her Songs Part 1..................*Part 2*	$5		MCA 40026
				all of above written (except #6, 8, 16, 17 & 19) and produced (except #13, 17 & 19) by **Sonny**			
				SONS OF CHAMPLIN BUB/AC/LP **'76**			
				Rock group from San Francisco, California: **Bill Champlin** (vocals, guitar), Terry Haggerty (guitar), Geoffrey Palmer (keyboards), David Schallock (bass) and James Preston (drums). Champlin joined **Chicago** in 1982.			
6/19/76	47	10		1 Hold On..................*Still In Love With You*	$5		Ariola America 7627
2/5/77	80	5		2 Here Is Where Your Love Belongs..................*Follow Your Heart*	$5		Ariola America 7653
				BILL CHAMPLIN:			
12/26/81+	55	8		3 Tonight Tonight..................*Without You*	$4		Elektra 47240
				based on the tune "My Everlasting Love"			
7/31/82	61	8		4 Sara..................*One Way Ticket*	$4		Elektra 47456
				SONS OF FUNK LP **'98**			
				R&B vocal group from Richmond, California: brothers G-Smooth and Dez with their cousins Renzo and Rico.			
9/6/97	25	20	●	1 I Miss My Homies..................S:15 *(2 versions) / Here We Go* (w/**Mystikal** & Fiend)	$3	▮	No Limit 53290
				MASTER P Featuring Pimp C, The Shocker, Mo B. Dick, O'Dell, Sons of Funk and Mercedes			
10/25/97	97	2		2 Pushin' Inside You..................*(2 versions) / How Ya Do Dat* (w/Young Bleed & C-Loc - R&B #29)	$4	▮	No Limit 53284
				SONS OF FUNK Featuring Master P, The Shocker, Young Bleed & C-Loc			
				from the movie *I'm 'Bout It* starring **Master P**			
4/11/98	16	20	●	3 I Got The Hook Up!..................S:11 *(2 versions) / From What I Was Told* (Soulja Slim)	$3	▮	No Limit 53311
				MASTER P Featuring: Sons Of Funk			
				title song from the movie starring **Master P**			
8/15/98	27	16		4 Goodbye To My Homies..................S:17 *(2 versions) / Homie Ride* (w/C-Murder)	$3	▮	No Limit 53326
				MASTER P Featuring Silkk the Shocker, Sons of Funk and Mo B. Dick			
				samples "It's So Hard To Say Goodbye To Yesterday" by **Boyz II Men**; clean version available on No Limit 53451			
				SO PLUSH **'99**			
				Female R&B vocal group: Raquel Campbell, Donielle Carter, TJ Lottie and Rhonda Roussel.			
11/6/99	35[S]	10		Damn (Should've Treated U Right)..................*(3 versions)*	$5	★	Darkchild/Epic 79283
				SO PLUSH Featuring Ja Rule			
				SOPWITH "CAMEL", The LP **'67**			
				Pop group from San Francisco, California: Peter Kraemer (vocals, sax), Terry MacNeil and William Sievers (guitars), Martin Beard (bass) and Norman Mayell (drums). Named after a type of airplane used in World War I.			
12/24/66+	26	10		1 Hello Hello..................*Treadin'*	$12		Kama Sutra 217
4/1/67	88	2		2 Postcard From Jamaica..................*Little Orphan Annie*	$12	■	Kama Sutra 224
				S.O.S. BAND, The R&B/BUB/LP **'80**			
				Funk-R&B-disco group from Atlanta, Georgia: Mary Davis (vocals, keyboards), Bruno Speight (guitar), Willie Killebrew (sax), Bill Ellis (flute), Jason Bryant (keyboards), John Simpson (bass) and James Earl Jones III (drums).			
5/31/80	3	21	▲	1 Take Your Time (Do It Right) Part 1..................RB[5] *Part 2*	$4		Tabu 5522
8/27/83	55	14		2 Just Be Good To Me..................*(instrumental)*	$4		Tabu 03955
11/19/83+	65	11		3 Tell Me If You Still Care..................*If You Want My Love*	$4		Tabu 04160
8/11/84	64	10		4 Just The Way You Like It..................*Body Break*	$4	■	Tabu 04523
5/17/86	44	13		5 The Finest..................S:39 *I Don't Want Nobody Else*	$4	■	Tabu 05848
				above 4 written and produced by Jimmy Jam and Terry Lewis			

DEBUT	PEAK	WKS	Gold	A-side (Chart Hit)...B-side	$	Sym	Label & Number
				SOUL, David LP '77			
				Born David Solberg on 8/28/43 in Chicago, Illinois. Actor/singer. Played "Joshua Bolt" on TV's *Here Come The Brides* and "Ken Hutchinson" on TV's *Starsky & Hutch*. Began career as a folk singer and appeared several times on *The Merv Griffin Show* as "The Covered Man" (wore a ski mask).			
1/29/77	❶[1]	19	●	1 **Don't Give Up On Us** ...AC[1] *Black Bean Soup*	$4		Private Stock 45,129
5/7/77	54	7		2 **Going In With My Eyes Open** ...*Topanga*	$4		Private Stock 45,150
9/10/77	52	12		3 **Silver Lady** ...*Rider*	$4		Private Stock 45,163
				SOUL, Jimmy BUB '63			
				Born James McCleese on 8/24/42 in Weldon, North Carolina. Died of a heart attack on 6/25/88 (age 45). R&B/calypso-styled singer.			
3/31/62	22	14		1 **Twistin' Matilda (and the channel)** ...*I Can't Hold Out Any Longer*	$15		S.P.Q.R. 3300
				twist version of the calypso song "Matilda" (popularized by **Harry Belafonte**)			
3/30/63	❶[2]	14		2 **If You Wanna Be Happy** ...RB[1] *Don't Release Me*	$15	■	S.P.Q.R. 3305
				based on the calypso song "Ugly Woman"			
				SOUL ASYLUM ROK/LP '93			
				Rock group from Minneapolis, Minnesota: Dave Pirner (vocals, guitar), Daniel Murphy (guitar), Karl Mueller (bass) and Grant Young (drums). Pirner appeared in the movie *Reality Bites*. Sterling Campbell (**Duran Duran**) replaced Young in 1995.			
6/12/93	5	26	●	1 **Runaway Train** ...S:5 / A:9 *Never Really Been (live)*	$3	▮	Columbia 74966
7/1/95	20	14		2 **Misery** ...MR[3] A:16 / S:30 *Hope*	$3	▮[V]	Columbia 77959 ■
2/17/96	63	5		3 **Promises Broken**...A:59 *Can't Even Tell (live)*	$3	▮[V]	Columbia 78215 ■
				SOUL BROTHERS SIX BUB '67			
				R&B group from Rochester, New York: John Ellison, Von Elle Benjamin, Lester Peleman, Joe Johnson, and brothers Charles and Harry Armstrong.			
6/24/67	91	1		**Some Kind Of Wonderful** ...*I'll Be Loving You*	$20		Atlantic 2406
				SOUL CHILDREN, The R&B/BUB/LP '74			
				R&B vocal group from Memphis, Tennessee: John Colbert, Anita Louis, Shelbra Bennett and Norman West. Colbert later recorded as **J. Blackfoot**.			
10/11/69	52	7		1 **The Sweeter He Is - Part I**...*Part II*	$8		Stax 0050
3/18/72	44	11		2 **Hearsay**...*Don't Take My Sunshine*	$8		Stax 0119
2/16/74	36	9		3 **I'll Be The Other Woman** ...*Come Back Kind Of Love*	$8		Stax 0182
				SOUL CLAN, The '68			
				Top soul stars: **Solomon Burke**, **Arthur Conley**, **Don Covay**, **Ben E. King** and **Joe Tex**.			
7/27/68	91	4		**Soul Meeting** ...*That's How It Feels*	$15	■	Atlantic 2530
				SOULDECISION BUB/LP '00			
				White male vocal trio from Vancouver, British Columbia, Canada: David Bowman, Ken Lewko and Trevor Guthrie.			
7/8/00	22	24		**Faded**...S:10 / A:32 *(radio edit)*	$4	★	MCA 156606
				SOULDECISION (Featuring Thrust)			
				SOUL FOR REAL R&B/BUB/LP '95			
				R&B vocal group from Long Island, New York: brothers Chris, Andre, Brian and Jason Dalyrimple.			
1/7/95	2[4]	25	●	1 **Candy Rain** ...RB[3] S:❶[3] / A:11 *(remix)*	$3	▮	Uptown/MCA 54906
5/6/95	17	26	●	2 **Every Little Thing I Do**...S:12 / A:20 *(instrumental)*	$3	▮	Uptown/MCA 55032
				samples "Outstanding" by **The Gap Band**; above 2 co-written/co-produced by **Heavy D.**			
				SOULFUL STRINGS, The LP '68			
				Instrumental studio group from Chicago, Illinois: Lennie Druss (oboe, flute), Bobby Christian (vibes), **Philip Upchurch** and Ron Steel (guitars). Arranged and conducted by Richard Evans.			
2/3/68	64	5		**Burning Spear**...*Within You Without You* [I]	$8		Cadet 5576
				SOULSISTER '89			
				Male pop vocal duo from Belgium: Jan Leyers and Paul Michiels.			
9/23/89	41	10		**The Way To Your Heart**...A:38 *(AC mix) / Heaven Sent You Here*	$3	▮	EMI 50217
				SOUL SISTERS BUB '64			
				R&B vocal duo: Thresia Cleveland and Ann Gissendanner.			
2/29/64	46	9		1 **I Can't Stand It** ...*Blueberry Hill*	$15		Sue 799
6/13/64	98	1		2 **Good Time Tonight**...*Foolish Dreamer*	$15		Sue 10-005
10/10/64	100	1		3 **Just A Moment Ago** ...*I Won't Be Your Fool Anymore*	$15		Sue 111
				SOULS OF MISCHIEF LP '93			
				Hip-hop group from Oakland, California: Tajai Massey, Opio Lindsey, Damani Thompson and Adam Carter.			
11/13/93	72	9		**93 'Til Infinity**...*(remix) / Disseshowedo*	$4	▮	Jive 42157
				samples "Heather" by Billy Cobham			
				SOUL SONIC FORCE — see BAMBAATAA, Afrika			
				SOUL SURVIVORS BUB/R&B/LP '67			
				Garage-rock band from New York and Philadelphia, Pennsylvania: vocals by Kenny Jeremiah and brothers Charles and Richard Ingui, with Edward Leonetti (guitar), Paul Venturini (organ) and Joey Forgione (drums).			
9/2/67	4	15		1 **Expressway To Your Heart** ...*Hey Gyp*	$12		Crimson 1010
12/23/67+	33	8		2 **Explosion In Your Soul** ...*Dathon's Theme*	$10		Crimson 1012
				actual title: "Explosion (In My Soul)"			
4/20/68	68	6		3 **Impossible Mission (Mission Impossible)** ...*Poor Man's Dream*	$10		Crimson 1016
				S.O.U.L. S.Y.S.T.E.M., The '93			
				Dance group assembled by Robert Clivilles and David Cole (**C & C Music Factory**). Featuring vocalist **Michelle Visage** (of **Seduction**).			
11/28/92+	34	16		**It's Gonna Be A Lovely Day** ...A:21 / S:43 *(2 versions)*	$4	▮	Arista 12486
				THE S.O.U.L. S.Y.S.T.E.M. Introducing Michelle Visage			
				from the movie *The Bodyguard* starring Kevin Costner and **Whitney Houston**; rap version of **Bill Withers**' 1978 hit "Lovely Day"			

DEBUT	PEAK	WKS	Gold	A-side (Chart Hit)...B-side	$	Sym	Label & Number
				SOUL II SOUL R&B/LP '89			
				R&B-dance group from London, England, led by the duo Beresford "DJ Jazzie B." Romeo and Nellee Hooper. Featured female vocalists **Caron Wheeler**, Do'Reen Waddell and Rose Windross, and musical backing by the Reggae Philharmonic Orchestra. Wheeler left in 1990. Waddell died after being struck by a car on 3/1/2002 (age 36).			
6/24/89	11	20	▲	1 **Keep On Movin'** RB^{2} S:8 / A:12 *(instrumental)*	$3	■	Virgin 99205
9/23/89	4	28	▲	2 **Back To Life** RB^{1} S:3 / A:5 *(instrumental)*	$3		Virgin 99171
4/14/90	54	11		3 **Get A Life** S:38 *Fairplay*	$3	▌	Virgin 98981
6/30/90	85	5		4 **A Dreams A Dream** *(instrumental)*	$3	▌	Virgin 98955
				SOUL TRAIN GANG R&B/BUB '76			
				Studio R&B-disco singers from the syndicated TV show *Soul Train*.			
12/6/75+	75	5		1 **Soul Train "75"** *(instrumental)*	$5		Soul Train 10400
8/13/77	92	3		2 **My Cherie Amour** *All My Life (I Wanna Live with You)*	$5		Soul Train 10995
				SOUND FACTORY BUB '93			
				Dance duo from Sweden: producers George Morels and Stonebridge.			
12/26/92+	58	17		**Understand This Groove** A:40 / S:75 *(original mix) / Take Me To The Top*	$3	▌	RCA 62437
				SOUNDGARDEN ROK/LP '94			
				Hard-rock group from Seattle, Washington: Chris Cornell (vocals), Kim Thayil (guitar), Ben Shepherd (bass) and Matt Cameron (drums). Cornell and Cameron also recorded with Temple Of The Dog. Group disbanded on 4/9/97. Cornell later joined **Audioslave**.			
5/28/94	24^{A}	23		1 **Black Hole Sun** AR^{7}		V	album cut
				"45": A&M 0766; B-side: "Spoonman" (ROK #3)			
9/17/94+	54^{A}	15		2 **Fell On Black Days**		V	album cut
				"45": A&M 0974; B-side: "My Wave" (ROK #11); above 2 from the album *Superunknown* on A&M 0198			
5/4/96	37^{A}	13		3 **Pretty Noose**			album cut
7/13/96	40^{A}	17		4 **Burden In My Hand** AR^{5}			album cut
11/9/96	53^{A}	13		5 **Blow Up The Outside World** AR^{4}			album cut
				above 3 from the album *Down On The Upside* on A&M 0526			
				SOUNDS OF BLACKNESS R&B/BUB/LP '94			
				Gospel group from Minneapolis, Minnesotal. Directed by Gary Hines. Featured vocalist is Ann Nesby.			
6/4/94	99	3		1 **I Believe** *(3 album snippets)*	$4	▌	Perspective 7446
				samples "Pain" by the **Ohio Players**			
5/31/97	70^{S}	2		2 **Spirit** BUB:102 *(remix)*	$4	▌	Perspective 7574
				SOUNDS OF BLACKNESS Featuring Craig Mack			
				SOUNDS OF SUNSHINE AC/LP '71			
				Adult Contemporary vocal trio from Los Angeles, California: brothers Walt, Warner and George Wilder. Also recorded as the Wilder Brothers.			
5/29/71	39	12		**Love Means (You Never Have To Say You're Sorry)** *Linda, The Untouchable*	$5		Ranwood 896
				song title taken from a line of dialogue in the 1970 movie *Love Story* starring Ali MacGraw and Ryan O'Neal			
				SOUNDS ORCHESTRAL AC/BUB/LP '65			
				Orchestral pop studio trio from England: John Pearson (piano), Tony Reeves (bass) and Ken Clare (drums).			
3/20/65	10	14		1 **Cast Your Fate To The Wind** AC^{3} *To Wendy With Love* [I]	$10		Parkway 942
7/31/65	76	4		2 **Canadian Sunset** *Have Faith In Your Love* [I]	$10		Parkway 958
				SOUP DRAGONS, The LP '92			
				Rock-dance fusion group from Glasgow, Scotland: Sean Dickson (vocals), Jim McCulloch (guitar), Sushil Dade (bass) and Paul Quinn (drums).			
11/17/90	79	5		1 **I'm Free** *Lovegod*	$3	▌	Big Life 877568
				Junior Reid (reggae rap); original version by **The Rolling Stones** (B-side of "Get Off Of My Cloud")			
8/8/92	35	16		2 **Divine Thing** S:39 / A:41 *(3 album snippets) / Driving*	$3	▌V	Big Life 865764
				"45": Big Life 865604			
12/12/92	69	8		3 **Pleasure** *(3 album snippets) / Dive Bomber*	$3	▌	Big Life 867416
				SOUTH, Joe BUB/LP '69			
				Born Joe Souter on 2/28/40 in Atlanta, Georgia. Pop-country singer/songwriter/guitarist. Wrote "Down In The Boondocks," "Hush," "Rose Garden" and "Yo-Yo."			
7/28/58	47	3		1 **The Purple People Eater Meets The Witch Doctor** S:47 / T:71 *My Fondest Memories* [N]	$25		NRC 5000
				written by the **Big Bopper**			
8/28/61	87	2		2 **You're The Reason** *Juke Box*	$20		Fairlane 21006
1/11/69	12	12		3 **Games People Play** *Mirror Of Your Mind*	$8		Capitol 2248
7/12/69	96	1		4 **Birds Of A Feather** *These Are Not My People*	$7		Capitol 2532
				originally "Bubbled Under" (#106) on 1/13/68 on Capitol 2060; above version has a "Games People Play" ending			
8/23/69	41	12		5 **Don't It Make You Want To Go Home** *Hearts Desire*	$7		Capitol 2592
1/3/70	12	11		6 **Walk A Mile In My Shoes** *Shelter*	$7		Capitol 2704
				JOE SOUTH and The Believers (above 2)			
3/21/70	51	7		7 **Children** *Clock Up On The Wall*	$7		Capitol 2755
11/6/71	78	7		8 **Fool Me** *Devil May Care*	$6		Capitol 3204
				SOUTH BOYZ CLICK '02			
				Male rap group from Flint, Michigan.			
10/19/02	64^{S}	1		**Make Em Jiggle** *(2 versions) / Ridin Dirty / My Neck My Back*	$8	T	TNL 35081
				SOUTH CENTRAL CARTEL LP '94			
				Rap group from Los Angeles, California: Cary Calvin, Austin Patterson, Brian West, Larry Sanders, Greg Scott and Perry Rayson. Sanders later recorded solo as **LV**.			
4/23/94	70^{S}	3		**Gang Stories** BUB:110 *(instrumental) / Servin' 'Em Heat*	$7	▌*	DJ West/Chaos 77367
				samples "The Hood Took Me Under" by **MC Eiht**			

DEBUT	PEAK	WKS	Gold	A-side (Chart Hit)...B-side	$	Sym	Label & Number
				SOUTHCOTE '74 Pop-rock group from Toronto, Ontario, Canada: Beau David (vocals), Charlie White (guitar), Breen LeBoeuf (bass) and Lance Wright (drums).			
3/9/74	80	4		**She**...*Right To The Top*	$6		Buddah 399
				SOUTHER, J.D. BUB/AC/C&W/LP '79 Born John David Souther on 11/2/45 in Detroit, Michigan; raised in Amarillo, Texas. Formed Longbranch Pennywhistle with **Glenn Frey**. Teamed with Chris Hillman and **Richie Furay** as **The Souther, Hillman, Furay Band** in 1974.			
8/24/74	27	10		1 **Fallin' In Love**...*Heavenly Fire* **THE SOUTHER, HILLMAN, FURAY BAND**	$5		Asylum 45201
9/8/79	7	21		2 **You're Only Lonely**...AC[5] *Songs Of Love*	$4		Columbia 11079
3/14/81	11	14		3 **Her Town Too**...*Believe It Or Not* (Taylor) **JAMES TAYLOR AND J.D. SOUTHER**	$4		Columbia 60514
				SOUTHERN, Jeri MEM/POP '51 Born Genevieve Hering on 8/5/26 in Royal, Nebraska. Died of pneumonia on 8/4/91 (one day before her 65th birthday). White jazz singer/pianist.			
11/12/55	89	2		**An Occasional Man**...T:89 *What Do You See In Her* Frank Merriweather (orch.); from the movie *The Girl Rush* starring Rosalind Russell	$12		Decca 29647
				SOUTH SHORE COMMISSION '75 R&B-funk group from Washington DC: Frank McCurry (male vocals), Sheryl Henry (female vocals), Sidney Lennear and Eugene Rogers (guitars), David Henderson (bass) and Warren Haygood (drums).			
6/28/75	61	7		1 **Free Man**...*(disco mix)*	$5		Wand 11287
1/10/76	94	4		2 **We're On The Right Track**...*I'd Rather Switch Than Fight*	$5		Wand 11291
2/28/76	86	4		3 **Train Called Freedom**...*(disco version)*	$5		Wand 11294
				SOUTHSIDE JOHNNY & THE JUKES ROK/BUB/R&B/LP '79 Born John Lyon on 12/4/48 in Neptune, New Jersey. Rock singer/harmonica player. Core members of The Jukes: Billy Rush (guitar), Kevin Kavanaugh (keyboards) and Alan Berger (drums). **Little Steven** Van Zandt was a founding member (left in 1975).			
9/22/79	71	4		1 **I'm So Anxious**...*Your Reply* **SOUTHSIDE JOHNNY AND THE ASBURY JUKES**	$4		Mercury 76007
8/16/86	98	5		2 **Walk Away Renee**...*I Can't Wait*	$3	■	Atlantic 89394
				SOUTH SIDE MOVEMENT, The R&B '73 R&B-funk group from Chicago, Illinois: Melvin Moore (vocals), Bobby Pointer (guitar), Morris Beeks (keyboards), Milton Johnson (sax), Steve Hawkins (trumpet), Bill McFarland (trombone), Ronald Simmons (bass) and Willie Hayes (drums).			
4/14/73	61	10		**I' Been Watchin' You**...*Have A Little Mercy*	$7		Wand 11251
				SOUTHSYDE B.O.I.Z. '96 R&B group is actually male solo artist Jan Styles from Phoenix. B.O.I.Z. stands for Beats Originated In the 'Zon (Arizona).			
10/19/96	96	2		**Get Ready, Here It Comes (It's The Choo-Choo)**...S:57 *(Southsyde mix)*	$4	▮V	LaFace 24157
				SOUTHWEST F.O.B. BUB '68 Psychedelic-pop group formed in Dallas, Texas: Dan Seals (vocals, sax), John Coley (keyboards), Larry Stevens (guitar), Mike Woolbright (bass) and Tony Durrell (drums). Seals and Coley later found success as **England Dan & John Ford Coley**.			
10/5/68	56	5		**Smell Of Incense**...*Green Skies* first released on GPC 1945 in 1968 ($20)	$10		HIP 8002
				SOVINE, Red C&W/BUB/LP '76 Born Woodrow Wilson Sovine on 7/17/18 in Charleston, West Virginia. Died of a heart attack on 4/4/80 (age 61). Country singer/songwriter/guitarist (charted 31 hits, 1955-80).			
1/8/66	82	3		1 **Giddyup Go**...CW[6] *Kiss And The Keys* [S]	$10		Starday 737
7/24/76	40	9	●	2 **Teddy Bear**...CW[3] *Daddy* [S] both are classic "truck-driving" songs	$5		Starday 142
				SPACE '79 French disco studio production featuring English session singer **Madeline Bell**.			
4/28/79	60	7		**My Love Is Music**...*Final Signal*	$5		Casablanca 974
				SPACE LP '97 Rock group from Liverpool, England: Tommy Scott (vocals, bass), Jamie Murphy (guitar), Franny Griffith (keyboards) and Andy Parle (drums).			
2/22/97	71[A]	5		**Female Of The Species**... from the album *Spiders* on Universal 53028			album cut
				SPACEHOG ROK/LP '96 Rock group from Leeds, England: Royston Langdon (vocals, bass), Richard Steel and Antony Langdon (guitars), and Jonny Cragg (drums). Langdon married actress Liv Tyler on 3/25/2003.			
4/6/96	32	20		**In The Meantime**...AR[4] A:25 / S:44 *To Be A Millionaire...Was It Likely? (live)*	$4	▮	Sire 64303
				SPACEMEN, The '59 R&B instrumental studio group: Panama Francis (**The Stylers**), Haywood Henry, Babe Clark and Sammy Benskin.			
10/19/59	41	14		**The Clouds**...RB[3] *The Lonely Jet Pilot* [I]	$25		Alton 254
				SPACE MONKEYS '98 Rock group from Manchester, England: Richard McNevin-Duff (vocals, guitar), Tony Pipes (keyboards), Dom Morrison (bass) and Chas Morrison (drums).			
1/24/98	58	4		**Sugar Cane**...A:69 *(unpopped remix)* samples "Bring The Noise" by **Public Enemy**	$5	▮	Chingón/Interscope 97022
				SPANDAU BALLET BUB/LP '83 Pop group formed in London, England: Tony Hadley (vocals), brothers Gary (guitar) and Martin (bass) Kemp, Steve Norman (sax) and John Keeble (drums). The Kemps starred in the 1990 movie *The Krays*. Gary Kemp was married to actress Sadie Frost from 1988-97.			
8/6/83	4	18		1 **True**...AC[1] *Gently* also see **PM Dawn**'s "Set Adrift On Memory Bliss"	$4	■	Chrysalis 42720
11/19/83+	29	12		2 **Gold**...*(live version)*	$4	■	Chrysalis 42743

DEBUT	PEAK	WKS	Gold	A-side (Chart Hit)..............B-side	$	Sym	Label & Number
				SPANDAU BALLET — Cont'd			
3/31/84	59	7		3 **Communication**..............*Code Of Love*	$4		Chrysalis 42770
7/28/84	34	12		4 **Only When You Leave**..............*Paint Me Down (live)*	$4	■	Chrysalis 42792
				SPANIELS, The R&B/MEM **'57** R&B doo-wop group from Gary, Indiana; James "**Pookie**" **Hudson**, lead singer. First recorded for Chance in 1953, then became the first artist to sign with Vee-Jay Records ("Baby, It's You" on Vee-Jay 101 in 1953). Bass singer Gerald Gregory died on 2/12/99 (age 64). Most famous recording was "Goodnite Sweetheart, Goodnite" in 1954 (R&B #5).			
7/1/57	69	3		**Everyone's Laughing**..............T:69 *I.O.U.* Al Smith (orch.)	$60		Vee-Jay 246
				SPANKY AND OUR GANG LP **'67** Folk-pop group formed in Chicago, Illinois: Elaine "Spanky" McFarlane (born on 6/19/42 in Peoria, Illinois), Malcolm Hale, Lefty Baker and Nigel Pickering (guitars), Kenny Hodges (bass) and John Seiter (drums). Spanky became the new lead singer of **The Mamas & The Papas** in the early 1980s. Named after the *Little Rascals* series. Hale died of liver failure on 10/31/68 (age 27). Baker died of liver failure on 8/11/71 (age 29).			
5/20/67	9	8		1 **Sunday Will Never Be The Same**..............*Distance*	$8		Mercury 72679
8/19/67	31	7		2 **Making Every Minute Count**..............*If You Could Only Be Me*	$8	■	Mercury 72714
10/14/67	14	11		3 **Lazy Day**..............*(It Ain't Necessarily) Byrd Avenue*	$8	■	Mercury 72732
1/6/68	30	8		4 **Sunday Mornin'**..............*Echoes*	$8	■	Mercury 72765
4/20/68	17	11		5 **Like To Get To Know You**..............*Three Ways From Tomorrow*	$8	■	Mercury 72795
8/3/68	43	8		6 **Give A Damn**..............*The Swingin' Gate*	$8		Mercury 72831
12/7/68	94	3		7 **Yesterday's Rain**..............*Without Rhyme Or Reason*	$8		Mercury 72871
2/15/69	86	3		8 **Anything You Choose**..............*Mecca Flat Blues*	$8		Mercury 72890
6/21/69	97	1		9 **And She's Mine**..............*Leopard Skin Phones*	$8		Mercury 72926
				SPARKLE R&B/LP **'98** Born in Harlem, New York. Female R&B singer.			
5/9/98	32^{A}	16		**Be Careful**..............RB^{6A} **SPARKLE featuring R. Kelly** from the album *Sparkle* on Rock Land 90149			album cut
				SPARKS BUB/LP **'83** Pop-rock-dance duo from Los Angeles, California: brothers Ron (born on 8/12/50) and Russell (born on 10/5/55) Mael. Appeared in the 1977 movie *Rollercoaster*.			
5/15/82	60	7		1 **I Predict**..............*Moustache*	$4	■	Atlantic 4030
4/16/83	49	12		2 **Cool Places**..............*Sports* **SPARKS AND JANE WIEDLIN**	$4	■	Atlantic 89866
				SPARXXX, Bubba R&B/LP **'01** Born Warren Mathis on 3/6/77 in LaGrange, Georgia. White rapper.			
9/1/01	15	20		**Ugly**..............A:13 / S:34 *(3 versions)* samples "Get Ur Freak On" by **Missy "Misdemeanor" Elliott**	$6	T	Beat Club 497602
				SPATS, The **'64** Rock group from Garden Grove, California: brothers Dick (vocals), Bud (guitar) and Ronnie (bass) Johnson, with Myron Caprino (guitar), Bob Dennis (sax), Chuck Scott (piano) and Mike Sulsona (drums).			
9/26/64	96	1		**Gator Tails And Monkey Ribs**..............*The Roach* **THE SPATS Featuring Dick Johnson** originally released on Enith 1268 in 1964 ($25); similar arrangement as "Louie Louie" by **The Kingsmen**	$15		ABC-Paramount 10585
				SPEARS, Billie Jo C&W **'75** Born Billie Jean Spears on 1/14/37 in Beaumont, Texas. Country singer/songwriter (charted 34 hits, 1968-84).			
4/26/69	80	4		1 **Mr. Walker, It's All Over**..............*Tips And Tables*	$6		Capitol 2436
5/17/75	78	5		2 **Blanket On The Ground**..............CW^{1} *Come On Home*	$5		United Artists 584
	★471★			**SPEARS, Britney** BUB/AC/LP **'99** Born on 12/2/81 in Kentwood, Louisiana. Teen pop singer/actress. Regular on TV's *The Mickey Mouse Club* (1992-93). Played "Lucy" in the movie *Crossroads*. *1)...Baby One More Time 2)Oops!...I Did It Again 3)(You Drive Me) Crazy*			
11/21/98+	❶[2]	32	▲	1 **...Baby One More Time**..............S:❶[4] / A:8 *Autumn Goodbye* "45" B-side: (same version)	$4	★[+V]	Jive 42545
5/22/99	21	20		2 **Sometimes**..............A:14		V	album cut
9/18/99	10	20		3 **(You Drive Me) Crazy**..............A:6 *(4 versions)* from the movie *Drive Me Crazy* starring Melissa Joan Hart	$6	T[V]	Jive 42606
1/29/00	14	20	▲	4 **From The Bottom Of My Broken Heart**........S:❶[1] / A:53 *(You Drive Me) Crazy (remix)* "45" issued for above 2 on Jive 42653; all of above from the album *...Baby One More Time* on Jive 41651	$4	★[V]	Jive 42653
4/22/00	9	20		5 **Oops!...I Did It Again**..............A:8 *(5 remixes)* "45": Jive 42696; B-side: (same version)	$6	T[V]	Jive 42700
8/12/00	23	11		6 **Lucky**..............A:18 *(4 versions)* "45": Jive 42745; B-side: (same version)	$6	T[V]	Jive 42742
12/2/00+	11	15	●	7 **Stronger**..............S:❶[1] / A:53 *(Pablo La Rosa's Tranceformation Edit)* "45": Jive 42762; B-side: (same version)	$4	★[V]	Jive 42861
10/20/01	27	14		8 **I'm A Slave 4 U**..............A:30 / S:73 *(instrumental)*	$6	T	Jive 42967
4/27/02	86	5		9 **Overprotected**..............*(5 versions)*	$6	T	Jive 40027
				SPECIAL DELIVERY R&B/BUB **'76** R&B vocal group featuring lead singer Terry Huff.			
5/29/76	75	8		**The Lonely One**..............*(instrumental)* **SPECIAL DELIVERY featuring TERRY HUFF**	$5		Mainstream 5581
				SPECIAL ED LP **'95** Born Edward Archer in Brooklyn, New York. Male rapper.			
7/8/95	75^{S}	1		**Neva Go Back**..............BUB:109 *Just A Killa* (w/**Bounty Killer**)	$5	▮	Profile 5433

DEBUT	PEAK	WKS	Gold	A-side (Chart Hit)...B-side	$	Sym	Label & Number
				SPECIAL GENERATION R&B '90			
				R&B vocal group from St. Petersburg, Florida. Charles Salter, Maurice Dowdell, Maquet Robinson, Chip Carter and Kendrick Washington are part of **M.C. Hammer**'s posse.			
12/8/90	91	4		**Love Me Just For Me**...*(2 versions)* — written by **M.C. Hammer**	$4	▮	Bust It/Capitol 44604
				SPECTOR, Ronnie — see RONETTES, The			
				SPELLBINDERS, The BUB '65			
				R&B vocal group from Jersey City, New Jersey: Bob Shivers, Jimmy Wright, Ben Grant, McArthur Munford and Elouise Pennington.			
11/27/65	93	1		1 **For You**...*Stone In Love*	$10		Columbia 43384
11/19/66	100	1		2 **Help Me (Get Myself Back Together Again)**...*Danny Boy*	$10		Columbia 43830
				SPELLBOUND '78			
				Pop group formed in San Francisco, California: Barry Flast (vocals), Bill Burgess (guitar), David Lenchner (keyboards), Ralph Carter (bass) and Joey Kluchar (drums).			
7/29/78	89	3		**Rumor At The Honky Tonk**...*A Taste Of The Devil*	$5		EMI America 8002
				SPELLMAN, Benny '62			
				Born on 12/11/31 in Pensacola, Florida. Worked with **Huey "Piano" Smith**. Frequent session work as an R&B backup singer. Bass vocalist on **Ernie K-Doe**'s "Mother-In-Law."			
5/5/62	80	6		**Lipstick Traces (On A Cigarette)**...*Fortune Teller*	$15		Minit 644
				SPENCE, Judson LP '88			
				Born on 4/29/65 in Pascagoula, Mississippi. Pop-rock singer/songwriter/multi-instrumentalist.			
10/15/88	32	14		**Yeah, Yeah, Yeah**...A:29 / S:34 *Dance With Me*	$3	■	Atlantic 88999
				SPENCER, Sonny '59			
				Born John Berry on 1/3/38 in Orangeburg, South Carolina. R&B singer/songwriter.			
11/16/59	82	4		**Gilee**...*Oh Boy*	$25		Memo 17984
				SPENCER, Tracie R&B/LP '91			
				Born on 7/12/76 in Waterloo, Iowa. R&B singer. Won the singing competition on TV's *Star Search* in 1986.			
10/1/88	38	16		1 **Symptoms Of True Love**...A:39 *(acappella version)*	$3	■	Capitol 44140
2/11/89	85	4		2 **Imagine**...*Hide And Seek*	$3	■	Capitol 44268
12/22/90+	3	23		3 **This House** S:4 / A:8 *(radio edit) / I Have A Song To Sing*	$3	▮	Capitol 44652
5/18/91	54	7		4 **This Time Make It Funky**...A:56 *(remix) / Tracie's Hideout*	$3	▮	Capitol 44699
10/19/91	42	20		5 **Tender Kisses**...RB[1] S:30 / A:37 *(album version)*	$3	▮	Capitol 44680
3/28/92	48	15		6 **Love Me**...A:33 / S:68 *(2 mixes)* — above 4 from the album *Make The Difference*	$3	▮	Capitol 44820
8/14/99	18	13		7 **It's All About You (Not About Me)**.....S:6 / A:68 *(2 remixes w/***The Roots***) / It's On Tonight* — "45": Capitol 58777	$4	★V	Capitol 58777
3/4/00	88	3		8 **Still In My Heart**...S:17 *If U Wanna Get Down*	$4	★V	Capitol 58807
				SPENCER & SPENCER '59			
				Duo of **Dickie Goodman** and **Mickey Shorr**.			
5/18/59	91	2		**Russian Band Stand**...*"Brass Wail"* [N] — **SPENCER & SPENCER with the Sonia Pryor Choir** — "break-in" record; parody of TV's *American Bandstand*	$30		Argo 5331
				SPERRY, Steve '77			
				Born on 10/3/41 in Fort Atkinson, Wisconsin. Pop singer/songwriter/jingle writer.			
7/16/77	91	3		**Flame**...*Comin' Through To You*	$5		Mercury 73905
	★458★			**SPICE GIRLS** BUB/LP '97			
				Female dance-pop vocal group from England: Victoria Adams (Posh Spice; born on 4/17/74), Melanie Brown (Scary Spice; born on 5/29/75), Emma Bunton (Baby Spice; born on 1/21/76), Geri Halliwell (Ginger Spice; born on 8/18/70) and **Melanie C**hisholm (Sporty Spice; born on 1/12/74) (see #8 below). Group starred in the movie *Spiceworld*. Halliwell left in May 1998. Adams married soccer star David Beckham on 7/4/99.			
1/25/97	❶[4]	23	▲	1 **Wannabe** S:❶[4] / A:6 *Bumper To Bumper* — "45": Virgin 19489	$3	▮V	Virgin 38579
5/24/97	3	21	●	2 **Say You'll Be There**...S:4 / A:6 *Take Me Home*	$3	▮	Virgin 38592
8/16/97	4	24	●	3 **2 Become 1**...A:5 / S:8 *One Of These Girls*	$3	▮	Virgin 38604
11/8/97	18	20	●	4 **Spice Up Your Life**...S:11 / A:72 *(2 versions) / Spice Invaders* — from the movie *Spiceworld* starring Spice Girls	$3	▮	Virgin 38620
2/14/98	9	20		5 **Too Much**...S:11 / A:36 *(2 versions) / Outer Space Girls*	$3	▮	Virgin 38630
6/20/98	16	19		6 **Stop**...S:11 / A:70 *Something Kinda Funny (Live In Istanbul)*	$3	▮	Virgin 38641
12/26/98	11	11	●	7 **Goodbye**...S:4 *Christmas Wrapping / Sisters Are Doin' It For Themselves (live) / We Are Family (live)*	$8	★*	Virgin 38652
3/31/01	43[S]	10		8 **I Turn To You**...BUB:114 *(3 mixes)* — **MELANIE C**	$8	★*	Virgin 38773
				SPIDER LP '80			
				Rock group formed in New York: South African native Amanda Blue (vocals), Keith Lentin (guitar), **Holly Knight** (keyboards), Jimmy Lowell (bass) and Anton Fig (drums). Knight, a prolific songwriter, later joined **Device** and then went solo. Fig joined the house band of TV's *Late Night With David Letterman*.			
4/19/80	39	11		1 **New Romance (It's A Mystery)**...*Crossfire*	$4	⊙	Dreamland 100
8/2/80	86	3		2 **Everything Is Alright**...*Shady Lady*	$4	■	Dreamland 103
5/30/81	43	10		3 **It Didn't Take Long**...*I Love*	$4		Dreamland 111
				SPIES, The '99			
				Pop trio from Fresno, California: brothers Mardo (bass) and Bob (drums), with Zig (guitar). All share vocals.			
2/6/99	58[S]	1		**You And Me**...*Forever? / Becka / Be The Same*	$8	★*	Fig 543222
				SPIN '76			
				Instrumental pop-jazz-rock session band from Holland: Hans Hollestelle (guitar), Rein van der Broek (trumpet), Jan Vennik (reeds), Hans Jansen (keyboards), Jan Hollestelle (bass) and Cees Kranenburg (drums).			
8/28/76	95	2		**Grasshopper**...*Spinning* [I]	$5		Ariola America 7632

SELECTED CD SINGLES

Aerosmith
Jaded

Christina Aguilera
Genie In A Bottle

Baha Men
Who Let The Dogs Out

Basement Jaxx
Where's Your Head At

BBMak
Back Here

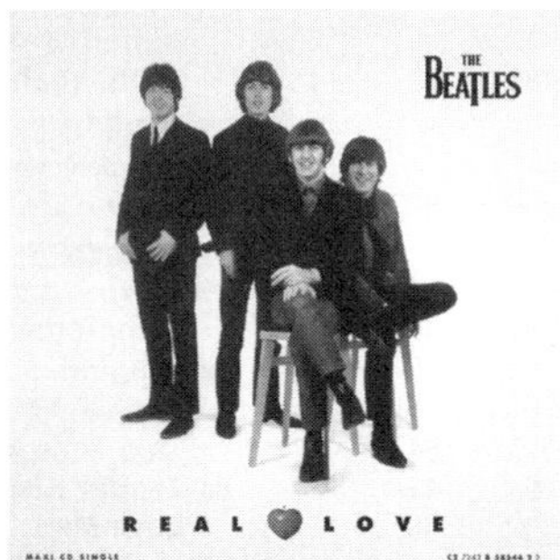

The Beatles
Real Love

B★Witched
C'est La Vie

Blink-182
I Won't Be Home For Christmas

Destiny's Child
Bills, Bills, Bills

Whitney Houston (Feat. Faith Evans & Kelly Price) — *Heartbreak Hotel*

Jewel
You Were Meant For Me

R. Kelly
If I Could Turn Back The Hands Of Time

SELECTED CD SINGLES

Luis Miguel
Sol, Arena y Mar

Chanté Moore
Chanté's Got A Man

No Doubt
Underneath It All

Pokémon
Pokémon Theme

Prince
Thieves In The Temple

Puff Daddy (Featuring R. Kelly)
Satisfy You

Red Hot Chili Peppers
Give It Away

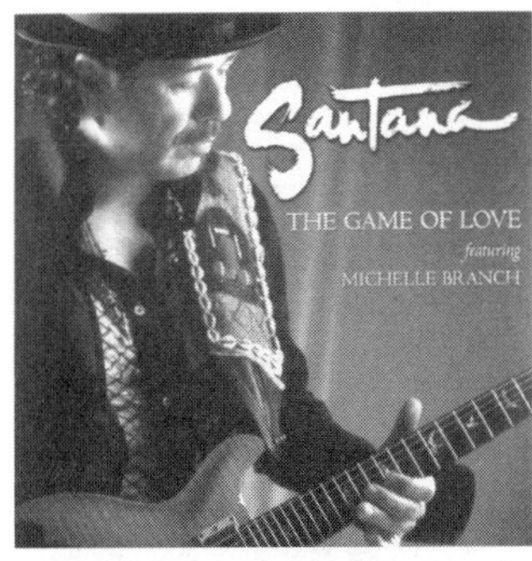

Santana featuring Michelle Branch
The Game Of Love

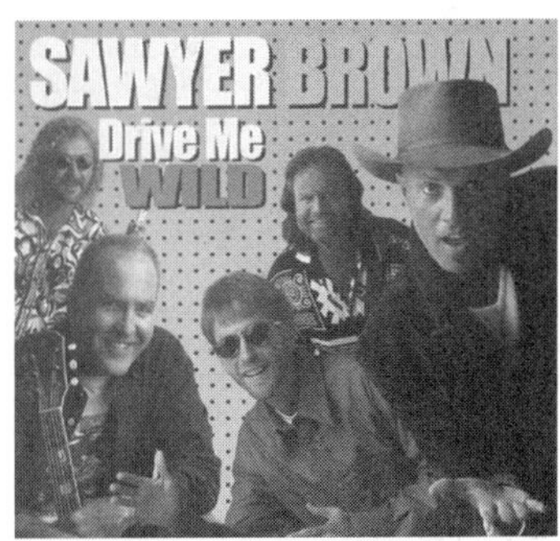

Sawyer Brown
Drive Me Wild

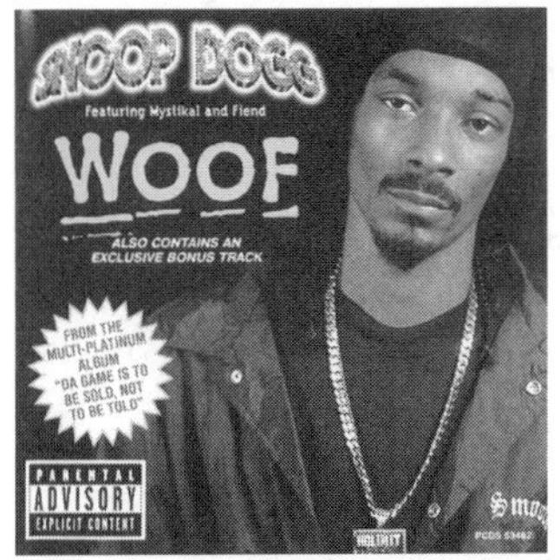

Snoop Dog Featuring Mystikal and Fiend
Woof

Sporty Thievz
No Pigeons

Rod Stewart
Leave Virginia Alone

DEBUT	PEAK	WKS	Gold	A-side (Chart Hit)	B-side	$	Sym	Label & Number

SPIN DOCTORS

ROK/BUB/LP **'93**

Rock group formed in New York: Christopher Barron (vocals), Eric Schenkman (guitar), Mark White (bass) and Aaron Comess (drums). Anthony Krizan replaced Schenkman in 1993.

DEBUT	PEAK	WKS	Gold	A-side (Chart Hit)	B-side	$	Sym	Label & Number
10/17/92	17	20		1 **Little Miss Can't Be Wrong** S:23 / A:24	*What Time Is It? (live)*	$3	▮V	Epic Associated 74473
1/30/93	7	29		2 **Two Princes** A:6 / S:14	*Off My Line (live)*	$3	▮V	Epic Associated 74804
				"45" issued for above 2 on Epic Associated 74473				
10/9/93	78	9		3 **Jimmy Olsen's Blues**	*Yo Mamas A Pajama*	$3	▮V	Epic Associated 74929
				Olsen: Daily Planet reporter in comic book series *Superman*				
6/18/94	84	3		4 **Cleopatra's Cat**	*Uranium Century*	$3	▮V	Epic 77525
7/16/94	42	10		5 **You Let Your Heart Go Too Fast** A:38	*Piece Of Glass*	$3	▮V	Epic 77600
				"45" B-side: "Cleopatra's Cat" (LP Version)				

SPINNERS ★90★

R&B/BUB/LP **'74**

R&B vocal group formed in Detroit, Michigan. Originally known as the Domingoes. Discovered by producer/lead singer of **The Moonglows**, **Harvey Fuqua**, and became the Spinners in 1961. First recorded on Fuqua's Tri-Phi label. Many personnel changes. G.C. Cameron was lead singer from 1968-72. 1972 hit lineup included Philippe Wynne (tenor; born on 4/3/41), Bobbie Smith (tenor; born on 4/10/46), Billy Henderson (tenor; born on 8/9/39), Henry Fambrough (baritone; born on 5/10/35) and Pervis Jackson (bass; born on 5/16/38). Wynne left group in 1977 and toured with **Parliament/Funkadelic**; replaced by John Edwards. Wynne died of a heart attack on 7/13/84 (age 43).

1)Then Came You 2)The Rubberband Man 3)Working My Way Back To You/Forgive Me, Girl 4)I'll Be Around 5)Could It Be I'm Falling In Love

DEBUT	PEAK	WKS	Gold	A-side (Chart Hit)	B-side	$	Sym	Label & Number
6/26/61	27	8		1 **That's What Girls Are Made For**	*Heebie Jeebie's*	$25		Tri-Phi 1001
11/20/61	91	1		2 **Love (I'm So Glad) I Found You**	*Subbuster*	$25		Tri-Phi 1004
7/17/65	35	7		3 **I'll Always Love You**	*Tomorrow May Never Come*	$15		Motown 1078
7/25/70	14	15		4 **It's A Shame**	*Together We Can Make Such Sweet Music*	$12		V.I.P. 25057
1/23/71	89	3		5 **We'll Have It Made**	*My Whole World Ended (The Moment You Left Me)*	$12		V.I.P. 25060
				above 2 written and produced by **Stevie Wonder**				
9/16/72	3	15	●	6 **I'll Be Around** / RB[5]				
				also see #30 below				
8/19/72	77	5		7 **How Could I Let You Get Away**		$6		Atlantic 2904
12/30/72+	4	15	●	8 **Could It Be I'm Falling In Love** RB[1]	*Just You And Me Baby*	$6		Atlantic 2927
4/28/73	11	15	●	9 **One Of A Kind (Love Affair)** RB[4]	*Don't Let The Green Grass Fool You*	$6		Atlantic 2962
5/12/73	91	5		10 **Together We Can Make Such Sweet Music**	*Bad, Bad Weather (Till You Come Home)*	$8		Motown 1235
				originally released as the B-side of #4 above				
8/18/73	29	8		11 **Ghetto Child**	*We Belong Together*	$6		Atlantic 2973
				#6-9 & 11: from the album *Spinners* (Atlantic 7256)				
1/26/74	20	15		12 **Mighty Love - Pt. 1** RB[2]	*Pt. II*	$6		Atlantic 3006
5/18/74	18	13		13 **I'm Coming Home**	*He'll Never Love You Like I Do*	$6		Atlantic 3027
7/27/74	❶[1]	19	●	14 **Then Came You**	*Just As Long As We Have Love*	$5		Atlantic 3202
				DIONNE WARWICKE AND SPINNERS				
				originally released on Atlantic 3029 earlier in 1974				
9/21/74	15	13		15 **Love Don't Love Nobody - Pt. I**	*Pt. II*	$5		Atlantic 3206
3/8/75	37	7		16 **Living A Little, Laughing A Little**	*Smile, We Have Each Other*	$5		Atlantic 3252
5/3/75	54	7		17 **Sadie**	*Lazy Susan*	$5		Atlantic 3268
8/9/75	5	18	●	18 **"They Just Can't Stop It" the (Games People Play)** RB[1]	*I Don't Want To Lose You*	$5		Atlantic 3284
				first pressings issued only as "Games People Play"				
12/27/75+	36	8		19 **Love Or Leave**	*You Made A Promise To Me*	$5		Atlantic 3309
7/17/76	56	5		20 **Wake Up Susan**	*If You Can't Be In Love*	$5		Atlantic 3341
9/11/76	2[3]	21	●	21 **The Rubberband Man** RB[1]	*Now That We're Together*	$5		Atlantic 3355
3/19/77	43	7		22 **You're Throwing A Good Love Away**	*You're All I Need In Life*	$5		Atlantic 3382
10/8/77	89	4		23 **Heaven On Earth (So Fine)**	*I'm Tired Of Giving*	$5		Atlantic 3425
7/29/78	49	6		24 **If You Wanna Do A Dance**	*Once In A Life Proposal*	$5		Atlantic 3493
				all of above Atlantic's produced and arranged by Thom Bell				
12/15/79+	2[2]	25	●	25 **Working My Way Back To You/Forgive Me, Girl**	*Disco Ride*	$4		Atlantic 3637
				although a medley, first pressings issued only as "Working My Way Back To You" ($8)				
5/17/80	4	19		26 **Cupid/I've Loved You For A Long Time**	*Pipedream*	$4		Atlantic 3664
2/14/81	52	8		27 **Yesterday Once More/Nothing Remains The Same**	*Be My Love*	$4		Atlantic 3798
				the second song on each of the above 3 medleys written by **Michael Zager**				
3/6/82	95	2		28 **Never Thought I'd Fall In Love**	*Send A Little Love*	$4		Atlantic 4007
12/11/82+	67	8		29 **Funny How Time Slips Away**	*I'm Calling You Now*	$4		Atlantic 89922
				written by **Willie Nelson**				
3/25/95	39	16		30 **I'll Be Around** S:26 / A:63	*Playaz Club (remix)* [R]	$3	▮	Chrysalis/EMI 58331
				RAPPIN' 4-TAY Featuring The Spinners				
				rap version featuring samples of #6 above				

SPIRAL STARECASE

BUB/LP **'69**

Pop-rock group from Sacramento, California: Pat Upton (vocals, guitar), Harvey Kaplan (organ), Dick Lopes (sax), Bobby Raymond (bass) and Vinny Parello (drums). Kaplan is the father of **Brenda K. Starr**.

DEBUT	PEAK	WKS	Gold	A-side (Chart Hit)	B-side	$	Sym	Label & Number
4/5/69	12	15		1 **More Today Than Yesterday**	*Broken-Hearted Man*	$8		Columbia 44741
8/30/69	52	7		2 **No One For Me To Turn To**	*Sweet Little Thing*	$6		Columbia 44924
2/7/70	72	6		3 **She's Ready**	*Judas To The Love We Knew*	$6		Columbia 45048
				SPIRAL STARECASE Featuring: Pat Upton				

SPIRIT

ROK/BUB/LP **'69**

Rock group from Los Angeles, California: **Jay Ferguson** (vocals), Randy California (guitar), John Locke (keyboards), Mark Andes (bass) and Ed Cassidy (drums). Ferguson and Andes left to form **Jo Jo Gunne** in mid-1971. Andes became an original member of **Firefall** in 1975; joined **Heart** in 1983. California drowned in Hawaii on 1/2/97 (age 45).

DEBUT	PEAK	WKS	Gold	A-side (Chart Hit)	B-side	$	Sym	Label & Number
1/18/69	25	12		1 **I Got A Line On You**	*She Smiles*	$10		Ode 115
2/7/70	69	9		2 **1984**	*Sweet Stella Baby*	$8		Ode 128

DEBUT	PEAK	WKS	Gold	A-side (Chart Hit)..........B-side	$	Sym	Label & Number
				SPIRIT — Cont'd			
9/12/70	97	1		3 **Animal Zoo**..........*Red Light Roll On*	$7		Epic 10648
10/20/73	92	2		4 **Mr. Skin**..........*Nature's Way* (#111)	$7		Epic 10701
				SPLENDER ROK/LP **'00**			
				Interracial rock group from New York: Waymon Boone (vocals), Jonathan Svec (guitar), James Cruz (bass) and Mark Slutsky (drums).			
6/10/00	62	12		**I Think God Can Explain**..........A:62			album cut
				produced by **Todd Rundgren**; from the album *Halfway Down The Sky* on Columbia 69144			
				SPLINTER LP **'75**			
				Pop-rock vocal duo from England: Bill Elliott and Bob Purvis.			
12/14/74+	77	8		**Costafine Town**..........*Elly-May*	$7	■	Dark Horse 10002
				George Harrison (production and bass guitar)			
				SPLIT ENZ ROK/BUB/LP **'80**			
				Pop-rock group from New Zealand: brothers Tim (vocals) and Neil (guitar, vocals) Finn, Eddy Rayner (keyboards), Noel Crombie (percussion), Nigel Griggs (bass) and Malcolm Green (drums). The Finns were later members of **Crowded House**.			
8/23/80	53	11		**I Got You**..........*Double Happy*	$6	■	A&M 2252
				"45" pressed on laser-etched vinyl			
				SPOKESMEN, The BUB **'65**			
				Pop-folk trio: Johnny Madara, David White and Roy Gilmore. White was with **Danny & The Juniors** (Madera wrote "At The Hop").			
9/18/65	36	7		**The Dawn Of Correction**..........*For You Babe*	$12		Decca 31844
				answer song to **Barry McGuire**'s "Eve Of Destruction"			
				SPONGE ROK/LP **'95**			
				Rock group from Detroit, Michigan: Vinnie Dombrowski (vocals), Mike Cross and Joe Mazzola (guitars), Tim Cross (bass) and Jimmy Paluzzi (drums). Charlie Grover replaced Paluzzi in early 1996.			
2/18/95	41^{A}	20		1 **Plowed**..........			album cut
8/12/95	55	18		2 **Molly (Sixteen Candles)**..........A:34 *I Hate Myself*	$4	▮	Work 77976
				above 2 from the album *Rotting Piñata* on Chaos 57800			
7/6/96	64^{A}	4		3 **Wax Ecstatic (To Sell Angelina)**..........			album cut
				from the album *Wax Ecstatic* on Columbia 67578			
				SPOOKS R&B **'00**			
				Rap group from Philadelphia, Pennsylvania: female singer Ming Xia with male rappers Mr. Booka, Aqua Dinero, Hypno and Vengeance.			
4/22/00	63^{S}	6		**Things I've Seen**..........*(crude mix) / (2 album snippets)*	$6	★	Antra 751027
				from the movie *Once In The Life* starring Laurence Fishburne			
				SPORTS, The LP **'79**			
				Rock group formed in Melbourne, Australia: Stephen Cummings (vocals), Andrew Pendlebury and Martin Armiger (guitars), James Niven (keyboards), Robert Glover (bass) and Paul Hitchins (drums).			
10/13/79	45	7		**Who Listens To The Radio**..........*Hit Single*	$5	■	Arista 0468
				SPORTY THIEVZ R&B/BUB **'99**			
				Rap trio from Brooklyn, New York: Marlon Brando, King Kirk and Big Dubez. Brando died in a car crash on 5/11/2001 (age 22).			
5/15/99	12	17	●	**No Pigeons**..........S:3 / A:40 *Even Cheaper*	$5	★	Roc-A-Blok 79190
				a parody of "No Scrubs" by **TLC**; originally released as a 12" single on AV 96			
	★250★			**SPRINGFIELD, Dusty** BUB/AC/LP **'64**			
				Born Mary O'Brien on 4/16/39 in London, England. Died of cancer on 3/2/99 (age 59). Pop singer. With brother Tom Springfield and Tim Field in folk trio **The Springfields** (see #1 & 2 below). Inducted into the Rock and Roll Hall of Fame in 1999.			
				1)You Don't Have To Say You Love Me 2)Wishin' And Hopin' 3)Son-Of-A Preacher Man 4)I Only Want To Be With You 5)All I See Is You			
8/4/62	20	10		1 **Silver Threads And Golden Needles**..........*Aunt Rhody*	$15		Philips 40038
11/3/62	95	3		2 **Dear Hearts And Gentle People**..........*Gotta Travel On* (#114)	$12		Philips 40072
				THE SPRINGFIELDS (above 2)			
				#2 hit for both **Bing Crosby** and **Dinah Shore** in 1950			
1/25/64	12	10		3 **I Only Want To Be With You**..........*Once Upon A Time*	$12		Philips 40162
3/28/64	38	7		4 **Stay Awhile**..........*Something Special*	$12	■	Philips 40180
6/20/64	6	13		5 **Wishin' And Hopin'**..........*Do Re Mi (Forget About The Do And Think About Me)*	$12		Philips 40207
9/26/64	41	7		6 **All Cried Out**..........*I Wish I'd Never Loved You*	$10	■	Philips 40229
3/13/65	91	4		7 **Losing You**..........*Here She Comes*	$10	■	Philips 40270
5/21/66	4	13		8 **You Don't Have To Say You Love Me**..........*Little By Little*	$12	■	Philips 40371
				picture sleeve issued with either a green or a yellow border; Italian song written in 1965 by Pino Donaggio			
9/17/66	20	8		9 **All I See Is You**..........*I'm Gonna Leave You*	$10	■	Philips 40396
3/18/67	40	8		10 **I'll Try Anything**..........*The Corrupt Ones*	$10	■	Philips 40439
7/22/67	22	15		11 **The Look Of Love /**			
				from the James Bond movie spoof *Casino Royale* starring David Niven and Peter Sellers			
7/1/67	76	4		12 **Give Me Time**..........	$10		Philips 40465
11/18/67	49	8		13 **What's It Gonna Be**..........*Small Town Girl*	$10	■	Philips 40498
11/30/68+	10	12		14 **Son-Of-A Preacher Man**..........*Just A Little Lovin' (Early In The Mornin')*	$8	■	Atlantic 2580
3/1/69	64	6		15 **Don't Forget About Me /**			
4/12/69	91	2		16 **Breakfast In Bed**..........	$8		Atlantic 2606
5/3/69	31	8		17 **The Windmills Of Your Mind**..........*I Don't Want To Hear It Anymore* (#105)	$8		Atlantic 2623
				from the movie *The Thomas Crown Affair* starring Steve McQueen; above 4 from the album *Dusty In Memphis*			
7/12/69	78	3		18 **Willie & Laura Mae Jones**..........*That Old Sweet Roll (Hi-De-Ho)*	$7		Atlantic 2647
				written by **Tony Joe White**			
11/8/69	24	12		19 **A Brand New Me**..........*Bad Case Of The Blues*	$7		Atlantic 2685

SPRINGFIELD, Dusty — Cont'd

DEBUT	PEAK	WKS	Gold	A-side (Chart Hit)	B-side	$	Sym	Label & Number
2/28/70	76	5		20 **Silly, Silly, Fool**	*Joe*	$7		Atlantic 2705
12/12/87+	2[2]	18		21 **What Have I Done To Deserve This?** S:❶[1] / A:4	*A New Life* (Pet Shop Boys)	$3	■	EMI-Manhattan 50107
				PET SHOP BOYS (and Dusty Springfield) also released on EMI America 50107 in 1987				

SPRINGFIELD, Rick ★133★ ROK/LP '81

Born Richard Springthorpe on 8/23/49 in Sydney, Australia. Pop-rock singer/songwriter/actor. Played "Noah Drake" on the TV soap opera *General Hospital*. Starred in the movie *Hard To Hold*.

1)Jessie's Girl 2)Don't Talk To Strangers 3)Love Somebody 4)I've Done Everything For You 5)Affair Of The Heart

DEBUT	PEAK	WKS	Gold	A-side (Chart Hit)	B-side	$	Sym	Label & Number
8/5/72	14	13		1 **Speak To The Sky**	*Why?*	$8	■	Capitol 3340
11/25/72	70	4		2 **What Would The Children Think**	*Come On Everybody*	$8	■	Capitol 3466
7/13/74	98	2		3 **American Girls**	*Weep No More*	$6		Columbia 46057
8/21/76	41	9		4 **Take A Hand**	*Archangel*	$6		Chelsea 3051
3/28/81	❶[2]	32	●	5 **Jessie's Girl**	*Carry Me Away*	$4	■	RCA 12201
8/22/81	8	22		6 **I've Done Everything For You** written by **Sammy Hagar**	*Red Hot And Blue Love*	$4	■	RCA 12166
12/5/81+	20	16		7 **Love Is Alright Tonite**	*Everybody's Girl*	$4	■	RCA 13008
3/6/82	2[4]	21		8 **Don't Talk To Strangers**	*Tonight*	$4	■	RCA 13070
6/5/82	21	12		9 **What Kind Of Fool Am I**	*How Do You Talk To Girls*	$4		RCA 13245
9/11/82	32	12		10 **I Get Excited**	*Kristina*	$4	■	RCA 13303
4/16/83	9	18		11 **Affair Of The Heart**	*Like Father, Like Son*	$4	■	RCA 13497
7/9/83	18	15		12 **Human Touch**	*Alyson*	$4		RCA 13576
10/15/83	23	15		13 **Souls**	*(live version)*	$4	■	RCA 13650
3/10/84	5	16		14 **Love Somebody**	*The Great Lost Art Of Conversation*	$3	■	RCA 13738
5/26/84	26	12		15 **Don't Walk Away**	*S.F.O.* [I]	$3	■	RCA 13813
8/18/84	20	15		16 **Bop 'Til You Drop /** A:16 / S:28				
11/17/84	59	10		17 **Taxi Dancing** **RICK SPRINGFIELD & RANDY CRAWFORD** above 4 from the album and movie *Hard To Hold* starring Springfield		$3	■	RCA 13861
11/17/84+	27	13		18 **Bruce** S:27 / A:27 recorded in 1978; an autobiographical song about Springfield being mistaken for **Bruce Springsteen**	*Guenevere* [N]	$4	■	Mercury 880405
4/6/85	26	11		19 **Celebrate Youth** S:24 / A:26	*Stranger In The House*	$3	■	RCA 14047
6/8/85	22	15		20 **State Of The Heart** S:20 / A:23	*The Power Of Love (The Tao of Love)*	$3	■	RCA 14120
2/6/88	22	15		21 **Rock Of Life** S:20 / A:21 all of above (except #6) written by Springfield	*The Language Of Love*	$3	■	RCA 6853

SPRINGFIELDS, The — see SPRINGFIELD, Dusty

SPRINGSTEEN, Bruce ★103★ ROK/LP '85

Born on 9/23/49 in Freehold, New Jersey. Rock and roll singer/songwriter/guitarist. Nicknamed "The Boss." Worked local clubs in New Jersey and Greenwich Village, mid-1960s. Own E-Street Band in 1973, consisted of **Clarence Clemons** (saxophone), David Sancious and Danny Federici (keyboards), Gary Tallent (bass) and Vini Lopez (drums). Sancious and Lopez replaced by Roy Bittan and Max Weinberg (became musical director for TV's *Late Night With Conan O'Brien* in 1993). Miami Steve Van Zandt (**Little Steven and the Disciples Of Soul**; guitar) joined group in 1975. Springsteen wrote **Manfred Mann's Earth Band**'s "Blinded By The Light" and the **Pointer Sisters**' "Fire." After *Born To Run*, a court injunction prevented the release of any new recordings until 1978. Married to model/actress Julianne Phillips from 1985-89. Appeared in the 1987 movie *Hail! Hail! Rock 'N' Roll*. Split from the E-Street Band in November 1989. Married Patti Scialfa, singer with the E-Street Band, on 6/8/91. Inducted into the Rock and Roll Hall of Fame in 1999. Reunited with the E-Street Band in 1999.

1)Dancing In The Dark 2)Hungry Heart 3)Glory Days 4)Brilliant Disguise 5)I'm On Fire

DEBUT	PEAK	WKS	Gold	A-side (Chart Hit)	B-side	$	Sym	Label & Number
9/20/75	23	11		1 **Born To Run** Springsteen's first 2 "45s": "Blinded By The Light"/"The Angel" (Columbia 45805 - $500) in 1972 and "Spirit In The Night"/"For You" (Columbia 45864 - $1000) in 1973	*Meeting Across The River*	$20		Columbia 10209
1/24/76	83	3		2 **Tenth Avenue Freeze-Out**	*She's The One*	$15		Columbia 10274
6/10/78	33	9		3 **Prove It All Night**	*Factory*	$12		Columbia 10763
8/19/78	42	8		4 **Badlands**	*Streets Of Fire*	$12		Columbia 10801
11/8/80	5	18		5 **Hungry Heart** Mark Volman and Howard Kaylan of **The Turtles** (backing vocals)	*Held Up Without A Gun*	$5	■	Columbia 11391
2/7/81	20	12		6 **Fade Away** first pressings list the B-side title as "To Be True" ($25)	*Be True* (ROK #42)	$5	■	Columbia 11431
5/26/84	2[4]	21	▲	7 **Dancing In The Dark** AR[6] B-side was a #5 hit for **Natalie Cole** in 1988	*Pink Cadillac* (ROK #27)	$4	■	Columbia 04463
8/11/84	7	18	●	8 **Cover Me** A:7 / S:9	*Jersey Girl*	$4	■	Columbia 04561
11/10/84+	9	17	●	9 **Born In The U.S.A.** S:9 / A:11	*Shut Out The Light*	$4	■	Columbia 04680
2/16/85	6	20		10 **I'm On Fire** A:5 / S:7	*Johnny Bye Bye*	$4	■	Columbia 04772
6/1/85	5	18		11 **Glory Days** A:4 / S:7	*Stand On It* (ROK #32)	$4	■	Columbia 04924
9/7/85	9	13		12 **I'm Goin' Down** S:8 / A:9	*Janey, Don't You Lose Heart*	$4	■	Columbia 05603
12/7/85+	6	15	●	13 **My Hometown /** AC[1] S:5 / A:7 #7-13: from the album *Born In The U.S.A.*				
12/21/85	❶[1X]	2		14 **Santa Claus Is Comin' To Town** [X-L] recorded on 12/12/75 at C.W. Post College in Greenvale, New York; promotional record issued in 1981 on Columbia AE7 1332 ($20) with a picture sleeve; #12 hit for George Hall in 1934		$4	■	Columbia 05728
11/22/86	8	12		15 **War** S:8 / A:12 recorded on 9/30/85 at the LA Coliseum; B-side was a #3 R&B hit in 1947 for **Charles Brown**	*Merry Christmas Baby* [L]	$4	■	Columbia 06432

DEBUT	PEAK	WKS	Gold	A-side (Chart Hit)...B-side	$	Sym	Label & Number
				SPRINGSTEEN, Bruce — Cont'd			
1/31/87	46	8		16 **Fire**...S:39 *Incident On 57th Street (live)* [L]	$4	■	Columbia 06657
				BRUCE SPRINGSTEEN & THE E STREET BAND (above 2) recorded on 12/16/78 at San Francisco's Winterland			
10/3/87	5	16		17 **Brilliant Disguise**...AR[1] S:5 / A:5 *Lucky Man*	$4	■	Columbia 07595
12/5/87+	9	16		18 **Tunnel Of Love**...AR[4] S:6 / A:15 *Two For The Road*	$4	■	Columbia 07663
2/27/88	13	15		19 **One Step Up**...S:11 / A:18 *Roulette* (ROK #45)	$4	■	Columbia 07726
3/21/92	16	16		20 **Human Touch** / AR[3] A:14 / S:27			
3/21/92		16		21 **Better Days**...	$4	■V	Columbia 74273
6/20/92	68	6		22 **57 Channels (And Nothin' On)**...*Part Man, Part Monkey*	$4	■V	Columbia 74354
2/19/94	9	20	●	23 **Streets Of Philadelphia**...A:7 / S:10 *If I Should Fall Behind*	$3	■V	Columbia 77384
				from the movie *Philadelphia* starring Tom Hanks and Denzel Washington			
4/29/95	63	7		24 **Secret Garden**...A:67 *Thunder Road (live)*	$3	■V	Columbia 77847 ■
3/22/97	19	16		25 **Secret Garden**...A:15 / S:26 *Thunder Road (live)* [R]	$3	■V	Columbia 77847 ■
				reissued due to inclusion in the movie *Jerry Maguire* starring Tom Cruise; above 2 are the same version			
8/3/02	52	11		26 **The Rising**...S:2 / A:72 *Land Of Hope And Dreams (live)*	$4	★	Columbia 79788
				all of above (except #14 & 15) written by Springsteen; all of above co-produced by Springsteen			
				SPRINGWELL '71			
				Rock quintet from Detroit, Michigan. Led by David Rule.			
9/18/71	60	10		**It's For You**...*Our Question*	$8		Parrot 359
				written by **John Lennon** and **Paul McCartney**			
				SPYRO GYRA AC/BUB/R&B/LP '79			
				Jazz-pop band formed in Buffalo, New York. Led by saxophonist Jay Beckenstein (born on 5/14/51). **The Brecker Brothers** were longtime members.			
6/17/78	90	5		1 **Shaker Song**...*Paw Prints* [I]	$5		Amherst 730
6/16/79	24	15		2 **Morning Dance**...AC[1] *Song For Lorraine* [I]	$5	■	Infinity 50,011
4/19/80	68	5		3 **Catching The Sun**...*Cockatoo* [I]	$4		MCA 41180
2/7/81	77	5		4 **Cafe Amore**...*Bittersweet* [I]	$4		MCA 51035
				SPYS LP '82			
				Rock group from New York: John Blanco (vocals), John DiGaudio (guitar), Al Greenwood (keyboards), Ed Gagliardi (bass) and Billy Milne (drums). Greenwood and Gagliardi were members of **Foreigner**.			
8/14/82	82	5		**Don't Run My Life**...*Ice Age*	$4		EMI America 8124
				SQUEEZE ROK/BUB/LP '87			
				New wave pop-rock group formed in London, England. Led by vocalists/guitarists Chris Difford and Glenn Tilbrook. Originally known as UK Squeeze due to confusion with American band Tight Squeeze. **Paul Carrack** (**Ace**, **Mike + The Mechanics**) was keyboardist/vocalist in 1981 of fluctuating lineup; re-joined in 1993.			
8/1/81	49	11		1 **Tempted**...*Trust*	$5	■	A&M 2345
				also see the B-side of **The Knack**'s 1994 version of "My Sharona"			
9/19/87	15	19		2 **Hourglass**...S:16 / A:16 *Wedding Bells*	$3	■	A&M 2967
12/19/87+	32	12		3 **853-5937**...S:30 / A:33 *Take Me I'm Yours (live)*	$3	■	A&M 2994
				SQUIER, Billy ROK/LP '81			
				Born on 5/12/50 in Wellesley Hills, Massachusetts. Hard-rock singer/songwriter/guitarist.			
				1)Rock Me Tonite 2)The Stroke 3)Everybody Wants You			
5/16/81	17	20		1 **The Stroke**...*Too Daze Gone*	$4	■	Capitol 5005
9/12/81	35	12		2 **In The Dark**...*Whadda You Want From Me*	$4	■	Capitol 5040
11/28/81+	45	10		3 **My Kinda Lover**...*Christmas Is The Time To Say I Love You*	$4	■	Capitol 5037
8/7/82	68	6		4 **Emotions In Motion**...*Catch 22*	$4	■	Capitol 5135
10/2/82	32	17		5 **Everybody Wants You**...AR[6] *Keep Me Satisfied* (ROK #46)	$4	■	Capitol 5163
2/5/83	75	6		6 **She's A Runner**...*In Your Eyes*	$4	■	Capitol 5202
7/7/84	15	16		7 **Rock Me Tonite** AR[2] *Can't Get Next To You* (ROK #51)	$3	■	Capitol 5370
10/27/84	75	3		8 **All Night Long**...*Calley Oh*	$3	■	Capitol 5422
12/8/84+	71	8		9 **Eye On You**...*Calley Oh*	$3	■	Capitol 5416
12/15/84	9[X]	1		10 **Christmas Is The Time To Say "I Love You"**...*White Christmas* [X]	$4	■	Capitol 5303
				originally released as the B-side of #3 above			
10/4/86	80	5		11 **Love Is The Hero**...*Learn How To Live (live)*	$3	■	Capitol 5619
6/24/89	58	15		12 **Don't Say You Love Me**...*Too Much*	$3	■V	Capitol 44420
				"45" promo: Capitol 79694; all of above written by Squier			
				SQUIRREL NUT ZIPPERS LP '97			
				Eclectic-jazz group from Chapel Hill, North Carolina: Jim Mathus (vocals, guitar, trombone), Katharine Whalen (vocals, banjo), Ken Mosher (guitar, sax), Tom Maxwell (sax, clarinet), Je Widenhouse (trumpet), Don Raleigh (bass) and Chris Phillips (drums). Group name taken from a brand of candy.			
5/3/97	72[A]	6		**Hell**...			album cut
				from the album *Hot* on Mammoth 0137			
				S.S.O. '76			
				Disco group featuring Douglas Lucas and the Sugar Sisters.			
1/10/76	99	4		**Tonight's The Night**...*(disco mix)*	$6		Shady Brook 019
				STABBING WESTWARD ROK/LP '96			
				Rock group from Chicago, Illinois: Christopher Hall (vocals, guitar), Walter Flakus (keyboards), Jim Sellers (bass) and Andy Kubiszewski (drums).			
3/2/96	60[A]	10		1 **What Do I Have To Do?**...			album cut
10/5/96	69[A]	2		2 **Shame**...			album cut
				above 2 from the album *Wither Blister Burn & Peel* on Columbia 66152			
				STABILIZERS '87			
				Pop-rock duo from Erie, Pennsylvania: Dave Christenson (vocals) and Rich Nevens (keyboards, guitar).			
4/4/87	93	3		**One Simple Thing**...*You Pull Me Down*	$4	■	Columbia 06700

DEBUT	PEAK	WKS	Gold	A-side (Chart Hit)...B-side	$	Sym	Label & Number
				STACEY Q LP **'86**			
				Born Stacey Swain on 11/30/58 in Los Angeles, California. Female dance singer.			
7/12/86	3	22		1 **Two Of Hearts** ...S:❶[1] / A:7 *Dancing Nowhere*	$3	■	Atlantic 89381
12/13/86+	35	19		2 **We Connect**...S:29 *Don't Break My Heart*	$3	■	Atlantic 89331
4/11/87	89	11		3 **Shy Girl**...*(same version)*	$6		On The Spot 110
				recorded in 1985			
2/27/88	66	8		4 **Don't Make A Fool Of Yourself** ...*Fly By Night*	$3	■	Atlantic 89135
				STACY, Clyde **'57**			
				Born on 8/11/36 in Eufala, Oklahoma; raised in Lubbock, Texas. Rockabilly singer.			
6/17/57	68	1		1 **So Young** *[CLYDE STACY & The Nitecaps]* ...T:68 *Hoy Hoy*	$40		Candlelight 1015
11/16/59	99	2		2 **So Young** ...*A Broken Heart* [R]	$30		Argyle 1001
				above 2 are the same version			
				STAFFORD, Jim C&W/BUB/LP **'74**			
				Born on 1/16/44 in Eloise, Florida. Pop-novelty singer/songwriter/guitarist. Hosted own summer variety TV show in 1975 and *Those Amazing Animals* from 1980-81. Married to **Bobbie Gentry** from 1978-79.			
5/12/73	39	12		1 **Swamp Witch** ...*Nifty Fifties Blues*	$6		MGM 14496
11/10/73+	3	23	●	2 **Spiders & Snakes** *Undecided*	$5		MGM 14648
4/20/74	12	15		3 **My Girl Bill**...*L.A. Mamma* [N]	$5		MGM 14718
7/6/74	7	14		4 **Wildwood Weed** ...*The Last Chant* [N]	$5		MGM 14737
				all of above from the album *Jim Stafford*			
12/21/74+	24	10		5 **Your Bulldog Drinks Champagne**...*A Real Good Time* [N]	$5		MGM 14775
8/16/75	37	9		6 **I Got Stoned And I Missed It**...*I Ain't Working* [N]	$5		MGM 14819
				all of above produced by **Lobo** and Phil Gernhard			
4/3/76	69	6		7 **Jasper**...*I Can't Find Nobody Home*	$5		Polydor 14309
1/29/77	98	2		8 **Turn Loose Of My Leg** ...*The Fight* [N]	$4		Warner/Curb 8299
				STAFFORD, Jo MEM/POP/BUB/LP **'52**			
				Born on 11/12/17 in Coalinga, California. Female singer. Sang with **Tommy Dorsey**'s band, both as a solo artist and with vocal group The Pied Pipers, 1940-43. Married to orchestra leader Paul Weston. Host of own TV musical series, 1954-55. Charted 70 hits, 1944-54, including 2 #1 hits: "You Belong To Me" and "Make Love To Me." Jo is the #1 ranked female vocalist of the 1940-1954 pre-rock era.			
11/20/54+	15	6		1 **Teach Me Tonight** ...A:15 / J:16 / S:23 *Suddenly*	$15		Columbia 40351
10/15/55	13	12		2 **Suddenly There's A Valley** A:13 / T:16 / J:18 / S:21 *The Night Watch*	$15		Columbia 40559
				Norman Luboff Choir (backing vocals)			
11/26/55+	14	20		3 **It's Almost Tomorrow**...J:14 / T:19 / A:20 / S:25 *If You Want To Love (You Have To Cry)*	$15		Columbia 40595
3/10/56	99	1		4 **All Night Long** ...T:99 *As I Love You*	$10		Columbia 40640
8/4/56	85	3		5 **With A Little Bit Of Luck** ...T:85 *One Little Kiss*	$10		Columbia 40718
				from the Lerner/Loewe Broadway musical *My Fair Lady* starring **Julie Andrews** and Rex Harrison			
11/17/56	62	2		6 **Love Me Good** ...T:62 *A Perfect Love*	$10		Columbia 40745
11/24/56	38	13		7 **On London Bridge**...T:38 *Bells Are Ringing*	$10		Columbia 40782
3/23/57	53	12		8 **Wind In The Willow** ...T:53 *King Of Paris*	$10		Columbia 40832
				Paul Weston (orch., all of above)			
				STAFFORD, Terry C&W/BUB/LP **'64**			
				Born on 11/22/41 in Hollis, Oklahoma; raised in Amarillo, Texas. Died on 3/17/96 (age 54). Pop-rock and roll singer/songwriter. **Elvis Presley** sound-alike. Moved to California in 1960. Appeared in the movie *Wild Wheels*.			
2/22/64	3	15		1 **Suspicion** ...*Judy*	$15		Crusader 101
				first recorded in 1962 by **Elvis Presley** for his *Pot Luck* album			
5/23/64	25	8		2 **I'll Touch A Star** ...*Playing With Fire*	$12		Crusader 105
				STAGE DOLLS ROK/LP **'89**			
				Rock trio from Trondheim, Norway: Torstein Flakne (vocals), Terje Storli (bass) and Steinar Krokstad (drums).			
7/29/89	46	13		**Love Cries** ...S:39 *Ammunition*	$4		Chrysalis 23366
				STAIND ROK/BUB/LP **'01**			
				Alternative-metal rock group from Boston, Massachusetts: **Aaron Lewis** (vocals), Mike Mushok (guitar), Johnny April (bass) and Jon Wysocki (drums).			
1/27/01	56	19		1 **Outside**...A:54 [L]			album cut
				AARON LEWIS from Staind (with Fred Durst from Limp Bizkit)			
				from the album *The Family Values Tour 1999* on Flawless 490641; Staind's original version "Bubbled Under" (#111 in 2001)			
4/14/01	5	46		2 **It's Been Awhile** ...AR[20] / MR[16] A:5			album cut
10/20/01	62	17		3 **Fade**...A:61			album cut
3/2/02	63	20		4 **For You**...A:61			album cut
				above 3 from the album *Break The Cycle* on Flip/Elektra 62626			
				STAIRSTEPS — see FIVE STAIRSTEPS			
				STALLION BUB/LP **'77**			
				Pop-rock group from Denver, Colorado: Buddy Stephens (vocals), Danny O'Neil (guitar), Wally Damrick (keyboards), Jorg Gonzalez (bass) and Larry Thompson (drums).			
3/12/77	37	9		**Old Fashioned Boy (You're The One)** ...*Woman*	$5		Casablanca 877
				STALLONE, Frank BUB/AC **'83**			
				Born on 7/30/50 in Philadelphia, Pennsylvania. Pop singer/songwriter/actor. Brother of actor Sylvester Stallone.			
9/27/80	67	6		1 **Case Of You**...*Sea Song*	$4		Scotti Brothers 603
				written by **Joni Mitchell** (on her 1971 album *Blues*); produced by Harry **Nilsson**			
7/30/83	10	16		2 **Far From Over** ...*Waking Up*	$4		RSO 815023
				from the movie *Staying Alive* starring **John Travolta** and directed by Sylvester Stallone			
5/5/84	81	4		3 **Darlin'** ...*Album Medley*	$4	■	Polydor 821382

DEBUT	PEAK	WKS	Gold	A-side (Chart Hit)..........B-side	$	Sym	Label & Number
				STAMPEDERS BUB/LP **'71**			
				Pop-rock trio from Calgary, Alberta, Canada: Rich Dodson (guitar), Ronnie King (bass) and Kim Berly (drums). All share vocals.			
8/14/71	8	14		1 **Sweet City Woman** ....*Gator Road*	$6		Bell 45,120
12/4/71+	61	7		2 **Devil You** ....*Giant In The Streets*	$6		Bell 45,154
2/28/76	40	8		3 **Hit The Road Jack** ....*Hard Lovin Woman* [N]	$6		Quality 501
				featuring a telephone conversation with **Wolfman Jack**			
				STAMPLEY, Joe — see UNIQUES, The			
				STAN & DOUG LP **'70**			
				Comedy duo from Seattle, Washington: Stan Boreson (born on 5/25/25) and Doug Setterberg.			
12/26/70	7^{X}	1		**Christmas Goose (Snowbird)** ....*Christmas Medley* [X-N]	$8		Golden Crest 550
				Scandinavian parody of **Anne Murray**'s 1970 hit "Snowbird"			
				STANDELLS, The BUB/LP **'66**			
				Early punk-rock group from Los Angeles, California: Dick Dodd (vocals, drums), Larry Tamblyn and Tony Valentino (guitars) and Gary Lane (bass). Dodd was an original Mouseketeer of TV's *The Mickey Mouse Club*. Tamblyn is the brother of actor Russ Tamblyn.			
4/23/66	11	16		1 **Dirty Water** ....*Rari*	$20		Tower 185
8/13/66	43	8		2 **Sometimes Good Guys Don't Wear White** ....*Why Did You Hurt Me*	$15		Tower 257
10/22/66	54	7		3 **Why Pick On Me** ....*Mr. Nobody*	$15		Tower 282
11/25/67	78	3		4 **Can't Help But Love You** ....*Ninety Nine And A Half*	$15	■	Tower 348
				all of above written (except #4) and produced by Ed Cobb of **The Four Preps**			
				STANLEY, Michael, Band ROK/LP **'81**			
				Born Michael Stanley Gee on 3/25/48 in Cleveland, Ohio. Rock singer/guitarist. His band: **Kevin Raleigh** (vocals, keyboards), Bob Pelander (keyboards), Gary Markshay (guitar), Rick Bell (sax), Mike Gismondi (bass) and Tom Dobeck (drums). Don Powers replaced Markshay in 1982.			
11/22/80+	33	16		1 **He Can't Love You** *Carolyn*	$4		EMI America 8063
				Clarence Clemons (sax solo)			
3/28/81	68	6		2 **Lover** ....*Save A Little Piece For Me*	$4		EMI America 8064
8/8/81	64	8		3 **Falling In Love Again** ....*Does It Hurt*	$4		EMI America 8090
9/11/82	78	4		4 **When I'm Holding You Tight** ....*In Between The Lines* (ROK #24)	$4		EMI America 8130
12/25/82+	81	5		5 **Take The Time** ....*Just A Little Bit Longer*	$4		EMI America 8146
10/1/83	39	10		6 **My Town** ....*Just How Good (A Bad Woman Feels)*	$4		EMI America 8178
12/24/83+	75	5		7 **Someone Like You** ....*Highlife*	$4		EMI America 8189
				STANLEY, Paul — see KISS			
				STANSFIELD, Lisa R&B/BUB/LP **'90**			
				Born on 4/11/66 in Roachdale, Manchester, England. Dance singer/songwriter. Lead singer of dance trio **Blue Zone U.K.** (see #1 below).			
8/13/88	54	9		1 **Jackie** ....*Chance It*	$4	■	Arista 9725
				BLUE ZONE U.K.			
2/3/90	3	22	▲	2 **All Around The World** RB[2] S:❶[1] / A:3 *Affection*	$3	▮V	Arista 9928 ■
5/26/90	14	14		3 **You Can't Deny It** ....RB[1] S:11 / A:18 *Lay Me Down*	$3	▮V	Arista 2024
8/18/90	21	13		4 **This Is The Right Time** ....A:20 / S:24 *Apple Heart*	$3	▮V	Arista 2049
11/2/91+	27	20		5 **Change** ....A:24 / S:40 *It's Got To Be Real*	$3	▮V	Arista 12362
				"45" B-side: "A Little More Love"			
3/7/92	56	17		6 **All Woman** ....RB[1] S:29 / A:59 *Everything Will Get Better*	$3	▮V	Arista 12398
8/9/97	74	9		7 **Never, Never Gonna Give You Up** ....S:58 *People Hold On*	$3	▮	Arista 13346
				#2, 4, 5 & 7: #1 Dance Club Play hits			
	★335★			**STAPLE SINGERS, The** R&B/BUB/LP **'72**			
				Family R&B group consisting of Roebuck "Pop" Staples (born on 12/28/15 in Winona, Mississippi), with his son Pervis (born on 11/18/35; left in 1971) and daughters Cleotha (born on 4/11/34), Yvonne (born on 1/19/43) and lead singer **Mavis Staples** (born on 6/20/40) (see #3 & 18 below). Roebuck was a blues guitarist in his teens, later with the Golden Trumpets gospel group. Moved to Chicago in 1935. Formed own gospel group in early '50s. First recorded for United in 1953. Mavis began solo career in 1970. Group inducted into the Rock and Roll Hall of Fame in 1999. Pop died on 12/19/2000 (age 84).			
				1)I'll Take You There 2)Let's Do It Again 3)If You're Ready (Come Go With Me)			
6/3/67	95	1		1 **Why? (Am I Treated So Bad)** ....*What Are They Doing? (In Heaven Today)*	$10		Epic 10158
9/23/67	66	4		2 **For What It's Worth** ....*Are You Sure*	$10		Epic 10220
9/5/70	87	4		3 **I Have Learned To Do Without You** ....*Since I Fell For You*	$7		Volt 4044
				MAVIS STAPLES			
2/6/71	27	12		4 **Heavy Makes You Happy (Sha-Na-Boom Boom)** ....*Love Is Plentiful* (R&B #31)	$7		Stax 0083
7/31/71	97	2		5 **You've Got To Earn It** ....*I'm A Lover*	$7		Stax 0093
				Bar-Kays (backing band); co-written by **Smokey Robinson**			
10/16/71	12	14	▲	6 **Respect Yourself** ....*You're Gonna Make Me Cry*	$6		Stax 0104
4/8/72	❶[1]	15		7 **I'll Take You There** RB[4] *I'm Just Another Soldier*	$6		Stax 0125
				also see #18 below			
8/5/72	38	7		8 **This World** ....*Are You Sure?*	$6		Stax 0137
3/10/73	33	9		9 **Oh La De Da** ....*We The People*	$6		Stax 0156
6/16/73	66	6		10 **Be What You Are** ....*I Like The Things About Me*	$6		Stax 0164
10/27/73	9	16	●	11 **If You're Ready (Come Go With Me)** ....RB[3] *Love Comes In All Colors*	$6		Stax 0179
12/8/73	2^{1X}	3		12 **Who Took The Merry Out Of Christmas** ....*(instrumental)* [X]	$8		Stax 0084
				first released in 1970			
2/23/74	23	13		13 **Touch A Hand, Make A Friend** ....*Tellin' Lies*	$5		Stax 0196
8/17/74	79	7		14 **City In The Sky** ....*That's What Friends Are For*	$5		Stax 0215
12/7/74	76	3		15 **My Main Man** ....*Who Made The Man*	$5		Stax 0227
				all of above Stax recordings produced by Al Bell			
10/25/75	❶[1]	15	●	16 **Let's Do It Again** ....RB[2] *After Sex*	$5		Curtom 0109

DEBUT	PEAK	WKS	Gold	A-side (Chart Hit)...B-side	$	Sym	Label & Number
				STAPLE SINGERS, The — Cont'd			
2/28/76	**70**	6		17 **New Orleans** ...*A Whole Lot Of Love*	$5		Curtom 0113
				above 2 written and produced by **Curtis Mayfield**; both from the movie *Let's Do It Again* starring Sidney Poitier and **Bill Cosby**			
1/4/92	**90**	6		18 **I'll Take You There**...RB[1] *(2 versions)* [R]	$4	▮	Capitol 44749
				BEBE + CECE WINANS (featuring Mavis Staples)			
				new version of #7 above			
				STAPLETON, Cyril, And His Orchestra '59			
				Born on 12/31/14 in Nottingham, England. Died on 2/25/74 (age 59). Orchestra leader.			
9/1/56	**25**	14		1 **The Italian Theme** ...T:25 *Tiger Tango* [I]	$12		London 1672
1/12/59	**13**	14		2 **The Children's Marching Song (Nick Nack Taddy Whack)** ...*(Theme From) The Inn Of The Sixth Happiness*	$12		London 1851
				based on the traditional nursery song "This Old Man"; featuring the children from the movie *The Inn Of The Sixth Happiness* starring Ingrid Bergman			
				STARBUCK LP '76			
				Pop-rock group from Atlanta, Georgia: Bruce Blackman (vocals, keyboards), Bo Wagner (marimbas), Sloan Hayes (keyboards), Tommy Strain and Ron Norris (guitars), Jimmy Cobb (bass) and Dave Snavely (drums). Strain, Norris and Snavely left after "Lucky Man," replaced by Darryl Kutz (guitar), David Shaver (keyboards) and Ken Crysler (drums). Also see **Eternity's Children** and **Korona**.			
4/17/76	**3**	22		1 **Moonlight Feels Right** *Lash LaRue*	$5		Private Stock 45,039
9/11/76	**43**	7		2 **I Got To Know** ...*The Slower You Go (The Longer It Lasts)*	$5		Private Stock 45,104
12/18/76	**73**	5		3 **Lucky Man** ...*So The Night Goes*	$5		Private Stock 45,125
4/16/77	**38**	8		4 **Everybody Be Dancin'**...*Gimme A Break*	$5		Private Stock 45,144
9/30/78	**58**	6		5 **Searching For A Thrill**...*Go Wild*	$4		United Artists 1245
				STARCHER, Buddy C&W/BUB '66			
				Born Oby Edgar Starcher on 3/16/06 in Ripley, West Virginia. Died on 11/2/2001 (age 95). Country singer/songwriter/DJ.			
4/9/66	**39**	7		**History Repeats Itself** ...*Sniper's Hill* [S]	$12		Boone 1038
				an accounting of "coincidental" parallels between the careers and deaths of Presidents Lincoln and Kennedy			
				STARDUST '98			
				Dance trio from Paris, France: Thomas Bangalter, Alan "Branxe" Queme and Benjamin "Diamond" Cohen. Bangalter was a member of **Daft Punk**.			
10/10/98	**62**	8		**Music Sounds Better With You** ...S:43 *(3 versions)*	$4	▮	Roulé/Virgin 38651
				samples "Fate" by **Chaka Khan**			
				STARGARD R&B/LP '78			
				Disco trio: Rochelle Runnells, Debra Anderson and Janice Williams. Appeared as "The Diamonds" in the movie *Sgt. Pepper's Lonely Hearts Club Band.*			
1/28/78	**21**	14		1 **Theme Song From "Which Way Is Up"** / RB[2]			
				from the movie *Which Way Is Up* starring Richard Pryor			
3/4/78	**88**	5		2 **Disco Rufus** ... [I]	$5		MCA 40825
				STARK & McBRIEN AC '75			
				Pop duo: Fred Stark and Rod McBrien.			
1/25/75	**85**	6		**Isn't It Lonely Together** ...*A Page Torn Out Of Me*	$5		RCA Victor 10109
				STARLAND VOCAL BAND AC/LP '76			
				Pop group formed in Washington DC: Bill and wife Taffy Danoff, John Carroll and future wife Margot Chapman. Bill and Taffy had fronted the folk group Fat City (backed **John Denver** on "Take Me Home, Country Roads). Group hosted own summer TV variety series in 1977. Won the 1976 Best New Artist Grammy.			
5/8/76	❶[2]	20	●	1 **Afternoon Delight**...*Starland*	$5		Windsong 10588
10/16/76	**66**	3		2 **California Day**...*War Surplus Baby*	$5		Windsong 10785
1/8/77	**71**	6		3 **Hail! Hail! Rock And Roll!** ...*Ain't It The Fall*	$5		Windsong 10855
2/23/80	**71**	6		4 **Loving You With My Eyes** ...*Apartment For Rent*	$4		Windsong 11899
				STARLETS, The '62			
				Female R&B vocal group from Chicago, Illinois: Dynetta Boone, Jane Hall, Maxine Edwards (sister of Earl Edwards of **The Dukays**), Mickey McKinney, Jeanette Miles and Bernice Williams. While under contract to PAM Records, The Starlets recorded "I Sold My Heart To The Junkman" on the Newtown label. Newtown credited one of its artists, **The Blue-Belles** (**Patti LaBelle**'s group), on the label.			
4/24/61	**38**	16		1 **Better Tell Him No** ...*You Are The One*	$25		PAM 1003
4/21/62	**15**	11		2 **I Sold My Heart To The Junkman** *[THE BLUE-BELLES]*...*Itty Bitty Twist*	$25		Newtown 5000
				vocal group is actually **The Starlets**; reissued on Peak 7042 with a picture sleeve			
				STARPOINT R&B/BUB/LP '85			
				Dance group from Maryland: brothers Ernesto, George, Orlando and Gregory Phillips, with Renee Diggs and Kayode Adeyemo.			
9/28/85	**25**	24		1 **Object Of My Desire** ...S:19 / A:30 *Send Me A Letter*	$3	■	Elektra 69621
3/22/86	**46**	12		2 **Restless**...*It's All Yours*	$3		Elektra 69561
3/14/87	**89**	7		3 **He Wants My Body** ...*Satisfy Me Lover*	$3	■	Elektra 69489
				STARR, Brenda K. R&B/BUB/LP '88			
				Born Brenda Kaplan on 10/15/66 in Manhattan, New York. R&B-dance singer/movie actress. Daughter of Harvey Kaplan (of **Spiral Starecase**).			
4/2/88	**13**	26		1 **I Still Believe**...S:10 / A:14 *All Tied Up*	$3	■	MCA 53288
8/6/88	**24**	13		2 **What You See Is What You Get** ...S:16 / A:26 *Giving You All My Love*	$3	■	MCA 53367
12/1/90+	**49**	16		3 **No Matter What**...*Without You* (LaMond)	$3	▮	Columbia 73603
				GEORGE LaMOND With BRENDA K. STARR			
	★556★			**STARR, Edwin** R&B/BUB/LP '70			
				Born Charles Hatcher on 1/21/42 in Nashville, Tennessee; raised in Cleveland, Ohio. Died of a heart attack on 4/2/2003 (age 61). R&B singer/songwriter. In the Futuretones vocal group; recorded for Tress in 1957. With **Bill Doggett** Combo from 1963-65. Recorded duets with Sandra "**Blinky**" Williams in 1969. Also see **The Holidays**.			
				1)War 2)Twenty-Five Miles 3)Agent Double-O-Soul			
8/7/65	**21**	11		1 **Agent Double-O-Soul**...*(instrumental)*	$15		Ric-Tic 103
12/11/65	**95**	2		2 **Back Street** ...*(instrumental)*	$15		Ric-Tic 107

DEBUT	PEAK	WKS	Gold	A-side (Chart Hit)...B-side	$	Sym	Label & Number
				STARR, Edwin — Cont'd			
2/19/66	48	8		3 **Stop Her On Sight (S.O.S.)** ... *I Have Faith In You*	$15		Ric-Tic 109
5/7/66	84	4		4 **Headline News** ... *Harlem*	$15		Ric-Tic 114
2/15/69	6	14		5 **Twenty-Five Miles** ... *Love Is My Destination*	$7		Gordy 7083
6/28/69	80	4		6 **I'm Still A Struggling Man** ... *Pretty Little Angel*	$7		Gordy 7087
8/16/69	92	2		7 **Oh How Happy** ... *Ooo Baby Baby* **BLINKY & EDWIN STARR**	$7		Gordy 7090
7/11/70	❶[3]	15		8 **War** *He Who Picks A Rose*	$7		Gordy 7101
12/19/70+	26	8		9 **Stop The War Now** ... *Gonna Keep On Tryin' Till I Win Your Love*	$7		Gordy 7104
4/24/71	64	6		10 **Funky Music Sho Nuff Turns Me On** ... *Cloud Nine*	$7		Gordy 7107
6/30/73	80	6		11 **There You Go** ... *(instrumental)*	$6		Soul 35103
2/7/76	98	2		12 **Abyssinia Jones** ... *Beginning*	$6		Granite 532
2/10/79	65	7		13 **Contact** ... *Don't Waste Your Time*	$5		20th Century 2396
8/4/79	79	5		14 **H.A.P.P.Y. Radio** ... *My Friend*	$5		20th Century 2408
	★557★			**STARR, Kay** MEM/POP/AC **'52** Born Katherine Starks on 7/21/22 in Dougherty, Oklahoma; raised in Dallas, Texas, and Memphis, Tennessee. With Joe Venuti's orchestra at age 15, and sang briefly with Glenn Miller, Charlie Barnet and Bob Crosby before launching solo career in 1945. In the movies *Make Believe Ballroom* and *When You're Smiling.* Charted 27 hits, 1948-54, including a 10-week stay at #1 in 1952 with "Wheel Of Fortune." *1)Rock And Roll Waltz 2)My Heart Reminds Me 3)Good And Lonesome*			
8/6/55	17	1		1 **Good And Lonesome** ... J:17 *Where, What Or When*	$15		RCA Victor 6146
12/31/55+	❶[6]	25	●	2 **Rock And Roll Waltz** / J:❶[6] / T:❶[4] / S:❶[1] / A:❶[1]			
2/4/56	73	4		3 **I've Changed My Mind A Thousand Times** ... T:73	$15		RCA Victor 6359
6/9/56	40	10		4 **Second Fiddle** / T:40			
8/11/56	89	1		5 **Love Ain't Right** ... T:89 **Joe Reisman** (orch. and chorus, above 2)	$12		RCA Victor 6541
9/8/56	89	4		6 **The Good Book** / T:89			
9/8/56	89	3		7 **The Things I Never Had** ... T:89 above 2 from the TV production *The Lord Don't Play Favorites*; Hal Mooney (orch. and chorus: #1, 6 & 7)	$12		RCA Victor 6617
4/20/57	54	5		8 **Jamie Boy** / T:54			
4/27/57	73	3		9 **A Little Loneliness** ... T:73 written by **Damita Jo**; **Hugo Winterhalter** (orch. and chorus: #2, 3, 8 & 9)	$12		RCA Victor 6864
9/2/57	9	12		10 **My Heart Reminds Me** ... A:9 / T:53 *Flim Flam Floo* Pete King (orch.); lyric version of the Italian instrumental "Autumn Concerto"	$12		RCA Victor 6981
3/20/61	49	9		11 **Foolin' Around** ... *Kay's Lament* Jimmie Haskell (orch.); #2 Country hit for **Buck Owens** in 1961	$10		Capitol 4542
6/19/61	94	3		12 **I'll Never Be Free** ... *Nobody* Jack Marshall (orch.); Starr and **Tennessee Ernie Ford**'s duet version was a #3 hit in 1950	$10		Capitol 4583
10/27/62	92	4		13 **Four Walls** ... *Oh, Lonesome Me* Billy Liebert (orch.)	$8	■	Capitol 4835
				STARR, Kenny C&W **'75** Born Kenneth Trebbe on 9/21/52 in Topeka, Kansas; raised in Burlingame, Kansas. Country singer/guitarist.			
12/6/75	58	5		**The Blind Man In The Bleachers** ... *Texas Proud*	$5		MCA 40474
				STARR, Lucille C&W **'64** Born Lucille Savoie in St. Boniface, Manitoba, Canada. Duo with husband Bob Regan as The Canadian Sweethearts.			
5/16/64	54	8		**The French Song (Quand Le Soleil Dit Bonjour Aux Montagnes)** ... *Sit Down And Write A Letter To Me (Wontcha', Baby)* [F] arranged by **Herb Alpert**	$10		Almo Int'l. 204
				STARR, Randy **'57** Born Warren Nadel on 7/2/30 in New York City, New York. Pop singer/songwriter/guitarist. Dentist since 1956. Wrote many tunes for **Elvis Presley**'s soundtracks. Formed instrumental duo, **The Islanders**, with Frank Metis.			
4/6/57	32	11		**After School** ... T:32 *Heaven High - (man so low)* "Bugs" Bower (orch.)	$25		Dale 100
	★316★			**STARR, Ringo** C&W/ROK/LP **'74** Born Richard Starkey on 7/7/40 in Dingle, Liverpool, England. Drummer with Rory Storm and the Hurricanes before joining **The Beatles** in 1962. First solo recording in 1970. Acted in several movies, including **Paul McCartney**'s *Give My Regards To Broad Street.* Played "Mr. Conductor" on PBS-TV's *Shining Time Station* from 1989-91. Married actress Barbara Bach on 4/27/81. Continues to tour with an ever-revolving lineup of top musicians ("The All-Star Band"). *1)You're Sixteen 2)Photograph 3)No No Song*			
11/7/70	87	5		1 **Beaucoups Of Blues** ... *Coochy - Coochy* label number shown erroneously as Apple 1826 on first pressings of the picture sleeve	$10	■	Apple 2969
5/1/71	4	12	●	2 **It Don't Come Easy** ... *Early 1970* **Badfinger** (harmony vocals)	$8	■	Apple 1831
4/1/72	9	10		3 **Back Off Boogaloo** ... *Blindman* above 2 produced by **George Harrison**	$8	■	Apple 1849
10/6/73	❶[1]	16	●	4 **Photograph** ... *Down And Out* **George Harrison** (harmony vocal, 12-string guitar)	$8	■	Apple 1865
12/15/73+	❶[1]	15	●	5 **You're Sixteen** *Devil Woman* **Nilsson** (backing vocal); **Paul McCartney** (kazoo)	$8	■	Apple 1870
3/9/74	5	14		6 **Oh My My** ... *Step Lightly* **Martha Reeves** and **Merry Clayton** (backing vocals); **Billy Preston** (keyboards); **Tom Scott** (sax)	$8		Apple 1872
11/16/74+	6	13		7 **Only You** ... AC[1] *Call Me*	$8	■	Apple 1876
2/8/75	3	14		8 **No No Song** / **Nilsson** (backing vocal); written by **Hoyt Axton**			
2/8/75		14		9 **Snookeroo** ... written by **Elton John** (also on piano and backing vocal)	$8		Apple 1880

DEBUT	PEAK	WKS	Gold	A-side (Chart Hit)	B-side	$	Sym	Label & Number
				STARR, Ringo — Cont'd				
6/14/75	31	7		10 **It's All Down To Goodnight Vienna /** written by **John Lennon** (also on piano)				
6/14/75		7		11 **Oo-Wee** **Dr. John** (piano); above 5 from the album *Goodnight Vienna*		$8	■	Apple 1882
10/2/76	26	9		12 **A Dose Of Rock 'N' Roll** **Melissa Manchester** (backing vocal); **Peter Frampton** (guitar)	*Cryin'*	$15		Atlantic 3361
1/29/77	74	3		13 **Hey Baby**	*Lady Gaye*	$25		Atlantic 3371
11/7/81	38	11		14 **Wrack My Brain** written and produced by **George Harrison** (also on guitar and backing vocal)	*Drumming Is My Madness*	$6	■	Boardwalk 130
				STARSHIP — see JEFFERSON STARSHIP				
				STARS on 45 BUB/R&B/LP **'81** Dutch session vocalists and musicians assembled by producer Jaap Eggermont. **John Lennon** vocals by Bas Muys, **Paul McCartney** vocals by Okkie Huysdens and **George Harrison** vocals by Hans Vermeulen.				
4/11/81	❶[1]	21	●	1 **Medley** Intro "Venus"/Sugar Sugar/No Reply/I'll Be Back/Drive My Car/Do You Want To Know A Secret/We Can Work It Out/I Should Have Known Better/Nowhere Man/You're Going To Lose That Girl/Stars on 45	*Stars on 45*	$5		Radio 3810
7/18/81	67	6		2 **Medley II** Stars on 45/Good Day Sunshine/My Sweet Lord/Here Comes The Sun/While My Guitar Gently Weeps/Tax Man/A Hard Day's Night/Please Please Me/From Me To You/I Wanna Hold Your Hand/Stars on 45	*Stars on 45 II*	$5		Radio 3830
9/26/81	55	7		3 **More Stars** Papa Was A Rolling Stone/Dance To The Music/Sugar Baby Love/Lets Go To San Francisco/A Horse With No Name/Monday Monday/Tears Of A Clown/Stop In The Name Of Love/Cracklin' Rosie/Do Wah Diddy-Diddy/A Lover's Concerto/Reach Out I'll Be There/Sounds Of Silence/Stars on 45	*45 Stars Get Ready*	$5		Radio 3863
3/27/82	28	10		4 **Stars on 45 III** **STARS ON (A Tribute To Stevie Wonder)** Uptight Everything's All Right/My Cherie Amour/Yester Me, Yester You/Master Blaster/You Are The Sunshine Of My Life/Isn't She Lovely/Stars On Jingle/Sir Duke/I Wish/I Was Made To Love Her/Superstition/Fingertips	*Stars on 45 Get Ready III*	$5		Radio 4019
				STARS ON 54 — see AMBER / ENRIQUEZ, Jocelyn / ULTRA NATÉ				
				STAR WARS INTERGALACTIC DROID CHOIR & CHORALE — see MECO				
				STARZ BUB/LP **'77** Hard-rock group formed in New York: Michael Lee Smith (vocals), Rich Ranno and Brendan Harkin (guitars), Piet Sweval (bass; **Looking Glass**) and Joe Dube (drums). Smith is the brother of **Rex Smith**. Sweval died on 1/23/90 (age 51).				
12/25/76+	95	3		1 (She's Just A) **Fallen Angel**	*Monkey Business*	$5	■	Capitol 4343
3/19/77	33	10		2 **Cherry Baby** promo "45" released with an insert describing tune as a "prisoner's lament for his lover"	*Rock Six Times*	$6	■	Capitol 4399
6/25/77	66	8		3 **Sing It, Shout It** above 2 issued on gold vinyl	*Subway Terror*	$6	■	Capitol 4434
3/11/78	79	4		4 (Any Way That You Want It) **I'll Be There**	*Texas*	$5	■	Capitol 4546
5/20/78	78	3		5 **Hold On To The Night**	*Texas*	$5		Capitol 4566
10/21/78	81	3		6 **So Young, So Bad**	*Coliseum Rock*	$5	■	Capitol 4637
				STATIC-X ROK/LP **'00** Alternative-metal rock group formed in Los Angeles, California: Wayne Static (vocals, guitar), Koichi Fukuda (keyboards), Tony Campos (bass) and Ken Jay (drums).				
2/5/00	57[S]	4		**Push It**	*(2 mixes) / Bled For Days (live) / Down*	$8	★*	Warner 44782
				STATLER BROTHERS, The C&W/BUB/AC/LP **'66** Country vocal group from Staunton, Virginia: brothers Harold (bass) and Don (lead) Reid, Phil Balsley (baritone) and Lew DeWitt (tenor). In 1983, Jimmy Fortune replaced DeWitt who died from Crohn's disease on 8/15/90 (age 52). Hosted their own Nashville Network cable TV variety show. Charted 66 Country hits, 1965-90.				
11/13/65+	4	13		1 **Flowers On The Wall**	*Billy Christian*	$10		Columbia 43315
1/16/71	58	9		2 **Bed Of Rose's**	*The Last Goodbye*	$6		Mercury 73141
11/1/75	93	4		3 **I'll Go To My Grave Loving You**	*You've Been Like A Mother To Me*	$6		Mercury 73687
				STATON, Candi R&B/BUB/LP **'70** Born Canzata Staton on 5/13/40 in Hanceville, Alabama. R&B singer. Formerly married to **Clarence Carter**. Own *Candi Staton-Sussewell* show on TBN TV. *1)Young Hearts Run Free 2)Stand By Your Man 3)I'd Rather Be An Old Man's Sweetheart*				
6/21/69	46	8		1 **I'd Rather Be An Old Man's Sweetheart** (Than A Young Man's Fool)	*For You*	$7		Fame 1456
1/3/70	56	8		2 **I'm Just A Prisoner** (Of Your Good Lovin')	*Heart On A String*	$7		Fame 1460
5/9/70	60	8		3 **Sweet Feeling**	*Evidence*	$7		Fame 1466
8/29/70	24	14		4 **Stand By Your Man**	*How Can I Put Out The Flame (When You Keep The Fire Burning)*	$7		Fame 1472
1/2/71	52	10		5 **He Called Me Baby** #47 hit for **Charlie Rich** in 1974 as "She Called Me Baby"; above 4 from the album *Stand By Your Man*	*What Would Become Of Me*	$7		Fame 1476
6/24/72	48	11		6 **In The Ghetto**	*Sure As Sin*	$6		Fame 91000
11/4/72	83	6		7 **Lovin' You, Lovin' Me**	*You Don't Love Me No More*	$6		Fame 91005
2/3/73	63	9		8 **Do It In The Name Of Love**	*The Thanks I Get For Loving You*	$6		Fame 91009
12/28/74+	51	6		9 **As Long As He Takes Care Of Home** **RCR** (Rhodes, Chalmers & Rhodes; backing vocals); all of above produced by Rick Hall	*(w/o rap)*	$5		Warner 8038
5/29/76	20	16		10 **Young Hearts Run Free** RB[1]	*I Know*	$5		Warner 8181
				STATUES, The **'60** White vocal trio based in Nashville, Tennessee: James "Buzz" Cason, Hugh Jarrett and Richard Williams. Also see **Garry Miles**.				
8/8/60	84	3		**Blue Velvet** #16 hit for **Tony Bennett** in 1951	*Keep The Hall Light Burning*	$25		Liberty 55245
				STATUS QUO, The LP **'68** Psychedelic-rock group from London, England: Francis Rossi (vocals), Rick Parfitt (guitar), Roy Lynes (organ), Alan Lancaster (bass) and John Coghlan (drums). Immensely popular in England where they've charted over 50 hits, 22 of which went Top 10.				
5/18/68	12	17		1 **Pictures Of Matchstick Men**	*Gentlemen Joe's Sidewalk Cafe*	$12		Cadet Concept 7001
9/28/68	70	3		2 **Ice In The Sun**	*When My Mind Is Not Live*	$12		Cadet Concept 7006

DEBUT	PEAK	WKS	Gold	A-side (Chart Hit)..........B-side	$	Sym	Label & Number
				STEALERS WHEEL LP '73			
				Pop-rock duo from Scotland: **Gerry Rafferty** (vocals, guitar) and Joe Egan (vocals, keyboards).			
3/3/73	6	18		1 **Stuck In The Middle With You**..........*Jose*	$5		A&M 1416
7/14/73	49	8		2 **Everyone's Agreed That Everything Will Turn Out Fine**..........*Next To Me*	$5		A&M 1450
1/5/74	29	14		3 **Star**..........*What More Could You Want*	$5	■	A&M 1483
				STEAM LP '69			
				Rock group from Bridgeport, Connecticut. "Na Na Hey Hey Kiss Him Goodbye" was recorded by the trio of Gary DeCarlo, Paul Leka and Dale Frashuer, and released as by Steam. After the song became a hit, Leka assembled an actual Steam group: Bill Steer (vocals), Jay Babins and Tom Zuke (guitars), Hank Schorz (keyboards), Mike Daniels (bass) and Ray Corries (drums).			
10/18/69	❶²	16	●	1 **Na Na Hey Hey Kiss Him Goodbye**..........*It's The Magic In You Girl*	$10	■	Fontana 1667
				reissued in 1976 as the Chicago White Sox theme with a picture sleeve on Mercury 30160			
1/24/70	46	7		2 **I've Gotta Make You Love Me**..........*One Good Woman*	$6		Mercury 73020
				STEEL BREEZE LP '82			
				Pop-rock group from Sacramento, California: Ric Jacobs (vocals), Ken Goorabian and Waylin Carpenter (guitars), Rod Toner (keyboards), Vinnie Pantleoni (bass) and Barry Lowenthal (drums).			
8/28/82	16	20		1 **You Don't Want Me Anymore**..........*Who's Gonna Love You Tonight*	$4		RCA 13283
1/15/83	30	13		2 **Dreamin' Is Easy**..........*Street Talkin'*	$4		RCA 13427
				STEELE, Jeffrey C&W '01			
				Born on 8/27/61 in Burbank, California; raised in North Hollywood. Country-rockabilly singer/songwriter/guitarist. Former member of Boy Howdy.			
9/15/01	71^S	1		**Somethin' In The Water**..........*How Long Am I Supposed To Wait For You*	$6	★	Monument 79625
				STEELE, Maureen '85			
				White pop-dance singer/songwriter.			
5/4/85	77	5		**Save The Night For Me**..........*Boys Will Be Boys*	$4	■	Motown 1787
				STEELE, Terry '02			
				Born in Los Angeles, California. Male R&B singer/songwriter/pianist.			
9/21/02	10^S	19		**Here And Now (Full Circle)**..........*(album edit)*	$5	★	JTS 01142
				STEELERS, The '69			
				R&B vocal group from Chicago, Illinois: Leonard "Red" Truss, Wales Wallace, Wes "Preach" Wells, Alonzo "Cool" Wells and George "Flue" Wells.			
11/15/69	56	6		**Get It From The Bottom**..........*I'm Sorry*	$8		Date 1642
				STEELHEART ROK/LP '91			
				Hard-rock group from Norwalk, Connecticut: Michael Matijevic (vocals), Chris Risola and Frank Dicostanzo (guitars), Jimmy Ward (bass) and John Fowler (drums).			
3/16/91	23	27		1 **I'll Never Let You Go (Angel Eyes)**..........S:11 / A:71 *(no B-side)*	$4	▮	MCA 53801
8/31/91	59	8		2 **She's Gone (Lady)**..........*(3 album snippets)*	$4	▮	MCA 54167
	★332★			**STEELY DAN** BUB/AC/LP '73			
				Jazz-rock group formed in Los Angeles, California, by **Donald Fagen** (keyboards, vocals; born on 1/10/48 in Passaic, New Jersey) and Walter Becker (bass, vocals; born on 2/20/50 in Manhattan, New York). Group, primarily known as a studio unit, featured Fagen and Becker with various studio musicians. Duo split from 1981-92. Inducted into the Rock and Roll Hall of Fame in 2001.			
				1)Rikki Don't Lose That Number 2)Do It Again 3)Hey Nineteen			
11/18/72+	6	17		1 **Do It Again**..........*Fire In The Hole*	$5		ABC 11338
3/10/73	11	16		2 **Reeling In The Years**..........*Only A Fool*	$5	⊙	ABC 11352
7/28/73	61	8		3 **Show Biz Kids**..........*Razor Boy*	$5		ABC 11382
11/3/73	63	9		4 **My Old School**..........*Pearl Of The Quarter*	$5		ABC 11396
5/11/74	4	19		5 **Rikki Don't Lose That Number** *Any Major Dude Will Tell You*	$5		ABC 11439
				also released on ABC 12014 in 1974			
10/12/74	57	5		6 **Pretzel Logic**..........*Through With Buzz*	$5		ABC 12033
5/24/75	37	7		7 **Black Friday**..........*Throw Back The Little Ones*	$5		ABC 12101
7/10/76	82	3		8 **Kid Charlemagne**..........*Green Earrings*	$4		ABC 12195
9/25/76	59	5		9 **The Fez**..........*Sign In Stranger*	$4		ABC 12222
11/19/77+	11	19		10 **Peg**..........*I Got The News*	$4		ABC 12320
				Michael McDonald (backing vocal)			
4/1/78	19	16		11 **Deacon Blues**..........*Home At Last*	$4		ABC 12355
6/3/78	22	10		12 **FM (No Static At All)**..........*(reprise)*	$4		MCA 40894
				Timothy B. Schmit (backing vocals); from the movie *FM* starring Michael Brandon			
8/26/78	26	11		13 **Josie**..........*Black Cow*	$4		ABC 12404
11/29/80+	10	19		14 **Hey Nineteen**..........*Bodhisattva (live)*	$4		MCA 51036
3/14/81	22	11		15 **Time Out Of Mind**..........*Bodhisattva (live)*	$4		MCA 51082
				Mark Knopfler of **Dire Straits** (guitar solo); all of above written by **Fagen** & Becker and produced by Gary Katz			
				STEIN, Lou '57			
				Born on 4/22/22 in Philadelphia, Pennsylvania. Died on 12/10/2002 (age 80). Session pianist.			
3/2/57	31	14		**Almost Paradise**..........T:31 *Soft Sands* [I]	$15		RKO Unique 385
				Bill Fontaine (orch.)			
				STEINER, Tommy Shane C&W/LP '02			
				Born in 1973 in Austin, Texas. Country singer/songwriter.			
2/23/02	39	20		**What If She's An Angel**..........A:36		V	album cut
				from the album *Then Came The Night* on RCA 67041; "45": RCA 69136; B-side: "The Mind Of John J. Blanchard"			
				STEINMAN, Jim LP '81			
				Born on 11/1/47 in Brooklyn, New York. Songwriter/pianist/producer. Wrote and produced songs for **Meat Loaf**, **Air Supply** and **Bonnie Tyler**.			
5/30/81	32	16		**Rock And Roll Dreams Come Through**..........*Love And Death And An American Guitar*	$5	□	Cleveland I./Epic 02111
				Rory Dodd (vocal); a promo record and picture sleeve issued on Cleveland International/Epic 1232			

DEBUT	PEAK	WKS	Gold	A-side (Chart Hit)..........B-side	$	Sym	Label & Number
				STEPHENS, Devyne, "The Entertainer" '00			
				Born in Atlanta, Georgia. Male rapper.			
8/19/00	51^{S}	6		**Un-Huh**..........*(instrumental) / (3 album snippets)*	$5	★	EastWest 67069
				STEPHENSON, Van LP '84			
				Born on 11/4/53 in Hamilton, Ohio. Died of cancer on 4/8/2001 (age 47). Pop-country singer/songwriter. Member of **BlackHawk**.			
9/12/81	79	4		1 **You've Got A Good Love Coming**..........*Hotter In The Night*	$5		Handshake 02140
4/21/84	22	17		2 **Modern Day Delilah**..........*Don't Do That*	$4	■	MCA 52376
8/4/84	45	9		3 **What The Big Girls Do**..........*Righteous Anger*	$4	■	MCA 52437
	★396★			**STEPPENWOLF** BUB/ROK/LP '68			
				Hard-rock group formed in Los Angeles, California: Joachim "**John Kay**" Krauledat (vocals, guitar; born on 4/12/44) (see #13 below), Michael Monarch (guitar; born on 7/5/50), John "Goldy McJohn" Goadsby (keyboards; born on 5/2/45) and Jerry "Edmonton" McCrohan (drums; born on 10/24/46). All but Monarch were members of Canadian group Sparrow. Many personnel changes except for Kay. Group named after a 1927 Herman Hesse novel. Edmonton died in a car crash on 11/28/93 (age 47).			
				1)Born To Be Wild 2)Magic Carpet Ride 3)Rock Me			
7/13/68	2^{3}	13	●	1 **Born To Be Wild**..........*Everybody's Next One*	$8		Dunhill/ABC 4138
10/5/68	3	16	●	2 **Magic Carpet Ride**..........*Sookie Sookie*	$8		Dunhill/ABC 4161
3/1/69	10	10		3 **Rock Me**..........*Jupiter Child*	$8		Dunhill/ABC 4182
5/10/69	51	5		4 **It's Never Too Late**..........*Happy Birthday*	$7		Dunhill/ABC 4192
8/16/69	31	9		5 **Move Over**..........*Power Play*	$7		Dunhill/ABC 4205
12/27/69+	39	8		6 **Monster**..........*Berry Rides Again*	$7		Dunhill/ABC 4221
4/11/70	35	8		7 **Hey Lawdy Mama**..........*Twisted*	$7		Dunhill/ABC 4234
				all of above produced by Gabriel Mekler			
8/22/70	62	7		8 **Screaming Night Hog**..........*Spiritual Fantasy*	$6		Dunhill/ABC 4248
11/14/70	54	6		9 **Who Needs Ya**..........*Earschplittenloudenboomer*	$6		Dunhill/ABC 4261
3/6/71	60	7		10 **Snow Blind Friend**..........*Hippo Stomp*	$6		Dunhill/ABC 4269
				written by **Hoyt Axton**			
7/17/71	52	8		11 **Ride With Me**..........*For Madmen Only*	$6	■	Dunhill/ABC 4283
				also released with "Black Pit" as the B-side			
11/6/71	64	7		12 **For Ladies Only**..........*Sparkle Eyes*	$6		Dunhill/ABC 4292
4/22/72	52	7		13 **I'm Movin' On**..........*Walk Beside Me*	$6		Dunhill/ABC 4309
				JOHN KAY			
				#1 Country hit for **Hank Snow** in 1950			
9/7/74	29	9		14 **Straight Shootin' Woman**..........*Justice Don't Be Slow*	$6	■	Mums 6031
				STEPS LP '00			
				Dance-pop vocal group from England: Lisa Scott-Lee, Ian Watkins, Claire Richards, Lee Latchford-Evans and Faye Tozer.			
3/4/00	25^{S}	17		**Tragedy**..........*Stay With Me*	$4	★	Jive 42652
				STEREO MC'S LP '93			
				Trio of dance remixers from Gee Street Records based in London, England: Rob Birch, Nick "The Head" Hallam and Owen "If" Rossiter. Features touring/video vocalist Cath Coffey.			
6/1/91	39	13		1 **Elevate My Mind**..........S:35 / A:41 *(12" version)*	$4	▮	4th & B'way 447519
3/27/93	20	20		2 **Connected**..........A:24 / S:29 *(3 album snippets)*	$4	▮	Gee Street 864744
				samples **Jimmy "Bo" Horne**'s R&B hit "Let Me (Let Me Be Your Lover)"			
7/10/93	58	13		3 **Step It Up**..........A:55 *(3 album snippets)*	$4	▮	Gee Street 862308
				STEREOS, The '61			
				R&B vocal group from Steubenville, Ohio: Bruce Robinson, Nathaniel Hicks, Sam Profit, George Otis and Ronnie Collins.			
9/25/61	29	9		**I Really Love You**..........*Please Come Back To Me*	$25		Cub 9095
				STEVENS, April — see TEMPO, Nino			
	★356★			**STEVENS, Cat** BUB/LP '71			
				Born Steven Georgiou on 7/21/47 in London, England. Pop-folk singer/songwriter/guitarist. Began career playing folk music at Hammersmith College in 1966. Contracted tuberculosis in 1968 and spent over a year recuperating. Adopted new style when he re-emerged. Lived in Brazil in the mid-1970s. Converted to Muslim religion in 1979; took name Yusuf Islam.			
				1)Morning Has Broken 2)Another Saturday Night 3)Peace Train			
2/13/71	11	13		1 **Wild World**..........*Miles From Nowhere*	$6		A&M 1231
6/26/71	30	11		2 **Moon Shadow**..........*I Think I See The Light*	$6	■	A&M 1265
9/25/71	7	12		3 **Peace Train**..........AC^{3} *Where Do The Children Play*	$6	■	A&M 1291
4/1/72	6	14		4 **Morning Has Broken** AC^{1} *I Want To Live In A Wigwam*	$6	■	A&M 1335
11/18/72+	16	11		5 **Sitting**..........*Crab Dance*	$6	■	A&M 1396
				all of above produced by Paul Samwell-Smith			
7/7/73	31	10		6 **The Hurt**..........*Silent Sunlight*	$5	■	A&M 1418
3/16/74	10	17		7 **Oh Very Young**..........*100 I Dream*	$5	■	A&M 1503
8/3/74	6	14		8 **Another Saturday Night**..........*Home In The Sky*	$5	■	A&M 1602
12/7/74+	26	10		9 **Ready**..........*I Think I See The Light*	$5		A&M 1645
7/19/75	33	9		10 **Two Fine People**..........*A Bad Penny*	$5	■	A&M 1700
2/7/76	41	6		11 **Banapple Gas**..........*Ghost Town*	$5	■	A&M 1785
6/25/77	33	10		12 (Remember The Days Of The) **Old Schoolyard**..........*Land O'Freelove & Goodbye*	$5	■	A&M 1948
11/19/77+	70	9		13 **Was Dog A Doughnut**..........*Sweet Jamaica* [I]	$5		A&M 1971
1/27/79	83	4		14 **Bad Brakes**..........*Nascimento*	$4		A&M 2109
				all of above (except #4 & 8) written by Stevens			
				STEVENS, Connie BUB '60			
				Born Concetta Ingolia on 8/8/38 in Brooklyn, New York. Pop singer/actress. Played "Cricket Blake" on TV's *Hawaiian Eye* from 1959-63. Appeared in many movies. Married to **Eddie Fisher** from 1967-69; singer **Tricia Leigh Fisher** is their daughter.			
4/20/59	4	13	●	1 **Kookie, Kookie (Lend Me Your Comb)**..........*You're The Top* (Brynes) [N]	$20	■	Warner 5047
				EDWARD BYRNES And CONNIE STEVENS			
2/1/60	3	24		2 **Sixteen Reasons**..........*Little Sister*	$15		Warner 5137

DEBUT	PEAK	WKS	Gold	A-side (Chart Hit)....B-side	$	Sym	Label & Number
				STEVENS, Connie — Cont'd			
7/4/60	71	5		3 **Too Young To Go Steady** ....*A Little Kiss Is A Kiss, Is A Kiss* from the musical *Strip For Action*; **Don Ralke** (orch., above 3)	$12	■	Warner 5159
5/5/62	52	11		4 **Why'd You Wanna Make Me Cry**....*Just One Kiss*	$12		Warner 5265
8/4/62	43	8		5 **Mr. Songwriter**....*I Couldn't Say No* **Perry Botkin Jr.** (orch., above 2)	$12		Warner 5289
4/24/65	53	7		6 **Now That You've Gone** ....*Lost In Wonderland* **Ernie Freeman** (orch.); written and recorded by **Petula Clark** on her 1965 album *Downtown*	$12		Warner 5610

STEVENS, Dodie

BUB '59

Born Geraldine Ann Pasquale on 2/17/46 in Chicago, Illinois; raised in California. Discovered while singing on **Art Linkletter**'s *House Party* TV show at age 8. First recorded as Geri Pace on Gold Star in 1954; also recorded as Geraldine Stevens ("Bubbled Under").

DEBUT	PEAK	WKS	Gold	A-side (Chart Hit)....B-side	$	Sym	Label & Number
2/16/59	3	19	●	1 **Pink Shoe Laces** *Coming Of Age* Bobby Hammack (orch.); Dodie was one day short of age 13 when this song debuted on the *Hot 100*	$20		Crystalette 724
6/1/59	79	3		2 **Yes - Sir - ee** /			
6/29/59	89	1		3 **The Five Pennies** .... title song from the movie starring Danny Kaye and **Louis Armstrong**	$20		Crystalette 728
8/8/60	73	8		4 **No**....*A Tisket A Tasket*	$15		Dot 16103
12/31/60+	60	6		5 **Yes, I'm Lonesome Tonight** ....*Too Young* **Billy Vaughn** (orch.); answer song to **Elvis Presley**'s "Are You Lonesome To-night?"	$15		Dot 16167

STEVENS, Ray ★160★

C&W/BUB/AC/LP '70

Born Harold Ray Ragsdale on 1/24/39 in Clarksdale, Georgia. Country-novelty singer/songwriter. Proficient on several instruments. Production work in the mid-1960s. Numerous appearances on the **Andy Williams** TV show in the late 1960s. Hosted own TV variety show in 1970. Also recorded as **Henhouse Five Plus Too**.

1)The Streak 2)Everything Is Beautiful 3)Ahab, The Arab 4)Gitarzan 5)Misty

DEBUT	PEAK	WKS	Gold	A-side (Chart Hit)....B-side	$	Sym	Label & Number
8/21/61	35	6		1 **Jeremiah Peabody's Poly Unsaturated Quick Dissolving Fast Acting Pleasant Tasting Green And Purple Pills**....*Teen Years* [N]	$15	■	Mercury 71843
6/30/62	5	11		2 **Ahab, The Arab** ....*It's Been So Long* [N]	$15	■	Mercury 71966
10/13/62	91	3		3 **Further More**....*Saturday Night At The Movies* [N]	$15		Mercury 72039
12/15/62	45	3		4 **Santa Claus Is Watching You** ....*Loved And Lost* [X-N] The Merry Melody Singers (backing vocals, above 3)	$15	■	Mercury 72058
3/30/63	81	3		5 **Funny Man**....*Just One Of Life's Little Tragedies* "Bubbled Under" (#122) in 1968 on Mercury 72816	$15		Mercury 72098
6/15/63	17	9		6 **Harry The Hairy Ape**....*Little Stone Statue* [N]	$15	■	Mercury 72125
10/12/63	59	3		7 **Speed Ball** ....*It's Party Time* [N]	$15		Mercury 72189
7/16/66	91	2		8 **Freddie Feelgood (And His Funky Little Five Piece Band)** ....*There's One In Every Crowd* [N]	$10		Monument 946
4/20/68	52	9		9 **Unwind**....*For He's A Jolly Good Fellow*	$8		Monument 1048
8/3/68	28	7		10 **Mr. Businessman**....*Face The Music*	$8		Monument 1083
4/5/69	8	13	●	11 **Gitarzan**....*Bagpipes-That's My Bag* [N]	$8		Monument 1131
6/28/69	27	8		12 **Along Came Jones**....*Yakety Yak* [N]	$8		Monument 1150
10/25/69	81	3		13 **Sunday Mornin' Comin' Down**....*The Minority* written by **Kris Kristofferson**	$8		Monument 1163
4/4/70	❶[2]	15	●	14 **Everything Is Beautiful** ....AC[3] *A Brighter Day* intro features the children's hymn "Jesus Loves The Little Children"	$6		Barnaby 2011
7/25/70	45	6		15 **America, Communicate With Me** ....*Monkey See, Monkey Do*	$6		Barnaby 2016
11/7/70	81	4		16 **Sunset Strip** ....*Islands*	$6		Barnaby 2021
12/19/70+	50	10		17 **Bridget The Midget (The Queen Of The Blues)** ....*Night People* [N]	$6	■	Barnaby 2024
5/1/71	82	3		18 **A Mama And A Papa**....*Melt*	$6		Barnaby 2029
8/28/71	70	6		19 **All My Trials** ....*Have A Little Talk With Myself* traditional West Indian lullaby	$6		Barnaby 2039
11/20/71	63	7		20 **Turn Your Radio On**....*Loving You On Paper* gospel song written in 1959 by Albert Brumley	$6		Barnaby 2048
4/13/74	❶[3]	17	●	21 **The Streak** *You've Got The Music Inside* [N]	$6		Barnaby 600
7/27/74	73	7		22 **Moonlight Special** ....*Just So Proud To Be Here* [N] parody of TV's *Midnight Special*	$6		Barnaby 604
4/26/75	14	16		23 **Misty**....*Sunshine* introduced by the Erroll Garner Trio in 1954 on Mercury 70442 ($15)	$6		Barnaby 614
10/11/75	68	5		24 **Indian Love Call** ....*Piece Of Paradise* #3 hit for Paul Whiteman in 1925	$6		Barnaby 616
1/24/76	93	2		25 **Young Love**....*Deep Purple*	$6		Barnaby 618
1/8/77	40	7		26 **In The Mood**....*Classical Cluck* [N] **HENHOUSE FIVE PLUS TOO** a chicken-clucking version of Glenn Miller's 1940 #1 hit	$6		Warner 8301
3/24/79	49	8		27 **I Need Your Help Barry Manilow** ....*Daydream Romance* [N]	$6	■	Warner 8785
2/2/02	8[S]	22		28 **Osama-Yo' Mama**....*United We Stand* [N] written by Stevens 3 months after "9/11"	$4	★	Curb 73130

STEVENS, Shakin'

'84

Born Michael Barratt on 3/4/48 in Ely, Wales. Rockabilly singer/songwriter.

DEBUT	PEAK	WKS	Gold	A-side (Chart Hit)....B-side	$	Sym	Label & Number
4/21/84	67	6		**I Cry Just A Little Bit**....*Love Me Tonight*	$5		Epic 04338

DEBUT	PEAK	WKS	Gold	A-side (Chart Hit)...B-side	$	Sym	Label & Number

STEVENSON, B.W. — AC/BUB/LP '73

Born Louis Stevenson on 10/5/49 in Dallas, Texas. Died of heart failure on 4/28/88 (age 38). Soft-rock singer/guitarist.

DEBUT	PEAK	WKS	Gold	A-side (Chart Hit)...B-side	$	Sym	Label & Number
5/12/73	66	8		1 **Shambala**...*My Feet Are So Weary*	$6		RCA Victor 0952
7/28/73	9	16		2 **My Maria** ...AC[1] *August Evening Lady* **Larry Carlton** (guitar)	$6		RCA Victor 0030
12/1/73+	53	7		3 **The River Of Love** ...*Lucky Touch*	$6		RCA Victor 0171
4/16/77	82	5		4 **Down To The Station** ...*May You Find Yourself In Heaven*	$5		Warner 8343

STEVIE B — R&B/LP '90

★419★

Born Steven Hill in Miami, Florida. Dance-pop singer/multi-instrumentalist. Also see **Jaya**.

1)Because I Love You 2)I'll Be By Your Side 3)Love & Emotion

DEBUT	PEAK	WKS	Gold	A-side (Chart Hit)...B-side	$	Sym	Label & Number
4/23/88	80	10		1 **Dreamin' Of Love**...*(dub version)*	$4		LMR 74001
7/9/88	43	18		2 **Spring Love (Come Back To Me)** ...S:34 *(long version)*	$4		LMR 74002
2/18/89	32	20		3 **I Wanna Be The One**...S:26 / A:37 *(extended mix)*	$4		LMR 74003
5/27/89	37	17		4 **In My Eyes** ...S:34 *(remix)*	$4		LMR 74004
10/7/89	56	15		5 **Girl I Am Searching For You**...*(remix)*	$4		LMR 74005
2/3/90	29	14		6 **Love Me For Life**...S:29 / A:30 *(same version)* above 4 from the album *In My Eyes*	$3	▮	LMR 84006
6/30/90	15	15		7 **Love & Emotion** ...A:14 / S:16 *(album version)* "45" B-side: "Come With Me"	$3	▮V	LMR/RCA 2645
10/6/90	❶[4]	23	●	8 **Because I Love You (The Postman Song)** AC[2] A:❶[5] / S:❶[1] *(album version)*	$3	▮V	LMR/RCA 2724
2/2/91	12	15		9 **I'll Be By Your Side**...A:11 / S:13 *(same version)*	$3	▮V	LMR/RCA 2758
10/26/91	96	4		10 **Forever More**...*(extended remix) / Spring Love* above 4 from the album *Love & Emotion*	$3	▮	LMR/RCA 62112
2/11/95	29	23		11 **Dream About You** / A:24 / S:45			
2/11/95		23		12 **Funky Melody**...S:flip "45" issued on white vinyl	$3	▮V	Emporia/Thump 2205

STEVIE V — see ADVENTURES OF

STEWART, Al — LP '77

Born on 9/5/45 in Glasgow, Scotland. Pop singer/songwriter/guitarist. Also see **Shot In The Dark**.

DEBUT	PEAK	WKS	Gold	A-side (Chart Hit)...B-side	$	Sym	Label & Number
12/11/76+	8	17		1 **Year Of The Cat** ...*Broadway Hotel* written about British comedian Tony Hancock	$6		Janus 266
4/23/77	42	9		2 **On The Border** ...*Flying Sorcery*	$5		Janus 267
9/30/78	7	18		3 **Time Passages** AC[10] *Almost Lucy*	$4		Arista 0362
1/27/79	29	9		4 **Song On The Radio** ...*A Man For All Seasons* all of above produced by **Alan Parsons**	$4		Arista 0389
8/30/80	24	13		5 **Midnight Rocks**...*Constantinople*	$4		Arista 0552

STEWART, Amii — R&B/LP '79

Born in 1956 in Washington DC. Disco singer/dancer/actress. In the Broadway musical *Bubbling Brown Sugar*. Aunt of singer **Sinitta**.

DEBUT	PEAK	WKS	Gold	A-side (Chart Hit)...B-side	$	Sym	Label & Number
1/27/79	❶[1]	20	▲	1 **Knock On Wood** ...*When You Are Beautiful*	$5		Ariola America 7736
6/23/79	69	6		2 **Light My Fire/137 Disco Heaven**...*Am I Losing You*	$5		Ariola America 7753
8/30/80	63	8		3 **My Guy/My Girl** ...*Now* **AMII STEWART & JOHNNY BRISTOL** medley of #1 tunes by **Mary Wells** and **The Temptations** (both written by **Smokey Robinson**)	$5		Handshake 5300

STEWART, Andy — '61

Born on 12/20/33 in Glasgow, Scotland. Died of a heart attack on 10/11/93 (age 59). Pop singer/actor/comedian.

DEBUT	PEAK	WKS	Gold	A-side (Chart Hit)...B-side	$	Sym	Label & Number
4/3/61	69	6		1 **A Scottish Soldier (Green Hills of Tyrol)**...*The Muckin 'O' Geordie's Byre* originally charted for 3 weeks (#88); re-entered on 6/19/61; melody dates back to the Crimean War	$15		Warwick 627
8/21/61	77	4		2 **Donald Where's Your Troosers?** ...*The Battle's O'er* [N] The White Heather Group (backing band); features an **Elvis Presley** impersonation	$20		Warwick 665

STEWART, Baron — '75

Pop-country singer/songwriter.

DEBUT	PEAK	WKS	Gold	A-side (Chart Hit)...B-side	$	Sym	Label & Number
8/16/75	91	6		**We Been Singin' Songs**...*Time*	$6		United Artists 686

STEWART, Billy — R&B/LP '66

Born on 3/24/37 in Washington DC. Died in a car crash on 1/17/70 (age 32). R&B singer/composer/keyboardist. Discovered by **Bo Diddley** in 1956. First recorded for Chess/Argo in 1956. Did not record from 1957-62. Nicknamed "Fat Boy." First cousin of Grace Ruffin of **The Jewels**.

1)Summertime 2)Sitting In The Park 3)I Do Love You

DEBUT	PEAK	WKS	Gold	A-side (Chart Hit)...B-side	$	Sym	Label & Number
7/21/62	79	5		1 **Reap What You Sow**...*Fat Boy*	$12		Chess 1820
9/28/63	70	6		2 **Strange Feeling** ...*Sugar And Spice*	$12		Chess 1868
3/27/65	26	10		3 **I Do Love You** ...*Keep Loving* also see #12 below	$10		Chess 1922
6/19/65	24	8		4 **Sitting In The Park**...*Once Again*	$10		Chess 1932
9/18/65	97	2		5 **How Nice It Is** ...*No Girl* all of above written by Stewart	$10		Chess 1941
1/22/66	96	2		6 **Because I Love You** /			
1/1/66	100	1		7 **Mountain Of Love** ...	$10		Chess 1948
7/16/66	10	10		8 **Summertime** *To Love To Love* from George Gershwin's 1935 folk opera *Porgy And Bess*; #12 hit for Billie Holiday in 1936	$12		Chess 1966
10/15/66	29	8		9 **Secret Love**...*Look Back And Smile* #1 hit for **Doris Day** in 1954	$10		Chess 1978
2/11/67	74	5		10 **Every Day I Have The Blues** ...*Ol' Man River*	$10		Chess 1991
12/2/67+	86	9		11 **Cross My Heart**...*Why (Do I Love You So) (R&B #49)*	$10		Chess 2002
2/22/69	94	3		12 **I Do Love You** ...*Keep Loving* [R] #3 (black label) and #12 (blue label) are the same version	$10		Chess 1922

DEBUT	PEAK	WKS	Gold	A-side (Chart Hit)...B-side	$	Sym	Label & Number

STEWART, Dave, & Barbara Gaskin '82

Duo from London, England: singer Gaskin and keyboardist Stewart (not to be confused with David A. Stewart of Eurythmics).

DEBUT	PEAK	WKS	Gold	A-side (Chart Hit)...B-side	$	Sym	Label & Number
12/19/81+	72	8		**It's My Party** ...*Waiting In The Wings*	$5		Platinum 4

STEWART, David A. '91

Born on 9/9/52 in Sunderland, England. Multi-instrumentalist/composer/producer. In **The Tourists**. Half of the **Eurythmics** duo. Married Siobhan Fahey (**Bananarama**, **Shakespear's Sister**) on 8/1/87.

DEBUT	PEAK	WKS	Gold	A-side (Chart Hit)...B-side	$	Sym	Label & Number
5/18/91	11	16		**Lily Was Here** ...A:26 / S:55 *Lily Robs The Bank / (DNA remix)* [I] **DAVID A. STEWART Introducing Candy Dulfer** (saxophonist from Amsterdam, Netherlands) from the Dutch movie *Lily Was Here* starring Marion Van Thijn	$3	■V	Arista 2187

STEWART, Jermaine R&B/LP '86

Born on 9/7/57 in Columbus, Ohio. Died of cancer on 3/17/97 (age 39). R&B-dance singer.

DEBUT	PEAK	WKS	Gold	A-side (Chart Hit)...B-side	$	Sym	Label & Number
2/2/85	41	15		1 **The Word Is Out** ...*Month Of Mondays*	$3		Arista 9256
5/17/86	5	22		2 **We Don't Have To Take Our Clothes Off** ...S:4 / A:5 *Give Your Love To Me*	$3	■	Arista 9424
9/20/86	42	9		3 **Jody** ...S:37 *Dance Floor*	$3	■	Arista 9476
3/19/88	27	12		4 **Say It Again** ...A:24 / S:26 *You Promise*	$3	■	Arista 9636

STEWART, John LP '79

Born on 9/5/39 in San Diego, California. Folk-pop singer/songwriter. Member of **The Kingston Trio** from 1961-67. Brother of Mike Stewart (drummer for **We Five**).

DEBUT	PEAK	WKS	Gold	A-side (Chart Hit)...B-side	$	Sym	Label & Number
9/6/69	74	3		1 **Armstrong** ...*Anna On A Memory*	$6		Capitol 2605
5/19/79	5	18		2 **Gold** ...*Comin' Out Of Nowhere*	$5		RSO 931
8/25/79	28	12		3 **Midnight Wind** ...*Somewhere Down The Line* **Stevie Nicks** (backing vocal, above 2); **Lindsey Buckingham** (guitar, above 2)	$5		RSO 1000
12/8/79+	34	13		4 **Lost Her In The Sun** ...*Heart Of The Dream*	$5		RSO 1016

STEWART, Rod ★13★ ROK/BUB/AC/LP '71

Born Roderick Stewart on 1/10/45 in Highgate, London, England. Pop-rock singer/songwriter. Worked as a folk singer in Europe in the early 1960s. Recorded for English Decca, 1964. With the Hoochie Coochie Men, Steampacket and Shotgun Express. Joined **Jeff Beck** Group, 1967-69. With **Faces** from 1969-75; also recorded solo during this time. Left Faces in December 1975. Won Grammy's Living Legends Award in 1989. Married to actress Alana Hamilton from 1979-84. Married supermodel Rachel Hunter on 12/15/90; separated January 1999. Inducted into the Rock and Roll Hall of Fame in 1994. One of the rock era's leading hit-makers for 28 consecutive years. Also see **Python Lee Jackson** and **Small Faces**.

1)Tonight's The Night 2)Maggie May 3)Da Ya Think I'm Sexy? 4)All For Love 5)Downtown Train

DEBUT	PEAK	WKS	Gold	A-side (Chart Hit)...B-side	$	Sym	Label & Number
8/14/71	❶ (5)	17	●	1 **Maggie May** / **Ron Wood** (guitar); Pete Sears (of **Jefferson Starship**; piano)			
7/17/71	62	21		2 **Reason To Believe** ... written by **Tim Hardin**; also see #48 below	$8		Mercury 73224
11/20/71	24	9		3 **(I Know) I'm Losing You** ...*Mandolin Wind* (Stewart) **ROD STEWART With Faces**	$8		Mercury 73244
2/12/72	42	6		4 **Handbags And Gladrags** ...*Man Of Constant Sorrow* first released on Mercury 73009 in 1969 ($10)	$8		Mercury 73031
8/26/72	13	10		5 **You Wear It Well** ...*True Blue*	$8	■	Mercury 73330
11/18/72	40	7		6 **Angel** ...*Lost Paraguayos* written by **Jimi Hendrix** (from his 1971 album *The Cry Of Love*)	$8		Mercury 73344
8/11/73	59	7		7 **Twisting The Night Away** ...*True Blue / Lady Day* written by **Sam Cooke**; also see #35 below	$8	■	Mercury 73412
10/13/73	59	8		8 **Oh! No Not My Baby** ...*Jodie* (Rod & **Faces**) picture sleeve has only a plaid pattern	$8	■	Mercury 73426
12/14/74	91	2		9 **Mine For Me** ...*Farewell* written by **Paul McCartney**	$6		Mercury 73636
10/18/75	58	7		10 **Sailing** ...*All In The Name Of Rock 'N' Roll*	$6		Warner 8146
1/10/76	83	4		11 **This Old Heart Of Mine** ...*Still Love You* also see #41 below	$6		Warner 8170
10/2/76	❶ (8)	23	●	12 **Tonight's The Night (Gonna Be Alright)** *Fool For You* French whispers by Rod's then-love, Swedish actress Britt Ekland	$5		Warner 8262
2/12/77	21	12		13 **The First Cut Is The Deepest** ...*The Balltrap* written by **Cat Stevens**	$5		Warner 8321
6/4/77	30	10		14 **The Killing Of Georgie (Part I And II)** ...*Rosie*	$5		Warner 8396
10/29/77+	4	22	●	15 **You're In My Heart (The Final Acclaim)** ...*You Got A Nerve*	$5		Warner 8475
2/11/78	28	11		16 **Hot Legs** ...*You're Insane*	$5	■	Warner 8535
4/29/78	22	12		17 **I Was Only Joking** ...*Born Loose*	$5	■	Warner 8568
12/23/78+	❶ (4)	21	▲	18 **Da Ya Think I'm Sexy?** ...*Scarred And Scared*	$4	■	Warner 8724
4/21/79	22	12		19 **Ain't Love A Bitch** ...*Last Summer*	$4	■	Warner 8810
12/22/79+	46	11		20 **I Don't Want To Talk About It** ...*The Best Days Of My Life* recorded in 1975; a new version by Stewart made the Adult Contemporary charts (#2) in 1990	$4	■	Warner 49138
11/22/80+	5	20		21 **Passion** ...*Better Off Dead*	$4	■	Warner 49617
3/21/81	71	5		22 **Somebody Special** ...*She Won't Dance With Me*	$4		Warner 49686
10/17/81	5	19		23 **Young Turks** ...*Sonny*	$4	■	Warner 49843
1/23/82	20	14		24 **Tonight I'm Yours (Don't Hurt Me)** ...*Tora, Tora, Tora (Out With The Boys)* (ROK #38)	$4	■	Warner 49886
4/24/82	49	9		25 **How Long** ...*Jealous* (ROK #44)	$4	■	Warner 50051
5/28/83	14	14		26 **Baby Jane** ...*Ready Now*	$4		Warner 29608
8/27/83	35	12		27 **What Am I Gonna Do (I'm So In Love With You)** ...*Dancin' Alone*	$4	■	Warner 29564
5/26/84	6	18		28 **Infatuation** ...*She Won't Dance With Me* **Jeff Beck** (guitar solo); also released with "Three Time Loser" as the B-side	$4	■	Warner 29256
8/25/84	10	17		29 **Some Guys Have All The Luck** ...A:8 / S:19 *I Was Only Joking*	$4	■	Warner 29215
12/15/84+	72	6		30 **All Right Now** ...*Dancin' Alone*	$4		Warner 29122
6/15/85	48	10		31 **People Get Ready** ...*Back On The Street* (Beck w/Karen Lawrence) **JEFF BECK and ROD STEWART**	$4	■	Epic 05416

DEBUT	PEAK	WKS	Gold	A-side (Chart Hit)........B-side	$	Sym	Label & Number
				STEWART, Rod — Cont'd			
5/31/86	6	18		32 **Love Touch** ....A:4 / S:7 *Heart Is On The Line* theme from the movie *Legal Eagles* starring Robert Redford and Debra Winger	$3	■	Warner 28668
8/30/86	52	9		33 **Another Heartache** ....*You're In My Heart (The Final Acclaim) (live)* co-written by **Bryan Adams**	$3	■	Warner 28631
11/29/86	83	6		34 **Every Beat Of My Heart** ....*Trouble*	$3	■	Warner 28625
7/18/87	80	4		35 **Twistin' The Night Away** ....*Let's Get Small* (Jerry Goldsmith) [R] new version of #7 above; featured in the movie *Innerspace* starring Dennis Quaid	$3	■	Geffen 28303
5/7/88	12	18		36 **Lost In You** ....S:9 / A:17 *Almost Illegal*	$3	■	Warner 27927
8/6/88	12	24		37 **Forever Young** ....S:13 / A:13 *Days Of Rage* **Andy Taylor** (guitar solo, above 2)	$3	■	Warner 27796
12/10/88+	4	25		38 **My Heart Can't Tell You No** ....A:3 / S:5 *The Wild Horse*	$3	■	Warner 27729
5/13/89	11	17		39 **Crazy About Her** ....S:10 / A:13 *Dynamite* (ROK #16) above 4 from the album *Out Of Order*	$3		Warner 27657
11/25/89+	3	18		40 **Downtown Train** ....AC[1] / AR[2] A:2 / S:3 *The Killing Of Georgie (Part I And II)* written by Tom Waits (from his 1985 album *Rain Dogs*)	$3	■	Warner 22685
3/24/90	10	16		41 **This Old Heart Of Mine (1989 Version)** ....AC[5] A:7 / S:15 *You're In My Heart* [R] **ROD STEWART (with Ronald Isley)** also see #11 above	$3	▮V	Warner 19983
3/16/91	5	18		42 **Rhythm Of My Heart** ....A:3 / S:9 *Moment Of Glory*	$3	▮V	Warner 19366
7/6/91	10	17		43 **The Motown Song** ....A:24 / S:36 *Sweet Soul Music (live)* **ROD STEWART (with The Temptations)**	$3	▮V	Warner 19322
10/19/91+	20	20		44 **Broken Arrow** ....A:19 / S:35 *The Wild Horse* written by Robbie Robertson (**The Band**); "45": Warner "Back to Back Hits" 15995; B-side: "Downtown Train"	$3	▮V	Warner 19274
4/25/92	48	9		45 **Your Song** ....A:59 *Mandolin Wind* written by **Elton John**; dedicated to the memory of **Freddie Mercury**; "45": Collectables 4947; B-side: "Twisting The Night Away" (Mercury version)	$3	▮V	Polydor 865944
12/12/92+	43[A]	20		46 **Have I Told You Lately** .... written by **Van Morrison**; #42-44 & 46: from the album *Vagabond Heart* on Warner 26300			album cut
4/24/93	5	22	●	47 **Have I Told You Lately** ....AC[5] S:6 / A:7 *Gasoline Alley* [L-R] above 2 are different versions: #46 is the original studio version; #47 is a "live" "unplugged" version	$3	▮V	Warner 18511
8/14/93	19	20		48 **Reason To Believe** ....A:12 / S:67 *It's All Over Now* [L-R] **ROD STEWART (with Ronnie Wood)** studio version on #2 above	$3	▮V	Warner 18427
11/27/93+	❶[3]	22	▲	49 **All For Love** ....S:❶[5] / A:3 *(instrumental)* **BRYAN ADAMS ROD STEWART STING** from the movie *The Three Musketeers* starring Kiefer Sutherland and Charlie Sheen	$3	▮V	A&M 0476
1/1/94	36	20		50 **Having A Party** ....A:31 *Sweet Little Rock And Roller* [L] **ROD STEWART With Ronnie Wood** above 4 (except #49) are from Stewart's MTV *Unplugged...And Seated* album	$3	▮V	Warner 18424
6/3/95	52	12		51 **Leave Virginia Alone** ....A:41 *Shock To The System* written by **Tom Petty**	$3	▮V	Warner 17847
3/16/96	71[A]	7		52 **So Far Away** .... from the album *Tapestry Revisited - A Tribute To Carole King* on Lava 92604			album cut
11/16/96+	54	20		53 **If We Fall In Love Tonight** ....A:50 *Tom Traubert's Blues (Waltzing Matilda)*	$3	▮V	Warner 17459
7/4/98	39	20		54 **Ooh La La** ....A:45 *A Night Like This* first recorded by **Rod Stewart & Faces** on the 1973 album *Ooh La La*	$3	▮V	Warner 17195
				STEWART, Sandy MEM/LP '63 Born Sandra Galitz on 7/10/37 in Philadelphia, Pennsylvania. Regular on the **Eddie Fisher** and **Perry Como** musical/variety TV shows.			
12/29/62+	20	10		**My Coloring Book** ....*I Heard You Cried Last Night* **Don Costa** (orch.)	$10	■	Colpix 669
				STEWART, Sandy — see NICKS, Stevie			
				STIGERS, Curtis AC/BUB/LP '91 Born on 10/18/65 in Boise, Idaho. Pop-jazz singer/saxophonist/songwriter.			
9/7/91	9	20		1 **I Wonder Why** ....A:28 / S:62 *Nobody Loves You Like I Do*	$3	▮	Arista 12331
3/7/92	98	1		2 **You're All That Matters To Me** ....*Count My Blessings*	$3	▮V	Arista 12391
6/20/92	96	1		3 **Sleeping With The Lights On** ....*People Like Us*	$3	▮	Arista 12430
				STILLS, Stephen BUB/LP '71 Born on 1/3/45 in Dallas, Texas. Singer/songwriter with **Buffalo Springfield** and **Crosby, Stills & Nash**. Manassas included Chris Hillman (guitar; **The Byrds**), Dallas Taylor (drums), Fuzzy Samuels (bass), Paul Harris (organ), Al Perkins (guitar) and Joe Lala (percussion). *1)Love The One You're With 2)Sit Yourself Down 3)Marianne*			
12/12/70+	14	11		1 **Love The One You're With** *To A Flame* **Rita Coolidge**, **David Crosby**, **Graham Nash** and **John Sebastian** (backing vocals)	$6		Atlantic 2778
3/13/71	37	6		2 **Sit Yourself Down** ....*We Are Not Helpless* **Rita Coolidge**, **David Crosby**, **Mama Cass**, **Graham Nash** and **John Sebastian** (backing vocals)	$5		Atlantic 2790
6/12/71	43	9		3 **Change Partners** ....*Relaxing Town* picture sleeve issued on either textured or glossy paper	$5	■	Atlantic 2806
8/21/71	42	8		4 **Marianne** ....*Nothin' To Do But Today* Nils Lofgren of **Grin** and **Eric Clapton** (guitars)	$5		Atlantic 2820
5/27/72	61	7		5 **It Doesn't Matter** ....*Rock & Roll Crazies Medley*	$5		Atlantic 2876
7/15/72	92	3		6 **Rock And Roll Crazies** *[STEPHEN STILLS & MANASSAS]* ....*Colorado*	$5		Atlantic 2888
4/28/73	56	8		7 **Isn't It About Time** *[STEPHEN STILLS & MANASSAS]* ....*So Many Times*	$5		Atlantic 2959
8/9/75	84	3		8 **Turn Back The Pages** ....*Shuffle Just As Bad*	$5		Columbia 10179
8/11/84	61	8		9 **Stranger** ....*No Hiding Place*	$4	■	Atlantic 89633
10/6/84	67	6		10 **Can't Let Go** ....*Grey To Green* (Stills) **STEPHEN STILLS FEATURING MICHAEL FINNIGAN**	$4		Atlantic 89611

DEBUT	PEAK	WKS	Gold	A-side (Chart Hit)..........B-side	$	Sym	Label & Number

STILLWATER '78

Rock group from Warner Robins, Georgia: Jimmy Hall (vocals; not to be confused with leader of Wet Willie), Bobby Golden, Michael Causey and Rob Walker (guitars), Bob Spearman (keyboards), Allison Scarborough (bass) and Sebie Lacey (drums).

DEBUT	PEAK	WKS	Gold	A-side (Chart Hit)..........B-side	$	Sym	Label & Number
11/19/77+	46	13		**Mind Bender** .... *Sunshine Blues* promo copies list artist as Arte Stillwater	$5		Capricorn 0280

STING ★197★ ROK/AC/BUB/LP '85

Born Gordon Sumner on 10/2/51 in Wallsend, England. Pop singer/songwriter/bassist. Lead singer of **The Police**. In the movies *Quadrophenia*, *Dune*, *The Bride*, *Plenty* and others. Married actress/producer Trudie Styler on 8/20/92. Nicknamed "Sting" because of a yellow and black jersey he liked to wear. Also see **Dire Strait**'s "Money For Nothing."

1)All For Love 2)If You Love Somebody Set Them Free 3)All This Time

DEBUT	PEAK	WKS	Gold	A-side (Chart Hit)..........B-side	$	Sym	Label & Number
6/8/85	3	18		1 **If You Love Somebody Set Them Free** .... AR[3] S:3 / A:3 *Another Day*	$3	■	A&M 2738
8/24/85	8	20		2 **Fortress Around Your Heart** .... AR[2] S:7 / A:7 *Consider Me Gone (live)*	$3	■	A&M 2767
11/9/85	17	13		3 **Love Is The Seventh Wave** .... A:17 / S:19 *The Dream Of The Blue Turtles*	$3	■	A&M 2787
1/18/86	16	13		4 **Russians** .... A:15 / S:17 *Gabriel's Message* samples "Romance" melody from Russian composer Sergei Prokofiev's *Lieutenant Kije Suite*; all of above from the album *The Dream Of The Blue Turtles*	$3	■	A&M 2799
10/10/87	7	18		5 **We'll Be Together** .... S:6 / A:8 *Conversation With A Dog*	$3	■	A&M 2983
1/16/88	15	14		6 **Be Still My Beating Heart** .... S:14 / A:15 *Ghost In The Strand*	$3	■	A&M 2992
4/16/88	84	4		7 **Englishman In New York** .... *If You There*	$3	■	A&M 1200
1/19/91	5	15		8 **All This Time** .... AR[7] / MR[2] S:8 / A:9 *I Miss You Kate*	$3	▮V	A&M 1541
2/20/93	17	20		9 **If I Ever Lose My Faith In You** .... A:14 / S:67 *All This Time (unplugged version)* "45": A&M 0530; B-side: "Shape Of My Heart"	$3	▮V	A&M 0111
6/5/93	23	20		10 **Fields Of Gold** .... A:12 / S:66 *(home video version)* "45" issued for #10 & #13 on A&M 0838	$3	▮V	A&M 0258
10/2/93	57	11		11 **Nothing 'Bout Me** .... A:51 *(album version)*	$3	▮	A&M 0350
11/27/93+	❶[3]	22	▲	12 **All For Love** .... S:❶[5] / A:3 *(instrumental)* **BRYAN ADAMS ROD STEWART STING** from the movie *The Three Musketeers* starring Kiefer Sutherland and Charlie Sheen	$3	▮V	A&M 0476
10/29/94	38	18		13 **When We Dance** .... A:40 / S:49 *Demolition Man*	$3	▮V	A&M 0846
3/2/96	86	5		14 **Let Your Soul Be Your Pilot** .... *The Bed's Too Big Without You*	$3	▮V	A&M 1456
5/18/96	60	13		15 **You Still Touch Me** .... A:51 *Twenty Five To Midnight* "45" issued for above 2 on A&M 1582	$3	▮V	A&M 1582 ■
11/2/96	94	3		16 **I'm So Happy I Can't Stop Crying** .... *This Was Never Meant To Be*	$4	▮V	A&M 1982
12/6/97	84	5		17 **I'm So Happy I Can't Stop Crying** .... S:67 *Jacky Don Tucker (Play By The Rules Miss All The Fun)* [R] **TOBY KEITH with Sting** above 2 are different versions	$4	▮V	Mercury 568114
12/27/97+	59	13		18 **Roxanne '97 - Puff Daddy Remix** .... S:34 *(2 versions) / Voices Inside My Head* **STING & THE POLICE Featuring Pras** **Full Force** (backing vocals); samples "Roxanne, Roxanne" by **UTFO** and "Kools Back Again" by **Kool & The Gang**; **The Police**'s original version of "Roxanne" hit #32 in 1979	$6	▮*	A&M 2449
5/13/00	17	26		19 **Desert Rose** .... S:17 / A:17 *(radio edit) / Brand New Day* (#103) **STING Featuring Cheb Mami** (male singer from Algeria) "45": A&M 497404; B-side: "After The Rain Has Fallen"; all of above (except #12) written by Sting	$4	★V	A&M 497321

STITES, Gary BUB '59

Born on 7/23/40 in Denver, Colorado. Pop singer/songwriter/guitarist.

DEBUT	PEAK	WKS	Gold	A-side (Chart Hit)..........B-side	$	Sym	Label & Number
4/13/59	24	14		1 **Lonely For You** .... *Shine That Ring* tune's arrangement is similar to **Conway Twitty**'s "It's Only Make Believe"	$20		Carlton 508
7/20/59	80	5		2 **A Girl Like You** .... *Hey Little Girl*	$20		Carlton 516
11/2/59	77	7		3 **Starry Eyed** .... *Without Your Love*	$20		Carlton 521
2/22/60	47	9		4 **Lawdy Miss Clawdy** .... *Don't Wanna Say Goodbye* #1 R&B hit for **Lloyd Price** in 1952; **Monty Kelly** (orch., all of above)	$20		Carlton 525

STOCKMAN, Shawn — see BOYZ II MEN

STOKES, Simon '74

Born on 4/3/45 in Reading, Massachusetts. R&B singer/songwriter.

DEBUT	PEAK	WKS	Gold	A-side (Chart Hit)..........B-side	$	Sym	Label & Number
12/20/69	90	2		1 **Voodoo Woman** .... *Can't Stop Now* **SIMON STOKES & THE NIGHTHAWKS**	$8		Elektra 45670
7/6/74	90	4		2 **Captain Howdy** .... *I Fell For Her, She Fell For Him & He Fell For Me* song title is the name given to Satan in the 1973 movie *The Exorcist* starring Linda Blair	$5	■	Casablanca 0007

STOLOFF, Morris '56

Born on 8/1/1898 in Philadelphia, Pennsylvania. Died on 4/16/80 (age 81). Composer/conductor/violinist. Became musical director for Columbia Pictures in 1936. Winner of three Academy Awards.

DEBUT	PEAK	WKS	Gold	A-side (Chart Hit)..........B-side	$	Sym	Label & Number
4/14/56	❶[3]	27	●	**Moonglow and Theme From "Picnic"** .... A:❶[3] / S:2 / T:2 / J:4 *Theme From "Picnic"* (George Duning) [I] **MORRIS STOLOFF Conducting The Columbia Pictures Orchestra** from the movie *Picnic* starring William Holden and Kim Novak; 4 Top 10 versions of "Moonglow" charted in 1934	$20		Decca 29888

STOMPERS, The '62

White rock and roll band from Medford, Massachusetts: Leonard Capizzi, Bill Capizzi (aka Chesley Uxbridge), Ron Deltorto, Lou Toscano and **Bobby "Boris" Pickett** (left for his own solo career; replaced by Don Squire). Formed as The Cordials.

DEBUT	PEAK	WKS	Gold	A-side (Chart Hit)..........B-side	$	Sym	Label & Number
3/3/62	100	1		**Quarter To Four Stomp** .... *Foolish One* promo "45" issued as "Surf Stompin'"	$30		Landa 684

STOMPERS, The BUB '83

Pop-rock group from Boston, Massachusetts: Sal Baglio (vocals, guitar), Dave Friedman (keyboards), Stephen Gilligan (bass) and Mark Cuccinello (drums).

DEBUT	PEAK	WKS	Gold	A-side (Chart Hit)..........B-side	$	Sym	Label & Number
6/18/83	88	4		**Never Tell An Angel (When Your Heart's On Fire)** .... *Your Sweet Love*	$5		Boardwalk 177

DEBUT	PEAK	WKS	Gold	A-side (Chart Hit)......B-side	$	Sym	Label & Number
				STONE, Angie R&B/LP **'02**			
				Born on 1/30/64 in Columbia, South Carolina. R&B singer. Former member of groups Sequence and **Vertical Hold**.			
12/25/99+	**56**	17		1 **No More Rain (In This Cloud)** A:49			album cut
				samples "Neither One Of Us" by **Gladys Knight & The Pips**; from the album *Black Diamond* on Arista 19092			
5/5/01	**59^{S}**	5		2 **U Make My Sun Shine**...... *When Will We B Paid?*	$5	★	NPG 05052
				PRINCE With ANGIE STONE			
				CD single released simultaneously on Wingspan 00102			
11/10/01+	**52**	20		3 **Brotha** ......A:50 / S:73 *(instrumental)*	$6	T	J Records 21104
3/23/02	**79**	19		4 **Wish I Didn't Miss You**...... *(2 versions)*	$6	T	J Records 21149
				samples "Back Stabbers" by **The O'Jays**			
				STONE, Cliffie, And His Orchestra C&W **'55**			
				Born Clifford Snyder on 3/1/17 in Burbank, California. Died on 1/16/98 (age 80). Square-dance bandleader/bassist/DJ/record company executive. Radio/TV personality in Los Angeles, from the 1940s-60s, hosting several country programs. An A&R executive for Capitol Records. Wrote many country hits. Elected to the Country Music Hall of Fame in 1989.			
8/13/55	**14**	4		**The Popcorn Song**......J:14 / S:25 *Barracuda* [N]	$15		Capitol 3131
				Bob Roubian (vocal)			
				STONE, Doug C&W/BUB/LP **'94**			
				Born Douglas Brooks on 6/19/56 in Marietta, Georgia. Country singer/guitarist. Changed name to avoid confusion with **Garth Brooks**. At age seven, opened on guitar for a **Loretta Lynn** concert. Starred in the 1995 movie *Gordy*.			
1/1/94	**81**	9		**I Never Knew Love** ......S:47 *This Empty House*	$4	▮V	Epic 77228
				STONE, Kirby, Four BUB/LP **'58**			
				Born on 4/27/18 in Manhattan, New York. Died in July 1981 (age 63). His vocal group included Eddie Hall, Larry Foster and Mike Gardner.			
7/28/58	**25**	3		**Baubles, Bangles And Beads** .....A:25 / H:50 *In The Good Old Summertime/Take The Lady*	$15		Columbia 41183
				Jimmy Carroll (orch.); from the musical *Kismet* starring Alfred Drake; introduced by **Peggy Lee** in 1953			
				STONE, Phoenix **'00**			
				Born on 2/10/76 in Tampa, Florida. Male pop singer/songwriter/multi-instrumentalist.			
2/26/00	**41^{S}**	4		**Nothing Good About Goodbye**...... *(3 album snippets)*	$5	★	Trans Continental 6699
				STONE, Sly — see SLY & THE FAMILY STONE			
				STONEBOLT **'78**			
				Pop group from Vancouver, British Columbia, Canada: David Willis (vocals), Ray Roper (guitar), John Webster (keyboards), Dan Atchison (bass) and Brian Lousley (drums).			
8/5/78	**29**	14		1 **I Will Still Love You**...... *Stay In Line*	$5		Parachute 512
2/10/79	**70**	5		2 **Love Struck** ...... *Was It You*	$5		Parachute 522
				STONE PONEYS — see RONSTADT, Linda			
				STONE ROSES, The ROK/LP **'95**			
				Alternative pop-rock group from Manchester, England: Ian Brown (vocal), John Squire (guitar), Gary Mournfield (bass) and Alan Wren (drums).			
12/31/94+	**55^{A}**	14		**Love Spreads**			album cut
				from the album *Second Coming* on Geffen 24503			
				STONE SOUR ROK/LP **'02**			
				Rock group formed by Slipknot members Corey Taylor (vocals) and Jim Root (guitar), with Josh Rand (guitar), Sid Wilson (bass) and Joel Ekman (drums).			
11/2/02	**56**	20		**Bother**......A:54			album cut
				from the album *Stone Sour* on Roadrunner 618425			
				STONE TEMPLE PILOTS ROK/BUB/LP **'94**			
				Rock group formed in San Diego, California: Scott Weiland (vocals), brothers Dean (guitar) and Robert (bass) DeLeo, and Eric Kretz (drums). Group originally known as Mighty Joe Young, then Shirley Temple's Pussy. Weiland also formed side project **The Magnificent Bastards** in 1995. The DeLeo brothers and Kretz formed side project Talk Show in 1997.			
				1)Interstate Love Song 2)Big Bang Baby 3)Trippin' On A Hole In A Paper Heart			
7/10/93	**39^{A}**	29		1 **Plush**......			album cut
1/29/94	**59^{A}**	4		2 **Creep**			album cut
				above 2 from the album *Core* on Atlantic 82418			
6/11/94	**50^{A}**	15		3 **Big Empty**......			album cut
7/9/94	**38^{A}**	15		4 **Vasoline** ......AR^{2}			album cut
9/10/94	**18^{A}**	30		5 **Interstate Love Song** AR^{15}			album cut
				above 3 from the album *Purple* on Atlantic 82607			
4/8/95	**63^{A}**	3		6 **Dancing Days**......			album cut
				from the album *Encomium: A Tribute To Led Zeppelin* on Atlantic 82731			
3/23/96	**28^{A}**	13		7 **Big Bang Baby**......AR^{1}			album cut
5/18/96	**36^{A}**	20		8 **Trippin' On A Hole In A Paper Heart**......AR^{4}			album cut
11/2/96	**53^{A}**	14		9 **Lady Picture Show** ......AR^{1}			album cut
				above 3 from the album *Tiny Music...Songs From The Vatican Gift Shop* on Atlantic 82871			
7/8/00	**78**	13		10 **Sour Girl**......A:73			album cut
				from the album *No.4* on Atlantic 83255			
12/15/01	**11^{S}**	18		11 **Revolution** ...... *(no B-side)*	$5	★	Atlantic 85200
				proceeds donated to the Twin Towers fund			
				STONEY — see MEAT LOAF			
				STOOKEY, Paul — see PETER, PAUL & MARY			
				STOREY SISTERS, The **'58**			
				Rock and roll duo from Philadelphia, Pennsylvania: Ann and Lillian Storey.			
3/3/58	**45**	7		**Bad Motorcycle**......S:45 / T:48 *Sweet Daddy*	$30		Cameo 126
				Al Browne (orch.); originally released on Peak 5001 in 1957 ($50 - as by The Twinkles)			

DEBUT	PEAK	WKS	Gold	A-side (Chart Hit)..........B-side	$	Sym	Label & Number

STORIES — BUB/LP '73

Rock group from Brooklyn, New York: **Ian Lloyd** (vocals, bass) (see #4 & 5 below), Michael Brown (keyboards; founding member of **The Left Banke**), Steve Love (guitar) and Bryan Madey (drums). Brown left group in 1973; replaced by Ken Aaronson (bass; later charted with **Sammy Hagar**) and Ken Bichel (keyboards).

DEBUT	PEAK	WKS	Gold	A-side (Chart Hit)..........B-side	$	Sym	Label & Number
6/17/72	42	12		1 **I'm Coming Home**..........*You Told Me* promo hard-cover picture sleeve featuring a photo of the group issued with a small-hole 45 rpm record	$6	□	Kama Sutra 545
6/23/73	❶^2	18	●	2 **Brother Louie**..........*What Comes After* originally recorded by **Hot Chocolate** in 1973 on RAK 4513 ($8)	$6		Kama Sutra 577
10/27/73	50	8		3 **Mammy Blue**..........*Traveling Underground*	$5		Kama Sutra 584
3/30/74	88	5		4 **If It Feels Good, Do It**..........*Circles* **IAN LLOYD & STORIES**	$5		Kama Sutra 588
10/13/79	50	9		5 **Slip Away**..........*Easy Money* **IAN LLOYD** written by **Ric Ocasek** of **The Cars**	$5		Scotti Brothers 505

STORM, The — ROK/LP '92

Rock group formed in San Francisco, California: Kevin Chalfant (vocals), Gregg Rolie (vocals, keyboards), Josh Ramos (guitar), Ross Valory (bass) and Steve Smith (drums). Rolie was a member of **Santana**. Rolie, Valory and Smith were members of **Journey**. Chalfant was a member of **707**.

DEBUT	PEAK	WKS	Gold	A-side (Chart Hit)..........B-side	$	Sym	Label & Number
10/26/91+	26	20		**I've Got A Lot To Learn About Love**..........A:26 *Gimme Love*	$4	▮	Interscope 98726

STORM, Billy — BUB '59

Born William Jones on 6/29/38 in Dayton, Ohio. Lead singer of the R&B vocal group **The Valiants**.

DEBUT	PEAK	WKS	Gold	A-side (Chart Hit)..........B-side	$	Sym	Label & Number
4/13/59	28	14		**I've Come Of Age**..........*This Is Always* **Frank DeVol** (orch.); melody is from "Tchaikowsky's 5th Symphony (2nd movement)"	$20		Columbia 41356

STORM, Gale — ★436★ — '56

Born Josephine Cottle on 4/5/22 in Bloomington, Texas. Pop singer/actress. Starred in several movie musicals. Star of TV's *My Little Margie* (1952-55) and *The Gale Storm Show* (1956-62).

1)I Hear You Knocking 2)Dark Moon 3)Memories Are Made Of This

DEBUT	PEAK	WKS	Gold	A-side (Chart Hit)..........B-side	$	Sym	Label & Number
10/22/55	2^3	18	●	1 **I Hear You Knocking** / J:2 / T:2 / S:3 / A:4 #2 R&B hit for Smiley Lewis in 1955			
10/15/55		1		2 **Never Leave Me**..........CU:flip	$20		Dot 15412
12/24/55+	5	16		3 **Memories Are Made Of This** / A:5 / T:16 / S:flip / J:flip			
12/24/55+	6	15		4 **Teen Age Prayer**..........A:6 / J:6 / T:9 / S:13	$15		Dot 15436
3/3/56	9	18		5 **Why Do Fools Fall In Love**..........A:9 / J:14 / S:15 / T:15 *I Walk Alone*	$15		Dot 15448
4/28/56	6	18		6 **Ivory Tower**..........A:6 / J:6 / T:10 / S:15 *I Ain't Gonna Worry*	$15		Dot 15458
6/30/56	52	6		7 **Tell Me Why**..........T:52 *Don't Be That Way (Please Listen to Me)*	$15		Dot 15474
9/15/56	59	7		8 **Now Is The Hour** / T:59 there were 7 Top 20 versions of this tune in 1948 (from the 1913 Australian song "Haere Ra")			
10/6/56	79	4		9 **A Heart Without A Sweetheart**..........T:79	$15		Dot 15492
3/16/57	74	4		10 **On Treasure Island** / T:74 #1 hit for **Tommy Dorsey** in 1935			
3/16/57	77	5		11 **Lucky Lips**..........T:77	$12		Dot 15539
4/20/57	4	23		12 **Dark Moon**..........J:4 / T:5 / S:6 / A:6 *A Little Too Late* **Billy Vaughn** (orch., all of above)	$12		Dot 15558

STORM, Warren — '58

Born Warren Schexnider on 2/18/37 in Abbeville, Louisiana. Swamp-pop singer/drummer.

DEBUT	PEAK	WKS	Gold	A-side (Chart Hit)..........B-side	$	Sym	Label & Number
8/25/58	81	2		**Prisoner's Song**..........H:81 *Mama Mama Mama (Look What Your Little Boy's Done)* #1 hit for Vernon Dalhart in 1925	$30		Nasco 6015

STOTT, Lally — '71

Born in Liverpool, England. Died in a bike accident in 1977. Pop singer/songwriter.

DEBUT	PEAK	WKS	Gold	A-side (Chart Hit)..........B-side	$	Sym	Label & Number
4/10/71	92	2		**Chirpy Chirpy, Cheep Cheep**..........*Henry James*	$6		Philips 40695

STRAIT, George — ★407★ — C&W/BUB/LP '99

Born on 5/18/52 in Poteet, Texas; raised in Pearsall, Texas. Country singer (charted 37 #1 singles, 1982-2002). Starred in the movie *Pure Country*.

1)She'll Leave You With A Smile 2)Living And Living Well 3)Write This Down

DEBUT	PEAK	WKS	Gold	A-side (Chart Hit)..........B-side	$	Sym	Label & Number
10/9/93	71	10		1 **Easy Come, Easy Go**..........CW^2 S:37 *She Lays It All On The Line*	$4	▮^{V}	MCA 54717
1/22/94	72^S	1		2 **I'd Like To Have That One Back**..........BUB:109 *That's Where My Baby Feels At Home*	$4	▮^{V}	MCA 54767
4/30/94	69^S	4		3 **Lovebug**..........BUB:114 *Just Look At Me* #6 Country hit for **George Jones** in 1965	$4	▮^{V}	MCA 54819
8/6/94	73^S	2		4 **The Man In Love With You**..........BUB:112 *We Must Be Loving Right*	$4	▮^{V}	MCA 54854
3/4/95	61^S	3		5 **You Can't Make A Heart Love Somebody**..........CW^1 BUB:111 *What Am I Waiting For*	$4	▮^{V}	MCA 54964
4/5/97	59	12		6 **One Night At A Time**..........CW^5 S:41 *Won't You Come Home (And Talk To A Stranger)*	$4	▮^{V}	MCA 55321
4/25/98	61	19		7 **I Just Want To Dance With You**..........CW^3 S:43 *Neon Row*	$4	▮^{V}	MCA 72046
12/5/98	44	5		8 **We Really Shouldn't Be Doing This**..........A:33 "45": MCA 72071; B-side: "Maria"; above 2 from the album *One Step At A Time* on MCA 70020		V	album cut
1/23/99	38	12		9 **Meanwhile**..........S:29 / A:32 *You Haven't Left Me Yet* (C&W #59)	$4	★^{V}	MCA 72084
4/24/99	27	20		10 **Write This Down**..........CW^4 A:18 "45": MCA 72095; B-side: "4 Minus 3 Equals Zero"		V	album cut
9/4/99	45	16		11 **What Do You Say To That**..........A:34 "45": MCA 72108; B-side: "4 Minus 3 Equals Zero"; above 3 from the album *Always Never The Same* on MCA 70050		V	album cut
1/29/00	31	20		12 **The Best Day**..........CW^3 A:24 from the album *Latest Greatest Straitest Hits* on MCA 170100; "45": MCA 172147; B-side: "I Can Still Make Cheyenne"		V	album cut
8/26/00	40	20		13 **Go On**..........A:33 "45": MCA 172169; B-side: "Murder On Music Row" (w/**Alan Jackson** - C&W #38)		V	album cut

DEBUT	PEAK	WKS	Gold	A-side (Chart Hit)	B-side	$	Sym	Label & Number

STRAIT, George — Cont'd

DEBUT	PEAK	WKS	Gold	A-side (Chart Hit)	B-side	$	Sym	Label & Number
4/14/01	**51**	18		14 **If You Can Do Anything Else**	A:42		V	album cut
				"45": MCA 172200; B-side: "Which Side Of The Glass"; above 2 from the album *George Strait* on MCA 170143				
10/27/01	**34**	20		15 **Run**	A:31		V	album cut
				"45": MCA 172221; B-side: "The Real Thing"				
4/6/02	**27**	20		16 **Living And Living Well** CW[2]	A:26		V	album cut
				"45": MCA 172238; B-side: "The Real Thing"				
10/5/02	**23**	20		17 **She'll Leave You With A Smile**	A:20		V	album cut
				"45": Mercury 172255; B-side: "Good Time Charley's"; above 3 from the album *The Road Less Traveled* on MCA 170220				

STRANGE, Billy — LP '65

Born on 9/29/30 in Long Beach, California. Session guitarist.

DEBUT	PEAK	WKS	Gold	A-side (Chart Hit)	B-side	$	Sym	Label & Number
8/22/64	**58**	10		1 **The James Bond Theme**	*007 Theme* [I]	$10		GNP Crescendo 320
				famous theme song from the James Bond series of movies				
1/23/65	**55**	9		2 **Goldfinger**	*(Theme From) The Munsters* [I]	$10		GNP Crescendo 334
				title song from the James Bond movie starring Sean Connery				

STRANGELOVES, The — BUB/LP '65

Writers/producers Bob Feldman, Jerry Goldstein and Richard Gottehrer. Team wrote/produced **The Angels**' "My Boyfriend's Back," produced **The McCoys**' "Hang On Sloopy" and **The Sheep**. Gottehrer became a partner in Sire Records and produced the **Go-Go's**' first two albums and **Blondie**'s debut album.

DEBUT	PEAK	WKS	Gold	A-side (Chart Hit)	B-side	$	Sym	Label & Number
6/26/65	**11**	10		1 **I Want Candy**	*It's About My Baby*	$15		Bang 501
9/18/65	**39**	8		2 **Cara-Lin**	*(Roll On) Mississippi*	$12		Bang 508
1/15/66	**30**	8		3 **Night Time**	*Rhythm Of Love*	$12		Bang 514
6/18/66	**100**	1		4 **Hand Jive**	*I Gotta Dance*	$12		Bang 524

STRANGERS, The — '59

Rock and roll instrumental group from San Diego, California: Joel Scott Hill (lead guitar), Harold Kirby, Ron Lynch and John Collard. Hill joined **Canned Heat** in 1972.

DEBUT	PEAK	WKS	Gold	A-side (Chart Hit)	B-side	$	Sym	Label & Number
8/31/59	**49**	7		**The Caterpillar Crawl**	*Rockin' Rebel* [I]	$30		Titan 1701

STRAWBERRY ALARM CLOCK — LP '67

Psychedelic-rock group formed in Los Angeles, California: Ed King (lead guitar), Mark Weitz (keyboards), Lee Freeman (guitar), Gary Lovetro (bass), George Bunnel (bass) and Randy Seol (drums). King joined **Lynyrd Skynyrd**, 1973-75. Originally known as Thee Sixpence.

DEBUT	PEAK	WKS	Gold	A-side (Chart Hit)	B-side	$	Sym	Label & Number
9/30/67	**1**[1]	16	●	1 **Incense And Peppermints**	*The Birdman Of Alkatrash*	$12		Uni 55018
				Greg Munford (16-year-old leader of L.A. band, the Shapes; lead vocal); originally released on All-American 373 in 1967 ($150)				
12/30/67+	**23**	10		2 **Tomorrow**	*Birds In My Tree*	$10		Uni 55046
3/16/68	**65**	5		3 **Sit With The Guru**	*Pretty Song From Psych-Out*	$10		Uni 55055
8/31/68	**67**	4		4 **Barefoot In Baltimore**	*An Angry Young Man*	$10		Uni 55076
5/24/69	**87**	2		5 **Good Morning Starshine**	*Me And The Township*	$10		Uni 55125
				from the off-Broadway musical *Hair* starring Steve Curry				

STRAY CATS — ROK/LP '83

Rockabilly trio from Long Island, New York: **Brian Setzer** (vocals, guitar; born on 4/10/60), Lee Rocker (string bass; born Leon Drucher) and Slim Jim Phantom (drums; born Jim McDonell). Recorded two albums in Britain in 1981 and 1982. Disbanded in 1984. Phantom and Rocker formed trio Phantom, Rocker & Slick in 1985. Setzer portrayed **Eddie Cochran** in the movie *La Bamba*. Phantom portrayed Charlie Parker's drummer in the movie *Bird*; married to actress Britt Ekland, 1984-93. Band reunited in 1988. Setzer formed own "jump" orchestra in 1998.

DEBUT	PEAK	WKS	Gold	A-side (Chart Hit)	B-side	$	Sym	Label & Number
9/18/82	**9**	21		1 **Rock This Town**	*You Can't Hurry Love*	$6	■	EMI America 8132
12/25/82+	**3**	19		2 **Stray Cat Strut**	*You Don't Believe Me*	$6	■	EMI America 8122
				originally "Bubbled Under" for 6 weeks beginning 7/17/82				
8/6/83	**5**	15		3 **(She's) Sexy + 17**	*Lookin' Better Every Beer*	$6	■	EMI America 8168
10/29/83	**35**	13		4 **I Won't Stand In Your Way**	*(acappella version)*	$6		EMI America 8185
1/28/84	**68**	5		5 **Look At That Cadillac**	*Lucky Charm*	$6	■	EMI America 8194
				all of above written by **Brian Setzer** and produced by **Dave Edmunds**				

STREEK — '81

Pop group from Los Angeles, California: Ron Abrams (guitar), Billy DeMartines (keyboards), Daniel Ricciardelli (sax), Randy Oviedo (bass) and Guivanni Bartoletto (drums).

DEBUT	PEAK	WKS	Gold	A-side (Chart Hit)	B-side	$	Sym	Label & Number
10/10/81	**47**	7		**One More Night**	*Gone Too Far*	$4		Columbia 02529

STREET, Janey — AC/LP '84

Born in Manhattan, New York. Pop-rock singer/songwriter.

DEBUT	PEAK	WKS	Gold	A-side (Chart Hit)	B-side	$	Sym	Label & Number
10/6/84	**68**	5		**Say Hello To Ronnie**	*In My Mind*	$4	□	Arista 9265

STREET PEOPLE — BUB '70

Studio group featuring **Rupert Holmes**.

DEBUT	PEAK	WKS	Gold	A-side (Chart Hit)	B-side	$	Sym	Label & Number
1/3/70	**36**	15		1 **Jennifer Tomkins**	*All Night Long*	$7		Musicor 1365
4/25/70	**96**	2		2 **Thank You Girl**	*The World Doesn't Matter Anymore*	$7		Musicor 1401

STREETS — LP '83

Rock group formed in Atlanta, Georgia: Steve Walsh (vocals, keyboards), Mike Slamer (guitar), Billy Greer (bass) and Tim Gehrt (drums). Walsh was co-founder of **Kansas**.

DEBUT	PEAK	WKS	Gold	A-side (Chart Hit)	B-side	$	Sym	Label & Number
12/3/83	**87**	5		**If Love Should Go**	*Fire*	$4		Atlantic 89760

DEBUT	PEAK	WKS	Gold	A-side (Chart Hit)..........B-side	$	Sym	Label & Number

STREISAND, Barbra ★43★ AC/BUB/C&W/LP '77

Born Barbara Joan Streisand on 4/24/42 in Brooklyn, New York. Made Broadway debut in *I Can Get It For You Wholesale*, 1962. Lead role in Broadway's *Funny Girl*, 1964. Movie debut in *Funny Girl* in 1968 (tied with Katharine Hepburn for Best Actress Oscar); also starred in *A Star Is Born, Hello Dolly, Funny Lady, The Way We Were* and many others. Produced/directed/starred in the movies *Yentl* and *Prince Of Tides*. Married to actor Elliott Gould from 1963-71. Married actor James Brolin on 7/2/98. Won Grammy's Lifetime Achievement Award in 1995. Has 8 #1 albums (only 3 artists have more).

1)Love Theme From "A Star Is Born" (Evergreen) 2)Woman In Love 3)The Way We Were 4)You Don't Bring Me Flowers 5)No More Tears (Enough Is Enough)

DEBUT	PEAK	WKS	Gold	A-side (Chart Hit)..........B-side	$	Sym	Label & Number
4/4/64	5	19		1 **People** ....AC[3] *I Am Woman* (#114)	$8		Columbia 42965
				from the Broadway musical *Funny Girl* starring Streisand			
9/12/64	44	9		2 **Funny Girl** ....*Absent Minded Me* (#123)	$8		Columbia 43127
				not from the Broadway musical; a different "Funny Girl" song was written for the 1968 movie version of the musical			
4/3/65	77	5		3 **Why Did I Choose You**..........*My Love*	$8		Columbia 43248
				from the Broadway musical *The Yearling*			
7/3/65	79	6		4 **My Man** ....*Where Is The Wonder*	$8		Columbia 43323
10/2/65	53	10		5 **He Touched Me**..........*I Like Him*	$8		Columbia 43403
				from the Broadway musical *Drat! The Cat!* starring Elliott Gould			
12/18/65+	32	9		6 **Second Hand Rose** ....*The Kind Of Man A Woman Needs*	$8		Columbia 43469
				#4 & 6 were hits in 1922 for Fanny Brice (the subject of *Funny Girl*)			
2/19/66	94	2		7 **Where Am I Going?**	$7		Columbia 43518
				from the Broadway musical *Sweet Charity* starring Gwen Verdon			
5/21/66	98	1		8 **Sam, You Made The Pants Too Long**	$7		Columbia 43612
				parody, written by Milton Berle in 1940, of "Lawd, You Made The Night Too Long"			
10/15/66	83	4		9 **Free Again** ....*I've Been Here*	$7		Columbia 43808
				a French version, "Non..C'est Rien," by Barbra made the Adult Contemporary charts (#15) earlier in 1966 on Columbia 43739			
12/10/66	❶[1X]	6		10 **Sleep In Heavenly Peace (Silent Night)** ....*Gounod's Ave Maria* [X]	$8	■	Columbia 43896
				X: 1/'66; 13/'67; a text-only sleeve and a promotional sleeve featuring a photo of Barbra were both released in 1966			
8/26/67	92	2		11 **Stout-Hearted Men** ....*Look*	$7		Columbia 44225
				from the 1928 Broadway musical *The New Moon* starring Evelyn Herbert			
10/31/70+	6	18		12 **Stoney End** ....*I'll Be Home*	$7		Columbia 45236
				original version by Peggy Lipton "Bubbled Under" (#121) in 1968			
3/20/71	51	7		13 **Time And Love** ....*No Easy Way Down*	$6		Columbia 45341
5/15/71	82	5		14 **Flim Flam Man**..........*Maybe*	$6		Columbia 45384
				above 3 written by **Laura Nyro**			
7/24/71	40	8		15 **Where You Lead**..........*Since I Fell For You*	$6		Columbia 45414
				also see #17 below for medley version			
10/16/71	79	5		16 **Mother** ....*The Summer Knows*	$6		Columbia 45471
				written by **John Lennon**			
6/24/72	37	12		17 **Sweet Inspiration/Where You Lead**..........*Didn't We* [L]	$5		Columbia 45626
9/30/72	94	3		18 **Sing A Song/Make Your Own Kind Of Music**..........*Starting Here, Starting Now* [L]	$5		Columbia 45686
12/9/72+	82	8		19 **Didn't We**..........*On A Clear Day (You Can See Forever)* [L]	$5		Columbia 45739
11/24/73+	❶[3]	23	▲	20 **The Way We Were**..........AC[2] *What Are You Doing The Rest Of Your Life?*	$4		Columbia 45944
				title song from the movie starring Streisand and Robert Redford			
3/30/74	63	5		21 **All In Love Is Fair**..........*My Buddy/How About Me*	$4		Columbia 46024
				written by **Stevie Wonder** (from his 1973 album *Innervisions*)			
12/11/76+	❶[3]	25	▲	22 **Love Theme From "A Star Is Born" (Evergreen)** AC[6] *I Believe In Love*	$4	■	Columbia 10450
				from the movie *A Star Is Born* starring Streisand and **Kris Kristofferson**			
5/21/77	4	17		23 **My Heart Belongs To Me**..........AC[4] *Answer Me*	$4		Columbia 10555
6/17/78	25	10		24 **Songbird**..........AC[2] *Honey Can I Put On Your Clothes*	$4		Columbia 10756
7/29/78	21	12		25 **Love Theme From "Eyes Of Laura Mars" (Prisoner)**...*Laura & Neville* (Artie Kane)	$4		Columbia 10777
				from the movie *Eyes Of Laura Mars* starring Faye Dunaway			
10/28/78	❶[2]	17	▲	26 **You Don't Bring Me Flowers** ....*(instrumental)*	$4		Columbia 10840
				BARBRA & NEIL			
				Streisand's solo version is on her 1978 album *Songbird*			
6/16/79	3	17	●	27 **The Main Event/Fight**..........*(instrumental)*	$4		Columbia 11008
				from the movie *The Main Event* starring Streisand and Ryan O'Neal			
10/20/79	❶[2]	15	▲	28 **No More Tears (Enough Is Enough)**..........*Wet* (Streisand)	$4	■	Columbia 11125
				BARBRA STREISAND/DONNA SUMMER			
				12" single available on Casablanca 20199			
1/12/80	37	11		29 **Kiss Me In The Rain**..........*I Ain't Gonna Cry Tonight*	$4		Columbia 11179
9/6/80	❶[3]	24	▲	30 **Woman In Love** ....AC[5] *Run Wild*	$4		Columbia 11364
11/1/80+	3	22	●	31 **Guilty**..........*Life Story* (Streisand)	$4		Columbia 11390
1/31/81	10	16		32 **What Kind Of Fool** ....AC[4] *The Love Inside* (Streisand)	$4		Columbia 11430
				BARBRA STREISAND & BARRY GIBB (above 2)			
5/23/81	48	9		33 **Promises** ....*Make It Like A Memory*	$4		Columbia 02065
				above 4 written and produced by **Barry Gibb** (**Bee Gees**), and from the album *Guilty*			
11/14/81+	11	16		34 **Comin' In And Out Of Your Life** ....*Lost Inside Of You*	$4		Columbia 02621
2/20/82	52	7		35 **Memory**..........*Evergreen (Love Theme From "A Star Is Born")*	$4		Columbia 02717
				theme from Andrew Lloyd Webber's musical *Cats* starring Betty Buckley			
10/22/83	40	15		36 **The Way He Makes Me Feel**..........AC[2] *(movie version)*	$4	■	Columbia 04177
				from the movie *Yentl* starring Streisand; promo picture sleeve features a different photo of Barbra			
9/22/84	50	12		37 **Left In The Dark**..........*Here We Are At Last*	$4	■	Columbia 04605
12/15/84+	51	10		38 **Make No Mistake, He's Mine** ....*Clear Sailing* (Streisand)	$3	■	Columbia 04695
				BARBRA STREISAND (WITH KIM CARNES)			
3/9/85	79	2		39 **Emotion**..........*Here We Are At Last*	$3	■	Columbia 04707
12/14/85+	43	14		40 **Somewhere** ....*Not While I'm Around*	$3	■	Columbia 05680
				from the Broadway musical *West Side Story*			
10/22/88	25	12		41 **Till I Loved You** ....S:22 / A:32 *Two People (Theme From "Nuts")* (Streisand)	$3	■	Columbia 08062
				BARBRA STREISAND AND DON JOHNSON			
				love theme from the Broadway musical *Goya*			

DEBUT	PEAK	WKS	Gold	A-side (Chart Hit)...B-side	$	Sym	Label & Number
				STREISAND, Barbra — Cont'd			
11/23/96	8	20	●	42 **I Finally Found Someone**....S:7 / A:20 *Evergreen (Spanish version - Streisand)* **BARBRA STREISAND and BRYAN ADAMS** from the movie *The Mirror Has Two Faces* starring Streisand	$3	▌	Columbia 78480
10/25/97	58^A	6		43 **Tell Him**.... **CELINE DION & BARBRA STREISAND** from the Streisand album *Higher Ground* on Columbia 66181			album cut
7/10/99	24^S	15		44 **I've Dreamed Of You**....*At The Same Time* Streisand's musical arrangers and conductors: Charlie Calello (#23), **Larry Carlton** (#24), **Don Costa** (#3, 5), Bill Cuomo (#38), **Nick DeCaro** (#21, 24), **Ray Ellis** (#10, 11), Bob Esty (#27), **Fanny** (#15), **David Foster** (#40, 42, 43), **Barry Gibb** (#30-33), Dave Grusin (#36), Don Hannah (#17, 18), Gary Klein (#25), **Michel Legrand** (#9), Alan Lindgren (#26), Greg Mathieson (#28, 29), Peter Matz (#1, 2, 4, 6, 8), Robert Mersey (#7), Claus Ogermann (#19), Gene Page (#12-14, 16), Marty Paich (#20), Richard Perry (#13, 16, 39), Phil Ramone (#22, 41), William Ross (#44), David Shire (#11, 18), **Jim Steinman** (#37) and Andrew Lloyd Webber (#34, 35)	$4	★	Columbia 79211
				STRIK 9INE '01 Hip-hop group from Cleveland, Ohio: Scott Jacobs ("Chief Body"), Warren Jones ("Dakota"), Otis Stathan ("Wild Wolf") and Myron Dixon ("Saige"). All four are African Americans who use Native American nicknames and costumes.			
11/10/01	7^S	31		**Dansin Wit Wolvez**....*Definition of the Trybe / Nyggaz & Hoez*	$8	★*	Fade 34239
				STRING-A-LONGS, The BUB '61 Guitar rock and roll instrumental group from Plainview, Texas: Keith McCormack, Aubrey Lee de Cordova, Richard Stephens and Jimmy Torres (guitars) and Don Allen (drums).			
1/9/61	3	16		1 **Wheels**....*Tell The World* [I] also released with "Am I Asking Too Much" as the B-side	$20		Warwick 603
3/27/61	35	7		2 **Brass Buttons**....*Panic Button* [I]	$15		Warwick 625
6/12/61	42	9		3 **Should I**....*Take A Minute* [I] #3 hit for the Arden-Ohman Orchestra in 1930	$15		Warwick 654
				STROKES, The ROK/BUB/LP '02 Rock group from Manhattan, New York: Julian Casablancas (vocals), Albert Hammond Jr. (son of **Albert Hammond**) and Nick Valensi (guitars), Nikolai Fraiture (bass) and Fab Moretti (drums).			
5/18/02	27^S	20		**Hard To Explain**....*New York City Cops / Take It Or Leave It / Trying Your Luck*	$5	★	RCA 60533
				STROLLERS, The '61 R&B vocal group.			
4/10/61	91	2		**Come On Over**....*There's No One But You*	$40		Carlton 546
				STRONG, Barrett R&B '60 Born on 2/5/41 in Mississippi. R&B singer/songwriter. Wrote many of **The Temptations**' hits with Norman Whitfield, including "Just My Imagination," "Papa Was A Rollin' Stone" and "Ball Of Confusion."			
2/1/60	23	17		**Money (That's what I want)**....*Oh I Apologize* also released on Tamla 54027 in 1960 ($50)	$30		Anna 1111
				STRUNK, Jud C&W/AC/LP '73 Born Justin Strunk on 6/11/36 in Jamestown, New York; raised in Farmington, Maine. Killed in a plane crash on 10/15/81 (age 45). Regular on TV's *Laugh In*.			
2/17/73	14	16		1 **Daisy A Day**....*The Searchers* **Mike Curb Congregation** (backing vocals)	$6		MGM 14463
9/28/74	59	4		2 **My Country**....*The Will* [S] produced by **Glen Campbell**	$6		Capitol 3960
7/5/75	50	6		3 **The Biggest Parakeets In Town**....*I Wasn't Wrong About You* [C-L]	$6		Melodyland 6015
				STRYPER LP '88 Christian heavy-metal band from Orange County, California: brothers Michael (vocals) and Robert (drums) Sweet, with Oz Fox (guitar; born Richard Martinez) and Tim Gaines (bass; born Tim Hagelganz). Michael Sweet left in mid-1992.			
11/7/87+	23	19		1 **Honestly**....S:22 / A:23 *Sing-Along-Song*	$4	■	Enigma 75009
7/23/88	71	8		2 **Always There For You**....*In God We Trust*	$4	■	Enigma 75019
11/5/88	88	5		3 **I Believe In You**....*Together Forever (live)*	$4		Enigma 75028
				STYLE COUNCIL, The LP '84 Techno-pop duo from England: Paul Weller (vocals) and Mick Talbot (keyboards).			
4/7/84	29	14		1 **My Ever Changing Moods**....*Mick's Company*	$4	■	Geffen 29359
7/14/84	76	5		2 **You're The Best Thing**....*The Big Boss Groove*	$4	■	Geffen 29248
				STYLERS, The '56 White pop vocal trio from Brooklyn, New York: Harry Boorows, brothers Tony (died of a heart attack in 1975) and Louis Colombo.			
11/24/56	72	5		**Confession Of A Sinner**....T:72 *Gonna Tell 'Em (I Love You)* Panama Francis (orch.)	$40		Jubilee 5253
				STYLES R&B/LP '02 Born David Styles on 4/4/72 in Yonkers, New York. Male rapper. Former member of **The Lox**.			
7/20/02	22	20		1 **Good Times**....A:21 samples "I Get High (On Your Memory)" by **Freda Payne**; from the album *A Gangster And A Gentleman* on Ruff Ryders 493339			album cut
10/12/02	3	20		2 **Jenny From The Block**....A:3 / S:16 *(4 versions)* **JENNIFER LOPEZ Featuring Jadakiss & Styles** samples "South Bronx" by Boogie Down Productions and "Hijack" by **Herbie Mann**	$6	T	Epic 79825
	★260★			**STYLISTICS, The** R&B/LP '72 R&B vocal group from Philadelphia, Pennsylvania: Russell Thompkins, Jr. (lead; born on 3/21/51), Airrion Love (born on 8/8/49), James Smith (born on 6/16/50), James Dunn (born on 2/4/50) and Herbie Murrell (born on 4/27/49). Thompkins, Love and Smith sang with the Percussions; Murrell and Dunn with the Monarchs from 1965-68. First recorded for Sebring in 1969. Also see **Glenn Medeiros**'s "Me - U = Blues." *1)You Make Me Feel Brand New 2)Betcha By Golly, Wow 3)Break Up To Make Up*			
1/9/71	73	7		1 **You're A Big Girl Now**....*Let The Junkie Bust The Pusher*	$6		Avco Embassy 4555
6/5/71	39	16		2 **Stop, Look, Listen (To Your Heart)**....*If I Love You*	$6		Avco Embassy 4572
11/6/71+	9	16	●	3 **You Are Everything**....*Country Living*	$5		Avco 4581

DEBUT	PEAK	WKS	Gold	A-side (Chart Hit)..........B-side	$	Sym	Label & Number

STYLISTICS, The — Cont'd

DEBUT	PEAK	WKS	Gold	A-side (Chart Hit)..........B-side	$	Sym	Label & Number
2/26/72	3	16	●	4 **Betcha By Golly, Wow**..........*Ebony Eyes* THE STYLISTICS featuring RUSSELL THOMPKINS, JR.	$5		Avco 4591
6/3/72	25	11		5 **People Make The World Go Round**..........*Point Of No Return* all of above from the album *The Stylistics* on Avco 33023	$5		Avco 4595
10/14/72	10	13	●	6 **I'm Stone In Love With You**..........*Make It Last*	$5		Avco 4603
2/10/73	5	14	●	7 **Break Up To Make Up**..........*You And Me*	$5		Avco 4611
5/19/73	23	10		8 **You'll Never Get To Heaven (If You Break My Heart)**..........*If You Don't Watch Out*	$5		Avco 4618
10/20/73	14	18		9 **Rockin' Roll Baby**..........*Pieces*	$5		Avco 4625
3/23/74	2^{2}	25	●	10 **You Make Me Feel Brand New** *Only For The Children* #2-10: produced by Thom Bell	$5		Avco 4634
7/27/74	18	12		11 **Let's Put It All Together**..........*I Take It Out On You*	$5		Avco 4640
10/19/74	41	11		12 **Heavy Fallin' Out**..........*Go Now*	$5		Avco 4647
1/18/75	47	7		13 **Star On A TV Show**..........*Hey Girl, Come And Get It*	$5		Avco 4649
4/19/75	70	6		14 **Thank You Baby**..........*Sing Baby Sing*	$5		Avco 4652
7/19/75	51	6		15 **Can't Give You Anything (But My Love)**..........*I'd Rather Be Hurt By You (Than Be Loved By Somebody Else)*	$5		Avco 4656
12/6/75+	76	9		16 **Funky Weekend**..........*If You Are There*	$5		Avco 4661
3/13/76	79	7		17 **You Are Beautiful**..........*Michael Or Me* #11-17: written and produced by **Hugo & Luigi**	$5	■	Avco 4664

STYX ★119★

BUB/ROK/AC/LP '79

Pop-rock group from Chicago, Illinois: **Dennis DeYoung** (vocals, keyboards; born on 2/18/47), **Tommy Shaw** (lead guitar; born on 9/11/53), James Young (guitar; born on 11/14/49), and twin brothers John (drums) and Chuck (bass) Panozzo (born on 9/20/48). Band earlier known as TW4. Shaw replaced John Curulewski in 1976. Most songs written by Dennis DeYoung and/or Tommy Shaw. Band broke up when DeYoung and Shaw went solo in 1984. Reunited in 1990 with guitarist **Glen Burtnick** (see #21 below) replacing Shaw, who joined **Damn Yankees**. John Panozzo died on 7/16/96 (age 47). In Greek mythology, Styx is a river in Hades.

1)Babe 2)The Best Of Times 3)Mr. Roboto 4)Show Me The Way 5)Lady

DEBUT	PEAK	WKS	Gold	A-side (Chart Hit)..........B-side	$	Sym	Label & Number
9/16/72	82	6		1 **Best Thing**..........*What Has Come Between Us*	$6		Wooden Nickel 0106
12/14/74+	6	17		2 **Lady**..........*Children Of The Land* first released on Wooden Nickel 0116 in 1973	$6		Wooden Nickel 10102
5/17/75	88	2		3 **You Need Love**..........*You Better Ask*	$6		Wooden Nickel 10272
2/14/76	27	14		4 **Lorelei**..........*Midnight Ride*	$5		A&M 1786
11/13/76	36	11		5 **Mademoiselle**..........*Light Up*	$5		A&M 1877
9/24/77+	8	22		6 **Come Sail Away**..........*Put Me On*	$5	■	A&M 1977
2/18/78	29	14		7 **Fooling Yourself (The Angry Young Man)**..........*The Grand Finale*	$5	■	A&M 2007
9/16/78	21	14		8 **Blue Collar Man (Long Nights)**..........*Superstars*	$5	■	A&M 2087
3/17/79	16	19		9 **Renegade /**			
1/6/79	41	8		10 **Sing For The Day**.......... first pressings issued with a different B-side ("Queen Of Spades") and with a different picture sleeve	$5	■	A&M 2110
10/6/79	❶^{2}	19	●	11 **Babe** *I'm O.K.*	$5		A&M 2188
12/15/79+	26	13		12 **Why Me**..........*Lights*	$5		A&M 2206
3/29/80	64	6		13 **Borrowed Time**..........*Eddie*	$5		A&M 2228
1/24/81	3	19		14 **The Best Of Times**..........*Lights*	$4	■	A&M 2300
3/21/81	9	19		15 **Too Much Time On My Hands**..........*Queen Of Spades*	$4		A&M 2323
7/11/81	54	8		16 **Nothing Ever Goes As Planned**..........*Never Say Never*	$4		A&M 2348
2/12/83	3	18	●	17 **Mr. Roboto**..........*Snowblind* (ROK #22)	$3	■	A&M 2525
4/30/83	6	16		18 **Don't Let It End**..........*(A.D. 1928) Rockin' The Paradise* (ROK #8)	$3	■	A&M 2543
8/13/83	48	7		19 **High Time**..........*Double Life*	$3		A&M 2568
5/5/84	40	9		20 **Music Time**..........*Heavy Metal Poisoning*	$3	■	A&M 2625
9/26/87	65	8		21 **Follow You**..........*Walls Came Down* **GLEN BURTNICK**	$3	■	A&M 2968
10/20/90	80	6		22 **Love Is The Ritual**..........*Homewrecker*	$3	▮	A&M 1525
12/8/90+	3	23		23 **Show Me The Way**..........S:5 / A:6 *Back To Chicago*	$3	▮V	A&M 1536
4/6/91	25	16		24 **Love At First Sight**..........A:25 *World Tonite* "45" issued for above 2 on A&M/Collectables 8696	$3	▮V	A&M 1548

SUAVE'

R&B/LP '88

Born on 2/22/66 in Los Angeles, California. R&B singer. Son of Waymond Anderson (of **GQ**).

DEBUT	PEAK	WKS	Gold	A-side (Chart Hit)..........B-side	$	Sym	Label & Number
3/12/88	20	15		**My Girl**..........S:16 / A:25 *(acappella version)*	$3	■	Capitol 44124

SUBLIME

ROK/LP '96

Ska-rock trio from Long Beach, California: Brad Nowell (vocals, guitar), Eric Wilson (bass) and Bud Gaugh (drums). Nowell died of a drug overdose on 5/25/96 (age 28).

DEBUT	PEAK	WKS	Gold	A-side (Chart Hit)..........B-side	$	Sym	Label & Number
9/7/96	29^{A}	24		1 **What I Got**..........MR^{3}			album cut
1/25/97	43^{A}	22		2 **Santeria**..........			album cut
6/28/97	47^{A}	21		3 **Wrong Way**..........			album cut
12/20/97+	87	7		4 **Doin' Time**..........*(3 versions)* samples "Summertime" by **Herbie Mann** and "Fight For Your Right" by **Beastie Boys**; all of above from the album *Sublime* on Gasoline Alley 11413	$6	★	Gasoline Alley 55390

SUBWAY

R&B/LP '95

Black teen vocal group from Chicago, Illinois: Eric McNeal, Roy Jones, Keith Thomas and Trerail Puckett.

DEBUT	PEAK	WKS	Gold	A-side (Chart Hit)..........B-side	$	Sym	Label & Number
2/4/95	15	20	●	1 **This Lil' Game We Play**..........S:7 / A:25 *(4 album snippets)* **SUBWAY featuring 702**	$3	▮	Biv 10 0252
6/24/95	91	4		2 **Fire**..........S:67 *Chi-Town Ride* (w/Easy & Tung Twista)	$3	▮	Biv 10 0338

DEBUT	PEAK	WKS	Gold	A-side (Chart Hit)...B-side	$	Sym	Label & Number
				SUDDEN CHANGE '94			
				Female R&B trio from New Jersey: Linne Mondestin, Jessie Mondestin and Katia Pinard.			
3/12/94	56	17		**Comin' On Strong** ...S:40 / A:67 *(instrumental)*	$3	▮	EastWest 98334
				samples "The Jam" by **Graham Central Station**			
				SUGA FREE R&B '97			
				Born in Oakland, California; raised in Compton, California. Male rapper.			
5/24/97	79	13		**If U Stay Ready** ...S:75 *Fly Fo Life (2 versions) / (remix)*	$3	▮	Island 854976
				written and produced by **DJ Quik**			
				SUGAR BEARS '72			
				Pop studio production by **Jimmy Bowen**. **Kim Carnes** wrote and performed vocals for the group. Based on General Foods' "Sugar Crisp" cereal character.			
3/11/72	51	13		**You Are The One**...*Someone Like You*	$6		Big Tree 122
				SUGARHILL GANG R&B/LP '79			
				Rap trio from Harlem, New York: Michael "Wonder Mike" Wright, Guy "Master Gee" O'Brien and Henry "Big Bank Hank" Jackson. The first commercially successful rap group.			
11/10/79+	36	12		1 **Rapper's Delight**...*(short version)*	$30	T^V	Sugar Hill 542
				the first "rap" record to make the *Hot 100*; rhythm track taken from **Chic**'s "Good Times"; "45" issued in 1980 as the B-side of "Here I Am" on Sugar Hill 755			
2/7/81	82	9		2 **8th Wonder**...*Sugar Hill Groove*	$10	T^V	Sugar Hill 553
				above 2 issued on 7" vinyl ("45s") for promotional use on Sugar Hill 752 & 753, respectively			
2/13/82	53	11		3 **Apache**...*Rapper's Delight*	$8		Sugar Hill 774
				samples Jorgen Ingmann's 1961 hit "Apache"; also see "Jump On It" by **Sir Mix-A-Lot**			
				SUGARLOAF BUB/LP '70			
				Rock group from Denver, Colorado: Jerry Corbetta (vocals, keyboards), Bob Webber (guitar), Bob Raymond (bass) and Bob MacVittie (drums). Robert Yeazel (guitar, vocals) joined in 1971. By 1974, Myron Pollock replaced MacVittie, and Yeazel had left.			
8/15/70	3	17		1 **Green-Eyed Lady** *West Of Tomorrow*	$6		Liberty 56183
3/6/71	55	8		2 **Tongue In Cheek**...*Woman*	$6	■	Liberty 56218
6/26/71	88	3		3 **Mother Nature's Wine**...*Bach Doors Man/Chest Fever*	$5		United Artists 50784
				SUGARLOAF/JERRY CORBETTA:			
12/7/74+	9	21		4 **Don't Call Us, We'll Call You**...*Texas Two-Lane*	$5		Claridge 402
				features brief snippet of **The Beatles**' "I Feel Fine"			
6/7/75	87	6		5 **Stars In My Eyes**...*Myra, Myra*	$5		Claridge 405
				all of above produced by **Frank Slay**			
	★598★			**SUGAR RAY** ROK/BUB/LP '99			
				Rock group from Los Angeles: Mark McGrath (vocals; born on 3/15/68), Craig Bullock (DJ; born on 12/17/70), Rodney Sheppard (guitar; born on 11/25/67), Murphy Karges (bass; born on 6/20/67) and Stan Frazier (drums; born on 4/23/68).			
7/5/97	1^{6A}	59		1 **Fly** MR^8			album cut
				SUGAR RAY Featuring Super Cat			
				from the album *Floored* on Lava/Atlantic 83006			
1/9/99	3	31	●	2 **Every Morning** ...MR^6 A:2 / S:4 *Even Though*	$4	$★^V$	Lava/Atlantic 84462
7/3/99	7	32		3 **Someday** ...A:4 / S:30 *(acoustic version) / Every Morning (acoustic version)*	$8	$★^{++}$	Lava/Atlantic 84536
1/15/00	29	20		4 **Falls Apart (Run Away)**...A:26			album cut
				above 3 from the album *14:59* on Lava/Atlantic 83151			
6/2/01	13	22		5 **When It's Over** ...A:12			album cut
				from the album *Sugar Ray* on Lava/Atlantic 83414			
				SUICIDE '00			
				Rap duo from Miami Beach, Florida: Earnest Jackson and Matthew Houston.			
11/4/00	49^S	8		**Big Doe** ...*(2 versions) / (3 album snippets)*	$7	★	Futurescope 3331
				SUM 41 ROK/LP '01			
				Punk-rock group from Ajax, Ontario, Canada: Deryck Whibley (vocals, guitar), Dave Baksh (guitar), Cone McCaslin (bass) and Steve Jocz (drums).			
9/1/01	66	12		1 **Fat Lip**...MR^1 A:61			album cut
3/30/02	28^S	4		2 **Motivation**...*All She's Got / Crazy Amanda Bunkface / What We're All About*	$10	$★^+$	Island 588995
				CD single packaged in a special black tin container with a skull drawing on top; above 2 from the album *All Killer, No Filler* on Island 548662			
				SUMMER, Donna ★48★ R&B/AC/BUB/LP '79			
				Born LaDonna Andrea Gaines on 12/31/48 in Boston, Massachusetts. "The Queen of Disco." With group Crow, played local clubs. In German production of *Hair*, European productions of *Godspell*, *The Me Nobody Knows* and *Porgy And Bess*. Settled in Germany, where she recorded "Love To Love You Baby." In the movie *Thank God It's Friday* in 1978. Married Bruce Sudano (**Alive And Kicking**, **Brooklyn Dreams**) on 7/16/80.			
				1)Bad Girls 2)Hot Stuff 3)MacArthur Park 4)No More Tears (Enough Is Enough) 5)Dim All The Lights			
12/6/75+	2^2	18	●	1 **Love To Love You Baby** ...*(short version)*	$6		Oasis 401
5/1/76	52	5		2 **Could It Be Magic**...*Whispering Waves*	$6		Oasis 405
				inspired by Chopin's "Prelude in C Minor"			
7/10/76	80	4		3 **Try Me, I Know We Can Make It**...*Wasted*	$6	■	Oasis 406
12/18/76+	58	8		4 **Spring Affair**...*Come With Me*	$5		Casablanca 872
1/15/77	43	10		5 **Winter Melody**...*Spring Affair*	$5		Casablanca 874
8/6/77	6	23	●	6 **I Feel Love** ...*Can't We Just Sit Down (And Talk It Over)* (R&B #20)	$5		Casablanca 884
12/17/77+	37	11		7 **I Love You**...*Once Upon A Time*	$5		Casablanca 907
3/4/78	53	9		8 **Rumour Has It** ...*Once Upon A Time*	$5		Casablanca 916

DEBUT	PEAK	WKS	Gold	A-side (Chart Hit)...B-side	$	Sym	Label & Number
				SUMMER, Donna — Cont'd			
5/13/78	3	21	●	9 **Last Dance** ...*With Your Love*	$5		Casablanca 926
				from the movie *Thank God It's Friday* starring Jeff Goldblum and Debra Winger			
9/9/78	1 (3)	20	●	10 **MacArthur Park** ...*Once Upon A Time*	$5		Casablanca 939
1/13/79	4	19	●	11 **Heaven Knows** ...*Only One Man* (Summer)	$5		Casablanca 959
				DONNA SUMMER with Brooklyn Dreams			
4/21/79	1 (3)	21	▲	12 **Hot Stuff** ...*Journey To The Centre Of Your Heart*	$4		Casablanca 978
5/26/79	1 (5)	20	▲	13 **Bad Girls** RB[1] *On My Honor*	$4		Casablanca 988
8/25/79	2 (2)	21	●	14 **Dim All The Lights** ...*There Will Always Be A You*	$4		Casablanca 2201
10/20/79	1 (2)	15	▲	15 **No More Tears (Enough Is Enough)**...*Wet* (Streisand)	$4	■	Columbia 11125
				BARBRA STREISAND/DONNA SUMMER			
				12" single available on Casablanca 20199			
1/12/80	5	17	●	16 **On The Radio** ...*There Will Always Be A You*	$4		Casablanca 2236
9/13/80	36	11		17 **Walk Away**...*Could It Be Magic*	$4		Casablanca 2300
				#12-14 & 17: from the album *Bad Girls*			
9/20/80	3	20	●	18 **The Wanderer** ...*Stop Me*	$4	■	Geffen 49563
11/29/80+	33	12		19 **Cold Love** ...*Grand Illusion*	$4	■	Geffen 49634
2/21/81	40	11		20 **Who Do You Think You're Foolin'** ...*Running For Cover*	$4		Geffen 49664
				all of above (except #15) produced by **Giorgio Moroder** and Pete Bellotte			
6/26/82	10	18		21 **Love Is In Control (Finger On The Trigger)**...*Sometimes Like Butterflies*	$4	■	Geffen 29982
10/2/82	41	10		22 **State Of Independence** ...*Love Is Just A Breath Away*	$4	■	Geffen 29895
				all-star choir includes: **James Ingram**, **Michael Jackson**, **Kenny Loggins**, **Lionel Richie**, **Dionne Warwick** and **Stevie Wonder**; written by **Jon & Vangelis**			
12/18/82+	33	16		23 **The Woman In Me** ...*Livin' In America*	$4	■	Geffen 29805
5/28/83	3	21		24 **She Works Hard For The Money**...RB[3] *I Do Believe (I Fell In Love)*	$4	■	Mercury 812370
9/3/83	43	8		25 **Unconditional Love** ...*Woman*	$4	■	Mercury 814088
				Musical Youth (background vocals)			
1/14/84	70	4		26 **Love Has A Mind Of Its Own** ...*Stop, Look And Listen*	$4		Mercury 814922
				DONNA SUMMER with Matthew Ward (of the Contemporary Christian group, 2nd Chapter of Acts)			
8/11/84	21	14		27 **There Goes My Baby** ...A:27 *Maybe It's Over*	$4	■	Geffen 29291
11/10/84	75	5		28 **Supernatural Love**...*Face The Music*	$4	■	Geffen 29142
8/22/87	48	11		29 **Dinner With Gershwin**...S:38 *(instrumental)*	$4	■	Geffen 28418
				written by **Brenda Russell**			
4/22/89	7	17	●	30 **This Time I Know It's For Real** ...S:4 / A:8 *If It Makes You Feel Good*	$3	■	Atlantic 88899
9/16/89	85	3		31 **Love's About To Change My Heart** ...(**Clivilles & Cole** mix)	$3		Atlantic 88840
8/17/91	77	5		32 **When Love Cries**...A:54 *(remix)*	$3	▮	Atlantic 87624
7/24/99	79	9		33 **I Will Go With You (Con Te Partiró)**...S:14 *(4 versions) / Love On & On*	$4	★V	Epic 79201
				recorded in Italian by Andrea Bocelli on his 1996 album *Romanza*			
11/18/00	75S	1		34 **The Power Of One** ...*The Legend Comes To Life*	$5	★	Atlantic 84930
				from the animated movie *Pokémon 2000*			
				SUMMER, Henry Lee ROK/LP **'88**			
				Born on 7/5/55 in Brazil, Indiana. Rock singer/songwriter/guitarist.			
2/13/88	20	18		1 **I Wish I Had A Girl**...AR[1] S:17 / A:24 *Wing Tip Shoes*	$3		CBS Associated 07720
5/28/88	57	8		2 **Darlin' Danielle Don't** ...*Lovin' Man*	$3	■	CBS Associated 07909
9/17/88	85	3		3 **Hands On The Radio**...*Just Another Day*	$3		CBS Associated 07986
5/20/89	18	18		4 **Hey Baby** A:15 / S:18 *Something Is Missing*	$3		CBS Associated 68891
8/10/91	51	10		5 **Till Somebody Loves You**...*I've Got The Fire*	$3	▮	Epic Associated 73893
				Michael Bolton (backing vocal)			
				SUN R&B/LP **'76**			
				Soul-funk group from Dayton, Ohio: Byron Byrd (vocals), Sheldon Reynolds and Anthony Thompson (guitars), Dean Francis (keyboards), Ernie Knisley (percussion), Robert Arnold, Gary King and Larry Hatchet (horns), Don Taylor (bass), and Robert "Mitch" Kinney (drums). Also see **Nikki**.			
9/25/76	76	6		**Wanna Make Love (Come Flick My BIC)**...*Love Is Never Sure*	$5	■	Capitol 4254
				SUN, Joe C&W **'80**			
				Born James Joseph Paulson on 9/25/43 in Rochester, Minnesota. Country singer. Began as a DJ. Later became promo man for Ovation Records, which led to recording career.			
5/31/80	71	6		**Shotgun Rider**...*Little Bit Of Push*	$5		Ovation 1141
				SUNDAY **'00**			
				Female R&B vocal group from Newark, New Jersey: sisters Tawanda, Notasha and Tiffany, with cousins Shakira and Stacey.			
12/30/00	98	2		**I Know** ...S:22 *(3 album snippets)*	$4	★	Better Place/Capitol 58898
				SUNDAYS, The ROK/LP **'97**			
				Pop-rock group from London, England: Harriet Wheeler (vocals), David Gavurin (guitar), Paul Brindley (bass) and Patrick Hannan (drums).			
9/27/97	50A	20		**Summertime**...			album cut
				from the album *Static & Silence* on DGC 25131			
				SUNDOWN COMPANY **'76**			
				Male/female studio group produced by Joe Beck.			
6/5/76	84	5		**Norma Jean Wants To Be A Movie Star** ...*Moon Beam Pie*	$5		Polydor 14312
				from the movie *Goodbye Norma Jean* starring Misty Rowe			

DEBUT	PEAK	WKS	Gold	A-side (Chart Hit)...B-side	$	Sym	Label & Number
				SUNNY & THE SUNGLOWS BUB/LP **'63**			
				Latin group from San Antonio, Texas: Sunny Ozuna, with brothers Jesse, Oscar and Ray Villanueva, Tony Tostado, Gilbert Fernandez and Alfred Luna.			
9/7/63	11	12		1 **Talk To Me** ...*Every Week, Every Month, Every Year* (Sunny & The Sunliners)	$20		Tear Drop 3014
11/16/63	45	7		2 **Rags To Riches** ***[SUNNY & The Sunliners]*** ...*Not Even Judgement Day*	$15		Tear Drop 3022
				#1 hit for **Tony Bennett** in 1953; above 2 originally released on Sunglow 110 and 111, respectively, in 1963 as by The Sunglows			
2/22/64	71	5		3 **Out Of Sight - Out Of Mind** ***[SUNNY & The Sunliners]*** ...*No One Else Will Do*	$15		Tear Drop 3027
5/8/65	64	4		4 **Peanuts (La Cacahuata)** ***[THE SUNGLOWS]*** ...*Happy Hippo* [I]	$15		Sunglow 107
				polka; originally released in 1962 as "La Cacahuata"; also released on Sunglow 107 with "Love Me (All My Love Belongs To You)" as the A-side			
				SUNNYSIDERS, The **'55**			
				Vocal group formed in New York: Freddy Morgan (banjo), Norman Milkin, Jad Paul and **Margie Rayburn**. Morgan and Paul were members of Spike Jones & The City Slickers from 1947-58. Morgan died of a heart attack on 12/21/70 (age 60). Rayburn died of a heart attack on 6/14/2000 (age 76).			
5/21/55	12	10		**Hey, Mr. Banjo** ...J:12 / A:19 / S:20 *Zoom, Zoom, Zoom*	$15		Kapp 113
				SUNRAYS, The **'66**			
				Rock and roll group from California: Rick Henn, Marty DiGiovanni, Byron Case, Eddie Medora and Vince Hozier. Produced by Murry Wilson (father and producer of **The Beach Boys**).			
9/4/65	51	10		1 **I Live For The Sun** ...*Bye Baby Bye*	$15		Tower 148
1/22/66	41	8		2 **Andrea** ...*You Don't Phase Me*	$15		Tower 191
5/7/66	93	2		3 **Still** ...*When You're Not Here*	$15		Tower 224
				SUNSCREEM LP **'93**			
				Techno-pop group from Essex, England: Lucia Holm (vocals), Darren Woodford (guitar), Paul Carnell (keyboards), Rob Fricker (bass) and Sean Wright (drums).			
2/27/93	36	19		**Love U More** ...A:28 *B/Doved Up*	$3	▮	Columbia 74769
				SUNSHINE COMPANY, The BUB/AC/LP **'67**			
				Pop group formed in Los Angeles, California: Mary Nance (vocals), Douglas "Red" Mark and Maury Manseau (guitars), Larry Sims (bass) and Merle Brigante (drums). Mark later formed **Redeye**.			
7/15/67	50	10		1 **Happy** ...*Blue May*	$10		Imperial 66247
10/21/67	36	7		2 **Back On The Street Again** ...*A Year Of Jaine Time*	$10		Imperial 66260
2/10/68	56	5		3 **Look, Here Comes The Sun** ...*It's Sunday*	$10		Imperial 66280
				SUPA NAT **'02**			
				Born Nathaniel Elder on 10/14/69 in Miami, Florida. Male rapper.			
8/31/02	36S	8		**Kick'n Ass** ...*(4 versions)*	$5	★	N'Da Hole 90207
				SUPERB **'01**			
				Rap duo from Atlanta, Georgia.			
6/16/01	65S	2		**Superb** ...*(2 versions) / U Can't Ride / (snippet presentation)*	$10	★*	FY Station 5690
				SUPERBS, The **'64**			
				R&B vocal group: Eleanor Green, Bobby Swayne, Ronnie Cook, Gordy Harmon and Walter White. Harmon later joined **The Whispers**. Eleanor later married pro baseball player Rudy May.			
10/3/64	83	5		**Baby Baby All The Time** ...*Raindrops, Memories, and Tears*	$30		Dore 715
				SUPER CAT R&B/BUB **'97**			
				Born William Maragh on 6/25/63 in Kingston, Jamaica (of East Indian heritage). Dance-hall reggae singer. Also see **Kris Kross**'s "Alright."			
10/7/95	99	1		1 **Girlstown** ...*(remix)*	$5	▮	Columbia 77850
				produced by **Erick Sermon**			
7/5/97	❶6A	59		2 **Fly** ...MR8			album cut
				SUGAR RAY Featuring Super Cat			
				from the **Sugar Ray** album *Floored* on Lava/Atlantic 83006			
				SUPERDRAG LP **'96**			
				Rock group from Knoxville, Tennessee: John Davis (vocals), Brandon Fisher (guitar), Tom Pappas (bass) and Don Coffey Jr. (drums).			
8/3/96	72A	1		**Sucked Out**...			album cut
				from the album *Regretfully Yours* on Elektra 61900			
	★442★			**SUPERTRAMP** ROK/AC/LP **'79**			
				Rock group formed in England: **Roger Hodgson** (vocals, guitar; born on 3/21/50) (see #10 below), Rick Davies (vocals, keyboards; born on 7/22/44), John Helliwell (sax; born on 2/15/45), Dougie Thomson (bass; born on 3/24/51; older brother of **Ali Thomson**) and Bob Siebenberg (drums). Hodgson went solo in 1983. Band formed in 1969 and took band name from a 1938 book by W.H. Davies, *The Autobiography Of A Supertramp*.			
				1)The Logical Song 2)Take The Long Way Home 3)It's Raining Again			
4/12/75	35	10		1 **Bloody Well Right** ...*Dreamer*	$6	■	A&M 1660
6/4/77	15	18		2 **Give A Little Bit** ...*Downstream*	$5	■	A&M 1938
3/24/79	6	21		3 **The Logical Song** *Just Another Nervous Wreck*	$5	■	A&M 2128
7/7/79	15	14		4 **Goodbye Stranger** ...*Even In The Quietest Moments*	$5	■	A&M 2162
10/13/79	10	15		5 **Take The Long Way Home** ...*Rudy*	$5	■	A&M 2193
				picture sleeve features a maze, issued in either orange, green or yellow ink			
9/20/80	15	14		6 **Dreamer** ...*From Now On* [L]	$5	■	A&M 2269
				studio version released on the B-side of #1 above and on A&M 1981 in 1977 with a picture sleeve			
12/13/80	62	8		7 **Breakfast In America** ...*You Started Laughing* [L]	$5		A&M 2292
				above 2 recorded on 11/29/79 at the Paris Pavillon			
10/30/82	11	13		8 **It's Raining Again** ...*Bonnie*	$5	■	A&M 2502
1/29/83	31	12		9 **My Kind Of Lady** ...*Know Who You Are*	$5	■	A&M 2517
10/13/84	48	15		10 **Had A Dream (Sleeping With The Enemy)** ...*(long version)*	$4		A&M 2678
				ROGER HODGSON			
5/25/85	28	12		11 **Cannonball** ...S:25 *Ever Open Door*	$4	■	A&M 2731

DEBUT	PEAK	WKS	Gold	A-side (Chart Hit)...B-side	$	Sym	Label & Number

SUPREMES, The ★25★ R&B/BUB/LP '64

R&B vocal group from Detroit, Michigan: lead singer **Diana Ross** (born on 3/26/44), Mary Wilson (born on 3/6/44), Florence Ballard (born on 6/30/43; died of cardiac arrest on 2/22/76, age 32) and Barbara Martin. Formed as the Primettes in 1959. Recorded for LuPine in 1960. Signed to Motown's Tamla label in 1960. Changed name to The Supremes in 1961; Martin left shortly thereafter. Worked as backing vocalists for Motown until 1964. Backed **Marvin Gaye** on "Can I Get A Witness" and "You're A Wonderful One." Ballard discharged from group in 1967; replaced by Cindy Birdsong, formerly with **Patti LaBelle's Blue Belles**. Ross left in 1969 for solo career; replaced by Jean Terrell. Birdsong left in 1972; replaced by Lynda Laurence. Terrell and Laurence left in 1973. Mary Wilson re-formed group with Scherrie Payne (sister of **Freda Payne**) and Cindy Birdsong. Birdsong left again in 1976; replaced by Susaye Greene. In 1978, Wilson toured England with Karen Ragland and Karen Jackson, but lost rights to the name "Supremes" thereafter. Group inducted into the Rock and Roll Hall of Fame in 1988. Diana Ross, Scherrie Payne and Lynda Laurence reunited in 2000 for a concert tour.

1)Baby Love 2)Love Child 3)Come See About Me 4)Where Did Our Love Go 5)You Can't Hurry Love

DEBUT	PEAK	WKS	Gold	#	A-side (Chart Hit)	B-side	$	Sym	Label & Number
8/11/62	95	3		1	**Your Heart Belongs To Me**	*(He's) Seventeen*	$30	■	Motown 1027
12/8/62+	90	6		2	**Let Me Go The Right Way**	*Time Changes Things*	$50		Motown 1034
7/27/63	75	7		3	**A Breath Taking Guy**	*(The Man With The) Rock And Roll Banjo Band*	$25		Motown 1044
					promo issue shows: "A Breath Taking, First Sight Soul Shaking, One Night Love Making, Next Day Heart Breaking Guy" ($75); #1 & 3: written and produced by **Smokey Robinson**				
11/30/63+	23	11		4	**When The Lovelight Starts Shining Through His Eyes**	*Standing At The Crossroads Of Love*	$25		Motown 1051
3/14/64	93	2		5	**Run, Run, Run**	*I'm Giving You Your Freedom*	$25		Motown 1054
7/11/64	❶ (2)	14		6	**Where Did Our Love Go** RB(2)	*He Means The World To Me*	$20	■	Motown 1060
10/3/64	❶ (4)	13	●	7	**Baby Love** RB(4)	*Ask Any Girl*	$20	■	Motown 1066
11/14/64	❶ (2)	14		8	**Come See About Me**	*Always In My Heart*	$20		Motown 1068
					above 6 from the album *Where Did Our Love Go*				
2/20/65	❶ (2)	12	●	9	**Stop! In The Name Of Love**	*I'm In Love Again*	$15	■	Motown 1074
5/1/65	❶ (1)	11		10	**Back In My Arms Again** RB(1)	*Whisper You Love Me Boy*	$15	■	Motown 1075
7/31/65	11	9		11	**Nothing But Heartaches**	*He Holds His Own*	$15	■	Motown 1080
10/30/65	❶ (2)	10		12	**I Hear A Symphony**	*Who Could Ever Doubt My Love*	$15		Motown 1083
12/18/65	5 X	7		13	**Twinkle Twinkle Little Me** / [X]				
					X: 5/'65; 26/'66; 10/'67				
12/11/65	7 X	3		14	**Children's Christmas Song** [X]		$20	■	Motown 1085
					children's chorus (backing vocals)				
1/15/66	5	11		15	**My World Is Empty Without You**	*Everything Is Good About You*	$15		Motown 1089
4/30/66	9	8		16	**Love Is Like An Itching In My Heart**	*He's All I Got*	$15		Motown 1094
8/13/66	❶ (2)	13		17	**You Can't Hurry Love** RB(2)	*Put Yourself In My Place*	$15	■	Motown 1097
10/29/66	❶ (2)	12		18	**You Keep Me Hangin' On** RB(4)	*Remove This Doubt*	$15	■	Motown 1101
1/28/67	❶ (1)	11		19	**Love Is Here And Now You're Gone** RB(2)	*There's No Stopping Us Now*	$12		Motown 1103
4/8/67	❶ (1)	11		20	**The Happening**	*All I Know About You*	$12		Motown 1107
					title song from the movie starring Anthony Quinn				
					DIANA ROSS AND THE SUPREMES:				
8/12/67	2 (2)	11		21	**Reflections**	*Going Down For The Third Time*	$12		Motown 1111
11/11/67	9	8		22	**In And Out Of Love**	*I Guess I'll Always Love You*	$12		Motown 1116
3/16/68	28	9		23	**Forever Came Today**	*Time Changes Things*	$10		Motown 1122
					#4-23: written by Eddie **Holland**, Lamont **Dozier** & Brian **Holland**				
6/8/68	30	7		24	**Some Things You Never Get Used To**	*You've Been So Wonderful To Me*	$10		Motown 1126
10/19/68	❶ (2)	16		25	**Love Child**	*Will This Be The Day*	$10		Motown 1135
12/7/68+	2 (2)	13	▲	26	**I'm Gonna Make You Love Me**	*A Place In The Sun*	$10	■	Motown 1137
					DIANA ROSS AND THE SUPREMES & THE TEMPTATIONS				
1/25/69	10	8		27	**I'm Livin' In Shame**	*I'm So Glad I Got Somebody (Like You Around)*	$10		Motown 1139
					some pressings show title as "I'm Living In Shame"				
3/15/69	25	7		28	**I'll Try Something New**	*The Way You Do The Things You Do*	$10		Motown 1142
					DIANA ROSS AND THE SUPREMES & THE TEMPTATIONS				
4/19/69	27	6		29	**The Composer**	*The Beginning Of The End*	$10		Motown 1146
5/31/69	31	6		30	**No Matter What Sign You Are** /				
8/2/69	69	5		31	**The Young Folks**		$10		Motown 1148
9/13/69	46	5		32	**The Weight**	*For Better Or Worse*	$10		Motown 1153
					DIANA ROSS AND THE SUPREMES & THE TEMPTATIONS				
11/8/69	❶ (1)	16	▲	33	**Someday We'll Be Together** RB(4)	*He's My Sunny Boy*	$10		Motown 1156
					Johnny Bristol (male vocal, co-writer, producer)				
					THE SUPREMES:				
3/7/70	10	11		34	**Up The Ladder To The Roof**	*Bill, When Are You Coming Home*	$10		Motown 1162
7/18/70	21	11		35	**Everybody's Got The Right To Love**	*But I Love You More*	$10		Motown 1167
11/7/70	7	14		36	**Stoned Love** RB(1)	*Shine On Me*	$10		Motown 1172
11/28/70+	14	10		37	**River Deep - Mountain High**	*Together We Can Make Such Sweet Music*	$10		Motown 1173
					THE SUPREMES & FOUR TOPS				
5/8/71	16	10		38	**Nathan Jones**	*Happy (Is A Bumpy Road)*	$10		Motown 1182
6/5/71	55	5		39	**You Gotta Have Love In Your Heart**	*I'm Glad About It*	$10		Motown 1181
					THE SUPREMES & FOUR TOPS				
10/9/71	71	4		40	**Touch**	*It's So Hard For Me To Say Good-Bye*	$8		Motown 1190
1/8/72	16	12		41	**Floy Joy**	*This Is The Story*	$8		Motown 1195
5/6/72	37	9		42	**Automatically Sunshine**	*Precious Little Things*	$8		Motown 1200
8/5/72	59	8		43	**Your Wonderful, Sweet Sweet Love**	*The Wisdom Of Time*	$8		Motown 1206
					above 3 written and produced by **Smokey Robinson**				
10/21/72	85	7		44	**I Guess I'll Miss The Man**	*Over And Over*	$8		Motown 1213
					from the Broadway musical *Pippin* starring Ben Vereen				
6/9/73	87	1		45	**Bad Weather**	*Oh Be My Love*	$8		Motown 1225
					written, produced and arranged by **Stevie Wonder**				

DEBUT	PEAK	WKS	Gold	A-side (Chart Hit)...B-side	$	Sym	Label & Number

SUPREMES, The — Cont'd

DEBUT	PEAK	WKS	Gold	A-side (Chart Hit)...B-side	$	Sym	Label & Number
5/29/76	40	14		46 **I'm Gonna Let My Heart Do The Walking** ... *Early Morning Love*	$6		Motown 1391
12/4/76	85	5		47 **You're My Driving Wheel** ... *You're What's Missing In My Life*	$6		Motown 1407

SURFACE — R&B/LP '91

R&B trio from New Jersey: Bernard Jackson (vocals), David Townsend (guitar, keyboards; son of producer/songwriter **Ed Townsend**) and Dave Conley (bass, sax; former horn player with **Mandrill**).

DEBUT	PEAK	WKS	Gold	A-side (Chart Hit)...B-side	$	Sym	Label & Number
5/23/87	20	14		1 **Happy** ...A:19 / S:21 *Let's Try Again*	$3		Columbia 06611
4/15/89	57	13		2 **Closer Than Friends** ...RB[2] *(jazz version)*	$3		Columbia 08537
7/1/89	5	19	●	3 **Shower Me With Your Love** ...RB[1] S:5 / A:6 *(instrumental)*	$3		Columbia 68746
11/4/89	84	5		4 **You Are My Everything** ...RB[2] *Feels So Good*	$3		Columbia 69016
11/3/90+	❶[2]	25	●	5 **The First Time** RB[1] / AC[2] A:❶[2] / S:2 *Closer Than Friends*	$3	▮[V]	Columbia 73502
4/27/91	17	17		6 **Never Gonna Let You Down** ...A:28 / S:47 *Gotta Make Love Tonight*	$3	▮[V]	Columbia 73643

SURFARIS, The — BUB/LP '63

Teen rock and roll-surf band from Glendora, California: Ron Wilson (drummer; died of an aneurysm, May 1989), Jim Fuller (lead guitar), Bob Berryhill (rhythm guitar), Pat Connolly (bass) and Jim Pash (sax, clarinet). Wilson was with **The New Establishment** in 1969.

DEBUT	PEAK	WKS	Gold	A-side (Chart Hit)...B-side	$	Sym	Label & Number
6/22/63	2[1]	16		1 **Wipe Out** / [I]			
				opening witch laugh and the words "Wipe Out" provided by their manager, Dale Smallin; also see #4 below			
8/31/63	62	6		2 **Surfer Joe** ...	$20		Dot 16479
				above 2 originally released on DFS 11/12 ($3000) and then on Princess 50 in 1963 ($300)			
9/28/63	49	8		3 **Point Panic** ... *Waikiki Run* [I]	$15		Decca 31538
7/30/66	16	14		4 **Wipe Out** ... *Surfer Joe* [I-R]	$10		Dot 144
				same version as #1 above; also "Bubbled Under" (#110) in 1970 on Dot/Paramount 144			

SURVIVALIST — '01

Rap group: Problemz, Preacha, Bookie, Jeebal and Sabatoj.

DEBUT	PEAK	WKS	Gold	A-side (Chart Hit)...B-side	$	Sym	Label & Number
9/8/01	37[S]	9		**Bounce** ... *(3 versions) / West*	$6	★	Fo' Life 356728

★237★ SURVIVOR — BUB/LP '82

Pop-rock group formed in Chicago, Illinois: Dave Bickler (vocals; former lead singer of **Jamestown Massacre**), Frankie Sullivan (guitar), Jim Peterik (keyboards; born on 11/11/50; former lead singer of **Ides Of March**), Stephan Ellis (bass) and Marc Droubay (drums). Bickler replaced by Jimi Jamison in early 1984. Droubay and Ellis left in early 1988.

1)Eye Of The Tiger 2)Burning Heart 3)The Search Is Over

DEBUT	PEAK	WKS	Gold	A-side (Chart Hit)...B-side	$	Sym	Label & Number
2/23/80	70	12		1 **Somewhere In America** ... *Freelance*	$5		Scotti Brothers 511
10/17/81	33	14		2 **Poor Man's Son** ... *Love Is On My Side*	$4		Scotti Brothers 02560
2/20/82	62	8		3 **Summer Nights** ... *Take You On A Saturday*	$4		Scotti Brothers 02700
6/5/82	❶[6]	25	▲[2]	4 **Eye Of The Tiger** AR[5] *Take You On A Saturday*	$4	■	Scotti Brothers 02912
				from the movie *Rocky III* starring Sylvester Stallone			
9/25/82	17	16		5 **American Heartbeat** ... *Silver Girl*	$4	■	Scotti Brothers 03213
1/22/83	74	6		6 **The One That Really Matters** ... *Hesitation Dance*	$4		Scotti Brothers 03485
10/22/83	77	5		7 **Caught In The Game** ... *Slander*	$4	■	Scotti Brothers 04074
6/16/84	63	7		8 **The Moment Of Truth** ... *It Doesn't Have To Be This Way*	$4		Casablanca 880053
				from the movie *The Karate Kid* starring Ralph Macchio			
9/15/84	13	23		9 **I Can't Hold Back** ...AR[3] A:11 / S:15 *I See You In Everyone*	$3	■	Scotti Brothers 04603
1/26/85	8	17		10 **High On You** ...A:8 / S:13 *Everlasting*	$3	■	Scotti Brothers 04685
4/20/85	4	21		11 **The Search Is Over** ...AC[4] A:4 / S:6 *It's The Singer Not The Song*	$3	■	Scotti Brothers 04871
8/17/85	53	9		12 **First Night** ... *Feels Like Love*	$3	■	Scotti Brothers 05579
				above 4 from the album *Vital Signs*			
11/2/85+	2[2]	22		13 **Burning Heart** ...S:❶[1] / A:2 *Feels Like Love*	$3	■	Scotti Brothers 05663
				from the movie *Rocky IV* starring Sylvester Stallone			
10/25/86+	9	19		14 **Is This Love** ...S:8 / A:8 *Can't Let You Go*	$3	■	Scotti Brothers 06381
2/21/87	51	9		15 **How Much Love** ... *Backstreet Love Affair*	$3		Scotti Brothers 06705
5/9/87	86	5		16 **Man Against The World** ... *Oceans*	$3	■	Scotti Brothers 07070
10/8/88	61	10		17 **Didn't Know It Was Love** ... *Rhythm Of The City*	$3		Scotti Brothers 08067
1/21/89	74	6		18 **Across The Miles** ... *Burning Bridges*	$3		Scotti Brothers 68526
				all of above (except #8) written or co-written by Jim Peterik			

SUTHERLAND BROTHERS AND QUIVER — LP '73

Rock and roll group formed in England: brothers Iain (vocals, guitar) and Gavin (vocals, bass) Sutherland, with their four-piece group Quiver: Tim Renwick (guitar), Pete Wood (keyboards), Bruce Thomas (bass) and Willie Wilson (drums; **Cochise**). Quiver disbanded in 1977 and Thomas joined **Elvis Costello**'s Attractions.

DEBUT	PEAK	WKS	Gold	A-side (Chart Hit)...B-side	$	Sym	Label & Number
8/18/73	48	12		1 (I Don't Want To Love You But) **You Got Me Anyway** ... *Rock And Roll Show*	$6		Island 1217
4/10/76	81	5		2 **Arms Of Mary** ... *Love On The Moon*	$5		Columbia 10284

SUTTON, Glenn — C&W '79

Born Royce Glenn Sutton on 9/28/37 in Hodge, Louisiana; raised in Henderson, Texas. Country singer/songwriter. Formerly married to **Lynn Anderson**.

DEBUT	PEAK	WKS	Gold	A-side (Chart Hit)...B-side	$	Sym	Label & Number
1/6/79	46	5		**The Football Card** ... *The Ballad Of The Blue Cyclone* [N]	$5		Mercury 55052

SUZY AND THE RED STRIPES — see McCARTNEY, Paul

SVALA — '01

Born Svala Björgvinsdottir in Iceland. Female pop singer.

DEBUT	PEAK	WKS	Gold	A-side (Chart Hit)...B-side	$	Sym	Label & Number
8/4/01	39[S]	11		**The Real Me** ... *(conversation w/Svala) / (2 album snippets)*	$5	★	Skifan/Priority 38762

SWALLOWS, The — R&B '58

R&B group from Baltimore, Maryland: **Bobby Hendricks** (lead singer), Eddie Rich, Leon Bailey, Henry Jackson, Oliver Lewis and Robert Pittman.

DEBUT	PEAK	WKS	Gold	A-side (Chart Hit)...B-side	$	Sym	Label & Number
9/22/58	100	1		**Itchy Twitchy Feeling** ...H:100 *Who Knows, Do You*	$75		Federal 12333
				also see **Bobby Hendricks**' solo version			

DEBUT	PEAK	WKS	Gold	A-side (Chart Hit)..........B-side	$	Sym	Label & Number
				SWAN, Billy C&W/LP '74			
				Born on 5/12/42 in Cape Girardeau, Missouri. Pop-country singer/songwriter/keyboardist/guitarist. Wrote "Lover Please" for **Clyde McPhatter**. Produced **Tony Joe White**'s first three albums. Toured with **Kris Kristofferson** from the early 1970s. Formed band Black Tie with **Randy Meisner** in 1986.			
9/28/74	1[2]	18	●	1 **I Can Help**..........CW[2] *Ways Of A Woman In Love*	$6		Monument 8621
3/15/75	53	4		2 **I'm Her Fool**..........*I'd Like To Work For You*	$6		Monument 8641
11/1/75	91	5		3 **Everything's The Same (Ain't Nothing Changed)**..........*Overnite Thing (Usually)*	$6		Monument 8661
				SWANN, Bettye R&B/BUB '67			
				Born Betty Champion on 10/24/44 in Shreveport, Louisiana. R&B singer.			
5/13/67	21	14		1 **Make Me Yours** RB[2] *I Will Not Cry*	$12		Money 126
9/23/67	67	5		2 **Fall In Love With Me**..........*Lonely Love*	$12		Money 129
3/8/69	38	10		3 **Don't Touch Me**..........*(My Heart Is) Closed For The Season*	$8	■	Capitol 2382
5/27/72	63	9		4 **Victim Of A Foolish Heart**..........*Cold Day (In Hell)*	$6		Atlantic 2869
1/27/73	46	7		5 **Today I Started Loving You Again**..........*I'd Rather Go Blind*	$6		Atlantic 2921
				co-written by **Merle Haggard** in 1968 (B-side of his #1 Country hit "The Legend Of Bonnie And Clyde")			
				SWANS, The '64			
				"Girl group." Backing vocalists for **The Sapphires**.			
2/29/64	85	4		**The Boy With The Beatle Hair**..........*Please Hurry Home* [N]	$40		Cameo 302
				SWAY & KING TECH LP '99			
				Male rap duo from San Francisco, California: rapper Sway and DJ King Tech.			
6/26/99	75[S]	1		**The Anthem**..........*(3 versions) / Underground Tactics* (**Heltah Skeltah**)	$7	★	Interscope 97054
				SWAY & KING TECH Featuring DJ Revolution			
				SWAYZE, Patrick '88			
				Born on 8/18/52 in Houston, Texas. Movie actor. Starred in *Red Dawn*, *Dirty Dancing*, *Road House*, *Ghost* and many others.			
12/19/87+	3	21		**She's Like The Wind**..........AC[2] S:2 / A:2 *Stay* (**Maurice Williams & The Zodiacs**)	$3	■	RCA 5363
				PATRICK SWAYZE (featuring Wendy Fraser)			
				from the movie *Dirty Dancing* starring Swayze and Jennifer Grey			
	★228★			**SWEAT, Keith** R&B/BUB/LP '96			
				Born on 7/22/61 in Harlem, New York. R&B singer/songwriter. Worked as a brokerage assistant on Wall Street. Also see **LSG**.			
				1)Twisted 2)Nobody 3)I Want Her			
1/16/88	5	20	●	1 **I Want Her**..........RB[3] S:5 / A:5 *(Part 2)*	$3	■	Vintertainment 69431
5/14/88	79	5		2 **Something Just Ain't Right**..........*(short version)*	$3		Vintertainment 69411
7/23/88	59	11		3 **Make It Last Forever**..........*(vocal beat version)*	$3		Vintertainment 69386
				KEITH SWEAT (with Jacci McGhee)			
1/13/90	71	7		4 **All Nite**..........*(acappella version)*	$3	▮[V]	Vintertainment 69260
				ENTOUCH (Featuring Keith Sweat)			
6/2/90	14	21	●	5 **Make You Sweat**..........RB[1] S:10 / A:14 *(The Love Pass version)*	$3	▮[V]	Vintertainment 64961
12/1/90+	7	20		6 **I'll Give All My Love To You**..........RB[1] S:4 / A:12 *I Want Her (remix)*	$3	▮[V]	Vintertainment 64915
				"45": Elektra Spun Gold 65923; B-side: "Why Me Baby? (Part 2)"			
6/15/91	71	9		7 **Your Love - Part 2**..........A:65 *Tell Me It's Me You Want*	$3	▮[V]	Vintertainment 64894
11/30/91+	17	20		8 **Keep It Comin'**..........RB[2] A:15 / S:45 *(smooth mix)*	$3	▮	Elektra 64812
				co-written by the members of **Joe Public**			
4/11/92	44	17		9 **Why Me Baby?**..........S:19 / A:45 *I Knew That You Were Cheatin*	$3	▮	Elektra 64777
3/26/94	48	20		10 **How Do You Like It?**..........S:27 / A:62 *(remix)*	$3	▮	Elektra 64555
				Lisa "Left Eye" Lopes (of **TLC**; rap)			
8/6/94	85	4		11 **When I Give My Love**..........S:57 *I'm Going For Mine*	$3	▮	Elektra 64525
10/15/94	62	16		12 **Get Up On It**..........S:27 *How Deep Is Your Love*	$3	▮	Elektra 64506
6/22/96	2[1]	38	▲	13 **Twisted** RB[3] S:2 / A:7 *(3 album snippets)*	$3	▮[V]	Elektra 64282
10/5/96	3	35	▲	14 **Nobody**..........RB[3] S:3 / A:10 *In The Mood*	$3	▮[V]	Elektra 64245
				KEITH SWEAT featuring Athena Cage			
				Kut Klose (backing vocals, above 3)			
6/14/97	68	11		15 **Come With Me**..........S:45 *Just A Touch*	$4	▮	Elektra 64175
				KEITH SWEAT Featuring Ronald Isley			
2/7/98	31	13		16 **Am I Dreaming**..........S:16 *(2 versions) / (3 album snippets)*	$4	▮	Universal 56163
				OL SKOOL [Featuring Keith Sweat and Xscape]			
10/24/98	12	15	●	17 **Come And Get With Me**..........S:4 *Yumi*	$4	★	Elektra 64080
				KEITH SWEAT Featuring Snoop Dogg			
3/13/99	16	10		18 **I'm Not Ready**..........S:5 *(radio edit w/rap w/Strings)*	$4	★	Elektra 64062
				SWEATHOG '71			
				Rock group: Lenny Goldsmith (vocals, keyboards), Bob Morris (guitar), Dave Johnson (bass) and Barry Frost (drums).			
11/13/71	33	10		**Hallelujah**..........*Still On The Road*	$6		Columbia 45492
				SWEDEN HEAVEN AND HELL Soundtrack — see UMILIANI, Piero			
				SWEENEY TODD '76			
				Canadian rock band founded by James McCulloch (guitar) and **Nick Gilder** (vocal), who was replaced by **Bryan Adams** in mid-1976. Gilder and Adams later scored as solo artists. Group named after the 19th century "Demon Barber of Fleet Street."			
8/21/76	90	2		1 **Roxy Roller**..........*Rue De Chance*	$8		London 240
				Nick Gilder (lead singer)			
9/18/76	99	1		2 **Roxy Roller**..........*Rue De Chance*	$8		London 244
				Bryan Adams (lead singer)			
	★594★			**SWEET** LP '75			
				Rock and roll band formed in England: Brian Connolly (vocals; born on 10/5/44), Andy Scott (guitar, keyboards; born on 7/30/49), Steve Priest (bass; born on 2/23/50) and Mick Tucker (drums; born on 7/17/48). Connolly died of liver failure on 2/10/97 (age 52). Tucker died of leukemia on 2/14/2002 (age 53).			
10/2/71	99	2		1 **Co-Co**..........*You're Not Wrong For Loving Me*	$6		Bell 45,126
1/20/73	3	23	●	2 **Little Willy** *Man From Mecca*	$6		Bell 45,251
6/16/73	73	7		3 **Blockbuster**..........*Need A Lot Of Lovin'*	$6		Bell 45,361

DEBUT	PEAK	WKS	Gold	A-side (Chart Hit)...B-side	$	Sym	Label & Number
				SWEET — Cont'd			
6/14/75	**5**	25		4 **Ballroom Blitz**...*Restless*	$5		Capitol 4055
11/15/75+	**5**	16	●	5 **Fox On The Run**...*Burn On The Flame*	$5		Capitol 4157
2/14/76	**20**	14		6 **Action**...*Medussa*	$5		Capitol 4220
8/13/77	**88**	5		7 **Funk It Up (David's Song)**...*Stairway To The Stars*	$5		Capitol 4454
2/18/78	**8**	25		8 **Love Is Like Oxygen**...*Cover Girl*	$5		Capitol 4549
8/12/78	**76**	4		9 **California Nights**...*Dream On*	$5		Capitol 4610
				SWEET, Matthew ROK/BUB/LP **'95**			
				Born on 10/6/64 in Lincoln, Nebraska. Pop-rock bassist/drummer/singer. Toured as guitarist with Lloyd Cole.			
5/27/95	**58**	20		**Sick Of Myself**...A:52 *Never Said Goodbye*	$4	▮	Zoo 14221
				SWEET, Rachel BUB/C&W/LP **'81**			
				Born on 7/28/62 in Akron, Ohio. Pop singer/actress.			
6/27/81	**32**	13		1 **Everlasting Love**...*Still Thinking Of You* (Smith) / *Billy And The Gun* (Sweet) **REX SMITH/RACHEL SWEET**	$4	■	Columbia 02169
2/5/83	**72**	5		2 **Voo Doo**...*American Girl*	$4		Columbia 03411
				SWEETBOX **'98**			
				Dance duo: German producer Geo and Maryland-born singer Tina Harris.			
10/10/98	**46**	8		**Everything's Gonna Be Alright**...A:58 *(3 versions)* featuring the German Symphony Orchestra at Babelsberg; melody is from Johann Sebastian Bach's "Air on the G String"	$6	T	RCA 65596
				SWEET DREAMS **'74**			
				Soul-reggae duo from England: **Polly Brown** and Tony Jackson. Brown was lead singer of **Pickettywitch**.			
8/31/74	**68**	7		**Honey Honey**...*I Surrender*	$5		ABC 12008
				SWEET INSPIRATIONS, The BUB/R&B/LP **'68**			
				R&B vocal group: **Cissy Houston**, Estelle Brown, Sylvia Shemwell and Myrna Smith. Spent nearly six years as a studio group, primarily for Atlantic. Work included backing **Aretha Franklin** and **Elvis Presley**. Houston, mother of **Whitney Houston** and aunt of **Dionne Warwick**, recorded solo in 1970. Also see **The Rascals**'s "Glory Glory."			
6/3/67	**57**	5		1 **Why (Am I Treated So Bad)**...*I Don't Want To Go On Without You*	$8		Atlantic 2410
7/22/67	**94**	2		2 **Let It Be Me**...*When Something Is Wrong With My Baby*	$8		Atlantic 2418
3/2/68	**18**	14		3 **Sweet Inspiration**...*I'm Blue*	$8		Atlantic 2476
7/6/68	**74**	4		4 **To Love Somebody**...*Where Did It Go*	$8		Atlantic 2529
8/31/68	**73**	5		5 **Unchained Melody**...*Am I Ever Gonna See My Baby Again*	$8		Atlantic 2551
				SWEET SABLE R&B **'94**			
				Born Ceybil Jeffries in Brooklyn, New York. Female R&B singer.			
5/14/94	**93**	3		**Old Times' Sake**...S:74 *(2 mixes)* from the movie *Above The Rim* starring **2Pac** and Duane Martin	$5	▮	Street Life 75380
				SWEET SENSATION LP **'75**			
				Soul group from Manchester, England: Marcel King (lead vocals), St. Clair Palmer, Vincent James and Junior Daye (backing vocals), Garry Shaughnessy (guitar), Leroy Smith (keyboards), Barry Johnson (bass) and Roy Flowers (drums).			
1/11/75	**14**	16		**Sad Sweet Dreamer**...*Surething, Yes I Do*	$6		Pye 71002
				SWEET SENSATION LP **'90**			
				Female dance trio from the Bronx, New York: Betty LeBron, and sisters Margie and Mari Fernandez. Sheila Bega replaced Mari in 1989.			
1/17/87	**64**	12		1 **Hooked On You**...*(long version)* also see #5 below	$4		Next Plateau 308
4/9/88	**57**	13		2 **Take It While It's Hot**...*(Spanish version)*	$3	■	Atco 99352
9/17/88	**58**	10		3 **Never Let You Go**...*(Spanish version)*	$3	■	Atco 99284
2/4/89	**14**	18		4 **Sincerely Yours**...S:9 / A:21 *(Spanish version)* featuring a short rap break by Romeo J.D.	$3	■	Atco 99246
6/3/89	**23**	16		5 **Hooked On You**...S:16 / A:25 *(version two)* [R] remix of #1 above; above 4 from the album *Take It While It's Hot*	$3	■	Atco 99210
3/17/90	**13**	15		6 **Love Child**...A:13 / S:16 *Child Of Love*	$3	▮V	Atco 98983
6/16/90	**❶**[1]	20		7 **If Wishes Came True**...A:2 / S:5 *LP Preview*	$3	▮V	Atco 98953
10/20/90	**59**	7		8 **Each And Every Time**...*Heartbreak*	$3	▮	Atco 98906
1/5/91	**72**A	2		9 **One Good Man**... above 4 from the album *Love Child* on Atco 91307			album cut
				SWINGING BLUE JEANS, The BUB/LP **'64**			
				Rock and roll group from Liverpool, England: Ray Ennis (vocals, guitar), Ralph Ellis (guitar), Les Braid (bass) and Norman Kuhlke (drums).			
3/7/64	**24**	8		1 **Hippy Hippy Shake**...*Now I Must Go*	$15		Imperial 66021
5/9/64	**43**	7		2 **Good Golly Miss Molly**...*Shaking Feeling*	$15		Imperial 66030
8/1/64	**97**	2		3 **You're No Good**...*Shake, Rattle And Roll*	$15		Imperial 66049
				SWINGIN' MEDALLIONS BUB/LP **'66**			
				Rock and roll group from Greenwood, South Carolina: John McElrath (vocals), Jimbo Dores (guitar), Brent Fortson (organ; **Pieces Of Eight**), Carroll Bledsoe, Charlie Webber and Steven Caldwell (horns; **Pieces Of Eight**), Jim Perkins (bass) and Joe Morris (drums). Caldwell died of cancer on 1/28/2002 (age 54). Webber died of cancer on 1/17/2003 (age 57).			
4/23/66	**17**	13		1 **Double Shot (Of My Baby's Love)**...*Here It Comes Again* originally released on 4 Sale 6230 in 1965 ($30)	$15		Smash 2033
8/20/66	**71**	5		2 **She Drives Me Out Of My Mind**...*You Gotta Have Faith*	$12		Smash 2050
				SWING OUT SISTER AC/LP **'87**			
				Pop-dance trio formed in England: Corinne Drewery (vocals), Andy Connell and Martin Jackson. Drewery was a fashion designer. Reduced to a duo in 1989 with the departure of Jackson.			
8/15/87	**6**	23		1 **Breakout**...AC[2] S:4 / A:5 *Dirty Money*	$3	■	Mercury 888016
12/19/87+	**31**	15		2 **Twilight World**...S:23 *Another Lost Weekend*	$3	■	Mercury 888484
6/3/89	**86**	4		3 **Waiting Game**...*Coney Island Man*	$3	■	Fontana 874190
9/12/92	**45**	12		4 **Am I The Same Girl**...AC[1] A:39 / S:67 *Break Out (remix)*	$3	▮	Fontana 864170

DEBUT	PEAK	WKS	Gold	A-side (Chart Hit)....B-side	$	Sym	Label & Number

SWIRL 360 — '98

Rock duo of twin brothers from Jacksonville, Florida: Denny and Kenny Scott.

DEBUT	PEAK	WKS	Gold	A-side (Chart Hit)....B-side	$	Sym	Label & Number
7/25/98	47	11		**Hey Now Now** ....S:62 / A:72 *Don't Shake My World*	$4	■V	Mercury 566028
				"45": Mercury 566234; B-side: "There"			

SWITCH — R&B/LP '78

Soul-funk group from Mansfield, Ohio: Philip Ingram (vocals), brothers Bobby (keyboards) and Tommy (bass) DeBarge, Greg Williams and Eddie Fluellen (horns), and Jody Sims (drums). Discovered by **Jermaine Jackson**. The DeBarges are brothers to the family group **DeBarge**. Bobby DeBarge died of AIDS on 8/16/95 (age 36).

DEBUT	PEAK	WKS	Gold	A-side (Chart Hit)....B-side	$	Sym	Label & Number
10/7/78	36	13		1 **There'll Never Be** ....*You Pulled A Switch*	$4		Gordy 7159
7/21/79	69	8		2 **Best Beat In Town** ....*It's So Real*	$4		Gordy 7168
11/3/79+	83	15		3 **I Call Your Name** ....*Best Beat In Town*	$4		Gordy 7175

SWV (Sisters With Voices) — R&B/BUB/LP '93

★284★

Female R&B vocal trio from Brooklyn, New York: Cheryl "**Coko**" Gamble (born on 6/13/74) (see #15 below), Tamara "Taj" Johnson and Leanne "Lelee" Lyons.

1)Weak 2)Right Here/Human Nature 3)You're The One

DEBUT	PEAK	WKS	Gold	A-side (Chart Hit)....B-side	$	Sym	Label & Number
1/2/93	92	5		1 **Right Here** ....S:75 *(3 mixes)*	$4	■	RCA 62355
				also see #4 below			
2/6/93	6	27	●	2 **I'm So Into You** ....S:5 / A:6 *(2 mixes) / SWV (In The House)*	$3	■V	RCA 62451
4/24/93	1 (2)	26	▲	3 **Weak** RB[2] S:2 / A:2 *(2 mixes)*	$3	■V	RCA 62521
				"45" issued for above 2 on RCA 62585			
7/17/93	2[3]	22	●	4 **Right Here/Human Nature** / RB[7] S:4 / A:5 [R]			
				new mix of #1 above, featuring excerpts from **Michael Jackson**'s 1983 hit "Human Nature"			
7/24/93		21		5 **Downtown** A:36	$3	■V	RCA 62614
1/8/94	54	17		6 **Always On My Mind** ....S:36 / A:66 *You're Always On My Mind*	$3	■V	RCA 62738
4/9/94	18	20		7 **Anything** ....A:16 / S:19 *(album remix)*	$3	■V	RCA 62834
				samples "Get Up And Dance"; from the movie *Above The Rim* starring **2 Pac** and Duane Martin; "45" issued for above 2 on RCA 62884; all of above (original mixes) from the album *It's About Time*			
8/19/95	80	7		8 **Tonight's The Night** ....S:43 *(remix w/SWV &* **Craig Mack***)*	$3	■	Interscope 98118
				BLACKstreet (featuring SWV)			
4/20/96	5	20	●	9 **You're The One** ....RB[1] S:2 / A:15 *(2 versions)*	$3	■	RCA 64516
8/17/96	22	20		10 **Use Your Heart** ....S:15 *You're The One (remix)*	$3	■	RCA 64607
1/18/97	61	15		11 **It's All About U** ....S:36 *(instrumental)*	$3	■	RCA 64735
7/26/97	19	20	●	12 **Someone** ....S:10 *Love Like This*	$3	■	RCA 64926
				SWV (Featuring Puff Daddy)			
				samples "Ten Crack Commandments" and "The World Is Filled" by **The Notorious B.I.G.**			
8/2/97	75	15		13 **Can We** ....A:28 *(5 versions)*	$6	T	Jive 42445
				Missy "Misdemeanor" Elliott (rap); from the movie *Booty Call* starring Jamie Foxx			
3/28/98	25	14		14 **Rain** ....S:16 / A:56 *Lose Myself*	$3	■	RCA 65402
7/24/99	70	12		15 **Sunshine** ....A:62 *(3 versions)*	$6	T	RCA 65751
				COKO			

SYBIL — R&B/LP '89

Born Sybil Lynch in Paterson, New Jersey. R&B singer/songwriter.

DEBUT	PEAK	WKS	Gold	A-side (Chart Hit)....B-side	$	Sym	Label & Number
9/23/89	20	23	●	1 **Don't Make Me Over** ....S:23 / A:24 *Falling In Love*	$4	■V	Next Plateau 325
1/27/90	74	6		2 **Walk On By** ....*(radio version) / Here Comes My Love*	$6	■*V	Next Plateau 50111
				"45" issued for above 2 on Next Plateau 327 (same number issued for "Walk On By" with "Here Comes My Love" on the B-side)			
4/17/93	90	2		3 **You're The Love Of My Life** / A:62			
4/17/93		2		4 **The Love I Lost**	$4	■	Next Plateau 857064

SYLK-E. FYNE — R&B/LP '98

Born in Los Angeles, California. Female rapper.

DEBUT	PEAK	WKS	Gold	A-side (Chart Hit)....B-side	$	Sym	Label & Number
2/14/98	6	20	●	**Romeo And Juliet** ....S:4 / A:42 *(instrumental)*	$3	■	RCA 64973
				SYLK-E. FYNE Featuring Chill			
				samples "You Don't Have To Cry" by **René & Angela**			

SYLVERS, The — R&B/LP '76

Family group of 9 brothers and sisters from Memphis, Tennessee: Olympia-Ann, Leon, Charmaine, James, Edmund, Ricky, Angelia, Pat and **Foster Sylvers** (born on 2/25/62) (see #3 & 5 below). Leon formed the group **Dynasty** in 1979.

1)Boogie Fever 2)Hot Line 3)High School Dance

DEBUT	PEAK	WKS	Gold	A-side (Chart Hit)....B-side	$	Sym	Label & Number
9/2/72	94	3		1 **Fool's Paradise** ....*I'm Truly Happy*	$6		Pride 1001
2/3/73	77	10		2 **Wish That I Could Talk To You** ....*How Love Hurts*	$6		Pride 1019
				above 2 produced by **Jerry Butler**			
6/2/73	22	13		3 **Misdemeanor** *[FOSTER SYLVERS]* ....*So Close*	$6		MGM 14580
				first released on Pride 1031 in 1973 ($6)			
8/18/73	89	3		4 **Stay Away From Me** ....*I'll Never Be Ashamed*	$6	■	Pride 1029
10/6/73	92	5		5 **Hey, Little Girl** *[FOSTER SYLVERS]* ....*I'll Get You In The End*	$6		MGM 14630
2/14/76	1 (1)	21	●	6 **Boogie Fever** RB[1] *Free Style*	$5		Capitol 4179
6/26/76	59	7		7 **Cotton Candy** ....*I Can Be For Real*	$5		Capitol 4255
10/9/76+	5	24	●	8 **Hot Line** ....*That's What Love Is Made Of*	$5		Capitol 4336
4/23/77	17	17		9 **High School Dance** ....*Lovin' You Is Like Lovin' The Wind*	$5		Capitol 4405
11/26/77	72	9		10 **Any Way You Want Me** ....*Lovin' Me Back*	$5		Capitol 4493

SYLVESTER — R&B/LP '78

Born Sylvester James on 9/6/47 in Los Angeles, California. Died of AIDS on 12/16/88 (age 41). Male disco singer/songwriter. To San Francisco in 1967. With vocal group the Cockettes. In movie *The Rose*. Backing vocals by **Martha Wash** and Izora Rhodes (later known as Two Tons O' Fun and **The Weather Girls**), and Jeanie Tracy.

DEBUT	PEAK	WKS	Gold	A-side (Chart Hit)....B-side	$	Sym	Label & Number
8/19/78	19	18		1 **Dance (Disco Heat)** ....*Was It Something That I Said*	$5		Fantasy 827
1/13/79	36	10		2 **You Make Me Feel (Mighty Real)** ....*Grateful*	$5	□	Fantasy 846
				promo record issued on pink vinyl with a pink picture sleeve stating "The Roxy December 22, 1978" and with an insert; above 2 released together on a 12" single (Fantasy 102 - #1 Dance Club Play hit for 6 weeks)			
4/7/79	40	7		3 **I (Who Have Nothing)** ....*I Need Somebody To Love Tonight*	$5		Fantasy 855
				all of above produced by **Harvey Fuqua** (of **The Moonglows**)			

DEBUT	PEAK	WKS	Gold	A-side (Chart Hit)..........B-side	$	Sym	Label & Number
				SYLVIA R&B/BUB/LP **'73**			
				Born Sylvia Vanderpool on 5/29/36 in Harlem, New York. R&B-disco singer/songwriter/producer. First recorded with Hot Lips Page for Columbia in 1950 as Little Sylvia. Half of **Mickey & Sylvia** duo. Married Joe Robinson, owner of All-Platinum/Vibration Records (later known as Sugar Hill). Their son Joey was leader of **West Street Mob**.			
3/24/73	3	21	●	1 **Pillow Talk** ....RB[2] *My Thing*	$6		Vibration 521
7/21/73	70	5		2 **Didn't I** ....*Had Any Lately*	$5		Vibration 524
9/8/73	99	2		3 **Soul Je T'Aime** ....*Sunday* (Sylvia) **SYLVIA AND RALFI PAGAN** disco version of "Je T'Aime...Moi Non Plus" by **Jane Birkin & Serge Gainsbourg**	$5		Vibration 525
6/8/74	80	4		4 **Sho Nuff Boogie (Part I)** ....*(Part II)* **SYLVIA & THE MOMENTS**	$5		All Platinum 2350
				SYLVIA C&W/AC/LP **'82**			
				Born Sylvia Kirby on 12/9/56 in Kokomo, Indiana. Country singer/songwriter.			
8/28/82	15	20	●	**Nobody** ....CW[1] *I'll Make It Right With You*	$4		RCA 13223
				SYMONÉ, Raven — see RAVEN-SYMONÉ			
				SYMS, Sylvia AC **'56**			
				Born on 12/2/17 in Brooklyn, New York. Died of a heart attack on 5/10/92 (age 74). SInger/actress. Dubbed the "world's greatest saloon singer" by **Frank Sinatra**. Discovered by actress Mae West in 1948. Star of several musical comedies.			
5/12/56	20	14		1 **I Could Have Danced All Night** ....A:20 / T:35 *The World In My Corner* from the Broadway musical *My Fair Lady* starring **Julie Andrews** and Rex Harrison	$12		Decca 29903
8/11/56	21	8		2 **English Muffins And Irish Stew** ....A:21 / T:51 *Walk Sweet*	$12		Decca 29969
12/22/56+	68	8		3 **Dancing Chandelier** ....T:68 *Each Day* **Jack Pleis** (orch., all of above)	$12		Decca 30143
				SYNCH **'89**			
				Pop-rock group from Wilkes-Barre, Pennsylvania: Jimmy Harnen (vocals), brothers Bill (keyboards) and Rich (drums) Kossuth, Jon Lorance (guitar), Chuck Yarmey (keyboards) and Mike Warner (bass).			
3/1/86	77	12		1 **Where Are You Now?** ....*Only For The Night* originally released on Micki 001 (B-side: "End The Game"; $15)	$4		Columbia 05788
2/25/89	10	24		2 **Where Are You Now?** *[JIMMY HARNEN W/SYNCH]* ...S:9 / A:12 *Only For The Night* [R] above 2 are the same version	$3		WTG 68625
				SYNDICATE OF SOUND LP **'66**			
				Garage-rock band from San Jose, California: Don Baskin (vocals), Jim Sawyers and John Sharkey (guitars), Bob Gonzalez (bass) and John Duckworth (drums).			
6/4/66	8	10		1 **Little Girl** ....*You* first released on Hush 228 in 1966 ($50)	$20		Bell 640
8/20/66	55	7		2 **Rumors** ....*The Upper Hand*	$15		Bell 646
3/28/70	73	5		3 **Brown Paper Bag** ....*Reverb Beat*	$10		Buddah 156
				SYREETA — see PRESTON, Billy			
				SYSTEM, The R&B/BUB/LP **'87**			
				Techno-funk-dance duo based in New York: Mic Murphy (vocals, guitar; born in Raleigh, North Carolina) and David Frank (synthesizer; born in Dayton, Ohio).			
3/5/83	64	8		1 **You Are In My System** ....*Now I Am Electric*	$4		Mirage 99937
4/11/87	4	21		2 **Don't Disturb This Groove** ....RB[1] S:4 / A:4 *Modern Girl*	$3	■	Atlantic 89320
7/9/88	91	5		3 **Coming To America (Part One)** ....*(Part Two)* from the movie *Coming To America* starring **Eddie Murphy**	$3	■	Atco 99320
				SYSTEM OF A DOWN ROK/LP **'02**			
				Alternative-metal rock group from Los Angeles, California: Serj Tankian (vocals), Daron Malakian (guitar), Shavo Odadjian (bass) and John Dulmayan (drums).			
1/5/02	76	20		1 **Chop Suey** A:71			album cut
5/4/02	70	13		2 **Toxicity** A:68			album cut
8/17/02	55	20		3 **Aerials** ....AR[1] / MR[3] A:53 all of above from the album *Toxicity* on American/Columbia 62240			album cut

T

DEBUT	PEAK	WKS	Gold	A-side (Chart Hit)..........B-side	$	Sym	Label & Number
				TACO LP **'83**			
				Born Taco Ockerse in 1955 in Jaharta, Indonesia (to Dutch parents). German-based techno-pop singer.			
6/25/83	4	21	●	**Puttin' On The Ritz** ....*Livin' In My Dream World* written in 1929 by Irving Berlin; #1 hit for Harry Richman in 1930	$4		RCA 13574
				TAG **'92**			
				Pop duo from Penzance, England: Treana Morris (lead singer) and Gareth Young. Tag is an acronym of Treana And Gareth.			
7/4/92	63	8		**The Way I Feel** ....A:68 *Keep On Moving*	$4	▮	Scotti Brothers 75315
				TAG TEAM R&B/LP **'93**			
				Hip-hop duo from Atlanta, Georgia: Cecil Glenn ("DC, The Brain Supreme") and Steve Gibson ("Steve Roll'n"). High school classmates in Denver, Colorado.			
5/29/93	2[7]	45	▲[4]	1 **Whoomp! (There It Is)** ....RB[1] S:❶[16] / A:9 *(instrumental)* samples **Kano**'s "I'm Ready"; also see #3 below	$3	▮	Life 79500
1/1/94	84	3		2 **Addams Family (Whoomp!)** ....S:53 *(TV mix)* samples "Addams Family Theme" from the TV series; from the movie *Addams Family Values* starring Raul Julia	$4	▮	Atlas 855138
1/14/95	97	1		3 **Whoomp! (There It Went)** ....S:69 *(instrumental)* [N] **TAG TEAM, MICKEY, MINNIE, and GOOFY** parody of #1 above	$4	▮	Life 79525
				TAKE 5 **'00**			
				White "boy band" from Orlando, Florida: brothers Clay and Ryan Goodell, TJ Christofore, Tilky Jones and Stevie Sculthorpe.			
7/15/00	19[S]	14		**Shake It Off** ....*(instrumental)*	$4	★	Trans Continental 70522

DEBUT	PEAK	WKS	Gold	A-side (Chart Hit)..........B-side	$	Sym	Label & Number
				TAKE THAT AC/BUB/LP **'95**			
				"Boy band" from England: **Gary Barlow** (lead; born on 1/20/71) (see #2 below), Howard Donald, Jason Orange, Mark Owen and **Robbie Williams** (left in early 1995). Disbanded in February 1996.			
8/12/95	7	30		1 **Back For Good**..........S:9 / A:12 *Love Ain't Here Anymore* live version is on the B-side of #2 below	$3	▮V	Arista 12848
10/18/97	44	20		2 **So Help Me Girl**..........S:46 / A:58 *Back For Good (live)* **GARY BARLOW**	$3	▮	Arista 13428
				TALENT **'01**			
				R&B vocal trio from Kansas City, Missouri. Member Ernest Dixon wrote **Joe**'s hit "Stutter."			
3/3/01	72S	1		**Celebrity**..........*(4 album snippets)* written, produced and arranged by **R. Kelly**	$6	★	Rock Land 497429
				TALKING HEADS ROK/BUB/LP **'83**			
				New-wave/rock group formed in New York: David Byrne (vocals, guitar), Jerry Harrison (keyboards, guitar), Tina Weymouth (bass) and Chris Frantz (drums). Formed as a trio of Byrne, Weymouth and Frantz at the Rhode Island School of Design in 1974. Harrison, earlier of The Modern Lovers, joined in 1977; Weymouth and Frantz married on 6/18/77. Weymouth and Frantz also formed **Tom Tom Club** (see #4 below). Much production work of other artists by each member. Disbanded in late 1991. Harrison, Weymouth and Frantz reunited in 1996. Group inducted into the Rock and Roll Hall of Fame in 2002.			
2/18/78	92	5		1 **Psycho Killer**..........*(acoustic version)*	$8	■	Sire 1013
11/4/78+	26	17		2 **Take Me To The River**..........*Thank You For Sending Me An Angel*	$5	■	Sire 1032
11/3/79	80	5		3 **Life During Wartime (This Ain't No Party...This Ain't No Disco... This Ain't No Foolin' Around)**..........*Electric Guitar*	$5		Sire 49075
1/23/82	31	17		4 **Genius Of Love**..........*Lorelei* [I] **TOM TOM CLUB** lyrics mention funk masters Bootsy Collins, **Hamilton Bohannon**, **Kurtis Blow** and **James Brown**	$5		Sire 49882
7/30/83	9	20		5 **Burning Down The House** *I Get Wild/Wild Gravity*	$4	■	Sire 29565
11/26/83	62	8		6 **This Must Be The Place (Naive Melody)**..........*Moon Rocks*	$4	■	Sire 29451
9/7/85	54	20		7 **And She Was**..........*(dub version)*	$4	■	Sire 28917
4/19/86	91	4		8 **Once In A Lifetime**..........*This Must Be The Place (Naive Melody) (live)* [L] from the concert movie *Stop Making Sense*; studio version "Bubbled Under" (#103) on 2/7/81 on Sire 49649; featured in the movie *Down And Out In Beverly Hills* starring Nick Nolte	$4	■	Sire 29163
9/6/86	25	21		9 **Wild Wild Life**..........S:23 / A:25 *People Like Us*	$3	■	Sire 28629
				TALK TALK LP **'84**			
				Techno-rock/dance group from England: Mark Hollis (vocals), Simon Brenner (keyboards), Paul Webb (bass) and Lee Harris (drums). Brenner left in 1983.			
10/16/82	75	7		1 **Talk Talk**..........*Mirror Man*	$4		EMI America 8136
3/24/84	31	14		2 **It's My Life**..........*Again, A Game...Again*	$4	■	EMI America 8195
6/30/84	89	3		3 **Such A Shame**..........*Call In The Night Boy*	$4		EMI America 8215
2/1/86	90	4		4 **Life's What You Make It**..........*It's Getting Late In The Evening*	$4	■	EMI America 8303
				TAMAR LP **'00**			
				Born Tamar (pronounced tay-mar) Braxton in Severn, Maryland. Female R&B singer. Sister of **Toni Braxton**.			
10/23/99	52S	9		1 **Get None**..........*(2 versions) / Don't Cry* **TAMAR featuring J.D. & Amil**	$4	★	DreamWorks 59025
3/25/00	89	6		2 **If You Don't Wanna Love Me**..........S:15 *(instrumental) / Can't Nobody*	$4	★	DreamWorks 59040
				TA MARA & THE SEEN R&B/LP **'85**			
				Dance group from Minneapolis, Minnesota: Margaret "Ta Mara" Cox (vocals), Oliver Leiber (guitar), Gina Fellicetta (keyboards), Keith Woodson (bass) and Jamie Chez (drums). Leiber is the son of songwriter Jerry Leiber (of Leiber & Stoller).			
10/12/85+	24	21		**Everybody Dance**..........A:22 / S:26 *Lonely Heart*	$3	■	A&M 2768
				TAMIA R&B/LP **'01**			
				Born Tamia Washington on 5/9/75 in Windsor, Ontario, Canada. Female R&B singer.			
12/30/95	98	4		1 **You Put A Move On My Heart**..........S:72 *The Secret Garden (instrumental)* **QUINCY JONES introducing TAMIA**	$3	▮V	Qwest 17751
4/20/96	68	9		2 **Slow Jams**..........S:43 *(remix)* **QUINCY JONES Featuring Babyface and Tamia with Portrait and Barry White**	$3	▮V	Qwest 17673
8/24/96	25	20		3 **Missing You**..........S:15 *(acappella version) / So Right, For Life* (Michael Speaks) **BRANDY, TAMIA, GLADYS KNIGHT & CHAKA KHAN** from the movie *Set It Off* starring Jada Pinkett and **Queen Latifah**	$3	▮V	EastWest 64262
3/21/98	37	20		4 **Imagination**..........S:33 / A:66 *(remix)* **Jermaine Dupri** (rap); samples "I Want You Back" by **The Jackson 5**	$3	▮V	Qwest 17253
7/18/98	30	20		5 **So Into You**..........S:20 *(4 album snippets)* **Mario Winans** (backing vocal); samples "Say Yeah" by **The Commodores**; "45" issued for above 2 on Qwest 17194	$3	▮V	Qwest 17194
7/3/99	21	22	●	6 **Spend My Life With You**..........RB² S:11 / A:34 *Georgy Porgy* (w/**Faith Evans**) **ERIC BENÉT featuring Tamia**	$4	★V	Warner 16958
9/16/00	84	5		7 **Can't Go For That**..........S:13 *Tell Me Who* (R&B #63) contains an interpolation of "I Can't Go For That (No Can Do)" by **Daryl Hall & John Oates**	$5	★+	Elektra 67083
1/13/01	10	21		8 **Stranger In My House** S:4 / A:29 *Un'h...To You*	$4	★	Elektra 67151
				TAMI SHOW **'91**			
				Pop group formed in Chicago, Illinois: sisters Cathy and Claire Massey (vocals), Tommy Gawenda (guitar), George McCrae (keyboards), Mark Jiaras (bass) and Ken Harck (drums). The *T.A.M.I. Show* is a 1964 movie of a superstar concert in Santa Monica, California.			
3/12/88	88	4		1 **She's Only 20**..........*Don't Say No*	$3	■	Chrysalis 43146
8/3/91	28	13		2 **The Truth**..........*(3 album snippets)*	$3	▮	RCA 2694
				TAMS, The BUB **'64**			
				R&B "beach music" group from Atlanta, Georgia: brothers Charles and Joseph (lead singer) Pope, with Robert Smith, Floyd Ashton and Horace Key. First recorded for Swan in 1960. Joseph Pope died on 3/16/96 (age 63).			
10/20/62	60	7		1 **Untie Me**..........*Disillusioned*	$20		Arlen 11
12/14/63+	9	14		2 **What Kind Of Fool (Do You Think I Am)** *Laugh It Off*	$15		ABC-Paramount 10502
3/21/64	70	5		3 **You Lied To Your Daddy** /			
4/4/64	79	3		4 **It's All Right (You're Just In Love)**..........	$15		ABC-Paramount 10533

DEBUT	PEAK	WKS	Gold	A-side (Chart Hit)..........B-side	$	Sym	Label & Number
				TAMS, The — Cont'd			
7/18/64	41	8		5 **Hey Girl Don't Bother Me** .... *Take Away* reissued in 1971 on Dunhill 4290 with a promo picture sleeve	$15		ABC-Paramount 10573
11/28/64	87	1		6 **Silly Little Girl** .... *Weep Little Girl* #1 & 6: written by **Joe South**	$15		ABC-Paramount 10601
6/22/68	61	6		7 **Be Young, Be Foolish, Be Happy** .... *That Same Old Song*	$12		ABC 11066
				TANEGA, Norma BUB '66 Born on 1/30/39 in Vallejo, California. White pop-folk singer/songwriter/pianist/guitarist.			
2/26/66	22	9		**Walkin' My Cat Named Dog** .... *I'm The Sky*	$12		New Voice 807
				TANGIER '89 Hard-rock group from Philadelphia, Pennsylvania: Bill Mattson (vocals), Doug Gordon and Gari Saint (guitars), Garry Nutt (bass) and Bobby Bender (drums).			
8/12/89	67	7		**On The Line** .... *Sweet Surrender*	$4	■	Atco 99208
				TANK R&B/BUB/LP '01 Born Durrell Babbs in Milwaukee, Wisconsin. Male R&B singer/songwriter.			
3/17/01	38	20		**Maybe I Deserve** .... A:31 from the album *Force Of Nature* on Blackground 50404			album cut
				TANNER, Gary '78 Pop singer/songwriter.			
5/27/78	69	5		**Over The Rainbow** .... *Piece Of Yesterday* #1 hit for Glenn Miller in 1939 (from the movie *The Wizard Of Oz* starring Judy Garland)	$5		20th Century 2373
				TANNER, Marc, Band LP '79 Born on 8/20/52 in Hollywood, California. Pop-rock singer/songwriter/guitarist.			
3/3/79	45	8		**Elena** .... *Lady In Blue*	$5		Elektra 46003
				TANTO METRO & DEVONTE BUB '02 Reggae duo: DJ Tanto Metro was born Mark Wolfe in Kingston, Jamaica; Devonte is a male singer from Jamaica.			
7/3/99	88	16		1 **Everyone Falls In Love** .... S:56 / BUB:115 *(3 mixes)*	$8	★*	Penthouse/VP 6278
3/23/02	85	20		2 **Give It To Her** .... *Bust It Up (Spragga Benz) / Shizzle My Nizzle (Elephant Man) / Keep It Blazin' (T.O.K.)* "45": VP 8674; B-side: "Tell Me What You Like" by Lady Saw	$7	T[V]	VP 6394
				TARNEY/SPENCER BAND, The LP '81 Pop-rock duo from Australia: Alan Tarney (vocals, guitar, keyboards) and Trevor Spencer (drums).			
7/22/78	86	6		1 **It's Really You** .... *Set The Minstrel Free*	$5		A&M 2049
5/19/79	84	6		2 **No Time To Lose** .... *Live Again*	$5		A&M 2124
9/19/81	74	4		3 **No Time To Lose** .... *Live Again* [R] same version (30 seconds shorter) as #2 above	$5		A&M 2366
				TARRIERS, The '57 Folk trio: Erik Darling (tenor, banjo), Bob Carey (bass, guitar) and future movie actor Alan Arkin (baritone, guitar). Darling replaced **Pete Seeger** in The Weavers, 1958-62, then formed **The Rooftop Singers**.			
10/13/56	9	19		1 **Cindy, Oh Cindy** .... J:9 / S:12 / T:12 / A:12 *Only If You Praise The Lord* **VINCE MARTIN With The Tarriers** adapted from a sailor's sea chantey	$25		Glory 247
12/22/56+	4	19		2 **The Banana Boat Song** .... J:4 / S:5 / T:6 / A:6 *No Hidin' Place* based on a Jamaican folk song brought to the U.S. in the late 1940s	$25		Glory 249
				TASSELS, The '59 White doo-wop group from New Jersey: John and sister Rochelle Gaudet (lead singer), Leo Joyce and Joe Intelisano.			
7/13/59	55	7		**To A Soldier Boy** .... *The Boy For Me*	$30		Madison 117
				TASTE OF HONEY, A R&B/LP '78 Disco group from Los Angeles, California: Janice Johnson (vocals, guitar), Hazel Payne (vocals, bass), Perry Kibble (keyboards) and Donald Johnson (drums). Re-formed in 1980 as a duo: Janice Johnson and Payne. Won the 1978 Best New Artist Grammy Award. Kibble died of heart failure in February 1999 (age 49).			
6/24/78	1[3]	23	▲	1 **Boogie Oogie Oogie** .... RB[1] *World Spin*	$4	■	Capitol 4565
8/11/79	79	4		2 **Do It Good** .... *I Love You*	$4		Capitol 4744
3/7/81	3	24	●	3 **Sukiyaki** .... RB[1] / AC[2] *Don't You Lead Me On*	$4	■	Capitol 4953
3/13/82	41	10		4 **I'll Try Something New** .... *Good-Bye Baby*	$4	■	Capitol 5099
				TA-TA + BRANDO '01 Hip-hop/reggae duo from Jamaica.			
8/11/01	31[S]	17		**Let's Be Friends** .... *(no B-side)* **TA-TA + BRANDO (Featuring Larry Poteat of The Donz)**	$5	★	Heartless 12726
				TATE, Grady — see BURRELL, Kenny / SMITH, Jimmy / WASHINGTON, Grover Jr.			
				TATE, Howard R&B/BUB '66 Born in 1930 in Macon, Georgia; raised in Philadelphia, Pennsylvania. R&B singer. Before going solo, sang with The **Bill Doggett** Band and The Gainors (founded by **Garnet Mimms**).			
8/20/66	63	7		1 **Ain't Nobody Home** .... *How Come My Bull Dog Don't Bark*	$10		Verve 10420
12/24/66+	67	7		2 **Look At Granny Run, Run** .... *Half A Man*	$10		Verve 10464
1/27/68	76	5		3 **Stop** .... *Shoot 'Em All Down*	$10		Verve 10573
4/4/70	100	1		4 **My Soul's Got A Hole In It** .... *It's Too Late* produced by **Lloyd Price** and **Johnny Nash**	$10		Turntable 1018
	★416★			**TAVARES** R&B/LP '75 Family R&B-disco vocal group from New Bedford, Massachusetts. Consisted of brothers Ralph (born on 12/10/48), Antone "Chubby" (born on 6/2/47), Feliciano "Butch" (born on 5/18/53), Arthur "Pooch" (born on 11/12/46) and Perry Lee "Tiny" (born on 10/24/54) Tavares. Worked as Chubby & The Turnpikes from 1964-69. Butch was married to actress/singer Lola Falana. *1)It Only Takes A Minute 2)Heaven Must Be Missing An Angel 3)Whodunit*			
9/22/73	35	12		1 **Check It Out** .... *The Judgement Day*	$5		Capitol 3674
2/2/74	70	7		2 **That's The Sound That Lonely Makes** .... *Little Girl*	$5		Capitol 3794

TAVARES — Cont'd

DEBUT	PEAK	WKS	Gold	A-side (Chart Hit)	B-side	$	Sym	Label & Number
6/1/74	59	7		3 **Too Late**	*Leave It Up To The Lady*	$5		Capitol 3882
10/5/74	50	16		4 **She's Gone**	RB[1] *To Love You*	$5		Capitol 3957
4/12/75	25	11		5 **Remember What I Told You To Forget /**				
4/12/75		6		6 **My Ship**		$5		Capitol 4010
				above 4 from the album *Hard Core Poetry*				
7/26/75	10	18		7 **It Only Takes A Minute**	RB[1] *I Hope She Chooses Me*	$5		Capitol 4111
12/6/75+	52	6		8 **Free Ride**	*In The Eyes Of Love*	$5		Capitol 4184
6/5/76	15	21	●	9 **Heaven Must Be Missing An Angel (Part 1)**	*(Part 2)*	$5		Capitol 4270
10/30/76	34	12		10 **Don't Take Away The Music**	*Guiding Star*	$5		Capitol 4348
3/26/77	22	15		11 **Whodunit**	RB[1] *Fool Of The Year*	$5		Capitol 4398
11/19/77+	32	21		12 **More Than A Woman**	*Keep In Touch*	$5		Capitol 4500
				from the movie *Saturday Night Fever* starring **John Travolta**; written by the **Bee Gees**				
1/5/80	47	10		13 **Bad Times**	*Got To Have Your Love*	$4		Capitol 4811
9/18/82	33	21		14 **A Penny For Your Thoughts**	*The Skin You're In*	$4		RCA 13292
				written and co-produced by **Kenny Nolan**				

TAYLOR, Andy — see DURAN DURAN

TAYLOR, Austin — see TAYLOR, Ted

TAYLOR, B.E., Group — ROK/BUB '84

Pop-rock group from Pittsburgh, Pennsylvania. Led by vocalist Taylor; includes former Crack The Sky members Rick Witkowski (guitar), Joe Macre (bass) and Joey D'Amico (drums), plus Nat Kerr (keyboards).

DEBUT	PEAK	WKS	Gold	A-side (Chart Hit)	B-side	$	Sym	Label & Number
1/28/84	66	8		1 **Vitamin L**	*Lonely At The Bottom*	$4		MCA/Sweet City 52311
5/31/86	94	2		2 **Karen**	*Take Me To Your Heart*	$3	■	Epic 05851

TAYLOR, Bobby, & The Vancouvers — R&B '68

Interracial R&B group based in Vancouver, British Columbia, Canada: Bobby Taylor (vocals), Thomas Chong (**Cheech & Chong**) and Edward Patterson (guitars), Robbie King (keyboards), Wes Henderson (bass) and Ted Lewis (drums). **Jimi Hendrix** played guitar for the group in 1963. Bobby Taylor discovered **The Jackson 5**.

DEBUT	PEAK	WKS	Gold	A-side (Chart Hit)	B-side	$	Sym	Label & Number
4/20/68	29	10		1 **Does Your Mama Know About Me**	*Fading Away*	$20	■	Gordy 7069
8/10/68	85	3		2 **I Am Your Man**	*If You Love Her*	$20		Gordy 7073
12/7/68+	48	7		3 **Malinda**	*It's Growing*	$20		Gordy 7079

TAYLOR, Debbie — R&B '69

R&B singer.

DEBUT	PEAK	WKS	Gold	A-side (Chart Hit)	B-side	$	Sym	Label & Number
4/26/69	86	6		1 **Never Gonna Let Him Know**	*Let's Prove Them Wrong*	$12		GWP 501
1/24/76	100	1		2 **I Don't Wanna Leave You**	*Just Don't Pay*	$6		Arista 0144

TAYLOR, Felice — '67

Born on 1/29/48 in Richmond, California. Female R&B singer.

DEBUT	PEAK	WKS	Gold	A-side (Chart Hit)	B-side	$	Sym	Label & Number
1/14/67	42	6		**It May Be Winter Outside (But In My Heart It's Spring)**	*Winter Again*	$15		Mustang 3024
				written and produced by **Barry White**				

TAYLOR, Gloria — R&B '69

R&B singer/songwriter.

DEBUT	PEAK	WKS	Gold	A-side (Chart Hit)	B-side	$	Sym	Label & Number
11/8/69	49	9		**You Got To Pay The Price**	*Loving You And Being Loved By You*	$10		Silver Fox 14
				first released on Glow-Wiz 1 in 1969; instrumental track is the same as **Al Kent**'s 1967 hit "You've Got To Pay The Price"				

TAYLOR, James ★171★ — AC/BUB/C&W/ROK/LP '71

Born on 3/12/48 in Boston, Massachusetts. Soft-rock singer/songwriter/guitarist. With older brother Alex in the Fabulous Corsairs in 1964. In New York group The Flying Machine in 1967, with friend Danny Kortchmar. Moved to England in 1968, recorded for Peter Asher. Married to **Carly Simon** from 1972-83. In movie *Two Lane Blacktop* with Dennis Wilson in 1973. Sister **Kate Taylor** and brothers Alex (died on 3/12/93) and **Livingston Taylor** also recorded. Their father, Isaac, was the dean of the University of North Carolina medical school until 1971. Recipient of *Billboard*'s Century Award in 1998. Inducted into the Rock and Roll Hall of Fame in 2000. Also see **Carly Simon**'s "Waterfall" and "You Belong To Me."

1)You've Got A Friend 2)Fire And Rain 3)Handy Man 4)How Sweet It Is (To Be Loved By You) 5)Mockingbird

DEBUT	PEAK	WKS	Gold	A-side (Chart Hit)	B-side	$	Sym	Label & Number
9/12/70	3	16		1 **Fire And Rain**	*Anywhere Like Heaven*	$8		Warner 7423
11/14/70	67	7		2 **Carolina In My Mind**	*Something's Wrong*	$10		Apple 1805
				originally "Bubbled Under" (#118) on 4/12/69; also issued with "Taking It In" as the B-side ($300)				
2/6/71	37	8		3 **Country Road**	*Sunny Skies*	$6		Warner 7460
6/5/71	1[1]	14	●	4 **You've Got A Friend**	AC[1] *You Can Close Your Eyes*	$6		Warner 7498
10/2/71	31	8		5 **Long Ago And Far Away**	*Let Me Ride*	$6		Warner 7521
				Joni Mitchell (backing vocal, above 2); **Carole King** (piano: #1, 3 & 5)				
12/2/72+	14	11		6 **Don't Let Me Be Lonely Tonight**	*Woh, Don't You Know*	$6		Warner 7655
3/3/73	67	4		7 **One Man Parade**	*Nobody But You*	$6		Warner 7682
2/2/74	5	16	●	8 **Mockingbird**	*Grownup* (Simon)	$6		Elektra 45880
				CARLY SIMON & JAMES TAYLOR				
				adapted from the same traditional folk lyrics as was the song "Bo Diddley"				
6/21/75	5	15		9 **How Sweet It Is (To Be Loved By You)**	AC[1] *Sarah Maria*	$5		Warner 8109
				David Sanborn (sax)				
10/4/75	49	8		10 **Mexico**	*Gorilla*	$5		Warner 8137
				David Crosby and **Graham Nash** (backing vocals)				
7/4/76	22	16		11 **Shower The People**	AC[1] *I Can Dream Of You*	$5		Warner 8222
				Carly Simon (harmony vocal: #9 & 11)				
6/18/77	4	20		12 **Handy Man**	AC[1] *Bartender's Blues* (C&W #88)	$5		Columbia 10557
10/1/77	20	17		13 **Your Smiling Face**	*If I Keep My Heart Out Of Sight*	$5		Columbia 10602
1/21/78	17	14		14 **(What A) Wonderful World**	AC[5] *Wooden Planes* (Garfunkel)	$5		Columbia 10676
				ART GARFUNKEL with JAMES TAYLOR & PAUL SIMON				
2/25/78	61	6		15 **Honey Don't Leave L.A.**	*Another Grey Morning*	$5		Columbia 10689
8/19/78	36	9		16 **Devoted To You**	*Boys In The Trees* (Simon)	$5		Elektra 45506
				CARLY SIMON and JAMES TAYLOR				

DEBUT	PEAK	WKS	Gold	A-side (Chart Hit)...B-side	$	Sym	Label & Number
				TAYLOR, James — Cont'd			
6/2/79	28	11		17 **Up On The Roof** ... *Chanson Francaise*	$5		Columbia 11005
3/14/81	11	14		18 **Her Town Too** ... *Believe It Or Not* (Taylor) **JAMES TAYLOR AND J.D. SOUTHER**	$4		Columbia 60514
6/13/81	72	5		19 **Hard Times** ... *Summer's Here* (AC #25)	$4	■	Columbia 02093
11/9/85	61	11		20 **Everyday** ... *Limousine Driver* original version is by **Buddy Holly** on the B-side of his 1957 hit "Peggy Sue"	$4	■	Columbia 05681
4/2/88	80	5		21 **Never Die Young** ... *Valentine's Day*	$4	■	Columbia 07616
8/2/97	70^A	4		22 **Little More Time With You** ... from the album *Hourglass* on Columbia 67912; all of above (except #4, 8, 9, 12, 14-17 & 20) written by Taylor			album cut

TAYLOR, John — see DURAN DURAN

★261★ TAYLOR, Johnnie — R&B/BUB/LP '76

Born on 5/5/38 in Crawfordsville, Arkansas. Died of a heart attack on 5/31/2000 (age 62). Soul singer. With gospel group the Highway QC's in Chicago, early 1950s. In vocal group The Five Echoes, recorded for Sabre in 1954. In the Soul Stirrers gospel group before going solo. First solo recording for SAR in 1961. Known as The Soul Philosopher.

1)Disco Lady 2)Who's Making Love 3)I Believe In You (You Believe In Me) 4)Cheaper To Keep Her 5)Take Care Of Your Homework

DEBUT	PEAK	WKS	Gold	A-side (Chart Hit)...B-side	$	Sym	Label & Number
11/30/63	98	1		1 **Baby, We've Got Love** ... *(I'll Always Be) In Love With You* written by **Sam Cooke**; vocal style is similar to Cooke on this tune	$20		Derby 1006
12/16/67	95	2		2 **Somebody's Sleeping In My Bed** ... *Strange Things (Happening in My Heart)*	$10		Stax 235
10/26/68	5	14	●	3 **Who's Making Love** ... RB[3] *I'm Trying*	$8		Stax 0009
1/18/69	20	9		4 **Take Care Of Your Homework** ... *Hold On This Time*	$8		Stax 0023
5/10/69	36	9		5 **Testify (I Wonna)** ... *I Had A Fight With Love*	$8		Stax 0033
8/9/69	48	8		6 **I Could Never Be President** ... *It's Amazing*	$8		Stax 0046
12/20/69+	43	10		7 **Love Bones** ... *Mr. Nobody Is Somebody*	$8		Stax 0055
6/6/70	37	10		8 **Steal Away** ... *Friday Night*	$7		Stax 0068
10/17/70	39	9		9 **I Am Somebody Part II** ... *Part I*	$7		Stax 0078
1/16/71	28	10		10 **Jody's Got Your Girl And Gone** ... RB[2] *A Fool Like Me*	$7		Stax 0085
5/22/71	86	3		11 **I Don't Wanna Lose You** ... *Party Life*	$7		Stax 0089
8/28/71	64	6		12 **Hijackin' Love** ... *Love In The Streets (Ain't Good As The Love At Home)*	$7		Stax 0096
1/22/72	74	7		13 **Standing In For Jody** ... *Shackin' Up*	$7		Stax 0114
6/23/73	11	16	●	14 **I Believe In You (You Believe In Me)** ... RB[2] *Love Depression*	$6		Stax 0161
10/13/73	15	11		15 **Cheaper To Keep Her** ... *I Can Read Between The Lines*	$6		Stax 0176
1/26/74	34	10		16 **We're Getting Careless With Our Love** ... *Poor Make Believer*	$6		Stax 0193
6/29/74	78	4		17 **I've Been Born Again** ... *At Night Time (My Pillow Tells A Tale On Me)*	$6		Stax 0208
2/7/76	❶[4]	19	▲	18 **Disco Lady** RB[6] *You're The Best In The World* first single certified platinum by R.I.A.A.	$5		Columbia 10281
6/5/76	33	7		19 **Somebody's Gettin' It** ... *Please Don't Stop (That Song From Playing)*	$5		Columbia 10334
2/26/77	77	7		20 **Love Is Better In The A.M. (Part 1)** ... *(Part 2)* all of above (except #1 & 2) produced by Don Davis	$5		Columbia 10478
10/1/77	86	2		21 **Disco 9000** ... *Right Now*	$5		Columbia 10610

TAYLOR, Kate — LP '77

Born on 8/15/49 in Boston, Massachusetts. Singer/songwriter/guitarist. Younger sister of **James Taylor**.

DEBUT	PEAK	WKS	Gold	A-side (Chart Hit)...B-side	$	Sym	Label & Number
9/3/77	49	7		**It's In His Kiss (The Shoop Shoop Song)** ... *Jason And Ida* produced and arranged by **James Taylor**	$5		Columbia 10596

TAYLOR, Ko Ko — '66

Born Cora Walton on 9/28/35 in Memphis, Tennessee. Female blues singer.

DEBUT	PEAK	WKS	Gold	A-side (Chart Hit)...B-side	$	Sym	Label & Number
4/23/66	58	8		**Wang Dang Doodle** ... *Blues Heaven* written, produced and backing vocal by Willie Dixon	$15		Checker 1135

TAYLOR, Little Johnny — R&B/BUB/LP '63

Born Johnny Merrett on 2/11/43 in Gregory, Arkansas; raised in Los Angeles, California. Died of diabetes on 5/17/2002 (age 59). Blues singer/songwriter/harmonica player. With **Mighty Clouds Of Joy** and Stars Of Bethel gospel groups. Duets with **Ted Taylor** (no relation) in the 1970s.

DEBUT	PEAK	WKS	Gold	A-side (Chart Hit)...B-side	$	Sym	Label & Number
8/17/63	19	13		1 **Part Time Love** ... RB[1] *Somewhere Down The Line*	$20		Galaxy 722
1/4/64	78	4		2 **Since I Found A New Love** ... *My Heart Is Filled With Pain*	$15		Galaxy 725
12/11/71+	60	8		3 **Everybody Knows About My Good Thing Pt. 1** ... *Pt. 2*	$10		Ronn 55

TAYLOR, Livingston — AC/C&W/LP '79

Born on 11/21/50 in Boston, Massachusetts. Singer/songwriter/guitarist. Younger brother of **James Taylor**. Hosted TV's *This Week's Music* in 1984.

DEBUT	PEAK	WKS	Gold	A-side (Chart Hit)...B-side	$	Sym	Label & Number
2/6/71	93	2		1 **Carolina Day** ... *Sit On Back*	$6		Capricorn 8012
2/5/72	97	2		2 **Get Out Of Bed** ... *(mono version)*	$6		Capricorn 8025
10/21/78+	30	14		3 **I Will Be In Love With You** *How Much Your Sweet Love Means To Me*	$4		Epic 50604
3/31/79	82	4		4 **I'll Come Running** ... *No Thank You Skycap*	$4		Epic 50667
7/26/80	38	10		5 **First Time Love** ... *Pajamas*	$4		Epic 50894

TAYLOR, R. Dean — BUB/C&W/LP '70

Born in 1939 in Toronto, Ontario, Canada. Pop singer/songwriter. First recorded for Barry in 1960. Co-wrote **The Supremes**' hit "Love Child."

DEBUT	PEAK	WKS	Gold	A-side (Chart Hit)...B-side	$	Sym	Label & Number
9/5/70	5	15		1 **Indiana Wants Me** ... *Love's Your Name* first pressings featured sirens on the intro	$6	□	Rare Earth 5013
2/13/71	66	5		2 **Ain't It A Sad Thing** ... *Back Street*	$6	■	Rare Earth 5023
4/17/71	67	4		3 **Gotta See Jane** ... *Back Street* originally released in 1968 on V.I.P. 25045 ($25) with "Don't Fool Around" as the B-side	$6		Rare Earth 5026
4/15/72	83	3		4 **Taos New Mexico** ... *Shadow*	$6		Rare Earth 5041

TAYLOR, Ted — R&B/BUB '60

Born Austin Taylor on 2/16/34 in Okmulgee, Oklahoma. Died in a car accident on 11/22/87 (age 53). R&B singer/songwriter. Formerly with Glory Bound Travellers and **Mighty Clouds Of Joy** gospel groups, and with **The Cadets/The Jacks**.

DEBUT	PEAK	WKS	Gold	A-side (Chart Hit)...B-side	$	Sym	Label & Number
11/14/60	90	2		1 **Push Push**...*A Heart That's True* **AUSTIN TAYLOR**	$15		Laurie 3067
12/4/65	99	2		2 **Stay Away From My Baby**...*Walking Out Of Your Life* promo record and sleeve issued as "Back-To-Back Hits" with **The Artistics**' "This Heart Of Mine" (R&B #25)	$12	□	Okeh 7231

T-BONES, The — LP '66

A Joe Saraceno studio production. Also see **Current**, **Hamilton, Joe Frank & Reynolds**, **The Routers** and **Tony And Joe**.

DEBUT	PEAK	WKS	Gold	A-side (Chart Hit)...B-side	$	Sym	Label & Number
12/11/65+	3	13		1 **No Matter What Shape (Your Stomach's In)**...*Feelin' Fine* [I] melody taken from an Alka Seltzer jingle	$12		Liberty 55836
3/26/66	62	5		2 **Sippin' 'N Chippin'**...*Moment Of Softness* [I] from the Nabisco Sip 'N Chip jingle	$10		Liberty 55867

T-BOZ — see DA BRAT / TLC

T.C.F. Featuring Asia Fernandez — R&B '91

Hip-hop vocal group from Queens, New York: Fola "Oo-Chile" Bell, Nicola "K.O." Bailey, her brother Shawn "Big Shawn B" Bailey and Kenny "Non-Chalant" Nealy. T.C.F. stands for The Chosen Four. Shawn and Kenny were dancers with **Kool G Rap & D.J. Polo**.

DEBUT	PEAK	WKS	Gold	A-side (Chart Hit)...B-side	$	Sym	Label & Number
7/20/91	43[S]	9		**If You Wanna Sex Me Up**...*(regular mix)* answer song to **Color Me Badd**'s "I Wanna Sex You Up"	$5	▮	Cold Chillin' 19238

TCHAIKOVSKY, Bram — see BRAM TCHAIKOVSKY

T-CONNECTION — R&B/BUB/LP '77

Black disco group from Nassau, Bahamas: brothers Theo (vocals, keyboards) and Kirk (bass) Coakley, Dave Mackey (guitar) and Tony Flolwers (drums).

DEBUT	PEAK	WKS	Gold	A-side (Chart Hit)...B-side	$	Sym	Label & Number
3/12/77	46	17		1 **Do What You Wanna Do**...*Mothers Love*	$5		Dash 5032
3/10/79	56	6		2 **At Midnight**...*Playin' Games*	$5		Dash 5048

TEARS FOR FEARS — ★423★ — BUB/ROK/LP '85

Synth-pop duo from England: Roland Orzabal (vocals, guitar, keyboards; born on 8/22/61) and Curt Smith (vocals, bass; born on 6/24/61). Adopted name from Arthur Janov's book *Prisoners Of Pain* in 1981. Smith left duo by 1992.

DEBUT	PEAK	WKS	Gold	A-side (Chart Hit)...B-side	$	Sym	Label & Number
8/6/83	73	6		1 **Change**...*The Conflict*	$4		Mercury 812677
3/16/85	❶[2]	24		2 **Everybody Wants To Rule The World**...S:❶[2] / A:❶[2] *Pharaohs*	$3		Mercury 880659
6/15/85	❶[3]	19	●	3 **Shout** A:❶[3] / S:❶[2] *The Big Chair* above 2: #1 Dance Club Play hits and Top 10 Rock hits	$3	■	Mercury 880294
9/14/85	3	20		4 **Head Over Heels**...A:2 / S:4 *When In Love With A Blind Man*	$3	■	Mercury 880899
4/12/86	27	12		5 **Mothers Talk**...S:26 / A:28 *Sea Song* above 4 from the album *Songs From The Big Chair*	$3	■	Mercury 884638
9/2/89	2[1]	15		6 **Sowing The Seeds Of Love**...MR[1] S:❶[2] / A:4 *Tears Roll Down*	$3	■	Fontana 874710
12/2/89+	36	14		7 **Woman In Chains**...S:25 *Always In The Past* **Oleta Adams** (female vocal); **Phil Collins** (drums)	$3	■	Fontana 876248
3/10/90	89	4		8 **Advice For The Young At Heart**...*Johnny Panic And The Bible Of Dreams*	$3	▮	Fontana 876894
7/17/93	25	20		9 **Break It Down Again**...MR[3] A:18 / S:61 *Bloodletting Go* "45": Mercury 862240	$3	▮V	Mercury 862330

TECHNIQUES — '57

White pop vocal group from Georgia: Jim Tinney, Jim Moore, Jim Falin and Buddy Funk. All were students at Georgia Tech University. Similar in style to **The Crew-Cuts**.

DEBUT	PEAK	WKS	Gold	A-side (Chart Hit)...B-side	$	Sym	Label & Number
11/18/57	29	13		**Hey! Little Girl**...S:29 / T:33 *In A Round About Way* first released on Stars 551 in 1957 ($50)	$30		Roulette 4030

TECHNOTRONIC — LP '90

Techno-dance studio group created by Belgian DJ/producer Thomas DeQuincey (born Jo Bogaert) featuring England-born rapper MC Eric and Zairean rapper **Ya Kid K** (**Hi Tek 3**; born Manuela Barbara Kamosi). Non-vocalist Felly, a model from Zaire, fronted the group for videos.

DEBUT	PEAK	WKS	Gold	A-side (Chart Hit)...B-side	$	Sym	Label & Number
10/14/89+	2[2]	24	▲	1 **Pump Up The Jam** ***[TECHNOTRONIC Featuring FELLY]*** S:❶[4] / A:6 *(instrumental)*	$3	■	SBK 07311
1/27/90	7	20	●	2 **Get Up! (Before The Night Is Over)**...S:5 / A:11 *Raw*	$3	▮V	SBK 07315
11/17/90	95	3		3 **Rockin' Over The Beat**...*Techno Medley* "45": SBK 17320 (green vinyl issued in 1993); B-side: "Tarzan Boy" by **Baltimora** (#51/'93)	$3	▮V	SBK 07338
6/13/92	6	23		4 **Move This** ***[TECHNOTRONIC featuring YA KID K]***...A:5 / S:10 *Rockin' Over The Beat* featured in a 1992 Revlon TV commercial; "45": SBK/EMI 57878; B-side: "Pump Up The Jam"; all of above from *Pump Up The Jam - The Album*	$3	▮V	SBK/EMI 50400
4/15/95	83	7		5 **Move It To The Rhythm** ***[TECHNOTRONIC featuring Ya Kid K]***...*(MCT edit)* "45": SBK/EMI 18481; B-side: "Recall"	$3	▮V	SBK/EMI 58397

TEDDY & The Twilights — '62

R&B group from Philadelphia, Pennsylvania. Lead vocals by Fred Cohen.

DEBUT	PEAK	WKS	Gold	A-side (Chart Hit)...B-side	$	Sym	Label & Number
5/19/62	59	8		**Woman Is A Man's Best Friend**...*Goodbye To Love*	$25		Swan 4102

TEDDY BEARS, The — '58

White doo-wop trio from Los Angeles, California: Phil Spector (born on 12/26/40 in the Bronx, New York), Carol Connors (lead singer; born Annette Kleinbard) and Marshall Leib (born on 1/26/39). Spector became a well-known writer and producer; owner of Philles Records. He was inducted into the Rock and Roll Hall of Fame in 1989. Connors co-wrote "Gonna Fly Now" (theme from the movie *Rocky*). Leib died of a heart attack on 3/15/2002 (age 63).

DEBUT	PEAK	WKS	Gold	A-side (Chart Hit)...B-side	$	Sym	Label & Number
9/22/58	❶[3]	23	●	1 **To Know Him, Is To Love Him**...H:❶[3] *Don't You Worry My Little Pet* **Sandy Nelson** (drums)	$30		Dore 503
3/9/59	91	2		2 **Oh Why /**			
2/16/59	98	1		3 **I Don't Need You Anymore**...	$25		Imperial 5562

DEBUT	PEAK	WKS	Gold	A-side (Chart Hit)......B-side	$	Sym	Label & Number
				TEE, Willie '65			
				Born Wilson Turbinton on 2/6/44 in New Orleans, Louisiana. R&B singer/pianist.			
3/20/65	**97**	2		**Teasin' You** ...... *Walking Up A One Way Street* originally released on Nola 708 in 1964 ($40)	$10		Atlantic 2273
				TEEGARDEN & VAN WINKLE '70			
				Rock and roll duo from Tulsa, Oklahoma: David Teegarden (drums) and Skip "Van Winkle" Knape (keyboards). Teegarden was a member of **Bob Seger**'s Silver Bullet Band from 1978-81.			
9/19/70	**22**	9		1 **God, Love And Rock & Roll** ...... *Work Me Tomorrow* first released on Plumm 68102 in 1970 ($20)	$6	■	Westbound 170
12/12/70	**84**	3		2 **Everything Is Going To Be Alright** ...... *You Do*	$6		Westbound 171
				TEENAGERS, The — see LYMON, Frankie			
				TEEN QUEENS, The '56			
				R&B teen doo-wop duo from Los Angeles, California: sisters Betty and Rosie Collins. Sisters of Aaron Collins of **The Cadets/The Jacks**.			
3/3/56	**14**	12		**Eddie My Love** ...... S:14 / J:16 / T:22 *Just Goofed*	$50		RPM 453
				TEE SET, The LP '70			
				Pop group from Delft, Holland: Peter Tetteroo (vocals), Hans Van Eijck (organ), Dill Bennink (guitar), Franklin Madjid (bass) and Joop Blom (drums). Tetteroo died of cancer on 9/5/2002 (age 55).			
1/24/70	**5**	12		1 **Ma Belle Amie** ...... *Angels Coming In The Holy Night*	$6	■	Colossus 107
5/9/70	**81**	4		2 **If You Do Believe In Love** ...... *Charmaine*	$6	■	Colossus 114
				TELA R&B/LP '97			
				Born in Memphis, Tennessee. Male rapper.			
3/29/97	**58**	8		**Sho Nuff** ...... S:40 *(clean version) / Suave House* **TELA Featuring Eightball & MJG, Crime Boss and The Suave House Family**	$5	▮	Suave House 1602
				TÉLÉPOPMUSIK '03			
				Dance trio of DJ/producers from France: Fabrice Dumont, Stephan Haeri and Christopher Hetier.			
12/28/02+	**78**	10		**Breathe** ...... *(remix) / Love Can Damage Your Health* Angela McCluskey (vocals); featured in a Mitsubishi Outlander SUV TV commercial	$7	T	Catalogue 77870
				TEMPO, Nino, & April Stevens POP/BUB/AC/LP '63			
				Brother-and-sister duo from Niagara Falls, New York: **Nino Tempo** (born Antonio Lo Tempio on 1/6/35) and **April Stevens** (born Carol Lo Tempio on 4/29/36). Prior to teaming up, Nino was a session saxophonist and April had recorded solo. April hit #6 in 1951 with "I'm In Love Again" (w/**Henri René** orch.). *1)Deep Purple 2)Whispering 3)All Strung Out*			
11/30/59	**86**	3		1 **Teach Me Tiger** *[APRIL STEVENS]* ...... *That Warm Afternoon* **Don Ralke** (orch.)	$15		Imperial 5626
7/7/62	**77**	4		2 **Sweet And Lovely** ...... *True Love (Means More Than Anything)* **APRIL STEVENS & NINO TEMPO** #1 hit for Gus Arnheim & His Orchestra in 1931	$12		Atco 6224
9/14/63	**1** (1)	15		3 **Deep Purple** *I've Been Carrying A Torch For You So Long That I Burned A Great Big Hole In My Heart* #1 hit for Larry Clinton & His Orchestra in 1939	$12		Atco 6273
12/21/63+	**11**	9		4 **Whispering** ...... *Tweedlee Dee* #1 hit for Paul Whiteman & His Orchestra in 1920	$10		Atco 6281
2/22/64	**32**	6		5 **Stardust** ...... *1-45* #1 hit for Isham Jones & His Orchestra in 1931	$10		Atco 6286
5/2/64	**56**	5		6 **Tea For Two** / #1 hit for Marion Harris in 1925			
4/25/64	**99**	1		7 **I'm Confessin' (That I Love You)** ...... #2 hit for Guy Lombardo & His Orchestra in 1930	$10		Atco 6294
9/10/66	**26**	8		8 **All Strung Out** ...... *I Can't Go On Living Baby Without You*	$8		White Whale 236
7/22/67	**86**	2		9 **I Can't Go On Livin' Baby Without You** ...... *Little Child* some pressings erroneously show title as "I Can't Go On Livin' Without You, Baby"	$8		White Whale 252
9/22/73	**53**	8		10 **Sister James** *[NINO TEMPO AND 5th AVE. SAX]* ...... *Clair De Lune (In Jazz)* [I]	$5		A&M 1461
6/15/74	**93**	4		11 **Wake Up And Love Me** *[APRIL]* ...... *Gotta Leave You Baby*	$5		A&M 1528
				TEMPOS, The '59			
				Pop vocal group from Pittsburgh, Pennsylvania: Mike Lazo, Gene Schachter, Jim Drake and Tom Minoto.			
6/29/59	**23**	14		**See You In September** ...... *Bless You My Love* **Billy Mure** (orch.)	$20		Climax 102
				TEMPREES, The R&B '72			
				R&B vocal trio: Del Juan Calvin, Harold "Scottie" Scott and Jasper "Jabbo" Phillips. Calvin replaced by William Norvell Johnson in 1972. In the movie *Wattstax* in 1972.			
10/7/72	**93**	2		**Dedicated To The One I Love** ...... *I Love You, You Love Me*	$10		We Produce 1808
				TEMPTATIONS, The '60			
				White doo-wop group from Flushing, New York: Neil Stevens, Larry Curtis, Artie Sands and Artie Marin.			
4/18/60	**29**	10		**Barbara** ...... *Someday*	$30		Goldisc 3001

DEBUT	PEAK	WKS	Gold	A-side (Chart Hit)......B-side	$	Sym	Label & Number

TEMPTATIONS, The ★21★ R&B/BUB/AC/LP '69

R&B vocal group from Detroit, Michigan: **Eddie Kendricks** (born on 12/17/39), Paul Williams (born on 7/2/39), Melvin Franklin (born on 10/12/42), Otis Williams (born on 10/30/41; not to be confused with the same-named member of the Charms) and Elbridge Bryant (who was replaced by **David Ruffin** (born on 1/18/41) in 1963. Originally called the Primes and Elgins; first recorded for Miracle in 1961. Ruffin (cousin of **Billy Stewart**) replaced by **Dennis Edwards** (ex-**Contours**) in 1968. Kendricks and Paul Williams left in 1971; replaced by Ricky Owens (ex-**Vibrations**) and Richard Street (**The Monitors**). Owens was replaced by Damon Harris. Harris left in 1975 to join **Impact**; replaced by Glenn Leonard. Edwards left group, 1977-79; replaced by Louis Price. Ali Ollie Woodson replaced Edwards from 1984-87. 1988 lineup: Otis Williams, Franklin, Street, Edwards and Ron Tyson. Charted 88 R&B hits, 1962-00. Recognized as America's all-time favorite R&B group. Paul Williams died of a self-inflicted gunshot on 8/17/73 (age 34). Ruffin died of a drug overdose on 6/1/91 (age 50). Kendricks died of cancer on 10/5/92 (age 52). Franklin died of heart failure on 2/23/95 (age 52). Inducted into the Rock and Roll Hall of Fame in 1989. Original member, Otis Williams, still recording with a lineup consisting of Ron Tyson, Harry McGilberry, Terry Weeks and Barrington Henderson.

1)I Can't Get Next To You 2)Just My Imagination (Running Away With Me) 3)My Girl 4)Papa Was A Rollin' Stone 5)I'm Gonna Make You Love Me

DEBUT	PEAK	WKS	Gold	A-side (Chart Hit)......B-side	$	Sym	Label & Number
2/29/64	11	11		1 **The Way You Do The Things You Do** ...... *Just Let Me Know*	$15		Gordy 7028
5/30/64	33	9		2 **I'll Be In Trouble** ...... *The Girl's Alright With Me* (#102)	$15		Gordy 7032
9/12/64	26	8		3 **Girl (Why You Wanna Make Me Blue)** ...... *Baby, Baby I Need You*	$15		Gordy 7035
1/16/65	1^{1}	13	▲	4 **My Girl** ...... RB^{6} *(Talking 'Bout) Nobody But My Baby*	$15	■	Gordy 7038
4/3/65	18	9		5 **It's Growing** ...... *What Love Has Joined Together*	$15		Gordy 7040
7/24/65	17	10		6 **Since I Lost My Baby** ...... *You've Got To Earn It* (#123/R&B #22)	$15		Gordy 7043
10/23/65	13	8		7 **My Baby** /			
12/18/65+	83	5		8 **Don't Look Back** ...... #2, 3 & 6-8: from the album *Temptin' Temptations*	$15		Gordy 7047
2/26/66	29	7		9 **Get Ready** ...... RB^{1} *Fading Away* all of above (except #3) written and produced by **Smokey Robinson**	$15		Gordy 7049
5/28/66	13	13	●	10 **Ain't Too Proud To Beg** ...... RB^{8} *You'll Lose A Precious Love*	$12		Gordy 7054
8/20/66	3	12	●	11 **Beauty Is Only Skin Deep** ...... RB^{5} *You're Not An Ordinary Girl*	$12	■	Gordy 7055
11/19/66	8	10	●	12 **(I Know) I'm Losing You** ...... RB^{2} *I Couldn't Cry If I Wanted To*	$12		Gordy 7057
4/29/67	8	10		13 **All I Need** ...... *Sorry Is A Sorry Word*	$12		Gordy 7061
7/29/67	6	12	●	14 **You're My Everything** ...... *I've Been Good To You* (#124)	$12		Gordy 7063
10/14/67	14	9		15 **(Loneliness Made Me Realize) It's You That I Need** ...... *Don't Send Me Away* above 4 from the album *With A Lot O' Soul*	$12		Gordy 7065
1/13/68	4	14	●	16 **I Wish It Would Rain** ...... RB^{3} *I Truly, Truly Believe* (#116; R&B #41)	$12		Gordy 7068
5/4/68	13	10	●	17 **I Could Never Love Another (After Loving You)** ...... RB^{1} *Gonna Give Her All The Love I've Got*	$12		Gordy 7072
8/3/68	26	7		18 **Please Return Your Love To Me** ...... *How Can I Forget*	$12		Gordy 7074
11/16/68+	6	12	●	19 **Cloud Nine** ...... *Why Did She Have To Leave Me (Why Did She Have To Go)*	$10		Gordy 7081
12/7/68+	2^{2}	13	▲	20 **I'm Gonna Make You Love Me** ...... *A Place In The Sun* **DIANA ROSS AND THE SUPREMES & THE TEMPTATIONS**	$10	■	Motown 1137
12/28/68	3^{X}	6		21 **Rudolph, The Red-Nosed Reindeer** / [X] X: 12/'68; 9/'69; 6/'70; 3/'71			
12/13/69	7^{X}	4		22 **Silent Night** ...... [X] X: 7/'69; 9/'85; new version issued on Gordy 1654 in 1982 and on Gordy 1713 in 1983 (B-side: "Everything For Christmas")	$15		Gordy 7082
2/15/69	6	12	●	23 **Run Away Child, Running Wild** ...... RB^{2} *I Need Your Lovin'*	$10		Gordy 7084
3/15/69	25	7		24 **I'll Try Something New** ...... *The Way You Do The Things You Do* **DIANA ROSS AND THE SUPREMES & THE TEMPTATIONS**	$10		Motown 1142
5/24/69	20	8		25 **Don't Let The Joneses Get You Down** ...... *Since I've Lost You*	$10		Gordy 7086
8/16/69	1^{2}	17	▲	26 **I Can't Get Next To You** RB^{5} *Running Away (Ain't Gonna Help You)*	$10		Gordy 7093
9/13/69	46	5		27 **The Weight** ...... *For Better Or Worse* **DIANA ROSS AND THE SUPREMES & THE TEMPTATIONS**	$10		Motown 1153
1/17/70	7	11	●	28 **Psychedelic Shack** ...... *That's The Way Love Is*	$8		Gordy 7096
5/23/70	3	15	▲	29 **Ball Of Confusion (That's What The World Is Today)** ...... *It's Summer*	$8	■	Gordy 7099
10/3/70	33	7		30 **Ungena Za Ulimwengu (Unite The World)** ...... *Hum Along And Dance* (R&B flip)	$8		Gordy 7102
2/6/71	1^{2}	15	▲	31 **Just My Imagination (Running Away With Me)** ...... RB^{3} *You Make Your Own Heaven And Hell Right Here On Earth*	$8		Gordy 7105
7/24/71	51	6		32 **It's Summer** ...... *I'm The Exception To The Rule* different version than the B-side of #29 above	$8		Gordy 7109
11/6/71	18	10	●	33 **Superstar (Remember How You Got Where You Are)** ...... *Gonna Keep On Tryin' Till I Win Your Love*	$7		Gordy 7111
3/4/72	30	8		34 **Take A Look Around** ...... *Smooth Sailing (From Now On)*	$7		Gordy 7115
7/1/72	92	4		35 **Mother Nature** ...... *Funky Music Sho Nuff Turns Me On* (R&B #27)	$7		Gordy 7119
10/14/72	1^{1}	16	▲	36 **Papa Was A Rollin' Stone** ...... *(instrumental)*	$7		Gordy 7121
2/24/73	7	14	●	37 **Masterpiece** ...... RB^{2} *(instrumental)*	$7		Gordy 7126
6/9/73	40	8		38 **The Plastic Man** ...... *Hurry Tomorrow*	$7		Gordy 7129
8/18/73	35	11		39 **Hey Girl (I Like Your Style)** ...... *Ma*	$7		Gordy 7131
12/22/73+	27	9		40 **Let Your Hair Down** ...... RB^{1} *Ain't No Justice*	$7		Gordy 7133
3/16/74	43	9		41 **Heavenly** ...... *Zoom*	$6		Gordy 7135
6/22/74	74	6		42 **You've Got My Soul On Fire** ...... *I Need You* #10-42 written (except #13, 20-22, 24, 27, & 35) and produced (except #13) by Norman Whitfield	$6		Gordy 7136
12/21/74+	40	10		43 **Happy People** ...... RB^{1} *(instrumental)* co-written by **Lionel Richie**	$6		Gordy 7138
3/22/75	26	14		44 **Shakey Ground** ...... RB^{1} *I'm A Bachelor*	$6		Gordy 7142
7/12/75	37	10		45 **Glasshouse** ...... *The Prophet*	$6		Gordy 7144
2/7/76	54	6		46 **Keep Holding On** ...... *What You Need Most (I Do Best Of All)*	$6		Gordy 7146
7/17/76	94	3		47 **Up The Creek (Without A Paddle)** ...... *Darling, Stand By Me (Song For My Woman)*	$6		Gordy 7150
5/10/80	43	9		48 **Power** ...... *(instrumental)*	$5		Gordy 7183
9/19/81	67	5		49 **Aiming At Your Heart** ...... *The Life Of A Cowboy*	$5		Gordy 7208

DEBUT	PEAK	WKS	Gold	A-side (Chart Hit)...B-side	$	Sym	Label & Number
				TEMPTATIONS, The — Cont'd			
5/8/82	66	8		50 **Standing On The Top-Part 1** ... *Part 2*	$4		Gordy 1616
				THE TEMPTATIONS FEATURING RICK JAMES			
4/16/83	88	3		51 **Love On My Mind Tonight** ... *Bringyourbodyhere (Exercise Chant)*	$4		Gordy 1666
4/7/84	54	8		52 **Sail Away** ... *Isn't The Night Fantastic*	$4		Gordy 1720
12/15/84+	48	14		53 **Treat Her Like A Lady** ... *Isn't The Night Fantastic*	$4		Gordy 1765
10/11/86	47	11		54 **Lady Soul** ... S:37 *Put Us Together Again*	$4		Gordy 1856
7/6/91	10	17		55 **The Motown Song** ... A:24 / S:36 *Sweet Soul Music (live)*	$3	▮V	Warner 19322
				ROD STEWART (with The Temptations)			

10cc — BUB/LP '75

Art-rock group formed in Manchester, England, that evolved from **Hotlegs**: Eric Stewart (guitar), Graham Gouldman (bass), Lol Creme (guitar, keyboards; born on 9/19/47) and Kevin Godley (drums; born on 10/7/45). Stewart and Gouldman were members of **The Mindbenders**. **Godley & Creme** left in 1976; replaced by drummer Paul Burgess. Added members Rick Fenn, Stuart Tosh and Duncan MacKay in 1978. Gouldman later in duo **Wax**.

DEBUT	PEAK	WKS	Gold	A-side (Chart Hit)...B-side	$	Sym	Label & Number
9/15/73	73	8		1 **Rubber Bullets** ... *Waterfall*	$6		UK 49015
5/17/75	2[3]	17		2 **I'm Not In Love** *Channel Swimmer*	$5	□	Mercury 73678
11/29/75	83	6		3 **Art For Art's Sake** ... *Get It While You Can*	$5	■	Mercury 73725
4/10/76	60	4		4 **I'm Mandy Fly Me** ... *How Dare You*	$5		Mercury 73779
1/8/77	5	19	●	5 **The Things We Do For Love** ... *Hot To Trot*	$5		Mercury 73875
5/21/77	40	7		6 **People In Love** ... *Don't Squeeze Me Like Toothpaste*	$5		Mercury 73917
8/6/77	69	8		7 **Good Morning Judge** ... *I'm So Laid Back I'm Laid Out*	$5		Mercury 73943
9/30/78	44	10		8 **Dreadlock Holiday** ... *Nothing Can Move Me*	$5		Polydor 14511
2/3/79	85	3		9 **For You And I** ... *Take These Chains*	$5		Polydor 14528
				from the movie *Moment By Moment* starring **John Travolta** and Lily Tomlin			

TENDER SLIM — '60

Studio project produced and directed by **Teddy Vann**.

DEBUT	PEAK	WKS	Gold	A-side (Chart Hit)...B-side	$	Sym	Label & Number
1/11/60	93	2		**Teenage Hayride** ... *Hey Joe!* [I]	$15		Grey Cliff 723
				rock and roll instrumental adapted from "Pop Goes The Weasel" and "Three Blind Mice"			

10,000 MANIACS — ROK/LP '94

Alternative-rock group formed in Jamestown, New York: **Natalie Merchant** (vocals), Robert Buck (guitar), Dennis Drew (keyboards), Steven Gustafson (bass) and Jerome Augustyniak (drums). Merchant left in August of 1993; replaced by Mary Ramsey. Original member John Lombardo left in 1986; returned in 1996. Buck died of liver failure on 12/19/2000 (age 42).

DEBUT	PEAK	WKS	Gold	A-side (Chart Hit)...B-side	$	Sym	Label & Number
5/7/88	68	8		1 **Like The Weather** ... *A Campfire Song*	$4	■	Elektra 69418
9/3/88	80	8		2 **What's The Matter Here?** ... *Cherry Tree*	$4	■	Elektra 69388
6/17/89	44	12		3 **Trouble Me** ... S:40 *The Lion's Share*	$4	■	Elektra 69298
11/28/92	66	11		4 **These Are Days** ... MR[2] A:70 *Circle Dream*	$4	▮	Elektra 64700
3/6/93	67	10		5 **Candy Everybody Wants** ... A:56 *I Hope That I Don't Fall In Love With You*	$4	▮	Elektra 64665
8/21/93	95	1		6 **Few & Far Between** ... S:73 *Candy Everybody Wants / To Sir With Love / Let The Mystery Be*	$8	★	Elektra 66296
				the first CD-only single to make the *Hot 100*			
11/6/93+	11	29		7 **Because The Night** A:8 / S:29 *Eat For Two* (ROK #12/'89) [L]	$3	▮V	Elektra 64595
7/12/97	25	18		8 **More Than This** ... A:29 / S:40 *(remix) / Beyond The Blue*	$3	▮	Geffen 19411
				"Bubbled Under" (#102) for **Roxy Music** in 1983			

TEN WHEEL DRIVE With Genya Ravan — LP '70

Jazz-rock group: **Genya Ravan** (vocals) (see #2 below), **Michael Zager** (keyboards), Aram Schefrin (guitar), Steve Satten, John Gatchell, Dave Liebman, John Eckert and Dennis Parisi (horns), Bob Piazza (bass) and Allen Herman (drums).

DEBUT	PEAK	WKS	Gold	A-side (Chart Hit)...B-side	$	Sym	Label & Number
7/25/70	74	7		1 **Morning Much Better** ... *Stay With Me*	$6		Polydor 14037
8/12/78	92	3		2 **Back In My Arms Again** ... *Do It Just For Me*	$5		20th Century 2374
				GENYA RAVAN			

TEN YEARS AFTER — ROK/LP '71

Blues-rock group formed in Nottingham, England: Alvin Lee (vocals, guitar), Chick Churchill (keyboards), Leo Lyons (bass) and Ric Lee (drums). Alvin Lee was also a top session guitarist.

DEBUT	PEAK	WKS	Gold	A-side (Chart Hit)...B-side	$	Sym	Label & Number
5/2/70	98	2		1 **Love Like A Man** ... *If You Should Love Me*	$7		Deram 7529
9/25/71	40	12		2 **I'd Love To Change The World** ... *Let The Sky Fall*	$6		Columbia 45457
1/15/72	61	5		3 **Baby Won't You Let Me Rock 'N Roll You** ... *Once There Was A Time*	$5		Columbia 45530
12/16/72+	89	6		4 **Choo Choo Mama** ... *You Can't Win Them All*	$5		Columbia 45736

TEPPER, Robert — LP '86

Born in Bayonne, New Jersey. Rock singer/songwriter.

DEBUT	PEAK	WKS	Gold	A-side (Chart Hit)...B-side	$	Sym	Label & Number
1/25/86	22	16		1 **No Easy Way Out** ... A:19 / S:23 *Domination*	$3	■	Scotti Brothers 05750
				from the movie *Rocky IV* starring Sylvester Stallone			
5/10/86	85	3		2 **Don't Walk Away** ... *Domination*	$3	■	Scotti Brothers 05879

★413★ TERRELL, Tammi — LP '68

Born Thomasina Montgomery on 4/29/45 in Philadelphia, Pennsylvania. Died of a brain tumor on 3/16/70 (age 24). R&B singer. First recorded for Wand in 1961. Worked with the **James Brown** Revue. Tumor diagnosed after collapsing on stage in 1967.

1)Your Precious Love 2)You're All I Need To Get By 3)Ain't Nothing Like The Real Thing

DEBUT	PEAK	WKS	Gold	A-side (Chart Hit)...B-side	$	Sym	Label & Number
8/17/63	99	1		1 **I Cried** *[TAMMY MONTGOMERY]* ... *If You Don't Think*	$30		Try Me 28001
				written and produced by **James Brown**			
1/8/66	72	5		2 **I Can't Believe You Love Me** ... *Hold Me Oh My Darling*	$12		Motown 1086
5/28/66	80	5		3 **Come On And See Me** ... *Baby Don'tcha Worry*	$12		Motown 1095
				MARVIN GAYE & TAMMI TERRELL:			
5/13/67	19	12		4 **Ain't No Mountain High Enough** ... *Give A Little Love*	$12		Tamla 54149
9/9/67	5	13		5 **Your Precious Love** *Hold Me Oh My Darling*	$12		Tamla 54156
12/2/67+	10	11		6 **If I Could Build My Whole World Around You** /			
3/2/68	68	6		7 **If This World Were Mine** ...	$12		Tamla 54161
				above 4 from the album *United*			
4/13/68	8	13		8 **Ain't Nothing Like The Real Thing** ... RB[1] *Little Ole Boy, Little Ole Girl*	$12		Tamla 54163
7/27/68	7	12		9 **You're All I Need To Get By** ... RB[5] *Two Can Have A Party*	$12		Tamla 54169

DEBUT	PEAK	WKS	Gold	A-side (Chart Hit)......B-side	$	Sym	Label & Number
				TERRELL, Tammi — Cont'd			
10/12/68	24	7		10 Keep On Lovin' Me Honey ......*You Ain't Livin' Till You're Lovin'*	$10		Tamla 54173
1/18/69	67	4		11 This Old Heart Of Mine (Is Weak For You) ......*Just Too Much To Hope For*	$10		Motown 1138
				TAMMI TERRELL			
2/1/69	30	7		12 Good Lovin' Ain't Easy To Come By ......*Satisfied Feelin'*	$10		Tamla 54179
11/29/69	49	8		13 What You Gave Me ......*How You Gonna Keep It (After You Get It)*	$10		Tamla 54187
4/18/70	50	7		14 The Onion Song /			
				Valerie Simpson actually sang the female part on above 3 due to Tammi's poor health			
4/25/70	56	6		15 California Soul	$10		Tamla 54192
				TERROR FABULOUS '94			
				Born Cecil Campbell in Kingston, Jamaica. Reggae rapper.			
7/23/94	43	20		Action ......S:40 / A:41 *No Ride*	$5	▮	EastWest 98260
				TERROR FABULOUS featuring Nadine Sutherland			
				TERRY, Helen — see PARKER, Ray Jr.			
				TERRY, Tony R&B/LP '91			
				Born on 3/12/64 in Pinehurst, North Carolina; raised in Washington DC. R&B-funk singer/songwriter. Former backing vocalist for **Sweet Sensation** and The Boogie Boys.			
11/28/87+	80	9		1 She's Fly ......*(dub mix)*	$3		Epic 07417
6/25/88	80	5		2 Forever Yours......*Here With Me*	$3	▆	Epic 07900
6/29/91	14	23		3 With You......A:16 / S:27 *Up & Down Love*	$3	▮V	Epic 73713
				"45" B-side: "Head Over Heels" (R&B #13)			
1/25/92	81	10		4 Everlasting Love ......S:69 *(instrumental)*	$3	▮V	Epic 74119
				Jodeci (backing vocals)			
				TESH, John AC/LP '98			
				Born on 7/9/52 in Garden City, New York. New Age/Contemporary Christian multi-instrumentalist. Former host of TV's *Entertainment Tonight.* Appeared in the movie *Shocker.* Married actress Connie Sellecca on 4/4/92.			
4/11/98	66^A	11		Give Me Forever (I Do)			album cut
				JOHN TESH Featuring James Ingram			
				from the album *Grand Passion* on GTSP 539804			
				TESLA ROK/LP '90			
				Hard-rock group formed in Sacramento, California: Jeff Keith (vocals), Frank Hannon and Tommy Skeoch (guitars), Brian Wheat (bass) and Troy Luccetta (drums). Band named after the inventor of the alternating current generator, Nikola Tesla.			
5/16/87	91	3		1 Little Suzi......*Cumin' Atcha Live*	$3	▆	Geffen 28353
9/30/89+	10	27	●	2 Love Song......S:4 / A:18 *I Ain't Superstitious*	$3	▮V	Geffen 22856
3/10/90	55	12		3 The Way It Is ......*Run Run Run*	$3	▮	Geffen 19948
1/5/91	8	22		4 Signs S:4 / A:15 *Down Fo' Boogie* [L]	$3	▮	Geffen 19653
				recorded on 7/2/90 at the Trocadero in Philadelphia, Pennsylvania			
4/18/92	86	6		5 What You Give ......S:69 *Cotton Fields*	$3	▮	Geffen 19117
				TEX, Joe ★183★ R&B/BUB/LP '65			
				Born Joseph Arrington Jr. on 8/8/33 in Rogers, Texas. Died of a heart attack on 8/13/82 (age 49). R&B singer/songwriter. Sang with local gospel groups. Won recording contract during Apollo Theater talent contest in 1954. First recorded for King in 1955. Converted to the Muslim faith; changed name to "Joseph Hazziez" in July 1972. Also see **The Soul Clan**.			
				1)I Gotcha 2)Hold What You've Got 3)Skinny Legs And All 4)Ain't Gonna Bump No More (With No Big Fat Woman) 5)I Want To (Do Everything For You)			
12/19/64+	5	11		1 Hold What You've Got......*Fresh Out Of Tears*	$12		Dial 4001
2/20/65	46	7		2 You Better Get It /			
2/27/65	51	6		3 You Got What It Takes	$10		Dial 4003
4/10/65	56	7		4 A Woman Can Change A Man /			
4/10/65	95	1		5 Don't Let Your Left Hand Know......	$10		Dial 4006
6/26/65	65	4		6 One Monkey Don't Stop No Show ......*Build Your Love (On A Solid Foundation)*	$10		Dial 4011
8/28/65	23	13		7 I Want To (Do Everything For You)......RB³ *Funny Bone*	$10		Dial 4016
12/4/65+	29	9		8 A Sweet Woman Like You ......RB¹ *Close The Door*	$10		Dial 4022
3/5/66	56	8		9 The Love You Save (May Be Your Own) ......*If Sugar Was As Sweet As You*	$10		Dial 4026
5/14/66	39	7		10 S.Y.S.L.J.F.M. (The Letter Song)......*I'm A Man*	$10		Dial 4028
				S.Y.S.L.J.F.M.: "Save Your Sweet Love Just For Me"			
7/23/66	67	5		11 I Believe I'm Gonna Make It ......*You Better Believe It Baby*	$10		Dial 4033
10/8/66	64	5		12 I've Got To Do A Little Bit Better......*What In The World*	$10		Dial 4045
12/17/66+	44	7		13 Papa Was Too......*The Truest Woman In The World*	$10		Dial 4051
3/4/67	35	8		14 Show Me......*A Woman Sees A Hard Time (When Her Man Is Gone)*	$10		Dial 4055
6/3/67	54	7		15 Woman Like That, Yeah ......*I'm Going And Get It*	$10		Dial 4059
8/5/67	63	5		16 A Woman's Hands ......*C.C. Rider*	$10		Dial 4061
10/28/67	10	15	●	17 Skinny Legs And All......*Watch The One (That Brings The Bad News)* [L]	$10		Dial 4063
12/16/67	15^X	3		18 I'll Make Every Day Christmas (For My Woman) ......*Don't Give Up* [X]	$12		Dial 4068
2/10/68	33	7		19 Men Are Gettin' Scarce ......*You're Gonna Thank Me, Woman*	$8		Dial 4069
5/18/68	59	5		20 I'll Never Do You Wrong ......*Wooden Spoon*	$8		Dial 4076
8/10/68	52	5		21 Keep The One You Got ......*Go Home And Do It*	$8		Dial 4083
10/12/68	81	3		22 You Need Me, Baby......*Baby, Be Good*	$8		Dial 4086
1/18/69	88	3		23 That's Your Baby......*Sweet, Sweet Woman*	$8		Dial 4089
4/12/69	47	8		24 Buying A Book......*Chicken Crazy* [S]	$8		Dial 4090
7/19/69	94	3		25 That's The Way ......*Anything You Wanna Know*	$8		Dial 4093
1/22/72	2²	21	●	26 I Gotcha RB¹ *A Mother's Prayer* (R&B #41)	$6		Dial 1010

DEBUT	PEAK	WKS	Gold	A-side (Chart Hit)...B-side	$	Sym	Label & Number
				TEX, Joe — Cont'd			
5/20/72	41	8		27 **You Said A Bad Word**...*It Ain't Gonna Work Baby*	$6		Dial 1012
				all of above written by Joe Tex			
4/2/77	12	18	●	28 **Ain't Gonna Bump No More (With No Big Fat Woman)**...*I Mess Up Everything I Get My Hands On*	$5		Epic 50313
				all of above produced by Buddy Killen			
				TEXANS, The — see BURNETTE, Johnny			
				TEXAS ROK/LP **'89**			
				Pop-rock group from Glasgow, Scotland: Sharleen Spiteri (vocals, guitar), Ally McErlaine (guitar), John McElhone (bass) and Stuart Kerr (drums). McElhone was a member of **Hipsway** and Altered Images. Kerr was an early member of **Love And Money**.			
9/9/89	77	6		**I Don't Want A Lover**...*Believe Me*	$3		Mercury 872350
				TG4 **'02**			
				Female R&B vocal group formed in Orlando, Florida: Ambee, Ashley, Davida and Keisha. TG4: Tom Girl 4.			
11/2/02	5^S	26		**Virginity**...*(3 album snippets)*	$4	★+	T.U.G./A&M 497811
				THEE MIDNITERS BUB **'65**			
				Mexican-American rock group from Los Angeles, California: Willie Garcia (vocals), Roy Marquez and George Dominguez (guitars), Ronnie Figueroa (organ), Romeo Prado (trombone), Larry Rendon (sax), Jimmy Espinoza (bass) and George Salazar (drums).			
3/13/65	67	4		**Land Of A Thousand Dances Part I**...*Part II* [L]	$15		Chattahoochee 666
				THEE PROPHETS BUB/LP **'69**			
				Pop-rock group from Milwaukee, Wisconsin: Brian Lake (vocals, keyboards), Jim Anderson (guitar), Dave Leslie (bass) and Chris Michaels (drums).			
3/8/69	49	8		**Playgirl**...*Patricia Ann*	$10		Kapp 962
				THEM BUB/LP **'65**			
				Rock group from Belfast, Northern Ireland: **Van Morrison** (vocals), brothers Jackie (piano) and Pat (drums) McAuley, Billy Harrison (guitar), Alan Henderson (bass) and **Pete Bardens** (keyboards). Disbanded in late 1966.			
5/22/65	93	1		1 **Gloria**...*Baby, Please Don't Go* (#102)	$20		Parrot 9727
5/29/65	24	10		2 **Here Comes The Night**...*All For Myself*	$20		Parrot 9749
10/30/65	33	8		3 **Mystic Eyes**...*If You And I Could Be As Two*	$20		Parrot 9796
4/23/66	71	6		4 **Gloria**...*Baby, Please Don't Go* [R]	$20		Parrot 9727
				same version as #1 above			
				THICKE **'02**			
				Born Robin Thicke in Los Angeles, California. "Blue-eyed soul" singer/songwriter. Son of actress **Gloria Loring** and actor Alan Thicke.			
11/2/02	8^S	30		**When I Get You Alone**...*(2 versions)*	$4	★	Nu America 497783
				samples "A Fifth Of Beethoven" by **Walter Murphy** (based on Beethoven's "Fifth Symphony")			
				THINK **'72**			
				Studio group assembled by producers Lou Stallman and Bobby Susser.			
12/4/71+	23	10		1 **Once You Understand**...*Gather*	$6		Laurie 3583
				featuring dialogue between a teenager and his parents			
3/9/74	53	8		2 **Once You Understand** *[THINK (Featuring LOU STALLMAN)]*...*Gather* [R]	$6		Big Tree 15000
				above 2 are the same version			
				THIN LIZZY ROK/LP **'76**			
				Rock group formed in Dublin, Ireland: Phil Lynott (vocals, bass; born on 8/20/51), Brian Robertson and Scott Gorham (guitars), and Brian Downey (drums). Lynott died on 1/4/86 (age 34).			
5/15/76	12	17		1 **The Boys Are Back In Town**...*Jailbreak*	$6		Mercury 73786
9/18/76	77	8		2 **Cowboy Song**...*Angel From The Coast*	$6		Mercury 73841
				3RD BASS R&B/LP **'91**			
				White rappers from Queens, New York: Prime Minister Pete Nice (Pete Nash) and **MC Serch** (Michael Berrin) (see #2 below). Supported by black DJ Richie Rich (Richard Lawson). Disbanded in early 1992. Nash and Lawson continued as the duo Prime Minister Pete Nice and DJ Daddy Rich; Berrin went solo.			
7/13/91	29	13	●	1 **Pop Goes The Weasel**...S:10 / A:48 *Derelict Of Dialect*	$3	▮	Def Jam 73728
				samples "Sledgehammer" by **Peter Gabriel**, "You Haven't Done Nothin'" by **Stevie Wonder** and "Eminence Front" by **The Who**			
10/17/92	71	10		2 **Here It Comes**...S:55 *Back To The Grill* (R&B flip)	$4	▮	Def Jam/Chaos 74414
				MC SERCH			
				THIRD EYE BLIND ROK/LP **'98**			
				Rock group from San Francisco, California: Stephan Jenkins (vocals), Kevin Cadogan (guitar), Arion Salazar (bass) and Brad Hargreaves (drums).			
7/5/97	4	43	●	1 **Semi-Charmed Life** MR⁸ A:❶³ / S:11 *Tattoo Of The Sun*	$3	▮	Elektra 64173
12/6/97+	9	52		2 **How's It Going To Be**...A:11 / S:20 *Horror Show*	$3	▮	Elektra 64130
12/5/98+	5	20		3 **Jumper**...A:5 / S:15 *Graduate* (ROK #14)	$6	★+V	Elektra 64058
				Hot 100 Airplay debut: 8/22/98			
1/22/00	14	22		4 **Never Let You Go**...A:11			album cut
9/2/00	69	12		5 **Deep Inside Of You**...A:66			album cut
				above 2 from the album *Blue* on Elektra 62415			
				3RD PARTY **'97**			
				Female techno-dance trio: Karmine, Maria Christensen and Elaine Borja.			
5/3/97	43	20		1 **Can U Feel It**...S:43 / A:55 *(LCD Galactica Edit)*	$4	▮	DV8/A&M 2084
9/27/97	61	11		2 **Love Is Alive**...S:64 *(remix)*	$4	▮	DV8/A&M 2348
				THIRD RAIL, The BUB **'67**			
				Studio project featuring lead singer Joey Levine (**Ohio Express** and **Reunion**).			
8/5/67	53	9		**Run, Run, Run**...*No Return*	$10		Epic 10191

DEBUT	PEAK	WKS	Gold	A-side (Chart Hit)...B-side	$	Sym	Label & Number

3RD STOREE — R&B/BUB '99

R&B vocal group from Los Angeles, California: Dante Clark, Gavin Rhone, Barry Reed, Jason Thomas and Kevontay Jackson.

DEBUT	PEAK	WKS	Gold	A-side (Chart Hit)...B-side	$	Sym	Label & Number
3/20/99	37^S	10		1 **If Ever**...BUB:115 *If They Only Knew* written by **Babyface**	$5	★	Yab Yum 64057
7/17/99	45^S	8		2 **Party Tonight**...*Is This The End* **3RD STOREE (Featuring RL of Next & Treach)** samples "They Don't Know" by **Jon B**	$5	★	Yab Yum 64036

3RD STRIKE — ROK/LP '02

Rock group from Los Angeles, California: Jim Karthe (vocals), Todd Deguchi and Erik Carlsson (guitars), Gabe Hammersmith (bass) and P.J. McMullan (drums).

DEBUT	PEAK	WKS	Gold	A-side (Chart Hit)...B-side	$	Sym	Label & Number
5/25/02+	37^S	5		**No Light**...*(no B-side)*	$8	◗	Hollywood 69010

THIRD WORLD — R&B/BUB/LP '79

Reggae fusion band from Jamaica: William "Bunny Rugs" Clarke (vocals), Stephen "Cat" Coore (guitar), Michael "Ibo" Cooper (keyboards), Richard Daley (bass), Willie Stewart (drums) and Irvin "Carrot" Jarrett (percussion). To England and the U.S. from 1975-76. Toured with **Stevie Wonder** in 1982.

DEBUT	PEAK	WKS	Gold	A-side (Chart Hit)...B-side	$	Sym	Label & Number
2/10/79	47	8		**Now That We Found Love**...*Night Heat* originally recorded by **The O'Jays** in 1973 on their album *Ship Ahoy*	$6		Island 8663

THIRTEENTH FLOOR ELEVATORS, The — BUB '66

Garage-rock band from Austin, Texas: Roky Erickson (vocals), Stacy Sutherland and Tommy Hall (guitars), Dan Galindo (bass) and Danny Thomas (drums). Sutherland was murdered on 8/24/78 (age 32). Galindo died of liver failure on 5/17/2001 (age 51).

DEBUT	PEAK	WKS	Gold	A-side (Chart Hit)...B-side	$	Sym	Label & Number
8/20/66	55	8		**You're Gonna Miss Me**...*Tried To Hide* originally released in 1966 on Zero 10002 as by The Spades ($400), then on Contact 5269 ($100) and then on HBR 492 ($200)	$30		IA 107

38 SPECIAL — ★333★ — ROK/LP '84

Southern-rock group formed in Jacksonville, Florida: Donnie Van Zant (vocals; born on 6/11/52; younger brother of **Lynyrd Skynyrd**'s Ronnie Van Zant), Don Barnes (guitar; born on 12/3/52), Jeff Carlisi (guitar; born on 7/15/52), Larry Junstrom (bass; born on 6/22/49), Steve Brookins (drums; born on 6/2/51) and Jack Grondin (drums; born on 10/3/51). By 1988, Barnes and Brookins replaced by Danny Chauncey (guitar) and Max Carl (keyboards). Barnes returned in 1992 to replace Carl.

1)Second Chance 2)Caught Up In You 3)Like No Other Night

DEBUT	PEAK	WKS	Gold	A-side (Chart Hit)...B-side	$	Sym	Label & Number
2/2/80	43	9		1 **Rockin' Into The Night**...*Robin Hood*	$5		A&M 2205
2/28/81	27	17		2 **Hold On Loosely**...*Throw Out The Line*	$4		A&M 2316
6/6/81	52	10		3 **Fantasy Girl**...*Honky Tonk Dancer*	$4	■	A&M 2330
5/1/82	10	17		4 **Caught Up In You**...AR^1 *Firestarter*	$4	■	A&M 2412
8/21/82	38	11		5 **You Keep Runnin' Away**...*Prisoners Of Rock 'N' Roll*	$4	■	A&M 2431
11/12/83+	19	16		6 **If I'd Been The One**...AR^4 *Twentieth Century Fox*	$4	■	A&M 2594
2/4/84	20	13		7 **Back Where You Belong**...*Undercover Lover*	$4	■	A&M 2615
9/29/84	25	12		8 **Teacher Teacher**...S:25 / A:27 *Twentieth Century Fox* from the movie *Teachers* starring Nick Nolte and JoBeth Williams	$4	■	Capitol 5405
5/3/86	14	16		9 **Like No Other Night**...A:11 / S:17 *Heart's On Fire* (ROK #30)	$4	■	A&M 2831
7/19/86	48	12		10 **Somebody Like You**...*Against The Night*	$4	■	A&M 2854
7/25/87	41	11		11 **Back To Paradise**...S:39 *Hold On Loosely* theme from the movie *Revenge Of The Nerds II* starring Robert Carradine; #8 & 11: co-written by **Bryan Adams**	$4	■	A&M 2955
10/29/88	67	8		12 **Rock & Roll Strategy** *[THIRTY EIGHT SPECIAL]*...*Love Strikes*	$3	■	A&M 1246
2/11/89	6	21		13 **Second Chance** *[THIRTY EIGHT SPECIAL]* AC^2 A:5 / S:9 *Comin' Down Tonight*	$3		A&M 1273
6/24/89	67	7		14 **Comin' Down Tonight** *[THIRTY EIGHT SPECIAL]*...*Chattahoochee* remix version of the B-side of #13 above	$3		A&M 1424
7/13/91	33	15		15 **The Sound Of Your Voice**...A:59 *Last Thing I Ever Do*	$3	▮	Charisma 98773

THOMAS, B.J. — ★142★ — C&W/AC/BUB/LP '70

Born Billy Joe Thomas on 8/7/42 in Hugo, Oklahoma; raised in Rosenberg, Texas. Pop-country singer. Joined band, The Triumphs, while in high school. Also recorded gospel music since 1976.

1)Raindrops Keep Fallin' On My Head 2)Another Somebody Done Somebody Wrong Song 3)Hooked On A Feeling 4)I'm So Lonesome I Could Cry 5)I Just Can't Help Believing

DEBUT	PEAK	WKS	Gold	A-side (Chart Hit)...B-side	$	Sym	Label & Number
2/19/66	8	13		1 **I'm So Lonesome I Could Cry** *[B.J. THOMAS AND THE TRIUMPHS]*...*Candy Baby* written in 1949 by Hank Williams; first released on Pacemaker 227 in 1964 ($20)	$10		Scepter 12129
5/14/66	22	8		2 **Mama**...*Wendy* first released on Pacemaker 231 in 1964 ($15)	$10		Scepter 12139
6/18/66	34	11		3 **Billy And Sue** *[B.J. THOMAS AND THE TRIUMPHS]*...*Never Tell* first released on Bragg 103 ($25), then on Warner 5491 ($20) in 1964	$12		Hickory 1395
7/30/66	75	4		4 **Bring Back The Time**...*I Don't Have A Mind Of My Own* first released on Pacemaker 234 in 1965 ($15)	$8		Scepter 12154
9/10/66	80	5		5 **Tomorrow Never Comes**...*Your Tears Leave Me Cold* first released on Pacemaker 239 in 1965 ($15); #3 Country hit for Ernest Tubb in 1945	$8		Scepter 12165
5/13/67	94	1		6 **I Can't Help It (If I'm Still In Love With You)**...*Baby Cried* first released on Pacemaker 256 in 1965 ($15); #2 Country hit for Hank Williams in 1951	$8		Scepter 12194
6/22/68	28	14		7 **The Eyes Of A New York Woman**...*I May Never Get To Heaven*	$7		Scepter 12219
11/16/68+	5	16	●	8 **Hooked On A Feeling**...*I've Been Down This Road Before*	$7		Scepter 12230
3/22/69	45	8		9 **It's Only Love**...*You Don't Love Me Anymore ("The Train Song")*	$7		Scepter 12244
7/12/69	97	3		10 **Pass The Apple Eve**...*Fairy Tale Of Time*	$7		Scepter 12255
11/1/69+	❶^4	22	●	11 **Raindrops Keep Fallin' On My Head** AC^7 *Never Had It So Good* from the movie *Butch Cassidy And The Sundance Kid* starring Paul Newman and Robert Redford	$6		Scepter 12265
3/28/70	26	9		12 **Everybody's Out Of Town**...*Living Again*	$6		Scepter 12277
6/20/70	9	13		13 **I Just Can't Help Believing**...AC^1 *Send My Picture To Scranton, PA.*	$6		Scepter 12283
11/28/70+	38	10		14 **Most Of All**...*The Mask*	$6		Scepter 12299
2/27/71	16	11		15 **No Love At All**...*Have A Heart*	$6		Scepter 12307

DEBUT	PEAK	WKS	Gold	A-side (Chart Hit)...B-side	$	Sym	Label & Number
				THOMAS, B.J. — Cont'd			
7/3/71	34	10		16 **Mighty Clouds Of Joy** ... *Life*	$6		Scepter 12320
11/6/71	61	7		17 **Long Ago Tomorrow** ... *Burnin' A Hole In My Mind*	$6		Scepter 12335
2/12/72	15	11		18 **Rock And Roll Lullaby** ... AC[1] *Are We Losing Touch* **Duane Eddy** (guitar); **The Blossoms** and Dave Somerville (of the **Diamonds**; backing vocals)	$6		Scepter 12344
7/15/72	74	6		19 **That's What Friends Are For** ... *I Get Enthused* **Paul Williams** (backing vocal)	$5		Scepter 12354
10/7/72	100	2		20 **Happier Than The Morning Sun** ... *We Have Got To Get Our Ship Together* **The Blossoms** (backing vocals); written by **Stevie Wonder** (Stevie also plays harmonica)	$5		Scepter 12364
2/1/75	❶[1]	18	●	21 **(Hey Won't You Play) Another Somebody Done Somebody Wrong Song** ... CW[1] / AC[1] *City Boys*	$5		ABC 12054
9/20/75	64	9		22 **Help Me Make It (To My Rockin' Chair)** ... *We Are Happy Together*	$5		ABC 12121
7/2/77	17	17		23 **Don't Worry Baby** ... *My Love*	$4		MCA 40735
11/12/77	77	4		24 **Still The Lovin' Is Fun** ... *Play Me A Little Traveling Music*	$4		MCA 40812
1/21/78	43	8		25 **Everybody Loves A Rain Song** ... *Dusty Roads*	$4		MCA 40854
5/21/83	93	2		26 **Whatever Happened To Old Fashioned Love** ... CW[1] *I Just Sing*	$4		Cleveland Int'l. 03492
				THOMAS, Carl R&B/LP **'00** Born in Chicago, Illinois. R&B singer/songwriter.			
3/25/00	20	20		1 **I Wish** ... RB[6] A:16 *(2 versions)*	$6	T	Bad Boy 79321
9/23/00	80	11		2 **Summer Rain** ... A:72 samples "Summer Soft" by **Stevie Wonder**; from the movie *Shaft* starring Samuel L. Jackson (soundtrack on LaFace 26080)			album cut
11/25/00	47	20		3 **Emotional** ... A:38 samples "Shape Of My Heart" by **Sting**; all of above from the album *Emotional* on Bad Boy 73025			album cut
5/5/01	56	20		4 **Can't Believe** ... A:48 / S:65 *(3 versions)* **FAITH EVANS Featuring Carl Thomas** samples "Phone Tap" by The Firm	$6	T	Bad Boy 79370
	★427★			**THOMAS, Carla** R&B/BUB/LP **'61** Born on 12/21/42 in Memphis, Tennessee. "The Queen of Memphis Soul." Daughter of **Rufus Thomas**; sister of R&B singer Vaneese Thomas. Sang with the Teentown Singers at age 10. First recorded with her father for Satellite in 1960. Recorded duets with her father, Rufus, and with **Otis Redding**. *1)Gee Whiz (Look At His Eyes) 2)B-A-B-Y 3)Tramp 4)Knock On Wood 5)I'll Bring It Home To You*			
1/30/61	10	14		1 **Gee Whiz (Look At His Eyes)** *For You* originally released on Satellite 104 in 1960 ($200)	$20		Atlantic 2086
5/8/61	56	6		2 **A Love Of My Own** ... *Promises*	$15		Atlantic 2101
10/13/62	41	8		3 **I'll Bring It Home To You** ... *I Can't Take It* answer song to **Sam Cooke**'s "Bring It On Home To Me"	$15		Atlantic 2163
7/20/63	93	2		4 **What A Fool I've Been** ... *The Life I Live*	$15		Atlantic 2189
12/28/63	23[X]	1		5 **Gee Whiz, It's Christmas** ... *All I Want For Christmas Is You* [X]	$20		Atlantic 2212
6/6/64	92	2		6 **That's Really Some Good /**			
6/20/64	94	1		7 **Night Time Is The Right Time** ... **RUFUS & CARLA** (above 2)	$15		Stax 151
8/1/64	67	9		8 **I've Got No Time To Lose** ... *A Boy Named Tom*	$15		Atlantic 2238
11/28/64	71	4		9 **A Woman's Love** ... *Don't Let The Love Light Leave*	$15		Atlantic 2258
7/3/65	92	3		10 **Stop! Look What You're Doing** ... *Every Ounce Of Strength*	$12		Stax 172
4/30/66	62	6		11 **Let Me Be Good To You** ... *Another Night Without My Man*	$12	■	Stax 188
8/20/66	14	16	●	12 **B-A-B-Y** ... *What Have You Got To Offer Me*	$12		Stax 195
12/10/66	11[X]	3		13 **All I Want For Christmas Is You** ... *Winter Snow* [X] new version of the B-side of #5 above	$15		Stax 206
1/14/67	74	7		14 **Something Good (Is Going To Happen To You)** ... *It's Starting To Grow*	$12		Stax 207
5/6/67	26	9		15 **Tramp** ... *Tell It Like It Is* **OTIS & CARLA**	$12		Stax 216
5/6/67	99	1		16 **When Tomorrow Comes** ... *Unchanging Love*	$12		Stax 214
6/17/67	85	4		17 **I'll Always Have Faith In You** ... *Stop Thief*	$12		Stax 222
8/12/67	30	9		18 **Knock On Wood** ... *Let Me Be Good To You* **OTIS & CARLA**	$12		Stax 228
12/30/67+	68	6		19 **Pick Up The Pieces** ... *Separation*	$12		Stax 239
2/10/68	60	6		20 **Lovey Dovey** ... *New Year's Resolution* **OTIS & CARLA** #2 R&B hit for **The Clovers** in 1954	$12		Stax 244
10/19/68	86	2		21 **Where Do I Go** ... *I've Fallen In Love* (#117/R&B #36) from the off-Broadway rock musical *Hair* starring Steve Curry	$10		Stax 0011
2/15/69	49	11		22 **I Like What You're Doing (To Me)** ... *Strung Out*	$10		Stax 0024
				THOMAS, Danny **'67** Born Muzyad Yakhoob on 1/6/12 in Deerfield, Michigan. Died of a heart attack on 2/6/91 (age 79). Actor. Star of TV's *Make Room For Daddy*. Father of actress Marlo Thomas and TV producer Tony Thomas. Founder of St. Jude's Children's Hospital in Memphis, Tennessee.			
12/23/67	24[X]	2		**The First Christmas** ... *Christmas Story* [X] Sid Feller (orch.); from the TV special *Cricket On The Hearth*	$15	■	RCA Victor 9342
				THOMAS, Dante **'01** Born on 1/7/78 in Salt Lake City, Utah. Pop-R&B singer. Discovered by **Pras Michel** of **The Fugees**.			
7/14/01	85	6		**Miss California** ... S:22 *(rap remix)* **DANTE THOMAS Featuring Pras**	$5	★	Rat Pack 67157
				THOMAS, Evelyn R&B **'84** Born on 8/22/53 in Chicago, Illinois. Disco singer.			
9/29/84	85	5		**High Energy** ... *(short version)* special remix versions issued on TSR 833 in 1984 with a picture sleeve	$5		TSR 106
				THOMAS, Gene — see GENE & DEBBE			

DEBUT	PEAK	WKS	Gold	A-side (Chart Hit)...B-side	$	Sym	Label & Number

THOMAS, Ian — '73

Born in Hamilton, Ontario, Canada. Pop singer/songwriter. Brother of comedian Dave Thomas ("**Doug McKenzie**").

DEBUT	PEAK	WKS	Gold	A-side (Chart Hit)...B-side	$	Sym	Label & Number
10/27/73+	34	14		**Painted Ladies** ...*Will You Still Love Me*	$6		Janus 224

THOMAS, Irma — BUB/R&B/LP '64

Born Irma Lee on 2/18/41 in Ponchatoula, Louisiana. R&B singer. Nicknamed "The Soul Queen of New Orleans."

DEBUT	PEAK	WKS	Gold	A-side (Chart Hit)...B-side	$	Sym	Label & Number
3/28/64	17	12		1 **Wish Someone Would Care**...*Break-A-Way*	$15		Imperial 66013
7/4/64	52	6		2 **Anyone Who Knows What Love Is (will understand)** ...*Time Is On My Side*	$12		Imperial 66041
11/7/64	98	2		3 **Times Have Changed**...*Moments To Remember*	$12		Imperial 66069
12/19/64+	63	8		4 **He's My Guy**...*(I Want A) True, True Love*	$12		Imperial 66080

THOMAS, Jamo — '66

Born in Chicago, Illinois. Soul singer/percussionist. Member of the **Bobby Peterson Quintet** from 1958-62.

DEBUT	PEAK	WKS	Gold	A-side (Chart Hit)...B-side	$	Sym	Label & Number
3/19/66	98	2		**I Spy (For The FBI)** ...*Snake Hip Mama* **JAMO THOMAS & His Party Brothers Orchestra**	$15	■	Thomas 303

THOMAS, Jon, and Orchestra — '60

Born in Cincinnati, Ohio. Blues singer/keyboardist. Staff musician at King Records, 1956-60. Died on 10/28/94 (age 76).

DEBUT	PEAK	WKS	Gold	A-side (Chart Hit)...B-side	$	Sym	Label & Number
6/6/60	48	10		**Heartbreak (It's Hurtin' Me)** ...*Teasin'*	$15		ABC-Paramount 10122

THOMAS, Nolan — R&B/BUB '85

Born Mark Kalfa on 8/24/66 in Jersey City, New Jersey; raised in Edison, New Jersey. R&B singer/songwriter.

DEBUT	PEAK	WKS	Gold	A-side (Chart Hit)...B-side	$	Sym	Label & Number
1/5/85	57	13		**Yo' Little Brother**...*(dub mix)*	$4		Mirage 99697

THOMAS, Pat — '62

Born in Chicago, Illinois. Black female pop-jazz vocalist.

DEBUT	PEAK	WKS	Gold	A-side (Chart Hit)...B-side	$	Sym	Label & Number
12/8/62	78	2		**Desafinado (Slightly Out Of Tune)** ...*One Note Samba* **Lalo Schifrin** (orch.); also released on Verve 10269 in 1962 ($8) with the same picture sleeve	$8	■	MGM 13102

THOMAS, Rob — see MATCHBOX TWENTY / SANTANA

THOMAS, Rufus — R&B/BUB/LP '63

Born on 3/26/17 in Cayce, Mississippi; raised in Memphis, Tennessee. Died on 12/15/2001 (age 84). R&B singer/songwriter/choreographer. Father of singers Vaneese and **Carla Thomas**. First recorded for Talent in 1950. DJ at WDIA-Memphis from 1953-74. Recorded for Alligator Records in the late '80s.

1)Walking The Dog 2)(Do The) Push And Pull 3)Do The Funky Chicken

DEBUT	PEAK	WKS	Gold	A-side (Chart Hit)...B-side	$	Sym	Label & Number
2/9/63	87	8		1 **The Dog**...*Did You Ever Love A Woman*	$15		Stax 130
10/5/63	10	14	●	2 **Walking The Dog** *You Said*	$15		Stax 140
2/1/64	48	9		3 **Can Your Monkey Do The Dog**...*I Want To Get Married*	$15		Stax 144
4/11/64	86	2		4 **Somebody Stole My Dog**...*I Want To Be Loved*	$15		Stax 149
6/6/64	92	2		5 **That's Really Some Good /**			
6/20/64	94	1		6 **Night Time Is The Right Time**... **RUFUS & CARLA** (above 2)	$15		Stax 151
10/10/64	49	7		7 **Jump Back**...*All Night Worker*	$15		Stax 157
2/7/70	28	12		8 **Do The Funky Chicken** ...*Turn Your Damper Down*	$8		Stax 0059
12/19/70+	25	13		9 **(Do The) Push And Pull Part I** ...RB[2] *Part II*	$8		Stax 0079
8/14/71	31	10		10 **The Breakdown (Part I)** ...*(Part II)*	$8		Stax 0098
12/25/71+	44	10		11 **Do The Funky Penguin Part I**...*Part II*	$8		Stax 0112

THOMAS, Tasha — '79

Born in 1950 in Jeutyn, Alaska. Died of cancer on 11/8/84 (age 34). Black disco singer. Moved to New York in 1970. Played "Auntie Em" in Broadway's *The Wiz*. Session singer for **Kiss**, **Cat Stevens**, **Diana Ross** and others.

DEBUT	PEAK	WKS	Gold	A-side (Chart Hit)...B-side	$	Sym	Label & Number
1/27/79	91	5		**Shoot Me (With Your Love)**...*(instrumental)* originally released on Orbit 2668 in 1978	$4		Atlantic 3542

THOMAS, Timmy — R&B/BUB/LP '73

Born on 11/13/44 in Evansville, Indiana. R&B-disco singer/songwriter/keyboardist. Studio musician at Gold Wax Records in Memphis. Moved to Miami in 1970. Session work for **Betty Wright** and **KC & The Sunshine Band**.

DEBUT	PEAK	WKS	Gold	A-side (Chart Hit)...B-side	$	Sym	Label & Number
11/25/72+	3	15		1 **Why Can't We Live Together** ...RB[2] *Funky Me*	$6		Glades 1703
4/7/73	75	5		2 **People Are Changin'**...*Rainbow Power*	$6		Glades 1709
6/2/84	80	3		3 **Gotta Give A Little Love (Ten Years After)**...*Same Ole Song*	$4		Gold Mountain 82004

THOMPSON, Chris — see NIGHT / WARNES, Jennifer

THOMPSON, Gina — R&B/BUB '96

Born in 1974 in Vineland, New Jersey. R&B singer. Also see **Crystal Waters**' "Say...If You Feel Alright."

DEBUT	PEAK	WKS	Gold	A-side (Chart Hit)...B-side	$	Sym	Label & Number
7/13/96	41	20		1 **The Things That You Do**...S:27 *(remix)* a special remix featuring **Raekwon** and **Craig Mack** released on Mercury 578712	$3	▮	Mercury 578158
10/2/99	26[S]	10		2 **Ya Di Ya**...BUB:124 *Take My Number Down* **GINA THOMPSON featuring Missy "Misdemeanor" Elliott**	$4	★	EastWest 64033

THOMPSON, Hank — C&W/BUB/MEM '60

Born on 9/3/25 in Waco, Texas. Country singer/songwriter (charted 79 hits, 1948-83).

DEBUT	PEAK	WKS	Gold	A-side (Chart Hit)...B-side	$	Sym	Label & Number
7/25/60	99	1		**She's Just A Whole Lot Like You** ...*There My Future Goes*	$20		Capitol 4386

THOMPSON, Kay — '56

Born on 11/9/13 in St. Louis, Missouri. Died on 7/2/98 (age 84). Wrote *Eloise* series of children's books. In the movie musical *Funny Face*, 1957.

DEBUT	PEAK	WKS	Gold	A-side (Chart Hit)...B-side	$	Sym	Label & Number
3/10/56	39	8		**Eloise**...T:39 *Just One Of Those Things* [N] **Archie Bleyer** (orch.); picture sleeve and record issued on Cadence Children's Series	$12	■	Cadence CCS 3

THOMPSON, Robbin, Band — LP '80

Pop-rock group from Virginia: Robbin Thompson (vocals, guitar), Velpo Robertson (guitar), Eric Heiberg (keyboards), Michael Lanning (bass) and Bob Antonelli (drums). Thompson played in **Bruce Springsteen**'s early Steel Mill band.

DEBUT	PEAK	WKS	Gold	A-side (Chart Hit)...B-side	$	Sym	Label & Number
10/18/80	66	9		**Brite Eyes** ...*That's Alright*	$5	⊙	Ovation 1157

DEBUT	PEAK	WKS	Gold	A-side (Chart Hit)....B-side	$	Sym	Label & Number
				THOMPSON, Sue C&W/BUB/AC/LP **'62**			
				Born Eva Sue McKee on 7/19/26 in Nevada, Missouri; raised in San Jose, California. Became a popular country singer in the 1970s; charted 9 hits with **Don Gibson**.			
9/4/61	5	14		1 **Sad Movies (Make Me Cry)**....AC[1] *Nine Little Teardrops*	$15		Hickory 1153
12/4/61+	3	16		2 **Norman** *Never Love Again*	$15		Hickory 1159
3/17/62	42	9		3 **Two Of A Kind**....*It Has To Be*	$12	⊙	Hickory 1166
				foldout promo insert features 3 photos of Sue printed in lavender ink			
6/16/62	31	11		4 **Have A Good Time**....*If The Boy Only Knew* (#112)	$12		Hickory 1174
9/29/62	17	10		5 **James (Hold The Ladder Steady)**....*My Hero*	$12		Hickory 1183
1/12/63	78	5		6 **Willie Can**....*Too Much In Love*	$12		Hickory 1196
1/2/65	23	10		7 **Paper Tiger**....*Mama, Don't Cry At My Wedding*	$12		Hickory 1284
				#1, 2, 5 & 7: written by **John D. Loudermilk**			
				THOMPSON, Tony — see HI-FIVE			
	★457★			**THOMPSON TWINS** R&B/ROK/LP **'84**			
				Synth-rock/dance trio from England: Tom Bailey (lead singer, synthesizer; born on 1/18/57), Alannah Currie (xylophone, percussion; born on 9/28/57; native of New Zealand) and Joe Leeway (conga, synthesizer; born on 11/15/57). Leeway left in 1986. Bailey and Currie recorded in 1993 as Babble.			
				1)Hold Me Now 2)Lay Your Hands On Me 3)King For A Day			
1/22/83	30	16		1 **Lies**....*Beach Culture*	$4		Arista 1024
4/30/83	45	9		2 **Love On Your Side**....*Love On Your Back*	$4	■	Arista 1056
				also released on Arista 9013 in 1983			
2/11/84	3	21		3 **Hold Me Now** *Let Loving Start*	$4	■	Arista 9164
5/26/84	11	16		4 **Doctor! Doctor!**....*Nurse Shark*	$4	■	Arista 9209
8/25/84	44	9		5 **You Take Me Up**....*Passion Planet*	$4	■	Arista 9244
11/10/84	69	6		6 **The Gap**....*Out Of The Gap (medley)*	$4		Arista 9290
				above 4 from the album *Into The Gap*			
9/21/85	6	20		7 **Lay Your Hands On Me**....A:5 / S:7 *The Lewis Carol (Adventures In Wonderland)*	$3	■	Arista 9396
1/18/86	8	16		8 **King For A Day**....A:7 / S:8 *Rollunder*	$3	■	Arista 9450
7/26/86	54	10		9 **Nothing In Common**....*Nothing To Lose*	$3	■	Arista 9511
				title song from the movie starring Tom Hanks			
3/28/87	31	11		10 **Get That Love**....S:27 / A:30 *Perfect Day*	$3	■	Arista 9577
9/23/89	28	12		11 **Sugar Daddy**....A:27 / S:31 *Monkey Man*	$3	■	Warner 22819
				THOMSON, Ali BUB/LP **'80**			
				Born in Glasgow, Scotland. Pop singer/songwriter. Younger brother of **Supertramp**'s Dougie Thomson.			
6/14/80	15	17		1 **Take A Little Rhythm**....*Jamie*	$4		A&M 2243
9/13/80	42	11		2 **Live Every Minute**....*Saturday Heartbreaker*	$4	■	A&M 2260
				THOMSON, Cyndi C&W/BUB/LP **'01**			
				Born on 10/19/76 in Tifton, Georgia. Country singer/songwriter.			
6/2/01	26	20		**What I Really Meant To Say**....CW[3] S:12 / A:23 *Things I Would Do*	$5	★+V	Capitol 58987
				THORNE, David **'62**			
				Black Adult Contemporary vocalist.			
10/20/62	76	4		**The Alley Cat Song**....*The Moon Was Yellow*	$12		Riverside 4530
				Richard Wolfe (orch.); vocal version of **Bent Fabric**'s instrumental hit "Alley Cat"			
				THOROGOOD, George, & The Destroyers ROK/BUB/LP **'85**			
				Born on 12/31/52 in Wilmington, Delaware. Blues-rock singer/guitarist. The Destroyers: Hank Carter (sax), Billy Blough (bass) and Jeff Simon (drums).			
6/15/85	63	8		**Willie And The Hand Jive**....*I Drink Alone* (ROK #13)	$5		EMI America 8270
				THORPE, Billy BUB/LP **'79**			
				Born on 3/29/46 in Manchester, England. Moved to Australia in 1964. Rock singer/guitarist. Superstar artist in Australia. Member of Mick Fleetwood's (of **Fleetwood Mac**) Zoo.			
7/28/79	41	10		**Children Of The Sun**....*Wrapped In The Chains Of Your Love*	$5		Capricorn 0321
				charted first 6 weeks on Capricorn 0321, 4 remaining weeks on Polydor 2018 ($5); both are the same version			
				THREE CHUCKLES, The **'54**			
				Pop vocal trio from Brooklyn, New York: **Teddy Randazzo** (accordion), Tom Romano (guitar) and Russ Gilberto (bass). Appeared in the movies *Rock Rock Rock* and *The Girl Can't Help It.*			
11/13/54	20	8		1 **Runaround**....S:20 *At Last You Understand*	$25		"X" 0066
				first released on Boulevard 100 in 1954 ($75)			
11/12/55	67	5		2 **Times Two, I Love You**....T:67 *Still Thinking Of You*	$25		"X" 0162
3/17/56	70	3		3 **And The Angels Sing**....T:70 *Tell Me (That Your Love Is For Me)*	$25		Vik 0194
				#1 hit for **Benny Goodman** in 1939; Marty Gold (orch., above 2)			
				THREE DEGREES, The R&B/BUB/AC/LP **'74**			
				Female R&B vocal trio from Philadelphia, Pennsylvania: Fayette Pinkney, Linda Turner and Shirley Porter. Turner and Porter replaced by Sheila Ferguson and Valerie Holiday in 1966. Discovered by **Richard Barrett**. Group appeared in the 1971 movie *The French Connection.*			
3/6/65	80	5		1 **Gee Baby (I'm Sorry)** *[THE 3° DEGREES]*....*Do What You're Supposed To Do*	$15		Swan 4197
1/1/66	97	1		2 **Look In My Eyes** *[THE 3° DEGREES]*....*Drivin' Me Mad*	$15		Swan 4235
6/6/70	29	12		3 **Maybe**....*Collage*	$7		Roulette 7079
9/12/70	48	9		4 **I Do Take You**....*You're The Fool*	$7		Roulette 7088
1/23/71	77	6		5 **You're The One**....*Stardust*	$7		Roulette 7097
5/8/71	98	2		6 **There's So Much Love All Around Me**....*Yours*	$7		Roulette 7102
				all of above produced by **Richard Barrett**			
3/2/74	❶[2]	18	●	7 **TSOP (The Sound Of Philadelphia)**....RB[1] / AC[2] *Something For Nothing* [I]	$6		Philadelphia I. 3540
				theme from the TV show *Soul Train*			
7/6/74	85	4		8 **Love Is The Message**....*My One And Only Love*	$6		Philadelphia I. 3547
				MFSB featuring The Three Degrees (above 2)			
9/28/74	2[1]	18	▲	9 **When Will I See You Again** AC[1] *Year Of Decision*	$6		Philadelphia I. 3550

DEBUT	PEAK	WKS	Gold	A-side (Chart Hit)...B-side	$	Sym	Label & Number

THREE DOG NIGHT ★92★ BUB/AC/LP '71

Pop-rock vocal trio formed in Los Angeles, California: Danny Hutton (born on 9/10/42), Cory Wells (born on 2/5/42) and Chuck Negron (born on 6/8/42). Named for the coldest night in the Australian outback. Disbanded in the mid-1970s. Re-formed in the mid-1980s.

1)Joy To The World 2)Mama Told Me (Not To Come) 3)Black & White 4)Shambala 5)An Old Fashioned Love Song

DEBUT	PEAK	WKS	Gold	A-side (Chart Hit)...B-side	$	Sym	Label & Number
2/8/69	29	12		1 **Try A Little Tenderness** ...*That No One Ever Hurt This Bad* #6 hit for Ted Lewis in 1933	$8		Dunhill/ABC 4177
5/3/69	5	16	●	2 **One**...*Chest Fever* written and recorded by **Nilsson** in 1968 on RCA Victor 9462 ($8)	$7		Dunhill/ABC 4191
8/9/69	4	13		3 **Easy To Be Hard**...*Dreaming Isn't Good For You* from the off-Broadway rock musical *Hair* starring Steve Curry	$7		Dunhill/ABC 4203
10/25/69	10	14		4 **Eli's Coming**...*Circle For A Landing* written by **Laura Nyro**	$7		Dunhill/ABC 4215
2/28/70	15	9		5 **Celebrate**...*Feeling Alright* all of above produced by Gabriel Mekler	$7		Dunhill/ABC 4229
5/23/70	❶²	15	●	6 **Mama Told Me (Not To Come)**...*Rock & Roll Widow* written by **Randy Newman**	$6	■	Dunhill/ABC 4239
8/29/70	15	11		7 **Out In The Country**...*Good Time Living*	$6		Dunhill/ABC 4250
11/21/70+	19	11		8 **One Man Band**...*It Ain't Easy*	$6		Dunhill/ABC 4262
3/13/71	❶⁶	17	●	9 **Joy To The World** *I Can Hear You Calling*	$5		Dunhill/ABC 4272
7/10/71	7	12		10 **Liar**...*Can't Get Enough Of It* written by **Russ Ballard**	$5		Dunhill/ABC 4282
11/13/71	4	11	●	11 **An Old Fashioned Love Song**...AC[1] *Jam*	$5		Dunhill/ABC 4294
12/25/71+	5	12		12 **Never Been To Spain**...*Peace Of Mind* #9 & 12: written by **Hoyt Axton**	$5		Dunhill/ABC 4299
3/25/72	12	9		13 **The Family Of Man**...*Going In Circles*	$5		Dunhill/ABC 4306
8/12/72	❶¹	11	●	14 **Black & White**...AC[1] *Freedom For The Stallion*	$5		Dunhill/ABC 4317
11/18/72+	19	14		15 **Pieces Of April**...*The Writings On The Wall*	$5		Dunhill/ABC 4331
5/19/73	3	16	●	16 **Shambala**...*Our "B" Side*	$5		Dunhill/ABC 4352
10/27/73	17	12		17 **Let Me Serenade You**...*Storybook Feeling* #6-17: produced by Richard Podolor	$5		Dunhill/ABC 4370
3/16/74	4	19	●	18 **The Show Must Go On**...*On The Way Back Home* written and recorded by **Leo Sayer** in 1973 on Warner 7768 ($8)	$5		Dunhill/ABC 4382
6/29/74	16	13		19 **Sure As I'm Sittin' Here**...*Anytime Babe*	$5		Dunhill/ABC 15001
9/28/74	33	12		20 **Play Something Sweet (Brickyard Blues)**...*I'd Be So Happy*	$5		Dunhill/ABC 15013
7/5/75	32	9		21 **Til The World Ends**...*Yo Te Quiero Hablar (Take you Down)*	$5		ABC 12114

3 DOORS DOWN ROK/BUB/LP '00

Rock group from Escatawpa, Mississippi: Brad Arnold (vocals), Matt Roberts (guitar), Todd Harrell (bass) and Chris Henderson (drums).

DEBUT	PEAK	WKS	Gold	A-side (Chart Hit)...B-side	$	Sym	Label & Number
4/8/00	3	53		1 **Kryptonite**...AR[9] / MR[11] A:❶⁶			album cut
10/21/00	55	20		2 **Loser**...AR[21] A:50			album cut
7/28/01	24	21		3 **Be Like That**...A:25 from the movie *American Pie 2* starring Jason Biggs; all of above from the album *The Better Life* on Republic 153920			album cut
11/23/02+	4	38↑		4 **When I'm Gone**...A:5 from the album *Away From The Sun* on Republic 064396; "45": Republic 156263; B-side: (same version)		V	album cut

311 ROK/BUB/LP '96

Rock-funk group from Omaha, Nebraska: Nicholas Hexum and Doug Martinez (vocals), Tim Mahoney (guitar), P-Nut (bass) and Chad Sexton (drums). 311 is the police code for indecent exposure. Pronounced: three eleven.

DEBUT	PEAK	WKS	Gold	A-side (Chart Hit)...B-side	$	Sym	Label & Number
7/20/96	37^A	20		1 **Down**...MR[4]			album cut
11/9/96+	36^A	20		2 **All Mixed Up**... above 2 from the album *311* on Capricorn 42041			album cut

3 FRIENDS, The '61

Black doo-wop trio from Compton, California: Julius Brown and brothers Clay and Walter Hammond (**The Olympics**).

DEBUT	PEAK	WKS	Gold	A-side (Chart Hit)...B-side	$	Sym	Label & Number
7/31/61	89	2		**Dedicated (To The Songs I Love)**...*Happy As A Man Can Be* [N] lyrics are made up from hit song titles	$30		Imperial 5763

THREE G'S, The '58

Pop vocal trio from the Los Angeles, California: brothers Ted, Robert and Jerry Glasser.

DEBUT	PEAK	WKS	Gold	A-side (Chart Hit)...B-side	$	Sym	Label & Number
8/4/58	55	3		**Let's Go Steady For The Summer**...H:55 *Wild Man*	$20		Columbia 41175

3LW R&B/LP '01

Female R&B vocal trio from New Jersey: Naturi Naughton, Kiely Williams and Adrienne Bailon. 3LW: 3 Little Women.

DEBUT	PEAK	WKS	Gold	A-side (Chart Hit)...B-side	$	Sym	Label & Number
11/4/00+	23	25		1 **No More (Baby I'ma Do Right)**...S:20 / A:21 *(3 versions) / I Can't Take It* (w/**Nas**)	$8	★*	Epic 79505
6/2/01	81	7		2 **Playas Gon' Play**...*(3 versions)*	$6	T	Epic 79595
3/30/02	53	20		3 **Feels Good (Don't Worry Bout A Thing)**...S:3 / A:64 *(3 remixes) / Rah Rah* **NAUGHTY BY NATURE Featuring 3LW** contains an interpolation of "Feels Good" by **Tony! Toni! Toné!**	$4	★	TVT 2344
8/3/02	58	14		4 **I Do (Wanna Get Close To You)**...S:41 / A:59 *(4 versions)* **3LW Featuring P. Diddy & Loon**	$6	T	Epic 79769

3 MAN ISLAND '88

Dance trio based in London, England: Tim Cox, Nigel Swanston and Mike Whitford.

DEBUT	PEAK	WKS	Gold	A-side (Chart Hit)...B-side	$	Sym	Label & Number
4/2/88	94	2		**Jack The Lad**...*(instrumental)*	$4	■	Chrysalis 43231

DEBUT	PEAK	WKS	Gold	A-side (Chart Hit)...B-side	$	Sym	Label & Number
				3 OF HEARTS C&W **'01**			
				Female country vocal trio from Fort Worth, Texas: Blaire Stroud, Katie McNeill and Deserea Wasdin.			
4/28/01	33^S	3		**Love Is Enough** ... *(3 album snippets)*	$5	★[+]	RCA 69034
				THREE PLAYMATES, The **'58**			
				Female R&B doo-wop trio from Newark, New Jersey: sisters Lucille and Alma Beatty with Gwen Brooks. Label credit similar to **The Playmates** (Donny-Morey-Chic): The Three Playmates (Lucille-Alma-Gwen).			
3/10/58	89	1		**Sugah Wooga** ... T:89 *Lovey Dovey Pair*	$25		Savoy 1528
				arrangement is similar to "Little Bitty Pretty One" by **Thurston Harris**			
				3T R&B/BUB/LP **'95**			
				R&B teen vocal trio from Los Angeles, California: brothers Taryll, T.J. and Taj Jackson. Sons of Tito Jackson (**The Jacksons**).			
10/7/95+	15	33	●	**Anything** ... S:9 / A:22 *(Urban mix) / What Will It Take*	$4	▮[V]	MJJ Music 77913
				"45": MJJ Music 78291; B-side: "Tease Me" (R&B #90)			
				THREE THE...— see G. DEP			
				THUNDER ROK/LP **'91**			
				Hard-rock group from England: Daniel Bowes (vocals), Luke Morley (guitar), Ben Matthews (keyboards), Mark Luckhurst (bass) and Gary James (drums).			
6/1/91	55	13		**Dirty Love** ... *Girl's Going Out Of Her Head*	$4	▮[V]	Geffen 19026
				THUNDER, Johnny BUB **'63**			
				Born Gil Hamilton on 8/15/41 in Leesburg, Florida. R&B singer. Discovered by producer **Teddy Vann**.			
12/22/62+	4	11		1 **Loop De Loop** ... *Don't Be Ashamed*	$15		Diamond 129
				based on the traditional children's song originally known as "Looby Loo"			
11/27/65	67	5		2 **Everybody Do The Sloopy** ... *Beautiful*	$15		Diamond 192
4/15/67	96	1		3 **Make Love To Me** ... *Teach Me Tonight*	$15		Diamond 218
				JOHNNY THUNDER & RUBY WINTERS			
				#1 hit for **Jo Stafford** in 1954			
				THUNDERCLAP NEWMAN LP **'69**			
				Rock trio formed in England: Andy Newman (keyboards), John "Speedy" Keene (vocals, drums) and Jimmy McCulloch (guitarist with **Wings**, 1975-77). McCulloch died of heart failure on 9/27/79 (age 26). Keene died on 3/21/2002 (age 56). Group assembled by **Pete Townshend**.			
9/6/69	37	10		**Something In The Air** ... *Wilhemina*	$10		Track 2656
				from the movie *The Magic Christian* starring Peter Sellers and **Ringo Starr**; "Bubbled Under" (#120) on 10/24/70 on Track 2769			
				THUNDERKLOUD, Billy, & The Chieftones C&W **'75**			
				Country group of Native American musicians from British Columbia, Canada: Vincent "Billy Thunderkloud" Clifford, Jack Wolf, Barry Littlestar and Richard Grayowl.			
6/28/75	92	3		**What Time Of Day** ... *When Love Is Right*	$5		20th Century 2181
				backing vocals by a children's chorus			
				TIA **'87**			
				Born in Lynbrook, Long Island, New York. Female disco singer. Discovered by producer Roy Be (**Ecstasy, Passion & Pain**).			
3/7/87	97	2		**Boy Toy** ... *(Toy Breakdown)*	$3	■	RCA 5107
				TIANA **'90**			
				Born on 5/2/67 in Vermont. Female dance singer.			
7/14/90	81	12		**First True Love** ... *(4 versions)*	$6	▮[*]	MicMac 2537
				TICO AND THE TRIUMPHS — see SIMON, Paul			
				TIERRA R&B/LP **'81**			
				Latin group formed in Los Angeles, California: brothers Steve (trombone, timbales) and Rudy (guitar) Salas, Joey Guerra (keyboards), Bobby Navarrete (reeds), Andre Baeza (congas), Steve Falomir (bass) and Phil Madayag (drums). The Salas brothers and Baeza were formerly with **El Chicano**.			
11/8/80+	18	21		1 **Together** ... *Zoot Suit Boogie/In The Mood Theme*	$4		Boardwalk 5702
				first released in 1980 on ASI 201			
3/14/81	62	8		2 **Memories** ... *Time To Dance*	$4		Boardwalk 70073
10/24/81	72	6		3 **La La Means I Love You** ... *Summer Daze*	$4		Boardwalk 129
				TIFFANY AC/LP **'87**			
				Born Tiffany Darwish on 10/2/71 in Norwalk, California. Teen pop singer.			
8/29/87	$❶^2$	24		1 **I Think We're Alone Now** ... S:$❶^2$ / A:$❶^2$ *No Rules*	$3	■	MCA 53167
11/28/87+	$❶^2$	20		2 **Could've Been** AC[1] A:$❶^3$ / S:$❶^2$ *The Heart Of Love*	$3	■	MCA 53231
2/27/88	7	14		3 **I Saw Him Standing There** ... S:2 / A:8 *Mr. Mambo*	$3	■	MCA 53285
				female version of **The Beatles**' "I Saw Her Standing There"			
6/11/88	50	9		4 **Feelings Of Forever** ... S:40 *Out Of My Heart*	$3	■	MCA 53325
				above 4 from the album *Tiffany*			
11/5/88+	6	21		5 **All This Time** ... S:7 / A:9 *Can't Stop A Heartbeat*	$3	■	MCA 53371
2/25/89	35	9		6 **Radio Romance** ... S:26 *I'll Be The Girl*	$3	■	MCA 53623
				all of above produced by George E. Tobin			
				TIGGI CLAY **'84**			
				Black trio: Debravon "Fizzy Qwick" Lewis (lead singer), Romeo McCall and Billy Peaches. Fizzy Qwick hit the R&B charts in 1986.			
2/25/84	86	3		**Flashes** ... *Roses For Lydia*	$5		Morocco 1716
				TIGHT FIT **'81**			
				Studio group assembled by British producer Ken Gold: Steve Grant, Denise Gyngell, Julie Harris, Vicki Pemberton, Carol Stevens and Roy Ward.			
10/10/81	89	3		**Back To The 60's** ... *Coco-Nite*	$5		Arista 0638
				Dancing In The Street/(I Can't Get No) Satisfaction/You Really Got Me/Do Wah Diddy Diddy/Black Is Black/Bend Me, Shape Me/When You Walk In The Room/Mony Mony			
				TIJUANA BRASS, The — see ALPERT, Herb			

DEBUT	PEAK	WKS	Gold	A-side (Chart Hit)	B-side	$	Sym	Label & Number

TILLMAN, Bertha — '62

Born in San Diego, California. R&B singer.

DEBUT	PEAK	WKS	Gold	A-side (Chart Hit)	B-side	$	Sym	Label & Number
5/5/62	61	9		**Oh My Angel**	*Lovin' Time*	$25		Brent 7029

TILLOTSON, Johnny ★155★ — BUB/C&W/LP '62

Born on 4/20/39 in Jacksonville, Florida; raised in Palatka, Florida. Teen idol pop singer/songwriter. On local radio *Young Folks Revue* from age nine. DJ on WWPF. Appeared on the *Toby Dowdy* TV show in Jacksonville, then own show. Signed by Cadence Records in 1958. In the movie *Just For Fun.*

1)Poetry In Motion 2)It Keeps Right On A-Hurtin' 3)Talk Back Trembling Lips 4)Without You 5)Send Me The Pillow You Dream On

DEBUT	PEAK	WKS	Gold	A-side (Chart Hit)	B-side	$	Sym	Label & Number
11/3/58+	63	9		1 **Dreamy Eyes /** also see #10 below				
10/6/58	87	3		2 **Well I'm Your Man**	H:87	$20		Cadence 1353
8/24/59	54	9		3 **True True Happiness**	*Love Is Blind*	$20		Cadence 1365
1/18/60	42	14		4 **Why Do I Love You So**	*Never Let Me Go*	$20		Cadence 1372
4/11/60	57	7		5 **Earth Angel /**				
4/11/60	63	6		6 **Pledging My Love**		$20	■	Cadence 1377
10/10/60	2^1	15		7 **Poetry In Motion**	*Princess, Princess*	$20		Cadence 1384
1/9/61	25	11		8 **Jimmy's Girl**	*(Little Sparrow) His True Love Said Goodbye*	$15	■	Cadence 1391
8/7/61	7	13		9 **Without You**	*Cutie Pie*	$15		Cadence 1404
12/4/61+	35	14		10 **Dreamy Eyes** same version as #1 above	*Well I'm Your Man* [R]	$15		Cadence 1409
5/12/62	3	14		11 **It Keeps Right On A-Hurtin'**	*She Gave Sweet Love To Me*	$15		Cadence 1418
8/11/62	17	9		12 **Send Me The Pillow You Dream On**	*What'll I Do* (#106)	$15		Cadence 1424
10/27/62	24	9		13 **I Can't Help It (If I'm Still In Love With You) /**				
12/1/62	89	1		14 **I'm So Lonesome I Could Cry** above 2 are classic country hits by Hank Williams		$15		Cadence 1432
3/2/63	24	10		15 **Out Of My Mind**	*Empty Feelin'*	$15		Cadence 1434
8/10/63	18	10		16 **You Can Never Stop Me Loving You**	*Judy, Judy, Judy*	$15		Cadence 1437
10/19/63	50	6		17 **Funny How Time Slips Away** written by **Willie Nelson**	*A Very Good Year For Girls*	$15		Cadence 1441
11/9/63+	7	13		18 **Talk Back Trembling Lips** #1 Country hit for Ernest Ashworth in 1963	*Another You*	$12	■	MGM 13181
2/22/64	37	7		19 **Worried Guy**	*Please Don't Go Away* (#112)	$10	■	MGM 13193
5/2/64	36	8		20 **I Rise, I Fall**	*I'm Watching My Watch*	$10	■	MGM 13232
7/18/64	45	10		21 **Worry**	*Sufferin' From A Heartache*	$10	■	MGM 13255
10/31/64	31	11		22 **She Understands Me** song charted in 1966 by **Bobby Vinton** as "Dum-De-Da"	*Tomorrow*	$10	■	MGM 13284
2/13/65	51	7		23 **Angel** from the Walt Disney movie *Those Calloways* starring Brian Keith and Vera Miles	*Little Boy*	$10	■	MGM 13316
6/5/65	86	4		24 **Then I'll Count Again**	*One's Yours, One's Mine*	$10	■	MGM 13344
8/28/65	35	8		25 **Heartaches By The Number** #2 Country hit for **Ray Price** in 1959	*Your Mem'ry Comes Along*	$10	■	MGM 13376
11/20/65	70	6		26 **Our World**	*(Wait 'Til You See) My Gidget*	$10		MGM 13408

'TIL TUESDAY — ROK/LP '85

Pop-rock group formed in Boston, Massachusetts: **Aimee Mann** (vocals, bass) (see #6 below), Robert Holmes (guitar), Joey Pesce (keyboards) and Michael Hausman (drums). Michael Montes replaced Pesce in 1988.

DEBUT	PEAK	WKS	Gold	A-side (Chart Hit)	B-side	$	Sym	Label & Number
4/13/85	8	21		1 **Voices Carry**	A:7 / S:9 *Are You Serious?*	$3	■	Epic 04795
8/24/85	61	5		2 **Looking Over My Shoulder**	*Don't Watch Me Bleed*	$3	■	Epic 04935
9/20/86	26	14		3 **What About Love**	S:24 / A:30 *Will She Just Fall Down*	$3	■	Epic 06289
1/10/87	59	10		4 **Coming Up Close**	*Angels Never Call*	$3	■	Epic 06571
1/21/89	95	3		5 **(Believed You Were) Lucky**	*Limits To Love*	$3	■	Epic 08059
1/21/95	93	6		6 **That's Just What You Are** **AIMEE MANN**	*I Should've Known*	$3	■	Imago 25086

TIMBALAND AND MAGOO — R&B/BUB/LP '97

Timbaland is male rapper/producer Timothy Mosley (born on 3/10/71). Magoo (born Melvin Barcliff) is a male rapper. Both were born in Norfolk, Virginia. Also see **Aaliyah**.

DEBUT	PEAK	WKS	Gold	A-side (Chart Hit)	B-side	$	Sym	Label & Number
7/19/97	12	20	●	1 **Up Jumps Da Boogie** *[MAGOO and TIMBALAND]* **Aaliyah** and **Missy Elliott** (guest vocals)	S:7 *(remix)*	$3	■	Blackground 98018
1/10/98	37^A	20		2 **Luv 2 Luv U**				album cut
5/2/98	37	14		3 **Clock Strikes** samples the theme from TV's *Knight Rider* starring David Hasselhoff; all of above from the album *Welcome To Our World* on Blackground 92772	S:27 *(album version)*	$3	■	Blackground 97995
12/5/98	92	4		4 **Here We Come** **TIMBALAND featuring Missy "Misdemeanor" Elliott & Magoo** from the album *Tim's Bio: Life From Da Bassment* on Blackground 92815	A:75			album cut
3/18/00	73	7		5 **Ryde Or Die, Chick** **LOX Featuring Timbaland and Eve** from the album *We Are The Streets* on Ruff Ryders 490599	A:65			album cut
6/2/01	59	16		6 **We Need A Resolution** **AALIYAH feat. Timbaland** "45" B-side: (instrumental)	A:50 *(3 versions)*	$6	T^V	Blackground 38781
12/7/02	46^S	2		7 **Ching Ching** **MS. JADE Featuring Timbaland & Nelly Furtado**	BUB:114 *(2 versions) / Jade's The Champ*	$7	T	Beat Club 497820

DEBUT	PEAK	WKS	Gold	A-side (Chart Hit)...B-side	$	Sym	Label & Number
				TIMBERLAKE, Justin LP **'03**			
				Born on 1/31/81 in Memphis, Tennessee. Member of ***NSYNC**. Regular on TV's *The Mickey Mouse Club* (1992-93).			
9/7/02	11	20		1 **Like I Love You**...A:11 / S:20 *(3 versions)* rap by **Clipse**	$6	T^V	Jive 40054
12/21/02+	3	20		2 **Cry Me A River**...S:2 / A:3 *(3 versions) / Like I Love You*	$8	★*	Jive 40073
				TIMBUK 3 ROK **'86**			
				Husband-and-wife alternative pop-rock duo from Austin, Texas: Patrick and Barbara MacDonald. Met while Barbara was attending the University of Wisconsin in 1978.			
10/25/86	19	16		**The Future's So Bright, I Gotta Wear Shades**...S:14 / A:24 *I'll Do All Right*	$4	■	I.R.S. 52940
				TIME, The R&B/BUB/LP **'90**			
				R&B-funk-dance group from Minneapolis, Minnesota: **Morris Day** (vocals) (see #6 & 7 below), **Jesse Johnson** (guitar), Jimmy "Jam" Harris and Monte Moir (keyboards), Terry Lewis (bass) and Jellybean Johnson (drums). Lewis, Harris and Moir left before band's featured role in movie *Purple Rain*. Paul "**St. Paul**" Peterson (**The Family** - see #5 below) and Lewis's half-brother, Jerome Benton, joined in 1984; group disbanded later that year. Day and Jesse Johnson went solo; Lewis and Harris became highly successful songwriting/producing team. Lewis married **Karyn White**. Original lineup plus Benton regrouped in 1990.			
1/30/82	90	7		1 **Cool (Part 1)**...*(Part II)*	$4		Warner 49864
10/9/82	88	3		2 **777-9311**...*Grace*	$4		Warner 29952
10/27/84+	20	25		3 **Jungle Love**...A:14 / S:23 *Oh, Baby*	$4		Warner 29181
2/23/85	36	13		4 **The Bird**...A:28 *My Drawers* above 2 from the movie *Purple Rain* starring **Prince** and **Apollonia** Kotero	$4		Warner 29094
9/28/85	63	6		5 **The Screams Of Passion**...*Yes* **THE FAMILY**	$3	■	Paisley Park 28953
9/28/85	65	12		6 **The Oak Tree**...*(dance instrumental)*	$3	■	Warner 28899
2/20/88	23	13		7 **Fishnet**...RB^2 S:15 / A:24 *Maybe* **MORRIS DAY** (above 2)	$3	■	Warner 28201
6/30/90	9	15	●	8 **Jerk-Out** RB^1 S:9 / A:9 *Mo' Jerk Out* #1-5 & 8: co-written by **Prince**	$3	▮^{V}	Paisley Park 19750
				TIMELORDS, The — see KLF			
				TIMES TWO R&B/LP **'88**			
				White male electro-pop duo of vocalists/keyboardists from Pt. Reyes, California: Shanti Jones and John Dollar.			
3/12/88	21	17		1 **Strange But True**...A:20 / S:21 *Come Over* picture sleeve is a foldout poster	$3	■	Reprise 27998
7/9/88	79	6		2 **Cecilia**...*Romeo*	$3	■	Reprise 27871
				TIMETONES, The BUB **'61**			
				Interracial doo-wop group from Glen Cove, Long Island, New York: Rodgers LaRue (lead), Glenn Williams, Claude "Sonny" Smith, Tom DeGeorge and Tom Glozek.			
5/8/61	51	5		**In My Heart**...*My Love* early pressings issued as "Here In My Heart"	$30		Times Square 421
				TIMEX SOCIAL CLUB R&B **'86**			
				R&B-funk-dance trio from Berkeley, California: Michael Marshall, Marcus Thompson and Alex Hill. Produced by Jay King, who later formed and fronted **Club Nouveau**.			
6/14/86	8	19		**Rumors**...RB^2 A:6 / S:8 *(same version)*	$5		Jay 7001
				TIMMY AND THE LORDS OF THE UNDERWORLD **'00**			
				Fictitious group based on an episode of the animated TV series *South Park*. The actual rock group consists of *South Park* creators Trey Parker (vocals) and Matt Stone (bass), with Bruce Howell (guitar), D.A. Young (keyboards) and Curt Bisquera (drums).			
9/23/00+	56^S	13		**Timmy And The Lords Of The Underworld**...*Timmy Livin' A Lie* [N]	$6	★	American 79489
				TIMMY -T- LP **'91**			
				Born Timmy Torres on 9/21/67 in Fresno, California. Dance-pop singer/songwriter.			
3/10/90	40	17		1 **Time After Time**...S:30 *(2 versions) / One More Try* "45": Quality 5003; B-side: (same version)	$6	▮*^{V}	Jam City 5003
7/21/90	96	4		2 **What Will I Do**...*(instrumental)*	$4	▮	Quality 15102
12/22/90+	❶^1	25	▲	3 **One More Try**...S:❶^5 / A:2 *(original version)*	$4	▮^{V}	Quality 15114
5/11/91	63	6		4 **Over and Over**...*(dance version)* all of above from the album *Time After Time*	$4	▮^{V}	Quality 15111
				TIM TAM And The Turn-Ons **'66**			
				Doo-wop/rock and roll group formed at Allen Park High in Allen Park, Michigan: Rick "Tim Tam" Wiesend and his brother Dan Wiesend with John Ogen, Don Gunderson, Earl Rennie and Nick Butsicaris.			
3/5/66	76	5		**Wait A Minute**...*Opelia* [I]	$25		Palmer 5002
				TIN TIN LP **'71**			
				Pop duo from Australia: Steve Kipner (keyboards) and Steve Groves (guitar). Disbanded in 1973. Kipner later co-wrote **Chicago**'s "Hard Habit To Break" and **Olivia Newton-John**'s "Physical" and "Twist Of Fate."			
4/3/71	20	11		1 **Toast And Marmalade For Tea**...*Manhattan Woman*	$8		Atco 6794
8/28/71	59	6		2 **Is That The Way**...*Swans On The Canal* above 2 produced by Maurice Gibb of the **Bee Gees**	$8		Atco 6821
				TINY TIM BUB/C&W/LP **'68**			
				Born Herbert Khaury on 4/12/30 in Brooklyn, New York. Died of heart failure on 11/30/96 (age 66). Novelty singer/ukulele player. Shot to national attention with appearances on TV's *Rowan & Martin's Laugh-In*. Married "Miss Vicki" on Johnny Carson's *Tonight Show* on 12/18/69; divorced in 1977.			
5/18/68	17	9		1 **Tip-Toe Thru' The Tulips With Me**...*Fill Your Heart* [N] #1 hit for Nick Lucas in 1929 (from the movie musical *Gold Diggers of Broadway*)	$8		Reprise 0679
8/24/68	95	2		2 **Bring Back Those Rockabye Baby Days**...*This Is All I Ask* also released with "Hello, Hello" as the B-side	$6		Reprise 0760
2/8/69	85	3		3 **Great Balls Of Fire**...*As Time Goes By*	$6		Reprise 0802

DEBUT	PEAK	WKS	Gold	A-side (Chart Hit)....B-side	$	Sym	Label & Number
				TIPPIN, Aaron C&W/BUB/LP '01 Born on 7/3/58 in Pensacola, Florida; raised in Travelers Rest, South Carolina. Country singer/songwriter.			
12/16/95	70^S	2		1 **That's As Close As I'll Get To Loving You**....CW² BUB:101 *She Feels Like A Brand New Man Tonight* (C&W #39)	$4	▮V	RCA 64392
10/10/98+	49	20		2 **For You I Will**....A:40 / S:45 *Back When I Knew Everything*	$4	★V	Lyric Street 64023
5/1/99	87	3		3 **I'm Leaving**....A:71 above 2 from the album *What This Country Needs* on Lyric Street 65003			album cut
8/26/00	42	20		4 **Kiss This**....CW² A:34 from the album *People Like Us* on Lyric Street 65014; "45": Lyric Street 11282; B-side: "People Like Us" (BUB #107/C&W #17)		V	album cut
10/20/01	20	20		5 **Where The Stars And Stripes And The Eagle Fly** S:3 / A:33 *You've Got To Stand For Something* proceeds donated to the Red Cross disaster relief fund	$4	★V	Lyric Street 64059
				TITIYO '91 Born in 1967 in Stockholm, Sweden. Female dance singer. Daughter of noted percussionist Ahmadu Jah. Pronounced: tee-tee-o.			
6/8/91	42	11		**My Body Says Yes**....A:34 *Peace And Quiet* **TITIYO Featuring Papa Dee**	$3	▮V	Arista 2224
				TJADER, Cal LP '65 Born Callen Tjader on 7/16/25 in St. Louis, Missouri. Died on 5/5/82 (age 56). Latin jazz vibraphonist.			
6/5/65+	88	5		**Soul Sauce (Guacha Guaro)**....*Somewhere In The Night* [I] written by jazz great Dizzy Gillespie	$10		Verve 10345
				TKA R&B/LP '92 Latin disco trio from Harlem, New York: Tony Ortiz, Louis "**K7**" Sharpe and Ralph Cruz.			
6/7/86	75	9		1 **One Way Love**....*(dub version)*	$4		Tommy Boy 866
6/3/89	91	7		2 **You Are The One**....*(radio dub version)* from the movie *Lean On Me* starring Morgan Freeman	$3	■	Warner 22946
8/11/90	65	8		3 **I Won't Give Up On You**....*(remix/edit)*	$4	▮	Tommy Boy 19730
12/1/90	80	7		4 **Crash (Have Some Fun)**....*You Are The One* **TKA (with Michelle Visage)**	$4	▮	Tommy Boy 19527
8/10/91	62	11		5 **Louder Than Love**....A:42 *(instrumental)*	$4	▮	Tommy Boy 7998
4/4/92	44	18		6 **Maria** A:35 / S:65 *(2 versions) / Tears May Fall*	$6	▮*	Tommy Boy 520
				TLC ★114★ R&B/BUB/LP '95 Female R&B trio from Atlanta, Georgia: Tionne "**T-Boz**" (see #11 below) Watkins (born on 4/26/70), Lisa "**Left Eye**" Lopes (born on 5/27/71) and Rozonda "Chilli" Thomas (born on 2/27/71). Founded and managed by **Pebbles**. Lopes was sentenced to five years probation for setting fire to the house of her boyfriend Andre Rison, an NFL football player, on 6/9/94. Group filed for Chapter 11 bankruptcy in 1995. T-Boz married **Mack 10** on 8/19/2000. Left Eye died in a car crash on 4/25/2002 (age 30). Also see **Da Brat**'s "Ghetto Love" and **Lil' Kim**'s "Not Tonight." *1)Waterfalls 2)Creep 3)No Scrubs*			
2/22/92	6	22	▲	1 **Ain't 2 Proud 2 Beg**....S:3 / A:9 *(album version)* samples "Escape-ism" by **James Brown**, "Jungle Boogie" by **Kool & The Gang**, "School Boy Crush" by **AWB**, "Fly, Robin, Fly" by **Silver Convention** and "Take Me To The Mardi Gras" by **Bob James**	$3	▮	LaFace 24008
6/6/92	2^6	33	▲	2 **Baby-Baby-Baby**....RB² A:❶² / S:3 *(instrumental)*	$3	▮	LaFace 24028
9/5/92	7	27	●	3 **What About Your Friends**....S:6 / A:7 *(2 versions)*	$3	▮	LaFace 24025
12/26/92+	43^A	4		4 **Sleigh Ride**.... [X] from the album *A LaFace Family Christmas* on LaFace 26011; #24 hit for the **Boston Pops Orchestra** in 1949			album cut
2/6/93	30	15		5 **Hat 2 Da Back**....S:24 / A:29 *(album version)* samples "Big Ole Butt" by **L.L. Cool J** and "What Makes You Happy" by **KC & The Sunshine Band**; all of above (except #4) from the album *Ooooooohhh...On The TLC Tip*	$4	▮	LaFace 24043
7/3/93	42	17		6 **Get It Up**....A:25 / S:37 *(album version)* written by **Prince**; from the movie *Poetic Justice* starring **Janet Jackson** and **2 Pac**	$4	▮	Epic Soundtrax 77059
11/12/94+	❶^4	32	▲	7 **Creep**....RB⁹ S:❶⁵ / A:3 *(instrumental)* samples "Hey Young World" by **Slick Rick**	$3	▮	LaFace 24082
3/4/95	2^3	22	●	8 **Red Light Special**....S:2 / A:4 *(instrumental)*	$3	▮V	LaFace 24097
6/10/95	❶^7	34	▲	9 **Waterfalls** S:❶³ / A:2 *(instrumental)*	$3	▮V	LaFace 24107 ■
11/18/95	5	20	●	10 **Diggin' On You**....S:5 / A:10 *(live remix)* #8 & 10: written and produced by **Babyface**; above 4 from the album *CrazySexyCool*	$3	▮	LaFace 24119
8/10/96	40	20		11 **Touch Myself**....S:24 *(instrumental)* **T-BOZ** samples "My Mike Sounds Nice" by **Salt-N-Pepa**; from the movie *Fled* starring Laurence Fishburne	$4	▮	Rowdy 35080
1/9/99	59	9		12 **Silly Ho**....A:51			album cut
2/20/99	❶^4	28	●	13 **No Scrubs**....RB⁵ A:❶¹³ / S:❶⁴ *(instrumental)*	$4	★	LaFace 24385
6/26/99	❶^3	32	●	14 **Unpretty**....S:2 / A:2 *(remix)*	$4	★	LaFace 24424
2/12/00	51	7		15 **Dear Lie**....A:48 above 4 from the album *Fanmail* on LaFace 26055			album cut
10/26/02	28	14		16 **Girl Talk**....A:31 / S:63 *(3 versions)*	$6	T	Arista 15171
				T.M.G. '79 Pop-rock group: Ted Mulry (vocals), Gary Dixon (guitar), Les Hall (bass) and Herm Kovac (drums). T.M.G.: Ted Mulry Group.			
3/3/79	91	4		**Lazy Eyes**....*Disturbing The Peace*	$5		Atco 7096t
				TO ..also see: TWO / 2			
				TOADIES ROK/LP '95 Rock group from Fort Worth, Texas: Todd Lewis (vocals, guitar), Darrel Herbert (guitar), Lisa Umbarger (bass) and Mark Reznicek (drums).			
9/30/95	40^A	20		**Possum Kingdom**.... from the album *Rubberneck* on Interscope 92402			album cut

DEBUT	PEAK	WKS	Gold	A-side (Chart Hit)...B-side	$	Sym	Label & Number
				TOAD THE WET SPROCKET ROK/LP **'92**			
				Alternative-rock group from Santa Barbara, California: Glen Phillips (vocals), Todd Nichols (guitar), Dean Dinning (bass) and Randy Guss (drums). Name taken from a Monty Python skit.			
6/27/92	15	25		1 **All I Want** A:8 / S:28 *All She Said*	$4	■V	Columbia 74355
11/14/92+	18	20		2 **Walk On The Ocean** A:21 / S:57 *(album version) / All In All* "45" issued for above 2 on Columbia 74706	$4	■V	Columbia 74706
6/4/94	33	17		3 **Fall Down** MR[6] A:31 *All Right*	$4	■V	Columbia 77474
10/1/94	41	20		4 **Something's Always Wrong** A:34 *Don't Go Away / Corporal Brown*	$4	■	Columbia 77639
10/14/95	23A	20		5 **Good Intentions** from the TV soundtrack album *Friends* on Reprise 46008			album cut
5/10/97	51A	9		6 **Come Down** from the album *Coil* on Columbia 67862			album cut
				TO BE CONTINUED... **'94**			
				Black funk trio from California: M&M Sweet, Spunky D and Wayne-Wayne.			
1/22/94	70	7		**One On One** A:64 *When The Lights Go Out*	$4	■	EastWest 98346
				TOBY BEAU BUB/LP **'78**			
				Pop group from Texas: Balde Silva (vocals, harmonica), Danny McKenna (guitar), Ron Rose (banjo), Steve Zipper (bass) and Rob Young (drums).			
6/3/78	13	17		1 **My Angel Baby** AC[1] *California*	$5		RCA 11250
8/11/79	57	9		2 **Then You Can Tell Me Goodbye** *Boogie Woogie Melody*	$5		RCA 11670
7/5/80	70	4		3 **If I Were You** *If You Believe*	$5		RCA 11964
				TODAY'S PEOPLE **'73**			
				Pop vocal group from France.			
9/1/73	90	6		**He** *I Didn't Know*	$5		20th Century 2032
				TODD, Art And Dotty **'58**			
				Pop vocal duo from Elizabeth, New Jersey. Art Todd was born on 3/11/20. Doris "Dotty" Todd was born on 6/22/13; died on 12/12/2000 (age 87). Married in 1941.			
4/14/58	6	16		**Chanson D'Amour (Song Of Love)** A:6 / S:13 / T:13 *Along The Trail With You*	$20		Era 1064
				TODD, Nick **'57**			
				Born Nicholas Boone on 6/1/35 in Jacksonville, Florida. Pop singer. Younger brother of **Pat Boone**.			
10/21/57	41	10		1 **Plaything** T:41 / S:45 *The Honey Song*	$20		Dot 15643
12/30/57+	21	6		2 **At The Hop** A:21 / T:70 *I Do* **Billy Vaughn** (orch., above 2)	$20		Dot 15675
	★516★			**TOKENS, The** BUB/AC/LP **'61**			
				Vocal group formed in Brooklyn, New York: Hank Medress (born on 11/19/38), **Neil Sedaka** (born on 3/13/39), Eddie Rabkin and Cynthia Zolitin. First recorded for Melba in 1956. Rabkin replaced in 1956 by Jay Siegel (born on 10/20/39). Zolitin and Sedaka left in 1958. Medress then formed Darrell & The Oxfords, 1958-59; then re-formed The Tokens with brothers Phil (born on 4/1/42) and Mitch (born on 5/25/47) Margo and recorded for Warwick in 1960. Formed own label, B.T. Puppy, in 1964 and produced **The Happenings**. Medress produced **Tony Orlando & Dawn**, and then left The Tokens, who continued as a trio (Siegel and the Margos) and recorded as **Cross Country** (see #12 below) in 1973. *1)The Lion Sleeps Tonight 2)Tonight I Fell In Love 3)I Hear Trumpets Blow*			
3/6/61	15	14		1 **Tonight I Fell In Love** *I'll Always Love You*	$30		Warwick 615
11/13/61	1[3]	15	●	2 **The Lion Sleeps Tonight** *Tina* #14 hit for The Weavers in 1952 (as "Wimoweh"); originally recorded in 1939 as "Mbube" by the South African Zulu group Solomon Linda & The Evening Birds; also see #13 below	$20		RCA Victor 7954
2/10/62	55	5		3 **B'wa Nina (Pretty Girl)** *Weeping River* picture sleeve printed in 2 variations: photo in either black and white or orange tint	$15	■	RCA Victor 7991
6/30/62	85	5		4 **La Bomba** *A Token Of Love* [F]	$15	■	RCA Victor 8052
8/24/63	94	4		5 **Hear The Bells** *A-B-C 1-2-3*	$15	■	RCA Victor 8210
8/8/64	43	8		6 **He's In Town** *Oh Kathy*	$12		B.T. Puppy 502
3/19/66	30	8		7 **I Hear Trumpets Blow** *Don't Cry, Sing Along With The Music*	$12	■	B.T. Puppy 518
4/15/67	36	8		8 **Portrait Of My Love** *She Comes And Goes*	$8	■	Warner 5900
7/22/67	69	4		9 **It's A Happening World** *How Nice?*	$8		Warner 7056
12/13/69+	61	7		10 **She Lets Her Hair Down (Early In The Morning)** *Oh To Get Away* tune originated as a TV jingle for a shampoo	$7		Buddah 151
3/7/70	95	2		11 **Don't Worry Baby** *Some People Sleep*	$7		Buddah 159
8/18/73	30	12		12 **In The Midnight Hour** *A Smile Song* **CROSS COUNTRY**	$7		Atco 6934
8/20/94	51	13		13 **The Lion Sleeps Tonight (Wimoweh)** S:19 *La Bamba* [R] from the animated movie *The Lion King*; same version as #2 above; "45": RCA Gold Standard 0702; B-side: "B'wa Nina"	$5	■V	RCA 62956
				TOLBERT, Israel "Popper Stopper" **'70**			
				Born on 10/28/34 in Memphis. R&B singer/songwriter/pianist. Blind since birth.			
10/31/70	61	9		**Big Leg Woman (With A Short Short Mini Skirt)** *I Got Love* (w/C.A. Warren Players)	$7		Warren 106
				TOM and JERRIO BUB **'65**			
				R&B dance duo: Robert "Tommy Dark" Tharp and Jerry "**Jerryo**" (see #2 below) Murray. Tharp was a baritone in The Ideals vocal group from 1952-65.			
5/1/65	47	8		1 **Boo-Ga-Loo** *Boomerang*	$10		ABC-Paramount 10638
9/16/67	51	9		2 **Karate-Boo-Ga-Loo** *The Pearl* **JERRYO**	$10		Shout 217
				TOM & JERRY — see SIMON & GARFUNKEL			
				TOMMY TUTONE BUB/LP **'82**			
				Rock group formed in San Francisco, California: Tommy Heath (vocals), Jim Keller (guitar), Jon Lyons (bass) and Victor Carberry (drums).			
5/24/80	38	8		1 **Angel Say No** *The Blame*	$4		Columbia 11278
1/23/82	4	27	●	2 **867-5309/Jenny** AR[3] *Not Say Goodbye*	$4		Columbia 02646

DEBUT	PEAK	WKS	Gold	A-side (Chart Hit)...B-side	$	Sym	Label & Number
				TOMS, Gary, Empire R&B/BUB/LP **'75**			
				Disco group formed in New York: Gary Toms (keyboards), Helen Jacobs (vocals), Rick Kenny (guitar), Eric Oliver (trumpet), Les Rose (sax), Warren Tesoro (percussion), John Freeman (bass) and Rick Murray (drums).			
6/21/75	**46**	17		1 **7-6-5-4-3-2-1 (Blow Your Whistle)** ...*(disco version)*	$6		p.i.p. 6504
11/22/75	**69**	5		2 **Drive My Car** ...*The New Empire*	$6		p.i.p. 6509
				tune first released on **The Beatles**' *Yesterday And Today* album in 1966			
				TOM TOM CLUB — see TALKING HEADS			
				TONE LŌC R&B/LP **'89**			
				Born Anthony Smith on 3/3/66 in Los Angeles, California. Male rapper/actor. Appeared in several movies. Stage name, pronounced: tone loke, derived from his Spanish nickname "Antonio Loco."			
12/3/88+	**2^{1}**	25	▲^{2}	1 **Wild Thing** ...S:❶^{2} / A:3 *Loc'ed After Dark*	$3		Delicious Vinyl 102
3/4/89	**3**	18	▲	2 **Funky Cold Medina** ...S:2 / A:5 *(instrumental)*	$3	■	Delicious Vinyl 104
12/14/91	**80**	7		3 **All Through The Night** ...S:56 *(remix)*	$3	▮^{V}	Delicious Vinyl 866104
				El DeBarge (guest vocal)			
				TONEY, Oscar Jr. BUB/LP **'67**			
				Born on 5/26/39 in Selma, Alabama; raised in Columbus, Georgia. R&B singer.			
5/27/67	**23**	9		1 **For Your Precious Love** ...*Ain't That True Love*	$10		Bell 672
8/12/67	**65**	6		2 **Turn On Your Love Light** ...*Any Day Now*	$10		Bell 681
1/13/68	**90**	3		3 **Without Love (There Is Nothing)** ...*A Love That Never Grows Cold*	$10		Bell 699
4/20/68	**95**	2		4 **Never Get Enough Of Your Love** ...*A Love That Never Grows Cold*	$10		Bell 714
				written by **Eddie Floyd**			
				TONIC ROK/BUB/LP **'97**			
				Rock group from Los Angeles, California: Emerson Hart (vocals, guitar), Jeff Russo (guitar), Dan Rothchild (bass) and Kevin Shepard (drums).			
5/10/97	**11^{A}**	63		1 **If You Could Only See** ...AR^{5}			album cut
4/18/98	**68^{A}**	2		2 **Open Up Your Eyes** ...			album cut
				#2 Mainstream Rock hit on 7/13/96; above 2 from the album *Lemon Parade* on Polydor 531042			
				TONY AND JOE **'58**			
				Rock and roll vocal duo: Tony Savonne and Joe Saraceno. Also see **Current** and **The T-Bones**.			
7/21/58	**33**	8		**The Freeze** ...H:33 / S:39 *Gonna Get A Little Kissin' Tonight*	$20		Era 1075
	★474★			**TONY! TONI! TONÉ!** R&B/BUB/LP **'93**			
				R&B-funk trio from Oakland, California: brothers Dwayne (born on 2/14/63) and Raphael (born on 5/14/66) Wiggins, with cousin Timothy Christian (born on 12/10/65). Raphael recorded as **Raphael Saadiq**. Appeared in the movie *House Party 2*. Dwayne produced **Simplē E**. Also see **Lucy Pearl**.			
				1)If I Had No Loot 2)Feels Good 3)Anniversary			
5/28/88	**47**	10		1 **Little Walter** ...RB^{1} *(instrumental)*	$4	■	Wing 887385
6/2/90	**46**	10		2 **The Blues** ...RB^{1} S:32 *(3 album snippets) / Jo-Jo*	$4	▮^{V}	Wing 873994
9/1/90	**9**	25	●	3 **Feels Good** ...RB^{2} S:5 / A:15 *(instrumental) / (3 album snippets)*	$3	▮^{V}	Wing 877436
				"45" B-side: (same version)			
12/22/90+	**34**	15		4 **It Never Rains (In Southern California)** ...RB^{2} S:19 *(3 album snippets)*	$3	▮^{V}	Wing 879068
				"45" A-side is a "live" version; B-side: "Jo-Jo"			
4/13/91	**48**	11		5 **Whatever You Want** ...RB^{2} S:35 *(3 album snippets) / (instrumental)*	$3	▮^{V}	Wing 879590
				above 4 from the album *The Revival*			
11/9/91	**46^{S}**	5		6 **House Party II (I Don't Know What You Come To Do)** ...*(instrumental)*	$3	▮	MCA 54170
				from the movie *House Party* starring **Kid 'N Play**			
				TONY TONI TONÉ:			
6/12/93	**7**	21	●	7 **If I Had No Loot** S:7 / A:9 *(3 album snippets)*	$3	▮^{V}	Wing 859056
				samples "The 'P' Is Free" by **KRS-1**, "The Wrong Nigga To Fuck Wit" by **Ice Cube** and "Knock On Wood" by **Eddie Floyd**			
9/25/93	**10**	20	●	8 **Anniversary** ...S:8 / A:11 *(3 album snippets)*	$3	▮^{V}	Wing 859566
1/15/94	**31**	15		9 **(Lay Your Head On My) Pillow** ...S:28 / A:28 *(same version)*	$3	▮^{V}	Wing 858260
5/14/94	**82**	5		10 **Leavin'** ...*(long version)*	$3	▮^{V}	Wing 855762
				above 4 from the album *Sons Of Soul*			
11/30/96+	**30^{A}**	21		11 **Let's Get Down** ...		V	album cut
5/10/97	**22**	20		12 **Thinking Of You** ...S:15 *Let's Get Down / (remix)*	$3	▮^{V}	Mercury 574382
				"45" issued for above 2 on Mercury 574226			
				TOOL ROK/LP **'01**			
				Hard-rock group from Los Angeles, California: Maynard James Keenan (vocals), Adam Jones (guitar), Justin Chancellor (bass) and Danny Carey (drums).			
6/23/01	**67**	20		**Schism** ...A:60			album cut
				from the album *Lateralus* on Volcano 31160			
				TOO $HORT R&B/BUB/LP **'99**			
				Born Todd Shaw on 4/28/66 in Los Angeles, California. The first West Coast rap star.			
				*1)The Ghetto 2)More Freaky Tales 3)2 B*tches*			
11/17/90+	**42**	14		1 **The Ghetto** S:26 *What Rap?*	$5	▮^{V}	Jive/RCA 1414
				"45": Jive 1397			
7/18/92	**69^{S}**	1		2 **I Want To Be Free (That's The Truth)** ...*Punk Bitch*	$5	▮	Jive 42069
				samples "I Want To Be Free" by **The Ohio Players**			
10/23/93	**85**	3		3 **I'm A Player** ...S:49 *(3 versions) / Only The Strong Survive*	$6	▮*	Jive 42152
				samples "Hollywood Squares" by Bootsy's Rubber Band			
2/19/94	**90**	3		4 **Money In The Ghetto** ...S:75 *(extended remix)*	$4	▮	Jive 42195
				samples "Hollywood Swinging" by **Kool & The Gang**			
1/21/95	**69**	9		5 **Cocktails** ...S:27 *The Loot* (Ant Banks) / *Whipped Cream, Nuts & Cherries* (Goldy)	$4	▮	Jive 42255
8/24/96	**68**	10		6 **Gettin' It** ...S:54 *(remix) / Never Talk Down* (w/**Rappin' 4-Tay** & **M.C. Breed**)	$3	▮	Jive 42409
				TOO $HORT featuring Parliament Funkadelic			
				samples "I'd Rather Be With You" by Bootsy's Rubber Band and "Inner City Blues" by **Marvin Gaye**			

DEBUT	PEAK	WKS	Gold	A-side (Chart Hit)...B-side	$	Sym	Label & Number
				TOO $HORT — Cont'd			
2/1/97	flip	14		7 **Rappers' Ball**...*Things'll Never Change* (**E-40** - #29) **E-40 featuring Too $hort and K-Ci** samples "Playboy $hort" by Too $hort	$4	▮	Sick Wid' It/Jive 42436
5/10/97	90	3		8 **Call Me**...*(radio version)* **TOO $HORT & LIL' KIM** from the movie *Booty Call* starring Jamie Foxx	$6	T	Jive 42447
9/26/98	51	10		9 **Invasion Of The Flat Booty Bitches**...S:29 *Don't Stop Rappin'* (w/Eightball & MJG) samples "Do The Do" by **Kurtis Blow**	$3	▮	$hort/Jive 42543
1/9/99	22^S	20		10 **More Freaky Tales**...BUB:121 *Couldn't Be A Better Player*	$4	★	$hort/Jive 42571
5/8/99	90	16		11 **Players Holiday**...S:37 *(2 versions)* **T.W.D.Y. featuring Too Short, Ant Banks, Rappin 4-Tay, Captain Save Em, Mac Mall** samples "Lovely Day" by **Bill Withers**	$4	★	Thump Street 2265
9/18/99	47^S	11		12 **Pimpin' Ain't No Illusion**...*Belts To Match* (w/Smitty & Sonji) **UGK Featuring Kool Ace & Too $hort**	$4	★	Jive 42633
6/10/00	24^S	16		13 **2 B*tches**...*2 Women (clean) / Pimp Sh*t*	$4	★	$hort/Jive 42701
9/2/00	46^S	7		14 **You Nasty**...*She Know* (w/The Nation Riders)	$4	★	$hort/Jive 42719
8/25/01	94	3		15 **Bia' Bia'**...*(2 versions)* **LIL JON & the East Side Boyz featuring Ludacris, Big Kap, Too $hort & Chyna**	$6	T	BME 7780
				TORA TORA ROK/LP **'89** Hard-rock group from Memphis, Tennessee: Anthony Corder (vocals), Keith Douglas (guitar), Patrick Francis (bass) and John Patterson (drums). Band name taken from a **Van Halen** song.			
8/12/89	86	6		**Walkin' Shoes**...*Dancing With A Gypsy*	$5	▮	A&M 1425
				TORME, Mel MEM/POP/AC/LP **'49** Born Melvin Howard on 9/13/25 in Chicago, Illinois. Died of a stroke on 6/5/99 (age 73). Jazz singer/songwriter/pianist/drummer/actor. Wrote "The Christmas Song." Frequently appeared as himself on TV's *Night Court.* Nicknamed "The Velvet Fog." Won Grammy's Lifetime Achievement Award in 1999. Hit #1 in 1949 with "Careless Hands."			
11/3/62	36	11		**Comin' Home Baby**...*Right Now* Claus Ogermann (orch.); song "Bubbled Under" (#101) for **Herbie Mann** earlier in 1962; also see **Travis Wammack**'s "Scratchy."	$12		Atlantic 2165
				TORNADOES, The BUB/LP **'62** Surf-rock instrumental group formed in England: Alan Caddy (lead guitar), George Bellamy (rhythm guitar), Roger Jackson (keyboards), Heinz Burt (bass) and Clem Cattini (drums). Burt died of muscular dystrophy on 4/7/2000 (age 57).			
11/3/62	❶^3	16		1 **Telstar**...*Jungle Fever* [I]	$25		London 9561
2/16/63	63	5		2 **Ridin' The Wind**...*The Breeze And I* [I]	$20		London 9581
				TOROK, Mitchell C&W/BUB/MEM **'59** Born on 10/28/29 in Houston, Texas. Pop-country singer/songwriter/guitarist.			
4/13/57	25	10		1 **Pledge Of Love**...S:25 / T:26 *What's Behind That Strange Door*	$20		Decca 30230
8/3/59	27	14		2 **Caribbean**...*Hootchy Kootchy Henry* (C&W #9/'54) alternate recording of Torok's #1 Country hit in 1953 on Abbott 140 ($30)	$20		Guyden 2018
5/9/60	60	9		3 **Pink Chiffon**...*What You Don't Know (Won't Hurt You)*	$15	■	Guyden 2034
				TORONTO BUB/LP **'82** Rock group from Toronto, Ontario, Canada: Holly Woods (vocals), Sheron Alton and Brian Allen (guitars), Scott Kreyer (keyboards) and Jim Fox (drums).			
8/7/82	77	8		**Your Daddy Don't Know**...*Why Can't We Talk?*	$4		Network 69986
				TORRENCE, George, & The Naturals **'68** Funk-R&B singer/songwriter.			
2/17/68	91	2		**(Mama Come Quick, and Bring Your) Lickin' Stick**...*So Long Goodbye* different song than **James Brown**'s 1968 hit "Licking Stick - Licking Stick"	$8		Shout 224
				TOSH, Peter R&B/LP **'78** Born Winston Hubert MacIntosh on 10/9/44 in Jamaica. Fatally shot during a robbery at his home in Kingston on 9/11/87 (age 42). Former member of **Bob Marley's Wailers.**			
11/4/78	81	5		1 **(You Got To Walk And) Don't Look Back**...*Soon Come* **PETER TOSH with Mick Jagger**	$6	■	Rolling Stones 19308
7/9/83	84	4		2 **Johnny B. Goode**...*Peace Treaty*	$5		EMI America 8159
	★496★			**TOTAL** R&B/LP **'96** Female R&B vocal trio from Harlem, New York: JaKima Raynor, Keisha Spivey and Pam Long. *1)Trippin' 2)What You Want 3)Kissin' You*			
4/8/95	13	20	●	1 **Can't You See**...S:9 / A:28 *(instrumental)* **TOTAL featuring The Notorious B.I.G.** samples "The Payback" by **James Brown**; from the movie *New Jersey Drive* starring Sharron Corley	$3	▮^{V}	Tommy Boy 7676
12/16/95+	22	20	●	2 **No One Else**...S:10 / A:51 *(radio edit)* **Da Brat** (rap); samples "South Bronx" by **KRS-One**; "45" issued for above 2 on Bad Boy 79050	$3	▮^{V}	Bad Boy 79042
5/4/96	12	22	●	3 **Kissin' You**...S:7 / A:43 *Tell Me*	$3	▮^{V}	Bad Boy 79056
10/26/96	61	4		4 **Do You Think About Us /** S:39 above 2 written and produced by **Raphael Saadiq (Tony! Toni! Toné!)**			
11/16/96	50	14		5 **When Boy Meets Girl**...S:35 **112** (backing vocals); samples the **Bee Gees**' "Love You Inside Out"; all of above from the album *Total*	$4	▮	Bad Boy 79074
8/30/97	16	24	●	6 **What About Us**...S:11 / A:47 *(instrumental)* from the movie *Soul Food* starring **Vanessa Williams**	$3	▮	LaFace 24272
1/31/98	6	24	●	7 **What You Want**...S:6 / A:26 *Will They Die 4 You?* (w/**Puff Daddy** & **Lil' Kim**) **MASE (FEATURING TOTAL)** samples "Right On For The Darkness" by **Curtis Mayfield**	$3	▮	Bad Boy 79141
11/7/98+	7	20	●	8 **Trippin'** S:6 / A:49 *(**Missy** mix)* **TOTAL (Feat. Missy Elliott)**	$4	★	Bad Boy 79185
4/10/99	42	14		9 **Sitting Home**...S:37 / A:42 *(3 versions) / Trippin'* (w/**DMX**) samples "Forget I Was A G" by **The Whitehead Brothers**	$8	★*	Bad Boy 79218
8/31/02	22^S	9		10 **Give It To Me**...*(2 versions)* **MAD LION featuring Total**	$6	★	Killah Pride 90429

DEBUT	PEAK	WKS	Gold	A-side (Chart Hit)	B-side	$	Sym	Label & Number

TOTAL COELO '83

Female dance group from England: Ros Holness, Anita Mahadervan, Lindsey Danvers, Lacey Bond and Sheen Doran. Also known as Toto Coelo.

DEBUT	PEAK	WKS	Gold	A-side (Chart Hit)	B-side	$	Sym	Label & Number
4/16/83	66	6		**I Eat Cannibals**	*Mucho Macho*	$5	■	Chrysalis 42669

TOTAL DEVASTATION '93

Hip-hop trio from San Francisco, California: Tuff Cut Tim, Tone and Freakin' Puertrican B-Fresh.

DEBUT	PEAK	WKS	Gold	A-side (Chart Hit)	B-side	$	Sym	Label & Number
10/30/93	75^S	1		**Many Clouds Of Smoke** BUB:103 first released on PGA 005 in 1993 (B-side: "Come Again!")	*(instrumental)*	$5	▮	PGA/Arista 12624

TOTO ★279★ ROK/BUB/AC/LP '82

Pop-rock group formed in Los Angeles, California: Bobby Kimball (vocals; born on 3/29/47), Steve Lukather (guitar; born on 10/21/57), David Paich (keyboards; born on 6/21/54), Steve Porcaro (keyboards; born on 9/2/57), David Hungate (bass) and Jeff Porcaro (drums; born on 4/1/54). Prominent session musicians, most notably behind **Boz Scaggs** in the late 1970s. Hungate was replaced by Mike Porcaro in 1983. (The Porcaros are brothers.) Kimball replaced by Fergie Fredericksen in 1984; Fredericksen replaced by Joseph Williams (conductor **John Williams**'s son) in 1986. Steve Porcaro left in 1988. Paich and his father, Marty, won an Emmy for writing the theme for the TV series *Ironside*. Kimball, Lukather and Paich with **Far Corporation** in 1986. Jeff Porcaro died of a heart attack on 8/5/92 (age 38).

1)Africa 2)Rosanna 3)Hold The Line

DEBUT	PEAK	WKS	Gold	A-side (Chart Hit)	B-side	$	Sym	Label & Number
10/7/78+	5	21	●	1 **Hold The Line**	*Takin' It Back*	$5		Columbia 10830
2/10/79	45	9		2 **I'll Supply The Love**	*You Are The Flower*	$5		Columbia 10898
4/28/79	48	10		3 **Georgy Porgy** **Cheryl Lynn** (backing vocal)	*Child's Anthem*	$5		Columbia 10944
12/22/79+	26	17		4 **99**	*Hydra*	$5		Columbia 11173
4/17/82	2^5	23	●	5 **Rosanna** written about Steve Porcaro's then-girlfriend, actress Rosanna Arquette; 1982 Grammy winner: Record of the Year	*It's A Feeling*	$4		Columbia 02811
8/7/82	30	13		6 **Make Believe**	*We Made It*	$4	■	Columbia 03143
10/30/82+	1^1	21	●	7 **Africa**	*Good For You*	$4		Columbia 03335
3/12/83	10	17		8 **I Won't Hold You Back** AC^3	*Afraid Of Love* (ROK #28)	$4	■	Columbia 03597
7/2/83	73	6		9 **Waiting For Your Love** above 5 from the album *Toto IV*	*Lovers In The Night* (ROK #57)	$4		Columbia 03981
10/27/84	30	15		10 **Stranger In Town** A:22	*Change Of Heart*	$4	■	Columbia 04672
2/9/85	71	5		11 **Holyanna**	*Mr. Friendly*	$4	■	Columbia 04752
8/30/86	11	23		12 **I'll Be Over You** AC^2 S:10 / A:11	*In A Word*	$3	■	Columbia 06280
12/27/86+	38	11		13 **Without Your Love** A:32	*Can't Stand It Any Longer*	$3	■	Columbia 06570
2/20/88	22	19		14 **Pamela** S:17 / A:20 all of above (except #8 & 12) written or co-written by David Paich	*The Seventh One*	$3	■	Columbia 07715

TOUCH '80

Rock group from Long Island, New York: Mark Mangold (vocals), Craig Brooks (guitar), Doug Howard (bass) and Glenn Kitchcart (drums).

DEBUT	PEAK	WKS	Gold	A-side (Chart Hit)	B-side	$	Sym	Label & Number
7/26/80	65	5		1 **(Call Me) When The Spirit Moves You**	*Yes (You Need To Rock N' Roll)*	$5		Atco 7222
1/31/81	69	6		2 **Don't You Know What Love Is**	*There's A Light*	$5		Atco 7311

TOURISTS, The '80

Rock group from London, England: **Annie Lennox** (vocals, keyboards), **David A. Stewart** and Peet Coombes (guitars), Eddie Chinn (bass) and Jim Toomey (drums). Lennox and Stewart formed **Eurythmics** in December 1980.

DEBUT	PEAK	WKS	Gold	A-side (Chart Hit)	B-side	$	Sym	Label & Number
5/17/80	83	4		**I Only Want To Be With You**	*In My Mind (There's Sorrow)*	$8		Epic 50850

TOWER OF POWER R&B/BUB/LP '73

Interracial R&B-funk group from Oakland, California: Lenny Williams (vocals), Willie Fulton (guitar), Greg Adams, Mic Gillette, Steve Kupka, Emilio Castillo and Lenny Pickett (horns), Chester Thompson (keyboards), Francis Prestia (bass) and David Garibaldi (drums).

DEBUT	PEAK	WKS	Gold	A-side (Chart Hit)	B-side	$	Sym	Label & Number
7/15/72	29	12		1 **You're Still A Young Man**	*Skating On Thin Ice*	$7		Warner 7612
10/21/72	66	8		2 **Down To The Nightclub**	*What Happened To The World That Day?*	$7		Warner 7635
5/5/73	17	18		3 **So Very Hard To Go**	*Clean Slate*	$6		Warner 7687
9/15/73	65	6		4 **This Time It's Real**	*Soul Vaccination*	$6		Warner 7733
2/23/74	91	2		5 **What Is Hip?**	*Clever Girl*	$6		Warner 7748
4/27/74	69	6		6 **Time Will Tell**	*Oakland Stroke...*	$6		Warner 7796
7/20/74	26	10		7 **Don't Change Horses (In The Middle Of A Stream)**	*I Got The Chop*	$6		Warner 7828
10/16/76	68	8		8 **You Ought To Be Havin' Fun**	*While We Went To The Moon*	$5		Columbia 10409

TOWER 32 '00

Studio dance group from Miami, Florida. Formed to cover the unavailable CD single of the **Eiffel 65** hit version.

DEBUT	PEAK	WKS	Gold	A-side (Chart Hit)	B-side	$	Sym	Label & Number
1/29/00	22^S	10		**Blue (Da Ba Dee)**	*(2 versions)*	$6	★	Groove 5113

TOWNES, Carol Lynn BUB/R&B '84

Born in Brooklyn, New York. Disco singer.

DEBUT	PEAK	WKS	Gold	A-side (Chart Hit)	B-side	$	Sym	Label & Number
7/7/84	77	9		**99 1/2** from the movie *Breakin'* starring Lucinda Dickey	*Reckless* (Chris "The Glove" Taylor & David Storrs)	$4		Polydor 881008

TOWNSELL, Lidell, & M.T.F. '92

Born in Chicago, Illinois. Black dance DJ/mixer. M.T.F. (More Than Friends): singer Martell and rapper Silk E.

DEBUT	PEAK	WKS	Gold	A-side (Chart Hit)	B-side	$	Sym	Label & Number
2/29/92	26	20		1 **Nu Nu** A:20 / S:25	*(new mix)*	$4	▮	Mercury 866780
8/15/92	78	8		2 **Get With U** A:48	*(remix)*	$4	▮	Mercury 864080

TOWNSEND, Ed BUB '58

Born on 4/16/29 in Fayetteville, Tennessee. R&B singer/songwriter. Son David is a member of **Surface**. Wrote **Marvin Gaye**'s "Let's Get It On."

DEBUT	PEAK	WKS	Gold	A-side (Chart Hit)	B-side	$	Sym	Label & Number
4/21/58	13	16		1 **For Your Love** A:13 / S:15 / T:15 Gerald Wilson (orch.)	*Over And Over Again*	$20		Capitol 3926
9/29/58	59	7		2 **When I Grow Too Old To Dream** H:59 Stan Applebaum (orch.); #1 hit for Glen Gray in 1935	*You Are My Everything*	$20		Capitol 4048

DEBUT	PEAK	WKS	Gold	A-side (Chart Hit)...B-side	$	Sym	Label & Number
				TOWNSHEND, Pete ROK/BUB/LP **'80**			
				Born on 5/19/45 in London, England. Rock singer/songwriter/guitarist. Member of **The Who**. First solo album *Who Came First*, 1972. Own publishing house, Eel Pie Press, mid-1970s. Currently plagued by a significant hearing loss.			
6/14/80	9	19		1 **Let My Love Open The Door** ... *And I Moved*	$4		Atco 7217
10/11/80	72	4		2 **A Little Is Enough** ... *Cat's In The Cupboard*	$4		Atco 7312
11/15/80	89	4		3 **Rough Boys** ... *Jools And Jim*	$4		Atco 7318
11/9/85+	26	16		4 **Face The Face** ... S:24 / A:27 *Hiding Out*	$3	■	Atco 99590
				TOYA LP **'01**			
				Born LeToya Luckett on 3/11/81 in Houston, Texas. R&B singer. Former member of **Destiny's Child**.			
6/2/01	16	39		1 **I Do!!** ... S:2 / A:20 *(instrumental)*	$4	★	Arista 13972
3/16/02	86	7		2 **No Matta What (Party All Night)** ... *(5 remixes - one w/**50 Cent** & **Loon**)*	$6	T	Arista 15108
8/31/02	3	21		3 **Hey Ma** ... A:3 / S:21 *(instrumental) / Boy Boy*	$6	T	Roc-A-Fella 063958
				CAM'RON (feat. Juelz Santana, Freekey Zekey and Toya)			
				TOY DOLLS, The **'63**			
				Female pre-teen pop duo from Los Angeles, California: Susan Leslie and Libby Redwine.			
12/29/62+	84	4		**Little Tin Soldier** ... *Fly Away*	$15		Era 3093
				TOYS, The BUB/R&B/LP **'65**			
				Female R&B vocal trio from Jamaica, Queens, New York: Barbara Harris, June Montiero and Barbara Parritt. Appearances on *Shindig* TV show in 1965. In the movie *The Girl In Daddy's Bikini*.			
9/11/65	2^3	15	●	1 **A Lover's Concerto** ... *This Night*	$15		DynoVoice 209
				adapted from Bach's *Minuet From The Anna Magdalena Notebook*			
12/18/65+	18	9		2 **Attack** ... *See How They Run*	$15		DynoVoice 214
4/2/66	85	3		3 **May My Heart Be Cast Into Stone** ... *On Backstreet*	$15		DynoVoice 218
9/3/66	76	4		4 **Baby Toys** ... *Happy Birthday Broken Heart*	$15		DynoVoice 222
				T'PAU LP **'87**			
				Pop-rock-dance group from Shrewsbury, England: Carol Decker (vocals), Dean Howard and Ronnie Rogers (guitars), Mick Chetwood (keyboards), Paul Jackson (bass) and Tim Burgess (drums). Band named after a Vulcan Princess in an episode of the TV series *Star Trek*.			
5/2/87	4	27		**Heart And Soul** ... A:3 / S:5 *On The Wing*	$3	■	Virgin 99466
				T.P.E. — see COLLAGE			
				TQ LP **'98**			
				Born Terrance Quaites in Mobile, Alabama; raised in Los Angeles, California. R&B singer/songwriter.			
10/3/98	12	16	●	1 **Westside** ... S:5 / A:69 *(instrumental) / Bye Bye Baby (snippet)*	$4	★	ClockWork 79022
				samples "The Breaks" by **Kurtis Blow** and "In All My Wildest Dreams" by Joe Sample			
6/5/99	59^S	4		2 **Better Days** ... *My Melody* (w/**DJ Quik**, Hi-C, James DeBarge, Playahamm, Supafree)	$4	★	ClockWork 79158
8/21/99	42^S	8		3 **Summertime** ... *I Can See You In My Mind*	$4	★	Arista 13696
				ANOTHER LEVEL featuring TQ			
8/5/00	16^S	14		4 **Daily** ... *(instrumental)*	$4	★	ClockWork 79439
				samples "Just A Friend" by **Biz Markie**			
				TRACTORS, The C&W/LP **'94**			
				Country-rock group formed in Tulsa, Oklahoma: Casey Van Beek (vocals), Steve Ripley (guitar), Walt Richmond (keyboards), Ron getman (bass) and Jamie Oldaker (drums).			
1/7/95-	91	1		**The Santa Claus Boogie** ... S:65 *Swingin' Home For Christmas* [X]	$4	▮V	Arista 12771
				TRADEWINDS, The **'59**			
				Pop group from New Jersey: Ralph Rizzoll, Phil Mehill, Sal Capriglione and Angel Cifelli.			
8/10/59	91	2		**Furry Murray** ... *Crossroads* [N]	$20		RCA Victor 7553
				"Furry Murray got a Yul Brynner haircut"			
				TRADE WINDS, The/THE INNOCENCE BUB **'65**			
				Pop singing/songwriting/production duo from New York: Pete Anders (Andreoli) and Vinnie Poncia. First recorded with group **The Videls**. Also recorded as **The Innocence**. Poncia produced several albums for **Ringo Starr** and **Melissa Manchester**. Also see **1910 Fruitgum Co.**'s "1, 2, 3, Red Light."			
				THE TRADE WINDS:			
2/6/65	32	8		1 **New York's A Lonely Town** ... *Club Seventeen*	$25		Red Bird 020
				a **Beach Boys** soundalike surf song			
9/3/66	51	9		2 **Mind Excursion** ... *Little Susan's Dreamin'*	$15		Kama Sutra 212
				THE INNOCENCE:			
12/3/66+	34	8		3 **There's Got To Be A Word!** ... *I Don't Wanna Be Around You*	$10		Kama Sutra 214
3/4/67	75	3		4 **Mairzy Doats** ... *A Lifetime Lovin' You*	$10		Kama Sutra 222
				#1 hit for The Merry Macs in 1944			
				TRAFFIC ROK/BUB/LP **'71**			
				Rock group formed in England. Original lineup: **Steve Winwood** (keyboards, guitar), **Dave Mason** (guitar), **Jim Capaldi** (drums) and Chris Wood (flute, sax; died on 7/12/83). Many personnel changes until the group disbanded in 1974. Winwood and Capaldi reunited in 1994.			
9/2/67	94	1		1 **Paper Sun** *[TRAFFIC featuring STEVIE WINWOOD]* ... *Giving To You*	$10		United Artists 50195
9/5/70	74	8		2 **Empty Pages** ... *Stranger To Himself*	$7		United Artists 50692
10/23/71	68	7		3 **Gimme Some Lovin'-Pt. 1** *[TRAFFIC, ETC.]* ... *Pt. 2* [L]	$7		United Artists 50841
				also see **The Spencer Davis Group**'s (feat. Winwood) 1967 hit version			
1/15/72	93	2		4 **Rock & Roll Stew...Part 1** ... *Part 2*	$6		Island 1201
				TRAGEDY • CAPONE • INFINITE **'98**			
				Male rap trio from New York.			
9/19/98	86	5		**'98 Thug Paradise** ... S:58 *(3 versions)*	$5	▮	H.O.L.A. 341077
				samples "Cramp Your Style" by **Ice-T**; from the movie *One Tough Cop* starring Stephen Baldwin			

TRAIN — ROK/BUB/LP '01

Rock group from San Francisco, California: Patrick Monahan (vocals), Rob Hotchkiss and Jimmy Stafford (guitars), Charlie Colin (bass) and Scott Underwood (drums).

DEBUT	PEAK	WKS	Gold	A-side (Chart Hit)..........B-side	$	Sym	Label & Number
10/9/99+	20	27		1 **Meet Virginia**..........A:17		V	album cut
				from the album *Train* on Aware/Columbia 38052			
3/17/01	5	53		2 **Drops Of Jupiter (Tell Me)**..........A:2		V	album cut
				from the album *Drops Of Jupiter* on Aware/Columbia 69888; "45" issued for above 2 on Columbia 79565			

TRAITS, The — see HEAD, Roy

TRAMMPS, The — R&B/BUB/LP '78

Disco group from Philadelphia, Pennsylvania: Jimmy Ellis (lead tenor), Earl Young (lead bass), Harold and Stanley Wade (tenors) and Robert Upchurch (baritone). Own Golden Fleece label in 1973.

DEBUT	PEAK	WKS	Gold	A-side (Chart Hit)..........B-side	$	Sym	Label & Number
7/8/72	64	11		1 **Zing Went The Strings Of My Heart**..........*Penguin At The Big Apple*	$8		Buddah 306
				later pressings show artist as The Tramps; #22 hit for Judy Garland in 1943 (from the 1935 musical revue *Thumbs Up*)			
1/17/76	35	10		2 **Hold Back The Night**..........*Tom's Song*	$6		Buddah 507
4/10/76	27	15		3 **That's Where The Happy People Go**..........*(long version)*	$5		Atlantic 3306
3/5/77	53	9		4 **Disco Inferno**..........*That's Where The Happy People Go*	$5	■	Atlantic 3389
2/18/78	11	20		5 **Disco Inferno** *You Touch My Hot Line* [R]	$5	■	Atlantic 3389
				above 2 are the same version; reissued because of inclusion in the movie *Saturday Night Fever* starring **John Travolta**			

TRANS-SIBERIAN ORCHESTRA — LP '97

Rock opera-styled project formed and produced by Paul O'Neill in Florida. "Christmas Eve (Sarajevo 12/24)" was originally released as by the hard-rock band **Savatage** in 1995. O'Neill then produced a Christmas rock opera album in 1996 under the name Trans-Siberian Orchestra and included the original Savatage recording on it.

DEBUT	PEAK	WKS	Gold	A-side (Chart Hit)..........B-side	$	Sym	Label & Number
1/6/96-	65^A	1		1 **Christmas Eve (Sarajevo 12/24)** *[SAVATAGE]*.......... [X-I]			album cut
				from the **Savatage** album *Dead Winter Dead* on Atlantic 82850			
1/4/97-	49^A	1		2 **Christmas Eve (Sarajevo 12/24)**.......... [X-I]			album cut
1/3/98-	49^A	2		3 **Christmas Eve/Sarajevo 12/24**.......... [X-I]			album cut
				above 2 from the album *Christmas Eve And Other Stories* on Lava/Atlantic 92736; above 3 are the exact same version			

TRANSVISION VAMP — ROK/LP '88

Pop-rock group from England: Wendy James (vocals), Nick Christian Sayer (guitar), Tex Axile (keyboards), Dave Parsons (bass) and Pol Burton (drums).

DEBUT	PEAK	WKS	Gold	A-side (Chart Hit)..........B-side	$	Sym	Label & Number
10/1/88	87	3		**Tell That Girl To Shut Up**..........*God Save The Royalties*	$5	■	Uni 50001
				originally recorded by Holly & The Italians in 1981			

TRANS-X — '86

Born Pascal Languirand in Montreal, Quebec, Canada. Techno-rock singer/songwriter.

DEBUT	PEAK	WKS	Gold	A-side (Chart Hit)..........B-side	$	Sym	Label & Number
5/10/86	61	12		**Living On Video**..........*(dub version)*	$5		Atco 99534

TRAPP • 2PAC • NOTORIOUS B.I.G. — R&B/LP '97

Trapp is male rapper John Parker. Founder of the Atlanta-based Deff Trapp record label.

DEBUT	PEAK	WKS	Gold	A-side (Chart Hit)..........B-side	$	Sym	Label & Number
4/26/97	77	7		**Stop The Gunfight**..........S:55 *(R&B version) / When I Come Down*	$5	▮	Deff Trapp 9269
				recorded in 1993; released after 2Pac and Biggy were shot to death within 6 months of each other			

TRASHMEN, The — BUB/LP '64

Garage-rock group from Minneapolis, Minnesota: Tony Andreason, Dal Winslow and Bob Reed (guitars), with Steve Wahrer (drums). Both hits taken from tunes by **The Rivingtons**: "Papa-Oom-Mow-Mow" and "The Bird's The Word." Wahrer died of cancer on 1/21/89 (age 47).

DEBUT	PEAK	WKS	Gold	A-side (Chart Hit)..........B-side	$	Sym	Label & Number
12/7/63+	4	13		1 **Surfin' Bird**..........*King Of The Surf*	$30		Garrett 4002
2/8/64	30	7		2 **Bird Dance Beat**..........*A-Bone*	$20		Garrett 4003

TRAVELING WILBURYS — ROK/LP '88

Supergroup masquerading as a band of brothers. Spearheaded by Nelson (**George Harrison**), with Lucky (**Bob Dylan**), Otis (**Jeff Lynne** of **ELO**), Lefty (**Roy Orbison**) and Charlie T. Junior (**Tom Petty**) Wilbury. Orbison died of a heart attack on 12/6/88 (age 52). Harrison died of cancer on 11/29/2001 (age 58).

DEBUT	PEAK	WKS	Gold	A-side (Chart Hit)..........B-side	$	Sym	Label & Number
10/29/88	45	14		1 **Handle With Care**..........S:31 *Margarita*	$10	■	Wilbury 27732
2/11/89	63	9		2 **End Of The Line**..........*Congratulations*	$15	■	Wilbury 27637

TRAVERS, Mary — see PETER, PAUL & MARY

TRAVERS, Pat — ROK/LP '80

Born on 4/12/54 in Toronto, Ontario, Canada. Rock singer/guitarist.

DEBUT	PEAK	WKS	Gold	A-side (Chart Hit)..........B-side	$	Sym	Label & Number
9/1/79	56	7		1 **Boom Boom (Out Go The Lights)**..........*Go All Night* [L]	$6		Polydor 2003
5/17/80	50	7		2 **Is This Love** *[PAT TRAVERS BAND]*..........*Love Will Make You Strong*	$6		Polydor 2080
				written by **Bob Marley** (on his 1978 album *Kaya*)			

TRAVIS, McKinley — '70

Born on 2/2/45 in Los Angeles, California. R&B singer.

DEBUT	PEAK	WKS	Gold	A-side (Chart Hit)..........B-side	$	Sym	Label & Number
7/18/70	91	2		**Baby, Is There Something On Your Mind**..........*You've Got It And I Want It*	$12		Pride 2

TRAVIS, Randy — C&W/BUB/LP '99

Born Randy Traywick on 5/4/59 in Marshville, North Carolina. Country singer/songwriter/guitarist/actor (charted 16 #1 hits, 1986-03). Acted in several movies and TV shows.

DEBUT	PEAK	WKS	Gold	A-side (Chart Hit)..........B-side	$	Sym	Label & Number
6/29/91	61^S	7		1 **Point Of Light**..........*Waiting On The Light To Change* (w/**B.B. King**)	$4		Warner 19283
4/25/98	64	10		2 **Out Of My Bones**..........S:46 *Brinks Truck*	$4	▮V	DreamWorks 59007
12/5/98+	42	14		3 **Spirit Of A Boy - Wisdom Of A Man** A:27			album cut
5/22/99	81	4		4 **Stranger In My Mirror**..........A:67			album cut
				above 3 from the album *You And You Alone* on DreamWorks 50034			
11/13/99	82	4		5 **A Man Ain't Made Of Stone**..........A:69			album cut
				from the album *A Man Ain't Made Of Stone* on DreamWorks 50119			
11/17/01	10^S	16		6 **America Will Always Stand**..........*Point Of Light*	$4	★	Relentless 51372
				all proceeds to benefit the American Red Cross			

TRAVIS & BOB — BUB '59

Pop-country duo from Jackson, Alabama: Travis Pritchett and Bob Weaver.

DEBUT	PEAK	WKS	Gold	A-side (Chart Hit)..........B-side	$	Sym	Label & Number
3/23/59	8	13		**Tell Him No**..........*We're Too Young*	$20		Sandy 1017

DEBUT	PEAK	WKS	Gold	A-side (Chart Hit)...B-side	$	Sym	Label & Number
				TRAVOLTA, Joey '78			
				Born on 10/14/50 in Englewood, New Jersey. Pop singer/actor/director/producer/screenwriter. Older brother of **John Travolta**.			
6/3/78	43	8		**I Don't Wanna Go** ... *Where Do We Go From Here*	$5	■	Millennium 615
				TRAVOLTA, John BUB/AC/LP '78			
				Born on 2/18/54 in Englewood, New Jersey. Actor/singer. Played "Vinnie Barbarino" on the TV series *Welcome Back Kotter*. Starred in many movies. Married actress Kelly Preston on 9/5/91.			
5/1/76	10	20		1 **Let Her In** ... *Big Trouble*	$6	■	Midland Int'l. 10623
				a promotional black-and-white picture sleeve was also issued with a different photo of Travolta			
10/30/76	38	6		2 **Whenever I'm Away From You** ... *Razzamatazz*	$6	■	Midland Int'l. 10780
2/19/77	34	8		3 **All Strung Out On You** ... *Easy Evil*	$6	■	Midland Int'l. 10907
4/1/78	1[1]	24	▲	4 **You're The One That I Want** *Alone At A Drive-In Movie* [I]	$5	■	RSO 891
				JOHN TRAVOLTA AND OLIVIA NEWTON-JOHN			
8/5/78	5	16	●	5 **Summer Nights** ... *Rock 'N' Roll Party Queen* (Louis St. Louis)	$5		RSO 906
				JOHN TRAVOLTA, OLIVIA NEWTON-JOHN & CAST			
9/30/78	47	8		6 **Greased Lightnin'** ... *Rock 'N' Roll Is Here To Stay* (**Sha-Na-Na**)	$5	■	RSO 909
				Jeff Conaway (backing vocal); above 3 from the movie *Grease* starring Travolta and Newton-John			
11/9/96	25[A]	16		7 **The Grease Megamix** ...			album cut
				JOHN TRAVOLTA & OLIVIA NEWTON-JOHN			
				from the album *Pure Disco* on Polydor 535877; medley of songs (#4-6 above) from the 1978 movie *Grease*			
				TRÉ '97			
				Female R&B vocal trio from Cleveland, Ohio: Rebecca Forsha, Kimberly Cromartie and Niko Williams.			
2/15/97	77	10		**Take Your Time** ... S:60 *Thug Devotion* (Mo Thugs Family)	$3	▮	Mo Thugs 1586
				TRÉ Featuring Krayzie Bone			
				TREACH — see L.V. / NAUGHTY BY NATURE			
				TREE SWINGERS, The '60			
				Pop-novelty duo from Asbury Park, New Jersey: Art Polhemus (born on 8/16/40) and Terry Byrnes (born on 5/6/40).			
8/15/60	73	6		**Kookie Little Paradise** ... *Teaching The Natives To Sing* [N]	$20		Guyden 2036
				TREMELOES, The BUB/LP '67			
				Pop-rock group from England: Len "Chip" Hawkes (vocals, bass), Alan Blakely and Ricky West (guitars), and Dave Munden (drums). Formed as backing band for British vocalist **Brian Poole** (born on 11/3/41 in England). Blakely is the brother of Mike Blakely of **Christie**. Hawkes is the father of singer **Chesney Hawkes**. Blakely died of cancer on 6/10/96 (age 54).			
9/12/64	97	2		1 **Someone, Someone** ... *(Meet Me) Where We Used To Meet*	$12		Monument 846
				BRIAN POOLE And The Tremeloes			
4/8/67	13	12		2 **Here Comes My Baby** ... *Gentleman Of Pleasure*	$10		Epic 10139
				written by **Cat Stevens**			
6/17/67	11	14		3 **Silence Is Golden** *Let Your Hair Hang Down*	$10	■	Epic 10184
				originally recorded by **The 4 Seasons** in 1964 (B-side of "Rag Doll"); promo picture sleeve also issued with **The Hollies**' "Carrie-Anne" on the flip side			
9/30/67	36	7		4 **Even The Bad Times Are Good** ... *Jenny's All Right*	$10	■	Epic 10233
2/17/68	44	10		5 **Suddenly You Love Me** ... *Suddenly Winter*	$10		Epic 10293
				TRESVANT, Ralph R&B/LP '91			
				Born on 5/16/68 in Roxbury, Massachusetts. R&B singer. Member of **New Edition**. Appeared in the movie *House Party 2*.			
11/3/90+	4	20	●	1 **Sensitivity** RB[1] S:3 / A:3 *(no B-side)*	$3	▮	MCA 53932
2/23/91	34	11		2 **Stone Cold Gentleman** ... S:32 / A:34 *(no B-side)*	$3	▮	MCA 54043
				Bobby Brown (guest rapper)			
6/15/91	54[S]	10		3 **Do What I Gotta Do** ... *(no B-side)*	$3	▮	MCA 54035
5/30/92	10	20		4 **The Best Things In Life Are Free** ... RB[1] A:5 / S:16 *(3 album snippets)*	$3	▮[V]	Perspective 0010
				LUTHER VANDROSS and JANET JACKSON with BBD and Ralph Tresvant			
				"45" B-side: (edit-no rap)			
7/18/92	54	12		5 **Money Can't Buy You Love** ... A:45 / S:51 *(LP version) / (3 album snippets)*	$3	▮	Perspective 0011
				above 2 from the movie *Mo' Money* starring Damon Wayans			
				T. REX LP '72			
				Glam-rock band from England: Marc Bolan (vocals, guitar; born Marc Feld on 7/30/47), Mickey Finn (guitar; born on 6/3/47), Steve Currie (bass) and Bill Legend (drums). Bolan died in a car crash on 9/16/77 (age 30). Finn died of liver failure on 1/11/2003 (age 55).			
1/23/71	76	6		1 **Ride A White Swan** *[TYRANNOSAURUS REX]* ... *Summertime Blues*	$8		Blue Thumb 121
5/8/71	72	6		2 **Hot Love** ... *One Inch Rock / Seagull Woman*	$7		Reprise 1006
1/1/72	10	15		3 **Bang A Gong (Get It On)** ... *Raw Ramp*	$7		Reprise 1032
				Howard Kaylan & Mark Volman of **The Turtles** (backing vocals)			
4/22/72	67	5		4 **Telegram Sam** ... *Cadillac*	$7		Reprise 1078
				TRIBE CALLED QUEST, A R&B/BUB/LP '94			
				Rap trio from Queens, New York: Jonathan "**Q-Tip**" Davis, Ali Shaheed Muhammad (**Lucy Pearl**) and Malik "**Phife Dawg**" Taylor (see #6 below).			
10/19/91	63[S]	9		1 **Check The Rhime** ... *(remix)*	$4	▮	Jive 42011
				samples "Love Your Life" by **Average White Band**			
6/6/92	57	15		2 **Scenario** ... S:35 / A:69 *(remix)*	$3	▮	Jive 42065
11/6/93+	47	18		3 **Award Tour** S:33 / A:50 *(instrumental) / The Chase, Part II*	$3	▮	Jive 42187
				Trugoy the Dove (**De La Soul**, backing vocal); samples "We Gettin' Down" by Weldon Irvine			
3/19/94	65	9		4 **Electric Relaxation (Relax Yourself Girl)** ... S:51 / A:67 *Midnight*	$3	▮	Jive 42197
9/12/98	71	7		5 **Find A Way** ... *(2 versions) / Steppin' It Up* (w/**Busta Rhymes** & **Redman**)	$6	T	Jive 42534
				samples "Dubnova" by Towa Tei			
9/30/00	38[S]	7		6 **Flawless** ... *Bend Ova*	$6	★	Groove Attack 067
				PHIFE DAWG			

DEBUT	PEAK	WKS	Gold	A-side (Chart Hit)..........B-side	$	Sym	Label & Number
				TRICK DADDY LP **'01**			
				Born Maurice Young in Miami, Florida. Male "thug" rapper/producer. Also see the B-side of **DJ Hurricane**'s "Come Get It."			
3/13/99	62	20		1 **Nann**..........S:30 / A:57 *Living In A World* (w/Society)	$4	★	Slip n Slide 247
				TRICK DADDY featuring: trina			
5/20/00	83	11		2 **Shut Up**..........*(3 versions)*	$6	T	Slip n Slide 84664
				TRICK DADDY Featuring Deuce Poppi, Trina & Co			
3/10/01	50	20		3 **Take It To Da House**..........A:43 *(3 versions)*	$6	T	Slip n Slide 85063
				TRICK DADDY featuring The SNS Express			
				samples "The Boss" by **James Brown** and "Boogie Shoes" by **KC And The Sunshine Band**			
7/21/01	17	20		4 **I'm A Thug** A:16 *(2 versions) / Can't F**k Wit Me* (w/J.V.)	$6	T	Slip n Slide 85141
				samples "Cheatin' Is" by **Millie Jackson**			
7/13/02	70	18		5 **In Da Wind**..........S:55 / A:66 *(3 versions)*	$6	T	Slip n Slide 85333
				TRICK DADDY feat. Cee-Lo & Big Boi			
12/21/02+	87	9		6 **Thug Holiday**..........*(2 versions) / Gangsta!* (w/**Baby** & **Scarface**)	$6	T	Slip n Slide 85404
				TRICK DADDY featuring LaTocha Scott			
				samples "Holiday" by Michael Sterling			
				TRICK PONY C&W/BUB/LP **'01**			
				Country trio formed in Nashville, Tennessee: Heidi Newfield (vocals), Keith Burns (guitar) and Ira Dean (bass).			
2/3/01	71	14		1 **Pour Me**..........S:23 / A:74 *If You Think You've Got Trouble*	$4	★^{V}	Warner 16816
7/28/01	47	20		2 **On A Night Like This**..........S:35 / A:47 *Pour Me (acoustic version)*	$4	★^{V}	Warner 16751
				TRILOGY BUB **'91**			
				Dance trio from the Bronx, New York: Duran Ramos, Angel DeLeon and Darrin Dewitt Henson. Choreography work for **New Kids On The Block**. Henson replaced by **Joey Kid**.			
3/30/91	82	7		**Love Me Forever Or Love Me Not**..........*(R&B radio mix)*	$3	▮	Atco 98876
				TRINA R&B/LP **'00**			
				Born Katrina Taylor in Miami, Florida. Female hardcore rapper. Discovered by **Trick Daddy**.			
3/13/99	62	20		1 **Nann**..........S:30 / A:57 *Living In A World* (w/Society)	$4	★	Slip n Slide 247
				TRICK DADDY featuring: trina			
5/20/00	83	11		2 **Shut Up**..........*(3 versions)*	$6	T	Slip n Slide 84664
				TRICK DADDY Featuring Deuce Poppi, Trina & Co			
9/9/00	93	4		3 **Pull Over**..........*(2 versions) / I Don't Need U* (w/**Trick Daddy**)	$6	T	Slip n Slide 84701
8/3/02	71^S	1		4 **No Panties**..........*(3 versions)*	$6	T	Slip n Slide 85367
				TRINA Featuring Tweet			
				TRINA & TAMARA **'97**			
				R&B vocal duo from Gary, Indiana: Trina and Tamara Powell. Sisters of **Jesse Powell**.			
8/30/97	4	26	●	1 **My Love Is The Shhh!**..........S:5 / A:17 *(instrumental)*	$3	▮	Warner 17327
				SOMETHIN' FOR THE PEOPLE featuring Trina & Tamara			
4/3/99	56	12		2 **What'd You Come Here For?**..........S:14 *(remix)*	$4	★	Columbia 79127
				samples "Car Wash" by **Rose Royce**			
				TRIPLETS, The AC/LP **'91**			
				Triplet sisters Diana, Sylvia and Vicky Villegas. Born on 4/18/65, seven minutes apart. Raised in Mexico by their American mother and Mexican father. Gained recognition after winning an *MTV Basement Tapes* competition in 1986.			
3/16/91	14	16		**You Don't Have To Go Home Tonight**..........A:12 / S:13 *(3 album snippets) / Pyramids Of Pleasure*	$3	▮^{V}	Mercury 878864
				TRIPPING DAISY ROK/LP **'95**			
				Pop-rock group from Dallas, Texas: Tim DeLaughter (vocals), Wes Berggren (guitar), Mark Pirro (bass) and Bryan Wakeland (drums). Berggren died on 10/27/99 (age 28).			
7/22/95	53^A	8		**I Got A Girl**..........			album cut
				from the album *I Am An Elastic Firecracker* on Island 524112			
				TRITT, Travis C&W/BUB/LP **'01**			
				Born James Travis Tritt on 2/9/63 in Marietta, Georgia. Country singer/songwriter/guitarist (charted 40 hits from 1989-03).			
6/19/93	72^S	2		1 **T-R-O-U-B-L-E**..........BUB:108 *(single version)*	$4	▮^{V}	Warner 18496
7/23/94	72^S	1		2 **Foolish Pride**..........CW^1 BUB:112 *No Vacation From The Blues*	$4	▮^{V}	Warner 18180
2/22/97	43	20	●	3 **Here's Your Sign (Get The Picture)**..........S:29 *Things Have Changed* [C]	$4	▮^{V}	Warner 17491
				BILL ENGVALL with Travis Tritt			
10/17/98	86	11		4 **If I Lost You**..........S:35 *Start The Car* (C&W #52)	$4	★^{V}	Warner 17152
8/19/00	27	22		5 **Best Of Intentions** CW^1 S:19 / A:24 *Southbound Train*	$4	★^{V}	Columbia 79404
3/3/01	33	20		6 **It's A Great Day To Be Alive**..........A:27		V	album cut
				"45" issued for above 2 on Columbia 79563			
9/15/01	39	20		7 **Love Of A Woman**..........A:34			album cut
3/30/02	55	11		8 **Modern Day Bonnie And Clyde**..........A:54		V	album cut
				"45": Columbia 79747; B-side: "It's A Great Day To Be Alive"; above 4 from the album *Down The Road I Go* on Columbia 62165			
				TRIUMPH ROK/BUB/LP **'86**			
				Hard-rock trio formed in Toronto, Ontario, Canada: Rik Emmett (guitar, vocals), Mike Levine (keyboards, bass) and Gil Moore (drums).			
6/16/79	38	14		1 **Hold On**..........*Just A Game*	$4	■	RCA 11569
11/3/79	86	7		2 **Lay It On The Line**..........*American Girls*	$4		RCA 11690
6/7/80	91	2		3 **I Can Survive**..........*Nature's Child*	$4		RCA 11945
10/3/81	51	11		4 **Magic Power**..........*Hot Time (In This City Tonight)*	$4		RCA 12298
3/9/85	88	2		5 **Follow Your Heart**..........*Stranger In A Strange Land*	$3	■	MCA 52540
8/30/86	27	15		6 **Somebody's Out There** S:20 / A:40 *What Rules My Heart*	$3	■	MCA 52898
				TRIUMPHS, The — see THOMAS, B.J.			

DEBUT	PEAK	WKS	Gold	A-side (Chart Hit)	B-side	$	Sym	Label & Number

TRIXTER — LP '91

Hard-rock group from Paramus, New Jersey: Peter Loran (vocals), Steve Brown (guitar), P.J. Farley (bass) and Mark Scott (drums).

DEBUT	PEAK	WKS	Gold	A-side (Chart Hit)	B-side	$	Sym	Label & Number
12/1/90+	65	9		1 **Give It To Me Good**	*(no B-side)*	$4	▮	Mechanic 53863
3/16/91	75	8		2 **One In A Million**	*(no B-side)*	$4	▮	Mechanic 54044
6/8/91	72	10		3 **Surrender**	*(no B-side)*	$4	▮	Mechanic 54105

TROCCOLI, Kathy — AC/BUB/LP '92

Born on 6/24/58 in Brooklyn, New York. Christian singer/songwriter.

DEBUT	PEAK	WKS	Gold	A-side (Chart Hit)	B-side	$	Sym	Label & Number
2/22/92	14	20		1 **Everything Changes** A:7 / S:50	*The Hard Days*	$4	▮	Reunion 19118
7/9/94	88	6		2 **Tell Me Where It Hurts**	*(3 album snippets)*	$3	▮	Reunion/RCA 62813

TROGGS, The — BUB/LP '66

Rock group from Andover, England: Reg Presley (vocals; born Reg Ball), Chris Britton (guitar), Pete Staples (bass) and Ronnie Bullis (drums). Bullis died on 11/13/92 (age 51).

DEBUT	PEAK	WKS	Gold	A-side (Chart Hit)	B-side	$	Sym	Label & Number
6/25/66	❶^2	11		1 **Wild Thing** / first recorded by The Wild Ones in 1965 on United Artists 947; also issued with "I Want You" as the B-side; also charted on Fontana 1548; B-side: "From Home" ($15)				
8/6/66	29	8		2 **With A Girl Like You** also charted on Fontana 1552; B-side: "I Want You" ($15)		$20		Atco 6415
10/15/66	43	6		3 **I Can't Control Myself** also charted on Fontana 1557; B-side: "Gonna Make You" ($15)	*Gonna Make You*	$15		Atco 6444
2/24/68	7	16		4 **Love Is All Around**	*When Will The Rain Come*	$15		Fontana 1607

TROLLS, The — BUB '66

Rock group from Lake Bluff, Illinois: Richard Clark (vocals, organ), Richard Gallagher (guitar), Max Jordan (bass) and Gary Aull (drums; replaced by Ken Cortese who died in the same plane crash that killed **Jim Croce** on 9/20/73).

DEBUT	PEAK	WKS	Gold	A-side (Chart Hit)	B-side	$	Sym	Label & Number
10/22/66	96	1		**Every Day And Every Night** arrangement similar to **The Shadows Of Knight**'s 1966 hit "Gloria"; original title is "Everyday, Everynight" on ABC Paramount 10823	*Are You The One?*	$12		ABC 10823

TROOP — R&B/LP '90

R&B vocal group from Pasadena, California: Steve Russell, Allen McNeil, Rodney Benford, John Harreld and Reggie Warren. Troop stands for Total Respect Of Other People. Group discovered by **Gerald Levert**.

DEBUT	PEAK	WKS	Gold	A-side (Chart Hit)	B-side	$	Sym	Label & Number
7/7/90	47	13		1 **All I Do Is Think Of You** RB^1 S:35	*My Music*	$3	▮	Atlantic 87952
6/20/92	63	5		2 **Whatever It Takes (To Make You Stay)** A:46	*(3 album snippets)*	$3	▮^{V}	Atlantic 87475
9/26/92	58	13		3 **Sweet November** RB^1 S:46 / A:64	*Strange Hotel*	$3	▮	Atlantic 87445

TROOPER — LP '78

Rock group from Vancouver, British Columbia, Canada: Ra McGuire (vocals, guitar), Brian Smith (guitar), Frank Ludwig (keyboards), Doni Underhill (bass) and Tommy Stewart (drums).

DEBUT	PEAK	WKS	Gold	A-side (Chart Hit)	B-side	$	Sym	Label & Number
8/5/78	59	8		**Raise A Little Hell** produced by Randy Bachman (**Bachman-Turner Overdrive**)	*A Fine Mess (You've Gotten Us Into)*	$6		MCA 40924

TROUTMAN, Roger — see ROGER

TROWER, Robin — ROK/BUB/LP '77

Born on 3/9/45 in London, England. Rock guitarist/songwriter. Original member of **Procol Harum**.

DEBUT	PEAK	WKS	Gold	A-side (Chart Hit)	B-side	$	Sym	Label & Number
12/4/76+	82	7		**Caledonia** James Dewar (vocal)	*Messin The Blues*	$6		Chrysalis 2122

TROY, Doris — BUB '63

Born Doris Higginson on 1/6/37 in Manhattan, New York. R&B singer/songwriter. Used Doris Payne as her pen name. The off-Broadway musical *Mama, I Want To Sing* is based on her life. Backing vocalist on **Pink Floyd**'s album *Dark Side Of The Moon.*

DEBUT	PEAK	WKS	Gold	A-side (Chart Hit)	B-side	$	Sym	Label & Number
6/8/63	10	14		**Just One Look**	*Bossa Nova Blues*	$15		Atlantic 2188

TROYER, Eric — '80

Born in Brooklyn, New York. Pop singer/songwriter.

DEBUT	PEAK	WKS	Gold	A-side (Chart Hit)	B-side	$	Sym	Label & Number
7/26/80	92	2		**Mirage**	*Meet Me At Midnight*	$4		Chrysalis 2445

TRU — R&B/BUB/LP '97

Rap group from New Orleans, Louisiana: brothers **Master P**, **Silkk the Shocker** and C-Murder, with **Mia X** and **Mo B Dick**. TRU stands for The Real Untouchables.

DEBUT	PEAK	WKS	Gold	A-side (Chart Hit)	B-side	$	Sym	Label & Number
2/8/97	71	15		1 **I Always Feel Like (Somebody's Watching Me)** S:40	*(3 versions) / Pimp Sh..* (**Silkk**) / *Eyes Of A Killa* (C-Murder)	$4	▮	No Limit 53261
7/3/99	24^S	13		2 **Tru Homies** BUB:122 samples "I'll Be Around" by the **Spinners**; clean version on No Limit 53493	*(2 versions)*	$4	★	No Limit 53494

TRUE, Andrea, Connection — LP '76

Born on 5/29/52 in Nashville, Tennessee. White female disco singer/actress. Appeared in several X-rated movies in the 1970s.

DEBUT	PEAK	WKS	Gold	A-side (Chart Hit)	B-side	$	Sym	Label & Number
3/13/76	4	25	●	1 **More, More, More Pt. 1**	*Pt. II*	$5		Buddah 515
8/7/76	80	4		2 **Party Line**	*Call Me*	$5		Buddah 538
2/19/77	27	11		3 **N.Y., You Got Me Dancing**	*Keep It Up Longer*	$5		Buddah 564
1/14/78	56	7		4 **What's Your Name, What's Your Number**	*Fill Me Up (Heart To Heart)*	$5		Buddah 582

TRUMPETEERS, The — '59

Big-band styled group directed by **Billy Mure** (guitarist with Leo Addeo's orchestra).

DEBUT	PEAK	WKS	Gold	A-side (Chart Hit)	B-side	$	Sym	Label & Number
4/27/59	64	9		**A String Of Trumpets** some pressings credit artist as: **BILLY MURE and The Trumpeteers**	*Tea And Trumpets* [I]	$15		Splash 800

TRUSTCOMPANY — ROK/LP '02

Rock group from Montgomery, Alabama: Kevin Palmer (vocals, guitar), James Fukai (guitar), Josh Moates (bass) and Jason Singleton (drums).

DEBUT	PEAK	WKS	Gold	A-side (Chart Hit)	B-side	$	Sym	Label & Number
10/19/02	91	4		**Downfall**	*Hover (decomposed)*	$4	★	Geffen 497786

TRUTH, The — LP '87

Rock duo from England: Dennis Greaves (lead vocals, guitar) and Mick Lister (vocals, guitar).

DEBUT	PEAK	WKS	Gold	A-side (Chart Hit)	B-side	$	Sym	Label & Number
5/9/87	65	9		**Weapons Of Love**	*This Way Forever*	$4	■	I.R.S. 53084

DEBUT	PEAK	WKS	Gold	A-side (Chart Hit)....B-side	$	Sym	Label & Number
				TRUTH HURTS R&B/LP **'02**			
				Born Shari Watson in Los Angeles, California. Female hip-hop singer.			
4/20/02	9	20		**Addictive** ....A:8 / S:23 *(2 versions)*	$6	T	Aftermath 497710
				Rakim (rap); co-produced by **Dr. Dre** and **DJ Quik**			
				TRYNIN, Jennifer **'95**			
				Born on 12/27/63 in New Jersey. Rock singer/songwriter/guitarist.			
7/29/95	74[A]	2		**Better Than Nothing**			album cut
				from the album *Cockamamie* on Squint 45931			
				T.S.U. TORONADOES, The **'69**			
				R&B band from Texas Southern University: Cal Thomas and Will Thomas (guitars), Robert Sanders (organ), Clarence Harper, Nelson Mills and Leroy Lewis (horns), Jerry Jenkins (bass) and Dwight Burns (drums). Similar in sound to **Archie Bell & The Drells**.			
1/18/69	75	6		**Getting The Corners** ....*What Good Am I?*	$10		Atlantic 2579
				TUBES, The ROK/BUB/LP **'83**			
				Pop-rock group from San Francisco, California: Fee Waybill (vocals), Bill Spooner and Roger Steen (guitars), Michael Cotton and Vince Welnick (keyboards), Rick Anderson (bass) and Prairie Prince (drums). Welnick joined **Grateful Dead** in 1990. Group appeared in the 1980 movie *Xanadu*.			
7/4/76	61	7		1 **Don't Touch Me There** ....*Proud To Be An American*	$5		A&M 1826
6/20/81	35	12		2 **Don't Want To Wait Anymore** ....*Think About Me*	$4	■	Capitol 5007
4/9/83	10	20		3 **She's A Beauty** AR[5] *When You're Ready To Come*	$4	■	Capitol 5217
7/23/83	52	7		4 **Tip Of My Tongue**....*Keyboard Kids*	$4		Capitol 5258
10/1/83	68	4		5 **The Monkey Time**....*Sports Fans*	$4	■	Capitol 5254
3/9/85	87	2		6 **Piece By Piece** ....*Night People*	$4	■	Capitol 5443
				written and produced by **Todd Rundgren**			
				TUCKER, Louise LP **'83**			
				Born in England. Classical-styled vocalist.			
6/18/83	46	13		**Midnight Blue**....*Voices In The Wind*	$4		Arista 9022
				Charlie Skarbek (male vocal); adaptation of Beethoven's *Sonata Pathetique*			
				TUCKER, Tanya C&W/BUB/LP **'75**			
				Born on 10/10/58 in Seminole, Texas; raised in Wilcox, Arizona. Country singer (charted 66 hits, 1972-02). Had her first chart hit at age 13. Bit part in the movie *Jeremiah Johnson* in 1972.			
7/1/72	72	7		1 **Delta Dawn** ....*I Love The Way He Loves Me*	$5	■	Columbia 45588
5/26/73	86	4		2 **What's Your Mama's Name** ....CW[1] *Rainy Girl*	$5		Columbia 45799
8/25/73	74	9		3 **Blood Red And Goin' Down**....CW[1] *The Missing Piece Of Puzzle*	$5		Columbia 45892
2/16/74	46	10		4 **Would You Lay With Me (In A Field of Stone)** ....CW[1] *No Man's Land*	$5		Columbia 45991
8/3/74	86	4		5 **The Man That Turned My Mama On**....*Satisfied With Missing You*	$5		Columbia 46047
5/3/75	37	9		6 **Lizzie And The Rainman** CW[1] *Traveling Salesman*	$5		MCA 40402
10/2/76	82	5		7 **Here's Some Love** ....CW[1] *Pride Of Franklin County*	$5		MCA 40598
1/20/79	70	4		8 **Not Fade Away**....*Texas (When I Die)* (C&W #5)	$5	■	MCA 40976
				Buddy Holly song first recorded by **The Crickets** in 1957 (B-side of "Oh, Boy!")			
				TUCKER, Tommy BUB **'64**			
				Born Robert Higginbotham on 3/5/39 in Springfield, Ohio. Died of poisoning on 1/22/82 (age 42). R&B singer/songwriter/pianist.			
2/8/64	11	11		1 **Hi-Heel Sneakers** ....*I Don't Want 'Cha*	$20		Checker 1067
5/16/64	96	2		2 **Long Tall Shorty**....*Mo' Shorty*	$15		Checker 1075
				TUESDAYS, The **'98**			
				Female pop group from Norway: Laila Samuels (vocals), Hege Solli (guitar), Kristin Werner (keyboards), Veslemoy Hole (bass) and Linda Gustafsson (drums).			
3/21/98	55	10		**It's Up To You** ....S:70 / A:75 *(3 album snippets)*	$4	▌	Arista 13469
				TUFANO & GIAMMARESE — see BUCKINGHAMS, The			
				TUNE ROCKERS, The **'58**			
				Instrumental rock and roll band from Buffalo, New York: Gene Strong (lead guitar), Fred Patton (guitar), Johnny Capello (sax), Tim Nolan (bass) and Mickey Vanderlip (drums).			
8/25/58	44	10		**The Green Mosquito** ....H:44 *Warm Up* [I-N]	$25		United Artists 139
				TUNE WEAVERS, The **'57**			
				R&B vocal group from Boston, Massachusetts: Margo Sylvia (lead), husband John Sylvia (bass), Gilbert Lopez (Margo's brother; tenor) and Charlotte Davis (Margo's cousin). Margo died of a heart attack on 10/25/91.			
9/16/57	5	19		**Happy, Happy Birthday Baby** ....T:5 / S:8 / A:12 *Ol Man River*	$40		Checker 872
				Frank Paul (orch.); first released on Casa Grande 4037 in 1957 ($100)			
				TURBANS, The BUB **'56**			
				R&B vocal group from Philadelphia, Pennsylvania: Al Banks, Matthew Platt, Charles Williams and Andrew Jones. Banks died in 1980 (age 43).			
11/12/55+	33	21		**When You Dance**....T:33 *Let Me Show You (Around My Heart)*	$75		Herald 458
				a new version by The Turbans "Bubbled Under" (#114) in 1961 on Parkway 820			
	★390★			**TURNER, Ike & Tina** BUB/R&B/LP **'71**			
				Husband-and-wife R&B duo: guitarist Ike Turner (born on 11/5/31 in Clarksdale, Mississippi) and vocalist **Tina Turner** (born Anna Mae Bullock on 11/26/38 in Brownsville, Tennessee). Married from 1958-76. At age 11, Ike was backing pianist for bluesmen Sonny Boy Williamson (Aleck Ford) and Robert Nighthawk (of the Nighthawks). Formed own band, the Kings of Rhythm, while in high school; backed Jackie Brenston's hit "Rocket '88'." Prolific session, production and guitar work during the 1950s. In 1960 developed a dynamic stage show around Tina; "The Ike & Tina Turner Revue" featuring her backing vocalists, **The Ikettes**, and Ike's Kings of Rhythm. Disbanded in 1974. In the mid-1980s, Tina emerged as a successful solo artist. Duo inducted into the Rock and Roll Hall of Fame in 1991.			
				1)Proud Mary 2)It's Gonna Work Out Fine 3)Nutbush City Limits 4)A Fool In Love 5)I Want To Take You Higher			
8/29/60	27	13		1 **A Fool In Love**....*The Way You Love Me*	$30		Sue 730
12/12/60	82	4		2 **I Idolize You**....*Letter From Tina*	$25		Sue 735
7/31/61	14	15		3 **It's Gonna Work Out Fine** ....*Won't You Forgive Me*	$25		Sue 749
				Mickey & Sylvia (backing vocals)			

DEBUT	PEAK	WKS	Gold	A-side (Chart Hit)...B-side	$	Sym	Label & Number
				TURNER, Ike & Tina — Cont'd			
11/27/61+	38	11		4 **Poor Fool** ... *You Can't Blame Me*	$20		Sue 753
3/24/62	50	7		5 **Tra La La La La** ... *Puppy Love*	$15		Sue 757
6/30/62	89	2		6 **You Should'a Treated Me Right** ... *Sleepless*	$15		Sue 765
10/3/64	95	3		7 **I Can't Believe What You Say (For Seeing What You Do)** ... *My Baby Now*	$15		Kent 402
				all of above written by Ike Turner			
5/28/66	88	4		8 **River Deep-Mountain High** ... *I'll Keep You Happy*	$20		Philles 131
				produced by Phil Spector; "Bubbled Under" (#112) in 1969 on A&M 1118			
4/26/69	68	7		9 **I've Been Loving You Too Long** ... *Grumbling*	$8		Blue Thumb 101
				"Bubbled Under" (#120) in 1971 on Blue Thumb 202			
5/10/69	98	2		10 **I'm Gonna Do All I Can (To Do Right By My Man)** ... *You've Got Too Many Ties That Bind*	$8		Minit 32060
8/2/69	93	2		11 **The Hunter** ... *Crazy 'Bout You Baby*	$8		Blue Thumb 102
12/20/69+	59	8		12 **Bold Soul Sister** ... *I Know (#126)*	$8		Blue Thumb 104
3/7/70	57	8		13 **Come Together** *[IKE & TINA TURNER & THE IKETTES]* ... *Honky Tonk Women*	$7		Minit 32087
5/23/70	34	18		14 **I Want To Take You Higher** *[IKE & TINA TURNER & THE IKETTES]* ... *Contact High*	$7		Liberty 56177
1/30/71	4	13	●	15 **Proud Mary** *Funkier Than A Mosquita's Tweeter*	$7		Liberty 56216
5/15/71	60	7		16 **Ooh Poo Pah Doo** ... *I Wanna Jump*	$6		United Artists 50782
2/26/72	83	4		17 **Up In Heah** ... *Doo Wah Ditty (Got To Get Ta)*	$6		United Artists 50881
9/8/73	22	15		18 **Nutbush City Limits** ... *Help Him*	$6		United Artists 298
				a "live" solo version by Tina is on the B-side of her "Private Dancer" single			
11/2/74	65	8		19 **Sexy Ida (Part 1)** ... *(Part 2)*	$6		United Artists 528
6/7/75	88	4		20 **Baby-Get It On** ... *(disco version)*	$6		United Artists 598

TURNER, Jesse Lee '59

Born in Bowling, Texas. Male rockabilly singer.

DEBUT	PEAK	WKS	Gold	A-side (Chart Hit)...B-side	$	Sym	Label & Number
1/5/59	20	12		**The Little Space Girl** ... *Shake, Baby, Shake* [N]	$35		Carlton 496

TURNER, Joe R&B/MEM/BUB '56

Born on 5/18/11 in Kansas City, Missouri. Died of a heart attack on 11/24/85 (age 74). Blues-R&B vocalist known as "Big Joe." Early in career teamed with boogie-woogie pianist Pete Johnson. Appeared in the movie *Shake, Rattle And Rock!* in 1957. Inducted into the Rock and Roll Hall of Fame in 1987 as a blues pioneer.

DEBUT	PEAK	WKS	Gold	A-side (Chart Hit)...B-side	$	Sym	Label & Number
5/12/56	41	10		1 **Corrine Corrina** ... T:41 *Boogie Woogie Country Girl* (R&B flip)	$35		Atlantic 1088
				The Cookies (backing vocals); first recorded by Turner in 1941 with the Art Tatum band (Decca 8563)			
12/28/59+	53	9		2 **Honey Hush** ... *Tomorrow Night*	$25		Atlantic 2044
				new version of Joe's #1 R&B hit in 1953 (Atlantic 1001)			

TURNER, Sammy '59

Born Samuel Black on 6/2/32 in Paterson, New Jersey. **Tommy Edwards**-styled vocalist.

DEBUT	PEAK	WKS	Gold	A-side (Chart Hit)...B-side	$	Sym	Label & Number
3/23/59	100	1		1 **Sweet Annie Laurie** *[SAMMY TURNER and THE TWISTERS]* ... *Thunderbolt*	$25		Big Top 3007
				#8 hit for John McCormack in 1910 (as "Annie Laurie")			
6/22/59	3	18		2 **Lavender-Blue** *Wrapped Up In A Dream*	$20		Big Top 3016
				originally released on Pacific 3016 ($40) in 1958; #4 hit for **Sammy Kaye** in 1949			
11/2/59	19	12		3 **Always** /			
				originally released on Pacific 3029 ($30) in 1959; 4 versions hit the Top 10 in 1926			
11/30/59	82	3		4 **Symphony** ...	$20		Big Top 3029
				5 versions hit the Top 10 in 1946			
2/15/60	46	11		5 **Paradise** ... *I'd Be A Fool Again*	$20		Big Top 3032
				#1 hit for both Leo Reisman and Guy Lombardo in 1932; all of above produced by Jerry Leiber and Mike Stoller			

TURNER, Spyder LP '67

Born Dwight Turner in 1947 in Beckley, West Virginia. R&B singer.

DEBUT	PEAK	WKS	Gold	A-side (Chart Hit)...B-side	$	Sym	Label & Number
12/17/66+	12	12		1 **Stand By Me** ... *You're Good Enough For Me* [N]	$15		MGM 13617
				vocal impressions of **Jackie Wilson**, **David Ruffin**, **Billy Stewart**, **Smokey Robinson** and **Chuck Jackson**			
3/25/67	95	2		2 **I Can't Make It Anymore** ... *Don't Hold Back*	$15		MGM 13692
				written by **Gordon Lightfoot**			

TURNER, Tina ★182★ R&B/AC/BUB/ROK/LP '84

Born Anna Mae Bullock on 11/26/38 in Brownsville, Tennessee. R&B-rock singer/actress. Half of **Ike & Tina Turner** duo, when married to Ike from 1958-76. In movies *Tommy* and *Mad Max-Beyond Thunderdome.* With Ike, inducted into the Rock and Roll Hall of Fame in 1991. Her autobiography, *What's Love Got To Do With It*, was made into a movie in 1993.

1)What's Love Got To Do With It 2)Typical Male 3)We Don't Need Another Hero

DEBUT	PEAK	WKS	Gold	A-side (Chart Hit)...B-side	$	Sym	Label & Number
1/21/84	26	15		1 **Let's Stay Together** ... *I Wrote A Letter*	$4	■	Capitol 5322
5/19/84	❶^{3}	28	●	2 **What's Love Got To Do With It** S:18 *Rock And Roll Widow*	$3	■	Capitol 5354
				1984 Grammy winner: Record of the Year			
9/15/84	5	21		3 **Better Be Good To Me** ... A:5 / S:6 *When I Was Young*	$3	■	Capitol 5387
1/19/85	7	18		4 **Private Dancer** ... S:7 / A:10 *Nutbush City Limits (live)*	$3	■	Capitol 5433
				Jeff Beck (guitar); written by Mark Knopfler (of **Dire Straits**)			
4/20/85	37	10		5 **Show Some Respect** ... *Let's Pretend We're Married*	$3	■	Capitol 5461
				above 5 from the album *Private Dancer*			
7/6/85	2^{1}	18		6 **We Don't Need Another Hero (Thunderdome)** ... S:3 / A:3 *(instrumental)*	$3	■	Capitol 5491
10/5/85	15	18		7 **One Of The Living** ... S:13 / A:14 *(dub version)*	$3	■	Capitol 5518
				above 2 from the movie *Mad Max-Beyond Thunderdome* starring Mel Gibson and Turner			
11/23/85+	15	14		8 **It's Only Love** ... A:14 / S:16 *The Only One* (Adams)	$5	■	A&M 2791
				BRYAN ADAMS/TINA TURNER			
8/30/86	2^{3}	16		9 **Typical Male** ... S:❶^{2} / A:2 *Don't Turn Around*	$3	■	Capitol 5615
11/22/86+	30	12		10 **Two People** ... S:27 / A:32 *Havin' A Party*	$3	■	Capitol 5644
2/7/87	13	14		11 **What You Get Is What You See** ... S:12 / A:16 *(live version)*	$3	■	Capitol 5668
5/9/87	74	5		12 **Break Every Rule** ... *Take Me To The River*	$3	■	Capitol 44003
				above 4 from the album *Break Every Rule*			

TURNER, Tina — Cont'd

DEBUT	PEAK	WKS	Gold	A-side (Chart Hit)...B-side	$	Sym	Label & Number
9/2/89	15	14		13 **The Best**.....S:12 / A:20 *Undercover Agent For The Blues* **Edgar Winter** (sax solo)	$3	■	Capitol 44442
11/25/89+	39	11		14 **Steamy Windows**.....S:32 *The Best* written by **Tony Joe White**; above 2 produced by **Dan Hartman**	$3	■	Capitol 44473
5/29/93	9	24		15 **I Don't Wanna Fight**.....AC[7] A:3 / S:28 *Tina's Wish* "45": Virgin 17401; co-written by **Lulu**	$3	■V	Virgin 12652
10/23/93	97	2		16 **Why Must We Wait Until Tonight?**.....*Shake A Tail Feather* co-written and co-produced by **Bryan Adams**; "45": Virgin 17498; above 2 from Tina's autobiographical movie *What's Love Got To Do With It* starring Angela Bassett and Laurence Fishburne	$4	■V	Virgin 12683
12/23/95	71[S]	1		17 **GoldenEye**.....BUB:102 *(3 mixes)* title song from the James Bond movie starring Pierce Brosnan; written by Bono & The Edge of **U2**	$5	■	Virgin 38524
10/5/96	84	9		18 **Missing You**.....S:73 *Do Something* "45": Virgin 19217	$4	■V	Virgin 38553

TURNER, Titus

R&B/BUB **'61**

Born on 5/11/33 in Atlanta, Georgia. Died on 9/13/84 (age 51). R&B singer/songwriter.

DEBUT	PEAK	WKS	Gold	A-side (Chart Hit)...B-side	$	Sym	Label & Number
11/23/59	83	6		1 **We Told You Not To Marry**.....*Taking Care Of Business* answer song to **Lloyd Price**'s "I'm Gonna Get Married"	$25		Glover 201
1/16/61	77	4		2 **Sound-Off**.....*Me And My Lonely Telephone* popular U.S. Army marching drill chant; #3 hit for **Vaughn Monroe** in 1951	$15		Jamie 1174

TURTLES, The

★298★ BUB/LP **'67**

Pop-rock group formed in Los Angeles, California: Mark Volman (vocals; born on 4/19/47), Howard Kaylan (vocals; born on 6/22/47), Jim Tucker (guitar; born on 10/17/46), Al Nichol (keyboards; born on 3/31/45), Chuck Portz (bass; born on 3/28/45) and Don Murray (drums; born on 11/8/45). Volman and Kaylan (under the names Flo and Eddie) later joined **Frank Zappa**'s Mothers. Murray died on 3/22/96 (age 50).

1)Happy Together 2)She'd Rather Be With Me 3)Elenore

DEBUT	PEAK	WKS	Gold	A-side (Chart Hit)...B-side	$	Sym	Label & Number
8/7/65	8	11		1 **It Ain't Me Babe**.....*Almost There* written by **Bob Dylan** (from his 1964 album *Another Side Of Bob Dylan*)	$12		White Whale 222
10/30/65	29	7		2 **Let Me Be**.....*Your Maw Said You Cried*	$12		White Whale 224
2/5/66	20	12		3 **You Baby**.....*Wanderin' Kind*	$12		White Whale 227
6/18/66	81	4		4 **Grim Reaper Of Love**.....*Come Back*	$15		White Whale 231
10/29/66	89	5		5 **Can I Get To Know You Better**.....*Like The Seasons* first recorded by Mark Wynter in 1965 on Scepter 1299	$15		White Whale 238
2/11/67	1[3]	15	●	6 **Happy Together** *Like The Seasons*	$10	■	White Whale 244
5/13/67	3	11		7 **She'd Rather Be With Me**.....*The Walking Song*	$10	■	White Whale 249
8/5/67	12	11		8 **You Know What I Mean**.....*Rugs Of Woods & Flowers*	$10	■	White Whale 254
11/11/67	14	10		9 **She's My Girl**.....*Chicken Little Was Right*	$10	■	White Whale 260
3/2/68	57	6		10 **Sound Asleep**.....*Umbassa The Dragon*	$8	■	White Whale 264
6/22/68	48	6		11 **The Story Of Rock And Roll**.....*Can't You Hear The Cows* written by **Nilsson**	$8	■	White Whale 273
9/21/68	6	12		12 **Elenore**.....*Surfer Dan*	$8	■	White Whale 276
1/4/69	6	12		13 **You Showed Me**.....*Buzz Saw* written and recorded by **The Byrds** in 1964	$8	■	White Whale 292
6/7/69	51	7		14 **You Don't Have To Walk In The Rain**.....*Come Over*	$8	■	White Whale 308
10/11/69	91	2		15 **Love In The City**.....*Bachelor Mother* above 2 produced by Ray Davies of **The Kinks**	$8	■	White Whale 326
12/6/69	78	4		16 **Lady-O**.....*Somewhere Friday Nite*	$8		White Whale 334
6/27/70	100	2		17 **Eve Of Destruction**.....*Wanderin' Kind* from the group's 1965 debut album *It Ain't Me Babe*; #2 & 17: written by **P.F. Sloan**	$8		White Whale 355

TUTONE, Tommy — see TOMMY TUTONE

TUXEDO JUNCTION

AC/BUB/LP **'78**

Female disco group: Jamie Edlin, Marilyn Jackson, Sue Allen and Marti McCall.

DEBUT	PEAK	WKS	Gold	A-side (Chart Hit)...B-side	$	Sym	Label & Number
4/22/78	32	17		**Chattanooga Choo Choo**.....*I Didn't Know About You* #1 hit for Glenn Miller in 1941 (from the movie *Sun Valley Serenade* starring Sonja Henie)	$5		Butterfly 1205

TWAIN, Shania

★312★ C&W/BUB/LP **'98**

Born Eileen Regina Edwards on 8/28/65 in Windsor, Ontario, Canada; raised in Timmins, Ontario, Canada. Country singer/songwriter (charted 29 hits, 1993-03). Adopted the name Shania which means "I'm on my way" in the Ojibwa Indian language. Married Robert John "Mutt" Lange (producer of **Def Leppard**, **The Cars**, **Foreigner** and many others) on 12/28/93.

1)You're Still The One 2)From This Moment On 3)That Don't Impress Me Much

DEBUT	PEAK	WKS	Gold	A-side (Chart Hit)...B-side	$	Sym	Label & Number
5/27/95	31	19	●	1 **Any Man Of Mine** / CW[2] S:13			
5/27/95	87	19		2 **Whose Bed Have Your Boots Been Under?**.....S:72 original cassette box only showed the above title on the front cover	$4	■V	Mercury 856448
12/16/95+	74	9		3 **(If You're Not In It For Love) I'm Outta Here!** / CW[2] S:43			
10/28/95	90	15		4 **The Woman In Me (Needs The Man In You)**.....S:53 "45" issued for above 2 on Mercury 852498	$4	■V	Mercury 852206
12/28/96+	75	5		5 **God Bless The Child**.....S:53 *If It Don't Take Two* Mark Kibble, Claude McKnight and Joel Kibble (of Take 6) (backing vocals); proceeds benefit hungry children throughout North America; "45" B-side: (If You're Not In It For Love) I'm Outta Here" (remix); all of above from the album *The Woman In Me*	$4	■V	Mercury 578748
10/11/97	25	20	●	6 **Love Gets Me Every Time**.....CW[5] S:12 *(dance mix)*	$4	■V	Mercury 568062
12/6/97+	40	16		7 **Don't Be Stupid (You Know I Love You)**.....S:24 *If It Don't Take Two*	$4	■V	Mercury 568242
2/14/98	2[9]	42	▲	8 **You're Still The One** CW[1] / AC[8] S:2 / A:2 *Don't Be Stupid (You Know I Love You) (remix)*	$4	■V	Mercury 568452
12/5/98	4	14		9 **From This Moment On**.....AC[1] S:5 / A:15 *(remix)* **Bryan White** (backing vocal); *Hot 100 Airplay* debut: 9/12/98	$4	★V	Mercury 566450
1/23/99	7	28		10 **That Don't Impress Me Much**.....A:5 / S:11 *(remix)* "45": Mercury 566220; B-side: "Honey, I'm Home" (C&W #1)	$4	★V	Mercury 172118
4/17/99	23	28		11 **Man! I Feel Like A Woman!**.....A:18		V	album cut
7/17/99	49	13		12 **You've Got A Way**.....A:42 from the movie *Notting Hill* starring Julia Roberts and Hugh Grant			album cut

DEBUT	PEAK	WKS	Gold	A-side (Chart Hit)...B-side	$	Sym	Label & Number
				TWAIN, Shania — Cont'd			
10/23/99	58	10		13 **Come On Over**...A:43 "45" issued for #11 & 13 on Mercury 172123; #7, 9, 11 & 13 all debuted on the Country charts on 11/15/97; #6-13: from the album *Come On Over* on Mercury 536003		V	album cut
10/19/02	34	20		14 **I'm Gonna Getcha Good!**...A:31 from the album *Up!* on Mercury 170314; "45": Mercury 172272; B-side: (pop version); all of above written by Twain and Mutt Lange (Lange produced all of above)		V	album cut
				T.W.D.Y. LP '99 Rap production presented by Ant Banks. T.W.D.Y.: The Who Damn Yey.			
5/8/99	90	16		1 **Players Holiday**...S:37 *(2 versions)* **T.W.D.Y. featuring Too Short, Ant Banks, Rappin 4-Tay, Captain Save Em, Mac Mall** samples "Lovely Day" by **Bill Withers**	$4	★	Thump Street 2265
8/28/99	71^S	1		2 **Drinks On Me**...*(album version) / Players Holiday*	$4	★	Thump Street 2267
				TWEET R&B/LP '02 Born Charlene Keys on 3/4/71 in Rochester, New York. Female R&B singer/songwriter.			
12/15/01+	45	20		1 **Take Away**...A:44 **MISSY "MISDEMEANOR" ELLIOTT (feat. Ginuwine & introducing Tweet)** from Elliott's album *Miss E...So Addictive* on Goldmind 62639			album cut
2/9/02	7	20		2 **Oops (Oh My)** RB^3 A:5 / S:15 *(5 versions w/***Fabolous** & **Bubba Sparxxx***)*	$6	T	Goldmind 67280
3/30/02	92	4		3 **Feel The Girl**...*(3 versions) / Dream* **MS. JADE Featuring Tweet**	$7	T	Beat Club 497687
6/1/02	31	19		4 **Call Me**...S:22 / A:31 *(2 versions) / 4 My People* (**Missy Elliott** w/**Eve**)	$6	T	Goldmind 67312
8/3/02	71^S	1		5 **No Panties**...*(3 versions)* **TRINA Featuring Tweet**	$6	T	Slip n Slide 85367
				12 GAUGE LP '94 Born Isiah Pinkney in Augusta, Georgia. Male hardcore rapper.			
1/8/94	28	21	●	**Dunkie Butt Please Please Please**...S:10 *(album version)*	$5	▮	Danzalot 75373
				TWENNYNINE FEATURING LENNY WHITE R&B/BUB/LP '80 R&B-funk band from New York: Donald Blackmon (vocals), Eddie Martinez and Nick Moroch (guitars), Denzil Miller (keyboards), Barry Johnson (bass) and Lenny White (drums).			
2/2/80	83	4		**Peanut Butter**...*Oh, Sylvie*	$4		Elektra 46552
				20 FINGERS featuring GILLETTE '94 Duo of Chicago-based dance producers Charles Babie and Manfred Mohr, with female rapper Sandra **Gillette**.			
9/10/94+	14	30	●	**Short Dick Man**...S:4 / A:55 *Short Dick (bass mix)* [N] clean version available on SOS/Zoo 14193 as "Short Short Man"	$3	▮	SOS/Zoo 14194
				21st CENTURY, The R&B '75 R&B vocal group from Chicago, Illinois: Fred Williams, Alphonso Smith, Tyrone Moores, Pierre Johnson and Alonzo Martin.			
5/31/75	100	1		**Remember The Rain?**...*You're My Only World*	$5		RCA Victor 10201
				TWILIGHT 22 R&B '84 An electro-dance-rap production led by New York synthesizer player Gordon Bahary (born in 1960). Worked with **Harry Chapin** in 1975, and with **Stevie Wonder** from 1976.			
12/17/83+	79	8		**Electric Kingdom**...*(instrumental)*	$4		Vanguard 35241
				TWILLEY, Dwight ROK/BUB/LP '75 Born on 6/6/51 in Tulsa, Oklahoma. Rock singer/songwriter/pianist. Formed the **Dwight Twilley Band** with **Phil Seymour** (bass, drums) in 1974.			
4/26/75	16	18		1 **I'm On Fire** *[DWIGHT TWILLEY BAND]*...*Did You See What Happened?*	$5	■	Shelter 40380
2/18/84	16	16		2 **Girls**...*To Get To You*	$4	■	EMI America 8196
5/19/84	77	4		3 **Little Bit Of Love**...*Max Dog*	$4	■	EMI America 8206
				TWINZ R&B/LP '95 Rap duo from Long Beach, California: identical twin brothers Deon ("Trip Locc") and DeWayne ("Wayniac") Williams.			
8/19/95	84	9		**Round & Round**...S:72 *4 Eyes 2 Heads* samples "Big Shipwreck" by Rudy Ray Moore; produced by **Warren G**	$5	▮	G Funk/RAL 579384
				TWISTA R&B/BUB/LP '96 Born in Chicago, Illinois. Male rapper. Known as Tung Twista in 1992 when he was recognized as the world's fastest rapper by the Guinness Book of World Records.			
8/3/96	22	20	●	1 **Po Pimp** S:10 *Promise* **DO OR DIE featuring Twista**	$4	▮	Rap-A-Lot 38559
6/21/97	69^S	2		2 **Emotions**...BUB:101 *(album version)*	$5	▮	Big Beat 98025
11/29/97	96	2		3 **Get It Wet**...S:75 *(instrumental)*	$5	▮	Creator's Way 98001
3/28/98	62	14		4 **Still Po' Pimpin'**...S:47 *(3 versions)* **DO OR DIE featuring Johnny P and Twista** "45": Virgin 19949; B-side: "Promise"	$4	▮V	Rap-A-Lot 38636
6/13/98	85	7		5 **Whatuon**...S:58 *(instrumental)* **LATANYA featuring Twista**	$5	▮	TVT 4402
7/25/98	73^S	2		6 **In Your World**...BUB:101 *(instrumental)* **TWISTA & THE SPEED KNOT MOBSTAZ** from the movie *Dr. Dolittle* starring **Eddie Murphy**	$4	▮	Atlantic 84122
12/16/00	50^S	4		7 **Peace Of Mind**...*(album version) / Grand Finale* (Legit Ballaz & Twista) **DARKSIDE BALLAZ Feat. Twista**	$10	★	Legit Ballin 25014
				TWISTED SISTER ROK/BUB/LP '84 Hard-rock group from Long Island, New York: Dee Snider (vocals), Jay French and Eddie Ojeda (guitars), Mark Mendosa (bass), and A.J. Pero (drums).			
7/28/84	21	15		1 **We're Not Gonna Take It**...*You Can't Stop Rock 'N' Roll*	$4	■	Atlantic 89641
10/20/84	68	7		2 **I Wanna Rock**...*The Kids Are Back*	$4	■	Atlantic 89617
11/30/85+	53	10		3 **Leader Of The Pack**...*I Wanna Rock*	$4	■	Atlantic 89478

DEBUT	PEAK	WKS	Gold	A-side (Chart Hit)..........B-side	$	Sym	Label & Number

TWITTY, Conway

★300★ — C&W/BUB/LP '58

Born Harold Jenkins on 9/1/33 in Friars Point, Mississippi; raised in Helena, Arkansas. Died of an abdominal aneurysm on 6/5/93 (age 59). Legendary country singer (charted 40 #1 hits, 1968-86). Formed own group, the Phillips County Ramblers, at age 10. Offered a professional baseball contract with the Philadelphia Phillies when drafted. With service band, Cimmarons, in Japan, early 1950s. Changed his name in 1957 (borrowed from Conway, Arkansas and Twitty, Texas) and first recorded for Sun (unissued recordings). In the movies *Sexpot Goes To College* and *College Confidential*. Switched from rock and roll to country music in 1965. Moved to Nashville in 1968.

1)It's Only Make Believe 2)Lonely Blue Boy 3)Danny Boy 4)You've Never Been This Far Before 5)C'est Si Bon (It's So Good)

DEBUT	PEAK	WKS	Gold	A-side (Chart Hit)..........B-side	$	Sym	Label & Number
5/20/57	93	1		1 **I Need Your Lovin'** ....T:93 *Born To Sing The Blues* originally recorded by Twitty for Sun Records as "Give Me Some Love" (unreleased)	$40		Mercury 71086
9/15/58	❶[2]	21	●	2 **It's Only Make Believe** H:❶[2] / S:30 *I'll Try*	$25		MGM 12677
1/26/59	28	12		3 **The Story Of My Love**..........*Make Me Know You're Mine*	$25		MGM 12748
5/18/59	87	2		4 **Hey Little Lucy! (Don'tcha Put No Lipstick On)**..........*When I'm Not With You*	$25		MGM 12785
7/20/59	29	12		5 **Mona Lisa** ....*Heavenly* #1 hit for **Nat "King" Cole** in 1950 (from the movie *Captain Carey, U.S.A.* starring Alan Ladd)	$25		MGM 12804
9/28/59	10	18		6 **Danny Boy** ....*Halfway To Heaven* based on the traditional Irish song "Londonderry Air" written in 1855	$25		MGM 12826
12/28/59+	6	15	●	7 **Lonely Blue Boy**..........*Star Spangled Heaven* originally recorded (unreleased) by **Elvis Presley** as "Danny" for the movie *King Creole*	$20		MGM 12857
3/28/60	26	11		8 **What Am I Living For**..........*The Hurt In My Heart*	$20	■	MGM 12886
6/13/60	35	11		9 **Is A Blue Bird Blue /**			
8/8/60	98	1		10 **She's Mine**..........	$20	■	MGM 12911
10/31/60	55	5		11 **Whole Lot Of Shakin' Going On**..........*The Flame*	$15		MGM 12962
12/31/60+	22	10		12 **C'est Si Bon (It's So Good)** ....*Don't You Dare Let Me Down* #21 hit for Danny Kaye in 1950	$15	■	MGM 12969
4/3/61	72	4		13 **The Next Kiss (Is The Last Goodbye)** ....*Man Alone*	$15	■	MGM 12998
1/20/62	98	2		14 **Portrait Of A Fool**..........*Tower Of Tears*	$15		MGM 13050
7/4/70	60	8		15 **Hello Darlin'** ....CW[4] *Girl At The Bar*	$7		Decca 32661
10/24/70	81	4		16 **Fifteen Years Ago** ....CW[1] *Up Comes The Bottle (Down Goes The Man)*	$7		Decca 32742
2/27/71	56	6		17 **After The Fire Is Gone**..........CW[2] *The One I Can't Live Without* **CONWAY TWITTY/LORETTA LYNN**	$7		Decca 32776
8/11/73	22	14		18 **You've Never Been This Far Before** ....CW[3] *You Make It Hard (To Take The Easy Way Out)*	$6		MCA 40094
2/22/75	61	8		19 **Linda On My Mind**..........CW[1] *She's Just Not Over You Yet*	$6		MCA 40339
12/20/75+	63	7		20 **Don't Cry Joni** .... Joni Lee (Twitty's daughter; guest vocal); similar to **Georgie Shaw**'s 1954 hit "Till We Two Are One"	$6		MCA 40407

II D EXTREME

R&B/BUB/LP '93

R&B trio from Washington DC: D'Extra Wiley, Randy Gill (brother of **Johnny Gill**) and his cousin Jermaine Mickey.

DEBUT	PEAK	WKS	Gold	A-side (Chart Hit)..........B-side	$	Sym	Label & Number
5/15/93	48	20		1 **Cry No More**..........S:23 / A:60 *(remix)*	$4	▮[V]	Gasoline Alley 54650
12/4/93	69[S]	4		2 **Up On The Roof** ....BUB:103 *(radio edit)*	$4	▮	Gasoline Alley 54738

2GE+HER

LP '00

Male vocal group formed for the same-named MTV series: Evan Farmer ("Jerry O'Keefe"), Michael Cuccione ("Jason McKnight"), Alex Solovitz ("Mickey Parke"), Noah Bastian ("Chad Linus") and Kevin Farley ("Doug Linus"). Farley is the younger brother of the late comedian Chris Farley. Cuccione died of respiratory failure on 1/13/2001 (age 16).

DEBUT	PEAK	WKS	Gold	A-side (Chart Hit)..........B-side	$	Sym	Label & Number
9/2/00	87	3		**The Hardest Part Of Breaking Up (Is Getting Back Your Stuff)** ....S:12 *That's When I'll Be Gone*	$5	★	TVT 6841

2 HYPED BROTHERS & A DOG

'92

2 Hyped Brothers are Frank "Doo Doo Brown" Ski (a DJ at Baltimore's V-103 FM) and Stanley Evans, Jr. Dog is Rhondo V. Haus Fokwulfe, Frank's German Shepherd.

DEBUT	PEAK	WKS	Gold	A-side (Chart Hit)..........B-side	$	Sym	Label & Number
3/21/92	90	5		**Doo Doo Brown**..........S:60 *(instrumental)*	$8	▮*	Deco/Warlock 108

2 IN A ROOM

LP '90

Dance duo from Washington Heights, New York: rapper Rafael "Dose" Vargas and remixer Roger "Rog Nice" Pauletta.

DEBUT	PEAK	WKS	Gold	A-side (Chart Hit)..........B-side	$	Sym	Label & Number
10/6/90	15	22	●	1 **Wiggle It**..........S:7 / A:24 *Take Me Away*	$4	▮	Cutting 98887
4/30/94	86	6		2 **El Trago "the drink"** ....*(3 versions)*	$6	▮*	Cutting 297

2 LIVE CREW/LUKE

R&B/BUB/LP '90

Rap group from Miami, Florida: David "Mr. Mixx" Hobbs, Chris "Kid-Ice" Wong Won, Mark "Brother Marquis" Ross and leader, Luther "**Luke** Skyywalker" Campbell (owner of Luke Records). Group's obscenity arrests sparked national censorship controversy in 1990. By 1994, group consisted of Campbell, Won and Larry "Verb" Dobson, with special appearances by Rudy Ray "Dolomite" Moore; changed name to The New 2 Live Crew. By 1996, Campbell split from group to record as Luke; group now a trio of Hobbs, Won and Ross.

DEBUT	PEAK	WKS	Gold	A-side (Chart Hit)..........B-side	$	Sym	Label & Number
9/9/89	26	30	●	1 **Me So Horny** *[THE 2 LIVE CREW]* ....S:18 *(same version)* samples "Firecracker" by **Mass Production**; "45" promo: Skyywalker 113	$5	▮[V]	Skyywalker 130
7/21/90	20	16	●	2 **Banned In The U.S.A.** *[LUKE Featuring 2 LIVE CREW]* S:8 *(instrumental)* rap protest song based on **Bruce Springsteen**'s 1985 hit "Born In The U.S.A."	$5	▮[V]	Luke 98915
11/2/91	58	13		3 **Pop That Coochie** *[THE 2 LIVE CREW]*..........S:30 *Mega Mix V*	$5	▮	Luke 98712
3/21/92	73	14		4 **I Wanna Rock** *[LUKE]*..........S:33 *Megamix*	$5	▮	Luke 98619
7/17/93	74[S]	1		5 **Work It Out!** *[LUKE]*..........BUB:107 *(dirty version)*	$5	▮	Luke 162
4/27/96	64	16		6 **Scarred** *[LUKE]*..........S:35 *Uncle Luke's Mega Mix* samples "Theme From Together Brothers" by **Love Unlimited Orchestra**; from the movie *Eddie* starring Whoopi Goldberg	$5	▮	Luther Campbell 164000
8/10/96	72	15		7 **Shake A Lil' Somethin'...** *[THE 2 LIVE CREW]* ....S:57 *(3 versions)*	$5	▮	Lil' Joe 890
3/28/98	26	20	●	8 **Raise The Roof**..........S:14 *(remix) / (instrumental)* **LUKE Featuring No Good But So Good** samples "Theme From King Kong" by **John Barry**	$4	▮	Luke/Island 572250
12/19/98	74[S]	1		9 **The Real One** ....BUB:103 *(clean version) / Shake Your Pants* **THE 2 LIVE CREW Featuring Ice-T**	$6	▮	Lil' Joe 899

DEBUT	PEAK	WKS	Gold	A-side (Chart Hit)......B-side	$	Sym	Label & Number

2nu — '91

Pop-novelty group from Seattle, Washington: Jock Blaney (vocals, production director of KPLZ-Seattle at time of hit), Mike Nealy, Tom Martin and Phil DeVault.

DEBUT	PEAK	WKS	Gold	A-side (Chart Hit)......B-side	$	Sym	Label & Number
12/22/90+	46	13		This Is Ponderous ......*She* [N]	$3	▮	Atlantic 87771

2 OF CLUBS — BUB '67

Female pop duo: Patti Valantine and Linda Parrish (former wife of Carl Edmonson, leader of **The Dolphins**).

DEBUT	PEAK	WKS	Gold	A-side (Chart Hit)......B-side	$	Sym	Label & Number
3/18/67	92	3		Walk Tall ......*So Blue Is Fall* some pressings show title as "Walk Tall Like A Man"; featured in the movie *Doctor, You've Got To Be Kidding* starring Sandra Dee	$12		Fraternity 975

2PAC — ★247★ — R&B/LP '96

Born Tupac Amaru Shakur on 6/16/71 in Brooklyn, New York (the son of 2 Black Panther members); raised in Oakland, California. Died on 9/13/96 (age 25) of wounds suffered on 9/7/96 in a shooting in Las Vegas, Nevada. Gangsta rapper/actor. Member of **Digital Underground** in 1991. Also recorded in 1996 as Makaveli. Appeared in the movies *Nothing But Trouble, Juice, Poetic Justice* and *Above The Rim.* Numerous run-ins with the law. Found guilty on 2/10/94 of the 1993 assault and battery of *Menace II Society* co-director Allen Hughes. Survived after being shot five times during a robbery in Manhattan on 11/29/94. Sentenced for up to four years in prison on 2/7/95 for a 1993 sexual assault; paroled in late 1995. Also see **M.C. Breed**'s "Gotta Get Mine."

1)How Do U Want It 2)California Love 3)Dear Mama

DEBUT	PEAK	WKS	Gold	A-side (Chart Hit)......B-side	$	Sym	Label & Number
7/3/93	11	25	●	1 I Get Around ......S:5 / A:24 *Nothing But Love* samples "Computer Love" by **Zapp**	$5	▮	Interscope 98372
7/10/93+	12	23	●	2 Keep Ya Head Up ......S:8 / A:15 *(edit)* samples "O-o-h Child" by **The Five Stairsteps** and "Be Alright" by **Roger**; originally charted as the B-side of the maxi-cassette "I Get Around" (Interscope 96036) for 3 weeks; re-entered on its own on 10/30/93; also see #17 below	$5	▮	Interscope 98345
4/9/94	87	2		3 Papa'z Song......*(instrumental)* duet with Mopreme of Thug Life; additional vocals by Poppi; samples "Soul Shadows" by **Bill Withers**	$5	▮	Interscope 98303
3/11/95	9	20	▲	4 Dear Mama / S:3 / A:39 samples "In My Wildest Dreams" by Joe Sample and "Sadie" by **The Spinners**			
6/3/95		8		5 Old School...... samples "We Share" by the Soul Searchers and "Dedication" by **Brand Nubian**	$4	▮	Interscope 98273
7/1/95	44	15		6 So Many Tears ......S:31 *Hard To Imagine* (Dramacydal) Thug Life and **Digital Underground** (backing vocals); samples "That Girl" by **Stevie Wonder**	$4	▮	Interscope 98145
9/30/95	68	6		7 Temptations ......S:39 *Me Against The World* samples "Computer Love" by **Zapp** and "Watch Your Nuggets" by **Redman**; above 4 from the album *Me Against The World*	$4	▮	Interscope 98120
6/15/96	❶^{2}	24	▲^{2}	8 How Do U Want It / RB^{3} S:❶^{4} / A:68 **2 PAC (featuring KC and JoJo)** samples "Body Heat" by **Quincy Jones**			
6/15/96	6	24		9 California Love ......S:3 / A:19 **2 PAC (featuring Dr. Dre and Roger Troutman)** samples "So Ruff So Tuff" by **Roger** and "Woman To Woman" by **Joe Cocker**	$3	▮	Death Row 854652
11/23/96	58^{A}	7		10 I Ain't Mad At Cha ...... above 3 from the album *All Eyez On Me* on Death Row 524204			album cut
2/1/97	81	14		11 Runnin'......S:57 *Is It A Dream* **2PAC, NOTORIOUS B.I.G., Radio, Dramacydal & Stretch**	$5	▮	Mergela/Solar 70134
4/26/97	77	7		12 Stop The Gunfight ......S:55 *(R&B version) / When I Come Down* **TRAPP · 2PAC · NOTORIOUS B.I.G.** recorded in 1993; released after 2Pac and Biggy were shot to death within 6 months of each other	$5	▮	Deff Trapp 9269
6/21/97	12	19	●	13 Smile ......S:4 / A:62 *(instrumental) / Untouchable* **SCARFACE Featuring 2 Pac & Johnny P**	$4	▮	Rap-A-Lot 38581
12/13/97	67	11		14 I Wonder If Heaven Got A Ghetto ......*(3 versions)* samples "The Two Of Us" by **Cameo**	$6	T	Amaru/Jive 42500
3/21/98	21	18	●	15 Do For Love......S:10 / A:66 *Brenda's Got A Baby* **2PAC Featuring Eric Williams of BLACKstreet** samples "What You Won't Do For Love" by **Bobby Caldwell**	$4	▮	Amaru/Jive 42516
12/5/98+	32	19		16 Changes ......A:21 samples "The Way It Is" by **Bruce Hornsby And The Range**; from the album *Greatest Hits* on Amaru/Jive 90301			album cut
2/26/00	72	7		17 Baby Don't Cry (Keep Ya Head Up II) ......A:65 **2PAC + OUTLAWZ** sequel to #2 above; from the album *Still I Rise* on Interscope 490413			album cut
4/21/01	52	14		18 Until The End Of Time......A:41 samples "Broken Wings" by **Mr. Mister**; from the album *Until The End Of Time* on Amaru 490840			album cut
12/7/02	19	20		19 Thugz Mansion ......A:18 from the album *Better Dayz* on Amaru 497070			album cut

2 UNLIMITED — BUB/LP '92

Techno-house dance duo from Amsterdam, Netherlands: Ray "Kid Ray" Slijngard (born on 6/28/71) and Anita Dells (born on 12/25/71).

DEBUT	PEAK	WKS	Gold	A-side (Chart Hit)......B-side	$	Sym	Label & Number
6/13/92	49	20		1 Twilight Zone......S:35 / A:47 *(instrumental)*	$5	▮	Radikal/Critique 15486
9/19/92	76	7		2 Get Ready For This ......A:59 *(orchestral mix)*	$5	▮	Radikal/Critique 15490
11/5/94+	38	27		3 Get Ready For This......A:33 *(orchestral mix)* [R] above 2 are the same version (cassette picture boxes are different)	$5	▮	Radikal/Critique 15535

TYCOON — LP '79

Pop-rock group from New York: Norman Mershon (vocals), Jon Gordon (guitar), Mark Rivera (sax), Michael Fonfara (keyboards), Mark Kreider (bass) and Richard Steinberg (drums).

DEBUT	PEAK	WKS	Gold	A-side (Chart Hit)......B-side	$	Sym	Label & Number
3/17/79	26	13		Such A Woman......*How Long (Can We Go On)*	$5		Arista 0398

TYLER, Bonnie — BUB/C&W/LP '83

Born Gaynor Hopkins on 6/8/53 in Swansea, Wales. Pop-rock singer. Worked local clubs until the mid-1970s. Distinctive raspy vocals caused by operation to remove throat nodules in 1976.

DEBUT	PEAK	WKS	Gold	A-side (Chart Hit)......B-side	$	Sym	Label & Number
3/25/78	3	21	●	1 It's A Heartache ......*It's About Time* Mike Gibbins of **Badfinger** (drums)	$5		RCA 11249
7/16/83	❶^{4}	29	▲	2 Total Eclipse Of The Heart *Straight From The Heart*	$4		Columbia 03906
12/3/83+	46	9		3 Take Me Back......*Getting So Excited*	$4	■	Columbia 04246
2/25/84	34	13		4 Holding Out For A Hero ......*Faster Than The Speed Of Night* from the movie *Footloose* starring Kevin Bacon and Lori Singer	$4	■	Columbia 04370

DEBUT	PEAK	WKS	Gold	A-side (Chart Hit)...B-side	$	Sym	Label & Number
				TYLER, Bonnie — Cont'd			
8/11/84	76	5		5 **Here She Comes** ...*Obsession* (**Giorgio Moroder**)	$4	■	Columbia 04548
				from the movie *Metropolis* starring Brigitte Helm (film restored from the original 1926 silent movie)			
4/12/86	77	6		6 **If You Were A Woman (And I Was A Man)**...*Under Suspicion*	$3	■	Columbia 05839
				Todd Rundgren (backing vocal); #2-4 & 6: produced by **Jim Steinman**			
				TYMES, The BUB/LP **'63**			
				R&B vocal group from Philadelphia, Pennsylvania: George Williams (lead), George Hilliard, Donald Banks, Albert Berry and Norman Burnett. First called the Latineers. Berry and Hilliard were replaced by female singers Terri Gonzalez and Melanie Moore in the early 1970s. Also see **Billy Abbott & The Jewels**.			
				1)So Much In Love 2)Wonderful! Wonderful! 3)You Little Trustmaker			
6/1/63	❶[1]	15		1 **So Much In Love** *Roscoe James McClain*	$15	■	Parkway 871
				originally titled "So In Love" ($25)			
8/17/63	7	11		2 **Wonderful! Wonderful!**...*Come With Me To The Sea*	$15	■	Parkway 884
12/7/63+	19	11		3 **Somewhere** ...*View From My Window*	$15	■	Parkway 891
3/14/64	78	4		4 **To Each His Own**...*Wonderland Of Love* (#124)	$15	■	Parkway 908
				#1 hit for **Eddy Howard**, Freddy Martin and the Ink Spots (all 3 in 1946)			
6/13/64	99	1		5 **The Magic of Our Summer Love**...*With All My Heart*	$15	■	Parkway 919
11/21/64	92	3		6 **Here She Comes** ...*Malibu*	$15	■	Parkway 924
11/16/68	39	8		7 **People** ...*For Love Of Ivy*	$8		Columbia 44630
				from the movie *Funny Girl* starring **Barbra Streisand**			
8/17/74	12	13		8 **You Little Trustmaker**...*The North Hills*	$6		RCA Victor 10022
12/21/74	91	4		9 **Ms. Grace**...*The Crutch*	$6		RCA Victor 10128
5/8/76	68	4		10 **It's Cool** ...*Good Morning Dear Lord*	$6		RCA Victor 10561
				TYRESE R&B/LP **'99**			
				Born Tyrese Gibson on 12/30/78 in Watts, California. Male R&B singer/songwriter/actor. Starred in the movies *Baby Boy* and *2 Fast 2 Furious*.			
8/22/98	36	15		1 **Nobody Else** ...S:22 *I Can't Go On*	$4	▮	RCA 65538
1/23/99	12	25		2 **Sweet Lady** A:8			album cut
6/19/99	56	13		3 **Lately**...A:44			album cut
				Juanita Wynn (backing vocal); above 3 from the album *Tyrese* on RCA 66901			
1/8/00	77	12		4 **The Best Man I Can Be**...A:67			album cut
				GINUWINE, R.L., TYRESE, CASE			
				from the movie *The Best Man* starring Taye Diggs (soundtrack on Columbia 69924)			
6/3/00	26	20		5 **What'Chu Like**...A:19 *(3 versions) / That's What I'm Looking For* (Da Brat - #56)	$6	T	So So Def 79330
				DA BRAT Featuring Tyrese			
4/7/01	48	19		6 **I Like Them Girls** ...A:43 *(5 versions)*	$6	T	RCA 60418
7/14/01	90	4		7 **Just A Baby Boy**...*(4 versions)*	$6	T	Universal 158986
				SNOOP DOGG feat. Tyrese & Mr. Tan			
				from the movie *Baby Boy* starring Tyrese			
9/29/01	71	18		8 **What Am I Gonna Do**...A:68			album cut
				from the album *2000 Watts* on RCA 68039			

U

DEBUT	PEAK	WKS	Gold	A-side (Chart Hit)...B-side	$	Sym	Label & Number
	★445★			**UB40** ROK/LP **'93**			
				Interracial reggae group formed in Birmingham, England: brothers Ali (vocals, guitar; born on 2/15/59) and Robin (guitar, vocals; born on 12/25/54) Campbell, Terence "Astro" Wilson (vocals; born on 6/24/57), Earl Falconer (bass; born on 1/223/59), Michael Virtue (keyboards; born on 1/19/57), Norman Hassan (percussion; born on 1/26/58), Brian Travers (sax; born on 2/7/59) and James Brown (drums; born on 11/20/57). Name taken from a British unemployment form.			
1/28/84	34	15		1 **Red Red Wine**...*Sufferin'*	$5		A&M 2600
				also see #3 below			
7/27/85	28	14		2 **I Got You Babe** ...S:24 *Nkomo A Go Go* (UB40)	$4	■	A&M 2758
				UB40 WITH CHRISSIE HYNDE			
				picture sleeve issued with either a green or a brown background			
8/13/88	❶[1]	25	●	3 **Red Red Wine** ...S:❶[2] / A:❶[1] *Sufferin'* [R]	$3		A&M 1244
				longer version than #1 above (includes rap by Astro)			
9/15/90	6	25	●	4 **The Way You Do The Things You Do** ...S:5 / A:10 *Splugen*	$3	▮[V]	Virgin 98978
3/23/91	7	25		5 **Here I Am (Come And Take Me)** ...A:9 / S:23 *Gator*	$3	▮[V]	Virgin 99141
				"45" issued for above 2 on Virgin 17448			
11/23/91	90	6		6 **Groovin'**...A:70 *Council House*	$4	▮	Virgin 98654
5/15/93	❶[7]	29	▲	7 **Can't Help Falling In Love** A:❶[4] / S:2 *Jungle Love*	$3	▮[V]	Virgin 12653
				from the movie *Sliver* starring Sharon Stone and William Baldwin; "45": Virgin 17402			
10/9/93+	45	20		8 **Higher Ground**...A:36 *Chronic*	$4	▮[V]	Virgin 12681
				"45": Virgin 17596 (clear vinyl)			
				UGGAMS, Leslie AC **'59**			
				Born on 5/25/43 in Harlem, New York. Black actress/singer. Played "Kizzy" in the TV mini-series *Roots*. Regular on TV's *Sing Along With Mitch*. Hosted own TV variety series in 1969.			
9/14/59	98	1		**One More Sunrise (Morgen)**...*The Eyes Of God*	$12		Columbia 41451
				English version of "Morgen" by **Ivo Robic**			
				UGK R&B/LP **'99**			
				Male rap duo: Chad "Pimp C" Butler and Bernard "Bun B" Freeman. Also recorded as Underground Kingz.			
9/18/99	47[S]	11		1 **Pimpin' Ain't No Illusion** ...*Belts To Match* (w/Smitty & Sonji)	$4	★	Jive 42633
				UGK Featuring Kool Ace & Too $hort			
4/22/00	18	20		2 **Big Pimpin'**...A:13 *Anything* (Jay-Z - #55)	$6	T	Roc-A-Fella 562670
				JAY-Z (featuring UGK)			

DEBUT	PEAK	WKS	Gold	A-side (Chart Hit)...B-side	$	Sym	Label & Number
				UGLY KID JOE ROK/LP '93			
				Rock group from Isla Vista, California: Whitfield Crane (vocals), Klaus Eichstadt and Dave Fortman (guitars), Cordell Crockett (bass), and Mark Davis (drums).			
4/4/92	9	20		1 **Everything About You.** ...S:5 / A:37 *(same version)*	$3	▮V	Mercury 866632
				from the movie *Wayne's World* starring Mike Myers and Dana Carvey (not on the soundtrack album)			
2/13/93	6	20	●	2 **Cats In The Cradle**...S:4 / A:27 *(3 album snippets) / Panhandlin' Prince*	$3	▮V	Stardog 864888
				U-GOD LP '99			
				Born Lamont Hawkins in Staten Island, New York. Male rapper. Member of **Wu-Tang Clan**.			
10/9/99	64S	4		**Bizarre** ...*(2 versions) / Shell Shock*	$6	★	Wu-Tang 53574
				samples "Far Cry" by **Marvin Gaye**; produced by **RZA**			
				U-KREW, The LP '90			
				Rap group from Portland, Oregon: Kevin Morse, Larry Bell, Lavell Alexander, James McClendon and Hakim Muhammad.			
1/27/90	24	22		1 **If U Were Mine**...S:17 / A:31 *(extended mix)*	$4	▮	Enigma 75051
6/9/90	68	8		2 **Let Me Be Your Lover** ...*(Fresh mix) / Pump Me Up*	$4	▮	Enigma 75069
				ULLMAN, Tracey LP '84			
				Born on 12/30/59 in Burnham, Buckinghamshire, England. Actress/singer/comedienne. Hosted own TV show from 1987-90. Acted in several movies.			
2/25/84	8	17		1 **They Don't Know** ...*You Broke My Heart In 17 Places*	$4	■	MCA/Stiff 52347
6/16/84	70	4		2 **Break-A-Way**...*Long Live Love*	$4	■	MCA/Stiff 52385
				co-written by **Jackie DeShannon**; B-side of **Irma Thomas**'s "Wish Someone Would Care"			
				ULTIMATE LP '79			
				Disco studio group assembled by producers Juliano Salerni and Bruce Weeden.			
4/21/79	82	3		**Touch Me Baby** ...*Music In My Heart*	$4		Casablanca 966
				ULTRAVOX ROK/BUB/LP '83			
				Electronic-rock group formed in London, England: **Midge Ure** (vocals, guitar; born James Ure on 10/10/53 in Glasgow, Scotland) (see #2 below), Billy Currie (synthesizer, piano), Chris Cross (bass) and Warren Cann (drums).			
4/9/83	71	5		1 **Reap The Wild Wind**...*Hosanna (In Excelsis Deo)*	$5		Chrysalis 42682
3/11/89	95	5		2 **Dear God** ...*Music #1*	$4	■	Chrysalis 43319
				MIDGE URE			
				UMILIANI, Piero '69			
				Born in 1925 in Florence, Italy. Died on 2/23/2001 (age 75). Composer/conductor.			
9/6/69	55	6		**Máh-Ná-Mah-Ná**...*You Tried To Warn Me* [I-N]	$10		Ariel 500
				from the movie *Sweden Heaven And Hell*; background tune used on TV's *Benny Hill Show*			
				UNCLE DOG '73			
				Rock group from England featuring vocalists Carol Grimes and David Skinner with Phil Crooks, John Porter, Sam Mitchell and Terry Stannard.			
3/3/73	86	7		**River Road** ...*Boogie With Me*	$5		MCA 40005
				UNCLE KRACKER LP '01			
				Born Matthew Shafer on 6/6/74 in Mount Clemens, Michigan. White pop-rock singer/DJ. Member of **Kid Rock**'s posse.			
3/10/01	5	33		1 **Follow Me** ...A:5		V	album cut
				co-produced by **Kid Rock**; from the album *Double Wide* on Lava/Atlantic 83279; "45": Lava/Atlantic 85184; B-side: "Yeah, Yeah, Yeah"			
11/2/02	59	20		2 **In A Little While** ...A:62			album cut
				from the album *No Stranger To Shame* on Lava 83542			
				UNCLE SAM R&B/LP '98			
				Born Sam Turner in Detroit, Michigan. R&B singer.			
11/8/97+	6	28	▲	**I Don't Ever Want To See You Again** ...S:4 / A:27 *(album version)*	$3	▮	Stonecreek 78689
				Michael McCary of **Boyz II Men** (monologue); Nathan Morris of **Boyz II Men** (backing vocal; producer)			
				UNDER COVER '01			
				Studio group from New Jersey. Formed to cover the unavailable CD single of the **Uncle Kracker** hit version.			
5/12/01	62S	6		**Follow Me**...*(4 mixes)*	$7	★*	National 71213
				UNDERGROUND SUNSHINE BUB/LP '69			
				Rock group from Montello, Wisconsin: brothers Egbert "Berty" (vocals, bass) and Frank (drums) Kohl, Chris Connors (guitar; born John Dahlberg) and Jane Little (keyboards). Actual last name of the German-born brothers is Koelbl.			
7/19/69	26	10		**Birthday** ...*All I Want Is You*	$12		Intrepid 75002
				originally recorded by **The Beatles** on their 1968 *White Album*			
				UNDERWORLD LP '89			
				Rock group from England: Karl Hyde (vocals, guitar), Alfie Thomas (guitar), Rick Smith (keyboards), Baz Allen (bass) and Pascal Console (drums).			
4/16/88	74	8		1 **Underneath The Radar** ...*Big Red X*	$3	■	Sire 27968
8/26/89	67	8		2 **Stand Up**...*Outskirts*	$3	■	Sire 22852
				UNDISPUTED TRUTH, The R&B/BUB/LP '71			
				R&B-disco vocal trio from Detroit, Michigan: Joe Harris, Billie Calvin and Brenda Evans.			
6/26/71	3	18		1 **Smiling Faces Sometimes** *You Got The Love I Need*	$6		Gordy 7108
12/18/71+	72	6		2 **You Make Your Own Heaven And Hell Right Here On Earth**...*Ball Of Confusion (That's What The World Is Today)*	$6		Gordy 7112
2/26/72	71	5		3 **What It Is**...*California Soul*	$6		Gordy 7114
6/10/72	63	5		4 **Papa Was A Rollin' Stone**...*Friendship Train*	$6		Gordy 7117
4/27/74	63	7		5 **Help Yourself**...*What's Going On*	$6		Gordy 7134
2/19/77	48	11		6 **You + Me = Love**...*(instrumental)*	$6		Whitfield 8231
				charted 2 weeks as Whitfield 8231, then 5 weeks as Whitfield 8306 (a 12" single with #7 below on the B-side); off charts for 4 weeks, then re-entered for 4 more weeks as Whitfield 8231			
2/19/77	flip	5		7 **Let's Go Down To The Disco** ...*Loose*	$6		Whitfield 8295
				charted for 5 weeks only as a flip side of #6 above; mistakenly listed as Whitfield 8231 for 2 weeks and correctly listed as Whitfield 8306 (a 12" single with #6 above on the A-side) for 3 weeks			

DEBUT	PEAK	WKS	Gold	A-side (Chart Hit)...B-side	$	Sym	Label & Number
				UNIFICS, The R&B **'68**			
				R&B vocal group from Washington DC: Al Johnson (lead), Michel Ward and Greg Cook (tenors), and Hal Worthington (baritone). Worthington was shot to death on 2/20/90 (age 42).			
9/21/68	**25**	9		1 **Court Of Love** ...*Which One Should I Choose*	$12		Kapp 935
12/14/68+	**36**	10		2 **The Beginning Of My End**...*Sentimental Man*	$12	■	Kapp 957
4/12/69	**97**	2		3 **It's A Groovy World!**...*Memories*	$12	■	Kapp 985
				UNION GAP, The — see PUCKETT, Gary			
				UNIPOP **'83**			
				Husband-and-wife pop duo from New York: Manny and Phyllis Loiacono.			
12/25/82+	**71**	8		**What If (I Said I Love You)** ...*Love At First Touch*	$5		Kat Family 03353
				UNIQUES, The C&W/BUB **'65**			
				Southern pop quintet featuring country star **Joe Stampley** (see #4 below).			
3/20/65	**66**	6		1 **Not Too Long Ago**...*Fast Way Of Living* **THE UNIQUES Featuring JOE STAMPLEY** produced by **Dale Hawkins**; also see Joe's solo version on the B-side of #4 below	$10		Paula 219
7/2/66	**97**	2		2 **All These Things** ...*Tell Me What To Do* "Bubbled Under" (#112) in 1970 on Paula 332; Stampley's solo version in 1976 was a #1 Country hit (ABC/Dot 17624)	$10		Paula 238
12/23/67	**32^{X}**	2		3 **Please Come Home For Christmas** ...*(instrumental)* [X]	$12		Paula 255
1/6/73	**37**	13		4 **Soul Song**...CW[1] *Not Too Long Ago* **JOE STAMPLEY**	$6	□	Dot 17442
				UNIT FOUR plus TWO BUB **'65**			
				Pop-rock group from Hertfordshire, England: Peter Moules (vocals), David Meikle and Howard Lubin (guitars), Thomas Moeller (keyboards), Rod Garwood (bass) and Hugh Halliday (drums).			
5/1/65	**28**	9		1 **Concrete And Clay** ...*When I Fall In Love* also released with "Wild As The Wind" as the B-side	$12		London 9751
7/17/65	**95**	2		2 **You've Never Been In Love Like This Before** ...*Tell Somebody You Know*	$12		London 9761
				UNIVERSAL ROBOT BAND **'77**			
				Interracial disco group from New York City, New York.			
5/14/77	**93**	6		**Dance And Shake Your Tambourine**...*(long version)*	$10		Red Greg 207
				UNKNOWNS, The **'66**			
				Star trio of **Steve Alaimo** with **Mark Lindsay** and Keith Allison, both of **Paul Revere & The Raiders**.			
9/24/66	**74**	4		**Melody For An Unknown Girl**...*Keith's Song* written by **Paul Revere** and **Mark Lindsay**	$20		Parrot 307
				UNV R&B/BUB/LP **'93**			
				R&B vocal group from Detroit, Michigan: brothers John and Shawn Powe, John Clay and Demetrius Peete. Clay also plays keyboards. UNV stands for Universal Nubian Voices. John and Shawn later charted as **The Poww Bros.**			
6/5/93	**29**	20		1 **Something's Goin' On** ...S:17 / A:36 *Flipside*	$3	▮V	Maverick/Sire 18564
6/3/95	**65**	13		2 **So In Love With You** ...S:61 *(R&B remix)*	$3	▮	Maverick/Sire 17889
				UNWRITTEN LAW ROK/BUB/LP **'01**			
				Hard-rock group from Poway, California: Scott Russo (vocals), Rob Brewer (guitar), Steve Morris (guitar), Wade Youman (drums) and "PK" (bass).			
12/1/01	**63^{S}**	1		**Up All Night**...*Darkside / Baby, Baby*	$5	★	Interscope 497647
				UPBEATS, The **'58**			
				Male Adult Contemporary vocal group.			
8/4/58	**75**	3		**Just Like In The Movies**...H:75 *My Foolish Heart* Earl Sheldon (orch. and chorus); tune is similar to "No, Not Much!" by **The Four Lads**	$20		Swan 4010
				UPCHURCH, Philip, Combo **'61**			
				Born on 7/19/41 in Chicago, Illinois. R&B guitarist. Session player for **George Benson**, **Quincy Jones**, **The Jacksons** and many others.			
6/19/61	**29**	8		**You Can't Sit Down Part 2**...*Part 1* [I]	$15		Boyd 3398
				UPTOWN **'87**			
				Female dance-disco trio from New York City, New York.			
12/27/86+	**80**	11		**(I Know) I'm Losing You** ...*Get Ready* (Robin Stanley)	$7		Oak Lawn 3810
				URBAN, Keith C&W/BUB/LP **'01**			
				Born on 10/26/67 in Whangarei, New Zealand; raised in Caboolture, Queensland, Australia. Country singer. Former member of The Ranch.			
7/15/00	**51**	16		1 **Your Everything**...A:43 "45": Capitol 58847; B-side: "If You Wanna Stay"		V	album cut
12/23/00+	**37**	20		2 **But For The Grace Of God** ...CW[1] A:31 "45": Capitol 58877; B-side: "I Thought You Knew"		V	album cut
6/16/01	**35**	20		3 **Where The Blacktop Ends**...A:30 "45": Capitol 58992; B-side: "Rollercoaster"; all of above from the album *Keith Urban* on Capitol 97591		V	album cut
8/17/02	**23**	20		4 **Somebody Like You**...CW[6] A:22 from the album *Golden Road* on Capitol 32936			album cut
				URBAN DANCE SQUAD **'91**			
				Rap-dance group from Amsterdam, Netherlands: Patrick "Rude Boy" Remington, Magic Stick, DNA, Silly Sil and Tres Manos.			
12/15/90+	**21**	18		**Deeper Shade Of Soul** ...S:8 *(live version)*	$4	▮V	Arista 2026
				URBAN RENEWAL PROGRAM **'02**			
				Hip-hop/electronica dance group: Dante "**Mos Def**" Smith, "Diverse" (trio of Matt Lux, Ted Sirota and Kenny Jenkins) and Scott "Prefuse 73" Herren.			
8/10/02	**47^{S}**	4		**Wylin Out** ...*(5 versions)*	$6	T	Chocolate Ind. 030
				URE, Midge — see ULTRAVOX			

DEBUT	PEAK	WKS	Gold	A-side (Chart Hit)...B-side	$	Sym	Label & Number
				URGENT '85			
				Rock quintet — Michael Kehr, lead singer.			
8/10/85	79	5		**Running Back** ... *Dedicated To Love* — produced by **Ian Hunter** and Mick Ronson (**Mott The Hoople**)	$4	■	Manhattan 50005
				URGE OVERKILL ROK/LP '94			
				Male pop-rock trio formed in 1986 in Chicago, Illinois: Nash Kato (guitar), "Eddie" King Roeser (bass) and Blackie Onassis (drums).			
11/19/94	59	11		**Girl, You'll Be A Woman Soon** ... A:42 *Bustin' Surfboards* (The Tornadoes - #102/'62) — from the movie *Pulp Fiction* starring **John Travolta**	$5	▮	MCA 54935
				URIAH HEEP BUB/ROK/LP '72			
				Hard-rock group from England. Core members: David Byron (vocals), Mick Box (guitar), Ken Hensley (keyboards; later with **Blackfoot**), Gary Thain (bass) and Keith Baker (drums). Thain died of a drug overdose on 3/19/76 (age 27). Byron died on 2/28/85 (age 38).			
7/29/72	39	12		1 **Easy Livin** ... *All My Life*	$8		Mercury 73307
1/20/73	91	3		2 **Sweet Lorraine** /			
1/20/73	97	1		3 **Blind Eye** ...	$7		Mercury 73349
10/13/73	91	7		4 **Stealin'** ... *Sunshine*	$7		Warner 7738
				USA FOR AFRICA LP '85			
				USA: United Support of Artists. Collection of top artists formed to help suffering people of Africa. Also see **Voices Of America**.			
3/23/85	❶⁴	18	▲⁴	**We Are The World** ... RB² / AC² S:❶⁵ / A:❶⁴ *Grace* (**Quincy Jones**) — soloists (in order of appearance): **Lionel Richie**, **Stevie Wonder**, **Paul Simon**, **Kenny Rogers**, **James Ingram**, **Tina Turner**, **Billy Joel**, **Michael Jackson**, **Diana Ross**, **Dionne Warwick**, **Willie Nelson**, **Al Jarreau**, **Bruce Springsteen**, **Kenny Loggins**, **Steve Perry**, **Daryl Hall**, **Huey Lewis**, **Cyndi Lauper**, **Kim Carnes**, **Bob Dylan**, and **Ray Charles**; written by **Michael Jackson** and **Lionel Richie**; 1985 Grammy winner: Record of the Year	$4	■	Columbia 04839

USHER ★192★ R&B/BUB/LP '01

Born Usher Raymond on 10/14/78 in Chattanooga, Tennessee. Male R&B singer/actor. Age 15 at the time of his chart debut. Played "Jeremy" on TV's *Moesha*. Acted in several movies. Also see **Jermaine Dupri**'s "The Party Continues."

1)U Got It Bad 2)U Remind Me 3)Nice & Slow

DEBUT	PEAK	WKS	Gold	A-side (Chart Hit)...B-side	$	Sym	Label & Number
9/3/94	59	16		1 **Can U Get Wit It** ... S:22 *(instrumental)* — written and produced by Devante Swing (**Jodeci**)	$4	▮	LaFace 24075
2/18/95	58	19		2 **Think Of You** ... S:23 *(instrumental)* — **Biz Markie** (rap); **Faith Evans** (backing vocal); samples "Tidal Wave" by **Ronnie Laws**	$4	▮	LaFace 24094
7/22/95	73ˢ	2		3 **The Many Ways** ... BUB:109 *(instrumental)* — **Al B. Sure!** (backing vocal)	$4	▮	LaFace 24105
8/23/97	2⁷	47	▲	4 **You Make Me Wanna...** ... RB¹¹ S:2 / A:4 *(instrumental)* — also see #9 below	$3	▮	LaFace 24265
1/24/98	❶²	23	▲	5 **Nice & Slow** ... RB⁸ S:❶⁴ / A:15 *(album version) / (instrumental)* — **Jagged Edge** (backing vocals)	$3	▮	LaFace 24290
6/20/98	2³	24	▲	6 **My Way** ... S:❶³ / A:29 *(instrumental)*	$3	▮	LaFace 24323
11/4/00	60	7		7 **Pop Ya Collar** ... A:59 — available as a promo CD single only on LaFace 4486 (not released on an album)			promo CD
6/16/01	❶⁴	24		8 **U Remind Me** ... RB⁴ S:❶³ / A:3 *(instrumental) / (5 album snippets)*	$4	★	Arista 13992
7/21/01	63ˢ	3		9 **You Make Me Wanna...** ... *(5 remixes)* [R] — reissue of #4 above on Arista's "Maximum Hits" series	$8	★*	LaFace 24269
9/22/01	❶⁶	32		10 **U Got It Bad** RB⁷ A:❶¹⁰ *(4 versions)*	$6	T	Arista 15036
2/9/02	3	26		11 **U Don't Have To Call** ... A:3 / S:10 *U Got It Bad*	$8	◗	Arista 15134
3/16/02	2⁴	23		12 **I Need A Girl (Part One)** ... A:2 / S:23 *(3 versions)* — **P. DIDDY Featuring Usher & Loon**	$6	T	Bad Boy 79436
9/7/02	30ˢ	1		13 **Can U Help Me** ... *(instrumental) / U Don't Have To Call*	$6	★	Arista 15184
				U.S. 1 '75			
				Bubblegum pop-rock studio creation of Joey Levine (**Ohio Express**).			
11/29/75	91	2		**Bye Bye Baby** ... *Creation*	$5		Private Stock 45,045
				US3 LP '94			
				Jazz-rap collaboration by London producers Mel Simpson (keyboards) and Geoff Wilkinson (samples). Samples of recordings from the Blue Note jazz record label serve as the backdrop for new rap solos and jazz playing by some of Britain's top players. Pronounced: us three.			
11/27/93+	9	27	●	**Cantaloop** ... S:6 / A:20 *(4 versions)* — Rahsaan (rap); Gerard Presencer (trumpet); samples "Cantaloupe Island" by **Herbie Hancock** and the introduction from "A Night In Birdland, Vol. 1" by the Art Blakey Quintet; "45": Blue Note 17707; B-side: "It's Like That"	$3	▮ᵛ	Blue Note 44945
				UTAH SAINTS LP '92			
				Techno-rave duo from England: Jez Willis and Tim Garbutt.			
11/21/92	98	1		**Something Good** ... *Anything Can Happen* — samples "Cloudbusting" by **Kate Bush**	$5	▮	London 869842
				UTFO R&B/LP '85			
				Rap group from Brooklyn, New York: Shawn Fequiere, Fred Reeves, Jeff Campbell and Maurice Bailey. UTFO: Untouchable Force Organization.			
3/9/85	77	5		**Roxanne, Roxanne** ... *The Real Roxanne* (Roxanne w/UTFO - R&B #44) — first released as a 12" single on Select 62254 (above B-side on Select 62256)	$10		Select 1182

DEBUT	PEAK	WKS	Gold	A-side (Chart Hit)...B-side	$	Sym	Label & Number

UTOPIA

ROK/LP **'80**

Pop-rock group: **Todd Rundgren** (vocals, guitar), Roger Powell (keyboards), Kasim Sulton (bass) and John Wilcox (drums).

DEBUT	PEAK	WKS	Gold	A-side (Chart Hit)...B-side	$	Sym	Label & Number
2/23/80	27	12		1 **Set Me Free** ... *Umbrella Man*	$5		Bearsville 49180
6/7/80	76	3		2 **The Very Last Time** ... *Love Alone*	$5		Bearsville 49247
1/8/83	82	6		3 **Feet Don't Fail Me Now** ... *There Goes My Inspiration*	$4		Network 69859

U2 ★94★

ROK/BUB/LP **'87**

Rock group formed in Dublin, Ireland: Paul "**Bono**" Hewson (vocals), Dave "The Edge" Evans (guitar), **Adam Clayton** (bass) and **Larry Mullen** (drums). Met while students at Dublin's Mount Temple High School. Emerged in 1987 as one of the world's leading rock acts. Released a concert tour documentary movie *Rattle And Hum* in 1988. Also see **Kirk Franklin**'s "Lean On Me." 2001 Grammy winner: Record of the Year — "Walk On" ("Bubbled Under" #118).

1)With Or Without You 2)I Still Haven't Found What I'm Looking For 3)Desire 4)Theme From Mission: Impossible 5)mysterious Ways

DEBUT	PEAK	WKS	Gold	A-side (Chart Hit)...B-side	$	Sym	Label & Number
4/2/83	53	12		1 **New Year's Day** ... *Treasure (Whatever happened to Pete the Chop)*	$8		Island 99915
1/14/84	81	5		2 **I Will Follow** ... *Two Hearts Beat As One* (ROK #12) [L] studio version released on Island 49716 in 1981 with a picture sleeve; B-side "Bubbled Under" in 1983 on Island 99861	$7		Island 99789
10/27/84	33	15		3 **Pride (In The Name Of Love)** ... *Boomerang II* a tribute to **Rev. Martin Luther King**	$6	■	Island 99704
3/21/87	❶[3]	18		4 **With Or Without You** AR[5] A:❶[3] / S:❶[1] *Luminous Times (Hold On To Love) / Walk To The Water*	$3	■	Island 99469
6/13/87	❶[2]	17		5 **I Still Haven't Found What I'm Looking For** ... A:❶[1] / S:2 *Spanish Eyes* (ROK #11) */ Deep In The Heart*	$3	■	Island 99430
9/12/87	13	14		6 **Where The Streets Have No Name** ... S:11 / A:16 *Silver And Gold / Sweetest Thing*	$3	■	Island 99408
12/5/87+	44	12		7 **In God's Country** ... S:35 *Bullet The Blue Sky* (ROK #14) */ Running To Stand Still* above 4 from the album *The Joshua Tree*; above 4 released simultaneously on Island 99453, 99431, 99407 and 99384, respectively, for juke boxes	$3	■	Island 99385
10/1/88	3	17	●	8 **Desire** ... AR[5] / MR[5] S:❶[1] / A:5 *Hallelujah Here She Comes*	$3	■	Island 99250
12/17/88+	14	15		9 **Angel Of Harlem** ... AR[6] S:11 / A:14 *A Room At The Heartbreak Hotel* a tribute to Billie Holiday	$3	■	Island 99254
4/1/89	68	7		10 **When Love Comes To Town** ... *Dancing Barefoot* (U2 - ROK #14) **U2 WITH B.B. KING**	$3	■	Island 99225
7/1/89	83	4		11 **All I Want Is You** ... *Unchained Melody* also see #20 below; above 4 from the U2 album and concert tour movie *Rattle And Hum*	$3	■	Island 99199
11/9/91	61	11		12 **The Fly** ... MR[2] S:13 *(remix) / Alex descends into Hell for a Bottle of Milk/Korova 1*	$4	▮	Island 868885
11/23/91+	9	20		13 **mysterious Ways** ... AR[12] / MR[9] A:11 / S:16 *(remix)*	$3	▮	Island 866188
3/14/92	10	20		14 **One** ... AR[2] / MR[1] A:7 / S:17 *Lady With The Spinning Head / Satellite Of Love*	$3	▮	Island 866533
7/11/92	32	15		15 **even better than the Real Thing** ... AR[3] A:43 / S:55 *Salomé / Where did it all go Wrong*	$3	▮	Island 866977
11/7/92	35	16		16 **Who's gonna ride your Wild Horses** ... S:42 / A:42 *paint it Black / Fortunate son* above 5 from the album *Achtung Baby*	$3	▮	Island 864521
7/10/93	61[A]	5		17 **Numb** ... a remix version was issued on the B-side of #25 below			album cut
10/16/93	71[A]	2		18 **Lemon** ... BUB:103 *(4 versions)*	$6	T	Island 862957
12/18/93+	61	13		19 **Stay (faraway, so close!)** ... S:55 / A:72 *I've Got You Under My Skin* (**Frank Sinatra** & Bono) above 3 from the album *Zooropa* on Island 518047	$4	▮[V]	Island 858076 ■
5/7/94	50[A]	18		20 **All I Want Is You** ... [R] from the movie *Reality Bites* starring Winona Ryder (soundtrack on RCA 66364); same version as #11 above			album cut
6/24/95	16	17		21 **Hold Me, Thrill Me, Kiss Me, Kill Me** ... AR[1] / MR[4] A:15 / S:19 *Themes From Batman Forever* from the movie *Batman Forever* starring Val Kilmer	$4	▮	Island 87131
5/11/96	7	20	●	22 **Theme From Mission: Impossible** ... S:4 / A:10 *(2 remixes)* [I] **ADAM CLAYTON & LARRY MULLEN** samples the original #41 hit by **Lalo Schifrin** from 1968; from the movie *Mission: Impossible* starring Tom Cruise	$3	▮	Mother/Island 576670
2/22/97	10	11	●	23 **Discothéque** ... MR[4] S:9 / A:22 *Holy Joe* samples "Fane" by Freeform	$3	▮[V]	Island 854774
4/26/97	26	18		24 **Staring At The Sun** ... MR[3] A:16 / S:36 *North And South Of The River*	$4	▮[V]	Island 854972
7/19/97	57	8		25 **Last Night On Earth** ... S:66 / A:74 *Pop Muzik / Happiness Is A Warm Gun / Numb* samples "Trayra Boia" by Colin Walcott, Don Cherry & Ed Blackwell	$8	★	Island 572053
12/5/98	63	17		26 **Sweetest Thing** ... A:43 recorded in 1987 (B-side of #6 above); from the album *The Best Of 1980-1990/The B-Sides* on Island 524612			album cut
10/2/99	41[S]	7		27 **New Day** ... *(clean version w/***Refugee Camp** *& guests)* **WYCLEF JEAN Featuring BONO**	$5	★	Ruffhouse 79274
10/7/00+	21	25		28 **Beautiful Day** ... A:19 *(same version)* 2000 Grammy winner: Record of the Year	$6	T	Island 562972
9/29/01	52	20		29 **Stuck In A Moment You Can't Get Out Of** ... A:53 above 2 from the album *All That You Can't Leave Behind* on Interscope 524653			album cut
9/28/02	77	7		30 **Electrical Storm** ... A:72 from the album *The Best Of 1990-2000* on Island 063361; all of above (except #22 & 27) written by U2			album cut

UWF ALL-STARS, The

'99

All-star funk group: **Bar-Kays**, **Con Funk Shun**, **Dazz Band**, **The Gap Band**, **The S.O.S. Band** and **Zapp**. UWF: United We Funk.

DEBUT	PEAK	WKS	Gold	A-side (Chart Hit)...B-side	$	Sym	Label & Number
11/20/99	62[S]	2		**Girls Night Out** ... *(instrumental) / United We Funk Medley* **THE UWF ALL-STARS Featuring The SOS Band**	$6	★	Major Label 74471

V

DEBUT	PEAK	WKS	Gold	A-side (Chart Hit)..................B-side	$	Sym	Label & Number
				VACELS, The '65 Rock group from Long Island, New York: Ricky Racano, Harvey Cooper, Vinnie Cappola, and brothers Vinnie and Peter Gutowski.			
7/24/65	63	5		**You're My Baby (And Don't You Forget It)**........*Hey Girl Stop Leading Me On*	$15		Kama Sutra 200
				VALADIERS '61 R&B vocal group featuring **Paul Kelly**.			
11/20/61	89	2		**Greetings (This is Uncle Sam)**........*Take A Chance* some pressings show title as just "Greetings"; produced by Motown owner Berry Gordy, Jr.	$50		Miracle 6
				VALE, Jerry AC/BUB/MEM/POP/LP '56 Born Genaro Vitaliano on 7/8/32 in the Bronx, New York. Adult Contemporary-ballad singer. First hit the pop charts in 1954 with "Two Purple Shadows" (#20).			
3/10/56	30	12		1 **Innamorata (Sweetheart)**........T:30 *Second Ending* from the movie *Artists & Models* starring **Dean Martin** and **Jerry Lewis**	$12		Columbia 40634
7/7/56	14	24		2 **You Don't Know Me** S:14 / T:14 / J:14 / A:15 *Enchanted*	$12		Columbia 40710
11/25/57	45	13		3 **Pretend You Don't See Her**........S:45 / T:52 *The Spreading Chestnut* written by **Steve Allen**; **Percy Faith** (orch., above 3)	$12		Columbia 41010
10/13/58	60	7		4 **Go Chase A Moonbeam**........H:60 *Around The Clock*	$12		Columbia 41238
12/19/64+	24	10		5 **Have You Looked Into Your Heart**........AC[1] *Andiamo*	$8	□	Columbia 43181
3/6/65	54	6		6 **For Mama**........*Ti Adoro* written by French actor/singer Charles Aznavour	$6		Columbia 43232
5/22/65	96	3		7 **Tears Keep On Falling**........*Now*	$6		Columbia 43252
8/7/65	99	1		8 **Where Were You When I Needed You**........*I Don't Wanna Go Home* Marty Manning (orch., above 4)	$6		Columbia 43337
10/8/66	93	2		9 **Dommage, Dommage (Too Bad, Too Bad)**........*Promises* Glenn Osser (orch.: #4 & 9)	$6		Columbia 43774
				VALENS, Ritchie LP '59 Born Richard Valenzuela on 5/13/41 in Pacoima, California. Killed in the plane crash that also took the lives of **Buddy Holly** and the **Big Bopper** on 2/3/59 (age 17). Latin rock and roll singer/songwriter/guitarist. In the movie *Go Johnny Go.* The 1987 movie *La Bamba* was based on his life. Inducted into the Rock and Roll Hall of Fame in 2001.			
9/22/58	42	13		1 **Come On, Let's Go**........H:42 *Framed*	$75		Del-Fi 4106
11/24/58+	2^{2}	23	●	2 **Donna /**			
12/29/58+	22	15		3 **La Bamba**........[F] above 2 reissued with a picture sleeve in 1961 on Kasey 7040	$40		Del-Fi 4110
4/6/59	55	8		4 **That's My Little Suzie**........*In A Turkish Town*	$40		Del-Fi 4114
7/13/59	92	2		5 **Little Girl**........*We Belong Together* special tribute label: "Limited Valens Memorial Series"; picture sleeve included an insert explaining the "Memorial Series"	$30	■	Del-Fi 4117
				VALENTE, Caterina '55 Born on 1/14/31 in Paris, France (of Italian parentage). Singer/dancer/actress. Sings in six languages.			
4/9/55	8	14		**The Breeze And I (Andalucia)**........A:8 / S:13 *Jalousie* Werner Müller (orch.); #1 hit for **Jimmy Dorsey** (Bob Eberly, vocal) in 1940	$15		Decca 29467
				VALENTI, John '76 Born **John LaVigni** in Chicago, Illinois. "Blue-eyed soul" singer/songwriter/drummer. Member of the group Puzzle in the early 1970s.			
10/18/75	83	6		1 **Machines** *[JOHN LiVIGNI]*........*Driving Back To You*	$6		Raintree 2204
9/4/76	37	12		2 **Anything You Want**........*That's The Way Life Goes*	$5		Ariola America 7625
				VALENTINO, Danny '60 Born on 2/19/41 in Flushing, New York. Teen pop singer.			
6/6/60	95	2		**Biology**........*A Million Tears* **Ray Ellis** (orch.)	$20		MGM 12881
				VALENTINO, Mark '62 Born Anthony Busillo on 3/12/42 in Philadelphia, Pennsylvania. Rock and roll singer; similar in style to **Freddy Cannon**.			
11/10/62	27	9		**The Push And Kick**........*Walking Alone* **Frank Slay** (orch.)	$15		Swan 4121
				VALENTINOS, The BUB '62 Family R&B group from Cleveland, Ohio: **Bobby Womack** and his brothers Cecil, Curtis, Friendly Jr. and Harris. Originated as the Womack Brothers gospel group. Also recorded as The Lovers. Signed to **Sam Cooke**'s SAR Records in 1962. Cecil married for a time to **Mary Wells**.			
8/18/62	72	8		1 **Lookin' For A Love**........*Somewhere There's A Girl* also see **Bobby Womack**'s solo version in 1974	$20		SAR 132
3/30/63	97	2		2 **I'll Make It Alright** *[THE VALENTINOS (The Lovers)]*........*Darling, Come Back Home*	$20		SAR 137
6/27/64	94	2		3 **It's All Over Now**........*Tired Of Livin' In The Country*	$20		SAR 152
				VALERIA '01 Born in 1978 in Los Angeles, California. Female dance singer.			
6/23/01+	30^{S}	15		**Ooh La La**........*I Think I'm Falling In Love*	$5	★	Interscope 75712
				VALERY, Dana '80 Born in Manhattan, New York. Pop session singer.			
6/19/76	95	4		1 **Will You Love Me Tomorrow**........*I Never Had It So Good*	$5		Phantom 10566
1/19/80	87	5		2 **I Don't Want To Be Lonely**........*Rainbow Connection*	$4		Scotti Brothers 509
				VALIANTS, The '58 R&B vocal group from Los Angeles, California: **Billy Storm**, Brice Coefield, Sheridan Spencer and Chester Pipkin.			
12/30/57+	69	7		**This Is The Nite**........T:69 *Good Golly Miss Molly* Bumps Blackwell (backing band)	$40		Keen 34004

VALINO, Joe — '56

Born Joseph Paolino on 3/9/29 in South Philadelphia, Pennsylvania. Died of a heart attack on 12/26/96 (age 67). Big band-styled singer.

DEBUT	PEAK	WKS	Gold	A-side (Chart Hit)	B-side	$	Sym	Label & Number
10/20/56	12	20		**Garden Of Eden** ... T:12 / A:12 / S:13 / J:13 George Siravo (orch.)	*Caravan*	$20		Vik 0226

VALJEAN — LP '62

Born Valjean Johns on 11/19/34 in Shattuck, Oklahoma. Male pianist.

DEBUT	PEAK	WKS	Gold	A-side (Chart Hit)	B-side	$	Sym	Label & Number
5/19/62	28	9		1 **Theme From Ben Casey** Jon Neel (orch.); from the TV series *Ben Casey* starring **Vince Edwards**	*Theme From Dr. Kildare* [I]	$10	■	Carlton 573
8/25/62	100	1		2 **Till There Was You** **Ernie Freeman** (orch.); from the movie *The Music Man* starring Robert Preston and **Shirley Jones**	*The Eighteenth Variation* [I]	$10	■	Carlton 576

VALLI, Frankie ★323★ — BUB/AC/LP '75

Born Francis Castellucio on 5/3/37 in Newark, New Jersey. Recorded his first solo single in 1953 as Frank Valley on the Corona label. Formed own group, the Variatones, in 1955 and changed its name to **The Four Lovers** in 1956, which evolved into **The 4 Seasons** by 1961. Began solo work in 1965. Suffered from a disease that caused hearing loss in the late 1970s; corrected by surgery.

1)Grease 2)My Eyes Adored You 3)Can't Take My Eyes Off You

DEBUT	PEAK	WKS	Gold	A-side (Chart Hit)	B-side	$	Sym	Label & Number
1/15/66	39	7		1 (You're Gonna) **Hurt Yourself**	*Night Hawk* (The Valli Boys)	$12		Smash 2015
11/12/66	68	6		2 **The Proud One**	*Ivy*	$10	■	Philips 40407
5/20/67	2[1]	16	●	3 **Can't Take My Eyes Off You**	*The Trouble With Me*	$10	■	Philips 40446
8/26/67	18	8		4 **I Make A Fool Of Myself**	*September Rain (Here Comes The Rain)*	$10	■	Philips 40484
12/30/67+	29	8		5 **To Give** (The Reason I Live)	*Watch Where You Walk*	$10	■	Philips 40510
6/14/69	52	7		6 **The Girl I'll Never Know (Angels Never Fly This Low)**	*A Face Without A Name*	$10	■	Philips 40622
11/23/74+	❶[1]	23	●	7 **My Eyes Adored You**	*Watch Where You Walk*	$6		Private Stock 45,003
5/17/75	6	14		8 **Swearin' To God** all of above produced by **Bob Crewe**	*Why*	$6		Private Stock 45,021
10/18/75	11	12		9 **Our Day Will Come**	*You Can Bet (I Ain't Goin' Nowhere)*	$6		Private Stock 45,043
4/3/76	36	8		10 **Fallen Angel**	*Carrie (I Would Marry You)*	$6		Private Stock 45,074
8/14/76	78	3		11 **We're All Alone** written by **Boz Scaggs**	*You To Me Are Everything*	$6		Private Stock 45,098
5/27/78	❶[2]	22	▲	12 **Grease** title song from the movie starring **John Travolta** and **Olivia Newton-John**; written and produced by **Barry Gibb**	*(instrumental)*	$5		RSO 897
1/27/79	77	4		13 **Fancy Dancer**	*Needing You*	$5		Warner/Curb 8734
7/19/80	90	4		14 **Where Did We Go Wrong** **FRANKIE VALLI Introducing Chris Forde**	*Doctor Dance*	$5		MCA/Curb 41253

VALLI, June — MEM/POP '53

Born on 6/30/30 in the Bronx, New York. Died on 3/12/93 (age 62). Co-star of *Lucky Strike Hit Parade* for three years in the 1950s. Voice for Chiquita Banana commercials. Married Chicago DJ Howard Miller. Hit #4 in 1953 with "Crying In The Chapel."

DEBUT	PEAK	WKS	Gold	A-side (Chart Hit)	B-side	$	Sym	Label & Number
5/14/55	29	1		1 **Unchained Melody** ... S:29 **Hugo Winterhalter** (orch.); from the movie *Unchained* starring football great Elroy "Crazylegs" Hirsch	*Tomorrow*	$15		RCA Victor 6078
11/24/58+	43	13		2 **The Wedding** **Bride: JUNE VALLI Groom: YOU Best Man: YOUR BEST FRIEND**	*Lunch Hour*	$10		Mercury 71382
3/2/59	71	5		3 **The Answer To A Maiden's Prayer** Chuck Sagle (orch., above 2)	*In His Arms*	$10		Mercury 71422
3/7/60	29	13		4 **Apple Green** Belford Hendricks (orch.)	*Oh Why*	$10		Mercury 71588

VAN, Harvie June — '67

Female pop singer.

DEBUT	PEAK	WKS	Gold	A-side (Chart Hit)	B-side	$	Sym	Label & Number
12/23/67	15[X]	2		**Natividad** (Nativity)	*Dasher* [X]	$20		Kapp 875

VANCE, Paul — see LEE and PAUL

VANDENBERG — ROK/LP '83

Born Adrian Vandenberg on 1/31/54 in Holland. Hard-rock guitarist. His group: Bert Heerink (vocals), Dick Kemper (bass) and Jos Zoomer (drums). Vandenberg later joined **Whitesnake**.

DEBUT	PEAK	WKS	Gold	A-side (Chart Hit)	B-side	$	Sym	Label & Number
1/8/83	39	14		**Burning Heart**	*Ready For You*	$4		Atco 99947

VANDROSS, Luther ★165★ — R&B/BUB/AC/LP '91

Born on 4/20/51 in the Bronx, New York. R&B singer/songwriter/producer. Commercial jingle singer, then a prolific session vocalist/arranger. Sang lead on a few of **Change**'s early albums. Appeared in the movie *The Meteor Man*. Much songwriting and production work for other artists. His older sister Patricia was a member of **The Crests**. Suffered a serious stroke on 4/16/2003.

1)Endless Love 2)Power Of Love/Love Power 3)Here And Now 4)Don't Want To Be A Fool 5)The Best Things In Life Are Free

DEBUT	PEAK	WKS	Gold	A-side (Chart Hit)	B-side	$	Sym	Label & Number
10/10/81	33	15		1 **Never Too Much** ... RB[2]	*You Stopped Loving Me*	$4		Epic 02409
10/30/82	55	12		2 **Bad Boy/Having A Party**	*Once You Know How*	$4		Epic 03205
10/8/83	27	13		3 **How Many Times Can We Say Goodbye** **DIONNE WARWICK AND LUTHER VANDROSS**	*What Can A Miracle Do* (Warwick)	$4		Arista 9073
4/28/84	87	4		4 **Superstar/Until You Come Back To Me (That's What I'm Gonna Do)** above medley only available as a 12" single; "45" issued on Epic 04441 as "Superstar (Don't you remember...)"	*I Wanted Your Love*	$8	T[V]	Epic 04969
3/16/85	29	16		5 **'Til My Baby Comes Home** ... S:26 **Billy Preston** (organ solo)	*(instrumental)*	$4	■	Epic 04760
8/23/86	57	11		6 **Give Me The Reason** from the movie *Ruthless People* starring Danny DeVito and **Bette Midler**	*Don't You Want My Love* (Nicole)	$4	■	Epic 06129
11/15/86+	15	19		7 **Stop To Love** ... RB[2] S:14 / A:14	*(instrumental)*	$3	■	Epic 06523

DEBUT	PEAK	WKS	Gold	A-side (Chart Hit)..........B-side	$	Sym	Label & Number
				VANDROSS, Luther — Cont'd			
3/14/87	50	14		8 **There's Nothing Better Than Love**..........RB[1] *(instrumental)*	$3	■	Epic 06978
				LUTHER VANDROSS (With Gregory Hines)			
10/8/88	44	13		9 **Any Love**..........RB[1] S:40 *(instrumental)*	$3		Epic 08047
1/28/89	30	12		10 **She Won't Talk To Me**..........A:33 / S:35 *(instrumental)*	$3		Epic 08513
12/23/89+	6	27	●	11 **Here And Now**..........RB[2] S:6 / A:7 *Come Back*	$3	▮V	Epic 73029
4/27/91	4	18		12 **Power Of Love/Love Power**..........RB[2] A:14 / S:22 *(instrumental)*	$3	▮V	Epic 73778
				Cissy Houston, **Darlene Love**, **Lisa Fischer** and others (backing vocals)			
8/3/91	9	20		13 **Don't Want To Be A Fool**..........A:21 *(instrumental)*	$3	▮V	Epic 73879
				"45" B-side: "Power Of Love/Love Power" (album version)			
1/4/92	73	7		14 **The Rush**..........A:67 *(radio edit)*	$3	▮	Epic 74049
5/30/92	10	20		15 **The Best Things In Life Are Free**..........RB[1] A:5 / S:16 *(3 album snippets)*	$3	▮V	Perspective 0010
				LUTHER VANDROSS and JANET JACKSON with BBD and Ralph Tresvant			
				from the movie *Mo' Money* starring Damon Wayans; "45" B-side: (edit-no rap)			
5/22/93	62	10		16 **Little Miracles (Happen Every Day)**..........S:57 / A:68 *I'm Gonna Start Today*	$3	▮V	Epic/LV 74945
9/18/93	94	3		17 **Heaven Knows**..........*I Want The Night To Stay*	$3	▮V	Epic/LV 74996
9/10/94	2[1]	20	●	18 **Endless Love** S:2 / A:5 *(instrumental)*	$3	▮V	Columbia 77629
				LUTHER VANDROSS & MARIAH CAREY			
12/10/94+	58	18		19 **Always And Forever**..........S:66 *Power Of Love/Love Power*	$3	▮V	Epic/LV 77735
4/22/95	95	2		20 **Love The One You're With /**			
4/22/95		2		21 **Going In Circles**..........	$3	▮V	Epic/LV 77754
				above 4 from the album *Songs*			
9/21/96	52	13		22 **Your Secret Love**..........S:28 *Please Come Home For Christmas / Power Of Love (Love Power)*	$3	▮V	Epic/LV 78400
12/21/96+	80	10		23 **I Can Make It Better**..........S:54 *This Time I'm Right / A Kiss For Christmas*	$3	▮V	Epic/LV 78466
7/21/01	26	17		24 **Take You Out**..........S:5 / A:75 *Let's Make Tonight The Night*	$4	★V	J Records 21084
				"45": J Records 21077; B-side: (instrumental)			
9/14/02	83	20		25 **I'd Rather**..........*(remix) / Wish I Didn't Miss You* (**Angie Stone** - #79/'02)	$4	★V	J Records 21220
				"45": J Records 21171; B-side: "Grown Thangs"			
				VAN DYK, Paul LP **'00**			
				Born on 12/16/71 in Eisenhuttenstadt, East Germany. Techno-dance DJ/producer.			
5/27/00	72[S]	1		**Tell Me Why (The Riddle)**..........*(5 mixes)*	$8	★*	Mute 9129
				PAUL VAN DYK feat. Saint Etienne			
				VAN DYKE, Dick — see ANDREWS, Julie			
				VAN DYKE, Leroy C&W/BUB **'61**			
				Born on 10/4/29 in Spring Fork, Missouri. Worked as a newspaper reporter. Served in U.S. Army in the early 1950s. Former livestock auctioneer. In the movie *What Am I Bid?* in 1967.			
11/24/56+	19	15		1 **Auctioneer**..........J:19 / S:21 / T:29 *I Fell In Love With A Pony-Tail*	$20		Dot 15503
				Andy Nelson (guitar)			
10/30/61	5	16		2 **Walk On By**..........CW[19] *My World Is Caving In*	$15		Mercury 71834
3/10/62	35	7		3 **If A Woman Answers (Hang Up The Phone)**..........*A Broken Promise*	$12		Mercury 71926
				The Merry Melody Singers (backing vocals, above 2)			
				VAN DYKES, The **'61**			
				Male R&B vocal group.			
1/16/61	91	2		1 **Gift Of Love** *[VAN DYKES]*..........*Guardian Angel*	$40		Donna 1333
				originally released on Spring 1113 in 1960 ($125)			
7/31/61	99	2		2 **The Bells Are Ringing**..........*Meaning Of Love*	$25		DeLuxe 6193
				originally released on King 5158 in 1958 ($75)			
				VAN DYKES, The R&B/BUB **'66**			
				R&B vocal trio from Fort Worth, Texas: Rondalis Tandy (lead), Wenzon Mosley (tenor) and James May (baritone).			
4/2/66	94	2		**No Man Is An Island**..........*I Won't Hold It Against You*	$15		Mala 520
				originally released on Hue 6501 in 1965 ($30)			
				VANGELIS LP **'82**			
				Born Evangelos Papathanassiou on 3/29/43 in Valos, Greece. Keyboardist/composer. Also see **Jon & Vangelis**.			
12/12/81+	❶[1]	28		**Chariots Of Fire - Titles**..........AC[5] *Eric's Theme* [I]	$5	■	Polydor 2189
				from the Academy Award-winning movie *Chariots Of Fire* starring Ian Charleson and Ben Cross; first pressings issued only as "Titles"			
				VAN HALEN ★139★ ROK/BUB/LP **'84**			
				Hard-rock group formed in Pasadena, California: **David Lee Roth** (vocals; born on 10/10/55), Eddie Van Halen (guitar; born on 1/26/55), Michael Anthony (bass; born on 6/20/54) and Alex Van Halen (drums; born on 5/8/53). The Van Halen brothers were born in Nijmegen, Netherlands; moved to Pasadena in 1968. **Sammy Hagar** replaced Roth as lead singer in 1985. Eddie married actress Valerie Bertinelli on 4/11/81 (since separated). Hagar left in June 1996; Roth rejoined briefly to record two new songs. Gary Cherone (**Extreme**) joined as lead singer in September 1996.			
				1)Jump 2)Why Can't This Be Love 3)When It's Love 4)(Oh) Pretty Woman 5)I'll Wait			
1/28/78	36	11		1 **You Really Got Me**..........*Atomic Punk*	$5		Warner 8515
5/6/78	84	4		2 **Runnin' With The Devil**..........*Eruption*	$5	■	Warner 8556
4/28/79	15	15		3 **Dance The Night Away**..........*Outta Love Again*	$5	■	Warner 8823
9/15/79	84	4		4 **Beautiful Girls**..........*D.O.A.*	$5		Warner 49035
5/24/80	55	7		5 **And The Cradle Will Rock...**..........*Could This Be Magic?*	$5		Warner 49501
2/6/82	12	16		6 **(Oh) Pretty Woman**..........AR[2] *Happy Trails*	$4	■	Warner 50003
				first pressings of record and picture sleeve show title as "Pretty Woman"			
5/22/82	38	11		7 **Dancing In The Street**..........*The Full Bug* (ROK #42)	$4		Warner 29986
1/14/84	❶[5]	21	●	8 **Jump** AR[8] *House Of Pain*	$4	■	Warner 29384
4/14/84	13	14		9 **I'll Wait**..........*Girl Gone Bad*	$4	■	Warner 29307
6/23/84	13	15		10 **Panama**..........*Drop Dead Legs*	$4	■	Warner 29250

DEBUT	PEAK	WKS	Gold	A-side (Chart Hit)...B-side	$	Sym	Label & Number
				VAN HALEN — Cont'd			
10/27/84	56	7		11 **Hot For Teacher**...*Little Dreamer*	$4	■	Warner 29199
				also issued with a foldout poster sleeve in a clear plastic die-cut sleeve; above 4 from the album *1984*; all of above produced by Ted Templeman; Roth, lead singer all of above; Hagar, lead singer all below			
3/15/86	3	16		12 **Why Can't This Be Love**...AR3 A:2 / S:7 *Get Up*	$3	■	Warner 28740
5/24/86	22	14		13 **Dreams**...A:18 / S:25 *Inside*	$3		Warner 28702
8/9/86	22	15		14 **Love Walks In**...A:15 / S:24 *Summer Nights* (ROK #33)	$3	■	Warner 28626
5/21/88	34	10		15 **Black And Blue**...AR3 S:29 *A Apolitical Blues*	$3	■	Warner 27891
7/2/88	5	19		16 **When It's Love**...AR1 A:4 / S:7 *Cabo Wabo* (ROK #31)	$3	■	Warner 27827
10/1/88	13	20		17 **Finish What Ya Started**...S:14 / A:16 *Sucker In A 3 Piece*	$3	■	Warner 27746
1/28/89	35	14		18 **Feels So Good**...A:35 *Sucker In A 3 Piece*	$3		Warner 27565
				above 4 from the album *OU812*			
10/12/91	27	19		19 **Top Of The World**...AR4 A:49 *Poundcake* (ROK #1)	$3	▮V	Warner 19151
2/8/92	55	13		20 **Right Now**...A:66 *Man On A Mission* (ROK #21)	$3	▮	Warner 19059
3/25/95	30	20		21 **Can't Stop Lovin' You**...A:32 / S:44 *Crossing Over*	$3	▮V	Warner 17909
8/19/95	97	3		22 **Not Enough**...*Amsterdam* (ROK #9)	$3	▮V	Warner 17810
				VANILLA FUDGE BUB/LP '68			
				Psychedelic-rock group formed in New York: Mark Stein (vocals, keyboards), Vinnie Martell (guitar), Tim Bogert (bass) and Carmine Appice (drums). Both Bogert and Appice also played with **Jeff Beck** and **Rod Stewart**'s backing bands.			
7/8/67	67	5		1 **You Keep Me Hanging On**...*Take Me For A Little While*	$12		Atco 6495
				also see #3 below; B-side charted on #4 below			
2/10/68	73	6		2 **Where Is My Mind**...*The Look Of Love*	$10		Atco 6554
7/13/68	6	12		3 **You Keep Me Hangin' On** *Come By Day, Come By Night* [R]	$10		Atco 6590
				#1 & 3: same 2:50 version (album version is 7:20)			
10/5/68	38	8		4 **Take Me For A Little While**...*Thoughts*	$10		Atco 6616
				"Bubbled Under" (#114) for **Evie Sands** in 1965			
12/21/68	65	3		5 **Season Of The Witch, Pt. 1**...*Pt. 2*	$10		Atco 6632
				written by **Donovan**; all of above produced by Shadow Morton			
3/8/69	68	5		6 **Shotgun**...*Good, Good Livin'*	$10		Atco 6655
				VANILLA ICE LP '90			
				Born Robert Van Winkle on 10/31/68 in Miami Lakes, Florida. White rapper. Starred in the movie *Cool As Ice*.			
9/8/90	❶1	21	▲	1 **Ice Ice Baby** S:❶4 / A:❶2 *Play That Funky Music*	$3	▮V	SBK 07335
				bass line sampled from "Under Pressure" by **Queen** & **David Bowie**			
12/8/90+	4	17	●	2 **Play That Funky Music**...S:2 / A:11 *Go Ill*	$3	▮V	SBK 07339
				"45" issued for above 2 on SBK 57394			
2/2/91	69A	3		3 **Satisfaction**...			album cut
				lead guitar riff sampled from "(I Can't Get No) Satisfaction" by **The Rolling Stones**; from the album *Hooked* on Ultra/Ichiban 4019			
2/23/91	52	7		4 **I Love You**...S:66 *Stop That Train*	$4	▮	SBK 07346
				VANILLA ICE Introducing Riff			
10/12/91	81	4		5 **Cool As Ice (Everybody Get Loose)**...*(2 versions)*	$4	▮	SBK 07369
				VANILLA ICE Featuring Naomi Campbell			
				from the movie *Cool As Ice* starring Vanilla Ice and Kristin Minter			
				VANITY R&B/BUB/LP '86			
				Born Denise Mathews on 1/3/63 in Niagara Falls, Ontario, Canada. Lead singer of Vanity 6 (assembled by **Prince**). Model/actress. Acted in the movies *The Last Dragon*, *52 Pick-Up*, *Action Jackson* and *Highlander II*. Married pro football player Anthony Smith on 3/26/95.			
9/8/84	75	7		1 **Pretty Mess**...*(instrumental)*	$4	■	Motown 1752
4/19/86	56	7		2 **Under The Influence**...*Wild Animal*	$4	■	Motown 1833
				VANITY FARE '70			
				Pop group from England: Trevor Brice (vocals), Tony Goulden (guitar), Barry Landeman (piano), Tony Jarrett (bass) and Dick Allix (drums).			
11/22/69+	12	13		1 **Early In The Morning**...*You Made Me Love You*	$8		Page One 21,027
3/21/70	5	22	●	2 **Hitchin' A Ride**...*Man Child*	$8		Page One 21,029
8/29/70	98	2		3 **(I Remember) Summer Morning**...*Megowd (Something Tells Me)*	$7		Page One 21,033
				VANN, Teddy BUB '61			
				Black singer/songwriter/producer. Wrote "Love Power" by **The Sandpebbles**. Also see **Tender Slim**.			
6/5/61	76	4		**The Lonely Crowd**...*I Was Born To Love You*	$15	⊙	Columbia 41996
				VANNELLI, Gino AC/LP '81			
				Born on 6/16/52 in Montreal, Quebec, Canada. Pop singer/songwriter. His brother Ross produced **Earth, Wind & Fire**, **Howard Hewett** and **The California Raisins**.			
				1)I Just Wanna Stop 2)Living Inside Myself 3)People Gotta Move			
9/21/74	22	13		1 **People Gotta Move**...*Son Of A New York Gun*	$5		A&M 1614
9/11/76	64	8		2 **Love Of My Life**...*Omens Of Love*	$5	■	A&M 1861
9/9/78	4	21		3 **I Just Wanna Stop** *The Surest Things Can Change*	$5	■	A&M 2072
2/17/79	78	5		4 **Wheels Of Life**...*Mardi Gras*	$5	■	A&M 2114
				picture sleeve is a foldout poster			
3/21/81	6	20		5 **Living Inside Myself**...*Stay With Me*	$4	■	Arista 0588
7/4/81	41	10		6 **Nightwalker**...*Sally (She Says The Sweetest Things)*	$4	■	Arista 0613
3/6/82	89	3		7 **The Longer You Wait**...*Bandito*	$4	■	Arista 0664
5/4/85	42	16		8 **Black Cars**...*Imagination*	$3	■	HME 04889
9/21/85	57	12		9 **Hurts To Be In Love**...*Here She Comes*	$3	■	CBS Associated 05586
4/18/87	55	15		10 **Wild Horses**...*Shape Me Like A Man*	$3	■	CBS Associated 06699

DEBUT	PEAK	WKS	Gold	A-side (Chart Hit)...B-side	$	Sym	Label & Number
				VANWARMER, Randy C&W/LP '79			
				Born Randall Van Wormer on 3/30/55 in Indian Hills, Colorado. Pop singer/songwriter/guitarist.			
3/24/79	**4**	20	●	1 **Just When I Needed You Most** ...AC[2] *Your Light*	$5		Bearsville 0334
8/2/80	**77**	3		2 **Whatever You Decide** ...*Doesn't Matter Anymore*	$4		Bearsville 49258
6/20/81	**55**	8		3 **Suzi**...*Babel*	$4		Bearsville 49752
				VAPORS, The ROK/LP '80			
				Pub-rock group from Guildford, Surrey, England: David Fenton (vocals), Ed Bazalgette (guitar), Steve Smith (bass) and Howard Smith (drums).			
9/27/80	**36**	17		**Turning Japanese** ...*Talk Talk* also released on Liberty 1364 in 1980	$4		United Artists 1364
				VASEL, Marianne, & Erich Storz '58			
				German yodeling duo.			
5/5/58	**46**	7		**The Little Train (Die Kleine Bimmelbahn)** ...S:46 / T:49 *Sunny Lane Walk* [F]	$15		Mercury 71286
				VASSAR, Phil LP '00			
				Born on 5/28/65 in Lynchburg, Virginia. Country singer/songwriter.			
3/4/00	**45**	20		1 **Carlene** ...A:37		V	album cut
9/30/00	**35**	20		2 **Just Another Day In Paradise** CW[1] A:26		V	album cut
4/28/01	**78**	4		3 **Rose Bouquet**...A:73 "45" issued for above 2 on Arista 69037		V	album cut
8/11/01	**56**	10		4 **Six-Pack Summer**...A:52 "45" issued for #1 & 4 on Arista 69084		V	album cut
2/23/02	**37**	20		5 **That's When I Love You**...A:36 all of above from the album *Phil Vassar* on Arista 18891			album cut
8/24/02	**48**	15		6 **American Child**...A:46 from the album *American Child* on Arista 67048			album cut
				VAUGHAN, Frankie '58			
				Born Frank Abelson on 2/3/28 in Liverpool, England. Died of heart failure on 9/17/99 (age 71). Popular entertainer in England. In movie *Let's Make Love* (1960). In London cast of *42nd Street* in 1985.			
7/28/58	**22**	1		**Judy** ...A:22 / H:100 *Am I Wasting My Time On You* Mark Jeffrey (orch.)	$20		Epic 9273
	★305★			**VAUGHAN, Sarah** MEM/POP/BUB/R&B/AC/LP '55			
				Born on 3/27/24 in Newark, New Jersey. Died of cancer on 4/3/90 (age 66). Jazz singer. Dubbed "The Divine One." Studied piano from 1931-39. Won amateur contest at the Apollo Theater in 1942, which led to her joining Earl Hines's band as vocalist/second pianist. First recorded solo for Continental in 1944. With **Billy Eckstine** from 1944-45. Married manager/trumpeter George Treadwell in 1947. Later husbands included pro football player Clyde Atkins and trumpeter Waymon Reed. Performed into the 1980s. Won Grammy's Lifetime Achievement Award in 1989. *1)Make Yourself Comfortable 2)Whatever Lola Wants 3)Broken-Hearted Melody 4)C'est La Vie 5)How Important Can It Be?*			
11/27/54+	**6**	15		1 **Make Yourself Comfortable** A:6 / S:8 / J:8 *Idle Gossip*	$15		Mercury 70469
2/26/55	**12**	9		2 **How Important Can It Be?**...A:12 / S:18 / J:20 *Waltzing Down The Aisle*	$15		Mercury 70534
4/23/55	**6**	11		3 **Whatever Lola Wants**...A:6 / J:9 / S:12 *Oh Yeah* from the Broadway musical *Damn Yankees* starring Gwen Verdon	$15		Mercury 70595
7/16/55	**14**	1		4 **Experience Unnecessary**...A:14 *Slowly With Feeling*	$15		Mercury 70646
11/19/55	**11**	15		5 **C'est La Vie** ...A:11 / T:22 *Never*	$15		Mercury 70727
2/11/56	**13**	19		6 **Mr. Wonderful** ...A:13 / T:38 *You Ought To Have A Wife* from the Broadway musical starring **Sammy Davis Jr.**	$15		Mercury 70777
6/9/56	**92**	2		7 **Hot And Cold Running Tears** ...T:92 *That's Not The Kind Of Love I Want*	$12		Mercury 70846
7/14/56	**19**	14		8 **Fabulous Character** / A:19 / T:27			
8/4/56	**86**	1		9 **The Other Woman** ...T:86	$12		Mercury 70885
10/6/56	**72**	9		10 **It Happened Again** ...T:72 *I Wanna Play House*	$12		Mercury 70947
12/29/56+	**19**	14		11 **The Banana Boat Song**...A:19 / T:31 *I've Got A New Heartache*	$12		Mercury 71020
3/2/57	**91**	1		12 **Leave It To Love** ...T:91 *The Bashful Matador*	$12		Mercury 71030
7/29/57	**82**	7		13 **Passing Strangers** ...T:82 *The Door Is Open* **SARAH VAUGHAN & BILLY ECKSTINE**	$12		Mercury 71122
5/4/59	**96**	1		14 **Separate Ways**...*Careless*	$12		Mercury 71433
7/20/59	**7**	19	●	15 **Broken-Hearted Melody** ...*Misty* (#106)	$12		Mercury 71477
11/2/59	**44**	9		16 **Smooth Operator**...*Maybe It's Because (I Love You Too Much)*	$12		Mercury 71519
2/8/60	**41**	8		17 **Eternally** / Charlie Chaplin penned melody, originally known as "Terry's Theme" from the 1952 movie *Limelight* starring Chaplin			
2/15/60	**87**	2		18 **You're My Baby**...	$12		Mercury 71562
10/10/60	**82**	6		19 **Serenata** ...*Let's* written as an instrumental in 1949 by Leroy Anderson	$10		Roulette 4285
4/2/66	**63**	6		20 **A Lover's Concerto** ...*First Thing Every Morning* adapted from Bach's *Minuet From The Anna Magdalena Notebook*; Vaughan's musical arrangers and conductors: **David Carroll** (#11), Luchi DeJesus (#20), **Ray Ellis** (#14), Belford Hendricks (#15-18), Hal Mooney (#7, 12), **Hugo** Peretti (#1-6, 8-10) and **Joe Reisman** (#19)	$8		Mercury 72543
				VAUGHAN BROTHERS, The ROK/LP '90			
				Blues-rock duo from Dallas, Texas: brothers Jimmie and Stevie Ray Vaughan. Jimmie was the lead guitarist of **The Fabulous Thunderbirds**. Stevie, the lead guitarist of own band, Double Trouble, was killed in a helicopter crash on 8/27/90 (age 35) after a concert at Alpine Valley, Wisconsin.			
10/20/90	**65**	9		**Tick Tock** ...*Brothers* "45": CBS Associated 73576	$5	▮V	Epic/Associated 73576

DEBUT	PEAK	WKS	Gold	A-side (Chart Hit)..........B-side	$	Sym	Label & Number

VAUGHN, Billy, and His Orchestra ★167★ BUB/AC/POP/LP '55

Born Richard Vaughn on 4/12/19 in Glasgow, Kentucky. Died of cancer on 9/26/91 (age 72). Organized **The Hilltoppers** vocal group in 1952. Music director for Dot Records. Arranger/conductor for **Pat Boone**, **Gale Storm**, **The Fontane Sisters** and many other Dot artists. Vaughn had more pop hits than any other orchestra leader during the rock era.

1)Melody Of Love 2)The Shifting Whispering Sands 3)Sail Along Silvery Moon 4)Raunchy 5)A Swingin' Safari

DEBUT	PEAK	WKS	Gold	A-side (Chart Hit)..........B-side	$	Sym	Label & Number
12/11/54+	2^1	27	●	1 **Melody Of Love** S:2 / A:2 / J:3 *Joy Ride* [I]	$15		Dot 15247
				music written in 1903; lyrics added in 1954 by **Tom Glazer**; above version inspired by the 1940 Wayne King arrangement on Victor 26695			
9/24/55	5	15		2 **The Shifting Whispering Sands Parts 1 & 2**..........A:5 / S:5 / T:5 / J:10 [S]	$15		Dot 15409
				Ken Nordine (narration); written in 1950			
2/4/56	37	13		3 **A Theme From (The Three Penny Opera) "Moritat" /** T:37 [I]			
				written in 1928; also known as "Mack The Knife"			
2/11/56	76	1		4 **Little Boy Blue**..........T:76 [S]	$15		Dot 15444
				Ken Nordine narrates the famous 1891 poem by Eugene Fields			
9/8/56	18	10		5 **When The White Lilacs Bloom Again**..........J:18 / A:21 / T:22 *Spanish Diary* [I]	$12		Dot 15491
				written in 1928			
12/15/56	83	3		6 **Petticoats Of Portugal**..........T:83 *La La Colette* [I]	$12		Dot 15506
4/13/57	95	1		7 **The Ship That Never Sailed**..........T:95 *Song Of The Nairobi Trio* [S]	$12		Dot 15546
				Ken Nordine (narration)			
12/23/57+	5	26	●	8 **Sail Along Silvery Moon /** S:5 / T:5 / A:6 [I]			
				#4 hit for **Bing Crosby** in 1937			
12/2/57	10	22		9 **Raunchy**..........A:10 / S:25 / T:33 [I]	$10		Dot 15661
4/7/58	30	11		10 **Tumbling Tumbleweeds /** S:30 / T:35 [I]			
				#13 hit for the Sons of The Pioneers in 1934			
4/14/58	77	4		11 **Trying**..........T:77 / S:flip [I]	$10		Dot 15710
				new version of **The Hilltoppers**' first hit (with Billy Vaughn) on Dot 15018 (#7) in 1952			
6/30/58	56	5		12 **Singing Hills**..........T:56 *Chimes Of Arcady* [I]	$8		Dot 15771
				#2 hit for **Bing Crosby** in 1940			
8/11/58	20	10		13 **La Paloma**..........S:20 / H:26 *Here Is My Love* [I]	$8		Dot 15795
				Spanish tango written in 1864			
10/20/58	44	10		14 **Cimarron (Roll On)**..........*You're My Baby Doll* [I]	$8	■	Dot 15836
				first appeared in the 1942 movie *Twilight On The Trail* starring William "Hopalong Cassidy" Boyd			
12/29/58+	37	10		15 **Blue Hawaii**..........*Tico Tico* [I]	$8		Dot 15879
				#5 hit for **Bing Crosby** in 1937 (from the movie *Waikiki Wedding* starring Crosby)			
3/30/59	89	1		16 **Hawaiian War Chant**..........*Trade Winds* [I]	$8	■	Dot 15900
				the classic Hawaiian song written in 1936			
4/27/59	82	5		17 **Your Cheatin' Heart**..........*Lights Out* [I]	$8		Dot 15936
				#1 Country hit for Hank Williams in 1953			
6/20/60	19	12		18 **Look For A Star**..........*He'll Have To Go* [I]	$8		Dot 16106
				from the British movie *Circus of Horrors* starring Donald Pleasence			
10/3/60	51	10		19 **The Sundowners**..........*Old Cape Cod* (#111) [I]	$8		Dot 16133
				title song from the movie starring **Robert Mitchum** and Deborah Kerr			
2/6/61	28	8		20 **Wheels /** [I]			
2/20/61	63	6		21 **Orange Blossom Special**.......... [I]	$8		Dot 16174
				bluegrass tune written in 1938			
6/12/61	84	5		22 **Blue Tomorrow**..........*Red Wing* [I]	$8		Dot 16220
9/18/61	61	7		23 **Berlin Melody /** [I]			
10/9/61	73	6		24 **Come September**.......... [I]	$8		Dot 16262
				title song from the movie starring **Bobby Darin** and Sandra Dee			
3/17/62	69	6		25 **Chapel By The Sea**..........*One Love, One Heartache* [I]	$7		Dot 16329
7/21/62	13	12		26 **A Swingin' Safari**..........*Indian Love Call* [I]	$7		Dot 16374
				written by **Bert Kaempfert**; theme song for the original *Match Game* TV quiz show			
4/17/65	94	2		27 **Mexican Pearls**..........*Woodpecker* [I]	$6	■	Dot 16706
1/8/66	77	6		28 **Michelle**..........*Elaine*	$6		Dot 16809
				originally recorded by **The Beatles** in 1965 on their album *Rubber Soul*			

VAUGHN, Denny '56

Born Charles Dennis Vaughn on 12/21/21 in Toronto, Ontario, Canada. Died of cancer on 10/2/72 (age 50). Adult Contemporary singer/songwriter/orchestra leader.

DEBUT	PEAK	WKS	Gold	A-side (Chart Hit)..........B-side	$	Sym	Label & Number
5/19/56	70	4		**Walk Hand In Hand**..........T:70 *Just Sing A Song*	$15		Kapp 143

VEE, Bobby ★111★ BUB/AC/LP '61

Born Robert Velline on 4/30/43 in Fargo, North Dakota. Pop singer. Formed The Shadows (not Cliff Richard's group) with his brother and a friend in 1959. After **Buddy Holly**'s death in a plane crash on 2/3/59, The Shadows filled in on Buddy's next scheduled show in Fargo. First recorded for Soma in 1959. In the movies *Swingin' Along*, *It's Trad Dad*, *Play It Cool*, *C'mon Let's Live A Little* and *Just For Fun*.

1)Take Good Care Of My Baby 2)Run To Him 3)Come Back When You Grow Up 4)The Night Has A Thousand Eyes 5)Devil Or Angel

DEBUT	PEAK	WKS	Gold	A-side (Chart Hit)..........B-side	$	Sym	Label & Number
8/31/59	77	4		1 **Suzie Baby**..........*Flyin' High*	$30		Liberty 55208
				BOBBY VEE and The Shadows			
				first released on Soma 1110 in 1959 ($75)			
4/4/60	93	2		2 **What Do You Want?**..........*My Love Loves Me*	$20		Liberty 55234

DEBUT	PEAK	WKS	Gold	A-side (Chart Hit)	B-side	$	Sym	Label & Number
				VEE, Bobby — Cont'd				
8/1/60	6	19		3 Devil Or Angel /				
				#3 R&B hit for **The Clovers** in 1956				
9/12/60	81	1		4 Since I Met You Baby		$20	■	Liberty 55270
11/28/60+	6	14		5 Rubber Ball	*Everyday*	$20	■	Liberty 55287
2/13/61	33	7		6 Stayin' In /				
2/27/61	61	5		7 More Than I Can Say		$15	■	Liberty 55296
5/29/61	63	4		8 How Many Tears	*Baby Face (#119)*	$15	■	Liberty 55325
8/7/61	1[3]	15	●	9 Take Good Care Of My Baby	*Bashful Bob*	$15		Liberty 55354
11/13/61	2[1]	15		10 Run To Him /				
11/27/61+	53	9		11 Walkin' With My Angel		$15		Liberty 55388
2/24/62	15	11		12 Please Don't Ask About Barbara /				
2/24/62	92	1		13 I Can't Say Goodbye		$15	■	Liberty 55419
5/19/62	15	10		14 Sharing You	*In My Baby's Eyes*	$15		Liberty 55451
9/1/62	20	8		15 Punish Her /				
9/22/62	99	2		16 Someday (When I'm Gone From You)		$20	■	Liberty 55479
				BOBBY VEE and THE CRICKETS				
12/8/62+	3	14		17 The Night Has A Thousand Eyes	*Anonymous Phone Call (Pop #110)*	$15		Liberty 55521
3/30/63	13	10		18 Charms	*Bobby Tomorrow*	$15	■	Liberty 55530
6/22/63	34	7		19 Be True To Yourself /				
6/29/63	85	2		20 A Letter From Betty		$12	■	Liberty 55581
11/9/63	55	7		21 Yesterday And You (Armen's Theme) /				
12/28/63	99	1		22 Never Love A Robin		$12		Liberty 55636
				The Johnny Mann Singers (backing vocals: #8-11, 13-15, 17-20 & 22)				
1/25/64	83	3		23 Stranger In Your Arms	*1963*	$12	■	Liberty 55654
2/22/64	52	8		24 I'll Make You Mine	*She's Sorry*	$12		Liberty 55670
				BOBBY VEE With The Eligibles				
5/30/64	63	8		25 Hickory, Dick And Doc	*I Wish You Were Mine Again*	$10		Liberty 55700
12/12/64+	84	5		26 (There'll Come A Day When) Ev'ry Little Bit Hurts /				
12/5/64	97	1		27 Pretend You Don't See Her		$10		Liberty 55751
				written by **Steve Allen**				
2/6/65	99	1		28 Cross My Heart	*This Is The End*	$10		Liberty 55761
				all of above (except #1) produced by Snuff Garrett				
5/8/65	85	5		29 Keep On Trying	*You Won't Forget Me*	$10		Liberty 55790
7/9/66	52	8		30 Look At Me Girl	*Save A Love*	$8		Liberty 55877
7/22/67	3	16	●	31 Come Back When You Grow Up	*Swahili Serenade*	$8		Liberty 55964
				also released on Liberty 55982 with "Growing Pains" as the B-side				
11/18/67	37	7		32 Beautiful People	*I May Be Gone*	$8		Liberty 56009
2/10/68	46	6		33 Maybe Just Today	*You're A Big Girl Now*	$8	■	Liberty 56014
				BOBBY VEE And The Strangers (above 4)				
4/20/68	35	9		34 My Girl/Hey Girl	*Just Keep It Up (And See What Happens)*	$7		Liberty 56033
8/31/68	83	4		35 Do What You Gotta Do	*Thank You*	$7		Liberty 56057
12/28/68	98	3		36 I'm Into Lookin' For Someone To Love Me	*Thank You*	$7		Liberty 56080
8/2/69	92	2		37 Let's Call It A Day Girl	*I'm Gonna Make It Up To You*	$7		Liberty 56124
11/21/70	88	3		38 Sweet Sweetheart	*Rock 'N' Roll Music And You*	$7		Liberty 56208
				VEGA, Suzanne ROK '87				
				Born on 7/11/59 in Sacramento, California. Folk-pop singer/songwriter/guitarist. Attended the New York High School of Performing Arts. Married record producer Mitchell Froom (ex-**Gamma**) on 3/17/95.				
6/6/87	3	19		1 Luka	S:2 / A:3 *Night Vision*	$3	■	A&M 2937
				Spanish version issued with a picture sleeve on A&M 35084				
9/12/87	94	3		2 Solitude Standing	*Tom's Diner*	$4	■	A&M 2960
10/6/90	5	21	●	3 Tom's Diner	S:2 / A:9 *(12" version)*	$3	■V	A&M 1529
				D.N.A. Featuring SUZANNE VEGA				
				remix by D.N.A. (2 DJs from Bristol, England) of Vega's original acappella recording (B-side of #2 above); "45": A&M Collectables 8699				
				VEJTABLES, The BUB '65				
				Rock group from San Francisco, California: Bob Bailey (vocals), Bob Cole (guitar), Ned Hollis (organ), Rick Dey (bass) and Jan Ashton (drums). One of the few rock groups with a female drummer.				
10/23/65	84	4		I Still Love You	*Anything*	$12		Autumn 15
				VELAIRES, The '61				
				Rock and roll group: Bob Dawdy, Danny Matousek, Jerry De Mers and Don Bourret. Originally known as The Screamers and then The Flairs. Changed name to avoid confusion with The Flares.				
8/14/61	51	7		Roll Over Beethoven	*Brazil*	$20		Jamie 1198
				first released on Palms 726 as by The Flairs ($50)				
				VELOURS, The '57				
				R&B vocal group from Brooklyn, New York: Jerome Ramos (lead), John Cheetom, Don Haywood, John Pearson and Charles Moffett. Also see **The Fantastics**.				
7/8/57	83	4		1 Can I Come Over Tonight	T:83 *Where There's A Will (There's A Way)*	$200		Onyx 512
3/17/58	83	3		2 Remember	T:83 *Can I Walk You Home*	$100		Onyx 520
				also released on Orbit 9001 ($60) in 1958; Sammy Lowe (orch., above 2)				
				VELS, The '85				
				Techno-rock/dance trio: Alice DeSoto, Chris Larkin and Charles Hanson.				
2/23/85	72	6		Look My Way	*Can't You Hear Me?*	$4		Mercury 880547
				VELVELETTES, The R&B/BUB '64				
				Female R&B vocal group from Detroit, Michigan: sisters Millie and Carol "Cal" Gill, cousins Bertha and Norma Barbee, and Betty Kelly (member of **Martha & The Vandellas**, 1964-67).				
10/17/64	45	8		1 Needle In A Haystack	*Should I Tell Them*	$25		V.I.P. 25007
1/30/65	64	6		2 He Was Really Sayin' Somthin'	*Throw A Farewell Kiss*	$25		V.I.P. 25013

DEBUT	PEAK	WKS	Gold	A-side (Chart Hit) ... B-side	$	Sym	Label & Number

VELVET, Jimmy
BUB '64

Born James Tennant in Memphis, Tennessee. Pop singer.

DEBUT	PEAK	WKS	Gold	A-side (Chart Hit) ... B-side	$	Sym	Label & Number
12/14/63+	75	7		1 **We Belong Together** ... *The History Of Love* released on Velvet 201 ($75) in 1961 by a different artist named Jimmy Velvit (James Mullins from Dallas) who, from 1976-77, recorded country music as Jimmy Velvet	$20		ABC-Paramount 10488
5/29/65	93	3		2 **It's Almost Tomorrow** ... *Blue Eyes (Don't Run Away)* first released on Velvet Tone 102 in 1964 ($25)	$15		Philips 40285

VELVETS, The
BUB '61

R&B doo-wop group from Odessa, Texas: Virgil Johnson, Will Soloman, Mark Prince, Clarence Rigby and Bob Thursby. Rigby died in a car crash in 1978.

DEBUT	PEAK	WKS	Gold	A-side (Chart Hit) ... B-side	$	Sym	Label & Number
5/29/61	26	9		1 **Tonight (Could Be The Night)** ... *Spring Fever*	$30		Monument 441
10/9/61	90	1		2 **Laugh** ... *Lana* written by **Roy Orbison**	$30		Monument 448

VENETIANS, The
'87

Rock group from Australia: Rick Swinn (vocals), Dave Skeet (guitar), Matt Hughes (keyboards), Pete Watson (bass) and Tim Powles (drums).

DEBUT	PEAK	WKS	Gold	A-side (Chart Hit) ... B-side	$	Sym	Label & Number
2/28/87	88	5		**So Much For Love** ... *Let It All Go*	$3	■	Chrysalis 43056

VENGABOYS
LP '99

Dance group assembled by Spanish producers Danski and DJ Delmundo: Kim, Robin, Deniece and Roy. Pronounced: bengaboys.

DEBUT	PEAK	WKS	Gold	A-side (Chart Hit) ... B-side	$	Sym	Label & Number
2/13/99	26	20		1 **We Like To Party!** ... S:17 / A:47 *(no B-side)*	$5	★	Groovilicious 071
8/7/99	84	6		2 **Boom, Boom, Boom, Boom!!** ... S:27 *(6 remixes)*	$8	★*	Groovilicious 089

VENTURES, The
★470★ BUB/AC/LP '60

Instrumental group from Seattle, Washington: guitarists Nokie Edwards (bass; born on 5/9/35), Bob Bogle (lead; born on 1/16/34) and Don Wilson (rhythm; born on 2/10/33), with drummer Howie Johnson. First recorded for own Blue Horizon label in 1959. Johnson suffered serious injuries in a 1961 car accident; replaced by Mel Taylor (born on 9/24/33). Taylor formed Mel Taylor & The Dynamics in 1973; returned in 1978. Edwards left in 1967; replaced by Gerry McGee. Edwards returned in 1972 and then left again in 1985. Added keyboardist John Durrill in 1969. Latest recordings featured Bogle, Wilson, Taylor and McGee. Group still active into the '00s; extremely popular in Japan. Johnson died in January 1988 (age 50). Taylor died of cancer and heart failure on 8/11/96 (age 62); his son, Leon Taylor, is now the drummer with the group. Charted 38 albums, 1960-72.

1)Walk -- Don't Run 2)Hawaii Five-O 3)Walk-Don't Run '64

DEBUT	PEAK	WKS	Gold	A-side (Chart Hit) ... B-side	$	Sym	Label & Number
7/18/60	2[1]	18		1 **Walk -- Don't Run** *Home* [I] first released on Blue Horizon 101 ($1500) in 1959; written by jazz guitarist Johnny Smith; also released with "The McCoy" as the B-side	$25		Dolton 25
10/31/60	15	13		2 **Perfidia** ... *No Trespassing* [I] #3 hit for Xavier Cugat in 1941	$20	■	Dolton 28
1/23/61	29	9		3 **Ram-Bunk-Shush** ... *Lonely Heart* [I] #10 R&B hit for **Bill Doggett** in 1957	$20		Dolton 32
4/24/61	69	5		4 **Lullaby Of The Leaves** ... *Ginchy* [I] #1 hit for George Olsen and his Music in 1932	$20		Dolton 41
8/28/61	83	3		5 **(Theme From) Silver City** ... *Bluer Than Blue* [I] **Hank Levine** (orchestral backing and the song's writer)	$20		Dolton 44
10/23/61	54	6		6 **Blue Moon** ... *Lady Of Spain* [I] #1 hit for Glen Gray & The Casa Loma Orchestra in 1935	$20		Dolton 47
8/4/62	61	7		7 **Lolita Ya-Ya** ... *Lucille* [I] co-written by **Nelson Riddle**; theme from the movie *Lolita* starring Sue Lyon (Lolita) and Peter Sellers	$20		Dolton 60
12/29/62+	91	4		8 **The 2,000 Pound Bee (Part 2)** ... *(Part 1)* [I]	$20		Dolton 67
7/11/64	8	11		9 **Walk-Don't Run '64** ... *The Cruel Sea* [I-R] new version of #1 above	$15	■	Dolton 96
10/24/64	35	7		10 **Slaughter On Tenth Avenue** ... *Rap City (#135)* [I] written by Richard Rodgers in 1936; #19 hit for Lennie Hayton in 1949	$15	■	Dolton 300
1/30/65	70	3		11 **Diamond Head** ... *Lonely Girl* [I]	$15		Dolton 303
2/26/66	54	7		12 **Secret Agent Man** ... *007-11* [I] theme from the CBS-TV series *Secret Agent* starring Patrick McGoohan	$15		Dolton 316
3/8/69	4	14		13 **Hawaii Five-O** ... *Soul Breeze* [I] theme from the TV series starring Jack Lord	$8		Liberty 56068
6/28/69	83	5		14 **Theme From "A Summer Place"** ... *A Summer Love* [I] title song from the 1959 movie starring Troy Donahue and Sandra Dee	$8		Liberty 56115

VENUS, Vik
'69

Born Jack Spector on 9/15/28 in Brooklyn, New York. Died of a heart attack on 3/8/94 (age 65). Popular New York radio personality.

DEBUT	PEAK	WKS	Gold	A-side (Chart Hit) ... B-side	$	Sym	Label & Number
6/14/69	38	10		**Moonflight** *[VIK VENUS Alias: Your Main Moon Man]* ... *Everybody's On Strike* [N] a **Dickie Goodman**-type recording of "bubblegum" hits	$10		Buddah 118

VERA, Billy
BUB/AC/C&W/LP '87

Born William McCord on 5/28/44 in Riverside, California; raised in Westchester County, New York. Wrote hit songs for many pop, R&B and country artists. In the movies *Buckaroo Banzai* and *The Doors*, and the HBO movie *Baja Oklahoma*. Formed The Beaters (an R&B-based, 10-piece band) in Los Angeles in 1979.

DEBUT	PEAK	WKS	Gold	A-side (Chart Hit) ... B-side	$	Sym	Label & Number
12/2/67+	54	9		1 **Storybook Children** ... *Really Together*	$10		Atlantic 2445
2/17/68	36	6		2 **Country Girl - City Man** ... *So Good (To Be Together)* **BILLY VERA & JUDY CLAY** (above 2)	$10		Atlantic 2480
<u>6/29/68</u>	43	6		3 **With Pen In Hand** ... *Good Morning Blues*	$10		Atlantic 2526
4/25/81	39	11		4 **I Can Take Care Of Myself** ... *Corner Of The Night* [L] promo copies issued with a foldout poster sleeve in a clear plastic holder	$6	□	Alfa 7002
<u>9/19/81</u>	79	3		5 **At This Moment** ... *Someone Will School You, Someone Will Cool You* [L] **BILLY & THE BEATERS** (above 2) above 2 recorded at the "Roxy" in January 1981	$6	■	Alfa 7005
11/8/86+	❶[2]	21	●	6 **At This Moment** AC[1] S:❶[2] / A:❶[1] *I Can Take Care Of Myself* [L-R] **BILLY VERA & THE BEATERS** re-charted due to play on the TV series *Family Ties* starring Michael J. Fox	$4		Rhino 74403

DEBUT	PEAK	WKS	Gold	A-side (Chart Hit)...B-side	$	Sym	Label & Number
				VERNE, Larry BUB '60 Born Larry Vern Erickson on 2/8/36 in Minneapolis, Minnesota. Photo studio worker-turned-singer by coincidence. A trio of California songwriters (see below) who worked in Verne's building selected him to record "Mr. Custer" because of his Southern drawl.			
8/29/60	❶[1]	13		1 **Mr. Custer**...*Okeefenokee Two Step* [N]	$15		Era 3024
12/19/60	75	3		2 **Mister Livingston**...*Roller Coaster* [N]	$12	■	Era 3034
				above 2 written by **Fred Darian**, **Al DeLory** and Joe Van Winkle			
				VERONICA R&B/BUB '97 Born in 1975 in the Bronx, New York (to Puerto Rican parents). Female R&B-dance singer.			
5/31/97	66	13		**No One But You**...S:63 *(remix)*	$4	▮	H.O.L.A. 341014
				VERONICA Featuring Craig Mack from the movie *BAPS* starring Halle Berry			
				VERTICAL HOLD '93 R&B vocal trio: Willie Bruno, David Bright and **Angie Stone** (former member of Sequence).			
6/19/93	73[A]	1		**Seems You're Much Too Busy**...BUB:108 *(remix)*	$5	▮	A&M 0140
				VERTICAL HORIZON ROK/LP '00 Rock group from Boston, Massachusetts: Matt Scannell (vocals), Keith Kane (guitar), Sean Hurley (bass) and Ed Toth (drums).			
1/22/00	❶[1]	41		1 **Everything You Want**...S:2 / A:2 *The Man Who Would Be Santa*	$4	★[V]	RCA 65981
8/26/00	23	21		2 **You're A God**...A:17		V	album cut
				"45" issued for above 2 on RCA 60231			
3/3/01	58	16		3 **Best I Ever Had (Grey Sky Morning)**...A:60			album cut
				all of above from the album *Everything You Want* on RCA 67818			
				VERUCA SALT ROK/LP '94 Rock group from Chicago, Illinois: Nina Gordon and Louise Post (vocals, guitar), with Steven Lack (bass) and Jim Shapiro (drums). Name taken from a character in the children's book *Charlie and The Chocolate Factory*.			
10/22/94+	53[A]	12		1 **Seether**...			album cut
				from the album *American Thighs* on Minty Fresh 24732			
2/22/97	59[A]	14		2 **Volcano Girls**...			album cut
				from the album *Eight Arms To Hold You* on Outpost 30001			
				VERVE, The ROK/LP '98 Rock group from Wigan, England: Richard Ashcroft (vocals), Nick McCabe (guitar), Simon Jones (bass) and Peter Salisbury (drums).			
3/28/98	12	20		**Bitter Sweet Symphony**...A:15 / S:17 *Lord I Guess I'll Never Know / So Sister / Echo Bass*	$3	▮	Hut/Virgin 38634
				theme song to a Nike shoes advertising campaign; samples an orchestral version of **The Rolling Stones**' "The Last Time" performed by The Andrew Loog Oldham Orchestra			
				VERVE PIPE, The ROK/LP '97 Rock group from East Lansing, Michigan: brothers Brian (vocals) and Brad (bass) Vander Ark, A.J. Dunning (guitar), Doug Corella (keyboards) and Donny Brown (drums).			
4/27/96	53[A]	11		1 **Photograph**...			album cut
2/22/97	5	42	●	2 **The Freshmen**...MR[3] S:8 / A:8 *(remix)*	$3	▮	RCA 64734
				above 2 from the album *Villains* on RCA 66809			
				VESTA R&B/LP '89 Born Vesta Williams in Coshocton, Ohio; raised in Los Angeles, California. Female R&B singer.			
9/9/89	55	8		**Congratulations**...*Once Bitten Twice Shy* (R&B #9/'86)	$3		A&M 1407
				VÍA, Angela BUB '00 Born on 12/29/81 in Raymondville, Texas; raised in Gresham, Oregon. Latin teen pop singer/songwriter.			
4/22/00	27[S]	20		1 **Picture Perfect**...BUB:125 *(4 album snippets)*	$4	★[V]	Lava/Atlantic 84621
				"45" B-side: (Spanish version)			
10/28/00	74[S]	2		2 **I Don't Care**...*A Good Time*	$5	★[+]	Lava/Atlantic 84933
				VIBRATIONS, The BUB/R&B '61 R&B vocal group from Los Angeles, California: James Johnson, Carlton Fisher, Richard Owens, Dave Govan and Don Bradley. Originally recorded as **The Jayhawks** (see #1 below) (Johnson, Fisher, Govan and Carver Bunkum). Also recorded the hit "Peanut Butter" as **The Marathons** (see #3 below). Owens joined **The Temptations** for a short time in 1971.			
6/30/56	18	11		1 **Stranded In The Jungle** S:18 / T:29 *My Only Darling* [N]	$40		Flash 109
				THE JAYHAWKS			
2/20/61	25	8		2 **The Watusi**...*Wallflower*	$25		Checker 969
				tune is similar to **Hank Ballard & The Midnighters**' "Let's Go, Let's Go, Let's Go"			
4/24/61	20	12		3 **Peanut Butter**...*Talkin' Trash*	$25		Arvee 5027
				THE MARATHONS same tune (different lyrics) as **The Olympics**' 1960 hit "(Baby) Hully Gully"; re-recorded on Argo 5389 in 1961 and labeled as: **"Vibrations Named by Others As MARATHONS"** ($20) and as **"Vibrations Recorded as MARATHONS"** ($20)			
3/28/64	26	9		4 **My Girl Sloopy**...*Daddy Woo-Woo*	$20		Atlantic 2221
				original title of "Hang On Sloopy" by **The McCoys**			
10/23/65	63	7		5 **Misty**...*Finding Out The Hard Way*	$15		Okeh 7230
				introduced by the Erroll Garner Trio in 1954			
4/20/68	93	2		6 **Love In Them There Hills**...*Remember The Rain*	$15		Okeh 7311
				VICIOUS '95 Born in Brooklyn, New York. Pre-teen male black rapper/dancehall singer.			
1/14/95	69	11		**Nika**...S:41 *(2 versions) / (3 album snippets)*	$4	▮	Epic Street 77804
				samples "Between The Sheets" by **The Isley Brothers**			
				VIDAL, Maria '84 Dance singer; formerly with **Desmond Child & Rouge**.			
9/8/84	48	12		**Body Rock**...*Do You Know Who I Am* (**Ashford & Simpson**)	$4	■	EMI America 8233
				main title from the movie starring **Lorenzo Lamas**			
				VIDELS, The '60 Pop vocal group from Providence, Rhode Island, featuring Pete Anders and Vinnie Poncia. Also see **The Trade Winds**.			
6/13/60	73	3		**Mister Lonely**...*I'll Forget You*	$30		JDS 5004

DEBUT	PEAK	WKS	Gold	A-side (Chart Hit)...B-side	$	Sym	Label & Number

VIGRASS & OSBORNE — AC '72

Folk-rock duo from England: Paul Vigrass and Gary Osborne.

DEBUT	PEAK	WKS	Gold	A-side (Chart Hit)...B-side	$	Sym	Label & Number
6/17/72	65	7		Men Of Learning ... *Forever Autumn*	$6		Uni 55330

VILLAGE PEOPLE — BUB/LP '79

Disco vocal group formed in New York: Victor Willis (policeman), Randy Jones (cowboy), David Hodo (construction worker), Felipe Rose (Indian chief), Glenn Hughes (biker) and Alexander Briley (G.I.). Willis replaced by Ray Simpson (brother of **Valerie Simpson** of **Ashford & Simpson**) in late 1979. Formed by French producer Jacques Morali (died of AIDS on 11/15/91, age 44). Appeared in the movie *Can't Stop The Music* (1980). Hughes died of cancer on 3/4/2001 (age 50).

DEBUT	PEAK	WKS	Gold	A-side (Chart Hit)...B-side	$	Sym	Label & Number
6/24/78	25	15	●	1 Macho Man ... *Key West*	$5		Casablanca 922
10/21/78+	2[3]	26	▲	2 Y.M.C.A. *The Women*	$5		Casablanca 945
3/17/79	3	18	●	3 In The Navy ... *Manhattan Woman*	$5	□	Casablanca 973
5/26/79	45	9		4 Go West ... *Citizens Of The World*	$5		Casablanca 984
11/3/79	52	9		5 Ready For The 80's ... *Sleazy*	$4		Casablanca 2220

VILLAGE SOUL CHOIR, The — '70

Ten-member, interracial group from Jamaica, Queens, New York. Managed by former opera singer Charles Matthews.

DEBUT	PEAK	WKS	Gold	A-side (Chart Hit)...B-side	$	Sym	Label & Number
2/21/70	55	10		The Cat Walk ... *The Country Walk*	$10		Abbott 2010

VILLAGE STOMPERS, The — BUB/AC/LP '63

Dixieland-styled band from Greenwich Village, New York: Dick Brady, Ralph Casale, Don Coates, Frank Hubbell, Mitchell May, Joe Muranyi, Al McManus and Lenny Pogan.

DEBUT	PEAK	WKS	Gold	A-side (Chart Hit)...B-side	$	Sym	Label & Number
9/21/63	2[1]	14		1 Washington Square ... AC[3] *Turkish Delight* [I]	$10	■	Epic 9617
4/25/64	81	6		2 From Russia With Love ... *The Bridges Of Budapest* [I] title song from the James Bond movie starring Sean Connery	$7		Epic 9674
12/5/64	97	2		3 Fiddler On The Roof ... *Moonlight On The Ganges* [I] title song from the Broadway musical starring Zero Mostel	$7		Epic 9740

VINCENT, Gene, and His Blue Caps — LP '56

Born Vincent Eugene Craddock on 2/11/35 in Norfolk, Virginia. Died of a bleeding ulcer on 10/12/71 (age 36). Innovative rock and roll singer/songwriter/guitarist. Injured left leg in motorcycle accident in 1953; had to wear steel brace thereafter. Formed the Blue Caps in Norfolk in 1956. Appeared in the movies *The Girl Can't Help It* and *Hot Rod Gang*. To England from 1960-67. Injured in car crash that killed **Eddie Cochran** in England in 1960. Inducted into the Rock and Roll Hall of Fame in 1998.

DEBUT	PEAK	WKS	Gold	A-side (Chart Hit)...B-side	$	Sym	Label & Number
6/16/56	7	20		1 Be-Bop-A-Lula S:7 / T:9 / J:10 / A:11 *Woman Love* promo record issued with a special half sleeve ("Capitol Introduces") and with a black-and-white insert featuring a photo of Vincent	$50	⊙	Capitol 3450
10/20/56	96	1		2 Race With The Devil ... T:96 *Gonna Back Up Baby*	$50		Capitol 3530
10/27/56	34[CU]	2		3 Bluejean Bop ... *Who Slapped John*	$50		Capitol 3558
8/19/57	13	19		4 Lotta Lovin' / S:13 / T:14 / A:18			
9/23/57		7		5 Wear My Ring ... S:flip co-written by **Bobby Darin**; insert has the same format as #1 above	$50	⊙	Capitol 3763
12/9/57+	23	9		6 Dance To The Bop ... A:23 / T:43 / S:44 *I Got It*	$50		Capitol 3839

VINTON, Bobby ★41★ — AC/BUB/C&W/LP '64

Born Stanley Robert Vinton on 4/16/35 in Canonsburg, Pennsylvania. Father was a bandleader. Formed own band while in high school; toured as leader of the backing band for Dick Clark's "Caravan of Stars" in 1960. Left band for a singing career in 1962. Own musical variety TV series from 1975-78. Dubbed "The Polish Prince."

1)Roses Are Red 2)There! I've Said It Again 3)Blue Velvet 4)Mr. Lonely 5)My Melody Of Love

DEBUT	PEAK	WKS	Gold	A-side (Chart Hit)...B-side	$	Sym	Label & Number
6/9/62	❶[4]	15	●	1 Roses Are Red (My Love) AC[4] *You And I* written by **Paul Evans**; issued with 2 different commercial picture sleeves and a special promotional sleeve	$12	■	Epic 9509
8/11/62	38	9		2 I Love You The Way You Are ... *You're My Girl* (Chuck & Johnny)	$15		Diamond 121
8/25/62	12	11		3 Rain Rain Go Away ... *Over And Over*	$10	■	Epic 9532
12/8/62+	33	9		4 Trouble Is My Middle Name /			
12/1/62+	38	9		5 Let's Kiss And Make Up ... also issued with a promotional picture sleeve	$10	■	Epic 9561
3/9/63	21	10		6 Over The Mountain (Across The Sea) ... *Faded Pictures*	$10	■	Epic 9577
5/18/63	3	13		7 Blue On Blue ... *Those Little Things*	$10	■	Epic 9593
8/10/63	❶[3]	15		8 Blue Velvet ... AC[8] *Is There A Place (Where I Can Go)* #16 hit for **Tony Bennett** in 1951	$10	■	Epic 9614
11/30/63+	❶[4]	13		9 There! I've Said It Again ... AC[5] *The Girl With The Bow In Her Hair* #1 hit for **Vaughn Monroe** in 1945; song introduced in 1941 by the Benny Carter Orch. (Bluebird 11090)	$10	■	Epic 9638
12/14/63	9[X]	3		10 Songs Of Christmas [EP] ... [X] 4-song EP: Silver Bells/White Christmas/O Holy Night/The Christmas Song (Chestnuts Roasting On An Open Fire)	$20	■	Epic EG 7215
2/29/64	9	9		11 My Heart Belongs To Only You ... *Warm And Tender* introduced by June Christy in 1953	$10	■	Epic 9662
5/23/64	13	8		12 Tell Me Why ... *Remembering* #2 hit for **The Four Aces** in 1952	$8	■	Epic 9687
8/8/64	17	8		13 Clinging Vine ... *Imagination Is A Magic Dream*	$8	■	Epic 9705
10/31/64	❶[1]	15		14 Mr. Lonely ... *It's Better To Have Loved* recorded in 1962 using the same music track as the **Buddy Greco** 1962 hit version on Epic; also issued with a promotional text sleeve	$8	■	Epic 9730
12/12/64	8[X]	3		15 Dearest Santa / [X] also issued with "Mr. Lonely" as a back-to-back promotional single with a text sleeve			
12/26/64	23[X]	1		16 The Bell That Couldn't Jingle ... [X]	$10	■	Epic 9741
3/6/65	17	7		17 Long Lonely Nights ... *Satin*	$8	■	Epic 9768
5/8/65	22	8		18 L-O-N-E-L-Y ... *Graduation Tears*	$8	■	Epic 9791
7/10/65	61	5		19 Theme From "Harlow" (Lonely Girl) ... *If I Should Lose Your Love* from the movie *Harlow* starring Carroll Baker	$8	■	Epic 9814
9/18/65	38	7		20 What Color (Is A Man) ... *Love Or Infatuation*	$7		Epic 9846

DEBUT	PEAK	WKS	Gold	A-side (Chart Hit)...B-side	$	Sym	Label & Number
				VINTON, Bobby — Cont'd			
12/4/65+	**23**	10		21 **Satin Pillows** ...*Careless* (#111)	$7	■	Epic 9869
2/26/66	**59**	5		22 **Tears** ...*Go Away Pain*	$7		Epic 9894
				#1 hit in England in 1965 for Ken Dodd ("Bubbled Under" at #107)			
4/30/66	**40**	6		23 **Dum-De-Da** ...*Blue Clarinet*	$7	■	Epic 10014
				song charted in 1964 by **Johnny Tillotson** as "She Understands Me"			
8/6/66	**81**	3		24 **Petticoat White (Summer Sky Blue)** ...*All The King's Horses (And All The King's Men)*	$7	■	Epic 10048
11/19/66+	**11**	12		25 **Coming Home Soldier** ...*Don't Let My Mary Go Around*	$7	■	Epic 10090
3/18/67	**66**	4		26 **For He's A Jolly Good Fellow** ...*Sweet Maria*	$7	■	Epic 10136
				based on the traditional 18th century tune			
5/20/67	**95**	2		27 **Red Roses For Mom** ...*College Town*	$7	■	Epic 10168
9/30/67	**6**	13		28 **Please Love Me Forever** ...*Miss America*	$7	■	Epic 10228
12/30/67+	**24**	8		29 **Just As Much As Ever** ...*Another Memory*	$6	■	Epic 10266
3/30/68	**33**	8		30 **Take Good Care Of My Baby** ...*Strange Sensations*	$6	■	Epic 10305
7/20/68	**23**	7		31 **Halfway To Paradise** ...*Kristie*	$6	■	Epic 10350
				issued with 2 different picture sleeves			
11/2/68	**9**	14	●	32 **I Love How You Love Me** ...*Little Barefoot Boy*	$6	■	Epic 10397
4/5/69	**34**	7		33 **To Know You Is To Love You** ...*The Beat Of My Heart*	$6	■	Epic 10461
6/14/69	**34**	8		34 **The Days Of Sand And Shovels** ...*So Many Lonely Girls*	$6	■	Epic 10485
2/7/70	**46**	9		35 **My Elusive Dreams** ...*Over And Over*	$6	■	Epic 10576
7/11/70	**93**	4		36 **No Arms Can Ever Hold You** ...*I've Got That Lovin' Feelin' (Back Again)*	$6	■	Epic 10629
1/29/72	**24**	16		37 **Every Day Of My Life** ...*You Can Do It To Me Anytime*	$6	■	Epic 10822
				also released as "Ev'ry Day Of My Life"			
6/10/72	**19**	14		38 **Sealed With A Kiss** ...*All My Life*	$6	■	Epic 10861
				first recorded by **The Four Voices** in 1960 on Columbia 41699			
12/30/72+	**82**	6		39 **But I Do** ...*When You Love*	$6	■	Epic 10936
9/21/74	**3**	17	●	40 **My Melody Of Love** ...AC[1] *I'll Be Loving You*	$5		ABC 12022
				sung partially in Polish			
3/15/75	**33**	9		41 **Beer Barrel Polka /**			
				#1 hit for **Will Glahe** in 1939			
3/15/75		9		42 **Dick And Jane** ...	$5		ABC 12056
6/21/75	**58**	5		43 **Wooden Heart** ...*Polka Pose*	$5		ABC 12100
5/1/76	**97**	2		44 **Moonlight Serenade** ...*Why Can't I Get Over You*	$4		ABC 12178
				#3 hit for Glenn Miller in 1939 (Miller's theme song)			
5/29/76	**75**	3		45 **Save Your Kisses For Me** ...*Love Shine*	$4		ABC 12186
6/4/77	**99**	2		46 **Only Love Can Break A Heart** ...*Once More With Feeling*	$4		ABC 12265
				#1, 3-24 & 40-46: produced by Bob Morgan			
1/5/80	**78**	4		47 **Make Believe It's Your First Time** ...*I Remember Loving You*	$5		Tapestry 002
				VIRTUES, The '59			
				Rock and roll instrumental band from Philadelphia, Pennsylvania: Frank "Virtue" Virtuoso (bass), Jimmy Bruno (guitar), John Renner (sax) and Joe Vespe (drums).			
3/9/59	**5**	16		1 **Guitar Boogie Shuffle** ...*Guitar In Orbit* [I]	$25		Hunt 324
				first released on Sure 501 ($80) in 1958; tune based on "Guitar Boogie" by Arthur Smith on MGM 10293 ('49-$25), and on "New Guitar Boogie Shuffle" recorded in 1953 by the Super-Sonics on Rainbow 214 ($40)			
3/24/62	**96**	1		2 **Guitar Boogie Shuffle Twist** ...*Guitar Boogie Stomp* [I-R]	$20		Sure 1733
				new version of #1 above			
				VISAGE, Michelle '93			
				Born Michelle Shupack on 9/20/68 in the Bronx, New York. Black dance singer. Member of **Seduction**. Sidekick on **RuPaul**'s TV talk show in 1996.			
12/1/90	**80**	7		1 **Crash (Have Some Fun)** ...*You Are The One*	$4	▮	Tommy Boy 19527
				TKA (with Michelle Visage)			
11/28/92+	**34**	16		2 **It's Gonna Be A Lovely Day** ...A:21 / S:43 *(2 versions)*	$4	▮	Arista 12486
				THE S.O.U.L. S.Y.S.T.E.M. Introducing Michelle Visage			
				from the movie *The Bodyguard* starring Kevin Costner and **Whitney Houston**; rap version of **Bill Withers**'s 1978 hit "Lovely Day"			
				VISCOUNTS, The BUB/LP '60			
				Rock and roll instrumental group from New Jersey: Harry Haller (tenor sax), brothers Bobby (guitar) and Joe (bass) Spievak, Larry Vecchio (organ) and Clark Smith (drums).			
12/28/59+	**52**	16		1 **Harlem Nocturne** ...*Dig* [I]	$20		Madison 123
				popular jazz intrumental written in 1940; also see #4 below; #24 hit for Herbie Fields & His Orchestra in 1953			
7/18/60	**82**	5		2 **Night Train** ...*Summertime* [I]	$15		Madison 133
				#1 R&B hit for Jimmy Forest in 1952 (riff borrowed from Duke Ellington's 1946 tune "Happy-Go-Lucky Local"); "Bubbled Under" (#122) in 1966 on Amy 949			
12/5/60+	**77**	7		3 **Wabash Blues** ...*So Slow* [I]	$15		Madison 140
				#1 hit for Isham Jones & His Orchestra in 1921			
10/30/65+	**39**	13		4 **Harlem Nocturne** ...*Dig* [I-R]	$15		Amy 940
				same version as #1 above			
				VITAMIN C BUB/LP '99			
				Born Colleen Fitzpatrick on 7/20/72 in Old Bridge, New Jersey. Former lead singer of Eve's Plum. Portrayed "Amber Von Tussle" in the 1988 movie *Hairspray*. Named for her orange hair.			
7/17/99	**18**	14	●	1 **Smile** ...S:7 *(remix)*	$5	★+	Elektra 64041
				VITAMIN C [featuring Lady Saw]			
12/11/99+	**27**[S]	20		2 **Me, Myself And I** ...BUB:120 *Money*	$4	★	Elektra 67001
				samples "No One To Depend On" by **Santana**			
4/15/00	**38**	12		3 **Graduation (Friends Forever)** ...A:39			album cut
				melody loosely based on Pachelbel's **Canon in D Major**; all of above from the album *Vitamin C* on Elektra 62406			
12/2/00	**45**	9		4 **The Itch** ...S:5 *Graduation (Friends Forever)*	$4	★	Elektra 67152
				VITAMIN Z LP '85			
				Pop group from Sheffield, Yorkshire, England: Geoff Barradale (vocals), Neil Hubbard and David Rhodes (guitars), Nick Lockwood (keyboards, bass) and Jerry Marotta (drums).			
6/15/85	**73**	7		**Burning Flame** ...*Don't Stop (To Listen To His Music)*	$3	■	Geffen 29039

DEBUT	PEAK	WKS	Gold	A-side (Chart Hit)....B-side	$	Sym	Label & Number
				VITO & THE SALUTATIONS '63			
				Male doo-wop group from Brooklyn, New York: Vito Balsamo (lead), Randy Silverman, Shelly Buchansky, Frankie Fox and Lenny Citrin.			
10/26/63	66	6		**Unchained Melody** ....*Hey, Hey, Baby*	$30		Herald 583
				VIXEN LP '89			
				Female hard-rock group formed in Los Angeles, California: Janet Gardner (vocals, guitar), Jan Kuehnemund (guitar), Share Pedersen (bass) and Roxy Petrucci (drums).			
9/17/88	26	21		1 **Edge Of A Broken Heart** ....S:21 / A:31 *Cruisin'*	$3	■	EMI-Manhattan 50141
				written, produced and arranged by **Richard Marx**; issued with a regular picture sleeve and a foldout poster sleeve			
1/28/89	22	13		2 **Cryin'** ....S:16 / A:30 *Desperate*	$3	■	EMI-Manhattan 50167
8/11/90	44	12		3 **How Much Love** ....S:37 *Wrecking Ball*	$3	▮	EMI 50302
11/10/90	71	6		4 **Love Is A Killer** ....*Bad Reputation*	$3	▮	EMI 50332
	★415★			**VOGUES, The** AC/BUB/LP '66			
				Pop/Adult Contemporary vocal group formed in Turtle Creek, Pennsylvania: Bill Burkette (lead), Hugh Geyer and Chuck Blasko (tenors), and Don Miller (baritone). Met in high school.			
				1)Five O'Clock World 2)You're The One 3)Turn Around, Look At Me			
9/18/65	4	12		1 **You're The One** ....*Some Words*	$12		Co & Ce 229
				first released on Blue Star 229 in 1965 ($30); written and recorded by **Petula Clark** in 1965			
11/27/65+	4	14		2 **Five O'Clock World** *Nothing To Offer You*	$12		Co & Ce 232
				later used as the theme for TV's *The Drew Carey SHow*			
2/26/66	21	9		3 **Magic Town**....*Humpty Dumpty*	$10		Co & Ce 234
6/4/66	29	8		4 **The Land Of Milk And Honey** ....*True Lovers*	$10		Co & Ce 238
9/24/66	48	8		5 **Please Mr. Sun** ....*Don't Blame The Rain*	$10		Co & Ce 240
				#6 hit for **Johnnie Ray** in 1952			
12/24/66	99	1		6 **That's The Tune**....*Midnight Dreams*	$10		Co & Ce 242
6/15/68	7	15	●	7 **Turn Around, Look At Me**....*Then*	$7		Reprise 0686
9/7/68	7	10	●	8 **My Special Angel** ....AC² *I Keep It Hid*	$7		Reprise 0766
11/23/68	27	6		9 **Till**....*I Will*	$6		Reprise 0788
3/8/69	34	5		10 **No, Not Much** /			
2/1/69	47	6		11 **Woman Helping Man**	$6		Reprise 0803
				originally issued with "I'll Know My Love" as the B-side			
4/19/69	42	6		12 **Earth Angel (Will You Be Mine)**....*P.S. I Love You*	$6		Reprise 0820
6/21/69	47	5		13 **Moments To Remember** ....*Once In A While*	$6		Reprise 0831
8/23/69	92	3		14 **Green Fields** ....*Easy To Say*	$6		Reprise 0844
				VOICE OF THE BEEHIVE ROK '91			
				Rock band formed in London by California-born sisters Melissa (vocals) and Tracey (vocals, guitar) Belland. British personnel include Mike Jones (guitar), Martin Brett (bass) and former **Madness** member Dan Woodgate (drums). The Bellands are the daughters of Bruce Belland of **The Four Preps**.			
11/2/91	74	7		1 **Monsters And Angels** ....*Only If You Want To*	$4	▮	London 869428
5/4/96	77	8		2 **Scary Kisses** ....*Blue In Paradise*	$4	▮	Discovery 74528
				VOICES R&B '92			
				Pre-teen R&B girl group from Los Angeles, California: Monique Wilson (age 12 in 1992), Arike Rice (age 10), and sisters LaToya (age 11) and LaPetra (age 10) McMoore. Rice went on to join **Before Dark**.			
9/5/92	72	8		**Yeah, Yeah, Yeah!**....A:51 *(dub version)*	$5	▮	Zoo 14051
				VOICES OF AMERICA '86			
				A project of the **USA for Africa** foundation.			
4/12/86	65	8		**Hands Across America**....*We Are The World*	$4	■	EMI America 8319
				theme for the 6 million Americans who joined hands from Los Angeles to New York on 5/25/86 to fight hunger and homelessness in America; registration/donation insert included with picture sleeve; B-side is the **USA for Africa** recording			
				VOICES OF THEORY R&B '98			
				Male Latino R&B vocal group from Philadelphia, Pennsylvania: James Cartagena, Mechi Cebollero, David Cordoba, Hector Ramos and Eric Serrano.			
4/4/98	10	31	●	1 **Say It**....S:11 / A:37 *Dímelo (Spanish version)*	$3	▮	H.O.L.A. 341032
10/17/98	36	16		2 **Wherever You Go** ....S:18 *Si Acaso (Te Vas)*	$4	★	H.O.L.A. 341075
				VOICES THAT CARE '91			
				Benefit spearheaded by **David Foster** and his fiancee Linda Thompson Jenner (ex-wife of Olympian Bruce Jenner) supporting the Persian Gulf allied troops and their families. Among superstar choir: Kevin Costner, Meryl Streep, **Billy Crystal**, Richard Gere, **Gloria Estefan**, Wayne Gretzky and many others.			
3/16/91	11	16	●	**Voices That Care** ....S:4 / A:19 *Messages Of Care*	$4	▮V	Giant 19350
				lead vocals: **Ralph Tresvant**, **Randy Travis**, **Celine Dion**, **Peter Cetera**, **Bobby Brown**, **Brenda Russell**, **Luther Vandross**, **Garth Brooks**, Kathy Mattea, **Nelson**, **Michael Bolton**, **Little Richard**, **Pointer Sisters**, **Fresh Prince**, Mark Knopfler, **Kenny G** and Warren Wiebe; co-written by Cetera, Foster, Jenner and Linda Thompson			
				VOICE V '00			
				Female R&B vocal group from San Francisco, California: Monica, Aimee, Meliossa, Mae and Marie.			
3/25/00	40S	12		**When U Think About Me**....*(instrumental)*	$3	★	Kamikaze/MCA 155677
				VOLUME'S, The BUB '62			
				R&B doo-wop group from Detroit, Michigan: Ed Union (lead), Elijah Davis, Larry Wright, Joe Truvillion and Ernest Newson.			
4/28/62	22	12		**I Love You** ....*Dreams*	$50		Chex 1002
				first pressings show artist as The Valume's ($300)			
				VONTASTICS, The '66			
				R&B group from Chicago, Illinois: Bobby Newsome, Kenneth Golar, Jose Holmes and Raymond Penn.			
9/3/66	100	1		**Day Tripper**....*My Baby*	$15		St. Lawrence 1014
				VOUDOURIS, Roger LP '79			
				Born on 12/29/54 in Sacramento, California. Pop singer/songwriter/guitarist.			
3/17/79	21	19		**Get Used To It** ....*The Next Time Around*	$4		Warner 8762

DEBUT	PEAK	WKS	Gold	A-side (Chart Hit)........B-side	$	Sym	Label & Number
				VOXPOPPERS, The '58			
				Pop-rock and roll group from Brooklyn, New York, featuring brothers Freddie, Sal and Harry Tamburo.			
4/14/58	18	8		**Wishing For Your Love**........A:18 / S:41 / T:44 *The Last Drag*	$20		Mercury 71282
				first released on Amp 3 1004 in 1958 ($30); B-side is a rock and roll "hot-rod" tune			
				VOYAGE R&B/BUB/LP '79			
				Disco group from Europe: Sylvia Mason (vocals), Slim Pezin (guitar), Marc Chantereau (keyboards), Sauver Mallin (bass) and Pierre-Alain Dahan (drums).			
2/17/79	41	9		**Souvenirs**........*Kechak Fantasy*	$5		Marlin 3330
				VOYCE '91			
				Dance trio of cousins from Brooklyn, New York: Carlos Colon (lead vocals), Danny Madera and Miguel Cordero.			
11/30/91	77	13		**Within My Heart**........A:60 *(radio mix)*	$4	▮	Atco 98759
				VYBE R&B/BUB '95			
				Female R&B vocal group from Los Angeles, California: Pam, Tanya, Debbie and Dove.			
8/5/95	81	5		**Warm Summer Daze**........*(Coolio mix) / Tell Me*	$5	▮	Island 854362
				contains elements of "Private Number" by **Judy Clay & William Bell**			

W

DEBUT	PEAK	WKS	Gold	A-side (Chart Hit)........B-side	$	Sym	Label & Number
				WACKERS, The BUB '72			
				Pop-rock group formed in Montreal, Quebec, Canada: Randy Bishop (vocals), Robert Segarini (guitar), J.P. Lauzon (keyboards), Bill "Kootch" Trochim (bass) and Spencer "Ernie" Earnshaw (drums).			
11/18/72	65	5		**Day And Night**........*Last Dance*	$6		Elektra 45816
				WADE, Adam BUB '61			
				Born on 3/17/37 in Pittsburgh, Pennsylvania. Black Adult Contemporary singer. Attended Virginia State College and worked as lab assistant with Dr. Jonas Salk team. TV actor/host of the 1975 game show *Musical Chairs*. Worked in *Guys & Dolls* musical in Las Vegas in 1978. TV talkshow host in Los Angeles in the 1980s.			
				1)The Writing On The Wall 2)Take Good Care Of Her 3)As If I Didn't Know			
1/11/60	66	7		1 **Tell Her For Me**........*Don't Cry, My Love*	$12		Coed 520
3/14/60	58	8		2 **Ruby**........*Too Far*	$12		Coed 526
				from the movie *Ruby Gentry* starring Charlton Heston; #3 hit for **Richard Hayman** in 1953			
6/20/60	64	7		3 **I Can't Help It**........*I Had The Craziest Dream*	$12	□	Coed 530
				#2 Country hit for Hank Williams in 1951; The Bel-Aire Singers (backing vocals, above 3)			
11/21/60	74	6		4 **Gloria's Theme**........*Dreamy*	$12	■	Coed 541
				theme from the movie *Butterfield 8* starring Elizabeth Taylor			
3/13/61	7	14		5 **Take Good Care Of Her**........*Sleepy Time Gal*	$10		Coed 546
5/15/61	5	11		6 **The Writing On The Wall /**			
6/19/61	85	4		7 **Point Of No Return**........	$10	■	Coed 550
7/24/61	10	10		8 **As If I Didn't Know**........*Playin' Around*	$10	■	Coed 553
9/18/61	61	7		9 **Tonight I Won't Be There /**			
				George Paxton (orch., all of above)			
10/2/61	94	1		10 **Linda**........	$10	■	Coed 556
				Joe Sherman (orch.); #1 hit for Buddy Clark with Ray Noble's orchestra in 1947			
1/30/65	88	3		11 **Crying In The Chapel**........*Broken Hearted Stranger*	$8		Epic 9752
				Teacho Wiltshire (orch.); #4 hit for June Valli in 1953			
				WADSWORTH MANSION '71			
				Pop-rock group formed in Los Angeles, California: brothers Steve (vocals) and Mike (drums) Jablecki, Wayne Gagnon (guitar) and John Poole (bass).			
12/26/70+	7	14		**Sweet Mary**........*What's On Tonight*	$6		Sussex 209
				WAGNER, Jack BUB/AC/LP '85			
				Born on 10/3/59 in Washington, Missouri. TV actor/singer. Played "Frisco Jones" on the TV soap opera *General Hospital* (1983-87). Also acted on several other TV soaps.			
10/20/84+	2^2	22		1 **All I Need**........AC^2 S:2 / A:2 *Tell Him (That You Won't Go)*	$3	■	Qwest 29238
5/25/85	76	8		2 **Lady Of My Heart**........*Premonition (#101)*	$3	■	Qwest 29085
10/26/85	52	14		3 **Too Young**........*Remember Me Laughing*	$3	■	Qwest 28931
5/9/87	67	6		4 **Weatherman Says**........*It's Been A Long Time*	$3	■	Qwest 28387
				WAGONER, Porter C&W/BUB/LP '69			
				Born on 8/12/27 in West Plains, Missouri. Country singer (charted 81 hits [includes duets with **Dolly Parton**], 1954-83). Host of his own TV variety series, 1960-79.			
1/25/69	92	4		**The Carroll County Accident**........*Sorrow Overtakes The Wine*	$8		RCA Victor 9651
				WAHLBERG, Donnie — see SEIKO			
				WAIKIKIS, The LP '65			
				Hawaiian music-styled instrumental group from Belgium.			
12/5/64+	33	9		1 **Hawaii Tattoo**........*Tahiti Tamoure* [I]	$8		Kapp 30
4/3/65	91	4		2 **Hawaii Honeymoon**........*Remember Boa-Boa* [I]	$8		Kapp 52
				above 2 released on Kapp's "Winners Circle Series" label			
				WAILERS, The BUB/LP '59			
				Teen rock and roll instrumental group from Tacoma, Washington: John Greek and Rich Dangel (guitars), Mark Marush (sax), Kent Morrill (piano) and Mike Burk (drums).			
5/18/59	36	13		1 **Tall Cool One**........*Road-Runner* [I]	$30		Golden Crest 518
8/17/59	68	5		2 **Mau-Mau**........*Dirty Robber* [I]	$30		Golden Crest 526
				above 2 feature a black and white photo of the group on the label			
4/11/64	38	10		3 **Tall Cool One**........*Roadrunner* [I-R]	$15		Golden Crest 518
				same version as #1 above			

DEBUT	PEAK	WKS	Gold	A-side (Chart Hit)...B-side	$	Sym	Label & Number

WAINWRIGHT, Loudon III — LP '73

Born on 9/5/46 in Chapel Hill, North Carolina. Satirical folk singer/songwriter. His father was the longtime editor of *Life* magazine. Played "Capt. Calvin Spaulding" in three episodes of TV's *M*A*S*H.* Appeared in the movies *The Slugger's Wife* and *Jacknife.* Married briefly to Kate McGarrigle (McGarrigle Sisters) in the mid-1970s, and Suzzy Roche (The Roches) in the 1980s.

DEBUT	PEAK	WKS	Gold	A-side / B-side	$	Sym	Label & Number
1/27/73	16	13		**Dead Skunk** ... *Needless To Say* [N]	$6		Columbia 45726

WAITE, John — BUB/AC/LP '84

Born on 7/4/55 in Lancaster, Lancashire, England. Lead singer of the rock groups **The Babys** and **Bad English**.

1)Missing You 2)Every Step Of The Way 3)Tears

DEBUT	PEAK	WKS	Gold	A-side / B-side	$	Sym	Label & Number
6/23/84	❶[1]	24		1 **Missing You** AR[2] S:8 / A:17 *For Your Love*	$3	■	EMI America 8212
10/20/84	37	13		2 **Tears** ... *Dreamtime/Shake It Up*	$3	■	EMI America 8238
1/26/85	59	8		3 **Restless Heart** ... *Euroshima*	$3	■	EMI America 8252
3/2/85	54	10		4 **Change** ... *White Heat* from the movie *Vision Quest* starring Matthew Modine (originally from Waite's 1982 album *Ignition*)	$3	■	Chrysalis 42606
8/10/85	25	12		5 **Every Step Of The Way** ... S:21 / A:24 *No Brakes*	$3	■	EMI America 8282
10/19/85	85	4		6 **Welcome To Paradise** ... *You're The One*	$3	■	EMI America 8278
6/28/86	76	6		7 **If Anybody Had A Heart** ... *Just Like Lovers* from the movie *About Last Night* starring Rob Lowe and Demi Moore	$3	■	EMI America 8315
6/20/87	53	16		8 **These Times Are Hard For Lovers** ... *Wild One*	$3	■	EMI America 43018
9/26/87	81	4		9 **Don't Lose Any Sleep** ... *Wild One*	$3	■	EMI America 43040
2/18/95	89	8		10 **How Did I Get By Without You?** ... *In Dreams / Extasy*	$3	▮	Imago 25091

WAITRESSES, The — LP '82

Rock group from Akron, Ohio: Patty Donahue (vocals; died of cancer on 12/9/96, age 40), Chris Butler (guitar), Dan Klayman (keyboards), Mars Williams (sax), Tracy Wormworth (bass) and Billy Ficca (drums; Television).

DEBUT	PEAK	WKS	Gold	A-side / B-side	$	Sym	Label & Number
5/8/82	62	6		**I Know What Boys Like** ... *It's My Car* first released on Antilles 4504 in 1980 with a picture sleeve (B-side: "No Guilt")	$4		Polydor 2196

WAKELIN, Johnny, & The Kinshasa Band — '75

Born in Brighton, Sussex, England. White reggae-styled singer/songwriter.

DEBUT	PEAK	WKS	Gold	A-side / B-side	$	Sym	Label & Number
3/8/75	21	27		**Black Superman - "Muhammad Ali"** ... *Bang The Drum* [N] refers to Ali's 10/30/74 knockout of George Foreman in Zaire, Africa	$6		Pye 71012

WAKELY, Jimmy — see CHANDLER, Karen

WALDEN, Narada Michael — R&B/BUB/LP '79

Born Michael Walden on 4/23/52 in Kalamazoo, Michigan. R&B singer/songwriter/drummer/producer. With John McLaughlin's Mahavishnu Orchestra from 1974-76. With **Jeff Beck** in 1975. Solo artist and much session work since 1976. Producer for **Whitney Houston**.

DEBUT	PEAK	WKS	Gold	A-side / B-side	$	Sym	Label & Number
3/31/79	47	11		1 **I Don't Want Nobody Else (To Dance With You)** ... *Will You Ever Know*	$5		Atlantic 3541
2/9/80	66	6		2 **I Shoulda Loved Ya** ... *Carry On*	$4		Atlantic 3631

WALDMAN, Wendy — '78

Born on 11/29/50 in Los Angeles, California. Folk-pop singer/songwriter/producer.

DEBUT	PEAK	WKS	Gold	A-side / B-side	$	Sym	Label & Number
8/19/78	76	4		**Long Hot Summer Nights** ... *You'll See*	$5		Warner 8617

WALKER, Billy — C&W/BUB '60

Born on 1/14/29 in Ralls, Texas. Country singer (charted 65 hits, 1954-88).

DEBUT	PEAK	WKS	Gold	A-side / B-side	$	Sym	Label & Number
2/15/60	83	1		**Forever** ... *Changed My Mind*	$15		Columbia 41548

WALKER, Boots — '67

Born on 3/24/38 in Marshall, Texas. Pop-novelty singer; produced by **Ernie Maresca**.

DEBUT	PEAK	WKS	Gold	A-side / B-side	$	Sym	Label & Number
6/10/67	77	2		**They're Here** ... *A Bum Can't Cry* [N] arrangement is similar to "They're Coming To Take Me Away, Ha-Haaa!" by **Napoleon XIV**	$10		Rust 5115

WALKER, Chris — R&B '92

Born in Houston, Texas. Male R&B singer/jazz bassist.

DEBUT	PEAK	WKS	Gold	A-side / B-side	$	Sym	Label & Number
3/14/92	29	18		**Take Time** ... A:28 *(w/o rap) / (4 album snippets)* Shazzy (female rapper)	$4	▮	Pendulum 64813

WALKER, Clay — C&W/BUB/LP '98

Born Ernest Clayton Walker on 8/19/69 in Beaumont, Texas. Country singer/songwriter/guitarist.

DEBUT	PEAK	WKS	Gold	A-side / B-side	$	Sym	Label & Number
10/9/93	73	15		1 **What's It To You** ... CW[1] S:37 *Where Do I Fit In The Picture*	$4	▮[V]	Giant 18450
2/7/98	65	18		2 **Then What?** ... S:45 *Country Boy And City Girl*	$4	▮[V]	Giant 17262
12/5/98	39	13		3 **You're Beginning To Get To Me** A:31 *Lose Your Memory*	$4	★[V]	Giant 17158
6/12/99	74	6		4 **She's Always Right** ... A:64			album cut
12/4/99+	74	11		5 **Live, Laugh, Love** ... A:58			album cut
4/15/00	40	20		6 **The Chain Of Love** ... A:34 above 3 from the album *Live, Laugh, Love* on Giant 24717			album cut

WALKER, Gloria — '68

R&B singer with her backing band, The Chevelles.

DEBUT	PEAK	WKS	Gold	A-side / B-side	$	Sym	Label & Number
11/2/68	60	7		1 **Talking About My Baby** ... *The Gallop* (The Chevelles)	$10		Flaming Arrow 35
1/25/69	98	2		2 **Please Don't Desert Me Baby** ... *Need Of You* **GLORIA WALKER & THE CHEVELLES**	$10		Flaming Arrow 36

WALKER, Jerry Jeff — C&W/LP '68

Born Ronald Clyde Crosby on 3/16/42 in Oneonta, New York. Country-folk-rock singer/songwriter. Wrote "Mr. Bojangles."

DEBUT	PEAK	WKS	Gold	A-side / B-side	$	Sym	Label & Number
7/27/68	77	5		1 **Mr. Bojangles** ... *Round And Round* a new version by Walker made the Country charts (#93) in 1977 on MCA 40760	$8		Atco 6594
7/28/73	98	3		2 **L.A. Freeway** ... *Charlie Dunn*	$6		MCA 40054

DEBUT	PEAK	WKS	Gold	A-side (Chart Hit)...B-side	$	Sym	Label & Number

WALKER, Jr., & The All Stars — R&B/BUB/LP '65

★227★

Born Autry DeWalt Walker on 6/14/31 in Blythesville, Arkansas. Died of cancer on 11/23/95 (age 64). R&B singer/saxophonist. The All Stars: Willie Woods (guitar), Vic Thomas (keyboards) and James Graves (drums). Woods died on 5/27/97 (age 60). First recorded for Harvey in 1962. Walker contributed sax solo to **Foreigner**'s 1981 hit "Urgent"; appeared in 1988 movie *Tapeheads*. His son Autry DeWalt, Jr. (drums) joined band in 1983.

1)Shotgun 2)What Does It Take (To Win Your Love) 3)These Eyes 4)How Sweet It Is (To Be Loved By You) 5)(I'm A) Road Runner

DEBUT	PEAK	WKS	Gold	A-side (Chart Hit)	B-side	$	Sym	Label & Number
2/13/65	4	14		1 **Shotgun** RB^{4}	*Hot Cha*	$15	■	Soul 35008
6/5/65	36	7		2 **Do The Boomerang**	*Tune Up*	$12		Soul 35012
7/31/65	29	8		3 **Shake And Fingerpop /**				
10/9/65	43	8		4 **Cleo's Back** [I]		$12		Soul 35013
1/15/66	50	6		5 **Cleo's Mood** [I] originally released on Harvey 117 ($20) in 1963 as by Jr. Walker All Stars	*Baby You Know You Ain't Right*	$12		Soul 35017
4/9/66	20	12		6 **(I'm A) Road Runner** all of above (and #10 below) from the album *Shotgun*	*Shoot Your Shot*	$12		Soul 35015
7/30/66	18	11		7 **How Sweet It Is (To Be Loved By You)**	*Nothing But Soul*	$10	■	Soul 35024
11/19/66	52	6		8 **Money (That's What I Want) Part 1**	*(Part 2)*	$10		Soul 35026
2/11/67	31	8		9 **Pucker Up Buttercup**	*Anyway You Wannta'*	$10		Soul 35030
7/22/67	44	7		10 **Shoot Your Shot** originally released as the B-side of #6 above	*Ain't That The Truth*	$10		Soul 35036
11/25/67+	24	11		11 **Come See About Me**	*Sweet Soul*	$10		Soul 35041
8/10/68	31	11		12 **Hip City - Pt. 2**	*Pt. 1*	$10		Soul 35048
1/18/69	42	6		13 **Home Cookin**	*Mutiny*	$10		Soul 35055
5/17/69	4	16		14 **What Does It Take (To Win Your Love)** RB^{2} above 4 from the album *Home Cookin'*	*Brainwasher (Part 1)*	$8		Soul 35062
10/25/69	16	13		15 **These Eyes**	*I've Got To Find A Way To Win Maria Back*	$8		Soul 35067
2/21/70	21	10		16 **Gotta Hold On To This Feeling**	*Clinging To The Thought That She's Coming Back*	$8		Soul 35070
7/11/70	32	10		17 **Do You See My Love (For You Growing)**	*Groove And Move*	$8		Soul 35073
12/26/70+	75	5		18 **Holly Holy**	*Carry Your Own Load (#117/R&B #50)*	$8		Soul 35081
8/7/71	50	9		19 **Take Me Girl, I'm Ready**	*Right On Brothers And Sisters*	$8		Soul 35084
12/11/71+	52	9		20 **Way Back Home**	*(instrumental)*	$8		Soul 35090
4/1/72	46	12		21 **Walk In The Night** [I]	*I Don't Want To Do Wrong*	$8		Soul 35095

WALKER, Mike — '02

Born in Columbus, Ohio; raised in Jackson, Tennessee. Country singer.

DEBUT	PEAK	WKS	Gold	A-side (Chart Hit)	B-side	$	Sym	Label & Number
8/3/02	54^{S}	1		**Honey Do** "45": DreamWorks 50881; B-side: "Stones In The Road"	*What Kind Of Love*	$5	★^{V}	DreamWorks 50914

WALKER BROS., The — '66

"Blue-eyed soul" trio from Los Angeles, California: Scott Engel, Gary Leeds and John Maus. More popular in England than the U.S. (charted 10 hits in the U.K.). Similar in style to **The Righteous Brothers**.

DEBUT	PEAK	WKS	Gold	A-side (Chart Hit)	B-side	$	Sym	Label & Number
10/16/65	16	10		1 **Make It Easy On Yourself** first released on Smash 2000 in 1965 (promo copies issued with a foldout picture sleeve and insert)	*Doin' The Jerk*	$12	■	Smash 2009
1/29/66	63	5		2 **My Ship Is Comin' In** first released by Jimmy Radcliffe in 1965 on Aurora 154	*You're All Around Me*	$12	■	Smash 2016
4/16/66	13	9		3 **The Sun Ain't Gonna Shine (Anymore)** song "Bubbled Under" (#128) for **Frankie Valli** in 1965	*After The Lights Go Out*	$12		Smash 2032

WALLACE, Jerry — C&W/BUB/MEM/LP '59

★560★

Born on 12/15/28 in Guilford, Missouri; raised in Glendale, Arizona. Pop-country singer/guitarist. First recorded for Allied in 1951. Charted 35 Country hits, 1965-80.

1)Primrose Lane 2)How The Time Flies 3)In The Misty Moonlight

DEBUT	PEAK	WKS	Gold	A-side (Chart Hit)	B-side	$	Sym	Label & Number
8/18/58	11	16		1 **How The Time Flies** H:11 / S:33	*With This Ring*	$20		Challenge 59013
12/8/58	78	4		2 **Diamond Ring** Ev Freeman Singers (backing vocals)	*All My Love Belongs To You*	$20		Challenge 59027
4/20/59	92	2		3 **A Touch Of Pink** from the movie *The Wild and The Innocent* starring Audie Murphy	*Off Stage*	$20		Challenge 59040
8/17/59	8	21	●	4 **Primrose Lane** *[JERRY WALLACE With the Jewels]*	*By Your Side*	$20		Challenge 59047
1/4/60	36	9		5 **Little Coco Palm**	*Mission Bell Blues*	$15	■	Challenge 59060
8/1/60	79	2		6 **Swingin' Down The Lane** #1 hit in 1923 for Isham Jones & His Orchestra	*Teardrop In The Rain*	$15		Challenge 59082
12/26/60+	26	10		7 **There She Goes** #3 Country hit for **Carl Smith** in 1955	*Angel On My Shoulder*	$15		Challenge 59098
5/8/61	91	1		8 **Life's A Holiday**	*I Can See An Angel Walking*	$15		Challenge 9107
11/17/62+	24	12		9 **Shutters And Boards** co-written by movie star Audie Murphy	*Am I That Easy To Forget*	$15		Challenge 9171
7/25/64	19	11		10 **In The Misty Moonlight** B-side "Bubbled Under" (#114) on 10/31/64 on Challenge 59265	*Even The Bad Times Are Good*	$15		Challenge 59246
8/15/64	99	1		11 **It's A Cotton Candy World**	*Keep A Lamp Burning*	$12		Mercury 72292
3/18/72	48	12		12 **To Get To You**	*Time*	$7		Decca 32914
8/19/72	38	9		13 **If You Leave Me Tonight I'll Cry** CW^{2} from TV's *Rod Serling's Night Gallery: The Tune In Dan's Cafe*	*What's He Doin' In My World*	$7		Decca 32989

WALLACE BROTHERS — BUB '64

R&B duo: Ernest and Johnny Wallace. Member Johnny Simon later joined The Naturals.

DEBUT	PEAK	WKS	Gold	A-side (Chart Hit)	B-side	$	Sym	Label & Number
8/29/64	97	2		**Lover's Prayer**	*Love Me Like I Love You*	$15		Sims 189

WALLFLOWERS, The — ROK/LP '97

Rock group formed in Los Angeles, California: Jakob Dylan (vocals), Michael Ward (guitar), Rami Jaffe (keyboards), Greg Richling (bass) and Mario Calire (drums). Dylan is the son of **Bob Dylan**.

DEBUT	PEAK	WKS	Gold	A-side (Chart Hit)	B-side	$	Sym	Label & Number
8/24/96	33^{A}	20		1 **6th Avenue Heartache**				album cut
1/4/97	2^{5A}	70		2 **One Headlight** AR^{5} / MR^{5}				album cut

DEBUT	PEAK	WKS	Gold	A-side (Chart Hit)...B-side	$	Sym	Label & Number
				WALLFLOWERS, The — Cont'd			
6/7/97	23[A]	21		3 **The Difference**			album cut
10/25/97	51[A]	9		4 **Three Marlenas**			album cut
				above 4 from the album *Bringing Down The Horse* on Interscope 90055			
5/2/98	27[A]	11		5 **Heroes**		□V	album cut
				written and first recorded by **David Bowie** in 1977; from the movie *Godzilla* starring Matthew Broderick (soundtrack on Epic 69338); promo "45" with picture sleeve: Epic 41025; B-side: (same)			
10/28/00	73	6		6 **Sleepwalker**...A:74			album cut
				from the album *(Breach)* on Interscope 490745			
				WALL OF VOODOO LP '83			
				Alternative-rock group formed in Los Angeles, California: Stan Ridgway (vocals), Marc Moreland (guitar), Chas T. Gray (bass) and Joe Nanini (drums). Moreland died of kidney failure on 3/13/2002 (age 44).			
3/19/83	58	9		**Mexican Radio**...*Call Of The West*	$5	■	I.R.S. 9912
				WALSH, James — see GYPSY			
				WALSH, Joe ROK/BUB/LP '78			
				Born on 11/20/47 in Wichita, Kansas. Rock singer/songwriter/guitarist. Member of **The James Gang** (1969-71) and the **Eagles** (1975-82, 1994). Own band (1972-75), Barnstorm, featured drummer Joe Vitale and bassist Kenny Passarelli.			
8/11/73	23	15		1 **Rocky Mountain Way**...*(Day Dream) Prayer*	$6		Dunhill/ABC 4361
1/12/74	89	4		2 **Meadows**...*Book Ends*	$6		Dunhill/ABC 4373
3/1/75	93	3		3 **Turn To Stone**...*All Night Laundry Mat Blues*	$6		Dunhill/ABC 15026
				Don Henley, **Glenn Frey** and **Randy Meisner** of the **Eagles** (backing vocals); "Bubbled Under" (#109) on 1/13/79 on ABC 12426			
6/10/78	12	15		4 **Life's Been Good** *Theme From Boat Weirdos*	$4		Asylum 45493
				from the movie *FM* starring Michael Brandon			
5/17/80	19	16		5 **All Night Long**...*Orange Blossom Special/Hoedown* (Gilley's "Urban Cowboy" Band)	$4	■	Full Moon 46639
				from the movie *Urban Cowboy* starring **John Travolta** and Debra Winger			
5/23/81	34	12		6 **A Life Of Illusion**...AR[1] *Rockets*	$4		Asylum 47144
6/11/83	52	8		7 **Space Age Whiz Kids**...*Theme From Island Weirdos*	$4	■	Full Moon 29611
				WALTERS, Jamie — see HEIGHTS, The			
				WAMMACK, Travis BUB '75			
				Born in 1946 in Walnut, Mississippi; raised in Memphis, Tennessee. Prolific session guitarist of the FAME studios in Muscle Shoals, Alabama.			
11/21/64	80	6		1 **Scratchy**...*Fire Fly* [I]	$12		ARA 204
				guitar instrumental version of **Mel Torme**'s 1962 hit "Comin' Home Baby"			
9/2/72	95	4		2 **Whatever Turns You On**...*Slip Away*	$6		Fame 91001
1/20/73	68	7		3 **How Can I Tell You**...*So Good*	$6		Fame 91008
				written by **Cat Stevens** (from his 1971 album *Teaser And The Firecat*)			
6/21/75	38	10		4 **(Shu-Doo-Pa-Poo-Poop) Love Being Your Fool** *Shotgun Woman*	$5		Capricorn 0239
9/27/75	72	6		5 **Easy Evil**...*Greenwood, Mississippi*	$5		Capricorn 0242
				WANDERERS, The BUB '62			
				R&B vocal group: Ray Pollard, Frank Joyner, Robert Yarborough and Sheppard Grant.			
5/15/61	93	2		1 **For Your Love**...*Sally Goodheart*	$30		Cub 9089
8/25/62	88	4		2 **There Is No Greater Love**...*As Time Goes By*	$20		MGM 13082
				first released on Cub 9109 in 1962 ($30); #20 hit in 1936 for Isham Jones & His Orchestra			
				WANDERLEY, Walter AC '66			
				Born on 5/12/32 in Recife, Brazil. Died of cancer on 9/4/86 (age 54). Samba organist.			
8/27/66	26	9		**Summer Samba (So Nice)**...*Call Me* [I]	$8		Verve 10421
				WANG CHUNG BUB '86			
				Pop-rock trio from London, England: Jack Hues (vocals, guitar, keyboards), Nick Feldman (bass, keyboards) and Darren Costin (drums). Costin left in 1985.			
2/4/84	38	11		1 **Don't Let Go**...*There Is A Nation*	$4	■	Geffen 29377
4/21/84	16	22		2 **Dance Hall Days**...*Ornamental Elephant*	$4	■	Geffen 29310
				a 12" remix version "Bubbled Under" (#107) in 1997 on Geffen 22301			
9/22/84	86	3		3 **Don't Be My Enemy**...*The Waves*	$4		Geffen 29193
10/12/85	41	18		4 **To Live And Die In L.A.**...*Black-Blue-White*	$3	■	Geffen 28891
				title song from the movie starring Willem Dafoe			
10/4/86	2[2]	21		5 **Everybody Have Fun Tonight** S:2 / A:2 *Fun Tonight: The Early Years*	$3	■	Geffen 28562
1/24/87	9	18		6 **Let's Go!**...A:6 / S:10 *The World In Which We Live*	$3	■	Geffen 28531
6/6/87	36	12		7 **Hypnotize Me**...A:33 *Lullaby*	$3	■	Geffen 28359
				from the movie *Innerspace* starring Dennis Quaid and Martin Short			
5/27/89	63	7		8 **Praying To A New God**...*Tall Trees In A Blue Sky*	$3	■	Geffen 22969
	★219★			**WAR** R&B/BUB/AC '73			
				Latin funk-rock band from Long Beach, California: Lonnie Jordan (keyboards; born on 11/21/48), Howard Scott (guitar; born on 3/15/46), Charles Miller (sax; born on 6/2/39), Morris "B.B." Dickerson (bass; born on 8/3/49), Harold Brown (drums; born on 3/17/46) and Thomas "Papa Dee" Allen (percussion; born on 7/19/31), and **Lee Oskar** (harmonica; born on 3/24/48) (see #12 below). **Eric Burdon**'s backup band until 1971. Alice Tweed Smyth (vocals) added in 1978. By 1979, Luther Rabb replaced Dickerson; Pat Rizzo (horns) and Ronnie Hammond (percussion; of R&B band Aalon) joined. Rabb and Hammond were members of **Ballin' Jack**. Miller was shot to death in June 1980 (age 41). Allen died of an aneurysm on 8/30/88 (age 57). Smyth left group in 1982. Lineup by 1994: Jordan, Scott, Brown and Hammond with Rae Valentine, Charles Green, Kerry Campbell, Tetsuya Nakamura and Sal Rodriguez.			
				1)The Cisco Kid 2)Why Can't We Be Friends? 3)Low Rider			
5/23/70	3	21	●	1 **Spill The Wine**...*Magic Mountain*	$8	■	MGM 14118
12/19/70+	50	8		2 **They Can't Take Away Our Music**...*Home Cookin'* (#108)	$8		MGM 14196
				ERIC BURDON AND WAR (above 2)			
				Sharon Scott (female vocal)			
8/7/71	35	11		3 **All Day Music**...*Get Down*	$7		United Artists 50815
1/22/72	16	22	●	4 **Slippin' Into Darkness**...*Nappy Head (Theme From "Ghetto Man")*	$6		United Artists 50867
11/18/72+	7	16	●	5 **The World Is A Ghetto**...*Four Cornered Room*	$6		United Artists 50975

DEBUT	PEAK	WKS	Gold	A-side (Chart Hit)...B-side	$	Sym	Label & Number
				WAR — Cont'd			
3/3/73	2[2]	15	●	6 The Cisco Kid ... *Beetles In The Bog*	$6		United Artists 163
7/21/73	8	13		7 Gypsy Man ... *Deliver The Word*	$6		United Artists 281
11/10/73+	15	15		8 Me And Baby Brother ... *In Your Eyes*	$6		United Artists 350
6/8/74	33	10		9 Ballero ... *Slippin' Into Darkness (live)* [I-L]	$6		United Artists 432
5/3/75	6	20	●	10 Why Can't We Be Friends? ... *In Mazatlan*	$6	■	United Artists 629
9/20/75	7	15		11 Low Rider ... RB[1] *So* also see #18 below; a 12" remix version made the R&B charts (#59) in 1987 on Priority 9364	$6	■	United Artists 706
6/26/76	59	6		12 BLT ... *(I Remember Home) The Immigrant* [I] **LEE OSKAR**	$6		United Artists 807
7/10/76	7	16	●	13 Summer ... AC[1] *All Day Music* released on the first day of summer, June 21, 1976	$6		United Artists 834
7/9/77	45	10		14 L.A. Sunshine ... *Slowly We Walk Together*	$5		Blue Note 1009
1/7/78	39	9		15 Galaxy ... *Part II*	$5	■	MCA 40820
4/3/82	66	6		16 You Got The Power ... *Cinco De Mayo*	$4		RCA 13061
7/10/82	94	3		17 Outlaw ... *I'm About Somebody* all of above produced by Jerry Goldstein	$4		RCA 13238
8/10/91	54	11		18 Lowrider (On The Boulevard) ... S:28 *Smooth Roughness* (Latin Alliance) [R] **LATIN ALLIANCE Featuring War** samples #11 above and **Santana**'s "Evil Ways"	$4	▌	Virgin 98751
				WARD, Anita LP **'79** Born on 12/20/57 in Memphis, Tennessee. Disco singer.			
5/12/79	❶[2]	21		1 Ring My Bell ... RB[5] *If I Could Feel That Old Feeling Again*	$5		Juana 3422
11/3/79	87	5		2 Don't Drop My Love ... *Spoiled By Your Love* above 2 written and produced by **Frederick Knight**	$5		Juana 3425
				WARD, Billy, And His Dominoes R&B/POP **'57** Born on 9/19/21 in Los Angeles, California. Died on 2/16/2002 (age 80). R&B pianist. His vocal group: Charlie White (tenor), Joe Lamont (baritone) and Bill Brown (bass). Signed by King/Federal in 1950. Lead singers, at various times: Clyde McPhatter (1950-53), **Jackie Wilson** (1953-57) and Eugene Mumford. Had 11 consecutive Top 10 R&B hits, 1951-53.			
8/11/56	13	15		1 St. Therese Of The Roses ... A:13 / S:20 / T:27 *Home Is Where You Hang Your Heart* **Jackie Wilson** (lead singer); **Jack Pleis** (orch.)	$50		Decca 29933
6/17/57	12	24	●	2 Star Dust ... A:12 / T:13 / S:14 *Lucinda* #1 hit for Isham Jones in 1931 and #2 hit versions for **Benny Goodman** in 1936 and Artie Shaw in 1941	$30	■	Liberty 55071
9/30/57	20	12		3 Deep Purple ... S:20 / T:22 *Do It Again* #1 hit for Larry Clinton's Orchestra in 1939; Vic Schoen (orch., above 2)	$30		Liberty 55099
6/2/58	55	5		4 Jennie Lee ... T:55 *Music, Maestro, Please!*	$30		Liberty 55136
				WARD, Dale C&W **'64** Male pop-country singer. Was not a member of The Crescendos, as rumored.			
12/28/63+	25	11		Letter From Sherry ... *Oh Julie* **Robin Ward** (female vocal; not related to Dale Ward)	$15		Dot 16520
				WARD, Joe **'55** Born in 1947 in Brooklyn, New York. Discovered by **Steve Allen**. On NBC-TV's *Juvenile Jury* from age five to nine. Prolific commercial songwriter/producer/arranger/singer as an adult.			
12/17/55	20	4		Nuttin For Xmas ... J:20 / S:22 / T:22 *Christmas Questions* [X-N] Dave Terry (orch.); verse melody based on traditional 19th-century French song "Vive La Companie"	$25	⊙	King 4854
				WARD, Matthew — see SUMMER, Donna			
				WARD, Robin BUB **'63** Born Jacqueline Eloise McDonnell in Hawaii; raised in Nebraska. Pop singer. Also see **Dale Ward**.			
11/2/63	14	10		Wonderful Summer ... *Dream Boy* **Perry Botkin, Jr.** (orch.)	$15		Dot 16530
				WARINER, Steve C&W/BUB/LP **'99** Born on 12/25/54 in Noblesville, Indiana. Country singer/songwriter/guitarist (charted 58 hits, 1978-2003).			
1/3/98	59	15		1 What If I Said ... CW[1] S:40 *Daddy Can You See Me* (Cochran - C&W #69)) **ANITA COCHRAN with Steve Wariner**	$4	▌V	Warner 17263
4/3/99	30	20		2 Two Teardrops ... A:21 co-written by **Bill Anderson**; "45": Capitol 58767; B-side: "Cry No More"		V	album cut
9/11/99	42	14		3 I'm Already Taken ... A:31 new version of Wariner's debut Country single in 1978; "45": Capitol 58786; B-side: Tattoos Of Life"; above 2 from the album *Two Teardrops* on Capitol 96139		V	album cut
2/19/00	44	20		4 Been There ... A:36 **CLINT BLACK with Steve Wariner** from Black's album *D'lectrified* on RCA 67823; "45": RCA 65966; B-side: "When I Said I Do" (w/Lisa Hartman Black - #31/'99)		V	album cut
	★506★			**WARNES, Jennifer** AC/BUB/C&W/LP **'82** Born on 3/3/47 in Seattle, Washington; raised in Orange County, California. Adult Contemporary singer/actress. Lead actress in the Los Angeles production of *Hair*. Also recorded as Jennifer Warren and simply as Jennifer.			
1/29/77	6	22		1 Right Time Of The Night ... AC[1] *Daddy Don't Go*	$5		Arista 0223
7/30/77	50	7		2 I'm Dreaming ... *Don't Lead Me On*	$5		Arista 0252
6/30/79	19	22		3 I Know A Heartache When I See One ... *Frankie In The Rain*	$4		Arista 0430
12/22/79+	67	7		4 Don't Make Me Over ... *I'm Restless*	$4		Arista 0455
4/5/80	45	8		5 When The Feeling Comes Around ... *Shot Through The Heart*	$4		Arista 0497
12/5/81+	47	10		6 Could It Be Love ... *I'm Restless*	$4		Arista 0611
8/21/82	❶[3]	23	▲	7 Up Where We Belong ... *Sweet Li'l Woman* (Cocker) **JOE COCKER and JENNIFER WARNES** love theme from the movie *An Officer And A Gentleman* starring Richard Gere and Debra Winger	$4	■	Island 99996

DEBUT	PEAK	WKS	Gold	A-side (Chart Hit)..........B-side	$	Sym	Label & Number

WARNES, Jennifer — Cont'd

DEBUT	PEAK	WKS	Gold	A-side (Chart Hit)..........B-side	$	Sym	Label & Number
11/12/83	85	4		8 **All The Right Moves** ......*Love Theme From All The Right Moves* (David Campbell) **JENNIFER WARNES/CHRIS THOMPSON** title song from the movie starring Tom Cruise	$4		Casablanca 814603
9/26/87	❶[1]	21	●	9 **(I've Had) The Time Of My Life**......AC[4] A:❶[2] / S:❶[1] *Love Is Strange* (**Mickey & Sylvia**) **BILL MEDLEY AND JENNIFER WARNES** love theme from the movie *Dirty Dancing* starring **Patrick Swayze** and Jennifer Grey	$3	■	RCA 5224

WARRANT

ROK/LP '89

Male hard-rock group from Los Angeles, California: Jani Lane (vocals), Erik Turner and Joey Allen (guitars), Jerry Dixon (bass) and Steven Sweet (drums).

DEBUT	PEAK	WKS	Gold	A-side (Chart Hit)..........B-side	$	Sym	Label & Number
4/29/89	27	16		1 **Down Boys**......A:26 / S:28 *Cold Sweat*	$3		Columbia 68606
7/22/89	2[2]	19	●	2 **Heaven** S:❶[1] / A:2 *In The Sticks*	$3		Columbia 68985
11/4/89	93	4		3 **Big Talk**......*D.R.F.S.R.*	$3		Columbia 73035
1/6/90	20	17		4 **Sometimes She Cries**......A:15 / S:23 *32 Pennies* "45": Columbia 73300; all of above from the album *Dirty Rotten Filthy Stinking Rich*	$3	▮V	Columbia 73095
9/8/90	10	19		5 **Cherry Pie**......S:6 / A:18 *Thin Disguise*	$3	▮V	Columbia 73510
12/1/90+	10	19		6 **I Saw Red**......A:11 / S:12 *(acoustic version)*	$3	▮V	Columbia 73597
4/20/91	78	6		7 **Uncle Tom's Cabin**......*Sure Feels Good To Me*	$3	▮V	Columbia 73644
6/29/91	88	6		8 **Blind Faith**......*Mr. Rainmaker* above 4 from the album *Cherry Pie*	$3	▮V	Columbia 73598
3/21/92	83	5		9 **We Will Rock You**......S:39 *Blind Faith (acoustic version)* from the movie *Gladiator* starring Brian Dennehy	$3	▮	Columbia 74207

WARREN G

★550★

R&B/LP '94

Born Warren Griffin on 11/10/71 in Long Beach, California. Male rapper. Also see **Slick Rick**'s "Behind Bars."

DEBUT	PEAK	WKS	Gold	A-side (Chart Hit)..........B-side	$	Sym	Label & Number
4/23/94	2[3]	20	▲	1 **Regulate** S:❶[2] / A:15 *(same version)* **WARREN G. & NATE DOGG** samples **Michael McDonald**'s "I Keep Forgettin'"; from the movie *Above The Rim* starring **2 Pac** and Duane Martin	$4	▮	Death Row 98280
7/23/94	9	20	●	2 **This DJ**......S:5 / A:20 *Regulate (remix)*	$4	▮	Violator/RAL 853236
12/3/94+	42	13		3 **Do You See**......S:20 *What's Next?* samples "Mama Used To Say" by **Junior**	$4	▮	Violator/RAL 853962
9/21/96	32	19		4 **What's Love Got To Do With It**......S:15 *(instrumental)* **WARREN G featuring Adina Howard** from the movie *Supercop* starring Jackie Chan	$4	▮	Interscope 97008
3/22/97	20	19	●	5 **I Shot The Sheriff**......S:9 *(**EPMD** radio remix) / What We Go Through* samples "Love's Gonna Get Cha" by Boogie Down Productions; written by **Bob Marley**	$4	▮	Def Jam 573564
6/21/97	35	14		6 **Smokin' Me Out**......S:21 *We Brings Heat* **WARREN G Featuring Ronald Isley** contains an interpolation of "Coolin' Me Out" by **The Isley Brothers**	$4	▮	Def Jam 571024
7/11/98	18	18		7 **Nobody Does It Better**......S:10 *(instrumental)* **NATE DOGG featuring WARREN G** samples "Let's Get Closer" by **Atlantic Starr**	$4	▮	Breakaway 4000
9/18/99	23	15	●	8 **I Want It All**......S:7 *(3 versions)* **WARREN G Featuring Mack 10** samples "I Like It" by **DeBarge**	$4	★	G-Funk 73721

WARWICK, Dee Dee

R&B/BUB '66

Born in 1945 in East Orange, New Jersey. R&B singer. Younger sister of **Dionne Warwick**; cousin of **Whitney Houston**. Sang in the gospel group the Drinkard Singers. Backup work for many artists. Also see **Maxine Brown**'s "Oh No Not My Baby."

DEBUT	PEAK	WKS	Gold	A-side (Chart Hit)..........B-side	$	Sym	Label & Number
8/7/65	96	1		1 **We're Doing Fine**......*I Want To Be With You*	$10		Blue Rock 4027
8/27/66	41	12		2 **I Want To Be With You** *Lover's Chant* from the Broadway musical *Golden Boy* starring **Sammy Davis, Jr.**; same version is on the B-side of #1 above	$8		Mercury 72584
11/26/66	88	3		3 **I'm Gonna Make You Love Me**......*Yours Until Tomorrow*	$8		Mercury 72638
5/6/67	92	1		4 **When Love Slips Away**......*House Of Gold*	$8		Mercury 72667
3/22/69	57	8		5 **Foolish Fool**......*Thank God* (w/Teaneck Choir)	$8		Mercury 72880
5/9/70	70	8		6 **She Didn't Know (She Kept On Talking)**......*Make Love To Me* The Dixie Flyers (backing vocals)	$6		Atco 6754
6/26/71	80	5		7 **Suspicious Minds**......*I'm Glad I'm A Woman* (w/The Dixie Flyers)	$6		Atco 6810

WARWICK, Dionne

★30★

AC/R&B/BUB/LP '68

Born Marie Dionne Warwick on 12/12/40 in East Orange, New Jersey. In church choir from age six. With the Drinkard Singers gospel group. Formed the Gospelaires trio with sister **Dee Dee Warwick** and their aunt **Cissy Houston**. Dionne is a cousin of **Whitney Houston**. Attended Hartt College Of Music, Hartford, Connecticut. Much backup studio work in New York during the late '50s. Added an "e" to her last name for a time in the early 1970s. Dionne was **Burt Bacharach**'s and Hal David's main "voice" for the songs they composed. Co-hosted TV's *Solid Gold* 1980-81, 1985-86. Beginning in the early 1990s, hosted TV infomercials for the Psychic Friends Network.

1)That's What Friends Are For 2)Then Came You 3)(Theme From) Valley Of The Dolls 4)I Say A Little Prayer 5)I'll Never Love This Way Again

DEBUT	PEAK	WKS	Gold	A-side (Chart Hit)..........B-side	$	Sym	Label & Number
12/8/62+	21	12		1 **Don't Make Me Over**......*I Smiled Yesterday*	$12		Scepter 1239
3/23/63	84	5		2 **This Empty Place**......*Wishin' And Hopin'* B-side was a #6 hit for **Dusty Springfield** in 1964	$12	■	Scepter 1247
8/3/63	81	4		3 **Make The Music Play**......*Please Make Him Love Me*	$12		Scepter 1253
12/7/63+	8	14		4 **Anyone Who Had A Heart**......*The Love Of A Boy* B-side was a #44 hit a year earlier for **Timi Yuro**	$12		Scepter 1262
4/25/64	6	13		5 **Walk On By**......*Any Old Time Of The Day*	$12		Scepter 1274
8/15/64	34	9		6 **You'll Never Get To Heaven (If You Break My Heart)** /			
8/1/64	71	6		7 **A House Is Not A Home**...... title song from the movie starring Shelley Winters	$10		Scepter 1282
10/24/64	20	8		8 **Reach Out For Me**......*How Many Days Of Sadness* above 4 from the album *Make Way For Dionne Warwick*	$10		Scepter 1285
2/27/65	62	6		9 **Who Can I Turn To**......*Don't Say I Didn't Tell You So* from the Broadway musical *The Roar of The Greasepaint* starring **Anthony Newley**	$10		Scepter 1298

DEBUT	PEAK	WKS	Gold	A-side (Chart Hit)...B-side	$	Sym	Label & Number
				WARWICK, Dionne — Cont'd			
3/13/65	**75**	6		10 **You Can Have Him** .... *Is There Another Way To Love Him*	$10		Scepter 1294
				female version of **Roy Hamilton**'s 1961 hit "You Can Have Her"			
7/3/65	**65**	8		11 **Here I Am** .... *They Long To Be Close To You*	$10		Scepter 12104
				from the movie *What's New Pussycat?* starring Peter Sellers and Peter O'Toole; B-side was a #1 hit for the **Carpenters** in 1970			
10/2/65	**64**	8		12 **Looking With My Eyes** .... *Only The Strong, Only The Brave*	$10		Scepter 12111
12/11/65+	**39**	10		13 **Are You There (With Another Girl)** .... *If I Ever Make You Cry*	$10		Scepter 12122
4/2/66	**8**	12		14 **Message To Michael** .... *Here Where There Is Love*	$10		Scepter 12133
				"Bubbled Under" (#104) in 1964 by Lou Johnson as "Kentucky Bluebird (Send A Message To Martha)"			
7/2/66	**22**	7		15 **Trains And Boats And Planes** .... *Don't Go Breaking My Heart*	$10		Scepter 12153
10/1/66	**26**	8		16 **I Just Don't Know What To Do With Myself** .... *In Between The Heartaches*	$10		Scepter 12167
				first recorded in 1962 by **Tommy Hunt** ("Bubbled Under" at #119 in 1964)			
12/24/66+	**49**	6		17 **Another Night** .... *Go With Love*	$10		Scepter 12181
4/8/67	**15**	17		18 **Alfie** /			
				title song from the movie starring Michael Caine			
3/18/67	**79**	3		19 **The Beginning Of Loneliness**	$10		Scepter 12187
7/29/67	**32**	9		20 **The Windows Of The World** .... *Walk Little Dolly*	$8		Scepter 12196
1/20/68	**2**[4]	13	●	21 **(Theme From) Valley Of The Dolls** /			
				from the movie *Valley Of The Dolls* starring Sharon Tate and **Patty Duke**			
10/21/67	**4**	13		22 **I Say A Little Prayer**	$8		Scepter 12203
4/13/68	**10**	12		23 **Do You Know The Way To San José** /			
6/8/68	**71**	5		24 **Let Me Be Lonely**	$8		Scepter 12216
8/24/68	**33**	9		25 **Who Is Gonna Love Me?** /			
8/31/68	**65**	5		26 **(There's) Always Something There To Remind Me**	$8		Scepter 12226
				#17, 19, 20, 22 & 26: from the album *The Windows Of The World*			
11/2/68	**19**	9		27 **Promises, Promises** .... *Whoever You Are, I Love You*	$8		Scepter 12231
				from the Broadway musical (also #32 below) starring Jerry Orbach			
2/1/69	**7**	12		28 **This Girl's In Love With You** .... *Dream Sweet Dreamer*	$8		Scepter 12241
				female version of **Herb Alpert**'s 1968 hit "This Guy's In Love With You"			
5/17/69	**37**	7		29 **The April Fools** .... *Slaves*	$8		Scepter 12249
				title song from the movie starring Jack Lemmon			
7/26/69	**43**	8		30 **Odds And Ends** .... *As Long As There's An Apple Tree*	$7		Scepter 12256
9/20/69	**16**	10		31 **You've Lost That Lovin' Feeling** .... *Window Wishing*	$7		Scepter 12262
12/27/69+	**6**	11		32 **I'll Never Fall In Love Again** .... AC[3] *What The World Needs Now Is Love*	$7		Scepter 12273
				a new version of the B-side charted on #56 below			
4/18/70	**32**	7		33 **Let Me Go To Him** .... *Loneliness Remembers What Happiness Forgets*	$6		Scepter 12276
7/11/70	**43**	7		34 **Paper Mache** .... *The Wine Is Young*	$6		Scepter 12285
10/3/70	**37**	8		35 **Make It Easy On Yourself** .... *Knowing When To Leave* [L]	$6		Scepter 12294
				recorded at the Garden State Arts Center; studio version recorded in 1964			
12/5/70+	**43**	9		36 **The Green Grass Starts To Grow** .... *They Don't Give Medals To Yesterday's Heroes*	$6		Scepter 12300
3/20/71	**57**	5		37 **Who Gets The Guy** .... *Walk The Way You Talk*	$6		Scepter 12309
8/7/71	**83**	5		38 **Amanda** *[DIONNE WARWICKE]* .... *He's Moving On*	$6		Scepter 12326
3/11/72	**84**	3		39 **If We Only Have Love** *[DIONNE WARWICKE]* .... *Close To You*	$6		Warner 7560
				all of above written (except #9, 10, 21, 31, 38 & 39) and produced by **Burt Bacharach** and Hal David			
7/27/74	❶[1]	19	●	40 **Then Came You** .... *Just As Long As We Have Love*	$5		Atlantic 3202
				DIONNE WARWICKE AND SPINNERS			
				originally released on Atlantic 3029 earlier in 1974			
1/10/76	**79**	5		41 **Once You Hit The Road** .... *World Of My Dreams*	$5		Warner 8154
6/23/79	**5**	24	●	42 **I'll Never Love This Way Again** .... *In Your Eyes*	$4		Arista 0419
11/10/79+	**15**	19		43 **Deja Vu** .... AC[1] *All The Time*	$4		Arista 0459
3/29/80	**65**	6		44 **After You** .... *Out Of My Hands*	$4		Arista 0498
				above 3 produced by **Barry Manilow** (backing vocals by Manilow and Ron Dante)			
7/26/80	**23**	16		45 **No Night So Long** .... AC[3] *Reaching For The Sky*	$4		Arista 0527
11/22/80	**62**	10		46 **Easy Love** .... *We Never Said Goodbye* (R&B #41)	$4		Arista 0572
6/20/81	**65**	6		47 **Some Changes Are For Good** .... *This Time Is Ours*	$4		Arista 0602
4/17/82	**38**	13		48 **Friends In Love** .... *What Is This* (Warwick)	$4		Arista 0673
				DIONNE WARWICK AND JOHNNY MATHIS			
10/9/82+	**10**	22		49 **Heartbreaker** .... AC[1] *I Can't See Anything (But You)*	$4		Arista 1015
2/26/83	**41**	13		50 **Take The Short Way Home** .... *Just One More Night*	$4		Arista 1040
				Barry Gibb (backing vocal, above 2)			
10/8/83	**27**	13		51 **How Many Times Can We Say Goodbye** .... *What Can A Miracle Do* (Warwick)	$4		Arista 9073
				DIONNE WARWICK AND LUTHER VANDROSS			
11/9/85+	❶[4]	23	●	52 **That's What Friends Are For** RB[3] / AC[2] S:❶[5] / A:❶[3] *Two Ships Passing In The Night* (Warwick)	$3	■	Arista 9422
				DIONNE & FRIENDS: Elton John, Gladys Knight and Stevie Wonder			
				song introduced by **Rod Stewart** on the 1982 movie soundtrack of *Night Shift*			
3/15/86	**72**	9		53 **Whisper In The Dark** .... *Extravagant Gestures*	$3	■	Arista 9460
7/11/87	**12**	14		54 **Love Power** .... AC[1] S:7 / A:14 *In A World Such As This* (Warwick)	$3	■	Arista 9567
				DIONNE WARWICK & JEFFREY OSBORNE			
10/31/87	**62**	7		55 **Reservations For Two** .... *For Everything You Are* (Warwick)	$3	■	Arista 9638
				DIONNE & KASHIF			
8/1/98	**87**	2		56 **What The World Needs Now Is Love** .... S:64 *(same version)*	$5	▮[V]	River North 3024
				DIONNE WARWICK and TheHipHopNationUnited			
				TheHipHopNationUnited: **Big Daddy Kane**, **Bobby Brown**, **Horace Brown**, Mike City, **Coolio**, Flesh-n-Bone, **Mic Geronimo**, Tony Grant, **Ray J.**, Mechalie Jamison, **Kurupt**, Royal Flush, **Tyrese** and **Veronica**; also see the B-side of #32 above			
				WASH, Martha — see WEATHER GIRLS, The			

DEBUT	PEAK	WKS	Gold	A-side (Chart Hit)...B-side	$	Sym	Label & Number
				WASHINGTON, Baby R&B/BUB **'63**			
				Born Justine Washington (aka: **Jeanette Washington**) on 11/13/40 in Bamberg, South Carolina; raised in Harlem, New York. R&B singer/pianist. Sang in vocal group **The Hearts**. First recorded solo for J&S in 1957.			
4/24/61	**60**	9		1 **Nobody Cares (about me)** ... *Money's Funny* **JEANETTE (BABY) WASHINGTON**	$20		Neptune 122
3/23/63	**40**	12		2 **That's How Heartaches Are Made** *There He Is*	$15		Sue 783
7/20/63	**62**	10		3 **Leave Me Alone** ... *You And The Night And The Music*	$15		Sue 790
10/12/63	**100**	1		4 **Hey Lonely One** ... *Doodlin*	$15		Sue 794
3/21/64	**93**	3		5 **I Can't Wait Until I See My Baby** ... *Who's Going To Take Care Of Me* (#125) **JUSTINE WASHINGTON**	$15		Sue 797
9/19/64	**100**	1		6 **The Clock** ... *Standing On The Pier*	$15		Sue 104
11/28/64	**98**	2		7 **It'll Never Be Over For Me** ... *Move On Drifter*	$15		Sue 114
7/24/65	**73**	9		8 **Only Those In Love** ... *The Ballad Of Bobby Dawn* music written by **Bert Kaempfert** (on his 1961 album *Dancing In Wonderland*)	$15		Sue 129
	★374★			**WASHINGTON, Dinah** R&B/MEM/POP/LP **'60**			
				Born Ruth Lee Jones on 8/29/24 in Tuscaloosa, Alabama. Died of an alcohol/pill overdose on 12/14/63 (age 39). All-time great jazz-blues vocalist/pianist. Moved to Chicago in 1927. With Sallie Martin Gospel Singers, 1940-41; local club work in Chicago, 1941-43. With Lionel Hampton, 1943-46. First recorded for Keynote in 1943. Solo touring from 1946. Charted 30 Top 10 R&B hits, 1944-55. Married seven times, once to singer Eddie Chamblee. Inducted into the Rock and Roll Hall of Fame in 1993 as an Early Influence.			
				1)Baby (You've Got What It Takes) 2)A Rockin' Good Way 3)What A Diff'rence A Day Makes 4)Unforgettable 5)September In The Rain			
5/25/59	**8**	20		1 **What A Diff'rence A Day Makes** ... *Come On Home* #5 hit for the Dorsey Brothers in 1934 as "What A Diff'rence A Day Made"	$20		Mercury 71435
10/5/59	**17**	13		2 **Unforgettable** ... *Nothing In The World* #12 hit for **Nat King Cole** in 1952	$20		Mercury 71508
1/25/60	**5**	15	●	3 **Baby (You've Got What It Takes)** RB^{10} *I Do* **DINAH WASHINGTON & BROOK BENTON**	$20		Mercury 71565
3/28/60	**53**	6		4 **It Could Happen To You** ... *The Age Of Miracles* #10 hit for **Jo Stafford** in 1944	$20		Mercury 71560
5/23/60	**7**	13		5 **A Rockin' Good Way (To Mess Around And Fall In Love)** ... RB^{4} *I Believe* **DINAH WASHINGTON & BROOK BENTON** tune first recorded by **The Spaniels** in 1958	$20	■	Mercury 71629
6/20/60	**24**	14		6 **This Bitter Earth** ... RB^{1} *I Understand*	$15	■	Mercury 71635
10/3/60	**30**	10		7 **Love Walked In** ... *I'm In Heaven Tonight* #1 hit for **Sammy Kaye**'s Orchestra in 1938	$15	■	Mercury 71696
12/26/60	**76**	3		8 **We Have Love** ... *Looking Back*	$15	■	Mercury 71744
3/13/61	**95**	1		9 **Early Every Morning (Early Every Evening Too)** ... *Do You Want It That Way*	$15	■	Mercury 71778
5/8/61	**89**	3		10 **Our Love Is Here To Stay** ... *Congratulations To Someone* both Larry Clinton and Red Norvo had Top 20 versions in 1938	$15	■	Mercury 71812
10/16/61	**23**	11		11 **September In The Rain** ... *Wake The Town And Tell The People* #1 hit for Guy Lombardo in 1937	$15	■	Mercury 71876
2/10/62	**71**	5		12 **Tears And Laughter** ... *If I Should Lose You*	$15	■	Mercury 71922
5/19/62	**36**	12		13 **Where Are You /** #5 hit for Mildred Bailey in 1937			
5/12/62	**87**	1		14 **You're Nobody 'Til Somebody Loves You** ... #14 hit for Russ Morgan in 1946	$12		Roulette 4424
5/12/62	**92**	2		15 **Dream** ... *Such A Night* new version of Dinah's #9 R&B hit in 1954 (Mercury 70439); #1 hit for The Pied Pipers in 1945	$10	■	Mercury 71958
8/18/62	**76**	4		16 **I Want To Be Loved** ... *Am I Blue* #1 R&B hit for Savannah Churchill and The Sentimentalists in 1947	$10		Mercury 72015
8/25/62	**88**	2		17 **For All We Know /** #3 hit for Hal Kemp in 1934			
9/1/62	**93**	1		18 **I Wouldn't Know (What To Do)** ...	$10		Roulette 4444
11/17/62	**96**	1		19 **Cold, Cold Heart** ... *I Don't Hurt Anymore* new version of Dinah's #3 R&B hit in 1951 (Mercury 5728)	$10	■	Mercury 72040
11/24/62	**98**	2		20 **You're A Sweetheart** ... *It's A Mean Old World* #1 hit for Dolly Dawn in 1938	$10		Roulette 4455
5/25/63	**92**	3		21 **Soulville** ... *Let Me Be The First To Know*	$10		Roulette 4490
				WASHINGTON, Ella **'69**			
				Born in Miami, Florida. R&B singer. First recorded for Octavia in 1965. Turned to gospel singing in 1973.			
1/18/69	**77**	3		**He Called Me Baby** ... *You're Gonna Cry, Cry, Cry* #1 Country hit for **Charlie Rich** in 1974 as "She Called Me Baby"	$8		Sound Stage 7 2621
				WASHINGTON, Grover Jr. R&B/BUB/LP **'81**			
				Born on 12/12/43 in Buffalo, New York. Died on 12/17/99 (age 56). Jazz-R&B saxophonist.			
<u>5/3/75</u>	**54**	10		1 **Mister Magic** ... *Black Frost* [I]	$6		Kudu 924
2/14/81	**2^3**	24		2 **Just The Two Of Us** ... *Make Me A Memory (Sad Samba)* (Washington, Jr.) **GROVER WASHINGTON, JR. (with Bill Withers)**	$4	■	Elektra 47103
2/6/82	**92**	4		3 **Be Mine (Tonight)** ... *Reaching Out* **Grady Tate** (vocal)	$4	■	Elektra 47246
				WASHINGTON, Keith R&B/LP **'91**			
				Born in Detroit, Michigan. R&B singer/songwriter.			
<u>5/25/91</u>	**40**	13		1 **Kissing You** ... RB^{1} S:41 / A:75 *We Can Work It Out*	$3	■^{V}	Qwest 19414
3/7/98	**63**	13		2 **Bring It On** ... S:44 *(instrumental)*	$3	■	Silas/MCA 55430

DEBUT	PEAK	WKS	Gold	A-side (Chart Hit)....B-side	$	Sym	Label & Number
				WAS (NOT WAS) R&B/BUB/LP **'89**			
				Interracial pop-dance-R&B group from Detroit, Michigan. Fronted by composer/bassist Don Fagenson ("Don Was") and lyricist/flutist David Weiss ("David Was"). Includes vocalists Sweet Pea Atkinson and Sir Harry Bowens. Group appeared in the movie *The Freshman.*			
10/1/88	16	17		1 **Spy In The House Of Love** ....S:9 / A:26 *Dad I'm In Jail*	$3	■	Chrysalis 43266
1/28/89	7	16		2 **Walk The Dinosaur** ....S:5 / A:10 *Wedding Vows In Vegas*	$3	■	Chrysalis 43331
5/6/89	75	6		3 **Anything Can Happen** ....*(R&B version)*	$3	■	Chrysalis 43365
				WATERFRONT AC/LP **'89**			
				Male pop-rock duo from Cardiff, Wales: Chris Duffy (vocals) and Phil Cillia (guitar).			
4/8/89	10	17		1 **Cry** ....S:8 / A:10 *Saved*	$3	■	Polydor 871110
7/29/89	70	5		2 **Nature Of Love** ....*Boy Inside The Man*	$3		Polydor 871414
				WATERS, Crystal R&B/BUB/LP **'91**			
				Born in 1964 in Philadelphia, Pennsylvania. Black dance singer/songwriter.			
5/4/91	8	16	●	1 **Gypsy Woman (She's Homeless)** S:8 / A:16 *(remix)*	$3	▮V	Mercury 868208
9/21/91	55^S	8		2 **Makin' Happy** ....A:58 *(album version) / (3 album snippets)*	$4	▮	Mercury 868762
5/28/94	11	45	●	3 **100% Pure Love** ....A:9 / S:13 *(remix) / (3 album snippets)*	$3	▮	Mercury 858485
3/4/95	82	4		4 **What I Need** ....*Ghetto Day* all of above: #1 Dance Club Play hits	$4	▮	Mercury 856404
2/22/97	40	15		5 **Say...If You Feel Alright** ....S:42 / A:52 *(3 versions)* samples "September" by **Earth, Wind & Fire**; "45": Mercury 574228; B-side: "You Bring The Sunshine" by **Gina Thompson** (R&B #53)	$4	▮V	Mercury 578943
	★296★			**WATLEY, Jody** R&B/BUB/AC/LP **'89**			
				Born on 1/30/59 in Chicago, Illinois. Female singer for the R&B-dance trio **Shalamar** (1977-84) and former dancer on TV's *Soul Train.* Goddaughter of **Jackie Wilson**. Won the 1987 Best New Artist Grammy Award. *1)Looking For A New Love 2)Real Love 3)Everything*			
3/7/87	2^4	19		1 **Looking For A New Love** RB^3 S:❶^3 / A:2 *(acappella version)* promotional foldout poster sleeve issued on MCA 17291	$3	■	MCA 52956
6/20/87	56	7		2 **Still A Thrill** ....*Looking For A New Love (acappella)*	$3	■	MCA 53081
10/3/87	6	23		3 **Don't You Want Me** ....S:5 / A:6 *(remix)*	$3	■	MCA 53162
1/30/88	10	17		4 **Some Kind Of Lover** ....A:9 / S:10 *(instrumental)*	$3	■	MCA 53235
4/30/88	60	11		5 **Most Of All** ....*(instrumental)* above 5 from the album *Jody Watley*	$3	■	MCA 53258
3/18/89	2^2	18	●	6 **Real Love** ....RB^1 S:❶^2 / A:3 *(instrumental)*	$3	■	MCA 53484
6/17/89	9	18		7 **Friends** ....S:5 / A:14 *Private Life* (Watley) **JODY WATLEY (With Eric B. & Rakim)**	$3		MCA 53660
10/14/89+	4	23		8 **Everything** ....A:5 / S:7 *(instrumental)*	$3	▮V	MCA 53714
3/24/90	87	3		9 **Precious Love** ....*(no B-side)* "45" B-side: (instrumental); above 4 from the album *Larger Than Life*	$3	▮V	MCA 53790
11/30/91+	61	15		10 **I Want You** ....A:51 *(3 album snippets)*	$3	▮	MCA 54137
3/7/92	19	17		11 **I'm The One You Need** ....A:14 *(3 album snippets)* "45": MCA/Collectables 90208; B-side: "Friends"	$3	▮V	MCA 54276
11/13/93	100	2		12 **Your Love Keeps Working On Me** ....*(instrumental)*	$3	▮	MCA 54744
10/26/96	6	20	▲	13 **This Is For The Lover In You** ....S:3 / A:37 *(remix)* **BABYFACE Featuring LL Cool J, Howard Hewett, Jody Watley and Jeffrey Daniels** #17 R&B hit for **Shalamar** in 1981 (Hewett, Watley and Daniels were members of **Shalamar**)	$3	▮V	Epic 78443
2/21/98	73	13		14 **Off The Hook** ....S:59 *(instrumental)* remix version featuring Rakim (**Eric B. & Rakim**) available on Atlantic 84100; all of above (except #8-10 & 13) were Top 10 Dance Club Play hits	$3	▮V	Atlantic 84071
				WATSON, Johnny "Guitar" R&B/BUB/LP **'77**			
				Born on 2/3/35 in Houston, Texas. Died of a heart attack on 5/17/96 (age 61) while performing at the Yokohama Blues café in Japan. R&B singer/songwriter/guitarist. First recorded for Federal in 1952. Member of the R&B group **The Shields**.			
2/25/67	96	4		1 **Mercy, Mercy, Mercy** ....*A Quitter Never Wins* **LARRY WILLIAMS & JOHNNY WATSON**	$15		Okeh 7274
10/4/75	99	4		2 **I Don't Want To Be A Lone Ranger** ....*You Can Stay But The Noise Must Go*	$6		Fantasy 739
7/9/77	41	12		3 **A Real Mother For Ya** ....*Nothing Left To Be Desired*	$6		DJM 1024
				WATTS, Noble "Thin Man" LP **'57**			
				Born in 1926 in DeLand, Florida. R&B saxophonist/songwriter.			
12/23/57	44	9		**Hard Times (The Slop)** ....S:44 / T:48 *I'm Walkin' The Floor Over You* [I] **NOBLE "THIN MAN" WATTS & His Rhythm Sparks**	$25		Baton 249
				WATTS 103rd STREET RHYTHM BAND — see WRIGHT, Charles			
				WA WA NEE LP **'87**			
				Pop group from Australia: brothers Paul (vocals, keyboards) and Mark (bass) Gray, with Steve Williams (guitar) and Chris Sweeney (drums).			
9/12/87	35	13		1 **Sugar Free** ....A:31 / S:34 *When The World Is A Home*	$3	■	Epic 07283
1/30/88	86	2		2 **Stimulation** ....*Headlines*	$3		Epic 07671
				WAX LP **'86**			
				Pop duo: **Andrew Gold** and Graham Gouldman (**10cc**). Credited later as Wax U.K.			
3/15/86	43	13		**Right Between The Eyes** ....*Only A Visitor*	$3		RCA 14306
				WAYLON & WILLIE — see JENNINGS, Waylon / NELSON, Willie			
				WAYNE, Thomas **'59**			
				Born Thomas Wayne Perkins on 7/22/40 in Battsville, Mississippi. Died in a car accident on 8/15/71 (age 31). Brother of guitarist Luther Perkins of **Johnny Cash**'s band. Backing vocals by the female group The DeLons.			
1/26/59	5	19		1 **Tragedy** ....*Saturday Date*	$30		Fernwood 109
5/11/59	92	1		2 **Eternally** ....*Scandalizing My Name* **THOMAS WAYNE With The DeLons** (above 2) above 2 produced by Scotty Moore (**Elvis Presley**'s former guitarist)	$30		Fernwood 111

DEBUT	PEAK	WKS	Gold	A-side (Chart Hit)..........B-side	$	Sym	Label & Number
				WC R&B/BUB/LP **'98**			
				Born William Calhoun in Los Angeles, California. Male rapper. Member of **Westside Connection**.			
9/30/95	88	10		1 **West Up!** ....*(instrumental)*	$4	▮	Payday 850258
				WC AND THE MAAD CIRCLE Featuring Ice Cube and Mack 10			
				samples "Reach For It" by **George Duke**			
12/13/97+	56	20		2 **Just Clownin'** ....S:42 *(instrumental)*	$4	▮	Payday 570043
10/17/98	64	7		3 **Better Days** ....S:36 *(instrumental) / Cheddar* (w/**Mack 10** & **Ice Cube**)	$4	▮	Payday 570258
				WC Featuring Jon B.			
				samples "We Are One" by **Maze Featuring Frankie Beverly**			
9/28/02	81	13		4 **The Streets** ....*(2 versions) / Wanna Ride* (w/**Ice Cube** & **MC Ren**)	$6	T	Def Jam 063974
				WC (feat. Nate Dogg)			
				WE ARE FAMILY **'01**			
				All-star group organized by producer Nile Rodgers (**Chic**) in response to the terrorist attacks in New York City. Featured performers include **Amber**, **Ashford & Simpson**, **Jackson Browne**, **Taylor Dayne**, **Faith Evans**, **Roberta Flack**, **Patti LaBelle**, **Stephanie Mills**, **Joan Osborne**, **Pointer Sisters**, **Diana Ross**, **Patty Smyth**, **Luther Vandross** and **Dionne Warwick**.			
11/17/01	29^{S}	9		**We Are Family** ....*(instrumental)*	$5	★	Tommy Boy 2331
				WEATHER GIRLS, The R&B/BUB/LP **'83**			
				R&B-disco duo from San Francisco, California: **Martha Wash** and Izora Redman. Formerly "Two Tons O' Fun." Backup singers for **Sylvester** in the late 1970s. Wash was the uncredited lead vocalist of "You're My One And Only (True Love)" by **Seduction**, "Everybody Everybody" by **Black Box** and "Gonna Make You Sweat" by **C & C Music Factory**.			
1/22/83	46	11		1 **It's Raining Men** ....*(long version)*	$4		Entertainment Co. 03354
3/13/93	90	2		2 **Give It To You** ....A:75 *(2 versions)*	$4	▮	RCA 62433
				MARTHA WASH			
				WEATHERLY, Jim C&W/AC/BUB/LP **'74**			
				Born on 3/17/43 in Pontotoc, Mississippi. Pop-country singer/songwriter. Wrote **Gladys Knight**'s hits "Neither One Of Us," "Midnight Train To Georgia" and "Best Thing That Ever Happened To Me." Played quarterback for the University of Mississippi.			
9/14/74	11	16		1 **The Need To Be** ....*Like Old Times Again*	$5	■	Buddah 420
1/25/75	87	5		2 **I'll Still Love You** ....*My First Day Without Her*	$5		Buddah 444
				WEBB, C. **'99**			
				Born Mayce Edward Christopher Webber III on 3/1/73 in Detroit, Michigan. Pro basketball player (Chris Webber).			
4/3/99	70^{S}	1		**Gangsta! Gangsta! (How U Do It)** ....*(4 versions)*	$10	★	Humility 54317
				C. WEBB Featuring Kurupt			
				samples "White Horse" by **Laid Back** and "Put Your Hands Where My Eyes Can See" by **Busta Rhymes**			
				WEBB, Paula **'75**			
				Born in Ypsilanti, Michigan. Ten years old in 1975.			
2/1/75	60	4		**Please, Mr. President** ....*Paula's Theme* (The Westbound Ensemble) [N]	$6		Westbound 5001
				WEBER, Joan **'55**			
				Born on 12/12/35 in Paulsboro, New Jersey. Died on 5/13/81 (age 45). Pop singer (19 years old in 1954).			
12/4/54+	❶^{4}	16	●	**Let Me Go Lover** ....A:❶^{4} / J:❶^{4} / S:❶^{2} *Marionette*	$15		Columbia 40366
				Jimmy Carroll (orch.); written in 1953 as "Let Me Go Devil" and first recorded by **Georgie Shaw**; Weber's version was an overnight sensation after being featured 6 times on the 11/15/54 *Studio One* CBS-TV production			
				WEDNESDAY **'74**			
				Pop group from Oshawa, Ontario, Canada: Mike O'Neil (vocals), Paul Andrew-Smith, John Dufek and Randy Begg.			
11/24/73+	34	18		1 **Last Kiss** ....*Without You*	$6		Sussex 507
5/11/74	79	4		2 **Teen Angel** ....*Taking Me Home*	$6		Sussex 515
				WEEZER ROK/BUB/LP **'95**			
				Rock group from Los Angeles, California: Rivers Cuomo (vocals, guitar), Brian Bell (guitar), Matt Sharp (bass) and Pat Wilson (drums). Also see **The Rentals**.			
10/1/94	57	16		1 **Undone-The Sweater Song** ....S:41 / A:74 *Holiday*	$5	▮V	DGC 19378
11/26/94+	18^{A}	21		2 **Buddy Holly**			album cut
7/1/95	51^{A}	14		3 **Say It Ain't So**			album cut
				all of above from the album *Weezer* on DGC 24629, and produced by **Ric Ocasek**			
				WE FIVE BUB/LP **'65**			
				Pop group from San Francisco, California: Beverly Bivens (vocals), Bob Jones and Jerry Burgan (guitars), Pete Fullerton (bass) and Mike Stewart (drums). Stewart (brother of **John Stewart**) died on 11/13/2002 (age 57).			
7/24/65	3	15		1 **You Were On My Mind** ....AC^{5} *Small World*	$10		A&M 770
				first released by Ian & Sylvia in 1964 on Vanguard 35025			
11/13/65	31	8		2 **Let's Get Together** ....*Cast Your Fate To The Wind*	$8		A&M 784
				chart hit for **The Youngbloods** in 1967 and 1969 as "Get Together"			
				WEIR, Bob — see GRATEFUL DEAD			
				WEISBERG, Tim — see FOGELBERG, Dan			
				WEISSBERG, Eric, & Steve Mandell C&W/LP **'73**			
				Prominent session musicians. Both had worked with **Judy Collins** and **John Denver**. Weissberg was a member of **The Tarriers** in the 1960s.			
1/13/73	2^{4}	14	●	**Dueling Banjos** ....AC^{2} *End Of A Dream* [I]	$6		Warner 7659
				tune written and recorded in 1955 as "Feuding Banjos" by Arthur "Guitar Boogie" Smith; from the movie *Deliverance* starring **Burt Reynolds**; some pressings credit artist as **ERIC WEISSBERG**, and others as **DELIVERANCE**			
				WELCH, Bob BUB/ROK/LP **'78**			
				Born on 7/31/46 in Los Angeles, California. Pop-rock singer/guitarist. Member of **Fleetwood Mac** from 1971-74.			
10/15/77+	8	18		1 **Sentimental Lady** *Hot Love, Cold World*	$4		Capitol 4479
				Christine McVie and **Lindsey Buckingham** (backing vocals)			
1/28/78	14	17		2 **Ebony Eyes** ....*Outskirts*	$4		Capitol 4543
6/3/78	31	10		3 **Hot Love, Cold World** ....*Danchiva*	$4	■	Capitol 4588
				originally released as the B-side of #1 above			

DEBUT	PEAK	WKS	Gold	A-side (Chart Hit)...B-side	$	Sym	Label & Number
				WELCH, Bob — Cont'd			
2/10/79	19	15		4 **Precious Love** ...*Something Strong*	$4		Capitol 4685
5/26/79	73	3		5 **Church**...*Here Comes The Night*	$4	■	Capitol 4719
				WELCH, Lenny BUB/R&B/AC/LP **'63**			
				Born on 5/15/38 in Asbury Park, New Jersey. Black Adult Contemporary singer.			
2/29/60	45	13		1 **You Don't Know Me**...*I Need Someone*	$15		Cadence 1373
				written and recorded by **Eddy Arnold** in 1956			
10/26/63	4	16		2 **Since I Fell For You** *Are You Sincere*	$15		Cadence 1439
				"Bubbled Under" (#134) in 1967 on Columbia 44007; #3 R&B hit for **Annie Laurie** & **Paul Gayten** in 1947			
3/21/64	25	9		3 **Ebb Tide** ...*Congratulations, Baby*	$20		Cadence 1422
				featured in the movie *Sweet Bird Of Youth* starring Paul Newman; #2 hit for **Frank Chacksfield**'s Orchestra in 1953			
7/4/64	92	2		4 **If You See My Love** ...*Father Sebastian*	$15		Cadence 1446
				written by **Seals & Crofts**; Archie Bleyer (orch., all of above)			
6/26/65	72	6		5 **Darling Take Me Back** ...*Time After Time*	$12		Kapp 662
8/21/65	61	8		6 **Two Different Worlds** ...*I Was There*	$12		Kapp 689
12/4/65	96	2		7 **Run To My Lovin' Arms**...*Coronet Blue*	$12		Kapp 712
				Alan Lorber (orch., above 3)			
1/10/70	34	10		8 **Breaking Up Is Hard To Do**...*Get Mommy To Come Back Home*	$8		Common. United 3004
				Charlie Calello (orch.)			
8/12/72	96	5		9 **A Sunday Kind Of Love**...*I Wish You Could Know Me (Naomi)*	$7		Atco 6894
				Thom Bell (orch.); co-written by **Louis Prima**; #15 hit for **Jo Stafford** in 1947			
	★348★			**WELK, Lawrence, And His Orchestra** MEM/POP/BUB/AC/C&W/LP **'61**			
				Born on 3/11/03 in Strasburg, North Dakota. Died of pneumonia on 5/17/92 (age 89). Accordion player and sweet band leader since the mid-1920s. Band's style labeled as "champagne music." Own national TV musical variety show began on 7/2/55 and ran on ABC until 9/4/71. New episodes in syndication from 1971 to 1982. Reruns still enjoy immense popularity. Hit #2 in 1944 with "Don't Sweetheart Me." Charted 42 albums, 1956-72.			
				1)Calcutta 2)Tonight You Belong To Me 3)The Poor People Of Paris 4)Moritat (A Theme From "The Threepenny Opera") 5)Last Date			
10/22/55	35CU	2		1 **Bonnie Blue Gal** ...*Sam, The Old Accordion Man*	$10		Coral 61515
				The Sparklers (vocals); adapted from the Civil War song "The Bonnie Blue Flag"			
2/18/56	17	11		2 **Moritat A Theme From "The Threepenny Opera"** .....J:17 / T:31 *Stompin' At The Savoy* [I]	$10		Coral 61574
				LAWRENCE WELK And His Sparkling Sextet			
3/17/56	17	13		3 **The Poor People Of Paris** ...J:17 / T:45 *Nobody Knows But The Lord* [I]	$10		Coral 61592
6/23/56	96	1		4 **On The Street Where You Live**...T:96 *I Could Have Danced All Night*	$10		Coral 61644
				Larry Deane (vocal); from the Broadway musical *My Fair Lady* starring **Julie Andrews**			
7/28/56	32	8		5 **Weary Blues** / T:32			
				THE McGUIRE SISTERS and LAWRENCE WELK And His Champagne Music			
				traditional tune first recorded in 1923 by The New Orleans Rhythm Kings			
8/4/56	63	5		6 **In The Alps** ...T:63	$10	■	Coral 61670
				LAWRENCE WELK AND HIS CHAMPAGNE MUSIC and THE McGUIRE SISTERS			
9/22/56	15	13		7 **Tonight You Belong To Me** / T:15 / S:16 / A:16 / J:17			
				LAWRENCE WELK And His Sparkling Strings (with The Lennon Sisters and The Sparklers)			
				#1 hit for **Gene Austin** in 1927			
9/15/56	70	10		8 **When The White Lilacs Bloom Again** ...T:70 [I]	$10		Coral 61701
				LAWRENCE WELK And His Sparkling Strings			
12/2/57	48	6		9 **Liechtenstein Polka** ...S:48 / T:62 *You Know Too Much* [F]	$10		Coral 61900
				LAWRENCE WELK And His Champagne Music (#1, 3, 4 & 9)			
				The Sparklers (vocals)			
10/24/60	21	11		10 **Last Date** ...*Remember Lolita* [I]	$8		Dot 16145
12/12/60+	❶2	17	●	11 **Calcutta** *My Grandfather's Clock* [I]	$8		Dot 16161
				written in Germany in 1958; above 2 feature Frank Scott (on piano and harpsichord, respectively)			
3/20/61	55	7		12 **Theme from My Three Sons** ...*Out Of A Clear Blue Sky* [I]	$8		Dot 16198
				from the TV series *My Three Sons* starring Fred MacMurray			
6/12/61	71	5		13 **Yellow Bird**...*Cruising Down The River* [I]	$8		Dot 16222
				adapted from a West Indian folk song			
9/25/61	87	3		14 **Riders In The Sky** ...*My Love For You* [I]	$8		Dot 16237
				#1 hit for **Vaughn Monroe** in 1949			
4/7/62	56	6		15 **Runaway** ...*Happy Love* [I]	$8		Dot 16336
6/9/62	48	16		16 **Baby Elephant Walk**...*Theme From The Brothers Grimm* [I]	$8		Dot 16364
				written by **Henry Mancini**; from the movie *Hatari!* starring John Wayne			
12/8/62	98	1		17 **Zero-Zero** ...*Night Theme* [I]	$6		Dot 16420
6/29/63	89	2		18 **Scarlett O'Hara** / [I]			
				title named after Vivien Leigh's character in the movie *Gone With The Wind*			
6/22/63	100	1		19 **Breakwater**... [I]	$6		Dot 16488
3/14/64	91	2		20 **Stockholm**...*The Girl From Barbados* [I]	$6		Dot 16582
4/10/65	75	4		21 **Apples And Bananas** ...*(Theme From) "The Addams Family"* [I]	$6		Dot 16697
				WELLS, Kitty C&W/MEM **'58**			
				Born Muriel Ellen Deason on 8/30/19 in Nashville, Tennessee. Singer/songwriter/guitarist. Known as "The Queen of Country Music" (charted 81 hits, 1952-79). Married Johnny Wright (of Johnnie & Jack) on 10/30/37. Won Grammy's Lifetime Achievement Award in 1991.			
7/14/58	78	5		**Jealousy** ...T:78 *I Can't Help Wondering*	$15		Decca 30662
	★224★			**WELLS, Mary** R&B/BUB/LP **'64**			
				Born on 5/13/43 in Detroit, Michigan. Died of cancer on 7/26/92 (age 49). R&B singer. At age 17, presented "Bye Bye Baby," a tune she had written for **Jackie Wilson**, to Wilson's producer, Berry Gordy, Jr. Gordy signed her to his newly formed label, Motown. Wells was the first artist to have a Top 10 and #1 single for that label. Married for a time to Cecil Womack (brother of **Bobby Womack**).			
				1)My Guy 2)Two Lovers 3)The One Who Really Loves You 4)You Beat Me To The Punch 5)Laughing Boy			
1/30/61	45	11		1 **Bye Bye Baby** ...*Please Forgive Me*	$40		Motown 1003
7/17/61	33	9		2 **I Don't Want To Take A Chance**...*I'm So Sorry*	$25	■	Motown 1011

DEBUT	PEAK	WKS	Gold	A-side (Chart Hit).....B-side	$	Sym	Label & Number
				WELLS, Mary — Cont'd			
3/24/62	8	18		3 The One Who Really Loves You ..... *I'm Gonna Stay*	$20	■	Motown 1024
8/11/62	9	12		4 You Beat Me To The Punch ..... RB[1] *Old Love (Let's Try It Again)*	$20	■	Motown 1032
12/1/62+	7	13		5 Two Lovers ..... RB[4] *Operator*	$20		Motown 1035
2/23/63	15	9		6 Laughing Boy /			
3/23/63	100	1		7 Two Wrongs Don't Make A Right	$20		Motown 1039
5/25/63	40	8		8 Your Old Stand By ..... *What Love Has Joined Together*	$20		Motown 1042
9/28/63	22	9		9 You Lost The Sweetest Boy /			
10/19/63+	29	17		10 What's Easy For Two Is So Hard For One	$20		Motown 1048
4/4/64	❶[2]	15		11 My Guy ..... RB[2] *Oh Little Boy (What Did You Do To Me)*	$20		Motown 1056
				#3-8, 10 & 11: written and produced by **Smokey Robinson**			
5/16/64	17	10		12 What's The Matter With You Baby /			
5/2/64	19	9		13 Once Upon A Time	$20	■	Motown 1057
				MARVIN GAYE & MARY WELLS (above 2)			
10/31/64	45	8		14 Ain't It The Truth /			
11/7/64	88	3		15 Stop Takin' Me For Granted	$15		20th Century 544
1/2/65	34	6		16 Use Your Head ..... *Everlovin' Boy*	$15		20th Century 555
3/20/65	54	6		17 Never, Never Leave Me ..... *Why Don't You Let Yourself Go* (#107)	$15		20th Century 570
6/19/65	74	4		18 He's A Lover ..... *I'm Learnin'*	$15	■	20th Century 590
9/11/65	95	2		19 Me Without You ..... *I'm Sorry*	$15	■	20th Century 606
2/12/66	51	8		20 Dear Lover /			
1/22/66	94	3		21 Can't You See (You're Losing Me)	$12		Atco 6392
7/2/66	99	2		22 Such A Sweet Thing ..... *Keep Me In Suspense*	$12		Atco 6423
5/18/68	65	8		23 The Doctor ..... *Two Lovers History*	$15		Jubilee 5621
				WENDY AND LISA R&B/LP **'87**			
				Pop duo from Los Angeles, California: Wendy Melvoin (born on 1/26/64) and Lisa Coleman (born on 6/8/60). Formerly with **Prince**'s band, The Revolution. Wendy is daughter of Mike Melvoin (The Plastic Cow); twin sister of Susannah Melvoin (**The Family**); sister of the late Jonathan Melvoin (touring keyboardist with **Smashing Pumpkins**).			
9/19/87	56	10		1 Waterfall ..... *The Life*	$3	■	Columbia 07243
12/19/92+	53[A]	4		2 The Closing Of The Year (Main Theme)		V	album cut
				THE MUSICAL CAST of TOYS FEATURING WENDY & LISA			
				from the movie *Toys* starring Robin Williams (soundtrack on Geffen 24505); "45": Geffen 19146; B-side: (instrumental)			
				WERNER, Max **'81**			
				Born in Holland. Lead singer of **Kayak**.			
5/16/81	74	6		Rain In May ..... *In The Winter*	$5		Radio 3821
				WESLEY, Fred — see JB's			
				WEST, Dottie C&W/AC/BUB/LP **'81**			
				Born Dorothy Marsh on 10/11/32 in McMinnville, Tennessee. Died on 9/4/91 (age 58) from injuries suffered in a car accident on 8/30/91. Country singer (charted 63 hits, 1963-85).			
1/20/73	97	3		1 If It's All Right With You ..... *Special Memory*	$6		RCA Victor 0828
9/29/73	49	11		2 Country Sunshine ..... *Wish I Didn't Love You Anymore*	$6		RCA Victor 0072
				The Jordanaires (backing vocals); adapted from a Coca-Cola jingle			
3/8/80	73	5		3 A Lesson In Leavin' ..... CW[1] *Love's So Easy For Two*	$5		United Artists 1339
3/28/81	14	20		4 What Are We Doin' In Love ..... CW[1] *Choosin' Means Losin'* (West)	$4		Liberty 1404
				DOTTIE WEST (with Kenny Rogers)			
				WEST COAST RAP ALL-STARS, The LP **'90**			
				Rap benefit for inner city youth: **Above The Law**, Body & Soul, Def Jef, **Digital Underground**, **Eazy-E**, **Ice-T**, **J.J. Fad**, King Tee, **M.C. Hammer**, **Michel'le**, N.W.A., **Oaktown's 3-5-7**, **Tone Loc** and **Young MC**			
6/23/90	35	16	●	We're All In The Same Gang ..... S:17 *Tellin' Time*	$4	▮	Warner 19819
				produced by **Dr. Dre**			
				WESTLIFE LP **'00**			
				"Boy band" from Dublin, Ireland: Nicky Byrne, Shane Filan, Kian Egan, Mark Feehily and Bryan McFadden.			
4/1/00	20	20	●	Swear It Again ..... S:2 *(4 album snippets)*	$3	★	Arista 13816
				WESTON, Kim R&B/BUB **'67**			
				Born Agatha Natalie Weston on 12/30/39 in Detroit, Michigan. R&B singer; previously sang in gospel groups.			
7/6/63	88	5		1 Love Me All The Way ..... *It Should Have Been Me*	$30		Tamla 54076
10/24/64	61	6		2 What Good Am I Without You ..... *I Want You 'Round*	$15		Tamla 54104
				MARVIN GAYE & KIM WESTON			
10/2/65	50	8		3 Take Me In Your Arms (Rock Me A Little While) ..... *Don't Compare Me With Her*	$15		Gordy 7046
3/12/66	56	7		4 Helpless ..... *A Love Like Yours (Don't Come Knocking Everyday)*	$15		Gordy 7050
1/7/67	14	12		5 It Takes Two ..... *It's Got To Be A Miracle (This Thing Called Love)*	$15		Tamla 54141
				MARVIN GAYE & KIM WESTON			
4/29/67	99	1		6 I Got What You Need ..... *Someone Like You*	$15	■	MGM 13720
				WESTSIDE CONNECTION R&B/LP **'96**			
				Collaboration of rap stars **Ice Cube**, **Mack 10** and WC (of **WC And The Maad Circle**).			
9/28/96	21	20		1 Bow Down ..... S:9 *Hoo Bangin'*	$5	▮	Lench Mob 53227
3/8/97	40	20		2 Gangstas Make The World Go Round .. S:28 *(clean version) / Bow Down / (instrumental)*	$5	▮	Lench Mob 53264
				samples "People Make The World Go Round" by **The Stylistics**			
				WEST STREET MOB R&B **'81**			
				Dance trio from Englewood, New Jersey: Joey Robinson, Warren Moore and Sebrina Gillison. Robinson is the son of **Sylvia**.			
9/12/81	88	3		1 Let's Dance (Make Your Body Move) ..... *Monster Jam*	$10	T	Sugar Hill 559
4/17/82	89	4		2 Sing A Simple Song ..... *Another Muther For Ya*	$10	T	Sugar Hill 576
				above 2 issued on 7" vinyl ("45s") for promotional use on Sugar Hill 763 and 780, respectively			

DEBUT	PEAK	WKS	Gold	A-side (Chart Hit)...B-side	$	Sym	Label & Number

WET WET WET
AC/LP **'94**

Pop-rock group from Glasgow, Scotland: Marti Pellow (vocals), Neil Mitchell (keyboards), Graeme Clark (bass) and Tom Cunningham (drums). Band name inspired from a line in the **Scritti Politti** song "Getting, Having, and Holding."

DEBUT	PEAK	WKS	Gold	A-side (Chart Hit)...B-side	$	Sym	Label & Number
5/28/88	**58**	8		1 **Wishing I Was Lucky** ...*Words Of Wisdom*	$3	■	Uni 50000
7/9/94	**41**	20		2 **Love Is All Around** ...S:39 / A:44 *I Can Give You Everything*	$4	▮V	London 857580
				from the movie *Four Weddings And A Funeral* starring Andie MacDowell; "45": London 856194; B-side: "Goodnight Girl"			

WET WILLIE
LP **'74**

Southern-rock band from Mobile, Alabama: brothers Jack (bass; born on 4/26/49) and **Jimmy Hall** (vocals) (see #9 & 10 below), Rick Hirsch (guitar), John Anthony (keyboards) and Lewis Ross (drums). Michael Duke (keyboards, vocals) joined in late 1975.

1)Keep On Smilin' 2)I'm Happy That Love Has Found You 3)Weekend

DEBUT	PEAK	WKS	Gold	A-side (Chart Hit)...B-side	$	Sym	Label & Number
5/25/74	**10**	19		1 **Keep On Smilin'** *Soul Jones*	$6		Capricorn 0043
				also released on Capricorn 0206 in 1974			
10/26/74	**66**	4		2 **Country Side Of Life** ...*Don't Wait Too Long*	$6		Capricorn 0212
				first released on Capricorn 0031 in 1973 with a promo picture sleeve			
3/1/75	**69**	5		3 **Leona** ...*Ain't He A Mess*	$5		Capricorn 0224
5/31/75	**96**	2		4 **Dixie Rock** ...*She's My Lady*	$5		Capricorn 0231
5/22/76	**66**	3		5 **Everything That 'Cha Do (Will Come Back To You)** ...*Walkin' By Myself*	$5		Capricorn 0254
12/3/77+	**30**	14		6 **Street Corner Serenade** ...*We Got Lovin'*	$4		Epic 50478
4/8/78	**45**	7		7 **Make You Feel Love Again** ...*Let It Shine*	$4		Epic 50528
5/26/79	**29**	12		8 **Weekend** ...*Mr. Streamline*	$4		Epic 50714
				JIMMY HALL:			
9/27/80	**27**	17		9 **I'm Happy That Love Has Found You** ...*Touch You*	$4		Epic 50931
5/1/82	**77**	3		10 **Fool For Your Love** ...*Cadillac Tracks*	$4		Epic 02857

WHAM! — see MICHAEL, George

WHAT IS THIS
LP **'85**

Pop-rock trio: Alain Johannes (vocals, guitar), Chris Hutchinson (bass) and Jack Irons (drums; **Red Hot Chili Peppers**, **Pearl Jam**).

DEBUT	PEAK	WKS	Gold	A-side (Chart Hit)...B-side	$	Sym	Label & Number
8/17/85	**62**	6		**I'll Be Around** ...*Whisper (To Natasha)*	$4		MCA 52593
				produced by **Todd Rundgren**			

WHATNAUTS
R&B **'71**

R&B vocal trio from Baltimore, Maryland: Billy Herndon (lead), Garnet Jones (tenor) and Gerald Pinkney (baritone).

DEBUT	PEAK	WKS	Gold	A-side (Chart Hit)...B-side	$	Sym	Label & Number
2/28/70	**99**	2		1 **Message From A Black Man** ...*Dance To The Music*	$8		A & I 001
				THE WHATNAUTS & THE WHATNAUT BAND			
4/17/71	**71**	7		2 **I'll Erase Away Your Pain** ...*Just Can't Lose Your Love*	$6		Stang 5023
9/4/71	**100**	1		3 **We're Friends By Day (And Lovers By Night)** ...*Just Can't Leave My Baby*	$6		Stang 5030

WHEELER, Billy Edd
C&W/LP **'65**

Born on 12/9/32 in Whitesville, West Virginia. Folk singer/songwriter/guitarist. Wrote "Reverend Mr. Black" for **The Kingston Trio** and "Coward Of The County" for **Kenny Rogers**. Co-owner of Sleepy Hollow Music.

DEBUT	PEAK	WKS	Gold	A-side (Chart Hit)...B-side	$	Sym	Label & Number
1/2/65	**50**	7		**Ode To The Little Brown Shack Out Back** ...*Sister Sara* [L-N]	$8		Kapp 617
				recorded at The Mountain State Art & Craft Fair in Ripley, West Virginia			

WHEELER, Caron
R&B/LP **'90**

Born on 1/19/63 in London, England (of Jamaican parents). Female R&B singer. Featured vocalist on **Soul II Soul**'s hits "Keep On Movin'" and "Back To Life." Backup singer for **Elvis Costello** in 1983.

DEBUT	PEAK	WKS	Gold	A-side (Chart Hit)...B-side	$	Sym	Label & Number
9/29/90	**53**	10		**Livin' In The Light** ...*(original mix)*	$4	▮	EMI 50286

WHEN IN ROME
LP **'88**

Electro-dance trio from England: Clive Farrington and Andrew Mann (vocals), with Michael Floreale (keyboards).

DEBUT	PEAK	WKS	Gold	A-side (Chart Hit)...B-side	$	Sym	Label & Number
9/3/88	**11**	25		1 **The Promise** ...S:9 / A:12 *(dub version)*	$3		Virgin 99323
2/18/89	**95**	2		2 **Heaven Knows** ...*Whatever The Weather*	$3	■	Virgin 99253

WHIRLWIND
'76

R&B-disco trio: Sandie Ancrum and her brothers Charles and Eddie Ancrum.

DEBUT	PEAK	WKS	Gold	A-side (Chart Hit)...B-side	$	Sym	Label & Number
10/23/76	**91**	4		**Full Time Thing (Between Dusk And Dawn)** ...*Don't Let Him Get The Best Of You*	$5		Roulette 7195

WHISPERS, The
R&B/BUB/LP **'87**

R&B-dance vocal group formed in Los Angeles, California: twin brothers Walter and Wallace "Scotty" Scott, Gordy Harmon (**The Superbs**), Marcus Hutson and Nicholas Caldwell. First recorded for Dore in 1964. Harmon replaced in 1973 by Leaveil Degree who was briefly a member of **The Friends Of Distinction**. Group founded the Black Tie record label.

1)Rock Steady 2)And The Beat Goes On 3)It's A Love Thing

DEBUT	PEAK	WKS	Gold	A-side (Chart Hit)...B-side	$	Sym	Label & Number
9/19/70	**50**	9		1 **Seems Like I Gotta Do Wrong** ...*Needle In A Haystack*	$10		Soul Clock 1004
5/29/71	**93**	2		2 **Your Love Is So Doggone Good** ...*Crackel Jack*	$7		Janus 150
1/27/73	**94**	4		3 **Somebody Loves You** ...*Can We Love Forever*	$7		Janus 200
2/9/74	**92**	4		4 **A Mother For My Children** ...*What More Can A Girl Ask For?*	$7		Janus 231
8/28/76	**88**	10		5 **One For The Money (Part 1)** ...*(Part 2)*	$6		Soul Train 10700
				also released on RCA 10700 in 1976			
8/13/77	**94**	4		6 **Make It With You** ...*You Are Number One*	$6		Soul Train 10996
2/9/80	**19**	15	●	7 **And The Beat Goes On** ...RB[5] *Can You Do The Boogie*	$4		Solar 11894
4/19/80	**28**	11		8 **Lady** ...*I Love You*	$4		Solar 11928
2/14/81	**28**	15		9 **It's A Love Thing** ...*Girl I Need You*	$4		Solar 12154
4/30/83	**84**	4		10 **Tonight** ...*Small Talkin'*	$4		Solar 69842
6/6/87	**7**	23		11 **Rock Steady** RB[1] A:5 / S:8 *Are You Going My Way*	$3		Solar 70006
8/4/90	**55**	11		12 **Innocent** ...*(2 remixes)*	$3	▮V	Capitol 44593
				"45" issued as a promo only on Capitol 79170; B-side: (club edit)			

DEBUT	PEAK	WKS	Gold	A-side (Chart Hit)..........B-side	$	Sym	Label & Number
				WHISTLE R&B/BUB '90			
				R&B vocal group from Brooklyn, New York: Brian Faust, Rickford Bennett, Kerry Hodge and Tarek Stevens.			
6/3/89	60	13		1 **Right Next To Me**..........*(instrumental)*	$10	▮	Select 2005
				above single and **De La Soul**'s "Me Myself And I" were the first two "Hot 100" hits available only as cassette singles			
4/7/90	35	15		2 **Always And Forever**..........S:31 / A:34 *Still My Girl*	$5	▮	Select 2014
				WHITCOMB, Ian BUB/LP '65			
				Born on 7/10/41 in Woking, Surrey, England. Pop singer/songwriter/author.			
3/13/65	100	1		1 **This Sporting Life**..........*Fizz*	$12		Tower 120
				first released on Jerden 747 in 1964 ($20)			
5/22/65	8	13		2 **You Turn Me On (Turn On Song)**..........*Poor But Honest*	$15		Tower 134
				IAN WHITCOMB And Bluesville (above 2)			
9/4/65	59	5		3 **N-E-R-V-O-U-S!**..........*The End* [N]	$12		Tower 155
	★233★			**WHITE, Barry** R&B/BUB/LP '74			
				Born on 9/12/44 in Galveston, Texas; raised in Los Angeles, California. Died of kidney failure on 7/4/2003 (age 58). Smooth soul singer/songwriter/keyboardist/producer/ arranger. With Upfronts vocal group, recorded for Lummtone in 1960. A&R man for Mustang/Bronco, 1966-67. Formed **Love Unlimited** in 1969, which included future wife Glodean James. Leader of 40-piece **Love Unlimited Orchestra**.			
				1)Can't Get Enough Of Your Love, Babe 2)You're The First, The Last, My Everything 3)I'm Gonna Love You Just A Little More Baby			
4/14/73	3	18	●	1 **I'm Gonna Love You Just A Little More Baby**..........RB[2] *Just A Little More Baby*	$5		20th Century 2018
8/4/73	32	11		2 **I've Got So Much To Give**..........*(instrumental)*	$5		20th Century 2042
10/27/73+	7	18	●	3 **Never, Never Gonna Give Ya Up**..........*(long version)*	$5		20th Century 2058
2/23/74	44	7		4 **Honey Please, Can't Ya See**..........*(instrumental)*	$5		20th Century 2077
8/3/74	❶[1]	12	●	5 **Can't Get Enough Of Your Love, Babe** RB[3] *Just Not Enough*	$5		20th Century 2120
11/2/74+	2[2]	15	●	6 **You're The First, The Last, My Everything**..........RB[1] *More Than Anything, You're My Everything*	$5		20th Century 2133
3/8/75	8	11		7 **What Am I Gonna Do With You**..........RB[1] *What Am I Gonna Do With You Baby*	$5		20th Century 2177
5/24/75	40	7		8 **I'll Do For You Anything You Want Me To**..........*Anything You Want Me To*	$5		20th Century 2208
12/27/75+	32	9		9 **Let The Music Play**..........*(instrumental)*	$5		20th Century 2265
7/24/76	92	2		10 **Baby, We Better Try To Get It Together**..........*If You Know, Won't You Tell Me*	$5		20th Century 2298
8/20/77	4	22	●	11 **It's Ecstasy When You Lay Down Next To Me**..........RB[5] *I Never Thought I'd Fall In Love With You*	$5		20th Century 2350
4/29/78	24	11		12 **Oh What A Night For Dancing**..........*You're So Good You're Bad*	$5		20th Century 2365
11/18/78	60	9		13 **Your Sweetness Is My Weakness**..........*It's Only Love Doing Its Thing*	$5		20th Century 2380
				all of above written (except #11) and produced by Barry White			
3/10/90	31	13	●	14 **The Secret Garden (Sweet Seduction Suite)**..........RB[1] S:20 *(instrumental)*	$3	▮V	Qwest 19992 ■
				QUINCY JONES/Al B. Sure!/James Ingram/El DeBarge/Barry White			
10/8/94	18	21	●	15 **Practice What You Preach**..........RB[3] S:9 *(instrumental)*	$3	▮V	A&M 0778
4/22/95	87	2		16 **Come On**..........S:74 *L.A. My Kinda Place*	$4	▮V	A&M 0972
				"45" issued for above 2 on A&M 0924			
4/20/96	68	9		17 **Slow Jams**..........S:43 *(remix)*	$3	▮V	Qwest 17673
				QUINCY JONES Featuring Babyface and Tamia with Portrait and Barry White			
10/16/99	40[S]	8		18 **Staying Power**..........*(album version)*	$5	★	Private Music 81021
				WHITE, Bryan C&W/BUB/LP '96			
				Born on 2/17/74 in Lawton, Oklahoma; raised in Oklahoma City, Oklahoma. Country singer/guitarist. Married actress Erika Page on 10/14/2000. Also see **Shania Twain**'s "From This Moment On."			
5/18/96	72[S]	3		1 **I'm Not Supposed To Love You Anymore**..........BUB:101 *Blindhearted*	$4	▮V	Asylum 64313
5/30/98	56	20		2 **One Heart At A Time**..........S:33 *(same version)*	$4	▮	Atlantic 84117
				GARTH BROOKS, BILLY DEAN, FAITH HILL, OLIVIA NEWTON-JOHN, NEAL McCOY, MICHAEL McDONALD, VICTORIA SHAW, BRYAN WHITE			
7/31/99	74[S]	2		3 **You're Still Beautiful To Me**..........*Shari Ann*	$4	★V	Asylum 64035
				written by **Bryan Adams** (from his 1996 album *18 Til I Die*)			
				WHITE, Danny '77			
				Born in New Jersey. Pop-disco singer.			
2/26/77	100	2		**Dance Little Lady Dance**..........*(instrumental)*	$6		RCR 19765
	★571★			**WHITE, Karyn** R&B/BUB/LP '89			
				Born on 10/14/65 in Los Angeles, California. R&B-dance singer. Touring vocalist with **O'Bryan** in 1984. Recorded with jazz-fusion keyboardist **Jeff Lorber** in 1986. Married to superproducer Terry Lewis (member of **The Time**).			
12/6/86+	27	16		1 **Facts Of Love**..........A:27 / S:29 *Sand Castles* (Lorber)	$3	■	Warner 28588
				JEFF LORBER Featuring Karyn White			
10/15/88+	7	25	●	2 **The Way You Love Me**..........RB[1] S:6 / A:7 *Love On The Line*	$3	■	Warner 27773
1/28/89	8	18	●	3 **Superwoman**..........RB[3] A:9 / S:10 *Language Of Love*	$3	■	Warner 27783
5/27/89	6	21		4 **Secret Rendezvous**..........S:6 / A:8 *Tell Me Tomorrow*	$3		Warner 27863
8/17/91	❶[1]	20		5 **Romantic** RB[1] A:2 / S:26 *(instrumental)*	$3	▮V	Warner 19319
11/30/91+	12	20		6 **The Way I Feel About You**..........A:7 / S:68 *(Spanish mix)*	$3	▮V	Warner 19088
9/24/94	78	7		7 **Hungah**..........*Ritual Of Love*	$3	▮V	Warner 18121
2/18/95	81	5		8 **Can I Stay With You**..........S:32 *How I Want You*	$3	▮V	Warner 18007
				WHITE, Kitty '56			
				Adult Contemporary singer.			
12/31/55+	68	6		**A Teen Age Prayer**..........T:68 *I'm Gonna Be A Fool Next Monday*	$15		Mercury 70750
				Hugo Peretti (of **Hugo & Luigi**; orch.)			
				WHITE, Lari C&W/BUB/LP '98			
				Born on 5/13/65 in Dunedin, Florida. Country singer. Pronounced: Laurie.			
7/11/98	73	12		**Stepping Stone**..........S:50 *Tired*	$4	▮V	Lyric Street 64019

WHITE, Maurice — see EARTH, WIND & FIRE

DEBUT	PEAK	WKS	Gold	A-side (Chart Hit)	B-side	$	Sym	Label & Number

WHITE, Tony Joe
BUB/C&W/LP '69

Born on 7/23/43 in Goodwill, Louisiana. Bayou-rock singer/songwriter. Wrote **Brook Benton**'s hit "Rainy Night In Georgia."

DEBUT	PEAK	WKS	Gold	A-side (Chart Hit)	B-side	$	Sym	Label & Number
7/5/69	8	12		1 Polk Salad Annie	*Aspen Colorado*	$8		Monument 1104
10/25/69	44	7		2 Roosevelt And Ira Lee (Night of the Mossacin)	*The Migrant*	$7		Monument 1169
8/8/70	94	2		3 Save Your Sugar For Me	*My Friend*	$7		Monument 1206
				above 3 produced by **Billy Swan**				
6/28/80	79	5		4 I Get Off On It	*Feelin' Loose*	$5		Casablanca 2279

WHITEHEAD BROS.
R&B '94

Duo of Kenny and Johnny Whitehead; sons of prolific songwriter John Whitehead of **McFadden & Whitehead**. Charted, while teens, in 1986 on the R&B singles chart as Kenny & Johnny Whitehead.

DEBUT	PEAK	WKS	Gold	A-side (Chart Hit)	B-side	$	Sym	Label & Number
8/27/94	76	10		Your Love Is A ... S:47 / A:65	*(4 album snippets)*	$4	▮	Motown 2253
				samples "Deep Cover" by **Dr. Dre** & **Snoop Doggy Dogg**				

WHITE LION
ROK '88

Rock group formed in Brooklyn, New York: Mike Tramp (vocals), Vito Bratta (guitar), James Lomenzo (bass) and Greg D'Angelo (drums).

DEBUT	PEAK	WKS	Gold	A-side (Chart Hit)	B-side	$	Sym	Label & Number
2/27/88	8	21		1 Wait S:7 / A:7	*Don't Give Up*	$3	■	Atlantic 89126
7/2/88	58	11		2 Tell Me	*All Join Our Hands*	$3	■	Atlantic 89051
11/5/88+	3	23		3 When The Children Cry S:3 / A:3	*Lady Of The Valley*	$3	■	Atlantic 89015
6/24/89	52	14		4 Little Fighter	*Let's Get Crazy*	$3	■	Atlantic 88874
9/23/89	59	13		5 Radar Love	*If My Mind Is Evil*	$3		Atlantic 88836

WHITE PLAINS
LP '70

Studio group from England. Featuring **Tony Burrows** (vocals), who was also with **The Brotherhood Of Man**, **Edison Lighthouse**, **First Class** and **The Pipkins**.

DEBUT	PEAK	WKS	Gold	A-side (Chart Hit)	B-side	$	Sym	Label & Number
4/18/70	13	15		1 My Baby Loves Lovin'	*Show Me Your Hand*	$7		Deram 85058
9/26/70	82	2		2 Lovin' You Baby	*Noises (In My Head)*	$7		Deram 85066

WHITESNAKE
ROK/BUB/LP '87

Former **Deep Purple** vocalist David Coverdale, who recorded solo as Whitesnake in 1977, formed British heavy-metal band in 1978. Coverdale fronted everchanging lineup. Early members included his Deep Purple bandmates, keyboardist Jon Lord (1978-84) and drummer Ian Paice (1979-81). Players in 1987 included John Sykes (guitar), Neil Murray (bass) and Aynsley Dunbar (former **Jefferson Starship** drummer). Sykes left in 1988 to form Blue Murder. Ex-Dio guitarist Vivian Campbell was a member from 1987-88, later with Riverdogs, Shadow King and **Def Leppard**. 1989 lineup included Steve Vai (**David Lee Roth**'s former guitarist), Adrian Vandenberg (former guitarist of **Vandenberg**), Rudy Sarzo (bass; **Quiet Riot**) and Tommy Aldridge (drums). Lineup in 1994: Coverdale, Vandenberg, Sarzo, Warren De Martini (guitar; **Ratt**), Paul Mirkovich (keyboards) and Denny Carmassi (drums; **Heart**). Coverdale married actress Tawny Kitaen on 2/17/89; divorced by 1992.

DEBUT	PEAK	WKS	Gold	A-side (Chart Hit)	B-side	$	Sym	Label & Number
8/2/80	53	8		1 Fool For Your Loving	*Black And Blue*	$5	■	Mirage 3672
				also see #6 below				
6/13/87	79	7		2 Still Of The Night	*Don't Turn Away*	$4		Geffen 28331
7/4/87	❶[1]	28		3 Here I Go Again S:❶[1] / A:❶[1]	*Children Of The Night*	$3	■	Geffen 28339
10/24/87	2[1]	19		4 Is This Love S:2 / A:2	*Bad Boys*	$3	■	Geffen 28233
2/13/88	48	11		5 Give Me All Your Love	*Straight For The Heart*	$3	■	Geffen 28103
				above 4 from the album *Whitesnake*				
11/4/89	37	14		6 Fool For Your Loving S:36 / A:39	*Slow Poke Music* [R]	$3	▮	Geffen 22715
				new version of #1 above				
1/20/90	28	14		7 The Deeper The Love A:25 / S:27	*Slip Of The Tongue*	$3	▮V	Geffen 19951
6/2/90	96	2		8 Now You're Gone	*Wings Of The Storm*	$3	▮	Geffen 19976

WHITE TOWN
LP '97

Born Jyoti Mishra on 7/30/66 in Rourkela, India; raised in England. Male synth-pop singer/multi-instrumentalist.

DEBUT	PEAK	WKS	Gold	A-side (Chart Hit)	B-side	$	Sym	Label & Number
3/29/97	23	20		Your Woman A:15 / S:36	*Theme For A Late-Night Documentary About The Dangers Of Drug Abuse*	$4	▮V	Chrysalis/EMI 58638
				"45": EMI 19526; B-side: "Wanted"				

WHITE ZOMBIE
ROK/LP '95

Hard-rock group formed in New York: Rob Zombie (vocals), Jay Yuenger (guitar), Sean Yseult (bass) and John Tempesta (drums). Band named after a 1932 Bela Lugosi movie.

DEBUT	PEAK	WKS	Gold	A-side (Chart Hit)	B-side	$	Sym	Label & Number
5/20/95	53[A]	11		More Human Than Human				album cut
				from the album *Astro Creep-2000* on Geffen 24806				

WHITFIELD, David
MEM/POP '54

Born on 2/2/26 in Hull, Yorkshire, England. Classical-styled tenor.

DEBUT	PEAK	WKS	Gold	A-side (Chart Hit)	B-side	$	Sym	Label & Number
8/14/54	10	18	●	1 Cara Mia S:10 / A:17	*How, When Or Where*	$20		London 1486
				DAVID WHITFIELD with MANTOVANI His Orchestra and Chorus				
1/1/55-	19	2		2 Santo Natale (Merry Christmas) A:19 / S:27	*Adeste Fideles (O Come All Ye Faithful)* [X]	$20		London 1508
				Stanley Black (orch.)				
2/4/56	62	8		3 When You Lose The One You Love T:62	*Angelus*	$15		London 1617
				DAVID WHITFIELD with MANTOVANI and his Orchestra and Chorus				

WHITING, Margaret
MEM/POP/AC/BUB/LP '49

Born on 7/22/24 in Detroit, Michigan; raised in Hollywood, California. Pop singer. Daughter of popular composer Richard Whiting ("Till We Meet Again"). One of the top female vocalists of the 1940s; charted 32 hits, 1945-52, including 2 #1s: "A Tree In The Meadow" and "Slipping Around" (w/**Jimmy Wakely**), and 2 #2s: "Far Away Places" and "Now Is The Hour."

DEBUT	PEAK	WKS	Gold	A-side (Chart Hit)	B-side	$	Sym	Label & Number
12/8/56	20	13		1 The Money Tree A:20 / T:49	*Maybe I Love Him*	$12		Capitol 3586
				Billy May (orch.)				
3/10/58	74	4		2 I Can't Help It (If I'm Still In Love With You) T:74	*That's Why I Was Born*	$10		Dot 15680
				Billy Vaughn (orch.); #2 Country hit for Hank Williams in 1951				
10/8/66	26	11		3 The Wheel Of Hurt AC[4]	*Nothing Lasts Forever*	$6		London 101
6/3/67	96	1		4 Only Love Can Break A Heart	*Where Do I Stand*	$6		London 108
				Arnold Goland (orch., above 2)				

WHITMAN, Slim
C&W/MEM/POP/BUB/LP '52

Born Otis Whitman on 1/20/24 in Tampa, Florida. Country balladeer/yodeller (charted 37 hits, 1952-81). Gained greatest fame with best-selling compilation albums sold exclusively over TV. Hit #9 in 1952 with "Indian Love Call."

DEBUT	PEAK	WKS	Gold	A-side (Chart Hit)	B-side	$	Sym	Label & Number
9/16/57	93	3		I'll Take You Home Again Kathleen T:93	*Lovesick Blues*	$15		Imperial 8310
				#3 hit for Walter Van Brunt in 1916				

DEBUT	PEAK	WKS	Gold	A-side (Chart Hit)..........B-side	$	Sym	Label & Number
				WHITNEY, Marva R&B/BUB '69			
				R&B-funk singer. Featured female singer with the **James Brown** Review, 1967-70.			
6/14/69	82	4		**It's My Thing (You Can't Tell Me Who To Sock It To)**..........*Ball Of Fire*	$10		King 6229
				produced by **James Brown**; answer song to **The Isley Brothers**' "It's Your Thing"			
				WHITTAKER, Roger AC/C&W/LP '75			
				Born on 3/22/36 in Nairobi, Kenya, Africa (of British parents). Adult Contemporary singer.			
4/5/75	19	15		**The Last Farewell**..........AC[1] *Paradise*	$5		RCA Victor 50030
				first released on Whittaker's 1971 album *A Special Kind Of Man*			
				WHO, The ★174★ ROK/BUB/LP '67			
				 Rock group formed in London, England: **Roger Daltrey** (vocals; born on 3/1/44), **Pete Townshend** (guitar, vocals; born on 5/19/45), John Entwistle (bass; born on 10/9/44) and Keith Moon (drums; born on 8/23/47). Originally known as the High Numbers in 1964. All but Moon had been in The Detours. Developed stage antics of destroying their instruments. 1969 rock opera album *Tommy* became a movie in 1975. Solo work by members began in 1972. Moon died of a drug overdose on 9/7/78; replaced by Kenney Jones (formerly with **Small Faces**). 1973 rock opera album *Quadrophenia* became a movie in 1979. The Who's biographical movie, *The Kids Are Alright*, was released in 1979. Eleven fans trampled to death at their concert in Cincinnati on 12/3/79. Disbanded in 1982. Regrouped at "Live Aid" in 1986. Daltrey, Townshend and Entwistle reunited with an ensemble of 15 for a U.S. tour in 1989 and again in 2000. Jones formed The Law with Paul Rodgers in 1991. Entwistle died of a heart attack on 6/27/2002 (age 57). Group inducted into the Rock and Roll Hall of Fame in 1990. Won Grammy's Lifetime Achievement Award in 2001.			
				1)I Can See For Miles 2)See Me, Feel Me 3)Who Are You 4)Won't Get Fooled Again 5)Squeeze Box			
3/27/65	93	2		1 **I Can't Explain**..........*Bald Headed Woman*	$30		Decca 31725
1/15/66	74	5		2 **My Generation**..........*Out In The Street (You're Going To Know Me)*	$40		Decca 31877
4/15/67	24	9		3 **Happy Jack**..........*Whiskey Man*	$30	■	Decca 32114
7/1/67	51	6		4 **Pictures Of Lily**..........*Doctor, Doctor*	$20		Decca 32156
10/14/67	9	11		5 **I Can See For Miles** *Mary-Anne With The Shaky Hands*	$20		Decca 32206
3/30/68	40	8		6 **Call Me Lightning**..........*Dr. Jekyll & Mr. Hyde*	$20		Decca 32288
8/10/68	25	9		7 **Magic Bus**..........*Someone's Coming*	$20		Decca 32362
4/5/69	19	11		8 **Pinball Wizard**..........*Dogs Part Two*	$12	■	Decca 32465
7/19/69	37	8		9 **I'm Free**..........*We're Not Gonna Take It*	$12		Decca 32519
4/18/70	44	7		10 **The Seeker**..........*Here For More*	$12		Decca 32670
7/11/70	27	9		11 **Summertime Blues**..........*Heaven And Hell* [L]	$12		Decca 32708
9/26/70	12	13		12 **See Me, Feel Me**..........*Overture From Tommy*	$12	■	Decca 32729
				#8, 9 & 12: from the group's 1969 rock opera album *Tommy*			
7/17/71	15	13		13 **Won't Get Fooled Again**..........*I Don't Even Know Myself*	$10		Decca 32846
				written for the aborted movie project *Lifehouse*			
11/6/71	34	11		14 **Behind Blue Eyes**..........*My Wife*	$10		Decca 32888
7/22/72	17	10		15 **Join Together**..........*Baby Don't You Do It*	$10		Decca 32983
12/9/72+	39	8		16 **The Relay**..........*Wasp Man*	$10		Track 33041
12/1/73	76	5		17 **Love, Reign O'er Me**..........*Water*	$8		Track 40152
2/2/74	92	3		18 **The Real Me**..........*I'm One*	$8		Track 40182
11/29/75+	16	16		19 **Squeeze Box**..........*Success Story*	$7	□	MCA 40475
				promo sleeve includes a lyric sheet insert			
8/26/78	14	15		20 **Who Are You**..........*Had Enough*	$7		MCA 40948
				song later used as the theme for TV's *CSI: Crime Scene Investigation*			
6/30/79	54	6		21 **Long Live Rock**..........*My Wife*	$5		MCA 41053
				from the group's biographical movie *The Kids Are Alright* (title song "Bubbled Under" at #106 on 8/13/66 on Decca 31988)			
9/29/79	45	7		22 **5:15**..........*I'm One*	$5	■	Polydor 2022
				from the movie *Quadrophenia* (based on the group's 1973 rock opera album)			
3/21/81	18	15		23 **You Better You Bet**..........AR[5] *The Quiet One*	$4	■	Warner 49698
6/27/81	84	4		24 **Don't Let Go The Coat**..........*You* (ROK #51)	$4		Warner 49743
9/4/82	28	14		25 **Athena**..........*It's Your Turn*	$4	■	Warner 29905
12/25/82+	68	6		26 **Eminence Front**..........*One At A Time*	$4		Warner 29814
				all of above (except #11) written by **Pete Townshend**			
				WHODINI R&B/BUB '85			
				Rap trio from Brooklyn, New York: Jalil Hutchins, John Fletcher and Drew Carter.			
1/5/85	87	3		1 **Friends /**			
1/5/85		3		2 **Five Minutes Of Funk**..........	$5		Jive 9276
				WIEDLIN, Jane LP '88			
				Born on 5/20/58 in Oconomowoc, Wisconsin; raised in California. Pop-rock singer/guitarist. Member of the **Go-Go's**.			
4/16/83	49	12		1 **Cool Places**..........*Sports*	$4	■	Atlantic 89866
				SPARKS AND JANE WIEDLIN			
9/28/85	77	9		2 **Blue Kiss**..........*My Traveling Heart*	$4	■	I.R.S. 52674
5/7/88	9	19		3 **Rush Hour**..........S:8 / A:13 *The End Of Love*	$3	■	EMI-Manhattan 50118
9/3/88	57	7		4 **Inside A Dream**..........*Song Of The Factory*	$3	■	EMI-Manhattan 50145
				WIER, Rusty C&W/LP '75			
				Born in Austin, Texas. Country-rock singer/songwriter/guitarist.			
9/6/75	82	4		**Don't It Make You Wanna Dance?**..........*I Believe In The Way That You Love Me*	$5		20th Century 2219
				WILCOX, Harlow, and the Oakies '69			
				Born on 1/28/43 in Norman, Oklahoma. Session guitarist.			
10/11/69	30	12		**Groovy Grubworm**..........*Moose Trot* [I]	$8	■	Plantation 28
				first released on Impel 002 in 1968 ($25)			
				WILD, Jack BUB '70			
				Born on 9/30/52 in Rayton, Manchester, England. Child actor. Played "The Artful Dodger" in the movie *Oliver!* and "Jimmy" on TV's *H.R. Pufnstuf*.			
5/30/70	92	4		**Some Beautiful**..........*Picture Of You*	$6	■	Capitol 2742

DEBUT	PEAK	WKS	Gold	A-side (Chart Hit)...B-side	$	Sym	Label & Number
				WILD BLUE '86			
				Pop group from Chicago, Illinois: Renee Varo (vocals), Mike Gorman, Ken Harck, Frank Barbalace and Joe Zanona.			
5/17/86	71	6		**Fire With Fire** ... *Taboo*	$3	■	Chrysalis 42985
				title song from the movie starring Craig Sheffer			
				WILD-CATS, The '59			
				Rock and roll instrumental trio from New Jersey: Dennis Gorgas (guitar), Frank Rainey (organ) and Pat Piccininno (drums). Discovered by guitarist **Billy Mure**.			
1/5/59	57	8		**Gazachstahagen** ... *Billy's Cha Cha* [I]	$25		United Artists 154
				WILD CHERRY LP '76			
				White funk group from Steubenville, Ohio: Robert Parissi (vocals, guitar), Bryan Bassett (guitar), Mark Avsec (keyboards; **Cellarful Of Noise**), Allen Wentz (bass) and Ron Beitle (drums).			
6/19/76	❶[3]	25	▲	1 **Play That Funky Music** RB[2] *The Lady Wants Your Money*	$5		Epic 50225
1/15/77	43	7		2 **Baby Don't You Know** ... *Get It Up*	$5		Epic 50306
5/14/77	95	2		3 **Hot To Trot** ... *Put Yourself In My Shoes*	$5		Epic 50362
9/3/77	61	6		4 **Hold On** ... *Are You Boogieing Around On Your Daddy*	$5		Epic 50401
2/25/78	69	8		5 **I Love My Music** ... *Don't Stop, Get Off*	$5		Epic 50500
				all of above written and produced by Robert Parissi			
				WILDE, Eugene R&B/LP '85			
				Born Ron Broomfield in Miami, Florida. R&B singer/songwriter. Member of the family group Life.			
1/12/85	83	8		1 **Gotta Get You Home Tonight** ... RB[1] *(long version)*	$3		Philly World 99710
12/7/85+	76	10		2 **Don't Say No Tonight** ... RB[3] *Gotta Get You Home Tonight*	$3	■	Philly World 99608
				WILDE, Kim ROK/LP '87			
				Born Kim Smith on 11/18/60 in Chiswick, London, England. Pop-rock-dance singer. Daughter of **Marty Wilde**.			
5/22/82	25	18		1 **Kids In America** ... *You'll Never Be So Wrong*	$4	■	EMI America 8110
1/19/85	65	7		2 **Go For It** ... *Lovers On A Beach*	$3	■	MCA 52513
				picture sleeve is a foldout poster			
3/28/87	❶[1]	21		3 **You Keep Me Hangin' On** S:❶[2] / A:❶[1] *Loving You*	$3	■	MCA 53024
7/18/87	44	8		4 **Say You Really Want Me** ... S:39 *She Hasn't Got Time For You*	$3	■	MCA 53130
				originally released on MCA 52952 in 1986 with a picture sleeve; from the movie *Running Scared* starring **Billy Crystal**			
9/17/88	41	10		5 **You Came** ... S:30 *Tell Me Where You Are*	$3	■	MCA 53370
				WILDE, Marty '60			
				Born Reginald Smith on 4/15/36 in London, England. Pop singer/songwriter. Father of **Kim Wilde**. Also recorded as **Shannon** (see #2 below).			
2/8/60	45	8		1 **Bad Boy** ... *Teenage Tears*	$15		Epic 9356
7/12/69	47	8		2 **Abergavenny** ... *Alice In Blue*	$8	■	Heritage 814
				SHANNON			
				Peter Knight (orch.); Abergavenny is a real town in South Wales			
				WILDER, Matthew AC/LP '84			
				Born on 1/24/53 in Manhattan, New York. White singer/songwriter/keyboardist. Session singer for **Rickie Lee Jones** and **Bette Midler**. Later produced group **No Doubt**.			
9/17/83+	5	29		1 **Break My Stride** ... *(instrumental)*	$4		Private I 04113
2/18/84	33	13		2 **The Kid's American** ... *Ladder Of Lovers*	$4		Private I 04363
9/22/84	52	9		3 **Bouncin' Off The Walls** ... *Love Of An Amazon*	$4	■	Private I 04617
				WILDFIRE '77			
				Pop vocal group formed in Atlanta, Georgia: Jack "Stack-A-Track" Grochmal, Scott Shannon, Ralph Penguinn and Herman Penguinn. Grochmal is a noted session musician. Shannon is a popular radio personality.			
6/18/77	49	7		**Here Comes Summer** ... *Weekend Love*	$5		Casablanca 885
				WILD ORCHID BUB/LP '97			
				White teen female vocal trio from Los Angeles, California: Stacy Ferguson, Stefanie Ridel and Renee Sandstrom. Both Ferguson (1984-89) and Sandstrom (1984-87) were regulars on the TV show *Kids Incorporated*.			
9/28/96	63	20		1 **At Night I Pray** ... S:50 *(remix w/**L.V.**)*	$3	▮	RCA 64628
3/1/97	48	15		2 **Talk To Me** ... S:47 / A:63 *Love Will Wait*	$3	▮	RCA 64777
8/23/97	70	6		3 **Supernatural** ... *(5 versions)*	$3	▮	RCA 64918
5/26/01	33[S]	7		4 **Stuttering (don't say)** ... *Lies*	$4	★	RCA 60414
				WILDWEEDS, The BUB '67			
				Garage-rock band from Connecticut: Al Anderson (guitar; **Clean Living**, **NRBQ**), Ray Zeiner (keyboards), Skip Yakitis (percussion), Bob Dudek (bass) and Andy Lepak (drums). Dudek died of heart failure on 6/2/2002 (age 57).			
5/27/67	88	4		**No Good To Cry** ... *Never Mind*	$10		Cadet 5561
				WILKINSONS, The C&W/LP '98			
				Country vocal trio from Belleville, Ontario, Canada: father Steve with children Amanda and Tyler Wilkinson.			
8/1/98	55	18		1 **26¢** ... S:32 *(3 album snipets)*	$4	▮[V]	Giant 17197
12/12/98+	53	15		2 **Fly (the angel song)** ... S:28 / A:64 *26¢ (acoustic version)*	$4	★[V]	Giant 17131
3/4/00	33[S]	19		3 **Jimmy's Got A Girlfriend** ... *Williamstown*	$4	★[V]	Giant 16887
				WILLIAMS, Andre R&B '67			
				Born in 1936 in Chicago, Illinois. R&B singer/songwriter/producer.			
1/29/66	94	1		1 **Rib Tip's (Part 1)** *[ANDRE WILLIAMS & HIS ORCH.]* ... *(Part 2)* [I]	$15		Avin 103
7/29/67	90	2		2 **Pearl Time** ... *Soul Groove*	$25		Sport 105

DEBUT	PEAK	WKS	Gold	A-side (Chart Hit)..........B-side	$	Sym	Label & Number

WILLIAMS, Andy ★47★ AC/BUB/LP '57

Born Howard Andrew Williams on 12/3/28 in Wall Lake, Iowa. Formed quartet with his brothers and eventually moved to Los Angeles. With **Bing Crosby** on hit "Swingin' On A Star," 1944. With comedienne **Kay Thompson** in the mid-1940s. Went solo in 1952. On **Steve Allen**'s *Tonight Show* from 1952-55. Own NBC-TV variety series from 1962-67, 1969-71. Appeared in the movie *I'd Rather Be Rich* in 1964. Married to singer/actress **Claudine Longet** from 1962-67. One of America's greatest Adult Contemporary singers. Andy's signature song "Moon River" was recorded in 1962, but was never released as a single.

1)Butterfly 2)Can't Get Used To Losing You 3)Are You Sincere 4)Lonely Street 5)Canadian Sunset

DEBUT	PEAK	WKS	Gold	A-side (Chart Hit)..........B-side	$	Sym	Label & Number
4/21/56	54	11		1 **Walk Hand In Hand** ....T:54 *Not Anymore*	$15		Cadence 1288
8/11/56	7	22		2 **Canadian Sunset** ....A:7 / T:8 / J:9 / S:10 *High Upon A Mountain*	$15		Cadence 1297
12/8/56	33	14		3 **Baby Doll**....T:33 *Since I've Found My Baby* title song from the movie starring Carroll Baker	$15		Cadence 1303
2/23/57	❶^{3}	20		4 **Butterfly** T:❶^{3} / A:❶^{2} / J:2 / S:4 *It Doesn't Take Very Long*	$15		Cadence 1308
5/20/57	8	20		5 **I Like Your Kind Of Love**....A:8 / T:9 / S:10 / J:19 *Stop Teasin' Me* Peggy Powers (female vocal)	$15		Cadence 1323
9/23/57	17	13		6 **Lips Of Wine**....A:17 / T:39 *Straight From My Heart*	$15		Cadence 1336
2/17/58	3	17		7 **Are You Sincere** ....A:3 / T:10 / S:11 *Be Mine Tonight*	$15		Cadence 1340
9/1/58	17	12		8 **Promise Me, Love**....H:17 *Your Hand, Your Heart, Your Love*	$15		Cadence 1351
12/29/58+	11	20		9 **The Hawaiian Wedding Song (Ke Kali Nei Au)** ....*The House Of Bamboo* song written in 1926, with new lyrics added	$15		Cadence 1358
9/7/59	5	16		10 **Lonely Street** ....*Summer Love*	$15		Cadence 1370
12/14/59+	7	13		11 **The Village Of St. Bernadette**....*I'm So Lonesome I Could Cry*	$15	■	Cadence 1374
3/21/60	50	8		12 **Wake Me When It's Over** ....*We Have A Date (Andy's Theme)* title song from the movie starring Dick Shawn	$12		Cadence 1378
7/4/60	70	7		13 **Do You Mind?**....*Dreamsville (from "Peter Gunn")* from the British movie *Let's Get Married* starring **Anthony Newley**	$12		Cadence 1381
12/12/60+	64	7		14 **You Don't Want My Love** ....*Don't Go To Strangers* some pressings issued as "In The Summertime (You Don't Want My Love)"; orignal version by **Roger Miller** made the Country charts (#14) in 1960	$12		Cadence 1389
4/24/61	37	10		15 **The Bilbao Song**....*How Wonderful To Know* new Johnny Mercer lyrics added to song from the 1929 German musical *Happy End*	$12		Cadence 1398
10/30/61	64	6		16 **Danny Boy** / based on the traditional Irish song "Londonderry Air" written in 1855			
11/6/61	82	2		17 **Fly By Night**....	$8	■	Columbia 42199
3/24/62	99	1		18 **The Wonderful World Of The Young** ....*Help Me*	$8	■	Columbia 42265
6/9/62	38	7		19 **Stranger On The Shore**....*I Want To Be Wanted*	$8	■	Columbia 42451
9/15/62	39	10		20 **Don't You Believe It** ....*Summertime*	$8	■	Columbia 42523
12/8/62	86	3		21 **Twilight Time** ....*So Rare* recorded on 2/10/59; #8 hit for The Three Suns in 1944	$10		Cadence 1433
3/2/63	2^{4}	15		22 **Can't Get Used To Losing You** / AC^{4}			
3/16/63	26	12		23 **Days Of Wine And Roses**.... title song from the movie starring Jack Lemmon and Lee Remick; issued with 2 different picture sleeves	$8	■	Columbia 42674
6/22/63	13	11		24 **Hopeless**....*The Peking Theme (So Little Time) (#115)* a promotional text sleeve was issued for the B-side	$8	□	Columbia 42784
11/30/63	❶^{5X}	7		25 **White Christmas**....*The Christmas Song* [X] X: 1/'63; 22/'67	$8	□	Columbia 42894
1/11/64	13	10		26 **A Fool Never Learns** /			
1/18/64	100	1		27 **Charade** .... title song from the movie starring Cary Grant and Audrey Hepburn	$8		Columbia 42950
4/18/64	34	9		28 **Wrong For Each Other** ....*Madrigal* a special promotional sleeve was issued for the B-side	$7	□	Columbia 43015
9/12/64	28	8		29 **On The Street Where You Live** / from the movie *My Fair Lady* starring Audrey Hepburn and Rex Harrison			
11/14/64	67	5		30 **Almost There**.... from the movie *I'd Rather Be Rich* starring Sandra Dee	$7		Columbia 43128
11/28/64+	24	11		31 **Dear Heart** ....*Emily* title song from the movie starring Glenn Ford and Angela Lansbury	$7		Columbia 43180
4/3/65	36	7		32 **.....And Roses And Roses**....*My Carousel*	$7	□	Columbia 43257
9/4/65	40	7		33 **Ain't It True** ....*Loved One*	$7		Columbia 43358
12/4/65	92	3		34 **Quiet Nights Of Quiet Stars** ....*I'll Remember You* lyric version of Antonio Carlos Jobim's Brazilian song "Corcovado"	$7		Columbia 43456
12/25/65	18^{X}	1		35 **Do You Hear What I Hear?** ....*Some Children See Him* [X]	$7		Columbia 43458
8/27/66	49	8		36 **In The Arms Of Love** ....AC^{2} *The Many Faces Of Love* from the movie *What Did You Do In The War, Daddy?* starring James Coburn	$7		Columbia 43737
3/25/67	34	8		37 **Music To Watch Girls By**....*The Face I Love* tune used in a Diet Pepsi commercial	$7		Columbia 44065
7/8/67	88	4		38 **More And More** ....*I Want To Be Free*	$7		Columbia 44202
6/8/68	75	6		39 **Sweet Memories** ....*You Are Where Everything Is* a different version is on the B-side of #42 below	$7		Columbia 44527
10/19/68	33	13		40 **Battle Hymn Of The Republic** ....*Ave Maria* **ANDY WILLIAMS with the St. Charles Borromeo Choir** recorded at St. Patrick's Cathedral on 6/8/68 as a eulogy to Senator Robert F. Kennedy	$7	■	Columbia 44650
4/12/69	22	11		41 **Happy Heart**....AC^{2} *Our Last Goodbye*	$6		Columbia 44818
2/28/70	88	3		42 **Can't Help Falling In Love**....*Sweet Memories*	$6		Columbia 45094
6/27/70	77	4		43 **One Day Of Your Life** ....*Long Time Blues* written by **Neil Sedaka**	$6		Columbia 45175
2/6/71	9	13		44 **(Where Do I Begin) Love Story** ....AC^{4} *Something* theme song from the movie *Love Story* starring Ryan O'Neal and Ali McGraw	$5		Columbia 45317

DEBUT	PEAK	WKS	Gold	A-side (Chart Hit)...B-side	$	Sym	Label & Number
				WILLIAMS, Andy — Cont'd			
8/21/71	**82**	4		45 **A Song For You** ... *You've Got A Friend*	$5		Columbia 45434
				written by **Leon Russell** (from his 1970 album *Leon Russell*)			
4/8/72	**34**	11		46 **Love Theme From "The Godfather" (Speak Softly Love)** ... *Home For Thee*	$5		Columbia 45579
				title song from the movie *The Godfather* starring Marlon Brando			
1/17/76	**72**	6		47 **Tell It Like It Is** ... *Goin' Through The Motions*	$5		Columbia 10263
				Williams's musical arrangers and conductors: **Archie Bleyer** (#1-15, 21), Al Capps (#41-43), **Nick DeCaro** (#37-39), **Ernie Freeman** (#45), Jimmie Haskell (#47), Richard Hazard (#44) and Robert Mersey (#18-20, 22-36)			
				WILLIAMS, Andy & David — see WILLIAMS BROTHERS			
				WILLIAMS, Anson '77			
				Born Anson William Heimlick on 9/25/52 in Los Angeles, California. Actor/singer. Played "Potsie Weber" on TV's *Happy Days*.			
4/2/77	**93**	4		**Deeply** ... *I Want To Believe In This One*	$5	■	Chelsea 3061
				WILLIAMS, Billy MEM/POP '57			
				Born on 12/28/10 in Waco, Texas. Died on 10/17/72 (age 61). Lead singer of The Charioteers from 1930-50. Formed own Billy Williams Quartet with Eugene Dixon, Claude Riddick and John Ball in 1950. Many appearances on TV, especially *Your Show Of Shows* with Sid Caesar. By the early 1960s, had lost voice due to diabetes. Moved to Chicago and worked as a social worker until his death.			
4/7/56	**49**	10		1 **A Crazy Little Palace (That's My Home)** *[BILLY WILLIAMS QUARTET]*..T:49 *Cry Baby*	$30		Coral 61576
3/23/57	**50**	4		2 **The Pied Piper** ... T:50 *Butterfly*	$25		Coral 61795
				Jimmy Haskelle (orch.)			
6/3/57	**3**	23	●	3 **I'm Gonna Sit Right Down And Write Myself A Letter /** A:3 / T:6 / S:7			
				#5 hit for Fats Waller in 1935			
8/26/57		5		4 **Date With The Blues** ... S:flip	$30		Coral 61830
11/11/57	**78**	4		5 **Got A Date With An Angel** ... T:78 *The Lord Will Understand (And Say "Well Done")*	$20		Coral 61886
				#13 hit for the Debroy Somers Band in 1932			
3/17/58	**78**	2		6 **Baby, Baby** *[BILLY WILLIAMS QUARTET]* ... T:78 *Don't Let Go*	$20		Coral 61932
7/28/58	**87**	2		7 **I'll Get By (As Long As I Have You)** ... T:87 *It's Prayin' Time*	$20		Coral 61999
				#3 hit for Ruth Etting in 1929; #1 hit for Harry James with **Dick Haymes** in 1944			
1/12/59	**39**	12		8 **Nola** ... *Tied To The Strings Of Your Heart*	$20		Coral 62069
				#3 instrumental hit for bandleader Vincent Lopez in 1922			
4/20/59	**75**	1		9 **Goodnight Irene** ... *Red Hot Love*	$30		Coral 62101
				written in 1933 by Leadbelly; #1 hit (13 weeks) for The Weavers in 1950; **Dick Jacobs** (orch., all of above - except #2)			
				WILLIAMS, Christopher R&B/BUB/LP '89			
				Born in Harlem, New York. R&B singer/songwriter. Nephew of jazz great **Ella Fitzgerald**.			
9/9/89	**49**	18		1 **Talk To Myself** ... *Sweet Memories*	$3	■	Geffen 22936
5/11/91	**89**	4		2 **I'm Dreamin'** ... RB^{1} *(radio mix with rap)*	$4	▮	Giant 19441
				from the movie *New Jack City* starring Wesley Snipes and **Ice-T**			
2/6/93	**72^{S}**	1		3 **All I See** ... BUB:104 *(instrumental)*	$4	▮^{V}	Uptown/MCA 54508
4/24/93	**75**	12		4 **Every Little Thing U Do** ... A:52 / S:64 *(instrumental)*	$4	▮^{V}	Uptown/MCA 54603
				WILLIAMS, Danny BUB/LP '64			
				Born on 1/7/42 in Port Elizabeth, South Africa. Black Adult Contemporary singer. Moved to England in 1960.			
3/7/64	**9**	14		1 **White On White** ... *The Comedy Is Ended*	$12		United Artists 685
6/20/64	**84**	4		2 **A Little Toy Balloon** ... *The Truth Hurts*	$10		United Artists 729
				Don Costa (orch., above 2)			
	★565★			**WILLIAMS, Deniece** R&B/BUB/AC/LP '84			
				Born Deniece Chandler on 6/3/51 in Gary, Indiana. R&B singer/songwriter. Recorded for Toddlin' Town, early 1960s. Member of Wonderlove, **Stevie Wonder**'s backup group, from 1972-75. Also a popular Inspirational artist.			
12/11/76+	**25**	20		1 **Free** ... *Cause You Love Me Baby* (R&B #74)	$5		Columbia 10429
4/1/78	**❶^{1}**	18	●	2 **Too Much, Too Little, Too Late** ... RB^{4} / AC^{1} *Emotion*	$5		Columbia 10693
7/29/78	**47**	8		3 **You're All I Need To Get By** ... *You're A Special Part Of My Life*	$5		Columbia 10772
				JOHNNY MATHIS/DENIECE WILLIAMS (above 2)			
8/18/79	**73**	5		4 **I've Got The Next Dance** ... *When Love Comes Calling*	$4		ARC 10971
8/15/81	**53**	10		5 **Silly** ... *My Melody*	$4		ARC 02406
4/3/82	**10**	17		6 **It's Gonna Take A Miracle** ... RB^{2} *A Part Of Love*	$4		ARC 02812
4/7/84	**❶^{2}**	19	▲	7 **Let's Hear It For The Boy** RB^{3} *(instrumental)*	$4	■	Columbia 04417
				from the movie *Footloose* starring Kevin Bacon and Lori Singer			
8/11/84	**81**	4		8 **Next Love** ... *Picking Up The Pieces*	$4	■	Columbia 04537
9/24/88	**66**	8		9 **I Can't Wait** ... *(instrumental)*	$3	■	Columbia 08014
				WILLIAMS, Diana '76			
				Born in Nashville, Tennessee. Country singer.			
9/4/76	**66**	6		**Teddy Bear's Last Ride** ... *If You Cared Enough To Cry* [S]	$5		Capitol 4317
				answer song to **Red Sovine**'s hit "Teddy Bear"			
				WILLIAMS, Don C&W/BUB/AC/LP '80			
				Born on 5/27/39 in Floydada, Texas. Country singer/songwriter/guitarist (charted 17 #1 hits, 1974-86). Leader of the **Pozo-Seco Singers**. In movies *W.W. & The Dixie Dancekings* and *Smokey & The Bandit II*.			
9/27/80	**24**	20		**I Believe In You** ... CW^{2} *It Only Rains On Me*	$4		MCA 41304
				WILLIAMS, Eric — see QUEEN PEN / 2 PAC			
				WILLIAMS, Freedom — see C & C MUSIC FACTORY			
				WILLIAMS, Geoffrey R&B '92			
				Born in 1965 in London, England (of West Indian parentage). R&B-dance singer/songwriter.			
3/21/92	**70**	9		**It's Not A Love Thing** ... A:51 *Let Me Be Your Baby*	$4	▮	Giant 19029

DEBUT	PEAK	WKS	Gold	A-side (Chart Hit)...B-side	$	Sym	Label & Number
				WILLIAMS, Hank Jr. C&W/BUB/LP **'64**			
				Born Randall Hank Williams on 5/26/49 in Shreveport, Louisiana; raised in Nashville, Tennessee. Country singer/ songwriter/ guitarist (charted 101 hits, 1964-02). Son of country music's first superstar, Hank Williams. Nicknamed "Bocephus" by his father. On the *Grand Ole Opry* since 1962. Injured in a climbing accident on 8/8/75 in Montana; returned to performing in 1977. Richard Thomas starred as Hank in his 1983 biographical TV movie *Living Proof: The Hank Williams, Jr. Story*. Sings the opening song for ABC's *Monday Night Football*.			
2/1/64	67	9		1 **Long Gone Lonesome Blues**...*Doesn't Anybody Know My Name*	$12	■	MGM 13208
				#1 Country hit for Hank Sr. in 1950			
12/5/64	90	4		2 **Endless Sleep**...*My Bucket's Got A Hole In It*	$12		MGM 13278
1/1/00	75	3		3 **A Country Boy Can Survive (Y2K Version)**...S:25 *Going The Distance*	$4	★V	Warner 16895
				CHAD BROCK (With Hank Williams, Jr. & George Jones)			
				#2 Country hit for Hank Williams, Jr. in 1982			
				WILLIAMS, John BUB/LP **'77**			
				Born on 2/8/32 in Flushing, Long Island, New York. Noted composer/conductor of many top box-office movie hits. Succeeded Arthur Fiedler as conductor of the **Boston Pops Orchestra** in 1980; resigned in 1993 but continued as music adviser. His son, Joseph, became a member of **Toto** in 1986.			
8/9/75	32	10		1 **Main Title (Theme From "Jaws")**...*End Title (Theme From "Jaws")* [I]	$5		MCA 40439
7/9/77	10	17		2 **Star Wars Main Title**...*Cantina Band* [I]	$5	■	20th Century 2345
12/24/77+	13	14		3 **Theme From "Close Encounters Of The Third Kind"**...*Nocturnal Pursuit* [I]	$5	■	Arista 0300
1/27/79	81	4		4 **Theme From Superman (Main Title)**...*Love Theme From Superman* [I]	$4	■	Warner 8729
				#2 & 4: performed by The London Symphony Orchestra; all of above from soundtracks composed by Williams			
				WILLIAMS, Johnny **'73**			
				Born on 1/15/42 in Tyler, Alabama. Died in December 1986 (age 44). R&B singer.			
1/6/73	78	7		**Slow Motion (Part 1)**...*Shall We Gather By The Water*	$5		Philadelphia I. 3518
				WILLIAMS, Larry R&B **'57**			
				Born on 5/10/35 in New Orleans, Louisiana. Committed suicide on 1/2/80 (age 44). R&B-rock and roll singer/songwriter/pianist. With **Lloyd Price** in the early 1950s. Convicted of narcotics dealing in 1960; jail term interrupted his career. **The Beatles** recorded his songs "Slow Down," "Dizzy Miss Lizzy" and "Bad Boy."			
6/24/57	5	21		1 **Short Fat Fannie** / RB[1] S:5 / T:6 / A:15			
8/12/57		5		2 **High School Dance**...S:flip	$40		Specialty 608
				LARRY WILLIAMS And His Band (above 2)			
11/11/57	14	18		3 **Bony Moronie** / S:14 / T:18			
11/11/57	45	11		4 **You Bug Me, Baby**...T:45 / S:flip	$40		Specialty 615
				#2 & 4: co-written by Sonny Bono (of **Sonny & Cher**)			
4/14/58	69	4		5 **Dizzy, Miss Lizzy**...T:69 *Slow Down*	$40	■	Specialty 626
				A- and B-sides recorded by **The Beatles** in 1965 and 1964, respectively			
2/25/67	96	4		6 **Mercy, Mercy, Mercy**...*A Quitter Never Wins*	$15		Okeh 7274
				LARRY WILLIAMS & JOHNNY WATSON			
				WILLIAMS, Mason AC/BUB/LP **'68**			
				Born on 8/24/38 in Abilene, Texas. Folk guitarist/songwriter/author/photographer/TV comedy writer (***The Smothers Brothers*** *Comedy Hour*, 1967-69; *Saturday Night Live*, 1980).			
6/22/68	2^{2}	14		1 **Classical Gas**...AC[3] *Long Time Blues* [I]	$6		Warner 7190
10/12/68	96	2		2 **Baroque-A-Nova**...*Wanderlove* [I]	$6		Warner 7235
2/1/69	99	1		3 **Saturday Night At The World**...*One Minute Commercial*	$6	□	Warner 7248
4/26/69	90	2		4 **Greensleeves**...*$13 Stella* [I]	$6		Warner 7272
				one of the oldest published songs (from 16th-century England)			
				WILLIAMS, Maurice, & The Zodiacs **'60**			
				Born on 4/26/38 in Lancaster, South Carolina. R&B singer. His group originally recorded as **The Gladiolas** (see #1 below); became The Zodiacs in 1959. Williams re-formed group with Wiley Bennett, Henry Gaston, Charles Thomas, Albert Hill and Little Willie Morrow in 1960.			
4/6/57	41	11		1 **Little Darlin'**...T:41 *Sweetheart Please Don't Go*	$75		Excello 2101
				THE GLADIOLAS			
10/3/60	❶[1]	18		2 **Stay**...*Do You Believe*	$25		Herald 552
1/16/61	86	3		3 **I Remember**...*Always*	$20		Herald 556
4/10/61	83	2		4 **Come Along**...*Do I*	$20		Herald 559
				WILLIAMS, Mike **'66**			
				Soul singer/songwriter.			
7/9/66	69	5		**Lonely Soldier**...*If This Isn't Love*	$10		Atlantic 2339
				Gene Barge (orch.)			
				WILLIAMS, Otis — see CHARMS			
				WILLIAMS, Paul AC/BUB/C&W/LP **'72**			
				Born on 9/19/40 in Omaha, Nebraska. Singer/songwriter/actor. Wrote "We've Only Just Begun" and "Rainy Days & Mondays" with partner Roger Nichols, and co-wrote "Evergreen" with **Barbra Streisand**. Acted in several movies.			
2/19/72	60	9		**Waking Up Alone**...*We've Only Just Begun*	$5		A&M 1325
				WILLIAMS, Robbie LP **'99**			
				Born on 2/13/74 in Port Vale, England. Pop-rock singer/songwriter. Former member of **Take That**.			
6/5/99	72	4		1 **Millennium**...A:74		V	album cut
				"45": Capital 58784; B-side: "South Of The Border"			
11/20/99+	53	19		2 **Angels**...A:45		V	album cut
				"45": Capitol 58795; B-side: "It's Only Us"; above 2 from the album *The Ego Has Landed* on Capitol 97726			

DEBUT	PEAK	WKS	Gold	A-side (Chart Hit)...B-side	$	Sym	Label & Number

★262★ WILLIAMS, Roger — AC/BUB/LP '55

Born Louis Weertz on 10/1/24 in Omaha, Nebraska. Pianist. Learned to play piano by age three. Educated at Drake University, Idaho State University, and Juilliard School of Music. Took lessons from Lenny Tristano and Teddy Wilson. Win on the TV show *Arthur Godfrey's Talent Scouts* led to recording contract.

1)Autumn Leaves 2)Born Free 3)Near You 4)Almost Paradise 5)Till

DEBUT	PEAK	WKS	Gold	A-side (Chart Hit)...B-side	$	Sym	Label & Number
8/20/55	❶⁴	26	●	1 **Autumn Leaves** S:❶⁴ / T:2 / J:2 / A:3 *Take Care* [I]	$15	■	Kapp 116
				from the 1947 French song "Les Feuilles' Mortes"; also see #17 below			
12/10/55+	38	10		2 **Wanting You**...T:38 *Night Wind* [I]	$12		Kapp 127
				from the 1928 musical *The New Moon* starring Evelyn Herbert			
3/3/56	37	9		3 **La Mer (Beyond The Sea)**...T:37 *Song Of Devotion* [I]	$12		Kapp 138
				#26 hit for **Benny Goodman** in 1948			
5/26/56	85	3		4 **Hi-Lili Hi-Lo**...T:85 *My Dream Sonata* [I]	$12		Kapp 144
				introduced by Leslie Caron and Mel Ferrer in the 1953 movie *Lili*			
8/25/56	60	8		5 **Tumbling Tumbleweeds**...T:60 *I'll Always Walk With You* [I]	$12		Kapp 156
				#10 hit for **Gene Autry** in 1935			
11/10/56	41	12		6 **Two Different Worlds**...T:41 *Nights In Verona* (Williams)	$12		Kapp 161
				ROGER WILLIAMS and JANE MORGAN			
3/2/57	15	20		7 **Almost Paradise**...A:15 / S:22 / T:26 *For The First Time* [I]	$10		Kapp 175
10/28/57	22	17	●	8 **Till**...A:22 / T:27 / S:28 *Big Town*	$10		Kapp 197
4/14/58	55	8		9 **Arrivederci, Roma**...T:55 *The Sentimental Touch*	$10		Kapp 210
8/18/58	10	17		10 **Near You**...H:10 / S:16 *The Merry Widow Waltz* [I]	$10		Kapp 233
				#1 hit (17 weeks) for Francis Craig in 1947			
12/8/58	71	3		11 **The World Outside**...*Tchaikovsky Piano Concerto No. 1*	$10		Kapp 246
				based on the *Warsaw Concerto*			
6/6/60	98	1		12 **La Montana (If She Should Come To You)**...*What Lies Over The Hill?* [I]	$8		Kapp 331
9/26/60	56	6		13 **Temptation**...*Homesick For New England* [I]	$8		Kapp 347
				#3 hit for **Bing Crosby** in 1934			
12/11/61+	48	8		14 **Maria**...*Eventide* [I]	$8	■	Kapp 437
				from the Broadway musical *West Side Story* starring Carol Lawrence (Maria)			
3/10/62	88	4		15 **Amor**...*Marie, Marie* [I]	$8		Kapp 447
				#2 hit for **Bing Crosby** in 1944			
4/10/65	97	2		16 **Try To Remember**...*Frenesi*	$8		Kapp 48
				from the off-Broadway musical *The Fantasticks* starring Jerry Orbach; label is Kapp's "Winners Circle Series"			
10/16/65	92	3		17 **Autumn Leaves - 1965**...*Autumn Leaves - 1955* [R]	$8		Kapp 707
				new version of #1 above; B-side is the original version; special commemorative gold label			
6/25/66	65	6		18 **Lara's Theme from "Dr. Zhivago"**...*Dulcinea* [I]	$6		Kapp 738
				from the movie *Dr. Zhivago* starring Omar Sharif and Julie Christie			
8/27/66	7	21		19 **Born Free**...AC⁶ *Jimmie's Train*	$6		Kapp 767
				title song from the movie starring Virginia McKenna			
1/28/67	84	5		20 **Sunrise, Sunset**...*Edelweiss*	$6		Kapp 801
				from the Broadway musical *Fiddler On The Roof* starring Zero Mostel			
5/6/67	60	5		21 **Love Me Forever**...*Sweet Pea*	$6		Kapp 821
7/13/68	55	7		22 **The Impossible Dream**...*If You Go (Si Tu Partais)* (AC #37) [I]	$6		Kapp 907
				from the Broadway musical *Man Of La Mancha* starring Richard Kiley			
6/7/69	99	2		23 **Galveston**...*Mini Minuet* [I]	$6		Kapp 2007
				Williams's orchestra conductors: Ralph Carmichael (#14-23), Marty Gold (#7, 8), Frank Hunter (#13), Hal Kanner (#5, 6, 9-11), Pete King (#12) and Glenn Osser (#1-3)			

WILLIAMS, Tené — '93

Born in Harlem, New York. Female R&B-dance singer.

DEBUT	PEAK	WKS	Gold	A-side (Chart Hit)...B-side	$	Sym	Label & Number
5/8/93	87	7		**Give Him A Love He Can Feel**...A:50 *(instrumental)*	$4	▮	Pendulum 64655
				Chantay Savage (backing vocal)			

★311★ WILLIAMS, Vanessa — R&B/AC/LP '92

Born on 3/18/63 in Tarrytown, New York. R&B singer/actress. In 1983, became the first black woman to win the Miss America pageant; relinquished crown after *Penthouse* magazine scandal. Married to Ramon Hervey (manager of **Babyface**) from 1987-97. Began hosting *Soul of VH-1* on the video music TV channel in 1991. Acted in several movies and Broadway shows. Married NBA player Rick Fox on 9/26/99.

1)Save The Best For Last 2)Love Is 3)Colors Of The Wind

DEBUT	PEAK	WKS	Gold	A-side (Chart Hit)...B-side	$	Sym	Label & Number
7/23/88	44	10		1 **The Right Stuff**...S:32 *(edited version)*	$3	■	Wing 887386
1/7/89	8	20		2 **Dreamin'**...RB² S:8 / A:10 *The Right Stuff (instrumental)*	$3	■	Wing 871078
6/3/89	88	4		3 **Darlin' I**...*The Right Stuff (1:10 version)*	$3	■	Wing 871936
8/10/91	18	21		4 **Running Back To You**...RB² A:17 / S:33 *(3 album snippets) / Better Off Now*	$4	▮ᵛ	Wing 867518
12/7/91+	62	12		5 **The Comfort Zone**...A:45 *(3 album snippets) / (instrumental)*	$4	▮ᵛ	Wing 865072
2/1/92	❶⁵	27	●	6 **Save The Best For Last** RB³ / AC³ A:❶⁸ / S:2 *Freedom Dance (Get Free!)*	$3	▮ᵛ	Wing 865136
5/23/92	26	19		7 **Just For Tonight**...A:27 / S:48 *(3 album snippets)*	$3	▮ᵛ	Wing 865888
				"45" B-side: (same as A-side)			
9/26/92	52	11		8 **Work To Do**...A:36 *(3 album snippets) / (radio mix w/rap)*	$3	▮ᵛ	Wing 863540
				VANESSA WILLIAMS (featuring Black Sheep)			
				above 5 from the album *The Comfort Zone*			
1/23/93	3	28		9 **Love Is**...AC³ A:2 / S:13 *(instrumental)*	$3	▮ᵛ	Giant 18630
				VANESSA WILLIAMS and BRIAN McKNIGHT			
				from the album *Beverly Hills, 90210 - The Soundtrack*			
11/12/94+	18	23		10 **The Sweetest Days**...S:21 / A:21 *Love Is (remix w/***Brian McKnight***)*	$3	▮ᵛ	Wing 851110
				"45" B-side: "Dreamin'"			
5/6/95	67	7		11 **The Way That You Love**...S:55 *(rhythm mix) / (3 album snippets)*	$3	▮	Wing 856766
6/24/95	4	23	●	12 **Colors Of The Wind**...S:4 / A:11 *(Spanish version)*	$3	▮ᵛ	Hollywood 64001
				from the Disney animated movie *Pocahontas*			
7/13/96	71	14		13 **Where Do We Go From Here**...*Erase*	$3	▮ᵛ	Mercury 578102
				theme song from the movie *Eraser* starring Arnold Schwarzenegger and Williams			

WILLIAMS, Vesta — see VESTA

DEBUT	PEAK	WKS	Gold	A-side (Chart Hit)........B-side	$	Sym	Label & Number

WILLIAMS BROTHERS, The — '92

Twin nephews of **Andy Williams**: Andrew and David Williams. Born on 2/22/59 in Henderson, Nevada.

DEBUT	PEAK	WKS	Gold	A-side (Chart Hit)........B-side	$	Sym	Label & Number
6/22/74	92	4		1 **What's Your Name** *[ANDY & DAVID WILLIAMS]*........*Say It Again*	$6		Barnaby 601
2/8/92	42	18		2 **Can't Cry Hard Enough**........S:41 / A:58 *Happy Man*	$3	▮V	Warner 19326

WILLIE D — see GETO BOYS, The

WILLIE MAX — '98

Female R&B vocal trio from Detroit, Michigan: sisters Rose, Sky and Lyric Smith.

DEBUT	PEAK	WKS	Gold	A-side (Chart Hit)........B-side	$	Sym	Label & Number
11/7/98	49	10		**Can't Get Enough**........S:22 *24* **WILLIE MAX Featuring Raphael Saadiq**	$4	★	Motown 860848

WILLI ONE BLOOD — '95

Born in Brooklyn, New York. White dancehall/reggae singer.

DEBUT	PEAK	WKS	Gold	A-side (Chart Hit)........B-side	$	Sym	Label & Number
1/21/95	62	11		**Whiney, Whiney (What Really Drives Me Crazy)**.......S:66 *Get Ready* (**The Proclaimers**) samples "Baby Elephant Walk" and "You Really Got Me"; from the movie *Dumb And Dumber* starring Jim Carrey; "45": RCA 64304; B-side: (instrumental)	$5	▮V	RCA 64265

WILLIS, Bruce — LP '87

Born Walter Bruce Willis on 3/19/55 in Idar-Oberstein, West Germany; raised in Penns Grove, New Jersey. Played "David Addison" on TV's *Moonlighting*. Starred in the *Die Hard* movies and many others. Married to actress Demi Moore from 1987-2000.

DEBUT	PEAK	WKS	Gold	A-side (Chart Hit)........B-side	$	Sym	Label & Number
1/17/87	5	14		1 **Respect Yourself**........S:5 / A:6 *Fun Time*	$3	■	Motown 1876
4/11/87	68	5		2 **Young Blood**........*Flirting With Disaster*	$3	■	Motown 1886
6/13/87	59	7		3 **Under The Boardwalk**........*Jackpot (Bruno's Bop)*	$3	■	Motown 1896

WILLIS, Chuck — R&B '58

Born on 1/31/28 in Atlanta, Georgia. Died of a bleeding ulcer on 4/10/58 (age 30). R&B singer/songwriter. Billed as the "King of the Stroll" and known as the "Sheik of The Blues" for the turban he wore while performing.

DEBUT	PEAK	WKS	Gold	A-side (Chart Hit)........B-side	$	Sym	Label & Number
4/20/57	12	26		1 **C. C. Rider**........RB[2] T:12 / S:13 *Ease The Pain* inspired the "Stroll" dance craze; #14 hit for Ma Rainey in 1925 (as "See See Rider Blues")	$30		Atlantic 1130
2/3/58	33	11		2 **Betty And Dupree**........S:33 / T:33 *My Crying Eyes* Jesse Stone (orch., above 2)	$30		Atlantic 1168
4/28/58	24	12		3 **Hang Up My Rock And Roll Shoes** / T:24 / S:flip Reggie Obrecht (orch., above 2)			
5/12/58	9	19	●	4 **What Am I Living For** RB[1] A:9 / S:15 / T:15	$30		Atlantic 1179
8/18/58	46	5		5 **My Life**........S:46 / H:56 *Thunder And Lightning*	$25		Atlantic 1192

WILLIS "THE GUARD" & VIGORISH — see BUCKNER & GARCIA

WILL-O-BEES, The — '68

Pop trio from New York: Janet Blossom, Steven Porter and Robert Merchanthouse.

DEBUT	PEAK	WKS	Gold	A-side (Chart Hit)........B-side	$	Sym	Label & Number
2/3/68	95	3		**It's Not Easy**........*Looking Glass*	$8		Date 1583

WILLOWS — BUB '56

R&B doo-wop group formed in Harlem, New York: Tony Middleton (lead), Richard Davis, Ralph Martin, Joseph Martin and Freddie Donovan (died on 5/13/97).

DEBUT	PEAK	WKS	Gold	A-side (Chart Hit)........B-side	$	Sym	Label & Number
4/7/56	62	11		**Church Bells May Ring**........T:62 *Baby Tell Me* **Neil Sedaka** (chimes); title also shown as "Church Bells Are Ringing" ($300); "Bubbled Under" (#114) on 3/6/61	$100		Melba 102

WILLS, Mark — C&W/BUB/LP '99

Born Daryl Mark Williams on 8/8/73 in Cleveland, Tennessee; raised in Blue Ridge, Georgia. Country singer.

DEBUT	PEAK	WKS	Gold	A-side (Chart Hit)........B-side	$	Sym	Label & Number
5/9/98	72	13		1 **I Do [Cherish You]**........S:49 *You Can't Go Wrong Loving Me*	$4	▮V	Mercury 568602
12/5/98	73	5		2 **Don't Laugh At Me**........A:60 "45": Mercury 566054; B-side: "I Can't Live With Myself"		V	album cut
3/6/99	34	20		3 **Wish You Were Here**........CW[1] A:22 co-written by **Bill Anderson**; "45": Mercury 566764; B-side: "Emily Harper"		V	album cut
9/11/99	60	10		4 **She's In Love**........A:47 "45": Mercury 566746; B-side: "Don't Think I Won't"; all of above from the album *Wish You Were Here* on Mercury 536317		V	album cut
1/15/00	36	20		5 **Back At One**........A:27 from the album *Permanently* on Mercury 546296; "45": Mercury 562530; B-side: "Because I Love You"		V	album cut
11/23/02+	23	20		6 **19 Somethin'** A:20 from the album *Greatest Hits* on Mercury 170313; "45": Mercury 172267; B-side: "When You Think Of Me"		V	album cut

WILL TO POWER — LP '88

Pop-dance trio from Florida: Bob Rosenberg, Dr. J. and Maria Mendez. Rosenberg is the son of singer **Gloria Mann**. By 1990, reduced to a duo of Rosenberg and Elin Michaels. Group name taken from the work of 19th-century German philosopher Friedrich Nietzsche.

DEBUT	PEAK	WKS	Gold	A-side (Chart Hit)........B-side	$	Sym	Label & Number
6/27/87	50	16		1 **Dreamin'**........*(original mix)*	$3		Epic 07199
6/18/88	49	14		2 **Say It's Gonna Rain**........*(instrumental)*	$3		Epic 07908
9/10/88	❶[1]	24	●	3 **Baby, I Love Your Way/Freebird Medley (Free Baby)** S:❶[1] / A:❶[1] *Anti-Social*	$3		Epic 08034
2/4/89	65	10		4 **Fading Away**........*(radio version II)* all of above from the album *Will To Power*	$3		Epic 68543
11/17/90+	7	18		5 **I'm Not In Love**........A:4 / S:7 *Fly Bird (Reprise)*	$3	▮V	Epic 73636

WILMER AND THE DUKES — BUB/LP '68

R&B-soul group from Rochester, New York. Led by Wilmer Alexander Jr.

DEBUT	PEAK	WKS	Gold	A-side (Chart Hit)........B-side	$	Sym	Label & Number
7/20/68	80	6		**Give Me One More Chance**........*Get It* incorporates the lyrics of the title of **Otis Redding**'s 1966 hit "Fa-Fa-Fa-Fa-Fa"	$8		Aphrodisiac 260

WILSON, Al — R&B/BUB/LP '74

Born on 6/19/39 in Meridian, Mississippi. R&B singer/drummer. Member of **The Rollers** from 1960-62.

DEBUT	PEAK	WKS	Gold	A-side (Chart Hit)........B-side	$	Sym	Label & Number
8/17/68	27	10		1 **The Snake**........*Getting Ready For Tomorrow*	$8		Soul City 767
1/18/69	75	4		2 **Poor Side Of Town**........*The Dolphins*	$8		Soul City 771
8/23/69	67	7		3 **Lodi**........*By The Time I Get Phoenix* above 3 produced by **Johnny Rivers** (owner of Soul City Records)	$8		Soul City 775
10/20/73+	❶[1]	22	●	4 **Show And Tell** *Listen To Me*	$6		Rocky Road 30073

DEBUT	PEAK	WKS	Gold	A-side (Chart Hit)...B-side	$	Sym	Label & Number
				WILSON, Al — Cont'd			
3/9/74	**57**	9		5 **Touch And Go**...*Settle Me Down*	$6		Rocky Road 30076
10/5/74	**30**	10		6 **La La Peace Song**...*Keep On Lovin' You*	$6		Rocky Road 30200
1/11/75	**70**	7		7 **I Won't Last A Day Without You/Let Me Be The One**...*Willoughby Brook* medley of songs written and recorded by **Paul Williams**	$6		Rocky Road 30202
3/27/76	**29**	10		8 **I've Got A Feeling (We'll Be Seeing Each Other Again)**...*Be Concerned*	$5		Playboy 6062
				WILSON, Ann — see HEART			
				WILSON, Brian — see BEACH BOYS, The			
				WILSON, Carl — see BEACH BOYS, The			
				WILSON, Charlie '00 Born in Tulsa, Oklahoma. Lead singer of **The Gap Band**.			
10/31/98	**41**	7		1 **Whatcha Wanna Do?**...S:20 *(instrumental) / I Can't Take The Heat* (w/**Snoop Dogg**) **MIA X Featuring Charlie Wilson** clean version available on No Limit 53460; produced by **Master P**	$3	■	No Limit 53459
11/11/00	**48[S]**	6		2 **Without You**...*(2 versions)*	$6	★	Major Hits 670004
				WILSON, Danny — see DANNY WILSON			
				WILSON, Hank — see RUSSELL, Leon			
				WILSON, J. Frank, and The Cavaliers BUB/LP '64 Born on 12/11/41 in Lufkin, Texas. Died on 10/4/91 (age 49). The Cavaliers: Sid Holmes (guitar), Lewis Elliott (bass) and Ray Smith (drums).			
9/5/64	**2[1]**	15		1 **Last Kiss**...*That's How Much I Love You* first released on Le Cam 722 ($30) and then on Tamara 761 ($30) in 1964; also see #3 below	$15		Josie 923
11/28/64	**85**	2		2 **Hey Little One**...*Speak To Me*	$10		Josie 926
12/22/73+	**92**	5		3 **Last Kiss**...*That's How Much I Love You* [R] same version as #1 above	$8		Virgo 506
				**WILSON, Jackie** ★53★ BUB/R&B/LP '60 Born on 6/9/34 in Detroit, Michigan. Died on 1/21/84 (age 49). One of the all-time great soul singers; dubbed "Mr. Excitement." Sang with local gospel groups; became an amateur boxer. Worked as a solo singer until 1953, then joined **Billy Ward And His Dominoes** as **Clyde McPhatter**'s replacement. Solo since 1957. Godfather of **Jody Watley**. Cousin of Hubert Johnson of **The Contours**. Wilson collapsed after suffering a stroke on stage at the Latin Casino in Cherry Hill, New Jersey on 9/29/75; spent the rest of his life in nursing homes. Inducted into the Rock and Roll Hall of Fame in 1987. *1)Night 2)Baby Workout 3)(Your Love Keeps Lifting Me) Higher And Higher 4)Lonely Teardrops 5)Alone At Last*			
11/4/57	**62**	10		1 **Reet Petite (The Finest Girl You Ever Want To Meet)**...T:62 *By The Light Of The Silvery Moon*	$30		Brunswick 55024
4/14/58	**22**	16		2 **To Be Loved**...T:22 / S:23 *Come Back To Me*	$30		Brunswick 55052
9/22/58	**93**	2		3 **We Have Love**...H:93 *Singing A Song*	$30		Brunswick 55086
11/24/58+	**7**	21		4 **Lonely Teardrops**...RB[7] *In The Blue Of Evening* a new version is on the B-side of #39 below	$30		Brunswick 55105
3/23/59	**13**	13		5 **That's Why (I Love You So)**...*Love Is All*	$25	■	Brunswick 55121
6/22/59	**20**	12		6 **I'll Be Satisfied**...*Ask* all of above written by Berry Gordy, Jr. and Tyran Carlo	$25		Brunswick 55136
9/7/59	**37**	10		7 **You Better Know It**...RB[1] *Never Go Away* from the movie *Go Johnny Go* starring Wilson and Alan Freed	$25		Brunswick 55149
11/23/59+	**34**	12		8 **Talk That Talk**...*Only You, Only Me*	$25	■	Brunswick 55165
3/21/60	**4**	17	●	9 **Night** / based on Saint-Saens' *Samson & Delilah* aria "My Heart At Thy Sweet Voice"			
4/4/60	**15**	16		10 **Doggin' Around**...RB[3]	$20	■	Brunswick 55166
7/11/60	**12**	13		11 **(You Were Made For) All My Love** /			
7/11/60	**15**	12		12 **A Woman, A Lover, A Friend**...RB[4]	$20		Brunswick 55167
10/10/60	**8**	15		13 **Alone At Last** / based on Tchaikovsky's "Piano Concerto in B Flat"			
10/24/60	**32**	10		14 **Am I The Man**...	$20	■	Brunswick 55170
1/9/61	**9**	9		15 **My Empty Arms** / based on "Vesti La Giubba" from the opera *I Pagliacci*			
1/23/61	**44**	7		16 **The Tear Of The Year**...	$20	■	Brunswick 55201
3/13/61	**20**	8		17 **Please Tell Me Why** /			
3/13/61	**40**	6		18 **Your One And Only Love**...	$20		Brunswick 55208
6/12/61	**19**	8		19 **I'm Comin' On Back To You** /			
6/12/61	**80**	1		20 **Lonely Life**...	$20		Brunswick 55216
8/21/61	**37**	6		21 **Years From Now** /			
10/2/61	**79**	3		22 **You Don't Know What It Means**...	$20		Brunswick 55219
10/23/61	**58**	6		23 **The Way I Am** /			
10/23/61	**65**	6		24 **My Heart Belongs To Only You**... #22 hit for June Christy in 1953	$20	■	Brunswick 55220
1/13/62	**34**	9		25 **The Greatest Hurt** /			
1/20/62	**75**	3		26 **There'll Be No Next Time**...	$20	■	Brunswick 55221
4/21/62	**93**	1		27 **I Found Love**...*There's Nothing Like Love* **JACKIE WILSON and LINDA HOPKINS**	$20		Brunswick 55224
4/28/62	**58**	6		28 **Hearts**...*Sing (And Tell The Blues So Long)*	$20		Brunswick 55225
7/7/62	**70**	4		29 **I Just Can't Help It**...*My Tale Of Woe*	$20		Brunswick 55229
9/22/62	**82**	4		30 **Forever And A Day**...*Baby, That's All* (#119)	$20		Brunswick 55233
3/9/63	**5**	12		31 **Baby Workout**...RB[3] *I'm Going Crazy (Gotta Get You Off My Mind)*	$20		Brunswick 55239

DEBUT	PEAK	WKS	Gold	A-side (Chart Hit)...B-side	$	Sym	Label & Number
				WILSON, Jackie — Cont'd			
5/25/63	42	7		32 **Shake A Hand**...*Say I Do*	$20		Brunswick 55243
				JACKIE WILSON and LINDA HOPKINS			
				#1 R&B hit for Faye Adams in 1953			
7/13/63	33	8		33 **Shake! Shake! Shake!**...*He's A Fool*	$15		Brunswick 55246
9/21/63	61	5		34 **Baby Get It (And Don't Quit It)**...*The New Breed*	$15		Brunswick 55250
5/23/64	94	1		35 **Big Boss Line**...*Be My Girl*	$15		Brunswick 55266
8/22/64	89	2		36 **Squeeze Her-Tease Her (But Love Her)**...*Give Me Back My Heart*	$15		Brunswick 55269
2/27/65	94	3		37 **Danny Boy**...*Soul Time*	$12		Brunswick 55277
				based on the traditional Irish song "Londonderry Air" written in 1855			
7/3/65	59	10		38 **No Pity (In The Naked City)**...*I'm So Lonely*	$12		Brunswick 55280
10/23/65	96	2		39 **I Believe I'll Love On**...*Lonely Teardrops*	$12		Brunswick 55283
1/15/66	93	1		40 **Think Twice**...*Please Don't Hurt Me (#128)*	$12		Brunswick 55287
				JACKIE WILSON And LaVERN BAKER			
10/15/66	11	12		41 **Whispers (Gettin' Louder)**...*The Fairest Of Them All*	$12		Brunswick 55300
3/4/67	84	3		42 **I Don't Want To Lose You /**			
2/11/67	91	3		43 **Just Be Sincere**...	$12		Brunswick 55309
5/6/67	82	4		44 **I've Lost You**...*Those Heartaches*	$12		Brunswick 55321
8/12/67	6	12		45 **(Your Love Keeps Lifting Me) Higher And Higher**...RB[1] *I'm The One To Do It*	$12		Brunswick 55336
11/25/67	32	6		46 **Since You Showed Me How To Be Happy**...*The Who Who Song*	$10		Brunswick 55354
2/17/68	49	7		47 **For Your Precious Love**...*Uptight (Everything's Alright)*	$10		Brunswick 55365
4/27/68	84	5		48 **Chain Gang**...*Funky Broadway*	$10		Brunswick 55373
				JACKIE WILSON And COUNT BASIE (above 2)			
7/20/68	34	8		49 **I Get The Sweetest Feeling**...*Nothing But Heartaches (Keep Haunting Me)*	$10		Brunswick 55381
11/2/68	70	3		50 **For Once In My Life**...*You Brought About A Change In Me*	$10		Brunswick 55392
5/16/70	91	2		51 **Let This Be A Letter (To My Baby)**...*Didn't I*	$8	■	Brunswick 55435
12/19/70+	56	11		52 **(I Can Feel Those Vibrations) This Love Is Real**...*Love Uprising*	$8		Brunswick 55443
11/27/71	95	3		53 **Love Is Funny That Way**...*Try It Again*	$8		Brunswick 55461
2/26/72	93	3		54 **You Got Me Walking**...*The Fountain*	$8		Brunswick 55467
				Wilson's musical conductors: Gil Askey (#35, 36), Benny Carter (#47, 48), Milton DeLugg (#2), **Willie Henderson** (#49-54), **Dick Jacobs** (#1, 3-22, 27-31, 34, 38), Alan Lorber (#32, 33), Bob Mersey (#23-26), Gerald Sims (#41-46), Dale Warren (#39, 40) and Teacho Wiltshire (#37)			
				WILSON, Meri '77			
				Born on 6/15/49 in Japan (father was a U.S. Air Force officer); raised in Marietta, Georgia. Died in a car crash on 12/28/2002 (age 53). Was the director of elementary education for Georgia.			
6/4/77	18	16	●	**Telephone Man**...*Itinerary* [N]	$5		GRT 127
				produced by **Boomer Castleman** and Jim Rutledge (of **Bloodrock**)			
				WILSON, Mike "Hitman" — see CHRISTOPHER, Shawn			
				WILSON, Nancy R&B/AC/BUB/LP '64			
				Born on 2/20/37 in Chillicothe, Ohio; raised in Columbus, Ohio. R&B/jazz-styled singer. Not to be confused with Nancy Wilson of Heart.			
				1)(You Don't Know) How Glad I Am 2)Face It Girl, It's Over 3)Can't Take My Eyes Off You			
8/24/63	73	6		1 **Tell Me The Truth**...*My Sweet Thing*	$8		Capitol 4991
12/14/63	6[X]	4		2 **That's What I Want For Christmas /** [X]			
				X: 6/'63; 26/'64			
12/25/65	17[X]	3		3 **What Are You Doing New Year's Eve**... [X]	$10		Capitol 5084
				X: 17/'65; 24/'67			
6/27/64	11	11		4 **(You Don't Know) How Glad I Am** *Never Less Than Yesterday*	$7		Capitol 5198
10/3/64	57	5		5 **I Wanna Be With You**...*It's Time For Me*	$7		Capitol 5254
				from the Broadway musical *Golden Boy* starring **Sammy Davis, Jr.**			
1/30/65	58	5		6 **Don't Come Running Back To Me**...*Love Has Many Faces*	$7	■	Capitol 5340
7/16/66	84	4		7 **Uptight (Everything's Alright)**...*You've Got Your Troubles (AC #20/R&B #48)*	$7		Capitol 5673
5/11/68	29	14		8 **Face It Girl, It's Over**...*The End Of Our Love*	$7		Capitol 2136
9/28/68	55	7		9 **Peace Of Mind**...*This Bitter Earth*	$6		Capitol 2283
11/22/69	52	10		10 **Can't Take My Eyes Off You**...*Do You Know Why*	$6		Capitol 2644
1/2/71	93	3		11 **Now I'm A Woman**...*The Real Me*	$6		Capitol 2934
				Wilson's musical arrangers and conductors: **H.B. Barnum** (#8), Sid Feller (#5, 6), **Jimmy Jones** (#9, 10), O.B. Masingill (#2), Oliver Nelson (#4, 7) and Gerald Wilson (#1, 3)			
				WILSON, Phill '61			
				Born on 6/19/40 in Sidney, Ohio. Pop singer/songwriter/actor/playwright. Acted in the movies *Mischief*, *Teachers* and *The Unseen Force*.			
7/10/61	91	2		**Wishin' On A Rainbow**...*Just Me*	$25		Huron 22000
				tune is similar to **Elvis Presley**'s "Pocketful of Rainbows" on his 1960 album *G.I. Blues*			
				WILSON, Shanice — see SHANICE			
				WILSON BROS. '79			
				Pop duo: Steve and Kelly Wilson.			
10/6/79	94	2		**Another Night**...*Shadows*	$4		Atco 7205
	★463★			**WILSON PHILLIPS** AC/BUB/LP '90			
				Pop-Adult Contemporary vocal trio formed in Los Angeles, California: sisters Carnie (born on 4/29/68) and Wendy (born on 10/16/69) Wilson, with Chynna Phillips (born on 2/12/68). Carnie and Wendy's father is **Brian Wilson** (**The Beach Boys**). Chynna, the daughter of Michelle and **John Phillips** (**The Mamas & The Papas**), acted in the movie *Caddyshack II*. Carnie became host of own TV talk show in 1995.			
3/17/90	❶[1]	25	●	1 **Hold On**...AC[1] S:2 / A:2 *Over And Over*	$3	▮[V]	SBK 07322 ■
6/30/90	❶[2]	22	●	2 **Release Me** AC[1] A:❶[3] / S:3 *Eyes Like Twins*	$3	▮[V]	SBK 07327
				"45": Collectables 6140; B-side: "Hold On"			
10/13/90	4	20		3 **Impulsive**...A:2 / S:8 *(album version)*	$3	▮[V]	SBK 07337
				Joe Walsh (rhythm & slide guitar)			

DEBUT	PEAK	WKS	Gold	A-side (Chart Hit)....B-side	$	Sym	Label & Number
				WILSON PHILLIPS — Cont'd			
2/9/91	❶[1]	19		4 **You're In Love**..........AC[4] A:❶[1] / S:2 *Hold On (live) / Release Me (live) / Morning Tea In Tokyo*	$3	▮	SBK 07343
6/1/91	12	14		5 **The Dream Is Still Alive**...A:29 *(Spanglish & Spanish versions) / Next To You (Someday I'll Be)* "45" issued for #3 & 5 on Collectables 6230; all of above from the album *Wilson Phillips*	$3	▮V	SBK 07356
5/9/92	20	16		6 **You Won't See Me Cry**..........S:22 / A:27 *This Doesn't Have To Be Love* "45": SBK 57743	$3	▮V	SBK 07385
8/8/92	30	11		7 **Give It Up**..........A:40 / S:42 *(2 mixes) / Daniel* "45": SBK 57896; all of above produced by Glen Ballard	$3	▮V	SBK 50398
				WILTON PLACE STREET BAND R&B '77 Studio disco group assembled in Los Angeles, California, by producer Trevor Lawrence (who resided on Wilton Place in L.A.).			
1/8/77	24	17		**Disco Lucy (I Love Lucy Theme)**..........*You Don't Even Know Who We Are* [I] discofied theme from the TV series *I Love Lucy* starring Lucille Ball	$5		Island 078
				WINANS, BeBe & CeCe R&B/BUB/AC/LP '96 Younger brother and sister of the Detroit gospel-singing family, The Winans: Benjamin "BeBe" and Priscilla "CeCe." They are the seventh and eighth children in a 10-sibling family.			
1/4/92	90	6		1 **I'll Take You There**..........RB[1] *(2 versions)* **BEBE + CECE WINANS (featuring Mavis Staples)** also see **The Staple Singers**' #1 hit version in 1972	$4	▮	Capitol 44749
3/23/96	8	20	●	2 **Count On Me**..........S:5 / A:29 *One Moment In Time* (Houston) **WHITNEY HOUSTON & CECE WINANS** from the movie *Waiting To Exhale* starring Houston	$3	▮V	Arista 12976
11/22/97	83	12		3 **In Harm's Way**..........S:64 *Stay* **BEBE WINANS**	$3	▮	Atlantic 84035
				WINANS, Mario R&B/BUB '02 Born in Detroit, Michigan. Singer/session drummer. Sibling, but not a member of **The Winans** singing group. Also see **Tamia**'s "So Into You."			
2/12/00	59	5		1 **Best Friend**..........S:8 *(instrumental)* **PUFF DADDY Featuring Mario Winans & Hezekiah Walker & The Love Fellowship Crusade Choir** samples "Sailing" by **Christopher Cross**	$5	★	Bad Boy 79318
6/8/02	4	26		2 **I Need A Girl (Part Two)**..........A:4 / S:17 *(instrumental) / So Complete* **P. DIDDY AND GINUWINE Featuring Loon, Mario Winans & Tammy Ruggeri**	$6	T	Bad Boy 79441
				WINBUSH, Angela — see ISLEY BROTHERS / RENÉ AND ANGELA			
				WINCHESTER, Jesse LP '81 Born on 5/17/44 in Shreveport, Louisiana. Pop singer/songwriter/guitarist.			
8/20/77	86	3		1 **Nothing But A Breeze**..........*Twigs And Seeds*	$4		Bearsville 0318
4/25/81	32	12		2 **Say What**..........*If Only*	$4		Bearsville 49711
				WIND — see ORLANDO, Tony			
				WINDING, Kai, & Orchestra BUB/LP '63 Born on 5/18/22 in Aarhus, Denmark. Died on 5/6/83 (age 60). Jazz trombonist. Moved to U.S. in 1934. With **Benny Goodman** and **Stan Kenton** in the mid-1940s.			
7/6/63	8	15		**More**..........*Comin' Home Baby* [I] theme from the Italian documentary movie *Mondo Cane*	$10		Verve 10295
				WINE, Toni '63 Female pop session singer. Backing vocalist for **The Archies**. Married record producer Chips Moman.			
12/28/63	22[X]	1		**My Boyfriend's Coming Home For Christmas**..........*What A Pity* [X] includes strains of "The First Noel"	$20		Colpix 715
				WING AND A PRAYER FIFE AND DRUM CORPS., The LP '76 Disco studio group assembled by producer Harold Wheeler. Vocals by Linda November, Vivian Cherry, Arlene Martell and Helen Miles.			
11/15/75+	14	20		**Baby Face**..........*(long version)* #1 hit for Jan Garber in 1926; #1 hit for **Art Mooney** in 1948	$6		Wing & A Prayer 103
				WINGER ROK/LP '89 Hard-rock group formed in New York: **Kip Winger** (vocals, bass) (see #4 below), Reb Beach (guitar), Paul Taylor (keyboards; left in 1992) and Rod Morgenstein (drums). Kip was a member of **Alice Cooper**'s band. Morgenstein was a member of Dixie Dregs.			
2/25/89	26	16		1 **Seventeen**..........S:24 / A:28 *Poison Angel*	$3	■	Atlantic 88958
6/3/89	19	18		2 **Headed For A Heartbreak**..........A:18 / S:20 *State Of Emergency*	$3	■	Atlantic 88922
9/23/89	85	6		3 **Hungry**..........*Time To Surrender*	$3	■	Atlantic 88859
11/25/89+	52	12		4 **Everything You Do (You're Sexing Me)**..........*Calling On You* **FIONA with Kip Winger**	$3	■	Atlantic 88823
7/28/90	42	15		5 **Can't Get Enuff**..........S:38 *In The Day We'll Never See*	$4	▮	Atlantic 87884
10/13/90+	12	22		6 **Miles Away**..........S:8 / A:14 *Rainbow In The Rose*	$4	▮	Atlantic 87824
2/9/91	41	11		7 **Easy Come Easy Go**..........A:35 *You Are The Saint, I Am The Sinner* all of above produced by Beau Hill	$4	▮	Atlantic 87773
				WINGFIELD, Pete BUB/LP '75 Born on 5/7/48 in Kiphook, Hampshire, England. Pop singer/keyboardist/producer. Also see **Band Of Gold**.			
8/23/75	15	19		**Eighteen With A Bullet**..........*Shadow Of A Doubt* hit #18 with a bullet on the 11/22/75 *Billboard* "Hot 100" chart	$6		Island 026
				WINGS — see McCARTNEY, Paul			
				WINSTONS, The BUB/LP '69 R&B group from Washington DC: Richard Spencer (vocals), Ray Maritano (sax), Quincy Mattison (guitar), Phil Tolotta (organ), Sonny Peckrol (bass) and G.C. Coleman (drums). Toured as backup band for **The Impressions**.			
5/24/69	7	13	●	1 **Color Him Father**..........*Amen, Brother*	$8		Metromedia 117
9/20/69	54	6		2 **Love Of The Common People**..........*Wheel Of Fortune*	$8		Metromedia 142

DEBUT	PEAK	WKS	Gold	A-side (Chart Hit)...B-side	$	Sym	Label & Number
				WINTER, Edgar, Group BUB/LP **'73**			
				Born on 12/28/46 in Beaumont, Texas. Rock singer/keyboardist/saxophonist. Younger brother of **Johnny Winter**. Group included **Dan Hartman** (1972-76), Ronnie Montrose (1972-74) and **Rick Derringer** (1974-76).			
12/18/71+	70	11		1 **Keep Playin' That Rock 'N' Roll** ...*Dying To Live*	$7		Epic 10788
5/6/72	81	4		2 **I Can't Turn You Loose** ...*Cool Fool*	$7		Epic 10855
				EDGAR WINTER'S WHITE TRASH (above 2)			
3/10/73	❶[1]	20	●	3 **Frankenstein** *Undercover Man* [I]	$6		Epic 10967
				Ronnie Montrose (lead guitar)			
8/11/73	14	15		4 **Free Ride** ...*When It Comes*	$6		Epic 11024
12/15/73+	65	7		5 **Hangin' Around** ...*We All Had A Real Good Time*	$5		Epic 11069
7/20/74	33	9		6 **River's Risin'** *[EDGAR WINTER]* ...*Animal*	$5		Epic 11143
10/26/74	83	4		7 **Easy Street** ...*Do Like Me*	$5		Epic 50034
				all of above produced by **Rick Derringer**			
				WINTER, Johnny ROK/BUB/LP **'71**			
				Born on 2/23/44 in Leland, Mississippi. Blues-rock singer/guitarist. Both Johnny and brother **Edgar Winter** are albinos. A prominent 1960s sessionman, Johnny toured with Muddy Waters and was a member of **The Traits**.			
1/10/70	92	3		1 **Johnny B. Goode** ...*I'm Not Sure*	$7		Columbia 45058
5/1/71	89	2		2 **Jumpin' Jack Flash** ...*Good Morning Little School Girl* [L]	$7		Columbia 45368
				WINTERHALTER, Hugo, and his Orchestra MEM/POP/AC **'56**			
				Born on 8/15/09 in Wilkes-Barre, Pennsylvania. Died of cancer on 9/17/73 (age 64). Conductor/arranger for RCA Records from 1950-63. Charted 22 hits, 1949-54. His orchestra backed more artists (17), who had chart hits, than any other conductor from 1940-54.			
12/18/54+	25	5		1 **Song Of The Barefoot Contessa** ...S:25 *Land Of Dreams* (Pop #30/'54 w/**Eddie Heywood**)	$15		RCA Victor 5888
				from the movie *The Barefoot Contessa* starring Humphrey Bogart and Ava Gardner			
1/28/56	62	5		2 **Memories Of You** ...T:62 *Autumn Rhapsody*	$12		RCA Victor 6339
				from the movie *The* **Benny Goodman** *Story* starring **Steve Allen**; #18 hit for **Louis Armstrong** in 1930			
4/7/56	41	3		3 **The Little Musicians** ...T:41 *Flaherty's Beguine* [I]	$12		RCA Victor 6459
6/23/56	2[2]	31	●	4 **Canadian Sunset** ...A:2 / T:2 / S:3 / J:3 *This Is Real (We're In Love, We're In Love, We're In Love)* [I]	$15		RCA Victor 6537
				HUGO WINTERHALTER and his Orchestra with EDDIE HEYWOOD			
				WINTERS, Ruby R&B/BUB **'69**			
				Born in Louisville, Kentucky; raised in Cincinnati, Ohio. R&B singer.			
4/15/67	96	1		1 **Make Love To Me** ...*Teach Me Tonight*	$15		Diamond 218
				JOHNNY THUNDER & RUBY WINTERS			
				#1 hit for **Jo Stafford** in 1954			
2/15/69	97	2		2 **I Don't Want To Cry** ...*Just Like A Yo Yo*	$15		Diamond 255
12/27/69	99	2		3 **Guess Who** ...*Sweetheart Things*	$15		Diamond 269
	★229★			**WINWOOD, Steve** ROK/AC/BUB/LP **'88**			
				Born on 5/12/48 in Birmingham, England. Rock singer/keyboardist/guitarist. Lead singer of **Spencer Davis Group**, Blind Faith and **Traffic**.			
				1)Roll With It 2)Higher Love 3)Don't You Know What The Night Can Do?			
2/7/81	7	18		1 **While You See A Chance** ...*Vacant Chair*	$4	■	Island 49656
5/9/81	48	9		2 **Arc Of A Diver** ...*Dust*	$4	■	Island 49726
8/7/82	47	10		3 **Still In The Game** ...*Dust*	$4		Island 29940
11/13/82	70	4		4 **Valerie** ...*Slowdown Sundown*	$4		Island 29879
				also see #9 below			
6/14/86	❶[1]	22		5 **Higher Love** ...AR[4] A:❶[2] / S:2 *And I Go*	$3	■	Island 28710
				Chaka Khan (backing vocal); 1986 Grammy winner: Record of the Year			
9/27/86	20	15		6 **Freedom Overspill** ...A:19 / S:21 *Help Me Angel*	$3	■	Island 28595
				Joe Walsh (slide guitar)			
2/7/87	8	23		7 **The Finer Things** ...AC[3] A:4 / S:9 *Night Train*	$3	■	Island 28498
5/30/87	13	21		8 **Back In The High Life Again** ...AC[3] A:10 / S:16 *Night Train*	$3	■	Island 28472
				James Taylor (backing vocal); above 4 from the album *Back In The High Life*			
10/10/87	9	20		9 **Valerie** ...A:7 / S:14 *Talking Back To The Night* [I] [R]	$3	■	Island 28231
				remixed version of #4 above			
2/13/88	57	10		10 **Talking Back To The Night** ...*There's A River*	$3	■	Island 28122
				remix of the title cut from his 1982 album			
6/11/88	❶[4]	18		11 **Roll With It** AC[2] / AR[4] A:❶[4] / S:❶[1] *The Morning Side*	$3	■	Virgin 99326
8/20/88	6	17		12 **Don't You Know What The Night Can Do?** ...AR[2] A:6 / S:8 *(instrumental)*	$3	■	Virgin 99290
				tune used in a Michelob TV commercial			
11/26/88+	11	17		13 **Holding On** ...AC[2] A:10 / S:13 *(instrumental)*	$3	■	Virgin 99261
3/18/89	53	9		14 **Hearts On Fire** ...*(instrumental)*	$3	■	Virgin 99234
				above 4 from the album *Roll With It*			
11/3/90	18	15		15 **One And Only Man** ...AR[2] A:16 / S:21 *Always*	$3	■[V]	Virgin 98892
				all of above co-written by Winwood (mostly with Will Jennings)			
				WISEGUYS, The LP **'01**			
				Techno-rock duo from England: Regal and Touché.			
8/4/01	31	12		**Start The Commotion** ...A:32			album cut
				samples "Wild Child" by **The Ventures**; from the album *The Antidote* on Mammoth 810015			
				WITCHDOCTOR — see COOL BREEZE			
				WITCH QUEEN LP **'79**			
				Studio disco group produced by Peter Alves and **Gino Soccio**.			
4/28/79	68	6		**Bang A Gong** ...*Witch Queen*	$5		Roadshow 11551

DEBUT	PEAK	WKS	Gold	A-side (Chart Hit)..........B-side	$	Sym	Label & Number

★320★ WITHERS, Bill — R&B/BUB/AC/LP '72

Born on 7/4/38 in Slab Fork, West Virginia. R&B singer/songwriter/guitarist. Married to actress Denise Nicholas.

1)Lean On Me 2)Use Me 3)Ain't No Sunshine

DEBUT	PEAK	WKS	Gold	A-side (Chart Hit)..........B-side	$	Sym	Label & Number
7/17/71	3	16	●	1 **Ain't No Sunshine** ....*Harlem*	$6		Sussex 219
10/30/71	42	8		2 **Grandma's Hands**..........*Sweet Wanomi*	$6		Sussex 227
				above 2 produced by Booker T. Jones (**Booker T. & The MG's**)			
4/22/72	$❶^3$	19	●	3 **Lean On Me** RB[1] *Better Off Dead*	$6		Sussex 235
8/26/72	2^2	12	●	4 **Use Me** ....*Let Me In Your Life*	$6		Sussex 241
12/9/72+	47	6		5 **Let Us Love** /			
12/9/72	5^X	2		6 **The Gift Of Giving** .... [X]	$6	■	Sussex 247
2/3/73	31	10		7 **Kissing My Love**..........*I Don't Know*	$6		Sussex 250
7/7/73	80	5		8 **Friend Of Mine**..........*Lonely Town, Lonely Street* [L]	$6		Sussex 257
4/13/74	50	13		9 **The Same Love That Made Me Laugh**..........*Make A Smile For Me*	$6		Sussex 513
12/28/74+	89	4		10 **Heartbreak Road**..........*Ruby Lee*	$6		Sussex 629
12/20/75+	76	8		11 **Make Love To Your Mind**..........*I Love You Dawn*	$5		Columbia 10255
12/10/77+	30	12		12 **Lovely Day**..........*It Ain't Because Of Me Baby*	$5		Columbia 10627
				all of above (except #10) written by Withers			
2/14/81	2^3	24		13 **Just The Two Of Us**..........*Make Me A Memory (Sad Samba)* (Washington, Jr.)	$4	■	Elektra 47103
				GROVER WASHINGTON, JR. (with Bill Withers)			
9/1/84	58	10		14 **In The Name Of Love**..........*Play Pen* (MacDonald)	$4		Polydor 881221
				RALPH MacDONALD (with Bill Withers)			

WITHERSPOON, Jimmy — R&B/LP '65

Born on 8/8/23 in Gurdon, Arkansas. Died on 9/18/97 (age 74). Blues singer/bassist. First recorded for Philo/Aladdin in 1945; has recorded for over two dozen labels. Hit #1 on the R&B charts in 1949 with "Ain't Nobody's Business."

DEBUT	PEAK	WKS	Gold	A-side (Chart Hit)..........B-side	$	Sym	Label & Number
3/6/65	98	1		**You're Next**..........*Some Of My Best Friends Are The Blues*	$15		Prestige 341
				Benny Golson (orch.)			

WITTER, Jimmy — '61

Pop singer; similar in style to **Bobby Rydell**.

DEBUT	PEAK	WKS	Gold	A-side (Chart Hit)..........B-side	$	Sym	Label & Number
5/1/61	89	4		**A Cross Stands Alone**..........*Pretty Little Girl*	$20		United Artists 301

WOLCOTT, Charles — POP '44

Born on 9/29/06 in Flint, Michigan. Died on 1/26/87 (age 80). Pianist/composer/arranger. With Paul Whiteman, Andre Kostelanetz and Jean Goldkette bands. Music director with MGM studios from 1950-60.

DEBUT	PEAK	WKS	Gold	A-side (Chart Hit)..........B-side	$	Sym	Label & Number
10/31/60	41	7		**Ruby Duby Du From Key Witness**..........*Leatherjacket Cowboy* [I]	$12		MGM 12944
				with the MGM Studio Orch.; from the movie *Key Witness* starring Jeffrey Hunter			

WOLF — '83

Born William Wolfer in Cheyenne, Wyoming. Keyboardist/synthesizer/vocorder player.

DEBUT	PEAK	WKS	Gold	A-side (Chart Hit)..........B-side	$	Sym	Label & Number
12/11/82+	55	9		**Papa Was A Rollin' Stone**..........*Window On A Dream*	$5	■	Constellation 69849

WOLF, Peter — ROK/LP '84

Born Peter Blankfield on 3/7/46 in the Bronx, New York. Lead singer of the **J. Geils Band**. Married to actress Faye Dunaway from 1974-79. Not to be confused with the producer of the same name.

DEBUT	PEAK	WKS	Gold	A-side (Chart Hit)..........B-side	$	Sym	Label & Number
7/14/84	12	14		1 **Lights Out** *Poor Girl's Heart*	$3	■	EMI America 8208
10/13/84	36	13		2 **I Need You Tonight**..........*Billy Bigtime*	$3	■	EMI America 8241
4/27/85	61	5		3 **Oo-Ee-Diddley-Bop!**..........*Crazy* (ROK #26)	$3	■	EMI America 8254
2/28/87	15	15		4 **Come As You Are**..........AR[1] S:13 / A:15 *Thick As Thieves*	$3	■	EMI America 8350
5/23/87	75	5		5 **Can't Get Started**..........*Mamma Said*	$3	■	EMI America 43012
3/17/90	78	4		6 **99 Worlds**..........*Are You A Boy Or Are You A Girl*	$3	■[V]	MCA 53726

WOLFMAN JACK — see FLASH CADILLAC / GUESS WHO / STAMPEDERS

★562★ WOMACK, Bobby — R&B/BUB/LP '74

Born on 3/4/44 in Cleveland, Ohio. R&B singer/guitarist/songwriter. Sang in family gospel group, the Womack Brothers. Group recorded for SAR as **The Valentinos** and The Lovers, 1962-64. Toured as guitarist with **Sam Cooke**. Backup guitarist on many sessions, including **Wilson Pickett**, **The Box Tops**, **Joe Tex**, **Aretha Franklin** and **Janis Joplin**. Nicknamed "The Preacher." Married for a time to Sam Cooke's widow, Barbara. Bobby's brother, Cecil, and Sam Cooke's daughter, Linda, recorded as Womack & Womack.

1)Lookin' For A Love 2)That's The Way I Feel About Cha 3)Nobody Wants You When You're Down And Out

DEBUT	PEAK	WKS	Gold	A-side (Chart Hit)..........B-side	$	Sym	Label & Number
8/17/68	52	13		1 **Fly Me To The Moon**..........*Take Me*	$10		Minit 32048
12/7/68+	43	9		2 **California Dreamin'**..........*Baby! You Oughta Think It Over*	$10		Minit 32055
12/13/69	93	2		3 **How I Miss You Baby**..........*Tried And Convicted*	$10		Minit 32081
4/25/70	90	4		4 **More Than I Can Stand**..........*Arkansas State Prison*	$10		Minit 32093
				"Bubbled Under" (#111) as part of a medley on 5/29/71 on United Artists 50773			
12/11/71+	27	13		5 **That's The Way I Feel About Cha**..........*Come L'Amore*	$6		United Artists 50847
				(The Preacher) BOBBY WOMACK (& Peace)			
5/6/72	60	9		6 **Woman's Gotta Have It**..........RB[1] *(If You Don't Want My Love) Give It Back*	$6		United Artists 50902
12/9/72+	31	12	●	7 **Harry Hippie** *[BOBBY WOMACK & Peace]* /			
8/26/72	51	9		8 **Sweet Caroline (Good Times Never Seemed So Good)**..........	$6		United Artists 50946
				BOBBY WOMACK & Peace			
3/24/73	56	6		9 **Across 110th Street** *[BOBBY WOMACK & Peace]*..........*Hang On In There*	$6		United Artists 196
				title song from the movie starring Anthony Quinn			
6/16/73	29	15		10 **Nobody Wants You When You're Down And Out**..........*I'm Through Trying To Prove My Love To You* (#101/R&B #80)	$6		United Artists 255
2/2/74	10	17	●	11 **Lookin' For A Love** RB[3] *Let It Hang Out*	$6		United Artists 375
				also see **The Valentinos**' (with Womack) 1962 hit version			
7/6/74	59	7		12 **You're Welcome, Stop On By**..........*I Don't Wanna Be Hurt By Ya Love Again*	$6		United Artists 439
4/12/75	91	3		13 **Check It Out**..........*Interlude #2*	$6		United Artists 621
3/24/84	88	5		14 **Love Has Finally Come At Last**..........*American Dream* (Womack)	$5		Beverly Glen 2012
				BOBBY WOMACK and PATTI LaBELLE			

DEBUT	PEAK	WKS	Gold	A-side (Chart Hit)...B-side	$	Sym	Label & Number

WOMACK, Lee Ann
C&W/BUB/LP **'01**

Born on 8/19/66 in Jacksonville, Texas. Country singer.

DEBUT	PEAK	WKS	Gold	A-side (Chart Hit)...B-side	$	Sym	Label & Number
10/10/98	43	10		1 **A Little Past Little Rock**..........A:36 / S:58 *If You're Ever Down In Dallas*	$4	★V	Decca 72068
2/27/99	38	20		2 **I'll Think Of A Reason Later**..........A:22 "45": Decca 72076; B-side: "I'd Rather Have What We Had"		V	album cut
8/7/99	72	11		3 **(Now You See Me) Now You Don't**..........A:59 "45": MCA 72111; B-side: "The Preacher Won't Have To Lie"; all of above from the album *Some Things I Know* on Decca 70040		V	album cut
5/13/00+	14	48	▲	4 **I Hope You Dance** CW[5] / AC[11] S:6 / A:14 *(album version)* Sons Of The Desert (backing vocals)	$4	★V	MCA 172185
12/9/00+	45	17		5 **Ashes By Now**..........A:40 "45": MCA 172182; B-side: "Lonely Too"		V	album cut
7/21/01	78	7		6 **Why They Call It Falling**..........A:74 "45": MCA 172203; B-side: "I Feel Like I'm Forgetting Something"; above 3 from the album *I Hope You Dance* on MCA 170099		V	album cut

WOMBLES, The
'74

Pop studio group from England. Creation of writer/producer/arranger Mike Batt. The Wombles were furry characters seen on British TV.

DEBUT	PEAK	WKS	Gold	A-side (Chart Hit)...B-side	$	Sym	Label & Number
8/3/74	55	7		**Wombling Summer Party**..........*Wimbledon Sunset*	$5		Columbia 10013

WOMENFOLK, The
BUB/LP **'64**

Female folk group from Pasadena, California: Elaine Gealer, Joyce James, Leni Ashmore, Babs Cooper and Judy Fine.

DEBUT	PEAK	WKS	Gold	A-side (Chart Hit)...B-side	$	Sym	Label & Number
4/18/64	83	3		**Little Boxes**..........*Love Come-A-Tricklin' Down* the shortest charted record (1:02) of the rock era; arranged by **Perry Botkin, Jr.**	$8		RCA Victor 8301

WONDER, Stevie ★5★
R&B/AC/BUB/LP **'73**

Born Steveland Morris on 5/13/50 in Saginaw, Michigan. R&B singer/songwriter/multi-instrumentalist/producer. Age 13 at the time of his first hit. Blind since birth. Signed to Motown in 1960, did backup work. First recorded in 1962, named "**Little Stevie Wonder**" by Berry Gordy, Jr. Married to **Syreeta** Wright from 1970-72. Near-fatal auto accident on 8/16/73. In the movies *Bikini Beach* and *Muscle Beach Party*. Inducted into the Rock and Roll Hall of Fame in 1989. Won Grammy's Lifetime Achievement Award in 1996.

1)I Just Called To Say I Love You 2)Sir Duke 3)Fingertips 4)I Wish 5)Part-Time Lover

DEBUT	PEAK	WKS	Gold	A-side (Chart Hit)...B-side	$	Sym	Label & Number
6/22/63	❶[3]	15		1 **Fingertips - Pt 2**..........RB[6] *Pt 1* [L]	$20	■	Tamla 54080
10/5/63	33	6		2 **Workout Stevie, Workout**..........*Monkey Talk*	$15		Tamla 54086
2/29/64	52	9		3 **Castles In The Sand**..........*Thank You For Loving Me All The Way* **LITTLE STEVIE WONDER** (above 3)	$15		Tamla 54090
6/13/64	29	8		4 **Hey Harmonica Man**..........*This Little Girl*	$15	■	Tamla 54096
8/28/65	59	7		5 **High Heel Sneakers**..........*Music Talk* [L] first released with "Funny How Time Slips Away" as the B-side	$15		Tamla 54119
12/18/65+	3	14		6 **Uptight (Everything's Alright)**..........RB[5] *Purple Rain Drops*	$15		Tamla 54124
4/16/66	20	7		7 **Nothing's Too Good For My Baby**..........*With A Child's Heart (#131; R&B #8)*	$15		Tamla 54130
7/23/66	9	10		8 **Blowin In The Wind**..........RB[1] *Ain't That Asking For Trouble* Clarence Paul (backing vocal; died on 5/6/95); written by **Bob Dylan** (from his 1963 album *The Freewheelin' Bob Dylan*)	$12	■	Tamla 54136
11/12/66	9	11		9 **A Place In The Sun**..........*Sylvia*	$12	■	Tamla 54139
12/17/66	24[X]	4		10 **Some Day At Christmas**..........*The Miracles Of Christmas* [X] X: 24/'66; 34/'67	$15		Tamla 54142
3/4/67	32	7		11 **Travlin' Man /**			
4/22/67	90	6		12 **Hey Love**..........	$10		Tamla 54147
6/10/67	2[2]	15		13 **I Was Made To Love Her**..........RB[4] *Hold Me*	$10		Tamla 54151
10/7/67	12	8		14 **I'm Wondering**..........*Every Time I See You I Go Wild*	$10		Tamla 54157
4/6/68	9	13		15 **Shoo-Be-Doo-Be-Doo-Da-Day**..........RB[1] *Why Don't You Lead Me To Love*	$10		Tamla 54165
7/20/68	35	7		16 **You Met Your Match**..........*My Girl*	$10		Tamla 54168
10/5/68	66	6		17 **Alfie**..........*More Than A Dream* [I] **EIVETS REDNOW** (Stevie Wonder spelled backwards) title song from the movie starring Michael Caine	$20		Gordy 7076
11/2/68	2[2]	14		18 **For Once In My Life**..........*Angie Girl*	$8		Tamla 54174
5/31/69	4	14		19 **My Cherie Amour /**			
2/15/69	39	7		20 **I Don't Know Why**.......... some pressings show title as "Don't Know Why I Love You"; #16 & 18-20: from the album *For Once In My Life*	$8		Tamla 54180
10/18/69	7	14		21 **Yester-Me, Yester-You, Yesterday**..........*I'd Be A Fool Right Now*	$8		Tamla 54188
2/7/70	26	7		22 **Never Had A Dream Come True**..........*Somebody Knows, Somebody Cares*	$8		Tamla 54191
6/27/70	3	14		23 **Signed, Sealed, Delivered I'm Yours**..........RB[6] *I'm More Than Happy (I'm Satisfied)*	$8		Tamla 54196
10/17/70	9	11		24 **Heaven Help Us All**..........*I Gotta Have A Song*	$8		Tamla 54200
3/13/71	13	11		25 **We Can Work It Out /** above 4 from the album *Signed Sealed & Delivered*			
6/19/71	78	4		26 **Never Dreamed You'd Leave In Summer**..........	$8		Tamla 54202
8/14/71	8	14		27 **If You Really Love Me**..........*Think Of Me As Your Soldier*	$7		Tamla 54208
5/20/72	33	11		28 **Superwoman (Where Were You When I Needed You)**..........*I Love Every Little Thing About You*	$7		Tamla 54216
9/16/72	90	3		29 **Keep On Running**..........*Evil*	$7		Tamla 54223
11/18/72+	❶[1]	16		30 **Superstition**..........RB[3] *You've Got It Bad Girl*	$6		Tamla 54226
3/17/73	❶[1]	17		31 **You Are The Sunshine Of My Life**..........AC[2] *Tuesday Heartbreak* **Jim Gilstrap** and Gloria Barley (first verse soloists)	$6		Tamla 54232
8/18/73	4	14		32 **Higher Ground**..........RB[1] *Too High*	$6		Tamla 54235
11/10/73+	8	17		33 **Living For The City**..........RB[2] *Visions*	$6		Tamla 54242
4/6/74	16	15		34 **Don't You Worry 'Bout A Thing**..........*Blame It On The Sun*	$6		Tamla 54245
8/3/74	❶[1]	19		35 **You Haven't Done Nothin**..........RB[2] *Big Brother* **The Jackson 5** (doo-doo-wop vocals)	$6		Tamla 54252
11/16/74+	3	17		36 **Boogie On Reggae Woman**..........RB[2] *Seems So Long*	$6		Tamla 54254

DEBUT	PEAK	WKS	Gold	A-side (Chart Hit)...B-side	$	Sym	Label & Number
				WONDER, Stevie — Cont'd			
12/4/76+	❶[1]	17		37 I Wish ... RB[5] *You And I*	$6		Tamla 54274
4/2/77	❶[3]	17		38 Sir Duke ... RB[1] *He's Misstra Know-It-All*	$6	■	Tamla 54281
				a tribute to Duke Ellington			
8/27/77	32	10		39 Another Star ... *Creepin'*	$5		Tamla 54286
11/5/77+	36	14		40 As ... *Contusion*	$5		Tamla 54291
				above 4 from the album *Songs In The Key Of Life* (a classic cut "Isn't She Lovely" was not released as a single)			
1/20/79	59	8		41 Pops, We Love You (A Tribute To Father) ... *(instrumental)*	$5		Motown 1455
				DIANA ROSS, MARVIN GAYE, SMOKEY ROBINSON & STEVIE WONDER			
				song commemorates Berry Gordy Sr.'s death at age 90			
11/3/79	4	18		42 Send One Your Love ... AC[4] *(instrumental)*	$5	■	Tamla 54303
3/1/80	52	7		43 Outside My Window ... *Same Old Story*	$5	■	Tamla 54308
9/20/80	5	23		44 Master Blaster (Jammin') ... RB[7] *(dub version)*	$5	■	Tamla 54317
				inspired by **Bob Marley**'s classic reggae tune "Jamming"			
12/13/80+	11	19		45 I Ain't Gonna Stand For It ... *Knocks Me Off My Feet*	$4		Tamla 54320
4/11/81	64	7		46 Lately ... *If It's Magic*	$4		Tamla 54323
1/16/82	4	18		47 That Girl ... RB[9] *All I Do*	$4		Tamla 1602
4/10/82	❶[7]	19	●	48 Ebony And Ivory ... AC[5] *Rainclouds* (McCartney)	$4	■	Columbia 02860
				PAUL McCARTNEY (with Stevie Wonder)			
5/29/82	13	14		49 Do I Do ... *Rocket Love*	$4		Tamla 1612
9/25/82	54	7		50 Ribbon In The Sky ... *Black Orchid*	$4	■	Tamla 1639
10/30/82	46	11		51 Used To Be ... *I Want To Come Back As A Song* (Charlene)	$4	□	Motown 1650
				CHARLENE & STEVIE WONDER			
8/18/84	❶[3]	26	●	52 I Just Called To Say I Love You RB[3] / AC[3] S:❶[3] / A:❶[3] *(instrumental)*	$4	□	Motown 1745
12/1/84+	17	16		53 Love Light In Flight ... A:15 / S:19 *It's More Than You*	$4	■	Motown 1769
				above 2 from the movie *The Woman In Red* starring Gene Wilder and Kelly LeBrock			
9/7/85	❶[1]	21		54 Part-Time Lover ... RB[6] / AC[3] A:❶[3] / S:2 *(instrumental)*	$3	■	Tamla 1808
				Luther Vandross (backing vocal); a special promotional full-color foldout insert was also issued			
11/9/85+	❶[4]	23	●	55 That's What Friends Are For ... RB[3] / AC[2] S:❶[5] / A:❶[3] *Two Ships Passing In The Night* (Warwick)	$3	■	Arista 9422
				DIONNE & FRIENDS: Elton John, Gladys Knight and Stevie Wonder			
				song introduced by **Rod Stewart** on the 1982 movie soundtrack of *Night Shift*			
11/23/85+	10	17		56 Go Home ... AC[1] S:11 / A:11 *(instrumental)*	$3	■	Tamla 1817
2/22/86	24	13		57 Overjoyed ... AC[2] S:18 / A:26 *(instrumental)*	$3	■	Tamla 1832
6/14/86	86	3		58 Land Of La La ... *(instrumental)*	$3	■	Tamla 1846
				#54 & 56-58: from the album *In Square Circle*			
10/17/87	19	16		59 Skeletons ... RB[2] S:11 / A:32 *(instrumental)*	$3	■	Motown 1907
2/6/88	77	6		60 You Will Know ... RB[1] *(instrumental)*	$3	■	Motown 1919
5/7/88	80	6		61 Get It ... *(instrumental)*	$3	■	Motown 1930
				STEVIE WONDER & MICHAEL JACKSON			
5/21/88	80	5		62 My Love ... *My Love* (Iglesias)	$3	■	Columbia 07781
				JULIO IGLESIAS FEATURING STEVIE WONDER			
7/20/91	92	3		63 Gotta Have You ... *Feeding Off The Love Of The Land*	$4	▮[V]	Motown 2081
				from the movie *Jungle Fever* starring Wesley Snipes			
3/4/95	53	14		64 For Your Love ... S:30 *(instrumental)*	$4	▮[V]	Motown 0290
				"45": Motown 0310; #28-64 (except #41, 48, 51 & 55): written solely by Wonder			
6/14/97	47[A]	11		65 How Come, How Long ...			album cut
				BABYFACE Featuring Stevie Wonder			
				from the *Babyface* album *The Day* on Epic 67293			
				WONDER BAND, The '79			
				Disco studio group assembled by producers Silvio Tancredi and Armando Noriega.			
3/3/79	87	2		Whole Lotta Love ... *Excerpts From The Wonderful Medley*	$15	T	Atco 4719
				the first 12"-only single to make the *Hot 100*			
				WONDER LAND — see ALICE			
				WONDERS, The '96			
				Fictitious band created for the movie *That Thing You Do!* Jonathan Schaech is "Jimmy" (vocals), Steve Zahn is "Lenny" (guitar), Ethan Embry is the nameless bass-player and Tom Everett Scott is "Guy" (drums). The actual recording is performed by studio musicians, including lead singer Mike Viola.			
10/12/96	41	15		That Thing You Do! ... A:34 / S:69 *Voyage Around The Moon* (The Saturn 5)	$5	▮[V]	Play-Tone/Epic 78401
				title song from the movie starring Tom Hanks; promo "45" issued with a picture sleeve on Play-Tone 8533; B-side: "Dance With Me Tonight"			
				WONDER WHO? — see 4 SEASONS			
				WON-G '01			
				Born Wondgy Bruny in Port-Au-Prince, Haiti; raised in Brooklyn, New York. Male rapper.			
10/20/01	9[S]	8		1 Nothing's Wrong ... *(3 versions)*	$5	★	TNO/EMG 70021
				WON-G Featuring DJ Quik			
5/18/02	50[S]	6		2 Put It Inside ... *(2 versions)*	$6	★	TNO/Orpheus 90412
				WON-G (featuring) Da Brat			
				WOOD, Bobby BUB/C&W '64			
				Born on 1/25/41 in Memphis, Tennessee. Pop-country singer/songwriter/pianist.			
8/8/64	74	5		If I'm A Fool For Loving You ... *(My Heart Went) Boing! Boing! Boing!*	$10		Joy 285
				WOOD, Brenton R&B/BUB/LP '67			
				Born Alfred Smith on 7/26/41 in Shreveport, Louisiana; raised in San Pedro, California. R&B singer/songwriter/pianist.			
4/15/67	34	12		1 The Oogum Boogum Song ... *I Like The Way You Love Me*	$10		Double Shot 111
8/12/67	9	15		2 Gimme Little Sign ... *I Think You've Got Your Fools Mixed Up*	$10		Double Shot 116
11/25/67	34	7		3 Baby You Got It ... *Catch You On The Rebound*	$10		Double Shot 121
3/9/68	99	2		4 Lovey Dovey Kinda Lovin' ... *Two-Time Loser*	$10		Double Shot 126

DEBUT	PEAK	WKS	Gold	A-side (Chart Hit)..........B-side	$	Sym	Label & Number
				WOOD, Lauren AC '79			
				Born in Pittsburgh, Pennsylvania. Pop singer/songwriter/keyboardist. Also see **Sam Harris**'s "I'd Do It All Again."			
9/22/79	24	15		**Please Don't Leave** ....*Where Did I Get These Tears*	$4	■	Warner 49043
				Michael McDonald (harmony vocal)			
				WOOD, Ronnie — see STEWART, Rod			
				WOODS, Stevie R&B/LP '81			
				Born in Columbus, Ohio. Male R&B singer/songwriter. Son of jazz great Rusty Bryant.			
9/12/81	25	21		1 **Steal The Night**..........*Read Between The Lines*	$4		Cotillion 46016
1/23/82	38	12		2 **Just Can't Win 'Em All** ....*Gotcha*	$4		Cotillion 46030
5/15/82	84	2		3 **Fly Away** ....*Wanna' Be Close To You*	$4		Cotillion 47006
				WOOLEY, Sheb C&W/BUB '58			
				Born Shelby Wooley on 4/10/21 near Erick, Oklahoma. Country singer/songwriter/actor. Played "Pete Nolan" on the TV series *Rawhide*. Appeared in several movies. Also made comical recordings under pseudonym **Ben Colder**.			
12/17/55	95	1		1 **Are You Satisfied?** ....T:95 *Humdinger*	$20		MGM 12114
6/2/58	❶[6]	14	●	2 **The Purple People Eater** S:❶[6] / T:❶[6] / A:❶[4] *I Can't Believe You're Mine* [N]	$20		MGM 12651
6/1/59	70	6		3 **Sweet Chile**..........*More*	$15		MGM 12781
1/6/62	51	11		4 **That's My Pa**..........CW[1] *Meet Mr. Lonely* [N]	$10		MGM 13046
				BEN COLDER:			
11/24/62	62	6		5 **Don't Go Near The Eskimos** ....*Louisiana Trapper* [N]	$10		MGM 13104
				parody of **Rex Allen**'s 1962 hit "Don't Go Near The Indians"			
7/20/63	98	2		6 **Still No. 2**..........*Goin' Surfin'* [N]	$15		MGM 13147
				parody of **Bill Anderson**'s 1963 hit "Still"			
10/12/63	90	1		7 **Detroit City No. 2**..........*Ring Of Smoke* [N]	$10		MGM 13167
				parody of **Bobby Bare**'s 1963 hit "Detroit City"			
10/1/66	58	6		8 **Almost Persuaded No. 2** ....*Packets Of Pencils* [N]	$10		MGM 13590
				parody of **David Houston**'s 1966 hit "Almost Persuaded"			
10/26/68	67	5		9 **Harper Valley P.T.A. (Later That Same Day)**..........*Folsom Prison Blues No. 1-1/2* [N]	$10		MGM 13997
				parody of **Jeannie C. Riley**'s 1968 hit "Harper Valley P.T.A."			
				WOOLIES, The '67			
				Garage-rock band from East Lansing, Michigan: Stormy Rice (vocals), brothers Bob (guitar) and Jeff (bass) Baldori, and Ron English (drums).			
3/11/67	95	3		**Who Do You Love**..........*Hey Girl*	$12		Dunhill/ABC 4052
				first released on Spirit 13 in 1966 ($25); written and introduced by **Bo Diddley** in 1956 on Checker 842 ($40)			
				WORLD CLASS WRECKIN CRU, The R&B '88			
				Rap-funk group from Los Angeles, California: Alonzo Williams, Andre "**Dr. Dre**" Young, Antoine "Yella" Carraby, Shakespeare and Michelle "**Michel'le**" Toussant.			
3/26/88	84	11		**Turn Off The Lights** ....*(same version)*	$7		Kru'-Cut 006
				WORLD PARTY ROK/LP '87			
				Group is actually rock singer/keyboardist Karl Wallinger (born on 10/19/57 in Prestatyn, Wales).			
2/14/87	27	15		**Ship Of Fools (Save Me From Tomorrow)** ....S:20 / A:37 *Holy Water*	$4	■	Chrysalis 43052
				WORLEY, Darryl C&W/BUB/LP '02			
				Born on 10/31/64 in Pyburn, Tennessee; raised in Savannah, Tennessee. Country singer/songwriter/guitarist.			
6/10/00	75	15		1 **When You Need My Love** ....S:44 / A:75 *Who's Gonna Get Me Over You?*	$4	★[V]	DreamWorks 59043
1/20/01	76	9		2 **A Good Day To Run** A:71			album cut
				above 2 from the album *Hard Rain Don't Last* on DreamWorks 50042			
6/15/02	28	20		3 **I Miss My Friend**..........CW[1] A:25		V	album cut
				from the album *I Miss My Friend* on DreamWorks 50351; "45": DreamWorks 50378; B-side: "Sideways" (C&W #41)			
				WORTH, Marion C&W '63			
				Born Mary Ann Ward on 7/4/30 in Birmingham, Alabama. Died of emphysema on 12/19/99 (age 69). Country singer.			
12/29/62+	42	8		**Shake Me I Rattle (Squeeze Me I Cry)** ....*Tennessee Teardrops*	$8	■	Columbia 42640
				first recorded in 1957 by **The Lennon Sisters** on Brunswick 55028 ($10)			
				WRAY, Bill '79			
				Born in Louisiana. Rock singer/songwriter.			
5/19/79	96	2		**Pinball, That's All**..........*My Music*	$6		ABC 12449
				from the movie *Tilt* starring Charles Durning and Brooke Shields			
				WRAY, Link, & His Ray Men LP '58			
				Born on 5/2/35 in Dunn, North Carolina. Rock and roll guitarist.			
4/28/58	16	14		1 **Rumble**..........S:16 / T:16 *The Swag* [I]	$40		Cadence 1347
1/26/59	23	13		2 **Raw-Hide** ***[LINK WRAY AND THE WRAYMEN]***..........*Dixie-Doodle* [I]	$25		Epic 9300
6/15/63	64	8		3 **Jack The Ripper** ....*The Black Widow* [I]	$20		Swan 4137
10/1/77	83	3		4 **Red Hot**..........*Sweet Surrender*	$7		Private Stock 45,156
				ROBERT GORDON With Link Wray			
				rockabilly song originally recorded in 1955 by Billy "The Kid" Emerson on Sun 219 ($150)			
				WRECKX-N-EFFECT R&B/BUB/LP '92			
				Male rap duo: Aqil Davidson and Markell Riley (brother of Teddy Riley of **Guy**).			
10/3/92	2[3]	28	▲[2]	1 **Rump Shaker** ....S:❶[3] / A:8 *(percapella mix)*	$3	▮[V]	MCA 54388
				samples "Back To The Hotel" by **N2Deep**			
2/20/93	72	11		2 **Knock-N-boots** ....S:28 *(radio mix)*	$4	▮[V]	MCA 54582
4/24/93	54[S]	6		3 **Wreckx Shop** ....BUB:101 *(album version)*	$4	▮[V]	MCA 54531
				WRIGHT, Betty R&B/BUB/LP '72			
				Born on 12/21/53 in Miami, Florida. R&B singer. In family gospel group, Echoes Of Joy, from 1956. First recorded for Deep City in 1966. Hosted own local TV talk show in Miami.			
				1)Clean Up Woman 2)Dance With Me 3)Girls Can't Do What The Guys Do			
8/3/68	33	8		1 **Girls Can't Do What The Guys Do** ....*Sweet Lovin' Daddy*	$8		Alston 4569
11/27/71+	6	14	●	2 **Clean Up Woman** *I'll Love You Forever*	$8		Alston 4601

DEBUT	PEAK	WKS	Gold	A-side (Chart Hit)...B-side	$	Sym	Label & Number

WRIGHT, Betty — Cont'd

DEBUT	PEAK	WKS	Gold	A-side (Chart Hit)...B-side	$	Sym	Label & Number
10/14/72	46	10		3 Baby Sitter ... *Outside Woman*	$7		Alston 4614
4/21/73	72	6		4 It's Hard To Stop (Doing Something When It's Good To You) ... *Who'll Be The Fool*	$7		Alston 4617
10/6/73	55	6		5 Let Me Be Your Lovemaker ... *Jealous Man*	$7		Alston 4619
7/13/74	62	8		6 Secretary ... *Value Your Love*	$7		Alston 4622
4/5/75	96	1		7 Where Is The Love ... *My Baby Ain't My Baby Anymore*	$6		Alston 3713
3/4/78	8	28		8 Dance With Me ... *For Your Love*	$6		Drive 6269
9/23/78	54	8		9 You Should Do It ... *Without Love*	$6		Drive 6272
				PETER BROWN with Betty Wright (above 2)			
3/31/90	67	7		10 How 'Bout Us ... *Finally Found A Friend* (Hugh)	$3	▮V	RCA 9163
				GRAYSON HUGH and BETTY WRIGHT			
				from the movie *True Love* starring Annabella Sciorra			

WRIGHT, Charles, And The Watts 103rd Street Rhythm Band — R&B/BUB/LP '70

Born in 1942 in Clarksdale, Mississippi. R&B singer/songwriter/pianist/guitarist/producer. Leader of an eight-man R&B-funk band from the Watts section of Los Angeles, California. Evolved from the Soul Runners. Big break came through assistance by comedian **Bill Cosby**.

DEBUT	PEAK	WKS	Gold	A-side (Chart Hit)...B-side	$	Sym	Label & Number
9/9/67	73	10		1 Spreadin' Honey ... *Charley* [I]	$12		Keymen 108
2/1/69	11	17		2 Do Your Thing ... *A Dance, A Kiss And A Song*	$8		Warner 7250
7/19/69	67	5		3 Till You Get Enough ... *Light My Fire*	$8		Warner 7298
				THE WATTS 103RD STREET RHYTHM BAND (above 3)			
4/11/70	16	17		4 Love Land ... *Sorry Charlie*	$7		Warner 7365
8/15/70	12	15		5 Express Yourself ... *Living On Borrowed Time*	$7		Warner 7417
1/23/71	96	1		6 Solution For Pollution ... *High As Apple Pie*	$7		Warner 7451
5/15/71	73	4		7 Your Love (Means Everything to Me) ... *What Can You Bring Me*	$7		Warner 7475
				CHARLES WRIGHT AND THE WATTS 103RD STREET BAND			

WRIGHT, Chely — C&W/BUB/LP '99

Born on 10/25/70 in Kansas City, Missouri. Female country singer/guitarist.

DEBUT	PEAK	WKS	Gold	A-side (Chart Hit)...B-side	$	Sym	Label & Number
5/15/99	36	20		1 Single White Female ... CW^1 A:25 / S:38 *Let Me In*	$4	★V	MCA 72092
3/4/00	64	10		2 It Was ... A:52		V	album cut
				"45": MCA 72113; B-side: "Rubbin' It In"; above 2 from the album *Single White Female* on MCA 70052			

WRIGHT, Dale — '58

Born Harlan Dale Riffe on 2/4/38 in Middletown, Ohio. Rock and roll singer/songwriter. Worked as a DJ in the Midwest.

DEBUT	PEAK	WKS	Gold	A-side (Chart Hit)...B-side	$	Sym	Label & Number
1/13/58	38	13		1 She's Neat ... S:38 / T:39 *Say That You Care*	$30		Fraternity 792
				DALE WRIGHT with the Rock-Its			
9/1/58	77	5		2 Please Don't Do It ... H:77 *Goody Goody Good-Bye*	$25	⊙	Fraternity 818
				DALE WRIGHT And The Wright Guys With the Dons			

WRIGHT, Gary — BUB/LP '76

Born on 4/26/43 in Creskill, New Jersey. Pop-rock singer/songwriter/keyboardist. Appeared in *Captain Video* TV series at age seven. In the Broadway play *Fanny*. Co-leader of the rock group Spooky Tooth.

DEBUT	PEAK	WKS	Gold	A-side (Chart Hit)...B-side	$	Sym	Label & Number
1/3/76	2^3	20	●	1 Dream Weaver ... *Let It Out*	$5		Warner 8167
4/17/76	2^2	27		2 Love Is Alive ... *Much Higher*	$5		Warner 8143
9/18/76	79	5		3 Made To Love You ... *Power Of Love*	$4		Warner 8250
3/5/77	43	7		4 Phantom Writer ... *Child Of Light*	$4		Warner 8331
1/21/78	73	3		5 Touch And Gone ... *Lost In My Emotions*	$4		Warner 8494
7/4/81	16	17		6 Really Wanna Know You ... *More Than A Heartache*	$4		Warner 49769

WRIGHT, O.V. — R&B/BUB '70

Born Overton Vertis Wright on 10/9/39 in Leno, Tennessee. Died of heart failure on 11/16/80 (age 41). Blues singer.

DEBUT	PEAK	WKS	Gold	A-side (Chart Hit)...B-side	$	Sym	Label & Number
8/7/65	86	5		1 You're Gonna Make Me Cry ... *Monkey Dog*	$10		Back Beat 548
5/13/67	80	3		2 Eight Men, Four Women ... *Fed Up With The Blues*	$8		Back Beat 580
11/14/70	54	8		3 Ace Of Spade ... *Afflicted*	$8		Back Beat 615

WRIGHT, Priscilla — '55

Born in 1941 in London, Ontario, Canada. Teen pop singer.

DEBUT	PEAK	WKS	Gold	A-side (Chart Hit)...B-side	$	Sym	Label & Number
6/25/55	16	9		The Man In The Raincoat ... A:16 / S:18 / J:20 *I Wanna Dance To A Mambo Combo*	$30		Unique 303
				PRISCILLA WRIGHT With Don Wright and The Septette			
				also issued with "Please Have Mercy" as the B-side			

WRIGHT, Ruby — '57

Born on 1/8/14 in Anderson, Indiana. Adult Contemporary singer.

DEBUT	PEAK	WKS	Gold	A-side (Chart Hit)...B-side	$	Sym	Label & Number
12/2/57	41	4		1 Let's Light The Christmas Tree ... S:41 / T:54 *Merry, Merry Christmas* [X]	$25		Fraternity 787
				The Dick Noel Singers with a children's chorus (backing vocals); Cliff Lash (orch.)			
5/4/59	99	1		2 Three Stars ... *I Only Have One Lifetime* [S]	$20		King 5192
				narration by Dick Pike (DJ in Cincinnati); a tribute to **Buddy Holly**, **Ritchie Valens** and the **Big Bopper**			

WU-TANG CLAN — R&B/BUB/LP '94

Rap group from Staten Island, New York: Gary Grice (**GZA/Genius**), Clifford Smith (**Method Man**), Russell Jones (**Ol Dirty Bastard**), Corey Woods (**Raekwon**), Jason Hunter (**Inspektah Deck**), Dennis Coles (**Ghostface Killah**), Lamont Hawkins (**U-God**), Robert Diggs (**RZA**) and Elgin Turner (Masta Killa). Diggs was also a member of **Gravediggaz**. Also see **Charli Baltimore**.

DEBUT	PEAK	WKS	Gold	A-side (Chart Hit)...B-side	$	Sym	Label & Number
10/9/93	69	14		1 Method Man ... S:54 / A:74 *Protect Ya Neck* (#105/R&B #86)	$8	▮	Loud/RCA 62544
3/12/94	60	16		2 C.R.E.A.M. (Cash Rules Everything Around Me) ... S:39 *Da Mystery Of Chessboxin'*	$5	▮	Loud/RCA 62829
				samples "As Long As I've Got You" by The Charmels			
11/4/00	51^S	2		3 Protect Ya Neck (The Jump Off) ... *(4 versions)*	$6	T	Loud 79524
				new version of the B-side of #1 above			
5/19/01	70^S	2		4 Gravel Pit ... *(3 versions) / Careful (Click, Click)*	$6	T	Loud 79530

DEBUT	PEAK	WKS	Gold	A-side (Chart Hit)..........B-side	$	Sym	Label & Number

WYATT, Keke — LP '02

Born Ketara Wyatt in Indianapolis, Indiana. Female R&B singer.

DEBUT	PEAK	WKS	Gold	A-side (Chart Hit)..........B-side	$	Sym	Label & Number
11/4/00	26	20		1 **My First Love** ....A:21 **AVANT Featuring Ketara Wyatt**			album cut
8/4/01	32[S]	24		2 **Used To Love** ....*(instrumental)*	$4	★	MCA 155844
1/5/02	27	20		3 **Nothing In This World** ....A:25 **KEKE WYATT featuring Avant** above 2 from the album *Soul Sista* on MCA 112609			album cut

WYMAN, Bill — see ROLLING STONES

WYNETTE, Tammy — C&W/BUB/AC/LP '69

Born Virginia Wynette Pugh on 5/5/42 in Itawamba County, Mississippi. Died of a blood clot on 4/6/98 (age 55). With 20 #1 Country hits from 1967-76, dubbed "The First Lady of Country Music." Married to **George Jones** from 1969-75.

1)Stand By Your Man 2)D-I-V-O-R-C-E 3)Kids Say The Darndest Things

DEBUT	PEAK	WKS	Gold	A-side (Chart Hit)..........B-side	$	Sym	Label & Number
7/8/67	89	5		1 **My Elusive Dreams** ....CW[2] *Marriage On The Rocks* **DAVID HOUSTON and TAMMY WYNETTE**	$10		Epic 10194
6/22/68	63	6		2 **D-I-V-O-R-C-E**..........CW[3] *Don't Make Me Now*	$10		Epic 10315
11/9/68+	19	16		3 **Stand By Your Man** CW[3] *I Stayed Long Enough* 2 weeks after Wynette's death, re-charted the Country chart (#56) for 1 week	$10		Epic 10398
4/12/69	75	5		4 **Singing My Song** ....CW[2] *Too Far Gone*	$10	■	Epic 10462
8/30/69	81	4		5 **The Ways To Love A Man**..........CW[2] *Still Around*	$10		Epic 10512
1/31/70	100	2		6 **I'll See Him Through**..........*Enough Of A Woman* The Jordanaires (backing vocals)	$10		Epic 10571
6/13/70	97	2		7 **He Loves Me All The Way** ....CW[3] *Our Last Night Together*	$10		Epic 10612
10/24/70	92	2		8 **Run, Woman, Run**..........CW[2] *My Daddy Doll*	$10		Epic 10653
1/29/72	86	4		9 **Bedtime Story**..........CW[1] *Reach Out Your Hand*	$10		Epic 10818
6/16/73	72	4		10 **Kids Say The Darndest Things** ....CW[1] *I Wish I Had A Mommy Like You*	$10		Epic 10969
5/1/76	84	5		11 **'Til I Can Make It On My Own**..........CW[1] *Love Is Something Good For Everybody* all of above produced by Billy Sherrill	$7		Epic 50196
2/1/92	11	18	●	12 **Justified & Ancient** ....S:10 / A:12 *(album version* w/o Wynette*)* **THE KLF (Featuring Tammy Wynette)**	$4	▮V	Arista 8657

WYNONNA — C&W/BUB/AC/LP '93

Born Christina Ciminella (her biological father was Charlie Jordan) on 5/30/64 in Ashland, Kentucky. Country singer. Half of The Judds duo with her mother, Naomi (they charted 14 #1 Country hits). Moved to Hollywood in 1968. Appeared in *More American Graffiti*. To Nashville in 1979. Naomi's chronic hepatitis forced duo to split at the end of 1991. Wynonna's half-sister is actress Ashley Judd.

DEBUT	PEAK	WKS	Gold	A-side (Chart Hit)..........B-side	$	Sym	Label & Number
10/24/92	83	12		1 **No One Else On Earth** CW[4] S:38 *(album version)*	$4	▮V	Curb/MCA 54449
6/12/93	43	11		2 **A Bad Goodbye**..........S:19 *The Hard Way* (Black) **CLINT BLACK (with Wynonna)**	$4	▮V	RCA 62503
7/3/93	77	4		3 **Tell Me Why**..........*A Little Bit Of Love* written by **Karla Bonoff**	$4	▮V	Curb/MCA 54606
10/9/93	63[S]	3		4 **Only Love**..........BUB:102 *Just Like New*	$4	▮V	Curb/MCA 54689
10/25/97	98	2		5 **When Love Starts Talkin'**..........*The Other Side*	$4	▮V	Curb/Universal 56095
12/4/99	65[S]	1		6 **Can't Nobody Love You (Like I Do)** ....*Help Me*	$5	★V	Curb/Mercury 72141

X

X-CON — '00

Born in Liberty City, Florida. Male rapper.

DEBUT	PEAK	WKS	Gold	A-side (Chart Hit)..........B-side	$	Sym	Label & Number
7/22/00	62[S]	3		**Whoa! Lil' Mama...**..........*(3 versions) / (7 album snippets)*	$10	★	First String 0312

X-ECUTIONERS, The — R&B/LP '02

Rap-DJ production group from Brooklyn, New York: Mista Sinista, Rob Swift, Total Eclipse and Roc Raida.

DEBUT	PEAK	WKS	Gold	A-side (Chart Hit)..........B-side	$	Sym	Label & Number
3/9/02	85	11		**It's Goin' Down** ....*(2 versions) / X-Ecutioners (Theme) Song* **X-ECUTIONERS Featuring Mike Shinoda and Mr. Hahn of Linkin Park** samples "Year 2000" by **Xzibit**	$7	T	Loud 9133

★301★ XSCAPE — R&B/BUB/LP '98

Female R&B vocal group formed in Atlanta, Georgia: sisters Tamika (born on 8/5/75) and **LaTocha Scott** (born on 10/2/72), with **Kandi** Burruss (born on 5/17/76) and Tameka Cottle (born on 7/14/75).

1)Just Kickin' It 2)The Arms Of The One Who Loves You 3)Understanding

DEBUT	PEAK	WKS	Gold	A-side (Chart Hit)..........B-side	$	Sym	Label & Number
9/18/93	2[1]	21	▲	1 **Just Kickin' It** RB[4] S:❶[1] / A:5 *W.S.S. Deez Nuts / (5 album snippets)*	$3	▮V	So So Def 77119
12/25/93+	8	20	●	2 **Understanding**..........RB[2] S:7 / A:15 *With You* "45" issued for above 2 on So So Def/Columbia 77341	$3	▮V	So So Def 77335
4/23/94	46	15		3 **Love On My Mind** ....S:44 / A:48 *(w/rap by* **Da Brat***)*	$4	▮V	So So Def 77438
6/24/95	32	18	●	4 **Feels So Good**..........S:15 *(5 album snippets)*	$3	▮	So So Def 77921
10/14/95	8	20	●	5 **Who Can I Run To?** ....RB[1] S:5 / A:29 *Feels So Good (remix)* originally recorded by **The Jones Girls** in 1979	$3	▮	So So Def 78056
3/9/96	50	16		6 **Do You Want To /** S:29			
4/13/96	56	11		7 **Can't Hang** ....S:52 **XSCAPE Featuring MC Lyte** above 4 from the album *Off The Hook*	$4	▮	So So Def 78263
3/16/96	10	20	●	8 **Keep On, Keepin' On**..........S:4 / A:42 *(instrumental)* **MC LYTE Featuring Xscape** samples "Liberian Girl" by **Michael Jackson**; from the movie *Sunset Park* starring Rhea Perlman	$3	▮	Flavor Unit 64302
2/7/98	31	13		9 **Am I Dreaming**..........S:16 *(2 versions) / (3 album snippets)* **OL SKOOL [Featuring Keith Sweat and Xscape]**	$4	▮	Universal 56163
5/2/98	7	20	●	10 **The Arms Of The One Who Loves You** ....S:5 / A:63 *(instrumental)* Sue Ann Carwell (backing vocal)	$3	▮V	So So Def 78788

DEBUT	PEAK	WKS	Gold	A-side (Chart Hit)...B-side	$	Sym	Label & Number
				XSCAPE — Cont'd			
10/24/98	9	14		11 **My Little Secret** ...S:3 / A:55 *(3 album snippets)*	$4	★V	So So Def 79036
				Jagged Edge (backing vocals); "45": So So Def 79078; B-side: "Softest Place On Earth" (#111/R&B #28)			
12/25/99+	34	17		12 **One Night Stand** ...S:9 / A:75 *(instrumental)*	$4	★	Slip n Slide 84489
				J-SHIN Featuring LaTocha Scott Of Xscape			
8/19/00	20	20		13 **Bounce With Me** ...RB[1] S:7 / A:29 *(4 versions w/***Lil Mo** & R.O.C.)	$7	★*	So So Def 79476
				LIL BOW WOW (featuring Xscape)			
				from the movie *Big Momma's House* starring Martin Lawrence			
				XTC ROK/BUB/LP '89			
				Alternative-rock trio formed in Wiltshire, England: Andy Partridge (guitar), Dave Gregory (keyboards) and Colin Moulding (bass). All share vocals.			
4/29/89	72	6		**The Mayor Of Simpleton**...MR[5] *One Of The Millions*	$4	■	Geffen 27552
				XYMOX ROK/LP '90			
				Techno-rock/dance trio formed in Amsterdam, Netherlands: Ronny Moorings (vocals, guitar, keyboards), Pieter Nooten (keyboards) and Anka Wolbert (bass, vocals, keyboards).			
3/3/90	85	3		**Imagination** ...*Senses Coalesce*	$5	▮	Wing 873000
				XZIBIT R&B/BUB/LP '98			
				Born Alvin Joyner on 9/18/74 in Detroit, Michigan; raised in New Mexico. Male rapper.			
7/20/96	83	6		1 **Paparazzi**...S:62 *(instrumental)*	$4	▮	Loud/RCA 64565
8/1/98	50	14		2 **What U See Is What U Get** S:29 *3 Card Molly*	$4	▮	Loud/RCA 65507
10/9/99	77	9		3 **B-Please** ...A:62			album cut
				SNOOP DOGG Featuring Xzibit and Nate Dogg			
				produced by **Dr. Dre**; from Snoop Dogg's album *No Limit Top Dogg* on No Limit 50052			
9/9/00	52S	8		4 **Connect** ...*(2 versions) / The Life* (w/**Kool G Rap**)	$5	★	TVT 6451
				DJ HURRICANE w/Xzibit, Big Gipp & Pharoahe Monch			
12/30/00+	76	10		5 **X** ...A:69 *(2 versions)*	$6	T	Loud 1968
				Snoop Dogg (ad libs)			

Y

DEBUT	PEAK	WKS	Gold	A-side (Chart Hit)...B-side	$	Sym	Label & Number
				YAKI-DA '95			
				Female pop-dance duo from Sweden: Linda Schonberg and Marie Knutsen.			
6/3/95	54	11		**I Saw You Dancing** ...S:64 / A:74 *(same version)*	$3	▮V	London 851880
				written and produced by Jonas "Joker" Berggren (**Ace Of Base**); "45": London 579798; B-side: "Rescue Me Tonight"			
				YA KID K — see HI TEK 3 / TECHNOTRONIC			
				Y&T ROK/LP '85			
				Hard-rock group from San Francisco, California: Dave Meniketti (vocals, guitar), Joey Alves (guitar), Philip Kennemore (bass) and Leonard Haze (drums). Band name stands for Yesterday & Today.			
7/13/85	55	10		**Summertime Girls** ...*(live version)*	$4		A&M 2748
				YANKEE GREY C&W '99			
				Country group from Cincinnati, Ohio: Tim Hunt (vocals, guitar), Matt Basford (guitar), Joe Caverlee (fiddle), Jerry Hughes (keyboards), Dave Buchanan (bass) and Kevin Griffin (drums).			
9/18/99	55	20		1 **All Things Considered**...A:42 / S:58 *Tell Me Something I Don't Know*	$4	★	Monument 79248
4/29/00	74	8		2 **Another Nine Minutes** ...A:66			album cut
				above 2 from the album *Untamed* on Monument 69085			
				YANKOVIC, "Weird Al" BUB/LP '84			
				Born on 10/23/59 in Lynwood, California. Novelty singer/accordionist. Specializes in song parodies. Starred in the movie *UHF*.			
4/30/83	63	8		1 **Ricky** ...*Buckingham Blues* [N]	$5	■	Rock 'n' Roll 03849
				Tress McNeil (voice of "Lucy"); parody of **Toni Basil**'s 1982 hit "Mickey" and TV's *I Love Lucy* show			
3/10/84	12	12	●	2 **Eat It** *That Boy Could Dance* [N]	$5	■	Rock 'n' Roll 04374
				Rick Derringer (guitar); parody of **Michael Jackson**'s 1983 hit "Beat It"			
5/5/84	62	6		3 **King Of Suede** ...*Nature Trail To Hell* [N]	$5	■	Rock 'n' Roll 04451
				parody of **Police**'s 1983 hit "King Of Pain"			
6/30/84	81	3		4 **I Lost On Jeopardy** ...*I'll Be Mellow When I'm Dead* [N]	$5	■	Rock 'n' Roll 04469
				parody of **Greg Kihn**'s 1983 hit "Jeopardy" and TV's *Jeopardy* game show			
6/22/85	47	8		5 **Like A Surgeon**...*Slime Creatures From Outer Space* [N]	$5	■	Rock 'n' Roll 04937
				parody of **Madonna**'s 1984 hit "Like A Virgin"			
5/21/88	99	2		6 **Fat**...*You Make Me* [N]	$4	■	Rock 'n' Roll 07769
				parody of **Michael Jackson**'s 1987 hit "Bad"; all of above produced by **Rick Derringer**			
4/25/92	35	11		7 **Smells Like Nirvana** ...S:12 *Waffle King* [N]	$4	▮	Scotti Brothers 75314
				parody of **Nirvana**'s 1992 hit "Smells Like Teen Spirit"			
3/30/96	53	16		8 **Amish Paradise**...S:22 *Everything You Know Is Wrong* [N]	$4	▮	Rock 'n' Roll 78061
				parody of **Coolio**'s 1995 hit "Gangsta's Paradise"			
6/8/96	71S	2		9 **Gump** ...BUB:102 *Spy Hard* [N]	$4	▮	Rock 'N' Roll 78073
				parody of **The Presidents Of The United States Of America**'s 1995 #1 Modern Rock hit "Lump" (and the movie *Forrest Gump*)			
				YARBROUGH, Glenn AC/LP '65			
				Born on 1/12/30 in Milwaukee, Wisconsin. Folk singer. Lead singer of **The Limeliters** (1959-63).			
3/13/65	12	14		1 **Baby The Rain Must Fall**...*I've Been To Town*	$10	■	RCA Victor 8498
				title song from the movie starring Lee Remick and Steve McQueen			
7/17/65	54	6		2 **It's Gonna Be Fine**...*She*	$8		RCA Victor 8619
				YARBROUGH & PEOPLES R&B/BUB/LP '81			
				Male/female R&B-funk duo from Dallas, Texas: Cavin Yarbrough and Alisa Peoples. Discovered by **The Gap Band**.			
2/7/81	19	16	●	1 **Don't Stop The Music** ...RB[5] *You're My Song*	$4		Mercury 76085
4/14/84	48	12		2 **Don't Waste Your Time**...RB[1] *(special dance mix)*	$4		Total Experience 2400
6/28/86	93	4		3 **I Wouldn't Lie**...*(short version)*	$3		Total Experience 2437

DEBUT	PEAK	WKS	Gold	A-side (Chart Hit)...B-side	$	Sym	Label & Number

YARDBIRDS, The — BUB/LP '65

Legendary rock group formed in Surrey, England: Keith Relf (vocals, harmonica; electrocuted on 5/14/76, age 33), Anthony "Top" Topham and Chris Dreja (guitars), Paul "Sam" Samwell-Smith (bass, keyboards) and Jim McCarty (drums). Formed as the Metropolitan Blues Quartet at Kingston Art School. Topham replaced by **Eric Clapton** in 1963. Clapton replaced by **Jeff Beck** in 1965. Samwell-Smith left in 1966; Dreja switched to bass and **Jimmy Page** (guitar) was added. Beck left in December 1966. Group disbanded in July 1968. Page formed the New Yardbirds in October 1968, which evolved into **Led Zeppelin**. Relf and McCarty formed Renaissance in 1969. Relf later in Armageddon, 1975; McCarty in Illusion, 1977. The Yardbirds were inducted into the Rock and Roll Hall of Fame in 1992.

DEBUT	PEAK	WKS	Gold	A-side (Chart Hit)...B-side	$	Sym	Label & Number
5/15/65	**6**	12		1 **For Your Love** ... *Got To Hurry*	$20		Epic 9790
7/31/65	**9**	12		2 **Heart Full Of Soul** ... *Steeled Blues* above 2 written by Graham Gouldman (**10cc**)	$20	■	Epic 9823
10/30/65	**17**	10		3 **I'm A Man** ... *Still I'm Sad* revival of **Bo Diddley**'s classic 1955 R&B hit	$20		Epic 9857
3/19/66	**11**	11		4 **Shapes Of Things** ... *New York City Blues* first released on Epic 9891 in 1966 ($20)	$20		Epic 10006
6/25/66	**13**	11		5 **Over Under Sideways Down** ... *Jeff's Boogie*	$20	■	Epic 10035
11/26/66	**30**	9		6 **Happenings Ten Years Time Ago** ... *The Nazz Are Blue*	$20	■	Epic 10094
4/22/67	**51**	6		7 **Little Games** ... *Puzzles*	$20		Epic 10156
8/5/67	**45**	7		8 **Ha Ha Said The Clown** ... *Tinker, Tailor, Soldier, Sailor*	$20		Epic 10204
11/18/67	**96**	2		9 **Ten Little Indians** ... *Drinking Muddy Water* written by **Nilsson**	$25		Epic 10248

YARROW, Peter — see PETER, PAUL & MARY

YASMEEN — '02

Born in Los Angeles, California. Female R&B singer.

DEBUT	PEAK	WKS	Gold	A-side (Chart Hit)...B-side	$	Sym	Label & Number
8/17/02	**97**	4		**Blue Jeans** ... S:8 *(instrumental)*	$5	★	Magic Johnson 155952

YASMIN — '91

Born Yasmin Jacobsen on 6/6/69 in Copenhagen, Denmark. Her mother is from the Faeroe Islands, and father is from Turkey.

DEBUT	PEAK	WKS	Gold	A-side (Chart Hit)...B-side	$	Sym	Label & Number
7/20/91	**76**	4		**Wanna Dance** ... A:67 *Slow*	$4	▮	Geffen 19022

YAVAHN — see RUFFNECK

YAZ — LP '83

Synth-dance duo from England: Genevieve **Alison Moyet** (vocals) and Vince Clarke (formerly of **Depeche Mode**; keyboards, synthesizers). Duo formerly named Yazoo. Clarke later formed **Erasure**, and Moyet went solo.

DEBUT	PEAK	WKS	Gold	A-side (Chart Hit)...B-side	$	Sym	Label & Number
9/18/82	**73**	8		1 **Situation** ... *(dub version)* first pressings credit artist as: YAZOO ($5)	$4	■	Sire 29953
2/26/83	**67**	8		2 **Only You** ... *Winter Kills*	$4		Sire 29844

YAZZ AND THE PLASTIC POPULATION — '88

Male/female techno-dance vocal duo. Yazz is U.K. female singer Yasmin Evans (of Jamaican descent).

DEBUT	PEAK	WKS	Gold	A-side (Chart Hit)...B-side	$	Sym	Label & Number
11/26/88	**96**	4		**The Only Way Is Up** ... *Bad House Music*	$4	■	Elektra 69365

YEAH YEAH YEAHS — LP '02

Punk-rock trio from Long Island, New York: Karen O (vocals), Nick Zinner (guitar) and Brian Chase (drums).

DEBUT	PEAK	WKS	Gold	A-side (Chart Hit)...B-side	$	Sym	Label & Number
11/23/02	**13**S	12		**Machine** ... *Graveyard / Pin*	$8	★*	Touch And Go 244

YEARWOOD, Trisha — C&W/BUB/LP '97

Born on 9/19/64 in Monticello, Georgia. Country singer. Backing singer on **Garth Brooks**'s first album. Married to Robert Reynolds of The Mavericks from 1994-99.

DEBUT	PEAK	WKS	Gold	A-side (Chart Hit)...B-side	$	Sym	Label & Number
11/27/93+	**82**	9		1 **The Song Remembers When** ... S:50 *Oh Lonesome You*	$4	▮V	MCA 54734
6/21/97	**23**	12		2 **How Do I Live** ... S:10 *(video version)* from the movie *Con Air* starring Nicolas Cage	$4	▮V	MCA 72015
7/18/98	**93**	2		3 **There Goes My Baby** ... S:64 *One More Chance*	$4	▮V	MCA 72048
1/23/99	**50**	12		4 **Powerful Thing** ... A:34 "45": MCA 72082; B-side: "Never Let You Go Again"		V	album cut
8/7/99	**65**	12		5 **I'll Still Love You More** ... A:51 *Wouldn't Any Woman* "45": MCA 72089; B-side: "Wouldn't Any Woman"; above 3 from the album *Where Your Road Leads* on MCA 70023		V	album cut
4/1/00	**81**	6		6 **Real Live Woman** ... A:66 from the album *Real Live Woman* on MCA 70102; "45": MCA 72146; B-side: "I'm Still Alive"		V	album cut
8/4/01	**44**	20		7 **I Would've Loved You Anyway** ... A:39 from the album *Inside Out* on MCA 70200; "45": MCA 72201; B-side: "Sad Eyes"		V	album cut

YELLO — BUB/LP '87

Computer/synthesizer-dance duo from Zurich, Switzerland: Dieter Meier and Boris Blank.

DEBUT	PEAK	WKS	Gold	A-side (Chart Hit)...B-side	$	Sym	Label & Number
8/8/87	**51**	11		**Oh Yeah** ... *(remix)* [I-N] featured in the movies *Ferris Bueller's Day Off* starring Matthew Broderick and *The Secret Of My Success* starring Michael J. Fox; issued with 2 different picture sleeves	$4	■	Mercury 884930

YELLOW BALLOON, The — BUB '67

Pop group formed in Los Angeles, California: Alex Valdez (vocals), Paul Canella (guitar), Frosty Green (keyboards), Don Braught (bass) and Don Grady (drums). Grady played "Robbie Douglas" on TV's *My Three Sons*.

DEBUT	PEAK	WKS	Gold	A-side (Chart Hit)...B-side	$	Sym	Label & Number
4/1/67	**25**	10		**Yellow Balloon** ... *Noollab Wolley* promotional record issued with a letter and a yellow balloon	$12	⊙	Canterbury 508

YELLOW MAGIC ORCHESTRA — LP '80

Electronic instrumental trio from Japan: Ryuichi Sakamoto, Yukihiro Takahashi and Haruomi Hosono.

DEBUT	PEAK	WKS	Gold	A-side (Chart Hit)...B-side	$	Sym	Label & Number
2/2/80	**60**	9		**Computer Game "Theme From The Circus"** ... *Yellow Magic (Tong Poo)* [I]	$5	■	Horizon 127

DEBUT	PEAK	WKS	Gold	A-side (Chart Hit)	B-side	$	Sym	Label & Number

YES — ★534★ — ROK/BUB/LP '84

Progressive-rock group formed in London, England: Jon Anderson (vocals; born on 10/25/44; **Jon & Vangelis**), Peter Banks (guitar), Tony Kaye (keyboards; born on 1/11/45), Chris Squire (bass; born on 3/4/48) and Bill Bruford (drums; born on 5/17/49). Banks, who went on to form **Flash** and **After The Fire**, replaced by Steve Howe in 1971. Kaye (joined **Badfinger** in 1979) replaced in 1971 by Rick Wakeman (born on 5/18/49). Bruford left to join **King Crimson**; replaced by Alan White in late 1972. Wakeman replaced by Patrick Moraz in 1974; re-joined in 1976 when Moraz left. Wakeman and Anderson left in 1980; replaced by **The Buggles**' Trevor Horn (guitar) and Geoff Downes (keyboards). Group disbanded in 1980. Howe and Downes joined **Asia**. Re-formed in 1983 with Anderson, Kaye, Squire, White and South African guitarist Trevor Rabin. Anderson left group in 1988. Anderson, Bruford, Wakeman and Howe formed self-named group in early 1989. Yes reunited in 1991 with Anderson, Bruford, Wakeman, Howe, Kaye, Squire, White and Rabin. Bruford, Wakeman and Howe had left group by 1994.

1)Owner Of A Lonely Heart 2)Roundabout 3)Leave It

DEBUT	PEAK	WKS	Gold	A-side (Chart Hit)	B-side	$	Sym	Label & Number
9/25/71	40	14		1 **Your Move**	*Clap*	$6		Atlantic 2819
2/12/72	13	13		2 **Roundabout**	*Long Distance Runaround*	$6		Atlantic 2854
8/12/72	46	7		3 **America**	*Total Mass Retain*	$6		Atlantic 2899
				written by **Paul Simon**; also released as the B-side of #10 below				
11/11/72	42	7		4 **And You And I (Part II)**	*(Part I)*	$6		Atlantic 2920
11/5/83+	❶[2]	23		5 **Owner Of A Lonely Heart** AR[4]	*Our Song* (ROK #32)	$4	■	Atco 99817
3/3/84	24	15		6 **Leave It**	*(acappella version)*	$4	■	Atco 99787
6/23/84	51	7		7 **It Can Happen**	*(live version)*	$4	■	Atco 99745
10/3/87	30	19		8 **Love Will Find A Way** AR[3] S:27 / A:30	*Holy Lamb*	$3	■	Atco 99449
12/19/87+	40	12		9 **Rhythm Of Love** S:40	*City Of Love*	$3	■	Atco 99419
6/1/91	86	5		10 **Lift Me Up** AR[6]	*America*	$4	▮V	Arista 2218
				"45" B-side: "Give & Take"				

YING YANG TWINS — R&B/BUB/LP '02

Rap duo from Atlanta, Georgia: D'Angelo Holmes and Eric Jackson. They are not related.

DEBUT	PEAK	WKS	Gold	A-side (Chart Hit)	B-side	$	Sym	Label & Number
3/18/00	74	14		1 **Whistle While You Twurk** S:19	*(2 versions) / Brang Yo Azz OutDoz*	$8	★*	ColliPark 1005
				due to legal action by Disney, a new recording, eliminating the sampling of "Whistle While You Work", was issued on the same label and number				
5/4/02	56	14		2 **Say I Yi Yi** A:55	*(2 versions) / Alley*	$6	T	Koch 8404

YIPES!! — LP '80

Rock group from Milwaukee, Wisconsin: Pat McCurdy (vocals), Andy Bartel and Mike Hoffmann (guitars), Pete Strand (bass) and Teddy Freese (drums).

DEBUT	PEAK	WKS	Gold	A-side (Chart Hit)	B-side	$	Sym	Label & Number
8/2/80	68	5		**Darlin'**	*Heartbreak Again*	$5		Millennium 11791

YOAKAM, Dwight — C&W/BUB/LP '99

Born on 10/23/56 in Pikeville, Kentucky. Country singer/songwriter/actor. Appeared in several movies.

DEBUT	PEAK	WKS	Gold	A-side (Chart Hit)	B-side	$	Sym	Label & Number
5/22/93	58[S]	6		1 **Ain't That Lonely Yet** BUB:101	*A Thousand Miles From Nowhere* (C&W #2)	$4	▮V	Reprise 18528
				"45": Reprise 18590; B-side: "Lonesome Roads"				
12/11/93+	70	10		2 **Fast As You** S:42	*Home For Sale*	$4	▮V	Reprise 18341
6/19/99	64	10		3 **Crazy Little Thing Called Love** A:55			V	album cut
				from the album *Last Chance For A Thousand Years* on Reprise 47389; "45": Reprise 16938; B-side: "Thinking About Leaving" (C&W #54)				

YOHANY — '02

Born in Miami, Florida. Female Latin dance singer. Pronounced: jo-ha-nee.

DEBUT	PEAK	WKS	Gold	A-side (Chart Hit)	B-side	$	Sym	Label & Number
6/15/02	34[S]	7		**Lose Control (Descontrólate)**	*(10 versions)*	$8	★*	Durmar 90200

YO LA TENGO — LP '02

Alternative-rock trio from Hoboken, New Jersey: Ira Kaplan (vocals, guitar), James McNew (bass) and Georgia Hubley (drums). Kaplan and Hubley are married. Name is Spanish for "I've got it."

DEBUT	PEAK	WKS	Gold	A-side (Chart Hit)	B-side	$	Sym	Label & Number
12/7/02	10[S]	11		Nuclear War	*(3 versions)*	$5	★	Matador 568

YORK, Dave, and The Beachcombers — '62

Born David Kinzie on 7/22/37 in Hammond, Indiana. The Beachcombers on "Beach Party" were **Glen Campbell** (guitar), Gary Paxton (piano, **Hollywood Argyles**), Steve Douglas (sax, **Duane Eddy**), Ray Polman (bass) and Jerry Reaple (drums).

DEBUT	PEAK	WKS	Gold	A-side (Chart Hit)	B-side	$	Sym	Label & Number
8/25/62	95	1		**Beach Party**	*I Wanna Go Surfin'*	$25		P-K-M 6700
				first released on Lancelot 6 in 1962 ($50)				

YORK, Rusty — '59

Born Charles Edward York on 5/24/35 in Harlan, Kentucky. Rock and roll singer.

DEBUT	PEAK	WKS	Gold	A-side (Chart Hit)	B-side	$	Sym	Label & Number
7/20/59	77	3		**Sugaree**	*Red Rooster (instrumental)*	$25		Chess 1730
				written by **Marty Robbins**; first released on P.J. 100 ($40) and then on Note 10021 ($40) in 1959				

YOST, Dennis — see CLASSICS IV

"YOU KNOW WHO" GROUP!, The — '65

Mysterious masked-and-caped rock group from New York.

DEBUT	PEAK	WKS	Gold	A-side (Chart Hit)	B-side	$	Sym	Label & Number
11/28/64+	43	9		**Roses Are Red My Love**	*Playboy*	$10		4 Corners 113

YOUNG, Barry — BUB/LP '66

Adult Contemporary singer.

DEBUT	PEAK	WKS	Gold	A-side (Chart Hit)	B-side	$	Sym	Label & Number
11/6/65+	13	11		**One Has My Name (The Other Has My Heart)**	*Show Me The Way*	$10		Dot 16756
				Ernie Freeman (arranger; similar to his **Dean Martin** arrangements); #1 Country hit for **Jimmy Wakely** in 1948				

YOUNG, Faron — C&W/BUB '61

Born on 2/25/32 in Shreveport, Louisiana. Died of a self-inflicted gunshot wound on 12/10/96 (age 64). Country singer/guitarist (charted 89 hits, 1953-89). In movies *The Young Sheriff*, *Daniel Boone* and *Hidden Guns*. Founder and one-time publisher of the *Music City News* magazine in Nashville.

DEBUT	PEAK	WKS	Gold	A-side (Chart Hit)	B-side	$	Sym	Label & Number
6/3/57	96	1		1 **The Shrine Of St. Cecilia** T:96	*He Was There*	$20		Capitol 3696
				the **Anita Kerr** Singers (backing vocals); #3 hit for the Andrews Sisters in 1941				
8/11/58	51	5		2 **Alone With You** CW[13] H:51	*Every Time I'm Kissing You* (C&W #10)	$25		Capitol 3982
1/4/60	83	3		3 **Riverboat**	*Face To The Wall* (C&W #10)	$20		Capitol 4291
				written by **Bill Anderson**				

DEBUT	PEAK	WKS	Gold	A-side (Chart Hit)..................B-side	$	Sym	Label & Number
				YOUNG, Faron — Cont'd			
4/10/61	12	15		4 **Hello Walls** CW[9] *Congratulations* (C&W #28)	$15		Capitol 4533
				written by **Willie Nelson**			
10/16/61	89	3		5 **Backtrack**..................*I Can't Find The Time*	$15	■	Capitol 4616
2/12/72	92	4		6 **It's Four In The Morning**..................CW[2] *It's Not The Miles*	$8		Mercury 73250
				YOUNG, Georgie, And The Rockin' Bocs '58			
				Rock and roll backing band on **Bobby Rydell**'s "Kissin' Time": Young (sax), Bob DeNardo (guitar), Bob McGraw (bass), Fred Bender (organ) and Pete Cozzi (drums).			
9/22/58	58	9		**Nine More Miles The "Faster-Faster" Song**..................H:58 *The Sneak (instrumental)*	$25		Cameo 150
				YOUNG, John Paul LP '78			
				Born on 6/21/50 in Glasgow, Scotland; raised in Sydney, Australia. Pop singer/songwriter/pianist.			
12/13/75+	42	9		1 **Yesterday's Hero**..................*The Next Time*	$5		Ariola America 7607
7/15/78	7	21		2 **Love Is In The Air**..................AC[2] *Where The Action Is*	$4		Scotti Brothers 402
12/9/78+	55	9		3 **Lost In Your Love**..................*The Day That My Heart Caught Fire*	$4		Scotti Brothers 405
				YOUNG, Karen '78			
				Born on 3/23/51 in Philadelphia, Pennsylvania. Died of a bleeding ulcer on 1/26/91 (age 39). Disco singer.			
9/16/78	67	13		**Hot Shot**..................*(long version)*	$6		West End 1211
				YOUNG, Kathy, with The Innocents BUB '60			
				Born on 10/21/45 in Santa Ana, California. Teen pop singer. Married for a time to a member of **The Walker Bros.** **The Innocents** were a trio consisting of James West (lead singer), Al Candelaria (bass) and Darron Stankey (guitar, tenor). First recorded as The Echoes for Andex in 1959.			
8/15/60	28	10		1 **Honest I Do** *[THE INNOCENTS]*..................*My Baby Hully Gullys*	$25		Indigo 105
10/24/60	3	17		2 **A Thousand Stars** *Eddie My Darling*	$30		Indigo 108
				originally recorded in 1954 by the R&B group The Rivileers on Baton 200 ($200)			
11/21/60+	28	11		3 **Gee Whiz** *[THE INNOCENTS]*..................*Please Mr. Sun*	$25		Indigo 111
2/20/61	30	10		4 **Happy Birthday Blues**..................*Someone To Love*	$20	■	Indigo 115
9/18/61	80	3		5 **Magic Is The Night**..................*Du Du'nt Du*	$20	■	Indigo 125
				YOUNG, Neil ROK/BUB/C&W/LP '72			
				Born on 11/12/45 in Toronto, Ontario, Canada. Rock singer/songwriter/guitarist. Joined Detroit rock band the Mynah Birds, featuring lead singer **Rick James** in 1965. To Los Angeles in 1966 and formed **Buffalo Springfield**. Went solo in 1969 with backing band Crazy Horse. Joined with **Crosby, Stills & Nash**, 1970-71. Appeared in the 1987 movie *Made In Heaven*. Reunited with Crosby, Stills & Nash in 1988 and again in 1999. Inducted into the Rock and Roll Hall of Fame in 1995.			
				1)Heart Of Gold 2)Old Man 3)Only Love Can Break Your Heart			
6/20/70	55	9		1 **Cinnamon Girl** *[NEIL YOUNG With Crazy Horse]*..................*Sugar Mountain (live)*	$7		Reprise 0911
10/24/70	33	12		2 **Only Love Can Break Your Heart**..................*Birds*	$6		Reprise 0958
4/10/71	93	1		3 **When You Dance I Can Really Love**..................*Sugar Mountain (live)*	$6		Reprise 0992
2/5/72	❶[1]	14	●	4 **Heart Of Gold** *Sugar Mountain (live)*	$6		Reprise 1065
				Linda Ronstadt and **James Taylor** (backing vocals)			
4/29/72	31	9		5 **Old Man**..................*The Needle And The Damage Done*	$6		Reprise 1084
7/1/72	61	6		6 **War Song**..................*The Needle And The Damage Done* (Young)	$6	⊙	Reprise 1099
				NEIL YOUNG and GRAHAM NASH			
7/13/74	69	7		7 **Walk On**..................*For The Turnstiles*	$5		Reprise 1209
2/3/79	61	7		8 **Four Strong Winds**..................*Human Highway*	$5		Reprise 1396
				Nicolette Larson (harmony vocal); Rufus Thibodeaux (fiddle); written by Canadian folk duo Ian & Sylvia			
10/13/79	79	5		9 **Rust Never Sleeps (Hey Hey, My My [Into The Black])**..................*(acoustic version)*	$5	■	Reprise 49031
12/26/81+	70	5		10 **Southern Pacific**..................*Motor City*	$4		Reprise 49870
				NEIL YOUNG & CRAZY HORSE (above 2)			
1/29/83	71	6		11 **Little Thing Called Love**..................*We R In Control* (ROK #42)	$4	■	Geffen 29887
				all of above (except #8) written by Neil Young			
	★568★			**YOUNG, Paul** AC/LP '85			
				Born on 1/17/56 in Bedfordshire, England. Pop-rock singer/songwriter/guitarist.			
10/1/83	70	7		1 **Wherever I Lay My Hat (That's My Home)**..................*Tender Trap*	$4	■	Columbia 04071
				written by **Marvin Gaye**			
2/4/84	22	15		2 **Come Back And Stay**..................*Yours*	$3	■	Columbia 04313
5/19/84	45	11		3 **Love Of The Common People**..................*Behind Your Smile (live)*	$3	■	Columbia 04453
5/11/85	❶[1]	23	●	4 **Everytime You Go Away** AC[2] S:❷[2] / A:❶[1] *This Means Anything*	$3	■	Columbia 04867
				written by **Daryl Hall** (from the **Hall & Oates**' 1980 album *Voices*)			
9/7/85	13	14		5 **I'm Gonna Tear Your Playhouse Down**..................S:13 / A:13 *Broken Man (live)*	$3	■	Columbia 05577
				original version by **Ann Peebles** "Bubbled Under" (#111) in 1973			
11/23/85+	56	11		6 **Everything Must Change**..................*Give Me My Freedom*	$3	■	Columbia 05712
11/15/86	65	10		7 **Some People**..................*Steps To Go*	$3	■	Columbia 06423
7/14/90	8	23		8 **Oh Girl**..................AC[3] A:6 / S:14 *Leaving Home*	$3	■V	Columbia 73377
				produced by **Pete Wingfield**; "45": Collectables 4685; B-side: "Don't Dream It's Over"			
2/1/92	22	14		9 **What Becomes Of The Brokenhearted**..................AC[2] A:26 / S:39 *Ghost Train (Main Title)* (Thomas Newman)	$4	■V	MCA 54331
				from the movie *Fried Green Tomatoes* starring Kathy Bates			
				YOUNG, Victor, And His Singing Strings MEM/POP '35			
				Born on 8/8/1900 in Chicago, Illinois. Died on 11/11/56 (age 56). Conductor/composer/violinist. Wrote "Stella By Starlight," "My Foolish Heart," "Blue Star," and many others. Composed the movie score for *Around The World In 80 Days*. Charted 25 hits, 1931-54, including the #1 hit in 1935 "She's A Latin From Manhattan."			
11/12/55	52	11		1 **Autumn Leaves**..................T:52 *Toy Tiger* [I]	$12		Decca 29653
				Ray Turner (piano solo)			
5/20/57	13	34		2 **(Main Theme) Around The World**..................A:13 / S:20 / T:26 *Around The World* (**Bing Crosby** - #25) [I]	$12	■	Decca 30262
				from the movie *Around The World In 80 Days* starring David Niven (soundtrack on Decca 79046)			

DEBUT	PEAK	WKS	Gold	A-side (Chart Hit)......B-side	$	Sym	Label & Number
				YOUNG & RESTLESS R&B/LP '90			
				Rap duo from Miami, Florida: Charles Trahan (born on 8/24/71) and Leon Johnson (born on 10/14/71).			
5/5/90	54	15		**"B" Girls**......S:40 *(3 versions)* [N]	$6	▮	Pandisc 10056
				YOUNG BLACK TEENAGERS LP '93			
				White rap group from New York: Firstborn, Kamron, A.T.A. and DJ Skribble.			
3/6/93	55	20		**Tap The Bottle**......S:33 / A:58 *(3 album snippets)*	$5	▮	MCA 54535
				YOUNGBLOOD, Sydney R&B/LP '90			
				Born Sydney Ford in San Antonio, Texas. R&B singer.			
8/25/90	46	11		**I'd Rather Go Blind**......A:40 *Could It Be (I'm In Love)*	$3	▮V	Arista 2055
				YOUNGBLOODS, The BUB/LP '69			
				Folk-rock group formed in Boston, Massachusetts: Jesse Colin Young (vocals, bass), Lowell Levinger and Jerry Corbitt (guitars), and Joe Bauer (drums; died in 1982).			
12/17/66+	52	10		1 **Grizzly Bear**......*Tears Are Falling*	$10	■	RCA Victor 9015
9/2/67	62	8		2 **Get Together**......*All My Dreams Blue*	$12		RCA Victor 9264
6/28/69	5	17	●	3 **Get Together**......*Beautiful* [R]	$8		RCA Victor 9752
				re-popularized as the theme for the National Conference of Christians & Jews; above 2 are the same version			
5/2/70	86	4		4 **Darkness, Darkness**......*On Sir Francis Drake*	$8		RCA Victor 0342
				originally "Bubbled Under" (#124) on 5/10/69 on RCA Victor 0129			
				YOUNGBLOODZ R&B/LP '99			
				Rap duo from Atlanta, Georgia: Sean Paul and J-Bo.			
8/14/99	27S	19		**U-Way (How We Do It)**......*(2 versions)*	$6	★	Ghet-O-Vision 24413
				YOUNG HEARTS R&B/BUB '68			
				R&B vocal group from Los Angeles, California: Ronald Preyer, Charles Ingersoll, Earl Carter and James Moore.			
11/16/68	94	3		**I've Got Love For My Baby**......*Takin' Care Of Business*	$20		Minit 32049
				YOUNG-HOLT UNLIMITED BUB/AC/R&B/LP '69			
				Soul-jazz instrumental group from Chicago, Illinois: Eldee Young (bass), Isaac "Red" Holt (drums; both of the **Ramsey Lewis Trio**) and Don Walker (piano). Walker left by 1968.			
12/17/66+	40	8		1 **Wack Wack** *[THE YOUNG HOLT TRIO]*......*This Little Light Of Mine* [I]	$8		Brunswick 55305
11/30/68+	3	13	●	2 **Soulful Strut**......*Country Slicker Joe* [I]	$8		Brunswick 55391
				instrumental track used for **Barbara Acklin**'s 1969 hit "Am I The Same Girl"			
3/1/69	57	4		3 **Who's Making Love**......*Just Ain't No Love* [I]	$7		Brunswick 55400
				YOUNG M.C. R&B/BUB/LP '89			
				Born Marvin Young on 5/10/67 in London, England; raised in Queens, New York. Rapper. Co-writer of **Tone Loc**'s "Wild Thing" and "Funky Cold Medina." Graduated with economics degree from University of Southern California.			
7/29/89	7	39	▲	1 **Bust A Move** S:2 / A:14 *Got More Rhymes*	$3	■	Delicious Vinyl 105
11/25/89+	33	14		2 **Principal's Office**......S:21 *(instrumental)*	$3	■	Delicious Vinyl 99137
3/24/90	75	5		3 **I Come Off**......*(album version)*	$4	▮V	Delicious Vinyl 98993 ■
8/3/91	54	7		4 **That's The Way Love Goes**......S:36 / A:71 *(2 remixes)*	$4	▮	Capitol 44740
10/5/02	6S	18		5 **Heatseeker**......*(remix)*	$6	★	Stimulus 680263
				YOUNG MILLIONAIRES, The '01			
				Rap trio formed in Atlanta, Georgia: Paul Reynolds, William Calhoun and Leroy Smith.			
5/26/01	55S	5		1 **All I Wanna Do**......*(3 versions)*	$6	★	Urban Spears 0003
				THE YOUNG MILLIONAIRES Featuring: Lil' One — The Young Millionairess			
9/15/01	49S	7		2 **Grippin Grain**......*(2 versions)*	$6	★	Urban Spears 0002
				YOUNG PHANTOM '01			
				Born in Los Angeles, California. Male rapper.			
8/11/01	42S	11		**All My Thugs**......*(no B-side)*	$8	★	Heartless 74268
				YOUNG RASCALS — see RASCALS			
				YOUNGSTOWN LP '99			
				"Boy band" from Youngstown, Ohio: Sammy Lopez, James Dallas and David Yeager.			
8/14/99	71	10		1 **I'll Be Your Everything**......S:9 *(3 album snippets)*	$4	★	Hollywood 64028
				from the movie *Inspector Gadget* starring Matthew Broderick			
6/23/01	24S	18		2 **Sugar**......*You Want What You Want*	$5	★+	Hollywood 64046
				YOUTH ASYLUM '00			
				Interracial "boy band" (ages 13-16): Kevin, Leo, Derek, Jason, Flashlight and Donnell.			
11/4/00	52S	6		**Jasmin**......*(2 album snippets)*	$5	★	Qwest 16841
				YO-YO R&B/BUB/LP '91			
				Born Yolanda Whitaker on 8/4/71 in Los Angeles, California. Female rapper.			
5/25/91	36	12		1 **You Can't Play With My Yo-Yo**......S:17 *Sisterland*	$5	▮	EastWest 98831
				YO-YO Featuring Ice Cube			
7/31/93	72	12		2 **The Bonnie And Clyde Theme** / S:56			
				YO YO (Featuring Ice Cube)			
				samples "Master Rocker" by Bernard Wright			
7/31/93		4		3 **IBWin' Wit My CREWin'**......	$5	▮	EastWest 98394
				samples "Buck Whylin'" by Terminator X			
8/13/94	55	16		4 **Romantic Call**......S:36 / A:66 *Love All The Men* (Patra)	$4	▮	Epic 77624
				PATRA Featuring Yo-Yo			
				samples "Bitches Brew" by Miles Davis			

YURO, Timi
BUB/AC/LP '61

Born Rosemarie Timothy Yuro on 8/4/40 in Chicago, Illinois; raised in Los Angeles, California. White female soul singer.

1)Hurt 2)What's A Matter Baby 3)Make The World Go Away

DEBUT	PEAK	WKS	Gold	A-side (Chart Hit)..........B-side	$	Sym	Label & Number
7/24/61	4	12		1 **Hurt /**			
				#8 R&B hit for **Roy Hamilton** in 1955			
10/9/61	72	3		2 **I Apologize**	$15		Liberty 55343
				#3 hit for **Bing Crosby** in 1931			
11/6/61	42	6		3 **Smile /**			
				written in 1936 by Charlie Chaplin for his movie *Modern Times*; #10 hit for **Nat King Cole** in 1954			
12/4/61	93	2		4 **She Really Loves You**	$12		Liberty 55375
2/3/62	66	5		5 **Let Me Call You Sweetheart** ..... *Satan Never Sleeps*	$12		Liberty 55410
				#1 hit for The Peerless Quartet in 1911			
7/14/62	12	11		6 **What's A Matter Baby (Is It Hurting You)** ..... *Thirteenth Hour*	$15		Liberty 55469
12/1/62+	44	8		7 **The Love Of A Boy** ..... *I Ain't Gonna Cry No More*	$12		Liberty 55519
3/30/63	81	1		8 **Insult To Injury** ..... *Just About The Time*	$12		Liberty 55552
7/20/63	24	11		9 **Make The World Go Away** ..... *Look Down*	$12		Liberty 55587
				#2 Country hit for **Ray Price** in 1963			
10/12/63	64	7		10 **Gotta Travel On** ..... *Down In The Valley*	$12		Liberty 55634
2/20/65	96	2		11 **You Can Have Him** ..... *Could This Be Magic*	$10		Mercury 72391
				female version of **Roy Hamilton**'s 1961 hit "You Can Have Her"; Yuro's musical arrangers and conductors: **Burt Bacharach** (#7), Belford Hendricks (#1-5, 9, 10), Bert Keyes (#6, 8) and **Jack Nitzsche** (#11)			

YUTAKA
LP '81

Born Yutaka Yokokura in Tokyo, Japan. Male jazz-pop keyboardist/singer.

DEBUT	PEAK	WKS	Gold	A-side (Chart Hit)..........B-side	$	Sym	Label & Number
7/18/81	81	3		**Love Light** ..... *Evening Star*	$5	■	Alfa 7004
				Yutaka and **Patti Austin** (vocals)			

YVONNE
'90

Born Yvonne Garcia in the Bronx, New York; raised in Miami, Florida. Dance singer.

DEBUT	PEAK	WKS	Gold	A-side (Chart Hit)..........B-side	$	Sym	Label & Number
1/27/90	88	9		**There's A Party Going On** ..... *What About Me*	$6	▮	Cutting 228

Z

ZABACH, Florian
MEM/POP '51

Born on 8/15/21 in Chicago, Illinois. Violinist/composer. Host of his own TV variety series in 1956. Hit #13 in 1951 with "The Hot Canary."

DEBUT	PEAK	WKS	Gold	A-side (Chart Hit)..........B-side	$	Sym	Label & Number
9/1/56	50	12		**When The White Lilacs Bloom Again** ..... T:50 *The Fiddler's Boogie* [I]	$12		Mercury 70936

ZACHARIAS, Helmut, And His Magic Violins
'56

Born on 1/27/20 in Germany. Died of lung failure on 2/28/2002 (age 82). Violinist.

DEBUT	PEAK	WKS	Gold	A-side (Chart Hit)..........B-side	$	Sym	Label & Number
9/1/56	12	14		**When The White Lilacs Bloom Again** ..... A:12 / T:16 / S:19 / J:19 *Blue Blues* [I]	$12		Decca 30039
				above 2 written in 1928 in Germany			

ZACHERLE, John, "The Cool Ghoul"
LP '58

Born on 9/26/18 in Philadelphia, Pennsylvania. Hosted horror movies on WCAU-TV in Philadelphia during the late '50s.

DEBUT	PEAK	WKS	Gold	A-side (Chart Hit)..........B-side	$	Sym	Label & Number
3/10/58	6	13		**Dinner With Drac Part 1** ..... T:6 / S:8 *Part 2* [N]	$35		Cameo 130
				The Applejacks (instrumental backing); Part 2 (B-side) is a less "gory" version; first released with "Igor" as the A-side ($40)			

ZADORA, Pia
C&W/BUB/LP '83

Born Pia Schipani on 5/4/54 in Hoboken, New Jersey. Singer/actress. Appeared in several movies.

DEBUT	PEAK	WKS	Gold	A-side (Chart Hit)..........B-side	$	Sym	Label & Number
3/27/82	45	9		1 **I'm In Love Again** ..... *It's Wrong For Me To Love You*	$4		Elektra/Curb 47428
12/11/82+	36	15		2 **The Clapping Song** ..... *Lovin' Things*	$4		Elektra/Curb 69889
2/2/85	54	11		3 **When The Rain Begins To Fall** ..... *Substitute* (Zadora)	$3	■	Curb/MCA 52521
				JERMAINE JACKSON/PIA ZADORA			
				from the movie *Voyage of the Rock Aliens* starring Zadora			

ZAGER, Michael, Band
R&B/LP '78

Born on 1/3/43 in Passaic, New Jersey. Disco keyboardist/producer. Member of **Ten Wheel Drive** from 1968-73.

DEBUT	PEAK	WKS	Gold	A-side (Chart Hit)..........B-side	$	Sym	Label & Number
3/20/76	94	3		1 **Do It With Feeling** ..... *This Is The Life*	$6		Bang 720
				MICHAEL ZAGER'S MOON BAND Featuring Peabo Bryson			
				re-entered the R&B charts (#76) in 1978 on Bang 737			
3/4/78	36	14		2 **Let's All Chant** ..... *Love Express* [I]	$5		Private Stock 45,184

ZAGER & EVANS
BUB/LP '69

Pop-folk duo from Lincoln, Nebraska: Denny Zager and Rick Evans (both sing and play guitar).

DEBUT	PEAK	WKS	Gold	A-side (Chart Hit)..........B-side	$	Sym	Label & Number
6/21/69	1 (6)	13	●	**In The Year 2525 (Exordium & Terminus)** ..... AC2 *Little Kids*	$6		RCA Victor 0174
				released regionally in 1968 on Truth 8082 ($15)			

ZAHND, Ricky, & The Blue Jeaners
'55

Born on 7/22/46 in Manhattan, New York. Lawyer since 1972. From 1979-86, was vice president of the New York Knicks basketball team and the New York Rangers hockey team.

DEBUT	PEAK	WKS	Gold	A-side (Chart Hit)..........B-side	$	Sym	Label & Number
12/17/55	21	4		**(I'm Gettin') Nuttin' For Christmas** ..... S:21 / T:40 *Something Barked On Christmas Morning* [X-N]	$20		Columbia 40576
				Tony Mottola (orch.); verse melody based on traditional 19th-century French song "Vive La Companie"; issued with a picture sleeve on Columbia Children's Series (J4-263)			

ZANDER, Robin — see WILSON, Ann

ZAPP — see ROGER

DEBUT	PEAK	WKS	Gold	A-side (Chart Hit)...B-side	$	Sym	Label & Number
				ZAPPA, Frank BUB/LP **'82**			
				Born on 12/21/40 in Baltimore, Maryland; raised in California. Died of cancer on 12/4/93 (age 52). Rock music's leading satirist. Singer/songwriter/guitarist/activist. Formed The Mothers Of Invention in 1965. In the movies *200 Motels* and *Baby Snakes*. Father of Dweezil and Moon Unit Zappa (both performed on the 1991 **Peace Choir**, "Give Peace A Chance"). Inducted into the Rock and Roll Hall of Fame in 1995. Won Grammy's Lifetime Achievement Award in 1997. Also see **Missing Persons**.			
10/19/74	86	4		1 **Don't Eat The Yellow Snow** ...*Cosmik Debris* [N]	$15		DiscReet 1312
4/14/79	45	8		2 **Dancin' Fool**...*Baby Snakes* [N]	$10		Zappa 10
7/17/82	32	12		3 **Valley Girl**...*You Are What You Is* [N]	$5	■	Barking Pumpkin 02972
				featuring Frank's daughter, Moon Unit Zappa; inspired the 1983 movie of the same title starring Nicolas Cage			
				ZAVARONI, Lena **'74**			
				Born on 11/4/63 in Rothesay, Scotland. Died of complications from anorexia nervosa on 10/1/99 (age 35). Pre-teen singer.			
7/13/74	91	4		**Ma! (He's Making Eyes At Me)**...*Rock-A-Bye Your Baby With A Dixie Melody*	$5		Stax 0206
				song introduced by Eddie Cantor in the 1921 musical *The Midnight Rounders*			
				ZEBRA ROK/BUB/LP **'83**			
				Rock trio from New Orleans, Louisiana: Randy Jackson (vocals, guitar), Felix Hanemann (bass) and Guy Gelso (drums).			
7/9/83	61	8		**Who's Behind The Door?** ...*As I Said Before*	$4		Atlantic 89821
				ZELLA, Danny, and his Zell Rocks **'59**			
				Born on 7/31/38 in Detroit, Michigan. Died on 1/27/2003 (age 64). Rock and roll singer/saxophonist.			
1/26/59	71	5		**Wicked Ruby** ...*Black Saxs* [I]	$40		Fox 10057
				ZENTNER, Si, And His Orchestra LP **'61**			
				Born Simon Zentner on 6/13/17 in Manhattan, New York. Died of leukemia on 1/31/2000 (age 82). Jazz trombonist.			
11/13/61	43	9		**Up A Lazy River** ...*Shufflin' Blues* [I]	$10		Liberty 55374
				#19 hit for Hoagy Carmichael in 1932			
				ZEVON, Warren ROK/LP **'78**			
				Born on 1/24/47 in Chicago, Illinois. Rock singer/songwriter/pianist. Parents were Russian immigrants. Recorded with female vocalist Tule Livingston as the duo **Lyme & Cybelle** in 1966. Worked as the keyboardist/bandleader for **The Everly Brothers**, shortly before their breakup. Wrote **Linda Ronstadt**'s "Poor Poor Pitiful Me." Recorded with three **R.E.M.** members as the Hindu Love Gods in 1990. Revealed in September 2002 that he has terminal cancer.			
3/25/78	21	12		1 **Werewolves Of London**...*Roland The Headless Thompson Gunner*	$6		Asylum 45472
				Fleetwood Mac's Mick Fleetwood (drums) and John McVie (bass guitar); produced by **Jackson Browne**			
3/8/80	57	7		2 **A Certain Girl** ...*Empty-Handed Heart*	$5		Asylum 46610
				Jackson Browne (backing vocal)			
				ZHANÉ R&B/BUB/LP **'93**			
				Female R&B-dance vocal duo from Philadelphia, Pennsylvania: Reneé Neufville and Jean Norris. Pronounced: jah-nay.			
8/28/93	6	24	●	1 **Hey Mr. D.J.** A:5 / S:6 *(7" remix)*	$3	▮	Flavor Unit 77177
				samples Michael Wycoff's "Looking Up To You"			
1/15/94	17	20		2 **Groove Thang** ...S:18 / A:20 *(instrumental)*	$4	▮	Motown 2228
5/21/94	40	20		3 **Sending My Love** ...S:36 / A:67 *(instrumental)*	$4	▮	Motown 2242
				above 3 co-written and produced by **Naughty By Nature**			
11/26/94	28	15		4 **Shame** ...A:31 / S:37 *(remix) / Zhané Flavor*	$4	▮	Hollywood 42269
				from the movie *A Low Down Dirty Shame* starring Keenan Ivory Wayans			
7/13/96	52	13		5 **It's a Party** ...S:32 *Ill Vibe* (w/**Q-Tip**)	$4	▮	Elektra 64268
				BUSTA RHYMES (featuring Zhané)			
3/15/97	39	12		6 **Request Line** ...S:30 / A:66 *(instrumental)*	$4	▮	Illtown/Motown 0614
				samples "It Seems To Hang On" by **Ashford & Simpson**			
7/3/99	10	17	●	7 **Jamboree** ...S:4 / A:58 *On The Run*	$4	★	Arista 13712
				NAUGHTY BY NATURE (Feat. Zhané)			
				samples "I'm Always Dancin' To The Music" by Benny Golson			
				ZILL, Pat **'61**			
				Born in Columbus, Ohio. Male pop-country singer.			
5/22/61	91	1		**Pick Me Up On Your Way Down**...*La Mirada*	$15		Indigo 119
				first released on Sand 336 ($20) in 1961; #2 Country hit for Charlie Walker in 1958			
				ZODIACS, The — see WILLIAMS, Maurice			
				ZOMBIE NATION **'00**			
				Techno-rock/rave/dance group is actually German dance producer Gnork Zomb (aka Splank).			
9/2/00	99	2		**Kernkraft 400**...S:44 *(2 versions)* [I]	$10	★*	Radikal 99027
				ZOMBIES, The BUB/LP **'64**			
				Rock group from Hertfordshire, England: Rod Argent (keyboards), Colin Blunstone (vocals), Paul Atkinson (guitar), Chris White (bass) and Hugh Grundy (drums). Disbanded in late 1967. Rod formed **Argent** in 1969.			
10/17/64	2[1]	15		1 **She's Not There** *You Make Me Feel So Good*	$15		Parrot 9695
1/9/65	6	11		2 **Tell Her No** ...*Leave Me Be*	$15	■	Parrot 9723
4/10/65	58	6		3 **She's Coming Home**...*I Must Move*	$12	■	Parrot 9747
6/26/65	95	3		4 **I Want You Back Again** ...*Remember When I Loved Her*	$12		Parrot 9769
2/8/69	3	13	●	5 **Time Of The Season** ...*Friends Of Mine*	$10		Date 1628
				recorded in 1967; all of above written by Rod Argent			
				ZWOL **'78**			
				Born Walter Zwol in Canada. Pop-rock singer/songwriter.			
9/16/78	76	8		1 **New York City** ...*A Little Bit Crazy*	$5	□	EMI America 8005
2/24/79	75	3		2 **Call Out My Name**...*It's So Real*	$5		EMI America 8009

DEBUT	PEAK	WKS	Gold	A-side (Chart Hit)...B-side	$	Sym	Label & Number

ZZ TOP ★351★ ROK/BUB/LP '86

Boogie-rock trio formed in Houston, Texas: Billy Gibbons (vocals, guitar; born on 12/16/49), Dusty Hill (vocals, bass; born on 5/19/49) and Frank Beard (drums; born on 6/11/49). Gibbons had been lead guitarist in Moving Sidewalks, a Houston psychedelic-rock band. Hill and Beard had played in American Blues, based in Dallas. Group appeared in the movie *Back To The Future III*. Gibbons and Hill are the long-bearded members.

1)Legs 2)Sleeping Bag 3)Tush

DEBUT	PEAK	WKS	Gold	A-side (Chart Hit)...B-side	$	Sym	Label & Number
5/20/72	**69**	9		1 **Francene**...*(Spanish version)*	$10		London 179
3/30/74	**41**	19		2 **La Grange**...*Just Got Paid*	$8		London 203
7/19/75	**20**	9		3 **Tush**...*Blue Jean Blues*	$8	■	London 220
9/11/76	**44**	11		4 **It's Only Love**...*Asleep In The Desert*	$8	■	London 241
3/26/77	**91**	6		5 **Arrested For Driving While Blind**...*It's Only Love*	$8		London 251
1/19/80	**34**	11		6 **I Thank You**...*A Fool For Your Stockings*	$4		Warner 49163
7/12/80	**89**	2		7 **Cheap Sunglasses**...*Esther Be The One*	$4		Warner 49220
10/3/81	**77**	4		8 **Leila**...*Don't Tease Me*	$4		Warner 49782
4/2/83	**37**	12		9 **Gimme All Your Lovin**...*If I Could Only Flag Her Down*	$4	■	Warner 29693
7/23/83	**56**	9		10 **Sharp Dressed Man**...*I Got The Six*	$4		Warner 29576
5/19/84	**8**	19		11 **Legs** *Bad Girl*	$4	■	Warner 29272
10/19/85	**8**	17		12 **Sleeping Bag**...AR[2] A:7 / S:10 *Party On The Patio*	$4	■	Warner 28884
1/18/86	**21**	12		13 **Stages**...AR[2] A:16 / S:27 *Can't Stop Rockin'* (ROK #8)	$4	■	Warner 28810
3/29/86	**22**	13		14 **Rough Boy**...A:17 / S:25 *Delirious* (ROK #16)	$4	■	Warner 28733
7/26/86	**35**	12		15 **Velcro Fly**...A:30 *Woke Up With Wood* (ROK #18) above 4 from the album *Afterburner*	$4		Warner 28650
5/19/90	**50**	11	▲	16 **Doubleback**...AR[5] *Planet Of Women* from the movie *Back To The Future III* starring Michael J. Fox	$4	▮V	Warner 26265 ■
2/9/91	**79**	5		17 **Give It Up**...*Concrete And Steel* (ROK #1) all of above (except #1 & 6) written by ZZ Top; all of above produced by Bill Ham	$4	▮	Warner 19470

HOT STARTS & STREAKS

This is a first-time listing of the artists in this book that have had the hottest and/or longest streaks of top hits. Some had a hot streak beginning with their very first chart hit, while others had their streaks later in their careers. All totals in the #1, Top 5, Top 10 and Top 20 columns were accumulated during the Streak Years shown in the far left column. (Christmas chart hits do not count in any of the totals.) A number in red indicates that the totals are for consecutive hits. A ^ symbol after an artist's name indicates that the streak began with their first chart hit in this book. Also shown are an artist's first-to-last hits during their streak. Starting with Gale Storm's debut of five consecutive Top 10 hits in 1955, and ending with Ashanti's debut of six consecutive Top 10 hits in 2001, here are the hottest "Hot Starts & Streaks" of the past 48 years.

Streak Years	#1	Top 5	Top 10	Top 20	Artist	First > Last Hit
55-56	—	2	5	5	Gale Storm ^	I Hear You Knocking > Ivory Tower
55-58	5	11	16	21	Pat Boone ^	Two Hearts > If Dreams Came True
55-58	3	7	10	19	Perry Como ^	Ko Ko Mo > Kewpie Doll
55-58	1	4	6	10	Frank Sinatra ^	Melody Of Love > Witchcraft
55-60	—	4	11	17	Fats Domino ^	Ain't It A Shame > My Girl Josephine
55-60	4	6	7	14	The Platters ^	Only You > Harbor Lights
56-59	1	3	6	9	Andy Williams	Canadian Sunset > The Village Of St. Bernadette
56-65	17	30	33	53	Elvis Presley ^	Heartbreak Hotel > Puppet On A String
57-58	1	3	5	7	Jimmie Rodgers ^	Honeycomb > Bimbombey
57-62	2	9	17	24	Ricky Nelson ^	A Teenager's Romance > It's Up To You
57-62	4	7	15	17	The Everly Brothers ^	Bye Bye Love > That's Old Fashioned
57-62	2	5	8	17	Paul Anka ^	Diana > Eso Beso
57-65	1	2	5	17	Sam Cooke ^	You Send Me > Shake
58-63	3	7	16	22	Connie Francis	Who's Sorry Now > Follow The Boys
58-63	1	6	9	13	Bobby Darin ^	Splish Splash > 18 Yellow Roses
58-63	1	6	10	12	Dion (& The Belmonts)	No One Knows > Drip Drop
59-61	—	1	4	11	Jackie Wilson	Lonely Teardrops > I'm Comin' On Back To You
59-62	—	4	7	15	Brook Benton	It's Just A Matter Of Time > Hotel Happiness
59-63	3	5	10	13	Ray Charles	What'd I Say > That Lucky Old Sun
59-63	—	4	6	14	Bobby Rydell ^	Kissin' Time > Forget Him
59-63	1	3	6	10	Neil Sedaka ^	The Diary > Alice In Wonderland
59-64	1	4	5	11	The Drifters	There Goes My Baby > Saturday Night At The Movies
60-63	2	7	12	16	Brenda Lee	Sweet Nothin's > As Usual
60-63	3	5	8	15	Chubby Checker	The Twist > Loddy Lo
60-63	1	3	5	9	Bobby Vee	Devil Or Angel > Charms
60-64	2	6	9	10	Roy Orbison	Only The Lonely > Oh, Pretty Woman
61-63	2	5	6	7	The Shirelles	Will You Love Me Tomorrow > Foolish Little Girl
62-63	—	3	5	5	Dee Dee Sharp ^	Slow Twistin' > Do The Bird
62-64	1	1	4	7	Mary Wells	The One Who Really Loves You > Once Upon A Time
62-67	4	7	13	19	The 4 Seasons	Sherry > C'mon Marianne
62-68	3	8	13	20	The Beach Boys	Surfin' Safari > Do It Again
62-68	4	5	8	13	Bobby Vinton ^	Roses Are Red > I Love How You Love Me
63-67	1	4	4	8	Lesley Gore ^	It's My Party > California Nights
63-69	1	3	11	17	Marvin Gaye	Pride And Joy > That's The Way Love Is
63-71	1	2	5	13	The Miracles	You've Really Got A Hold On Me > I Don't Blame You At All
63-87	10	20	28	36	Stevie Wonder ^	Fingertips > Skeletons
64-67	2	8	11	14	Herman's Hermits ^	I'm Into Something Good > Don't Go Out Into The Rain
64-67	1	5	8	14	Dave Clark Five ^	Glad All Over > You Got What It Takes
64-67	1	4	7	11	Johnny Rivers ^	Memphis > Summer Rain
64-68	2	4	5	12	Four Tops ^	Baby I Need Your Loving > If I Were A Carpenter
64-70	20	29	32	38	The Beatles ^	I Want To Hold Your Hand > The Long And Winding Road
64-70	—	2	8	12	Dionne Warwick	Anyone Who Had A Heart > I'll Never Fall In Love Again

HOT STARTS & STREAKS (cont'd)

Streak Years	#1	Top 5	Top 10	Top 20	Artist	First > Last Hit
64-72	12	15	20	24	The Supremes	Where Did Our Love Go > Floy Joy
64-73	4	8	15	24	The Temptations ^	The Way You Do The Things You Do > Masterpiece
64-83	8	13	21	28	The Rolling Stones	Time Is On My Side > Undercover Of The Night
65-66	1	5	7	9	Gary Lewis & The Playboys ^	This Diamond Ring > Paint Me A Picture
65-67	1	3	7	9	The Lovin' Spoonful ^	Do You Believe In Magic > Six O'Clock
65-68	2	5	6	9	Petula Clark ^	Downtown > Kiss Me Goodbye
65-72	—	1	6	14	James Brown	Papa's Got A Brand New Bag > Get On The Good Foot
66-67	1	6	6	7	The Mamas & The Papas ^	California Dreamin' > Twelve Thirty
66-68	3	6	6	9	The Monkees ^	Last Train To Clarksville > D.W. Washburn
66-70	3	6	7	11	Simon & Garfunkel ^	The Sounds Of Silence > El Condor Pasa
66-82	3	8	13	25	Neil Diamond	Cherry, Cherry > Heartlight
67-74	1	7	14	24	Aretha Franklin	I Never Loved A Man > I'm In Love
67-75	1	6	7	13	Gladys Knight & The Pips	I Heard It Through The Grapevine > The Way We Were/Try To Remember
67-79	9	11	14	23	Bee Gees ^	New York Mining Disaster 1941 > Love You Inside Out
68-69	—	3	5	6	Gary Puckett & The Union Gap ^	Woman, Woman > This Girl Is A Woman Now
68-71	—	7	9	11	Creedence Clearwater Revival ^	Suzie Q. > Sweet Hitch-Hiker
68-73	3	4	5	6	Sly & The Family Stone ^	Dance To The Music > If You Want Me To Stay
69-70	—	3	3	4	Blood, Sweat & Tears ^	You've Made Me So Very Happy > Hi-De-Ho
69-74	3	9	11	18	Three Dog Night	One > Sure As I'm Sittin' Here
70-75	4	7	8	13	The Jackson 5 ^	I Want You Back > I Am Love
70-76	3	11	12	16	Carpenters	(They Long To Be) Close To You > There's A Kind Of Hush
70-80	1	7	7	12	Spinners	It's A Shame > Cupid/I've Loved You For A Long Time
70-85	6	7	12	20	Diana Ross ^	Reach Out And Touch > Missing You
70-89	3	13	20	28	Chicago	Make Me Smile > What Kind Of Man Would I Be?
71-75	2	7	12	19	The Osmonds (+ Donny & Marie) ^	One Bad Apple > Deep Purple
71-75	1	4	7	10	Al Green	Tired Of Being Alone > L.O.V.E. (Love)
71-75	2	5	7	7	Ringo Starr	It Don't Come Easy > No No Song
71-76	4	7	8	10	John Denver ^	Take Me Home, Country Roads > Fly Away
71-77	3	4	6	11	Helen Reddy ^	I Don't Know How To Love Him > You're My World
71-85	9	15	22	25	Paul McCartney ^	Another Day > Spies Like Us
71-93	4	11	16	24	Rod Stewart ^	Maggie May > All For Love
71-97	10	20	28	41	Elton John	Your Song > Candle In The Wind 1997
72-75	2	4	6	7	America ^	A Horse With No Name > Daisy Jane
73-81	5	8	9	10	Barbra Streisand	The Way We Were > Comin' In And Out Of Your Life
73-85	5	13	15	21	Olivia Newton-John	Let Me Be There > Soul Kiss
74-80	1	2	4	10	Abba ^	Waterloo > The Winner Takes It All
74-81	3	4	11	16	Barry Manilow ^	Mandy > The Old Songs
75-79	5	7	7	7	KC & The Sunshine Band ^	Get Down Tonight > Yes, I'm Ready
75-79	2	6	7	8	Captain & Tennille ^	Love Will Keep Us Together > Do That To Me One More Time
75-80	5	7	9	11	Eagles	Best Of My Love > I Can't Tell You Why
75-80	1	5	8	10	Linda Ronstadt	You're No Good > Hurt So Bad
75-81	2	7	9	11	Commodores	Slippery When Wet > Oh No
75-83	—	1	7	14	Electric Light Orchestra	Can't Get It Out Of My Head > Rock 'N' Roll Is King
75-87	1	5	9	16	Fleetwood Mac	Over My Head > Everywhere
76-83	4	11	13	13	Donna Summer ^	Love To Love You Baby > She Works Hard For The Money
76-90	6	11	16	22	Daryl Hall & John Oates	Sara Smile > So Close
77-80	3	5	6	8	Andy Gibb ^	I Just Want To Be Your Everything > Time Is Time
77-84	2	7	9	16	Kenny Rogers	Lucille > What About Me?
77-88	1	7	9	14	Foreigner ^	Feels Like The First Time > I Don't Want To Live Without You
78-93	3	7	13	23	Billy Joel	Just The Way You Are > The River Of Dreams
79-81	4	4	4	4	Blondie ^	Heart Of Glass > Rapture
79-87	1	4	10	13	Kool & The Gang	Ladies Night > Stone Love

HOT STARTS & STREAKS (cont'd)

Streak Years	#1	Top 5	Top 10	Top 20	Artist	First > Last Hit
79-95	12	17	24	26	Michael Jackson	Don't Stop 'Til You Get Enough > You Are Not Alone
80-85	1	8	8	9	Air Supply ^	Lost In Love > Just As I Am
80-94	—	4	12	15	Bruce Springsteen	Hungry Heart > Streets Of Philadelphia
80-95	5	11	19	23	Prince	I Wanna Be Your Lover > I Hate U
81-84	1	3	5	8	Rick Springfield	Jessie's Girl > Bop 'Til You Drop
81-87	5	9	13	14	Lionel Richie ^	Endless Love > Se La
81-90	7	12	14	16	Phil Collins ^	I Missed Again > Something Happened On The Way To Heaven
81-96	1	4	10	17	John Mellencamp	Ain't Even Done With The Night > Key West Intermezzo
82-88	3	5	12	13	Huey Lewis & The News ^	Do You Believe In Love > Perfect World
83-86	1	4	6	9	Culture Club ^	Do You Really Want To Hurt Me > Move Away
83-88	2	8	9	11	Duran Duran ^	Hungry Like The Wolf > I Don't Want Your Love
83-96	4	6	11	17	Bryan Adams	Straight From The Heart > I Finally Found Someone
83-02	12	27	35	41	Madonna ^	Holiday > Die Another Day
84-88	3	6	7	9	Billy Ocean	Caribbean Queen > The Colour Of Love
84-89	2	6	8	9	Cyndi Lauper ^	Girls Just Want To Have Fun > I Drove All Night
84-89	1	4	5	9	Tina Turner	What's Love Got To Do With It > The Best
84-92	10	15	19	19	George Michael	Wake Me Up Before You Go-Go > Too Funky
85-91	3	6	10	11	Gloria Estefan ^	Conga > Coming Out Of The Dark
85-99	11	19	22	26	Whitney Houston	You Give Good Love > My Love Is Your Love
86-90	2	2	5	9	Steve Winwood	Higher Love > One And Only Man
86-95	5	7	11	13	Bon Jovi	You Give Love A Bad Name > This Ain't A Love Song
86-01	10	25	28	29	Janet Jackson	What Have You Done For Me Lately > Someone To Call My Lover
87-89	2	5	5	7	Debbie Gibson ^	Only In My Dreams > No More Rhyme
87-93	2	4	7	13	Michael Bolton	That's What Love Is All About > Said I Loved You...But I Lied
87-93	1	5	7	9	Taylor Dayne ^	Tell It To My Heart > Can't Get Enough Of Your Love
87-93	1	3	8	9	Exposé ^	Come Go With Me > I'll Never Get Over You
87-94	3	7	9	14	Richard Marx ^	Don't Mean Nothing > The Way She Loves Me
88-90	3	5	9	9	New Kids On The Block ^	Please Don't Go Girl > Tonight
88-93	2	6	9	10	Bobby Brown ^	Don't Be Cruel > Get Away
89-90	3	5	5	5	Milli Vanilli ^	Girl You Know It's True > All Or Nothing
89-91	4	6	6	7	Roxette ^	The Look > Fading Like A Flower
89-92	6	7	8	10	Paula Abdul	Straight Up > Will You Marry Me?
90-92	3	4	4	6	Wilson Phillips ^	Hold On > You Won't See Me Cry
90-01	15	21	22	26	Mariah Carey ^	Vision Of Love > Loverboy
91-92	2	3	3	6	Color Me Badd ^	I Wanna Sex You Up > Forever Love
91-98	5	9	10	11	Boyz II Men ^	Motownphilly > A Song For Mama
91-99	4	8	10	11	Celine Dion ^	Where Does My Heart Beat Now > That's The Way It Is
92-99	4	7	9	9	TLC ^	Ain't 2 Proud 2 Beg > Unpretty
93-02	2	9	10	15	R. Kelly	Sex Me > Ignition
95-99	3	5	7	7	Monica ^	Don't Take It Personal > Angel Of Mine
96-01	1	4	4	8	112 ^	Only You > Peaches & Cream
96-02	3	8	10	15	Puff Daddy ^	No Time > Trade It All
97-98	1	3	4	7	Spice Girls ^	Wannabe > Goodbye
97-00	—	4	7	7	Backstreet Boys	Quit Playing Games (With My Heart) > Shape Of My Heart
97-01	4	7	8	8	Destiny's Child ^	No, No, No > Emotion
97-02	3	7	7	7	Usher	You Make Me Wanna... > I Need A Girl (Part One)
98-01	1	1	3	5	Britney Spears ^	...Baby One More Time > Stronger
99-02	4	6	6	8	Christina Aguilera ^	Genie In A Bottle > Beautiful
99-03	4	6	8	9	Jennifer Lopez ^	If You Had My Love > All I Have
00-02	2	6	7	8	Nelly ^	(Hot S**t) Country Grammar > Air Force Ones
00-02	1	3	6	7	P!nk ^	There You Go > Family Portrait
01-03	2	4	6	7	Ashanti ^	Always On Time > Mesmerize

SONG TITLE SECTION

Lists, alphabetically, all charted titles from the artist section. The artist's name is listed with each title along with the highest position attained and the year the song first peaked on the chart.

For songs that hit the charts listed below but did not hit the Hot 100 chart, the following letter designations appear to the right of their peak positions:

A - Hot 100 Airplay or Top 40 Radio Monitor
S - Hot 100 Singles Sales
X - Christmas Singles
H - Honor Roll Of Hits
C - Coming Up Strong

Some titles show the letter **F** as a position, indicating that the title was listed on the charts as a flip side and did not make it on its own.

A song with more than one charted version is listed once, with the artists' names listed below in chronological order. Many songs that have the same title, but are different tunes, are listed separately, with the most popular title listed first. This will make it easy to determine which songs are the same composition, the number of charted versions of a particular song, and which of these were the most popular.

Cross-references have been used throughout to aid in finding a title.

The Song Title Section now includes special key word headings — such as "Rock," "Love," "How," "Let" — that help you quickly find sections of listings in which multiple titles begin with that word or a variation of it. Also, all Top 10 peak positions are highlighted in red type.

Here are some tips when searching for titles:

Titles such as "G.T.O.," "I.O.U.," and "O.P.P." will be found at the beginning of their respective letters; however, titles such as "L-O-N-E-L-Y" and "T-R-O-U-B-L-E," which are spellings of words, are listed with their regular spellings.

Titles beginning with a numeral would be found under the spelling of the number. ["911 Is A Joke" would be found under the letter "N" (Nine One One)]

Two-word titles which have the exact same spelling as one-word titles are listed together alphabetically. ("Dream Lover" is listed directly before "Dreamlover.")

Articles (A, An, The, Tha) at the beginning of a title are dropped and the title can be found alphabetically under the subsequent word. ["The Sound Of My Tears" would be found under the letter "S" (Sound Of My Tears)]

Titles which are identical, except for an apostrophized word in one of the titles, are shown together. ("Holdin' On" appears immediately above "Holding On.")

A

28/66 **"A" Team** *SSgt Barry Sadler*
1/70 **ABC** *Jackson 5*
46/93 **abc-123** *Levert*
77/56 **ABC's Of Love** *Frankie Lymon*
27/01 **AM To PM** *Christina Milian*
35/97 **ATLiens** *OutKast*
35/00 **Aaron's Party (Come Get It)** *Aaron Carter*
26/82 **Abacab** *Genesis*
67/85 **Abadabadango** *Kim Carnes*
47/69 **Abergavenny** *Shannon*
16/64 **Abigail Beecher** *Freddy Cannon*
15/63 **Abilene** *George Hamilton IV*
22A/94 **About A Girl** *Nirvana*
31/60 **About This Thing Called Love** *Fabian*
51S/00 **Above The Clouds** *Amber*
59/62 **Above The Stars** *Mr. Acker Bilk*
32/74 **Abra-Ca-Dabra** *DeFranco Family*
1/82 **Abracadabra** *Steve Miller Band*
Abraham, Martin And John
4/68 *Dion*
33/69 *Miracles*
35/69 *Moms Mabley*
8/71 *Tom Clay (medley)*
83/98 **Absence Of The Heart** *Deana Carter*
53/86 **Absolute Beginners** *David Bowie*
48S/02 **Absolutely Everybody** *Vanessa Amorosi*
26/71 **Absolutely Right** *Five Man Electrical Band*
6/00 **Absolutely (Story Of A Girl)** *Ninedays*
44A/97 **Abuse Me** *Silverchair*
98/76 **Abyssinia Jones** *Edwin Starr*
54/70 **Ace Of Spade** *O.V. Wright*
4/92 **Achy Breaky Heart** *Billy Ray Cyrus*
56/73 **Across 110th Street** *Bobby Womack*
74/89 **Across The Miles** *Survivor*
18/90 **Across The River** *Bruce Hornsby*
98/64 **Across The Street** *Lenny O'Henry*
47/65 **Act Naturally** *Beatles*
13/65 **Action** *Freddy Cannon*
20/76 **Action** *Sweet*
43/94 **Action** *Terror Fabulous*
75/84 **Action** *Evelyn "Champagne" King*
69/75 **Action Speaks Louder Than Words** *Chocolate Milk*
75/98 **Actual, The** *All City*
90/60 **Adam And Eve** *Paul Anka*
64/70 **Add Some Music To Your Day** *Beach Boys*
84/94 **Addams Family (Whoomp!)** *Tag Team*
7/92 **Addams Groove** *Hammer*
1/86 **Addicted To Love** *Robert Palmer*
9/02 **Addictive** *Truth Hurts*
45/60 **Adeste Fideles** *Bing Crosby*
3/98 **Adia** *Sarah McLachlan*
90/62 **Adios Amigo** *Jim Reeves*
Admiral Halsey ..see: Uncle Albert
71/55 **Adorable** *Fontane Sisters*
93/71 **Adrienne** *Tommy James*
8/84 **Adult Education** *Daryl Hall - John Oates*
Adventures In Paradise ..see: Theme From
89/90 **Advice For The Young At Heart** *Tears For Fears*
55/02 **Aerials** *System Of A Down*
49A/96 **Aeroplane** *Red Hot Chili Peppers*
9/83 **Affair Of The Heart** *Rick Springfield*
16/57 **Affair To Remember (Our Love Affair)** *Vic Damone*
1/83 **Africa** *Toto*
41/61 **African Waltz** *Cannonball Adderley*
Africanism ..see: Gimme Some Lovin'
42/62 **Afrikaan Beat** *Bert Kaempfert*
57/94 **Afro Puffs** *Lady Of Rage*
49/72 **Afro-Strut** *Nite-Liters*

AFTER:

6/89 **After All** *Cher & Peter Cetera*
69/84 **After All** *Al Jarreau*
71/72 **After All This Time** *Merry Clayton*
48/83 **After I Cry Tonight** *Lanier & Co.*
95/65 **After Loving You** *Della Reese*
After Midnight
18/70 *Eric Clapton*
42/72 *J.J. Cale*
97/74 *Maggie Bell*
44/01 **After Party** *Koffee Brown*
32/57 **After School** *Randy Starr*
92/56 **After School** *Tommy Charles*
74/76 **After The Dance** *Marvin Gaye*
23/83 **After The Fall** *Journey*
89/70 **After The Feeling Is Gone** *Five Flights Up*
48/85 **After The Fire** *Roger Daltrey*
56/71 **After The Fire Is Gone** *Conway Twitty/Loretta Lynn*
32/82 **After The Glitter Fades** *Stevie Nicks*
22/74 **After The Goldrush** *Prelude*
10/56 **After The Lights Go Down Low** *Al Hibbler*
2/79 **After The Love Has Gone** *Earth, Wind & Fire*
8/77 **After The Lovin'** *Engelbert Humperdinck*
6/91 **After The Rain** *Nelson*
41/91 **After The Summer's Gone** *PC Quest*
51/97 **After 12, Before 6** *Sam Salter*
65/80 **After You** *Dionne Warwick*
1/76 **Afternoon Delight** *Starland Vocal Band*
66/94 **Afternoons & Coffeespoons** *Crash Test Dummies*
1/93 **Again** *Janet Jackson*
4/01 **Again** *Lenny Kravitz*
36/92 **Again Tonight** *John Mellencamp*
1/84 **Against All Odds (Take A Look At Me Now)** *Phil Collins*
5/80 **Against The Wind** *Bob Seger*
75/95 **Age Ain't Nothing But A Number** *Aaliyah*
47/61 **Age For Love** *Jimmy Charles*
21/65 **Agent Double-O-Soul** *Edwin Starr*
36/75 **Agony And The Ecstasy** *Smokey Robinson*
29/81 **Ah! Leah!** *Donnie Iris*
5/62 **Ahab, The Arab** *Ray Stevens*
20S/02 **Ahh!! Dee!! Ahh!!** *Sandman*
28/81 **Ai No Corrida** *Quincy Jones*
67/81 **Aiming At Your Heart** *Temptations*

AIN'T:

49/64 **Ain't Doing Too Bad** *Bobby Bland*
17/81 **Ain't Even Done With The Night** *John Cougar*
74/60 **Ain't Gonna Be That Way** *Marv Johnson*
12/77 **Ain't Gonna Bump No More (With No Big Fat Woman)** *Joe Tex*
77/66 **Ain't Gonna Cry No More** *Brenda Lee*
Ain't Gonna Eat Out My Heart Anymore ..see: I Ain't Gonna
Ain't Gonna' Hurt Nobody
92/78 *Brick*
51/92 *Kid 'N Play*
81/63 **Ain't Gonna Kiss Ya** *Ribbons*
39/66 **Ain't Gonna Lie** *Keith*
87/67 **Ain't Gonna Rest (Till I Get You)** *Five Stairsteps*
53/64 **Ain't Gonna Tell Anybody** *Jimmy Gilmer/Fireballs*
Ain't Got No Home
20/57 *Clarence "Frog Man" Henry*
73/73 *Band*
94/69 **Ain't Got No; I Got Life** *Nina Simone*
30A/94 **Ain't Got Nothing If You Ain't Got Love** *Michael Bolton*
53/71 **Ain't Got Time** *Impressions*
66/71 **Ain't It A Sad Thing** *R. Dean Taylor*
91/65 **Ain't It A Shame** *Major Lance*
(also see: Ain't That A Shame)
49/61 **Ain't It, Baby** *Miracles*
24/70 **Ain't It Funky Now** *James Brown*
1/02 **Ain't It Funny** *Jennifer Lopez*
45/64 **Ain't It The Truth** *Mary Wells*
40/65 **Ain't It True** *Andy Williams*
22/79 **Ain't Love A Bitch** *Rod Stewart*
66/92 **Ain't No Future In Yo' Frontin'** *M.C. Breed & DFC*
91/74 **Ain't No Love In The Heart Of The City** *Bobby Bland*
Ain't No Mountain High Enough
19/67 *Marvin Gaye & Tammi Terrell*
1/70 *Diana Ross*
50/96 **Ain't No Nigga** *Jay-Z*
73/96 **Ain't No Playa Like...** *Rappin' 4-Tay*
13/79 **Ain't No Stoppin' Us Now** *McFadden & Whitehead*
Ain't No Sunshine
3/71 *Bill Withers*
95/92 *Kid Frost*
93/65 **Ain't No Telling** *Bobby Bland*
16/68 **Ain't No Way** *Aretha Franklin*
8/75 **Ain't No Way To Treat A Lady** *Helen Reddy*
4/73 **Ain't No Woman (Like The One I've Got)** *Four Tops*
Ain't Nobody
22/83 *Rufus & Chaka Khan*
94/96 *Diana King*
46/97 *LL Cool J*
67/96 **Ain't Nobody** *Faith Evans*
F/96 **Ain't Nobody** *Monica*
Ain't Nobody Home
63/66 *Howard Tate*
46/72 *B.B. King*
84/92 **Ain't Nobody Like You** *Miki Howard*
21S/02 **Ain't Nobody (We Got It Locked!)** *Rawlo Boys*
Ain't Nothin' ..also see: Ain't Nuthin' / T'ain't Nothin'
87/68 **Ain't Nothin' But A House Party** *Show Stoppers*
42/86 **Ain't Nothin' Goin' On But The Rent** *Gwen Guthrie*
25/01 **Ain't Nothing 'Bout You** *Brooks & Dunn*
43/78 **Ain't Nothing Gonna Keep Me From You** *Teri DeSario*

Ain't Nothing Like The Real Thing
8/68 *Marvin Gaye & Tammi Terrell*
47/74 *Aretha Franklin*
21/77 *Donny & Marie Osmond*
88/82 *Chris Christian with Amy Holland (medley)*
20/64 **Ain't Nothing You Can Do** *Bobby Bland*
38/95 **Ain't Nuthin' But A She Thing** *Salt-N-Pepa*
83/94 **Ain't Seen Love Like That** *Mr. Big*
19/64 **Ain't She Sweet** *Beatles*
51/87 **Ain't So Easy** *David & David*
42/66 **Ain't That A Groove** *James Brown*
Ain't That A Shame
1/55 *Pat Boone*
10/55 *Fats Domino*
22/63 *4 Seasons*
35/79 *Cheap Trick*
89/79 **Ain't That Enough For You** *John Davis*
33/61 **Ain't That Just Like A Woman** *Fats Domino*
61/64 **Ain't That Just Like Me** *Searchers*
63/98 **Ain't That Just The Way** *Lutricia McNeal*
58S/93 **Ain't That Lonely Yet** *Dwight Yoakam*
93/65 **Ain't That Love** *Four Tops*
86/62 **Ain't That Loving You** *Bobby Bland*
16/64 **Ain't That Loving You Baby** *Elvis Presley*
Ain't That Loving You (For More Reasons Than One)
45/70 *Luther Ingram*
86/72 *Isaac Hayes & David Porter*
Ain't That Peculiar
8/65 *Marvin Gaye*
85/72 *Fanny*
44/75 *Diamond Reo*
6/92 **Ain't 2 Proud 2 Beg** *TLC*
Ain't Too Proud To Beg
13/66 *Temptations*
17/74 *Rolling Stones*
89/89 *Rick Astley*
21/72 **Ain't Understanding Mellow** *Jerry Butler & Brenda Lee Eager*
77/72 **Ain't Wastin' Time No More** *Allman Brothers Band*
81/74 **Air Disaster** *Albert Hammond*
3/03 **Air Force Ones** *Nelly*
6/74 **Air That I Breathe** *Hollies*
99/62 **Air Travel** *Ray & Bob*
46/67 **Airplane Song (My Airplane)** *Royal Guardsmen*
31/70 **Airport Love Theme** *Vincent Bell*
68/72 **Ajax Airlines** *Hudson & Landry*
43/71 **Ajax Liquor Store** *Hudson & Landry*
Al Di La'
6/62 *Emilio Pericoli*
90/63 *Connie Francis*
29/64 *Ray Charles Singers*
57/65 **Al's Place** *Al Hirt*
Alabam
47/60 *Pat Boone*
63/60 *Cowboy Copas*
68/80 **Alabama Getaway** *Grateful Dead*
14/55 **Alabama Jubilee** *Ferko String Band*
62/72 **Alabama Wild Man** *Jerry Reed*
92/62 **Aladdin** *Bobby Curtola*
(Aladdin's Theme) ..see: Whole New World

Alamo ..see: Ballad Of The
70S/02 **Alaska** *Fairweather*
29/71 **Albert Flasher** *Guess Who*
Alfie
32/66 *Cher*
95/66 *Cilla Black*
15/67 *Dionne Warwick*
66/68 *Eivets Rednow (Stevie Wonder)*
29/84 **Alibis** *Sergio Mendes*
72/93 **Alibis** *Tracy Lawrence*
17/63 **Alice In Wonderland** *Neil Sedaka*
27/68 **Alice Long (You're Still My Favorite Girlfriend)** *Tommy Boyce & Bobby Hart*
97/69 **Alice's Rock & Roll Restaurant** *Arlo Guthrie*
29/81 **Alien** *Atlanta Rhythm Section*
97/59 **Alimony** *Frankie Ford*
34/72 **Alive** *Bee Gees*
41/02 **Alive** *P.O.D.*
14/78 **Alive Again** *Chicago*
3/85 **Alive & Kicking** *Simple Minds*

ALL:

35/67 **All** *James Darren*
50/63 **All About My Girl** *Jimmy McGriff*
29/93 **All About Soul** *Billy Joel*
96/91 **All About You** *Pretty In Pink*
3/62 **All Alone Am I** *Brenda Lee*
83/92 **All Alone On Christmas** *Darlene Love*
70/96 **All Along** *Blessid Union Of Souls*
20/68 **All Along The Watchtower** *Jimi Hendrix Experience*
2/59 **All American Boy** *Bill Parsons*
79/81 **All American Girls** *Sister Sledge*
45A/94 **All Apologies** *Nirvana*
3/90 **All Around The World** *Lisa Stansfield*
11/56 **All At Once You Love Her** *Perry Como*
All By Myself
2/76 *Eric Carmen*
4/97 *Celine Dion*
All Cried Out
8/86 *Lisa Lisa & Cult Jam*
72/96 *Denine*
4/97 *Allure*
41/64 **All Cried Out** *Dusty Springfield*
7/65 **All Day And All Of The Night** *Kinks*
35/71 **All Day Music** *War*
69/02 **All Eyez On Me** *Monica*
65/85 **All Fall Down** *Five Star*
19/88 **All Fired Up** *Pat Benatar*
1/92 **All 4 Love** *Color Me Badd*
1/94 **All For Love** *Bryan Adams/Rod Stewart/Sting*
1/01 **All For You** *Janet Jackson*
11/97 **All For You** *Sister Hazel*
95/69 **All God's Children Got Soul** *Dorothy Morrison*
96/00 **All Good?** *De La Soul*
98/64 **All Grown Up** *Crystals*
92/72 **All His Children** *Charley Pride with Henry Mancini*
33/60 **All I Could Do Was Cry** *Etta James*
47/98 **All I Do** *Somethin' For The People*
47/90 **All I Do Is Think Of You** *Troop*
7/71 **All I Ever Need Is You** *Sonny & Chér*
1/03 **All I Have** *Jennifer Lopez*
56/71 **All I Have** *Moments*

All I Have To Do Is Dream
1/58 *Everly Brothers*
96/61 *Everly Brothers*
14/63 *Richard Chamberlain*
27/70 *Bobbie Gentry & Glen Campbell*
66/75 *Nitty Gritty Dirt Band*
51/81 *Andy Gibb & Victoria Principal*
5/99 **All I Have To Give** *Backstreet Boys*
91/69 **All I Have To Offer You (Is Me)** *Charley Pride*
9/73 **All I Know** *Garfunkel*
52S/99 **All I Know** *Rahzel*
62A/96 **All I Know** *Screaming Trees*
93/87 **All I Know Is The Way I Feel** *Pointer Sisters*
2/85 **All I Need** *Jack Wagner*
8/67 **All I Need** *Temptations*
5/86 **All I Need Is A Miracle** *Mike + The Mechanics*
61/73 **All I Need Is Time** *Gladys Knight*
46/91 **All I Need Is You** *Blue Train*
All I Need To Know ..see: Don't Know Much
65A/95 **All I Really Want** *Alanis Morissette*
All I Really Want To Do
15/65 *Chér*
40/65 *Byrds*
66/96 **All I See** *A+*
72S/93 **All I See** *Christopher Williams*
20/66 **All I See Is You** *Dusty Springfield*
41/78 **All I See Is Your Face** *Dan Hill*
2/94 **All I Wanna Do** *Sheryl Crow*
55S/01 **All I Wanna Do** *Young Millionaires*
2/90 **All I Wanna Do Is Make Love To You** *Heart*
15/92 **All I Want** *Toad The Wet Sprocket*
35/97 **All I Want** *702*
65A/97 **All I Want** *Offspring*
76/87 **All I Want** *Howard Jones*
77/97 **All I Want** *Susanna Hoffs*
11X/66 **All I Want For Christmas Is You** *Carla Thomas*
All I Want For Christmas Is You
12A/94 *Mariah Carey*
35A/95 *Mariah Carey*
35A/96 *Mariah Carey*
83/99 *Mariah Carey*
54/88 **All I Want Is You** *Carly Simon*
All I Want Is You
83/89 *U2*
50A/94 *U2*
19/87 **All I Wanted** *Kansas*
32/90 **All I'm Missing Is You** *Glenn Medeiros*
63/74 **All In Love Is Fair** *Barbra Streisand*
19/61 **All In My Mind** *Maxine Brown*
76/90 **All Lips N' Hips** *Electric Boys*
36A/97 **All Mixed Up** *311*
93/71 **All My Hard Times** *Joe Simon*
1/98 **All My Life** *K-Ci & JoJo*
11/90 **All My Life** *Linda Ronstadt/Aaron Neville*
37/83 **All My Life** *Kenny Rogers*
43/02 **All My Life** *Foo Fighters*
28/98 **All My Love** *Queen Pen*
(also see: You Were Made For)
All My Loving
45/64 *Beatles*
93/64 *Hollyridge Strings*
42S/01 **All My Thugs** *Young Phantom*
All My Trials
89/64 *Dick & DeeDee*
70/71 *Ray Stevens*

64/99 **All N My Grill** *Missy "Misdemeanor" Elliott*
9/99 **All Night Long** *Faith Evans*
19/80 **All Night Long** *Joe Walsh*
47S/01 **All Night Long** *Montgomery Gentry*
75/62 **All Night Long** *Sandy Nelson*
75/84 **All Night Long** *Billy Squier*
99/56 **All Night Long** *Jo Stafford*
(also see: Touch Me)
1/83 **All Night Long (All Night)** *Lionel Richie*
45/80 **All Night Thing** *Invisible Man's Band*
69/82 **All Night With Me** *Laura Branigan*
71/90 **All Nite** *Entouch*
(All of a Sudden) My Heart Sings
15/59 *Paul Anka*
38/65 *Mel Carter*
70/61 **All Of Everything** *Frankie Avalon*
51/85 **All Of Me For All Of You** *9.9*
65/97 **All Of My Days** *Changing Faces*
71/65 **All Of My Life** *Lesley Gore*
77/82 **All Of My Love** *Bobby Caldwell*
19/84 **All Of You** *Julio Iglesias & Diana Ross*
3/01 **All Or Nothing** *O-Town*
4/90 **All Or Nothing** *Milli Vanilli*
38S/99 **All Or Nothing** *Cher*
68/66 **All Or Nothing** *Patti LaBelle*
28/82 **All Our Tomorrows** *Eddie Schwartz*
2/80 **All Out Of Love** *Air Supply*
38/58 **All Over Again** *Johnny Cash*
13/80 **All Over The World** *Electric Light Orchestra*
42/63 **All Over The World** *Nat King Cole*
33A/95 **All Over You** *Live*
12/83 **All Right** *Christopher Cross*
(also see: Alright)
All Right Now
4/70 *Free*
92/75 *Lea Roberts*
72/85 *Rod Stewart*
66/88 *Pepsi & Shirlie*
97/76 **All Roads (Lead Back To You)** *Donny Most*
22/89 **All She Wants Is** *Duran Duran*
9/85 **All She Wants To Do Is Dance** *Don Henley*
58/92 **All She Wrote** *Firehouse*
All Shook Up
1/57 *Elvis Presley*
85/74 *Suzi Quatro*
92/92 *Billy Joel*
4/99 **All Star** *Smash Mouth*
All Strung Out
26/66 *Nino Tempo & April Stevens*
34/77 *John Travolta*
49/90 **All That Glitters Isn't Gold** *Cover Girls*
41/66 **All That I Am** *Elvis Presley*
44/99 **All That I Can Say** *Mary J. Blige*
2/93 **All That She Wants** *Ace Of Base*
94/77 **All The Kids On The Street** *Hollywood Stars*
26/72 **All The King's Horses** *Aretha Franklin*
61/86 **All The Kings Horses** *Firm*
63/60 **All The Love I've Got** *Marv Johnson*
19/86 **All The Love In The World** *Outfield*
1/91 **All The Man That I Need** *Whitney Houston*
26/98 **All The Places (I Will Kiss You)** *Aaron Hall*
85/83 **All The Right Moves** *Jennifer Warnes/Chris Thompson*
6/00 **All The Small Things** *Blink 182*
28/86 **All The Things She Said** *Simple Minds*
11/96 **All The Things (Your Man Won't Do)** *Joe*
21/58 **All The Time** *Johnny Mathis*
54/79 **All The Time In The World** *Dr. Hook*
2/58 **All The Way** *Frank Sinatra*
63/90 **All The Way** *Calloway*
63/56 **All The Way 'Round The World** *Mills Brothers*
37/72 **All The Young Dudes** *Mott The Hoople*
97/66 **All These Things** *Uniques*
78/79 **All Things Are Possible** *Dan Peek*
55/99 **All Things Considered** *Yankee Grey*
17/83 **All This Love** *DeBarge*
5/91 **All This Time** *Sting*
6/89 **All This Time** *Tiffany*
41/83 **All Those Lies** *Glenn Frey*
2/81 **All Those Years Ago** *George Harrison*
5/84 **All Through The Night** *Cyndi Lauper*
80/91 **All Through The Night** *Tone Loc*
36/83 **All Time High** *Rita Coolidge*
58/83 **All Touch** *Rough Trade*
43/91 **All True Man** *Alexander O'Neal*
56/92 **All Woman** *Lisa Stansfield*
35/77 **All You Get From Love Is A Love Song** *Carpenters*
1/67 **All You Need Is Love** *Beatles*
6/02 **All You Wanted** *Michelle Branch*
58/85 **All You Zombies** *Hooters*
56/92 **All You've Got** *RTZ*
80/67 **All Your Goodies Are Gone (The Loser's Seat)** *Parliaments*
2/56 **Allegheny Moon** *Patti Page*
17/83 **Allentown** *Billy Joel*
44/83 **Allergies** *Paul Simon*
Alley Cat
7/62 *Bent Fabric*
76/62 *David Thorne*
Alley-Oop
1/60 *Hollywood Argyles*
15/60 *Danté & the Evergreens*
59/60 *Dyna-Sores*
83/83 **Allies** *Heart*
93/67 **Alligator Bogaloo** *Lou Donaldson*
24A/94 **Allison Road** *Gin Blossoms*
54/84 **Allnighter, The** *Glenn Frey*
61/63 **Ally Ally Oxen Free** *Kingston Trio*
16/99 **Almost Doesn't Count** *Brandy*
32/59 **Almost Grown** *Chuck Berry*
50/90 **Almost Hear You Sigh** *Rolling Stones*
85/99 **Almost Home** *Mary Chapin Carpenter*
95/68 **Almost In Love** *Elvis Presley*
78/58 **Almost In Your Arms** *Johnny Nash*
32/78 **Almost Like Being In Love** *Michael Johnson*
25/84 **Almost Over You** *Sheena Easton*
Almost Paradise
15/57 *Roger Williams*
31/57 *Lou Stein*
56/57 *Norman Petty Trio*
7/84 **Almost Paradise...Love Theme From Footloose** *Mike Reno & Ann Wilson*
Almost Persuaded
24/66 *David Houston*
58/66 *Ben Colder*
79/69 *Etta James*
Almost Saturday Night
78/75 *John Fogerty*
54/81 *Dave Edmunds*
28/78 **Almost Summer** *Celebration*
27S/02 **Almost There** *Gabbie Nolen*
67/64 **Almost There** *Andy Williams*
94/93 **Almost Unreal** *Roxette*
1/87 **Alone** *Heart*
28/97 **Alone** *Bee Gees*
64/85 **Alone Again** *Dokken*
1/72 **Alone Again (Naturally)** *Gilbert O'Sullivan*
99/70 **Alone Again Or** *Love*
8/60 **Alone At Last** *Jackie Wilson*
Alone (Why Must I Be Alone)
18/57 *Shepherd Sisters*
28/64 *Four Seasons*
48/64 **Alone With You** *Brenda Lee*
51/58 **Alone With You** *Faron Young*
72/92 **Alone With You** *Tevin Campbell*
Along Came Jones
9/59 *Coasters*
27/69 *Ray Stevens*
14/85 **Along Comes A Woman** *Chicago*
Along Comes Mary
7/66 *Association*
96/67 *Baja Marimba Band*
8/88 **Alphabet St.** *Prince*
32/74 **Already Gone** *Eagles*
75/95 **Already Missing You** *Gerald & Eddie Levert, Sr.*
4/90 **Alright** *Janet Jackson*
19/93 **Alright** *Kris Kross*
78/97 **Alright** *Jamiroquai*
91/70 **Alright In The City** *Dunn & McCashen*
68/59 **Alright, Okay, You Win** *Peggy Lee*
Also Sprach Zarathustra (2001)
90/70 *Berlin Philharmonic*
2/73 *Deodato*
95/60 **Alvin For President** *David Seville/The Chipmunks*
74/75 **Alvin Stone (The Birth & Death Of A Gangster)** *Fantastic Four*
40/62 **Alvin Twist** *David Seville/The Chipmunks*
74/66 **Alvin's Boo-Ga-Loo** *Alvin Cash*
Alvin's Harmonica
3/59 *David Seville/The Chipmunks*
73/61 *David Seville/The Chipmunks*
87/62 *David Seville/The Chipmunks*
33/60 **Alvin's Orchestra** *David Seville/The Chipmunks*

ALWAYS:

1/87 **Always** *Atlantic Starr*
4/94 **Always** *Bon Jovi*
19/59 **Always** *Sammy Turner*
20/94 **Always** *Erasure*
51/03 **Always** *Saliva*
59/83 **Always** *Firefall*
64/73 **Always** *Luther Ingram*
Always And Forever
18/78 *Heatwave*
35/90 *Whistle*
58/95 *Luther Vandross*
1/96 **Always Be My Baby** *Mariah Carey*
20/94 **Always In My Heart** *Tevin Campbell*
82/64 **Always In My Heart** *Los Indios Tabajaras*
56/60 **Always It's You** *Everly Brothers*

Always On My Mind
5/82 *Willie Nelson*
4/88 *Pet Shop Boys*
54/94 **Always On My Mind** *SWV*
1/02 **Always On Time** *Ja Rule*
Always Something There To Remind Me ..see: (There's)
30/92 **Always The Last To Know** *Del Amitri*
71/88 **Always There For You** *Stryper*
18/68 **Always Together** *Dells*
33/64 **Always Together** *Al Martino*
81/92 **Always Tomorrow** *Gloria Estefan*
31^{S}/99 **Always You** *Jennifer Paige*
79/73 **Am I Black Enough For You** *Billy Paul*
31/98 **Am I Dreaming** *Ol' Skool*
90/86 **Am I Forgiven** *Isle Of Man*
71/67 **Am I Grooving You** *Freddie Scott*
31/60 **Am I Losing You** *Jim Reeves*
59/72 **Am I Losing You** *Partridge Family*
Am I That Easy To Forget
25/60 *Debbie Reynolds*
18/68 *Engelbert Humperdinck*
32/60 **Am I The Man** *Jackie Wilson*
Am I The Same Girl
79/69 *Barbara Acklin*
45/92 *Swing Out Sister*
(also see: Soulful Strut)
83/94 **Am I Wrong** *Love Spit Love*
1/86 **Amanda** *Boston*
54/79 **Amanda** *Waylon Jennings*
83/71 **Amanda** *Dionne Warwicke*
63/60 **Amapola** *Jacky Noguez*
44/77 **Amarillo** *Neil Sedaka*
1/00 **Amazed** *Lonestar*
24/94 **Amazing** *Aerosmith*
Amazing Grace
15/71 *Judy Collins*
11/72 *Royal Scots Dragoon Guards*
72/76 **Amazing Grace (Used To Be Her Favorite Song)** *Amazing Rhythm Aces*
75/76 **Amber Cascades** *America*
52/59 **Ambrose** *Linda Laurie*
37/68 **Ame Caline (Soul Coaxing)** *Raymond Lefevre*
Amen
7/65 *Impressions*
36/68 *Otis Redding*

AMERICA:

8/81 **America** *Neil Diamond*
America
46/72 *Yes*
97/72 *Simon & Garfunkel*
46/85 **America** *Prince*
45/70 **America, Communicate With Me** *Ray Stevens*
52/68 **America Is My Home** *James Brown*
83/70 **America/Standing** *Five Stairsteps*
6^{S}/01 **America The Beautiful** *Elvis Presley*
10^{S}/01 **America Will Always Stand** *Randy Travis*
59/68 **American Boys** *Petula Clark*
48/02 **American Child** *Phil Vassar*
27/72 **American City Suite** *Cashman & West*
13/80 **American Dream** *Dirt Band*
91/87 **American Dream** *Simon F.*
98/74 **American Girls** *Rick Springfield*
17/82 **American Heartbeat** *Survivor*
72/83 **American Made** *Oak Ridge Boys*
80/81 **American Memories** *Shamus M'Cool*
16/82 **American Music** *Pointer Sisters*
79/72 **Amerikan Music** *Steve Alaimo*
American Pie
1/72 *Don McLean*
29/00 *Madonna*
13/86 **American Storm** *Bob Seger*
American Trilogy
26/72 *Mickey Newbury*
66/72 *Elvis Presley*
35/74 **American Tune** *Paul Simon*
American Woman
1/70 *Guess Who*
49/99 *Lenny Kravitz*
Americans
4/74 *Byron MacGregor*
24/74 *Gordon Sinclair*
90/74 *Tex Ritter*
27/75 **Amie** *Pure Prairie League*
53/96 **Amish Paradise** *"Weird Al" Yankovic*
60^{A}/98 **Amnesia** *Chumbawamba*
73/84 **Amnesia** *Shalamar*
7/59 **Among My Souvenirs** *Connie Francis*
Amor
18/61 *Ben E. King*
88/62 *Roger Williams*
(Amos & Andy Song) ..see: Like A Sunday In Salem
8/71 **Amos Moses** *Jerry Reed*
38/55 **Amukiriki (The Lord Willing)** *Les Paul & Mary Ford*
65/63 **Amy** *Paul Petersen*
(also see: Ame / Amie)
77/64 **Anaheim, Azusa & Cucamonga Sewing Circle, Book Review And Timing Association** *Jan & Dean*
37/57 **Anastasia** *Pat Boone*
66/89 **Anchorage** *Michelle Shocked*

AND:

22/67 **And Get Away** *Esquires*
And I Am Telling You I'm Not Going
22/82 *Jennifer Holliday*
66^{S}/01 *Rosabel with Jennifer Holliday*
And I Love Her (Him)
12/64 *Beatles*
54/65 *Esther Phillips*
And I Love You So
83/71 *Bobby Goldsboro*
29/73 *Perry Como*
59/81 **And Love Goes On** *Earth, Wind & Fire*
64/70 **And My Heart Sang (Tra La La)** *Brenda & The Tabulations*
69/60 **And Now** *Della Reese*
F/94 **And On And On** *Janet Jackson*
21/94 **And Our Feelings** *Babyface*
36/65 **And Roses And Roses** *Andy Williams*
54/85 **And She Was** *Talking Heads*
97/69 **And She's Mine** *Spanky & Our Gang*
37/90 **And So It Goes** *Billy Joel*
45/68 **And Suddenly** *Cherry People*
And That Reminds Me
9/57 *Kay Starr*
12/57 *Della Reese*
45/69 *4 Seasons*
70/56 **And The Angels Sing** *Three Chuckles*
19/80 **And The Beat Goes On** *Whispers*
55/80 **And The Cradle Will Rock...** *Van Halen*
44/70 **And The Grass Won't Pay No Mind** *Mark Lindsay*
84/61 **And The Heavens Cried** *Ronnie Savoy*
75/89 **And The Night Stood Still** *Dion*
65/62 **And Then There Were Drums** *Sandy Nelson*
21/85 **And We Danced** *Hooters*
2/69 **And When I Die** *Blood, Sweat & Tears*
42/72 **And You And I** *Yes*
69^{S}/00 **And You Know That** *D-Don*
41/66 **Andrea** *Sunrays*
63^{A}/96 **Aneurysm** *Nirvana*

ANGEL:

1/01 **Angel** *Shaggy*
3/88 **Angel** *Aerosmith*
4/99 **Angel** *Sarah McLachlan*
5/85 **Angel** *Madonna*
18/93 **Angel** *Jon Secada*
20/73 **Angel** *Aretha Franklin*
40/72 **Angel** *Rod Stewart*
51/65 **Angel** *Johnny Tillotson*
70/01 **Angel** *Lionel Richie*
Angel Baby
5/61 *Rosie & The Originals*
29/92 *Angelica*
30/58 **Angel Baby** *Dean Martin*
57/71 **Angel Baby** *Dusk*
5/89 **Angel Eyes** *Jeff Healey Band*
(also see: I'll Never Let You Go)
64/79 **Angeleyes** *Abba*
47/59 **Angel Face** *Jimmy Darren*
40/82 **Angel In Blue** *J. Geils Band*
72/99 **Angel In Disguise** *Brandy*
92/86 **Angel In My Pocket** *One To One*
6/77 **Angel In Your Arms** *Hot*
14/89 **Angel Of Harlem** *U2*
1/99 **Angel Of Mine** *Monica*
Angel Of The Morning
7/68 *Merrilee Rush*
4/81 *Juice Newton*
22/61 **Angel On My Shoulder** *Shelby Flint*
81/56 **Angel Pie (Postillon!)** *Peggy King*
38/80 **Angel Say No** *Tommy Tutone*
33/58 **Angel Smile** *Nat "King" Cole*
30/89 **Angel Song** *Great White*
(also see: Fly)
79/75 **Angel (What In The World's Come Over Us)** *Atlanta Rhythm Section*
27/60 **Angela Jones** *Johnny Ferguson*
4/89 **Angelia** *Richard Marx*
97/70 **Angelica** *Oliver*
58/80 **Angeline** *Allman Brothers Band*
67/96 **Angeline Is Coming Home** *Badlees*
43/64 **Angelito** *Rene & Rene*
53/00 **Angels** *Robbie Williams*
11/56 **Angels In The Sky** *Crew Cuts*
73/01 **Angels In Waiting** *Tammy Cochran*
22/59 **Angels Listened In** *Crests*
45^{A}/96 **Angels Of The Silences** *Counting Crows*
51/99 **Angels Would Fall** *Melissa Etheridge*
1/73 **Angie** *Rolling Stones*
(also see: Different Worlds)
1/74 **Angie Baby** *Helen Reddy*
70/57 **Angry** *Frank Pizani*
38/01 **Angry All The Time** *Tim McGraw*
60^{A}/96 **Angry Johnny** *Poe*
(Angry Young Man) ..see: Fooling Yourself
19/87 **Animal** *Def Leppard*
73/79 **Animal House** *Stephen Bishop*

43/85 **Animal Instinct** *Commodores*
19/99 **Animal Song** *Savage Garden*
76/71 **Animal Trainer And The Toad** *Mountain*
97/70 **Animal Zoo** *Spirit*
86/63 **Ann-Marie** *Belmonts*
54/61 **Anna** *Jorgen Ingmann*
68/62 **Anna (Go To Him)** *Arthur Alexander*
93/58 **Anna Marie** *Jim Reeves*
46/71 **Annabella** *Hamilton, Joe Frank & Reynolds*
86/72 **Annabelle** *Daniel Boone*
47/65 **Annie Fanny** *Kingsmen*
51/62 **Annie Get Your Yo-Yo** *Little Junior Parker*
1/74 **Annie's Song** *John Denver*
10/93 **Anniversary** *Tony Toni Tone*
89/61 **Anniversary Of Love** *Caslons*

ANOTHER:

1/80 **Another Brick In The Wall** *Pink Floyd*
47/64 **Another Cup Of Coffee** *Brook Benton*
5/71 **Another Day** *Paul McCartney*
45/67 **Another Day, Another Heartache** *5th Dimension*
1/89 **Another Day In Paradise** *Phil Collins*
27/00 **Another Dumb Blonde** *Hoku*
52/86 **Another Heartache** *Rod Stewart*
66/91 **Another Like My Lover** *Jasmine Guy*
5X/84 **Another Lonely Christmas** *Prince*
13/88 **Another Lover** *Giant Steps*
75/92 **Another Minute** *Cause & Effect*
3/94 **Another Night** *Real McCoy*
22/86 **Another Night** *Aretha Franklin*
49/67 **Another Night** *Dionne Warwick*
Another Night
71/75 *Hollies*
94/79 *Wilson Bros.*
74/00 **Another Nine Minutes** *Yankee Grey*
1/80 **Another One Bites The Dust** *Queen*
32/74 **Another Park, Another Sunday** *Doobie Brothers*
11/88 **Another Part Of Me** *Michael Jackson*
97/68 **Another Place Another Time** *Jerry Lee Lewis*
65/72 **Another Puff** *Jerry Reed*
32/76 **Another Rainy Day In New York City** *Chicago*
7/93 **Another Sad Love Song** *Toni Braxton*
Another Saturday Night
10/63 *Sam Cooke*
6/74 *Cat Stevens*
22/60 **Another Sleepless Night** *Jimmy Clanton*
44/82 **Another Sleepless Night** *Anne Murray*
67/91 **Another Sleepless Night** *Shawn Christopher*
Another Somebody Done Somebody Wrong Song ..see: (Hey Won't You Play)
32/77 **Another Star** *Stevie Wonder*
78/81 **Another Ticket** *Eric Clapton*
20/58 **Another Time, Another Place** *Patti Page*
43/71 **Another Time, Another Place** *Engelbert Humperdinck*
100/99 **Another Way** *Tevin Campbell*
91/97 **Another You, Another Me** *Brady Seals*
63/86 **Anotherloverholenyohead** *Prince*
71/59 **Answer To A Maiden's Prayer** *June Valli*
89/66 **Answer To My Prayer** *Neil Sedaka*
32/80 **Answering Machine** *Rupert Holmes*
65S/95 **Answering Service** *Gerald Levert*
63S/01 **Ante Up (Remix)** *M.O.P.*
65/73 **Anthem** *Wayne Newton*
75S/99 **Anthem, The** *Sway & King Tech*
60/59 **Anthony Boy** *Chuck Berry*
(Anthony's Song) ..see: Movin' Out
13/72 **Anticipation** *Carly Simon*
83/63 **Antony And Cleopatra Theme** *Ferrante & Teicher*
21A/95 **Ants Marching** *Dave Matthews Band*

ANY:

Any Day Now
23/62 *Chuck Jackson*
86/69 *Percy Sledge*
14/82 *Ronnie Milsap*
44/88 **Any Love** *Luther Vandross*
31/95 **Any Man Of Mine** *Shania Twain*
Any Number Can Win ..see: Theme From
72/02 **Any Other Night** *Sharissa*
81/63 **Any Other Way** *Chuck Jackson*
(also see: If There Was)
Any Time ..also see: Anytime
2/94 **Any Time, Any Place** *Janet Jackson*
Any Way ..also see: Anyway
79/78 **(Any Way That You Want It) I'll Be There** *Starz*
Any Way That You Want Me
98/66 *Liverpool Five*
88/68 *American Breed*
53/69 *Evie Sands*
14/65 **Any Way You Want It** *Dave Clark Five*
23/80 **Any Way You Want It** *Journey*
72/77 **Any Way You Want Me** *Sylvers*
31/61 **Anybody But Me** *Brenda Lee*
31/60 **Anymore** *Teresa Brewer*
42/82 **Anyone Can See** *Irene Cara*
37/99 **Anyone Else** *Collin Raye*
64/68 **Anyone For Tennis** *Cream*
8/64 **Anyone Who Had A Heart** *Dionne Warwick*
52/64 **Anyone Who Knows What Love Is (will understand)** *Irma Thomas*
15/96 **Anything** *3T*
18/94 **Anything** *SWV*
28/02 **Anything** *Jaheim*
55/00 **Anything** *Jay-Z*
80/68 **Anything** *Animals*
49/92 **Anything At All** *Mitch Malloy*
49/99 **Anything But Down** *Sheryl Crow*
75/89 **Anything Can Happen** *Was (Not Was)*
1/88 **Anything For You** *Gloria Estefan*
43/67 **Anything Goes** *Harpers Bizarre*
29/90 **Anything I Want** *Kevin Paige*
26/91 **Anything Is Possible** *Debbie Gibson*
31/62 **Anything That's Part Of You** *Elvis Presley*
86/69 **Anything You Choose** *Spanky & Our Gang*
37/76 **Anything You Want** *John Valenti*
6A/98 **Anytime** *Brian McKnight*
69/90 **Anytime** *McAuley Schenker Group*
83/78 **Anytime** *Journey*
46/65 **Anytime At All** *Frank Sinatra*
Anytime (I'll Be There)
75/75 *Frank Sinatra*
33/76 *Paul Anka*
12/94 **Anytime You Need A Friend** *Mariah Carey*
28S/02 **Anyway (men are from mars)** *Amber*
50/60 **Anyway The Wind Blows** *Doris Day*
20/56 **Anyway You Want Me (That's How I Will Be)** *Elvis Presley*
15/99 **Anywhere** *112*
86/84 **Anywhere With You** *Rubber Rodeo*
Apache
2/61 *Jorgen Ingmann*
87/61 *Sonny James*
64/65 *Davie Allan ('65)*
53/82 *Sugar Hill Gang*
Apartment ..see: Theme From The
81/70 **Apartment 21** *Bobbie Gentry*
24/56 **Ape Call** *Nervous Norvus*
45/71 **Apeman** *Kinks*
79/68 **Apologize** *Ed Ames*
Apple Blossom Time ..see: (I'll Be With You In)
29/60 **Apple Green** *June Valli*
32/65 **Apple Of My Eye** *Roy Head*
75/65 **Apples And Bananas** *Lawrence Welk*
6/67 **Apples, Peaches, Pumpkin Pie** *Jay & The Techniques*
46/69 **Apricot Brandy** *Rhinoceros*
37/69 **April Fools** *Dionne Warwick*
April In Paris
28/56 *Count Basie*
97/56 *Modernaires*
1/57 **April Love** *Pat Boone*
89/79 **Aqua Boogie** *Parliament*
1/69 **Aquarius/Let The Sunshine In (The Flesh Failures)** *5th Dimension*
48/81 **Arc Of A Diver** *Steve Winwood*

ARE:

29/98 **Are U Still Down** *Jon B.*
96/02 **Are We Cuttin'** *Pastor Troy*
15/84 **Are We Ourselves?** *Fixx*
55/65 **Are You A Boy Or Are You A Girl** *Barbarians*
73/70 **Are You Getting Any Sunshine?** *Lou Christie*
65/83 **Are You Getting Enough Happiness** *Hot Chocolate*
39/69 **Are You Happy** *Jerry Butler*
13/98 **Are You Jimmy Ray?** *Jimmy Ray*
39/67 **Are You Lonely For Me** *Freddy Scott*
Are You Lonesome Tonight
65/59 *Jaye P. Morgan*
1/60 *Elvis Presley*
14/74 *Donny Osmond*
(also see: Yes, I'm Lonesome Tonight)
15/73 **Are You Man Enough** *Four Tops*
72/71 **Are You My Woman? (Tell Me So)** *Chi-Lites*
59/67 **Are You Never Coming Home** *Sandy Posey*
87/71 **Are You Old Enough** *Mark Lindsay*
14/70 **Are You Ready?** *Pacific Gas & Electric*
(also see: R U Ready)
63A/92 **Are You Ready To Fly?** *Rozalla*
10/58 **Are You Really Mine** *Jimmie Rodgers*

Are You Satisfied?
95/55 *Sheb Wooley*
11/56 *Rusty Draper*
78/56 *Toni Arden*
57/83 **Are You Serious** *Tyrone Davis*
Are You Sincere
3/58 *Andy Williams*
85/65 *Trini Lopez*
91/65 **Are You Still My Baby** *Shirelles*
41/88 **Are You Sure** *So*
60/75 **Are You Sure Hank Done It This Way** *Waylon Jennings*
4[A]/98 **Are You That Somebody?** *Aaliyah*
39/66 **Are You There (With Another Girl)** *Dionne Warwick*
24/01 **Area Codes** *Ludacris*
26/77 **Ariel** *Dean Friedman*
10/70 **Arizona** *Mark Lindsay*
3/89 **Armageddon It** *Def Leppard*
28/73 **Armed And Extremely Dangerous** *First Choice*
Armen's Theme
46/56 *Joe Reisman*
42/57 *David Seville*
55/63 *Bobby Vee (Yesterday And You)*
Arms Of Mary
81/76 *Sutherland Brothers & Quiver*
67/78 *Chilliwack*
36/89 **Arms Of Orion** *Prince with Sheena Easton*
7/98 **Arms Of The One Who Loves You** *Xscape*
74/69 **Armstrong** *John Stewart*
Around ..also see: Round
91/65 **Around The Corner** *Duprees*
9/91 **Around The Way Girl** *LL Cool J*
61/97 **Around The World** *Daft Punk*
Around The World In 80 Days
12/57 *Mantovani*
13/57 *Victor Young*
25/57 *Bing Crosby*
73/57 *McGuire Sisters*
28/01 **Around The World (La La La La La)** *ATC*
91/77 **Arrested For Driving While Blind** *ZZ Top*
Arrivederci, Roma
51/55 *Georgia Gibbs*
55/58 *Roger Williams*
97/58 *Mario Lanza*
80/57 **Arrow Of Love** *Six Teens*
29/79 **Arrow Through Me** *Wings*
83/75 **Art For Art's Sake** *10cc*
1/81 **Arthur's Theme (Best That You Can Do)** *Christopher Cross*
20/60 **Artificial Flowers** *Bobby Darin*
36/78 **As** *Stevie Wonder*
42[S]/01 **As I Come Back** *Busta Rhymes*
6/95 **As I Lay Me Down** *Sophie B. Hawkins*
10/61 **As If I Didn't Know** *Adam Wade*
51/75 **As Long As He Takes Care Of Home** *Candi Staton*
55/93 **As Long As I Can Dream** *Exposé*
47/63 **As Long As I Know He's Mine** *Marvelettes*
75/96 **As Long As It Matters** *Gin Blossoms*
59/63 **As Long As She Needs Me** *Sammy Davis Jr.*
43/89 **As Long As You Follow** *Fleetwood Mac*
4[A]/98 **As Long As You Love Me** *Backstreet Boys*

As Tears Go By
22/65 *Marianne Faithfull*
6/66 *Rolling Stones*
31/70 **As The Years Go By** *Mashmakhan*
As Time Goes By
43/59 *Johnny Nash*
86/73 *Nilsson*
12/64 **As Usual** *Brenda Lee*
As We Lay
23/87 *Shirley Murdock*
59/97 *Dana*
65/00 *Kelly Price*
36/96 **Ascension (Don't Ever Wonder)** *Maxwell*
96/77 **Ashes And Sand** *Johnny Rivers*
Ashes By Now
37/80 *Rodney Crowell*
45/01 *Lee Ann Womack*
52/73 **Ashes To Ashes** *5th Dimension*
55/66 **Ashes To Ashes** *Mindbenders*
8/61 **Asia Minor** *Kokomo*
12/64 **Ask Me** *Elvis Presley*
18/56 **Ask Me** *Nat "King" Cole*
52/74 **Ask Me** *Ecstasy, Passion & Pain*
75/63 **Ask Me** *Maxine Brown*
91/64 **Ask Me** *Inez Foxx*
40/71 **Ask Me No Questions** *B.B. King*
27/72 **Ask Me What You Want** *Millie Jackson*
19/95 **Ask Of You** *Raphael Saadiq*
24/65 **Ask The Lonely** *Four Tops*
91/75 **Astral Man** *Nektar*
19/61 **Astronaut, The** *Jose Jimenez*
47/61 **At Last** *Etta James*
56/79 **At Midnight** *T-Connection*
30/77 **At Midnight (My Love Will Lift You Up)** *Rufus, Feat. Chaka Khan*
At My Front Door
7/55 *Pat Boone*
17/55 *El Dorados*
56/60 *Dee Clark*
63/96 **At Night I Pray** *Wild Orchid*
3/75 **At Seventeen** *Janis Ian*
45/98 **At The Beginning** *Donna Lewis & Richard Marx*
43/65 **At The Club** *Drifters*
44/62 **At The Club** *Ray Charles*
(At The Copa) ..see: Copacabana
At The Hop
1/58 *Danny & The Juniors*
21/58 *Nick Todd*
18/66 **At The Scene** *Dave Clark Five*
97/63 **At The Shore** *Johnny Caswell*
78/99 **At The Stars** *Better Than Ezra*
83/68 **At The Top Of The Stairs** *Formations*
16/67 **At The Zoo** *Simon & Garfunkel*
At This Moment
79/81 *Billy & The Beaters*
1/87 *Billy Vera & The Beaters*
6/94 **At Your Best (You Are Love)** *Aaliyah*
28/82 **Athena** *Who*
27/81 **Atlanta Lady (Something About Your Love)** *Marty Balin*
7/69 **Atlantis** *Donovan*
39/80 **Atomic** *Blondie*
18/66 **Attack** *Toys*
70/82 **Attack Of The Name Game** *Stacy Lattisaw*
(also see: Name Game)
21/75 **Attitude Dancing** *Carly Simon*
15/73 **Aubrey** *Bread*

Auctioneer
59/56 *Chuck Miller*
19/57 *Leroy Van Dyke*
Auld Lang Syne
7/00 *Kenny G (Millennium Mix)*
2[S]/03 *Kenny G (Freedom Mix)*
(also see: Christmas / I Understand)
85/68 **Aunt Dora's Love Soul Shack** *Arthur Conley*
18/01 **Austin** *Blake Shelton*
15/84 **Authority Song** *John Cougar Mellencamp*
25/75 **Autobahn** *Kraftwerk*
52/80 **Autograph** *John Denver*
5/84 **Automatic** *Pointer Sisters*
53[S]/99 **Automatic** *MC Eiht*
52/95 **Automatic Lover (Call For Love)** *Real McCoy*
34/83 **Automatic Man** *Michael Sembello*
37/72 **Automatically Sunshine** *Supremes*
Autumn Leaves
1/55 *Roger Williams*
35/55 *Steve Allen/George Cates*
41/55 *Mitch Miller*
50/55 *Jackie Gleason*
52/55 *Victor Young*
55/55 *Ray Charles Singers*
92/65 *Roger Williams (1965)*
19/68 **Autumn Of My Life** *Bobby Goldsboro*
18/56 **Autumn Waltz** *Tony Bennett*
42/98 **Ava Adore** *Smashing Pumpkins*
Avenging Annie
78/73 *Andy Pratt*
88/77 *Roger Daltrey*
35/97 **Avenues** *Refugee Camp All-Stars*
93/62 **Aw Shucks, Hush Your Mouth** *Jimmy Reed*
88/95 **Awake** *Letters To Cleo*
47/94 **Award Tour** *Tribe Called Quest*
77/56 **Away All Boats** *Al Hibbler*
51/02 **Awnaw** *Nappy Roots*
3/85 **Axel F** *Harold Faltermeyer*

B

48[S]/99 **B-Boy Document 99** *High & Mighty*
54/90 **"B" Girls** *Young & Restless*
77/99 **B-Please** *Snoop Dogg*
98/68 **B.B. Jones** *B.B. King*
26/90 **B.B.D. (I Thought It Was Me)?** *Bell Biv DeVoe*
59/76 **BLT** *Lee Oskar*
1/79 **Babe** *Styx*

BABY:

4/95 **Baby** *Brandy*
14/66 **B-A-B-Y** *Carla Thomas*
15/02 **Baby** *Ashanti*
28/03 **Baby, The** *Blake Shelton*
57[S]/99 **Baby** *Before Dark*
1/91 **Baby Baby** *Amy Grant*
57/95 **Baby Baby** *Corona*
78/58 **Baby, Baby** *Billy Williams Quartet*
84/89 **Baby Baby**, *Eighth Wonder*
83/64 **Baby Baby All The Time** *Superbs*
2/92 **Baby-Baby-Baby** *TLC*
52/64 **Baby Baby Baby** *Anna King-Bobby Byrd*
66/63 **Baby, Baby, Baby** *Sam Cooke*
34[C]/56 **(Baby, Baby) Be Good To Me** *McGuire Sisters*
8/69 **Baby, Baby Don't Cry** *Miracles*

79/76 **Baby, Baby I Love You** *Terry Cashman*
51/64 **Baby Be Mine** *Jelly Beans*
83/98 **Baby Be There** *Nu Flavor*
12/61 **Baby Blue** *Echoes*
14/72 **Baby Blue** *Badfinger*
60/76 **Baby Boy** *Mary Kay Place*
48/88 **Baby Can I Hold You** *Tracy Chapman*
44/85 **Baby Come And Get It** *Pointer Sisters*
1/78 **Baby Come Back** *Player*
32/68 **Baby, Come Back** *Equals*
52/84 **Baby Come Back** *Billy Rankin*
83/85 **Baby Come Back To Me (The Morse Code Of Love)** *Manhattan Transfer*
27/74 **Baby Come Close** *Smokey Robinson*
75/64 **Baby Come Home** *Ruby & The Romantics*
96/66 **Baby Come On Home** *Solomon Burke*
49/01 **Baby, Come Over (This Is Our Night)** *Samantha Mumba*
1/83 **Baby, Come To Me** *Patti Austin (with James Ingram)*
60/89 **Baby Come To Me** *Regina Belle*
63/66 **Baby, Do The Philly Dog** *Olympics*
(also see: Philly Dog)
33/56 **Baby Doll** *Andy Williams*
72/69 **Baby, Don't Be Looking In My Mind** *Joe Simon*
52/77 **Baby Don't Change Your Mind** *Gladys Knight*
72/00 **Baby Don't Cry (Keep Ya Head Up II)** *2Pac + Outlawz*
1/89 **Baby Don't Forget My Number** *Milli Vanilli*
1/72 **Baby Don't Get Hooked On Me** *Mac Davis*
8/65 **Baby Don't Go** *Sonny & Cher*
69/80 **Baby Don't Go** *Karla Bonoff*
96/70 **Baby Don't Take Your Love** *Faith, Hope & Charity*
39/64 **Baby, Don't You Cry (The New Swingova Rhythm)** *Ray Charles*
Baby Don't You Do It
27/64 *Marvin Gaye*
34/72 *Band*
43/77 **Baby Don't You Know** *Wild Cherry*
30/63 **Baby Don't You Weep** *Garnet Mimms*
Baby Elephant Walk
48/62 *Lawrence Welk*
87/62 *Miniature Men*
Baby Face
41/58 *Little Richard*
42/62 *Bobby Darin*
14/76 *Wing & Prayer Fife & Drum Corps*
61/63 **Baby Get It (And Don't Quit It)** *Jackie Wilson*
88/75 **Baby-Get It On** *Ike & Tina Turner*
1/92 **Baby Got Back** *Sir Mix-A-Lot*
75/87 **Baby Grand** *Billy Joel/Ray Charles*
50/75 **Baby, Hang Up The Phone** *Carl Graves*
62/62 **Baby Has Gone Bye Bye** *George Maharis*
87/67 **Baby, Help Me** *Percy Sledge*
11/78 **Baby Hold On** *Eddie Money*
35/70 **Baby Hold On** *Grass Roots*
37/92 **Baby Hold On To Me** *Gerald Levert (with Eddie Levert)*
72/60 **(Baby) Hully Gully** *Olympics*
66/92 **Baby, I Believe In You** *George LaMond*

70/63 **Baby I Do Love You** *Galens*
26/84 **Baby I Lied** *Deborah Allen*
4/67 **Baby I Love You** *Aretha Franklin*
Baby, I Love You
24/64 *Ronettes*
9/69 *Andy Kim*
Baby I Love You
98/66 *Jimmy Holiday*
82/70 *Little Milton*
Baby, I Love Your Way
12/76 *Peter Frampton*
1/88 *Will To Power (medley)*
6/94 *Big Mountain*
96/66 **Baby I Need You** *Manhattans*
Baby I Need Your Loving
11/64 *Four Tops*
3/67 *Johnny Rivers*
52/70 *O.C. Smith*
62/79 *Eric Carmen*
47/79 **Baby I Want You** *Funky Communication Committee*
58/76 **Baby, I'll Give It To You** *Seals & Crofts*
3/71 **Baby I'm - A Want You** *Bread*
25/79 **Baby I'm Burnin'** *Dolly Parton*
Baby I'm For Real
14/69 *Originals*
55/92 *After 7 (medley)*
76/84 **Baby, I'm Hooked (Right Into Your Love)** *Con Funk Shun*
70/67 **Baby I'm Lonely** *Intruders*
10/93 **Baby I'm Yours** *Shai*
Baby, I'm Yours
11/65 *Barbara Lewis*
91/71 *Jody Miller*
F/78 *Debby Boone*
(also see: Yours)
41/73 **Baby I've Been Missing You** *Independents*
18S/00 **Baby If You're Ready** *Doggys Angels*
91/70 **Baby, Is There Something On Your Mind** *McKinley Travis*
91/62 **Baby It's Cold Outside** *Ray Charles & Betty Carter*
16/90 **Baby, It's Tonight** *Jude Cole*
Baby It's You
8/62 *Shirelles*
5/69 *Smith*
67/95 *Beatles*
14/83 **Baby Jane** *Rod Stewart*
29/71 **Baby Let Me Kiss You** *King Floyd*
24/72 **Baby Let Me Take You (In My Arms)** *Detroit Emeralds*
35/69 **Baby Let's Wait** *Royal Guardsmen*
1/64 **Baby Love** *Supremes*
10/86 **Baby Love** *Regina*
58/77 **Baby Love** *Mother's Finest*
65/96 **Baby Luv** *Groove Theory*
87/70 **Baby Make It Soon** *Flying Machine*
64/68 **Baby Make Your Own Sweet Music** *Jay & The Techniques*
25/82 **Baby Makes Her Blue Jeans Talk** *Dr. Hook*
11/68 **Baby, Now That I've Found You** *Foundations*
21/61 **Baby Oh Baby** *Shells*
1/99 **Baby One More Time** *Britney Spears*
61/67 **Baby Please Come Back Home** *J.J. Barnes*
16/66 **Baby Scratch My Back** *Slim Harpo*
46/72 **Baby Sitter** *Betty Wright*
6/61 **Baby Sittin' Boogie** *Buzz Clifford*
50/82 **Baby Step Back** *Gordon Lightfoot*

23/70 **Baby Take Me In Your Arms** *Jefferson*
10/59 **Baby Talk** *Jan & Dean*
68/86 **Baby Talk** *Alisha*
38/80 **Baby Talks Dirty** *Knack*
50/87 **(Baby Tell Me) Can You Dance** *Shanice Wilson*
26/75 **Baby That's Backatcha** *Smokey Robinson*
12/65 **Baby The Rain Must Fall** *Glenn Yarbrough*
76/66 **Baby Toys** *Toys*
56/70 **(Baby) Turn On To Me** *Impressions*
89/00 **Baby U Are** *Gerald Levert*
92/76 **Baby, We Better Try To Get It Together** *Barry White*
98/63 **Baby, We've Got Love** *Johnnie Taylor*
4/77 **Baby, What A Big Surprise** *Chicago*
83/83 **Baby, What About You** *Crystal Gayle*
74/66 **Baby What Do You Want Me To Do** *Barbara Lewis*
62/66 **Baby What I Mean** *Drifters*
Baby What You Want Me To Do
37/60 *Jimmy Reed*
82/64 *Etta James*
93/63 **Baby, What's Wrong** *Lonnie Mack*
61/72 **Baby Won't You Let Me Rock 'N Roll You** *Ten Years After*
5/63 **Baby Workout** *Jackie Wilson*
59/68 **Baby You Come Rollin' Across My Mind** *Peppermint Trolley Company*
34/67 **Baby You Got It** *Brenton Wood*
76/97 **Baby You Know** *O'Jays*
65/77 **Baby, You Look Good To Me Tonight** *John Denver*
34/67 **Baby You're A Rich Man** *Beatles*
100/63 **Baby, You're Driving Me Crazy** *Joey Dee*
49/61 **Baby, You're Right** *James Brown*
52/61 **Baby You're So Fine** *Mickey & Sylvia*
86/68 **Baby You're So Right For Me** *Brenda & The Tabulations*
5/60 **Baby (You've Got What It Takes)** *Dinah Washington & Brook Benton*
62/91 **Baby's Coming Back** *Jellyfish*
26/61 **Baby's First Christmas** *Connie Francis*
84/64 **Baby's Gone** *Gene Thomas*
21S/02 **Baby's Got A Temper** *Prodigy*
57/01 **Babylon** *David Gray*
99/64 **Bachelor Boy** *Cliff Richard*
43/60 **Baciare Baciare (Kissing Kissing)** *Dorothy Collins*

BACK:

5/94 **Back & Forth** *Aaliyah*
50/87 **Back And Forth** *Cameo*
Back At One
2/99 *Brian McKnight*
36/00 *Mark Wills*
63/63 **Back At The Chicken Shack** *Jimmy Smith*
66/61 **Back Beat No. 1** *Rondels*
59/69 **Back Door Man** *Derek*
4X/68 **Back Door Santa** *Clarence Carter*
72/73 **Back For A Taste Of Your Love** *Syl Johnson*
7/95 **Back For Good** *Take That*
13/00 **Back Here** *BBMak*
5/74 **Back Home Again** *John Denver*
37/81 **Back In Black** *AC/DC*
57/68 **Back In Love Again** *Buckinghams*

Back In My Arms Again
1/65 *Supremes*
92/78 *Genya Ravan*
88/85 **Back In Stride** *Maze Feat. Frankie Beverly*
26/94 **Back In The Day** *Ahmad*
13/87 **Back In The High Life Again** *Steve Winwood*
38/77 **Back In The Saddle** *Aerosmith*
Back In The U.S.A.
37/59 *Chuck Berry*
16/78 *Linda Ronstadt*
82/69 **Back In The U.S.S.R.** *Chubby Checker*
84/80 **Back Of My Hand (I've Got Your Number)** *Jags*
9/72 **Back Off Boogaloo** *Ringo Starr*
34/89 **Back On Holiday** *Robbie Nevil*
33/80 **Back On My Feet Again** *Babys*
59/68 **Back On My Feet Again** *Foundations*
5/83 **Back On The Chain Gang** *Pretenders*
36/67 **Back On The Street Again** *Sunshine Company*
42/93 **Back Seat (Of My Jeep)** *LL Cool J*
3/72 **Back Stabbers** *O'Jays*
95/65 **Back Street** *Edwin Starr*
19/99 **Back That Azz Up** *Juvenile*
24/99 **Back 2 Good** *Matchbox 20*
4/89 **Back To Life** *Soul II Soul*
41/87 **Back To Paradise** *38 Special*
36/57 **Back To School Again** *Timmie Rogers*
71/82 **Back To School Again** *Four Tops*
63/89 **Back To The Bullet** *Saraya*
80/61 **Back To The Hop** *Danny & The Juniors*
14/93 **Back To The Hotel** *N2Deep*
53/76 **Back To The Island** *Leon Russell*
89/81 **Back To The 60's (medley)** *Tight Fit*
47/96 **Back To The World** *Tevin Campbell*
42[A]/98 **Back To You** *Bryan Adams*
28/77 **Back Together Again** *Daryl Hall & John Oates*
56/80 **Back Together Again** *Roberta Flack w/Donny Hathaway*
85/94 **Back Up Off Me!** *Doctor Dre & Ed Lover*
41/68 **Back Up Train** *Al Greene*
40/73 **Back When My Hair Was Short** *Gunhill Road*
20/84 **Back Where You Belong** *38 Special*
10/69 **Backfield In Motion** *Mel & Tim*
43/81 **Backfired** *Debbie Harry*
25/66 **Backstage** *Gene Pitney*
89/61 **Backtrack** *Faron Young*
47/94 **Backwater** *Meat Puppets*
73/91 **Backyard** *Pebbles With Salt-N-Pepa*
37/97 **Backyard Boogie** *Mack 10*

BAD:

1/87 **Bad** *Michael Jackson*
(also see: Fat)
88/83 **Bad, Bad Billy** *Snuff*
98/92 **Bad Bad Boys** *Midi Maxi & Efti*
Bad, Bad Leroy Brown
1/73 *Jim Croce*
83/74 *Frank Sinatra*
1/75 **Bad Blood** *Neil Sedaka*
8/86 **Bad Boy** *Miami Sound Machine*
35/83 **Bad Boy** *Ray Parker Jr.*
36/57 **Bad Boy** *Jive Bombers*
45/60 **Bad Boy** *Marty Wilde*
55/82 **Bad Boy (medley)** *Luther Vandross*
33/01 **Bad Boy For Life** *P. Diddy, Black Rob & Mark Curry*
8/93 **Bad Boys** *Inner Circle*
60/83 **Bad Boys** *Wham! U.K.*
57/00 **Bad Boyz** *Shyne*
83/79 **Bad Brakes** *Cat Stevens*
14/79 **Bad Case Of Loving You (Doctor, Doctor)** *Robert Palmer*
64/01 **Bad Day** *Fuel*
45/57 **(Bad Donkey) Pum-Pa-Lum** *Steve Lawrence*
92/66 **Bad Eye** *Willie Mitchell*
33/63 **Bad Girl** *Neil Sedaka*
36/93 **Bad Girl** *Madonna*
93/59 **Bad Girl** *Miracles*
1/79 **Bad Girls** *Donna Summer*
43/93 **Bad Goodbye** *Clint Black (with Wynonna)*
91/66 **Bad Little Woman** *Shadows Of Knight*
88/90 **Bad Love** *Eric Clapton*
Bad Luck
15/75 *Harold Melvin*
94/76 *Atlanta Disco Band*
37/60 **Bad Man Blunder** *Kingston Trio*
1/88 **Bad Medicine** *Bon Jovi*
55/66 **Bad Misunderstanding** *Critters*
2/69 **Bad Moon Rising** *Creedence Clearwater Revival*
45/58 **Bad Motorcycle** *Storey Sisters*
25/90 **Bad Of The Heart** *George LaMond*
54/95 **Bad Reputation** *Freedy Johnston*
4/75 **Bad Time** *Grand Funk*
47/80 **Bad Times** *Tavares*
9/64 **Bad To Me** *Billy J. Kramer*
52/00 **Bad Touch** *Bloodhound Gang*
58/71 **Bad Water** *Raeletts*
87/73 **Bad Weather** *Supremes*
60/69 **Badge** *Cream*
42/78 **Badlands** *Bruce Springsteen*
6/00 **Bag Lady** *Erykah Badu*
53/57 **Bahama Mama** *Four Aces*
1/99 **Bailamos** *Enrique Iglesias*
94/63 **Baja** *Astronauts*
2/78 **Baker Street** *Gerry Rafferty*
48/62 **Balboa Blue** *Marketts*
57/70 **Ball And Chain** *Tommy James*
3/70 **Ball Of Confusion (That's What The World Is Today)** *Temptations*
19/69 **Ball Of Fire** *Tommy James*
74/59 **Ballad Of A Girl And Boy** *Graduates*
14/58 **Ballad Of A Teenage Queen** *Johnny Cash*
7/68 **Ballad Of Bonnie And Clyde** *Georgie Fame*
(also see: Bonnie And Clyde Theme / Foggy Mountain Breakdown)
Ballad Of Davy Crockett
1/55 *Bill Hayes*
5/55 *"Tennessee" Ernie Ford*
5/55 *Fess Parker*
14/55 *Walter Schumann*
65/69 **Ballad Of Easy Rider** *Byrds*
Ballad Of Francis Powers ..see: There's A Star Spangled Banner Waving
34/66 **Ballad Of Irving** *Frank Gallop*
33/90 **Ballad of Jayne** *L.A. Guns*
44/63 **Ballad Of Jed Clampett** *Lester Flatt & Earl Scruggs*
8/69 **Ballad Of John And Yoko** *Beatles*
33/62 **Ballad Of Paladin** *Duane Eddy*
(Ballad Of Sleeping Beauty) ..see: Only Love
Ballad Of The Alamo
34/60 *Marty Robbins*
64/60 *Bud & Travis*
1/66 **Ballad Of The Green Berets** *SSgt Barry Sadler*
(also see: He Wore The Green Beret)
Ballad Of Thunder Road
62/58 *Robert Mitchum*
65/62 *Robert Mitchum*
48/68 **Ballad Of Two Brothers** *Autry Inman*
42/67 **Ballad Of You & Me & Pooneil** *Jefferson Airplane*
63/91 **Ballad Of Youth** *Richie Sambora*
58[S]/02 **Baller** *Richard Burton*
18/57 **Ballerina** *Nat "King" Cole*
7/87 **Ballerina Girl** *Lionel Richie*
33/74 **Ballero** *War*
60[S]/00 **Ballers (Up In Here)** *Ram Squad*
3[S]/02 **Ballin' Boy** *No Good*
95/01 **Ballin' Out Of Control** *Jermaine Dupri*
5/75 **Ballroom Blitz** *Sweet*
82/64 **Bama Lama Bama Loo** *Little Richard*
Banana Boat (Day-O)/Banana Boat Song
4/57 *Tarriers*
5/57 *Harry Belafonte*
13/57 *Fontane Sisters*
18/57 *Steve Lawrence*
19/57 *Sarah Vaughan*
25/57 *Stan Freberg*
41/76 **Banapple Gas** *Cat Stevens*
3/70 **Band Of Gold** *Freda Payne*
Band Of Gold
11/55 *Kit Carson*
4/56 *Don Cherry*
93/56 *Hi-Fi Four*
32/66 *Mel Carter*
1/74 **Band On The Run** *Paul McCartney*
35/67 **Banda, A** *Herb Alpert*
18/55 **Bandit (O'Cangaceiro)** *Eddie Barclay*
65/62 **Bandit Of My Dreams** *Eddie Hodges*
71[A]/96 **Banditos** *Refreshments*
Bang A Gong (Get It On)
10/72 *T. Rex*
68/79 *Witch Queen*
9/85 *Power Station*
19/95 **Bang And Blame** *R.E.M.*
49/90 **Bang Bang** *Danger Danger*
Bang Bang
63/66 *Joe Cuba Sextet*
53/92 *David Sanborn*
2/66 **Bang Bang (My Baby Shot Me Down)** *Cher*
8[S]/02 **Bang My Hit** *Rozelly Presents Da Fam*
22/68 **Bang-Shang-A-Lang** *Archies*
63/83 **Bang The Drum All Day** *Todd Rundgren*
31/84 **Bang Your Head (Metal Health)** *Quiet Riot*
23/71 **Bangla-Desh** *George Harrison*
Banjo Boy
58/60 *Jan & Kjeld*
79/60 *Dorothy Collins*
100/60 *Art Mooney*
15/55 **Banjo's Back In Town** *Teresa Brewer*
94/71 **Banks Of The Ohio** *Olivia Newton-John*

20/90 **Banned In The U.S.A.** *Luke Feat. 2 Live Crew*
93/63 **Banzai Pipeline** *Henry Mancini*
29/60 **Barbara** *Temptations*
Barbara-Ann
13/61 *Regents*
2/66 *Beach Boys*
78/70 **Barbara, I Love You** *New Colony Six*
7/97 **Barbie Girl** *Aqua*
67/68 **Barefoot In Baltimore** *Strawberry Alarm Clock*
9[X]/66 **Barefoot Santa Claus** *Sonny James*
7/66 **Barefootin'** *Robert Parker*
16/97 **Barely Breathing** *Duncan Sheik*
Baretta's Theme ("Keep Your Eye On The Sparrow")
45/75 *Merry Clayton*
20/76 *Rhythm Heritage*
96/68 **Baroque-A-Nova** *Mason Williams*
11/77 **Barracuda** *Heart*
59/65 **Barracuda, The** *Alvin Cash*
47/97 **Barrel Of A Gun** *Depeche Mode*
Baseball Game ..see: (Love Is Like)
94/62 **Basie Twist** *Count Basie*
26[A]/94 **Basket Case** *Green Day*
71/85 **Basketball** *Kurtis Blow*
15/73 **Basketball Jones Featuring Tyrone Shoelaces** *Cheech & Chong*
1/89 **Batdance** *Prince*
66/66 **Batman** *Jan & Dean*
70/66 **Batman & His Grandmother** *Dickie Goodman*
Batman Theme
17/66 *Marketts*
35/66 *Neal Hefti*
37/71 **Battle Hymn Of Lt. Calley** *C Company*
Battle Hymn Of The Republic
13/59 *Mormon Tabernacle Choir*
33/68 *Andy Williams*
(also see: Ballad Of Two Brothers / Leave Me Alone (Let Me Cry) / Young Abe Lincoln)
100/61 **Battle Of Gettysburg** *Fred Darian*
14/59 **Battle Of Kookamonga** *Homer & Jethro*
Battle Of New Orleans
1/59 *Johnny Horton*
87/59 *Vaughn Monroe*
95/68 *Harpers Bizarre*
72/74 *Nitty Gritty Dirt Band*
86/87 **Battleship Chains** *Georgia Satellites*
25/58 **Baubles, Bangles And Beads** *Kirby Stone Four*

BE:

34/73 **Be** *Neil Diamond*
Be Anything (But Be Mine)
25/64 *Connie Francis*
88/64 *Gloria Lynne*
Be-Bop-A-Lula
7/56 *Gene Vincent*
74/60 *Everly Brothers*
3/57 **Be-Bop Baby** *Ricky Nelson*
32[A]/98 **Be Careful** *Sparkle*
31/63 **Be Careful Of Stones That You Throw** *Dion*
95/57 **Be Careful With A Fool** *B.B. King*
97/71 **Be Good To Me Baby** *Luther Ingram*
9/86 **Be Good To Yourself** *Journey*
29/94 **Be Happy** *Mary J. Blige*
99/02 **Be Here** *Raphael Saadiq*
66/69 **Be-In (medley)** *Happenings*
24/01 **Be Like That** *3 Doors Down*
64/63 **Be Mad Little Girl** *Bobby Darin*
35/82 **Be Mine Tonight** *Neil Diamond*
92/82 **Be Mine (Tonight)** *Grover Washington, Jr.*
Be My Baby
2/63 *Ronettes*
17/70 *Andy Kim*
92/71 *Cissy Houston*
87/65 **Be My Baby** *Dick & DeeDee*
73/94 **Be My Baby Tonight** *John Michael Montgomery*
56/61 **Be My Boy** *Paris Sisters*
53/77 **Be My Girl** *Dramatics*
75/64 **Be My Girl** *Four-Evers*
8/59 **Be My Guest** *Fats Domino*
28/82 **Be My Lady** *Jefferson Starship*
78/77 **Be My Lady** *Meters*
6/96 **Be My Lover** *La Bouche*
49/72 **Be My Lover** *Alice Cooper*
9/85 **Be Near Me** *ABC*
71/71 **Be Nice To Me** *Runt-Todd Rundgren*
15/88 **Be Still My Beating Heart** *Sting*
4/74 **Be Thankful For What You Got** *William DeVaughn*
42/87 **Be There** *Pointer Sisters*
6/63 **Be True To Your School** *Beach Boys*
34/63 **Be True To Yourself** *Bobby Vee*
78/92 **Be True To Yourself** *2nd II None*
66/73 **Be What You Are** *Staple Singers*
1/00 **Be With You** *Enrique Iglesias*
30/89 **Be With You** *Bangles*
61/68 **Be Young, Be Foolish, Be Happy** *Tams*
61/85 **Be Your Man** *Jesse Johnson's Revue*
4/74 **Beach Baby** *First Class*
12/81 **Beach Boys Medley** *Beach Boys*
72/64 **Beach Girl** *Pat Boone*
60/62 **Beach Party** *King Curtis*
95/62 **Beach Party** *Dave York*
64/59 **Beach Time** *Roger Smith*
100/60 **Beachcomber** *Bobby Darin*
30/64 **Beans In My Ears** *Serendipity Singers*
Beast Of Burden
8/78 *Rolling Stones*
71/84 *Bette Midler*
57/59 **Beat, The** *Rockin R's*
6/67 **Beat Goes On** *Sonny & Chér*
1/83 **Beat It** *Michael Jackson*
(also see: Eat It)
81/72 **Beat Me Daddy Eight To The Bar** *Commander Cody*
41/85 **Beat Of A Heart** *Scandal*
46/87 **Beat Patrol** *Starship*
86/84 **Beat Street Breakdown** *Grandmaster Melle Mel*
92/67 **Beat The Clock** *McCoys*
41[S]/02 **Beat Your Chest!!** *Lifer's*
17/86 **Beat's So Lonely** *Charlie Sexton*
Beatles E.P.'s ..see: Four By The Beatles
12/82 **Beatles' Movie Medley** *Beatles*
15/60 **Beatnik Fly** *Johnny & The Hurricanes*
87/70 **Beaucoups Of Blues** *Ringo Starr*
82/64 **Beautician Blues** *B.B. King*
2/03 **Beautiful** *Christina Aguilera*
58/72 **Beautiful** *Gordon Lightfoot*
21/01 **Beautiful Day** *U2*
81/58 **Beautiful Delilah** *Chuck Berry*
74/56 **Beautiful Friendship** *Ella Fitzgerald*
46/93 **Beautiful Girl** *INXS*
84/79 **Beautiful Girls** *Van Halen*
19/94 **Beautiful In My Eyes** *Joshua Kadison*
15/95 **Beautiful Life** *Ace Of Base*
28/02 **Beautiful Mess** *Diamond Rio*
3/68 **Beautiful Morning** *Rascals*
89/60 **Beautiful Obsession** *Sir Chauncey*
Beautiful People
37/67 *Bobby Vee*
38/67 *Kenny O'Dell*
67/71 **Beautiful People** *New Seekers*
53/67 **Beautiful Story** *Sonny & Chér*
19/99 **Beautiful Stranger** *Madonna*
15/72 **Beautiful Sunday** *Daniel Boone*
79/99 **Beauty** *Dru Hill*
9/92 **Beauty And The Beast** *Celine Dion & Peabo Bryson*
3/66 **Beauty Is Only Skin Deep** *Temptations*
3/64 **Because** *Dave Clark Five*
(also see: Cuz)
Because I Got High
13/01 *Afroman*
33[S]/01 *CoverVersions.com*
96/66 **Because I Love You** *Billy Stewart*
F/70 **Because I Love You** *Five Stairsteps*
1/90 **Because I Love You (The Postman Song)** *Stevie B*
10/94 **Because Of Love** *Janet Jackson*
3/98 **Because Of You** *98°*
27/88 **Because Of You** *Cover Girls*
71/67 **Because Of You** *Chris Montez*
Because The Night
13/78 *Patti Smith Group*
11/94 *10,000 Maniacs*
4/60 **Because They're Young** *Duane Eddy*
53/00 **Because You Love Me** *Jo Dee Messina*
1/96 **Because You Loved Me** *Celine Dion*
62/59 **Because You're Young** *Jimmie Rodgers*
70/72 **Bed And Board** *Barbara Mason*
58/71 **Bed Of Rose's** *Statler Brothers*
10/93 **Bed Of Roses** *Bon Jovi*
22[S]/01 **Bedrock, The** *Club Drama*
17/88 **Beds Are Burning** *Midnight Oil*
42/95 **Bedtime Story** *Madonna*
86/72 **Bedtime Story** *Tammy Wynette*
Beechwood 4-5789
17/62 *Marvelettes*
74/82 *Carpenters*
4/98 **Been Around The World** *Puff Daddy & The Family*
24/58 **Been So Long** *Pastels*
44/00 **Been There** *Clint Black with Steve Wariner*
24/73 **Been To Canaan** *Carole King*
98/71 **Been Too Long On The Road** *Mark Lindsay*
4/58 **Beep Beep** *Playmates*
33/75 **Beer Barrel Polka** *Bobby Vinton*
50/65 **(Bees Are For The Birds) The Birds Are For The Bees** *Newbeats*
17/65 **Before And After** *Chad & Jeremy*
68/86 **Before I Go** *Starship*
84/60 **Before I Grow Too Old** *Fats Domino*
7/95 **Before I Let You Go** *BLACKstreet*

23/78 **Before My Heart Finds Out** *Gene Cotton*
1/75 **Before The Next Teardrop Falls** *Freddy Fender*
83/65 **Before You Go** *Buck Owens*
7/95 **Before You Walk Out Of My Life** *Monica*
29/67 **Beg, Borrow And Steal** *Ohio Express*
79/83 **Beg, Borrow Or Steal** *Hughes/Thrall*
45/64 **Beg Me** *Chuck Jackson*
81/72 **Beg, Steal Or Borrow** *New Seekers*
16/67 **Beggin'** *4 Seasons*
74/63 **Begging To You** *Marty Robbins*
79/67 **Beginning Of Loneliness** *Dionne Warwick*
36/69 **Beginning Of My End** *Unifics*
92/71 **Beginning To Feel The Pain** *Mac Davis*
7/71 **Beginnings** *Chicago*
87/94 **Behind Bars** *Slick Rick*
34/71 **Behind Blue Eyes** *Who*
15/73 **Behind Closed Doors** *Charlie Rich*
97/66 **Behind The Door** *Cher*
61/88 **Behind The Wheel (medley)** *Depeche Mode*
69/59 **Bei Mir Bist Du Schön** *Louis Prima & Keely Smith*
2/81 **Being With You** *Smokey Robinson*
1/99 **Believe** *Cher*
13/95 **Believe** *Elton John*
60/93 **Believe** *Lenny Kravitz*
94/75 **Believe Half Of What You See (And None Of What You Hear)** *Leon Haywood*
28/73 **Believe In Humanity** *Carole King*
58S/94 **Believe In Love** *Teddy Pendergrass*
48/84 **Believe In Me** *Dan Fogelberg*
92/67 **Believe In Me Baby** *Jesse James*
26/59 **Believe Me** *Royal Teens*
4/58 **Believe What You Say** *Ricky Nelson*
95/89 **(Believed You Were) Lucky** *'Til Tuesday*
Bell Bottom Blues
91/71 *Derek & The Dominos*
78/73 *Eric Clapton*
23X/64 **Bell That Couldn't Jingle** *Bobby Vinton*
28/69 **Bella Linda** *Grassroots*
83/78 **Belle** *Al Green*
34/84 **Belle Of St. Mark** *Sheila E.*
Bells, The
68/60 *James Brown*
12/70 *Originals*
99/61 **Bells Are Ringing** *Van Dykes*
88/59 **Bells, Bells, Bells (The Bell Song)** *Billie & Lillie*
13/58 **Belonging To Someone** *Patti Page*
1/72 **Ben** *Michael Jackson*
Ben Casey ..see: Theme From
Ben Crazy - Dr. Ben Basey
44/62 *Dickie Goodman*
60/62 *Mickey Shorr*
(also see: Callin' Doctor Casey)
5/68 **Bend Me, Shape Me** *American Breed*
1/74 **Bennie And The Jets** *Elton John*
1/00 **Bent** *Matchbox Twenty*
61/61 **Berlin Melody** *Billy Vaughn*
70/62 **Bermuda** *Linda Scott*
4/67 **Bernadette** *Four Tops*
14/57 **Bernardine** *Pat Boone*
16/75 **Bertha Butt Boogie** *Jimmy Castor Bunch*
79/58 **Bertha Lou** *Clint Miller*
70/60 **Besame Mucho** *Coasters*
15/89 **Best, The** *Tina Turner*
69/79 **Best Beat In Town** *Switch*
31/00 **Best Day** *George Strait*
17/76 **Best Disco In Town** *Ritchie Family*
34/95 **Best Friend** *Brandy*
59/00 **Best Friend** *Puff Daddy*
58/01 **Best I Ever Had (Grey Sky Morning)** *Vertical Horizon*
77/00 **Best Man I Can Be** *Ginuwine, R.L., Tyrese, Case*
61/87 **Best Man In The World** *Ann Wilson*
32/68 **Best Of Both Worlds** *Lulu*
62/59 **Best Of Everything** *Johnny Mathis*
27/00 **Best Of Intentions** *Travis Tritt*
65A/97 **Best Of Love** *Michael Bolton*
50/00 **Best Of Me** *Mya*
80/86 **Best Of Me** *David Foster & Olivia Newton-John*
1/77 **Best Of My Love** *Emotions*
1/75 **Best Of My Love** *Eagles*
3/81 **Best Of Times** *Styx*
59/88 **Best Of Times** *Peter Cetera*
39/64 **(Best Part Of) Breakin' Up** *Ronettes*
82/72 **Best Thing** *Styx*
Best Thing That Ever Happened To Me
82/73 *Ray Price*
3/74 *Gladys Knight*
85/74 *Persuaders*
10/92 **Best Things In Life Are Free** *Luther Vandross & Janet Jackson*
54/81 **Bet Your Heart On Me** *Johnny Lee*
Betcha By Golly, Wow
3/72 *Stylistics*
31A/96 *Prince*
(Betcha Got A Chick On The Side) ..see: How Long
36/87 **Betcha Say That** *Gloria Estefan*
49/83 **Betcha She Don't Love You** *Evelyn King*
70/94 **Betcha'll Never Find** *Chantay Savage*
7/76 **Beth** *Kiss*
1/81 **Bette Davis Eyes** *Kim Carnes*
5/84 **Better Be Good To Me** *Tina Turner*
42/88 **Better Be Home Soon** *Crowded House*
99/75 **Better By The Pound** *Funkadelic*
59S/99 **Better Days** *TQ*
64/98 **Better Days** *WC*
71/76 **Better Days** *Melissa Manchester*
F/92 **Better Days** *Bruce Springsteen*
25/99 **Better Days (and the bottom drops out)** *Citizen King*
18/91 **Better Love** *Londonbeat*
12/80 **Better Love Next Time** *Dr. Hook*
13A/95 **Better Man** *Pearl Jam*
27/00 **Better Off Alone** *Alice Deejay*
86/76 **Better Place To Be** *Harry Chapin*
38/61 **Better Tell Him No** *Starlets*
99/99 **Better Than Me** *Terry Dexter*
74A/95 **Better Than Nothing** *Jennifer Trynin*
36/93 **Better Than You** *Lisa Keith*
92/82 **Better Things** *Kinks*
89/63 **Better To Give Than Receive** *Joe Hinton*
54/66 **Better Use Your Head** *Little Anthony & The Imperials*
33/58 **Betty And Dupree** *Chuck Willis*
50/63 **Betty In Bermudas** *Dovells*
37/58 **Betty Lou Got A New Pair Of Shoes** *Bobby Freeman*
90/59 **Betty My Angel** *Jerry Fuller*
77/89 **(Between A) Rock And A Hard Place** *Cutting Crew*
57/74 **Between Her Goodbye And My Hello** *Gladys Knight*
11/00 **Between Me And You** *Ja Rule*
Beverly Hillbillies ..see: Ballad Of Jed Clampett
75/96 **Beware Of My Crew** *L.B.C. Crew*
Bewildered
57/58 *Mickey & Sylvia*
40/61 *James Brown*
50/58 **Bewitched** *Betty Smith Group*
50/80 **Beyond** *Herb Alpert*
80/74 **Beyond The Blue Horizon** *Lou Christie*
81/96 **Beyond The Invisible** *Enigma*
Beyond The Sea
37/56 *Roger Williams*
6/60 *Bobby Darin*
71/59 **Beyond The Sunset** *Pat Boone*
94/01 **Bia' Bia'** *Lil Jon & East Side Boyz*
Bible Tells Me So
7/55 *Don Cornell*
22/55 *Nick Noble*
24/79 **Bicycle Race** *Queen*

BIG:

1/61 **Big Bad John** *Jimmy Dean*
53/97 **Big Bad Mamma** *Foxy Brown*
28A/96 **Big Bang Baby** *Stone Temple Pilots*
26/58 **Big Beat** *Fats Domino*
87/57 **Big Beat** *Dick Jacobs*
55S/02 **Big Big** *Kage*
58/61 **Big Big World** *Johnny Burnette*
92/98 **Big Big World** *Emilia*
93/63 **Big Boat** *Peter, Paul & Mary*
38/58 **Big Bopper's Wedding** *Big Bopper*
94/64 **Big Boss Line** *Jackie Wilson*
Big Boss Man
78/61 *Jimmy Reed*
92/64 *Gene Chandler (Soul Hootenanny)*
38/67 *Elvis Presley*
50/60 **Big Boy Pete** *Olympics*
(also see: Jolly Green Giant)
84/58 **Big Brown Eyes** *Redjacks*
97/69 **Big Bruce** *Steve Greenberg*
23/73 **Big City Miss Ruth Ann** *Gallery*
19/61 **Big Cold Wind** *Pat Boone*
54/84 **Big Crash** *Eddie Money*
18/97 **Big Daddy** *Heavy D*
96/58 **Big Daddy** *Jill Corey*
23/00 **Big Deal** *LeAnn Rimes*
49S/00 **Big Doe** *Suicide*
61/62 **Big Draft (medley)** *Four Preps*
50A/94 **Big Empty** *Stone Temple Pilots*
21/82 **Big Fun** *Kool & The Gang*
1/62 **Big Girls Don't Cry** *4 Seasons*
46/58 **Big Guitar** *Owen Bradley Quintet*
65/93 **Big Gun** *AC/DC*
1/59 **Big Hunk O' Love** *Elvis Presley*
Big Hurt
3/59 *Miss Toni Fisher*
94/66 *Del Shannon*
66/85 **Big In Japan** *Alphaville*
100/69 **Big In Vegas** *Buck Owens*
26/60 **Big Iron** *Marty Robbins*
21/61 **Big John** *Shirelles*
61/70 **Big Leg Woman (With A Short Short Mini Skirt)** *Israel Tolbert*
20/83 **Big Log** *Robert Plant*
5/87 **Big Love** *Fleetwood Mac*
74/62 **Big Love** *Joe Henderson*

64/02 **Big Machine** *Goo Goo Dolls*
3/58 **Big Man** *Four Preps*
20/64 **Big Man In Town** *4 Seasons*
13A/96 **Big Me** *Foo Fighters*
61/87 **Big Mistake** *Peter Cetera*
45/86 **Big Money** *Rush*
97/64 **Big Party** *Barbara & The Browns*
18/00 **Big Pimpin'** *Jay-Z*
Big Poppa
6/95 *Notorious B.I.G.*
38S/01 *Notorious B.I.G.*
F/58 **Big River** *Johnny Cash*
82/61 **Big River, Big Man** *Claude King*
14/79 **Big Shot** *Billy Joel*
93/89 **Big Talk** *Warrant*
8/87 **Big Time** *Peter Gabriel*
95/66 **Big Time** *Lou Christie*
81/73 **Big Time Operator** *Keith Hampshire*
88/94 **Big Time Sensuality** *Björk*
75/60 **Big Time Spender** *Cornbread & Biscuits*
51/63 **Big Wide World** *Teddy Randazzo*
Big Yellow Taxi
29/70 *Neighborhood*
67/70 *Joni Mitchell*
24/75 *Joni Mitchell (live)*
67/95 *Amy Grant*
25S/01 **Bigacts Littleacts** *Afu-Ra*
57/76 **Bigfoot** *Bro Smith*
32S/02 **Bigger Than Life** *C.3.O*
50/75 **Biggest Parakeets In Town** *Jud Strunk*
3/80 **Biggest Part Of Me** *Ambrosia*
37/61 **Bilbao Song** *Andy Williams*
87/97 **Bill** *Peggy Scott-Adams*
Bill Bailey ..see: Won't You Come Home
84/64 **Billie Baby** *Lloyd Price*
Billie Jean
1/83 *Michael Jackson*
75/83 *Club House (medley)*
57/73 **Billion Dollar Babies** *Alice Cooper*
1/99 **Bills, Bills, Bills** *Destiny's Child*
7/58 **Billy** *Kathy Linden*
34/66 **Billy And Sue** *B.J. Thomas*
95/58 **Billy Bayou** *Jim Reeves*
Billy, Don't Be A Hero
1/74 *Bo Donaldson*
96/74 *Paper Lace*
Billy Goat ..see: (You Hit The Wrong Note)
Billy Jack ..see: One Tin Soldier
92/68 **Billy You're My Friend** *Gene Pitney*
11/58 **Bimbombey** *Jimmie Rodgers*
78/95 **Biological Didn't Bother** *Shaquille O'Neal*
95/60 **Biology** *Danny Valentino*
91/68 **Biplane, Ever More** *Irish Rovers*
36/85 **Bird, The** *Time*
(also see: Bossa Nova / Do The)
30/64 **Bird Dance Beat** *Trashmen*
1/58 **Bird Dog** *Everly Brothers*
64/62 **Bird Man** *Highwaymen*
34/58 **Bird On My Head** *David Seville*
52/63 **Bird's The Word** *Rivingtons*
(also see: Surfin' Bird)
12/63 **Birdland** *Chubby Checker*
3/65 **Birds And The Bees** *Jewel Akens*
Birds Of A Feather
96/69 *Joe South*
23/71 *Raiders*
89/67 **Birds Of Britain** *Bob Crewe Generation*
43/96 **Birmingham** *Amanda Marshall*

(Birth & Death Of A Gangster) ..see: Alvin Stone
75/62 **Birth Of The Beat** *Sandy Nelson*
17/55 **Birth Of The Boogie** *Bill Haley*
26/69 **Birthday** *Underground Sunshine*
40/63 **Birthday Party** *Pixies Three*
74/57 **Birthday Party** *Sil Austin*
36/89 **Birthday Suit** *Johnny Kemp*
85/90 **Biscuit's In The House** *Biscuit*
78/85 **Bit By Bit** *Stephanie Mills*
2/97 **Bitch** *Meredith Brooks*
4/74 **Bitch Is Back** *Elton John*
21S/00 **Bitch With No Man** *Somethin' For The People*
28/77 **Bite Your Lip (Get up and dance!)** *Elton John*
4/64 **Bits And Pieces** *Dave Clark Five*
36/73 **Bitter Bad** *Melanie*
88/99 **Bitter End** *Deryl Dodd*
12/98 **Bitter Sweet Symphony** *Verve*
46/91 **Bitter Tears** *INXS*
76/56 **Bitter With The Sweet** *Billy Eckstine*
46/96 **Bittersweet Me** *R.E.M.*
64S/99 **Bizarre** *U-God*
Bizarre Love Triangle
49/94 *Frente!*
98/95 *New Order*
15/01 **Bizounce** *Olivia*

BLACK:

34/88 **Black And Blue** *Van Halen*
1/72 **Black & White** *Three Dog Night*
16/99 **Black Balloon** *Goo Goo Dolls*
79/69 **Black Berries** *Isley Brothers*
18/77 **Black Betty** *Ram Jam*
88/73 **Black Byrd** *Donald Byrd*
42/85 **Black Cars** *Gino Vannelli*
1/90 **Black Cat** *Janet Jackson*
98/63 **Black Cloud** *Chubby Checker*
57/95 **Black Coffee** *Heavy D & The Boyz*
Black Denim Trousers
6/55 *Cheers*
38/55 *Vaughn Monroe*
Black Dog
15/72 *Led Zeppelin*
80/87 *Newcity Rockers*
F/71 **Black-Eyed Blues** *Joe Cocker*
41/74 **Black-Eyed Boys** *Paper Lace*
56/70 **Black Fox** *Freddy Robinson*
37/75 **Black Friday** *Steely Dan*
79/70 **Black Hands White Cotton** *Caboose*
24A/94 **Black Hole Sun** *Soundgarden*
50/98 **Black Ice (Sky High)** *Goodie Mob.*
4/66 **Black Is Black** *Los Bravos*
81/85 **Black Kisses (Never Make You Blue)** *Curtie & The Boombox*
Black Land Farmer
82/61 *Frankie Miller*
85/61 *Wink Martindale*
55/74 **Black Lassie (Featuring Johnny Stash)** *Cheech & Chong*
98/88 **Black Leather** *Kings Of The Sun*
4/71 **Black Magic Woman** *Santana*
66/70 **Black Night** *Deep Purple*
99/65 **Black Night** *Bobby Bland*
91/66 **Black Nights** *Lowell Fulsom*
1/91 **Black Or White** *Michael Jackson*
13/69 **Black Pearl** *Sonny Charles & The Checkmates, Ltd.*
97/71 **Black Seeds Keep On Growing** *Main Ingredient*
68/67 **Black Sheep** *Sam The Sham & The Pharaohs*
17/57 **Black Slacks** *Joe Bennett*

63/84 **Black Stations/White Stations** *M+M*
77/02 **Black Suits Comin' (Nod Ya Head)** *Will Smith*
21/75 **Black Superman - "Muhammad Ali"** *Johnny Wakelin*
1/90 **Black Velvet** *Alannah Myles*
1/75 **Black Water** *Doobie Brothers*
53/96 **Blackberry Molasses** *Mista*
57/59 **Blah, Blah, Blah** *Nicola Paone*
48/83 **Blame It On Love** *Smokey Robinson & Barbara Mitchell*
Blame It On The Boogie
54/78 *Jacksons*
61/78 *Mick Jackson*
7/63 **Blame It On The Bossa Nova** *Eydie Gorme*
88/86 **Blame It On The Radio** *John Parr*
1/89 **Blame It On The Rain** *Milli Vanilli*
78/75 **Blanket On The Ground** *Billie Jo Spears*
36S/01 **Blast, The** *Talib Kweli & Hi-Tek*
1/90 **Blaze Of Glory** *Jon Bon Jovi*
66/81 **Blaze Of Glory** *Kenny Rogers*
39/64 **Bless Our Love** *Gene Chandler*
Bless The Beasts And Children
67/72 *Carpenters*
82/77 *Barry DeVorzon & Perry Botkin, Jr.*
15/61 **Bless You** *Tony Orlando*
53/71 **Bless You** *Martha & The Vandellas*
31/02 **Blessed** *Martina McBride*
34/95 **Blessed** *Elton John*
34/81 **Blessed Are The Believers** *Anne Murray*
97/68 **Blessed Are The Lonely** *Robert Knight*
45/69 **Blessed Is The Rain** *Brooklyn Bridge*
97/73 **Blind Eye** *Uriah Heep*
88/91 **Blind Faith** *Warrant*
48/94 **Blind Man** *Aerosmith*
Blind Man
78/65 *Bobby Bland*
86/65 *Little Milton*
(Blind Man In The Bleachers) ..see: Last Game Of The Season
76/92 **Blinded By Love** *Rythm Syndicate*
1/77 **Blinded By The Light** *Manfred Mann's Earth Band*
36/99 **Bling Bling** *B.G.*
82/58 **Blip Blop** *Bill Doggett*
91/99 **Bliss** *Tori Amos*
50/69 **Blistered** *Johnny Cash*
62/61 **Blizzard, The** *Jim Reeves*
41/78 **Bloat On (Featuring the Bloaters)** *Cheech & Chong*
33/58 **Blob, The** *Five Blobs*
72/00 **Block Is Hot** *Lil Wayne*
73/73 **Blockbuster** *Sweet*
43/74 **Blood Is Thicker Than Water** *William DeVaughn*
42/97 **Blood On The Dance Floor** *Michael Jackson*
74/73 **Blood Red And Goin' Down** *Tanya Tucker*
35/75 **Bloody Well Right** *Supertramp*
2/55 **Blossom Fell** *Nat "King" Cole*
16/79 **Blow Away** *George Harrison*
53A/96 **Blow Up The Outside World** *Soundgarden*
Blowin' In The Wind
2/63 *Peter, Paul & Mary*
9/66 *Stevie Wonder*
21/70 **Blowing Away** *5th Dimension*
6/91 **Blowing Kisses In The Wind** *Paula Abdul*

BLUE:

26/96 **Blue** *LeAnn Rimes*
9/60 **Blue Angel** *Roy Orbison*
35/67 **Blue Autumn** *Bobby Goldsboro*
Blue Bayou
29/63 *Roy Orbison*
3/77 *Linda Ronstadt*
20/58 **Blue Blue Day** *Don Gibson*
45/58 **Blue Boy** *Jim Reeves*
Blue Christmas
97/60 *Browns*
1X/64 *Elvis Presley*
68/73 **Blue Collar** *Bachman-Turner Overdrive*
21/78 **Blue Collar Man (Long Nights)** *Styx*
Blue (Da Ba Dee)
6/00 *Eiffel 65*
22S/00 *Tower 32*
12/82 **Blue Eyes** *Elton John*
21/75 **Blue Eyes Crying In The Rain** *Willie Nelson*
42/63 **Blue Guitar** *Richard Chamberlain*
94/76 **Blue Guitar** *Justin Hayward & John Lodge*
37/59 **Blue Hawaii** *Billy Vaughn*
8/84 **Blue Jean** *David Bowie*
97/02 **Blue Jeans** *Yasmeen*
77/85 **Blue Kiss** *Jane Wiedlin*
62/84 **Blue Light** *David Gilmour*
14H/55 **Blue Mirage (Don't Go)** *Ralph Marterie*
5/57 **Blue Monday** *Fats Domino*
Blue Monday
68/88 *New Order (1988)*
56/99 *Orgy*
23/71 **Blue Money** *Van Morrison*
Blue Moon
55/56 *Elvis Presley*
1/61 *Marcels*
50/61 *Herb Lance*
54/61 *Ventures*
15/79 **Blue Morning, Blue Day** *Foreigner*
78/98 **Blue On Black** *Kenny Wayne Shepherd*
3/63 **Blue On Blue** *Bobby Vinton*
50/58 **Blue Ribbon Baby** *Tommy Sands*
95/66 **Blue River** *Elvis Presley*
97/65 **Blue Shadows** *B.B. King*
81/80 **Blue Side** *Crystal Gayle*
59/66 **Blue Side Of Lonesome** *Jim Reeves*
57/75 **Blue Sky** *Joan Baez*
47/90 **Blue Sky Mine** *Midnight Oil*
Blue Star
29/55 *Felicia Sanders*
F/55 *Les Baxter*
Blue Suede Shoes
2/56 *Carl Perkins*
20/56 *Elvis Presley*
63/56 *Boyd Bennett*
38/73 *Johnny Rivers*
16/60 **Blue Tango** *Bill Black's Combo*
84/61 **Blue Tomorrow** *Billy Vaughn*
Blue Velvet
84/60 *Statues*
1/63 *Bobby Vinton*
68/62 **Blue Water Line** *Brothers Four*
24/64 **Blue Winter** *Connie Francis*
62/83 **Blue World** *Moody Blues*
94/58 **Bluebell** *Mitch Miller*
Blueberry Hill
29/56 *Louis Armstrong & Gordon Jenkins*
2/57 *Fats Domino*
35/75 **Bluebird** *Helen Reddy*
58/67 **Bluebird** *Buffalo Springfield*
54/59 **Bluebird, The Buzzard & The Oriole** *Bobby Day*
Bluebirds Over The Mountain
75/58 *Ersel Hickey*
61/68 *Beach Boys*
34C/56 **Bluejean Bop** *Gene Vincent*
12/78 **Bluer Than Blue** *Michael Johnson*
46/90 **Blues, The** *Tony! Toni! Toné!*
51/83 **Blues, The** *Randy Newman & Paul Simon*
94/90 **Blues Before And After** *Smithereens*
76/80 **Blues Power** *Eric Clapton*
36/62 **Blues (Stay Away From Me)** *Ace Cannon*
37/67 **Blue's Theme** *Davie Allan*
5/02 **Blurry** *Puddle Of Mudd*
Bo Weevil
17/56 *Teresa Brewer*
35/56 *Fats Domino*
(also see: Boll Weevil)
88/78 **Boats Against The Current** *Eric Carmen*
12/82 **Bobbie Sue** *Oak Ridge Boys*
58/61 **Bobby** *Neil Scott*
8/59 **Bobby Sox To Stockings** *Frankie Avalon*
3/62 **Bobby's Girl** *Marcie Blane*
47/84 **Body** *Jacksons*
36/94 **Body & Soul** *Anita Baker*
5/98 **Body Bumpin' Yippie-Yi-Yo** *Public Announcement*
86/79 **Body Heat** *Alicia Bridges*
88/77 **Bodyheat** *James Brown*
11/82 **Body Language** *Queen*
48/84 **Body Rock** *Maria Vidal*
F/94 **Body Rock** *K7*
77/84 **Body Talk** *Deele*
Bohemian Rhapsody
9/76 *Queen*
2/92 *Queen*
42/96 *Braids*
59/70 **Bold Soul Sister** *Ike & Tina Turner*
2/61 **Boll Weevil Song** *Brook Benton*
64S/01 **Bomb Bomb Girl** *J.A.G.*
49/95 **Bomb! (These Sounds Fall Into My Mind)** *Bucketheads*
70/78 **Bombs Away** *Bob Weir*
84/95 **Bomdigi** *Erick Sermon*
63/81 **Bon Bon Vie (Gimme The Good Life)** *T.S. Monk*
55/64 **Bon-Doo-Wah** *Orlons*
46/57 **Bon Voyage** *Janice Harper*
Bonanza
19/61 *Al Caiola*
94/62 *Johnny Cash*
50/59 **Bonaparte's Retreat** *Billy Grammer*
84/85 **Bongo Bongo** *Steve Miller Band*
78/60 **Bongo Bongo Bongo** *Preston Epps*
Bongo Rock
14/59 *Preston Epps*
57/73 *Incredible Bongo Band*
33/62 **Bongo Stomp** *Little Joey & The Flips*
72/93 **Bonnie And Clyde Theme** *Yo-Yo*
(also see: Ballad Of / Foggy Mountain Breakdown)
Bonnie Blue Gal
35C/55 *Lawrence Welk*
51/55 *Mitch Miller*
26/60 **Bonnie Came Back** *Duane Eddy*
(also see: My Bonnie)
Bony Moronie
14/57 *Larry Williams*
62/63 *Appalachians*
70/73 **Boo, Boo, Don't 'Cha Be Blue** *Tommy James*
49/59 **Boo Boo Stick Beat** *Chet Atkins*
47/65 **Boo-Ga-Loo** *Tom & Jerrio*
(also see: Karate-Boo-Ga-Loo)
7/67 **Boogaloo Down Broadway** *Fantastic Johnny C*
93/66 **Boogaloo Party** *Flamingos*
72/74 **Boogie Bands And One Night Stands** *Kathy Dalton*
73/59 **Boogie Bear** *Boyd Bennett*
12/77 **Boogie Child** *Bee Gees*
2/74 **Boogie Down** *Eddie Kendricks*
77/83 **Boogie Down** *Al Jarreau*
1/76 **Boogie Fever** *Sylvers*
2/77 **Boogie Nights** *Heatwave*
3/75 **Boogie On Reggae Woman** *Stevie Wonder*
1/78 **Boogie Oogie Oogie** *Taste Of Honey*
35/78 **Boogie Shoes** *KC & The Sunshine Band*
6/79 **Boogie Wonderland** *Earth, Wind & Fire/The Emotions*
89/61 **Boogie Woogie** *B. Bumble & The Stingers*
(also see: Jay-Dee's)
8/73 **Boogie Woogie Bugle Boy** *Bette Midler*
56/79 **Boogie Woogie Dancin' Shoes** *Claudja Barry*
68/73 **Boogie Woogie Man** *Paul Davis*
Book Of Love
5/58 *Monotones*
62/64 *Raindrops*
60S/01 **Boom** *Richard Lugo*
83/59 **Boom-A-Dip-Dip** *Stan Robinson*
87/96 **Boom Biddy Bye Bye** *Cypress Hill*
Boom Boom
60/62 *John Lee Hooker*
43/65 *Animals*
65/95 **Boom Boom Boom** *Outhere Brothers*
84/99 **Boom, Boom, Boom, Boom!!** *Vengaboys*
17/55 **Boom Boom Boomerang** *DeCastro Sisters*
43/87 **Boom Boom (Let's Go Back To My Room)** *Paul Lekakis*
56/79 **Boom Boom (Out Go The Lights)** *Pat Travers*
90/98 **Boom Bye Yae** *Reiss*
61/92 **Boom! I Got Your Boyfriend** *M.C. Lucious*
84/94 **Boom Shak A-Tack** *Born Jamericans*
13/93 **Boom! Shake The Room** *Jazzy Jeff & Fresh Prince*
53/88 **Boom! There She Was** *Scritti Politti*
3/95 **Boombastic** *Shaggy*
Boomerang ..see: Do The
48/90 **Boomin' System** *LL Cool J*
58/65 **Boot-Leg** *Booker T. & The MG's*
50/92 **Boot Scootin' Boogie** *Brooks & Dunn*
34/94 **Booti Call** *BLACKstreet*
75S/02 **Boottee** *Benzino*
36/71 **Booty Butt** *Ray Charles*
1/01 **Bootylicious** *Destiny's Child*
42/86 **Bop** *Dan Seals*
Bop Gun ..see: One Nation Under A Groove
20/84 **Bop 'Til You Drop** *Rick Springfield*

63/58 **Bop-A-Lena** *Ronnie Self*
70/56 **Boppin' The Blues** *Carl Perkins*
33/83 **Border, The** *America*
Border Song
37/70 *Aretha Franklin*
92/70 *Elton John*
10/84 **Borderline** *Madonna*
38/85 **Borderlines, The** *Jeffrey Osborne*
12/66 **Born A Woman** *Sandy Posey*
92/69 **Born Again** *Sam & Dave*
49S/91 **Born And Raised In Compton** *DJ Quik*
Born Free
7/66 *Roger Williams*
38/68 *Hesitations*
48/85 **Born In East L.A.** *Cheech & Chong*
9/85 **Born In The U.S.A.** *Bruce Springsteen*
(also see: Banned In The U.S.A.)
16/79 **Born To Be Alive** *Patrick Hernandez*
3/89 **Born To Be My Baby** *Bon Jovi*
52/65 **Born To Be Together** *Ronettes*
Born To Be Wild
2/68 *Steppenwolf*
64/69 *Wilson Pickett*
Born To Be With You
5/56 *Chordettes*
81/68 *Sonny James*
89/93 **Born 2 B.R.E.E.D.** *Monie Love*
34/00 **Born To Fly** *Sara Evans*
41/62 **Born To Lose** *Ray Charles*
23/94 **Born To Roll** *Masta Ace Incorporated*
23/75 **Born To Run** *Bruce Springsteen*
17/71 **Born To Wander** *Rare Earth*
7/58 **Born Too Late** *Poni-Tails*
60/58 **Borrowed Dreams** *Bobby Helms*
71/91 **Borrowed Love** *Bingoboys*
64/80 **Borrowed Time** *Styx*
19/79 **Boss, The** *Diana Ross*
87/63 **Boss** *Rumblers*
28/63 **Boss Guitar** *Duane Eddy*
Bossa Nova ..also see: Fly Me To The Moon
8/63 **Bossa Nova Baby** *Elvis Presley*
97/62 **(Bossa Nova) Bird** *Dells*
69/63 **Bossa Nova U.S.A.** *Dave Brubeck Quartet*
Both Sides Now
8/68 *Judy Collins*
91/69 *Dion*
25/93 **Both Sides Of The Story** *Phil Collins*
56/02 **Bother** *Stone Sour*
9/68 **Bottle Of Wine** *Fireballs*
19/80 **Boulevard** *Jackson Browne*
37S/00 **Bounce** *Miracle*
37S/01 **Bounce** *Survivalist*
40/63 **Bounce, The** *Olympics*
54/90 **Bounce Back** *Alisha*
81/80 **Bounce, Rock, Skate, Roll** *Vaughan Mason*
20/00 **Bounce With Me** *Lil Bow Wow*
37/02 **Bouncin' Back (Bumpin' Me Against The Wall)** *Mystikal*
52/84 **Bouncin' Off The Walls** *Matthew Wilder*
93/01 **Bouncing Off The Ceiling (Upside Down)** *A*Teens*
46A/96 **Bound For The Floor** *Local H*
54S/02 **Bout It Bout It** *Diplomats*
21/96 **Bow Down** *Westside Connection*
21/01 **Bow Wow (That's My Name)** *Lil Bow Wow*
89/93 **Bow Wow Wow** *Funkdoobiest*
40/67 **Bowling Green** *Everly Brothers*
7/69 **Boxer, The** *Simon & Garfunkel*

BOY:

63S/01 **Boy** *Book Of Love*
71/87 **Boy Blue** *Cyndi Lauper*
Boy From New York City
8/65 *Ad Libs*
7/81 *Manhattan Transfer*
57S/02 **Boy (I Need You)** *Mariah Carey*
Boy I'm Gonna Marry ..see: (Today I Met)
48/88 **Boy, I've Been Told** *Sa-Fire*
26/85 **Boy In The Box** *Corey Hart*
86/87 **Boy In The Bubble** *Paul Simon*
1/98 **Boy Is Mine** *Brandy & Monica*
2/69 **Boy Named Sue** *Johnny Cash*
18/63 **Boy Next Door** *Secrets*
97/87 **Boy Toy** *Tia*
85/64 **Boy With The Beatle Hair** *Swans*
10/59 **Boy Without A Girl** *Frankie Avalon*
12/76 **Boys Are Back In Town** *Thin Lizzy*
37/84 **Boys Do Fall In Love** *Robin Gibb*
Boys In The Band ..see: (How Bout A Little Hand For)
25/87 **Boys Night Out** *Timothy B. Schmit*
49/62 **Boys' Night Out** *Patti Page*
Boys Of Summer
5/85 *Don Henley*
52S/03 *DJ Sammy*
42S/91 **Boys To Men** *New Edition*
74/02 **Braid My Hair** *Mario*
35A/96 **Brain Stew/Jaded** *Green Day*
69/92 **Brainstorming** *M.C. Brains*
1/71 **Brand New Key** *Melanie*
61/75 **Brand New Love Affair** *Chicago*
66/76 **Brand New Love Affair** *Jigsaw*
15/87 **Brand New Lover** *Dead Or Alive*
Brand New Me
24/69 *Dusty Springfield*
F/71 *Aretha Franklin*
79/78 **Brandy** *O'Jays*
(also see: Mandy)
1/72 **Brandy (You're A Fine Girl)** *Looking Glass*
35/61 **Brass Buttons** *String-A-Longs*
14/80 **Brass In Pocket (I'm Special)** *Pretenders*
48/87 **Brass Monkey** *Beastie Boys*
11/75 **Brazil** *Ritchie Family*
Bread And Butter
2/64 *Newbeats*
68/83 *Robert John*

BREAK:

70/84 **Break-A-Way** *Tracey Ullman*
39/76 **Break Away** *Art Garfunkel*
63/69 **Break Away** *Beach Boys*
60/88 **Breakaway** *Big Pig*
40/65 **Break Away (From That Boy)** *Newbeats*
74/87 **Break Every Rule** *Tina Turner*
51S/01 **Break 4 Love** *Peter Rauhofer & The Pet Shop Boys*
25/93 **Break It Down Again** *Tears For Fears*
Break It To Me Gently
4/62 *Brenda Lee*
11/82 *Juice Newton*
85/77 **Break It To Me Gently** *Aretha Franklin*
85/78 **Break It To Them Gently** *Burton Cummings*
26/82 **Break It Up** *Foreigner*
5/84 **Break My Stride** *Matthew Wilder*
62/66 **Break Out** *Mitch Ryder*
6/87 **Breakout** *Swing Out Sister*
52/58 **Break-Up** *Jerry Lee Lewis*
95/65 **Break Up** *Del Shannon*
Break Up To Make Up
5/73 *Stylistics*
70/91 *Cynthia*
98/99 **Break Ups 2 Make Ups** *Method Man*
26/02 **Break Ya Neck** *Busta Rhymes*
35/68 **Break Your Promise** *Delfonics*
76/93 **Breakadawn** *De La Soul*
8/84 **Breakdance** *Irene Cara*
31/71 **Breakdown, The** *Rufus Thomas*
40/78 **Breakdown** *Tom Petty*
53A/98 **Breakdown** *Mariah Carey*
67/94 **Breakdown** *FU-Schnickens'*
82/90 **Breakdown** *Seduction*
15/80 **Breakdown Dead Ahead** *Boz Scaggs*
94/76 **Breaker - Breaker** *Outlaws*
5/96 **Breakfast At Tiffany's** *Deep Blue Something*
92/76 **Breakfast For Two** *Country Joe McDonald*
62/80 **Breakfast In America** *Supertramp*
91/69 **Breakfast In Bed** *Dusty Springfield*
43/82 **Breakin' Away** *Al Jarreau*
22/81 **Breaking Away** *Balance*
7/61 **Breakin' In A Brand New Broken Heart** *Connie Francis*
6/92 **Breakin' My Heart (Pretty Brown Eyes)** *Mint Condition*
9/84 **Breakin'...There's No Stopping Us** *Ollie & Jerry*
Breakin' Up ..see: (Best Part Of)
31/66 **Breakin' Up Is Breakin' My Heart** *Roy Orbison*
32/97 **Breaking All The Rules** *She Moves*
70/84 **Breaking Up Is Hard On You (a/k/a Don't Take Ma Bell Away From Me)** *American Comedy Network*
Breaking Up Is Hard To Do
1/62 *Neil Sedaka*
67/68 *Happenings*
34/70 *Lenny Welch*
28/72 *Partridge Family*
8/76 *Neil Sedaka (new version)*
69/59 **Breaking Up Is Hard To Do** *Jivin' Gene*
91/73 **Breaking Up Somebody's Home** *Albert King*
18/83 **Breaking Us In Two** *Joe Jackson*
87/80 **Breaks, The** *Kurtis Blow*
15/81 **Breakup Song (They Don't Write 'Em)** *Greg Kihn Band*
100/63 **Breakwater** *Lawrence Welk*
75/63 **Breath Taking Guy** *Supremes*
2/00 **Breathe** *Faith Hill*
78/03 **Breathe** *Télépopmusik*
3/94 **Breathe Again** *Toni Braxton*
71/00 **Breathe And Stop** *Q-Tip*
70S/02 **Breathe Your Name** *Sixpence None The Richer*
7/58 **Breathless** *Jerry Lee Lewis*
34/01 **Breathless** *Corrs*
8/55 **Breeze And I (Andalucia)** *Caterina Valente*
63/76 **Breezin'** *George Benson*
57/63 **Brenda** *Cupids*
68/98 **Brian Wilson** *Barenaked Ladies*
56/72 **Brian's Song** *Michel LeGrand*
19A/98 **Brick** *Ben Folds Five*
5/77 **Brick House** *Commodores*
50/61 **Bridge Of Love** *Joe Dowell*

Bridge Over Troubled Water
1/70 *Simon & Garfunkel*
6/71 *Aretha Franklin*
41/79 *Linda Clifford*
50/71 **Bridget The Midget** *Ray Stevens*
81/60 **Brigade Of Broken Hearts** *Paul Evans*
Bright ..also see: Brite
Bright Lights Big City
58/61 *Jimmy Reed*
91/71 *Sonny James*
92/63 **Brightest Smile In Town** *Ray Charles*
82/70 **Brighton Hill** *Jackie DeShannon*
5/87 **Brilliant Disguise** *Bruce Springsteen*
51/68 **Bring A Little Lovin'** *Los Bravos*
66/65 **Bring A Little Sunshine (To My Heart)** *Vic Dana*
87/74 **Bring Back The Love Of Yesterday** *Dells*
75/66 **Bring Back The Time** *B.J. Thomas*
95/68 **Bring Back Those Rockabye Baby Days** *Tiny Tim*
49/89 **Bring Down The Moon** *Boy Meets Girl*
22S/00 **Bring It All Back** *S Club 7*
87/89 **Bring It All Back** *Grayson Hugh*
5/00 **Bring It All To Me** *Blaque (Feat. *NSYNC)*
96/72 **Bring It Home (And Give It To Me)** *Hot Sauce*
63/98 **Bring It On** *Keith Washington*
Bring It On Home To Me
13/62 *Sam Cooke*
32/65 *Animals*
17/68 *Eddie Floyd*
96/70 *Lou Rawls*
(also see: I'll Bring It Home To You)
29/67 **Bring It Up** *James Brown*
36/02 **Bring On The Rain** *Jo Dee Messina with Tim McGraw*
12/71 **Bring The Boys Home** *Freda Payne*
45/94 **Bring The Pain** *Method Man*
83/65 **Bring Your Love To Me** *Righteous Brothers*
61/84 **Bringin' On The Heartbreak** *Def Leppard*
65/75 **Bringing It Back** *Elvis Presley*
73/79 **(Bringing Out) The Girl In Me** *Maxine Nightingale*
82/67 **Brink Of Disaster** *Lesley Gore*
2/61 **Bristol Stomp** *Dovells*
27/62 **Bristol Twistin' Annie** *Dovells*
66/80 **Brite Eyes** *Robbin Thompson Band*
24/00 **Broadway** *Goo Goo Dolls*
55/71 **Broken** *Guess Who*
20/92 **Broken Arrow** *Rod Stewart*
81/62 **Broken Heart** *Fiestas*
91/61 **Broken Heart And A Pillow Filled With Tears** *Patti Page*
97/61 **Broken Hearted** *Miracles*
9/95 **Brokenhearted** *Brandy*
12/79 **Broken Hearted Me** *Anne Murray*
7/59 **Broken-Hearted Melody** *Sarah Vaughan*
95/88 **Broken Land** *Adventures*
61/97 **Broken Wing** *Martina McBride*
1/85 **Broken Wings** *Mr. Mister*
75/60 **Brontosaurus Stomp** *Piltdown Men*
74/77 **Brooklyn** *Cody Jameson*
54/81 **Brooklyn Girls** *Robbie Dupree*
58/68 **Brooklyn Roads** *Neil Diamond*
54/95 **Brooklyn Zoo** *Ol Dirty Bastard*
53/66 **Broomstick Cowboy** *Bobby Goldsboro*
52/02 **Brotha** *Angie Stone*
84/61 **Brother-In-Law (He's A Moocher)** *Paul Peek*
1/73 **Brother Louie** *Stories*
22/69 **Brother Love's Travelling Salvation Show** *Neil Diamond*
32/70 **Brother Rapp** *James Brown*
67/73 **Brother's Gonna Work It Out** *Willie Hutch*
91/69 **Brown Arms In Houston** *Orpheus*
Brown Eyed Girl
10/67 *Van Morrison*
45/72 *El Chicano*
43/68 **Brown Eyed Woman** *Bill Medley*
73/70 **Brown Paper Bag** *Syndicate Of Sound*
56S/01 **Brown Skin** *India.Arie*
1/71 **Brown Sugar** *Rolling Stones*
27/95 **Brown Sugar** *D'Angelo*
55S/02 **Brown Sugar (Extra Sweet)** *Mos Def*
66/71 **Brownsville** *Joy Of Cooking*
27/85 **Bruce** *Rick Springfield*
71S/95 **Bubba Hyde** *Diamond Rio*
74/69 **Bubble Gum Music** *Rock & Roll Double Bubble*
80/56 **Buchanan and Goodman On Trial** *Buchanan & Goodman*
60/65 **Buckaroo** *Buck Owens*
54/65 **Bucket "T"** *Ronny & The Daytonas*
93/94 **Bucktown** *Smif-N-Wessun*
18A/95 **Buddy Holly** *Weezer*
43/93 **Buddy X** *Neneh Cherry*
86/70 **Buffalo Soldier** *Flamingos*
3/89 **Buffalo Stance** *Neneh Cherry*
33/99 **Bug A Boo** *Destiny's Child*
3/69 **Build Me Up Buttercup** *Foundations*
58/57 **Build Your Love (On A Strong Foundation)** *Johnnie Ray*
13/97 **Building A Mystery** *Sarah McLachlan*
24/60 **Bulldog** *Fireballs*
22/96 **Bullet With Butterfly Wings** *Smashing Pumpkins*
90/84 **Bullish** *Herb Alpert*
62A/96 **Bulls On Parade** *Rage Against The Machine*
83/58 **Bullwhip Rock** *Cyclones*
Bumble Bee
46/60 *LaVern Baker*
21/65 *Searchers*
21/61 **Bumble Boogie** *B. Bumble & The Stingers*
1/03 **Bump, Bump, Bump** *B2K*
80/75 **Bump Me Baby** *Dooley Silverspoon*
1/94 **Bump N' Grind** *R. Kelly*
12/75 **Bungle In The Jungle** *Jethro Tull*
18S/02 **Bunny Hop** *Da En Tourage*
70/59 **Bunny Hop** *Applejacks*
40A/96 **Burden In My Hand** *Soundgarden*
42/01 **Burn** *Jo Dee Messina*
52/98 **Burn** *Militia*
99/02 **Burn** *Mobb Deep*
84/81 **Burn Rubber (Why You Wanna Hurt Me)** *Gap Band*
Burn That Candle
86/55 *Cues*
9/56 *Bill Haley*
40/81 **Burnin' For You** *Blue Öyster Cult*
78/77 **Burnin' Sky** *Bad Company*
53/75 **Burnin' Thing** *Mac Davis*
60/02 **Burnin' Up** *Faith Evans*
3/60 **Burning Bridges** *Jack Scott*
34/71 **Burning Bridges** *Mike Curb Congregation*
64/82 **Burning Down One Side** *Robert Plant*
9/83 **Burning Down The House** *Talking Heads*
73/85 **Burning Flame** *Vitamin Z*
2/86 **Burning Heart** *Survivor*
39/83 **Burning Heart** *Vandenberg*
72/88 **Burning Like A Flame** *Dokken*
2/72 **Burning Love** *Elvis Presley*
53/62 **Burning Of Atlanta** *Claude King*
64/68 **Burning Spear** *Soulful Strings*
5/66 **Bus Stop** *Hollies*
17/56 **Bus Stop Song (A Paper Of Pins)** *Four Lads*
7/89 **Bust A Move** *Young MC*
25/63 **Bust Out** *Busters*
4/63 **Busted** *Ray Charles*
14S/01 **Buster** *Dennis Da Menace*
96/65 **Buster Browne** *Willie Mitchell*
34/79 **Bustin' Loose** *Chuck Brown*
71/79 **Bustin' Out** *Rick James*
46/99 **Busy Man** *Billy Ray Cyrus*
36A/96 **But Anyway** *Blues Traveler*
69/57 **(But As They Say) That's Life** *Jack Pleis*
69/70 **But For Love** *Jerry Naylor*
37/01 **But For The Grace Of God** *Keith Urban*
But I Do
4/61 *Clarence Henry*
82/73 *Bobby Vinton*
But It's Alright
22/66 *J.J. Jackson*
45/69 *J.J. Jackson*
54/94 *Huey Lewis*
41/62 **But Not For Me** *Ketty Lester*
72/62 **But On The Other Hand Baby** *Ray Charles*
But You Know I Love You
19/69 *First Edition*
41/81 *Dolly Parton*
15/65 **But You're Mine** *Sonny & Cher*
91/92 **Butt Naked** *Charm*
16/97 **Butta Love** *Next*
29/75 **Butter Boy** *Fanny*
14/02 **Butterflies** *Michael Jackson*
Butterfly
1/57 *Charlie Gracie*
1/57 *Andy Williams*
61/57 *Bob Carroll*
1/01 **Butterfly** *Crazy Town*
16A/97 **Butterfly** *Mariah Carey*
78/72 **Butterfly** *Danyel Gerard*
23/63 **Butterfly Baby** *Bobby Rydell*
Butterfly Kisses
10A/97 *Bob Carlisle*
22/97 *Raybon Bros.*
93/56 **Butternut** *Jimmy Heap*
91/88 **Button Off My Shirt** *Paul Carrack*
45/67 **Buy For Me The Rain** *Nitty Gritty Dirt Band*
40/00 **Buy Me A Rose** *Kenny Rogers*
47/69 **Buying A Book** *Joe Tex*
51/61 **Buzz Buzz A-Diddle-It** *Freddy Cannon*
11/58 **Buzz-Buzz-Buzz** *Hollywood Flames*
91/72 **Buzzy Brown** *Tim Davis*
55/62 **B'wa Nina (Pretty Girl)** *Tokens*
50/58 **By The Light Of The Silvery Moon** *Jimmy Bowen*

By The Time I Get To Phoenix

26/67 *Glen Campbell*

37/69 *Isaac Hayes*

84/69 *Mad Lads*

81/71 *Glen Campbell/Anne Murray (medley)*

25/93 **By The Time This Night Is Over** *Kenny G with Peabo Bryson*

34/02 **By The Way** *Red Hot Chili Peppers*

43/57 **By You, By You, By You** *Jim Lowe*

75/01 **By Your Side** *Sade*

43/98 **Bye Bye** *Jo Dee Messina*

15^{S}/01 **Bye-Bye Baby** *Brandy Moss-Scott*

45/61 **Bye Bye Baby** *Mary Wells*

91/75 **Bye Bye Baby** *U.S. 1*

12/65 **Bye, Bye, Baby (Baby, Goodbye)** *4 Seasons*

53/64 **Bye Bye Barbara** *Johnny Mathis*

54/66 **Bye Bye Blues** *Bert Kaempfert*

4/00 **Bye Bye Bye** **NSYNC*

Bye Bye Love

2/57 *Everly Brothers*

73/57 *Webb Pierce*

C

12/97 **C U When U Get There** *Coolio*

C'mon ..see: Come On

67/77 **C.B. Savage** *Rod Hart*

C.C. Rider

12/57 *Chuck Willis*

34/63 *LaVern Baker*

10/66 *Animals*

76/66 *Bobby Powell*

(also see: Jenny Take A Ride)

2/87 **C'est La Vie** *Robbie Nevil*

9/99 **C'est La Vie** *B*Witched*

C'est La Vie

11/55 *Sarah Vaughan*

85/55 *Sunny Gale*

97/55 *DeJohn Sisters*

91/77 **C'est La Vie** *Greg Lake*

22/61 **C'est Si Bon (It's So Good)** *Conway Twitty*

C'mon ..see: Come On

22/57 **Ca, C'est L'amour** *Tony Bennett*

47/78 **Ca Plane Pour Moi** *Plastic Bertrand*

23/68 **Cab Driver** *Mills Brothers*

72/68 **Cabaret** *Herb Alpert*

77/81 **Cafe Amore** *Spyro Gyra*

22/62 **Cajun Queen** *Jimmy Dean*

Calcutta

1/61 *Lawrence Welk*

96/61 *Four Preps*

95/64 **Caldonia** *James Brown*

82/77 **Caledonia** *Robin Trower*

4/61 **Calendar Girl** *Neil Sedaka*

50/78 **California** *Debby Boone*

72/64 **California Bound** *Ronny & The Daytonas*

66/76 **California Day** *Starland Vocal Band*

California Dreamin'

4/66 *Mama's & The Papa's*

43/69 *Bobby Womack*

56/79 *America*

57/86 *Beach Boys*

67/68 **California Earthquake** *Mama Cass*

93/71 **California Earthquake** *Norman Greenbaum*

45/70 **California Girl** *Eddie Floyd*

92/69 **California Girl (And The Tennessee Square)** *Tompall & The Glaser Brothers*

California Girls

3/65 *Beach Boys*

3/85 *David Lee Roth*

72/71 **California Kid And Reemo** *Lobo*

6/96 **California Love** *2Pac*

75/74 **California My Way** *Main Ingredient*

16/67 **California Nights** *Lesley Gore*

76/78 **California Nights** *Sweet*

96/71 **California On My Mind** *Morning Mist*

84/73 **California Saga (On My Way To Sunny Californ-i-a)** *Beach Boys*

California Soul

25/69 *5th Dimension*

56/70 *Marvin Gaye & Tammi Terrell*

California Sun

89/61 *Joe Jones*

5/64 *Rivieras*

69/00 **Californication** *Red Hot Chili Peppers*

CALL:

52/01 **Call, The** *Backstreet Boys*

91/76 **Call, The** *Anne Murray*

18/89 **Call It Love** *Poco*

44/91 **Call It Poison** *Escape Club*

53/91 **Call It Rock N' Roll** *Great White*

1/80 **Call Me** *Blondie*

13/70 **Call Me** *Aretha Franklin*

21/58 **Call Me** *Johnny Mathis*

22/66 **Call Me** *Chris Montez*

26/82 **Call Me** *Skyy*

31/02 **Call Me** *Tweet*

35/97 **Call Me** *Le Click*

54/85 **Call Me** *Go West*

54/86 **Call Me** *Dennis DeYoung*

90/97 **Call Me** *Too $hort & Lil' Kim*

22^{S}/01 **Call Me Claus** *Garth Brooks*

10/73 **Call Me (Come Back Home)** *Al Green*

44^{S}/01 **Call Me E.S.** *7L & Esoteric*

Call Me Irresponsible

75/63 *Jack Jones*

78/63 *Frank Sinatra*

40/68 **Call Me Lightning** *Who*

19/62 **Call Me Mr. In-Between** *Burl Ives*

95/71 **Call Me Up In Dreamland** *Van Morrison*

65/80 **(Call Me) When The Spirit Moves You** *Touch*

99/75 **(Call Me Your) Anything Man** *Bobby Moore*

52/71 **Call My Name, I'll Be There** *Wilson Pickett*

6/74 **Call On Me** *Chicago*

22/63 **Call On Me** *Bobby Bland*

75/79 **Call Out My Name** *Zwol*

15/85 **Call To The Heart** *Giuffria*

83/62 **Callin' Doctor Casey** *John D. Loudermilk*

21/00 **Callin' Me** *Lil' Zane*

60/82 **Calling All Girls** *Queen*

18/86 **Calling America** *Electric Light Orchestra*

16/77 **Calling Dr. Love** *Kiss*

53/89 **Calling It Love** *Animotion*

31^{S}/02 **Calling My Name** *Ren with Christina Sanchez*

Calling Occupants Of Interplanetary Craft

32/77 *Carpenters*

F/77 *Klaatu*

2/75 **Calypso** *John Denver*

42/57 **Calypso Melody** *David Rose*

100/69 **Camel Back** *A.B. Skhy*

91/66 **Campfire Girls** *Billy Joe Royal*

CAN:

67^{S}/93 **Can He Love U Like This** *After 7*

22^{S}/03 **Can I** *Prince EP*

58/91 **Can I Call You My Girl?** *PC Quest*

5/69 **Can I Change My Mind** *Tyrone Davis*

83/57 **Can I Come Over Tonight** *Velours*

19/99 **Can I Get A...** *Jay-Z*

Can I Get A Witness

22/63 *Marvin Gaye*

39/71 *Lee Michaels*

18^{S}/02 **Can I Get That?!!?** *Bear Witnez!*

89/66 **Can I Get To Know You Better** *Turtles*

35^{S}/00 **Can I Get Your Number** *No Authority*

81/95 **Can I Stay With You** *Karyn White*

15/57 **Can I Steal A Little Love** *Frank Sinatra*

27/95 **Can I Touch You...There?** *Michael Bolton*

49/66 **Can I Trust You?** *Bachelors*

56/76 **Can The Can** *Suzi Quatro*

31/74 **Can This Be Real** *Natural Four*

43/97 **Can U Feel It** *3rd Party*

59/94 **Can U Get Wit It** *Usher*

30^{S}/02 **Can U Help Me** *Usher*

75/97 **Can We** *SWV*

(Can We Rock?) ..see: What's Up Doc?

Can We Still Be Friends

29/78 *Todd Rundgren*

52/80 *Robert Palmer*

9/94 **Can We Talk** *Tevin Campbell*

Can You ..also see: Can U

Can You Dance ..see: (Baby Tell Me)

Can You Do It

41/64 *Contours*

45/76 *Grand Funk Railroad*

75/70 **Can You Feel It** *Bobby Goldsboro*

77/81 **Can You Feel It** *Jacksons*

92/96 **Can You Feel Me** *Dru Down*

69/85 **Can You Feel The Beat** *Lisa Lisa & Cult Jam*

4/94 **Can You Feel The Love Tonight** *Elton John*

16/56 **Can You Find It In Your Heart** *Tony Bennett*

38/78 **Can You Fool** *Glen Campbell*

93/50 **Can You Get To That** *Funkadelic*

49/74 **Can You Handle It?** *Graham Central Station*

47/65 **Can You Jerk Like Me** *Contours*

58/66 **Can You Please Crawl Out Your Window?** *Bob Dylan*

52/79 **Can You Read My Mind** *Maureen McGovern*

44/89 **Can You Stand The Rain** *New Edition*

52/91 **Can You Stop The Rain** *Peabo Bryson*

48/64 **Can Your Monkey Do The Dog** *Rufus Thomas*

CAN'T:

87/96 **Can't Be Really Gone** *Tim McGraw*

65/96 **Can't Be Wasting My Time** *Mona Lisa*

56/01 **Can't Believe** *Faith Evans*

1/64 **Can't Buy Me Love** *Beatles*

91/76 **Can't Change My Heart** *Cate Bros.*

36/95 **Can't Cry Anymore** *Sheryl Crow*

42/92 **Can't Cry Hard Enough** *Williams Brothers*

25/01 **Can't Deny It** *Fabolous*

Can't Fight The Moonlight
71/00 *LeAnn Rimes*
11/02 *LeAnn Rimes*
1/85 **Can't Fight This Feeling** *REO Speedwagon*
Can't Find The Time
80/69 *Orpheus*
54/71 *Rose Colored Glass*
43/91 **Can't Forget You** *Gloria Estefan*
5/74 **Can't Get Enough** *Bad Company*
49/98 **Can't Get Enough** *Willie Max*
96/99 **Can't Get Enough** *Patty Loveless*
42/90 **Can't Get Enuff** *Winger*
Can't Get Enough Of You, Baby
56/67 *? (Question Mark) & The Mysterians*
27[A]/98 *Smash Mouth*
Can't Get Enough Of Your Love, Babe
1/74 *Barry White*
20/93 *Taylor Dayne*
9/75 **Can't Get It Out Of My Head** *Electric Light Orchestra*
98/70 **Can't Get Over Losing You** *Donnie Elbert*
87/64 **Can't Get Over (The Bossa Nova)** *Eydie Gorme*
75/87 **Can't Get Started** *Peter Wolf*
2/63 **Can't Get Used To Losing You** *Andy Williams*
62/96 **Can't Get You Off My Mind** *Lenny Kravitz*
7/02 **Can't Get You Out Of My Head** *Kylie Minogue*
79/97 **Can't Get You Out Of My Mind** *Lil Suzy*
51/75 **Can't Give You Anything (But My Love)** *Stylistics*
84/00 **Can't Go For That** *Tamia*
(also see: I Can't Go For That)
56/96 **Can't Hang** *Xscape*
78/67 **Can't Help But Love You** *Standells*
Can't Help Falling In Love
2/62 *Elvis Presley*
51/70 *Al Martino*
88/70 *Andy Williams*
24/87 *Corey Hart*
1/93 *UB40*
100/61 **Can't Help Lovin' That Girl Of Mine** *Excels*
98/94 **Can't Help Myself** *Gerald Levert*
39/76 **Can't Hide Love** *Earth, Wind & Fire*
89/82 **Can't Hold Back (Your Loving)** *Kano*
63/79 **Can't Keep A Good Man Down** *Eddie Money*
73/96 **Can't Knock The Hustle** *Jay-Z*
2/92 **Can't Let Go** *Mariah Carey*
55/97 **Can't Let Go** *Laurneá*
67/84 **Can't Let Go** *Stephen Stills*
91/65 **Can't Let You Out Of My Sight** *Chuck Jackson & Maxine Brown*
1/90 **(Can't Live Without Your) Love And Affection** *Nelson*
1/97 **Can't Nobody Hold Me Down** *Puff Daddy*
66/63 **Can't Nobody Love You** *Solomon Burke*
65[S]/99 **Can't Nobody Love You (Like I Do)** *Wynonna*
62/80 **Can't Put A Price On Love** *Knack*
65/66 **Can't Satisfy** *Impressions*
88/74 **Can't Say Nothin'** *Curtis Mayfield*
41/67 **Can't Seem To Make You Mine** *Seeds*
29/83 **Can't Shake Loose** *Agnetha Fältskog*
51/79 **Can't Sleep** *Rockets*
3/78 **Can't Smile Without You** *Barry Manilow*
84/00 **Can't Stay** *Dave Hollister*
6/88 **Can't Stay Away From You** *Gloria Estefan*
6/90 **Can't Stop** *After 7*
50/85 **Can't Stop** *Rick James*
13/77 **Can't Stop Dancin'** *Captain & Tennille*
12/90 **Can't Stop Fallin' Into Love** *Cheap Trick*
52/76 **Can't Stop Groovin' Now, Wanna Do It Some More** *B.T. Express*
30/95 **Can't Stop Lovin' You** *Van Halen*
25/70 **Can't Stop Loving You** *Tom Jones*
78/67 **Can't Stop Loving You** *Last Word*
99/95 **Can't Stop My Heart From Loving You (The Rain Song)** *Aaron Neville*
2/91 **Can't Stop This Thing We Started** *Bryan Adams*
Can't Take My Eyes Off You
2/67 *Frankie Valli*
7/68 *Lettermen (medley)*
52/69 *Nancy Wilson*
35[A]/98 *Lauryn Hill*
50/91 **Can't Truss It** *Public Enemy*
94/95 **Can't Wait** *Redman*
66/84 **Can't Wait All Night** *Juice Newton*
41/86 **Can't Wait Another Minute** *Five Star*
42/57 **Can't Wait For Summer** *Steve Lawrence*
Can't We Try
6/87 *Dan Hill (with Vonda Sheppard)*
59/98 *Rockell (With Collage)*
52/80 **Can't We Try** *Teddy Pendergrass*
54/68 **Can't You Find Another Way (Of Doing It)** *Sam & Dave*
2/65 **Can't You Hear My Heartbeat** *Herman's Hermits*
48/72 **Can't You Hear The Song?** *Wayne Newton*
96/65 **Can't You Just See Me** *Aretha Franklin*
13/95 **Can't You See** *Total*
Can't You See
97/76 *Waylon Jennings*
75/77 *Marshall Tucker Band*
52/68 **Can't You See Me Cry** *New Colony Six*
4/64 **Can't You See That She's Mine** *Dave Clark Five*
94/66 **Can't You See (You're Losing Me)** *Mary Wells*
20/87 **Can'tcha Say (You Believe In Me)/Still In Love** *Boston*
Canadian Sunset
2/56 *Hugo Winterhalter/Eddie Heywood*
7/56 *Andy Williams*
91/61 *Etta Jones*
76/65 *Sounds Orchestral*
3/70 **Candida** *Dawn*
Candle In The Wind
6/88 *Elton John*
1/97 *Elton John (1997)*
(Candles In The Rain) ..see: Lay Down
21/87 **Candy** *Cameo*
28/91 **Candy** *Iggy Pop*
41/99 **Candy** *Mandy Moore*
59[S]/01 **Candy** *Foxy Brown*
63/65 **Candy** *Astors*
97/59 **Candy Apple Red** *Bonnie Guitar*
67/93 **Candy Everybody Wants** *10,000 Maniacs*
3/63 **Candy Girl** *Four Seasons*
46/83 **Candy Girl** *New Edition*
1/72 **Candy Man** *Sammy Davis, Jr.*
25/61 **Candy Man** *Roy Orbison*
2/95 **Candy Rain** *Soul For Real*
72/60 **Candy Sweet** *Pat Boone*
58/64 **Candy To Me** *Eddie Holland*
91/74 **Candy's Going Bad** *Golden Earring*
46/70 **Canned Ham** *Norman Greenbaum*
58[S]/99 **Canned Heat** *Jamiroquai*
15/58 **Cannonball** *Duane Eddy*
28/85 **Cannonball** *Supertramp*
44/94 **Cannonball** *Breeders*
9/94 **Cantaloop** *US3*
92/83 **Canvas Of Life** *Minor Detail*
45/59 **Cap And Gown** *Marty Robbins*
90/74 **Captain Howdy** *Simon Stokes*
16/86 **Captain Of Her Heart** *Double*
94/94 **Captain Save A Hoe** *E-40*
57/70 **Capture The Moment** *Jay & The Americans*
88/77 **Capture Your Heart** *Blue*
1/77 **Car Wash** *Rose Royce*
39/65 **Cara-Lin** *Strangeloves*
Cara Mia
10/54 *David Whitfield with Mantovani*
4/65 *Jay & The Americans*
18/02 **Caramel** *City High*
48/60 **Caravan** *Santo & Johnny*
51/86 **Caravan Of Love** *Isley Jasper Isley*
10/74 **Carefree Highway** *Gordon Lightfoot*
60/62 **Careless Love** *Ray Charles*
1/85 **Careless Whisper** *Wham!*
93/71 **Carey** *Joni Mitchell*
27/59 **Caribbean** *Mitchell Torok*
79/92 **Caribbean Blue** *Enya*
55/75 **Caribbean Festival** *Kool & The Gang*
1/84 **Caribbean Queen (No More Love On The Run)** *Billy Ocean*
45/00 **Carlene** *Phil Vassar*
51/68 **Carmen** *Herb Alpert*
10/95 **Carnival** *Natalie Merchant*
Carol
18/58 *Chuck Berry*
61/64 *Tommy Roe*
93/71 **Carolina Day** *Livingston Taylor*
Carolina In My Mind
67/70 *James Taylor*
73/70 *Crystal Mansion*
21/75 **Carolina In The Pines** *Michael Murphey*
32/66 **Caroline, No** *Brian Wilson*
58/72 **Carolyn** *Merle Haggard*
29/68 **Carpet Man** *5th Dimension*
3/87 **Carrie** *Europe*
34/80 **Carrie** *Cliff Richard*
9/67 **Carrie-Anne** *Hollies*
81/83 **Carrie's Gone** *Le Roux*
92/69 **Carroll County Accident** *Porter Wagoner*
52/75 **Carry Me** *David Crosby/Graham Nash*
26/69 **Carry Me Back** *Rascals*
71/72 **Carry Me, Carrie** *Dr. Hook*
11/77 **Carry On Wayward Son** *Kansas*
9/80 **Cars** *Gary Numan*
54/88 **Cars With The Boom** *L'Trimm*
5/87 **Casanova** *Levert*
2/00 **Case Of The Ex (Whatcha Gonna Do)** *Mya*
67/80 **Case Of You** *Frank Stallone*

27/67 **Casino Royale** *Herb Alpert*
51/67 **Casonova (Your Playing Days Are Over)** *Ruby Andrews*
Cast Your Fate To The Wind
22/63 *Vince Guaraldi Trio*
10/65 *Sounds Orchestral*
89/65 *Steve Alaimo*
61/66 *Shelby Flint*
52/59 **Castin' My Spell** *Johnny Otis Show*
Castles In The Air
F/72 *Don McLean*
36/81 *Don McLean*
52/64 **Castles In The Sand** *Little Stevie Wonder*
91/01 **Castles In The Sky** *Ian Van Dahl*
25/56 **Casual Look** *Six Teens*
67/64 **Cat, The** *Jimmy Smith*
26/67 **Cat In The Window (The Bird In The Sky)** *Petula Clark*
67/82 **Cat People (Putting Out Fire)** *David Bowie*
30/77 **Cat Scratch Fever** *Ted Nugent*
55/70 **Cat Walk** *Village Soul Choir*
90/72 **Cat's Eye In The Window** *Tommy James*
Cat's In The Cradle
1/74 *Harry Chapin*
6/93 *Ugly Kid Joe*
1/58 **Catch A Falling Star** *Perry Como*
8/87 **Catch Me (I'm Falling)** *Pretty Poison*
40/84 **Catch Me I'm Falling** *Real Life*
50/84 **Catch My Fall** *Billy Idol*
23/65 **Catch The Wind** *Donovan*
4/65 **Catch Us If You Can** *Dave Clark Five*
68/80 **Catching The Sun** *Spyro Gyra*
23/62 **Caterina** *Perry Como*
49/59 **Caterpillar Crawl** *Strangers*
71/76 **Catfish** *Four Tops*
94/76 **Cathedrals** *D.C. LaRue*
1/60 **Cathy's Clown** *Everly Brothers*
Cats In The Cradle ..see: Cat's
Cattle Call
69/55 *Eddy Arnold*
92/57 *Dinah Shore*
60/96 **Caught A Lite Sneeze** *Tori Amos*
94/71 **Caught In A Dream** *Alice Cooper*
77/83 **Caught In The Game** *Survivor*
54/00 **Caught Out There** *Kelis*
37/87 **Caught Up In The Rapture** *Anita Baker*
10/82 **Caught Up In You** *38 Special*
2/87 **Causing A Commotion** *Madonna*
(Cavalleria Rusticana) ..see: Theme From Raging Bull
(Cave Man) ..see: Troglodyte
Cecilia
4/70 *Simon & Garfunkel*
79/88 *Times Two*
15/70 **Celebrate** *Three Dog Night*
26/85 **Celebrate Youth** *Rick Springfield*
1/81 **Celebration** *Kool & The Gang*
88/96 **Celebration** *Fun Factory*
95/72 **Celebration** *Tommy James*
72^{S}/01 **Celebrity** *Talent*
56^{A}/98 **Celebrity Skin** *Hole*
84/71 **Celia Of The Seals** *Donovan*
39/95 **Cell Therapy** *Goodie Mob.*
86/83 **Celtic Soul Brothers** *Dexys Midnight Runners*
44/85 **Centerfield** *John Fogerty*
1/82 **Centerfold** *J. Geils Band*
24/84 **Centipede** *Rebbie Jackson*
83/88 **Century's End** *Donald Fagen*

Certain Girl
71/61 *Ernie K-Doe*
57/80 *Warren Zevon*
14/58 **Certain Smile** *Johnny Mathis*
97/87 **Certain Things Are Likely** *KTP*
Cerveza
23/58 *Boots Brown*
73/61 *Bert Kaempfert*
53/81 **Ch Ch Cherie** *Johnny Average Band*
10/62 **Cha-Cha-Cha** *Bobby Rydell*
83/01 **Cha-Cha Slide** *Mr C The Slide Man*
74^{S}/02 **Cha Cha Slide Pt. III: Roll Like This** *Mr. C. The Slide Man*
Cha-Hua-Hua
34/58 *Pets*
74/58 *Eddie Platt*
Chain Gang
2/60 *Sam Cooke*
84/68 *Jackie Wilson & Count Basie*
63/76 *Jim Croce (Medley)*
Chain Gang
13/56 *Bobby Scott*
78/56 *Len Dresslar*
Chain Of Fools
2/68 *Aretha Franklin*
100/68 *Jimmy Smith*
88/90 *Little Caesar*
40/00 **Chain Of Love** *Clay Walker*
Chain Reaction
95/85 *Diana Ross*
66/86 *Diana Ross (new mix)*
32/68 **Chained** *Marvin Gaye*
70/64 **Chained And Bound** *Otis Redding*
17/62 **Chains** *Cookies*
38/96 **Chains** *Tina Arena*
45/70 **Chains And Things** *B.B. King*
44/92 **Chains Around My Heart** *Richard Marx*
Chains Of Love
10/56 *Pat Boone*
60/69 *Bobby Bland*
12/88 **Chains Of Love** *Erasure*
90/65 **Chains Of Love** *Drifters*
42/71 **Chairman Of The Board** *Chairmen Of The Board*
42/74 **Chameleon** *Herbie Hancock*
43/78 **Champagne Jam** *Atlanta Rhythm Section*
20^{A}/96 **Champagne Supernova** *Oasis*
16^{S}/01 **Champion** *Oleander*
76/84 **Chance For Heaven** *Christopher Cross*
1/57 **Chances Are** *Johnny Mathis*
27/92 **Change** *Lisa Stansfield*
54/85 **Change** *John Waite*
73/83 **Change** *Tears For Fears*
Change Is Gonna Come
31/65 *Sam Cooke*
60/70 *5th Dimension (medley)*
75^{S}/96 **Change My Mind** *John Berry*
3/87 **Change Of Heart** *Cyndi Lauper*
19/78 **Change Of Heart** *Eric Carmen*
21/83 **Change Of Heart** *Tom Petty*
49/69 **Change Of Heart** *Classics IV*
43/71 **Change Partners** *Stephen Stills*
86/01 **Change The Game** *Jay-Z, Beanie Sigel & Memphis Bleek*
5/96 **Change The World** *Eric Clapton*
46/75 **Change With The Times** *Van McCoy*
19^{A}/97 **Change Would Do You Good** *Sheryl Crow*
59/00 **Change Your Mind** *Sister Hazel*
32/99 **Changes** *2Pac*

Changes
66/72 *David Bowie*
41/75 *David Bowie*
57/66 **Changes** *Crispian St. Peters*
84/75 **Changes** *Loggins & Messina*
37/77 **Changes In Latitudes, Changes In Attitudes** *Jimmy Buffett*
Chanson D'Amour (Song Of Love)
6/58 *Art & Dotty Todd*
12/58 *Fontane Sisters*
10/99 **Chanté's Got A Man** *Chanté Moore*
19/57 **Chantez-Chantez** *Dinah Shore*
Chantilly Lace
6/58 *Big Bopper*
87/68 *Mitch Ryder (medley)*
43/72 *Jerry Lee Lewis*
Chanukah Song
10^{A}/95 *Adam Sandler*
46^{A}/96 *Adam Sandler*
25^{A}/97 *Adam Sandler*
80/98 *Adam Sandler*
69/62 **Chapel By The Sea** *Billy Vaughn*
Chapel In The Moonlight
32/65 *Bachelors*
25/67 *Dean Martin*
74/59 **Chapel Of Dreams** *Dubs*
Chapel Of Love
1/64 *Dixie Cups*
F/73 *Bette Midler*
Charade
36/64 *Sammy Kaye*
36/64 *Henry Mancini*
100/64 *Andy Williams*
69/61 **Charanga, The** *Merv Griffin*
59/58 **Chariot Rock** *Champs*
1/82 **Chariots Of Fire - Titles** *Vangelis*
40/71 **Charity Ball** *Fanny*
84/61 **Charlena** *Sevilles*
47/61 **Charleston, The** *Ernie Fields*
2/59 **Charlie Brown** *Coasters*
Charlies Angels ..see: Theme From
68/85 **Charm The Snake** *Christopher Cross*
69/56 **Charmaine** *Four Freshmen*
91/75 **Charmer** *Tim Moore*
13/63 **Charms** *Bobby Vee*
33/79 **Chase** *Giorgio Moroder*
96/75 **Chase The Clouds Away** *Chuck Mangione*
39/91 **Chasin' The Wind** *Chicago*
46/93 **Chattahoochee** *Alan Jackson*
Chattanooga Choo Choo
54/60 *Ernie Fields*
36/62 *Floyd Cramer*
45/67 *Harpers Bizarre*
32/78 *Tuxedo Junction*
34/60 **Chattanooga Shoe Shine Boy** *Freddy Cannon*
89/80 **Cheap Sunglasses** *ZZ Top*
15/73 **Cheaper To Keep Her** *Johnnie Taylor*
74/56 **Cheat, A** *Sanford Clark*
74/98 **Cheated (To All The Girls)** *Wyclef Jean*
12/66 **Cheater, The** *Bob Kuban*
59^{S}/01 **Cheatin' On Me** *Kandi*
14/88 **Check It Out** *John Cougar Mellencamp*
35/73 **Check It Out** *Tavares*
91/75 **Check It Out** *Bobby Womack*
28/70 **Check Out Your Mind** *Impressions*
63^{S}/91 **Check The Rhime** *Tribe Called Quest*
20/93 **Check Yo Self** *Ice Cube*

97/70 **Check Yourself** *I.A.P. CO.*
12/55 **Chee Chee-oo Chee (Sang the Little Bird)** *Perry Como & Jaye P. Morgan*
65/72 **Cheer** *Potliquor*
78/64 **Cheer Leader** *Paul Petersen*
38/98 **Cheers 2 U** *Playa*
32/78 **Cheeseburger In Paradise** *Jimmy Buffett*
78/69 **Chelsea Morning** *Judy Collins*
67/99 **Chemicals Between Us** *Bush*
Cherchez La Femme ..see: Whispering
98/00 **Cherchez LaGhost** *Ghostface Killah*
54/61 **Cherié** *Bobby Rydell*
63/58 **Cherie, I Love You** *Pat Boone*
Cherish
1/66 *Association*
9/71 *David Cassidy*
2/85 **Cherish** *Kool & The Gang*
2/89 **Cherish** *Madonna*
44/71 **Cherish What Is Dear To You (While It's Near to You)** *Freda Payne*
72/87 **Cherokee** *Europe*
33/77 **Cherry Baby** *Starz*
99/61 **Cherry Berry Wine** *Charlie McCoy*
8/88 **Cherry Bomb** *John Cougar Mellencamp*
Cherry, Cherry
6/66 *Neil Diamond*
31/73 *Neil Diamond (Live)*
15/69 **Cherry Hill Park** *Billy Joe Royal*
10/90 **Cherry Pie** *Warrant*
11/60 **Cherry Pie** *Skip & Flip*
Cherry Pink And Apple Blossom White
1/55 *Perez Prado*
14/55 *Alan Dale*
56/61 *Jerry Murad's Harmonicats*
62/59 **Cherrystone** *Addrisi Brothers*
64/71 **Cheryl Moana Marie** *John Rowles*
5/75 **Chevy Van** *Sammy Johns*
15/68 **Chewy Chewy** *Ohio Express*
35/71 **Chicago** *Graham Nash*
84/57 **Chicago** *Frank Sinatra*
100/59 **Chick, The** *Lee & Paul*
9/71 **Chick-A-Boom (Don't Ya Jes' Love It)** *Daddy Dewdrop*
89/57 **Chicken, Baby, Chicken** *Tony Harris*
63/63 **Chicken Feed** *Bent Fabric*
50/70 **Chicken Strut** *Meters*
69/98 **Chickenhead** *Wyclef Jean*
87/01 **Chickenhead** *Project Pat*
96/75 **Chico And The Man** *José Feliciano*
55/93 **Chief Rocka** *Lords Of The Underground*
69/96 **Child (Inside)** *Qkumba Zoo*
31/67 **Child Of Clay** *Jimmie Rodgers*
95/60 **Child Of God** *Bobby Darin*
72/65 **Child Of Our Times** *Barry McGuire*
F/95 **Childhood** *Michael Jackson*
21/96 **Children** *Robert Miles*
51/70 **Children** *Joe South*
13/90 **Children Of The Night** *Richard Marx*
41/79 **Children Of The Sun** *Billy Thorpe*
7X/65 **Children's Christmas Song** *Supremes*
Children's Marching Song
13/59 *Cyril Stapleton*
16/59 *Mitch Miller*
48/75 *Purple Reign*
20S/01 **Chillin' In Your Benz** *Exhale*

72/61 **Chills And Fever** *Ronnie Love*
81/65 **Chim, Chim, Cheree** *New Christy Minstrels*
53/83 **China** *Red Rockers*
38/60 **China Doll** *Ames Brothers*
10/83 **China Girl** *David Bowie*
15/73 **China Grove** *Doobie Brothers*
58/63 **China Nights (Shina No Yoru)** *Kyu Sakamoto*
59/56 **Chincherinchee** *Perry Como*
78/63 **Chinese Checkers** *Booker T. & The MG's*
98/75 **Chinese Kung Fu** *Banzaii*
87/56 **Chinese Rock And Egg Roll** *Buddy Hackett*
46S/02 **Ching Ching** *Ms. Jade*
77/79 **Chip Away The Stone** *Aerosmith*
10/62 **Chip Chip** *Gene McDaniels*
97/59 **Chip Off The Old Block** *Eddy Arnold*
F/80 **Chip Off The Old Block** *Chic*
Chipmunk Song
1/58 *David Seville/The Chipmunks*
41/59 *David Seville/The Chipmunks*
45/60 *David Seville/The Chipmunks*
39/61 *David Seville/The Chipmunks*
40/62 *David Seville/The Chipmunks*
29/80 **Chiquitita** *Abba*
Chirpy Chirpy Cheep Cheep
20/71 *Mac & Katie Kissoon*
92/71 *Lally Stott*
76/69 **Chitty Chitty Bang Bang** *Paul Mauriat*
34/81 **Chloe** *Elton John*
92/75 **Chocolate Chip** *Isaac Hayes*
94/75 **Chocolate City** *Parliament*
94/68 **Choice, The** *O'Jays*
57/92 **Choice Is Yours** *Black Sheep*
21/69 **Choice Of Colors** *Impressions*
13/69 **Chokin' Kind** *Joe Simon*
Choo Choo ..also see: Do The
FC/56 **Choo Choo Ch'Boogie** *Bill Haley*
89/73 **Choo Choo Mama** *Ten Years After*
26/68 **Choo Choo Train** *Box Tops*
23/94 **Choose** *Color Me Badd*
F/55 **Chop Chop Boom** *Crew-Cuts*
76/02 **Chop Suey** *System Of A Down*
83/91 **Chorus (Fishes In The Sea)** *Erasure*
25/77 **Christine Sixteen** *Kiss*

CHRISTMAS:

51/60 **Christmas Auld Lang Syne** *Bobby Darin*
18X/68 **Christmas Blues** *Canned Heat*
17X/64 **Christmas Celebration** *B.B. King*
92/74 **Christmas Dream** *Perry Como*
Christmas Eve (Sarajevo 12/24)
65A/95 *Savatage*
49A/96 *Trans-Siberian Orchestra*
49A/97 *Trans-Siberian Orchestra*
58/75 **Christmas For Cowboys** *John Denver*
7X/70 **Christmas Goose (Snowbird)** *Stan & Doug*
37S/02 **Christmas in America** *Pat Benatar*
3X/83 **Christmas In Dixie** *Alabama*
11X/70 **Christmas In My Home Town** *Charley Pride*
7X/68 **Christmas Is For Children** *Glen Campbell*
9X/84 **Christmas Is The Time To Say "I Love You"** *Billy Squier*
20X/63 **Christmas Love** *Johnny Kaye*
33X/67 **Christmas Lullaby** *Cary Grant*
42/01 **Christmas Shoes** *Newsong*

5X/68 **Christmas Shopping** *Buck Owens*
Christmas Song
80/60 *Nat "King" Cole*
65/62 *Nat "King" Cole*
12X/66 *James Brown*
1X/68 *Herb Alpert*
18/99 *Christina Aguilera*
(also see: Children's)
12X/64 **Christmas Tears** *Freddy King*
4X/85 **Christmas Time** *Bryan Adams*
24X/64 **Christmas Will Be Just Another Lonely Day** *Brenda Lee*
11X/68 **Christmas Wish** *Bobby Goldsboro*
FX/70 **Christmas Won't Be The Same This Year** *Jackson 5*
4/79 **Chuck E.'s In Love** *Rickie Lee Jones*
9/64 **Chug-A-Lug** *Roger Miller*
73/79 **Church** *Bob Welch*
Church Bells May Ring
14/56 *Diamonds*
62/56 *Willows*
10/83 **Church Of The Poison Mind** *Culture Club*
36/92 **Church Of Your Heart** *Roxette*
62/71 **Church Street Soul Revival** *Tommy James*
Ciao, Ciao Bambina (Chiow, Chiow, Bambeena)
24/59 *Jacky Noguez*
97/59 *Domenico Modugno (Piove)*
93/63 **Cigarettes And Coffee Blues** *Marty Robbins*
44/58 **Cimarron (Roll On)** *Billy Vaughn*
Cinco Robles (Five Oaks)
22/57 *Russell Arms*
35/57 *Les Paul & Mary Ford*
16/62 **Cinderella** *Jack Ross*
34/77 **Cinderella** *Firefall*
69/58 **Cinderella** *Four Preps*
70/61 **Cinderella** *Paul Anka*
68/68 **Cinderella Rockefella** *Esther & Abi Ofarim*
58/68 **Cinderella Sunshine** *Paul Revere & The Raiders*
48/73 **Cindy Incidentally** *Faces*
Cindy, Oh Cindy
9/56 *Vince Martin/The Tarriers*
10/56 *Eddie Fisher*
8/62 **Cindy's Birthday** *Johnny Crawford*
72/63 **Cindy's Gonna Cry** *Johnny Crawford*
11/69 **Cinnamon** *Derek*
25/63 **Cinnamon Cinder (It's A Very Nice Dance)** *Pastel Six*
Cinnamon Girl
52/70 *Gentrys*
55/70 *Neil Young & Crazy Horse*
48/89 **Circle** *Edie Brickell*
7/88 **Circle In The Sand** *Belinda Carlisle*
33/78 **Circle Is Small (I Can See It In Your Eyes)** *Gordon Lightfoot*
18/94 **Circle Of Life** *Elton John*
55/82 **Circle Of Love** *Steve Miller Band*
38/82 **Circles** *Atlantic Starr*
87/72 **Circles** *New Seekers*
Circus, The ..see: Computer Game
2/73 **Cisco Kid** *War*
23/69 **Cissy Strut** *Meters*
18/85 **C-I-T-Y** *John Cafferty*
90/61 **City Girl Stole My Country Boy** *Patti Page*
79/74 **City In The Sky** *Staple Singers*
52/98 **City Is Mine** *Jay-Z*

City Lights
71/58 *Ray Price*
92/59 *Ivory Joe Hunter*
55/60 *Debbie Reynolds*
19/56 **City Of Angels** *Highlights*
18/72 **City Of New Orleans** *Arlo Guthrie*
2/72 **Clair** *Gilbert O'Sullivan*
Clam ..see: Do The
6/74 **Clap For The Wolfman** *Guess Who*
45/60 **Clap Your Hands** *Beau-Marks*
Clapping Song (Clap Pat Clap Slap)
8/65 *Shirley Ellis*
36/83 *Pia Zadora*
38/59 **Class, The** *Chubby Checker*
(Class Cutter) ..see: Yea-Yea
2/68 **Classical Gas** *Mason Williams*
30/58 **Claudette** *Everly Brothers*
72/56 **Clay Idol** *Betty Johnson*
6/72 **Clean Up Woman** *Betty Wright*
35/69 **Clean Up Your Own Back Yard** *Elvis Presley*
4/02 **Cleanin' Out My Closet** *Eminem*
68/84 **Cleanin' Up The Town** *Bus Boys*
Clementine
21/60 *Bobby Darin*
65/60 *Jan & Dean*
43/65 **Cleo's Back** *Jr. Walker*
50/66 **Cleo's Mood** *Jr. Walker*
Cleopatra Jones ..see: Theme From
84/94 **Cleopatra's Cat** *Spin Doctors*
26/98 **Cleopatra's Theme** *Cleopatra*
28/58 **Click-Clack** *Dickey Doo & The Don'ts*
Clickity Clack Song ..see: Four Little Heels
65/65 **Climb, The** *Kingsmen*
Climb Every Mountain
74/60 *Tony Bennett*
90/68 *Hesitations*
17/64 **Clinging Vine** *Bobby Vinton*
57/01 **Clint Eastwood** *Gorillaz*
100/64 **Clock, The** *Baby Washington*
37/98 **Clock Strikes** *Timbaland & Magoo*
72S/96 **Clones** *Roots*
40/80 **Clones (We're All)** *Alice Cooper*

CLOSE:

Close Encounters ..see: Theme From
65/82 **Close Enough To Perfect** *Alabama*
8/89 **Close My Eyes Forever** *Lita Ford/Ozzy Osbourne*
25/78 **Close The Door** *Teddy Pendergrass*
27C/55 **Close The Door** *Jim Lowe*
12/62 **Close To Cathy** *Mike Clifford*
97/91 **Close To Me** *Cure*
1/90 **Close To You** *Maxi Priest*
46/95 **Close To You** *Fun Factory*
(also see: They Long To Be)
68/61 **Close Together** *Jimmy Reed*
8/67 **Close Your Eyes** *Peaches & Herb*
37/73 **Close Your Eyes** *Edward Bear*
41/94 **Closer** *Nine Inch Nails*
66/93 **Closer** *Remedy*
2/78 **Closer I Get To You** *Roberta Flack w/Donny Hathaway*
57/89 **Closer Than Friends** *Surface*
52/89 **Closer To Fine** *Indigo Girls*
16/96 **Closer To Free** *BoDeans*
22/70 **Closer To Home** *Grand Funk Railroad*
43/92 **Closer To Me** *Outfield*
Closer To The Heart
76/77 *Rush*
69/82 *Rush (Live)*
Closer Walk ..see: Just A Closer Walk
38/83 **Closer You Get** *Alabama*
67/85 **(Closest Thing To) Perfect** *Jermaine Jackson*
98/02 **Closet Freak** *Cee-Lo*
53A/93 **Closing Of The Year (Main Theme)** *Wendy & Lisa*
11A/98 **Closing Time** *Semisonic*
Cloud Nine
6/69 *Temptations*
32/69 *Mongo Santamaria*
41/59 **Clouds, The** *Spacemen*
47/73 **Clouds** *David Gates*
62/66 **Cloudy Summer Afternoon (Raindrops)** *Barry McGuire*
28/90 **Club At The End Of The Street** *Elton John*
75S/02 **Club Banger** *Petey Pablo*
66/84 **Club Michelle** *Eddie Money*
18S/01 **Cluck Cluck** *Product G&B*
59A/98 **Clumsy** *Our Lady Peace*
C'mon ..see: Come On
99/71 **Co-Co** *Sweet*
83/70 **Coal Miner's Daughter** *Loretta Lynn*
F/80 **Cocaine** *Eric Clapton*
69/02 **Cochise** *Audioslave*
69/95 **Cocktales** *Too $hort*
21/97 **Coco Jamboo** *Mr. President*
44/78 **Cocomotion** *El Coco*
8/72 **Coconut** *Nilsson*
25/57 **Cocoanut Woman** *Harry Belafonte*
6/77 **Cold As Ice** *Foreigner*
40/83 **Cold Blooded** *Rick James*
F/74 **Coldblooded** *James Brown*
96/62 **Cold, Cold Heart** *Dinah Washington*
79/64 **Cold Cold Winter** *Pixies Three*
65/00 **Cold Day In July** *Dixie Chicks*
67/68 **Cold Feet** *Albert King*
1/89 **Cold Hearted** *Paula Abdul*
33/81 **Cold Love** *Donna Summer*
11/97 **Cold Rock A Party** *MC Lyte*
90/92 **Cold Shower** *Erin Cruise*
7/67 **Cold Sweat** *James Brown*
30/70 **Cold Turkey** *Plastic Ono Band*
97/95 **Cold World** *Genius/GZA*
47/72 **Coldest Days Of My Life** *Chi-Lites*
91/70 **Cole, Cooke & Redding** *Wilson Pickett*
42/58 **College Man** *Bill Justis*
Colonel Bogey ..see: March From The River Kwai
7/69 **Color Him Father** *Winstons*
16/67 **Color My World** *Petula Clark*
66/72 **Colorado** *Danny Holien*
70/88 **Colors** *Ice-T*
4/95 **Colors Of The Wind** *Vanessa Williams*
F/71 **Colour My World** *Chicago*
17/88 **Colour Of Love** *Billy Ocean*
74/97 **Colour Of Love** *Amber*
68/69 **Colour Of My Love** *Jefferson*
61/65 **Colours** *Donovan*
71/61 **Comancheros, The** *Claude King*

COME:

3/64 **Come A Little Bit Closer** *Jay & The Americans*
53S/01 **Come A Little Closer** *Lila McCann*
50/91 **Come Again** *Damn Yankees*
83/61 **Come Along** *Maurice Williams*
83/75 **Come An' Get Yourself Some** *Leon Haywood*
7/70 **Come And Get It** *Badfinger*
83/66 **Come And Get Me** *Jackie de Shannon*
29/63 **Come And Get These Memories** *Martha & The Vandellas*
12/98 **Come And Get With Me** *Keith Sweat*
Come And Get Your Love
5/74 *Redbone*
19/95 *Real McCoy*
68/75 **Come And Get Your Love** *Roger Daltrey*
26/65 **Come And Stay With Me** *Marianne Faithfull*
11/92 **Come & Talk To Me** *Jodeci*
15/87 **Come As You Are** *Peter Wolf*
32/92 **Come As You Are** *Nirvana*
18/93 **Come Baby Come** *K7*
32/80 **Come Back** *J. Geils Band*
61/63 **Come Back** *Johnny Mathis*
61/66 **Come Back** *Five Stairsteps*
62/95 **Come Back** *Londonbeat*
63/60 **Come Back** *Jimmy Clanton*
22/84 **Come Back And Stay** *Paul Young*
86/65 **Come Back Baby** *Roddie Joy*
69/71 **Come Back Home** *Bobby Goldsboro*
17/62 **Come Back Silly Girl** *Lettermen*
2/90 **Come Back To Me** *Janet Jackson*
3/67 **Come Back When You Grow Up** *Bobby Vee*
88/94 **Come Clean** *Jeru The Damaja*
65/03 **Come Close To Me** *Common*
38/58 **Come Closer To Me (Acercate Mas)** *Nat "King" Cole*
76/63 **Come Dance With Me** *Jay & The Americans*
6/83 **Come Dancing** *Kinks*
51A/97 **Come Down** *Toad The Wet Sprocket*
57S/99 **Come Get It** *DJ Hurricane*
21/73 **Come Get To This** *Marvin Gaye*
58/83 **Come Give Your Love To Me** *Janet Jackson*
Come Go With Me
4/57 *Dell-Vikings*
48/63 *Dion*
18/82 *Beach Boys*
5/87 **Come Go With Me** *Exposé*
84/78 **Come Go With Me** *Pockets*
14/65 **Come Home** *Dave Clark Five*
92/55 **Come Home** *Bubber Johnson*
69/89 **Come Home With Me Baby** *Dead Or Alive*
61/77 **Come In From The Rain** *Captain & Tennille*
55/93 **Come In Out Of The Rain** *Wendy Moten*
66/58 **Come In Stranger** *Johnny Cash*
33/93 **Come Inside** *Intro*
20/59 **Come Into My Heart** *Lloyd Price*
89/70 **Come Into My Life** *Jimmy Cliff*
91/03 **Come Into My World** *Kylie Minogue*
Come Live With Me
82/73 *Ray Charles*
89/73 *Roy Clark*
30/74 **Come Monday** *Jimmy Buffett*
36/64 **Come On** *Tommy Roe*
44/97 **Come On** *Billy Lawrence*
69/71 **C'mon** *Poco*
87/95 **Come On** *Barry White*
(also see: Cum On)
29/59 **Come On And Get Me** *Fabian*

10/90 **C'mon And Get My Love** *D Mob/Cathy Dennis*
61/70 **Come On And Say It** *Grass Roots*
80/66 **Come On And See Me** *Tammi Terrell*
5/64 **C'mon And Swim** *Bobby Freeman*
98/62 **Come On Baby** *Bruce Channel*
50/65 **Come On Do The Jerk** *Miracles*
6/67 **Come On Down To My Boat** *Every Mothers' Son*
1/83 **Come On Eileen** *Dexys Midnight Runners*
35/59 **C'mon Everybody** *Eddie Cochran*
Come On Let's Go
42/58 *Ritchie Valens*
22/66 *McCoys*
21/87 *Los Lobos*
28/62 **Come On Little Angel** *Belmonts*
C'mon Marianne
9/67 *4 Seasons*
38/76 *Donny Osmond*
3/96 **C'Mon N' Ride It (The Train)** *Quad City DJ's*
23/76 **Come On Over** *Olivia Newton-John*
58/99 **Come On Over** *Shania Twain*
91/61 **Come On Over** *Strollers*
Come On Over Baby (all I want is you)
1/00 *Christina Aguilera*
FS/01 *Christina Aguilera*
60/65 **Come On Over To My Place** *Drifters*
63/68 **Come On, React!** *Fireballs*
76/85 **(Come On) Shout** *Alex Brown*
97/67 **Come On Sock It To Me** *Syl Johnson*
43/66 **Come On Up** *Young Rascals*
38A/94 **Come Out And Play** *Offspring*
82/89 **Come Out Fighting** *Easterhouse*
81/98 **Come Over To My Place** *Davina*
Come Prima
67/58 *Polly Bergen*
60/59 *Tony Dallara*
Come Rain Or Come Shine
83/60 *Ray Charles*
98/68 *Ray Charles*
51S/00 **Come Ride With Me** *Jahari*
17/66 **(Come 'Round Here) I'm The One You Need** *Miracles*
39/70 **Come Running** *Van Morrison*
35/66 **Come Running Back** *Dean Martin*
8/78 **Come Sail Away** *Styx*
17/70 **Come Saturday Morning** *Sandpipers*
40/65 **Come See** *Major Lance*
Come See About Me
1/64 *Supremes*
74/64 *Nella Dodds*
24/68 *Jr. Walker*
33/97 **Come See Me** *112*
73/61 **Come September** *Billy Vaughn*
96/66 **Come Share The Good Times With Me** *Julie Monday*
Come Softly To Me
1/59 *Fleetwoods*
45/59 *Ronnie Height*
95/73 *New Seekers*
15/79 **Come To Me** *France Joli*
22/58 **Come To Me** *Johnny Mathis*
30/59 **Come To Me** *Marv Johnson*
47/70 **Come To Me** *Tommy James*
69/64 **Come To Me** *Otis Redding*
84/81 **Come To Me** *Aretha Franklin*
76/68 **Come To Me Softly** *Jimmy James*
25/94 **Come To My Window** *Melissa Etheridge*
37/67 **Come To The Sunshine** *Harpers Bizarre*
Come Together
1/69 *Beatles*
57/70 *Ike & Tina Turner*
23/78 *Aerosmith*
50/65 **Come Tomorrow** *Manfred Mann*
7/93 **Come Undone** *Duran Duran*
43/58 **Come What May** *Clyde McPhatter*
4/98 **Come With Me** *Puff Daddy*
43/95 **Come With Me** *Shai*
68/97 **Come With Me** *Keith Sweat*
30/95 **Comedown** *Bush*
62/92 **Comfort Zone** *Vanessa Williams*
10/93 **Comforter** *Shai*

COMIN'/COMING:

67/89 **Comin' Down Tonight** *Thirty Eight Special*
69/60 **Comin' Down With Love** *Mel Gadson*
84/70 **Comin' Home** *Delaney & Bonnie/Eric Clapton*
20/89 **Coming Home** *Cinderella*
36/62 **Comin' Home Baby** *Mel Torme*
11/82 **Comin' In And Out Of Your Life** *Barbra Streisand*
41/64 **Comin' In The Back Door** *Baja Marimba Band*
67/64 **Comin' On** *Bill Black's Combo*
56/94 **Comin' On Strong** *Sudden Change*
11/66 **Coming On Strong** *Brenda Lee*
65/65 **Comin' On Too Strong** *Wayne Newton*
18/87 **Coming Around Again** *Carly Simon*
99/64 **Coming Back To You** *Maxine Brown*
42/80 **Coming Down From Love** *Bobby Caldwell*
11/67 **Coming Home Soldier** *Bobby Vinton*
74S/93 **Coming Home To Love** *Coming Of Age*
60/90 **Coming Of Age** *Damn Yankees*
1/91 **Coming Out Of The Dark** *Gloria Estefan*
91/88 **Coming To America** *System*
1/80 **Coming Up** *Paul McCartney*
59/87 **Coming Up Close** *'Til Tuesday*
74/88 **Coming Up You** *Cars*
96/93 **Commitment Of The Heart** *Clive Griffin*
75A/96 **Common Disaster** *Cowboy Junkies*
30/69 **Commotion** *Creedence Clearwater Revival*
(also see: Kommotion)
34/85 **Communication** *Power Station*
59/84 **Communication** *Spandau Ballet*
60/67 **Communication Breakdown** *Roy Orbison*
85/70 **Compared To What** *Les McCann & Eddie Harris*
75/68 **Competition Ain't Nothin'** *Carl Carlton*
32/94 **Completely** *Michael Bolton*
2/02 **Complicated** *Avril Lavigne*
59/01 **Complicated** *Carolyn Dawn Johnson*
27/69 **Composer, The** *Supremes*
60/80 **Computer Game** *Yellow Magic Orchestra*
63/84 **Concealed Weapons** *J. Geils Band*
48S/00 **Concertina** *Tori Amos*
Concrete And Clay
28/65 *Unit Four plus Two*
35/65 *Eddie Rambeau*
46/69 **Condition Red** *Goodees*
51/63 **Coney Island Baby** *Excellents*
72/56 **Confession Of A Sinner** *Stylers*
17/56 **Confidential** *Sonny Knight*
37/79 **Confusion** *Electric Light Orchestra*
10/86 **Conga** *Miami Sound Machine*
55/89 **Congratulations** *Vesta*
63/64 **Congratulations** *Rick Nelson*
99/68 **Congratulations** *Cliff Richard*
52S/00 **Connect** *DJ Hurricane*
20/93 **Connected** *Stereo MC's*
53/95 **Connection** *Elastica*
16/72 **Conquistador** *Procol Harum*
11/62 **Conscience** *James Darren*
38/92 **Constant Craving** *k.d. lang*
71/67 **Constant Rain (Chove Chuva)** *Sergio Mendes*
16/95 **Constantly** *Immature*
65/79 **Contact** *Edwin Starr*
19/01 **Contagious** *Isley Brothers*
Continental Walk
33/61 *Hank Ballard*
80/61 *Rollers*
(also see: Do The New)
5/87 **Control** *Janet Jackson*
68/01 **Control** *Puddle Of Mudd*
51/73 **Control Of Me** *Les Emmerson*
70/81 **Controversy** *Prince*
8/72 **Convention '72** *Delegates*
65/91 **Conviction Of The Heart** *Kenny Loggins*
1/76 **Convoy** *C.W. McCall*
84/68 **Coo Coo** *Big Brother & The Holding Company*
98/59 **CooCoo-U** *Kingston Trio*
32/73 **Cook With Honey** *Judy Collins*
92/62 **Cookin'** *Al Casey Combo*
90/82 **Cool** *Time*
29/71 **Cool Aid** *Paul Humphrey*
81/91 **Cool As Ice (Everybody Get Loose)** *Vanilla Ice*
10/80 **Cool Change** *Little River Band*
4/85 **Cool It Now** *New Edition*
7/66 **Cool Jerk** *Capitols*
13/81 **Cool Love** *Pablo Cruise*
57/82 **Cool Magic** *Steve Miller Band*
11/82 **Cool Night** *Paul Davis*
49/83 **Cool Places** *Sparks & Jane Wiedlin*
12/57 **Cool Shake** *Del Vikings*
85/60 **Cool Water** *Jack Scott*
8/78 **Copacabana (At The Copa)** *Barry Manilow*
92/62 **Copy Cat** *Gary (U.S.) Bonds*
92/58 **Coquette** *Fats Domino*
37/73 **Corazón** *Carole King*
53A/95 **Corduroy** *Pearl Jam*
Corinna, Corinna
41/56 *Joe Turner*
9/61 *Ray Peterson*
83/66 **Corner In The Sun** *Walter Jackson*
18/72 **Corner Of The Sky** *Jackson 5*
83/73 **Cosmic Sea** *Mystic Moods*
77/75 **Costafine Town** *Splinter*
56/70 **Cottage Cheese** *Crow*
63/60 **Cottage For Sale** *Little Willie John*
15/64 **Cotton Candy** *Al Hirt*
59/76 **Cotton Candy** *Sylvers*
25/95 **Cotton Eye Joe** *Rednex*
Cotton Fields
13/62 *Highwaymen*
67/63 *Ace Cannon*
71/72 **Cotton Jenny** *Anne Murray*

76/77 **Could Heaven Ever Be Like This** *Idris Muhammad*
52/80 **Could I Be Dreaming** *Pointer Sisters*
60/71 **Could I Forget You** *Tyrone Davis*
33/80 **Could I Have This Dance** *Anne Murray*
52/00 **Could I Have This Kiss Forever** *Whitney Houston & Enrique Iglesias*
26/01 **Could It Be** *Jaheim*
37/72 **Could It Be Forever** *David Cassidy*
4/73 **Could It Be I'm Falling In Love** *Spinners*
47/82 **Could It Be Love** *Jennifer Warnes*
Could It Be Magic
6/75 *Barry Manilow*
52/76 *Donna Summer*
11/90 **Could This Be Love** *Seduction*
23/57 **Could This Be Magic** *Dubs*
92/73 **Could You Ever Love Me Again** *Gary & Dave*
1/88 **Could've Been** *Tiffany*
72/92 **Could've Been Me** *Billy Ray Cyrus*
3/77 **Couldn't Get It Right** *Climax Blues Band*
93/72 **Couldn't I Just Tell You** *Todd Rundgren*
43/00 **Couldn't Last A Moment** *Collin Raye*
91/66 **Count Down** *Dave "Baby" Cortez*
Count Every Star
73/58 *Rivieras*
35/61 *Donnie & The Dreamers*
41/62 *Linda Scott*
2/65 **Count Me In** *Gary Lewis*
51/85 **Count Me Out** *New Edition*
8/78 **Count On Me** *Jefferson Starship*
8/96 **Count On Me** *Whitney Houston & CeCe Winans*
85/83 **Count On Me** *Gerard McMahon*
Count The Days ..see: (1-2-3-4-5-6-7)
84/86 **Count Your Blessings** *Ashford & Simpson*
5/55 **Count Your Blessings (Instead of Sheep)** *Eddie Fisher*
15/96 **Counting Blue Cars** *Dishwalla*
70/90 **Counting The Days** *Joey Kid*
25/60 **Country Boy** *Fats Domino*
75/00 **Country Boy Can Survive (Y2K Version)** *Chad Brock*
11/76 **Country Boy (You Got Your Feet In L.A.)** *Glen Campbell*
54/00 **Country Comes To Town** *Toby Keith*
36/68 **Country Girl - City Man** *Billy Vera & Judy Clay*
86/70 **Country Preacher** *Cannonball Adderley*
37/71 **Country Road** *James Taylor*
66/74 **Country Side Of Life** *Wet Willie*
49/73 **Country Sunshine** *Dottie West*
51/72 **Country Wine** *Raiders*
88/72 **Country Woman** *Magic Lantern*
11/91 **Couple Days Off** *Huey Lewis*
25/68 **Court Of Love** *Unifics*
80/70 **Court Of The Crimson King** *King Crimson*
61/71 **Court Room** *Clarence Carter*
25/02 **Courtesy Of The Red, White And Blue (The Angry American)** *Toby Keith*
31/64 **Cousin Of Mine** *Sam Cooke*
2/89 **Cover Girl** *New Kids On The Block*
7/84 **Cover Me** *Bruce Springsteen*
42/68 **Cover Me** *Percy Sledge*
31/89 **Cover Of Love** *Michael Damian*
6/73 **Cover Of "Rolling Stone"** *Dr. Hook*
91/98 **Cover You In Kisses** *John Michael Montgomery*
3/80 **Coward Of The County** *Kenny Rogers*
82/99 **Cowboy** *Kid Rock*
66/81 **Cowboy And The Lady** *John Denver*
95/63 **Cowboy Boots** *Dave Dudley*
33/02 **Cowboy In Me** *Tim McGraw*
94/61 **Cowboy Jimmy Joe (Die Sterne Der Prarie)** *Lolita*
77/76 **Cowboy Song** *Thin Lizzy*
27/00 **Cowboy Take Me Away** *Dixie Chicks*
6/68 **Cowboys To Girls** *Intruders*
8/72 **Cowboys Work Is Never Done** *Sonny & Chér*
19/77 **Crackerbox Palace** *George Harrison*
62/59 **Crackin Up** *Bo Diddley*
1/70 **Cracklin' Rosie** *Neil Diamond*
2/90 **Cradle Of Love** *Billy Idol*
7/60 **Cradle Of Love** *Johnny Preston*
86/79 **Crank It Up (Funk Town)** *Peter Brown*
24/00 **Crash And Burn** *Savage Garden*
80/90 **Crash (Have Some Fun)** *TKA (with Michelle Visage)*
19A/97 **Crash Into Me** *Dave Matthews Band*
34S/01 **Crave** *4Shades*
10S/02 **Crawl To Me** *Kemi*
79/01 **Crawling** *Linkin Park*
46/65 **Crawling Back** *Roy Orbison*
68/02 **Crawling In The Dark** *Hoobastank*
51/95 **Craziest** *Naughty By Nature*

CRAZY:

53/86 **Crazay** *Jesse Johnson*
7/91 **Crazy** *Seal*
9/61 **Crazy** *Patsy Cline*
11/01 **Crazy** *K-Ci & JoJo*
14/88 **Crazy** *Icehouse*
17/94 **Crazy** *Aerosmith*
29/90 **Crazy** *Boys*
72/83 **Crazy** *Manhattans*
73/91 **Crazy** *Daisy Dee*
79/85 **Crazy** *Kenny Rogers*
F/58 **Crazy** *Hollywood Flames*
(also see: Krazy / You Drive Me)
11/89 **Crazy About Her** *Rod Stewart*
56/71 **Crazy About The La La La** *Miracles*
Crazy Arms
27H/56 *Ray Price*
36/60 *Bob Beckham*
58/95 **Crazy Cool** *Paula Abdul*
87/58 **Crazy Country Hop** *Johnny Otis*
65/87 **Crazy Crazy Nights** *Kiss*
Crazy Downtown ..see: Downtown
40/58 **Crazy Eyes For You** *Bobby Hamilton*
54/78 **Crazy Feelin'** *Jefferson Starship*
15/01 **Crazy For This Girl** *Evan & Jaron*
1/85 **Crazy For You** *Madonna*
14/72 **Crazy Horses** *Osmonds*
15/85 **Crazy In The Night (Barking At Airplanes)** *Kim Carnes*
42/82 **Crazy (Keep On Falling)** *John Hall Band*
Crazy Little Mama ..see: At My Front Door
49/56 **Crazy Little Palace (That's My Home)** *Billy Williams Quartet*
Crazy Little Thing Called Love
1/80 *Queen*
64/99 *Dwight Yoakam*
15/58 **Crazy Love** *Paul Anka*
17/79 **Crazy Love** *Poco*
29/79 **Crazy Love** *Allman Brothers Band*
45/95 **Crazy Love** *Brian McKnight*
51/71 **Crazy Love** *Helen Reddy*
60/57 **Crazy Love** *Frank Sinatra*
97/92 **Crazy Love** *CeCe Peniston*
22/72 **Crazy Mama** *J.J. Cale*
Crazy On You
35/76 *Heart*
62/78 *Heart*
2/55 **Crazy Otto (medley)** *Johnny Maddox*
98/75 **Crazy Talk** *Chilliwack*
Crazy With Love
53/56 *Guy Mitchell*
73/56 *Teresa Brewer*
71/87 **Crazy World** *Big Trouble*
1/91 **Cream** *Prince*
60/94 **C.R.E.A.M. (Cash Rules Everything Around Me)** *Wu-Tang Clan*
85/57 **Creature, The** *Buchanan & Ancell*
1/95 **Creep** *TLC*
34/93 **Creep** *Radiohead*
59A/94 **Creep** *Stone Temple Pilots*
5/67 **Creeque Alley** *Mamas & The Papas*
41S/02 **Crew Deep** *Skillz*
16/71 **Cried Like A Baby** *Bobby Sherman*
21/97 **Criminal** *Fiona Apple*
F/95 **Criminology** *Raekwon*
Crimson And Clover
1/69 *Tommy James*
7/82 *Joan Jett*
89/95 *SF Spanish Fly*
70/87 **Criticize** *Alexander O'Neal*
Croce Di Oro (Cross Of Gold)
16/55 *Patti Page*
55/55 *Joan Regan*
1/73 **Crocodile Rock** *Elton John*
(Crooked Little Man) ..see: Don't Let The Rain Come Down
75S/93 **Crooked Officer** *Geto Boys*
60/94 **Crooklyn** *Crooklyn Dodgers*
7/87 **Cross My Broken Heart** *Jets*
56/89 **Cross My Heart** *Eighth Wonder*
69/82 **Cross My Heart** *Lee Ritenour*
86/68 **Cross My Heart** *Billy Stewart*
99/65 **Cross My Heart** *Bobby Vee*
Cross Of Gold ..see: Croce Di Oro
89/61 **Cross Stands Alone** *Jimmy Witter*
98/01 **Cross The Border** *Philly's Most Wanted*
19/63 **Cross Fire!** *Orlons*
23/59 **Crossfire** *Johnny & The Hurricanes*
92/63 **Crossfire Time** *Dee Clark*
42/92 **Crossover** *EPMD*
1/96 **Crossroads, Tha** *Bone thugs-n-harmony*
28/69 **Crossroads** *Cream*
90/89 **Crossroads** *Tracy Chapman*
52/68 **Crosstown Traffic** *Jimi Hendrix Experience*
26/62 **Crowd, The** *Roy Orbison*
64/68 **Crown Of Creation** *Jefferson Airplane*
91/74 **Crude Oil Blues** *Jerry Reed*
91/79 **Cruel Shoes** *Steve Martin*
Cruel Summer
9/84 *Bananarama*
10/98 *Ace Of Base*

12/79 **Cruel To Be Kind** *Nick Lowe*
52/66 **Cruel War** *Peter, Paul & Mary*
Cruisin'
4/80 *Smokey Robinson*
53/95 *D'Angelo*
29/90 **Cruising For Bruising** *Basia*
9/83 **Crumblin' Down** *John Cougar Mellencamp*
59/69 **Crumbs Off The Table** *Glass House*
F/71 **Crunchy Granola Suite** *Neil Diamond*
3/98 **Crush** *Jennifer Paige*
75/99 **Crush** *Dave Matthews Band*
3/86 **Crush On You** *Jets*
52^{A}/97 **Crush On You** *Lil' Kim*
77/02 **Crush Tonight** *Fat Joe*
88/65 **Crusher, The** *Novas*

CRY:

10/89 **Cry** *Waterfront*
16/85 **Cry** *Godley & Creme*
Cry
53/59 *Knightsbridge Strings*
58/65 *Ray Charles*
18/66 *Ronnie Dove*
71/72 *Lynn Anderson*
33/02 **Cry** *Faith Hill*
Cry Baby
4/63 *Garnet Mimms*
42/71 *Janis Joplin*
18/56 **Cry Baby** *Bonnie Sisters*
28/00 **Crybaby** *Mariah Carey*
38/62 **Cry Baby Cry** *Angels*
71/60 **Cry Cry Cry** *Bobby Bland*
91/75 **Cry Cry Cry** *Shirley & Company*
7/91 **Cry For Help** *Rick Astley*
15/94 **Cry For You** *Jodeci*
78/80 **Cry Just A Little** *Paul Davis*
Cry Like A Baby
2/68 *Box Tops*
44/80 *Kim Carnes*
3/03 **Cry Me A River** *Justin Timberlake*
Cry Me A River
9/55 *Julie London*
91/60 *Janice Harper*
11/70 *Joe Cocker*
99/62 **Cry Myself To Sleep** *Del Shannon*
27^{S}/01 **Cry No More** *Donz*
48/93 **Cry No More** *II D Extreme*
95/66 **Cry Softly** *Nancy Ames*
52/67 **Cry Softly Lonely One** *Roy Orbison*
Cry To Me
44/62 *Solomon Burke*
23/63 *Betty Harris*
70/67 *Freddie Scott*
68/75 **Cry To Me** *Loleatta Holloway*
50/87 **Cry Wolf** *A-Ha*
12/93 **Cryin'** *Aerosmith*
22/89 **Cryin'** *Vixen*
Crying
2/61 *Roy Orbison*
25/66 *Jay & The Americans*
5/81 *Don McLean*
61/70 **Cryin' In The Streets** *George Perkins*
Crying Game
87/65 *Brenda Lee*
15/93 *Boy George*
Crying In The Chapel
3/65 *Elvis Presley*
88/65 *Adam Wade*
6/62 **Crying In The Rain** *Everly Brothers*
6/66 **Crying Time** *Ray Charles*

19^{S}/01 **Crystal** *New Order*
2/69 **Crystal Blue Persuasion** *Tommy James*
51/65 **Crystal Chandelier** *Vic Dana*
(Cuando Calienta El Sol) ..see: Love Me With All Of Your Heart
81/79 **Cuba** *Gibson Brothers*
25/89 **Cuddly Toy (Feel For Me)** *Roachford*
13/89 **Cult Of Personality** *Living Colour*
Cum On Feel The Noize
98/73 *Slade*
5/83 *Quiet Riot*
39/96 **Cumbersome** *Seven Mary Three*
Cup Of Life
60/98 *Ricky Martin*
45/99 *Ricky Martin*
Cupid
17/61 *Sam Cooke*
76/65 *Johnny Rivers*
39/70 *Johnny Nash*
22/76 *Tony Orlando & Dawn*
4/80 *Spinners (medley)*
13/97 **Cupid** *112*
Curious Mind ..see: Um, Um, Um, Um, Um, Um
97/69 **Curly** *Jimmy Clanton*
15/84 **Curly Shuffle** *Jump 'N The Saddle*
85/64 **Custom Machine** *Bruce & Terry*
10/75 **Cut The Cake** *AWB*
47^{S}/01 **Cut Throat** *John Got'ti*
61/82 **Cutie Pie** *One Way*
44/90 **Cuts Both Ways** *Gloria Estefan*
15/83 **Cuts Like A Knife** *Bryan Adams*
55/90 **Cuts You Up** *Peter Murphy*
71/78 **Cuz It's You, Girl** *James Walsh Gypsy Band*
23/68 **Cycles** *Frank Sinatra*

D

19/68 **D. W. Washburn** *Monkees*
20/73 **D'yer Mak'er** *Led Zeppelin*
49^{A}/97 **D'You Know What I Mean?** *Oasis*
86/96 **DJ Girl** *Katalina*
84/97 **DJ Keep Playin' (Get Your Music On)** *Yvette Michele*
36/71 **D.O.A.** *Bloodrock*
46^{S}/01 **Da B.O.M.B.** *Caponiac*
35/88 **Da'Butt** *E.U.*
Da' Dip
15/97 *Freak Nasty*
82/97 *MC Luscious*
Da Doo Ron Ron
3/63 *Crystals*
96/72 *Ian Matthews*
1/77 *Shaun Cassidy*
1/79 **Da Ya Think I'm Sexy?** *Rod Stewart*
(also see: Do You Think I'm Disco)
65/77 **Daddy Cool** *Boney M*
F/57 **Daddy Cool** *Rays*
19/73 **Daddy Could Swear, I Declare** *Gladys Knight*
4/72 **Daddy Don't You Walk So Fast** *Wayne Newton*
Daddy-O
11/55 *Fontane Sisters*
14/55 *Bonnie Lou*
42/69 **Daddy Sang Bass** *Johnny Cash*
41/74 **Daddy What If** *Bobby Bare*
79/00 **Daddy Won't Sell The Farm** *Montgomery Gentry*

19^{X}/73 **Daddy's Drinking Up Our Christmas** *Commander Cody*
Daddy's Home
2/61 *Shep & The Limelites*
91/67 *Chuck Jackson & Maxine Brown*
9/73 *Jermaine Jackson*
23/82 *Cliff Richard*
42/67 **Daddy's Little Girl** *Al Martino*
48^{S}/91 **Daddy's Little Girl** *Nikki D*
(also see: One More Year Of)
34/69 **Daddy's Little Man** *O.C. Smith*
16^{S}/00 **Daily** *TQ*
14/73 **Daisy A Day** *Jud Strunk*
20/75 **Daisy Jane** *America*
41/72 **Daisy Mae** *Hamilton, Joe Frank & Reynolds*
15/64 **Daisy Petal Pickin'** *Jimmy Gilmer/Fireballs*
61^{A}/98 **Dammit (Growing Up)** *Blink-182*
86/69 **Dammit Isn't God's Last Name** *Frankie Laine*
5/92 **Damn I Wish I Was Your Lover** *Sophie B. Hawkins*
73/75 **Damn It All** *Gene Cotton*
35^{S}/99 **Damn (Should've Treated U Right)** *So Plush*
27/79 **Damned If I Do** *Alan Parsons Project*

DANCE:

59/87 **Dance** *Ratt*
(also see: Mojo Workout)
38/78 **Dance Across The Floor** *Jimmy "Bo" Horne*
93/77 **Dance And Shake Your Tambourine** *Universal Robot Band*
44/79 **Dance Away** *Roxy Music*
47/60 **Dance By The Light Of The Moon** *Olympics*
8/64 **Dance, Dance, Dance** *Beach Boys*
84/72 **Dance, Dance, Dance** *New Seekers*
89/63 **Dance, Dance, Dance** *Joey Dee*
6/78 **Dance, Dance, Dance (Yowsah, Yowsah, Yowsah)** *Chic*
19/78 **Dance (Disco Heat)** *Sylvester*
99/63 **Dance, Everybody, Dance** *Dartells*
31/58 **Dance Everyone Dance** *Betty Madigan*
16/84 **Dance Hall Days** *Wang Chung*
45/96 **Dance Into The Light** *Phil Collins*
100/77 **Dance Little Lady Dance** *Danny White*
30/88 **Dance Little Sister** *Terence Trent D'Arby*
73/74 **Dance Master** *Willie Henderson*
41/94 **Dance Naked** *John Mellencamp*
10/61 **Dance On Little Girl** *Paul Anka*
19/58 **Dance Only With Me** *Perry Como*
48/75 **Dance The Kung Fu** *Carl Douglas*
24/61 **(Dance The) Mess Around** *Chubby Checker*
15/79 **Dance The Night Away** *Van Halen*
(Dance Till You Can't Dance No More!) ..see: Keep It Comin'
23/58 **Dance To The Bop** *Gene Vincent*
8/68 **Dance To The Music** *Sly & The Family Stone*
36/00 **Dance Tonight** *Lucy Pearl*
39/76 **Dance Wit Me** *Rufus Feat. Chaka Khan*
64/82 **Dance Wit' Me** *Rick James*
6/75 **Dance With Me** *Orleans*
8/78 **Dance With Me** *Peter Brown with Betty Wright*
8/01 **Dance With Me** *Debelah Morgan*

14S/02 **Dance With Me** *Jaimie Lee*
15/59 **Dance With Me** *Drifters*
39/01 **Dance With Me** *112*
61/65 **Dance With Me** *Mojo Men*
95/60 **Dance With Me Georgie** *Bobbettes*
1/55 **Dance With Me Henry (Wallflower)** *Georgia Gibbs*
98/62 **Dance With Mr. Domino** *Fats Domino*
49/74 **Dance With The Devil** *Cozy Powell*
12/62 **(Dance With The) Guitar Man** *Duane Eddy*
70/79 **Dance With You** *Carrie Lucas*
90/97 **Dancehall Queen** *Beenie Man*
48/79 **Dancer** *Gino Soccio*

DANCIN'/DANCING:

19/00 **Dancin'** *Guy*
42/77 **Dancin'** *Crown Heights Affair*
76/57 **Dancin'** *Perry Como*
83/79 **Dancin'** *Grey & Hanks*
(also see: Dansin)
72/78 **Dancin' Fever** *Claudja Barry*
28/75 **Dancin' Fool** *Guess Who*
45/79 **Dancin' Fool** *Frank Zappa*
86/63 **Dancin' Holiday** *Olympics*
91/86 **Dancin In My Sleep** *Secret Ties*
68/85 **Dancin' In The Key Of Life** *Steve Arrington*
60/76 **Dancin' Kid** *Disco Tex & The Sex-O-Lettes*
72/80 **Dancin' Like Lovers** *Mary MacGregor*
23/77 **Dancin' Man** *Q*
93/74 **Dancin' (On A Saturday Night)** *Flash Cadillac & The Continental Kids*
87/67 **Dancin' Out Of My Heart** *Ronnie Dove*
12/62 **Dancin' Party** *Chubby Checker*
82/79 **Dancin' 'Round And 'Round** *Olivia Newton-John*
Dancin' Shoes
18/79 *Nigel Olsson*
54/79 *Faith Band*
91/62 **Dancin' The Strand** *Maureen Gray*
88/87 **Dancin' With My Mirror** *Corey Hart*
51/68 **Dancing Bear** *Mamas & The Papas*
68/57 **Dancing Chandelier** *Sylvia Syms*
63A/95 **Dancing Days** *Stone Temple Pilots*
75/89 **Dancing In Heaven (Orbital Be-Bop)** *Q-Feel*
91/78 **Dancing In Paradise** *El Coco*
43/79 **Dancing In The City** *Marshall Hain*
2/84 **Dancing In The Dark** *Bruce Springsteen*
13/73 **Dancing In The Moonlight** *King Harvest*
85/83 **Dancing In The Shadows** *After The Fire*
17/84 **Dancing In The Sheets** *Shalamar*
Dancing In The Street
2/64 *Martha & The Vandellas*
73/67 *Mamas & The Papas*
84/67 *Ramsey Lewis*
66/80 *Teri DeSario with K.C.*
38/82 *Van Halen*
7/85 *Mick Jagger/David Bowie*
2/74 **Dancing Machine** *Jackson 5*
2/86 **Dancing On The Ceiling** *Lionel Richie*
Dancing Queen
1/77 *Abba*
95/00 *A*Teens*
61/73 **Dancing To Your Music** *Archie Bell*
68/88 **Dancing Under A Latin Moon** *Candi*

50/58 **Dancing With My Shadow** *Four Voices*
97/80 **Dancing With The Mountains** *John Denver*
14/67 **Dandelion** *Rolling Stones*
5/66 **Dandy** *Herman's Hermits*
7/64 **Dang Me** *Roger Miller*
46/95 **Danger** *Blahzay Blahzay*
96/63 **Danger** *Vic Dana*
14/01 **Danger (Been So Long)** *Mystikal*
12/55 **Danger! Heartbreak Ahead** *Jaye P. Morgan*
61/65 **Danger Heartbreak Dead Ahead** *Marvelettes*
89/67 **Danger! She's A Stranger** *Five Stairsteps*
2/86 **Danger Zone** *Kenny Loggins*
2/90 **Dangerous** *Roxette*
9/98 **Dangerous** *Busta Rhymes*
57/85 **Dangerous** *Natalie Cole*
65/85 **Dangerous** *Loverboy*
59A/91 **Dangerous On The Dancefloor** *Musto & Bones*
25/66 **Dangling Conversation** *Simon & Garfunkel*
Dangling On A String ..see: (You've Got Me)
2/73 **Daniel** *Elton John*
13/63 **Danke Schoen** *Wayne Newton*
Danny Boy
10/59 *Conway Twitty*
59/59 *Sil Austin*
64/61 *Andy Williams*
76/65 *Patti LaBelle*
94/65 *Jackie Wilson*
60/67 *Ray Price*
7/73 **Danny's Song** *Anne Murray*
7S/01 **Dansin Wit Wolvez** *Strik 9ine*
11/85 **Dare Me** *Pointer Sisters*
32/90 **Dare To Fall In Love** *Brent Bourgeois*
Dark At The Top Of The Stairs ..see: Theme From The
77/67 **Dark End Of The Street** *James Carr*
15/75 **Dark Horse** *George Harrison*
1/74 **Dark Lady** *Chér*
Dark Moon
4/57 *Gale Storm*
6/57 *Bonnie Guitar*
77/63 **Darkest Street In Town** *Jimmy Clanton*
86/70 **Darkness, Darkness** *Youngbloods*
Darlin'
19/68 *Beach Boys*
51/78 *Paul Davis*
68/80 *Yipes!!*
81/84 **Darlin'** *Frank Stallone*
57/88 **Darlin' Danielle Don't** *Henry Lee Summer*
72/77 **Darlin' Darlin' Baby (Sweet, Tender, Love)** *O'Jays*
88/89 **Darlin' I** *Vanessa Williams*
72/66 **Darling Baby** *Elgins*
Darling Be Home Soon
15/67 *Lovin' Spoonful*
93/67 *Bobby Darin*
67/73 **Darling Come Back Home** *Eddie Kendricks*
100/70 **Darling Dear** *Miracles*
63/59 **Darling, I Love You** *Al Martino*
48/57 **Darling It's Wonderful** *Lovers*
7/55 **Darling Je Vous Aime Beaucoup** *Nat "King" Cole*
46/60 **Darling Lorraine** *Knockouts*

72/65 **Darling Take Me Back** *Lenny Welch*
92/64 **Dartell Stomp** *Mustangs*
F/57 **Date With The Blues** *Billy Williams*
61/63 **Daughter** *Blenders*
97/96 **Daughter** *Pearl Jam*
13/70 **Daughter Of Darkness** *Tom Jones*
Davy Crockett ..see: Ballad Of
62/63 **Dawn** *David Rockingham Trio*
3/64 **Dawn (Go Away)** *Four Seasons*
36/65 **Dawn Of Correction** *Spokesmen*

DAY:

4/72 **Day After Day** *Badfinger*
57/69 **Day After Day (It's Slippin' Away)** *Shango*
65/72 **Day And Night** *Wackers*
98/02 **Day + Night** *Isyss*
Day At The Beach ..see: (How I Spent My Summer Vacation)
13/72 **Day By Day** *Godspell*
18/86 **Day By Day** *Hooters*
72/55 **Day By Day** *Four Freshmen*
84/71 **Day By Day (Every Minute of The Hour)** *Continental 4*
5/72 **Day Dreaming** *Aretha Franklin*
(also see: Daydreamin')
35/66 **Day For Decision** *Johnny Sea*
81/58 **Day I Died** *Playmates*
23/72 **Day I Found Myself** *Honey Cone*
21/87 **Day-In Day-Out** *David Bowie*
49/91 **Day In My Life (Without You)** *Lisette Melendez*
62/66 **Day In The Life Of A Fool** *Jack Jones*
Day Is Done
21/69 *Peter, Paul & Mary*
98/70 *Brooklyn Bridge*
Day-O ..see: Banana Boat
86/98 **Day That She Left Tulsa (In A Chevy)** *Wade Hayes*
Day The Rains Came
21/58 *Jane Morgan*
30/58 *Raymond Lefevre*
17/99 **Day The World Went Away** *Nine Inch Nails*
Day Tripper
5/66 *Beatles*
100/66 *Vontastics*
74/67 *Ramsey Lewis*
59/75 *Anne Murray*
23/77 **Daybreak** *Barry Manilow*
39/74 **Daybreak** *Nilsson*
(also see: Storybook Children)
87/74 **Daybreaker** *Electric Light Orchestra*
2/66 **Daydream** *Lovin' Spoonful*
Daydream Believer
1/67 *Monkees*
12/80 *Anne Murray*
79/86 *Monkees*
91/76 **Daydreamer** *C.C. & Company*
6/98 **Daydreamin'** *Tatyana Ali*
70/61 **Daydreams** *Johnny Crawford*
73/56 **Daydreams** *Art Mooney*
63/76 **Daylight** *Vicki Sue Robinson*
75/78 **Daylight And Darkness** *Smokey Robinson*
51A/97 **Daylight Fading** *Counting Crows*
36S/02 **Daylight In Your Eyes** *No Angels*
79/67 **Daylight Savin' Time** *Keith*
71/85 **Days Are Numbers (The Traveller)** *Alan Parsons Project*
14/02 **Days Go By** *Dirty Vegas*
80/84 **Days Gone By** *Poco*

17/79 **Days Gone Down (Still Got The Light In Your Eyes)** *Gerry Rafferty*
64/90 **Days Like These** *Asia*
39A/96 **Days Of Our Livez** *Bone Thugs-N-Harmony*
34/69 **Days Of Sand And Shovels** *Bobby Vinton*
Days Of Wine And Roses
26/63 *Andy Williams*
33/63 *Henry Mancini*
57/98 **Daysleeper** *R.E.M.*
28/77 **Daytime Friends** *Kenny Rogers*
51/73 **Daytime Night-Time** *Keith Hampshire*
3/77 **Dazz** *Brick*
12/93 **Dazzey Duks** *Duice*
10/81 **De Do Do Do, De Da Da Da** *Police*
19/78 **Deacon Blues** *Steely Dan*
29/67 **Dead End Street** *Lou Rawls*
73/67 **Deadend Street** *Kinks*
22/83 **Dead Giveaway** *Shalamar*
53/88 **Dead Heart** *Midnight Oil*
55S/02 **Dead Light** *El-P*
8/64 **Dead Man's Curve** *Jan & Dean*
F/96 **Dead Presidents** *Jay-Z*
16/73 **Dead Skunk** *Loudon Wainwright III*
30/90 **Deadbeat Club** *B-52's*
79/98 **Deadly Zone** *Bounty Killer*

DEAR:

94/63 **Dear Abby** *Hearts*
93/70 **Dear Ann** *George Baker Selection*
95/65 **Dear Dad** *Chuck Berry*
98/68 **Dear Delilah** *Grapefruit*
50/67 **Dear Eloise** *Hollies*
87/56 **Dear Elvis** *Audrey*
12S/02 **Dear God** *Willie D*
95/89 **Dear God** *Midge Ure*
Dear Heart
24/65 *Andy Williams*
30/65 *Jack Jones*
77/65 *Henry Mancini*
95/62 **Dear Hearts And Gentle People** *Springfields*
24/62 **Dear Ivan** *Jimmy Dean*
44/60 **Dear John** *Pat Boone*
9/62 **Dear Lady Twist** *Gary (U.S.) Bonds*
51/00 **Dear Lie** *TLC*
13/62 **Dear Lonely Hearts** *Nat King Cole*
51/66 **Dear Lover** *Mary Wells*
9/95 **Dear Mama** *2Pac*
95/61 **Dear Mr. D.J. Play It Again** *Tina Robin*
61/88 **Dear Mr. Jesus** *Powersource*
91/66 **Dear Mrs. Applebee** *Flip Cartridge*
11/62 **Dear One** *Larry Finnegan*
Dear Prudence
66/70 *5 Stairsteps*
62/75 *Katfish*
59/63 **Dearer Than Life** *Brook Benton*
85/57 **Dearest** *Mickey & Sylvia*
8X/64 **Dearest Santa** *Bobby Vinton*
42/64 **Death Of An Angel** *Kingsmen*
20/95 **December** *Collective Soul*
December, 1963 (Oh, What a Night)
1/76 *Four Seasons*
14/94 *Four Seasons (remix)*
7/59 **Deck Of Cards** *Wink Martindale*
61/00 **Deck The Halls** *SheDaisy*
64/70 **Declaration, The** *5th Dimension*
7/58 **DeDe Dinah** *Frankie Avalon*
31/93 **Dedicated** *R. Kelly*
36/66 **Dedicated Follower Of Fashion** *Kinks*
Dedicated To The One I Love
83/59 *Shirelles*
3/61 *Shirelles*
81/61 *"5" Royales*
2/67 *Mamas & The Papas*
93/72 *Temprees*
65/81 *Bernadette Peters*
89/61 **Dedicated (To The Songs I Love)** *3 Friends*
60/77 **Dedication** *Bay City Rollers*
41/66 **Dedication Song** *Freddy Cannon*

DEEP:

F/71 **Deep Blue** *George Harrison*
67/57 **Deep Blue Sea** *Jimmy Dean*
57S/92 **Deep Cover** *Dr. Dre & Snoop Doggy Dogg*
69/91 **Deep, Deep Trouble** *Simpsons*
73/71 **Deep Enough For Me** *Ocean*
90/64 **Deep In The Heart Of Harlem** *Clyde McPhatter*
78/62 **Deep In The Heart Of Texas** *Duane Eddy*
63/00 **Deep Inside** *Mary J. Blige*
22/80 **Deep Inside My Heart** *Randy Meisner*
69/00 **Deep Inside Of You** *Third Eye Blind*
Deep Purple
20/57 *Billy Ward*
1/63 *Nino Tempo & April Stevens*
14/76 *Donny & Marie Osmond*
71/87 **Deep River Woman** *Lionel Richie with Alabama*
32S/02 **Deep Space 9mm** *El-P*
65/93 **Deeper** *Boss*
7/93 **Deeper And Deeper** *Madonna*
24/70 **Deeper & Deeper** *Freda Payne*
64/70 **Deeper (In Love With You)** *O'Jays*
Deeper Love
44/92 *Clivilles & Cole*
63/94 *Aretha Franklin*
21/91 **Deeper Shade Of Soul** *Urban Dance Squad*
11/79 **Deeper Than The Night** *Olivia Newton-John*
28/90 **Deeper The Love** *Whitesnake*
93/77 **Deeply** *Anson Williams*
60/98 **Definition** *Mos Def & Kweli are Black Star*
77/02 **Defy You** *Offspring*
15/80 **Deja Vu** *Dionne Warwick*
9/98 **Deja Vu (Uptown Baby)** *Lord Tariq & Peter Gunz*
22/60 **Delaware** *Perry Como*
66/60 **Delia Gone** *Pat Boone*
74/93 **Delicate** *Terence Trent D'Arby*
40/58 **Delicious!** *Jim Backus*
66/98 **Delicious** *Pure Sugar*
15/68 **Delilah** *Tom Jones*
Delilah Jones ..see: Man With The Golden Arm
8/83 **Delirious** *Prince*
Delta Dawn
72/72 *Tanya Tucker*
1/73 *Helen Reddy*
84/74 **Delta Dirt** *Larry Gatlin*
69/69 **Delta Lady** *Joe Cocker*
86/73 **Delta Queen** *Don Fardon*
10/63 **Denise** *Randy & The Rainbows*
67/75 **Department Of Youth** *Alice Cooper*
25/79 **Dependin' On You** *Doobie Brothers*
5/83 **Der Kommissar** *After The Fire*
Desafinado
15/62 *Stan Getz/Charlie Byrd*
78/62 *Pat Thomas*
94/71 **Desdemona** *Searchers*
88/57 **Deserie** *Charts*
(also see: Desiree)
10/84 **Desert Moon** *Dennis DeYoung*
33/63 **Desert Pete** *Kingston Trio*
17/00 **Desert Rose** *Sting*
8/71 **Desiderata** *Les Crane*
(also see: Deteriorata)
3/88 **Desire** *U2*
4/80 **Desire** *Andy Gibb*
70/80 **Desire** *Rockets*
47/58 **Desire Me** *Sam Cooke*
16/78 **Desirée** *Neil Diamond*
98/67 **Desiree'** *Left Banke*
66/83 **Desperate But Not Serious** *Adam Ant*
48/97 **Desperately Wanting** *Better Than Ezra*
63/68 **Destination: Anywhere** *Marvelettes*
42/82 **Destination Unknown** *Missing Persons*
47/98 **Destiny** *Myron*
83/70 **Destiny** *José Feliciano*
85/81 **Destroyer** *Kinks*
91/72 **Deteriorata** *National Lampoon*
Detroit City
16/63 *Bobby Bare*
90/63 *Ben Colder*
27/67 *Tom Jones*
F/76 **Detroit Rock City** *Kiss*
46/91 **Devil Came Up To Michigan** *K.M.C. Kru*
79/84 **Devil In A Fast Car** *Sheena Easton*
Devil In Disguise ..see: (You're the)
54/75 **Devil In The Bottle** *T.G. Sheppard*
2/88 **Devil Inside** *INXS*
79/83 **Devil Made Me Do It** *Golden Earring*
6/60 **Devil Or Angel** *Bobby Vee*
3/79 **Devil Went Down To Georgia** *Charlie Daniels Band*
(also see: Devil Came Up To Michigan)
Devil With A Blue Dress On
4/66 *Mitch Ryder (medley)*
71/76 *Pratt & McClain*
6/76 **Devil Woman** *Cliff Richard*
16/62 **Devil Woman** *Marty Robbins*
61/72 **Devil You** *Stampeders*
97/67 **Devil's Angels** *Davie Allen*
36/77 **Devil's Gun** *C.J. & Co.*
94/96 **Devils Haircut** *Beck*
Devoted To You
10/58 *Everly Brothers*
36/78 *Carly Simon & James Taylor*
33/74 **Devotion** *Earth, Wind & Fire*
82/58 **Devotion** *Janice Harper*
13/89 **Dial My Heart** *Boys*
24/72 **Dialogue** *Chicago*
6/73 **Diamond Girl** *Seals & Crofts*
70/65 **Diamond Head** *Ventures*
78/58 **Diamond Ring** *Jerry Wallace*
5/87 **Diamonds** *Herb Alpert (with Janet Jackson)*
44/79 **Diamonds** *Chris Rea*
3/92 **Diamonds And Pearls** *Prince*
18/60 **Diamonds And Pearls** *Paradons*
35/75 **Diamonds And Rust** *Joan Baez*
57/72 **Diamonds Are Forever** *Shirley Bassey*
Diana
1/57 *Paul Anka*
98/65 *Bobby Rydell*

Diane
97/63 *Joe Harnell*
10/64 *Bachelors*
69/66 **Dianne, Dianne** *Ronny & The Daytonas*
14/59 **Diary, The** *Neil Sedaka*
15/72 **Diary** *Bread*
82/94 **Diary Of A Madman** *Gravediggaz*
F/75 **Dick And Jane** *Bobby Vinton*
85/98 **Did I Shave My Legs For This?** *Deana Carter*
9/82 **Did It In A Minute** *Daryl Hall & John Oates*
60S/01 **Did That!** *812 Souljaz*
29/76 **Did You Boogie (With Your Baby)** *Flash Cadillac & The Continental Kids*
74/65 **Did You Ever** *Hullaballoos*
2/66 **Did You Ever Have To Make Up Your Mind?** *Lovin' Spoonful*
79/62 **Did You Ever See A Dream Walking** *Fats Domino*
27/99 **Did You Ever Think** *R. Kelly*
89/63 **Did You Have A Happy Birthday?** *Paul Anka*
32/69 **Did You See Her Eyes** *Illusion*
53/62 **Diddle-Dee-Dum (What Happens When Your Love Has Gone)** *Belmonts*
66/01 **Diddy** *P. Diddy*
70/73 **Didn't I** *Sylvia*
Didn't I (Blow Your Mind This Time)
10/70 *Delfonics*
8/89 *New Kids On The Block*
81/71 **Didn't It Look So Easy** *Stairsteps*
61/88 **Didn't Know It Was Love** *Survivor*
Didn't We
63/69 *Richard Harris*
82/73 *Barbra Streisand*
1/87 **Didn't We Almost Have It All** *Whitney Houston*
63/69 **Didn't You Know (You'd Have To Cry Sometime)** *Gladys Knight*
8/02 **Die Another Day** *Madonna*
Died In Your Arms ..see: (I Just)
23A/97 **Difference, The** *Wallflowers*
4/01 **Differences** *Ginuwine*
7/86 **Different Corner** *George Michael*
13/68 **Different Drum** *Linda Ronstadt*
11S/02 **Different Kind Of Love Song** *Cher*
61/89 **Different Story (World Of Lust And Crime)** *Peter Schilling*
95/67 **Different Strokes** *Syl Johnson*
18/79 **Different Worlds** *Maureen McGovern*
42S/01 **Dig** *Mudvayne*
31/01 **Dig In** *Lenny Kravitz*
42/80 **Dig The Gold** *Joyce Cobb*
5/95 **Diggin' On You** *TLC*
52/92 **Digging in the Dirt** *Peter Gabriel*
14/86 **Digging Your Scene** *Blow Monkeys*
21/86 **Digital Display** *Ready For The World*
1/02 **Dilemma** *Nelly*
2/79 **Dim All The Lights** *Donna Summer*
11/55 **Dim, Dim The Lights (I Want Some Atmosphere)** *Bill Haley*
86/72 **Dinah Flo** *Boz Scaggs*
18/60 **Ding-A-Ling** *Bobby Rydell*
56/98 **Ding-A-Ling** *Hi-Town DJ's*
(also see: My Ding-A-Ling)
25/58 **Ding Dong** *McGuire Sisters*
36/75 **Ding Dong; Ding Dong** *George Harrison*
11/67 **Ding Dong! The Witch Is Dead** *Fifth Estate*
6/58 **Dinner With Drac** *John Zacherle*
48/87 **Dinner With Gershwin** *Donna Summer*
48/02 **Dirrty** *Christina Aguilera*
56S/99 **Dirty Bird Groove** *ATL All-Stars*
25/90 **Dirty Cash (Money Talks)** *Adventures Of Stevie V*
66/94 **Dirty Dawg** *NKOTB*
36/90 **Dirty Deeds** *Joan Jett*
1/88 **Dirty Diana** *Michael Jackson*
3/83 **Dirty Laundry** *Don Henley*
90/83 **Dirty Looks** *Juice Newton*
55/91 **Dirty Love** *Thunder*
68/67 **Dirty Man** *Laura Lee*
92/96 **Dirty South** *Goodie Mob.*
Dirty Water
11/66 *Standells*
51/80 *Inmates*
61/87 **Dirty Water** *Rock & Hyde*
12/79 **Dirty White Boy** *Foreigner*
36/67 **Dis-Advantages Of You** *Brass Ring*
56/77 **Dis-Gorilla** *Rick Dees*
8/91 **Disappear** *INXS*
48A/94 **Disarm** *Smashing Pumpkins*
82/85 **Discipline Of Love (Why Did You Do It)** *Robert Palmer*
1/76 **Disco Duck** *Rick Dees*
Disco Inferno
53/77 *Trammps*
11/78 *Trammps*
1/76 **Disco Lady** *Johnnie Taylor*
24/77 **Disco Lucy (I Love Lucy Theme)** *Wilton Place Street Band*
12/79 **Disco Nights (Rock-Freak)** *GQ*
86/77 **Disco 9000** *Johnnie Taylor*
28/75 **Disco Queen** *Hot Chocolate*
(Disco 'Round) ..see: I Love The Nightlife
88/78 **Disco Rufus** *Stargard*
91/76 **Disco Sax** *Houston Person*
100/77 **Discomania** *Lovers*
10/97 **Discothèque** *U2*
40S/01 **Discretion Grove** *Stephen Malkmus*
29/02 **Disease** *Matchbox Twenty*
35A/96 **Distance, The** *Cake*
45/66 **Distant Drums** *Jim Reeves*
28/74 **Distant Lover** *Marvin Gaye*
30/66 **Distant Shores** *Chad & Jeremy*
10/93 **Ditty** *Paperboy*
79/86 **Divided Hearts** *Kim Carnes*
35/92 **Divine Thing** *Soup Dragons*
63/68 **D-I-V-O-R-C-E** *Tammy Wynette*
Dixie ..see: Theme From
30/55 **Dixie Danny** *Laurie Sisters*
96/75 **Dixie Rock** *Wet Willie*
1/69 **Dizzy** *Tommy Roe*
69/58 **Dizzy, Miss Lizzy** *Larry Williams*

DO:

Do ..also see: Doo
2/91 **Do Anything** *Natural Selection*
74/64 **Do Anything You Wanna** *Harold Betters*
74/93 **Do Da What** *1 Of The Girls*
21/98 **Do For Love** *2Pac*
57/97 **Do G's Get To Go To Heaven?** *Richie Rich*
13/82 **Do I Do** *Stevie Wonder*
11/92 **Do I Have To Say The Words?** *Bryan Adams*
67/58 **Do I Like It** *Nat "King" Cole*
34/64 **Do I Love You?** *Ronettes*
53/71 **Do I Love You** *Paul Anka*
Do I Love You (Because You're Beautiful)
62/57 *Vic Damone*
82/57 *Tony Martin*
96/65 **Do I Make Myself Clear** *Etta James & Sugar Pie DeSanto*
36/70 **Do It** *Neil Diamond*
Do It Again
6/73 *Steely Dan*
75/83 *Club House (medley)*
20/68 **Do It Again** *Beach Boys*
41/85 **Do It Again** *Kinks*
18/67 **Do It Again A Little Bit Slower** *Jon & Robin & The In Crowd*
65/00 **Do It Again (Put Ya Hands Up)** *Jay-Z*
11/75 **Do It Any Way You Wanna** *Peoples Choice*
13/74 **Do It Baby** *Miracles*
69/74 **Do It, Fluid** *Blackbyrds*
29/85 **Do It For Love** *Sheena Easton*
79/79 **Do It Good** *Taste Of Honey*
60/75 **Do It In The Name Of Love** *Ben E. King*
63/73 **Do It In The Name Of Love** *Candi Staton*
19/79 **Do It Or Die** *Atlanta Rhythm Section*
51/63 **Do It - Rat Now** *Bill Black's Combo*
67/65 **Do It Right** *Brook Benton*
2/74 **Do It ('Til You're Satisfied)** *B.T. Express*
21/92 **Do It To Me** *Lionel Richie*
43/77 **Do It To My Mind** *Johnny Bristol*
94/76 **Do It With Feeling** *Michael Zager Band*
3/90 **Do Me!** *Bell Biv DeVoe*
46/86 **Do Me Baby** *Meli'sa Morgan*
43/71 **Do Me Right** *Detroit Emeralds*
73S/91 **Do Me Right** *Guy*
62/92 **Do Not Pass Me By** *Hammer*
27/62 **Do-Re-Mi** *Lee Dorsey*
Do-Re-Mi
70/59 *Mitch Miller*
94/59 *Anita Bryant*
23/80 **Do Right** *Paul Davis*
38/68 **Do Something To Me** *Tommy James*
33/03 **Do That...** *Baby*
1/80 **Do That To Me One More Time** *Captain & Tennille*
11A/91 **Do The Bartman** *Simpsons*
93/68 **Do The Best You Can** *Hollies*
10/63 **Do The Bird** *Dee Dee Sharp*
36/65 **Do The Boomerang** *Jr. Walker*
44/68 **Do The Choo Choo** *Archie Bell*
21/65 **Do The Clam** *Elvis Presley*
18/65 **Do The Freddie** *Freddie & The Dreamers*
(also see: Freddie / Let's Do The Freddie)
28/70 **Do The Funky Chicken** *Rufus Thomas*
44/72 **Do The Funky Penguin** *Rufus Thomas*
(Do The) Mashed Potatoes ..see: Mashed Potatoes
92/63 **Do The Monkey** *King Curtis*
37/62 **(Do The New) Continental** *Dovells*
25/71 **(Do The) Push And Pull** *Rufus Thomas*
80/67 **Do The Thing** *Lou Courtney*
Do They Know It's Christmas?
13/84 *Band Aid*
49A/97 *Band Aid*

84/01 **Do U Wanna Roll** *R.L., Snoop Dogg & Lil' Kim*
73/68 **Do Unto Me** *James & Bobby Purify*
31/65 **Do-Wacka-Do** *Roger Miller*
Do Wah Diddy Diddy
1/64 *Manfred Mann*
78/64 *Exciters*
54[S]/91 **Do What I Gotta Do** *Ralph Tresvant*
57/58 **Do What You Did** *Thurston Harris*
13/85 **Do What You Do** *Jermaine Jackson*
52/65 **Do What You Do Do Well** *Ned Miller*
69/00 **Do What You Gotta Do** *Garth Brooks*
Do What You Gotta Do
83/68 *Nina Simone*
83/68 *Bobby Vee*
64/72 **Do What You Set Out To Do** *Bobby Bland*
37/70 **Do What You Wanna Do** *Five Flights Up*
46/77 **Do What You Wanna Do** *T-Connection*
39/76 **Do What You Want, Be What You Are** *Daryl Hall & John Oates*
Do Ya
93/72 *Move*
24/77 *Electric Light Orchestra*
87/87 **Do Ya Do Ya (Wanna Please Me)** *Samantha Fox*
Do Ya Think I'm Sexy? ..see: Da Ya
18/77 **Do Ya Wanna Get Funky With Me** *Peter Brown*
13[S]/02 **Do Yo Thang** *Beelow*
89/98 **Do You** *Heather B.*
91/00 **Do You** *Funkmaster Flex*
(also see: Do U / Do Ya / D'You / D'yer)
7/82 **Do You Believe In Love** *Huey Lewis*
Do You Believe In Magic
9/65 *Lovin' Spoonful*
31/78 *Shaun Cassidy*
72/89 **Do You Believe In Shame?** *Duran Duran*
13/92 **Do You Believe In Us** *Jon Secada*
64/83 **Do You Compute?** *Donnie Iris*
98/92 **Do You Everynite** *Joe Public*
63/78 **Do You Feel All Right** *KC & The Sunshine Band*
73/91 **Do You Feel Like I Feel?** *Belinda Carlisle*
10/76 **Do You Feel Like We Do** *Peter Frampton*
44[S]/99 **Do You Feel Me? (...Freak You)** *Men Of Vizion*
Do You Hear What I Hear?
2[X]/63 *Bing Crosby*
18[X]/65 *Andy Williams*
87/62 **Do You Know How To Twist** *Hank Ballard*
10/68 **Do You Know The Way To San José** *Dionne Warwick*
6/71 **Do You Know What I Mean** *Lee Michaels*
7/97 **Do You Know (What It Takes)** *Robyn*
62/71 **Do You Know What Time It Is?** *P-Nut Gallery*
Do You Know Where You're Going To ..see: Theme From Mahogany
31/97 **Do You Like This** *Rome*
Do You Love Me
3/62 *Contours*
11/64 *Dave Clark Five*
82/84 *Andy Fraser*
11/88 *Contours*
30/80 **Do You Love What You Feel** *Rufus & Chaka*
Do You Mind?
70/60 *Andy Williams*
91/60 *Anthony Newley*
49/96 **Do You Miss Me** *Jocelyn Enriquez*
32[A]/98 **Do You Really Want Me (Show Respect)** *Robyn*
2/83 **Do You Really Want To Hurt Me** *Culture Club*
4/90 **Do You Remember?** *Phil Collins*
71/86 **Do You Remember Me?** *Jermaine Jackson*
42/95 **Do You See** *Warren G*
32/70 **Do You See My Love (For You Growing)** *Jr. Walker*
18/95 **Do You Sleep?** *Lisa Loeb*
61/96 **Do You Think About Us** *Total*
58/79 **Do You Think I'm Disco?** *Steve Dahl*
49/85 **Do You Wanna Get Away** *Shannon*
40/94 **Do You Wanna Get Funky** *C+C Music Factory*
50/79 **Do You Wanna Go Party** *KC & The Sunshine Band*
77/83 **Do You Wanna Hold Me?** *Bow Wow Wow*
5/77 **Do You Wanna Make Love** *Peter McCann*
80/98 **(Do You) Wanna Ride** *Reel Tight*
20/82 **Do You Wanna Touch Me (Oh Yeah)** *Joan Jett*
37/85 **Do You Want Crying** *Katrina & The Waves*
94/92 **Do You Want It Right Now** *Degrees Of Motion*
21/91 **Do You Want Me** *Salt-N-Pepa*
50/96 **Do You Want To** *Xscape*
Do You Want To Dance
5/58 *Bobby Freeman*
43/64 *Del Shannon*
12/65 *Beach Boys*
76/68 *Mamas & The Papas*
17/73 *Bette Midler*
86/78 *Ramones*
2/64 **Do You Want To Know A Secret** *Beatles*
39/77 **Do Your Dance** *Rose Royce*
99/68 **Do Your Own Thing** *Brook Benton*
11/69 **Do Your Thing** *Watts 103rd Street Rhythm Band*
30/72 **Do Your Thing** *Isaac Hayes*
50/98 **Do Your Thing** *7 Mile*
Dock Of The Bay ..see: (Sittin' On)
9/89 **Doctor, The** *Doobie Brothers*
65/68 **Doctor, The** *Mary Wells*
Dr. Ben Basey ..see: Ben Crazy
Doctor Detroit ..see: Theme From
11/84 **Doctor! Doctor!** *Thompson Twins*
(also see: Bad Case Of Loving You)
66/62 **Doctor Feel-Good** *Dr. Feelgood & The Interns*
6/89 **Dr. Feelgood** *Mötley Crüe*
72/98 **Dr. Greenthumb** *Cypress Hill*
28/83 **Dr. Heckyll & Mr. Jive** *Men At Work*
87/68 **Dr. Jon (The Medicine Man)** *Jon & Robin & The In Crowd*
Doctor Kildare ..see: Theme From
41/77 **Doctor Love** *First Choice*
8/72 **Doctor My Eyes** *Jackson Browne*
Doctor Tarr ..see: (System Of)
Dr. Zhivago ..see: Somewhere My Love
11/75 **Doctor's Orders** *Carol Douglas*
66/89 **Doctorin' The Tardis** *Timelords*
83/64 **Dodo, The** *Jumpin' Gene Simmons*
38/69 **Does Anybody Know I'm Here** *Dells*
38/91 **Does Anybody Really Fall In Love Anymore?** *Kane Roberts*
7/71 **Does Anybody Really Know What Time It Is?** *Chicago*
98/62 **Does He Mean That Much To You?** *Eddy Arnold*
87/65 **Does He Really Care For Me** *Ruby & The Romantics*
36/83 **Does It Make You Remember** *Kim Carnes*
74/77 **Does She Do It Like She Dances** *Addrisi Brothers*
34/91 **Does She Love That Man?** *Breathe*
5/61 **Does Your Chewing Gum Lose It's Flavor (On The Bedpost Over Night)** *Lonnie Donegan*
29/68 **Does Your Mama Know About Me** *Bobby Taylor*
19/79 **Does Your Mother Know** *Abba*
F/55 **Doesn't Anybody Love Me?** *McGuire Sisters*
1/00 **Doesn't Really Matter** *Janet Jackson*
6/71 **Doesn't Somebody Want To Be Wanted** *Partridge Family*
87/63 **Dog, The** *Rufus Thomas*
34/79 **Dog & Butterfly** *Heart*
64/77 **Dog Days** *Atlanta Rhythm Section*
91/76 **Dog Eat Dog** *Ted Nugent*
66[S]/99 **Dog Food** *Forshé*
30/55 **Dogface Soldier** *Russ Morgan*
Doggin' Around
15/60 *Jackie Wilson*
50/83 *Klique*
32/69 **Doggone Right** *Miracles*
46[A]/94 **Doggy Dogg World** *Snoop Doggy Dogg*
9/96 **Doin It** *LL Cool J*
46/69 **Doin' Our Thing** *Clarence Carter*
93/62 **Doin' The Continental Walk** *Danny & The Juniors*
90/90 **Doin' The Do** *Betty Boo*
93/60 **(Doin' The) Lovers Leap** *Webb Pierce*
87/98 **Doin' Time** *Sublime*
6/87 **Doing It All For My Baby** *Huey Lewis*
22/73 **Doing It To Death** *JB's*
31/60 **Doll House** *Donnie Brooks*
58/95 **Doll Parts** *Hole*
60/61 **Dollar Down** *Limeliters*
34[S]/01 **Dollaz, Drank & Dank** *Mr. Short Khop*
74/71 **Dolly Dagger** *Jimi Hendrix*
78/99 **Dolphin's Cry** *Live*
13/55 **Domani (Tomorrow)** *Julius LaRosa*
1/63 **Dominique** *Singing Nun*
9/71 **Domino** *Van Morrison*
18/88 **Domino Dancing** *Pet Shop Boys*
14/87 **Dominoes** *Robbie Nevil*
Dommage, Dommage (Too Bad, Too Bad)
93/66 *Jerry Vale*
97/66 *Paul Vance*
56/86 **Don Quichotte** *Magazine 60*

DON'T:

1/58 **Don't** *Elvis Presley*
15/84 **Don't Answer Me** *Alan Parsons Project*

72/66 **Don't Answer The Door** *B.B. King*
48/62 **Don't Ask Me To Be Friends** *Everly Brothers*
72/57 **Don't Ask Me (To Be Lonely)** *Dubs*
19/80 **Don't Ask Me Why** *Billy Joel*
25/58 **Don't Ask Me Why** *Elvis Presley*
40/89 **Don't Ask Me Why** *Eurythmics*
44/77 **Don't Ask My Neighbors** *Emotions*
50/66 **Don't Be A Drop-Out** *James Brown*
44/92 **Don't Be Afraid** *Aaron Hall*
93/68 **Don't Be Afraid (Do As I Say)** *Frankie Karl*
26/63 **Don't Be Afraid, Little Darlin'** *Steve Lawrence*
74/88 **Don't Be Afraid Of The Dark** *Robert Cray Band*
Don't Be Angry
14/55 *Crew-Cuts*
25/55 *Nappy Brown*
Don't Be Cruel
1/56 *Elvis Presley*
11/60 *Bill Black's Combo*
93/63 *Barbara Lynn*
4/88 *Cheap Trick*
8/88 **Don't Be Cruel** *Bobby Brown*
86/84 **Don't Be My Enemy** *Wang Chung*
40/98 **Don't Be Stupid (You Know I Love You)** *Shania Twain*
41/61 **Don't Believe Him, Donna** *Lenny Miles*
9/61 **Don't Bet Money Honey** *Linda Scott*
20/61 **Don't Blame Me** *Everly Brothers*
37/67 **Don't Blame The Children** *Sammy Davis, Jr.*
73/88 **Don't Break My Heart** *Romeo's Daughter*
1/62 **Don't Break The Heart That Loves You** *Connie Francis*
4/79 **Don't Bring Me Down** *Electric Light Orchestra*
12/66 **Don't Bring Me Down** *Animals*
F/74 **Don't Burn Down The Bridge** *Gladys Knight*
79/73 **Don't Burn Me** *Paul Kelly*
88/00 **Don't Call Me Baby** *Madison Avenue*
83/57 **Don't Call Me Sweetie (Cause I'm Bitter)** *Eileen Rodgers*
9/75 **Don't Call Us, We'll Call You** *Sugarloaf/jerry Corbetta*
Don't Cha ..also see: Don't You / Doncha'
78/75 **Don't Cha Love It** *Miracles*
17/02 **dontchange** *Musiq*
80/83 **Don't Change** *INXS*
26/74 **Don't Change Horses (In The Middle Of A Stream)** *Tower Of Power*
36/71 **Don't Change On Me** *Ray Charles*
59/68 **Don't Change Your Love** *Five Stairsteps*
11/89 **Don't Close Your Eyes** *Kix*
13/85 **Don't Come Around Here No More** *Tom Petty*
21/60 **Don't Come Knockin'** *Fats Domino*
58/65 **Don't Come Running Back To Me** *Nancy Wilson*
79/78 **Don't Cost You Nothing** *Ashford & Simpson*
35/73 **Don't Cross The River** *America*
10/83 **Don't Cry** *Asia*
10/91 **Don't Cry** *Guns N' Roses*
33/96 **Don't Cry** *Seal*
83/56 **Don't Cry** *Frankie Laine with Paul Weston*
Don't Cry, Baby
39/61 *Etta James*
92/62 *Aretha Franklin*
6/70 **Don't Cry Daddy** *Elvis Presley*
Don't Cry For Me Argentina
72/80 *Festival*
8/97 *Madonna*
63/76 **Don't Cry Joni** *Conway Twitty*
71/68 **Don't Cry My Love** *Impressions*
55/57 **Don't Cry My Love (The Faithful Hussar)** *Vera Lynn*
71/61 **Don't Cry No More** *Bobby Bland*
10/79 **Don't Cry Out Loud** *Melissa Manchester*
62/60 **Don't Deceive Me** *Ruth Brown*
94/59 **Don't Destroy Me** *Crash Craddock*
4/87 **Don't Disturb This Groove** *System*
75/67 **Don't Do It** *Micky Dolenz*
(also see: Baby Don't You Do It)
90/84 **Don't Do Me** *Randy Bell*
10/80 **Don't Do Me Like That** *Tom Petty*
2/87 **Don't Dream It's Over** *Crowded House*
50^A/98 **Don't Drink The Water** *Dave Matthews Band*
87/79 **Don't Drop My Love** *Anita Ward*
86/74 **Don't Eat The Yellow Snow** *Frank Zappa*
23/72 **Don't Ever Be Lonely (A Poor Little Fool Like Me)** *Cornelius Brothers & Sister Rose*
85/62 **Don't Ever Leave Me** *Bob & Earl*
42/64 **Don't Ever Leave Me** *Connie Francis*
90/57 **Don't Ever Love Me** *Harry Belafonte*
100/72 **Don't Ever Take Away My Freedom** *Peter Yarrow*
40/79 **Don't Ever Wanna Lose Ya** *New England*
8/73 **Don't Expect Me To Be Your Friend** *Lobo*
4/80 **Don't Fall In Love With A Dreamer** *Kenny Rogers with Kim Carnes*
12/76 **(Don't Fear) The Reaper** *Blue Öyster Cult*
Don't Fence Me In
45/60 *Tommy Edwards*
93/63 *George Maharis*
17/82 **Don't Fight It** *Kenny Loggins/Steve Perry*
53/65 **Don't Fight It** *Wilson Pickett*
72/76 **Don't Fight The Hands (That Need You)** *Hamilton, Joe Frank & Dennison*
1/57 **Don't Forbid Me** *Pat Boone*
Don't Forget About Me
91/66 *Barbara Lewis*
64/69 *Dusty Springfield*
96/61 **Don't Forget I Love You** *Butanes*
19/65 **Don't Forget I Still Love You** *Bobbi Martin*
2/86 **Don't Forget Me (When I'm Gone)** *Glass Tiger*
29/83 **Don't Forget To Dance** *Kinks*
73/69 **Don't Forget To Remember** *Bee Gees*
Don't Get Around Much Anymore
74/57 *Tab Hunter*
57/61 *Belmonts*
10/86 **Don't Get Me Wrong** *Pretenders*
69/83 **Don't Girls Get Lonely** *Glenn Shorrock*
15/69 **Don't Give In To Him** *Gary Puckett*
26/81 **Don't Give It Up** *Robbie Patton*
37/68 **Don't Give Up** *Petula Clark*
72/87 **Don't Give Up** *Peter Gabriel/Kate Bush*
1/77 **Don't Give Up On Us** *David Soul*
62/97 **Don't Go** *Le Click*
35^A/97 **Don't Go Away** *Oasis*
93/96 **Don't Go Away** *Fun Factory*
19/90 **Don't Go Away Mad (Just Go Away)** *Mötley Crüe*
Don't Go Breaking My Heart
1/76 *Elton John & Kiki Dee*
92/94 *Elton John & RuPaul*
22/58 **Don't Go Home** *Playmates*
62/62 **Don't Go Near The Eskimos** *Ben Colder*
17/62 **Don't Go Near The Indians** *Rex Allen*
18/67 **Don't Go Out Into The Rain (You're Going To Melt)** *Herman's Hermits*
Don't Go To Strangers
38/56 *Vaughn Monroe*
36/60 *Etta Jones*
4/62 **Don't Hang Up** *Orlons*
26/01 **Don't Happen Twice** *Kenny Chesney*
93/65 **Don't Have To Shop Around** *Mad Lads*
46/72 **Don't Hide Your Love** *Chér*
21/79 **Don't Hold Back** *Chanson*
41/91 **Don't Hold Back Your Love** *Daryl Hall/John Oates*
2/77 **Don't It Make My Brown Eyes Blue** *Crystal Gayle*
82/75 **Don't It Make You Wanna Dance?** *Rusty Wier*
Don't It Make You Want To Go Home
41/69 *Joe South*
45/70 *Brook Benton*
8/65 **Don't Just Stand There** *Patty Duke*
90/97 **Don't Keep Wastin' My Time** *Teddy Pendergrass*
Don't Knock My Love
13/71 *Wilson Pickett*
46/74 *Diana Ross & Marvin Gaye*
30^C/56 **Don't Knock The Rock** *Bill Haley*
Don't Know Much
88/81 *Bill Medley*
77/83 *Bette Midler (All I Need To Know)*
2/89 *Linda Ronstadt/Aaron Neville*
12/88 **Don't Know What You Got (Till It's Gone)** *Cinderella*
30/03 **Don't Know Why** *Norah Jones*
73/98 **Don't Laugh At Me** *Mark Wills*
12^A/97 **Don't Leave Me** *BLACKstreet*
91/75 **Don't Leave Me In The Morning** *Odia Coates*
52/73 **Don't Leave Me Starvin' For Your Love** *Holland-Dozier*
Don't Leave Me This Way
1/77 *Thelma Houston*
40/87 *Communards*
Don't Let Go
13/58 *Roy Hamilton*
56/75 *Commander Cody*
18/80 *Isaac Hayes*
38/84 **Don't Let Go** *Wang Chung*
2/97 **Don't Let Go (Love)** *En Vogue*
84/81 **Don't Let Go The Coat** *Who*
64/63 **Don't Let Her Be Your Baby** *Contours*
24/81 **Don't Let Him Go** *REO Speedwagon*
39/82 **Don't Let Him Know** *Prism*
92/61 **Don't Let Him Shop Around** *Debbie Dean*
(also see: Shop Around)

45/69 **Don't Let Him Take Your Love From Me** *Four Tops*
6/83 **Don't Let It End** *Styx*
56/73 **Don't Let It End ('Til You Let It Begin)** *Miracles*
86/73 **Don't Let It Get You Down** *Crusaders*
54/98 **Don't Let It Go To Your Head** *Brand Nubian*
92/78 **Don't Let It Show** *Alan Parsons Project*
44/69 **Don't Let Love Hang You Up** *Jerry Butler*
85/60 **Don't Let Love Pass Me By** *Frankie Avalon*
14/73 **Don't Let Me Be Lonely Tonight** *James Taylor*
Don't Let Me Be Misunderstood
15/65 *Animals*
15/78 *Santa Esmeralda*
88/63 **Don't Let Me Cross Over** *Carl Butler & Pearl*
35/69 **Don't Let Me Down** *Beatles with Billy Preston*
8/02 **Don't Let Me Get Me** *P!nk*
63/82 **Don't Let Me In** *Sneaker*
68/77 **Don't Let The Flame Burn Out** *Jackie DeShannon*
17/71 **Don't Let The Green Grass Fool You** *Wilson Pickett*
20/69 **Don't Let The Joneses Get You Down** *Temptations*
100/70 **Don't Let The Music Slip Away** *Archie Bell*
6/64 **Don't Let The Rain Come Down (Crooked Little Man)** *Serendipity Singers*
39/67 **Don't Let The Rain Fall Down On Me** *Critters*
95/60 **Don't Let The Sun Catch You Cryin'** *Ray Charles*
4/64 **Don't Let The Sun Catch You Crying** *Gerry & The Pacemakers*
Don't Let The Sun Go Down On Me
2/74 *Elton John*
1/92 *George Michael/Elton John*
76/98 **Don't Let This Moment End** *Gloria Estefan*
95/65 **Don't Let Your Left Hand Know** *Joe Tex*
Don't Look Any Further
72/84 *Dennis Edwards*
64/88 *Kane Gang*
4/78 **Don't Look Back** *Boston*
11/89 **Don't Look Back** *Fine Young Cannibals*
(also see: You Got To Walk And)
55/96 **Don't Look Back In Anger** *Oasis*
39/87 **Don't Look Down - The Sequel** *Go West*
81/87 **Don't Lose Any Sleep** *John Waite*
4/85 **Don't Lose My Number** *Phil Collins*
71/92 **Don't Lose the Magic** *Shawn Christopher*
66/88 **Don't Make A Fool Of Yourself** *Stacey Q*
75/83 **Don't Make Me Do It** *Patrick Simmons*
Don't Make Me Over
21/63 *Dionne Warwick*
77/70 *Brenda & The Tabulations*
67/80 *Jennifer Warnes*
20/89 *Sybil*
62/71 **Don't Make Me Pay For His Mistakes** *Z.Z. Hill*
15/87 **Don't Make Me Wait For Love** *Kenny G*
51/63 **Don't Make My Baby Blue** *Frankie Laine*
79/68 **Don't Make The Good Girls Go Bad** *Della Humphrey*
3/87 **Don't Mean Nothing** *Richard Marx*
94/63 **Don't Mention My Name** *Shepherd Sisters*
33/65 **Don't Mess Up A Good Thing** *Fontella Bass & Bobby McClure*
7/66 **Don't Mess With Bill** *Marvelettes*
8/02 **Don't Mess With My Man** *Nivea*
42S/00 **Don't Mess With My Man** *Lucy Pearl*
90/01 **Don't Mess With The Radio** *Nivea*
55/80 **Don't Misunderstand Me** *Rossington Collins Band*
37/87 **Don't Need A Gun** *Billy Idol*
20S/01 **Don't Need You To (Tell Me I'm Pretty)** *Samantha Mumba*
91/68 **Don't Pat Me On The Back And Call Me Brother** *Kasandra*
34/83 **Don't Pay The Ferryman** *Chris DeBurgh*
40/59 **Don't Pity Me** *Dion & The Belmonts*
83/65 **Don't Pity Me** *Peter & Gordon*
Don't Play That Song
11/62 *Ben E. King*
11/70 *Aretha Franklin*
Don't Pull Your Love
4/71 *Hamilton, Joe Frank & Reynolds*
27/76 *Glen Campbell (medley)*
49/80 **Don't Push It Don't Force It** *Leon Haywood*
65/61 **Don't Read The Letter** *Patti Page*
98/67 **Don't Rock The Boat** *Eddie Floyd*
82/82 **Don't Run My Life** *Spys*
91/96 **Don't Rush** *Silk*
2/89 **Don't Rush Me** *Taylor Dayne*
68/97 **Don't Say** *Jon B*
41/02 **Don't Say Goodbye** *Paulina Rubio*
71/95 **Don't Say Goodbye Girl** *Tevin Campbell*
26/63 **Don't Say Goodnight And Mean Goodbye** *Shirelles*
39/80 **Don't Say Goodnight (It's Time For Love)** *Isley Brothers*
68/80 **Don't Say No** *Billy Burnette*
96/02 **Don't Say No, Just Say Yes** *Avant*
76/86 **Don't Say No Tonight** *Eugene Wilde*
7/63 **Don't Say Nothin' Bad (About My Baby)** *Cookies*
15/72 **Don't Say You Don't Remember** *Beverly Bremers*
21/00 **Don't Say You Love Me** *M2M*
58/89 **Don't Say You Love Me** *Billy Squier*
57/74 **Don't Send Nobody Else** *Ace Spectrum*
20/63 **Don't Set Me Free** *Ray Charles*
9/88 **Don't Shed A Tear** *Paul Carrack*
18/89 **Don't Shut Me Out** *Kevin Paige*
96/68 **Don't Sign The Paper Baby (I Want You Back)** *Jimmy Delphs*
5/67 **Don't Sleep In The Subway** *Petula Clark*
1A/96 **Don't Speak** *No Doubt*
93/64 **Don't Spread It Around** *Barbara Lynn*
Don't Stand So Close To Me
10/81 *Police*
46/86 *Police ('86)*
F/55 **Don't Stay Away Too Long** *Eddie Fisher*
3/77 **Don't Stop** *Fleetwood Mac*
44/84 **Don't Stop** *Jeffrey Osborne*
9/81 **Don't Stop Believin'** *Journey*
33/76 **Don't Stop Believin'** *Olivia Newton-John*
6S/02 **Don't Stop Dancing** *Creed*
42/76 **Don't Stop It Now** *Hot Chocolate*
61/82 **Don't Stop Me Baby (I'm On Fire)** *Boys Band*
86/79 **Don't Stop Me Now** *Queen*
67/97 **Don't Stop Movin'** *Livin' Joy*
48/70 **Don't Stop Now** *Eddie Holman*
63A/91 **Don't Stop Now** *Cover Girls*
19/81 **Don't Stop The Music** *Yarbrough & Peoples*
73/97 **Don't Stop The Music** *Playa*
99/62 **Don't Stop The Wedding** *Ann Cole*
1/79 **Don't Stop 'Til You Get Enough** *Michael Jackson*
83/82 **Don't Stop Trying** *Rodway*
56/93 **Don't Take Away My Heaven** *Aaron Neville*
34/76 **Don't Take Away The Music** *Tavares*
64/90 **Don't Take It Personal** *Jermaine Jackson*
2/95 **Don't Take It Personal (just one of dem days)** *Monica*
27/68 **Don't Take It So Hard** *Paul Revere & The Raiders*
17/94 **Don't Take The Girl** *Tim McGraw*
98/59 **Don't Take The Stars** *Mystics*
32/59 **Don't Take Your Guns To Town** *Johnny Cash*
37/75 **Don't Take Your Love** *Manhattans*
76/64 **Don't Take Your Love From Me** *Gloria Lynne*
58/01 **Don't Talk** *Jon B.*
81/82 **Don't Talk** *Larry Lee*
76/92 **Don't Talk Just Kiss** *Right Said Fred*
2/82 **Don't Talk To Strangers** *Rick Springfield*
52/65 **Don't Talk To Strangers** *Beau Brummels*
4/01 **Don't Tell Me** *Madonna*
27/75 **Don't Tell Me Goodnight** *Lobo*
10/89 **Don't Tell Me Lies** *Breathe*
83/56 **Don't Tell Me Not To Love You** *Joni James*
80/87 **Don't Tell Me The Time** *Martha Davis*
40/83 **Don't Tell Me You Love Me** *Night Ranger*
85/59 **Don't Tell Me Your Troubles** *Don Gibson*
73/69 **Don't Tell Your Mama (Where You've Been)** *Eddie Floyd*
43/76 **Don't Think....Feel** *Neil Diamond*
24/00 **Don't Think I'm Not** *Kandi*
Don't Think Twice, It's All Right
9/63 *Peter, Paul & Mary*
12/65 *Wonder Who?*
22/60 **Don't Throw Away All Those Teardrops** *Frankie Avalon*
Don't Throw It All Away ..see: (Our Love)
16/64 **Don't Throw Your Love Away** *Searchers*
Don't Touch Me
85/66 *Jeannie Seely*
38/69 *Bettye Swann*
61/76 **Don't Touch Me There** *Tubes*
19/91 **Don't Treat Me Bad** *Firehouse*
53/63 **Don't Try To Fight It, Baby** *Eydie Gorme*

(Don't Try To Lay No Boogie Woogie On The) "King Of Rock & Roll"

52/70 *Crow*

73/71 *John Baldry*

68/83 **Don't Try To Stop It** *Roman Holliday*

4/94 **Don't Turn Around** *Ace Of Base*

57/77 **Don't Turn The Light Out** *Cliff Richard*

83/84 **Don't Wait For Heroes** *Dennis DeYoung*

54/63 **Don't Wait Too Long** *Tony Bennett*

54/69 **Don't Wake Me Up In The Morning, Michael** *Peppermint Rainbow*

4/93 **Don't Walk Away** *Jade*

26/84 **Don't Walk Away** *Rick Springfield*

72/88 **Don't Walk Away** *Toni Childs*

85/86 **Don't Walk Away** *Robert Tepper*

21/97 **Don't Wanna Be A Player** *Joe*

2/90 **Don't Wanna Fall In Love** *Jane Child*

53/71 **Don't Wanna Live Inside Myself** *Bee Gees*

1/89 **Don't Wanna Lose You** *Gloria Estefan*

39/96 **Don't Wanna Lose You** *Lionel Richie*

58A/92 **Don't Wanna Love You** *Shanice*

68/63 **Don't Wanna Think About Paula** *Dickey Lee*

79/81 **Don't Want No-Body** *J.D. Drews*

9/91 **Don't Want To Be A Fool** *Luther Vandross*

21/78 **Don't Want To Live Without It** *Pablo Cruise*

86/72 **Don't Want To Say Goodbye** *Raspberries*

35/81 **Don't Want To Wait Anymore** *Tubes*

81/69 **Don't Waste My Time** *John Mayall*

48/84 **Don't Waste Your Time** *Yarbrough & Peoples*

3/61 **Don't Worry** *Marty Robbins*

Don't Worry Baby

24/64 *Beach Boys*

95/70 *Tokens*

17/77 *B.J. Thomas*

1/88 **Don't Worry Be Happy** *Bobby McFerrin*

72/62 **Don't Worry 'Bout Me** *Vincent Edwards*

29/71 **(Don't Worry) If There's A Hell Below We're All Going To Go** *Curtis Mayfield*

67/66 **Don't Worry Mother, Your Son's Heart Is Pure** *McCoys*

Don't Ya Wanna Play This Game No More ..see: (Sartorial Eloquence)

Don't You ..also see: Don't Cha / Doncha'

39/62 **Don't You Believe It** *Andy Williams*

6/67 **Don't You Care** *Buckinghams*

70/90 **Don't You Come Cryin'** *Linear*

1/85 **Don't You (Forget About Me)** *Simple Minds*

30/02 **Don't You Forget It** *Glenn Lewis* *(also see: I Love You)*

25/83 **Don't You Get So Mad** *Jeffrey Osborne*

9/58 **Don't You Just Know It** *Huey (Piano) Smith*

2/59 **Don't You Know** *Della Reese*

58/83 **Don't You Know How Much I Love You** *Ronnie Milsap*

69/81 **Don't You Know What Love Is** *Touch*

6/88 **Don't You Know What The Night Can Do?** *Steve Winwood*

56/59 **Don't You Know Yockomo** *Huey "Piano" Smith*

78/90 **Don't You Love Me** *49ers*

68/67 **Don't You Miss Me A Little Bit Baby** *Jimmy Ruffin*

86/90 **Don't You Wanna Be Mine** *Denise Lopez*

1/82 **Don't You Want Me** *Human League*

6/87 **Don't You Want Me** *Jody Watley*

66/62 **Don't You Worry** *Don Gardner & Dee Dee Ford*

16/74 **Don't You Worry 'Bout A Thing** *Stevie Wonder*

(Don't You Worry 'Bout Me) ..see: Opus 17

33/79 **Don't You Write Her Off** *McGuinn, Clark & Hillman*

77/61 **Donald Where's Your Troosers?** *Andy Stewart*

15/58 **Doncha' Think It's Time** *Elvis Presley*

47/58 **¿Dònde Està Santa Claus? (Where Is Santa Claus?)** *Augie Rios*

65/71 **Done Too Soon** *Neil Diamond*

2/59 **Donna** *Ritchie Valens*

6/63 **Donna The Prima Donna** *Dion*

62/64 **Donnie** *Bermudas*

90/92 **Doo Doo Brown** *2 Hyped Brothers & A Dog*

15/74 **Doo Doo Doo Doo Doo (Heartbreaker)** *Rolling Stones*

1/98 **Doo Wop (That Thing)** *Lauryn Hill*

71/77 **Doodle Song** *Frankie Miller*

94/61 **Dooley** *Olympics*

92/62 **Door Is Open** *Tommy Hunt*

Door Is Still Open To My Heart

F/55 *Don Cornell*

6/64 *Dean Martin*

85/61 **Door To Paradise** *Bobby Rydell*

62/74 **Door To Your Heart** *Dramatics*

35/74 **Doraville** *Atlanta Rhythm Section*

26/76 **Dose Of Rock 'N' Roll** *Ringo Starr*

39/58 **Dottie** *Danny & The Juniors*

22/71 **Double Barrel** *Dave & Ansil Collins*

30/81 **Double Dutch Bus** *Frankie Smith*

91/91 **Double Good Everything** *Smokey Robinson*

14/71 **Double Lovin'** *Osmonds*

89/65 **Double-O-Seven** *Detergents*

17/66 **Double Shot (Of My Baby's Love)** *Swingin' Medallions*

80/76 **Double Trouble** *Lynyrd Skynyrd*

2/78 **Double Vision** *Foreigner*

50/90 **Doubleback** *ZZ Top*

DOWN:

37A/96 **Down** *311*

50/73 **Down And Out In New York City** *James Brown*

21/02 **Down A** Chick** *Ja Rule*

33/68 **Down At Lulu's** *Ohio Express*

9/63 **(Down At) Papa Joe's** *Dixiebelles*

35S/00 **Down Bottom** *Drag-On*

27/89 **Down Boys** *Warrant*

4/72 **Down By The Lazy River** *Osmonds*

Down By The River

68/70 *Buddy Miles*

91/70 *Brooklyn Bridge*

91/72 **Down By The River** *Albert Hammond*

60/60 **Down By The Riverside** *Les Compagnons De La Chanson*

13/60 **Down By The Station** *Four Preps*

48A/95 **Down By The Water** *PJ Harvey*

6/02 **Down 4 U** *Inc.*

92/95 **Down 4 Whateva** *Nuttin' Nyce*

69/97 **Down For Yours** *Nastyboy Klick*

69/68 **Down Here On The Ground** *Lou Rawls*

75/70 **Down In The Alley** *Ronnie Hawkins*

9/65 **Down In The Boondocks** *Billy Joe Royal*

71/62 **Down In The Valley** *Solomon Burke*

93/58 **Down In Virginia** *Jimmy Reed*

4/96 **Down Low (Nobody Has To Know)** *R. Kelly*

54/85 **Down On Love** *Foreigner*

Down On Me

43/68 *Big Brother & The Holding Company*

91/72 *Janis Joplin*

3/69 **Down On The Corner** *Creedence Clearwater Revival*

59/99 **Down So Long** *Jewel*

91/60 **Down The Aisle** *Ike Clanton*

18/58 **Down The Aisle Of Love** *Quin-Tones*

37/63 **Down The Aisle (Wedding Song)** *Patti LaBelle*

65/77 **Down The Hall** *Four Seasons*

85/60 **Down The Street To 301** *Johnny Cash*

47/76 **Down To Love Town** *Originals*

43/76 **Down To The Line** *Bachman-Turner Overdrive*

66/72 **Down To The Nightclub** *Tower Of Power*

82/77 **Down To The Station** *B.W. Stevenson*

1/83 **Down Under** *Men At Work*

21/93 **Down With The King** *Run-D.M.C.*

48/60 **Down Yonder** *Johnny & The Hurricanes*

57/90 **Downeaster "Alexa"** *Billy Joel*

91/02 **Downfall** *TrustCompany*

46/01 **Downtime** *Jo Dee Messina*

Downtown

1/65 *Petula Clark*

40/65 *Allan Sherman (Crazy Downtown)*

82/66 *Mrs. Miller*

80/84 *Dolly Parton*

37/89 **Downtown** *One 2 Many*

F/93 **Downtown** *SWV*

31/88 **Downtown Life** *Daryl Hall/John Oates*

Downtown Train

95/87 *Patty Smyth*

3/90 *Rod Stewart*

48/95 **Downtown Venus** *P.M. Dawn*

Dr. ..see: Doctor

10/64 **Drag City** *Jan & Dean*

77/90 **Drag My Bad Name Down** *4 Of Us*

4/71 **Draggin' The Line** *Tommy James*

28/81 **Draw Of The Cards** *Kim Carnes*

42/77 **Draw The Line** *Aerosmith*

8/93 **Dre Day** *Dr. Dre*

44/78 **Dreadlock Holiday** *10 CC*

DREAM:

Dream

19/58 *Betty Johnson*

55/61 *Etta James*

92/62 *Dinah Washington*

72/97 **Dream** *Forest For The Trees*

12/68 **Dream A Little Dream Of Me** *Mama Cass*

29/95 **Dream About You** *Stevie B*

85/56 **Dream Along With Me (I'm On My Way To A Star)** *Perry Como*

Dream Baby (How Long Must I Dream)
4/62 Roy Orbison
31/71 Glen Campbell
87/61 Dream Boy Annette
53/90 Dream Boy-Dream Girl Cynthia & Johnny 'O'
69/74 Dream Goes On Forever Todd Rundgren
37/84 Dream (Hold On To Your Dream) Irene Cara
60S/95 Dream Is A Wish Your Heart Makes Linda Ronstadt
12/91 Dream Is Still Alive Wilson Phillips
Dream Lover
2/59 Bobby Darin
91/64 Paris Sisters
42/91 Dream Lover Rebel Pebbles
75/78 Dream Lover Marshall Tucker Band
1/93 Dreamlover Mariah Carey
73/73 Dream Me Home Mac Davis
Dream Merchant
38/67 Jerry Butler
36/75 New Birth
48/78 Dream Never Dies Cooper Brothers
Dream On
59/73 Aerosmith
6/76 Aerosmith
32/74 Dream On Righteous Brothers
85/01 Dream On Depeche Mode
51/94 Dream on Dreamer Brand New Heavies
25/65 Dream On Little Dreamer Perry Como
26/79 Dream Police Cheap Trick
2/76 Dream Weaver Gary Wright
Dreamboat ..see: (He's My)
42/77 Dreamboat Annie Heart
15/80 Dreamer Supertramp
47/63 Dreamer, The Neil Sedaka
66/81 Dreamer Association
Dreamer
72/95 Livin' Joy
95/96 Livin' Joy
86/56 Dreamer Four Aces
8/89 Dreamin' Vanessa Williams
Dreamin'
11/60 Johnny Burnette
45/82 John Schneider
50/87 Dreamin' Will To Power
72/77 Dreamin Loleatta Holloway
10/80 Dreaming Cliff Richard
16/88 Dreaming Orchestral Manoeuvres In The Dark
27/79 Dreaming Blondie
30/83 Dreamin' Is Easy Steel Breeze
80/88 Dreamin' Of Love Stevie B
43/75 Dreaming A Dream Crown Heights Affair
22/95 Dreaming Of You Selena
1/77 Dreams Fleetwood Mac
22/86 Dreams Van Halen
26/94 Dreams Gabrielle
42/94 Dreams Cranberries
86/70 Dreams Buddy Miles
85/90 Dreams A Dream Soul II Soul
83/74 Dreams Are Ten A Penny First Class
Dreams Of The Everyday Housewife
32/68 Glen Campbell
60/68 Wayne Newton
5/86 Dreamtime Daryl Hall

Dreamy Eyes
63/59 Johnny Tillotson
35/62 Johnny Tillotson
56/57 Dreamy Eyes Four Preps
21/73 Dreidel Don McLean
5/85 Dress You Up Madonna
14/89 Dressed For Success Roxette
61/02 Drift & Die Puddle Of Mudd
5/73 Drift Away Dobie Gray
96/68 Driftin' Blues Bobby Bland
59/78 Driftwood Moody Blues
86/97 Drink, Swear, Steal & Lie Michael Peterson
98/65 Drinking Man's Diet Allan Sherman
41/73 Drinking Wine Spo-Dee O'Dee Jerry Lee Lewis
71S/99 Drinks On Me T.W.D.Y.
Drip Drop
58/58 Drifters
6/63 Dion
3/84 Drive Cars
9/01 Drive Incubus
28/92 Drive R.E.M.
28/02 Drive (For Daddy Gene) Alan Jackson
82/57 Drive In Show Eddie Cochran
44/99 Drive Me Wild Sawyer Brown
Drive My Car
93/66 Bob Kuban
69/75 Gary Toms Empire
55/89 Driven Out Fixx
15/79 Driver's Seat Sniff 'n' the Tears
87/61 Drivin' Home Duane Eddy
5/80 Drivin' My Life Away Eddie Rabbitt
34/77 Drivin' Wheel Foghat
85/61 Driving Wheel Junior Parker
93/96 Drop Pharcyde
78/70 Drop By My Place Carl Carlton
93/97 Drop Dead Gorgeous Republica
78/83 Drop The Pilot Joan Armatrading
5/01 Drops Of Jupiter (Tell Me) Train
100/62 Drown In My Own Tears Don Shirley
36/63 Drownin' My Sorrows Connie Francis
28/01 Drowning Backstreet Boys
11/72 Drowning In The Sea Of Love Joe Simon
72/92 Drowning In Your Eyes Ephraim Lewis
29/71 Drum, The Bobby Sherman
86/62 Drum Stomp Sandy Nelson
98/69 Drummer Man Nancy Sinatra
67/62 Drummin' Up A Storm Sandy Nelson
100/67 Drums Jon & Robin
29/62 Drums Are My Beat Sandy Nelson
20/67 Dry Your Eyes Brenda & The Tabulations
Dub Be Good To Me ..see: Just Be Good To Me
96/62 Duchess Of Earl Pearlettes
14/66 Duck, The Jackie Lee
35S/02 Duck Season Beatnuts
14/87 Dude (Looks Like A Lady) Aerosmith
2/73 Dueling Banjos Eric Weissberg & Steve Mandell
Dueling Bikes ..see: One Sunny Day
92/73 Dueling Tubas Martin Mull
1/62 Duke Of Earl Gene Chandler (also see: Duchess Of Earl)
Dukes Of Hazzard ..see: Theme From The

Dum-De-Da ..see: She Understands Me
4/61 Dum Dum Brenda Lee
77/63 Dum Dum Dee Dum Johnny Cymbal
50/64 Dumb Head Ginny Arnell
Dumplin's
69/57 Doc Bagby
75/57 Ernie Freeman
52/72 Duncan Paul Simon
7/56 Dungaree Doll Eddie Fisher
28/94 Dunkie Butt (Please Please Please) 12 Gauge
58/93 Dur Dur D'Etre Bébé! (It's Tough To Be A Baby!) Jordy
18/77 Dusic Brick
6/78 Dust In The Wind Kansas
55/65 Dusty Rag Dolls
30/60 Dutchman's Gold Walter Brennan/Billy Vaughn
15/84 Dynamite Jermaine Jackson
72/57 Dynamite Brenda Lee
83/69 Dynamite Woman Sir Douglas Quintet
Dynasty ..see: Theme From
10/75 Dynomite Bazuka

E

49/96 E-Bow The Letter R.E.M.
15/01 E.I. Nelly
E.T. ..see: Theme From
59/90 Each And Every Time Sweet Sensation
89/84 Each Word's A Beat Of My Heart Mink Deville
82/87 Eagles Fly Sammy Hagar
9/74 Earache My Eye (Featuring Alice Bowie) Cheech & Chong
95/61 Early Every Morning (Early Every Evening Too) Dinah Washington
12/70 Early In The Morning Vanity Fare
Early In The Morning
24/58 Rinky-Dinks
32/58 Buddy Holly
Early In The Morning
24/82 Gap Band
19/88 Robert Palmer
68/74 Early Morning Love Sammy Johns
91/65 Early Morning Rain Peter, Paul & Mary
Earth Angel
3/55 Crew-Cuts
8/55 Penguins
18/55 Gloria Mann
57/60 Johnny Tillotson
42/69 Vogues
21/86 New Edition
21/96 Earth, The Sun, The Rain Color Me Badd
Earthbound
46/56 Sammy Davis, Jr.
53/56 Mario Lanza
61/69 Ease Back Meters
45/94 Ease My Mind Arrested Development
Ease On Down The Road
42/75 Consumer Rapport
41/78 Diana Ross/Michael Jackson
1/63 Easier Said Than Done Essex
62/96 East 1999 Bone thugs-n-harmony
East Of Eden ..see: Theme From
73/95 East Side Rendezvous Frost

27/66 **East West** *Herman's Hermits*

EASY:

Easy
4/77 *Commodores*
58/93 *Faith No More*
54/76 **Easy As Pie** *Billy "Crash" Craddock*
9/70 **Easy Come, Easy Go** *Bobby Sherman*
41/91 **Easy Come Easy Go** *Winger*
71/93 **Easy Come, Easy Go** *George Strait*
60/79 **Easy Driver** *Kenny Loggins*
72/75 **Easy Evil** *Travis Wammack*
54/83 **Easy For You To Say** *Linda Ronstadt*
39/72 **Easy Livin** *Uriah Heep*
62/80 **Easy Love** *Dionne Warwick*
2/85 **Easy Lover** *Philip Bailey with Phil Collins*
70/60 **Easy Lovin'** *Wade Flemons*
17/71 **Easy Loving** *Freddie Hart*
Easy Question ..see: (Such An)
Easy Rider ..see: Ballad Of
66/70 **Easy Rider (Let The Wind Pay The Way)** *Iron Butterfly*
83/74 **Easy Street** *Edgar Winter Group*
48/70 **Easy To Be Free** *Rick Nelson*
Easy To Be Hard
4/69 *Three Dog Night*
64/79 *Cheryl Barnes*
36/78 **Easy To Love** *Leo Sayer*
12/84 **Eat It** *Weird Al Yankovic*
75/84 **Eat My Shorts** *Rick Dees*
77/85 **Eaten Alive** *Diana Ross*
Ebb Tide
93/59 *Bobby Freeman*
56/60 *Platters*
25/64 *Lenny Welch*
5/66 *Righteous Brothers*
1/82 **Ebony And Ivory** *Paul McCartney/Stevie Wonder*
8/61 **Ebony Eyes** *Everly Brothers*
14/78 **Ebony Eyes** *Bob Welch*
43/84 **Ebony Eyes** *Rick James*
76/63 **Echo** *Emotions*
40/69 **Echo Park** *Keith Barbour*
66/77 **Echoes Of Love** *Doobie Brothers*
31/73 **Ecstasy** *Ohio Players*
56/62 **Ecstasy** *Ben E. King*
Eddie My Love
11/56 *Fontane Sisters*
14/56 *Chordettes*
14/56 *Teen Queens*
77/72 **Eddie's Love** *Eddie Kendricks*
74A/90 **Eddy Steady Go** *Rozlyne Clarke*
26/88 **Edge Of A Broken Heart** *Vixen*
38A/87 **Edge Of A Broken Heart** *Bon Jovi*
69/84 **Edge Of A Dream** *Joe Cocker*
10/86 **Edge Of Heaven** *Wham!*
11/82 **Edge Of Seventeen (Just Like The White Winged Dove)** *Stevie Nicks*
26/77 **Edge Of The Universe** *Bee Gees*
93/89 **Edie (Ciao Baby)** *Cult*
76/83 **Eenie Meenie** *Jeffrey Osborne*
52/66 **Eggplant That Ate Chicago** *Dr. West's Medicine Show*
34/78 **Ego** *Elton John*
72/76 **Eh! Cumpari** *Gaylord & Holiday*
53/63 **8 X 10** *Bill Anderson*
1/65 **Eight Days A Week** *Beatles*
32/88 **853-5937** *Squeeze*
80/67 **Eight Men, Four Women** *O.V. Wright*
14/66 **Eight Miles High** *Byrds*
8/99 **808** *Blaque*
4/82 **867-5309/Jenny** *Tommy Tutone*
21/71 **Eighteen** *Alice Cooper*
4/89 **18 And Life** *Skid Row*
15/75 **Eighteen With A Bullet** *Pete Wingfield*
10/63 **18 Yellow Roses** *Bobby Darin*
82/81 **8th Wonder** *Sugarhill Gang*
51/65 **81, The** *Candy & The Kisses*
Ein Schiff Wird Kommen ..see: Never On Sunday
45A/94 **Einstein On The Beach (For An Eggman)** *Counting Crows*
43/75 **El Bimbo** *Bimbo Jet*
18/70 **El Condor Pasa** *Simon & Garfunkel*
32/60 **El Matador** *Kingston Trio*
1/60 **El Paso** *Marty Robbins*
97/65 **El Pussy Cat** *Mongo Santamaria*
30/58 **El Rancho Rock** *Champs*
86/94 **El Trago "the drink"** *2 in a Room*
17/63 **El Watusi** *Ray Barretto*
(also see: Wah Watusi / Watusi)
Eleanor Rigby
11/66 *Beatles*
35/68 *Ray Charles*
17/69 *Aretha Franklin*
26/72 **Elected** *Alice Cooper*
6/85 **Election Day** *Arcadia*
2/83 **Electric Avenue** *Eddy Grant*
52/97 **Electric Barbarella** *Duran Duran*
7/88 **Electric Blue** *Icehouse*
51/90 **Electric Boogie** *Marcia Griffiths*
79/84 **Electric Kingdom** *Twilight 22*
65/94 **Electric Relaxation (Relax Yourself Girl)** *Tribe Called Quest*
61/69 **Electric Stories** *4 Seasons*
Electric Surfboard ..see: Theme From
11/89 **Electric Youth** *Debbie Gibson*
77/02 **Electrical Storm** *U2*
74/82 **Electricland** *Bad Company*
96/97 **Electrolite** *R.E.M.*
96/71 **Electronic Magnetism** *Solomon Burke*
27A/97 **Elegantly Wasted** *INXS*
45/79 **Elena** *Marc Tanner Band*
6/68 **Elenore** *Turtles*
64/63 **Elephant Walk** *Donald Jenkins*
39/91 **Elevate My Mind** *Stereo MC's*
12/96 **Elevators (me & you)** *OutKast*
11th Hour Melody
21/56 *Al Hibbler*
35/56 *Lou Busch*
10/69 **Eli's Coming** *Three Dog Night*
39/56 **Eloise** *Kay Thompson*
86/69 **Eloise** *Barry Ryan*
5/66 **Elusive Butterfly** *Bob Lind*
Elvira
72/66 *Dallas Frazier*
5/81 *Oak Ridge Boys*
71/82 **Elvis Medley** *Elvis Presley*
18/85 **Emergency** *Kool & The Gang*
68/83 **Eminence Front** *Who*
8/75 **Emma** *Hot Chocolate*
Emotion
3/78 *Samantha Sang*
10/01 *Destiny's Child*
22/75 **Emotion** *Helen Reddy*
79/85 **Emotion** *Barbra Streisand*
15/86 **Emotion In Motion** *Ric Ocasek*
47/00 **Emotional** *Carl Thomas*
3/80 **Emotional Rescue** *Rolling Stones*
1/91 **Emotions** *Mariah Carey*
7/61 **Emotions** *Brenda Lee*
51/95 **Emotions** *H-Town*
69S/97 **Emotions** *Twista*
68/82 **Emotions In Motion** *Billy Squier*
60/90 **Emperor's New Clothes** *Sinéad O'Connor*
18/80 **Empire Strikes Back (medley)** *Meco*
Empty Arms
13/57 *Teresa Brewer*
43/57 *Ivory Joe Hunter*
93/71 *Sonny James*
72/90 **Empty Beach** *Tricia Leigh Fisher*
13/82 **Empty Garden (Hey Hey Johnny)** *Elton John*
74/70 **Empty Pages** *Traffic*
66/63 **Enamorado** *Keith Colley*
12/59 **Enchanted** *Platters*
12/58 **Enchanted Island** *Four Lads*
Enchanted Sea
15/59 *Islanders*
28/59 *Martin Denny*
69/84 **Encore** *Cheryl Lynn*
7/58 **End, The** *Earl Grant*
42/76 **End Is Not In Sight (The Cowboy Tune)** *Amazing Rhythm Aces*
50A/97 **End Is The Beginning Is The End** *Smashing Pumpkins*
End Of Our Road
15/68 *Gladys Knight*
40/70 *Marvin Gaye*
8/89 **End Of The Innocence** *Don Henley*
63/89 **End Of The Line** *Traveling Wilburys*
1/92 **End of the Road** *Boyz II Men*
2/63 **End Of The World** *Skeeter Davis*
52/56 **Endless** *McGuire Sisters*
Endless Love
1/81 *Diana Ross & Lionel Richie*
2/94 *Luther Vandross & Mariah Carey*
21/87 **Endless Nights** *Eddie Money*
Endless Sleep
5/58 *Jody Reynolds*
90/64 *Hank Williams, Jr.*
2/88 **Endless Summer Nights** *Richard Marx*
12/59 **Endlessly** *Brook Benton*
70/96 **Energy** *Devoné*
33/74 **Energy Crisis '74** *Dickie Goodman*
7/65 **Engine Engine #9** *Roger Miller*
14/70 **Engine Number 9** *Wilson Pickett*
8/65 **England Swings** *Roger Miller*
21/56 **English Muffins And Irish Stew** *Sylvia Syms*
84/88 **Englishman In New York** *Sting*
8/90 **Enjoy The Silence** *Depeche Mode*
6/77 **Enjoy Yourself** *Jacksons*
10S/01 **Enjoy Yourself** *Allure*
63/98 **Enjoy Yourself** *A+*
50/82 **Enough Is Enough** *April Wine*
(also see: No More Tears)
16/91 **Enter Sandman** *Metallica*
3/74 **Entertainer, The** *Marvin Hamlisch/"The Sting"*
31/65 **Entertainer, The** *Tony Clarke*
34/75 **Entertainer, The** *Billy Joel*
38S/02 **Envious** *Dawn Robinson*
85/96 **Envy** *Fat Joe*
9/90 **Epic** *Faith No More*
19/67 **Epistle To Dippy** *Donovan*
9/74 **Eres Tu (Touch The Wind)** *Mocedades*
3/92 **Erotica** *Madonna*
74/96 **Esa Nena Linda** *Artie The 1 Man Party*
58/83 **Escalator Of Life** *Robert Hazard*
1/90 **Escapade** *Janet Jackson*
12/02 **Escape** *Enrique Iglesias*
1/79 **Escape (The Pina Colada Song)** *Rupert Holmes*

35/71 **Escape-ism** *James Brown*
19/62 **Eso Beso (That Kiss!)** *Paul Anka*
1/89 **Eternal Flame** *Bangles*
Eternally
41/60 *Sarah Vaughan*
77/63 *Chantels*
92/59 **Eternally** *Thomas Wayne*
(also see: Limelight)
79/69 **Eternity** *Vikki Carr*
67/83 **Europa And The Pirate Twins** *Thomas Dolby*
91/72 **Eve** *Jim Capaldi*
Eve Of Destruction
1/65 *Barry McGuire*
100/70 *Turtles*
(also see: Dawn Of Correction / Day For Decision)
68/93 **Even A Fool Can See** *Peter Cetera*
32/92 **Even Better Than The Real Thing** *U2*
33/80 **Even It Up** *Heart*
12/83 **Even Now** *Bob Seger*
19/78 **Even Now** *Barry Manilow*
36/67 **Even The Bad Times Are Good** *Tremeloes*
5/82 **Even The Nights Are Better** *Air Supply*
63/59 **Evening Rain** *Earl Grant*
56/61 **Eventually** *Brenda Lee*
63/57 **Ever Lovin' Fingers** *Jimmy Bowen*
75/88 **Ever Since The World Began** *Tommy Shaw*
72/96 **Ever Since You Went Away** *Art N' Soul*
60S/92 **Ever So Clear** *Bushwick Bill*
60/60 **Everglades** *Kingston Trio*
Evergreen ..see: Love Theme From A Star Is Born
5/78 **Everlasting Love** *Andy Gibb*
Everlasting Love
13/67 *Robert Knight*
6/74 *Carl Carlton*
32/81 *Rex Smith/Rachel Sweet*
27/95 *Gloria Estefan*
12/89 **Everlasting Love** *Howard Jones*
81/92 **Everlasting Love** *Tony Terry*
42A/97 **Everlong** *Foo Fighters*
16/61 **Everlovin'** *Rick Nelson*

EVERY:

Every Beat Of My Heart
6/61 *Pips*
45/61 *Gladys Knight*
99/63 *James Brown*
83/76 **Every Beat Of My Heart** *Crown Heights Affair*
83/86 **Every Beat Of My Heart** *Rod Stewart*
(also see: With Every Beat Of My Heart)
42/61 **Every Breath I Take** *Gene Pitney*
1/83 **Every Breath You Take** *Police*
Every Day ..also see: Everyday
96/66 **Every Day And Every Night** *Trolls*
60/96 **EveryDay & EveryNight** *Yvette Michele*
74/67 **Every Day I Have The Blues** *Billy Stewart*
Every Day I Have To Cry Some
46/63 *Steve Alaimo*
77/66 *Gentrys*
45/75 *Arthur Alexander*
Every Day Of My Life
37/56 *McGuire Sisters*
24/72 *Bobby Vinton*
20/95 **Every Day Of The Week** *Jade*

55/76 **Every Face Tells A Story** *Olivia Newton-John*
2/91 **Every Heartbeat** *Amy Grant*
Every Home Should Have One
62/82 *Patti Austin*
69/83 *Patti Austin*
16/78 **Every Kinda People** *Robert Palmer*
78/97 **Every Light In The House** *Trace Adkins*
13/64 **Every Little Bit Hurts** *Brenda Holloway*
Every Little Kiss
72/86 *Bruce Hornsby*
14/87 *Bruce Hornsby*
3/89 **Every Little Step** *Bobby Brown*
17/95 **Every Little Thing I Do** *Soul For Real*
48/59 **Every Little Thing I Do** *Dion & The Belmonts*
3/81 **Every Little Thing She Does Is Magic** *Police*
75/93 **Every Little Thing U Do** *Christopher Williams*
82/82 **Every Love Song** *Greg Kihn Band*
3/99 **Every Morning** *Sugar Ray*
91/65 **Every Night, Every Day** *Jimmy McCracklin*
39/58 **Every Night (I Pray)** *Chantels*
46/62 **Every Night (Without You)** *Paul Anka*
Every 1's A Winner ..see: Everyone's
Every Other Day ..see: Everyotherday
44/01 **Every Other Time** *LFO*
75/02 **Every River** *Brooks & Dunn*
78/92 **Every Road Leads Back To You** *Bette Midler*
1/88 **Every Rose Has Its Thorn** *Poison*
25/85 **Every Step Of The Way** *John Waite*
30/63 **Every Step Of The Way** *Johnny Mathis*
Every Time ..also see: Everytime
6/97 **Every Time I Close My Eyes** *Babyface*
87/56 **Every Time (I Feel His Spirit)** *Patti Page*
13/79 **Every Time I Think Of You** *Babys*
4/77 **(Every Time I Turn Around) Back In Love Again** *L.T.D.*
19/75 **Every Time You Touch Me (I Get High)** *Charlie Rich*
30/79 **Every Which Way But Loose** *Eddie Rabbitt*
5/81 **Every Woman In The World** *Air Supply*

EVERYBODY:

3/63 **Everybody** *Tommy Roe*
4/98 **Everybody (Backstreet's Back)** *Backstreet Boys*
38/77 **Everybody Be Dancin'** *Starbuck*
82/96 **Everybody Be Somebody** *Ruffneck*
24/86 **Everybody Dance** *Ta Mara & The Seen*
38/78 **Everybody Dance** *Chic*
67/65 **Everybody Do The Sloopy** *Johnny Thunder*
81/01 **Everybody Doesn't** *Amanda*
8/90 **Everybody Everybody** *Black Box*
(Everybody Get Loose) ..see: Cool As Ice
80/63 **Everybody Go Home** *Eydie Gorme*
73/68 **Everybody Got To Believe In Somebody** *Sam & Dave*

2/86 **Everybody Have Fun Tonight** *Wang Chung*
29/93 **Everybody Hurts** *R.E.M.*
F/70 **Everybody Is A Star** *Sly & The Family Stone*
43/68 **Everybody Knows** *Dave Clark Five*
72/64 **Everybody Knows** *Steve Lawrence*
60/72 **Everybody Knows About My Good Thing** *Little Johnny Taylor*
15/64 **Everybody Knows (I Still Love You)** *Dave Clark Five*
52/69 **Everybody Knows Matilda** *Duke Baxter*
31/59 **Everybody Likes To Cha Cha Cha** *Sam Cooke*
4/65 **Everybody Loves A Clown** *Gary Lewis*
63/72 **Everybody Loves A Love Song** *Mac Davis*
Everybody Loves A Lover
6/58 *Doris Day*
19/63 *Shirelles*
96/66 **Everybody Loves A Nut** *Johnny Cash*
43/78 **Everybody Loves A Rain Song** *B.J. Thomas*
95/67 **Everybody Loves A Winner** *William Bell*
6/62 **Everybody Loves Me But You** *Brenda Lee*
1/64 **Everybody Loves Somebody** *Dean Martin*
52/63 **Everybody Monkey** *Freddy Cannon*
90/91 **Everybody Move** *Cathy Dennis*
32/78 **Everybody Needs Love** *Stephen Bishop*
39/67 **Everybody Needs Love** *Gladys Knight*
Everybody Needs Somebody To Love
58/64 *Solomon Burke*
29/67 *Wilson Pickett*
(also see: Life)
75/77 **Everybody Ought To Be In Love** *Paul Anka*
Everybody Plays The Fool
3/72 *Main Ingredient*
8/91 *Aaron Neville*
92/74 **(Everybody Wanna Get Rich) Rite Away** *Dr. John*
92/75 **Everybody Wants To Find A Bluebird** *Randy Edelman*
1/85 **Everybody Wants To Rule The World** *Tears For Fears*
32/82 **Everybody Wants You** *Billy Squier*
100/61 **Ev'rybody's Cryin'** *Jimmie Beaumont*
12/71 **Everybody's Everything** *Santana*
37/92 **Everybody's Free (To Feel Good)** *Rozalla*
45/99 **everybody's free (to wear Sunscreen) The Speech Song** *Baz Luhrmann*
Everybody's Got A Home But Me
20/55 *Eddie Fisher*
42/56 *Roy Hamilton*
21/70 **Everybody's Got The Right To Love** *Supremes*
18/80 **Everybody's Got To Learn Sometime** *Korgis*
52/61 **Everybody's Gotta Pay Some Dues** *Miracles*
62/73 **Everybody's Had The Blues** *Merle Haggard*
26/70 **Everybody's Out Of Town** *B.J. Thomas*

1/60 **Everybody's Somebody's Fool** *Connie Francis*
78/57 **Everybody's Somebody's Fool** *Heartbeats*
6/69 **Everybody's Talkin'** *Nilsson*
75/62 **Ev'rybody's Twistin'** *Frank Sinatra*
24/94 **Everyday** *Phil Collins*
44S/02 **Everyday** *Kim English*
Everyday
81/72 *John Denver*
61/85 *James Taylor*
36/83 **Everyday I Write The Book** *Elvis Costello*
11/97 **Everyday Is A Winding Road** *Sheryl Crow*
Everyday People
1/69 *Sly & The Family Stone*
37/83 *Joan Jett*
(also see: People Everyday)
19/69 **Everyday With You Girl** *Classics IV*
62/76 **Everyday Without You** *Hamilton, Joe Frank & Reynolds*
70S/02 **Everyday's A Party** *Damozel*
88/99 **Everyone Falls In Love** *Tanto Metro & Devonte*
96/58 **Everyone Was There** *Bob Kayli*
6/79 **Every 1's A Winner** *Hot Chocolate*
49/73 **Everyone's Agreed That Everything Will Turn Out Fine** *Stealers Wheel*
17/65 **Everyone's Gone To The Moon** *Jonathan King*
69/57 **Everyone's Laughing** *Spaniels*
46/91 **Everyotherday** *Or-N-More*

EVERYTHING:

4/90 **Everything** *Jody Watley*
24/97 **Everything** *Mary J. Blige*
52/70 **Everything A Man Could Ever Need** *Glen Campbell*
9/92 **Everything About You.** *Ugly Kid Joe*
14/92 **Everything Changes** *Kathy Troccoli*
Everything Falls Apart
14A/96 *Dog's Eye View*
66/96 *Dog's Eye View (Live)*
45/72 **Everything Good Is Bad** *100 Proof (Aged In Soul)*
95/69 **Everything I Do Gonh Be Funky (From Now On)** *Lee Dorsey*
1/91 **(Everything I Do) I Do It For You** *Bryan Adams*
47/85 **Everything I Need** *Men At Work*
5/72 **Everything I Own** *Bread*
30/86 **Everything In My Heart** *Corey Hart*
86/80 **Everything Is Alright** *Spider*
1/70 **Everything Is Beautiful** *Ray Stevens*
35/99 **Everything Is Everything** *Lauryn Hill*
84/70 **Everything Is Going To Be Alright** *Teegarden & Van Winkle*
74/71 **Everything Is Good About You** *Lettermen*
56/86 **Everything Must Change** *Paul Young*
F/96 **Everything Remains Raw** *Busta Rhymes*
1/85 **Everything She Wants** *Wham!*
66/76 **Everything That 'Cha Do (Will Come Back To You)** *Wet Willie*
10/68 **Everything That Touches You** *Association*
43A/97 **Everything To Everyone** *Everclear*
8S/01 **Everything U R** *Lindsay Pagano*
44/80 **Everything Works If You Let It** *Cheap Trick*
52/90 **Everything You Do (You're Sexing Me)** *Fiona with Kip Winger*
1/00 **Everything You Want** *Vertical Horizon*
83/97 **Everything You Want** *Ray J*
3/88 **Everything Your Heart Desires** *Daryl Hall John Oates*
40A/95 **Everything Zen** *Bush*
16/64 **Everything's Alright** *Newbeats*
Everything's Alright
92/71 *Yvonne Elliman*
99/71 *Kimberlys (medley)*
70/73 **Everything's Been Changed** *5th Dimension*
95/98 **Everything's Changed** *Lonestar*
49/76 **Everything's Coming Up Love** *David Ruffin*
37/93 **Everything's Gonna Be Alright** *Father MC*
53/92 **Everything's Gonna Be Alright** *Naughty By Nature*
46/98 **Everything's Gonna Be Alright** *Sweetbox*
91/75 **Everything's The Same (Ain't Nothing Changed)** *Billy Swan*
38/70 **Everything's Tuesday** *Chairman Of The Board*
31S/99 **Everytime** *Tatyana Ali*
69/99 **Everytime I Cry** *Terri Clark*
66/86 **Everytime You Cry** *Outfield*
1/85 **Everytime You Go Away** *Paul Young*
12/01 **Everywhere** *Michelle Branch*
14/88 **Everywhere** *Fleetwood Mac*
50/73 **Evil** *Earth, Wind & Fire*
72/74 **Evil Boll-Weevil** *Grand Canyon*
Evil Ways
9/70 *Santana*
84/72 *Carlos Santana & Buddy Miles*
10/76 **Evil Woman** *Electric Light Orchestra*
19/70 **Evil Woman Don't Play Your Games With Me** *Crow*
52/66 **Evol-Not Love** *Five Americans*
60/83 **Ewok Celebration** *Meco*
21/99 **Ex-Factor** *Lauryn Hill*
62/60 **Exclusively Yours** *Carl Dobkins, Jr.*
42/91 **Exclusivity** *Damian Dame*
1/95 **Exhale (Shoop Shoop)** *Whitney Houston*
Exodus
2/61 *Ferrante & Teicher*
31/61 *Mantovani*
36/61 *Eddie Harris*
64/61 *Pat Boone*
Exorcist, Theme From ..see: Tubular Bells
98/68 **Expecting To Fly** *Buffalo Springfield*
14/55 **Experience Unnecessary** *Sarah Vaughan*
61/56 **Experiments With Mice** *Johnny Dankworth*
33/68 **Explosion (In Your Soul)** *Soul Survivors*
4/75 **Express** *B.T. Express*
66S/00 **Express, The** *Talib Kweli & Hi-Tek*
2/89 **Express Yourself** *Madonna*
12/70 **Express Yourself** *Charles Wright*
26/90 **Expression** *Salt-N-Pepa*
4/67 **Expressway (To Your Heart)** *Soul Survivors*
49A/97 **Eye** *Smashing Pumpkins*
3/82 **Eye In The Sky** *Alan Parsons Project*
1/82 **Eye Of The Tiger** *Survivor*
81/86 **Eye Of The Zombie** *John Fogerty*
71/85 **Eye On You** *Billy Squier*
73/85 **Eye To Eye** *Go West*
28/68 **Eyes Of A New York Woman** *B.J. Thomas*
Eyes Of Laura Mars ..see: Love Theme From
52/74 **Eyes Of Silver** *Doobie Brothers*
79/84 **Eyes That See In The Dark** *Kenny Rogers*
4/84 **Eyes Without A Face** *Billy Idol*

F

22/78 **FM (No Static At All)** *Steely Dan*
37/94 **Fa All Y'all** *Da Brat*
29/66 **Fa-Fa-Fa-Fa-Fa (Sad Song)** *Otis Redding*
Fabulous
16/57 *Charlie Gracie*
71/57 *Steve Lawrence*
28/03 **Fabulous** *Jaheim*
19/56 **Fabulous Character** *Sarah Vaughan*
46/90 **Face In The Crowd** *Tom Petty*
29/68 **Face It Girl, It's Over** *Nancy Wilson*
26/86 **Face The Face** *Pete Townshend*
49/91 **Face The Music** *RTZ*
88/92 **Faces Of Love** *Nia Peeples*
27/87 **Facts Of Love** *Jeff Lorber Feat. Karyn White*
62/01 **Fade** *Staind*
20/81 **Fade Away** *Bruce Springsteen*
82/83 **Fade Away** *Loz Netto*
44/94 **Fade Into You** *Mazzy Star*
22/00 **Faded** *SoulDecision*
Faded Love
96/63 *Patsy Cline*
97/63 *Jackie de Shannon*
10/99 **Faded Pictures** *Case & Joe*
54/56 **Faded Summer Love** *Georgie Shaw*
65/89 **Fading Away** *Will To Power*
2/91 **Fading Like A Flower (Every Time You Leave)** *Roxette*
43/77 **Fair Game** *Crosby, Stills & Nash*
28/90 **Fairweather Friend** *Johnny Gill*
FC/55 **Fairy Tale** *Frank Sinatra*
13/74 **Fairytale** *Pointer Sisters*
1/87 **Faith** *George Michael*
14/93 **Faithful** *Go West*
52/56 **Faithful Hussar** *Ted Heath*
(also see: Don't Cry My Love)
25S/03 **Faithful To** *Poww Bros.*
12/83 **Faithfully** *Journey*
25/87 **Fake** *Alexander O'Neal*
35/83 **Fake Friends** *Joan Jett*
65A/95 **Fake Plastic Trees** *Radiohead*
23/67 **Fakin' It** *Simon & Garfunkel*

FALL:

75/91 **Fall At Your Feet** *Crowded House*
33/94 **Fall Down** *Toad The Wet Sprocket*
54/92 **Fall In Love Again** *Eddie Money*
17/83 **Fall In Love With Me** *Earth, Wind & Fire*
67/67 **Fall In Love With Me** *Bettye Swann*
34/03 **Fall Into Me** *Emerson Drive*
94/86 **Fall On Me** *R.E.M.*
12/88 **Fallen Angel** *Poison*
36/76 **Fallen Angel** *Frankie Valli*
99/60 **Fallen Angel** *Webb Pierce*
(also see: She's Just A)

Fallen Star
20/57 *Nick Noble*
23/57 *Jimmy Newman*
47/57 *Ferlin Husky*
58/57 *Hilltoppers*
1/01 **Fallin'** *Alicia Keys*
30/58 **Fallin'** *Connie Francis*
13/78 **Falling** *LeBlanc & Carr*
22/63 **Falling** *Roy Orbison*
Fallin' In Love
1/75 *Hamilton, Joe Frank & Reynolds*
97/93 *New Born*
35A/96 *La Bouche*
27/74 **Fallin' In Love** *Souther, Hillman, Furay Band*
58/82 **Falling In Love** *Balance*
18/96 **Falling** *Montell Jordan*
49/76 **Falling Apart At The Seams** *Marmalade*
64/81 **Falling In Love Again** *Michael Stanley Band*
35/97 **Falling In Love (Is Hard On The Knees)** *Aerosmith*
25/87 **Falling In Love (Uh-Oh)** *Miami Sound Machine*
91/89 **Falling Out Of Love** *Ivan Neville*
92/90 **Falling To Pieces** *Faith No More*
29/00 **Falls Apart (Run Away)** *Sugar Ray*
1/75 **Fame** *David Bowie*
4/80 **Fame** *Irene Cara*
42S/02 **Fame** *GZA/Genius*
17/60 **Fame And Fortune** *Elvis Presley*
Family Affair
1/71 *Sly & The Family Stone*
84/94 *Shabba Ranks*
1/01 **Family Affair** *Mary J. Blige*
6/83 **Family Man** *Daryl Hall & John Oates*
90/88 **Family Man** *Fleetwood Mac*
12/72 **Family Of Man** *Three Dog Night*
20/03 **Family Portrait** *P!nk*
42/83 **Fanatic, The** *Felony*
31/70 **Fancy** *Bobbie Gentry*
39/77 **Fancy Dancer** *Commodores*
77/79 **Fancy Dancer** *Frankie Valli*
71/75 **Fancy Lady** *Billy Preston*
71/59 **Fancy Nancy** *Skip & Flip*
47/65 **Fancy Pants** *Al Hirt*
38/60 **Fannie Mae** *Buster Brown*
12/76 **Fanny (Be Tender With My Love)** *Bee Gees*
Fantastic Voyage
55/81 *Lakeside*
3/94 *Coolio*
1/95 **Fantasy** *Mariah Carey*
23/82 **Fantasy** *Aldo Nova*
32/78 **Fantasy** *Earth, Wind & Fire*
52/81 **Fantasy Girl** *.38 Special*
18/94 **Far Behind** *Candlebox*
72/60 **Far, Far Away** *Don Gibson*
10/83 **Far From Over** *Frank Stallone*
81/97 **Far From Yours** *O.C.*
90/61 **Faraway Star** *Chordettes*
89/73 **Farewell Andromeda (Welcome To My Morning)** *John Denver*
86/69 **Farewell Love Scene** *Romeo & Juliet Soundtrack*
38/84 **Farewell My Summer Love** *Michael Jackson*
19/64 **Farmer John** *Premiers*
56/70 **Farther On Down The Road** *Joe Simon*
43/57 **Farther Up The Road** *Bobby "Blue" Bland*
21/87 **Fascinated** *Company B*
Fascination
7/57 *Jane Morgan*
15/57 *Dinah Shore*
17/57 *Dick Jacobs*
56/57 *David Carroll*
(also see: Keep Falling)
46/89 **Fascination Street** *Cure*
70/81 **Fashion** *David Bowie*
70/94 **Fast As You** *Dwight Yoakam*
6/88 **Fast Car** *Tracy Chapman*
74/95 **Fast Life** *Kool G Rap*
8/96 **Fastlove** *George Michael*
99/88 **Fat** *"Weird Al" Yankovic*
F/79 **Fat Bottomed Girls** *Queen*
69/95 **Fat Boy** *Max-A-Million*
66/01 **Fat Lip** *Sum 41*
18/98 **Father** *LL Cool J*
93/70 **Father Come On Home** *Pacific Gas & Electric*
1/88 **Father Figure** *George Michael*
100/62 **Father Knows Best** *Radiants*
92/68 **Father Of Girls** *Perry Como*
46A/98 **Father Of Mine** *Everclear*
86/64 **Father Sebastian** *Ramblers*
87/01 **Fatty Girl** *Ludacris, LL Cool J & Keith Murray*
78/83 **Favorite Waste Of Time** *Bette Midler*
95/93 **Feed The Tree** *Belly*

FEEL:

Feel It
56/61 *Sam Cooke*
95/66 *Sam Cooke*
34/86 **Feel It Again** *Honeymoon Suite*
28/02 **Feel It Boy** *Beenie Man*
48/82 **Feel Like A Number** *Bob Seger*
Feel Like Makin' Love
1/74 *Roberta Flack*
88/74 *Bob James*
10/75 **Feel Like Makin' Love** *Bad Company*
17/95 **Feel Me Flow** *Naughty By Nature*
Feel So Bad ..see: I Feel So Bad
Feel So Fine
14/60 *Johnny Preston*
22/67 *Bunny Sigler (medley)*
5/97 **Feel So Good** *Mase*
67/95 **Feel So High** *Des'ree*
67/79 **Feel That You're Feelin'** *Maze Feat. Frankie Beverly*
61/77 **Feel The Beat (Everybody Disco)** *Ohio Players*
46/95 **Feel The Funk** *Immature*
92/02 **Feel The Girl** *Ms. Jade*
66/91 **Feel The Groove** *Cartouche*
73/86 **Feel The Heat** *Jean Beauvoir*
73/96 **Feel The Music** *Planet Soul*
Feel The Need
90/77 *Detroit Emeralds*
57/79 *Leif Garrett*
62A/94 **Feel The Pain** *Dinosaur Jr.*
Feelin' Groovy ..see: 59th Street Bridge
79/97 **Feelin' It** *Jay-Z*
36/01 **Feelin' On Yo Booty** *R. Kelly*
46/79 **Feelin' Satisfied** *Boston*
51/00 **Feelin' So Good** *Jennifer Lopez*
53/69 **Feelin' So Good (S.k.o.o.b.y-D.o.o)** *Archies*
10/73 **Feelin' Stronger Every Day** *Chicago*
76/75 **Feelin' That Glow** *Roberta Flack*
Feeling Alright
69/69 *Joe Cocker*
96/69 *Mongo Santamaria*
54/71 *Grand Funk Railroad*
33/72 *Joe Cocker*
91/64 **Feeling Is Gone** *Bobby Bland*
65/69 **Feeling Is Right** *Clarence Carter*
Feelings
6/75 *Morris Albert*
93/77 *Walter Jackson*
93/70 **Feelings** *Barry Mann*
50/88 **Feelings Of Forever** *Tiffany*
9/90 **Feels Good** *Tony! Toni! Toné!*
53/02 **Feels Good (Don't Worry Bout A Thing)** *Naughty By Nature*
71/93 **Feels Like Heaven** *Peter Cetera with Chaka Khan*
52/00 **Feels Like Love** *Vince Gill*
4/77 **Feels Like The First Time** *Foreigner*
4/78 **Feels So Good** *Chuck Mangione*
32/95 **Feels So Good** *Xscape*
35/89 **Feels So Good** *Van Halen*
35/96 **Feels So Good (Show Me Your Love)** *Lina Santiago*
78/84 **Feels So Real (Won't Let Go)** *Patrice Rushen*
20/81 **Feels So Right** *Alabama*
25/94 **Feenin'** *Jodeci*
82/83 **Feet Don't Fail Me Now** *Utopia*
94/67 **Felicidad** *Sally Field*
70A/97 **Feliz Navidad** *José Feliciano*
45/73 **Fell For You** *Dramatics*
32/61 **Fell In Love On Monday** *Fats Domino*
54A/95 **Fell On Black Days** *Soundgarden*
71/86 **Female Intuition** *Mai Tai*
71A/97 **Female Of The Species** *Space*
52/73 **Fencewalk** *Mandrill*
13/76 **Fernando** *Abba*
72/64 **Ferris Wheel** *Everly Brothers*
6/65 **Ferry Cross The Mersey** *Gerry & The Pacemakers*
Fever
24/56 *Little Willie John*
8/58 *Peggy Lee*
7/65 *McCoys*
76/73 *Rita Coolidge*
95/93 **Few & Far Between** *10,000 Maniacs*
59/76 **Fez, The** *Steely Dan*
23/78 **Ffun** *Con Funk Shun*
39/58 **Fibbin'** *Patti Page*
93/66 **Fiddle Around** *Jan & Dean*
97/64 **Fiddler On The Roof** *Village Stompers*
52/84 **Fields Of Fire** *Big Country*
23/93 **Fields Of Gold** *Sting*
69/93 **Fields Of Gray** *Bruce Hornsby*
96/62 **Fiesta** *Dave "Baby" Cortez*
6/01 **Fiesta Remix** *R. Kelly*
53/66 **Fife Piper** *Dynatones*
27/99 **15 Minutes** *Marc Nelson*
81/70 **Fifteen Years Ago** *Conway Twitty*
1/76 **Fifth Of Beethoven** *Walter Murphy*
13/67 **59th Street Bridge Song (Feelin' Groovy)** *Harpers Bizarre*
44S/01 **50 Playaz Deep** *Drunken Master*
68/92 **57 Channels (And Nothin' On)** *Bruce Springsteen*
1/76 **50 Ways To Leave Your Lover** *Paul Simon*
Fight ..see: Main Event
58/83 **Fight Fire With Fire** *Kansas*
Fight For Your Right (To Party!) ..see: (You Gotta)

4/75 **Fight The Power** *Isley Brothers*
92/70 **Fightin' Side Of Me** *Merle Haggard*
92/90 **Figure Of Eight** *Paul McCartney*
15/01 **Fill Me In** *Craig David*
(Final Acclaim) ..see: You're In My Heart
8/87 **Final Countdown** *Europe*
5/92 **Finally** *Ce Ce Peniston*
58/82 **Finally** *T.G. Sheppard*
17/74 **Finally Got Myself Together (I'm A Changed Man)** *Impressions*
29/85 **Find A Way** *Amy Grant*
71/98 **Find A Way** *Tribe Called Quest*
16/82 **Find Another Fool** *Quarterflash*
27/61 **Find Another Girl** *Jerry Butler*
94/76 **Find 'Em, Fool 'Em & Forget 'Em** *Dobie Gray*
98/65 **Find My Way Back Home** *Nashville Teens*
29/81 **Find Your Way Back** *Jefferson Starship*
59/73 **Finder's Keepers** *Chairman Of The Board*
96/65 **Finders Keepers, Losers Weepers** *Nella Dodds*
61/03 **Fine Again** *Seether*
53/63 **Fine Fine Boy** *Darlene Love*
22/84 **Fine Fine Day** *Tony Carey*
8/87 **Finer Things** *Steve Winwood*
44/86 **Finest, The** *S.O.S. Band*
7/60 **Finger Poppin' Time** *Hank Ballard*
1/63 **Fingertips** *Little Stevie Wonder*
13/88 **Finish What Ya Started** *Van Halen*
35/79 **Fins** *Jimmy Buffett*

FIRE:

1/75 **Fire** *Ohio Players*
2/68 **Fire** *Arthur Brown*
Fire
2/79 *Pointer Sisters*
46/87 *Bruce Springsteen*
52/68 **Fire** *Five By Five*
91/95 **Fire** *Subway*
93/76 **Fire** *Mother's Finest*
17/81 **Fire And Ice** *Pat Benatar*
Fire And Rain
3/70 *James Taylor*
82/70 *R.B. Greaves*
94/70 *Johnny Rivers*
24/72 **Fire And Water** *Wilson Pickett*
28/74 **Fire, Baby I'm On Fire** *Andy Kim*
86/98 **Fire Escape** *Fastball*
32/80 **Fire In The Morning** *Melissa Manchester*
76/81 **Fire In The Sky** *Dirt Band*
70^S/00 **Fire It Up** *Self*
6/80 **Fire Lake** *Bob Seger*
66/58 **Fire Of Love** *Jody Reynolds*
38/75 **Fire On The Mountain** *Marshall Tucker Band*
89/77 **Fire Sign** *Cory*
71/86 **Fire With Fire** *Wild Blue*
46/89 **Fire Woman** *Cult*
43/79 **Firecracker** *Mass Production*
80/97 **Fired Up!** *Funky Green Dogs*
60/81 **Fireflies** *Fleetwood Mac*
20/58 **Firefly** *Tony Bennett*
30/97 **Firestarter** *Prodigy*
76/96 **Firewater** *Fat Joe*

FIRST:

42/59 **First Anniversary** *Cathy Carr*
53/80 **First...Be A Woman** *Lenore O'Malley*
46/56 **First Born** *"Tennessee" Ernie Ford*
24^X/67 **First Christmas** *Danny Thomas*
First Cut Is The Deepest
70/73 *Keith Hampshire*
21/77 *Rod Stewart*
25/57 **First Date, First Kiss, First Love** *Sonny James*
60/63 **First Day Back At School** *Paul & Paula*
33/84 **First Day Of Summer** *Tony Carey*
81/69 **First Hymn From Grand Terrace** *Mark Lindsay*
57/65 **First I Look At The Purse** *Contours*
81/57 **First Kiss** *Norman Petty Trio*
59/59 **First Love, First Tears** *Duane Eddy*
20/60 **First Name Initial** *Annette*
1/98 **First Night** *Monica*
53/85 **First Night** *Survivor*
59/64 **First Night Of The Full Moon** *Jack Jones*
37/69 **First Of May** *Bee Gees*
14/95 **1st Of Tha Month** *Bone thugs-n-harmony*
27/63 **First Quarrel** *Paul & Paula*
53/61 **First Taste Of Love** *Ben E. King*
91/65 **First Thing Ev'ry Morning (And The Last Thing Ev'ry Night)** *Jimmy Dean*
1/91 **First Time** *Surface*
1/72 **First Time Ever I Saw Your Face** *Roberta Flack*
(First Time I Was A Fool) ..see: Third Time Lucky
38/80 **First Time Love** *Livingston Taylor*
81/90 **First True Love** *Tiana*
25/61 **Fish, The** *Bobby Rydell*
26/74 **Fish Ain't Bitin'** *Lamont Dozier*
(Fishin' Song) ..see: I'm Gonna Miss Her
23/88 **Fishnet** *Morris Day*
71/56 **Five** *Sammy Davis, Jr.*
74/60 **Five Brothers** *Marty Robbins*
44/66 **5 D (Fifth Dimension)** *Byrds*
64^S/99 **Five Fathoms** *Everything But The Girl*
76/59 **Five Feet High And Rising** *Johnny Cash*
45/79 **5:15** *Who*
72/94 **5-4-3-2 (Yo! Time Is Up)** *Jade*
73/56 **Five Hundred Guys** *Frank Sinatra*
Five Hundred Miles
79/72 *Heaven Bound*
97/89 *Hooters*
(also see: I'm Gonna Be)
10/63 **500 Miles Away From Home** *Bobby Bare*
39/97 **5 Miles To Empty** *Brownstone*
F/85 **Five Minutes Of Funk** *Whodini*
24/96 **5 O'Clock** *Nonchalant*
4/66 **Five O'Clock World** *Vogues*
(Five Oaks) ..see: Cinco Robles
89/59 **Five Pennies** *Dodie Stevens*
27/78 **5.7.0.5.** *City Boy*
11/70 **5-10-15-20 (25-30 Years Of Love)** *Presidents*
58/97 **Fix** *BLACKstreet*
38^A/98 **Flagpole Sitta** *Harvey Danger*
73/02 **Flake** *Jack Johnson*
20^S/00 **Flamboyant** *Big L*
1/88 **Flame, The** *Cheap Trick*
91/77 **Flame** *Steve Sperry*
36/87 **Flames Of Paradise** *Jennifer Rush (with Elton John)*
14/61 **Flaming Star** *Elvis Presley*
74/76 **Flaming Youth** *Kiss*
Flamingo
98/58 *Gaylords (L'Amore)*
28/66 *Herb Alpert*
82/61 **Flamingo Express** *Royaltones*
16/78 **Flash Light** *Parliament*
42/81 **Flash's Theme aka Flash** *Queen*
82/74 **Flashback** *5th Dimension*
1/83 **Flashdance...What A Feeling** *Irene Cara*
86/84 **Flashes** *Tiggi Clay*
9/94 **Flava In Ya Ear** *Craig Mack*
41/01 **Flavor Of The Weak** *American Hi-Fi*
38^S/00 **Flawless** *Phife Dawg*
54/71 **Flesh And Blood** *Johnny Cash*
29/84 **Flesh For Fantasy** *Billy Idol*
13/93 **Flex** *Mad Cobra*
44/76 **Flight '76** *Walter Murphy*
82/71 **Flim Flam Man** *Barbra Streisand*
Flintstones ..see: (Meet) The
87/58 **Flip Flop And Bop** *Floyd Cramer*
46/58 **Flip Top Box** *Dicky Doo & The Don'ts*
42/80 **Flirtin' With Disaster** *Molly Hatchet*
92/61 **Float, The** *Hank Ballard*
2/77 **Float On** *Floaters*
(also see: Bloat On)
47/96 **Floatin' On Your Love** *Isley Brothers*
37/96 **Flood** *Jars Of Clay*
56/93 **Floor, The** *Johnny Gill*
89/93 **Flow Joe** *Fat Joe*
79/59 **Flower Of Love** *Crests*
87/76 **Flowers** *Emotions*
18^S/00 **Flowers For The Dead** *Cuban Link*
21/56 **Flowers Mean Forgiveness** *Frank Sinatra*
Flowers On The Wall
4/66 *Statler Brothers*
50/00 *Eric Heatherly*
16/72 **Floy Joy** *Supremes*

FLY:

1^A/97 **Fly** *Sugar Ray*
7/61 **Fly, The** *Chubby Checker*
61/91 **Fly, The** *U2*
75/77 **Fly At Night** *Chilliwack*
12/99 **Fly Away** *Lenny Kravitz*
13/76 **Fly Away** *John Denver*
42/81 **Fly Away** *Blackfoot*
Fly Away
55/81 *Peter Allen*
84/82 *Stevie Woods*
68^S/02 **Fly Away From Here (Graduation Day)** *Dropline*
82/61 **Fly By Night** *Andy Williams*
88/77 **Fly By Night/In The Mood** *Rush*
47/90 **Fly High Michelle** *Enuff Z'Nuff*
Fly Like An Eagle
2/77 *Steve Miller*
10/97 *Seal*
95/71 **Fly Little White Dove Fly** *Bells*
Fly Me To The Moon
14/63 *Joe Harnell (Bossa Nova)*
84/65 *LaVern Baker*
84/65 *Tony Bennett*
98/66 *Sam & Bill*
52/68 *Bobby Womack*
1/75 **Fly, Robin, Fly** *Silver Convention*
53/99 **Fly (the angel song)** *Wilkinsons*
19/90 **Fly To The Angels** *Slaughter*
79/83 **Flyer** *Saga*
53/78 **Flyin'** *Prism*
70/75 **Flyin' High** *Blackbyrds*
38/78 **Flying High** *Commodores*
45/62 **Flying Circle** *Frank Slay*
3/56 **Flying Saucer** *Buchanan & Goodman*
18/57 **Flying Saucer The 2nd** *Buchanan & Goodman*

71/95 **Foe Life** *Mack 10*
41/95 **Foe Tha Love Of $** *Bone Thugs N Harmony*
93/59 **Fog Cutter** *Frantics*
Foggy Mountain Breakdown
55/68 *Flatt & Scruggs (Theme From Bonnie & Clyde)*
55/68 *Flatt & Scruggs*
84/63 **Folk Singer** *Tommy Roe*
Follow Me
5/01 *Uncle Kracker*
62S/01 *Under Cover*
56/71 **Follow Me** *Mary Travers*
65/66 **Follow Me** *Lyme & Cybelle*
91/65 **Follow Me** *Drifters*
72/90 **Follow My Heartbeat** *A'me Lorain*
15/62 **Follow That Dream** *Elvis Presley*
17/63 **Follow The Boys** *Connie Francis*
68S/00 **Follow The Leader** *Soca Boys*
65/87 **Follow You** *Glen Burtnick*
9/96 **Follow You Down** *Gin Blossoms*
23/78 **Follow You Follow Me** *Genesis*
61/73 **Follow Your Daughter Home** *Guess Who*
88/85 **Follow Your Heart** *Triumph*
92/66 **Follow Your Heart** *Manhattans*
32/68 **Folsom Prison Blues** *Johnny Cash*
91/76 **Fonz Song** *Heyettes*

FOOL:

Fool, The
7/56 *Sanford Clark*
62/56 *Gallahads*
F/73 **Fool** *Elvis Presley*
75/59 **Fool And The Angel** *Bobby Helms*
52/80 **Fool For A Pretty Face (Hurt By Love)** *Humble Pie*
45/76 **Fool For The City** *Foghat*
22/68 **Fool For You** *Impressions*
77/82 **Fool For Your Love** *Jimmy Hall*
Fool For Your Loving
53/80 *Whitesnake*
37/89 *Whitesnake*
12/78 **Fool (If You Think It's Over)** *Chris Rea*
27/60 **Fool In Love** *Ike & Tina Turner*
25/81 **Fool In Love With You** *Jim Photoglo*
21/80 **Fool In The Rain** *Led Zeppelin*
93/73 **Fool Like You** *Tim Moore*
78/71 **Fool Me** *Joe South*
46/83 **Fool Moon Fire** *Walter Egan*
13/64 **Fool Never Learns** *Andy Williams*
3/61 **Fool #1** *Brenda Lee*
6/68 **Fool On The Hill** *Sergio Mendes*
Fool Such As I
2/59 *Elvis Presley*
55/74 *Bob Dylan*
46/81 **Fool That I Am** *Rita Coolidge*
50/61 **Fool That I Am** *Etta James*
10/76 **Fool To Cry** *Rolling Stones*
20/55 **Fooled** *Perry Como*
3/76 **Fooled Around And Fell In Love** *Elvin Bishop*
89/79 **Fooled By A Feeling** *Barbara Mandrell*
28/83 **Foolin'** *Def Leppard*
38/95 **Foolin' Around** *Changing Faces*
49/61 **Foolin' Around** *Kay Starr*
65/82 **Foolin' Yourself** *Aldo Nova*
29/78 **Fooling Yourself (The Angry Young Man)** *Styx*
1/02 **Foolish** *Ashanti*
1/88 **Foolish Beat** *Debbie Gibson*
57/69 **Foolish Fool** *Dee Dee Warwick*
7/97 **Foolish Games** *Jewel*

Foolish Heart
18/85 *Steve Perry*
90/89 *Sharon Bryant*
4/63 **Foolish Little Girl** *Shirelles*
33/86 **Foolish Pride** *Daryl Hall*
72S/94 **Foolish Pride** *Travis Tritt*
69/57 **Fools Fall In Love** *Drifters*
82/83 **Fools Game** *Michael Bolton*
29/59 **Fools Hall Of Fame** *Pat Boone*
85/85 **Fools Like Me** *Lorenzo Lamas*
58/58 **Fool's Paradise** *Crickets*
94/72 **Fool's Paradise** *Sylvers*
Fools Rush In
24/60 *Brook Benton*
87/62 *Etta James*
12/63 *Rick Nelson*
98/75 **Foot Stompin Music** *Hamilton Bohannon*
29/72 **Footstompin' Music** *Grand Funk Railroad*
25/61 **Foot Stomping** *Flares*
46/79 **Football Card** *Glenn Sutton*
1/84 **Footloose** *Kenny Loggins*
7/60 **Footsteps** *Steve Lawrence*
30/76 **Fopp** *Ohio Players*

FOR:

For ..also see: Fa / Foe
60S/95 **For A Change** *Neal McCoy*
63/76 **For A Dancer** *Prelude*
37/99 **For A Little While** *Tim McGraw*
23/59 **For A Penny** *Pat Boone*
45/84 **For A Rocker** *Jackson Browne*
90/77 **For A While** *Mary MacGregor*
72/02 **For All Time** *Soluna*
3/71 **For All We Know** *Carpenters*
88/62 **For All We Know** *Dinah Washington*
30/86 **For America** *Jackson Browne*
100/77 **For Elise** *Philarmonics*
53/72 **For Emily, Whenever I May Find Her** *Simon & Garfunkel*
26/71 **(For God's Sake) Give More Power To The People** *Chi-Lites*
66/67 **For He's A Jolly Good Fellow** *Bobby Vinton*
64/71 **For Ladies Only** *Steppenwolf*
43/60 **For Love** *Lloyd Price*
83/79 **For Love** *Pousette-Dart Band*
30/65 **For Lovin' Me** *Peter, Paul & Mary*
For Mama
48/65 *Connie Francis*
54/65 *Jerry Vale*
98/67 **For Me** *Sergio Mendes*
71/61 **For Me And My Gal** *Freddy Cannon*
28/61 **For My Baby** *Brook Benton*
23/58 **For My Good Fortune** *Pat Boone*
F/73 **For Ol' Times Sake** *Elvis Presley*
For Once In My Life
91/67 *Tony Bennett*
2/68 *Stevie Wonder*
70/68 *Jackie Wilson*
72A/97 **For Once In Our Lives** *Paul Carrack*
For Sentimental Reasons ..see: (I Love You)
81/93 **For The Cool In You** *Babyface*
60A/97 **For The First Time** *Kenny Loggins*
11/71 **For The Good Times** *Ray Price*
F/76 **For The Heart** *Elvis Presley*
13/70 **For The Love Of Him** *Bobbi Martin*
81/68 **For The Love Of Ivy** *Mamas & The Papas*
For The Love Of Money
9/74 *O'Jays*
78/89 *Bulletboys*

For The Love Of You
22/75 *Isley Brothers*
F/76 *Houston Person*
66/96 **For The Love Of You** *Jordan Hill*
32/86 **For Tonight** *Nancy Martinez*
For What It's Worth
7/67 *Buffalo Springfield*
66/67 *Staple Singers*
87/67 *King Curtis*
6/64 **For You** *Rick Nelson*
21/91 **For You** *Outfield*
33/97 **For You** *Kenny Lattimore*
60/91 **For You** *Michael W. Smith*
63/02 **For You** *Staind*
93/65 **For You** *Spellbinders*
85/79 **For You And I** *10 cc*
F/70 **For You Blue** *Beatles*
4/97 **For You I Will** *Monica*
49/99 **For You I Will** *Aaron Tippin*
4/81 **For Your Eyes Only** *Sheena Easton*
6/65 **For Your Love** *Yardbirds*
For Your Love
13/58 *Ed Townsend*
93/61 *Wanderers*
95/65 *Sam & Bill*
20/67 *Peaches & Herb*
91/75 *Christopher Paul & Shawn*
53/95 **For Your Love** *Stevie Wonder*
86/91 **For Your Mind** *Robbie Nevil*
For Your Precious Love
11/58 *Jerry Butler & The Impressions*
26/64 *Garnet Mimms*
99/66 *Jerry Butler*
23/67 *Oscar Toney, Jr.*
49/68 *Jackie Wilson & Count Basie*
74/72 *Linda Jones*
86/64 **For Your Sweet Love** *Cascades*
74/93 **Foreplay** *Raab*

FOREVER:

8/90 **Forever** *Kiss*
Forever
9/60 *Little Dippers*
83/60 *Billy Walker*
25/64 *Pete Drake*
79/69 *Mercy*
40/85 **Forever** *Kenny Loggins*
60/57 **Forever** *Sam Cooke*
63/83 **Forever** *Little Steven*
78/63 **Forever** *Marvelettes*
9A/96 **Forever** *Mariah Carey*
77/91 **Forever Amo'r** *D'zyre*
82/62 **Forever And A Day** *Jackie Wilson*
47/78 **Forever Autumn** *Justin Hayward*
Forever Came Today
28/68 *Supremes*
60/75 *Jackson 5*
35/56 **Forever Darling** *Ames Brothers*
20/79 **Forever In Blue Jeans** *Neil Diamond*
18/93 **Forever In Love** *Kenny G*
81/92 **Forever In Your Eyes** *Mint Condition*
19/86 **(Forever) Live And Die** *Orchestral Manoeuvres In The Dark*
15/92 **Forever Love** *Color Me Badd*
76/76 **Forever Lovers** *Mac Davis*
26/85 **Forever Man** *Eric Clapton*
28/80 **Forever Mine** *O'Jays*
60/82 **Forever Mine** *Motels*
63/96 **Forever More** *Puff Johnson*
96/91 **Forever More** *Stevie B*
25/91 **Forever My Lady** *Jodeci*

Forever Tonight ..see: (I Wanna Take)
12/88 **Forever Young** *Rod Stewart*
Forever Young
93/85 *Alphaville*
65/88 *Alphaville*
1/89 **Forever Your Girl** *Paula Abdul*
80/88 **Forever Yours** *Tony Terry*
Forget Domani
78/65 *Frank Sinatra*
79/65 *Connie Francis*
4/64 **Forget Him** *Bobby Rydell*
81/67 **Forget It** *Sandpebbles*
12/58 **Forget Me Not** *Kalin Twins*
45/89 **Forget Me Not** *Bad English*
93/68 **Forget Me Not** *Martha & The Vandellas*
23/82 **Forget Me Nots** *Patrice Rushen*
F/69 **Forget To Remember** *Frank Sinatra*
71/02 **Forgive** *Rebecca Lynn Howard*
61/65 **Forgive Me** *Al Martino*
49/88 **Forgive Me For Dreaming** *Elisa Fiorillo*
2/80 **Forgive Me Girl (medley)** *Spinners*
13/55 **Forgive My Heart** *Nat "King" Cole*
30C/55 **Forgive This Fool** *Roy Hamilton*
25/00 **Forgot About Dre** *Dr. Dre*
71S/01 **Formal Invite** *Ray J*
8/85 **Fortress Around Your Heart** *Sting*
4/99 **Fortunate** *Maxwell*
14/69 **Fortunate Son** *Creedence Clearwater Revival*
97/67 **Fortune Teller** *Hardtimes*
41/62 **Fortuneteller** *Bobby Curtola*
70/57 **Forty Cups Of Coffee** *Bill Haley*
45/59 **Forty Days** *Ronnie Hawkins*
9/59 **Forty Miles Of Bad Road** *Duane Eddy*
49/56 **49 Shades Of Green** *Ames Brothers*
36/79 **Found A Cure** *Ashford & Simpson*
88/60 **Found Love** *Jimmy Reed*
64A/90 **Found Love** *Double Dee*
25/94 **Found Out About You** *Gin Blossoms*
90/59 **Fountain Of Youth** *Four Lads*
4-By The Beatles [E.P.]
92/64 *Beatles*
68/65 *Beatles*
21/99 **4,5,6** *Solé*
56/64 **442 Glenwood Avenue** *Pixies Three*
19/85 **Four In The Morning (I Can't Take Any More)** *Night Ranger*
63/97 **Four Leaf Clover** *Abra Moore*
86/83 **Four Little Diamonds** *ELO*
73/60 **Four Little Heels** *Brian Hyland*
76/62 **409** *Beach Boys*
59A/97 **4 Page Letter** *Aaliyah*
1/97 **4 Seasons Of Loneliness** *Boyz II Men*
Four Strong Winds
60/64 *Bobby Bare*
61/79 *Neil Young*
75/97 **4, 3, 2, 1** *LL Cool J*
Four Walls
11/57 *Jim Reeves*
15/57 *Jim Lowe*
92/62 *Kay Starr*
70/57 **1492** *Betty Johnson*
36/68 **1432 Franklin Pike Circle Hero** *Bobby Russell*
84/74 **Fox Hunt** *Herb Alpert*
5/76 **Fox On The Run** *Sweet*
97/69 **Fox On The Run** *Manfred Mann*
67/68 **Foxey Lady** *Jimi Hendrix*
49/76 **Foxy Lady** *Crown Heights Affair*
41/76 **Framed** *Cheech & Chong*
69/72 **Francene** *ZZ Top*
Francis Powers, Ballad Of ..see: There's A Star Spangled Banner Waving
1/73 **Frankenstein** *Edgar Winter Group*
9/59 **Frankie** *Connie Francis*
75/85 **Frankie** *Sister Sledge*
Frankie And Johnny
57/59 *Johnny Cash*
20/61 *Brook Benton*
14/63 *Sam Cooke*
75/64 *Greenwood County Singers*
25/66 *Elvis Presley*
Fraulein
36/57 *Bobby Helms*
54/57 *Steve Lawrence*
Freak ..also see: Freek
90/85 **Freak-A-Ristic** *Atlantic Starr*
66/83 **Freak-A-Zoid** *Midnight Star*
70/97 **[Freak] And U Know It** *Adina Howard*
2/95 **Freak Like Me** *Adina Howard*
1/93 **Freak Me** *Silk*
60/95 **Freak Me Baby** *Dis 'N' Dat*
63/98 **Freak Out** *Nutta Butta*
99/00 **Freakin' It** *Will Smith*
43/93 **Freakit** *DAS EFX*
73A/97 **Freaks** *Live*
73/84 **Freakshow On The Dance Floor** *Bar-Kays*
96/77 **Freddie** *Charlene*
(also see: Do The / Let's Do The)
91/66 **Freddie Feelgood (And His Funky Little Five Piece Band)** *Ray Stevens*
4/72 **Freddie's Dead** *Curtis Mayfield*
90/79 **Frederick** *Patti Smith Group*

FREE:

20/71 **Free** *Chicago*
23/56 **Free** *Tommy Leonetti*
25/77 **Free** *Deniece Williams*
42/01 **Free** *Mya*
75/97 **Free** *Ultra Naté*
83/66 **Free Again** *Barbra Streisand*
6/96 **Free As A Bird** *Beatles*
Free Bird
19/75 *Lynyrd Skynyrd*
38/77 *Lynyrd Skynyrd (Live)*
48/73 **Free Electric Band** *Albert Hammond*
7/90 **Free Fallin'** *Tom Petty*
61/75 **Free Man** *South Shore Commission*
22/74 **Free Man In Paris** *Joni Mitchell*
53/80 **Free Me** *Roger Daltrey*
97/61 **Free Me** *Johnny Preston*
58/79 **Free Me From My Freedom/Tie Me To A Tree (Handcuff Me)** *Bonnie Pointer*
Free Ride
14/73 *Edgar Winter Group*
52/76 *Tavares*
85/76 **Free Spirit** *Atlanta Rhythm Section*
75/70 **Free The People** *Delaney & Bonnie*
94/70 **Free To Carry On** *Sandpipers*
48/96 **Free To Decide** *Cranberries*
F/74 **Free Wheelin'** *Bachman-Turner Overdrive*
8/92 **Free Your Mind** *En Vogue*
3/85 **Freedom** *Wham!*
8/90 **Freedom** *George Michael*
45/95 **Freedom** *Panther Soundtrack*
59/71 **Freedom** *Jimi Hendrix*
59/85 **Freedom** *Pointer Sisters*
72/71 **Freedom** *Isley Brothers*
97/01 **Freedom** *Paul McCartney*
47/70 **Freedom Blues** *Little Richard*
72/71 **Freedom Comes, Freedom Goes** *Fortunes*
63/73 **Freedom For The Stallion** *Hues Corporation*
20/86 **Freedom Overspill** *Steve Winwood*
14/95 **Freek 'n You** *Jodeci*
28S/01 **Freelove** *Depeche Mode*
3/85 **Freeway Of Love** *Aretha Franklin*
33/58 **Freeze, The** *Tony & Joe*
4/82 **Freeze-Frame** *J. Geils Band*
Freight Train
6/57 *Rusty Draper*
40/57 *Chas. McDevitt*
61/59 **French Foreign Legion** *Frank Sinatra*
50/89 **French Kiss** *Lil Louis*
57/87 **French Kissin** *Debbie Harry*
54/64 **French Song (Quand Le Soleil Dit Bonjour Aux Montagnes)** *Lucille Starr*
9/85 **Fresh** *Kool & The Gang*
49/70 **Fresh Air** *Quicksilver Messenger Service*
54/71 **Fresh As A Daisy** *Emitt Rhodes*
50S/02 **Fresh From Yard** *Beenie Man & Lil' Kim*
5/97 **Freshmen, The** *Verve Pipe*
18/92 **Friday I'm In Love** *Cure*
52S/02 **Friday Night** *Mr. Cheeks*
(Friday Night) ..see: Livin' It Up
16/67 **Friday On My Mind** *Easybeats*
36/66 **Friday's Child** *Nancy Sinatra*
73/59 **Fried Eggs** *Intruders*
96/58 **Fried Onions** *Lord Rockingham's XI*
99/73 **Friend And A Lover** *Partridge Family*
90/70 **Friend In The City** *Andy Kim*
47/69 **Friend, Lover, Woman, Wife** *O.C. Smith*
80/73 **Friend Of Mine** *Bill Withers*
72/75 **Friend Of Mine Is Going Blind** *John Dawson Read*
12/98 **Friend of Mine** *Kelly Price*
Friendly Persuasion (Thee I Love)
5/56 *Pat Boone*
45/56 *Four Aces*
9/89 **Friends** *Jody Watley (w/Eric B. & Rakim)*
34/71 **Friends** *Elton John*
40/73 **Friends** *Bette Midler*
47/68 **Friends** *Beach Boys*
69/97 **Friends** *John Michael Montgomery*
79/70 **Friends** *Feather*
87/85 **Friends** *Whodini*
2/86 **Friends And Lovers** *Gloria Loring & Carl Anderson*
38/82 **Friends In Love** *Dionne Warwick & Johnny Mathis*
82/95 **Friends Of P.** *Rentals*
47/71 **Friends With You** *John Denver*
17/69 **Friendship Train** *Gladys Knight*
91/85 **Fright Night** *J. Geils Band*
79/73 **Frisky** *Sly & The Family Stone*
32/61 **Frogg** *Brothers Four*
63/95 **Froggy Style** *Nuttin' Nyce*

FROM:

2/90 **From A Distance** *Bette Midler*
6/63 **From A Jack To A King** *Ned Miller*
56S/01 **From A Lover To A Friend** *Paul McCartney*
79/56 **From A School Ring To A Wedding Ring** *Rover Boys*
From A Window
23/64 *Billy J. Kramer*
97/65 *Chad & Jeremy*
From Both Sides Now ..see: Both Sides Now
58/77 **From Graceland To The Promised Land** *Merle Haggard*
65/02 **From Her Mama (Mama Got A**)** *Juvenile*
28/75 **From His Woman To You** *Barbara Mason*
From Me To You
77/63 *Del Shannon*
41/64 *Beatles*
81/64 **From Russia With Love** *Village Stompers*
77/02 **From Tha Chuuuch To Da Palace** *Snoop Dogg*
39/72 **From The Beginning** *Emerson, Lake & Palmer*
14/00 **From The Bottom Of My Broken Heart** *Britney Spears*
FC/56 **From The Bottom Of My Heart** *Don Cornell*
91/63 **From The Bottom Of My Heart (Dammi, Dammi, Dammi)** *Dean Martin*
93/65 **From The Bottom Of My Heart (I Love You)** *Moody Blues*
11/56 **From The Candy Store On The Corner To The Chapel On The Hill** *Tony Bennett*
57/68 **From The Teacher To The Preacher** *Gene Chandler & Barbara Acklin*
4/98 **From This Moment On** *Shania Twain*
65/83 **Front Page Story** *Neil Diamond*
2/98 **Frozen** *Madonna*
29/96 **Fu-Gee-La** *Fugees (Refugee Camp)*
72S/02 **F**k Off 2000** *Jayne County*
87/67 **Full Measure** *Lovin' Spoonful*
67S/02 **Full Mode** *N.O.R.E.*
18/02 **Full Moon** *Brandy*
28/75 **Full Of Fire** *Al Green*
55/81 **Full Of Fire** *Shalamar*
53/97 **Full Of Smoke** *Christión*
96/92 **Full Term Love** *Monie Love*
91/76 **Full Time Thing (Between Dusk And Dawn)** *Whirlwind*
90/97 **Fulton St.** *Leschea*
Fun ..also see: Ffun
5/64 **Fun, Fun, Fun** *Beach Boys*
46S/00 **Fun Of Your Love** *Jennifer Day*
43/78 **Fun Time** *Joe Cocker*
97/66 **Function At The Junction** *Shorty Long*

FUNK:

75S/01 **Funk** *Empty Mynd*
55/91 **Funk Boutique** *Cover Girls*
63/94 **(Funk Dat)** *Sagat*
58/72 **Funk Factory** *Wilson Pickett*
88/77 **Funk It Up (David's Song)** *Sweet*
59/70 **Funk # 49** *James Gang*
6/94 **Funkdafied** *Da Brat*
81/96 **Funkorama** *Redman*
Funky ..also see: Phuncky
Funky Broadway
8/67 *Wilson Pickett*
65/67 *Dyke & The Blazers*
91/70 **Funky Chicken** *Willie Henderson*
(also see: Do The)
74/93 **Funky Child** *Lords Of The Underground*
3/89 **Funky Cold Medina** *Tone Loc*
87/67 **Funky Donkey** *Pretty Purdie*
51/70 **Funky Drummer** *James Brown*
88/68 **Funky Fever** *Clarence Carter*
79/75 **Funky Gibbon** *Goodies*
39/68 **Funky Judge** *Bull & The Matadors*
87/70 **Funky Man** *Kool & the Gang*
F/95 **Funky Melody** *Stevie B*
64/71 **Funky Music Sho Nuff Turns Me On** *Edwin Starr*
15/71 **Funky Nassau** *Beginning Of The End*
91/68 **Funky North Philly** *Bill Cosby*
99/74 **Funky Party** *Clarence Reid*
Funky Penguin ..see: Do The
44/74 **Funky President (People It's Bad)** *James Brown*
14/68 **Funky Street** *Arthur Conley*
29/73 **Funky Stuff** *Kool & The Gang*
67/68 **Funky Walk** *Dyke & The Blazers*
72/68 **Funky Way** *Calvin Arnold*
76/76 **Funky Weekend** *Stylistics*
15/73 **Funky Worm** *Ohio Players*
40/94 **Funky Y-2-C** *Puppies*
Funkytown
1/80 *Lipps, Inc.*
6/87 *Pseudo Echo*
59/70 **Funniest Thing** *Classics IV*
25/61 **Funny** *Maxine Brown*
Funny
81/59 *Jesse Belvin*
99/62 *Gene McDaniels*
5/73 **Funny Face** *Donna Fargo*
49/67 **Funny Familiar Forgotten Feelings** *Tom Jones*
94/69 **Funny Feeling** *Delfonics*
44/64 **Funny Girl** *Barbra Streisand*
74/75 **Funny How Love Can Be** *First Class*
90/95 **Funny How Time Flies** *Intro*
Funny How Time Slips Away
22/62 *Jimmy Elledge*
50/63 *Johnny Tillotson*
13/64 *Joe Hinton*
58/76 *Dorothy Moore*
67/83 *Spinners*
77/65 **Funny Little Butterflies** *Patty Duke*
81/63 **Funny Man** *Ray Stevens*
10/62 **Funny Way Of Laughin'** *Burl Ives*
17S/01 **Furniture** *Fugazi*
91/59 **Furry Murray** *Tradewinds*
91/62 **Further More** *Ray Stevens*
39/73 **Future Shock** *Curtis Mayfield*
71/75 **Future Shock** *Hello People*
19/86 **Future's So Bright, I Gotta Wear Shades** *Timbuk 3*

G

47/00 **G'd Up** *Eastsidaz*
4/64 **G.T.O.** *Ronny & The Daytonas*
91/56 **Gal With The Yaller Shoes** *Four Aces*
54A/95 **Galaxie** *Blind Melon*
39/78 **Galaxy** *War*
89/92 **Galileo** *Indigo Girls*
29/67 **Gallant Men** *Senator Everett McKinley Dirksen*
Galveston
4/69 *Glen Campbell*
99/69 *Roger Williams*
16/79 **Gambler, The** *Kenny Rogers*
79/76 **Game Is Over (What's The Matter With You)** *Brown Sugar*
1/65 **Game Of Love** *Wayne Fontana & The Mindbenders*
5/02 **Game Of Love** *Santana feat. Michelle Branch*
27/71 **Games** *Redeye*
46/81 **Games** *Phoebe Snow*
68/92 **Games** *Chuckii Booker*
58A/91 **Games** *NKOTB*
Games People Play
12/69 *Joe South*
84/94 *Inner Circle*
16/81 **Games People Play** *Alan Parsons Project*
(also see: They Just Can't Stop It)
Games That Lovers Play
45/66 *Eddie Fisher*
86/66 *Wayne Newton*
48/80 **Games Without Frontiers** *Peter Gabriel*
70S/94 **Gang Stories** *South Central Cartel*
85/70 **Gangs Back Again** *Kool & The Gang*
21/93 **Gangsta** *Bell Biv DeVoe*
67/93 **Gangsta Bitch** *Apache*
70S/99 **Gangsta! Gangsta! (How U Do It)** *C. Webb*
4/93 **Gangsta Lean** *D.R.S.*
2/02 **Gangsta Lovin'** *Eve*
Gangsta's Paradise
1/95 *Coolio*
F/96 *L.V.*
(also see: Amish Paradise)
40/97 **Gangstas Make The World Go Round** *Westside Connection*
53S/02 **Gantz Graf** *Autechre*
69/84 **Gap, The** *Thompson Twins*
97/64 **Garden In The Rain** *Vic Dana*
12/56 **Garden Of Eden** *Joe Valino*
6/72 **Garden Party** *Rick Nelson*
81/83 **Garden Party** *Herb Alpert*
81/70 **Gas Lamps And Clay** *Blues Image*
81/58 **Gas Money** *Jan & Arnie*
96/64 **Gator Tails And Monkey Ribs** *Spats*
57/59 **Gazachstahagen** *Wild-Cats*
73/59 **Gee** *George Hamilton IV*
Gee
81/60 *Jan & Dean*
87/64 *Pixies Three*
81/75 **Gee Baby** *Peter Shelley*
80/65 **Gee Baby (I'm Sorry)** *3° Degrees*
21/58 **Gee, But It's Lonely** *Pat Boone*
19/56 **Gee Whittakers!** *Pat Boone*
28/61 **Gee Whiz** *Innocents*
23X/63 **Gee Whiz, It's Christmas** *Carla Thomas*
Gee Whiz (Look At His Eyes)
10/61 *Carla Thomas*
31/80 *Bernadette Peters*
27A/95 **Geek Stink Breath** *Green Day*
66/58 **Geisha Girl** *Hank Locklin*
49A/95 **Gel** *Collective Soul*
12/81 **Gemini Dream** *Moody Blues*
33/81 **General Hospi-Tale** *Afternoon Delights*
Genie In A Bottle
1/99 *Christina Aguilera*
17S/01 *Christina Aguilera*

31/82 **Genius Of Love** *Tom Tom Club*
31/91 **Gentle** *Dino*
Gentle On My Mind
62/67 *Glen Campbell*
39/68 *Glen Campbell*
66/68 *Patti Page*
76/69 *Aretha Franklin*
33/72 **George Jackson** *Bob Dylan*
98/01 **Georgia** *Carolyn Dawn Johnson*
Georgia On My Mind
1/60 *Ray Charles*
62/66 *Righteous Brothers*
91/68 *Wes Montgomery*
84/78 *Willie Nelson*
36/90 *Michael Bolton*
81/67 **Georgia Pines** *Candymen*
93/74 **Georgia Porcupine** *George Fischoff*
68/77 **Georgia Rhythm** *Atlanta Rhythm Section*
89/66 **Georgia Rose** *Tony Bennett*
88/70 **Georgia Took Her Back** *R.B. Greaves*
68/65 **Georgie Porgie** *Jewel Akens*
Georgy Girl
2/67 *Seekers*
98/67 *Baja Marimba Band*
Georgy Porgy
48/79 *Toto*
55/99 *Eric Benét*
96/58 **Geraldine** *Jack Scott*
37/72 **Geronimo's Cadillac** *Michael Murphey*

GET:

Get A Job
1/58 *Silhouettes*
21/58 *Mills Brothers*
14/91 **Get A Leg Up** *John Mellencamp*
54/90 **Get A Life** *Soul II Soul*
46/79 **Get A Move On** *Eddie Money*
39/98 **Get At Me Dog** *DMX*
14/93 **Get Away** *Bobby Brown*
48S/02 **Get Away** *Mobb Deep*
70/66 **Get Away** *Georgie Fame*
12/76 **Getaway** *Earth, Wind & Fire*
Get Back
1/69 *Beatles with Billy Preston*
86/78 *Billy Preston*
88/66 **Get Back** *Roy Head*
6/76 **Get Closer** *Seals & Crofts*
29/82 **Get Closer** *Linda Ronstadt*
93/01 **Get Crunked Up** *Iconz*
10/75 **Get Dancin'** *Disco-Tex & The Sex-O-Lettes*
7/73 **Get Down** *Gilbert O'Sullivan*
38/95 **Get Down** *Craig Mack*
53/79 **Get Down** *Gene Chandler*
69/71 **Get Down** *Curtis Mayfield*
79/67 **Get Down** *Harvey Scales*
8/75 **Get Down, Get Down (Get On The Floor)** *Joe Simon*
10/82 **Get Down On It** *Kool & The Gang*
88/70 **Get Down People** *Fabulous Counts*
1/75 **Get Down Tonight** *KC & The Sunshine Band*
13/99 **Get Gone** *Ideal*
5/91 **Get Here** *Oleta Adams*
76/63 **Get Him** *Exciters*
89/70 **Get Into Something** *Isley Brothers*
67/99 **Get Involved** *Raphael Saadiq & Q-Tip*
80/88 **Get It** *Stevie Wonder & Michael Jackson*
56/69 **Get It From The Bottom** *Steelers*
24/71 **Get It On** *Chase*
69/88 **Get It On** *Kingdom Come*
(also see: Bang A Gong)
4/00 **Get It On...Tonite** *Montell Jordan*
61/83 **Get It Right** *Aretha Franklin*
21/79 **Get It Right Next Time** *Gerry Rafferty*
10/97 **Get It Together** *702*
28/73 **Get It Together** *Jackson 5*
40/67 **Get It Together** *James Brown*
69S/94 **Get It Together** *Beastie Boys*
42/93 **Get It Up** *TLC*
43/79 **Get It Up** *Ronnie Milsap*
96/97 **Get It Wet** *Twista*
78/71 **Get It While You Can** *Janis Joplin*
71/95 **Get Lifted** *Keith Murray*
42A/97 **Get Me Home** *Foxy Brown*
56S/02 **Get Me Off** *Basement Jaxx*
89/56 **Get Me To The Church On Time** *Julius LaRosa*
27/67 **Get Me To The World On Time** *Electric Prunes*
14S/01 **Get Mo** *Sherm*
17/96 **Get Money** *Junior M.A.F.I.A.*
52S/99 **Get None** *Tamar*
9/78 **Get Off** *Foxy*
(also see: Gett Off)
74/69 **Get Off My Back Woman** *B.B. King*
1/65 **Get Off Of My Cloud** *Rolling Stones*
18/72 **Get On The Good Foot** *James Brown*
11/67 **Get On Up** *Esquires*
22/96 **Get On Up** *Jodeci*
11/89 **Get On Your Feet** *Gloria Estefan*
Get Out ..see: G.H.E.T.T.O.U.T.
48/68 **Get Out Now** *Tommy James*
97/72 **Get Out Of Bed** *Livingston Taylor*
80/74 **Get Out Of Denver** *Bob Seger*
44/66 **Get Out Of My Life, Woman** *Lee Dorsey*
1/88 **Get Outta My Dreams, Get Into My Car** *Billy Ocean*
31/94 **Get Over It** *Eagles*
8/01 **Get Over Yourself** *Eden's Crush*
Get Ready
29/66 *Temptations*
4/70 *Rare Earth*
Get Ready For This
76/92 *2 Unlimited*
38/95 *2 Unlimited*
96/96 **Get Ready, Here It Comes (It's The Choo-Choo)** *Southsyde B.O.I.Z.*
95/98 **Get Ready To Bounce** *Brooklyn Bounce*
60/69 **Get Rhythm** *Johnny Cash*
76/91 **Get Serious** *Cut 'N' Move*
70/74 **Get That Gasoline Blues** *NRBQ*
31/87 **Get That Love** *Thompson Twins*
50/75 **Get The Cream Off The Top** *Eddie Kendricks*
30/76 **Get The Funk Out Ma Face** *Brothers Johnson*
91/67 **Get The Message** *Brian Hyland*
4/01 **Get The Party Started** *P!nk*
Get Together
31/65 *We Five*
62/67 *Youngbloods*
5/69 *Youngbloods*
44/96 *Big Mountain*
42S/00 **Get Up** *Jessica*
58S/01 **Get Up** *Cocoa Brovaz*
60/97 **Get Up** *Lost Boyz*
97/00 **Get Up** *Amel Larrieux*
(also see: Git Up)
2/76 **Get Up And Boogie (That's Right)** *Silver Convention*
(Get up and dance!) ..see: Bite Your Lip
78/72 **Get Up And Get Down** *Dramatics*
50/82 **Get Up And Go** *Go-Go's*
7/90 **Get Up! (Before The Night Is Over)** *Technotronic*
34/71 **Get Up, Get Into It, Get Involved** *James Brown*
83/56 **Get Up! Get Up! (You Sleepyhead)** *Jaye P. Morgan*
Get Up I Feel Like Being A Sex Machine ..see: Sex Machine
83/93 **Get Up (Move Boy Move)** *AB Logic*
45/76 **Get Up Offa That Thing** *James Brown*
62/94 **Get Up On It** *Keith Sweat*
7/01 **Get Ur Freak On** *Missy Elliott*
21/79 **Get Used To It** *Roger Voudouris*
78/92 **Get With U** *Lidell Townsell & M.T.F.*
91/97 **Get Your Groove On** *Gyrl*
26/85 **Getcha Back** *Beach Boys*
21/91 **Gett Off** *Prince*
68/96 **Gettin' It** *Too $hort*
Gettin' Jiggy Wit It
1/98 *Will Smith*
30S/02 *Will Smith*
27/78 **Gettin' Ready For Love** *Diana Ross*
18/67 **Gettin' Together** *Tommy James*
38/90 **Getting Away With It** *Electronic*
20/79 **Getting Closer** *Wings*
93/72 **Getting It On** *Dennis Coffey*
65/65 **Getting Mighty Crowded** *Betty Everett*
88/62 **Getting Ready For The Heartbreak** *Chuck Jackson*
75/69 **Getting The Corners** *T.S.U. Toronadoes*
7/94 **Getto Jam** *Domino*
Ghetto, The
87/70 *Donny Hathaway*
42/91 *Too $hort*
29/73 **Ghetto Child** *Spinners*
15/99 **Ghetto Cowboy** *Mo Thugs Family & Bone Thugs N Harmony*
91/01 **Ghetto Girls** *Lil Bow Wow*
16/97 **Ghetto Love** *Da Brat*
53S/02 **Ghetto Millionaire** *Dem Ghetto Playa$*
15/98 **Ghetto Supastar (That Is What You Are)** *Pras Michel*
68/71 **Ghetto Woman** *B.B. King*
8/97 **G.H.E.T.T.O.U.T.** *Changing Faces*
45/79 **Ghost Dancer** *Addrisi Brothers*
59/84 **Ghost In You** *Psychedelic Furs*
(Ghost) Riders In The Sky
30/61 *Ramrods*
87/61 *Lawrence Welk*
52/66 *Baja Marimba Band*
31/81 *Outlaws*
63S/02 **Ghost Showers** *Ghostface Killah*
22/56 **Ghost Town** *Don Cherry*
33/88 **Ghost Town** *Cheap Trick*
1/84 **Ghostbusters** *Ray Parker Jr.*
Giant
63/56 *Les Baxter*
77/56 *Art Mooney*
91/56 *Jack Pleis*
82/66 **Giddyup Go** *Red Sovine*
41/59 **Gidget** *Jimmy Darren*
65A/98 **Gift, The** *Collin Raye with Jim Brickman*
5X/72 **Gift Of Giving** *Bill Withers*
91/61 **Gift Of Love** *Van Dykes*
88/58 **Gigi** *Vic Damone*
57/82 **Gigolo, The** *O'Bryan*

82/59 **Gilee** *Sonny Spencer*
37/83 **Gimme All Your Lovin** *ZZ Top*
9/70 **Gimme Dat Ding** *Pipkins*
12/69 **Gimme Gimme Good Lovin'** *Crazy Elephant*
9/67 **Gimme Little Sign** *Brenton Wood*
Gimme Shelter
73/70 *Merry Clayton*
61/71 *Grand Funk Railroad*
46/97 **Gimme Some Love** *Gina G*
Gimme Some Lovin'
7/67 *Spencer Davis Group*
68/71 *Traffic, Etc.*
84/78 *Kongas*
18/80 *Blues Brothers*
67/72 **Gimme Some More** *JB's*
Gimme The Light
7/02 *Sean Paul*
17S/02 *Sean Paul (Remix)*
84/89 **Gimme Your Good Lovin'** *Diving For Pearls*
70/76 **Gimme Your Money Please** *Bachman-Turner Overdrive*
8/94 **Gin & Juice** *Snoop Doggy Dogg*
6/62 **Gina** *Johnny Mathis*
9/58 **Ginger Bread** *Frankie Avalon*
38/61 **Ginnie Bell** *Paul Dino*
21/62 **Ginny Come Lately** *Brian Hyland*

GIRL:

Girl And Boy ..see: Ballad Of
17/86 **Girl Can't Help It** *Journey*
49/57 **Girl Can't Help It** *Little Richard*
30/65 **Girl Come Running** *4 Seasons*
66/67 **Girl Don't Care** *Gene Chandler*
42/65 **Girl Don't Come** *Sandie Shaw*
55/80 **Girl, Don't Let It Get You Down** *O'Jays*
5/64 **Girl From Ipanema** *Stan Getz/Astrud Gilberto*
73/65 **Girl From Peyton Place** *Dickey Lee*
28S/00 **Girl From The Gutter** *Kina*
81/62 **Girl Has To Know** *G-Clefs*
56/89 **Girl I Am Searching For You** *Stevie B*
39/67 **Girl I Knew Somewhere** *Monkees*
69/67 **Girl I Need You** *Artistics*
27/90 **Girl I Used To Know** *Brother Beyond*
52/69 **Girl I'll Never Know (Angels Never Fly This Low)** *Frankie Valli*
1/89 **Girl I'm Gonna Miss You** *Milli Vanilli*
19/93 **Girl, I've Been Hurt** *Snow*
21/66 **Girl In Love** *Outsiders*
Girl In Me ..see: (Bringing Out)
Girl In My Dreams
45/56 *Cliques*
92/61 *Capris*
35/84 **Girl In Trouble (Is A Temporary Thing)** *Romeo Void*
2/83 **Girl Is Mine** *Michael Jackson/Paul McCartney*
10/67 **Girl Like You** *Young Rascals*
32/95 **Girl Like You** *Edwyn Collins*
38/90 **Girl Like You** *Smithereens*
80/59 **Girl Like You** *Gary Stites*
55/68 **Girl Most Likely** *Jeannie C. Riley*
85/01 **Girl Next Door** *Musiq Soulchild*
19/61 **Girl Of My Best Friend** *Ral Donner*
37/79 **Girl Of My Dreams** *Bram Tchaikovsky*
28/66 **Girl On A Swing** *Gerry & The Pacemakers*
52/59 **Girl On Page 44** *Four Lads*
10/99 **Girl On TV** *LFO*
96/65 **Girl On The Billboard** *Del Reeves*
28/02 **Girl Talk** *TLC*
66/66 **Girl That Stood Beside Me** *Bobby Darin*
5/68 **Girl Watcher** *O'Kaysions*
87/71 **Girl Who Loved Me When** *Glass Bottle*
26/64 **Girl (Why You Wanna Make Me Blue)** *Temptations*
13/57 **Girl With The Golden Braids** *Perry Como*
55/80 **Girl With The Hungry Eyes** *Jefferson Starship*
85/60 **Girl With The Story In Her Eyes** *Safaris*
98/67 **Girl (You Captivate Me)** *? (Question Mark) & The Mysterians*
26/93 **Girl U For Me** *Silk*
2/89 **Girl You Know It's True** *Milli Vanilli*
87/73 **Girl You Need A Change Of Mind** *Eddie Kendricks*
Girl, You'll Be A Woman Soon
10/67 *Neil Diamond*
59/94 *Urge Overkill*
59/69 **Girl You're Too Young** *Archie Bell*
5/88 **Girlfriend** *Pebbles*
5/02 **Girlfriend** **NSYNC*
57/87 **Girlfriend** *Bobby Brown*
47/99 **Girlfriend/Boyfriend** *BLACKstreet With Janet*
16/84 **Girls** *Dwight Twilley*
68/64 **Girls** *Major Lance*
64/61 **Girl's A Devil** *Dukays*
57/88 **Girls Ain't Nothing But Trouble** *DJ Jazzy Jeff & The Fresh Prince*
59/94 **Girls & Boys** *Blur*
34/85 **Girls Are More Fun** *Ray Parker Jr.*
92/67 **Girls Are Out To Get You** *Fascinations*
52/99 **Girls' Best Friend** *Jay-Z*
34/80 **Girls Can Get It** *Dr. Hook*
33/68 **Girls Can't Do What The Guys Do** *Betty Wright*
54/00 **Girls Dem Sugar** *Beenie Man*
12/87 **Girls, Girls, Girls** *Mötley Crüe*
17/01 **Girls, Girls, Girls** *Jay-Z*
96/61 **Girls Girls Girls** *Coasters*
14/62 **(Girls, Girls, Girls) Made To Love** *Eddie Hodges*
33/64 **Girls Grow Up Faster Than Boys** *Cookies*
39/67 **Girls In Love** *Gary Lewis*
68/69 **Girls It Ain't Easy** *Honey Cone*
Girls Just Want To Have Fun
2/84 *Cyndi Lauper*
87/95 *Cyndi Lauper (Hey Now)*
62S/99 **Girls Night Out** *UWF All-Stars*
6/90 **Girls Nite Out** *Tyler Collins*
33/78 **Girls' School** *Wings*
43/70 **Girls' Song** *5th Dimension*
65/79 **Girls Talk** *Dave Edmunds*
75/70 **Girls Will Be Girls, Boys Will Be Boys** *Isley Brothers*
33/84 **Girls With Guns** *Tommy Shaw*
89/59 **Girl's Work Is Never Done** *Chordettes*
99/95 **Girlstown** *Super Cat*
75S/94 **Git Up, Git Out** *OutKast*
8/69 **Gitarzan** *Ray Stevens*
74S/00 **Gittin' What I Want** *Gwen McCrae*
50/98 **Gitty Up** *Salt N'Pepa*

GIVE:

13S/01 **Give** *Donz*
67/84 **Give** *Missing Persons*
43/68 **Give A Damn** *Spanky & Our Gang*
15/77 **Give A Little Bit** *Supertramp*
41/81 **Give A Little Bit More** *Cliff Richard*
97/70 **Give A Woman Love** *Bobbi Martin*
68/65 **Give All Your Love To Me** *Gerry & The Pacemakers*
91/67 **Give Everybody Some** *Bar-Kays*
18/65 **Give Him A Great Big Kiss** *Shangri-Las*
87/93 **Give Him A Love He Can Feel** *Tené Williams*
21/72 **Give Ireland Back To The Irish** *Wings*
18/80 **Give It All You Got** *Chuck Mangione*
73/92 **Give It Away** *Red Hot Chili Peppers*
88/69 **Give It Away** *Chi-Lites*
85/02 **Give It To Her** *Tanto Metro & Devonte*
22S/02 **Give It To Me** *Mad Lion*
30/73 **Give It To Me** *J. Geils Band*
71/71 **Give It To Me** *Mob*
40/81 **Give It To Me Baby** *Rick James*
65/91 **Give It To Me Good** *Trixter*
20/74 **Give It To The People** *Righteous Brothers*
10/99 **Give It To You** *Jordan Knight*
26/95 **Give It To You** *Da Brat*
90/93 **Give It To You** *Martha Wash*
18/84 **Give It Up** *KC*
30/92 **Give It Up** *Wilson Phillips*
33/94 **Give It Up** *Public Enemy*
60/83 **Give It Up** *Steve Miller Band*
71/93 **Give It Up** *Goodmen*
79/91 **Give It Up** *ZZ Top*
15/69 **Give It Up Or Turnit A Loose** *James Brown*
15/93 **Give It Up, Turn It Loose** *En Vogue*
38/76 **Give It Up (Turn It Loose)** *Tyrone Davis*
40/75 **Give It What You Got** *B.T. Express*
Give Me ..also see: Gimme
61/57 **Give Me** *Eileen Rodgers*
78/96 **Give Me...A Reason** *Buffy*
71/74 **Give Me A Reason To Be Gone** *Maureen McGovern*
61/87 **Give Me All Night** *Carly Simon*
48/88 **Give Me All Your Love** *Whitesnake*
67/79 **Give Me An Inch** *Ian Matthews*
66A/98 **Give Me Forever (I Do)** *John Tesh*
3/70 **Give Me Just A Little More Time** *Chairmen Of The Board*
2/00 **Give Me Just One Night (Una Noche)** *98°*
95/55 **Give Me Love** *McGuire Sisters*
1/73 **Give Me Love - (Give Me Peace On Earth)** *George Harrison*
80/68 **Give Me One More Chance** *Wilmer & The Dukes*
3/96 **Give Me One Reason** *Tracy Chapman*
47/89 **Give Me The Keys (And I'll Drive You Crazy)** *Huey Lewis*
4/80 **Give Me The Night** *George Benson*
57/86 **Give Me The Reason** *Luther Vandross*
76/67 **Give Me Time** *Dusty Springfield*
46/84 **Give Me Tonight** *Shannon*
68/00 **Give Me You** *Mary J. Blige*
31/73 **Give Me Your Love** *Barbara Mason*
82/59 **Give Me Your Love** *Nat "King" Cole*

Give More Power To The People ..see: (For God's Sake)
93/68 **Give My Love A Try** *Linda Jones*
46/58 **Give Myself A Party** *Don Gibson*
Give Peace A Chance
14/69 *Plastic Ono Band*
54/91 *Peace Choir*
45/75 **Give The People What They Want** *O'Jays*
23/87 **Give To Live** *Sammy Hagar*
29/92 **Give U My Heart** *Babyface*
84/71 **Give Up Your Guns** *Buoys*
30/56 **Give Us This Day** *Joni James*
Give Us Your Blessings
70/63 *Ray Peterson*
29/65 *Shangri-Las*
71/99 **Give You What You Want (Fa Sure)** *Chico DeBarge*
34/73 **Give Your Baby A Standing Ovation** *Dells*
21/98 **Given To Fly** *Pearl Jam*
Giving Him Something He Can Feel ..see: Something He Can Feel
83/73 **Giving It All Away** *Roger Daltrey*
8/81 **Giving It Up For Your Love** *Delbert McClinton*
Giving Up
38/64 *Gladys Knight*
81/72 *Donny Hathaway*
38/89 **Giving Up On Love** *Rick Astley*
56/64 **Giving Up On Love** *Jerry Butler*
4/90 **Giving You The Benefit** *Pebbles*
3/88 **Giving You The Best That I Got** *Anita Baker*
43/95 **Glaciers Of Ice** *Raekwon*
6/64 **Glad All Over** *Dave Clark Five*
19/55 **Glad Rag Doll** *Crazy Otto*
100/59 **Glad Rags** *Tennessee Ernie Ford*
61/69 **Glad She's A Woman** *Bobby Goldsboro*
26/67 **Glad To Be Unhappy** *Mamas & The Papas*
7/84 **Glamorous Life** *Sheila E.*
31/89 **Glamour Boys** *Living Colour*
37/75 **Glasshouse** *Temptations*
8/56 **Glendora** *Perry Como*
55/80 **Glide** *Pleasure*
72/92 **Globe, The** *Big Audio Dynamite II*
2/82 **Gloria** *Laura Branigan*
Gloria
93/65 *Them*
10/66 *Shadows Of Knight*
71/66 *Them*
71/84 *Doors*
25/77 **Gloria** *Enchantment*
74/60 **Gloria's Theme** *Adam Wade*
34/72 **Glory Bound** *Grass Roots*
5/85 **Glory Days** *Bruce Springsteen*
58/70 **Glory Glory** *Rascals*
1/86 **Glory Of Love** *Peter Cetera*
Glory Of Love
49/61 *Roommates*
75/62 *Don Gardner & Dee Dee Ford*
60/67 *Otis Redding*
92/71 *Dells*
28/96 **Glycerine** *Bush*

GO:

46/86 **Go** *Asia*
30/66 **Go Ahead And Cry** *Righteous Brothers*
5/72 **Go All The Way** *Raspberries*
85/97 **Go Away** *Lorrie Morgan*
89/65 **Go Away From My World** *Marianne Faithfull*
Go Away Little Girl
1/63 *Steve Lawrence*
12/66 *Happenings*
1/71 *Donny Osmond*
36/70 **Go Back** *Crabby Appleton*
60/58 **Go Chase A Moonbeam** *Jerry Vale*
28A/98 **Go Deep** *Janet Jackson*
85/85 **Go Down Easy** *Dan Fogelberg*
32/71 **Go Down Gamblin'** *Blood, Sweat & Tears*
65/85 **Go For It** *Kim Wilde*
66/91 **Go For It! (Heart And Fire)** *Joey B. Ellis & Tynetta Hare*
86/85 **Go For Soda** *Kim Mitchell*
Go-Go ..see: (See You At The)
62/67 **Go-Go Girl** *Lee Dorsey*
10/86 **Go Home** *Stevie Wonder*
23/84 **Go Insane** *Lindsey Buckingham*
5/60 **Go, Jimmy, Go** *Jimmy Clanton*
10/65 **Go Now!** *Moody Blues*
40/00 **Go On** *George Strait*
42/62 **Go On Home** *Patti Page*
Go On With The Wedding
11/56 *Patti Page*
39/56 *Kitty Kallen & Georgie Shaw*
89/87 **Go See The Doctor** *Kool Moe Dee*
24/97 **Go The Distance** *Michael Bolton*
45/79 **Go West** *Village People*
16/67 **Go Where You Wanna Go** *5th Dimension*
78/67 **Go With Me** *Gene & Debbe*
10/77 **Go Your Own Way** *Fleetwood Mac*
72/94 **God** *Tori Amos*
72S/97 **G.O.D.** *Mobb Deep*
God Bless America
36/59 *Connie Francis*
12S/01 *LeAnn Rimes*
99/01 *Daniel Rodriguez*
65/68 **God Bless Our Love** *Ballads*
75/97 **God Bless The Child** *Shania Twain*
God Bless The USA
30S/91 *Lee Greenwood*
16/01 *Lee Greenwood*
18S/01 *Jump 5*
53/71 **God Bless Whoever Sent You** *Originals*
55/94 **God Blessed Texas** *Little Texas*
18/61 **God, Country And My Baby** *Johnny Burnette*
74/78 **God Knows** *Debby Boone*
97/69 **God Knows I Love You** *Nancy Sinatra*
22/70 **God, Love And Rock & Roll** *Teegarden & Van Winkle*
(God Must Have Spent) A Little More Time On You
8/99 **NSYNC*
29/99 *Alabama (featuring *NSYNC)*
God Only Knows
39/66 *Beach Boys*
61/78 *Marilyn Scott*
Godfather ..see: Love Theme From

GOIN'/GOING:

79/68 **Goin' Away** *Fireballs*
89/67 **Goin' Back** *Byrds*
66/86 **Goin' Crazy!** *David Lee Roth*
17/82 **Goin' Down** *Greg Guidry*
57/72 **Goin' Down (On The Road To L.A.)** *Terry Black & Laurel Ward*
69/74 **Goin' Down Slow** *Bobby Blue Bland*
36/73 **Goin' Home** *Osmonds*
56/90 **Going Home** *Kenny G*
83/80 **Goin' On** *Beach Boys*
Goin' Out Of My Head
6/64 *Little Anthony & The Imperials*
7/68 *Lettermen (medley)*
79/69 *Frank Sinatra*
52/77 **Goin' Places** *Jacksons*
16/57 **Goin' Steady** *Tommy Sands*
65/86 **Goin' To The Bank** *Commodores*
70S/96 **Goin' Up Yonder** *M.C. Hammer*
26/98 **Going Back To Cali** *Notorious B.I.G.*
31/88 **Going Back To Cali** *LL Cool J*
89/64 **Going Back To Louisiana** *Bruce Channel*
61/75 **Going Down Slowly** *Pointer Sisters*
35/64 **Going Going Gone** *Brook Benton*
Going In Circles
15/69 *Friends Of Distinction*
F/95 *Luther Vandross*
54/77 **Going In With My Eyes Open** *David Soul*
91/66 **Going Nowhere** *Los Bravos*
52/91 **Going Through The Motions** *Aftershock*
53/79 **Going Through The Motions** *Hot Chocolate*
Going To A Go-Go
11/66 *Miracles*
25/82 *Rolling Stones*
100/58 **Going To Chicago Blues** *Count Basie*
69/70 **Going To The Country** *Steve Miller Band*
11/69 **Going Up The Country** *Canned Heat*
5/79 **Gold** *John Stewart*
29/84 **Gold** *Spandau Ballet*
88/95 **Gold** *Prince*
91/93 **Gold Diggin' Girls** *MC Nas-D & DJ Freaky Fred*
96/74 **Golden Age Of Rock 'N' Roll** *Mott The Hoople*
96/68 **Golden Gate Park** *Rejoice!*
10/76 **Golden Years** *David Bowie*
71S/95 **GoldenEye** *Tina Turner*
Goldfinger
8/65 *Shirley Bassey*
55/65 *Billy Strange*
72/65 *John Barry*
96/65 *Jack LaForge*
33/86 **Goldmine** *Pointer Sisters*
Gone
4/57 *Ferlin Husky*
24/72 *Joey Heatherton*
11/01 **Gone** **NSYNC*
88/63 **Gone** *Rip Chords*
23/75 **Gone At Last** *Paul Simon/Phoebe Snow*
50A/97 **Gone Away** *Offspring*
43/99 **Gone Crazy** *Alan Jackson*
31/64 **Gone, Gone, Gone** *Everly Brothers*
56/79 **Gone, Gone, Gone** *Bad Company*
73/79 **Gone Long Gone** *Chicago*
7/98 **Gone Till November** *Wyclef Jean*
23/77 **Gone Too Far** *England Dan & John Ford Coley*
82/80 **Gone Too Far** *Eddie Rabbitt*
89/63 **Gone With The Wind** *Duprees*
(Gong-Gong Song) ..see: I'm Blue
84/71 **Gonna Be Alright Now** *Gayle McCormick*
79/91 **Gonna Catch You** *Lonnie Gordon*
Gonna Find Me A Bluebird
18/57 *Marvin Rainwater*
51/57 *Eddy Arnold*
84/57 *Joyce Hahn*

Gonna Fly Now (Theme From 'Rocky')
1/77 *Bill Conti*
28/77 *Maynard Ferguson*
94/77 *Current*
94/77 *Rhythm Heritage*
Gonna Get Along Without Ya Now
11/56 *Patience & Prudence*
48/64 *Skeeter Davis*
51/64 *Tracey Dey*
93/67 *Trini Lopez*
Gonna Give Her All The Love I've Got
29/67 *Jimmy Ruffin*
67/70 *Marvin Gaye*
72^A/92 **Gonna Have A Good Time** *Marky Mark & The Funky Bunch*
71/77 **Gonna Love You More** *George Benson*
87/94 **Gonna Love You Right** *After 7*
71/89 **Gonna Make It** *Sa-Fire*
1/91 **Gonna Make You Sweat (Everybody Dance Now)** *C & C Music Factory*
73/62 **Gonna Raise A Rukus Tonight** *Jimmy Dean*
Gonna Send You Back To Georgia
41/64 *Timmy Shaw*
57/64 *Animals (Walker)*
43/60 **Gonzo** *James Booker*
36/69 **Goo Goo Barabajagal (Love Is Hot)** *Donovan/Jeff Beck Group*

GOOD:

30/95 **Good** *Better Than Ezra*
17/55 **Good And Lonesome** *Kay Starr*
89/56 **Good Book** *Kay Starr*
82/69 **Good Clean Fun** *Monkees*
56/68 **Good Combination** *Sonny & Cher*
100/67 **Good Day Sunshine** *Claudine Longet*
76/01 **Good Day To Run** *Darryl Worley*
7/92 **Good Enough** *Bobby Brown*
77/94 **Good Enough** *Sarah McLachlan*
97/71 **Good Enough To Be Your Wife** *Jeannie C. Riley*
Good Foot ..see: Get On The
8/92 **Good For Me** *Amy Grant*
39/79 **Good Friend** *Mary MacGregor*
85/86 **Good Friends** *Joni Mitchell*
11/79 **Good Girls Don't** *Knack*
Good Golly, Miss Molly
10/58 *Little Richard*
43/64 *Swinging Blue Jeans*
4/66 *Mitch Ryder (medley)*
43/61 **Good, Good Lovin'** *Chubby Checker*
45/70 **Good Guys Only Win In The Movies** *Mel & Tim*
74/86 **Good Heart** *Feargal Sharkey*
81/91 **Good Heart** *Starship*
25/76 **Good Hearted Woman** *Waylon Jennings & Willie Nelson*
23^A/95 **Good Intentions** *Toad The Wet Sprocket*
18/63 **Good Life** *Tony Bennett*
73/89 **Good Life** *Inner City*
67/80 **Good Lord Loves You** *Neil Diamond*
77/62 **Good Lover** *Jimmy Reed*
Good Lovin'
81/65 *Olympics*
1/66 *Young Rascals*
30/69 **Good Lovin' Ain't Easy To Come By** *Marvin Gaye & Tammi Terrell*
36/75 **Good Lovin' Gone Bad** *Bad Company*
1/62 **Good Luck Charm** *Elvis Presley*
85/73 **Good Morning** *Michael Redway*
29/02 **Good Morning Beautiful** *Steve Holy*
94/70 **Good Morning Freedom** *Daybreak*
55/80 **Good Morning Girl/Stay Awhile** *Journey*
34/73 **Good Morning Heartache** *Diana Ross*
69/77 **Good Morning Judge** *10cc*
Good Morning Starshine
3/69 *Oliver*
87/69 *Strawberry Alarm Clock*
83/86 **Good Music** *Joan Jett*
11/64 **Good News** *Sam Cooke*
(Good Ol' Boys) ..see: Theme From The Dukes Of Hazzard
78/93 **Good Ol' Days** *Levert*
Good Night ..see: Goodnight
21/69 **Good Old Rock 'N Roll (medley)** *Cat Mother & the All Night News Boys*
11^A/98 **Good Riddance (Time Of Your Life)** *Green Day*
49/59 **Good Rockin' Tonight** *Pat Boone* (also see: Rockin' At Midnight)
22/02 **Good Stuff** *Kenny Chesney*
28/92 **Good Stuff** *the B-52's*
2/68 **Good, The Bad And The Ugly** *Hugo Montenegro*
1/89 **Good Thing** *Fine Young Cannibals*
4/67 **Good Thing** *Paul Revere & The Raiders*
92/77 **Good Thing Man** *Frank Lucas*
93/74 **Good Things Don't Last Forever** *Ecstasy, Passion & Pain*
85/91 **Good Time** *Ziggy Marley*
11/61 **Good Time Baby** *Bobby Rydell*
75/66 **Good Time Charlie** *Bobby Bland*
9/72 **Good Time Charlie's Got The Blues** *Danny O'Keefe*
65/68 **Good Time Girl** *Nancy Sinatra*
97/65 **Good Time Music** *Beau Brummels*
67/72 **Good Time Sally** *Rare Earth*
98/64 **Good Time Tonight** *Soul Sisters*
1/79 **Good Times** *Chic*
11/64 **Good Times** *Sam Cooke*
22/02 **Good Times** *Styles*
47/87 **Good Times** *INXS & Jimmy Barnes*
60/94 **Good Times** *Edie Brickell*
64/65 **Good Times** *Jerry Butler*
92/65 **Good Times** *Gene Chandler*
80/69 **Good Times Bad Times** *Led Zeppelin*
41/75 **Good Times, Rock & Roll** *Flash Cadillac & The Continental Kids*
41/79 **Good Times Roll** *Cars*
59/93 **Good Times With Bad Boys** *Boy Krazy*
3/60 **Good Timin'** *Jimmy Jones*
40/79 **Good Timin'** *Beach Boys*
44^S/02 **Good To You** *Kweli*
Good Vibrations
1/66 *Beach Boys*
34/76 *Todd Rundgren*
1/91 **Good Vibrations** *Marky Mark & The Funky Bunch*

GOODBYE:

11/98 **Goodbye** *Spice Girls*
13/69 **Goodbye** *Mary Hopkin*
17/86 **Goodbye** *Night Ranger*
58/01 **Goodbye** *Jagged Edge*
85/92 **Goodbye** *Tevin Campbell* (also see: Gudbuy / Kiss Off)
88/72 **Goodbye Again** *John Denver* (also see: Theme From)
8/59 **Goodbye Baby** *Jack Scott*
33/64 **Goodbye Baby (Baby Goodbye)** *Solomon Burke*
53/68 **Goodbye Baby (I Don't Want To See You Cry)** *Tommy Boyce & Bobby Hart*
90/59 **Goodbye Charlie** *Patti Page*
80/69 **Goodbye Columbus** *Association*
3/61 **Goodbye Cruel World** *James Darren*
100/62 **Goodbye Dad** *Castle Sisters*
19/00 **Goodbye Earl** *Dixie Chicks*
15/78 **Goodbye Girl** *David Gates*
43/79 **Goodbye, I Love You** *Firefall*
33/86 **Goodbye Is Forever** *Arcadia*
11/59 **Goodbye Jimmy, Goodbye** *Kathy Linden*
97/77 **Goodbye My Friend** *Engelbert Humperdinck*
31/68 **Goodbye My Love** *James Brown*
52/65 **Goodbye My Lover Goodbye** *Searchers*
73^S/94 **Goodbye Says It All** *BlackHawk*
15/79 **Goodbye Stranger** *Supertramp*
7/72 **Goodbye To Love** *Carpenters*
27/98 **Goodbye To My Homies** *Master P*
Goodbye To Rome ..see: Arrivederci, Roma
21/02 **Goodbye To You** *Michelle Branch*
65/82 **Goodbye To You** *Scandal*
2/73 **Goodbye Yellow Brick Road** *Elton John*
21/65 **Goodnight** *Roy Orbison*
51/64 **Good Night Baby** *Butterflys*
Goodnight Irene
75/59 *Billy Williams*
79/62 *Jerry Reed*
Goodnight My Love
32/57 *McGuire Sisters*
64/59 *Ray Peterson*
32/63 *Fleetwoods*
91/66 *Ben E. King*
27/69 *Paul Anka*
51/67 **Goodnight My Love** *Happenings*
70/80 **Goodnight My Love** *Mike Pinera*
56/83 **Goodnight Saigon** *Billy Joel*
30^C/55 **Goodnight, Sweet Dreams** *Gordon Jenkins*
5/79 **Goodnight Tonight** *Wings*
20/57 **Goody Goody** *Frankie Lymon*
53/94 **Goody Goody** *Lisette Melendez*
37/68 **Goody Goody Gumdrops** *1910 Fruitgum Co.*
12/83 **Goody Two Shoes** *Adam Ant*
56/76 **Goofus** *Carpenters*
10/85 **Goonies 'R' Good Enough** *Cyndi Lauper*
8/03 **Gossip Folks** *Missy Elliott*

GOT:

78/57 **Got A Date With An Angel** *Billy Williams*
24/60 **Got A Girl** *Four Preps*
10/84 **Got A Hold On Me** *Christine McVie*
40/91 **Got A Love For You** *Jomanda*
Got A Match?
39/58 *Daddy-O's*
57/58 *Frank Gallup*
86/88 **Got A New Love** *Good Question*
99/00 **Got Beef** *Eastsidaz*
88/00 **Got It All** *Eve & Jadakiss*

69/89 **Got It Made** *Crosby, Stills, Nash & Young*
20/94 **Got Me Waiting** *Heavy D & The Boyz*
70^A/91 **Got My Eye On You** *Pajama Party*
1/88 **Got My Mind Set On You** *George Harrison*
51/66 **Got My Mojo Working** *Jimmy Smith*
54/59 **Got The Feeling** *Fabian*
36^A/97 **Got 'Til It's Gone** *Janet Jackson*
Got To ..also see: Gotta
12/79 **Got To Be Real** *Cheryl Lynn*
Got To Be There
4/71 *Michael Jackson*
67/83 *Chaka Khan*
80/70 **Got To Believe In Love** *Robin McNamara*
48/90 **Got To Get** *Leila K with Rob 'n' Raz*
40/00 **Got To Get It** *Sisqó*
Got To Get You Into My Life
62/75 *Blood, Sweat & Tears*
7/76 *Beatles*
9/78 *Earth, Wind & Fire*
22/65 **Got To Get You Off My Mind** *Solomon Burke*
43/79 **Got To Give In To Love** *Bonnie Boyer*
1/77 **Got To Give It Up** *Marvin Gaye*
44/78 **Got To Have Loving** *Don Ray*
93/67 **Got To Have You Back** *Isley Brothers*
82/90 **Got To Have Your Love** *Mantronix (Feat. Wondress)*
64/80 **Got To Love Somebody** *Sister Sledge*
76/81 **Got To Rock On** *Kansas*
62/70 **Got To See If I Can't Get Mommy (To Come Back Home)** *Jerry Butler*
66/90 **Got To Tell Me Something** *Ana*
87/02 **Got Ur Self A...** *Nas*
56/68 **Got What You Need** *Fantastic Johnny C*
94/63 **Got You On My Mind** *Cookie & His Cupcakes*
33/99 **Got Your Money** *Ol' Dirty Bastard*
9/97 **Gotham City** *R. Kelly*
34/02 **Gots Ta Be** *B2K*

GOTTA:

23/98 **Gotta Be** *Jagged Edge*
90/98 **Gotta Be...Movin' On Up** *Prince Be*
53/76 **Gotta Be The One** *Maxine Nightingale*
68/73 **Gotta Find A Way** *Moments*
58^A/95 **Gotta Get Away** *Offspring*
45/70 **Gotta Get Back To You** *Tommy James*
96/93 **Gotta Get Mine** *MC Breed*
10/02 **Gotta Get Thru This** *Daniel Bedingfield*
91/69 **Gotta Get To Know You** *Bobby Bland*
77/57 **Gotta Get To Your House** *David Seville*
83/85 **Gotta Get You Home Tonight** *Eugene Wilde*
80/84 **Gotta Give A Little Love (Ten Years After)** *Timmy Thomas*
52^S/01 **Gotta Have It** *Chocolate Bandit*
47/80 **Gotta Have More Love** *Climax Blues Band*
63/58 **Gotta Have Rain** *Eydie Gorme*
92/91 **Gotta Have You** *Stevie Wonder*
77/65 **Gotta Have Your Love** *Sapphires*
21/70 **Gotta Hold On To This Feeling** *Jr. Walker*
74^A/93 **Gotta Know (Your Name)** *Malaika*
74/63 **Gotta Lotta Love** *Steve Alaimo*
26/99 **Gotta Man** *Eve*
82/59 **Gotta New Girl** *Bobby Day*
67/71 **Gotta See Jane** *R. Dean Taylor*
24/79 **Gotta Serve Somebody** *Bob Dylan*
4/00 **Gotta Tell You** *Samantha Mumba*
Gotta Travel On
4/59 *Billy Grammer*
64/63 *Timi Yuro*
81/87 **Graceland** *Paul Simon*
Graduation Day
16/56 *Rover Boys*
17/56 *Four Freshmen*
88/63 *Bobby Pickett*
59/67 *Arbors*
(also see: Fly Away From Here)
Graduation (Friends Forever)
38/00 *Vitamin C*
69^S/00 *Class 2000*
34/61 **(Graduation Song...) Pomp And Circumstance** *Adrian Kimberly*
39/59 **Graduation's Here** *Fleetwoods*
64/61 **Granada** *Frank Sinatra*
90/93 **Grand Tour** *Aaron Neville*
95/75 **Granddaddy** *New Birth*
Grandma Got Run Over By A Reindeer
1^X/83 *Elmo & Patsy*
1^X/84 *Elmo & Patsy*
87/97 *Elmo & Patsy*
42/71 **Grandma's Hands** *Bill Withers*
72/77 **Grandmother's Song** *Steve Martin*
49/95 **Grapevyne** *Brownstone*
17/63 **Grass Is Greener** *Brenda Lee*
95/76 **Grasshopper** *Spin*
70^S/01 **Gravel Pit** *Wu-Tang Clan*
93/86 **Gravity** *James Brown*
9/62 **Gravy (For My Mashed Potatoes)** *Dee Dee Sharp*
64/63 **Gravy Waltz** *Steve Allen*
Grazing In The Grass
1/68 *Hugh Masekela*
3/69 *Friends Of Distinction*
1/78 **Grease** *Frankie Valli*
25^A/96 **Grease Megamix** *John Travolta & Olivia Newton-John*
47/78 **Greased Lightnin'** *John Travolta*
98/68 **Greasy Heart** *Jefferson Airplane*
20/66 **Great Airplane Strike** *Paul Revere & The Raiders*
Great Balls Of Fire
2/58 *Jerry Lee Lewis*
85/69 *Tiny Tim*
57/00 **Great Beyond** *R.E.M.*
59/89 **Great Commandment** *Camouflage*
42/86 **Great Gosh A'Mighty! (It's A Matter Of Time)** *Little Richard*
Great Imposter ..see: (He's) The / Theme From The
1/56 **Great Pretender** *Platters*
Greatest American Hero ..see: Theme From
81/84 **Greatest Gift Of All** *Kenny Rogers & Dolly Parton*
34/62 **Greatest Hurt** *Jackie Wilson*
67/69 **Greatest Love** *Dorsey Burnette*
Greatest Love Of All
24/77 *George Benson*
1/86 *Whitney Houston*
63/99 **Greatest Romance Ever Sold** *Prince*
41^A/97 **Greedy Fly** *Bush*

GREEN:

Green Berets ..see: Ballad Of
44/58 **Green Chritma** *Stan Freberg*
1/56 **Green Door** *Jim Lowe*
3/70 **Green-Eyed Lady** *Sugarloaf*
Green Fields ..see: Greenfields
8/66 **Green Grass** *Gary Lewis*
100/61 **Green Grass Of Texas** *Texans*
43/71 **Green Grass Starts To Grow** *Dionne Warwick*
14/63 **Green, Green** *New Christy Minstrels*
11/67 **Green, Green Grass Of Home** *Tom Jones*
Green Leaves Of Summer
65/60 *Brothers Four*
87/62 *Kenny Ball*
39/68 **Green Light** *American Breed*
44/58 **Green Mosquito** *Tune Rockers*
3/62 **Green Onions** *Booker T. & The MG's*
2/69 **Green River** *Creedence Clearwater Revival*
1/68 **Green Tambourine** *Lemon Pipers*
21/63 **Greenback Dollar** *Kingston Trio*
Greenfields
2/60 *Brothers Four*
92/69 *Vogues*
Greensleeves
41/57 *Beverly Sisters*
90/69 *Mason Williams*
(also see: Stay Away)
85/70 **Greenwood Mississippi** *Little Richard*
Greetings (This is Uncle Sam)
89/61 *Valadiers*
100/66 *Monitors*
81/66 **Grim Reaper Of Love** *Turtles*
30/02 **Grindin'** *Clipse*
49^S/01 **Grippin Grain** *Young Millionaires*
73/69 **Grits Ain't Groceries (All Around The World)** *Little Milton*
52/67 **Grizzly Bear** *Youngbloods*
4/90 **Groove Is In The Heart** *Deee-Lite*
7/78 **Groove Line** *Heatwave*
Groove Me
6/71 *King Floyd*
54/79 *Fern Kinney*
17/94 **Groove Thang** *Zhané*
78/69 **Grooviest Girl In The World** *Fun & Games*
Groovin'
1/67 *Young Rascals*
21/67 *Booker T. & The M.G.'s*
90/91 **Groovin'** *UB40*
63/92 **Groovin' In The Midnight** *Maxi Priest*
82/70 **Groovin' (Out On Life)** *Newbeats*
89/70 **Groovin' With Mr. Bloe** *Cool Heat*
55/63 **Groovy Baby** *Billy Abbott*
30/69 **Groovy Grubworm** *Harlow Wilcox*
Groovy Kind Of Love
2/66 *Mindbenders*
1/88 *Phil Collins*
64/76 **Groovy People** *Lou Rawls*
12/70 **Groovy Situation** *Gene Chandler*
74/67 **Groovy Summertime** *Love Generation*
70/60 **Groovy Tonight** *Bobby Rydell*
41/91 **Groovy Train** *Farm*
97/61 **Ground Hog** *Browns*
28^S/01 **Ground Zero (In Our Hearts You Will Remain)** *Cash & Computa*
70/70 **Grover Henson Feels Forgotten** *Bill Cosby*

99/62 **Grow Closer Together** *Impressions*
14/76 **Grow Some Funk Of Your Own** *Elton John*
52/75 **Growin'** *Loggins & Messina*
67/76 **Growin' Up** *Dan Hill*
62S/91 **Growin' Up In The Hood** *Compton's Most Wanted*
25/01 **Grown Men Don't Cry** *Tim McGraw*
53/58 **Guaglione** *Perez Prado*
Guantanamera
9/66 *Sandpipers*
62A/97 *Wyclef Jean*
69/87 **Guaranteed For Life** *Millions Like Us*
68/73 **Gudbuy T' Jane** *Slade*
69/99 **Guerrilla Radio** *Rage Against The Machine*
93/58 **Guess I've Been Around Too Long** *Carl Smith*
11/58 **Guess Things Happen That Way** *Johnny Cash*
Guess Who
31/59 *Jesse Belvin*
99/69 *Ruby Winters*
62/72 *B.B. King*
79/02 **Guess Who's Back** *Scarface*
3/81 **Guilty** *Barbra Streisand & Barry Gibb*
69/72 **Guilty** *Al Green*
86/96 **Guilty** *Gravity Kills*
91/63 **Guilty** *Jim Reeves*
94/61 **Guilty Of Loving You** *Jerry Fuller*
82/01 **Guilty Until Proven Innocent** *Jay-Z*
5/59 **Guitar Boogie Shuffle** *Virtues*
96/62 **Guitar Boogie Shuffle Twist** *Virtues*
11/72 **Guitar Man** *Bread*
Guitar Man
43/68 *Elvis Presley*
28/81 *Elvis Presley*
(also see: Dance With The)
10/55 **Gum Drop** *Crew-Cuts*
71S/96 **Gump** *"Weird Al" Yankovic*
84/83 **Guns For Hire** *AC/DC*
70/72 **Guns, Guns, Guns** *Guess Who*
74/61 **Guns Of Navarone** *Joe Reisman*
72/96 **Guys Do It All The Time** *Mindy McCready*
12/82 **Gypsy** *Fleetwood Mac*
24/63 **Gypsy Cried** *Lou Christie*
8/73 **Gypsy Man** *War*
62/71 **Gypsy Queen** *Gypsy*
51/89 **Gypsy Road** *Cinderella*
42/61 **Gypsy Rover** *Highwaymen*
89/80 **Gypsy Spirit** *Pendulum*
Gypsy Woman
20/61 *Impressions*
3/70 *Brian Hyland*
62/63 **Gypsy Woman** *Rick Nelson*
8/91 **Gypsy Woman (She's Homeless)** *Crystal Waters*
1/71 **Gypsys, Tramps & Thieves** *Chér*

H

68/99 **"Ha"** *Juvenile*
51/77 **Ha Cha Cha (Funktion)** *Brass Construction*
91/57 **Ha! Ha! Ha! (Chella Lla!)** *Kay Armen*
45/67 **Ha Ha Said The Clown** *Yardbirds*
48/84 **Had A Dream (Sleeping With The Enemy)** *Roger Hodgson*
69A/96 **Hail, Hail** *Pearl Jam*
71/77 **Hail! Hail! Rock And Roll!** *Starland Vocal Band*
97/62 **Hail To The Conquering Hero** *James Darren*
2/69 **Hair** *Cowsills*
22/66 **Hair On My Chinny Chin Chin** *Sam The Sham & The Pharoahs*
14/54 **Hajji Baba (Persian Lament)** *Nat "King" Cole*
87/73 **Half A Million Miles From Home** *Albert Hammond*
1/73 **Half-Breed** *Chér*
66/59 **Half-Breed** *Marvin Rainwater*
16/02 **halfcrazy** *Musiq*
12/63 **Half Heaven - Half Heartache** *Gene Pitney*
72/80 **Half Moon Silver** *Hotel*
15/79 **Half The Way** *Crystal Gayle*
Halfway To Paradise
39/61 *Tony Orlando*
23/68 *Bobby Vinton*
75/89 **Halleluiah Man** *Love & Money*
33/71 **Hallelujah** *Sweathog*
28/73 **Hallelujah Day** *Jackson 5*
77/59 **Hallelujah, I Love Him So** *Peggy Lee*
92/69 **Hallways Of My Mind** *Dells*
41S/00 **Hampsterdance Song** *Hampton The Hampster*
89/70 **Hand Clapping Song** *Meters*
15A/95 **Hand In My Pocket** *Alanis Morissette*
92/64 **Hand It Over** *Chuck Jackson*
Hand Jive ..see: Willie And The Hand Jive
17/70 **Hand Me Down World** *Guess Who*
72S/92 **Hand On The Pump** *Cypress Hill*
19/83 **Hand To Hold On To** *John Cougar*
Handbags And Gladrags
84/71 *Chase*
42/72 *Rod Stewart*
45/88 **Handle With Care** *Traveling Wilburys*
6/99 **Hands** *Jewel*
65/86 **Hands Across America** *Voices Of America*
91/84 **Hands Across The Sea** *Modern English*
23/02 **Hands Clean** *Alanis Morissette*
47/99 **Hands Of A Working Man** *Ty Herndon*
85/88 **Hands On The Radio** *Henry Lee Summer*
41/84 **Hands Tied** *Scandal*
2/88 **Hands To Heaven** *Breathe*
Handy Man
2/60 *Jimmy Jones*
22/64 *Del Shannon*
4/77 *James Taylor*
Hang 'Em High
82/68 *Hugo Montenegro*
9/69 *Booker T. & The MG's*
98/96 **Hang 'Em High** *Sadat X*
20/82 **Hang Fire** *Rolling Stones*
23/91 **Hang In Long Enough** *Phil Collins*
83/73 **Hang Loose** *Mandrill*
95/61 **Hang On** *Floyd Cramer*
8/74 **Hang On In There Baby** *Johnny Bristol*
78/83 **Hang On Now** *Kajagoogoo*
Hang On Sloopy
26/64 *Vibrations (My Girl Sloopy)*
1/65 *McCoys*
11/65 *Ramsey Lewis Trio*
50/65 *Little Caesar & The Consuls (My Girl Sloopy)*
93/70 *Lettermen*
94/75 *Rick Derringer*
43/71 **Hang On To Your Life** *Guess Who*
24/58 **Hang Up My Rock And Roll Shoes** *Chuck Willis*
65/74 **Hangin' Around** *Edgar Winter Group*
28/00 **Hanginaround** *Counting Crows*
Hangin' On ..see: (You Keep Me)
43/85 **Hangin' On A String (Contemplating)** *Loose Ends*
1/89 **Hangin' Tough** *New Kids On The Block*
2/01 **Hanging By A Moment** *Lifehouse*
35/86 **Hanging On A Heart Attack** *Device*
38/59 **Hanging Tree** *Marty Robbins*
1/66 **Hanky Panky** *Tommy James*
10/90 **Hanky Panky** *Madonna*
98/93 **Happenin' All Over Again** *Lonnie Gordon*
Happening, The
1/67 *Supremes*
32/67 *Herb Alpert*
30/66 **Happenings Ten Years Time Ago** *Yardbirds*
60/77 **Happier** *Paul Anka*
100/72 **Happier Than The Morning Sun** *B.J. Thomas*
11/72 **Happiest Girl In The Whole U.S.A.** *Donna Fargo*
15/99 **Happily Ever After** *Case*
30/79 **Happiness** *Pointer Sisters*
56/58 **Happiness** *Billy & Lillie*
78/66 **Happiness** *Shades Of Blue*
87/94 **Happiness** *Billy Lawrence*
35/74 **Happiness Is Just Around The Bend** *Main Ingredient*
62/74 **Happiness Is Me And You** *Gilbert O'Sullivan*
Happiness Street
20/56 *Georgia Gibbs*
38/56 *Tony Bennett*

HAPPY:

8/02 **Happy** *Ashanti*
20/87 **Happy** *Surface*
22/72 **Happy** *Rolling Stones*
Happy
50/67 *Sunshine Company*
87/67 *Blades Of Grass*
66/75 **Happy** *Eddie Kendricks*
67/73 **Happy** *Bobby Darin*
68/93 **Happy** *Legacy Of Sound*
73A/98 **Happy** *Sister Hazel*
74/68 **Happy** *Nancy Sinatra*
86/69 **Happy** *Paul Anka*
98/71 **Happy** *Hog Heaven*
98/67 **Happy And Me** *Don & The Goodtimes*
16/78 **Happy Anniversary** *Little River Band*
Happy Anniversary
77/59 *Four Lads*
57/60 *Jane Morgan*
30/61 **Happy Birthday Blues** *Kathy Young*
15X/67 **Happy Birthday, Jesus (A Child's Prayer)** *Patti Page*
6/62 **Happy Birthday, Sweet Sixteen** *Neil Sedaka*

Happy Christmas ..see: Happy Xmas
5/76 **Happy Days** *Pratt & McClain*
58/61 **Happy Days** *Marv Johnson*
86/93 **Happy Days** *Silk*
57/84 **Happy Ending** *Joe Jackson*
57/77 **Happy Girls** *Helen Reddy*
10/60 **Happy-Go-Lucky-Me** *Paul Evans*
82/64 **Happy Guy** *Rick Nelson*
5/57 **Happy, Happy Birthday Baby** *Tune Weavers*
Happy Heart
22/69 *Andy Williams*
62/69 *Petula Clark*
70/82 **Happy Hour** *Deodato*
24/67 **Happy Jack** *Who*
57/62 **Happy Jose (Ching-Ching)** *Jack Ross*
62/82 **Happy Man** *Greg Kihn Band*
94/76 **Happy Man (Pt. I)** *Impact*
58/60 **Happy Muleteer** *Ivo Robic*
19/76 **Happy Music** *Blackbyrds*
1/59 **Happy Organ** *Dave 'Baby' Cortez*
40/75 **Happy People** *Temptations*
79/79 **H.A.P.P.Y. Radio** *Edwin Starr*
34/59 **Happy Reindeer** *Dancer, Prancer & Nervous*
83/60 **Happy Shades Of Blue** *Freddie Cannon*
25/68 **Happy Song (Dum-Dum)** *Otis Redding*
27/66 **Happy Summer Days** *Ronnie Dove*
82/61 **Happy Times (Are Here To Stay)** *Tony Orlando*
Happy Together
1/67 *Turtles*
79/72 *Dawn Feat. Tony Orlando (medley)*
53/80 *Captain & Tennille*
75/87 *Nylons*
95/59 **Happy Vacation** *Jackie Lee*
67/62 **Happy Weekend** *Dave "Baby" Cortez*
6/56 **Happy Whistler** *Don Robertson*
78/97 **Happy With You** *Samantha Cole*
3[X]/71 **Happy Xmas (War Is Over)** *John Lennon & Yoko Ono*
73/58 **Happy Years** *Diamonds*
8/60 **Harbor Lights** *Platters*

HARD:

Hard Day's Night
1/64 *Beatles*
29/66 *Ramsey Lewis Trio*
3/84 **Hard Habit To Break** *Chicago*
1/58 **Hard Headed Woman** *Elvis Presley*
15/99 **Hard Knock Life (Ghetto Anthem)** *Jay-Z*
97/67 **Hard Lovin' Loser** *Judy Collins*
Hard Luck Woman
15/77 *Kiss*
45[A]/94 *Garth Brooks*
30/77 **Hard Rock Cafe** *Carole King*
54[S]/02 **Hard Times** *Pharcyde/Jurassic 5*
58/77 **Hard Times** *Boz Scaggs*
72/81 **Hard Times** *James Taylor*
66/79 **Hard Times For Lovers** *Judy Collins*
69/85 **Hard Times For Lovers** *Jennifer Holliday*
44/57 **Hard Times (The Slop)** *Noble "Thin Man" Watts*
27[S]/02 **Hard To Explain** *Strokes*
4/55 **Hard To Get** *Gisele MacKenzie*
Hard To Handle
51/68 *Otis Redding*
93/68 *Patti Drew*
45/90 *Black Crowes*
26/91 *Black Crowes*
7/81 **Hard To Say** *Dan Fogelberg*
Hard To Say I'm Sorry
1/82 *Chicago*
8/97 *Az Yet*
46/76 **Hard Work** *John Handy*
3/82 **Harden My Heart** *Quarterflash*
50/72 **Harder I Try (The Bluer I Get)** *Free Movement*
84/80 **Hardest Part** *Blondie*
87/00 **Hardest Part Of Breaking Up (Is Getting Back Your Stuff)** *2Ge+ther*
5/99 **Hardest Thing** *98°*
55/60 **Hardhearted Hannah** *Ray Charles*
66/69 **Hare Krishna (medley)** *Happenings*
67/57 **Harem Dance** *Armenian Jazz Sextet* (also see: Shish-Kebab)
Harlem Nocturne
52/60 *Viscounts*
39/66 *Viscounts*
Harlem Shuffle
44/64 *Bob & Earl*
94/66 *Traits*
5/86 *Rolling Stones*
Harlow ..see: Theme From
99/99 **Harmless** *Mulberry Lane*
91/60 **Harmony** *Billy Bland*
Harper Valley P.T.A.
1/68 *Jeannie C. Riley*
67/68 *Ben Colder*
93/68 *King Curtis*
31/73 **Harry Hippie** *Bobby Womack*
17/63 **Harry The Hairy Ape** *Ray Stevens*
13/75 **Harry Truman** *Chicago*
63/76 **Harvest For The World** *Isley Brothers*
78/58 **Harvey's Got A Girl Friend** *Royal Teens*
60/86 **Has Anyone Ever Written Anything For You** *Stevie Nicks*
30/93 **Hat 2 Da Back** *TLC*
Hatari ..see: Theme From
62/99 **Hate Me Now** *Nas*
86/02 **Hate To Say I Told You So** *Hives*
5/61 **Hats Off To Larry** *Del Shannon*
11/64 **Haunted House** *Gene Simmons*
Hava Nagila ..see: Dance Everyone Dance / Flying Circle / Now!
66/97 **Havana** *Kenny G*

HAVE:

31/62 **Have A Good Time** *Sue Thompson*
49/90 **Have A Heart** *Bonnie Raitt*
98/68 **Have A Little Faith** *David Houston*
46/97 **Have A Little Mercy** *4.0*
73/58 **Have Faith** *Gene Allison*
86/98 **Have Fun, Go Mad** *Blair*
76/96 **Have I Never** *Few Good Men*
94/64 **Have I Stayed Away Too Long** *Bobby Bare*
49/66 **Have I Stayed Too Long** *Sonny & Cher*
5/64 **Have I The Right?** *Honeycombs*
Have I Told You Lately
5/93 *Rod Stewart (Live)*
43[A]/93 *Rod Stewart*
29/57 **Have I Told You Lately That I Love You?** *Ricky Nelson*
Have Mercy Baby
66/60 *Bobbettes*
92/65 *James Brown*
1/99 **Have You Ever?** *Brandy*
Have You Ever Been Lonely (Have You Ever Been Blue)
84/60 *Teresa Brewer*
94/64 *Caravelles*
69/87 **Have You Ever Loved Somebody** *Freddie Jackson*
94/66 **Have You Ever Loved Somebody** *Searchers*
12/92 **Have You Ever Needed Someone So Bad** *Def Leppard*
1/95 **Have You Ever Really Loved A Woman?** *Bryan Adams*
8/71 **Have You Ever Seen The Rain** *Creedence Clearwater Revival*
18/63 **Have You Heard** *Duprees*
24/65 **Have You Looked Into Your Heart** *Jerry Vale*
1/75 **Have You Never Been Mellow** *Olivia Newton-John*
Have You Seen Her
3/71 *Chi-Lites*
4/90 *M.C. Hammer*
74/67 **Have You Seen Her Face** *Byrds*
(Have You Seen My Wife Mr. Jones) ..see: New York Mining Disaster 1941
9/66 **Have You Seen Your Mother, Baby, Standing In The Shadow?** *Rolling Stones*
14/74 **Haven't Got Time For The Pain** *Carly Simon*
26/79 **Haven't Stopped Dancing Yet** *Gonzalez*
42/80 **Haven't You Heard** *Patrice Rushen*
42/61 **Havin' Fun** *Dion*
Having A Party
17/62 *Sam Cooke*
56/73 *Ovations (medley)*
55/82 *Luther Vandross (medley)*
36/94 *Rod Stewart (with Ronnie Wood)*
Having My Baby ..see: (You're)
4/69 **Hawaii Five-O** *Ventures*
91/65 **Hawaii Honeymoon** *Waikikis*
33/65 **Hawaii Tattoo** *Waikikis*
89/59 **Hawaiian War Chant** *Billy Vaughn*
11/59 **Hawaiian Wedding Song (Ke Kali Nei Au)** *Andy Williams*
73/55 **Hawk-Eye** *Frankie Laine*
18/96 **Hay** *Crucial Conflict*
9/92 **Hazard** *Richard Marx*
Hazy Shade Of Winter
13/66 *Simon & Garfunkel*
2/88 *Bangles*

HE:

He
4/55 *Al Hibbler*
10/55 *McGuire Sisters*
18/66 *Righteous Brothers*
90/73 **He** *Today's People*
100/67 **He Ain't Give You None** *Freddie Scott*
He Ain't Heavy, He's My Brother
7/70 *Hollies*
20/70 *Neil Diamond*
F/76 *Olivia Newton-John*
100/65 **He Ain't No Angel** *Ad Libs*
He [She] Called Me Baby
77/69 *Ella Washington*
52/71 *Candi Staton*
47/74 *Charlie Rich*
15/00 **He Can't Love U** *Jagged Edge*

33/81 **He Can't Love You** *Michael Stanley Band*
74/82 **He Could Be The One** *Josie Cotton*
He Cried ..see: She Cried
20S/00 **He Did That** *Silkk The Shocker*
75/73 **He Did With Me** *Vickie Lawrence*
30/99 **He Didn't Have To Be** *Brad Paisley*
He Don't Love You (Like I Love You)
7/60 *Jerry Butler*
91/66 *Righteous Brothers*
1/75 *Tony Orlando & Dawn*
92/68 **He Don't Really Love You** *Delfonics*
59/82 **He Got You** *Ronnie Milsap*
90/03 **He Is** *Heather Headley*
(He Knew) ..see: Portrait
34/62 **He Knows I Love Him Too Much** *Paris Sisters*
97/70 **He Loves Me All The Way** *Tammy Wynette*
2/00 **He Loves U Not** *Dream*
71/70 **He Made A Woman Out Of Me** *Bobbie Gentry*
47/64 **He Says The Same Things To Me** *Skeeter Davis*
He [She] Thinks I Still Care
57/62 *Connie Francis*
F/77 *Elvis Presley*
53/65 **He Touched Me** *Barbra Streisand*
66/64 **He Walks Like A Man** *Jody Miller*
89/87 **He Wants My Body** *Starpoint*
64/65 **He Was Really Sayin' Somthin'** *Velvelettes*
2/00 **He Wasn't Man Enough** *Toni Braxton*
He Will Break Your Heart ..see: He Don't Love You
89/66 **He Wore The Green Beret** *Nancy Ames*
83/71 **He'd Rather Have The Rain** *Heaven Bound*
He'll Have To Go (Stay)
2/60 *Jim Reeves*
4/60 *Jeanne Black*
51/64 *Solomon Burke*
25/86 **He'll Never Love You (Like I Do)** *Freddie Jackson*

HE'S:

94/63 **He's A Bad Boy** *Carole King*
36/76 **He's A Friend** *Eddie Kendricks*
55/64 **He's A Good Guy (Yes He Is)** *Marvelettes*
30/81 **He's A Liar** *Bee Gees*
74/65 **He's A Lover** *Mary Wells*
82/83 **He's A Pretender** *High Inergy*
1/62 **He's A Rebel** *Crystals*
98/72 **He's An Indian Cowboy In The Rodeo** *Buffy Sainte-Marie*
71/57 **He's Gone** *Chantels*
70/71 **He's Gonna Step On You Again** *John Kongos*
79/65 **He's Got No Love** *Searchers*
57/63 **He's Got The Power** *Exciters*
He's Got The Whole World (In His Hands)
1/58 *Laurie London*
69/58 *Mahalia Jackson*
43/64 **He's In Town** *Tokens*
7/95 **He's Mine** *MoKenStef*
16/57 **He's Mine** *Platters*
62/63 **He's Mine (I Love Him, I Love Him, I Love Him)** *Alice Wonder Land*
14/61 **(He's My) Dreamboat** *Connie Francis*
79/87 **He's My Girl** *David Hallyday*
63/65 **He's My Guy** *Irma Thomas*
90/66 **(He's) Raining In My Sunshine** *Jay & The Americans*
He's So Fine
1/63 *Chiffons*
53/71 *Jody Miller*
70/78 *Kristy & Jimmy McNichol*
77/78 *Jane Olivor*
73/63 **He's So Heavenly** *Brenda Lee*
3/80 **He's So Shy** *Pointer Sisters*
11/63 **He's Sure The Boy I Love** *Crystals*
30/61 **(He's) The Great Impostor** *Fleetwoods*
9/79 **He's The Greatest Dancer** *Sister Sledge*
77/79 **Head First** *Babys*
14/79 **Head Games** *Foreigner*
3A/96 **Head Over Feet** *Alanis Morissette*
3/85 **Head Over Heels** *Tears For Fears*
11/84 **Head Over Heels** *Go-Go's*
35/97 **Head Over Heels** *Allure*
1/87 **Head To Toe** *Lisa Lisa & Cult Jam*
35/80 **Headed For A Fall** *Firefall*
19/89 **Headed For A Heartbreak** *Winger*
53/86 **Headed For The Future** *Neil Diamond*
84/66 **Headline News** *Edwin Starr*
69/86 **Headlines** *Midnight Star*
27/93 **Heal The World** *Michael Jackson*
13/89 **Healing Hands** *Elton John*
(Hear My Voice) ..see: Oye Mi Canto
94/63 **Hear The Bells** *Tokens*
18/01 **Heard It All Before** *Sunshine Anderson*
14/77 **Heard It In A Love Song** *Marshall Tucker Band*
44/72 **Hearsay** *Soul Children*

HEART:

Heart
6/55 *Eddie Fisher*
13/55 *Four Aces*
Heart
64/63 *Kenny Chandler*
82/63 *Wayne Newton*
73/90 **Heart** *Neneh Cherry*
4/87 **Heart And Soul** *T'Pau*
8/83 **Heart And Soul** *Huey Lewis*
Heart And Soul
57/56 *Johnny Maddox*
18/61 *Cleftones*
25/61 *Jan & Dean*
87/87 **Heart and Soul** *Monkees*
3/82 **Heart Attack** *Olivia Newton-John*
89/67 **Heart Be Still** *Lorraine Ellison*
Heart Breaker ..see: Heartbreaker
59/88 **Heart Don't Fail Me Now** *Holly Knight*
56/84 **Heart Don't Lie** *La Toya Jackson*
9/65 **Heart Full Of Soul** *Yardbirds*
67/56 **Heart Hideaway** *Cathy Carr*
21/80 **Heart Hotels** *Dan Fogelberg*
15/62 **Heart In Hand** *Brenda Lee*
66/81 **Heart In New York** *Art Garfunkel*
75/86 **Heart Is Not So Smart** *El DeBarge*
24/81 **Heart Like A Wheel** *Steve Miller Band*
32/90 **Heart Like A Wheel** *Human League*
1/79 **Heart Of Glass** *Blondie*
1/72 **Heart Of Gold** *Neil Young*
35/88 **Heart Of Mine** *Boz Scaggs*
6/84 **Heart Of Rock & Roll** *Huey Lewis*
12/90 **Heart Of Stone** *Taylor Dayne*
19/65 **Heart Of Stone** *Rolling Stones*
20/90 **Heart Of Stone** *Cher*
21/90 **Heart Of The Matter** *Don Henley*
20/79 **Heart Of The Night** *Poco*
25/83 **Heart Of The Night** *Juice Newton*
Heart On My Sleeve
67/76 *Gallagher & Lyle*
86/76 *Bryan Ferry*
15/83 **Heart To Heart** *Kenny Loggins*
65/79 **Heart To Heart** *Errol Sober*
56/88 **Heart Turns To Stone** *Foreigner*
79/56 **Heart Without A Sweetheart** *Gale Storm*
88/66 **Heart's Desire** *Billy Joe Royal*
76/86 **Heart's On Fire** *John Cafferty*
(also see: Hearts On Fire)
78/87 **Heartache** *Pepsi & Shirlie*
55/86 **Heartache All Over The World** *Elton John*
56/86 **Heartache Away** *Don Johnson*
1/79 **Heartache Tonight** *Eagles*
Heartaches
71/56 *Somethin' Smith & The Redheads*
7/61 *Marcels*
73/62 *Patsy Cline*
60/79 **Heartaches** *BTO*
Heartaches By The Number
1/59 *Guy Mitchell*
35/65 *Johnny Tillotson*
5/86 **Heartbeat** *Don Johnson*
13/90 **Heartbeat** *Seduction*
82/59 **Heartbeat** *Buddy Holly*
3/73 **Heartbeat - It's A Lovebeat** *DeFranco Family*
26/87 **Heartbreak Beat** *Psychedelic Furs*
99/64 **Heartbreak Hill** *Fats Domino*
Heartbreak Hotel
1/56 *Elvis Presley*
79/56 *Stan Freberg*
84/66 *Roger Miller*
72/71 *Frijid Pink*
2/99 **Heartbreak Hotel** *Whitney Houston*
22/81 **Heartbreak Hotel** *Jacksons*
Heartbreak (It's Hurtin' Me)
38/60 *Little Willie John*
48/60 *Jon Thomas*
39/74 **Heartbreak Kid** *Bo Donaldson*
89/75 **Heartbreak Road** *Bill Withers*
44/91 **Heartbreak Station** *Cinderella*
87/62 **Heart Breaker** *Dean Christie*
1/99 **Heartbreaker** *Mariah Carey*
10/83 **Heartbreaker** *Dionne Warwick*
23/80 **Heartbreaker** *Pat Benatar*
37/78 **Heartbreaker** *Dolly Parton*
72/70 **Heartbreaker** *Grand Funk Railroad*
(also see: Doo Doo Doo Doo Doo)
47/72 **Heartbroken Bopper** *Guess Who*
24/78 **Heartless** *Heart*
99/55 **Heartless** *Tommy Leonetti*
5/82 **Heartlight** *Neil Diamond*
92/85 **Heartline** *Robin George*
8/81 **Hearts** *Marty Balin*
58/62 **Hearts** *Jackie Wilson*
90/87 **Hearts Away** *Night Ranger*
28/92 **Hearts Don't Think (They Feel)!** *Natural Selection*
92/95 **Hearts Filthy Lesson** *David Bowie*
75/90 **Hearts In Trouble** *Chicago*
Hearts Of Stone
1/55 *Fontane Sisters*
15/55 *Charms*
20/61 *Bill Black's Combo*
37/73 *Blue Ridge Rangers*
19/81 **Hearts On Fire** *Randy Meisner*
26/87 **Hearts On Fire** *Bryan Adams*

53/89 **Hearts On Fire** *Steve Winwood* (also see Heart's On Fire)
85/96 **Heartspark Dollarsign** *Everclear*
2/85 **Heat Is On** *Glenn Frey*
55/86 **Heat Of Heat** *Patti Austin*
4/82 **Heat Of The Moment** *Asia*
Heat Of The Moment
74/89 *After 7*
19/91 *After 7*
6/87 **Heat Of The Night** *Bryan Adams*
Heat Wave
4/63 *Martha & The Vandellas*
5/75 *Linda Ronstadt*
29/69 **Heather Honey** *Tommy Roe*
6S/02 **Heatseeker** *Young M.C.*

HEAVEN:

Heaven
1/85 *Bryan Adams*
8/02 *DJ Sammy & Yanou*
61S/02 *Eyra Gail*
2/89 **Heaven** *Warrant*
27/98 **Heaven** *Nu Flavor*
39/69 **Heaven** *Rascals*
42/95 **Heaven** *Solo*
52A/96 **Heaven Beside You** *Alice In Chains*
80/94 **Heaven Help** *Lenny Kravitz*
5/89 **Heaven Help Me** *Deon Estus (with George Michael)*
9/70 **Heaven Help Us All** *Stevie Wonder*
58/91 **Heaven In The Back Seat** *Eddie Money*
86/81 **Heaven In Your Arms** *Dan Hartman*
12/86 **Heaven In Your Eyes** *Loverboy*
66/90 **Heaven Is A 4 Letter Word** *Bad English*
1/87 **Heaven Is A Place On Earth** *Belinda Carlisle*
4/79 **Heaven Knows** *Donna Summer with Brooklyn Dreams*
24/69 **Heaven Knows** *Grass Roots*
94/93 **Heaven Knows** *Luther Vandross*
95/89 **Heaven Knows** *When In Rome*
15/76 **Heaven Must Be Missing An Angel** *Tavares*
65/84 **Heaven (Must Be There)** *Eurogliders*
Heaven Must Have Sent You
50/66 *Elgins*
11/79 *Bonnie Pointer*
F/94 **Heaven 'N Hell** *Salt-N-Pepa*
39/56 **Heaven On Earth** *Platters*
89/77 **Heaven On Earth (So Fine)** *Spinners*
6/77 **Heaven On The 7th Floor** *Paul Nicholas*
69/77 **Heaven's Just A Sin Away** *Kendalls*
49/84 **Heaven's On Fire** *Kiss*
27/98 **Heaven's What I Feel** *Gloria Estefan*
43/74 **Heavenly** *Temptations*
40/59 **Heavenly Lover** *Teresa Brewer*
73/99 **Heavy** *Collective Soul*
41/74 **Heavy Fallin' Out** *Stylistics*
47/76 **Heavy Love** *David Ruffin*
27/71 **Heavy Makes You Happy (Sha-Na-Boom Boom)** *Staple Singers*
43/81 **Heavy Metal (Takin' A Ride)** *Don Felder*
33/70 **Heed The Call** *Kenny Rogers & The First Edition*
94/70 **Heighdy-Ho Princess** *Neon Philharmonic*
50/56 **Held For Questioning** *Rusty Draper*
10/74 **Helen Wheels** *Paul McCartney*
72A/97 **Hell** *Squirrel Nut Zippers*
70/76 **Hell Cat** *Bellamy Brothers*
59/79 **Hell On Wheels** *Cher*
13/02 **Hella Good** *No Doubt*

HELLO:

1/84 **Hello** *Lionel Richie*
65A/97 **Hello** *Poe*
6/81 **Hello Again** *Neil Diamond*
20/84 **Hello Again** *Cars*
60/70 **Hello Darlin'** *Conway Twitty*
Hello, Dolly!
1/64 *Louis Armstrong*
79/65 *Bobby Darin*
1/67 **Hello Goodbye** *Beatles*
51S/01 **Hello, Goodbye, Hello** *BSK*
26/63 **Hello Heartache, Goodbye Love** *Little Peggy March*
Hello Hello
26/67 *Sopwith "Camel"*
91/67 *Claudine Longet*
69/79 **Hello, Hello, Hello** *New England*
35/73 **Hello Hurray** *Alice Cooper*
1/68 **Hello, I Love You** *Doors*
Hello It's Me
71/69 *Nazz*
66/70 *Nazz*
5/73 *Todd Rundgren*
97/63 **Hello Jim** *Paul Anka*
71/99 **Hello L.O.V.E.** *John Michael Montgomery*
9/61 **Hello Mary Lou** *Ricky Nelson*
Hello Mudduh, Hello Fadduh! (A Letter From Camp)
2/63 *Allan Sherman*
59/64 *Allan Sherman (1964)*
24/76 **Hello Old Friend** *Eric Clapton*
54/65 **Hello Pretty Girl** *Ronnie Dove*
Hello Stranger
3/63 *Barbara Lewis*
100/73 *Fire & Rain*
15/77 *Yvonne Elliman*
12/61 **Hello Walls** *Faron Young*
23/60 **Hello Young Lovers** *Paul Anka*
53/92 **Helluva** *Brotherhood Creed*
1/65 **Help!** *Beatles*
14/77 **Help Is On Its Way** *Little River Band*
7/74 **Help Me** *Joni Mitchell*
50/80 **Help Me!** *Marcy Levy & Robin Gibb*
92/70 **Help Me Find A Way (To Say I Love You)** *Little Anthony & The Imperials*
100/66 **Help Me (Get Myself Back Together Again)** *Spellbinders*
Help Me Girl
29/66 *Animals*
37/66 *Outsiders*
Help Me Make It Through The Night
8/71 *Sammi Smith*
69/71 *Joe Simon*
91/71 *O.C. Smith*
33/72 *Gladys Knight*
64/75 **Help Me Make It (To My Rockin' Chair)** *B.J. Thomas*
Help Me, Rhonda
1/65 *Beach Boys*
22/75 *Johnny Rivers*
80/02 **Help Me Understand** *Trace Adkins*
Help The Poor
98/64 *B.B. King*
90/71 *B.B. King*
70/76 **Help Wanted** *Hudson Brothers*
Help Yourself
35/68 *Tom Jones*
63/74 *Undisputed Truth*
94/68 **Help Yourself (To All Of My Lovin')** *James & Bobby Purify*
56/58 **Helpless** *Platters*
56/66 **Helpless** *Kim Weston*
30/01 **Hemorrhage (In My Hands)** *Fuel*
47/58 **Henrietta** *Jimmy Dee*
6/62 **Her Royal Majesty** *James Darren*
11/81 **Her Town Too** *James Taylor & J.D. Souther*

HERE:

6/90 **Here And Now** *Luther Vandross*
56/95 **Here & Now** *Letters To Cleo*
10S/02 **Here And Now (Full Circle)** *Terry Steele*
88/68 **Here Come Da Judge** *Buena Vistas*
54/68 **Here Come The Judge** *Magistrates*
8/68 **Here Comes The Judge** *Shorty Long*
19/68 **Here Comes The Judge** *Pigmeat Markham*
93/93 **Here Come The Lords** *Lords Of The Underground*
23/77 **Here Come Those Tears Again** *Jackson Browne*
91/67 **Here Comes Heaven** *Eddy Arnold*
13/67 **Here Comes My Baby** *Tremeloes*
59/80 **Here Comes My Girl** *Tom Petty*
Here Comes Summer
14/59 *Jerry Keller*
49/77 *Wildfire*
89/62 **Here Comes That Feelin'** *Brenda Lee*
15/71 **Here Comes That Rainy Day Feeling Again** *Fortunes*
93/63 **Here Comes The Boy** *Tracey Dey*
54/91 **Here Comes The Hammer** *M.C. Hammer*
1/94 **Here Comes The Hotstepper** *Ini Kamoze*
24/65 **Here Comes The Night** *Them*
44/78 **Here Comes The Night** *Nick Gilder*
44/79 **Here Comes The Night** *Beach Boys*
81/61 **Here Comes The Night** *Ben E. King*
4/84 **Here Comes The Rain Again** *Eurythmics*
74/68 **Here Comes The Rain, Baby** *Eddy Arnold*
16/71 **Here Comes The Sun** *Richie Havens*
65/65 **Here I Am** *Dionne Warwick*
44/68 **Here I Am Baby** *Marvelettes*
Here I Am (Come And Take Me)
10/73 *Al Green*
7/91 *UB40*
5/81 **Here I Am (Just When I Thought I Was Over You)** *Air Supply*
60S/99 **Here I Go** *Infamous Syndicate*
1/87 **Here I Go Again** *Whitesnake*
37/69 **Here I Go Again** *Miracles*
76/79 **Here I Go (Fallin' In Love Again)** *Frannie Golde*
Here I Stand
80/59 *Wade Flemons*
51/63 *Rip Chords*
59A/97 **Here In My Heart** *Chicago*
86/61 **Here In My Heart** *Al Martino*
47A/96 **Here In Your Bedroom** *Goldfinger*

18/02 **Here Is Gone** *Goo Goo Dolls*
80/77 **Here Is Where Your Love Belongs** *Sons Of Champlin*
71/92 **Here It Comes** *MC Serch*
27/65 **Here It Comes Again** *Fortunes*
76/84 **Here She Comes** *Bonnie Tyler*
92/64 **Here She Comes** *Tymes*
65/76 **Here, There And Everywhere** *Emmylou Harris*
56/65 **(Here They Come) From All Over The World** *Jan & Dean*
65/82 **Here To Love You** *Doobie Brothers*
72/02 **Here To Stay** *Korn*
6/90 **Here We Are** *Gloria Estefan*
92/98 **Here We Come** *Timbaland*
3/91 **Here We Go** *C + C Music Factory*
72/98 **Here We Go** *Funkmaster Flex*
11/93 **Here We Go Again!** *Portrait*
Here We Go Again
15/67 *Ray Charles*
98/69 *Nancy Sinatra*
76/98 **Here We Go Again** *Aretha Franklin*
20/88 **Here With Me** *REO Speedwagon*
3/78 **Here You Come Again** *Dolly Parton*
89/64 **Here's A Heart** *Diplomats*
97/61 **Here's My Confession** *Wyatt (Earp) McPherson*
82/76 **Here's Some Love** *Tanya Tucker*
30/01 **Here's To The Night** *Eve 6*
76/68 **Here's To You** *Hamilton Camp*
43/97 **Here's Your Sign (Get The Picture)** *Bill Engvall with Travis Tritt*
Hero
1/93 *Mariah Carey*
81/01 *Mariah Carey (medley)*
3/01 **Hero** *Enrique Iglesias*
3/02 **Hero** *Chad Kroeger*
44/93 **Hero** *David Crosby & Phil Collins*
60/97 **Hero Of The Day** *Metallica*
27A/98 **Heroes** *Wallflowers*
54/80 **Heroes** *Commodores*
12/67 **Heroes And Villains** *Beach Boys*

HEY:

Hey! Baby
1/62 *Bruce Channel*
71/69 *José Feliciano*
74/77 *Ringo Starr*
5/02 **Hey Baby** *No Doubt*
18/89 **Hey Baby** *Henry Lee Summer*
72/76 **Hey Baby** *Ted Nugent*
96/76 **Hey Baby** *J.J. Cale*
12/67 **Hey Baby (They're Playing Our Song)** *Buckinghams*
19/72 **Hey Big Brother** *Rare Earth*
23/64 **Hey, Bobba Needle** *Chubby Checker*
92/68 **Hey Boy Take A Chance On Love** *Ruby Andrews*
43/94 **Hey D.J.** *Lighter Shade Of Brown*
69/65 **Hey-Da-Da-Dow** *Dolphins*
7/78 **Hey Deanie** *Shaun Cassidy*
13/91 **Hey Donna** *Rythm Syndicate*
Hey, Girl
10/63 *Freddie Scott*
35/68 *Bobby Vee (medley)*
9/72 *Donny Osmond*
41/64 **Hey Girl Don't Bother Me** *Tams*
61/58 **Hey Girl - Hey Boy** *Oscar McLollie & Jeanette Baker*
35/73 **Hey Girl (I Like Your Style)** *Temptations*
29/64 **Hey Harmonica Man** *Stevie Wonder*
22S/01 **Hey Hey** *Athena Cage*
57/68 **Hey Hey Bunny** *John Fred*

3/57 **Hey! Jealous Lover** *Frank Sinatra*
25/93 **Hey Jealousy** *Gin Blossoms*
32/64 **Hey Jean, Hey Dean** *Dean & Jean*
Hey Joe
31/66 *Leaves*
94/67 *Chér*
59/69 *Wilson Pickett*
Hey Jude
1/68 *Beatles*
23/69 *Wilson Pickett*
36/89 **Hey Ladies** *Beastie Boys*
35/70 **Hey Lawdy Mama** *Steppenwolf*
33/99 **Hey Leonardo (she likes me for me)** *Blessid Union Of Souls*
31/67 **Hey, Leroy, Your Mama's Callin' You** *Jimmy Castor*
20/62 **Hey, Let's Twist** *Joey Dee*
4/64 **Hey Little Cobra** *Rip Chords*
13/63 **Hey Little Girl** *Major Lance*
Hey Little Girl
20/59 *Dee Clark*
92/73 *Foster Sylvers*
29/57 **Hey! Little Girl** *Techniques*
38/62 **Hey! Little Girl** *Del Shannon*
87/59 **Hey Little Lucy! (Don'tcha Put No Lipstick On)** *Conway Twitty*
Hey Little One
48/60 *Dorsey Burnette*
85/64 *J. Frank Wilson*
54/68 *Glen Campbell*
100/63 **Hey Lonely One** *Baby Washington*
52/71 **Hey! Love** *Delfonics*
90/67 **Hey Love** *Stevie Wonder*
3/95 **Hey Lover** *LL Cool J*
81/63 **Hey Lover** *Debbie Dovale*
58/02 **Hey Luv (Anything)** *Mobb Deep*
3/02 **Hey Ma** *Cam'ron*
90/88 **Hey Mambo** *Barry Manilow/Kid Creole*
76/95 **Hey Man Nice Shot** *Filter*
12/55 **Hey, Mr. Banjo** *Sunnysiders*
6/93 **Hey Mr. D.J.** *Zhané*
77/64 **Hey, Mr. Sax Man** *Boots Randolph*
24/70 **Hey, Mister Sun** *Bobby Sherman*
10/81 **Hey Nineteen** *Steely Dan*
76/64 **Hey Now** *Lesley Gore*
47/98 **Hey Now Now** *Swirl 360*
76/00 **Hey Papi** *Jay-Z*
1/63 **Hey Paula** *Paul & Paula*
49/58 **Hey, Schoolgirl** *Tom & Jerry*
59S/02 **Hey Sexy Lady** *Shaggy w/ Sean Paul*
48/76 **Hey Shirley (This Is Squirrely)** *Shirley & Squirrely*
76/79 **Hey, St. Peter** *Flash & The Pan*
78/91 **Hey Stoopid** *Alice Cooper*
1/54 **Hey There** *Rosemary Clooney*
67/75 **Hey There Little Firefly** *Firefly*
Hey There Lonely Girl (Boy)
27/63 *Ruby & The Romantics*
2/70 *Eddie Holman*
31/80 *Robert John*
F/71 **Hey Tonight** *Creedence Clearwater Revival*
16/68 **Hey, Western Union Man** *Jerry Butler*
1/75 **(Hey Won't You Play) Another Somebody Done Somebody Wrong Song** *B.J. Thomas*
21/75 **Hey You** *Bachman-Turner Overdrive*
43/73 **Hey You! Get Off My Mountain** *Dramatics*
76/66 **Hey You! Little Boo-Ga-Loo** *Chubby Checker*
87/72 **Hey, You Love** *Mouth & MacNeal*

14/70 **Hi-De-Ho** *Blood, Sweat & Tears*
98/63 **Hi Diddle Diddle** *Inez Foxx*
Hi-Heel Sneakers
11/64 *Tommy Tucker*
91/64 *Jerry Lee Lewis*
59/65 *Stevie Wonder*
70/66 *Ramsey Lewis Trio*
25/68 *José Feliciano*
(also see: Slip-In Mules)
96/66 **Hi Hi Hazel** *Gary & The Hornets*
10/73 **Hi, Hi, Hi** *Wings*
Hi-Lili, Hi-Lo
78/56 *Dick Hyman*
85/56 *Roger Williams*
64/63 *Richard Chamberlain*
63/64 **Hickory, Dick And Doc** *Bobby Vee*
50S/01 **Hidden Place** *Björk*
Hide & Go Seek
33/62 *Bunker Hill*
58/66 *Sheep*
73/90 **Hide And Seek** *Pajama Party*
29/61 **Hide Away** *Freddy King*
21/58 **Hideaway** *Four Esquires*
95/76 **Hideaway** *John Sebastian*
20/62 **Hide 'Nor Hair** *Ray Charles*
68S/01 **Hide U** *Suzanne Palmer*
66/89 **Hide Your Heart** *Kiss*

HIGH:

42/92 **High** *Cure*
78/96 **High & Dry** *Radiohead*
85/84 **High Energy** *Evelyn Thomas*
3/91 **High Enough** *Damn Yankees*
High-Heel ..see: Hi-Heel
30/59 **High Hopes** *Frank Sinatra*
77/64 **High On A Hill** *Scott English*
44/84 **High On Emotion** *Chris DeBurgh*
94/66 **High On Love** *Knickerbockers*
8/85 **High On You** *Survivor*
70/80 **High On Your Love** *Debbie Jacobs*
72/79 **High On Your Love Suite** *Rick James*
76/76 **High Out Of Time** *Carole King*
21/58 **High School Confidential** *Jerry Lee Lewis*
17/77 **High School Dance** *Sylvers*
F/57 **High School Dance** *Larry Williams*
91/85 **High School Nights** *Dave Edmunds*
80/57 **High School Romance** *George Hamilton IV*
28/59 **High School U.S.A. (Area)** *Tommy Facenda*
37/58 **High Sign** *Diamonds*
48/83 **High Time** *Styx*
22/71 **High Time We Went** *Joe Cocker*
7/00 **Higher** *Creed*
Higher & Higher ..see: (Your Love Keeps Lifting Me)
4/73 **Higher Ground** *Stevie Wonder*
45/94 **Higher Ground** *UB40*
1/86 **Higher Love** *Steve Winwood*
37/74 **Higher Plane** *Kool & The Gang*
47/91 **Higher Than Hope** *Daryl Braithwaite*
68/76 **Highfly** *John Miles*
26/79 **Highway Song** *Blackfoot*
47/79 **Highway To Hell** *AC/DC*
57/91 **Highwire** *Rolling Stones*
14/75 **Hijack** *Herbie Mann*
64/71 **Hijackin' Love** *Johnnie Taylor*
Hill Street Blues ..see: Theme From
76/71 **Hill Where The Lord Hides** *Chuck Mangione*
62/99 **Hillbilly Shoes** *Montgomery Gentry*

6/80 **Him** *Rupert Holmes*
5/67 **Him Or Me - What's It Gonna Be?** *Paul Revere & The Raiders*
31/68 **Hip City** *Jr. Walker*
66/97 **Hip Hop Drunkies** *Alkaholiks*
8/93 **Hip Hop Hooray** *Naughty By Nature*
61S/91 **Hip Hop Junkies** *Nice & Smooth*
68/94 **Hip Hop Ride** *Da Youngsta's*
81/97 **Hip-Hopera** *Bounty Killer*
37/67 **Hip Hug-Her** *Booker T. & The M.G.'s*
3/86 **Hip To Be Square** *Huey Lewis*
Hippy Hippy Shake
24/64 *Swinging Blue Jeans*
45/88 *Georgia Satellites*
14/90 **Hippychick** *Soho*
89/64 **His Kiss** *Betty Harris*
His Latest Flame ..see: (Marie's the Name)
History Repeats Itself
39/66 *Buddy Starcher*
89/66 *Cab Calloway*
90/94 **Hit By Love** *Ce Ce Peniston*
2/01 **Hit 'Em Up Style (Oops!)** *Blu Cantrell*
3/96 **Hit Me Off** *New Edition*
9/80 **Hit Me With Your Best Shot** *Pat Benatar*
45/62 **Hit Record** *Brook Benton* *(also see: Overnight Sensation)*
86/02 **Hit The Freeway** *Toni Braxton*
Hit The Road Jack
1/61 *Ray Charles*
40/76 *Stampeders*
30/63 **Hitch Hike** *Marvin Gaye*
34/68 **Hitch It To The Horse** *Fantastic Johnny C*
77/68 **Hitchcock Railway** *José Feliciano*
(Hitchhiker, The) ..see: Popeye
5/70 **Hitchin' A Ride** *Vanity Fare*
59A/97 **Hitchin' A Ride** *Green Day*
58/60 **Hither And Thither And Yon** *Brook Benton*
60/92 **Hitman, The** *AB Logic*
69/63 **Hobo Flats** *Jimmy Smith*
9/73 **Hocus Pocus** *Focus*

HOLD:

Hold Back The Night
35/76 *Trammps*
58/77 *Graham Parker*
78/61 **Hold Back The Tears** *Delacardos*
84/57 **Hold 'Em Joe** *Harry Belafonte*
14/72 **Hold Her Tight** *Osmonds*
92/58 **Hold It** *Bill Doggett*
4/82 **Hold Me** *Fleetwood Mac*
35/99 **Hold Me** *Brian McKnight*
46/84 **Hold Me** *Teddy Pendergrass (with Whitney Houston)*
62/85 **Hold Me** *Menudo*
68/87 **Hold Me** *Sheila E.*
Hold Me
70/64 *P.J. Proby*
88/69 *Baskerville Hounds*
82/85 **Hold Me** *Laura Branigan*
99/87 **Hold Me** *Colin James Hay*
3/84 **Hold Me Now** *Thompson Twins*
8/65 **Hold Me, Thrill Me, Kiss Me** *Mel Carter*
16/95 **Hold Me, Thrill Me, Kiss Me, Kill Me** *U2*
5/68 **Hold Me Tight** *Johnny Nash*
40/83 **Hold Me 'Til The Mornin' Comes** *Paul Anka*
46/78 **Hold Me, Touch Me** *Paul Stanley*
2/54 **Hold My Hand** *Don Cornell*
10/95 **Hold My Hand** *Hootie & The Blowfish*
1/90 **Hold On** *Wilson Phillips*
2/90 **Hold On** *En Vogue*
15/82 **Hold On** *Santana*
16/95 **Hold On** *Jamie Walters*
18/79 **Hold On** *Ian Gomm*
38/79 **Hold On** *Triumph*
40/80 **Hold On** *Kansas*
47/76 **Hold On** *Sons Of Champlin*
51/70 **Hold On** *Rascals*
56/81 **Hold On** *Badfinger*
61/77 **Hold On** *Wild Cherry*
68/68 **Hold On** *Radiants*
73/89 **Hold On** *Donny Osmond*
Hold On! I'm A Comin'
21/66 *Sam & Dave*
91/67 *Chuck Jackson & Maxine Brown*
27/81 **Hold On Loosely** *.38 Special*
12/92 **Hold On My Heart** *Genesis*
10/81 **Hold On Tight** *ELO*
79/92 **Hold On (Tighter To Love)** *Clubland*
33/99 **Hold On To Me** *John Michael Montgomery*
10/80 **Hold On To My Love** *Jimmy Ruffin*
78/78 **Hold On To The Night** *Starz*
80/79 **Hold On To The Night** *Hotel*
1/88 **Hold On To The Nights** *Richard Marx*
5/79 **Hold The Line** *Toto*
67/77 **Hold Tight** *Vicki Sue Robinson*
89/81 **Hold Tight** *Change*
5/65 **Hold What You've Got** *Joe Tex*
3/91 **Hold You Tight** *Tara Kemp*
5/72 **Hold Your Head Up** *Argent*
37/82 **Holdin' On** *Tané Cain*
11/89 **Holding On** *Steve Winwood*
75/80 **Holdin' On For Dear Love** *Lobo*
17/75 **Holdin' On To Yesterday** *Ambrosia*
1/86 **Holding Back The Years** *Simply Red*
93/90 **Holding My Heart** *Bang*
49/78 **Holding On (When Love Is Gone)** *L.T.D.*
34/84 **Holding Out For A Hero** *Bonnie Tyler*
4/91 **Hole Hearted** *Extreme*
54/88 **Hole In My Heart** *Cyndi Lauper*
51/97 **Hole In My Soul** *Aerosmith*
43/65 **Hole In The Wall** *Packers*
16/67 **Holiday** *Bee Gees*
16/84 **Holiday** *Madonna*
29/87 **Holiday** *Other Ones*
66/87 **Holiday** *Kool & The Gang*
87/80 **Holiday** *Nazareth*
94/67 **Holiday For Clowns** *Brian Hyland*
84/57 **Holiday For Trombones** *David Rose*
19X/63 **Holiday Hootenanny** *Paul & Paula*
82/83 **Holiday Road** *Lindsey Buckingham*
65S/02 **Holla At A Playa** *Jim Crow*
35/99 **Holla Holla** *Ja Rule*
Holly Holy
6/69 *Neil Diamond*
75/71 *Jr. Walker*
13X/64 **Holly Jolly Christmas** *Burl Ives*
32/77 **Hollywood** *Rufus, Feat. Chaka Khan*
42/61 **Hollywood** *Connie Francis*
49/78 **Hollywood** *Boz Scaggs*
70/82 **Hollywood** *Shooting Star*
55/75 **Hollywood Hot** *Eleventh Hour*
12/78 **Hollywood Nights** *Bob Seger*
6/74 **Hollywood Swinging** *Kool & The Gang*
23/66 **Holy Cow** *Lee Dorsey*
Holy Holy ..see: Wholy Holy
67/70 **Holy Man** *Diane Kolby*
58A/97 **Holy River** *Prince*
89/90 **Holy Water** *Bad Company*
71/85 **Holyanna** *Toto*
34/67 **Homburg** *Procol Harum*
88/97 **Home** *Depeche Mode*
65/98 **Home Alone** *R. Kelly*
28/79 **Home And Dry** *Gerry Rafferty*
70/78 **Home Bound** *Ted Nugent*
42/69 **Home Cookin** *Jr. Walker*
88/57 **Home Of The Blues** *Johnny Cash*
Home Of The Brave
25/65 *Jody Miller*
77/65 *Bonnie & The Treasures*
Home Sweet Home
89/85 *Mötley Crüe*
37/92 *Mötley Crüe ('91)*
45/99 **Home To You** *John Michael Montgomery*
97/69 **Home To You** *Earth Opera*
71/76 **Home Tonight** *Aerosmith*
41/76 **Homecoming, The** *Hagood Hardy*
54/74 **Homely Girl** *Chi-Lites*
5/66 **Homeward Bound** *Simon & Garfunkel*
57/93 **Homies** *Lighter Shade Of Brown*
28/60 **Honest I Do** *Innocents*
32/57 **Honest I Do** *Jimmy Reed*
23/88 **Honestly** *Stryper*
65/59 **Honestly And Truly** *Tommy Edwards*
24/79 **Honesty** *Billy Joel*
Honey
1/68 *Bobby Goldsboro*
44/69 *O.C. Smith*
1/97 **Honey** *Mariah Carey*
6/55 **Honey-Babe** *Art Mooney*
59/76 **Honey Child** *Bad Company*
11/67 **Honey Chile** *Martha & The Vandellas*
19/70 **Honey Come Back** *Glen Campbell*
71S/93 **Honey Dip** *Portrait*
54S/02 **Honey Do** *Mike Walker*
61/78 **Honey Don't Leave L.A.** *James Taylor*
Honey, Honey
27/74 *Abba*
68/74 *Sweet Dreams*
59/80 **Honey, Honey** *David Hudson*
53/60 **Honey Hush** *Joe Turner*
65/76 **Honey I** *George McCrae*
39/92 **Honey Love** *R. Kelly*
90/60 **Honey Love** *Narvel Felts*
44/74 **Honey Please, Can't Ya See** *Barry White*
F/57 **Honey Rock** *Barney Kessel*
98/75 **Honey Trippin'** *Mystic Moods*
1/57 **Honeycomb** *Jimmie Rodgers*
19/87 **Honeythief, The** *Hipsway*
8/72 **Honky Cat** *Elton John*
Honky Tonk
2/56 *Bill Doggett (Parts 1 & 2)*
57/61 *Bill Doggett (Part 2)*
78/65 *Lonnie Mack*
44/72 *James Brown*
92/60 **Honky-Tonk Girl** *Johnny Cash*
96/62 **Honky-Tonk Man** *Johnny Horton*
1/69 **Honky Tonk Women** *Rolling Stones*
92/61 **Honky Train** *Bill Black's Combo*
11/63 **Honolulu Lulu** *Jan & Dean*

34A/98 **Hooch** *Everything*
23/61 **Hoochi Coochi Coo** *Hank Ballard*
23/96 **Hook** *Blues Traveler*
73/69 **Hook And Sling** *Eddie Bo*
FC/57 **Hook, Line And Sinker** *Bill Haley*
17/64 **Hooka Tooka** *Chubby Checker*
Hooked On A Feeling
5/69 *B.J. Thomas*
1/74 *Blue Swede*
71/98 *Baby Talk*
61/82 **Hooked On Big Bands** *Frank Barber*
10/82 **Hooked On Classics** *Royal Philharmonic Orchestra*
31/82 **Hooked On Swing (medley)** *Larry Elgart*
54/95 **Hooked On You** *Silk*
60/77 **Hooked On You** *Bread*
Hooked On You
64/87 *Sweet Sensation*
23/89 *Sweet Sensation*
95/96 **Hoop N Yo Face** *69 Boyz*
56/58 **Hoopa Hoola** *Betty Johnson*
6/66 **Hooray For Hazel** *Tommy Roe*
6X/64 **Hooray For Santa Claus** *Al Hirt*
71/67 **Hooray For The Salvation Army Band** *Bill Cosby*
38/63 **Hootenanny** *Glencoves*
89/63 **Hootenanny Saturday Night** *Brothers Four*
88/98 **Hop, Tha** *Kinsu*
90/61 **Hop Scotch** *Santo & Johnny*
67S/99 **Hope** *Shaggy*
83/93 **Hope Of Deliverance** *Paul McCartney*
42/75 **Hope That We Can Be Together Soon** *Sharon Paige & Harold Melvin*
36/82 **Hope You Love Me Like You Say You Do** *Huey Lewis*
13/63 **Hopeless** *Andy Williams*
28/93 **Hopelessly** *Rick Astley*
3/78 **Hopelessly Devoted To You** *Olivia Newton-John*
65/75 **Hoppy, Gene And Me** *Roy Rogers*
42/80 **Horizontal Bop** *Bob Seger*
2/68 **Horse, The** *Cliff Nobles & Co.*
41/98 **Horse & Carriage** *Cam'ron*
68/68 **Horse Fever** *Cliff Nobles & Co.*
1/72 **Horse With No Name** *America*

HOT:

70S/00 **Hot** *Toni Estes*
92/56 **Hot And Cold Running Tears** *Sarah Vaughan*
3/78 **Hot Blooded** *Foreigner*
5/00 **Hot Boyz** *Missy "Misdemeanor" Elliott*
91/63 **Hot Cakes! 1st Serving** *Dave "Baby" Cortez*
1/78 **Hot Child In The City** *Nick Gilder*
50/75 **Hot Dawgit** *Ramsey Lewis/Earth, Wind & Fire*
1/56 **Hot Diggity (Dog Ziggity Boom)** *Perry Como*
60/56 **Hot Dog Buddy Buddy** *Bill Haley*
56/84 **Hot For Teacher** *Van Halen*
Hot Fun In The Summertime
2/69 *Sly & The Family Stone*
58/82 *Dayton*
60S/00 **Hot Gal Today (Haffi Get De Gal Yah)** *Sean Paul & Mr. Vegas*
11/83 **Hot Girls In Love** *Loverboy*
45/88 **Hot Hot Hot** *Buster Poindexter*
65/88 **Hot Hot Hot!!!** *Cure*
1/02 **Hot In Herre** *Nelly*
Hot In The City
23/82 *Billy Idol*
48/88 *Billy Idol*
28/78 **Hot Legs** *Rod Stewart*
5/77 **Hot Line** *Sylvers*
72/71 **Hot Love** *T. Rex*
31/78 **Hot Love, Cold World** *Bob Welch*
52/72 **Hot 'N' Nasty** *Humble Pie*
21/79 **Hot Number** *Foxy*
15/71 **Hot Pants** *James Brown*
54/71 **Hot Pants** *Salvage*
85/71 **Hot Pants** *Bobby Byrd*
11/63 **Hot Pastrami** *Dartells*
36/63 **Hot Pastrami With Mashed Potatoes** *Joey Dee*
63/62 **Hot Pepper** *Floyd Cramer*
15/80 **Hot Rod Hearts** *Robbie Dupree*
Hot Rod Lincoln
26/60 *Johnny Bond*
33/60 *Charlie Ryan*
9/72 *Commander Cody*
7/00 **(Hot S**t) Country Grammar** *Nelly*
67/78 **Hot Shot** *Karen Young*
87/66 **Hot Shot** *Buena Vistas*
14/69 **Hot Smoke & Sasafrass** *Bubble Puppy*
91/99 **Hot Spot** *Foxy Brown*
1/79 **Hot Stuff** *Donna Summer*
49/76 **Hot Stuff** *Rolling Stones*
Hot Summer Nights
55/78 *Walter Egan*
18/79 *Night*
63/88 **Hot Thing** *Prince*
95/77 **Hot To Trot** *Wild Cherry*
87/86 **Hot Water** *Level 42*
71/73 **Hot Wire** *Al Green*
1/77 **Hotel California** *Eagles*
3/63 **Hotel Happiness** *Brook Benton*
25S/01 **Hottie** *Ashley Ballard*
100/62 **Houdini** *Walter Brennan*
1/56 **Hound Dog** *Elvis Presley*
9/59 **Hound Dog Man** *Fabian*
58/77 **Hound Dog Man (Play It Again)** *Lenny LeBlanc*
15/87 **Hourglass** *Squeeze*
House, A Car And A Wedding Ring
88/58 *Dale Hawkins*
93/58 *Mike Preston*
53/71 **House At Pooh Corner** *Nitty Gritty Dirt Band*
69/91 **House Full Of Reasons** *Jude Cole*
House Is Not A Home
71/64 *Dionne Warwick*
75/64 *Brook Benton*
67/96 **House Keeper** *Men Of Vizion*
88/60 **House Of Bamboo** *Earl Grant*
9/55 **House Of Blue Lights** *Chuck Miller*
83/90 **House Of Broken Love** *Great White*
56/90 **House Of Fire** *Alice Cooper*
37/95 **House Of Love** *Amy Grant with Vince Gill*
92/59 **House Of Love** *Scott Garrett*
28/90 **House Of Pain** *Faster Pussycat*
93/75 **House Of Strangers** *Jim Gilstrap*
House Of The Rising Sun
1/64 *Animals*
7/70 *Frijid Pink*
78/78 *Santa Esmeralda*
77/81 *Dolly Parton*
46S/91 **House Party II (I Don't Know What You Come To Do)** *Tony! Toni! Toné!*
6/68 **House That Jack Built** *Aretha Franklin*
16/56 **House With Love In It** *Four Lads*
37/91 **Housecall (Your Body Can't Lie To Me)** *Shabba Ranks*
21/65 **Houston** *Dean Martin*
68/74 **Houston (I'm Comin' To See You)** *Glen Campbell*
36S/02 **Hovi Baby** *Jay-Z*

HOW:

33/60 **How About That** *Dee Clark*
38/92 **How About That** *Bad Company*
How Am I Supposed To Live Without You
12/83 *Laura Branigan*
1/90 *Michael Bolton*
22/58 **How Are Ya' Fixed For Love?** *Frank Sinatra & Keely Smith*
48/90 **How Bad Do You Want It?** *Don Henley*
4A/97 **How Bizarre** *OMC*
97/64 **How Blue Can You Get** *B.B. King*
48/70 **(How Bout A Little Hand For) The Boys In The Band** *Boys In The Band*
How 'Bout Us
12/81 *Champaign*
67/90 *Grayson Hugh & Betty Wright*
How Can I Be Sure
4/67 *Young Rascals*
25/72 *David Cassidy*
11/91 **How Can I Ease The Pain** *Lisa Fischer*
3/88 **How Can I Fall?** *Breathe*
41/70 **How Can I Forget** *Marvin Gaye*
How Can I Forget
57/63 *Jimmy Holiday*
85/63 *Ben E. King*
60/88 **How Can I Forget You** *Elisa Fiorillo*
44/78 **How Can I Leave You Again** *John Denver*
71/82 **How Can I Live Without Her** *Christopher Atkins*
75/62 **How Can I Meet Her?** *Everly Brothers*
44/83 **How Can I Refuse** *Heart*
22/73 **How Can I Tell Her** *Lobo*
60/70 **How Can I Tell My Mom & Dad** *Lovelites*
68/73 **How Can I Tell You** *Travis Wammack*
63/71 **How Can I Unlove You** *Lynn Anderson*
92/61 **(How Can I Write On Paper) What I Feel In My Heart** *Jim Reeves*
3/90 **How Can We Be Lovers** *Michael Bolton*
93/91 **How Can You Expect To Be Taken Seriously?** *Pet Shop Boys*
86/82 **How Can You Love Me** *Ambrosia*
1/71 **How Can You Mend A Broken Heart** *Bee Gees*
96/67 **How Can You Mistreat The One You Love** *Jean & The Darlings*
47A/97 **How Come, How Long** *Babyface*
59/02 **How Come You Don't Call Me** *Alicia Keys*
77/72 **How Could I Let You Get Away** *Spinners*
88/79 **How Could This Go Wrong** *Exile*
53/96 **How Could You** *K-Ci & JoJo*
93/60 **How Deep Is The Ocean** *Miss Toni Fisher*
How Deep Is Your Love
1/77 *Bee Gees*
93/95 *Portrait*
3/98 **How Deep Is Your Love** *Dru Hill*

89/95 **How Did I Get By Without You?** *John Waite*
85/71 **How Did We Lose It Baby** *Jerry Butler*
59/99 **How Do I Deal** *Jennifer Love Hewitt*
How Do I Live
2/97 *LeAnn Rimes*
23/97 *Trisha Yearwood*
10/80 **How Do I Make You** *Linda Ronstadt*
63/98 **How Do I Say I'm Sorry** *Tami Davis*
22/80 **How Do I Survive** *Amy Holland*
1/96 **How Do U Want It** *2Pac*
27/67 **How Do You Catch A Girl** *Sam The Sham & The Pharoahs*
8/72 **How Do You Do?** *Mouth & MacNeal*
58/92 **How Do You Do!** *Roxette*
9/64 **How Do You Do It?** *Gerry & The Pacemakers*
82/98 **How Do You Fall In Love** *Alabama*
77/74 **How Do You Feel The Morning After** *Millie Jackson*
45/83 **How Do You Keep The Music Playing** *James Ingram & Patti Austin*
48/94 **How Do You Like It?** *Keith Sweat*
31/00 **How Do You Like Me Now?!** *Toby Keith*
67/98 **How Do You Sleep At Night** *Wade Hayes*
1/92 **How Do You Talk To An Angel** *Heights*
30/80 **How Does It Feel To Be Back** *Daryl Hall & John Oates*
7/66 **How Does That Grab You, Darlin'?** *Nancy Sinatra*
27/99 **How Forever Feels** *Kenny Chesney*
How Glad I Am ..see: (You Don't Know)
13/95 **How High** *Redman/Method Man*
How High The Moon
76/60 *Ella Fitzgerald*
75/75 *Gloria Gaynor*
77/92 **How I Could Just Kill A Man** *Cypress Hill*
93/69 **How I Miss You Baby** *Bobby Womack*
54/75 **(How I Spent My Summer Vacation) Or A Day At The Beach With Pedro & Man** *Cheech & Chong*
57/93 **How I'm Comin'** *LL Cool J*
How Important Can It Be?
2/55 *Joni James*
12/55 *Sarah Vaughan*
F/55 *Teresa Brewer*
42/62 **How Is Julie?** *Lettermen*
13/56 **(How Little It Matters) How Little We Know** *Frank Sinatra*
How Long
3/75 *Ace*
49/82 *Rod Stewart*
26S/00 **How Long** *LV*
20/75 **How Long (Betcha' Got A Chick On The Side)** *Pointer Sisters*
97/57 **How Lovely Is Christmas** *Bing Crosby*
70/56 **How Lucky You Are** *Joni James*
75/00 **How Many Licks?** *Lil' Kim*
46/63 **How Many Teardrops** *Lou Christie*
63/61 **How Many Tears** *Bobby Vee*
27/83 **How Many Times Can We Say Goodbye** *Dionne Warwick & Luther Vandross*
35/94 **How Many Ways** *Toni Braxton*
92/64 **How Much Can A Lonely Heart Stand** *Skeeter Davis*
3/78 **How Much I Feel** *Ambrosia*
35/91 **How Much Is Enough** *Fixx*
69/63 **How Much Is That Doggie In The Window** *Baby Jane & The Rockabyes*
17/77 **How Much Love** *Leo Sayer*
44/90 **How Much Love** *Vixen*
51/87 **How Much Love** *Survivor*
72S/00 **How Much You Want Me** *Havana*
97/65 **How Nice It Is** *Billy Stewart*
86/68 **How Sweet It Is, Montage From** *Love Generation*
How Sweet It Is (To Be Loved By You)
6/65 *Marvin Gaye*
18/66 *Jr. Walker*
5/75 *James Taylor*
11/58 **How The Time Flies** *Jerry Wallace*
20/86 **(How To Be A) Millionaire** *ABC*
25/91 **How To Dance** *Bingoboys/Princessa*
64/60 **How To Handle A Woman** *Johnny Mathis*
14S/01 **How We Do** *Big Lew Betta*
64S/00 **How We Roll** *69 Boyz*
1/86 **How Will I Know** *Whitney Houston*
12/78 **How You Gonna See Me Now** *Alice Cooper*
1/01 **How You Remind Me** *Nickelback*
21/68 **How'd We Ever Get This Way** *Andy Kim*
70/98 **How's It Goin' Down?** *DMX*
9/98 **How's It Going To Be** *Third Eye Blind*
61/76 **Howzat** *Sherbet*
14/60 **Hucklebuck, The** *Chubby Checker*
Hula Hoop Song
32/58 *Georgia Gibbs*
38/58 *Teresa Brewer*
9/57 **Hula Love** *Buddy Knox*
Hully Gully ..also see: (Baby)
54/61 **Hully Gully Again** *Little Caesar & The Romans*
25/62 **Hully Gully Baby** *Dovells*
99/62 **Hully Gully Guitar** *Jerry Reed*
54/70 **Hum A Song (From Your Heart)** *Lulu with The Dixie Flyers*
1/86 **Human** *Human League*
48/61 **Human** *Tommy Hunt*
7/83 **Human Nature** *Michael Jackson*
46/95 **Human Nature** *Madonna* (also see: Right Here)
16/92 **Human Touch** *Bruce Springsteen*
18/83 **Human Touch** *Rick Springfield*
48/93 **Human Wheels** *John Mellencamp*
59/60 **Humdinger** *Freddy Cannon*
Hummingbird
7/55 *Les Paul & Mary Ford*
17/55 *Frankie Laine*
20/73 **Hummingbird** *Seals & Crofts*
48/70 **Hummingbird** *B.B. King*
78/70 **Humphrey The Camel** *Jack Blanchard & Misty Morgan*
3/92 **Humpin' Around** *Bobby Brown*
84/93 **Humps For The Blvd.** *Rodney -O- & Joe Cooley*
11/90 **Humpty Dance** *Digital Underground*
71/57 **Humpty Dumpty Heart** *LaVern Baker*
Hunch, The
68/59 *Paul Gayten*
71/59 *Bobby Peterson Quintet*
Hundred ..also see: One Hundred
3/61 **Hundred Pounds Of Clay** *Gene McDaniels*
47/65 **Hung On You** *Righteous Brothers*
58/67 **Hung Up In Your Eyes** *Brian Hyland*
78/94 **Hungah** *Karyn White*
6/66 **Hungry** *Paul Revere & The Raiders*
85/89 **Hungry** *Winger*
98/90 **Hungry** *Lita Ford*
4/88 **Hungry Eyes** *Eric Carmen*
27/65 **Hungry For Love** *San Remo Golden Strings*
5/80 **Hungry Heart** *Bruce Springsteen*
3/83 **Hungry Like The Wolf** *Duran Duran*
82/76 **Hungry Years** *Wayne Newton*
85/86 **Hunter, The** *GTR*
93/69 **Hunter, The** *Ike & Tina Turner*
13/67 **Hunter Gets Captured By The Game** *Marvelettes*
57/84 **Hunters Of The Night** *Mr. Mister*
5/68 **Hurdy Gurdy Man** *Donovan*
33/76 **Hurricane** *Bob Dylan*
63/95 **Hurricane** *Click*
81/75 **Hurricane Is Coming Tonite** *Carol Douglas*
19X/68 **Hurry Home For Christmas** *Robert Goulet*
60/77 **Hurry Sundown** *Outlaws*
58/81 **Hurry Up And Wait** *Isley Brothers*
Hurt
4/61 *Timi Yuro*
51/66 *Little Anthony & The Imperials*
97/75 *Manhattans*
28/76 *Elvis Presley*
31/73 **Hurt, The** *Cat Stevens*
82/84 **Hurt** *Re-Flex*
54A/95 **Hurt** *Nine Inch Nails*
54/64 **Hurt By Love** *Inez Foxx*
Hurt So Bad
10/65 *Little Anthony & The Imperials*
12/69 *Lettermen*
76/70 *Jackie DeShannon (medley)*
8/80 *Linda Ronstadt*
Hurt Yourself ..see: (You're Gonna)
78/59 **Hurtin' Inside** *Brook Benton*
2/72 **Hurting Each Other** *Carpenters*
46/90 **Hurting Kind (I've Got My Eyes On You)** *Robert Plant*
2/82 **Hurts So Good** *John Cougar*
24/73 **Hurts So Good** *Millie Jackson*
57/85 **Hurts To Be In Love** *Gino Vannelli*
Husbands And Wives
26/66 *Roger Miller*
36/98 *Brooks & Dunn*
Hush
52/67 *Billy Joe Royal*
4/68 *Deep Purple*
61/75 *Blue Swede (medley)*
75/60 **Hush-Hush** *Jimmy Reed*
8/65 **Hush, Hush, Sweet Charlotte** *Patti Page*
63/02 **Hush Lil' Lady** *Corey*
Hushabye
20/59 *Mystics*
62/69 *Jay & The Americans*
99/72 *Robert John*
1/75 **Hustle, The** *Van McCoy*
30S/02 **Hyde Ha** *Big Logic*
91/71 **Hymn 43** *Jethro Tull*
33/86 **Hyperactive** *Robert Palmer*
62/84 **Hyperactive** *Thomas Dolby*
1/97 **Hypnotize** *Notorious B.I.G.*
36/87 **Hypnotize Me** *Wang Chung*
21/67 **Hypnotized** *Linda Jones*
79/57 **Hypnotized** *Drifters*
10/88 **Hysteria** *Def Leppard*

I

F/93 **IBWin' Wit My CREWin'** *Yo Yo*
26/82 **I.G.Y. (What A Beautiful World)** *Donald Fagen*
69/95 **INC Ride** *Masta Ace Incorporated*
94/70 **I.O.I.O.** *Bee Gees*
35/76 **I.O.U.** *Jimmy Dean*
53/83 **I.O.U.** *Lee Greenwood*
93/92 **I O U** *Arthur Baker/Nikeeta*

I:

25/63 **I Adore Him** *Angels*
1/91 **I Adore Mi Amor** *Color Me Badd*
I Ain't Gonna Eat Out My Heart Anymore
52/66 *Young Rascals*
44/78 *Angel*
11/81 **I Ain't Gonna Stand For It** *Stevie Wonder*
I Ain't Got Nobody ..see: Just A Gigolo
36/71 **I Ain't Got Time Anymore** *Glass Bottle*
57/68 **I Ain't Got To Love Nobody Else** *Masqueraders*
80/98 **I Ain't Havin' That** *Heltah Skeltah*
58A/96 **I Ain't Mad At Cha** *2Pac*
I Ain't Never
24/59 *Webb Pierce*
79/59 *Four Preps*
71S/99 **I Ain't The One** *Profyle*
1/56 **I Almost Lost My Mind** *Pat Boone*
38A/95 **I Alone** *Live*
71/97 **I Always Feel Like (Somebody's Watching Me)** *Tru*
93/57 **I Am** *Tony Bennett*
3/66 **I Am A Rock** *Simon & Garfunkel*
71/63 **I Am A Witness** *Tommy Hunt*
18/86 **I Am By Your Side** *Corey Hart*
56/75 **I Am I Am** *Smokey Robinson*
4/71 **I Am...I Said** *Neil Diamond*
15/75 **I Am Love** *Jackson 5*
49/83 **I Am Love** *Jennifer Holliday*
43/02 **I Am Mine** *Pearl Jam*
39/70 **I Am Somebody** *Johnnie Taylor*
94/76 **I Am Somebody** *Jimmy James*
(I Am The Japanese Sandman) ..see: Rang Tang Ding Dong
56/67 **I Am The Walrus** *Beatles*
64/74 **I Am What I Am** *Lois Fletcher*
1/72 **I Am Woman** *Helen Reddy*
85/68 **I Am Your Man** *Bobby Taylor*
72/61 **I Apologize** *Timi Yuro*
74/95 **I Apologize** *Anita Baker*
97/71 **I Been Moved** *Andy Kim*
61/73 **I' Been Watchin' You** *South Side Movement*
8/58 **I Beg Of You** *Elvis Presley*
15/89 **I Beg Your Pardon** *Kon Kan*
(also see: Rose Garden)
8/95 **I Believe** *Blessid Union Of Souls*
33/64 **I Believe** *Bachelors*
33/82 **I Believe** *Chilliwack*
99/94 **I Believe** *Sounds Of Blackness*
2/96 **I Believe I Can Fly** *R. Kelly*
96/65 **I Believe I'll Love On** *Jackie Wilson*
47/75 **I Believe I'm Gonna Love You** *Frank Sinatra*
67/66 **I Believe I'm Gonna Make It** *Joe Tex*
95/75 **I Believe In Father Christmas** *Greg Lake*
66/77 **I Believe In Love** *Kenny Loggins*
22/72 **I Believe In Music** *Gallery*
24/80 **I Believe In You** *Don Williams*
88/88 **I Believe In You** *Stryper*
93/58 **I Believe In You** *Robert & Johnny*
4/97 **I Believe In You And Me** *Whitney Houston*
11/73 **I Believe In You (You Believe In Me)** *Johnnie Taylor*
15/75 **(I Believe) There's Nothing Stronger Than Our Love** *Paul Anka/Odia Coates*
I Believe You
27/77 *Dorothy Moore*
68/78 *Carpenters*
96/67 **I Believed It All** *Pozo Seco Singers*
27/75 **I Belong To You** *Love Unlimited*
28/95 **I Belong To You** *Toni Braxton*
71/00 **I Belong To You** *Lenny Kravitz*
6/97 **I Belong To You (Every Time I See Your Face)** *Rome*
92/71 **I Bet He Don't Love You (Like I Love You)** *Intruders*
35/02 **I Breathe In, I Breathe Out** *Chris Cagle*
96/68 **I Call It Love** *Manhattans*
75/70 **I Call My Baby Candy** *Jaggerz*
83/80 **I Call Your Name** *Switch*

I CAN:

I Can Dance ..see: Long Tall Glasses
14/98 **I Can Do That** *Montell Jordan*
6/84 **I Can Dream About You** *Dan Hartman*
56/71 **(I Can Feel Those Vibrations) This Love Is Real** *Jackie Wilson*
97/68 **(I Can Feel Your Love) Slipping Away** *Barbara Mason*
71/94 **I Can Go Deep** *Silk*
I Can Hear Music
100/66 *Ronettes*
24/69 *Beach Boys*
1/74 **I Can Help** *Billy Swan*
28/97 **I Can Love You** *Mary J. Blige*
77/98 **I Can Love You Better** *Dixie Chicks*
5/95 **I Can Love You Like That** *All-4-One*
80/97 **I Can Make It Better** *Luther Vandross*
81/73 **I Can Make It Thru The Days (But Oh Those Lonely Nights)** *Ray Charles*
I Can Make It With You
32/66 *Pozo-Seco Singers*
68/66 *Jackie DeShannon*
6/65 **I Can Never Go Home Anymore** *Shangri-Las*
51/68 **I Can Remember** *James & Bobby Purify*
I Can See Clearly Now
1/72 *Johnny Nash*
18/94 *Jimmy Cliff*
9/67 **I Can See For Miles** *Who*
(I Can See It In Your Eyes) ..see: Circle Is Small
22/69 **I Can Sing A Rainbow (medley)** *Dells*
91/80 **I Can Survive** *Triumph*
39/81 **I Can Take Care Of Myself** *Billy & The Beaters*
22/68 **I Can Take Or Leave Your Loving** *Herman's Hermits*
35/73 **I Can Understand It** *New Birth*

I CAN'T:

80/76 **I Can't Ask For Anymore Than You** *Cliff Richard*
89/69 **I Can't Be All Bad** *Johnny Adams*
90/70 **I Can't Be You (You Can't Be Me)** *Glass House*
60/68 **I Can't Believe I'm Losing You** *Frank Sinatra*
71/70 **I Can't Believe That You've Stopped Loving Me** *Charley Pride*
95/64 **I Can't Believe What You Say (For Seeing What You Do)** *Ike & Tina Turner*
72/66 **I Can't Believe You Love Me** *Tammi Terrell*
43/66 **I Can't Control Myself** *Troggs*
7/92 **I Can't Dance** *Genesis*
42/68 **I Can't Dance To That Music You're Playin'** *Martha & The Vandellas*
98/69 **I Can't Do Enough** *Dells*
87/61 **I Can't Do It By Myself** *Anita Bryant*
26/84 **I Can't Drive 55** *Sammy Hagar*
93/65 **I Can't Explain** *Who*
78/89 **I Can't Face The Fact** *Gina Go-Go*
I Can't Get Next To You
1/69 *Temptations*
60/71 *Al Green*
(I Can't Get No) Satisfaction
1/65 *Rolling Stones*
31/66 *Otis Redding*
69A/91 *Vanilla Ice*
51/99 **I Can't Get Over You** *Brooks & Dunn*
I Can't Get You Out Of My Heart
44/59 *Al Martino*
99/64 *Al Martino*
100/66 **I Can't Give You Anything But Love** *Bert Kaempfert*
1/82 **I Can't Go For That (No Can Do)** *Daryl Hall & John Oates*
86/67 **I Can't Go On Livin' Baby Without You** *Nino Tempo & April Stevens*
34/66 **I Can't Grow Peaches On A Cherry Tree** *Just Us*
66/64 **I Can't Hear You** *Betty Everett*
29/76 **I Can't Hear You No More** *Helen Reddy*
12/80 **I Can't Help It** *Andy Gibb & Olivia Newton-John*
47/88 **I Can't Help It** *Bananarama*
I Can't Help It (If I'm Still In Love With You)
74/58 *Margaret Whiting*
64/60 *Adam Wade*
24/62 *Johnny Tillotson*
94/67 *B.J. Thomas*
97/69 *Al Martino*
I Can't Help Myself
1/65 *Four Tops*
22/72 *Donnie Elbert*
40/80 *Bonnie Pointer*
77/77 **I Can't Help Myself** *Eddie Rabbitt*
39/60 **(I Can't Help You) I'm Falling Too** *Skeeter Davis*
(also see: Please Help Me I'm Falling)
13/84 **I Can't Hold Back** *Survivor*
76/78 **I Can't Hold On** *Karla Bonoff*
50/74 **I Can't Leave You Alone** *George McCrae*
42/70 **I Can't Leave Your Love Alone** *Clarence Carter*
I Can't Let Go
42/66 *Hollies*
31/80 *Linda Ronstadt*

46/76 **I Can't Live A Dream** *Osmonds*
22/56 **I Can't Love You Enough** *LaVern Baker*
I Can't Make It Alone
95/68 *Bill Medley*
63/69 *Lou Rawls*
95/67 **I Can't Make It Anymore** *Spyder Turner*
18/92 **I Can't Make You Love Me** *Bonnie Raitt*
67/69 **I Can't Quit Her** *Arbors*
90/60 **I Can't Say Goodbye** *Fireflies*
92/62 **I Can't Say Goodbye** *Bobby Vee*
88/81 **I Can't Say Goodbye To You** *Helen Reddy*
78/69 **I Can't Say No To You** *Betty Everett*
28/69 **I Can't See Myself Leaving You** *Aretha Franklin*
94/59 **I Can't Sit Down** *Marie & Rex*
5/96 **I Can't Sleep Baby (If I)** *R. Kelly*
10/81 **I Can't Stand It** *Eric Clapton*
46/64 **I Can't Stand It** *Soul Sisters*
14/79 **I Can't Stand It No More** *Peter Frampton*
28/68 **I Can't Stand Myself (When You Touch Me)** *James Brown*
48/83 **I Can't Stand Still** *Don Henley*
I Can't Stand The Rain
38/73 *Ann Peebles*
18/78 *Eruption*
45/73 **I Can't Stand To See You Cry** *Miracles*
80/67 **I Can't Stay Away From You** *Impressions*
7/63 **I Can't Stay Mad At You** *Skeeter Davis*
48/65 **I Can't Stop** *Honeycombs*
96/71 **I Can't Stop** *Osmond Brothers*
9/68 **I Can't Stop Dancing** *Archie Bell*
I Can't Stop Loving You
81/58 *Don Gibson*
1/62 *Ray Charles*
77/63 *Count Basie*
35/64 **I Can't Stop Talking About You** *Steve & Eydie*
77/80 **I Can't Stop The Feelin'** *Pure Prairie League*
46/65 **I Can't Stop Thinking Of You** *Bobbi Martin*
92/61 **I Can't Take It** *Mary Ann Fisher*
I Can't Take My Eyes Off You ..see: Can't Take My Eyes Off You
82/70 **I Can't Tell The Bottom From The Top** *Hollies*
I Can't Tell You Why
8/80 *Eagles*
54/95 *Brownstone*
I Can't Turn You Loose
37/68 *Chambers Brothers*
81/72 *Edgar Winter's White Trash*
3/86 **I Can't Wait** *Nu Shooz*
16/86 **I Can't Wait** *Stevie Nicks*
66/88 **I Can't Wait** *Deniece Williams*
8/91 **I Can't Wait Another Minute** *Hi-Five*
80/78 **I Can't Wait Any Longer** *Bill Anderson*
93/64 **I Can't Wait Until I See My Baby** *Justine Washington*
60/65 **I Can't Work No Longer** *Billy Butler*
79/83 **I Cannot Believe It's True** *Phil Collins*
16/02 **I Care 4 U** *Aaliyah*
23/97 **I Care 'Bout You** *Milestone*
92/77 **I Caught Your Act** *Hues Corporation*
60/76 **I Cheat The Hangman** *Doobie Brothers*
32/66 **I Chose To Sing The Blues** *Ray Charles*
75/90 **I Come Off** *Young M.C.*
80/66 **I Confess** *New Colony Six*
52/80 **I Could Be Good For You** *707*
56/67 **I Could Be So Good To You** *Don & The Goodtimes*
93/67 **I Could Be So Happy** *Magnificent Men*
8^{A}/95 **I Could Fall In Love** *Selena*
I Could Have Danced All Night
20/56 *Sylvia Syms*
49/56 *Rosemary Clooney*
93/56 *Dinah Shore*
72/63 *Ben E. King*
72/76 *Biddu Orchestra*
57/62 **I Could Have Loved You So Well** *Ray Peterson*
93/72 **I Could Never Be Happy** *Emotions*
48/69 **I Could Never Be President** *Johnnie Taylor*
50/69 **I Could Never Lie To You** *New Colony Six*
13/68 **I Could Never Love Another (After Loving You)** *Temptations*
18/81 **I Could Never Miss You (More Than I Do)** *Lulu*
10/88 **I Could Never Take The Place Of Your Man** *Prince*
I Could Not Ask For More
37/99 *Edwin McCain*
35/01 *Sara Evans*
67/95 **(I Could Only) Whisper Your Name** *Harry Connick, Jr.*
46/70 **I Could Write A Book** *Jerry Butler*
9/66 **I Couldn't Live Without Your Love** *Petula Clark*
32/83 **I Couldn't Say No** *Robert Ellis Orrall w/Carlene Carter*
17/61 **I Count The Tears** *Drifters*
I Cried
99/63 *Tammy Montgomery*
50/71 *James Brown*
91/59 **I Cried** *Joe Damiano*
6/59 **I Cried A Tear** *LaVern Baker*
68/63 **(I Cried at) Laura's Wedding** *Barbara Lynn*
69/61 **I Cried My Last Tear** *Ernie K-Doe*
40/01 **I Cry** *Ja Rule*
67/84 **I Cry Just A Little Bit** *Shakin' Stevens*
71/01 **I Did It** *Dave Matthews Band*
75/88 **I Did It For Love** *Night Ranger*
I Didn't Get To Sleep At All ..see: (Last Night)
35/72 **I Didn't Know I Loved You (Till I Saw You Rock And Roll)** *Gary Glitter*
92/64 **I Didn't Know What Time It Was** *Crampton Sisters*
75/89 **I Didn't Mean To Stay All Night** *Starship*
I Didn't Mean To Turn You On
79/84 *Cherrelle*
2/86 *Robert Palmer*
23/90 **I Didn't Want To Need You** *Heart*
83/71 **I Dig Everything About You** *Mob*
46/59 **I Dig Girls** *Bobby Rydell*
83/67 **I Dig Girls** *J.J. Jackson*
9/67 **I Dig Rock And Roll Music** *Peter, Paul & Mary*
60/67 **I Dig You Baby** *Jerry Butler*
76/00 **I Disappear** *Metallica*

I DO:

16/01 **I Do!!** *Toya*
17/98 **I Do** *Lisa Loeb*
I Do
37/65 *Marvelows*
24/83 *J. Geils Band*
62/69 **I Do** *Moments*
63^{S}/96 **I Do** *Paul Brandt*
(also see: Give Me Forever)
84/79 **I Do Believe In You** *Pages*
58^{S}/00 **I Do Both Jay & Jane** *La Rissa*
I Do [Cherish You]
72/98 *Mark Wills*
13/99 *98°*
15/76 **I Do, I Do, I Do, I Do, I Do** *Abba*
I Do It For You ..see: (Everything I Do)
I Do Love You
26/65 *Billy Stewart*
94/69 *Billy Stewart*
20/79 *GQ*
48/70 **I Do Take You** *Three Degrees*
91/79 **I Do The Rock** *Tim Curry*
(I Do The) Shimmy Shimmy
37/60 *Bobby Freeman*
66/64 *Orlons*
58/02 **I Do (Wanna Get Close To You)** *3LW*
29/84 **I Do'wanna Know** *REO Speedwagon*
23/86 **I Do What I Do...(Theme for 9 1/2 Weeks)** *John Taylor Jonathan Elias*
20/87 **I Do You** *Jets*

I DON'T:

18/71 **I Don't Blame You At All** *Miracles*
I Don't Care
73^{S}/99 *No Question*
28^{S}/00 *No Question*
55/93 **I Don't Care** *Shakespear's Sister*
74^{S}/00 **I Don't Care** *Angela Vía*
39/83 **I Don't Care Anymore** *Phil Collins*
74/56 **I Don't Care If The Sun Don't Shine** *Elvis Presley*
92/64 **I Don't Care (Just as Long as You Love Me)** *Buck Owens*
62/59 **(I Don't Care) Only Love Me** *Steve Lawrence*
6/98 **I Don't Ever Want To See You Again** *Uncle Sam*
1/90 **I Don't Have The Heart** *James Ingram*
35/02 **I Don't Have To Be Me ('Til Monday)** *Steve Azar*
64/59 **I Don't Know** *Ruth Brown*
81/89 **I Don't Know** *Michael Morales*
23/91 **I Don't Know Anybody Else** *Black Box*
I Don't Know How To Love Him
13/71 *Helen Reddy*
28/71 *Yvonne Elliman*
99/71 *Kimberlys (medley)*
23/79 **I Don't Know If It's Right** *Evelyn "Champagne" King*
61/60 **I Don't Know What It Is** *Bluenotes*
67/73 **I Don't Know What It Is, But It Sure Is Funky** *Ripple*
66^{S}/00 **I Don't Know What You Want But I Can't Give It Any More** *Pet Shop Boys*
92/65 **I Don't Know What You've Got But It's Got Me** *Little Richard*
35/82 **I Don't Know Where To Start** *Eddie Rabbitt*
12/61 **I Don't Know Why** *Linda Scott*

I Don't Know Why
39/69 *Stevie Wonder*
42/75 *Rolling Stones*
(also see: But I Do)
72/61 **I Don't Like It Like That** *Bobbettes*
(also see: I Like It Like That)
73/80 **I Don't Like Mondays** *Boomtown Rats*
8/75 **I Don't Like To Sleep Alone** *Paul Anka/Odia Coates*
41/77 **I Don't Love You Anymore** *Teddy Pendergrass*
76/90 **I Don't Love You Anymore** *London Quireboys*
47/62 **I Don't Love You No More (I Don't Care About You)** *Jimmy Norman*
47/61 **I Don't Mind** *James Brown*
95/95 **I Don't Mind** *Immature*
38/87 **I Don't Mind At All** *Bourgeois Tagg*
I Don't Need No Doctor
72/66 *Ray Charles*
73/71 *Humble Pie*
81/72 *New Riders Of The Purple Sage*
3/81 **I Don't Need You** *Kenny Rogers*
56/81 **I Don't Need You** *Rupert Holmes*
86/80 **I Don't Need You Anymore** *Jackie DeShannon*
98/59 **I Don't Need You Anymore** *Teddy Bears*
69/96 **I Don't Need Your Love** *Angelina*
5S/02 **I Don't Really Know** *Brandy Moss-Scott*
47/74 **I Don't See Me In Your Eyes Anymore** *Charlie Rich*
68/87 **I Don't Think That Man Should Sleep Alone** *Ray Parker Jr.*
35/00 **I Don't Wanna** *Aaliyah*
37/64 **I Don't Wanna Be A Loser** *Lesley Gore*
89/96 **I Don't Wanna Be Alone** *Shai*
1/91 **I Don't Wanna Cry** *Mariah Carey*
53/83 **I Don't Wanna Dance** *Eddy Grant*
9/93 **I Don't Wanna Fight** *Tina Turner*
43/78 **I Don't Wanna Go** *Joey Travolta*
95/98 **I Don't Wanna Go On** *Innerlude*
2/88 **I Don't Wanna Go On With You Like That** *Elton John*
61/00 **I Don't Wanna Kiss You Goodnight** *LFO*
100/76 **I Don't Wanna Leave You** *Debbie Taylor*
3/88 **I Don't Wanna Live Without Your Love** *Chicago*
42/79 **I Don't Wanna Lose You** *Daryl Hall & John Oates*
86/71 **I Don't Wanna Lose You** *Johnnie Taylor*
35/65 **I Don't Wanna Lose You Baby** *Chad & Jeremy*
I Don't Wanna Lose Your Love
51/76 *Emotions*
54/91 *B Angie B*
25S/99 **I Don't Wanna See** *Link*
73/91 **I Don't Wanna See You** *Michael Morales*
77/89 **I Don't Want A Lover** *Texas*
47/79 **I Don't Want Nobody Else (To Dance With You)** *Narada Michael Walden*
20/69 **I Don't Want Nobody To Give Me Nothing** *James Brown*
I Don't Want Nobody (To Have My Love But You)
75/56 *Woody Herman*
78/61 *Ella Johnson with Buddy Johnson*
19/97 **I Don't Want To** *Toni Braxton*
(also see: I Don't Wanna)

31/88 **I Don't Want To Be A Hero** *Johnny Hates Jazz*
99/75 **I Don't Want To Be A Lone Ranger** *Johnny "Guitar" Watson*
22/64 **I Don't Want To Be Hurt Anymore** *Nat King Cole*
87/80 **I Don't Want To Be Lonely** *Dana Valery*
I Don't Want To Be Right ..see: (If Loving You Is Wrong)
I Don't Want To Cry
36/61 *Chuck Jackson*
97/69 *Ruby Winters*
50/70 *Ronnie Dyson*
17/71 **I Don't Want To Do Wrong** *Gladys Knight*
95/64 **I Don't Want To Hear Anymore** *Jerry Butler*
65/81 **I Don't Want To Know Your Name** *Glen Campbell*
5/88 **I Don't Want To Live Without You** *Foreigner*
84/67 **I Don't Want To Lose You** *Jackie Wilson*
I Don't Want To Lose Your Love ..see: I Don't Wanna
48/73 **(I Don't Want To Love You But) You Got Me Anyway** *Sutherland Brothers & Quiver*
91/73 **I Don't Want To Make You Wait** *Delfonics*
I Don't Want To Miss A Thing
1/98 *Aerosmith*
17/99 *Mark Chesnutt*
10S/02 *Aerosmith*
34/64 **I Don't Want To See Tomorrow** *Nat King Cole*
16/64 **I Don't Want To See You Again** *Peter & Gordon*
(I Don't Want To See You Cry) ..see: Goodbye Baby
39/65 **I Don't Want To Spoil The Party** *Beatles*
33/61 **I Don't Want To Take A Chance** *Mary Wells*
46/80 **I Don't Want To Talk About It** *Rod Stewart*
11/98 **I Don't Want To Wait** *Paula Cole*
I Don't Want To Walk Without You
79/64 *Phyllis McGuire*
36/80 *Barry Manilow*
54/02 **I Don't Want You To Go** *Carolyn Dawn Johnson*
4/88 **I Don't Want Your Love** *Duran Duran*
9/57 **I Dreamed** *Betty Johnson*
47/75 **I Dreamed Last Night** *Justin Hayward & John Lodge*
20/61 **I Dreamed Of A Hill-Billy Heaven** *Tex Ritter*
67/99 **I Drive Myself Crazy** **NSYNC*
I Drove All Night
6/89 *Cyndi Lauper*
74S/92 *Roy Orbison*
66/83 **I Eat Cannibals** *Total Coelo*
76/86 **I Engineer** *Animotion*
12/61 **I Fall To Pieces** *Patsy Cline*
38S/03 **I Farted On Santa's Lap (Now Christmas Is Gonna Stink For Me)** *Little Stinkers*
97/66 **I Feel A Sin Coming On** *Solomon Burke*
21/74 **I Feel A Song (In My Heart)** *Gladys Knight*
1/64 **I Feel Fine** *Beatles*
3/84 **I Feel For You** *Chaka Khan*
88/88 **I Feel Free** *Belinda Carlisle*

38/57 **I Feel Good** *Shirley & Lee*
64/67 **I Feel Good (I Feel Bad)** *Lewis & Clarke Expedition*
F/76 **I Feel Like A Bullet (In The Gun Of Robert Ford)** *Elton John*
6/77 **I Feel Love** *Donna Summer*
32S/01 **I Feel Loved** *Depeche Mode*
75/74 **I Feel Sanctified** *Commodores*
I Feel So Bad
5/61 *Elvis Presley*
91/67 *Little Milton*
68/71 *Ray Charles*
84/57 **I Feel The Beat** *Jim Lowe*
I Feel The Earth Move
F/71 *Carole King*
25/89 *Martika*
82/86 **I Feel The Magic** *Belinda Carlisle*
37/93 **I Feel You** *Depeche Mode*
61/97 **I Fell In Love** *Rockell*
8/96 **I Finally Found Someone** *Barbra Streisand & Bryan Adams*
45/67 **I Fooled You This Time** *Gene Chandler*
80/60 **I Forgot More Than You'll Ever Know** *Sonny James*
I Forgot To Be Your Lover ..see: To Be A Lover
I Fought The Law
9/66 *Bobby Fuller Four*
54/75 *Sam Neely*
30/65 **I Found A Girl** *Jan & Dean*
I Found A Love
75/62 *Falcons & Band*
32/67 *Wilson Pickett*
67/65 **I Found A Love Oh What A Love** *Jo Ann & Troy*
90/62 **I Found A New Baby** *Bobby Darin*
42/68 **I Found A True Love** *Wilson Pickett*
79/90 **I Found Love** *Party*
93/62 **I Found Love** *Jackie Wilson & Linda Hopkins*
78/72 **I Found My Dad** *Joe Simon*
31/82 **I Found Somebody** *Glenn Frey*
I Found Someone
90/86 *Laura Branigan*
10/88 *Cher*
47/73 **I Found Sunshine** *Chi-Lites*
F/70 **I Found That Girl** *Jackson 5*
1/64 **I Get Around** *Beach Boys*
11/93 **I Get Around** *2Pac*
32/82 **I Get Excited** *Rick Springfield*
52/75 **I Get High On You** *Sly Stone*
37/75 **I Get Lifted** *George McCrae*
3/98 **I Get Lonely** *Janet Jackson*
79/80 **I Get Off On It** *Tony Joe White*
34/68 **I Get The Sweetest Feeling** *Jackie Wilson*
2/88 **I Get Weak** *Belinda Carlisle*
42/59 **I Go Ape** *Neil Sedaka*
13A/96 **I Go Blind** *Hootie & The Blowfish*
7/78 **I Go Crazy** *Paul Davis*
6/90 **I Go To Extremes** *Billy Joel*
I Go To Pieces
9/65 *Peter & Gordon*
66/75 *Cotton, Lloyd & Christian*
46/79 **I Go To Rio** *Pablo Cruise*

I GOT:

44/72 **I Got A Bag Of My Own** *James Brown*
10/58 **I Got A Feeling** *Ricky Nelson*
53A/95 **I Got A Girl** *Tripping Daisy*
25/69 **I Got A Line On You** *Spirit*
14/93 **I Got A Man** *Positive K*
10/73 **I Got A Name** *Jim Croce*
95/70 **I Got A Problem** *Jesse Anderson*

73/68 **I Got A Sure Thing** *Ollie & The Nightingales*
27/93 **I Got A Thang 4 Ya!** *Lo-Key?*
I Got A Thing About You Baby ..see: I've Got A Thing
80/70 **I Got A Thing, You Got A Thing, Everybody's Got A Thing** *Funkadelic*
24/59 **I Got A Wife** *Mark IV*
I Got A Woman
20/62 *Jimmy McGriff*
48/63 *Freddie Scott*
49/63 *Rick Nelson*
79/65 *Ray Charles*
27/73 **I Got Ants In My Pants** *James Brown*
93/94 **I Got Cha Opin** *Black Moon*
8/95 **I Got 5 On It** *Luniz*
7/95 **I Got Id** *Pearl Jam*
42[S]/02 **I Got It 2** *Jagged Edge*
I Got Life ..see: Ain't Got No
69[S]/01 **I Got Love** *Nate Dogg*
20/79 **I Got My Mind Made Up (You Can Get It Girl)** *Instant Funk*
3/67 **I Got Rhythm** *Happenings*
92/72 **I Got Some Help I Don't Need** *B.B. King*
37/75 **I Got Stoned And I Missed It** *Jim Stafford*
43/59 **I Got Stripes** *Johnny Cash*
8/58 **I Got Stung** *Elvis Presley*
6/68 **I Got The Feelin'** *James Brown*
56/87 **I Got The Feelin' (It's Over)** *Gregory Abbott*
16/66 **I Got The Feelin' (Oh No No)** *Neil Diamond*
16/98 **I Got The Hook Up!** *Master P*
I Got To ..also see: I Gotta
69/67 **I Got To Go Back (And Watch That Little Girl Dance)** *McCoys*
74/66 **I Got To Handle It** *Capitols*
43/76 **I Got To Know** *Starbuck*
96/71 **I Got To Tell Somebody** *Betty Everett*
28/63 **I Got What I Wanted** *Brook Benton*
99/67 **I Got What You Need** *Kim Weston*
53/80 **I Got You** *Split Enz*
(also see: I Gotcha)
I Got You Babe
1/65 *Sonny & Cher*
69/68 *Etta James*
28/85 *UB40 With Chrissie Hynde*
3/65 **I Got You (I Feel Good)** *James Brown*
2/72 **I Gotcha** *Joe Tex*
35/64 **I Gotta Dance To Keep From Crying** *Miracles*
19[H]/55 **I Gotta Go Get My Baby** *Teresa Brewer*
64/77 **I Gotta Keep Dancin'** *Carrie Lucas*
20/60 **I Gotta Know** *Elvis Presley*
93/70 **I Gotta Let You Go** *Martha & The Vandellas*
44/82 **I Gotta Try** *Michael McDonald*
I Gotta Woman ..see: I Got A Woman
61/66 **I Guess I'll Always Love You** *Isley Brothers*
55/68 **I Guess I'll Have To Cry, Cry, Cry** *James Brown*
85/72 **I Guess I'll Miss The Man** *Supremes*
82/64 **I Guess I'm Crazy** *Jim Reeves*
4/84 **I Guess That's Why They Call It The Blues** *Elton John*
34/69 **I Guess The Lord Must Be In New York City** *Nilsson*
17/67 **I Had A Dream** *Paul Revere & The Raiders*
41/64 **I Had A Talk With My Man** *Mitty Collier*
61/72 **I Had It All The Time** *Tyrone Davis*
44/98 **I Had No Right** *PM Dawn*
11/67 **I Had Too Much To Dream (Last Night)** *Electric Prunes*
67/74 **I Hate Hate** *Razzy*
67[A]/96 **I Hate My Generation** *Cracker*
8/88 **I Hate Myself For Loving You** *Joan Jett*
12/95 **I Hate U** *Prince*
36/64 **I Have A Boyfriend** *Chiffons*
50/75 **I Have A Dream** *Donny Osmond*
88/68 **I Have A Dream** *Rev. Martin Luther King*
91/65 **I Have Dreamed** *Chad & Jeremy*
87/70 **I Have Learned To Do Without You** *Mavis Staples*
4/93 **I Have Nothing** *Whitney Houston*
61/81 **I Have The Skill** *Sherbs*
1/65 **I Hear A Symphony** *Supremes*
53/71 **I Hear Those Church Bells Ringing** *Dusk*
30/66 **I Hear Trumpets Blow** *Tokens*
I Hear You Knocking
2/55 *Gale Storm*
67/61 *Fats Domino*
4/71 *Dave Edmunds*
58/80 **I Hear You Now** *Jon & Vangelis*
4/87 **I Heard A Rumour** *Bananarama*
I Heard It Through The Grapevine
2/67 *Gladys Knight*
1/68 *Marvin Gaye*
83/68 *King Curtis*
43/76 *Creedence Clearwater Revival*
79/81 *Roger*
84/88 *California Raisins*
(also see: Paper)
99/70 **I Heard The Voice Of Jesus** *Turley Richards*
I Honestly Love You
1/74 *Olivia Newton-John*
48/77 *Olivia Newton-John*
67/98 *Olivia Newton-John*
91/76 **I Hope We Get To Love In Time** *Marilyn McCoo & Billy Davis Jr.*
14/01 **I Hope You Dance** *Lee Ann Womack*
82/60 **I Idolize You** *Ike & Tina Turner*

I JUST:

1/84 **I Just Called To Say I Love You** *Stevie Wonder*
65/79 **I Just Can't Control Myself** *Nature's Divine*
62/74 **I Just Can't Get You Out Of My Mind** *Four Tops*
9/70 **I Just Can't Help Believing** *B.J. Thomas*
70/62 **I Just Can't Help It** *Jackie Wilson*
94/64 **I Just Can't Say Goodbye** *Bobby Rydell*
95/75 **I Just Can't Say Goodbye** *Philly Devotions*
42/77 **I Just Can't Say No To You** *Parker McGee*
1/87 **I Just Can't Stop Loving You** *Michael Jackson*
71/83 **I Just Can't Walk Away** *Four Tops*
(I Just) Died In Your Arms
1/87 *Cutting Crew*
86/95 *Intonation feat. Joee*
17/57 **I Just Don't Know** *Four Lads*
I Just Don't Know What To Do With Myself
26/66 *Dionne Warwick*
61/70 *Gary Puckett*
17/61 **I Just Don't Understand** *Ann-Margret*
12/79 **I Just Fall In Love Again** *Anne Murray*
85/58 **I Just Thought You'd Like To Know** *Johnny Cash*
27/03 **I Just Wanna Be Mad** *Terri Clark*
93/72 **I Just Wanna Be Your Friend** *Lighthouse*
51/70 **I Just Wanna Keep It Together** *Paul Davis*
11/00 **I Just Wanna Love U (Give It 2 Me)** *Jay-Z*
4/78 **I Just Wanna Stop** *Gino Vannelli*
1/77 **I Just Want To Be Your Everything** *Andy Gibb*
7/71 **I Just Want To Celebrate** *Rare Earth*
61/98 **I Just Want To Dance With You** *George Strait*
I Just Want To Make Love To You
83/72 *Foghat*
33/77 *Foghat (Live)*
I Keep Forgettin'
55/62 *Chuck Jackson*
4/82 *Michael McDonald*
35/02 **I Keep Looking** *Sara Evans*
46/76 **I Kinda Miss You** *Manhattans*
67/95 **I Kissed A Girl** *Jill Sobule*
I Kissed You ..see: ('Til)
85/59 **I Kneel At Your Throne** *Joe Medlin*
1/00 **I Knew I Loved You** *Savage Garden*
53/64 **I Knew It All The Time** *Dave Clark Five*
45/73 **I Knew Jesus (Before He Was A Star)** *Glen Campbell*
77/86 **I Knew The Bride (When She Use To Rock And Roll)** *Nick Lowe*
1/87 **I Knew You Were Waiting (For Me)** *Aretha Franklin & George Michael*
I Knew You When
14/65 *Billy Joe Royal*
F/72 *Donny Osmond*
37/83 *Linda Ronstadt*
4/95 **I Know** *Dionne Farris*
47/59 **I Know** *Perry Como*
98/00 **I Know** *Sunday*
19/79 **I Know A Heartache When I See One** *Jennifer Warnes*
3/65 **I Know A Place** *Petula Clark*
35/93 **(I Know I Got) Skillz** *Shaquille O'Neal*
96/63 **I Know I Know** *"Pookie" Hudson*
49/71 **I Know I'm In Love** *Chee-Chee & Peppy*
(I Know) I'm Losing You
8/66 *Temptations*
7/70 *Rare Earth*
24/71 *Rod Stewart With Faces*
80/87 *Uptown*
82/60 **I Know One** *Jim Reeves*
13/83 **I Know There's Something Going On** *Frida*
62/82 **I Know What Boys Like** *Waitresses*
81/60 **I Know What God Is** *Perry Como*
9/87 **I Know What I Like** *Huey Lewis*
43/58 **I Know Where I'm Goin'** *George Hamilton IV*
36/98 **I Know Where It's At** *All Saints*
56/66 **I Know You Better Than That** *Bobby Goldsboro*

3/62 **I Know (You Don't Love Me No More)** *Barbara George*
30/88 **I Know You're Out There Somewhere** *Moody Blues*
27/00 **I Learned From The Best** *Whitney Houston*
19/62 **I Left My Heart In San Francisco** *Tony Bennett*
74/62 **I Left My Heart In The Balcony** *Linda Scott*
96/61 **I Lied To My Heart** *Enchanters*

I LIKE:

28/96 **I Like** *Montell Jordan*
34/95 **I Like** *Kut Klose*
70/89 **I Like** *Guy*
84/83 **I Like** *Men Without Hats*
I Like Dem Girlz ..see: I Like Them
3/77 **I Like Dreamin'** *Kenny Nolan*
7/89 **I Like It** *Dion*
17/64 **I Like It** *Gerry & The Pacemakers*
24/00 **I Like It** *Sammie*
25/97 **I Like It** *Blackout Allstars*
I Like It
31/83 *DeBarge*
83/93 *Jomanda*
25/95 **I Like It, I Love It** *Tim McGraw*
91/95 **I Like It (I Wanna Be Where You Are)** *Grand Puba*
I Like It Like That
2/61 *Chris Kenner*
7/65 *Dave Clark Five*
84/75 *Loggins & Messina*
27/64 **I Like It Like That** *Miracles*
(also see: I Don't Like It Like That)
25/67 **I Like The Way** *Tommy James*
1/91 **I Like The Way (The Kissing Game)** *Hi-Five*
35[S]/00 **I Like Dem Girlz** *Lil Jon & The East Side Boyz*
48/01 **I Like Them Girls** *Tyrese*
37/77 **I Like To Do It** *KC & The Sunshine Band*
28/74 **I Like To Live The Love** *B.B. King*
89/94 **I Like To Move It** *Reel 2 Real*
86/80 **I Like To Rock** *April Wine*
70/71 **I Like What You Give** *Nolan*
49/69 **I Like What You're Doing (To Me)** *Carla Thomas*
61/86 **I Like You** *Phyllis Nelson*
66/73 **I Like You** *Donovan*
56[A]/91 **I Like You** *Culture Beat*
8/57 **I Like Your Kind Of Love** *Andy Williams*
72/70 **I Like Your Lovin'** *Chi-Lites*
38/71 **I Likes To Do It** *People's Choice*
31/89 **I Live By The Groove** *Paul Carrack*
51/65 **I Live For The Sun** *Sunrays*
13/88 **I Live For Your Love** *Natalie Cole*
26/95 **I Live My Life For You** *Firehouse*
66/56 **I Look At You** *Lassies*
100/59 **I Looked At Heaven** *Tommy Edwards*
34/00 **I Lost It** *Kenny Chesney*
61/62 **I Lost My Baby** *Joey Dee*
81/84 **I Lost On Jeopardy** *"Weird Al" Yankovic*

I LOVE:

12/74 **I Love** *Tom T. Hall*
1/81 **I Love A Rainy Night** *Eddie Rabbitt*
66/59 **I Love An Angel** *Little Bill & The Bluenotes*
I Love How You Love Me
5/61 *Paris Sisters*
9/68 *Bobby Vinton*
I Love Lucy ..see: Disco Lucy
50/75 **I Love Makin' Love To You** *Evie Sands*
F/97 **I Love Me Some Him** *Toni Braxton*
87/56 **I Love Mickey** *Mickey Mantle & Teresa Brewer*
I Love Music
5/76 *O'Jays*
76/94 *Rozalla*
94/69 **I Love My Baby** *Archie Bell*
21/57 **I Love My Baby (My Baby Loves Me)** *Jill Corey*
24/74 **I Love My Friend** *Charlie Rich*
I Love My Girl
62/57 *Cozy Morley*
75/57 *Hilltoppers*
69/78 **I Love My Music** *Wild Cherry*
94/81 **I Love My Truck** *Glen Campbell*
63/66 **I Love Onions** *Susan Christie*
1/82 **I Love Rock 'N Roll** *Joan Jett*
5/78 **I Love The Nightlife (Disco 'Round)** *Alicia Bridges*
9/60 **I Love The Way You Love** *Marv Johnson*
60/93 **I Love The Way You Love Me** *John Michael Montgomery*
68/89 **I Love To Bass** *Bardeux*
90/80 **I Love Women** *Jim Hurt*
12/81 **I Love You** *Climax Blues Band*
14/68 **I Love You** *People*
14/02 **I Love You** *Faith Evans*
22/62 **I Love You** *Volume's*
24/99 **I Love You** *Martina McBride*
37/78 **I Love You** *Donna Summer*
52/91 **I Love You** *Vanilla Ice*
63/70 **I Love You** *Otis Leavill*
65/95 **I Love You** *Mary J. Blige*
2/96 **I Love You Always Forever** *Donna Lewis*
97/57 **I Love You, Baby** *Paul Anka*
(also see: I Luv U Baby)
3/63 **I Love You Because** *Al Martino*
54/99 **I Love You Came Too Late** *Joey McIntyre*
39/63 **(I Love You) Don't You Forget It** *Perry Como*
30/66 **I Love You Drops** *Vic Dana*
21/71 **I Love You For All Seasons** *Fuzz*
(I Love You) For Sentimental Reasons
17/58 *Sam Cooke*
60/61 *Cleftones*
81/78 **I Love You, I Love You, I Love You** *Ronnie McDowell*
40/60 **I Love You In The Same Old Way** *Paul Anka*
64/71 **I Love You Lady Dawn** *Bells*
28/55 **I Love You Madly** *Four Coins*
56/68 **I Love You Madly** *Fantastic Four*
9/64 **I Love You More And More Every Day** *Al Martino*
78/67 **I Love You More Than Words Can Say** *Otis Redding*
60/72 **I Love You More Than You'll Ever Know** *Donny Hathaway*
31/66 **I Love You 1000 Times** *Platters*
26/93 **I Love You Period.** *Dan Baird*
42/58 **I Love You So** *Chantels*
70/65 **I Love You So** *Bobbi Martin*
(also see: Ko Ko Mo)
71/57 **I Love You So Much It Hurts** *Charlie Gracie*
38/62 **I Love You The Way You Are** *Bobby Vinton*
98/61 **I Love You Yes I Do** *Bull Moose Jackson*
2/92 **I Love Your Smile** *Shanice*
61/68 **I Loved And I Lost** *Impressions*
37/81 **I Loved 'Em Every One** *T.G. Sheppard*
18/59 **I Loves You, Porgy** *Nina Simone*
66/96 **I Luv U Baby** *Original*
10/81 **I Made It Through The Rain** *Barry Manilow*
18/67 **I Make A Fool Of Myself** *Frankie Valli*
69/63 **I May Not Live To See Tomorrow** *Brian Hyland*
I Melt With You
78/83 *Modern English*
76/90 *Modern English*
37/68 **I Met Her In Church** *Box Tops*
68[S]/01 **I Met Her In Miami** *Liberty City FLA.*
49/58 **I Met Him On A Sunday** *Shirelles*
28/02 **I Miss My Friend** *Darryl Worley*
25/97 **I Miss My Homies** *Master P*
5/85 **I Miss You** *Klymaxx*
14/94 **I Miss You** *Aaron Hall*
22/95 **I Miss You** *N II U*
55/92 **I Miss You** *Joe Public*
58/72 **I Miss You** *Harold Melvin*
60/74 **I Miss You** *Dells*
86/02 **I Miss You** *DMX*
95/73 **I Miss You Baby** *Millie Jackson*
56/96 **I Miss You (Come Back Home)** *Monifa*
I Miss You So
34/57 *Chris Connor*
33/59 *Paul Anka*
34/65 *Little Anthony & The Imperials*
19/81 **I Missed Again** *Phil Collins*
44/60 **I Missed Me** *Jim Reeves*
63/92 **I Missed The Bus** *Kris Kross*
52/86 **I Must Be Dreaming** *Giuffria*
69/59 **I Must Be Dreaming** *Nat "King" Cole*
31/65 **I Must Be Seeing Things** *Gene Pitney*

I NEED:

2/02 **I Need A Girl (Part One)** *P. Diddy*
4/02 **I Need A Girl (Part Two)** *P. Diddy & Ginuwine*
65/00 **I Need A Hot Girl** *Hot Boy$*
28/79 **I Need A Lover** *John Cougar*
46/88 **I Need A Man** *Eurythmics*
83/77 **I Need A Man** *Grace Jones*
69/70 **I Need Help (I Can't Do It Alone)** *Bobby Byrd*
14/87 **I Need Love** *LL Cool J*
96/92 **I Need Love** *Olivia Newton-John*
98/66 **I Need Love** *Barbara Mason*
61/92 **I Need Money** *Marky Mark & The Funky Bunch*
75/62 **I Need Some One** *Belmonts*
22/66 **I Need Somebody** *? (Question Mark) & The Mysterians*
86/71 **I Need Someone (To Love Me)** *Z.Z. Hill*
25/76 **I Need To Be In Love** *Carpenters*
3/99 **I Need To Know** *Marc Anthony*
41/78 **I Need To Know** *Tom Petty*
9/72 **I Need You** *America*
11/00 **I Need You** *LeAnn Rimes*
37/82 **I Need You** *Paul Carrack*
48/83 **I Need You** *Pointer Sisters*
64/65 **I Need You** *Impressions*
75/65 **I Need You** *Chuck Jackson*
79/71 **I Need You** *Friends Of Distinction*
81/79 **I Need You** *Euclid Beach Band*
83/63 **I Need You** *Rick Nelson*
95/86 **I Need You** *Maurice White*

I Need You Now
1/54 *Eddie Fisher*
98/60 *Joni James*
93/69 *Ronnie Dove*
98/65 **I Need You So**
Chuck Jackson & Maxine Brown
85/57 **I Need You So Bad** *B.B. King*
36/84 **I Need You Tonight** *Peter Wolf*
60S/95 **I Need You Tonight**
Junior M.A.F.I.A.
49/79 **I Need Your Help Barry Manilow**
Ray Stevens
51/94 **I Need Your Love** *Boston*
4/59 **I Need Your Love Tonight**
Elvis Presley
37/81 **I Need Your Lovin'** *Teena Marie*
62/59 **I Need Your Lovin'** *Roy Hamilton*
93/57 **I Need Your Lovin'** *Conway Twitty*
20/62 **I Need Your Loving**
Don Gardner & Dee Dee Ford
44/87 **I Need Your Loving** *Human League*
12/77 **I Never Cry** *Alice Cooper*
78/59 **I Never Felt Like This** *Jack Scott*
45S/02 **I Never Knew** *Gloria Gaynor*
56/61 **I Never Knew** *Clyde McPhatter*
81/94 **I Never Knew Love** *Doug Stone*
9/67 **I Never Loved A Man (The Way I Love You)** *Aretha Franklin*
61/73 **I Never Said Goodbye**
Engelbert Humperdinck
84/79 **I Never Said I Love You** *Orsa Lia*
37/95 **I Never Seen A Man Cry (aka I Seen A Man Die)** *Scarface*
I Only Have Eyes For You
11/59 *Flamingos*
72/66 *Lettermen*
85/72 *Jerry Butler*
18/75 *Art Garfunkel*
22/56 **I Only Know I Love You** *Four Aces*
I Only Want To Be With You
12/64 *Dusty Springfield*
12/76 *Bay City Rollers*
83/80 *Tourists*
53/82 *Nicolette Larson*
31/89 *Samantha Fox*
I Pity The Fool
46/61 *Bobby Bland*
85/71 *Ann Peebles*
25/71 **I Play And Sing** *Dawn*
19/80 **I Pledge My Love** *Peaches & Herb*
60/82 **I Predict** *Sparks*
74/84 **I Pretend** *Kim Carnes*
57/56 **I Promise To Remember**
Frankie Lymon
62/68 **I Promise To Wait My Love**
Martha & The Vandellas
I Put A Spell On You
80/66 *Alan Price Set*
58/68 *Creedence Clearwater Revival*
9/82 **I Ran (So Far Away)**
Flock Of Seagulls
39/82 **I Really Don't Need No Light**
Jeffrey Osborne
I Really Don't Want To Know
18/60 *Tommy Edwards*
93/62 *Solomon Burke*
61/63 *Esther Phillips*
22/66 *Ronnie Dove*
21/71 *Elvis Presley*
29/61 **I Really Love You** *Stereos*
78/65 **I Really Love You** *Dee Dee Sharp*
90/72 **I Received A Letter** *Delbert & Glen*
46/96 **I Remember** *Boyz II Men*
86/61 **I Remember** *Maurice Williams*
8/89 **I Remember Holding You**
Boys Club
98/70 **(I Remember) Summer Morning**
Vanity Fare
5/62 **I Remember You** *Frank Ifield*
6/90 **I Remember You** *Skid Row*
36/64 **I Rise, I Fall** *Johnny Tillotson*
42/74 **I Saw A Man And He Danced With His Wife** *Chér*
51/56 **I Saw Esau** *Ames Brothers*
5/66 **I Saw Her Again**
Mamas & The Papas
I Saw Her (Him) Standing There
14/64 *Beatles*
7/88 *Tiffany*
89/94 **I Saw It Cummin'** *PMD*
14/63 **I Saw Linda Yesterday** *Dickey Lee*
19X/64 **I Saw Mommy Kissing Santa Claus**
Four Seasons
10/91 **I Saw Red** *Warrant*
16/72 **I Saw The Light** *Todd Rundgren*
54/95 **I Saw You Dancing** *Yaki Da*
I Say A Little Prayer
4/67 *Dionne Warwick*
10/68 *Aretha Franklin*
81/71 *Glen Campbell/Anne Murray (medley)*
38/97 *Diana King*
72/68 **I Say Love** *Royal Guardsmen*
24S/01 **I Say Yeah** *Dream Street*
4/67 **I Second That Emotion** *Miracles*
84/94 **I See It Now** *Tracy Lawrence*
51S/02 **I See Right Through To You**
DJ Encore (feat.) Engelina
26/66 **I See The Light** *Five Americans*
82/64 **I See You** *Cathy & Joe*
69S/00 **I See You Baby** *Groove Armada*
48/93 **I See Your Smile** *Gloria Estefan*
77/84 **I Send A Message** *INXS*
67/69 **I Shall Be Released** *Box Tops*
38/74 **I Shall Sing** *Art Garfunkel*
52/60 **I Shot Mr. Lee** *Bobbettes*
I Shot The Sheriff
1/74 *Eric Clapton*
20/97 *Warren G*
25/03 **I Should Be...** *Dru Hill*
86/93 **I Should Be Laughing** *Patty Smyth*
35/02 **I Should Be Sleeping**
Emerson Drive
28/88 **I Should Be So Lucky**
Kylie Minogue
64/64 **I Should Care** *Gloria Lynne*
72/98 **I Should Cheat On You** *J'Son*
53/64 **I Should Have Known Better**
Beatles
66/80 **I Shoulda Loved Ya**
Narada Michael Walden
40S/91 **I Shouldn't Have Done It** *Slick Rick*
15/62 **I Sold My Heart To The Junkman**
Blue-Belles
98/66 **I Spy (For The FBI)** *Jamo Thomas*
I Stand Accused
61/64 *Jerry Butler*
42/70 *Isaac Hayes*
74/67 **I Stand Accused (Of Loving You)**
Glories
6/69 **I Started A Joke** *Bee Gees*
86/70 **I Started Loving You Again**
Al Martino
I Still Believe
13/88 *Brenda K. Starr*
4/99 *Mariah Carey*
70/69 **I Still Believe In Tomorrow**
John & Anne Ryder
12/84 **I Still Can't Get Over Loving You**
Ray Parker Jr.
51/59 **I Still Get A Thrill (Thinking Of You)** *Joni James*
I Still Get Jealous
63/59 *Joni James*
45/64 *Louis Armstrong*
39/79 **I Still Have Dreams** *Richie Furay*
1/87 **I Still Haven't Found What I'm Looking For** *U2*
14/98 **I Still Love You** *Next*
79/57 **I Still Love You** *Fats Domino*
84/65 **I Still Love You** *Vejtables*
94/98 **I Still Love You** *Lil Suzy*
87/86 **I Still Want You** *Del Fuegos*
98/66 **I Struck It Rich** *Len Barry*
71/81 **I Surrender** *Arlan Day*
78/66 **I Surrender** *Fontella Bass*
87/62 **I Surrender, Dear** *Aretha Franklin*
I Swear
1/94 *All-4-One*
42/94 *John Michael Montgomery*
75/69 **I Take A Lot Of Pride In What I Am**
Dean Martin
12/67 **I Take It Back** *Sandy Posey*
41/67 **I Take What I Want**
James & Bobby Purify
77/59 **I Talk To The Trees** *Edmundo Ros*
13/67 **I Thank The Lord For The Night Time** *Neil Diamond*
I Thank You
9/68 *Sam & Dave*
34/80 *ZZ Top*
94/72 **I Thank You**
Donny Hathaway & June Conquest
62/00 **I Think God Can Explain** *Splender*
58/89 **I Think I Can Beat Mike Tyson**
D.J. Jazzy Jeff & The Fresh Prince
1/70 **I Think I Love You** *Partridge Family*
97/70 **I Think I Love You Again**
Brenda Lee
55/59 **I Think I'm Gonna Kill Myself**
Buddy Knox
21/00 **I Think I'm In Love With You**
Jessica Simpson
70A/98 **I Think I'm Paranoid** *Garbage*
16/86 **I Think It's Love** *Jermaine Jackson*
53/71 **I Think Of You** *Perry Como*
I Think We're Alone Now
4/67 *Tommy James*
45/77 *Rubinoos*
1/87 *Tiffany*
94/83 **I Think You'll Remember Tonight**
Axe
47/76 **I Thought It Took A Little Time**
Diana Ross
85/69 **I Threw It All Away** *Bob Dylan*
70/59 **I Told Myself A Lie**
Clyde McPhatter
81/62 **I Told The Brook** *Marty Robbins*
94/02 **I Told Y'all** *Petey Pablo*
85/61 **I Told You So** *Jimmy Jones*
4/91 **I Touch Myself** *Divinyls*
5/00 **I Try** *Macy Gray*
3/00 **I Turn To You** *Christina Aguilera*
43S/01 **I Turn To You** *Melanie C*
23/69 **I Turned You On** *Isley Brothers*
I Understand (Just How You Feel)
9/61 *G-Clefs*
36/65 *Freddie & The Dreamers*
33/59 **I Waited Too Long** *LaVern Baker*
59/61 **I Wake Up Crying** *Chuck Jackson*
65/68 **I Walk Alone** *Marty Robbins*
I Walk The Line
17/56 *Johnny Cash*
59/59 *Don Costa*
66/60 *Jaye P. Morgan*

I WANNA:

F/57 **I Wanna** *Platters*

12/86 **I Wanna Be A Cowboy** *Boys Don't Cry*
14/63 **I Wanna Be Around** *Tony Bennett*
22/01 **I Wanna Be Bad** *Willa Ford*
6/94 **I Wanna Be Down** *Brandy*
94/71 **I Wanna Be Free** *Loretta Lynn*
20/59 **I Wanna Be Loved** *Ricky Nelson*
58/89 **I Wanna Be Loved** *House Of Lords*
91/64 **I Wanna Be Loved** *Dean & Jean*
2/90 **I Wanna Be Rich** *Calloway*
32/89 **I Wanna Be The One** *Stevie B*
39/97 **I Wanna Be There** *Blessid Union Of Souls*
16/72 **I Wanna Be Where You Are** *Michael Jackson*
45/95 **I Wanna B With U** *Fun Factory*
16/73 **I Wanna Be With You** *Raspberries*
24/00 **I Wanna Be With You** *Mandy Moore*
I Wanna Be With You
57/64 *Nancy Wilson*
41/66 *Dee Dee Warwick*
68/65 **I Wanna Be (Your Everything)** *Manhattans*
46/92 **I Wanna Be Your Girl** *Icy Blu*
11/80 **I Wanna Be Your Lover** *Prince*
23/75 **I Wanna Dance Wit' Choo** *Disco Tex & The Sex-O-Lettes*
1/87 **I Wanna Dance With Somebody (Who Loves Me)** *Whitney Houston*
71/59 **(I Wanna) Dance With The Teacher** *Olympics*
51/77 **I Wanna Do It To You** *Jerry Butler*
69/90 **I Wanna Get Back With You** *Louie Louie*
I Wanna Get Next To You
10/77 *Rose Royce*
86/98 *Christión*
50/90 **I Wanna Get With U** *Guy*
66A/91 **(i wanna give you) Devotion** *Nomad*
I Wanna Go Back
78/84 *Billy Satellite*
14/87 *Eddie Money*
75/55 **I Wanna Go Where You Go** *Eddie Fisher*
8/89 **I Wanna Have Some Fun** *Samantha Fox*
35/85 **I Wanna Hear It From Your Lips** *Eric Carmen*
4/00 **I Wanna Know** *Joe*
81/70 **I Wanna Know If It's Good To You?** *Funkadelic*
60/73 **I Wanna Know Your Name** *Intruders*
44/75 **I Wanna Learn A Love Song** *Harry Chapin*
36/68 **I Wanna Live** *Glen Campbell*
9/64 **I Wanna Love Him So Bad** *Jelly Beans*
59/95 **I Wanna Love Like That** *Tony Thompson*
39/61 **(I Wanna) Love My Life Away** *Gene Pitney*
16/92 **I Wanna Love You** *Jade*
3/99 **I Wanna Love You Forever** *Jessica Simpson*
73/92 **I Wanna Make Love To You** *Rhythm Syndicate*
85/66 **I Wanna Meet You** *Cryan Shames*
68/84 **I Wanna Rock** *Twisted Sister*
73/92 **I Wanna Rock** *Luke*
2/91 **I Wanna Sex You Up** *Color Me Badd*
(also see: If You Wanna Sex Me Up)
49/76 **I Wanna Stay With You** *Gallagher & Lyle*
86/95 **(I Wanna Take) Forever Tonight** *Peter Cetera with Crystal Bernard*
28/01 **I Wanna Talk About Me** *Toby Keith*
(I Wanna) Testify
20/67 *Parliaments*
36/69 *Johnnie Taylor*
21/61 **I Wanna Thank You** *Bobby Rydell*
91/64 **I Wanna Thank You** *Enchanters*

I WANT:

6/84 **I Want A New Drug** *Huey Lewis*
50/87 **I Want Action** *Poison*
I Want Candy
11/65 *Strangeloves*
62/82 *Bow Wow Wow*
5/88 **I Want Her** *Keith Sweat*
23/99 **I Want It All** *Warren G*
50/89 **I Want It All** *Queen*
6/99 **I Want It That Way** *Backstreet Boys*
92/65 **I Want My Baby Back** *Jimmy Cross*
76/85 **I Want My Girl** *Jesse Johnson's Revue*
74/66 **I Want Someone** *Mad Lads*
I Want To ..also see: I Wanna / I Want'a
44/75 **I Want To Be Free** *Ohio Players*
69S/92 **I Want To Be Free (That's The Truth)** *Too $hort*
I Want To Be Happy Cha Cha
48/58 *Enoch Light*
70/58 *Tommy Dorsey*
76/62 **I Want To Be Loved** *Dinah Washington*
1/60 **I Want To Be Wanted** *Brenda Lee*
3/88 **I Want To Be Your Man** *Roger*
66/88 **I Want To Be Your Property** *Blue Mercedes*
45/84 **I Want To Break Free** *Queen*
22/96 **I Want To Come Over** *Melissa Etheridge*
84/75 **I Want To Dance With You (Dance With Me)** *Ritchie Family*
I Want To (Do Everything For You)
23/65 *Joe Tex*
96/70 *Raeletts*
36/66 **I Want To Go With You** *Eddy Arnold*
I Want To Hold Your Hand
1/64 *Beatles*
55/64 *Boston Pops Orchestra*
1/85 **I Want To Know What Love Is** *Foreigner*
55/78 **I Want To Live** *John Denver*
81/69 **I Want To Love You Baby** *Peggy Scott & Jo Jo Benson*
54/67 **I Want To Love You For What You Are** *Ronnie Dove*
97/86 **I Want To Make The World Turn Around** *Steve Miller Band*
72/65 **I Want To Meet Him** *Royalettes*
95/71 **I Want To Pay You Back (For Loving Me)** *Chi-Lites*
28/63 **I Want To Stay Here** *Steve & Eydie*
I Want To Take You Higher
60/69 *Sly & The Family Stone*
34/70 *Ike & Tina Turner*
38/70 *Sly & The Family Stone*
98/67 **I Want To Talk About You** *Ray Charles*
8/59 **I Want To Walk You Home** *Fats Domino*
39S/99 **I Want U** *Reel Tight*
4/97 **I Want You** *Savage Garden*
I Want You
15/76 *Marvin Gaye*
16/91 *Robert Palmer (medley)*
20/66 **I Want You** *Bob Dylan*
40/90 **I Want You** *Shana*
44/94 **I Want You** *Juliet Roberts*
61/92 **I Want You** *Jody Watley*
84/86 **I Want You** *Animotion*
1/70 **I Want You Back** *Jackson 5*
13/98 **I Want You Back** *'N Sync*
95/65 **I Want You Back Again** *Zombies*
37/81 **I Want You, I Need You** *Chris Christian*
1/56 **I Want You, I Need You, I Love You** *Elvis Presley*
49/88 **I Want You So Bad** *Heart*
55/78 **I Want You To Be Mine** *Kayak*
I Want You To Be My Baby
14/55 *Georgia Gibbs*
18/55 *Lillian Briggs*
83/67 *Ellie Greenwich*
I Want You To Be My Girl (Boy)
13/56 *Frankie Lymon*
98/65 *Exciters*
32/58 **I Want You To Know** *Fats Domino*
65/69 **I Want You To Know** *New Colony Six*
43/64 **I Want You To Meet My Baby** *Eydie Gorme*
7/79 **I Want You To Want Me** *Cheap Trick*
19/79 **I Want You Tonight** *Pablo Cruise*
7/79 **I Want Your Love** *Chic*
2/87 **I Want Your Sex** *George Michael*
15/75 **I Want'a Do Something Freaky To You** *Leon Haywood*
42/62 **(I was) Born To Cry** *Dion*
76/85 **I Was Born To Love You** *Freddie Mercury*
29/73 **I Was Checkin' Out She Was Checkin' In** *Don Covay*
20/67 **I Was Kaiser Bill's Batman** *Whistling Jack Smith*
78/80 **I Was Looking For Someone To Love** *Leif Garrett*
10/79 **I Was Made For Dancin'** *Leif Garrett*
11/79 **I Was Made For Lovin' You** *Kiss*
I Was Made To Love Her
2/67 *Stevie Wonder*
76/68 *King Curtis*
22/78 **I Was Only Joking** *Rod Stewart*
I Was Such A Fool (To Fall In Love With You)
71/60 *Flamingos*
24/62 *Connie Francis*
19/56 **I Was The One** *Elvis Presley*
100/71 **I Was Wondering** *Poppy Family*
54A/96 **I Was Wrong** *Social Distortion*
88/74 **I Wash My Hands Of The Whole Damn Deal** *New Birth*
19/66 **(I Washed My Hands In) Muddy Water** *Johnny Rivers*
93/88 **I Wasn't The One (Who Said Goodbye)** *Agnetha Fältskog & Peter Cetera*
85/98 **I Wasn't With It** *Jesse Powell*
I (Who Have Nothing)
29/63 *Ben E. King*
46/67 *Terry Knight*
14/70 *Tom Jones*
82/70 *Liquid Smoke*
40/79 *Sylvester*

I WILL:

I Will ..also see: I'll

I Will
47/62 *Vic Dana*
10/65 *Dean Martin*
I Will Always Love You
53/82 *Dolly Parton*
1/92 *Whitney Houston*
22/68 **I Will Always Think About You** *New Colony Six*
27/92 **I Will Be Here For You** *Michael W. Smith*
30/79 **I Will Be In Love With You** *Livingston Taylor*
34/87 **I Will Be There** *Glass Tiger*
66S/99 **I Will Be There For You** *Jessica Andrews*
73S/00 **I Will Be Waiting** *D-Cru*
41/78 **(I Will Be Your) Shadow In The Street** *Allan Clarke*
43/00 **I Will...But** *SheDaisy*
33A/98 **I Will Buy You A New Life** *Everclear*
9/97 **I Will Come To You** *Hanson*
81/84 **I Will Follow** *U2*
1/63 **I Will Follow Him** *Little Peggy March*
32/99 **I Will Get There** *Boyz II Men*
79/99 **I Will Go With You (Con Te Partiró)** *Donna Summer*
85/63 **I Will Live My Life For You** *Tony Bennett*
32/00 **I Will Love Again** *Lara Fabian*
65/63 **I Will Love You** *Richard Chamberlain*
61/72 **I Will Never Pass This Way Again** *Glen Campbell*
I Will Remember You
65/96 *Sarah McLachlan*
14/99 *Sarah McLachlan (Live)*
20/92 **I Will Remember You** *Amy Grant*
71S/98 **I Will Stand** *Kenny Chesney*
29/78 **I Will Still Love You** *Stonebolt*
I Will Survive
1/79 *Gloria Gaynor*
53/90 *Safire*
24/96 *Chantay Savage*
18A/98 **I Will Wait** *Hootie & The Blowfish*
1/77 **I Wish** *Stevie Wonder*
13/95 **I Wish** *Skee-Lo*
14/01 **I Wish** *R. Kelly*
20/00 **I Wish** *Carl Thomas*
42/58 **I Wish** *Platters*
52/94 **I Wish** *Gabrielle*
20/88 **I Wish I Had A Girl** *Henry Lee Summer*
68/68 **I Wish I Knew** *Solomon Burke*
49/80 **I Wish I Was Eighteen Again** *George Burns*
62/71 **I Wish I Were** *Andy Kim*
32/63 **I Wish I Were A Princess** *Little Peggy March*
52/60 **I Wish I'd Never Been Born** *Patti Page*
57/74 **I Wish It Was Me** *Tyrone Davis*
94/74 **I Wish It Was Me You Loved** *Dells*
I Wish It Would Rain
4/68 *Temptations*
41/68 *Gladys Knight*
3/90 **I Wish It Would Rain Down** *Phil Collins*
16/62 **I Wish That We Were Married** *Ronnie & The Hi-Lites*
28/92 **I Wish The Phone Would Ring** *Exposé*
70/67 **I Wish You Could Be Here** *Cyrkle*
28/64 **I Wish You Love** *Gloria Lynne*
72/56 **I Woke Up Crying** *Joni James*
13/71 **I Woke Up In Love This Morning** *Partridge Family*
12/89 **I Won't Back Down** *Tom Petty*
34S/02 **I Won't Be Home For Christmas** *Blink-182*
79/83 **I Won't Be Home Tonight** *Tony Carey*
13/87 **I Won't Forget You** *Poison*
93/64 **I Won't Forget You** *Jim Reeves*
65/90 **I Won't Give Up On You** *TKA*
10/83 **I Won't Hold You Back** *Toto*
I Won't Last A Day Without You
89/73 *Maureen McGovern*
11/74 *Carpenters*
70/75 *Al Wilson (medley)*
80/65 **I Won't Love You Anymore (Sorry)** *Lesley Gore*
42/71 **I Won't Mention It Again** *Ray Price*
35/83 **I Won't Stand In Your Way** *Stray Cats*
25/63 **I Wonder** *Brenda Lee*
67/97 **I Wonder If Heaven Got A Ghetto** *2Pac*
F/57 **I Wonder If I Care As Much** *Everly Brothers*
34/85 **I Wonder If I Take You Home** *Lisa-Lisa & Cult Jam*
84/61 **I Wonder (If Your Love Will Ever Belong To Me)** *Pentagons*
8/68 **I Wonder What She's Doing Tonite** *Tommy Boyce & Bobby Hart*
21/63 **I Wonder What She's Doing Tonight** *Barry & The Tamerlanes*
93/64 **I Wonder Who's Kissing Her Now** *Bobby Darin*
9/91 **I Wonder Why** *Curtis Stigers*
22/58 **I Wonder Why** *Dion & The Belmonts*
98/68 **I Worry About You** *Joe Simon*
88/70 **I Would Be In Love (Anyway)** *Frank Sinatra*
8/85 **I Would Die 4 U** *Prince*
(also see: *I'd Die Without You*)
44/01 **I Would've Loved You Anyway** *Trisha Yearwood*
64/82 **I Wouldn't Beg For Water** *Sheena Easton*
20/82 **I Wouldn't Have Missed It For The World** *Ronnie Milsap*
93/62 **I Wouldn't Know (What To Do)** *Dinah Washington*
22/56 **I Wouldn't Know Where To Begin** *Eddy Arnold*
93/86 **I Wouldn't Lie** *Yarbrough & Peoples*
69/64 **I Wouldn't Trade You For The World** *Bachelors*
88/74 **I Wouldn't Treat A Dog (The Way You Treated Me)** *Bobby Bland*
36/77 **I Wouldn't Want To Be Like You** *Alan Parsons*
1/76 **I Write The Songs** *Barry Manilow*
77/72 **I Wrote A Simple Song** *Billy Preston*

I'D:

3/92 **I'd Die Without You** *PM Dawn*
1/93 **I'd Do Anything For Love (But I Won't Do That)** *Meat Loaf*
52/86 **I'd Do It All Again** *Sam Harris*
28/94 **I'd Give Anything** *Gerald Levert*
88/74 **(I'd Know You) Anywhere** *Ashford & Simpson*
13/95 **I'd Lie For You (And That's The Truth)** *Meat Loaf*
72S/94 **I'd Like To Have That One Back** *George Strait*
I'd Like To Teach The World To Sing (In Perfect Harmony)
7/72 *New Seekers*
13/72 *Hillside Singers*
40/71 **I'd Love To Change The World** *Ten Years After*
2/72 **I'd Love You To Want Me** *Lobo*
83/02 **I'd Rather** *Luther Vandross*
62/73 **I'd Rather Be A Cowboy** *John Denver*
44/95 **I'd Rather Be Alone** *IV Xample*
46/69 **I'd Rather Be An Old Man's Sweetheart** *Candi Staton*
91/63 **I'd Rather Be Here In Your Arms** *Duprees*
70/71 **I'd Rather Be Sorry** *Ray Price*
46/90 **I'd Rather Go Blind** *Sydney Youngblood*
38/80 **I'd Rather Leave While I'm In Love** *Rita Coolidge*
79/71 **I'd Rather Love You** *Charley Pride*
2/76 **I'd Really Love To See You Tonight** *England Dan & John Ford Coley*
18/87 **I'd Still Say Yes** *Klymaxx*
15/69 **I'd Wait A Million Years** *Grass Roots*

I'LL:

I'll ..also see: I Will

65/56 **I'll Always Be In Love With You** *Jack Pleis*
59A/97 **I'll Always Be Right There** *Bryan Adams*
62/77 **I'll Always Call Your Name** *Little River Band*
85/67 **I'll Always Have Faith In You** *Carla Thomas*
36/73 **I'll Always Love My Mama** *Intruders*
3/88 **I'll Always Love You** *Taylor Dayne*
35/65 **I'll Always Love You** *Spinners*
60/64 **I'll Always Love You** *Brenda Holloway*
5/98 **I'll Be** *Edwin McCain*
7/97 **I'll Be** *Foxy Brown*
51/00 **I'll Be** *Reba McEntire*
14/87 **I'll Be Alright Without You** *Journey*
I'll Be Around
3/72 *Spinners*
62/85 *What Is This*
39/95 *Rappin' 4-Tay*
78/56 **I'll Be Around** *Don Cherry*
12/91 **I'll Be By Your Side** *Stevie B*
8/65 **I'll Be Doggone** *Marvin Gaye*
92/66 **I'll Be Gone** *Pozo Seco Singers*
47/85 **I'll Be Good** *René & Angela*
I'll Be Good To You
3/76 *Brothers Johnson*
18/90 *Quincy Jones*
85/75 **I'll Be Holding On** *Al Downing*
I'll Be Home
4/56 *Pat Boone*
97/66 *Platters*
96/71 **I'll Be Home** *Vikki Carr*
26X/66 **I'll Be Home For Christmas** *Brothers Four*
33/64 **I'll Be In Trouble** *Temptations*
56/94 **I'll Be Loving You** *Collage*
1/89 **I'll Be Loving You (Forever)** *New Kids On The Block*
I'll Be Missing You
1/97 *Puff Daddy & Faith Evans*
56S/01 *Puff Daddy & Faith Evans*
11/86 **I'll Be Over You** *Toto*

53/70 **I'll Be Right Here** *Tyrone Davis*
20/59 **I'll Be Satisfied** *Jackie Wilson*
I'll Be Seeing You
51/59 *Tommy Sands*
87/59 *Poni-Tails*
79/60 *Five Satins*
58/61 *Frank Sinatra*
67/77 **I'll Be Standing By** *Foghat*
66/68 **I'll Be Sweeter Tomorrow** *O'Jays*
36/74 **I'll Be The Other Woman** *Soul Children*
I'll Be There
1/70 *Jackson 5*
1/92 *Mariah Carey*
54[S]/02 *Mariah Carey*
8/91 **I'll Be There** *Escape Club*
12/61 **I'll Be There** *Damita Jo*
I'll Be There
79/60 *Bobby Darin*
14/65 *Gerry & The Pacemakers*
70/90 **I'll Be There** *Joyce "Fenderella" Irby*
88/85 **I'll Be There** *Kenny Loggins*
(also see: Stand By Me)
1/89 **I'll Be There For You** *Bon Jovi*
3/95 **I'll Be There For You (medley)** *Method Man*
17/95 **I'll Be There For You (Theme from "Friends")** *Rembrandts*
(I'll Be With You In) Apple Blossom Time
31/59 *Tab Hunter*
52/65 *Wayne Newton*
51/89 **I'll Be You** *Replacements*
1/90 **I'll Be Your Everything** *Tommy Page*
62/74 **I'll Be Your Everything** *Percy Sledge*
71/99 **I'll Be Your Everything** *Youngstown*
4/90 **I'll Be Your Shelter** *Taylor Dayne*
40/73 **I'll Be Your Shelter (In Time Of Storm)** *Luther Ingram*
63/69 **I'll Bet You** *Funkadelic*
41/62 **I'll Bring It Home To You** *Carla Thomas*
(also see: Bring It On Home To Me)
82/79 **I'll Come Running** *Livingston Taylor*
18/58 **I'll Come Running Back To You** *Sam Cooke*
25/64 **I'll Cry Instead** *Beatles*
20/91 **I'll Do 4 U** *Father M.C.*
40/75 **I'll Do For You Anything You Want Me To** *Barry White*
77/67 **I'll Do It For You** *Toussaint McCall*
58/82 **I'll Drink To You** *Duke Jupiter*
71/71 **I'll Erase Away Your Pain** *Whatnauts*
43/82 **I'll Fall In Love Again** *Sammy Hagar*
51/82 **I'll Find My Way Home** *Jon & Vangelis*
78/01 **I'll Fly With You (L'Amour Toujours)** *Gigi D'Agostino*
21/92 **I'll Get By** *Eddie Money*
87/58 **I'll Get By (As Long As I Have You)** *Billy Williams*
71/76 **I'll Get Over You** *Crystal Gayle*
7/91 **I'll Give All My Love To You** *Keith Sweat*
65/99 **I'll Go Crazy** *Andy Griggs*
73/66 **I'll Go Crazy** *James Brown*
93/75 **I'll Go To My Grave Loving You** *Statler Brothers*
9/74 **I'll Have To Say I Love You In A Song** *Jim Croce*
45/69 **I'll Hold Out My Hand** *Clique*
84/61 **I'll Just Have A Cup Of Coffee (Then I'll Go)** *Claude Gray*
34/65 **I'll Keep Holding On** *Marvelettes*
30/64 **I'll Keep You Satisfied** *Billy J. Kramer*
87/56 **I'll Know** *Sammy Davis, Jr.*
79/79 **I'll Know Her When I See Her** *Cooper Brothers Band*
63/66 **I'll Love You Forever** *Holidays*
21/65 **I'll Make All Your Dreams Come True** *Ronnie Dove*
15[X]/67 **I'll Make Every Day Christmas (For My Woman)** *Joe Tex*
72/67 **I'll Make Him Love Me** *Barbara Lewis*
85/58 **I'll Make It All Up To You** *Jerry Lee Lewis*
97/63 **I'll Make It Alright** *Valentinos (The Lovers)*
1/94 **I'll Make Love To You** *Boyz II Men*
52/64 **I'll Make You Mine** *Bobby Vee*
63/72 **I'll Make You Music** *Beverly Bremers*
9/71 **I'll Meet You Halfway** *Partridge Family*
94/61 **I'll Never Be Free** *Kay Starr*
4[A]/98 **I'll Never Break Your Heart** *Backstreet Boys*
14/62 **I'll Never Dance Again** *Bobby Rydell*
59/68 **I'll Never Do You Wrong** *Joe Tex*
I'll Never Fall In Love Again
49/67 *Tom Jones*
6/69 *Tom Jones*
I'll Never Fall In Love Again
93/69 *Burt Bacharach*
6/70 *Dionne Warwick*
75/59 **I'll Never Fall In Love Again** *Johnnie Ray*
I'll Never Find Another You
4/65 *Seekers*
97/67 *Sonny James*
8/93 **I'll Never Get Over You (Getting Over Me)** *Exposé*
52/56 **I'll Never Know** *Four Lads*
23/91 **I'll Never Let You Go (Angel Eyes)** *Steelheart*
5/79 **I'll Never Love This Way Again** *Dionne Warwick*
24/57 **I'll Never Say "Never Again" Again** *Dinah Shore*
25/61 **I'll Never Smile Again** *Platters*
13/55 **I'll Never Stop Loving You** *Doris Day*
62/96 **I'll Never Stop Loving You** *J'Son*
83/61 **I'll Never Stop Wanting You** *Brian Hyland*
18/75 **I'll Play For You** *Seals & Crofts*
80/76 **I'll Play The Fool** *Dr. Buzzard's Original "Savannah" Band*
2/94 **I'll Remember** *Madonna*
(also see: In The Still Of The Nite)
80/62 **I'll Remember Carol** *Tommy Boyce*
23/57 **I'll Remember Today** *Patti Page*
34/58 **I'll Remember Tonight** *Pat Boone*
55/94 **I'll Remember You** *Atlantic Starr*
93/59 **I'll Sail My Ship Alone** *Jerry Lee Lewis*
22/60 **I'll Save The Last Dance For You** *Damita Jo*
(also see: Save The Last Dance For Me)
77/68 **I'll Say Forever My Love** *Jimmy Ruffin*
90/63 **I'll Search My Heart** *Johnny Mathis*
100/70 **I'll See Him Through** *Tammy Wynette*
20/90 **I'll See You In My Dreams** *Giant*
32/62 **I'll See You In My Dreams** *Pat Boone*
97/93 **I'll Sleep When I'm Dead** *Bon Jovi*
16/94 **I'll Stand By You** *Pretenders*
51[A]/95 **I'll Stick Around** *Foo Fighters*
33/87 **I'll Still Be Loving You** *Restless Heart*
87/75 **I'll Still Love You** *Jim Weatherly*
65/99 **I'll Still Love You More** *Trisha Yearwood*
45/79 **I'll Supply The Love** *Toto*
89/60 **I'll Take Care Of You** *Bobby Bland*
39/67 **I'll Take Care Of Your Cares** *Frankie Laine*
30/66 **I'll Take Good Care Of You** *Garnet Mimms*
62/94 **I'll Take Her** *Ill Al Skratch*
65/57 **I'll Take Romance** *Eydie Gorme*
25/63 **I'll Take You Home** *Drifters*
68/62 **I'll Take You Home** *Corsairs*
93/57 **I'll Take You Home Again Kathleen** *Slim Whitman*
I'll Take You There
1/72 *Staple Singers*
90/92 *BeBe & CeCe Winans*
22/94 *General Public*
51/65 **I'll Take You Where The Music's Playing** *Drifters*
38/99 **I'll Think Of A Reason Later** *Lee Ann Womack*
25/64 **I'll Touch A Star** *Terry Stafford*
40/67 **I'll Try Anything** *Dusty Springfield*
I'll Try Something New
39/62 *Miracles*
25/69 *Supremes & Temptations*
41/82 *Taste Of Honey*
9/83 **I'll Tumble 4 Ya** *Culture Club*
76/67 **I'll Turn To Stone** *Four Tops*
13/84 **I'll Wait** *Van Halen*
94/56 **I'll Wait** *Betty Johnson*
15/58 **I'll Wait For You** *Frankie Avalon*
I'll Walk The Line ..see: I Walk The Line

I'M:

I'm ..also see: I Am
I'm A Believer
1/66 *Monkees*
51/71 *Neil Diamond*
25/01 *Smash Mouth*
56/89 **I'm A Believer** *Giant*
38/69 **I'm A Better Man** *Engelbert Humperdinck*
46/69 **I'm A Drifter** *Bobby Goldsboro*
17/65 **I'm A Fool** *Dino, Desi & Billy*
97/67 **I'm A Fool For You** *James Carr*
I'm A Fool To Care
24/61 *Joe Barry*
94/61 *Oscar Black*
84/65 *Ray Charles*
35/71 **I'm A Greedy Man** *James Brown*
36/65 **I'm A Happy Man** *Jive Five*
38/59 **I'm A Hog For You** *Coasters*
I'm A Man
10/67 *Spencer Davis Group*
49/71 *Chicago*
17/65 **I'm A Man** *Yardbirds*
31/59 **I'm A Man** *Fabian*
24/68 **I'm A Midnight Mover** *Wilson Pickett*
57/66 **I'm A Nut** *Leroy Pullins*
85/93 **I'm A Player** *Too $hort*

75/74 **I'm A Ramblin' Man** *Waylon Jennings*
20/66 **(I'm A) Road Runner** *Jr. Walker*
94/73 **I'm A Rocker** *Raspberries*
27/01 **I'm A Slave 4 U** *Britney Spears*
76/73 **I'm A Stranger Here** *Five Man Electrical Band*
49/01 **I'm A Survivor** *Reba McEntire*
25/61 **I'm A Telling You** *Jerry Butler*
17/01 **I'm A Thug** *Trick Daddy*
31/74 **I'm A Train** *Albert Hammond*
I'm A Woman
54/63 *Peggy Lee*
12/75 *Maria Muldaur*
61/74 **(I'm A) YoYo Man** *Rick Cunha*
66/97 **I'm Afraid Of Americans** *David Bowie*
63/63 **I'm Afraid To Go Home** *Brian Hyland*
16/80 **I'm Alive** *Electric Light Orchestra*
35/83 **I'm Alive** *Neil Diamond*
60/80 **I'm Alive** *Gamma*
61/75 **I'm Alive (medley)** *Blue Swede*
34/80 **I'm Almost Ready** *Pure Prairie League*
42/99 **I'm Already Taken** *Steve Wariner*
24/01 **I'm Already There** *Lonestar*
7/80 **I'm Alright** *Kenny Loggins*
43/98 **I'm Alright** *Jo Dee Messina*
20/55 **(I'm Always Hearing) Wedding Bells** *Eddie Fisher*
9/57 **I'm Available** *Margie Rayburn*
84/87 **I'm Bad** *LL Cool J*
60S/99 **I'm Beautiful** *Bette Midler*
91/70 **I'm Better Off Without You** *Main Ingredient*
19/62 **I'm Blue (The Gong-Gong Song)** *Ikettes*
40/71 **I'm Comin' Home** *Tommy James*
75/71 **I'm Comin' Home** *Dave Edmunds*
I'm Coming Home
75/73 *Johnny Mathis*
18/74 *Spinners*
42/72 **I'm Coming Home** *Stories*
57/68 **I'm Coming Home** *Tom Jones*
82/59 **I'm Coming Home** *Marv Johnson*
94/62 **I'm Coming Home** *Paul Anka*
39/66 **I'm Comin' Home, Cindy** *Trini Lopez*
19/61 **I'm Comin' On Back To You** *Jackie Wilson*
5/80 **I'm Coming Out** *Diana Ross*
I'm Confessin' (That I Love You)
58/63 *Frank Ifield*
99/64 *Nino Tempo & April Stevens*
77/63 **I'm Crazy 'Bout My Baby** *Marvin Gaye*
19/64 **I'm Crying** *Animals*
42S/00 **I'm Diggin' It** *Alecia Elliott*
17/73 **I'm Doin' Fine Now** *New York City*
95/63 **I'm Down To My Last Heartbreak** *Wilson Pickett*
89/91 **I'm Dreamin'** *Christopher Williams*
50/77 **I'm Dreaming** *Jennifer Warnes*
17/76 **I'm Easy** *Keith Carradine*
I'm Every Woman
21/78 *Chaka Khan*
4/93 *Whitney Houston*
96/77 **I'm Falling In Love (medley)** *Hodges, James & Smith*
86/74 **I'm Falling In Love With You** *Little Anthony & The Imperials*
I'm Falling Too ..see: (I Can't Help You)
90/86 **I'm For Real** *Howard Hewett*
27/93 **I'm Free** *Jon Secada*
37/69 **I'm Free** *Who*
79/90 **I'm Free** *Soup Dragons*
22/84 **I'm Free (Heaven Helps The Man)** *Kenny Loggins*
63/98 **I'm From The Country** *Tracy Byrd*
(I'm Gettin') ..also see: Nuttin' For Christmas
37/60 **I'm Gettin' Better** *Jim Reeves*
51S/01 **I'm Ghetto** *Baby S*
88/71 **I'm Girl Scoutin'** *Intruders*
9/85 **I'm Goin' Down** *Bruce Springsteen*
22/95 **I'm Goin' Down** *Mary J. Blige*
70/77 **I'm Going Down** *Rose Royce*
52/62 **I'm Going Back To School** *Dee Clark*
81/75 **(I'm Going By) The Stars In Your Eyes** *Dramatics*
98/71 **I'm Gonna Be A Country Girl Again** *Buffy Sainte-Marie*
17/59 **I'm Gonna Be A Wheel Some Day** *Fats Domino*
10/02 **I'm Gonna Be Alright** *Jennifer Lopez*
3/93 **I'm Gonna Be (500 Miles)** *Proclaimers*
9/64 **I'm Gonna Be Strong** *Gene Pitney*
18/63 **I'm Gonna' Be Warm This Winter** *Connie Francis*
95/62 **I'm Gonna Change Everything** *Jim Reeves*
63/59 **I'm Gonna Change Him** *Cathy Carr*
98/69 **I'm Gonna Do All I Can (To Do Right By My Man)** *Ike & Tina Turner*
74/68 **I'm Gonna Do What They Do To Me** *B.B. King*
3/59 **I'm Gonna Get Married** *Lloyd Price*
(also see: We Told You Not To Marry)
47/93 **I'm Gonna Get You** *Bizarre Inc*
34/02 **I'm Gonna Getcha Good!** *Shania Twain*
76/69 **I'm Gonna Hold On Long As I Can** *Marvelettes*
12/61 **I'm Gonna Knock On Your Door** *Eddie Hodges*
57/56 **I'm Gonna Laugh You Right Out Of My Life** *Nat "King" Cole*
40/76 **I'm Gonna Let My Heart Do The Walking** *Supremes*
84/81 **I'm Gonna Love Her For Both Of Us** *Meat Loaf*
84/56 **I'm Gonna Love You** *Ames Brothers*
86/70 **I'm Gonna Love You** *Intrigues*
3/73 **I'm Gonna Love You Just A Little More Baby** *Barry White*
56/65 **I'm Gonna Love You Too** *Hullaballoos*
I'm Gonna Make You Love Me
88/66 *Dee Dee Warwick*
26/68 *Madeline Bell*
2/69 *Supremes & Temptations*
91/78 **I'm Gonna Make You Love Me** *Blend*
10/69 **I'm Gonna Make You Mine** *Lou Christie*
90/66 **I'm Gonna Make You Mine** *Shadows Of Knight*
29/02 **I'm Gonna Miss Her (The Fishin' Song)** *Brad Paisley*
55/67 **I'm Gonna Miss You** *Artistics*
82/88 **I'm Gonna Miss You** *Kenny Loggins*
84/61 **I'm Gonna Move To The Outskirts Of Town** *Ray Charles*
3/57 **I'm Gonna Sit Right Down And Write Myself A Letter** *Billy Williams*
28/78 **I'm Gonna Take Care Of Everything** *Rubicon*
13/85 **I'm Gonna Tear Your Playhouse Down** *Paul Young*
85/62 **I'm Hanging Up My Heart For You** *Solomon Burke*
87/58 **I'm Happy** *Four Dates*
I'm Happy Just To Dance With You
95/64 *Beatles*
64/80 *Anne Murray*
27/80 **I'm Happy That Love Has Found You** *Jimmy Hall*
1/65 **I'm Henry VIII, I Am** *Herman's Hermits*
53/75 **I'm Her Fool** *Billy Swan*
76/62 **I'm Here To Get My Baby Out Of Jail** *Everly Brothers*
47S/01 **I'm Hot** *Erick Sermon*
27/61 **I'm Hurtin'** *Roy Orbison*
98/68 **I'm Hypnotized** *Anthony & The Imperials*
66S/00 **I'm In** *Kinleys*
51/68 **I'm In A Different World** *Four Tops*
82/93 **I'm In A Philly Mood** *Daryl Hall*
I'm In Love
45/67 *Wilson Pickett*
19/74 *Aretha Franklin*
40/81 **I'm In Love** *Evelyn King*
84/94 **I'm In Love** *Lisa Keith*
64/93 **I'm In Luv** *Joe*
I'm In Love Again
3/56 *Fats Domino*
38/56 *Fontane Sisters*
67/63 *Rick Nelson*
45/82 **I'm In Love Again** *Pia Zadora*
57/56 **I'm In Love With You** *Pat Boone*
32/94 **I'm In The Mood** *Ce Ce Peniston*
38/61 **I'm In The Mood For Love** *Chimes*
2/77 **I'm In You** *Peter Frampton*
81/67 **I'm Indestructible** *Jack Jones*
98/68 **I'm Into Lookin' For Someone To Love Me** *Bobby Vee*
I'm Into Something Good
13/64 *Herman's Hermits*
38/64 *Earl-Jean*
I'm Just A Country Boy
FC/57 *Harry Belafonte*
55/63 *George McCurn*
87/56 **I'm Just A Dancing Partner** *Platters*
88/66 **(I'm Just A) Fool For You** *Gene Chandler*
56/70 **I'm Just A Prisoner (Of Your Good Lovin')** *Candi Staton*
12/73 **I'm Just A Singer (In A Rock And Roll Band)** *Moody Blues*
94/71 **I'm Just Me** *Charley Pride*
27/01 **I'm Just Talkin' About Tonight** *Toby Keith*
60/81 **I'm Just Too Shy** *Jermaine Jackson*
33/61 **I'm Learning About Love** *Brenda Lee*
36/71 **I'm Leavin'** *Elvis Presley*
87/99 **I'm Leaving** *Aaron Tippin*
99/73 **I'm Leavin' You** *Engelbert Humperdinck*
I'm Leaving It Up To You
1/63 *Dale & Grace*
4/74 *Donny & Marie Osmond*
9/01 **I'm Like A Bird** *Nelly Furtado*
10/69 **I'm Livin' In Shame** *Supremes*
99/66 **I'm Living In Two Worlds** *Bonnie Guitar*

79/93 **I'm Looking For The One (To Be With Me)** *Jazzy Jeff & Fresh Prince*
I'm Losing You ..see: (I Know)
60/76 **I'm Mandy Fly Me** *10cc*
I'm Movin' On
40/59 *Ray Charles*
56/63 *Matt Lucas*
52/72 *John Kay*
41/02 **I'm Movin' On** *Rascal Flatts*
37/73 **I'm Never Gonna Be Alone Anymore** *Cornelius Brothers & Sister Rose*
71/90 **I'm Never Gonna Give You Up** *Brat Pack*
88/82 **I'm Never Gonna Say Goodbye** *Billy Preston*
36/59 **I'm Never Gonna Tell** *Jimmie Rodgers*
49/87 **I'm No Angel** *Gregg Allman Band*
69/97 **I'm Not A Fool** *Immature*
92/63 **I'm Not A Fool Anymore** *T.K. Hulin*
57/97 **I'm Not A Player** *Big Punisher*
27/60 **I'm Not Afraid** *Ricky Nelson*
44/97 **I'm Not Feeling You** *Yvette Michele*
40/97 **I'm Not Giving You Up** *Gloria Estefan*
66/79 **I'm Not Gonna Cry Anymore** *Nancy Brooks*
14/78 **I'm Not Gonna Let It Bother Me Tonight** *Atlanta Rhythm Section*
I'm Not In Love
2/75 *10cc*
7/91 *Will To Power*
60S/00 *Olive*
4/75 **I'm Not Lisa** *Jessi Colter*
34/70 **I'm Not My Brothers Keeper** *Flaming Ember*
41/94 **I'm Not Over You** *Ce Ce Peniston*
69/87 **I'm Not Perfect (But I'm Perfect For You)** *Grace Jones*
16/99 **I'm Not Ready** *Keith Sweat*
90/90 **I'm Not Satisfied** *Fine Young Cannibals*
66S/95 **I'm Not Strong Enough To Say No** *BlackHawk*
72S/96 **I'm Not Supposed To Love You Anymore** *Bryan White*
54/89 **I'm Not The Man I Used To Be** *Fine Young Cannibals*
32/86 **I'm Not The One** *Cars*
74/88 **I'm Not Your Man** *Tommy Conwell*
63/91 **I'm Not Your Puppet** *Hi-C*
20/67 **(I'm Not Your) Steppin' Stone** *Monkees*
6/85 **I'm On Fire** *Bruce Springsteen*
16/75 **I'm On Fire** *Dwight Twilley Band*
I'm On Fire
26/75 *5000 Volts*
78/75 *Jim Gilstrap*
98/64 **I'm On Fire** *Jerry Lee Lewis*
74/78 **I'm On My Way** *Captain & Tennille*
90/62 **I'm On My Way** *Highwaymen*
15/64 **I'm On The Outside (Looking In)** *Little Anthony & The Imperials*
47/94 **I'm Outstanding** *Shaquille O'Neal*
I'm Outta Here! ..see: (If You're Not In It For Love)
92/00 **I'm Outta Love** *Anastacia*
93/65 **I'm Over You** *Jan Bradley*
86/92 **I'm Overjoyed** *Nona Gaye*
9/94 **I'm Ready** *Tevin Campbell*
16/59 **I'm Ready** *Fats Domino*
9/66 **I'm Ready For Love** *Martha & The Vandellas*
1/01 **I'm Real** *Jennifer Lopez*
84/93 **I'm Real** *Kris Kross*
89/65 **I'm Satisfied** *San Remo Golden Strings*
41/63 **I'm Saving My Love** *Skeeter Davis*
61/77 **I'm Scared** *Burton Cummings*
74/57 **I'm Serious** *Hilltoppers*
74/69 **(I'm So) Afraid Of Losing You Again** *Charley Pride*
71/79 **I'm So Anxious** *Southside Johnny & The Asbury Jukes*
I'm So Excited
30/82 *Pointer Sisters*
9/84 *Pointer Sisters*
95/71 **I'm So Glad** *Fuzz*
53/70 **I'm So Glad I Fell For You** *David Ruffin*
97/81 **I'm So Glad I'm Standing Here Today** *Crusaders*
I'm So Happy I Can't Stop Crying
94/96 *Sting*
84/97 *Toby Keith with Sting*
6/93 **I'm So Into You** *SWV*
I'm So Lonesome I Could Cry
89/62 *Johnny Tillotson*
8/66 *B.J. Thomas*
F/73 *Hank Wilson*
91/76 *Terry Bradshaw*
I'm So Proud
14/64 *Impressions*
49/71 *Main Ingredient*
74/65 **I'm So Thankful** *Ikettes*
I'm Sorry
1/60 *Brenda Lee*
87/73 *Joey Heatherton*
1/75 **I'm Sorry** *John Denver*
11/57 **I'm Sorry** *Platters*
42/68 **I'm Sorry** *Delfonics*
97/71 **I'm Sorry** *Bobby Bland*
36/58 **I'm Sorry I Made You Cry** *Connie Francis*
55/84 **I'm Stepping Out** *John Lennon*
I'm Stickin' With You
14/57 *Jimmy Bowen*
72/57 *Fontane Sisters*
72/56 **I'm Still A King To You** *Don Cherry*
80/69 **I'm Still A Struggling Man** *Edwin Starr*
I'm Still In Love With You
3/72 *Al Green*
F/94 *Al B. Sure!*
7/97 **I'm Still In Love With You** *New Edition*
31/88 **I'm Still Searching** *Glass Tiger*
12/83 **I'm Still Standing** *Elton John*
63/71 **I'm Still Waiting** *Diana Ross*
85/92 **I'm Still Waiting** *Jodeci*
10/72 **I'm Stone In Love With You** *Stylistics*
1/65 **I'm Telling You Now** *Freddie & The Dreamers*
15/89 **I'm That Type Of Guy** *LL Cool J*
38/62 **(I'm The Girl On) Wolverton Mountain** *Jo Ann Campbell*
48/74 **I'm The Leader Of The Gang** *Brownsville Station*
92/64 **I'm The Lonely One** *Cliff Richard*
42/82 **I'm The One** *Roberta Flack*
82/64 **I'm The One** *Gerry & The Pacemakers*
73/63 **I'm The One Who Loves You** *Impressions*
19/92 **I'm The One You Need** *Jody Watley*
(also see: Come 'Round Here)
8/95 **I'm The Only One** *Melissa Etheridge*
F/71 **I'm The Only One** *Lobo*
87/85 **I'm Through With Love** *Eric Carmen*
74/69 **I'm Tired** *Savoy Brown*
62/66 **I'm Too Far Gone (To Turn Around)** *Bobby Bland*
1/92 **I'm Too Sexy** *R*S*F (Right Said Fred)*
98/62 **I'm Tossin' And Turnin' Again** *Bobby Lewis*
44/01 **I'm Tryin'** *Trace Adkins*
27/57 **I'm Waiting Just For You** *Pat Boone*
17S/01 **I'm Waking Up To Us** *Belle & Sebastian*
I'm Walkin'
4/57 *Fats Domino*
4/57 *Ricky Nelson*
I'm Walking The Floor Over You
92/57 *Georgia Gibbs*
44/60 *Pat Boone*
84/64 **(I'm Watching) Every Little Move You Make** *Little Peggy March*
4/03 **I'm With You** *Avril Lavigne*
12/67 **I'm Wondering** *Stevie Wonder*
1/98 **I'm Your Angel** *R. Kelly & Celine Dion*
1/90 **I'm Your Baby Tonight** *Whitney Houston*
1/77 **I'm Your Boogie Man** *KC & The Sunshine Band*
21S/01 **I'm Your Girl** *Dena Cali*
94/66 **I'm Your Hoochie Cooche Man** *Jimmy Smith*
3/86 **I'm Your Man** *Wham!*
86/86 **I'm Your Man** *Barry Manilow*
6/66 **I'm Your Puppet** *James & Bobby Purify*
(also see: I'm Not Your Puppet)
93/81 **I'm Your Superman** *All Sports Band*
11/65 **I'm Yours** *Elvis Presley*

I'VE:

I've ..also see: I Have
33/59 **I've Been Around** *Fats Domino*
78/74 **I've Been Born Again** *Johnnie Taylor*
68/62 **I've Been Everywhere** *Hank Snow*
35/69 **I've Been Hurt** *Bill Deal*
9/87 **I've Been In Love Before** *Cutting Crew*
27/72 **I've Been Lonely For So Long** *Frederick Knight*
16/67 **I've Been Lonely Too Long** *Young Rascals*
88/60 **I've Been Loved Before** *Shirley & Lee*
81/76 **I've Been Lovin' You** *Easy Street*
I've Been Loving You Too Long (To Stop Now)
21/65 *Otis Redding*
68/69 *Ike & Tina Turner*
48S/02 **I've Been Real** *Brill*
9/74 **(I've Been) Searchin' So Long** *Chicago*
53/59 **I've Been There** *Tommy Edwards*
1/91 **I've Been Thinking About You** *Londonbeat*
80/94 **I've Been Thinking About You** *Jocelyn Enriquez*
34/75 **I've Been This Way Before** *Neil Diamond*
42/91 **I've Been Waiting For You** *Guys Next Door*
48/81 **I've Been Waiting For You All Of My Life** *Paul Anka*

73/56 **I've Changed My Mind A Thousand Times** *Kay Starr*
28/59 **I've Come Of Age** *Billy Storm*
94/65 **I've Cried My Last Tear** *O'Jays*
8/81 **I've Done Everything For You** *Rick Springfield*
24S/99 **I've Dreamed Of You** *Barbra Streisand*
5/71 **I've Found Someone Of My Own** *Free Movement*
29/76 **I've Got A Feeling (We'll Be Seeing Each Other Again)** *Al Wilson*
26/92 **I've Got A Lot To Learn About Love** *Storm*
18/83 **I've Got A Rock N' Roll Heart** *Eric Clapton*
I've Got A Thing About You Baby
93/72 *Billy Lee Riley*
39/74 *Elvis Presley*
25/65 **I've Got A Tiger By The Tail** *Buck Owens*
I've Got A Woman ..see: I Got A Woman
18/62 **(I've Got) Bonnie** *Bobby Rydell*
41/68 **I've Got Dreams To Remember** *Otis Redding*
99/65 **I've Got Five Dollars And It's Saturday Night** *George Jones & Gene Pitney*
93/56 **I've Got Love** *Julius LaRosa*
94/68 **I've Got Love For My Baby** *Young Hearts*
5/77 **I've Got Love On My Mind** *Natalie Cole*
91/92 **I've Got Mine** *Glenn Frey*
66/61 **I've Got News For You** *Ray Charles*
67/64 **I've Got No Time To Lose** *Carla Thomas*
33/64 **I've Got Sand In My Shoes** *Drifters*
32/73 **I've Got So Much To Give** *Barry White*
71/61 **(I've Got) Spring Fever** *Little Willie John*
12/74 **I've Got The Music In Me** *Kiki Dee Band*
73/79 **I've Got The Next Dance** *Deniece Williams*
89/64 **I've Got The Skill** *Jackie Ross*
I've Got To ..also see: I've Gotta
38/66 **I've Got To Be Somebody** *Billy Joe Royal*
64/66 **I've Got To Do A Little Bit Better** *Joe Tex*
44/67 **I've Got To Have A Reason** *Dave Clark Five*
77/72 **I've Got To Have You** *Sammi Smith*
4/74 **I've Got To Use My Imagination** *Gladys Knight*
81/02 **I've Got You** *Marc Anthony*
I've Got You Under My Skin
95/59 *Louis Prima & Keely Smith*
9/66 *4 Seasons*
11/69 **I've Gotta Be Me** *Sammy Davis, Jr.*
8/68 **I've Gotta Get A Message To You** *Bee Gees*
46/70 **I've Gotta Make You Love Me** *Steam*
I've Grown Accustomed To Your Face
70/56 *Rosemary Clooney*
96/56 *Gordon MacRae*
25/78 **I've Had Enough** *Wings*
I've Had It
6/59 *Bell Notes*
79/74 *Fanny*
1/87 **(I've Had) The Time Of My Life** *Bill Medley & Jennifer Warnes*
87/80 **I've Just Begun To Love You** *Dynasty*
58/69 **I've Lost Everything I've Ever Loved** *David Ruffin*
32/70 **I've Lost You** *Elvis Presley*
82/67 **I've Lost You** *Jackie Wilson*
4/80 **I've Loved You For A Long Time (medley)** *Spinners*
44/79 **I've Never Been In Love** *Suzi Quatro*
I've Never Been To Me
97/77 *Charlene*
3/82 *Charlene*
40/68 **I've Never Found A Girl (To Love Me Like You Do)** *Eddie Floyd*
17/67 **I've Passed This Way Before** *Jimmy Ruffin*
3/61 **I've Told Every Little Star** *Linda Scott*
Ice Castles ..see: Theme From
37/95 **Ice Cream** *Chef Raekwon*
59/69 **Ice Cream Song** *Dynamics*
1/90 **Ice Ice Baby** *Vanilla Ice*
70/68 **Ice In The Sun** *Status Quo*
90/62 **Ida Jane** *Fats Domino*
95/69 **Idaho** *4 Seasons*
64/57 **Idol With The Golden Head** *Coasters*
9/91 **Iesha** *Another Bad Creation*

IF:

4/71 **If** *Bread*
4/93 **If** *Janet Jackson*
82/61 **If** *Paragons*
32/62 **If A Man Answers** *Bobby Darin*
35/62 **If A Woman Answers (Hang Up The Phone)** *Leroy Van Dyke*
76/86 **If Anybody Had A Heart** *John Waite*
14/83 **If Anyone Falls** *Stevie Nicks*
7/58 **If Dreams Came True** *Pat Boone*
37S/99 **If Ever** *3rd Storee*
24/78 **If Ever I See You Again** *Roberta Flack*
10/84 **If Ever You're In My Arms Again** *Peabo Bryson*
2X/66 **If Every Day Was Like Christmas** *Elvis Presley*
68/00 **If I Am** *Ninedays*
12/69 **If I Can Dream** *Elvis Presley*
If I Can't Have You
1/78 *Yvonne Elliman*
70/98 *LFO*
52/60 **If I Can't Have You** *Etta James & Harvey Fuqua*
52/93 **If I Could** *Regina Belle*
10/68 **If I Could Build My Whole World Around You** *Marvin Gaye & Tammi Terrell*
60/97 **If I Could Change** *Master P*
76/82 **If I Could Get You (into my Life)** *Gene Cotton*
15/02 **If I Could Go!** *Angie Martinez*
89/73 **If I Could Only Be Sure** *Nolan Porter*
58/75 **If I Could Only Win Your Love** *Emmylou Harris*
10/72 **If I Could Reach You** *5th Dimension*
79/72 **If I Could See The Light** *8th Day*
27/97 **If I Could Teach The World** *Bone Thugs-N-Harmony*
12/99 **If I Could Turn Back The Hands Of Time** *R. Kelly*
3/89 **If I Could Turn Back Time** *Cher*
58/62 **If I Cried Every Time You Hurt Me** *Wanda Jackson*
If I Didn't Care
22/59 *Connie Francis*
30/61 *Platters*
44/70 *Moments*
58/62 **If I Didn't Have A Dime (To Play The Jukebox)** *Gene Pitney*
46/65 **If I Didn't Love You** *Chuck Jackson*
2/92 **If I Ever Fall In Love** *Shai*
17/93 **If I Ever Lose My Faith In You** *Sting*
39/75 **If I Ever Lose This Heaven** *AWB*
38/01 **If I Fall You're Going Down With Me** *Dixie Chicks*
53/64 **If I Fell** *Beatles*
If I Give My Heart To You
3/54 *Doris Day*
34/59 *Kitty Kallen*
31/60 **If I Had A Girl** *Rod Lauren*
If I Had A Hammer
10/62 *Peter, Paul & Mary*
3/63 *Trini Lopez*
88/85 **If I Had A Rocket Launcher** *Bruce Cockburn*
36/82 **If I Had My Wish Tonight** *David Lasley*
7/93 **If I Had No Loot** *Tony Toni Tone*
83/98 **If I Had The Chance** *Cynthia*
93/77 **If I Have To Go Away** *Jigsaw*
86/61 **If I Knew** *Nat King Cole*
86/98 **If I Lost You** *Travis Tritt*
23/65 **If I Loved You** *Chad & Jeremy*
8/55 **If I May** *Nat "King" Cole/Four Knights*
47/70 **If I Never Knew Your Name** *Vic Dana*
67/98 **If I Never Stop Loving You** *David Kersh*
74/76 **If I Only Could** *Rowans*
95/69 **If I Only Had Time** *Nick DeCaro*
65/76 **If I Only Knew** *Ozark Mountain Daredevils*
34/65 **If I Ruled The World** *Tony Bennett*
53/96 **If I Ruled The World** *Nas*
39/79 **If I Said You Have A Beautiful Body Would You Hold It Against Me** *Bellamy Brothers*
63/91 **If I Say** *Kingofthehill*
67/87 **If I Say Yes** *Five Star*
62/62 **If I Should Lose You** *Dreamlovers*
16/95 **If I Wanted To** *Melissa Etheridge*
67/87 **If I Was Your Girlfriend** *Prince*
If I Were A Carpenter
8/66 *Bobby Darin*
20/68 *Four Tops*
36/70 *Johnny Cash & June Carter*
76/72 *Bob Seger*
73/74 *Leon Russell*
71/73 **If I Were Only A Child Again** *Curtis Mayfield*
If I Were You
70/80 *Toby Beau*
44/82 *Lulu*
9/71 **If I Were Your Woman** *Gladys Knight*
19/84 **If I'd Been The One** *38 Special*
74/64 **If I'm A Fool For Loving You** *Bobby Wood*
47/82 **If It Ain't One Thing...It's Another** *Richard "Dimples" Fields*
75/78 **If It Don't Fit, Don't Force It** *Kellee Patterson*
88/74 **If It Feels Good, Do It** *Stories*

7/88 **If It Isn't Love** *New Edition*
10/97 **If It Makes You Happy** *Sheryl Crow*
77/69 **If It Wasn't For Bad Luck** *Ray Charles & Jimmy Lewis*
If It's Alright With You
95/71 *Rose Colored Glass*
97/73 *Dottie West*
69/71 **If It's Real What I Feel** *Jerry Butler*
47/77 **If It's The Last Thing I Do** *Thelma Houston*
48/82 **If Looks Could Kill** *Player*
54/86 **If Looks Could Kill** *Heart*
86/68 **If Love Is In Your Heart** *Friend & Lover*
78/76 **If Love Must Go** *Dobie Gray*
87/83 **If Love Should Go** *Streets*
(If Loving You Is Wrong) I Don't Want To Be Right
3/72 *Luther Ingram*
42/75 *Millie Jackson*
31/79 *Barbara Mandrell*
88/63 **If Mary's There** *Brian Hyland*
54/78 **If My Friends Could See Me Now** *Linda Clifford*
98/70 **If My Heart Could Speak** *Manhattans*
39/01 **If My Heart Had Wings** *Faith Hill*
23/63 **If My Pillow Could Talk** *Connie Francis*
25/71 **If Not For You** *Olivia Newton-John*
55/76 **If Not You** *Dr. Hook*
91/70 **If Only I Had My Mind On Something Else** *Bee Gees*
46/84 **If Only You Knew** *Patti LaBelle*
29/86 **If She Knew What She Wants** *Bangles*
If She Should Come To You (La Montana)
67/60 *Anthony Newley*
77/60 *Frank DeVol*
98/60 *Roger Williams*
17/87 **If She Would Have Been Faithful...** *Chicago*
67/64 **If Somebody Told You** *Anna King*
73/94 **If That's Your Boyfriend (He Wasn't Last Night)** *Me'shell Ndegéocello*
28/82 **If The Love Fits Wear It** *Leslie Pearl*
35/91 **(If There Was) Any Other Way** *Celine Dion*
If There's A Hell Below ..see: (Don't Worry)
6/84 **If This Is It** *Huey Lewis*
60/67 **If This Is Love (I'd Rather Be Lonely)** *Precisions*
68/68 **If This World Were Mine** *Marvin Gaye & Tammi Terrell*
51/97 **If Tomorrow Never Comes** *Joose*
79/97 **If U Stay Ready** *Suga Free*
24/90 **If U Were Mine** *U-Krew*
71/70 **If Walls Could Talk** *Little Milton*
54/97 **If We Fall In Love Tonight** *Rod Stewart*
28/73 **If We Make It Through December** *Merle Haggard*
48/89 **If We Never Meet Again** *Tommy Conwell*
84/72 **If We Only Have Love** *Dionne Warwicke*
58/73 **If We Try** *Don McLean*
1/90 **If Wishes Came True** *Sweet Sensation*

IF YOU:

If You ..also see: If U
54/75 **(If You Add) All The Love In The World** *Mac Davis*
If You Asked Me To
79/89 *Patti LaBelle*
4/92 *Celine Dion*
68^{S}/00 **If You Can** *Tammy Cochran*
65/72 **If You Can Beat Me Rockin' (You Can Have My Chair)** *Laura Lee*
51/01 **If You Can Do Anything Else** *George Strait*
62/56 **If You Can Dream** *Four Aces*
11/68 **If You Can Want** *Miracles*
45/79 **If You Can't Give Me Love** *Suzi Quatro*
100/63 **If You Can't Rock Me** *Ricky Nelson*
11^{A}/97 **If You Could Only See** *Tonic*
If You Could Read My Mind
5/71 *Gordon Lightfoot*
52/98 *Stars On 54*
33/59 **(If You Cry) True Love, True Love** *Drifters*
81/70 **If You Do Believe In Love** *Tee Set*
If You Don't Know Me By Now
3/72 *Harold Melvin*
1/89 *Simply Red*
85/65 **If You Don't (Love Me, Tell Me So)** *Barbara Mason*
89/00 **If You Don't Wanna Love Me** *Tamar*
12/55 **If You Don't Want My Love** *Jaye P. Morgan*
49/68 **If You Don't Want My Love** *Robert John*
67/59 **If You Don't Want My Lovin'** *Carl Dobkins, Jr.*
60/98 **If You Ever Have Forever In Mind** *Vince Gill*
92/68 **If You Ever Leave Me** *Jack Jones*
94/88 **If You Feel It** *Denise Lopez*
10/94 **If You Go** *Jon Secada*
16/92 **If You Go Away** *NKOTB*
If You Go Away
68/67 *Damita Jo*
68/74 *Terry Jacks*
63/73 **If You Gotta Break Another Heart** *Albert Hammond*
If You Gotta Make A Fool Of Somebody
22/62 *James Ray*
63/66 *Maxine Brown*
1/99 **If You Had My Love** *Jennifer Lopez*
11/76 **If You Know What I Mean** *Neil Diamond*
4/86 **If You Leave** *Orchestral Manoeuvres In The Dark*
1/76 **If You Leave Me Now** *Chicago*
44/90 **If You Leave Me Now** *Jaya*
38/72 **If You Leave Me Tonight I'll Cry** *Jerry Wallace*
66/72 **If You Let Me** *Eddie Kendricks*
8/70 **(If You Let Me Make Love To You Then) Why Can't I Touch You?** *Ronnie Dyson*
68/87 **If You Let Me Stay** *Terence Trent D'Arby*
8/95 **If You Love Me** *Brownstone*
30/99 **If You Love Me** *Mint Condition*
79/59 **If You Love Me** *LaVern Baker*
5/74 **If You Love Me (Let Me Know)** *Olivia Newton-John*
3/85 **If You Love Somebody Set Them Free** *Sting*
13/99 **If You (Lovin' Me)** *Silk*

If You Need Me
37/63 *Solomon Burke*
64/63 *Wilson Pickett*
98/60 **If You Need Me** *Fats Domino*
16/91 **If You Needed Somebody** *Bad Company*
48/76 **If You Only Believe (Jesus For Tonite)** *Michel Polnareff*
4^{S}/02 **If You Only Knew** *Prymary Colorz*
8/71 **If You Really Love Me** *Stevie Wonder*
59^{S}/99 **If You Really Wanna Know** *Marc Dorsey*
97/65 **If You Really Want Me To, I'll Go** *Ron-Dels*
17/79 **If You Remember Me** *Chris Thompson & Night*
92/64 **If You See My Love** *Lenny Welch*
38/80 **If You Should Sail** *Nielsen/Pearson*
17/74 **If You Talk In Your Sleep** *Elvis Presley*
30/98 **If You Think I'm Jiggy** *Lox*
96/75 **If You Think You Know How To Love Me** *Smokey*
17/95 **If You Think You're Lonely Now** *K-Ci Hailey*
75/65 **If You Wait For Love** *Bobby Goldsboro*
1/63 **If You Wanna Be Happy** *Jimmy Soul*
25^{S}/00 **If You Wanna Dance** *Nobody's Angel*
49/78 **If You Wanna Do A Dance** *Spinners*
67/83 **If You Wanna Get Back Your Lady** *Pointer Sisters*
25/74 **If You Wanna Get To Heaven** *Ozark Mountain Daredevils*
89/56 **If You Wanna See Mamie Tonight** *Ames Brothers*
43^{S}/91 **If You Wanna Sex Me Up** *T.C.F.*
37/79 **If You Want It** *Niteflyte*
64/92 **If You Want It** *2nd II None*
98/75 **(If You Want It) Do It Yourself** *Gloria Gaynor*
12/73 **If You Want Me To Stay** *Sly & The Family Stone*
45/82 **If You Want My Love** *Cheap Trick*
71/64 **If You Want This Love** *Sonny Knight*
67/62 **If You Were A Rock And Roll Record** *Freddy Cannon*
77/86 **If You Were A Woman (And I Was A Man)** *Bonnie Tyler*
41/71 **If You Were Mine** *Ray Charles*
(also see: If U Were Mine)
5/01 **If You're Gone** *Matchbox Twenty*
43/78 **If You're Not Back In Love By Monday** *Millie Jackson*
74/96 **(If You're Not In It For Love) I'm Outta Here!** *Shania Twain*
9/73 **If You're Ready (Come Go With Me)** *Staple Singers*
88/91 **If You're Serious** *Riff*
60/65 **If You've Got A Heart** *Bobby Goldsboro*
96/70 **If You've Got A Heart** *Bobby Bland*
88/77 **If You've Got The Time** *Babys*
11/96 **If Your Girl Only Knew** *Aaliyah*
57/86 **If Your Heart Isn't In It** *Atlantic Starr*
95/59 **Igmoo (The Pride Of South Central High)** *Stonewall Jackson*
66^{S}/02 **Ign'ant** *Al-Shid*
2/03 **Ignition** *R. Kelly*

Iko Iko
20/65 *Dixie Cups*
71/72 *Dr. John*
14/89 *Belle Stars*
44/84 **Illegal Alien** *Genesis*
98/61 **Image** *Hank Levine*
6/60 **Image Of A Girl** *Safaris*
7/78 **Imaginary Lover** *Atlanta Rhythm Section*
37/98 **Imagination** *Tamia*
85/90 **Imagination** *Xymox*
88/85 **Imagination** *Belouis Some*
Imagine
3/71 *John Lennon*
85/89 *Tracie Spencer*
90/62 **Imagine That** *Patsy Cline*
98/00 **Imagine That** *LL Cool J*
83/01 **Imitation Of Life** *R.E.M.*
22/75 **Immigrant, The** *Neil Sedaka*
16/71 **Immigrant Song** *Led Zeppelin*
36/72 **Immigration Man** *Graham Nash & David Crosby*
29/02 **Impossible, The** *Joe Nichols*
95/61 **Impossible** *Gloria Lynne*
Impossible Dream
35/66 *Jack Jones*
42/68 *Hesitations*
55/68 *Roger Williams*
57/63 **Impossible Happened** *Little Peggy March*
68/68 **Impossible Mission (Mission Impossible)** *Soul Survivors*
(also see: Theme From Mission: Impossible)
23A/97 **Impression That I Get** *Mighty Mighty Bosstones*
4/90 **Impulsive** *Wilson Phillips*

IN:

17/83 **In A Big Country** *Big Country*
56/72 **In A Broken Dream** *Python Lee Jackson*
72/98 **In A Dream** *Rockell*
In-A-Gadda-Da-Vida
30/68 *Iron Butterfly*
68/69 *Iron Butterfly*
49/56 **In A Little Spanish Town ('Twas On A Night Like This)** *Bing Crosby & Buddy Cole*
59/02 **In A Little While** *Uncle Kracker*
31/69 **In A Moment** *Intrigues*
27/56 **In A Shanty In Old Shanty Town** *Somethin' Smith & The Redheads*
11/80 **In America** *Charlie Daniels Band*
9/67 **In And Out Of Love** *Supremes*
69/85 **In And Out Of Love** *Bon Jovi*
87/68 **In Another Land** *Bill Wyman*
66/02 **In Another World** *Joe Diffie*
99/86 **In Between Days (Without You)** *Cure*
84/61 **In Between Tears** *Lenny Miles*
'In' Crowd
5/65 *Ramsey Lewis Trio*
13/65 *Dobie Gray*
70/02 **In Da Wind** *Trick Daddy*
7/63 **In Dreams** *Roy Orbison*
86/78 **In For The Night** *Dirt Band*
66/76 **In France They Kiss On Main Street** *Joni Mitchell*
44/88 **In God's Country** *U2*
83/97 **In Harm's Way** *BeBe Winans*
49/72 **In Heaven There Is No Beer** *Clean Living*
75/80 **In It For Love** *England Dan & John Ford Coley*
70/87 **In Love With Love** *Debbie Harry*
55/97 **In My Arms** *Erasure*
4/97 **In My Bed** *Dru Hill*
19/87 **In My Dreams** *REO Speedwagon*
In My Dreams
77/86 *Dokken*
34/92 *Party*
37/89 **In My Eyes** *Stevie B*
51/61 **In My Heart** *Timetones*
7/85 **In My House** *Mary Jane Girls*
10/60 **In My Little Corner Of The World** *Anita Bryant*
44/64 **In My Lonely Room** *Martha & The Vandellas*
63S/02 **In My Memory** *DJ Tiësto*
83/93 **In My Nature** *Nuttin' Nyce*
In My Room
23/63 *Beach Boys*
86/69 *Sagittarius*
62/66 **In My Room (El Amor)** *Verdelle Smith*
54/68 **In Need Of A Friend** *Cowsills*
38/85 **In Neon** *Elton John*
46/66 **In Our Time** *Nancy Sinatra*
64/92 **In Paradise** *Laissez Faire*
In Real Life..see: (It Never Happens)
99/68 **In Some Time** *Ronnie Dove*
65S/02 **In Tha Ghetto** *Infinity - Tha Ghetto Child*
In The ..also see: In Da
19/81 **In The Air Tonight** *Phil Collins*
63/56 **In The Alps** *Lawrence Welk & The McGuire Sisters*
49/66 **In The Arms Of Love** *Andy Williams*
51/69 **In The Bad, Bad Old Days** *Foundations*
97/66 **In The Basement** *Etta James & Sugar Pie DeSanto*
48A/95 **In The Blood** *Better Than Ezra*
46/74 **In The Bottle** *Brother To Brother*
58/78 **In The Bush** *Musique*
In The Chapel In The Moonlight ..see: Chapel
6/92 **In The Closet** *Michael Jackson*
35/81 **In The Dark** *Billy Squier*
72/82 **In The Driver's Seat** *John Schneider*
2/02 **In The End** *Linkin Park*
65S/99 **In The Game** *O*
In The Ghetto
3/69 *Elvis Presley*
48/72 *Candi Staton*
76/93 **In The Heart Of A Woman** *Billy Ray Cyrus*
33/67 **In The Heat Of The Night** *Ray Charles*
79/96 **In The Hood** *Donell Jones*
14/95 **In The House Of Stone And Light** *Martin Page*
32/96 **In The Meantime** *Spacehog*
97/65 **In The Meantime** *Georgie Fame*
75/77 **In The Middle** *Tim Moore*
27/61 **In The Middle Of A Heartache** *Wanda Jackson*
In The Middle Of An Island
9/57 *Tony Bennett*
23/57 *Tennessee Ernie Ford*
In The Middle Of The House
11/56 *Vaughn Monroe*
20/56 *Rusty Draper*
In The Midnight Hour
21/65 *Wilson Pickett*
45/68 *Mirettes*
30/73 *Cross Country*
88/79 *Samantha Sang*
In The Misty Moonlight
19/64 *Jerry Wallace*
46/67 *Dean Martin*
In The Mood
4/59 *Ernie Fields*
51/74 *Bette Midler*
40/77 *Henhouse Five Plus Too*
(also see: Fly By Night / Swing The Mood)
39/84 **In The Mood** *Robert Plant*
58/84 **In The Name Of Love** *Ralph MacDonald (w/Bill Withers)*
(also see: What)
3/79 **In The Navy** *Village People*
69/72 **In The Quiet Morning** *Joan Baez*
5/72 **In The Rain** *Dramatics*
70/86 **In The Shape Of A Heart** *Jackson Browne*
38/60 **In The Still Of The Night** *Dion & The Belmonts*
In The Still Of The Nite
24/56 *Five Satins*
81/60 *Five Satins*
99/61 *Five Satins*
58/64 *Santo & Johnny*
64/69 *Paul Anka*
3/93 *Boyz II Men*
58/79 **In The Stone** *Earth, Wind & Fire*
46/64 **In The Summer Of His Years** *Connie Francis*
In The Summertime
3/70 *Mungo Jerry*
F/95 *Shaggy*
96/69 **In The Time Of Our Lives** *Iron Butterfly*
1/69 **In The Year 2525 (Exordium & Terminus)** *Zager & Evans*
74/79 **In Thee** *Blue Öyster Cult*
27/93 **In These Arms** *Bon Jovi*
70/71 **In These Changing Times** *Four Tops*
69/72 **In Time** *Engelbert Humperdinck*
94/61 **In Time** *Steve Lawrence*
(also see: Where)
3/87 **In Too Deep** *Genesis*
84/94 **In Walked Love** *Exposé*
79/91 **In Your Arms** *Little Caesar*
In Your Eyes
26/86 *Peter Gabriel*
41/89 *Peter Gabriel*
20/81 **In Your Letter** *REO Speedwagon*
5/89 **In Your Room** *Bangles*
38/88 **In Your Soul** *Corey Hart*
73S/98 **In Your World** *Twista*
71/96 **Incarcerated Scarfaces** *Chef Raekwon*
1/67 **Incense And Peppermints** *Strawberry Alarm Clock*
1/00 **Incomplete** *Sisqó*
1/00 **Independent Women** *Destiny's Child*
33/67 **Indescribably Blue** *Elvis Presley*
35/88 **Indestructible** *Four Tops*
5/69 **Indian Giver** *1910 Fruitgum Co.*
10/68 **Indian Lake** *Cowsills*
Indian Love Call
59/58 *Ernie Freeman*
68/75 *Ray Stevens*
15/94 **Indian Outlaw** *Tim McGraw*
Indian Reservation
20/68 *Don Fardon*
1/71 *Raiders*
50/77 **Indian Summer** *Poco*
74/71 **Indian Summer** *Audience*
5/70 **Indiana Wants Me** *R. Dean Taylor*
56/93 **Indo Smoke** *Mista Grimm*

75/83 **Industrial Disease** *Dire Straits*
6/84 **Infatuation** *Rod Stewart*
92/94 **Infatuation** *Jamie Foxx*
87/85 **Information** *Eric Martin*
1/93 **Informer** *Snow*
91/85 **Injured In The Game Of Love** *Donnie Iris*
84/65 **Inky Dinky Spider** *Kids Next Door*
Innamorata
27/56 *Dean Martin*
30/56 *Jerry Vale*
9/71 **Inner City Blues (Make Me Wanna Holler)** *Marvin Gaye*
96/68 **Inner Light** *Beatles*
55/90 **Innocent** *Whispers*
57S/01 **Innocente** *Delerium*
50/92 **Innocent Child** *Colourhaus*
84/86 **Innocent Eyes** *Graham Nash*
10/84 **Innocent Man** *Billy Joel*
19/93 **Insane In The Brain** *Cypress Hill*
77/92 **Insatiable** *Prince*
77/02 **Insatiable** *Darren Hayes*
12/96 **Insensitive** *Jann Arden*
32/76 **Inseparable** *Natalie Cole*
71A/96 **Inside** *Patti Rothberg*
57/88 **Inside A Dream** *Jane Wiedlin*
34/66 **Inside-Looking Out** *Animals*
43/83 **Inside Love (So Personal)** *George Benson*
76/75 **Inside My Love** *Minnie Riperton*
76/80 **Inside Of You** *Ray, Goodman & Brown*
28/98 **Inside Out** *Eve 6*
55/88 **Inside Outside** *Cover Girls*
94/92 **Inside That I Cried** *CeCe Peniston*
62/97 **Insomnia** *Faithless*
3/70 **Instant Karma** *John Ono Lennon*
29/79 **Instant Replay** *Dan Hartman*
81/63 **Insult To Injury** *Timi Yuro*
28/98 **Intergalactic** *Beastie Boys*
61/58 **Intermission Riff** *Bernie Lowe*
18A/94 **Interstate Love Song** *Stone Temple Pilots*
92/82 **Into My Love** *Greg Guidry*
97/87 **Into My Secret** *Alisha*
92/91 **Into The Great Wide Open** *Tom Petty*
51/70 **Into The Mystic** *Johnny Rivers*
Into The Night
11/80 *Benny Mardones*
20/89 *Benny Mardones*
82/56 **Into The Night** *Dream Weavers*
58/89 **Into You** *Giant Steps*
67/93 **Into Your Arms** *Lemonheads*
51/98 **Invasion Of The Flat Booty Bitches** *Too $hort*
10/85 **Invincible** *Pat Benatar*
31/85 **Invisible** *Alison Moyet*
40/83 **Invisible Hands** *Kim Carnes*
12/97 **Invisible Man** *98°*
57/64 **Invisible Tears** *Ray Conniff Singers*
1/86 **Invisible Touch** *Genesis*
68/85 **Invitation To Dance** *Kim Carnes*
92/58 **Invitation To The Blues** *Ray Price*
1A/98 **Iris** *Goo Goo Dolls*
52/72 **Iron Man** *Black Sabbath*
4/96 **Ironic** *Alanis Morissette*
15/01 **Irresistible** *Jessica Simpson*
61/93 **Irresistible** *Cathy Dennis*
F/84 **Irresistible Bitch** *Prince*
Irresistible You
96/60 *Bobby Peterson*
15/62 *Bobby Darin*
Irving ..see: Ballad Of

IS:

35/60 **Is A Blue Bird Blue** *Conway Twitty*
70/70 **Is Anybody Goin' To San Antone** *Charley Pride*
68/70 **Is It Because I'm Black** *Syl Johnson*
32/92 **Is It Good To You** *Heavy D & The Boyz*
8/86 **Is It Love** *Mr. Mister*
92/88 **Is It Love** *J.J. Fad*
70/75 **Is It Love That We're Missin'** *Quincy Jones*
97/66 **Is It Me?** *Barbara Mason*
26S/00 **Is It Really Like That?** *Absolute*
79/65 **Is It Really Over?** *Jim Reeves*
34/69 **Is It Something You've Got** *Tyrone Davis*
17/64 **Is It True** *Brenda Lee*
Is It Wrong (For Loving You)
61/57 *Warner Mack*
69/60 *Webb Pierce*
15/81 **Is It You** *Lee Ritenour*
21/79 **Is She Really Going Out With Him?** *Joe Jackson*
11/69 **Is That All There Is** *Peggy Lee*
70/86 **Is That It?** *Katrina & The Waves*
59/71 **Is That The Way** *Tin Tin*
68/01 **Is That Your Chick** *Memphis Bleek*
31/60 **Is There Any Chance** *Marty Robbins*
87/56 **Is There Somebody Else** *Dream Weavers*
4/83 **Is There Something I Should Know** *Duran Duran*
89/61 **Is There Something On Your Mind** *Jack Scott*
2/87 **Is This Love** *Whitesnake*
9/87 **Is This Love** *Survivor*
50/80 **Is This Love** *Pat Travers Band*
85/83 **Is This The End** *New Edition*
75/65 **Is This What I Get For Loving You?** *Ronettes*
81/60 **Is You Is Or Is You Ain't My Baby** *Buster Brown*
1/75 **Island Girl** *Elton John*
92/62 **Island In The Sky** *Troy Shondell*
30/57 **Island In The Sun** *Harry Belafonte*
37/82 **Island Of Lost Souls** *Blondie*
1/83 **Islands In The Stream** *Kenny Rogers with Dolly Parton*
F/70 **Isn't It A Pity** *George Harrison*
56/73 **Isn't It About Time** *Stephen Stills-Manassas*
100/60 **Isn't It Amazing** *Crests*
Isn't It Lonely Together
63/68 *O.C. Smith*
97/68 *Robert Knight*
85/75 **Isn't It Lonely Together** *Stark & McBrien*
13/77 **Isn't It Time** *Babys*
29/72 **Isn't Life Strange** *Moody Blues*
9/69 **Israelites** *Desmond Dekker*

IT:

97/77 **It Ain't Easy Comin' Down** *Charlene*
17/84 **It Ain't Enough** *Corey Hart*
91/94 **It Ain't Hard To Tell** *Nas*
92/77 **It Ain't Love** *Tom Powers*
It Ain't Me, Babe
58/64 *Johnny Cash & June Carter*
8/65 *Turtles*
18/99 **It Ain't My Fault 2** *Silkk The Shocker & Mystikal*
91/65 **It Ain't No Big Thing** *Radiants*
94/75 **It Ain't No Fun** *Shirley Brown*
68/64 **It Ain't No Use** *Major Lance*
2/91 **It Ain't Over 'Til It's Over** *Lenny Kravitz*
68/57 **It All Depends On You** *Jerry Lewis*
59/78 **It Amazes Me** *John Denver*
42S/01 **It Began In Afrika** *Chemical Brothers*
51/84 **It Can Happen** *Yes*
85/67 **It Could Be We're In Love** *Cryan' Shames*
53/60 **It Could Happen To You** *Dinah Washington*
46/74 **It Could Have Been Me** *Sami Jo*
43/81 **It Didn't Take Long** *Spider*
98/75 **It Do Feel Good** *Donna Fargo*
97/61 **It Do Me So Good** *Ann-Margret*
64/73 **It Doesn't Have To Be That Way** *Jim Croce*
61/72 **It Doesn't Matter** *Stephen Stills*
88/92 **It Doesn't Matter** *Tyler Collins*
It Doesn't Matter Anymore
13/59 *Buddy Holly*
47/75 *Linda Ronstadt*
4/71 **It Don't Come Easy** *Ringo Starr*
89/58 **It Don't Hurt No More** *Nappy Brown*
10/70 **It Don't Matter To Me** *Bread*
8/00 **It Feels So Good** *Sonique*
66/77 **It Feels So Good To Be Loved So Bad** *Manhattans*
55/65 **It Feels So Right** *Elvis Presley*
72/56 **It Happened Again** *Sarah Vaughan*
59/59 **It Happened Today** *Skyliners*
48S/01 **It Happens Every Time** *Dream Street*
21/91 **It Hit Me Like A Hammer** *Huey Lewis*
29/64 **It Hurts Me** *Elvis Presley*
70/66 **It Hurts Me** *Bobby Goldsboro*
70S/93 **It Hurts Me** *Jacci McGhee*
56/79 **It Hurts So Bad** *Kim Carnes*
It Hurts To Be In Love
7/64 *Gene Pitney*
72/81 *Dan Hartman*
61/57 **It Hurts To Be In Love** *Annie Laurie*
45/63 **It Hurts To Be Sixteen** *Andrea Carroll*
75/80 **It Hurts Too Much** *Eric Carmen*
41/89 **It Isn't, It Wasn't, It Ain't Never Gonna Be** *Aretha Franklin & Whitney Houston*
13/56 **It Isn't Right** *Platters*
32S/02 **It Just Happened** *Nikie Batey*
23/61 **It Keeps Rainin'** *Fats Domino*
3/62 **It Keeps Right On A-Hurtin'** *Johnny Tillotson*
It Keeps You Runnin'
46/76 *Carly Simon*
37/77 *Doobie Brothers*
60/76 **It Makes Me Giggle** *John Denver*
74/96 **It Matters To Me** *Faith Hill*
It May Be Winter Outside (But In My Heart It's Spring)
42/67 *Felice Taylor*
83/73 *Love Unlimited*
11/55 **It May Sound Silly** *McGuire Sisters*
22/62 **It Might As Well Rain Until September** *Carole King*
25/83 **It Might Be You** *Stephen Bishop*
3/67 **It Must Be Him** *Vikki Carr*
32/79 **It Must Be Love** *Alton McClain & Destiny*
33/83 **It Must Be Love** *Madness*
37/00 **It Must Be Love** *Alan Jackson*
38/98 **It Must Be Love** *Ty Herndon*
91/97 **It Must Be Love** *Robin S.*

1/90 **It Must Have Been Love** *Roxette*
46/61 **(It Never Happens) In Real Life** *Chuck Jackson*
5/72 **It Never Rains In Southern California** *Albert Hammond*
34/91 **It Never Rains (In Southern California)** *Tony! Toni! Toné!*
38/60 **It Only Happened Yesterday** *Jack Scott*
11/56 **It Only Hurts For A Little While** *Ames Brothers*
81/74 **It Only Hurts When I Try To Smile** *Dawn Feat. Tony Orlando*
10/75 **It Only Takes A Minute** *Tavares*
59A/94 **It Seems Like You're Ready** *R. Kelly*
It Should Have Been Me
40/68 *Gladys Knight*
85/76 *Yvonne Fair*
29/62 **It Started All Over Again** *Brenda Lee*
27/73 **It Sure Took A Long, Long Time** *Lobo*
79/80 **It Takes Time** *Marshall Tucker Band*
14/67 **It Takes Two** *Marvin Gaye & Kim Weston*
36/88 **It Takes Two** *Rob Base & D.J. E-Z Rock*
20/66 **It Tears Me Up** *Percy Sledge*
64/00 **It Was** *Chely Wright*
15/93 **It Was A Good Day** *Ice Cube*
It Was A Very Good Year
28/66 *Frank Sinatra*
99/66 *Della Reese*
16/77 **It Was Almost Like A Song** *Ronnie Milsap*
11/59 **It Was I** *Skip & Flip*
1/01 **It Wasn't Me** *Shaggy*
It Will Stand
61/62 *Showmen*
80/64 *Showmen*
89/63 **It Won't Be This Way (Always)** *King Pins*
63/66 **It Won't Be Wrong** *Byrds*
10/88 **It Would Take A Strong Strong Man** *Rick Astley*
98/64 **It'll Never Be Over For Me** *Baby Washington*

IT'S:

99/64 **It's A Cotton Candy World** *Jerry Wallace*
37/77 **It's A Crazy World** *Mac McAnally*
44/71 **It's A Cryin' Shame** *Gayle McCormick*
90/79 **It's A Disco Night (Rock Don't Stop)** *Isley Brothers*
It's A Funky Thing ..see: Memphis Underground
33/01 **It's A Great Day To Be Alive** *Travis Tritt*
97/69 **It's A Groovy World!** *Unifics*
93/66 **It's-A-Happening** *Magic Mushrooms*
93/67 **It's A Happening Thing** *Peanut Butter Conspiracy*
69/67 **It's A Happening World** *Tokens*
72/84 **It's A Hard Life** *Queen*
It's A Heartache
3/78 *Bonnie Tyler*
86/78 *Juice Newton*
20/78 **It's A Laugh** *Daryl Hall & John Oates*
64/63 **It's A Lonely Town** *Gene McDaniels*
28/76 **It's A Long Way There** *Little River Band*
28/81 **It's A Love Thing** *Whispers*
92/63 **It's A Mad, Mad, Mad, Mad World** *Shirelles*
67/65 **It's A Man Down There** *G.L. Crockett*
8/66 **It's A Man's Man's Man's World** *James Brown*
12/75 **It's A Miracle** *Barry Manilow*
13/84 **It's A Miracle** *Culture Club*
6/83 **It's A Mistake** *Men At Work*
32/70 **It's A New Day** *James Brown*
67/80 **It's A Night For Beautiful Girls** *Fools*
52/96 **It's a Party** *Busta Rhymes*
14/70 **It's A Shame** *Spinners*
26/91 **It's A Shame (My Sister)** *Monie Love*
9/87 **It's A Sin** *Pet Shop Boys*
It's A Sin To Tell A Lie
7/55 *Somethin' Smith & The Redheads*
99/64 *Tony Bennett*
F/75 **It's A Sin When You Love Somebody** *Joe Cocker*
92/71 **It's About Time** *Dillards*
6/98 **It's All About Me** *Mya With Sisqo*
2/98 **It's All About The Benjamins** *Puff Daddy & The Family*
61/97 **It's All About U** *SWV*
18/99 **It's All About You (Not About Me)** *Tracie Spencer*
50/61 **It's All Because** *Linda Scott*
44/99 **It's All Been Done** *Barenaked Ladies*
2/96 **It's All Coming Back To Me Now** *Celine Dion*
31/75 **It's All Down To Goodnight Vienna** *Ringo Starr*
46/94 **It's All Good** *Hammer*
41/79 **It's All I Can Do** *Cars*
53/81 **It's All I Can Do** *Anne Murray*
It's All In The Game
1/58 *Tommy Edwards*
25/64 *Cliff Richard*
24/70 *Four Tops*
51/70 **It's All In Your Mind** *Clarence Carter*
65/73 **It's All Over** *Independents*
67/64 **It's All Over** *Walter Jackson*
72/64 **It's All Over** *Ben E. King*
It's All Over Now
26/64 *Rolling Stones*
94/64 *Valentinos*
65/67 **It's All Over Now** *Casinos*
It's All Right
4/63 *Impressions*
37A/93 *Huey Lewis*
55/75 **It's All Right** *Jim Capaldi*
93/61 **It's All Right** *Sam Cooke*
(also see: It's Alright)
79/64 **It's All Right (You're Just In Love)** *Tams*
29/96 **It's All The Way Live (Now)** *Coolio*
94/72 **It's All Up To You** *Dells*
It's Almost Tomorrow
20/55 *David Carroll*
20/55 *Snooky Lanson*
7/56 *Dream Weavers*
14/56 *Jo Stafford*
93/65 *Jimmy Velvet*
31/65 **It's Alright** *Adam Faith*
61/98 **It's Alright** *Memphis Bleek & Jay-Z*
68/92 **It's Alright** *Classic Example*
76/97 **It's Alright** *Queen Latifah*
92/75 **It's Alright** *Graham Central Station*
78/86 **It's Alright (Baby's Coming Back)** *Eurythmics*
57/97 **It's Alright, It's OK** *Leah Andreone*
57/00 **It's Always Somethin'** *Joe Diffie*
88/66 **It's An Uphill Climb To The Bottom** *Walter Jackson*
92/67 **It's Been A Long Long Time** *Elgins*
66/74 **It's Been A Long Time** *New Birth*
96/69 **It's Been A Long Time** *Betty Everett*
20/58 **(It's Been A Long Time) Pretty Baby** *Gino & Gina*
5/01 **It's Been Awhile** *Staind*
60/56 **It's Better In The Dark** *Tony Martin*
63/74 **It's Better To Have (And Don't Need)** *Don Covay*
95/65 **It's Better To Have It** *Barbara Lynn*
68/67 **It's Cold Outside** *Choir*
68/76 **It's Cool** *Tymes*
88/68 **It's Crazy** *Eddie Harris*
4/77 **It's Ecstasy When You Lay Down Next To Me** *Barry White*
46/80 **It's For You** *Player*
57/93 **It's For You** *Shanice*
It's For You
79/64 *Cilla Black*
60/71 *Springwell*
68/73 **It's Forever** *Ebonys*
92/72 **It's Four In The Morning** *Faron Young*
82/85 **It's Gettin' Late** *Beach Boys*
30/69 **It's Getting Better** *Mama Cass*
85/02 **It's Goin' Down** *X-Ecutioners*
12/72 **It's Going To Take Some Time** *Carpenters*
34/93 **It's Gonna Be A Lovely Day** *S.O.U.L. S.Y.S.T.E.M.*
(also see: Lovely Day)
23/65 **It's Gonna Be Alright** *Gerry & The Pacemakers*
56/65 **It's Gonna Be Alright** *Maxine Brown*
54/65 **It's Gonna Be Fine** *Glenn Yarbrough*
1/00 **It's Gonna Be Me** **NSYNC*
82/84 **It's Gonna Be Special** *Patti Austin*
It's Gonna Take A Miracle
41/65 *Royalettes*
10/82 *Deniece Williams*
14/61 **It's Gonna Work Out Fine** *Ike & Tina Turner*
48/66 **It's Good News Week** *Hedgehoppers Anonymous*
68/95 **It's Good To Be King** *Tom Petty*
41/65 **It's Got The Whole World Shakin'** *Sam Cooke*
63/67 **It's Got To Be Mellow** *Leon Haywood*
67/65 **It's Gotta Last Forever** *Billy J. Kramer*
18/65 **It's Growing** *Temptations*
43/80 **It's Hard To Be Humble** *Mac Davis*
87/69 **It's Hard To Get Along** *Joe Simon*
72/73 **It's Hard To Stop (Doing Something When It's Good To You)** *Betty Wright*
82/74 **It's Her Turn To Live** *Smokey Robinson*
It's Impossible
10/71 *Perry Como*
52/71 *New Birth*
(It's In His Kiss) ..see: Shoop Shoop Song
77/97 **It's In Your Eyes** *Phil Collins*
38/83 **It's Inevitable** *Charlie*
45/61 **It's Just A House Without You** *Brook Benton*

45/65 **It's Just A Little Bit Too Late** *Wayne Fontana & The Mindbenders*
It's Just A Matter Of Time
3/59 *Brook Benton*
87/70 *Sonny James*
47/59 **It's Just About Time** *Johnny Cash*
83/81 **It's Just The Sun** *Don McLean*
(It's Just) The Way That You Love Me
88/88 *Paula Abdul*
3/89 *Paula Abdul*
9/59 **It's Late** *Ricky Nelson*
74/78 **It's Late** *Queen*
95/96 **It's Like That (My Big Brother)** *Redman*
63/80 **It's Like We Never Said Goodbye** *Crystal Gayle*
91/62 **It's Magic** *Platters*
60/88 **It's Money That Matters** *Randy Newman*
96/92 **It's My Cadillac (Got That Bass)** *MC Nas-D & DJ Fred*
57/81 **It's My Job** *Jimmy Buffett*
23/66 **It's My Life** *Animals*
31/84 **It's My Life** *Talk Talk*
33/00 **It's My Life** *Bon Jovi*
88/93 **It's My Life** *Dr. Alban*
It's My Party
1/63 *Lesley Gore*
72/82 *Dave Stewart & Barbara Gaskin*
82/69 **It's My Thing** *Marva Whitney*
9/81 **It's My Turn** *Diana Ross*
51/69 **It's Never Too Late** *Steppenwolf*
51/68 **It's Nice To Be With You** *Monkees*
7/89 **It's No Crime** *Babyface*
38/97 **It's No Good** *Depeche Mode*
37/89 **It's No Secret** *Kylie Minogue*
74/64 **(It's No) Sin** *Duprees*
70/92 **It's Not A Love Thing** *Geoffrey Williams*
51/80 **It's Not A Wonder** *Little River Band*
95/68 **It's Not Easy** *Will-O-Bees*
12/89 **It's Not Enough** *Starship*
5/57 **It's Not For Me To Say** *Johnny Mathis*
9/87 **It's Not Over ('Til It's Over)** *Starship*
It's Not Right But It's Okay
4/99 *Whitney Houston*
63S/01 *Whitney Houston*
78/60 **It's Not The End Of Everything** *Tommy Edwards*
92/66 **It's Not The Same** *Anthony & The Imperials*
10/65 **It's Not Unusual** *Tom Jones*
89/86 **It's Not You, It's Not Me** *KBC Band*
It's Now Or Never
1/60 *Elvis Presley*
14/81 *John Schneider*
23/67 **It's Now Winters Day** *Tommy Roe*
18S/00 **It's OK** *Slimm Calhoun*
29/76 **It's O.K.** *Beach Boys*
94/55 **It's Obdacious** *Buddy Johnson*
74/93 **It's On** *Naughty By Nature*
20/72 **It's One Of Those Nights (Yes Love)** *Partridge Family*
15/86 **It's Only Love** *Bryan Adams/Tina Turner*
31/66 **It's Only Love** *Tommy James*
44/76 **It's Only Love** *ZZ Top*
It's Only Love
45/69 *B.J. Thomas*
51/71 *Elvis Presley*
57/89 **It's Only Love** *Simply Red*
It's Only Make Believe
1/58 *Conway Twitty*
10/70 *Glen Campbell*
16/74 **It's Only Rock 'N Roll (But I Like It)** *Rolling Stones*
42/59 **It's Only The Beginning** *Kalin Twins*
86/59 **It's Only The Good Times** *Tommy Edwards*
9/64 **It's Over** *Roy Orbison*
It's Over
37/66 *Jimmie Rodgers*
74/68 *Eddy Arnold*
38/76 **It's Over** *Boz Scaggs*
75/78 **It's Over** *Electric Light Orchestra*
It's Over Now
6/01 *One Twelve*
55S/02 *One Twelve*
62/92 **It's Over Now** *L.A. Guns*
70S/97 **It's Over Now** *Danny Boy*
70/99 **It's Over Now** *Deborah Cox*
67/94 **It's Over Now (It's Alright)** *Cause & Effect*
(It's Party Time) ..see: Theme
11/82 **It's Raining Again** *Supertramp*
46/83 **It's Raining Men** *Weather Girls*
93/58 **It's Raining Outside** *Platters*
86/78 **It's Really You** *Tarney/Spencer Band*
21/77 **It's Sad To Belong** *England Dan & John Ford Coley*
5/77 **It's So Easy** *Linda Ronstadt*
FC/57 **It's So Easy To Forget** *Four Lads*
75/00 **It's So Hard** *Big Pun*
79/67 **It's So Hard Being A Loser** *Contours*
88/71 **It's So Hard For Me To Say Good-Bye** *Eddie Kendricks*
2/91 **It's So Hard To Say Goodbye To Yesterday** *Boyz II Men*
84/70 **It's So Nice** *Jackie DeShannon*
1/80 **It's Still Rock And Roll To Me** *Billy Joel*
51/71 **It's Summer** *Temptations*
91/66 **It's That Time Of The Year** *Len Barry*
69/88 **Its The End Of The World As We Know It** *R.E.M.*
50/67 **It's The Little Things** *Sonny & Chér*
81/71 **It's The Real Thing** *Electric Express*
93/72 **It's The Same Old Love** *Courtship*
It's The Same Old Song
5/65 *Four Tops*
35/78 *KC & The Sunshine Band*
53/98 **It's The Things You Do** *Five*
53/72 **(It's The Way) Nature Planned It** *Four Tops*
6S/02 **It's The Weekend** *Lil' J*
94/75 **It's Time For Love** *Chi-Lites*
4/59 **It's Time To Cry** *Paul Anka*
1/71 **It's Too Late** *Carole King*
23/66 **It's Too Late** *Bobby Goldsboro*
49/63 **It's Too Late** *Wilson Pickett*
56/65 **It's Too Late, Baby Too Late** *Arthur Prysock*
It's Too Soon To Know
4/58 *Pat Boone*
54/61 *Etta James*
(It's Tough To Be A Baby!) ..see: Dur Dur D'Etre Bebe!
57/87 **It's Tricky** *Run-D.M.C.*
69/61 **It's Unbelievable** *Larks*
80/77 **It's Uncanny** *Daryl Hall/John Oates*
6/63 **It's Up To You** *Rick Nelson*
55/98 **It's Up To You** *Tuesdays*
72/71 **It's Up To You Petula** *Edison Lighthouse*
20/68 **It's Wonderful** *Young Rascals*
61/65 **It's Wonderful To Be In Love** *Ovations*
52/86 **It's You** *Bob Seger*
6/57 **It's You I Love** *Fats Domino*
33/78 **It's You That I Need** *Enchantment*
43/97 **It's Your Body** *Johnny Gill*
85/70 **It's Your Life** *Andy Kim*
7/97 **It's Your Love** *Tim McGraw with Faith Hill*
67/98 **It's Your Love** *She Moves*
62/98 **It's Your Song** *Garth Brooks*
2/69 **It's Your Thing** *Isley Brothers*
96/99 **It's Your Thing** *Mercedes*
51/61 **It's Your World** *Marty Robbins*
74/56 **It's Yours** *DeCastro Sisters*
25/56 **Italian Theme** *Cyril Stapleton*
45/00 **Itch** *Vitamin C*
Itchy Twitchy Feeling
25/58 *Bobby Hendricks*
100/58 *Swallows*
16/68 **Itchycoo Park** *Small Faces*
1/60 **Itsy Bitsy Teenie Weenie Yellow Polkadot Bikini** *Brian Hyland*
41/62 **Itty Bitty Pieces** *James Ray*
97/69 **Ivory** *Bob Seger*
Ivory Tower
2/56 *Cathy Carr*
6/56 *Gale Storm*
11/56 *Charms*
FC/57 **Ivy League** *Tennessee Ernie Ford*
18/57 **Ivy Rose** *Perry Como*
8/01 **Izzo (H.O.V.A.)** *Jay-Z*

J

22A/95 **J.A.R. (Jason Andrew Relva)** *Green Day*
86/61 **Ja-Da** *Johnny & The Hurricanes*
1/82 **Jack & Diane** *John Cougar*
8/78 **Jack And Jill** *Raydio*
53/69 **Jack And Jill** *Tommy Roe*
73/97 **Jack-Ass** *Beck*
96/59 **Jack O'Diamonds** *Ruth Brown*
94/88 **Jack The Lad** *3 Man Island*
64/63 **Jack The Ripper** *Link Wray*
54/88 **Jackie** *Blue Zone U.K.*
3/75 **Jackie Blue** *Ozark Mountain Daredevils*
48/89 **Jackie Brown** *John Cougar Mellencamp*
61/72 **Jackie Wilson Said (I'm In Heaven When You Smile)** *Van Morrison*
54/98 **Jackie's Strength** *Tori Amos*
14/67 **Jackson** *Nancy Sinatra & Lee Hazlewood*
1/87 **Jacob's Ladder** *Huey Lewis*
63/58 **Jacqueline** *Bobby Helms*
7/01 **Jaded** *Aerosmith*
94/64 **Jailer, Bring Me Water** *Trini Lopez*
1/57 **Jailhouse Rock** *Elvis Presley*
26/92 **Jam** *Michael Jackson*
29/62 **Jam, The** *Bobby Gregg*
63/76 **Jam, The** *Graham Central Station*
80/75 **Jam Band** *Disco Tex & The Sex-O-Lettes*
Jam On It
56/84 *Newcleus*
50S/01 *Mos Def*
32/87 **Jam Tonight** *Freddie Jackson*
8/70 **Jam Up Jelly Tight** *Tommy Roe*

82/81 **Jam Was Moving** *Debbie Harry*
14/57 **Jamaica Farewell** *Harry Belafonte*
98/64 **Jamaica Ska** *Ska Kings*
Jambalaya (On The Bayou)
90/60 *Bobby Comstock*
30/62 *Fats Domino*
84/72 *Nitty Gritty Dirt Band*
16/73 *Blue Ridge Rangers*
10/99 **Jamboree** *Naughty By Nature*
58/64 **James Bond Theme** *Billy Strange*
59/92 **James Brown Is Dead** *L.A. Style*
77/74 **James Dean** *Eagles*
17/62 **James (Hold The Ladder Steady)** *Sue Thompson*
14/85 **Jamie** *Ray Parker Jr.*
30/62 **Jamie** *Eddie Holland*
54/57 **Jamie Boy** *Kay Starr*
81/85 **Jammin** *Teena Marie*
18/87 **Jammin' Me** *Tom Petty*
14/80 **Jane** *Jefferson Starship*
93/62 **Jane, Jane, Jane** *Kingston Trio*
77/87 **Jane's Getting Serious** *Jon Astley*
87/85 **Janet** *Commodores*
4/90 **Janie's Got A Gun** *Aerosmith*
87/76 **January** *Pilot*
52/56 **Japanese Farewell Song** *Kay Cee Jones*
Jar ..see: J.A.R.
52^{S}/00 **Jasmin** *Youth Asylum*
69/76 **Jasper** *Jim Stafford*
Java
49/63 *Floyd Cramer*
4/64 *Al Hirt*
Jaws ..see: Theme From / Mr. Jaws
77/57 **Jay-Dee's Boogie Woogie** *Jimmy Dorsey*
Jayne ..see: Ballad of
2/74 **Jazzman** *Carole King*
52/97 **Jazzy Belle** *OutKast*
Je T'Aime...Moi Non Plus
58/70 *Jane Birkin & Serge Gainsbourg*
99/73 *Sylvia & Ralfi Pagan (Soul)*
68/90 **Jealous** *Gene Loves Jezebel*
75/90 **Jealous Again** *Black Crowes*
80/88 **Jealous Guy** *John Lennon*
Jealous Heart
62/58 *Tab Hunter*
94/58 *Fontane Sisters*
47/65 *Connie Francis*
20/69 **Jealous Kind Of Fella** *Garland Green*
50/68 **Jealous Love** *Wilson Pickett*
Jealous Lover ..see: Theme From The Apartment
19/60 **Jealous Of You** *Connie Francis*
23/96 **Jealousy** *Natalie Merchant*
73/76 **Jealousy** *Major Harris*
78/58 **Jealousy** *Kitty Wells*
89/98 **Jealousy** *Kim Sanders*
94/91 **Jealousy** *Adventures Of Stevie V*
2/69 **Jean** *Oliver*
71/72 **Jean Genie** *David Bowie*
94/58 **Jeannie Jeannie Jeannie** *Eddie Cochran*
17/77 **Jeans On** *David Dundas*
Jed Clampett ..see: Ballad Of
67/95 **Jeeps, Lex Coups, Bimaz & Benz** *Lost Boyz*
51/68 **Jelly Jungle (Of Orange Marmalade)** *Lemon Pipers*
82/63 **Jellybread** *Booker T. & The MG's*
72/96 **Jellyhead** *Crush*
Jennie Lee
8/58 *Jan & Arnie*
55/58 *Billy Ward*
60/71 **Jennifer** *Bobby Sherman*
40/68 **Jennifer Eccles** *Hollies*
26/68 **Jennifer Juniper** *Donovan*
36/70 **Jennifer Tomkins** *Street People*
75^{S}/01 **Jenny & The Ess-Dog** *Stephen Malkmus*
Jenny ..see: 867-5309
84/63 **Jenny Brown** *Smothers Brothers*
3/02 **Jenny From The Block** *Jennifer Lopez*
10/57 **Jenny, Jenny** *Little Richard*
67/60 **Jenny Lou** *Sonny James*
10/66 **Jenny Take A Ride!** *Mitch Ryder*
2/83 **Jeopardy** *Greg Kihn Band*
(also see: I Lost On Jeopardy)
35/61 **Jeremiah Peabody's Poly Unsaturated Pills** *Ray Stevens*
79/95 **Jeremy** *Pearl Jam*
7/65 **Jerk, The** *Larks*
85/65 **Jerk And Twine** *Jackie Ross*
9/90 **Jerk-Out** *Time*
74/70 **Jerusalem** *Herb Alpert*
11/80 **Jesse** *Carly Simon*
30/73 **Jesse** *Roberta Flack*
54/85 **Jesse** *Julian Lennon*
98/68 **Jesse Brady** *McCoys*
65/74 **Jessica** *Allman Brothers Band*
26/94 **Jessie** *Joshua Kadison*
1/81 **Jessie's Girl** *Rick Springfield*
Jesus Christ Superstar ..see: Superstar
23/92 **Jesus He Knows Me** *Genesis*
28/69 **Jesus Is A Soul Man** *Lawrence Reynolds*
Jesus Is Just Alright
97/70 *Byrds*
35/73 *Doobie Brothers*
7/96 **Jesus To A Child** *George Michael*
91/72 **Jesus Was A Capricorn** *Kris Kristofferson*
7/74 **Jet** *Paul McCartney*
8/77 **Jet Airliner** *Steve Miller Band*
66/02 **Jigga** *Jay-Z*
28/99 **Jigga My Nigga** *Jay-Z*
84/99 **Jigga What?** *Jay-Z*
52/67 **Jill** *Gary Lewis*
Jim Dandy
17/57 *LaVerne Baker*
25/74 *Black Oak Arkansas*
76/57 **Jim Dandy Got Married** *LaVern Baker*
95/59 **Jimmy Kiss And Run** *Diane Maxwell*
28/87 **Jimmy Lee** *Aretha Franklin*
Jimmy Loves Mary-Anne
33/73 *Looking Glass*
82/84 *Josie Cotton*
Jimmy Mack
10/67 *Martha & The Vandellas*
65/86 *Sheena Easton*
51/61 **Jimmy Martinez** *Marty Robbins*
78/93 **Jimmy Olsen's Blues** *Spin Doctors*
25/61 **Jimmy's Girl** *Johnny Tillotson*
33^{S}/00 **Jimmy's Got A Girlfriend** *Wilkinsons*
Jingle Bell Rock
6/57 *Bobby Helms*
35/58 *Bobby Helms*
36/60 *Bobby Helms*
21/61 *Bobby Rydell/Chubby Checker*
41/61 *Bobby Helms*
56/62 *Bobby Helms*
92/62 *Bobby Rydell/Chubby Checker*
8^{X}/64 *Brenda Lee*
73^{A}/97 *Bobby Helms*
Jingle Bells
74/57 *Perry Como*
21^{X}/65 *Ramsey Lewis Trio*
20^{X}/66 *Booker T. & The M.G.'s*
1^{X}/71 *Singing Dogs*
(also see: Twistin' Bells)
10/70 **Jingle Jangle** *Archies*
56/69 **Jingo** *Santana*
8^{X}/63 **Jingo Jango** *Bert Kaempfert*
82/62 **Jitterbug, The** *Dovells*
66/63 **Jive Samba** *Cannonball Adderley*
1/75 **Jive Talkin'** *Bee Gees*
47/74 **Jive Turkey** *Ohio Players*
71/62 **Jivin' Around** *Al Casey Combo*
19/58 **Jo-Ann** *Playmates*
17/80 **JoJo** *Boz Scaggs*
73/59 **Jo-Jo The Dog-Faced Boy** *Annette*
78/61 **Joanie** *Frankie Calen*
2/84 **Joanna** *Kool & The Gang*
21/70 **Joanne** *Michael Nesmith*
31/97 **Jock Jam** *ESPN Presents*
42/86 **Jody** *Jermaine Stewart*
28/71 **Jody's Got Your Girl And Gone** *Johnnie Taylor*
83/58 **Joe Joe Gun** *Chuck Berry*
19/90 **Joey** *Concrete Blonde*
91/62 **Joey Baby** *Anita & Th' So-And-So's*
76/56 **Joey, Joey, Joey** *Peggy Lee*
46/59 **Joey's Song** *Bill Haley*

JOHN:

John And Yoko ..see: Ballad Of
99/62 **John Birch Society** *Chad Mitchell Trio*
69/94 **John Deere Green** *Joe Diffie*
95/01 **John Doe** *Public Announcement*
100/55 **Johnnie's Comin' Home** *Johnnie Ray*
1/62 **Johnny Angel** *Shelley Fabares*
61/87 **Johnny B** *Hooters*
Johnny B. Goode
8/58 *Chuck Berry*
71/64 *Dion*
92/70 *Johnny Winter*
84/83 *Peter Tosh*
42/82 **Johnny Can't Read** *Don Henley*
81/56 **Johnny Casanova** *Jaye P. Morgan*
76/86 **Johnny Come Home** *Fine Young Cannibals*
75/56 **Johnny Concho Theme (Wait For Me)** *Frank Sinatra*
72/76 **Johnny Cool** *Steve Gibbons Band*
69/60 **Johnny Freedom** *Johnny Horton*
7/62 **Johnny Get Angry** *Joanie Sommers*
54/92 **Johnny Have You Seen Her?** *Rembrandts*
21/62 **Johnny Jingo** *Hayley Mills*
21/62 **Johnny Loves Me** *Shelley Fabares*
41/69 **Johnny One Time** *Brenda Lee*
54/59 **Johnny Reb** *Johnny Horton*
35/62 **Johnny Will** *Pat Boone*
96/61 **Johnny Willow** *Fred Darian*
17/72 **Join Together** *Who*
94/97 **Joint** *EPMD*
1/74 **Joker, The** *Steve Miller Band*
93/78 **Joker, The** *Snail*
Joker (That's What They Call Me)
22/57 *Hilltoppers*
25/57 *Billy Myles*
20/66 **Joker Went Wild** *Brian Hyland*
97/67 **Jokers, The** *Peter & Gordon*
65/81 **Jolé Blon** *Gary U.S. Bonds*
60/74 **Jolene** *Dolly Parton*
4/65 **Jolly Green Giant** *Kingsmen*
(also see: Big Boy Pete)

30S/01 **Jonathan David** *Belle & Sebastian*
39/81 **Jones Vs. Jones** *Kool & The Gang*
18/60 **Josephine** *Bill Black's Combo*
26/78 **Josie** *Steely Dan*
63/72 **Josie** *Kris Kristofferson*
81/60 **Journey Of Love** *Crests*
16/68 **Journey To The Center Of The Mind** *Amboy Dukes*
6/72 **Joy** *Apollo 100*
30/74 **"Joy"** *Isaac Hayes*
41/67 **Joy** *Mitch Ryder*
43/95 **Joy** *BLACKstreet*
77/88 **Joy** *Teddy Pendergrass*
58/89 **Joy And Pain** *Rob Base & D.J. E-Z Rock*
1/71 **Joy To The World** *Three Dog Night*
1/91 **Joyride** *Roxette*
61/84 **Joystick** *Dazz Band*
26/65 **Ju Ju Hand** *Sam The Sham & the Pharaohs*
59/66 **Juanita Banana** *Peels*
65/72 **Jubilation** *Paul Anka*
22/58 **Judy** *Frankie Vaughan*
78/67 **Judy** *Elvis Presley*
86/59 **Judy** *David Seville*
Judy Blue Eyes ..see: Suite
1/68 **Judy In Disguise (With Glasses)** *John Fred*
95/64 **Judy Loves Me** *Johnny Crawford*
33/75 **Judy Mae** *Boomer Castleman*
5/63 **Judy's Turn To Cry** *Lesley Gore*
96/92 **Juice (know the ledge)** *Eric B. & Rakim*
27/94 **Juicy** *Notorious B.I.G.*
45/83 **Juicy Fruit** *Mtume*
10/56 **Juke Box Baby** *Perry Como*
26/82 **Juke Box Hero** *Foreigner*
57/61 **Juke Box Saturday Night** *Nino & The Ebb Tides*
82/76 **Jukin** *Atlanta Rhythm Section*
76/69 **Julia** *Ramsey Lewis*
64/56 **Julie** *Doris Day*
(also see: Oh, Julie)
5/70 **Julie, Do Ya Love Me** *Bobby Sherman*
40S/01 **Juliet** *LMNT*
85/70 **July 12, 1939** *Charlie Rich*
100/69 **July You're A Woman** *Pat Boone*
57/68 **Jumbo** *Bee Gees*
1/84 **Jump** *Van Halen*
Jump
1/92 *Kris Kross*
64S/02 *Kris Kross*
53/92 **Jump!** *Movement*
72/76 **Jump** *Aretha Franklin*
3/92 **Jump Around** *House Of Pain*
Jump Back
49/64 *Rufus Thomas*
63/67 *King Curtis*
F/76 **Jump For Joy** *Biddu Orchestra*
3/84 **Jump (For My Love)** *Pointer Sisters*
27/72 **Jump Into The Fire** *Nilsson*
23A/98 **Jump Jive An' Wail** *Brian Setzer Orchestra*
97/96 **Jump On It** *Sir Mix-A-Lot*
28/60 **Jump Over** *Freddy Cannon*
13/87 **Jump Start** *Natalie Cole*
24/82 **Jump To It** *Aretha Franklin*
29S/02 **Jump Up In The Air** *Original P*
5/99 **Jumper** *Third Eye Blind*
Jumpin' Jack Flash
3/68 *Rolling Stones*
89/71 *Johnny Winter*
21/86 *Aretha Franklin*
3/00 **Jumpin', Jumpin'** *Destiny's Child*

21/57 **June Night** *Jimmy Dorsey*
94/67 **Jungle, The** *B.B. King*
4/74 **Jungle Boogie** *Kool & The Gang*
52/86 **Jungle Boy** *John Eddie*
8/72 **Jungle Fever** *Chakachas*
20/85 **Jungle Love** *Time*
23/77 **Jungle Love** *Steve Miller Band*
3/75 **Junior's Farm** *Paul McCartney*
9/76 **Junk Food Junkie** *Larry Groce*
81/59 **Jupiter-C** *Pat & the Satellites*
51S/99 **Jupiter (Swallow The Moon)** *Jewel*
37/61 **Jura (I Swear I Love You)** *Les Paul & Mary Ford*
62/92 **Jus Lyke Compton** *DJ Quik*

JUST:

90/01 **Just A Baby Boy** *Snoop Dogg*
Just A Closer Walk With Thee
44/60 *Jimmie Rodgers*
93/60 *Pete Fountain*
4/58 **Just A Dream** *Jimmy Clanton*
9/90 **Just A Friend** *Biz Markie*
4/02 **Just A Friend 2002** *Mario*
12/85 **Just A Gigolo/I Ain't Got Nobody** *David Lee Roth*
23/96 **Just A Girl** *No Doubt*
8/65 **Just A Little** *Beau Brummels*
40/60 **Just A Little** *Brenda Lee*
Just A Little Bit
64/60 *Rosco Gordon*
39/65 *Roy Head*
92/68 **Just A Little Bit** *Blue Cheer*
97/69 **Just A Little Bit** *Little Milton*
7/65 **Just A Little Bit Better** *Herman's Hermits*
62/91 **Just A Little Bit Longer** *Maxi Priest*
23/75 **Just A Little Bit Of You** *Michael Jackson*
76/69 **Just A Little Love** *B.B. King*
85/66 **Just A Little Misunderstanding** *Contours*
9/59 **Just A Little Too Much** *Ricky Nelson*
100/64 **Just A Moment Ago** *Soul Sisters*
90/75 **Just A Smile** *Pilot*
7/77 **Just A Song Before I Go** *Crosby, Stills & Nash*
50/91 **Just A Touch Of Love** *C & C Music Factory*
54/64 **Just Ain't Enough Love** *Eddie Holland*
67/69 **Just Ain't No Love** *Barbara Acklin*
68/97 **Just Another Case** *Cru*
5/92 **Just Another Day** *Jon Secada*
46/97 **Just Another Day** *John Mellencamp*
54/94 **Just Another Day...** *Queen Latifah*
85/86 **Just Another Day** *Oingo Boingo*
35/00 **Just Another Day In Paradise** *Phil Vassar*
46/82 **Just Another Day In Paradise** *Bertie Higgins*
9/91 **Just Another Dream** *Cathy Dennis*
64/01 **Just Another Girl** *Monica*
88/91 **Just Another Girlfriend** *Hi-Five*
12/85 **Just Another Night** *Mick Jagger*
68/79 **Just Another Night** *Ian Hunter*
19/85 **Just As I Am** *Air Supply*
76/56 **Just As Long As I'm With You** *Pat Boone*
84/72 **Just As Long As You Need Me** *Independents*
Just As Much As Ever
32/59 *Bob Beckham*
24/68 *Bobby Vinton*
88/91 **Just Ask Me To** *Tevin Campbell*

7/59 **Just Ask Your Heart** *Frankie Avalon*
32/00 **Just Be A Man About It** *Toni Braxton*
Just Be Good To Me
55/83 *S.O.S. Band*
76/90 *Beats International*
67/81 **Just Be My Lady** *Larry Graham*
91/67 **Just Be Sincere** *Jackie Wilson*
57/98 **Just Be Straight With Me** *Silkk The Shocker*
19/64 **Just Be True** *Gene Chandler*
14/89 **Just Because** *Anita Baker*
29/57 **Just Because** *Lloyd Price*
99/61 **Just Because** *McGuire Sisters*
78/96 **Just Because I Love You** *Lina Santiago*
6/90 **Just Between You And Me** *Lou Gramm*
8/57 **Just Between You And Me** *Chordettes*
21/81 **Just Between You And Me** *April Wine*
29/96 **Just Between You And Me** *DC Talk*
12/57 **Just Born (To Be Your Baby)** *Perry Como*
79/60 **Just Call Me (And I'll Understand)** *Lloyd Price*
78/80 **Just Can't Wait** *J. Geils Band*
38/82 **Just Can't Win 'Em All** *Stevie Woods*
56/98 **Just Clownin'** *WC*
35/60 **Just Come Home** *Hugo & Luigi*
36S/99 **Just Don't Give A F***** *Eminem*
Just Don't Want To Be Lonely
60/73 *Ronnie Dyson*
10/74 *Main Ingredient*
5/68 **Just Dropped In (To See What Condition My Condition Was In)** *First Edition*
20/61 **Just For Old Time's Sake** *McGuire Sisters*
82/80 **Just For The Moment** *Ray Kennedy*
26/92 **Just For Tonight** *Vanessa Williams*
31/00 **Just Friends (Sunny)** *Musiq*
96/60 **Just Give Me A Ring** *Clyde McPhatter*
36/83 **Just Got Lucky** *JoBoxers*
10/88 **Just Got Paid** *Johnny Kemp*
64/62 **Just Got To Know** *Jimmy McCracklin*
52/01 **Just In Case** *Jaheim*
46/56 **Just In Time** *Tony Bennett*
18/59 **Just Keep It Up** *Dee Clark*
2/93 **Just Kickin' It** *Xscape*
69/70 **Just Let It Come** *Alive 'N Kickin'*
64/02 **Just Let Me Be In Love** *Tracy Byrd*
Just Like ..see: Jus Lyke
8/02 **Just Like A Pill** *P!nk*
33/66 **Just Like A Woman** *Bob Dylan*
40/88 **Just Like Heaven** *Cure*
75/58 **Just Like In The Movies** *Upbeats*
8/89 **Just Like Jesse James** *Cher*
11/66 **Just Like Me** *Paul Revere & The Raiders*
6/88 **Just Like Paradise** *David Lee Roth*
86/81 **Just Like Paradise** *Larry John McNally*
(Just Like) Romeo & Juliet
6/64 *Reflections*
55/75 *Sha Na Na*
1/80 **(Just Like) Starting Over** *John Lennon*
25/91 **Just Like You** *Robbie Nevil*

69/67 **Just Look What You've Done** *Brenda Holloway*
97/56 **Just Love Me** *Jaye P. Morgan*
26/58 **Just Married** *Marty Robbins*
1/71 **Just My Imagination** *Temptations*
17/81 **Just Once** *Quincy Jones*
97/67 **Just Once In A Lifetime** *Brenda & The Tabulations*
9/65 **Just Once In My Life** *Righteous Brothers*
76/65 **Just One Kiss From You** *Impressions*
Just One Look
10/63 *Doris Troy*
98/64 *Hollies*
44/67 *Hollies*
86/74 *Anne Murray*
44/79 *Linda Ronstadt*
85/65 **Just One More Day** *Otis Redding*
70/84 **Just One More Time** *Headpins*
64/67 **Just One Smile** *Gene Pitney*
29/60 **Just One Time** *Don Gibson*
Just Out Of Reach (Of My Two Open Arms)
24/61 *Solomon Burke*
66/67 *Percy Sledge*
11/77 **Just Remember I Love You** *Firefall*
88/95 **Just Roll** *Fabu*
40/71 **Just Seven Numbers (Can Straighten Out My Life)** *Four Tops*
82/70 **Just Seventeen** *Raiders*
39/81 **Just So Lonely** *Get Wet*
45/96 **Just Tah Let U Know** *Eazy-E*
16/92 **Just Take My Heart** *Mr. Big*
55/62 **Just Tell Her Jim Said Hello** *Elvis Presley*
58/79 **Just The Same Way** *Journey*
Just The Two Of Us
2/81 *Grover Washington, Jr. (with Bill Withers)*
20/98 *Will Smith*
14/91 **Just The Way It Is, Baby** *Rembrandts*
85/96 **Just The Way (Playas Play)** *Alfonzo Hunter*
3/78 **Just The Way You Are** *Billy Joel*
64/84 **Just The Way You Like It** *S.O.S. Band*
93/97 **Just The Way You Like It** *Tasha Holiday*
7/76 **Just To Be Close To You** *Commodores*
69/59 **Just To Be With You** *Passions*
26/57 **Just To Hold My Hand** *Clyde McPhatter*
52/82 **Just To Satisfy You** *Waylon Jennings & Willie Nelson*
8/87 **Just To See Her** *Smokey Robinson*
30/75 **Just Too Many People** *Melissa Manchester*
2/56 **Just Walking In The Rain** *Johnnie Ray*
34/91 **Just Want To Hold You** *Jasmine Guy*
27/78 **Just What I Needed** *Cars*
4/79 **Just When I Needed You Most** *Randy Vanwarmer*
73/65 **Just Yesterday** *Jack Jones*
77/66 **Just Yesterday** *Al Martino*
20/65 **Just You** *Sonny & Cher*
27/76 **Just You And I** *Melissa Manchester*
4/73 **Just You 'N' Me** *Chicago*
Just Young
69/58 *Andy Rose*
80/58 *Paul Anka*
11/92 **Justified & Ancient** *KLF*
1/91 **Justify My Love** *Madonna*
85/65 **Justine** *Righteous Brothers*

K

39/71 **K-Jee** *Nite-Liters*
Ka-Ding Dong
24/56 *G-Clefs*
35/56 *Diamonds*
38/56 *Hilltoppers*
55/74 **Kalimba Story** *Earth, Wind & Fire*
Kansas City
1/59 *Wilbert Harrison*
60/59 *Rocky Olson*
72/59 *Hank Ballard*
95/59 *Little Richard*
23/64 *Trini Lopez*
55/67 *James Brown*
31/65 **Kansas City Star** *Roger Miller*
55/67 **Karate** *Emperor's*
51/67 **Karate-Boo-Ga-Loo** *Jerryo*
94/86 **Karen** *B.E. Taylor Group*
1/84 **Karma Chameleon** *Culture Club*
69[A]/98 **Karma Police** *Radiohead*
75/72 **Kate** *Johnny Cash*
16/58 **Kathy-O** *Diamonds*
43/75 **Katmandu** *Bob Seger*
66/59 **Katy Too** *Johnny Cash*
83/69 **Kay** *John Wesley Ryles*
74/85 **Kayleigh** *Marillion*
16/69 **Keem-O-Sabe** *Electric Indian*

KEEP:

8/57 **Keep A Knockin'** *Little Richard*
64/67 **Keep A Light In The Window Till I Come Home** *Solomon Burke*
12/91 **Keep Coming Back** *Richard Marx*
8/83 **(Keep Feeling) Fascination** *Human League*
54/76 **Keep Holding On** *Temptations*
17/92 **Keep It Comin'** *Keith Sweat*
83/92 **Keep It Comin' (Dance Till You Can't Dance No More!)** *C + C Music Factory*
2/77 **Keep It Comin' Love** *KC & The Sunshine Band*
91/83 **Keep It Confidential** *Nona Hendryx*
50/74 **Keep It In The Family** *Leon Haywood*
17[S]/01 **Keep It Real** *Kelli Mack*
78/83 **Keep It Tight** *Single Bullet Theory*
8/90 **Keep It Together** *Madonna*
37/77 **Keep Me Cryin'** *Al Green*
41/79 **Keep On Dancin'** *Gary's Gang*
4/65 **Keep On Dancing** *Gentrys*
66/61 **Keep On Dancing** *Hank Ballard*
66/68 **Keep On Dancing** *Alvin Cash*
75/70 **Keep On Doin'** *Isley Brothers*
88/72 **Keep On Doin' What You're Doin'** *Bobby Byrd*
10/96 **Keep On, Keepin' On** *MC Lyte*
77/72 **Keep On Keeping On** *N.F. Porter*
24/68 **Keep On Lovin' Me Honey** *Marvin Gaye & Tammi Terrell*
89/70 **Keep On Loving Me (You'll See The Change)** *Bobby Bland*
1/81 **Keep On Loving You** *REO Speedwagon*
11/89 **Keep On Movin'** *Soul II Soul*
10/64 **Keep On Pushing** *Impressions*
76/66 **Keep On Running** *Spencer Davis Group*
90/72 **Keep On Running** *Stevie Wonder*
81/79 **Keep On Running Away** *Lazy Racer*
Keep On Singing
50/73 *Austin Roberts*
15/74 *Helen Reddy*
10/74 **Keep On Smilin'** *Wet Willie*
1/73 **Keep On Truckin'** *Eddie Kendricks*
50/75 **Keep On Tryin'** *Poco*
85/65 **Keep On Trying** *Bobby Vee*
15/92 **Keep On Walkin'** *Ce Ce Peniston*
90/75 **Keep Our Love Alive** *Paul Davis*
70/72 **Keep Playin' That Rock 'N' Roll** *Edgar Winter's White Trash*
9/65 **Keep Searchin'** *Del Shannon*
Keep The Ball Rollin'
14/67 *Jay & The Techniques*
100/68 *Al Hirt*
71/71 **Keep The Customer Satisfied** *Gary Puckett*
29/92 **Keep The Faith** *Bon Jovi*
36/80 **Keep The Fire** *Kenny Loggins*
7/82 **Keep The Fire Burnin'** *REO Speedwagon*
52/68 **Keep The One You Got** *Joe Tex*
10/95 **Keep Their Heads Ringin'** *Dr. Dre*
62/81 **Keep This Train A-Rollin'** *Doobie Brothers*
64/96 **Keep Tryin'** *Groove Theory*
97/91 **Keep Warm** *Jinny*
12/94 **Keep Ya Head Up** *2Pac*
46/87 **Keep Your Eye On Me** *Herb Alpert*
Keep Your Eye On The Sparrow **..see: Baretta's Theme**
88/62 **Keep Your Hands In Your Pockets** *Playmates*
12/62 **Keep Your Hands Off My Baby** *Little Eva*
75/61 **Keep Your Hands Off Of Him** *Damita Jo*
2/87 **Keep Your Hands To Yourself** *Georgia Satellites*
52/74 **Keep Your Head To The Sky** *Earth, Wind & Fire*
58/62 **Keep Your Love Locked (Deep In Your Heart)** *Paul Petersen*
10/73 **Keeper Of The Castle** *Four Tops*
83/95 **Keeper Of The Flame** *Martin Page*
68/95 **Keeper Of The Stars** *Tracy Byrd*
69/99 **Keepin' Up** *Alabama*
50/82 **Keeping Our Love Alive** *Henry Paul Band*
18/85 **Keeping The Faith** *Billy Joel*
20/55 **Kentuckian Song** *Hilltoppers*
85/76 **Kentucky Moonrunner** *Cledus Maggard*
16/70 **Kentucky Rain** *Elvis Presley*
Kentucky Woman
22/67 *Neil Diamond*
38/68 *Deep Purple*
99/00 **Kernkraft 400** *Zombie Nation*
Ketchup Song
30[S]/02 *Hines Girls*
54/02 *Las Ketchup*
6/58 **Kewpie Doll** *Perry Como*
8/82 **Key Largo** *Bertie Higgins*
82/56 **Key To My Heart** *Rosemary Clooney*
14/96 **Key West Intermezzo (I Saw You First)** *John Mellencamp*
50[S]/00 **Keys** *LaTanya*
68[S]/94 **Kick A Little** *Little Texas*
79/77 **Kick It Out** *Heart*
82/69 **Kick Out The Jams** *MC5*
61/64 **Kick That Little Foot Sally Ann** *Round Robin*

67/87 **Kick The Wall** *Jimmy Davis & Junction*
36[S]/02 **Kick'n Ass** *Supa Nat*
45/92 **Kickin' It** *After 7*
4/66 **Kicks** *Paul Revere & The Raiders*
27/90 **Kickstart My Heart** *Mötley Crüe*
82/76 **Kid Charlemagne** *Steely Dan*
55/81 **Kid Is Hot Tonite** *Loverboy*
95/73 **Kid Stuff** *Barbara Fairchild*
33/84 **Kid's American** *Matthew Wilder*
7/60 **Kiddio** *Brook Benton*
25/82 **Kids In America** *Kim Wilde*
72/73 **Kids Say The Darndest Things** *Tammy Wynette*
79/64 **Kiko** *Jimmy McGriff*
Killer
100/92 *Seal*
69/93 *George Michael (medley)*
60/79 **Killer Cut** *Charlie*
Killer Joe
16/63 *Rocky Fellers*
77/66 *Kingsmen*
74/70 **Killer Joe** *Quincy Jones*
12/75 **Killer Queen** *Queen*
28/81 **Killin' Time** *Fred Knoblock & Susan Anton*
Killing Me Softly With His Song
1/73 *Roberta Flack*
80/88 *Al B. Sure!*
2[A]/96 *Fugees*
30/77 **Killing Of Georgie** *Rod Stewart*
18[A]/98 **Kind & Generous** *Natalie Merchant*
1/67 **Kind Of A Drag** *Buckinghams*
17/63 **Kind Of Boy You Can't Forget** *Raindrops*
42/86 **Kind Of Magic** *Queen*

KING:

8/86 **King For A Day** *Thompson Twins*
40/72 **King Heroin** *James Brown*
13/77 **King Is Gone** *Ronnie McDowell*
69/75 **King Kong** *Jimmy Castor Bunch*
(also see: Theme From / Kong)
51/67 **King Midas In Reverse** *Hollies*
90/97 **King Nothing** *Metallica*
45/62 **King Of Clowns** *Neil Sedaka*
62[A]/96 **King Of New Orleans** *Better Than Ezra*
60/74 **King Of Nothing** *Seals & Crofts*
3/83 **King Of Pain** *Police*
(also see: King Of Suede)
King Of Rock & Roll ..see: (Don't Try To Lay No Boogie Woogie On The)
62/84 **King Of Suede** *"Weird Al" Yankovic*
(also see: King Of Pain)
36/80 **King Of The Hill** *Rick Pinette & Oak*
4/65 **King Of The Road** *Roger Miller*
(also see: Queen Of The House)
30/62 **King Of The Whole Wide World** *Elvis Presley*
8/90 **King Of Wishful Thinking** *Go West*
17/78 **King Tut** *Steve Martin*
70/78 **Kings And Queens** *Aerosmith*
31/74 **Kings Of The Party** *Brownsville Station*

KISS:

Kiss
1/86 *Prince*
31/89 *Art Of Noise*
21/72 **Kiss An Angel Good Mornin'** *Charley Pride*
88/56 **Kiss And Run** *Peggy King*
1/76 **Kiss And Say Goodbye** *Manhattans*
31/88 **Kiss And Tell** *Bryan Ferry*
48/87 **Kiss And Tell** *Breakfast Club*
63/85 **Kiss And Tell** *Isley, Jasper, Isley*
25/65 **Kiss Away** *Ronnie Dove*
1/95 **Kiss From A Rose** *Seal*
Kiss Him Goodbye ..see: Na Na Hey Hey
37/79 **Kiss In The Dark** *Pink Lady*
2/99 **Kiss Me** *Sixpence None The Richer*
30/56 **Kiss Me Another** *Georgia Gibbs*
12/88 **Kiss Me Deadly** *Lita Ford*
15/68 **Kiss Me Goodbye** *Petula Clark*
37/80 **Kiss Me In The Rain** *Barbra Streisand*
34/64 **Kiss Me Quick** *Elvis Presley*
29/64 **Kiss Me Sailor** *Diane Renay*
78/93 **Kiss Of Life** *Sade*
28[S]/01 **Kiss Off (Goodbye)** *Brooke Allison*
1/81 **Kiss On My List** *Daryl Hall & John Oates*
25/83 **Kiss The Bride** *Elton John*
15/98 **Kiss The Rain** *Billie Myers*
23/91 **Kiss Them For Me** *Siouxsie & The Banshees*
42/00 **Kiss This** *Aaron Tippin*
35/90 **Kiss This Thing Goodbye** *Del Amitri*
Kiss You All Over
1/78 *Exile*
80/97 *No Mercy*
40/92 **Kiss You Back** *Digital Underground*
72/87 **Kiss You (When It's Dangerous)** *Eight Seconds*
64/91 **Kisses In The Night** *Brandon*
8/89 **Kisses On The Wind** *Neneh Cherry*
3/57 **Kisses Sweeter Than Wine** *Jimmie Rodgers*
91/60 **Kissin' And Twistin'** *Fabian*
12/64 **Kissin' Cousins** *Elvis Presley*
82/61 **Kissin Game** *Dion*
35/61 **Kissin' On The Phone** *Paul Anka*
Kissin' Time
11/59 *Bobby Rydell*
83/74 *Kiss*
12/96 **Kissin' You** *Total*
40/91 **Kissing You** *Keith Washington*
F/96 **Kissing You** *Faith Evans*
97/88 **K.I.S.S.I.N.G.** *Siedah Garrett*
5/88 **Kissing A Fool** *George Michael*
(Kissing Game) ..see: I Like The Way
31/73 **Kissing My Love** *Bill Withers*
76/92 **Kissing The Wind** *Nia Peeples*
60/59 **Kissing Tree** *Billy Grammer*
67[A]/95 **Kitty** *Presidents Of The United States Of America*
51/95 **Kitty Kitty** *69 Boyz*
Knee Deep ..see: (not just)
16/57 **Knee Deep In The Blues** *Guy Mitchell*
15/67 **Knight In Rusty Armour** *Peter & Gordon*
20[S]/01 **Knives Out** *Radiohead*
98/02 **Knoc** *Knoc-Turn'al*
65[S]/02 **Knock Knock** *GZA/Genius*
64/64 **Knock! Knock! (Who's There?)** *Orlons*
92/72 **Knock Knock Who's There** *Mary Hopkin*
Knock On Wood
28/66 *Eddie Floyd*
30/67 *Otis & Carla*
1/79 *Amii Stewart*
1/71 **Knock Three Times** *Dawn*
41/88 **Knocked Out** *Paula Abdul*
9/90 **Knockin' Boots** *Candyman*
72/93 **Knock-N-boots** *Wreckx-N-Effect*
3/93 **Knockin' Da Boots** *H-Town*
12/73 **Knockin' On Heaven's Door** *Bob Dylan*
61/85 **Knocking At Your Back Door** *Deep Purple*
49/97 **Knocks Me Off My Feet** *Donell Jones*
76/98 **Know What You Mean** *Sister 7*
14/77 **Knowing Me, Knowing You** *Abba*
76/67 **Knucklehead** *Bar-Kays*
51/71 **Ko-Ko Joe** *Jerry Reed*
Ko Ko Mo (I Love You So)
2/55 *Perry Como*
6/55 *Crew-Cuts*
92/61 *Flamingos*
2/73 **Kodachrome** *Paul Simon*
1/88 **Kokomo** *Beach Boys*
78/60 **Kommotion** *Duane Eddy*
48/77 **Kong** *Dickie Goodman*
4/59 **Kookie, Kookie (Lend Me Your Comb)** *Edward Byrnes & Connie Stevens*
Kookie Little Paradise
61/60 *Jo Ann Campbell*
73/60 *Tree Swingers*
59/69 **Kool And The Gang** *Kool & The Gang*
41/69 **Kozmic Blues** *Janis Joplin*
91/94 **Krazy** *Blackgirl*
3/00 **Kryptonite** *3 Doors Down*
93/73 **Kufanya Mapenzi (Making Love)** *Ramsey Lewis*
54/69 **Kum Ba Yah** *Tommy Leonetti*
40/74 **Kung Fu** *Curtis Mayfield*
1/74 **Kung Fu Fighting** *Carl Douglas*
1/86 **Kyrie** *Mr. Mister*

L

52/68 **L. David Sloane** *Michele Lee*
15[S]/02 **L'Italiano** *Sicilians*
71/97 **L-L-Lies** *Diana King*
98/73 **L.A. Freeway** *Jerry Jeff Walker*
73/71 **L.A. Goodbye** *Ides Of March*
54/71 **L.A. International Airport** *Susan Raye*
90/00 **L.A. Song** *Beth Hart*
45/77 **L.A. Sunshine** *War*
52/90 **L.A. Woman** *Billy Idol*
72[A]/92 **LSI (Love, Sex, Intelligence)** *Shamen*
La Bamba
22/59 *Ritchie Valens*
85/62 *Tokens*
86/66 *Trini Lopez*
1/87 *Los Lobos*
70/01 **La Bomba** *Azul Azul*
9/58 **La Dee Dah** *Billy & Lillie*
78/81 **La-Di-Da** *Sad Café*
32/58 **La-Do-Dada** *Dale Hawkins*
81/61 **La Dolce Vita (The Sweet Life)** *Ray Ellis*
77/96 **La Familia** *Frost*
41/74 **La Grange** *ZZ Top*
4/87 **La Isla Bonita** *Madonna*
90/66 **La La La** *Gerry & The Pacemakers*
9/70 **La La La (If I Had You)** *Bobby Sherman*
62/64 **La La La La La** *Blendells*
86/93 **La La Love** *Bobby Ross Avila*
La-La Means I Love You
4/68 *Delfonics*
72/81 *Tierra*

La La Peace Song
30/74 *Al Wilson*
62/74 *O.C. Smith*
La Mer ..see: Beyond The Sea
La Montana ..see: If She Should Come To You
87/61 **La Pachanga** *Audrey Arno*
La Paloma
20/58 *Billy Vaughn*
72/62 *Chubby Checker (Twist)*
86/59 **La Plume De Ma Tante** *Hugo & Luigi*
42/90 **La Raza** *Kid Frost*
62S/92 **La Schmoove** *Fu-Schnickens'*
8/80 **Ladies Night** *Kool & The Gang*

LADY:

1/80 **Lady** *Kenny Rogers*
6/75 **Lady** *Styx*
10/79 **Lady** *Little River Band*
10/96 **Lady** *D'Angelo*
28/80 **Lady** *Whispers*
39/67 **Lady** *Jack Jones*
90/97 **Lady** *Mista*
(also see: She's Gone)
20/67 **Lady Bird** *Nancy Sinatra & Lee Hazlewood*
14/75 **Lady Blue** *Leon Russell*
48/76 **Lady Bump** *Penny McLean*
62/67 **Lady Came From Baltimore** *Bobby Darin*
76/83 **Lady Down On Love** *Alabama*
82/72 **Lady Eleanor** *Lindisfarne*
82/67 **Lady Friend** *Byrds*
6/66 **Lady Godiva** *Peter & Gordon*
81/01 **Lady (hear me tonight)** *Modjo*
3/87 **Lady In Red** *Chris DeBurgh*
24/66 **Lady Jane** *Rolling Stones*
86/83 **Lady, Lady, Lady** *Joe "Bean" Esposito*
24/78 **Lady Love** *Lou Rawls*
95/70 **Lady Love** *Klowns*
30/83 **Lady Love Me (One More Time)** *George Benson*
14/60 **Lady Luck** *Lloyd Price*
Lady Madonna
4/68 *Beatles*
100/68 *Fats Domino*
Lady Marmalade
1/75 *LaBelle*
1/01 *Christina Aguilera, Lil' Kim, Mya & P!nk*
78/69 **Lady-O** *Turtles*
76/85 **Lady Of My Heart** *Jack Wagner*
53A/96 **Lady Picture Show** *Stone Temple Pilots*
46/77 **Lady (Put The Light On Me)** *Brownsville Station*
Lady Sings The Blues, Love Theme ..see: Happy
47/86 **Lady Soul** *Temptations*
2/68 **Lady Willpower** *Gary Puckett*
45/79 **Lady Writer** *Dire Straits*
8/81 **Lady (You Bring Me Up)** *Commodores*
61/94 **Laid** *James*
91/76 **Laid Back Love** *Major Harris*
35A/97 **Lakini's Juice** *Live*
33/68 **Lalena** *Donovan*
46/90 **Lambada** *Kaoma*
(Lament Of Cherokee) ..see: Indian Reservation
71/74 **Lamplight** *David Essex*
4/87 **Land Of Confusion** *Genesis*
Land Of Hope And Glory ..see: (Graduation Song)
86/86 **Land Of La La** *Stevie Wonder*
86/77 **Land Of Make Believe** *Chuck Mangione*
29/66 **Land Of Milk And Honey** *Vogues*
Land Of 1000 Dances
77/63 *Chris Kenner*
30/65 *Cannibal & The Headhunters*
67/65 *Thee Midniters*
6/66 *Wilson Pickett*
95/69 *Electric Indian*
60/83 *J. Geils Band*
46/80 **Landlord** *Gladys Knight*
Landslide
51/98 *Fleetwood Mac*
7/03 *Dixie Chicks*
30A/94 **Landslide** *Smashing Pumpkins*
52/82 **Landslide** *Olivia Newton-John*
13/84 **Language Of Love** *Dan Fogelberg*
32/61 **Language Of Love** *John D. Loudermilk*
100/71 **Language Of Love** *Intrigues*
94/67 **Lapland** *Baltimore & Ohio Marching Band*
Lara's Theme ..see: Somewhere My Love
60/01 **Laredo** *Chris Cagle*
79/56 **Large Large House** *Mike Pedicin Quintet*
25/99 **Larger Than Life** *Backstreet Boys*

LAST:

82/60 **Last Chance** *Collay & the Satellites*
13/65 **Last Chance To Turn Around** *Gene Pitney*
21/76 **Last Child** *Aerosmith*
58A/97 **Last Christmas** *Wham!*
3/78 **Last Dance** *Donna Summer*
99/60 **Last Dance** *McGuire Sisters*
Last Date
2/60 *Floyd Cramer*
21/60 *Lawrence Welk*
(also see: My Last Date With You)
89/95 **Last Dayz** *Onyx*
19/75 **Last Farewell** *Roger Whittaker*
Last Game Of The Season (A Blind Man In The Bleachers)
18/75 *David Geddes*
58/75 *Kenny Starr*
Last Kiss
2/64 *J. Frank Wilson*
34/74 *Wednesday*
92/74 *J. Frank Wilson*
2/99 *Pearl Jam*
60/63 **Last Leaf** *Cascades*
36/89 **Last Mile** *Cinderella*
99/63 **Last Minute** *Jimmy McGriff*
99/67 **Last Minute Miracle** *Shirelles*
3/61 **Last Night** *Mar-Keys*
9/96 **Last Night** *Az Yet*
8/72 **(Last Night) I Didn't Get To Sleep At All** *5th Dimension*
57/97 **Last Night On Earth** *U2*
46/97 **Last Night's Letter** *K-Ci & JoJo*
42/79 **Last Of The Singing Cowboys** *Marshall Tucker Band*
96/60 **Last One To Know** *Fleetwoods*
57/00 **Last Resort** *Papa Roach*
77/82 **Last Safe Place On Earth** *Le Roux*
3/73 **Last Song** *Edward Bear*
23/92 **Last Song** *Elton John*
77/73 **Last Tango In Paris** *Herb Alpert*
56/73 **Last Thing On My Mind** *Neil Diamond*
9/65 **Last Time** *Rolling Stones*
40/84 **Last Time I Made Love** *Joyce Kennedy & Jeffrey Osborne*
61/71 **Last Time I Saw Her** *Glen Campbell*
14/74 **Last Time I Saw Him** *Diana Ross*
1/66 **Last Train To Clarksville** *Monkees*
39/80 **Last Train To London** *Electric Light Orchestra*
25/67 **Last Waltz** *Engelbert Humperdinck*
40/66 **Last Word In Lonesome Is Me** *Eddy Arnold*
21/89 **Last Worthless Evening** *Don Henley*
27/57 **Lasting Love** *Sal Mineo*
57/80 **Late At Night** *England Dan Seals*
89/61 **Late Date** *Parkays*
6/80 **Late In The Evening** *Paul Simon*
1/98 **Lately** *Divine*
Lately
64/81 *Stevie Wonder*
4/93 *Jodeci*
56/99 **Lately** *Tyrese*
59/91 **Latin Active** *Lighter Shade Of Brown*
90/61 **Laugh** *Velvets*
10/65 **Laugh At Me** *Sonny*
15/65 **Laugh, Laugh** *Beau Brummels*
98/70 **Laughin And Clownin** *Ray Charles*
10/69 **Laughing** *Guess Who*
15/63 **Laughing Boy** *Mary Wells*
1/75 **Laughter In The Rain** *Neil Sedaka*
Laura, What's He Got That I Ain't Got
66/67 *Frankie Laine*
78/67 *Brook Benton*
14/65 **Laurie (Strange Things Happen)** *Dickey Lee*
3/59 **Lavender-Blue** *Sammy Turner*
LaVerne & Shirley Theme ..see: Making Our Dreams Come True
Lawdy Miss Clawdy
47/60 *Gary Stites*
41/67 *Buckinghams*
Lawrence Of Arabia ..see: Theme From
13/83 **Lawyers In Love** *Jackson Browne*
11/70 **Lay A Little Lovin' On Me** *Robin McNamara*
83/89 **Lay All Your Love On Me** *Information Society*
54/72 **Lay-Away** *Isley Brothers*
6/70 **Lay Down (Candles In The Rain)** *Melanie/Edwin Hawkins Singers*
3/78 **Lay Down Sally** *Eric Clapton*
Lay Down Your Arms
16/56 *Chordettes*
59/56 *Anne Shelton*
56/89 **Lay Down Your Arms** *Graces*
40/85 **Lay It Down** *Ratt*
86/79 **Lay It On The Line** *Triumph*
Lay Lady Lay
7/69 *Bob Dylan*
99/70 *Ferrante & Teicher*
71/72 *Isley Brothers*
50/01 **Lay Low** *Snoop Dogg*
55/67 **Lay Some Happiness On Me** *Dean Martin*
6/85 **Lay Your Hands On Me** *Thompson Twins*
7/89 **Lay Your Hands On Me** *Bon Jovi*
31/94 **(Lay Your Head On My) Pillow** *Tony Toni Tone*
66/84 **Layin' It On The Line** *Jefferson Starship*
Layla
51/71 *Derek & The Dominos*
10/72 *Derek & The Dominos*
12/92 *Eric Clapton (Live)*

14/67 **Lazy Day** *Spanky & Our Gang*
40/64 **Lazy Elsie Molly** *Chubby Checker*
91/79 **Lazy Eyes** *T.M.G.*
86/64 **Lazy Lady** *Fats Domino*
12/58 **Lazy Mary (Luna Mezzo Mare)** *Lou Monte*
Lazy River
57/56 *Roberta Sherwood*
14/61 *Bobby Darin*
43/61 *Si Zentner (Up A)*
21/58 **Lazy Summer Night** *Four Preps*
54/86 **Le Bel Age** *Pat Benatar*
1/78 **Le Freak** *Chic*
58/78 **Le Spank** *Le Pamplemousse*
75/96 **LeFlaur LeFlah Eshkoshka** *Fabulous Five*
68/86 **Lead A Double Life** *Loverboy*
5/79 **Lead Me On** *Maxine Nightingale*
96/88 **Lead Me On** *Amy Grant*
9/82 **Leader Of The Band** *Dan Fogelberg*
19/65 **Leader Of The Laundromat** *Detergents*
Leader Of The Pack
1/64 *Shangri-Las*
53/86 *Twisted Sister*
25/62 **Léah** *Roy Orbison*
67/58 **Lean Jean** *Bill Haley*
Lean On Me
1/72 *Bill Withers*
1/87 *Club Nouveau*
79/98 **Lean On Me** *Kirk Franklin*
9/66 **Leaning On The Lamp Post** *Herman's Hermits*
92/57 **Leap Frog** *Chuck Alaimo Quartet*
61A/95 **Learn To Be Still** *Eagles*
19/00 **Learn To Fly** *Foo Fighters*
1/55 **Learnin' The Blues** *Frank Sinatra*
28/91 **Learning To Fly** *Tom Petty*
70/87 **Learning To Fly** *Pink Floyd*
61/55 **Learning To Love** *Peggy King*
6/82 **Leather And Lace** *Stevie Nicks (with Don Henley)*
11/89 **Leave A Light On** *Belinda Carlisle*
27/84 **Leave A Tender Moment Alone** *Billy Joel*
24/84 **Leave It** *Yes*
91/57 **Leave It To Love** *Sarah Vaughan*
62/63 **Leave Me Alone** *Baby Washington*
44/58 **Leave Me Alone (Let Me Cry)** *Dicky Doo & The Don'ts*
3/73 **Leave Me Alone (Ruby Red Dress)** *Helen Reddy*
Leave My Kitten Alone
60/59 *Little Willie John*
60/61 *Little Willie John*
73/61 *Johnny Preston*
52/95 **Leave Virginia Alone** *Rod Stewart*
82/94 **Leavin'** *Tony Toni Tone*
88/97 **Leavin'** *Tony Rich Project*
83/63 **Leavin' On Your Mind** *Patsy Cline*
76/64 **Leaving Here** *Eddie Holland*
71/80 **Leaving L.A.** *Deliverance*
60/94 **Leaving Las Vegas** *Sheryl Crow*
21/73 **Leaving Me** *Independents*
1/69 **Leaving On A Jet Plane** *Peter, Paul & Mary*
64/84 **Lebanon, The** *Human League*
70/00 **Left & Right** *D'Angelo*
82/56 **Left Arm Of Buddha** *Les Baxter*
50/84 **Left In The Dark** *Barbra Streisand*
9/58 **Left Right Out Of Your Heart** *Patti Page*
84/89 **Left To My Own Devices** *Pet Shop Boys*
73/00 **Left/Right** *Drama*

87/75 **Leftovers** *Millie Jackson*
47S/00 **Legal Man** *Belle & Sebastian*
81/83 **Legal Tender** *B-52's*
50/72 **Legend In Your Own Time** *Carly Simon*
36/97 **Legend Of A Cowgirl** *Imani Coppola*
(Legend Of Billy Jack) ..see: One Tin Soldier
31/80 **Legend Of Wooley Swamp** *Charlie Daniels Band*
8/84 **Legs** *ZZ Top*
77/81 **Leila** *ZZ Top*
71A/93 **Lemon** *U2*
Lemon Tree
35/62 *Peter, Paul & Mary*
20/65 *Trini Lopez*
69/75 **Leona** *Wet Willie*
81/67 **Leopard-Skin Pill-Box Hat** *Bob Dylan*
11/58 **Leroy** *Jack Scott*
31/68 **Les Bicyclettes De Belsize** *Engelbert Humperdinck*
34/68 **Lesson, The** *Vikki Carr*
Lesson In Leavin'
73/80 *Dottie West*
28/99 *Jo Dee Messina*
12/87 **Lessons In Love** *Level 42*
40/00 **Lessons Learned** *Tracy Lawrence*

LET:

Let A Man Come In And Do The Popcorn
21/69 *James Brown (Part One)*
40/70 *James Brown (Part Two)*
36/69 **Let A Woman Be A Woman - Let A Man Be A Man** *Dyke & The Blazers*
3/76 **Let 'Em In** *Wings*
34/89 **Let Go** *Sharon Bryant*
9/95 **Let Her Cry** *Hootie & The Blowfish*
10/76 **Let Her In** *John Travolta*
39/85 **Let Him Go** *Animotion*
84/84 **Let It All Blow** *Dazz Band*
Let It Be
1/70 *Beatles*
49/71 *Joan Baez*
Let It Be Me
57/57 *Jill Corey with Jimmy Carroll*
7/60 *Everly Brothers*
5/64 *Betty Everett & Jerry Butler*
94/67 *Sweet Inspirations*
36/69 *Glen Campbell & Bobbie Gentry*
40/82 *Willie Nelson*
F/96 **Let It Flow** *Toni Braxton*
25/97 **Let It Go** *Ray J*
(also see: Letitgo)
45/78 **Let It Go, Let It Flow** *Dave Mason*
12/67 **Let It Out (Let It All Hang Out)** *Hombres*
48/72 **Let It Rain** *Eric Clapton*
23/74 **Let It Ride** *Bachman-Turner Overdrive*
51/56 **Let It Ring** *Doris Day*
64/60 **Let It Rock** *Chuck Berry*
30/76 **Let It Shine** *Olivia Newton-John*
77/76 **Let It Shine** *Santana*
32/93 **Let It Snow** *Boyz II Men*
5/82 **Let It Whip** *Dazz Band*
23/67 **Let Love Come Between Us** *James & Bobby Purify*
89/90 **Let Love Rule** *Lenny Kravitz*
20/69 **Let Me** *Paul Revere & The Raiders*
58/70 **Let Me Back In** *Tyrone Davis*
29/65 **Let Me Be** *Turtles*
43/80 **Let Me Be** *Korona*

62/66 **Let Me Be Good To You** *Carla Thomas*
71/68 **Let Me Be Lonely** *Dionne Warwick*
31/80 **Let Me Be The Clock** *Smokey Robinson*
94/69 **Let Me Be The Man My Daddy Was** *Chi-Lites*
7/87 **Let Me Be The One** *Exposé*
29/95 **Let Me Be The One** *Blessid Union Of Souls*
59/86 **Let Me Be The One** *Five Star*
70/75 **Let Me Be The One (medley)** *Al Wilson*
72S/00 **Let Me Be The One** *Ram-Z*
Let Me Be The One
87/62 *Paris Sisters*
74/69 *Peaches & Herb*
6/74 **Let Me Be There** *Olivia Newton-John*
21/80 **Let Me Be Your Angel** *Stacy Lattisaw*
55/73 **Let Me Be Your Lovemaker** *Betty Wright*
68/90 **Let Me Be Your Lover** *U-Krew*
1/57 **(Let Me Be Your) Teddy Bear** *Elvis Presley*
20/61 **Let Me Belong To You** *Brian Hyland*
2/01 **Let Me Blow Ya Mind** *Eve*
66/62 **Let Me Call You Sweetheart** *Timi Yuro*
30/97 **Let Me Clear My Throat** *DJ Kool*
80/76 **Let Me Down Easy** *American Flyer*
86/86 **Let Me Down Easy** *Roger Daltrey*
96/73 **Let Me Down Easy** *Cornelius Brothers & Sister Rose*
96/62 **Let Me Entertain You** *Ray Anthony*
80/74 **Let Me Get To Know You** *Paul Anka*
38/82 **Let Me Go** *Ray Parker Jr.*
74/83 **Let Me Go** *Heaven 17*
75/81 **Let Me Go** *Rings*
35/80 **Let Me Go, Love** *Nicolette Larson*
Let Me Go, Lover!
8/54 *Patti Page*
1/55 *Joan Weber*
6/55 *Teresa Brewer with The Lancers*
17/55 *Sunny Gale*
90/63 **Let Me Go The Right Way** *Supremes*
32/70 **Let Me Go To Him** *Dionne Warwick*
4/62 **Let Me In** *Sensations*
36/73 **Let Me In** *Osmonds*
60/89 **Let Me In** *Eddie Money*
86/76 **Let Me In** *Derringer*
99/99 **Let Me Know** *Cam'ron*
42/79 **Let Me Know (I Have A Right)** *Gloria Gaynor*
33/98 **Let Me Let Go** *Faith Hill*
94/69 **Let Me Love You** *Ray Charles*
48/81 **Let Me Love You Once** *Greg Lake*
10/80 **Let Me Love You Tonight** *Pure Prairie League*
75/75 **Let Me Make Love To You** *O'Jays*
43/78 **Let Me Party With You** *Bunny Sigler*
82/98 **Let Me Return The Favor** *Andrea Martin*
34/93 **Let Me Ride** *Dr. Dre*
87/93 **Let Me Roll** *Scarface*
17/73 **Let Me Serenade You** *Three Dog Night*
88/80 **Let Me Sleep Alone** *Cugini*
87/75 **Let Me Start Tonite** *Lamont Dozier*
44/80 **Let Me Talk** *Earth, Wind & Fire*
90/66 **Let Me Tell You, Babe** *Nat King Cole*

18/82 **Let Me Tickle Your Fancy** *Jermaine Jackson*
63/73 **Let Me Try Again (Laisse Moi Le Temps)** *Frank Sinatra*
9/80 **Let My Love Open The Door** *Pete Townshend*
37/91 **Let The Beat Hit 'Em** *Lisa Lisa & Cult Jam*
16/58 **Let The Bells Keep Ringing** *Paul Anka*
51/89 **Let The Day Begin** *Call*
42/82 **Let The Feeling Flow** *Peabo Bryson*
Let The Four Winds Blow
29/57 *Roy Brown*
15/61 *Fats Domino*
Let The Good Times Roll
20/56 *Shirley & Lee*
48/60 *Shirley & Lee*
81/65 *Roy Orbison*
22/67 *Bunny Sigler (medley)*
63^{S}/02 **Let The Good Times Roll** *RJD2*
78/60 **Let The Good Times Roll** *Ray Charles*
(also see: Good Times Roll)
88/68 **Let The Heartaches Begin** *Long John Baldry*
7/60 **Let The Little Girl Dance** *Billy Bland*
60/98 **Let The Music Heal Your Soul** *Bravo All Stars*
8/84 **Let The Music Play** *Shannon*
32/76 **Let The Music Play** *Barry White*
78/70 **Let The Music Take Your Mind** *Kool & The Gang*
49/89 **Let The River Run** *Carly Simon*
91/78 **Let The Song Last Forever** *Dan Hill*
Let The Sunshine In ..see: Aquarius
Let Them ..also see: Let 'Em
100/60 **Let Them Talk** *Little Willie John*
7/61 **Let There Be Drums** *Sandy Nelson*
55/75 **Let There Be Music** *Orleans*
69/57 **Let There Be You** *Five Keys*
88/74 **Let This Be A Lesson To You** *Independents*
91/70 **Let This Be A Letter (To My Baby)** *Jackie Wilson*
73/61 **Let True Love Begin** *Nat King Cole*
47/73 **Let Us Love** *Bill Withers*
27/74 **Let Your Hair Down** *Temptations*
1/76 **Let Your Love Flow** *Bellamy Brothers*
28/71 **Let Your Love Go** *Bread*
86/96 **Let Your Soul Be Your Pilot** *Sting*
57/73 **Let Your Yeah Be Yeah** *Brownsville Station*
46/67 **Let Yourself Go** *James Brown*
63/69 **Let Yourself Go** *Friends Of Distinction*
71/68 **Let Yourself Go** *Elvis Presley*

LET'S:

36/78 **Let's All Chant** *Michael Zager Band*
31^{S}/01 **Let's Be Friends** *Ta-Ta + Brando*
87/58 **Let's Be Lovers** *Playmates*
65/80 **Let's Be Lovers Again** *Eddie Money/Valerie Carter*
55/76 **Let's Be Young Tonight** *Jermaine Jackson*
Let's Call It A Day Girl
77/66 *Razor's Edge*
92/69 *Bobby Vee*
41/91 **Let's Chill** *Guy*
91/77 **Let's Clean Up The Ghetto** *Philadelphia International All Stars*
1/83 **Let's Dance** *David Bowie*
Let's Dance
4/62 *Chris Montez*
92/69 *Ola & The Janglers*
81/87 **Let's Dance** *Chris Rea*
88/81 **Let's Dance (Make Your Body Move)** *West Street Mob*
1/75 **Let's Do It Again** *Staple Singers*
88/80 **Let's Do Something Cheap And Superficial** *Burt Reynolds*
40/65 **Let's Do The Freddie** *Chubby Checker*
(also see: Do The Freddie / Freddie)
66/60 **(Let's Do) The Hully Gully Twist** *Bill Doggett*
21/67 **Let's Fall In Love** *Peaches & Herb*
71/98 **Let's Forget About It** *Lisa Loeb*
72/78 **Let's Get Crazy Tonight** *Rupert Holmes*
97/01 **Let's Get Dirty (I Can't Get In Da Club)** *Redman*
30^{A}/97 **Let's Get Down** *Tony Toni Toné*
74^{A}/93 **Let's Get Into Something Sexy** *Erik Hicks*
80/01 **Let's Get It** *Three The...*
1/73 **Let's Get It On** *Marvin Gaye*
81/95 **Let's Get It On** *Shabba Ranks*
61/76 **Lets Get It Together** *El Coco*
44/82 **Let's Get It Up** *AC/DC*
11/00 **Let's Get Married** *Jagged Edge*
32/74 **Let's Get Married** *Al Green*
15/92 **Let's Get Rocked** *Def Leppard*
9/80 **Let's Get Serious** *Jermaine Jackson*
53/96 **Let's Get The Mood Right** *Johnny Gill*
8/61 **Let's Get Together** *Hayley Mills*
(also see: Get Together)
41/70 **Let's Give Adam And Eve Another Chance** *Gary Puckett*
9/87 **Let's Go!** *Wang Chung*
14/79 **Let's Go** *Cars*
19/62 **Let's Go (pony)** *Routers*
90/62 **Let's Go** *Floyd Cramer*
39/61 **Let's Go Again** *Hank Ballard*
7/86 **Let's Go All The Way** *Sly Fox*
(Let's Go Back To My Room) ..see: Boom Boom
53/57 **Let's Go Calypso** *Rusty Draper*
1/84 **Let's Go Crazy** *Prince*
30/83 **Let's Go Dancin' (Ooh La, La, La)** *Kool & The Gang*
F/77 **Let's Go Down To The Disco** *Undisputed Truth*
31/66 **Let's Go Get Stoned** *Ray Charles*
6/60 **Let's Go, Let's Go, Let's Go** *Hank Ballard*
88/85 **Let's Go Out Tonight** *Nile Rodgers*
53/80 **Let's Go 'Round Again** *Average White Band*
26/63 **Let's Go Steady Again** *Neil Sedaka*
97/66 **Let's Go Steady Again** *Sam Cooke*
55/58 **Let's Go Steady For The Summer** *Three G's*
65/93 **Let's Go Through The Motions** *Jodeci*
60/62 **Let's Go Trippin'** *Dick Dale*
77/84 **Let's Go Up** *Diana Ross*
3/81 **Let's Groove** *Earth, Wind & Fire*
Let's Hang On!
3/65 *4 Seasons*
32/82 *Barry Manilow*
Let's Have A Party
37/60 *Wanda Jackson*
99/64 *Rivieras*
1/84 **Let's Hear It For The Boy** *Deniece Williams*
38/63 **Let's Kiss And Make Up** *Bobby Vinton*
93/96 **Let's Lay Together** *Isley Brothers*
41/57 **Let's Light The Christmas Tree** *Ruby Wright*
20/63 **Let's Limbo Some More** *Chubby Checker*
8/67 **Let's Live For Today** *Grass Roots*
Let's Live Together
35/76 *Road Apples*
70/78 *Cazz*
11/65 **Let's Lock The Door** *Jay & The Americans*
44/59 **Let's Love** *Johnny Mathis*
83/76 **Let's Make A Baby** *Billy Paul*
24/96 **Let's Make A Night To Remember** *Bryan Adams*
75/68 **Let's Make A Promise** *Peaches & Herb*
98/70 **Let's Make Each Other Happy** *Illusion*
54/00 **Let's Make Love** *Faith Hill with Tim McGraw*
98/63 **Let's Make Love Tonight** *Bobby Rydell*
13^{X}/67 **Let's Make This Christmas Mean Something This Year** *James Brown*
88/65 **Let's Move & Groove (Together)** *Johnny Nash*
45/96 **Let's Play House** *Dogg Pound*
35/73 **Let's Pretend** *Raspberries*
52/84 **Let's Pretend We're Married** *Prince*
18/74 **Let's Put It All Together** *Stylistics*
81/81 **Let's Put The Fun Back In Rock N Roll** *Freddy Cannon & The Belmonts*
97/89 **Let's Put The X In Sex** *Kiss*
2/98 **Let's Ride** *Montell Jordan*
67/97 **Let's Ride** *Richie Rich*
92/76 **Let's Rock** *Ellison Chase*
55/67 **Let's Spend The Night Together** *Rolling Stones*
20/66 **Let's Start All Over Again** *Ronnie Dove*
68/01 **Let's Stay Home Tonight** *Joe*
Let's Stay Together
1/72 *Al Green*
48/72 *Isaac Hayes*
26/84 *Tina Turner*
57/63 **Let's Stomp** *Bobby Comstock*
31/74 **Let's Straighten It Out** *Latimore*
56/85 **Let's Talk About Me** *Alan Parsons Project*
13/91 **Let's Talk About Sex** *Salt-N-Pepa*
7/60 **Let's Think About Living** *Bob Luman*
48/60 **Let's Try Again** *Clyde McPhatter*
53/90 **Let's Try It Again** *New Kids On The Block*
20/63 **Let's Turkey Trot** *Little Eva*
8/61 **Let's Twist Again** *Chubby Checker*
2/87 **Let's Wait Awhile** *Janet Jackson*
39/87 **Let's Work** *Mick Jagger*
Let's Work Together
26/70 *Canned Heat*
32/70 *Wilbert Harrison*
31/94 **Letitgo** *Prince*
Letter, The
1/67 *Box Tops*
20/69 *Arbors*
7/70 *Joe Cocker with Leon Russell*
75/65 **Letter, The** *Sonny & Cher*
85/63 **Letter From Betty** *Bobby Vee*

25/64 **Letter From Sherry** *Dale Ward*
19/62 **Letter Full Of Tears** *Gladys Knight*
Letter Song ..see: S.Y.S.L.J.F.M.
25/58 **Letter To An Angel** *Jimmy Clanton*
93/67 **Letter To Dad**
Every Father's Teenage Son
60/73 **Letter To Lucille** *Tom Jones*
33/73 **Letter To Myself** *Chi-Lites*
85/64 **Letter To The Beatles** *Four Preps*
39/75 **Letting Go** *Wings*
Levon
24/72 *Elton John*
64A/92 *Jon Bon Jovi*
7/71 **Liar** *Three Dog Night*
14/00 **Liar** *Profyle*
12/65 **Liar, Liar** *Castaways*
Liberty Valance ..see: (Man Who Shot)
32/89 **Licence To Chill** *Billy Ocean*
72/95 **Lick It** *Roula*
66/83 **Lick It Up** *Kiss*
74S/01 **Lick Shots**
Missy "Misdemeanor" Elliott
67/93 **Lick U Up** *H-Town*
14/68 **Licking Stick - Licking Stick**
James Brown
(also see: Mama Come Quick)
11/77 **Lido Shuffle** *Boz Scaggs*
13/62 **Lie To Me** *Brook Benton*
88/95 **Lie To Me** *Bon Jovi*
Liechtensteiner Polka
16/57 *Will Glahé*
48/57 *Lawrence Welk*
18/91 **Lies.** *EMF*
20/66 **Lies** *Knickerbockers*
27/87 **Lies** *Jonathan Butler*
30/83 **Lies** *Thompson Twins*
38/90 **Lies** *En Vogue*
42/72 **Lies** *J.J. Cale*

LIFE:

53/71 **Life** *Elvis Presley*
60/99 **Life** *K-Ci & JoJo*
93/68 **Life** *Sly & The Family Stone*
68/73 **Life Ain't Easy** *Dr. Hook*
81/98 **Life Ain't Easy** *Cleopatra*
52/72 **Life And Breath** *Climax*
Life And Death In G & A
74/69 *Abaco Dream*
90/75 *Love Childs Afro Cuban Blues Band*
80/79 **Life During Wartime** *Talking Heads*
41/94 **Life (Everybody Needs Somebody To Love)** *Haddaway*
94/83 **Life Gets Better** *Graham Parker*
35/91 **Life Goes On** *Poison*
7/86 **Life In A Northern Town**
Dream Academy
70/98 **Life In Mono** *Mono*
19/85 **Life In One Day** *Howard Jones*
11/77 **Life In The Fast Lane** *Eagles*
72/71 **Life Is A Carnival** *Band*
6/92 **Life Is A Highway** *Tom Cochrane*
8/74 **Life Is A Rock (But The Radio Rolled Me)** *Reunion*
54/74 **Life Is A Song Worth Singing**
Johnny Mathis
40S/02 **Life Is Good** *LFO*
34/81 **Life Of Illusion** *Joe Walsh*
98/92 **Life Of Riley** *Lightning Seeds*
91/61 **Life's A Holiday** *Jerry Wallace*
12/78 **Life's Been Good** *Joe Walsh*
87/62 **Life's Too Short** *Lafayettes*
90/86 **Life's What You Make It** *Talk Talk*
91/95 **LifestyLes Of The Rich And ShameLess** *Lost Boyz*

20/03 **Lifestyles Of The Rich And Famous** *Good Charlotte*
22/01 **Lifetime** *Maxwell*
66/65 **Lifetime Of Loneliness**
Jackie DeShannon
32/92 **Lift Me Up** *Howard Jones*
86/91 **Lift Me Up** *Yes*
44/00 **Light** *Common*
48/98 **Light In Your Eyes**
Blessid Union Of Souls
Light My Fire
1/67 *Doors*
3/68 *Jose Feliciano*
87/68 *Doors*
69/79 *Amii Stewart (medley)*
87/77 **Light Of A Clear Blue Morning**
Dolly Parton
33/87 **Light Of Day** *Barbusters (Joan Jett)*
63/58 **Light Of Love** *Peggy Lee*
44/71 **Light Sings** *5th Dimension*
66/78 **Light The Sky On Fire**
Jefferson Starship
67/76 **Light Up The World With Sunshine**
Hamilton, Joe Frank & Dennison
42S/00 **Light Years** *Pearl Jam*
67S/99 **Lighthouse** *New Direction*
1/66 **Lightnin' Strikes** *Lou Christie*
12A/95 **Lightning Crashes** *Live*
86/99 **Lightning Does The Work**
Chad Brock
24/67 **Lightning's Girl** *Nancy Sinatra*
Lights
68/78 *Journey*
74/93 *Journey (Live)*
14/02 **Lights, Camera, Action!**
Mr. Cheeks
93/70 **Lights Of Tucson** *Jim Campbell*
12/84 **Lights Out** *Peter Wolf*
11/67 **(Lights Went Out In) Massachusetts** *Bee Gees*

LIKE:

27/66 **Like A Baby** *Len Barry*
67/65 **Like A Child** *Julie Rogers*
67/88 **Like A Child** *Noel*
1/89 **Like A Prayer** *Madonna*
12/86 **Like A Rock** *Bob Seger*
2/65 **Like A Rolling Stone** *Bob Dylan*
36/76 **Like A Sad Song** *John Denver*
40/78 **Like A Sunday In Salem (The Amos & Andy Song)**
Gene Cotton
63/75 **Like A Sunday Morning**
Lana Cantrell
47/85 **Like A Surgeon**
"Weird Al" Yankovic
1/84 **Like A Virgin** *Madonna*
41/96 **Like A Woman** *Tony Rich Project*
24/67 **Like An Old Time Movie**
Scott McKenzie
77/71 **Like An Open Door** *Fuzz*
96/64 **Like Columbus Did** *Reflections*
82/86 **Like Flames** *Berlin*
72/96 **Like I Do** *For Real*
11/02 **Like I Love You** *Justin Timberlake*
42/59 **Like I Love You** *Edd Byrnes*
38/61 **Like, Long Hair**
Paul Revere & The Raiders
14/86 **Like No Other Night** *38 Special*
22/60 **Like Strangers** *Everly Brothers*
66S/01 **Like That** *Domino*
55/63 **Like The Big Guys Do**
Rocky Fellers
42/95 **Like The Way I Do**
Melissa Etheridge
68/88 **Like The Weather** *10,000 Maniacs*

72/75 **Like They Say In L.A.**
East L.A. Car Pool
F/95 **Like This And Like That** *Monica*
17/68 **Like To Get To Know You**
Spanky & Our Gang
49/85 **Like To Get To Know You Well**
Howard Jones
99/01 **Like, Wow!** *Leslie Carter*
46/59 **Like Young**
Andre Previn With David Rose
43S/02 **Lil Buddy** *Que Bo Gold*
10X/63 **L'il Elfy** *Ray Bolger*
87/68 **Lili Marlene** *Al Martino*
11/91 **Lily Was Here**
David A. Stewart & Candy Dulfer
99/62 **Limbo** *Capris*
97/62 **Limbo Dance** *Champs*
Limbo Rock
2/62 *Chubby Checker*
40/62 *Champs*
55/81 **Limelight** *Rush*
92/62 **Limelight** *Mr. Acker Bilk*
(also see: Eternally)
28/63 **Linda** *Jan & Dean*
94/61 **Linda** *Adam Wade*
46/59 **Linda Lu** *Ray Sharpe*
61/75 **Linda On My Mind** *Conway Twitty*
36S/02 **Line 'Em Up** *Freeway*
Ling, Ting, Tong
28/54 *Five Keys*
26/55 *Charms*
65/61 *Buddy Knox*
(also see: Big Brown Eyes)
8/94 **Linger** *Cranberries*
Lion Sleeps Tonight
1/61 *Tokens*
3/72 *Robert John*
51/94 *Tokens*
84/65 **Lip Sync (To The Tongue Twisters)** *Len Barry*
17/57 **Lips Of Wine** *Andy Williams*
51/81 **Lipstick** *Suzi Quatro*
61/76 **Lipstick** *Michel Polnareff*
15/56 **Lipstick And Candy And Rubbersole Shoes**
Julius LaRosa
5/59 **Lipstick On Your Collar**
Connie Francis
Lipstick Traces (On A Cigarette)
80/62 *Benny Spellman*
48/65 *O'Jays*
10/01 **Liquid Dreams** *O-Town*
48/95 **Liquid Swords** *Genius/GZA*
43/60 **Lisa** *Jeanne Black*
98/62 **Lisa** *Ferrante & Teicher*
73/71 **Lisa, Listen To Me**
Blood, Sweat & Tears
Lisbon Antigua
1/56 *Nelson Riddle*
19/56 *Mitch Miller*
72/97 **Listen** *Collective Soul*
Listen Here
45/68 *Eddie Harris*
100/70 *Brian Auger & The Trinity*
54/86 **Listen Like Thieves** *INXS*
62/64 **Listen Lonely Girl** *Johnny Mathis*
88/95 **Listen Me Tic (Woyoi)** *Ini Kamoze*
3/66 **Listen People** *Herman's Hermits*
92/68 **Listen, They're Playing My Song**
Ray Charles
59/78 **Listen To Her Heart** *Tom Petty*
63/69 **Listen To The Band** *Monkees*
96/76 **Listen To The Buddha** *Ozo*
11/72 **Listen To The Music**
Doobie Brothers

1/75 **Listen To What The Man Said** *Wings*
1/89 **Listen To Your Heart** *Roxette*
64/92 **Lithium** *Nirvana*

LITTLE:

Little ..also see: Lil'
45/61 **Little Altar Boy** *Vic Dana*
16/68 **Little Arrows** *Leapy Lee*
21/63 **Little Band Of Gold** *James Gilreath*
2X/67 **Little Becky's Christmas Wish** *Becky Lamb*
51/65 **Little Bell** *Dixie Cups*
47S/99 **Little Bird** *Sherrié Austin*
49/93 **Little Bird** *Annie Lennox*
91/73 **Little Bit Like Magic** *King Harvest*
2/67 **Little Bit Me, A Little Bit You** *Monkees*
11/76 **Little Bit More** *Dr. Hook*
Little Bit Now
63/62 *Majors*
67/67 *Dave Clark Five*
55/97 **Little Bit Of Ecstasy** *Jocelyn Enriquez*
16/65 **Little Bit Of Heaven** *Ronnie Dove*
81/85 **Little Bit Of Heaven** *Natalie Cole*
77/84 **Little Bit Of Love** *Dwight Twilley*
38/86 **Little Bit Of Love (Is All It Takes)** *New Edition*
Little Bit Of Soap
12/61 *Jarmels*
95/65 *Garnet Mimms*
58/66 *Exciters*
52/70 *Paul Davis*
34/79 *Nigel Olsson*
2/67 **Little Bit O' Soul** *Music Explosion*
58/97 **Little Bitty** *Alan Jackson*
19/60 **Little Bitty Girl** *Bobby Rydell*
Little Bitty Pretty One
6/57 *Thurston Harris*
57/57 *Bobby Day*
58/60 *Frankie Lymon*
25/62 *Clyde McPhatter*
13/72 *Jackson 5*
Little Bitty Tear
9/62 *Burl Ives*
84/62 *Wanda Jackson*
29/62 **Little Black Book** *Jimmy Dean*
85/67 **Little Black Egg** *Nightcrawlers*
17/58 **Little Blue Man** *Betty Johnson*
Little Boxes
70/64 *Pete Seeger*
83/64 *Womenfolk*
52/64 **Little Boy** *Tony Bennett*
92/64 **Little Boy** *Crystals*
76/56 **Little Boy Blue** *Billy Vaughn*
88/59 **Little Boy Blue** *Huelyn Duvall*
60/66 **Little Boy (In Grown Up Clothes)** *Four Seasons*
17/61 **Little Boy Sad** *Johnny Burnette*
78/58 **Little Brass Band** *David Seville*
36/85 **Little By Little** *Robert Plant*
Little By Little
55/57 *Micki Marlo*
57/57 *Nappy Brown*
Little Child
56/56 *Eddie Albert & Sondra Lee*
62/56 *Lael & Cab Calloway*
7/64 **Little Children** *Billy J. Kramer*
36/60 **Little Coco Palm** *Jerry Wallace*
Little Darlin'
2/57 *Diamonds*
41/57 *Gladiolas*
49/82 **Little Darlin'** *Sheila*

Little Darling, I Need You
47/66 *Marvin Gaye*
48/77 *Doobie Brothers*
15/63 **Little Deuce Coupe** *Beach Boys*
11/61 **Little Devil** *Neil Sedaka*
8/62 **Little Diane** *Dion*
30/59 **Little Dipper** *Robert Maxwell (Mickey Mozart Quintet)*
71/61 **Little Dog Cried** *Jimmie Rodgers*
93/64 **Little Donna** *Rivieras*
Little Drummer Boy
13/58 *Harry Simeone Chorale*
15/59 *Harry Simeone Chorale*
63/59 *Johnny Cash*
24/60 *Harry Simeone Chorale*
22/61 *Harry Simeone Chorale*
96/61 *Jack Halloran Singers*
28/62 *Harry Simeone Chorale*
11X/63 *Johnny Mathis*
16X/66 *Joan Baez*
2X/67 *Lou Rawls*
21X/67 *Kenny Burrell*
95/75 *Moonlion*
58S/00 *David Bowie & Bing Crosby (medley)*
75S/01 *David Bowie & Bing Crosby (medley)*
43S/02 *David Bowie & Bing Crosby (medley)*
76/63 **Little Eeefin Annie** *Joe Perkins*
23/61 **Little Egypt (Ying-Yang)** *Coasters*
91/61 **Little Feeling (Called Love)** *Jack Scott*
52/89 **Little Fighter** *White Lion*
51/67 **Little Games** *Yardbirds*
75/00 **Little Gasoline** *Terri Clark*
8/66 **Little Girl** *Syndicate Of Sound*
35/00 **Little Girl** *John Michael Montgomery*
92/59 **Little Girl** *Ritchie Valens*
57/73 **Little Girl Gone** *Donna Fargo*
20/66 **Little Girl I Once Knew** *Beach Boys*
57/56 **Little Girl Of Mine** *Cleftones*
43/99 **Little Good-Byes** *SheDaisy*
74/83 **Little Good News** *Anne Murray*
Little Green Apples
2/68 *O.C. Smith*
39/68 *Roger Miller*
96/68 *Patti Page*
21/70 **Little Green Bag** *George Baker Selection*
67/58 **Little Gypsy** *Ames Brothers*
Little Honda
9/64 *Hondells*
65/64 *Beach Boys*
17/81 **Little In Love** *Cliff Richard*
72/80 **Little Is Enough** *Pete Townshend*
29/89 **Little Jackie Wants To Be A Star** *Lisa Lisa & Cult Jam*
3/80 **Little Jeannie** *Elton John*
68/84 **Little Lady** *Duke Jupiter*
Little Latin Lupe Lu
49/63 *Righteous Brothers*
46/64 *Kingsmen*
17/66 *Mitch Ryder*
Little Less Conversation
69/68 *Elvis Presley*
50/02 *Elvis vs JXL*
19/89 **Little Liar** *Joan Jett*
4/87 **Little Lies** *Fleetwood Mac*
73/57 **Little Loneliness** *Kay Starr*
42/65 **Little Lonely One** *Tom Jones*
37/90 **Little Love** *Corey Hart*

44/84 **Little Love** *Juice Newton*
33/56 **Little Love Can Go A Long, Long Way** *Dream Weavers*
61/79 **Little Lovin' (Keeps The Doctor Away)** *Raes*
21/66 **Little Man** *Sonny & Chér*
39/99 **Little Man** *Alan Jackson*
54/64 **Little Marie** *Chuck Berry*
48/58 **Little Mary** *Fats Domino*
62/93 **Little Miracles (Happen Every Day)** *Luther Vandross*
96/60 **Little Miss Blue** *Dion*
17/92 **Little Miss Can't Be Wrong** *Spin Doctors*
74/65 **Little Miss Sad** *Five Emprees*
70/61 **Little Miss Stuck-Up** *Playmates*
99/67 **Little Miss Sunshine** *Tommy Roe*
3/79 **Little More Love** *Olivia Newton-John*
70A/97 **Little More Time With You** *James Taylor*
41/56 **Little Musicians** *Hugo Winterhalter*
3/64 **Little Old Lady (From Pasadena)** *Jan & Dean*
Little Old Wine Drinker, Me
38/67 *Dean Martin*
96/67 *Robert Mitchum*
4/67 **Little Ole Man (Uptight-Everything's Alright)** *Bill Cosby*
44/78 **Little One** *Chicago*
43/98 **Little Past Little Rock** *Lee Ann Womack*
76/61 **Little Pedro** *Olympics*
45/58 **Little Pigeon** *Sal Mineo*
72/58 **Little Pixie** *Moe Koffman Quartet*
62/77 **Little Queen** *Heart*
Little Queenie
80/59 *Chuck Berry*
73/64 *Bill Black's Combo*
87/68 **Little Rain Must Fall** *Epic Splendor*
6/83 **Little Red Corvette** *Prince*
23/62 **Little Red Rented Rowboat** *Joe Dowell*
2/66 **Lil' Red Riding Hood** *Sam The Sham & The Pharoahs*
72/58 **Little Red Riding Hood** *Big Bopper*
11/63 **Little Red Rooster** *Sam Cooke*
14/89 **Little Respect** *Erasure*
3X/63 **Little Saint Nick** *Beach Boys*
32/57 **Little Sandy Sleighfoot** *Jimmy Dean*
Little Serenade (Piccolissima Serenata)
66/58 *Teddy Randazzo*
98/58 *Ames Brothers*
86/85 **Little Sheila** *Slade*
5/61 **Little Sister** *Elvis Presley*
55S/01 **Little Sister** *Big Jim*
20/59 **Little Space Girl** *Jesse Lee Turner*
1/58 **Little Star** *Elegants*
95/63 **Little Star** *Bobby Callender*
91/87 **Little Suzi** *Tesla*
71/83 **Little Thing Called Love** *Neil Young*
13/65 **Little Things** *Bobby Goldsboro*
46A/95 **Little Things** *Bush*
89/02 **Little Things** *India.Arie*
35/60 **Little Things Mean A Lot** *Joni James*
84/63 **Little Tin Soldier** *Toy Dolls*
20/83 **Little Too Late** *Pat Benatar*
77/62 **Little Too Much** *Clarence Henry*
12/63 **Little Town Flirt** *Del Shannon*
84/64 **Little Toy Balloon** *Danny Williams*

46/58 **Little Train**
Marianne Vasel & Erich Storz
95/61 **Little Turtle Dove** *Charms*
47/88 **Little Walter** *Tony! Toni! Toné!*
99/64 **Little White Cloud That Cried**
Wayne Newton
25/57 **Little White Lies** *Betty Johnson*
3/73 **Little Willy** *Sweet*
3/69 **Little Woman** *Bobby Sherman*
F/72 **Little Woman Love** *Wings*
48/65 **Little You** *Freddie & The Dreamers*
96/62 **Little Young Lover** *Impressions*

LIVE:

63/67 **Live** *Merry-Go-Round*
65S/95 **Live!!!** *Onyx*
Live And Die ..see: (Forever)
72/96 **Live And Die For Hip Hop**
Kris Kross
4/92 **Live And Learn** *Joe Public*
Live And Let Die
2/73 *Wings*
33/92 *Guns N' Roses*
48S/02 **Live Big** *Sacario*
42/80 **Live Every Minute** *Ali Thomson*
34/85 **Live Every Moment**
REO Speedwagon
99/67 **Live For Life** *Jack Jones*
22/91 **Live For Loving You** *Gloria Estefan*
39A/95 **Live Forever** *Oasis*
32/86 **Live Is Life** *Opus*
52/74 **Live It Up** *Isley Brothers*
91/88 **Live It Up** *Gardner Cole*
74/00 **Live, Laugh, Love** *Clay Walker*
40/88 **Live My Life** *Boy George*
1/86 **Live To Tell** *Madonna*
42/64 **Live Wire** *Martha & The Vandellas*
89/75 **Live Your Life Before You Die**
Pointer Sisters

LIVIN'/LIVING:

76/66 **Livin' Above Your Head**
Jay & The Americans
42/76 **Livin' Ain't Livin'** *Firefall*
97/60 **Livin' Dangerously**
McGuire Sisters
20/76 **Livin' For The Weekend** *O'Jays*
19/74 **Livin' For You** *Al Green*
87/66 **Living For You** *Sonny & Chér*
31/84 **Livin' In Desperate Times**
Olivia Newton-John
40/77 **Livin' In The Life** *Isley Brothers*
53/90 **Livin' In The Light** *Caron Wheeler*
6/01 **Livin' It Up** *Ja Rule*
15/79 **Livin' It Up (Friday Night)**
Bell & James
Livin' La Vida Loca
1/99 *Ricky Martin*
70S/02 *Ricky Martin*
1/87 **Livin' On A Prayer** *Bon Jovi*
54S/94 **Livin' On Love** *Alan Jackson*
18/93 **Livin' On The Edge** *Aerosmith*
75/83 **Living On The Edge** *Jim Capaldi*
90/89 **Livin' Right** *Glenn Frey*
13/77 **Livin' Thing** *Electric Light Orchestra*
22/63 **Living A Lie** *Al Martino*
37/75 **Living A Little, Laughing A Little**
Spinners
27/02 **Living And Living Well**
George Strait
Living Doll
30/59 *Cliff Richard*
92/59 *David Hill*
45/81 **Living Eyes** *Bee Gees*
Living For The City
8/74 *Stevie Wonder*
91/75 *Ray Charles*
17/87 **Living In A Box** *Living In A Box*
57/87 **Living In A Dream** *Pseudo Echo*
23/81 **Living In A Fantasy** *Leo Sayer*
22/72 **Living In A House Divided** *Chér*
4/86 **Living In America** *James Brown*
20/94 **Living In Danger** *Ace Of Base*
65/90 **Living In Oblivion** *Anything Box*
9/89 **Living In Sin** *Bon Jovi*
87/86 **Living In The Background**
Baltimora
11/73 **Living In The Past** *Jethro Tull*
Living In The U.S.A.
94/68 *Steve Miller Band*
49/74 *Steve Miller Band*
6/81 **Living Inside Myself** *Gino Vannelli*
72/76 **Living It Down** *Freddy Fender*
65/70 **Living Loving Maid** *Led Zeppelin*
25/77 **Living Next Door To Alice** *Smokie*
61/86 **Living On Video** *Trans-X*
32/73 **Living Together, Growing Together** *5th Dimension*
69/72 **Living Without You**
Manfred Mann's Earth Band
1/89 **Living Years**
Mike & The Mechanics
52/78 **Livingston Saturday Night**
Jimmy Buffett
37/75 **Lizzie And The Rainman**
Tanya Tucker
44/62 **Lizzie Borden** *Chad Mitchell Trio*
14/69 **Lo Mucho Que Te Quiero**
Rene & Rene
F/78 **Load-Out, The** *Jackson Browne*
97/01 **Loaded** *Ricky Martin*
44/63 **Locking Up My Heart** *Marvelettes*
Loco-Motion, The
1/62 *Little Eva*
1/74 *Grand Funk*
3/88 *Kylie Minogue*
62/76 **Locomotive Breath** *Jethro Tull*
12/63 **Loddy Lo** *Chubby Checker*
Lodi
52/69 *Creedence Clearwater Revival*
67/69 *Al Wilson*
63A/94 **Lodi Dodi** *Snoop Doggy Dogg*
6/79 **Logical Song** *Supertramp*
(also see: Topical Song)
Lola
9/70 *Kinks*
81/80 *Kinks (Live)*
Lola's Theme
67/56 *Muir Mathieson*
75/56 *Steve Allen*
61/62 **Lolita Ya-Ya** *Ventures*
Lollipop
2/58 *Chordettes*
20/58 *Ronald & Ruby*
23/98 **Lollipop (Candyman)** *Aqua*
Lollipops And Roses
54/62 *Paul Petersen*
66/62 *Jack Jones*
39/78 **London Town** *Wings*
69/74 **Lone Ranger** *Oscar Brown Jr.*
97/63 **Lone Teen Ranger** *Jerry Landis*
89/78 **Loneliest Man On The Moon**
David Castle
65/64 **Loneliest Night** *Dale & Grace*
14/67 **(Loneliness Made Me Realize) It's You That I Need** *Temptations*

LONELY:

22/65 **L-O-N-E-L-Y** *Bobby Vinton*
87/67 **Lonely Again** *Eddy Arnold*
46/99 **Lonely And Gone**
Montgomery Gentry
6/60 **Lonely Blue Boy** *Conway Twitty*
66/61 **Lonely Blue Nights** *Rosie*
Lonely Boy
1/59 *Paul Anka*
F/72 *Donny Osmond*
7/77 **Lonely Boy** *Andrew Gold*
82/63 **Lonely Boy, Lonely Guitar**
Duane Eddy
6/62 **Lonely Bull (El Solo Torro)**
Herb Alpert
88/57 **Lonely Chair** *Lloyd Price*
76/61 **Lonely Crowd** *Teddy Vann*
3/71 **Lonely Days** *Bee Gees*
Lonely Drifter
93/63 *O'Jays*
59/67 *Pieces Of Eight*
41/80 **Lonely Eyes** *Robert John*
24/59 **Lonely For You** *Gary Stites*
50/59 **Lonely Guitar** *Annette*
57/85 **Lonely In Love** *Giuffria*
93/68 **Lonely Is The Name**
Sammy Davis, Jr.
76/86 **Lonely Is The Night** *Air Supply*
26/58 **Lonely Island** *Sam Cooke*
80/61 **Lonely Life** *Jackie Wilson*
32/61 **Lonely Man** *Elvis Presley*
57/72 **Lonely Man** *Chi-Lites*
3/76 **Lonely Night (Angel Face)**
Captain & Tennille
84/82 **Lonely Nights** *Bryan Adams*
6/85 **Lonely Ol' Night**
John Cougar Mellencamp
23/59 **Lonely One** *Duane Eddy*
75/76 **Lonely One** *Special Delivery*
5/75 **Lonely People** *America*
72/59 **Lonely Saturday Night** *Don French*
60/85 **Lonely School** *Tommy Shaw*
57/75 **Lonely School Year**
Hudson Brothers
69/66 **Lonely Soldier** *Mike Williams*
5/59 **Lonely Street** *Andy Williams*
57/61 **Lonely Street** *Clarence Henry*
72/66 **Lonely Summer** *Shades Of Blue*
39/63 **Lonely Surfer** *Jack Nitzsche*
Lonely Teardrops
7/59 *Jackie Wilson*
54/71 *Brian Hyland*
62/76 *Narvel Felts*
12/60 **Lonely Teenager** *Dion*
45/81 **Lonely Together** *Barry Manilow*
22/60 **Lonely Weekends** *Charlie Rich*
60/79 **Lonely Wind** *Kansas*
54/60 **Lonely Winds** *Drifters*
67/88 **Lonely Won't Leave Me Alone**
Glenn Medeiros
6X/64 **Lonesome Christmas**
Lowell Fulson
6/79 **Lonesome Loser** *Little River Band*
93/56 **Lonesome Lover Blues**
Fontane Sisters
75/72 **Lonesome Mary** *Chilliwack*
59/61 **Lonesome Number One**
Don Gibson
71/59 **Lonesome Old House** *Don Gibson*
89/67 **Lonesome Road** *Wonder Who?*
7/58 **Lonesome Town** *Ricky Nelson*
88/61 **Lonesome Whistle Blues**
Freddy King

LONG:

31/71 **Long Ago And Far Away** *James Taylor*
61/71 **Long Ago Tomorrow** *B.J. Thomas*
68/88 **Long And Lasting Love** *Glenn Medeiros*
75/70 **Long And Lonesome Road** *Shocking Blue*
1/70 **Long And Winding Road** *Beatles*
F/70 **Long As I Can See The Light** *Creedence Clearwater Revival*
62/62 **Long As The Rose Is Red** *Florraine Darlin*
2/72 **Long Cool Woman (In A Black Dress)** *Hollies*
26/72 **Long Dark Road** *Hollies*
6A/97 **Long December** *Counting Crows*
67/64 **Long Gone Lonesome Blues** *Hank Williams, Jr.*
39/02 **Long Goodbye** *Brooks & Dunn*
73/69 **Long Green** *Fireballs*
56/75 **Long Haired Country Boy** *Charlie Daniels Band*
38/72 **Long Haired Lover From Liverpool** *Little Jimmy Osmond*
77/58 **Long Hot Summer** *Jimmie Rodgers*
76/78 **Long Hot Summer Nights** *Wendy Waldman*
63/67 **Long Legged Girl (With The Short Dress On)** *Elvis Presley*
79/69 **Long Line Rider** *Bobby Darin*
97/65 **Long Live Love** *Sandie Shaw*
33/66 **Long Live Our Love** *Shangri-Las*
54/79 **Long Live Rock** *Who*
Long Lonely Nights
45/57 *Lee Andrews*
49/57 *Clyde McPhatter*
17/65 *Bobby Vinton*
74/70 *Dells*
20/70 **Long Lonesome Highway** *Michael Parks*
25/70 **Long Long Time** *Linda Ronstadt*
20/78 **Long, Long Way From Home** *Foreigner*
(Long Nights) ..see: Blue Collar Man
89/71 **Long Promised Road** *Beach Boys*
F/95 **Long Road** *Pearl Jam*
8/80 **Long Run** *Eagles*
9/75 **Long Tall Glasses (I Can Dance)** *Leo Sayer*
Long Tall Sally
6/56 *Little Richard*
8/56 *Pat Boone*
96/64 **Long Tall Shorty** *Tommy Tucker*
51/63 **Long Tall Texan** *Murry Kellum*
22/77 **Long Time** *Boston*
92/71 **Long Time, A Long Way To Go** *Runt-Todd Rundgren*
7/02 **Long Time Gone** *Dixie Chicks*
85/81 **Long Time Lovin' You** *McGuffey Lane*
93/72 **Long Time To Be Alone** *New Colony Six*
8/73 **Long Train Runnin'** *Doobie Brothers*
36A/94 **Long View** *Green Day*
43/01 **Long Walk** *Jill Scott*
F/71 **Long Way Around** *Linda Ronstadt*
91/73 **Long Way Home** *Neil Diamond*
100/88 **Long Way To Love** *Britny Fox*
2/80 **Longer** *Dan Fogelberg*
89/82 **Longer You Wait** *Gino Vannelli*
14/84 **Longest Time** *Billy Joel*
6/55 **Longest Walk** *Jaye P. Morgan*
5/74 **Longfellow Serenade** *Neil Diamond*

LOOK:

1/89 **Look, The** *Roxette*
67/67 **Look At Granny Run, Run** *Howard Tate*
91/63 **Look At Me** *Dobie Gray*
52/66 **Look At Me Girl** *Bobby Vee*
39/75 **Look At Me (I'm In Love)** *Moments*
89/69 **Look At Mine** *Petula Clark*
68/84 **Look At That Cadillac** *Stray Cats*
59/01 **Look At Us** *Sarina Paris*
95/75 **Look At You** *George McCrae*
1/88 **Look Away** *Chicago*
73/64 **Look Away** *Garnet Mimms*
Look For A Star
16/60 *Garry Miles*
19/60 *Billy Vaughn*
26/60 *Garry Mills*
29/60 *Deane Hawley*
56/68 **Look, Here Comes The Sun** *Sunshine Company*
Look Homeward Angel
55/56 *Four Esquires*
36/57 *Johnnie Ray*
47/64 *Monarchs*
Look In My Eyes
14/61 *Chantels*
97/66 *3° Degrees*
11/75 **Look In My Eyes Pretty Woman** *Tony Orlando & Dawn*
4/97 **Look Into My Eyes** *BONE thugs-n-harmony*
63/90 **Look Into My Eyes** *George LaMond*
Look Into Your Heart
82/77 *Aretha Franklin*
68A/94 *Whitney Houston*
56/70 **Look-Ka Py Py** *Meters*
72/85 **Look My Way** *Vels*
Look Of Love
22/67 *Dusty Springfield*
4/68 *Sergio Mendes*
79/71 *Isaac Hayes*
18/83 **Look Of Love** *ABC*
27/65 **Look Of Love** *Lesley Gore*
35/88 **Look Out Any Window** *Bruce Hornsby*
89/68 **Look Over Your Shoulder** *O'Jays*
32/66 **Look Through Any Window** *Hollies*
24/66 **Look Through My Window** *Mamas & The Papas*
49/68 **Look To Your Soul** *Johnny Rivers*
Look What They've Done To My Song Ma
14/70 *New Seekers*
65/72 *Ray Charles*
4/72 **Look What You Done For Me** *Al Green*
32/67 **Look What You've Done** *Pozo Seco Singers*
14/80 **Look What You've Done To Me** *Boz Scaggs*
51/77 **Look What You've Done To My Heart** *Marilyn McCoo & Billy Davis Jr.*
58/58 **Look Who's Blue** *Don Gibson*
8/98 **Lookin' At Me** *Mase*
96/71 **Lookin' Back** *Bob Seger*
Looking Back
5/58 *Nat "King" Cole*
70/69 *Joe Simon*
Lookin' For A Love
72/62 *Valentinos*
39/72 *J. Geils Band*
10/74 *Bobby Womack*
5/80 **Lookin' For Love** *Johnny Lee*
94/66 **Lookin' For Love** *Ray Conniff*
45/64 **Looking For Love** *Connie Francis*
65/76 **Lookin' Out For #1** *Bachman-Turner Overdrive*
2/70 **Lookin' Out My Back Door** *Creedence Clearwater Revival*
16/72 **Lookin' Through The Windows** *Jackson 5*
62/68 **Looking For A Fox** *Clarence Carter*
2/87 **Looking For A New Love** *Jody Watley*
39/83 **Looking For A Stranger** *Pat Benatar*
69/93 **Looking For Mr. Do Right** *Jade*
29/76 **Looking For Space** *John Denver*
61/85 **Looking Over My Shoulder** *'Til Tuesday*
6/93 **Looking Through Patient Eyes** *PM Dawn*
Looking Through The Eyes Of Love
28/65 *Gene Pitney*
39/73 *Partridge Family*
18/98 **Looking Through Your Eyes** *LeAnn Rimes*
64/65 **Looking With My Eyes** *Dionne Warwick*
41/80 **Looks Like Love Again** *Dann Rogers*
1/77 **Looks Like We Made It** *Barry Manilow*
54/84 **Looks That Kill** *Mötley Crüe*
98/70 **Looky Looky (Look At Me Girl)** *O'Jays*
80/66 **Loop, The** *Johnny Lytle*
4/63 **Loop De Loop** *Johnny Thunder*
84/74 **Loose Booty** *Sly & The Family Stone*
64/73 **Lord Knows I'm Drinking** *Cal Smith*
68/73 **Lord, Mr. Ford** *Jerry Reed*
4/74 **Lord's Prayer** *Sister Janet Mead*
27/76 **Lorelei** *Styx*
76/77 **Lose Again** *Linda Ronstadt*
F/93 **Lose Control** *Silk*
34S/02 **Lose Control (Descontrólate)** *Yohany*
69/62 **Lose Her** *Bobby Rydell*
1/02 **Lose Yourself** *Eminem*
10/94 **Loser** *Beck*
55/00 **Loser** *3 Doors Down*
72/65 **Loser, The** *Skyliners*
43/67 **Loser (With A Broken Heart)** *Gary Lewis*
94/70 **Losers Weepers** *Etta James*
86/93 **Losin' Myself** *Debbie Gibson*
4/91 **Losing My Religion** *R.E.M.*
6/63 **Losing You** *Brenda Lee*
91/65 **Losing You** *Dusty Springfield*
99/92 **Losing You** *SGH Mocca Soul*
89/61 **Losing Your Love** *Jim Reeves*

LOST:

62/68 **Lost** *Jerry Butler*
34/80 **Lost Her In The Sun** *John Stewart*
63/73 **Lost Horizon** *Shawn Phillips*
1/87 **Lost In Emotion** *Lisa Lisa & Cult Jam*
3/80 **Lost In Love** *Air Supply*
35/85 **Lost In Love** *New Edition*
53/98 **Lost In Love** *Nastyboy Klick*

69/56 **Lost In The Shuffle** *Jaye P. Morgan*
5/99 **Lost In You** *Garth Brooks As Chris Gaines*
12/88 **Lost In You** *Rod Stewart*
1/89 **Lost In Your Eyes** *Debbie Gibson*
91/93 **Lost In Your Eyes** *Jeff Healey Band*
55/79 **Lost In Your Love** *John Paul Young*
58/56 **Lost John** *Lonnie Donegan*
35/61 **Lost Love** *H.B. Barnum*
77/62 **Lost Penny** *Brook Benton*
Lost Someone
48/62 *James Brown*
94/66 *James Brown*
84/90 **Lost Soul** *Bruce Hornsby/Shawn Colvin*
9/77 **Lost Without Your Love** *Bread*
55/02 **Lot Of Things Different** *Kenny Chesney*
8/79 **Lotta Love** *Nicolette Larson*
13/57 **Lotta Lovin'** *Gene Vincent*
62/91 **Louder Than Love** *TKA*
Louie Louie
2/63 *Kingsmen*
30/66 *Sandpipers*
97/66 *Kingsmen*
89/78 *John Belushi*
89/88 *Fat Boys*
78/75 **Louisiana Lou And Three Card Monty John** *Allman Brothers Band*
Louisiana Man
97/67 *Pozo Seco Singers*
100/68 *Bobbie Gentry*
62/72 **Louisianna** *Mike Kennedy*
3/96 **Loungin** *LL Cool J*

LOVE:

Love ..also see: Luv
24/01 **Love** *Musiq Soulchild*
42/71 **Love** *Lettermen*
81/64 **L-O-V-E** *Nat King Cole*
F/57 **Love Affair** *Sal Mineo*
85/84 **Love Again** *John Denver & Sylvie Vartan*
68/99 **Love Ain't Like That** *Faith Hill*
89/56 **Love Ain't Right** *Kay Starr*
46/81 **Love All The Hurt Away** *Aretha Franklin & George Benson*
43/86 **Love Always** *El DeBarge*
Love And Affection ..see: (Can't Live Without Your)
70/79 **Love And Desire** *Arpeggio*
15/90 **Love & Emotion** *Stevie B*
58/73 **Love And Happiness** *Earnest Jackson*
94/72 **Love And Liberty** *Laura Lee*
78/80 **Love And Loneliness** *Motors*
Love And Marriage
5/55 *Frank Sinatra*
20/55 *Dinah Shore*
55/85 **Love & Pride** *King*
92/86 **Love And Rock And Roll** *Greg Kihn*
17/91 **Love And Understanding** *Cher*
77/76 **Love And Understanding (Come Together)** *Kool & The Gang*
23/02 **Love At First Sight** *Kylie Minogue*
25/91 **Love At First Sight** *Styx*
99/66 **Love Attack** *James Carr*
Love Ballad
20/76 *L.T.D.*
18/79 *George Benson*

Love Being Your Fool ..see: (Shu-Doo-Pa-Poo-Poop)
1/88 **Love Bites** *Def Leppard*
11/86 **Love Bizarre** *Sheila E.*
43/70 **Love Bones** *Johnnie Taylor*
Love Bug
71/66 *Jack Jones*
69S/94 *George Strait*
92/77 **Love Bug** *Bumble Bee Unlimited*
78/58 **Love Bug Crawl** *Jimmy Edwards*
25/67 **Love Bug Leave My Heart Alone** *Martha & The Vandellas*
10/62 **Love Came To Me** *Dion*
2/69 **Love (Can Make You Happy)** *Mercy*
36/93 **Love Can Move Mountains** *Celine Dion*
69/62 **Love Can't Wait** *Marty Robbins*
23/88 **Love Changes (Everything)** *Climie Fisher*
91/88 **Love Changes Everything** *Honeymoon Suite*
Love Child
1/68 *Supremes*
13/90 *Sweet Sensation*
17/82 **Love Come Down** *Evelyn King*
62/86 **Love Comes Quickly** *Pet Shop Boys*
62/75 **Love Corporation** *Hues Corporation*
75/91 **Love Crazy** *Atlantic Starr*
46/89 **Love Cries** *Stage Dolls*
49/91 **Love Desire** *Sandée*
3/01 **Love Don't Cost A Thing** *Jennifer Lopez*
Love Don't Live Here Anymore
32/79 *Rose Royce*
78/96 *Madonna*
15/74 **Love Don't Love Nobody** *Spinners*
36/93 **Love Don't Love You** *En Vogue*
92/75 **Love Don't You Go Through No Changes On Me** *Sister Sledge*
92/68 **Love Explosion** *Troy Keyes*
15/67 **Love Eyes** *Nancy Sinatra*
47/75 **Love Finds It's Own Way** *Gladys Knight*
30/76 **Love Fire** *Jigsaw*
86/98 **Love For Free** *Rell*
53/93 **Love For Love** *Robin S*
43/63 **Love For Sale** *Arthur Lyman Group*
25/97 **Love Gets Me Every Time** *Shania Twain*
92/91 **Love Gets Rough** *Troy Newman*
64/72 **Love Gonna Pack Up (And Walk Out)** *Persuaders*
89/85 **Love Grammar** *John Parr*
5/70 **Love Grows (Where My Rosemary Goes)** *Edison Lighthouse*
61/77 **Love Gun** *Kiss*
Love Hangover
1/76 *Diana Ross*
80/76 *5th Dimension*
70/84 **Love Has A Mind Of Its Own** *Donna Summer w/Matthew Ward*
88/84 **Love Has Finally Come At Last** *Bobby Womack & Patti LaBelle*
51/74 **Love Has No Pride** *Linda Ronstadt*
64/89 **Love Has Taken Its Toll** *Saraya*
11/71 **Love Her Madly** *Doors*
Love Hurts
97/75 *Jim Capaldi*
8/76 *Nazareth*
Love I Lost
7/73 *Harold Melvin*
F/93 *Sybil*

20/67 **Love I Saw In You Was Just A Mirage** *Miracles*
91/61 **Love (I'm So Glad) I Found You** *Spinners*
79/56 **Love In A Home** *Doris Day*
5/89 **Love In An Elevator** *Aerosmith*
Love In 'C' Minor
36/77 *Cerrone*
46/77 *Heart & Soul Orchestra*
60/68 **Love In Every Room** *Paul Mauriat*
88/86 **Love In Siberia** *Laban*
22/83 **Love In Store** *Fleetwood Mac*
91/69 **Love In The City** *Turtles*
15/82 **Love In The First Degree** *Alabama*
48/88 **Love In The First Degree** *Bananarama*
16/76 **Love In The Shadows** *Neil Sedaka*
93/68 **Love In Them There Hills** *Vibrations*
24/89 **Love In Your Eyes** *Eddie Money*
3/93 **Love Is** *Vanessa Williams & Brian McKnight*
36/90 **Love Is** *Alannah Myles*
20X/67 **Love Is** *Lise Miller*
5/83 **Love Is A Battlefield** *Pat Benatar*
97/67 **Love Is A Doggone Good Thing** *Eddie Floyd*
66/65 **Love Is A 5-Letter Word** *James Phelps*
10/57 **Love Is A Golden Ring** *Frankie Laine*
78/87 **Love Is A House** *Force M.D.'s*
13/66 **Love Is A Hurtin' Thing** *Lou Rawls*
71/90 **Love Is A Killer** *Vixen*
Love Is A Many-Splendored Thing
1/55 *Four Aces*
26/55 *Don Cornell*
54/55 *David Rose*
79/55 *Woody Herman*
96/55 *Don, Dick N' Jimmy*
65/90 **Love Is A Rock** *REO Speedwagon*
63/75 **Love Is A Rose** *Linda Ronstadt*
23/83 **Love Is A Stranger** *Eurythmics*
4/91 **Love Is A Wonderful Thing** *Michael Bolton*
Love Is Alive
2/76 *Gary Wright*
61/97 *3rd Party*
91/73 **Love Is All** *Engelbert Humperdinck*
Love Is All Around
7/68 *Troggs*
41/94 *Wet Wet Wet*
65/69 **Love Is All I Have To Give** *Checkmates, Ltd.*
Love Is All We Need
15/58 *Tommy Edwards*
53/64 *Vic Dana*
50/66 *Mel Carter*
43A/97 **Love Is All We Need** *Mary J. Blige*
89/78 **Love Is All You Need** *High Inergy*
20/82 **Love Is Alright Tonite** *Rick Springfield*
77/77 **Love Is Better In The A.M.** *Johnnie Taylor*
34/00 **Love Is Blind** *Eve*
Love Is Blue
1/68 *Paul Mauriat*
57/68 *Al Martino*
71/68 *Claudine Longet*
96/68 *Manny Kellem*
22/69 *Dells (medley)*
62/87 **Love Is Contagious** *Taja Sevelle*
33S/01 **Love Is Enough** *3 Of Hearts*
(Love Is Everywhere) ..see: Revival
16/86 **Love Is Forever** *Billy Ocean*

95/71 **Love Is Funny That Way** *Jackie Wilson*
69/79 **Love Is Gonna Come At Last** *Badfinger*
1/67 **Love Is Here And Now You're Gone** *Supremes*
10/82 **Love Is In Control (Finger On The Trigger)** *Donna Summer*
7/78 **Love Is In The Air** *John Paul Young*
86/69 **Love Is Just A Four-Letter Word** *Joan Baez*
93/71 **Love Is Life** *Earth, Wind & Fire*
26/68 **(Love Is Like A) Baseball Game** *Intruders*
37/82 **Love Is Like A Rock** *Donnie Iris*
9/66 **Love Is Like An Itching In My Heart** *Supremes*
8/78 **Love Is Like Oxygen** *Sweet*
66/66 **Love Is Me, Love Is You** *Connie Francis*
12/92 **Love Is On The Way** *Saigon Kick*
Love Is Strange
11/57 *Mickey & Sylvia*
13/67 *Peaches & Herb*
91/94 **Love Is Strong** *Rolling Stones*
10/79 **Love Is The Answer** *England Dan & John Ford Coley*
30/76 **Love Is The Drug** *Roxy Music*
80/86 **Love Is The Hero** *Billy Squier*
80/83 **Love Is The Key** *Maze Feat. Frankie Beverly*
85/74 **Love Is The Message** *MFSB feat. The Three Degrees*
80/90 **Love Is The Ritual** *Styx*
17/85 **Love Is The Seventh Wave** *Sting*
86/62 **Love Is The Sweetest Thing** *Saverio Saridis*
7/56 **(Love Is) The Tender Trap** *Frank Sinatra*
1/78 **(Love Is) Thicker Than Water** *Andy Gibb*
55/73 **Love Is What You Make It** *Grass Roots*
18S/01 **Love It** *Bilal*
16/73 **Love Jones** *Brighter Side Of Darkness* *(also see: Basketball Jones)*
69/84 **Love Kills** *Freddie Mercury*
16/70 **Love Land** *Charles Wright*
Love Letters
5/62 *Ketty Lester*
19/66 *Elvis Presley*
1/57 **Love Letters In The Sand** *Pat Boone*
97/76 **Love Lifted Me** *Kenny Rogers*
81/81 **Love Light** *Yutaka*
17/85 **Love Light In Flight** *Stevie Wonder*
98/70 **Love Like A Man** *Ten Years After*
7/98 **Love Like This** *Faith Evans*
13/75 **L-O-V-E (Love)** *Al Green*
Love, Love, Love
30/56 *Clovers*
30/56 *Diamonds*
44/73 **Love, Love, Love** *Donny Hathaway*
1/76 **Love Machine** *Miracles*
76/68 **Love Machine** *O'Kaysions*
15/68 **Love Makes A Woman** *Barbara Acklin*
70/66 **Love (Makes Me Do Foolish Things)** *Martha & The Vandellas*
Love Makes The World Go Round
11/66 *Deon Jackson*
83/71 *Odds & Ends*
87/71 *Kiki Dee*
26/63 **Love (Makes the World Go 'Round)** *Paul Anka*
33/58 **Love Makes The World Go 'Round** *Perry Como*
13/91 **Love Makes Things Happen** *Pebbles*
72/69 **Love Man** *Otis Redding*
2/57 **Love Me** *Elvis Presley*
14/76 **Love Me** *Yvonne Elliman*
17/98 **Love Me** *112*
48/92 **Love Me** *Tracie Spencer*
84/67 **Love Me** *Bobby Hebb*
94/71 **Love Me** *Impressions*
95/71 **Love Me** *Rascals*
64/83 **Love Me Again** *John Hall Band*
68/78 **Love Me Again** *Rita Coolidge*
88/63 **Love Me All The Way** *Kim Weston*
26/92 **Love Me All Up** *Stacy Earl*
54/62 **Love Me As I Love You** *George Maharis*
100/65 **Love Me As Though There Were No Tomorrow** *Sonny Knight*
1/64 **Love Me Do** *Beatles*
10/74 **Love Me For A Reason** *Osmonds*
29/90 **Love Me For Life** *Stevie B*
86/73 **Love Me For What I Am** *Lobo*
Love Me Forever
24/57 *Eydie Gorme*
25/57 *Four Esquires*
60/67 *Roger Williams*
82/91 **Love Me Forever Or Love Me Not** *Trilogy*
61/98 **Love Me Good** *Michael W. Smith*
62/56 **Love Me Good** *Jo Stafford*
45/84 **Love Me In A Special Way** *DeBarge*
100/59 **Love Me In The Daytime** *Doris Day*
91/90 **Love Me Just For Me** *Special Generation*
46/72 **Love Me, Love Me Love** *Frank Mills*
86/72 **(Love Me) Love The Life I Lead** *Fantastics*
100/65 **Love Me Now** *Brook Benton*
79/77 **Love Me One More Time** *Karen Nelson & Billy T*
Love Me Or Leave Me
12/55 *Sammy Davis, Jr.*
19/55 *Lena Horne*
92/93 **Love Me Or Leave Me Alone** *Brand Nubian*
80/78 **Love Me Right** *Denise LaSalle*
Love Me Tender
1/56 *Elvis Presley*
44/56 *Henri René*
21/62 *Richard Chamberlain*
40/67 *Percy Sledge*
97/93 **Love Me The Right Way** *Rapination & Kym Mazelle*
11/57 **Love Me To Pieces** *Jill Corey*
22/82 **Love Me Tomorrow** *Chicago*
13/69 **Love Me Tonight** *Tom Jones*
54/76 **Love Me Tonight** *Head East*
62/79 **Love Me Tonight** *Blackjack*
75A/92 **Love Me Tonight** *Cynthia*
25/68 **Love Me Two Times** *Doors*
12/62 **Love Me Warm And Tender** *Paul Anka*
Love Me With All Your Heart
85/63 *Steve Allen (Cuando Calienta)*
3/64 *Ray Charles Singers*
38/66 *Bachelors*
39/71 **Love Means (You Never Have To Say You're Sorry)** *Sounds Of Sunshine*
84/70 **Love Minus Zero-No Limit** *Turley Richards*
97/73 **Love Music** *Raiders*
Love My Life Away ..see: (I Wanna)
44/83 **Love My Way** *Psychedelic Furs*
59/83 **Love Never Fails** *Greg Kihn Band*
44/93 **Love No Limit** *Mary J. Blige*
44/63 **Love Of A Boy** *Timi Yuro*
5/91 **Love Of A Lifetime** *Firehouse*
53/86 **Love Of A Lifetime** *Chaka Khan*
39/01 **Love Of A Woman** *Travis Tritt*
40/58 **Love Of My Life** *Everly Brothers*
51/01 **Love Of My Life** *Brian McKnight*
64/76 **Love Of My Life** *Gino Vannelli*
85/98 **Love Of My Life** *Sammy Kershaw*
9/03 **Love Of My Life (An Ode To Hip Hop)** *Erykah Badu*
21/63 **Love Of My Man** *Theola Kilgore*
56/61 **Love Of My Own** *Carla Thomas*
Love Of The Common People
54/69 *Winstons*
45/84 *Paul Young*
40/91 **Love On A Rooftop** *Desmond Child*
55/80 **Love On A Shoestring** *Captain & Tennille*
Love On A Two-Way Street
3/70 *Moments*
26/81 *Stacy Lattisaw*
46/94 **Love On My Mind** *Xscape*
88/83 **Love On My Mind Tonight** *Temptations*
87/81 **Love On The Airwaves** *Night*
87/80 **Love On The Phone** *Suzanne Fellini*
2/81 **Love On The Rocks** *Neil Diamond*
45/83 **Love On Your Side** *Thompson Twins*
36/76 **Love Or Leave** *Spinners*
Love Or Let Me Be Lonely
6/70 *Friends Of Distinction*
40/82 *Paul Davis*
32/78 **Love Or Something Like It** *Kenny Rogers*
13/88 **Love Overboard** *Gladys Knight*
34/79 **Love Pains** *Yvonne Elliman*
36/86 **Love Parade** *Dream Academy*
96/70 **Love, Peace And Happiness** *Chambers Brothers*
37/82 **Love Plus One** *Haircut One Hundred*
Love Potion Number Nine
23/59 *Clovers*
3/65 *Searchers*
76/72 *Coasters*
Love Power
22/68 *Sandpebbles*
4/91 *Luther Vandross (medley)*
12/87 **Love Power** *Dionne Warwick & Jeffrey Osborne*
41/75 **Love Power** *Willie Hutch*
22/76 **Love Really Hurts Without You** *Billy Ocean*
76/73 **Love, Reign O'er Me** *Who*
82/85 **Love Resurrection** *Alison Moyet*
Love Rollercoaster
1/76 *Ohio Players*
40A/97 *Red Hot Chili Peppers*
65A/97 **Love Scene** *Joe*
91/00 **Love Sets You Free** *Kelly Price*
3/89 **Love Shack** *B-52's*
31/63 **Love She Can Count On** *Miracles*
33/93 **Love Shoulda Brought You Home** *Toni Braxton*
72A/94 **Love Sign** *Nona Gaye & Prince*
19/94 **Love Sneakin' Up On You** *Bonnie Raitt*
40/63 **Love So Fine** *Chiffons*
3/76 **Love So Right** *Bee Gees*

5/84 **Love Somebody** *Rick Springfield*
2/89 **Love Song** *Cure*
10/90 **Love Song** *Tesla*
12/74 **Love Song** *Anne Murray*
47/82 **Love Song** *Kenny Rogers*
60S/99 **Love Song** *Sky*
67/72 **Love Song** *Tommy James*
Love Songs Are Back Again ..see: Medley
55A/95 **Love Spreads** *Stone Roses*
38/80 **Love Stinks** *J. Geils Band*
Love Story ..see: Theme From
70/79 **Love Struck** *Stonebolt*
78/88 **Love Struck** *Jesse Johnson*
44/81 **Love T.K.O.** *Teddy Pendergrass*
77/66 **Love Takes A Long Time Growing** *Deon Jackson*
1/90 **Love Takes Time** *Mariah Carey*
11/79 **Love Takes Time** *Orleans*
50/80 **Love That Got Away** *Firefall*
98/74 **Love That Really Counts** *Natural Four*
82/67 **Love That's Real** *Intruders*
Love The One You're With
14/71 *Stephen Stills*
18/71 *Isley Brothers*
95/95 *Luther Vandross*
79/98 **Love The Way** *E.O.L.*
14/80 **Love The World Away** *Kenny Rogers*
1/77 **Love Theme From A Star Is Born (Evergreen)** *Barbra Streisand*
Love Theme From "Eyes Of Laura Mars" (Prisoner)
86/77 *L.A. Jets*
21/78 *Barbra Streisand*
Love Theme From Lady Sings The Blues ..see: Happy
37/61 **(Love Theme From) One Eyed Jacks** *Ferrante & Teicher*
Love Theme From One On One ..see: My Fair Share
Love Theme From Romeo & Juliet
1/69 *Henry Mancini*
96/69 *Johnny Mathis*
15/85 **Love Theme From St. Elmo's Fire** *David Foster*
70/80 **Love Theme From Shogun (Mariko's Theme)** *Meco*
Love Theme From The Godfather
34/72 *Andy Williams*
66/72 *Carlo Savina*
80/72 *Al Martino*
Love Theme From The Sandpiper ..see: Shadow Of Your Smile
10/91 **Love...Thy Will Be Done** *Martika*
61/80 **Love X Love** *George Benson*
82/97 **Love II Love** *Damage*
2/76 **Love To Love You Baby** *Donna Summer*
91/77 **Love To The World** *L.T.D.*
6/86 **Love Touch** *Rod Stewart*
1/73 **Love Train** *O'Jays*
65/89 **Love Train** *Holly Johnson*
89/88 **Love, Truth & Honesty** *Bananarama*
31/96 **Love U 4 Life** *Jodeci*
36/93 **Love U More** *Sunscreem*
72/70 **Love Uprising** *Otis Leaville*
Love Walked In
88/59 *Flamingos*
30/60 *Dinah Washington*
22/86 **Love Walks In** *Van Halen*
30/71 **Love We Had (Stays On My Mind)** *Dells*

9/86 **Love Will Conquer All** *Lionel Richie*
6/78 **Love Will Find A Way** *Pablo Cruise*
30/87 **Love Will Find A Way** *Yes*
40/69 **Love Will Find A Way** *Jackie DeShannon*
22A/95 **Love Will Keep Us Alive** *Eagles*
Love Will Keep Us Together
1/75 *Captain & Tennille*
49/75 *Captain & Tennille (Por Amor Viviremos)*
1/90 **Love Will Lead You Back** *Taylor Dayne*
1/91 **Love Will Never Do (Without You)** *Janet Jackson*
9/88 **Love Will Save The Day** *Whitney Houston*
30/84 **Love Will Show Us How** *Christine McVie*
13/82 **Love Will Turn You Around** *Kenny Rogers*
62/64 **Love With The Proper Stranger** *Jack Jones*
5/75 **Love Won't Let Me Wait** *Major Harris*
Love X ..see: Love Times
Love You ..also see: Love U / Luv U
68/92 **Love You All My Lifetime** *Chaka Khan*
Love You Down
9/87 *Ready For The World*
25/98 *Inoj*
1/79 **Love You Inside Out** *Bee Gees*
24/81 **Love You Like I Never Loved Before** *John O'Banion*
26/58 **Love You Most Of All** *Sam Cooke*
1/70 **Love You Save** *Jackson 5*
56/66 **Love You Save (May Be Your Own)** *Joe Tex*
7/60 **Love You So** *Ron Holden*
61/67 **Love You So Much** *New Colony Six*
10/86 **Love Zone** *Billy Ocean*
85/89 **Love's About To Change My Heart** *Donna Summer*
7/82 **Love's Been A Little Bit Hard On Me** *Juice Newton*
75/69 **Love's Been Good To Me** *Frank Sinatra*
59/83 **Love's Got A Line On You** *Scandal*
20/77 **Love's Grown Deep** *Kenny Nolan*
19/71 **Love's Lines, Angles And Rhymes** *5th Dimension*
Love's Made A Fool Of You
26/66 *Bobby Fuller Four*
96/71 *Cochise*
83/80 **Love's Only Love** *Engelbert Humperdinck*
89/72 **Love's Street And Fool's Road** *Solomon Burke*
86/93 **Love's Taken Over** *Chanté Moore*
42/00 **Love's The Only House** *Martina McBride*
1/74 **Love's Theme** *Love Unlimited Orchestra*
Lovebug ..see: Love Bug
97/61 **Lovedrops** *Mickey & Sylvia*
2A/97 **Lovefool** *Cardigans*
60/82 **Loveline** *Dr. Hook*
30/78 **Lovely Day** *Bill Withers*
45/56 **Lovely Lies** *Manhattan Brothers & Miriam Makeba*
70/65 **Lovely, Lovely (Loverly, Loverly)** *Chubby Checker*
12/80 **Lovely One** *Jacksons*
20/56 **Lovely One** *Four Voices*

LOVER:

68/81 **Lover** *Michael Stanley Band*
98/62 **Lover Come Back** *Doris Day*
75/85 **Lover Come Back To Me** *Dead Or Alive*
95/62 **Lover Come Back To Me** *Cleftones*
2/89 **Lover In Me** *Sheena Easton*
7/62 **Lover Please** *Clyde McPhatter*
Lover's Concerto
2/65 *Toys*
63/66 *Sarah Vaughan*
95/66 *Mrs. Miller*
64S/96 **Lover's Groove** *Immature*
31/68 **Lover's Holiday** *Peggy Scott & Jo Jo Benson*
40/80 **Lover's Holiday** *Change*
31/61 **Lover's Island** *Blue Jays*
59/87 **Lover's Lane** *Georgio*
73/59 **Lover's Prayer** *Dion & The Belmonts*
97/64 **Lover's Prayer** *Wallace Brothers*
Lover's Question
6/59 *Clyde McPhatter*
98/61 *Ernestine Anderson*
48/69 *Otis Redding*
89/75 *Loggins & Messina*
2/85 **Loverboy** *Billy Ocean*
2/01 **Loverboy** *Mariah Carey*
88/84 **Loverboy** *Karen Kamon*
4/85 **Lovergirl** *Teena Marie*
54/81 **Lovers After All** *Melissa Manchester & Peabo Bryson*
89/64 **Lovers Always Forgive** *Gladys Knight*
36/62 **Lovers By Night, Strangers By Day** *Fleetwoods*
52/59 **Lovers Never Say Goodbye** *Flamingos*
3/62 **Lovers Who Wander** *Dion*
2/73 **Loves Me Like A Rock** *Paul Simon*
Lovesick Blues
87/62 *Floyd Cramer*
44/63 *Frank Ifield*
Lovey Dovey
49/59 *Clyde McPhatter*
25/61 *Buddy Knox*
86/67 *Bunny Sigler (medley)*
60/68 *Otis & Carla*
99/68 **Lovey Dovey Kinda Lovin'** *Brenton Wood*

LOVIN'/LOVING:

38S/02 **Lovin' Each Day** *Ronan Keating*
9/85 **Lovin' Every Minute Of It** *Loverboy*
54/65 **Lovin' Place** *Gale Garnett*
81/68 **Lovin' Season** *Gene & Debbe*
45/81 **Lovin' The Night Away** *Dillman Band*
49/69 **Lovin' Things** *Grassroots*
84/60 **Lovin' Touch** *Mark Dinning*
16/79 **Lovin', Touchin', Squeezin'** *Journey*
47S/01 **Lovin' You** *Kristine W*
(also see: Loving You)
82/70 **Lovin' You Baby** *White Plains*
83/72 **Lovin' You, Lovin' Me** *Candi Staton*
Loving Arms
61/73 *Dobie Gray*
86/74 *Kris Kristofferson & Rita Coolidge*
96/93 **Loving Arms** *Darden Smith*
26/71 **Loving Her Was Easier (Than Anything I'll Ever Do Again)** *Kris Kristofferson*
1/75 **Lovin' You** *Minnie Riperton*
32/67 **Lovin' You** *Bobby Darin*
20/57 **Loving You** *Elvis Presley*

88/82 **Loving You** *Chris Rea*
91/74 **Loving You** *Johnny Nash*
51/68 **Loving You Has Made Me Bananas** *Guy Marks*
87/70 **Loving You Is A Natural Thing** *Ronnie Milsap*
45/66 **Loving You Is Sweeter Than Ever** *Four Tops*
29/72 **Loving You Just Crossed My Mind** *Sam Neely*
65/64 **Loving You More Every Day** *Etta James*
71/80 **Loving You With My Eyes** *Starland Vocal Band*
64/94 **Low** *Cracker*
3/76 **Lowdown** *Boz Scaggs*
35/71 **Lowdown** *Chicago*
41/69 **Lowdown Popcorn** *James Brown*
7/75 **Low Rider** *War*
57[S]/02 **Lowrider** *Cypress Hill*
54/91 **Lowrider (On The Boulevard)** *Latin Alliance Feat. War*
Lt. Calley ..see: Battle Hymn Of
75/82 **Luanne** *Foreigner*
29/94 **Lucas With The Lid Off** *Lucas*
50/97 **Luchini aka (this is it)** *Camp Lo*
84/70 **Lucifer** *Bob Seger*
5/77 **Lucille** *Kenny Rogers*
Lucille
21/57 *Little Richard*
21/60 *Everly Brothers*
25/77 **Luckenbach, Texas** *Waylon Jennings*
23/00 **Lucky** *Britney Spears*
30/85 **Lucky** *Greg Kihn*
88/83 **Lucky** *Eye To Eye*
25/60 **Lucky Devil** *Carl Dobkins, Jr.*
79/01 **Lucky 4 You (Tonight I'm Just Me)** *SheDaisy*
64/81 **Lucky Guy** *Rickie Lee Jones*
38/85 **Lucky In Love** *Mick Jagger*
14/59 **Lucky Ladybug** *Billy & Lillie*
Lucky Lips
25/57 *Ruth Brown*
77/57 *Gale Storm*
62/63 *Cliff Richard*
30/96 **Lucky Love** *Ace Of Base*
Lucky Man
48/71 *Emerson, Lake & Palmer*
51/73 *Emerson, Lake & Palmer*
73/76 **Lucky Man** *Starbuck*
42/80 **Lucky Me** *Anne Murray*
98/71 **Lucky Me** *Moments*
18/94 **Lucky One** *Amy Grant*
20/84 **Lucky One** *Laura Branigan*
4/84 **Lucky Star** *Madonna*
29/70 **Lucretia Mac Evil** *Blood, Sweat & Tears*
1/75 **Lucy In The Sky With Diamonds** *Elton John*
3/87 **Luka** *Suzanne Vega*
7/99 **Lullaby** *Shawn Mullins*
74/89 **Lullaby** *Cure*
16/56 **Lullaby Of Birdland** *Blue Stars*
69[S]/00 **Lullaby Of Clubland** *Everything But The Girl*
23/61 **Lullaby Of Love** *Frank Gari*
56/66 **Lullaby Of Love** *Poppies*
69/61 **Lullaby Of The Leaves** *Ventures*
77/94 **Lullabye (Goodnight, My Angel)** *Billy Joel*
53/64 **Lumberjack** *Brook Benton*
21[A]/95 **Lump** *Presidents Of The United States Of America*
95/69 **Luna Trip** *Dickie Goodman*
53[S]/99 **Luv At First Sight** *Chilldrin Of Da Ghetto*
63[S]/94 **Luv 4 Dem Gangsta'z** *Eazy-E*
76/98 **Luv Me, Luv Me** *Shaggy*
37[A]/98 **Luv 2 Luv U** *Timbaland & Magoo*
4/02 **Luv U Better** *LL Cool J*
2/75 **Lyin' Eyes** *Eagles*
27/90 **Lyin' To Myself** *David Cassidy*
74/86 **Lying** *Peter Frampton*

M

95/63 **M.G. Blues** *Jimmy McGriff*
57/95 **MC's Act Like They Don't Know** *KRS-One*
1/97 **MMMBop** *Hanson*
15/59 **M.T.A.** *Kingston Trio*
96/77 **Ma Baker** *Boney M*
5/70 **Ma Belle Amie** *Tee Set*
91/74 **Ma! (He's Making Eyes At Me)** *Lena Zavaroni*
97/58 **Ma Ma Ma Marie** *Gaylords*
MacArthur Park
2/68 *Richard Harris*
93/69 *Waylon Jennings*
38/71 *Four Tops*
1/78 *Donna Summer*
Macarena
1/96 *Los Del Rio (bayside boys mix)*
23/96 *Los Del Rio (non stop)*
71/96 *Los Del Mar*
57/96 **Macarena Christmas** *Los Del Rio*
68[A]/96 **Mach 5** *Presidents Of The United States Of America*
13[S]/02 **Machine** *Yeah Yeah Yeahs*
22/74 **Machine Gun** *Commodores*
43/96 **Machinehead** *Bush*
57/82 **Machinery** *Sheena Easton*
83/75 **Machines** *John LiVigni*
25/78 **Macho Man** *Village People*
Mack The Knife
8/56 *Dick Hyman*
11/56 *Richard Hayman & Jan August*
17/56 *Lawrence Welk*
20/56 *Louis Armstrong*
37/56 *Billy Vaughn*
49/56 *Les Paul*
1/59 *Bobby Darin*
27/60 *Ella Fitzgerald*
3/86 **Mad About You** *Belinda Carlisle*
54/95 **Mad Izm** *Channel Live*
29[S]/99 **Mad Professor** *Insane Clown Posse*
48/01 **Mad Season** *Matchbox Twenty*
52/95 **Made In England** *Elton John*
Made To Love ..see: (Girls, Girls, Girls)
79/76 **Made To Love You** *Gary Wright*
82/91 **Made Up My Mind** *Safire*
32/03 **Made You Look** *Nas*
50/56 **Madeira** *Mitch Miller*
36/76 **Mademoiselle** *Styx*
23/60 **Madison, The** *Al Brown*
30/60 **Madison Time** *Ray Bryant Combo*
85/59 **Madrid** *Nat "King" Cole*
45/71 **Maggie** *Redbone*
1/71 **Maggie May** *Rod Stewart*

MAGIC:

1/80 **Magic** *Olivia Newton-John*
5/75 **Magic** *Pilot*
12/84 **Magic** *Cars*
25/68 **Magic Bus** *Who*
3/68 **Magic Carpet Ride** *Steppenwolf*
58/95 **Magic Carpet Ride** *Mighty Dub Kats*
81/88 **Magic Carpet Ride** *Bardeux*
52/55 **Magic Fingers** *Eddie Fisher*
80/61 **Magic Is The Night** *Kathy Young*
9/76 **Magic Man** *Heart*
79/81 **Magic Man** *Herb Alpert*
96/55 **Magic Melody** *Les Paul & Mary Ford*
4/58 **Magic Moments** *Perry Como*
49/61 **Magic Moon** *Rays*
99/64 **Magic of Our Summer Love** *Tymes*
51/81 **Magic Power** *Triumph*
Magic Touch ..see: (You've Got)
21/66 **Magic Town** *Vogues*
91/62 **Magic Wand** *Don & Juan*
60/73 **Magic Woman Touch** *Hollies*
73/85 **Magical** *John Parr*
39/77 **Magical Mystery Tour** *Ambrosia*
8/78 **Magnet And Steel** *Walter Egan*
57/83 **Magnetic** *Earth, Wind & Fire*
35/61 **Magnificent Seven** *Al Caiola*
Magnum P.I. ..see: Theme From
55/69 **Máh-Ná-Mah-Ná** *Piero Umiliani*
Mahogany ..see: Theme From
3/79 **Main Event/Fight** *Barbra Streisand*
Main Theme From Exodus ..see: Exodus
Main Title And Molly-O ..see: Man With The Golden Arm
24/77 **Mainstreet** *Bob Seger*
75/67 **Mairzy Doats** *Innocence*
36/61 **Majestic, The** *Dion*
93/57 **Majesty Of Love** *Marvin Rainwater & Connie Francis*
14/83 **Major Tom (Coming Home)** *Peter Schilling*

MAKE:

97/67 **Make A Little Love** *Lowell Fulsom*
25/80 **Make A Little Magic** *Dirt Band*
5/82 **Make A Move On Me** *Olivia Newton-John*
28/69 **Make Believe** *Wind*
30/82 **Make Believe** *Toto*
78/80 **Make Believe It's Your First Time** *Bobby Vinton*
98/61 **Make Believe Wedding** *Castells*
64[S]/02 **Make Em Jiggle** *South Boyz Click*
16/98 **Make Em' Say Uhh!** *Master P*
54/85 **Make It Better (Forget About Me)** *Tom Petty*
46/03 **Make It Clap** *Busta Rhymes*
Make It Easy On Yourself
20/62 *Jerry Butler*
16/65 *Walker Bros.*
37/70 *Dionne Warwick*
Make It Funky
22/71 *James Brown*
68/71 *James Brown (My Part)*
5/92 **Make It Happen** *Mariah Carey*
5/98 **Make It Hot** *Nicole*
69/79 **Make It Last** *Brooklyn Dreams*
59/88 **Make It Last Forever** *Keith Sweat (with Jacci McGhee)*
43/90 **Make It Like It Was** *Regina Belle*
86/87 **Make It Mean Something** *Rob Jungklas*
4/88 **Make It Real** *Jets*
37[S]/01 **Make It Vibrate** *Rising Son*
Make It With You
1/70 *Bread*
94/77 *Whispers*

95/57 **Make Like A Bunny, Honey** *Jill Corey with Jimmy Carroll*
36/92 **Make Love Like A Man** *Def Leppard*
29/83 **Make Love Stay** *Dan Fogelberg*
57S/93 **Make Love 2 Me** *Lorenzo*
60/79 **Make Love To Me** *Helen Reddy*
96/67 **Make Love To Me** *Johnny Thunder & Ruby Winters*
76/76 **Make Love To Your Mind** *Bill Withers*
16/58 **Make Me A Miracle** *Jimmie Rodgers*
28/66 **Make Me Belong To You** *Barbara Lewis*
43/64 **Make Me Forget** *Bobby Rydell*
80/71 **Make Me Happy** *Bobby Bloom*
3/88 **Make Me Lose Control** *Eric Carmen*
9/70 **Make Me Smile** *Chicago*
96/76 **Make Me Smile (Come Up And See Me)** *Steve Harley*
27/72 **Make Me The Woman That You Go Home To** *Gladys Knight*
93/73 **Make Me Twice The Man** *New York City*
11/65 **Make Me Your Baby** *Barbara Lewis*
21/67 **Make Me Yours** *Bettye Swann*
62/84 **Make My Day** *T.G. Sheppard w/Clint Eastwood*
51/85 **Make No Mistake, He's Mine** *Barbra Streisand (w/Kim Carnes)*
80/60 **Make Someone Happy** *Perry Como*
60/81 **Make That Move** *Shalamar*
81/63 **Make The Music Play** *Dionne Warwick*
Make The World Go Away
24/63 *Timi Yuro*
100/63 *Ray Price*
6/65 *Eddy Arnold*
44/75 *Donny & Marie Osmond*
75A/94 **Make This Last Forever** *Jocelyn Enriquez*
71/82 **Make Up Your Mind** *Aurra*
98/73 **Make Up Your Mind** *J. Geils Band*
69/58 **(Make With) The Shake** *Mark IV*
45/78 **Make You Feel Love Again** *Wet Willie*
69S/02 **Make You Feel That Way** *Blackalicious*
14/90 **Make You Sweat** *Keith Sweat*
Make Your Own Kind Of Music
36/69 *Mama Cass Elliot*
94/72 *Barbra Streisand (medley)*
Make Yourself Comfortable
6/55 *Sarah Vaughan*
26/55 *Andy Griffith*
30/55 *Peggy King*
91/76 **Makes You Blind** *Glitter Band*
27/02 **Makin' Good Love** *Avant*
55S/91 **Makin' Happy** *Crystal Waters*
5/79 **Makin' It** *David Naughton*
20/59 **Makin' Love** *Floyd Robinson*
91/78 **Makin' Love** *Climax Blues Band*
13/82 **Making Love** *Roberta Flack*
(also see: Kufanya Mapenzi)
85/74 **Makin' The Best Of A Bad Situation** *Dick Feller*
46/65 **Makin' Whoopee** *Ray Charles*
87/77 **Making A Good Thing Better** *Olivia Newton-John*
31/67 **Making Every Minute Count** *Spanky & Our Gang*
35/87 **Making Love In The Rain** *Herb Alpert*
2/83 **Making Love Out Of Nothing At All** *Air Supply*
35/67 **Making Memories** *Frankie Laine*
25/76 **Making Our Dreams Come True** *Cyndi Grecco*
42/60 **Malaguena** *Connie Francis*
85/68 **Malayisha** *Miriam Makeba*
81/99 **Malibu** *Hole*
48/69 **Malinda** *Bobby Taylor*

MAMA:

8/60 **Mama** *Connie Francis*
22/66 **Mama** *B.J. Thomas*
73/83 **Mama** *Genesis*
(also see: Mamma)
82/71 **Mama And A Papa** *Ray Stevens*
9/79 **Mama Can't Buy You Love** *Elton John*
91/68 **(Mama Come Quick, and Bring Your) Lickin' Stick** *George Torrence*
14/63 **Mama Didn't Lie** *Jan Bradley*
55/63 **Mama Don't Allow** *Rooftop Singers*
11/56 **Mama From The Train** *Patti Page*
Mama Guitar
47/57 *Don Cornell*
98/57 *Julius LaRosa*
99/62 **Mama (He Treats Your Daughter Mean)** *Ruth Brown*
28/92 **Mama, I'm Coming Home** *Ozzy Osbourne*
72/78 **Mama Let Him Play** *Doucette*
F/70 **Mama Liked The Roses** *Elvis Presley*
11/57 **Mama Look At Bubu** *Harry Belafonte*
4/61 **Mama Said** *Shirelles*
17/91 **Mama Said Knock You Out** *LL Cool J*
Mama Sang A Song
32/62 *Stan Kenton*
38/62 *Walter Brennan*
89/62 *Bill Anderson*
34/56 **Mama, Teach Me To Dance** *Eydie Gorme*
Mama Told Me (Not To Come)
1/70 *Three Dog Night*
99/72 *Wilson Pickett*
30/82 **Mama Used To Say** *Junior*
77/73 **Mama Was A Rock And Roll Singer** *Sonny & Chér*
Mama Weer All Crazee Now
76/73 *Slade*
51/84 *Quiet Riot*
18S/02 **Mama's Baby, Poppa's Maybe** *Green Eyez*
2/71 **Mama's Pearl** *Jackson 5*
39/01 **Mamacita** *Public Announcement*
71/75 **Mamacita** *Grass Roots*
9/54 **Mambo Italiano** *Rosemary Clooney*
Mambo No. 5 (A Little Bit Of...)
3/99 *Lou Bega*
33S/99 *Latin Lou & The Mambo All-Stars*
40S/02 *Lou Bega*
18/55 **Mambo Rock** *Bill Haley*
Mame
19/66 *Herb Alpert*
53/66 *Bobby Darin*
81/66 *Louis Armstrong*
Mamma Mia
32/76 *Abba*
63S/00 *A*Teens*
42/78 **Mammas Don't Let Your Babies Grow Up To Be Cowboys** *Waylon Jennings & Willie Nelson*
Mammy Blue
57/71 *Pop-Tops*
50/73 *Stories*

MAN:

72/65 **Man, The** *Lorne Greene*
86/87 **Man Against The World** *Survivor*
82/99 **Man Ain't Made Of Stone** *Randy Travis*
42/68 **Man And A Half** *Wilson Pickett*
88/66 **Man And A Woman** *Tamiko Jones with Herbie Mann*
F/72 **Man & The Woman** *Chi-Lites*
Man And Woman ..see: Suite
84/98 **Man Behind The Music** *Queen Pen*
16/55 **Man Chases A Girl** *Eddie Fisher*
81/98 **Man Holdin' On (To A Woman Lettin' Go)** *Ty Herndon*
23/99 **Man! I Feel Like A Woman!** *Shania Twain*
31/79 **Man I'll Never Be** *Boston*
58/71 **Man In Black** *Johnny Cash*
73S/94 **Man In Love With You** *George Strait*
1/88 **Man In The Mirror** *Michael Jackson*
Man In The Raincoat
14/55 *Marion Marlowe*
16/55 *Priscilla Wright*
63/68 **Man Needs A Woman** *James Carr*
85/70 **Man Of Constant Sorrow** *Ginger Baker's Air Force*
40/82 **Man On The Corner** *Genesis*
30/93 **Man On The Moon** *R.E.M.*
14/82 **Man On Your Mind** *Little River Band*
15/86 **Man Size Love** *Klymaxx*
55/72 **Man Sized Job** *Denise LaSalle*
63/77 **Man Smart, Woman Smarter** *Robert Palmer*
86/74 **Man That Turned My Mama On** *Tanya Tucker*
4/62 **(Man Who Shot) Liberty Valance** *Gene Pitney*
39A/95 **Man Who Sold The World** *Nirvana*
3X/64 **Man With All The Toys** *Beach Boys*
85/79 **Man With The Child In His Eyes** *Kate Bush*
Man With The Golden Arm (Main Title/Molly-O/Delilah Jones)
14/56 *Richard Maltby*
16/56 *Elmer Bernstein*
22/56 *Dick Jacobs*
37/56 *McGuire Sisters*
49/56 *Billy May*
56/56 *Les Elgart*
82/56 *Buddy Morrow*
19/68 **Man Without Love (Quando M'innamoro)** *Engelbert Humperdinck*
71/63 **Man's Temptation** *Gene Chandler*
84/78 **Mañana** *Jimmy Buffett*
4/87 **Mandolin Rain** *Bruce Hornsby*
47/58 **Mandolins In The Moonlight** *Perry Como*
94/71 **Mandrill** *Mandrill*
Mandy
91/72 *Scott English (Brandy)*
1/75 *Barry Manilow*
1/82 **Maneater** *Daryl Hall & John Oates*
10/57 **Mangos** *Rosemary Clooney*
Manhattan Spiritual
10/59 *Reg Owen*
56/75 *Mike Post*
1/83 **Maniac** *Michael Sembello*
2/86 **Manic Monday** *Bangles*
97/58 **Many A Time** *Steve Lawrence*
84/60 **Many A Wonderful Moment** *Rosemary Clooney*

75S/93 **Many Clouds Of Smoke** *Total Devastation*
7/60 **Many Tears Ago** *Connie Francis*
73S/95 **Many Ways** *Usher*
80/66 **Marble Breaks And Iron Bends** *Drafi*
March From The River Kwai and Colonel Bogey
20/58 *Mitch Miller*
75/58 *Edmundo Ros*
88/58 *Art Mooney*
59/94 **March Of The Pigs** *Nine Inch Nails*
88/62 **March Of The Siamese Children** *Kenny Ball*
96/63 **Marching Thru Madrid** *Herb Alpert*
96/71 **Mare, Take Me Home** *Matthews' Southern Comfort*
8/77 **Margaritaville** *Jimmy Buffett*
51/59 **Margie** *Fats Domino*
44/92 **Maria** *TKA*
Maria
78/60 *Johnny Mathis*
48/62 *Roger Williams*
88/62 *Johnny Mathis*
82/99 **Maria** *Blondie*
88/96 **Maria** *Ricky Martin*
6/63 **Maria Elena** *Los Indios Tabajaras*
Maria Maria
1/00 *Santana Feat. The Product G&B*
59S/01 *Santana Feat. The Product G&B*
97/71 **Maria (You Were The Only One)** *Jimmy Ruffin*
86/62 **Marianna** *Johnny Mathis*
Marianne
3/57 *Hilltoppers*
4/57 *Terry Gilkyson & The Easy Riders*
64/57 *Lane Brothers*
84/57 *Burl Ives*
42/71 **Marianne** *Stephen Stills*
15/65 **Marie** *Bachelors*
4/61 **(Marie's the Name) His Latest Flame** *Elvis Presley*
82/56 **Marimba Charleston** *Marimba Chiapas*
Marina
31/59 *Rocco Granata*
42/59 *Willy Alberti*
87/59 *Jacky Noguez*
36/63 **Marlena** *Four Seasons*
70/69 **Marley Purt Drive** *José Feliciano*
28/69 **Marrakesh Express** *Crosby, Stills & Nash*
75/56 **Married I Can Always Get** *Teddi King*
64/65 **Married Man** *Richard Burton*
40/79 **Married Men** *Bette Midler*
73/78 **Martha (Your Lovers Come And Go)** *Gabriel*
59/77 **Martian Boogie** *Brownsville Station*
16/63 **Martian Hop** *Ran-Dells*
93/92 **Martika's Kitchen** *Martika*
88/59 **Martinique** *Martin Denny*
43/64 **Marvelous Toy** *Chad Mitchell Trio*
39/62 **Mary Ann Regrets** *Burl Ives*
90/59 **Mary Ann Thomas** *Bobby Freeman*
41/60 **Mary Don't You Weep** *Stonewall Jackson*
28/72 **Mary Had A Little Lamb** *Wings*
79/76 **Mary Hartman, Mary Hartman (Theme)** *Deadly Nightshade*
27/67 **Mary In The Morning** *Al Martino*
41/79 **Mary Jane** *Rick James*
14/94 **Mary Jane's Last Dance** *Tom Petty*
26/59 **Mary Lou** *Ronnie Hawkins*
75/88 **Mary, Mary** *Run-D.M.C.*
Mary's Boy Child
12/56 *Harry Belafonte*
85/78 *Boney M (medley)*
39/62 **Mary's Little Lamb** *James Darren*
23/87 **Mary's Prayer** *Danny Wilson*
47/66 **Mas Que Nada** *Sergio Mendes*
M*A*S*H ..see: Song From
2/62 **Mashed Potato Time** *Dee Dee Sharp*
Mashed Potatoes
84/60 *Nat Kendrick (Do The)*
81/62 *Steve Alaimo*
82/62 **Mashed Potatoes U.S.A.** *James Brown*
82/83 **Masquerade** *Berlin*
67/94 **Mass Appeal** *Gang Starr*
Massachusetts ..see: (Lights Went Out In)
87/85 **Master And Servant** *Depeche Mode*
Master Blaster (Jammin')
5/80 *Stevie Wonder*
71S/01 *Darrell Labrado*
18/68 **Master Jack** *Four Jacks & A Jill*
33/73 **Master Of Eyes** *Aretha Franklin*
3/92 **Masterpiece** *Atlantic Starr*
7/73 **Masterpiece** *Temptations*
20/64 **Matador, The** *Major Lance*
44/63 **Matador, The** *Johnny Cash*
17/64 **Matchbox** *Beatles*
2/85 **Material Girl** *Madonna*
74/85 **Mathematics** *Melissa Manchester*
47/59 **Matilda** *Cookie & His Cupcakes*
(also see: Twistin' Matilda)
10/86 **Matter Of Trust** *Billy Joel*
52S/01 **Matthew, Mark, Luke and Earnhardt** *Shane Sellers*
68/59 **Mau-Mau** *Wailers*
39/69 **May I** *Bill Deal*
63/68 **May I Take A Giant Step (Into Your Heart)** *1910 Fruitgum Co.*
85/66 **May My Heart Be Cast Into Stone** *Toys*
15/65 **May The Bird Of Paradise Fly Up Your Nose** *"Little" Jimmy Dickens*
May You Always
11/59 *McGuire Sisters*
26X/65 *Harry Harrison*
9S/01 **Maybe** *Mpress*
Maybe
15/58 *Chantels*
91/65 *Shangri-Las*
29/70 *Three Degrees*
17/58 **Maybe Baby** *Crickets*
38/01 **Maybe I Deserve** *Tank*
14/64 **Maybe I Know** *Lesley Gore*
22/79 **Maybe I'm A Fool** *Eddie Money*
10/77 **Maybe I'm Amazed** *Wings*
46/68 **Maybe Just Today** *Bobby Vee*
57/94 **Maybe Love Will Change Your Mind** *Stevie Nicks*
86/99 **Maybe Not Tonight** *Sammy Kershaw & Lorrie Morgan*
61/69 **Maybe The Rain Will Fall** *Cascades*
87/83 **Maybe This Day** *Kissing The Pink*
20/71 **Maybe Tomorrow** *Jackson 5*
67/69 **Maybe Tomorrow** *Iveys*
88/64 **Maybe Tonight** *Shirelles*
Maybellene
5/55 *Chuck Berry*
12/64 *Johnny Rivers*
72/89 **Mayor Of Simpleton** *XTC*

ME:

35A/98 **Me** *Paula Cole*
Me About You
83/67 *Mojo Men*
91/69 *Lovin' Spoonful*
15/74 **Me And Baby Brother** *War*
Me And Bobby McGee
1/71 *Janis Joplin*
40/72 *Jerry Lee Lewis*
98/72 **Me And Jesus** *Tom T. Hall*
22/72 **Me And Julio Down By The Schoolyard** *Paul Simon*
Me And Mrs. Jones
1/72 *Billy Paul*
47/75 *Dramatics*
34/71 **Me And My Arrow** *Nilsson*
86/72 **Me And My Baby Got A Good Thing Going** *Lyn Collins*
52/97 **Me And My Crazy World** *Lost Boyz*
64/62 **Me And My Shadow** *Frank Sinatra & Sammy Davis Jr.*
74/96 **Me And Those Dreamin' Eyes Of Mine** *D'Angelo*
5/71 **Me And You And A Dog Named Boo** *Lobo*
74/64 **Me Japanese Boy I Love You** *Bobby Goldsboro*
78/90 **Me - U = Blue** *Glenn Medeiros*
27S/00 **Me, Myself And I** *Vitamin C*
34/89 **Me Myself And I** *De La Soul*
85/00 **Me Neither** *Brad Paisley*
26/89 **Me So Horny** *2 Live Crew*
53/68 **Me, The Peaceful Heart** *Lulu*
22S/02 **Me U Want** *Kya-Pi*
40/81 **Me (Without You)** *Andy Gibb*
95/65 **Me Without You** *Mary Wells*
54S/91 **Mea Culpa** *Enigma*
89/74 **Meadows** *Joe Walsh*
92/72 **Mean Little Woman, Rosalie** *Tommy Roe*
47/71 **Mean Mistreater** *Grand Funk Railroad*
96/65 **Mean Old World** *Rick Nelson*
5/63 **Mean Woman Blues** *Roy Orbison*
38/99 **Meanwhile** *George Strait*
80/00 **Meanwhile Back At The Ranch** *Clark Family Experience*
12/63 **Mecca** *Gene Pitney*
"Medic" Theme ..see: Blue Star
22/69 **Medicine Man** *Buchanan Brothers*
65/84 **Medicine Song** *Stephanie Mills*
Meditation (Meditacao)
66/63 *Charlie Byrd*
91/63 *Pat Boone*
98/66 *Claudine Longet*
95/60 **Mediterranean Moon** *Rays*
1/81 **Medley** *Stars On 45*
67/81 **Medley II** *Stars On 45*
64/84 **Medley: Love Songs Are Back Again** *Band Of Gold*
70/87 **Meet El Presidente** *Duran Duran*
63/62 **Meet Me At The Twistin' Place** *Johnnie Morisette*
11/87 **Meet Me Half Way** *Kenny Loggins*
33/94 **(Meet) The Flintstones** *B-52's*
20/00 **Meet Virginia** *Train*
62/99 **Meeting In My Bedroom** *Silk*
59/85 **Meeting In The Ladies Room** *Klymaxx*
48/65 **Meeting Over Yonder** *Impressions*
62/82 **Mega Force** *707*
54/93 **Mega Medley** *Zapp & Roger*
43/67 **Melancholy Music Man** *Righteous Brothers*
87/70 **Melanie Makes Me Smile** *Tony Burrows*

86/72 **Melissa** *Allman Brothers Band*
65/78 **Mellow Lovin'** *Judy Cheeks*
92/68 **Mellow Moonlight** *Leon Haywood*
Mellow Yellow
2/66 *Donovan*
99/67 *Senator Bobby & Senator McKinley*
5/57 **Melodie D'Amour (Melody of Love)** *Ames Brothers*
74/66 **Melody For An Unknown Girl** *Unknowns*
Melody Of Love
2/55 *Billy Vaughn*
3/55 *Four Aces*
8/55 *David Carroll*
19/55 *Frank Sinatra & Ray Anthony*
30/55 *Leo Diamond*
69/91 **Melt In Your Mouth** *Candyman*
45/71 **Melting Pot** *Booker T. & The M.G.'s*
Memories
35/69 *Elvis Presley*
47/70 *Lettermen (medley)*
62/81 **Memories** *Tierra*
Memories Are Made Of This
1/56 *Dean Martin*
5/56 *Gale Storm*
53/56 *Mindy Carson*
48/66 *Drifters*
71/82 **Memories Of Days Gone By** *Five Satins*
74/62 **Memories Of Maria** *Jerry Byrd*
Memories Of You
22/55 *Four Coins*
20/56 *Benny Goodman/Rosemary Clooney*
62/56 *Hugo Winterhalter*
60/80 **Memorize Your Number** *Leif Garrett*
Memory
52/82 *Barbra Streisand*
39/83 *Barry Manilow*
63/63 **Memory Lane** *Hippies*
28/97 **Memory Remains** *Metallica*
Memphis
5/63 *Lonnie Mack*
2/64 *Johnny Rivers*
85/83 **Memphis** *Joe Jackson*
90/61 **Memphis** *Donnie Brooks*
33/67 **Memphis Soul Stew** *King Curtis*
100/69 **Memphis Train** *Buddy Miles*
Memphis Underground
44/69 *Herbie Mann*
95/69 *Herbie Mann*
Men ..see: Theme From The
80/86 **Men All Pause** *Klymaxx*
33/68 **Men Are Gettin' Scarce** *Joe Tex*
1^{A}/97 **Men In Black** *Will Smith*
6/66 **Men In My Little Girl's Life** *Mike Douglas*
65/72 **Men Of Learning** *Vigrass & Osborne*
82/97 **Men Of Steel** *Shaquille O'Neal, Ice Cube, B Real, Peter Gunz & KRS-One*
94/72 **Mendelssohn's 4th (Second Movement)** *Apollo 100*
27/69 **Mendocino** *Sir Douglas Quintet*
29/95 **Mental Picture** *Jon Secada*
14/90 **Mentirosa** *Mellow Man Ace*
Mercedes Benz ..see: (Oh Lord Won't You Buy Me A)
2/88 **Mercedes Boy** *Pebbles*
30/69 **Mercy** *Ohio Express*
35/64 **Mercy, Mercy** *Don Covay*
Mercy Mercy Me (The Ecology)
4/71 *Marvin Gaye*
16/91 *Robert Palmer (medley)*
Mercy, Mercy, Mercy
5/67 *Buckinghams*
11/67 *"Cannonball" Adderley*
58/67 *Marlena Shaw*
96/67 *Larry Williams & Johnny Watson*
52/81 **Mercy, Mercy, Mercy** *Phoebe Snow*
Merry Christmas Baby
71/58 *Chuck Berry*
4^{X}/64 *Charles Brown*
2^{X}/65 *Charles Brown*
9^{X}/68 *Otis Redding*
2^{X}/73 *Charles Brown*
1^{X}/70 **Merry Christmas Darling** *Carpenters*
82/80 **Merry Christmas In The NFL** *Willis "The Guard" & Vigorish*
61/61 **Merry-Go-Round** *Marv Johnson*
2/03 **Mesmerize** *Ja Rule*
89/61 **Mess Around** *Bobby Freeman*
32/60 **Mess Of Blues** *Elvis Presley*
48/73 **Message, The** *Cymande*
62/82 **Message, The** *Grand Master Flash*
75/92 **Message, The** *Sofia Shinas*
99/70 **Message From A Black Man** *Whatnauts*
75/68 **Message From Maria** *Joe Simon*
74/79 **Message In A Bottle** *Police*
49/76 **Message In Our Music** *O'Jays*
8/66 **Message To Michael** *Dionne Warwick*
66^{S}/00 **Messed Around** *Boyz-N-Girlz United*
69/93 **Method Man** *Wu-Tang Clan*
5/85 **Method Of Modern Love** *Daryl Hall/John Oates*
58/83 **Metro, The** *Berlin*
77/64 **Mexican Drummer Man** *Herb Alpert*
16/58 **Mexican Hat Rock** *Applejacks*
94/65 **Mexican Pearls** *Billy Vaughn*
58/83 **Mexican Radio** *Wall Of Voodoo*
85/64 **Mexican Shuffle** *Herb Alpert*
7/61 **Mexico** *Bob Moore*
49/75 **Mexico** *James Taylor*
50/57 **Mi Casa, Su Casa** *Perry Como*
Miami
17/99 *Will Smith*
61^{S}/99 *Slick*
67/59 **Miami** *Eugene Church*
70/86 **Miami** *Bob Seger*
1/85 **Miami Vice Theme** *Jan Hammer*
Michael
1/61 *Highwaymen*
100/63 *Steve Alaimo*
42/64 *Trini Lopez*
41/66 **Michael** *C.O.D.'s*
Michelle
18/66 *David & Jonathan*
65/66 *Bud Shank*
77/66 *Billy Vaughn*
1/82 **Mickey** *Toni Basil*
(also see: Ricky)
8/63 **Mickey's Monkey** *Miracles*
86/96 **Microphone Master** *DAS EFX*
42/86 **Midas Touch** *Midnight Star*
5/02 **Middle, The** *Jimmy Eat World*
19/84 **Middle Of The Road** *Pretenders*

MIDNIGHT:

Midnight ..also see: Midnite
58/69 **Midnight** *Classics IV*
69/58 **Midnight** *Paul Anka*
76/62 **Midnight** *Johnny Gibson*
(also see: Midnite)
6/74 **Midnight At The Oasis** *Maria Muldaur*
5/87 **Midnight Blue** *Lou Gramm*
6/75 **Midnight Blue** *Melissa Manchester*
46/83 **Midnight Blue** *Louise Tucker*
5/68 **Midnight Confessions** *Grass Roots*
10/70 **Midnight Cowboy** *Ferrante & Teicher*
55/74 **Midnight Flower** *Four Tops*
51/59 **Midnight Flyer** *Nat "King" Cole*
Midnight Hour ..see: In The
57^{A}/97 **Midnight In Chelsea** *Jon Bon Jovi*
2/62 **Midnight In Moscow** *Kenny Ball*
Midnight Lace
84/60 *Ray Ellis*
92/60 *Ray Conniff*
98/60 *David Carroll*
91/78 **Midnight Light** *LeBlanc & Carr*
80/71 **Midnight Man** *James Gang*
10/64 **Midnight Mary** *Joey Powers*
55/59 **Midnight Oil** *Charlie Blackwell*
74/80 **Midnight Rain** *Poco*
72/80 **Midnight Rendezvous** *Babys*
Midnight Rider
27/72 *Joe Cocker*
19/74 *Gregg Allman*
24/80 **Midnight Rocks** *Al Stewart*
73/75 **Midnight Sky** *Isley Brothers*
Midnight Special
16/60 *Paul Evans*
20/65 *Johnny Rivers*
69/62 **Midnight Special** *Jimmy Smith*
35/59 **Midnight Stroll** *Revels*
1/73 **Midnight Train To Georgia** *Gladys Knight*
28/79 **Midnight Wind** *John Stewart*
94/58 **Midnighter** *Champs*
71/84 **Midnite Maniac** *Krokus*
88/01 **Midwest Swing** *St. Lunatics*
91/74 **Might Just Take Your Life** *Deep Purple*
34/71 **Mighty Clouds Of Joy** *B.J. Thomas*
38/59 **Mighty Good** *Ricky Nelson*
51/61 **Mighty Good Lovin'** *Miracles*
69/76 **Mighty High** *Mighty Clouds Of Joy*
43/70 **Mighty Joe** *Shocking Blue*
70^{A}/96 **Mighty K.C.** *For Squirrels*
20/74 **Mighty Love** *Spinners*
29/74 **Mighty Mighty** *Earth, Wind & Fire*
10/68 **Mighty Quinn (Quinn The Eskimo)** *Manfred Mann*
12/91 **Miles Away** *Winger*
63/78 **Miles Away** *Fotomaker*
73/71 **Military Madness** *Graham Nash*
79/61 **Milk Cow Blues** *Ricky Nelson*
90/70 **Mill Valley** *Miss Abrams*
72/99 **Millennium** *Robbie Williams*
33/64 **Miller's Cave** *Bobby Bare*
Million And One
41/66 *Dean Martin*
71/66 *Vic Dana*
82/83 **Million Miles Away** *Plimsouls*
82/58 **Million Miles From Nowhere** *Brook Benton*

Million To One
5/60 *Jimmy Charles*
68/68 *Five Stairsteps*
90/69 *Brian Hyland*
23/73 *Donny Osmond*
95/75 **Millionaire, The** *Dr. Hook*
(also see: How To Be A)
Milord
74/61 *Teresa Brewer*
88/61 *Edith Piaf*
45/64 *Bobby Darin*
46/78 **Mind Bender** *Stillwater*
75/95 **Mind Blowin'** *Smooth*
26/69 **Mind, Body and Soul** *Flaming Ember*
51/66 **Mind Excursion** *Trade Winds*
18/73 **Mind Games** *John Lennon*
23/92 **Mind Playing Tricks On Me** *Geto Boys*
99/66 **Mine Exclusively** *Olympics*
91/74 **Mine For Me** *Rod Stewart*
50/69 **Mini-Skirt Minnie** *Wilson Pickett*
41/83 **Minimum Love** *Mac McAnally*
88/75 **Minnesota** *Northern Light*
38/69 **Minotaur, The** *Dick Hyman*
79/75 **Minstrel In The Gallery** *Jethro Tull*
58/96 **Mint Car** *Cure*
14/79 **Minute By Minute** *Doobie Brothers*
48/69 **Minute Of Your Time** *Tom Jones*
95/63 **Minute You're Gone** *Sonny James*
74/60 **Mio Amore** *Flamingos*
9/91 **Miracle** *Whitney Houston*
12/90 **Miracle** *Jon Bon Jovi*
75/62 **Miracle, A** *Frankie Avalon*
Miracle Of Love
18/56 *Eileen Rodgers*
68/56 *Ginny Gibson*
3/75 **Miracles** *Jefferson Starship*
40/83 **Miracles** *Stacy Lattisaw*
10/67 **Mirage** *Tommy James*
92/80 **Mirage** *Eric Troyer*
30/83 **Mirror Man** *Human League*
8/82 **Mirror, Mirror** *Diana Ross*
62/00 **Mirror Mirror** *M2M*
81/79 **Mirror Star** *Fabulous Poodles*
22/73 **Misdemeanor** *Foster Sylvers*
20/95 **Misery** *Soul Asylum*
44/63 **Misery** *Dynamics*
42/87 **Misfit** *Curiosity Killed The Cat*
38/95 **Mishale** *Andru Donalds*
10/85 **Misled** *Kool & The Gang*
23/94 **Misled** *Celine Dion*

MISS:

Miss ..also see: Ms.
44/70 **Miss America** *Mark Lindsay*
56/57 **Miss Ann** *Little Richard*
92/78 **Miss Broadway** *Belle Epoque*
85/01 **Miss California** *Dante Thomas*
69/61 **Miss Fine** *New Yorkers*
5/84 **Miss Me Blind** *Culture Club*
14/81 **Miss Sun** *Boz Scaggs*
1/78 **Miss You** *Rolling Stones*
3/03 **Miss You** *Aaliyah*
78/59 **Miss You** *Jaye P. Morgan*
39/94 **Miss You In A Heartbeat** *Def Leppard*
7/89 **Miss You Like Crazy** *Natalie Cole*
1/89 **Miss You Much** *Janet Jackson*
66/57 **Miss You So** *Lillian Offitt*
29/88 **Missed Opportunity** *Daryl Hall/John Oates*
2/96 **Missing** *Everything But The Girl*
44/56 **Missing** *McGuire Sisters*
Missing You
1/84 *John Waite*
84/96 *Tina Turner*
75/99 *Brooks & Dunn*
4/01 **Missing You** *Case*
10/85 **Missing You** *Diana Ross*
23/82 **Missing You** *Dan Fogelberg*
25/96 **Missing You** *Brandy, Tamia, Gladys Knight & Chaka Khan*
29/61 **Missing You** *Ray Peterson*
74/94 **Missing You** *Steve Perry*
12/92 **Missing You Now** *Michael Bolton Feat. Kenny G*
7/60 **Mission Bell** *Donnie Brooks*
Mission-Impossible ..see: Theme From
14/86 **Missionary Man** *Eurythmics*
32/70 **Mississippi** *John Phillips*
70/74 **Mississippi Cotton Picking Delta Town** *Charley Pride*
97/70 **Mississippi Mama** *Owen B.*
21/70 **Mississippi Queen** *Mountain*
42/90 **Missunderstanding** *Al B. Sure!*
33/85 **Mistake No. 3** *Culture Club*
60/81 **Mistaken Identity** *Kim Carnes*
Mister ..see: Mr.
5X/73 **Mistletoe And Me** *Isaac Hayes*
49/79 **Mistrusted Love** *Mistress*
Misty
12/59 *Johnny Mathis*
21/63 *Lloyd Price*
63/65 *Vibrations*
44/66 *"Groove" Holmes*
14/75 *Ray Stevens*
Misty Blue
57/67 *Eddy Arnold*
91/72 *Joe Simon*
3/76 *Dorothy Moore*
14/80 **Misunderstanding** *Genesis*
(also see: Missunderstanding)
5/89 **Mixed Emotions** *Rolling Stones*
73/71 **Mixed Up Guy** *Joey Scarbury*
37/64 **Mixed-Up, Shook-Up, Girl** *Patty & The Emblems*
4/94 **Mmm Mmm Mmm Mmm** *Crash Test Dummies*
Mo Money Mo Problems
1/97 *Notorious B.I.G.*
63S/01 *Notorious B.I.G.*
97/64 **Mo-Onions** *Booker T. & The MG's*
76/98 **Moan & Groan** *Mark Morrison*
Mocking Bird, The
67/56 *Four Lads*
32/58 *Four Lads*
(also see: Sweet Bird Of Youth)
Mockingbird
7/63 *Inez Foxx (with Charlie Foxx)*
94/67 *Aretha Franklin*
5/74 *Carly Simon & James Taylor*
66A/95 **Mockingbird Girl** *Magnificent Bastards*
20/61 **Model Girl** *Johnny Mastro*
55/02 **Modern Day Bonnie And Clyde** *Travis Tritt*
22/84 **Modern Day Delilah** *Van Stephenson*
18/81 **Modern Girl** *Sheena Easton*
14/83 **Modern Love** *David Bowie*
32S/02 **Modern Man's Hustle** *Atmosphere*
10/86 **Modern Woman** *Billy Joel*
21/65 **Mohair Sam** *Charlie Rich*
90/60 **Mojo Workout (Dance)** *Larry Bright*
70/63 **Molly** *Bobby Goldsboro*
Molly-O ..see: Man With The Golden Arm
55/95 **Molly (Sixteen Candles)** *Sponge*
58/61 **Mom And Dad's Waltz** *Patti Page*
63/96 **Moment, The** *Kenny G*
59/79 **Moment By Moment** *Yvonne Elliman*
1/02 **Moment Like This** *Kelly Clarkson*
63/84 **Moment Of Truth** *Survivor*
50/62 **Moments** *Jennell Hawkins*
Moments To Remember
2/55 *Four Lads*
47/69 *Vogues*
Mona Lisa
25/59 *Carl Mann*
29/59 *Conway Twitty*
1/66 **Monday, Monday** *Mama's & The Papa's*

MONEY:

13/73 **Money** *Pink Floyd*
48/68 **Money** *Lovin' Spoonful*
50/75 **Money** *Gladys Knight*
70A/98 **Money** *Charli Baltimore*
75S/01 **Money** *Jelleestone*
52/98 **Money Ain't A Thang** *JD*
72/72 **Money Back Guarantee** *Five Man Electrical Band*
54/92 **Money Can't Buy You Love** *Ralph Tresvant*
27/85 **Money Changes Everything** *Cyndi Lauper*
23/92 **Money Don't Matter 2 Night** *Prince*
1/85 **Money For Nothing** *Dire Straits*
9/76 **Money Honey** *Bay City Rollers*
76/56 **Money Honey** *Elvis Presley*
90/94 **Money In The Ghetto** *Too $hort*
56/77 **Money, Money, Money** *Abba*
17/98 **Money, Power & Respect** *Lox*
57/72 **Money Runner** *Quincy Jones*
23/91 **Moneytalks** *AC/DC*
Money (That's what I want)
23/60 *Barrett Strong*
16/64 *Kingsmen*
52/66 *Jr. Walker*
50/80 *Flying Lizards*
Money Tree
20/56 *Margaret Whiting*
73/57 *Patience & Prudence*
53/66 **Money Won't Change You** *James Brown*
54/98 **Money's Just A Touch Away** *Mack 10*
28/86 **Money$ Too Tight (To Mention)** *Simply Red*
50/70 **Mongoose** *Elephant's Memory*
77/00 **Monica** *Before Dark*
1/88 **Monkey** *George Michael*
(also see: Do The)
65S/91 **Monkey Business** *Skid Row*
47/63 **Monkey-Shine** *Bill Black's Combo*
Monkey Time
8/63 *Major Lance*
68/83 *Tubes*
58A/97 **Monkey Wrench** *Foo Fighters*
39/70 **Monster** *Steppenwolf*
85/91 **Monster** *Fred Schneider*
Monster Mash
1/62 *Bobby "Boris" Pickett*
91/70 *Bobby "Boris" Pickett*
10/73 *Bobby "Boris" Pickett*
74/91 **Monsters And Angels** *Voice Of The Beehive*
30/62 **Monsters' Holiday** *Bobby "Boris" Pickett*
Montage From ..see: How Sweet It Is

Montego Bay
8/70 *Bobby Bloom*
90/87 *Amazulu*
15/68 **Monterey** *Animals*
Mony Mony
3/68 *Tommy James*
1/87 *Billy Idol*
31/77 **Moody Blue** *Elvis Presley*
1/61 **Moody River** *Pat Boone*
24/69 **Moody Woman** *Jerry Butler*

MOON:

59/65 **Moon Over Naples** *Bert Kaempfert*
Moon River
11/61 *Jerry Butler*
11/61 *Henry Mancini*
30/71 **Moon Shadow** *Cat Stevens*
28/58 **Moon Talk** *Perry Como*
54/70 **Moon Walk** *Joe Simon*
99/62 **Moon Was Yellow** *Frank Sinatra*
92/77 **Moondance** *Van Morrison*
38/69 **Moonflight** *Vik Venus*
Moonglow and Theme From "Picnic"
1/56 *Morris Stoloff*
4/56 *George Cates*
13/56 *McGuire Sisters (Picnic)*
64/56 *Ralph Marterie (Picnic)*
51/65 **Moonlight And Roses** *Vic Dana*
72/58 **Moonlight Bay** *Drifters*
3/76 **Moonlight Feels Right** *Starbuck*
3/57 **Moonlight Gambler** *Frankie Laine*
42/56 **Moonlight Love** *Perry Como*
Moonlight On Water
60/89 *Kevin Raleigh*
59/90 *Laura Branigan*
Moonlight Serenade
47/59 *Rivieras*
97/76 *Bobby Vinton*
87/69 **Moonlight Sonata** *Henry Mancini*
73/74 **Moonlight Special** *Ray Stevens*
Moonlight Swim
24/57 *Tony Perkins*
37/57 *Nick Noble*
23/87 **Moonlighting (Theme)** *Al Jarreau*
72/58 **Moovin' N' Groovin'** *Duane Eddy*

MORE:

More ..also see: Mo
4/56 **More** *Perry Como*
More
8/63 *Kai Winding*
42/63 *Vic Dana*
65/00 **More** *Trace Adkins*
17/93 **More And More** *Captain Hollywood Project*
88/67 **More And More** *Andy Williams*
94/75 **More And More** *Carly Simon*
86/80 **More Bounce To The Ounce** *Zapp*
22S/99 **More Freaky Tales** *Too $hort*
53A/95 **More Human Than Human** *White Zombie*
(More I Love You) ..see: Lo Mucho Que Te Quiero
16/66 **More I See You** *Chris Montez*
More Love
23/67 *Miracles*
10/80 *Kim Carnes*
17/61 **More Money For You And Me** *Four Preps*
4/76 **More, More, More** *Andrea True Connection*
55/81 **More Stars** *More Stars on 45*
(also see: Medley / Stars On 45 III)
5/76 **More Than A Feeling** *Boston*
25/02 **More Than A Woman** *Aaliyah*
32/78 **More Than A Woman** *Tavares*
14/91 **More Than Ever** *Nelson*
More Than I Can Say
61/61 *Bobby Vee*
2/80 *Leo Sayer*
90/70 **More Than I Can Stand** *Bobby Womack*
34/82 **More Than Just The Two Of Us** *Sneaker*
73/86 **More Than Physical** *Bananarama*
27/01 **More Than That** *Backstreet Boys*
54/67 **More Than The Eye Can See** *Al Martino*
25/97 **More Than This** *10,000 Maniacs*
1/91 **More Than Words** *Extreme*
2/90 **More Than Words Can Say** *Alias*
18/89 **More Than You Know** *Martika*
12/69 **More Today Than Yesterday** *Spiral Starecase*
62/76 **More You Do It (The More I Like It Done To Me)** *Ronnie Dyson*
46/94 **More You Ignore Me, The Closer I Get** *Morrissey*
56/84 **More You Live, The More You Love** *Flock Of Seagulls*
Morgen
13/59 *Ivo Robic*
98/59 *Leslie Uggams (One More Sunrise)*
Moritat ..see: Mack The Knife

MORNIN'/MORNING:

21/83 **Mornin'** *Al Jarreau*
47/70 **Morning** *Jim Ed Brown*
14/75 **Mornin' Beautiful** *Tony Orlando & Dawn*
74/68 **Mornin' Glory** *Bobbie Gentry & Glen Campbell*
78/70 **Mornin Mornin** *Bobby Goldsboro*
1/73 **Morning After** *Maureen McGovern*
60/61 **Morning After** *Mar-Keys*
24/79 **Morning Dance** *Spyro Gyra*
72/85 **Morning Desire** *Kenny Rogers*
52/68 **Morning Dew** *Lulu*
17/69 **Morning Girl** *Neon Philharmonic*
6/72 **Morning Has Broken** *Cat Stevens*
68/80 **Morning Man** *Rupert Holmes*
74/70 **Morning Much Better** *Ten Wheel Drive w/Genya Ravan*
60/71 **Morning Of Our Lives** *Arkade*
44/93 **Morning Papers** *Prince*
Morning Side Of The Mountain
27/59 *Tommy Edwards*
8/75 *Donny & Marie Osmond*
1/81 **Morning Train (Nine To Five)** *Sheena Easton*
44/67 **Morningtown Ride** *Seekers*
85/72 **Mosquito, The** *Doors*
1/73 **Most Beautiful Girl** *Charlie Rich*
70S/98 **Most Beautiful Girl** *Raheem*
3/94 **Most Beautiful Girl In The World** *Prince*
67/61 **Most Beautiful Words** *Della Reese*
50/94 **Most Beautifullest Thing In This World** *Keith Murray*
4/00 **Most Girls** *P!nk*
66/74 **Most Likely You Go Your Way (And I'll Go Mine)** *Bob Dylan/The Band*
14/55 **Most Of All** *Don Cornell*
38/71 **Most Of All** *B.J. Thomas*
60/88 **Most Of All** *Jody Watley*
27/62 **Most People Get Married** *Patti Page*
74A/97 **Most Precarious** *Blues Traveler*
31/56 **Mostly Martha** *Crew Cuts*

MOTHER:

9S/02 **Mother** *Ray Charles*
Mother
43/71 *John Lennon*
79/71 *Barbra Streisand*
43/94 **Mother** *Danzig*
4/72 **Mother And Child Reunion** *Paul Simon*
92/74 **Mother For My Children** *Whispers*
37/71 **Mother Freedom** *Bread*
Mother-In-Law
1/61 *Ernie K-Doe*
80/73 *Clarence Carter*
(also see: Son-In-Law)
32A/96 **Mother Mother** *Tracy Bonham*
92/72 **Mother Nature** *Temptations*
53/65 **Mother Nature, Father Time** *Brook Benton*
88/71 **Mother Nature's Wine** *Sugarloaf*
88/63 **Mother, Please!** *Jo Ann Campbell*
11/69 **Mother Popcorn** *James Brown*
46/91 **Mother's Pride** *George Michael*
8/66 **Mothers Little Helper** *Rolling Stones*
27/86 **Mothers Talk** *Tears For Fears*
87/88 **Motion Of Love** *Gene Loves Jezebel*
28S/02 **Motivation** *Sum 41*
99/62 **Motorcycle** *Tico & The Triumphs*
12/72 **Motorcycle Mama** *Sailcat*
36/87 **Motortown** *Kane Gang*
67/79 **Motown Review** *Philly Cream*
10/91 **Motown Song** *Rod Stewart (w/The Temptations)*
3/91 **Motownphilly** *Boyz II Men*
90/66 **Moulty** *Barbarians*
Mountain Of Love
21/60 *Harold Dorman*
9/64 *Johnny Rivers*
67/68 *Ronnie Dove*
100/66 **Mountain Of Love** *Billy Stewart*
2/61 **Mountain's High** *Dick & DeeDee*
23/86 **Mountains** *Prince*
51/97 **Mourn You Til I Join You** *Naughty By Nature*
76/65 **Mouse, The** *Soupy Sales*
4/96 **Mouth** *Merril Bainbridge*
63A/97 **Mouth** *Bush*

MOVE:

38/92 **Move Any Mountain (Progen 91)** *Shamen*
12/86 **Move Away** *Culture Club*
10/02 **Move B***h** *Ludacris*
59/72 **Move 'Em Out** *Delaney & Bonnie*
58/69 **Move In A Little Closer, Baby** *Mama Cass*
5S/02 **Move It Like This** *Baha Men*
54/95 **Move It Like This** *K7*
83/95 **Move It To The Rhythm** *Technotronic*
99/70 **Move Me, O Wondrous Music** *Ray Charles Singers*
31/69 **Move Over** *Steppenwolf*
81/91 **Move Right Out** *Rick Astley*
26S/00 **Move Somethin'** *Talib Kweli & Hi-Tek*
6/92 **Move This** *Technotronic*
Move Two Mountains ..see: (You've Got To)
57/80 **Move Your Boogie Body** *Bar-Kays*
65/95 **Mover La Colita** *Artie The 1 Man Party*
Movin' ..also see: Moovin'
14/76 **Movin'** *Brass Construction*
41/61 **Movin'** *Bill Black's Combo*

19/75 **Movin' On** *Bad Company*

34/98 **Movin' On** *Mya*

83/96 **Movin' On** *CeCe Peniston*

17/78 **Movin' Out (Anthony's Song)** *Billy Joel*

34/94 **Moving On Up** *M People*

54/76 **Mozambique** *Bob Dylan*

67/71 **Mozart Symphony No. 40 In G Minor** *Waldo De Los Rios*

MR:

16/63 **Mr. Bass Man** *Johnny Cymbal*

2/71 **Mr. Big Stuff** *Jean Knight*

1/59 **Mr. Blue** *Fleetwoods*

35/78 **Mr. Blue Sky** *Electric Light Orchestra*

Mr. Bojangles

77/68 *Jerry Jeff Walker*

79/68 *Bobby Cole*

9/71 *Nitty Gritty Dirt Band*

90/67 **Mr. Bus Driver** *Bruce Channel*

28/68 **Mr. Businessman** *Ray Stevens*

38/72 **Mister Can't You See** *Buffy Sainte-Marie*

1/60 **Mr. Custer** *Larry Verne*

53/75 **Mr. D.J. (5 For The D.J.)** *Aretha Franklin*

17/66 **Mr. Dieingly Sad** *Critters*

Mr. Dream Merchant ..see: Dream Merchant

86/67 **Mr. Farmer** *Seeds*

71/57 **Mister Fire Eyes** *Bonnie Guitar*

57/61 **Mr. Happiness** *Johnny Maestro*

90/96 **Mr. Ice Cream Man** *Master P*

4/75 **Mr. Jaws** *Dickie Goodman*

5[A]/94 **Mr. Jones** *Counting Crows*

6/57 **Mr. Lee** *Bobbettes*

97/69 **Mr. Limousine Driver** *Grand Funk Railroad*

75/60 **Mister Livingston** *Larry Verne*

Mr. Lonely

64/62 *Buddy Greco*

1/64 *Bobby Vinton*

73/60 **Mister Lonely** *Videls*

40/92 **Mr. Loverman** *Shabba Ranks*

21/60 **Mr. Lucky** *Henry Mancini*

54/75 **Mister Magic** *Grover Washington, Jr.*

98/73 **Mr. Magic Man** *Wilson Pickett*

49/76 **Mr. Melody** *Natalie Cole*

93/74 **Mr. Natural** *Bee Gees*

96/68 **Mister Nico** *Four Jacks & A Jill*

63/72 **Mr. Penguin** *Lunar Funk*

42/95 **Mr. Personality** *Gillette*

41/65 **Mr. Pitiful** *Otis Redding*

80/67 **Mr. Pleasant** *Kinks*

73/74 **Mr. President** *Dickie Goodman*

91/61 **Mr. Pride** *Chuck Jackson*

3/83 **Mr. Roboto** *Styx*

Mister Sandman

1/54 *Chordettes*

5/55 *Four Aces*

37/81 *Emmylou Harris*

92/73 **Mr. Skin** *Spirit*

43/62 **Mr. Songwriter** *Connie Stevens*

36/66 **Mr. Spaceman** *Byrds*

41/58 **Mr. Success** *Frank Sinatra*

18/69 **Mr. Sun, Mr. Moon** *Paul Revere & The Raiders*

1/65 **Mr. Tambourine Man** *Byrds*

12/85 **Mr. Telephone Man** *New Edition*

76/00 **Mr. Too Damn Good** *Gerald Levert*

17/94 **Mr. Vain** *Culture Beat*

80/69 **Mr. Walker, It's All Over** *Billie Jo Spears*

6/93 **Mr. Wendal** *Arrested Development*

92/63 **Mr. Wishing Well** *Nat King Cole*

Mr. Wonderful

13/56 *Sarah Vaughan*

14/56 *Peggy Lee*

18/56 *Teddi King*

69/68 **Mrs. Bluebird** *Eternity's Children*

1/65 **Mrs. Brown You've Got A Lovely Daughter** *Herman's Hermits*

Mrs. Robinson

1/68 *Simon & Garfunkel*

37/69 *Booker T. & The M.G.'s*

44/01 **Mrs. Steven Rudy** *Mark McGuinn*

91/74 **Ms. Grace** *Tymes*

1/01 **Ms. Jackson** *OutKast*

95/98 **Much Better** *Club 69*

53/69 **Muddy Mississippi Line** *Bobby Goldsboro*

41/69 **Muddy River** *Johnny Rivers*

Muddy Water ..see: (I Washed My Hands In)

Muhammad Ali ..see: Black Superman

82/68 **Mule** *James Boys*

5/60 **Mule Skinner Blues** *Fendermen*

30/62 **Multiplication** *Bobby Darin*

80/60 **Mumblin' Mosie** *Johnny Otis Show*

18/98 **Mummers' Dance** *Loreena McKennitt*

39/59 **Mummy, The** *Bob McFadden & Dor*

39[S]/02 **Murder On The Dancefloor** *Sophie Ellis Bextor*

57/93 **Murder She Wrote** *Chaka Demus & Pliers*

67[A]/94 **Murder Was The Case** *Snoop Doggy Dogg*

39/82 **Murphy's Law** *Cheri*

10/82 **Muscles** *Diana Ross*

39/67 **Museum** *Herman's Hermits*

1/00 **Music** *Madonna*

22/01 **Music** *Erick Sermon*

88/76 **Music** *John Miles*

75/79 **Music Box** *Evelyn "Champagne" King*

3/79 **Music Box Dancer** *Frank Mills*

68/73 **Music Everywhere** *Tufano & Giammarese*

95/74 **Music Eyes** *Heartsfield*

84/72 **Music From Across The Way** *James Last*

57/78 **Music, Harmony And Rhythm** *Brooklyn Dreams*

92/75 **Music In My Bones** *Joe Simon*

95/71 **Music Is Love** *David Crosby*

F/76 **Music Is My Life** *Helen Reddy*

51/96 **Music Makes Me High** *Lost Boyz*

Music, Music, Music

54/61 *Sensations*

96/68 *Happenings*

81/75 **Music Never Stopped** *Grateful Dead*

2/99 **Music Of My Heart** **NSYNC & Gloria Estefan*

62/98 **Music Sounds Better With You** *Stardust*

40/84 **Music Time** *Styx*

Music To Watch Girls By

15/67 *Bob Crewe Generation*

34/67 *Andy Williams*

82/61 **Muskrat** *Everly Brothers*

Muskrat Love

67/73 *America*

4/76 *Captain & Tennille*

54/61 **Muskrat Ramble** *Freddy Cannon*

54/74 **Must Be Love** *James Gang*

83/79 **Must Have Been Crazy** *Chicago*

12/75 **Must Of Got Lost** *J. Geils Band*

8/66 **Must To Avoid** *Herman's Hermits*

23/66 **Mustang Sally** *Wilson Pickett*

Mutual Admiration Society

21/56 *Teresa Brewer*

47/56 *Eddy Arnold & Jaye P. Morgan*

62/86 **Mutual Surrender (What A Wonderful World)** *Bourgeois Tagg*

57[A]/96 **Muzzle** *Smashing Pumpkins*

MY:

My Airplane ..see: Airplane Song

1/98 **My All** *Mariah Carey*

13/78 **My Angel Baby** *Toby Beau*

92/66 **My Answer** *Jimmy McCracklin*

50/67 **My Babe** *Ronnie Dove*

75/63 **My Babe** *Righteous Brothers*

99/66 **My Babe** *Roy Head*

3/01 **My Baby** *Lil' Romeo*

13/65 **My Baby** *Temptations*

64/87 **My Baby** *Pretenders*

10/97 **MyBabyDaddy** *B-Rock & The Bizz*

51/64 **My Baby Don't Dig Me** *Ray Charles*

(My Baby Don't Love Me) ..see: No More

31/56 **My Baby Left Me** *Elvis Presley*

13/70 **My Baby Loves Lovin'** *White Plains*

22/66 **My Baby Loves Me** *Martha & The Vandellas*

94/97 **My Baby Mama** *QT*

17/68 **My Baby Must Be A Magician** *Marvelettes*

(My Baby Shot Me Down) ..see: Bang Bang

70/00 **My Baby You** *Marc Anthony*

45/79 **My Baby's Baby** *Liquid Gold*

32[C]/56 **My Baby's Got Such Lovin' Ways** *McGuire Sisters*

30/67 **My Back Pages** *Byrds*

34[S]/02 **My Bad** *Rayvon*

87/69 **My Balloon's Going Up** *Archie Bell*

49/56 **My Believing Heart** *Joni James*

29/00 **My Best Friend** *Tim McGraw*

35/78 **My Best Friend's Girl** *Cars*

80/77 **My Best Friend's Wife** *Paul Anka*

67/63 **My Block** *Four Pennies*

My Blue Heaven

19/56 *Fats Domino*

50/61 *Duane Eddy*

4/97 **My Body** *LSG*

42/91 **My Body Says Yes** *Titiyo*

11/55 **My Bonnie Lassie** *Ames Brothers* *(also see: Theme From Tunes Of Glory)*

26/64 **My Bonnie (My Bonnie Lies Over The Ocean)** *Beatles/Tony Sheridan* *(also see: Bonnie Came Back)*

31/96 **My Boo** *Ghost Town DJ's*

21/62 **My Boomerang Won't Come Back** *Charlie Drake*

My Boy

41/72 *Richard Harris*

20/75 *Elvis Presley*

My Boy - Flat Top

16/55 *Dorothy Collins*

39/55 *Boyd Bennett*

2/64 **My Boy Lollipop** *Millie Small*

83/64 **My Boyfriend Got A Beatle Haircut** *Donna Lynn*

1/63 **My Boyfriend's Back** *Angels* *(also see: Your Boyfriend's Back)*

22[X]/63 **My Boyfriend's Coming Home For Christmas** *Toni Wine*

25/89 **My Brave Face** *Paul McCartney*

12/58 **My Bucket's Got A Hole In It** *Ricky Nelson*
87/65 **My Buddy Seat** *Hondells*
26^{S}/00 **My Cellmate Thinks I'm Sexy** *Cledus T. Judd*
(also see: She Thinks My Tractor's Sexy)
88/65 **My Cherie** *Al Martino*
My Cherie Amour
4/69 *Stevie Wonder*
92/77 *Soul Train Gang*
68/61 **My Claire De Lune** *Steve Lawrence*
My Coloring Book
18/63 *Kitty Kallen*
20/63 *Sandy Stewart*
59/74 **My Country** *Jud Strunk*
F/73 **My Crew** *Rita Coolidge*
8/67 **My Cup Runneth Over** *Ed Ames*
6/63 **My Dad** *Paul Petersen*
67/62 **My Daddy Is President** *Little Jo Ann*
67/63 **My Daddy Knows Best** *Marvelettes*
34/60 **My Dearest Darling** *Etta James*
1/72 **My Ding-A-Ling** *Chuck Berry*
(also see: Ding-A-Ling)
7^{S}/02 **My Dogs** *Chuck-N-Blood*
24/57 **My Dream** *Platters*
83/61 **My Dream Come True** *Jack Scott*
59/56 **My Dream Sonata** *Nat "King" Cole*
85/64 **My Dreams** *Brenda Lee*
My Elusive Dreams
89/67 *David Houston & Tammy Wynette*
46/70 *Bobby Vinton*
49/75 *Charlie Rich*
9/61 **My Empty Arms** *Jackie Wilson*
86/60 **My Empty Room** *Little Anthony & The Imperials*
29/84 **My Ever Changing Moods** *Style Council*
34/01 **My Everything** *98°*
1/75 **My Eyes Adored You** *Frankie Valli*
97/77 **My Eyes Get Blurry** *Kenny Nolan*
28/77 **My Fair Share** *Seals & Crofts*
54/91 **My Fallen Angel** *Coro*
62/89 **My Fantasy** *Teddy Riley*
16^{A}/98 **My Father's Eyes** *Eric Clapton*
39/99 **My Favorite Girl** *Dave Hollister*
9^{A}/98 **My Favorite Mistake** *Sheryl Crow*
45/68 **My Favorite Things** *Herb Alpert*
94/75 **My First Day Without Her** *Classics IV*
80/56 **My First Formal Gown** *Patti Page*
26/00 **My First Love** *Avant*
50^{S}/02 **My First Love** *Kevin Ceballo*
28/99 **My First Night With You** *Mya*
62/89 **My First Night Without You** *Cyndi Lauper*
95/63 **My Foolish Heart** *Demensions*
43/79 **My Forbidden Lover** *Chic*
27^{A}/95 **My Friends** *Red Hot Chili Peppers*
85/02 **My Friends Over You** *New Found Glory*
74/66 **My Generation** *Who*
My Girl
1/65 *Temptations*
35/68 *Bobby Vee (medley)*
20/85 *Daryl Hall/John Oates (medley)*
20/88 *Suave'*
25/82 **My Girl** *Donnie Iris*
12/74 **My Girl Bill** *Jim Stafford*
22/81 **My Girl (Gone, Gone, Gone)** *Chilliwack*
14/65 **My Girl Has Gone** *Miracles*
My Girl Josephine
14/60 *Fats Domino*
29/67 *Jerry Jaye*

My Girl Sloopy ..see: Hang On Sloopy
My Guy
1/64 *Mary Wells*
70/72 *Petula Clark*
63/80 *Amii Stewart & Johnny Bristol (My Guy/My Girl)*
23/82 *Sister Sledge*
2/59 **My Happiness** *Connie Francis*
74/59 **My Heart Became Of Age** *Annette*
4/77 **My Heart Belongs To Me** *Barbra Streisand*
My Heart Belongs To Only You
65/61 *Jackie Wilson*
9/64 *Bobby Vinton*
28/91 **My Heart Belongs To You** *Russ Irwin*
4/89 **My Heart Can't Tell You No** *Rod Stewart*
38/64 **My Heart Cries For You** *Ray Charles*
1/60 **My Heart Has A Mind Of Its Own** *Connie Francis*
3/59 **My Heart Is An Open Book** *Carl Dobkins, Jr.*
77/97 **My Heart Is Calling** *Whitney Houston*
25/91 **My Heart Is Failing Me** *Riff*
48/02 **My Heart Is Lost To You** *Brooks & Dunn*
98/71 **My Heart Is Yours** *Wilbert Harrison*
92/73 **My Heart Just Keeps On Breakin'** *Chi-Lites*
My Heart Reminds Me ..see: And That Reminds Me
My Heart Sings ..see: (All Of A Sudden)
38/89 **My Heart Skips A Beat** *Cover Girls*
94/64 **My Heart Skips A Beat** *Buck Owens*
My Heart Will Go On (Love Theme From 'Titanic')
1/98 *Celine Dion*
58/98 *Deja Vu*
52/65 **My Heart Would Know** *Al Martino*
90/61 **My Heart's On Fire** *Billy Bland*
13/66 **My Heart's Symphony** *Gary Lewis*
59^{A}/98 **My Hero** *Foo Fighters*
78/60 **My Hero** *Blue Notes*
44/80 **My Heroes Have Always Been Cowboys** *Willie Nelson*
8/60 **My Home Town** *Paul Anka*
6/86 **My Hometown** *Bruce Springsteen*
55/70 **My Honey And Me** *Luther Ingram*
18/61 **My Kind Of Girl** *Matt Monro*
31/83 **My Kind Of Lady** *Supertramp*
30/90 **My Kinda Girl** *Babyface*
45/82 **My Kinda Lover** *Billy Squier*
93/68 **M'Lady** *Sly & The Family Stone*
My Last Date (With You)
26/61 *Skeeter Davis*
38/61 *Joni James*
(also see: Last Date)
3/79 **My Life** *Billy Joel*
41^{S}/01 **My Life** *Kool G Rap*
46/58 **My Life** *Chuck Willis*
26/02 **My List** *Toby Keith*
22/56 **My Little Angel** *Four Lads*
48/57 **My Little Baby** *Perry Como*
99/69 **My Little Chickadee** *Foundations*
57/75 **My Little Lady** *Bloodstone*
84/60 **My Little Marine** *Jamie Horton*
52/66 **My Little Red Book** *Love*
9/98 **My Little Secret** *Xscape*
9/75 **My Little Town** *Simon & Garfunkel*
1/66 **My Love** *Petula Clark*

My Love
1/73 *Paul McCartney*
69/74 *Margie Joseph*
5/83 **My Love** *Lionel Richie*
47/60 **My Love** *Nat King Cole-Stan Kenton*
80/88 **My Love** *Julio Iglesias & Stevie Wonder*
83/94 **My Love** *Little Texas*
47/60 **My Love For You** *Johnny Mathis*
16/65 **My Love, Forgive Me** *Robert Goulet*
76/00 **My Love Goes On And On** *Chris Cagle*
21/90 **My Love Is A Fire** *Donny Osmond*
28/95 **My Love Is For Real** *Paula Abdul*
60/79 **My Love Is Music** *Space*
4/97 **My Love Is The Shhh!** *Somethin' For The People*
4/00 **My Love Is Your Love** *Whitney Houston*
62/57 **My Love Song** *Tommy Sands*
61/66 **My Lover's Prayer** *Otis Redding*
2/92 **My Lovin' (You're Never Gonna Get It)** *En Vogue*
73/58 **My Lucky Love** *Doug Franklin*
76/74 **My Main Man** *Staple Singers*
13/67 **My Mammy** *Happenings*
My Man
81/59 *Peggy Lee*
79/65 *Barbra Streisand*
42/72 **My Man, A Sweet Man** *Millie Jackson*
My Maria
9/73 *B.W. Stevenson*
79/96 *Brooks & Dunn*
43/70 **My Marie** *Engelbert Humperdinck*
My Melancholy Baby
26/59 *Tommy Edwards*
58/62 *Marcels*
3/74 **My Melody Of Love** *Bobby Vinton*
79/61 **My Memories Of You** *Donnie & The Dreamers*
77/73 **My Merry-Go-Round** *Johnny Nash*
81/80 **My Mistake** *Kingbees*
19/74 **My Mistake (Was To Love You)** *Diana Ross & Marvin Gaye*
23^{X}/65 **My Mom And Santa Claus** *George Jones*
39/81 **My Mother's Eyes** *Bette Midler*
16/73 **My Music** *Loggins & Messina*
10/90 **My, My, My** *Johnny Gill*
36/99 **My Name Is** *Eminem*
20/91 **My Name Is Not Susan** *Whitney Houston*
36/92 **My Name Is Prince** *Prince*
42/02 **My Neck, My Back (Lick It)** *Khia*
27/00 **My Next Thirty Years** *Tim McGraw*
88/88 **My Obsession** *Icehouse*
37/84 **My Oh My** *Slade*
97/67 **My Old Car** *Lee Dorsey*
63/73 **My Old School** *Steely Dan*
49/64 **My One And Only, Jimmy Boy** *Girlfriends*
My One Sin
24/55 *Nat "King" Cole*
28/57 *Four Coins*
97/89 **My One Temptation** *Mica Paris*
54^{A}/98 **My Own Prison** *Creed*
My Own True Love
33/59 *Jimmy Clanton*
13/62 *Duprees*
74/77 **My Own Way To Rock** *Burton Cummings*
51/99 **My Own Worst Enemy** *Lit*
72/89 **My Paradise** *Outfield*

97/77 **My Pearl** *Automatic Man*
21/57 **My Personal Possession** *Nat "King" Cole/Four Knights*
14/69 **My Pledge Of Love** *Joe Jeffrey Group*
My Prayer
1/56 *Platters*
47/80 *Ray, Goodman & Brown*
1/89 **My Prerogative** *Bobby Brown*
51/73 **My Pretending Days Are Over** *Dells*
81/01 **My Projects** *Coo Coo Cal*
59/62 **My Real Name** *Fats Domino*
4/02 **My Sacrifice** *Creed*
My Sharona
1/79 *Knack*
91/94 *Knack*
F/75 **My Ship** *Tavares*
63/66 **My Ship Is Comin' In** *Walker Bros.*
My Shoes Keep Walking Back To You
63/57 *Ray Price*
45/60 *Guy Mitchell*
73/68 **My Shy Violet** *Mills Brothers*
30/91 **My Side Of The Bed** *Susanna Hoffs*
(My Sister) ..see: It's A Shame
31/69 **My Song** *Aretha Franklin*
100/70 **My Soul's Got A Hole In It** *Howard Tate*
My Special Angel
7/57 *Bobby Helms*
7/68 *Vogues*
My Special Prayer
87/67 *Joe Simon*
93/69 *Percy Sledge*
16/63 **My Summer Love** *Ruby & The Romantics*
My Sweet Lady
17/74 *Cliff DeYoung*
32/77 *John Denver*
My Sweet Lord
1/70 *George Harrison*
90/71 *Billy Preston*
94/02 *George Harrison*
85/66 **My Sweet Potato** *Booker T. & The M.G.'s*
48/76 **My Sweet Summer Suite** *Love Unlimited Orchestra*
50/60 **My Tani** *Brothers Four*
29/74 **My Thang** *James Brown*
My Three Sons ..see: Theme From
98/62 **My Time For Cryin'** *Maxine Brown*
50/85 **My Toot Toot** *Jean Knight*
39/83 **My Town** *Michael Stanley Band*
40/02 **My Town** *Montgomery Gentry*
32/65 **My Town, My Guy And Me** *Lesley Gore*
31/56 **My Treasure** *Hilltoppers*
49/64 **My True Carrie, Love** *Nat King Cole*
22/63 **My True Confession** *Brook Benton*
3/58 **My True Love** *Jack Scott*
3/61 **My True Story** *Jive Five*
58/66 **My Uncle Used To Love Me But She Died** *Roger Miller*
68/95 **My Up And Down** *Adina Howard*
2/98 **My Way** *Usher*
My Way
27/69 *Frank Sinatra*
72/70 *Brook Benton*
22/77 *Elvis Presley*
75/01 **My Way** *Limp Bizkit*
64/68 **My Way Of Life** *Frank Sinatra*
9/69 **My Whole World Ended (The Moment You Left Me)** *David Ruffin*
24/63 **My Whole World Is Falling Down** *Brenda Lee*
57/63 **My Wife Can't Cook** *Lonnie Russ*
91/69 **My Wife, My Dog, My Cat** *Maskman & The Agents*
52/70 **My Wife, The Dancer** *Eddie & Dutch*
12/59 **My Wish Came True** *Elvis Presley*
42/70 **My Woman, My Woman, My Wife** *Marty Robbins*
16/72 **My World** *Bee Gees*
70/67 **My World Fell Down** *Sagittarius*
My World Is Empty Without You
5/66 *Supremes*
87/69 *José Feliciano*
9/92 **Mysterious Ways** *U2*
24/85 **Mystery Lady** *Billy Ocean*
33/65 **Mystic Eyes** *Them*

N

73/00 **n 2 gether now** *Limp Bizkit*
Na Na Hey Hey Kiss Him Goodbye
1/69 *Steam*
12/87 *Nylons*
8/76 **Nadia's Theme (The Young And The Restless)** *Barry DeVorzon & Perry Botkin, Jr.*
F/70 **Nadine** *Dells*
23/64 **Nadine (Is It You?)** *Chuck Berry*
25/61 **"Nag"** *Halos*
48/86 **Nail It To The Wall** *Stacy Lattisaw*
47A/96 **Naked** *Goo Goo Dolls*
36/97 **Naked Eye** *Luscious Jackson*
5/96 **Name** *Goo Goo Dolls*
97/89 **Name And Number** *Big Noise*
3/65 **Name Game** *Shirley Ellis*
12/78 **Name Of The Game** *Abba*
65/56 **Namely You** *Don Cherry*
91/73 **Names, Tags, Numbers & Labels** *Association*
62/99 **Nann** *Trick Daddy*
49/94 **Nappy Heads** *Fugees*
86/99 **Nas Is Like** *Nas*
8/67 **Nashville Cats** *Lovin' Spoonful*
92/99 **Nastradamus** *Nas*
3/86 **Nasty** *Janet Jackson*
55S/99 **Nasty Trick** *Gangsta Boo*
16/71 **Nathan Jones** *Supremes*
53/60 **National City** *Joiner, Arkansas Junior High School Band*
Native Girl ..see: Elephant Walk
21/78 **Native New Yorker** *Odyssey*
15X/67 **Natividad (Nativity)** *Harvie June Van*
15S/00 **Natural** *S Club 7*
75S/00 **Natural Blues** *Moby*
38/60 **Natural Born Lover** *Fats Domino*
Natural High
10/73 *Bloodstone*
55/92 *After 7 (medley)*
66/82 **Natural Love** *Petula Clark*
17/71 **Natural Man** *Lou Rawls*
29/96 **Natural One** *Folk Implosion*
Natural Woman
8/67 *Aretha Franklin*
95/95 *Mary J. Blige*
40/68 **Naturally Stoned** *Avant-Garde*
40/61 **Nature Boy** *Bobby Darin*
70/89 **Nature Of Love** *Waterfront*
Nature Planned It ..see: (It's The Way)
3/88 **Naughty Girls (Need Love Too)** *Samantha Fox*
Naughty Lady Of Shady Lane
3/54 *Ames Brothers*
17/55 *Archie Bleyer*
23/85 **Naughty Naughty** *John Parr*
6/64 **Navy Blue** *Diane Renay*
22/70 **Neanderthal Man** *Hotlegs*
10/58 **Near You** *Roger Williams*
96/71 **Near You** *Boz Scaggs*
85/67 **Nearer To You** *Betty Harris*
40/58 **Nee Nee Na Na Na Na Nu Nu** *Dicky Doo & The Don'ts*
45/89 **Need A Little Taste Of Love** *Doobie Brothers*
11/74 **Need To Be** *Jim Weatherly*
30S/02 **Need To Be Naked** *Amber*
31/64 **Need To Belong** *Jerry Butler*
25/58 **Need You** *Donnie Owens*
84/79 **Need You Bad** *Ted Nugent*
1/88 **Need You Tonight** *INXS*
54/58 **Need Your Love** *Bobby Freeman*
70/97 **Need Your Love** *Big Bub*
44/80 **Need Your Loving Tonight** *Queen*
45/64 **Needle In A Haystack** *Velvelettes*
Needles And Pins
84/63 *Jackie DeShannon*
13/64 *Searchers*
68/77 *Smokie*
37/86 *Tom Petty with Stevie Nicks*
65/66 **Neighbor, Neighbor** *Jimmy Hughes*
2/73 **Neither One Of Us (Wants To Be The First To Say Goodbye)** *Gladys Knight*
Nel Blu Dipinto Di Blu ..see: Volare
57/94 **Neon Moonlight** *Rosco Martinez*
42/77 **Neon Nites** *Atlanta Rhythm Section*
24/67 **Neon Rainbow** *Box Tops*
59/65 **N-E-R-V-O-U-S!** *Ian Whitcomb*
68/57 **Nervous Boogie** *Paul Gayten*
6/85 **Neutron Dance** *Pointer Sisters*
75S/95 **Neva Go Back** *Special Ed*
70/71 **Nevada Fighter** *Michael Nesmith*

NEVER:

4/85 **Never** *Heart*
79/02 **Never** *Amanda Perez*
21/93 **Never A Time** *Genesis*
48/95 **Never Alone (Eeyore's Lullaby)** *Tyler Collins*
20/86 **Never As Good As The First Time** *Sade*
6/59 **Never Be Anyone Else But You** *Ricky Nelson*
15/80 **Never Be The Same** *Christopher Cross*
68/75 **Never Been Any Reason** *Head East*
28/82 **Never Been In Love** *Randy Meisner*
89/99 **Never Been Kissed** *Sherrié Austin*
5/72 **Never Been To Spain** *Three Dog Night*
Never Can Say Goodbye
2/71 *Jackson 5*
22/71 *Isaac Hayes*
9/75 *Gloria Gaynor*
51/88 *Communards*
91/69 **Never Comes The Day** *Moody Blues*
80/88 **Never Die Young** *James Taylor*
78/71 **Never Dreamed You'd Leave In Summer** *Stevie Wonder*

13/71 **Never Ending Song Of Love** *Delaney & Bonnie*
17/85 **Never Ending Story** *Limahl*
61/87 **Never Enough** *Patty Smyth*
72/90 **Never Enough** *Cure*
4/98 **Never Ever** *All Saints*
53/95 **Never Find Someone Like You** *Keith Martin*
F/94 **Never Forget You** *Mariah Carey*
56/78 **Never Get Enough Of Your Love** *L.T.D.*
95/68 **Never Get Enough Of Your Love** *Oscar Toney, Jr.*
46/83 **Never Give Up** *Sammy Hagar*
52/82 **Never Give Up On A Good Thing** *George Benson*
20/68 **Never Give You Up** *Jerry Butler*
73/68 **Never Going Back** *Lovin' Spoonful*
11/76 **Never Gonna Fall In Love Again** *Eric Carmen*
1/88 **Never Gonna Give You Up** *Rick Astley*
86/69 **Never Gonna Let Him Know** *Debbie Taylor*
17/91 **Never Gonna Let You Down** *Surface*
4/83 **Never Gonna Let You Go** *Sergio Mendes*
17/99 **Never Gonna Let You Go** *Faith Evans*
10/01 **Never Had A Dream Come True** *S Club 7*
26/70 **Never Had A Dream Come True** *Stevie Wonder*
75/89 **Never Had A Lot To Lose** *Cheap Trick*
87/78 **Never Had A Love** *Pablo Cruise*
56/62 **Never In A Million Years** *Linda Scott*
15/94 **Never Keeping Secrets** *Babyface*
28/88 **Never Knew Love Like This** *Alexander O'Neal/Cherrelle*
6/80 **Never Knew Love Like This Before** *Stephanie Mills*
FC/55 **Never Leave Me** *Gale Storm*
33/96 **Never Leave Me Alone** *Nate Dogg*
29/75 **Never Let Her Go** *David Gates*
67/78 **Never Let Her Slip Away** *Andrew Gold*
27/87 **Never Let Me Down** *David Bowie*
63/88 **Never Let Me Down Again** *Depeche Mode*
79/56 **Never Let Me Go** *Nat "King" Cole*
82/60 **Never Let Me Go** *Lloyd Price*
14/00 **Never Let You Go** *Third Eye Blind*
43/73 **Never Let You Go** *Bloodstone*
58/88 **Never Let You Go** *Sweet Sensation*
5/94 **Never Lie** *Immature*
99/63 **Never Love A Robin** *Bobby Vee*
7/97 **Never Make A Promise** *Dru Hill*
Never My Love
2/67 *Association*
98/68 *Sandpebbles*
12/71 *5th Dimension*
7/74 *Blue Swede*
80/77 *Addrisi Brothers*
74/61 **Never, Never** *Jive Five*
Never, Never Gonna Give Ya Up
7/74 *Barry White*
74/97 *Lisa Stansfield*
54/65 **Never, Never Leave Me** *Mary Wells*
48/73 **Never, Never, Never (Grande, Grande, Grande)** *Shirley Bassey*

Never On Sunday
19/60 *Don Costa*
13/61 *Chordettes*
88/61 *Lale Anderson (Ein Schiff)*
64/92 **Never Satisfied** *Good 2 Go*
73/83 **Never Say Die (Give A Little Bit More)** *Cliff Richard*
28A/87 **Never Say Goodbye** *Bon Jovi*
30/93 **Never Should've Let You Go** *Hi-Five*
54/91 **Never Stop** *Brand New Heavies*
(Never Stop Givin' You Love) ..see: Shoop Shoop
3/85 **Never Surrender** *Corey Hart*
7/88 **Never Tear Us Apart** *INXS*
88/83 **Never Tell An Angel (When Your Heart's On Fire)** *Stompers*
78/99 **Never There** *Cake*
95/82 **Never Thought I'd Fall In Love** *Spinners*
43/88 **Never Thought (That I Could Love)** *Dan Hill*
89/96 **Never Too Busy** *Kenny Lattimore*
81/01 **Never Too Far (Medley)** *Mariah Carey*
33/81 **Never Too Much** *Luther Vandross*
61/90 **Never 2 Much Of U** *Dino*
90/64 **Never Trust A Woman** *B.B. King*
22/56 **Never Turn Back** *Al Hibbler*
67/75 **Nevertheless** *Allman Brothers Band*

NEW:

New ..also see: Nu
27/95 **New Age Girl** *Deadeye Dick*
17/85 **New Attitude** *Patti LaBelle*
41S/99 **New Day** *Wyclef Jean Feat. Bono*
53/89 **New Day For You** *Basia*
22/02 **New Day Has Come** *Celine Dion*
70/83 **New Frontier** *Donald Fagen*
37/64 **New Girl In School** *Jan & Dean*
57/84 **New Girl Now** *Honeymoon Suite*
47/60 **(New In) The Ways Of Love** *Tommy Edwards*
67/91 **New Jack Hustler (Nino's Theme)** *Ice-T*
1/77 **New Kid In Town** *Eagles*
New Lovers ..see: (Welcome)
36/63 **New Mexican Rose** *Four Seasons*
10/84 **New Moon On Monday** *Duran Duran*
New Orleans
6/60 *U.S. Bonds*
44/65 *Eddie Hodges*
51/68 *Neil Diamond*
70/76 **New Orleans** *Staple Singers*
59/78 **New Orleans Ladies** *Le Roux*
78/97 **New Pollution** *Beck*
64/90 **New Power Generation** *Prince*
39/80 **New Romance (It's A Mystery)** *Spider*
3/88 **New Sensation** *INXS*
27/84 **New Song** *Howard Jones*
67/89 **New Thing** *Enuff Z'Nuff*
42/70 **New World Coming** *Mama Cass Elliot*
21/82 **New World Man** *Rush*
53/83 **New Year's Day** *U2*
76/78 **New York City** *Zwol*
53S/99 **New York City Boy** *Pet Shop Boys*
13/79 **New York Groove** *Ace Frehley*
14/67 **New York Mining Disaster 1941** *Bee Gees*
48/90 **New York Minute** *Don Henley*
New York, New York ..see: Theme From

27/77 **New York, You Got Me Dancing** *Andrea True Connection*
32/65 **New York's A Lonely Town** *Trade Winds*
59/56 **New York's My Home** *Sammy Davis, Jr.*
97/74 **Newsy Neighbors** *First Choice*
5/62 **Next Door To An Angel** *Neil Sedaka*
71/62 **Next Door To The Blues** *Etta James*
23/00 **Next Episode** *Dr. Dre*
49/78 **Next Hundred Years** *Al Martino*
99/57 **Next In Line** *Johnny Cash*
72/61 **Next Kiss (Is The Last Goodbye)** *Conway Twitty*
61A/97 **Next Lifetime** *Erykah Badu*
81/84 **Next Love** *Deniece Williams*
17/67 **Next Plane To London** *Rose Garden*
F/70 **Next Step Is Love** *Elvis Presley*
1/86 **Next Time I Fall** *Peter Cetera w/Amy Grant*
75/56 **Next Time It Happens** *Carmen McRae*
74/57 **Next Time You See Me** *Little Junior Parker*
82/81 **Next Time You'll Know** *Sister Sledge*
91/87 **Niagara Falls** *Chicago*
1/98 **Nice & Slow** *Usher*
37/82 **Nice Girls** *Eye To Eye*
42/83 **Nice Girls** *Melissa Manchester*
60/60 **Nice 'N' Easy** *Frank Sinatra*
30/76 **Nice 'N' Naasty** *Salsoul Orchestra*
61/88 **Nice 'N' Slow** *Freddie Jackson*
63/75 **Nice, Nice, Very Nice** *Ambrosia*
4/72 **Nice To Be With You** *Gallery*
29/90 **Nicety** *Michel'le*
92/90 **Nick Of Time** *Bonnie Raitt*
95/63 **Nick Teen And Al K. Hall** *Rolf Harris*
Nickel Song
81/71 *New Seekers*
35/72 *Melanie*
39/81 **Nicole** *Point Blank*

NIGHT:

Night ..also see: Nite
4/60 **Night** *Jackie Wilson*
48/83 **Night, The** *Animals*
62/91 **Night And Day** *Bette Midler*
82/67 **Night And Day** *Sergio Mendes*
1/74 **Night Chicago Died** *Paper Lace*
74/79 **Night Dancin'** *Taka Boom*
61S/02 **Night Disappear With You** *Brian McComas*
1/78 **Night Fever** *Bee Gees*
75/68 **Night Fo' Last** *Shorty Long*
3/63 **Night Has A Thousand Eyes** *Bobby Vee*
71/94 **Night In My Veins** *Pretenders*
72S/95 **Night Is Fallin' In My Heart** *Diamond Rio*
34/85 **Night Is Still Young** *Billy Joel*
57/63 **Night Life** *Rusty Draper*
11/56 **Night Lights** *Nat "King" Cole*
4/77 **Night Moves** *Bob Seger*
28/86 **Night Moves** *Marilyn Martin*
6/81 **Night Owls** *Little River Band*
92/83 **Night Pulse** *Double Image*
60/82 **Night Shift** *Quarterflash*
3/85 **Nightshift** *Commodores*
Night Stood Still ..see: And The Night
1/73 **Night The Lights Went Out In Georgia** *Vicki Lawrence*

75/60 **Night Theme** *Mark II*
3/71 **Night They Drove Old Dixie Down** *Joan Baez*
30/66 **Night Time** *Strangeloves*
100/62 **Night Time** *Pete Antell*
36/88 **Nightime** *Pretty Poison*
Night Time Is The Right Time
95/59 *Ray Charles*
94/64 *Rufus & Carla*
Night To Remember
44/82 *Shalamar*
38/99 *Joe Diffie*
Night Train
82/60 *Viscounts*
80/61 *Richard Hayman*
35/62 *James Brown*
93/89 **Nightrain** *Guns N' Roses*
96/76 **Night Walk** *Van McCoy*
68S/98 **Night Wind** *Tony Mascolo*
33/84 **Nightbird** *Stevie Nicks/Sandy Stewart*
91/91 **Nightgown** *Candyman*
9/75 **Nightingale** *Carole King*
15/88 **Nightmare On My Street** *DJ Jazzy Jeff & The Fresh Prince*
10/76 **Nights Are Forever Without You** *England Dan & John Ford Coley*
2/72 **Nights In White Satin** *Moody Blues*
24/91 **Nights Like This** *After 7*
7/75 **Nights On Broadway** *Bee Gees*
41/81 **Nightwalker** *Gino Vannelli*
69/95 **Nika** *Vicious*
23/67 **Niki Hoeky** *P.J. Proby*
7/86 **Nikita** *Elton John*
57/72 **992 Arguments** *O'Jays*
52/77 **9,999,999 Tears** *Dickey Lee*
58/58 **Nine More Miles** *Georgie Young*
38/00 **911** *Wyclef Jean*
34S/90 **911 Is A Joke** *Public Enemy*
70/67 **Nine Pound Steel** *Joe Simon*
1/81 **9 To 5** *Dolly Parton*
15/85 **19** *Paul Hardcastle*
48/66 **Nineteen Days** *Dave Clark Five*
69/70 **1984** *Spirit*
88/68 **1941** *Tom Northcott*
33/71 **1900 Yesterday** *Liz Damon's Orient Express*
1999
12/83 *Prince*
40/99 *Prince*
56S/00 *Prince*
(also see: One-Nine-Nine-Nine)
12/96 **1979** *Smashing Pumpkins*
23/03 **19 Somethin'** *Mark Wills*
88/71 **1927 Kansas City** *Mike Reilly*
2/66 **19th Nervous Breakdown** *Rolling Stones*
71/94 **90's Girl** *Blackgirl*
7/67 **98.6** *Keith*
86/98 **'98 Thug Paradise** *Tragedy · Capone · Infinite*
26/80 **99** *Toto*
77/84 **99 1/2** *Carol Lynn Townes*
53/66 **Ninety-Nine And A Half (Won't Do)** *Wilson Pickett*
59/98 **Ninety Nine (Flash The Message)** *John Forté*
2/84 **99 Luftballons** *Nena*
91/75 **99 Miles From L.A.** *Albert Hammond*
11/57 **Ninety-Nine Ways** *Tab Hunter*
78/90 **99 Worlds** *Peter Wolf*
23/56 **Ninety Nine Years (Dead Or Alive)** *Guy Mitchell*
96 Tears
1/66 *? (Question Mark) & The Mysterians*
96/67 *Big Maybelle*
66/81 *Garland Jeffreys*
72/93 **93 'Til Infinity** *Souls Of Mischief*
(Nino's Theme) ..see: New Jack Hustler
80/94 **9th Wonder (blackitolism)** *Digable Planets*
7/88 **Nite And Day** *Al B. Sure!*
Nite Owl
73/62 *Dukays*
88/62 *Dukays*
Nitty Gritty
8/64 *Shirley Ellis*
90/68 *Ricardo Ray*
19/69 *Gladys Knight*

NO:

44/72 **No** *Bulldog*
73/60 **No** *Dodie Stevens*
No Arms Can Ever Hold You
23/55 *Georgie Shaw*
26/55 *Pat Boone*
67/55 *Gaylords*
27/65 *Bachelors*
93/70 *Bobby Vinton*
82/89 **No Big Deal** *Love & Rockets*
50/79 **No Chance** *Moon Martin*
No Charge
39/74 *Melba Montgomery*
91/75 *Shirley Caesar*
23/58 **No Chemise, Please** *Gerry Granahan*
1/96 **No Diggity** *BLACKstreet*
56S/99 **No Doubt** *Imajin*
75/94 **No Doubt About It** *Neal McCoy*
22/86 **No Easy Way Out** *Robert Tepper*
66S/01 **No Escapin' This** *Beatnuts*
48A/94 **No Excuses** *Alice In Chains*
51/67 **No Fair At All** *Association*
91/65 **No Faith, No Love** *Mitty Collier*
57/98 **No Fool No More** *En Vogue*
87/86 **No Frills Love** *Jennifer Holliday*
No Gettin' Over Me ..see: (There's)
No Good To Cry
88/67 *Wildweeds*
84/71 *Poppy Family*
94/94 **No Guns, No Murder** *Rayvon*
54S/95 **No Hook** *Shaquille O'Neal*
40/60 **No If's - No And's** *Lloyd Price*
74/00 **No Leaf Clover** *Metallica*
37S/03 **No Light** *3rd Strike*
34/85 **No Lookin' Back** *Michael McDonald*
16/71 **No Love At All** *B.J. Thomas*
21/58 **No Love (But Your Love)** *Johnny Mathis*
54/60 **No Love Have I** *Webb Pierce*
94/66 **No Man Is An Island** *Van Dykes*
86/02 **No Matta What (Party All Night)** *Toya*
8/70 **No Matter What** *Badfinger*
49/91 **No Matter What** *George LaMond With Brenda K. Starr*
3/66 **No Matter What Shape (Your Stomach's In)** *T-Bones*
31/69 **No Matter What Sign You Are** *Supremes*
60/00 **No Matter What They Say** *Lil' Kim*
77/00 **No Me Dejes De Querer** *Gloria Estefan*
92/00 **No Mercy** *Ty Herndon*
35/67 **No Milk Today** *Herman's Hermits*
33/93 **No Mistakes** *Patty Smyth*
5/00 **No More** *Ruff Endz*
No More
6/55 *DeJohn Sisters*
17/55 *McGuire Sisters*
23/01 **No More (Baby I'ma Do Right)** *3LW*
15/02 **No More Drama** *Mary J. Blige*
92/96 **No More Games** *Skin Deep*
23/95 **No More "I Love You's"** *Annie Lennox*
7/90 **No More Lies** *Michel'le*
6/84 **No More Lonely Nights** *Paul McCartney*
25/73 **No More Mr. Nice Guy** *Alice Cooper*
56/00 **No More Rain (In This Cloud)** *Angie Stone*
17/89 **No More Rhyme** *Debbie Gibson*
71/92 **No More Tears** *Ozzy Osbourne*
1/79 **No More Tears (Enough Is Enough)** *Barbra Streisand/Donna Summer*
23/84 **No More Words** *Berlin*
13/90 **No Myth** *Michael Penn*
23/80 **No Night So Long** *Dionne Warwick*
55/58 **No, No** *Fats Domino*
60/76 **No, No, Joe** *Silver Convention*
3/98 **No, No, No** *Destiny's Child*
41/61 **No, No, No** *Chanters*
56S/01 **No! No! No!** *Sunni Black*
3/75 **No No Song** *Ringo Starr*
No, Not Much!
2/56 *Four Lads*
34/69 *Vogues*
85/69 *Smoke Ring*
No One
34/61 *Connie Francis*
21/63 *Ray Charles*
98/65 *Brenda Lee*
93/69 **No One Better Than You** *Petula Clark*
66/97 **No One But You** *Veronica*
45/58 **No One But You (In My Heart)** *Ames Brothers*
78/83 **No One Can Love You More Than Me** *Melissa Manchester*
22/96 **No One Else** *Total*
83/92 **No One Else On Earth** *Wynonna*
52/69 **No One For Me To Turn To** *Spiral Starecase*
44/87 **No One In The World** *Anita Baker*
4/86 **No One Is To Blame** *Howard Jones*
19/58 **No One Knows** *Dion & The Belmonts*
51/03 **No One Knows** *Queens Of The Stone Age*
96/68 **No One Knows** *Every Mother's Son*
65/82 **No One Like You** *Scorpions*
55/64 **No One To Cry To** *Ray Charles*
36/72 **No One To Depend On** *Santana*
43/62 **No One Will Ever Know** *Jimmie Rodgers*
28/93 **No Ordinary Love** *Sade*
No Other Arms ..also see: No Arms Can Ever Hold You
No Other Arms, No Other Lips
27/59 *Chordettes*
74/59 *Four Aces*
65/56 **No Other One** *Eddie Fisher*
71S/02 **No Panties** *Trina*
81/84 **No Parking (On The Dance Floor)** *Midnight Star*
10/64 **No Particular Place To Go** *Chuck Berry*
12/99 **No Pigeons** *Sporty Thievz*

59/65 **No Pity (In The Naked City)** *Jackie Wilson*
37/99 **No Place That Far** *Sara Evans*
79/86 **No Promises** *Icehouse*
20/93 **No Rain** *Blind Melon*
90/59 **No Regrets** *Jimmy Barnes*
29/81 **No Reply At All** *Genesis*
62/72 **No Sad Song** *Helen Reddy*
49/68 **No Sad Songs** *Joe Simon*
1/99 **No Scrubs** *TLC*
12/92 **No Son Of Mine** *Genesis*
95/89 **No Souvenirs** *Melissa Etheridge*
13/02 **No Such Thing** *John Mayer*
F/70 **No Sugar Tonight** *Guess Who*
No Sunshine..see: Ain't No Sunshine
14/79 **No Tell Lover** *Chicago*
42/97 **No Tengo Dinero** *Los Umbrellos*
5/70 **No Time** *Guess Who*
18/97 **No Time** *Lil' Kim*
33/83 **No Time For Talk** *Christopher Cross*
96/67 **No Time Like The Right Time** *Blues Project*
No Time To Lose
84/79 *Tarney/Spencer Band*
74/81 *Tarney/Spencer Band*
23/84 **No Way Out** *Jefferson Starship*
38A/96 **No Woman, No Cry** *Fugees*

NOBODY:

3/96 **Nobody** *Keith Sweat*
15/82 **Nobody** *Sylvia*
58/74 **Nobody** *Doobie Brothers*
8/68 **Nobody But Me** *Human Beinz*
21/59 **Nobody But You** *Dee Clark*
86/72 **Nobody But You** *Loggins & Messina*
40/69 **Nobody But You Babe** *Clarence Reid*
60/61 **Nobody Cares (about me)** *Jeanette Washington*
2/77 **Nobody Does It Better** *Carly Simon*
18/98 **Nobody Does It Better** *Nate Dogg*
36/98 **Nobody Else** *Tyrese*
12/64 **Nobody I Know** *Peter & Gordon*
2/96 **Nobody Knows** *Tony Rich Project*
49/65 **Nobody Knows What's Goin' On** *Chiffons*
93/60 **Nobody Knows You When You're Down And Out** *Nina Simone*
30/60 **Nobody Loves Me Like You** *Flamingos*
18/82 **Nobody Said It Was Easy** *Le Roux*
5/84 **Nobody Told Me** *John Lennon*
13/01 **Nobody Wants To Be Lonely** *Ricky Martin w/Christina Aguilera*
29/73 **Nobody Wants You When You're Down And Out** *Bobby Womack*
21/81 **Nobody Wins** *Elton John*
70/73 **Nobody Wins** *Brenda Lee*
66/92 **Nobody Wins In This War** *Mitch Malloy*
60/66 **Nobody's Baby Again** *Dean Martin*
8/88 **Nobody's Fool** *Kenny Loggins*
13/87 **Nobody's Fool** *Cinderella*
63/88 **Nobody's Perfect** *Mike + The Mechanics*
2/98 **Nobody's Supposed To Be Here** *Deborah Cox*
Nola
39/59 *Billy Williams*
50/59 *Morgan Brothers*
45/58 **Non Dimenticar (Don't Forget)** *Nat "King" Cole*
48/00 **None Of Ur Friends Business** *Ginuwine*
32/94 **None Of Your Business** *Salt-N-Pepa*
16S/01 **None Tonight** *Lil' Zane*
80/99 **Nookie** *Limp Bizkit*
84/76 **Norma Jean Wants To Be A Movie Star** *Sundown Company*
3/62 **Norman** *Sue Thompson*
4/60 **North To Alaska** *Johnny Horton*

NOT:

36/02 **Not A Day Goes By** *Lonestar*
82/96 **Not A Dry Eye In The House** *Meat Loaf*
92/98 **Not About Romance** *Inner Circle*
56A/97 **Not An Addict** *K's Choice*
18S/01 **[Not Enough]** *Outsiderz 4 Life*
97/95 **Not Enough** *Van Halen*
43/68 **Not Enough Indians** *Dean Martin*
34/85 **Not Enough Love In The World** *Don Henley*
28/92 **Not Enough Time** *INXS*
Not Fade Away
48/64 *Rolling Stones*
70/79 *Tanya Tucker*
73/81 *Eric Hine*
100/63 **Not For All The Money In The World** *Shirelles*
2/96 **Not Gon' Cry** *Mary J. Blige*
26/88 **Not Just Another Girl** *Ivan Neville*
77/79 **(not just) Knee Deep** *Funkadelic*
12/63 **Not Me** *Orlons*
57/69 **Not On The Outside** *Moments*
97/95 **Not On Your Love** *Jeff Carson*
48/56 **Not One Goodbye** *Jaye P. Morgan*
16/60 **Not One Minute More** *Della Reese*
58/66 **Not Responsible** *Tom Jones*
95/67 **Not So Sweet Martha Lorraine** *Country Joe & The Fish*
25/65 **Not The Lovin' Kind** *Dino, Desi & Billy*
34/92 **Not The Only One** *Bonnie Raitt*
6/97 **Not Tonight** *Lil' Kim*
66/65 **Not Too Long Ago** *Uniques*
63/63 **Not Too Young To Get Married** *Bob B. Soxx & The Blue Jeans*
90/98 **Note, The** *Daryle Singletary*

NOTHIN'/NOTHING:

Nothin' ..also see: Nuthin' / Nuttin'
10/02 **Nothin'** *N.O.R.E.*
10/86 **Nothin' At All** *Heart*
6/88 **Nothin' But A Good Time** *Poison*
38/97 **Nothin' But The Cavi Hit** *Mack 10 & Dogg Pound*
77/75 **Nothin' Heavy** *David Bellamy*
70/98 **Nothin' Move But The Money** *Mic Geronimo*
19/93 **Nothin' My Love Can't Fix** *Joey Lawrence*
64/58 **Nothin' Shakin'** *Eddie Fontaine*
77/89 **Nothin (That Compares 2 U)** *Jacksons*
39/90 **Nothin' To Hide** *Poco*
41/71 **Nothing To Hide** *Tommy James*
Nothin' Yet ..see: (We Ain't Got)
49/00 **Nothing As It Seems** *Pearl Jam*
57/93 **Nothing 'Bout Me** *Sting*
29/92 **Nothing Broken But My Heart** *Celine Dion*
86/77 **Nothing But A Breeze** *Jesse Winchester*
34/69 **Nothing But A Heartache** *Flirtations*
49/61 **Nothing But Good** *Hank Ballard*
11/65 **Nothing But Heartaches** *Supremes*
12/62 **Nothing Can Change This Love** *Sam Cooke*
18/65 **Nothing Can Stop Me** *Gene Chandler*
74/69 **Nothing Can Take The Place Of You** *Brook Benton*
1/90 **Nothing Compares 2 U** *Sinéad O'Connor*
34/92 **Nothing Else Matters** *Metallica*
72/56 **Nothing Ever Changes My Love For You** *Nat "King" Cole*
54/81 **Nothing Ever Goes As Planned** *Styx*
Nothing For Xmas ..see: Nuttin'
1/74 **Nothing From Nothing** *Billy Preston*
87/63 **Nothing Goes Up (Without Coming Down)** *Nat King Cole*
41S/00 **Nothing Good About Goodbye** *Phoenix Stone*
54/86 **Nothing In Common** *Thompson Twins*
99/58 **Nothing In The World** *Nat "King" Cole*
27/02 **Nothing In This World** *Keke Wyatt*
84/57 **Nothing Is Too Good For You** *Harvey Boys*
74A/95 **Nothing Left Behind Us** *Richard Marx*
77/62 **Nothing New (Same Old Thing)** *Fats Domino*
93/99 **Nothing Really Matters** *Madonna*
52/81 **Nothing Remains The Same (medley)** *Spinners*
62/70 **Nothing Succeeds Like Success** *Bill Deal*
52/67 **Nothing Takes The Place Of You** *Toussaint McCall*
12/87 **Nothing's Gonna Change My Love For You** *Glenn Medeiros*
80/87 **Nothing's Gonna Stop Me Now** *Samantha Fox*
1/87 **Nothing's Gonna Stop Us Now** *Starship*
20/66 **Nothing's Too Good For My Baby** *Stevie Wonder*
9S/01 **Nothing's Wrong** *Won-G*
21/90 **Notice Me** *Nikki*
2/87 **Notorious** *Duran Duran*
38/87 **Notorious** *Loverboy*
82/99 **Notorious B.I.G.** *Notorious B.I.G.*
3/92 **November Rain** *Guns N' Roses*
39A/96 **Novocaine For The Soul** *Eels*

NOW:

92/63 **Now!** *Lena Horne*
25/58 **Now And For Always** *George Hamilton IV*
7/94 **Now and Forever** *Richard Marx*
48/61 **Now And Forever** *Bert Kaempfert*
92/86 **Now And Forever (You And Me)** *Anne Murray*
(Now And Then There's) A ..see: Fool Such As I
73/67 **Now I Know** *Jack Jones*
93/71 **Now I'm A Woman** *Nancy Wilson*
59/56 **Now Is The Hour** *Gale Storm*
68A/91 **Now Is Tomorrow** *Definition Of Sound*
74/84 **Now It's My Turn** *Berlin*
64/82 **Now Or Never** *Axe*
46/72 **Now Run And Tell That** *Denise LaSalle*
55S/00 **Now That I Found You** *Mytown*
72/98 **Now That I Found You** *Terri Clark*
Now That We Found Love
47/79 *Third World*
11/91 *Heavy D & The Boyz*
72A/92 **Now That You're Gone** *Corina*

53/65 **Now That You've Gone** *Connie Stevens*
88/56 **Now You Has Jazz** *Bing Crosby & Louis Armstrong*
93/61 **Now You Know** *Little Willie John*
72/99 **(Now You See Me) Now You Don't** *Lee Ann Womack*
96/90 **Now You're Gone** *Whitesnake*
93/89 **Now You're In Heaven** *Julian Lennon*
3/66 **Nowhere Man** *Beatles*
40/96 **Nowhere To Go** *Melissa Etheridge*
8/65 **Nowhere To Run** *Martha & The Vandellas*
66/82 **Nowhere To Run** *Santana*
26/92 **Nu Nu** *Lidell Townsell & M.T.F.*
10S/02 **Nuclear War** *Yo La Tengo*
91/56 **Nuevo Laredo** *Les Paul & Mary Ford*
61A/93 **Numb** *U2*
9/75 **#9 Dream** *John Lennon*
22/01 **#1** *Nelly*
97/78 **Number One** *Eloise Laws*
29A/97 **#1 Crush** *Garbage*
82/78 **#1 Dee Jay** *Goody Goody*
52/62 **Number One Man** *Bruce Channel*
95/55 **Number One Street** *Bob Corley*
95/72 **Number Wonderful** *Rock Flowers*
93/76 **Nursery Rhymes** *People's Choice*
Nutbush City Limits
22/73 *Ike & Tina Turner*
69/76 *Bob Seger*
2/93 **Nuthin' But A "G" Thang** *Dr. Dre*
Nutrocker
23/62 *B. Bumble & The Stingers*
70/72 *Emerson, Lake & Palmer*
40/94 **Nuttin' But Love** *Heavy D & The Boyz*
Nuttin For Xmas
6/55 *Art Mooney/Barry Gordon*
20/55 *Joe Ward*
21/55 *Ricky Zahnd*
36/55 *Fontane Sisters*
53/55 *Stan Freberg*

O

O ..also see: Oh
9X/64 **O' Bambino (One Cold And Blessed Winter)** *Harry Simeone Chorale*
10/60 **O Dio Mio** *Annette*
83/59 **O' Falling Star** *Four Knights*
4/02 **'03 Bonnie & Clyde** *Jay-Z*
6/91 **O.P.P.** *Naughty By Nature*
65/85 **Oak Tree** *Morris Day*
Ob-La-Di, Ob-La-Da
51/69 *Arthur Conley*
49/76 *Beatles*
25/85 **Object Of My Desire** *Starpoint*
55/02 **Objection (Tango)** *Shakira*
38/94 **Objects In The Rear View Mirror May Appear Closer Than They Are** *Meat Loaf*
35/84 **Obscene Phone Caller** *Rockwell*
6/85 **Obsession** *Animotion*
92/91 **Obvious Child** *Paul Simon*
89/55 **Occasional Man** *Jeri Southern*
43/69 **Odds And Ends** *Dionne Warwick*
Ode To Billie Joe
1/67 *Bobbie Gentry*
28/67 *Kingpins*
89/67 *Ray Bryant*
54/76 *Bobbie Gentry*
65/76 *Bobbie Gentry (Main Title)*
39A/95 **Ode To My Family** *Cranberries*
50/65 **Ode To The Little Brown Shack Out Back** *Billy Edd Wheeler*
56/55 **Of This I'm Sure** *Four Aces*
45/88 **Off On Your Own (Girl)** *Al B. Sure!*
86/97 **Off The Books** *Beatnuts*
73/98 **Off The Hook** *Jody Watley*
10/80 **Off The Wall** *Michael Jackson*
94/66 **Off To Dublin In The Green** *Abbey Tavern Singers*

OH:

Oh ..also see: O
3/73 **Oh, Babe, What Would You Say?** *Hurricane Smith*
69/64 **Oh! Baby** *Barbara Lynn*
57/57 **Oh Baby Doll** *Chuck Berry*
23/64 **Oh Baby Don't You Weep** *James Brown*
4/02 **Oh Boy** *Cam'ron*
10/58 **Oh, Boy!** *Crickets*
9/59 **Oh! Carol** *Neil Sedaka*
59/93 **Oh Carolina** *Shaggy*
(Oh, Come, All Ye Faithful) ..see: Adeste Fideles
58/89 **Oh Daddy** *Adrian Belew*
15/78 **Oh! Darling** *Robin Gibb*
20/90 **Oh Father** *Madonna*
Oh Girl
1/72 *Chi-Lites*
8/90 *Paul Young*
39/85 **Oh Girl** *Boy Meets Girl*
Oh Happy Day
4/69 *Edwin Hawkins' Singers*
40/70 *Glen Campbell*
45/79 **Oh Honey** *Delegation*
Oh How Happy
12/66 *Shades Of Blue*
92/69 *Blinky & Edwin Starr*
63/61 **Oh, How I Miss You Tonight** *Jeanne Black*
59/68 **Oh, How It Hurts** *Barbara Mason*
Oh Julie
5/58 *Crescendos*
23/58 *Sammy Salvo*
38/82 **Oh Julie** *Barry Manilow*
33/73 **Oh La De Da** *Staple Singers*
34/60 **Oh, Little One** *Jack Scott*
Oh Lonesome Me
7/58 *Don Gibson*
93/61 *Johnny Cash*
78/68 **Oh Lord, Why Lord** *Los Pop Tops*
64/72 **(Oh Lord Won't You Buy Me A) Mercedes Benz** *Goose Creek Symphony*
48/75 **Oh Me, Oh My (Dreams In My Arms)** *Al Green*
Oh Me Oh My (I'm A Fool For You Baby)
22/70 *Lulu*
73/72 *Aretha Franklin*
94/61 **Oh Mein Papa** *Dick Lee*
61/62 **Oh My Angel** *Bertha Tillman*
85/78 **Oh My Lord (medley)** *Boney M*
80/56 **Oh My Maria** *Eddie Fisher*
5/74 **Oh My My** *Ringo Starr*
98/70 **Oh My My** *Monkees*
4/81 **Oh No** *Commodores*
83/01 **Oh No** *Mos Def & Pharoahe Monch*
Oh No Not My Baby
24/65 *Maxine Brown*
59/73 *Rod Stewart*
72/73 *Merry Clayton*
7/58 **Oh-Oh, I'm Falling In Love Again** *Jimmie Rodgers*
29/86 **Oh, People** *Patti LaBelle*
Oh, Pretty Woman
1/64 *Roy Orbison*
12/82 *Van Halen*
93/64 **Oh, Rock My Soul** *Peter, Paul & Mary*
1/85 **Oh Sheila** *Ready For The World*
3/84 **Oh Sherrie** *Steve Perry*
74/71 **Oh, Singer** *Jeannie C. Riley*
22/55 **Oh! Susanna** *Singing Dogs*
54/67 **Oh That's Good, No That's Bad** *Sam The Sham & The Pharoahs*
10/74 **Oh Very Young** *Cat Stevens*
54A/96 **Oh Virginia** *Blessid Union Of Souls*
Oh Well
55/70 *Fleetwood Mac*
30/79 *Rockets*
43/70 **Oh What A Day** *Dells*
86/59 **Oh, What A Fool** *Impalas*
10/69 **Oh, What A Night** *Dells*
(also see: December, 1963)
24/78 **Oh What A Night For Dancing** *Barry White*
91/62 **Oh! What It Seemed To Be** *Castells*
91/59 **Oh Why** *Teddy Bears*
F/71 **Oh Woman Oh Why** *Paul McCartney*
39/66 **Oh Yeah** *Shadows Of Knight*
46/02 **Oh Yeah!** *Big Tymers*
51/87 **Oh Yeah** *Yello*
62/67 **Oh Yeah!** *Joe Cuba Sextet*
14/70 **Ohio** *Crosby, Stills, Nash & Young*
45/77 **O-H-I-O** *Ohio Players*
Oíche Chiún (Silent Night)
71S/00 *Enya*
29S/01 *Enya*
11S/02 *Enya*
43/59 **Okefenokee** *Freddie Cannon*
41/70 **Okie From Muskogee** *Merle Haggard*
63/01 **Oklahoma** *Billy Gilman*
54/67 **Okolona River Bottom Band** *Bobbie Gentry*

OL'/OLD:

82/62 **Ol' Man River** *Jimmy Smith*
83/68 **Ol' Race Track** *Mills Brothers*
88/97 **Old Apartment** *Barenaked Ladies*
3/57 **Old Cape Cod** *Patti Page*
5/75 **Old Days** *Chicago*
94/63 **Old Enough To Love** *Ricky Nelson*
20/80 **Old-Fashion Love** *Commodores*
37/77 **Old Fashioned Boy (You're The One)** *Stallion*
60/82 **Old Fashioned Love** *Smokey Robinson*
4/71 **Old Fashioned Love Song** *Three Dog Night*
54/74 **Old Home Filler-Up An' Keep On-A-Truckin' Cafe** *C.W. McCall*
5/60 **Old Lamplighter** *Browns*
Old MacDonald
95/58 *Chargers*
25/60 *Frank Sinatra*
31/72 **Old Man** *Neil Young*
13/96 **Old Man & Me (When I Get To Heaven)** *Hootie & The Blowfish*
10/85 **Old Man Down The Road** *John Fogerty*

73/60 **Old Oaken Bucket** *Tommy Sands*
99/60 **Old Payola Roll Blues** *Stan Freberg*
34/56 **Old Philosopher** *Eddie Lawrence*
5/62 **Old Rivers** *Walter Brennan*
F/95 **Old School** *2Pac*
Old Schoolyard ..see: (Remember The Days Of The)
Old Shep
47/56 *Elvis Presley*
91/59 *Ralph DeMarco*
48/63 **Old Smokey Locomotion** *Little Eva*
15/81 **Old Songs** *Barry Manilow*
76/59 **Old Spanish Town** *Bell Notes*
Old Time Rock & Roll
28/79 *Bob Seger*
48/83 *Bob Seger*
93/94 **Old Times' Sake** *Sweet Sable*
59/94 **Old To The New** *Nice & Smooth*
13X/67 **Old Toy Trains** *Roger Miller*
25/61 **Ole Buttermilk Sky** *Bill Black's Combo*
94/71 **Olena** *Don Nix*
76/62 **Oliver Twist** *Rod McKuen*
58/84 **Olympia** *Sergio Mendes*
88/67 **Omaha** *Moby Grape*

ON:

On A Carousel
11/67 *Hollies*
50/82 *Glass Moon*
98/65 **On A Clear Day You Can See Forever** *Johnny Mathis*
44/74 **On A Night Like This** *Bob Dylan*
47/01 **On A Night Like This** *Trick Pony*
92/67 **On A Saturday Night** *Eddie Floyd*
39/92 **On A Sunday Afternoon** *Lighter Shade Of Brown*
59/59 **On An Evening In Roma** *Dean Martin*
90/73 **On And Off** *Anacostia*
5/74 **On And On** *Gladys Knight*
11/77 **On And On** *Stephen Bishop*
12/97 **On&On** *Erykah Badu*
89/94 **On And On** *Shyheim*
90/81 **On And On And On** *Abba*
1/94 **On Bended Knee** *Boyz II Men*
64/61 **On Bended Knees** *Clarence Henry*
On Broadway
9/63 *Drifters*
7/78 *George Benson*
45/69 **On Campus** *Dickie Goodman*
38/56 **On London Bridge** *Jo Stafford*
1/86 **On My Own** *Patti LaBelle & Michael McDonald*
39/97 **On My Own** *Peach Union*
(On My Way To Sunny Californ-i-a) ..see: California Saga
20/57 **On My Word Of Honor** *Platters*
2/89 **On Our Own** *Bobby Brown*
85/94 **On Point** *House Of Pain*
47/60 **On The Beach** *Frank Chacksfield*
54/70 **On The Beach (In The Summertime)** *5th Dimension*
42/77 **On The Border** *Al Stewart*
On The Dark Side
64/83 *Eddie & The Cruisers*
7/84 *John Cafferty*
73/95 **On The Down Low** *Brian McKnight*
87/66 **On The Good Ship Lollipop** *Wonder Who?*
67/89 **On The Line** *Tangier*
26/83 **On The Loose** *Saga*
5/80 **On The Radio** *Donna Summer*
4/61 **On The Rebound** *Floyd Cramer*
58/80 **On The Rebound** *Russ Ballard*
16/68 **On The Road Again** *Canned Heat*
20/80 **On The Road Again** *Willie Nelson*
38/78 **On The Shelf** *Donny & Marie Osmond*
On The Street Where You Live
4/56 *Vic Damone*
18/56 *Eddie Fisher*
96/56 *Lawrence Welk*
28/64 *Andy Williams*
67/78 **On The Strip** *Paul Nicholas*
82/68 **On The Way Home** *Buffalo Springfield*
27/82 **On The Way To The Sky** *Neil Diamond*
27/91 **On The Way Up** *Elisa Fiorillo*
50/84 **On The Wings Of A Nightingale** *Everly Brothers*
29/82 **On The Wings Of Love** *Jeffrey Osborne*
82/78 **On The Wrong Track** *Kevin Lamb*
47/66 **On This Side Of Goodbye** *Righteous Bros.*
14/63 **On Top Of Spaghetti** *Tom Glazer* *(also see: Old Smokey Locomotion)*
74/57 **On Treasure Island** *Gale Storm*
82/76 **Once A Fool** *Kiki Dee*
94/81 **Once A Night** *Jackie English*
5/89 **Once Bitten Twice Shy** *Great White*
91/86 **Once In A Lifetime** *Talking Heads*
11/61 **Once In Awhile** *Chimes*
19/64 **Once Upon A Time** *Marvin Gaye & Mary Wells*
26/61 **Once Upon A Time** *Rochell & The Candles*
10/75 **Once You Get Started** *Rufus Feat. Chaka Khan*
79/76 **Once You Hit The Road** *Dionne Warwick*
Once You Understand
23/72 *Think*
53/74 *Think*

ONE:

5/69 **One** *Three Dog Night*
7/89 **One** *Bee Gees*
9/92 **One, The** *Elton John*
10/92 **One** *U2*
30/00 **One, The** *Backstreet Boys*
35/89 **One** *Metallica*
37/02 **One, The** *Gary Allan*
42S/99 **One, The** *Aaron Skyy*
70/99 **One** *Creed*
54/96 **One And One** *Robert Miles*
10/91 **One And Only** *Chesney Hawkes*
18/90 **One And Only Man** *Steve Winwood*
1/71 **One Bad Apple** *Osmonds*
(One Banana, Two Banana) ..see: Tra La La Song
48/75 **One Beautiful Day** *Ecstasy, Passion & Pain*
66S/02 **One Big Trip** *Del The Funky Homosapien*
54/60 **One Boy** *Joanie Sommers*
87/95 **One Boy, One Girl** *Collin Raye*
96/63 **One Boy Too Late** *Mike Clifford*
11/63 **One Broken Heart For Sale** *Elvis Presley*
52/96 **One By One** *Cher*
71/67 **One By One** *Blues Magoos*
One Chain Don't Make No Prison
41/74 *Four Tops*
59/79 *Santana*
(One Cold And Blessed Winter) ..see: O' Bambino
37/74 **One Day At A Time** *Marilyn Sellars*
55/81 **One Day In Your Life** *Michael Jackson*
77/70 **One Day Of Your Life** *Andy Williams*
34/65 **One Dyin' And A Buryin'** *Roger Miller*
95/69 **One Eye Open** *Maskman & The Agents*
One Eyed Jacks ..see: Love Theme From
One Fine Day
5/63 *Chiffons*
93/76 *Julie*
66/79 *Rita Coolidge*
12/80 *Carole King*
24/71 **One Fine Morning** *Lighthouse*
76/85 **One Foot Back In Your Door** *Roman Holliday*
81/92 **1-4-All-4-1** *East Coast Family*
49/57 **One For My Baby** *Tony Bennett*
38/87 **One For The Mockingbird** *Cutting Crew*
62/96 **One For The Money** *Horace Brown*
88/76 **One For The Money** *Whispers*
31S/00 **One Four Love** *Hip Hop For Respect*
67/64 **One Girl** *Garnet Mimms*
72A/91 **One Good Man** *Sweet Sensation*
28/88 **One Good Reason** *Paul Carrack*
47S/02 **One Good Reason** *Nicole J. McCloud*
4/88 **One Good Woman** *Peter Cetera*
13/66 **One Has My Name (The Other Has My Heart)** *Barry Young*
2A/97 **One Headlight** *Wallflowers*
56/98 **One Heart At A Time** *Garth Brooks, Billy Dean, Faith Hill, Olivia Newton-John, Neal McCoy, Michael McDonald, Victoria Shaw, Bryan White*
10/87 **One Heartbeat** *Smokey Robinson*
11/74 **One Hell Of A Woman** *Mac Davis*
28/86 **One Hit (To The Body)** *Rolling Stones*
54/99 **One Honest Heart** *Reba McEntire*
One Hundred ..also see: Hundred
11/94 **100% Pure Love** *Crystal Waters*
14/82 **One Hundred Ways** *Quincy Jones/James Ingram*
69/68 **100 Years** *Nancy Sinatra*
76/67 **One Hurt Deserves Another** *Raelets*
9/97 **One I Gave My Heart To** *Aaliyah*
9/87 **One I Love** *R.E.M.*
20/57 **One In A Million** *Platters*
37/84 **One In A Million** *Romantics*
75/91 **One In A Million** *Trixter*
85/85 **One In A Million** *Eddie & The Tide*
25A/97 **One In A Million** *Aaliyah*
9/80 **One In A Million You** *Larry Graham*
14/65 **One Kiss For Old Times' Sake** *Ronnie Dove*
73/56 **One Kiss Led To Another** *Coasters*
6/02 **One Last Breath** *Creed*
13/93 **One Last Cry** *Brian McKnight*
35/79 **One Last Kiss** *J. Geils Band*
78/73 **One Last Time** *Glen Campbell*
2/70 **One Less Bell To Answer** *5th Dimension*
37/73 **One Less Set Of Footsteps** *Jim Croce*
92/80 **One Life To Live** *Wayne Massey*
94/70 **One Light Two Lights** *Satisfactions*
19/85 **One Lonely Night** *REO Speedwagon*

25/76 **One Love In My Lifetime** *Diana Ross*
82/59 **One Love, One Heart** *Four Coins*
58/87 **One Lover At A Time** *Atlantic Starr*
71/95 **1-Luv** *E-40*
19/71 **One Man Band** *Three Dog Night*
96/75 **One Man Band** *Leo Sayer*
28/73 **One Man Band (Plays All Alone)** *Ronnie Dyson*
67/73 **One Man Parade** *James Taylor*
7/75 **One Man Woman/One Woman Man** *Paul Anka/Odia Coates*
96/71 **One Man's Leftovers** *100 Proof Aged in Soul*
43/02 **One Mic** *Nas*
One Mint Julep
82/60 *Chet Atkins*
8/61 *Ray Charles*
15/01 **One Minute Man** *Missy Elliott*
5/88 **One Moment In Time** *Whitney Houston*
15/72 **One Monkey Don't Stop No Show** *Honey Cone*
65/65 **One Monkey Don't Stop No Show** *Joe Tex*
31S/99 **One More Chance** *Julio Iglesias Jr.*
74/59 **One More Chance** *Rod Bernard*
76/72 **One More Chance** *Ocean*
79/81 **One More Chance** *Diana Ross*
One More Chance/Stay With Me
2/95 *Notorious B.I.G.*
35S/01 *Notorious B.I.G.*
29/01 **One More Day** *Diamond Rio*
61/97 **One More Day** *New Edition*
29/66 **One More Heartache** *Marvin Gaye*
49/79 **One More Minute** *Saint Tropez*
45/67 **One More Mountain To Climb** *Ronnie Dove*
1/85 **One More Night** *Phil Collins*
47/81 **One More Night** *Streek*
58/98 **One More Night** *Amber*
One More Sunrise ..see: Morgen
97/64 **One More Tear** *Raindrops*
27/97 **One More Time** *Real McCoy*
32/65 **One More Time** *Ray Charles Singers*
61/01 **One More Time** *Daft Punk*
52/80 **One More Time For Love** *Billy Preston & Syreeta*
93/75 **One More Tomorrow** *Henry Gross*
97/62 **One More Town** *Kingston Trio*
One More Try
1/88 *George Michael*
29/99 *Divine*
1/91 **One More Try** *Timmy -T-*
78/96 **One More Try** *Kristine W*
81/76 **(One More Year Of) Daddy's Little Girl** *Ray Sawyer*
One Nation Under A Groove
28/78 *Funkadelic*
23/94 *Ice Cube (Bop Gun)*
4/58 **One Night** *Elvis Presley*
One Night Affair
68/69 *O'Jays*
52/72 *Jerry Butler*
59/97 **One Night At A Time** *George Strait*
One Night In Bangkok
3/85 *Murray Head*
77/85 *Robey*
13/85 **One Night Love Affair** *Bryan Adams*
34/00 **One Night Stand** *J-Shin*
74/71 **One Night Stand** *Magic Lanterns*
35S/99 **One-Nine-Nine-Nine** *Common*
11/73 **One Of A Kind (Love Affair)** *Spinners*
96/73 **One Of The Boys** *Mott The Hoople*
15/85 **One Of The Living** *Tina Turner*
62/60 **One Of The Lucky Ones** *Anita Bryant*
74/98 **One Of These Days** *Tim McGraw*
92/69 **(One Of These Days) Sunday's Gonna' Come On Tuesday** *New Establishment*
1/75 **One Of These Nights** *Eagles*
72/03 **One Of Those Days** *Whitney Houston*
4/96 **One Of Us** *Joan Osborne*
31/60 **One Of Us (Will Weep Tonight)** *Patti Page*
7/83 **One On One** *Daryl Hall & John Oates*
70/94 **One On One** *To Be Continued...*
One On One, Love Theme From ..see: My Fair Share
46/66 **One On The Right Is On The Left** *Johnny Cash*
29/76 **One Piece At A Time** *Johnny Cash*
96/64 **One Piece Topless Bathing Suit** *Rip Chords*
75/59 **One Rose (That's Left In My Heart)** *Teresa Brewer*
93/87 **One Simple Thing** *Stabilizers*
43/57 **One Step At A Time** *Brenda Lee*
55/65 **One Step At A Time** *Maxine Brown*
24/81 **One Step Closer** *Doobie Brothers*
75/01 **One Step Closer** *Linkin Park*
22/86 **One Step Closer To You** *Gavin Christopher*
13/88 **One Step Up** *Bruce Springsteen*
93/57 **One Suit** *"Tennessee" Ernie Ford*
One Summer Night
7/58 *Danleers*
22/61 *Diamonds*
96/86 **One Sunny Day/Dueling Bikes From Quicksilver** *Ray Parker, Jr. & Helen Terry*
One Sweet Day
1/95 *Mariah Carey & Boyz II Men*
35S/02 *Mariah Carey & Boyz II Men*
71/74 **One Tear** *Eddie Kendricks*
74/83 **One That Really Matters** *Survivor*
1/81 **One That You Love** *Air Supply*
30/83 **One Thing** *INXS*
4/83 **One Thing Leads To Another** *Fixx*
69/79 **137 Disco Heaven (medley)** *Amii Stewart*
91/78 **1,000 Laughs** *Eloise Laws*
22S/99 **1000 Oceans** *Tori Amos*
One Tin Soldier (The Legend Of Billy Jack)
34/70 *Original Caste*
26/71 *Coven*
79/73 *Coven*
73/74 *Coven*
45/82 **One To One** *Carole King*
10/71 **One Toke Over The Line** *Brewer & Shipley*
95/66 **One Too Many Mornings** *Beau Brummels*
9/61 **One Track Mind** *Bobby Lewis*
46/66 **One Track Mind** *Knickerbockers*
40/80 **One-Trick Pony** *Paul Simon*
1-2-3
2/65 *Len Barry*
67/67 *Ramsey Lewis*
3/88 **1-2-3** *Gloria Estefan*
59S/99 **1*2*3** *Amyth*
86/90 **1-2-3** *Chimes*
5/68 **1, 2, 3, Red Light** *1910 Fruitgum Company*
5/96 **1,2,3,4 (Sumpin' New)** *Coolio*
76/68 **(1-2-3-4-5-6-7) Count The Days** *Inez & Charlie Foxx*
61/86 **One Vision** *Queen*
38/00 **One Voice** *Billy Gilman*
56/64 **One Way Love** *Drifters*
75/86 **One Way Love** *TKA*
77/79 **One Way Love** *Bandit*
24/79 **One Way Or Another** *Blondie*
86/72 **One Way Out** *Allman Brothers Band*
94/72 **One Way Sunday** *Mark-Almond*
75/71 **One-Way Ticket** *Tyrone Davis*
1/98 **One Week** *Barenaked Ladies*
8/62 **One Who Really Loves You** *Mary Wells*
22/93 **One Woman** *Jade*
89/69 **One Woman** *Johnny Rivers*
44/01 **One Woman Man** *Dave Hollister*
15/82 **One You Love** *Glenn Frey*
97/02 **One You Love** *Paulina Rubio*
50/70 **Onion Song** *Marvin Gaye & Tammi Terrell*

ONLY:

35S/99 **Only A Dream** *EYC*
36/80 **Only A Lonely Heart Sees** *Felix Cavaliere*
92/88 **Only A Memory** *Smithereens*
65/57 **Only Because** *Platters*
F/71 **Only Believe** *Elvis Presley*
56/84 **Only Flame In Town** *Elvis Costello*
51/85 **Only For Love** *Limahl*
19/00 **Only God Knows Why** *Kid Rock*
55/96 **Only Happy When It Rains** *Garbage*
88/98 **Only If...** *Enya*
25/63 **Only In America** *Jay & The Americans*
33/01 **Only In America** *Brooks & Dunn*
4/87 **Only In My Dreams** *Debbie Gibson*
62/73 **Only In Your Heart** *America*
54/85 **Only Lonely** *Bon Jovi*
63S/93 **Only Love** *Wynonna*
86/73 **Only Love** *Bill Quateman*
Only Love Can Break A Heart
2/62 *Gene Pitney*
96/67 *Margaret Whiting*
99/77 *Bobby Vinton*
Only Love Can Break Your Heart
33/70 *Neil Young*
97/92 *St. Etienne*
94/65 **Only Love (Can Save Me Now)** *Solomon Burke*
28/76 **Only Love Is Real** *Carole King*
49/96 **Only Love (The Ballad Of Sleeping Beauty)** *Sophie B. Hawkins*
89/90 **Only My Heart Talkin'** *Alice Cooper*
60A/98 **Only One For Me** *Brian McKnight*
33/57 **Only One Love** *George Hamilton IV*
63/78 **Only One Love In My Life** *Ronnie Milsap*
93/95 **Only One Road** *Celine Dion*
91/75 **Only One Woman** *Nigel Olsson*
68/82 **Only One You** *T.G. Sheppard*
Only Sixteen
28/59 *Sam Cooke*
6/76 *Dr. Hook*
24/78 **Only The Good Die Young** *Billy Joel*
Only The Lonely
2/60 *Roy Orbison*
92/69 *Sonny James*
9/82 **Only The Lonely** *Motels*
91/80 **Only The Lonely (Have A Reason To Be Sad)** *La Flavour*
82/77 **Only The Lucky** *Walter Egan*

4/69 **Only The Strong Survive** *Jerry Butler*
9/85 **Only The Young** *Journey*
52/96 **Only Thing That Looks Good On Me Is You** *Bryan Adams*
73/65 **Only Those In Love** *Baby Washington*
10/01 **Only Time** *Enya*
17/82 **Only Time Will Tell** *Asia*
28/91 **Only Time Will Tell** *Nelson*
6/95 **Only Wanna Be With You** *Hootie & The Blowfish*
96/88 **Only Way Is Up** *Yazz & The Plastic Population*
64/82 **Only Way Out** *Cliff Richard*
61/98 **Only When I Lose Myself** *Depeche Mode*
34/84 **Only When You Leave** *Spandau Ballet*
96/66 **Only When You're Lonely** *Grass Roots*
Only Women
12/75 *Alice Cooper*
69/90 *Favorite Angel*
4/75 **Only Yesterday** *Carpenters*
Only You
5/55 *Platters*
8/55 *Hilltoppers*
9/59 *Franck Pourcel's French Fiddles*
77/63 *Mr. Acker Bilk*
95/69 *Bobby Hatfield*
6/75 *Ringo Starr*
13/96 **Only You** *112*
54/83 **Only You** *Commodores*
67/83 **Only You** *Yaz*
87/78 **Only You** *Loleatta Holloway & Bunny Sigler*
93/98 **Only You** *Tami Davis*
53/75 **Only You Can** *Fox*
Only You Know And I Know
42/70 *Dave Mason*
20/71 *Delaney & Bonnie*
61/85 **Oo-Ee-Diddley-Bop!** *Peter Wolf*
61/67 **O-O, I Love You** *Dells*
99/63 **Oo-La-La-Limbo** *Danny & The Juniors*
F/75 **Oo-Wee** *Ringo Starr*
23/65 **Oo Wee Baby, I Love You** *Fred Hughes*
59/56 **Ooby Dooby** *Roy Orbison*
21/92 **Oochie Coochie** *MC Brains*
26/01 **Oochie Wally** *QB Finest*
34/67 **Oogum Boogum Song** *Brenton Wood*
12/97 **Ooh Aah...Just A Little Bit** *Gina G*
25/73 **Ooh Baby** *Gilbert O'Sullivan*
65/67 **Ooh Baby** *Deon Jackson*
88/67 **Ooh Baby** *Bo Diddley*
Ooh Baby Baby
16/65 *Miracles*
63/67 *Five Stairsteps*
7/79 *Linda Ronstadt*
83/55 **Ooh Bang Jiggilly Jang** *Doris Day*
72/78 **Ooh Boy** *Rose Royce*
O-o-h Child
8/70 *5 Stairsteps*
27/93 *Dino*
30S/02 **Ooh La La** *Valeria*
39/98 **Ooh La La** *Rod Stewart*
51/91 **Ooh La La** *David Hallyday*
10/90 **Ooh La La (I Can't Get Over You)** *Perfect Gentlemen*
31/58 **Ooh! My Soul** *Little Richard*
36/85 **Ooh Ooh Song** *Pat Benatar*

Ooh Poo Pah Doo
28/60 *Jessie Hill*
60/71 *Ike & Tina Turner*
85/88 **Ooo La La La** *Teena Marie*
68S/00 **Oooh.** *De La Soul*
90/91 **Oooh This I Need** *Elisa Fiorillo*
63/01 **Ooohhhwee** *Master P*
35/90 **Ooops Up** *Snap!*
7/02 **Oops (Oh My)** *Tweet*
9/00 **Oops!...I Did It Again** *Britney Spears*
88/65 **Oowee, Oowee** *Perry Como*
69/58 **Op** *Honeycones*
81/76 **Open** *Smokey Robinson*
2/82 **Open Arms** *Journey*
82/89 **Open Letter (To A Landlord)** *Living Colour*
10/67 **Open Letter To My Teenage Son** *Victor Lundberg*
(also see: Letter To Dad)
57/00 **Open My Heart** *Yolanda Adams*
55/77 **Open Sesame** *Kool & The Gang*
90/72 **Open The Door (Song For Judith)** *Judy Collins*
27/66 **Open The Door To Your Heart** *Darrell Banks*
51/70 **Open Up My Heart** *Dells*
55/67 **(Open Up The Door) Let The Good Times In** *Dean Martin*
99/66 **Open Up Your Door** *Richard & The Young Lions*
68A/98 **Open Up Your Eyes** *Tonic*
8/55 **Open Up Your Heart (And Let The Sunshine In)** *Cowboy Church Sunday School*
1/87 **Open Your Heart** *Madonna*
18/85 **Operator** *Midnight Star*
22/75 **Operator** *Manhattan Transfer*
78/65 **Operator** *Brenda Holloway*
97/62 **Operator** *Gladys Knight*
17/72 **Operator (That's Not the Way it Feels)** *Jim Croce*
62/76 **Ophelia** *Band*
10/86 **Opportunities (Let's Make Lots Of Money)** *Pet Shop Boys*
64/64 **Opportunity** *Jewels*
1/90 **Opposites Attract** *Paula Abdul*
78/82 **Opposites Do Attract** *All Sports Band*
56S/01 **Opticon** *Orgy*
13/66 **Opus 17 (Don't You Worry 'Bout Me)** *4 Seasons*
Orange Blossom Special
63/61 *Billy Vaughn*
80/65 *Johnny Cash*
30/02 **Ordinary Day** *Vanessa Carlton*
39/99 **Ordinary Life** *Chad Brock*
3/93 **Ordinary World** *Duran Duran*
92/65 **Organ Grinder's Swing** *Jimmy Smith, Kenny Burrell, Grady Tate*
76/63 **Organ Shout** *Dave "Baby" Cortez*
70/00 **Original Prankster** *Offspring*
58/84 **Original Sin** *INXS*
24/89 **Orinoco Flow (Sail Away)** *Enya*
8S/02 **Osama-Yo' Mama** *Ray Stevens*
11/83 **Other Guy** *Little River Band*
31/67 **Other Man's Grass Is Always Greener** *Petula Clark*
22/90 **Other Side** *Aerosmith*
14/00 **Otherside** *Red Hot Chili Peppers*
58/86 **Other Side Of Life** *Moody Blues*
100/66 **Other Side Of This Life** *Peter, Paul & Mary*
4/82 **Other Woman** *Ray Parker Jr.*
81/75 **Other Woman** *Vicki Lawrence*

86/56 **Other Woman** *Sarah Vaughan*
Otherside ..see: Other Side

OUR:

59/62 **Our Anniversary** *Shep & The Limelites*
Our Day Will Come
1/63 *Ruby & The Romantics*
11/75 *Frankie Valli*
64/64 **Our Everlasting Love** *Ruby & The Romantics*
7/83 **Our House** *Madness*
30/70 **Our House** *Crosby, Stills, Nash & Young*
95/75 **Our Last Song Together** *Bo Donaldson*
20/81 **Our Lips Are Sealed** *Go-Go's*
10/78 **Our Love** *Natalie Cole*
43/56 **Our Love Affair** *Tommy Charles*
(also see: Affair To Remember)
9/78 **(Our Love) Don't Throw It All Away** *Andy Gibb*
89/61 **Our Love Is Here To Stay** *Dinah Washington*
51/79 **Our Love Is Insane** *Desmond Child & Rouge*
80/78 **Our Night** *Shaun Cassidy*
92/67 **Our Song** *Jack Jones*
Our Winter Love
9/63 *Bill Pursell*
72/67 *Lettermen*
64/70 **Our World** *Blue Mink*
70/65 **Our World** *Johnny Tillotson*

OUT:

39/67 **Out & About** *Tommy Boyce & Bobby Hart*
19/80 **Out Here On My Own** *Irene Cara*
15/70 **Out In The Country** *Three Dog Night*
53/65 **Out In The Streets** *Shangri-Las*
Out Of ..see: Outa
59/67 **Out Of Left Field** *Percy Sledge*
3/64 **Out Of Limits** *Marketts*
37/86 **Out Of Mind Out Of Sight** *Models*
64/98 **Out Of My Bones** *Randy Travis*
20/99 **Out Of My Head** *Fastball*
56/02 **Out Of My Heart (Into Your Head)** *BBMak*
24/63 **Out Of My Mind** *Johnny Tillotson*
22S/01 **Out Of Nowhere** *Gloria Estefan*
24/64 **Out Of Sight** *James Brown*
Out Of Sight, Out Of Mind
23/56 *Five Keys*
71/64 *Sunny & The Sunliners*
52/69 *Little Anthony & The Imperials*
97/98 **Out Of Sight (Yo)** *Rufus Blaq*
60/94 **Out Of Tears** *Rolling Stones*
3/88 **Out Of The Blue** *Debbie Gibson*
43/67 **Out Of The Blue** *Tommy James*
89/76 **Out Of The Darkness** *David Crosby/Graham Nash*
17/73 **Out Of The Question** *Gilbert O'Sullivan*
67/66 **Out Of This World** *Chiffons*
81/75 **Out Of Time** *Rolling Stones*
1/84 **Out Of Touch** *Daryl Hall John Oates*
21/82 **Out Of Work** *Gary U.S. Bonds*
2/72 **Outa-Space** *Billy Preston*
94/82 **Outlaw** *War*
Outlaw Man
59/73 *Eagles*
94/73 *David Blue*
56/01 **Outside** *Aaron Lewis*
28/60 **Outside My Window** *Fleetwoods*

52/80 **Outside My Window** *Stevie Wonder*
45/66 **Outside The Gates Of Heaven** *Lou Christie*
34/74 **Outside Woman** *Bloodstone*
51/83 **Outstanding** *Gap Band*
Over And Over
41/58 *Bobby Day*
96/58 *Thurston Harris*
1/65 *Dave Clark Five*
58/71 **Over And Over** *Delfonics*
59/89 **Over And Over** *Pajama Party*
63/91 **Over and Over** *Timmy -T-*
20/76 **Over My Head** *Fleetwood Mac*
81/84 **Over My Head** *Toni Basil*
51/73 **Over The Hills And Far Away** *Led Zeppelin*
91/82 **Over The Line** *Eddie Schwartz*
Over The Mountain; Across The Sea
8/57 *Johnnie & Joe*
89/60 *Johnnie & Joe*
21/63 *Bobby Vinton*
Over The Rainbow
16/60 *Demensions*
69/78 *Gary Tanner*
62/58 **Over The Weekend** *Playboys*
8^{S}/02 **Over The Years** *Good Bad Ugly*
13/66 **Over Under Sideways Down** *Yardbirds*
7/68 **Over You** *Gary Puckett*
80/80 **Over You** *Roxy Music*
24/86 **Overjoyed** *Stevie Wonder*
3/83 **Overkill** *Men At Work*
18/74 **Overnight Sensation (Hit Record)** *Raspberries*
86/02 **Overprotected** *Britney Spears*
16/70 **Overture From Tommy (A Rock Opera)** *Assembled Multitude*
57/86 **Own The Night** *Chaka Khan*
1/84 **Owner Of A Lonely Heart** *Yes*
77/89 **Owwww!** *Chunky A*
45^{S}/02 **Oxygen** *Krumb Snatcha*
13/71 **Oye Como Va** *Santana*
48/90 **Oye Mi Canto (Hear My Voice)** *Gloria Estefan*

P

46^{S}/99 **P.E. 2000** *Puff Daddy*
10/64 **P.S. I Love You** *Beatles*
8/62 **P.T. 109** *Jimmy Dean*
10/83 **P.Y.T. (Pretty Young Thing)** *Michael Jackson*
9/82 **Pac-Man Fever** *Buckner & Garcia*
13/58 **Padre** *Toni Arden*
64/72 **Pain** *Ohio Players*
89/66 **Pain Gets A Little Deeper** *Darrow Fletcher*
61/64 **Pain In My Heart** *Otis Redding*
1/66 **Paint It, Black** *Rolling Stones*
Paint Me A Picture ..see: (You Don't Have To)
34/74 **Painted Ladies** *Ian Thomas*
82/87 **Painted Moon** *Silencers*
70/83 **Painted Picture** *Commodores*
15/63 **Painted, Tainted Rose** *Al Martino*
81/66 **Painter** *Lou Christie*
65/73 **Palace Guard** *Rick Nelson*
Paladin ..see: Ballad Of
3/62 **Palisades Park** *Freddy Cannon*
26/76 **Paloma Blanca** *George Baker Selection*
22/88 **Pamela** *Toto*
55/57 **Pamela Throws A Party** *Joe Reisman*
13/84 **Panama** *Van Halen*
35/66 **Pandora's Golden Heebie Jeebies** *Association*
99/61 **Panic** *Charms*
Papa Don't Preach
1/86 *Madonna*
74/02 *Kelly Osbourne*
31/74 **Papa Don't Take No Mess** *James Brown*
Papa Joe's ..see: (Down At)
4/54 **Papa Loves Mambo** *Perry Como*
48/62 **Papa-Oom-Mow-Mow** *Rivingtons*
Papa Was A Rollin' Stone
1/72 *Temptations*
63/72 *Undisputed Truth*
55/83 *Wolf*
44/67 **Papa Was Too** *Joe Tex*
Papa's Got A Brand New Bag
8/65 *James Brown*
21/69 *Otis Redding*
87/94 **Papa'z Song** *2Pac*
83/96 **Paparazzi** *Xzibit*
50/98 **Paper** *Queen Latifah*
34/67 **Paper Cup** *5th Dimension*
28/92 **Paper Doll** *PM Dawn*
9/87 **Paper In Fire** *John Cougar Mellencamp*
43/70 **Paper Mache** *Dionne Warwick*
Paper Roses
5/60 *Anita Bryant*
5/73 *Marie Osmond*
72/55 **Paper Roses** *Lola Dee*
94/67 **Paper Sun** *Traffic*
23/65 **Paper Tiger** *Sue Thompson*
1/66 **Paperback Writer** *Beatles*
32/82 **Paperlate** *Genesis*
16/88 **Paradise** *Sade*
36/03 **Paradise** *LL Cool J*
46/60 **Paradise** *Sammy Turner*
50^{S}/01 **Paradise** *Kaci*
80/81 **Paradise** *Change*
39/78 **Paradise By The Dashboard Light** *Meat Loaf*
5/89 **Paradise City** *Guns N' Roses*
59/57 **Paralyzed** *Elvis Presley*
61/70 **Paranoid** *Black Sabbath*
34/86 **Paranoimia** *Art Of Noise with Max Headroom*
51/73 **Pardon Me Sir** *Joe Cocker*
12/88 **Parents Just Don't Understand** *D.J. Jazzy Jeff & The Fresh Prince*
95/58 **Paris** *Perez Prado*
71/73 **Parrty** *Maceo & The Macks*
38/58 **Part Of Me** *Jimmy Clanton*
55/91 **Part Of Me, Part Of You** *Glenn Frey*
98/80 **Part Of Me That Needs You Most** *Jay Black*
31/75 **Part Of The Plan** *Dan Fogelberg*
94/71 **Part Of You** *Brenda & The Tabulations*
Part Time Love
19/63 *Little Johnny Taylor*
45/70 *Ann Peebles*
22/75 **Part Time Love** *Gladys Knight*
22/78 **Part-Time Love** *Elton John*
97/77 **Part Time Love** *Kerry Chater*
1/85 **Part-Time Lover** *Stevie Wonder*
57/94 **Part Time Lover** *H-Town*
72/02 **Part II** *Method Man & Redman*

PARTY:

69/76 **Party** *Van McCoy*
71^{S}/94 **Party** *Dis 'N' Dat*
(also see: Parrty)
74/98 **Party Ain't A Party** *Queen Pen*
60^{S}/95 **Party All Night** *Jeff Foxworthy with Little Texas*
2/85 **Party All The Time** *Eddie Murphy*
29/98 **Party Continues** *JD & Da Brat*
Party Doll
1/57 *Buddy Knox*
5/57 *Steve Lawrence*
56/57 *Wingy Manone*
89/57 *Roy Brown*
47/64 **Party Girl** *Bernadette Carroll*
85/64 **Party Girl** *Tommy Roe*
5/62 **Party Lights** *Claudine Clark*
79/77 **Party Lights** *Natalie Cole*
80/76 **Party Line** *Andrea True Connection*
78/75 **Party Music** *Pat Lundi*
45/57 **Party Time** *Sal Mineo*
45^{S}/99 **Party Tonight** *3rd Storee*
27/00 **Party Up (Up In Here)** *DMX*
63/57 **Party's Over** *Doris Day*
34/81 **Party's Over (Hopelessly In Love)** *Journey*
18/89 **Partyman** *Prince*
93/65 **Pass Me By** *Peggy Lee*
97/69 **Pass The Apple Eve** *B.J. Thomas*
11/02 **Pass The Courvoisier** *Busta Rhymes*
10/83 **Pass The Dutchie** *Musical Youth*
95/72 **Pass The Peas** *JB's*
52/93 **Passin' Me By** *Pharcyde*
82/57 **Passing Strangers** *Sarah Vaughan & Billy Eckstine*
2/91 **P.A.S.S.I.O.N** *Rythm Syndicate*
5/81 **Passion** *Rod Stewart*
98/97 **Passion** *K5*
80/73 **Passion Play (Edit #8)** *Jethro Tull*
57/93 **Passionate Kisses** *Mary-Chapin Carpenter*
59/66 **Past, Present And Future** *Shangri-Las*
12/67 **Pata Pata** *Miriam Makeba*
F/70 **Patch It Up** *Elvis Presley*
94/70 **Patch Of Blue** *4 Seasons*
4/70 **Patches** *Clarence Carter*
6/62 **Patches** *Dickey Lee*
4/89 **Patience** *Guns N' Roses*
Patricia
1/58 *Perez Prado*
65/62 *Perez Prado (Twist)*
65/60 **Patsy** *Jack Scott*
43/62 **Patti Ann** *Johnny Crawford*
65/63 **Patty Baby** *Freddy Cannon*
78/63 **Pay Back** *Etta James*
26/74 **Payback, The** *James Brown*
67/81 **Pay The Devil (Ooo, Baby, Ooo)** *Knack*
13/71 **Pay To The Piper** *Chairmen Of The Board*
Pay You Back With Interest
28/67 *Hollies*
70/81 *Gary O'*
39/68 **Paying The Cost To Be The Boss** *B.B. King*
74/93 **Paying The Price Of Love** *Bee Gees*
85/59 **Peace** *McGuire Sisters*
48/68 **Peace Brother Peace** *Bill Medley*
11/90 **Peace In Our Time** *Eddie Money*
75^{A}/91 **Peace (In The Valley)** *Sabrina Johnston*
(also see: There'll Be)

38/77 **Peace Of Mind** *Boston*
42/67 **Peace Of Mind** *Paul Revere & The Raiders*
50S/00 **Peace Of Mind** *Darkside Ballaz*
55/68 **Peace Of Mind** *Nancy Wilson*
66/60 **Peace Of Mind** *Teresa Brewer*
95/92 **Peace Of Mind (Love Goes On)** *One 2 One*
Peace On Earth (medley)
58S/00 *David Bowie & Bing Crosby*
75S/01 *David Bowie & Bing Crosby*
43S/02 *David Bowie & Bing Crosby*
31/75 **Peace Pipe** *B.T. Express*
7/71 **Peace Train** *Cat Stevens*
32/70 **Peace Will Come (According To Plan)** *Melanie*
12/73 **Peaceful** *Helen Reddy*
22/73 **Peaceful Easy Feeling** *Eagles*
80/73 **Peacemaker, The** *Albert Hammond*
29/96 **Peaches** *Presidents Of The United States Of America*
Peaches & Cream
4/01 *One Twelve*
38S/02 *One Twelve*
36/65 **Peaches "N" Cream** *Ikettes*
97/66 **Peak Of Love** *Bobby McClure*
20/61 **Peanut Butter** *Marathons*
83/80 **Peanut Butter** *Twennynine Feat. Lenny White*
Peanuts
22/57 *Little Joe & The Thrillers*
60/61 *Rick & The Keens*
64/65 **Peanuts (La Cacahuata)** *Sunglows*
50/70 **Pearl** *Tommy Roe*
90/67 **Pearl Time** *Andre Williams*
60/64 **Pearly Shells (Popo O Ewa)** *Burl Ives*
(also see: First Night Of The Full Moon)
92/67 **Peas 'N' Rice** *Freddie McCoy*
28/59 **Peek-A-Boo** *Cadillacs*
53/88 **Peek-A-Boo** *Siouxsie & The Banshees*
72/67 **Peek-A-Boo** *New Vaudeville Band*
11/78 **Peg** *Steely Dan*
64/64 **Peg O' My Heart** *Robert Maxwell*
Peggy Sue
3/57 *Buddy Holly*
59/78 *Beach Boys*
18/64 **Penetration** *Pyramids*
24/60 **Pennies From Heaven** *Skyliners*
95/67 **Penny Arcade** *Cyrkle*
33/82 **Penny For Your Thoughts** *Tavares*
1/67 **Penny Lane** *Beatles*
42/57 **Penny Loafers And Bobby Socks** *Joe Bennett*
8/84 **Penny Lover** *Lionel Richie*
People
5/64 *Barbra Streisand*
100/64 *Nat King Cole*
39/68 *Tymes*
75/73 **People Are Changin'** *Timmy Thomas*
13/85 **People Are People** *Depeche Mode*
35/91 **People Are Still Having Sex** *LaTour*
12/67 **People Are Strange** *Doors*
74/95 **People Don't Believe (a.k.a. Hand Of The Dead Body)** *Scarface*
8/92 **People Everyday** *Arrested Development*
People Get Ready
14/65 *Impressions*
48/85 *Jeff Beck & Rod Stewart*

People Got To Be Free
1/68 *Rascals*
60/70 *5th Dimension (medley)*
22/74 **People Gotta Move** *Gino Vannelli*
40/77 **People In Love** *10cc*
66/67 **People In Me** *Music Machine*
97/67 **People Like You** *Eddie Fisher*
25/72 **People Make The World Go Round** *Stylistics*
23/79 **People Of The South Wind** *Kansas*
12/64 **People Say** *Dixie Cups*
58/68 **People Sure Act Funny** *Arthur Conley*
92/72 **People Tree** *Sammy Davis, Jr.*
94/68 **People World** *Jim & Jean*
18/61 **"Pepe"** *Duane Eddy*
5/63 **Pepino The Italian Mouse** *Lou Monte*
78/63 **Pepino's Friend Pasqual (The Italian Pussy-Cat)** *Lou Monte*
26A/96 **Pepper** *Butthole Surfers*
76/74 **Pepper Box** *Peppers*
Pepper Hot Baby
60/55 *Gisele MacKenzie*
14/56 *Jaye P. Morgan*
1/62 **Peppermint Twist** *Joey Dee*
54/61 **Peppermint Twist** *Danny Peppermint*
85/65 **Percolatin'** *Willie Mitchell*
10/62 **Percolator (Twist)** *Billy Joe & The Checkmates*
54/98 **Perfect** *Smashing Pumpkins*
80/89 **Perfect** *Fairground Attraction*
(also see: Closest Thing To)
75/84 **Perfect Combination** *Stacy Lattisaw & Johnny Gill*
46/97 **Perfect Drug** *Nine Inch Nails*
47/61 **Perfect Love** *Frankie Avalon*
11/85 **Perfect Way** *Scritti Politti*
3/88 **Perfect World** *Huey Lewis*
90/91 **Perfect World** *Alias*
15/60 **Perfidia** *Ventures*
59/82 **Perhaps Love** *Plácido Domingo & John Denver*
28/90 **Personal Jesus** *Depeche Mode*
Personality
2/59 *Lloyd Price*
87/68 *Mitch Ryder (medley)*
19/82 **Personally** *Karla Bonoff*
62/55 **Pet Me, Poppa** *Rosemary Clooney*
28H/55 **Pete Kelly's Blues** *Ray Anthony*
Peter Gunn
8/59 *Ray Anthony*
27/60 *Duane Eddy*
84/76 *Deodato*
50/86 *Art Of Noise*
48/79 **Peter Piper** *Frank Mills*
45/66 **Peter Rabbit** *Dee Jay & The Runaways*
Petite Fleur
5/59 *Chris Barber's Jazz Band*
59/65 *Lou Johnson (Time To Love)*
67/93 **Pets** *Porno For Pyros*
81/66 **Petticoat White (Summer Sky Blue)** *Bobby Vinton*
Petticoats Of Portugal
16/56 *Dick Jacobs*
83/56 *Billy Vaughn*
43/77 **Phantom Writer** *Gary Wright*
55/97 **Phenomenon** *LL Cool J*
64/75 **Philadelphia** *B.B. King*
1/75 **Philadelphia Freedom** *Elton John Band*

Philadelphia U.S.A.
26/58 *Nu Tornados*
89/58 *Art Lund*
Philly Dog
89/66 *Mar-Keys*
93/66 *Herbie Mann*
(also see: Baby, Do The)
49/66 **Philly Freeze** *Alvin Cash*
32/66 **Phoenix Love Theme (Senza Fine)** *Brass Ring*
1/73 **Photograph** *Ringo Starr*
12/83 **Photograph** *Def Leppard*
53A/96 **Photograph** *Verve Pipe*
94/92 **Phuncky Feel One** *Cypress Hill*
1/81 **Physical** *Olivia Newton-John*
87/96 **Physical Funk** *Domino*
6/88 **Piano In The Dark** *Brenda Russell*
25/74 **Piano Man** *Billy Joel*
90/92 **Pick It Up Pick It Up** *Home Team*
91/61 **Pick Me Up On Your Way Down** *Pat Zill*
1/75 **Pick Up The Pieces** *AWB*
68/68 **Pick Up The Pieces** *Carla Thomas*
27/68 **Pickin' Wild Mountain Berries** *Peggy Scott & Jo Jo Benson*
99/58 **Pickle Up A Doodle** *Teresa Brewer*
60/95 **Pickup Man** *Joe Diffie*
Picnic ..see: Moonglow
4/03 **Picture** *Kid Rock*
27S/00 **Picture Perfect** *Angela Vía*
84/94 **Picture Postcards From L.A.** *Joshua Kadison*
77/62 **Pictures In The Fire** *Pat Boone*
51/67 **Pictures Of Lily** *Who*
12/68 **Pictures Of Matchstick Men** *Status Quo*
71/90 **Pictures Of You** *Cure*
32C/55 **Piddily Patter Patter** *Patti Page*
87/85 **Piece By Piece** *Tubes*
7/91 **Piece Of My Heart** *Tara Kemp*
Piece Of My Heart
62/67 *Erma Franklin*
12/68 *Big Brother & The Holding Company*
73/82 *Sammy Hagar*
72/97 *Shaggy*
45/72 **Piece Of Paper** *Gladstone*
19/73 **Pieces Of April** *Three Dog Night*
31/83 **Pieces Of Ice** *Diana Ross*
50/57 **Pied Piper** *Billy Williams*
Pied Piper
87/65 *Changin' Times*
4/66 *Crispian St. Peters*
70/75 **Pill, The** *Loretta Lynn*
Pillow ..see: (Lay Your Head On My)
3/73 **Pillow Talk** *Sylvia*
13/80 **Pilot Of The Airwaves** *Charlie Dore*
65/95 **Pimp Of The Year** *Dru Down*
47S/99 **Pimpin' Ain't No Illusion** *UGK*
72S/02 **Pimps/Players** *Skip*
54/63 **Pin A Medal On Joey** *James Darren*
74/71 **Pin The Tail On The Donkey** *Newcomers*
91/66 **Pin The Tail On The Donkey** *Paul Peek*
(Pina Colada Song) ..see: Escape
60/75 **Pinball** *Brian Protheroe*
96/79 **Pinball, That's All** *Bill Wray*
Pinball Wizard
19/69 *Who*
29/73 *New Seekers (medley)*
15/00 **Pinch Me** *Barenaked Ladies*

99/69 **Pinch Me (Baby, Convince Me)** *Ohio Express*
11/60 **Pineapple Princess** *Annette*
27/98 **Pink** *Aerosmith*
5/88 **Pink Cadillac** *Natalie Cole*
50/93 **Pink Cashmere** *Prince*
60/60 **Pink Chiffon** *Mitchell Torok*
96/93 **Pink Cookies In A Plastic Bag Getting Crushed By Buildings** *LL Cool J*
69/64 **Pink Dominos** *Crescents*
8/84 **Pink Houses** *John Cougar Mellencamp*
31/64 **Pink Panther Theme** *Henry Mancini*
91/58 **Pink Pedal Pushers** *Carl Perkins*
3/59 **Pink Shoe Laces** *Dodie Stevens*
Piove ..see: Ciao, Ciao Bambina
60/67 **Pipe Dream** *Blues Magoos*
82/59 **Pipe Dreams** *Jimmy Beck*
4/63 **Pipeline** *Chantay's*
93/77 **Pirate** *Cher*
76/61 **Pitter-Patter** *Four Sportsmen*
9/66 **Place In The Sun** *Stevie Wonder*
42/77 **Place In The Sun** *Pablo Cruise*
6/91 **Place In This World** *Michael W. Smith*
34/94 **Place Where You Belong** *Shai*
38/59 **Plain Jane** *Bobby Darin*
77/79 **Plain Jane** *Sammy Hagar*
48/82 **Planet Rock** *Afrika Bambaataa*
36S/01 **Planets Of The Universe** *Stevie Nicks*
19/55 **Plantation Boogie** *Lenny Dee*
40/73 **Plastic Man** *Temptations*
74/67 **Plastic Man** *Sonny & Chér*
63/77 **Platinum Heroes** *Bruce Foster*

PLAY:

18/01 **Play** *Jennifer Lopez*
41S/99 **Play Around** *Lil' Cease*
79/56 **Play For Keeps** *Jaye P. Morgan*
11/72 **Play Me** *Neil Diamond*
6/55 **Play Me Hearts And Flowers (I Wanna Cry)** *Johnny Desmond*
72/94 **Play My Funk** *Simple E*
49/76 **Play On Love** *Jefferson Starship*
33/74 **Play Something Sweet (Brickyard Blues)** *Three Dog Night*
Play That Funky Music
1/76 *Wild Cherry*
63/88 *Roxanne*
4/91 *Vanilla Ice*
42/80 **Play The Game** *Queen*
17/82 **Play The Game Tonight** *Kansas*
95/62 **Play The Thing** *Marlowe Morris Quintet*
13S/02 **Play Wit It** *DSD*
96/65 **Play With Fire** *Rolling Stones*
65S/95 **Playa Hata** *Luniz*
52S/00 **Playa No More** *Crystal Sierra*
61S/01 **Playa Playa (playing the game right)** *Minott*
81/01 **Playas Gon' Play** *3LW*
36/94 **Playaz Club** *Rappin' 4-Tay*
7/62 **Playboy** *Marvelettes*
17/68 **Playboy** *Gene & Debbe*
70/74 **Player, The** *First Choice*
13/95 **Player's Anthem** *Junior M.A.F.I.a.*
37/94 **Player's Ball** *OutKast*
90/99 **Players Holiday** *T.W.D.Y.*
49/69 **Playgirl** *Thee Prophets*
10/91 **Playground** *Another Bad Creation*
2/73 **Playground In My Mind** *Clint Holmes*
21/57 **Playing For Keeps** *Elvis Presley*
60/85 **Playing To Win** *LRB*
71/81 **Playing With Lightning** *Shot In The Dark*
60/86 **Playing With The Boys** *Kenny Loggins*
F/55 **Playmates** *Fontane Sisters*
Plaything
41/57 *Nick Todd*
45/57 *Ted Newman*
74/58 **Plea, The** *Jesters*
3/67 **Pleasant Valley Sunday** *Monkees*

PLEASE:

67/97 **Please** *Kinleys*
71/64 **Please** *Frank Ifield*
63/82 **Please Be The One** *Karla Bonoff*
Please Come Home For Christmas
76/61 *Charles Brown*
32X/67 *Uniques*
18/78 *Eagles*
5/74 **Please Come To Boston** *Dave Loggins*
69/73 **Please, Daddy** *John Denver*
15/62 **Please Don't Ask About Barbara** *Bobby Vee*
98/69 **Please Don't Desert Me Baby** *Gloria Walker/Chevelles*
77/58 **Please Don't Do It** *Dale Wright*
59/66 **Please Don't Ever Leave Me** *Cyrkle*
60/66 **Please Don't Fight It** *Dino, Desi & Billy*
Please Don't Go
1/80 *KC & The Sunshine Band*
6/92 *K.W.S.*
21/97 **Please Don't Go** *No Mercy*
36/96 **Please Don't Go** *Immature*
39/61 **Please Don't Go** *Ral Donner*
49/92 **Please Don't Go** *Boyz II Men*
10/88 **Please Don't Go Girl** *New Kids On The Block*
100/63 **Please Don't Kiss Me Again** *Charmettes*
24/79 **Please Don't Leave** *Lauren Wood*
55/56 **Please Don't Leave Me** *Fontane Sisters*
64/66 **Please Don't Sell My Daddy No More Wine** *Greenwoods*
45/66 **Please Don't Stop Loving Me** *Elvis Presley*
31/63 **Please Don't Talk To The Lifeguard** *Diane Ray*
95/74 **Please Don't Tell Me How The Story Ends** *Ronnie Milsap*
7/93 **Please Forgive Me** *Bryan Adams*
Please Help Me, I'm Falling
8/60 *Hank Locklin*
54/60 *Rusty Draper*
(also see: I Can't Help You)
52/65 **Please Let Me Wonder** *Beach Boys*
Please Love Me Forever
61/58 *Tommy Edwards*
12/61 *Cathy Jean & The Roommates*
6/67 *Bobby Vinton*
3/75 **Please Mr. Please** *Olivia Newton-John*
Please Mr. Postman
1/61 *Marvelettes*
1/75 *Carpenters*
82/83 *Gentle Persuasion*
60/75 **Please, Mr. President** *Paula Webb*
Please Mr. Sun
11/59 *Tommy Edwards*
48/66 *Vogues*
48/75 **Please Pardon Me (You Remind Me Of A Friend)** *Rufus feat. Chaka Khan*
3/64 **Please Please Me** *Beatles*
95/64 **Please, Please, Please** *James Brown*
10/99 **Please Remember Me** *Tim McGraw*
26/68 **Please Return Your Love To Me** *Temptations*
64/66 **Please Say You're Fooling** *Ray Charles*
73/57 **Please Send Me Someone To Love** *Moonglows*
14/61 **Please Stay** *Drifters*
84/75 **Please Tell Him That I Said Hello** *Debbie Campbell*
20/61 **Please Tell Me Why** *Jackie Wilson*
28/66 **Please Tell Me Why** *Dave Clark Five*
69/92 **Pleasure** *Soup Dragons*
76/86 **Pleasure And Pain** *Divinyls*
14/87 **Pleasure Principle** *Janet Jackson*
44/69 **Pledge Of Allegiance** *Red Skelton*
Pledge Of Love
12/57 *Ken Copeland*
25/57 *Mitchell Torok*
42/57 *Dick Contino*
63/57 *Johnny Janis*
74/82 **Pledge Pin** *Robert Plant*
Pledging My Love
17/55 *Johnny Ace*
17/55 *Teresa Brewer*
45/58 *Roy Hamilton*
63/60 *Johnny Tillotson*
69/59 **Plenty Good Lovin'** *Connie Francis*
41A/95 **Plowed** *Sponge*
39A/93 **Plush** *Stone Temple Pilots*
21/02 **Po' Folks** *Nappy Roots*
18X/68 **Po' Folks' Christmas** *Bill Anderson*
22/96 **Po Pimp** *Do Or Die*
25S/01 **Po' Punch** *Po' White Trash*
34/62 **Pocketful Of Miracles** *Frank Sinatra*
93/61 **Pocketful Of Rainbows** *Deane Hawley*
48/59 **Poco-Loco** *Gene & Eunice*
2/60 **Poetry In Motion** *Johnny Tillotson*
5/75 **Poetry Man** *Phoebe Snow*
37/70 **Point It Out** *Miracles*
28/78 **Point Of Know Return** *Kansas*
61S/91 **Point Of Light** *Randy Travis*
5/87 **Point Of No Return** *Exposé*
21/62 **Point Of No Return** *Gene McDaniels*
28/86 **Point Of No Return** *Nu Shooz*
85/61 **Point Of No Return** *Adam Wade*
49/63 **Point Panic** *Surfaris*
93/59 **Pointed Toe Shoes** *Carl Perkins*
3/90 **Poison** *Bell Biv DeVoe*
7/89 **Poison** *Alice Cooper*
25/83 **Poison Arrow** *ABC*
7/59 **Poison Ivy** *Coasters*
62S/00 **Pokémon Theme** *Pokémon*
15/90 **Policy Of Truth** *Depeche Mode*
24/84 **Politics Of Dancing** *Re-Flex*
8/69 **Polk Salad Annie** *Tony Joe White*
Pomp & Circumstance ..see: Graduation Song
6/96 **Pony** *Ginuwine*
60/61 **Pony Express** *Danny & The Juniors*
Pony Time
1/61 *Chubby Checker*
60/61 *Goodtimers*
93/67 **Pony With The Golden Mane** *Every Mothers' Son*

42/72 **Pool Of Bad Luck** *Joe Simon*
Poor ..also see: Po
44/68 **Poor Baby** *Cowsills*
17/58 **Poor Boy** *Royaltones*
24/57 **Poor Boy** *Elvis Presley*
52/72 **Poor Boy** *Casey Kelly*
38/62 **Poor Fool** *Ike & Tina Turner*
83/92 **Poor Georgie** *MC Lyte*
22/59 **Poor Jenny** *Everly Brothers*
1/58 **Poor Little Fool** *Ricky Nelson*
91/62 **Poor Little Puppet** *Cathy Carroll*
27/63 **Poor Little Rich Girl** *Steve Lawrence*
14/57 **Poor Man's Roses (Or A Rich Man's Gold)** *Patti Page*
33/81 **Poor Man's Son** *Survivor*
55/65 **Poor Man's Son** *Reflections*
Poor People Of Paris
1/56 *Les Baxter*
17/56 *Lawrence Welk*
19/56 *Russ Morgan*
52/56 *Chet Atkins*
31/78 **Poor Poor Pitiful Me** *Linda Ronstadt*
Poor Side Of Town
1/66 *Johnny Rivers*
75/69 *Al Wilson*
19/01 **Pop** **NSYNC*
43/00 **Pop A Top** *Alan Jackson*
Pop-Eye ..see: Popeye
35/82 **Pop Goes The Movies** *Meco*
29/91 **Pop Goes The Weasel** *3rd Bass*
85/62 **Pop Goes The Weasel** *Anthony Newley*
20/88 **Pop Goes The World** *Men Without Hats*
7/85 **Pop Life** *Prince*
1/79 **Pop Muzik** *M*
35/62 **Pop Pop Pop - Pie** *Sherrys*
15/89 **Pop Singer** *John Cougar Mellencamp*
86/89 **Pop Song 89** *R.E.M.*
58/91 **Pop That Coochie** *2 Live Crew*
24/72 **Pop That Thang** *Isley Brothers*
60/00 **Pop Ya Collar** *Usher*
9/72 **Popcorn** *Hot Butter*
30/69 **Popcorn, The** *James Brown*
14/55 **Popcorn Song** *Cliffie Stone*
51/62 **Pop-Eye** *Huey Smith*
99/62 **Popeye Joe** *Ernie K-Doe*
94/62 **Pop-Eye Stroll** *Mar-Keys*
10/62 **Popeye (The Hitchhiker)** *Chubby Checker*
75/63 **Popeye Waddle** *Don Covay*
59/79 **Pops, We Love You (A Tribute To Father)** *Diana Ross, Marvin Gaye, Smokey Robinson & Stevie Wonder*
21/66 **Popsicle** *Jan & Dean*
43/76 **Popsicle Toes** *Michael Franks*
3/64 **Popsicles And Icicles** *Murmaids*
51A/96 **Popular** *Nada Surf*
Por Amor Viviremos ..see: Love Will Keep Us Together
73/55 **Por Favor** *Vic Damone*
62/68 **Porpoise Song** *Monkees*
20/56 **Port Au Prince** *Nelson Riddle*
64/78 **Portrait (He Knew)** *Kansas*
98/62 **Portrait Of A Fool** *Conway Twitty*
Portrait Of My Love
9/61 *Steve Lawrence*
36/67 *Tokens*
19/56 **Portuguese Washerwomen** *Joe "Fingers" Carr*
Poseidon Adventure ..see: Morning After
7/65 **Positively 4th Street** *Bob Dylan*
70/89 **Posse' On Broadway** *Sir Mix-A-Lot*
21/90 **Possession** *Bad English*
73/94 **Possession** *Sarah McLachlan*
30/85 **Possession Obsession** *Daryl Hall/John Oates*
40A/95 **Possum Kingdom** *Toadies*
88/67 **Postcard From Jamaica** *Sopwith "Camel"*
89/62 **Potato Peeler** *Bobby Gregg*
71/01 **Pour Me** *Trick Pony*
2/88 **Pour Some Sugar On Me** *Def Leppard*
85/66 **Pouring Water On A Drowning Man** *James Carr*
65/66 **Poverty** *Bobby Bland*
76/79 **Pow Wow** *Cory Daye*
54/72 **Powder Blue Mercedes Queen** *Raiders*
2/90 **Power, The** *Snap!*
43/80 **Power** *Temptations*
84/87 **Power** *Kansas*
24/78 **Power Of Gold** *Dan Fogelberg/Tim Weisberg*
11/98 **Power Of Good-Bye** *Madonna*
1/85 **Power Of Love** *Huey Lewis*
4/91 **Power Of Love (medley)** *Luther Vandross*
Power Of Love
11/72 *Joe Simon*
76/74 *Martha Reeves*
Power Of Love
68/85 *Air Supply*
57/86 *Jennifer Rush*
26/88 *Laura Branigan*
1/94 *Celine Dion*
47/91 **Power Of Love** *Deee-Lite*
75S/00 **Power Of One** *Donna Summer*
96/82 **Power Play** *Molly Hatchet*
11/71 **Power To The People** *John Lennon*
35/91 **Power Windows** *Billy Falcon*
65/88 **Powerful Stuff** *Fabulous Thunderbirds*
50/99 **Powerful Thing** *Trisha Yearwood*
18/94 **Practice What You Preach** *Barry White*
36/99 **Praise You** *Fatboy Slim*
2/90 **Pray** *M.C. Hammer*
58/02 **Prayer** *Disturbed*
81/59 **Prayer And A Juke Box** *Little Anthony & The Imperials*
21/94 **Prayer For The Dying** *Seal*
45/68 **Prayer Meetin'** *Willie Mitchell*
38/00 **Prayin' For Daylight** *Rascal Flatts*
1/90 **Praying For Time** *George Michael*
63/89 **Praying To A New God** *Wang Chung*
92/63 **Preacherman** *Charlie Russo*
62S/02 **Precious** *B.I.*
3/72 **Precious And Few** *Climax*
65/97 **Precious Declaration** *Collective Soul*
19/79 **Precious Love** *Bob Welch*
87/90 **Precious Love** *Jody Watley*
67/67 **Precious Memories** *Romeos*
30/71 **Precious, Precious** *Jackie Moore*
22/81 **Precious To Me** *Phil Seymour*
77/88 **Presence Of Love** *Alarm*
88/56 **President On The Dollar** *Mitch Miller*
21/86 **Press** *Paul McCartney*
20/82 **Pressure** *Billy Joel*
Pretend
89/57 *Tab Smith*
57/59 *Carl Mann*
Pretend You Don't See Her
45/57 *Jerry Vale*
97/64 *Bobby Vee*
58/77 **Pretender, The** *Jackson Browne*
55/89 **Pretending** *Eric Clapton*

PRETTY:

60/72 **Pretty As You Feel** *Jefferson Airplane*
Pretty Baby ..see: (It's Been A Long Time)
15/67 **Pretty Ballerina** *Left Banke*
9/60 **Pretty Blue Eyes** *Steve Lawrence*
98/63 **Pretty Boy Lonely** *Patti Page*
90/88 **Pretty Boys And Pretty Girls** *Book Of Love*
(Pretty Brown Eyes) ..see: Breakin' My Heart
29/66 **Pretty Flamingo** *Manfred Mann*
Pretty Fly (For A White Guy)
53/99 *Offspring*
68S/99 *Obscure*
25/95 **Pretty Girl** *Jon B.*
39/79 **Pretty Girls** *Melissa Manchester*
36/59 **Pretty Girls Everywhere** *Eugene Church*
41/86 **Pretty In Pink** *Psychedelic Furs*
53/73 **Pretty Lady** *Lighthouse*
7/61 **Pretty Little Angel Eyes** *Curtis Lee*
25/65 **Pretty Little Baby** *Marvin Gaye*
75/84 **Pretty Mess** *Vanity*
37A/96 **Pretty Noose** *Soundgarden*
15/63 **Pretty Paper** *Roy Orbison*
Pretty Woman ..see: Oh, Pretty Woman
62/69 **Pretty World** *Sergio Mendes*
57/74 **Pretzel Logic** *Steely Dan*
57/64 **Price, The** *Solomon Burke*
5/90 **Price Of Love** *Bad English*
(also see: World)
63/77 **Pride, The** *Isley Brothers*
10/63 **Pride And Joy** *Marvin Gaye*
66/89 **Pride & Passion** *John Cafferty*
Pride (In The Name Of Love)
33/84 *U2*
54/92 *Clivilles & Cole*
63/91 **Primal Scream** *Mötley Crüe*
34/84 **Prime Time** *Alan Parsons Project*
71/87 **Primitive Love Rites** *Mondo Rock*
Primrose Lane
8/59 *Jerry Wallace*
86/70 *O.C. Smith*
30/61 **Princess** *Frank Gari*
78/76 **Princess And The Punk** *Barry Mann*
37/65 **Princess In Rags** *Gene Pitney*
33/90 **Principal's Office** *Young M.C.*
20/56 **Priscilla** *Eddie Cooley*
30/89 **Prisoner, The** *Howard Jones*
(also see: Love Theme From Eyes Of Laura Mars)
18/63 **Prisoner Of Love** *James Brown*
27/78 **Prisoner Of Your Love** *Player*
81/58 **Prisoner's Song** *Warren Storm*
7/85 **Private Dancer** *Tina Turner*
67/00 **Private Emotion** *Ricky Martin*
95/59 **Private Eye** *Olympics*
1/81 **Private Eyes** *Daryl Hall & John Oates*
74/80 **Private Idaho** *B-52's*
47/86 **Private Number** *Jets*
75/68 **Private Number** *Judy Clay & William Bell*
80/71 **Problem Child** *Mark Lindsay*
2/58 **Problems** *Everly Brothers*

13S/02 **Product Of Our Environment** *Born Predators*
47/01 **Project Chick** *Cash Money Millionaires*
9/01 **Promise** *Jagged Edge*
11/88 **Promise, The** *When In Rome*
74/66 **Promise Her Anything** *Tom Jones*
69/98 **Promise I Make** *Dakota Moon*
40/88 **Promise Me** *Cover Girls*
62/95 **Promise Me** *Lil Suzy*
78/60 **Promise Me A Rose (A Slight Detail)** *Anita Bryant*
17/58 **Promise Me, Love** *Andy Williams*
1/91 **Promise Of A New Day** *Paula Abdul*
Promised Land
41/65 *Chuck Berry*
14/74 *Elvis Presley*
9/79 **Promises** *Eric Clapton*
48/81 **Promises** *Barbra Streisand*
63/96 **Promises Broken** *Soul Asylum*
38/81 **Promises In The Dark** *Pat Benatar*
11/83 **Promises, Promises** *Naked Eyes*
19/68 **Promises, Promises** *Dionne Warwick*
75/69 **Prophecy Of Daniel and John The Divine (Six-Six-Six)** *Cowsills*
51S/00 **Protect Ya Neck (The Jump Off)** *Wu-Tang Clan*
29/63 **Proud** *Johnny Crawford*
68/81 **Proud** *Joe Chemay Band*
Proud Mary
2/69 *Creedence Clearwater Revival*
45/69 *Solomon Burke*
69/69 *Checkmates, Ltd. feat. Sonny Charles*
4/71 *Ike & Tina Turner*
Proud One
68/66 *Frankie Valli*
22/75 *Osmonds*
Proud Ones ..see: Theme From
33/78 **Prove It All Night** *Bruce Springsteen*
95/86 **Prove Me Wrong** *David Pack*
7/88 **Prove Your Love** *Taylor Dayne*
7/70 **Psychedelic Shack** *Temptations*
73/60 **Psycho** *Bobby Hendricks*
92/78 **Psycho Killer** *Talking Heads*
57/82 **Psychobabble** *Alan Parsons Project*
5/66 **Psychotic Reaction** *Count Five*
31/67 **Pucker Up Buttercup** *Jr. Walker*
43/63 **Puddin N' Tain (Ask Me Again, I'll Tell You the Same)** *Alley Cats*
96/71 **Puff Of Smoke** *Roy Head*
2/63 **Puff (The Magic Dragon)** *Peter, Paul & Mary*
71/68 **Puffin' On Down The Track** *Hugh Masekela*
93/00 **Pull Over** *Trina*
60/95 **Pull Up To The Bumper** *Patra*
Pum-Pa-Lum ..see: Bad Donkey
78/91 **Pump It (Nice An' Hard)** *Icy Blu*
2/90 **Pump Up The Jam** *Technotronic*
13/88 **Pump Up The Volume** *M/A/R/R/S*
26/94 **Pumps And A Bump** *Hammer*
20/62 **Punish Her** *Bobby Vee*
77/93 **Punks Jump Up To Get Beat Down** *Brand Nubian*
Puppet Man
24/70 *5th Dimension*
26/71 *Tom Jones*
14/65 **Puppet On A String** *Elvis Presley*
56/60 **Puppet Song** *Frankie Avalon*
75/68 **(Puppet Song) Whiskey On A Sunday** *Irish Rovers*
Puppy Love
2/60 *Paul Anka*
3/72 *Donny Osmond*
38/64 **Puppy Love** *Barbara Lewis*
75/01 **Puppy Love** *Lil Bow Wow*
31/90 **Pure** *Lightning Seeds*
72A/95 **Pure Massacre** *Silverchair*
26/00 **Purest Of Pain (A Puro Dolor)** *Son By Four*
Purple Haze
65/67 *Jimi Hendrix Experience*
63/69 *Dion*
66A/93 *Cure*
19/01 **Purple Hills** *D-12*
84/95 **Purple Medley** *Prince*
1/58 **Purple People Eater** *Sheb Wooley*
47/58 **Purple People Eater Meets The Witch Doctor** *Joe South*
2/84 **Purple Rain** *Prince*
5A/97 **Push** *Matchbox 20*
27/62 **Push And Kick** *Mark Valentino*
Push And Pull ..see: (Do The)
19/88 **Push It** *Salt-N-Pepa*
52/98 **Push It** *Garbage*
57S/00 **Push It** *Static-X*
90/60 **Push Push** *Austin Taylor*
80/93 **Push The Feeling On** *Nightcrawlers*
44/71 **Pushbike Song** *Mixtures*
97/97 **Pushin' Inside You** *Sons Of Funk*
36/67 **Pushin' Too Hard** *Seeds*
26/99 **Pushin' Weight** *Ice Cube*
92/62 **Pushin' Your Luck** *Sleepy King*
25/63 **Pushover** *Etta James*
58/89 **Puss N' Boots/These Boots (Are Made For Walkin')** *Kon Kan*
17/58 **Pussy Cat** *Ames Brothers*
8/58 **Put A Light In The Window** *Four Lads*
73/74 **Put A Little Love Away** *Emotions*
Put A Little Love In Your Heart
4/69 *Jackie Deshannon*
9/89 *Annie Lennox & Al Green*
32/58 **Put A Ring On My Finger** *Les Paul & Mary Ford*
71/82 **Put Away Your Love** *Alessi*
40/83 **Put It In A Magazine** *Sonny Charles*
50S/02 **Put It Inside** *Won-G*
8/01 **Put It On Me** *Ja Rule*
52/72 **Put It Where You Want It** *Crusaders*
98/02 **Put Me Down** *Donell Jones*
46/74 **Put Out The Light** *Joe Cocker*
74/88 **Put This Love To The Test** *Jon Astley*
29S/02 **Put Yo Sets Up** *Redd Eyezz*
8S/01 **Put Your Arms Around Me** *Natural*
Put Your Arms Around Me Honey
58/60 *Fats Domino*
91/60 *Ray Smith*
76/00 **Put Your Hand In Mine** *Tracy Byrd*
2/71 **Put Your Hand In The Hand** *Ocean*
10/74 **Put Your Hands Together** *O'Jays*
37A/97 **Put Your Hands Where My Eyes Could See** *Busta Rhymes*
Put Your Head On My Shoulder
2/59 *Paul Anka*
44/68 *Lettermen*
58/78 *Leif Garrett*
46/67 **Put Your Mind At Ease** *Every Mothers' Son*
27/89 **Put Your Mouth On Me** *Eddie Murphy*
92/66 **Put Yourself In My Place** *Elgins*
4/83 **Puttin' On The Ritz** *Taco*
78/65 **Puzzle Song (A Puzzle In Song)** *Shirley Ellis*

Q

74S/00 **Quality Control** *Jurrassic 5*
38/93 **Quality Time** *Hi-Five*
95/62 **Quando, Quando, Quando (Tell Me When)** *Pat Boone*
100/62 **(Quarter To Four) Stomp** *Stompers*
1/61 **Quarter To Three** *U.S. Bonds*
Que Sera, Sera (Whatever Will Be, Will Be)
2/56 *Doris Day*
47/63 *High Keyes*
77/70 *Mary Hopkin*
71/85 **Que Te Quiero** *Katrina & The Waves*
66/76 **Queen Of Clubs** *KC & The Sunshine Band*
2/81 **Queen Of Hearts** *Juice Newton*
79/62 **Queen Of My Heart** *René & Ray*
40/76 **Queen Of My Soul** *Average White Band*
34/83 **Queen Of The Broken Hearts** *Loverboy*
9/58 **Queen Of The Hop** *Bobby Darin*
12/65 **Queen Of The House** *Jody Miller*
(also see: King Of The Road)
36A/94 **Queen Of The Night** *Whitney Houston*
89/73 **Queen Of The Roller Derby** *Leon Russell*
39/57 **Queen Of The Senior Prom** *Mills Brothers*
57A/95 **Queer** *Garbage*
13/69 **Quentin's Theme** *Charles Randolph Grean Sounde*
19/60 **Question** *Lloyd Price*
21/70 **Question** *Moody Blues*
37/68 **Question Of Temperature** *Balloon Farm*
90/72 **Questions** *Bang*
92/66 **Questions And Answers** *In Crowd*
Questions 67 And 68
71/69 *Chicago*
24/71 *Chicago*
79/74 **Quick, Fast, In A Hurry** *New York City*
25/68 **Quick Joey Small (Run Joey Run)** *Kasenetz-Katz Singing Orchestral Circus*
8/64 **Quicksand** *Martha & The Vandellas*
92/65 **Quiet Nights Of Quiet Stars** *Andy Williams*
78/64 **Quiet Place** *Garnet Mimms*
61/76 **Quiet Storm** *Smokey Robinson*
46/59 **Quiet Three** *Duane Eddy*
4/59 **Quiet Village** *Martin Denny*
2/97 **Quit Playing Games (With My Heart)** *Backstreet Boys*
74/02 **Quítame Ese Hombre** *Pilar Montenegro*
27/61 **Quite A Party** *Fireballs*
90/00 **Quittin' Kind** *Joe Diffie*

R

61A/97 **R U Ready** *Salt-N-Pepa*
43S/00 **R.N.S.** *Freddie Foxxx*
69S/02 **RPM Revolutions Per Minute** *Slug & El-P*
65/77 **Race Among The Ruins** *Gordon Lightfoot*
Race Is On
15/65 *Jack Jones*
96/65 *George Jones*
96/56 **Race With The Devil** *Gene Vincent*
Radar Love
13/74 *Golden Earring*
59/89 *White Lion*
71A/97 **Radiation Vibe** *Fountains Of Wayne*
78/83 **Radio Free Europe** *R.E.M.*
16/84 **Radio Ga-Ga** *Queen*
35/89 **Radio Romance** *Tiffany*
28/85 **Radioactive** *Firm*
47/79 **Radioactive** *Gene Simmons*
1/64 **Rag Doll** *4 Seasons*
17/88 **Rag Doll** *Aerosmith*
52/75 **Rag Doll** *Sammy Johns*
57/70 **Rag Mama Rag** *Band*
Raging Bull ..see: Theme From
Rags To Riches
45/63 *Sunny & The Sunliners*
F/71 *Elvis Presley*
16/59 **Ragtime Cowboy Joe** *David Seville/The Chipmunks*

RAIN:

9/86 **Rain, The** *Oran "Juice" Jones*
14/93 **Rain** *Madonna*
23/66 **Rain** *Beatles*
25/98 **Rain** *SWV*
76/69 **Rain** *José Feliciano*
88/84 **Rain** *Dragon*
19/71 **Rain Dance** *Guess Who*
68A/92 **Rain Falls** *Frankie Knuckles*
57/85 **Rain Forest** *Paul Hardcastle*
74/81 **Rain In May** *Max Werner*
62/69 **Rain In My Heart** *Frank Sinatra*
71/88 **Rain In The Summertime** *Alarm*
66A/94 **Rain King** *Counting Crows*
76/76 **Rain, Oh Rain** *Fools Gold*
10/66 **Rain On The Roof** *Lovin' Spoonful*
21/86 **Rain On The Scarecrow** *John Cougar Mellencamp*
12/62 **Rain Rain Go Away** *Bobby Vinton*
51A/97 **Rain (Supa Dupa Fly)** *Missy "Misdemeanor" Elliott*
2/67 **Rain, The Park & Other Things** *Cowsills*
4/57 **Rainbow** *Russ Hamilton*
Rainbow
47/63 *Gene Chandler*
69/66 *Gene Chandler ('65)*
51/70 **Rainbow** *Marmalade*
62/62 **Rainbow At Midnight** *Jimmie Rodgers*
25/79 **Rainbow Connection** *Kermit (Jim Henson)*
52/76 **Rainbow In Your Eyes** *Leon & Mary Russell*
49/69 **Rainbow Ride** *Andy Kim*
52/83 **Rainbow's End** *Sergio Mendes*
2/61 **Raindrops** *Dee Clark*
(also see: Cloudy Summer Afternoon)
1/70 **Raindrops Keep Fallin' On My Head** *B.J. Thomas*
34/61 **Rainin' In My Heart** *Slim Harpo*
Raining In My Heart
88/59 *Buddy Holly*
47/78 *Leo Sayer*
Raining In My Sunshine ..see: (He's)
Rains Came
74/62 *Big Sambo*
31/66 *Sir Douglas Quintet*
Raintree County ..see: (Song Of)
26/75 **Rainy Day People** *Gordon Lightfoot*
2/66 **Rainy Day Women #12 & 35** *Bob Dylan*
93/95 **Rainy Days** *General Public*
12/02 **Rainy Dayz** *Mary J. Blige*
2/71 **Rainy Days And Mondays** *Carpenters*
52/71 **Rainy Jane** *Davy Jones*
4/70 **Rainy Night In Georgia** *Brook Benton*
59/78 **Raise A Little Hell** *Trooper*
26/98 **Raise The Roof** *Luke*
25/01 **Raise Up** *Petey Pablo*
79/67 **Raise Your Hand** *Eddie Floyd*
65/74 **Raised On Robbery** *Joni Mitchell*
41/73 **Raised On Rock** *Elvis Presley*
Ram-Bunk-Shush
67/57 *Bill Doggett*
29/61 *Ventures*
21/61 **Rama Lama Ding Dong** *Edsels*
91/81 **Rambler, The** *Molly Hatchet*
17/69 **Ramblin' Gamblin' Man** *Bob Seger*
2/73 **Ramblin Man** *Allman Brothers Band*
2/62 **Ramblin' Rose** *Nat King Cole*
73/60 **Rambling** *Ramblers*
72/60 **Ramona** *Blue Diamonds*
27/58 **Ramrod** *Duane Eddy*
62/57 **Rang Tang Ding Dong (I Am The Japanese Sandman)** *Cellos*
2/70 **Rapper, The** *Jaggerz*
Rapper's Delight
36/80 *Sugarhill Gang*
51A/98 *Erick Sermon, Keith Murray & Redman*
F/97 **Rappers' Ball** *E-40*
83/84 **Rappin' Rodney** *Rodney Dangerfield*
1/81 **Rapture** *Blondie*
46/02 **Rapture (Tastes So Sweet)** *iio*
(Rapture's Delight) ..see: Step Into A World
68A/97 **Rascal King** *Mighty Mighty Bosstones*
70/59 **Raspberries, Strawberries** *Kingston Trio*
2/85 **Raspberry Beret** *Prince*
38S/98 **Raspberry Swirl** *Tori Amos*
71/63 **Rat Race** *Drifters*
90/76 **Rattlesnake** *Ohio Players*
Raunchy
2/57 *Bill Justis*
4/57 *Ernie Freeman*
10/57 *Billy Vaughn*
37/58 **Rave On** *Buddy Holly*
80/76 **Raven, The** *Alan Parsons Project*
23/59 **Raw-Hide** *Link Wray*
24/69 **Ray Of Hope** *Rascals*
5/98 **Ray Of Light** *Madonna*
15/55 **Razzle-Dazzle** *Bill Haley*
88/00 **Re-Arranged** *Limp Bizkit*
65S/02 **Re-Rewind** *Artful Dodger UK*
42/96 **Reach** *Gloria Estefan*
51/77 **Reach** *Orleans*
54/78 **Reach For It** *George Duke*
83/92 **Reach For The Sky** *Firehouse*
81/84 **Reach Out** *Giorgio Moroder*
20/70 **Reach Out And Touch (Somebody's Hand)** *Diana Ross*
Reach Out For Me
74/63 *Lou Johnson*
20/64 *Dionne Warwick*
Reach Out I'll Be There
1/66 *Four Tops*
79/68 *Merrilee Rush*
29/71 *Diana Ross*
60/75 *Gloria Gaynor*
73A/92 *Michael Bolton*
10/68 **Reach Out Of The Darkness** *Friend & Lover*
77/71 **Reach Out Your Hand** *Brotherhood Of Man*
74/77 **Reaching For The World** *Harold Melvin*
36/02 **React** *Erick Sermon*
54/85 **Reaction To Action** *Foreigner*
18/84 **Read 'Em And Weep** *Barry Manilow*
26/75 **Ready** *Cat Stevens*
45S/00 **Ready** *N-Toon*
92/81 **Ready For Love** *Silverado*
52/79 **Ready For The 80's** *Village People*
52/78 **Ready For The Times To Get Better** *Crystal Gayle*
42/61 **Ready For Your Love** *Shep & The Limelites*
7/90 **Ready Or Not** *After 7*
54/87 **Ready Or Not** *Lou Gramm*
69A/96 **Ready Or Not** *Fugees*
73/78 **Ready Or Not** *Helen Reddy*
35/69 **Ready Or Not Here I Come (Can't Hide From Love)** *Delfonics*
44/56 **Ready Teddy** *Little Richard*
56/96 **Ready To Go** *Republica*
39/99 **Ready To Run** *Dixie Chicks*
11/78 **Ready To Take A Chance Again** *Barry Manilow*
84/68 **Ready, Willing and Able** *American Breed*

REAL:

83/84 **Real End** *Rickie Lee Jones*
61/95 **Real Hip-Hop** *DAS EFX*
80/66 **Real Humdinger** *J.J. Barnes*
77/65 **Real Live Girl** *Steve Alaimo*
81/00 **Real Live Woman** *Trisha Yearwood*
2/89 **Real Love** *Jody Watley*
5/80 **Real Love** *Doobie Brothers*
7/92 **Real Love** *Mary J. Blige*
11/96 **Real Love** *Beatles*
24/91 **Real Love** *Bob Seger*
47/90 **Real Love** *Skyy*
69/92 **Real Love** *Slaughter*
79/80 **Real Love** *Cretones*
91/85 **Real Love** *Dolly Parton (with Kenny Rogers)*
83/75 **Real Man** *Todd Rundgren*
39S/01 **Real Me** *Svala*
92/74 **Real Me** *Who*
19X/65 **Real Meaning Of Christmas** *Ray Conniff*
41/77 **Real Mother For Ya** *Johnny Guitar Watson*
42/94 **Real Muthaphuckkin G's** *Eazy-E*
74S/98 **Real One** *2 Live Crew*
79/80 **Real People** *Chic*
4/91 **Real, Real, Real** *Jesus Jones*
4/00 **Real Slim Shady** *Eminem*
67/81 **Real Thing** *Brothers Johnson*
82/87 **Real Thing** *Jellybean*
68/58 **Real Wild Child** *Ivan*
9A/98 **Real World** *Matchbox 20*
84/89 **Realistic** *Shirley Lewis*

75/98 **Reality** *Elusion*
80/75 **Reality** *James Brown*
54/93 **Really Doe** *Ice Cube*
89/92 **Really Into You** *Around The Way*
16/81 **Really Wanna Know You** *Gary Wright*
71/83 **Reap The Wild Wind** *Ultravox*
79/62 **Reap What You Sow** *Billy Stewart*
Reaper, The ..see: (Don't Fear)
58S/02 **Reason** *Ian Van Dahl*
98/58 **Reason, The** *5 Chanels*
52/79 **Reason To Be** *Kansas*
Reason To Believe
62/71 *Rod Stewart*
19/93 *Rod Stewart (with Ronnie Wood)*
64/88 **Reason To Live** *Kiss*
87/88 **Reason To Try** *Eric Carmen*
48/57 **Rebel** *Carol Jarvis*
64/74 **Rebel Rebel** *David Bowie*
6/58 **Rebel-'Rouser** *Duane Eddy*
46/84 **Rebel Yell** *Billy Idol*
74/85 **Rebels** *Tom Petty*
61/80 **Rebels Are We** *Chic*
15/93 **Rebirth Of Slick (Cool Like Dat)** *Digable Planets*
Reconsider Me
28/69 *Johnny Adams*
67/75 *Narvel Felts*
84/65 **Record (Baby I Love You)** *Ben E. King*
82/59 **Record Hop Blues** *Quarter Notes*
74S/95 **Record Jock** *Dana Dane*
55/98 **Recover Your Soul** *Elton John*
37/66 **Recovery** *Fontella Bass*

RED:

56/03 **Red, The** *Chevelle*
89/67 **Red And Blue** *Dave Clark Five*
96/73 **Red Back Spider** *Brownsville Station*
78/71 **Red Eye Blues** *Red Eye*
Red Hot
82/66 *Sam The Sham & The Pharoahs*
83/77 *Robert Gordon/Link Wray*
77/83 **Red Hot** *Herb Alpert*
41/80 **Red Light** *Linda Clifford*
2/95 **Red Light Special** *TLC*
78/63 **Red Pepper I** *Roosevelt Fountain*
40/02 **Red Rag Top** *Tim McGraw*
Red Red Wine
62/68 *Neil Diamond*
72/70 *Vic Dana*
34/84 *UB40*
1/88 *UB40*
5/59 **Red River Rock** *Johnny & The Hurricanes*
37/59 **Red River Rose** *Ames Brothers*
Red Roses For A Blue Lady
10/65 *Vic Dana*
11/65 *Bert Kaempfert*
23/65 *Wayne Newton*
95/67 **Red Roses For Mom** *Bobby Vinton*
2/66 **Red Rubber Ball** *Cyrkle*
Red Sails In The Sunset
57/57 *Tab Hunter*
36/60 *Platters*
35/63 *Fats Domino*
85/73 **Redneck Friend** *Jackson Browne*
66/96 **Redneck Games** *Jeff Foxworthy with Alan Jackson*
75/95 **Redneck Stomp** *Jeff Foxworthy*
98/72 **Redwood Tree** *Van Morrison*
Reelin' And Rockin'
23/65 *Dave Clark Five*
27/73 *Chuck Berry*
11/73 **Reeling In The Years** *Steely Dan*
62/57 **Reet Petite (The Finest Girl You Ever Want To Meet)** *Jackie Wilson*
2/67 **Reflections** *Supremes*
10/70 **Reflections Of My Life** *Marmalade*
1/84 **Reflex, The** *Duran Duran*
69S/95 **Refried Dreams** *Tim McGraw*
15/80 **Refugee** *Tom Petty*
28/93 **Regret** *New Order*
72/94 **Regular Thang** *Ovis*
2/94 **Regulate** *Warren G. & Nate Dogg*
Relax
67/84 *Frankie Goes To Hollywood*
10/85 *Frankie Goes To Hollywood*
88/97 **Relax & Party** *Ivory*
39/73 **Relay, The** *Who*
1/90 **Release Me** *Wilson Phillips*
Release Me
8/62 *Esther Phillips*
4/67 *Engelbert Humperdinck*
93/67 *Esther Phillips*
82/68 *Johnny Adams*
52/96 **Release Me** *Angelina*
98/95 **Release Yo' Delf** *Method Man*
48/92 **Remedy** *Black Crowes*
61S/02 **Remedy, The** *Proof*
57/55 **Rememb'ring** *Peter Lind Hayes & Mary Healy*

REMEMBER:

83/58 **Remember** *Velours*
91/63 **Remember Baby** *Shep & The Limelites*
53/73 **Remember (Christmas)** *Nilsson*
39/63 **Remember Diana** *Paul Anka*
16/71 **Remember Me** *Diana Ross*
26/64 **Remember Me** *Rita Pavone*
67/76 **Remember Me** *Willie Nelson*
32/65 **(Remember Me) I'm The One Who Loves You** *Dean Martin*
80/95 **Remember Me This Way** *Jordan Hill*
72/91 **Remember My Name** *House Of Lords*
33/77 **(Remember The Days Of The) Old Schoolyard** *Cat Stevens*
36/84 **Remember The Nights** *Motels*
64/66 **Remember The Rain** *Bob Lind*
100/75 **Remember The Rain?** *21st Century*
3/92 **Remember The Time** *Michael Jackson*
24/63 **Remember Then** *Earls*
Remember (Walkin' in the Sand)
5/64 *Shangri-Las*
43/79 *Louise Goffin*
67/80 *Aerosmith*
25/75 **Remember What I Told You To Forget** *Tavares*
81/84 **Remember What You Like** *Jenny Burton*
Remember When
41/59 *Platters*
48/98 *Color Me Badd*
69/65 **Remember When** *Wayne Newton*
6/57 **Remember You're Mine** *Pat Boone*
57/92 **Reminisce** *Mary J. Blige*
3/78 **Reminiscing** *Little River Band*
81/85 **Remo's Theme (What If)** *Tommy Shaw*
89/80 **Remote Control** *Reddings*
26/75 **Rendezvous** *Hudson Brothers*
33/96 **Renee** *Lost Boyz*
16/79 **Renegade** *Styx*
39/76 **Renegade** *Michael Murphey*
53/57 **Repeat After Me** *Patti Page*
76/89 **Repetition** *Information Society*
39/97 **Request Line** *Zhané*
63/01 **Request Line** *Black Eyed Peas*
100/67 **Requiem For The Masses** *Association*
Rescue Me
4/65 *Fontella Bass*
78/76 *Melissa Manchester*
9/91 **Rescue Me** *Madonna*
62/87 **Reservations For Two** *Dionne Warwick & Kashif*
Respect
35/65 *Otis Redding*
92/66 *Rationals*
1/67 *Aretha Franklin*
66S/01 **R.E.S.P.E.C.T.** *4th Avenue Jones'*
Respect Yourself
12/71 *Staple Singers*
5/87 *Bruce Willis*
15/66 **Respectable** *Outsiders*
50S/99 **Respiration** *Mos Def & Talib Kweli Are Black Star*
96/92 **Rest In Peace** *Extreme*
70/97 **Rest Of Mine** *Trace Adkins*
46/86 **Restless** *Starpoint*
35/92 **Restless Heart** *Peter Cetera*
59/85 **Restless Heart** *John Waite*
Resurrection Shuffle
38/71 *Tom Jones*
40/71 *Ashton, Gardner & Dyke*
96/95 **Return Of The Crooklyn Dodgers** *Crooklyn Dodgers '95*
2/97 **Return Of The Mack** *Mark Morrison*
15/67 **Return Of The Red Baron** *Royal Guardsmen*
4/94 **Return To Innocence** *Enigma*
4/58 **Return To Me** *Dean Martin*
2/62 **Return To Sender** *Elvis Presley*
Reuben ..see: Ruben
1/79 **Reunited** *Peaches & Herb*
86/87 **Rev It Up** *Newcity Rockers*
25/59 **Reveille Rock** *Johnny & The Hurricanes*
15/62 **Revenge** *Brook Benton*
8/63 **Reverend Mr. Black** *Kingston Trio*
97/60 **Revival** *Johnny & The Hurricanes*
92/71 **Revival (Love Is Everywhere)** *Allman Brothers Band*
Revolution
12/68 *Beatles*
11S/01 *Stone Temple Pilots*
90/93 **Revolution** *Arrested Development*
70/65 **Revolution Kind** *Sonny*
41/73 **Rhapsody In Blue** *Deodato*
16/66 **Rhapsody In The Rain** *Lou Christie*
63/74 **Rhapsody In White** *Love Unlimited Orchestra*
11/76 **Rhiannon (Will You Ever Win)** *Fleetwood Mac*
1/75 **Rhinestone Cowboy** *Glen Campbell*
47/79 **Rhumba Girl** *Nicolette Larson*
63/75 **Rhyme Tyme People** *Kool And The Gang*
24/64 **Rhythm** *Major Lance*
32/00 **Rhythm Divine** *Enrique Iglesias*
5/93 **Rhythm Is A Dancer** *Snap!*
5/87 **Rhythm Is Gonna Get You** *Gloria Estefan*
F/55 **Rhythm 'N' Blues (Mama's Got The Rhythm - Papa's Got The Blues)** *McGuire Sisters*
2/90 **Rhythm Nation** *Janet Jackson*
40/88 **Rhythm Of Love** *Yes*
53/97 **Rhythm Of Love** *DJ Company*
75/88 **Rhythm Of Love** *Scorpions*

5/91 **Rhythm Of My Heart** *Rod Stewart*
3/85 **Rhythm Of The Night** *DeBarge*
11/95 **Rhythm Of The Night** *Corona*
Rhythm Of The Rain
3/63 *Cascades*
63/69 *Gary Lewis*
94/66 **Rib Tip's** *Andre Williams*
Ribbon In The Sky
54/82 *Stevie Wonder*
72S/94 *Intro*
46/68 **Rice Is Nice** *Lemon Pipers*
1/77 **Rich Girl** *Daryl Hall & John Oates*
89/81 **Rich Man** *Terri Gibbs*
99/55 **Richest Man (In the World)** *Eddy Arnold*
63/83 **Ricky** *"Weird Al" Yankovic*
7/91 **Rico Suave** *Gerardo*
92/00 **Riddle** *En Vogue*
56/95 **Riddler, The** *Method Man*

RIDE:

5/62 **Ride!** *Dee Dee Sharp*
76/71 **Ride A White Swan** *Tyrannosaurus Rex*
25/65 **Ride Away** *Roy Orbison*
4/70 **Ride Captain Ride** *Blues Image*
23/75 **Ride 'Em Cowboy** *Paul Davis*
2/80 **Ride Like The Wind** *Christopher Cross*
61/68 **Ride My See-Saw** *Moody Blues*
37/67 **Ride, Ride, Ride** *Brenda Lee*
F/72 **Ride, Sally, Ride** *Dennis Coffey*
84/74 **Ride The Tiger** *Jefferson Starship*
16/64 **Ride The Wild Surf** *Jan & Dean*
38/91 **Ride The Wind** *Poison*
3/01 **Ride Wit Me** *Nelly*
52/71 **Ride With Me** *Steppenwolf*
28/65 **Ride Your Pony** *Lee Dorsey*
Riders In The Sky ..see: (Ghost)
14/71 **Riders On The Storm** *Doors*
47/96 **Ridin' Low** *L.A.D. Ft. Darvy Traylor*
70/73 **Ridin' My Thumb To Mexico** *Johnny Rodriguez*
94/77 **Ridin' The Storm Out** *REO Speedwagon*
63/63 **Ridin' The Wind** *Tornadoes*
36/01 **Riding With Private Malone** *David Ball*

RIGHT:

89/90 **Right And Hype** *Abstrac'*
63/81 **Right Away** *Hawks*
73/82 **Right Away** *Kansas*
Right Back Where We Started From
2/76 *Maxine Nightingale*
84/89 *Sinitta*
45/83 **Right Before Your Eyes** *America*
56/94 **Right Beside You** *Sophie B. Hawkins*
43/86 **Right Between The Eyes** *Wax*
59/60 **Right By My Side** *Ricky Nelson*
29/84 **Right By Your Side** *Eurythmics*
54/90 **Right Combination** *Seiko & Donny Wahlberg*
12/78 **Right Down The Line** *Gerry Rafferty*
90/91 **Right Down To It** *Damian Dame*
65/77 **Right Feeling At The Wrong Time** *Hot*
Right Here
2/93 *SWV (Human Nature)*
92/93 *SWV*
58/82 **Right Here And Now** *Bill Medley*
2/91 **Right Here, Right Now** *Jesus Jones*
1/89 **Right Here Waiting** *Richard Marx*
14/93 **Right Kind Of Love** *Jeremy Jordan*
56/82 **Right Kind Of Love** *Quarterflash*
61/94 **Right Kinda Lover** *Patti LaBelle*
80/87 **Right Next Door (Because of Me)** *Robert Cray Band*
60/89 **Right Next To Me** *Whistle*
47/92 **Right Now** *Al B. Sure!*
55/92 **Right Now** *Van Halen*
99/65 **Right Now And Not Later** *Shangri-Las*
43/99 **Right On The Money** *Alan Jackson*
23/71 **Right On The Tip Of My Tongue** *Brenda & The Tabulations*
7/87 **Right On Track** *Breakfast Club*
Right Or Wrong
29/61 *Wanda Jackson*
14/64 *Ronnie Dove*
9/73 **Right Place Wrong Time** *Dr. John*
61/68 **Right Relations** *Johnny Rivers*
84/62 **Right String But The Wrong Yo-Yo** *Dr. Feelgood & The Interns*
44/88 **Right Stuff** *Vanessa Williams*
77/82 **Right The First Time** *Gamma*
27/87 **Right Thing** *Simply Red*
17/73 **Right Thing To Do** *Carly Simon*
81/94 **Right Time** *I To I*
6/77 **Right Time Of The Night** *Jennifer Warnes*
42/01 **Right Where I Need To Be** *Gary Allan*
55/70 **Riki Tiki Tavi** *Donovan*
4/74 **Rikki Don't Lose That Number** *Steely Dan*
50/57 **Ring-A-Ding-A-Ding** *Tommy Sands*
32/59 **Ring-A-Ling-A-Lario** *Jimmie Rodgers*
33/65 **Ring Dang Doo** *Sam The Sham & The Pharoahs*
Ring My Bell
1/79 *Anita Ward*
20/91 *D.J. Jazzy Jeff & The Fresh Prince*
45S/99 *Inoj*
F/57 **Ring My Phone** *Tommy Sands*
17/63 **Ring Of Fire** *Johnny Cash*
84/61 **Ring Of Fire** *Duane Eddy*
31/72 **Ring The Living Bell** *Melanie*
1/64 **Ringo** *Lorne Greene*
53/64 **Ringo's Theme (This Boy)** *George Martin*
Rings
17/71 *Cymarron*
43/74 *Lobo*
86/74 *Reuben Howell*
10/62 **Rinky Dink** *Baby Cortez*
14/83 **Rio** *Duran Duran*
55/69 **Riot** *Hugh Masekela*
Rip It Up
17/56 *Little Richard*
25/56 *Bill Haley*
68/72 **Rip Off** *Laura Lee*
36/64 **Rip Van Winkle** *Devotions*
1/79 **Rise** *Herb Alpert*
58S/91 **Rise 'N' Shine** *Kool Moe Dee*
81/90 **Rise To It** *Kiss*
52/02 **Rising** *Bruce Springsteen*
38/88 **Ritual** *Dan Reed Network*
99/77 **Ritzy Mambo** *Salsoul Orchestra*
62/73 **River** *Joe Simon*
River Deep-Mountain High
88/66 *Ike & Tina Turner*
53/69 *Deep Purple*
14/71 *Supremes & Four Tops*
River Is Wide
45/67 *Forum*
31/69 *Grassroots*
River Kwai March ..see: March From
3/93 **River Of Dreams** *Billy Joel*
53/74 **River Of Love** *B.W. Stevenson*
86/73 **River Road** *Uncle Dog*
82/60 **River, Stay 'Way From My Door** *Frank Sinatra*
99/63 **River's Invitation** *Percy Mayfield*
33/74 **River's Risin'** *Edgar Winter*
83/60 **Riverboat** *Faron Young*
30/78 **Rivers Of Babylon** *Boney M*
65/62 **Road Hog** *John D. Loudermilk*
Road Runner
75/60 *Bo Diddley*
46/65 *Gants*
(also see: I'm A)
100/72 **Road We Didn't Take** *Freda Payne*
F/70 **Roadhouse Blues** *Doors*
3/90 **Roam** *B-52's*
25/59 **Robbin' The Cradle** *Tony Bellus*
95/84 **Robert DeNiro's Waiting** *Bananarama*
94/72 **Roberta** *Bones*
70A/95 **Robi-Rob's Boriqua Anthem** *C & C Music Factory*
74/58 **Roc-A-Chicka** *Warner Mack*
55/02 **Roc The Mic** *Beanie Sigel & Freeway*

ROCK:

16/56 **R-O-C-K** *Bill Haley*
23/55 **Rock-A-Beatin' Boogie** *Bill Haley*
10/57 **Rock-A-Billy** *Guy Mitchell*
Rock-A-Bye Your Baby With A Dixie Melody
10/56 *Jerry Lewis*
37/61 *Aretha Franklin*
23/62 **Rock-A-Hula Baby ("Twist" Special)** *Elvis Presley*
82/87 **Rock-A-Lott** *Aretha Franklin*
23/89 **Rock And A Hard Place** *Rolling Stones*
(also see: Between A)
93/57 **Rock And Cry** *Clyde McPhatter*
Rock And Roll ..also see: Rock 'N' Roll / Rockin' Roll
47/72 **Rock And Roll** *Led Zeppelin*
7/72 **Rock And Roll** *Gary Glitter*
Rock And Roll All Nite
68/75 *Kiss*
12/76 *Kiss (Live)*
92/72 **Rock And Roll Crazies** *Stephen Stills & Manassas*
53/79 **Rock And Roll Dancin'** *Beckmeier Brothers*
Rock And Roll Dreams Come Through
32/81 *Jim Steinman*
13/94 *Meat Loaf*
20/85 **Rock And Roll Girls** *John Fogerty*
3/74 **Rock And Roll Heaven** *Righteous Brothers*
23/74 **Rock And Roll, Hoochie Koo** *Rick Derringer*
75/95 **Rock And Roll Is Dead** *Lenny Kravitz*
19/58 **Rock And Roll Is Here To Stay** *Danny & The Juniors*
28/76 **Rock And Roll Love Letter** *Bay City Rollers*
15/72 **Rock And Roll Lullaby** *B.J. Thomas*

Rock And Roll Music
8/57 *Chuck Berry*
5/76 *Beach Boys*
41/77 **Rock And Roll Never Forgets** *Bob Seger*
66/58 **Rock And Roll Rhapsody** *Four Aces*
71/75 **Rock And Roll Runaway** *Ace*
83/77 **Rock And Roll Star** *Champagne*
93/72 **Rock & Roll Stew** *Traffic*
67/88 **Rock And Roll Strategy** *Thirty Eight Special*
1/56 **Rock And Roll Waltz** *Kay Starr*
66/56 **Rock And Roll Wedding** *Sunny Gale*
52/56 **Rock Around Mother Goose** *Barry Gordon*
Rock Around The Clock
1/55 *Bill Haley*
39/74 *Bill Haley*
93/76 **Rock Creek Park** *Blackbyrds*
30S/02 **Rock Em** *Boobakaw*
Rock In America ..see: (You Can Still)
2/86 **R.O.C.K. In The U.S.A. (A Salute To 60's Rock)** *John Cougar Mellencamp*
Rock Island Line
8/56 *Lonnie Donegan*
59/56 *Don Cornell*
93/70 *Johnny Cash*
64/80 **Rock It** *Lipps, Inc.*
71/83 **Rockit** *Herbie Hancock*
56/80 **Rock Lobster** *B-52's*
13/55 **Rock Love** *Fontane Sisters*
10/69 **Rock Me** *Steppenwolf*
57/79 **Rock Me** *Nick Gilder*
60/87 **Rock Me** *Great White*
1/86 **Rock Me Amadeus** *Falco*
34/64 **Rock Me Baby** *B.B. King*
38/72 **Rock Me Baby** *David Cassidy*
1/74 **Rock Me Gently** *Andy Kim*
43/63 **Rock Me In The Cradle Of Love** *Dee Dee Sharp*
Rock Me On The Water
48/72 *Jackson Browne*
85/72 *Linda Ronstadt*
18/85 **Rock Me Tonight (For Old Times Sake)** *Freddie Jackson*
15/84 **Rock Me Tonite** *Billy Squier*
97/94 **Rock My World (Little Country Girl)** *Brooks & Dunn*
Rock 'N' Roll ..also see: Rock And Roll / Rockin' Roll
13/79 **Rock 'N' Roll Fantasy** *Bad Company*
30/78 **Rock 'N' Roll Fantasy** *Kinks*
Rock 'N' Roll (I Gave You The Best Years Of My Life)
73/73 *Kevin Johnson*
97/74 *Terry Jacks*
15/75 *Mac Davis*
19/83 **Rock 'N' Roll Is King** *ELO*
29/72 **Rock 'N Roll Soul** *Grand Funk Railroad*
68/86 **Rock 'N' Roll To The Rescue** *Beach Boys*
44/67 **Rock 'N' Roll Woman** *Buffalo Springfield*
16/83 **Rock Of Ages** *Def Leppard*
22/88 **Rock Of Life** *Rick Springfield*
Rock On
5/74 *David Essex*
1/89 *Michael Damian*
36/56 **Rock Right** *Georgia Gibbs*
71/01 **Rock Show** *Blink-182*
7/87 **Rock Steady** *Whispers*
9/71 **Rock Steady** *Aretha Franklin*
73/95 **Rock Steady** *Bonnie Raitt & Bryan Adams*
1/74 **Rock The Boat** *Hues Corporation*
14/01 **Rock The Boat** *Aaliyah*
8/83 **Rock The Casbah** *Clash*
30/87 **Rock The Night** *Europe*
82/02 **Rock The Party** *Benzino*
9/82 **Rock This Town** *Stray Cats*
7/89 **Rock Wit'cha** *Bobby Brown*
1/80 **Rock With You** *Michael Jackson*
98/93 **Rock With You** *Inner Circle*
25/84 **Rock You Like A Hurricane** *Scorpions*
1/74 **Rock Your Baby** *George McCrae*
17/57 **Rock Your Little Baby To Sleep** *Buddy Knox*
38/59 **Rocka-Conga** *Applejacks*
67S/94 **Rockafella** *Redman*
Rockafeller Skank
78/98 *Fatboy Slim*
76/00 *Fatboy Slim*
66/78 **Rockaway Beach** *Ramones*
12/89 **Rocket** *Def Leppard*
6/72 **Rocket Man** *Elton John*
39/78 **Rocket Ride** *Kiss*
6/88 **Rocket 2 U** *Jets*
10/75 **Rockford Files** *Mike Post*
79/58 **Rockhouse** *Ray Charles*

ROCKIN':

27/75 **Rockin' All Over The World** *John Fogerty*
91/75 **Rockin' And Rollin' On The Streets Of Hollywood** *Buddy Miles*
Rockin' Around The Christmas Tree
14/60 *Brenda Lee*
50/61 *Brenda Lee*
59/62 *Brenda Lee*
25/85 **Rockin' At Midnight** *Honeydrippers*
(also see: Good Rockin' Tonight)
83/61 **Rockin' Bicycle** *Fats Domino*
9/75 **Rockin' Chair** *Gwen McCrae*
Rockin' Crickets
57/59 *Hot-Toddys*
87/63 *Rockin' Rebels*
61/56 **Rockin' Ghost** *Archie Bleyer*
7/60 **Rockin' Good Way (To Mess Around And Fall In Love)** *Dinah Washington & Brook Benton*
78/59 **Rockin' In The Jungle** *Eternals*
58/69 **Rockin' In The Same Old Boat** *Bobby Bland*
43/80 **Rockin' Into The Night** *38-Special*
22/60 **Rockin' Little Angel** *Ray Smith*
1/76 **Rockin' Me** *Steve Miller*
95/90 **Rockin' Over The Beat** *Technotronic*
Rockin' Pneumonia And The Boogie Woogie Flu
52/57 *Huey Smith*
6/73 *Johnny Rivers*
64/60 **Rockin' Red Wing** *Sammy Masters*
Rockin' Robin
2/58 *Bobby Day*
96/64 *Rivieras*
2/72 *Michael Jackson*
Rockin' Roll ..also see: Rock And Roll / Rock 'N' Roll
14/73 **Rockin' Roll Baby** *Stylistics*
87/60 **Rockin', Rollin' Ocean** *Hank Snow*
64/57 **Rockin' Shoes** *Ames Brothers*
18/74 **Rockin' Soul** *Hues Corporation*
78/56 **Rockin' Through The Rye** *Bill Haley*
88/72 **Rockin' With The King** *Canned Heat*
60/60 **Rocking Goose** *Johnny & The Hurricanes*
9/75 **Rocky** *Austin Roberts*
82/79 **Rocky II Disco** *Maynard Ferguson*
9/73 **Rocky Mountain High** *John Denver*
76/76 **Rocky Mountain Music** *Eddie Rabbitt*
23/73 **Rocky Mountain Way** *Joe Walsh*
Rocky, Theme From ..see: Gonna Fly Now
62S/02 **Rocky Top** *Osborne Brothers*
45S/01 **Rodeo, Tha'** *Phenomenon*
77/95 **Rodeo** *95 South*
83/73 **Roland The Roadie And Gertrude The Groupie** *Dr. Hook*
30/79 **Rolene** *Moon Martin*
78/73 **Roll In My Sweet Baby's Arms** *Hank Wilson*
27/83 **Roll Me Away** *Bob Seger*
56/71 **Roll On** *New Colony Six*
(also see: Cimarron)
14/75 **Roll On Down The Highway** *Bachman-Turner Overdrive*
Roll Over Beethoven
29/56 *Chuck Berry*
51/61 *Velaires*
68/64 *Beatles*
42/73 *Electric Light Orchestra*
10/95 **Roll To Me** *del Amitri*
23S/02 **Roll Wit Me** *Pretty Willie*
86/93 **Roll Wit Tha Flava** *Flavor Unit MCs*
1/88 **Roll With It** *Steve Winwood*
58/78 **Roll With The Changes** *REO Speedwagon*
54S/01 **Rolla Man** *Suave Gotti*
34/79 **Roller** *April Wine*
92/66 **Roller Coaster** *Ides Of March*
67/99 **Rollercoaster** *B*Witched*
66/79 **Roller-Skatin' Mate** *Peaches & Herb*
13/55 **Rollin' Stone** *Fontane Sisters*
65/00 **Rollin' (Urban Assault Vehicle)** *Limp Bizkit*
92/75 **Rolling Down A Mountainside** *Main Ingredient*
17/02 **Rollout (My Business)** *Ludacris*
74/62 **Roly Poly** *Joey Dee*
26/84 **Romancing The Stone** *Eddy Grant*
1/91 **Romantic** *Karyn White*
55/94 **Romantic Call** *Patra*
99/64 **Rome Will Never Leave You** *Richard Chamberlain*
6/90 **Romeo** *Dino*
50/93 **Romeo** *Dolly Parton*
75/61 **Romeo** *Janie Grant*
87/77 **Romeo** *Mr. Big*
6/98 **Romeo And Juliet** *Sylk-E. Fyne*
27/92 **Romeo & Juliet** *Stacy Earl*
(also see: Farewell Love Theme / (Just Like) / Love Theme)
11/80 **Romeo's Tune** *Steve Forbert*
3/89 **Roni** *Bobby Brown*
6/64 **Ronnie** *4 Seasons*
81/61 **Ronnie** *Marcy Joe*
72/63 **Ronnie, Call Me When You Get A Chance** *Shelley Fabares*
93/87 **Ronnies Rapp** *Ron & The D.C. Crew*
17/90 **Room At The Top** *Adam Ant*
50/74 **Room Full Of Roses** *Mickey Gilley*
72/61 **Room Full Of Tears** *Drifters*
9/89 **Room To Move** *Animotion*

16/89 **Rooms On Fire** *Stevie Nicks*
44/69 **Roosevelt And Ira Lee (Night of the Mossacin)** *Tony Joe White*
57/77 **"Roots" Medley** *Quincy Jones*
51/76 **Roots, Rock, Reggae** *Bob Marley*
61/88 **Rooty Toot Toot** *John Cougar Mellencamp*
63S/94 **Rope The Moon** *John Michael Montgomery*
55/99 **Rosa Parks** *OutKast*
43/73 **Rosalie** *Sam Neely*
(also see: Rosealia / Rosie Lee)
2/82 **Rosanna** *Toto*
95/73 **Rosanna** *Classics IV*
91/68 **Rosanna's Going Wild** *Johnny Cash*
3/80 **Rose, The** *Bette Midler*
6/56 **Rose And A Baby Ruth** *George Hamilton IV*
78/01 **Rose Bouquet** *Phil Vassar*
3/71 **Rose Garden** *Lynn Anderson*
(also see: I Beg Your Pardon)
26/98 **Rose Is Still A Rose** *Aretha Franklin*
94/76 **Rose Of Cimarron** *Poco*
79/55 **Rose Tattoo** *Perry Como*
71/95 **Rosealia** *Better Than Ezra*
73/65 **Roses And Rainbows** *Danny Hutton*
Roses And Roses ..see: And Roses
1/62 **Roses Are Red (My Love)** *Bobby Vinton*
43/65 **Roses Are Red My Love** *"You Know Who" Group!*
(also see: Long As The Rose Is Red)
24/57 **Rosie Lee** *Mello-Tones*
30/80 **Rotation** *Herb Alpert*
22/86 **Rough Boy** *ZZ Top*
89/80 **Rough Boys** *Pete Townshend*
94/62 **Rough Lover** *Aretha Franklin*
Rough Neck ..see: RuffNeck
1/57 **Round And Round** *Perry Como*
12/84 **Round And Round** *Ratt*
12/91 **Round And Round** *Tevin Campbell*
64/89 **Round & round** *New Order*
84/95 **Round & Round** *Twinz*
62/02 **Round and Round Remix** *Jonell*
21/65 **Round Every Corner** *Petula Clark*
31A/94 **Round Here** *Counting Crows*
91/96 **'Round We Go** *Big Sister*
13/72 **Roundabout** *Yes*
80/65 **Roundabout** *Connie Francis*
Route 66
78/82 *Manhattan Transfer*
61/88 *Depeche Mode (medley)*
30/62 **Route 66 Theme** *Nelson Riddle*
37/82 **Route 101** *Herb Alpert*
60/56 **Rovin' Gambler** *"Tennessee" Ernie Ford*
Roxanne
32/79 *Police*
59/98 *Sting & The Police*
77/85 **Roxanne, Roxanne** *UTFO*
Roxy Roller
90/76 *Sweeney Todd*
99/76 *Sweeney Todd*
54/80 **Royal Mile (Sweet Darlin')** *Gerry Rafferty*
Rub It In
65/71 *Layng Martine*
16/74 *Billy "Crash" Craddock*
3/90 **Rub You The Right Way** *Johnny Gill*
6/61 **Rubber Ball** *Bobby Vee*
37/79 **Rubber Biscuit** *Blues Brothers*
73/73 **Rubber Bullets** *10 C.C.*
16/70 **Rubber Duckie** *Ernie (Jim Henson)*
88/93 **Rubberband Girl** *Kate Bush*
2/76 **Rubberband Man** *Spinners*
F/70 **Rubberneckin'** *Elvis Presley*
26/69 **Ruben James** *Kenny Rogers & The First Edition*
Ruby
28/60 *Ray Charles*
58/60 *Adam Wade*
18/62 **Ruby Ann** *Marty Robbins*
Ruby Baby
2/63 *Dion*
33/75 *Billy "Crash" Craddock*
6/69 **Ruby, Don't Take Your Love To Town** *Kenny Rogers & The First Edition*
Ruby Duby Du
30/60 *Tobin Mathews & Co.*
41/60 *Charles Wolcott*
(Ruby Red Dress) ..see: Leave Me Alone
63A/96 **Ruby Soho** *Rancid*
Ruby Tuesday
1/67 *Rolling Stones*
52/71 *Melanie*
Rudolph The Red-Nosed Reindeer
70/57 *Gene Autry*
21/60 *David Seville/The Chipmunks*
71/60 *Melodeers*
47/61 *David Seville/The Chipmunks*
77/62 *David Seville/The Chipmunks*
3X/68 *Temptations*
34/56 **Rudy's Rock** *Bill Haley*
94/99 **Ruff Ryders' Anthem** *DMX*
35/93 **RuffNeck** *MC Lyte*
66/64 **Rules Of Love** *Orlons*
Rumble
16/58 *Link Wray*
91/63 *Jack Nitzsche*
28/86 **Rumbleseat** *John Cougar Mellencamp*
89/78 **Rumor At The Honky Tonk** *Spellbound*
8/86 **Rumors** *Timex Social Club*
12/62 **Rumors** *Johnny Crawford*
55/66 **Rumors** *Syndicate Of Sound*
62/88 **Rumour, The** *Olivia Newton-John*
53/78 **Rumour Has It** *Donna Summer*
2/92 **Rump Shaker** *Wreckx-N-Effect*

RUN:

34/01 **Run** *George Strait*
76/99 **Run** *Collective Soul*
Run Away .. also see: Runaway
6/69 **Run Away Child, Running Wild** *Temptations*
12/65 **Run, Baby Run (Back Into My Arms)** *Newbeats*
33/78 **Run For Home** *Lindisfarne*
18/82 **Run For The Roses** *Dan Fogelberg*
16S/02 **Run 4 Us** *Mark Lane*
71/79 **Run Home Girl** *Sad Café*
4/75 **Run Joey Run** *David Geddes*
53/80 **Run Like Hell** *Pink Floyd*
36/60 **Run Red Run** *Coasters*
69/58 **Run Rudolph Run** *Chuck Berry*
25/66 **Run, Run, Look And See** *Brian Hyland*
27/72 **Run Run Run** *Jo Jo Gunne*
44/64 **Run, Run, Run** *Gestures*
53/67 **Run, Run, Run** *Third Rail*
75/61 **Run, Run, Run** *Ronny Douglas*
93/64 **Run, Run, Run** *Supremes*
20/84 **Run Runaway** *Slade*
76/70 **Run Sally Run** *Cuff Links*
28/60 **Run Samson Run** *Neil Sedaka*
93/75 **Run Tell The People** *Daniel Boone*
F/70 **Run Through The Jungle** *Creedence Clearwater Revival*
2/61 **Run To Him** *Bobby Vee*
16/72 **Run To Me** *Bee Gees*
68/81 **Run To Me** *Savoy Brown*
96/65 **Run To My Lovin' Arms** *Lenny Welch*
80/89 **Run To Paradise** *Choirboys*
6/85 **Run To You** *Bryan Adams*
31/93 **Run To You** *Whitney Houston*
92/70 **Run, Woman, Run** *Tammy Wynette*
8/95 **Run-Around** *Blues Traveler*
Runaround
20/54 *Three Chuckles*
23/60 *Fleetwoods*
28/61 **Runaround** *Regents*
Runaround Sue
1/61 *Dion*
13/78 *Leif Garrett*
3/95 **Run Away** *Real McCoy*
Runaway
1/61 *Del Shannon*
56/62 *Lawrence Welk*
79/72 *Dawn Feat. Tony Orlando (medley)*
46/75 *Charlie Kulis*
57/77 *Bonnie Raitt*
83/86 *Luis Cardenas*
3/95 **Runaway** *Janet Jackson*
12/78 **Runaway** *Jefferson Starship*
39/84 **Runaway** *Bon Jovi*
68/95 **Runaway** *Corrs*
97/02 **Runaway** *NB-Ridaz*
51/93 **Runaway Love** *En Vogue*
76/78 **Runaway Love** *Linda Clifford*
87/94 **Runaway Love** *Johnny O*
84/81 **Runaway Rita** *Leif Garrett*
5/93 **Runaway Train** *Soul Asylum*
22/84 **Runner** *Manfred Mann's Earth Band*
55/95 **Runnin'** *Pharcyde*
81/97 **Runnin'** *2Pac & Notorious B.I.G.*
23/72 **Runnin' Away** *Sly & The Family Stone*
44/02 **Running Away** *Hoobastank*
96/72 **Runnin' Back To Saskatoon** *Guess Who*
64/69 **Runnin' Blue** *Doors*
23/89 **Runnin' Down A Dream** *Tom Petty*
57/64 **Runnin' Out Of Fools** *Aretha Franklin*
84/78 **Runnin' With The Devil** *Van Halen*
91/82 **Running** *Chubby Checker*
78/80 **Running Back** *Eddie Money*
79/85 **Running Back** *Urgent*
18/91 **Running Back To You** *Vanessa Williams*
Running Bear
1/60 *Johnny Preston*
94/69 *Sonny James*
83/87 **Running In The Family** *Level 42*
11/78 **Running On Empty** *Jackson Browne*
Running Scared
1/61 *Roy Orbison*
50/81 *Fools*
30/85 **Running Up That Hill** *Kate Bush*
7/84 **Running With The Night** *Lionel Richie*
39/72 **Runway, The** *Grass Roots*
32/91 **Rush** *Big Audio Dynamite II*
73/92 **Rush, The** *Luther Vandross*
9/88 **Rush Hour** *Jane Wiedlin*
Rush On Me ..see: (You're Puttin')
1/91 **Rush, Rush** *Paula Abdul*

91/59 **Russian Band Stand** *Spencer & Spencer*
16/86 **Russians** *Sting*
79/79 **Rust Never Sleeps (Hey Hey, My My [Into The Black])** *Neil Young & Crazy Horse*
33/65 **Rusty Bells** *Brenda Lee*
51/86 **Ruthless People** *Mick Jagger*
73/00 **Ryde Or Die, Chick** *Lox*

S

73/57 **'S Wonderful** *Ray Conniff*
15/75 **S.O.S.** *Abba*
(also see: Same Ol' Situation / Stop Her On Sight)
39/66 **S.Y.S.L.J.F.M. (The Letter Song)** *Joe Tex*
20/61 **Sacred** *Castells*
13/89 **Sacred Emotion** *Donny Osmond*
18/90 **Sacrifice** *Elton John*
98/92 **Sad But True** *Metallica*
74^{A}/96 **Sad Caper** *Hootie & The Blowfish*
1/79 **Sad Eyes** *Robert John*
63/77 **Sad Eyes** *Brooklyn Dreams*
88/61 **Sad Eyes (Don't You Cry)** *Echoes*
Sad Girl
47/69 *Intruders*
93/82 *GQ*
83/77 **Sad Girl** *Carl Graves*
84/82 **Sad Hearts** *Four Tops*
29/60 **Sad Mood** *Sam Cooke*
Sad Movies (Make Me Cry)
5/61 *Sue Thompson*
56/61 *Lennon Sisters*
83/92 **Sad New Day** *Me Phi Me*
27/65 **Sad, Sad Girl** *Barbara Mason*
84/63 **Sad, Sad Girl And Boy** *Impressions*
5/84 **Sad Songs (Say So Much)** *Elton John*
14/75 **Sad Sweet Dreamer** *Sweet Sensation*
94/65 **Sad Tomorrows** *Trini Lopez*
5/91 **Sadeness** *Enigma*
54/75 **Sadie** *Spinners*
52/56 **Sadie's Shawl** *Bob Sharples*
81/95 **Safe + Sound** *DJ Quik*
100/66 **Safe And Sound** *Fontella Bass*
53/68 **Safe In My Garden** *Mamas & The Papas*
3/83 **Safety Dance** *Men Without Hats*
85/64 **Saginaw, Michigan** *Lefty Frizzell*
6/94 **Said I Loved You...But I Lied** *Michael Bolton*
64/66 **Said I Wasn't Gonna Tell Nobody** *Sam & Dave*
5/58 **Sail Along Silvery Moon** *Billy Vaughn*
50/73 **Sail Around The World** *David Gates*
54/84 **Sail Away** *Temptations*
84/77 **Sail Away** *Sam Neely*
(also see: Orinoco Flow)
4/79 **Sail On** *Commodores*
Sail On Sailor
79/73 *Beach Boys*
49/75 *Beach Boys*
1/80 **Sailing** *Christopher Cross*
58/75 **Sailing** *Rod Stewart*
55/77 **Sailing Ships** *Mesa*
81/64 **Sailor Boy** *Chiffons*
5/60 **Sailor (Your Home Is The Sea)** *Lolita*

Saint ..also see: St.
94/98 **Saint Of Me** *Rolling Stones*
Saints Rock 'N Roll ..see: When The Saints Go Marchin' In
69/76 **Sally** *Grand Funk Railroad*
17/75 **Sally G** *Paul McCartney*
2/63 **Sally, Go 'Round The Roses** *Jaynetts*
95/68 **Sally Had A Party** *Flavor*
Sally Was A Good Old Girl
99/64 *Fats Domino*
99/68 *Trini Lopez*
81/59 **Sal's Got A Sugar Lip** *Johnny Horton*
76/75 **Salsoul Hustle** *Salsoul Orchestra*
36/83 **Salt In My Tears** *Martin Briley*
93/63 **Saltwater Taffy** *Morty Jay*
21^{A}/96 **Salvation** *Cranberries*
20/77 **Sam** *Olivia Newton-John*
98/66 **Sam, You Made The Pants Too Long** *Barbra Streisand*
92/67 **Sam's Place** *Buck Owens*
94/62 **Sam's Song** *Dean Martin & Sammy Davis Jr.*
69/88 **Samantha (What You Gonna Do?)** *Cellarful Of Noise*
87/89 **Same Love** *Jets*
50/74 **Same Love That Made Me Laugh** *Bill Withers*
67^{A}/98 **Same Ol' G** *Ginuwine*
33^{S}/01 **Same Ol' Same Ol'** *PYT*
90/93 **Same Ol' Shit** *MC Ren*
78/90 **Same Ol' Situation (S.O.S.)** *Mötley Crüe*
91/63 **Same Old Hurt** *Burl Ives*
9/81 **Same Old Lang Syne** *Dan Fogelberg*
78/90 **Same Old Look** *Jimmy Ryser*
51/60 **Same Old Me** *Guy Mitchell*
13/55 **Same Old Saturday Night** *Frank Sinatra*
25^{S}/02 **Same Old Song** *Sev*
44/87 **Same Ole Love (365 Days A Year)** *Anita Baker*
16/60 **Same One** *Brook Benton*
70/00 **Same Script, Different Cast** *Whitney Houston & Deborah Cox*
61^{A}/91 **Same Song** *Digital Underground*
75/75 **Same Thing It Took** *Impressions*
8/61 **San Antonio Rose** *Floyd Cramer*
100/71 **San Bernadino** *Christie*
9/67 **San Franciscan Nights** *Animals*
4/67 **San Francisco (Be Sure To Wear Flowers In Your Hair)** *Scott McKenzie*
91/68 **San Francisco Girls (Return of the Native)** *Fever Tree*
79/69 **San Francisco Is A Lonely Town** *Joe Simon*
47/61 **San-Ho-Zay** *Freddy King*
14/86 **Sanctify Yourself** *Simple Minds*
23/55 **Sand And The Sea** *Nat "King" Cole*
Sandpiper, Love Theme From ..see: Shadow Of Your Smile
83/01 **Sandstorm** *Darude*
15/60 **Sandy** *Larry Hall*
21/63 **Sandy** *Dion*
27/66 **Sandy** *Ronny & The Daytonas*
85/75 **Sandy** *Hollies*
32/57 **Santa And The Satellite** *Buchanan & Goodman*
99/61 **Santa & The Touchables** *Dickie Goodman*
3^{X}/71 **Santa Claus And His Old Lady** *Cheech & Chong*
91/94 **Santa Claus Boogie** *Tractors*

4^{X}/68 **Santa Claus Go Straight To The Ghetto** *James Brown*
Santa Claus Is Coming To Town
23/62 *4 Seasons*
1^{X}/70 *Jackson 5*
1^{X}/85 *Bruce Springsteen*
7^{X}/70 **Santa Claus Is Definitely Here To Stay** *James Brown*
45/62 **Santa Claus Is Watching You** *Ray Stevens*
2^{X}/65 **Santa Looked A Lot Like Daddy** *Buck Owens*
29^{A}/96 **Santa Monica (Watch The World Die)** *Everclear*
67/97 **Santa's A Fat Bitch** *Insane Clown Posse*
11^{X}/73 **Santa's Little Helper, Dingo** *Richard Doyle (Shamus M'Cool)*
43^{A}/97 **Santeria** *Sublime*
19/54 **Santo Natale (Merry Christmas)** *David Whitfield*
1/86 **Sara** *Starship*
7/80 **Sara** *Fleetwood Mac*
61/82 **Sara** *Bill Champlin*
4/76 **Sara Smile** *Daryl Hall & John Oates*
39/80 **(Sartorial Eloquence) Don't Ya Wanna Play This Game No More?** *Elton John*
61/87 **Satellite** *Hooters*
55^{A}/96 **Satellite** *Dave Matthews Band*
23/66 **Satin Pillows** *Bobby Vinton*
97/70 **Satin Red And Black Velvet Woman** *Dave Mason*
28/73 **Satin Sheets** *Jeanne Pruett*
73/76 **Satin Sheets** *Bellamy Brothers*
22/75 **Satin Soul** *Love Unlimited Orchestra*
27/03 **Satisfaction** *Eve*
49/72 **Satisfaction** *Smokey Robinson & The Miracles*
(also see: I Can't Get No)
73/85 **Satisfaction Guaranteed** *Firm*
58/74 **Satisfaction Guaranteed (Or Take Your Love Back)** *Harold Melvin*
1/89 **Satisfied** *Richard Marx*
81/84 **Satisfied Man** *Molly Hatchet*
39/66 **Satisfied Mind** *Bobby Hebb*
50/66 **Satisfied With You** *Dave Clark Five*
64/84 **Satisfy Me** *Billy Satellite*
2/99 **Satisfy You** *Puff Daddy*
3/72 **Saturday In The Park** *Chicago*
26/86 **Saturday Love** *Cherrelle with Alexander O'Neal*
28/71 **Saturday Morning Confusion** *Bobby Russell*
1/76 **Saturday Night** *Bay City Rollers*
29/63 **Saturday Night** *New Christy Minstrels*
35/79 **Saturdaynight** *Herman Brood*
21/77 **Saturday Nite** *Earth, Wind & Fire*
18/64 **Saturday Night At The Movies** *Drifters*
99/69 **Saturday Night At The World** *Mason Williams*
27/75 **Saturday Night Special** *Lynyrd Skynyrd*
34/79 **Saturday Night, Sunday Morning** *Thelma Houston*
12/73 **Saturday Night's Alright For Fighting** *Elton John*
22/02 **Saturday (Oooh! Ooooh!)** *Ludacris*
93/63 **Saturday Sunshine** *Burt Bacharach*
Sausalito
86/69 *Ohio Express*
99/69 *Al Martino*
25/81 **Sausalito Summernight** *Diesel*
34/80 **Savannah Nights** *Tom Johnston*

SAVE:

16/85 **Save A Prayer** *Duran Duran*
53/62 **Save All Your Lovin' For Me** *Brenda Lee*
22/77 **Save It For A Rainy Day** *Stephen Bishop*
10/64 **Save It For Me** *4 Seasons*
33/90 **Save Me** *Fleetwood Mac*
Save Me
54/77 *Merrilee Rush*
90/77 *Donna McDaniel*
71/80 **Save Me** *Dave Mason*
74/91 **Save Me** *Lisa Fischer*
73/59 **Save My Soul** *Jack Scott*
15/91 **Save Some Love** *Keedy*
1/92 **Save The Best For Last** *Vanessa Williams*
Save The Country
27/70 *5th Dimension*
74/70 *Thelma Houston*
Save The Last Dance For Me
1/60 *Drifters*
18/74 *DeFranco Family*
45/84 *Dolly Parton*
(also see: I'll Save The Last Dance)
77/85 **Save The Night For Me** *Maureen Steele*
66/83 **Save The Overtime (For Me)** *Gladys Knight*
5/99 **Save Tonight** *Eagle-Eye Cherry*
37/92 **Save Up All Your Tears** *Cher*
2/65 **Save Your Heart For Me** *Gary Lewis*
Save Your Kisses For Me
27/76 *Brotherhood Of Man*
75/76 *Bobby Vinton*
57/88 **Save Your Love** *Great White*
81/93 **Save Your Love** *Bad Boys Blue*
94/70 **Save Your Sugar For Me** *Tony Joe White*
37/61 **Saved** *LaVern Baker*
20/83 **Saved By Zero** *Fixx*
50/88 **Savin' Myself** *Eria Fachin*
1/85 **Saving All My Love For You** *Whitney Houston*
4/93 **Saving Forever For You** *Shanice*
94/73 **Saw A New Morning** *Bee Gees*
65/63 **Sax Fifth Avenue** *Johnny Beecher*

SAY:

21/90 **Say A Prayer** *Breathe*
17/81 **Say Goodbye To Hollywood** *Billy Joel*
85/80 **Say Goodbye To Little Jo** *Steve Forbert*
3/73 **Say, Has Anybody Seen My Sweet Gypsy Rose** *Dawn feat. Tony Orlando*
68/84 **Say Hello To Ronnie** *Janey Street*
21/66 **Say I Am (What I Am)** *Tommy James*
56/02 **Say I Yi Yi** *Ying Yang Twins*
40/97 **Say...If You Feel Alright** *Crystal Waters*
10/98 **Say It** *Voices Of Theory*
27/88 **Say It Again** *Jermaine Stewart*
46/85 **Say It Again** *Santana*
51A/95 **Say It Ain't So** *Weezer*
2/83 **Say It Isn't So** *Daryl Hall - John Oates*
98/57 **Say It Isn't So** *Teddi King*
10/68 **Say It Loud - I'm Black And I'm Proud** *James Brown*
70/86 **Say It, Say It** *E.G. Daily*
49/88 **Say It's Gonna Rain** *Will To Power*
20/59 **Say Man** *Bo Diddley*
55/79 **Say Maybe** *Neil Diamond*
1/00 **Say My Name** *Destiny's Child*
20S/00 **Say No More** *Innosense*
1/83 **Say Say Say** *Paul McCartney & Michael Jackson*
22/65 **Say Something Funny** *Patty Duke*
32/81 **Say What** *Jesse Winchester*
Say Wonderful Things
81/63 *Patti Page*
91/63 *Ronnie Carroll*
40/64 **Say You** *Ronnie Dove*
11/76 **Say You Love Me** *Fleetwood Mac*
58/69 **Say You Love Me** *Impressions*
98/76 **Say You Love Me** *D.J. Rogers*
44/87 **Say You Really Want Me** *Kim Wilde*
1/85 **Say You, Say Me** *Lionel Richie*
6/88 **Say You Will** *Foreigner*
20/81 **Say You'll Be Mine** *Christopher Cross*
3/97 **Say You'll Be There** *Spice Girls*
59/98 **Say You'll Stay** *Kai*
15/77 **Say You'll Stay Until Tomorrow** *Tom Jones*
39/65 **(Say) You're My Girl** *Roy Orbison*
21/85 **Say You're Wrong** *Julian Lennon*
31/88 **Sayin' Sorry (Don't Make It Right)** *Denise Lopez*
94/80 **Scandal** *RCR*
72S/96 **Scandalous** *Click*
9/99 **Scar Tissue** *Red Hot Chili Peppers*
Scarborough Fair
11/68 *Simon & Garfunkel*
16/68 *Sergio Mendes*
94/83 **Scarlet Fever** *Kenny Rogers*
13/59 **Scarlet Ribbons (For Her Hair)** *Browns*
89/63 **Scarlett O'Hara** *Lawrence Welk*
64/96 **Scarred** *Luke*
77/96 **Scary Kisses** *Voice Of The Beehive*
60/95 **Scatman (Ski-Ba-Bop-Ba-Dop-Bop)** *Scatman John*
98/63 **Scavenger, The** *Dick Dale*
57/92 **Scenario** *Tribe Called Quest*
82/96 **Scent Of Attraction** *Patra with Aaron Hall*
67/01 **Schism** *Tool*
33/75 **School Boy Crush** *AWB*
3/57 **School Day** *Chuck Berry*
28/61 **School Is In** *Gary (U.S.) Bonds*
5/61 **School Is Out** *Gary (U.S.) Bonds*
91/72 **School Teacher** *Kenny Rogers & The First Edition*
School's Out
7/72 *Alice Cooper*
67/86 *Krokus*
80/85 **Scientific Love** *Midnight Star*
73A/96 **Scooby Snacks** *Fun Lovin' Criminals*
6/72 **Scorpio** *Dennis Coffey*
81/62 **Scotch And Soda** *Kingston Trio*
75/76 **Scotch On The Rocks** *Band Of The Black Watch*
69/61 **Scottish Soldier (Green Hills of Tyrol)** *Andy Stewart*
81/74 **Scratch** *Crusaders*
80/64 **Scratchy** *Travis Wammack*
5/95 **Scream** *Michael Jackson & Janet Jackson*
62/70 **Screaming Night Hog** *Steppenwolf*
63/85 **Screams Of Passion** *Family*
20/87 **Se La** *Lionel Richie*
Se Si Bon ..see: Whispering
Sea Cruise
14/59 *Frankie Ford*
84/71 *Johnny Rivers*
21/61 **Sea Of Heartbreak** *Don Gibson*
Sea Of Love
2/59 *Phil Phillips*
33/82 *Del Shannon*
3/85 *Honeydrippers*
53/91 **Seal Our Fate** *Gloria Estefan*
Sealed With A Kiss
3/62 *Brian Hyland*
19/68 *Gary Lewis*
19/72 *Bobby Vinton*
96/59 **Search, The** *Dean Reed*
4/85 **Search Is Over** *Survivor*
Searchin'
3/57 *Coasters*
83/61 *Jack Eubanks*
84/64 *Ace Cannon*
81/55 **Searching** *Hilltoppers*
16A/98 **Searchin' My Soul** *Vonda Shepard*
Searchin' So Long ..see: (I've Been)
58/78 **Searching For A Thrill** *Starbuck*
27/66 **Searching For My Love** *Bobby Moore & The Rhythm Aces*
94/62 **Searching Is Over** *Joe Henderson*
59/77 **Seaside Woman** *Suzy & The Red Stripes*
65/68 **Season Of The Witch** *Vanilla Fudge*
75/81 **Seasons** *Charles Fox*
95/80 **Seasons** *Grace Slick*
(also see: Oh Lord, Why Lord)
1/88 **Seasons Change** *Exposé*
1/74 **Seasons In The Sun** *Terry Jacks*
82/82 **Seasons Of Gold** *Gidea Park*
78/82 **Seasons Of The Heart** *John Denver*
38/69 **Seattle** *Perry Como*
Second Avenue
34/74 *Garfunkel*
58/74 *Tim Moore*
6/89 **Second Chance** *Thirty Eight Special*
53/90 **Second Chance** *Tyler Collins*
40/56 **Second Fiddle** *Kay Starr*
63/62 **Second Fiddle Girl** *Barbara Lynn*
7/62 **Second Hand Love** *Connie Francis*
32/66 **Second Hand Rose** *Barbra Streisand*
79/60 **Second Honeymoon** *Johnny Cash*
39/85 **Second Nature** *Dan Hartman*
28/98 **Second Round K.O.** *Canibus*
8/80 **Second Time Around** *Shalamar*
50/61 **Second Time Around** *Frank Sinatra*
3/94 **Secret** *Madonna*
18/58 **Secret, The** *Gordon MacRae*
63/86 **Secret** *Orchestral Manoeuvres In The Dark*
64/91 **Secret** *Heart*
Secret Agent Man
3/66 *Johnny Rivers*
54/66 *Ventures*
Secret Garden
63/95 *Bruce Springsteen*
19/97 *Bruce Springsteen*
31/90 **Secret Garden (Sweet Seduction Suite)** *Quincy Jones/Al B. Sure!/James Ingram/El DeBarge/Barry White*
46/82 **Secret Journey** *Police*
Secret Love
29/66 *Billy Stewart*
99/66 *Richard "Groove" Holmes*
20/75 *Freddy Fender*

3/86 **Secret Lovers** *Atlantic Starr*
46/99 **Secret Of Life** *Faith Hill*
88/60 **Secret Of Love** *Elton Anderson*
64/87 **Secret Of My Success** *Night Ranger*
6/89 **Secret Rendezvous** *Karyn White*
19/86 **Secret Separation** *Fixx*
62/74 **Secretary** *Betty Wright*
Secretly
3/58 *Jimmie Rodgers*
64/65 *Lettermen*
76/81 **Secrets** *Mac Davis*
Security
97/64 *Otis Redding*
35/68 *Etta James*
72/81 **Seduced** *Leon Redbone*
28/80 **Seduction, The** *James Last Band*
27/69 **See** *Rascals*
See Me, Feel Me
12/70 *Who*
29/73 *New Seekers (medley)*
75/69 **See Ruby Fall** *Johnny Cash*
See Saw
25/56 *Moonglows*
57/56 *Don Cornell*
See Saw
44/65 *Don Covay*
14/68 *Aretha Franklin*
See See ..see: C.C.
9/64 **See The Funny Little Clown** *Bobby Goldsboro*
95/70 **See The Light** *Flame*
40/91 **See The Lights** *Simple Minds*
89/85 **See What Love Can Do** *Eric Clapton*
See You ..also see: C U
69/65 **(See You At The) "Go-Go"** *Dobie Gray*
See You In September
23/59 *Tempos*
3/66 *Happenings*
6/56 **See You Later, Alligator** *Bill Haley*
66/77 **See You When I Git There** *Lou Rawls*
46/65 **Seein' The Right Love Go Wrong** *Jack Jones*
62/89 **Seeing Is Believing** *Mike + The Mechanics*
44/70 **Seeker, The** *Who*
50/70 **Seems Like I Gotta Do Wrong** *Whispers*
73A/93 **Seems You're Much Too Busy** *Vertical Hold*
53A/95 **Seether** *Veruca Salt*
4/84 **Self Control** *Laura Branigan*
45A/94 **Self Esteem** *Offspring*
11/64 **Selfish One** *Jackie Ross*
69A/97 **Sell Out** *Reel Big Fish*
43/94 **Selling The Drama** *Live*
4/97 **Semi-Charmed Life** *Third Eye Blind*
72/73 **Send A Little Love My Way** *Anne Murray*
6/57 **Send For Me** *Nat "King" Cole*
96/62 **Send For Me (If you need some Lovin)** *Barbara George*
23/83 **Send Her My Love** *Journey*
Send In The Clowns
36/75 *Judy Collins*
19/77 *Judy Collins*
50/93 **Send Me A Lover** *Taylor Dayne*
Send Me An Angel
29/84 *Real Life*
26/89 *Real Life ('89)*
44/92 **Send Me An Angel** *Scorpions*
72/95 **Send Me On My Way** *Rusted Root*

Send Me Some Lovin'
54/57 *Little Richard*
13/63 *Sam Cooke*
Send Me The Pillow You Dream On
77/58 *Hank Locklin*
56/60 *Browns*
17/62 *Johnny Tillotson*
22/65 *Dean Martin*
94/68 **Send My Baby Back** *Freddie Hughes*
72/98 **Send My Love/Send One Your Love** *Born Americans*
4/79 **Send One Your Love** *Stevie Wonder*
88/88 **Sendin' All My Love** *Jets*
5/90 **Sending All My Love** *Linear*
40/94 **Sending My Love** *Zhané*
56/81 **Sensitive Kind** *Santana*
4/91 **Sensitivity** *Ralph Tresvant*
27/95 **Sentimental** *Deborah Cox*
72/93 **Sentimental** *Kenny G*
8/78 **Sentimental Lady** *Bob Welch*
8/85 **Sentimental Street** *Night Ranger*
(Senza Fine) ..see: Phoenix Love Theme
87/60 **Senza Mamma (With No One)** *Connie Francis*
1/85 **Separate Lives** *Phil Collins & Marilyn Martin*
20/73 **Separate Ways** *Elvis Presley*
96/59 **Separate Ways** *Sarah Vaughan*
8/83 **Separate Ways (Worlds Apart)** *Journey*
23/00 **Separated** *Avant*
8/79 **September** *Earth, Wind & Fire*
23/61 **September In The Rain** *Dinah Washington*
17/80 **September Morn'** *Neil Diamond*
51/63 **September Song** *Jimmy Durante*
23/80 **Sequel** *Harry Chapin*
88/97 **Serenade** *Shades*
82/60 **Serenata** *Sarah Vaughan*
Sergeant ..see: Sgt.
21/87 **Serious** *Donna Allen*
75/89 **Serious Kinda Girl** *Christopher Max*
99/59 **Sermonette** *Della Reese*
13/78 **Serpentine Fire** *Earth, Wind & Fire*
36S/02 **Serve The Ego** *Jewel*
60/92 **Sesame's Treet** *Smart E's*
1/91 **Set Adrift On Memory Bliss** *PM Dawn*
65/01 **Set It Off** *Juvenile*
23/65 **Set Me Free** *Kinks*
27/80 **Set Me Free** *Utopia*
90/92 **Set Me Free** *Clubland*
71/81 **Set The Night On Fire** *Oak*
6/91 **Set The Night To Music** *Roberta Flack with Maxi Priest*
26/96 **Set U Free** *Planet Soul*
79/66 **Set You Free This Time** *Byrds*
80/97 **Setting Sun** *Chemical Brothers*
56/63 **Settle Down (Goin' Down That Highway)** *Peter, Paul & Mary*

SEVEN:

7/93 **7** *Prince*
33/66 **7 And 7 Is** *Love*
21/81 **Seven Bridges Road** *Eagles*
95/61 **Seven Day Fool** *Etta James*
27/62 **Seven Day Weekend** *Gary (US) Bonds*
10/02 **7 Days** *Craig David*

Seven Days
17/56 *Dorothy Collins*
18/56 *Crew Cuts*
44/56 *Clyde McPhatter*
71A/98 **Seven Days** *Mary J. Blige*
30/58 **"7-11" (Mambo No. 5)** *Gone All Stars*
45/65 **Seven Letters** *Ben E. King*
9/59 **(Seven Little Girls) Sitting In The Back Seat** *Paul Evans*
71/75 **Seven Lonely Nights** *Four Tops*
85/58 **Seven Minutes In Heaven** *Poni-Tails*
14/67 **7 Rooms Of Gloom** *Four Tops*
98/94 **7 Seconds** *Youssou N'Dour & Neneh Cherry*
88/82 **777-9311** *Time*
46/75 **7-6-5-4-3-2-1 (Blow Your Whistle)** *Gary Toms Empire*
96/68 **7:30 Guided Tour** *Five Americans*
48A/94 **Seven Whole Days** *Toni Braxton*
19/87 **Seven Wonders** *Fleetwood Mac*
22/81 **Seven Year Ache** *Rosanne Cash*
84/69 **Seven Years** *Impressions*
7/65 **Seventh Son** *Johnny Rivers*
Seventeen
3/55 *Fontane Sisters*
5/55 *Boyd Bennett*
18/55 *Rusty Draper*
72/61 *Frankie Ford*
26/89 **Seventeen** *Winger*
36/84 **17** *Rick James*
F/94 **70's Love Groove** *Janet Jackson*
69/59 **77 Sunset Strip** *Don Ralke*

SEX:

8/98 **Sex and Candy** *Marcy Playground*
28/86 **Sex As A Weapon** *Pat Benatar*
62/83 **Sex (I'm A...)** *Berlin*
Sex Machine
15/70 *James Brown*
61/75 *James Brown*
20/93 **Sex Me** *R. Kelly*
6S/02 **Sex, Money, & Music** *Above The Law*
85/84 **Sex Shooter** *Apollonia 6*
58/87 **Sexappeal** *Georgio*
81/84 **Sexcrime (Nineteen Eighty-Four)** *Eurythmics*
74/92 **Sexual** *Goddess*
Sexual Healing
3/83 *Marvin Gaye*
60/95 *Max-A-Million*
42/00 **Sexual (Li Da Di)** *Amber*
42/75 **Sexy** *MFSB*
Sexy + 17 ..see: (She's)
5/80 **Sexy Eyes** *Dr. Hook*
20/84 **Sexy Girl** *Glenn Frey*
65/74 **Sexy Ida** *Ike & Tina Turner*
66/92 **Sexy M.F.** *Prince*
17/74 **Sexy Mama** *Moments*
50/73 **Sexy, Sexy, Sexy** *James Brown*
71/78 **Sgt. Pepper's Lonely Hearts Club Band (medley)** *Beatles*
Sha-La-La
69/64 *Shirelles*
12/65 *Manfred Mann*
7/74 **Sha-La-La (Make Me Happy)** *Al Green*
91/75 **Shackin' Up** *Barbara Mason*
28/00 **Shackles (Praise You)** *Mary Mary*
53/81 **Shaddap You Face** *Joe Dolce*
88/70 **Shades Of Green** *Flaming Ember*
1/78 **Shadow Dancing** *Andy Gibb*
94/68 **Shadow Of Your Love** *Five Stairsteps*

Shadow Of Your Smile
95/65 *Tony Bennett*
93/67 *Boots Randolph*
67/96 **Shadowboxin'** *Genius/GZA*
87/59 **Shadows** *5 Satins*
25/79 **Shadows In The Moonlight** *Anne Murray*
40S/02 **Shadows In The Night** *Michael Damian*
83/60 **Shadows Of Love** *LaVern Baker*
13/82 **Shadows Of The Night** *Pat Benatar*
19/62 **Shadrack** *Brook Benton*
12S/02 **Shady** *Big "C"*
Shaft ..see:, Theme From
53/59 **Shag (Is Totally Cool)** *Billy Graves*
38/64 **Shaggy Dog** *Mickey Lee Lane*

SHAKE:

Shake
7/65 *Sam Cooke*
47/67 *Otis Redding*
46/68 **Shake** *Shadows Of Knight*
77/90 **Shake** *Andrew Ridgeley*
Shake A Hand
71/58 *Mike Pedicin Quintet*
97/62 *Ruth Brown*
42/63 *Jackie Wilson & Linda Hopkins*
72/96 **Shake A Lil' Somethin'...** *2 Live Crew*
Shake A Tail Feather
51/63 *Five Du-Tones*
25/67 *James & Bobby Purify*
60/78 **Shake And Dance With Me** *Con Funk Shun*
29/65 **Shake And Fingerpop** *Jr. Walker*
28/89 **Shake For The Sheik** *Escape Club*
92/66 **Shake Hands (And Come Out Crying)** *Newbeats*
95/67 **Shake Hands And Walk Away Cryin'** *Lou Christie*
13/79 **Shake It** *Ian Matthews*
53S/00 **Shake It Like A Dog** *Kane & Abel*
74/91 **Shake It (Like A White Girl)** *Jesse Jaymes*
19S/00 **Shake It Off** *Take 5*
4/82 **Shake It Up** *Cars*
82/89 **Shake It Up** *Bad Company*
70/81 **Shake It Up Tonight** *Cheryl Lynn*
76/77 **Shake It Well** *Dramatics*
42/63 **Shake Me I Rattle (Squeeze Me I Cry)** *Marion Worth*
18/66 **Shake Me, Wake Me (When It's Over)** *Four Tops*
98/72 **Shake Off The Demon** *Brewer & Shipley*
Shake, Rattle And Roll
7/54 *Bill Haley*
31/67 *Arthur Conley*
33/63 **Shake! Shake! Shake!** *Jackie Wilson*
1/76 **(Shake, Shake, Shake) Shake Your Booty** *KC & The Sunshine Band*
43/63 **Shake Sherry** *Contours*
13/00 **Shake Ya Ass** *Mystikal*
1/87 **Shake You Down** *Gregory Abbott*
7/79 **Shake Your Body (Down To The Ground)** *Jacksons*
22/00 **Shake Your Bon-Bon** *Ricky Martin*
5/79 **Shake Your Groove Thing** *Peaches & Herb*
4/87 **Shake Your Love** *Debbie Gibson*
23/77 **Shake Your Rump To The Funk** *Bar-Kays*
1/87 **Shakedown** *Bob Seger*
31/79 **Shakedown Cruise** *Jay Ferguson*
90/78 **Shaker Song** *Spyro Gyra*

Shakey Ground
26/75 *Temptations*
70/77 *Phoebe Snow*
63/82 **Shakin'** *Eddie Money*
22/65 **Shakin' All Over** *Guess Who?*
Shambala
3/73 *Three Dog Night*
66/73 *B.W. Stevenson*
Shame
9/78 *Evelyn "Champagne" King*
28/94 *Zhané*
21/85 **Shame** *Motels*
69A/96 **Shame** *Stabbing Westward*
Shame On Me
23/62 *Bobby Bare*
76/67 *Chuck Jackson*
2/83 **Shame On The Moon** *Bob Seger*
42A/97 **Shame On You** *Indigo Girls*
29/68 **Shame, Shame** *Magic Lanterns*
12/75 **Shame, Shame, Shame** *Shirley (& Company)*
52/63 **Shame, Shame, Shame** *Jimmy Reed*
65/93 **Shamrocks And Shenanigans (Boom Shalock Lock Boom)** *House Of Pain*
47/80 **Shandi** *Kiss*
31/82 **Shanghai Breezes** *John Denver*
Shangri-La
11/57 *Four Coins*
15/64 *Robert Maxwell*
27/64 *Vic Dana*
64/69 *Lettermen*
57/84 **Shangri-La** *Steve Miller Band*
6/76 **Shannon** *Henry Gross*
80/59 **Shape I'm In** *Johnny Restivo*
9/00 **Shape Of My Heart** *Backstreet Boys*
22/68 **Shape Of Things To Come** *Max Frost*
67/79 **Shape Of Things To Come** *Headboys*
11/66 **Shapes Of Things** *Yardbirds*
10/70 **Share The Land** *Guess Who*
Share Your Love With Me
42/64 *Bobby Bland*
13/69 *Aretha Franklin*
14/81 *Kenny Rogers*
91/81 **Sharing The Love** *Rufus With Chaka Khan*
6/79 **Sharing The Night Together** *Dr. Hook*
15/62 **Sharing You** *Bobby Vee*
97/66 **Sharing You** *Mitty Collier*
56/83 **Sharp Dressed Man** *ZZ Top*
31/79 **Shattered** *Rolling Stones*
2/88 **Shattered Dreams** *Johnny Hates Jazz*
48/87 **Shattered Glass** *Laura Branigan*
30/75 **Shaving Cream** *Benny Bell*
43S/02 **Shawty** *P-Lo*
45/60 **Shazam!** *Duane Eddy*

SHE:

23/70 **She** *Tommy James*
80/74 **She** *Southcote*
41A/95 **She** *Green Day*
86/92 **She Ain't Pretty** *Northern Pikes*
61S/00 **She Ain't The Girl For You** *Kinleys*
1/90 **She Ain't Worth It** *Glenn Medeiros & Bobby Brown*
12/00 **She Bangs** *Ricky Martin*
5/79 **She Believes In Me** *Kenny Rogers*
33/70 **She Belongs To Me** *Rick Nelson*
45/66 **She Blew A Good Thing** *Poets*

5/83 **She Blinded Me With Science** *Thomas Dolby*
3/84 **She Bop** *Cyndi Lauper*
She Called Me Baby ..see: He
30/70 **She Came In Through The Bathroom Window** *Joe Cocker*
19/62 **She Can't Find Her Keys** *Paul Petersen*
She Comes To Me ..see: (When She Needs Good Lovin')
37/01 **She Couldn't Change Me** *Montgomery Gentry*
She Cried
5/62 *Jay & The Americans*
65/66 *Shangri-Las (He Cried)*
73/70 *Lettermen*
She Did It
23/77 *Eric Carmen*
69/81 *Michael Damian*
46/71 **She Didn't Do Magic** *Lobo*
70/70 **She Didn't Know (She Kept On Talking)** *Dee Dee Warwick*
48/84 **She Don't Know Me** *Bon Jovi*
84/87 **She Don't Look Back** *Dan Fogelberg*
55/95 **She Don't Use Jelly** *Flaming Lips*
1/89 **She Drives Me Crazy** *Fine Young Cannibals*
71/66 **She Drives Me Out Of My Mind** *Swingin' Medallions*
57/82 **She Got The Goldmine (I Got The Shaft)** *Jerry Reed*
13/02 **She Hates Me** *Puddle Of Mudd*
27/67 **She Is Still A Mystery** *Lovin' Spoonful*
She Lets Her Hair Down (Early In The Morning)
61/70 *Tokens*
89/70 *Gene Pitney*
67/82 **She Looks A Lot Like You** *Clocks*
76/02 **She Loves Me Not** *Papa Roach*
84/84 **She Loves My Car** *Ronnie Milsap*
54/78 **She Loves To Be In Love** *Charlie*
She Loves You
1/64 *Beatles*
97/64 *Die Beatles (Sie Liebt Dich)*
59/01 **She Misses Him** *Tim Rushlow*
93/61 **She Really Loves You** *Timi Yuro*
68/70 **She Said Yes** *Wilson Pickett*
18/59 **She Say (Oom Dooby Doom)** *Diamonds*
95/67 **She Shot A Hole In My Soul** *Clifford Curry*
30/91 **She Talks To Angels** *Black Crowes*
65S/94 **She Thinks His Name Was John** *Reba McEntire*
She Thinks I Still Care ..see: He Thinks
74/99 **She Thinks My Tractor's Sexy** *Kenny Chesney*
(also see: My Cellmate Thinks I'm Sexy)
92/67 **She Took You For A Ride** *Aaron Neville*
She Understands Me
31/64 *Johnny Tillotson*
40/66 *Bobby Vinton (Dum-De-Da)*
50/64 **She Wants T' Swim** *Chubby Checker*
6/89 **She Wants To Dance With Me** *Rick Astley*
49S/99 **She Wants You** *Billie*
62/02 **She Was** *Mark Chesnutt*
44/84 **She Was Hot** *Rolling Stones*
27/58 **She Was Only Seventeen (He Was One Year More)** *Marty Robbins*

30/89 **She Won't Talk To Me** *Luther Vandross*
3/83 **She Works Hard For The Money** *Donna Summer*
3/67 **She'd Rather Be With Me** *Turtles*
99/68 **She'll Be There** *Vikki Carr*
23/02 **She'll Leave You With A Smile** *George Strait*
47/63 **She'll Never Know** *Brenda Lee*

SHE'S:

22/81 **She's A Bad Mama Jama (She's Built, She's Stacked)** *Carl Carlton*
10/83 **She's A Beauty** *Tubes*
90/99 **She's A Bitch** *Missy "Misdemeanor" Elliott*
5/63 **She's A Fool** *Lesley Gore*
16/68 **She's A Heartbreaker** *Gene Pitney*
2/71 **She's A Lady** *Tom Jones*
84/69 **She's A Lady** *John Sebastian*
25/68 **She's A Rainbow** *Rolling Stones*
52/95 **She's A River** *Simple Minds*
75/83 **She's A Runner** *Billy Squier*
83/62 **She's A Troublemaker** *Majors*
She's A Very Lovely Woman
94/67 *Merry-Go-Round*
70/71 *Linda Ronstadt*
4/64 **She's A Woman** *Beatles*
She's About A Mover
13/65 *Sir Douglas Quintet*
97/68 *Otis Clay*
2/99 **She's All I Ever Had** *Ricky Martin*
26/01 **She's All I Got** *Jimmy Cozier*
She's All I Got
39/71 *Freddie North*
91/71 *Johnny Paycheck*
17/78 **She's Always A Woman** *Billy Joel*
74/99 **She's Always Right** *Clay Walker*
58/65 **She's Coming Home** *Zombies*
63[S]/91 **She's Dope!** *Bell Biv DeVoe*
18/62 **She's Everything (I Wanted You To Be)** *Ral Donner*
80/88 **She's Fly** *Tony Terry*
She's Gone
50/74 *Tavares*
60/74 *Daryl Hall & John Oates*
7/76 *Daryl Hall & John Oates*
59/91 **She's Gone (Lady)** *Steelheart*
23/82 **She's Got A Way** *Billy Joel*
87/79 **She's Got A Whole Number** *Keith Herman*
56/63 **She's Got Everything** *Essex*
83/69 **She's Got Love** *Thomas & Richard Frost*
57/95 **(She's Got) Skillz** *All-4-One*
59/92 **She's Got That Vibe** *R. Kelly*
93/73 **She's Got To Be A Saint** *Ray Price*
14/62 **She's Got You** *Patsy Cline*
60/99 **She's In Love** *Mark Wills*
41/80 **She's In Love With You** *Suzi Quatro*
95/77 **(She's Just A) Fallen Angel** *Starz*
99/60 **She's Just A Whole Lot Like You** *Hank Thompson*
3/66 **She's Just My Style** *Gary Lewis*
3/88 **She's Like The Wind** *Patrick Swayze*
15/68 **She's Lookin' Good** *Wilson Pickett*
21/84 **She's Mine** *Steve Perry*
98/60 **She's Mine** *Conway Twitty*
37/00 **She's More** *Andy Griggs*
14/67 **She's My Girl** *Turtles*
99/64 **She's My Girl** *Bobby Shafto*
38/58 **She's Neat** *Dale Wright*
70/93 **She's Not Cryin' Anymore** *Billy Ray Cyrus*
11/71 **She's Not Just Another Woman** *8th Day*
She's Not There
2/64 *Zombies*
27/77 *Santana*
5/62 **She's Not You** *Elvis Presley*
48/88 **She's On The Left** *Jeffrey Osborne*
88/88 **She's Only 20** *TAMI Show*
10/80 **She's Out Of My Life** *Michael Jackson*
5/92 **She's Playing Hard To Get** *Hi-Five*
72/70 **She's Ready** *Spiral Starecase*
5/83 **(She's) Sexy + 17** *Stray Cats*
26/80 **She's So Cold** *Rolling Stones*
14/99 **She's So High** *Tal Bachman*
(She's) Some Kind Of Wonderful ..see: Some Kind
47/84 **She's Strange** *Cameo*
33/64 **She's The One** *Chartbusters*
65/82 **She's Tight** *Cheap Trick*
65/84 **She's Trouble** *Musical Youth*
92/65 **She's With Her Other Love** *Leon Hayward*
81/77 **Sheena Is A Punk Rocker** *Ramones*
54/58 **Sheik Of Araby (Italian Style)** *Lou Monte*
1/62 **Sheila** *Tommy Roe*
47/87 **Shelter** *Lone Justice*
36/91 **Shelter Me** *Cinderella*
91/86 **Shelter Me** *Joe Cocker*
17/64 **Shelter Of Your Arms** *Sammy Davis Jr.*
Sherry
1/62 *4 Seasons*
70/80 *Robert John*
84/76 **Sherry** *Keane Brothers*
52/68 **Sherry Don't Go** *Lettermen*
45[A]/94 **Shhh** *Tevin Campbell*
92/93 **Shifftee** *Onyx*
Shifting, Whispering Sands
3/55 *Rusty Draper*
5/55 *Billy Vaughn*
24/70 **Shilo** *Neil Diamond*
42/98 **Shimmer** *Fuel*
42/60 **Shimmy Like Kate** *Olympics*
Shimmy Shimmy ..see: (I Do The)
24/60 **Shimmy, Shimmy, Ko-Ko-Bop** *Little Anthony & The Imperials*
88/62 **Shimmy, Shimmy Walk** *Megatons*
62/95 **Shimmy Shimmy Ya** *Ol' Dirty Bastard*
11/94 **Shine** *Collective Soul*
96/01 **Shine** *Lil Wayne*
8/79 **Shine A Little Love** *Electric Light Orchestra*
40/81 **Shine On** *L.T.D.*
41/82 **Shine On** *George Duke*
37/84 **Shine Shine** *Barry Gibb*
11/74 **Shinin' On** *Grand Funk*
1/75 **Shining Star** *Earth, Wind & Fire*
5/80 **Shining Star** *Manhattans*
10/91 **Shiny Happy People** *R.E.M.*
74/83 **Shiny Shiny** *Haysi Fantayzee*
84/88 **Ship Of Fools** *Robert Plant*
27/87 **Ship Of Fools (Save Me From Tomorrow)** *World Party*
Ship That Never Sailed
65/57 *David Carroll*
95/57 *Billy Vaughn*
71/83 **Ship To Shore** *Chris DeBurgh*
9/79 **Ships** *Barry Manilow*
58/63 **Shirl Girl** *Wayne Newton*
82/59 **Shirley** *John Fred*
91/57 **Shirley** *Schoolboys*
10/57 **Shish-Kebab** *Ralph Marterie*
(also see: Harem Dance)
31[S]/01 **$#!* On You** *D-12*
81/80 **Shiver And Shake** *Silencers*
58/97 **Sho Nuff** *Tela*
80/74 **Sho Nuff Boogie** *Sylvia & The Moments*
84/85 **Shock** *Motels*
29/83 **Shock The Monkey** *Peter Gabriel*
68/74 **Shoe Shoe Shine** *Dynamic Superiors*
67/71 **Shoes** *Brook Benton*
92/75 **Shoes** *Reparata*
18/75 **Shoeshine Boy** *Eddie Kendricks*
Shoo ..also see: Shu
9/68 **Shoo-Be-Doo-Be-Doo-Da-Day** *Stevie Wonder*
59/95 **Shook Ones** *Mobb Deep*
4/93 **Shoop** *Salt-N-Pepa*
(Shoop Shoop) ..see: Exhale
67/93 **Shoop Shoop (Never Stop Givin' You Love)** *Michael Cooper*
Shoop Shoop Song (It's In His Kiss)
6/64 *Betty Everett*
49/77 *Kate Taylor*
33/91 *Cher*
50/83 **Shoot For The Moon** *Poco*
66/55 **Shoot It Again** *Teresa Brewer*
91/79 **Shoot Me (With Your Love)** *Tasha Thomas*
44/67 **Shoot Your Shot** *Jr. Walker*
31/68 **Shoot'em Up, Baby** *Andy Kim*
83/84 **Shooting Shark** *Blue Öyster Cult*
74/80 **Shooting Star** *Dollar*
Shop Around
2/61 *Miracles*
4/76 *Captain & Tennille*
(also see: Don't Let Him Shop Around)
83/60 **Shoppin' For Clothes** *Coasters*
77/83 **Shoppin' From A To Z** *Toni Basil*
14/95 **Short Dick Man** *20 Fingers*
5/57 **Short Fat Fannie** *Larry Williams*
2/78 **Short People** *Randy Newman*
3/58 **Short Shorts** *Royal Teens*
Shortnin' Bread
82/60 *Paul Chaplain*
96/60 *Bell Notes*
25/98 **Shorty (You Keep Playin' With My Mind)** *Imajin*
68/86 **Shot In The Dark** *Ozzy Osbourne*
97/64 **Shot In The Dark** *Henry Mancini*
45/91 **Shot Of Poison** *Lita Ford*
Shotgun
4/65 *Jr. Walker*
68/69 *Vanilla Fudge*
Shotgun Rider
71/80 *Joe Sun*
70/81 *Delbert McClinton*
88/75 **Shotgun Shuffle** *Sunshine Band*
42/61 **Should I** *String-A-Longs*
13/82 **Should I Do It** *Pointer Sisters*
82/83 **Should I Love You** *Cee Farrow*
41/88 **Should I Say Yes?** *Nu Shooz*
69/87 **Should I See** *Frozen Ghost*
Should I Stay Or Should I Go
45/82 *Clash*
50/83 *Clash*
F/58 **Should We Tell Him** *Everly Brothers*
93/93 **Should've Been A Cowboy** *Toby Keith*
3/87 **Should've Known Better** *Richard Marx*

19/80 **Should've Never Let You Go** *Neil Sedaka & Dara Sedaka*
29/89 **Shoulder To Cry On** *Tommy Page*
1/85 **Shout** *Tears For Fears*
Shout
47/59 *Isley Brothers*
6/62 *Joey Dee*
94/62 *Isley Brothers*
94/64 *Lulu*
96/67 *Lulu*
83/69 *Chambers Brothers*
36S/03 **Shout** *Lilian Garcia*
(also see: Come On)
61/62 **Shout And Shimmy** *James Brown*
54/67 **Shout Bamalama** *Mickey Murray*
Shout It Out Loud
31/76 *Kiss*
54/78 *Kiss (Live)*
6/62 **Shout! Shout! (Knock Yourself Out)** *Ernie Maresca*
1/74 **Show And Tell** *Al Wilson*
61/73 **Show Biz Kids** *Steely Dan*
45/67 **Show Business** *Lou Rawls*
28/84 **Show Me** *Pretenders*
35/67 **Show Me** *Joe Tex*
44/87 **Show Me** *Cover Girls*
62/90 **Show Me** *Howard Hewett*
52/72 **Show Me How** *Emotions*
5/93 **Show Me Love** *Robin S*
7/97 **Show Me Love** *Robyn*
6/00 **Show Me The Meaning Of Being Lonely** *Backstreet Boys*
3/91 **Show Me The Way** *Styx*
6/76 **Show Me The Way** *Peter Frampton*
68/87 **Show Me The Way** *Regina Belle*
4/74 **Show Must Go On** *Three Dog Night*
37/85 **Show Some Respect** *Tina Turner*
89/68 **Show Time** *Detroit Emeralds*
28/77 **Show You The Way To Go** *Jacksons*
Showdown
53/74 *Electric Light Orchestra*
71/75 *Odia Coates*
59/76 *Electric Light Orchestra*
5/89 **Shower Me With Your Love** *Surface*
22/76 **Shower The People** *James Taylor*
78/87 **Showing Out (Get Fresh at the Weekend)** *Mel & Kim*
96/57 **Shrine Of St. Cecilia** *Faron Young*
38/75 **(Shu-Doo-Pa-Poo-Poop) Love Being Your Fool** *Travis Wammack*
32/61 **Shu Rah** *Fats Domino*
23/63 **Shut Down** *Beach Boys*
83/00 **Shut Up** *Trick Daddy*
90/94 **Shut Up And Kiss Me** *Mary Chapin Carpenter*
24/63 **Shutters And Boards** *Jerry Wallace*
71/61 **Shy Away** *Jerry Fuller*
83/83 **Shy Boy (Don't It Make You Feel Good)** *Bananarama*
94/87 **Shy Boys** *Ana*
89/87 **Shy Girl** *Stacey Q*
91/63 **Shy Girl** *Cascades*
13/95 **Shy Guy** *Diana King*
22/58 **Sick And Tired** *Fats Domino*
18/03 **Sick Of Being Lonely** *Field Mob*
58/95 **Sick Of Myself** *Matthew Sweet*
76/83 **Side By Side** *Earth, Wind & Fire*
84/60 **Side Car Cycle** *Charlie Ryan*
8/74 **Sideshow** *Blue Magic*
25/64 **Sidewalk Surfin'** *Jan & Dean*
18/86 **Sidewalk Talk** *Jellybean*
81/65 **Sidewinder, The** *Lee Morgan*

Sie Liebt Dich ..see: She Loves You
1/94 **Sign, The** *Ace Of Base*
32/84 **Sign Of Fire** *Fixx*
57/81 **Sign Of The Gypsy Queen** *April Wine*
3/87 **Sign 'O' The Times** *Prince*
11/66 **Sign Of The Times** *Petula Clark*
75/83 **Sign Of The Times** *Belle Stars*
4/88 **Sign Your Name** *Terence Trent D'Arby*
Signed, Sealed And Delivered
91/61 *Rusty Draper*
77/63 *James Brown*
Signed, Sealed, Delivered I'm Yours
3/70 *Stevie Wonder*
18/77 *Peter Frampton*
Signs
3/71 *Five Man Electrical Band*
8/91 *Tesla*
58S/01 **Silence** *Delerium*
96/65 **Silence, The (Il Silenzio)** *Al Hirt*
62/93 **Silence Is Broken** *Damn Yankees*
11/67 **Silence Is Golden** *Tremeloes*
65/97 **Silent All These Years** *Tori Amos*
68/57 **Silent Lips** *Georgia Gibbs*
9/91 **Silent Lucidity** *Queensrÿche*
47/87 **Silent Morning** *Noel*
Silent Night
54/57 *Bing Crosby*
54/60 *Bing Crosby*
99/62 *Mahalia Jackson*
1X/66 *Barbra Streisand*
7X/69 *Temptations*
(also see: Oíche Chiún)
31/92 **Silent Prayer** *Shanice*
6/86 **Silent Running (On Dangerous Ground)** *Mike + The Mechanics*
13/89 **Silhouette** *Kenny G*
Silhouettes
3/57 *Rays*
10/57 *Diamonds*
63/57 *Steve Gibson*
5/65 *Herman's Hermits*
53/81 **Silly** *Deniece Williams*
81/62 **Silly Boy (She Doesn't Love You)** *Lettermen*
59/99 **Silly Ho** *TLC*
87/64 **Silly Little Girl** *Tams*
1/76 **Silly Love Songs** *Wings*
71/74 **Silly Milly** *Blue Swede*
92/64 **Silly Ol' Summertime** *New Christy Minstrels*
76/70 **Silly, Silly, Fool** *Dusty Springfield*
63/73 **Silly Wasn't I** *Valerie Simpson*
Silver Bells
78/57 *Bing Crosby & Carol Richards*
6X/64 *Al Martino*
3X/66 *Earl Grant*
25/70 **Silver Bird** *Mark Lindsay*
Silver City ..see: (Theme From)
20/55 **Silver Dollar** *Teresa Brewer*
53/78 **Silver Dreams** *Babys*
95/76 **Silver Heels** *Blaze*
52/77 **Silver Lady** *David Soul*
62/79 **Silver Lining** *Player*
42/71 **Silver Moon** *Michael Nesmith*
41A/97 **Silver Springs** *Fleetwood Mac*
38/76 **Silver Star** *Four Seasons*
Silver Threads And Golden Needles
20/62 *Springfields*
54/65 *Jody Miller*
74/69 *Cowsills*
67/74 *Linda Ronstadt*

63/91 **Silver Thunderbird** *Marc Cohn*
94/89 **Similar Features** *Melissa Etheridge*
4/68 **Simon Says** *1910 Fruitgum Co.*
97/99 **Simon Says** *Pharoahe Monch*
91/65 **Simpel Gimpel** *Horst Jankowski*
81/84 **Simple** *Johnny Mathis*
90/72 **Simple Game** *Four Tops*
38/00 **Simple Kind Of Life** *No Doubt*
60A/95 **Simple Lessons** *Candlebox*
30/93 **Simple Life** *Elton John*
56/72 **Simple Man** *Lobo*
Simple Song Of Freedom
50/69 *Tim Hardin*
84/72 *Buckwheat*
75/70 **Simply Call It Love** *Gene Chandler*
2/88 **Simply Irresistible** *Robert Palmer*
Sin ..see: (It's No)
80/98 **Sin So Well** *Rebekah*
Since I Don't Have You
12/59 *Skyliners*
47/64 *Chuck Jackson*
F/70 *Eddie Holman*
53/79 *Art Garfunkel*
23/81 *Don McLean*
69/94 *Guns N' Roses*
Since I Fell For You
4/63 *Lenny Welch*
76/72 *Laura Lee*
71/76 *Charlie Rich*
96/77 *Hodges, James & Smith (medley)*
78/64 **Since I Found A New Love** *Little Johnny Taylor*
17/65 **Since I Lost My Baby** *Temptations*
90/66 **Since I Lost The One I Love** *Impressions*
93/60 **Since I Made You Cry** *Rivieras*
Since I Met You Baby
12/56 *Ivory Joe Hunter*
34/57 *Mindy Carson*
81/60 *Bobby Vee*
65/69 *Sonny James*
45/75 *Freddy Fender*
Since You Been Gone
46/78 *Head East*
57/79 *Rainbow*
32/67 **Since You Showed Me How To Be Happy** *Jackie Wilson*
41/82 **Since You're Gone** *Cars*
31/87 **Since You've Been Gone** *Outfield*
38/59 **Since You've Been Gone** *Clyde McPhatter*
95/79 **Since You've Been Gone** *Cherie & Marie Currie*
(also see: Sweet Sweet Baby)
Sincerely
1/55 *McGuire Sisters*
20/55 *Moonglow's*
75/64 *Four Seasons*
80/69 *Paul Anka*
14/89 **Sincerely Yours** *Sweet Sensation*
58/77 **Sing** *Tony Orlando & Dawn*
Sing
94/72 *Barbra Streisand (medley)*
3/73 *Carpenters*
Sing A Simple Song
89/69 *Sly & The Family Stone*
89/82 *West Street Mob*
5/76 **Sing A Song** *Earth, Wind & Fire*
55/70 **Sing A Song For Freedom** *Frijid Pink*
91/67 **Sing Along With Me** *Tommy Roe*
24/58 **Sing Boy Sing** *Tommy Sands*
41/79 **Sing For The Day** *Styx*
83/71 **Sing High - Sing Low** *Anne Murray*
66/77 **Sing It, Shout It** *Starz*

54/83 **Sing Me Away** *Night Ranger*
99/70 **Sing Out The Love (In My Heart)** *Arkade*
46/58 **Sing Sing Sing** *Bernie Lowe*
56/58 **Singing Hills** *Billy Vaughn*
75/69 **Singing My Song** *Tammy Wynette*
Singing The Blues
1/56 *Guy Mitchell*
17/56 *Marty Robbins*
71/02 **Single For The Rest Of My Life** *Isyss*
12/66 **Single Girl** *Sandy Posey*
36/99 **Single White Female** *Chely Wright*
3/60 **Sink The Bismarck** *Johnny Horton*
54/65 **Sinner Man** *Trini Lopez*
71/79 **Sinner Man** *Sarah Dash*
82/56 **Sinner Man** *Les Baxter*
87/65 **Sins Of A Family** *P.F. Sloan*
62/66 **Sippin' 'N Chippin'** *T-Bones*
1/77 **Sir Duke** *Stevie Wonder*
Sissy ..see: Cissy
48A/96 **Sister** *Nixons*
5/84 **Sister Christian** *Night Ranger*
1/75 **Sister Golden Hair** *America*
53/73 **Sister James** *Nino Tempo & 5th Ave. Sax*
24/74 **Sister Mary Elephant (Shudd-Up!)** *Cheech & Chong*
18/85 **Sisters Are Doin' It For Themselves** *Eurythmics & Aretha Franklin*
86/80 **Sisters Of The Moon** *Fleetwood Mac*
36/67 **Sit Down, I Think I Love You** *Mojo Men*
46A/93 **Sit Down You're Rockin' The Boat** *Don Henley*
65/68 **Sit With The Guru** *Strawberry Alarm Clock*
37/71 **Sit Yourself Down** *Stephen Stills*
54S/95 **Sittin' In My Car** *Slick Rick/Doug E. Fresh*
Sittin' In The Balcony
18/57 *Eddie Cochran*
38/57 *Johnny Dee*
19/90 **Sittin' In The Lap Of Luxury** *Louie Louie*
96/72 **Sittin' On A Time Bomb (Waitin' For The Hurt To Come)** *Honey Cone*
84/95 **Sittin' On Chrome** *Masta Ace Incorporated*
(Sittin' On) The Dock Of The Bay
1/68 *Otis Redding*
84/68 *King Curtis*
42/69 *Dells*
66/69 *Sergio Mendes*
65/79 *Sammy Hagar*
55/82 *Reddings*
11/88 *Michael Bolton*
30/96 **Sittin' On Top Of The World** *Da Brat*
2/96 **Sittin' Up In My Room** *Brandy*
16/73 **Sitting** *Cat Stevens*
27/83 **Sitting At The Wheel** *Moody Blues*
42/99 **Sitting Home** *Total*
74/78 **Sitting In Limbo** *Don Brown*
24/65 **Sitting In The Park** *Billy Stewart*
73/82 **Situation** *Yaz*

SIX:

62/59 **Six Boys And Seven Girls** *Anita Bryant*
10S/02 **Six Days** *DJ Shadow*
32/63 **Six Days On The Road** *Dave Dudley*
40/93 **Six Feet Deep** *Geto Boys*
47/68 **Six Man Band** *Association*
95/91 **6 Minutes Of Pleasure** *LL Cool J*
28/59 **Six Nights A Week** *Crests*
18/67 **Six O'Clock** *Lovin' Spoonful*
56/01 **Six-Pack Summer** *Phil Vassar*
93/77 **Six Packs A Day** *Billy Lemmons*
13/66 **634-5789 (Soulsville, U.S.A.)** *Wilson Pickett*
(also see: Beechwood 4-5789)
45/97 **6 Underground** *Sneaker Pimps*
79/70 **Six White Horses** *Tommy Cash*
2/59 **16 Candles** *Crests*
Sixteen Reasons
3/60 *Connie Stevens*
65/76 *Laverne & Shirley*
Sixteen Tons
1/55 *"Tennessee" Ernie Ford*
17/55 *Johnny Desmond*
68/67 *Tom Jones*
47/76 *Don Harrison Band*
33A/96 **6th Avenue Heartache** *Wallflowers*
6/82 **'65 Love Affair** *Paul Davis*
65/73 **Sixty Minute Man** *Clarence Carter*
80/91 **Skat Strut** *MC Skat Kat & The Stray Mob*
71/67 **Skate Now** *Lou Courtney*
58/81 **Skateaway** *Dire Straits*
10/02 **Sk8er Boi** *Avril Lavigne*
19/87 **Skeletons** *Stevie Wonder*
50/59 **Ski King** *E.C. Beatty*
18S/02 **Skills** *Gang Starr*
Skillz ..see: (I Know I Got) / (She's Got)
79/88 **Skin Deep** *Cher*
13/74 **Skin Tight** *Ohio Players*
39/87 **Skin Trade** *Duran Duran*
10/67 **Skinny Legs And All** *Joe Tex*
22/58 **Skinny Minnie** *Bill Haley*
25/68 **Skip A Rope** *Henson Cargill*
70/60 **Skokiaan (South African Song)** *Bill Haley*
3/75 **Sky High** *Jigsaw*
14/68 **Sky Pilot** *Animals*
60/97 **Sky's The Limit** *Notorious B.I.G.*
49/75 **Skybird** *Tony Orlando & Dawn*
75/74 **Skybird** *Neil Diamond*
92/57 **Skyliner** *Carmen McRae*
4/93 **Slam** *Onyx*
86/99 **Slam Dunk** *Five*
50/72 **Slaughter** *Billy Preston*
35/64 **Slaughter On Tenth Avenue** *Ventures*
82/99 **Slave To The Habit** *Shane Minor*
1/86 **Sledgehammer** *Peter Gabriel*
13/60 **Sleep** *Little Willie John*
Sleep Walk
1/59 *Santo & Johnny*
74/82 *Larry Carlton*
70/74 **Sleepin'** *Diana Ross*
8/85 **Sleeping Bag** *ZZ Top*
Sleeping Beauty ..see: To A
50/94 **Sleeping In My Car** *Roxette*
32/93 **Sleeping Satellite** *Tasmin Archer*
96/92 **Sleeping With The Lights On** *Curtis Stigers*
78/93 **Sleeping With You** *Firehouse*
48/77 **Sleepwalker** *Kinks*
73/00 **Sleepwalker** *Wallflowers*
54/61 **Sleepy-Eyed John** *Johnny Horton*
61/68 **Sleepy Joe** *Herman's Hermits*
65/60 **Sleepy Lagoon** *Platters*
Sleigh Ride
6X/84 *Dolly Parton (medley)*
43A/93 *TLC*
65/73 **Slick** *Willie Hutch*
8/99 **Slide** *Goo Goo Dolls*
32/77 **Slide** *Slave*
70/67 **Slim Jenkin's Place** *Booker T. & The M.G.'s*
6/68 **Slip Away** *Clarence Carter*
50/79 **Slip Away** *Ian Lloyd*
75/81 **Slip Away** *Pablo Cruise*
48/64 **Slip-In Mules (No High Heel Sneakers)** *Sugar Pie DeSanto*
5/78 **Slip Slidin' Away** *Paul Simon*
84/71 **Slipped, Tripped And Fell In Love** *Clarence Carter*
19/75 **Slippery When Wet** *Commodores*
Slippin' And Slidin'
33/56 *Little Richard*
96/64 *Jim & Monica*
96/67 *Willie Mitchell*
81/73 **Slippin' Away** *Jean Shepard*
39/83 **Slipping Away** *Dave Edmunds*
16/72 **Slippin' Into Darkness** *War*
4X/72 **Slipping Into Christmas** *Leon Russell*
70/80 **Slipstream** *Allan Clarke*
Sloop John B
64/60 *Jimmie Rodgers*
3/66 *Beach Boys*
(Slop, The) ..see: Hard Times
97/63 **Slop Time** *Sherrys*
43/94 **Slow And Easy** *Zapp & Roger*
33/93 **Slow And Sexy** *Shabba Ranks*
13S/02 **Slow Dance** *Lou Mosley*
43/92 **Slow Dance (Hey Mr. DJ)** *R. Kelly*
82/84 **Slow Dancin'** *Peabo Bryson*
20/77 **Slow Dancin' Don't Turn Me On** *Addrisi Bros.*
Slow Dancin' (Swayin' To The Music)
10/77 *Johnny Rivers*
61/77 *Funky Kings*
25/64 **Slow Down** *Beatles*
34/77 **Slowdown** *John Miles*
54/68 **Slow Drag** *Intruders*
2/81 **Slow Hand** *Pointer Sisters*
68/96 **Slow Jams** *Quincy Jones*
51/90 **Slow Love** *Doc Box & B. Fresh*
18/92 **Slow Motion** *Color Me Badd*
78/73 **Slow Motion** *Johnny Williams*
20/76 **Slow Ride** *Foghat*
3/62 **Slow Twistin'** *Chubby Checker (with Dee Dee Sharp)*
Slow Walk
17/56 *Sil Austin*
26/57 *Bill Doggett*
52/92 **Slowly** *Stacy Earl*
88/69 **Slum Baby** *Booker T. & The M.G.'s*
30/70 **Sly, Slick, And The Wicked** *Lost Generation*
52/64 **Smack Dab In The Middle** *Ray Charles*
89/98 **Smack My Bitch Up** *Prodigy*
F/71 **Smackwater Jack** *Carole King*
29/72 **Small Beginnings** *Flash*
87/80 **Small Paradise** *John Cougar*
21/62 **Small Sad Sam** *Phil McLean*
6/85 **Small Town** *John Cougar Mellencamp*
64/85 **Small Town Girl** *John Cafferty*
F/96 **Small Wonders** *Dog's Eye View*
20/59 **Small World** *Johnny Mathis*
25/88 **Small World** *Huey Lewis*
48/85 **Smalltown Boy** *Bronski Beat*
56/73 **Smarty Pants** *First Choice*
47A/95 **Smash It Up** *Offspring*
56/68 **Smell Of Incense** *Southwest F.O.B.*

35/92 **Smells Like Nirvana** *"Weird Al" Yankovic*
6/92 **Smells Like Teen Spirit** *Nirvana*
12/97 **Smile** *Scarface*
18/99 **Smile** *Vitamin C*
39/00 **Smile** *Lonestar*
Smile
73/59 *Tony Bennett*
42/61 *Timi Yuro*
94/62 *Ferrante & Teicher*
42/65 *Betty Everett & Jerry Butler*
5/69 **Smile A Little Smile For Me** *Flying Machine*
34/83 **Smile Has Left Your Eyes** *Asia*
84/97 **Smile Like Yours** *Natalie Cole*
21/55 **Smiles** *Crazy Otto*
42/72 **Smilin'** *Sly & The Family Stone*
3/71 **Smiling Faces Sometimes** *Undisputed Truth*
52/83 **Smiling Islands** *Robbie Patton*
9/77 **Smoke From A Distant Fire** *Sanford/Townsend Band*
Smoke Gets In Your Eyes
94/58 *Richard Barrett*
1/59 *Platters*
27/73 *Blue Haze*
4/73 **Smoke On The Water** *Deep Purple*
76/00 **Smoke Rings In The Dark** *Gary Allan*
94/73 **Smoke! Smoke! Smoke! (That Cigarette)** *Commander Cody*
79/55 **Smokey Joe's Cafe** *Robins*
77/66 **Smokey Joe's La La** *Googie Rene Combo*
Smokie
17/60 *Bill Black's Combo*
95/60 *Bill Doggett*
Smokin' In The Boy's Room
3/74 *Brownsville Station*
16/85 *Mötley Crüe*
35/97 **Smokin' Me Out** *Warren G*
91/75 **Smokin' Room** *Carl Carlton*
22/87 **Smoking Gun** *Robert Cray Band*
24/81 **Smoky Mountain Rain** *Ronnie Milsap*
12/62 **Smoky Places** *Corsairs*
1/99 **Smooth** *Santana Feat. Rob Thomas*
Smooth Criminal
7/89 *Michael Jackson*
23/01 *Alien Ant Farm*
5/85 **Smooth Operator** *Sade*
44/59 **Smooth Operator** *Sarah Vaughan*
71/89 **Smooth Up** *Bulletboys*
12/85 **Smuggler's Blues** *Glenn Frey*
27/68 **Snake, The** *Al Wilson*
67/81 **Snake Eyes** *Alan Parsons Project*
91/81 **Snap Shot** *Slave*
Snap Your Fingers
8/62 *Joe Henderson*
71/64 *Barbara Lewis*
95/96 **Snapshot** *RuPaul*
31/69 **Snatching It Back** *Clarence Carter*
58/75 **Sneakin' Up Behind You** *Brecker Brothers*
55/75 **Sneaky Snake** *Tom T. Hall*
F/75 **Snookeroo** *Ringo Starr*
77/01 **Snoop Dogg (What's My Name)** *Snoop Dogg*
85/68 **Snoopy For President** *Royal Guardsmen*
2/66 **Snoopy Vs. The Red Baron** *Royal Guardsmen*
(also see: Return Of The Red Baron)
1X/67 **Snoopy's Christmas** *Royal Guardsmen*
30X/67 **Snow** *Claudine Longet*
60/71 **Snow Blind Friend** *Steppenwolf*
66/66 **Snow Flake** *Jim Reeves*
8/70 **Snowbird** *Anne Murray*
(also see: Christmas Goose)
84/55 **Snowbound For Christmas** *DeCastro Sisters*

SO:

3/89 **So Alive** *Love & Rockets*
31/93 **So Alone** *Men At Large*
16/99 **So Anxious** *Ginuwine*
23/84 **So Bad** *Paul McCartney*
11/90 **So Close** *Daryl Hall/John Oates*
38/59 **So Close** *Brook Benton*
40/83 **So Close** *Diana Ross*
49/70 **So Close** *Jake Holmes*
95/93 **So Close** *Dina Carroll*
52/62 **So Deep** *Brenda Lee*
1/88 **So Emotional** *Whitney Houston*
54/70 **So Excited** *B.B. King*
So Far Away
14/71 *Carole King*
71A/96 *Rod Stewart*
19/86 **So Far Away** *Dire Straits*
91/64 **So Far Away** *Hank Jacobs*
43/86 **So Far So Good** *Sheena Easton*
So Fine
11/59 *Fiestas*
76/82 *Oak Ridge Boys*
44S/00 **So Flossy** *Midwest Mafia*
30/01 **So Fresh, So Clean** *OutKast*
60/97 **So Good** *Davina*
94/74 **So Good** *Eleventh Hour*
30/79 **So Good, So Right** *Brenda Russell*
36/69 **So Good Together** *Andy Kim*
62/90 **So Hard** *Pet Shop Boys*
62/78 **So Hard Livin' Without You** *Airwaves*
So Help Me Girl
84/95 *Joe Diffie*
44/97 *Gary Barlow*
59S/02 **So High** *Gada*
89/77 **So High (Rock Me Baby And Roll Me Away)** *Dave Mason*
52/59 **So High So Low** *LaVern Baker*
(also see: Oh, Rock My Soul)
39/69 **So I Can Love You** *Emotions*
26/85 **So In Love** *Orchestral Manoeuvres In The Dark*
67/75 **So In Love** *Curtis Mayfield*
25/01 **So In Love With Two** *Mikaila*
65/95 **So In Love With You** *U.N.V.*
7/77 **So In To You** *Atlanta Rhythm Section*
30/98 **So Into You** *Tamia*
44/56 **So-Long** *Fats Domino*
48/78 **So Long** *Firefall*
86/65 **So Long Babe** *Nancy Sinatra*
28/61 **So Long Baby** *Del Shannon*
56/64 **So Long Dearie** *Louis Armstrong*
44/72 **So Long Dixie** *Blood, Sweat & Tears*
72/57 **So Long I'm Gone** *Warren Smith*
74/57 **So Long, My Love** *Frank Sinatra*
87/98 **So Long (Well, Well, Well)** *Phajja*
81/72 **So Many People** *Chase*
44/95 **So Many Tears** *2Pac*
6/59 **So Many Ways** *Brook Benton*
83/96 **So Many Ways** *Braxtons*
87/58 **So Much** *Little Anthony & The Imperials*
88/87 **So Much For Love** *Venetians*
So Much In Love
1/63 *Tymes*
59/82 *Timothy B. Schmit*
5/94 *All-4-One*
51/70 **So Much Love** *Faith Hope & Charity*
55A/92 **So Much Love** *Malaika*
So Much Love
92/66 *Steve Alaimo*
96/66 *Ben E. King*
48A/96 **So Much To Say** *Dave Matthews Band*
2/57 **So Rare** *Jimmy Dorsey*
47/76 **So Sad The Song** *Gladys Knight*
7/60 **So Sad (To Watch Good Love Go Bad)** *Everly Brothers*
100/57 **So Strange** *Jesters*
81/87 **So The Story Goes** *Living In A Box*
21/62 **So This Is Love** *Castells*
So Tough
42/58 *Original Casuals*
76/58 *Kuf-Linx*
17/73 **So Very Hard To Go** *Tower Of Power*
So What
78/62 *Bill Black's Combo*
89/65 *Bill Black's Combo*
93/92 **So What 'Cha Want** *Beastie Boys*
30/83 **So Wrong** *Patrick Simmons*
85/62 **So Wrong** *Patsy Cline*
21/74 **So You Are A Star** *Hudson Brothers*
58/84 **So You Ran** *Orion The Hunter*
29/67 **So You Want To Be A Rock 'N' Roll Star** *Byrds*
31/77 **So You Win Again** *Hot Chocolate*
So Young
68/57 *Clyde Stacy*
99/59 *Clyde Stacy*
81/78 **So Young, So Bad** *Starz*
17/02 **Soak Up The Sun** *Sheryl Crow*
15X/63 **Soalin', A** *Peter, Paul & Mary*
91/64 **Society Girl** *Rag Dolls*
14/67 **Society's Child (Baby I've Been Thinking)** *Janis Ian*
12/97 **Sock It 2 Me** *Missy "Misdemeanor" Elliott*
6/67 **Sock It To Me-Baby!** *Mitch Ryder*
71/67 **Sockin' 1-2-3-4** *John Roberts*
35/57 **Soft** *Bill Doggett*
92/78 **Soft And Wet** *Prince*
73/57 **Soft Sands** *Chordettes*
Soft Summer Breeze
11/56 *Eddie Heywood*
34/56 *Diamonds*
27/64 **Softly, As I Leave You** *Frank Sinatra*
F/55 **Softly, Softly** *Jaye P. Morgan*
29/72 **Softly Whispering I Love You** *English Congregation*
67S/99 **Sol, Arena y Mar** *Luis Miguel*
50/89 **Sold Me Down The River** *Alarm*
1/62 **Soldier Boy** *Shirelles*
(also see: To A)
2/89 **Soldier Of Love** *Donny Osmond*
87/59 **Soldier's Joy** *Hawkshaw Hawkins*
90/71 **Soldier's Last Letter** *Merle Haggard*
Soldiers ..see: Souljas
58/64 **Sole Sole Sole** *Siw Malmkvist-Umberto Marcato*
12/85 **Solid** *Ashford & Simpson*
71/83 **Solid Rock** *Goanna*
7/83 **Solitaire** *Laura Branigan*
17/75 **Solitaire** *Carpenters*
52/80 **Solitaire** *Peter McIan*

Solitary Man
55/66 *Neil Diamond*
21/70 *Neil Diamond*
100/76 *T.G. Sheppard*
72/95 **Solitude** *Edwin McCain*
94/87 **Solitude Standing** *Suzanne Vega*
91/71 **Solo** *Billie Sans*
Solsbury Hill
68/77 *Peter Gabriel*
84/83 *Peter Gabriel (Live)*
96/71 **Solution For Pollution** *Charles Wright*

SOME:

92/70 **Some Beautiful** *Jack Wild*
65/81 **Some Changes Are For Good** *Dionne Warwick*
Some Day ..also see: Someday
24ˣ/66 **Some Day At Christmas** *Stevie Wonder*
94/57 **Some Day Soon** *Eddie Fisher*
34/64 **Some Day We're Gonna Love Again** *Searchers*
36/81 **Some Days Are Diamonds (Some Days Are Stone)** *John Denver*
55/02 **Some Days You Gotta Dance** *Dixie Chicks*
Some Enchanted Evening
13/65 *Jay & The Americans*
91/77 *Jane Olivor*
Some Guys Have All The Luck
39/73 *Persuaders*
10/84 *Rod Stewart*
37/59 **Some Kind-A Earthquake** *Duane Eddy*
26/83 **Some Kind Of Friend** *Barry Manilow*
10/88 **Some Kind Of Lover** *Jody Watley*
Some Kind Of Wonderful
91/67 *Soul Brothers Six*
87/68 *Fantastic Johnny C*
3/75 *Grand Funk*
44/94 *Huey Lewis*
32/61 **Some Kind Of Wonderful** *Drifters*
43/63 **Some Kinda Fun** *Chris Montez*
6/85 **Some Like It Hot** *Power Station*
64/71 **Some Of Shelly's Blues** *Nitty Gritty Dirt Band*
65/86 **Some People** *Paul Young*
67/85 **Some People** *Belouis Some*
Some Things ..also see: Somethings
18/85 **Some Things Are Better Left Unsaid** *Daryl Hall/John Oates*
58/00 **Some Things Never Change** *Tim McGraw*
30/68 **Some Things You Never Get Used To** *Supremes*
26/68 **Some Velvet Morning** *Nancy Sinatra & Lee Hazlewood*

SOMEBODY:

11/85 **Somebody** *Bryan Adams*
53/68 **Somebody Cares** *Tommy James*
53/65 **Somebody Else Is Taking My Place** *Al Martino*
75/84 **Somebody Else's Guy** *Jocelyn Brown*
70/62 **Somebody Have Mercy** *Sam Cooke*
47/67 **Somebody Help Me** *Spencer Davis Group*
53/66 **Somebody Like Me** *Eddy Arnold*
23/02 **Somebody Like You** *Keith Urban*
48/86 **Somebody Like You** *38 Special*
63/89 **Somebody Like You** *Robbie Nevil*
71/93 **Somebody Love Me** *Michael W. Smith*
72/69 **Somebody Loves You** *Delfonics*
94/73 **Somebody Loves You** *Whispers*
57ˢ/92 **Somebody Loves You Baby (You Know Who It Is)** *Patti LaBelle*
Somebody New
93/64 *Chuck Jackson*
71ˢ/94 *Billy Ray Cyrus*
66/87 **Somebody Save Me** *Cinderella*
55/81 **Somebody Send My Baby Home** *Lenny LeBlanc*
82/86 **Somebody Somewhere** *Platinum Blonde*
55/66 **Somebody (Somewhere) Needs You** *Darrell Banks*
71/81 **Somebody Special** *Rod Stewart*
86/64 **Somebody Stole My Dog** *Rufus Thomas*
5/67 **Somebody To Love** *Jefferson Airplane*
Somebody To Love
13/77 *Queen*
30/93 *George Michael & Queen*
45/60 **Somebody To Love** *Bobby Darin*
22/58 **Somebody Touched Me** *Buddy Knox*
18/56 **Somebody Up There Likes Me** *Perry Como*
7/82 **Somebody's Baby** *Jackson Browne*
8/70 **Somebody's Been Sleeping** *100 Proof Aged in Soul*
45/95 **Somebody's Crying** *Chris Isaak*
33/76 **Somebody's Gettin' It** *Johnnie Taylor*
96/83 **Somebody's Gonna Love You** *Lee Greenwood*
13/81 **Somebody's Knockin'** *Terri Gibbs*
27/86 **Somebody's Out There** *Triumph*
64/99 **Somebody's Out There Watching** *Kinleys*
95/67 **Somebody's Sleeping In My Bed** *Johnnie Taylor*
2/84 **Somebody's Watching Me** *Rockwell*
32/71 **Somebody's Watching You** *Little Sister*
Someday ..also see: Some Day
1/91 **Someday** *Mariah Carey*
7/87 **Someday** *Glass Tiger*
7/99 **Someday** *Sugar Ray*
30/96 **Someday** *All-4-One*
57/74 **Someday** *Dave Loggins*
85/76 **Someday (I Didn't Want To Have to be the One)** *Henry Gross*
81/69 **Someday Man** *Monkees*
25/72 **Someday Never Comes** *Creedence Clearwater Revival*
49/00 **Someday Out Of The Blue (Theme From El Dorado)** *Elton John*
Someday, Someway
76/81 *Robert Gordon*
36/82 *Marshall Crenshaw*
55/69 **Someday Soon** *Judy Collins*
1/69 **Someday We'll Be Together** *Supremes*
99/62 **Someday (When I'm Gone From You)** *Bobby Vee*
Someday You'll Want Me To Want You
95/58 *Jodie Sands*
56/60 *Della Reese*
93/60 *Brook Benton*

SOMEONE:

19/97 **Someone** *SWV*
35/59 **Someone** *Johnny Mathis*
70/87 **Someone** *El DeBarge*
78/91 **Someone** *Rembrandts*
49/83 **Someone Belonging To Someone** *Bee Gees*
15/82 **Someone Could Lose A Heart Tonight** *Eddie Rabbitt*
89/65 **Someone Is Watching** *Solomon Burke*
57/87 **Someone Like You** *Daryl Hall*
75/84 **Someone Like You** *Michael Stanley Band*
91/60 **Someone Loves You, Joe** *Singing Belles*
77/55 **Someone On Your Mind** *Champ Butler with George Cates*
4/75 **Someone Saved My Life Tonight** *Elton John*
97/64 **Someone, Someone** *Brian Poole*
95/63 **Someone Somewhere** *Junior Parker*
21/80 **Someone That I Used To Love** *Natalie Cole*
3/01 **Someone To Call My Lover** *Janet Jackson*
78/59 **Someone To Come Home To** *Ames Brothers*
19/92 **Someone To Hold** *Trey Lorenz*
42/77 **Someone To Lay Down Beside Me** *Linda Ronstadt*
10/95 **Someone To Love** *Jon B.*
47/56 **Someone To Love** *Four Aces*
78/87 **Someone To Love Me For Me** *Lisa Lisa & Cult Jam*
49/02 **Someone To Love You** *Ruff Endz*
51/71 **Someone Who Cares** *Kenny Rogers & The First Edition*
13/55 **Someone You Love** *Nat "King" Cole*
37/98 **Someone You Used To Know** *Collin Raye*

SOMETHIN'/SOMETHING:

37/77 **Somethin' 'Bout 'Cha** *Latimore*
42/80 **Somethin' 'Bout You Baby I Like** *Glen Campbell & Rita Coolidge*
58/59 **Somethin Else** *Eddie Cochran*
21/95 **Somethin' 4 Da Honeyz** *Montell Jordan*
71ˢ/01 **Somethin' In The Water** *Jeffrey Steele*
1/67 **Somethin' Stupid** *Nancy Sinatra & Frank Sinatra*
Something
3/69 *Beatles*
55/70 *Shirley Bassey*
76/70 *Booker T. & The M.G.'s*
85/74 *Johnny Rodriguez*
35/03 **Something** *Lasgo*
F/97 **Something About The Way You Look Tonight** *Elton John*
7/86 **Something About You** *Level 42*
Something About You
19/65 *Four Tops*
48/77 *LeBlanc & Carr*
13/75 **Something Better To Do** *Olivia Newton-John*
76/95 **Something For The Pain** *Bon Jovi*
98/92 **Something Good** *Utah Saints*
74/67 **Something Good (Is Going To Happen To You)** *Carla Thomas*
23/91 **Something Got Me Started** *Simply Red*
41/60 **Something Happened** *Paul Anka*

4/90 **Something Happened On The Way To Heaven** *Phil Collins*
Something He Can Feel
28/76 *Aretha Franklin*
6/92 *En Vogue*
79/66 **Something I Want To Tell You** *Johnny & The Expressions*
32A/93 **Something In Common** *Bobby Brown & Whitney Houston*
31/91 **Something In My Heart** *Michel'le*
85/87 **Something In My House** *Dead Or Alive*
37/69 **Something In The Air** *Thunderclap Newman*
38/93 **Something In Your Eyes** *Bell Biv DeVoe*
79/88 **Something Just Ain't Right** *Keith Sweat*
28/99 **Something Like That** *Tim McGraw*
77/63 **Something Old, Something New** *Paul & Paula*
29/87 **Something Real (Inside Me/Inside You)** *Mr. Mister*
7/87 **Something So Strong** *Crowded House*
76/97 **Something That We Do** *Clint Black*
4/90 **Something To Believe In** *Poison*
47/83 **Something To Grab For** *Ric Ocasek*
42/94 **Something To Ride To (Fonky Expedition)** *Conscious Daughters*
5/91 **Something To Talk About** *Bonnie Raitt*
Something You Got
52/64 *Alvin Robinson*
63/64 *Ramsey Lewis Trio*
55/65 *Chuck Jackson & Maxine Brown*
41/94 **Something's Always Wrong** *Toad The Wet Sprocket*
11/70 **Something's Burning** *Kenny Rogers & The First Edition*
29/93 **Something's Goin' On** *U.N.V.*
37/62 **Something's Got A Hold On Me** *Etta James*
Something's Gotta Give
5/55 *McGuire Sisters*
9/55 *Sammy Davis, Jr.*
88/68 **Something's Missing** *Five Stairsteps*
98/69 **Something's On Her Mind** *4 Seasons*
79/84 **Something's On Your Mind** *"D" Train*
12/72 **Something's Wrong With Me** *Austin Roberts*
53/61 **Sometime** *Gene Thomas*
21/99 **Sometimes** *Britney Spears*
31/77 **Sometimes** *Facts Of Life*
88/97 **Sometimes** *Brand New Heavies*
36/80 **Sometimes A Fantasy** *Billy Joel*
96/94 **Sometimes Always** *Jesus & Mary Chain*
43/66 **Sometimes Good Guys Don't Wear White** *Standells*
95/95 **Sometimes I Miss You So Much (dedicated to the christ-consciousness)** *P.M. Dawn*
44/92 **Sometimes I Rhyme Slow** *Nice & Smooth*
86/64 **Sometimes I Wish I Were A Boy** *Lesley Gore*
64/64 **Sometimes I Wonder** *Major Lance*
56/91 **Sometimes It's A Bitch** *Stevie Nicks*

2/92 **Sometimes Love Just Ain't Enough** *Patty Smyth with Don Henley*
20/90 **Sometimes She Cries** *Warrant*
3/78 **Sometimes When We Touch** *Dan Hill*
56/63 **Sometimes You Gotta Cry A Little** *Bobby Bland*
19/64 **Somewhere** *Tymes*
Somewhere
91/65 *P.J. Proby*
26/66 *Len Barry*
43/86 *Barbra Streisand*
67/61 **Somewhere Along The Way** *Steve Lawrence*
81/74 **Somewhere Between Love And Tomorrow** *Roy Clark*
21/82 **Somewhere Down The Road** *Barry Manilow*
70/80 **Somewhere In America** *Survivor*
Somewhere In The Night
69/75 *Batdorf & Rodney*
19/76 *Helen Reddy*
9/79 *Barry Manilow*
32/65 **Somewhere In Your Heart** *Frank Sinatra*
Somewhere, My Love
9/66 *Ray Conniff*
65/66 *Roger Williams (Lara's Theme)*
2/87 **Somewhere Out There** *Linda Ronstadt & James Ingram*
44/02 **Somewhere Out There** *Our Lady Peace*
32/66 **Somewhere There's A Someone** *Dean Martin*
76/61 **Son-In-Law** *Louise Brown*
79/61 **Son-In-Law** *Blossoms*
28/01 **Son Of A Gun (I Betcha Think This Song Is About You)** *Janet Jackson*
61/69 **Son Of A Lovin' Man** *Buchanan Brothers*
Son Of A Preacher Man
10/69 *Dusty Springfield*
F/70 *Aretha Franklin*
92/69 **Son Of A Travelin' Man** *Ed Ames*
40/68 **Son Of Hickory Holler's Tramp** *O.C. Smith*
Son Of My Father
46/72 *Giorgio*
91/72 *Chicory*
97/64 **Son Of Rebel Rouser** *Duane Eddy*
28/74 **Son Of Sagittarius** *Eddie Kendricks*
53/72 **Son Of Shaft** *Bar-Kays*

SONG:

8/56 **Song For A Summer Night** *Mitch Miller*
7/98 **Song For Mama** *Boyz II Men*
85/02 **Song For The Lonely** *Cher*
82/71 **Song For You** *Andy Williams*
70/70 **Song From M*A*S*H** *Al DeLory*
49/73 **Song I'd Like To Sing** *Kris Kristofferson & Rita Coolidge*
14/70 **Song Of Joy (Himno A La Alegria)** *Miguel Rios*
(also see: Joy)
F/57 **(Song Of) Raintree County** *Nat "King" Cole*
25/55 **Song Of The Barefoot Contessa** *Hugo Winterhalter*
86/57 **Song Of The Barefoot Mailman** *Billy Leach*
11/55 **Song Of The Dreamer** *Eddie Fisher*
29/79 **Song On The Radio** *Al Stewart*
Song Of The Sparrow ..see: (Theme From)

82/94 **Song Remembers When** *Trisha Yearwood*
96/72 **Song Seller** *Raiders*
1/72 **Song Sung Blue** *Neil Diamond*
99/70 **Song That Never Comes** *Mama Cass Elliot*
55A/97 **Song 2** *Blur*
4/87 **Songbird** *Kenny G*
25/78 **Songbird** *Barbra Streisand*
59/73 **Songman** *Cashman & West*
9X/63 **Songs Of Christmas [EP]** *Bobby Vinton*
30/70 **Soolaimón (African Trilogy II)** *Neil Diamond*
21/96 **Soon As I Get Home** *Faith Evans*
77/63 **Soon (I'll Be Home Again)** *4 Seasons*
89/64 **Soon I'll Wed My Love** *John Gary*
9/71 **Sooner Or Later** *Grass Roots*
68/75 **Sooner Or Later** *Impressions*
84/63 **Sooner Or Later** *Johnny Mathis*
56S/99 **Soopaman Lover** *Chico DeBarge*
Soothe Me
42/61 *Sims Twins*
56/67 *Sam & Dave*
34/69 **Sophisticated Cissy** *Meters*
25/76 **Sophisticated Lady (She's A Different Lady)** *Natalie Cole*
71/77 **Sorry** *Grace Jones*
2/59 **Sorry (I Ran All the Way Home)** *Impalas*
6/76 **Sorry Seems To Be The Hardest Word** *Elton John*
56/69 **Sorry Suzanne** *Hollies*

SOUL:

Soul And Inspiration ..see: (You're My)
27/87 **Soul City** *Partland Brothers*
(Soul Coaxing) ..see: Ame Caline
55/67 **Soul Dance Number Three** *Wilson Pickett*
18/69 **Soul Deep** *Box Tops*
95/64 **Soul Dressing** *Booker T. & The MG's*
85/68 **Soul Drippin'** *Mauds*
75/69 **Soul Experience** *Iron Butterfly*
17/67 **Soul Finger** *Bar-Kays*
64/96 **Soul Food** *Goodie Mob.*
99/65 **Soul Heaven** *Dixie Drifter*
Soul Hootenanny ..see: Big Boss Man
72/90 **Soul Inspiration** *Anita Baker*
Soul Je T'Aime ..see: Je T'Aime
20/85 **Soul Kiss** *Olivia Newton-John*
17/68 **Soul-Limbo** *Booker T. & The M.G.'s*
Soul Makossa
35/73 *Manu Dibango*
47/73 *Afrique*
Soul Man
2/67 *Sam & Dave*
49/67 *Ramsey Lewis*
14/79 *Blues Brothers*
91/68 **Soul Meeting** *Soul Clan*
29/71 **Soul Power** *James Brown*
17/89 **Soul Provider** *Michael Bolton*
88/50 **Soul Sauce (Guacha Guaro)** *Cal Tjader*
Soul Serenade
51/64 *King Curtis*
23/68 *Willie Mitchell*
Soul Shake ..see: Soulshake
71/01 **Soul Sista** *Bilal*
41/69 **Soul Sister, Brown Sugar** *Sam & Dave*
37/73 **Soul Song** *Joe Stampley*

67/67 **Soul Time** *Shirley Ellis*
22/93 **Soul To Squeeze** *Red Hot Chili Peppers*
90/68 **Soul Train** *Classics IV*
75/76 **Soul Train "75"** *Soul Train Gang*
17/62 **Soul Twist** *King Curtis*
3/69 **Soulful Strut** *Young-Holt Unlimited* *(also see: Am I The Same Girl)*
98/00 **Souljas** *Master P*
23/83 **Souls** *Rick Springfield*
Soulshake
37/69 *Peggy Scott & Jo Jo Benson*
43/70 *Delaney & Bonnie*
(Soulsville, U.S.A.) ..see: 634-5789
Soulville
92/63 *Dinah Washington*
83/68 *Aretha Franklin*
69/77 **Sound And Vision** *David Bowie*
57/68 **Sound Asleep** *Turtles*
89/94 **Sound Of Da Police** *KRS-One*
84/83 **Sound Of Goodbye** *Crystal Gayle*
36/67 **Sound Of Love** *Five Americans*
90/60 **Sound Of Music** *Patti Page*
97/97 **Sound Of My Tears** *Deborah Cox*
33/91 **Sound Of Your Voice** *38 Special*
77/61 **Sound-Off** *Titus Turner*
Sounds Of Silence
1/66 *Simon & Garfunkel*
100/71 *Peaches & Herb*
94/85 **Sounds Of Your Voice** *Jon Butcher Axis*
80/82 **Soup For One** *Chic*
78/00 **Sour Girl** *Stone Temple Pilots*
50/72 **Sour Suite** *Guess Who*
53/95 **Sour Times (Nobody Loves Me)** *Portishead*
85/84 **so. Central Rain (I'm Sorry)** *R.E.M.*
14/01 **South Side** *Moby*
3/63 **South Street** *Orlons*
29/75 **South's Gonna Do It** *Charlie Daniels Band*
55[A]/98 **Southampton** *James Horner*
99/72 **Southbound Train** *Graham Nash & David Crosby*
18/82 **Southern Cross** *Crosby, Stills & Nash*
76/99 **Southern Gul** *Erykah Badu*
23/01 **Southern Hospitality** *Ludacris*
1/77 **Southern Nights** *Glen Campbell*
70/82 **Southern Pacific** *Neil Young/Crazy Horse*
74/94 **Southernplayalisticadillacmuzik** *OutKast*
71[S]/98 **Southside** *Lil' Keke*
15/64 **Southtown, U.S.A.** *Dixiebelles*
41/79 **Souvenirs** *Voyage*
2/89 **Sowing The Seeds Of Love** *Tears For Fears*
30/83 **Space Age Love Song** *Flock Of Seagulls*
52/83 **Space Age Whiz Kids** *Joe Walsh*
22/01 **Space Between** *Dave Matthews Band*
37/97 **Space Jam** *Quad City DJ's*
15/73 **Space Oddity** *David Bowie*
4/73 **Space Race** *Billy Preston*
23/72 **Spaceman** *Nilsson*
82/77 **Spaceship Superstar** *Prism*
40/85 **Spanish Eddie** *Laura Branigan*
15/66 **Spanish Eyes** *Al Martino* *(also see: Moon Over Naples)*
27/66 **Spanish Flea** *Herb Alpert*
98/00 **Spanish Guitar** *Toni Braxton*
Spanish Harlem
10/61 *Ben E. King*
89/66 *King Curtis*
2/71 *Aretha Franklin*
31/62 **Spanish Lace** *Gene McDaniels*
99/66 **Spanish Nights And You** *Connie Francis*
49/98 **Spark** *Tori Amos*
100/70 **Sparkle And Shine** *Clique*
89/67 **Speak Her Name** *Walter Jackson*
(Speak Softly Love) ..see: Love Theme From The Godfather
14/72 **Speak To The Sky** *Rick Springfield*
52/99 **Special** *Garbage*
38/69 **Special Delivery** *1910 Fruitgum Co.*
39[S]/01 **Special Delivery** *G. Dep*
5/80 **Special Lady** *Ray, Goodman, & Brown*
26/68 **Special Occasion** *Miracles*
64/72 **Special Someone** *Heywoods*
72/87 **Special Way** *Kool & The Gang*
74/93 **Speed** *Alpha Team*
59/63 **Speed Ball** *Ray Stevens*
17/56 **Speedoo** *Cadillacs*
6/62 **Speedy Gonzales** *Pat Boone*
39/91 **Spend My Life** *Slaughter*
21/99 **Spend My Life With You** *Eric Benét*
93/77 **Spend Some Time** *Elvin Bishop*
91/80 **Spend The Night In Love** *Four Seasons*
32/92 **Spending My Time** *Roxette*
63[S]/01 **Spente Le Stelle** *Opera Trance*
40/83 **Spice Of Life** *Manhattan Transfer*
18/97 **Spice Up Your Life** *Spice Girls*
87/75 **Spider Jiving** *Andy Fairweather Low*
3/74 **Spiders & Snakes** *Jim Stafford*
18[A]/96 **Spiderwebs** *No Doubt*
7/86 **Spies Like Us** *Paul McCartney*
Spill The Wine
3/70 *Eric Burdon & War*
49/71 *Isley Brothers*
71/02 **Spin** *Lifehouse*
87/97 **Spin Spin Sugar** *Sneaker Pimps*
69/90 **Spin That Wheel** *Hi Tek 3*
58/94 **Spin The Black Circle** *Pearl Jam*
97/94 **Spin The Bottle** *Juliana Hatfield*
52/71 **Spinning Around (I Must Be Falling In Love)** *Main Ingredient*
F/94 **Spinning Around Over You** *Lenny Kravitz*
Spinning Wheel
2/69 *Blood, Sweat & Tears*
90/71 *James Brown*
40/66 **Spinout** *Elvis Presley*
70[S]/97 **Spirit** *Sounds Of Blackness*
23/70 **Spirit In The Dark** *Aretha Franklin*
Spirit In The Night
97/76 *Manfred Mann's Earth Band*
40/77 *Manfred Mann's Earth Band*
Spirit In The Sky
3/70 *Norman Greenbaum*
99/70 *Dorothy Morrison*
69/86 *Doctor & The Medics*
42/99 **Spirit Of A Boy - Wisdom Of A Man** *Randy Travis*
51/80 **Spirit Of Radio** *Rush*
35/75 **Spirit Of The Boogie** *Kool & The Gang*
11/82 **Spirits In The Material World** *Police*
27/98 **Splackavellie** *Pressha*
3/58 **Splish Splash** *Bobby Darin*
Spooky
57/67 *Mike Sharpe*
3/68 *Classics IV*
17/79 *Atlanta Rhythm Section*
78/60 **Spoonful** *Etta James & Harvey Fuqua*
32[A]/88 **Spotlight** *Madonna*
50/66 **Spread It On Thick** *Gentrys*
73/67 **Spreadin' Honey** *Watts 103rd St. Rhythm Band*
94/63 **Spring** *Birdlegs & Pauline*
58/77 **Spring Affair** *Donna Summer*
92/63 **Spring In Manhattan** *Tony Bennett*
98/87 **Spring Love** *Cover Girls*
43/88 **Spring Love (Come Back To Me)** *Stevie B*
39/77 **Spring Rain** *Silvetti*
50/60 **Spring Rain** *Pat Boone*
94/68 **Springfield Plane** *Kenny O'Dell*
37/76 **Springtime Mama** *Henry Gross*
44/95 **Sprinkle Me** *E-40*
16/88 **Spy In The House Of Love** *Was (Not Was)*
50/81 **Square Biz** *Teena Marie*
80/85 **Square Rooms** *Al Corley*
16/76 **Squeeze Box** *Who*
89/64 **Squeeze Her-Tease Her (But Love Her)** *Jackie Wilson*
64/76 **St. Charles** *Jefferson Starship*
1/85 **St. Elmo's Fire (Man In Motion)** *John Parr* *(also see: Love Theme)*
100/69 **St. Louis** *Easybeats*
13/56 **St. Therese Of The Roses** *Billy Ward*
80/86 **Stacy** *Fortune*
21/86 **Stages** *ZZ Top*
Stagger Lee
1/59 *Lloyd Price*
22/67 *Wilson Pickett*
25/71 *Tommy Roe*
68/58 **Stairway Of Love** *Marty Robbins*
9/60 **Stairway To Heaven** *Neil Sedaka*
79/96 **Stairway To Heaven** *Pure Soul*
89/86 **Stairway To Heaven** *Far Corporation*
51/00 **Stan** *Eminem*

STAND:

6/89 **Stand** *R.E.M.*
22/69 **Stand!** *Sly & The Family Stone*
50/93 **Stand** *Poison*
75[A]/93 **Stand Above Me** *Orchestral Manoeuvres In The Dark*
5/83 **Stand Back** *Stevie Nicks*
76/87 **Stand Back** *Fabulous Thunderbirds*
34/99 **Stand Beside Me** *Jo Dee Messina*
54/83 **Stand By** *Roman Holliday*
Stand By Me
4/61 *Ben E. King*
75/65 *Earl Grant*
12/67 *Spyder Turner*
61/70 *David & Jimmy Ruffin*
20/75 *John Lennon*
22/80 *Mickey Gilley*
50/85 *Maurice White*
9/86 *Ben E. King*
82/98 *4 The Cause* *(also see: I'll Be There)*
76/91 **Stand By My Woman** *Lenny Kravitz*
Stand By Your Man
19/69 *Tammy Wynette*
24/70 *Candi Staton*
95/66 **Stand In For Love** *O'Jays*
76/82 **Stand Or Fall** *Fixx*
10/77 **Stand Tall** *Burton Cummings*

54S/99 **Stand Up** *Charli Baltimore*
64/88 **Stand Up** *David Lee Roth*
67/89 **Stand Up** *Underworld*
89/97 **Stand Up** *Love Tribe*
34/93 **Stand Up (Kick Love Into Motion)** *Def Leppard*
Standing ..see: America
37/74 **Standing At The End Of The Line** *Lobo*
74/72 **Standing In For Jody** *Johnnie Taylor*
6/67 **Standing In The Shadows Of Love** *Four Tops*
Standing On The Corner
3/56 *Four Lads*
22/56 *Dean Martin*
57/56 *Mills Brothers*
66/82 **Standing On The Top** *Temptations*
10A/96 **Standing Outside A Broken Phone Booth With Money In My Hand** *Primitive Radio Gods*
25/02 **Standing Still** *Jewel*

STAR:

13S/03 **Star** *702*
29/74 **Star** *Stealers Wheel*
64/80 **Star** *Earth, Wind & Fire*
39/74 **Star Baby** *Guess Who*
38S/02 **Star Guitar** *Chemical Brothers*
Star Is Born ..see: Love Theme From A
68/60 **Star Is Born (A Love Has Died)** *Mark Dinning*
62/79 **Star Love** *Cheryl Lynn*
75/59 **Star Love** *Playmates*
47/75 **Star On A TV Show** *Stylistics*
74A/95 **Star 69** *R.E.M.*
62S/01 **Star 69 (What The F**k)** *Fatboy Slim*
Star-Spangled Banner
50/68 *José Feliciano*
20/91 *Whitney Houston*
6/01 *Whitney Houston*
Star Wars Theme
1/77 *Meco*
10/77 *John Williams*
42/56 **Star You Wished Upon Last Night** *Gisele MacKenzie*
25/60 **Starbright** *Johnny Mathis*
Stardust
12/57 *Billy Ward*
79/57 *Nat "King" Cole*
98/62 *Frank Sinatra*
32/64 *Nino Tempo & April Stevens*
59/80 **Stargazer** *Peter Brown*
26/97 **Staring At The Sun** *U2*
80/61 **Starlight** *Preludes Five*
44/61 **Starlight, Starbright** *Linda Scott*
65/72 **Starman** *David Bowie*
77/59 **Starry Eyed** *Gary Stites*
41/02 **Starry Eyed Surprise** *Oakenfold*
56/79 **Starry Eyes** *Records*
44/92 **Stars** *Simply Red*
72A/95 **Stars** *Hum*
87/75 **Stars In My Eyes** *Sugarloaf/Jerry Corbetta*
28/82 **Stars on 45 III** *Stars On*
(also see: Medley / More Stars)
97/82 **Start It All Over** *McGuffey Lane*
2/81 **Start Me Up** *Rolling Stones*
9/57 **Start Movin' (In My Direction)** *Sal Mineo*
71/92 **Start The Car** *Jude Cole*
31/01 **Start The Commotion** *Wiseguys*
73/77 **Started Out Dancing, Ended Up Making Love** *Alan O'Day*
19/72 **Starting All Over Again** *Mel & Tim*
Starting Over ..see: (Just Like)
36/80 **Starting Over Again** *Dolly Parton*
41/82 **State Of Independence** *Donna Summer*
70S/94 **State Of Mind** *Clint Black*
3/84 **State Of Shock** *Jacksons*
22/85 **State Of The Heart** *Rick Springfield*
81/83 **State Of The Nation** *Industry*
5A/91 **State Of The World** *Janet Jackson*

STAY:

Stay
1/60 *Maurice Williams*
16/64 *4 Seasons*
20/78 *Jackson Browne*
4/92 **Stay** *Shakespear's Sister*
19/94 **Stay** *Eternal*
38/78 **Stay** *Rufus/Chaka Khan*
41/92 **Stay** *Jodeci*
90/58 **Stay** *Ames Brothers*
82/69 **Stay And Love Me All Summer** *Brian Hyland*
60/81 **Stay Awake** *Ronnie Laws*
67/68 **Stay Away ('Greensleeves' melody)** *Elvis Presley*
89/73 **Stay Away From Me** *Sylvers*
67/70 **Stay Away From Me (I Love You Too Much)** *Major Lance*
99/65 **Stay Away From My Baby** *Ted Taylor*
7/71 **Stay Awhile** *Bells*
Stay Awhile
38/64 *Dusty Springfield*
90/78 *Continental Miniatures*
(also see: Good Morning Girl)
91/68 **Stay Close To Me** *Five Stairsteps*
61/94 **Stay (Faraway, So Close!)** *U2*
52/93 **Stay Forever** *Joey Lawrence*
1/94 **Stay (I Missed You)** *Lisa Loeb*
10/68 **Stay In My Corner** *Dells*
51/80 **Stay In Time** *Off Broadway USA*
76/00 **Stay Or Let It Go** *Brian McKnight*
92/93 **Stay Real** *Erick Sermon*
16/84 **Stay The Night** *Chicago*
23/00 **Stay The Night** *IMx*
24/87 **Stay The Night** *Benjamin Orr*
50/79 **Stay The Night** *Faragher Bros.*
10/99 **Stay The Same** *Joey McIntyre*
66/67 **Stay Together Young Lovers** *Brenda & The Tabulations*
94/86 **Stay True** *Sly Fox*
44A/98 **Stay (Wasting Time)** *Dave Matthews Band*
17/72 **Stay With Me** *Faces*
64/66 **Stay With Me** *Lorraine Ellison*
81/64 **Stay With Me** *Frank Sinatra*
(also see: One More Chance)
30/84 **Stay With Me Tonight** *Jeffrey Osborne*
Stayin' Alive
1/78 *Bee Gees*
62/96 *n-trance*
33/61 **Stayin' In** *Bobby Vee*
40S/99 **Staying Power** *Barry White*
22/88 **Staying Together** *Debbie Gibson*
37/81 **Staying With It** *Firefall*
57/85 **Steady** *Jules Shear*
67S/92 **Steady Mobbin'** *Ice Cube*
6/80 **Steal Away** *Robbie Dupree*
Steal Away
17/64 *Jimmy Hughes*
37/70 *Johnnie Taylor*
9/99 **Steal My Sunshine** *Len*
25/81 **Steal The Night** *Stevie Woods*
49/71 **Stealer** *Free*
91/73 **Stealin'** *Uriah Heep*
49/70 **Stealing In The Name Of The Lord** *Paul Kelly*
Steam
32/93 *Peter Gabriel*
83/99 *Ty Herndon*
17/73 **Steamroller Blues** *Elvis Presley*
39/90 **Steamy Windows** *Tina Turner*
16A/92 **Steel Bars** *Michael Bolton*
13/62 **Steel Guitar And A Glass Of Wine** *Paul Anka*
41/62 **Steel Men** *Jimmy Dean*
32/96 **Steelo** *702*

STEP:

1/90 **Step By Step** *New Kids On The Block*
5/81 **Step By Step** *Eddie Rabbitt*
14/60 **Step By Step** *Crests*
15/97 **Step By Step** *Whitney Houston*
37/73 **Step By Step** *Joe Simon*
70/97 **Step Into A World (Rapture's Delight)** *KRS-One*
1X/73 **Step Into Christmas** *Elton John*
58/93 **Step It Up** *Stereo MC's*
57/91 **'Step On' Remix '91** *Happy Mondays*
81/72 **Step Out** *Mamas & The Papas*
24/67 **Step Out Of Your Mind** *American Breed*
88/99 **Step To This** *Master P*
39/78 **Steppin' In A Slide Zone** *Moody Blues*
6/82 **Steppin' Out** *Joe Jackson*
36/76 **Steppin' Out** *Neil Sedaka*
46/65 **Steppin' Out** *Paul Revere & The Raiders*
89/82 **Steppin' Out** *Kool & The Gang*
7/74 **Steppin' Out (Gonna Boogie Tonight)** *Tony Orlando & Dawn*
Steppin' Stone ..see: (I'm Not Your)
73/98 **Stepping Stone** *Lari White*
86/61 **Steps 1 And 2** *Jack Scott*
82/86 **Stereotomy** *Alan Parsons Project*
88/02 **Steve McQueen** *Sheryl Crow*
35/63 **Stewball** *Peter, Paul & Mary*
32/86 **Stick Around** *Julian Lennon*
25/61 **Stick Shift** *Duals*
11/71 **Stick-Up** *Honey Cone*
41/61 **Stick With Me Baby** *Everly Brothers*
40/60 **Sticks And Stones** *Ray Charles*

STILL:

Still
1/79 *Commodores*
69/81 *John Schneider*
Still
8/63 *Bill Anderson*
98/63 *Ben Colder*
93/66 *Sunrays*
Still
86/56 *Fontane Sisters*
97/57 *LaVern Baker*
19/98 **Still A G Thang** *Snoop Dogg*
56/87 **Still A Thrill** *Jody Watley*
40/76 **Still Crazy After All These Years** *Paul Simon*
93/89 **Still Cruisin'** *Beach Boys*
93/99 **Still D.R.E.** *Dr. Dre*
11/02 **Still Fly** *Big Tymers*
97/91 **Still Got The Blues** *Gary Moore*
Still In Love ..see: Can'tcha Say (You Believe In Me)
88/00 **Still In My Heart** *Tracie Spencer*

22/82 **Still In Saigon** *Charlie Daniels Band*
47/82 **Still In The Game** *Steve Winwood*
64/84 **Still Loving You** *Scorpions*
24/98 **Still Not A Player** *Big Punisher*
9S/02 **Still Not Over You** *Exhale*
79/87 **Still Of The Night** *Whitesnake*
54/01 **Still On Your Side** *BBMak*
62/98 **Still Po' Pimpin'** *Do Or Die*
28/81 **Still Right Here In My Heart** *Pure Prairie League*
76/83 **Still Taking Chances** *Michael Murphey*
77/77 **Still The Lovin' Is Fun** *B.J. Thomas*
5/76 **Still The One** *Orleans*
4/78 **Still The Same** *Bob Seger*
19/82 **Still They Ride** *Journey*
11/70 **Still Water (Love)** *Four Tops*
57/97 **Still Waters (Run Deep)** *Bee Gees*
89/62 **Still Waters Run Deep** *Brook Benton*
71/79 **Stillsane** *Carolyne Mas*
86/88 **Stimulation** *Wa Wa Nee*
50/63 **Sting Ray** *Routers*
33/02 **Stingy** *Ginuwine*
12/73 **Stir It Up** *Johnny Nash*
41/85 **Stir It Up** *Patti LaBelle*
50/70 **Stir It Up And Serve It** *Tommy Roe*
91/64 **Stockholm** *Lawrence Welk*
27/02 **Stole** *Kelly Rowland*
73/56 **Stolen Love** *Dinah Shore*
7/80 **Stomp!** *Brothers Johnson*
52A/97 **Stomp** *God's Property (feat. Kirk Franklin)*
36/78 **Stone Blue** *Foghat*
40/82 **Stone Cold** *Rainbow*
34/91 **Stone Cold Gentleman** *Ralph Tresvant*
65/77 **Stone Cold Sober** *Crawler*
10/87 **Stone Love** *Kool & The Gang*
77/70 **Stoned Cowboy** *Fantasy*
7/70 **Stoned Love** *Supremes*
30/73 **Stoned Out Of My Mind** *Chi-Lites*
3/68 **Stoned Soul Picnic** *5th Dimension*
58/74 **Stoned To The Bone** *James Brown*
14/71 **Stones** *Neil Diamond*
6/71 **Stoney End** *Barbra Streisand*
2/58 **Stood Up** *Ricky Nelson*

STOP:

16/98 **Stop** *Spice Girls*
65/89 **Stop** *Sam Brown*
76/68 **Stop** *Howard Tate*
97/89 **Stop!** *Erasure*
98/66 **Stop!** *Moody Blues*
9/74 **Stop And Smell The Roses** *Mac Davis*
8/64 **Stop And Think It Over** *Dale & Grace*
92/67 **Stop! And Think It Over** *Perry Como*
79/98 **Stop Being Greedy** *DMX*
Stop Doggin' Me Around ..see: Doggin' Around
3/81 **Stop Draggin' My Heart Around** *Stevie Nicks (with Tom Petty)*
80/66 **Stop! Get A Ticket** *Clefs Of Lavender Hill*
48/66 **Stop Her On Sight (S.O.S.)** *Edwin Starr*
Stop! In The Name Of Love
1/65 *Supremes*
96/71 *Margie Joseph*
29/83 *Hollies*
85/66 **Stop, Look And Listen** *Chiffons*
39/71 **Stop, Look, Listen (To Your Heart)** *Stylistics*
92/65 **Stop! Look What You're Doing** *Carla Thomas*
94/63 **Stop Monkeyin' Aroun'** *Dovells*
33S/02 **Stop Playin'** *LeVert Agee*
7/66 **Stop Stop Stop** *Hollies*
88/64 **Stop Takin' Me For Granted** *Mary Wells*
77/97 **Stop The Gunfight** *Trapp · 2Pac · Notorious B.I.G.*
36/62 **Stop The Music** *Shirelles*
26/71 **Stop The War Now** *Edwin Starr*
34/62 **Stop The Wedding** *Etta James*
95/93 **Stop The World** *Extreme*
48/80 **Stop This Game** *Cheap Trick*
15/87 **Stop To Love** *Luther Vandross*
74/74 **Stop To Start** *Blue Magic*
91/73 **Stop, Wait & Listen** *Circus*
65/80 **Stop Your Sobbing** *Pretenders*
Stormy
5/68 *Classics IV*
32/79 *Santana*
43/62 **Stormy Monday Blues** *Bobby Bland*
23/71 **Story In Your Eyes** *Moody Blues*
15/58 **Story Of My Life** *Marty Robbins*
16/61 **Story Of My Love** *Paul Anka*
28/59 **Story Of My Love** *Conway Twitty*
93/59 **Story Of Our Love** *Johnny Mathis*
48/68 **Story Of Rock And Roll** *Turtles*
88/64 **(Story Of) Woman, Love And A Man** *Tony Clarke*
16/55 **Story Untold** *Crew-Cuts*
54/68 **Storybook Children** *Billy Vera & Judy Clay*
57/78 **Storybook Children (Daybreak)** *Bette Midler*
92/67 **Stout-Hearted Men** *Barbra Streisand*
Straight ..also see: Strait / Streiht
84/60 **Straight A's In Love** *Johnny Cash*
91/59 **Straight Flush** *Frantics*
10/83 **Straight From The Heart** *Bryan Adams*
39/81 **Straight From The Heart** *Allman Brothers Band*
66/84 **Straight From The Heart (Into Your Life)** *Coyote Sisters*
36/68 **Straight Life** *Bobby Goldsboro*
15/78 **Straight On** *Heart*
29/74 **Straight Shootin' Woman** *Steppenwolf*
42/91 **Straight To Your Heart** *Bad English*
1/89 **Straight Up** *Paula Abdul*
83/00 **Straight Up** *Chanté Moore*
73/58 **Straighten Up & Fly Right** *DeJohn Sisters*
43/63 **Straighten Up Your Heart** *Barbara Lewis*
72A/97 **Strait Playin'** *Shaquille O'Neal*
13/90 **Stranded** *Heart*
Stranded In The Jungle
15/56 *Cadets*
18/56 *Jayhawks*
39/56 *Gadabouts*
72/67 **Stranded In The Middle Of Noplace** *Righteous Brothers*
97/62 **Strange** *Patsy Cline*
80/58 **Strange Are The Ways Of Love** *Gogi Grant*
21/88 **Strange But True** *Times Two*
47/95 **Strange Currencies** *R.E.M.*
70/63 **Strange Feeling** *Billy Stewart*
49/63 **Strange I Know** *Marvelettes*
14/76 **Strange Magic** *Electric Light Orchestra*
99/64 **Strange Things Happening** *Little Jr. Parker*
11/78 **Strange Way** *Firefall*
Strangelove
76/87 *Depeche Mode*
50/88 *Depeche Mode*
61/84 **Stranger** *Stephen Stills*
48/81 **Stranger** *Jefferson Starship*
90/60 **Stranger From Durango** *Richie Allen*
91/97 **Stranger In Moscow** *Michael Jackson*
81/80 **Stranger In My Home Town** *Foghat*
10/01 **Stranger In My House** *Tamia*
23/83 **Stranger In My House** *Ronnie Milsap*
81/99 **Stranger In My Mirror** *Randy Travis*
30/65 **Stranger In Town** *Del Shannon*
30/84 **Stranger In Town** *Toto*
83/64 **Stranger In Your Arms** *Bobby Vee*
70/63 **Stranger In Your Town** *Shacklefords*
Stranger On The Shore
1/62 *Mr. Acker Bilk*
38/62 *Andy Williams*
73/62 *Drifters*
52/90 **Stranger To Love** *St. Paul*
54/84 **Strangers In A Strange World** *Jenny Burton & Patrick Jude*
1/66 **Strangers In The Night** *Frank Sinatra*
93/56 **Strangest Romance** *Patti Page*
81/86 **Stranglehold** *Paul McCartney*
85/87 **Strap Me In** *Cars*
49/98 **Strawberries** *Smooth*
83/98 **Strawberry** *Nicole Renée*
8/67 **Strawberry Fields Forever** *Beatles*
Strawberry Letter 23
5/77 *Brothers Johnson*
53/92 *Tevin Campbell*
39/68 **Strawberry Shortcake** *Jay & The Techniques*
65/96 **Strawberry Wine** *Deana Carter*
3/83 **Stray Cat Strut** *Stray Cats*
59S/00 **Strayed Away** *Terry Dexter*
1/74 **Streak, The** *Ray Stevens*
56/82 **Street Corner** *Ashford & Simpson*
30/78 **Street Corner Serenade** *Wet Willie*
22/97 **Street Dreams** *Nas*
48/68 **Street Fighting Man** *Rolling Stones*
36/79 **Street Life** *Crusaders*
93/98 **Street Mix** *Mag 7*
12/91 **Street Of Dreams** *Nia Peeples*
60/83 **Street Of Dreams** *Rainbow*
27/76 **Street Singin'** *Lady Flash*
56/76 **Street Talk** *Bob Crewe Generation*
81/02 **Streets, The** *WC*
9/94 **Streets Of Philadelphia** *Bruce Springsteen*
72/93 **Streiht Up Menace** *MC Eiht*
61/86 **Strength** *Alarm*
8/91 **Strike It Up** *Black Box*
String Along
39/60 *Fabian*
25/63 *Rick Nelson*
64/59 **String Of Trumpets** *Trumpeteers*
42/84 **Strip** *Adam Ant*
1/62 **Stripper, The** *David Rose*
80/92 **Strobelite Honey** *Black Sheep*
17/81 **Stroke, The** *Billy Squier*
3/94 **Stroke You Up** *Changing Faces*
4/58 **Stroll, The** *Diamonds*

5/95 **Strong Enough** *Sheryl Crow*
57/99 **Strong Enough** *Cher*
89/76 **Strong Enough To Be Gentle** *Black Oak Arkansas*
11/01 **Stronger** *Britney Spears*
65S/00 **Stronger** *Kristine W*
30/81 **Stronger Than Before** *Carole Bayer Sager*
40/84 **Strung Out** *Steve Perry*
7/84 **Strut** *Sheena Easton*
22/75 **Struttin'** *Billy Preston*
68/76 **Struttin' My Stuff** *Elvin Bishop*
46/62 **Stubborn Kind Of Fellow** *Marvin Gaye*
52/01 **Stuck In A Moment You Can't Get Out Of** *U2*
6/73 **Stuck In The Middle With You** *Stealers Wheel*
1/60 **Stuck On You** *Elvis Presley*
3/84 **Stuck On You** *Lionel Richie*
1/86 **Stuck With You** *Huey Lewis*
21/78 **Stuff Like That** *Quincy Jones*
4/79 **Stumblin' In** *Suzi Quatro & Chris Norman*
14/58 **Stupid Cupid** *Connie Francis*
24/96 **Stupid Girl** *Garbage*
1/01 **Stutter** *Joe*
67/95 **Stutter** *Elastica*
33S/01 **Stuttering (don't say)** *Wild Orchid*
18/72 **Suavecito** *Malo*
84/98 **Suavemente** *Elvis Crespo*
62/77 **Sub-Rosa Subway** *Klaatu*
67/78 **Substitute** *Clout*
39/65 **Subterranean Homesick Blues** *Bob Dylan*
70/87 **Suburbia** *Pet Shop Boys*
Such A Day
89/56 *Rita Raines*
96/56 *Vera Lynn*
64A/91 **Such A Good Feeling** *Brothers In Rhythm*
16/64 **Such A Night** *Elvis Presley*
42/73 **Such A Night** *Dr. John*
89/84 **Such A Shame** *Talk Talk*
99/66 **Such A Sweet Thing** *Mary Wells*
26/79 **Such A Woman** *Tycoon*
11/65 **(Such An) Easy Question** *Elvis Presley*
72A/96 **Sucked Out** *Superdrag*
63/68 **Sudden Stop** *Percy Sledge*
4/85 **Suddenly** *Billy Ocean*
20/81 **Suddenly** *Olivia Newton-John & Cliff Richard*
90/60 **Suddenly** *Nickey DeMatteo*
96/65 **Suddenly I'm All Alone** *Walter Jackson*
9/83 **Suddenly Last Summer** *Motels*
Suddenly There's A Valley
9/55 *Gogi Grant*
13/55 *Jo Stafford*
20/55 *Julius LaRosa*
45/55 *Mills Brothers*
69/55 *Patty Andrews*
44/68 **Suddenly You Love Me** *Tremeloes*
71/63 **Sue's Gotta Be Mine** *Del Shannon*

SUGAR:

68S/99 **Suga Suga** *Monifah*
(also see: Sugar, Sugar)
89/58 **Sugah Wooga** *Three Playmates*
24S/01 **Sugar** *Youngstown*
Sugar And Spice
44/64 *Searchers*
49/66 *Cryan Shames*
99/62 **Sugar Babe** *Buster Brown*
37/74 **Sugar Baby Love** *Rubettes*
80/61 **Sugar Bee** *Cleveland Crochet*
92/62 **Sugar Blues** *Ace Cannon*
58/98 **Sugar Cane** *Space Monkeys*
10/72 **Sugar Daddy** *Jackson 5*
28/89 **Sugar Daddy** *Thompson Twins*
36/84 **Sugar Don't Bite** *Sam Harris*
32/65 **Sugar Dumpling** *Sam Cooke*
35/87 **Sugar Free** *Wa Wa Nee*
25/95 **Sugar Hill** *AZ*
64/97 **Sugar Honey Ice Tea** *Goodfellaz*
30/64 **Sugar Lips** *Al Hirt*
91/73 **Sugar Magnolia** *Grateful Dead*
5/58 **Sugar Moon** *Pat Boone*
22/69 **Sugar On Sunday** *Clique*
47/75 **Sugar Pie Guy** *Joneses*
95/62 **Sugar Plum** *Ike Clanton*
1/63 **Sugar Shack** *Jimmy Gilmer/Fireballs*
Sugar, Sugar
1/69 *Archies*
25/70 *Wilson Pickett*
(also see: Suga Suga)
5/66 **Sugar Town** *Nancy Sinatra*
9/85 **Sugar Walls** *Sheena Easton*
77/59 **Sugaree** *Rusty York*
94/72 **Sugaree** *Jerry Garcia*
96/02 **Sugarhigh** *Jade Anderson*
1/58 **Sugartime** *McGuire Sisters*
63S/01 **Suicidal Failure** *Cage*
9/90 **Suicide Blonde** *INXS*
21/69 **Suite: Judy Blue Eyes** *Crosby, Stills & Nash*
97/72 **Suite: Man And Woman** *Tony Cole*
Sukiyaki
1/63 *Kyu Sakamoto*
3/81 *Taste Of Honey*
8/95 *4 P.M. (For Positive Music)*
4/79 **Sultans Of Swing** *Dire Straits*
64S/95 **Sultry Funk** *M.C. Hammer*

SUMMER:

7/76 **Summer** *War*
65/67 **Summer And Sandy** *Lesley Gore*
Summer Breeze
6/72 *Seals & Crofts*
60/74 *Isley Brothers*
55/94 **Summer Bunnies** *R. Kelly*
55/59 **Summer Dreams** *McGuire Sisters*
81/81 **Summer '81 medley** *Cantina Band*
3/99 **Summer Girls** *LFO*
1/66 **Summer In The City** *Lovin' Spoonful*
97/57 **Summer Love** *Joni James*
F/75 **Summer Madness** *Kool & The Gang*
72/64 **Summer Means Fun** *Bruce & Terry*
Summer Night ..see: Song For A
5/78 **Summer Nights** *John Travolta & Olivia Newton-John*
24/65 **Summer Nights** *Marianne Faithfull*
62/82 **Summer Nights** *Survivor*
Summer Of '42 ..see: Theme From
5/85 **Summer Of '69** *Bryan Adams*
Summer Place ..see: Theme From A
14/68 **Summer Rain** *Johnny Rivers*
30/90 **Summer Rain** *Belinda Carlisle*
80/00 **Summer Rain** *Carl Thomas*
26/66 **Summer Samba (So Nice)** *Walter Wanderley*
33/71 **Summer Sand** *Dawn*
30/60 **Summer Set** *Monty Kelly*
98/71 **Summer Side Of Life** *Gordon Lightfoot*
7/64 **Summer Song** *Chad & Jeremy*
58/65 **Summer Sounds** *Robert Goulet*
68/61 **Summer Souvenirs** *Karl Hammel, Jr.*
90/72 **Summer Sun** *Jamestown Massacre*
67/56 **Summer Sweetheart** *Ames Brothers*
21/73 **Summer (The First Time)** *Bobby Goldsboro*
Summer Time ..see: In The Summertime
Summer Vacation
72/90 *Party*
86/91 *Party*
Summer Wind
78/65 *Wayne Newton*
25/66 *Frank Sinatra*
49/67 **Summer Wine** *Nancy Sinatra with Lee Hazlewood*
49/63 **Summer's Comin'** *Kirby St. Romain*
11/60 **Summer's Gone** *Paul Anka*
93/59 **Summer's Love** *Richard Barrett/Chantels*
50/88 **Summergirls** *Dino*
4/91 **Summertime** *D.J. Jazzy Jeff & The Fresh Prince*
Summertime
81/57 *Sam Cooke*
78/61 *Marcels*
89/62 *Rick Nelson*
93/63 *Chris Columbo Quintet*
10/66 *Billy Stewart*
42S/99 **Summertime** *Another Level*
50A/97 **Summertime** *Sundays*
Summertime Blues
8/58 *Eddie Cochran*
14/68 *Blue Cheer*
27/70 *Who*
60S/94 *Alan Jackson*
55/85 **Summertime Girls** *Y&T*
54/95 **Summertime In The LBC** *Dove Shack*
F/58 **Summertime Lies** *Four Preps*
Summertime, Summertime
26/58 *Jamies*
38/62 *Jamies*
Summertime, Summertime
84/87 *Nocera*
86/97 *Corina*
Sun Ain't Gonna Shine (Anymore)
13/66 *Walker Bros.*
56/81 *Nielsen/Pearson*
20/86 **Sun Always Shines On T.V.** *A-Ha*
72/84 **Sun And The Rain** *Madness*
61/63 **Sun Arise** *Rolf Harris*
38/85 **Sun City** *Artists United Against Apartheid*
50S/01 **Sun God** *Hi-Tek*
44/75 **Sun Goddess** *Ramsey Lewis/Earth, Wind & Fire*
65/57 **Sun Is Shining** *Jimmy Reed*
75S/00 **Sun Is Shining** *Bob Marley Vs. Funkstar De Luxe*
96/76 **Sun...Sun...Sun** *Ja-Kki*
86/94 **Sun's Gonna Rise** *Sass Jordan*
90/69 **Sunday** *Moments*
18/65 **Sunday And Me** *Jay & The Americans*
97/58 **Sunday Barbecue** *Tennessee Ernie Ford*
31/67 **Sunday For Tea** *Peter & Gordon*
Sunday Kind Of Love
95/62 *Jan & Dean*
96/72 *Lenny Welch*
Sunday Mornin'
30/68 *Spanky & Our Gang*
35/69 *Oliver*

53/93 **Sunday Morning** *Earth, Wind & Fire*
Sunday Morning Coming Down
81/69 *Ray Stevens*
46/70 *Johnny Cash*
75/72 **Sunday Morning Sunshine** *Harry Chapin*
68/68 **Sunday Sun** *Neil Diamond*
98/75 **Sunday Sunrise** *Anne Murray*
9/67 **Sunday Will Never Be The Same** *Spanky & Our Gang*
1/74 **Sundown** *Gordon Lightfoot*
Sundowners ..see: Theme From The
39/77 **Sunflower** *Glen Campbell*
7/84 **Sunglasses At Night** *Corey Hart*
2/66 **Sunny** *Bobby Hebb*
86/64 **Sunny** *Neil Sedaka*
(also see: Just Friends)
14/66 **Sunny Afternoon** *Kinks*
7/97 **Sunny Came Home** *Shawn Colvin*
34/72 **Sunny Days** *Lighthouse*
34/76 **Sunrise** *Eric Carmen*
84/67 **Sunrise, Sunset** *Roger Williams*
22/85 **Sunset Grill** *Don Henley*
81/70 **Sunset Strip** *Ray Stevens*
4/72 **Sunshine** *Jonathan Edwards*
23/89 **Sunshine** *Dino*
45/77 **Sunshine** *Enchantment*
48/75 **Sunshine** *O'Jays*
57/70 **Sunshine** *Archies*
70/99 **Sunshine** *Coko*
87/73 **Sunshine** *Mickey Newbury*
95/97 **Sunshine** *Jay-Z*
63/67 **Sunshine Games** *Music Explosion*
20/67 **Sunshine Girl** *Parade*
94/57 **Sunshine Girl** *Eddie Fisher*
69/84 **Sunshine In The Shade** *Fixx*
13/65 **Sunshine, Lollipops And Rainbows** *Lesley Gore*
5/68 **Sunshine Of Your Love** *Cream*
1/74 **Sunshine On My Shoulders** *John Denver*
79/74 **Sunshine Roses** *Gene Cotton*
1/66 **Sunshine Superman** *Donovan*

SUPER:

85/95 **Supa Star** *Group Home*
13/70 **Super Bad** *James Brown*
66/65 **Super-cali-fragil-istic-expi-ali-docious** *Julie Andrews & Dick Van Dyke*
31/73 **Super Fly Meets Shaft** *John & Ernest*
16/81 **Super Freak** *Rick James*
93/71 **Super Highway** *Ballin' Jack*
36/98 **SuperThug (What What)** *Noreaga*
45/81 **Super Trouper** *Abba*
65S/01 **Superb** *Superb*
41/86 **Superbowl Shuffle** *Chicago Bears Shufflin' Crew*
8/73 **Superfly** *Curtis Mayfield*
(also see: Freddie's Dead)
88/98 **Superhero** *Daze*
Superman
41/77 *Celi Bee*
26/79 *Herbie Mann*
41/73 **Superman** *Donna Fargo*
64/70 **Superman** *Ides Of March*
94/66 **Superman** *Dino, Desi & Billy*
(also see: Theme From / Wish I Could Fly Like)
14/01 **Superman (It's Not Easy)** *Five For Fighting*
Superman Lover ..see: Soopaman Lover
74A/97 **Superman's Dead** *Our Lady Peace*
56/91 **Superman's Song** *Crash Test Dummies*
45/93 **Supermodel (You Better Work)** *RuPaul*
70/97 **Supernatural** *Wild Orchid*
75/84 **Supernatural Love** *Donna Summer*
5/75 **Supernatural Thing** *Ben E. King*
70/78 **Supernature** *Cerrone*
78/94 **Supernova** *Liz Phair*
29S/00 **Supersonic** *Jamiroquai*
30/88 **Supersonic** *J.J. Fad*
Superstar
2/71 *Carpenters*
87/84 *Luther Vandross (medley)*
35/76 **Superstar** *Paul Davis*
89/96 **Superstar** *Charm Farm*
Superstar - Jesus Christ Superstar
74/70 *Murray Head*
14/71 *Murray Head*
95/71 *Assembled Multitude*
18/71 **Superstar (Remember How You Got Where You Are)** *Temptations*
1/73 **Superstition** *Stevie Wonder*
31/88 **Superstitious** *Europe*
8/89 **Superwoman** *Karyn White*
11/01 **Superwoman** *Lil' Mo*
33/72 **Superwoman (Where Were You When I Needed You)** *Stevie Wonder*
Sure ..also see: Sho
16/74 **Sure As I'm Sittin' Here** *Three Dog Night*
83/75 **Sure Feels Good** *Elvin Bishop*
9/66 **Sure Gonna Miss Her** *Gary Lewis*
47/79 **Sure Know Something** *Kiss*
54/91 **Sure Lookin'** *Donny Osmond*
1/63 **Surf City** *Jan & Dean*
55/63 **Surf Party** *Chubby Checker*
7/63 **Surfer Girl** *Beach Boys*
62/63 **Surfer Joe** *Surfaris*
93/63 **Surfer Street** *Allisons*
31/62 **Surfer's Stomp** *Mar-Kets*
75/62 **Surfin** *Beach Boys*
4/64 **Surfin' Bird** *Trashmen*
(also see: Bird's The Word)
48/63 **Surfin' Hootenanny** *Al Casey*
14/62 **Surfin' Safari** *Beach Boys*
Surfin' U.S.A.
3/63 *Beach Boys*
36/74 *Beach Boys*
20/77 *Leif Garrett*
1/61 **Surrender** *Elvis Presley*
38/71 **Surrender** *Diana Ross*
43S/02 **Surrender** *Laura Pausini*
62/78 **Surrender** *Cheap Trick*
72/91 **Surrender** *Trixter*
6/89 **Surrender To Me** *Ann Wilson & Robin Zander*
74A/98 **Surrounded** *Chantal Kreviazuk*
69/95 **Survival Of The Fittest** *Mobb Deep*
77/80 **Survive** *Jimmy Buffett*
2/01 **Survivor** *Destiny's Child*
56/79 **Survivor** *Cindy Bullens*
11/68 **Susan** *Buckinghams*
Susie Darlin'
5/58 *Robin Luke*
35/62 *Tommy Roe*
3/64 **Suspicion** *Terry Stafford*
13/79 **Suspicions** *Eddie Rabbitt*
55/66 **Suspicions** *Sidekicks*
Suspicious Minds
1/69 *Elvis Presley*
80/71 *Dee Dee Warwick*
1/85 **Sussudio** *Phil Collins*
17/86 **Suzanne** *Journey*
56/67 **Suzanne** *Noel Harrison*
55/81 **Suzi** *Randy Vanwarmer*
77/59 **Suzie Baby** *Bobby Vee*
Suzie-Q
27/57 *Dale Hawkins*
11/68 *Creedence Clearwater Revival*
84/70 *José Feliciano*
90/90 **Swalk, The** *Notorious*
27A/96 **Swallowed** *Bush*
39/73 **Swamp Witch** *Jim Stafford*
F/55 **Swanee** *Jaye P. Morgan*
34/57 **Swanee River Rock (Talkin' 'Bout That River)** *Ray Charles*
S.W.A.T. ..see: Theme From
14/60 **Sway** *Bobby Rydell*
(Swayin' To The Music) ..see: Slow Dancin'
80/85 **Swear** *Sheena Easton*
20/00 **Swear It Again** *Westlife*
6/75 **Swearin' To God** *Frankie Valli*
16/93 **Sweat (A La La La La Long)** *Inner Circle*

SWEET:

Sweet And Gentle
10/55 *Alan Dale*
12/55 *Georgia Gibbs*
7/71 **Sweet And Innocent** *Donny Osmond*
77/62 **Sweet And Lovely** *April Stevens & Nino Tempo*
100/59 **Sweet Annie Laurie** *Sammy Turner*
19/81 **Sweet Baby** *Stanley Clarke/George Duke*
92/72 **Sweet Baby** *Donnie Elbert*
96/59 **Sweet Bird Of Youth** *Nat "King" Cole*
(also see: Mocking Bird)
13/68 **Sweet Blindness** *5th Dimension*
Sweet Caroline (Good Times Never Seemed So Good)
4/69 *Neil Diamond*
51/72 *Bobby Womack*
42/73 **Sweet Charlie Babe** *Jackie Moore*
7/69 **Sweet Cherry Wine** *Tommy James*
1/88 **Sweet Child O' Mine** *Guns N' Roses*
70/59 **Sweet Chile** *Sheb Wooley*
8/71 **Sweet City Woman** *Stampeders*
28/69 **Sweet Cream Ladies, Forward March** *Box Tops*
80/68 **Sweet Darlin'** *Martha & The Vandellas*
5/82 **Sweet Dreams** *Air Supply*
13/96 **Sweet Dreams** *La Bouche*
Sweet Dreams
93/60 *Don Gibson*
44/63 *Patsy Cline*
15/66 *Tommy McLain*
1/83 **Sweet Dreams (Are Made of This)** *Eurythmics*
91/58 **Sweet Elizabeth** *Will Glahé*
36/75 **Sweet Emotion** *Aerosmith*
60/70 **Sweet Feeling** *Candi Staton*
7/86 **Sweet Freedom** *Michael McDonald*
100/62 **Sweet Georgia Brown** *Carroll Bros.*
48/73 **Sweet Harmony** *Smokey Robinson*
42/56 **Sweet Heartaches** *Eddie Fisher*
6/71 **Sweet Hitch-Hiker** *Creedence Clearwater Revival*
8/74 **Sweet Home Alabama** *Lynyrd Skynyrd*
91/98 **Sweet Honesty** *M:G*
70/63 **Sweet Impossible You** *Brenda Lee*

Sweet Inspiration
18/68 *Sweet Inspirations*
37/72 *Barbra Streisand (medley)*
52A/94 **Sweet Jane** *Cowboy Junkies*
76/55 **Sweet Kentucky Rose** *Kitty Kallen*
12/99 **Sweet Lady** *Tyrese*
94/88 **Sweet Lies** *Robert Palmer*
17/78 **Sweet Life** *Paul Davis*
85/56 **Sweet Lips** *Jaye P. Morgan*
8X/66 **Sweet Little Baby Boy** *James Brown*
100/61 **Sweet Little Kathy** *Ray Peterson*
47/58 **Sweet Little Rock And Roll** *Chuck Berry*
Sweet Little Sixteen
2/58 *Chuck Berry*
95/62 *Jerry Lee Lewis*
59/61 **Sweet Little You** *Neil Sedaka*
91/73 **Sweet Lorraine** *Uriah Heep*
5/76 **Sweet Love** *Commodores*
8/86 **Sweet Love** *Anita Baker*
66A/96 **Sweet Lover Hangover** *Love & Rockets*
93/76 **Sweet Loving Man** *Morris Albert*
36/79 **Sweet Lui-Louise** *Ironhorse*
78/94 **Sweet Lullaby** *Deep Forest*
7/71 **Sweet Mary** *Wadsworth Mansion*
40/75 **Sweet Maxine** *Doobie Brothers*
75/68 **Sweet Memories** *Andy Williams*
80/81 **Sweet Merilee** *Donnie Iris*
44/78 **Sweet Music Man** *Kenny Rogers*
4/60 **Sweet Nothin's** *Brenda Lee*
58/92 **Sweet November** *Troop*
7/56 **Sweet Old Fashioned Girl** *Teresa Brewer*
91/93 **Sweet On U** *Lo-Key?*
8/66 **Sweet Pea** *Tommy Roe*
27/94 **Sweet Potatoe Pie** *Domino*
80/87 **Sweet Rachel** *Beau Coup*
9/72 **Sweet Seasons** *Carole King*
52/80 **Sweet Sensation** *Stephanie Mills*
80/94 **Sweet Sensual Love** *Big Mountain*
62/97 **Sweet Sexy Thing** *Nu Flavor*
20/87 **Sweet Sixteen** *Billy Idol*
93/72 **Sweet Sixteen** *B.B. King*
55/62 **Sweet Sixteen Bars** *Earl Grant*
87/59 **Sweet Someone** *Eddie & Betty*
Sweet Soul Music
2/67 *Arthur Conley*
90/67 *Magnificent Men (Medley)*
33/75 **Sweet Sticky Thing** *Ohio Players*
83/57 **Sweet Stuff** *Guy Mitchell*
97/59 **Sweet Sugar Lips** *Kalin Twins*
77/79 **Sweet Summer Lovin'** *Dolly Parton*
94/76 **Sweet Summer Music** *Attitudes*
13/75 **Sweet Surrender** *John Denver*
15/72 **Sweet Surrender** *Bread*
28/98 **Sweet Surrender** *Sarah McLachlan*
73/85 **Sweet, Sweet Baby (I'm Falling)** *Lone Justice*
(Sweet Sweet Baby) Since You've Been Gone
5/68 *Aretha Franklin*
98/68 *Ramsey Lewis*
70/67 **Sweet, Sweet Lovin'** *Platters*
44/78 **Sweet, Sweet Smile** *Carpenters*
88/70 **Sweet Sweetheart** *Bobby Vee*
10/66 **Sweet Talkin' Guy** *Chiffons*
17/78 **Sweet Talkin' Woman** *Electric Light Orchestra*
Sweet Thing
5/76 *Rufus Feat. Chaka Khan*
28/93 *Mary J. Blige*
84/93 **Sweet Thing** *Mick Jagger*
99/62 **Sweet Thursday** *Johnny Mathis*
26/82 **Sweet Time** *REO Speedwagon*
33/73 **Sweet Understanding Love** *Four Tops*
40/64 **Sweet William** *Millie Small*
29/66 **Sweet Woman Like You** *Joe Tex*
83/68 **Sweet Young Thing Like You** *Ray Charles*
52/69 **Sweeter He Is** *Soul Children*
96/69 **Sweeter Than Sugar** *Ohio Express*
9/59 **Sweeter Than You** *Ricky Nelson*
18/95 **Sweetest Days** *Vanessa Williams*
86/57 **Sweetest One** *Crests*
88/67 **Sweetest One** *Metros*
5/86 **Sweetest Taboo** *Sade*
61A/97 **Sweetest Thing** *Refugee Camp All-Stars*
63/98 **Sweetest Thing** *U2*
7/82 **Sweetest Thing (I've Ever Known)** *Juice Newton*
32/67 **Sweetest Thing This Side Of Heaven** *Chris Bartley*
10/81 **Sweetheart** *Franke & The Knockouts*
47/70 **Sweetheart** *Engelbert Humperdinck*
98/58 **Sweetheart** *Peggy Lee*
55/84 **Sweetheart Like You** *Bob Dylan*
75/02 **Sweetness** *Jimmy Eat World*
Sweets For My Sweet
16/61 *Drifters*
54/79 *Tony Orlando*
19/84 **Swept Away** *Diana Ross*
56/64 **S-W-I-M** *Bobby Freeman*
6/98 **Swing My Way** *K.P. & Envyi*
11/90 **Swing The Mood (medley)** *Jive Bunny & the Mastermixers*
55/75 **Swing Your Daddy** *Jim Gilstrap*
43/83 **Swingin'** *John Anderson*
80/58 **Swingin' Daddy** *Buddy Knox*
79/60 **Swingin' Down The Lane** *Jerry Wallace*
44/62 **Swingin' Gently** *Earl Grant*
39/60 **Swingin' On A Rainbow** *Frankie Avalon*
13/62 **Swingin' Safari** *Billy Vaughn*
5/60 **Swingin' School** *Bobby Rydell*
Swingin' Shepherd Blues
23/58 *Moe Koffman Quartette*
43/58 *Johnny Pate Quintet*
47/58 *David Rose*
85/69 **Swingin' Tight** *Bill Deal*
38/63 **Swinging On A Star** *Big Dee Irwin/Little Eva*
52/57 **Swinging Sweethearts** *Ron Goodwin*
17/77 **Swingtown** *Steve Miller Band*
64/62 **Swiss Maid** *Del Shannon*
26/61 **Switch-A-Roo** *Hank Ballard*
93/69 **Switch It On** *Cliff Nobles & Co.*
43/80 **Switchin' To Glide** *Kings*
89/73 **Sylvia** *Focus*
5/72 **Sylvia's Mother** *Dr. Hook*
55/95 **Sympathy For The Devil** *Guns N' Roses*
82/59 **Symphony** *Sammy Turner*
51/66 **Symphony For Susan** *Arbors*
71/92 **Symphony Of Destruction** *Megadeth*
38/88 **Symptoms Of True Love** *Tracie Spencer*
16/83 **Synchronicity II** *Police*
37/76 **(System Of) Doctor Tarr And Professor Fether** *Alan Parsons Project*
60/87 **System Of Survival** *Earth, Wind & Fire*

T

30/92 **T.L.C.** *Linear*
24/60 **T.L.C. Tender Love And Care** *Jimmie Rodgers*
1/74 **TSOP (The Sound Of Philadelphia)** *MFSB feat. The Three Degrees*
64/76 **TVC 15** *David Bowie*
95/00 **Ta Da** *Lil' Mo*
23/60 **Ta Ta** *Clyde McPhatter*
55/59 **Taboo** *Arthur Lyman*
46A/96 **Tahitian Moon** *Porno For Pyros*
64/64 **T'ain't Nothin' To Me** *Coasters*
87/02 **Tainted** *Slum Village*
Tainted Love
8/82 *Soft Cell*
59S/99 *Soft Cell vs. Club 69*

TAKE:

1/95 **Take A Bow** *Madonna*
Take A Chance On Me
3/78 *Abba*
51A/92 *Erasure*
90/73 **Take A Closer Look At The Woman You're With** *Wilson Pickett*
71/61 **Take A Fool's Advice** *Nat King Cole*
41/76 **Take A Hand** *Rick Springfield*
2/69 **Take A Letter Maria** *R.B. Greaves*
45S/99 **Take A Lick** *Akinyele*
15/80 **Take A Little Rhythm** *Ali Thomson*
56/67 **Take A Look** *Aretha Franklin*
74/96 **Take A Look** *J'Son*
30/72 **Take A Look Around** *Temptations*
43/70 **Take A Look Around** *Smith*
89/02 **Take A Message** *Remy Shand*
16/59 **Take A Message To Mary** *Everly Brothers*
12/00 **Take A Picture** *Filter*
58/83 **Take Another Picture** *Quarterflash*
45/02 **Take Away** *Missy Elliott*
91/83 **Take Away** *Big Ric*
20/69 **Take Care Of Your Homework** *Johnnie Taylor*
25/61 **Take Five** *Dave Brubeck Quartet*
Take Good Care Of Her
7/61 *Adam Wade*
78/66 *Mel Carter*
F/74 *Elvis Presley*
Take Good Care Of My Baby
1/61 *Bobby Vee*
33/68 *Bobby Vinton*
10/82 **Take It Away** *Paul McCartney*
67/79 **Take It Back** *J. Geils Band*
73/94 **Take It Back** *Pink Floyd*
12/72 **Take It Easy** *Eagles*
24/86 **Take It Easy** *Andy Taylor*
69/94 **Take It Easy** *Mad Lion*
10/82 **Take It Easy On Me** *Little River Band*
33/76 **Take It Like A Man** *Bachman-Turner Overdrive*
94/70 **Take It Off Him And Put It On Me** *Clarence Carter*
5/81 **Take It On The Run** *REO Speedwagon*
64/72 **Take It Slow (Out In The Country)** *Lighthouse*
50/01 **Take It To Da House** *Trick Daddy*
98/90 **Take It To Heart** *Michael McDonald*
4/76 **Take It To The Limit** *Eagles*
34/97 **Take It To The Streets** *Rampage*
57/88 **Take It While It's Hot** *Sweet Sensation*

53/76 **Take Me** *Grand Funk Railroad*
16/65 **Take Me Back**
Little Anthony & The Imperials
46/84 **Take Me Back** *Bonnie Tyler*
47/57 **Take Me Back Baby** *Guy Mitchell*
97/72 **Take Me Bak 'Ome** *Slade*
63/78 **Take Me Back To Chicago**
Chicago
47/56 **Take Me Back To Toyland**
Nat "King" Cole
18/82 **Take Me Down** *Alabama*
Take Me For A Little While
89/67 *Patti LaBelle*
38/68 *Vanilla Fudge*
76/66 **Take Me For What I'm Worth**
Searchers
50/71 **Take Me Girl, I'm Ready** *Jr. Walker*
7/86 **Take Me Home** *Phil Collins*
8/79 **Take Me Home** *Cher*
2/71 **Take Me Home, Country Roads**
John Denver
4/86 **Take Me Home Tonight**
Eddie Money
88/78 **Take Me I'm Yours**
Michael Henderson
67/92 **Take Me In Your Arms** *Lil Suzy*
98/67 **Take Me In Your Arms And Love Me** *Gladys Knight*
Take Me In Your Arms (Rock Me)
50/65 *Kim Weston*
11/75 *Doobie Brothers*
49/67 **Take Me (Just As I Am)**
Solomon Burke
62/81 **Take Me Now** *David Gates*
14/99 **Take Me There** *BLACKstreet & Mya*
14/83 **Take Me To Heart** *Quarterflash*
59/78 **Take Me To The Kaptin** *Prism*
Take Me To The River
48/75 *Syl Johnson*
26/79 *Talking Heads*
25/85 **Take Me With U** *Prince*
86/92 **Take My Advice** *Kym Sims*
Take My Breath Away
1/86 *Berlin*
60A/92 *Berlin*
91/71 **Take My Hand**
Kenny Rogers & The First Edition
17/81 **Take My Heart (You Can Have It If You Want It)** *Kool & The Gang*
87/61 **Take My Love (I Want To Give It All To You)** *Little Willie John*
78/85 **Take No Prisoners (In The Game Of Love)** *Peabo Bryson*
16/82 **Take Off** *Bob & Doug McKenzie*
1/85 **Take On Me** *A-Ha*
66/66 **Take Some Time Out For Love**
Isley Brothers
41S/01 **Take That** *Da Beatminerz*
86/00 **Take That** *Torrey Carter*
79/79 **Take That To The Bank** *Shalamar*
52/82 **Take The L.** *Motels*
10/79 **Take The Long Way Home**
Supertramp
11/76 **Take The Money And Run**
Steve Miller
41/83 **Take The Short Way Home**
Dionne Warwick
81/83 **Take The Time**
Michael Stanley Band
8/63 **Take These Chains From My Heart**
Ray Charles
20/92 **Take This Heart** *Richard Marx*
44/66 **Take This Heart Of Mine**
Marvin Gaye
97/64 **Take This Hurt Off Me** *Don Covay*
29/92 **Take Time** *Chris Walker*

11/68 **Take Time To Know Her**
Percy Sledge
72/02 **Take Ya Home** *Lil Bow Wow*
81/02 **Take You Home With Me A.K.A. Body** *R. Kelly & Jay-Z*
26/01 **Take You Out** *Luther Vandross*
76/95 **Take You There**
Pete Rock & C.L. Smooth
67/80 **Take You Tonight**
Ozark Mountain Daredevils
F/96 **Take Your Chance** *Fun Factory*
Take Your Time (Do It Right)
3/80 *S.O.S. Band*
64/95 *Max-A-Million*
77/97 *Tré*
32/86 **Taken In** *Mike + The Mechanics*
94/70 **Taker, The** *Waylon Jennings*
21A/97 **Takes A Little Time** *Amy Grant*
100/66 **Takin' All I Can Get** *Mitch Ryder*
12/74 **Takin' Care Of Business**
Bachman-Turner Overdrive
92/80 **Takin' It Back** *Breathless*
79/78 **Takin' It Easy** *Seals & Crofts*
13/76 **Takin' It To The Streets**
Doobie Brothers
11/99 **Taking Everything** *Gerald Levert*
50/84 **Taking It All Too Hard** *Genesis*
58/00 **Taking You Home** *Don Henley*
56S/95 **Tales From The Hood** *Domino*

TALK:

97/65 **Talk About Love** *Adam Faith*
7/64 **Talk Back Trembling Lips**
Johnny Tillotson
9/87 **Talk Dirty To Me** *Poison*
19/89 **Talk It Over** *Grayson Hugh*
57/71 **Talk It Over In The Morning**
Anne Murray
85/59 **Talk Of The School** *Sonny James*
88/99 **Talk Show Shhh!** *Shae Jones*
15/67 **Talk Talk** *Music Machine*
75/82 **Talk Talk** *Talk Talk*
34/60 **Talk That Talk** *Jackie Wilson*
4/86 **Talk To Me** *Stevie Nicks*
21/87 **Talk To Me** *Chico DeBarge*
38/59 **Talk To Me** *Frank Sinatra*
44/90 **Talk To Me** *Anita Baker*
48/97 **Talk To Me** *Wild Orchid*
64/85 **Talk To Me** *Fiona*
83/85 **Talk To Me** *Quarterflash*
92/60 **Talk To Me Baby** *Annette*
94/64 **Talk To Me Baby** *Barry Mann*
Talk To Me, Talk To Me
20/58 *Little Willie John*
11/63 *Sunny & The Sunglows*
49/89 **Talk To Myself**
Christopher Williams
75/88 **Talkin' Bout A Revolution**
Tracy Chapman
51/02 **Talkin' To Me** *Amerie*
15/57 **Talkin' To The Blues** *Jim Lowe*
12/64 **Talking About My Baby**
Impressions
60/68 **Talking About My Baby**
Gloria Walker
57/88 **Talking Back To The Night**
Steve Winwood
3/84 **Talking In Your Sleep** *Romantics*
18/78 **Talking In Your Sleep**
Crystal Gayle
64/71 **Talking In Your Sleep**
Gordon Lightfoot
27/72 **Talking Loud And Saying Nothing**
James Brown
65/81 **Talking Out Of Turn** *Moody Blues*
25/88 **Tall Cool One** *Robert Plant*

Tall Cool One
36/59 *Wailers*
38/64 *Wailers*
Tall Oak Tree ..see: (There Was A)
7/59 **Tall Paul** *Annette*
6/59 **Tallahassee Lassie** *Freddy Cannon*
Tammy
1/57 *Debbie Reynolds*
5/57 *Ames Brothers*
18/76 **Tangerine** *Salsoul Orchestra*
31/75 **Tangled Up In Blue** *Bob Dylan*
44/56 **Tango Of The Drums** *Les Baxter*
83/72 **Taos New Mexico** *R. Dean Taylor*
55/93 **Tap The Bottle**
Young Black Teenagers
34/68 **Tapioca Tundra** *Monkees*
38/66 **Tar And Cement** *Verdelle Smith*
75S/02 **Tarantula** *Mystikal*
Taras Bulba ..see: Theme From
55/71 **Tarkio Road** *Brewer & Shipley*
Tarzan Boy
13/86 *Baltimora*
51/93 *Baltimora*
Taste Of Honey
50/62 *Martin Denny*
88/62 *Victor Feldman Quartet*
94/64 *Tony Bennett*
7/65 *Herb Alpert*
87/64 **Taste Of Tears** *Johnny Mathis*
41/86 **Tasty Love** *Freddie Jackson*
63A/96 **Tattva** *Kula Shaker*
18/72 **Taurus** *Dennis Coffey*
24/72 **Taxi** *Harry Chapin*
90/84 **Taxi** *J. Blackfoot*
59/84 **Taxi Dancing**
Rick Springfield & Randy Crawford
70/56 **Te Amo** *Dick Jacobs*
53/61 **Te-Ta-Te-Ta-Ta** *Ernie K-Doe*
Tea For Two
7/58 *Tommy Dorsey (Cha Cha)*
56/64 *Nino Tempo & April Stevens*
86/59 **Teach Me Tiger** *April Stevens*
Teach Me Tonight
2/55 *DeCastro Sisters*
15/55 *Jo Stafford*
76/59 *DeCastro Sisters (Cha Cha)*
25/62 *George Maharis*
70/82 *Al Jarreau*
16/70 **Teach Your Children**
Crosby, Stills, Nash & Young
21/58 **Teacher, Teacher** *Johnny Mathis*
25/84 **Teacher Teacher** *38 Special*
51/81 **Teacher Teacher** *Rockpile*
56/58 **Teacher's Pet** *Doris Day*

TEAR:

31/61 **Tear, A** *Gene McDaniels*
23/59 **Tear Drop** *Santo & Johnny*
56/69 **Tear Drop City** *Monkees*
20/57 **Tear Drops** *Lee Andrews*
Tear Fell
5/56 *Teresa Brewer*
50/64 *Ray Charles*
44/61 **Tear Of The Year** *Jackie Wilson*
15/76 **Tear The Roof Off The Sucker (Give Up The Funk)** *Parliament*
Teardrops In My Heart
64/57 *Teresa Brewer*
63/61 *Joe Barry*
87/59 **Teardrops On Your Letter**
Hank Ballard
61/59 **Teardrops Will Fall**
Dicky Doo & The Don'ts
15A/98 **Tearin' Up My Heart** **NSYNC*
37/84 **Tears** *John Waite*

55/97 **Tears** *Isley Brothers*
59/66 **Tears** *Bobby Vinton*
71/62 **Tears And Laughter** *Dinah Washington*
20/64 **Tears And Roses** *Al Martino*
51/85 **Tears Are Falling** *Kiss*
77/62 **Tears From An Angel** *Troy Shondell*
2/92 **Tears In Heaven** *Eric Clapton*
96/65 **Tears Keep On Falling** *Jerry Vale*
Tears Of A Clown
1/70 *Miracles*
61S/00 *Brandy Moss-Scott*
85/63 **Tears Of Joy** *Chuck Jackson*
4/58 **Tears On My Pillow** *Little Anthony & The Imperials*
59/61 **Tears On My Pillow** *McGuire Sisters*
67/89 **Tears Run Rings** *Marc Almond*
93/67 **Tears, Tears, Tears** *Ben E. King*
85/59 **Teasable, Pleasable You** *Buddy Knox*
70/66 **Teaser, The** *Bob Kuban*
39/59 **Teasin'** *Quaker City Boys*
97/65 **Teasin' You** *Willie Tee*
17/60 **Teddy** *Connie Francis*
40/76 **Teddy Bear** *Red Sovine*
73/93 **Teddy Bear** *G-Wiz*
(also see: Let Me Be Your)
32/73 **Teddy Bear Song** *Barbara Fairchild*
66/76 **Teddy Bear's Last Ride** *Diana Williams*

TEEN:

Teen Age ..also see: Teenage
2/57 **Teen-Age Crush** *Tommy Sands*
81/58 **Teen-Age Doll** *Tommy Sands*
45/56 **Teen Age Goodnight** *Chordettes*
5/62 **Teen Age Idol** *Rick Nelson*
Teen Age Prayer
6/56 *Gale Storm*
19/56 *Gloria Mann*
68/56 *Kitty White*
90/55 **Teen-Ager's Waltz** *Eddy Howard*
Teen Angel
1/60 *Mark Dinning*
79/74 *Wednesday*
Teen Beat
4/59 *Sandy Nelson*
44/64 *Sandy Nelson ('65)*
29/59 **Teen Commandments** *Paul Anka-Geo. Hamilton IV-Johnny Nash*
47/60 **Teen-Ex** *Browns*
92/62 **Teen Queen Of The Week** *Freddy Cannon*
75/63 **Teenage Cleopatra** *Tracey Dey*
93/60 **Teenage Hayride** *Tender Slim*
58/63 **Teenage Heaven** *Johnny Cymbal*
99/59 **Teenage Heaven** *Eddie Cochran*
48/74 **Teenage Lament '74** *Alice Cooper*
80/74 **Teenage Love Affair** *Rick Derringer*
80/56 **Teenage Meeting (Gonna Rock It Up Right)** *Don Cornell*
Teenage Queen ..see: Ballad Of
50/60 **Teenage Sonata** *Sam Cooke*
94/60 **Teenager Feels It Too** *Denny Reed*
5/59 **Teenager In Love** *Dion & The Belmonts*
68/56 **Teenager's Mother (Are You Right?)** *Bill Haley*
66/66 **Teenager's Prayer** *Joe Simon*
2/57 **Teenager's Romance** *Ricky Nelson*
73/60 **Teensville** *Chet Atkins*
9/83 **Telefone (Long Distance Love Affair)** *Sheena Easton*
67/72 **Telegram Sam** *T. Rex*
7/77 **Telephone Line** *Electric Light Orchestra*
18/77 **Telephone Man** *Meri Wilson*

TELL:

57/69 **Tell All The People** *Doors*
89/72 **Tell 'Em Willie Boy's A'Comin'** *Tommy James*
39/01 **Tell Her** *Lonestar*
(also see: Tell Him)
1/83 **Tell Her About It** *Billy Joel*
66/60 **Tell Her For Me** *Adam Wade*
50/74 **Tell Her Love Has Felt The Need** *Eddie Kendricks*
Tell Her No
6/65 *Zombies*
27/83 *Juice Newton*
40/73 **Tell Her She's Lovely** *El Chicano*
57/65 **Tell Her (You Love Her Every Day)** *Frank Sinatra*
Tell Him [Her]
4/63 *Exciters*
97/66 *Dean Parrish*
76/89 *Kenny Loggins*
58A/97 **Tell Him** *Celine Dion & Barbra Streisand*
Tell Him
90/64 *Drew-Vels*
85/67 *Patti Drew*
42/63 **Tell Him I'm Not Home** *Chuck Jackson*
Tell Him No
8/59 *Travis & Bob*
42/59 *Dean & Marc*
17/70 **Tell It All Brother** *Kenny Rogers & The First Edition*
Tell It Like It Is
2/67 *Aaron Neville*
72/76 *Andy Williams*
8/81 *Heart*
33/64 **Tell It On The Mountain** *Peter, Paul & Mary*
7/88 **Tell It To My Heart** *Taylor Dayne*
10/67 **Tell It To The Rain** *4 Seasons*
Tell Laura I Love Her
7/60 *Ray Peterson*
94/74 *Johnny T. Angel*
23/68 **Tell Mama** *Etta James*
83/71 **Tell Mama** *Savoy Brown*
5/95 **Tell Me** *Groove Theory*
18/96 **Tell Me** *Dru Hill*
22/62 **Tell Me** *Dick & DeeDee*
58/88 **Tell Me** *White Lion*
21/74 **Tell Me A Lie** *Sami Jo*
69/64 **Tell Me Baby** *Garnet Mimms*
55A/97 **Tell Me Do U Wanna** *Ginuwine*
46S/00 **Tell Me How You Feel** *Joy Enriquez*
50/96 **Tell Me (I'll Be Around)** *Shades*
60/89 **Tell Me I'm Not Dreaming** *Robert Palmer*
65/84 **Tell Me If You Still Care** *S.O.S. Band*
Tell Me It's Real
2/99 *K-Ci & JoJo*
47S/02 *K-Ci & JoJo*
85/64 **Tell Me Mamma** *Christine Quaite*
31/90 **Tell Me Something** *Indecent Obsession*
3/74 **Tell Me Something Good** *Rufus*
83/74 **Tell Me That I'm Wrong** *Blood, Sweat & Tears*
51/60 **Tell Me That You Love Me** *Fats Domino*
73/63 **Tell Me The Truth** *Nancy Wilson*
86/72 **Tell Me This Is A Dream** *Delfonics*
37/67 **Tell Me To My Face** *Keith*
33/82 **Tell Me Tomorrow** *Smokey Robinson*
43/93 **Tell Me What You Dream** *Restless Heart*
6/92 **Tell Me What You Want Me To Do** *Tevin Campbell*
91/02 **Tell Me What's It Gonna Be** *Brian McKnight*
31/95 **Tell Me When** *Human League*
(also see: Quando, Quando, Quando)
88/94 **Tell Me Where It Hurts** *Kathy Troccoli*
9/90 **Tell Me Why** *Exposé*
13/64 **Tell Me Why** *Bobby Vinton*
18/61 **Tell Me Why** *Belmonts*
Tell Me Why
45/56 *Crew Cuts*
52/56 *Gale Storm*
33/66 *Elvis Presley*
77/93 **Tell Me Why** *Wynonna*
98/71 **Tell Me Why** *Matthews' Southern Comfort*
72S/00 **Tell Me Why (The Riddle)** *Paul van Dyk*
24/64 **Tell Me (You're Coming Back)** *Rolling Stones*
92/68 **Tell Someone You Love Them** *Dino, Desi & Billy*
87/88 **Tell That Girl To Shut Up** *Transvision Vamp*
57/93 **Tell The Truth** *Jude Cole*
94/76 **Tell The World How I Feel About 'Cha Baby** *Harold Melvin*
50/59 **Telling Lies** *Fats Domino*
1/62 **Telstar** *Tornadoes*
39/70 **Temma Harbour** *Mary Hopkin*
66S/00 **Temperamental** *Everything But The Girl*
39/91 **Temple Of Love** *Harriet*
6/91 **Temptation** *Corina*
Temptation
56/60 *Roger Williams*
27/61 *Everly Brothers*
93/67 *Boots Randolph*
70/65 **Temptation 'Bout To Get Me** *Knight Bros.*
15/71 **Temptation Eyes** *Grass Roots*
68/95 **Temptations** *2Pac*
49/81 **Tempted** *Squeeze*
81/67 **Ten Commandments** *Prince Buster*
(also see: Teen Commandments)
Ten Commandments Of Love
22/58 *Harvey & The Moonglows*
94/63 *James MacArthur*
55/68 *Peaches & Herb*
82/69 *Little Anthony & The Imperials*
43/65 **10 Little Bottles** *Johnny Bond*
49/63 **Ten Little Indians** *Beach Boys*
96/67 **Ten Little Indians** *Yardbirds*
45/62 **Ten Lonely Guys** *Pat Boone*
38/84 **10-9-8** *Face To Face*
20S/02 **10 Out Of 10** *Louchie Lou & Michie One*
54/76 **Ten Percent** *Double Exposure*
26/02 **Ten Rounds With José Cuervo** *Tracy Byrd*
43/59 **Ten Thousand Drums** *Carl Smith*
68/77 **Ten To Eight** *David Castle*
25/83 **Tender Is The Night** *Jackson Browne*
42/91 **Tender Kisses** *Tracie Spencer*
10/86 **Tender Love** *Force M.D.'s*
Tender, Love and Care ..see: T.L.C.
14/90 **Tender Lover** *Babyface*
Tender Trap ..see: (Love Is)

Tender Years
78/84 *John Cafferty*
31/85 *John Cafferty*
76/61 **Tender Years** *George Jones*
31/61 **Tenderly** *Bert Kaempfert*
27/85 **Tenderness** *General Public*
6/92 **Tennessee** *Arrested Development*
69/62 **Tennessee** *Jan & Dean*
23/70 **Tennessee Bird Walk** *Jack Blanchard & Misty Morgan*
84/61 **Tennessee Flat-Top Box** *Johnny Cash*
48/59 **Tennessee Stud** *Eddy Arnold*
Tennessee Waltz
52/59 *Bobby Comstock*
63/59 *Jerry Fuller*
35/64 *Sam Cooke*
83/76 **Tenth Avenue Freeze-Out** *Bruce Springsteen*
Tequila
1/58 *Champs*
20/58 *Eddie Platt*
99/62 *Champs (Twist)*
91/64 *Bill Black's Combo*
48/92 *A.L.T. & The Lost Civilization*
64/73 **Tequila Sunrise** *Eagles*
70/98 **Tequila Sunrise** *Cypress Hill*
Terms Of Endearment ..see: Theme From
71/85 **Test Of Time** *Romantics*
Testify ..see: (I Wanna)
85/61 **Texan And A Girl From Mexico** *Anita Bryant*
91/76 **Texas** *Charlie Daniels Band*
51/80 **Texas In My Rear View Mirror** *Mac Davis*
91/56 **Texas Lady** *Les Paul & Mary Ford*

THANK:

90/70 **Thank God And Greyhound** *Roy Clark*
97/72 **Thank God For You Baby** *PG&E*
1/00 **Thank God I Found You** *Mariah Carey With Joe & 98°*
1/75 **Thank God I'm A Country Boy** *John Denver*
22/78 **Thank God It's Friday** *Love & Kisses*
2A/98 **Thank U** *Alanis Morissette*
3/01 **Thankyou** *Dido*
21/95 **Thank You** *Boyz II Men*
75/92 **Thank You** *Cover Girls*
93/02 **Thank You** *Lil Bow Wow*
84/63 **Thank You And Goodnight** *Angels*
63/64 **Thank You Baby** *Shirelles*
70/75 **Thank You Baby** *Stylistics*
1/70 **Thank You (Falettinme Be Mice Elf Agin)** *Sly & The Family Stone*
25/78 **Thank You For Being A Friend** *Andrew Gold*
57/01 **Thank You For Loving Me** *Bon Jovi*
35/64 **Thank You Girl** *Beatles*
96/70 **Thank You Girl** *Street People*
80/01 **Thank You In Advance** *Boyz II Men*
16/59 **Thank You Pretty Baby** *Brook Benton*
69/68 **Thank U Very Much** *Scaffold*
45/65 **Thanks A Lot** *Brenda Lee*
32/88 **Thanks For My Child** *Cheryl Pepsii Riley*
37/74 **Thanks For Saving My Life** *Billy Paul*
61/75 **Thanks For The Smiles** *Charlie Ross*
67A/96 **Thanksgiving Song** *Adam Sandler*

THAT:

70/67 **That Acapulco Gold** *Rainy Daze*
16/87 **That Ain't Love** *REO Speedwagon*
64/64 **That Boy John** *Raindrops*
69/81 **That Didn't Hurt Too Bad** *Dr. Hook*
7/99 **That Don't Impress Me Much** *Shania Twain*
97/71 **That Evil Child** *B.B. King*
4/82 **That Girl** *Stevie Wonder*
20/96 **That Girl** *Maxi Priest*
49/64 **That Girl Belongs To Yesterday** *Gene Pitney*
22/80 **That Girl Could Sing** *Jackson Browne*
74/62 **That Greasy Kid Stuff** *Janie Grant*
67/62 **That Happy Feeling** *Bert Kaempfert*
76/68 **That Kind Of Woman** *Merrilee Rush*
(That Kiss!) ..see: Eso Beso
6/73 **That Lady** *Isley Brothers*
55/80 **That Lovin' You Feelin' Again** *Roy Orbison & Emmylou Harris*
20/64 **That Lucky Old Sun** *Ray Charles*
77/77 **That Magic Touch** *Angel*
That Old Black Magic
13/55 *Sammy Davis, Jr.*
18/58 *Louis Prima & Keely Smith*
21/61 *Bobby Rydell*
55/60 **That Old Feeling** *Kitty Kallen*
21/81 **That Old Song** *Ray Parker Jr.*
47/78 **That Once In A Lifetime** *Demis Roussos*
64/00 **That Other Woman** *Changing Faces*
That Same Old Feeling
62/70 *Fortunes*
67/70 *Pickettywitch*
56S/00 **That Smut** *Smut Peddlers*
63/74 **That Song Is Driving Me Crazy** *Tom T. Hall*
28/62 **That Stranger Used To Be My Girl** *Trade Martin*
12/63 **That Sunday, That Summer** *Nat King Cole*
41/96 **That Thing You Do!** *Wonders*
5S/02 **That Was Then** *Roy Jones Jr.*
89/84 **That Was Then But This Is Now** *ABC*
20/86 **That Was Then, This Is Now** *Monkees*
12/85 **That Was Yesterday** *Foreigner*
That'll Be The Day
1/57 *Crickets*
11/76 *Linda Ronstadt*

THAT'S:

64/68 **That's A Lie** *Ray Charles*
6/84 **That's All!** *Genesis*
17/56 **That's All** *"Tennessee" Ernie Ford*
48/63 **That's All** *Rick Nelson*
98/59 **That's All I Want** *Bobby Day*
That's All I Want From You
3/55 *Jaye P. Morgan*
86/57 *Silva-Tones*
16/56 **That's All There Is To That** *Nat "King" Cole/Four Knights*
6/60 **That's All You Gotta Do** *Brenda Lee*
78/58 **That's Alright** *Little Junior Parker*
70S/95 **That's As Close As I'll Get To Loving You** *Aaron Tippin*
62/66 **That's Enough** *Rosco Robinson*
64/87 **That's Freedom** *Tom Kimmel*
That's How Heartaches Are Made
40/63 *Baby Washington*
97/69 *Marvelettes*
96/01 **That's How I Beat Shaq** *Aaron Carter*
88/63 **That's How It Goes** *George Maharis*
F/75 **That's How Long** *Chi-Lites*
46/72 **That's How Love Goes** *Jermaine Jackson*
74/60 **That's How Much** *Brian Hyland*
39/58 **That's How Much I Love You** *Pat Boone*
74/65 **That's How Strong My Love Is** *Otis Redding*
31/61 **That's It - I Quit - I'm Movin' On** *Sam Cooke*
76/02 **That's Just Jessie** *Kevin Denney*
93/95 **That's Just What You Are** *Aimee Mann*
That's Life
4/66 *Frank Sinatra*
85/86 *David Lee Roth*
51/62 **That's Life (That's Tough)** *Gabriel & The Angels*
28/83 **That's Love** *Jim Capaldi*
69/62 **That's My Desire** *Yvonne Baker*
55/59 **That's My Little Suzie** *Ritchie Valens*
51/62 **That's My Pa** *Sheb Wooley*
77/90 **That's Not Her Style** *Billy Joel*
82/74 **That's Not How It Goes** *Bloodstone*
9/62 **That's Old Fashioned (That's The Way Love Should Be)** *Everly Brothers*
92/64 **That's Really Some Good** *Rufus & Carla*
51/97 **That's Right** *DJ Taz*
3/77 **That's Rock 'N' Roll** *Shaun Cassidy*
92/67 **That's Someone You Never Forget** *Elvis Presley*
71/00 **That's The Kind Of Mood I'm In** *Patty Loveless*
88/63 **That's The Only Way** *Four Seasons*
70/74 **That's The Sound That Lonely Makes** *Tavares*
F/77 **That's The Trouble** *Grace Jones*
99/66 **That's The Tune** *Vogues*
16/89 **That's The Way** *Katrina & The Waves*
25/00 **That's The Way** *Jo Dee Messina*
94/69 **That's The Way** *Joe Tex*
62/71 **That's The Way A Woman Is** *Messengers*
12/64 **That's The Way Boys Are** *Lesley Gore*
That's The Way God Planned It
62/69 *Billy Preston*
65/72 *Billy Preston*
27/72 **That's The Way I Feel About Cha** *Bobby Womack*
1/75 **That's The Way (I Like It)** *KC & The Sunshine Band*
93/70 **That's The Way I Want Our Love** *Joe Simon*
10/71 **That's The Way I've Always Heard It Should Be** *Carly Simon*
6/00 **That's The Way It Is** *Celine Dion*
1/93 **That's The Way Love Goes** *Janet Jackson*
54/91 **That's The Way Love Goes** *Young M.C.*
7/69 **That's The Way Love Is** *Marvin Gaye*
33/63 **That's The Way Love Is** *Bobby Bland*
57/93 **That's The Way Love Is** *Bobby Brown*

12/75 **That's The Way Of The World** *Earth, Wind & Fire*

59/90 **That's The Way Of The World** *D Mob w/Cathy Dennis*

44[S]/01 **That's The Way We Roll** *Alley Life*

59/61 **That's The Way With Love** *Piero Soffici*

1/86 **That's What Friends Are For** *Dionne Warwick*

74/72 **That's What Friends Are For** *B.J. Thomas*

27/61 **That's What Girls Are Made For** *Spinners*

7[S]/02 **That's What Girls Do** *No Secrets*

69/90 **That's What I Like (medley)** *Jive Bunny & the Mastermixers*

6[X]/63 **That's What I Want For Christmas** *Nancy Wilson*

56/00 **That's What I'm Looking For** *Da Brat*

68/93 **That's What Little Girls Are Made Of** *Raven-Symoné*

18/93 **That's What Love Can Do** *Boy Krazy*

19/87 **That's What Love Is All About** *Michael Bolton*

7/91 **That's What Love Is For** *Amy Grant*

35/64 **That's What Love Is Made Of** *Miracles*

59/72 **That's What Love Will Make You Do** *Little Milton*

72/64 **(That's) What The Nitty Gritty Is** *Shirley Ellis*

83/60 **That's When I Cried** *Jimmy Jones*

37/02 **That's When I Love You** *Phil Vassar*

100/89 **That's When I Think Of You** *1927*

63/64 **That's When It Hurts** *Ben E. King*

27/75 **That's When The Music Takes Me** *Neil Sedaka*

58/57 **That's When Your Heartaches Begin** *Elvis Presley*

29/70 **That's Where I Went Wrong** *Poppy Family*

93/64 **That's Where It's At** *Sam Cooke*

27/76 **That's Where The Happy People Go** *Trammps*

55/91 **That's Why** *Party*

88/59 **That's Why I Cry** *Buddy Knox*

68/76 **That's Why I Love You** *Andrew Gold*

13/59 **That's Why (I Love You So)** *Jackie Wilson*

84/57 **That's Why I Was Born** *Janice Harper*

79/98 **That's Why I'm Here** *Kenny Chesney*

82/73 **That's Why You Remember** *Kenny Karen*

88/69 **That's Your Baby** *Joe Tex*

48/56 **That's Your Mistake** *Otis Williams*

50/78 **That's Your Secret** *Sea Level*

Them Changes
81/70 *Buddy Miles*
62/71 *Buddy Miles*
F/72 *Carlos Santana & Buddy Miles*

58/61 **Them That Got** *Ray Charles*

THEME:

35/60 **Theme For Young Lovers** *Percy Faith*

Theme From A Summer Place
1/60 *Percy Faith*
64/62 *Dick Roman*
16/65 *Lettermen*
83/69 *Ventures*

97/60 **Theme From Adventures In Paradise** *Jerry Byrd*

96/63 **Theme From Any Number Can Win** *Jimmy Smith*

28/62 **Theme From Ben Casey** *Valjean*

Theme From Bonnie & Clyde ..see: Foggy Mountain Breakdown

45/77 **(Theme from) Charlie's Angels** *Henry Mancini*

18/73 **Theme From Cleopatra Jones** *Joe Simon*

Theme From Close Encounters
13/78 *John Williams*
25/78 *Meco*

39/61 **Theme From Dixie** *Duane Eddy*

59/83 **Theme From Doctor Detroit** *Devo*

10/62 **Theme From Dr. Kildare (Three Stars Will Shine Tonight)** *Richard Chamberlain*

52/82 **Theme From Dynasty** *Bill Conti*

73/56 **Theme From East Of Eden** *Dick Jacobs*

(Theme From El Dorado) ..see: Someday Out Of The Blue

95/69 **Theme From Electric Surfboard** *Brother Jack McDuff*

Theme From Exorcist ..see: Tubular Bells

85/61 **(Theme From) "Goodbye Again"** *Ferrante & Teicher*

2/81 **Theme From Greatest American Hero (Believe It Or Not)** *Joey Scarbury*

61/65 **Theme From Harlow (Lonely Girl)** *Bobby Vinton*

95/62 **Theme From Hatari!** *Henry Mancini*

10/81 **Theme From Hill Street Blues** *Mike Post*

76/79 **Theme From Ice Castles (Through The Eyes Of Love)** *Melissa Manchester*

32/75 **Theme From Jaws (Main Title)** *John Williams*

68/77 **Theme From King Kong** *Love Unlimited Orchestra*

84/63 **Theme From Lawrence Of Arabia** *Ferrante & Teicher*

Theme From Love Story
9/71 *Andy Williams (Where Do I Begin)*
13/71 *Henry Mancini*
31/71 *Francis Lai*

25/82 **(Theme From) Magnum P.I.** *Mike Post*

1/76 **Theme From Mahogany (Do You Know Where You're Going To)** *Diana Ross*

Theme From Mission: Impossible
41/68 *Lalo Schifrin*
7/96 *Adam Clayton & Larry Mullen*
(also see: Impossible Mission)

Theme from Moonlighting ..see: Moonlighting

55/61 **Theme From My Three Sons** *Lawrence Welk*

32/80 **Theme From New York, New York** *Frank Sinatra*

Theme From Picnic ..see: Moonglow

Theme From Pink Panther ..see: Pink Panther Theme

82/81 **Theme From Raging Bull (Cavalleria Rusticana)** *Joel Diamond*

Theme From Rocky ..see: Gonna Fly Now

91/88 **Theme From S-Express** *S-Express*

1/71 **Theme From Shaft** *Isaac Hayes*

83/61 **(Theme From) Silver City** *Ventures*

94/56 **(Theme from) Song Of The Sparrow** *Mitch Miller*

Theme From Summer Of '42
21/71 *Peter Nero*
57/75 *Biddu Orchestra*

Theme From Superfly ..see: Freddie's Dead

81/79 **Theme From Superman (Main Title)** *John Williams*

1/76 **Theme From S.W.A.T.** *Rhythm Heritage*

100/62 **Theme From Taras Bulba (The Wishing Star)** *Jerry Butler*

84/84 **Theme From Terms Of Endearment** *Michael Gore*

10/60 **Theme From The Apartment** *Ferrante & Teicher*

Theme From The Circus ..see: Computer Game

70/60 **Theme From The Dark At The Top Of The Stairs** *Ernie Freeman*

21/80 **Theme From The Dukes Of Hazzard (Good Ol' Boys)** *Waylon Jennings*

90/61 **(Theme from) The Great Impostor** *Henry Mancini*

Theme From The Man With The Golden Arm ..see: Man With The Golden Arm

38/72 **Theme From The Men** *Isaac Hayes*

Theme From The Proud Ones
39/56 *Nelson Riddle*
72/56 *Lionel Newman*
95/56 *LeRoy Holmes*

Theme From The Sundowners
51/60 *Billy Vaughn*
70/60 *Felix Slatkin*
93/60 *Mantovani*

Theme From The Three Penny Opera ..see: Mack The Knife

27/60 **Theme From The Unforgiven (The Need For Love)** *Don Costa*

99/66 **Theme From The Wild Angels** *Davie Allan*

Theme From Tunes Of Glory
60/61 *Cambridge Strings & Singers*
88/61 *Mitch Miller*

Theme From Valley Of The Dolls
2/68 *Dionne Warwick*
83/68 *King Curtis*

21/78 **Theme From Which Way Is Up** *Stargard*

55/97 **Theme (It's Party Time)** *Tracey Lee*

47/82 **Themes From E.T. (The Extra-Terrestrial)** *Walter Murphy*

35/78 **Themes From The Wizard Of Oz** *Meco*

1/74 **Then Came You** *Dionne Warwicke & Spinners*

91/91 **Then Came You** *T.P.E.*

6/63 **Then He Kissed Me** *Crystals*

86/65 **Then I'll Count Again** *Johnny Tillotson*

94/70 **Then She's A Lover** *Roy Clark*

11/00 **Then The Morning Comes** *Smash Mouth*

65/98 **Then What?** *Clay Walker*

Then You Can Tell Me Goodbye
6/67 *Casinos*
84/68 *Eddy Arnold*
27/76 *Glen Campbell (medley)*
57/79 *Toby Beau*

THERE:

68/73 **There Ain't No Way** *Lobo*
50/65 **There But For Fortune** *Joan Baez*
77/79 **There But For The Grace Of God Go I** *Machine*
71/59 **There Comes A Time** *Jack Scott*
34/75 **There Goes Another Love Song** *Outlaws*
There Goes My Baby
2/59 *Drifters*
21/84 *Donna Summer*
93/98 **There Goes My Baby** *Trisha Yearwood*
There Goes My Everything
20/67 *Engelbert Humperdinck*
65/67 *Jack Greene*
F/71 *Elvis Presley*
19/58 **There Goes My Heart** *Joni James*
59/63 **There Goes (My Heart Again)** *Fats Domino*
98/67 **There Goes The Lover** *Gene Chandler*
There, I've Said It Again
81/59 *Sam Cooke*
1/64 *Bobby Vinton*
20/68 **There Is** *Dells*
11/67 **There Is A Mountain** *Donovan*
(There Is Love) ..see: Wedding Song
40/01 **There Is No Arizona** *Jamie O'Neal*
28X/68 **There Is No Christmas Like A Home Christmas** *Perry Como*
88/62 **There Is No Greater Love** *Wanderers*
91/71 **There It Goes Again** *Barbara & The Uniques*
32/73 **There It Is** *Tyrone Davis*
43/72 **There It Is** *James Brown*
66/01 **There It Is** *Ginuwine*
There Must Be A Way
33/59 *Joni James*
93/67 *Jimmy Roselli*
22/85 **There Must Be An Angel (Playing With My Heart)** *Eurythmics*
77/69 **There Never Was A Time** *Jeannie C. Riley*
47/57 **There Oughta Be A Law** *Mickey & Sylvia*
26/61 **There She Goes** *Jerry Wallace*
31/01 **There She Goes** *Babyface*
There She Goes
49/91 *La's*
32/99 *Sixpence None The Richer*
54/55 **There Should Be Rules (Protecting Fools Who Fall In Love)** *Betty Madigan*
23/60 **(There Was A) Tall Oak Tree** *Dorsey Burnette*
There Was A Time
36/68 *James Brown*
82/68 *Gene Chandler*
42/77 **There Will Come A Day (I'm Gonna Happen To You)** *Smokey Robinson*
31/92 **There Will Never Be Another Tonight** *Bryan Adams*
33/66 **There Will Never Be Another You** *Chris Montez*
63/74 **There Will Never Be Any Peace (Until God Is Seated At The Conference Table)** *Chi-Lites*
8X/65 **There Won't Be Any Snow (Christmas In The Jungle)** *Derrik Roberts*
18/74 **There Won't Be Anymore** *Charlie Rich*
73/76 **There Won't Be No Country Music (There Won't Be No Rock 'N' Roll)** *C.W. McCall*
57/98 **There You Are** *Sam Salter*
60/00 **There You Are** *Martina McBride*
7/00 **There You Go** *P!nk*
80/73 **There You Go** *Edwin Starr*
41/99 **There You Have It** *BlackHawk*
10/01 **There You'll Be** *Faith Hill*
75/62 **There'll Be No Next Time** *Jackie Wilson*
25/57 **(There'll Be) Peace In The Valley (For Me)** *Elvis Presley*
1/86 **There'll Be Sad Songs (To Make You Cry)** *Billy Ocean*
84/65 **(There'll Come A Day When) Ev'ry Little Bit Hurts** *Bobby Vee*
26/69 **There'll Come A Time** *Betty Everett*
36/78 **There'll Never Be** *Switch*

THERE'S:

81/67 **There's A Chance We Can Make It** *Blues Magoos*
97/59 **There's A Girl** *Jan & Dean*
14/57 **There's A Gold Mine In The Sky** *Pat Boone*
There's A Kind Of Hush (All Over The World)
4/67 *Herman's Hermits*
12/76 *Carpenters*
3/61 **There's A Moon Out Tonight** *Capris*
88/90 **There's A Party Going On** *Yvonne*
74/64 **There's A Place** *Beatles*
64/60 **There's A Star Spangled Banner Waving #2 (The Ballad Of Francis Powers)** *Red River Dave*
56/67 **There's Always Me** *Elvis Presley*
(There's) Always Something There To Remind Me
49/64 *Lou Johnson*
52/65 *Sandie Shaw*
65/68 *Dionne Warwick*
27/70 *R.B. Greaves*
8/83 *Naked Eyes*
21/69 **There's Gonna Be A Showdown** *Archie Bell*
34/67 **There's Got To Be A Word!** *Innocence*
88/74 **There's Got To Be Rain In Your Life (To Appreciate The Sunshine)** *Dorothy Norwood*
58/84 **There's No Easy Way** *James Ingram*
68/59 **There's No Fool Like A Young Fool** *Tab Hunter*
5/81 **(There's) No Gettin' Over Me** *Ronnie Milsap*
50/66 **There's No Living Without Your Loving** *Peter & Gordon*
43/73 **There's No Me Without You** *Manhattans*
20/62 **There's No Other (Like My Baby)** *Crystals*
82/92 **There's No Other Way** *Blur*
8/54 **(There's No Place Like) Home For The Holidays** *Perry Como*
50/87 **There's Nothing Better Than Love** *Luther Vandross*
47/64 **There's Nothing I Can Say** *Rick Nelson*
There's Nothing Stronger Than Our Love ..see: (I Believe)
10/58 **There's Only One Of You** *Four Lads*
77/57 **There's Only You** *Don Rondo*
98/71 **There's So Much Love All Around Me** *Three Degrees*
There's Something On Your Mind
44/59 *Big Jay McNeely*
31/60 *Bobby Marchan*
69/66 *Baby Ray*
12/88 **There's The Girl** *Heart*
36/98 **There's Your Trouble** *Dixie Chicks*
66/92 **These Are Days** *10,000 Maniacs*
55/69 **These Are Not My People** *Johnny Rivers*
64/02 **These Are The Days** *O-Town*
21/99 **These Are The Times** *Dru Hill*
85/63 **These Arms Of Mine** *Otis Redding*
1/66 **These Boots Are Made For Walkin'** *Nancy Sinatra*
(also see: Puss N' Boots)
23/02 **These Days** *Rascal Flatts*
1/86 **These Dreams** *Heart*
These Eyes
6/69 *Guess Who?*
16/69 *Jr. Walker*
55/63 **These Foolish Things** *James Brown*
81/56 **These Hands** *Len Dresslar*
63/65 **These Hands (Small But Mighty)** *Bobby Bland*
53/87 **These Times Are Hard For Lovers** *John Waite*
50/71 **They Can't Take Away Our Music** *Eric Burdon & War*
30/96 **They Don't Care About Us** *Michael Jackson*
7/98 **They Don't Know** *Jon B*
8/84 **They Don't Know** *Tracey Ullman*
99/68 **They Don't Make Love Like They Used To** *Eddy Arnold*
5/75 **They Just Can't Stop It the (Games People Play)** *Spinners*
35/97 **They Like It Slow** *H-Town*
(They Long To Be) Close To You
1/70 *Carpenters*
91/72 *Jerry Butler & Brenda Lee Eager*
82/76 *B.T. Express*
53/63 **They Remind Me Too Much Of You** *Elvis Presley*
58/92 **They Reminisce Over You (T.R.O.Y.)** *Pete Rock & C.L. Smooth*
37S/02 **They-Say Vision** *Res*
25/92 **They Want EFX** *DAS EFX*
They're Coming To Take Me Away, Ha-Haaa!
3/66 *Napoleon XIV*
87/73 *Napoleon XIV*
77/67 **They're Here** *Boots Walker*
Thicker Than Water ..see: (Love Is)
86/84 **Thief Of Hearts** *Melissa Manchester*
6/90 **Thieves In The Temple** *Prince*
Thin Line Between Love & Hate
15/71 *Persuaders*
83/84 *Pretenders*
37/96 *H-Town*
Thing ..also see: Do The Thing
41/61 **Thing Of The Past** *Shirelles*
Things
3/62 *Bobby Darin*
89/76 *Anne Murray*
5/85 **Things Can Only Get Better** *Howard Jones*
60/58 **Things I Love** *Fidelity's*
89/56 **Things I Never Had** *Kay Starr*
23/67 **Things I Should Have Said** *Grass Roots*

16/69 **Things I'd Like To Say** *New Colony Six*
63^S/00 **Things I've Seen** *Spooks*
86/64 **Things In This House** *Bobby Darin*
56/97 **Things Just Ain't The Same** *Deborah Cox*
99/64 **Things That I Used To Do** *James Brown*
4/91 **Things That Make You Go Hmmmm...** *C + C Music Factory*
41/96 **Things That You Do** *Gina Thompson*
46/62 **Things We Did Last Summer** *Shelley Fabares*
5/77 **Things We Do For Love** *10 CC*
95/96 **Things We Do For Love** *Horace Brown*
29/97 **Things'll Never Change** *E-40*

THINK:

7/68 **Think** *Aretha Franklin*
25/64 **Think** *Brenda Lee*
28/90 **Think** *Information Society*
Think
66/57 *"5" Royales*
33/60 *James Brown*
100/67 *Vicki Anderson & James Brown*
77/73 *James Brown*
80/73 *James Brown*
95/65 **Think** *Jimmy McCracklin*
66/72 **Think (About It)** *Lyn Collins*
20/80 **Think About Me** *Fleetwood Mac*
87/70 **Think About Your Children** *Mary Hopkin*
27^S/02 **Think Big** *Crimewave*
65/71 **Think His Name** *Johnny Rivers*
30/66 **Think I'll Go Somewhere And Cry Myself To Sleep** *Al Martino*
16/82 **Think I'm In Love** *Eddie Money*
27/58 **Think It Over** *Crickets*
34/78 **Think It Over** *Cheryl Ladd*
66/60 **Think Me A Kiss** *Clyde McPhatter*
9/84 **Think Of Laura** *Christopher Cross*
74/66 **Think Of Me** *Buck Owens*
57/65 **Think Of The Good Times** *Jay & The Americans*
58/95 **Think Of You** *Usher*
11/61 **Think Twice** *Brook Benton*
93/66 **Think Twice** *Jackie Wilson & LaVern Baker*
95/94 **Think Twice** *Celine Dion*
16/92 **Thinkin' Back** *Color Me Badd*
12/98 **Thinkin' Bout It** *Gerald Levert*
40/94 **Thinkin' Problem** *David Ball*
12/89 **Thinking Of You** *Sa-Fire*
18/73 **Thinking Of You** *Loggins & Messina*
22/97 **Thinking Of You** *Tony Toni Toné*
45/76 **Thinking Of You** *Paul Davis*
67/88 **Thinking Of You** *Earth, Wind & Fire*
85/91 **Thinking Of You** *Grandmaster Slice*
82/57 **Third Finger - Left Hand** *Eileen Rodgers*
47/65 **3rd Man Theme** *Herb Alpert*
Third Rate Romance
14/75 *Amazing Rhythm Aces*
66^S/94 *Sammy Kershaw*
84/94 **Third Rock From The Sun** *Joe Diffie*
23/80 **Third Time Lucky (First Time I Was A Fool)** *Foghat*
49/71 **13 Questions** *Seatrain*
44/96 **13th, The** *Cure*
97/63 **31 Flavors** *Shirelles*
69/69 **30-60-90** *Willie Mitchell*
39/97 **Thirty-Three** *Smashing Pumpkins*
37/98 **32 Flavors** *Alana Davis*

THIS:

14/95 **This Ain't A Love Song** *Bon Jovi*
53/90 **This & That** *Michael Penn*
F/80 **This Beat Goes On** *Kings*
72/91 **This Beat Is Hot** *B.G. The Prince Of Rap*
This Bitter Earth
24/60 *Dinah Washington*
96/70 *Satisfactions*
(This Boy) ..see: Ringo's Theme
57/66 **This Can't Be True** *Eddie Holman*
11^X/72 **This Christmas** *Donny Hathaway*
10/86 **This Could Be The Night** *Loverboy*
87/92 **This Could Be The One** *Bad Company*
58/84 **This Could Be The Right One** *April Wine*
1/65 **This Diamond Ring** *Gary Lewis*
9/94 **This DJ** *Warren G*
12/66 **This Door Swings Both Ways** *Herman's Hermits*
84/63 **This Empty Place** *Dionne Warwick*
56/01 **This Everyday Love** *Rascal Flatts*
12/59 **This Friendly World** *Fabian*
49/99 **This Gift** *98°*
46/77 **This Girl (Has Turned Into A Woman)** *Mary MacGregor*
9/69 **This Girl Is A Woman Now** *Gary Puckett*
82/66 **This Golden Ring** *Fortunes*
This Guy's (Girl's) In Love With You
1/68 *Herb Alpert*
7/69 *Dionne Warwick*
24/74 **This Heart** *Gene Redding*
3/91 **This House** *Tracie Spencer*
F/95 **This House Is Not A Home** *Rembrandts*
5/00 **This I Promise You** **NSYNC*
26/59 **This I Swear** *Skyliners*
35^A/95 **This Is A Call** *Foo Fighters*
This Is All I Ask
67/63 *Burl Ives*
70/63 *Tony Bennett*
6/96 **This Is For The Lover In You** *Babyface*
1/95 **This Is How We Do It** *Montell Jordan*
51/98 **This Is How We Party** *S.O.A.P.*
11/80 **This Is It** *Kenny Loggins*
88/65 **This Is It** *Jim Reeves*
91/76 **This Is It** *Melba Moore*
91/79 **This Is It** *Dan Hartman*
35/78 **This Is Love** *Paul Anka*
58/79 **This Is Love** *Oak*
39/01 **This Is Me** *Dream*
25/69 **This Is My Country** *Impressions*
85/70 **This Is My Love Song** *Intruders*
60/85 **This Is My Night** *Chaka Khan*
5^S/03 **This Is My Party** *Fabolous*
60/63 **This Is My Prayer** *Theola Kilgore*
72/65 **This Is My Prayer** *Ray Charles Singers*
3/67 **This Is My Song** *Petula Clark*
100/60 **This Is My Story** *Mickey & Sylvia*
32/85 **This Is Not America** *David Bowie/Pat Metheny Group*
46/91 **This Is Ponderous** *2nu*
70/92 **This Is The Last Time** *Laura Enea*
69/58 **This Is The Nite** *Valiants*
21/90 **This Is The Right Time** *Lisa Stansfield*
65/68 **This Is The Thanks I Get** *Barbara Lynn*
18/87 **This Is The Time** *Billy Joel*
93/86 **This Is The Time** *Dennis DeYoung*
39/77 **This Is The Way That I Feel** *Marie Osmond*
86/92 **This Is The Way We Roll** *Hammer*
82/87 **This Is The World Calling** *Bob Geldof*
24/97 **This Is Your Night** *Amber*
86/73 **This Is Your Song** *Don Goodwin*
7/98 **This Kiss** *Faith Hill*
This Land Is Your Land
93/62 *New Christy Minstrels*
97/62 *Ketty Lester*
15/95 **This Lil' Game We Play** *Subway*
32/65 **This Little Bird** *Marianne Faithfull*
11/81 **This Little Girl** *Gary U.S. Bonds*
21/63 **This Little Girl** *Dion*
26/58 **This Little Girl Of Mine** *Everly Brothers*
24/58 **This Little Girl's Gone Rockin'** *Ruth Brown*
85/86 **This Love** *Bad Company*
This Magic Moment
16/60 *Drifters*
6/69 *Jay & The Americans*
33/82 **This Man Is Mine** *Heart*
10/76 **This Masquerade** *George Benson*
58/79 **This Moment In Time** *Engelbert Humperdinck*
62/83 **This Must Be The Place (Naive Melody)** *Talking Heads*
This Night Won't Last Forever
65/78 *Bill Labounty*
19/79 *Michael Johnson*
78/75 **This Ol' Cowboy** *Marshall Tucker Band*
79/60 **This Old Heart** *James Brown*
This Old Heart Of Mine
12/66 *Isley Brothers*
67/69 *Tammi Terrell*
83/76 *Rod Stewart*
10/90 *Rod Stewart (with Ronald Isley)*
This Old Man ..see: Children's Marching Song
This Ole House
1/54 *Rosemary Clooney*
26/54 *Stuart Hamblen*
94/89 **This One** *Paul McCartney*
7/89 **This One's For The Children** *New Kids On The Block*
29/76 **This One's For You** *Barry Manilow*
20/59 **This Should Go On Forever** *Rod Bernard*
25/77 **This Song** *George Harrison*
100/65 **This Sporting Life** *Ian Whitcomb*
30^S/99 **This Thing Called Love** *EYC*
6/61 **This Time** *Troy Shondell*
24/83 **This Time** *Bryan Adams*
27/80 **This Time** *John Cougar*
78/89 **This Time** *Kiara (with Shanice Wilson)*
81/85 **This Time** *INXS*
20/00 **This Time Around** *Hanson*
21^S/99 **This Time Around** *Michael Fredo*
7/89 **This Time I Know It's For Real** *Donna Summer*
42/74 **This Time I'm Gone For Good** *Bobby Blue Bland*
10/78 **This Time I'm In It For Love** *Player*
65/73 **This Time It's Real** *Tower Of Power*
54/91 **This Time Make It Funky** *Tracie Spencer*

This Time Of The Year
66/59 *Brook Benton*
12X/64 *Brenda Lee*
53/67 **This Town** *Frank Sinatra*
1/92 **This Used To Be My Playground** *Madonna*
6/75 **This Will Be** *Natalie Cole*
90/77 **This Will Be A Night To Remember** *Eddie Holman*
23/84 **This Woman** *Kenny Rogers*
57/00 **This Woman Needs** *SheDaisy*
58/02 **This Woman's Work** *Maxwell*
38/72 **This World** *Staple Singers*
90/61 **This World We Love In (Il Cielo In Una Stanza)** *Mina*
3/00 **Thong Song** *Sisqó*
80/92 **Thorn In My Pride** *Black Crowes*
68/86 **Thorn In My Side** *Eurythmics*
63/82 **Those Good Old Dreams** *Carpenters*
6/63 **Those Lazy-Hazy-Crazy Days Of Summer** *Nat King Cole*
9/61 **Those Oldies But Goodies (Remind Me Of You)** *Little Caesar & The Romans*
2/68 **Those Were The Days** *Mary Hopkin*
43/72 **Those Were The Days** *Carroll O'Connor & Jean Stapleton*
Thou Shalt Not Steal
73/62 *John D. Loudermilk*
13/65 *Dick & DeeDee*
13/92 **Thought I'd Died And Gone To Heaven** *Bryan Adams*
84/69 **Thought Of Loving You** *Crystal Mansion*
5/02 **Thousand Miles** *Vanessa Carlton*
Thousand Miles Away
53/57 *Heartbeats*
96/60 *Heartbeats*
72/67 **Thousand Shadows** *Seeds*
3/60 **Thousand Stars** *Kathy Young*
98/67 **Thread The Needle** *Clarence Carter*

THREE:

3A/98 **3 AM** *Matchbox 20*
5/91 **3 A.M. Eternal** *KLF*
Three Bells
1/59 *Browns*
23/59 *Dick Flood*
Three Hearts In A Tangle
35/61 *Roy Drusky*
93/62 *James Brown*
68/92 **360° (What Goes Around)** *Grand Puba*
24/67 **Three Little Fishes (medley)** *Mitch Ryder*
17/93 **Three Little Pigs** *Green Jellÿ*
89/00 **3 Little Words** *Nuflavor*
51A/97 **Three Marlenas** *Wallflowers*
15/60 **Three Nights A Week** *Fats Domino*
Three O'Clock In The Morning
33/65 *Bert Kaempfert*
83/65 *Lou Rawls*
Three Penny Opera ..see: Mack The Knife
36/74 **Three Ring Circus** *Blue Magic*
Three Stars
11/59 *Tommy Dee with Carol Kay*
99/59 *Ruby Wright*
(Three Stars Will Shine Tonight) ..see: Theme From Dr. Kildare
58/61 **Three Steps From The Altar** *Shep & The Limelites*
94/75 **Three Steps From True Love** *Reflections*
99/66 **3000 Miles** *Brian Hyland*
1/78 **Three Times A Lady** *Commodores*
19/80 **Three Times In Love** *Tommy James*
52/92 **3-2-1 Pump** *Redhead Kingpin & The F.B.I.*
28/64 **Three Window Coupe** *Rip Chords*
15/70 **Thrill Is Gone** *B.B. King*
4/84 **Thriller** *Michael Jackson*
66A/93 **Throb** *Janet Jackson*
(Through The Eyes Of Love) ..see: Theme From Ice Castles
60/85 **Through The Fire** *Chaka Khan*
81/03 **Through The Rain** *Mariah Carey*
90/94 **Through The Rain** *Tanya Blount*
16/89 **Through The Storm** *Aretha Franklin & Elton John*
13/82 **Through The Years** *Kenny Rogers*
14S/02 **Throw It Up** *Illicit Biznez*
45S/03 **Throw Up** *Racket City*
81/93 **Throw Ya Gunz** *Onyx*
63/96 **Throw Your Hands Up** *L.V.*
45/95 **Throw Your Set In The Air** *Cypress Hill*
67/87 **Throwaway** *Mick Jagger*
4/86 **Throwing It All Away** *Genesis*
87/03 **Thug Holiday** *Trick Daddy*
14S/02 **Thug Lady** *Dyshon & Squabble*
42/02 **Thug Lovin'** *Ja Rule*
22/94 **thuggish-ruggish-Bone** *Bone Thugs-N-Harmony*
19/02 **Thugz Mansion** *2Pac*
17/72 **Thunder And Lightning** *Chi Coltrane*
56/80 **Thunder And Lightning** *Chicago*
38/77 **Thunder In My Heart** *Leo Sayer*
9/78 **Thunder Island** *Jay Ferguson*
Thunder Road ..see: Ballad Of
25/66 **Thunderball** *Tom Jones*
55/84 **Ti Amo** *Laura Branigan*
14/90 **Tic-Tac-Toe** *Kyper*
81/98 **Tic Tic Tac** *Fruit De La Passion*
73/95 **Tic Toc** *Lords Of The Underground*
92/58 **Tic Toc** *Lee Allen*
65/90 **Tick Tock** *Vaughan Brothers*
Ticket To Ride
1/65 *Beatles*
54/70 *Carpenters*
70/65 **Tickle Me (EP)** *Elvis Presley*
Tide Is High
1/81 *Blondie*
89/97 *Angelina*
1/73 **Tie A Yellow Ribbon Round The Ole Oak Tree** *Dawn Feat. Tony Orlando*
3/63 **Tie Me Kangaroo Down, Sport** *Rolf Harris*
Tie Me To A Tree (Handcuff Me) ..see: Free Me From My Freedom
49/77 **Tie Your Mother Down** *Queen*
38/83 **Tied Up** *Olivia Newton-John*
37/60 **Ties That Bind** *Brook Benton*
3/59 **Tiger** *Fabian*
88/57 **Tiger Lily** *Rusty Draper*
11/72 **Tight Rope** *Leon Russell*
69S/02 **Tight Whips** *504 Boyz*
1/68 **Tighten Up** *Archie Bell*
7/70 **Tighter, Tighter** *Alive & Kicking*
71/71 **Tightrope Ride** *Doors*
12/59 **Tijuana Jail** *Kingston Trio*
38/66 **Tijuana Taxi** *Herb Alpert*

'TIL/TILL:

84/76 **'Til I Can Make It On My Own** *Tammy Wynette*
11/96 **Til I Hear It From You** *Gin Blossoms*
4/59 **('Til) I Kissed You** *Everly Brothers*
44/76 **'Til It's Time To Say Goodbye** *Jonathan Cain*
29/85 **'Til My Baby Comes Home** *Luther Vandross*
32/75 **Til The World Ends** *Three Dog Night*
77/83 **Til You And Your Lover Are Lovers Again** *Engelbert Humperdinck*
31/95 **'Til You Do Me Right** *After 7*
Till
22/57 *Roger Williams*
63/57 *Percy Faith*
14/62 *Angels*
27/68 *Vogues*
41/71 *Tom Jones*
26/62 **Till Death Do Us Part** *Bob Braun*
25/88 **Till I Loved You** *Barbra Streisand & Don Johnson*
51/91 **Till Somebody Loves You** *Henry Lee Summer*
50/66 **Till The End Of The Day** *Kinks*
83/64 **Till The End Of Time** *Ray Charles Singers*
20/63 **Till Then** *Classics*
Till There Was You
30/59 *Anita Bryant*
100/62 *Valjean*
67/69 **Till You Get Enough** *Watts 103rd Street Rhythm Band*
78/95 **Till You Love Me** *Reba McEntire*

TIME:

14/96 **Time** *Hootie & The Blowfish*
15/81 **Time** *Alan Parsons Project*
47/66 **Time** *Pozo-Seco Singers*
Time After Time
1/84 *Cyndi Lauper*
6/98 *Inoj*
40/90 **Time After Time** *Timmy -T-*
Time After Time
75/60 *Frankie Ford*
36/66 *Chris Montez*
75A/98 **Time Ago** *Black Lab*
94/67 **Time Alone Will Tell** *Connie Francis*
23/93 **Time And Chance** *Color Me Badd*
51/71 **Time And Love** *Barbra Streisand*
30/60 **Time And The River** *Nat King Cole*
26/88 **Time And Tide** *Basia*
83/77 **Time Bomb** *Lake*
48A/95 **Time Bomb** *Rancid*
2/83 **Time (Clock Of The Heart)** *Culture Club*
32/90 **Time For Letting Go** *Jude Cole*
32/74 **Time For Livin'** *Sly & The Family Stone*
39/68 **Time For Livin'** *Association*
Time For Me To Fly
56/78 *REO Speedwagon*
77/80 *REO Speedwagon*
(Time For Us) ..see: Love Theme From Romeo & Juliet
11/68 **Time Has Come Today** *Chambers Brothers*
1/73 **Time In A Bottle** *Jim Croce*
95/77 **Time Is Movin'** *Blackbyrds*
6/64 **Time Is On My Side** *Rolling Stones*
6/69 **Time Is Tight** *Booker T. & The M.G.'s*

15/81 **Time Is Time** *Andy Gibb*
7/91 **Time, Love And Tenderness** *Michael Bolton*
48/69 **Time Machine** *Grand Funk Railroad*
73/60 **Time Machine** *Danté & the Evergreens*
84/59 **Time Marches On** *Roy Hamilton*
Time Of My Life ..see: (I've Had)
3/69 **Time Of The Season** *Zombies*
22/81 **Time Out Of Mind** *Steely Dan*
7/78 **Time Passages** *Al Stewart*
100/67 **Time Seller** *Spencer Davis Group*
61/67 **Time, Time** *Ed Ames*
33/73 **Time To Get Down** *O'Jays*
96/70 **Time To Get It Together** *Country Coalition*
77/70 **Time To Kill** *Band*
Time To Love-A Time To Cry ..see: Petite Fleur
60/70 **Time Waits For No One** *Friends Of Distinction*
45/61 **Time Was** *Flamingos*
67/69 **Time Was** *Canned Heat*
18/84 **Time Will Reveal** *DeBarge*
69/74 **Time Will Tell** *Tower Of Power*
5/66 **Time Won't Let Me** *Outsiders*
85/90 **Timeless Love** *Saraya*
98/64 **Times Have Changed** *Irma Thomas*
7/76 **Times Of Your Life** *Paul Anka*
67/55 **Times Two, I Love You** *Three Chuckles*
56S/01 **Timmy And The Lords Of The Underworld** *Timmy & The Lords Of The Underworld*
17/71 **Timothy** *Buoys*
4/74 **Tin Man** *America*
73/68 **Tin Soldier** *Small Faces*
96/57 **Tina** *Easy Riders*
96/87 **Tina Cherry** *Georgio*
5/55 **Tina Marie** *Perry Como*
57/67 **Tiny Bubbles** *Don Ho*
41/72 **Tiny Dancer** *Elton John*
63/59 **Tiny Tim** *LaVern Baker*
Tip Of My Fingers
45/63 *Roy Clark*
43/66 *Eddy Arnold*
52/83 **Tip Of My Tongue** *Tubes*
83/67 **Tip Toe** *Robert Parker*
17/68 **Tip-Toe Thru' The Tulips With Me** *Tiny Tim*
44/66 **Tippy Toeing** *Harden Trio*
11/71 **Tired Of Being Alone** *Al Green*
70/85 **Tired Of Being Blonde** *Carly Simon*
79/66 **Tired Of Being Lonely** *Sharpees*
8/80 **Tired Of Toein' The Line** *Rocky Burnette*
6/65 **Tired Of Waiting For You** *Kinks*
86/68 **Tit For Tat (Ain't No Taking Back)** *James Brown*

TO:

To ..also see: Too / Two
26/62 **To A Sleeping Beauty** *Jimmy Dean*
55/59 **To A Soldier Boy** *Tassels*
5/84 **To All The Girls I've Loved Before** *Julio Iglesias & Willie Nelson*
To Be A Lover
45/69 *William Bell*
6/86 *Billy Idol*
94/67 **To Be A Lover** *Gene Chandler*
40S/01 **To Be Able To Love** *Jessica Folker*
22/58 **To Be Loved** *Jackie Wilson*
48/61 **To Be Loved (Forever)** *Pentagons*
1/92 **To Be With You** *Mr. Big*
84/57 **To Be With You** *Highlights*
76/70 **To Be Young, Gifted And Black** *Nina Simone*
62/82 **To Dream The Dream** *Frankie Miller*
To Each His Own
21/60 *Platters*
78/64 *Tymes*
82/68 *Frankie Laine*
50/75 **To Each His Own** *Faith Hope & Charity*
(To Everything There Is A Season) ..see: Turn! Turn! Turn!
48/72 **To Get To You** *Jerry Wallace*
29/68 **To Give (The Reason I Live)** *Frankie Valli*
To Know You [Him] Is To Love You [Him]
1/58 *Teddy Bears*
24/65 *Peter & Gordon*
34/69 *Bobby Vinton*
38/73 **To Know You Is To Love You** *B.B. King*
41/85 **To Live And Die In L.A.** *Wang Chung*
43/56 **To Love Again** *Four Aces*
To Love Somebody
17/67 *Bee Gees*
74/68 *Sweet Inspirations*
11/92 *Michael Bolton*
11A/98 **To Love You More** *Celine Dion*
95/66 **To Make A Big Man Cry** *Roy Head*
50/97 **To Make You Feel My Love** *Billy Joel*
68/67 **To Share Your Love** *Fantastic Four*
98/66 **To Show I Love You** *Peter & Gordon*
To Sir With Love
1/67 *Lulu*
93/67 *Herbie Mann*
35/69 **To Susan On The West Coast Waiting** *Donovan*
25/57 **To The Aisle** *Five Satins*
17/75 **To The Door Of The Sun (Alle Porte Del Sole)** *Al Martino*
25/56 **To The Ends Of The Earth** *Nat "King" Cole*
To The Moon And Back
37/97 *Savage Garden*
24/98 *Savage Garden*
61S/01 **To The Music** *A*Teens*
50/70 **To The Other Woman (I'm The Other Woman)** *Doris Duke*
51/68 **To Wait For Love** *Herb Alpert*
To You, My Love
27/56 *Nick Noble*
70/56 *Georgie Shaw*
20/71 **Toast And Marmalade For Tea** *Tin Tin*
67/72 **Toast To The Fool** *Dramatics*
Tobacco Road
14/64 *Nashville Teens*
93/70 *Jamul*
78/75 **Toby** *Chi-Lites*
99/00 **Toca's Miracle** *Fragma*
83/81 **Toccata** *Sky*
17/64 **Today** *New Christy Minstrels*
69A/94 **Today** *Smashing Pumpkins*
39/63 **(Today I Met) The Boy I'm Gonna Marry** *Darlene Love*
46/73 **Today I Started Loving You Again** *Bettye Swann*
60/80 **Today Is The Day** *Bar-Kays*
54/64 **Today's Teardrops** *Rick Nelson*
23/76 **Today's The Day** *America*
6/61 **Together** *Connie Francis*
Together
48/67 *Intruders*
18/81 *Tierra*
80/70 **Together** *Illusion*
1/98 **Together Again** *Janet Jackson*
19/66 **Together Again** *Ray Charles*
91/72 **Together Again** *Bobby Sherman*
86/72 **Together Alone** *Melanie*
1/88 **Together Forever** *Rick Astley*
35/91 **Together Forever** *Lisette Melendez*
37/72 **Together Let's Find Love** *5th Dimension*
91/73 **Together We Can Make Such Sweet Music** *Spinners*
26/60 **Togetherness** *Frankie Avalon*
20/63 **Tom Cat** *Rooftop Singers*
1/58 **Tom Dooley** *Kingston Trio*
44/81 **Tom Sawyer** *Rush*
5/90 **Tom's Diner** *D.N.A. Feat. Suzanne Vega*
29/59 **Tomboy** *Perry Como*
96/68 **Tomboy** *Ronnie Dove*
92/65 **Tommy** *Reparata & The Delrons*
(also see: Overture From Tommy)
23/68 **Tomorrow** *Strawberry Alarm Clock*
28A/95 **Tomorrow** *Silverchair*
75/90 **Tomorrow (A Better You, Better Me)** *Quincy Jones*
26/86 **Tomorrow Doesn't Matter Tonight** *Starship*
80/66 **Tomorrow Never Comes** *B.J. Thomas*
39/88 **Tomorrow People** *Ziggy Marley*
54/69 **Tomorrow Tomorrow** *Bee Gees*
55/71 **Tongue In Cheek** *Sugarloaf*

TONIGHT:

Tonight ..also see: Tonite
7/90 **Tonight** *New Kids On The Block*
Tonight
8/61 *Ferrante & Teicher*
44/61 *Eddie Fisher*
13/84 **Tonight** *Kool & The Gang*
53/84 **Tonight** *David Bowie*
62/93 **Tonight** *Def Leppard*
69/73 **Tonight** *Raspberries*
84/83 **Tonight** *Whispers*
26/61 **Tonight (Could Be The Night)** *Velvets*
16/83 **Tonight, I Celebrate My Love** *Peabo Bryson/Roberta Flack*
15/61 **Tonight I Fell In Love** *Tokens*
52/02 **Tonight I Wanna Be Your Man** *Andy Griggs*
61/61 **Tonight I Won't Be There** *Adam Wade*
50/69 **Tonight I'll Be Staying Here With You** *Bob Dylan*
45/70 **Tonight I'll Say A Prayer** *Eydie Gorme*
53S/02 **Tonight I'm Gonna Let Go** *Syleena Johnson*
20/82 **Tonight I'm Yours (Don't Hurt Me)** *Rod Stewart*
Tonight Is The Night
89/95 *Le Click*
68/97 *Le Click*
80/84 **Tonight Is What It Means To Be Young** *Fire Inc.*
44/85 **Tonight It's You** *Cheap Trick*
96/57 **Tonight My Heart Will Be Crying** *Eddie Fisher*
13/61 **Tonight My Love, Tonight** *Paul Anka*
7/86 **Tonight She Comes** *Cars*
46/99 **Tonight The Heartache's On Me** *Dixie Chicks*

36/96 **Tonight, Tonight** *Smashing Pumpkins*
55/82 **Tonight Tonight** *Bill Champlin*
3/87 **Tonight, Tonight, Tonight** *Genesis*
Tonight You Belong To Me
4/56 *Patience & Prudence*
15/56 *Lawrence Welk/Lennon Sisters*
49/56 *Karen Chandler & Jimmy Wakely*
57/64 **Tonight You're Gonna Fall In Love With Me** *Shirelles*
28/65 **Tonight's The Night** *Solomon Burke*
Tonight's The Night
39/60 *Shirelles*
76/60 *Chiffons*
99/76 **Tonight's The Night** *S.S.O.*
80/95 **Tonight's The Night** *BLACKstreet*
1/76 **Tonight's The Night (Gonna Be Alright)** *Rod Stewart*
49/91 **Tonite** *DJ Quik*
Tonite, Tonite
77/57 *Mello-Kings*
95/61 *Mello-Kings*
12/96 **Tonite's Tha Night** *Kris Kross*
83/67 **Tony Rome** *Nancy Sinatra*

TOO:

42/02 **Too Bad** *Nickelback*
88/62 **Too Bad** *Ben E. King*
86/72 **Too Beautiful To Last** *Engelbert Humperdinck*
38/92 **Too Blind To See It** *Kym Sims*
4/69 **Too Busy Thinking About My Baby** *Marvin Gaye*
Too Close
1/98 *Next*
69[S]/01 *Next*
39/56 **Too Close For Comfort** *Eydie Gorme*
95/69 **Too Experienced** *Eddie Lovette*
10/92 **Too Funky** *George Michael*
33/97 **Too Gone, Too Long** *En Vogue*
77/82 **Too Good To Turn Back Now** *Rick Bowles*
Too Hot
5/80 *Kool & The Gang*
24/96 *Coolio*
84/90 **Too Hot** *Loverboy*
24/78 **Too Hot Ta Trot** *Commodores*
93/65 **Too Hot To Hold** *Major Lance*
74/77 **Too Hot To Stop** *Bar-Kays*
59/74 **Too Late** *Tavares*
70/80 **Too Late** *Journey*
75/57 **Too Late** *Gene Austin*
75/79 **Too Late** *Shoes*
5/85 **Too Late For Goodbyes** *Julian Lennon*
66/56 **Too Late Now** *DeCastro Sisters*
12/90 **Too Late To Say Goodbye** *Richard Marx*
2/72 **Too Late To Turn Back Now** *Cornelius Brothers & Sister Rose*
43/64 **Too Late To Turn Back Now** *Brook Benton*
76/62 **Too Late To Worry - Too Blue To Cry** *Glen Campbell*
41/97 **Too Late, Too Soon** *Jon Secada*
5/92 **2 Legit 2 Quit** *Hammer*
86/01 **Too Little Too Late** *Barenaked Ladies*
94/69 **Too Many Cooks (Spoil The Soup)** *100 Proof (Aged In Soul)*
Too Many Fish In The Sea
25/65 *Marvelettes*
24/67 *Mitch Ryder (medley)*
13/65 **Too Many Rivers** *Brenda Lee*
72/61 **Too Many Rules** *Connie Francis*
8/91 **Too Many Walls** *Cathy Dennis*
1/57 **Too Much** *Elvis Presley*
9/98 **Too Much** *Spice Girls*
39[A]/96 **Too Much** *Dave Matthews Band*
95/91 **Too Much** *Tara Kemp*
91/88 **Too Much Ain't Enough Love** *Jimmy Barnes*
1/79 **Too Much Heaven** *Bee Gees*
45/93 **Too Much Information** *Duran Duran*
69/83 **Too Much Love To Hide** *Crosby, Stills & Nash*
35/67 **Too Much Of Nothing** *Peter, Paul & Mary*
37/92 **Too Much Passion** *Smithereens*
19/68 **Too Much Talk** *Paul Revere & The Raiders*
30/60 **Too Much Tequila** *Champs*
9/81 **Too Much Time On My Hands** *Styx*
1/78 **Too Much, Too Little, Too Late** *Johnny Mathis/Deniece Williams*
42/60 **Too Pooped To Pop ("Casey")** *Chuck Berry*
5/83 **Too Shy** *Kajagoogoo*
91/66 **Too Slow** *Impressions*
68/66 **Too Soon To Know** *Roy Orbison*
40/81 **Too Tight** *Con Funk Shun*
13/69 **Too Weak To Fight** *Clarence Carter*
13/72 **Too Young** *Donny Osmond*
52/85 **Too Young** *Jack Wagner*
90/84 **Too Young To Fall In Love** *Mötley Crüe*
Too Young To Go Steady
21/56 *Nat "King" Cole*
73/56 *Patti Page*
71/60 *Connie Stevens*
30/78 **Took The Last Train** *David Gates*
8/95 **Tootsee Roll** *69 Boyz*
84/71 **Top Forty** *Sha Na Na*
81/61 **Top Forty, News, Weather And Sports** *Mark Dinning*
Top Of The World
1/73 *Carpenters*
74/73 *Lynn Anderson*
44[A]/98 *Brandy*
27/91 **Top Of The World** *Van Halen*
98/75 **Top Of The World (Make My Reservation)** *Canyon*
70/79 **Topical Song** *Barron Knights*
75[S]/98 **Tops Drop** *Fat Pat*
27/58 **Topsy I** *Cozy Cole*
3/58 **Topsy II** *Cozy Cole*
Torero
18/58 *Renato Carosone*
21/58 *Julius LaRosa*
Torn
1[A]/98 *Natalie Imbruglia*
72[S]/02 *Natalie Imbruglia*
1/77 **Torn Between Two Lovers** *Mary MacGregor*
39/59 **Torquay** *Fireballs*
17/84 **Torture** *Jacksons*
20/62 **Torture** *Kris Jensen*
40[S]/01 **Torture** *Screwball*
92/93 **Toss-Up** *N2Deep*
Tossin' And Turnin'
1/61 *Bobby Lewis*
97/73 *Bunny Sigler*
83/65 **Tossing & Turning** *Ivy League*
Total Eclipse Of The Heart
1/83 *Bonnie Tyler*
2/95 *Nicki French*
52/79 **Totally Hot** *Olivia Newton-John*

TOUCH:

71/71 **Touch** *Supremes*
87/83 **Touch A Four Leaf Clover** *Atlantic Starr*
23/74 **Touch A Hand, Make A Friend** *Staple Singers*
37/80 **Touch And Go** *Cars*
57/74 **Touch And Go** *Al Wilson*
60/86 **Touch And Go** *Emerson, Lake & Powell*
98/76 **Touch And Go** *Ecstasy, Passion & Pain*
73/78 **Touch And Gone** *Gary Wright*
9/98 **Touch It** *Monifah*
3/69 **Touch Me** *Doors*
19/74 **Touch Me** *Fancy*
59/98 **Touch Me** *Solo*
2/91 **Touch Me (All Night Long)** *Cathy Dennis*
82/79 **Touch Me Baby** *Ultimate*
60/75 **Touch Me Baby (Reaching Out For Your Love)** *Tamiko Jones*
4/87 **Touch Me (I Want Your Body)** *Samantha Fox*
1/73 **Touch Me In The Morning** *Diana Ross*
14/96 **Touch Me Tease Me** *Case*
67/89 **Touch Me Tonight** *Shooting Star*
Touch Me When We're Dancing
86/79 *Bama*
16/81 *Carpenters*
51/93 **Touch My Light** *Big Mountain*
40/96 **Touch Myself** *T-Boz*
9/87 **Touch Of Grey** *Grateful Dead*
92/59 **Touch Of Pink** *Jerry Wallace*
50/70 **Touch Of You** *Brenda & The Tabulations*
57[A]/97 **Touch, Peel And Stand** *Days Of The New*
84/89 **Touch The Fire** *Icehouse*
Touch The Wind ..see: Eres Tu
60/61 **Touchables, The** *Dickie Goodman*
42/61 **Touchables In Brooklyn** *Dickie Goodman*
Tough ..also see: Tuff
22/85 **Tough All Over** *John Cafferty*
57/82 **Tough World** *Donnie Iris*
57/95 **Tour** *Capleton*
5/61 **Tower Of Strength** *Gene McDaniels*
(also see: You Don't Have To Be A)
73/57 **Tower's Trot (And Then You Do That Step)** *Dick Jacobs*
13/62 **Town Without Pity** *Gene Pitney*
70/02 **Toxicity** *System Of A Down*
64/65 **Toy Soldier** *4 Seasons*
1/89 **Toy Soldiers** *Martika*
Toys In The Attic
85/63 *Joe Sherman*
92/63 *Jack Jones*
Tra La La
24/56 *Georgia Gibbs*
94/56 *LaVerne Baker*
50/62 **Tra La La La La** *Ike & Tina Turner*
35/64 **Tra La La La Suzy** *Dean & Jean*
96/69 **Tra La La Song (One Banana, Two Banana)** *Banana Splits*
Traces
2/69 *Classics IV*
47/70 *Lettermen (medley)*
Tracks Of My Tears
16/65 *Miracles*
10/67 *Johnny Rivers*
71/69 *Aretha Franklin*
25/76 *Linda Ronstadt*

9/69 **Tracy** *Cuff Links*
13/60 **Tracy's Theme** *Spencer Ross*
20/02 **Trade It All** *Fabolous*
Tragedy
1/79 *Bee Gees*
25S/00 *Steps*
Tragedy
5/59 *Thomas Wayne*
10/61 *Fleetwoods*
56/69 *Brian Hyland*
39/85 **Tragedy** *John Hunter*
57/69 **Train, The** *1910 Fruitgum Co.* *(also see: C'Mon N' Ride It)*
86/76 **Train Called Freedom** *South Shore Commission*
23/80 **Train In Vain (Stand By Me)** *Clash*
36/60 **Train Of Love** *Annette*
27/74 **Train Of Thought** *Chér*
38/79 **Train, Train** *Blackfoot*
Trains And Boats And Planes
47/65 *Billy J. Kramer*
22/66 *Dionne Warwick*
Tramp
26/67 *Otis Redding & Carla Thomas*
52/67 *Lowell Fulsom*
38/75 **Trampled Under Foot** *Led Zeppelin*
67/78 **Trans-Europe Express** *Kraftwerk*
8/56 **Transfusion** *Nervous Norvus*
35/61 **Transistor Sister** *Freddy Cannon*
13/71 **Trapped By A Thing Called Love** *Denise LaSalle*
2/70 **Travelin' Band** *Creedence Clearwater Revival*
1/61 **Travelin' Man** *Ricky Nelson*
77/74 **Travelin' Prayer** *Billy Joel*
61/74 **Travelin' Shoes** *Elvin Bishop*
32/67 **Travlin' Man** *Stevie Wonder*
73/80 **Treasure** *Brothers Johnson*
16/56 **Treasure Of Love** *Clyde McPhatter*
26/58 **Treasure Of Your Love** *Eileen Rodgers*
95/91 **Treat 'Em Right** *Chubb Rock*
3/71 **Treat Her Like A Lady** *Cornelius Brothers & Sister Rose*
48/85 **Treat Her Like A Lady** *Temptations*
63/00 **Treat Her Like A Lady** *Joe*
2/65 **Treat Her Right** *Roy Head*
18/57 **Treat Me Nice** *Elvis Presley*
18/81 **Treat Me Right** *Pat Benatar*
43/63 **Treat My Baby Good** *Bobby Darin*
Trees
92/57 *Al Hibbler*
62/61 *Platters*
18/94 **Tremor Christ** *Pearl Jam*
35/96 **Tres Delinquentes** *Delinquent Habits*
29/61 **Triangle** *Janie Grant*
68/71 **Triangle Of Love (Hey Diddle Diddle)** *Presidents*
52/89 **Tribute (Right On)** *Pasadenas*
86/68 **Tribute To A King [Otis Redding]** *William Bell*
76/87 **Trick Of The Night** *Bananarama*
45S/01 **Trickin'** *Ram-Z*
73/80 **Trickle Trickle** *Manhattan Transfer*
Tricky
79/56 *Gus Jinkins*
25/57 *Ralph Marterie*
Tricky Tricky
74/00 *Lou Bega*
FS/02 *Lou Bega*
41/78 **Tried To Love** *Peter Frampton*
7/99 **Trippin'** *Total*
36A/96 **Trippin' On A Hole In A Paper Heart** *Stone Temple Pilots*

6/72 **Troglodyte (Cave Man)** *Jimmy Castor Bunch*
9/82 **Trouble** *Lindsey Buckingham*
T-R-O-U-B-L-E
35/75 *Elvis Presley*
72S/93 *Travis Tritt*
35/88 **Trouble** *Nia Peeples*
92/67 **Trouble Down Here Below** *Lou Rawls*
99/64 **Trouble I've Had** *Clarence Ashe*
Trouble In Mind
92/61 *Nina Simone*
86/63 *Aretha Franklin*
50/72 **Trouble In My Home** *Joe Simon*
20/60 **Trouble In Paradise** *Crests*
63/83 **Trouble In Paradise** *Al Jarreau*
33/63 **Trouble Is My Middle Name** *Bobby Vinton*
7/73 **Trouble Man** *Marvin Gaye*
44/89 **Trouble Me** *10,000 Maniacs*
Trouble With Harry
44/56 *Alfi & Harry*
80/56 *Les Baxter*
(T.R.O.Y.) ..see: They Reminisce Over You
24S/99 **Tru Homies** *Tru*
71/69 **Truck Stop** *Jerry Smith*
64/71 **Truckin'** *Grateful Dead*

TRUE:

4/83 **True** *Spandau Ballet*
3/86 **True Blue** *Madonna*
99/63 **True Blue Lou** *Tony Bennett*
40/90 **True Blue Love** *Lou Gramm*
True Colors
1/86 *Cyndi Lauper*
66A/98 *Phil Collins*
80/91 **True Companion** *Marc Cohn*
32/87 **True Faith** *New Order*
68/58 **True, Fine Mama** *Little Richard*
35/69 **True Grit** *Glen Campbell*
True Love
3/56 *Bing Crosby & Grace Kelly*
15/56 *Jane Powell*
98/63 *Richard Chamberlain*
56/93 *Elton John & Kiki Dee*
13/88 **True Love** *Glenn Frey*
66/64 **True Love Goes On And On** *Burl Ives*
78/57 **True Love Gone (Come On Home)** *Betty Madigan*
21/63 **True Love Never Runs Smooth** *Gene Pitney*
True Love, True Love ..see: (If You Cry)
True Love Ways
14/65 *Peter & Gordon*
66/80 *Mickey Gilley*
75/87 **True To You** *Ric Ocasek*
54/59 **True True Happiness** *Johnny Tillotson*
90/61 **True, True Love** *Frankie Avalon*
1/82 **Truly** *Lionel Richie*
65/66 **Truly Julie's Blues (I'll Be There)** *Bob Lind*
Truly Madly Deeply
1/98 *Savage Garden*
29S/02 *Savage Garden*
54/65 **Truly, Truly, True** *Brenda Lee*
18S/02 **Truly Yours** *Narée*
Trust In Me
95/57 *Chris Connor*
43/59 *Patti Page*
30/61 *Etta James*
90/80 **Trust Me** *Cindy Bullens*

19S/01 **Trust Your Love** *Koda*
28/91 **Truth, The** *TAMI Show*

TRY:

23/69 **Try A Little Kindness** *Glen Campbell*
Try A Little Tenderness
100/62 *Aretha Franklin*
25/67 *Otis Redding*
29/69 *Three Dog Night*
67/91 *Commitments*
1/00 **Try Again** *Aaliyah*
23/83 **Try Again** *Champaign*
83/68 **Try It** *Ohio Express*
15/64 **Try It Baby** *Marvin Gaye*
97/77 **Try It On** *Exile*
Try Me
48/59 *James Brown*
65/64 *Jimmy Hughes*
63/65 *James Brown*
80/76 **Try Me, I Know We Can Make It** *Donna Summer*
97/66 **Try My Love Again** *Bobby Moore & The Rhythm Aces*
77/71 **Try Some, Buy Some** *Ronnie Spector*
33/58 **Try The Impossible** *Lee Andrews*
81/90 **Try To Find Me** *Gorky Park*
Try To Remember
73/65 *Ed Ames*
91/65 *Brothers Four*
97/65 *Roger Williams*
11/75 *Gladys Knight (medley)*
12/66 **Try Too Hard** *Dave Clark Five*
88/74 **Try (Try To Fall In Love)** *Cooker*
95/75 **Tryin' To Beat The Morning Home** *T.G. Sheppard*
88/94 **Tryin' To Get Over You** *Vince Gill*
10/76 **Tryin' To Get The Feeling Again** *Barry Manilow*
5/81 **Tryin' To Live My Life Without You** *Bob Seger*
10/77 **Tryin' To Love Two** *William Bell*
77/58 **Trying** *Billy Vaughn*
15/74 **Trying To Hold On To My Woman** *Lamont Dozier*
40/70 **Trying To Make A Fool Of Me** *Delfonics*
Tubthumping
6/97 *Chumbawamba*
87/98 *Chucklebutt*
Tubular Bells
7/74 *Mike Oldfield*
98/76 *Champs' Boys Orchestra*
58/98 **Tuck Me In** *Kimberly Scott*
38/96 **Tucker's Town** *Hootie & The Blowfish*
32/59 **Tucumcari** *Jimmie Rodgers*
24/68 **Tuesday Afternoon (Forever Afternoon)** *Moody Blues*
17/62 **Tuff** *Ace Cannon*
10/86 **Tuff Enuff** *Fabulous Thunderbirds*
53/82 **Tug Of War** *Paul McCartney*
86/71 **Tulsa** *Billy Joe Royal*
30/80 **Tulsa Time** *Eric Clapton*
Tumbling Dice
7/72 *Rolling Stones*
32/78 *Linda Ronstadt*
Tumbling Tumbleweeds
60/56 *Roger Williams*
30/58 *Billy Vaughn*
Tunes Of Glory ..see: Theme From
9/88 **Tunnel Of Love** *Bruce Springsteen*
43/58 **Tunnel Of Love** *Doris Day*
47/72 **Tupelo Honey** *Van Morrison*

TURN:

42/80 **Turn And Walk Away** *Babys*
27/64 **Turn Around** *Dick & DeeDee*
62/84 **Turn Around** *Neil Diamond*
96/69 **Turn Around And Love You** *Rita Coolidge*
Turn Around, Look At Me
62/61 *Glen Campbell*
7/68 *Vogues*
3/70 **Turn Back The Hands Of Time** *Tyrone Davis*
84/75 **Turn Back The Pages** *Stephen Stills*
49A/98 **Turn Back Time** *Aqua*
16/66 **Turn-Down Day** *Cyrkle*
58/80 **Turn It On Again** *Genesis*
66/91 **Turn It Up** *Oaktown's 3.5.7*
10/98 **Turn It Up [Remix]/Fire It Up** *Busta Rhymes*
98/77 **Turn Loose Of My Leg** *Jim Stafford*
9/59 **Turn Me Loose** *Fabian*
35/81 **Turn Me Loose** *Loverboy*
45A/97 **Turn My Head** *Live*
5/01 **Turn Off The Light** *Nelly Furtado*
48/79 **Turn Off The Lights** *Teddy Pendergrass*
84/88 **Turn Off The Lights** *World Class Wreckin Cru*
58/69 **Turn On A Dream** *Box Tops*
Turn On To Me ..see: (Baby)
Turn On Your Love Light
28/62 *Bobby Bland*
65/67 *Oscar Toney, Jr.*
80/68 *Human Beinz*
82/68 *Bill Black's Combo*
95/72 *Jerry Lee Lewis*
64/82 **Turn On Your Radar** *Prism*
Turn The Beat Around
10/76 *Vicki Sue Robinson*
13/94 *Gloria Estefan*
66/67 **Turn The World Around** *Eddy Arnold*
13/78 **Turn To Stone** *Electric Light Orchestra*
93/75 **Turn To Stone** *Joe Walsh*
32/84 **Turn To You** *Go-Go's*
Turn! Turn! Turn!
1/65 *Byrds*
69/69 *Judy Collins*
29/85 **Turn Up The Radio** *Autograph*
5/82 **Turn Your Love Around** *George Benson*
63/71 **Turn Your Radio On** *Ray Stevens*
42/89 **Turned Away** *Chuckii Booker*
36/80 **Turning Japanese** *Vapors*
96/77 **Turning To You** *Charlie*
13/90 **Turtle Power!** *Partners In Kryme*
36/58 **Turvy II** *Cozy Cole*
20/75 **Tush** *ZZ Top*
8/79 **Tusk** *Fleetwood Mac*
Tutti' Frutti
12/56 *Pat Boone*
17/56 *Little Richard*
82/60 **Tuxedo Junction** *Frankie Avalon*
Tweedlee Dee
2/55 *Georgia Gibbs*
14/55 *LaVern Baker*
59/73 *Little Jimmy Osmond*
Twelfth Of Never
9/57 *Johnny Mathis*
8/73 *Donny Osmond*
5X/63 **Twelve Gifts Of Christmas** *Allan Sherman*
68/57 **Twelve O'Clock Tonight** *Doris Day*
20/67 **Twelve Thirty (Young Girls Are Coming To The Canyon)** *Mamas & The Papas*
6/69 **Twenty-Five Miles** *Edwin Starr*
25 Or 6 To 4
4/70 *Chicago*
48/86 *Chicago*
74/55 **24 Hours A Day (365 A Year)** *Georgia Gibbs*
17/63 **Twenty Four Hours From Tulsa** *Gene Pitney*
10/99 **24/7** *Kevon Edmonds*
42/89 **24/7** *Dino*
68S/99 **24-7** *Liberty City Fla.*
15/63 **Twenty Miles** *Chubby Checker*
31/64 **20-75** *Willie Mitchell*
55/98 **26¢** *Wilkinsons*
2/58 **26 Miles (Santa Catalina)** *Four Preps*
48/85 **20/20** *George Benson*
91/59 **Twice As Nice** *Clyde McPhatter*
38/81 **Twilight** *ELO*
Twilight Time
1/58 *Platters*
86/62 *Andy Williams*
31/88 **Twilight World** *Swing Out Sister*
10/83 **Twilight Zone** *Golden Earring*
49/92 **Twilight Zone** *2 Unlimited*
30/80 **Twilight Zone/Twilight Tone** *Manhattan Transfer*
14/65 **Twine Time** *Alvin Cash*
39/66 **Twinkle Toes** *Roy Orbison*
5X/65 **Twinkle Twinkle Little Me** *Supremes*
Twist, The
1/60 *Chubby Checker*
28/60 *Hank Ballard*
1/62 *Chubby Checker*
93/62 *Ernie Freeman*
16/88 *Fat Boys/Chubby Checker (Yo, Twist!)*
(also see: Percolator)
Twist And Shout
17/62 *Isley Brothers*
2/64 *Beatles*
23/86 *Beatles*
26/62 **Twist-Her** *Bill Black's Combo*
25/63 **Twist It Up** *Chubby Checker*
83/86 **Twist My Arm** *Pointer Sisters*
5/84 **Twist Of Fate** *Olivia Newton-John*
("Twist" Special) ..see: Rock-A-Hula Baby
9/62 **Twist, Twist Senora** *Gary (U.S.) Bonds*
2/96 **Twisted** *Keith Sweat*
68/62 **Twistin' All Night Long** *Danny & The Juniors*
49/60 **Twistin' Bells** *Santo & Johnny*
22/62 **Twistin' Matilda (and the channel)** *Jimmy Soul*
(also see: Matilda)
34/62 **Twistin' Postman** *Marvelettes*
Twistin' The Night Away
9/62 *Sam Cooke*
59/73 *Rod Stewart*
80/87 *Rod Stewart*
Twistin' U.S.A.
27/60 *Danny & The Juniors*
68/61 *Chubby Checker*
Twistin' White Silver Sands ..see: White Silver Sands
54/62 **Twistin' With Linda** *Isley Brothers*
17/59 **Twixt Twelve And Twenty** *Pat Boone*

TWO:

4/97 **2 Become 1** *Spice Girls*
66/68 **Two-Bit Manchild** *Neil Diamond*
24S/00 **2 B*tches** *Too $hort*
90/59 **Two Brothers** *David Hill*
(also see: Ballad Of)
Two Different Worlds
11/56 *Don Rondo*
41/56 *Roger Williams & Jane Morgan*
80/56 *Dick Haymes*
61/65 *Lenny Welch*
16/71 **Two Divided By Love** *Grass Roots*
19/78 **Two Doors Down** *Dolly Parton*
6/63 **Two Faces Have I** *Lou Christie*
33/75 **Two Fine People** *Cat Stevens*
54/59 **Two Fools** *Frankie Avalon*
1/89 **Two Hearts** *Phil Collins*
16/55 **Two Hearts** *Pat Boone*
40/81 **Two Hearts** *Stephanie Mills/ Teddy Pendergrass*
F/55 **Two Hound Dogs** *Bill Haley*
19S/00 **Two In A Million** *S Club 7*
99/67 **Two In The Afternoon** *Dino, Desi & Billy*
50/63 **Two Kind Of Teardrops** *Del Shannon*
97/75 **Two Lane Highway** *Pure Prairie League*
38/83 **Two Less Lonely People In The World** *Air Supply*
31/68 **Two Little Kids** *Peaches & Herb*
18/55 **Two Lost Souls** *Perry Como & Jaye P. Morgan*
7/63 **Two Lovers** *Mary Wells*
10/88 **Two Occasions** *Deele*
42/62 **Two Of A Kind** *Sue Thompson*
3/86 **Two Of Hearts** *Stacey Q*
11/78 **Two Out Of Three Ain't Bad** *Meat Loaf*
30/87 **Two People** *Tina Turner*
51/01 **Two People Fell In Love** *Brad Paisley*
30/80 **Two Places At The Same Time** *Ray Parker Jr.*
7/93 **Two Princes** *Spin Doctors*
38/84 **Two Sides Of Love** *Sammy Hagar*
63/63 **Two Sides (To Every Story)** *Etta James*
12/93 **Two Steps Behind** *Def Leppard*
30/99 **Two Teardrops** *Steve Wariner*
78/63 **Two-Ten, Six-Eighteen (Doesn't Anybody Know My Name)** *Jimmie Rodgers*
2001 Space Odyssey ..see: Also Sprach Zarathustra
67/60 **Two Thousand, Two Hundred, Twenty-Three Miles** *Patti Page*
22/78 **Two Tickets To Paradise** *Eddie Money*
32/63 **Two Tickets To Paradise** *Brook Benton*
2/90 **Two To Make It Right** *Seduction*
43/84 **Two Tribes** *Frankie Goes To Hollywood*
41S/02 **2-Way** *Rayvon*
62/98 **2 Way Street** *Missjones*
28/02 **Two Wrongs** *Wyclef Jean*
100/63 **Two Wrongs Don't Make A Right** *Mary Wells*
91/63 **2,000 Pound Bee** *Ventures*
2/86 **Typical Male** *Tina Turner*
64/93 **Typical Reasons (Swing My Way)** *Prince Markie Dee*
62A/97 **Tyrone** *Erykah Badu*

U

U ..also see: You
8/90 **U Can't Touch This** *M.C. Hammer*
3/02 **U Don't Have To Call** *Usher*
93/93 **U Don't Hear Me Tho'** *Rodney O & Joe Cooley*
79/99 **U Don't Know Me (Like U Used To)** *Brandy*
62/00 **U Don't Love Me** *Kumbia Kings*
68S/00 **U Got It** *Cleopatra*
1/01 **U Got It Bad** *Usher*
2/87 **U Got The Look** *Prince*
38S/01 **U Know U Ghetto** *Bishop*
7/99 **U Know What's Up** *Donell Jones*
59S/01 **U Make My Sun Shine** *Prince With Angie Stone*
1/01 **U Remind Me** *Usher*
33/94 **U Send Me Swingin'** *Mint Condition*
83/00 **U Understand** *Juvenile*
27S/99 **U-Way (How We Do It)** *Youngbloodz*
28/94 **U Will Know** *BMU (Black Men United)*
28/68 **U.S. Male** *Elvis Presley*
86/74 **U.S. Of A** *Donna Fargo*
15/01 **Ugly** *Bubba Sparxxx*
37/02 **Uh Huh** *B2K*
92/57 **Uh-Huh--mm** *Sonny James*
73/58 **Uh-Huh, Oh Yeah** *Steve Lawrence*
Uh! Oh!
14/59 *Nutty Squirrels (Part 2)*
45/59 *Nutty Squirrels (Part 1)*
16/92 **Uhh Ahh** *Boyz II Men*
42S/01 **Uhhnnh** *Bad Seed*
Um, Um, Um, Um, Um, Um
5/64 *Major Lance*
41/78 *Johnny Rivers*
51S/00 **Un-Huh** *Devyne Stephens*
1/91 **Unbelievable** *EMF*
36/99 **Unbelievable** *Diamond Rio*
F/94 **Unbelievable** *Notorious B.I.G.*
66/74 **Unborn Child** *Seals & Crofts*
1/96 **Un-Break My Heart** *Toni Braxton*
25S/00 **Unbreakable Heart** *Jessica Andrews*
26/02 **Unbroken** *Tim McGraw*
73S/02 **Unbroken By You** *Kortney Kayle*
Unchain My Heart
9/62 *Ray Charles*
81/68 *Herbie Mann*
Unchained Melody
1/55 *Les Baxter*
3/55 *Al Hibbler*
6/55 *Roy Hamilton*
29/55 *June Valli*
66/63 *Vito & The Salutations*
4/65 *Righteous Brothers*
73/68 *Sweet Inspirations*
83/81 *Heart*
13/90 *Righteous Brothers*
19/90 *Righteous Brothers (new version)*
1/71 **Uncle Albert/Admiral Halsey** *Paul & Linda McCartney*
69/70 **Uncle John's Band** *Grateful Dead*
78/91 **Uncle Tom's Cabin** *Warrant*
49/00 **Unconditional** *Clay Davidson*
43/83 **Unconditional Love** *Donna Summer*
92/93 **Unconditional Love** *Hi-Five*
73/90 **Undeniable** *Ms. Adventures*

UNDER:

15S/02 **Under God** *Pat Boone*
59/72 **Under My Wheels** *Alice Cooper*
29/82 **Under Pressure** *Queen & David Bowie*
Under The Boardwalk
4/64 *Drifters*
82/78 *Billy Joe Royal*
59/87 *Bruce Willis*
2/92 **Under The Bridge** *Red Hot Chili Peppers*
71/81 **Under The Covers** *Janis Ian*
48/80 **Under The Gun** *Poco*
56/86 **Under The Influence** *Vanity*
76/74 **Under The Influence Of Love** *Love Unlimited*
24/88 **Under The Milky Way** *Church*
46/61 **Under The Moon Of Love** *Curtis Lee*
91/97 **Under The Water** *Merril Bainbridge*
35/66 **Under Your Spell Again** *Johnny Rivers*
1/77 **Undercover Angel** *Alan O'Day*
9/83 **Undercover Of The Night** *Rolling Stones*
3/02 **Underneath It All** *No Doubt*
74/88 **Underneath The Radar** *Underworld*
9/02 **Underneath Your Clothes** *Shakira*
58/93 **Understand This Groove** *Sound Factory*
35/64 **Understand Your Man** *Johnny Cash*
8/94 **Understanding** *Xscape*
17/85 **Understanding** *Bob Seger*
46/68 **Understanding** *Ray Charles*
44/61 **Underwater** *Frogmen*
57/94 **Undone-The Sweater Song** *Weezer*
22/69 **Undun** *Guess Who*
9/73 **Uneasy Rider** *Charlie Daniels*
87/84 **Unfaithfully Yours (One Love)** *Stephen Bishop*
Unforgettable
17/59 *Dinah Washington*
14/91 *Natalie Cole with Nat "King" Cole*
35/92 **Unforgiven, The** *Metallica*
(also see: Theme From)
59/98 **Unforgiven II** *Metallica*
33/70 **Ungena Za Ulimwengu (Unite The World)** *Temptations*
7/68 **Unicorn, The** *Irish Rovers*
4A/98 **Uninvited** *Alanis Morissette*
24/76 **Union Man** *Cate Bros.*
3/83 **Union Of The Snake** *Duran Duran*
United
78/66 *Intruders (We'll Be)*
46/68 *Peaches & Herb*
78/68 *Music Makers*
56/81 **United Together** *Aretha Franklin*
13/70 **United We Stand** *Brotherhood Of Man*
23/94 **U.N.I.T.Y.** *Queen Latifah*
84/95 **Universal Heart-Beat** *Juliana Hatfield*
Universal Soldier
45/65 *Glen Campbell*
53/65 *Donovan*
39/68 **Unknown Soldier** *Doors*
99/64 **Unless You Care** *Terry Black*
1/99 **Unpretty** *TLC*
58/99 **Unsent** *Alanis Morissette*
3/90 **Unskinny Bop** *Poison*
74/62 **Unsquare Dance** *Dave Brubeck Quartet*
14H/55 **Unsuspecting Heart** *Sunny Gale*
60/62 **Untie Me** *Tams*
21A/94 **Until I Fall Away** *Gin Blossoms*
42/97 **Until I Find You Again** *Richard Marx*
10/96 **Until It Sleeps** *Metallica*
Until It's Time For You To Go
53/70 *Neil Diamond*
40/72 *Elvis Presley*
97/73 *New Birth*
72/78 **Until Now** *Bobby Arvon*
42/95 **Until The End Of Time** *Foreigner*
52/01 **Until The End Of Time** *2Pac*
Until You Come Back To Me (That's What I'm Gonna Do)
3/74 *Aretha Franklin*
87/84 *Luther Vandross (medley)*
75S/99 **Until You Loved Me** *Moffatts*
26/92 **Until Your Love Comes Back Around** *RTZ*
25/00 **Untitled (How Does It Feel)** *D'Angelo*
52/68 **Unwind** *Ray Stevens*

UP:

Up A Lazy River ..see: Lazy River
85/64 **Up Above My Head (I Hear Music In The Air)** *Al Hirt*
27/90 **Up All Night** *Slaughter*
63S/01 **Up All Night** *Unwritten Law*
46/66 **Up And Down** *McCoys*
92/97 **Up & Down** *Billy Lawrence*
67S/02 **Up & Down (In & Out)** *Deborah Cox*
4/70 **Up Around The Bend** *Creedence Clearwater Revival*
63/74 **Up For The Down Stroke** *Parliament*
82/68 **Up From The Skies** *Jimi Hendrix Experience*
91/68 **Up-Hard** *Willie Mitchell*
16/75 **Up In A Puff Of Smoke** *Polly Brown*
83/72 **Up In Heah** *Ike & Tina Turner*
12/97 **Up Jumps Da Boogie** *Magoo & Timbaland*
25/70 **Up On Cripple Creek** *Band*
Up On The Roof
5/63 *Drifters*
85/68 *Cryan' Shames*
92/70 *Laura Nyro*
28/79 *James Taylor*
69S/93 *II D Extreme*
94/76 **Up The Creek (Without A Paddle)** *Temptations*
10/70 **Up The Ladder To The Roof** *Supremes*
93/68 **Up Tight, Good Man** *Laura Lee*
93/68 **Up To My Neck In High Muddy Water** *Linda Ronstadt*
72/60 **Up Town** *Roy Orbison*
13/62 **Uptown** *Crystals*
81/58 **Up Until Now** *Johnnie Ray*
Up-Up And Away
7/67 *5th Dimension*
91/67 *Johnny Mann Singers*
71/68 *Hugh Masekela*
1/82 **Up Where We Belong** *Joe Cocker & Jennifer Warnes*
91/77 **Up Your Nose** *Gabriel Kaplan*
22/67 **Ups And Downs** *Paul Revere & The Raiders*
73/72 **Upsetter** *Grand Funk Railroad*
1/80 **Upside Down** *Diana Ross*

Uptight (Everything's Alright)
3/66 *Stevie Wonder*
49/66 *Ramsey Lewis*
84/66 *Nancy Wilson*
95/66 *Jazz Crusaders*
(also see: Little Ole Man)
80/76 **Uptown & Country** *Tom Scott*
65S/92 **Uptown Anthem** *Naughty By Nature*
25/77 **Uptown Festival (Motown Medley)** *Shalamar*
3/83 **Uptown Girl** *Billy Joel*
60/60 **Urge, The** *Freddy Cannon*
4/81 **Urgent** *Foreigner*
10S/02 **Us Against The World** *Play*
44/80 **Us And Love (We Go Together)** *Kenny Nolan*
81/91 **Use It Up And Wear It Out** *Pat & Mick*
2/72 **Use Me** *Bill Withers*
4/78 **Use Ta Be My Girl** *O'Jays*
34/65 **Use Your Head** *Mary Wells*
22/96 **Use Your Heart** *SWV*
46/82 **Used To Be** *Charlene & Stevie Wonder*
32S/01 **Used To Love** *Keke Wyatt*
27/61 **Utopia** *Frank Gari*

V

8/82 **Vacation** *Go-Go's*
9/62 **Vacation** *Connie Francis*
Vado Via ..see: Words (Are Impossible)
84/72 **Vahevala** *Loggins & Messina*
50/97 **Valentine** *Martina McBride w/Jim Brickman*
97/76 **Valentine Love** *Norman Connors*
Valerie
70/82 *Steve Winwood*
9/87 *Steve Winwood*
96/71 **Valerie** *Cymarron*
3/68 **Valleri** *Monkees*
32/82 **Valley Girl** *Frank Zappa*
8/57 **Valley Of Tears** *Fats Domino*
Valley Of The Dolls ..see: Theme From
5/88 **Valley Road** *Bruce Hornsby*
53/56 **Valley Valparaiso** *Percy Faith*
9/85 **Valotte** *Julian Lennon*
80/68 **Vance** *Roger Miller*
76/72 **Vanilla Ólay** *Jackie DeShannon*
90/64 **Vanishing Point** *Marketts*
91/86 **Vanity Kills** *ABC*
99/60 **Vaquero (Cowboy)** *Fireballs*
60/87 **Variety Tonight** *REO Speedwagon*
38A/94 **Vasoline** *Stone Temple Pilots*
Vaya Con Dios
43/64 *Drifters*
95/72 *Dawn Feat. Tony Orlando*
59/76 *Freddy Fender*
2/70 **Vehicle** *Ides Of March*
35/86 **Velcro Fly** *ZZ Top*
51/59 **Velvet Waters** *Megatrons*
48/79 **Vengeance** *Carly Simon*
8/72 **Ventura Highway** *America*
Venus
1/59 *Frankie Avalon*
46/76 *Frankie Avalon (disco)*
Venus
1/70 *Shocking Blue*
1/86 *Bananarama*
12/75 **Venus And Mars Rock Show** *Wings*
7/62 **Venus In Blue Jeans** *Jimmy Clanton*
19/89 **Veronica** *Elvis Costello*
84/82 **Very Best In You** *Change*
76/80 **Very Last Time** *Utopia*
Very Lovely Woman ..see: She's A
23/58 **Very Precious Love** *Ames Brothers*
31/93 **Very Special** *Big Daddy Kane*
90/81 **Very Special** *Debra Laws*
Very Special Love
94/57 *Mitch Miller*
20/58 *Debbie Reynolds*
23/58 *Johnny Nash*
11/74 **Very Special Love Song** *Charlie Rich*
Very Thought Of You
61/61 *Little Willie John*
26/64 *Rick Nelson*
16/92 **Vibeology** *Paula Abdul*
56/95 **Vibin'** *Boyz II Men*
63/72 **Victim Of A Foolish Heart** *Bettye Swann*
31/79 **Victim Of Love** *Elton John*
32/87 **Victim Of Love** *Bryan Adams*
68/92 **Victim Of The Ghetto** *College Boyz*
62/70 **Victoria** *Kinks*
10/87 **Victory** *Kool & The Gang*
19/98 **Victory** *Puff Daddy & The Family*
79/86 **Victory Line** *Limited Warranty*
Video
47/01 *India.Arie*
59/02 *India.Arie*
85/84 **Video!** *Jeff Lynne*
40/79 **Video Killed The Radio Star** *Buggles*
18/86 **Vienna Calling** *Falco*
1/85 **View To A Kill** *Duran Duran*
22/62 **Village Of Love** *Nathaniel Mayer*
7/60 **Village Of St. Bernadette** *Andy Williams*
12/72 **Vincent** *Don McLean*
64/90 **Violence Of Summer (Love's Taking Over)** *Duran Duran*
56/74 **Virgin Man** *Smokey Robinson*
59/74 **Virginia (Touch Me Like You Do)** *Bill Amesbury*
5S/02 **Virginity** *TG4*
1/90 **Vision Of Love** *Mariah Carey*
45/96 **Visions Of A Sunset** *Shawn Stockman*
63/82 **Visitors, The** *Abba*
66/84 **Vitamin L** *B.E. Taylor Group*
Viva Las Vegas
29/64 *Elvis Presley*
92/64 *Elvis Presley (EP)*
28/70 **Viva Tirado** *El Chicano*
26/99 **Vivrant Thing** *Q-Tip*
1/90 **Vogue** *Madonna*
15/81 **Voice, The** *Moody Blues*
88/58 **Voice In My Heart** *Eydie Gorme*
80/68 **Voice In The Choir** *Al Martino*
62/86 **Voice Of America's Sons** *John Cafferty*
71/80 **Voice Of Freedom** *Jim Kirk*
74/93 **Voice Of Freedom** *Freedom Williams*
63/82 **Voice On The Radio** *Conductor*
51/65 **Voice Your Choice** *Radiants*
32/80 **Voices** *Cheap Trick*
47/56 **Voices** *Fontane Sisters*
8/85 **Voices Carry** *'Til Tuesday*
25/89 **Voices Of Babylon** *Outfield*
11/91 **Voices That Care** *Voices That Care*
Volare (Nel Blu Dipinto Di Blu)
1/58 *Domenico Modugno*
12/58 *Dean Martin*
80/58 *McGuire Sisters*
4/60 *Bobby Rydell*
33/75 *Al Martino*
66/80 **Volcano** *Jimmy Buffett*
59A/97 **Volcano Girls** *Veruca Salt*
65/69 **Volunteers** *Jefferson Airplane*
72/83 **Voo Doo** *Rachel Sweet*
27/65 **Voodoo Woman** *Bobby Goldsboro*
90/69 **Voodoo Woman** *Simon Stokes*
80/79 **Voulez-Vous** *Abba*
97/95 **Vow** *Garbage*
29/85 **Vox Humana** *Kenny Loggins*
29/82 **Voyeur** *Kim Carnes*

W

65/81 **WKRP In Cincinnati (Main Theme)** *Steve Carlisle*
59S/00 **W.O.E. Is Me (World Of Entertainment)** *Jurassic 5*
36/74 **WOLD** *Harry Chapin*
45/00 **www.memory** *Alan Jackson*
77/61 **Wabash Blues** *Viscounts*
40/67 **Wack Wack** *Young Holt Trio*
Wade In The Water
19/66 *Ramsey Lewis*
37/67 *Herb Alpert*
2/62 **Wah Watusi** *Orlons*
(also see: El Watusi / Watusi)

WAIT:

8/88 **Wait** *White Lion*
91/60 **Wait** *Jimmy Clanton*
30/01 **Wait A Minute** *Ray-J*
37/61 **Wait A Minute** *Coasters*
76/66 **Wait A Minute** *Tim Tam & The Turn-Ons*
23/57 **Wait And See** *Fats Domino*
18/80 **Wait For Me** *Daryl Hall & John Oates*
37/60 **Wait For Me** *Playmates*
55/90 **Wait For You** *Bonham*
79/88 **Wait On Love** *Michael Bolton*
26/63 **Wait Til' My Bobby Gets Home** *Darlene Love*
33S/99 **Wait Till I Get Home** *C Note*
39S/02 **Waitin' For The DJ** *Talib Kweli*
18/58 **Waitin' In School** *Ricky Nelson*
57/66 **Waitin' In Your Welfare Line** *Buck Owens*
19/81 **Waiting, The** *Tom Petty*
54/71 **Waiting At The Bus Stop** *Bobby Sherman*
2/81 **Waiting For A Girl Like You** *Foreigner*
5/88 **Waiting For A Star To Fall** *Boy Meets Girl*
13/91 **Waiting For Love** *Alias*
27/91 **Waiting For That Day** *George Michael*
8/99 **Waiting For Tonight** *Jennifer Lopez*
83/96 **Waiting For Wednesday** *Lisa Loeb*
73/83 **Waiting For Your Love** *Toto*
86/89 **Waiting Game** *Swing Out Sister*
13/82 **Waiting On A Friend** *Rolling Stones*
51/60 **Wake Me, Shake Me** *Coasters*
1/84 **Wake Me Up Before You Go-Go** *Wham!*

50/60 **Wake Me When It's Over** *Andy Williams*
Wake The Town And Tell The People
5/55 *Les Baxter*
13/55 *Mindy Carson*
92/69 **Wake Up** *Chambers Brothers*
86/77 **Wake Up And Be Somebody** *Brainstorm*
93/74 **Wake Up And Love Me** *April Stevens*
12/76 **Wake Up Everybody** *Harold Melvin*
Wake Up Little Susie
1/57 *Everly Brothers*
27/82 *Simon & Garfunkel*
53/82 **Wake Up My Love** *George Harrison*
39/85 **Wake Up (Next To You)** *Graham Parker*
56/76 **Wake Up Susan** *Spinners*
68/67 **Wake Up, Wake Up** *Grass Roots*
60/72 **Waking Up Alone** *Paul Williams*

WALK:

7/58 **Walk, The** *Jimmy McCracklin*
12/70 **Walk A Mile In My Shoes** *Joe South*
23/65 **Walk Away** *Matt Monro*
36/80 **Walk Away** *Donna Summer*
51/71 **Walk Away** *James Gang*
9/76 **Walk Away From Love** *David Ruffin*
Walk Away Renee
5/66 *Left Banke*
14/68 *Four Tops*
98/86 *Southside Johnny & The Jukes*
Walk Don't Run
2/60 *Ventures*
8/64 *Ventures ('64)*
93/71 **Walk Easy My Son** *Jerry Butler*
Walk Hand In Hand
10/56 *Tony Martin*
54/56 *Andy Williams*
70/56 *Denny Vaughn*
12/65 **Walk In The Black Forest** *Horst Jankowski*
46/72 **Walk In The Night** *Jr. Walker*
54/95 **Walk In The Sun** *Bruce Hornsby*
Walk Like A Man
1/63 *4 Seasons*
41/86 *Mary Jane Girls*
19/74 **Walk Like A Man** *Grand Funk*
1/86 **Walk Like An Egyptian** *Bangles*
7/86 **Walk Of Life** *Dire Straits*
69/74 **Walk On** *Neil Young*
5/61 **Walk On By** *Leroy Van Dyke*
Walk On By
6/64 *Dionne Warwick*
30/69 *Isaac Hayes*
98/75 *Gloria Gaynor*
92/79 *AWB*
74/90 *Sybil*
18/93 **Walk On The Ocean** *Toad The Wet Sprocket*
16/73 **Walk On The Wild Side** *Lou Reed*
Walk On The Wild Side
21/62 *Jimmy Smith*
43/62 *Brook Benton*
(also see: Wildside)
9/88 **Walk On Water** *Eddie Money*
17/72 **Walk On Water** *Neil Diamond*
91/62 **Walk On With The Duke** *Duke Of Earl*
7/61 **Walk Right Back** *Everly Brothers*
Walk Right In
1/63 *Rooftop Singers*
82/63 *Moments*
46/77 *Dr. Hook*
73/81 **Walk Right Now** *Jacksons*
81/71 **Walk Right Up To The Sun** *Delfonics*
48/60 **Walk Slow** *Little Willie John*
92/67 **Walk Tall** *2 Of Clubs*
7/89 **Walk The Dinosaur** *Was (Not Was)*
Walk This Way
10/77 *Aerosmith*
4/86 *Run-D.M.C.*
63A/95 **Walk This World** *Heather Nova*
28/91 **Walk Through Fire** *Bad Company*
83/67 **Walk With Faith In Your Heart** *Bachelors*

WALKIN'/WALKING:

12/57 **Walkin' After Midnight** *Patsy Cline*
100/61 **Walkin' Back To Happiness** *Helen Shapiro*
Walkin' In The Rain
23/64 *Ronettes*
19/70 *Jay & The Americans*
14/72 **Walkin' In The Rain With The One I Love** *Love Unlimited*
Walkin' In The Sand ..see: Remember
37/67 **Walkin' In The Sunshine** *Roger Miller*
12/63 **Walkin' Miracle** *Essex*
22/66 **Walkin' My Cat Named Dog** *Norma Tanega*
2A/98 **Walkin' On The Sun** *Smash Mouth*
98/67 **Walkin' Proud** *Pete Klint Quintet*
26/63 **Walking Proud** *Steve Lawrence*
86/89 **Walkin' Shoes** *Tora Tora*
96/59 **Walkin' To Mother's** *Ray Anthony*
54/58 **Walkin' With Mr. Lee** *Lee Allen*
53/62 **Walkin' With My Angel** *Bobby Vee*
29/58 **Walking Along** *Diamonds*
9/89 **Walking Away** *Information Society*
44/02 **Walking Away** *Craig David*
70A/96 **Walking Contradiction** *Green Day*
11/87 **Walking Down Your Street** *Bangles*
70/83 **Walking In L.A.** *Missing Persons*
13/91 **Walking In Memphis** *Marc Cohn*
69/93 **Walking In My Shoes** *Depeche Mode*
62/84 **Walking In My Sleep** *Roger Daltrey*
6/75 **Walking In Rhythm** *Blackbyrds*
53S/02 **Walking In The Sky** *DJ Encore (feat.) Engelina*
84/81 **Walking Into Sunshine** *Central Line*
18/84 **Walking On A Thin Line** *Huey Lewis*
14/92 **Walking On Broken Glass** *Annie Lennox*
9/85 **Walking On Sunshine** *Katrina & The Waves*
46/85 **Walking On The Chinese Wall** *Philip Bailey*
58/81 **Walking On Thin Ice** *Yoko Ono*
10/63 **Walking The Dog** *Rufus Thomas*
Walking The Floor ..see: I'm Walking
44/70 **Walking Through The Country** *Grass Roots*
81/89 **Walking Through Walls** *Escape Club*
92/95 **Walking To Jerusalem** *Tracy Byrd*
6/60 **Walking To New Orleans** *Fats Domino*
32/80 **Walks Like A Lady** *Journey*
Wall, The
43/57 *Patti Page*
62/57 *Eileen Rodgers*
69/96 **Walls** *Tom Petty*
74/83 **Walls Came Down** *Call*
77/59 **Walls Have Ears** *Patti Page*
94/62 **Waltz You Saved For Me** *Ferlin Husky*
41/60 **Waltzing Matilda** *Jimmie Rodgers*
Wanderer, The
2/62 *Dion*
49/78 *Leif Garrett*
3/80 **Wanderer, The** *Donna Summer*
Wang Dang Doodle
58/66 *Ko Ko Taylor*
61/74 *Pointer Sisters*
62/59 **Wang Dang Taffy-Apple Tango (Mambo Cha Cha Cha)** *Pat Boone*
86/80 **Wango Tango** *Ted Nugent*
13/03 **Wanksta** *50 Cent*
70/99 **Wanna Be A Baller** *Lil' Troy*
5/83 **Wanna Be Startin' Somethin'** *Michael Jackson*
51/82 **Wanna Be With You** *Earth, Wind & Fire*
76/91 **Wanna Dance** *Yasmin*
76/76 **Wanna Make Love (Come Flick My BIC)** *Sun*
1/97 **Wannabe** *Spice Girls*
28/93 **Wannagirl** *Jeremy Jordan*
1/71 **Want Ads** *Honey Cone*
72/81 **(Want You) Back In My Life Again** *Carpenters*
79/87 **Want You For My Girlfriend** *4 By Four*
96/70 **Want You To Know** *Rotary Connection*
7/87 **Wanted Dead Or Alive** *Bon Jovi*
87/84 **Wanted Man** *Ratt*
84/67 **Wanted: Lover, No Experience Necessary** *Laura Lee*
38/56 **Wanting You** *Roger Williams*
War
1/70 *Edwin Starr*
8/86 *Bruce Springsteen*
59/56 **War And Peace** *Vic Damone*
45/83 **War Games** *Crosby, Stills & Nash*
(War Is Over) ..see: Happy Xmas
17/84 **War Song** *Culture Club*
61/72 **War Song** *Neil Young & Graham Nash*
17/66 **Warm And Tender Love** *Percy Sledge*
13/92 **Warm It Up** *Kris Kross*
39/78 **Warm Ride** *Rare Earth*
81/95 **Warm Summer Daze** *Vybe*
57/57 **Warm Up To Me Baby** *Jimmy Bowen*
25/62 **Warmed Over Kisses (Left Over Love)** *Brian Hyland*
Warning
F/95 *Notorious B.I.G.*
FS/01 *Notorious B.I.G.*
41A/95 **Warped** *Red Hot Chili Peppers*
7/84 **Warrior, The** *Scandal*
96/94 **Warrior's Drum (Hay-Ya Hay-Ya Hay-Ya Ho!)** *King Just*
70/78 **Was Dog A Doughnut** *Cat Stevens*
83/69 **Was It Good To You** *Isley Brothers*
24/90 **Was It Nothing At All** *Michael Damian*
56/67 **Washed Ashore (On A Lonely Island In The Sea)** *Platters*
88/92 **Washed Away** *Tom Cochrane*

2/63 **Washington Square**
Village Stompers
49/79 **Wasn't It Good** *Cher*
37/81 **Wasn't That A Party** *Rovers*
89/61 **Wasn't The Summer Short?**
Johnny Mathis
8/75 **Wasted Days And Wasted Nights**
Freddy Fender
9/82 **Wasted On The Way**
Crosby, Stills & Nash
88/92 **Wasted Time** *Skid Row*
13/02 **Wasting My Time** *Default*
52/77 **Watch Closely Now**
Kris Kristofferson
73/99 **Watch For The Hook** *Cool Breeze*
61/67 **Watch Her Ride** *Jefferson Airplane*
32/97 **Watch Me Do My Thing** *Immature*
40/79 **Watch Out For Lucy** *Eric Clapton*
84/99 **Watch Out Now** *Beatnuts*
30/67 **Watch The Flowers Grow**
4 Seasons
51/61 **Watch Your Step** *Bobby Parker*
58/64 **Watch Your Step** *Brooks O'Dell*
80/87 **Watching Over You**
Glenn Medeiros
11/71 **Watching Scotty Grow**
Bobby Goldsboro
41/71 **Watching The River Flow**
Bob Dylan
71/74 **Watching The River Run**
Loggins & Messina
10/81 **Watching The Wheels**
John Lennon
83/56 **Watching The World Go By**
Dean Martin
78/81 **Watching You** *Slave*
40/61 **Water Boy** *Don Shirley Trio*
2/95 **Water Runs Dry** *Boyz II Men*
56/87 **Waterfall** *Wendy & Lisa*
78/75 **Waterfall** *Carly Simon*
1/95 **Waterfalls** *TLC*
42/73 **Watergrate** *Dickie Goodman*
4/59 **Waterloo** *Stonewall Jackson*
6/74 **Waterloo** *Abba*
81/94 **Watermelon Crawl** *Tracy Byrd*
Watermelon Man
10/63 *Mongo Santamaria Band*
62/65 *Gloria Lynne*
87/57 **Watermelon Song**
"Tennessee" Ernie Ford
25/61 **Watusi, The** *Vibrations*
(also see: El Watusi / Wah Watusi)
42/78 **Wavelength** *Van Morrison*
64A/96 **Wax Ecstatic (To Sell Angelina)**
Sponge

WAY:

5A/98 **Way, The** *Fastball*
60/01 **Way, The** *Jill Scott*
Way Back Home
90/71 *Jazz Crusaders*
52/72 *Jr. Walker*
75/89 **Way Cool Jr.** *Ratt*
18/77 **Way Down** *Elvis Presley*
3/60 **Way Down Yonder In New Orleans**
Freddie Cannon
40/83 **Way He Makes Me Feel**
Barbra Streisand
58/61 **Way I Am** *Jackie Wilson*
58/00 **Way I Am** *Eminem*
63/92 **Way I Feel** *Tag*
12/92 **Way I Feel About You** *Karyn White*
24/78 **Way I Feel Tonight** *Bay City Rollers*
35/59 **Way I Walk** *Jack Scott*
4/75 **Way I Want To Touch You**
Captain & Tennille
1/86 **Way It Is** *Bruce Hornsby*
55/90 **Way It Is** *Tesla*
42/69 **Way It Used To Be**
Engelbert Humperdinck
44/60 **Way Of A Clown** *Teddy Randazzo*
71/02 **Way Of Life** *Lil Wayne*
Way Of Love
88/65 *Kathy Kirby*
7/72 *Chér*
61/88 **Way Out** *J.J. Fad*
94/62 **Way Over There** *Miracles*
20/94 **Way She Loves Me** *Richard Marx*
67/95 **Way That You Love**
Vanessa Williams
Way That You Love Me ..see: (It's Just)
65/97 **Way That You Talk** *Jagged Edge*
41/89 **Way To Your Heart** *Soulsister*
Way We Were
1/74 *Barbra Streisand*
11/75 *Gladys Knight (medley)*
Way You Do The Things You Do
11/64 *Temptations*
20/78 *Rita Coolidge*
20/85 *Daryl Hall John Oates/David Ruffin/Eddie Kendrick (medley)*
6/90 *UB40*
13/61 **Way You Look Tonight** *Lettermen*
6/01 **Way You Love Me** *Faith Hill*
7/89 **Way You Love Me** *Karyn White*
1/88 **Way You Make Me Feel**
Michael Jackson
24/58 **Ways Of A Woman In Love**
Johnny Cash
54/93 **Ways Of The Wind** *PM Dawn*
71/85 **Ways To Be Wicked** *Lone Justice*
81/69 **Ways To Love A Man**
Tammy Wynette
Wayward Wind
1/56 *Gogi Grant*
28/56 *Tex Ritter*
50/61 *Gogi Grant*

WE:

89/73 **We** *Shawn Phillips*
65/94 **We Ain't Goin' Out Like That**
Cypress Hill
5/67 **(We Ain't Got) Nothin' Yet**
Blues Magoos
97/75 **We All Gotta Stick Together**
Four Tops
67/56 **We All Need Love** *Percy Faith*
(We All Shine On) ..see: Instant Karma
14/88 **We All Sleep Alone** *Cher*
We Are Family
2/79 *Sister Sledge*
29S/01 *We Are Family*
70/71 **We Are Neighbors** *Chi-Lites*
We Are The Champions (medley)
4/78 *Queen*
52/92 *Queen*
1/85 **We Are The World** *USA for Africa*
25/84 **We Are The Young** *Dan Hartman*
53/87 **We Are What We Are** *Other Ones*
56A/98 **We Be Clubbin'** *Ice Cube*
58S/99 **We Be Puttin' It Down** *Bad Azz*
91/75 **We Been Singin' Songs**
Baron Stewart
5/85 **We Belong** *Pat Benatar*
We Belong Together
32/58 *Robert & Johnny*
75/64 *Jimmy Velvet*
1/85 **We Built This City** *Starship*
21/68 **We Can Fly** *Cowsills*
75/97 **We Can Get Down** *Myron*
62/81 **We Can Get Together** *Icehouse*
55/89 **We Can Last Forever** *Chicago*
74/70 **We Can Make It Baby** *Originals*
68/72 **We Can Make It Together**
Steve & Eydie/The Osmonds
49/70 **We Can Make Music** *Tommy Roe*
We Can Work It Out
1/66 *Beatles*
13/71 *Stevie Wonder*
8/99 **We Can't Be Friends**
Deborah Cox with R.L.
8/90 **We Can't Go Wrong** *Cover Girls*
36/76 **We Can't Hide It Anymore**
Larry Santos
41/85 **We Close Our Eyes** *Go West*
35/87 **We Connect** *Stacey Q*
41/64 **We Could** *Al Martino*
71/89 **We Could Be Together**
Debbie Gibson
29/00 **We Danced** *Brad Paisley*
72/97 **We Danced Anyway** *Deana Carter*
95/73 **We Did It** *Syl Johnson*
1/89 **We Didn't Start The Fire** *Billy Joel*
5/86 **We Don't Have To Take Our Clothes Off** *Jermaine Stewart*
2/85 **We Don't Need Another Hero (Thunderdome)** *Tina Turner*
7/80 **We Don't Talk Anymore**
Cliff Richard
80/78 **We Fell In Love While Dancing**
Bill Brandon
95/93 **We Getz Buzy** *Illegal*
53/60 **We Go Together** *Jan & Dean*
69S/01 **We Gonna Make It** *Jadakiss*
82/71 **We Got A Dream** *Ocean*
20/92 **We Got A Love Thang**
Ce Ce Peniston
65/66 **We Got A Thing That's In The Groove** *Capitols*
37/96 **We Got It** *Immature*
6/59 **We Got Love** *Bobby Rydell*
35/69 **We Got More Soul**
Dyke & The Blazers
2/82 **We Got The Beat** *Go-Go's*
100/66 **We Got The Winning Hand**
Little Milton
86/71 **We Got To Live Together**
Buddy Miles
50/69 **We Gotta All Get Together**
Paul Revere & The Raiders
13/65 **We Gotta Get Out Of This Place**
Animals
20/71 **We Gotta Get You A Woman** *Runt*
72/67 **We Had A Good Thing Goin'**
Cyrkle
76/60 **We Have Love** *Dinah Washington*
93/58 **We Have Love** *Jackie Wilson*
12/77 **We Just Disagree** *Dave Mason*
76/66 **We Know We're In Love**
Lesley Gore
26/99 **We Like To Party!** *Vengaboys*
47S/00 **We Live** *Bosson*
27/80 **We Live For Love** *Pat Benatar*
50/67 **We Love You** *Rolling Stones*
39/64 **We Love You Beatles** *Carefrees*
42/69 **We Love You, Call Collect**
Art Linkletter
83/75 **We May Never Love Like This Again** *Maureen McGovern*
21/73 **We May Never Pass This Way (Again)** *Seals & Crofts*
65/95 **We Must Be In Love** *Pure Soul*
88/69 **We Must Be In Love**
Five Stairsteps
59/01 **We Need A Resolution** *Aaliyah*
61/72 **We Need Order** *Chi-Lites*
93/77 **We Never Danced To A Love Song**
Manhattans

44/98 **We Really Shouldn't Be Doing This** *George Strait*
36S/01 **We Right Here** *DMX*
90/63 **We Shall Overcome** *Joan Baez*
90/87 **We Should Be Sleeping** *Eddie Money*
15/02 **We Thuggin** *Fat Joe*
83/59 **We Told You Not To Marry** *Titus Turner*
45/97 **We Trying To Stay Alive** *Wyclef Jean*
22/83 **We Two** *Little River Band*
16/91 **We Want The Funk** *Gerardo*
61/71 **We Were Always Sweethearts** *Boz Scaggs*
31/80 **We Were Meant To Be Lovers** *Photoglo*
We Will Rock You (medley)
4/78 *Queen*
52/92 *Queen*
83/92 *Warrant*
7/87 **We'll Be Together** *Sting*
(We'll Be) United ..see: United
73/69 **We'll Cry Together** *Maxine Brown*
89/71 **We'll Have It Made** *Spinners*
9/78 **We'll Never Have To Say Goodbye Again** *England Dan & John Ford Coley*
4/64 **We'll Sing In The Sunshine** *Gale Garnett*

WE'RE:

14/68 **We're A Winner** *Impressions*
We're All Alone
78/76 *Frankie Valli*
7/77 *Rita Coolidge*
93/71 **We're All Goin' Home** *Bobby Bloom*
35/90 **We're All In The Same Gang** *West Coast Rap All-Stars*
48/70 **We're All Playing In The Same Band** *Bert Sommer*
54/75 **We're Almost There** *Michael Jackson*
1/73 **We're An American Band** *Grand Funk*
96/65 **We're Doing Fine** *Dee Dee Warwick*
40/72 **We're Free** *Beverly Bremers*
100/71 **We're Friends By Day (And Lovers By Night)** *Whatnauts*
34/74 **We're Getting Careless With Our Love** *Johnnie Taylor*
48/84 **We're Going All The Way** *Jeffrey Osborne*
(We're Gonna) ..see: Rock Around The Clock
93/73 **We're Gonna Have A Good Time** *Rare Earth*
25/65 **We're Gonna Make It** *Little Milton*
15/81 **We're In This Love Together** *Al Jarreau*
21/84 **We're Not Gonna Take It** *Twisted Sister*
13/98 **We're Not Making Love No More** *Dru Hill*
44/72 **We're On Our Way** *Chris Hodge*
94/76 **We're On The Right Track** *South Shore Commission*
9/87 **We're Ready** *Boston*
59/68 **We're Rolling On** *Impressions*
100/72 **We're Together** *Hillside Singers*
46/72 **We've Come Too Far To End It Now** *Miracles*
56/69 **(We've Got) Honey Love** *Martha & The Vandellas*
69/95 **We've Got It Goin' On** *Backstreet Boys*
44/79 **We've Got Love** *Peaches & Herb*
25/72 **We've Got To Get It On Again** *Addrisi Brothers*
We've Got Tonite
13/79 *Bob Seger*
6/83 *Kenny Rogers & Sheena Easton*
2/70 **We've Only Just Begun** *Carpenters*
66/87 **We've Only Just Begun (The Romance Is Not Over)** *Glenn Jones*
47/89 **We've Saved The Best For Last** *Kenny G (with Smokey Robinson)*
1/93 **Weak** *SWV*
65/87 **Weapons Of Love** *Truth*
44/68 **Wear It On Our Face** *Dells*
F/57 **Wear My Ring** *Gene Vincent*
2/58 **Wear My Ring Around Your Neck** *Elvis Presley*
91/71 **Wear This Ring (With Love)** *Detroit Emeralds*
23/67 **Wear Your Love Like Heaven** *Donovan*
32/56 **Weary Blues** *McGuire Sisters & Lawrence Welk*
Weatherman
95/86 *Nick Jameson*
67/87 *Jack Wagner*
10/65 **Wedding, The** *Julie Rogers*
43/59 **Wedding, The** *June Valli*
91/56 **Wedding, The** *Chordettes*
1/69 **Wedding Bell Blues** *5th Dimension*
Wedding Bells ..see: (I'm Always Hearing)
91/69 **Wedding Cake** *Connie Francis*
Wedding Song (There Is Love)
24/71 *Paul Stookey*
61/72 *Petula Clark*
81/78 *Mary MacGregor*
(also see: Down The Aisle)
97/67 **Wednesday** *Royal Guardsmen*
35/58 **Week End** *Kingsmen*
29/79 **Weekend** *Wet Willie*
10/77 **Weekend In New England** *Barry Manilow*
70/94 **Weekend Love** *Queen Latifah*
57/78 **Weekend Lover** *Odyssey*
90/97 **Weekend Thang** *Alfonzo Hunter*
Weight, The
55/68 *Jackie DeShannon*
63/68 *Band*
19/69 *Aretha Franklin*
46/69 *Supremes & Temptations*
74A/95 **Weird-Out** *Dandelion*
45/85 **Weird Science** *Oingo Boingo*
1/76 **Welcome Back** *John Sebastian*
68/61 **Welcome Home** *Sammy Kaye*
95/65 **Welcome Home** *Walter Jackson*
22/62 **Welcome Home Baby** *Shirelles*
48/69 **Welcome Me Love** *Brooklyn Bridge*
18/60 **(Welcome) New Lovers** *Pat Boone*
35/02 **Welcome To Atlanta** *Jermaine Dupri & Ludacris*
24/83 **Welcome To Heartlight** *Kenny Loggins*
(Welcome To My Morning) ..see: Farewell Andromeda
45/75 **Welcome To My Nightmare** *Alice Cooper*
35S/02 **Welcome To New York City** *Cam'ron*
68/77 **Welcome To Our World (Of Merry Music)** *Mass Production*
85/85 **Welcome To Paradise** *John Waite*
56A/94 **Welcome To Paradise** *Green Day*
37/86 **Welcome To The Boomtown** *David & David*
7/88 **Welcome To The Jungle** *Guns N' Roses*
48/85 **Welcome To The Pleasuredome** *Frankie Goes To Hollywood*
49/90 **Welcome To The Real World** *Jane Child*
63/70 **Welfare Cadilac** *Guy Drake*
77/61 **Well-A, Well-A** *Shirley & Lee*
69/78 **Well All Right** *Santana*
92/56 **Well Did You Evah?** *Bing Crosby & Frank Sinatra*
29/61 **Well. I Told You** *Chantels*
87/58 **Well I'm Your Man** *Johnny Tillotson*
13/66 **Well Respected Man** *Kinks*
44/64 **Wendy** *Beach Boys*
72/58 **Wendy, Wendy** *Four Coins*
64/74 **Werewolf** *Five Man Electrical Band*
83/60 **Werewolf** *Frantics*
21/78 **Werewolves Of London** *Warren Zevon*
64/83 **West Coast Summer Nights** *Tony Carey*
79/73 **West Coast Woman** *Painter*
1/86 **West End Girls** *Pet Shop Boys*
37/62 **West Of The Wall** *Toni Fisher*
84/00 **West Side Story** *LFO*
88/95 **West Up!** *WC & The Maad Circle*
24/70 **Westbound #9** *Flaming Ember*
8/58 **Western Movies** *Olympics*
5/67 **Western Union** *Five Americans*
12/98 **Westside** *TQ*
61/84 **Wet My Whistle** *Midnight Star*
24/63 **Wham!** *Lonnie Mack*
16/76 **Wham Bam** *Silver*

WHAT:

F/95 **What, The** *Notorious B.I.G. & Method Man*
What A Beautiful World ..see: I.G.Y.
88/70 **What A Bummer** *Jaggerz*
What A Diff'rence A Day Makes
8/59 *Dinah Washington*
20/75 *Esther Phillips*
80/78 **What A Difference You've Made In My Life** *Ronnie Milsap*
What A Feeling ..see: Flashdance
1/79 **What A Fool Believes** *Doobie Brothers*
93/63 **What A Fool I've Been** *Carla Thomas*
1/00 **What A Girl Wants** *Christina Aguilera*
41/63 **What A Guy** *Raindrops*
93/75 **What A Man, My Man Is** *Lynn Anderson*
22/61 **What A Party** *Fats Domino*
22/61 **What A Price** *Fats Domino*
60/91 **What A Price To Pay** *Michael Damian*
74/62 **(What A Sad Way) To Love Someone** *Ral Donner*
82/73 **What A Shame** *Foghat*
33/61 **What A Surprise** *Johnny Maestro*
54/61 **What A Sweet Thing That Was** *Shirelles*
77/61 **What A Walk** *Bobby Lewis*
31/67 **What A Woman In Love Won't Do** *Sandy Posey*
78/72 **What A Wonderful Thing We Have** *Fabulous Rhinestones*
What A Wonderful World
32/88 *Louis Armstrong*
53S/99 *Louis Armstrong With Kenny G*
(also see: Wonderful World)
10/85 **What About Love?** *Heart*

26/86 **What About Love** *'Til Tuesday*
15/84 **What About Me?**
Kenny Rogers/Kim Carnes/James Ingram
What About Me
29/83 *Moving Pictures*
46/89 *Moving Pictures*
64/73 **What About Me** *Anne Murray*
100/61 **What About Me** *Don Gibson*
100/71 **What About Me**
Quicksilver Messenger Service
30/00 **What About Now** *Lonestar*
7/02 **What About Us?** *Brandy*
16/97 **What About Us** *Total*
47/60 **What About Us** *Coasters*
74S/94 **What About Us** *Jodeci*
7/92 **What About Your Friends** *TLC*
39/72 **What Am I Crying For?** *Classics IV*
71/66 **What Am I Going To Do Without Your Love**
Martha & The Vandellas
50/61 **What Am I Gonna Do**
Jimmy Clanton
71/01 **What Am I Gonna Do** *Tyrese*
73/70 **What Am I Gonna Do** *Smith*
35/83 **What Am I Gonna Do (I'm So In Love With You)** *Rod Stewart*
8/75 **What Am I Gonna Do With You**
Barry White
What Am I Living For
9/58 *Chuck Willis*
26/60 *Conway Twitty*
91/67 *Percy Sledge*
54/72 *Ray Charles*
82/62 **What Am I Supposed To Do**
Ann-Margret
53/63 **What Are Boys Made Of** *Percells*
14/81 **What Are We Doin' In Love**
Dottie West (with Kenny Rogers)
93/65 **What Are We Going To Do?**
David Jones
17X/65 **What Are You Doing New Year's Eve** *Nancy Wilson*
39/71 **What Are You Doing Sunday**
Dawn Feat. Tony Orlando
96/90 **What Are You Doing With A Fool Like Me** *Joe Cocker*
What Becomes Of The Brokenhearted
7/66 *Jimmy Ruffin*
22/92 *Paul Young*
61/57 **What Can I Do** *Donnie Elbert*
48/75 **What Can I Do For You?** *LaBelle*
50/79 **What Can I Do With This Broken Heart**
England Dan & John Ford Coley
42/76 **What Can I Say** *Boz Scaggs*
69/80 **What Can You Get A Wookiee For Christmas (When He Already Owns A Comb?)** *Star Wars Intergalactic Droid Choir & Chorale*
What Cha ..also see: What You / Whatcha / What U / What'Chu
53/81 **What Cha' Gonna Do For Me**
Chaka Khan
What Cha Gonna Do With My Lovin'
22/79 *Stephanie Mills*
76/90 *Inner City*
38/65 **What Color (Is A Man)**
Bobby Vinton
19/91 **What Comes Naturally**
Sheena Easton
94/62 **What Did Daddy Do**
Shep & The Limelites
59/82 **What Do All The People Know**
Monroes

52/58 **What Do I Care** *Johnny Cash*
60A/96 **What Do I Have To Do?**
Stabbing Westward
31/00 **What Do You Say** *Reba McEntire*
45/99 **What Do You Say To That**
George Strait
93/60 **What Do You Want?** *Bobby Vee*
61A/97 **What Do You Want From Me?**
Monaco
51/65 **What Do You Want With Me**
Chad & Jeremy
53/63 **What Does A Girl Do?** *Shirelles*
82/63 **What Does A Girl Do?**
Marcie Blane
52/86 **What Does It Take**
Honeymoon Suite
4/69 **What Does It Take (To Win Your Love)** *Jr. Walker*
47/92 **What Goes Around Comes Around**
Giggles
81/66 **What Goes On** *Beatles*
87/78 **What Goes Up**
Alan Parsons Project
89/74 **What Goes Up (Must Come Down)**
Tyrone Davis
61/64 **What Good Am I Without You**
Marvin Gaye & Kim Weston
2/88 **What Have I Done To Deserve This?**
Pet Shop Boys/Dusty Springfield
43/64 **What Have I Got Of My Own**
Trini Lopez
29/65 **What Have They Done To The Rain**
Searchers
4/86 **What Have You Done For Me Lately** *Janet Jackson*
7/89 **What I Am** *Edie Brickell*
58/98 **What I Didn't Know** *Athenaeum*
29A/96 **What I Got** *Sublime*
What I Like About You
49/80 *Romantics*
28/89 *Michael Morales*
82/95 **What I Need** *Crystal Waters*
56/00 **What I Need To Do** *Kenny Chesney*
26/01 **What I Really Meant To Say**
Cyndi Thomson
56S/99 **What I Wanna Do** *No Authority*
50/98 **What If** *Reba McEntire*
80/01 **What If** *Babyface*
(also see: Remo's Theme)
63/02 **What If A Woman** *Joe*
72S/97 **What If I Do** *Mindy McCready*
59/98 **What If I Said**
Anita Cochran with Steve Wariner
71/83 **What If (I Said I Love You)** *Unipop*
39/02 **What If She's An Angel**
Tommy Shane Steiner
39/84 **(What) In The Name Of Love**
Naked Eyes
5/60 **What In The World's Come Over You** *Jack Scott*
53/69 **What Is A Man** *Four Tops*
96/57 **What Is A Teenage Boy?**
Tom Edwards
57/57 **What Is A Teenage Girl?**
Tom Edwards
56/56 **What Is A Wife** *Steve Allen*
91/74 **What Is Hip?** *Tower Of Power*
10/71 **What Is Life** *George Harrison*
11/93 **What Is Love** *Haddaway*
15/59 **What Is Love?** *Playmates*
33/84 **What Is Love?** *Howard Jones*
19/70 **What Is Truth** *Johnny Cash*
55/74 **What It Comes Down To**
Isley Brothers
23/01 **What It Feels Like For A Girl**
Madonna

63/01 **What It Is** *Busta Rhymes*
71/72 **What It Is** *Undisputed Truth*
9/90 **What It Takes** *Aerosmith*
13/99 **What It's Like** *Everlast*
10/81 **What Kind Of Fool**
Barbra Streisand & Barry Gibb
What Kind Of Fool Am I
17/62 *Sammy Davis Jr.*
85/62 *Anthony Newley*
89/62 *Robert Goulet*
21/82 **What Kind Of Fool Am I**
Rick Springfield
What Kind Of Fool Do You Think I Am
9/64 *Tams*
23/69 *Bill Deal*
18/62 **What Kind Of Love Is This**
Joey Dee
5/90 **What Kind Of Man Would I Be?**
Chicago
17/96 **What Kind Of Man Would I Be**
Mint Condition
79/58 **What Little Girl** *Frankie Avalon*
63/83 **What Love Is** *Marty Balin*
90/95 **What Mattered Most** *Ty Herndon*
83/00 **What Means The World To You**
Cam'ron
74/94 **What Might Have Been** *Little Texas*
56/73 **What My Baby Needs Now Is A Little More Lovin'**
James Brown-Lyn Collins
40/65 **What Now** *Gene Chandler*
What Now My Love
14/66 *Sonny & Cher*
24/66 *Herb Alpert*
96/66 *"Groove" Holmes*
30/67 *Mitch Ryder*
61/81 **What She Does To Me (The Diana Song)** *Producers*
54S/01 **What Side You On** *Crimewave*
45/84 **What The Big Girls Do**
Van Stephenson
What The World Needs Now Is Love
7/65 *Jackie DeShannon*
8/71 *Tom Clay (medley)*
87/98 *Dionne Warwick*
34/97 **What They Do** *Roots*
67/62 **What Time Is It?** *Jive Five*
57/91 **What Time Is Love?** *KLF*
92/75 **What Time Of Day**
Billy Thunderkloud
68/63 **What To Do With Laurie**
Mike Clifford
50/98 **What U See Is What U Get** *Xzibit*
96/90 **What Will I Do** *Timmy -T-*
What Will I Tell My Heart
64/57 *Fats Domino*
96/61 *Harptones*
9/63 **What Will Mary Say** *Johnny Mathis*
46/98 **What Would Happen**
Meredith Brooks
46/61 **What Would I Do** *Mickey & Sylvia*
70/72 **What Would The Children Think**
Rick Springfield
8/01 **What Would You Do?** *City High*
65S/02 **What Would You Do?** *Nine20*
73/61 **What Would You Do?** *Jim Reeves*
22A/95 **What Would You Say**
Dave Matthews Band
29/99 **What Ya Want** *Eve & Nokio*
What You ..also see: What Cha / Whatcha / What U / What'Chu
72/83 **What You Do To Me** *Carl Wilson*
8/89 **What You Don't Know** *Exposé*

49/69 **What You Gave Me** *Marvin Gaye & Tammi Terrell*
13/87 **What You Get Is What You See** *Tina Turner*
86/92 **What You Give** *Tesla*
95/75 **What You Got** *Duke & The Drivers*
5/86 **What You Need** *INXS*
24/88 **What You See Is What You Get** *Brenda K. Starr*
71/71 **What You See Is What You Get** *Stoney & Meatloaf*
6/98 **What You Want** *Mase*
49/00 **What You Want** *DMX*
What You Won't Do For Love
9/79 *Bobby Caldwell*
55/93 *Go West*
81/83 **What You're Missing** *Chicago*
26/00 **What'Chu Like** *Da Brat*
What'd I Say
6/59 *Ray Charles*
30/61 *Jerry Lee Lewis*
24/62 *Bobby Darin*
21/64 *Elvis Presley*
61/72 *Rare Earth*
56/99 **What'd You Come Here For?** *Trina & Tamara*

WHAT'S:

What's ..also see: Wot's
What's A Matter Baby
12/62 *Timi Yuro*
92/79 *Ellen Foley*
61/98 **What's Clef** *Wyclef Jean*
29/64 **What's Easy For Two Is So Hard For One** *Mary Wells*
19/82 **What's Forever For** *Michael Murphey*
What's Going On
2/71 *Marvin Gaye*
12/87 *Cyndi Lauper*
27/01 *Artists Against AIDS*
43S/02 **What's Golden?** *Jurassic 5*
45/62 **What's Gonna Happen When Summer's Done** *Freddy Cannon*
57/75 **What's Happened To Blue Eyes** *Jessi Colter*
94/60 **What's Happening** *Wade Flemons*
60/65 **What's He Doing In My World** *Eddy Arnold*
3/99 **What's It Gonna Be?!** *Busta Rhymes*
49/67 **What's It Gonna Be** *Dusty Springfield*
90/91 **What's It Gonna Be** *Jellybean*
73/93 **What's It To You** *Clay Walker*
What's Love Got To Do With It
1/84 *Tina Turner*
32/96 *Warren G*
2/02 **What's Luv?** *Fat Joe*
94/68 **What's Made Milwaukee Famous (Has Made A Loser Out Of Me)** *Jerry Lee Lewis*
58/99 **What's My Age Again?** *Blink 182*
8/94 **What's My Name?** *Snoop Doggy Dog*
67/00 **What's My Name** *DMX*
53/83 **What's New** *Linda Ronstadt & Nelson Riddle*
3/65 **What's New Pussycat?** *Tom Jones*
21/97 **What's On Tonight** *Montell Jordan*
3/88 **What's On Your Mind (Pure Energy)** *Information Society*
86/83 **What's She Got** *Liquid Gold*
49/99 **What's So Different?** *Ginuwine*
35/62 **What's So Good About Good-by** *Miracles*
73/97 **What's Stopping You** *O'Jays*
21/94 **What's The Frequency, Kenneth?** *R.E.M.*
80/88 **What's The Matter Here?** *10,000 Maniacs*
17/64 **What's The Matter With You Baby** *Marvin Gaye & Mary Wells*
69/76 **What's The Name Of This Funk (Spider Man)** *Ramsey Lewis*
What's The Reason
50/57 *Fats Domino*
71/62 *Bobby Edwards*
20/69 **What's The Use Of Breaking Up** *Jerry Butler*
79/87 **What's Too Much** *Smokey Robinson*
What's Up
14/93 *4 Non Blondes*
58/94 *DJ Miko*
39/93 **What's Up Doc? (Can We Rock?)** *Fu-Schnickens w/Shaquille O'Neal*
21/00 **What's Your Fantasy** *Ludacris*
89/80 **What's Your Hurry Darlin'** *Ironhorse*
86/73 **What's Your Mama's Name** *Tanya Tucker*
What's Your Name
7/62 *Don & Juan*
92/74 *Andy & David Williams*
13/78 **What's Your Name** *Lynyrd Skynyrd*
56/78 **What's Your Name, What's Your Number** *Andrea True Connection*
61/67 **What've I Done (To Make You Mad)** *Linda Jones*
Whatcha ..also see: What Cha / What You / What U / What'Chu
23/98 **Whatcha Gone Do?** *Link*
6/77 **Whatcha Gonna Do** *Pablo Cruise*
41/82 **Whatcha Gonna Do** *Chilliwack*
92/60 **Whatcha Gonna Do** *Nat King Cole*
9/71 **Whatcha See Is Whatcha Get** *Dramatics*
41/98 **Whatcha Wanna Do?** *Mia X*
50S/01 **Whatcha Wants To Do** *Blocka Boyz*
96/02 **Whatchulookinat** *Whitney Houston*
42/97 **Whateva Man** *Redman*
16/97 **Whatever** *En Vogue*
47/00 **Whatever** *Ideal*
1/74 **Whatever Gets You Thru The Night** *John Lennon*
71/78 **Whatever Happened To Benny Santini?** *Chris Rea*
7X/68 **Whatever Happened To Christmas?** *Frank Sinatra*
93/83 **Whatever Happened To Old Fashioned Love** *B.J. Thomas*
63/92 **Whatever It Takes (To Make You Stay)** *Troop*
Whatever Lola Wants
6/55 *Sarah Vaughan*
12/55 *Dinah Shore*
95/72 **Whatever Turns You On** *Travis Wammack*
(Whatever Will Be, Will Be) ..see: Que Sera, Sera
77/80 **Whatever You Decide** *Randy Vanwarmer*
38/74 **Whatever You Got, I Want** *Jackson 5*
37/99 **Whatever You Say** *Martina McBride*
48/91 **Whatever You Want** *Tony! Toni! Toné!*
68/63 **Whatever You Want** *Jerry Butler*
3/94 **Whatta Man** *Salt 'N' Pepa with En Vogue*
85/98 **Whatuon** *LaTanya*
57/78 **Wheel In The Sky** *Journey*
Wheel Of Fortune
88/59 *Knightsbridge Strings*
83/60 *LaVern Baker*
Wheel Of Hurt
26/66 *Margaret Whiting*
59/66 *Al Martino*
Wheels
3/61 *String-A-Longs*
28/61 *Billy Vaughn*
87/76 **Wheels Of Fortune** *Doobie Brothers*
78/79 **Wheels Of Life** *Gino Vannelli*

WHEN:

5/58 **When** *Kalin Twins*
When A Boy Falls In Love
44/63 *Mel Carter*
52/65 *Sam Cooke*
53/74 **When A Child Is Born** *Michael Holm*
When A Man (Woman) Loves A Woman (Man)
1/66 *Percy Sledge*
73/66 *Esther Phillips*
35/80 *Bette Midler*
1/91 *Michael Bolton*
22/99 **When A Woman's Fed Up** *R. Kelly*
27/82 **When All Is Said And Done** *Abba*
90/55 **When All The Streets Are Dark** *Somethin' Smith & The Redheads*
50/96 **When Boy Meets Girl** *Total*
4/94 **When Can I See You** *Babyface*
1/84 **When Doves Cry** *Prince*
64/01 **When God-Fearin' Women Get The Blues** *Martina McBride*
30/82 **When He Shines** *Sheena Easton*
49/69 **When He Touches Me (Nothing Else Matters)** *Peaches & Herb*
12/99 **When I Close My Eyes** *Shanice*
6A/95 **When I Come Around** *Green Day*
18/69 **When I Die** *Motherlode*
41/97 **When I Die** *No Mercy*
84/79 **When I Dream** *Crystal Gayle*
42/90 **When I Dream Of You** *Tommy Page*
When I Fall In Love
65/61 *Etta Jones*
7/62 *Lettermen*
55/73 *Donny Osmond*
95/88 *Natalie Cole*
23/93 *Celine Dion & Clive Griffin*
70S/00 **When I Get Close To You** *Jocelyn Enriquez*
53/62 **When I Get Thru With You (You'll Love Me Too)** *Patsy Cline*
(When I Get To Heaven) ..see: Old Man & Me
8S/02 **When I Get You Alone** *Thicke*
85/94 **When I Give My Love** *Keith Sweat*
59/58 **When I Grow Too Old To Dream** *Ed Townsend*
9/64 **When I Grow Up (To Be A Man)** *Beach Boys*
8/92 **When I Look Into Your Eyes** *Firehouse*
10/89 **When I Looked At Him** *Exposé*
1/77 **When I Need You** *Leo Sayer*
31/99 **When I Said I Do** *Clint Black (w/Lisa Hartman Black)*
29/57 **When I See You** *Fats Domino*
1/89 **When I See You Smile** *Bad English*

35/01 **When I Think About Angels** *Jamie O'Neal*
1/86 **When I Think Of You** *Janet Jackson*
78/79 **When I Think Of You** *Leif Garrett*
20/80 **When I Wanted You** *Barry Manilow*
15/67 **When I Was Young** *Animals*
7/90 **When I'm Back On My Feet Again** *Michael Bolton*
47/71 **When I'm Dead And Gone** *McGuinness Flint*
4/03 **When I'm Gone** *3 Doors Down*
25/65 **When I'm Gone** *Brenda Holloway*
78/82 **When I'm Holding You Tight** *Michael Stanley Band*
When I'm With You
61/83 *Sheriff*
1/89 *Sheriff*
5/88 **When It's Love** *Van Halen*
13/01 **When It's Over** *Sugar Ray*
26/82 **When It's Over** *Loverboy*
94/64 **When Joanna Loved Me** *Tony Bennett*
41/70 **When Julie Comes Around** *Cuff Links*
18/66 **When Liking Turns To Loving** *Ronnie Dove*
58/96 **When Love & Hate Collide** *Def Leppard*
68/89 **When Love Comes To Town** *U2 With B.B. King*
77/91 **When Love Cries** *Donna Summer*
41/76 **When Love Has Gone Away** *Richard Cocciante*
64/77 **When Love Is New** *Arthur Prysock*
92/67 **When Love Slips Away** *Dee Dee Warwick*
98/97 **When Love Starts Talkin'** *Wynonna*
19/56 **When My Blue Moon Turns To Gold Again** *Elvis Presley*
14/56 **When My Dreamboat Comes Home** *Fats Domino*
When My Little Girl Is Smiling
28/62 *Drifters*
72/71 *Steve Alaimo*
48/57 **When Rock And Roll Come To Trinidad** *Nat "King" Cole*
11/93 **When She Cries** *Restless Heart*
49/81 **When She Dances** *Joey Scarbury*
37/66 **(When She Needs Good Lovin') She Comes To Me** *Chicago Loop*
11/81 **When She Was My Girl** *Four Tops*
5/87 **When Smokey Sings** *ABC*
52/01 **When Somebody Loves You** *Alan Jackson*
When Something Is Wrong With My Baby
42/67 *Sam & Dave*
78/90 *Linda Ronstadt/Aaron Neville*
10/62 **When The Boy In Your Arms (Is The Boy In Your Heart)** *Connie Francis*
95/63 **When The Boy's Happy (The Girl's Happy Too)** *Four Pennies*
94/62 **When The Boys Get Together** *Joanie Sommers*
19/58 **When The Boys Talk About The Girls** *Valerie Carr*
3/89 **When The Children Cry** *White Lion*
45/80 **When The Feeling Comes Around** *Jennifer Warnes*
2/86 **When The Going Gets Tough, The Tough Get Going** *Billy Ocean*
98/67 **When The Good Sun Shines** *Elmo & Almo*

14/86 **When The Heart Rules The Mind** *GTR*
76/84 **When The Lady Smiles** *Golden Earring*
19/02 **When The Last Time** *Clipse*
37/83 **When The Lights Go Out** *Naked Eyes*
98/91 **When The Lights Go Out** *Gerardo*
10/98 **When The Lights Go Out** *Five*
23/64 **When The Lovelight Starts Shining Through His Eyes** *Supremes*
54/74 **When The Morning Comes** *Hoyt Axton*
11/90 **When The Night Comes** *Joe Cocker*
71/70 **When The Party Is Over** *Robert John*
81/89 **When The Radio Is On** *Paul Shaffer*
54/85 **When The Rain Begins To Fall** *Jermaine Jackson/Pia Zadora*
73/86 **When The Rain Comes Down** *Andy Taylor*
When The Saints Go Marching In
18/56 *Bill Haley*
50/59 *Fats Domino*
91/65 **When The Ship Comes In** *Peter, Paul & Mary*
98/67 **When The Snow Is On The Roses** *Ed Ames*
80/57 **When The Swallows Come Back To Capistrano** *Pat Boone*
75/56 **When The Tide Is High** *Gogi Grant*
When The White Lilacs Bloom Again
12/56 *Helmut Zacharias*
18/56 *Billy Vaughn*
50/56 *Florian Zabach*
59/56 *LeRoy Holmes*
70/56 *Lawrence Welk*
45/71 **When There's No You** *Engelbert Humperdinck*
87/80 **When Things Go Wrong** *Robin Lane*
99/67 **When Tomorrow Comes** *Carla Thomas*
40S/00 **When U Think About Me** *Voice V*
38/94 **When We Dance** *Sting*
When We Get Married
10/61 *Dreamlovers*
45/70 *Intruders*
76/80 *Larry Graham*
36/88 **When We Kiss** *Bardeux*
72/84 **When We Make Love** *Alabama*
23/88 **When We Was Fab** *George Harrison*
83/88 **When Will I Be Famous?** *Bros*
When Will I Be Loved
8/60 *Everly Brothers*
2/75 *Linda Ronstadt*
65/58 **When Will I Know** *George Hamilton IV*
2/74 **When Will I See You Again** *Three Degrees*
63/91 **When Will I See You Smile Again?** *Bell Biv DeVoe*
When You ..also see: When U
15/99 **When You Believe** *Whitney Houston & Mariah Carey*
14/84 **When You Close Your Eyes** *Night Ranger*
When You Dance
33/56 *Turbans*
70/69 *Jay & The Americans*
93/71 **When You Dance I Can Really Love** *Neil Young*

91/78 **When You Feel Love** *Bob McGilpin*
When You Get Right Down To It
53/70 *Delfonics*
94/71 *Ronnie Dyson*
54/02 **When You Lie Next To Me** *Kellie Coffey*
62/56 **When You Lose The One You Love** *David Whitfield/Mantovani*
12/96 **When You Love A Woman** *Journey*
47/64 **When You Loved Me** *Brenda Lee*
75/00 **When You Need My Love** *Darryl Worley*
32/72 **When You Say Love** *Sonny & Chér*
53/95 **When You Say Nothing At All** *Alison Krauss & Union Station*
56/97 **When You Talk About Love** *Patti LaBelle*
When You Walk In The Room
35/64 *Searchers*
99/64 *Jackie de Shannon*
90/88 *Paul Carrack*
87/83 **When You Were Mine** *Mitch Ryder*
30/60 **When You Wish Upon A Star** *Dion & The Belmonts*
99/79 **When You're #1** *Gene Chandler*
22/97 **When You're Gone** *Cranberries*
58/67 **When You're Gone** *Brenda & The Tabulations*
9/71 **When You're Hot, You're Hot** *Jerry Reed*
6/79 **When You're In Love With A Beautiful Woman** *Dr. Hook*
When You're Young And In Love
48/64 *Ruby & The Romantics*
23/67 *Marvelettes*
91/75 *Choice Four*
95/75 *Ralph Carter*
35/85 **When Your Heart Is Weak** *Cock Robin*
(When Your Heart's On Fire) ..see: Smoke Gets In Your Eyes
60/65 **Whenever A Teenager Cries** *Reparata & The Delrons*
Whenever He (She) Holds You
39/64 *Bobby Goldsboro*
64/66 *Patty Duke*
5/78 **Whenever I Call You "Friend"** *Kenny Loggins*
38/76 **Whenever I'm Away From You** *John Travolta*
6/01 **Whenever, Wherever** *Shakira*
72/94 **Whenever You Come Around** *Vince Gill*
76/98 **Whenever You're Near Me** *Ace Of Base*

WHERE:

44/59 **Where** *Platters* (also see: In Time)
94/66 **Where Am I Going?** *Barbra Streisand*
80/74 **Where Are All My Friends** *Harold Melvin*
84/71 **Where Are We Going** *Bobby Bloom*
32/60 **Where Are You** *Frankie Avalon*
36/62 **Where Are You** *Dinah Washington*
65/00 **Where Are You Christmas?** *Faith Hill*
39/02 **Where Are You Going** *Dave Matthews Band*
95/70 **Where Are You Going** *Jerry Butler*
61/70 **Where Are You Going To My Love** *Brotherhood Of Man*
Where Are You Now?
77/86 *Synch*
10/89 *Jimmy Harnen w/Synch*
30A/93 **Where Are You Now** *Janet Jackson*

69/70 **Where Did All The Good Times Go** *Classics IV*
82/64 **Where Did I Go Wrong** *Dee Dee Sharp*
Where Did Our Love Go
1/64 *Supremes*
15/71 *Donnie Elbert*
68/76 *J. Geils Band*
93/63 **Where Did The Good Times Go** *Dick & DeeDee*
33/71 **Where Did They Go, Lord** *Elvis Presley*
90/80 **Where Did We Go Wrong** *Frankie Valli & Chris Forde*
50/86 **Where Did Your Heart Go?** *Wham!*
1/88 **Where Do Broken Hearts Go** *Whitney Houston*
(Where Do I Begin) ..see: Theme From Love Story
Where Do I Go
86/68 *Carla Thomas*
66/69 *Happenings (medley)*
38/86 **Where Do The Children Go** *Hooters*
48/96 **Where Do We Go From Here** *Deborah Cox*
71/96 **Where Do We Go From Here** *Vanessa Williams*
94/02 **Where Do We Go From Here** *Filter*
99/62 **Where Do You Come From** *Elvis Presley*
5/96 **Where Do You Go** *No Mercy*
25/65 **Where Do You Go** *Cher*
70/69 **Where Do You Go To (My Lovely)** *Peter Sarstedt*
50/96 **Where Do U Want Me To Put It** *Solo*
82/64 **Where Does Love Go** *Freddie Scott*
4/91 **Where Does My Heart Beat Now** *Celine Dion*
59/92 **Where Does That Leave Love** *George LaMond*
46/80 **Where Does The Lovin' Go** *David Gates*
52/95 **Where Ever You Are** *Terry Ellis*
83/83 **Where Everybody Knows Your Name (The Theme From "Cheers")** *Gary Portnoy*
45/71 **Where Evil Grows** *Poppy Family*
93/70 **Where Have All Our Heroes Gone** *Bill Anderson*
8/97 **Where Have All The Cowboys Gone?** *Paula Cole*
Where Have All The Flowers Gone
21/62 *Kingston Trio*
26/65 *Johnny Rivers*
100/75 **Where Have They Gone** *Jimmy Beaumont & The Skyliners*
58/62 **Where Have You Been (All My Life)** *Arthur Alexander*
81/78 **Where Have You Been All My Life** *Fotomaker*
34/01 **Where I Come From** *Alan Jackson*
74/61 **Where I Fell In Love** *Capris*
29/00 **Where I Wanna Be** *Donell Jones*
95/00 **Where I Wanna Be** *Shade Sheist*
79/95 **Where I Wanna Be Boy** *Missjones*
68S/93 **Where I'm From** *Digable Planets*
68S/94 **Where Is My Love?** *El DeBarge*
73/68 **Where Is My Mind** *Vanilla Fudge*
(Where Is Santa Claus?) ..see: Dònde Està Santa Claus?
5/72 **Where Is The Love** *Roberta Flack & Donny Hathaway*
96/75 **Where Is The Love** *Betty Wright*
90/67 **Where Is The Party** *Helena Ferguson*
61/96 **Where It's At** *Beck*
62/64 **Where Love Has Gone** *Jack Jones*
4/99 **Where My Girls At?** *702*
59S/94 **Where My Homiez? (Come Around My Way)** *Ill Al Skratch*
Where Or When
3/60 *Dion & The Belmonts*
98/64 *Lettermen*
28/73 **Where Peaceful Waters Flow** *Gladys Knight*
Where The Action Is ..see: Action
35/01 **Where The Blacktop Ends** *Keith Urban*
76/58 **Where The Blue Of The Night** *Tommy Mara*
4/61 **Where The Boys Are** *Connie Francis*
79/98 **Where The Green Grass Grows** *Tim McGraw*
3/01 **Where The Party At** *Jagged Edge*
20/01 **Where The Stars And Stripes And The Eagle Fly** *Aaron Tippin*
Where The Streets Have No Name
13/87 *U2*
72/91 *Pet Shop Boys (medley)*
97/66 **Where The Sun Has Never Shone** *Jonathan King*
99/72 **Where There's A Will There's A Way** *Delaney & Bonnie*
75/56 **Where There's Life** *George Cates*
23/59 **Where Were You (On Our Wedding Day)?** *Lloyd Price*
28/66 **Where Were You When I Needed You** *Grass Roots*
99/65 **Where Were You When I Needed You** *Jerry Vale*
23/79 **Where Were You When I Was Falling In Love** *Lobo*
28/02 **Where Were You (When The World Stopped Turning)** *Alan Jackson*
21/67 **Where Will The Words Come From** *Gary Lewis*
63/79 **Where Will Your Heart Take You** *Buckeye*
45/02 **Where Would You Be** *Martina McBride*
62/00 **Where You Are** *Jessica Simpson*
20/92 **Where You Goin' Now** *Damn Yankees*
Where You Lead
40/71 *Barbra Streisand*
37/72 *Barbra Streisand (medley)*
27A/97 **Where's The Love** *Hanson*
26/69 **Where's The Playground Susie** *Glen Campbell*
88/81 **Where's Your Angel?** *Lani Hall*
43S/02 **Where's Your Head At** *Basement Jaxx*
70/83 **Wherever I Lay My Hat (That's My Home)** *Paul Young*
82/92 **Wherever I May Roam** *Metallica*
50/90 **Wherever Would I Be** *Cheap Trick*
36/98 **Wherever You Go** *Voices Of Theory*
5/02 **Wherever You Will Go** *Calling*
Which Way Is Up ..see: Theme From
2/70 **Which Way You Goin' Billy?** *Poppy Family*
96/60 **Whiffenpoof Song** *Bob Crewe*
89/77 **While I'm Alone** *Maze Feat. Frankie Beverly*
60/01 **While You Loved Me** *Rascal Flatts*
7/81 **While You See A Chance** *Steve Winwood*
62/69 **While You're Out Looking For Sugar?** *Honey Cone*
62/95 **Whiney, Whiney (What Really Drives Me Crazy)** *Willi One Blood*
6/90 **Whip Appeal** *Babyface*
14/80 **Whip It** *Devo*
91/60 **Whip It On Me** *Jessie Hill*
65/94 **Whipped** *Jon Secada*
68/65 **Whipped Cream** *Herb Alpert*
28/83 **Whirly Girl** *Oxo*
Whiskey On A Sunday ..see: (Puppet Song)
72/86 **Whisper In The Dark** *Dionne Warwick*
37/84 **Whisper To A Scream (Birds Fly)** *Icicle Works*
Whisper Your Name ..see: (I Could Only)
Whispering
11/64 *Nino Tempo & April Stevens*
27/77 *Dr. Buzzard's Original "Savannah" Band (medley)*
9/57 **Whispering Bells** *Dell-Vikings*
51/91 **Whispers** *Corina*
11/66 **Whispers (Gettin' Louder)** *Jackie Wilson*
55S/00 **Whispers In The Dark** *Profyle*
67A/91 **Whistle Song** *Frankie Knuckles*
74/00 **Whistle While You Twurk** *Ying Yang Twins*
59/77 **Whistler, The** *Jethro Tull*
61/59 **Whistling Organ** *Dave 'Baby' Cortez*

WHITE:

89/77 **White Bird** *David Laflamme*
74/58 **White Bucks And Saddle Shoes** *Bobby Pedrick, Jr.*
White Christmas
13/54 *Bing Crosby*
7/55 *Bing Crosby*
80/55 *Drifters*
65/56 *Bing Crosby*
34/57 *Bing Crosby*
66/58 *Bing Crosby*
59/59 *Bing Crosby*
26/60 *Bing Crosby*
96/60 *Drifters*
12/61 *Bing Crosby*
38/62 *Bing Crosby*
88/62 *Drifters*
1X/63 *Andy Williams*
12X/68 *Otis Redding*
73A/93 *Michael Bolton*
71A/95 **White, Discussion** *Live*
26/84 **White Horse** *Laid Back*
48/80 **White Hot** *Red Rider*
67/68 **White Houses** *Animals*
19/76 **White Knight** *Cledus Maggard*
75/72 **White Lies** *Grin*
28/72 **White Lies, Blue Eyes** *Bullet*
73/59 **White Lightning** *George Jones*
67A/95 **White Lines** *Duran Duran*
90/92 **White Men Can't Jump** *Riff*
9/64 **White On White** *Danny Williams*
8/67 **White Rabbit** *Jefferson Airplane*
6/68 **White Room** *Cream*
61/62 **White Rose Of Athens** *David Carroll*
White Silver Sands
7/57 *Don Rondo*
18/57 *Owen Bradley Quintet*
22/57 *Dave Gardner*
9/60 *Bill Black's Combo*
92/62 *Bill Black's Combo (Twistin')*

White Sport Coat (And A Pink Carnation)
2/57 *Marty Robbins*
62/57 *Johnny Desmond*
36/83 **White Wedding** *Billy Idol*
20X/65 **White World Of Winter** *Bing Crosby*
Whiter Shade Of Pale
5/67 *Procol Harum*
100/68 *Hesitations*
82/70 *R.B. Greaves*
94/84 *Hagar, Schon, Aaronson, Shrieve*
66S/95 *Annie Lennox*
34S/01 *Sarah Brightman*

WHO:

21/66 **Who Am I** *Petula Clark*
40/98 **Who Am I "Sim Simma"** *Beenie Man*
99/58 **Who Are They To Say** *DeCastro Sisters*
62/56 **Who Are We** *Gogi Grant*
14/78 **Who Are You** *Who*
78/74 **Who Are You** *B.B. King*
FC/56 **Who Can Explain?** *Frankie Lymon*
99/61 **Who Can I Count On** *Patsy Cline*
8/95 **Who Can I Run To?** *Xscape*
Who Can I Turn To
33/64 *Tony Bennett*
62/65 *Dionne Warwick*
1/82 **Who Can It Be Now?** *Men At Work*
Who Cares
43/59 *Don Gibson*
63/64 *Fats Domino*
5/99 **Who Dat** *JT Money*
17/96 **Who Do U Love** *Deborah Cox*
68/79 **Who Do Ya Love** *KC & The Sunshine Band*
15/89 **Who Do You Give Your Love To?** *Michael Morales*
25/64 **Who Do You Love** *Sapphires*
Who Do You Love
95/67 *Woolies*
91/69 *Quicksilver Messenger Service*
15/74 **Who Do You Think You Are** *Bo Donaldson*
91/66 **Who Do You Think You Are** *Shindogs*
40/81 **Who Do You Think You're Foolin'** *Donna Summer*
82/61 **Who Else But You** *Frankie Avalon*
16/87 **Who Found Who** *Jellybean/Elisa Fiorillo*
57/71 **Who Gets The Guy** *Dionne Warwick*
86/93 **Who Got The Props** *Black Moon*
28/01 **Who I Am** *Jessica Andrews*
33/68 **Who Is Gonna Love Me?** *Dionne Warwick*
69/74 **Who Is He And What Is He To You** *Creative Source*
14/93 **Who Is It** *Michael Jackson*
Who Let The Dogs Out
40/00 *Baha Men*
32S/01 *Bahama Mama's*
45/79 **Who Listens To The Radio** *Sports*
3/75 **Who Loves You** *Four Seasons*
47/76 **Who Loves You Better** *Isley Brothers*
65/99 **Who Needs Pictures** *Brad Paisley*
54/70 **Who Needs Ya** *Steppenwolf*
9/57 **Who Needs You** *Four Lads*
7/61 **Who Put The Bomp (In The Bomp, Bomp, Bomp)** *Barry Mann*
73/91 **Who Said I Would** *Phil Collins*
79/86 **Who Says** *Device*
67/80 **Who Shot J.R.?** *Gary Burbank*
93/59 **Who Shot Sam** *George Jones*
55/63 **Who Stole The Keeshka?** *Matys Bros.*
2X/73 **Who Took The Merry Out Of Christmas** *Staple Singers*
27S/02 **Who U Rollin' Wit** *Lil' Tykes*
8S/02 **Who Wants This?** *Smilez & Southstar*
49/73 **Who Was It?** *Hurricane Smith*
60/01 **Who We Be** *DMX*
16/84 **Who Wears These Shoes?** *Elton John*
49/80 **Who Were You Thinkin' Of** *Doolittle Band*
19/68 **Who Will Answer?** *Ed Ames*
11/96 **Who Will Save Your Soul** *Jewel*
76/62 **Who Will The Next Fool Be** *Bobby Bland*
7/87 **Who Will You Run To** *Heart*
31/96 **Who You Are** *Pearl Jam*
84/97 **Who You Wit** *Jay-Z*
18/76 **Who'd She Coo?** *Ohio Players*
29/80 **Who'll Be The Fool Tonight** *Larsen-Feiten Band*
34/65 **Who'll Be The Next In Line** *Kinks*
F/70 **Who'll Stop The Rain** *Creedence Clearwater Revival*

WHO'S:

72/64 **Who's Afraid Of Virginia Woolf?** *Jimmy Smith*
100/64 **Who's Been Sleeping In My Bed?** *Linda Scott*
61/83 **Who's Behind The Door?** *Zebra*
43/65 **Who's Cheating Who?** *Little Milton*
4/81 **Who's Crying Now** *Journey*
26S/01 **Who's Gonna Love Ya'** *Bigga Figgaz*
35/92 **Who's Gonna Ride Your Wild Horses** *U2*
46/70 **Who's Gonna Take The Blame** *Miracles*
95/92 **Who's Got Your Love** *Nyasia*
6/85 **Who's Holding Donna Now** *DeBarge*
27/73 **Who's In The Strawberry Patch With Sally** *Tony Orlando & Dawn*
3/86 **Who's Johnny** *El DeBarge*
66/67 **Who's Lovin' You** *Brenda & The Tabulations*
Who's Making Love
5/68 *Johnnie Taylor*
57/69 *Young-Holt Unlimited*
39/81 *Blues Brothers*
60S/00 **Who's She Lovin' Now?** *Liberty City Fla.*
Who's Sorry Now
4/58 *Connie Francis*
40/75 *Marie Osmond*
1/87 **Who's That Girl** *Madonna*
21/84 **Who's That Girl?** *Eurythmics*
47/01 **Who's That Girl?** *Eve*
71/59 **Who's That Knocking** *Genies*
50S/94 **Who's That Man** *Toby Keith*
56S/93 **Who's The Man?** *Heavy D & The Boyz*
96/93 **Who's The Man?** *House Of Pain*
40/70 **Who's Your Baby?** *Archies*
22/02 **Who's Your Daddy?** *Toby Keith*
7/85 **Who's Zoomin' Who** *Aretha Franklin*
43/00 **Whoa!** *Black Rob*
62S/00 **Whoa! Lil' Mama...** *X-Con*
98/02 **Whoa Now** *B Rich*
22/77 **Whodunit** *Tavares*
53/70 **Whoever Finds This, I Love You** *Mac Davis*
67A/96 **Whoever You Are** *Geggy Tah*
70S/99 **Whole Lot Of Gangstas Die** *Flexx G.*
Whole Lot Of Shakin' Going On
3/57 *Jerry Lee Lewis*
42/60 *Chubby Checker*
55/60 *Conway Twitty*
46/66 **Whole Lot Of Shakin' In My Heart (Since I Met You)** *Miracles*
Whole Lotta Love
4/70 *Led Zeppelin*
58/71 *C.C.S.*
64/71 *King Curtis*
87/79 *Wonder Band*
6/59 **Whole Lotta Loving** *Fats Domino*
60/58 **Whole Lotta Woman** *Marvin Rainwater*
73/67 **Whole Lotta Woman** *Arthur Conley*
1/93 **Whole New World (Aladdin's Theme)** *Peabo Bryson & Regina Belle*
9/90 **Whole Wide World** *A'me Lorain*
19/02 **Whole World** *OutKast*
63/67 **Whole World Is A Stage** *Fantastic Four*
71/71 **Wholesale Love** *Buddy Miles*
81/72 **Wholy Holy** *Aretha Franklin*
2/93 **Whoomp! (There It Is)** *Tag Team*
(also see: Addams Family)
97/95 **Whoomp! (There It Went)** *Tag Team, Mickey, Minnie, & Goofy*
11/93 **Whoot, There It Is** *95 South*
87/95 **Whose Bed Have Your Boots Been Under?** *Shania Twain*
43/65 **Whose Heart Are You Breaking Tonight** *Connie Francis*
50/95 **Whutcha Want?** *Nine*

WHY:

Why
1/59 *Frankie Avalon*
13/72 *Donny Osmond*
34/92 **Why** *Annie Lennox*
74/82 **Why** *Carly Simon*
77/57 **Why** *Cues*
88/64 **Why** *Beatles/Tony Sheridan*
Why (Am I Treated So Bad)
57/67 *Sweet Inspirations*
73/67 *"Cannonball" Adderley*
91/67 *Bobby Powell*
95/67 *Staple Singers*
5/57 **Why Baby Why** *Pat Boone*
54/87 **Why Can't I Be You?** *Cure*
33/85 **Why Can't I Have You** *Cars*
Why Can't I Touch You ..see: (If You Let Me Make Love To You Then)
3/86 **Why Can't This Be Love** *Van Halen*
60/87 **Why Can't This Night Go On Forever** *Journey*
6/75 **Why Can't We Be Friends?** *War*
57/72 **Why Can't We Be Lovers** *Holland-Dozier*
3/73 **Why Can't We Live Together** *Timmy Thomas*
63/66 **Why Can't You Bring Me Home** *Jay & The Americans*
78/91 **Why Can't You Come Home** *Ex-Girlfriend*
77/65 **Why Did I Choose You** *Barbra Streisand*
68/62 **Why Did You Leave Me?** *Vince Edwards*

Why Do Fools Fall In Love
6/56 *Frankie Lymon*
9/56 *Gale Storm*
12/56 *Diamonds*
59/56 *Gloria Mann*
41/67 *Happenings*
7/81 *Diana Ross*
42/60 **Why Do I Love You So** *Johnny Tillotson*
97/63 **Why Do Kids Grow Up** *Randy & The Rainbows*
38/63 **Why Do Lovers Break Each Other's Heart?** *Bob B. Soxx & The Blue Jeans*
73/77 **Why Do Lovers (Break Each Other's Heart?)** *Daryl Hall & John Oates*
26/96 **Why Does It Hurt So Bad** *Whitney Houston*
10/58 **Why Don't They Understand** *George Hamilton IV*
23/02 **Why Don't We Fall In Love** *Amerie*
37/63 **Why Don't You Believe Me** *Duprees*
74/99 **Why Don't You Get A Job?** *Offspring*
Why Don't You Write Me
30C/55 *Snooky Lanson*
82/55 *Jacks*
92/64 **Why (Doncha Be My Girl)** *Chartbusters*
50S/94 **Why Haven't I Heard From You** *Reba McEntire*
73/02 **Why I Love You** *B2K*
9/96 **Why I Love You So Much** *Monica*
61/69 **Why I Sing The Blues** *B.B. King*
83/60 **Why I'm Walkin'** *Stonewall Jackson*
98/69 **Why Is The Wine Sweeter (On The Other Side)** *Eddie Floyd*
55/79 **Why Leave Us Alone** *Five Special*
13/83 **Why Me?** *Irene Cara*
16/73 **Why Me** *Kris Kristofferson*
26/80 **Why Me** *Styx*
64/83 **Why Me?** *Planet P*
44/92 **Why Me Baby?** *Keith Sweat*
97/93 **Why Must We Wait Until Tonight?** *Tina Turner*
18/80 **Why Not Me** *Fred Knoblock*
92/61 **Why Not Now** *Matt Monro*
90/67 **Why Not Tonight** *Jimmy Hughes*
64S/99 **Why-O-Why** *B.C.*
54/66 **Why Pick On Me** *Standells*
58/87 **Why Should I Cry?** *Nona Hendryx*
61/70 **Why Should I Cry** *Gentrys*
78/01 **Why They Call It Falling** *Lee Ann Womack*
39/87 **Why You Treat Me So Bad** *Club Nouveau*
66/82 **Why You Wanna Try Me** *Commodores*
52/62 **Why'd You Wanna Make Me Cry** *Connie Stevens*
Wichita Lineman
3/69 *Glen Campbell*
95/69 *Sergio Mendes*
55/92 **Wicked** *Ice Cube*
6/91 **Wicked Game** *Chris Isaak*
71/59 **Wicked Ruby** *Danny Zella*
41/98 **Wide Open Spaces** *Dixie Chicks*
64/93 **Wide River** *Steve Miller Band*
57/66 **Wiederseh'n** *Al Martino*
7/00 **Wifey** *Next*
15/90 **Wiggle It** *2 In A Room*
51/59 **Wiggle, Wiggle** *Accents*
22/63 **Wiggle Wobble** *Les Cooper*
41/70 **Wigwam** *Bob Dylan*

WILD:

33/63 **Wild!** *Dee Dee Sharp*
73/89 **Wild Again** *Starship*
42/85 **Wild And Crazy Love** *Mary Jane Girls*
Wild Angels ..see: Theme From The
2/84 **Wild Boys** *Duran Duran*
29/56 **Wild Cherry** *Don Cherry*
31/67 **Wild Honey** *Beach Boys*
28/71 **Wild Horses** *Rolling Stones*
50/01 **Wild Horses** *Garth Brooks*
55/87 **Wild Horses** *Gino Vannelli*
26/61 **Wild In The Country** *Elvis Presley*
87/78 **Wild In The Streets** *British Lions*
22/57 **Wild Is The Wind** *Johnny Mathis*
70/84 **Wild Life** *Bananarama*
Wild Night
28/71 *Van Morrison*
3/94 *John Mellencamp Me'Shell Ndegéocello*
2/60 **Wild One** *Bobby Rydell*
34/65 **Wild One** *Martha & The Vandellas*
Wild Thing
1/66 *Troggs*
20/67 *Senator Bobby*
14/74 *Fancy*
2/89 **Wild Thing** *Tone Loc*
8/63 **Wild Weekend** *Rebels*
25/86 **Wild Wild Life** *Talking Heads*
1/88 **Wild, Wild West** *Escape Club*
1/99 **Wild Wild West** *Will Smith*
62/88 **Wild, Wild West** *Kool Moe Dee*
34/90 **Wild Women Do** *Natalie Cole*
Wild World
11/71 *Cat Stevens*
97/71 *Gentrys*
25/89 *Maxi Priest*
27/93 *Mr. Big*
3/75 **Wildfire** *Michael Murphey*
Wildflower
9/73 *Skylark*
45/74 *New Birth*
10/91 **Wildside** *Marky Mark & The Funky Bunch*
17/63 **Wildwood Days** *Bobby Rydell*
7/74 **Wildwood Weed** *Jim Stafford*
23S/02 **Will Destroy** *Lil Ru*
55S/02 **Will I?** *Ian Van Dahl*
1/73 **Will It Go Round In Circles** *Billy Preston*
72/63 **Will Power** *Cookies*
78/85 **Will The Wolf Survive?** *Los Lobos*
25/99 **Will 2K** *Will Smith*
32/69 **Will You Be Staying After Sunday** *Peppermint Rainbow*
7/93 **Will You Be There** *Michael Jackson*
39/94 **Will You Be There (In The Morning)** *Heart*
Will You Love Me Tomorrow
1/61 *Shirelles*
24/68 *4 Seasons*
76/72 *Roberta Flack*
82/73 *Melanie*
95/76 *Dana Valery*
39/78 *Dave Mason*
19/92 **Will You Marry Me?** *Paula Abdul*
3/87 **Will You Still Love Me?** *Chicago*
35C/56 **Will You, Willyum** *Janis Martin*
78/69 **Willie & Laura Mae Jones** *Dusty Springfield*
Willie And The Hand Jive
9/58 *Johnny Otis Show*
100/66 *Strangeloves*
26/74 *Eric Clapton*
63/85 *George Thorogood*
78/63 **Willie Can** *Sue Thompson*
26/94 **Willing To Forgive** *Aretha Franklin*
15/65 **Willow Weep For Me** *Chad & Jeremy*
96/72 **Willpower Weak, Temptation Strong** *Bullet*
97/64 **Willyam, Willyam** *Dee Dee Sharp*
21S/01 **Win** *Brian McKnight*
22/58 **Win Your Love For Me** *Sam Cooke*
Winchester Cathedral
1/66 *New Vaudeville Band*
71/66 *Dana Rollin*
Wind Beneath My Wings
65/83 *Lou Rawls*
1/89 *Bette Midler*
71S/96 *Gerald Levert & Eddie Levert, Sr.*
64/83 **Wind Him Up** *Saga*
53/57 **Wind In The Willow** *Jo Stafford*
4/91 **Wind Of Change** *Scorpions*
31/69 **Windmills Of Your Mind** *Dusty Springfield*
63/83 **Windows** *Missing Persons*
32/67 **Windows Of The World** *Dionne Warwick*
38/83 **Winds Of Change** *Jefferson Starship*
Windy
1/67 *Association*
44/67 *Wes Montgomery*
78/58 **Windy** *Paul Gayten*
12/61 **Wings Of A Dove** *Ferlin Husky*
79/95 **Wings Of The Morning** *Capleton*
91/94 **Wink** *Neal McCoy*
Winkin', Blinkin' And Nod
73/64 *Simon Sisters*
76/81 *Doobie Brothers*
50/56 **Winner Take All** *Platters*
8/81 **Winner Takes It All** *Abba*
54/87 **Winner Takes It All** *Sammy Hagar*
21/76 **Winners And Losers** *Hamilton, Joe Frank & Reynolds*
17/81 **Winning** *Santana*
85/88 **Winter Games** *David Foster*
43/77 **Winter Melody** *Donna Summer*
Winter Wonderland
23X/66 *Ramsey Lewis*
6X/84 *Dolly Parton (medley)*
16/70 **Winter World Of Love** *Engelbert Humperdinck*
Wipe Out
2/63 *Surfaris*
16/66 *Surfaris*
12/87 *Fat Boys (with The Beach Boys)*
71/81 **Wired For Sound** *Cliff Richard*
35/57 **Wisdom Of A Fool** *Five Keys*
66/85 **Wise Up** *Amy Grant*

WISH:

41/79 **(Wish I Could Fly Like) Superman** *Kinks*
79/02 **Wish I Didn't Miss You** *Angie Stone*
61/59 **Wish It Were Me** *Platters*
63/67 **Wish Me A Rainbow** *Gunter Kallmann Chorus*
17/64 **Wish Someone Would Care** *Irma Thomas*
77/73 **Wish That I Could Talk To You** *Sylvers*
38/67 **Wish You Didn't Have To Go** *James & Bobby Purify*

34/99 **Wish You Were Here** *Mark Wills*
60/01 **Wish You Were Here** *Incubus*
49/66 **Wish You Were Here, Buddy** *Pat Boone*
86/96 **Wishes** *Nathan Morris*
44/69 **Wishful Sinful** *Doors*
79/59 **Wishful Thinking** *Little Anthony & The Imperials*
6/64 **Wishin' And Hopin'** *Dusty Springfield*
91/61 **Wishin' On A Rainbow** *Phill Wilson*
18/58 **Wishing For Your Love** *Voxpoppers*
58/88 **Wishing I Was Lucky** *Wet Wet Wet*
Wishing I Was There
25A/98 *Natalie Imbruglia*
FS/02 *Natalie Imbruglia*
26/83 **Wishing (If I Had A Photograph Of You)** *Flock Of Seagulls*
57/65 **Wishing It Was You** *Connie Francis*
9/92 **Wishing On A Star** *Cover Girls*
86/91 **Wishing On The Same Star** *Keedy*
(Wishing Star) ..see: Theme From Taras Bulba
1/88 **Wishing Well** *Terence Trent D'Arby*
11/74 **Wishing You Were Here** *Chicago*
47/98 **Wishlist** *Pearl Jam*
79/70 **Witch, The** *Rattles*
1/58 **Witch Doctor** *David Seville*
21/72 **Witch Queen Of New Orleans** *Redbone*
6/58 **Witchcraft** *Frank Sinatra*
32/63 **Witchcraft** *Elvis Presley*
69/69 **Witchi Tai To** *Everything Is Everything*
9/72 **Witchy Woman** *Eagles*

WITH:

50/73 **With A Child's Heart** *Michael Jackson*
29/66 **With A Girl Like You** *Troggs*
With A Little Bit Of Luck
82/56 *Percy Faith*
85/56 *Jo Stafford*
With A Little Help From My Friends
68/68 *Joe Cocker*
71/78 *Beatles (medley)*
1/78 **With A Little Luck** *Wings*
With All My Heart
15/57 *Jodie Sands*
76/57 *Judy Scott*
82/59 **With All Of My Heart** *Brook Benton*
1/00 **With Arms Wide Open** *Creed*
5/89 **With Every Beat Of My Heart** *Taylor Dayne*
63/01 **With Me** *Lonestar*
With My Eyes Wide Open I'm Dreaming
59/59 *Patti Page*
99/59 *Enoch Light*
39/59 **With Open Arms** *Jane Morgan*
1/87 **With Or Without You** *U2*
With Pen In Hand
43/68 *Billy Vera*
35/69 *Vikki Carr*
94/72 *Bobby Goldsboro*
21/59 **With The Wind And The Rain In Your Hair** *Pat Boone*
27/65 **With These Hands** *Tom Jones*
14/67 **With This Ring** *Platters*
14/91 **With You** *Tony Terry*
41/99 **With You** *Lila McCann*
98/96 **With You** *Somethin' For The People*
51/86 **With You All The Way** *New Edition*
4/80 **With You I'm Born Again** *Billy Preston & Syreeta*
30/57 **With You On My Mind** *Nat "King" Cole*
12/76 **With Your Love** *Jefferson Starship*
28/58 **With Your Love** *Jack Scott*
77/91 **Within My Heart** *Voyce*
73S/94 **Without A Doubt** *Black Sheep*
77/55 **Without A Song** *Roy Hamilton*
63/69 **Without Her** *Herb Alpert*
41/97 **Without Love** *Donna Lewis*
45/74 **Without Love** *Aretha Franklin*
Without Love (There Is Nothing)
19/57 *Clyde McPhatter*
29/63 *Ray Charles*
90/68 *Oscar Toney, Jr.*
5/70 *Tom Jones*
2/02 **Without Me** *Eminem*
43/64 **Without The One You Love (Life's Not Worth While)** *Four Tops*
Without You
1/72 *Nilsson*
3/94 *Mariah Carey*
7/61 **Without You** *Johnny Tillotson*
8/90 **Without You** *Mötley Crüe*
31/00 **Without You** *Dixie Chicks*
41/56 **Without You** *Eddie Fisher*
43S/01 **Without You** *Digital Allies*
48S/00 **Without You** *Charlie Wilson*
73/84 **Without You** *David Bowie*
89/88 **Without You** *Peabo Bryson & Regina Belle*
64/73 **Without You In My Life** *Tyrone Davis*
24/82 **Without You (Not Another Lonely Night)** *Franke & The Knockouts*
20/80 **Without Your Love** *Roger Daltrey*
38/87 **Without Your Love** *Toto*
82/97 **Without Your Love** *Angelina*
42/76 **Without Your Love (Mr. Jordan)** *Charlie Ross*
14/64 **Wives And Lovers** *Jack Jones*
45/58 **Wizard, The** *Jimmie Rodgers*
54/61 **Wizard Of Love** *Ly - Dells*
Wizard Of Oz ..see: Themes From The
17/00 **Wobble Wobble** *504 Boyz*
40/75 **Wolf Creek Pass** *C.W. McCall*
6/62 **Wolverton Mountain** *Claude King*
(also see: I'm The Girl On)

WOMAN:

2/81 **Woman** *John Lennon*
14/66 **Woman** *Peter & Gordon*
15/60 **Woman, A Lover, A Friend** *Jackie Wilson*
56/65 **Woman Can Change A Man** *Joe Tex*
53/72 **Woman Don't Go Astray** *King Floyd*
60/73 **Woman From Tokyo** *Deep Purple*
47/69 **Woman Helping Man** *Vogues*
94/68 **Woman I Love** *B.B. King*
36/90 **Woman In Chains** *Tears For Fears*
1/80 **Woman In Love** *Barbra Streisand*
Woman In Love
14/55 *Four Aces*
19/55 *Frankie Laine*
79/81 **Woman In Love (It's Not Me)** *Tom Petty*
33/83 **Woman In Me** *Donna Summer*
76/81 **Woman In Me** *Crystal Gayle*
90/95 **Woman In Me (Needs The Man In You)** *Shania Twain*
24/83 **Woman In You** *Bee Gees*
59/62 **Woman Is A Man's Best Friend** *Teddy & The Twilights*
57/72 **Woman Is The Nigger Of The World** *John Lennon*
54/67 **Woman Like That, Yeah** *Joe Tex*
4/81 **Woman Needs Love (Just Like You Do)** *Ray Parker Jr.*
Woman To Woman
22/74 *Shirley Brown*
92/78 *Barbara Mandrell*
56/73 **Woman To Woman** *Joe Cocker*
72/95 **Woman To Woman** *Jewell*
44/76 **Woman Tonight** *America*
4/68 **Woman, Woman** *Gary Puckett*
29/65 **Woman's Got Soul** *Impressions*
60/72 **Woman's Gotta Have It** *Bobby Womack*
63/67 **Woman's Hands** *Joe Tex*
71/64 **Woman's Love** *Carla Thomas*
7/02 **Woman's Worth** *Alicia Keys*
94/70 **Womans' Way** *Rozetta Johnson*
55/74 **Wombling Summer Party** *Wombles*
41/80 **Women** *Foreigner*
80/87 **Women** *Def Leppard*
36/71 **Women's Love Rights** *Laura Lee*
76/61 **Won't Be Long** *Aretha Franklin*
57/70 **Won't Find Better (Than Me)** *New Hope*
15/71 **Won't Get Fooled Again** *Who*
76/90 **Won't Talk About It** *Beats International*
Won't You Come Home Bill Bailey
19/60 *Bobby Darin*
98/61 *Della Reese*
75/63 *Ella Fitzgerald*

WONDER:

20/96 **Wonder** *Natalie Merchant*
87/70 **Wonder Could I Live There Anymore** *Charley Pride*
11/61 **Wonder Like You** *Rick Nelson*
Wonder Of You
25/59 *Ray Peterson*
70/64 *Ray Peterson*
9/70 *Elvis Presley*
11/00 **Wonderful** *Everclear*
39/95 **Wonderful** *Adam Ant*
71/74 **Wonderful** *Isaac Hayes*
89/69 **Wonderful** *Blackwell*
93/75 **Wonderful Baby** *Don McLean*
10X/84 **Wonderful Christmastime** *Paul McCartney*
22/62 **Wonderful Dream** *Majors*
14/63 **Wonderful Summer** *Robin Ward*
4/58 **Wonderful Time Up There** *Pat Boone*
16/78 **Wonderful Tonight** *Eric Clapton*
Wonderful! Wonderful!
14/57 *Johnny Mathis*
7/63 *Tymes*
(also see: Wun'erful Wun'erful)
Wonderful World
12/60 *Sam Cooke*
4/65 *Herman's Hermits*
17/78 *Art Garfunkel w/James Taylor & Paul Simon*
(also see: What A)
25/70 **Wonderful World, Beautiful People** *Jimmy Cliff*
99/62 **Wonderful World Of The Young** *Andy Williams*
40/59 **Wonderful You** *Jimmie Rodgers*
12/57 **Wondering** *Patti Page*
21/80 **Wondering Where The Lions Are** *Bruce Cockburn*

25/80 **Wonderland** *Commodores*
86/84 **Wonderland** *Big Country*
Wonderland By Night
1/61 *Bert Kaempfert*
15/61 *Louis Prima*
18/61 *Anita Bryant*
8/96 **Wonderwall** *Oasis*
43/59 **Wont'cha Come Home** *Lloyd Price*
8/96 **Woo-Hah!! Got You All In Check** *Busta Rhymes*
16/59 **Woo-Hoo** *Rock-A-Teens*
Woo Woo Song ..see: You Should Be Mine
38S/01 **Wood, The** *Papa Seville*
91/86 **Wood Beez (pray like aretha franklin)** *Scritti Politti*
51/58 **Woodchopper's Ball** *Hutch Davie*
Wooden Heart
1/61 *Joe Dowell*
58/75 *Bobby Vinton*
Woodstock
11/70 *Crosby, Stills, Nash & Young*
79/70 *Assembled Multitude*
23/71 *Matthews' Southern Comfort*
62/99 **Woof** *Snoop Dogg*
31/98 **Woof Woof** *69 Boyz*
2/65 **Wooly Bully** *Sam The Sham & the Pharaohs*
19/88 **Word In Spanish** *Elton John*
94/94 **Word Is Bond** *Brand Nubian*
41/85 **Word Is Out** *Jermaine Stewart*
78/91 **Word Of Mouth** *Mike & The Mechanics*
78/91 **Word To The Badd!!** *Jermaine Jackson*
37A/91 **Word To The Mutha!** *Bell Biv DeVoe*
6/86 **Word Up** *Cameo*
11/67 **Words** *Monkees*
15/68 **Words** *Bee Gees*
42/82 **Words** *Missing Persons*
62/83 **Words** *F.R. David*
94/60 **Words** *Pat Boone*
Words (Are Impossible)
88/73 *Drupi (Vado Via)*
91/75 *Margie Joseph*
87/76 *Donny Gerrard*
5/86 **Words Get In The Way** *Miami Sound Machine*
5/67 **Words Of Love** *Mamas & The Papas*
13/57 **Words Of Love** *Diamonds*
35/02 **Work In Progress** *Alan Jackson*
2/02 **Work It** *Missy Elliott*
74S/93 **Work It Out!** *Luke*
18/66 **Work Song** *Herb Alpert*
44/82 **Work That Body** *Diana Ross*
Work To Do
51/72 *Isley Brothers*
52/92 *Vanessa Williams*
53/94 **Worker Man** *Patra*
32/74 **Workin' At The Car Wash Blues** *Jim Croce*
41/82 **Workin' For A Livin'** *Huey Lewis*
33/62 **Workin' For The Man** *Roy Orbison*
Workin' On A Groovy Thing
62/68 *Patti Drew*
20/69 *5th Dimension*
97/73 **Working Class Hero** *Tommy Roe*
74/86 **Working Class Man** *Jimmy Barnes*
29/82 **Working For The Weekend** *Loverboy*
Working In The Coal Mine
8/66 *Lee Dorsey*
43/81 *Devo*
74/68 **Working Man's Prayer** *Arthur Prysock*
Working My Way Back To You
9/66 *4 Seasons*
2/80 *Spinners (medley)*
73/89 **Working On It** *Chris Rea*
33/63 **Workout Stevie, Workout** *Little Stevie Wonder*
37/69 **World** *James Brown*
19/96 **World I Know** *Collective Soul*
51/64 **World I Used To Know** *Jimmie Rodgers*
52/90 **World In My Eyes** *Depeche Mode*
World Is A Ghetto
7/73 *War*
82/96 *Geto Boys*
49/66 **World Of Fantasy** *Five Stairsteps*
59/64 **World Of Lonely People** *Anita Bryant*
19/65 **World Of Our Own** *Seekers*
World Outside
21/58 *Four Coins*
63/58 *Four Aces*
71/58 *Roger Williams*
84/87 **World Shut Your Mouth** *Julian Cope*
92/93 **World (The Price Of Love)** *New Order*
76/65 **World Through A Tear** *Neil Sedaka*
64/97 **World Tonight** *Paul McCartney*
30/67 **World We Knew (Over And Over)** *Frank Sinatra*
65/87 **World Where You Live** *Crowded House*
56/82 **World Without Heroes** *Kiss*
World Without Love
1/64 *Peter & Gordon*
80/64 *Bobby Rydell*
90/70 **World Without Music** *Archie Bell*
34/02 **World's Greatest** *R. Kelly*
97/68 **Worm, The** *Jimmy McGriff*
37/64 **Worried Guy** *Johnny Tillotson*
20/59 **Worried Man** *Kingston Trio*
74/62 **Worried Mind** *Ray Anthony*
45/64 **Worry** *Johnny Tillotson*
69/59 **Worryin' Kind** *Tommy Sands*
80/74 **Worse Comes To Worst** *Billy Joel*
3/69 **Worst That Could Happen** *Brooklyn Bridge*
10/87 **Wot's It To Ya** *Robbie Nevil*
5/85 **Would I Lie To You?** *Eurythmics*
13/92 **Would I Lie To You?** *Charles & Eddie*
64/63 **Would It Make Any Difference To You** *Etta James*
46/74 **Would You Lay With Me (In A Field of Stone)** *Tanya Tucker*
46/84 **Wouldn't It Be Good** *Nik Kershaw*
8/66 **Wouldn't It Be Nice** *Beach Boys*
95/76 **Wow** *Andre Gagnon*
41/64 **Wow Wow Wee (He's The Boy For Me)** *Angels*
38/81 **Wrack My Brain** *Ringo Starr*
20/85 **Wrap Her Up** *Elton John*
Wrap It Up
93/70 *Archie Bell*
50/86 *Fabulous Thunderbirds*
84/91 **Wrap My Body Tight** *Johnny Gill*
48/78 **Wrap Your Arms Around Me** *KC & The Sunshine Band*
35/02 **Wrapped Around** *Brad Paisley*
8/84 **Wrapped Around Your Finger** *Police*
46/01 **Wrapped Up In You** *Garth Brooks*
2/76 **Wreck Of The Edmund Fitzgerald** *Gordon Lightfoot*
Wreck Of The "John B" ..see: Sloop John B
54S/93 **Wreckx Shop** *Wreckx-N-Effect*
Wringle Wrangle
12/57 *Fess Parker*
33/57 *Bill Hayes*
27/99 **Write This Down** *George Strait*
5/61 **Writing On The Wall** *Adam Wade*
16/91 **Written All Over Your Face** *Rude Boys*
29/99 **Written In The Stars** *Elton John & LeAnn Rimes*
61/57 **Written On The Wind** *Four Aces*
93/93 **Written On Ya Kitten** *Naughty By Nature*
68/96 **Wrong** *Everything But The Girl*
36/99 **Wrong Again** *Martina McBride*
34/64 **Wrong For Each Other** *Andy Williams*
64/02 **Wrong Impression** *Natalie Imbruglia*
52/99 **Wrong Night** *Reba McEntire*
64A/97 **Wrong Number** *Cure*
47A/97 **Wrong Way** *Sublime*
69S/97 **Wu-Renegades** *Killarmy*
60/96 **Wu-Wear: The Garment Renaissance** *RZA*
32/57 **Wun'erful, Wun'erful!** *Stan Freberg*
47S/02 **Wylin Out** *Urban Renewal Program*
Wynken, Blynken And Nod ..see: Winkin', Blinkin' And Nod
62A/95 **Wynona's Big Brown Beaver** *Primus*

X

76/01 **X** *Xzibit*
8/80 **Xanadu** *Olivia Newton-John/ Electric Light Orchestra*

Y

2/79 **Y.M.C.A.** *Village People*
26S/99 **Ya Di Ya** *Gina Thompson*
7/61 **Ya Ya** *Lee Dorsey*
19/84 **Yah Mo B There** *James Ingram (with Michael McDonald)*
Yakety Sax (Axe)
35/63 *Boots Randolph*
98/65 *Chet Atkins*
1/58 **Yakety Yak** *Coasters*
75S/00 **Y'all Can't Never Hurt Us** *Philly's Most Wanted*
61S/01 **Y'all Don't Wanna** *Skillz*
58/78 **Yank Me, Crank Me** *Ted Nugent*
16/86 **Yankee Rose** *David Lee Roth*
64/68 **Yard Went On Forever** *Richard Harris*
52/59 **Yea - Yea (Class Cutter)** *Dale Hawkins*
73/58 **Yea, Yea** *Kendall Sisters*
26S/00 **Yeah That's Us** *Major Figgas*
32/88 **Yeah, Yeah, Yeah** *Judson Spence*
72/92 **Yeah, Yeah, Yeah!** *Voices*
42/60 **Year Ago Tonight** *Crests*
8/77 **Year Of The Cat** *Al Stewart*
42/71 **Year That Clayton Delaney Died** *Tom T. Hall*
60/81 **Yearning For Your Love** *Gap Band*
35/80 **Years** *Wayne Newton*
37/61 **Years From Now** *Jackie Wilson*

51/80 **Years From Now** *Dr. Hook*
Yeh, Yeh
92/63 *Mongo Santamaria*
21/65 *Georgie Fame*
48/01 **Yellow** *Coldplay*
25/67 **Yellow Balloon** *Yellow Balloon*
Yellow Bird
70/59 *Mills Brothers*
4/61 *Arthur Lyman Group*
71/61 *Lawrence Welk*
Yellow Dog Blues
43/58 *Joe Darensbourg*
87/58 *Johnny Maddox*
Yellow Ledbetter
F/95 *Pearl Jam*
F/96 *Pearl Jam (Live)*
23/70 **Yellow River** *Christie*
Yellow Rose Of Texas
1/55 *Mitch Miller*
3/55 *Johnny Desmond*
16/55 *Stan Freberg*
2/66 **Yellow Submarine** *Beatles*
99/60 **Yen Yet Song** *Gary Cane*
30/59 **"Yep!"** *Duane Eddy*
22/00 **Yes!** *Chad Brock*
33S/01 **Yes!** *Amber*
45/88 **Yes** *Merry Clayton*
92/64 **Yes I Do** *Solomon Burke*
94/58 **Yes I Want You** *Ivory Joe Hunter*
Yes, I'm Lonesome Tonight
55/61 *Thelma Carpenter*
60/61 *Dodie Stevens*
(also see: Are You Lonesome Tonight)
Yes, I'm Ready
5/65 *Barbara Mason*
2/80 *Teri DeSario with K.C.*
69/62 **Yes Indeed** *Pete Fountain*
46/65 **Yes It Is** *Beatles*
55/58 **Yes, My Darling** *Fats Domino*
84/84 **Yes Or No** *Go-Go's*
14X/65 **Yes, Patricia, There Is A Santa Claus** *Jimmy Dean*
34/60 **Yes Sir, That's My Baby** *Ricky Nelson*
12/57 **Yes Tonight, Josephine** *Johnnie Ray*
11/73 **Yes We Can Can** *Pointer Sisters*
46/76 **Yes, Yes, Yes** *Bill Cosby*
60/62 **Yessiree** *Linda Scott*
79/59 **Yes - Sir - ee** *Dodie Stevens*
31/68 **Yester Love** *Miracles*
7/69 **Yester-Me, Yester-You, Yesterday** *Stevie Wonder*
Yesterday
1/65 *Beatles*
25/67 *Ray Charles*
73A/92 *En Vogue*
56/98 **Yesterday** *Debelah Morgan*
Yesterday And You ..see: Armens Theme
63/73 **Yesterday I Had The Blues** *Harold Melvin*
94/66 **Yesterday Man** *Chris Andrews*
Yesterday Once More
2/73 *Carpenters*
52/81 *Spinners (medley)*
19/69 **Yesterday, When I Was Young** *Roy Clark*
49/68 **Yesterday's Dreams** *Four Tops*
Yesterday's Gone
21/64 *Chad & Jeremy*
75/64 *Overlanders*
Yesterday's Hero
42/76 *John Paul Young*
54/77 *Bay City Rollers*
64/64 **Yesterday's Hero** *Gene Pitney*
94/68 **Yesterday's Rain** *Spanky & Our Gang*
11/82 **Yesterday's Songs** *Neil Diamond*
72/92 **Yesterdays** *Guns N' Roses*
77/64 **Yet...I Know (Et Pourtant)** *Steve Lawrence*
56/62 **Yield Not To Temptation** *Bobby Bland*
57/85 **Yo' Little Brother** *Nolan Thomas*
75/89 **Yo No Se'** *Pajama Party*
3/71 **Yo-Yo** *Osmonds*
35S/02 **Yo-Yo** *Mulberry Lane*
Yo Yo Man ..see: (I'm A)
8/60 **Yogi** *Ivy Three*
72/93 **Yolanda** *Reality*

YOU:

You ..also see: U
10/99 **You** *Jesse Powell*
20/75 **You** *George Harrison*
21/58 **You** *Aquatones*
25/78 **You** *Rita Coolidge*
32/96 **You** *Monifah*
34/68 **You** *Marvin Gaye*
45/78 **You** *McCrarys*
48/80 **You** *Earth, Wind & Fire*
78/94 **You** *Candlebox*
92/94 **You** *Bonnie Raitt*
74/68 **You Ain't Going Nowhere** *Byrds*
64/75 **You Ain't Never Been Loved (Like I'm Gonna Love You)** *Jessi Colter*
You Ain't Seen Nothing Yet
1/74 *Bachman-Turner Overdrive*
67/89 *Figures On A Beach*
94/01 **You All Dat** *Baha Men*
86/73 **You Always Come Back (To Hurting Me)** *Johnny Rodriguez*
96/67 **You Always Hurt Me** *Impressions*
12/61 **You Always Hurt The One You Love** *Clarence Henry*
7/83 **You And I** *Eddie Rabbitt with Crystal Gayle*
13/78 **You And I** *Rick James*
48/74 **You And I** *Johnny Bristol*
9/77 **You And Me** *Alice Cooper*
58S/99 **You And Me** *Spies*
80/80 **You And Me** *Rockie Robbins*
92/79 **You And Me** *Liner*
F/70 **You And Me** *Aretha Franklin*
9/74 **You And Me Against The World** *Helen Reddy*
You & Me & Pooneil ..see: Ballad Of
54/87 **You And Me Tonight** *Déja*
96/75 **You And Your Baby Blues** *Solomon Burke*
91/71 **You And Your Folks, Me And My Folks** *Funkadelic*
58/79 **You Angel You** *Manfred Mann's Earth Band*
4/83 **You Are** *Lionel Richie*
87/75 **You Are A Song** *Batdorf & Rodney*
60/59 **You Are Beautiful** *Johnny Mathis*
79/76 **You Are Beautiful** *Stylistics*
9/72 **You Are Everything** *Stylistics*
84/99 **You Are Everything** *Dru Hill*
59/81 **You Are Forever** *Smokey Robinson*
You Are In My System
64/83 *System*
78/83 *Robert Palmer*
26/62 **You Are Mine** *Frankie Avalon*
7/58 **You Are My Destiny** *Paul Anka*
84/89 **You Are My Everything** *Surface*
65/57 **You Are My First Love** *Nat "King" Cole*
47/80 **You Are My Heaven** *Roberta Flack w/Donny Hathaway*
12/85 **You Are My Lady** *Freddie Jackson*
6/55 **You Are My Love** *Joni James*
27/76 **You Are My Starship** *Norman Connors*
You Are My Sunshine
29C/55 *Ferko String Band*
91/60 *Johnny & The Hurricanes*
7/62 *Ray Charles*
88/67 *Mitch Ryder*
1/95 **You Are Not Alone** *Michael Jackson*
49/77 **You Are On My Mind** *Chicago*
87/66 **You Are She** *Chad & Jeremy*
5/75 **You Are So Beautiful** *Joe Cocker*
17/87 **You Are The Girl** *Cars*
51/72 **You Are The One** *Sugar Bears*
58/92 **You Are The One** *Chris Cuevas*
91/89 **You Are The One** *TKA*
25/61 **You Are The Only One** *Ricky Nelson*
1/73 **You Are The Sunshine Of My Life** *Stevie Wonder*
9/76 **You Are The Woman** *Firefall*
20/66 **You Baby** *Turtles*
78/56 **You Baby You** *Cleftones*
29/86 **You Be Illin'** *Run-D.M.C.*
9/62 **You Beat Me To The Punch** *Mary Wells*
You Belong To Me
6/78 *Carly Simon*
79/83 *Doobie Brothers*
7/62 **You Belong To Me** *Duprees*
2/85 **You Belong To The City** *Glenn Frey*
59/89 **You Better Dance** *Jets*
46/65 **You Better Get It** *Joe Tex*
78/65 **You Better Go** *Derek Martin*
37/59 **You Better Know It** *Jackie Wilson*
90/60 **(You Better) Know What You're Doin'** *Lloyd Price*
24/62 **You Better Move On** *Arthur Alexander*
You Better Run
20/66 *Young Rascals*
42/80 *Pat Benatar*
9/67 **You Better Sit Down Kids** *Chér*
72/70 **You Better Think Twice** *Poco*
29/94 **You Better Wait** *Steve Perry*
18/81 **You Better You Bet** *Who*
57/95 **You Bring Me Joy** *Mary J. Blige*
26/97 **You Bring Me Up** *K-Ci & JoJo*
52/71 **You Brought The Joy** *Freda Payne*
You Brought The Woman Out Of Me
50/75 *Evie Sands*
71/78 *Hot*
45/57 **You Bug Me, Baby** *Larry Williams*
41/88 **You Came** *Kim Wilde*
35S/00 **You Came Along** *Beverly*
77/82 **You Can** *Madleen Kane*
55/67 **You Can Bring Me All Your Heartaches** *Lou Rawls*
23/87 **You Can Call Me Al** *Paul Simon*
86/80 **You Can Call Me Blue** *Michael Johnson*
6/61 **You Can Depend On Me** *Brenda Lee*
35/00 **You Can Do It** *Ice Cube*
37/79 **You Can Do It** *Dobie Gray*
8/82 **You Can Do Magic** *America*

84/73 **You Can Do Magic** *Limmie & Family Cookin'*
You Can Have Her (Him)
12/61 *Roy Hamilton*
67/65 *Righteous Brothers*
75/65 *Dionne Warwick*
96/65 *Timi Yuro*
34/74 *Sam Neely*
70/96 **You Can Make History (Young Again)** *Elton John*
36/58 **You Can Make It If You Try** *Gene Allison*
18/63 **You Can Never Stop Me Loving You** *Johnny Tillotson*
63/62 **You Can Run (But You Can't Hide)** *Jerry Butler*
51/84 **(You Can Still) Rock In America** *Night Ranger*
42/73 **You Can't Always Get What You Want** *Rolling Stones*
57/74 **You Can't Be A Beacon (If Your Light Don't Shine)** *Donna Fargo*
You Can't Be True Dear
75/59 *Mary Kaye Trio*
94/65 *Patti Page*
9/79 **You Can't Change That** *Raydio*
49/78 **You Can't Dance** *England Dan & John Ford Coley*
14/90 **You Can't Deny It** *Lisa Stansfield*
48/64 **You Can't Do That** *Beatles*
82/90 **You Can't Get Away** *Shana*
99/59 **You Can't Get To Heaven On Roller Skates** *Betty Johnson*
15/84 **You Can't Get What You Want (Till You Know What You Want)** *Joe Jackson*
9S/02 **You Can't Go Home Again!** *DJ Shadow*
38/03 **You Can't Hide Beautiful** *Aaron Lines*
You Can't Hurry Love
1/66 *Supremes*
10/83 *Phil Collins*
92/65 **You Can't Hurt Me No More** *Gene Chandler*
48/62 **You Can't Judge A Book By The Cover** *Bo Diddley*
(You Can't Let The Boy Overpower) The Man In You
59/64 *Miracles*
94/68 *Chuck Jackson*
90/62 **You Can't Lie To A Liar** *Ketty Lester*
61S/95 **You Can't Make A Heart Love Somebody** *George Strait*
36/91 **You Can't Play With My Yo-Yo** *Yo-Yo*
40/66 **You Can't Roller Skate In A Buffalo Herd** *Roger Miller*
20/56 **You Can't Run Away From It** *Four Aces*
55/83 **You Can't Run From Love** *Eddie Rabbitt*
You Can't Sit Down
29/61 *Philip Upchurch Combo*
3/63 *Dovells*
70/67 **You Can't Stand Alone** *Wilson Pickett*
96/65 **You Can't Take It Away** *Fred Hughes*
12/77 **You Can't Turn Me Off (In The Middle Of Turning Me On)** *High Inergy*
81/79 **You Can't Win** *Michael Jackson*
You Cheated
12/58 *Shields*
42/58 *Slades*

29/91 **You Could Be Mine** *Guns N' Roses*
32/72 **You Could Have Been A Lady** *April Wine*
15/82 **You Could Have Been With Me** *Sheena Easton*
32/81 **You Could Take My Heart Away** *Silver Condor*
7/79 **You Decorated My Life** *Kenny Rogers*
10/66 **You Didn't Have To Be So Nice** *Lovin' Spoonful*
54/83 **You Don't Believe** *Alan Parsons Project*
1/78 **You Don't Bring Me Flowers** *Barbra Streisand & Neil Diamond*
You Don't Have To Be A Baby To Cry
78/56 *"Tennessee" Ernie Ford*
3/63 *Caravelles*
1/77 **You Don't Have To Be A Star** *Marilyn McCoo & Billy Davis, Jr.*
100/61 **You Don't Have To Be A Tower Of Strength** *Gloria Lynne*
75/86 **You Don't Have To Cry** *René & Angela*
14/91 **You Don't Have To Go Home Tonight** *Triplets*
32/97 **You Don't Have To Hurt No More** *Mint Condition*
82/97 **You Don't Have To Love Me** *Monifah*
15/66 **(You Don't Have To) Paint Me A Picture** *Gary Lewis*
You Don't Have To Say You Love Me
4/66 *Dusty Springfield*
89/68 *Four Sonics*
11/70 *Elvis Presley*
51/69 **You Don't Have To Walk In The Rain** *Turtles*
63/94 **You Don't Have To Worry** *Mary J. Blige*
57A/91 **You Don't Have To Worry** *En Vogue*
20/88 **You Don't Know** *Scarlett & Black*
92/59 **You Don't Know Girls** *Kathy Linden*
(You Don't Know) How Glad I Am
11/64 *Nancy Wilson*
74/75 *Kiki Dee*
13/95 **You Don't Know How It Feels** *Tom Petty*
90/66 **You Don't Know Like I Know** *Sam & Dave*
You Don't Know Me
14/56 *Jerry Vale*
45/60 *Lenny Welch*
2/62 *Ray Charles*
44/67 *Elvis Presley*
55/81 *Mickey Gilley*
88/94 **You Don't Know Nothin'** *For Real*
79/61 **You Don't Know What It Means** *Jackie Wilson*
48/68 **You Don't Know What You Mean To Me** *Sam & Dave*
4/61 **You Don't Know What You've Got (Until You Lose It)** *Ral Donner*
53/78 **You Don't Love Me Anymore** *Eddie Rabbitt*
47/63 **You Don't Love Me Anymore (And I Can Tell)** *Rick Nelson*
58/94 **You Don't Love Me (No, No, No)** *Dawn Penn*
8/72 **You Don't Mess Around With Jim** *Jim Croce*
95/62 **You Don't Miss Your Water** *William Bell*

84/69 **You Don't Need Me For Anything Anymore** *Brenda Lee*
10/57 **You Don't Owe Me A Thing** *Johnnie Ray*
2/64 **You Don't Own Me** *Lesley Gore*
16/82 **You Don't Want Me Anymore** *Steel Breeze*
64/61 **You Don't Want My Love** *Andy Williams*
10/99 **(You Drive Me) Crazy** *Britney Spears*
31/82 **You Dropped A Bomb On Me** *Gap Band*
49/58 **You Excite Me** *Frankie Avalon*
24/69 **You Gave Me A Mountain** *Frankie Laine*
55/67 **You Gave Me Something (And Everything's Alright)** *Fantastic Four*
36/99 **You Get What You Give** *New Radicals*
38/01 **You Gets No Love** *Faith Evans*
3/85 **You Give Good Love** *Whitney Houston*
1/86 **You Give Love A Bad Name** *Bon Jovi*
38/79 **You Gonna Make Me Love Somebody Else** *Jones Girls*
You Got It
9/89 *Roy Orbison*
33/95 *Bonnie Raitt*
49/78 **You Got It** *Diana Ross*
3/87 **You Got It All** *Jets*
3/89 **You Got It (The Right Stuff)** *New Kids On The Block*
20/83 **You Got Lucky** *Tom Petty*
39/99 **You Got Me** *Roots*
You Got Me Hummin'
77/67 *Sam & Dave*
52/70 *Cold Blood*
93/72 **You Got Me Walking** *Jackie Wilson*
58/69 **You Got Soul** *Johnny Nash*
69/78 **You Got That Right** *Lynyrd Skynyrd*
94/58 **You Got That Touch** *Sonny James*
11/74 **You Got The Love** *Rufus feat. Chaka Khan*
88/68 **You Got The Love** *Professor Morrison's Lollipop*
87/76 **You Got The Magic** *John Fogerty*
66/82 **You Got The Power** *War*
83/74 **You Got To Be The One** *Chi-Lites*
18/67 **You Got To Me** *Neil Diamond*
You Got To Pay The Price ..see: You've Got
(You Got To Walk And) Don't Look Back
83/66 *Temptations*
81/78 *Peter Tosh with Mick Jagger*
You Got What It Takes
10/60 *Marv Johnson*
7/67 *Dave Clark Five*
51/65 **You Got What It Takes** *Joe Tex*
40/69 **You Got Yours And I'll Get Mine** *Delfonics*
5/95 **You Gotta Be** *Des'ree*
49/92 **You Gotta Believe** *Marky Mark & The Funky Bunch*
7/87 **(You Gotta) Fight For Your Right (To Party!)** *Beastie Boys*
55/71 **You Gotta Have Love In Your Heart** *Supremes & Four Tops*
43/91 **You Gotta Love Someone** *Elton John*
53/76 **You Gotta Make Your Own Sunshine** *Neil Sedaka*

34/99 **You Had Me From Hello**
Kenny Chesney
64/88 **You Have Placed A Chill In My Heart** *Eurythmics*
61/95 **You Have The Right To Remain Silent** *Perfect Stranger*
1/74 **You Haven't Done Nothin**
Stevie Wonder
60/57 **(You Hit The Wrong Note) Billy Goat** *Bill Haley*
24/69 **You, I** *Rugbys*
94/71 **You Just Can't Win (By Making The Same Mistake)** *Gene & Jerry*
56/78 **You Keep Me Dancing**
Samantha Sang
You Keep Me Hangin' On
1/66 *Supremes*
67/67 *Vanilla Fudge*
6/68 *Vanilla Fudge*
92/69 *Wilson Pickett*
96/70 *Jackie DeShannon (medley)*
1/87 *Kim Wilde*
25/68 **(You Keep Me) Hangin' On**
Joe Simon
94/71 **You Keep Me Holding On**
Tyrone Davis
38/82 **You Keep Runnin' Away**
38 Special
19/67 **You Keep Running Away**
Four Tops
92/70 **You Keep Tightening Up On Me**
Box Tops
30/94 **You Know How We Do It** *Ice Cube*
17/86 **You Know I Love You...Don't You?**
Howard Jones
88/63 **You Know It Ain't Right** *Joe Hinton*
74/77 **You Know Like I Know**
Ozark Mountain Daredevils
76/98 **You Know My Steez** *Gang Starr*
35/80 **You Know That I Love You**
Santana
54/02 **You Know That I Love You**
Donell Jones
12/67 **You Know What I Mean** *Turtles*
83/83 **You Know What To Do**
Carly Simon
45/02 **You Know You're Right** *Nirvana*
6/96 **You Learn** *Alanis Morissette*
42/94 **You Let Your Heart Go Too Fast**
Spin Doctors
32/92 **You Lied To Me** *Cathy Dennis*
70/64 **You Lied To Your Daddy** *Tams*
You Light Up My Life
1/77 *Debby Boone*
80/77 *Kacey Cisyk*
34/97 *LeAnn Rimes*
67/73 **You Light Up My Life** *Carole King*
50/81 **You Like Me Don't You**
Jermaine Jackson
12/74 **You Little Trustmaker** *Tymes*
58/85 **You Look Marvelous** *Billy Crystal*
22/63 **You Lost The Sweetest Boy**
Mary Wells
96/69 **You Made A Believer (Out Of Me)**
Ruby Andrews
10/77 **You Made Me Believe In Magic**
Bay City Rollers
45/59 **You Made Me Love You**
Nat "King" Cole
9/77 **You Make Loving Fun**
Fleetwood Mac
62/78 **You Make Me Crazy** *Sammy Hagar*
2/74 **You Make Me Feel Brand New**
Stylistics
1/77 **You Make Me Feel Like Dancing**
Leo Sayer

You Make Me Feel (Mighty Real)
36/79 *Sylvester*
87/90 *Jimmy Somerville*
53/66 **(You Make Me Feel) So Good**
McCoys
50/70 **You Make Me Real** *Doors*
You Make Me Sick
33/01 *P!nk*
45S/02 *P!nk*
You Make Me Wanna...
2/97 *Usher*
63S/01 *Usher*
85/88 **You Make Me Work** *Cameo*
5/81 **You Make My Dreams**
Daryl Hall & John Oates
54/84 **You Make My Heart Beat Faster**
Kim Carnes
72/72 **You Make Your Own Heaven And Hell Right Here On Earth**
Undisputed Truth
7/80 **You May Be Right** *Billy Joel*
83/84 **You, Me And He** *Mtume*
68/70 **You, Me And Mexico** *Edward Bear*
17/60 **You Mean Everything To Me**
Neil Sedaka
84/59 **You Mean Everything To Me**
Fleetwoods
7/94 **You Mean The World To Me**
Toni Braxton
75/67 **You Mean The World To Me**
David Houston
35/68 **You Met Your Match**
Stevie Wonder
54/80 **You Might Need Somebody**
Turley Richards
7/84 **You Might Think** *Cars*
15/64 **You Must Believe Me** *Impressions*
You Must Have Been A Beautiful Baby
5/61 *Bobby Darin*
35/67 *Dave Clark Five*
18/96 **You Must Love Me** *Madonna*
46S/00 **You Nasty** *Too $hort*
36S/99 **You Need A Man** *Shanice*
40/79 **You Need A Woman Tonight**
Captain & Tennille
11/58 **You Need Hands** *Eydie Gorme*
88/75 **You Need Love** *Styx*
25/70 **You Need Love Like I Do (Don't You)** *Gladys Knight*
81/68 **You Need Me, Baby** *Joe Tex*
1/78 **You Needed Me** *Anne Murray*
14/64 **You Never Can Tell** *Chuck Berry*
10/78 **You Never Done It Like That**
Captain & Tennille
73/63 **You Never Miss Your Water (Till The Well Runs Dry)**
Esther Phillips & Big Al Downing
83/67 **You, No One But You**
Frankie Laine
65/98 **You Only Have To Say You Love Me** *Hannah Jones*
44/67 **You Only Live Twice**
Nancy Sinatra
68/76 **You Ought To Be Havin' Fun**
Tower Of Power
3/72 **You Ought To Be With Me**
Al Green
You Oughta Know
13A/95 *Alanis Morissette*
F/96 *Alanis Morissette (Live)*
59/00 **You Owe Me** *Nas*
48/77 **You + Me = Love** *Undisputed Truth*
98/95 **You Put A Move On My Heart**
Quincy Jones
82/68 **You Put It On Me** *B.B. King*

81/83 **You Put The Beat In My Heart**
Eddie Rabbitt
You Really Got A Hold On Me
..see: You've Really
You Really Got Me
7/64 *Kinks*
36/78 *Van Halen*
27/65 **You Really Know How To Hurt A Guy** *Jan & Dean*
29/92 **You Remind Me** *Mary J. Blige*
4/95 **You Remind Me Of Something**
R. Kelly
10/01 **You Rock My World**
Michael Jackson
83/96 **You Said** *Mona Lisa*
41/72 **You Said A Bad Word** *Joe Tex*
2/00 **You Sang To Me** *Marc Anthony*
37/81 **You Saved My Soul**
Burton Cummings
72/79 **You Says It All** *Randy Brown*
You Send Me
1/57 *Sam Cooke*
8/57 *Teresa Brewer*
56/68 *Aretha Franklin*
78/71 *Ponderosa Twins + One*
81/85 *Manhattans*
3/76 **You Sexy Thing** *Hot Chocolate*
35/80 **You Shook Me All Night Long**
AC/DC
1/76 **You Should Be Dancing** *Bee Gees*
17/97 **You Should Be Mine (Don't Waste Your Time)** *Brian McKnight*
13/86 **You Should Be Mine (The Woo Woo Song)** *Jeffrey Osborne*
54/78 **You Should Do It**
Peter Brown with Betty Wright
39/64 **You Should Have Seen The Way He Looked At Me** *Dixie Cups*
5/82 **You Should Hear How She Talks About You** *Melissa Manchester*
89/62 **You Should'a Treated Me Right**
Ike & Tina Turner
64/00 **You Should've Told Me** *Kelly Price*
F/57 **You Shouldn't Do That** *Sal Mineo*
32/01 **You Shouldn't Kiss Me Like This**
Toby Keith
You Showed Me
6/69 *Turtles*
47/92 *Salt-N-Pepa*
11/85 **You Spin Me Round (Like A Record)** *Dead Or Alive*
You Stepped Into My Life
47/79 *Melba Moore*
90/79 *Wayne Newton*
60/96 **You Still Touch Me** *Sting*
89/94 **You Suck** *Murmurs*
50/74 **You Sure Love To Ball**
Marvin Gaye
44/84 **You Take Me Up** *Thompson Twins*
10/79 **You Take My Breath Away**
Rex Smith
52/77 **You Take My Heart Away**
James Darren
46/62 **You Talk About Love**
Barbara George
You Talk Too Much
3/60 *Joe Jones*
87/60 *Frankie Ford*
38/65 **You Tell Me Why** *Beau Brummels*
38/92 **You Think You Know Her**
Cause & Effect
57/71 **You Think You're Hot Stuff**
Jean Knight
49/62 **You Threw A Lucky Punch**
Gene Chandler
40/79 **You Thrill Me** *Exile*

77/55 **You Tickle Me Baby** *Royal Jokers*
You To Me Are Everything
64/76 *Real Thing*
86/76 *Broadway*
98/76 *Revelation*
39/79 **You Took The Words Right Out Of My Mouth** *Meat Loaf*
8/65 **You Turn Me On** *Ian Whitcomb*
25/73 **You Turn Me On, I'm A Radio** *Joni Mitchell*
83/74 **You Turned My World Around** *Frank Sinatra*
24/95 **You Used To Love Me** *Faith*
94/66 **You Waited Too Long** *Five Stairsteps*
93/97 **You Walked In** *Lonestar*
36/72 **You Want It, You Got It** *Detroit Emeralds*
8/94 **You Want This** *Janet Jackson*
48/67 **You Wanted Someone To Play With (I Wanted Someone To Love)** *Frankie Laine*
13/72 **You Wear It Well** *Rod Stewart*
46/85 **You Wear It Well** *El DeBarge with DeBarge*
72/59 **You Went Back On Your Word** *Clyde McPhatter*
93/73 **You Were Always There** *Donna Fargo*
94/60 **You Were Born To Be Loved** *Billy Bland*
12/60 **(You Were Made For) All My Love** *Jackie Wilson*
21/65 **You Were Made For Me** *Freddie & The Dreamers*
You Were Made For Me
27/58 *Sam Cooke*
93/72 *Luther Ingram*
78/84 **You Were Made For Me** *Irene Cara*
2/97 **You Were Meant For Me** *Jewel*
21/59 **You Were Mine** *Fireflies*
34/99 **You Were Mine** *Dixie Chicks*
You Were On My Mind
3/65 *We Five*
36/67 *Crispian St. Peters*
30/65 **You Were Only Fooling (While I Was Falling In Love)** *Vic Damone*
100/64 **You Were Wrong** *Z.Z. Hill*
77/88 **You Will Know** *Stevie Wonder* *(also see: U Will Know)*
75/87 **You Win Again** *Bee Gees*
You Win Again
92/55 *Paulette Sisters*
95/58 *Jerry Lee Lewis*
22/62 *Fats Domino*
80/00 **You Won't Be Lonely Now** *Billy Ray Cyrus*
28/99 **You Won't Ever Be Lonely** *Andy Griggs*
48/98 **You Won't Forget Me** *La Bouche*
8/74 **You Won't See Me** *Anne Murray*
20/92 **You Won't See Me Cry** *Wilson Phillips*
42/66 **You Wouldn't Listen** *I'des Of March*
49/66 **You You You** *Mel Carter*
50/58 **You'd Be Surprised** *Kathy Linden*
77/73 **You'd Better Believe It** *Manhattans*
22/65 **You'd Better Come Home** *Petula Clark*
50/61 **You'd Better Come Home** *Russell Byrd*
14/80 **You'll Accomp'ny Me** *Bob Seger*
55/00 **You'll Always Be Loved By Me** *Brooks & Dunn*
64/65 **You'll Always Be The One I Love** *Dean Martin*
46/61 **You'll Answer To Me** *Patti Page*
21/99 **You'll Be In My Heart** *Phil Collins*
70/96 **You'll Be Mine (Party Time)** *Gloria Estefan*
67/56 **You'll Get Yours** *Frank Sinatra*
You'll Lose A Good Thing
8/62 *Barbara Lynn*
32/76 *Freddy Fender*
71/78 **You'll Love Again** *Hotel*
91/65 **You'll Miss Me (When I'm Gone)** *Fontella Bass & Bobby McClure*
2/76 **You'll Never Find Another Love Like Mine** *Lou Rawls*
You'll Never Get To Heaven (If You Break My Heart)
34/64 *Dionne Warwick*
23/73 *Stylistics*
11/56 **You'll Never Never Know** *Platters*
You'll Never Walk Alone
34/64 *Patti LaBelle*
48/65 *Gerry & The Pacemakers*
90/68 *Elvis Presley*
51/69 *Brooklyn Bridge*
6/95 **You'll See** *Madonna*

YOU'RE:

You're ..also see: Your
73/71 **You're A Big Girl Now** *Stylistics*
18/86 **You're A Friend Of Mine** *Clarence Clemons & Jackson Browne*
23/00 **You're A God** *Vertical Horizon*
You're A Lady
50/73 *Peter Skellern*
70/73 *Dawn Feat. Tony Orlando*
You're A Part Of Me
90/75 *Susan Jacks*
36/78 *Gene Cotton with Kim Carnes*
12/73 **You're A Special Part Of Me** *Diana Ross & Marvin Gaye*
You're A Sweetheart
66/58 *Little Willie John*
98/62 *Dinah Washington*
You're A Very Lovely Woman ..see: She's A Very
15/64 **You're A Wonderful One** *Marvin Gaye*
83/87 **You're All I Need** *Mötley Crüe*
88/67 **You're All I Need** *Bobby Bland*
You're All I Need To Get By
7/68 *Marvin Gaye & Tammi Terrell*
19/71 *Aretha Franklin*
34/75 *Tony Orlando & Dawn*
47/78 *Johnny Mathis & Deniece Williams*
88/82 *Chris Christian (medley)*
3/95 *Method Man (medley)*
3x/63 **You're All I Want For Christmas** *Brook Benton*
98/92 **You're All That Matters To Me** *Curtis Stigers*
28/91 **You're Amazing** *Robert Palmer*
39/98 **You're Beginning To Get To Me** *Clay Walker*
25/57 **You're Cheatin' Yourself (If You're Cheatin' On Me)** *Frank Sinatra*
35/83 **You're Driving Me Out Of My Mind** *Little River Band*
40/98 **You're Easy On The Eyes** *Terri Clark*
92/61 **You're Following Me** *Perry Como*
87/76 **You're Fooling You** *Dramatics*
73/80 **You're Gonna Get What's Coming** *Bonnie Raitt*
39/66 **(You're Gonna) Hurt Yourself** *Frankie Valli*
86/65 **You're Gonna Make Me Cry** *O.V. Wright*
34/59 **You're Gonna Miss Me** *Connie Francis*
55/66 **You're Gonna Miss Me** *Thirteenth Floor Elevators*
80/61 **You're Gonna Need Magic** *Roy Hamilton*
65/63 **You're Gonna Need Me** *Barbara Lynn*
49/63 **You're Good For Me** *Solomon Burke*
1/74 **(You're) Having My Baby** *Paul Anka/Odia Coates*
79/73 **You're In Good Hands** *Jermaine Jackson*
1/91 **You're In Love** *Wilson Phillips*
69/56 **You're In Love** *Gogi Grant*
89/85 **You're In Love** *Ratt*
4/78 **You're In My Heart (The Final Acclaim)** *Rod Stewart*
91/66 **You're Just About To Lose Your Clown** *Ray Charles*
88/76 **You're Just The Right Size** *Salsoul Orchestra*
43/60 **You're Looking Good** *Dee Clark*
58/84 **You're Looking Like Love To Me** *Peabo Bryson/Roberta Flack*
1/96 **You're Makin' Me High** *Toni Braxton*
50/58 **You're Making A Mistake** *Platters*
76/57 **You're Mine** *Four Aces*
100/56 **You're Mine** *Dream Weavers*
68/81 **You're Mine Tonight** *Pure Prairie League*
You're Movin' Out Today
42/77 *Bette Midler*
69/77 *Carole Bayer Sager*
87/60 **You're My Baby** *Sarah Vaughan*
63/65 **You're My Baby (And Don't You Forget It)** *Vacels*
16/76 **You're My Best Friend** *Queen*
77/80 **You're My Blessing** *Lou Rawls*
85/76 **You're My Driving Wheel** *Supremes*
6/67 **You're My Everything** *Temptations*
58/76 **You're My Everything** *Lee Garrett*
27/81 **You're My Girl** *Franke & The Knockouts* *(also see: Say)*
43/82 **You're My Latest, My Greatest Inspiration** *Teddy Pendergrass*
63/71 **You're My Man** *Lynn Anderson*
14/57 **You're My One And Only Love** *Ricky Nelson*
23/89 **You're My One And Only (True Love)** *Seduction*
48/64 **You're My Remedy** *Marvelettes*
(You're My) Soul And Inspiration
1/66 *Righteous Brothers*
38/78 *Donny & Marie Osmond*
76/79 **You're My Weakness** *Faith Band*
You're My World
26/64 *Cilla Black*
18/77 *Helen Reddy*
(You're Never Gonna Get It) ..see: My Lovin'
98/65 **You're Next** *Jimmy Witherspoon*
You're No Good
51/64 *Betty Everett*
97/64 *Swinging Blue Jeans*
1/75 *Linda Ronstadt*

You're Nobody Till Somebody Loves You
87/62 *Dinah Washington*
25/65 *Dean Martin*
96/66 *Wonder Who?*
You're Not Alone
10/89 *Chicago*
56/97 *Olive*
95/88 You're Not My Kind Of Girl *New Edition*
9/85 You're Only Human (Second Wind) *Billy Joel*
7/79 You're Only Lonely *J.D. Souther*
85/87 (You're Puttin') A Rush On Me *Stephanie Mills*
52/56 You're Sensational *Frank Sinatra*
You're Sixteen
8/60 *Johnny Burnette*
1/74 *Ringo Starr*
58/81 You're So Easy To Love *Tommy James*
You're So Fine
17/59 *Falcons*
86/67 *Bunny Sigler (medley)*
91/55 You're So Nice To Be Near *Loreleis*
47/82 (You're So Square) Baby, I Don't Care *Joni Mitchell*
48/74 You're So Unique *Billy Preston*
1/73 You're So Vain *Carly Simon*
29/72 You're Still A Young Man *Tower Of Power*
74S/99 You're Still Beautiful To Me *Bryan White*
2/98 You're Still The One *Shania Twain*
34/80 You're Supposed To Keep Your Love For Me *Jermaine Jackson*
62/56 You're The Apple Of My Eye *Four Lovers*
76/84 You're The Best Thing *Style Council*
(also see: Best Thing)
81/61 You're The Boss *LaVern Baker & Jimmy Ricks*
3/63 (You're the) Devil In Disguise *Elvis Presley*
2/75 You're The First, The Last, My Everything *Barry White*
73/58 You're The Greatest *Billy Scott*
You're The Inspiration
3/85 *Chicago*
77/97 *Peter Cetera*
18/78 You're The Love *Seals & Crofts*
90/93 You're The Love Of My Life *Sybil*
50/72 You're The Man *Marvin Gaye*
F/58 You're The Nearest Thing To Heaven *Johnny Cash*
4/65 You're The One *Vogues*
5/96 You're The One *SWV*
You're The One
22/70 *Little Sister*
77/71 *Three Degrees*
48/66 You're The One *Marvelettes*
71/71 You're The One For Me *Joe Simon*
55A/91 You're The One For Me *April*
1/78 You're The One That I Want *John Travolta & Olivia Newton-John*
84/85 You're The Only Love *Paul Hyde*
59/79 You're The Only One *Dolly Parton*
83/77 You're The Only One *Geils*
You're The Only Woman (You & I)
13/80 *Ambrosia*
36/90 *Brat Pack*
91/64 You're The Only World I Know *Sonny James*
You're The Reason
11/61 *Bobby Edwards*
87/61 *Joe South*
3/63 You're The Reason I'm Living *Bobby Darin*
51/71 You're The Reason Why *Ebonys*
74/91 You're The Story Of My Life *Desmond Child*
82/90 You're The Voice *John Farnham*
43/77 You're Throwing A Good Love Away *Spinners*
59/74 You're Welcome, Stop On By *Bobby Womack*

YOU'VE:

33/66 You've Been Cheatin' *Impressions*
36/65 You've Been In Love Too Long *Martha & The Vandellas*
64/70 You've Been My Inspiration *Main Ingredient*
(You've Got) ..see: Personality
You've Got A Friend
1/71 *James Taylor*
29/71 *Roberta Flack & Donny Hathaway*
79/81 You've Got A Good Love Coming *Van Stephenson*
49/99 You've Got A Way *Shania Twain*
67/82 You've Got Another Thing Comin' *Judas Priest*
54/79 You've Got Another Thing Coming *Hotel*
38/70 (You've Got Me) Dangling On A String *Chairmen Of The Board*
33/77 You've Got Me Runnin' *Gene Cotton*
63/66 You've Got My Mind Messed Up *James Carr*
74/74 You've Got My Soul On Fire *Temptations*
4/56 (You've Got) The Magic Touch *Platters*
86/60 You've Got The Power *James Brown*
91/69 You've Got The Power *Esquires*
58/68 You've Got To Be Loved *Montanas*
28/71 You've Got To Crawl (Before You Walk) *8th Day*
97/71 You've Got To Earn It *Staple Singers*
10/65 You've Got To Hide Your Love Away *Silkie*
93/61 You've Got To Love Her With A Feeling *Freddy King*
20/60 (You've Got To) Move Two Mountains *Marv Johnson*
You've Got To Pay The Price
49/67 *Al Kent*
49/69 *Gloria Taylor*
46/73 You've Got To Take It (If You Want It) *Main Ingredient*
76/80 You've Got What I Need *Shooting Star*
(You've Got What It Takes) ..see: Baby
7/65 You've Got Your Troubles *Fortunes*
You've Lost That Lovin' Feelin'
1/65 *Righteous Brothers*
16/69 *Dionne Warwick*
71/71 *Roberta Flack & Donny Hathaway*
89/79 *Long John Baldry & Kathi MacDonald*
12/80 *Daryl Hall & John Oates*
You've Made Me So Very Happy
39/67 *Brenda Holloway*
2/69 *Blood, Sweat & Tears*
95/70 *Lou Rawls*
95/65 You've Never Been In Love Like This Before *Unit Four plus Two*
22/73 You've Never Been This Far Before *Conway Twitty*
You've Really Got A Hold On Me
8/63 *Miracles*
98/72 *Gayle McCormick*
72/79 *Eddie Money*
60/68 You've Still Got A Place In My Heart *Dean Martin*

YOUNG:

35/02 Young *Kenny Chesney*
Young Abe Lincoln
25/55 *Don Cornell*
90/55 *Hugo & Luigi*
28/75 Young Americans *David Bowie*
17/63 Young And In Love *Dick & DeeDee*
53/64 Young And In Love *Chris Crosby*
Young And The Restless ..see: Nadia's Theme
23/58 Young And Warm And Wonderful *Tony Bennett*
99/68 Young Birds Fly *Cryan' Shames*
Young Blood
8/57 *Coasters*
20/76 *Bad Company*
68/87 *Bruce Willis*
40/79 Young Blood *Rickie Lee Jones*
86/68 Young Boy *Barbara Greene*
66/61 Young Boy Blues *Ben E. King*
12/60 Young Emotions *Ricky Nelson*
69/69 Young Folks *Supremes*
2/68 Young Girl *Gary Puckett*
51/66 Young Girl *Noel Harrison*
20/76 Young Hearts Run Free *Candi Staton*
74/59 Young Ideas *Chico Holiday*
Young Love
1/57 *Tab Hunter*
1/57 *Sonny James*
17/57 *Crew-Cuts*
50/66 *Lesley Gore*
25/73 *Donny Osmond*
93/76 *Ray Stevens*
38/82 Young Love *Air Supply*
64/83 Young Love *Janet Jackson*
6/63 Young Lovers *Paul & Paula*
(also see: Theme For)
80/72 Young New Mexican Puppeteer *Tom Jones*
75/98 Young, Sad And Blue *Lysette*
92/58 Young School Girl *Fats Domino*
71/84 Young Thing, Wild Dreams (Rock Me) *Red Rider*
5/81 Young Turks *Rod Stewart*
47/63 Young Wings Can Fly (Higher Than You Know) *Ruby & The Romantics*
5/62 Young World *Rick Nelson*
33/02 Young'n (Holla Back) *Fabolous*
80/82 Younger Days *Joe Fagin*
Younger Girl
42/66 *Critters*
52/66 *Hondells*

YOUR:

Your ..also see: You're

17/90 **Your Baby Never Looked Good In Blue** *Exposé*
93/63 **Your Baby's Gone Surfin'** *Duane Eddy*
18/03 **Your Body Is A Wonderland** *John Mayer*
13/94 **Your Body's Callin'** *R. Kelly*
98/63 **Your Boyfriend's Back** *Bobby Comstock*
(also see: My Boyfriend's Back)
24/75 **Your Bulldog Drinks Champagne** *Jim Stafford*
51/74 **Your Cash Ain't Nothin' But Trash** *Steve Miller Band*
Your Cheatin' Heart
72/58 *George Hamilton IV*
82/59 *Billy Vaughn*
29/62 *Ray Charles*
77/82 **Your Daddy Don't Know** *Toronto*
51/00 **Your Everything** *Keith Urban*
34/61 **Your Friends** *Dee Clark*
Your Good Thing (Is About To End)
95/66 *Mable John*
18/69 *Lou Rawls*
95/62 **Your Heart Belongs To Me** *Supremes*
91/68 **Your Heart Is Free Just Like The Wind** *Vikki Carr*
46/69 **Your Husband - My Wife** *Brooklyn Bridge*
33/82 **Your Imagination** *Daryl Hall & John Oates*
53/57 **Your Kisses Kill Me** *Eydie Gorme*
63/61 **Your Last Goodbye** *Floyd Cramer*
62A/98 **Your Life Is Now** *John Mellencamp*
47A/95 **Your Little Secret** *Melissa Etheridge*
6/86 **Your Love** *Outfield*
15/77 **Your Love** *Marilyn McCoo & Billy Davis Jr.*
38/75 **Your Love** *Graham Central Station*
71/91 **Your Love** *Keith Sweat*
60/57 **Your Love For Me** *Frank Sinatra*
76/94 **Your Love Is A ...** *Whitehead Bros.*
13/83 **Your Love Is Driving Me Crazy** *Sammy Hagar*
54/85 **Your Love Is King** *Sade*
66/94 **Your Love Is So Divine** *Miranda*
93/71 **Your Love Is So Doggone Good** *Whispers*
49/78 **Your Love Is So Good For Me** *Diana Ross*
(Your Love Keeps Lifting Me) Higher And Higher
6/67 *Jackie Wilson*
2/77 *Rita Coolidge*
100/93 **Your Love Keeps Working On Me** *Jody Watley*
73/71 **Your Love (Means Everything to Me)** *Charles Wright*
Your Loving Arms
87/95 *Billie Ray Martin*
46/96 *Billie Ray Martin*
24/61 **Your Ma Said You Cried In Your Sleep Last Night** *Kenny Dino*
Your Mama Don't Dance
4/73 *Loggins & Messina*
10/89 *Poison*
40/71 **Your Move** *Yes*
80/58 **Your Name Is Beautiful** *Carl Smith*
14/62 **Your Nose Is Gonna Grow** *Johnny Crawford*
40/63 **Your Old Stand By** *Mary Wells*
40/61 **Your One And Only Love** *Jackie Wilson*
28/63 **Your Other Love** *Connie Francis*
54/61 **Your Other Love** *Flamingos*
75/70 **Your Own Back Yard** *Dion*
62/77 **Your Own Special Way** *Genesis*
86/86 **Your Personal Touch** *Evelyn "Champagne" King*
5/67 **Your Precious Love** *Marvin Gaye & Tammi Terrell*
(also see: For Your Precious Love)
52/96 **Your Secret Love** *Luther Vandross*
88/73 **Your Side Of The Bed** *Mac Davis*
62/86 **Your Smile** *René & Angela*
20/77 **Your Smiling Face** *James Taylor*
Your Song
8/71 *Elton John*
48/92 *Rod Stewart*
60/78 **Your Sweetness Is My Weakness** *Barry White*
68/63 **Your Teenage Dreams** *Johnny Mathis*
72/68 **Your Time Hasn't Come Yet, Baby** *Elvis Presley*
40/71 **Your Time To Cry** *Joe Simon*
67/57 **Your True Love** *Carl Perkins*
33/67 **Your Unchanging Love** *Marvin Gaye*
32/63 **Your Used To Be** *Brenda Lee*
20/57 **Your Wild Heart** *Joy Layne*
9/86 **Your Wildest Dreams** *Moody Blues*
23/97 **Your Woman** *White Town*
59/72 **Your Wonderful, Sweet Sweet Love** *Supremes*
63/94 **Yours** *Shai*
(also see: Baby, I'm Yours)
78/70 **Yours Love** *Joe Simon*
99/89 **Youth Gone Wild** *Skid Row*
28/02 **Youth Of The Nation** *P.O.D.*
(Yowsah, Yowsah, Yowsah) ..see: Dance, Dance, Dance
4/68 **Yummy Yummy Yummy** *Ohio Express*

Z

52/68 **Zabadak** *Dave Dee, Dozy, Beaky, Mick & Tich*
75/56 **Zambezi** *Lou Busch*
78/69 **Zazueira (Za-zoo-wher-a)** *Herb Alpert*
49/02 **Zephyr Song** *Red Hot Chili Peppers*
49A/96 **Zero** *Smashing Pumpkins*
98/62 **Zero-Zero** *Lawrence Welk*
Zing! Went The Strings Of My Heart
92/63 *Furys*
64/72 *Trammps*
91/75 **Zip, The** *MFSB*
8/63 **Zip-A-Dee Doo-Dah** *Bob B. Soxx & The Blue Jeans*
36/67 **Zip Code** *Five Americans*
16/57 **Zip Zip** *Diamonds*
22A/94 **Zombie** *Cranberries*
41A/98 **Zoot Suit Riot** *Cherry Poppin' Daddies*
11/66 **Zorba The Greek** *Herb Alpert*
17/58 **Zorro** *Chordettes*
61/94 **Zunga Zeng** *K7*

TOP ARTISTS

This section ranks the Top 600 pop artists from 1955-2002. Each artist's accumulated point total is shown to the right of their name. This ranking includes all titles that peaked prior to 2003.

A picture of each Top 200 artist is shown next to their listing in the artist section of this book.

HEADINGS AND SPECIAL SYMBOLS

Old Rank: Artist ranking in *Top Pop Singles 1955-1999*

New Rank: Artist ranking in *Top Pop Singles 1955-2002*

● = **Deceased Solo Artist or Group Member**

✪ = **Super Hot Artist**
Had significant chart activity since the previous edition with an increase of at least 400 points and a minimum of 5 chart hits from 2000-2002.

★ = **Hot Artist**
Had significant chart activity since the previous edition with an increase of at least 200 points and a minimum of 3 chart hits from 2000-2002.

▼ = **Pioneer Artist**
Had earlier pop chart hits (as found in *Pop Hits Singles & Albums 1940-1954*)

— = Newly ranked artist in the Top 600

POINT SYSTEM

Points are awarded according to the following formula:

1. Each artist's *Hot 100* singles are given points based on their highest charted position:

#1	=	100 points for its first week at #1, plus 10 points for each additional week at #1
#2	=	90 points for its first week at #2, plus 5 points for each additional week at #2
#3	=	80 points for its first week at #3, plus 3 points for each additional week at #3
#4-5	=	70 points
#6-10	=	60 points
#11-15	=	55 points
#16-20	=	50 points
#21-30	=	45 points
#31-40	=	40 points
#41-50	=	35 points
#51-60	=	30 points
#61-70	=	25 points
#71-80	=	20 points
#81-90	=	15 points
#91-100	=	10 points

2. Points awarded for *Hot 100 Airplay* hits:

#1	=	85 points for its first week at #1, plus 5 points for each additional week at #1
#2	=	75 points for its first week at #2, plus 3 points for each additional week at #2
#3	=	65 points for its first week at #3, plus 2 points for each additional week at #3
#4-5	=	55 points
#6-10	=	45 points
#11-15	=	40 points
#16-20	=	35 points
#21-30	=	30 points
#31-40	=	25 points
#41-50	=	20 points
#51-60	=	15 points
#61-75	=	10 points

POINT SYSTEM (Cont'd)

3. Points awarded for *Hot 100 Sales* hits:

#1	=	40 points for its first week at #1, plus 5 points for each additional week at #1
#2	=	40 points for its first week at #2, plus 3 points for each additional week at #2
#3	=	40 points for its first week at #3, plus 2 points for each additional week at #3
#4-5	=	40 points
#6-10	=	30 points
#11-20	=	25 points
#21-30	=	20 points
#31-40	=	15 points
#41-50	=	10 points
#51-75	=	5 points

4. Points awarded for *Christmas* and *Honor Roll* hits:

#1-10	=	25 points
#11-20	=	20 points
#21-30	=	15 points
#31-40	=	10 points

5. All *Coming Up* hits get 5 points no matter what position they reach.

6. Total weeks charted are added in.

In the case of a tie, the artist listed first is determined by the following tie-breaker rules:

1) Most charted singles
2) Most Top 40 singles
3) Most Top 10 singles

When two or more artists combine for a hit single, such as Bryan Adams/Tina Turner, the full point value is given to each artist. Duos, such as Simon & Garfunkel, are considered regular recording teams, and their points are not shared by either artist individually.

TOP 600 ARTISTS (#1-119)

Old Rank	New Rank	Artist	Points
(1)	1.	**Elvis Presley** ●	9,761
(2)	2.	**The Beatles** ●●	5,398
(3)	3.	**Elton John**	5,226
(6)	✪4.	**Madonna**	4,517
(4)	5.	**Stevie Wonder**	4,470
(5)	6.	**James Brown**	4,152
(9)	7.	**Michael Jackson**	3,930
(7)	8.	**The Rolling Stones** ●	3,819
(23)	✪9.	**Janet Jackson**	3,811
(8)	10.	**Aretha Franklin**	3,782
(10)	11.	Pat Boone	3,733
(11)	12.	Marvin Gaye ●	3,540
(12)	13.	Rod Stewart	3,489
(27)	★14.	Mariah Carey	3,467
(26)	15.	Bee Gees ●	3,425
(28)	★16.	Whitney Houston	3,367
(13)	17.	The Beach Boys ●●	3,360
(15)	18.	Ray Charles	3,353
(14)	19.	Paul McCartney/Wings	3,347
(21)	20.	Prince	3,227
(16)	21.	The Temptations ●●●●	3,224
(18)	22.	Chicago ●	3,193
(17)	23.	Fats Domino	3,182
(19)	24.	Neil Diamond	3,177
(20)	25.	The Supremes ●	3,176
(22)	26.	Ricky Nelson ●	3,122
(24)	27.	Connie Francis	3,076
(25)	28.	Frank Sinatra ▼ ●	3,073
(29)	29.	Paul Anka	2,933
(30)	30.	Dionne Warwick	2,905
(31)	31.	The 4 Seasons ●	2,816
(33)	32.	Olivia Newton-John	2,793
(32)	33.	Brenda Lee	2,779
(36)	34.	Billy Joel	2,761
(37)	35.	Diana Ross	2,721
(34)	36.	Nat "King" Cole ▼ ●	2,680
(38)	37.	Daryl Hall & John Oates	2,662
(35)	38.	Perry Como ▼ ●	2,610
(39)	39.	George Michael/Wham!	2,565
(44)	40.	Kenny Rogers/First Edition	2,494
(40)	41.	Bobby Vinton	2,473
(41)	42.	Gladys Knight & The Pips	2,473
(42)	43.	Barbra Streisand	2,463
(43)	44.	The Miracles ●	2,444
(45)	45.	The Everly Brothers	2,383
(46)	46.	Brook Benton ●	2,373
(47)	47.	Andy Williams	2,307
(49)	48.	Donna Summer	2,293
(48)	49.	Four Tops ●	2,292
(50)	50.	Sam Cooke ●	2,278
(51)	51.	The Platters ●●●●	2,278
(53)	52.	Phil Collins	2,197
(52)	53.	Jackie Wilson ●	2,194
(56)	54.	Cher	2,187
(54)	55.	The Jackson 5/Jacksons	2,183
(55)	56.	Bobby Darin ●	2,154
(63)	57.	Boyz II Men	2,133
(59)	58.	Bryan Adams	2,100
(57)	59.	Johnny Mathis	2,091
(58)	60.	Carpenters ●	2,082
(70)	61.	Heart	2,077
(60)	62.	Linda Ronstadt	2,069
(95)	★63.	R. Kelly	2,047
(61)	64.	John Cougar Mellencamp	2,034
(66)	65.	Gloria Estefan/Miami Sound Machine	2,032
(126)	✪66.	**Puff Daddy**	2,024
(62)	67.	Chubby Checker	2,023
(65)	68.	Jefferson Airplane/Starship ●●	2,010
(86)	69.	The Isley Brothers ●	2,004
(64)	70.	Kool & The Gang ●	1,990
(67)	71.	Barry Manilow	1,915
(79)	72.	Aerosmith	1,914
(75)	73.	Earth, Wind & Fire	1,911
(68)	74.	Roy Orbison ●	1,892
(82)	75.	Bon Jovi	1,891
(69)	76.	Glen Campbell	1,885
(71)	77.	Dion (Dion & The Belmonts)	1,870
(72)	78.	Bob Seger	1,865
(73)	79.	Herb Alpert/The Tijuana Brass	1,860
(74)	80.	Neil Sedaka	1,858
(76)	81.	John Denver ●	1,826
(78)	82.	The 5th Dimension ●	1,810
(81)	83.	Tommy James & The Shondells	1,747
(77)	84.	Patti Page ▼	1,743
(80)	85.	Johnny Cash	1,741
(85)	86.	Lionel Richie	1,728
(106)	87.	Duran Duran	1,714
(109)	88.	Celine Dion	1,709
(83)	89.	The Drifters ●●●	1,691
(84)	90.	Spinners ●	1,686
(87)	91.	Pointer Sisters	1,671
(88)	92.	Three Dog Night	1,668
(97)	93.	Queen ●	1,664
(113)	94.	U2	1,651
(296)	✪95.	**Jay-Z**	1,648
(93)	96.	Huey Lewis & The News	1,647
(89)	97.	Tom Jones	1,644
(90)	98.	The Impressions ●	1,641
(91)	99.	Commodores	1,634
(92)	100.	Wilson Pickett	1,632
(94)	101.	Foreigner	1,630
(111)	102.	The Doobie Brothers ●	1,620
(100)	103.	Bruce Springsteen	1,619
(98)	104.	Fleetwood Mac	1,619
(96)	105.	Jerry Butler	1,618
(102)	106.	Eagles	1,598
(99)	107.	Johnny Rivers	1,587
(103)	108.	Eric Clapton	1,583
(101)	109.	Dean Martin ▼ ●	1,577
(107)	110.	Electric Light Orchestra	1,576
(104)	111.	Bobby Vee	1,566
(105)	112.	Journey	1,562
(108)	113.	Bobby Rydell	1,548
(129)	114.	TLC ●	1,526
(110)	115.	Tony Orlando (& Dawn)	1,524
(231)	✪116.	**Mary J. Blige**	1,522
(174)	★117.	Santana	1,503
(112)	118.	Genesis	1,476
(118)	119.	Styx ●	1,471

TOP 600 ARTISTS (#120-240)

Old Rank	New Rank	Artist	Points
(114)	120.	Richard Marx	1,471
(121)	121.	Michael Bolton	1,459
(119)	122.	David Bowie	1,449
(115)	123.	Chuck Berry	1,443
(116)	124.	The McGuire Sisters ▼	1,441
(117)	125.	Dave Clark Five	1,441
(120)	126.	Tom Petty & The Heartbreakers ●	1,435
(122)	127.	Al Martino ▼	1,403
(123)	128.	Herman's Hermits ●	1,397
(136)	129.	Carly Simon	1,392
(124)	130.	Simon & Garfunkel	1,392
(125)	131.	Jimmie Rodgers	1,381
(164)	132.	Abba	1,371
(127)	133.	Rick Springfield	1,363
(130)	134.	John Lennon ●	1,339
(137)	135.	Kenny Loggins	1,333
(131)	136.	Frankie Avalon	1,331
(132)	137.	Chaka Khan/Rufus	1,328
(128)	138.	Bill Haley (& His Comets) ▼ ●	1,327
(133)	139.	Van Halen	1,323
(134)	140.	Helen Reddy	1,317
(209)★	141.	Toni Braxton	1,316
(135)	142.	B.J. Thomas	1,312
(138)	143.	Sheena Easton	1,303
(139)	144.	KC & The Sunshine Band ●	1,300
(140)	145.	Paul Revere & The Raiders	1,298
(141)	146.	The O'Jays ●	1,295
(145)	147.	The Righteous Brothers	1,295
(186)	148.	Kiss ●	1,288
(142)	149.	Paula Abdul	1,288
(202)	150.	The Cars ●	1,287
(143)	151.	Roberta Flack	1,287
(144)	152.	The Monkees	1,282
(146)	153.	The Shirelles ●	1,276
(147)	154.	Petula Clark	1,275
(148)	155.	Johnny Tillotson	1,274
(149)	156.	Marty Robbins ●	1,274
(150)	157.	Anne Murray	1,273
(151)	158.	Duane Eddy	1,268
(152)	159.	Def Leppard ●	1,268
(165)	160.	Ray Stevens	1,265
(153)	161.	Gene Pitney	1,263
(154)	162.	Jan & Dean	1,261
(155)	163.	Al Green	1,261
(167)	164.	The Rascals	1,259
(177)	165.	Luther Vandross	1,256
(193)	166.	The Notorious B.I.G. ●	1,255
(156)	167.	Billy Vaughn ●	1,249
(157)	168.	Otis Redding ●	1,245
(224)	169.	New Kids On The Block	1,244
(158)	170.	Creedence Clearwater Revival ●	1,241
(159)	171.	James Taylor	1,240
(191)	172.	LL Cool J	1,233
(179)	173.	The Hollies	1,229
(160)	174.	The Who ●	1,226
(161)	175.	Smokey Robinson	1,223
(162)	176.	Donny Osmond	1,219
(163)	177.	Bobby Goldsboro	1,214
(166)	178.	Tony Bennett ▼	1,211
(225)	179.	Brandy	1,210
(168)	180.	Paul Simon	1,198
— ✪	181.	Destiny's Child	1,194
(171)	182.	Tina Turner	1,190
(169)	183.	Joe Tex ●	1,189
(170)	184.	REO Speedwagon	1,188
(299)★	185.	Faith Evans	1,186
(207)	186.	The Moody Blues	1,175
(172)	187.	Martha & The Vandellas	1,175
(173)	188.	The Guess Who ●	1,175
(212)	189.	En Vogue	1,173
(175)	190.	Eddie Money	1,168
(181)	191.	Sly & The Family Stone	1,162
— ✪	192.	Usher	1,162
(176)	193.	Bob Dylan	1,159
(486)✪	194.	Tim McGraw	1,159
(192)	195.	Bobby Brown	1,157
(178)	196.	Steve Miller Band	1,156
(206)	197.	Sting	1,149
(180)	198.	Steve Lawrence ▼	1,147
— ✪	199.	Ja Rule	1,135
(182)	200.	Tommy Roe	1,134
(183)	201.	The Marvelettes ●	1,125
(184)	202.	Bobby Bland	1,123
(185)	203.	Joe Simon	1,123
(187)	204.	The Kinks	1,122
(188)	205.	The Four Lads ▼	1,122
— ✪	206.	Missy "Misdemeanor" Elliott	1,121
(356)★	207.	112	1,119
(211)	208.	Little River Band	1,115
(189)	209.	Dr. Hook ●	1,110
(196)	210.	Pat Benatar	1,109
(195)	211.	INXS ●	1,108
(190)	212.	The Animals ● ●	1,104
(198)	213.	America	1,103
(245)	214.	Peter, Paul & Mary	1,101
(419)★	215.	Backstreet Boys	1,099
(227)	216.	Don Henley	1,097
(221)	217.	Grand Funk Railroad	1,094
(194)	218.	Kim Carnes	1,093
(216)	219.	War ●	1,092
— ✪	220.	*NSYNC	1,092
(200)	221.	George Harrison ●	1,088
(235)	222.	Monica	1,086
(199)	223.	The Grass Roots	1,077
(201)	224.	Mary Wells ●	1,076
(203)	225.	Billy Ocean	1,076
(204)	226.	Air Supply	1,075
(205)	227.	Jr. Walker & The All Stars ● ●	1,074
(208)	228.	Keith Sweat	1,070
(210)	229.	Steve Winwood	1,063
(213)	230.	Teresa Brewer ▼	1,059
(214)	231.	Cyndi Lauper	1,059
(217)	232.	Sonny & Cher ●	1,055
(220)	233.	Barry White ●	1,055
(218)	234.	Gary Lewis & The Playboys	1,052
(219)	235.	Alice Cooper	1,051
(257)	236.	Babyface	1,050
(222)	237.	Survivor	1,049
(215)	238.	David Seville(/The Chipmunks) ●	1,043
(232)	239.	The Coasters ● ●	1,043
(223)	240.	The Diamonds ●	1,042

TOP 600 ARTISTS (#241-361)

Old Rank	New Rank		Points
(226)	241.	Natalie Cole	1,034
(228)	242.	Nancy Sinatra	1,029
(229)	243.	Four Aces ▼	1,029
(230)	244.	B.B. King	1,026
(233)	245.	Captain & Tennille	1,019
(234)	246.	Lesley Gore	1,017
(297)	247.	2Pac ●	1,013
(258)	248.	R.E.M.	1,012
(237)	249.	Freddy Cannon	1,011
(259)	250.	Dusty Springfield ●	1,011
(238)	251.	Ray Parker, Jr./Raydio	1,011
(256)	252.	Mamas & The Papas ● ●	1,009
—	✪253.	Jennifer Lopez	1,006
(239)	254.	Carole King	1,003
(240)	255.	Little Richard	1,002
(241)	256.	Dolly Parton	1,002
(242)	257.	Joe Cocker	998
(243)	258.	Culture Club	996
(244)	259.	Roxette	996
(246)	260.	The Stylistics	989
(247)	261.	Johnnie Taylor ●	984
(248)	262.	Roger Williams	983
(249)	263.	Etta James	979
—	✪264.	Aaliyah ●	977
(411)	★265.	Snoop Dogg	972
(250)	266.	The Police	970
(251)	267.	Engelbert Humperdinck	969
(252)	268.	Bette Midler	967
—	✪269.	Christina Aguilera	966
(284)	270.	Gene Chandler	965
—	✪271.	Faith Hill	963
(253)	272.	Lloyd Price	961
(254)	273.	Andy Gibb ●	960
(255)	274.	Donovan	959
(261)	275.	Mase	959
—	✪276.	Nelly	959
(260)	277.	Jay & The Americans	952
(197)	278.	Eddie Fisher ▼	943
(262)	279.	Toto ●	935
(263)	280.	Brian Hyland	932
(264)	281.	Bread	928
(271)	282.	Stevie Nicks	923
(268)	283.	Amy Grant	923
(285)	284.	SWV (Sisters With Voices)	921
(265)	285.	The Fontane Sisters ▼	915
(266)	286.	Jackson Browne	912
(236)	287.	The Ames Brothers ▼ ●	910
(269)	288.	Patti LaBelle	908
(267)	289.	Cheap Trick	908
(270)	290.	Clyde McPhatter ●	905
(272)	291.	J. Geils Band	902
(273)	292.	Poison	902
(274)	293.	The Doors ●	901
(275)	294.	The Lovin' Spoonful ●	897
(276)	295.	Robert Palmer	896
(277)	296.	Jody Watley	896
(279)	297.	Billy Preston	893
(281)	298.	The Turtles ●	890
(282)	299.	Exposé	888
(283)	300.	Conway Twitty ●	887

Old Rank	New Rank		Points
(343)	301.	Xscape	885
(286)	302.	The Dells ●	879
(287)	303.	Ben E. King	878
(288)	304.	Eurythmics	875
(289)	305.	Sarah Vaughan ▼ ●	874
(290)	306.	Ronnie Dove	873
(291)	307.	Taylor Dayne	872
(292)	308.	Billy Idol	870
(293)	309.	Cliff Richard	869
(294)	310.	Peaches & Herb	865
(295)	311.	Vanessa Williams	864
(323)	312.	Shania Twain	863
(298)	313.	Dan Fogelberg	859
(338)	314.	Bangles	858
(301)	315.	New Edition	856
(300)	316.	Ringo Starr	853
(349)	317.	K-Ci & JoJo	851
(395)	318.	Brian McKnight	850
(302)	319.	The Osmonds	850
(303)	320.	Bill Withers	847
—	✪321.	Joe	847
(304)	322.	Jermaine Jackson	843
(305)	323.	Frankie Valli	842
(306)	324.	Color Me Badd	840
(307)	325.	Debbie Gibson	838
(308)	326.	Del Shannon ●	837
(319)	327.	James Ingram	837
(309)	328.	Eddie Rabbitt ●	836
(310)	329.	Jack Scott	834
(311)	330.	The Lettermen	833
(312)	331.	Sammy Davis, Jr. ▼ ●	826
(313)	332.	Steely Dan	825
(314)	333.	38 Special	825
(315)	334.	Solomon Burke	818
(316)	335.	The Staple Singers ●	818
(317)	336.	The Chi-Lites	816
(318)	337.	Ohio Players ● ●	816
(320)	338.	Blondie	808
(321)	339.	The Kingston Trio ●	807
(322)	340.	Roger Miller ●	806
(359)	341.	Depeche Mode	805
(278)	342.	Bing Crosby ▼ ●	804
(324)	343.	Bad Company	802
(325)	344.	Guns N' Roses	802
(326)	345.	The Alan Parsons Project	798
(369)	346.	Loverboy ●	793
(340)	347.	BLACKstreet	793
(327)	348.	Lawrence Welk ▼ ●	789
(328)	349.	George Benson	788
(329)	350.	The Association ●	788
(330)	351.	ZZ Top	786
—	✪352.	Mya	785
(331)	353.	Paul Davis	783
(332)	354.	Lou Rawls	782
(333)	355.	Christopher Cross	782
(334)	356.	Cat Stevens	780
(459)	357.	Alanis Morissette	778
(335)	358.	Lobo	777
(336)	359.	Peter Cetera	775
(337)	360.	Jaye P. Morgan	774
(421)	361.	Sheryl Crow	774

Old Rank	New Rank		Points
—	★362.	Matchbox Twenty	769
—	✪363.	Eminem	768
(339)	364.	Bill Black's Combo ●	765
(345)	365.	Salt-N-Pepa	764
—	✪366.	Alan Jackson	761
(341)	367.	Laura Branigan	760
(342)	368.	Peter & Gordon	759
—	★369.	Busta Rhymes	758
(344)	370.	Eddie Kendricks ●	757
—	✪371.	Ginuwine	757
(430)	372.	Montell Jordan	754
(346)	373.	Boz Scaggs	753
(347)	374.	Dinah Washington ▼ ●	752
—	★375.	Lil' Kim	751
(348)	376.	Charlie Rich ●	751
(442)	377.	Pearl Jam	748
—	✪378.	Ashanti	747
(350)	379.	Georgia Gibbs ▼	746
(457)	380.	Dr. Dre	746
(351)	381.	Booker T. & The MG's ●	743
(477)	382.	Master P	740
(352)	383.	Ace Of Base	740
(354)	384.	DeBarge/El DeBarge	739
(353)	385.	Jim Reeves ●	737
—	★386.	Savage Garden	737
(451)	387.	Da Brat	736
(400)	388.	Bone Thugs-N-Harmony	734
(355)	389.	The Byrds ● ● ●	732
(357)	390.	Ike & Tina Turner	730
(358)	391.	Crosby, Stills & Nash (& Young)	730
(412)	392.	Kenny G	730
—	★393.	LeAnn Rimes	730
(360)	394.	Little Anthony & The Imperials	728
(368)	395.	Dru Hill	728
(389)	396.	Steppenwolf ● ●	725
(361)	397.	Guy Mitchell ▼ ●	724
(362)	398.	Tommy Edwards ▼ ●	723
(363)	399.	Leo Sayer	723
(364)	400.	Glenn Frey	722
(365)	401.	Eydie Gorme	720
(375)	402.	Pet Shop Boys	720
—	✪403.	Dixie Chicks	719
(366)	404.	LaVern Baker ●	718
(367)	405.	Eric Carmen	718
—	✪406.	Jagged Edge	715
—	★407.	George Strait	712
(280)	408.	The Chordettes ●	712
(370)	409.	Eddy Arnold ▼	711
(371)	410.	Isaac Hayes	710
(372)	411.	Jerry Lee Lewis	708
(373)	412.	Jim Croce ●	708
(374)	413.	Tammi Terrell ●	707
(376)	414.	Gary (U.S.) Bonds	706
(378)	415.	The Vogues	703
(377)	416.	Tavares	703
(379)	417.	Buddy Holly (/The Crickets) ●	703
—	418.	Goo Goo Dolls	703
(380)	419.	Stevie B	702
—	★420.	No Doubt	702
(381)	421.	Mac Davis	700
(384)	422.	Jodeci	699
(382)	423.	Tears For Fears	699
—	✪424.	Eve	697
(385)	425.	Melissa Manchester	696
(386)	426.	Joan Jett & The Blackhearts	696
(387)	427.	Carla Thomas	695
—	★428.	Nas	694
(388)	429.	Dickie Goodman ●	690
—	★430.	Red Hot Chili Peppers	688
(390)	431.	Howard Jones	687
—	★432.	98°	685
(391)	433.	Seals & Crofts	682
(397)	434.	M.C. Hammer	682
(392)	435.	Peabo Bryson	680
(402)	436.	Gale Storm	680
(393)	437.	The Fleetwoods	680
(394)	438.	Rita Coolidge	679
—	✪439.	P!nk	678
(398)	440.	Ramsey Lewis	677
(399)	441.	Manfred Mann	677
(435)	442.	Supertramp	677
(401)	443.	Juice Newton	676
(403)	444.	Boston	675
(404)	445.	UB40	674
(405)	446.	Jack Jones	673
(406)	447.	Mitch Miller ▼	673
(407)	448.	Atlanta Rhythm Section	669
—	449.	Ice Cube	667
(408)	450.	Kansas	666
(422)	451.	Tevin Campbell	666
(409)	452.	Joni James ▼	665
(410)	453.	Jimmy Dean	665
—	★454.	Ricky Martin	663
(481)	455.	England Dan & John Ford Coley	661
—	456.	Will Smith	661
(413)	457.	Thompson Twins	659
(429)	458.	Spice Girls	659
(414)	459.	Gordon Lightfoot	658
(415)	460.	Frankie Laine ▼	657
(416)	461.	Jeffrey Osborne	657
—	★462.	OutKast	657
(417)	463.	Wilson Phillips	657
(418)	464.	Clarence Carter	656
—	✪465.	Ludacris	655
(432)	466.	Chic ●	655
(420)	467.	Ronnie Milsap	652
(479)	468.	Atlantic Starr	651
(423)	469.	The Crew-Cuts ▼	651
(424)	470.	The Ventures ● ●	647
—	★471.	Britney Spears	647
(450)	472.	Hootie & The Blowfish	646
(425)	473.	The Jets	645
(438)	474.	Tony! Toni! Toné!	643
(426)	475.	Henry Mancini ●	642
(427)	476.	Chuck Jackson	641
(439)	477.	Sergio Mendes & Brasil '66	639
(428)	478.	Rick Astley	639
(431)	479.	Tyrone Davis	637
—	✪480.	Mystikal	637
(433)	481.	Johnny Nash	633
(434)	482.	Mötley Crüe	632

TOP 600 ARTISTS (#483-600)

Old Rank	New Rank		Points
—	483.	The Crests	632
—	484.	Lenny Kravitz	630
(436)	485.	Irene Cara	625
(437)	486.	Wayne Newton	624
(446)	487.	Gary Puckett & The Union Gap	624
(440)	488.	The Four Preps ● ●	620
(494)	489.	The Pretenders ● ●	620
(441)	490.	The Delfonics	616
(456)	491.	The Cure	615
(443)	492.	Blood, Sweat & Tears	614
(444)	493.	Corey Hart	613
(445)	494.	The Box Tops	612
(447)	495.	Nilsson ●	611
(474)	496.	Total	611
(448)	497.	The Searchers	609
(449)	498.	Willie Nelson	609
—	★499.	Shaggy	608
(452)	500.	Meat Loaf	607
(453)	501.	Bruce Hornsby & The Range	606
(454)	502.	Belinda Carlisle	604
(455)	503.	The Moments ●	603
—	504.	Metallica	600
(458)	505.	Bachman-Turner Overdrive	599
(460)	506.	Jennifer Warnes	599
(383)	507.	Doris Day ▼	598
(461)	508.	Firefall ●	595
—	509.	After 7	594
(462)	510.	Percy Sledge	593
(463)	511.	Classics IV	593
(464)	512.	The Manhattans ● ●	592
(465)	513.	Quincy Jones	592
(466)	514.	The Fireballs ●	592
(467)	515.	Peter Gabriel	591
(468)	516.	The Tokens	590
(469)	517.	Andy Kim	587
(470)	518.	Milli Vanilli ●	586
(471)	519.	Jimmy Clanton	585
—	520.	C & C Music Factory ●	585
(472)	521.	The Human League	584
(473)	522.	Night Ranger	582
(475)	523.	Anita Baker	581
(478)	524.	Dee Dee Sharp	579
—	✪525.	Creed	579
—	526.	Method Man	578
(476)	527.	Vic Dana	578
—	528.	Gerald Levert	578
—	529.	Parliament/Funkadelic	577
(496)	530.	Lou Christie	576
(480)	531.	Bobby Sherman	576
(482)	532.	Lisa Lisa & Cult Jam	574
(488)	533.	The Cover Girls	573
(483)	534.	Yes	572
(484)	535.	Jon Secada	572
—	✪536.	Enrique Iglesias	571
(490)	537.	Coolio	570
(485)	538.	Hank Ballard & The Midnighters ●	568
—	539.	The Smashing Pumpkins	567
(487)	540.	The Chiffons ●	567
(489)	541.	Harold Melvin & The Bluenotes ●	564
—	542.	Bell Biv DeVoe	564
—	543.	Men At Work	564
(491)	544.	Bert Kaempfert ●	562
(492)	545.	Gerry & The Pacemakers	562
(493)	546.	Rick James	561
(495)	547.	Sam & Dave ●	559
(497)	548.	Crystal Gayle	558
—	549.	Silkk The Shocker	558
(498)	550.	Warren G	558
(499)	551.	Fabian	557
—	552.	The Allman Brothers Band ● ● ● ●	556
(500)	553.	The Partridge Family	556
—	554.	"Tennessee" Ernie Ford ▼ ●	555
—	555.	Sarah McLachlan	555
—	556.	Edwin Starr ●	554
—	557.	Kay Starr ▼	554
—	558.	Peter Frampton	552
—	559.	Rusty Draper ▼ ●	551
—	560.	Jerry Wallace	550
—	561.	Deborah Cox	550
—	562.	Bobby Womack	549
—	563.	The Shangri-Las ● ●	549
—	564.	Johnny Gill	549
—	565.	Deniece Williams	549
—	★566.	Nate Dogg	548
—	567.	Don McLean	548
—	568.	Paul Young	548
—	★569.	Redman	547
—	570.	Dave Matthews Band	547
—	571.	Karyn White	547
—	572.	Poco	546
—	573.	Naughty By Nature	544
—	✪574.	Toby Keith	540
—	575.	Michael McDonald	540
—	576.	The Orlons ●	539
—	577.	PM Dawn	539
—	✪578.	Lonestar	538
—	★579.	Kenny Chesney	537
—	580.	Major Lance ●	536
—	581.	Sammy Hagar	535
—	582.	George Hamilton IV	535
—	583.	Jewel	535
—	584.	Don Gibson	534
—	585.	Melissa Etheridge	534
—	586.	Dee Clark ●	532
—	587.	All-4-One	531
—	588.	Alabama	530
—	589.	Bay City Rollers	530
—	590.	Mitch Ryder & The Detroit Wheels	529
—	★591.	DMX	526
—	592.	Little Willie John ●	524
—	593.	Donny Hathaway ●	524
—	594.	Sweet ● ●	522
—	595.	The Buckinghams ●	521
—	596.	Wyclef Jean	520
—	597.	Led Zeppelin ●	520
—	598.	Sugar Ray	520
—	599.	Scandal	519
—	600.	The Intruders ●	517

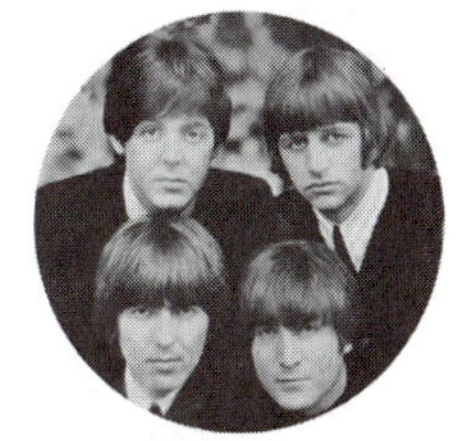

A–Z (Top 600 Artists)

TOP 600 ARTIST DEBUTS

The following lists, in chronological order, the chart debut dates of the Top 600 pop artists. The debut dates shown for artists that debuted on the pop charts prior to 1955 are taken from our *Pop Hits Singles & Albums 1940-1954* book.

	DEBUT		ARTIST (RANK)	[AGE]
1.	11/25/39		**Bing Crosby** (342)	[36]
2.	3/28/42		**Frank Sinatra** (28)	[26]
3.	10/16/43		**Perry Como** (38)	[31]
4.	12/11/43		**Nat "King" Cole** (36)	[26]
5.	2/5/44		**Lawrence Welk** (348)	[40]
6.	3/29/47		**Frankie Laine** (460)	[33]
7.	5/15/48		**Eddy Arnold** (409)	[30]
8.	5/29/48		**Doris Day** (507)	[26]
9.	6/12/48	▲	**Eddie Fisher** (278)	[19]
10.	6/26/48		**Patti Page** (84)	[20]
11.	7/3/48		**Sarah Vaughan** (305)	[24]
12.	8/21/48		**The Ames Brothers** (287)	[21-24]
13.	12/4/48		**Dean Martin** (109)	[31]
14.	12/4/48		**Kay Starr** (557)	[26]
15.	11/26/49		**"Tennessee" Ernie Ford** (554)	[30]
16.	2/4/50	▲	**Teresa Brewer** (230)	[18]
17.	3/25/50		**Georgia Gibbs** (379)	[29]
18.	6/3/50		**The Fontane Sisters** (285)	
19.	6/17/50		**Dinah Washington** (374)	[25]
20.	7/15/50		**Mitch Miller** (447)	[39]
21.	12/9/50		**Guy Mitchell** (397)	[23]
22.	6/23/51		**Tony Bennett** (178)	[24]
23.	7/28/51		**Tommy Edwards** (398)	[29]
24.	9/15/51		**Four Aces** (243)	[19-23]
25.	11/24/51		**The Four Lads** (205)	
26.	5/17/52		**Al Martino** (127)	[24]
27.	6/14/52	▲	**Steve Lawrence** (198)	[16]
28.	10/18/52		**Joni James** (452)	[22]
29.	2/28/53		**Rusty Draper** (559)	[28]
30.	5/23/53		**Bill Haley (& His Comets)** (138)	[27]
31.	5/8/54		**The Crew-Cuts** (469)	[20-23]
32.	6/26/54		**The McGuire Sisters** (124)	[23-28]
33.	8/21/54		**Sammy Davis Jr.** (331)	[28]
34.	10/30/54		**The Chordettes** (408)	
35.	11/27/54		**Jaye P. Morgan** (360)	[22]
36.	12/11/54		**Billy Vaughn** (167)	[35]
37.	1/15/55		**LaVern Baker** (404)	[25]
38.	4/2/55		**Pat Boone** (11)	[20]
39.	7/16/55		**Fats Domino** (23)	[27]
40.	8/20/55		**Chuck Berry** (123)	[28]
41.	8/20/55		**Roger Williams** (262)	[30]
42.	10/1/55		**The Platters** (51)	[24-27]
43.	10/15/55		**Gale Storm** (436)	[33]
	12/10/55		**The Coasters/The Robins** – see 9/22/56	
	12/31/55		**The Drifters** – see 6/1/59	
44.	1/14/56		**Little Richard** (255)	[23]
45.	1/28/56		**David Seville (The Chipmunks)** (238)	[37]
46.	2/4/56		**Clyde McPhatter** (290)	[23]
47.	2/18/56		**The Diamonds** (240)	[20-21]
48.	3/3/56		**Elvis Presley** (1)	[21]
49.	4/21/56		**Andy Williams** (47)	[27]
50.	4/21/56		**Eydie Gorme** (401)	[24]
	5/26/56		**The Four Lovers** – see 8/25/62 (4 Seasons)	
51.	6/16/56		**Roy Orbison** (74)	[20]
52.	7/7/56	▲	**Little Willie John** (592)	[18]
53.	8/4/56		**Dickie Goodman (Buchanan & Goodman)** (429)	[22]
54.	9/15/56		**Johnny Cash** (85)	[24]
55.	9/22/56		**The Coasters** (239)	[18-31]
56.	11/3/56		**Marty Robbins** (156)	[31]
57.	11/3/56	▲	**George Hamilton IV** (582)	[19]
58.	12/22/56		**The Four Preps** (488)	
59.	2/9/57		**Johnny Mathis** (59)	[21]
60.	3/2/57	▲	**Brenda Lee** (33)	[12]
61.	3/2/57		**Lloyd Price** (272)	[23]
62.	4/29/57		**Jim Reeves** (385)	[32]
63.	5/6/57	▲	**Ricky Nelson** (26)	[17]
64.	5/20/57		**The Everly Brothers** (45)	[18 & 20]
65.	5/20/57		**Conway Twitty** (300)	[23]
66.	6/24/57		**Jerry Lee Lewis** (411)	[21]
67.	7/15/57	▲	**Paul Anka** (29)	[15]
68.	7/15/57	▲	**The Crests (Johnny Maestro)** (483)	[18]
69.	7/22/57		**B.B. King** (244)	[31]
70.	8/5/57		**Bobby Bland** (202)	[27]
71.	8/12/57		**Jimmie Rodgers** (131)	[23]
72.	8/12/57		**Buddy Holly (The Crickets)** (417)	[20]
73.	10/14/57		**Jimmy Dean** (453)	[29]
74.	10/21/57		**Sam Cooke** (50)	[26]
75.	10/28/57		**Ray Charles** (18)	[27]
76.	11/4/57		**Jackie Wilson** (53)	[23]
77.	12/2/57	▲	**Connie Francis** (27)	[18]
	12/23/57		**Tom & Jerry** – see 11/20/65 (Simon & Garfunkel)	
78.	12/30/57	▲	**Johnny Nash** (481)	[17]
79.	1/20/58	▲	**Frankie Avalon** (136)	[18]
80.	2/24/58		**Don Gibson** (584)	[29]
81.	3/10/58		**Brook Benton** (46)	[26]
82.	3/17/58	▲	**Duane Eddy** (158)	[19]
83.	4/21/58	▲	**The Shirelles** (153)	[16-18]
84.	5/19/58	▲	**Dion (& The Belmonts)** (77)	[18]
85.	5/19/58	▲	**Jan & Dean (Jan & Arnie)** (162)	[17 & 18]
86.	6/9/58		**Jack Scott** (329)	[22]
	6/16/58		**Jerry Butler** – see 10/31/60 and **The Impressions** – see 10/16/61	
87.	6/23/58		**Bobby Darin** (56)	[22]
88.	7/14/58	▲	**Jimmy Clanton** (519)	[17]
89.	8/11/58	▲	**Little Anthony (The Imperials)** (394)	[18]
90.	8/18/58		**Jerry Wallace** (560)	[29]
91.	9/29/58		**The Kingston Trio** (339)	[23-25]
92.	10/6/58	▲	**Johnny Tillotson** (155)	[19]
93.	12/1/58		**Dee Clark** (586)	[20]
	12/1/58		**The Chipmunks** – see 1/28/56	
94.	12/8/58	▲	**Neil Sedaka** (80)	[19]
95.	12/15/58		**James Brown** (6)	[25]
96.	1/12/59	▲	**Fabian** (551)	[15]
97.	3/9/59	▲	**The Fleetwoods** (437)	[all 19]
98.	3/9/59		**Hank Ballard (The Midnighters)** (538)	[22]
99.	5/11/59	▲	**Freddy Cannon** (249)	[19]
100.	5/18/59	▲	**Chubby Checker** (67)	[17]

TOP 600 ARTIST DEBUTS (cont'd)

	DEBUT		ARTIST (RANK)	[AGE]
101.	6/1/59		**The Drifters** (89)	[20-24]
102.	6/29/59	▲	**Bobby Rydell** (113)	[17]
103.	8/31/59	▲	**Bobby Vee** (111)	[16]
104.	9/21/59		**The Isley Brothers** (69)	[18-21]
105.	9/28/59	▲	**Cliff Richard** (309)	[18]
106.	9/28/59		**The Fireballs** (514)	[18-20]
107.	10/5/59		**The Miracles** (44)	[19-20]
108.	11/30/59		**Bill Black('s Combo)** (364)	[33]
109.	3/14/60		**Charlie Rich** (376)	[28]
110.	4/4/60		**Henry Mancini** (475)	[35]
111.	5/2/60		**Etta James** (263)	[22]
112.	7/4/60	▲	**Brian Hyland** (280)	[16]
113.	7/18/60		**The Ventures** (470)	[25-27]
114.	8/29/60		**Ike & Tina Turner** (390)	[28 & 21]
115.	9/12/60	▲	**The Chiffons** (540)	[13-14]
	10/3/60		**The Blue Notes** – see 7/1/72	
116.	10/17/60		**Gary (U.S.) Bonds** (414)	[21]
117.	10/31/60		**Jerry Butler** (105)	[20]
118.	11/14/60		**Bert Kaempfert** (544)	[37]
119.	12/31/60		**Ben E. King** (303)	[22]
120.	1/30/61	▲	**Gene Pitney** (161)	[19]
121.	1/30/61	▲	**Mary Wells** (224)	[17]
122.	1/30/61	▲	**Carla Thomas** (427)	[18]
123.	2/20/61		**Chuck Jackson** (476)	[23]
	2/20/61		**Dickie Goodman** – see 8/4/56	
124.	2/27/61	▲	**Aretha Franklin** (10)	[18]
125.	3/6/61		**Del Shannon** (326)	[26]
126.	3/6/61		**The Tokens** (516)	[13-22]
127.	3/27/61		**Paul Revere & The Raiders** (145)	[19-23]
128.	5/1/61	▲	**Tony Orlando (& Dawn)** (115)	[17]
129.	5/15/61	▲	**Gladys Knight (& The Pips)** (42)	[16]
	5/15/61		**The Dukays** – see 1/13/62 (Gene Chandler)	
	6/26/61		**Spinners** – see 9/16/72	
130.	8/21/61		**Ray Stevens** (160)	[22]
131.	9/4/61		**The Marvelettes** (201)	
132.	9/4/61		**The Lettermen** (330)	[22-25]
133.	9/18/61		**Solomon Burke** (334)	[25]
134.	10/16/61		**The Impressions** (98)	[19-22]
135.	10/30/61		**Glen Campbell** (76)	[25]
136.	11/27/61	▲	**Vic Dana** (527)	[19]
	1/6/62		**Tico & The Triumphs** – see 2/5/72 (Paul Simon)	
137.	1/13/62		**Gene Chandler** (270)	[21]
138.	2/17/62		**The Beach Boys** (17)	[15-26]
139.	3/3/62		**Jack Jones** (446)	[24]
140.	3/3/62	▲	**Dee Dee Sharp** (524)	[16]
141.	3/17/62		**Jay & The Americans** (277)	[18-21]
142.	4/21/62	▲	**Patti LaBelle (& Her Blue-Belles)** (288)	[17]
143.	5/5/62		**Peter, Paul & Mary** (214)	[23-24]
144.	6/9/62		**Bobby Vinton** (41)	[27]
145.	6/9/62	▲	**The Orlons** (576)	[17-19]
146.	7/28/62		**Tommy Roe** (200)	[20]
	8/4/62		**The Springfields** – see 1/25/64 (Dusty Springfield)	
147.	8/11/62	▲	**The Supremes** (25)	[18-19]
148.	8/11/62	▲	**Booker T. (& The MG's)** (381)	[17]
149.	8/25/62		**4 Seasons** (31)	[19-34]
150.	8/25/62		**Carole King** (254)	[20]
151.	10/20/62		**Marvin Gaye** (12)	[23]
152.	10/27/62		**Herb Alpert (& The Tijuana Brass)** (79)	[27]
153.	12/8/62		**Dionne Warwick** (30)	[21]
154.	12/22/62		**Bobby Goldsboro** (177)	[21]
155.	12/22/62		**The Dells** (302)	[25-28]
156.	1/5/63	▲	**Lou Christie** (530)	[19]
157.	4/6/63		**Martha & The Vandellas** (187)	[18-21]
158.	4/27/63		**Wayne Newton** (486)	[21]
159.	5/4/63		**Wilson Pickett** (100)	[22]
160.	5/11/63		**The Righteous Brothers** (147)	[both 22]
161.	5/11/63	▲	**Lesley Gore** (246)	[17]
162.	5/25/63		**Otis Redding** (168)	[21]
163.	6/22/63	▲	**Stevie Wonder** (5)	[13]
164.	7/13/63		**Major Lance** (580)	[21]
165.	8/17/63	▲	**Tammi Terrell (Tammy Montgomery)** (413)	[17]
166.	9/14/63		**The O'Jays** (146)	[all 21]
167.	11/30/63		**Johnnie Taylor** (261)	[25]
168.	1/18/64		**The Beatles** (2)	[20-23]
169.	1/25/64		**Dusty Springfield** (250)	[24]
170.	2/15/64		**Dave Clark Five** (125)	[19-21]
171.	2/29/64		**The Temptations** (21)	[21-24]
172.	3/7/64		**The Searchers** (497)	[21-23]
173.	4/4/64		**Barbra Streisand** (43)	[21]
	4/25/64		**The Simon Sisters** – see 4/17/71 (Carly Simon)	
174.	5/2/64		**The Rolling Stones** (8)	[20-27]
175.	5/9/64	▲	**Peter & Gordon** (368)	[19 & 18]
176.	5/16/64		**The Hollies** (173)	[20-22]
177.	5/23/64		**Gerry & The Pacemakers** (545)	[21-23]
178.	5/30/64		**Johnny Rivers** (107)	[21]
179.	6/13/64		**Roger Miller** (340)	[28]
180.	7/18/64		**Ronnie Dove** (306)	[28]
181.	8/8/64		**The Animals** (212)	[21-25]
182.	8/15/64		**Four Tops** (49)	[26-28]
183.	8/22/64		**The Shangri-Las** (563)	
184.	9/5/64		**Manfred Mann** (441)	[22-23]
185.	9/26/64		**The Kinks** (204)	[17-20]
186.	10/10/64		**Ramsey Lewis** (440)	[29]
187.	10/17/64	▲	**Herman's Hermits** (128)	[16-19]
188.	12/19/64		**Petula Clark** (154)	[32]
189.	12/19/64		**Joe Tex** (183)	[31]
190.	1/16/65	▲	**Gary Lewis (& The Playboys)** (234)	[19]
191.	1/16/65		**The Manhattans** (512)	[21-23]
192.	2/13/65		**Jr. Walker (& The All Stars)** (227)	[33]
193.	2/20/65		**The Moody Blues (w/Hayward & Lodge)** (186)	[20-25]
194.	3/27/65		**The Who** (174)	[17-21]
195.	4/3/65		**Bob Dylan** (193)	[23]
196.	4/10/65		**Tom Jones** (97)	[24]
197.	5/8/65		**The Guess Who** (188)	[19-21]
198.	5/15/65	▲	**Donovan** (274)	[19]
199.	5/15/65		**The Byrds** (389)	[20-23]
200.	6/5/65		**Lou Rawls** (354)	[29]
201.	7/3/65	▲	**Cher** (54)	[19]
202.	7/10/65		**Sonny & Cher** (232)	[30 & 19]
203.	8/7/65	▲	**The Turtles (Volman & Kaylan)** (298)	[18]
204.	8/7/65		**Edwin Starr** (556)	[23]
205.	8/21/65		**The Lovin' Spoonful** (294)	[20-22]
206.	9/18/65		**The Vogues** (415)	

	DEBUT	ARTIST (RANK)	[AGE]
207.	10/16/65	**Nancy Sinatra** (242)	[25]
208.	11/20/65	**Simon & Garfunkel** (130)	[23 & 24]
209.	12/11/65	**Mitch Ryder** (& The Detroit Wheels) (590)	[20]
210.	12/25/65	**The Rascals** (Young Rascals) (164)	[19-21]
211.	1/8/66	**The Mamas & The Papas** (252)	[20-30]
212.	1/15/66	**Frankie Valli** (323)	[28]
213.	1/15/66	**Sam & Dave** (547)	[30 & 28]
214.	2/19/66	**B.J. Thomas** (142)	[23]
215.	4/9/66	**Percy Sledge** (510)	[25]
216.	5/21/66	**Neil Diamond** (24)	[25]
217.	6/4/66	▲ **Tommy James** (& The Shondells) (83)	[19]
218.	6/4/66	**The Association** (350)	[22-26]
219.	6/18/66	**Joe Simon** (203)	[22]
220.	6/18/66	**The Grass Roots** (223)	[18-23]
221.	7/16/66	**The Intruders** (600)	[23-26]
222.	9/10/66	**The Monkees** (152)	[20-23]
223.	9/24/66	**Sergio Mendes** (& Brasil '66) (477)	[25]
	11/12/66	Terry Knight – see 9/27/69 (Grand Funk Railroad)	
224.	12/31/66	**Peaches & Herb** (310)	[19 & 24]
225.	12/31/66	**The Buckinghams** (595)	[19-20]
226.	1/14/67	**The 5th Dimension** (82)	[22-26]
227.	4/1/67	**Jefferson Airplane** (Starship) (68)	[22-27]
228.	4/8/67	**Engelbert Humperdinck** (267)	[30]
229.	5/27/67	▲ **Bee Gees** (15)	[17-19]
230.	6/3/67	**The Doors** (293)	[21-32]
231.	6/3/67	**The Staple Singers** (335)	[26-51]
232.	6/24/67	**Clarence Carter** (464)	[31]
	7/1/67	Parliaments – see 10/4/69	
233.	8/12/67	▲ **The Box Tops** (Alex Chilton) (494)	[16]
234.	11/11/67	**Linda Ronstadt** (62)	[21]
235.	11/18/67	**Gary Puckett** (& The Union Gap) (487)	[25]
236.	12/9/67	**Al Green** (163)	[21]
237.	12/23/67	**Classics IV** (Dennis Yost) (511)	
238.	2/3/68	**The Delfonics** (490)	[20-23]
239.	2/10/68	**Kenny Rogers** (First Edition) (40)	[29]
240.	2/10/68	**Sly** (& The Family Stone) (191)	[23]
241.	5/4/68	**Andy Kim** (517)	[21]
242.	7/13/68	**Steppenwolf** (396)	[18-24]
243.	8/17/68	**Bobby Womack** (562)	[24]
244.	9/7/68	**Creedence Clearwater Revival** (170)	[23-26]
245.	11/16/68	**Joe Cocker** (257)	[24]
246.	11/23/68	**Steve Miller** (Band) (196)	[25]
247.	12/21/68	**Bob Seger** (78)	[23]
248.	12/21/68	**Tyrone Davis** (479)	[30]
249.	12/28/68	**The Moments** (503)	[21-22]
250.	2/8/69	**Three Dog Night** (92)	[26-27]
251.	3/1/69	**The Chi-Lites** (Eugene Record) (336)	[28]
252.	3/1/69	**Blood, Sweat & Tears** (492)	[21-27]
253.	3/29/69	**Led Zeppelin** (597)	[20-25]
254.	5/10/69	**Rita Coolidge** (438)	[25]
255.	7/19/69	**Crosby, Stills & Nash** (& Young) (391)	[24-27]
256.	7/26/69	**John Lennon** (134)	[28]
257.	8/2/69	**Billy Preston** (297)	[22]
258.	8/9/69	**Chicago** (22)	[20-24]
259.	8/16/69	**Nilsson** (495)	[28]
260.	8/23/69	**Isaac Hayes** (410)	[27]
261.	8/23/69	**Bobby Sherman** (531)	[26]
262.	9/13/69	**Kool & The Gang** (70)	[17-21]
263.	9/27/69	**Grand Funk Railroad** (217)	[18-21]
264.	10/4/69	**Parliament/Funkadelic** (George Clinton) (529)	[26]
265.	10/25/69	**Santana** (117)	[22]
266.	11/15/69	▲ **The Jackson 5** (55)	[11-18]
267.	1/17/70	**Donny Hathaway** (593)	[24]
	1/31/70	Fleetwood Mac – see 11/8/75	
268.	2/14/70	**Carpenters** (60)	[19 & 23]
269.	2/21/70	**Eric Clapton** (108)	[24]
270.	4/18/70	**Paul Davis** (353)	[21]
271.	4/25/70	**Diana Ross** (35)	[26]
272.	5/16/70	**Mac Davis** (421)	[28]
273.	5/16/70	**Quincy Jones** (513)	[37]
274.	5/23/70	**War** (219)	[20-38]
275.	6/13/70	**Bread** (David Gates) (281)	[29]
276.	7/18/70	**Anne Murray** (157)	[25]
	7/25/70	Dawn – see 5/1/61	
277.	8/15/70	**Elton John** (3)	[23]
278.	9/12/70	**James Taylor** (171)	[22]
279.	9/12/70	**Ronnie Milsap** (467)	[24]
280.	10/3/70	**Poco** (572)	[22-26]
281.	10/10/70	**The Partridge Family** (David Cassidy) (553)	[20]
282.	11/7/70	**Ringo Starr** (316)	[30]
283.	11/28/70	**George Harrison** (221)	[27]
284.	12/26/70	**Gordon Lightfoot** (459)	[32]
285.	1/2/71	**The Osmonds** (319)	[13-21]
286.	1/9/71	**The Stylistics** (260)	[20-21]
287.	1/9/71	**The Allman Brothers Band** (552)	[22-27]
288.	2/13/71	**Cat Stevens** (356)	[23]
289.	2/20/71	**Helen Reddy** (140)	[29]
290.	2/20/71	**Alice Cooper** (235)	[23]
291.	3/6/71	**Paul McCartney** (Wings) (19)	[28]
292.	3/27/71	▲ **Donny Osmond** (176)	[13]
293.	4/3/71	**Lobo** (358)	[27]
294.	4/10/71	**John Denver** (81)	[27]
295.	4/17/71	**Carly Simon** (129)	[25]
296.	4/17/71	**Boz Scaggs** (373)	[26]
297.	5/22/71	**Meat Loaf** (500)	[23]
298.	5/29/71	**Olivia Newton-John** (32)	[22]
299.	5/29/71	**Eddie Kendricks** (370)	[31]
300.	6/12/71	**Roberta Flack** (151)	[32]
301.	7/3/71	**Earth, Wind & Fire** (73)	[19-26]
302.	7/17/71	**Rod Stewart** (13)	[26]
303.	7/17/71	**Bill Withers** (320)	[33]
304.	9/25/71	**Yes** (534)	[22-26]
305.	10/2/71	**Sweet** (594)	[21-26]
306.	10/30/71	▲ **Michael Jackson** (7)	[13]
307.	11/27/71	**Don McLean** (567)	[26]
308.	12/4/71	**J. Geils Band** (291)	[20-29]
309.	12/25/71	**Ohio Players** (337)	[29-32]
310.	2/5/72	**Paul Simon** (180)	[30]
311.	2/19/72	**America** (213)	[19-21]
312.	3/18/72	**Jackson Browne** (286)	[23]

TOP 600 ARTIST DEBUTS (cont'd)

	DEBUT	ARTIST (RANK)	[AGE]
313.	4/1/72	Dr. Hook (209)	[22-35]
314.	4/15/72	David Bowie (122)	[25]
	4/15/72	Loggins & Messina – see 7/30/77	
315.	5/20/72	ZZ Top (351)	[21-23]
316.	6/3/72	Eagles (106)	[23-26]
317.	7/1/72	Jim Croce (412)	[29]
318.	7/1/72	Harold Melvin (& The Blue Notes) (541)	[33]
319.	8/5/72	Rick Springfield (133)	[22]
320.	9/2/72	The Doobie Brothers (102)	[21-24]
321.	9/9/72	Seals & Crofts (433)	[30 & 32]
322.	9/16/72	Spinners (90)	[26-37]
323.	9/16/72	Styx (119)	[19-25]
324.	9/16/72 ^	Jermaine Jackson (322)	[17]
325.	10/28/72	Electric Light Orchestra (110)	[24-25]
326.	11/18/72	Steely Dan (332)	[22 & 24]
327.	12/23/72	Bette Midler (268)	[27]
328.	4/14/73	Barry White (233)	[28]
329.	7/7/73	Smokey Robinson (175)	[33]
330.	8/18/73	Pointer Sisters (91)	[18-27]
331.	9/22/73	Tavares (416)	[18-26]
332.	10/20/73	Aerosmith (72)	[21-25]
333.	12/1/73	Bachman-Turner Overdrive (505)	[20-30]
334.	1/26/74	Dolly Parton (256)	[28]
335.	2/9/74	Daryl Hall & John Oates (37)	[25 & 24]
336.	2/23/74	Billy Joel (34)	[24]
337.	5/25/74	Kiss (148)	[23-26]
338.	6/1/74	Abba (132)	[24-29]
339.	6/15/74	Commodores (99)	[23-27]
340.	6/15/74	Chaka Khan (Rufus) (137)	[21]
341.	8/17/74	Bad Company (343)	[24-30]
342.	10/5/74	Atlanta Rhythm Section (448)	[25-30]
343.	11/16/74	Barry Manilow (71)	[28]
	11/16/74	Jefferson Starship – see 4/1/67	
344.	2/1/75	Dan Fogelberg (313)	[23]
345.	2/8/75	Queen (93)	[23-27]
346.	2/22/75	Leo Sayer (399)	[26]
347.	4/12/75	Supertramp (442)	[24-30]
348.	4/19/75	Captain & Tennille (245)	[32 & 31]
349.	5/10/75	Melissa Manchester (425)	[24]
350.	7/12/75	KC (& The Sunshine Band) (144)	[24]
351.	8/30/75	Natalie Cole (241)	[25]
352.	8/30/75	Willie Nelson (498)	[42]
353.	9/20/75	Bruce Springsteen (103)	[25]
354.	10/11/75	Bay City Rollers (589)	[18-22]
355.	11/8/75	Fleetwood Mac (104)	[27-32]
356.	12/6/75	Donna Summer (48)	[26]
357.	12/20/75	Eric Carmen (405)	[26]
358.	2/21/76	Peter Frampton (558)	[25]
	3/13/76	Kenny Rogers – see 2/10/68	
359.	3/20/76	Peabo Bryson (435)	[24]
360.	4/3/76	Billy Ocean (225)	[26]
361.	4/17/76	Heart (61)	[22-26]
362.	6/5/76	Firefall (508)	[24-30]
363.	6/12/76	George Benson (349)	[33]
364.	6/12/76	England Dan & John Ford Coley (455)	[28 & 27]
365.	6/12/76	Crystal Gayle (548)	[25]
366.	7/24/76	Eddie Rabbitt (328)	[34]
367.	7/24/76	Alan Parsons (Project) (345)	[26]
368.	9/18/76	Little River Band (208)	[22-32]
369.	9/18/76	Boston (444)	[24-29]
370.	12/4/76	Robert Palmer (295)	[27]
371.	12/11/76	Deniece Williams (565)	[25]
372.	12/25/76	Kansas (450)	[25-27]
373.	1/29/77	Jennifer Warnes (506)	[29]
374.	3/12/77	Genesis (118)	[all 26]
375.	3/26/77	Foreigner (101)	[25-32]
376.	4/23/77 ^	Andy Gibb (273)	[19]
377.	4/30/77	Peter Gabriel (515)	[27]
378.	5/28/77	REO Speedwagon (184)	[24-30]
379.	7/30/77	Kenny Loggins (135)	[30]
380.	10/29/77	Chic (466)	[24-25]
381.	11/5/77	Tom Petty (& The Heartbreakers) (126)	[24]
382.	12/10/77	Sammy Hagar (581)	[30]
383.	1/14/78	Ray Parker Jr. (Raydio) (251)	[23]
384.	1/28/78	Van Halen (139)	[22-24]
385.	2/25/78	Eddie Money (190)	[28]
386.	4/8/78	Journey (112)	[24-32]
387.	4/8/78	Juice Newton (443)	[26]
388.	6/17/78	The Cars (150)	[24-30]
389.	6/17/78	Kim Carnes (218)	[32]
390.	7/1/78	Rick James (546)	[26]
391.	7/22/78	Cheap Trick (289)	[26-31]
392.	10/7/78	Toto (279)	[20-31]
	10/7/78	Chaka Khan – see 6/15/74	
393.	11/4/78	Prince (20)	[20]
394.	2/17/79	Blondie (338)	[23-33]
395.	2/24/79	The Police (266)	[26-36]
396.	10/13/69	John Cougar Mellencamp (64)	[28]
397.	12/22/79	Pat Benatar (210)	[26]
398.	2/2/80	38 Special (333)	[28-31]
399.	2/9/80	Air Supply (226)	[29 & 30]
400.	2/16/80	Christopher Cross (355)	[28]
401.	2/16/80	The Pretenders (Chrissie Hynde) (489)	[28]
402.	2/23/80	Survivor (237)	
403.	6/14/80	Irene Cara (485)	[21]
404.	1/31/81	Loverboy (346)	[25-34]
405.	2/7/81	Steve Winwood (229)	[32]
406.	2/14/81	Sheena Easton (143)	[21]
407.	3/21/81	Phil Collins (52)	[30]
408.	6/6/81	Alabama (588)	[26-31]
409.	7/11/81	Lionel Richie (86)	[32]
410.	7/25/81	Stevie Nicks (282)	[33]
411.	8/15/81	James Ingram (327)	[25]
412.	10/10/81	Luther Vandross (165)	[30]
413.	10/24/81	Don Henley (216)	[34]
414.	2/6/82	Huey Lewis (& The News) (96)	[31]
415.	2/6/82	Joan Jett (& The Blackhearts) (426)	[21]
416.	3/6/82	The Human League (521)	[18-26]
417.	3/13/82	Bryan Adams (58)	[22]
418.	3/20/82	Laura Branigan (367)	[24]
419.	3/27/82	Atlantic Starr (468)	[23-25]
420.	6/5/82	Glenn Frey (400)	[33]

TOP 600 ARTIST DEBUTS (cont'd)

	DEBUT		ARTIST (RANK)	[AGE]
421.	6/5/82		**Jeffrey Osborne** (461)	[34]
422.	7/3/82		**Billy Idol** (308)	[26]
423.	7/10/82		**Men At Work** (543)	[24-29]
424.	8/7/82		**Michael McDonald** (575)	[30]
425.	11/13/82		**Scandal (Patty Smyth)** (599)	[25]
426.	12/4/82		**Culture Club** (258)	[21-25]
427.	12/18/82	^	**Janet Jackson** (9)	[16]
428.	12/25/82		**Duran Duran** (87)	[20-24]
429.	1/15/83		**Night Ranger** (522)	[25-30]
430.	1/22/83		**Thompson Twins** (457)	[25-26]
431.	2/5/83		**DeBarge (El DeBarge)** (384)	[19-27]
432.	3/12/83		**Def Leppard** (159)	[19-25]
433.	3/26/83		**INXS** (211)	[21-25]
434.	4/2/83		**U2** (94)	[21-23]
435.	5/7/83	^	**New Edition** (315)	[14-15]
436.	5/14/83		**Michael Bolton** (121)	[30]
437.	5/14/83		**Eurythmics** (304)	[28 & 30]
438.	7/23/83		**R.E.M.** (248)	[23-26]
439.	8/6/83		**Tears For Fears** (423)	[21 & 22]
440.	8/20/83		**George Michael (Wham!)** (39)	[20]
441.	10/1/83		**Paul Young** (568)	[27]
442.	10/29/83		**Madonna** (4)	[25]
443.	12/17/83		**Cyndi Lauper** (231)	[30]
444.	1/21/84		**Tina Turner** (182) (also see 8/29/60)	[45]
445.	1/21/84		**Howard Jones** (431)	[28]
446.	1/28/84		**UB40** (445)	[24-29]
447.	2/4/84		**Mötley Crüe** (482)	[21-28]
448.	2/25/84		**Bon Jovi** (75)	[21-30]
449.	3/10/84	^	**Johnny Gill** (564)	[17]
450.	5/26/84		**Corey Hart** (493)	[21]
451.	6/9/84		**Whitney Houston** (16)	[20]
452.	5/18/85		**Amy Grant** (283)	[24]
453.	5/25/85		**Depeche Mode** (341)	[23-25]
454.	6/8/85		**Sting** (197)	[33]
455.	6/8/85	^	**Lisa Lisa (& Cult Jam)** (532)	[18]
	9/7/85		**Starship** – see 4/1/67	
456.	10/19/85		**Gloria Estefan (& Miami Sound Machine)** (65)	[27]
457.	1/25/86		**Bangles** (314)	[28-30]
458.	2/15/86		**The Cure** (491)	[26-27]
459.	3/1/86		**Pet Shop Boys** (402)	[26 & 31]
460.	4/12/86		**The Jets** (473)	[12-20]
461.	5/17/86		**Belinda Carlisle** (502)	[27]
462.	6/7/86		**Peter Cetera** (359)	[41]
463.	7/26/86		**Bruce Hornsby (& The Range)** (501)	[31]
464.	8/16/86		**Anita Baker** (523)	[28]
465.	12/6/86		**Karyn White** (571)	[21]
466.	12/20/86	^	**Bobby Brown** (195)	[17]
467.	1/24/87		**Exposé** (299)	[20-21]
468.	2/28/87		**The Cover Girls** (533)	
469.	3/7/87		**Jody Watley** (296)	[28]
470.	3/14/87		**Poison** (292)	[23-25]
471.	4/4/87		**Kenny G** (392)	[30]
472.	5/9/87	^	**Debbie Gibson** (325)	[16]
473.	6/13/87		**Richard Marx** (120)	[23]
474.	7/11/87	^	**LL Cool J** (172)	[18]

	DEBUT		ARTIST (RANK)	[AGE]
475.	8/15/87		**Gerald Levert (Levert)** (528)	[21]
476.	10/10/87		**Taylor Dayne** (307)	[24]
477.	11/21/87		**Salt-N-Pepa** (365)	[23-26]
478.	12/19/87		**Rick Astley** (478)	[21]
479.	1/16/88		**Keith Sweat** (228)	[26]
480.	4/23/88		**Stevie B** (419)	
481.	5/28/88		**Tony! Toni! Toné!** (474)	[22-25]
482.	6/18/88		**Paula Abdul** (149)	[25]
483.	6/25/88	^	**New Kids On The Block** (169)	[15-19]
484.	6/25/88		**Guns N' Roses** (344)	[22-26]
485.	7/23/88		**Vanessa Williams** (311)	[25]
486.	1/7/89		**Milli Vanilli** (518)	[22 & 23]
487.	2/11/89		**Roxette** (259)	[29 & 30]
488.	2/18/89		**Metallica** (504)	[25-26]
489.	4/8/89		**Melissa Etheridge** (585)	[27]
490.	8/12/89		**Babyface** (236)	[30]
491.	10/21/89		**After 7** (509)	
492.	1/27/90		**Lenny Kravitz** (484)	[25]
493.	3/17/90		**Wilson Phillips** (463)	[20-21]
494.	4/7/90		**Bell Biv DeVoe** (542)	[21-22]
495.	4/28/90		**M.C. Hammer** (434)	[27]
496.	5/5/90		**En Vogue** (189)	[21-24]
497.	5/26/90	^	**Tevin Campbell** (451)	[11]
498.	6/2/90		**Mariah Carey** (14)	[20]
499.	11/17/90		**C & C Music Factory (Clivilles & Cole)** (520)	[26 & 28]
500.	12/8/90		**Celine Dion** (88)	[22]
501.	4/6/91		**Color Me Badd** (324)	[20-21]
502.	5/25/91		**Ice Cube** (449)	[22]
503.	6/15/91	^	**Boyz II Men** (57)	[16-18]
504.	9/7/91		**Naughty By Nature** (573)	[21-22]
505.	10/19/91		**PM Dawn** (577)	[20 & 21]
506.	10/26/91		**Jodeci** (422)	[20-22]
507.	12/21/91		**Red Hot Chili Peppers** (430)	[21-29]
508.	2/22/92		**TLC** (114)	[20-21]
509.	3/14/92		**R. Kelly** (63)	[23]
510.	4/18/92		**Jon Secada** (535)	[28]
511.	6/6/92	^	**Snoop Dogg** (265)	[19]
512.	6/6/92		**Dr. Dre** (380)	[27]
513.	6/20/92		**Mary J. Blige** (116)	[21]
514.	7/25/92		**Toni Braxton** (141)	[23]
515.	1/2/93	^	**SWV** (284)	[18]
516.	1/23/93		**Brian McKnight** (318)	[23]
517.	6/26/93		**Toby Keith** (574)	[31]
518.	7/3/93		**2Pac** (247)	[22]
519.	7/10/93		**Alan Jackson** (366)	[34]
520.	8/14/93		**Shaggy** (499)	[24]
521.	8/28/93		**Joe** (321)	[21]
522.	9/18/93		**Xscape** (301)	[17-20]
523.	9/18/93		**Ace Of Base** (383)	[21-26]
524.	10/9/93		**George Strait** (407)	[41]
525.	12/25/93		**The Smashing Pumpkins** (539)	[25-29]
526.	1/1/94		**All-4-One** (587)	[20-22]
527.	2/26/94	^	**OutKast** (462)	[18 & 19]
528.	3/5/94		**Tim McGraw** (194)	[26]
529.	4/16/94		**Nas** (428)	[20]

TOP 600 ARTIST DEBUTS (cont'd)

	DEBUT		ARTIST (RANK)	[AGE]
530.	4/23/94		**Sheryl Crow** (361)	[31]
531.	4/23/94		**Warren G** (550)	[22]
532.	4/23/94		**Nate Dogg** (566)	
533.	4/30/94	^	**Aaliyah** (264)	[15]
534.	5/7/94		**Sarah McLachlan** (555)	[26]
535.	6/4/94		**Da Brat** (387)	[21]
536.	6/4/94		**Coolio** (537)	[30]
537.	6/25/94		**BLACKstreet** (347)	
538.	8/27/94		**The Notorious B.I.G.** (166)	[22]
539.	9/3/94	^	**Usher** (192)	[15]
540.	9/17/94		**Bone Thugs-N-Harmony** (388)	[17-20]
541.	10/1/94	^	**Brandy** (179)	[15]
542.	10/8/94		**Hootie & The Blowfish** (472)	[27-30]
543.	11/12/94		**Method Man** (526)	[24]
544.	11/19/94		**Pearl Jam** (377)	[26-31]
545.	11/19/94		**Redman** (569)	[24]
546.	2/18/95		**K-Ci & JoJo** (317)	[23 & 25]
547.	2/25/95		**Montell Jordan** (372)	[26]
548.	4/1/95		**Dave Matthews (Band)** (570)	[28]
549.	4/8/95		**Total** (496)	
550.	4/29/95	^	**Monica** (222)	[14]
551.	5/27/95		**Shania Twain** (312)	[29]
552.	6/17/95		**Alanis Morissette** (357)	[21]
553.	7/1/95		**Faith Evans** (185)	[22]
554.	9/9/95		**Deborah Cox** (561)	[21]
555.	10/14/95		**Goo Goo Dolls** (418)	[29-32]
556.	10/28/95		**Backstreet Boys** (215)	[15-24]
557.	12/16/95		**No Doubt** (420)	[25-27]
558.	12/23/95		**Faith Hill** (271)	[28]
559.	3/9/96		**Busta Rhymes** (369)	[23]
560.	4/6/96		**Jay-Z** (95)	[25]
561.	4/27/96		**Lil' Kim** (375)	[20]
562.	4/27/96		**Master P** (382)	[25]
563.	6/1/96		**112** (207)	[19-21]
564.	6/1/96		**Jewel** (583)	[22]
565.	6/22/96	^	**LeAnn Rimes** (393)	[13]
566.	7/20/96		**Ricky Martin** (454)	[24]
567.	8/31/96	^	**Dru Hill** (395)	[17-18]
568.	9/7/96		**Ginuwine** (371)	[20]
569.	11/9/96		**Puff Daddy** (66)	[26]
570.	1/25/97		**Mase** (275)	[26]
571.	1/25/97		**Spice Girls** (458)	[21-26]
572.	3/1/97		**Savage Garden** (386)	[23 & 24]
573.	6/7/97		**Matchbox Twenty** (362)	[21-33]
574.	6/14/97		**Wyclef Jean** (596)	[26]
575.	6/28/97		**Will Smith** (456) (as "Fresh Prince" on 5/21/88; age 19)	[28]
576.	7/5/97		**Missy "Misdemeanor" Elliott** (206)	[26]
577.	7/5/97		**Sugar Ray** (598)	[26-30]
578.	7/12/97		**98°** (432)	[20-24]
579.	9/6/97	^	**Silkk The Shocker** (549)	[17]
580.	9/20/97		**Jagged Edge** (406)	
581.	11/22/97		**Lonestar** (578)	[23-35]
582.	11/29/97	^	**Destiny's Child** (181)	[all 16]
583.	12/27/97		**DMX** (591)	[27]
584.	1/31/98		**Dixie Chicks** (403)	[23-28]
585.	1/31/98		**Mystikal** (480)	[22]
586.	2/21/98		**Creed** (525)	[23-25]
587.	3/7/98		***NSYNC** (220)	[17-26]
588.	3/14/98	^	**Mýa** (352)	[18]
589.	5/9/98		**Kenny Chesney** (579)	[30]
590.	11/21/98	^	**Britney Spears** (471)	[16]
591.	1/23/99		**Eminem** (363)	[26]
592.	4/3/99		**Ja Rule** (199)	[23]
593.	5/15/99		**Jennifer Lopez** (253)	[28]
594.	7/3/99	^	**Christina Aguilera** (269)	[18]
595.	7/3/99		**Eve** (424)	[20]
596.	7/10/99		**Enrique Iglesias** (536)	[24]
597.	3/4/00		**P!nk** (439)	[20]
598.	4/29/00		**Nelly** (276)	[25]
599.	9/30/00		**Ludacris** (465)	[22]
600.	11/17/01		**Ashanti** (378)	[21]

Artist's Top 600 ranking is shown in parentheses after name.

The name of the highest ranking artist of the Top 600 debuting that year (or half-decade in the case of pre-1955 artists) is shown in red.

The name of the #1 artist of each half-decade is shown in white with a red-shaded background.

The age of nearly every Top 600 Artist at the time of their chart debut is shown in *red italics*.

^ = Teenager(s) at the time of their chart debut (except Tevin Campbell [11] and Brenda Lee [12]).

Age column is blank for artists whose birth dates are unknown. If part of an artist's name is in parentheses: Gary Lewis (& The Playboys), the age is for the individual's name only: Gary Lewis. If a person's name is in parentheses after a group name: Bread (David Gates), the age is for the person: David Gates.

TOP 30 ARTISTS

1955-1959

1. Elvis Presley (60s #2 / 70s #10) ... 3,704
2. Pat Boone ... 2,851
3. Perry Como ... 2,042
4. Fats Domino ... 1,908
5. Nat "King" Cole ... 1,797
6. The Platters ... 1,682
7. Frank Sinatra (60s #27) ... 1,448
8. Ricky Nelson (60s #25) ... 1,437
9. The McGuire Sisters ... 1,286
10. Bill Haley & His Comets ... 1,242
11. Patti Page ... 1,136
12. Johnny Mathis ... 1,135
13. The Four Lads ... 1,122
14. The Everly Brothers ... 1,105
15. Four Aces ... 1,029

16. The Diamonds ... 988
17. Jimmie Rodgers ... 942
18. Teresa Brewer ... 930
19. Paul Anka ... 926
20. The Fontane Sisters ... 915
21. Chuck Berry ... 902
22. Little Richard ... 863
23. The Ames Brothers ... 857
24. Billy Vaughn ... 849
25. Eddie Fisher ... 845
26. Connie Francis (60s #9) ... 818
27. Frankie Avalon ... 817
28. Andy Williams ... 780
29. Sarah Vaughan ... 762
30. Georgia Gibbs ... 746

1960s

1. The Beatles ... 4,711
2. Elvis Presley (50s #1 / 70s #10) ... 4,279
3. Ray Charles ... 2,684
4. Brenda Lee ... 2,664
5. The Supremes ... 2,530
6. The Beach Boys ... 2,355
7. The 4 Seasons ... 2,348
8. James Brown (70s #7) ... 2,323
9. Connie Francis (50s #26) ... 2,258
10. Marvin Gaye (70s #20) ... 2,084
11. Bobby Vinton ... 2,005
12. Chubby Checker ... 1,896
13. The Temptations (70s #29) ... 1,761
14. Brook Benton ... 1,747
15. Jackie Wilson ... 1,746

16. The Rolling Stones ... 1,734
17. Roy Orbison ... 1,732
18. The Miracles ... 1,714
19. Dionne Warwick ... 1,569
20. Sam Cooke ... 1,545
21. Bobby Darin ... 1,530
22. Bobby Vee ... 1.524
23. Dion ... 1,495
24. Aretha Franklin (70s #24) ... 1,493
25. Ricky Nelson (50s #8) ... 1,477
26. Dave Clark Five ... 1,441
27. Frank Sinatra (50s #7) ... 1,410
28. Herman's Hermits ... 1,397
29. Bobby Rydell ... 1,358
30. The Drifters ... 1,332

1970s

1. Elton John (80s #7 / 90s #10) ... 2,202
2. Paul McCartney (80s #28) ... 2,147
3. Bee Gees ... 2,074
4. Carpenters ... 1,935
5. Chicago (80s #24) ... 1,795
6. The Jackson 5 ... 1,768
7. James Brown (60s #8) ... 1,680
8. Stevie Wonder (80s #11) ... 1,615
9. Neil Diamond ... 1,589
10. Elvis Presley (50s #1 / 60s #2) ... 1,572
11. John Denver ... 1,546
12. Olivia Newton-John (80s #26) ... 1,520
13. Diana Ross (80s #18) ... 1,467
14. Three Dog Night ... 1,368
15. Gladys Knight & The Pips ... 1,355

16. Tony Orlando & Dawn ... 1,337
17. Donna Summer ... 1,303
18. Helen Reddy ... 1,299
19. Earth, Wind & Fire ... 1,295
20. Marvin Gaye (60s #10) ... 1,284
21. Rod Stewart (80s #23 / 90s #19) ... 1,271
22. Eagles ... 1,261
23. Linda Ronstadt ... 1,254
24. Aretha Franklin (60s #24) ... 1,239
25. Barry Manilow ... 1,229
26. Spinners ... 1,227
27. Barbra Streisand ... 1,171
28. Al Green ... 1,137
29. The Temptations (60s #13) ... 1,128
30. The Doobie Brothers ... 1,114

TOP 30 ARTISTS

1980s

1. Michael Jackson (90s #22) 2,100
2. Prince (90s #13) 2,056
3. Madonna (90s #3) 1,996
4. Daryl Hall & John Oates 1,928
5. George Michael & Wham! 1,794
6. Billy Joel 1,631
7. Elton John (70s #1 / 90s #10) 1,614
8. Lionel Richie 1,565
9. Phil Collins 1,492
10. John Cougar Mellencamp 1,476
11. Stevie Wonder (70s #8) 1,437
12. Kenny Rogers 1,428
13. Kool & The Gang 1,403
14. Duran Duran 1,388
15. Huey Lewis and the News 1,383

16. Journey 1,258
17. Whitney Houston (90s #5) 1,255
18. Diana Ross (70s #13) 1,254
19. Sheena Easton 1,238
20. Heart 1,211
21. Rick Springfield 1,210
22. Pointer Sisters 1,206
23. Rod Stewart (70s #21 / 90s #19) ...1,186
24. Chicago (70s #5) 1,186
25. Starship 1,169
26. Olivia Newton-John (70s #12) ...1,128
27. Bruce Springsteen 1,121
28. Paul McCartney (70s #2) 1,110
29. Kenny Loggins 1,101
30. Bob Seger 1,100

1990s

1. Mariah Carey 3,120
2. Janet Jackson (00s #19) 2,370
3. Madonna (80s #3) 2,090
4. Boyz II Men 2,076
5. Whitney Houston (80s #17) 1,779
6. R. Kelly 1,651
7. Celine Dion 1,556
8. TLC 1,430
9. Puff Daddy (00s #13) 1,386
10. Elton John (70s #1 / 80s #7) 1,360
11. Michael Bolton 1,201
12. Bryan Adams 1,159
13. Prince (80s #2) 1,139
14. En Vogue 1,130
15. The Notorious B.I.G. 1,096

16. Toni Braxton 1,082
17. Brandy 1,056
18. Mary J. Blige (00s #25) 1,048
19. Rod Stewart (70s #21 / 80s #23) ...1,032
20. Monica 1,016
21. Gloria Estefan 1,015
22. Michael Jackson (80s #1) 986
23. Mase 952
24. SWV (Sisters With Voices) 921
25. Keith Sweat 914
26. LL Cool J 888
27. Babyface 882
28. 2Pac 872
29. Aerosmith 868
30. Jay-Z (00s #4) 860

2000-2002

1. Ja Rule 1,050
2. Nelly 959
3. Destiny's Child 853
4. Jay-Z (90s #30) 788
5. Jennifer Lopez 761
6. Christina Aguilera 747
7. Ashanti 747
8. Eminem 692
9. P!nk 678
10. Missy "Misdemeanor" Elliott 664
11. *NSYNC 657
12. Ludacris 655
13. Puff Daddy (90s #9) 638
14. Usher 636
15. Jagged Edge 620

16. Tim McGraw 589
17. Eve 571
18. Faith Hill 553
19. Janet Jackson (90s #2) 543
20. Lonestar 512
21. Joe 510
22. Creed 506
23. Ginuwine 501
24. Toby Keith 490
25. Mary J. Blige (90s #18) 474
26. Alan Jackson 458
27. Aaliyah 457
28. Mystikal 455
29. Enrique Iglesias 441
30. Mya 438

TOP ARTISTS BY YEAR & CATEGORY

YEAR	MALE	FEMALE	GROUP / DUO
55	Nat "King" Cole	Jaye P. Morgan	Bill Haley & His Comets
56	Elvis Presley	Gale Storm	The Platters
57	Elvis Presley	Patti Page	The Platters
58	Elvis Presley	Connie Francis	The Everly Brothers
59	Lloyd Price	Connie Francis	The Fleetwoods
60	Elvis Presley	Connie Francis	The Everly Brothers
61	Elvis Presley	Brenda Lee	The Shirelles
62	Elvis Presley	Brenda Lee	Joey Dee & The Starliters
63	Dion	Brenda Lee	The Beach Boys
64	Elvis Presley	Mary Wells	The Beatles
65	Elvis Presley	Petula Clark	The Beatles
66	Johnny Rivers	Nancy Sinatra	The Beatles
67	Wilson Pickett	Nancy Sinatra	The Monkees
68	Marvin Gaye	Aretha Franklin	Gary Puckett & The Union Gap
69	James Brown	Aretha Franklin	Creedence Clearwater Revival
70	Neil Diamond	Aretha Franklin	The Jackson 5
71	James Brown	Aretha Franklin	Three Dog Night
72	Al Green	Roberta Flack	The Stylistics
73	Elton John	Helen Reddy	Gladys Knight & The Pips
74	John Denver	Olivia Newton-John	Gladys Knight & The Pips
75	Elton John	Linda Ronstadt	Paul McCartney & Wings
76	Elton John	Diana Ross	Bay City Rollers
77	Leo Sayer	Linda Ronstadt	Fleetwood Mac
78	Andy Gibb	Donna Summer	Bee Gees
79	Kenny Rogers	Donna Summer	Bee Gees
80	Kenny Rogers	Olivia Newton-John	Queen
81	Kenny Rogers	Diana Ross	Daryl Hall & John Oates
82	Stevie Wonder	Juice Newton	Daryl Hall & John Oates
83	Michael Jackson	Irene Cara	Culture Club
84	Prince	Cyndi Lauper	Culture Club
85	Phil Collins	Madonna	Tears For Fears
86	Billy Ocean	Madonna	Bangles
87	George Michael	Madonna	U2
88	George Michael	Whitney Houston	INXS
89	Bobby Brown	Paula Abdul	New Kids On The Block
90	Michael Bolton	Janet Jackson	Wilson Phillips
91	Bryan Adams	Mariah Carey	C & C Music Factory
92	Elton John	Mariah Carey	Boyz II Men
93	Dr. Dre	Janet Jackson	SWV (Sisters With Voices)
94	R. Kelly	Mariah Carey	Boyz II Men
95	The Notorious B.I.G.	Mariah Carey	TLC
96	R. Kelly	Toni Braxton	Los Del Rio
97	Puff Daddy	Da Brat	112
98	Puff Daddy	Monica	Next
99	Jay-Z	Faith Evans	TLC
00	Sisqó	Christina Aguilera	Destiny's Child
01	Ja Rule	Jennifer Lopez	Destiny's Child
02	Ja Rule	Ashanti	No Doubt

TOP ARTISTS BY DECADE & CATEGORY

1955-59

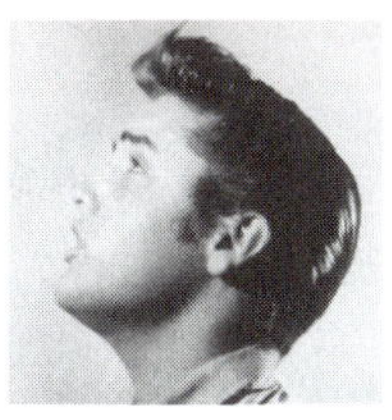

MALE

1. **Elvis Presley**
2. Pat Boone
3. Perry Como
4. Fats Domino
5. Nat "King" Cole

FEMALE

1. **Patti Page**
2. Teresa Brewer
3. Connie Francis
4. Sarah Vaughan
5. Georgia Gibbs

GROUPS/DUOS/ORCH.

1. **The Platters**
2. The McGuire Sisters
3. Bill Haley And His Comets
4. The Four Lads
5. The Everly Brothers

SIXTIES

MALE

1. **Elvis Presley**
2. Ray Charles
3. James Brown
4. Marvin Gaye
5. Bobby Vinton

FEMALE

1. **Brenda Lee**
2. Connie Francis
3. Dionne Warwick
4. Aretha Franklin
5. Petula Clark

GROUPS/DUOS/ORCH.

1. **The Beatles**
2. The Supremes
3. The Beach Boys
4. The 4 Seasons
5. The Temptations

SEVENTIES

MALE

1. **Elton John**
2. Paul McCartney
3. James Brown
4. Stevie Wonder
5. Neil Diamond

FEMALE

1. **Olivia Newton-John**
2. Diana Ross
3. Donna Summer
4. Helen Reddy
5. Linda Ronstadt

GROUPS/DUOS

1. **Bee Gees**
2. Carpenters
3. Chicago
4. The Jackson 5
5. Three Dog Night

TOP ARTISTS BY DECADE & CATEGORY (cont'd)

EIGHTIES

MALE

1. **Michael Jackson**
2. Prince
3. George Michael
4. Billy Joel
5. Elton John

FEMALE

1. **Madonna**
2. Whitney Houston
3. Diana Ross
4. Sheena Easton
5. Olivia Newton-John

GROUPS/DUOS

1. **Hall & Oates**
2. Kool & The Gang
3. Duran Duran
4. Huey Lewis and the News
5. Journey

NINETIES

MALE

1. **R. Kelly**
2. Puff Daddy
3. Elton John
4. Michael Bolton
5. Bryan Adams

FEMALE

1. **Mariah Carey**
2. Janet Jackson
3. Madonna
4. Whitney Houston
5. Celine Dion

GROUPS/DUOS

1. **Boyz II Men**
2. TLC
3. En Vogue
4. SWV (Sisters With Voices)
5. Aerosmith

2000-02

MALE

1. **Ja Rule**
2. Nelly
3. Jay-Z
4. Eminem
5. Ludacris

FEMALE

1. **Jennifer Lopez**
2. Christina Aguilera
3. Ashanti
4. P!nk
5. Missy "Misdemeanor" Elliott

GROUPS/DUOS

1. **Destiny's Child**
2. *NSYNC
3. Jagged Edge
4. Lonestar
5. Creed

TOP ARTIST ACHIEVEMENTS

MOST CHART HITS

1. Elvis Presley 153
2. James Brown 99
3. Ray Charles............................77
4. Aretha Franklin 76
5. The Beatles 73
6. Elton John 70
7. Frank Sinatra..........................68
8. Fats Domino 66
9. Stevie Wonder.........................65
10. Pat Boone 61
11. The Beach Boys.......................60
12. Nat "King" Cole 60
13. The Rolling Stones 57
14. Marvin Gaye 57
15. Neil Diamond..........................56
16. Connie Francis........................56
17. Dionne Warwick......................56
18. The Temptations.....................55
19. Brenda Lee 55
20. Rod Stewart............................54
21. Ricky Nelson 54
22. Jackie Wilson 54
23. Prince.....................................53
24. Paul Anka 53
25. Chicago 50
26. Perry Como 50
27. Brook Benton..........................50

MOST TOP 40 HITS

1. Elvis Presley 104
2. Elton John 57
3. The Beatles 51
4. Stevie Wonder 46
5. Madonna.................................45
6. James Brown 44
7. Aretha Franklin 43
8. The Rolling Stones 41
9. Marvin Gaye 41
10. Pat Boone...............................38
11. The Temptations.....................38
12. Michael Jackson 37
13. Fats Domino...........................37
14. Neil Diamond 37
15. The Beach Boys 36
16. Janet Jackson..........................35
17. Bee Gees 35
18. Paul McCartney 35
19. Ricky Nelson...........................35
20. Connie Francis 35
21. Rod Stewart 34
22. Chicago 34
23. Ray Charles............................33
24. The Supremes.........................33
25. Paul Anka 33
26. Billy Joel.................................33
27. Whitney Houston....................32
28. Prince 32

MOST TOP 10 HITS

1. Elvis Presley 38
2. Madonna.................................35
3. The Beatles 34
4. Janet Jackson..........................29
5. Stevie Wonder 28
6. Michael Jackson.....................28
7. Elton John...............................27
8. The Rolling Stones 23
9. Whitney Houston....................23
10. Mariah Carey..........................22
11. Paul McCartney 22
12. George Michael.......................21
13. Chicago 20
14. The Supremes.........................20
15. Prince 19
16. Ricky Nelson...........................19
17. Pat Boone...............................18
18. Marvin Gaye 18
19. Aretha Franklin 17
20. Bee Gees 17
21. Rod Stewart 16
22. The Temptations.....................16
23. Connie Francis 16
24. Daryl Hall & John Oates.........16
25. The Beach Boys 15
26. The 4 Seasons 15
27. Olivia Newton-John................15
28. The Everly Brothers 15

MOST #1 HITS

1. The Beatles 20
2. Elvis Presley 18
3. Mariah Carey..........................15
4. Michael Jackson.....................13
5. Madonna.................................12
6. The Supremes.........................12
7. Whitney Houston....................11
8. Stevie Wonder 10
9. Janet Jackson..........................10
10. George Michael.......................10
11. Elton John.................................9
12. Bee Gees...................................9
13. Paul McCartney 9
14. The Rolling Stones...................8
15. Phil Collins................................7
16. Pat Boone..................................6
17. Diana Ross................................6
18. Daryl Hall & John Oates............6
19. Paula Abdul...............................6

MOST #2 HITS

1. Elvis Presley.............................6
2. Madonna 6
3. Carpenters................................5
4. Creedence Clearwater Revival * .5
5. Elton John 4
6. Janet Jackson 4
7. The Beatles...............................3
8. Mariah Carey 3
9. Prince.......................................3
10. Puff Daddy...............................3
11. The Jackson 5 3
12. R. Kelly....................................3
13. Linda Ronstadt.........................3
14. En Vogue * 3
15. Usher.......................................3
16. Blood, Sweat & Tears *............3

* Never had a #1 hit.

MOST WEEKS AT THE #1 POSITION

1. Elvis Presley 80
2. Mariah Carey.......................... 61
3. The Beatles 59
4. Boyz II Men............................ 50
5. Michael Jackson..................... 37
6. Elton John 34
7. Janet Jackson......................... 33
8. Madonna................................ 32
9. Whitney Houston.................... 31
10. Paul McCartney 30
11. Bee Gees 27
12. Stevie Wonder 25
13. George Michael...................... 23
14. The Supremes......................... 22
15. Santana 22
16. Monica 22
17. Pat Boone.............................. 21
18. Lionel Richie 21

Only "Most Chart Hits" include songs that hit exclusively on *Billboard's Christmas* singles chart and *Billboard's Hot 100 Sales* chart after *Billboard* introduced a new methodology to the *Hot 100* on 12/5/98. Ties are broken according to rank in the *Top 600 Artists* section.

TOP ARTIST ACHIEVEMENTS (cont'd)

MOST CONSECUTIVE #1 HITS

1.	10	**Elvis Presley** (1956-58)
2.	7	**Whitney Houston** (1985-88)
3.	6	**The Beatles** (1964-66)
4.	6	**Bee Gees** (1977-79)
5.	6	**Paula Abdul** (1988-91)
6.	5	**Michael Jackson** (1987-88)
7.	5	**The Supremes** (1964-65)
8.	5	**Mariah Carey** (1990-91)
9.	4	**George Michael** (1987-88)
10.	4	**The Jackson 5** (1970)

Excludes Christmas hits, re-issues, B-sides, and duos (unless they add to the streak).

MOST CONSECUTIVE TOP 10 HITS

1.	30	**Elvis Presley** (1956-62)
2.	24	**The Beatles** (1964-76)
3.	23	**Janet Jackson** (1989-01)
4.	17	**Michael Jackson** (1979-88)
5.	17	**Madonna** (1984-89)
6.	14	**Pat Boone** (1956-58)
7.	13	**Whitney Houston** (1985-91)
8.	13	**Phil Collins** (1984-90)
9.	13	**Lionel Richie** (1981-87)
10.	11	**Mariah Carey** (1990-94)

Excludes Christmas hits, re-issues, B-sides, and duos (unless they add to the streak).

ARTISTS WITH LONGEST CHART CAREERS (ROCK ERA)

Dates			Artist (Years/Months/Weeks)
4/2/55	–	3/8/03	**Pat Boone** (47/11/1)
12/25/54	–	1/11/03	**Bing Crosby** (47/0/2)
3/3/56	–	9/7/02	**Elvis Presley** (46/6/1)
1/28/57	–	9/28/02	**Ray Charles** (45/8/0)
2/11/56	–	1/8/00	**Louis Armstrong** (43/11/0)
9/21/59	–	11/17/01	**The Isley Brothers** (42/2/0)
7/15/57	–	1/4/97	**Bobby Helms** (39/5/3)
8/21/61	–	7/20/02	**Ray Stevens** (40/11/0)
5/4/59	–	1/15/00	**George Jones** (40/8/2)
10/20/62	–	10/13/01	**Marvin Gaye** (38/11/3)
5/26/56	–	2/11/95	**Frankie Valli (The 4 Seasons)** (38/8/2)
4/25/64	–	2/9/02	**Carly Simon** (37/11/2)
2/27/61	–	9/26/98	**Aretha Franklin** (37/7/0)
7/3/65	–	11/23/02	**Cher** (37/4/3)

ARTISTS WITH LONGEST SPAN BETWEEN CHART HITS

Dates			Artist (Years/Months/Weeks)
12/26/64	–	1/1/00	**Hank Williams Jr.** (35/0/1)
12/25/65	–	12/23/00	**Bing Crosby** (35/0/0)
12/25/65	–	1/1/00	**George Jones** (34/0/1)
12/29/62	–	1/4/97	**Bobby Helms** (34/0/1)
4/26/69	–	11/23/02	**Pat Boone** (33/7/0)
11/23/63	–	1/2/93	**Darlene Love** (29/1/1)
5/24/69	–	3/29/97	**Peggy Scott-Adams** (27/10/1)
8/27/66	–	7/13/91	**Nat "King" Cole** (24/10/2)
3/14/70	–	8/20/94	**The Tokens** (24/5/1)
3/28/70	–	11/6/93	**Jimmy Cliff** (23/7/1)
2/1/75	–	1/10/98	**Jose Feliciano** (22/11/1)
5/12/79	–	2/2/02	**Ray Stevens** (22/8/3)
4/15/67	–	9/30/89	**Aaron Neville** (22/5/2)
1/11/64	–	5/17/86	**Duane Eddy** (22/4/1)

MOST 2-SIDED HITS

52	**Elvis Presley**
26	**The Beatles**
24	**Fats Domino**
21	**Pat Boone**
21	**Nat "King" Cole**
20	**Ricky Nelson**
17	**Brenda Lee**
16	**Ray Charles**
14	**Perry Como**
13	**Connie Francis**
13	**The Everly Brothers**
12	**Brook Benton**
11	**Aretha Franklin**
11	**Sam Cooke**
10	**The Platters**
10	**Jackie Wilson**
9	**Frank Sinatra**
9	**Chubby Checker**

MOST PLATINUM HITS

1.	**Elvis Presley**	28
2.	**Michael Jackson**	9
3.	**Mariah Carey**	8
4.	**Boyz II Men**	8
5.	**Whitney Houston**	7
6.	**The Notorious B.I.G.**	7
7.	**The Beatles**	6
8.	**Elton John**	6
9.	**The Temptations**	6
10.	**Puff Daddy**	6
11.	**R. Kelly**	6
12.	**Monica**	6

MOST GOLD HITS *

1.	**Elvis Presley**	24
2.	**Madonna**	19
3.	**The Beatles**	18
4.	**Janet Jackson**	17
5.	**Aretha Franklin**	15
6.	**Whitney Houston**	14

*Totals do not include gold hits later certified platinum.

TOP ARTISTS WHO NEVER HIT #1 (POP)

	Rank	
1.	6	**James Brown**
2.	23	**Fats Domino**
3.	46	**Brook Benton**
4.	53	**Jackie Wilson**
5.	69	**The Isley Brothers**
6.	85	**Johnny Cash**
7.	91	**Pointer Sisters**
8.	97	**Tom Jones**
9.	98	**The Impressions**
10.	100	**Wilson Pickett**
11.	103	**Bruce Springsteen**
12.	105	**Jerry Butler**
13.	110	**Electric Light Orchestra**
14.	112	**Journey**
15.	113	**Bobby Rydell**
16.	126	**Tom Petty**
17.	137	**Chaka Khan**
18.	148	**Kiss**
19.	150	**The Cars**

To qualify, artist must rank in the Top 150. Excludes Christmas hits.

HOT 100 HITS OF THE ROCK ERA:

1955-1989
1990-2002

The rankings on the following two pages begin with America's first #1 rock & roll hit "Rock Around The Clock" in the summer of 1955 and run through the year 2002. There are two rankings (of 50 titles each) because *Billboard* changed its chart methodology on 11/30/91 by using Broadcast Data Systems and SoundScan, resulting in songs having much longer runs at #1 than ever before. ("Cherry Pink And Apple Blossom White" and "Sincerely" debuted prior to "Rock Around The Clock" and therefore are not included in any of the following rankings.)

The rankings are based on the most weeks a title held the #1 position (WKS @ #1). Ties are broken in this order: total weeks in the Top 10, total weeks in the Top 40; and, finally, total weeks charted. The superscript "A" in the WKS @ #1 column indicates the total weeks at #1 is from *Billboard's Hot 100 Airplay* chart (prior to *Billboard* allowing airplay-only hits to make the main *Hot 100* chart).

TOP 20 #1 HITS:

1955-59
1960s
1970s
1980s
1990s
2000-02

SINGLES OF LONGEVITY:

1955-59
1960s
1970s
1980s
1990s
2000-02

HOT 100 HITS OF THE ROCK ERA 1955-1989

Peak Year	Wks Chr	Wks T40	Wks T10	Wks @ #1	Rank	Title	Artist
56	28	23	21	11	1.	Don't Be Cruel / Hound Dog	Elvis Presley
56	26	22	17	10	2.	Singing The Blues	Guy Mitchell
81	26	21	15	10	3.	Physical	Olivia Newton-John
77	25	21	14	10	4.	You Light Up My Life	Debby Boone
59	26	22	16	9	5.	Mack The Knife	Bobby Darin
57	30	22	15	9	6.	All Shook Up	Elvis Presley
81	26	20	14	9	7.	Bette Davis Eyes	Kim Carnes
68	19	19	14	9	8.	Hey Jude	The Beatles
81	27	19	13	9	9.	Endless Love	Diana Ross & Lionel Richie
60	21	17	12	9	10.	The Theme From "A Summer Place"	Percy Faith
55	24	24	19	8	11.	Rock Around The Clock	Bill Haley & His Comets
56	28	22	16	8	12.	The Wayward Wind	Gogi Grant
55	22	19	16	8	13.	Sixteen Tons	"Tennessee" Ernie Ford
56	27	22	15	8	14.	Heartbreak Hotel	Elvis Presley
83	22	20	13	8	15.	Every Breath You Take	The Police
78	20	18	13	8	16.	Night Fever	Bee Gees
76	23	17	11	8	17.	Tonight's The Night (Gonna Be Alright)	Rod Stewart
57	34	24	17	7	18.	Love Letters In The Sand	Pat Boone
57	27	19	15	7	19.	Jailhouse Rock	Elvis Presley
57	25	18	14	7	20.	Let Me Be Your Teddy Bear	Elvis Presley
78	25	19	12	7	21.	Shadow Dancing	Andy Gibb
58	21	18	12	7	22.	At The Hop	Danny & The Juniors
61	23	17	12	7	23.	Tossin' And Turnin'	Bobby Lewis
82	20	16	12	7	24.	I Love Rock 'N Roll	Joan Jett & The Blackhearts
82	19	15	12	7	25.	Ebony And Ivory	Paul McCartney & Stevie Wonder
64	15	14	12	7	26.	I Want To Hold Your Hand	The Beatles
66	15	13	12	7	27.	I'm A Believer	The Monkees
83	24	17	11	7	28.	Billie Jean	Michael Jackson
68	15	15	11	7	29.	I Heard It Through The Grapevine	Marvin Gaye
55	21	21	17	6	30.	Love Is A Many-Splendored Thing	Four Aces
56	25	20	16	6	31.	Rock And Roll Waltz	Kay Starr
56	24	20	16	6	32.	The Poor People Of Paris	Les Baxter
55	19	19	16	6	33.	The Yellow Rose Of Texas	Mitch Miller
78	25	19	15	6	34.	Le Freak	Chic
56	24	19	15	6	35.	Memories Are Made Of This	Dean Martin
82	25	18	15	6	36.	Eye Of The Tiger	Survivor
83	25	20	14	6	37.	Flashdance...What A Feeling	Irene Cara
57	26	19	14	6	38.	April Love	Pat Boone
80	25	19	13	6	39.	Lady	Kenny Rogers
83	22	18	13	6	40.	Say Say Say	Paul McCartney & Michael Jackson
59	21	18	13	6	41.	The Battle Of New Orleans	Johnny Horton
57	21	17	13	6	42.	Young Love	Tab Hunter
82	25	20	12	6	43.	Centerfold	The J. Geils Band
80	25	19	12	6	44.	Call Me	Blondie
58	22	19	12	6	45.	It's All In The Game	Tommy Edwards
79	22	16	12	6	46.	My Sharona	The Knack
69	17	16	11	6	47.	Aquarius/Let The Sunshine In	The 5th Dimension
72	18	15	11	6	48.	The First Time Ever I Saw Your Face	Roberta Flack
72	18	15	11	6	49.	Alone Again (Naturally)	Gilbert O'Sullivan
71	17	15	11	6	50.	Joy To The World	Three Dog Night

HOT 100 HITS OF THE ROCK ERA 1990-2002

Peak Year	Wks Chr	Wks T40	Wks T10	Wks @ #1	Rank	Title	Artist
98	47	45	29	18 [A]	1.	Iris	Goo Goo Dolls
96	63	52	28	16 [A]	2.	Don't Speak	No Doubt
95	27	26	19	16	3.	One Sweet Day	Mariah Carey & Boyz II Men
96	60	37	23	14	4.	Macarena	Los Del Rio
94	33	31	22	14	5.	I'll Make Love To You	Boyz II Men
97	42	28	17	14	6.	Candle In The Wind 1997 / Something About The Way You Look Tonight	Elton John
92	26	24	16	14	7.	I Will Always Love You	Whitney Houston
92	32	28	19	13	8.	End of the Road	Boyz II Men
98	27	27	18	13	9.	The Boy Is Mine	Brandy & Monica
99	58	50	30	12	10.	Smooth	Santana Featuring Rob Thomas
02	23	21	16	12	11.	Lose Yourself	Eminem
98	44	43	32	11 [A]	12.	Torn	Natalie Imbruglia
96	42	37	25	11	13.	Un-Break My Heart	Toni Braxton
94	30	26	18	11	14.	I Swear	All-4-One
97	33	29	17	11	15.	I'll Be Missing You	Puff Daddy & Faith Evans & 112
00	28	25	17	11	16.	Independent Women	Destiny's Child
02	29	27	19	10	17.	Dilemma	Nelly Featuring Kelly Rowland
00	26	24	18	10	18.	Maria Maria	Santana Featuring The Product G&B
02	32	26	17	10	19.	Foolish	Ashanti
95	25	23	16	8	20.	Fantasy	Mariah Carey
93	29	26	14	8	21.	Dreamlover	Mariah Carey
93	23	20	14	8	22.	That's The Way Love Goes	Janet Jackson
92	21	18	13	8	23.	Jump	Kris Kross
96	20	16	12	8	24.	Tha Crossroads	Bone Thugs-N-Harmony
95	34	28	18	7	25.	Waterfalls	TLC
02	26	25	18	7	26.	Hot In Herre	Nelly
95	30	27	15	7	27.	Take A Bow	Madonna
93	29	23	15	7	28.	Can't Help Falling In Love	UB40
95	29	24	14	7	29.	This Is How We Do It	Montell Jordan
01	22	20	14	7	30.	All For You	Janet Jackson
93	25	19	13	7	31.	Informer	Snow
91	22	17	10	7	32.	(Everything I Do) I Do It For You	Bryan Adams
91	20	15	10	7	33.	Black Or White	Michael Jackson
97	59	50	25	6 [A]	34.	Fly	Sugar Ray
94	41	33	21	6	35.	The Sign	Ace Of Base
01	32	29	20	6	36.	U Got It Bad	Usher
01	41	36	19	6	37.	Family Affair	Mary J. Blige
96	33	30	19	6	38.	Because You Loved Me	Celine Dion
01	34	29	19	6	39.	Fallin'	Alicia Keys
94	27	25	17	6	40.	On Bended Knee	Boyz II Men
97	28	26	16	6	41.	Can't Nobody Hold Me Down	Puff Daddy & Mase
02	27	23	15	6	42.	Ain't It Funny	Jennifer Lopez featuring Ja Rule
98	18	15	10	6	43.	I'm Your Angel	R. Kelly & Celine Dion
98	53	49	23	5	44.	Too Close	Next
01	31	29	19	5	45.	I'm Real	Jennifer Lopez featuring Ja Rule
98	23	23	16	5	46.	The First Night	Monica
92	28	24	15	5	47.	Baby Got Back	Sir Mix-A-Lot
99	25	20	15	5	48.	If You Had My Love	Jennifer Lopez
99	25	23	14	5	49.	Genie In A Bottle	Christina Aguilera
93	22	18	14	5	50.	I'd Do Anything For Love	Meat Loaf

TOP 20 #1 HITS — 1955-59

Peak Year	Wks Chr	Wks T40	Wks T10	Wks @ #1	Rank	Title	Artist
56	28	23	21	11	1.	Don't Be Cruel / Hound Dog	Elvis Presley
56	26	22	17	10	2.	Singing The Blues	Guy Mitchell
59	26	22	16	9	3.	Mack The Knife	Bobby Darin
57	30	22	15	9	4.	All Shook Up	Elvis Presley
55	24	24	19	8	5.	Rock Around The Clock	Bill Haley & His Comets
56	28	22	16	8	6.	The Wayward Wind	Gogi Grant
55	22	19	16	8	7.	Sixteen Tons	"Tennessee" Ernie Ford
56	27	22	15	8	8.	Heartbreak Hotel	Elvis Presley
57	34	24	17	7	9.	Love Letters In The Sand	Pat Boone
57	27	19	15	7	10.	Jailhouse Rock	Elvis Presley
57	25	18	14	7	11.	Let Me Be Your Teddy Bear	Elvis Presley
58	21	18	12	7	12.	At The Hop	Danny & The Juniors
55	21	21	17	6	13.	Love Is A Many-Splendored Thing	Four Aces
56	25	20	16	6	14.	Rock And Roll Waltz	Kay Starr
56	24	20	16	6	15.	The Poor People Of Paris	Les Baxter
55	19	19	16	6	16.	The Yellow Rose Of Texas	Mitch Miller
56	24	19	15	6	17.	Memories Are Made Of This	Dean Martin
57	26	19	14	6	18.	April Love	Pat Boone
59	21	18	13	6	19.	The Battle Of New Orleans	Johnny Horton
57	21	17	13	6	20.	Young Love	Tab Hunter

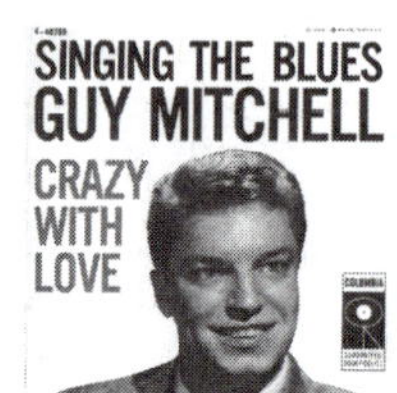

TOP 20 #1 HITS — 1960s

Peak Year	Wks Chr	Wks T40	Wks T10	Wks @ #1	Rank	Title	Artist
68	19	19	14	9	1.	Hey Jude	The Beatles
60	21	17	12	9	2.	The Theme From "A Summer Place"	Percy Faith
61	23	17	12	7	3.	Tossin' And Turnin'	Bobby Lewis
64	15	14	12	7	4.	I Want To Hold Your Hand	The Beatles
66	15	13	12	7	5.	I'm A Believer	The Monkees
68	15	15	11	7	6.	I Heard It Through The Grapevine	Marvin Gaye
69	17	16	11	6	7.	Aquarius/Let The Sunshine In	The 5th Dimension
60	16	14	11	6	8.	Are You Lonesome To-night?	Elvis Presley
69	13	12	9	6	9.	In The Year 2525	Zager & Evans
60	20	16	11	5	10.	It's Now Or Never	Elvis Presley
62	18	14	11	5	11.	I Can't Stop Loving You	Ray Charles
68	18	15	10	5	12.	Love Is Blue	Paul Mauriat
62	16	14	10	5	13.	Big Girls Don't Cry	The 4 Seasons
61	16	13	10	5	14.	Big Bad John	Jimmy Dean
63	15	13	10	5	15.	Sugar Shack	Jimmy Gilmer & The Fireballs
68	15	13	10	5	16.	Honey	Bobby Goldsboro
67	17	15	9	5	17.	To Sir With Love	Lulu
60	17	13	9	5	18.	Cathy's Clown	The Everly Brothers
68	14	13	9	5	19.	People Got To Be Free	The Rascals
69	12	12	9	5	20.	Get Back	The Beatles

TOP 20 #1 HITS — 1970s

Peak Year	Wks Chr	Wks T40	Wks T10	Wks @ #1	Rank	Title	Artist
77	25	21	14	10	1.	You Light Up My Life	Debby Boone
78	20	18	13	8	2.	Night Fever	Bee Gees
76	23	17	11	8	3.	Tonight's The Night (Gonna Be Alright)	Rod Stewart
78	25	19	12	7	4.	Shadow Dancing	Andy Gibb
78	25	19	15	6	5.	Le Freak	Chic
79	22	16	12	6	6.	My Sharona	The Knack
72	18	15	11	6	7.	The First Time Ever I Saw Your Face	Roberta Flack
72	18	15	11	6	8.	Alone Again (Naturally)	Gilbert O'Sullivan
71	17	15	11	6	9.	Joy To The World	Three Dog Night
70	14	13	10	6	10.	Bridge Over Troubled Water	Simon & Garfunkel
77	23	17	12	5	11.	Best Of My Love	Emotions
70	16	16	11	5	12.	I'll Be There	The Jackson 5
76	19	15	11	5	13.	Silly Love Songs	Paul McCartney & Wings
71	17	15	11	5	14.	Maggie May	Rod Stewart
79	20	15	10	5	15.	Bad Girls	Donna Summer
71	17	15	10	5	16.	It's Too Late	Carole King
73	16	13	9	5	17.	Killing Me Softly With His Song	Roberta Flack
71	15	12	9	5	18.	One Bad Apple	The Osmonds
77	31	23	16	4	19.	I Just Want To Be Your Everything	Andy Gibb
78	27	22	13	4	20.	Stayin' Alive	Bee Gees

TOP 20 #1 HITS — 1980s

Peak Year	Wks Chr	Wks T40	Wks T10	Wks @ #1	Rank	Title	Artist
81	26	21	15	10	1.	Physical	Olivia Newton-John
81	26	20	14	9	2.	Bette Davis Eyes	Kim Carnes
81	27	19	13	9	3.	Endless Love	Diana Ross & Lionel Richie
83	22	20	13	8	4.	Every Breath You Take	The Police
82	20	16	12	7	5.	I Love Rock 'N Roll	Joan Jett & The Blackhearts
82	19	15	12	7	6.	Ebony And Ivory	Paul McCartney & Stevie Wonder
83	24	17	11	7	7.	Billie Jean	Michael Jackson
82	25	18	15	6	8.	Eye Of The Tiger	Survivor
83	25	20	14	6	9.	Flashdance...What A Feeling	Irene Cara
80	25	19	13	6	10.	Lady	Kenny Rogers
83	22	18	13	6	11.	Say Say Say	Paul McCartney & Michael Jackson
82	25	20	12	6	12.	Centerfold	The J. Geils Band
80	25	19	12	6	13.	Call Me	Blondie
84	19	14	9	6	14.	Like A Virgin	Madonna
80	22	19	14	5	15.	(Just Like) Starting Over	John Lennon
84	21	16	11	5	16.	When Doves Cry	Prince
84	21	15	10	5	17.	Jump	Van Halen
80	29	17	14	4	18.	Upside Down	Diana Ross
83	24	17	13	4	19.	All Night Long (All Night)	Lionel Richie
82	23	17	13	4	20.	Maneater	Daryl Hall & John Oates

TOP 20 #1 HITS — 1990s

Peak Year	Wks Chr	Wks T40	Wks T10	Wks @ #1	Rank	Title	Artist
98	47	45	29	18 [A]	1.	Iris	Goo Goo Dolls
96	63	52	28	16 [A]	2.	Don't Speak	No Doubt
95	27	26	19	16	3.	One Sweet Day	Mariah Carey & Boyz II Men
96	60	37	23	14	4.	Macarena	Los Del Rio
94	33	31	22	14	5.	I'll Make Love To You	Boyz II Men
97	42	28	17	14	6.	Candle In The Wind 1997 / Something About The Way You Look Tonight	Elton John
92	26	24	16	14	7.	I Will Always Love You	Whitney Houston
92	32	28	19	13	8.	End of the Road	Boyz II Men
98	27	27	18	13	9.	The Boy Is Mine	Brandy & Monica
99	58	50	30	12	10.	Smooth	Santana Featuring Rob Thomas
98	44	43	32	11 [A]	11.	Torn	Natalie Imbruglia
96	42	37	25	11	12.	Un-Break My Heart	Toni Braxton
94	30	26	18	11	13.	I Swear	All-4-One
97	33	29	17	11	14.	I'll Be Missing You	Puff Daddy & Faith Evans & 112
95	25	23	16	8	15.	Fantasy	Mariah Carey
93	29	26	14	8	16.	Dreamlover	Mariah Carey
93	23	20	14	8	17.	That's The Way Love Goes	Janet Jackson
92	21	18	13	8	18.	Jump	Kris Kross
96	20	16	12	8	19.	Tha Crossroads	Bone Thugs-N-Harmony
95	34	28	18	7	20.	Waterfalls	TLC

TOP 20 #1 HITS — 2000-02

Peak Year	Wks Chr	Wks T40	Wks T10	Wks @ #1	Rank	Title	Artist
02	23	21	16	12	1.	Lose Yourself	Eminem
00	28	25	17	11	2.	Independent Women	Destiny's Child
02	29	27	19	10	3.	Dilemma	Nelly Featuring Kelly Rowland
00	26	24	18	10	4.	Maria Maria	Santana Featuring The Product G&B
02	32	26	17	10	5.	Foolish	Ashanti
02	26	25	18	7	6.	Hot In Herre	Nelly
01	22	20	14	7	7.	All For You	Janet Jackson
01	32	29	20	6	8.	U Got It Bad	Usher
01	41	36	19	6	9.	Family Affair	Mary J. Blige
01	34	29	19	6	10.	Fallin'	Alicia Keys
02	27	23	15	6	11.	Ain't It Funny	Jennifer Lopez featuring Ja Rule
01	31	29	19	5	12.	I'm Real	Jennifer Lopez featuring Ja Rule
01	20	17	12	5	13.	Lady Marmalade	Christina Aguilera, Lil' Kim, Mya & P!nk
01	49	40	23	4	14.	How You Remind Me	Nickelback
00	33	28	17	4	15.	I Knew I Loved You	Savage Garden
01	24	22	16	4	16.	U Remind Me	Usher
01	26	23	14	4	17.	Stutter	Joe featuring Mystikal
00	24	22	12	4	18.	Music	Madonna
00	21	16	8	4	19.	Come On Over Baby (all I want is you)	Christina Aguilera
00	24	20	12	3	20.	Doesn't Really Matter	Janet Jackson

SINGLES OF LONGEVITY

Peak Year	Peak Pos	Peak Wks	Total Wks	Title	Artist
				1955-59	
56	2	3	39 *	1. Honky Tonk (Parts 1 & 2) ..... (includes 10 wks. in '61)	*Bill Doggett*
57	14	1	39	2. Wonderful! Wonderful!	*Johnny Mathis*
57	2	4	38	3. So Rare	*Jimmy Dorsey*
57	1	7	34	4. Love Letters In The Sand	*Pat Boone*
57	5	1	34	5. It's Not For Me To Say	*Johnny Mathis*
57	13	1	34	6. (Main Theme) Around The World	*Victor Young*
57	12	1	32	7. Around The World	*Mantovani*
57	1	5	31	8. Tammy	*Debbie Reynolds*
				1960s	
60	1	3	39 *	1. The Twist ..... (18 wks. in '60 / 21 wks. in '61 & 62)	*Chubby Checker*
60	1	3	27	2. Running Bear	*Johnny Preston*
68	5	1	26	3. Sunshine Of Your Love	*Cream*
60	7	2	26	4. Finger Poppin' Time	*Hank Ballard And The Midnighters*
61	11	1	26	5. Moon River	*Henry Mancini*
60	19	1	26	6. Never On Sunday	*Don Costa*
60	3	1	24	7. Sixteen Reasons	*Connie Stevens*
60	4	1	24	8. Sweet Nothin's	*Brenda Lee*
				1970s	
76	1	3	54 *	1. December 1963 (Oh, What A Night) ..... (includes 27 wks. in '94)	*Four Seasons*
78	4	3	41 *	2. We Will Rock You/We Are The Champions ..... (includes 14 wks. in '92)	*Queen*
78	7	3	40	3. I Go Crazy	*Paul Davis*
73	16	1	38	4. Why Me	*Kris Kristofferson*
77	1	3	33	5. How Deep Is Your Love	*Bee Gees*
78	1	3	32	6. Baby Come Back	*Player*
75	6	1	32	7. Feelings	*Morris Albert*
77	1	4	31	8. I Just Want To Be Your Everything	*Andy Gibb*
				1980s	
82	8	2	43	1. Tainted Love	*Soft Cell*
83	29	2	43 *	2. What About Me ..... (includes 17 wks. in '89)	*Moving Pictures*
88	1	1	40 *	3. Red Red Wine ..... (includes 15 wks. in '84)	*UB40*
84	9	1	40 *	4. I'm So Excited ..... (includes 16 wks. in '82)	*Pointer Sisters*
89	7	1	39	5. Bust A Move	*Young MC*
82	2	3	36	6. Gloria	*Laura Branigan*
81	1	2	32	7. Jessie's Girl	*Rick Springfield*
83	1	2	32	8. Baby, Come To Me	*Patti Austin (with James Ingram)*
				1990s	
97	2	5	70	1. One Headlight *(Air)*	*The Wallflowers*
97	2	4	69	2. How Do I Live	*LeAnn Rimes*
97	2	2	65	3. You Were Meant For Me	*Jewel*
96	1	16	63	4. Don't Speak *(Air)*	*No Doubt*
97	11	1	63	5. If You Could Only See *(Air)*	*Tonic*
96	1	14	60	6. Macarena	*Los Del Rio*
98	2	1	60	7. Walkin' On The Sun *(Air)*	*Smash Mouth*
97	1	6	59	8. Fly *(Air)*	*Sugar Ray Featuring Super Cat*
				2000-02	
02	10	1	65	1. Us Against The World *(Sales)*	*Play*
00	7	2	57	2. Higher	*Creed*
01	6	1	56	3. The Way You Love Me	*Faith Hill*
00	1	2	55	4. Amazed	*Lonestar*
01	2	4	54	5. Hanging By A Moment	*Lifehouse*
00	2	5	53	6. Breathe	*Faith Hill*
00	3	3	53	7. Kryptonite	*3 Doors Down*
01	5	2	53	8. Drops Of Jupiter (Tell Me)	*Train*

(Air) *Airplay* chart only
(Sales) *Sales* chart only

* Singles which charted more than once (at least 6 months apart). To qualify, the recharted hit must be the original recording (or remix of original recording) and not a re-recording.

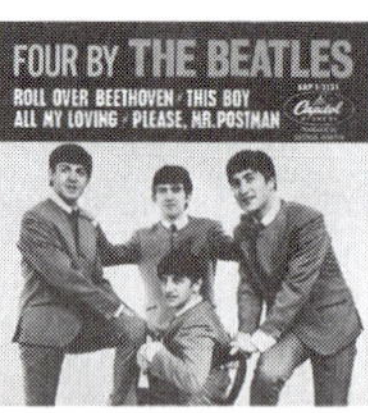

MVP'S (Most Valuable Platters)

Following is a list of records in this book valued at $80 or more.

Year	Value	Title	Artist.Label & Number
		"45s"	
62	$250	**Surfin**	*Beach Boys*...Candix 331
58	$200	**Real Wild Child**	*Ivan*...Coral 62017
57	$200	**Can I Come Over Tonight**	*The Velours*...Onyx 512
64	$150	**Why**	*The Beatles With Tony Sheridan*...MGM 13227
64	$150	**Sie Liebt Dich (She Loves You)**	*Die Beatles*...Swan 4182
55	$150	**Earth Angel** (Will You Be Mine)	*The Penguins*...DooTone 348
57	$125	**Don't Ask Me** (To Be Lonely)	*The Dubs*...Gone 5002
57	$125	**Could This Be Magic**	*The Dubs*...Gone 5011
56	$100	**Dear Elvis (Pages 1 & 2)**	*Audrey*...Plus 104
55	$100	**Hearts Of Stone**	*The Charms*...DeLuxe 6062
57	$100	**Deserie**	*The Charts*...Everlast 5001
60	$100	**Tonight's The Night**	*The Chiffons*...Big Deal 6003
61	$100	**What Will I Tell My Heart**	*The Harptones*...Companion 103
61	$100	**Ain't It, Baby**	*The Miracles*...Tamla 54036
56	$100	**Ooby Dooby**	*Roy Orbison and Teen Kings*...Sun 242
62	$100	**Motorcycle**	*Tico And The Triumphs*...Amy 835
58	$100	**Remember**	*The Velours*...Onyx 520
56	$100	**Church Bells May Ring**	*Willows*...Melba 102
55	$80	**Why Don't You Write Me?**	*The Jacks*...RPM 428
56	$80	**Speedo**	*The Cadillacs*...Josie 785
56	$80	**A Thousand Miles Away**	*The Heartbeats*...Rama 216
57	$80	**Everybody's Somebody's Fool**	*The Heartbeats*...Rama 231
65	$80	**The Crusher**	*The Novas*...Parrot 45005
		EPs	
64	$400	**Four By The Beatles**	*The Beatles*...Capitol EAP 1-2121
65	$275	**4 – By The Beatles**	*The Beatles*...Capitol R-5365
56	$125	**Elvis Presley ("Blue Suede Shoes")**	*Elvis Presley*...RCA Victor EPA-747
56	$125	**Heartbreak Hotel ("Money Honey")**	*Elvis Presley*...RCA Victor EPA-821
56	$100	**Elvis ("Love Me")**	*Elvis Presley*...RCA Victor EPA-992
56	$100	**Elvis, Volume II ("Old Shep")**	*Elvis Presley*...RCA Victor EPA-993
57	$100	**Love Me Tender ("Poor Boy")**	*Elvis Presley*...RCA Victor EPA-4006
57	$100	**Peace In The Valley**	*Elvis Presley*...RCA Victor EPA-4054
64	$100	**Viva Las Vegas**	*Elvis Presley*...RCA Victor EPA-4382
61	$80	**Elvis By Request ("Flaming Star")**	*Elvis Presley*...RCA Victor LPC-128

Although the research for this book begins in 1955, there were four rare and important pre-1955 R&B/Rock & Roll hits that blazed a trail on the Pop charts:

8/25/51 "Sixty Minute Man" by The Dominoes (#17)...$500
5/23/53 "Crazy Man, Crazy" by Bill Haley With Haley's Comets (#12)...$75
4/10/54 "Gee" by The Crows (#14)...$125
7/3/54 "Sh-Boom" by The Chords (#5)...$125

TOP POPular RECORDINGS

TOP INSTRUMENTAL

PEAK YEAR	WKS CHR	WKS T40	WKS T10	PEAK POS	RANK	TITLE	ARTIST
55	26	26	20	1^{10}	1.	Cherry Pink And Apple Blossom White	*Perez "Prez" Prado*
60	21	17	12	1^{9}	2.	The Theme From "A Summer Place"	*Percy Faith*
56	24	20	16	1^{6}	3.	The Poor People Of Paris	*Les Baxter*
58	19	16	11	1^{5}	4.	Tequila	*The Champs*
68	18	15	10	1^{5}	5.	Love Is Blue	*Paul Mauriat*
55	26	26	18	1^{4}	6.	Autumn Leaves	*Roger Williams*
56	29	24	17	1^{4}	7.	Lisbon Antigua	*Nelson Riddle*
56	27	22	15	1^{3}	8.	Moonglow and Theme From "Picnic"	*Morris Stoloff*
61	17	15	10	1^{3}	9.	Wonderland By Night	*Bert Kaempfert*
62	16	13	8	1^{3}	10.	Telstar	*The Tornadoes*
75	17	13	7	1^{3}	11.	Fly, Robin, Fly	*Silver Convention*
79	25	15	9	1^{2}	12.	Rise	*Herb Alpert*

TOP NOVELTY *

PEAK YEAR	WKS CHR	WKS T40	WKS T10	PEAK POS	RANK	TITLE	ARTIST
58	14	14	10	1^{6}	1.	The Purple People Eater	*Sheb Wooley*
58	19	18	12	1^{3}	2.	Witch Doctor	*David Seville*
74	17	12	8	1^{3}	3.	The Streak	*Ray Stevens*
62	14	12	7	1^{2}	4.	Monster Mash	*Bobby "Boris" Pickett And The Crypt-Kickers*
72	17	12	6	1^{2}	5.	My Ding-A-Ling	*Chuck Berry*
76	25	16	10	1^{1}	6.	Disco Duck (Part I)	*Rick Dees And His Cast Of Idiots*
60	15	13	8	1^{1}	7.	Itsy Bitsy Teenie Weenie Yellow Polkadot Bikini	*Brian Hyland*
60	15	12	8	1^{1}	8.	Alley-Oop	*Hollywood Argyles*
76	16	11	7	1^{1}	9.	Convoy	*C.W. McCall*
60	13	10	7	1^{1}	10.	Mr. Custer	*Larry Verne*
66	12	11	8	2^{4}	11.	Snoopy Vs. The Red Baron	*The Royal Guardsmen*
63	10	8	6	2^{3}	12.	Hello Mudduh, Hello Fadduh! (A Letter From Camp)	*Allan Sherman*

* excluding holiday and foreign language recordings

TOP SPOKEN

PEAK YEAR	WKS CHR	WKS T40	WKS T10	PEAK POS	RANK	TITLE	ARTIST
61	16	13	10	1^{5}	1.	Big Bad John	*Jimmy Dean*
64	12	10	7	1^{1}	2.	Ringo	*Lorne Greene*
74	12	9	4	4^{1}	3.	Americans	*Byron MacGregor*
55	15	15	8	5^{4}	4.	The Shifting Whispering Sands Parts 1 & 2	*Billy Vaughn with Ken Nordini*
62	11	9	4	5^{1}	5.	Old Rivers	*Walter Brennan*
59	17	12	5	7^{3}	6.	Deck Of Cards	*Wink Martindale*
00	5	2	2	7^{1}	7.	Auld Lang Syne (The Millennium Mix)	*Kenny G*
71	12	10	3	8^{1}	8.	Desiderata	*Les Crane*
71	9	7	3	8^{1}	9.	What The World Needs Now Is Love/Abraham, Martin and John	*Tom Clay*
67	6	4	2	10^{2}	10.	An Open Letter To My Teenage Son	*Victor Lundberg*
59	12	8		11^{1}	11.	Three Stars	*Tommy Dee With Carol Kay*
70	8	6		19^{1}	12.	What Is Truth	*Johnny Cash*

TOP POPular RECORDINGS (cont'd)

TOP FOREIGN

PEAK YEAR	WKS CHR	WKS T40	WKS T10	PEAK POS	RANK	TITLE	ARTIST
96	60	37	23	1^{14}	1.	Macarena (bayside boys mix)	*Los Del Rio*
58	16	13	10	1^{5}	2.	Nel Blu Dipinto Di Blue (Volaré)	*Domenico Modugno*
63	13	12	9	1^{4}	3.	Dominique	*The Singing Nun (Soeur Sourire)*
63	14	12	8	1^{3}	4.	Sukiyaki	*Kyu Sakamoto*
87	21	14	7	1^{3}	5.	La Bamba	*Los Lobos*
84	23	13	6	2^{1}	6.	99 Luftballons	*Nena*
91	18	11	5	5^{2}	7.	Sadeness Part 1	*Enigma*
60	18	14	4	5^{1}	8.	Sailor (Your Home Is The Sea)	*Lolita*
62	14	10	3	6^{1}	9.	Al Di La'	*Emilio Pericoli*
74	17	11	2	9^{2}	10.	Eres Tu (Touch The Wind)	*Mocedades*
66	11	9	2	9^{1}	11.	Guantanamera	*The Sandpipers*
58	18	11		12^{1}	12.	Lazy Mary (Luna Mezzo Mare)	*Lou Monte*

TOP CHRISTMAS/HOLIDAY (Pop charts only)

PEAK YEAR	WKS CHR	WKS T40	WKS T10	PEAK POS	RANK	TITLE	ARTIST
58	28*	13*	6	1^{4}	1.	The Chipmunk Song	*The Chipmunks With David Seville*
55	4	4	3	6^{1}	2.	Nuttin' For Christmas	*Barry Gordon with Art Mooney*
57	22*	8*	2	6^{1}	3.	Jingle Bell Rock	*Bobby Helms*
89	16	10	4	7^{2}	4.	This One's For The Children	*New Kids On The Block*
64	11	7	2	7^{1}	5.	Amen	*The Impressions*
55	23*	10*	1	7^{1}	6.	White Christmas	*Bing Crosby*
95	10*	4*	1	10^{1}	7.	The Chanukah Song *(Air)*	*Adam Sandler*
56	5	3		12^{1}	8.	Mary's Boy Child	*Harry Belafonte*
94	7*	5*		12^{1}	9.	All I Want For Christmas Is You *(Air)*	*Mariah Carey*
58	28*	17*		13^{1}	10.	The Little Drummer Boy	*The Harry Simeone Chorale*
84	11*	4		13^{1}	11.	Do They Know It's Christmas?	*Band Aid*
60	11*	3		14^{1}	12.	Rockin' Around The Christmas Tree	*Brenda Lee*

TOP CHRISTMAS (Christmas charts only)

PEAK YEAR	WKS CHR	WKS T40	WKS T10	PEAK POS	RANK	TITLE	ARTIST
67	7	7	5	1^{5}	1.	Snoopy's Christmas	*The Royal Guardsmen*
63	7	7	5	1^{5}	2.	White Christmas	*Andy Williams*
83	6*	6*	6*	1^{4}	3.	Grandma Got Run Over By A Reindeer	*Elmo & Patsy*
70	12	12	10	1^{3}	4.	Merry Christmas Darling	*Carpenters*
68	4	4	4	1^{3}	5.	The Christmas Song	*Herb Alpert*
64	34	34	25	1^{2}	6.	Blue Christmas	*Elvis Presley*
70	5	5	4	1^{2}	7.	Santa Claus Is Comin' To Town	*The Jackson 5*
71	11	11	11	1^{1}	8.	Jingle Bells	*The Singing Dogs*
66	6	6	3	1^{1}	9.	Sleep In Heavenly Peace (Silent Night)	*Barbra Streisand*
73	3	3	3	1^{1}	10.	Step Into Christmas	*Elton John*
85	2	2	2	1^{1}	11.	Santa Claus Is Comin' To Town	*Bruce Springsteen*
64	23*	23*	17*	2^{2}	12.	Merry Christmas Baby	*Charles Brown*

* Totals are a combination of all entries for title.

SINGLES WITH LONGEST TITLES

# of Char.	Title	Artist
104	**Jeremiah Peabody's Poly Unsaturated Quick Dissolving Fast Acting Pleasant Tasting Green And Purple Pills**	Ray Stevens
94	**Life During Wartime** (This Ain't No Party...This Ain't No Disco...This Ain't No Foolin' Around)	Talking Heads
86	**(How I Spent My Summer Vacation)** Or **A Day At The Beach With Pedro & Man - Parts I & II**	Cheech & Chong
80	**The Anaheim, Azusa & Cucamonga Sewing Circle, Book Review And Timing Association**	Jan & Dean
77	**I Don't Want Nobody To Give Me Nothing (Open Up The Door, I'll Get It Myself)**	James Brown
76	**Theme Music For The Film "2001" A Space Odyssey from Also Sprach Zarathustra**	Berlin Philharmonic
75	**There Will Never Be Any Peace** (Until God Is Seated At The Conference Table)	The Chi-Lites
72	**Mama Was A Rock And Roll Singer, Papa Used To Write All Her Songs Part 1**	Sonny & Cher
71	**There's A Star Spangled Banner Waving #2 (The Ballad Of Francis Powers)**	Red River Dave
71	**What Can You Get A Wookiee For Christmas (When He Already Owns A Comb?)**	Meco
68	**Sometimes I Miss You So Much (dedicated to the christ-consciousness)**	PM Dawn
67	**Hot Pants Pt. 1** (She Got To Use What She Got To Get What She Wants)	James Brown
66	**Indian Reservation** (The Lament Of The Cherokee Reservation Indian)	Raiders
66	**Breaking Up Is Hard On You (a/k/a Don't Take Ma Bell Away From Me)**	The American Comedy Network
65	**Does Your Chewing Gum Lose Its Flavor** (On The Bedpost Over Night)	Lonnie Donegan And His Skiffle Group
65	**There Won't Be No Country Music (There Won't Be No Rock 'N' Roll)**	C.W. McCall

SONGS WITH MOST CHARTED VERSIONS

Total Versions*	Title	Songwriter(s)
9	**Unchained Melody**	Hy Zaret/Alex North
9	**The Little Drummer Boy**	Katherine Davis/Henry Onorati/Harry Simeone
8	**Mack The Knife**	Kurt Weill/Marc Blitzstein
8	**Stand By Me**	Ben E. King/Jerry Leiber/Mike Stoller
7	**Autumn Leaves**	Johnny Mercer/Joseph Kosma
7	**Man With The Golden Arm**	Sammy Cahn/James Van Heusen
7	**(Sittin' On) The Dock Of The Bay**	Otis Redding/Steve Cropper
6	**Banana Boat (Day-O)/Banana Boat Song**	Erik Darling/Bob Carey/Alan Arkin
6	**Dancing In The Street**	William Stevenson/Marvin Gaye
6	**Danny Boy**	Fred Weatherly
6	**Do You Want To Dance**	Bobby Freeman
6	**Earth Angel**	Jesse Belvin
6	**For Your Precious Love**	Arthur Brooks/Richard Brooks/Jerry Butler
6	**Hang On Sloopy/My Girl Sloopy**	Wes Farrell/Bert Russell
6	**I Heard It Through The Grapevine**	Norman Whitfield/Barrett Strong
6	**Kansas City**	Jerry Leiber/Mike Stoller
6	**Land Of 1000 Dances**	Chris Kenner
6	**Let It Be Me**	Mann Curtis/Gilbert Becaud
6	**Only You**	Buck Ram/Ande Rand
6	**Runaway**	Del Shannon/Max Crook
6	**Since I Don't Have You**	James Beaumont/Walter Lester/Lennie Martin/Joseph Rock/John Taylor/Joseph Verscharen/Janet Vogel
6	**Why Do Fools Fall In Love**	Frankie Lymon/George Goldner
6	**Will You Love Me Tomorrow**	Gerry Goffin/Carole King
6	**You're All I Need To Get By**	Nicholas Ashford/Valerie Simpson
6	**Young Love**	Carole Joyner/Ric Cartey

* Total does not include re-entries of the same version by an artist; however, new versions are counted.

TOP 50 RECORD LABELS

		Total Hits
1.	**Columbia**	1,655
2.	**RCA**	1,285
3.	**Capitol**	1,245
4.	**Atlantic**	984
5.	**Epic**	822
6.	**Warner**	810
7.	**Mercury**	735
8.	**MCA**	652
9.	**A&M**	600
10.	**Arista**	533
11.	**ABC**	490
12.	**Elektra**	396
13.	**MGM**	353
14.	**Decca**	347
15.	**Reprise**	339
16.	**Motown**	337
17.	**Atco**	312
18.	**United Artists**	261
19.	**Polydor**	257
20.	**EMI America**	256
21.	**Dot**	244
22.	**Imperial**	217
23.	**Tamla**	217
24.	**Liberty**	216
25.	**Geffen**	212
26.	**Virgin**	197
27.	**Jive**	186
28.	**Chrysalis**	153
29.	**London**	141
30.	**Roulette**	135
31.	**Kapp**	134
32.	**Coral**	133
33.	**Gordy**	133
34.	**Island**	128
35.	**Sire**	124
36.	**Dunhill**	121
37.	**King**	117
38.	**Stax**	112
39.	**Asylum**	111
40.	**Scepter**	107
41.	**Casablanca**	105
42.	**Curb**	105
43.	**Def Jam**	102
44.	**Brunswick**	100
45.	**Bell**	95
46.	**RSO**	94
47.	**Buddah**	89
48.	**20th Century**	89
49.	**Cadence**	85
50.	**Philips**	83

LABEL ABBREVIATIONS

Almo Int'l.	Almo International
Alpha Int'l.	Alpha International
American Int'l.	American International
CBS Assoc./Curb	CBS Associated/Curb
Chocolate Ind.	Chocolate Industries
Cleveland I./Epic	Cleveland International/Epic
Common. United	Commonwealth United
Empire/Metro.	Empire/Metropolitan
Epic/Phil. Int.	Epic/Philadelphia International
Grand R./Cap.	Grand Royal/Capitol
Gut R./Univ.	Gut Reaction/Universal
Hiero Imp.	Hiero Imperium
Int'l. Artists	International Artists
London Int'l.	London International
Midland Int'l.	Midland International
Midsong Int'l.	Midsong International
Music Fac./Atco	Music Factory/Atco
Philadelphia I.	Philadelphia International
Roadshow/U.A.	Roadshow/United Artists
Shocking V.	Shocking Vibes
United Art./Jet	United Artists/Jet

ROCK & ROLL HALL OF FAME INDUCTEES

1986

Performers

Chuck Berry
James Brown
Ray Charles
Sam Cooke
Fats Domino
The Everly Brothers
Buddy Holly
Jerry Lee Lewis
Little Richard
Elvis Presley

Early Influences

Robert Johnson
Jimmie Rodgers
Jimmy Yancey

Non-Performers

Alan Freed
John Hammond (LA)
Sam Phillips

1987

Performers

The Coasters
Eddie Cochran
Bo Diddley
Aretha Franklin
Marvin Gaye
Bill Haley
B.B. King
Clyde McPhatter
Ricky Nelson
Roy Orbison
Carl Perkins
Smokey Robinson
Big Joe Turner
Muddy Waters
Jackie Wilson

Early Influences

Louis Jordan
T-Bone Walker
Hank Williams

Non-Performers

Leonard Chess
Ahmet Ertegun
Jerry Leiber & Mike Stoller
Jerry Wexler

1988

Performers

The Beach Boys
The Beatles
The Drifters
Bob Dylan
The Supremes

Early Influences

Woody Guthrie
Leadbelly
Les Paul

Non-Performer

Berry Gordy, Jr.

1989

Performers

Dion
Otis Redding
The Rolling Stones
The Temptations
Stevie Wonder

Early Influences

The Ink Spots
Bessie Smith
The Soul Stirrers

Non-Performer

Phil Spector

1990

Performers

Hank Ballard
Bobby Darin
The 4 Seasons
Four Tops
The Kinks
The Platters
Simon & Garfunkel
The Who

Early Influences

Louis Armstrong
Charlie Christian
Ma Rainey

Non-Performers

Gerry Goffin & Carole King
Holland-Dozier-Holland

1991

Performers

LaVern Baker
The Byrds
John Lee Hooker
The Impressions
Wilson Pickett
Jimmy Reed
Ike & Tina Turner

Early Influence

Howlin' Wolf

Non-Performers

Dave Bartholomew
Ralph Bass
Nesuhi Ertegun (LA)

1992

Performers

Bobby "Blue" Bland
Booker T. & The MG's
Johnny Cash
Jimi Hendrix Experience
The Isley Brothers
Sam & Dave
The Yardbirds

Early Influences

Elmore James
Professor Longhair

Non-Performers

Leo Fender
Bill Graham
Doc Pomus

1993

Performers

Ruth Brown
Cream
The Doors
Etta James
Creedence Clearwater Revival
Frankie Lymon/Teenagers
Van Morrison
Sly & The Family Stone

Early Influence

Dinah Washington

Non-Performers

Dick Clark
Milt Gabler

1994

Performers

The Animals
The Band
Duane Eddy
The Grateful Dead
Elton John
John Lennon
Bob Marley
Rod Stewart

Early Influence

Willie Dixon

Non-Performer

Johnny Otis

1995

Performers

The Allman Brothers Band
Al Green
Janis Joplin
Led Zeppelin
Martha & The Vandellas
Neil Young
Frank Zappa

Early Influence

The Orioles

Non-Performer

Paul Ackerman

1996

Performers

David Bowie
Jefferson Airplane
Little Willie John
Gladys Knight & The Pips
Pink Floyd
The Shirelles
The Velvet Underground

Early Influence

Pete Seeger

Non-Performer

Tom Donahue

1997

Performers

Bee Gees
The Buffalo Springfield
Crosby, Stills & Nash
The Jackson 5
Joni Mitchell
Parliament/Funkadelic
The (Young) Rascals

Early Influences

Mahalia Jackson
Bill Monroe

Non-Performer

Syd Nathan

1998

Performers

Eagles
Fleetwood Mac
The Mamas & The Papas
Lloyd Price
Santana
Gene Vincent

Early Influence

Jelly Roll Morton

Non-Performer

Allen Toussaint

1999

Performers

Billy Joel
Curtis Mayfield
Paul McCartney
Del Shannon
Dusty Springfield
Bruce Springsteen
The Staple Singers

Early Influences

Bob Wills/Texas Playboys
Charles Brown

Non-Performer

George Martin

2000

Performers

Eric Clapton
Earth, Wind & Fire
The Lovin' Spoonful
The Moonglows
Bonnie Raitt
James Taylor

Early Influences

Nat "King" Cole
Billie Holiday

Non-Performer

Clive Davis

Sidemen

Hal Blaine
James Jamerson
King Curtis
Scotty Moore
Earl Palmer

2001

Performers

Aerosmith
Solomon Burke
The Flamingos
Michael Jackson
Queen
Paul Simon
Steely Dan
Ritchie Valens

Non-Performer

Chris Blackwell

Sidemen

James Burton
Johnnie Johnson

2002

Performers

Isaac Hayes
Brenda Lee
Tom Petty/Heartbreakers
Gene Pitney
The Ramones
Talking Heads

Non-Performer

Jim Stewart

Sideman

Chet Atkins

2003

Performers

AC/DC
The Clash
Elvis Costello/Attractions
The Police
The Righteous Brothers

Non-Performer

Mo Ostin

Sidemen

Benny Benjamin
Floyd Cramer
Steve Douglas

A–Z LISTING OF INDUCTEES

Inductee	Year
AC/DC	2003
Ackerman, Paul (NP)	1995
Aerosmith	2001
Allman Brothers Band, The	1995
Animals, The	1994
Armstrong, Louis (EI)	1990
Atkins, Chet (S)	2002
Baker, LaVern	1991
Ballard, Hank	1990
Band, The	1994
Bartholomew, Dave (NP)	1991
Bass, Ralph (NP)	1991
Beach Boys, The	1988
Beatles, The	1988
Bee Gees	1997
Benjamin, Benny (S)	2003
Berry, Chuck	1986
Blackwell, Chris (NP)	2001
Blaine, Hal (S)	2000
Bland, Bobby "Blue"	1992
Booker T. & The MG's	1992
Bowie, David	1996
Brown, Charles (EI)	1999
Brown, James	1986
Brown, Ruth	1993
Burke, Solomon	2001
Buffalo Springfield	1997
Burton, James (S)	2001
Byrds, The	1991
Cash, Johnny	1992
Charles, Ray	1986
Chess, Leonard (NP)	1987
Christian, Charlie (EI)	1990
Clapton, Eric	2000
Clark, Dick (NP)	1993
Clash, The	2003
Coasters, The	1987
Cochran, Eddie	1987
Cole, Nat "King" (EI)	2000
Cooke, Sam	1986
Costello, Elvis/Attractions	2003
Cramer, Floyd (S)	2003
Cream	1993
Creedence Clearwater Revival	1993
Crosby, Stills & Nash	1997
Darin, Bobby	1990
Davis, Clive (NP)	2000
Diddley, Bo	1987
Dion	1989
Dixon, Willie (EI)	1994
Domino, Fats	1986
Donahue, Tom (NP)	1996
Doors, The	1993
Douglas, Steve (S)	2003
Dozier, Lamont (NP)	1990
Drifters, The	1988
Dylan, Bob	1988
Eagles	1998
Earth, Wind & Fire	2000
Eddy, Duane	1994
Ertegun, Ahmet (NP)	1987
Ertegun, Nesuhi (LA-NP)	1991
Everly Brothers, The	1986
Fender, Leo (NP)	1992
Flamingos, The	2001
Fleetwood Mac	1998
4 Seasons, The	1990
Four Tops	1990

Inductee	Year
Franklin, Aretha	1987
Freed, Alan (NP)	1986
Gabler, Milt (NP)	1993
Gaye, Marvin	1987
Goffin, Gerry (NP)	1990
Gordy, Berry Jr. (NP)	1988
Graham, Bill (NP)	1992
Grateful Dead, The	1994
Green, Al	1995
Guthrie, Woody (EI)	1988
Haley, Bill	1987
Hammond, John (LA-NP)	1986
Hayes, Isaac	2002
Hendrix, Jimi, Experience	1992
Holiday, Billie (EI)	2000
Holland, Brian (NP)	1990
Holland, Eddie (NP)	1990
Holly, Buddy	1986
Hooker, John Lee	1991
Howlin' Wolf (EI)	1991
Impressions, The	1991
Ink Spots, The (EI)	1989
Isley Brothers, The	1992
Jackson, Mahalia (EI)	1997
Jackson, Michael	2001
Jackson 5, The	1997
Jamerson, James (S)	2000
James, Elmore (EI)	1992
James, Etta	1993
Jefferson Airplane	1996
Joel, Billy	1999
John, Elton	1994
John, Little Willie	1996
Johnson, Johnnie (S)	2001
Johnson, Robert (EI)	1986
Joplin, Janis	1995
Jordan, Louis (EI)	1987
King, B.B.	1987
King, Carole (NP)	1990
King Curtis (S)	2000
Kinks, The	1990
Knight, Gladys, & The Pips	1996
Leadbelly (EI)	1988
Led Zeppelin	1995
Lee, Brenda	2002
Leiber, Jerry (NP)	1987
Lennon, John	1994
Lewis, Jerry Lee	1986
Little Richard	1986
Lovin' Spoonful, The	2000
Lymon, Frankie/Teenagers	1993
Mamas & The Papas, The	1998
Marley, Bob	1994
Martha & The Vandellas	1995
Martin, George (NP)	1999
Mayfield, Curtis	1999
McCartney, Paul	1999
McPhatter, Clyde	1987
Mitchell, Joni	1997
Monroe, Bill (EI)	1997
Moonglows, The	2000
Moore, Scotty (S)	2000
Morrison, Van	1993
Morton, Jelly Roll (EI)	1998
Nathan, Syd (NP)	1997
Nelson, Ricky	1987
Orbison, Roy	1987
Orioles, The (EI)	1995

Inductee	Year
Ostin, Mo (NP)	2003
Otis, Johnny (NP)	1994
Palmer, Earl (S)	2000
Parliament/Funkadelic	1997
Paul, Les (EI)	1988
Perkins, Carl	1987
Petty, Tom/Heartbreakers	2002
Phillips, Sam (NP)	1986
Pickett, Wilson	1991
Pink Floyd	1996
Pitney, Gene	2002
Platters, The	1990
Police, The	2003
Pomus, Doc (NP)	1992
Presley, Elvis	1986
Price, Lloyd	1998
Professor Longhair (EI)	1992
Queen	2001
Rainey, Ma (EI)	1990
Raitt, Bonnie	2000
Ramones, The	2002
Rascals, The (Young)	1997
Redding, Otis	1989
Reed, Jimmy	1991
Righteous Brothers, The	2003
Robinson, Smokey	1987
Rodgers, Jimmie (EI)	1986
Rolling Stones, The	1989
Sam & Dave	1992
Santana	1998
Seeger, Pete (EI)	1996
Shannon, Del	1999
Shirelles, The	1996
Simon, Paul	2001
Simon & Garfunkel	1990
Sly & The Family Stone	1993
Smith, Bessie (EI)	1989
Soul Stirrers, The (EI)	1989
Spector, Phil (NP)	1989
Springfield, Dusty	1999
Springsteen, Bruce	1999
Staple Singers, The	1999
Steely Dan	2001
Stewart, Jim (NP)	2002
Stewart, Rod	1994
Stoller, Mike (NP)	1987
Supremes, The	1988
Talking Heads	2002
Taylor, James	2000
Temptations, The	1989
Toussaint, Allen (NP)	1998
Turner, Big Joe	1987
Turner, Ike & Tina	1991
Valens, Ritchie	2001
Velvet Underground, The	1996
Vincent, Gene	1998
Walker, T-Bone (EI)	1987
Washington, Dinah (EI)	1993
Waters, Muddy	1987
Wexler, Jerry (NP)	1987
Who, The	1990
Williams, Hank (EI)	1987
Wills, Bob/Texas Playboys (EI)	1999
Wilson, Jackie	1987
Wonder, Stevie	1989
Yancey, Jimmy (EI)	1986
Yardbirds, The	1992
Young, Neil	1995
Zappa, Frank	1995

EI = Early Influence NP = Non-Performer LA = Lifetime Achievement S = Sideman

#1 HITS

This section lists, in chronological order, all 967 singles which hit #1 on *Billboard's Hot 100* chart and pre-*Hot 100* pop singles charts (*Best Sellers In Stores, Most Played By Jockeys, Most Played In Juke Boxes* and *Top 100*) from 1955 through 2003. "The Twist," which hit #1 in 1960 and again in 1962, is counted twice. There have been 896 #1 hits on the *Hot 100* chart since its debut in 1958.

From January 1, 1955 through October 13, 1958, when *Billboard* published more than one weekly pop chart, the chart designation and #1 weeks on each chart are listed beneath the record title. The chart designations are:

BS: Best Sellers
JY: Jockeys
JB: Juke Box
TP: Top 100
HT: Hot 100

The date shown is the earliest date that a record hit #1 on any of the pop charts. The weeks column lists the total weeks at #1, from whichever chart it achieved its highest total. This total is not a combined total from the various pop charts.

Because of the multiple charts used for this research, some dates are duplicated, as certain #1 hits may have peaked on the same week on different charts. *Billboard* also showed ties at #1 on some of these charts; therefore, the total weeks for each year may calculate out to more than 52.

Billboard has not published an issue for the last week of the year since 1976. For the years 1976 through 1991, *Billboard* considered the charts listed in the last published issue of the year to be "frozen" and all chart positions remained the same for the unpublished week. This frozen chart data is included in our tabulations. Since 1992, *Billboard* has compiled a pop chart for the last week of the year, even though an issue is not published. This chart is only available through *Billboard's* Web site or by mail. Our tabulations include this unpublished chart data.

See the introduction pages of this book for more details on researching the pop charts.

DATE: Date single first peaked at the #1 position

WKS: Total weeks single held the #1 position

↕ : Indicates single hit #1, dropped down, and then returned to the #1 spot

❶: Indicates title debuted at #1

16A: A superscript 'A' next to the peak weeks indicates a Hot 100 Airplay hit (five Airplay hits are included in this section, all of which peaked at #1 on the Hot 100 Airplay chart prior to *Billboard* including Airplay hits on the Hot 100 on 12/5/98)

The chronological position [such as (1 of 4)] is listed after the artist name of each #1 hit to indicate the artist's total string of #1s. (Ex.: **April Love** *Pat Boone* (5 of 6) indicates that "April Love" is Pat Boone's fifth #1 of his six #1 hits.)

The top hit of each year is shown in **red**. The top hit is determined by most weeks at the #1 position, followed by total weeks in the Top 10, Top 40, and total weeks charted.

Hot New #1 Artist: The first #1 hit by an artist with a minimum of four #1 hits is underlined and highlighted in **bold red** type.

#1 HITS

1955

DATE WKS

1. 1/1 **4** **Let Me Go Lover** *Joan Weber* (1)
JY: 4↕ / JB: 4 / BS: 2
2. 2/5 **3** **Hearts Of Stone** *The Fontane Sisters* (1)
JB: 3 / BS: 1
3. 2/12 **10** **Sincerely** *The McGuire Sisters* (1 of 2)
JY: 10 / JB: 7 / BS: 6
4. 3/26 **5** **The Ballad Of Davy Crockett** *Bill Hayes* (1)
BS: 5 / JY: 3 / JB: 3
5. 4/30 **10** **Cherry Pink And Apple Blossom White** *Perez "Prez" Prado* (1 of 2)
BS: 10 / JB: 8 / JY: 6↕
6. 5/14 **3** **Dance With Me Henry (Wallflower)** *Georgia Gibbs* (2 of 2)
JB: 3
7. 5/14 **2↕** **Unchained Melody** *Les Baxter* (1 of 2)
JY: 2↕
8. 7/9 **8** **(We're Gonna) Rock Around The Clock** *Bill Haley & His Comets* (1)
BS: 8 / JB: 7 / JY: 6↕
9. 7/9 **2↕** **Learnin' The Blues** *Frank Sinatra* (4 of 6)
JY: 2↕
(total #1s do not include his three #1 hits with Tommy Dorsey)
10. 9/3 **6** **The Yellow Rose Of Texas** *Mitch Miller* (1)
BS: 6↕ / JY: 6 / JB: 6
11. 9/17 **2** **Ain't That A Shame** *Pat Boone* (1 of 6)
JB: 2
12. 10/8 **6** **Love Is A Many-Splendored Thing** *Four Aces* (2 of 2)
JY: 6 / TP: 3 / JB: 3 / BS: 2↕
13. 10/29 **4** **Autumn Leaves** *Roger Williams* (1)
BS: 4

11/12/55: Billboard's "Top 100" chart debuts.

14. 11/26 **8** **Sixteen Tons** *"Tennessee" Ernie Ford* (1)
JB: 8 / BS: 7 / TP: 6 / JY: 6

1956

DATE WKS

1. 1/7 **6** **Memories Are Made Of This** *Dean Martin* (1 of 2)
JY: 6 / BS: 5 / TP: 5 / JB: 4
2. 2/18 **6** **Rock And Roll Waltz** *Kay Starr* (2 of 2)
JB: 6 / TP: 4 / BS: 1 / JY: 1
3. 2/18 **2** **The Great Pretender** *The Platters* (1 of 4)
TP: 2 / JY: 2 / JB: 1
4. 2/25 **4** **Lisbon Antigua** *Nelson Riddle* (1)
BS: 4 / JY: 2↕
5. 3/17 **6** **The Poor People Of Paris** *Les Baxter* (2 of 2)
TP: 6 / JY: 6↕ / BS: 4 / JB: 3
6. 4/21 **8** **Heartbreak Hotel** *Elvis Presley* (1 of 18)
BS: 8 / JB: 8 / TP: 7 / JY: 3
7. 5/5 **1** **Hot Diggity (Dog Ziggity Boom)** *Perry Como* (12 of 14)
JY: 1
8. 6/2 **3** **Moonglow and Theme From "Picnic"** *Morris Stoloff* (1)
JY: 3
9. 6/16 **8** **The Wayward Wind** *Gogi Grant* (1)
JY: 8 / TP: 7 / BS: 6 / JB: 4

1956 (cont'd)

10. 7/28 **4** **I Almost Lost My Mind** *Pat Boone* (2 of 6)
JB: 4 / TP: 2
11. 7/28 **1** **I Want You, I Need You, I Love You** *Elvis Presley* (2 of 18)
BS: 1
12. 8/4 **5** **My Prayer** *The Platters* (2 of 4)
TP: 5 / JY: 3 / BS: 2 / JB: 1
13. 8/18 **11** **Don't Be Cruel /** (3 of 18)
BS: 11 / JB: 11 / JY: 8 / TP: 7
14. **Hound Dog** *Elvis Presley* (4 of 18)
BS: 11 / JB: 11
15. 11/3 **5** **Love Me Tender** *Elvis Presley* (5 of 18)
BS: 5 / JY: 5 / TP: 4↕ / JB: 1
16. 11/3 **3** **The Green Door** *Jim Lowe* (1)
TP: 3 / JB: 3
17. 12/8 **10** **Singing The Blues** *Guy Mitchell* (1 of 2)
JB: 10 / BS: 9 / TP: 9 / JY: 9

1957

DATE WKS

1. 2/9 **3** **Too Much** *Elvis Presley* (6 of 18)
BS: 3 / JB: 1
2. 2/9 **1** **Don't Forbid Me** *Pat Boone* (3 of 6)
TP: 1 / JB: 1
3. 2/9 **1** **Young Love** *Sonny James* (1)
JY: 1
4. 2/16 **6** **Young Love** *Tab Hunter* (1)
TP: 6 / JY: 6 / JB: 5↕ / BS: 4
5. 3/30 **3** **Butterfly** *Andy Williams* (1)
TP: 3 / JY: 2
6. 3/30 **1** **Party Doll** *Buddy Knox* (1)
BS: 1
7. 4/6 **2** **Round And Round** *Perry Como* (13 of 14)
JY: 2 / BS: 1 / TP: 1
8. 4/13 **9** **All Shook Up** *Elvis Presley* (7 of 18)
JB: 9 / BS: 8 / TP: 8 / JY: 7
9. 4/13 **2** **Butterfly** *Charlie Gracie* (1)
JB: 2
10. 6/3 **7** **Love Letters In The Sand** *Pat Boone* (4 of 6)
JY: 7 / BS: 5 / TP: 5

6/17/57: Billboard's last "Juke Box" chart.

11. 7/8 **7** **(Let Me Be Your) Teddy Bear** *Elvis Presley* (8 of 18)
BS: 7 / TP: 7 / JY: 3
12. 8/19 **5** **Tammy** *Debbie Reynolds* (1)
TP: 5 / JY: 5 / BS: 3↕
13. 9/9 **1** **Diana** *Paul Anka* (1 of 3)
BS: 1
14. 9/23 **4** **Honeycomb** *Jimmie Rodgers* (1)
JY: 4 / BS: 2 / TP: 2
15. 9/23 **1** **That'll Be The Day** *The Crickets* (1)
BS: 1
16. 10/14 **4** **Wake Up Little Susie** *The Everly Brothers* (1 of 4)
JY: 4 / TP: 2 / BS: 1
17. 10/21 **7** **Jailhouse Rock** *Elvis Presley* (9 of 18)
BS: 7↕ / TP: 6 / JY: 2
18. 10/21 **1** **Chances Are** *Johnny Mathis* (1 of 2)
JY: 1
19. 12/2 **3** **You Send Me** *Sam Cooke* (1)
TP: 3 / BS: 2 / JY: 1

#1 HITS

1957 (cont'd)

20. 12/16 6 **April Love** *Pat Boone* (5 of 6)
JY: 6 / BS: 2 / TP: 1

DATE WKS 1958

1. 1/6 7 **At The Hop** *Danny & The Juniors* (1)
TP: 7 / BS: 5 / JY: 3
2. 2/10 5 **Don't** *Elvis Presley* (10 of 18)
BS: 5 / TP: 1 / JY: 1
3. 2/17 4 **Sugartime** *The McGuire Sisters* (2 of 2)
JY: 4
4. 2/24 2 **Get A Job** *The Silhouettes* (1)
TP: 2
5. 3/17 5 **Tequila** *The Champs* (1)
BS: 5 / TP: 5 / JY: 2
6. 3/24 1 **Catch A Falling Star** *Perry Como* (14 of 14)
JY: 1
7. 4/14 4 **He's Got The Whole World (In His Hands)** *Laurie London* (1)
JY: 4
8. 4/21 1 **Twilight Time** *The Platters* (3 of 4)
BS: 1 / TP: 1 / JY: 1
9. 4/28 3 **Witch Doctor** *David Seville* (1 of 2)
TP: 3 / BS: 2
10. 5/12 5 **All I Have To Do Is Dream** *The Everly Brothers* (2 of 4)
JY: 5 / BS: 4 / TP: 3
11. 6/9 6 **The Purple People Eater** *Sheb Wooley* (1)
BS: 6 / TP: 6 / JY: 4
12. 7/21 2 **Hard Headed Woman** *Elvis Presley* (11 of 18)
BS: 2 / JY: 1
13. 7/21 1 **Yakety Yak** *The Coasters* (1)
TP: 1
14. 7/28 1 **Patricia** *Perez Prado* (2 of 2)
TP: 1 / JY: 1

7/28/58: Billboard's last "Jockeys" and "Top 100" charts.

8/4/58: Billboard's "Hot 100" chart debuts.

15. 8/4 2 **Poor Little Fool** *Ricky Nelson* (1 of 2)
HT: 2 / BS: 2
16. 8/18 5 **Nel Blu Dipinto Di Blu (Volare)** *Domenico Modugno* (1)
HT: 5↕ / BS: 5↕
17. 8/25 1 **Little Star** *The Elegants* (1)
HT: 1
18. 8/25 1 **Bird Dog** *The Everly Brothers* (3 of 4)
BS: 1
19. 9/29 6 **It's All In The Game** *Tommy Edwards* (1)
HT: 6 / BS: 3

10/13/58: Billboard's last "Best Sellers" chart.

20. 11/10 2↕ **It's Only Make Believe** *Conway Twitty* (1)
21. 11/17 1 **Tom Dooley** *The Kingston Trio* (1)
22. 12/1 3 **To Know Him, Is To Love Him** *The Teddy Bears* (1)
23. 12/22 4 **The Chipmunk Song** *David Seville* (2 of 2) & *The Chipmunks* (1)

DATE WKS 1959

1. 1/19 3 **Smoke Gets In Your Eyes** *The Platters* (4 of 4)
2. 2/9 4 **Stagger Lee** *Lloyd Price* (1)
3. 3/9 5 **Venus** *Frankie Avalon* (1 of 2)
4. 4/13 4 **Come Softly To Me** *Fleetwoods* (1 of 2)
5. 5/11 1 **The Happy Organ** *Dave 'Baby' Cortez* (1)
6. 5/18 2 **Kansas City** *Wilbert Harrison* (1)
7. 6/1 6 **The Battle Of New Orleans** *Johnny Horton* (1)
8. 7/13 4 **Lonely Boy** *Paul Anka* (2 of 3)
9. 8/10 2 **A Big Hunk O' Love** *Elvis Presley* (12 of 18)
10. 8/24 4 **The Three Bells** *The Browns* (1)
11. 9/21 2 **Sleep Walk** *Santo & Johnny* (1)
12. 10/5 9↕ **Mack The Knife** *Bobby Darin* (1)
13. 11/16 1 **Mr. Blue** *The Fleetwoods* (2 of 2)
14. 12/14 2 **Heartaches By The Number** *Guy Mitchell* (2 of 2)
15. 12/28 1 **Why** *Frankie Avalon* (2 of 2)

DATE WKS 1960

1. 1/4 2 **El Paso** *Marty Robbins* (1)
2. 1/18 3 **Running Bear** *Johnny Preston* (1)
3. 2/8 2 **Teen Angel** *Mark Dinning* (1)
4. 2/22 9 **The Theme From "A Summer Place"** *Percy Faith* (3 of 3)
5. 4/25 4 **Stuck On You** *Elvis Presley* (13 of 18)
6. 5/23 5 **Cathy's Clown** *The Everly Brothers* (4 of 4)
7. 6/27 2 **Everybody's Somebody's Fool** *Connie Francis* (1 of 3)
8. 7/11 1 **Alley-Oop** *Hollywood Argyles* (1)
9. 7/18 3 **I'm Sorry** *Brenda Lee* (1 of 2)
10. 8/8 1 **Itsy Bitsy Teenie Weenie Yellow Polkadot Bikini** *Brian Hyland* (1)
11. 8/15 5 **It's Now Or Never** *Elvis Presley* (14 of 18)
12. 9/19 1 **The Twist** *Chubby Checker* (1 of 3)
re-entered #1 position on 1/13/62
13. 9/26 2 **My Heart Has A Mind Of Its Own** *Connie Francis* (2 of 3)
14. 10/10 1 **Mr. Custer** *Larry Verne* (1)
15. 10/17 3↕ **Save The Last Dance For Me** *The Drifters* (1)
16. 10/24 1 **I Want To Be Wanted** *Brenda Lee* (2 of 2)
17. 11/14 1 **Georgia On My Mind** *Ray Charles* (1 of 3)
18. 11/21 1 **Stay** *Maurice Williams & The Zodiacs* (1)
19. 11/28 6 **Are You Lonesome To-night?** *Elvis Presley* (15 of 18)

DATE WKS 1961

1. 1/9 3 **Wonderland By Night** *Bert Kaempfert* (1)
2. 1/30 2 **Will You Love Me Tomorrow** *The Shirelles* (1 of 2)
3. 2/13 2 **Calcutta** *Lawrence Welk* (1)
4. 2/27 3 **Pony Time** *Chubby Checker* (2 of 3)
5. 3/20 2 **Surrender** *Elvis Presley* (16 of 18)
6. 4/3 3 **Blue Moon** *The Marcels* (1)
7. 4/24 4 **Runaway** *Del Shannon* (1)

1961 (cont'd)

8. 5/22 1 **Mother-In-Law** *Ernie K-Doe* (1)
9. 5/29 2↕ **Travelin' Man** *Ricky Nelson* (2 of 2)
10. 6/5 1 **Running Scared** *Roy Orbison* (1 of 2)
11. 6/19 1 **Moody River** *Pat Boone* (6 of 6)
12. 6/26 2 **Quarter To Three** *U.S. Bonds* (1)
13. 7/10 7 **Tossin' And Turnin'** *Bobby Lewis* (1)
14. 8/28 1 **Wooden Heart** *Joe Dowell* (1)
15. 9/4 2 **Michael** *The Highwaymen* (1)
16. 9/18 3 **Take Good Care Of My Baby** *Bobby Vee* (1)
17. 10/9 2 **Hit The Road Jack** *Ray Charles* (2 of 3)
18. 10/23 2 **Runaround Sue** *Dion* (1)
19. 11/6 5 **Big Bad John** *Jimmy Dean* (1)
20. 12/11 1 **Please Mr. Postman** *The Marvelettes* (1)
21. 12/18 3 **The Lion Sleeps Tonight** *The Tokens* (1)

DATE WKS 1962

1. 1/13 2 **The Twist** *Chubby Checker* (3 of 3)
first entered #1 position on 9/19/60
2. 1/27 3 **Peppermint Twist - Part I** *Joey Dee & the Starliters* (1)
3. 2/17 3 **Duke Of Earl** *Gene Chandler* (1)
4. 3/10 3 **Hey! Baby** *Bruce Channel* (1)
5. 3/31 1 **Don't Break The Heart That Loves You** *Connie Francis* (3 of 3)
6. 4/7 2 **Johnny Angel** *Shelley Fabares* (1)
7. 4/21 2 **Good Luck Charm** *Elvis Presley* (17 of 18)
8. 5/5 3 **Soldier Boy** *The Shirelles* (2 of 2)
9. 5/26 1 **Stranger On The Shore** *Mr. Acker Bilk* (1)
10. 6/2 5 **I Can't Stop Loving You** *Ray Charles* (3 of 3)
11. 7/7 1 **The Stripper** *David Rose* (1)
12. 7/14 4 **Roses Are Red (My Love)** ***Bobby Vinton*** (1 of 4)
13. 8/11 2 **Breaking Up Is Hard To Do** *Neil Sedaka* (1 of 3)
14. 8/25 1 **The Loco-Motion** *Little Eva* (1)
15. 9/1 2 **Sheila** *Tommy Roe* (1 of 2)
16. 9/15 5 **Sherry** ***The 4 Seasons*** (1 of 5)
17. 10/20 2 **Monster Mash** *Bobby "Boris" Pickett & The Crypt-Kickers* (1)
18. 11/3 2 **He's A Rebel** *The Crystals* (1)
19. 11/17 5 **Big Girls Don't Cry** *The 4 Seasons* (2 of 5)
20. 12/22 3 **Telstar** *The Tornadoes* (1)

DATE WKS 1963

1. 1/12 2 **Go Away Little Girl** *Steve Lawrence* (1)
2. 1/26 2 **Walk Right In** *The Rooftop Singers* (1)
3. 2/9 3 **Hey Paula** *Paul & Paula* (1)
4. 3/2 3 **Walk Like A Man** *The 4 Seasons* (3 of 5)
5. 3/23 1 **Our Day Will Come** *Ruby & The Romantics* (1)
6. 3/30 4 **He's So Fine** *The Chiffons* (1)
7. 4/27 3 **I Will Follow Him** *Little Peggy March* (1)
8. 5/18 2 **If You Wanna Be Happy** *Jimmy Soul* (1)
9. 6/1 2 **It's My Party** *Lesley Gore* (1)
10. 6/15 3 **Sukiyaki** *Kyu Sakamoto* (1)
11. 7/6 2 **Easier Said Than Done** *The Essex* (1)

1963 (cont'd)

12. 7/20 2 **Surf City** *Jan & Dean* (1)
13. 8/3 1 **So Much In Love** *The Tymes* (1)
14. 8/10 3 **Fingertips - Pt 2** ***Little Stevie Wonder*** (1 of 10)
15. 8/31 3 **My Boyfriend's Back** *The Angels* (1)
16. 9/21 3 **Blue Velvet** *Bobby Vinton* (2 of 4)
17. 10/12 5 **Sugar Shack** *Jimmy Gilmer & The Fireballs* (1)
18. 11/16 1 **Deep Purple** *Nino Tempo & April Stevens* (1)
19. 11/23 2 **I'm Leaving It Up To You** *Dale & Grace* (1)
20. 12/7 4 **Dominique** *The Singing Nun* (1)

DATE WKS 1964

1. 1/4 4 **There! I've Said It Again** *Bobby Vinton* (3 of 4)
2. 2/1 7 **I Want To Hold Your Hand** ***The Beatles*** (1 of 20)
3. 3/21 2 **She Loves You** *The Beatles* (2 of 20)
4. 4/4 5 **Can't Buy Me Love** *The Beatles* (3 of 20)
5. 5/9 1 **Hello, Dolly!** *Louis Armstrong* (2 of 2)
Armstrong's first #1 was "All Of Me" in 1932
6. 5/16 2 **My Guy** *Mary Wells* (1)
7. 5/30 1 **Love Me Do** *The Beatles* (4 of 20)
8. 6/6 3 **Chapel Of Love** *The Dixie Cups* (1)
9. 6/27 1 **A World Without Love** *Peter & Gordon* (1)
10. 7/4 2 **I Get Around** ***The Beach Boys*** (1 of 4)
11. 7/18 2 **Rag Doll** *The 4 Seasons* (4 of 5)
12. 8/1 2 **A Hard Day's Night** *The Beatles* (5 of 20)
13. 8/15 1 **Everybody Loves Somebody** *Dean Martin* (2 of 2)
14. 8/22 2 **Where Did Our Love Go** ***The Supremes*** (1 of 12)
15. 9/5 3 **The House Of The Rising Sun** *The Animals* (1)
16. 9/26 3 **Oh, Pretty Woman** *Roy Orbison* (2 of 2)
17. 10/17 2 **Do Wah Diddy Diddy** *Manfred Mann* (1 of 2)
18. 10/31 4 **Baby Love** *The Supremes* (2 of 12)
19. 11/28 1 **Leader Of The Pack** *The Shangri-Las* (1)
20. 12/5 1 **Ringo** *Lorne Greene* (1)
21. 12/12 1 **Mr. Lonely** *Bobby Vinton* (4 of 4)
22. 12/19 2↕ **Come See About Me** *The Supremes* (3 of 12)
23. 12/26 3 **I Feel Fine** *The Beatles* (6 of 20)

DATE WKS 1965

1. 1/23 2 **Downtown** *Petula Clark* (1 of 2)
2. 2/6 2 **You've Lost That Lovin' Feelin'** *The Righteous Brothers* (1 of 2)
3. 2/20 2 **This Diamond Ring** *Gary Lewis & The Playboys* (1)
4. 3/6 1 **My Girl** ***The Temptations*** (1 of 4)
5. 3/13 2 **Eight Days A Week** *The Beatles* (7 of 20)
6. 3/27 2 **Stop! In The Name Of Love** *The Supremes* (4 of 12)
7. 4/10 2 **I'm Telling You Now** *Freddie & The Dreamers* (1)

#1 HITS

1965 (cont'd)

8. 4/24 1 **Game Of Love** *Wayne Fontana & The Mindbenders* (1)
9. 5/1 3 **Mrs. Brown You've Got A Lovely Daughter** *Herman's Hermits* (1 of 2)
10. 5/22 1 **Ticket To Ride** *The Beatles* (8 of 20)
11. 5/29 2 **Help Me, Rhonda** *The Beach Boys* (2 of 4)
12. 6/12 1 **Back In My Arms Again** *The Supremes* (5 of 12)
13. 6/19 2↕ **I Can't Help Myself** *Four Tops* (1 of 2)
14. 6/26 1 **Mr. Tambourine Man** *The Byrds* (1 of 2)
15. 7/10 4 **(I Can't Get No) Satisfaction** ***The Rolling Stones*** (1 of 8)
16. 8/7 1 **I'm Henry VIII, I Am** *Herman's Hermits* (2 of 2)
17. 8/14 3 **I Got You Babe** *Sonny & Cher* (1)
   see 11/6/71 for Cher's solo #1 total
18. 9/4 3 **Help!** *The Beatles* (9 of 20)
19. 9/25 1 **Eve Of Destruction** *Barry McGuire* (1)
20. 10/2 1 **Hang On Sloopy** *The McCoys* (1)
21. 10/9 4 **Yesterday** *The Beatles* (10 of 20)
22. 11/6 2 **Get Off Of My Cloud** *The Rolling Stones* (2 of 8)
23. 11/20 2 **I Hear A Symphony** *The Supremes* (6 of 12)
24. 12/4 3 **Turn! Turn! Turn! (To Everything There Is A Season)** *The Byrds* (2 of 2)
25. 12/25 1 **Over And Over** *The Dave Clark Five* (1)

DATE WKS 1966

1. 1/1 2↕ **The Sounds Of Silence** *Simon & Garfunkel* (1 of 3)
   Simon had a solo #1 on 2/7/76
2. 1/8 3↕ **We Can Work It Out** *The Beatles* (11 of 20)
3. 2/5 2 **My Love** *Petula Clark* (2 of 2)
4. 2/19 1 **Lightnin' Strikes** *Lou Christie* (1)
5. 2/26 1 **These Boots Are Made For Walkin'** *Nancy Sinatra* (1 of 2)
6. 3/5 5 **The Ballad Of The Green Berets** *SSgt Barry Sadler* (1)
7. 4/9 3 **(You're My) Soul And Inspiration** *The Righteous Brothers* (2 of 2)
8. 4/30 1 **Good Lovin'** *The Young Rascals* (1 of 3)
9. 5/7 3 **Monday, Monday** *The Mama's & The Papa's* (1)
10. 5/28 2 **When A Man Loves A Woman** *Percy Sledge* (1)
11. 6/11 2 **Paint It, Black** *The Rolling Stones* (3 of 8)
12. 6/25 2↕ **Paperback Writer** *The Beatles* (12 of 20)
13. 7/2 1 **Strangers In The Night** *Frank Sinatra* (5 of 6)
14. 7/16 2 **Hanky Panky** *Tommy James & The Shondells* (1 of 2)
15. 7/30 2 **Wild Thing** *The Troggs* (1)
16. 8/13 3 **Summer In The City** *The Lovin' Spoonful* (1)
17. 9/3 1 **Sunshine Superman** *Donovan* (1)
18. 9/10 2 **You Can't Hurry Love** *The Supremes* (7 of 12)
19. 9/24 3 **Cherish** *The Association* (1 of 2)
20. 10/15 2 **Reach Out I'll Be There** *Four Tops* (2 of 2)

1966 (cont'd)

21. 10/29 1 **96 Tears** *? & The Mysterians* (1)
22. 11/5 1 **Last Train To Clarksville** *The Monkees* (1 of 3)
23. 11/12 1 **Poor Side Of Town** *Johnny Rivers* (1)
24. 11/19 2 **You Keep Me Hangin' On** *The Supremes* (8 of 12)
25. 12/3 3↕ **Winchester Cathedral** *The New Vaudeville Band* (1)
26. 12/10 1 **Good Vibrations** *The Beach Boys* (3 of 4)
27. 12/31 7 **I'm A Believer** *The Monkees* (2 of 3)

DATE WKS 1967

1. 2/18 2 **Kind Of A Drag** *The Buckinghams* (1)
2. 3/4 1 **Ruby Tuesday** *The Rolling Stones* (4 of 8)
3. 3/11 1 **Love Is Here And Now You're Gone** *The Supremes* (9 of 12)
4. 3/18 1 **Penny Lane** *The Beatles* (13 of 20)
5. 3/25 3 **Happy Together** *The Turtles* (1)
6. 4/15 4 **Somethin' Stupid** *Nancy Sinatra* (2 of 2) & *Frank Sinatra* (6 of 6)
7. 5/13 1 **The Happening** *The Supremes* (10 of 12)
8. 5/20 4↕ **Groovin'** *The Young Rascals* (2 of 3)
9. 6/3 2 **Respect** *Aretha Franklin* (1 of 2)
10. 7/1 4 **Windy** *The Association* (2 of 2)
11. 7/29 3 **Light My Fire** *The Doors* (1 of 2)
12. 8/19 1 **All You Need Is Love** *The Beatles* (14 of 20)
13. 8/26 4 **Ode To Billie Joe** *Bobbie Gentry* (1)
14. 9/23 4 **The Letter** *The Box Tops* (1)
15. 10/21 5 **To Sir With Love** *Lulu* (1)
16. 11/25 1 **Incense And Peppermints** *Strawberry Alarm Clock* (1)
17. 12/2 4 **Daydream Believer** *The Monkees* (3 of 3)
18. 12/30 3 **Hello Goodbye** *The Beatles* (15 of 20)

DATE WKS 1968

1. 1/20 2 **Judy In Disguise (With Glasses)** *John Fred & His Playboy Band* (1)
2. 2/3 1 **Green Tambourine** *The Lemon Pipers* (1)
3. 2/10 5 **Love Is Blue** *Paul Mauriat* (1)
4. 3/16 4 **(Sittin' On) The Dock Of The Bay** *Otis Redding* (1)
5. 4/13 5 **Honey** *Bobby Goldsboro* (1)
6. 5/18 2 **Tighten Up** *Archie Bell & The Drells* (1)
7. 6/1 3 **Mrs. Robinson** *Simon & Garfunkel* (2 of 3)
8. 6/22 4 **This Guy's In Love With You** *Herb Alpert* (1 of 2)
9. 7/20 2 **Grazing In The Grass** *Hugh Masekela* (1)
10. 8/3 2 **Hello, I Love You** *The Doors* (2 of 2)
11. 8/17 5 **People Got To Be Free** *The Rascals* (3 of 3)
12. 9/21 1 **Harper Valley P.T.A.** *Jeannie C. Riley* (1)
13. 9/28 9 **Hey Jude** *The Beatles* (16 of 20)
14. 11/30 2 **Love Child** *Diana Ross & The Supremes* (11 of 12)
15. 12/14 7 **I Heard It Through The Grapevine** *Marvin Gaye* (1 of 3)

#1 HITS

1969

#	DATE	WKS	Title / Artist
1.	2/1	2	**Crimson And Clover** *Tommy James & The Shondells* (2 of 2)
2.	2/15	4	**Everyday People** *Sly & The Family Stone* (1 of 3)
3.	3/15	4	**Dizzy** *Tommy Roe* (2 of 2)
4.	4/12	6	**Aquarius/Let The Sunshine In (The Flesh Failures)** *The 5th Dimension* (1 of 2)
5.	5/24	5	**Get Back** *The Beatles* (17 of 20)
6.	6/28	2	**Love Theme From Romeo & Juliet** *Henry Mancini* (1)
7.	7/12	6	**In The Year 2525 (Exordium & Terminus)** *Zager & Evans* (1)
8.	8/23	4	**Honky Tonk Women** *The Rolling Stones* (5 of 8)
9.	9/20	4	**Sugar, Sugar** *The Archies* (1)
10.	10/18	2	**I Can't Get Next To You** *The Temptations* (2 of 4)
11.	11/1	1	**Suspicious Minds** *Elvis Presley* (18 of 18)
12.	11/8	3	**Wedding Bell Blues** *The 5th Dimension* (2 of 2)
13.	11/29	1	**Come Together** *The Beatles* (18 of 20)
14.	12/6	2	**Na Na Hey Hey Kiss Him Goodbye** *Steam* (1)
15.	12/20	1	**Leaving On A Jet Plane** *Peter, Paul & Mary* (1)
16.	12/27	1	**Someday We'll Be Together** *Diana Ross & The Supremes* (12 of 12) see 9/19/70 for Ross's solo #1 total

1970

#	DATE	WKS	Title / Artist
1.	1/3	4	**Raindrops Keep Fallin' On My Head** *B.J. Thomas* (1 of 2)
2.	1/31	1	**I Want You Back** *The Jackson 5* (1 of 4)
3.	2/7	1	**Venus** *The Shocking Blue* (1)
4.	2/14	2	**Thank You (Falettinme Be Mice Elf Agin)** *Sly & The Family Stone* (2 of 3)
5.	2/28	6	**Bridge Over Troubled Water** *Simon & Garfunkel* (3 of 3)
6.	4/11	2	**Let It Be** *The Beatles* (19 of 20)
7.	4/25	2	**ABC** *The Jackson 5* (2 of 4)
8.	5/9	3	**American Woman** *The Guess Who* (1)
9.	5/30	2	**Everything Is Beautiful** *Ray Stevens* (1 of 2)
10.	6/13	2	**The Long And Winding Road** *The Beatles* (20 of 20)
11.	6/27	2	**The Love You Save** *The Jackson 5* (3 of 4)
12.	7/11	2	**Mama Told Me (Not To Come)** *Three Dog Night* (1 of 3)
13.	7/25	4	**(They Long To Be) Close To You** *Carpenters* (1 of 3)
14.	8/22	1	**Make It With You** *Bread* (1)
15.	8/29	3	**War** *Edwin Starr* (1)
16.	9/19	3	**Ain't No Mountain High Enough** *Diana Ross* (1 of 6)
17.	10/10	1	**Cracklin' Rosie** *Neil Diamond* (1 of 3)
18.	10/17	5	**I'll Be There** *The Jackson 5* (4 of 4)
19.	11/21	3	**I Think I Love You** *The Partridge Family* (1)

1970 (cont'd)

#	DATE	WKS	Title / Artist
20.	12/12	2	**The Tears Of A Clown** *Smokey Robinson & The Miracles* (1 of 2)
21.	12/26	4	**My Sweet Lord** *George Harrison* (1 of 3)

1971

#	DATE	WKS	Title / Artist
1.	1/23	3	**Knock Three Times** *Dawn* (1 of 3)
2.	2/13	5	**One Bad Apple** *The Osmonds* (1)
3.	3/20	2	**Me And Bobby McGee** *Janis Joplin* (1)
4.	4/3	2	**Just My Imagination (Running Away With Me)** *The Temptations* (3 of 4)
5.	4/17	6	**Joy To The World** *Three Dog Night* (2 of 3)
6.	5/29	2	**Brown Sugar** *The Rolling Stones* (6 of 8)
7.	6/12	1	**Want Ads** *The Honey Cone* (1)
8.	6/19	5	**It's Too Late** *Carole King* (1)
9.	7/24	1	**Indian Reservation** *Raiders* (1)
10.	7/31	1	**You've Got A Friend** *James Taylor* (1)
11.	8/7	4	**How Can You Mend A Broken Heart** *The Bee Gees* (1 of 9)
12.	9/4	1	**Uncle Albert/Admiral Halsey** *Paul McCartney* (1 of 9)
13.	9/11	3	**Go Away Little Girl** *Donny Osmond* (1)
14.	10/2	5	**Maggie May** *Rod Stewart* (1 of 4)
15.	11/6	2	**Gypsys, Tramps & Thieves** *Cher* (1 of 4)
16.	11/20	2	**Theme From Shaft** *Isaac Hayes* (1)
17.	12/4	3	**Family Affair** *Sly & The Family Stone* (3 of 3)
18.	12/25	3	**Brand New Key** *Melanie* (1)

1972

#	DATE	WKS	Title / Artist
1.	1/15	4	**American Pie - Parts I & II** *Don McLean* (1)
2.	2/12	1	**Let's Stay Together** *Al Green* (1)
3.	2/19	4	**Without You** *Nilsson* (1)
4.	3/18	1	**Heart Of Gold** *Neil Young* (1)
5.	3/25	3	**A Horse With No Name** *America* (1 of 2)
6.	4/15	6	**The First Time Ever I Saw Your Face** *Roberta Flack* (1 of 3)
7.	5/27	1	**Oh Girl** *Chi-Lites* (1)
8.	6/3	1	**I'll Take You There** *The Staple Singers* (1 of 2)
9.	6/10	3	**The Candy Man** *Sammy Davis, Jr.* (1)
10.	7/1	1	**Song Sung Blue** *Neil Diamond* (2 of 3)
11.	7/8	3	**Lean On Me** *Bill Withers* (1)
12.	7/29	6↕	**Alone Again (Naturally)** *Gilbert O'Sullivan* (1)
13.	8/26	1	**Brandy (You're A Fine Girl)** *Looking Glass* (1)
14.	9/16	1	**Black & White** *Three Dog Night* (3 of 3)
15.	9/23	3	**Baby Don't Get Hooked On Me** *Mac Davis* (1)
16.	10/14	1	**Ben** *Michael Jackson* (1 of 13)
17.	10/21	2	**My Ding-A-Ling** *Chuck Berry* (1)
18.	11/4	4	**I Can See Clearly Now** *Johnny Nash* (1)
19.	12/2	1	**Papa Was A Rollin' Stone** *The Temptations* (4 of 4)
20.	12/9	1	**I Am Woman** *Helen Reddy* (1 of 3)
21.	12/16	3	**Me And Mrs. Jones** *Billy Paul* (1)

#1 HITS

1973

	DATE	WKS	
1.	1/6	3	**You're So Vain** *Carly Simon* (1)
2.	1/27	1	**Superstition** *Stevie Wonder* (2 of 10)
3.	2/3	3	**Crocodile Rock** *Elton John* (1 of 9)
4.	2/24	5↕	**Killing Me Softly With His Song** *Roberta Flack* (2 of 3)
5.	3/24	1	**Love Train** *O'Jays* (1)
6.	4/7	2	**The Night The Lights Went Out In Georgia** *Vicki Lawrence* (1)
7.	4/21	4	**Tie A Yellow Ribbon Round The Ole Oak Tree** *Dawn Featuring Tony Orlando* (2 of 3)
8.	5/19	1	**You Are The Sunshine Of My Life** *Stevie Wonder* (3 of 10)
9.	5/26	1	**Frankenstein** *The Edgar Winter Group* (1)
10.	6/2	4	**My Love** *Paul McCartney & Wings* (2 of 9)
11.	6/30	1	**Give Me Love - (Give Me Peace On Earth)** *George Harrison* (2 of 3)
12.	7/7	2	**Will It Go Round In Circles** *Billy Preston* (1 of 2)
13.	7/21	2	**Bad, Bad Leroy Brown** *Jim Croce* (1 of 2)
14.	8/4	2	**The Morning After** *Maureen McGovern* (1)
15.	8/18	1	**Touch Me In The Morning** *Diana Ross* (2 of 6)
16.	8/25	2	**Brother Louie** *Stories* (1)
17.	9/8	2↕	**Let's Get It On** *Marvin Gaye* (2 of 3)
18.	9/15	1	**Delta Dawn** *Helen Reddy* (2 of 3)
19.	9/29	1	**We're An American Band** *Grand Funk* (1 of 2)
20.	10/6	2	**Half-Breed** *Cher* (2 of 4)
21.	10/20	1	**Angie** *The Rolling Stones* (7 of 8)
22.	10/27	2	**Midnight Train To Georgia** *Gladys Knight & The Pips* (1 of 2)
23.	11/10	2	**Keep On Truckin' (Part 1)** *Eddie Kendricks* (1)
24.	11/24	1	**Photograph** *Ringo Starr* (1 of 2)
25.	12/1	2	**Top Of The World** *Carpenters* (2 of 3)
26.	12/15	2	**The Most Beautiful Girl** *Charlie Rich* (1)
27.	12/29	2	**Time In A Bottle** *Jim Croce* (2 of 2)

1974

	DATE	WKS	
1.	1/12	1	**The Joker** *Steve Miller Band* (1 of 3)
2.	1/19	1	**Show And Tell** *Al Wilson* (1)
3.	1/26	1	**You're Sixteen** *Ringo Starr* (2 of 2)
4.	2/2	3↕	**The Way We Were** *Barbra Streisand* (1 of 5)
5.	2/9	1	**Love's Theme** *Love Unlimited Orchestra* (1)
6.	3/2	3	**Seasons In The Sun** *Terry Jacks* (1)
7.	3/23	1	**Dark Lady** *Cher* (3 of 4)
8.	3/30	1	**Sunshine On My Shoulders** *John Denver* (1 of 4)
9.	4/6	1	**Hooked On A Feeling** *Blue Swede* (1)
10.	4/13	1	**Bennie And The Jets** *Elton John* (2 of 9)
11.	4/20	2	**TSOP (The Sound Of Philadelphia)** *MFSB* (1) *feat. The Three Degrees* (1)
12.	5/4	2	**The Loco-Motion** *Grand Funk* (2 of 2)
13.	5/18	3	**The Streak** *Ray Stevens* (2 of 2)
14.	6/8	1	**Band On The Run** *Paul McCartney & Wings* (3 of 9)

1974 (cont'd)

	DATE	WKS	
15.	6/15	2	**Billy, Don't Be A Hero** *Bo Donaldson & The Heywoods* (1)
16.	6/29	1	**Sundown** *Gordon Lightfoot* (1)
17.	7/6	1	**Rock The Boat** *The Hues Corporation* (1)
18.	7/13	2	**Rock Your Baby** *George McCrae* (1)
19.	7/27	2	**Annie's Song** *John Denver* (2 of 4)
20.	8/10	1	**Feel Like Makin' Love** *Roberta Flack* (3 of 3)
21.	8/17	1	**The Night Chicago Died** *Paper Lace* (1)
22.	8/24	3	**(You're) Having My Baby** *Paul Anka* (3 of 3)
23.	9/14	1	**I Shot The Sheriff** *Eric Clapton* (1)
24.	9/21	1	**Can't Get Enough Of Your Love, Babe** *Barry White* (1)
25.	9/28	1	**Rock Me Gently** *Andy Kim* (1)
26.	10/5	2	**I Honestly Love You** *Olivia Newton-John* (1 of 5)
27.	10/19	1	**Nothing From Nothing** *Billy Preston* (2 of 2)
28.	10/26	1	**Then Came You** *Dionne Warwicke* (1 of 2) *& Spinners* (1)
29.	11/2	1	**You Haven't Done Nothin** *Stevie Wonder* (4 of 10)
30.	11/9	1	**You Ain't Seen Nothing Yet** *Bachman-Turner Overdrive* (1)
31.	11/16	1	**Whatever Gets You Thru The Night** *John Lennon/Plastic Ono Band* (1 of 2)
32.	11/23	2	**I Can Help** *Billy Swan* (1)
33.	12/7	2	**Kung Fu Fighting** *Carl Douglas* (1)
34.	12/21	1	**Cat's In The Cradle** *Harry Chapin* (1)
35.	12/28	1	**Angie Baby** *Helen Reddy* (3 of 3)

1975

	DATE	WKS	
1.	1/4	2	**Lucy In The Sky With Diamonds** *Elton John* (3 of 9)
2.	1/18	1	**Mandy** *Barry Manilow* (1 of 3)
3.	1/25	1	**Please Mr. Postman** *Carpenters* (3 of 3)
4.	2/1	1	**Laughter In The Rain** *Neil Sedaka* (2 of 3)
5.	2/8	1	**Fire** *Ohio Players* (1 of 2)
6.	2/15	1	**You're No Good** *Linda Ronstadt* (1)
7.	2/22	1	**Pick Up The Pieces** *AWB* (1)
8.	3/1	1	**Best Of My Love** *Eagles* (1 of 5)
9.	3/8	1	**Have You Never Been Mellow** *Olivia Newton-John* (2 of 5)
10.	3/15	1	**Black Water** *The Doobie Brothers* (1 of 2)
11.	3/22	1	**My Eyes Adored You** *Frankie Valli* (1 of 2)
12.	3/29	1	**Lady Marmalade** *LaBelle* (1 of 2) total includes Patti LaBelle's #1 hit on 6/14/86
13.	4/5	1	**Lovin' You** *Minnie Riperton* (1)
14.	4/12	2	**Philadelphia Freedom** *The Elton John Band* (4 of 9)
15.	4/26	1	**(Hey Won't You Play) Another Somebody Done Somebody Wrong Song** *B.J. Thomas* (2 of 2)
16.	5/3	3	**He Don't Love You (Like I Love You)** *Tony Orlando & Dawn* (3 of 3)
17.	5/24	1	**Shining Star** *Earth, Wind & Fire* (1)
18.	5/31	1	**Before The Next Teardrop Falls** *Freddy Fender* (1)

1975 (cont'd)

	DATE	WKS	Title / Artist
19.	6/7	1	**Thank God I'm A Country Boy** *John Denver* (3 of 4)
20.	6/14	1	**Sister Golden Hair** *America* (2 of 2)
21.	6/21	4	**Love Will Keep Us Together** *The Captain & Tennille* (1 of 2)
22.	7/19	1	**Listen To What The Man Said** *Wings (Paul McCartney)* (4 of 9)
23.	7/26	1	**The Hustle** *Van McCoy/The Soul City Symphony* (1)
24.	8/2	1	**One Of These Nights** *Eagles* (2 of 5)
25.	8/9	2	**Jive Talkin'** *Bee Gees* (2 of 9)
26.	8/23	1	**Fallin' In Love** *Hamilton, Joe Frank & Reynolds* (1)
27.	8/30	1	**Get Down Tonight** *K.C. & The Sunshine Band* (1 of 5)
28.	9/6	2	**Rhinestone Cowboy** *Glen Campbell* (1 of 2)
29.	9/20	2↕	**Fame** *David Bowie* (1 of 2)
30.	9/27	1	**I'm Sorry** *John Denver* (4 of 4)
31.	10/11	3	**Bad Blood** *Neil Sedaka* (3 of 3)
32.	11/1	3	**Island Girl** *Elton John* (5 of 9)
33.	11/22	2↕	**That's The Way (I Like It)** *KC & The Sunshine Band* (2 of 5)
34.	11/29	3	**Fly, Robin, Fly** *Silver Convention* (1)
35.	12/27	1	**Let's Do It Again** *The Staple Singers* (2 of 2)

1976

	DATE	WKS	Title / Artist
1.	1/3	1	**Saturday Night** *Bay City Rollers* (1)
2.	1/10	1	**Convoy** *C.W. McCall* (1)
3.	1/17	1	**I Write The Songs** *Barry Manilow* (2 of 3)
4.	1/24	1	**Theme From Mahogany (Do You Know Where You're Going To)** *Diana Ross* (3 of 6)
5.	1/31	1	**Love Rollercoaster** *Ohio Players* (2 of 2)
6.	2/7	3	**50 Ways To Leave Your Lover** *Paul Simon* (1)
7.	2/28	1	**Theme From S.W.A.T.** *Rhythm Heritage* (1)
8.	3/6	1	**Love Machine (Part 1)** *The Miracles* (2 of 2)
9.	3/13	3	**December, 1963 (Oh, What a Night)** *The Four Seasons* (5 of 5)
10.	4/3	4	**Disco Lady** *Johnnie Taylor* (1)
11.	5/1	1	**Let Your Love Flow** *Bellamy Brothers* (1)
12.	5/8	1	**Welcome Back** *John Sebastian* (1)
13.	5/15	1	**Boogie Fever** *Sylvers* (1)
14.	5/22	5↕	**Silly Love Songs** *Wings (Paul McCartney)* (5 of 9)
15.	5/29	2	**Love Hangover** *Diana Ross* (4 of 6)
16.	7/10	2	**Afternoon Delight** *Starland Vocal Band* (1)
17.	7/24	2	**Kiss And Say Goodbye** *Manhattans* (1)
18.	8/7	4	**Don't Go Breaking My Heart** *Elton John* (6 of 9) & *Kiki Dee* (1)
19.	9/4	1	**You Should Be Dancing** *Bee Gees* (3 of 9)
20.	9/11	1	**(Shake, Shake, Shake) Shake Your Booty** *KC & The Sunshine Band* (3 of 5)
21.	9/18	3	**Play That Funky Music** *Wild Cherry* (1)
22.	10/9	1	**A Fifth Of Beethoven** *Walter Murphy & The Big Apple Band* (1)

1976 (cont'd)

	DATE	WKS	Title / Artist
23.	10/16	1	**Disco Duck (Part 1)** *Rick Dees & His Cast Of Idiots* (1)
24.	10/23	2	**If You Leave Me Now** *Chicago* (1 of 3)
25.	11/6	1	**Rock'n Me** *Steve Miller* (2 of 3)
26.	11/13	8	**Tonight's The Night (Gonna Be Alright)** *Rod Stewart* (2 of 4)

1977

	DATE	WKS	Title / Artist
1.	1/8	1	**You Don't Have To Be A Star (To Be In My Show)** *Marilyn McCoo & Billy Davis, Jr.* (1)
2.	1/15	1	**You Make Me Feel Like Dancing** *Leo Sayer* (1 of 2)
3.	1/22	1	**I Wish** *Stevie Wonder* (5 of 10)
4.	1/29	1	**Car Wash** *Rose Royce* (1)
5.	2/5	2	**Torn Between Two Lovers** *Mary MacGregor* (1)
6.	2/19	1	**Blinded By The Light** *Manfred Mann's Earth Band* (2 of 2)
7.	2/26	1	**New Kid In Town** *Eagles* (3 of 5)
8.	3/5	3	**Love Theme From "A Star Is Born" (Evergreen)** *Barbra Streisand* (2 of 5)
9.	3/26	2	**Rich Girl** *Daryl Hall & John Oates* (1 of 6)
10.	4/9	1	**Dancing Queen** *Abba* (1)
11.	4/16	1	**Don't Give Up On Us** *David Soul* (1)
12.	4/23	1	**Don't Leave Me This Way** *Thelma Houston* (1)
13.	4/30	1	**Southern Nights** *Glen Campbell* (2 of 2)
14.	5/7	1	**Hotel California** *Eagles* (4 of 5)
15.	5/14	1	**When I Need You** *Leo Sayer* (2 of 2)
16.	5/21	3	**Sir Duke** *Stevie Wonder* (6 of 10)
17.	6/11	1	**I'm Your Boogie Man** *KC & The Sunshine Band* (4 of 5)
18.	6/18	1	**Dreams** *Fleetwood Mac* (1)
19.	6/25	1	**Got To Give It Up (Pt. I)** *Marvin Gaye* (3 of 3)
20.	7/2	1	**Gonna Fly Now** *Bill Conti* (1)
21.	7/9	1	**Undercover Angel** *Alan O'Day* (1)
22.	7/16	1	**Da Doo Ron Ron** *Shaun Cassidy* (1)
23.	7/23	1	**Looks Like We Made It** *Barry Manilow* (3 of 3)
24.	7/30	4↕	**I Just Want To Be Your Everything** *Andy Gibb* (1 of 3)
25.	8/20	5↕	**Best Of My Love** *Emotions* (1)
26.	10/1	2	**Star Wars Theme/Cantina Band** *Meco* (1)
27.	10/15	10	**You Light Up My Life** *Debby Boone* (1)
28.	12/24	3	**How Deep Is Your Love** *Bee Gees* (4 of 9)

1978

	DATE	WKS	Title / Artist
1.	1/14	3	**Baby Come Back** *Player* (1)
2.	2/4	4	**Stayin' Alive** *Bee Gees* (5 of 9)
3.	3/4	2	**(Love Is) Thicker Than Water** *Andy Gibb* (2 of 3)
4.	3/18	8	**Night Fever** *Bee Gees* (6 of 9)
5.	5/13	1	**If I Can't Have You** *Yvonne Elliman* (1)

#1 HITS

1978 (cont'd)

6. 5/20 2 **With A Little Luck** *Wings (Paul McCartney)* (6 of 9)
7. 6/3 1 **Too Much, Too Little, Too Late** *Johnny Mathis* (2 of 2)/*Deniece Williams* (1 of 2)
8. 6/10 1 **You're The One That I Want** *John Travolta* (1) *& Olivia Newton-John* (3 of 5)
9. 6/17 7 **Shadow Dancing** *Andy Gibb* (3 of 3)
10. 8/5 1 **Miss You** *The Rolling Stones* (8 of 8)
11. 8/12 2 **Three Times A Lady** *Commodores* (1 of 2)
12. 8/26 2 **Grease** *Frankie Valli* (2 of 2)
13. 9/9 3 **Boogie Oogie Oogie** *A Taste Of Honey* (1)
14. 9/30 4 **Kiss You All Over** *Exile* (1)
15. 10/28 1 **Hot Child In The City** *Nick Gilder* (1)
16. 11/4 1 **You Needed Me** *Anne Murray* (1)
17. 11/11 3 **MacArthur Park** ***Donna Summer*** (1 of 4)
18. 12/2 2↕ **You Don't Bring Me Flowers** *Barbra Streisand* (3 of 5) *& Neil Diamond* (3 of 3)
19. 12/9 6↕ **Le Freak** *Chic* (1 of 2)

1979

DATE WKS

1. 1/6 2 **Too Much Heaven** *Bee Gees* (7 of 9)
2. 2/10 4 **Da Ya Think I'm Sexy?** *Rod Stewart* (3 of 4)
3. 3/10 3↕ **I Will Survive** *Gloria Gaynor* (1)
4. 3/24 2 **Tragedy** *Bee Gees* (8 of 9)
5. 4/14 1 **What A Fool Believes** *The Doobie Brothers* (2 of 2)
6. 4/21 1 **Knock On Wood** *Amii Stewart* (1)
7. 4/28 1 **Heart Of Glass** ***Blondie*** (1 of 4)
8. 5/5 4 **Reunited** *Peaches & Herb* (1)
9. 6/2 3↕ **Hot Stuff** *Donna Summer* (2 of 4)
10. 6/9 1 **Love You Inside Out** *Bee Gees* (9 of 9)
11. 6/30 2 **Ring My Bell** *Anita Ward* (1)
12. 7/14 5 **Bad Girls** *Donna Summer* (3 of 4)
13. 8/18 1 **Good Times** *Chic* (2 of 2)
14. 8/25 6 **My Sharona** *The Knack* (1)
15. 10/6 1 **Sad Eyes** *Robert John* (1)
16. 10/13 1 **Don't Stop 'Til You Get Enough** *Michael Jackson* (2 of 13)
17. 10/20 2 **Rise** *Herb Alpert* (2 of 2)
18. 11/3 1 **Pop Muzik** *M* (1)
19. 11/10 1 **Heartache Tonight** *Eagles* (5 of 5)
20. 11/17 1 **Still** *Commodores* (2 of 2)
21. 11/24 2 **No More Tears (Enough Is Enough)** *Barbra Streisand* (4 of 5)/*Donna Summer* (4 of 4)
22. 12/8 2 **Babe** *Styx* (1)
23. 12/22 3↕ **Escape (The Pina Colada Song)** *Rupert Holmes* (1)

1980

DATE WKS

1. 1/5 1 **Please Don't Go** *K.C. & The Sunshine Band* (5 of 5)
2. 1/19 4 **Rock With You** *Michael Jackson* (3 of 13)
3. 2/16 1 **Do That To Me One More Time** *The Captain & Tennille* (2 of 2)

1980 (cont'd)

4. 2/23 4 **Crazy Little Thing Called Love** *Queen* (1 of 2)
5. 3/22 4 **Another Brick In The Wall (Part II)** *Pink Floyd* (1)
6. 4/19 6 **Call Me** *Blondie* (2 of 4)
7. 5/31 4 **Funkytown** *Lipps, Inc.* (1)
8. 6/28 3 **Coming Up (Live at Glasgow)** *Paul McCartney & Wings* (7 of 9)
9. 7/19 2 **It's Still Rock And Roll To Me** *Billy Joel* (1 of 3)
10. 8/2 4 **Magic** *Olivia Newton-John* (4 of 5)
11. 8/30 1 **Sailing** *Christopher Cross* (1 of 2)
12. 9/6 4 **Upside Down** *Diana Ross* (5 of 6)
13. 10/4 3 **Another One Bites The Dust** *Queen* (2 of 2)
14. 10/25 3 **Woman In Love** *Barbra Streisand* (5 of 5)
15. 11/15 6 **Lady** *Kenny Rogers* (1 of 2)
16. 12/27 5 **(Just Like) Starting Over** *John Lennon* (2 of 2)

1981

DATE WKS

1. 1/31 1 **The Tide Is High** *Blondie* (3 of 4)
2. 2/7 2 **Celebration** *Kool & The Gang* (1)
3. 2/21 2 **9 To 5** *Dolly Parton* (1 of 2)
4. 2/28 2 **I Love A Rainy Night** *Eddie Rabbitt* (1)
5. 3/21 1 **Keep On Loving You** *REO Speedwagon* (1 of 2)
6. 3/28 2 **Rapture** *Blondie* (4 of 4)
7. 4/11 3 **Kiss On My List** *Daryl Hall & John Oates* (2 of 6)
8. 5/2 2 **Morning Train (Nine To Five)** *Sheena Easton* (1)
9. 5/16 9↕ **Bette Davis Eyes** *Kim Carnes* (1)
10. 6/20 1 **Medley** *Stars on 45* (1)
11. 7/25 1 **The One That You Love** *Air Supply* (1)
12. 8/1 2 **Jessie's Girl** *Rick Springfield* (1)
13. 8/15 9 **Endless Love** *Diana Ross* (6 of 6) *&* ***Lionel Richie*** (1 of 5)
14. 10/17 3 **Arthur's Theme (Best That You Can Do)** *Christopher Cross* (2 of 2)
15. 11/7 2 **Private Eyes** *Daryl Hall & John Oates* (3 of 6)
16. 11/21 10 **Physical** *Olivia Newton-John* (5 of 5)

1982

DATE WKS

1. 1/30 1 **I Can't Go For That (No Can Do)** *Daryl Hall & John Oates* (4 of 6)
2. 2/6 6 **Centerfold** *The J. Geils Band* (1)
3. 3/20 7 **I Love Rock 'N Roll** *Joan Jett & The Blackhearts* (1)
4. 5/8 1 **Chariots Of Fire - Titles** *Vangelis* (1)
5. 5/15 7 **Ebony And Ivory** *Paul McCartney* (8 of 9) *with Stevie Wonder* (7 of 10)
6. 7/3 3 **Don't You Want Me** *The Human League* (1 of 2)
7. 7/24 6 **Eye Of The Tiger** *Survivor* (1)
8. 9/4 2↕ **Abracadabra** *The Steve Miller Band* (3 of 3)
9. 9/11 2 **Hard To Say I'm Sorry** *Chicago* (2 of 3)

#1 HITS

1982 (cont'd)

10. 10/2 4 **Jack & Diane** *John Cougar* (1)
11. 10/30 1 **Who Can It Be Now?** *Men At Work* (1 of 2)
12. 11/6 3 **Up Where We Belong** *Joe Cocker* (1) *& Jennifer Warnes* (1 of 2)
13. 11/27 2 **Truly** *Lionel Richie* (2 of 5)
14. 12/11 1 **Mickey** *Toni Basil* (1)
15. 12/18 4 **Maneater** *Daryl Hall & John Oates* (5 of 6)

1983

DATE WKS

1. 1/15 4↕ **Down Under** *Men At Work* (2 of 2)
2. 2/5 1 **Africa** *Toto* (1)
3. 2/19 2 **Baby, Come To Me** *Patti Austin* (1) *with James Ingram* (1 of 2)
4. 3/5 7 **Billie Jean** *Michael Jackson* (4 of 13)
5. 4/23 1 **Come On Eileen** *Dexys Midnight Runners* (1)
6. 4/30 3 **Beat It** *Michael Jackson* (5 of 13)
7. 5/21 1 **Let's Dance** *David Bowie* (2 of 2)
8. 5/28 6 **Flashdance...What A Feeling** *Irene Cara* (1)
9. 7/9 8 **Every Breath You Take** *The Police* (1)
10. 9/3 1 **Sweet Dreams (Are Made of This)** *Eurythmics* (1)
11. 9/10 2 **Maniac** *Michael Sembello* (1)
12. 9/24 1 **Tell Her About It** *Billy Joel* (2 of 3)
13. 10/1 4 **Total Eclipse Of The Heart** *Bonnie Tyler* (1)
14. 10/29 2 **Islands In The Stream** *Kenny Rogers* (2 of 2) *with Dolly Parton* (2 of 2)
15. 11/12 4 **All Night Long (All Night)** *Lionel Richie* (3 of 5)
16. 12/10 6 **Say Say Say** *Paul McCartney* (9 of 9) *& Michael Jackson* (6 of 13)

1984

DATE WKS

1. 1/21 2 **Owner Of A Lonely Heart** *Yes* (1)
2. 2/4 3 **Karma Chameleon** *Culture Club* (1)
3. 2/25 5 **Jump** *Van Halen* (1)
4. 3/31 3 **Footloose** *Kenny Loggins* (1)
5. 4/21 3 **Against All Odds (Take A Look At Me Now)** *Phil Collins* (1 of 7)
6. 5/12 2 **Hello** *Lionel Richie* (4 of 5)
7. 5/26 2 **Let's Hear It For The Boy** *Deniece Williams* (2 of 2)
8. 6/9 2 **Time After Time** *Cyndi Lauper* (1 of 2)
9. 6/23 2 **The Reflex** *Duran Duran* (1 of 2)
10. 7/7 5 **When Doves Cry** *Prince* (1 of 5)
11. 8/11 3 **Ghostbusters** *Ray Parker Jr.* (1)
12. 9/1 3 **What's Love Got To Do With It** *Tina Turner* (1)
13. 9/22 1 **Missing You** *John Waite* (1)
14. 9/29 2 **Let's Go Crazy** *Prince & the Revolution* (2 of 5)
15. 10/13 3 **I Just Called To Say I Love You** *Stevie Wonder* (8 of 10)
16. 11/3 2 **Caribbean Queen (No More Love On The Run)** *Billy Ocean* (1 of 3)

1984 (cont'd)

17. 11/17 3 **Wake Me Up Before You Go-Go** *Wham! (George Michael)* (1 of 10)
18. 12/8 2 **Out Of Touch** *Daryl Hall & John Oates* (6 of 6)
19. 12/22 6 **Like A Virgin** *Madonna* (1 of 12)

1985

DATE WKS

1. 2/2 2 **I Want To Know What Love Is** *Foreigner* (1)
2. 2/16 3 **Careless Whisper** *Wham! Featuring George Michael* (2 of 10)
3. 3/9 3 **Can't Fight This Feeling** *REO Speedwagon* (2 of 2)
4. 3/30 2 **One More Night** *Phil Collins* (2 of 7)
5. 4/13 4 **We Are The World** *USA for Africa* (1)
6. 5/11 1 **Crazy For You** *Madonna* (2 of 12)
7. 5/18 1 **Don't You (Forget About Me)** *Simple Minds* (1)
8. 5/25 2 **Everything She Wants** *Wham! (George Michael)* (3 of 10)
9. 6/8 2 **Everybody Wants To Rule The World** *Tears For Fears* (1 of 2)
10. 6/22 2 **Heaven** *Bryan Adams* (1 of 4)
11. 7/6 1 **Sussudio** *Phil Collins* (3 of 7)
12. 7/13 2 **A View To A Kill** *Duran Duran* (2 of 2)
13. 7/27 1 **Everytime You Go Away** *Paul Young* (1)
14. 8/3 3 **Shout** *Tears For Fears* (2 of 2)
15. 8/24 2 **The Power Of Love** *Huey Lewis & the News* (1 of 3)
16. 9/7 2 **St. Elmo's Fire (Man In Motion)** *John Parr* (1)
17. 9/21 3 **Money For Nothing** *Dire Straits* (1)
18. 10/12 1 **Oh Sheila** *Ready For The World* (1)
19. 10/19 1 **Take On Me** *A-Ha* (1)
20. 10/26 1 **Saving All My Love For You** *Whitney Houston* (1 of 11)
21. 11/2 1 **Part-Time Lover** *Stevie Wonder* (9 of 10)
22. 11/9 1 **Miami Vice Theme** *Jan Hammer* (1)
23. 11/16 2 **We Built This City** *Starship* (1 of 3)
24. 11/30 1 **Separate Lives** *Phil Collins* (4 of 7) *& Marilyn Martin* (1)
25. 12/7 2 **Broken Wings** *Mr. Mister* (1 of 2)
26. 12/21 4 **Say You, Say Me** *Lionel Richie* (5 of 5)

1986

DATE WKS

1. 1/18 4 **That's What Friends Are For** *Dionne (Warwick)* (2 of 2) *& Friends: Elton John* (7 of 9), *Gladys Knight* (2 of 2) *& Stevie Wonder* (10 of 10)
2. 2/15 2 **How Will I Know** *Whitney Houston* (2 of 11)
3. 3/1 2 **Kyrie** *Mr. Mister* (2 of 2)
4. 3/15 1 **Sara** *Starship* (2 of 3)
5. 3/22 1 **These Dreams** *Heart* (1 of 2)
6. 3/29 3 **Rock Me Amadeus** *Falco* (1)
7. 4/19 2 **Kiss** *Prince & The Revolution* (3 of 5)
8. 5/3 1 **Addicted To Love** *Robert Palmer* (1)
9. 5/10 1 **West End Girls** *Pet Shop Boys* (1)
10. 5/17 3 **Greatest Love Of All** *Whitney Houston* (3 of 11)

#1 HITS

1986 (cont'd)

11. 6/7 **1** **Live To Tell** *Madonna* (3 of 12)
12. 6/14 **3** **On My Own** *Patti LaBelle* (2 of 2) *& Michael McDonald* (1)
13. 7/5 **1** **There'll Be Sad Songs (To Make You Cry)** *Billy Ocean* (2 of 3)
14. 7/12 **1** **Holding Back The Years** *Simply Red* (1 of 2)
15. 7/19 **1** **Invisible Touch** *Genesis* (1)
16. 7/26 **1** **Sledgehammer** *Peter Gabriel* (1)
17. 8/2 **2** **Glory Of Love** *Peter Cetera* (1 of 2)
18. 8/16 **2** **Papa Don't Preach** *Madonna* (4 of 12)
19. 8/30 **1** **Higher Love** *Steve Winwood* (1 of 2)
20. 9/6 **1** **Venus** *Bananarama* (1)
21. 9/13 **1** **Take My Breath Away** *Berlin* (1)
22. 9/20 **3** **Stuck With You** *Huey Lewis & the News* (2 of 3)
23. 10/11 **2** **When I Think Of You** *Janet Jackson* (1 of 10)
24. 10/25 **2** **True Colors** *Cyndi Lauper* (2 of 2)
25. 11/8 **2** **Amanda** *Boston* (1)
26. 11/22 **1** **Human** *Human League* (2 of 2)
27. 11/29 **1** **You Give Love A Bad Name** *Bon Jovi* (1 of 5)
28. 12/6 **1** **The Next Time I Fall** *Peter Cetera* (2 of 2) *w/Amy Grant* (1 of 2)
29. 12/13 **1** **The Way It Is** *Bruce Hornsby & The Range* (1)
30. 12/20 **4** **Walk Like An Egyptian** *Bangles* (1 of 2)

1987

DATE WKS

1. 1/17 **1** **Shake You Down** *Gregory Abbott* (1)
2. 1/24 **2** **At This Moment** *Billy Vera & The Beaters* (1)
3. 2/7 **1** **Open Your Heart** *Madonna* (5 of 12)
4. 2/14 **4** **Livin' On A Prayer** *Bon Jovi* (2 of 5)
5. 3/14 **1** **Jacob's Ladder** *Huey Lewis & the News* (3 of 3)
6. 3/21 **2** **Lean On Me** *Club Nouveau* (1)
7. 4/4 **2** **Nothing's Gonna Stop Us Now** *Starship* (3 of 3)
8. 4/18 **2** **I Knew You Were Waiting (For Me)** *Aretha Franklin* (2 of 2) *& George Michael* (4 of 10)
9. 5/2 **2** **(I Just) Died In Your Arms** *Cutting Crew* (1)
10. 5/16 **3** **With Or Without You** *U2* (1 of 2)
11. 6/6 **1** **You Keep Me Hangin' On** *Kim Wilde* (1)
12. 6/13 **1** **Always** *Atlantic Starr* (1)
13. 6/20 **1** **Head To Toe** *Lisa Lisa & Cult Jam* (1 of 2)
14. 6/27 **2** **I Wanna Dance With Somebody (Who Loves Me)** *Whitney Houston* (4 of 11)
15. 7/11 **3** **Alone** *Heart* (2 of 2)
16. 8/1 **1** **Shakedown** *Bob Seger* (1)
17. 8/8 **2** **I Still Haven't Found What I'm Looking For** *U2* (2 of 2)
18. 8/22 **1** **Who's That Girl** *Madonna* (6 of 12)
19. 8/29 **3** **La Bamba** *Los Lobos* (1)
20. 9/19 **1** **I Just Can't Stop Loving You** *Michael Jackson* (7 of 13)

1987 (cont'd)

21. 9/26 **2** **Didn't We Almost Have It All** *Whitney Houston* (5 of 11)
22. 10/10 **1** **Here I Go Again** *Whitesnake* (1)
23. 10/17 **1** **Lost In Emotion** *Lisa Lisa & Cult Jam* (2 of 2)
24. 10/24 **2** **Bad** *Michael Jackson* (8 of 13)
25. 11/7 **2** **I Think We're Alone Now** *Tiffany* (1 of 2)
26. 11/21 **1** **Mony Mony "Live"** *Billy Idol* (1)
27. 11/28 **1** **(I've Had) The Time Of My Life** *Bill Medley* (1) *& Jennifer Warnes* (2 of 2)
28. 12/5 **1** **Heaven Is A Place On Earth** *Belinda Carlisle* (1)
29. 12/12 **4** **Faith** *George Michael* (5 of 10)

1988

DATE WKS

1. 1/9 **1** **So Emotional** *Whitney Houston* (6 of 11)
2. 1/16 **1** **Got My Mind Set On You** *George Harrison* (3 of 3)
3. 1/23 **1** **The Way You Make Me Feel** *Michael Jackson* (9 of 13)
4. 1/30 **1** **Need You Tonight** *INXS* (1)
5. 2/6 **2** **Could've Been** *Tiffany* (2 of 2)
6. 2/20 **1** **Seasons Change** *Exposé* (1)
7. 2/27 **2** **Father Figure** *George Michael* (6 of 10)
8. 3/12 **2** **Never Gonna Give You Up** *Rick Astley* (1 of 2)
9. 3/26 **2** **Man In The Mirror** *Michael Jackson* (10 of 13)
10. 4/9 **2** **Get Outta My Dreams, Get Into My Car** *Billy Ocean* (3 of 3)
11. 4/23 **2** **Where Do Broken Hearts Go** *Whitney Houston* (7 of 11)
12. 5/7 **1** **Wishing Well** *Terence Trent D'Arby* (1)
13. 5/14 **2** **Anything For You** *Gloria Estefan & Miami Sound Machine* (1 of 3)
14. 5/28 **3** **One More Try** *George Michael* (7 of 10)
15. 6/18 **1** **Together Forever** *Rick Astley* (2 of 2)
16. 6/25 **1** **Foolish Beat** *Debbie Gibson* (1 of 2)
17. 7/2 **1** **Dirty Diana** *Michael Jackson* (11 of 13)
18. 7/9 **2** **The Flame** *Cheap Trick* (1)
19. 7/23 **1** **Hold On To The Nights** *Richard Marx* (1 of 3)
20. 7/30 **4** **Roll With It** *Steve Winwood* (2 of 2)
21. 8/27 **2** **Monkey** *George Michael* (8 of 10)
22. 9/10 **2** **Sweet Child O' Mine** *Guns N' Roses* (1)
23. 9/24 **2** **Don't Worry Be Happy** *Bobby McFerrin* (1)
24. 10/8 **1** **Love Bites** *Def Leppard* (1)
25. 10/15 **1** **Red Red Wine** *UB40* (1 of 2)
26. 10/22 **2** **Groovy Kind Of Love** *Phil Collins* (5 of 7)
27. 11/5 **1** **Kokomo** *The Beach Boys* (4 of 4)
28. 11/12 **1** **Wild, Wild West** *The Escape Club* (1)
29. 11/19 **2** **Bad Medicine** *Bon Jovi* (3 of 5)
30. 12/3 **1** **Baby, I Love Your Way/Freebird Medley (Free Baby)** *Will To Power* (1)
31. 12/10 **2** **Look Away** *Chicago* (3 of 3)
32. 12/24 **3** **Every Rose Has Its Thorn** *Poison* (1)

#1 HITS

1989

	DATE	WKS	
1.	1/14	1	**My Prerogative** *Bobby Brown* (1 of 2)
2.	1/21	2	**Two Hearts** *Phil Collins* (6 of 7)
3.	2/4	1	**When I'm With You** *Sheriff* (1)
4.	2/11	3	**Straight Up** *Paula Abdul* (1 of 6)
5.	3/4	3	**Lost In Your Eyes** *Debbie Gibson* (2 of 2)
6.	3/25	1	**The Living Years** *Mike & The Mechanics* (1)
7.	4/1	1	**Eternal Flame** *Bangles* (2 of 2)
8.	4/8	1	**The Look** *Roxette* (1 of 4)
9.	4/15	1	**She Drives Me Crazy** *Fine Young Cannibals* (1 of 2)
10.	4/22	3	**Like A Prayer** *Madonna* (7 of 12)
11.	5/13	1	**I'll Be There For You** *Bon Jovi* (4 of 5)
12.	5/20	2	**Forever Your Girl** *Paula Abdul* (2 of 6)
13.	6/3	1	**Rock On** *Michael Damian* (1)
14.	6/10	1	**Wind Beneath My Wings** *Bette Midler* (1)
15.	6/17	1	**I'll Be Loving You (Forever)** *New Kids On The Block* (1 of 3)
16.	6/24	1	**Satisfied** *Richard Marx* (2 of 3)
17.	7/1	1	**Baby Don't Forget My Number** *Milli Vanilli* (1 of 3)
18.	7/8	1	**Good Thing** *Fine Young Cannibals* (2 of 2)
19.	7/15	1	**If You Don't Know Me By Now** *Simply Red* (2 of 2)
20.	7/22	2	**Toy Soldiers** *Martika* (1)
21.	8/5	1	**Batdance** *Prince* (4 of 5)
22.	8/12	3	**Right Here Waiting** *Richard Marx* (3 of 3)
23.	9/2	1	**Cold Hearted** *Paula Abdul* (3 of 6)
24.	9/9	1	**Hangin' Tough** *New Kids On The Block* (2 of 3)
25.	9/16	1	**Don't Wanna Lose You** *Gloria Estefan* (2 of 3)
26.	9/23	2	**Girl I'm Gonna Miss You** *Milli Vanilli* (2 of 3)
27.	10/7	4	**Miss You Much** *Janet Jackson* (2 of 10)
28.	11/4	1	**Listen To Your Heart** *Roxette* (2 of 4)
29.	11/11	2	**When I See You Smile** *Bad English* (1)
30.	11/25	2	**Blame It On The Rain** *Milli Vanilli* (3 of 3)
31.	12/9	2	**We Didn't Start The Fire** *Billy Joel* (3 of 3)
32.	12/23	4	**Another Day In Paradise** *Phil Collins* (7 of 7)

1990

	DATE	WKS	
1.	1/20	3	**How Am I Supposed To Live Without You** *Michael Bolton* (1 of 2)
2.	2/10	3	**Opposites Attract** *Paula Abdul* (4 of 6)
3.	3/3	3	**Escapade** *Janet Jackson* (3 of 10)
4.	3/24	2	**Black Velvet** *Alannah Myles* (1)
5.	4/7	1	**Love Will Lead You Back** *Taylor Dayne* (1)
6.	4/14	1	**I'll Be Your Everything** *Tommy Page* (1)
7.	4/21	4	**Nothing Compares 2 U** *Sinéad O'Connor* (1)
8.	5/19	3	**Vogue** *Madonna* (8 of 12)
9.	6/9	1	**Hold On** *Wilson Phillips* (1 of 3)
10.	6/16	2	**It Must Have Been Love** *Roxette* (3 of 4)
11.	6/30	3	**Step By Step** *New Kids On The Block* (3 of 3)
12.	7/21	2	**She Ain't Worth It** *Glenn Medeiros* (1) *Feat. Bobby Brown* (2 of 2)

1990 (cont'd)

	DATE	WKS	
13.	8/4	4	**Vision Of Love** *Mariah Carey* (1 of 15)
14.	9/1	1	**If Wishes Came True** *Sweet Sensation* (1)
15.	9/8	1	**Blaze Of Glory** *Jon Bon Jovi* (5 of 5)
16.	9/15	2	**Release Me** *Wilson Phillips* (2 of 3)
17.	9/29	1	**(Can't Live Without Your) Love And Affection** *Nelson* (1)
18.	10/6	1	**Close To You** *Maxi Priest* (1)
19.	10/13	1	**Praying For Time** *George Michael* (9 of 10)
20.	10/20	1	**I Don't Have The Heart** *James Ingram* (2 of 2)
21.	10/27	1	**Black Cat** *Janet Jackson* (4 of 10)
22.	11/3	1	**Ice Ice Baby** *Vanilla Ice* (1)
23.	11/10	3	**Love Takes Time** *Mariah Carey* (2 of 15)
24.	12/1	1	**I'm Your Baby Tonight** *Whitney Houston* (8 of 11)
25.	12/8	4	**Because I Love You (The Postman Song)** *Stevie B* (1)

1991

	DATE	WKS	
1.	1/5	2	**Justify My Love** *Madonna* (9 of 12)
2.	1/19	1	**Love Will Never Do (Without You)** *Janet Jackson* (5 of 10)
3.	1/26	2	**The First Time** *Surface* (1)
4.	2/9	2	**Gonna Make You Sweat (Everybody Dance Now)** *C & C Music Factory* (1)
5.	2/23	2	**All The Man That I Need** *Whitney Houston* (9 of 11)
6.	3/9	2	**Someday** *Mariah Carey* (3 of 15)
7.	3/23	1	**One More Try** *Timmy -T-* (1)
8.	3/30	2	**Coming Out Of The Dark** *Gloria Estefan* (3 of 3)
9.	4/13	1	**I've Been Thinking About You** *Londonbeat* (1)
10.	4/20	1	**You're In Love** *Wilson Phillips* (3 of 3)
11.	4/27	2	**Baby Baby** *Amy Grant* (2 of 2)
12.	5/11	1	**Joyride** *Roxette* (4 of 4)
13.	5/18	1	**I Like The Way (The Kissing Game)** *Hi-Five* (1)
14.	5/25	2	**I Don't Wanna Cry** *Mariah Carey* (4 of 15)
15.	6/8	1	**More Than Words** *Extreme* (1)
16.	6/15	5	**Rush, Rush** *Paula Abdul* (5 of 6)
17.	7/20	1	**Unbelievable** *EMF* (1)
18.	7/27	7	**(Everything I Do) I Do It For You** *Bryan Adams* (2 of 4)
19.	9/14	1	**The Promise Of A New Day** *Paula Abdul* (6 of 6)
20.	9/21	2	**I Adore Mi Amor** *Color Me Badd* (1 of 2)
21.	10/5	1	**Good Vibrations** *Marky Mark & The Funky Bunch* (1) *Featuring Loleatta Holloway* (1)
22.	10/12	3	**Emotions** *Mariah Carey* (5 of 15)
23.	11/2	1	**Romantic** *Karyn White* (1)
24.	11/9	2	**Cream** *Prince And The N.P.G.* (5 of 5)
25.	11/23	1	**When A Man Loves A Woman** *Michael Bolton* (2 of 2)

11/30/91: Billboard begins compiling "Hot 100" from data provided by BDS and SoundScan.

	DATE	WKS	
26.	11/30	1	**Set Adrift On Memory Bliss** *PM Dawn* (1)
27.	12/7	7	**Black Or White** *Michael Jackson* (12 of 13)

#1 HITS

1992

	DATE	WKS	
1.	1/25	1	**All 4 Love** *Color Me Badd* (2 of 2)
2.	2/1	1	**Don't Let The Sun Go Down On Me** *George Michael* (10 of 10)/*Elton John* (8 of 9)
3.	2/8	3	**I'm Too Sexy** *R*S*F (Right Said Fred)* (1)
4.	2/29	3	**To Be With You** *Mr. Big* (1)
5.	3/21	5	**Save The Best For Last** *Vanessa Williams* (1)
6.	4/25	8	**Jump** *Kris Kross* (1)
7.	6/20	2	**I'll Be There** *Mariah Carey* (6 of 15)
8.	7/4	5	**Baby Got Back** *Sir Mix-A-Lot* (1)
9.	8/8	1	**This Used To Be My Playground** *Madonna* (10 of 12)
10.	8/15	13	**End of the Road** ***Boyz II Men*** (1 of 5)
11.	11/14	2	**How Do You Talk To An Angel** *The Heights* (1)
12.	11/28	14	**I Will Always Love You** *Whitney Houston* (10 of 11)

1993

	DATE	WKS	
1.	3/6	1	**A Whole New World (Aladdin's Theme)** *Peabo Bryson* (1) & *Regina Belle* (1)
2.	3/13	7	**Informer** *Snow* (1)
3.	5/1	2	**Freak Me** *Silk* (1)
4.	5/15	8	**That's The Way Love Goes** *Janet Jackson* (6 of 10)
5.	7/10	2	**Weak** *SWV (Sisters With Voices)* (1)
6.	7/24	7	**Can't Help Falling In Love** *UB40* (2 of 2)
7.	9/11	8	**Dreamlover** *Mariah Carey* (7 of 15)
8.	11/6	5	**I'd Do Anything For Love (But I Won't Do That)** *Meat Loaf* (1)
9.	12/11	2	**Again** *Janet Jackson* (7 of 10)
10.	12/25	4	**Hero** *Mariah Carey* (8 of 15)

1994

	DATE	WKS	
1.	1/22	3	**All For Love** *Bryan Adams* (3 of 4)/ *Rod Stewart* (4 of 4)/*Sting* (1)
2.	2/12	4	**The Power Of Love** ***Celine Dion*** (1 of 4)
3.	3/12	6↕	**The Sign** *Ace Of Base* (1)
4.	4/9	4	**Bump N' Grind** *R. Kelly* (1 of 2)
5.	5/21	11	**I Swear** *All-4-One* (1)
6.	8/6	3	**Stay (I Missed You)** *Lisa Loeb & Nine Stories* (1)
7.	8/27	14	**I'll Make Love To You** *Boyz II Men* (2 of 5)
8.	12/3	6↕	**On Bended Knee** *Boyz II Men* (3 of 5)
9.	12/17	2	**Here Comes The Hotstepper** *Ini Kamoze* (1)

1995

	DATE	WKS	
1.	1/28	4	**Creep** ***TLC*** (1 of 4)
2.	2/25	7	**Take A Bow** *Madonna* (11 of 12)
3.	4/15	7	**This Is How We Do It** *Montell Jordan* (1)
4.	6/3	5	**Have You Ever Really Loved A Woman?** *Bryan Adams* (4 of 4)
5.	7/8	7	**Waterfalls** *TLC* (2 of 4)
6.	8/26	1	**Kiss From A Rose** *Seal* (1)
7.	9/2	1 ❶	**You Are Not Alone** *Michael Jackson* (13 of 13)

1995 (cont'd)

	DATE	WKS	
8.	9/9	3	**Gangsta's Paradise** *Coolio* (1) *Featuring L.V.* (1)
9.	9/30	8 ❶	**Fantasy** *Mariah Carey* (9 of 15)
10.	11/25	1 ❶	**Exhale (Shoop Shoop)** *Whitney Houston* (11 of 11)
11.	12/2	16 ❶	**One Sweet Day** *Mariah Carey* (10 of 15) & *Boyz II Men* (4 of 5)

1996

	DATE	WKS	
1.	3/23	6	**Because You Loved Me** *Celine Dion* (2 of 4)
2.	5/4	2	**Always Be My Baby** *Mariah Carey* (11 of 15)
3.	5/18	8	**Tha Crossroads** *Bone thugs-n-harmony* (1)
4.	7/13	2	**How Do U Want It** *2 Pac* (1) *(featuring KC & JoJo)* (1 of 2)
5.	7/27	1	**You're Makin' Me High** *Toni Braxton* (1 of 2)
6.	8/3	14	**Macarena (bayside boys mix)** *Los Del Rio* (1)
7.	11/9	4	**No Diggity** *BLACKstreet* (1) *(Featuring Dr. Dre)* (1)
8.	12/7	16[A]	**Don't Speak** *No Doubt* (1)
9.	12/7	11	**Un-Break My Heart** *Toni Braxton* (2 of 2)

1997

	DATE	WKS	
1.	2/22	4	**Wannabe** *Spice Girls* (1)
2.	3/22	6	**Can't Nobody Hold Me Down** ***Puff Daddy*** (1 of 4) *Featuring Mase* (1 of 2)
3.	5/3	3	**Hypnotize** *The Notorious B.I.G.* (1 of 2)
4.	5/24	3	**MMMBop** *Hanson* (1)
5.	6/14	11 ❶	**I'll Be Missing You** *Puff Daddy* (2 of 4) *& Faith Evans* (1) *(featuring 112)* (1)
6.	8/9	4[A]	**Men In Black** *Will Smith* (1 of 3)
7.	8/30	2	**Mo Money Mo Problems** *The Notorious B.I.G.* (2 of 2) *Featuring Puff Daddy* (3 of 4) & Mase (2 of 2)
8.	9/13	3 ❶	**Honey** *Mariah Carey* (12 of 15)
9.	10/4	1	**4 Seasons Of Loneliness** *Boyz II Men* (5 of 5)
10.	10/11	14 ❶	**Candle In The Wind 1997 / Something About The Way You Look Tonight** *Elton John* (9 of 9)
11.	10/18	6[A]	**Fly** *Sugar Ray* (1)

1998

	DATE	WKS	
1.	1/17	2	**Truly Madly Deeply** *Savage Garden* (1 of 2)
2.	1/31	2	**Together Again** *Janet Jackson* (8 of 10)
3.	2/14	2	**Nice & Slow** *Usher* (1 of 3)
4.	2/28	2 ❶	**My Heart Will Go On (Love Theme From 'Titanic')** *Celine Dion* (3 of 4)
5.	3/14	3	**Gettin' Jiggy Wit It** *Will Smith* (2 of 3)
6.	4/4	3	**All My Life** *K-Ci & JoJo* (2 of 2)
7.	4/25	5↕	**Too Close** *Next* (1)
8.	5/16	11[A]	**Torn** *Natalie Imbruglia* (1)
9.	5/23	1	**My All** *Mariah Carey* (13 of 15)

#1 HITS

1998 (cont'd)

10. 6/6 **13** **The Boy Is Mine** *Brandy (1 of 2) & Monica (1 of 3)*
11. 8/1 **18A** **Iris** *Goo Goo Dolls (1)*
12. 9/5 **4 ❶** **I Don't Want To Miss A Thing** *Aerosmith (1)*
13. 10/3 **5↕** **The First Night** *Monica (2 of 3)*
14. 10/17 **1** **One Week** *Barenaked Ladies (1)*
15. 11/14 **2 ❶** **Doo Wop (That Thing)** *Lauryn Hill (1)*
16. 11/28 **1** **Lately** *Divine (1)*
17. 12/5 **6 ❶** **I'm Your Angel** *R. Kelly (2 of 2) & Celine Dion (4 of 4)*

DATE WKS 1999

1. 1/16 **2** **Have You Ever?** *Brandy (2 of 2)*
2. 1/30 **2** **...Baby One More Time** *Britney Spears (1)*
3. 2/13 **4** **Angel Of Mine** *Monica (3 of 3)*
4. 3/13 **4** **Believe** *Cher (4 of 4)*
5. 4/10 **4** **No Scrubs** *TLC (3 of 4)*
6. 5/8 **5** **Livin' La Vida Loca** *Ricky Martin (1)*
7. 6/12 **5** **If You Had My Love** *Jennifer Lopez (1 of 4)*
8. 7/17 **1** **Bills, Bills, Bills** *Destiny's Child (1 of 4)*
9. 7/24 **1** **Wild Wild West** *Will Smith (3 of 3) featuring Dru Hill (1) & Kool Mo Dee (1)*
10. 7/31 **5** **Genie In A Bottle** *Christina Aguilera (1 of 4)*
11. 9/4 **2** **Bailamos** *Enrique Iglesias (1 of 2)*
12. 9/18 **3** **Unpretty** *TLC (4 of 4)*
13. 10/9 **2** **Heartbreaker** *Mariah Carey (14 of 15) (Featuring Jay-Z) (1 of 2)*
14. 10/23 **12** **Smooth** *Santana (1 of 2) Feat. Rob Thomas (1)*

DATE WKS 2000

1. 1/15 **2** **What A Girl Wants** *Christina Aguilera (2 of 4)*
2. 1/29 **4↕** **I Knew I Loved You** *Savage Garden (2 of 2)*
3. 2/19 **1** **Thank God I Found You** *Mariah (Carey) (15 of 15) With Joe (1 of 2) & 98° (1)*
4. 3/4 **2** **Amazed** *Lonestar (1)*
5. 3/18 **3** **Say My Name** *Destiny's Child (2 of 4)*
6. 4/8 **10** **Maria Maria** *Santana (2 of 2) Featuring The Product G&B (1)*
7. 6/17 **1** **Try Again** *Aaliyah (1)*
8. 6/24 **3** **Be With You** *Enrique Iglesias (2 of 2)*
9. 7/15 **1** **Everything You Want** *Vertical Horizon (1)*
10. 7/22 **1** **Bent** *Matchbox Twenty (1)*
11. 7/29 **2** **It's Gonna Be Me** **NSYNC (1)*
12. 8/12 **2** **Incomplete** *Sisqó (1)*
13. 8/26 **3** **Doesn't Really Matter** *Janet (Jackson) (9 of 10)*
14. 9/16 **4** **Music** *Madonna (12 of 12)*
15. 10/14 **4** **Come On Over Baby (all I want is you)** *Christina Aguilera (3 of 4)*

2000 (cont'd)

16. 11/11 **1** **With Arms Wide Open** *Creed (1)*
17. 11/18 **11** **Independent Women Part I** *Destiny's Child (3 of 4)*

DATE WKS 2001

1. 2/3 **2** **It Wasn't Me** *Shaggy (1 of 2) (Featuring Ricardo "RikRok" Ducent) (1)*
2. 2/17 **1** **Ms. Jackson** *OutKast (1)*
3. 2/24 **4** **Stutter** *Joe (2 of 2) (featuring Mystikal) (1)*
4. 3/24 **2↕** **Butterfly** *Crazy Town (1)*
5. 3/31 **1** **Angel** *Shaggy (2 of 2) Featuring Rayvon (1)*
6. 4/14 **7** **All For You** *Janet Jackson (10 of 10)*
7. 6/2 **5** **Lady Marmalade** *Christina Aguilera (4 of 4), Lil' Kim (1), Mýa (1) and P!nk (1)*
8. 7/7 **4** **U Remind Me** *Usher (2 of 3)*
9. 8/4 **2** **Bootylicious** *Destiny's Child (4 of 4)*
10. 8/18 **6↕** **Fallin'** *Alicia Keys (1)*
11. 9/8 **5↕** **I'm Real** *Jennifer Lopez (2 of 4) featuring Ja Rule (1 of 3)*
12. 11/3 **6** **Family Affair** *Mary J. Blige (1)*
13. 12/15 **6↕** **U Got It Bad** *Usher (3 of 3)*
14. 12/22 **4** **How You Remind Me** *Nickelback (1)*

DATE WKS 2002

1. 2/23 **2** **Always On Time** *Ja Rule (2 of 3) (feat. Ashanti) (1 of 2)*
2. 3/9 **6** **Ain't It Funny** *Jennifer Lopez (3 of 4) featuring Ja Rule (3 of 3)*
3. 4/20 **10** **Foolish** *Ashanti (2 of 2)*
4. 6/29 **7** **Hot In Herre** *Nelly (1 of 2)*
5. 8/17 **10↕** **Dilemma** *Nelly (2 of 2) Featuring Kelly Rowland (1)*
6. 10/5 **2** **A Moment Like This** *Kelly Clarkson (1)*
7. 11/9 **12** **Lose Yourself** *Eminem (1)*

DATE WKS 2003

1. 2/1 **1** **Bump, Bump, Bump** *B2K (1) & P. Diddy (4 of 4)*
2. 2/8 **4** **All I Have** *Jennifer Lopez (4 of 4) Featuring LL Cool J (1)*
3. 3/8 **9** **In Da Club** *50 Cent (1 of 2)*
4. 5/10 **3** **Get Busy** *Sean Paul (1)*
5. 5/31 **4** **21 Questions** *50 Cent (2 of 2) Feat. Nate Dogg (1)*
6. 6/28 **2 ❶** **This Is The Night** *Clay Aiken (1)*
7. 7/12 **5+** **Crazy In Love** *Beyoncé (1) (Featuring Jay-Z) (2 of 2)*

\+ still #1 as of 8/9/03 cut-off date

The Charts From Top To Bottom

When the talk turns to music, more people turn to Joel Whitburn's Record Research Collection than to any other reference source.

TOP POP SINGLES 1955-2002

Over 25,000 pop singles — every "Hot 100" hit — arranged by artist. Features thousands of artist biographies and countless titles notes. Also includes the B-side title of every "Hot 100" hit. 1,024 pages. Hardcover. $79.95.

POP ANNUAL 1955-1999

A year-by-year ranking, based on chart performance, of over 23,000 pop hits. Also includes, for the first time, the songwriters for every "Hot 100" hit. 912 pages. $79.95 Hardcover / $69.95 Softcover.

POP HITS SINGLES & ALBUMS 1940-1954

Four big books in one: an artist-by-artist anthology of early pop classics, a year-by year ranking of Pop's early hits, the complete story of the early pop albums and the top 10 singles charts of every *Billboard* "Best Selling Singles" chart. Filled with artist bios, title notes, and many special sections. 576 pages. Hardcover. $69.95.

POP MEMORIES 1890-1954

Unprecedented in depth and dimension. An artist-by-artist, title-by-title chronicle of the 65 formative years of recorded popular music. Fascinating facts and statistics on over 1,600 artists and 12,000 recordings, compiled directly from America's popular music charts, surveys and record listings. 660 pages. Hardcover. $59.95.

TOP POP ALBUMS 1955-2001

An artist-by-artist history of the over 22,000 albums that ever appeared on *Billboard's* pop albums charts, with a complete A-Z listing below each artist of tracks from every charted album by that artist. 1,208 pages. Hardcover. $99.95.

ALBUM CUTS 1955-2001

A companion guide to our Top Pop Albums 1955-2001 book — an A-Z list of cut titles along with the artist name and chart debut year of the album on which the cut is first found. 720 pages. Hardcover. $44.95.

BILLBOARD HOT 100/POP SINGLES CHARTS:

THE NINETIES 1990-1999
THE EIGHTIES 1980-1989
THE SEVENTIES 1970-1979
THE SIXTIES 1960-1969

Four complete collections of the actual weekly "Hot 100" charts from each decade; black-and-white reproductions at 70% of original size. Over 550 pages each. Deluxe Hardcover. $79.95 each.

POP CHARTS 1955-1959

Reproductions of every weekly pop singles chart *Billboard* published from 1955 through 1959 ("Best Sellers," "Jockeys," "Juke Box," "Top 100" and "Hot 100"). 496 pages. Deluxe Hardcover. $59.95.

BILLBOARD POP ALBUM CHARTS 1965-1969

The greatest of all album eras...straight off the pages of *Billboard*! Every weekly *Billboard* pop albums chart, shown in its entirety, from 1965 through 1969. Black-and-white reproductions at 70% of original size. 496 pages. Deluxe Hardcover. $59.95.

TOP ADULT CONTEMPORARY 1961-2001

Artist-by-artist listing of the nearly 8,000 singles and over 1,900 artists that appeared on *Billboard's* "Easy Listening" and "Hot Adult Contemporary" singles charts from July 17, 1961 through December 29, 2001. 352 pages. Hardcover. $44.95.

TOP COUNTRY SINGLES 1944-2001

The complete history of the most genuine of American musical genres, with an artist-by-artist listing of every "Country" single ever charted. 608 pages. Hardcover. $69.95.

COUNTRY ANNUAL 1944-1997

A year-by-year ranking, based on chart performance, of over 16,000 Country hits. 704 pages. Hardcover. $64.95.

TOP COUNTRY ALBUMS 1964-1997

A music industry first and a Record Research exclusive — features an artist-by-artist listing of every album to appear on *Billboard's* Top Country Albums chart from its first appearance in 1964 through September, 1997. Includes complete listings of all tracks from every Top 10 Country album. 304 pages. Hardcover. $49.95.

A CENTURY OF POP MUSIC

Chronicles the biggest Pop hits of the past 100 years, in yearly rankings of the Top 40 songs of every year from 1900 through 1999. Includes complete artist and title sections, pictures of the top artists, top hits and top artists by decade, and more. 256 pages. Softcover. $39.95.

TOP R&B SINGLES 1942-1999

Revised edition of our R&B bestseller — loaded with new features! Every "Soul," "Black," "Urban Contemporary" and "Rhythm & Blues" charted single, listed by artist. 688 pages. Hardcover. $69.95.

TOP R&B ALBUMS 1965-1998
First edition! An artist-by-artist listing of each of the 2,177 artists and 6,940 albums to appear on *Billboard's* "Top R&B Albums" chart. Includes complete listings of all tracks from every Top 10 R&B album. 360 pages. Hardcover. $49.95.

ROCK TRACKS 2002 Edition
Two separate artist-by-artist listings of of every title and artist that appeared on *Billboard's* "Mainstream (Album) Rock Tracks" chart from March, 1981 through October, 2002 and every title and artist that appeared on *Billboard's* "Modern Rock Tracks" chart from September, 1988 through October, 2002. 336 pages. Hardcover. $49.95.

BUBBLING UNDER SINGLES AND ALBUMS 1998 Edition
All "Bubbling Under The Hot 100" (1959-1997) and "Bubbling Under The Top Pop Albums" (1970-1985) charts covered in ful; organized artist by artist. Also features a photo section of every EP that hit *Billboard's* "Best Selling Pop EP's" chart (1957-1960). 416 pages. Softcover. $49.95.

BILLBOARD TOP 10 SINGLES CHARTS 1955-2000
A complete listing of each weekly Top 10 singles chart from *Billboard's* "Best Sellers" chart (1955-July 28, 1958) and "Hot 100" chart from its inception (August 4, 1958) through 2000. Each chart shows each single's current and previous week's positions, total weeks charted on the entire chart, original label & number, and more. 712 pages. Hardcover. $49.95.

BILLBOARD TOP 10 ALBUM CHARTS 1963-1998
This books contains more than 1,800 individual Top 10 charts from over 35 years of *Billboard's* weekly Top Albums chart (currently titled The Billboard 200). Each chart shows each album's current and previous week's positions, total weeks charted on the entire Top Albums chart, original label & number, and more. 536 pages. Hardcover. $39.95.

BILLBOARD SINGLES REVIEWS 1958
Reproductions of every weekly 1958 record review *Billboard* published for 1958. Reviews of nearly 10,000 record sides by 3,465 artists. 280 pages. Softcover. $29.95.

MUSIC YEARBOOKS 2002/2001/2000/1999/1998/1997/1996/1995/1994/1993/1992/1991/1990
A complete review of each year's charted music — as well as a superb supplemental update of our Record Research Pop Singles and Albums, Country Singles, R&B Singles, Adult Contemporary Singles, and Bubbling Under Singles books. Various page lengths. Softcover. 1999 thru 2002 editions $39.95 each / 1995 thru 1998 editions $34.95 each / 1990 thru 1994 editions $29.95 each.

Order Information

Shipping/Handling Extra — If you do not order through our online Web site (see below), please contact us for shipping rates.

Order By:

U.S. Toll-Free: 1-800-827-9810
(orders only please – Mon-Fri 8 AM-12 PM, 1 PM-5 PM CST)
Foreign Orders: 1-262-251-5408
Questions?: 1-262-251-5408 or **Email**: books@recordresearch.com

Online at our Web site: www.recordresearch.com

Fax (24 hours): 1-262-251-9452

Mail: Record Research Inc.
P.O. Box 200
Menomonee Falls, WI 53052-0200
U.S.A.

U.S. orders are shipped **via UPS**; please allow **7-10 business days** for delivery.

Canadian and **Foreign** orders are shipped **via surface mail**; please allow **8-12 weeks** for delivery. Orders must be paid in U.S. dollars and drawn on a U.S. bank.

For faster delivery, contact us for other shipping options/rates. We now offer
UPS Worldwide Express service for Canadian and Foreign orders as well as **airmail** service through the postal system.

Payment methods accepted: MasterCard, VISA, American Express, Money Order, or Check (personal checks may be held up to 10 days for bank clearance).